Peterson's Graduate Programs in Engineering & Applied Sciences

2013

PETERSON'S
Publishing

About Peterson's Publishing

Peterson's Publishing provides the accurate, dependable, high-quality education content and guidance you need to succeed. No matter where you are on your academic or professional path, you can rely on Peterson's print and digital publications for the most up-to-date education exploration data, expert test-prep tools, and top-notch career success resources—everything you need to achieve your goals.

Visit us online at **www.petersonspublishing.com** and let Peterson's help you achieve your goals.

For more information, contact Peterson's Publishing, 2000 Lenox Drive, Lawrenceville, NJ 08648; 800-338-3282 Ext. 54229; or find us on the World Wide Web at www.petersonspublishing.com.

Bernadette Webster, Managing Editor; Jill C. Schwartz, Editor; Ken Britschge, Research Project Manager; Amanda Ortiz, Amy L. Weber, Research Associates; Phyllis Johnson, Software Engineer; Ray Golaszewski, Publishing Operations Manager; Linda M. Williams, Composition Manager; Carrie Hansen, Christine Lucht, Bailey Williams, Client Fulfillment Team

ISSN 1093-8443
ISBN-13: 978-0-7689-3624-7
ISBN-10: 0-7689-3624-1

Printed in the United States of America

10 9 8 7 6 5 4 3 2 1   15 14 13

Forty-seventh Edition

By producing this book on recycled paper (40% post-consumer waste) 49 trees were saved.

Sustainability—Its Importance to Peterson's Publishing

What does sustainability mean to Peterson's Publishing? As a leading publisher, we are aware that out business has a direct impact on vital resources—most especially the trees that are used to make out books. Peterson's Publishing is proud that its products are certified to the Sustainable Forestry Initiative (SFI) chain-of-custody standard and that all of its books are printed on paper that is 40 percent post-consumer waste using vegetable-based ink.

Being a part of the Sustainable Forestry Initiative (SFI) means that all of out vendors—from paper suppliers to printers—have undergone rigorous audits to demonstrate that they are maintaining a sustainable environment.

Peterson's Publishing continuously strives to find new ways to incorporate sustainability throughout all aspects of its business.

CONTENTS

CONTENTS

A Note from the Peterson's Editors

The six volumes of Peterson's *Graduate and Professional Programs*, the only annually updated reference work of its kind, provide wideranging information on the graduate and professional programs offered by accredited colleges and universities in the United States, U.S. territories, and Canada and by those institutions outside the United States that are accredited by U.S. accrediting bodies. Nearly 36,000 individual academic and professional programs at more than 2,200 institutions are listed. Peterson's *Graduate and Professional Programs* have been used for more than forty years by prospective graduate and professional students, placement counselors, faculty advisers, and all others interested in postbaccalaureate education.

Graduate & Professional Programs: An Overview contains information on institutions as a whole, while the other books in the series are devoted to specific academic and professional fields:

Graduate Programs in the Humanities, Arts & Social Sciences
Graduate Programs in the Biological/Biomedical Sciences & Health-Related Medical Professions
Graduate Programs in the Physical Sciences, Mathematics, Agricultural Sciences, the Environment & Natural Resources
Graduate Programs in Engineering & Applied Sciences
Graduate Programs in Business, Education, Information Studies, Law & Social Work

The books may be used individually or as a set. For example, if you have chosen a field of study but do not know what institution you want to attend or if you have a college or university in mind but have not chosen an academic field of study, it is best to begin with the Overview guide.

Graduate & Professional Programs: An Overview presents several directories to help you identify programs of study that might interest you; you can then research those programs further in the other books in the series by using the Directory of Graduate and Professional Programs by Field, which lists 500 fields and gives the names of those institutions that offer graduate degree programs in each.

For geographical or financial reasons, you may be interested in attending a particular institution and will want to know what it has to offer. You should turn to the Directory of Institutions and Their Offerings, which lists the degree programs available at each institution. As in the Directory of Graduate and Professional Programs by Field, the level of degrees offered is also indicated. All books in the series include advice on graduate education, including topics such as admissions tests, financial aid, and accreditation. **The Graduate Adviser** includes two essays and

information about accreditation. The first essay, "The Admissions Process," discusses general admission requirements, admission tests, factors to consider when selecting a graduate school or program, when and how to apply, and how admission decisions are made. Special information for international students and tips for minority students are also included. The second essay, "Financial Support," is an overview of the broad range of support available at the graduate level. Fellowships, scholarships, and grants; assistantships and internships; federal and private loan programs, as well as Federal Work-Study; and the GI bill are detailed. This essay concludes with advice on applying for need-based financial aid. "Accreditation and Accrediting Agencies" gives information on accreditation and its purpose and lists institutional accrediting agencies first and then specialized accrediting agencies relevant to each volume's specific fields of study.

With information on more than 44,000 graduate programs in more than 500 disciplines, Peterson's *Graduate and Professional Programs* give you all the information you need about the programs that are of interest to you in three formats: **Profiles** (capsule summaries of basic information), **Displays** (information that an institution or program wants to emphasize), and **Close-Ups** (written by administrators, with more expansive information than the **Profiles**, emphasizing different aspects of the programs). By using these various formats of program information, coupled with **Appendixes** and **Indexes** covering directories and subject areas for all six books, you will find that these guides provide the most comprehensive, accurate, and up-to-date graduate study information available.

Find Us on Facebook®

Join the grad school conversation on Facebook® at www.facebook.com/petersonspublishing. Peterson's expert resources are available to help you as you search for the right graduate program for you.

Peterson's publishes a full line of resources with information you need to guide you through the graduate admissions process. Peterson's publications can be found at college libraries and career centers and your local bookstore or library—or visit us on the Web at www.petersonspublishing.com. Peterson's books are now also available as eBooks.

Colleges and universities will be pleased to know that Peterson's helped you in your selection. Admissions staff members are more than happy to answer questions, address specific problems, and help in any way they can. The editors at Peterson's wish you great success in your graduate program search!

THE GRADUATE ADVISER

The Admissions Process

Generalizations about graduate admissions practices are not always helpful because each institution has its own set of guidelines and procedures. Nevertheless, some broad statements can be made about the admissions process that may help you plan your strategy.

Factors Involved in Selecting a Graduate School or Program

Selecting a graduate school and a specific program of study is a complex matter. Quality of the faculty; program and course offerings; the nature, size, and location of the institution; admission requirements; cost; and the availability of financial assistance are among the many factors that affect one's choice of institution. Other considerations are job placement and achievements of the program's graduates and the institution's resources, such as libraries, laboratories, and computer facilities. If you are to make the best possible choice, you need to learn as much as you can about the schools and programs you are considering before you apply.

The following steps may help you narrow your choices.

- Talk to alumni of the programs or institutions you are considering to get their impressions of how well they were prepared for work in their fields of study.
- Remember that graduate school requirements change, so be sure to get the most up-to-date information possible.
- Talk to department faculty members and the graduate adviser at your undergraduate institution. They often have information about programs of study at other institutions.
- Visit the Web sites of the graduate schools in which you are interested to request a graduate catalog. Contact the department chair in your chosen field of study for additional information about the department and the field.
- Visit as many campuses as possible. Call ahead for an appointment with the graduate adviser in your field of interest and be sure to check out the facilities and talk to students.

General Requirements

Graduate schools and departments have requirements that applicants for admission must meet. Typically, these requirements include undergraduate transcripts (which provide information about undergraduate grade point average and course work applied toward a major), admission test scores, and letters of recommendation. Most graduate programs also ask for an essay or personal statement that describes your personal reasons for seeking graduate study. In some fields, such as art and music, portfolios or auditions may be required in addition to other evidence of talent. Some institutions require that the applicant have an undergraduate degree in the same subject as the intended graduate major.

Most institutions evaluate each applicant on the basis of the applicant's total record, and the weight accorded any given factor varies widely from institution to institution and from program to program.

The Application Process

You should begin the application process at least one year before you expect to begin your graduate study. Find out the application deadline for each institution (many are provided in the **Profile** section of this guide). Go to the institution's Web site and find out if you can apply online. If not, request a paper application form. Fill out this form thoroughly and neatly. Assume that the school needs all the information it is requesting and that the admissions officer will be sensitive to the neatness and overall quality of what you submit. Do not supply more information than the school requires.

The institution may ask at least one question that will require a three- or four-paragraph answer. Compose your response on the assumption that the admissions officer is interested in both what you think and how you express yourself. Keep your statement brief and to the point, but, at the same time, include all pertinent information about your past experiences and your educational goals. Individual statements vary greatly in style and content, which helps admissions officers differentiate among applicants. Many graduate departments give considerable weight to the statement in making their admissions decisions, so be sure to take the time to prepare a thoughtful and concise statement.

If recommendations are a part of the admissions requirements, carefully choose the individuals you ask to write them. It is generally best to ask current or former professors to write the recommendations, provided they are able to attest to your intellectual ability and motivation for doing the work required of a graduate student. It is advisable to provide stamped, preaddressed envelopes to people being asked to submit recommendations on your behalf.

Completed applications, including references, transcripts, and admission test scores, should be received at the institution by the specified date.

Be advised that institutions do not usually make admissions decisions until all materials have been received. Enclose a self-addressed postcard with your application, requesting confirmation of receipt. Allow at least ten days for the return of the postcard before making further inquiries.

If you plan to apply for financial support, it is imperative that you file your application early.

ADMISSION TESTS

The major testing program used in graduate admissions is the Graduate Record Examinations (GRE) testing program, sponsored by the GRE Board and administered by Educational Testing Service, Princeton, New Jersey.

The Graduate Record Examinations testing program consists of a General Test and eight Subject Tests. The General Test measures critical thinking, verbal reasoning, quantitative reasoning, and analytical writing skills. It is offered as an Internet-based test (iBT) in the United States, Canada, and many other countries.

The Graduate Record Examinations testing program consists of the revised General Test and eight Subject Tests. The GRE® revised General Test, introduced in August 2011, features a new test-taker friendly design and new question types. It reflects the kind of thinking students need to do in graduate or business school and demonstrates that students are indeed ready for graduate-level work.

- **Verbal Reasoning**—Measures ability to analyze and evaluate written material and synthesize information obtained from it, analyze relationships among component parts of sentences, and recognize relationships among words and concepts.
- **Quantitative Reasoning**—Measures problem-solving ability, focusing on basic concepts of arithmetic, algebra, geometry, and data analysis.
- **Analytical Writing**—Measures critical thinking and analytical writing skills, specifically the ability to articulate and support complex ideas clearly and effectively.

The GRE® revised General Test is available at about 700 test centers in more than 160 countries. It is offered as a computer-based test year-round at most locations around the world and as a paper-based test up to three times a year in areas where computer-based testing is not available.

Three scores are reported on the revised General Test:

1. A **Verbal Reasoning score** is reported on a 130–170 score scale, in 1-point increments.
2. A **Quantitative Reasoning score** is reported on a 130–170 score scale, in 1-point increments.

3 An **Analytical Writing score** is reported on a 0–6 score level, in half-point increments.

The GRE Subject Tests measure achievement and assume undergraduate majors or extensive background in the following eight disciplines:

- Biochemistry, Cell and Molecular Biology
- Biology
- Chemistry
- Computer Science
- Literature in English
- Mathematics
- Physics
- Psychology

The Subject Tests are available three times per year as paper-based administrations around the world. Testing time is approximately 2 hours and 50 minutes. You can obtain more information about the GRE by visiting the ETS Web site at www.ets.org or consulting the *GRE Information and Registration Bulletin*. The *Bulletin* can be obtained at many undergraduate colleges. You can also download it from the ETS Web site or obtain it by contacting Graduate Record Examinations, Educational Testing Service, P.O. Box 6000, Princeton, NJ 08541-6000; phone: 609-771-7670.

If you expect to apply for admission to a program that requires any of the GRE tests, you should select a test date well in advance of the application deadline. Scores on the computer-based General Test are reported within ten to fifteen days; scores on the paper-based Subject Tests are reported within six weeks.

Another testing program, the Miller Analogies Test (MAT), is administered at more than 500 Controlled Testing Centers, licensed by Harcourt Assessment, Inc., in the United States, Canada, and other countries. The MAT computer-based test is now available. Testing time is 60 minutes. The test consists of 120 partial analogies. You can obtain the *Candidate Information Booklet,* which contains a list of test centers and instructions for taking the test, from http://www.milleranalogies.com or by calling 800-622-3231 (toll-free).

Check the specific requirements of the programs to which you are applying.

How Admission Decisions Are Made

The program you apply to is directly involved in the admissions process. Although the final decision is usually made by the graduate dean (or an associate) or the faculty admissions committee, recommendations from faculty members in your intended field are important. At some institutions, an interview is incorporated into the decision process.

A Special Note for International Students

In addition to the steps already described, there are some special considerations for international students who intend to apply for graduate study in the United States. All graduate schools require an indication of competence in English. The purpose of the Test of English as a Foreign Language (TOEFL) is to evaluate the English proficiency of people who are nonnative speakers of English and want to study at colleges and universities where English is the language of instruction. The TOEFL is administered by Educational Testing Service (ETS) under the general direction of a policy board established by the College Board and the Graduate Record Examinations Board.

The TOEFL iBT assesses the four basic language skills: listening, reading, writing, and speaking. It was administered for the first time in September 2005, and ETS continues to introduce the TOEFL iBT in selected cities. The Internet-based test is administered at secure, official test centers. The testing time is approximately 4 hours. Because the TOEFL iBT includes a speaking section, the Test of Spoken English (TSE) is no longer needed.

The TOEFL is also offered in the paper-based format in areas of the world where Internet-based testing is not available. The paper-based TOEFL consists of three sections—listening comprehension, structure and written expression, and reading comprehension. The testing time is approximately 3 hours. The Test of Written English (TWE) is also given. The TWE is a 30-minute essay that measures the examinee's ability to compose in English. Examinees receive a TWE score separate from their TOEFL score. The *Information Bulletin* contains information on local fees and registration procedures.

The TOEFL® paper-based test (TOEFL PBT) began being phased out in mid-2012. For those who may have taken the TOEFL PBT, scores remain valid for two years after the test date. The Test of Written English (TWE) is also given. The TWE is a 30-minute essay that measures the examinee's ability to compose in English. Examinees receive a TWE score separate from their TOEFL score. The Information Bulletin contains information on local fees and registration procedures.

Additional information and registration materials are available from TOEFL Services, Educational Testing Service, P.O. Box 6151, Princeton, New Jersey 08541-6151. Phone: 609-771-7100. Web site: www.toefl.org.

International students should apply especially early because of the number of steps required to complete the admissions process. Furthermore, many United States graduate schools have a limited number of spaces for international students, and many more students apply than the schools can accommodate.

International students may find financial assistance from institutions very limited. The U.S. government requires international applicants to submit a certification of support, which is a statement attesting to the applicant's financial resources. In addition, international students *must* have health insurance coverage.

Tips for Minority Students

Indicators of a university's values in terms of diversity are found both in its recruitment programs and its resources directed to student success. Important questions: Does the institution vigorously recruit minorities for its graduate programs? Is there funding available to help with the costs associated with visiting the school? Are minorities represented in the institution's brochures or Web site or on their faculty rolls? What campus-based resources or services (including assistance in locating housing or career counseling and placement) are available? Is funding available to members of underrepresented groups?

At the program level, it is particularly important for minority students to investigate the "climate" of a program under consideration. How many minority students are enrolled and how many have graduated? What opportunities are there to work with diverse faculty and mentors whose research interests match yours? How are conflicts resolved or concerns addressed? How interested are faculty in building strong and supportive relations with students? "Climate" concerns should be addressed by posing questions to various individuals, including faculty members, current students, and alumni.

Information is also available through various organizations, such as the Hispanic Association of Colleges & Universities (HACU), and publications such as *Diverse Issues in Higher Education* and *Hispanic Outlook* magazine. There are also books devoted to this topic, such as *The Multicultural Student's Guide to Colleges* by Robert Mitchell.

Financial Support

The range of financial support at the graduate level is very broad. The following descriptions will give you a general idea of what you might expect and what will be expected of you as a financial support recipient.

Fellowships, Scholarships, and Grants

These are usually outright awards of a few hundred to many thousands of dollars with no service to the institution required in return. Fellowships and scholarships are usually awarded on the basis of merit and are highly competitive. Grants are made on the basis of financial need or special talent in a field of study. Many fellowships, scholarships, and grants not only cover tuition, fees, and supplies but also include stipends for living expenses with allowances for dependents. However, the terms of each should be examined because some do not permit recipients to supplement their income with outside work. Fellowships, scholarships, and grants may vary in the number of years for which they are awarded.

In addition to the availability of these funds at the university or program level, many excellent fellowship programs are available at the national level and may be applied for before and during enrollment in a graduate program. A listing of many of these programs can be found at the Council of Graduate Schools' Web site: http://www. cgsnet.org. There is a wealth of information in the "Programs" and "Awards" sections.

Assistantships and Internships

Many graduate students receive financial support through assistantships, particularly involving teaching or research duties. It is important to recognize that such appointments should not be viewed simply as employment relationships but rather should constitute an integral and important part of a student's graduate education. As such, the appointments should be accompanied by strong faculty mentoring and increasingly responsible apprenticeship experiences. The specific nature of these appointments in a given program should be considered in selecting that graduate program.

TEACHING ASSISTANTSHIPS

These usually provide a salary and full or partial tuition remission and may also provide health benefits. Unlike fellowships, scholarships, and grants, which require no service to the institution, teaching assistantships require recipients to provide the institution with a specific amount of undergraduate teaching, ideally related to the student's field of study. Some teaching assistants are limited to grading papers, compiling bibliographies, taking notes, or monitoring laboratories. At some graduate schools, teaching assistants must carry lighter course loads than regular full-time students.

RESEARCH ASSISTANTSHIPS

These are very similar to teaching assistantships in the manner in which financial assistance is provided. The difference is that recipients are given basic research assignments in their disciplines rather than teaching responsibilities. The work required is normally related to the student's field of study; in most instances, the assistantship supports the student's thesis or dissertation research.

ADMINISTRATIVE INTERNSHIPS

These are similar to assistantships in application of financial assistance funds, but the student is given an assignment on a part-time basis, usually as a special assistant with one of the university's administrative offices. The assignment may not necessarily be directly related to the recipient's discipline.

RESIDENCE HALL AND COUNSELING ASSISTANTSHIPS

These assistantships are frequently assigned to graduate students in psychology, counseling, and social work, but they may be offered to students in other disciplines, especially if the student has worked in this capacity during his or her undergraduate years. Duties can vary from being available in a dean's office for a specific number of hours for consultation with undergraduates to living in campus residences and being responsible for both counseling and administrative tasks or advising student activity groups. Residence hall assistantships often include a room and board allowance and, in some cases, tuition assistance and stipends. Contact the Housing and Student Life Office for more information.

Health Insurance

The availability and affordability of health insurance is an important issue and one that should be considered in an applicant's choice of institution and program. While often included with assistantships and fellowships, this is not always the case and, even if provided, the benefits may be limited. It is important to note that the U.S. government requires international students to have health insurance.

The GI Bill

This provides financial assistance for students who are veterans of the United States armed forces. If you are a veteran, contact your local Veterans Administration office to determine your eligibility and to get full details about benefits. There are a number of programs that offer educational benefits to current military enlistees. Some states have tuition assistance programs for members of the National Guard. Contact the VA office at the college for more information.

Federal Work-Study Program (FWS)

Employment is another way some students finance their graduate studies. The federally funded Federal Work-Study Program provides eligible students with employment opportunities, usually in public and private nonprofit organizations. Federal funds pay up to 75 percent of the wages, with the remainder paid by the employing agency. FWS is available to graduate students who demonstrate financial need. Not all schools have these funds, and some only award them to undergraduates. Each school sets its application deadline and workstudy earnings limits. Wages vary and are related to the type of work done. You must file the Free Application for Federal Student Aid (FAFSA) to be eligible for this program.

Loans

Many graduate students borrow to finance their graduate programs when other sources of assistance (which do not have to be repaid) prove insufficient. You should always read and understand the terms of any loan program before submitting your application.

FEDERAL DIRECT LOANS

Federal Direct Stafford Loans. The Federal Direct Stafford Loan Program offers 6.8 percent interest rate loans to students with the Department of Education acting as the lender.

There are two components of the Federal Stafford Loan program. Under the *subsidized* component (for loans with enrollment prior to July 1, 2012) of the program, the federal government pays the interest on the loan while you are enrolled in graduate school on at least a half-time basis, as well as during any period of deferment. Under the *unsubsidized* component of the program, you pay the interest on the loan from the day proceeds are issued. Eligibility for the federal subsidy is based on demonstrated financial need as determined by the financial aid office from the information you provide on the FAFSA. A cosigner is not required, since the loan is not based on creditworthiness.

Although *unsubsidized* Federal Direct Stafford Loans may not be as desirable as *subsidized* Federal Direct Stafford Loans from the student's perspective, they are a useful source of support for those who may not qualify for the subsidized loans or who need additional financial assistance.

Graduate students may borrow up to $20,500 per year through the Direct Stafford Loan Program, up to a cumulative maximum of $138,500, including undergraduate borrowing. This may include up to $8,500 in *subsidized* Direct Stafford Loans annually, depending on eligibility, up to a cumulative maximum of $65,500, including undergraduate borrowing. The amount of the loan borrowed through the *unsubsidized* Direct Stafford Loan Program equals the total amount of the loan (as much as $20,500) minus your eligibility for a *subsidized* Direct Loan (as much as $8,500). You may borrow up to the cost of attendance at the school in which you are enrolled or will attend, minus estimated financial assistance from other federal, state, and private sources, up to a maximum of $20,500.

Direct Stafford Graduate Loans made on or after July 1, 2006, carry a fixed interest rate of 6.8% both for in-school and in-repayment borrowers.

A fee is deducted from the loan proceeds upon disbursement. Loans with a first disbursement on or after July 1, 2010 but before July 1, 2012, have a borrower origination fee of 1 percent. For loans disbursed after July 1, 2012, these fee deductions no longer apply. The Budget Control Act of 2011, signed into law on August 2, 2011, eliminates Direct Subsidized Loan eligibility for graduate and professional students for periods of enrollment beginning on or after July 1, 2012 and terminates the authority of the Department of Education to offer most repayment incentives to Direct Loan borrowers for loans disbursed on or after July 1, 2012.

Under the *subsidized* Federal Direct Stafford Loan Program, repayment begins six months after your last date of enrollment on at least a half-time basis. Under the *unsubsidized* program, repayment of interest begins within thirty days from disbursement of the loan proceeds, and repayment of the principal begins six months after your last enrollment on at least a half-time basis. Some borrowers may choose to defer interest payments while they are in school. The accrued interest is added to the loan balance when the borrower begins repayment. There are several repayment options.

Federal Perkins Loans. The Federal Perkins Loan is available to students demonstrating financial need and is administered directly by the school. Not all schools have these funds, and some may award them to undergraduates only. Eligibility is determined from the information you provide on the FAFSA. The school will notify you of your eligibility.

Eligible graduate students may borrow up to $6,000 per year, up to a maximum of $40,000, including undergraduate borrowing (even if your previous Perkins Loans have been repaid). The interest rate for Federal Perkins Loans is 5 percent, and no interest accrues while you remain in school at least half-time. There are no guarantee, loan, or disbursement fees. Repayment begins nine months after your last date of enrollment on at least a half-time basis and may extend over a maximum of ten years with no prepayment penalty.

Federal Direct Graduate PLUS Loans. Effective July 1, 2006, graduate and professional students are eligible for Graduate PLUS loans. This program allows students to borrow up to the cost of attendance, less any other aid received. These loans have a fixed interest rate of 7.9 percent, and interest begins to accrue at the time of disbursement. The PLUS loans do involve a credit check; a PLUS borrower may obtain a loan with a cosigner if his or her credit is not good enough. Grad PLUS loans may be deferred while a student in school and for the six months following a drop below half-time enrollment. For more information, contact your college financial aid office.

Deferring Your Federal Loan Repayments. If you borrowed under the Federal Direct Stafford Loan Program, Federal Direct PLUS Loan Program, or the Federal Perkins Loan Program for previous undergraduate or graduate study, your payments may be deferred when you return to graduate school, depending on when you borrowed and under which program.

There are other deferment options available if you are temporarily unable to repay your loan. Information about these deferments is provided at your entrance and exit interviews. If you believe you are eligible for a deferment of your loan payments, you must contact your lender or loan servicer to request a deferment. The deferment must be filed prior to the time your payment is due, and it must be refiled when it expires if you remain eligible for deferment at that time.

SUPPLEMENTAL (PRIVATE) LOANS

Many lending institutions offer supplemental loan programs and other financing plans, such as the ones described here, to students seeking additional assistance in meeting their education expenses. Some loan programs target all types of graduate students; others are designed specifically for business, law, or medical students. In addition, you can use private loans not specifically designed for education to help finance your graduate degree.

If you are considering borrowing through a supplemental or private loan program, you should carefully consider the terms and be sure to "read the fine print." Check with the program sponsor for the most current terms that will be applicable to the amounts you intend to borrow for graduate study. Most supplemental loan programs for graduate study offer unsubsidized, credit-based loans. In general, a credit-ready borrower is one who has a satisfactory credit history or no credit history at all. A creditworthy borrower generally must pass a credit test to be eligible to borrow or act as a cosigner for the loan funds.

Many supplemental loan programs have minimum and maximum annual loan limits. Some offer amounts equal to the cost of attendance minus any other aid you will receive for graduate study. If you are planning to borrow for several years of graduate study, consider whether there is a cumulative or aggregate limit on the amount you may borrow. Often this cumulative or aggregate limit will include any amounts you borrowed and have not repaid for undergraduate or previous graduate study.

The combination of the annual interest rate, loan fees, and the repayment terms you choose will determine how much you will repay over time. Compare these features in combination before you decide which loan program to use. Some loans offer interest rates that are adjusted monthly, some quarterly, some annually. Some offer interest rates that are lower during the in-school, grace, and deferment periods and then increase when you begin repayment. Some programs include a loan "origination" fee, which is usually deducted from the principal amount you receive when the loan is disbursed and must be repaid along with the interest and other principal when you graduate, withdraw from school, or drop below half-time study. Sometimes the loan fees are reduced if you borrow with a qualified cosigner. Some programs allow you to defer interest and/or principal payments while you are enrolled in graduate school. Many programs allow you to capitalize your interest payments; the interest due on your loan is added to the outstanding balance of your loan, so you don't have to repay immediately, but this increases the amount you owe. Other programs allow you to pay the interest as you go, which reduces the amount you later have to repay. The private loan market is very competitive, and your financial aid office can help you evaluate these programs.

Applying for Need-Based Financial Aid

Schools that award federal and institutional financial assistance based on need will require you to complete the FAFSA and, in some cases, an institutional financial aid application.

If you are applying for federal student assistance, you **must** complete the FAFSA. A service of the U.S. Department of Education, the FAFSA is free to all applicants. Most applicants apply online at www.fafsa.ed.gov. Paper applications are available at the financial aid office of your local college.

After your FAFSA information has been processed, you will receive a Student Aid Report (SAR). If you provided an e-mail address on the FAFSA, this will be sent to you electronically; otherwise, it will be mailed to your home address.

Follow the instructions on the SAR if you need to correct information reported on your original application. If your situation changes after you file your FAFSA, contact your financial aid officer to discuss amending your information. You can also appeal your financial aid award if you have extenuating circumstances.

If you would like more information on federal student financial aid, visit the FAFSA Web site or download the most recent version of *Funding Education Beyond High School: The Guide to Federal Student Aid* at http://studentaid.ed.gov/students/publications/student_guide/index.html. This guide is also available in Spanish.

The U.S. Department of Education also has a toll-free number for questions concerning federal student aid programs. The number is 1-800-4-FED AID (1-800-433-3243). If you are hearing impaired, call toll-free, 1-800-730-8913.

Summary

Remember that these are generalized statements about financial assistance at the graduate level. Because each institution allots its aid differently, you should communicate directly with the school and the specific department of interest to you. It is not unusual, for example, to find that an endowment vested within a specific department supports one or more fellowships. You may fit its requirements and specifications precisely.

Accreditation and Accrediting Agencies

Colleges and universities in the United States, and their individual academic and professional programs, are accredited by nongovernmental agencies concerned with monitoring the quality of education in this country. Agencies with both regional and national jurisdictions grant accreditation to institutions as a whole, while specialized bodies acting on a nationwide basis—often national professional associations— grant accreditation to departments and programs in specific fields.

Institutional and specialized accrediting agencies share the same basic concerns: the purpose an academic unit—whether university or program—has set for itself and how well it fulfills that purpose, the adequacy of its financial and other resources, the quality of its academic offerings, and the level of services it provides. Agencies that grant institutional accreditation take a broader view, of course, and examine university-wide or college-wide services with which a specialized agency may not concern itself.

Both types of agencies follow the same general procedures when considering an application for accreditation. The academic unit prepares a self-evaluation, focusing on the concerns mentioned above and usually including an assessment of both its strengths and weaknesses; a team of representatives of the accrediting body reviews this evaluation, visits the campus, and makes its own report; and finally, the accrediting body makes a decision on the application. Often, even when accreditation is granted, the agency makes a recommendation regarding how the institution or program can improve. All institutions and programs are also reviewed every few years to determine whether they continue to meet established standards; if they do not, they may lose their accreditation.

Accrediting agencies themselves are reviewed and evaluated periodically by the U.S. Department of Education and the Council for Higher Education Accreditation (CHEA). Recognized agencies adhere to certain standards and practices, and their authority in matters of accreditation is widely accepted in the educational community.

This does not mean, however, that accreditation is a simple matter, either for schools wishing to become accredited or for students deciding where to apply. Indeed, in certain fields the very meaning and methods of accreditation are the subject of a good deal of debate. For their part, those applying to graduate school should be aware of the safeguards provided by regional accreditation, especially in terms of degree acceptance and institutional longevity. Beyond this, applicants should understand the role that specialized accreditation plays in their field, as this varies considerably from one discipline to another. In certain professional fields, it is necessary to have graduated from a program that is accredited in order to be eligible for a license to practice, and in some fields the federal government also makes this a hiring requirement. In other disciplines, however, accreditation is not as essential, and there can be excellent programs that are not accredited. In fact, some programs choose not to seek accreditation, although most do.

Institutions and programs that present themselves for accreditation are sometimes granted the status of candidate for accreditation, or what is known as "preaccreditation." This may happen, for example, when an academic unit is too new to have met all the requirements for accreditation. Such status signifies initial recognition and indicates that the school or program in question is working to fulfill all requirements; it does not, however, guarantee that accreditation will be granted.

Institutional Accrediting Agencies—Regional

MIDDLE STATES ASSOCIATION OF COLLEGES AND SCHOOLS
Accredits institutions in Delaware, District of Columbia, Maryland, New Jersey, New York, Pennsylvania, Puerto Rico, and the Virgin Islands.
Dr. Elizabeth Sibolski, President
Middle States Commission on Higher Education
3624 Market Street, Second Floor West
Philadelphia, Pennsylvania 19104
Phone: 267-284-5000
Fax: 215-662-5501
E-mail: info@msche.org
Web: www.msche.org

NEW ENGLAND ASSOCIATION OF SCHOOLS AND COLLEGES
Accredits institutions in Connecticut, Maine, Massachusetts, New Hampshire, Rhode Island, and Vermont.
Barbara E. Brittingham, Director
Commission on Institutions of Higher Education
209 Burlington Road, Suite 201
Bedford, Massachusetts 01730-1433
Phone: 781-271-0022
Fax: 781-271-0950
E-mail: kwillis@neasc.org
Web: http://cihe.neasc.org

NORTH CENTRAL ASSOCIATION OF COLLEGES AND SCHOOLS
Accredits institutions in Arizona, Arkansas, Colorado, Illinois, Indiana, Iowa, Kansas, Michigan, Minnesota, Missouri, Nebraska, New Mexico, North Dakota, Ohio, Oklahoma, South Dakota, West Virginia, Wisconsin, and Wyoming.
Dr. Sylvia Manning, President
The Higher Learning Commission
230 South LaSalle Street, Suite 7-500
Chicago, Illinois 60604-1413
Phone: 312-263-0456
Fax: 312-263-7462
E-mail: smanning@hlcommission.org
Web: www.ncahlc.org

NORTHWEST COMMISSION ON COLLEGES AND UNIVERSITIES
Accredits institutions in Alaska, Idaho, Montana, Nevada, Oregon, Utah, and Washington.
Dr. Sandra E. Elman, President
8060 165th Avenue, NE, Suite 100
Redmond, Washington 98052
Phone: 425-558-4224
Fax: 425-376-0596
E-mail: selman@nwccu.org
Web: www.nwccu.org

SOUTHERN ASSOCIATION OF COLLEGES AND SCHOOLS
Accredits institutions in Alabama, Florida, Georgia, Kentucky, Louisiana, Mississippi, North Carolina, South Carolina, Tennessee, Texas, and Virginia.
Belle S. Wheelan, President
Commission on Colleges
1866 Southern Lane
Decatur, Georgia 30033-4097
Phone: 404-679-4500
Fax: 404-679-4558
E-mail: questions@sacscoc.org
Web: www.sacscoc.org

WESTERN ASSOCIATION OF SCHOOLS AND COLLEGES
Accredits institutions in California, Guam, and Hawaii.
Ralph A. Wolff, President and Executive Director
Accrediting Commission for Senior Colleges and Universities
985 Atlantic Avenue, Suite 100
Alameda, California 94501
Phone: 510-748-9001
Fax: 510-748-9797
E-mail: wascsr@wascsenior.org
Web: www.wascweb.org/org

Institutional Accrediting Agencies—Other

ACCREDITING COUNCIL FOR INDEPENDENT COLLEGES AND SCHOOLS
Albert C. Gray, Ph.D., Executive Director and CEO
750 First Street, NE, Suite 980
Washington, DC 20002-4241
Phone: 202-336-6780
Fax: 202-842-2593
E-mail: info@acics.org
Web: www.acics.org

DISTANCE EDUCATION AND TRAINING COUNCIL (DETC)
Accrediting Commission
Michael P. Lambert, Executive Director
1601 18th Street, NW, Suite 2
Washington, DC 20009
Phone: 202-234-5100
Fax: 202-332-1386
E-mail: Brianna@detc.org
Web: www.detc.org

Specialized Accrediting Agencies

ACUPUNCTURE AND ORIENTAL MEDICINE
William W. Goding, M.Ed., RRT, Interim Executive Director
Accreditation Commission for Acupuncture and Oriental Medicine
14502 Greenview Drive, Suite 300B
Laurel, Maryland 20708
Phone: 301-313-0855
Fax: 301-313-0912
E-mail: coordinator@acaom.org
Web: www.acaom.org

ART AND DESIGN
Samuel Hope, Executive Director
Karen P. Moynahan, Associate Director
National Association of Schools of Art and Design (NASAD)
Commission on Accreditation
11250 Roger Bacon Drive, Suite 21
Reston, Virginia 20190-5243
Phone: 703-437-0700
Fax: 703-437-6312
E-mail: info@arts-accredit.org
Web: http://nasad.arts-accredit.org/

BUSINESS
Jerry Trapnell, Executive Vice President/Chief Accreditation Officer
AACSB International—The Association to Advance Collegiate Schools of Business
777 South Harbour Island Boulevard, Suite 750
Tampa, Florida 33602
Phone: 813-769-6500
Fax: 813-769-6559
E-mail: jerryt@aacsb.edu
Web: www.aacsb.edu

CHIROPRACTIC
S. Ray Bennett, Director of Accreditation Services
Council on Chiropractic Education (CCE)
Commission on Accreditation
8049 North 85th Way
Scottsdale, Arizona 85258-4321
Phone: 480-443-8877
Fax: 480-483-7333
E-mail: cce@cce-usa.org
Web: www.cce-usa.org

CLINICAL LABORATORY SCIENCES
Dianne M. Cearlock, Ph.D., Chief Executive Officer
National Accrediting Agency for Clinical Laboratory Sciences
5600 North River Road, Suite 720
Rosemont, Illinois 60018-5119
Phone: 773-714-8880
Fax: 773-714-8886
E-mail: info@naacls.org
Web: www.naacls.org

CLINICAL PASTORAL EDUCATION
Deryck Durston, Interim Executive Director
Association for Clinical Pastoral Education, Inc.
1549 Claremont Road, Suite 103
Decatur, Georgia 30033-4611
Phone: 404-320-1472
Fax: 404-320-0849
E-mail: acpe@acpe.edu
Web: www.acpe.edu

DANCE
Samuel Hope, Executive Director
Karen P. Moynahan, Associate Director
National Association of Schools of Dance (NASD)
Commission on Accreditation
11250 Roger Bacon Drive, Suite 21
Reston, Virginia 20190-5248
Phone: 703-437-0700
Fax: 703-437-6312
E-mail: info@arts-accredit.org
Web: http://nasd.arts-accredit.org

DENTISTRY
Anthony Ziebert, Director
Commission on Dental Accreditation
American Dental Association
211 East Chicago Avenue, Suite 1900
Chicago, Illinois 60611
Phone: 312-440-4643
E-mail: accreditation@ada.org
Web: www.ada.org

DIETETICS
Ulric K. Chung, Ph.D., Executive Director
American Dietetic Association
Commission on Accreditation for Dietetics Education (CADE-ADA)
120 South Riverside Plaza, Suite 2000
Chicago, Illinois 60606-6995
Phone: 800-877-1600
Fax: 312-899-4817
E-mail: cade@eatright.org
Web: www.eatright.org/cade

ENGINEERING
Michael Milligan, Ph.D., PE, Executive Director
Accreditation Board for Engineering and Technology, Inc. (ABET)
111 Market Place, Suite 1050
Baltimore, Maryland 21202
Phone: 410-347-7700
Fax: 410-625-2238
E-mail: accreditation@abet.org
Web: www.abet.org

FORESTRY
Carol L. Redelsheimer
Director of Science and Education
5400 Grosvenor Lane
Bethesda, Maryland 20814-2198
Phone: 301-897-8720 Ext. 123
Fax: 301-897-3690
E-mail: redelsheimerc@safnet.org
Web: www.safnet.org

HEALTH SERVICES ADMINISTRATION
Commission on Accreditation of Healthcare Management Education (CAHME)
John S. Lloyd, President and CEO
2111 Wilson Boulevard, Suite 700
Arlington, Virginia 22201
Phone: 703-351-5010
Fax: 703-991-5989
E-mail: info@cahme.org
Web: www.cahme.org

INTERIOR DESIGN
Holly Mattson, Executive Director
Council for Interior Design Accreditation
206 Grandview Avenue, Suite 350
Grand Rapids, Michigan 49503-4014
Phone: 616-458-0400
Fax: 616-458-0460
E-mail: info@accredit-id.org
Web: www.accredit-id.org

JOURNALISM AND MASS COMMUNICATIONS
Susanne Shaw, Executive Director
Accrediting Council on Education in Journalism and Mass Communications (ACEJMC)
School of Journalism
Stauffer-Flint Hall
University of Kansas
1435 Jayhawk Boulevard
Lawrence, Kansas 66045-7575
Phone: 785-864-3973
Fax: 785-864-5225
E-mail: sshaw@ku.edu
Web: www2.ku.edu/~acejmc

LANDSCAPE ARCHITECTURE
Ronald C. Leighton, Executive Director
Landscape Architectural Accreditation Board (LAAB)
American Society of Landscape Architects (ASLA)
636 Eye Street, NW
Washington, DC 20001-3736
Phone: 202-898-2444
Fax: 202-898-1185
E-mail: info@asla.org
Web: www.asla.org

LAW
Hulett H. Askew, Consultant on Legal Education
American Bar Association
321 North Clark Street, 21st Floor
Chicago, Illinois 60654
Phone: 312-988-6738
Fax: 312-988-5681
E-mail: legaled@americanbar.org
Web: www.abanet.org/legaled/

LIBRARY
Karen O'Brien, Director
Office for Accreditation
American Library Association
50 East Huron Street
Chicago, Illinois 60611
Phone: 800-545-2433 Ext. 2432
Fax: 312-280-2433
E-mail: accred@ala.org
Web: www.ala.org/accreditation/

MARRIAGE AND FAMILY THERAPY
Tanya A. Tamarkin, Director of Educational Affairs
Commission on Accreditation for Marriage and Family Therapy Education
American Association for Marriage and Family Therapy
112 South Alfred Street
Alexandria, Virginia 22314-3061
Phone: 703-838-9808
Fax: 703-838-9805
E-mail: coamfte@aamft.org
Web: www.aamft.org

MEDICAL ILLUSTRATION
Commission on Accreditation of Allied Health Education Programs (CAAHEP)
Kathleen Megivern, Executive Director
1361 Park Street
Clearwater, Florida 33756
Phone: 727-210-2350
Fax: 727-210-2354
E-mail: mail@caahep.org
Web: www.caahep.org

MEDICINE
Liaison Committee on Medical Education (LCME)
In odd-numbered years beginning each July 1, contact:
Barbara Barzansky, Ph.D., LCME Secretary
American Medical Association
Council on Medical Education
515 North State Street
Chicago, Illinois 60654
Phone: 312-464-4933
Fax: 312-464-5830
E-mail: cme@aamc.org
Web: www.ama-assn.org

In even-numbered years beginning each July 1, contact:
Dan Hunt, M.D., LCME Secretary
Association of American Medical Colleges
2450 N Street, NW Washington, DC 20037
Phone: 202-828-0596
Fax: 202-828-1125
E-mail: dhunt@aamc.org
Web: www.lcme.org

MUSIC
Samuel Hope, Executive Director
Karen P. Moynahan, Associate Director
National Association of Schools of Music (NASM)
Commission on Accreditation
11250 Roger Bacon Drive, Suite 21
Reston, Virginia 20190-5248
Phone: 703-437-0700
Fax: 703-437-6312
E-mail: info@arts-accredit.org
Web: http://nasm.arts-accredit.org/

NATUROPATHIC MEDICINE
Daniel Seitz, J.D., Ed.D., Executive Director
Council on Naturopathic Medical Education
P.O. Box 178
Great Barrington, Massachusetts 01230
Phone: 413-528-8877
Fax: 413-528-8880
E-mail: council@cnme.org
Web: www.cnme.org

NURSE ANESTHESIA
Francis R. Gerbasi, Executive Director
Council on Accreditation of Nurse Anesthesia Educational Programs
American Association of Nurse Anesthetists
222 South Prospect Avenue, Suite 304
Park Ridge, Illinois 60068
Phone: 847-692-7050 Ext. 1154
Fax: 847-692-6968
E-mail: fgerbasi@aana.com
Web: http://home.coa.us.com

NURSE EDUCATION
Jennifer L. Butlin, Director
Commission on Collegiate Nursing Education (CCNE)
One Dupont Circle, NW, Suite 530
Washington, DC 20036-1120
Phone: 202-887-6791
Fax: 202-887-8476
E-mail: jbutlin@aacn.nche.edu
Web: www.aacn.nche.edu/accreditation

NURSE MIDWIFERY
Lorrie Kaplan, Executive Director
Accreditation Commission for Midwifery Education
American College of Nurse-Midwives
Nurse-Midwifery Program
8403 Colesville Road, Suite 1550
Silver Spring, Maryland 20910
Phone: 240-485-1800
Fax: 240-485-1818
E-mail: lkaplan@acnm.org
Web: www.midwife.org/acme.cfm

Jo Anne Myers-Ciecko, MPH, Executive Director
Midwifery Education Accreditation Council
P.O. Box 984
La Conner, Washington 98257
Phone: 360-466-2080
Fax: 480-907-2936
E-mail: info@meacschools.org
Web: www.meacschools.org

NURSE PRACTITIONER
Gay Johnson, Acting CEO
National Association of Nurse Practitioners in Women's Health
Council on Accreditation
505 C Street, NE Washington, DC 20002
Phone: 202-543-9693 Ext. 1
Fax: 202-543-9858
E-mail: info@npwh.org
Web: www.npwh.org

NURSING
Sharon J. Tanner, Ed.D., RN, Executive Director
National League for Nursing Accrediting Commission (NLNAC)
3343 Peachtree Road, NE, Suite 500
Atlanta, Georgia 30326
Phone: 404-975-5000
Fax: 404-975-5020
E-mail: nlnac@nlnac.org
Web: www.nlnac.org

OCCUPATIONAL THERAPY
Neil Harvison, Ph.D., OTR/L
Director of Accreditation and Academic Affairs
The American Occupational Therapy Association
4720 Montgomery Lane
P.O. Box 31220
Bethesda, Maryland 20824-1220
Phone: 301-652-2682 Ext. 2912
Fax: 301-652-7711
E-mail: accred@aota.org
Web: www.aota.org

OPTOMETRY
Joyce L. Urbeck, Administrative Director
Accreditation Council on Optometric Education
American Optometric Association (AOA)
243 North Lindbergh Boulevard
St. Louis, Missouri 63141
Phone: 314-991-4000 Ext. 246
Fax: 314-991-4101
E-mail: acoe@aoa.org
Web: www.theacoe.org

OSTEOPATHIC MEDICINE
Konrad C. Miskowicz-Retz, Ph.D., CAE
Director, Department of Education
Commission on Osteopathic College Accreditation
American Osteopathic Association
142 East Ontario Street
Chicago, Illinois 60611
Phone: 312-202-8048
Fax: 312-202-8202
E-mail: kretz@osteopathic.org
Web: www.osteopathic.org

PHARMACY
Peter H. Vlasses, Executive Director
Accreditation Council for Pharmacy Education
20 North Clark Street, Suite 2500
Chicago, Illinois 60602-5109
Phone: 312-664-3575
Fax: 312-664-4652
E-mail: csinfo@acpe-accredit.org
Web: www.acpe-accredit.org

PHYSICAL THERAPY
Mary Jane Harris, Director
Commission on Accreditation in Physical Therapy Education (CAPTE)
American Physical Therapy Association (APTA)
1111 North Fairfax Street
Alexandria, Virginia 22314
Phone: 703-706-3245
Fax: 703-706-3387
E-mail: accreditation@apta.org
Web: www.capteonline.org

PHYSICIAN ASSISTANT STUDIES
John E. McCarty, Executive Director
Accreditation Review Commission on Education for the Physician
    Assistant, Inc. (ARC-PA)
12000 Findley Road, Suite 150
Johns Creek, Georgia 30097
Phone: 770-476-1224
Fax: 770-476-1738
E-mail: arc-pa@arc-pa.org
Web: www.arc-pa.org

PLANNING
Shonagh Merits, Executive Director
American Institute of Certified Planners/Association of Collegiate
    Schools of Planning/American Planning Association
Planning Accreditation Board (PAB)
53 W. Jackson Boulevard, Suite 1315
Chicago, Illinois 60604
Phone: 312-334-1271
Fax: 312-334-1273
E-mail: smerits@planningaccreditationboard.org
Web: www.planningaccreditationboard.org

PODIATRIC MEDICINE
Alan R. Tinkleman, Executive Director
Council on Podiatric Medical Education (CPME)
American Podiatric Medical Association
9312 Old Georgetown Road
Bethesda, Maryland 20814-1621
Phone: 301-571-9200
Fax: 301-571-4903
E-mail: artinkleman@apma.org
Web: www.cpme.org

PSYCHOLOGY AND COUNSELING
Susan Zlotlow, Executive Director
Office of Program Consultation and Accreditation
American Psychological Association
750 First Street, NE Washington, DC 20002-4242
Phone: 202-336-5979
Fax: 202-336-5978
E-mail: apaaccred@apa.org
Web: www.apa.org/ed/accreditation

Carol L. Bobby, Executive Director
Council for Accreditation of Counseling and Related Educational
    Programs (CACREP)
1001 North Fairfax Street, Suite 510
Alexandria, Virginia 22314
Phone: 703-535-5990
Fax: 703-739-6209
E-mail: cacrep@cacrep.org
Web: www.cacrep.org

PUBLIC AFFAIRS AND ADMINISTRATION
Crystal Calarusse, Executive Director
Commission on Peer Review and Accreditation
National Association of Schools of Public Affairs and Administration
1029 Vermont Avenue, NW, Suite 1100
Washington, DC 20005
Phone: 202-628-8965
Fax: 202-626-4978
E-mail: copra@naspaa.org
Web: www.naspaa.org

PUBLIC HEALTH
Laura Rasar King, M.P.H., CHES, Executive Director
Council on Education for Public Health
800 Eye Street, NW, Suite 202
Washington, DC 20001-3710
Phone: 202-789-1050
Fax: 202-789-1895
E-mail: Lking@ceph.org
Web: www.ceph.org

REHABILITATION EDUCATION
Dr. Tom Evenson, Executive Director
Council on Rehabilitation Education (CORE)
Commission on Standards and Accreditation
1699 Woodfield Road, Suite 300
Schaumburg, Illinois 60173
Phone: 847-944-1345
Fax: 847-944-1324
E-mail: evenson@unt.edu
Web: www.core-rehab.org

SOCIAL WORK
Stephen M. Holloway, Director of Accreditation
Commission on Accreditation
Council on Social Work Education
1701 Duke Street, Suite 200
Alexandria, Virginia 22314
Phone: 703-683-8080
Fax: 703-683-8099
E-mail: sholloway@cswe.org
Web: www.cswe.org

SPEECH-LANGUAGE PATHOLOGY AND AUDIOLOGY
Patrima L. Tice, Director of Credentialing
American Speech-Language-Hearing Association
Council on Academic Accreditation in Audiology and SpeechLanguage
    Pathology
2200 Research Boulevard
Rockville, Maryland 20850-3289
Phone: 301-296-5796
Fax: 301-296-8750
E-mail: ptice@asha.org
Web: www.asha.org/academic/accreditation/default.htm

TECHNOLOGY
Michale S. McComis, Ed.D., Executive Director
Accrediting Commission of Career Schools and Colleges
2101 Wilson Boulevard, Suite 302
Arlington, Virginia 22201
Phone: 703-247-4212
Fax: 703-247-4533
E-mail: mccomis@accsc.org
Web: www.accsc.org

TEACHER EDUCATION
James G. Cibulka, President
National Council for Accreditation of Teacher Education
2010 Massachusetts Avenue, NW, Suite 500
Washington, DC 20036-1023
Phone: 202-466-7496
Fax: 202-296-6620
E-mail: ncate@ncate.org
Web: www.ncate.org

Mark LaCelle-Peterson, President
Teacher Education Accreditation Council (TEAC)
Accreditation Committee
One Dupont Circle, Suite 320
Washington, DC 20036-0110
Phone: 202-831-0400
Fax: 202-831-3013
E-mail: teac@teac.org
Web: www.teac.org

THEATER
Samuel Hope, Executive Director
Karen P. Moynahan, Associate Director
National Association of Schools of Theatre Commission on
    Accreditation
11250 Roger Bacon Drive, Suite 21
Reston, Virginia 20190
Phone: 703-437-0700
Fax: 703-437-6312
E-mail: info@arts-accredit.org
Web: http://nast.arts-accredit.org/

THEOLOGY
Bernard Fryshman, Executive Vice President
Association of Advanced Rabbinical and Talmudic Schools (AARTS)
Accreditation Commission
11 Broadway, Suite 405
New York, New York 10004
Phone: 212-363-1991
Fax: 212-533-5335
E-mail: BFryshman@nyit.edu

Daniel O. Aleshire, Executive Director
Association of Theological Schools in the United States and Canada
   (ATS)
Commission on Accrediting
10 Summit Park Drive
Pittsburgh, Pennsylvania 15275-1110
Phone: 412-788-6505
Fax: 412-788-6510
E-mail: ats@ats.edu
Web: www.ats.edu

Paul Boatner, President
Transnational Association of Christian Colleges and Schools (TRACS)
Accreditation Commission
15935 Forest Road
Forest, Virginia 24551
Phone: 434-525-9539
Fax: 434-525-9538
E-mail: info@tracs.org
Web: www.tracs.org

VETERINARY MEDICINE
Dave Granstrom, Executive Director
Education and Research Division
American Veterinary Medical Association (AVMA)
Council on Education
1931 North Meacham Road, Suite 100
Schaumburg, Illinois 60173
Phone: 847-925-8070 Ext. 6674
Fax: 847-925-9329
E-mail: info@avma.org
Web: www.avma.org

How to Use These Guides

As you identify the particular programs and institutions that interest you, you can use both the *Graduate & Professional Programs: An Overview* volume and the specialized volumes in the series to obtain detailed information.

- *Graduate Programs in the Physical Sciences, Mathematics, Agricultural Sciences, the Environment & Natural Resources*
- *Graduate Programs in Engineering & Applied Sciences*
- *Graduate Programs the Humanities, Arts & Social Sciences*
- *Graduate Programs in the Biological/Biomedical Sciences & Health-Related Professions*
- *Graduate Programs in Business, Education, Information Studies, Law & Social Work*

Each of the specialized volumes in the series is divided into sections that contain one or more directories devoted to programs in a particular field. If you do not find a directory devoted to your field of interest in a specific volume, consult "Directories and Subject Areas" (located at the end of each volume). After you have identified the correct volume, consult the "Directories and Subject Areas in This Book" index, which shows (as does the more general directory) what directories cover subjects not specifically named in a directory or section title.

Each of the specialized volumes in the series has a number of general directories. These directories have entries for the largest unit at an institution granting graduate degrees in that field. For example, the general Engineering and Applied Sciences directory in the *Graduate Programs in Engineering & Applied Sciences* volume consists of **Profiles** for colleges, schools, and departments of engineering and applied sciences.

General directories are followed by other directories, or sections, that give more detailed information about programs in particular areas of the general field that has been covered. The general Engineering and Applied Sciences directory, in the previous example, is followed by nineteen sections with directories in specific areas of engineering, such as Chemical Engineering, Industrial/Management Engineering, and Mechanical Engineering.

Because of the broad nature of many fields, any system of organization is bound to involve a certain amount of overlap. Environmental studies, for example, is a field whose various aspects are studied in several types of departments and schools. Readers interested in such studies will find information on relevant programs in the *Graduate Programs in the Biological/Biomedical Sciences & Health-Related Professions* volume under Ecology and Environmental Biology and Environmental and Occupational Health; in the *Graduate Programs in the Physical Sciences, Mathematics, Agricultural Sciences, the Environment & Natural Resources* volume under Environmental Management and Policy and Natural Resources; and in the *Graduate Programs in Engineering & Applied Sciences* volume under Energy Management and Policy and Environmental Engineering. To help you find all of the programs of interest to you, the introduction to each section within the specialized volumes includes, if applicable, a paragraph suggesting other sections and directories with information on related areas of study.

Directory of Institutions with Programs in Engineering & Applied Sciences

This directory lists institutions in alphabetical order and includes beneath each name the academic fields in which each institution offers graduate programs. The degree level in each field is also indicated, provided that the institution has supplied that information in response to Peterson's Annual Survey of Graduate and Professional Institutions.

An M indicates that a master's degree program is offered; a D indicates that a doctoral degree program is offered; a P indicates that the first professional degree is offered; an O signifies that other advanced

degrees (e.g., certificates or specialist degrees) are offered; and an * (asterisk) indicates that a **Close-Up** and/or **Display** is located in this volume. See the index, "Close-Ups and Displays," for the specific page number.

Profiles of Academic and Professional Programs in the Specialized Volumes

Each section of **Profiles** has a table of contents that lists the Program Directories, **Displays**, and **Close-Ups**. Program Directories consist of the **Profiles** of programs in the relevant fields, with **Displays** following if programs have chosen to include them. **Close-Ups,** which are more individualized statements, again if programs have chosen to submit them, are also listed.

The **Profiles** found in the 500 directories in the specialized volumes provide basic data about the graduate units in capsule form for quick reference. To make these directories as useful as possible, **Profiles** are generally listed for an institution's smallest academic unit within a subject area. In other words, if an institution has a College of Liberal Arts that administers many related programs, the **Profile** for the individual program (e.g., Program in History), not the entire College, appears in the directory.

There are some programs that do not fit into any current directory and are not given individual **Profiles**. The directory structure is reviewed annually in order to keep this number to a minimum and to accommodate major trends in graduate education.

The following outline describes the **Profile** information found in the guides and explains how best to use that information. Any item that does not apply to or was not provided by a graduate unit is omitted from its listing. The format of the **Profiles** is constant, making it easy to compare one institution with another and one program with another.

Identifying Information. The institution's name, in boldface type, is followed by a complete listing of the administrative structure for that field of study. (For example, University of Akron, Buchtel College of Arts and Sciences, Department of Theoretical and Applied Mathematics, Program in Mathematics.) The last unit listed is the one to which all information in the **Profile** pertains. The institution's city, state, and zip code follow.

Offerings. Each field of study offered by the unit is listed with all postbaccalaureate degrees awarded. Degrees that are not preceded by a specific concentration are awarded in the general field listed in the unit name. Frequently, fields of study are broken down into subspecializations, and those appear following the degrees awarded; for example, "Offerings in secondary education (M.Ed.), including English education, mathematics education, science education." Students enrolled in the M.Ed. program would be able to specialize in any of the three fields mentioned.

Professional Accreditation. Some **Profiles** indicate whether a program is professionally accredited. Because it is possible for a program to receive or lose professional accreditation at any time, students entering fields in which accreditation is important to a career should verify the status of programs by contacting either the chairperson or the appropriate accrediting association.

Jointly Offered Degrees. Explanatory statements concerning programs that are offered in cooperation with other institutions are included in the list of degrees offered. This occurs most commonly on a regional basis (for example, two state universities offering a cooperative Ph.D. in special education) or where the specialized nature of the institutions encourages joint efforts (a J.D./M.B.A. offered by a law school at an institution with no formal business programs and an institution with a business school but lacking a law school). Only programs that are truly cooperative are listed; those involving only limited course work at another institution are not. Interested students should contact the heads of such units for further information.

Part-Time and Evening/Weekend Programs. When information regarding the availability of part-time or evening/weekend study appears in the **Profile**, it means that students are able to earn a degree exclusively through such study.

Postbaccalaureate Distance Learning Degrees. A post-baccalaureate distance learning degree program signifies that course requirements can be fulfilled with minimal or no on-campus study.

Faculty. Figures on the number of faculty members actively involved with graduate students through teaching or research are separated into full- and part-time as well as men and women whenever the information has been supplied.

Students. Figures for the number of students enrolled in graduate and professional programs pertain to the semester of highest enrollment from the 2011–12 academic year. These figures are broken down into full- and part-time and men and women whenever the data have been supplied. Information on the number of matriculated students enrolled in the unit who are members of a minority group or are international students appears here. The average age of the matriculated students is followed by the number of applicants, the percentage accepted, and the number enrolled for fall 2011.

Degrees Awarded. The number of degrees awarded in the calendar year is listed. Many doctoral programs offer a terminal master's degree if students leave the program after completing only part of the requirements for a doctoral degree; that is indicated here. All degrees are classified into one of four types: master's, doctoral, first professional, and other advanced degrees. A unit may award one or several degrees at a given level; however, the data are only collected by type and may therefore represent several different degree programs.

Degree Requirements. The information in this section is also broken down by type of degree, and all information for a degree level pertains to all degrees of that type unless otherwise specified. Degree requirements are collected in a simplified form to provide some very basic information on the nature of the program and on foreign language, thesis or dissertation, comprehensive exam, and registration requirements. Many units also provide a short list of additional requirements, such as fieldwork or an internship. For complete information on graduation requirements, contact the graduate school or program directly.

Entrance Requirements. Entrance requirements are broken down into the four degree levels of master's, doctoral, first professional, and other advanced degrees. Within each level, information may be provided in two basic categories: entrance exams and other requirements. The entrance exams are identified by the standard acronyms used by the testing agencies, unless they are not well known. Other entrance requirements are quite varied, but they often contain an undergraduate or graduate grade point average (GPA). Unless otherwise stated, the GPA is calculated on a 4.0 scale and is listed as a minimum required for admission. Additional exam requirements/recommendations for international students may be listed here. Application deadlines for domestic and international students, the application fee, and whether electronic applications are accepted may be listed here. Note that the deadline should be used for reference only; these dates are subject to change, and students interested in applying should always contact the graduate unit directly about application procedures and deadlines.

Expenses. The typical cost of study for the 2011–12 academic year is given in two basic categories: tuition and fees. Cost of study may be quite complex at a graduate institution. There are often sliding scales for part-time study, a different cost for first-year students, and other variables that make it impossible to completely cover the cost of study for each graduate program. To provide the most usable information, figures are given for full-time study for a full year where available and for part-time study in terms of a per-unit rate (per credit, per semester hour, etc.). Occasionally, variances may be noted in tuition and fees for reasons such as the type of program, whether courses are taken during the day or evening, whether courses are at the master's or doctoral level, or other institution-specific reasons. Expenses are usually subject to change; for exact costs at any given time, contact your chosen schools and programs directly. Keep in mind that the tuition of Canadian institutions is usually given in Canadian dollars.

Financial Support. This section contains data on the number of awards administered by the institution and given to graduate students during the 2011–12 academic year. The first figure given represents the total number of students receiving financial support enrolled in that unit. If the unit has provided information on graduate appointments, these are broken down into three major categories: fellowships give money to graduate students to cover the cost of study and living expenses and are not based on a work obligation or research commitment, research assistantships provide stipends to graduate students for assistance in a formal research project with a faculty member, and teaching assistantships provide stipends to graduate students for teaching or for assisting faculty members in teaching undergraduate classes. Within each category, figures are given for the total number of awards, the average yearly amount per award, and whether full or partial tuition reimbursements are awarded. In addition to graduate appointments, the availability of several other financial aid sources is covered in this section. Tuition waivers are routinely part of a graduate appointment, but units sometimes waive part or all of a student's tuition even if a graduate appointment is not available. Federal WorkStudy is made available to students who demonstrate need and meet the federal guidelines; this form of aid normally includes 10 or more hours of work per week in an office of the institution. Institutionally sponsored loans are low-interest loans available to graduate students to cover both educational and living expenses. Career-related internships or fieldwork offer money to students who are participating in a formal off-campus research project or practicum. Grants, scholarships, traineeships, unspecified assistantships, and other awards may also be noted. The availability of financial support to part-time students is also indicated here.

Some programs list the financial aid application deadline and the forms that need to be completed for students to be eligible for financial awards. There are two forms: FAFSA, the Free Application for Federal Student Aid, which is required for federal aid, and the CSS PROFILE®.

Faculty Research. Each unit has the opportunity to list several keyword phrases describing the current research involving faculty members and graduate students. Space limitations prevent the unit from listing complete information on all research programs. The total expenditure for funded research from the previous academic year may also be included.

Unit Head and Application Contact. The head of the graduate program for each unit is listed with academic title and telephone and fax numbers and e-mail address if available. In addition to the unit head, many graduate programs list a separate contact for application and admission information, which follows the listing for the unit head. If no unit head or application contact is given, you should contact the overall institution for information on graduate admissions.

Displays and Close-Ups

The **Displays** and **Close-Ups** are supplementary insertions submitted by deans, chairs, and other administrators who wish to offer an additional, more individualized statement to readers. A number of graduate school and program administrators have attached a **Display** ad near the **Profile** listing. Here you will find information that an institution or program wants to emphasize. The **Close-Ups** are by their very nature more expansive and flexible than the **Profiles**, and the administrators who have written them may emphasize different aspects of their programs. All of the **Close-Ups** are organized in the same way (with the exception of a few that describe research and training opportunities instead of degree programs), and in each one you will find information on the same basic topics, such as programs of study, research facilities, tuition and fees, financial aid, and application procedures. If an institution or program has submitted a **Close-Up**, a boldface cross-reference appears below its **Profile**. As with the **Displays**, all of the **Close-Ups** in the guides have been submitted by choice; the absence of a **Display** or **Close-Up** does not reflect any type of editorial judgment on the part of Peterson's, and their presence in the guides should not be taken as an indication of status, quality, or approval. Statements regarding a university's objectives and accomplishments are a reflection of its own beliefs and are not the opinions of the Peterson's editors.

Appendixes

This section contains two appendixes. The first, "Institutional Changes Since the 2012 Edition," lists institutions that have closed, merged, or changed their name or status since the last edition of the guides. The second, "Abbreviations Used in the Guides," gives abbreviations of degree names, along with what those abbreviations stand for. These appendixes are identical in all six volumes of *Peterson's Graduate and Professional Programs*.

Indexes

There are three indexes presented here. The first index, "Close-Ups and Displays," gives page references for all programs that have chosen to place **Close-Ups** and **Displays** in this volume. It is arranged alphabetically by institution; within institutions, the arrangement is alphabetical by subject area. It is not an index to all programs in the book's directories of **Profiles**; readers must refer to the directories themselves for **Profile** information on programs that have not submitted the additional, more individualized statements. The second index, "Directories and Subject Areas in Other Books in This Series", gives book references for the directories in the specialized volumes and also includes cross-references for subject area names not used in the directory structure, for example, "Computing Technology (see Computer Science)." The third index, "Directories and Subject Areas in This Book," gives page references for the directories in this volume and cross-references for subject area names not used in this volume's directory structure.

Data Collection Procedures

The information published in the directories and **Profiles** of all the books is collected through Peterson's Annual Survey of Graduate and Professional Institutions. The survey is sent each spring to nearly 2,400 institutions offering postbaccalaureate degree programs, including accredited institutions in the United States, U.S. territories, and Canada and those institutions outside the United States that are accredited by U.S. accrediting bodies. Deans and other administrators complete these surveys, providing information on programs in the 500 academic and professional fields covered in the guides as well as overall institutional information. While every effort has been made to ensure the accuracy and completeness of the data, information is sometimes unavailable or changes occur after publication deadlines. All usable information received in time for publication has been included. The omission of any particular item from a directory or **Profile** signifies either that the item is not applicable to the institution or program or that information was not available. **Profiles** of programs scheduled to begin during the 2012–13 academic year cannot, obviously, include statistics on enrollment or, in many cases, the number of faculty members. If no usable data were submitted by an institution, its name, address, and program name appear in order to indicate the availability of graduate work.

Criteria for Inclusion in This Guide

To be included in this guide, an institution must have full accreditation or be a candidate for accreditation (preaccreditation) status by an institutional or specialized accrediting body recognized by the U.S. Department of Education or the Council for Higher Education Accreditation (CHEA). Institutional accrediting bodies, which review each institution as a whole, include the six regional associations of schools and colleges (Middle States, New England, North Central, Northwest, Southern, and Western), each of which is responsible for a specified portion of the United States and its territories. Other institutional accrediting bodies are national in scope and accredit specific kinds of institutions (e.g., Bible colleges, independent colleges, and rabbinical and Talmudic schools). Program registration by the New York State Board of Regents is considered to be the equivalent of institutional accreditation, since the board requires that all programs offered by an institution meet its standards before recognition is granted. A Canadian institution must be chartered and authorized to grant degrees by the provincial government, affiliated with a chartered institution, or accredited by a recognized U.S. accrediting body. This guide also includes institutions outside the United States that are accredited by these U.S. accrediting bodies. There are recognized specialized or professional accrediting bodies in more than fifty different fields, each of which is authorized to accredit institutions or specific programs in its particular field. For specialized institutions that offer programs in one field only, we designate this to be the equivalent of institutional accreditation. A full explanation of the accrediting process and complete information on recognized institutional (regional and national) and specialized accrediting bodies can be found online at www.chea.org or at www.ed.gov/admins/finaid/accred/index.html.

DIRECTORY OF INSTITUTIONS WITH PROGRAMS IN ENGINEERING & APPLIED SCIENCES

ACADEMY OF ART UNIVERSITY
Game Design and Development — M
Modeling and Simulation — M

ACADIA UNIVERSITY
Computer Science — M

AIR FORCE INSTITUTE OF TECHNOLOGY
Aerospace/Aeronautical Engineering — M,D
Computer Engineering — M,D
Computer Science — M,D
Electrical Engineering — M,D
Engineering and Applied
   Sciences—General — M,D
Engineering Management — M
Engineering Physics — M,D
Environmental Engineering — M
Management of Technology — M,D
Materials Sciences — M,D
Nuclear Engineering — M,D
Operations Research — M
Systems Engineering — M,D

ALABAMA AGRICULTURAL AND MECHANICAL UNIVERSITY
Computer Science — M
Engineering and Applied
   Sciences—General — M
Materials Sciences — M,D

ALASKA PACIFIC UNIVERSITY
Telecommunications Management — M

ALBANY COLLEGE OF PHARMACY AND HEALTH SCIENCES
Biotechnology — M

ALCORN STATE UNIVERSITY
Computer Science — M
Information Science — M

ALFRED UNIVERSITY
Bioengineering — M,D
Ceramic Sciences and Engineering — M,D
Electrical Engineering — M,D
Engineering and Applied
   Sciences—General — M,D
Materials Sciences — M,D
Mechanical Engineering — M,D

AMERICAN INTERCONTINENTAL UNIVERSITY ATLANTA
Information Science — M

AMERICAN INTERCONTINENTAL UNIVERSITY ONLINE
Computer and Information
   Systems Security — M
Information Science — M

AMERICAN INTERCONTINENTAL UNIVERSITY SOUTH FLORIDA
Computer and Information
   Systems Security — M
Information Science — M

AMERICAN PUBLIC UNIVERSITY SYSTEM
Aerospace/Aeronautical Engineering — M
Computer and Information
   Systems Security — M
Software Engineering — M

AMERICAN SENTINEL UNIVERSITY
Computer Science — M
Health Informatics — M

AMERICAN UNIVERSITY
Applied Science and Technology — M,O
Biotechnology — M
Computer Science — M,O

THE AMERICAN UNIVERSITY IN CAIRO
Computer Science — M,O.
Construction Engineering — M
Engineering and Applied
   Sciences—General — M,D,O
Mechanical Engineering — M

THE AMERICAN UNIVERSITY IN DUBAI
Construction Management — M

THE AMERICAN UNIVERSITY OF ATHENS
Computer Science — M
Engineering and Applied
   Sciences—General — M
Systems Engineering — M
Telecommunications — M

AMERICAN UNIVERSITY OF BEIRUT
Civil Engineering — M,D
Computer Engineering — M,D
Computer Science — M
Electrical Engineering — M,D
Engineering and Applied
   Sciences—General — M,D
Engineering Management — M,D
Mechanical Engineering — M,D
Water Resources Engineering — M,D

AMERICAN UNIVERSITY OF SHARJAH
Chemical Engineering — M
Civil Engineering — M
Computer Engineering — M
Electrical Engineering — M
Mechanical Engineering — M

ANDREWS UNIVERSITY
Engineering and Applied
   Sciences—General — M
Software Engineering — M

ANNA MARIA COLLEGE
Fire Protection Engineering — M

APPALACHIAN STATE UNIVERSITY
Computer Science — M
Energy and Power Engineering — M
Engineering Physics — M

ARIZONA STATE UNIVERSITY
Aerospace/Aeronautical Engineering — M,D
Bioinformatics — M,D
Biomedical Engineering — M,D
Biotechnology — M,D
Chemical Engineering — M,D
Civil Engineering — M,D
Computer Science — M,D
Construction Engineering — M,D
Construction Management — M,D
Electrical Engineering — M,D,O
Engineering and Applied
   Sciences—General — M,D,O
Environmental Engineering — M,D
Ergonomics and Human Factors — M
Geological Engineering — M,D
Industrial/Management Engineering — M,D
Information Science — M
Management of Technology — M
Manufacturing Engineering — M
Materials Engineering — M,D
Materials Sciences — M,D
Mechanical Engineering — M,D
Medical Informatics — M,D
Modeling and Simulation — M,D
Nanotechnology — M,D
Nuclear Engineering — M,D,O
Reliability Engineering — M
Software Engineering — M
Systems Engineering — M
Systems Science — M
Technology and Public Policy — M
Transportation and Highway
   Engineering — M,D,O

ARKANSAS STATE UNIVERSITY
Biotechnology — M,O
Computer Science — M
Engineering and Applied
   Sciences—General — M
Engineering Management — M

ARKANSAS TECH UNIVERSITY
Engineering and Applied
   Sciences—General — M
Health Informatics — M
Information Science — M

ARMSTRONG ATLANTIC STATE UNIVERSITY
Computer Science — M

ASPEN UNIVERSITY
Information Science — M,O

ATHABASCA UNIVERSITY
Information Science — M
Management of Technology — M,O

AUBURN UNIVERSITY
Aerospace/Aeronautical Engineering — M,D
Biosystems Engineering — M,D
Chemical Engineering — M,D
Civil Engineering — M,D
Computer Engineering — M,D
Computer Science — M,D
Construction Engineering — M,D
Construction Management — M
Electrical Engineering — M,D
Engineering and Applied
   Sciences—General — M,D,O
Environmental Engineering — M,D
Geotechnical Engineering — M,D
Hydraulics — M,D
Industrial/Management Engineering — M,D,O
Materials Engineering — M,D
Mechanical Engineering — M,D
Polymer Science and Engineering — M,D
Software Engineering — M,D
Structural Engineering — M,D
Systems Engineering — M,D,O
Textile Sciences and Engineering — D
Transportation and Highway
   Engineering — M,D

BALL STATE UNIVERSITY
Computer Science — M
Information Science — M
Telecommunications — M

BARRY UNIVERSITY
Health Informatics — O
Information Science — M

BAYLOR COLLEGE OF MEDICINE
Bioengineering — D
Biomedical Engineering — D

BAYLOR UNIVERSITY
Biomedical Engineering — M,D
Computer Engineering — M,D
Computer Science — M
Electrical Engineering — M,D
Engineering and Applied
   Sciences—General — M,D
Mechanical Engineering — M,D

BELLEVUE UNIVERSITY
Information Science — M

BENEDICTINE UNIVERSITY
Computer and Information
   Systems Security — M
Health Informatics — M

BENTLEY UNIVERSITY
Ergonomics and Human Factors — M
Information Science — M

BOISE STATE UNIVERSITY
Civil Engineering — M
Computer Engineering — M,D
Computer Science — M
Electrical Engineering — M,D
Engineering and Applied
   Sciences—General — M,D
Materials Engineering — M
Mechanical Engineering — M

BOSTON UNIVERSITY
Bioinformatics — M,D
Biomedical Engineering — M,D
Computer and Information
   Systems Security — M
Computer Engincoring — M
Computer Science — M,D
Database Systems — M
Electrical Engineering — M,D
Engineering and Applied
   Sciences—General — M,D
Health Informatics — M
Management of Technology — M
Manufacturing Engineering — M,D
Materials Engineering — M,D
Materials Sciences — M,D
Mechanical Engineering — M,D
Systems Engineering — M,D
Telecommunications Management — M
Telecommunications — M

BOWIE STATE UNIVERSITY
Computer Science — M,D

BOWLING GREEN STATE UNIVERSITY
Computer Science — M
Construction Management — M
Manufacturing Engineering — M
Operations Research — M
Software Engineering — M

BRADLEY UNIVERSITY
Civil Engineering — M
Computer Science — M
Construction Engineering — M
Electrical Engineering — M
Engineering and Applied
   Sciences—General — M
Industrial/Management Engineering — M
Information Science — M
Manufacturing Engineering — M
Mechanical Engineering — M

BRANDEIS UNIVERSITY
Bioinformatics — M
Biotechnology — M
Computer and Information
   Systems Security — M
Computer Science — M,D,O
Health Informatics — M
Software Engineering — M

BRIDGEWATER STATE UNIVERSITY
Computer Science — M

BRIGHAM YOUNG UNIVERSITY
Biotechnology — M,D
Chemical Engineering — M,D
Civil Engineering — M,D
Computer Engineering — M,D
Computer Science — M,D
Construction Management — M
Electrical Engineering — M,D
Engineering and Applied
   Sciences—General — M,D
Information Science — M
Mechanical Engineering — M,D

BROCK UNIVERSITY
Biotechnology — M,D
Computer Science — M

BROOKLYN COLLEGE OF THE CITY UNIVERSITY OF NEW YORK
Computer Science — M,D,O
Information Science — M,D,O

BROWN UNIVERSITY
Biomedical Engineering — M,D
Biotechnology — M,D
Chemical Engineering — M,D
Computer Engineering — M,D
Computer Science — M,D
Electrical Engineering — M,D
Engineering and Applied
   Sciences—General — M,D
Materials Sciences — M,D
Mechanical Engineering — M,D
Mechanics — M,D

BUCKNELL UNIVERSITY
Chemical Engineering — M
Civil Engineering — M
Electrical Engineering — M
Engineering and Applied
   Sciences—General — M
Mechanical Engineering — M

BUFFALO STATE COLLEGE, STATE UNIVERSITY OF NEW YORK
Industrial/Management Engineering — M

CALIFORNIA INSTITUTE OF TECHNOLOGY
Aerospace/Aeronautical Engineering — M,D,O
Bioengineering — M,D
Chemical Engineering — M,D
Civil Engineering — M,D,O
Computer Science — M,D
Electrical Engineering — M,D,O
Engineering and Applied
   Sciences—General — M,D,O
Environmental Engineering — M,D
Materials Sciences — M,D
Mechanical Engineering — M,D,O
Mechanics — M,D
Systems Engineering — M,D

CALIFORNIA LUTHERAN UNIVERSITY
Management of Technology — M,O

CALIFORNIA MARITIME ACADEMY
Engineering Management — M

CALIFORNIA MIRAMAR UNIVERSITY
Telecommunications Management — M
Telecommunications — M

CALIFORNIA NATIONAL UNIVERSITY FOR ADVANCED STUDIES
Engineering and Applied
   Sciences—General — M
Engineering Management — M

CALIFORNIA POLYTECHNIC STATE UNIVERSITY, SAN LUIS OBISPO
Aerospace/Aeronautical Engineering — M
Civil Engineering — M
Computer Science — M
Electrical Engineering — M
Engineering and Applied
   Sciences—General — M
Environmental Engineering — M
Industrial/Management Engineering — M
Mechanical Engineering — M
Polymer Science and Engineering — M

CALIFORNIA STATE POLYTECHNIC UNIVERSITY, POMONA
Aerospace/Aeronautical Engineering — M
Biotechnology — M
Civil Engineering — M
Computer Science — M
Electrical Engineering — M
Engineering Management — M
Mechanical Engineering — M

CALIFORNIA STATE UNIVERSITY CHANNEL ISLANDS
Bioinformatics — M
Biotechnology — M
Computer Science — M

CALIFORNIA STATE UNIVERSITY, CHICO
Computer Engineering — M
Computer Science — M
Electrical Engineering — M
Engineering and Applied
   Sciences—General — M

CALIFORNIA STATE UNIVERSITY, DOMINGUEZ HILLS
Bioinformatics — M
Computer Science — M

CALIFORNIA STATE UNIVERSITY, EAST BAY
Computer Science — M
Construction Management — M
Engineering and Applied
   Sciences—General — M
Engineering Management — M

CALIFORNIA STATE UNIVERSITY, FRESNO
Civil Engineering — M
Computer Science — M
Electrical Engineering — M
Engineering and Applied
   Sciences—General — M
Industrial/Management Engineering — M
Mechanical Engineering — M

CALIFORNIA STATE UNIVERSITY, FULLERTON
Civil Engineering — M
Computer Science — M
Electrical Engineering — M
Engineering and Applied
   Sciences—General — M
Information Science — M
Mechanical Engineering — M
Mechanics — M
Software Engineering — M
Systems Engineering — M

CALIFORNIA STATE UNIVERSITY, LONG BEACH
Aerospace/Aeronautical Engineering — M
Chemical Engineering — M
Civil Engineering — M
Computer Engineering — M
Computer Science — M
Electrical Engineering — M
Engineering Management — M,D
Ergonomics and Human Factors — M
Mechanical Engineering — M,D

CALIFORNIA STATE UNIVERSITY, LOS ANGELES
Civil Engineering — M
Computer Science — M
Electrical Engineering — M
Engineering and Applied
   Sciences—General — M
Management of Technology — M
Mechanical Engineering — M

CALIFORNIA STATE UNIVERSITY, NORTHRIDGE
Artificial Intelligence/Robotics — M
Civil Engineering — M
Computer Science — M
Electrical Engineering — M
Engineering and Applied
   Sciences—General — M
Engineering Management — M
Ergonomics and Human Factors — M
Industrial/Management Engineering — M
Manufacturing Engineering — M
Materials Engineering — M
Mechanical Engineering — M
Software Engineering — M
Structural Engineering — M
Systems Engineering — M

CALIFORNIA STATE UNIVERSITY, SACRAMENTO
Civil Engineering — M
Computer Science — M
Electrical Engineering — M
Engineering and Applied
   Sciences—General — M

Mechanical Engineering M
Software Engineering M

CALIFORNIA STATE UNIVERSITY, SAN BERNARDINO
Computer and Information Systems Security M
Computer Science M

CALIFORNIA STATE UNIVERSITY, SAN MARCOS
Computer Science M

CAMBRIDGE COLLEGE
Management of Technology M
Medical Informatics M

CAPELLA UNIVERSITY
Computer and Information Systems Security M,D,O
Management of Technology M,D,O

CAPITOL COLLEGE
Computer and Information Systems Security M
Computer Science M
Electrical Engineering M
Information Science M
Telecommunications Management M

CARLETON UNIVERSITY
Aerospace/Aeronautical Engineering M,D
Biomedical Engineering M
Civil Engineering M,D
Computer Science M,D
Electrical Engineering M,D
Engineering and Applied Sciences—General M,D
Environmental Engineering M,D
Information Science M,D
Management of Technology M
Materials Engineering M,D
Mechanical Engineering M,D
Systems Engineering M,D
Systems Science M,D

CARLOW UNIVERSITY
Computer and Information Systems Security M
Management of Technology M

CARNEGIE MELLON UNIVERSITY
Architectural Engineering M,D
Artificial Intelligence/Robotics M,D
Bioengineering M,D
Biomedical Engineering M,D
Biotechnology M,D
Chemical Engineering M,D
Civil Engineering M,D
Computer and Information Systems Security M
Computer Engineering M,D
Computer Science M,D
Construction Management M,D
Electrical Engineering M,D
Environmental Engineering M,D
Human-Computer Interaction M,D
Information Science M,D
Management of Technology M,D
Materials Engineering M,D
Materials Sciences M,D
Mechanical Engineering M,D
Mechanics M,D
Operations Research D
Polymer Science and Engineering M,D
Software Engineering M,D
Systems Engineering M
Technology and Public Policy M,D
Telecommunications Management M

CARROLL UNIVERSITY
Software Engineering M

CASE WESTERN RESERVE UNIVERSITY
Aerospace/Aeronautical Engineering M,D
Biomedical Engineering M,D*
Chemical Engineering M,D
Civil Engineering M,D
Computer Engineering M,D
Computer Science M,D
Electrical Engineering M,D
Engineering and Applied Sciences—General M,D
Engineering Management M
Information Science M,D
Materials Engineering M,D
Materials Sciences M,D
Mechanical Engineering M,D
Operations Research M
Polymer Science and Engineering M,D
Systems Engineering M,D

THE CATHOLIC UNIVERSITY OF AMERICA
Biomedical Engineering M,D
Civil Engineering M,D
Computer Science M,D
Electrical Engineering M,D
Engineering and Applied Sciences—General M,D,O
Engineering Management M,O
Environmental Engineering M,D
Ergonomics and Human Factors M,D
Materials Engineering M
Materials Sciences M
Mechanical Engineering M,D

CENTRAL CONNECTICUT STATE UNIVERSITY
Computer Science M,O
Construction Management M,O
Engineering and Applied Sciences—General M,O
Management of Technology M,O

CENTRAL MICHIGAN UNIVERSITY
Computer Science M
Engineering and Applied Sciences—General M
Materials Sciences D

CENTRAL WASHINGTON UNIVERSITY
Engineering and Applied Sciences—General M
Industrial/Management Engineering M

CHAMPLAIN COLLEGE
Management of Technology M

CHICAGO STATE UNIVERSITY
Computer Science M

CHRISTIAN BROTHERS UNIVERSITY
Engineering and Applied Sciences—General M

CHRISTOPHER NEWPORT UNIVERSITY
Computer Science M

THE CITADEL, THE MILITARY COLLEGE OF SOUTH CAROLINA
Civil Engineering M
Computer Science M
Engineering Management M
Information Science M

CITY COLLEGE OF THE CITY UNIVERSITY OF NEW YORK
Biomedical Engineering M,D
Chemical Engineering M,D
Civil Engineering M,D
Computer Science M,D
Electrical Engineering M,D
Engineering and Applied Sciences—General M,D
Mechanical Engineering M,D

CITY UNIVERSITY OF SEATTLE
Computer and Information Systems Security M,O
Computer Science M,O
Management of Technology M,O

CLAFLIN UNIVERSITY
Biotechnology M

CLAREMONT GRADUATE UNIVERSITY
Financial Engineering M
Health Informatics M,D,O
Information Science M,D,O
Operations Research M,D
Systems Science M,D,O
Telecommunications M,D,O

CLARK ATLANTA UNIVERSITY
Computer Science M
Information Science M

CLARKSON UNIVERSITY
Biotechnology D
Chemical Engineering M,D
Civil Engineering M,D
Computer Engineering M,D
Computer Science M,D
Electrical Engineering M,D
Engineering and Applied Sciences—General M,D*
Engineering Management M
Environmental Engineering M,D
Information Science M
Materials Engineering D
Materials Sciences D
Mechanical Engineering M,D

CLARK UNIVERSITY
Information Science M

CLEMSON UNIVERSITY
Automotive Engineering M,D
Bioengineering M,D
Biosystems Engineering M,D
Chemical Engineering M,D
Civil Engineering M,D
Computer Engineering M,D
Computer Science M,D
Construction Management M
Electrical Engineering M,D
Engineering and Applied Sciences—General M,D
Environmental Engineering M,D
Ergonomics and Human Factors D
Human-Computer Interaction D
Industrial/Management Engineering M,D
Manufacturing Engineering M
Materials Engineering M,D
Materials Sciences M,D
Mechanical Engineering M,D
Operations Research M,D

CLEVELAND STATE UNIVERSITY
Biomedical Engineering D
Chemical Engineering M,D
Civil Engineering M,D
Computer Science M,D
Electrical Engineering M,D
Engineering and Applied Sciences—General M,D
Environmental Engineering M,D
Industrial/Management Engineering M,D
Information Science M,D
Mechanical Engineering M,D
Software Engineering M,D

COLEMAN UNIVERSITY
Information Science M
Management of Technology M

COLLEGE OF CHARLESTON
Computer Science M

THE COLLEGE OF SAINT ROSE
Computer Science M
Information Science M

THE COLLEGE OF ST. SCHOLASTICA
Health Informatics M,O

COLLEGE OF STATEN ISLAND OF THE CITY UNIVERSITY OF NEW YORK
Computer Science M

THE COLLEGE OF WILLIAM AND MARY
Applied Science and Technology M,D
Computer Science M,D
Operations Research M

COLORADO CHRISTIAN UNIVERSITY
Computer and Information Systems Security M

COLORADO SCHOOL OF MINES
Bioengineering M,D
Chemical Engineering M,D
Computer Science M,D
Electronic Materials M,D
Engineering and Applied Sciences—General M,D,O
Engineering Management M,D
Environmental Engineering M,D
Geological Engineering M,D
Management of Technology M,D
Materials Engineering M,D
Materials Sciences M,D
Metallurgical Engineering and Metallurgy M,D
Mineral/Mining Engineering M,D
Nuclear Engineering M,D
Petroleum Engineering M,D
Systems Engineering M,D

COLORADO STATE UNIVERSITY
Biomedical Engineering M,D
Chemical Engineering M,D
Civil Engineering M,D
Computer Science M,D
Construction Management M
Electrical Engineering M,D
Engineering and Applied Sciences—General M,D
Mechanical Engineering M,D

COLORADO STATE UNIVERSITY–PUEBLO
Applied Science and Technology M
Engineering and Applied Sciences—General M
Industrial/Management Engineering M
Systems Engineering M

COLORADO TECHNICAL UNIVERSITY COLORADO SPRINGS
Computer and Information Systems Security M,D
Computer Engineering M
Computer Science M,D
Database Systems M,D
Electrical Engineering M
Management of Technology M,D
Software Engineering M,D
Systems Engineering M

COLORADO TECHNICAL UNIVERSITY DENVER SOUTH
Computer and Information Systems Security M
Computer Engineering M
Computer Science M
Database Systems M
Electrical Engineering M
Management of Technology M
Software Engineering M
Systems Engineering M

COLORADO TECHNICAL UNIVERSITY SIOUX FALLS
Computer and Information Systems Security M
Computer Science M
Management of Technology M
Software Engineering M

COLUMBIA UNIVERSITY
Biomedical Engineering M,D
Chemical Engineering M,D
Civil Engineering M,D,O
Computer Engineering M,D,O
Computer Science M,D,O*
Construction Engineering M,D,O
Construction Management M,D,O
Electrical Engineering M,D,O*
Engineering and Applied Sciences—General M,D,O
Environmental Engineering M,D,O
Financial Engineering M,D,O
Industrial/Management Engineering M,D,O
Management of Technology M
Materials Engineering M,D,O
Materials Sciences M,D,O
Mechanical Engineering M,D,O
Mechanics M,D,O
Medical Informatics M,D,O
Metallurgical Engineering and Metallurgy M,D,O
Mineral/Mining Engineering M,D,O
Operations Research M,D,O

COLUMBUS STATE UNIVERSITY
Computer Science M,O
Modeling and Simulation M,O

CONCORDIA UNIVERSITY (CANADA)
Aerospace/Aeronautical Engineering M
Biotechnology M,D,O
Civil Engineering M,D,O
Computer and Information Systems Security M,O
Computer Engineering M,D
Computer Science M,D,O
Construction Engineering M,D,O
Electrical Engineering M,D
Engineering and Applied Sciences—General M,D,O
Environmental Engineering M,D,O
Game Design and Development M,O
Industrial/Management Engineering M,D,O
Mechanical Engineering M,D,O
Software Engineering M,D,O
Systems Engineering M,O
Telecommunications Management M,O

CONCORDIA UNIVERSITY COLLEGE OF ALBERTA
Computer and Information Systems Security M

COOPER UNION FOR THE ADVANCEMENT OF SCIENCE AND ART
Chemical Engineering M
Civil Engineering M
Electrical Engineering M
Engineering and Applied Sciences—General M
Mechanical Engineering M

CORNELL UNIVERSITY
Aerospace/Aeronautical Engineering M,D
Agricultural Engineering M,D
Artificial Intelligence/Robotics M,D
Biochemical Engineering M,D
Bioengineering M,D
Biomedical Engineering M,D
Chemical Engineering M,D
Civil Engineering M,D
Computer Engineering M,D
Computer Science M,D
Electrical Engineering M,D
Engineering and Applied Sciences—General M,D
Engineering Management M,D
Engineering Physics M,D
Environmental Engineering M,D
Ergonomics and Human Factors M
Geotechnical Engineering M,D
Human-Computer Interaction D
Industrial/Management Engineering M,D
Information Science D
Manufacturing Engineering M,D
Materials Engineering M,D
Materials Sciences M,D
Mechanical Engineering M,D
Mechanics M,D
Operations Research M,D
Polymer Science and Engineering M,D
Structural Engineering M,D
Systems Engineering M
Textile Sciences and Engineering M,D
Transportation and Highway Engineering M,D
Water Resources Engineering M,D

DAKOTA STATE UNIVERSITY
Information Science M,D*

DALHOUSIE UNIVERSITY
Agricultural Engineering M,D
Bioengineering M,D
Bioinformatics M,D
Biomedical Engineering M,D
Chemical Engineering M,D
Civil Engineering M,D
Computer Engineering M,D
Computer Science M,D
Electrical Engineering M,D
Engineering and Applied Sciences—General M,D
Environmental Engineering M,D
Human-Computer Interaction M
Industrial/Management Engineering M,D
Materials Engineering M,D
Mechanical Engineering M,D
Medical Informatics M,D
Mineral/Mining Engineering M,D

DALLAS BAPTIST UNIVERSITY
Engineering Management M
Management of Technology M

DARTMOUTH COLLEGE
Biochemical Engineering M,D
Biomedical Engineering M,D
Biotechnology M,D
Computer Engineering M,D
Computer Science M,D
Electrical Engineering M,D
Engineering and Applied Sciences—General M,D
Engineering Management M
Engineering Physics M,D
Environmental Engineering M,D
Materials Engineering M,D
Materials Sciences M,D
Mechanical Engineering M,D

DAVENPORT UNIVERSITY
Computer and Information Systems Security M

DAVENPORT UNIVERSITY
Computer and Information Systems Security M

DAVENPORT UNIVERSITY
Computer and Information Systems Security M

DEPAUL UNIVERSITY
Computer and Information Systems Security M,D

*M—master's degree; P—first professional degree; D—doctorate; O—other advanced degree; *—Close-Up and/or Display*

Computer Science M,D
Game Design and Development M,D
Human-Computer Interaction M,D
Information Science M,D
Management of Technology M,D
Polymer Science and Engineering M
Software Engineering M,D

DESALES UNIVERSITY
Information Science M

DIGIPEN INSTITUTE OF TECHNOLOGY
Computer Science M

DREXEL UNIVERSITY
Architectural Engineering M,D
Biochemical Engineering M
Biomedical Engineering M,D
Chemical Engineering M,D
Civil Engineering M,D
Computer Engineering M
Computer Science M,D
Construction Management M
Electrical Engineering M
Engineering and Applied Sciences—General M,D,O
Engineering Management M,O
Environmental Engineering M,D
Geotechnical Engineering M,D
Health Informatics M
Hydraulics M,D
Information Science M,D
Materials Engineering M,D
Mechanical Engineering M,D
Mechanics M,D
Software Engineering M
Structural Engineering M,D
Telecommunications M

DUKE UNIVERSITY
Bioinformatics D,O
Biomedical Engineering M,D
Civil Engineering M,D
Computer Engineering M,D
Computer Science M,D
Electrical Engineering M,D*
Engineering and Applied Sciences—General M
Engineering Management M
Environmental Engineering M,D
Materials Engineering M
Materials Sciences M,D
Mechanical Engineering M,D

DUQUESNE UNIVERSITY
Biotechnology M

EAST CAROLINA UNIVERSITY
Biotechnology M
Computer Science M,D,O
Industrial/Management Engineering M,D,O
Management of Technology M,D,O
Manufacturing Engineering M,D,O
Software Engineering M

EASTERN ILLINOIS UNIVERSITY
Computer and Information Systems Security M,O
Computer Science M,O
Engineering and Applied Sciences—General M,O
Systems Science M,O

EASTERN KENTUCKY UNIVERSITY
Industrial/Management Engineering M
Manufacturing Engineering M

EASTERN MICHIGAN UNIVERSITY
Artificial Intelligence/Robotics M,O
Computer and Information Systems Security M,O
Computer Science M,O
Construction Management M
Engineering and Applied Sciences—General M
Engineering Management M
Management of Technology D
Polymer Science and Engineering M
Technology and Public Policy M

EASTERN WASHINGTON UNIVERSITY
Computer Science M

EAST STROUDSBURG UNIVERSITY OF PENNSYLVANIA
Computer Science M

EAST TENNESSEE STATE UNIVERSITY
Computer Science M
Information Science M
Manufacturing Engineering M,O

ÉCOLE POLYTECHNIQUE DE MONTRÉAL
Aerospace/Aeronautical Engineering M,D,O
Biomedical Engineering M,D,O
Chemical Engineering M,D,O
Civil Engineering M,D,O
Computer Engineering M,D,O
Computer Science M,D,O
Electrical Engineering M,D,O
Engineering and Applied Sciences—General M,D,O
Engineering Physics M,D,O
Environmental Engineering M,D,O
Geotechnical Engineering M,D,O
Hydraulics M,D,O
Industrial/Management Engineering M,D,O
Management of Technology M,D,O
Mechanical Engineering M,D,O
Mechanics M,D,O
Nuclear Engineering M,D,O
Operations Research M,D,O
Structural Engineering M,D,O
Transportation and Highway Engineering M,D,O

EMBRY-RIDDLE AERONAUTICAL UNIVERSITY–DAYTONA
Aerospace/Aeronautical Engineering M
Computer Engineering M
Electrical Engineering M
Engineering Physics M,D
Ergonomics and Human Factors M
Mechanical Engineering M
Software Engineering M
Systems Engineering M

EMBRY-RIDDLE AERONAUTICAL UNIVERSITY–PRESCOTT
Safety Engineering M

EMBRY-RIDDLE AERONAUTICAL UNIVERSITY–WORLDWIDE
Aerospace/Aeronautical Engineering M,O
Aviation D
Management of Technology M
Modeling and Simulation M,O
Systems Engineering M

EMORY UNIVERSITY
Bioinformatics M,D
Computer Science M,D
Health Informatics M,D

EVERGLADES UNIVERSITY
Aviation M
Information Science M

EXCELSIOR COLLEGE
Computer and Information Systems Security M,O
Management of Technology M,O
Medical Informatics O

FAIRFIELD UNIVERSITY
Computer Engineering M
Electrical Engineering M
Engineering and Applied Sciences—General M
Management of Technology M
Mechanical Engineering M
Software Engineering M

FAIRLEIGH DICKINSON UNIVERSITY, COLLEGE AT FLORHAM
Chemical Engineering M,O
Computer Science M
Management of Technology M,O

FAIRLEIGH DICKINSON UNIVERSITY, METROPOLITAN CAMPUS
Computer Engineering M
Computer Science M
Electrical Engineering M
Engineering and Applied Sciences—General M
Systems Science M

FERRIS STATE UNIVERSITY
Computer and Information Systems Security M
Database Systems M

FITCHBURG STATE UNIVERSITY
Computer Science M

FLORIDA AGRICULTURAL AND MECHANICAL UNIVERSITY
Biomedical Engineering M,D
Chemical Engineering M,D
Civil Engineering M,D
Electrical Engineering M,D
Engineering and Applied Sciences—General M,D
Environmental Engineering M,D
Industrial/Management Engineering M,D
Mechanical Engineering M,D
Software Engineering M

FLORIDA ATLANTIC UNIVERSITY
Civil Engineering M
Computer Engineering M,D
Computer Science M,D
Electrical Engineering M,D
Engineering and Applied Sciences—General M,D
Mechanical Engineering M,D
Ocean Engineering M,D

FLORIDA GULF COAST UNIVERSITY
Computer Science M
Information Science M

FLORIDA INSTITUTE OF TECHNOLOGY
Aerospace/Aeronautical Engineering M,D
Biomedical Engineering M,D
Biotechnology M,D
Chemical Engineering M,D
Civil Engineering M,D
Computer and Information Systems Security M
Computer Engineering M,D
Computer Science M,D
Electrical Engineering M,D
Engineering and Applied Sciences—General M,D
Engineering Management M,D
Ergonomics and Human Factors M,D
Management of Technology M
Mechanical Engineering M,D
Ocean Engineering M,D
Operations Research M,D
Software Engineering M,D
Systems Engineering M,D

FLORIDA INTERNATIONAL UNIVERSITY
Biomedical Engineering M,D
Civil Engineering M,D
Computer Engineering M
Computer Science M,D
Construction Management M
Electrical Engineering M,D
Engineering and Applied Sciences—General M,D*
Environmental Engineering M
Information Science M,D
Materials Engineering M,D
Materials Sciences M,D
Mechanical Engineering M,D
Telecommunications M,D

FLORIDA STATE UNIVERSITY
Bioinformatics M,D
Biomedical Engineering M,D
Chemical Engineering M,D
Civil Engineering M,D
Computer and Information Systems Security M,D
Computer Science M,D
Electrical Engineering M,D
Energy and Power Engineering M,D
Engineering and Applied Sciences—General M,D
Environmental Engineering M,D
Industrial/Management Engineering M,D
Manufacturing Engineering M,D
Materials Engineering M,D
Materials Sciences M,D
Mechanical Engineering M,D
Polymer Science and Engineering M,D

FORDHAM UNIVERSITY
Computer Science M,O

FRANKLIN PIERCE UNIVERSITY
Energy Management and Policy M,D,O
Telecommunications M,D,O

FRANKLIN UNIVERSITY
Computer Science M

FROSTBURG STATE UNIVERSITY
Computer Science M

FULL SAIL UNIVERSITY
Game Design and Development M

GANNON UNIVERSITY
Computer Science M
Electrical Engineering M
Engineering Management M
Environmental Engineering M
Information Science M
Mechanical Engineering M
Software Engineering M

GEORGE MASON UNIVERSITY
Bioinformatics M,D,O
Civil Engineering M,D,O
Computer and Information Systems Security M,D,O
Computer Engineering M,D,O
Computer Science M,D,O
Database Systems M,D,O
Electrical Engineering M,D,O
Engineering and Applied Sciences—General M,D,O
Engineering Physics M,D,O
Game Design and Development M,D,O
Health Informatics M,O
Information Science M,D,O
Management of Technology M,D
Modeling and Simulation M,D,O
Operations Research M,D,O
Software Engineering M,D,O
Systems Engineering M,D,O
Telecommunications Management M,D,O
Telecommunications M,D,O
Water Resources Engineering M,D,O

GEORGETOWN UNIVERSITY
Bioinformatics M
Computer Science M
Materials Sciences D

THE GEORGE WASHINGTON UNIVERSITY
Aerospace/Aeronautical Engineering M,D,O
Bioinformatics M
Biotechnology M
Civil Engineering M,D,O
Computer Engineering M,D
Computer Science M,D
Electrical Engineering M,D
Engineering and Applied Sciences—General M,D,O
Engineering Management M,D,O
Environmental Engineering M,D,O
Management of Technology M,D
Materials Sciences M,D
Mechanical Engineering M,D,O
Systems Engineering M,D,O
Technology and Public Policy M
Telecommunications M,D

GEORGIA HEALTH SCIENCES UNIVERSITY
Health Informatics M

GEORGIA INSTITUTE OF TECHNOLOGY
Aerospace/Aeronautical Engineering M,D
Bioengineering M,D
Bioinformatics M,D
Biomedical Engineering D
Chemical Engineering M,D
Civil Engineering M,D
Computer and Information Systems Security M,D
Computer Engineering M,D
Computer Science M,D
Electrical Engineering M,D
Engineering and Applied Sciences—General M,D
Environmental Engineering M,D
Ergonomics and Human Factors M,D
Human-Computer Interaction M
Industrial/Management Engineering M,D
Management of Technology M,O
Materials Engineering M,D
Mechanical Engineering M,D
Mechanics M,D
Nuclear Engineering M,D
Operations Research M,D
Polymer Science and Engineering M,D
Systems Engineering M,D
Textile Sciences and Engineering M,D

GEORGIA SOUTHERN UNIVERSITY
Computer Science M
Electrical Engineering M,O
Mechanical Engineering M,O

GEORGIA SOUTHWESTERN STATE UNIVERSITY
Computer Science M
Information Science M

GEORGIA STATE UNIVERSITY
Computer Science M,D
Information Science M
Operations Research M,D

GOLDEN GATE UNIVERSITY
Health Informatics M,D,O
Management of Technology M,D,O

GOVERNORS STATE UNIVERSITY
Computer Science M

GRADUATE SCHOOL AND UNIVERSITY CENTER OF THE CITY UNIVERSITY OF NEW YORK
Biomedical Engineering D
Chemical Engineering D
Civil Engineering D
Computer Science D
Electrical Engineering D
Engineering and Applied Sciences—General D
Mechanical Engineering D

GRAND CANYON UNIVERSITY
Health Informatics M

GRAND VALLEY STATE UNIVERSITY
Bioinformatics M
Computer Engineering M
Computer Science M
Electrical Engineering M
Engineering and Applied Sciences—General M
Information Science M
Manufacturing Engineering M
Mechanical Engineering M
Medical Informatics M
Software Engineering M

HAMPTON UNIVERSITY
Computer Science M

HARDING UNIVERSITY
Management of Technology M

HARRISBURG UNIVERSITY OF SCIENCE AND TECHNOLOGY
Construction Management M
Management of Technology M
Systems Engineering M

HARVARD UNIVERSITY
Applied Science and Technology M,O
Biomedical Engineering D
Biotechnology M,O
Computer Science M,D
Engineering and Applied Sciences—General M,D
Information Science M,D,O
Management of Technology D

HAWAI'I PACIFIC UNIVERSITY
Software Engineering M
Telecommunications Management M

HEC MONTREAL
Financial Engineering M
Operations Research M

HENLEY-PUTNAM UNIVERSITY
Computer and Information Systems Security M

HERZING UNIVERSITY ONLINE
Management of Technology M

HOFSTRA UNIVERSITY
Computer and Information Systems Security M
Computer Science M
Internet Engineering M

HOLY NAMES UNIVERSITY
Energy Management and Policy M

HOOD COLLEGE
Biotechnology M,O
Computer and Information Systems Security M,O
Computer Science M,O
Information Science M,O
Systems Science M

HOWARD UNIVERSITY
Biotechnology M,D
Chemical Engineering M
Civil Engineering M
Computer Science M
Electrical Engineering M,D
Engineering and Applied Sciences—General M,D
Mechanical Engineering M,D

HUMBOLDT STATE UNIVERSITY
Hazardous Materials Management M

IDAHO STATE UNIVERSITY
Civil Engineering M
Engineering and Applied Sciences—General M,D,O
Environmental Engineering M
Hazardous Materials Management M
Management of Technology M
Mechanical Engineering M
Nuclear Engineering M,D
Operations Research M

ILLINOIS INSTITUTE OF TECHNOLOGY
Aerospace/Aeronautical Engineering — M,D
Agricultural Engineering — M,D
Architectural Engineering — M,D
Bioengineering — M,D
Biomedical Engineering — D
Biotechnology — M,D
Chemical Engineering — M,D
Civil Engineering — M,D
Computer Engineering — M,D
Computer Science — M,D
Construction Engineering — M,D
Construction Management — M,D
Electrical Engineering — M,D
Engineering and Applied
   Sciences—General — M,D
Environmental Engineering — M,D
Geotechnical Engineering — M,D
Manufacturing Engineering — M,D
Materials Engineering — M,D
Materials Sciences — M,D
Mechanical Engineering — M,D
Software Engineering — M,D
Structural Engineering — M,D
Telecommunications — M,D
Transportation and Highway
   Engineering — M,D

ILLINOIS STATE UNIVERSITY
Biotechnology — M
Industrial/Management Engineering — M
Management of Technology — M

INDIANA STATE UNIVERSITY
Computer Engineering — M
Computer Science — M
Engineering and Applied
   Sciences—General — M
Industrial/Management Engineering — M
Management of Technology — D

INDIANA UNIVERSITY BLOOMINGTON
Bioinformatics — M,D
Biotechnology — M,D
Computer Science — M,D
Energy Management and Policy — M,D,O
Ergonomics and Human Factors — M,D
Hazardous Materials Management — M,D,O
Health Informatics — M,D
Human-Computer Interaction — M,D
Information Science — M,D,O
Materials Sciences — M,D
Safety Engineering — M,D
Telecommunications — M
Water Resources Engineering — M,D

INDIANA UNIVERSITY–PURDUE UNIVERSITY FORT WAYNE
Computer Engineering — M
Computer Science — M
Construction Management — M
Electrical Engineering — M
Engineering and Applied
   Sciences—General — M,O
Industrial/Management Engineering — M
Information Science — M
Mechanical Engineering — M
Operations Research — M,O
Systems Engineering — M

INDIANA UNIVERSITY–PURDUE UNIVERSITY INDIANAPOLIS
Artificial Intelligence/Robotics — M,D
Biomedical Engineering — M,D,O
Computer Engineering — M,D
Computer Science — M,D
Electrical Engineering — M,D
Information Science — M,D
Mechanical Engineering — M,D,O

INDIANA UNIVERSITY SOUTH BEND
Computer Science — M

INSTITUTO CENTROAMERICANO DE ADMINISTRACIÓN DE EMPRESAS
Management of Technology — M

INSTITUTO TECNOLOGICO DE SANTO DOMINGO
Construction Management — M,O
Energy and Power Engineering — M,D,O
Energy Management and Policy — M,D,O
Engineering and Applied
   Sciences—General — M,O
Environmental Engineering — M,O
Industrial/Management Engineering — M,O
Information Science — M,O
Software Engineering — M,O
Structural Engineering — M,O
Telecommunications — M,O

INSTITUTO TECNOLÓGICO Y DE ESTUDIOS SUPERIORES DE MONTERREY, CAMPUS CENTRAL DE VERACRUZ
Computer Science — M
Management of Technology — M

INSTITUTO TECNOLÓGICO Y DE ESTUDIOS SUPERIORES DE MONTERREY, CAMPUS CHIHUAHUA
Computer Engineering — M,O
Electrical Engineering — M,O
Engineering Management — M,O
Industrial/Management Engineering — M,O
Mechanical Engineering — M,O
Systems Engineering — M,O

INSTITUTO TECNOLÓGICO Y DE ESTUDIOS SUPERIORES DE MONTERREY, CAMPUS CIUDAD DE MÉXICO
Computer Science — M,D

INSTITUTO TECNOLÓGICO Y DE ESTUDIOS SUPERIORES DE MONTERREY, CAMPUS CIUDAD OBREGÓN
Engineering and Applied
   Sciences—General — M
Telecommunications Management — M

INSTITUTO TECNOLÓGICO Y DE ESTUDIOS SUPERIORES DE MONTERREY, CAMPUS CUERNAVACA
Computer Science — M,D
Information Science — M,D
Management of Technology — M,D

INSTITUTO TECNOLÓGICO Y DE ESTUDIOS SUPERIORES DE MONTERREY, CAMPUS ESTADO DE MÉXICO
Computer Science — M,D
Information Science — M,D
Materials Engineering — M,D
Materials Sciences — M,D
Telecommunications Management — M,D

INSTITUTO TECNOLÓGICO Y DE ESTUDIOS SUPERIORES DE MONTERREY, CAMPUS IRAPUATO
Computer Science — M,D
Information Science — M,D
Management of Technology — M,D
Telecommunications Management — M,D

INSTITUTO TECNOLÓGICO Y DE ESTUDIOS SUPERIORES DE MONTERREY, CAMPUS LAGUNA
Industrial/Management Engineering — M

INSTITUTO TECNOLÓGICO Y DE ESTUDIOS SUPERIORES DE MONTERREY, CAMPUS MONTERREY
Agricultural Engineering — M,D
Artificial Intelligence/Robotics — M,D
Biotechnology — M,D
Chemical Engineering — M,D
Civil Engineering — M,D
Computer Science — M,D
Electrical Engineering — M,D
Engineering and Applied
   Sciences—General — M,D
Environmental Engineering — M,D
Industrial/Management Engineering — M,D
Information Science — M,D
Manufacturing Engineering — M,D
Mechanical Engineering — M,D
Systems Engineering — M,D

INSTITUTO TECNOLÓGICO Y DE ESTUDIOS SUPERIORES DE MONTERREY, CAMPUS SONORA NORTE
Information Science — M

INTER AMERICAN UNIVERSITY OF PUERTO RICO, BAYAMÓN CAMPUS
Biotechnology — M

INTER AMERICAN UNIVERSITY OF PUERTO RICO, GUAYAMA CAMPUS
Computer and Information
   Systems Security — M
Computer Science — M

INTER AMERICAN UNIVERSITY OF PUERTO RICO, METROPOLITAN CAMPUS
Computer Science — M

INTER AMERICAN UNIVERSITY OF PUERTO RICO, SAN GERMÁN CAMPUS
Information Science — M,D

INTERNATIONAL TECHNOLOGICAL UNIVERSITY
Computer Engineering — M
Computer Science — M
Electrical Engineering — M,D
Engineering Management — M
Software Engineering — M,D

THE INTERNATIONAL UNIVERSITY OF MONACO
Financial Engineering — M

IONA COLLEGE
Computer Science — M
Management of Technology — M,O

IOWA STATE UNIVERSITY OF SCIENCE AND TECHNOLOGY
Aerospace/Aeronautical Engineering — M,D
Agricultural Engineering — M,D
Bioinformatics — M,D
Chemical Engineering — M,D
Civil Engineering — M,D
Computer Engineering — M,D
Computer Science — M,D
Construction Engineering — M,D
Electrical Engineering — M,D
Environmental Engineering — M,D
Geotechnical Engineering — M,D
Human-Computer Interaction — M,D
Industrial/Management Engineering — M,D
Information Science — M,D
Materials Engineering — M,D
Materials Sciences — M,D
Mechanical Engineering — M,D
Mechanics — M,D
Operations Research — M,D
Structural Engineering — M,D

JACKSON STATE UNIVERSITY
Computer Science — M
Materials Sciences — M

JACKSONVILLE STATE UNIVERSITY
Computer Science — M
Software Engineering — M

JAMES MADISON UNIVERSITY
Applied Science and Technology — M
Computer Science — M

JOHN MARSHALL LAW SCHOOL
Computer and Information
   Systems Security — M,D

THE JOHNS HOPKINS UNIVERSITY
Bioengineering — M,D
Bioinformatics — M,D,O
Biomedical Engineering — M,D,O*
Biotechnology — M
Chemical Engineering — M,D
Civil Engineering — M,D
Computer and Information
   Systems Security — M,O
Computer Engineering — M,D,O
Computer Science — M,D,O
Electrical Engineering — M,D,O
Engineering and Applied
   Sciences—General — M,D,O
Engineering Management — M,D
Environmental Engineering — M,D,O
Health Informatics — M
Information Science — M
Management of Technology — M
Materials Engineering — M,D
Materials Sciences — M,D
Mechanical Engineering — M,D
Mechanics — M
Nanotechnology — M
Operations Research — M,D
Systems Engineering — M,O
Telecommunications — M,O

JONES INTERNATIONAL UNIVERSITY
Computer and Information
   Systems Security — M
Management of Technology — M

KANSAS STATE UNIVERSITY
Agricultural Engineering — M,D
Architectural Engineering — M
Bioengineering — M,D
Chemical Engineering — M,D
Civil Engineering — M,D
Computer Science — M,D
Electrical Engineering — M,D
Engineering and Applied
   Sciences—General — M,D*
Engineering Management — M,D
Industrial/Management Engineering — M,D
Information Science — M,D
Management of Technology — M
Manufacturing Engineering — M,D
Mechanical Engineering — M,D
Nuclear Engineering — M,D
Operations Research — M,D
Software Engineering — M,D

KAPLAN UNIVERSITY, DAVENPORT CAMPUS
Computer and Information
   Systems Security — M

KEAN UNIVERSITY
Biotechnology — M

KENNESAW STATE UNIVERSITY
Computer Science — M
Information Science — M

KENT STATE UNIVERSITY
Computer Science — M,D
Engineering and Applied
   Sciences—General — M
Information Science — M

KENTUCKY STATE UNIVERSITY
Computer Science — M

KETTERING UNIVERSITY
Electrical Engineering — M
Engineering Management — M
Manufacturing Engineering — M
Mechanical Engineering — M

KNOWLEDGE SYSTEMS INSTITUTE
Computer Science — M
Information Science — M

KUTZTOWN UNIVERSITY OF PENNSYLVANIA
Computer Science — M

LAKEHEAD UNIVERSITY
Computer Engineering — M
Computer Science — M
Electrical Engineering — M
Engineering and Applied
   Sciences—General — M
Environmental Engineering — M

LAMAR UNIVERSITY
Chemical Engineering — M,D
Civil Engineering — M,D
Computer Science — M
Electrical Engineering — M,D
Engineering and Applied
   Sciences—General — M,D
Engineering Management — M
Environmental Engineering — M,D
Industrial/Management Engineering — M,D

JACKSON STATE UNIVERSITY appears under column — Systems Engineering — M
Transportation and Highway
   Engineering — M,D

LA SALLE UNIVERSITY
Computer Science — M
Management of Technology — M

LAURENTIAN UNIVERSITY
Engineering and Applied
   Sciences—General — M,D
Mineral/Mining Engineering — M,D

LAWRENCE TECHNOLOGICAL UNIVERSITY
Architectural Engineering — M
Automotive Engineering — M,D
Civil Engineering — M,D
Computer Engineering — M,D
Computer Science — M
Construction Engineering — M,D
Electrical Engineering — M,D
Engineering and Applied
   Sciences—General — M,D
Engineering Management — M,D
Industrial/Management Engineering — M,D
Management of Technology — M,D
Manufacturing Engineering — M,D
Mechanical Engineering — M,D

LEBANESE AMERICAN UNIVERSITY
Computer Science — M

LEHIGH UNIVERSITY
Bioengineering — M,D
Chemical Engineering — M,D
Civil Engineering — M,D
Computer Engineering — M,D
Computer Science — M,D
Electrical Engineering — M,D
Energy and Power Engineering — M
Engineering and Applied
   Sciences—General — M,D
Engineering Management — M,D
Environmental Engineering — M,D
Industrial/Management Engineering — M,D
Information Science — M
Manufacturing Engineering — M
Materials Engineering — M,D
Materials Sciences — M,D
Mechanical Engineering — M,D
Mechanics — M,D
Polymer Science and Engineering — M,D
Structural Engineering — M,D
Systems Engineering — M,D

LEHMAN COLLEGE OF THE CITY UNIVERSITY OF NEW YORK
Computer Science — M

LETOURNEAU UNIVERSITY
Engineering and Applied
   Sciences—General — M

LEWIS UNIVERSITY
Aviation — M
Computer and Information
   Systems Security — M
Management of Technology — M

LIPSCOMB UNIVERSITY
Health Informatics — M

LONG ISLAND UNIVERSITY–BROOKLYN CAMPUS
Computer Science — M

LONG ISLAND UNIVERSITY–C. W. POST CAMPUS
Computer Science — M
Engineering Management — M
Information Science — M

LOUISIANA STATE UNIVERSITY AND AGRICULTURAL AND MECHANICAL COLLEGE
Agricultural Engineering — M,D
Applied Science and Technology — M
Bioengineering — M,D
Chemical Engineering — M,D
Civil Engineering — M,D
Computer Engineering — M,D
Computer Science — M,D
Electrical Engineering — M,D
Engineering and Applied
   Sciences—General — M,D
Environmental Engineering — M,D
Geotechnical Engineering — M,D
Industrial/Management Engineering — M,D
Mechanical Engineering — M,D
Mechanics — M,D
Petroleum Engineering — M,D
Structural Engineering — M,D
Systems Science — M,D
Transportation and Highway
   Engineering — M,D
Water Resources Engineering — M,D

LOUISIANA STATE UNIVERSITY IN SHREVEPORT
Computer Science — M
Systems Science — M

LOUISIANA TECH UNIVERSITY
Biomedical Engineering — M,D
Chemical Engineering — M,D
Civil Engineering — M,D
Computer Science — M,D
Electrical Engineering — M,D
Engineering and Applied
   Sciences—General — M,D
Industrial/Management Engineering — M
Mechanical Engineering — M,D
Modeling and Simulation — M,D

Environmental Engineering — M,D
Industrial/Management Engineering — M,D
Telecommunications Management — M

---

*M—master's degree; P—first professional degree; D—doctorate; O—other advanced degree; *—Close-Up and/or Display*

LOYOLA MARYMOUNT UNIVERSITY
Civil Engineering M
Engineering Management M
Mechanical Engineering M
Systems Engineering M

LOYOLA UNIVERSITY CHICAGO
Computer Science M
Information Science M
Software Engineering M

LOYOLA UNIVERSITY MARYLAND
Computer Science M
Software Engineering M

MAHARISHI UNIVERSITY OF MANAGEMENT
Computer Science M

MANHATTAN COLLEGE
Chemical Engineering M
Civil Engineering M
Computer Engineering M
Electrical Engineering M
Engineering and Applied Sciences—General M
Environmental Engineering M
Mechanical Engineering M

MARIST COLLEGE
Computer Science M,O
Management of Technology M,O
Software Engineering M,O

MARLBORO COLLEGE
Information Science M,O

MARQUETTE UNIVERSITY
Bioinformatics M,D
Biomedical Engineering M,D
Civil Engineering M,D,O
Computer Engineering M,D,O
Computer Science M,D
Construction Engineering M,D,O
Construction Management M,D,O
Electrical Engineering M,D,O
Engineering and Applied Sciences—General M,D,O
Engineering Management M,D,O
Environmental Engineering M,D,O
Geotechnical Engineering M,D,O
Hazardous Materials Management M,D,O
Management of Technology M,D
Mechanical Engineering M,D,O
Structural Engineering M,D,O
Transportation and Highway Engineering M,D,O
Water Resources Engineering M,D,O

MARSHALL UNIVERSITY
Engineering and Applied Sciences—General M
Engineering Management M
Environmental Engineering M
Health Informatics M
Information Science M
Management of Technology M

MARYLHURST UNIVERSITY
Energy and Power Engineering M

MARYMOUNT UNIVERSITY
Computer and Information Systems Security M,O
Medical Informatics M,O

MARYWOOD UNIVERSITY
Biotechnology M

MASSACHUSETTS INSTITUTE OF TECHNOLOGY
Aerospace/Aeronautical Engineering M,D,O
Bioengineering M,D
Biomedical Engineering M,D
Chemical Engineering M,D
Civil Engineering M,D,O
Computer Engineering M,D,O
Computer Science M,D,O
Construction Engineering M,D,O
Electrical Engineering M,D,O
Engineering and Applied Sciences—General M,D,O
Engineering Management M,D
Environmental Engineering M,D,O
Geotechnical Engineering M,D,O
Information Science M,D,O
Manufacturing Engineering M,D,O
Materials Engineering M,D,O
Materials Sciences M,D,O
Mechanical Engineering M,D,O
Mechanics M,D,O
Nuclear Engineering M,D,O
Ocean Engineering M,D,O
Operations Research M,D
Structural Engineering M,D,O
Systems Engineering M,D
Technology and Public Policy M,D
Transportation and Highway Engineering M,D,O
Water Resources Engineering M,D,O

MAYO GRADUATE SCHOOL
Biomedical Engineering D

MCGILL UNIVERSITY
Aerospace/Aeronautical Engineering M,D
Agricultural Engineering M,D
Bioengineering M,D
Bioinformatics M,D
Biomedical Engineering M,D
Biotechnology M,D,O
Chemical Engineering M,D
Civil Engineering M,D
Computer Engineering M,D
Computer Science M,D
Electrical Engineering M,D
Engineering and Applied Sciences—General M,D,O
Environmental Engineering M,D
Geotechnical Engineering M,D
Hydraulics M,D
Materials Engineering M,D,O
Mechanical Engineering M,D
Mechanics M,D
Mineral/Mining Engineering M,D,O
Structural Engineering M,D
Water Resources Engineering M,D

MCMASTER UNIVERSITY
Chemical Engineering M,D
Civil Engineering M,D
Computer Science M,D
Electrical Engineering M,D
Engineering and Applied Sciences—General M,D
Engineering Physics M,D
Materials Engineering M,D
Materials Sciences M,D
Mechanical Engineering M,D
Nuclear Engineering M,D
Software Engineering M,D

MCNEESE STATE UNIVERSITY
Chemical Engineering M,O
Civil Engineering M,O
Computer Science M
Electrical Engineering M,O
Engineering and Applied Sciences—General M,O
Engineering Management M,O
Mechanical Engineering M,O

MEDICAL COLLEGE OF WISCONSIN
Bioinformatics M
Medical Informatics M

MEMORIAL UNIVERSITY OF NEWFOUNDLAND
Civil Engineering M,D
Computer Engineering M,D
Computer Science M,D
Electrical Engineering M,D
Engineering and Applied Sciences—General M,D
Environmental Engineering M
Mechanical Engineering M,D
Ocean Engineering M,D

MERCER UNIVERSITY
Biomedical Engineering M
Computer Engineering M
Electrical Engineering M
Engineering and Applied Sciences—General M
Engineering Management M
Environmental Engineering M
Management of Technology M
Mechanical Engineering M
Software Engineering M

MERCY COLLEGE
Computer and Information Systems Security M

MERRIMACK COLLEGE
Engineering and Applied Sciences—General M

METROPOLITAN STATE UNIVERSITY
Computer and Information Systems Security M,D,O
Computer Science M
Database Systems M,D,O
Health Informatics M,D,O

MIAMI UNIVERSITY
Engineering and Applied Sciences—General M,O
Paper and Pulp Engineering M
Software Engineering M,O
Systems Science M

MICHIGAN STATE UNIVERSITY
Biosystems Engineering M,D
Chemical Engineering M,D
Civil Engineering M,D
Computer Science M,D
Construction Management M,D
Electrical Engineering M,D
Engineering and Applied Sciences—General M,D
Environmental Engineering M,D
Game Design and Development M
Manufacturing Engineering M,D
Materials Engineering M,D
Materials Sciences M,D
Mechanical Engineering M,D
Mechanics M,D
Telecommunications M

MICHIGAN TECHNOLOGICAL UNIVERSITY
Biomedical Engineering D
Chemical Engineering M,D
Civil Engineering M,D
Computer Engineering M,D,O
Computer Science M,D
Electrical Engineering M,D,O
Engineering and Applied Sciences—General M,D,O
Engineering Physics M,D
Environmental Engineering M,D
Ergonomics and Human Factors M,D
Geological Engineering M,D
Materials Engineering M,D
Mechanical Engineering M,D,O
Mechanics M,D,O
Metallurgical Engineering and Metallurgy M,D
Mineral/Mining Engineering M,D

MIDDLE TENNESSEE STATE UNIVERSITY
Aerospace/Aeronautical Engineering M
Computer Science M
Medical Informatics M

MIDWESTERN STATE UNIVERSITY
Computer Science M

MILLS COLLEGE
Computer Science M,O

MILWAUKEE SCHOOL OF ENGINEERING
Civil Engineering M
Engineering and Applied Sciences—General M
Engineering Management M
Environmental Engineering M
Medical Informatics M
Structural Engineering M

MINNESOTA STATE UNIVERSITY MANKATO
Automotive Engineering M
Database Systems M,O
Electrical Engineering M
Manufacturing Engineering M

MISSISSIPPI COLLEGE
Computer Science M

MISSISSIPPI STATE UNIVERSITY
Aerospace/Aeronautical Engineering M,D
Bioengineering M,D
Biomedical Engineering M,D
Chemical Engineering M,D
Civil Engineering M,D
Computer Engineering M,D
Computer Science M,D
Electrical Engineering M,D
Engineering and Applied Sciences—General M,D
Industrial/Management Engineering M,D
Mechanical Engineering M,D
Systems Engineering M,D

MISSISSIPPI VALLEY STATE UNIVERSITY
Bioinformatics M

MISSOURI STATE UNIVERSITY
Applied Science and Technology M
Computer Science M
Construction Management M
Materials Sciences M

MISSOURI UNIVERSITY OF SCIENCE AND TECHNOLOGY
Aerospace/Aeronautical Engineering M,D
Ceramic Sciences and Engineering M,D
Chemical Engineering M,D
Civil Engineering M,D
Computer Engineering M,D
Computer Science M,D
Construction Engineering M,D
Electrical Engineering M,D
Engineering and Applied Sciences—General M,D
Engineering Management M,D
Environmental Engineering M,D
Geological Engineering M,D
Geotechnical Engineering M,D
Hydraulics M,D
Information Science M
Manufacturing Engineering M,D
Mechanical Engineering M,D
Mechanics M,D
Metallurgical Engineering and Metallurgy M,D
Mineral/Mining Engineering M,D
Nuclear Engineering M,D
Petroleum Engineering M,D
Systems Engineering M,D

MISSOURI WESTERN STATE UNIVERSITY
Engineering and Applied Sciences—General M
Ergonomics and Human Factors M

MONMOUTH UNIVERSITY
Computer Science M
Software Engineering M,O

MONTANA STATE UNIVERSITY
Chemical Engineering M,D
Civil Engineering M,D
Computer Engineering M,D
Computer Science M,D
Construction Engineering M,D
Electrical Engineering M,D
Engineering and Applied Sciences—General M,D
Environmental Engineering M,D
Industrial/Management Engineering M,D
Mechanical Engineering M,D
Mechanics M,D

MONTANA TECH OF THE UNIVERSITY OF MONTANA
Electrical Engineering M
Engineering and Applied Sciences—General M
Environmental Engineering M
Geological Engineering M
Health Informatics O
Industrial/Management Engineering M
Metallurgical Engineering and Metallurgy M
Mineral/Mining Engineering M
Petroleum Engineering M

MONTCLAIR STATE UNIVERSITY
Computer Science M,O
Information Science M,O

MOREHEAD STATE UNIVERSITY
Industrial/Management Engineering M

MORGAN STATE UNIVERSITY
Bioinformatics M
Civil Engineering M,D
Electrical Engineering M,D
Engineering and Applied Sciences—General M,D
Industrial/Management Engineering M,D
Telecommunications Management M
Transportation and Highway Engineering M

MURRAY STATE UNIVERSITY
Management of Technology M
Safety Engineering M
Telecommunications Management M

NATIONAL UNIVERSITY
Computer and Information Systems Security M
Computer Science M
Engineering and Applied Sciences—General M,O
Engineering Management M,O
Environmental Engineering M,O
Health Informatics M,O
Information Science M
Safety Engineering M,O
Telecommunications M,O

NAVAL POSTGRADUATE SCHOOL
Aerospace/Aeronautical Engineering M,D,O
Applied Science and Technology M,D
Computer and Information Systems Security M,D
Computer Engineering M,D,O
Computer Science M,D,O
Electrical Engineering M,D,O
Engineering Management M,D,O
Information Science M,D,O
Mechanical Engineering M,D,O
Modeling and Simulation M,D
Operations Research M,D
Software Engineering M,D
Systems Engineering M,D,O

NEW JERSEY INSTITUTE OF TECHNOLOGY
Bioinformatics M
Biomedical Engineering M,D
Chemical Engineering M,D
Civil Engineering M,D
Computer and Information Systems Security M
Computer Engineering M,D
Computer Science M,D
Electrical Engineering M,D
Energy and Power Engineering M
Engineering and Applied Sciences—General M,D
Engineering Management M
Environmental Engineering M,D
Industrial/Management Engineering M,D
Information Science M,D
Internet Engineering M
Management of Technology M
Manufacturing Engineering M
Materials Engineering M,D
Materials Sciences M,D
Mechanical Engineering M,D
Pharmaceutical Engineering M
Safety Engineering M
Software Engineering M
Systems Engineering M
Systems Science M
Telecommunications M
Transportation and Highway Engineering M,D

NEW MEXICO HIGHLANDS UNIVERSITY
Computer Science M

NEW MEXICO INSTITUTE OF MINING AND TECHNOLOGY
Computer Science M,D
Electrical Engineering M
Engineering Management M
Environmental Engineering M
Hazardous Materials Management M
Materials Engineering M,D
Mechanical Engineering M
Mechanics M
Mineral/Mining Engineering M
Operations Research M,D
Petroleum Engineering M,D
Systems Engineering M
Water Resources Engineering M

NEW MEXICO STATE UNIVERSITY
Bioinformatics M,D
Biotechnology M,D
Chemical Engineering M,D
Civil Engineering M,D
Computer Engineering M,D
Computer Science M,D
Electrical Engineering M,D
Engineering and Applied Sciences—General M,D,O
Environmental Engineering M,D
Industrial/Management Engineering M,D,O
Mechanical Engineering M,D
Systems Engineering M,D,O

NEW YORK INSTITUTE OF TECHNOLOGY
Computer and Information Systems Security M
Computer Engineering M
Computer Science M
Electrical Engineering M
Energy and Power Engineering M,O
Energy Management and Policy M,O
Engineering and Applied Sciences—General M,O
Environmental Engineering M

NEW YORK UNIVERSITY
Agricultural Engineering M,D
Computer Science M,D
Construction Management M,O
Database Systems M,O
Ergonomics and Human Factors M,D

NICHOLLS STATE UNIVERSITY

Computer Science	M

NORFOLK STATE UNIVERSITY

Computer Engineering	M
Computer Science	M
Electrical Engineering	M
Materials Sciences	M

NORTH CAROLINA AGRICULTURAL AND TECHNICAL STATE UNIVERSITY

Bioengineering	M
Chemical Engineering	M
Civil Engineering	M
Computer Engineering	M,D
Computer Science	M
Construction Management	M
Electrical Engineering	M,D
Energy and Power Engineering	M,D
Engineering and Applied Sciences—General	M,D
Industrial/Management Engineering	M,D
Management of Technology	M
Mechanical Engineering	M,D
Systems Engineering	M,D

NORTH CAROLINA STATE UNIVERSITY

Aerospace/Aeronautical Engineering	M,D
Agricultural Engineering	M,D,O
Bioengineering	M,D,O
Bioinformatics	M,D
Biomedical Engineering	M,D
Biotechnology	M
Chemical Engineering	M,D
Civil Engineering	M,D
Computer Engineering	M,D
Computer Science	M,D
Electrical Engineering	M,D
Engineering and Applied Sciences—General	M,D*
Ergonomics and Human Factors	D
Financial Engineering	M
Industrial/Management Engineering	M,D
Management of Technology	D
Manufacturing Engineering	M
Materials Engineering	M,D
Materials Sciences	M,D
Mechanical Engineering	M,D
Nuclear Engineering	M,D
Operations Research	M,D
Paper and Pulp Engineering	M,D
Polymer Science and Engineering	D
Textile Sciences and Engineering	M,D

NORTH CENTRAL COLLEGE

Computer Science	M

NORTH DAKOTA STATE UNIVERSITY

Agricultural Engineering	M,D
Bioinformatics	M,D
Biosystems Engineering	M,D
Civil Engineering	M,D
Computer Engineering	M,D
Computer Science	M,D,O
Construction Management	M
Electrical Engineering	M,D
Engineering and Applied Sciences—General	M,D
Environmental Engineering	M,D
Industrial/Management Engineering	M,D
Manufacturing Engineering	M,D
Materials Sciences	D
Mechanical Engineering	M,D
Mechanics	M,D
Nanotechnology	D
Operations Research	M,D,O
Polymer Science and Engineering	M,D
Software Engineering	M,D,O

NORTHEASTERN ILLINOIS UNIVERSITY

Computer Science	M

NORTHEASTERN UNIVERSITY

Bioinformatics	M
Biotechnology	M
Chemical Engineering	M,D
Civil Engineering	M,D
Computer Engineering	M,D
Computer Science	M,D
Electrical Engineering	M,D
Energy and Power Engineering	M
Engineering and Applied Sciences—General	M,D,O
Engineering Management	M,D
Environmental Engineering	M,D
Health Informatics	M,D
Industrial/Management Engineering	M,D
Information Science	M,D,O
Manufacturing Engineering	M,D
Mechanical Engineering	M,D
Operations Research	M,D
Telecommunications Management	M

NORTHERN ARIZONA UNIVERSITY

Civil Engineering	M
Computer Science	M
Electrical Engineering	M
Engineering and Applied Sciences—General	M,D,O
Environmental Engineering	M
Mechanical Engineering	M

NORTHERN ILLINOIS UNIVERSITY

Computer Science	M
Electrical Engineering	M
Engineering and Applied Sciences—General	M
Industrial/Management Engineering	M
Mechanical Engineering	M

NORTHERN KENTUCKY UNIVERSITY

Computer and Information Systems Security	M,O
Computer Science	M,O
Health Informatics	M,O
Information Science	M,O
Management of Technology	M
Software Engineering	M,O

NORTHWESTERN POLYTECHNIC UNIVERSITY

Computer Engineering	M
Computer Science	M
Electrical Engineering	M
Engineering and Applied Sciences—General	M

NORTHWESTERN UNIVERSITY

Biomedical Engineering	M,D
Biotechnology	M,D
Chemical Engineering	M,D
Civil Engineering	M,D
Computer and Information Systems Security	M
Computer Engineering	M,D
Database Systems	M
Electrical Engineering	M,D
Electronic Materials	M,D,O
Engineering and Applied Sciences—General	M,D,O
Engineering Design	M
Engineering Management	M
Environmental Engineering	M,D
Geotechnical Engineering	M,D
Industrial/Management Engineering	M,D
Information Science	M
Materials Engineering	M,D,O
Materials Sciences	M,D,O
Mechanical Engineering	M,D
Mechanics	M,D
Medical Informatics	M
Software Engineering	M
Structural Engineering	M,D
Transportation and Highway Engineering	M,D

NORTHWEST MISSOURI STATE UNIVERSITY

Computer Science	M,O

NORWICH UNIVERSITY

Civil Engineering	M
Computer and Information Systems Security	M
Construction Management	M
Environmental Engineering	M
Geotechnical Engineering	M
Structural Engineering	M
Water Resources Engineering	M

NOTRE DAME COLLEGE (OH)

Computer Science	M,O

NOTRE DAME DE NAMUR UNIVERSITY

Computer Science	M
Information Science	M

NOVA SOUTHEASTERN UNIVERSITY

Bioinformatics	M,D,O
Computer and Information Systems Security	M,D
Computer Science	M,D
Health Informatics	M,D,O
Information Science	M,D
Medical Informatics	M,D,O

OAKLAND UNIVERSITY

Computer Engineering	M
Computer Science	M
Electrical Engineering	M
Engineering and Applied Sciences—General	M,D
Engineering Management	M
Mechanical Engineering	M,D
Software Engineering	M
Systems Engineering	M,D
Systems Science	M

THE OHIO STATE UNIVERSITY

Agricultural Engineering	M,D
Bioengineering	M,D
Biomedical Engineering	M,D
Chemical Engineering	M,D
Civil Engineering	M,D
Computer Engineering	M,D
Computer Science	M,D
Electrical Engineering	M,D
Engineering and Applied Sciences—General	M,D
Industrial/Management Engineering	M,D
Information Science	M,D
Materials Engineering	M,D
Materials Sciences	M,D
Mechanical Engineering	M,D
Metallurgical Engineering and Metallurgy	M,D
Nuclear Engineering	M,D
Operations Research	M
Surveying Science and Engineering	M,D
Systems Engineering	M,D

OHIO UNIVERSITY

Biomedical Engineering	M
Chemical Engineering	M,D
Civil Engineering	M,D
Computer Science	M,D
Construction Engineering	M,D
Electrical Engineering	M,D
Engineering and Applied Sciences—General	M,D
Environmental Engineering	M,D
Geotechnical Engineering	M,D
Industrial/Management Engineering	M,D
Mechanical Engineering	M,D
Mechanics	M,D
Structural Engineering	M,D
Systems Engineering	M
Telecommunications	M
Transportation and Highway Engineering	M,D
Water Resources Engineering	M,D

OKLAHOMA CITY UNIVERSITY

Computer Science	M
Energy Management and Policy	M

OKLAHOMA STATE UNIVERSITY

Agricultural Engineering	M,D
Applied Science and Technology	M,D,O
Bioengineering	M,D
Chemical Engineering	M,D
Civil Engineering	M,D
Computer Engineering	M,D
Computer Science	M,D
Electrical Engineering	M,D
Engineering and Applied Sciences—General	M,D*
Environmental Engineering	M,D
Fire Protection Engineering	M,D
Industrial/Management Engineering	M,D
Information Science	M,D
Mechanical Engineering	M,D
Telecommunications Management	M,D

OLD DOMINION UNIVERSITY

Aerospace/Aeronautical Engineering	M,D
Biomedical Engineering	D
Civil Engineering	M,D
Computer Engineering	M,D
Computer Science	M,D
Electrical Engineering	M,D
Engineering and Applied Sciences—General	M,D
Engineering Management	M,D
Environmental Engineering	M,D
Ergonomics and Human Factors	D
Information Science	D
Management of Technology	M
Mechanical Engineering	M,D
Modeling and Simulation	M,D
Systems Engineering	M,D

OREGON HEALTH & SCIENCE UNIVERSITY

Biomedical Engineering	M,D
Computer Engineering	M,D
Computer Science	M,D
Electrical Engineering	M,D
Environmental Engineering	M,D
Health Informatics	M,D,O
Medical Informatics	M,D,O

OREGON STATE UNIVERSITY

Bioengineering	M,D
Chemical Engineering	M,D
Civil Engineering	M,D
Computer Engineering	M,D
Computer Science	M,D
Construction Engineering	M,D
Electrical Engineering	M,D
Engineering and Applied Sciences—General	M,D
Environmental Engineering	M,D
Geotechnical Engineering	M,D
Industrial/Management Engineering	M,D
Manufacturing Engineering	M,D
Materials Sciences	M,D
Mechanical Engineering	M,D
Nanotechnology	M,D
Nuclear Engineering	M,D
Ocean Engineering	M,D
Operations Research	M,D
Paper and Pulp Engineering	M,D
Structural Engineering	M,D
Systems Engineering	M,D
Transportation and Highway Engineering	M,D
Water Resources Engineering	M,D

OUR LADY OF THE LAKE UNIVERSITY OF SAN ANTONIO

Computer and Information Systems Security	M

PACE UNIVERSITY

Computer and Information Systems Security	M,D,O
Computer Science	M,D,O
Information Science	M,D,O
Software Engineering	M,D,O
Telecommunications	M,D,O

PACIFIC LUTHERAN UNIVERSITY

Management of Technology	M

PACIFIC STATES UNIVERSITY

Computer Science	M
Management of Technology	M,D

PENN STATE ERIE, THE BEHREND COLLEGE

Engineering and Applied Sciences—General	M

PENN STATE GREAT VALLEY

Engineering and Applied Sciences—General	M
Engineering Management	M
Information Science	M
Software Engineering	M
Systems Engineering	M

PENN STATE HARRISBURG

Computer Science	M
Electrical Engineering	M
Engineering and Applied Sciences—General	M
Engineering Management	M
Environmental Engineering	M

PENN STATE UNIVERSITY PARK

Aerospace/Aeronautical Engineering	M,D
Agricultural Engineering	M,D
Architectural Engineering	M,D
Bioengineering	M,D
Biotechnology	M,D
Chemical Engineering	M,D
Civil Engineering	M,D
Computer Engineering	M,D
Computer Science	M,D
Electrical Engineering	M,D
Engineering and Applied Sciences—General	M,D
Environmental Engineering	M,D
Geotechnical Engineering	M,D
Industrial/Management Engineering	M,D
Information Science	M,D
Materials Engineering	M,D
Materials Sciences	M,D
Mechanical Engineering	M,D
Mechanics	M,D
Mineral/Mining Engineering	M,D
Nuclear Engineering	M,D

PHILADELPHIA UNIVERSITY

Construction Management	M
Textile Sciences and Engineering	M,D

PITTSBURG STATE UNIVERSITY

Construction Engineering	M
Engineering and Applied Sciences—General	M

POINT PARK UNIVERSITY

Engineering Management	M

POLYTECHNIC INSTITUTE OF NEW YORK UNIVERSITY

Bioinformatics	M
Biomedical Engineering	M,D
Biotechnology	M
Chemical Engineering	M,D
Civil Engineering	M,D
Computer and Information Systems Security	O
Computer Engineering	M,O
Computer Science	M,D
Construction Management	M,D,O
Electrical Engineering	M,D
Engineering Physics	M
Environmental Engineering	M
Financial Engineering	M,O
Industrial/Management Engineering	M
Management of Technology	M,D,O
Manufacturing Engineering	M
Mechanical Engineering	M,D
Polymer Science and Engineering	M
Software Engineering	O
Systems Engineering	M
Telecommunications Management	M
Telecommunications	M
Transportation and Highway Engineering	M,D

POLYTECHNIC INSTITUTE OF NYU, LONG ISLAND GRADUATE CENTER

Aerospace/Aeronautical Engineering	M
Bioinformatics	M
Chemical Engineering	M
Civil Engineering	M
Computer Engineering	M
Computer Science	M
Construction Management	M
Electrical Engineering	M
Engineering Design	M
Engineering Physics	M
Environmental Engineering	M
Financial Engineering	M,O
Industrial/Management Engineering	M
Management of Technology	M
Manufacturing Engineering	M
Mechanical Engineering	M
Systems Engineering	M
Telecommunications	M
Transportation and Highway Engineering	M

POLYTECHNIC INSTITUTE OF NYU, WESTCHESTER GRADUATE CENTER

Computer Engineering	M
Computer Science	M
Construction Management	M
Electrical Engineering	M
Information Science	M
Management of Technology	M
Telecommunications	M

POLYTECHNIC UNIVERSITY OF PUERTO RICO

Civil Engineering	M
Computer Engineering	M
Computer Science	M
Electrical Engineering	M
Engineering Management	M
Management of Technology	M
Manufacturing Engineering	M
Mechanical Engineering	M

POLYTECHNIC UNIVERSITY OF PUERTO RICO, MIAMI CAMPUS

Construction Management	M
Environmental Engineering	M

POLYTECHNIC UNIVERSITY OF PUERTO RICO, ORLANDO CAMPUS

Construction Management	M
Engineering Management	M
Environmental Engineering	M
Management of Technology	M

PONTIFICIA UNIVERSIDAD CATOLICA MADRE Y MAESTRA

Engineering and Applied Sciences—General	M
Structural Engineering	M

*M—master's degree; P—first professional degree; D—doctorate; O—other advanced degree; *—Close-Up and/or Display*

PORTLAND STATE UNIVERSITY
Artificial Intelligence/Robotics M,D,O
Civil Engineering M,D,O
Computer Engineering M,D
Computer Science M,D
Electrical Engineering M,D
Engineering and Applied
  Sciences—General M,D,O
Engineering Management M,D,O
Environmental Engineering M,D
Management of Technology M,D
Manufacturing Engineering M,D
Mechanical Engineering M,D,O
Modeling and Simulation M,D,O
Software Engineering M,D
Systems Engineering M,O
Systems Science M,D,O

PRAIRIE VIEW A&M UNIVERSITY
Computer Science M,D
Electrical Engineering M,D
Engineering and Applied
  Sciences—General M,D

PRINCETON UNIVERSITY
Aerospace/Aeronautical Engineering M,D
Chemical Engineering M,D
Civil Engineering M,D
Computer Science M,D
Electrical Engineering M,D
Electronic Materials D
Engineering and Applied
  Sciences—General M,D
Financial Engineering M,D
Materials Sciences D
Mechanical Engineering M,D
Ocean Engineering D
Operations Research M,D

PURDUE UNIVERSITY
Aerospace/Aeronautical Engineering M,D
Agricultural Engineering M,D
Biomedical Engineering M,D
Biotechnology D
Chemical Engineering M,D
Civil Engineering M,D
Computer and Information
  Systems Security M
Computer Engineering M,D
Computer Science M,D
Electrical Engineering M,D
Engineering and Applied
  Sciences—General M,D,O
Ergonomics and Human Factors M,D
Industrial/Management Engineering M,D
Materials Engineering M,D
Mechanical Engineering M,D,O
Nuclear Engineering M,D

PURDUE UNIVERSITY CALUMET
Biotechnology M
Computer Engineering M
Computer Science M
Electrical Engineering M
Engineering and Applied
  Sciences—General M
Mechanical Engineering M

QUEENS COLLEGE OF THE CITY UNIVERSITY OF NEW YORK
Computer Science M

QUEEN'S UNIVERSITY AT KINGSTON
Chemical Engineering M,D
Civil Engineering M,D
Computer Engineering M,D
Computer Science M,D
Electrical Engineering M,D
Engineering and Applied
  Sciences—General M,D
Mechanical Engineering M,D
Mineral/Mining Engineering M,D

REGIS COLLEGE (MA)
Biotechnology M

REGIS UNIVERSITY
Computer and Information
  Systems Security M,O
Computer Science M,O
Database Systems M,O
Health Informatics M,D,O
Information Science M,O
Management of Technology M,O
Software Engineering M,O
Systems Engineering M,O

RENSSELAER AT HARTFORD
Computer Engineering M
Computer Science M
Electrical Engineering M
Engineering and Applied
  Sciences—General M
Information Science M
Mechanical Engineering M
Systems Science M

RENSSELAER POLYTECHNIC INSTITUTE
Aerospace/Aeronautical Engineering M,D
Bioengineering M,D
Biomedical Engineering M,D
Ceramic Sciences and Engineering M,D
Chemical Engineering M,D
Civil Engineering M,D
Computer Engineering M,D
Computer Science M,D
Electrical Engineering M,D
Engineering and Applied
  Sciences—General M,D
Engineering Management M,D
Engineering Physics M,D
Environmental Engineering M,D
Financial Engineering M,D
Geotechnical Engineering M,D
Human-Computer Interaction M
Industrial/Management Engineering M,D

Information Science M
Materials Engineering M,D
Materials Sciences M,D
Mechanical Engineering M,D
Metallurgical Engineering and
  Metallurgy M,D
Nuclear Engineering M,D
Polymer Science and Engineering M,D
Structural Engineering M,D
Systems Engineering M,D
Technology and Public Policy M,D
Transportation and Highway
  Engineering M,D

RICE UNIVERSITY
Bioengineering M,D
Bioinformatics M,D
Biomedical Engineering M,D
Chemical Engineering M,D
Civil Engineering M,D
Computer Engineering M,D
Computer Science M,D
Electrical Engineering M,D
Engineering and Applied
  Sciences—General M,D
Environmental Engineering M,D
Materials Sciences M,D
Mechanical Engineering M,D

RIVIER UNIVERSITY
Computer Science M

ROBERT MORRIS UNIVERSITY
Computer and Information
  Systems Security M,D
Engineering and Applied
  Sciences—General M
Engineering Management M
Information Science M,D

ROCHESTER INSTITUTE OF TECHNOLOGY
Bioinformatics M
Computer and Information
  Systems Security M,O
Computer Engineering M
Computer Science M,D,O
Database Systems M,O
Electrical Engineering M
Engineering and Applied
  Sciences—General M,D,O
Engineering Management M
Game Design and Development M
Human-Computer Interaction M
Industrial/Management Engineering M
Information Science M,D
Manufacturing Engineering M
Materials Engineering M
Materials Sciences M
Mechanical Engineering M
Medical Informatics M
Safety Engineering M
Software Engineering M
Systems Engineering M,D
Technology and Public Policy M
Telecommunications M

ROGER WILLIAMS UNIVERSITY
Construction Management M

ROLLINS COLLEGE
Management of Technology M

ROOSEVELT UNIVERSITY
Biotechnology M
Computer Science M
Telecommunications M

ROSE-HULMAN INSTITUTE OF TECHNOLOGY
Biomedical Engineering M
Chemical Engineering M
Civil Engineering M
Computer Engineering M
Electrical Engineering M
Engineering and Applied
  Sciences—General M
Engineering Management M
Environmental Engineering M
Mechanical Engineering M
Software Engineering M

ROWAN UNIVERSITY
Chemical Engineering M
Civil Engineering M
Construction Management M
Electrical Engineering M
Engineering and Applied
  Sciences—General M
Engineering Management M
Mechanical Engineering M

ROYAL MILITARY COLLEGE OF CANADA
Chemical Engineering M,D
Civil Engineering M,D
Computer Engineering M,D
Computer Science M
Electrical Engineering M,D
Engineering and Applied
  Sciences—General M,D
Environmental Engineering M,D
Materials Sciences M,D
Mechanical Engineering M,D
Nuclear Engineering M,D
Software Engineering M,D

RUTGERS, THE STATE UNIVERSITY OF NEW JERSEY, CAMDEN
Computer Science M

RUTGERS, THE STATE UNIVERSITY OF NEW JERSEY, NEWARK
Management of Technology D

RUTGERS, THE STATE UNIVERSITY OF NEW JERSEY, NEW BRUNSWICK
Aerospace/Aeronautical Engineering M,D

Biochemical Engineering M,D
Biomedical Engineering M,D
Chemical Engineering M,D
Civil Engineering M,D
Computer Engineering M,D
Computer Science M,D
Electrical Engineering M,D
Environmental Engineering M,D
Hazardous Materials Management M,D
Industrial/Management Engineering M,D
Materials Engineering M,D
Materials Sciences M,D
Mechanical Engineering M,D
Mechanics M,D
Operations Research D
Systems Engineering M,D

SACRED HEART UNIVERSITY
Computer and Information
  Systems Security M,O
Computer Science M,O
Database Systems M,O
Health Informatics M
Information Science M,O

ST. AMBROSE UNIVERSITY
Management of Technology M

ST. CLOUD STATE UNIVERSITY
Biomedical Engineering M
Computer and Information
  Systems Security M
Computer Science M
Electrical Engineering M
Engineering and Applied
  Sciences—General M
Engineering Management M
Mechanical Engineering M
Technology and Public Policy M

ST. FRANCIS XAVIER UNIVERSITY
Computer Science M

ST. JOHN'S UNIVERSITY (NY)
Biotechnology M

SAINT JOSEPH'S UNIVERSITY
Computer Science M,O
Health Informatics M,O

SAINT LEO UNIVERSITY
Computer and Information
  Systems Security M

SAINT LOUIS UNIVERSITY
Biomedical Engineering M,D

SAINT MARTIN'S UNIVERSITY
Civil Engineering M
Engineering Management M

SAINT MARY'S UNIVERSITY (CANADA)
Applied Science and Technology M

ST. MARY'S UNIVERSITY (UNITED STATES)
Computer Engineering M
Computer Science M
Electrical Engineering M
Engineering and Applied
  Sciences—General M
Engineering Management M
Industrial/Management Engineering M
Information Science M
Operations Research M
Software Engineering M

SAINT MARY'S UNIVERSITY OF MINNESOTA
Telecommunications M

SAINT XAVIER UNIVERSITY
Computer Science M

SALEM INTERNATIONAL UNIVERSITY
Computer and Information
  Systems Security M

SALVE REGINA UNIVERSITY
Computer and Information
  Systems Security M

SAM HOUSTON STATE UNIVERSITY
Computer and Information
  Systems Security M
Computer Science M
Information Science M

SAN DIEGO STATE UNIVERSITY
Aerospace/Aeronautical Engineering M,D
Civil Engineering M
Computer Science M
Electrical Engineering M
Engineering and Applied
  Sciences—General M,D
Engineering Design M,D
Mechanical Engineering M,D
Mechanics M,D
Telecommunications Management M

SAN FRANCISCO STATE UNIVERSITY
Biotechnology M
Computer Science M
Engineering and Applied
  Sciences—General M
Software Engineering M

SAN JOSE STATE UNIVERSITY
Aerospace/Aeronautical Engineering M
Chemical Engineering M
Civil Engineering M
Computer Engineering M
Computer Science M
Electrical Engineering M
Engineering and Applied
  Sciences—General M
Industrial/Management Engineering M
Materials Engineering M
Mechanical Engineering M
Software Engineering M
Systems Engineering M

SANTA CLARA UNIVERSITY
Civil Engineering M
Computer Engineering M,D,O
Computer Science M,D,O
Electrical Engineering M,D,O
Energy and Power Engineering M,D,O
Energy Management and Policy M,D,O
Engineering and Applied
  Sciences—General M,D,O
Engineering Design M,D,O
Engineering Management M
Management of Technology M
Materials Engineering M,D,O
Mechanical Engineering M,D,O
Software Engineering M,D,O

SAVANNAH COLLEGE OF ART AND DESIGN
Game Design and Development M,O

SCHOOL OF THE ART INSTITUTE OF CHICAGO
Materials Sciences M

SEATTLE UNIVERSITY
Engineering and Applied
  Sciences—General M
Software Engineering M

SETON HALL UNIVERSITY
Management of Technology M

SHIPPENSBURG UNIVERSITY OF PENNSYLVANIA
Computer Science M

SILICON VALLEY UNIVERSITY
Computer Engineering M
Computer Science M

SIMMONS COLLEGE
Information Science M,D,O

SIMON FRASER UNIVERSITY
Biotechnology M
Computer Science M,D
Engineering and Applied
  Sciences—General M,D
Information Science M,D
Management of Technology M,D

SOUTH CAROLINA STATE UNIVERSITY
Civil Engineering M
Mechanical Engineering M
Transportation and Highway
  Engineering M

SOUTH DAKOTA SCHOOL OF MINES AND TECHNOLOGY
Artificial Intelligence/Robotics M
Bioengineering D
Biomedical Engineering M,D
Chemical Engineering M,D
Civil Engineering M
Construction Management M
Electrical Engineering M
Engineering and Applied
  Sciences—General M,D
Engineering Management M
Geological Engineering M,D
Management of Technology M
Materials Engineering M,D
Materials Sciences M,D
Mechanical Engineering D
Nanotechnology D

SOUTH DAKOTA STATE UNIVERSITY
Agricultural Engineering M,D
Biosystems Engineering M,D
Civil Engineering M
Electrical Engineering M,D
Engineering and Applied
  Sciences—General M,D
Industrial/Management Engineering M
Mechanical Engineering M

SOUTHEASTERN LOUISIANA UNIVERSITY
Applied Science and Technology M

SOUTHEASTERN OKLAHOMA STATE UNIVERSITY
Aviation M
Biotechnology M

SOUTHEAST MISSOURI STATE UNIVERSITY
Management of Technology M

SOUTHERN ARKANSAS UNIVERSITY–MAGNOLIA
Computer Science M

SOUTHERN CONNECTICUT STATE UNIVERSITY
Computer Science M

SOUTHERN ILLINOIS UNIVERSITY CARBONDALE
Biomedical Engineering M
Civil Engineering M
Computer Engineering M,D
Computer Science M,D
Electrical Engineering M,D
Energy and Power Engineering D
Engineering and Applied
  Sciences—General M,D
Manufacturing Engineering M
Mechanical Engineering M
Mechanics M,D
Mineral/Mining Engineering M

SOUTHERN ILLINOIS UNIVERSITY EDWARDSVILLE
Biotechnology M
Civil Engineering M
Computer Science M
Electrical Engineering M

Engineering and Applied
  Sciences—General M
Industrial/Management Engineering M
Mechanical Engineering M
Operations Research M

SOUTHERN METHODIST UNIVERSITY
Applied Science and Technology M,D
Civil Engineering M,D
Computer Engineering M,D
Computer Science M,D
Electrical Engineering M,D
Engineering and Applied
  Sciences—General M,D
Engineering Management M,D
Environmental Engineering M,D
Information Science M,D
Manufacturing Engineering M,D
Mechanical Engineering M,D
Operations Research M,D
Software Engineering M,D
Systems Engineering M,D
Systems Science M,D
Telecommunications M,D

SOUTHERN OREGON UNIVERSITY
Computer Science M

SOUTHERN POLYTECHNIC STATE UNIVERSITY
Computer and Information
  Systems Security M,O
Computer Engineering M
Computer Science M,O
Construction Management M
Electrical Engineering M
Engineering and Applied
  Sciences—General M,O
Health Informatics M,O
Industrial/Management Engineering M,O
Information Science M,O
Software Engineering M,O
Systems Engineering M,O

SOUTHERN UNIVERSITY AND AGRICULTURAL AND MECHANICAL COLLEGE
Computer Science M
Engineering and Applied
  Sciences—General M

STANFORD UNIVERSITY
Aerospace/Aeronautical Engineering M,D,O
Bioengineering M,D
Biomedical Engineering M
Chemical Engineering M,D,O
Civil Engineering M,D,O
Computer Science M,D
Electrical Engineering M,D,O
Engineering and Applied
  Sciences—General M,D,O
Engineering Design M
Engineering Management M,D
Environmental Engineering M,D,O
Industrial/Management Engineering M,D
Materials Engineering M,D,O
Materials Sciences M,D,O
Mechanical Engineering M,D,O
Medical Informatics M,D
Petroleum Engineering M,D

STATE UNIVERSITY OF NEW YORK AT BINGHAMTON
Biomedical Engineering M,D
Computer Science M,D
Electrical Engineering M,D
Engineering and Applied
  Sciences—General M,D
Industrial/Management Engineering M,D
Materials Engineering M,D
Materials Sciences M,D
Mechanical Engineering M,D
Systems Science M,D

STATE UNIVERSITY OF NEW YORK AT NEW PALTZ
Computer Science M
Electrical Engineering M

STATE UNIVERSITY OF NEW YORK AT OSWEGO
Human-Computer Interaction M

STATE UNIVERSITY OF NEW YORK COLLEGE OF ENVIRONMENTAL SCIENCE AND FORESTRY
Construction Management M,D
Environmental Engineering M,D
Materials Sciences M,D
Paper and Pulp Engineering M,D
Water Resources Engineering M,D

STATE UNIVERSITY OF NEW YORK DOWNSTATE MEDICAL CENTER
Biomedical Engineering M,D

STATE UNIVERSITY OF NEW YORK INSTITUTE OF TECHNOLOGY
Computer Science M
Information Science M
Management of Technology M
Telecommunications M

STEPHEN F. AUSTIN STATE UNIVERSITY
Biotechnology M
Computer Science M

STEPHENS COLLEGE
Health Informatics M,O

STEVENS INSTITUTE OF TECHNOLOGY
Aerospace/Aeronautical Engineering M,D
Bioinformatics M,D,O
Biomedical Engineering M,O
Chemical Engineering M,D,O

Civil Engineering M,D,O
Computer and Information
  Systems Security M,D,O
Computer Engineering M,D,O
Computer Science M,D,O
Construction Engineering M,O
Construction Management M,O
Database Systems M,D,O
Electrical Engineering M,D,O
Engineering and Applied
  Sciences—General M,D,O
Engineering Design M
Engineering Management M,D
Engineering Physics M,D,O
Environmental Engineering M,D,O
Financial Engineering M
Health Informatics M,D,O
Information Science M,O
Management of Technology M,D,O
Manufacturing Engineering M
Materials Engineering M,D
Mechanical Engineering M,D,O
Modeling and Simulation M,D,O
Ocean Engineering M,D
Polymer Science and Engineering M,D
Software Engineering M,D,O
Structural Engineering M,D,O
Systems Engineering M,D,O
Systems Science M,D,O
Telecommunications Management M,D,O
Telecommunications M,D,O
Water Resources Engineering M,D,O

STEVENSON UNIVERSITY
Management of Technology M

STONY BROOK UNIVERSITY, STATE UNIVERSITY OF NEW YORK
Biomedical Engineering M,D,O
Computer Engineering M,D,O
Computer Science M,D,O
Electrical Engineering M,D
Engineering and Applied
  Sciences—General M,D,O
Hazardous Materials Management M,O
Management of Technology M,O
Materials Engineering M,D
Materials Sciences M,D
Mechanical Engineering M,D
Software Engineering M,D,O
Systems Engineering M
Technology and Public Policy D

STRATFORD UNIVERSITY (VA)
Computer and Information
  Systems Security M
Software Engineering M
Telecommunications M

STRAYER UNIVERSITY
Computer and Information
  Systems Security M
Information Science M
Software Engineering M
Systems Science M
Telecommunications Management M

SUFFOLK UNIVERSITY
Computer Science M

SYRACUSE UNIVERSITY
Aerospace/Aeronautical Engineering M,D
Bioengineering M,D
Chemical Engineering M,D
Civil Engineering M,D
Computer and Information
  Systems Security O
Computer Engineering M,D,O
Computer Science M
Electrical Engineering M,D,O
Engineering and Applied
  Sciences—General M,D,O
Engineering Management M
Environmental Engineering M
Information Science D,O
Mechanical Engineering M,D
Systems Engineering O
Telecommunications Management M,O
Telecommunications M

TEACHERS COLLEGE, COLUMBIA UNIVERSITY
Management of Technology M

T\U00E9 L\U00E9 -UNIVERSIT\U00E9
Computer Science M,D

TEMPLE UNIVERSITY
Civil Engineering M
Computer Engineering M
Computer Science M,D
Electrical Engineering M
Engineering and Applied
  Sciences—General M,D
Financial Engineering M
Health Informatics M
Information Science M,D
Mechanical Engineering M

TENNESSEE STATE UNIVERSITY
Engineering and Applied
  Sciences—General M,D

TENNESSEE TECHNOLOGICAL UNIVERSITY
Chemical Engineering M
Civil Engineering M
Computer Science M
Electrical Engineering M
Engineering and Applied
  Sciences—General M,D
Mechanical Engineering M
Software Engineering M

TEXAS A&M UNIVERSITY
Aerospace/Aeronautical Engineering M,D
Agricultural Engineering M,D
Bioengineering M,D
Biomedical Engineering M,D
Chemical Engineering M,D
Civil Engineering M,D
Computer Engineering M,D
Computer Science M,D
Construction Engineering M,D
Construction Management M,D
Electrical Engineering M,D
Engineering and Applied
  Sciences—General M,D
Environmental Engineering M,D
Geotechnical Engineering M,D
Industrial/Management Engineering M,D
Manufacturing Engineering M
Materials Engineering M,D
Mechanical Engineering M,D
Nuclear Engineering M,D
Ocean Engineering M,D
Petroleum Engineering M,D
Structural Engineering M,D
Transportation and Highway
  Engineering M,D
Water Resources Engineering M,D

TEXAS A&M UNIVERSITY–COMMERCE
Computer Science M
Management of Technology M

TEXAS A&M UNIVERSITY–CORPUS CHRISTI
Computer Science M

TEXAS A&M UNIVERSITY–KINGSVILLE
Chemical Engineering M
Civil Engineering M
Computer Science M
Electrical Engineering M
Engineering and Applied
  Sciences—General M,D
Environmental Engineering M,D
Industrial/Management Engineering M
Mechanical Engineering M
Petroleum Engineering M

TEXAS A&M UNIVERSITY–SAN ANTONIO
Computer and Information
  Systems Security M

TEXAS SOUTHERN UNIVERSITY
Computer Science M
Industrial/Management Engineering M
Transportation and Highway
  Engineering M

TEXAS STATE UNIVERSITY–SAN MARCOS
Computer Science M
Industrial/Management Engineering M
Management of Technology M
Materials Engineering D
Materials Sciences M,D
Software Engineering M

TEXAS TECH UNIVERSITY
Biotechnology M
Chemical Engineering M,D
Civil Engineering M,D
Computer Science M,D
Electrical Engineering M,D
Engineering and Applied
  Sciences—General M,D
Engineering Management M,D
Environmental Engineering M,D
Industrial/Management Engineering M,D
Mechanical Engineering M,D
Petroleum Engineering M,D
Software Engineering M,D
Systems Engineering M,D

TEXAS TECH UNIVERSITY HEALTH SCIENCES CENTER
Biotechnology M

THOMAS EDISON STATE COLLEGE
Applied Science and Technology O

THOMAS JEFFERSON UNIVERSITY
Biomedical Engineering D
Biotechnology D

TOWSON UNIVERSITY
Computer and Information
  Systems Security M,D,O
Computer Science M
Database Systems M,D,O
Information Science M,D,O
Software Engineering M,D,O

TOYOTA TECHNOLOGICAL INSTITUTE OF CHICAGO
Computer Science D

TRENT UNIVERSITY
Computer Science M
Materials Sciences M
Modeling and Simulation M,D

TREVECCA NAZARENE UNIVERSITY
Information Science M
Management of Technology M

TRIDENT UNIVERSITY INTERNATIONAL
Computer and Information
  Systems Security M,D
Health Informatics M,D,O

TRINE UNIVERSITY
Civil Engineering M
Engineering and Applied
  Sciences—General M
Mechanical Engineering M

TROY UNIVERSITY
Computer Science M

TUFTS UNIVERSITY
Bioengineering M,D;O
Bioinformatics M,D
Biomedical Engineering M,D
Biotechnology M,D,O
Chemical Engineering M,D
Civil Engineering M,D
Computer Science M,D,O
Electrical Engineering M,D,O
Engineering and Applied
  Sciences—General M
Engineering Management M
Environmental Engineering M,D
Ergonomics and Human Factors M,D
Geotechnical Engineering M,D
Hazardous Materials Management M,D
Human-Computer Interaction O
Manufacturing Engineering O
Mechanical Engineering M,D
Structural Engineering M,D
Water Resources Engineering M,D

TULANE UNIVERSITY
Biomedical Engineering M,D
Chemical Engineering D

TUSKEGEE UNIVERSITY
Electrical Engineering M
Engineering and Applied
  Sciences—General M,D
Materials Engineering D
Mechanical Engineering M

UNION GRADUATE COLLEGE
Computer Science M
Electrical Engineering M
Engineering and Applied
  Sciences—General M
Engineering Management M
Mechanical Engineering M

UNIVERSIDAD AUTONOMA DE GUADALAJARA
Computer Science M,D
Energy and Power Engineering M,D
Manufacturing Engineering M,D
Systems Science M,D

UNIVERSIDAD CENTRAL DEL ESTE
Environmental Engineering M

UNIVERSIDAD DE LAS AMÉRICAS–PUEBLA
Biotechnology M
Chemical Engineering M
Computer Science M,D
Construction Management M
Electrical Engineering M
Engineering and Applied
  Sciences—General M,D
Industrial/Management Engineering M
Manufacturing Engineering M

UNIVERSIDAD DEL ESTE
Computer and Information
  Systems Security M

UNIVERSIDAD DEL TURABO
Telecommunications M

UNIVERSIDAD NACIONAL PEDRO HENRIQUEZ URENA
Environmental Engineering M

UNIVERSITÉ DE MONCTON
Civil Engineering M
Computer Science M,O
Electrical Engineering M
Engineering and Applied
  Sciences—General M
Industrial/Management Engineering M
Mechanical Engineering M

UNIVERSITÉ DE MONTRÉAL
Bioinformatics M,D
Biomedical Engineering M,D,O
Computer Science M,D
Ergonomics and Human Factors O

UNIVERSITÉ DE SHERBROOKE
Chemical Engineering M,D
Civil Engineering M,D
Computer and Information
  Systems Security M
Electrical Engineering M,D
Engineering and Applied
  Sciences—General M,D,O
Engineering Management M,O
Environmental Engineering M,O
Information Science M,D
Mechanical Engineering M,D

UNIVERSITÉ DU QUÉBEC À CHICOUTIMI
Engineering and Applied
  Sciences—General M,D

UNIVERSITÉ DU QUÉBEC À MONTRÉAL
Ergonomics and Human Factors O

UNIVERSITÉ DU QUÉBEC À RIMOUSKI
Engineering and Applied
  Sciences—General M

UNIVERSITÉ DU QUÉBEC À TROIS-RIVIÈRES
Computer Science M
Electrical Engineering M,D
Industrial/Management Engineering M,D

UNIVERSITÉ DU QUÉBEC, ÈCOLE DE TECHNOLOGIE SUPÉRIEURE
Engineering and Applied
  Sciences—General M,D,O

---

*M—master's degree; P—first professional degree; D—doctorate; O—other advanced degree; *—Close-Up and/or Display*

UNIVERSITÉ DU QUÉBEC EN ABITIBI-TÉMISCAMINGUE
Engineering and Applied Sciences—General M,O
Mineral/Mining Engineering M,O

UNIVERSITÉ DU QUÉBEC EN OUTAOUAIS
Computer Science M,D
Software Engineering O

UNIVERSITÉ DU QUÉBEC, INSTITUT NATIONAL DE LA RECHERCHE SCIENTIFIQUE
Energy Management and Policy M,D
Materials Sciences M,D
Telecommunications M,D

UNIVERSITÉ LAVAL
Aerospace/Aeronautical Engineering M
Agricultural Engineering M
Chemical Engineering M,D
Civil Engineering M,D,O
Computer Science M,D
Electrical Engineering M,D
Engineering and Applied Sciences—General M,D,O
Environmental Engineering M,D
Industrial/Management Engineering O
Mechanical Engineering M,D
Metallurgical Engineering and Metallurgy M,D
Mineral/Mining Engineering M,D
Modeling and Simulation M,O
Software Engineering O

UNIVERSITY AT ALBANY, STATE UNIVERSITY OF NEW YORK
Computer Science M,D
Information Science M,D,O
Management of Technology M
Nanotechnology M,D

UNIVERSITY AT BUFFALO, THE STATE UNIVERSITY OF NEW YORK
Aerospace/Aeronautical Engineering M,D
Bioengineering M,D
Biotechnology M
Chemical Engineering M,D
Civil Engineering M,D
Computer Science M,D,O
Electrical Engineering M,D
Engineering and Applied Sciences—General M,D,O*
Environmental Engineering M,D
Financial Engineering M,D
Health Informatics O
Industrial/Management Engineering M,D
Materials Sciences M
Mechanical Engineering M,D
Medical Informatics O
Modeling and Simulation M,D,O
Structural Engineering M,D

UNIVERSITY OF ADVANCING TECHNOLOGY
Computer and Information Systems Security M
Computer Science M
Game Design and Development M
Management of Technology M

THE UNIVERSITY OF AKRON
Biomedical Engineering M,D
Chemical Engineering M,D
Civil Engineering M,D
Computer Engineering M,D
Computer Science M
Electrical Engineering M,D
Engineering and Applied Sciences—General M,D
Engineering Management M
Management of Technology M
Mechanical Engineering M,D
Polymer Science and Engineering M,D

THE UNIVERSITY OF ALABAMA
Aerospace/Aeronautical Engineering M,D
Chemical Engineering M,D
Civil Engineering M,D
Computer Engineering M,D
Computer Science M,D
Construction Engineering M,D
Electrical Engineering M,D
Engineering and Applied Sciences—General M,D
Environmental Engineering M,D
Ergonomics and Human Factors M
Materials Engineering M,D
Materials Sciences D
Mechanical Engineering M,D
Mechanics M,D
Metallurgical Engineering and Metallurgy M,D

THE UNIVERSITY OF ALABAMA AT BIRMINGHAM
Biomedical Engineering M,D
Civil Engineering M,D
Computer and Information Systems Security M
Computer Engineering D
Computer Science M,D
Construction Engineering M
Electrical Engineering M
Engineering and Applied Sciences—General M,D
Health Informatics M
Information Science M,D
Materials Engineering M,D
Materials Sciences D
Mechanical Engineering M
Safety Engineering M

THE UNIVERSITY OF ALABAMA IN HUNTSVILLE
Aerospace/Aeronautical Engineering M,D
Biotechnology D
Chemical Engineering M
Civil Engineering M,D
Computer and Information Systems Security M,D,O
Computer Engineering M,D,O
Computer Science M,D,O
Electrical Engineering M,D
Engineering and Applied Sciences—General M,D
Environmental Engineering M,D
Geotechnical Engineering M,D
Industrial/Management Engineering M,D
Management of Technology M,O
Materials Sciences M,D
Mechanical Engineering M,D
Modeling and Simulation M,D,O
Operations Research M,D
Software Engineering M,D,O
Structural Engineering M,D
Systems Engineering M,D
Transportation and Highway Engineering M,D
Water Resources Engineering M,D

UNIVERSITY OF ALASKA ANCHORAGE
Civil Engineering M,O
Engineering and Applied Sciences—General M,O
Engineering Management M
Environmental Engineering M
Geological Engineering M
Ocean Engineering M,O

UNIVERSITY OF ALASKA FAIRBANKS
Civil Engineering M,D,O
Computer Engineering M,D
Computer Science M
Construction Management M,D,O
Electrical Engineering M,D
Engineering and Applied Sciences—General M,D
Engineering Management M,D
Environmental Engineering M,D
Geological Engineering M,D
Mechanical Engineering M,D
Mineral/Mining Engineering M
Petroleum Engineering M,D
Software Engineering M

UNIVERSITY OF ALBERTA
Biomedical Engineering M,D
Biotechnology M,D
Chemical Engineering M,D
Civil Engineering M,D
Computer Engineering M,D
Computer Science M,D
Construction Engineering M,D
Electrical Engineering M,D
Energy and Power Engineering M,D
Engineering Management M,D
Environmental Engineering M,D
Geotechnical Engineering M,D
Materials Engineering M,D
Mechanical Engineering M,D
Mineral/Mining Engineering M,D
Nanotechnology M,D
Petroleum Engineering M,D
Structural Engineering M,D
Systems Engineering M,D
Telecommunications M,D
Water Resources Engineering M,D

THE UNIVERSITY OF ARIZONA
Aerospace/Aeronautical Engineering M,D
Agricultural Engineering M,D
Biomedical Engineering M,D
Biosystems Engineering M,D
Chemical Engineering M,D
Civil Engineering M,D
Computer Engineering M,D
Computer Science M,D
Electrical Engineering M,D
Engineering and Applied Sciences—General M,D,O
Environmental Engineering M,D
Geological Engineering M,D,O
Industrial/Management Engineering M,D
Materials Engineering M,D
Materials Sciences M,D
Mechanical Engineering M,D
Mechanics M,D
Medical Informatics M,D,O
Mineral/Mining Engineering M,O
Reliability Engineering M
Systems Engineering M,D

UNIVERSITY OF ARKANSAS
Agricultural Engineering M,D
Bioengineering M
Biomedical Engineering M
Chemical Engineering M,D
Civil Engineering M,D
Computer Engineering M,D
Computer Science M,D
Electrical Engineering M,D
Electronic Materials M,D
Engineering and Applied Sciences—General M,D
Environmental Engineering M
Industrial/Management Engineering M,D
Mechanical Engineering M,D
Operations Research M,D
Telecommunications M,D
Transportation and Highway Engineering M,D

UNIVERSITY OF ARKANSAS AT LITTLE ROCK
Applied Science and Technology M,D
Bioinformatics M,D
Computer Science M
Construction Management M,O
Information Science M
Management of Technology M,O
Systems Engineering O

UNIVERSITY OF ATLANTA
Computer Science M,D,O

UNIVERSITY OF BALTIMORE
Human-Computer Interaction M,D
Information Science M,D

UNIVERSITY OF BRIDGEPORT
Biomedical Engineering M
Computer Engineering M,D
Computer Science M,D
Electrical Engineering M
Engineering and Applied Sciences—General M,D
Management of Technology M
Mechanical Engineering M

THE UNIVERSITY OF BRITISH COLUMBIA
Chemical Engineering M,D
Civil Engineering M,D
Computer Engineering M,D
Computer Science M,D
Electrical Engineering M,D
Engineering and Applied Sciences—General M,D
Geological Engineering M,D
Materials Engineering M,D
Materials Sciences M,D
Mechanical Engineering M,D
Metallurgical Engineering and Metallurgy M,D
Mineral/Mining Engineering M,D
Operations Research M
Software Engineering M

UNIVERSITY OF CALGARY
Biomedical Engineering M,D
Biotechnology M
Chemical Engineering M,D
Civil Engineering M,D
Computer Engineering M,D
Computer Science M,D
Electrical Engineering M,D
Engineering and Applied Sciences—General M,D
Geotechnical Engineering M,D
Manufacturing Engineering M,D
Mechanical Engineering M,D
Petroleum Engineering M,D
Software Engineering M,D

UNIVERSITY OF CALIFORNIA, BERKELEY
Applied Science and Technology D
Bioengineering D
Chemical Engineering M,D
Civil Engineering M,D
Computer Science M,D
Construction Management O
Electrical Engineering M,D
Energy Management and Policy M,D
Engineering and Applied Sciences—General M,D,O
Engineering Management M,D
Environmental Engineering M,D
Financial Engineering M
Geotechnical Engineering M,D
Industrial/Management Engineering M,D
Materials Engineering M,D
Materials Sciences M,D
Mechanical Engineering M,D
Mechanics M,D
Nuclear Engineering M,D
Operations Research M,D
Structural Engineering M,D
Transportation and Highway Engineering M,D
Water Resources Engineering M,D

UNIVERSITY OF CALIFORNIA, DAVIS
Aerospace/Aeronautical Engineering M,D,O
Applied Science and Technology M,D
Bioengineering M,D
Biomedical Engineering M,D
Chemical Engineering M,D
Civil Engineering M,D,O
Computer Engineering M,D
Computer Science M,D
Electrical Engineering M,D
Engineering and Applied Sciences—General M,D,O
Environmental Engineering M,D,O
Materials Engineering M,D
Materials Sciences M,D
Mechanical Engineering M,D,O
Medical Informatics M
Transportation and Highway Engineering M,D

UNIVERSITY OF CALIFORNIA, IRVINE
Aerospace/Aeronautical Engineering M,D
Biochemical Engineering M,D
Biomedical Engineering M,D
Biotechnology M
Chemical Engineering M,D
Civil Engineering M,D
Computer Science M,D
Electrical Engineering M,D
Engineering and Applied Sciences—General M,D
Environmental Engineering M,D
Information Science M,D
Materials Engineering M,D
Materials Sciences M,D
Mechanical Engineering M,D
Transportation and Highway Engineering M,D

UNIVERSITY OF CALIFORNIA, LOS ANGELES
Aerospace/Aeronautical Engineering M,D
Bioinformatics M,D
Biomedical Engineering M,D
Chemical Engineering M,D
Civil Engineering M,D
Computer Science M,D
Electrical Engineering M,D
Engineering and Applied Sciences—General M,D
Environmental Engineering M,D
Financial Engineering M,D
Manufacturing Engineering M
Materials Engineering M,D
Materials Sciences M,D
Mechanical Engineering M,D

UNIVERSITY OF CALIFORNIA, MERCED
Bioengineering M,D
Computer Science M,D
Electrical Engineering M,D
Engineering and Applied Sciences—General M,D
Mechanical Engineering M,D
Mechanics M,D

UNIVERSITY OF CALIFORNIA, RIVERSIDE
Artificial Intelligence/Robotics M,D
Bioengineering M,D
Bioinformatics D
Chemical Engineering M,D
Computer Engineering M,D
Computer Science M,D
Electrical Engineering M,D
Environmental Engineering M,D
Materials Engineering M,D
Materials Sciences M,D
Mechanical Engineering M,D
Nanotechnology M,D

UNIVERSITY OF CALIFORNIA, SAN DIEGO
Aerospace/Aeronautical Engineering M,D
Artificial Intelligence/Robotics M,D
Bioengineering M,D
Bioinformatics D
Chemical Engineering M,D
Computer Engineering M,D
Computer Science M,D
Electrical Engineering M,D
Engineering Physics M,D
Materials Sciences M,D
Mechanical Engineering M,D
Mechanics M,D
Modeling and Simulation M,D
Ocean Engineering M,D
Structural Engineering M,D
Telecommunications M,D

UNIVERSITY OF CALIFORNIA, SAN FRANCISCO
Bioengineering D
Bioinformatics D
Medical Informatics D

UNIVERSITY OF CALIFORNIA, SANTA BARBARA
Bioengineering D
Chemical Engineering M,D
Computer Engineering M,D
Computer Science M,D
Electrical Engineering M,D
Engineering and Applied Sciences—General M,D
Materials Engineering M,D
Materials Sciences M,D
Mechanical Engineering M,D

UNIVERSITY OF CALIFORNIA, SANTA CRUZ
Bioinformatics M,D
Computer Engineering M,D
Computer Science M,D
Electrical Engineering M,D
Engineering and Applied Sciences—General M,D
Management of Technology M,D
Telecommunications M,D

UNIVERSITY OF CENTRAL ARKANSAS
Computer Science M

UNIVERSITY OF CENTRAL FLORIDA
Aerospace/Aeronautical Engineering M
Biotechnology M,D
Civil Engineering M,D,O
Computer Engineering M,D
Computer Science M,D
Construction Engineering M,D,O
Electrical Engineering M,D,O
Engineering and Applied Sciences—General M,D,O
Engineering Design M,D,O
Engineering Management M,D,O
Environmental Engineering M,D
Ergonomics and Human Factors M,D,O
Game Design and Development M
Health Informatics M,O
Industrial/Management Engineering M,D,O
Materials Engineering M,D
Materials Sciences M,D
Mechanical Engineering M,D
Modeling and Simulation M,D,O
Operations Research M,D,O
Structural Engineering M,D,O
Systems Engineering M,D,O
Transportation and Highway Engineering M,D,O

UNIVERSITY OF CENTRAL MISSOURI
Aerospace/Aeronautical Engineering M,D
Computer Science M,D
Information Science M,D,O
Management of Technology M,D

UNIVERSITY OF CENTRAL OKLAHOMA
Computer Science M
Engineering and Applied Sciences—General M

UNIVERSITY OF CHICAGO
Computer Science M

UNIVERSITY OF CINCINNATI
Aerospace/Aeronautical Engineering M,D
Bioinformatics D
Biomedical Engineering D
Chemical Engineering M,D
Civil Engineering M,D
Computer Engineering M,D
Computer Science M,D
Electrical Engineering M,D
Engineering and Applied Sciences—General M,D
Environmental Engineering M,D
Ergonomics and Human Factors M,D
Industrial/Management Engineering M,D
Materials Engineering M,D
Materials Sciences M,D
Mechanical Engineering M,D
Mechanics M,D
Nuclear Engineering M,D

UNIVERSITY OF COLORADO AT COLORADO SPRINGS
Aerospace/Aeronautical Engineering M
Applied Science and Technology M,D
Computer Science M,D
Electrical Engineering M,D
Engineering and Applied Sciences—General M,D
Engineering Management M
Information Science M
Manufacturing Engineering M
Mechanical Engineering M
Software Engineering M

UNIVERSITY OF COLORADO BOULDER
Aerospace/Aeronautical Engineering M,D
Architectural Engineering M,D
Chemical Engineering M,D
Civil Engineering M,D
Computer Engineering M,D
Computer Science M,D
Construction Engineering M,D
Electrical Engineering M,D
Engineering and Applied Sciences—General M,D
Engineering Management M
Environmental Engineering M,D
Geotechnical Engineering M,D
Mechanical Engineering M,D
Operations Research M
Structural Engineering M,D
Telecommunications Management M
Telecommunications M
Water Resources Engineering M,D

UNIVERSITY OF COLORADO DENVER
Applied Science and Technology M
Bioengineering M,D
Bioinformatics D
Civil Engineering M,D
Computer Science M,D
Electrical Engineering M,D
Energy Management and Policy M
Engineering and Applied Sciences—General M,D
Environmental Engineering M,D
Geotechnical Engineering M,D
Hazardous Materials Management M
Hydraulics M,D
Information Science M,D
Management of Technology M,D
Mechanical Engineering M,D
Mechanics M
Medical Informatics M,D
Operations Research M,D
Structural Engineering M,D
Transportation and Highway Engineering M,D

UNIVERSITY OF CONNECTICUT
Biomedical Engineering M,D
Chemical Engineering M,D
Civil Engineering M,D
Computer Science M,D
Electrical Engineering M,D
Engineering and Applied Sciences—General M,D
Environmental Engineering M,D
Materials Engineering M,D
Materials Sciences M,D
Mechanical Engineering M,D
Metallurgical Engineering and Metallurgy M,D
Polymer Science and Engineering M,D
Software Engineering M,D

UNIVERSITY OF DALLAS
Management of Technology M

UNIVERSITY OF DAYTON
Aerospace/Aeronautical Engineering M,D
Agricultural Engineering M
Bioengineering M
Biosystems Engineering M
Chemical Engineering M
Civil Engineering M
Computer and Information Systems Security M
Computer Engineering M,D
Computer Science M
Electrical Engineering M,D
Engineering Management M
Environmental Engineering M
Materials Engineering M,D
Mechanical Engineering M,D
Mechanics M
Structural Engineering M
Transportation and Highway Engineering M
Water Resources Engineering M

UNIVERSITY OF DELAWARE
Biotechnology M,D
Chemical Engineering M,D
Civil Engineering M,D
Computer Engineering M,D
Computer Science M,D
Electrical Engineering M,D
Energy Management and Policy M,D
Engineering and Applied Sciences—General M,D
Environmental Engineering M,D
Geotechnical Engineering M,D
Information Science M,D
Management of Technology M
Materials Engineering M,D
Materials Sciences M,D
Mechanical Engineering M,D
Ocean Engineering M,D
Operations Research M
Structural Engineering M,D
Transportation and Highway Engineering M,D
Water Resources Engineering M,D

UNIVERSITY OF DENVER
Bioengineering M,D
Computer and Information Systems Security M,O
Computer Engineering M,D
Computer Science M,D
Construction Management M
Database Systems M,O
Electrical Engineering M,D
Energy Management and Policy M,O
Engineering and Applied Sciences—General M,D
Engineering Management M,D
Internet Engineering M,O
Management of Technology M,O
Materials Engineering M,D
Materials Sciences M,D
Mechanical Engineering M,D
Software Engineering M,O
Systems Engineering M,D
Telecommunications M,O

UNIVERSITY OF DETROIT MERCY
Architectural Engineering M
Civil Engineering M,D
Computer Engineering M,D
Computer Science M
Electrical Engineering M,D
Engineering and Applied Sciences—General M,D
Engineering Management M
Environmental Engineering M,D
Information Science M
Mechanical Engineering M,D
Software Engineering M

UNIVERSITY OF EVANSVILLE
Computer Science M
Electrical Engineering M
Engineering and Applied Sciences—General M

UNIVERSITY OF FLORIDA
Aerospace/Aeronautical Engineering M,D,O
Agricultural Engineering M,D,O
Bioengineering M,D,O
Biomedical Engineering M,D,O
Chemical Engineering M,D
Civil Engineering M,D,O
Computer Engineering M,D,O
Computer Science M,D
Construction Engineering M
Construction Management M
Electrical Engineering M,D,O
Engineering and Applied Sciences—General M,D,O
Environmental Engineering M,D,O
Industrial/Management Engineering M,D,O
Information Science M,D
Materials Engineering M,D,O
Materials Sciences M,D,O
Mechanical Engineering M,D,O
Nuclear Engineering M,D,O
Ocean Engineering M,D,O
Systems Engineering M,D,O

UNIVERSITY OF GEORGIA
Agricultural Engineering M,D
Artificial Intelligence/Robotics M
Biochemical Engineering M
Bioengineering M,D
Bioinformatics M,D,O
Computer Science M,D
Environmental Engineering M

UNIVERSITY OF GUELPH
Bioengineering M,D
Biotechnology M,D
Computer Science M,D
Engineering and Applied Sciences—General M,D
Environmental Engineering M,D
Water Resources Engineering M,D

UNIVERSITY OF HARTFORD
Engineering and Applied Sciences—General M

UNIVERSITY OF HAWAII AT MANOA
Bioengineering M
Civil Engineering M,D
Computer Science M,D,O
Electrical Engineering M,D
Engineering and Applied Sciences—General M,D
Environmental Engineering M,D
Financial Engineering M
Geological Engineering M,D
Information Science M,D
Mechanical Engineering M,D
Ocean Engineering M,D
Telecommunications O

UNIVERSITY OF HOUSTON
Biomedical Engineering D
Chemical Engineering M,D
Civil Engineering M,D
Computer and Information Systems Security M
Computer Science M,D
Construction Management M
Electrical Engineering M,D
Engineering and Applied Sciences—General M,D
Industrial/Management Engineering M,D
Information Science M,D
Mechanical Engineering M,D
Petroleum Engineering M,D
Telecommunications M

UNIVERSITY OF HOUSTON–CLEAR LAKE
Biotechnology M
Computer Engineering M
Computer Science M
Information Science M
Software Engineering M
Systems Engineering M

UNIVERSITY OF HOUSTON–VICTORIA
Computer Science M

UNIVERSITY OF IDAHO
Agricultural Engineering M,D
Bioengineering M,D
Bioinformatics M,D
Chemical Engineering M,D
Civil Engineering M,D
Computer Engineering M
Computer Science M,D
Electrical Engineering M,D
Engineering and Applied Sciences—General M,D
Engineering Management M
Environmental Engineering M
Geological Engineering M
Management of Technology M,D
Materials Sciences M,D
Metallurgical Engineering and Metallurgy M,D
Nuclear Engineering M,D

UNIVERSITY OF ILLINOIS AT CHICAGO
Bioengineering M,D
Biotechnology D
Chemical Engineering M,D
Civil Engineering M,D
Computer Engineering M,D
Computer Science M,D
Electrical Engineering M,D
Engineering and Applied Sciences—General M,D
Health Informatics M
Industrial/Management Engineering M,D
Materials Engineering M,D
Mechanical Engineering M,D
Operations Research D

UNIVERSITY OF ILLINOIS AT SPRINGFIELD
Computer Science M

UNIVERSITY OF ILLINOIS AT URBANA–CHAMPAIGN
Aerospace/Aeronautical Engineering M,D
Agricultural Engineering M,D
Aviation M
Bioengineering M,D
Bioinformatics M,D,O
Chemical Engineering M,D
Civil Engineering M,D
Computer Engineering M,D
Computer Science M,D
Electrical Engineering M,D
Energy Management and Policy M
Engineering and Applied Sciences—General M,D
Environmental Engineering M,D
Ergonomics and Human Factors M
Financial Engineering M
Health Informatics M,D,O
Human-Computer Interaction M,D,O
Industrial/Management Engineering M,D
Information Science M,D,O
Management of Technology M,D
Materials Engineering M,D
Materials Sciences M,D
Mechanical Engineering M,D
Mechanics M,D
Medical Informatics M,D,O
Nuclear Engineering M,D
Systems Engineering M,D

THE UNIVERSITY OF IOWA
Biochemical Engineering M,D
Biomedical Engineering M,D
Chemical Engineering M,D
Civil Engineering M,D
Computer Engineering M,D
Computer Science M,D
Electrical Engineering M,D
Engineering and Applied Sciences—General M,D*
Environmental Engineering M,D
Ergonomics and Human Factors M,D
Health Informatics M,D,O
Industrial/Management Engineering M,D
Information Science M,D,O
Manufacturing Engineering M,D
Mechanical Engineering M,D
Operations Research M,D

THE UNIVERSITY OF KANSAS
Aerospace/Aeronautical Engineering M,D
Architectural Engineering M
Bioengineering M,D
Biotechnology M
Chemical Engineering M,D
Civil Engineering M,D
Computer Engineering M
Computer Science M,D
Construction Management M
Electrical Engineering M,D
Engineering and Applied Sciences—General M,D
Engineering Management M
Environmental Engineering M,D
Health Informatics M
Mechanical Engineering M,D
Medical Informatics M,D,O
Petroleum Engineering M,D

UNIVERSITY OF KENTUCKY
Agricultural Engineering M,D
Biomedical Engineering M,D
Chemical Engineering M,D
Civil Engineering M,D
Computer Science M,D
Electrical Engineering M,D
Engineering and Applied Sciences—General M,D
Information Science M
Manufacturing Engineering M
Materials Sciences M,D
Mechanical Engineering M,D
Mineral/Mining Engineering M,D

UNIVERSITY OF LA VERNE
Health Informatics M

UNIVERSITY OF LETHBRIDGE
Computer Science M,D

UNIVERSITY OF LOUISIANA AT LAFAYETTE
Architectural Engineering M
Chemical Engineering M
Civil Engineering M
Computer Engineering M,D
Computer Science M,D*
Engineering Management M
Mechanical Engineering M
Petroleum Engineering M
Telecommunications M

UNIVERSITY OF LOUISVILLE
Chemical Engineering M,D
Civil Engineering M,D
Computer and Information Systems Security M,D,O
Computer Engineering M,D,O
Computer Science M,D,O
Electrical Engineering M,D
Engineering and Applied Sciences—General M,D,O
Engineering Management M,D,O
Environmental Engineering M,D
Industrial/Management Engineering M,D,O
Mechanical Engineering M,D

UNIVERSITY OF MAINE
Bioengineering M,D
Biomedical Engineering D
Chemical Engineering M,D
Civil Engineering M,D
Computer Engineering M,D
Computer Science M,D
Electrical Engineering M,D
Engineering and Applied Sciences—General M,D
Engineering Physics M
Mechanical Engineering M,D
Ocean Engineering D
Water Resources Engineering M,D

UNIVERSITY OF MANAGEMENT AND TECHNOLOGY
Computer Science M,O
Information Science M,O
Software Engineering M,O

THE UNIVERSITY OF MANCHESTER
Aerospace/Aeronautical Engineering M,D
Biochemical Engineering M,D
Bioinformatics M,D
Biotechnology M,D
Chemical Engineering M,D
Civil Engineering M,D
Computer Science M,D
Electrical Engineering M,D
Engineering Management M,D
Environmental Engineering M,D
Hazardous Materials Management M,D
Materials Sciences M,D
Mechanical Engineering M,D
Metallurgical Engineering and Metallurgy M,D
Modeling and Simulation M,D
Nuclear Engineering M,D
Paper and Pulp Engineering M,D
Polymer Science and Engineering M,D
Structural Engineering M,D

UNIVERSITY OF MANITOBA
Biosystems Engineering M,D
Civil Engineering M,D
Computer Engineering M,D
Computer Science M,D
Electrical Engineering M,D
Engineering and Applied Sciences—General M,D
Industrial/Management Engineering M,D
Manufacturing Engineering M,D
Mechanical Engineering M,D

UNIVERSITY OF MARYLAND, BALTIMORE COUNTY
Biochemical Engineering M,D,O
Biotechnology M,O
Chemical Engineering M,D

*M—master's degree; P—first professional degree; D—doctorate; O—other advanced degree; *—Close-Up and/or Display*

Civil Engineering	M,D
Computer and Information Systems Security	M,O
Computer Engineering	M,D
Computer Science	M,D
Electrical Engineering	M,D
Engineering and Applied Sciences—General	M,D,O
Engineering Management	M,O
Information Science	M,D
Mechanical Engineering	M,D,O
Systems Engineering	M,O

UNIVERSITY OF MARYLAND, COLLEGE PARK

Aerospace/Aeronautical Engineering	M,D
Bioengineering	M,D
Bioinformatics	D
Chemical Engineering	M,D
Civil Engineering	M,D
Computer Engineering	M,D
Computer Science	M,D
Electrical Engineering	M,D
Engineering and Applied Sciences—General	M
Environmental Engineering	M,D
Fire Protection Engineering	M
Manufacturing Engineering	M,D
Materials Engineering	M,D
Materials Sciences	M,D
Mechanical Engineering	M,D
Mechanics	M,D
Nuclear Engineering	M,D
Reliability Engineering	M,D
Systems Engineering	M
Telecommunications	M

UNIVERSITY OF MARYLAND EASTERN SHORE

Computer Science	M

UNIVERSITY OF MARYLAND UNIVERSITY COLLEGE

Biotechnology	M,O
Computer and Information Systems Security	M,O
Health Informatics	M,O
Information Science	M,O
Management of Technology	M,O

UNIVERSITY OF MASSACHUSETTS AMHERST

Architectural Engineering	M,D
Biotechnology	M,D
Chemical Engineering	M,D
Civil Engineering	M,D
Computer Engineering	M,D
Computer Science	M,D
Electrical Engineering	M,D
Engineering and Applied Sciences—General	M,D
Engineering Management	
Environmental Engineering	M,D
Geotechnical Engineering	M,D
Industrial/Management Engineering	M,D
Mechanical Engineering	M,D
Mechanics	M,D
Operations Research	M,D
Polymer Science and Engineering	M,D
Structural Engineering	M,D
Transportation and Highway Engineering	M,D
Water Resources Engineering	M,D

UNIVERSITY OF MASSACHUSETTS BOSTON

Biotechnology	M
Computer Science	M,D

UNIVERSITY OF MASSACHUSETTS DARTMOUTH

Biomedical Engineering	M,D
Biotechnology	M,D
Civil Engineering	M
Computer Engineering	M,D,O
Electrical Engineering	M,D,O
Engineering and Applied Sciences—General	M,D,O
Environmental Engineering	M
Mechanical Engineering	M
Software Engineering	M,O
Telecommunications	M,D,O
Textile Sciences and Engineering	M

UNIVERSITY OF MASSACHUSETTS LOWELL

Biotechnology	M,D
Chemical Engineering	M,D
Civil Engineering	M,D,O
Computer Engineering	M
Computer Science	M,D
Electrical Engineering	M,D
Energy and Power Engineering	M,D
Engineering and Applied Sciences—General	M,D,O
Environmental Engineering	M,D,O
Ergonomics and Human Factors	M,D,O
Health Informatics	M,O
Industrial/Management Engineering	M,D,O
Materials Engineering	M,D,O
Mechanical Engineering	M,D
Mechanics	M,D
Nuclear Engineering	M,D
Polymer Science and Engineering	M,D,O

UNIVERSITY OF MASSACHUSETTS WORCESTER

Bioinformatics	M,D

UNIVERSITY OF MEDICINE AND DENTISTRY OF NEW JERSEY

Bioinformatics	M,D
Biomedical Engineering	M,D,O
Medical Informatics	M,D,O

UNIVERSITY OF MEMPHIS

Biomedical Engineering	M,D
Civil Engineering	M,D
Computer Engineering	M,D
Computer Science	M,D
Electrical Engineering	M,D
Energy and Power Engineering	M,D
Engineering and Applied Sciences—General	M,D
Environmental Engineering	M,D
Industrial/Management Engineering	M,D
Manufacturing Engineering	M
Mechanical Engineering	M,D
Structural Engineering	M,D
Transportation and Highway Engineering	M,D
Water Resources Engineering	M,D

UNIVERSITY OF MIAMI

Aerospace/Aeronautical Engineering	M,D
Architectural Engineering	M,D
Biomedical Engineering	M,D
Civil Engineering	M,D
Computer Engineering	M,D
Computer Science	M,D
Electrical Engineering	M,D
Engineering and Applied Sciences—General	M,D
Ergonomics and Human Factors	M
Industrial/Management Engineering	M,D
Management of Technology	M,D
Mechanical Engineering	M,D

UNIVERSITY OF MICHIGAN

Aerospace/Aeronautical Engineering	M,D
Artificial Intelligence/Robotics	M,D
Automotive Engineering	M,D
Bioinformatics	M,D
Biomedical Engineering	M,D
Chemical Engineering	M,D,O
Civil Engineering	M,D,O
Computer Engineering	M,D
Computer Science	M,D
Construction Engineering	M,D,O
Electrical Engineering	M,D
Energy and Power Engineering	M,D
Engineering and Applied Sciences—General	M,D,O
Environmental Engineering	M,D,O
Financial Engineering	M,D
Health Informatics	M,D
Human-Computer Interaction	M,D
Industrial/Management Engineering	M,D
Information Science	M,D
Manufacturing Engineering	M,D
Materials Engineering	M,D
Materials Sciences	M,D*
Mechanical Engineering	M,D
Nuclear Engineering	M,D,O
Ocean Engineering	M,D,O
Operations Research	M,D
Pharmaceutical Engineering	M,D
Structural Engineering	M,D,O

UNIVERSITY OF MICHIGAN–DEARBORN

Automotive Engineering	M,D
Computer Engineering	M
Computer Science	M
Electrical Engineering	M
Engineering and Applied Sciences—General	M,D
Industrial/Management Engineering	M
Information Science	M
Manufacturing Engineering	M
Mechanical Engineering	M
Software Engineering	M
Systems Engineering	M,D

UNIVERSITY OF MICHIGAN–FLINT

Computer Science	M
Information Science	M

UNIVERSITY OF MINNESOTA, DULUTH

Computer Engineering	M
Computer Science	M
Electrical Engineering	M
Engineering Management	M
Safety Engineering	M

UNIVERSITY OF MINNESOTA, TWIN CITIES CAMPUS

Aerospace/Aeronautical Engineering	M,D
Biomedical Engineering	M,D
Biosystems Engineering	M,D
Biotechnology	M
Chemical Engineering	M,D
Civil Engineering	M,D,O
Computer and Information Systems Security	M
Computer Engineering	M,D
Computer Science	M,D
Electrical Engineering	M,D
Engineering and Applied Sciences—General	M,D,O
Geological Engineering	M,D,O
Health Informatics	M,D
Industrial/Management Engineering	M,D
Management of Technology	M
Materials Engineering	M,D
Materials Sciences	M,D
Mechanical Engineering	M,D
Mechanics	M,D
Software Engineering	M,D
Systems Engineering	M
Technology and Public Policy	M

UNIVERSITY OF MISSISSIPPI

Applied Science and Technology	M,D
Engineering and Applied Sciences—General	M,D

UNIVERSITY OF MISSOURI

Aerospace/Aeronautical Engineering	M,D
Agricultural Engineering	M,D
Bioengineering	M,D
Bioinformatics	D
Chemical Engineering	M,D
Civil Engineering	M,D
Computer Science	M,D
Electrical Engineering	M,D
Engineering and Applied Sciences—General	M,D
Environmental Engineering	M,D
Geotechnical Engineering	M,D
Health Informatics	M,D,O
Industrial/Management Engineering	M,D
Manufacturing Engineering	M,D
Mechanical Engineering	M,D
Nuclear Engineering	M,D
Structural Engineering	M,D
Transportation and Highway Engineering	M,D
Water Resources Engineering	M,D

UNIVERSITY OF MISSOURI–KANSAS CITY

Bioinformatics	M,D
Civil Engineering	M,D
Computer Engineering	M,D
Computer Science	M,D
Electrical Engineering	M,D
Engineering and Applied Sciences—General	M,D
Mechanical Engineering	M,D
Polymer Science and Engineering	M,D
Software Engineering	M,D
Telecommunications	M,D

UNIVERSITY OF MISSOURI–ST. LOUIS

Biotechnology	M,D,O
Computer Science	M,D

THE UNIVERSITY OF MONTANA

Computer Science	M

UNIVERSITY OF NEBRASKA AT OMAHA

Artificial Intelligence/Robotics	M,O
Computer and Information Systems Security	M,D,O
Computer Science	M,O
Information Science	M,D,O
Systems Engineering	M,O

UNIVERSITY OF NEBRASKA–LINCOLN

Agricultural Engineering	M,D
Architectural Engineering	M,D
Bioengineering	M,D
Bioinformatics	M,D
Chemical Engineering	M,D
Civil Engineering	M,D
Computer Engineering	M,D
Computer Science	M,D
Electrical Engineering	M,D
Engineering and Applied Sciences—General	M,D
Engineering Management	M,D
Environmental Engineering	M,D
Industrial/Management Engineering	M,D
Information Science	M,D
Manufacturing Engineering	M,D
Materials Engineering	M,D
Materials Sciences	M,D
Mechanical Engineering	M,D
Mechanics	M,D
Metallurgical Engineering and Metallurgy	M,D

UNIVERSITY OF NEVADA, LAS VEGAS

Aerospace/Aeronautical Engineering	M,D
Biomedical Engineering	M,D
Civil Engineering	M,D
Computer Engineering	M,D
Computer Science	M,D
Construction Management	M
Electrical Engineering	M,D
Energy and Power Engineering	M,D,O
Engineering and Applied Sciences—General	M,D
Environmental Engineering	M,D
Information Science	M,D
Materials Engineering	M,D
Mechanical Engineering	M,D
Nuclear Engineering	M,D
Transportation and Highway Engineering	M,D

UNIVERSITY OF NEVADA, RENO

Biomedical Engineering	M,D
Biotechnology	M
Chemical Engineering	M,D
Civil Engineering	M,D
Computer Engineering	M,D
Computer Science	M,D
Electrical Engineering	M,D
Engineering and Applied Sciences—General	M,D
Geological Engineering	M,D
Materials Engineering	M,D
Mechanical Engineering	M,D
Metallurgical Engineering and Metallurgy	M,D
Mineral/Mining Engineering	M

UNIVERSITY OF NEW BRUNSWICK FREDERICTON

Chemical Engineering	M,D
Civil Engineering	M,D
Computer Engineering	M,D
Computer Science	M,D
Construction Engineering	M,D
Electrical Engineering	M,D
Engineering and Applied Sciences—General	M,D,O
Engineering Management	M
Environmental Engineering	M,D
Geotechnical Engineering	M,D
Materials Sciences	M,D
Mechanical Engineering	M,D
Mechanics	M,D
Structural Engineering	M,D
Surveying Science and Engineering	M,D,O
Transportation and Highway Engineering	M,D

UNIVERSITY OF NEW HAMPSHIRE

Chemical Engineering	M,D
Civil Engineering	M,D
Computer Science	M,D,O
Electrical Engineering	M,D
Management of Technology	M
Materials Sciences	M,D
Mechanical Engineering	M,D
Ocean Engineering	M,D,O
Software Engineering	M,D,O

UNIVERSITY OF NEW HAVEN

Computer and Information Systems Security	M,O
Computer Engineering	M
Computer Science	M,D,O
Database Systems	M,O
Electrical Engineering	M
Engineering and Applied Sciences—General	M,O
Engineering Management	M
Environmental Engineering	M
Fire Protection Engineering	M,O
Hazardous Materials Management	M
Industrial/Management Engineering	M,O
Information Science	M,O
Mechanical Engineering	M
Software Engineering	M,O
Systems Engineering	M,O
Telecommunications Management	M,O

UNIVERSITY OF NEW MEXICO

Biomedical Engineering	D
Chemical Engineering	M,D
Civil Engineering	M,D
Computer and Information Systems Security	M
Computer Engineering	M,D,O
Computer Science	M,D
Construction Management	M
Electrical Engineering	M,D,O*
Engineering and Applied Sciences—General	M,D,O
Management of Technology	M
Manufacturing Engineering	M
Mechanical Engineering	M,D
Nanotechnology	M,D
Nuclear Engineering	M,D

UNIVERSITY OF NEW ORLEANS

Computer Science	M
Engineering and Applied Sciences—General	M,D,O
Engineering Management	M,O
Mechanical Engineering	M

THE UNIVERSITY OF NORTH CAROLINA AT CHAPEL HILL

Bioinformatics	D
Biomedical Engineering	M,D
Computer Science	M,D*
Environmental Engineering	M,D
Materials Sciences	M,D
Operations Research	M,D

THE UNIVERSITY OF NORTH CAROLINA AT CHARLOTTE

Bioinformatics	M,D,O
Civil Engineering	M,D
Computer and Information Systems Security	M,D,O
Computer Engineering	M,D
Computer Science	M,O
Database Systems	M,O
Electrical Engineering	M,D
Engineering and Applied Sciences—General	M,D
Environmental Engineering	M,D
Game Design and Development	M,D,O
Health Informatics	M,D,O
Information Science	M,D,O
Management of Technology	M
Mechanical Engineering	M,D
Systems Engineering	M,D

THE UNIVERSITY OF NORTH CAROLINA AT GREENSBORO

Computer Science	M

THE UNIVERSITY OF NORTH CAROLINA WILMINGTON

Computer Science	M
Systems Science	M

UNIVERSITY OF NORTH DAKOTA

Aviation	M
Chemical Engineering	M
Civil Engineering	M
Computer Science	M,D
Electrical Engineering	M
Engineering and Applied Sciences—General	D
Environmental Engineering	M
Geological Engineering	M
Management of Technology	M
Mechanical Engineering	M
Mineral/Mining Engineering	M
Structural Engineering	M

UNIVERSITY OF NORTHERN BRITISH COLUMBIA

Computer Science	M,D,O

UNIVERSITY OF NORTHERN IOWA

Biotechnology	M
Computer Science	M
Modeling and Simulation	M

UNIVERSITY OF NORTH FLORIDA

Civil Engineering	M
Computer Science	M
Construction Management	M
Electrical Engineering	M
Mechanical Engineering	M
Software Engineering	M

UNIVERSITY OF NORTH TEXAS

Computer Engineering	M,D
Computer Science	M,D
Electrical Engineering	M

Engineering and Applied
   Sciences—General — M
Materials Sciences — M,D

UNIVERSITY OF NORTH TEXAS HEALTH SCIENCE CENTER AT FORT WORTH
Biotechnology — M,D

UNIVERSITY OF NOTRE DAME
Aerospace/Aeronautical Engineering — M,D
Bioengineering — M,D
Chemical Engineering — M,D
Civil Engineering — M,D
Computer Engineering — M,D
Computer Science — M,D
Electrical Engineering — M,D
Engineering and Applied
   Sciences—General — M,D
Environmental Engineering — M,D
Mechanical Engineering — M,D

UNIVERSITY OF OKLAHOMA
Aerospace/Aeronautical Engineering — M,D
Bioengineering — M,D
Bioinformatics — M,D
Chemical Engineering — M,D
Civil Engineering — M,D
Computer Engineering — M,D
Computer Science — M,D
Construction Management — M
Electrical Engineering — M,D
Engineering and Applied
   Sciences—General — M,D
Engineering Management — M,D
Engineering Physics — M,D
Environmental Engineering — M,D
Geological Engineering — M,D
Industrial/Management Engineering — M,D
Mechanical Engineering — M,D
Petroleum Engineering — M,D
Telecommunications — M

UNIVERSITY OF OREGON
Computer Science — M,D
Information Science — M,D

UNIVERSITY OF OTTAWA
Aerospace/Aeronautical Engineering — M,D
Bioengineering — M,D
Biomedical Engineering — M
Chemical Engineering — M,D
Civil Engineering — M,D
Computer Engineering — M,D
Computer Science — M,D
Electrical Engineering — M,D
Engineering and Applied
   Sciences—General — M,D,O
Engineering Management — M,O
Information Science — M,O
Mechanical Engineering — M,D
Systems Science — M,D,O

UNIVERSITY OF PENNSYLVANIA
Bioengineering — M,D
Biotechnology — M
Chemical Engineering — M,D
Computer Science — M,D
Electrical Engineering — M,D
Engineering and Applied
   Sciences—General — M,D,O*
Information Science — M,D
Management of Technology — M
Materials Engineering — M,D
Materials Sciences — M,D
Mechanical Engineering — M,D
Mechanics — M,D
Systems Engineering — M,D
Telecommunications Management — M
Telecommunications — M

UNIVERSITY OF PHOENIX–ATLANTA CAMPUS
Management of Technology — M

UNIVERSITY OF PHOENIX–AUGUSTA CAMPUS
Management of Technology — M

UNIVERSITY OF PHOENIX–AUSTIN CAMPUS
Management of Technology — M

UNIVERSITY OF PHOENIX–BAY AREA CAMPUS
Energy Management and Policy — M,D
Management of Technology — M,D

UNIVERSITY OF PHOENIX–BIRMINGHAM CAMPUS
Health Informatics — M
Management of Technology — M

UNIVERSITY OF PHOENIX–BOSTON CAMPUS
Management of Technology — M

UNIVERSITY OF PHOENIX–CENTRAL FLORIDA CAMPUS
Management of Technology — M

UNIVERSITY OF PHOENIX–CENTRAL MASSACHUSETTS CAMPUS
Management of Technology — M

UNIVERSITY OF PHOENIX–CENTRAL VALLEY CAMPUS
Management of Technology — M

UNIVERSITY OF PHOENIX–CHARLOTTE CAMPUS
Health Informatics — M
Management of Technology — M

UNIVERSITY OF PHOENIX–CHATTANOOGA CAMPUS
Management of Technology — M

UNIVERSITY OF PHOENIX–CHEYENNE CAMPUS
Management of Technology — M

UNIVERSITY OF PHOENIX–CHICAGO CAMPUS
Management of Technology — M

UNIVERSITY OF PHOENIX–CINCINNATI CAMPUS
Information Science — M
Management of Technology — M

UNIVERSITY OF PHOENIX–CLEVELAND CAMPUS
Management of Technology — M

UNIVERSITY OF PHOENIX–COLUMBIA CAMPUS
Management of Technology — M

UNIVERSITY OF PHOENIX–COLUMBUS GEORGIA CAMPUS
Management of Technology — M

UNIVERSITY OF PHOENIX–COLUMBUS OHIO CAMPUS
Management of Technology — M

UNIVERSITY OF PHOENIX–DALLAS CAMPUS
Management of Technology — M

UNIVERSITY OF PHOENIX–DENVER CAMPUS
Management of Technology — M

UNIVERSITY OF PHOENIX–DES MOINES CAMPUS
Health Informatics — M,D
Management of Technology — M

UNIVERSITY OF PHOENIX–EASTERN WASHINGTON CAMPUS
Management of Technology — M

UNIVERSITY OF PHOENIX–HARRISBURG CAMPUS
Management of Technology — M

UNIVERSITY OF PHOENIX–HAWAII CAMPUS
Management of Technology — M

UNIVERSITY OF PHOENIX–HOUSTON CAMPUS
Management of Technology — M

UNIVERSITY OF PHOENIX–IDAHO CAMPUS
Management of Technology — M

UNIVERSITY OF PHOENIX–INDIANAPOLIS CAMPUS
Management of Technology — M

UNIVERSITY OF PHOENIX–JERSEY CITY CAMPUS
Management of Technology — M

UNIVERSITY OF PHOENIX–KANSAS CITY CAMPUS
Management of Technology — M

UNIVERSITY OF PHOENIX–LAS VEGAS CAMPUS
Management of Technology — M

UNIVERSITY OF PHOENIX–LOUISIANA CAMPUS
Management of Technology — M

UNIVERSITY OF PHOENIX–MADISON CAMPUS
Management of Technology — M

UNIVERSITY OF PHOENIX–MARYLAND CAMPUS
Management of Technology — M

UNIVERSITY OF PHOENIX–MEMPHIS CAMPUS
Management of Technology — M

UNIVERSITY OF PHOENIX–MILWAUKEE CAMPUS
Health Informatics — M,D

UNIVERSITY OF PHOENIX–MINNEAPOLIS/ST. LOUIS PARK CAMPUS
Management of Technology — M

UNIVERSITY OF PHOENIX–NASHVILLE CAMPUS
Management of Technology — M

UNIVERSITY OF PHOENIX–NEW MEXICO CAMPUS
Management of Technology — M

UNIVERSITY OF PHOENIX–NORTHERN NEVADA CAMPUS
Management of Technology — M

UNIVERSITY OF PHOENIX–NORTHWEST ARKANSAS CAMPUS
Management of Technology — M

UNIVERSITY OF PHOENIX–OKLAHOMA CITY CAMPUS
Management of Technology — M

UNIVERSITY OF PHOENIX–OMAHA CAMPUS
Management of Technology — M

UNIVERSITY OF PHOENIX–ONLINE CAMPUS
Energy Management and Policy — M,O
Health Informatics — M,O
Management of Technology — M,O

UNIVERSITY OF PHOENIX–OREGON CAMPUS
Management of Technology — M

UNIVERSITY OF PHOENIX–PHILADELPHIA CAMPUS
Management of Technology — M

UNIVERSITY OF PHOENIX–PHOENIX MAIN CAMPUS
Energy Management and Policy — M,O
Health Informatics — M,O
Management of Technology — M,O

UNIVERSITY OF PHOENIX–PITTSBURGH CAMPUS
Management of Technology — M

UNIVERSITY OF PHOENIX–PUERTO RICO CAMPUS
Energy Management and Policy — M
Management of Technology — M

UNIVERSITY OF PHOENIX–RALEIGH CAMPUS
Health Informatics — M,D
Management of Technology — M

UNIVERSITY OF PHOENIX–RICHMOND CAMPUS
Management of Technology — M

UNIVERSITY OF PHOENIX–SACRAMENTO VALLEY CAMPUS
Management of Technology — M

UNIVERSITY OF PHOENIX–SAN ANTONIO CAMPUS
Management of Technology — M

UNIVERSITY OF PHOENIX–SAN DIEGO CAMPUS
Management of Technology — M

UNIVERSITY OF PHOENIX–SAVANNAH CAMPUS
Management of Technology — M

UNIVERSITY OF PHOENIX–SOUTHERN ARIZONA CAMPUS
Management of Technology — M

UNIVERSITY OF PHOENIX–SOUTHERN CALIFORNIA CAMPUS
Energy Management and Policy — M
Management of Technology — M

UNIVERSITY OF PHOENIX–SOUTHERN COLORADO CAMPUS
Management of Technology — M

UNIVERSITY OF PHOENIX–SPRINGFIELD CAMPUS
Management of Technology — M

UNIVERSITY OF PHOENIX–TULSA CAMPUS
Management of Technology — M

UNIVERSITY OF PHOENIX–UTAH CAMPUS
Management of Technology — M

UNIVERSITY OF PHOENIX–VANCOUVER CAMPUS
Management of Technology — M

UNIVERSITY OF PHOENIX–WASHINGTON D.C. CAMPUS
Health Informatics — M,D

UNIVERSITY OF PHOENIX–WEST FLORIDA CAMPUS
Management of Technology — M

UNIVERSITY OF PITTSBURGH
Artificial Intelligence/Robotics — M,D
Bioengineering — M,D
Bioinformatics — M,D,O
Chemical Engineering — M,D
Civil Engineering — M,D
Computer Engineering — M,D
Computer Science — M,D
Electrical Engineering — M,D
Engineering and Applied
   Sciences—General — M,D
Environmental Engineering — M,D
Health Informatics — M
Industrial/Management Engineering — M,D
Information Science — M,D,O
Materials Sciences — M,D
Mechanical Engineering — M,D
Petroleum Engineering — M,D
Telecommunications — M,D,O

UNIVERSITY OF PORTLAND
Engineering and Applied
   Sciences—General — M
Management of Technology — M

UNIVERSITY OF PUERTO RICO, MAYAGÜEZ CAMPUS
Chemical Engineering — M,D
Civil Engineering — M,D
Computer Engineering — M,D
Computer Science — M,D
Electrical Engineering — M,D
Engineering and Applied
   Sciences—General — M,D
Industrial/Management Engineering — M

Information Science — M,D
Mechanical Engineering — M,D

UNIVERSITY OF PUERTO RICO, MEDICAL SCIENCES CAMPUS
Health Informatics — M

UNIVERSITY OF PUERTO RICO, RIO PIEDRAS
Information Science — M,O

UNIVERSITY OF REGINA
Computer Engineering — M,D
Computer Science — M,D
Engineering and Applied
   Sciences—General — M,D
Environmental Engineering — M,D
Industrial/Management Engineering — M,D
Petroleum Engineering — M,D
Software Engineering — M,D
Systems Engineering — M,D

UNIVERSITY OF RHODE ISLAND
Biomedical Engineering — M,D,O
Biotechnology — M,D
Chemical Engineering — M,D
Civil Engineering — M,D
Computer Engineering — M,D,O
Computer Science — M,D,O
Electrical Engineering — M,D,O
Engineering and Applied
   Sciences—General — M,D,O
Environmental Engineering — M,D
Ocean Engineering — M,D

UNIVERSITY OF ROCHESTER
Biomedical Engineering — M,D
Chemical Engineering — M,D*
Computer Engineering — M,D
Computer Science — M,D
Electrical Engineering — M,D
Energy and Power Engineering — M
Energy Management and Policy — M
Engineering and Applied
   Sciences—General — M,D
Materials Sciences — M,D
Mechanical Engineering — M,D

UNIVERSITY OF ST. THOMAS (MN)
Computer and Information
   Systems Security — M,O
Engineering and Applied
   Sciences—General — M,O
Engineering Management — M,O
Management of Technology — M,O
Manufacturing Engineering — M,O
Mechanical Engineering — M,O
Software Engineering — M,O
Systems Engineering — M,O

UNIVERSITY OF SAN DIEGO
Health Informatics — M,D

UNIVERSITY OF SAN FRANCISCO
Biotechnology — M
Computer Science — M
Database Systems — M
Internet Engineering — M
Telecommunications Management — M

UNIVERSITY OF SASKATCHEWAN
Agricultural Engineering — M,D
Biomedical Engineering — M,D
Biotechnology — M
Chemical Engineering — M,D
Civil Engineering — M,D
Computer Science — M,D
Electrical Engineering — M,D
Engineering and Applied
   Sciences—General — M,D,O
Engineering Physics — M,D
Environmental Engineering — M,D,O
Mechanical Engineering — M,D

THE UNIVERSITY OF SCRANTON
Software Engineering — M

UNIVERSITY OF SOUTH AFRICA
Chemical Engineering — M
Engineering and Applied
   Sciences—General — M
Information Science — M,D
Technology and Public Policy — M,D
Telecommunications Management — M,D

UNIVERSITY OF SOUTH ALABAMA
Chemical Engineering — M
Civil Engineering — M
Computer Science — M
Electrical Engineering — M
Engineering and Applied
   Sciences—General — M
Information Science — M
Mechanical Engineering — M

UNIVERSITY OF SOUTH CAROLINA
Chemical Engineering — M,D
Civil Engineering — M,D
Computer Engineering — M,D
Computer Science — M,D
Electrical Engineering — M,D
Engineering and Applied
   Sciences—General — M,D
Hazardous Materials Management — M,D
Mechanical Engineering — M,D
Nuclear Engineering — M,D
Software Engineering — M,D

THE UNIVERSITY OF SOUTH DAKOTA
Computer Science — M,D

UNIVERSITY OF SOUTHERN CALIFORNIA
Aerospace/Aeronautical Engineering — M,D,O
Artificial Intelligence/Robotics — M,D
Bioinformatics — D

Biomedical Engineering	M,D
Chemical Engineering	M,D,O
Civil Engineering	M,D,O
Computer and Information Systems Security	M,D
Computer Engineering	M,D,O
Computer Science	M,D
Construction Management	M,D,O
Electrical Engineering	M,D,O
Engineering and Applied Sciences—General	M,D,O
Engineering Management	M,D,O
Environmental Engineering	M,D,O
Game Design and Development	M,D
Hazardous Materials Management	M,D,O
Industrial/Management Engineering	M,D,O
Manufacturing Engineering	M,D,O
Materials Engineering	M,D,O
Materials Sciences	M,D,O
Mechanical Engineering	M,D,O
Mechanics	M,D,O
Modeling and Simulation	M,D
Operations Research	M,D,O
Petroleum Engineering	M,D,O
Safety Engineering	M,D,O
Software Engineering	M,D
Systems Engineering	M,D,O
Telecommunications	M,D,O
Transportation and Highway Engineering	M,D,O

UNIVERSITY OF SOUTHERN INDIANA

Engineering and Applied Sciences—General	M

UNIVERSITY OF SOUTHERN MAINE

Computer Science	M
Manufacturing Engineering	M

UNIVERSITY OF SOUTHERN MISSISSIPPI

Computer Science	M,D
Construction Engineering	M
Polymer Science and Engineering	M,D

UNIVERSITY OF SOUTH FLORIDA

Bioinformatics	M,D
Biomedical Engineering	M,D
Biotechnology	M,D
Chemical Engineering	M,D
Civil Engineering	M,D
Computer Engineering	M,D
Computer Science	M,D
Electrical Engineering	M,D
Engineering and Applied Sciences—General	M,D
Engineering Management	M,D
Environmental Engineering	M,D
Industrial/Management Engineering	M,D
Mechanical Engineering	M,D
Polymer Science and Engineering	M,D

THE UNIVERSITY OF TENNESSEE

Aerospace/Aeronautical Engineering	M,D
Agricultural Engineering	M
Aviation	M
Biomedical Engineering	M,D
Biosystems Engineering	M,D
Chemical Engineering	M,D
Civil Engineering	M,D
Computer Engineering	M,D
Computer Science	M,D
Electrical Engineering	M,D
Energy and Power Engineering	D
Engineering and Applied Sciences—General	M,D
Engineering Management	M,D
Environmental Engineering	M
Industrial/Management Engineering	M,D
Information Science	M,D
Materials Engineering	M,D
Materials Sciences	M,D
Mechanical Engineering	M,D
Nuclear Engineering	M,D
Polymer Science and Engineering	M,D
Reliability Engineering	M,D

THE UNIVERSITY OF TENNESSEE AT CHATTANOOGA

Chemical Engineering	M
Civil Engineering	M
Computer Science	M,O
Electrical Engineering	M
Energy and Power Engineering	M,O
Engineering and Applied Sciences—General	M,D,O
Engineering Management	M,O
Industrial/Management Engineering	M
Mechanical Engineering	M
Medical Informatics	M,D,O

THE UNIVERSITY OF TENNESSEE SPACE INSTITUTE

Aerospace/Aeronautical Engineering	M,D
Aviation	M
Computer Science	M,D
Electrical Engineering	M,D
Engineering and Applied Sciences—General	M,D
Engineering Management	M,D
Materials Engineering	M
Materials Sciences	M
Mechanical Engineering	M,D
Mechanics	M,D

THE UNIVERSITY OF TEXAS AT ARLINGTON

Aerospace/Aeronautical Engineering	M,D
Bioengineering	M,D
Civil Engineering	M,D
Computer Engineering	M,D
Computer Science	M,D
Electrical Engineering	M,D
Engineering and Applied Sciences—General	M,D
Engineering Management	M
Industrial/Management Engineering	M,D
Materials Engineering	M,D
Materials Sciences	M,D
Mechanical Engineering	M,D
Software Engineering	M,D
Systems Engineering	M

THE UNIVERSITY OF TEXAS AT AUSTIN

Aerospace/Aeronautical Engineering	M,D
Architectural Engineering	M
Biomedical Engineering	M,D
Chemical Engineering	M,D
Civil Engineering	M,D
Computer Engineering	M,D
Computer Science	M,D
Electrical Engineering	M,D
Engineering and Applied Sciences—General	M,D
Environmental Engineering	M,D
Geotechnical Engineering	M,D
Industrial/Management Engineering	M,D
Materials Engineering	M,D
Materials Sciences	M,D
Mechanical Engineering	M,D
Mechanics	M,D
Mineral/Mining Engineering	M
Operations Research	M,D
Petroleum Engineering	M,D
Technology and Public Policy	M
Textile Sciences and Engineering	M
Water Resources Engineering	M,D

THE UNIVERSITY OF TEXAS AT DALLAS

Bioinformatics	M,D
Biomedical Engineering	M,D
Biotechnology	M,D
Computer and Information Systems Security	M
Computer Engineering	M,D
Computer Science	M,D
Electrical Engineering	M,D
Engineering and Applied Sciences—General	M,D
Financial Engineering	M
Materials Engineering	M,D
Materials Sciences	M,D
Mechanical Engineering	M
Software Engineering	M,D
Systems Engineering	M,D
Telecommunications	M,D

THE UNIVERSITY OF TEXAS AT EL PASO

Bioinformatics	M,D
Civil Engineering	M,D,O
Computer Engineering	M,D
Computer Science	M,D
Construction Management	M,D,O
Electrical Engineering	M,D
Engineering and Applied Sciences—General	M,D,O
Environmental Engineering	M,D,O
Industrial/Management Engineering	M,O
Information Science	M,D
Manufacturing Engineering	M,O
Materials Engineering	M,D
Materials Sciences	M,D
Mechanical Engineering	M
Metallurgical Engineering and Metallurgy	M,D
Systems Engineering	M,O

THE UNIVERSITY OF TEXAS AT SAN ANTONIO

Biomedical Engineering	M,D
Biotechnology	M,D
Civil Engineering	M,D
Computer and Information Systems Security	M,D
Computer Engineering	M,D
Computer Science	M,D
Construction Management	M
Electrical Engineering	M,D
Engineering and Applied Sciences—General	M,D
Environmental Engineering	M,D
Information Science	M,D
Management of Technology	M,D
Manufacturing Engineering	M,D
Materials Engineering	M,D
Mechanical Engineering	M,D

THE UNIVERSITY OF TEXAS AT TYLER

Civil Engineering	M
Computer Science	M
Electrical Engineering	M
Environmental Engineering	M
Mechanical Engineering	M
Structural Engineering	M
Transportation and Highway Engineering	M
Water Resources Engineering	M

THE UNIVERSITY OF TEXAS HEALTH SCIENCE CENTER AT HOUSTON

Health Informatics	M,D,O

THE UNIVERSITY OF TEXAS MEDICAL BRANCH

Bioinformatics	D

THE UNIVERSITY OF TEXAS OF THE PERMIAN BASIN

Computer Science	M

THE UNIVERSITY OF TEXAS–PAN AMERICAN

Computer Science	M
Electrical Engineering	M
Engineering Management	M
Manufacturing Engineering	M
Mechanical Engineering	M
Systems Engineering	M

THE UNIVERSITY OF TEXAS SOUTHWESTERN MEDICAL CENTER

Biomedical Engineering	M,D

UNIVERSITY OF THE DISTRICT OF COLUMBIA

Computer Science	M
Electrical Engineering	M
Engineering and Applied Sciences—General	M

UNIVERSITY OF THE SACRED HEART

Information Science	O

UNIVERSITY OF THE SCIENCES IN PHILADELPHIA

Bioinformatics	M
Biotechnology	M,D

THE UNIVERSITY OF TOLEDO

Bioengineering	M,D
Bioinformatics	M,O
Biomedical Engineering	D
Chemical Engineering	M,D
Civil Engineering	M,D
Computer Science	M,D
Electrical Engineering	M,D
Engineering and Applied Sciences—General	M
Industrial/Management Engineering	M,D
Materials Sciences	M,D
Mechanical Engineering	M,D

UNIVERSITY OF TORONTO

Aerospace/Aeronautical Engineering	M,D
Biomedical Engineering	M,D
Biotechnology	M
Chemical Engineering	M,D
Civil Engineering	M,D
Computer Engineering	M,D
Computer Science	M,D
Electrical Engineering	M,D
Engineering and Applied Sciences—General	M,D
Health Informatics	M
Industrial/Management Engineering	M,D
Management of Technology	M
Manufacturing Engineering	M
Materials Engineering	M,D
Materials Sciences	M,D
Mechanical Engineering	M,D

UNIVERSITY OF TULSA

Chemical Engineering	M,D
Computer Science	M,D
Electrical Engineering	M
Energy Management and Policy	M
Engineering and Applied Sciences—General	M,D
Engineering Physics	M
Financial Engineering	M
Mechanical Engineering	M,D
Petroleum Engineering	M,D

UNIVERSITY OF UTAH

Bioengineering	M,D*
Bioinformatics	M,D,O
Biotechnology	M
Chemical Engineering	M,D
Civil Engineering	M,D
Computer Science	M,D
Electrical Engineering	M,D
Engineering and Applied Sciences—General	M,D
Environmental Engineering	M,D
Geological Engineering	M,D
Materials Engineering	M,D
Materials Sciences	M,D
Mechanical Engineering	M,D
Metallurgical Engineering and Metallurgy	M,D
Mineral/Mining Engineering	M,D
Nuclear Engineering	M,D

UNIVERSITY OF VERMONT

Biomedical Engineering	M
Civil Engineering	M,D
Computer Science	M,D
Electrical Engineering	M,D
Engineering and Applied Sciences—General	M,D
Environmental Engineering	M,D
Materials Sciences	M,D
Mechanical Engineering	M,D

UNIVERSITY OF VICTORIA

Computer Engineering	M,D
Computer Science	M,D
Electrical Engineering	M,D
Engineering and Applied Sciences—General	M,D
Health Informatics	M
Mechanical Engineering	M,D

UNIVERSITY OF VIRGINIA

Aerospace/Aeronautical Engineering	M,D
Biomedical Engineering	M,D
Chemical Engineering	M,D
Civil Engineering	M,D
Computer Engineering	M,D
Computer Science	M,D
Electrical Engineering	M,D
Engineering and Applied Sciences—General	M,D
Engineering Physics	M,D
Health Informatics	M
Materials Sciences	M,D
Mechanical Engineering	M,D
Systems Engineering	M,D

UNIVERSITY OF WASHINGTON

Aerospace/Aeronautical Engineering	M,D
Bioengineering	M,D
Bioinformatics	M,D
Biomedical Engineering	M,D
Biotechnology	D
Ceramic Sciences and Engineering	M,D
Chemical Engineering	M,D
Civil Engineering	M,D
Computer Science	M,D
Construction Engineering	M,D
Construction Management	M
Electrical Engineering	M,D
Energy Management and Policy	M,D
Engineering and Applied Sciences—General	M,D
Environmental Engineering	M,D
Geotechnical Engineering	M,D
Health Informatics	M,D
Industrial/Management Engineering	M,D
Information Science	M,D
Management of Technology	M,D
Materials Engineering	M,D
Materials Sciences	M,D
Mechanical Engineering	M,D
Medical Informatics	M,D
Nanotechnology	M,D
Structural Engineering	M,D
Transportation and Highway Engineering	M,D
Water Resources Engineering	M,D

UNIVERSITY OF WASHINGTON, BOTHELL

Computer Engineering	M
Software Engineering	M

UNIVERSITY OF WASHINGTON, TACOMA

Computer Engineering	M
Software Engineering	M

UNIVERSITY OF WATERLOO

Chemical Engineering	M,D
Civil Engineering	M,D
Computer Engineering	M,D
Computer Science	M,D
Electrical Engineering	M,D
Engineering and Applied Sciences—General	M,D
Engineering Management	M,D
Environmental Engineering	M,D
Information Science	M,D
Management of Technology	M,D
Mechanical Engineering	M,D
Operations Research	M,D
Software Engineering	M,D
Systems Engineering	M,D

THE UNIVERSITY OF WESTERN ONTARIO

Biochemical Engineering	M,D
Chemical Engineering	M,D
Civil Engineering	M,D
Computer Engineering	M,D
Computer Science	M,D
Electrical Engineering	M,D
Engineering and Applied Sciences—General	M,D
Environmental Engineering	M,D
Materials Engineering	M,D
Mechanical Engineering	M,D

UNIVERSITY OF WEST FLORIDA

Biotechnology	M
Computer Science	M
Database Systems	M,O
Software Engineering	M,O

UNIVERSITY OF WEST GEORGIA

Computer Science	M

UNIVERSITY OF WINDSOR

Civil Engineering	M,D
Computer Science	M,D
Electrical Engineering	M,D
Engineering and Applied Sciences—General	M,D
Environmental Engineering	M,D
Industrial/Management Engineering	M,D
Manufacturing Engineering	M,D
Materials Engineering	M,D
Mechanical Engineering	M,D

UNIVERSITY OF WISCONSIN–LA CROSSE

Software Engineering	M

UNIVERSITY OF WISCONSIN–MADISON

Agricultural Engineering	M,D
Bioengineering	M,D
Biomedical Engineering	M,D
Chemical Engineering	M,D
Civil Engineering	M,D
Computer and Information Systems Security	M
Computer Science	M,D
Electrical Engineering	M,D
Energy and Power Engineering	M,D
Engineering and Applied Sciences—General	M,D
Engineering Physics	M,D
Environmental Engineering	M,D
Geological Engineering	M,D
Industrial/Management Engineering	M,D
Management of Technology	M
Manufacturing Engineering	M
Materials Engineering	M,D
Materials Sciences	M,D
Mechanical Engineering	M,D
Mechanics	M,D
Nuclear Engineering	M,D
Polymer Science and Engineering	M,D
Systems Engineering	M,D

UNIVERSITY OF WISCONSIN–MILWAUKEE

Civil Engineering	M,D,O
Computer Engineering	M,D,O
Computer Science	M,D
Electrical Engineering	M,D,O
Engineering and Applied Sciences—General	M,D,O
Engineering Management	M,D,O
Ergonomics and Human Factors	M,D,O
Health Informatics	M,O
Industrial/Management Engineering	M,D,O
Manufacturing Engineering	M,D,O

Materials Engineering — M,D,O
Mechanical Engineering — M,D,O
Mechanics — M,D,O
Medical Informatics — D

UNIVERSITY OF WISCONSIN–PARKSIDE
Computer Science — M
Information Science — M

UNIVERSITY OF WISCONSIN–PLATTEVILLE
Computer Science — M
Engineering and Applied
  Sciences—General — M

UNIVERSITY OF WISCONSIN–STOUT
Industrial/Management Engineering — M
Information Science — M
Management of Technology — M
Manufacturing Engineering — M
Telecommunications Management — M

UNIVERSITY OF WISCONSIN–WHITEWATER
Management of Technology — M

UNIVERSITY OF WYOMING
Biotechnology — D
Chemical Engineering — M,D
Civil Engineering — M,D
Computer Science — M,D
Electrical Engineering — M,D
Engineering and Applied
  Sciences—General — M,D
Environmental Engineering — M
Mechanical Engineering — M,D
Petroleum Engineering — M,D

UTAH STATE UNIVERSITY
Aerospace/Aeronautical Engineering — M,D
Agricultural Engineering — M,D
Civil Engineering — M,D,O
Computer Science — M,D
Electrical Engineering — M,D
Engineering and Applied
  Sciences—General — M,D,O
Environmental Engineering — M,D,O
Mechanical Engineering — M,D
Water Resources Engineering — M,D

UTICA COLLEGE
Computer and Information
  Systems Security — M

VALPARAISO UNIVERSITY
Engineering Management — M,O

VANDERBILT UNIVERSITY
Bioinformatics — M,D
Biomedical Engineering — M,D
Chemical Engineering — M,D
Civil Engineering — M,D
Computer Science — M,D
Electrical Engineering — M,D
Engineering and Applied
  Sciences—General — M,D
Environmental Engineering — M,D
Materials Sciences — M,D
Mechanical Engineering — M,D

VILLANOVA UNIVERSITY
Artificial Intelligence/Robotics — M,O
Biochemical Engineering — M,O
Chemical Engineering — M,O
Civil Engineering — M
Computer Engineering — M,O
Computer Science — M,O
Electrical Engineering — M,O
Engineering and Applied
  Sciences—General — M,D,O
Environmental Engineering — M,O
Manufacturing Engineering — M,O
Mechanical Engineering — M,O
Software Engineering — M
Water Resources Engineering — M,O

VIRGINIA COMMONWEALTH UNIVERSITY
Bioengineering — M,D
Bioinformatics — M,D
Biomedical Engineering — M,D
Chemical Engineering — M,D
Computer Science — M,D
Electrical Engineering — M,D
Engineering and Applied
  Sciences—General — M,D
Mechanical Engineering — M,D
Modeling and Simulation — M,D
Nanotechnology — M,D
Operations Research — M,D

VIRGINIA INTERNATIONAL UNIVERSITY
Computer Science — M

VIRGINIA POLYTECHNIC INSTITUTE AND STATE UNIVERSITY
Aerospace/Aeronautical Engineering — M,D,O
Agricultural Engineering — M,D
Bioengineering — M,D
Bioinformatics — D

Biomedical Engineering — M,D
Biotechnology — M
Chemical Engineering — M,D
Civil Engineering — M,D,O
Computer and Information
  Systems Security — M,D,O
Computer Engineering — M,D,O
Computer Science — M,O
Construction Engineering — M,D
Electrical Engineering — M,D,O
Engineering and Applied
  Sciences—General — M,D,O
Engineering Management — M,O
Environmental Engineering — M,D,O
Hazardous Materials Management — M,D,O
Human-Computer Interaction — M,D,O
Industrial/Management Engineering — M,D
Materials Engineering — M,D
Materials Sciences — M,D
Mechanical Engineering — M,D
Mechanics — M,D,O
Mineral/Mining Engineering — M,D
Ocean Engineering — M,O
Software Engineering — M,O
Systems Engineering — M,D,O
Transportation and Highway
  Engineering — M,D,O
Water Resources Engineering — M,D,O

VIRGINIA STATE UNIVERSITY
Computer Science — M

WAKE FOREST UNIVERSITY
Biomedical Engineering — M,D
Computer Science — M

WALDEN UNIVERSITY
Health Informatics — M,D,O
Management of Technology — M,D,O

WASHINGTON STATE UNIVERSITY
Agricultural Engineering — M,D
Bioengineering — M,D
Chemical Engineering — M,D
Civil Engineering — M,D
Computer Engineering — M,D
Computer Science — M,D
Electrical Engineering — M,D
Engineering and Applied
  Sciences—General — M,D
Environmental Engineering — M
Materials Engineering — M
Materials Sciences — M
Mechanical Engineering — M,D

WASHINGTON STATE UNIVERSITY SPOKANE
Engineering Management — M

WASHINGTON STATE UNIVERSITY TRI-CITIES
Computer Science — M,D
Electrical Engineering — M,D
Engineering and Applied
  Sciences—General — M,D
Mechanical Engineering — M,D

WASHINGTON STATE UNIVERSITY VANCOUVER
Computer Science — M
Engineering and Applied
  Sciences—General — M
Mechanical Engineering — M

WASHINGTON UNIVERSITY IN ST. LOUIS
Aerospace/Aeronautical Engineering — M,D
Biomedical Engineering — M,D
Chemical Engineering — M,D
Computer Engineering — M,D
Computer Science — M,D
Electrical Engineering — M,D
Engineering and Applied
  Sciences—General — M,D
Environmental Engineering — M,D
Mechanical Engineering — M,D
Structural Engineering — M,D
Systems Science — M,D

WAYNE STATE UNIVERSITY
Automotive Engineering — M,O
Biomedical Engineering — M,D
Chemical Engineering — M,D
Civil Engineering — M,D
Computer Engineering — M,D
Computer Science — M,D,O
Electrical Engineering — M,D
Energy and Power Engineering — M,D,O
Engineering and Applied
  Sciences—General — M,D,O
Engineering Management — M,O
Industrial/Management Engineering — M,D
Manufacturing Engineering — M
Materials Engineering — M,D,O
Materials Sciences — M,D,O
Mechanical Engineering — M,D
Polymer Science and Engineering — M,D,O
Systems Engineering — M,D,O

WEBSTER UNIVERSITY
Aerospace/Aeronautical Engineering — M,D,O
Computer Science — M,O
Engineering Management — M
Telecommunications Management — M,D,O

WENTWORTH INSTITUTE OF TECHNOLOGY
Construction Management — M

WESLEYAN UNIVERSITY
Bioinformatics — D
Computer Science — M,D

WEST CHESTER UNIVERSITY OF PENNSYLVANIA
Computer and Information
  Systems Security — M,O
Computer Science — M,O

WESTERN CAROLINA UNIVERSITY
Computer Science — M
Construction Management — M
Industrial/Management Engineering — M

WESTERN GOVERNORS UNIVERSITY
Computer and Information
  Systems Security — M

WESTERN ILLINOIS UNIVERSITY
Computer Science — M
Manufacturing Engineering — M

WESTERN INTERNATIONAL UNIVERSITY
Systems Engineering — M

WESTERN KENTUCKY UNIVERSITY
Computer Science — M
Management of Technology — M

WESTERN MICHIGAN UNIVERSITY
Chemical Engineering — M,D
Civil Engineering — M
Computer Engineering — M,D
Computer Science — M,D
Construction Engineering — M
Construction Management — M
Electrical Engineering — M,D
Engineering and Applied
  Sciences—General — M,D
Engineering Management — M
Industrial/Management Engineering — M,D
Manufacturing Engineering — M
Mechanical Engineering — M,D
Paper and Pulp Engineering — M,D
Structural Engineering — M
Transportation and Highway
  Engineering — M

WESTERN NEW ENGLAND UNIVERSITY
Electrical Engineering — M
Engineering and Applied
  Sciences—General — M
Engineering Management — M,D
Industrial/Management Engineering — M,D
Manufacturing Engineering — M
Mechanical Engineering — M

WESTERN WASHINGTON UNIVERSITY
Computer Science — M

WESTMINSTER COLLEGE (UT)
Management of Technology — M,O

WEST TEXAS A&M UNIVERSITY
Engineering and Applied
  Sciences—General — M

WEST VIRGINIA STATE UNIVERSITY
Biotechnology — M

WEST VIRGINIA UNIVERSITY
Aerospace/Aeronautical Engineering — M,D
Chemical Engineering — M,D
Civil Engineering — M,D
Computer Engineering — D
Computer Science — M,D
Electrical Engineering — M,D
Engineering and Applied
  Sciences—General — M,D,O
Environmental Engineering — M,D
Game Design and Development — O
Industrial/Management Engineering — M,D
Mechanical Engineering — M,D
Mineral/Mining Engineering — M,D
Petroleum Engineering — M,D
Safety Engineering — M
Software Engineering — M

WICHITA STATE UNIVERSITY
Aerospace/Aeronautical Engineering — M,D
Computer Engineering — M,D
Computer Science — M,D
Electrical Engineering — M,D
Engineering and Applied
  Sciences—General — M,D
Engineering Management — M,D
Industrial/Management Engineering — M,D
Manufacturing Engineering — M,D
Mechanical Engineering — M,D

WIDENER UNIVERSITY
Chemical Engineering — M
Civil Engineering — M
Computer Engineering — M
Engineering and Applied
  Sciences—General — M
Engineering Management — M
Mechanical Engineering — M
Software Engineering — M
Telecommunications — M

WILFRID LAURIER UNIVERSITY
Management of Technology — M,D

WILKES UNIVERSITY
Electrical Engineering — M
Engineering and Applied
  Sciences—General — M
Engineering Management — M
Mechanical Engineering — M

WILLIAM PATERSON UNIVERSITY OF NEW JERSEY
Biotechnology — M

WILMINGTON UNIVERSITY
Computer and Information
  Systems Security — M
Internet Engineering — M

WINSTON-SALEM STATE UNIVERSITY
Computer Science — M

WINTHROP UNIVERSITY
Software Engineering — M,O

WOODS HOLE OCEANOGRAPHIC INSTITUTION
Ocean Engineering — D

WORCESTER POLYTECHNIC INSTITUTE
Artificial Intelligence/Robotics — M,D,O
Biomedical Engineering — M,D,O
Biotechnology — M,D
Chemical Engineering — M,D
Civil Engineering — M,D,O
Computer Engineering — M,D,O
Computer Science — M,D,O
Construction Management — M,D,O
Electrical Engineering — M,D,O
Energy and Power Engineering — M,D
Engineering and Applied
  Sciences—General — M,D,O
Engineering Design — M,O
Environmental Engineering — M,D,O
Fire Protection Engineering — M,D,O
Game Design and Development — M
Manufacturing Engineering — M,D
Materials Engineering — M,D
Materials Sciences — M,D
Mechanical Engineering — M,D,O
Modeling and Simulation — M,D
Systems Engineering — M,D,O

WORCESTER STATE UNIVERSITY
Biotechnology — M

WRIGHT STATE UNIVERSITY
Biomedical Engineering — M
Computer Engineering — M,D
Computer Science — M,D
Electrical Engineering — M
Engineering and Applied
  Sciences—General — M,D
Ergonomics and Human Factors — M,D
Materials Engineering — M
Materials Sciences — M
Mechanical Engineering — M

YALE UNIVERSITY
Bioinformatics — D
Biomedical Engineering — M,D
Chemical Engineering — M,D
Computer Science — M,D
Electrical Engineering — M,D
Engineering and Applied
  Sciences—General — M,D*
Engineering Physics — M,D
Environmental Engineering — M,D
Mechanical Engineering — M,D

YORK UNIVERSITY
Computer Science — M,D

YOUNGSTOWN STATE UNIVERSITY
Civil Engineering — M
Computer Engineering — M
Computer Science — M
Electrical Engineering — M
Engineering and Applied
  Sciences—General — M
Environmental Engineering — M
Industrial/Management Engineering — M
Information Science — M
Mechanical Engineering — M

*M—master's degree; P—first professional degree; D—doctorate; O—other advanced degree; *—Close-Up and/or Display*

ACADEMIC AND PROFESSIONAL PROGRAMS IN ENGINEERING & APPLIED SCIENCES

Section 1
Engineering and Applied Sciences

This section contains a directory of institutions offering graduate work in engineering and applied sciences, followed by in-depth entries submitted by institutions that chose to prepare detailed program descriptions. Additional information about programs listed in the directory but not augmented by an in-depth entry may be obtained by writing directly to the dean of a graduate school or chair of a department at the address given in the directory.

For programs in specific areas of engineering, see all other sections in this book. In the other guides in this series:

Graduate Programs in the Humanities, Arts & Social Sciences

See *Applied Arts and Design (Industrial Design)* and *Architecture (Environmental Design)*

Graduate Programs in the Biological/Biomedical Sciences & Health-Related Medical Professions

See *Ecology, Environmental Biology,* and *Evolutionary Biology*

Graduate Programs in the Physical Sciences, Mathematics, Agricultural Sciences, the Environment & Natural Resources

See *Agricultural and Food Sciences* and *Natural Resources*

CONTENTS

Engineering and Applied Sciences—General

Air Force Institute of Technology, Graduate School of Engineering and Management, Dayton, OH 45433-7765. Offers MS, PhD. *Accreditation:* ABET (one or more programs are accredited). Part-time programs available. *Degree requirements:* For master's, thesis; for doctorate, thesis/dissertation. *Entrance requirements:* For master's, GRE General Test, minimum GPA of 3.0; for doctorate, GRE General Test.

Alabama Agricultural and Mechanical University, School of Graduate Studies, School of Engineering and Technology, Huntsville, AL 35811. Offers M Ed, MS. Part-time and evening/weekend programs available. *Degree requirements:* For master's, comprehensive exam, thesis optional. *Entrance requirements:* For master's, GRE General Test. Additional exam requirements/recommendations for international students: Required—TOEFL (minimum score 500 paper-based; 173 computer-based; 61 iBT). Electronic applications accepted. *Faculty research:* Ionized gases, hypersonic flow phenomenology, robotics systems development.

Alfred University, Graduate School, New York State College of Ceramics, School of Engineering, Alfred, NY 14802-1205. Offers biomedical materials engineering science (MS); ceramic engineering (MS); ceramics (PhD); electrical engineering (MS); glass science (MS, PhD); materials science and engineering (MS, PhD); mechanical engineering (MS). *Degree requirements:* For master's, thesis; for doctorate, thesis/dissertation. *Entrance requirements:* Additional exam requirements/recommendations for international students: Required—TOEFL (minimum score 590 paper-based; 243 computer-based). Electronic applications accepted. *Expenses:* Contact institution. *Faculty research:* Fine-particle technology, x-ray diffraction, superconductivity, electronic materials.

The American University in Cairo, School of Sciences and Engineering, New Cairo 11835, Egypt. Offers M Chem, M Comp, M Eng, MS, PhD, Graduate Diploma. Part-time programs available. *Faculty:* 40 full-time (6 women), 8 part-time/adjunct (1 woman). *Students:* 90 full-time (47 women), 243 part-time (117 women). 378 applicants, 57% accepted, 88 enrolled. In 2011, 41 master's awarded. *Degree requirements:* For master's, thesis (for some programs); for doctorate, thesis/dissertation. *Entrance requirements:* Additional exam requirements/recommendations for international students: Required—TOEFL (minimum score 450 paper-based; 133 computer-based; 45 iBT). *Application deadline:* For fall admission, 2/1 priority date for domestic students, 2/1 for international students; for spring admission, 11/1 priority date for domestic students, 11/1 for international students. Applications are processed on a rolling basis. Application fee: $50. Electronic applications accepted. *Expenses: Tuition:* Part-time $932 per credit hour. Tuition and fees vary according to course load, degree level and program. *Financial support:* Fellowships with partial tuition reimbursements, teaching assistantships, scholarships/grants, and unspecified assistantships available. Financial award application deadline: 5/12. *Faculty research:* Construction management and technology, structural engineering, public works engineering. *Unit head:* Dr. Ezzat Fahmy, Dean, 20-2-2615-2926, E-mail: ezzat@aucegypt.edu. *Application contact:* Wesley Clark, Director of North American Admissions and Financial Aid, 212-646-810-9433 Ext. 4547, E-mail: wclark@aucnyo.edu. Web site: http://www.aucegypt.edu/sse/Pages/default.aspx.

The American University of Athens, School of Graduate Studies, Athens, Greece. Offers biomedical sciences (MS); business (MBA); business communication (MA); computer sciences (MS); engineering and applied sciences (MS); politics and policy making (MA); systems engineering (MS); telecommunications (MS). *Entrance requirements:* For master's, resume, 2 recommendation letters. Additional exam requirements/recommendations for international students: Required—TOEFL (minimum score 550 paper-based; 213 computer-based). *Faculty research:* Nanotechnology, environmental sciences, rock mechanics, human skin studies, Monte Carlo algorithms and software.

American University of Beirut, Graduate Programs, Faculty of Engineering and Architecture, Beirut, Lebanon. Offers applied energy (MME); civil engineering (ME, PhD); electrical and computer engineering (ME, PhD); engineering management (MEM); environmental and water resources (ME); environmental and water resources engineering (PhD); environmental technology (MSES); mechanical engineering (ME, PhD); urban design (MUD); urban planning and policy (MUP). Part-time programs available. *Faculty:* 53 full-time (8 women), 10 part-time/adjunct (2 women). *Students:* 290 full-time (101 women), 59 part-time (18 women). Average age 25. 336 applicants, 80% accepted, 83 enrolled. In 2011, 72 master's, 5 doctorates awarded. *Degree requirements:* For master's, one foreign language, comprehensive exam, thesis (for some programs); for doctorate, one foreign language, comprehensive exam, thesis/dissertation, publications. *Entrance requirements:* For master's, GRE (for electrical and computer engineering), letters of recommendation; for doctorate, GRE, letters of recommendation, master's degree, transcripts, curriculum vitae, interview. Additional exam requirements/recommendations for international students: Required—TOEFL (minimum score 600 paper-based; 250 computer-based; 100 iBT), IELTS (minimum score 7.5). *Application deadline:* For fall admission, 2/5 priority date for domestic students, 2/5 for international students; for spring admission, 11/1 priority date for domestic students, 11/1 for international students. Applications are processed on a rolling basis. Application fee: $50. Electronic applications accepted. *Expenses: Tuition:* Full-time $12,780; part-time $710 per credit. *Required fees:* $528; $528 per credit. Tuition and fees vary according to course load and program. *Financial support:* In 2011–12, 9 fellowships with full tuition reimbursements (averaging $24,800 per year), 33 research assistantships with full tuition reimbursements (averaging $24,800 per year), 74 teaching assistantships with full tuition reimbursements (averaging $9,800 per year) were awarded; career-related internships or fieldwork, institutionally sponsored loans, scholarships/grants, health care benefits, and unspecified assistantships also available. *Total annual research expenditures:* $1.1 million. *Unit head:* Prof. Makram T. Suidan, Dean, 961-135-0000 Ext. 3400, Fax: 961-174-4462, E-mail: msuidan@aub.edu.lb. *Application contact:* Dr. Salim Kanaan, Director, Admissions Office, 961-135-0000 Ext. 2594, Fax: 961-175-0775, E-mail: sk00@aub.edu.lb. Web site: http://staff.aub.edu.lb/~webfea.

Andrews University, School of Graduate Studies, College of Technology, Berrien Springs, MI 49104. Offers MS. *Faculty:* 6 full-time (1 woman). *Students:* 7 full-time (1 woman), 2 part-time (0 women); includes 1 minority (Black or African American, non-Hispanic/Latino), 6 international. Average age 31. 9 applicants, 56% accepted, 4 enrolled. In 2011, 3 master's awarded. *Entrance requirements:* For master's, minimum GPA of 2.6. Additional exam requirements/recommendations for international students: Required—TOEFL (minimum score 550 paper-based). *Application deadline:* Applications are processed on a rolling basis. Application fee: $40. *Unit head:* Dr. Verlyn Benson, Head, 269-471-3413. *Application contact:* Carolyn Hurst, Supervisor of Graduate Admission, 800-253-2874, Fax: 269-471-6321, E-mail: graduate@andrews.edu.

Arizona State University, College of Technology and Innovation, Mesa, AZ 85212. Offers MCST, MS, PhD. Part-time and evening/weekend programs available. *Degree requirements:* For master's, thesis, interactive Program of Study (iPOS) submitted before completing 50 percent of required credit hours. *Entrance requirements:* For master's, GRE, minimum GPA of 3.0 or equivalent in last 2 years of work leading to bachelor's degree. Additional exam requirements/recommendations for international students: Required—TOEFL (minimum score 83 iBT), TOEFL, IELTS, or Pearson Test of English. Electronic applications accepted. *Expenses:* Contact institution.

Arizona State University, Ira A. Fulton School of Engineering, Tempe, AZ 85287-9309. Offers M Eng, MA, MCS, MS, MSE, PhD, Graduate Certificate. Part-time and evening/weekend programs available. Postbaccalaureate distance learning degree programs offered (minimal on-campus study). Terminal master's awarded for partial completion of doctoral program. *Degree requirements:* For master's, comprehensive exam (for some programs), thesis (for some programs), interactive Program of Study (iPOS) submitted before completing 50 percent of required credit hours; for doctorate, comprehensive exam, thesis/dissertation, interactive Program of Study (iPOS) submitted before completing 50 percent of required credit hours. *Entrance requirements:* For master's and doctorate, GRE, minimum GPA of 3.0 or equivalent in last 2 years of work leading to bachelor's degree. Additional exam requirements/recommendations for international students: Required—TOEFL (minimum score 80 iBT), TOEFL, IELTS, or Pearson Test of English. Electronic applications accepted. *Expenses:* Contact institution.

Arkansas State University, Graduate School, College of Engineering, Jonesboro, State University, AR 72467. Offers MEM. Part-time programs available. *Faculty:* 7 full-time (0 women). *Students:* 5 full-time (0 women), 15 part-time (1 woman); includes 2 minority (1 Black or African American, non-Hispanic/Latino; 1 Asian, non-Hispanic/Latino), 15 international. Average age 26. 24 applicants, 79% accepted, 10 enrolled. In 2011, 6 master's awarded. *Degree requirements:* For master's, comprehensive exam. *Entrance requirements:* For master's, GRE, appropriate bachelor's degree, official transcript, letters of recommendation, resume, immunization records. Additional exam requirements/recommendations for international students: Required—TOEFL (minimum score 550 paper-based; 213 computer-based; 79 iBT), IELTS (minimum score 6), PTE: Pearson Test of English Academic (minimum score 56). *Application deadline:* For fall admission, 6/1 for domestic and international students; for spring admission, 10/15 for domestic and international students. Applications are processed on a rolling basis. Application fee: $30 ($40 for international students). Electronic applications accepted. *Expenses:* Contact institution. *Financial support:* In 2011–12, 4 students received support. Career-related internships or fieldwork, scholarships/grants, and unspecified assistantships available. Financial award application deadline: 7/1; financial award applicants required to submit FAFSA. *Unit head:* Dr. David Beasley, Dean, 870-972-2088, Fax: 870-972-3539, E-mail: dbbeasley@astate.edu. *Application contact:* Dr. Andrew Sustich, Dean of the Graduate School, 870-972-3029, Fax: 870-972-3857, E-mail: sustich@astate.edu. Web site: http://www.astate.edu/engr/.

Arkansas Tech University, Center for Leadership and Learning, College of Applied Sciences, Russellville, AR 72801. Offers emergency management (MS); engineering (M Engr); information technology (MS). Part-time programs available. Postbaccalaureate distance learning degree programs offered (no on-campus study). *Students:* 81 full-time (29 women), 53 part-time (15 women); includes 15 minority (7 Black or African American, non-Hispanic/Latino; 1 American Indian or Alaska Native, non-Hispanic/Latino; 1 Asian, non-Hispanic/Latino; 2 Hispanic/Latino; 1 Native Hawaiian or other Pacific Islander, non-Hispanic/Latino; 3 Two or more races, non-Hispanic/Latino), 55 international. Average age 30. In 2011, 52 master's awarded. *Degree requirements:* For master's, comprehensive exam (for some programs), thesis (for some programs), internship. *Entrance requirements:* For master's, GRE General Test. Additional exam requirements/recommendations for international students: Required—TOEFL (minimum score 550 paper-based; 213 computer-based; 79 iBT), IELTS (minimum score 6). *Application deadline:* For fall admission, 3/1 priority date for domestic students, 5/1 for international students; for spring admission, 10/1 priority date for domestic students, 10/1 for international students. Applications are processed on a rolling basis. Application fee: $25 ($75 for international students). Electronic applications accepted. *Expenses: Tuition,* state resident: full-time $4968; part-time $207 per credit hour. Tuition, nonresident: full-time $9936; part-time $414 per credit hour. *Required fees:* $375 per semester. Tuition and fees vary according to course load. *Financial support:* In 2011–12, teaching assistantships with full tuition reimbursements (averaging $4,800 per year) were awarded; research assistantships with full tuition reimbursements, career-related internships or fieldwork, Federal Work-Study, scholarships/grants, health care benefits, and unspecified assistantships also available. Support available to part-time students. Financial award application deadline: 4/15; financial award applicants required to submit FAFSA. *Unit head:* Dr. William Hoefler, Dean, 479-968-0353 Ext. 501, E-mail: whoeflerjr@atu.edu. *Application contact:* Dr. Mary B. Gunter, Dean of Graduate College, 479-968-0398, Fax: 479-964-0542, E-mail: gradcollege@atu.edu. Web site: http://www.atu.edu/appliedsci/.

Auburn University, Graduate School, Ginn College of Engineering, Auburn University, AL 36849. Offers M Ch E, M Mtl E, MAE, MCE, MEE, MISE, MME, MS, MSWE, PhD, Graduate Certificate. Part-time programs available. *Faculty:* 116 full-time (11 women), 10 part-time/adjunct (1 woman). *Students:* 427 full-time (103 women), 407 part-time (96 women); includes 65 minority (35 Black or African American, non-Hispanic/Latino; 1 American Indian or Alaska Native, non-Hispanic/Latino; 19 Asian, non-Hispanic/Latino; 10 Hispanic/Latino), 438 international. Average age 27. 1,312 applicants, 55% accepted, 188 enrolled. In 2011, 185 master's, 62 doctorates, 16 other advanced degrees awarded. *Degree requirements:* For master's, thesis (for some programs); for doctorate, thesis/dissertation. *Entrance requirements:* For master's and doctorate, GRE General Test. *Application deadline:* For fall admission, 7/7 for domestic students; for spring admission, 11/24 for domestic students. Applications are processed on a rolling basis. Application fee: $50 ($60 for international students). Electronic applications accepted. *Expenses:* Tuition, state resident: full-time $7290; part-time $405 per credit hour. Tuition, nonresident: full-time $21,870; part-time $1215 per credit hour. *International tuition:* $22,000 full-time. *Required fees:* $1402. *Financial support:* Fellowships, research assistantships, teaching assistantships, and Federal Work-Study available. Support available to part-time students. Financial award application deadline: 3/15; financial award applicants required to submit FAFSA. *Unit head:* Dr. Chris Roberts, Dean, 334-844-2308. *Application contact:* Dr. George Flowers, Dean of the Graduate School, 334-844-2125. Web site: http://www.eng.auburn.edu/.

Baylor University, Graduate School, School of Engineering and Computer Science, Department of Engineering, Waco, TX 76798. Offers biomedical engineering (MSBE); electrical and computer engineering (MSECE, PhD); engineering (ME); mechanical engineering (MSME). *Faculty:* 14 full-time (1 woman). *Students:* 25 full-time (2 women), 7 part-time (1 woman); includes 6 minority (2 Black or African American, non-Hispanic/Latino; 1 Asian, non-Hispanic/Latino; 1 Hispanic/Latino; 2 Two or more races, non-

Hispanic/Latino), 6 international. In 2011, 19 master's awarded. *Unit head:* Dr. Mike Thompson, Graduate Director, 254-710-4188. *Application contact:* Linda Keer, Administrative Assistant, 254-710-4188, Fax: 254-710-3870, E-mail: linda_kerr@baylor.edu. Web site: http://www.ecs.baylor.edu/engineering.

Boise State University, Graduate College, College of Engineering, Boise, ID 83725-0399. Offers M Engr, MS, PhD. Part-time programs available. Postbaccalaureate distance learning degree programs offered (no on-campus study). *Entrance requirements:* For master's, minimum GPA of 3.0. Electronic applications accepted.

Boston University, College of Engineering, Boston, MA 02215. Offers M Eng, MS, PhD, MD/PhD, MS/MBA. Part-time programs available. Postbaccalaureate distance learning degree programs offered (no on-campus study). *Faculty:* 112 full-time (12 women), 9 part-time/adjunct (1 woman). *Students:* 668 full-time (145 women), 79 part-time (19 women); includes 112 minority (4 Black or African American, non-Hispanic/Latino; 1 American Indian or Alaska Native, non-Hispanic/Latino; 74 Asian, non-Hispanic/Latino; 24 Hispanic/Latino; 9 Two or more races, non-Hispanic/Latino), 348 international. Average age 26. 1,931 applicants, 25% accepted, 245 enrolled. In 2011, 148 master's, 65 doctorates awarded. Terminal master's awarded for partial completion of doctoral program. *Degree requirements:* For master's, thesis (for some programs); for doctorate, comprehensive exam, thesis/dissertation. *Entrance requirements:* For master's and doctorate, GRE General Test. Additional exam requirements/recommendations for international students: Required—TOEFL (minimum score 550 paper-based; 213 computer-based; 84 iBT) or IELTS (minimum score 6.5); Recommended—TOEFL. *Application deadline:* For fall admission, 3/15 for domestic and international students; for spring admission, 10/1 for domestic and international students. Application fee: $70. Electronic applications accepted. *Expenses: Tuition:* Full-time $40,848; part-time $1276 per credit hour. *Required fees:* $572; $286 per semester. *Financial support:* In 2011–12, 458 students received support, including 70 fellowships with full tuition reimbursements available (averaging $28,950 per year), 241 research assistantships with full tuition reimbursements available (averaging $19,300 per year), 62 teaching assistantships with full tuition reimbursements available (averaging $19,300 per year); career-related internships or fieldwork, Federal Work-Study, institutionally sponsored loans, scholarships/grants, traineeships, health care benefits, and tuition waivers (full and partial) also available. Financial award application deadline: 1/15; financial award applicants required to submit FAFSA. *Faculty research:* Photonics, bioengineering, computer and information systems, nanotechnology, materials science and engineering. *Unit head:* Dr. Kenneth R. Lutchen, Dean, 617-353-2800, Fax: 617-358-3468, E-mail: klutch@bu.edu. *Application contact:* Stephen Doherty, Director of Graduate Programs, 617-353-9760, Fax: 617-353-0259, E-mail: enggrad@bu.edu. Web site: http://www.bu.edu/eng/.

Bradley University, Graduate School, College of Engineering and Technology, Peoria, IL 61625-0002. Offers MSCE, MSEE, MSIE, MSME, MSMFE. Part-time and evening/weekend programs available. *Degree requirements:* For master's, comprehensive exam, thesis optional. *Entrance requirements:* For master's, minimum GPA of 3.0, 2 letters of recommendation. Additional exam requirements/recommendations for international students: Required—TOEFL (minimum score 550 paper-based; 213 computer-based; 79 iBT). *Expenses:* Contact institution.

Brigham Young University, Graduate Studies, Ira A. Fulton College of Engineering and Technology, Provo, UT 84602. Offers MS, PhD. *Faculty:* 105 full-time (1 woman), 21 part-time/adjunct (3 women). *Students:* 374 full-time (29 women), 38 part-time (7 women); includes 62 minority (1 Black or African American, non-Hispanic/Latino; 1 American Indian or Alaska Native, non-Hispanic/Latino; 34 Asian, non-Hispanic/Latino; 21 Hispanic/Latino; 5 Native Hawaiian or other Pacific Islander, non-Hispanic/Latino), 33 international. Average age 27. 227 applicants, 74% accepted, 123 enrolled. In 2011, 115 master's, 28 doctorates awarded. *Degree requirements:* For master's, comprehensive exam, thesis (for some programs); for doctorate, comprehensive exam, thesis/dissertation. *Entrance requirements:* For master's, GRE, at least 3 letters of recommendation, transcripts from each institution attended, ecclesiastical endorsement; for doctorate, GRE, at least 3 letters of recommendation, ecclesiastical endorsement. Additional exam requirements/recommendations for international students: Required—TOEFL (minimum score 580 paper-based; 237 computer-based; 85 iBT), IELTS (minimum score 7). *Application deadline:* For fall admission, 1/15 for domestic and international students; for winter admission, 6/15 for domestic and international students; for spring admission, 1/15 for domestic and international students. Application fee: $50. Electronic applications accepted. *Expenses: Tuition:* Full-time $5760; part-time $320 per credit. Tuition and fees vary according to student's religious affiliation. *Financial support:* In 2011–12, 204 students received support, including 95 fellowships with full and partial tuition reimbursements available (averaging $26,752 per year), 172 research assistantships with full and partial tuition reimbursements available (averaging $55,096 per year), 97 teaching assistantships with full and partial tuition reimbursements available (averaging $38,982 per year); career-related internships or fieldwork, institutionally sponsored loans, scholarships/grants, and unspecified assistantships also available. Support available to part-time students. Financial award application deadline: 3/1; financial award applicants required to submit FAFSA. *Faculty research:* Combustion, microwave remote sensing, structural optimization, biomedical engineering, networking. *Total annual research expenditures:* $10 million. *Unit head:* Dr. Alan R. Parkinson, Dean, 801-422-4327, Fax: 801-422-0218, E-mail: college@et.byu.edu. *Application contact:* Claire A. DeWitt, Adviser, 801-422-4541, Fax: 801-422-0270, E-mail: gradstudies@byu.edu. Web site: http://www.et.byu.edu/.

Brown University, Graduate School, Division of Engineering, Providence, RI 02912. Offers biomedical engineering (Sc M, PhD); electrical sciences and computer engineering (Sc M, PhD); fluid, thermal and chemical processes (Sc M, PhD); materials science and engineering (Sc M, PhD); mechanics of solids (Sc M, PhD). *Degree requirements:* For doctorate, thesis/dissertation, preliminary exam.

Bucknell University, Graduate Studies, College of Engineering, Lewisburg, PA 17837. Offers MS Ch E, MSCE, MSEE, MSEV, MSME. Part-time programs available. *Faculty:* 45 full-time (8 women). *Students:* 11 full-time (2 women), 1 part-time, 1 international. 17 applicants, 47% accepted, 3 enrolled. In 2011, 15 master's awarded. *Degree requirements:* For master's, thesis. *Entrance requirements:* For master's, GRE General Test, minimum GPA of 3.0. Additional exam requirements/recommendations for international students: Required—TOEFL (minimum score 600 paper-based). *Application deadline:* For fall admission, 2/1 priority date for domestic students, 1/1 for international students. Application fee: $25. *Financial support:* In 2011–12, 11 students received support, including 11 research assistantships with full tuition reimbursements available (averaging $28,000 per year); unspecified assistantships also available. Financial award application deadline: 2/1. *Unit head:* Dr. James Rice, Dean, 570-577-3117. *Application contact:* Gretchen H. Fegley, Coordinator, 570-577-3655, Fax: 570-577-3760, E-mail: gfegley@bucknell.edu. Web site: http://www.bucknell.edu/.

California Institute of Technology, Division of Engineering and Applied Science, Pasadena, CA 91125. Offers aeronautics (MS, PhD, Engr); applied and computational mathematics (MS, PhD); applied mechanics (MS, PhD); applied physics (MS, PhD); bioengineering (MS, PhD); civil engineering (MS, PhD, Engr); computation and neural systems (MS, PhD); computer science (MS, PhD); control and dynamical systems (MS, PhD); electrical engineering (MS, PhD, Engr); environmental science and engineering (MS, PhD); materials science (MS, PhD); mechanical engineering (MS, PhD, Engr). Terminal master's awarded for partial completion of doctoral program. *Degree requirements:* For doctorate, thesis/dissertation. *Entrance requirements:* For master's and doctorate, GRE (strongly recommended), minimum GPA of 3.5. Additional exam requirements/recommendations for international students: Required—TOEFL; Recommended—TWE (minimum score 5). Electronic applications accepted.

California National University for Advanced Studies, College of Engineering, Northridge, CA 91325. Offers MS Eng. Part-time programs available. Postbaccalaureate distance learning degree programs offered (no on-campus study). *Degree requirements:* For master's, thesis or alternative, project. *Entrance requirements:* For master's, minimum GPA of 3.0. Electronic applications accepted.

California Polytechnic State University, San Luis Obispo, College of Engineering, Department of Biomedical and General Engineering, San Luis Obispo, CA 93407. Offers MS, MBA/MS, MCRP/MS. Part-time programs available. *Faculty:* 5 full-time (2 women). *Students:* 139 full-time (42 women), 29 part-time (8 women); includes 57 minority (2 Black or African American, non-Hispanic/Latino; 1 American Indian or Alaska Native, non-Hispanic/Latino; 34 Asian, non-Hispanic/Latino; 15 Hispanic/Latino; 2 Native Hawaiian or other Pacific Islander, non-Hispanic/Latino; 3 Two or more races, non-Hispanic/Latino), 4 international. Average age 24. 112 applicants, 61% accepted, 51 enrolled. In 2011, 75 master's awarded. *Degree requirements:* For master's, comprehensive exam (for some programs), thesis (for some programs). *Entrance requirements:* For master's, minimum GPA of 3.0 in last 90 quarter units of course work. Additional exam requirements/recommendations for international students: Required—TOEFL (minimum score 550 paper-based; 213 computer-based), TWE (minimum score 4.5). *Application deadline:* For fall admission, 7/1 for domestic students, 11/30 for international students; for winter admission, 11/1 for domestic students, 6/30 for international students; for spring admission, 2/1 for domestic students. Applications are processed on a rolling basis. Application fee: $55. Electronic applications accepted. *Expenses:* Tuition, state resident: full-time $6738. Tuition, nonresident: full-time $17,898. *Required fees:* $2449. *Financial support:* Fellowships, research assistantships, teaching assistantships, Federal Work-Study, and scholarships/grants available. Support available to part-time students. Financial award application deadline: 3/2; financial award applicants required to submit FAFSA. *Faculty research:* Biomedical engineering, materials engineering, water engineering, stem cell research. *Unit head:* Dr. David Clague, Graduate Coordinator, 805-756-5145, Fax: 805-756-6424, E-mail: dclague@calpoly.edu. *Application contact:* Dr. James Maraviglia, Associate Vice Provost for Marketing and Enrollment Development, 805-756-2311, Fax: 805-756-5400, E-mail: admissions@calpoly.edu. Web site: http://ceng.calpoly.edu/academic/masters/programs/.

California State University, Chico, Office of Graduate Studies, College of Engineering, Computer Science, and Technology, Chico, CA 95929-0722. Offers MS. Part-time programs available. Postbaccalaureate distance learning degree programs offered. *Faculty:* 8 full-time (0 women). *Students:* 19 full-time (3 women), 17 part-time (1 woman); includes 2 minority (1 Asian, non-Hispanic/Latino; 1 Hispanic/Latino), 23 international. Average age 26. 124 applicants, 66% accepted, 14 enrolled. In 2011, 26 master's awarded. *Degree requirements:* For master's, thesis or project. *Entrance requirements:* For master's, GRE. Additional exam requirements/recommendations for international students: Required—TOEFL (minimum score 550 paper-based; 213 computer-based; 80 iBT), IELTS (minimum score 6.5), Pearson Test of English (minimum score 59). *Application deadline:* For fall admission, 3/1 priority date for domestic students, 3/1 for international students; for spring admission, 9/15 priority date for domestic students, 9/15 for international students. Application fee: $55. Electronic applications accepted. Tuition and fees vary according to class time, course load and degree level. *Financial support:* Fellowships, research assistantships, teaching assistantships, career-related internships or fieldwork, Federal Work-Study, scholarships/grants, and traineeships available. Support available to part-time students. Financial award application deadline: 3/1; financial award applicants required to submit FAFSA. *Unit head:* Dr. Mike Ward, Dean, 530-898-5963, Fax: 530-898-4070, E-mail: ecc@csuchico.edu. *Application contact:* Judy L. Rice, Graduate Admissions Counselor, 530-898-5416, Fax: 530-898-3342, E-mail: jlrice@csuchico.edu. Web site: http://www.ecst.csuchico.edu.

California State University, East Bay, Office of Academic Programs and Graduate Studies, College of Science, Engineering Department, Hayward, CA 94542-3000. Offers construction management (MS); engineering management (MS). *Faculty:* 6 full-time (2 women), 2 part-time/adjunct (0 women). *Students:* 22 full-time (7 women), 75 part-time (22 women); includes 29 minority (4 Black or African American, non-Hispanic/Latino; 10 Asian, non-Hispanic/Latino; 14 Hispanic/Latino; 1 Two or more races, non-Hispanic/Latino), 27 international. Average age 33. 118 applicants, 64% accepted, 41 enrolled. In 2011, 18 master's awarded. *Degree requirements:* For master's, comprehensive exam (for some programs), research project or exam. *Entrance requirements:* For master's, GRE or GMAT, minimum GPA of 2.5; personal statement; 2 letters of recommendation; resume; college algebra/trigonometry or equivalent. Additional exam requirements/recommendations for international students: Required—TOEFL (minimum score 550 paper-based; 213 computer-based). *Application deadline:* For fall admission, 6/30 for domestic and international students. Application fee: $55. Electronic applications accepted. *Expenses:* Tuition, state resident: full-time $6738; part-time $1302 per quarter. Tuition, nonresident: full-time $12,690; part-time $2294 per quarter. *Required fees:* $449 per quarter. Tuition and fees vary according to degree level, program and reciprocity agreements. *Financial support:* Federal Work-Study and institutionally sponsored loans available. Support available to part-time students. Financial award application deadline: 3/2; financial award applicants required to submit FAFSA. *Faculty research:* Operations resesarch, production planning, simulation, human factors/ergonomics, quality assurance, sustainability. *Unit head:* Dr. Saeid Motavalli, Chair/Graduate Advisor, 510-885-2654, Fax: 510-885-2678, E-mail: saeid.motavalli@csueastbay.edu. Web site: http://www20.csueastbay.edu/csci/departments/engineering/.

California State University, Fresno, Division of Graduate Studies, College of Engineering and Computer Science, Fresno, CA 93740-8027. Offers MS. Part-time and evening/weekend programs available. *Degree requirements:* For master's, thesis or alternative. *Entrance requirements:* For master's, GRE General Test, minimum GPA of 2.7. Additional exam requirements/recommendations for international students: Required—TOEFL. Electronic applications accepted. *Faculty research:* Exhaust emission, blended fuel testing, waste management.

California State University, Fullerton, Graduate Studies, College of Engineering and Computer Science, Fullerton, CA 92834-9480. Offers MS. Part-time programs available.

Students: 242 full-time (53 women), 446 part-time (96 women); includes 252 minority (17 Black or African American, non-Hispanic/Latino; 163 Asian, non-Hispanic/Latino; 54 Hispanic/Latino; 18 Two or more races, non-Hispanic/Latino), 247 international. Average age 29. 1,173 applicants, 68% accepted, 234 enrolled. In 2011, 273 master's awarded. *Degree requirements:* For master's, comprehensive exam, project or thesis. *Entrance requirements:* For master's, minimum undergraduate GPA of 2.5. Application fee: $55. *Financial support:* Career-related internships or fieldwork, Federal Work-Study, institutionally sponsored loans, and scholarships/grants available. Support available to part-time students. Financial award application deadline: 3/1; financial award applicants required to submit FAFSA. *Unit head:* Dr. Raman Unnikrishnan, Dean, 657-278-3362. *Application contact:* Admissions/Applications, 657-278-2371.

California State University, Los Angeles, Graduate Studies, College of Engineering, Computer Science, and Technology, Los Angeles, CA 90032-8530. Offers MA, MS. Part-time and evening/weekend programs available. *Faculty:* 10 full-time (0 women), 17 part-time/adjunct (3 women). *Students:* 124 full-time (33 women), 230 part-time (38 women); includes 191 minority (20 Black or African American, non-Hispanic/Latino; 1 American Indian or Alaska Native, non-Hispanic/Latino; 84 Asian, non-Hispanic/Latino; 83 Hispanic/Latino; 1 Native Hawaiian or other Pacific Islander, non-Hispanic/Latino; 2 Two or more races, non-Hispanic/Latino), 101 international. Average age 30. 380 applicants, 58% accepted, 99 enrolled. In 2011, 230 master's awarded. *Entrance requirements:* Additional exam requirements/recommendations for international students: Required—TOEFL (minimum score 550 paper-based). *Application deadline:* For fall admission, 5/1 for domestic and international students. Applications are processed on a rolling basis. Application fee: $55. Electronic applications accepted. *Expenses:* Tuition, state resident: full-time $8225. *Financial support:* Federal Work-Study available. Support available to part-time students. Financial award application deadline: 3/1. *Unit head:* Dr. Keith Moo-Young, Dean, 323-343-4500, Fax: 323-343-4555, E-mail: kmooyou@exchange.calstatela.edu. *Application contact:* Dr. Karin Brown, Acting Associate Dean of Graduate Studies, 323-343-3820, Fax: 323-343-5653, E-mail: kbrown5@calstatela.edu. Web site: http://www.calstatela.edu/academic/ecst/.

California State University, Northridge, Graduate Studies, College of Engineering and Computer Science, Northridge, CA 91330. Offers MS. Part-time and evening/weekend programs available. *Entrance requirements:* For master's, GRE General Test, minimum GPA of 2.5. Additional exam requirements/recommendations for international students: Required—TOEFL.

California State University, Sacramento, Office of Graduate Studies, College of Engineering and Computer Science, Sacramento, CA 95819-6029. Offers MS. Part-time and evening/weekend programs available. *Faculty:* 48 full-time (9 women), 40 part-time/adjunct (8 women). *Students:* 157 full-time, 185 part-time; includes 101 minority (15 Black or African American, non-Hispanic/Latino; 43 Asian, non-Hispanic/Latino; 22 Hispanic/Latino; 9 Native Hawaiian or other Pacific Islander, non-Hispanic/Latino; 12 Two or more races, non-Hispanic/Latino), 121 international. Average age 27. 518 applicants, 60% accepted, 146 enrolled. In 2011, 192 master's awarded. *Degree requirements:* For master's, writing proficiency exam. *Entrance requirements:* Additional exam requirements/recommendations for international students: Required—TOEFL. *Application deadline:* Applications are processed on a rolling basis. Application fee: $55. Electronic applications accepted. *Financial support:* Research assistantships, teaching assistantships, career-related internships or fieldwork, and Federal Work-Study available. Support available to part-time students. Financial award application deadline: 3/1; financial award applicants required to submit FAFSA. *Unit head:* Dr. Emir Jose Macari, Dean, 916-278-6127, Fax: 916-278-5949, E-mail: emacari@csus.edu. *Application contact:* Jose Martinez, Outreach and Graduate Diversity Coordinator, 916-278-6470, Fax: 916-278-5669, E-mail: martinj@skymail.csus.edu. Web site: http://www.hera.ecs.csus.edu.

Carleton University, Faculty of Graduate Studies, Faculty of Engineering and Design, Ottawa, ON K1S 5B6, Canada. Offers M Arch, M Des, M Eng, M Sc, MA Sc, PhD. *Degree requirements:* For doctorate, thesis/dissertation. *Entrance requirements:* For master's, honors degree; for doctorate, MA Sc or M Eng. Additional exam requirements/recommendations for international students: Required—TOEFL.

Case Western Reserve University, School of Graduate Studies, Case School of Engineering, Cleveland, OH 44106. Offers ME, MEM, MS, PhD, MD/MS, MD/PhD. Part-time and evening/weekend programs available. Postbaccalaureate distance learning degree programs offered (minimal on-campus study). *Faculty:* 107 full-time (13 women). *Students:* 537 full-time (133 women), 69 part-time (15 women); includes 68 minority (13 Black or African American, non-Hispanic/Latino; 1 American Indian or Alaska Native, non-Hispanic/Latino; 42 Asian, non-Hispanic/Latino; 8 Hispanic/Latino; 4 Two or more races, non-Hispanic/Latino), 298 international. 1,542 applicants, 23% accepted, 143 enrolled. In 2011, 103 master's, 78 doctorates awarded. Terminal master's awarded for partial completion of doctoral program. *Degree requirements:* For master's, thesis (for some programs); for doctorate, thesis/dissertation, qualifying exam, teaching experience. *Entrance requirements:* For master's and doctorate, GRE General Test. Additional exam requirements/recommendations for international students: Required—TOEFL (minimum score 550 paper-based; 213 computer-based; 79 iBT), IELTS (minimum score 6.5). *Application deadline:* Applications are processed on a rolling basis. Application fee: $50. Electronic applications accepted. *Financial support:* In 2011–12, 389 students received support. Fellowships with full and partial tuition reimbursements available, research assistantships with full and partial tuition reimbursements available, teaching assistantships, career-related internships or fieldwork, Federal Work-Study, and institutionally sponsored loans available. Support available to part-time students. Financial award applicants required to submit FAFSA. *Faculty research:* Advanced materials, biomedical engineering and human health, electrical engineering and computer science, civil engineering, engineering management. *Total annual research expenditures:* $38.7 million. *Unit head:* Jeffrey L. Duerk, Dean/Professor, 216-368-4436, Fax: 216-368-6939, E-mail: duerk@case.edu. *Application contact:* Dr. Patrick Crago, Associate Dean and Professor of Biomedical Engineering, 216-368-4436, Fax: 216-368-6939, E-mail: cseinfo@case.edu. Web site: http://www.engineering.case.edu.

The Catholic University of America, School of Engineering, Washington, DC 20064. Offers MBE, MCE, MEE, MME, MS, MSCS, MSE, D Engr, PhD, Certificate. Part-time programs available. *Faculty:* 29 full-time (4 women), 29 part-time/adjunct (1 woman). *Students:* 56 full-time (19 women), 122 part-time (37 women); includes 33 minority (16 Black or African American, non-Hispanic/Latino; 7 Asian, non-Hispanic/Latino; 10 Hispanic/Latino), 63 international. Average age 32. 174 applicants, 56% accepted, 51 enrolled. In 2011, 49 master's, 6 doctorates awarded. *Degree requirements:* For master's, thesis optional; for doctorate, comprehensive exam, thesis/dissertation. *Entrance requirements:* For master's and doctorate, statement of purpose, official copies of academic transcripts, three letters of recommendation. Additional exam requirements/recommendations for international students: Required—TOEFL (minimum score 580 paper-based; 237 computer-based). *Application deadline:* For fall admission, 8/1 priority date for domestic students, 7/15 for international students; for spring admission, 12/1 priority date for domestic students, 10/15 for international students. Applications are processed on a rolling basis. Application fee: $55. Electronic applications accepted. *Expenses:* Contact institution. *Financial support:* Fellowships, research assistantships, teaching assistantships, Federal Work-Study, scholarships/grants, tuition waivers (full and partial), and unspecified assistantships available. Financial award application deadline: 2/1; financial award applicants required to submit FAFSA. *Faculty research:* Rehabilitation engineering, cardiopulmonary biomechanics, geotechnical engineering, signal and image processing, fluid mechanics. *Total annual research expenditures:* $2.1 million. *Unit head:* Dr. Charles C. Nguyen, Dean, 202-319-5160, Fax: 202-319-4499, E-mail: nguyen@cua.edu. *Application contact:* Andrew Woodall, Director of Graduate Admissions, 202-319-5057, Fax: 202-319-6533, E-mail: cua-admissions@cua.edu. Web site: http://engineering.cua.edu/.

Central Connecticut State University, School of Graduate Studies, School of Technology, Department of Engineering, New Britain, CT 06050-4010. Offers MS. Part-time and evening/weekend programs available. *Faculty:* 14 full-time (1 woman), 12 part-time/adjunct (2 women). *Students:* 2 full-time (1 woman), 29 part-time (3 women); includes 6 minority (1 Black or African American, non-Hispanic/Latino; 4 Asian, non-Hispanic/Latino; 1 Hispanic/Latino), 2 international. Average age 35. 8 applicants, 63% accepted, 3 enrolled. In 2011, 4 master's awarded. *Degree requirements:* For master's, comprehensive exam, thesis or alternative. *Entrance requirements:* For master's, minimum undergraduate GPA of 2.7. Additional exam requirements/recommendations for international students: Required—TOEFL (minimum score 550 paper-based; 213 computer-based). *Application deadline:* For fall admission, 6/1 for domestic students, 5/1 for international students; for spring admission, 11/1 for domestic and international students. Applications are processed on a rolling basis. Application fee: $50. Electronic applications accepted. *Expenses: Tuition, area resident:* Full-time $5137; part-time $482 per credit. Tuition, state resident: full-time $7707; part-time $494 per credit. Tuition, nonresident: full-time $14,311; part-time $494 per credit. *Required fees:* $3865. One-time fee: $62 part-time. *Financial support:* In 2011–12, 1 student received support. Career-related internships or fieldwork, Federal Work-Study, scholarships/grants, and unspecified assistantships available. Support available to part-time students. Financial award application deadline: 4/15; financial award applicants required to submit FAFSA. *Unit head:* Dr. Alfred Gates, Chair, 860-832-1815, E-mail: gatesa@ccsu.edu. *Application contact:* Patricia Gardner, Associate Director of Graduate Studies, 860-832-2350, Fax: 860-832-2352, E-mail: graduateadmissions@ccsu.edu. Web site: http://www.ccsu.edu/page.cfm?p=6496.

Central Connecticut State University, School of Graduate Studies, School of Technology, Department of Technology Engineering Education, New Britain, CT 06050-4010. Offers MS, Certificate. Part-time and evening/weekend programs available. *Faculty:* 5 full-time (1 woman), 1 part-time/adjunct (0 women). *Students:* 3 full-time (2 women), 19 part-time (1 woman); includes 4 minority (1 Black or African American, non-Hispanic/Latino; 1 Asian, non-Hispanic/Latino; 1 Hispanic/Latino; 1 Two or more races, non-Hispanic/Latino). Average age 35. 11 applicants, 82% accepted, 4 enrolled. In 2011, 8 master's, 2 other advanced degrees awarded. *Degree requirements:* For master's, comprehensive exam, thesis or alternative; for Certificate, qualifying exam. *Entrance requirements:* For master's, minimum undergraduate GPA of 2.7. Additional exam requirements/recommendations for international students: Required—TOEFL (minimum score 550 paper-based; 213 computer-based). *Application deadline:* For fall admission, 6/1 for domestic students, 5/1 for international students; for spring admission, 11/1 for domestic and international students. Applications are processed on a rolling basis. Application fee: $50. Electronic applications accepted. *Expenses: Tuition, area resident:* Full-time $5137; part-time $482 per credit. Tuition, state resident: full-time $7707; part-time $494 per credit. Tuition, nonresident: full-time $14,311; part-time $494 per credit. *Required fees:* $3865. One-time fee: $62 part-time. *Financial support:* In 2011–12, 1 student received support, including 1 research assistantship; career-related internships or fieldwork, Federal Work-Study, scholarships/grants, and unspecified assistantships also available. Support available to part-time students. Financial award application deadline: 4/15; financial award applicants required to submit FAFSA. *Faculty research:* Instruction, curriculum development, administration, occupational training. *Unit head:* Dr. James DeLaura, Chair, 860-832-1850, E-mail: delaura@ccsu.edu. *Application contact:* Patricia Gardner, Associate Director of Graduate Studies, 860-832-2350, Fax: 860-832-2352, E-mail: graduateadmissions@ccsu.edu. Web site: http://www.ccsu.edu/page.cfm?p=6498.

Central Michigan University, College of Graduate Studies, College of Science and Technology, Department of Engineering Technology, Mount Pleasant, MI 48859. Offers industrial management and technology (MA). Part-time programs available. *Degree requirements:* For master's, thesis or alternative. Electronic applications accepted. *Faculty research:* Computer applications, manufacturing process control, mechanical engineering automation, industrial technology.

Central Washington University, Graduate Studies and Research, College of Education and Professional Studies, Department of Industrial and Engineering Technology, Ellensburg, WA 98926. Offers engineering technology (MS). Part-time programs available. *Faculty:* 18 full-time (0 women). *Students:* 23 full-time (5 women), 16 part-time (0 women); includes 14 minority (1 Black or African American, non-Hispanic/Latino; 12 Asian, non-Hispanic/Latino; 1 Native Hawaiian or other Pacific Islander, non-Hispanic/Latino). 20 applicants, 90% accepted, 18 enrolled. In 2011, 24 master's awarded. *Degree requirements:* For master's, thesis or alternative. *Entrance requirements:* For master's, minimum GPA of 3.0. Additional exam requirements/recommendations for international students: Required—TOEFL (minimum score 550 paper-based; 213 computer-based; 79 iBT), IELTS (minimum score 6.5). *Application deadline:* For fall admission, 2/1 priority date for domestic students; for winter admission, 10/1 for domestic students; for spring admission, 1/1 for domestic students. Applications are processed on a rolling basis. Application fee: $50. Electronic applications accepted. *Expenses:* Tuition, state resident: full-time $8112; part-time $270 per credit. Tuition, nonresident: full-time $18,069; part-time $602 per credit. *Required fees:* $924. *Financial support:* In 2011–12, 4 teaching assistantships with full and partial tuition reimbursements (averaging $9,234 per year) were awarded; career-related internships or fieldwork, Federal Work-Study, and health care benefits also available. *Unit head:* Dr. Darren Olson, Graduate Coordinator, 509-963-1756. *Application contact:* Justine Eason, Admissions Program Coordinator, 509-963-3103, Fax: 509-963-1799, E-mail: masters@cwu.edu. Web site: http://www.cwu.edu/~iet/.

Christian Brothers University, School of Engineering, Memphis, TN 38104-5581. Offers MEM, MSEM. Part-time and evening/weekend programs available. Postbaccalaureate distance learning degree programs offered (no on-campus study). *Degree requirements:* For master's, engineering management project. *Entrance requirements:* For master's, GRE. Additional exam requirements/recommendations for international students: Required—TOEFL.

City College of the City University of New York, Graduate School, Grove School of Engineering, New York, NY 10031-9198. Offers ME, MS, PhD. Part-time programs available. Terminal master's awarded for partial completion of doctoral program. *Degree requirements:* For master's, thesis optional; for doctorate, one foreign language, comprehensive exam, thesis/dissertation. *Entrance requirements:* For master's, GRE General Test, minimum B average in undergraduate coursework; for doctorate, GRE General Test, minimum GPA of 3.5. Additional exam requirements/recommendations for international students: Required—TOEFL (minimum score 500 paper-based; 173 computer-based; 61 iBT). *Faculty research:* Robotics, network systems, structures.

Clarkson University, Graduate School, Wallace H. Coulter School of Engineering, Potsdam, NY 13699. Offers ME, MS, PhD. Part-time programs available. *Faculty:* 89 full-time (14 women), 9 part-time/adjunct (4 women). *Students:* 182 full-time (31 women), 2 part-time (1 woman); includes 11 minority (2 Black or African American, non-Hispanic/Latino; 3 Asian, non-Hispanic/Latino; 5 Hispanic/Latino; 1 Two or more races, non-Hispanic/Latino), 91 international. Average age 27. 304 applicants, 80% accepted, 51 enrolled. In 2011, 43 master's, 19 doctorates awarded. Terminal master's awarded for partial completion of doctoral program. *Degree requirements:* For master's, thesis; for doctorate, comprehensive exam, thesis/dissertation, departmental qualifying exam. *Entrance requirements:* For master's and doctorate, GRE, transcripts of all college coursework, resume, personal statement, three letters of recommendation. Additional exam requirements/recommendations for international students: Required—TOEFL (minimum score 550 paper-based; 213 computer-based; 80 iBT), IELTS (minimum score 6.5). *Application deadline:* For fall admission, 1/30 priority date for domestic students, 1/30 for international students; for spring admission, 9/1 priority date for domestic students, 9/1 for international students. Applications are processed on a rolling basis. Application fee: $25 ($35 for international students). Electronic applications accepted. *Expenses: Tuition:* Full-time $14,376; part-time $1198 per credit hour. *Required fees:* $295 per semester. *Financial support:* In 2011–12, 160 students received support, including 6 fellowships with full tuition reimbursements available (averaging $21,999 per year), 87 research assistantships with full tuition reimbursements available (averaging $21,999 per year), 66 teaching assistantships with full tuition reimbursements available (averaging $21,999 per year); scholarships/grants, tuition waivers (partial), and unspecified assistantships also available. *Faculty research:* Advanced materials processing, renewable energy rehabilitation, environmental issues. *Total annual research expenditures:* $8.4 million. *Unit head:* Dr. Goodarz Ahmadi, Dean, 315-268-6446, Fax: 315-268-4494, E-mail: gahmadi@clarkson.edu. *Application contact:* Kelly Sharlow, Assistant to the Dean, 315-268-7929, Fax: 315-268-4494, E-mail: ksharlow@clarkson.edu. Web site: http://www.clarkson.edu/engineering/.

See Display below and Close-Up on page 73.

Clemson University, Graduate School, College of Engineering and Science, Clemson, SC 29634. Offers M Eng, M Engr, MFA, MS, PhD. Part-time programs available. *Faculty:* 11 full-time (0 women), 9 part-time/adjunct (0 women). *Students:* 125 full-time (7 women), 4 part-time; includes 6 minority (2 Black or African American, non-Hispanic/Latino; 1 Asian, non-Hispanic/Latino; 1 Hispanic/Latino; 2 Two or more races, non-Hispanic/Latino), 92 international. Average age 26. 233 applicants, 73% accepted, 58 enrolled. In 2011, 30 master's, 4 doctorates awarded. *Degree requirements:* For doctorate, thesis/dissertation. *Entrance requirements:* For master's and doctorate, GRE General Test. Additional exam requirements/recommendations for international students: Required—TOEFL. Application fee: $70 ($80 for international students). Electronic applications accepted. *Financial support:* In 2011–12, 43 students received support, including 32 research assistantships with partial tuition reimbursements available (averaging $16,875 per year), 6 teaching assistantships with partial tuition reimbursements available (averaging $14,777 per year); fellowships with full and partial tuition reimbursements available, career-related internships or fieldwork, institutionally sponsored loans, scholarships/grants, health care benefits, and unspecified assistantships also available. Support available to part-time students. Financial award applicants required to submit FAFSA. *Total annual research expenditures:* $1.4 million. *Unit head:* Dr. Esin Gulari, Dean, 864-656-3202. *Application contact:* Dr. R. Larry Dooley, Associate Dean for Research and Graduate Studies, 864-656-3200, Fax: 864-656-4466, E-mail: dooley@eng.clemson.edu. Web site: http://www.clemson.edu/ces/.

Cleveland State University, College of Graduate Studies, Fenn College of Engineering, Cleveland, OH 44115. Offers MS, D Eng. Part-time and evening/weekend programs available. *Faculty:* 54 full-time (5 women), 12 part-time/adjunct (0 women). *Students:* 129 full-time (31 women), 242 part-time (36 women); includes 19 minority (9 Black or African American, non-Hispanic/Latino; 8 Asian, non-Hispanic/Latino; 2 Hispanic/Latino), 238 international. Average age 27. 686 applicants, 52% accepted, 80 enrolled. In 2011, 147 master's, 11 doctorates awarded. *Degree requirements:* For master's, thesis or alternative; for doctorate, thesis/dissertation, candidacy and qualifying exams. *Entrance requirements:* For master's, GRE General Test, BS in engineering, minimum GPA of 3.0 (2.75 for students from ABET/EAC-accredited programs from the U.S. and Canada); for doctorate, GRE General Test, MS in engineering, minimum GPA of 3.25. Additional exam requirements/recommendations for international students: Required—TOEFL (minimum score 525 paper-based; 197 computer-based). *Application deadline:* For fall admission, 7/15 for domestic students, 5/15 for international students; for spring admission, 12/5 for domestic students, 11/1 for international students. Applications are processed on a rolling basis. Application fee: $30. Electronic applications accepted. *Expenses:* Tuition, state resident: full-time $6416; part-time $494 per credit hour. Tuition, nonresident: full-time $12,074; part-time $929 per credit hour. *Financial support:* In 2011–12, 93 students received support, including 1 fellowship with full tuition reimbursement available, 120 research assistantships with full and partial tuition reimbursements available (averaging $8,694 per year), 20 teaching assistantships with full and partial tuition reimbursements available (averaging $8,082 per year); career-related internships or fieldwork, institutionally sponsored loans, scholarships/grants, tuition waivers (full and partial), and unspecified assistantships also available. Support available to part-time students. Financial award application deadline: 3/30. *Faculty research:* Structural analysis and design, dynamic system and controls, applied biomedical engineering, transportation, water resources, telecommunication, power electronics, computer engineering, industrial automation, engineering management, mechanical design, thermodynamics and fluid mechanics, material engineering, tribology. *Total annual research expenditures:* $7.2 million. *Unit head:* Dr. Paul P. Lin, Associate Dean, 216-687-2556, Fax: 216-687-9280, E-mail: p.lin@csuohio.edu. *Application contact:* Deborah L. Brown, Interim Assistant Director, Graduate Admissions, 216-523-7572, Fax: 216-687-9214, E-mail: d.l.brown@csuohio.edu. Web site: http://www.csuohio.edu/engineering/.

Colorado School of Mines, Graduate School, Golden, CO 80401-1887. Offers ME, MIPER, MS, PMS, PhD, Graduate Certificate. Part-time programs available. *Faculty:* 325 full-time (70 women), 102 part-time/adjunct (30 women). *Students:* 1,167 full-time (298 women), 176 part-time (43 women); includes 133 minority (14 Black or African American, non-Hispanic/Latino; 9 American Indian or Alaska Native, non-Hispanic/Latino; 35 Asian, non-Hispanic/Latino; 65 Hispanic/Latino; 1 Native Hawaiian or other

Pacific Islander, non-Hispanic/Latino; 9 Two or more races, non-Hispanic/Latino), 369 international. Average age 28. 2,075 applicants, 47% accepted, 459 enrolled. In 2011, 310 master's, 50 doctorates awarded. *Degree requirements:* For master's, thesis (for some programs); for doctorate, comprehensive exam, thesis/dissertation. *Entrance requirements:* For master's, doctorate, and Graduate Certificate, GRE General Test. Additional exam requirements/recommendations for international students: Required—TOEFL (minimum score 550 paper-based; 213 computer-based; 80 iBT). *Application deadline:* For fall admission, 1/15 priority date for domestic students, 1/15 for international students; for spring admission, 10/15 priority date for domestic students, 10/15 for international students. Application fee: $50 ($70 for international students). Electronic applications accepted. *Expenses:* Tuition, state resident: full-time $12,585; part-time $699 per credit. Tuition, nonresident: full-time $27,270; part-time $1516 per credit. *Required fees:* $1864.20; $670 per semester. *Financial support:* In 2011–12, 755 students received support, including 81 fellowships with full tuition reimbursements available (averaging $20,000 per year), 488 research assistantships with full tuition reimbursements available (averaging $20,000 per year), 186 teaching assistantships with full tuition reimbursements available (averaging $20,000 per year); career-related internships or fieldwork, Federal Work-Study, institutionally sponsored loans, scholarships/grants, health care benefits, and unspecified assistantships also available. Financial award application deadline: 1/15; financial award applicants required to submit FAFSA. *Faculty research:* Energy, environment, materials, minerals, engineering systems. *Total annual research expenditures:* $35 million. *Unit head:* Dr. Tom M. Boyd, Dean of Graduate Studies, 303-273-3020, Fax: 303-273-3244, E-mail: tboyd@mines.edu. *Application contact:* Kay Leaman, Graduate Admissions Coordinator, 303-273-3249, Fax: 303-273-3244, E-mail: grad-app@mines.edu. Web site: http://mines.edu/graduate_admissions.

Colorado State University, Graduate School, College of Engineering, Fort Colllins, CO 80523-1301. Offers ME, MEE, MS, PhD. *Accreditation:* ABET. Part-time programs available. *Faculty:* 91 full-time (13 women), 9 part-time/adjunct (0 women). *Students:* 297 full-time (72 women), 427 part-time (93 women); includes 70 minority (7 Black or African American, non-Hispanic/Latino; 1 American Indian or Alaska Native, non-Hispanic/Latino; 16 Asian, non-Hispanic/Latino; 32 Hispanic/Latino; 1 Native Hawaiian or other Pacific Islander, non-Hispanic/Latino; 13 Two or more races, non-Hispanic/Latino), 220 international. Average age 29. 834 applicants, 46% accepted, 166 enrolled. In 2011, 104 master's, 40 doctorates awarded. *Degree requirements:* For doctorate, thesis/dissertation. *Entrance requirements:* For master's, GRE General Test, minimum GPA of 3.0, 3 letters of recommendation; for doctorate, GRE General Test, minimum GPA of 3.0, transcripts, 3 letters of recommendation, statement of purpose with interests. Additional exam requirements/recommendations for international students: Required—TOEFL (minimum score 550 paper-based; 213 computer-based; 80 iBT), IELTS (minimum score 6.5). *Application deadline:* For fall admission, 2/1 priority date for domestic students, 2/1 for international students; for spring admission, 9/1 priority date for domestic students, 9/1 for international students. Applications are processed on a rolling basis. Application fee: $50. Electronic applications accepted. *Expenses:* Tuition, state resident: full-time $7992. Tuition, nonresident: full-time $19,592. *Required fees:* $1735; $58 per credit. *Financial support:* In 2011–12, 306 students received support, including 40 fellowships with full tuition reimbursements available (averaging $33,025 per year), 217 research assistantships with full tuition reimbursements available (averaging $18,660 per year), 49 teaching assistantships with full tuition reimbursements available (averaging $9,639 per year); career-related internships or fieldwork, Federal Work-Study, institutionally sponsored loans, scholarships/grants, traineeships, health care benefits, and unspecified assistantships also available. Financial award application deadline: 1/15; financial award applicants required to submit FAFSA. *Faculty research:* Atmospheric science, biological engineering, civil and environmental engineering, electrical and computer engineering, mechanical and biomedical engineering. *Total annual research expenditures:* $62.2 million. *Unit head:* Dr. Sandra L. Woods, Dean, 970-491-3366, Fax: 970-491-5569, E-mail: sandra.woods@colostate.edu. *Application contact:* Dr. Tom Siller, Associate Dean, 970-491-6220, Fax: 970-491-3429, E-mail: thomas.siller@colostate.edu. Web site: http://www.engr.colostate.edu/.

Colorado State University–Pueblo, College of Education, Engineering and Professional Studies, Pueblo, CO 81001-4901. Offers M Ed, MS. Part-time and evening/weekend programs available. *Degree requirements:* For master's, thesis optional. *Entrance requirements:* For master's, GRE General Test. Additional exam requirements/recommendations for international students: Required—TOEFL (minimum score 500 paper-based; 173 computer-based). Electronic applications accepted. *Expenses:* Contact institution. *Faculty research:* Nanotechnology, applied operations, research transportation, decision analysis.

Columbia University, The Fu Foundation School of Engineering and Applied Science, New York, NY 10027. Offers MS, Eng Sc D, PhD, Engr, MS/MBA. Part-time programs available. Postbaccalaureate distance learning degree programs offered (no on-campus study). *Faculty:* 199 full-time (24 women), 124 part-time/adjunct (9 women). *Students:* 1,470 full-time (369 women), 766 part-time (196 women); includes 215 minority (11 Black or African American, non-Hispanic/Latino; 1 American Indian or Alaska Native, non-Hispanic/Latino; 149 Asian, non-Hispanic/Latino; 10 Hispanic/Latino; 1 Native Hawaiian or other Pacific Islander, non-Hispanic/Latino; 43 Two or more races, non-Hispanic/Latino), 1,526 international. Average age 27. 6,587 applicants, 25% accepted, 963 enrolled. In 2011, 732 master's, 97 doctorates, 5 other advanced degrees awarded. Terminal master's awarded for partial completion of doctoral program. *Degree requirements:* For master's, comprehensive exam (for some programs), thesis (for some programs); for doctorate, comprehensive exam (for some programs), thesis/dissertation, qualifying exam; for Engr, thesis optional. *Entrance requirements:* For master's and Engr, GRE General Test; for doctorate, GRE General Test, GRE Subject Test (computer science and applied physics programs only). Additional exam requirements/recommendations for international students: Required—TOEFL, IELTS. *Application deadline:* For fall admission, 12/1 priority date for domestic students, 12/1 for international students; for spring admission, 10/1 priority date for domestic students, 10/1 for international students. Application fee: $95. Electronic applications accepted. *Financial support:* In 2011–12, 586 students received support, including 55 fellowships with full and partial tuition reimbursements available (averaging $26,833 per year), 404 research assistantships with full tuition reimbursements available (averaging $30,426 per year), 127 teaching assistantships with full tuition reimbursements available (averaging $28,828 per year); career-related internships or fieldwork, traineeships, health care benefits, tuition waivers, and unspecified assistantships also available. Financial award application deadline: 12/1; financial award applicants required to submit FAFSA. *Total annual research expenditures:* $125.4 million. *Unit head:* Dr. Feniosky Pena-Mora, Dean, 212-854-2993, Fax: 212-864-0104, E-mail: dean@seas.columbia.edu. *Application contact:* Jocelyn Morales, Assistant Director, 212-854-6901, Fax: 212-854-5900, E-mail: seasgradmit@columbia.edu. Web site: http://www.engineering.columbia.edu/.

Concordia University, School of Graduate Studies, Faculty of Engineering and Computer Science, Montréal, QC H3G 1M8, Canada. Offers M App Comp Sc, M Comp Sc, M Eng, MA Sc, PhD, Certificate, Diploma. *Degree requirements:* For doctorate, comprehensive exam, thesis/dissertation. *Expenses:* Contact institution.

Cooper Union for the Advancement of Science and Art, Albert Nerken School of Engineering, New York, NY 10003-7120. Offers chemical engineering (ME); civil engineering (ME); electrical engineering (ME); mechanical engineering (ME). Part-time programs available. *Faculty:* 27 full-time (1 woman), 15 part-time/adjunct (2 women). *Students:* 39 full-time (10 women), 17 part-time (3 women); includes 18 minority (1 Black or African American, non-Hispanic/Latino; 1 American Indian or Alaska Native, non-Hispanic/Latino; 15 Asian, non-Hispanic/Latino; 1 Hispanic/Latino), 11 international. *Degree requirements:* For master's, thesis. *Entrance requirements:* For master's, GRE, BE, minimum GPA of 3.5. Additional exam requirements/recommendations for international students: Required—TOEFL (minimum score 600 paper-based; 250 computer-based; 100 iBT). *Application deadline:* For fall admission, 2/15 for domestic and international students. Application fee: $65. *Expenses: Tuition:* Full-time $37,500. *Required fees:* $825 per semester. *Financial support:* Fellowships with full tuition reimbursements, career-related internships or fieldwork, Federal Work-Study, tuition waivers (full), and full-tuition scholarships for all admitted students available. Support available to part-time students. Financial award application deadline: 5/1; financial award applicants required to submit CSS PROFILE or FAFSA. *Faculty research:* Civil infrastructure, imaging and sensing technology, biomedical engineering, encryption technology, process engineering. *Unit head:* Dr. Simon Ben-Avi, Acting Dean, 212-353-4286, E-mail: benavi@cooper.edu. *Application contact:* Student Contact, 212-353-4120, E-mail: admissions@cooper.edu. Web site: http://cooper.edu/engineering.

Cornell University, Graduate School, Graduate Fields of Engineering, Ithaca, NY 14853-0001. Offers M Eng, MPS, MS, PhD, M Eng/MBA. *Faculty:* 579 full-time (70 women). *Students:* 1,661 full-time (475 women); includes 285 minority (41 Black or African American, non-Hispanic/Latino; 1 American Indian or Alaska Native, non-Hispanic/Latino; 184 Asian, non-Hispanic/Latino; 59 Hispanic/Latino), 807 international. Average age 25. 7,075 applicants, 28% accepted, 884 enrolled. In 2011, 779 master's, 111 doctorates awarded. *Degree requirements:* For doctorate, comprehensive exam, thesis/dissertation. *Entrance requirements:* Additional exam requirements/recommendations for international students: Required—TOEFL. Application fee: $95. Electronic applications accepted. *Financial support:* In 2011–12, 740 students received support, including 212 fellowships with full tuition reimbursements available, 467 research assistantships with full tuition reimbursements available, 173 teaching assistantships with full tuition reimbursements available; career-related internships or fieldwork, institutionally sponsored loans, scholarships/grants, health care benefits, tuition waivers (full and partial), and unspecified assistantships also available. Financial award applicants required to submit FAFSA. *Unit head:* Dr. Barbara Knuth, Dean, 607-255-5417. *Application contact:* Graduate School Application Requests, 607-255-5816. Web site: http://www.engineering.cornell.edu/.

Dalhousie University, Faculty of Engineering, Halifax, NS B3H 4R2, Canada. Offers M Eng, M Sc, MA Sc, PhD, M Eng/M Plan, MA Sc/M Plan, MBA/M Eng. *Entrance requirements:* Additional exam requirements/recommendations for international students: Required—1 of 5 approved tests: TOEFL, IELTS, CANTEST, CAEL, Michigan English Language Assessment Battery.

Dartmouth College, Thayer School of Engineering, Hanover, NH 03755. Offers MEM, MS, PhD, MBA/MEM. *Faculty:* 50 full-time (7 women), 38 part-time/adjunct (4 women). *Students:* 203 full-time (68 women); includes 17 minority (3 Black or African American, non-Hispanic/Latino; 2 American Indian or Alaska Native, non-Hispanic/Latino; 9 Asian, non-Hispanic/Latino; 2 Hispanic/Latino; 1 Two or more races, non-Hispanic/Latino), 107 international. Average age 24. 630 applicants, 26% accepted, 86 enrolled. In 2011, 61 master's, 18 doctorates awarded. *Degree requirements:* For doctorate, thesis/dissertation, candidacy oral exam. *Entrance requirements:* For master's and doctorate, GRE General Test. Additional exam requirements/recommendations for international students: Required—TOEFL. *Application deadline:* For fall admission, 1/1 priority date for domestic students, 1/1 for international students. Applications are processed on a rolling basis. Application fee: $45. Electronic applications accepted. *Financial support:* In 2011–12, 187 students received support, including 10 fellowships with full tuition reimbursements available (averaging $23,520 per year), 83 research assistantships with full tuition reimbursements available (averaging $23,580 per year), 60 teaching assistantships with partial tuition reimbursements available (averaging $7,200 per year); career-related internships or fieldwork, institutionally sponsored loans, scholarships/grants, and tuition waivers (full and partial) also available. Financial award application deadline: 2/15; financial award applicants required to submit CSS PROFILE. *Faculty research:* Biomedical engineering, biotechnology and biochemical engineering, electrical and computer engineering, engineering physics, environmental engineering, materials science and engineering, mechanical systems engineering. *Unit head:* Dr. Joseph J. Helbie, Dean, 603-646-2238, Fax: 603-646-2580, E-mail: joseph.j.helbie@dartmouth.edu. *Application contact:* Candace S. Potter, Graduate Admissions Administrator, 603-646-3844, Fax: 603-646-1620, E-mail: candace.potter@dartmouth.edu. Web site: http://engineering.dartmouth.edu/.

Drexel University, College of Engineering, Philadelphia, PA 19104-2875. Offers MS, MSEE, MSSE, PhD, Certificate. Part-time and evening/weekend programs available. *Degree requirements:* For doctorate, thesis/dissertation. *Entrance requirements:* Additional exam requirements/recommendations for international students: Required—TOEFL. Electronic applications accepted.

Drexel University, Goodwin College of Professional Studies, School of Technology and Professional Studies, Philadelphia, PA 19104-2875. Offers construction management (MS); engineering technology (MS); food science (MS); hospitality management (MS); professional studies: creativity studies (MS); professional studies: e-learning leadership (MS); professional studies: homeland security management (MS); project management (MS); property management (MS); sport management (MS). Postbaccalaureate distance learning degree programs offered.

Duke University, Graduate School, Pratt School of Engineering, Master of Engineering Program, Durham, NC 27708-0271. Offers biomedical engineering (M Eng); civil engineering (M Eng); electrical and computer engineering (M Eng); environmental engineering (M Eng); materials science and engineering (M Eng); mechanical engineering (M Eng); photonics and optical sciences (M Eng). Part-time programs available. *Entrance requirements:* For master's, GRE General Test, resume, 3 letters of recommendation, statement of purpose. Additional exam requirements/recommendations for international students: Required—TOEFL. *Expenses: Tuition:* Full-time $40,720. *Required fees:* $3107.

Eastern Illinois University, Graduate School, Lumpkin College of Business and Applied Sciences, School of Technology, Charleston, IL 61920-3099. Offers computer technology (Certificate); quality systems (Certificate); technology (MS); technology security (Certificate); work performance improvement (Certificate). Part-time and evening/weekend programs available. *Expenses:* Tuition, state resident: part-time $279 per credit hour. Tuition, nonresident: part-time $670 per credit hour. *Required fees:* $179.07 per credit hour. $1253 per semester.

Eastern Michigan University, Graduate School, College of Technology, School of Engineering Technology, Programs in Computer Aided Engineering, Ypsilanti, MI 48197. Offers CAD/CAM (MS); computer aided technology (MS). Part-time and evening/weekend programs available. Postbaccalaureate distance learning degree programs offered (minimal on-campus study). *Students:* 5 full-time (1 woman), 13 part-time (0 women); includes 1 minority (Asian, non-Hispanic/Latino), 10 international. Average age 30. 14 applicants, 71% accepted, 7 enrolled. In 2011, 5 degrees awarded. *Entrance requirements:* Additional exam requirements/recommendations for international students: Required—TOEFL. *Application deadline:* Applications are processed on a rolling basis. Application fee: $35. *Expenses:* Tuition, state resident: full-time $10,367; part-time $432 per credit hour. Tuition, nonresident: full-time $20,435; part-time $851 per credit hour. *Required fees:* $39 per credit hour. $46 per semester. One-time fee: $100. Tuition and fees vary according to course level, degree level and reciprocity agreements. *Financial support:* Fellowships, research assistantships with full tuition reimbursements, teaching assistantships with full tuition reimbursements, and tuition waivers (partial) available. Financial award applicants required to submit FAFSA. *Unit head:* Dr. Tony Fukuo Shay, Program Coordinator, 734-487-2040, Fax: 734-487-8755, E-mail: tony.shay@emich.edu. *Application contact:* Graduate Admissions, 734-487-2400, Fax: 734-487-6559, E-mail: graduate.admissions@emich.edu.

École Polytechnique de Montréal, Graduate Programs, Montréal, QC H3C 3A7, Canada. Offers M Eng, M Sc A, PhD, DESS. Part-time and evening/weekend programs available. Terminal master's awarded for partial completion of doctoral program. *Degree requirements:* For master's, one foreign language, thesis; for doctorate, one foreign language, thesis/dissertation. *Entrance requirements:* For master's, minimum GPA of 2.75; for doctorate, minimum GPA of 3.0. Electronic applications accepted. *Faculty research:* Chemical engineering, environmental engineering, microelectronics and communications, biomedical engineering, engineering physics.

Fairfield University, School of Engineering, Fairfield, CT 06824-5195. Offers electrical and computer engineering (MS); management of technology (MS); mechanical engineering (MS); software engineering (MS). Part-time and evening/weekend programs available. *Faculty:* 10 full-time (2 women), 11 part-time/adjunct. *Students:* 44 full-time (15 women), 86 part-time (22 women); includes 19 minority (4 Black or African American, non-Hispanic/Latino; 8 Asian, non-Hispanic/Latino; 4 Hispanic/Latino; 1 Native Hawaiian or other Pacific Islander, non-Hispanic/Latino; 2 Two or more races, non-Hispanic/Latino), 21 international. Average age 34. 100 applicants, 76% accepted, 27 enrolled. In 2011, 38 master's awarded. *Degree requirements:* For master's, thesis, capstone course. *Entrance requirements:* For master's, interview, minimum GPA of 2.8, resume, 2 recommendations. Additional exam requirements/recommendations for international students: Required—TOEFL (minimum score 550 paper-based; 213 computer-based; 80 iBT)or IELTS (minimum score 6.5). *Application deadline:* For fall admission, 5/15 for international students; for spring admission, 10/15 for international students. Applications are processed on a rolling basis. Application fee: $60. Electronic applications accepted. *Expenses:* Contact institution. *Financial support:* In 2011–12, 50 students received support. Scholarships/grants and unspecified assistantships available. Financial award applicants required to submit FAFSA. *Faculty research:* Vehicle dynamics, image processing, multimedia in instruction, thermal packaging, character recognition, photovoltaics and nanotechnology, Web technology. *Unit head:* Dr. Jack Beal, Dean, 203-254-4000 Ext. 4147, Fax: 203-254-4013, E-mail: jwbeal@fairfield.edu. *Application contact:* Marianne Gumpper, Director of Graduate and Continuing Studies Admission, 203-254-4184, Fax: 203-254-4073, E-mail: gradadmis@fairfield.edu. Web site: http://www.fairfield.edu/soe/soe_grad_1.html.

Fairleigh Dickinson University, Metropolitan Campus, University College: Arts, Sciences, and Professional Studies, School of Computer Sciences and Engineering, Teaneck, NJ 07666-1914. Offers computer engineering (MS); computer science (MS); e-commerce (MS); electrical engineering (MSEE); management information systems (MS); mathematical foundation (MS).

Florida Agricultural and Mechanical University, Division of Graduate Studies, Research, and Continuing Education, FAMU-FSU College of Engineering, Tallahassee, FL 32307-3200. Offers MS, PhD. College administered jointly by Florida State University. *Entrance requirements:* For master's, GRE General Test, minimum GPA of 3.0. Additional exam requirements/recommendations for international students: Required—TOEFL (minimum score 550 paper-based; 213 computer-based).

Florida Atlantic University, College of Engineering and Computer Science, Boca Raton, FL 33431-0991. Offers MS, PhD. Part-time and evening/weekend programs available. Postbaccalaureate distance learning degree programs offered (minimal on-campus study). *Faculty:* 68 full-time (10 women), 8 part-time/adjunct (1 woman). *Students:* 152 full-time (37 women), 151 part-time (27 women); includes 105 minority (24 Black or African American, non-Hispanic/Latino; 1 American Indian or Alaska Native, non-Hispanic/Latino; 24 Asian, non-Hispanic/Latino; 49 Hispanic/Latino; 5 Native Hawaiian or other Pacific Islander, non-Hispanic/Latino; 2 Two or more races, non-Hispanic/Latino), 68 international. Average age 32. 285 applicants, 42% accepted, 55 enrolled. In 2011, 96 master's, 7 doctorates awarded. Terminal master's awarded for partial completion of doctoral program. *Degree requirements:* For master's, thesis optional; for doctorate, thesis/dissertation, qualifying exam. *Entrance requirements:* For master's, GRE General Test, minimum GPA of 3.0; for doctorate, GRE General Test. Additional exam requirements/recommendations for international students: Required—TOEFL. *Application deadline:* For fall admission, 7/1 for domestic students, 2/15 for international students; for spring admission, 11/1 for domestic students, 7/15 for international students. Applications are processed on a rolling basis. Application fee: $30. *Expenses: Tuition, area resident:* Part-time $343.02 per credit hour. Tuition, state resident: full-time $8232. Tuition, nonresident: full-time $23,931; part-time $997.14 per credit hour. *Financial support:* In 2011–12, research assistantships with partial tuition reimbursements (averaging $15,000 per year), teaching assistantships with partial tuition reimbursements (averaging $15,000 per year) were awarded; fellowships, career-related internships or fieldwork, Federal Work-Study, and unspecified assistantships also available. Support available to part-time students. Financial award applicants required to submit FAFSA. *Faculty research:* Automated underwater vehicles, communication systems, computer networks, materials, neural networks. *Unit head:* Dr. Mohammad Ilyas, Interim Dean, 561-297-3400, Fax: 561-297-2659, E-mail: ilyas@fau.edu. *Application contact:* Joanna Arlington, Manager, Graduate Admissions, 561-297-2428, Fax: 561-297-2117, E-mail: arlingto@fau.edu. Web site: http://www.eng.fau.edu/.

Florida Institute of Technology, Graduate Programs, College of Engineering, Melbourne, FL 32901-6975. Offers MS, PhD. Part-time and evening/weekend programs available. *Faculty:* 58 full-time (3 women), 18 part-time/adjunct (1 woman). *Students:* 341 full-time (81 women), 220 part-time (47 women); includes 43 minority (15 Black or African American, non-Hispanic/Latino; 10 Asian, non-Hispanic/Latino; 14 Hispanic/Latino; 4 Two or more races, non-Hispanic/Latino), 292 international. Average age 29. 1,154 applicants, 61% accepted, 155 enrolled. In 2011, 151 master's, 11 doctorates awarded. Terminal master's awarded for partial completion of doctoral program. *Degree requirements:* For master's, comprehensive exam (for some programs), thesis (for some programs); for doctorate, comprehensive exam (for some programs), thesis/dissertation. *Entrance requirements:* For master's, GRE, minimum GPA of 3.0, 3 letters of recommendation, resume, statement of objectives; for doctorate, GRE, minimum GPA of 3.2, 3 letters of recommendation, resume, statement of objectives. Additional exam requirements/recommendations for international students: Required—TOEFL (minimum score 550 paper-based; 213 computer-based; 79 iBT). *Application deadline:* For fall admission, 4/1 for international students; for spring admission, 9/30 for international students. Applications are processed on a rolling basis. Electronic applications accepted. *Expenses: Tuition:* Full-time $19,620; part-time $1090 per credit hour. Tuition and fees vary according to campus/location. *Financial support:* In 2011–12, 5 fellowships with full and partial tuition reimbursements (averaging $7,240 per year); 20 research assistantships with full and partial tuition reimbursements (averaging $6,680 per year), 46 teaching assistantships with full and partial tuition reimbursements (averaging $6,457 per year) were awarded; career-related internships or fieldwork, institutionally sponsored loans, unspecified assistantships, and tuition remissions also available. Support available to part-time students. Financial award application deadline: 3/1; financial award applicants required to submit FAFSA. *Faculty research:* Electrical and computer science and engineering; aerospace, chemical, civil, mechanical, and ocean engineering; environmental science and oceanography. *Total annual research expenditures:* $4.1 million. *Unit head:* Dr. Fredric M. Ham, Interim Dean, 321-674-8138, Fax: 321-674-7270, E-mail: fmh@fit.edu. *Application contact:* Cheryl A. Brown, Associate Director of Graduate Admissions, 321-674-7581, Fax: 321-723-9468, E-mail: cbrown@fit.edu. Web site: http://coe.fit.edu.

Florida International University, College of Engineering and Computing, Miami, FL 33175. Offers MS, PhD. Part-time and evening/weekend programs available. Postbaccalaureate distance learning degree programs offered. Terminal master's awarded for partial completion of doctoral program. *Degree requirements:* For master's, thesis (for some programs); for doctorate, comprehensive exam, thesis/dissertation. *Entrance requirements:* For master's, GRE (depending on program), minimum GPA of 3.0; for doctorate, GRE General Test, minimum GPA of 3.0. Additional exam requirements/recommendations for international students: Required—TOEFL (minimum score 550 paper-based; 80 iBT). Electronic applications accepted. *Faculty research:* Databases, informatics, computing systems, software engineering, security, biosensors, imaging, tissue engineering, biomaterials and bionanotechnology, transportation, wind engineering, hydrology, environmental engineering, engineering management, sustainability and green construction, risk management and decision systems, infrastructure systems, digital signal processing, power systems, nanophotonics, embedded systems, image processing, nanotechnology.

See Display on next page and Close-Up on page 75.

Florida State University, The Graduate School, FAMU-FSU College of Engineering, Tallahassee, FL 32310-6046. Offers M Eng, MS, PhD. Part-time programs available. *Faculty:* 78 full-time (9 women), 12 part-time/adjunct (1 woman). *Students:* 250 full-time (54 women), 27 part-time (4 women); includes 45 minority (30 Black or African American, non-Hispanic/Latino; 3 Asian, non-Hispanic/Latino; 12 Hispanic/Latino), 125 international. Average age 25. 552 applicants, 42% accepted, 75 enrolled. In 2011, 69 master's, 18 doctorates awarded. *Degree requirements:* For master's, thesis (for some programs); for doctorate, comprehensive exam, thesis/dissertation, preliminary exam, qualifying exam. *Entrance requirements:* For master's and doctorate, GRE General Test. Additional exam requirements/recommendations for international students: Required—TOEFL (minimum score 550 paper-based; 213 computer-based; 80 iBT). *Application deadline:* Applications are processed on a rolling basis. Application fee: $30. *Expenses:* Tuition, state resident: full-time $9474; part-time $350.88 per credit hour. Tuition, nonresident: full-time $16,236; part-time $601.34 per credit hour. *Required fees:* $630 per semester. One-time fee: $20. Tuition and fees vary according to course load and campus/location. *Financial support:* In 2011–12, 236 students received support, including 10 fellowships with full tuition reimbursements available (averaging $23,000 per year), 129 research assistantships with full tuition reimbursements available (averaging $18,000 per year), 76 teaching assistantships with full tuition reimbursements available (averaging $17,000 per year); career-related internships or fieldwork, institutionally sponsored loans, scholarships/grants, tuition waivers (full), and unspecified assistantships also available. *Total annual research expenditures:* $8.4 million. *Unit head:* Dr. John Collier, Interim Dean and Professor, 850-410-6161, Fax: 850-410-6546, E-mail: dean@eng.fsu.edu. *Application contact:* Melanie Booker, Associate Director for Graduate Admissions, 850-644-3420, Fax: 850-644-0197, E-mail: mbooker@admin.fsu.edu. Web site: http://www.eng.fsu.edu/.

George Mason University, Volgenau School of Engineering, Fairfax, VA 22030. Offers MS, PhD, Certificate, Engr. Part-time and evening/weekend programs available. Postbaccalaureate distance learning degree programs offered. *Faculty:* 145 full-time (30 women), 155 part-time/adjunct (21 women). *Students:* 545 full-time (148 women), 1,076 part-time (224 women); includes 351 minority (78 Black or African American, non-Hispanic/Latino; 4 American Indian or Alaska Native, non-Hispanic/Latino; 195 Asian, non-Hispanic/Latino; 58 Hispanic/Latino; 2 Native Hawaiian or other Pacific Islander, non-Hispanic/Latino; 14 Two or more races, non-Hispanic/Latino), 473 international. Average age 31. 1,770 applicants, 60% accepted, 408 enrolled. In 2011, 410 master's, 26 doctorates, 94 other advanced degrees awarded. *Degree requirements:* For master's, thesis optional; for doctorate, thesis/dissertation, comprehensive oral and written exams. *Entrance requirements:* For master's, minimum GPA of 3.0 in last 60 hours of course work; for doctorate, GRE General Test, minimum graduate GPA of 3.5. Additional exam requirements/recommendations for international students: Required—TOEFL (minimum score 575 paper-based; 230 computer-based; 88 iBT), IELTS, Pearson Test of English. Application fee: $65 ($80 for international students). Electronic applications accepted. *Expenses:* Tuition, state resident: full-time $8750; part-time $364.58 per credit. Tuition, nonresident: full-time $24,092; part-time $1003.83 per credit. *Required fees:* $2514; $104.75 per credit. *Financial support:* In 2011–12, 267 students received support, including 12 fellowships with full tuition reimbursements available (averaging $18,000 per year), 102 research assistantships with full and partial tuition reimbursements available (averaging $15,482 per year), 153 teaching assistantships with full and partial tuition reimbursements available (averaging $11,438 per year); career-related internships or fieldwork, Federal Work-Study, scholarships/grants, unspecified assistantships, and health care benefits (full-time research or teaching assistantship recipients) also available. Support available to part-time students. Financial award application deadline: 3/1; financial award applicants required to submit FAFSA. *Faculty research:* Systems management, quality assurance, decision support systems, cognitive ergonomics. *Total annual research expenditures:* $18.5 million. *Unit*

head: Lloyd Griffiths, Dean, 703-993-1500, Fax: 703-993-1734, E-mail: lgriff@gmu.edu. *Application contact:* Jade T. Perez, Graduate Admission and Enrollment Services Director, 703-993-3932, Fax: 703-993-1242, E-mail: jperezc@gmu.edu. Web site: http://volgenau.gmu.edu.

The George Washington University, School of Engineering and Applied Science, Washington, DC 20052. Offers MS, D Sc, App Sc, Engr, Graduate Certificate. Part-time and evening/weekend programs available. *Faculty:* 87 full-time (11 women), 69 part-time/adjunct (11 women). *Students:* 496 full-time (136 women), 1,342 part-time (333 women); includes 360 minority (179 Black or African American, non-Hispanic/Latino; 7 American Indian or Alaska Native, non-Hispanic/Latino; 109 Asian, non-Hispanic/Latino; 52 Hispanic/Latino; 6 Native Hawaiian or other Pacific Islander, non-Hispanic/Latino; 7 Two or more races, non-Hispanic/Latino), 481 international. Average age 33. 1,528 applicants, 85% accepted, 486 enrolled. In 2011, 586 master's, 55 doctorates, 272 other advanced degrees awarded. *Degree requirements:* For master's, thesis optional; for doctorate, thesis/dissertation, qualifying exam. *Entrance requirements:* For master's, appropriate bachelor's degree; for doctorate, GRE (if highest earned degree is BS), appropriate bachelor's or master's degree; for other advanced degree, appropriate master's degree. Additional exam requirements/recommendations for international students: Required—TOEFL or The George Washington University English as a Foreign Language Test. *Application deadline:* For fall admission, 3/1 for domestic students; for spring admission, 10/1 for domestic students. Applications are processed on a rolling basis. Application fee: $75. *Financial support:* In 2011–12, 216 students received support. Fellowships with full and partial tuition reimbursements available, research assistantships with full and partial tuition reimbursements available, teaching assistantships with full and partial tuition reimbursements available, career-related internships or fieldwork, Federal Work-Study, institutionally sponsored loans, and tuition waivers (full and partial) available. Financial award application deadline: 3/1; financial award applicants required to submit FAFSA. *Faculty research:* Fatigue fracture and structural reliability, computer-integrated manufacturing, materials engineering, artificial intelligence and expert systems, quality assurance. *Total annual research expenditures:* $6.3 million. *Unit head:* David S. Dolling, Dean, 202-994-6080, E-mail: dolling@gwu.edu. *Application contact:* Adina Lav, Marketing, Recruiting and Admissions, 202-994-5827, Fax: 202-994-0909, E-mail: engineering@gwu.edu. Web site: http://www.seas.gwu.edu/.

Georgia Institute of Technology, Graduate Studies and Research, College of Engineering, Atlanta, GA 30332-0001. Offers MS, MS Bio E, MS Ch E, MS Env E, MS Poly, MS Stat, MSAE, MSCE, MSEE, MSESM, MSHS, MSIE, MSME, MSNE, MSOR, PhD, MD/PhD. *Accreditation:* ABET (one or more programs are accredited). Part-time programs available. Postbaccalaureate distance learning degree programs offered. Terminal master's awarded for partial completion of doctoral program. *Degree requirements:* For doctorate, thesis/dissertation. *Entrance requirements:* Additional exam requirements/recommendations for international students: Required—TOEFL. Electronic applications accepted.

Graduate School and University Center of the City University of New York, Graduate Studies, Program in Engineering, New York, NY 10016-4039. Offers biomedical engineering (PhD); chemical engineering (PhD); civil engineering (PhD); electrical engineering (PhD); mechanical engineering (PhD). *Degree requirements:* For doctorate, thesis/dissertation. *Entrance requirements:* For doctorate, GRE General Test. Additional exam requirements/recommendations for international students: Required—TOEFL. Electronic applications accepted.

Grand Valley State University, Padnos College of Engineering and Computing, School of Engineering, Allendale, MI 49401-9403. Offers electrical and computer engineering (MSE); manufacturing operations (MSE); mechanical engineering (MSE); product design and manufacturing engineering (MSE). Part-time and evening/weekend programs available. *Degree requirements:* For master's, project or thesis. *Entrance requirements:* For master's, engineering degree, minimum GPA of 3.0. Additional exam requirements/recommendations for international students: Required—TOEFL. Electronic applications accepted. *Faculty research:* Digital signal processing, computer aided design, computer aided manufacturing, manufacturing simulation, biomechanics, product design.

Harvard University, Graduate School of Arts and Sciences, School of Engineering and Applied Sciences, Cambridge, MA 02138. Offers applied mathematics (ME, SM, PhD); applied physics (ME, SM, PhD); computer science (ME, SM, PhD); engineering science (ME); engineering sciences (SM, PhD). Part-time programs available. Terminal master's awarded for partial completion of doctoral program. *Degree requirements:* For master's, thesis optional; for doctorate, comprehensive exam, thesis/dissertation. *Entrance requirements:* For master's and doctorate, GRE General Test, GRE Subject Test (recommended), 3 letters of recommendation. Additional exam requirements/recommendations for international students: Required—TOEFL (minimum score 80 iBT). Electronic applications accepted. *Expenses: Tuition:* Full-time $36,304. *Required fees:* $1186. Full-time tuition and fees vary according to program. *Faculty research:* Applied mathematics, applied physics, computer science and electrical engineering, environmental engineering, mechanical and biomedical engineering.

Howard University, College of Engineering, Architecture, and Computer Sciences, School of Engineering and Computer Science, Washington, DC 20059-0002. Offers M Eng, MCS, MS, PhD. Part-time programs available. Terminal master's awarded for partial completion of doctoral program. *Degree requirements:* For doctorate, one foreign language, thesis/dissertation, preliminary exam. *Entrance requirements:* For master's and doctorate, GRE General Test, minimum GPA of 3.0. Additional exam requirements/recommendations for international students: Required—TOEFL. Electronic applications accepted. *Faculty research:* Environmental engineering, solid-state electronics, dynamics and control of large flexible space structures, power systems, reaction kinetics.

Idaho State University, Office of Graduate Studies, College of Science and Engineering, Pocatello, ID 83209-8060. Offers MA, MNS, MS, DA, PhD, Postbaccalaureate Certificate. *Accreditation:* ABET. Part-time programs available. *Degree requirements:* For master's, comprehensive exam (for some programs), thesis, thesis project, 2 semesters of seminar; for doctorate, comprehensive exam, thesis/dissertation, oral presentation and defense of research, oral examination; for Postbaccalaureate Certificate, comprehensive exam (for some programs), thesis optional, oral exam or thesis defense. *Entrance requirements:* For master's, GRE General Test, minimum GPA of 3.0 in upper-division undergraduate classes; for doctorate, GRE General Test, master's degree in engineering or physics, 1-page statement of research interests, resume, 3 letters of reference, 1-page statement of career interests; for Postbaccalaureate Certificate, GRE (if GPA between 2.0 and 3.0), bachelor's degree, minimum GPA of 3.0 in upper-division courses. Additional exam requirements/recommendations for international students: Required—TOEFL (minimum score 550 paper-based; 213 computer-based; 80 iBT). Electronic applications accepted.

Faculty research: Nuclear engineering, biomedical engineering, robotics, measurement and control, structural systems.

Illinois Institute of Technology, Graduate College, Armour College of Engineering, Chicago, IL 60616-3793. Offers M Arch E, M Ch E, M Env E, M Geoenv E, M Trans E, MBE, MBMI, MCEM, MECE, MEM, MFPE, MGE, MMAE, MME, MMME, MNE, MPE, MPW, MS, MSE, MTSE, MVM, PhD. Part-time and evening/weekend programs available. Postbaccalaureate distance learning degree programs offered (no on-campus study). Terminal master's awarded for partial completion of doctoral program. *Degree requirements:* For master's, comprehensive exam (for some programs), thesis (for some programs); for doctorate, comprehensive exam, thesis/dissertation. *Entrance requirements:* For master's and doctorate, GRE General Test, minimum undergraduate GPA of 3.0. Additional exam requirements/recommendations for international students: Required—TOEFL (minimum score 523 paper-based; 70 iBT); Recommended—IELTS (minimum score 5.5). Electronic applications accepted.

Indiana State University, College of Graduate and Professional Studies, College of Technology, Terre Haute, IN 47809. Offers MS, MA/MS. *Entrance requirements:* For master's, bachelor's degree in industrial technology or related field. Additional exam requirements/recommendations for international students: Required—TOEFL. Electronic applications accepted.

Indiana University–Purdue University Fort Wayne, College of Engineering, Technology, and Computer Science, Fort Wayne, IN 46805-1499. Offers MS, MSE, Certificate. Part-time programs available. *Faculty:* 54 full-time (6 women), 3 part-time/adjunct (0 women). *Students:* 17 full-time (5 women), 97 part-time (32 women); includes 17 minority (7 Black or African American, non-Hispanic/Latino; 7 Asian, non-Hispanic/Latino; 3 Hispanic/Latino), 9 international. Average age 32. 55 applicants, 93% accepted, 34 enrolled. In 2011, 33 master's awarded. *Entrance requirements:* For master's, GRE General Test, minimum GPA of 3.0. Additional exam requirements/recommendations for international students: Required—TOEFL (minimum score 550 paper-based; 213 computer-based; 77 iBT); Recommended—TWE. *Application deadline:* For fall admission, 7/15 for domestic students, 5/15 for international students; for spring admission, 12/1 for domestic students, 10/15 for international students. Applications are processed on a rolling basis. Application fee: $55 ($60 for international students). Electronic applications accepted. *Financial support:* In 2011–12, 7 research assistantships with partial tuition reimbursements (averaging $12,930 per year), 8 teaching assistantships with partial tuition reimbursements (averaging $12,930 per year) were awarded; career-related internships or fieldwork, scholarships/grants, and unspecified assistantships also available. Support available to part-time students. Financial award application deadline: 3/1; financial award applicants required to submit FAFSA. *Faculty research:* Manufacturing applications, multimodal approaches in classrooms, secure virtual environments. *Total annual research expenditures:* $249,820. *Unit head:* Dr. Max Yen, Dean, 260-481-6839, Fax: 260-481-5734, E-mail: yens@ipfw.edu. *Application contact:* Susan Humphrey, Graduate Applications Coordinator, 260-481-6145, Fax: 260-481-6880, E-mail: ask@ipfw.edu. Web site: http://www.ipfw.edu/etcs.

Instituto Tecnologico de Santo Domingo, Graduate School, Area of Engineering, Santo Domingo, Dominican Republic. Offers construction administration (MS, Certificate); data telecommunications (M Eng, MS, Certificate); industrial engineering (M Eng, Certificate); industrial management (M Mgmt); information technology (Certificate); maintenance engineering (M Eng); occupational hazard prevention (M Mgmt); production management (Certificate); quantitative methods (Certificate); sanitary and environmental engineering (M Eng); structural engineering (M Eng); systems engineering and electronic data processing (Certificate); transportation (Certificate).

Instituto Tecnológico y de Estudios Superiores de Monterrey, Campus Ciudad Obregón, Program in Engineering, Ciudad Obregón, Mexico. Offers ME.

Instituto Tecnológico y de Estudios Superiores de Monterrey, Campus Monterrey, Graduate and Research Division, Programs in Engineering, Monterrey, Mexico. Offers applied statistics (M Eng); artificial intelligence (PhD); automation engineering (M Eng); chemical engineering (M Eng); civil engineering (M Eng); electrical engineering (M Eng); electronic engineering (M Eng); environmental engineering (M Eng); industrial engineering (M Eng, PhD); manufacturing engineering (M Eng); mechanical engineering (M Eng); systems and quality engineering (M Eng). M Eng program offered jointly with University of Waterloo; PhD in industrial engineering with Texas A&M University. Part-time and evening/weekend programs available. Terminal master's awarded for partial completion of doctoral program. *Degree requirements:* For master's, one foreign language, thesis; for doctorate, one foreign language, thesis/dissertation. *Entrance requirements:* For master's, EXADEP; for doctorate, GRE, master's degree in related field. Additional exam requirements/recommendations for international students: Required—TOEFL. *Faculty research:* Flexible manufacturing cells, materials, statistical methods, environmental prevention, control and evaluation.

The Johns Hopkins University, Engineering Program for Professionals, Elkridge, MD 21075. Offers M Ch E, M Mat SE, MCE, MEE, MME, MS, MSE, Graduate Certificate, Post-Master's Certificate. Part-time and evening/weekend programs available. Electronic applications accepted.

The Johns Hopkins University, Whiting School of Engineering, Baltimore, MD 21218-2699. Offers M Ch E, M Mat SE, MA, MCE, MEE, MME, MS, MSE, MSEM, MSSI, PhD, Certificate, Post-Master's Certificate. Terminal master's awarded for partial completion of doctoral program. *Degree requirements:* For master's, comprehensive exam (for some programs), thesis (for some programs); for doctorate, comprehensive exam, thesis/dissertation, oral exam. *Entrance requirements:* For master's, GRE General Test, letters of recommendation, transcripts; for doctorate, GRE General Test, letters of recommendation. Additional exam requirements/recommendations for international students: Required—TOEFL (minimum score 600 paper-based; 250 computer-based; 100 iBT) or IELTS (minimum score 7). Electronic applications accepted. *Faculty research:* Biomedical engineering, environmental systems and engineering, materials science and engineering, signal and image processing, structural dynamics and geomechanics.

Kansas State University, Graduate School, College of Engineering, Manhattan, KS 66506. Offers MEM, MS, MSE, PhD. Part-time programs available. Postbaccalaureate distance learning degree programs offered (minimal on-campus study). *Faculty:* 109 full-time (16 women), 20 part-time/adjunct (2 women). *Students:* 292 full-time (80 women), 201 part-time (32 women); includes 40 minority (14 Black or African American, non-Hispanic/Latino; 9 Asian, non-Hispanic/Latino; 10 Hispanic/Latino; 7 Two or more races, non-Hispanic/Latino), 205 international. Average age 29. 842 applicants, 30% accepted, 70 enrolled. In 2011, 150 master's, 19 doctorates awarded. *Degree requirements:* For doctorate, thesis/dissertation. *Entrance requirements:* For master's and doctorate, GRE. Additional exam requirements/recommendations for international students: Required—TOEFL. *Application deadline:* For fall admission, 2/1 priority date for domestic students,

2/1 for international students; for spring admission, 8/1 priority date for domestic students, 8/1 for international students. Applications are processed on a rolling basis. Application fee: $40 ($55 for international students). Electronic applications accepted. *Financial support:* In 2011–12, 184 research assistantships (averaging $17,889 per year), 47 teaching assistantships (averaging $14,919 per year) were awarded; career-related internships or fieldwork, Federal Work-Study, institutionally sponsored loans, and scholarships/grants also available. Support available to part-time students. Financial award application deadline: 3/1; financial award applicants required to submit FAFSA. *Total annual research expenditures:* $20.3 million. *Unit head:* John English, Dean, 785-532-5590, Fax: 785-532-7810, E-mail: jenglish@ksu.edu. *Application contact:* Maureen Lockhart, Administrative Assistant to the Dean, 785-532-5441, Fax: 785-532-7810, E-mail: maureen@ksu.edu. Web site: http://www.engg.ksu.edu/.
See Display on next page and Close-Up on page 77.

Kent State University, College of Technology, Kent, OH 44242-0001. Offers MT. Part-time programs available. Postbaccalaureate distance learning degree programs offered. *Degree requirements:* For master's, thesis optional. *Entrance requirements:* For master's, GRE, minimum GPA of 2.75. Electronic applications accepted. *Expenses:* Tuition, state resident: full-time $8136; part-time $452 per credit hour. Tuition, nonresident: full-time $14,292; part-time $794 per credit hour. *Faculty research:* Automation, robotics, CAD, CAM, CIM.

Lakehead University, Graduate Studies, Faculty of Engineering, Thunder Bay, ON P7B 5E1, Canada. Offers control engineering (M Sc Engr); electrical/computer engineering (M Sc Engr); environmental engineering (M Sc Engr). Part-time programs available. *Degree requirements:* For master's, thesis. *Entrance requirements:* For master's, bachelor's degree in chemical, electrical or mechanical engineering, minimum B average. Additional exam requirements/recommendations for international students: Required—TOEFL. *Faculty research:* Pulp and paper, adaptive/process control, robust/interactive learning control, vibration control.

Lamar University, College of Graduate Studies, College of Engineering, Beaumont, TX 77710. Offers ME, MEM, MES, MS, DE, PhD. Part-time and evening/weekend programs available. *Faculty:* 40 full-time (3 women), 2 part-time/adjunct (1 woman). *Students:* 172 full-time (29 women), 107 part-time (18 women); includes 19 minority (5 Black or African American, non-Hispanic/Latino; 10 Asian, non-Hispanic/Latino; 4 Hispanic/Latino), 236 international. Average age 27. 286 applicants, 74% accepted, 54 enrolled. In 2011, 270 master's, 9 doctorates awarded. Terminal master's awarded for partial completion of doctoral program. *Degree requirements:* For doctorate, thesis/dissertation. *Entrance requirements:* For master's and doctorate, GRE General Test. Additional exam requirements/recommendations for international students: Required—TOEFL. *Application deadline:* For fall admission, 5/15 priority date for domestic students; for spring admission, 10/1 priority date for domestic students. Applications are processed on a rolling basis. Application fee: $25 ($50 for international students). *Expenses:* Tuition, state resident: full-time $5430; part-time $272 per credit hour. Tuition, nonresident: full-time $11,540; part-time $577 per credit hour. Required fees: $1916. *Financial support:* In 2011–12, fellowships with partial tuition reimbursements (averaging $6,000 per year), research assistantships with partial tuition reimbursements (averaging $7,500 per year), teaching assistantships with partial tuition reimbursements (averaging $7,500 per year) were awarded; career-related internships or fieldwork, Federal Work-Study, institutionally sponsored loans, scholarships/grants, tuition waivers (full and partial), and laboratory assistantships also available. Support available to part-time students. Financial award application deadline: 4/1. *Faculty research:* Energy alternatives; process analysis, design, and control; pollution prevention. *Unit head:* Dr. Jack Hopper, Chair, 409-880-8784, Fax: 409-880-2197, E-mail: che_dept@hal.lamar.edu. *Application contact:* Sandy Drane, Coordinator of Graduate Admissions, 409-880-8356, Fax: 409-880-8414, E-mail: gradmissions@hal.lamar.edu.

Laurentian University, School of Graduate Studies and Research, School of Engineering, Sudbury, ON P3E 2C6, Canada. Offers mineral resources engineering (M Eng, MA Sc); natural resources engineering (PhD). Part-time programs available. *Faculty research:* Mining engineering, rock mechanics (tunneling, rockbursts, rock support), metallurgy (mineral processing, hydro and pyrometallurgy), simulations and remote mining, simulations and scheduling.

Lawrence Technological University, College of Engineering, Southfield, MI 48075-1058. Offers architectural engineering (MS); automotive engineering (MS); civil engineering (MA, MS); construction engineering management (MA); electrical and computer engineering (MS); engineering management (MEM); industrial engineering (MS); manufacturing systems (ME, DE); mechanical engineering (MS, DE); mechatronic systems engineering (MS). Part-time and evening/weekend programs available. *Faculty:* 25 full-time (4 women), 20 part-time/adjunct (1 woman). *Students:* 8 full-time (0 women), 332 part-time (52 women); includes 58 minority (21 Black or African American, non-Hispanic/Latino; 1 American Indian or Alaska Native, non-Hispanic/Latino; 32 Asian, non-Hispanic/Latino; 2 Hispanic/Latino; 2 Two or more races, non-Hispanic/Latino), 84 international. Average age 32. 652 applicants, 44% accepted, 70 enrolled. In 2011, 127 master's, 2 doctorates awarded. *Degree requirements:* For master's, thesis (for some programs). *Entrance requirements:* Additional exam requirements/recommendations for international students: Required—TOEFL (minimum score 550 paper-based; 213 computer-based; 79 iBT). *Application deadline:* For fall admission, 7/27 priority date for domestic students, 5/23 for international students; for spring admission, 11/15 priority date for domestic students, 11/15 for international students. Applications are processed on a rolling basis. Application fee: $50. Electronic applications accepted. *Financial support:* In 2011–12, 68 students received support, including 6 research assistantships (averaging $8,078 per year); Federal Work-Study and institutionally sponsored loans also available. Support available to part-time students. Financial award application deadline: 4/1; financial award applicants required to submit FAFSA. *Faculty research:* Advanced composite materials in bridges, strengthening existing bridges with carbon and glass fiber sheets, development of drive shafts using composite materials. *Unit head:* Dr. Nabil Grace, Dean, 248-204-2500, Fax: 248-204-2509, E-mail: engrdean@ltu.edu. *Application contact:* Jane Rohrback, Director of Admissions, 248-204-3160, Fax: 248-204-2228, E-mail: admissions@ltu.edu. Web site: http://www.ltu.edu/engineering/index.asp.

Lehigh University, P.C. Rossin College of Engineering and Applied Science, Bethlehem, PA 18015. Offers M Eng, MS, PhD, MBA/E. Part-time programs available. Postbaccalaureate distance learning degree programs offered (no on-campus study). *Faculty:* 118 full-time (16 women), 6 part-time/adjunct (0 women). *Students:* 490 full-time (111 women), 177 part-time (47 women); includes 38 minority (9 Black or African American, non-Hispanic/Latino; 17 Asian, non-Hispanic/Latino; 11 Hispanic/Latino; 1 Two or more races, non-Hispanic/Latino), 375 international. Average age 27. 2,648 applicants, 23% accepted, 162 enrolled. In 2011, 169 master's, 42 doctorates awarded. Terminal master's awarded for partial completion of doctoral program. *Degree requirements:* For master's, comprehensive exam (for some programs), thesis (for some programs); for doctorate, comprehensive exam (for some programs), thesis/dissertation.

KANSAS STATE ENGINEERING

Kansas State College of Engineering graduate programs offer state-of-the-art facilities that support nationally and internationally recognized research endeavors. Faculty, staff and students share a keen focus on creating a supportive environment and optimal educational experience for all participants in its eight doctorate and 12 master's degree programs.

Graduate Degree Programs

http://www.engg.ksu.edu/graduate_programs2.php

- Architectural Engineering, M.S.
- Biological and Agricultural Engineering, M.S./Ph.D.
- Chemical Engineering, M.S/Ph.D.
- Civil Engineering, M.S./Ph.D.
- Computer Science, M.S./Ph.D.
- Electrical Engineering, M.S./Ph.D.
- Engineering Management, M.E.M.
- Industrial Engineering, M.S./Ph.D.
- Mechanical Engineering, M.S./Ph.D.
- Nuclear Engineering, M.S./Ph.D.
- Operations Research, M.S.
- Software Engineering, M.S.E.

KANSAS STATE UNIVERSITY

Entrance requirements: For master's and doctorate, GRE General Test, BS. Additional exam requirements/recommendations for international students: Required—TOEFL (minimum score 550 paper-based; 213 computer-based; 79 iBT). *Application deadline:* For fall admission, 7/15 for domestic and international students; for spring admission, 12/1 for domestic and international students. Applications are processed on a rolling basis. Application fee: $75. Electronic applications accepted. *Expenses:* Contact institution. *Financial support:* In 2011–12, 361 students received support, including 36 fellowships with full and partial tuition reimbursements available (averaging $18,360 per year), 201 research assistantships with full and partial tuition reimbursements available (averaging $21,960 per year), 64 teaching assistantships with full and partial tuition reimbursements available (averaging $18,819 per year); career-related internships or fieldwork, institutionally sponsored loans, scholarships/grants, health care benefits, tuition waivers (full and partial), and unspecified assistantships also available. Financial award application deadline: 1/15. *Faculty research:* Advanced materials and nanotechnology, life sciences and bioengineering, environmental science and energy, information science and technology, large structural systems, optical technologies. *Unit head:* Dr. John P. Coulter, Associate Dean of Graduate Studies and Research, 610-758-6310, Fax: 610-758-5623, E-mail: john.coulter@lehigh.edu. *Application contact:* Brianne Lisk, Manager of Graduate Programs, 610-758-6310, Fax: 610-758-5623, E-mail: brc3@lehigh.edu. Web site: http://www3.lehigh.edu/engineering/.

LeTourneau University, School of Graduate and Professional Studies, Longview, TX 75607-7001. Offers business administration (MBA); counseling (MA); education (M Ed); engineering (M Sc); health care administration (MS); psychology (MA); strategic leadership (MSL). Part-time and evening/weekend programs available. Postbaccalaureate distance learning degree programs offered (no on-campus study). *Faculty:* 19 full-time (5 women), 62 part-time/adjunct (25 women). *Students:* 12 full-time (6 women), 347 part-time (273 women); includes 191 minority (162 Black or African American, non-Hispanic/Latino; 2 American Indian or Alaska Native, non-Hispanic/Latino; 3 Asian, non-Hispanic/Latino; 20 Hispanic/Latino; 1 Native Hawaiian or other Pacific Islander, non-Hispanic/Latino; 3 Two or more races, non-Hispanic/Latino), 1 international. Average age 37. 138 applicants, 90% accepted, 120 enrolled. In 2011, 129 master's awarded. *Degree requirements:* For master's, thesis (for some programs). *Entrance requirements:* For master's, GRE (for counseling and engineering programs), minimum GPA of 2.8 (3.0 for counseling and engineering programs). Additional exam requirements/recommendations for international students: Required—TOEFL. *Application deadline:* Applications are processed on a rolling basis. Electronic applications accepted. *Expenses: Tuition:* Full-time $13,020; part-time $620 per credit hour. *Financial support:* In 2011–12, 15 students received support, including 5 research assistantships (averaging $9,600 per year); institutionally sponsored loans and unspecified assistantships also available. *Unit head:* Dr. Carol Green, Vice President, 903-233-4010, Fax: 903-233-3227, E-mail: carolgreen@letu.edu. *Application contact:* Chris Fontaine, Assistant Vice President for Enrollment Management and Marketing, 903-233-4071, Fax: 903-233-3227, E-mail: chrisfontaine@letu.edu. Web site: http://www.adults.letu.edu/.

Louisiana State University and Agricultural and Mechanical College, Graduate School, College of Agriculture, Department of Biological and Agricultural Engineering, Baton Rouge, LA 70803. Offers biological and agricultural engineering (MSBAE); engineering science (MS, PhD). Part-time programs available. *Faculty:* 11 full-time (2 women). *Students:* 16 full-time (4 women), 2 part-time (1 woman); includes 7 minority (3 Black or African American, non-Hispanic/Latino; 3 Asian, non-Hispanic/Latino; 1 Hispanic/Latino), 6 international. Average age 26. 9 applicants, 56% accepted, 2 enrolled. In 2011, 7 master's awarded. Terminal master's awarded for partial completion of doctoral program. *Degree requirements:* For master's, thesis; for doctorate, thesis/dissertation. *Entrance requirements:* For master's and doctorate, GRE General Test, minimum GPA of 3.0. Additional exam requirements/recommendations for international students: Required—TOEFL (minimum score 550 paper-based; 213 computer-based; 79 iBT) or IELTS (minimum score 6.5). *Application deadline:* For fall admission, 1/25 priority date for domestic students, 5/15 for international students; for spring admission, 10/15 for international students. Applications are processed on a rolling basis. Application fee: $50 ($70 for international students). Electronic applications accepted. *Financial support:* In 2011–12, 16 students received support, including 1 fellowship (averaging $6,300 per year), 14 research assistantships with partial tuition reimbursements available (averaging $17,956 per year); teaching assistantships with partial tuition reimbursements available, career-related internships or fieldwork, Federal Work-Study, institutionally sponsored loans, scholarships/grants, health care benefits, and unspecified assistantships also available. Financial award application deadline: 7/1; financial award applicants required to submit FAFSA. *Faculty research:* Bioenergy, bioprocess engineering, cellular and molecular engineering, drug delivery using nanotechnology, environmental engineering. *Total annual research expenditures:* $87,691. *Unit head:* Dr. Dan Thomas, Head, 225-578-3153, Fax: 225-578-3492, E-mail: dthomas@agcenter.lsu.edu. *Application contact:* Dr. Steven Hall, Graduate Coordinator, 225-578-1058, Fax: 225-578-3492, E-mail: sghall@agcenter.lsu.edu. Web site: http://www.bae.lsu.edu/.

Louisiana State University and Agricultural and Mechanical College, Graduate School, College of Engineering, Department of Construction Management and Industrial Engineering, Baton Rouge, LA 70803. Offers engineering science (PhD); industrial engineering (MSIE). *Faculty:* 11 full-time (5 women), 1 part-time/adjunct (0 women). *Students:* 11 full-time (3 women), 3 part-time (0 women); includes 1 minority (Black or African American, non-Hispanic/Latino), 8 international. Average age 27. 20 applicants, 55% accepted, 1 enrolled. In 2011, 3 master's awarded. Terminal master's awarded for partial completion of doctoral program. *Degree requirements:* For master's, thesis; for doctorate, thesis/dissertation. *Entrance requirements:* For master's and doctorate, GRE General Test, minimum GPA of 3.0. Additional exam requirements/recommendations for international students: Required—TOEFL (minimum score 550 paper-based; 213 computer-based; 79 iBT) or IELTS (minimum score 6.5). *Application deadline:* For fall admission, 1/25 priority date for domestic students, 5/15 for international students; for spring admission, 10/15 for international students. Applications are processed on a rolling basis. Application fee: $50 ($70 for international students). Electronic applications accepted. *Financial support:* In 2011–12, 9 students received support, including 5 research assistantships with partial tuition reimbursements available (averaging $10,240 per year), 2 teaching assistantships with partial tuition reimbursements available (averaging $12,400 per year); fellowships, Federal Work-Study, institutionally sponsored loans, health care benefits, and unspecified assistantships also available. Financial award application deadline: 5/1; financial award applicants required to submit FAFSA. *Faculty research:* Ergonomics and occupational health, information technology, production systems, supply management, construction safety and methods. *Total annual research expenditures:* $434,200. *Unit head:* Dr. Craig Harvey, Chair, 225-578-5112, Fax: 225-578-5109, E-mail: harvey@lsu.edu. *Application contact:* Dr. Pius Egbelu, Graduate Adviser, 225-578-5112, Fax: 225-578-5109, E-mail: pegbelu@eng.lsu.edu. Web site: http://www.cm.lsu.edu/.

Louisiana State University and Agricultural and Mechanical College, Graduate School, College of Engineering, Interdepartmental Program in Engineering Science, Baton Rouge, LA 70803. Offers engineering science (MSES, PhD). Part-time and evening/weekend programs available. *Students:* 49 full-time (20 women), 10 part-time (4 women); includes 9 minority (7 Black or African American, non-Hispanic/Latino; 1 Asian, non-Hispanic/Latino; 1 Hispanic/Latino), 27 international. Average age 32. 37 applicants, 41% accepted, 7 enrolled. In 2011, 16 master's, 5 doctorates awarded. Terminal master's awarded for partial completion of doctoral program. *Degree requirements:* For master's, thesis optional; for doctorate, thesis/dissertation. *Entrance requirements:* For master's and doctorate, GRE General Test, minimum GPA of 3.0. Additional exam requirements/recommendations for international students: Required—TOEFL (minimum score 550 paper-based; 213 computer-based; 79 iBT) or IELTS (minimum score 6.5). *Application deadline:* For fall admission, 1/25 priority date for domestic students, 5/15 for international students; for spring admission, 10/15 for international students. Applications are processed on a rolling basis. Application fee: $50 ($70 for international students). *Financial support:* In 2011–12, 48 students received support, including 5 fellowships (averaging $14,795 per year), 23 research assistantships with full and partial tuition reimbursements available (averaging $17,676 per year), 10 teaching assistantships with full and partial tuition reimbursements available (averaging $12,140 per year); Federal Work-Study, scholarships/grants, health care benefits, tuition waivers (full and partial), and unspecified assistantships also available. Support available to part-time students. Financial award application deadline: 3/1; financial award applicants required to submit FAFSA. *Faculty research:* Environmental engineering, transportation engineering, enhanced oil recovery, microelectrical-mechanical systems, manufacturing. *Total annual research expenditures:* $1.2 million. *Unit head:* Dr. Warren Waggenspack, Associate Dean for Academic Programs, 225-578-5701, Fax: 225-578-9162, E-mail: mewagg@me.lsu.edu. *Application contact:* Dr. Warren Waggenspack, Associate Dean for Academic Programs, 225-578-5701, Fax: 225-578-9162, E-mail: mewagg@me.lsu.edu. Web site: http://www.eng.lsu.edu/academics/gradprogs/engrsci/overview.

Louisiana Tech University, Graduate School, College of Engineering and Science, Ruston, LA 71272. Offers MS, PhD. Part-time programs available. Terminal master's awarded for partial completion of doctoral program. *Degree requirements:* For doctorate, thesis/dissertation. *Entrance requirements:* For master's, GRE General Test, minimum GPA of 3.0 in last 60 hours. Additional exam requirements/recommendations for international students: Required—TOEFL. *Faculty research:* Trenchless technology, micromanufacturing, radionuclide transport, microbial liquefaction, hazardous waste treatment.

Manhattan College, Graduate Division, School of Engineering, Riverdale, NY 10471. Offers chemical engineering (MS), including chemical engineering, cosmetic engineering; civil engineering (MS); computer engineering (MS); electrical engineering (MS); environmental engineering (ME, MS); mechanical engineering (MS). Part-time and evening/weekend programs available. *Faculty:* 34 full-time (4 women), 25 part-time/adjunct (0 women). *Students:* 46 full-time (12 women), 111 part-time (39 women); includes 48 minority (14 Black or African American, non-Hispanic/Latino; 12 Asian, non-Hispanic/Latino; 14 Hispanic/Latino; 8 Two or more races, non-Hispanic/Latino), 3 international. Average age 25. 95 applicants, 86% accepted, 63 enrolled. In 2011, 49 master's awarded. *Degree requirements:* For master's, thesis or alternative. *Entrance requirements:* For master's, GRE (recommended), minimum GPA of 3.0. Additional exam requirements/recommendations for international students: Required—TOEFL (minimum score 550 paper-based; 213 computer-based; 80 iBT), IELTS (minimum score 6). *Application deadline:* For fall admission, 8/10 priority date for domestic students, 8/10 for international students; for spring admission, 1/7 for domestic and international students. Applications are processed on a rolling basis. Application fee: $50. *Expenses:* Contact institution. *Financial support:* In 2011–12, 31 students received support, including 33 teaching assistantships with partial tuition reimbursements available (averaging $4,000 per year); career-related internships or fieldwork, Federal Work-Study, scholarships/grants, and laboratory assistantships also available. Support available to part-time students. Financial award application deadline: 2/1. *Faculty research:* Environmental/water, nucleation, environmental/management, heat transfer. *Total annual research expenditures:* $400,000. *Unit head:* Dr. Tim J. Ward, Dean, 718-862-7281, Fax: 718-862-8015, E-mail: deanengr@manhattan.edu. *Application contact:* Sheila M. Halpin, Information Contact, 718-862-7281, Fax: 718-862-8015, E-mail: deanengr@manhattan.edu. Web site: http://www.manhattan.edu/academics/engineering/.

Marquette University, Graduate School, College of Engineering, Milwaukee, WI 53201-1881. Offers ME, MS, MSEM, PhD, Certificate. Part-time and evening/weekend programs available. *Faculty:* 59 full-time (8 women), 17 part-time/adjunct (2 women). *Students:* 119 full-time (29 women), 97 part-time (18 women); includes 22 minority (3 Black or African American, non-Hispanic/Latino; 10 Asian, non-Hispanic/Latino; 6 Hispanic/Latino; 1 Native Hawaiian or other Pacific Islander, non-Hispanic/Latino; 2 Two or more races, non-Hispanic/Latino), 72 international. Average age 27. 311 applicants, 53% accepted, 50 enrolled. In 2011, 57 master's, 13 doctorates, 2 other advanced degrees awarded. *Degree requirements:* For doctorate, thesis/dissertation. *Entrance requirements:* For master's, minimum GPA of 3.0; for doctorate, GRE General Test, minimum GPA of 3.0. Additional exam requirements/recommendations for international students: Required—TOEFL (minimum score 530 paper-based; 78 computer-based). *Application deadline:* Applications are processed on a rolling basis. Application fee: $50. Electronic applications accepted. *Expenses: Tuition:* Full-time $17,010; part-time $945 per credit hour. Tuition and fees vary according to program. *Financial support:* In 2011–12, 63 students received support, including 9 fellowships with partial tuition reimbursements available, 5 research assistantships with full tuition reimbursements available, 31 teaching assistantships with full tuition reimbursements available; scholarships/grants, health care benefits, tuition waivers (partial), and unspecified assistantships also available. Support available to part-time students. Financial award application deadline: 2/15. *Faculty research:* Urban watershed management, microsensors for environmental pollutants, orthopedic rehabilitation engineering, telemedicine, ergonomics. *Total annual research expenditures:* $5.6 million. *Unit head:* Dr. Robert Bishop, Dean, 414-288-6591, Fax: 414-288-7082, E-mail: robert.bishop@marquette.edu. *Application contact:* Craig Pierce, Director of Graduate Admissions, 414-288-5740, Fax: 414-288-1902, E-mail: craig.pierce@marquette.edu. Web site: http://www.marquette.edu/engineering/grad.shtml.

Marshall University, Academic Affairs Division, College of Information Technology and Engineering, Huntington, WV 25755. Offers MS, MSE. Part-time and evening/weekend programs available. *Faculty:* 17 full-time (2 women), 5 part-time/adjunct (2 women). *Students:* 78 full-time (21 women), 115 part-time (25 women); includes 17 minority (10 Black or African American, non-Hispanic/Latino; 5 Asian, non-Hispanic/Latino; 2 Hispanic/Latino), 29 international. Average age 32. In 2011, 58 master's awarded. *Degree requirements:* For master's, final project, oral exam. Application fee: $40. *Expenses:* Contact institution. *Financial support:* Fellowships and tuition waivers (full) available. Support available to part-time students. Financial award application deadline: 8/1; financial award applicants required to submit FAFSA. *Unit head:* Dr. Wael Zatar, Interim Dean, 304-696-6043, E-mail: zatar@marshall.edu. *Application contact:* Information Contact, 304-746-1900, Fax: 304-746-1902, E-mail: services@marshall.edu. Web site: http://www.marshall.edu/cite/.

Marshall University, Academic Affairs Division, College of Information Technology and Engineering, Weisberg Division of Engineering and Computer Science, Program in Engineering, Huntington, WV 25755. Offers MSE. *Students:* 5 full-time (1 woman), 32 part-time (5 women); includes 4 minority (2 Black or African American, non-Hispanic/Latino; 2 Asian, non-Hispanic/Latino), 1 international. Average age 33. In 2011, 12 master's awarded. *Unit head:* Dr. Eldon R. Larsen, Professor, 304-746-2047, E-mail: larsen@marshall.edu. *Application contact:* Information Contact, 304-746-1900, Fax: 304-746-1902, E-mail: services@marshall.edu.

Massachusetts Institute of Technology, School of Engineering, Cambridge, MA 02139. Offers M Eng, SM, PhD, Sc D, CE, EAA, ECS, EE, Mat E, Mech E, NE, Naval E, SM/MBA. *Faculty:* 371 full-time (62 women), 1 part-time/adjunct (0 women). *Students:* 2,811 full-time (729 women), 7 part-time (2 women); includes 509 minority (42 Black or African American, non-Hispanic/Latino; 4 American Indian or Alaska Native, non-Hispanic/Latino; 315 Asian, non-Hispanic/Latino; 107 Hispanic/Latino; 41 Two or more races, non-Hispanic/Latino), 1,201 international. Average age 27. 7,676 applicants, 18% accepted, 919 enrolled. In 2011, 721 master's, 304 doctorates, 17 other advanced degrees awarded. Terminal master's awarded for partial completion of doctoral program. *Degree requirements:* For master's, thesis (for some programs); for doctorate, comprehensive exam, thesis/dissertation; for other advanced degree, thesis. Application fee: $75. Electronic applications accepted. *Expenses: Tuition:* Full-time $40,460; part-time $630 per credit hour. *Required fees:* $272. *Financial support:* In 2011–12, 2,458 students received support, including 659 fellowships (averaging $32,400 per year), 1,570 research assistantships (averaging $29,900 per year), 241 teaching assistantships (averaging $31,600 per year); career-related internships or fieldwork, Federal Work-Study, institutionally sponsored loans, scholarships/grants, traineeships, health care benefits, and unspecified assistantships also available. *Total annual research expenditures:* $332.5 million. *Unit head:* Prof. Ian A. Waitz, Dean, 617-253-3291, Fax: 617-253-8549. *Application contact:* Graduate Admissions, 617-253-2917, Fax: 617-687-9174, E-mail: mitgrad@mit.edu. Web site: http://engineering.mit.edu/.

McGill University, Faculty of Graduate and Postdoctoral Studies, Faculty of Engineering, Montréal, QC H3A 2T5, Canada. Offers M Arch I, M Arch II, M Eng, M Sc, MMM, MUP, PhD, Diploma.

McGill University, Faculty of Graduate and Postdoctoral Studies, Faculty of Science, Department of Mathematics and Statistics, Montréal, QC H3A 2T5, Canada. Offers computational science and engineering (M Sc); mathematics and statistics (M Sc, MA, PhD), including applied mathematics (M Sc, MA), pure mathematics (M Sc, MA), statistics (M Sc, MA).

McMaster University, School of Graduate Studies, Faculty of Engineering, Hamilton, ON L8S 4M2, Canada. Offers M Eng, M Sc, MA Sc, PhD. Part-time programs available. *Degree requirements:* For doctorate, comprehensive exam, thesis/dissertation. *Entrance requirements:* Additional exam requirements/recommendations for international students: Required—TOEFL (minimum score 550 paper-based; 213 computer-based). *Faculty research:* Computer process control, water resources engineering, elasticity, flow induced vibrations, microelectronics.

McNeese State University, Doré School of Graduate Studies, College of Engineering and Engineering Technology, Lake Charles, LA 70609. Offers chemical engineering (M Eng); civil engineering (M Eng); electrical engineering (M Eng); engineering management (M Eng); mechanical engineering (M Eng); pump reliability engineering (Postbaccalaureate Certificate). Part-time and evening/weekend programs available. *Faculty:* 13 full-time (1 woman). *Students:* 21 full-time (4 women), 18 part-time (5 women); includes 5 minority (4 Black or African American, non-Hispanic/Latino; 1 American Indian or Alaska Native, non-Hispanic/Latino), 23 international. In 2011, 28 master's awarded. *Degree requirements:* For master's, thesis or alternative. *Entrance requirements:* For master's, GRE, minimum undergraduate GPA of 3.0. Additional exam requirements/recommendations for international students: Required—TOEFL (minimum score 560 paper-based; 220 computer-based; 83 iBT). *Application deadline:* For fall admission, 5/15 priority date for domestic students, 5/15 for international students; for spring admission, 10/15 priority date for domestic students, 10/15 for international students. Applications are processed on a rolling basis. Application fee: $20 ($30 for international students). *Expenses:* Tuition, state resident: part-time $519 per credit hour. Tuition and fees vary according to course load. *Financial support:* Federal Work-Study available. Support available to part-time students. Financial award application deadline: 5/1. *Unit head:* Dr. Nikos Kiritsis, Dean, 337-475-5875, Fax: 337-475-5237, E-mail: nikosk@mcneese.edu. *Application contact:* Dr. George F. Mead, Jr., Interim Dean of Dore' School of Graduate Studies, 337-475-5396, Fax: 337-475-5397, E-mail: admissions@mcneese.edu.

Memorial University of Newfoundland, School of Graduate Studies, Faculty of Engineering and Applied Science, St. John's, NL A1C 5S7, Canada. Offers civil engineering (M Eng, PhD); electrical and computer engineering (M Eng, PhD); mechanical engineering (M Eng, PhD); ocean and naval architecture engineering (M Eng, PhD). Part-time programs available. *Degree requirements:* For master's, thesis; for doctorate, comprehensive exam, thesis/dissertation, oral thesis defense. *Entrance requirements:* For master's, 2nd class degree; for doctorate, master's degree in engineering. Electronic applications accepted. *Faculty research:* Engineering analysis, environmental and hydrotechnical studies, manufacturing and robotics, mechanics, structures and materials.

Mercer University, Graduate Studies, Macon Campus, School of Engineering, Macon, GA 31207-0003. Offers biomedical engineering (MSE); computer engineering (MSE); electrical engineering (MSE); engineering management (MSE); environmental engineering (MSE); environmental systems (MS); mechanical engineering (MSE); software engineering (MSE); software systems (MS); technical communications management (MS); technical management (MS). Part-time and evening/weekend programs available. Postbaccalaureate distance learning degree programs offered (no on-campus study). *Faculty:* 17 full-time (3 women), 1 part-time/adjunct (0 women). *Students:* 12 full-time (3 women), 113 part-time (28 women); includes 23 minority (13 Black or African American, non-Hispanic/Latino; 9 Asian, non-Hispanic/Latino; 1 Hispanic/Latino). Average age 31. In 2011, 44 master's awarded. *Degree requirements:* For master's, thesis or alternative. *Entrance requirements:* For master's, minimum undergraduate GPA of 3.0. Additional exam requirements/recommendations for international students: Required—TOEFL. *Application deadline:* For fall admission, 7/1 for domestic students; for spring admission, 11/15 for domestic students. Applications are processed on a rolling basis. Application fee: $35 ($50 for international students). Electronic applications accepted. *Expenses:* Contact institution. *Financial support:* Federal Work-Study available. *Unit head:* Dr. Wade H. Shaw, Dean, 478-301-2459,

Fax: 478-301-5593, E-mail: shaw_wh@mercer.edu. *Application contact:* Greg Lofton, Graduate Program Coordinator, 478-301-5480, Fax: 478-301-5434, E-mail: lofton_g@mercer.edu. Web site: http://engineering.mercer.edu/.

Merrimack College, School of Science and Engineering, North Andover, MA 01845-5800. Offers engineering (MS). Part-time and evening/weekend programs available. *Degree requirements:* For master's, variable foreign language requirement, comprehensive exam (for some programs), thesis optional. *Entrance requirements:* Additional exam requirements/recommendations for international students: Recommended—TOEFL (minimum score 80 iBT), IELTS (minimum score 6.5). *Application deadline:* For fall admission, 8/1 priority date for domestic students, 7/15 for international students; for winter admission, 12/1 priority date for domestic students, 11/15 for international students; for spring admission, 3/1 priority date for domestic students, 2/15 for international students. *Expenses: Tuition:* Part-time $475 per credit. *Required fees:* $62.50 per semester. *Financial support:* Application deadline: 5/1; applicants required to submit FAFSA. *Unit head:* Mary Noonan, Interim Dean, Science and Engineering, 978-837-5145, E-mail: noonanm@merrimack.edu. *Application contact:* 978-837-5073, E-mail: graduate@merrimack.edu. Web site: http://www.merrimack.edu/academics/science_engineering/graduate/mse/.

Miami University, School of Engineering and Applied Science, Oxford, OH 45056. Offers chemical and paper engineering (MS); computational science and engineering (MS); computer science and software engineering (MCS), including computer science; software development (Certificate). *Entrance requirements:* For master's, GRE, minimum undergraduate GPA of 3.0 during previous 2 years or 2.75 overall. Additional exam requirements/recommendations for international students: Required—TOEFL. *Expenses:* Tuition, state resident: full-time $12,023; part-time $501 per credit hour. Tuition, nonresident: full-time $26,554; part-time $1107 per credit hour. *Required fees:* $528. *Unit head:* Dr. Marek Dollar, Dean, 513-529-0700, E-mail: seasfyi@muohio.edu. *Application contact:* Graduate Admission Coordinator, 513-529-3734, Fax: 513-529-3734, E-mail: gradschool@muohio.edu. Web site: http://www.eas.muohio.edu/.

Michigan State University, The Graduate School, College of Engineering, East Lansing, MI 48824. Offers MS, PhD. Part-time programs available. Electronic applications accepted.

Michigan Technological University, Graduate School, College of Engineering, Houghton, MI 49931. Offers M Eng, MS, PhD, Graduate Certificate. Part-time programs available. Postbaccalaureate distance learning degree programs offered (minimal on-campus study). *Faculty:* 198 full-time (67 women), 41 part-time/adjunct (12 women). *Students:* 587 full-time (117 women), 150 part-time (28 women); includes 39 minority (11 Black or African American, non-Hispanic/Latino; 9 Asian, non-Hispanic/Latino; 18 Hispanic/Latino; 1 Two or more races, non-Hispanic/Latino), 417 international. Average age 27. 1,881 applicants, 45% accepted, 230 enrolled. In 2011, 173 master's, 31 doctorates, 3 other advanced degrees awarded. Terminal master's awarded for partial completion of doctoral program. *Degree requirements:* For master's, comprehensive exam (for some programs), thesis (for some programs); for doctorate, comprehensive exam, thesis/dissertation. *Entrance requirements:* For master's and doctorate, GRE, statement of purpose, official transcripts, 2-3 letters of recommendation. Additional exam requirements/recommendations for international students: Required—TOEFL or IELTS. *Application deadline:* Applications are processed on a rolling basis. Electronic applications accepted. *Expenses:* Tuition, state resident: full-time $12,636; part-time $702 per credit. Tuition, nonresident: full-time $12,636; part-time $702 per credit. *Required fees:* $226; $226 per year. *Financial support:* In 2011–12, 508 students received support, including 29 fellowships with full tuition reimbursements available (averaging $6,065 per year), 173 research assistantships with full tuition reimbursements available (averaging $6,065 per year), 69 teaching assistantships with full tuition reimbursements available (averaging $6,065 per year); Federal Work-Study, health care benefits, and cooperative program also available. Financial award applicants required to submit FAFSA. *Faculty research:* Design and dynamic systems, energy and thermal fluids, solid mechanics, manufacturing and industrial, communications. *Total annual research expenditures:* $14.2 million. *Unit head:* Dr. Carl Anderson, Chair, 906-487-2005, Fax: 906-487-2782, E-mail: carl@mtu.edu. *Application contact:* Carol T. Wingerson, Senior Staff Assistant, 906-487-2327, Fax: 906-487-2463, E-mail: gradadms@mtu.edu. Web site: http://www.mtu.edu/engineering/.

Milwaukee School of Engineering, Department of Electrical Engineering and Computer Science, Program in Engineering, Milwaukee, WI 53202-3109. Offers MS. Part-time and evening/weekend programs available. *Faculty:* 2 full-time (0 women), 3 part-time/adjunct (1 woman). *Students:* 4 full-time (0 women), 24 part-time (3 women); includes 3 minority (1 Black or African American, non-Hispanic/Latino; 2 Asian, non-Hispanic/Latino), 3 international. Average age 25. 27 applicants, 56% accepted, 6 enrolled. In 2011, 8 master's awarded. *Degree requirements:* For master's, thesis, design project or capstone. *Entrance requirements:* For master's, GRE General Test or GMAT, BS in engineering, 2 letters of recommendation. Additional exam requirements/recommendations for international students: Required—TOEFL (minimum score 79 iBT) or IELTS. *Application deadline:* Applications are processed on a rolling basis. Electronic applications accepted. Application fee is waived when completed online. *Expenses: Tuition:* Full-time $17,550; part-time $650 per credit hour. *Financial support:* In 2011–12, 7 students received support, including 4 research assistantships (averaging $15,000 per year); career-related internships or fieldwork also available. Support available to part-time students. Financial award applicants required to submit FAFSA. *Faculty research:* Microprocessors, materials, thermodynamics, artificial intelligence, fluid power/hydraulics. *Unit head:* Dr. Subha Kumpaty, Director, 414-277-7466, Fax: 414-277-2222, E-mail: kumpaty@msoe.edu. *Application contact:* Katie Gassenhuber, Graduate Program Associate, 800-321-6763, Fax: 414-277-7208, E-mail: gassenhuber@msoe.edu. Web site: http://www.msoe.edu/.

Mississippi State University, Bagley College of Engineering, Mississippi State, MS 39762. Offers MS, PhD. Part-time programs available. Postbaccalaureate distance learning degree programs offered (no on-campus study). *Faculty:* 103 full-time (14 women), 13 part-time/adjunct (1 woman). *Students:* 354 full-time (73 women), 206 part-time (34 women); includes 78 minority (44 Black or African American, non-Hispanic/Latino; 15 Asian, non-Hispanic/Latino; 16 Hispanic/Latino; 1 Native Hawaiian or other Pacific Islander, non-Hispanic/Latino; 2 Two or more races, non-Hispanic/Latino), 192 international. Average age 29. 720 applicants, 27% accepted, 106 enrolled. In 2011, 79 master's, 44 doctorates awarded. *Degree requirements:* For master's, comprehensive exam (for some programs), thesis; for doctorate, comprehensive exam (for some programs), thesis/dissertation. *Entrance requirements:* For master's, GRE General Test, minimum GPA of 2.75; for doctorate, GRE General Test. Additional exam requirements/recommendations for international students: Required—TOEFL (minimum score 475 paper-based; 153 computer-based; 53 iBT); Recommended—IELTS (minimum score 4.5). *Application deadline:* For fall admission, 7/1 for domestic students, 5/1 for international students; for spring admission, 11/1 for domestic students, 9/1 for international students. Applications are processed on a rolling basis. Application fee: $40. Electronic applications accepted. *Expenses:* Tuition, state resident: full-time $5805; part-time $322.50 per credit hour. Tuition, nonresident: full-time $14,670; part-time $815 per credit hour. *Financial support:* In 2011–12, 112 research assistantships with full tuition reimbursements (averaging $14,693 per year), 49 teaching assistantships with full tuition reimbursements (averaging $13,202 per year) were awarded; Federal Work-Study, institutionally sponsored loans, scholarships/grants, and unspecified assistantships also available. Financial award application deadline: 4/1; financial award applicants required to submit FAFSA. *Faculty research:* Fluid dynamics, combustion, composite materials, computer design, high-voltage phenomena. *Total annual research expenditures:* $60.8 million. *Unit head:* Dr. Sarah A. Rajala, Jr., Dean, 662-325-2270, Fax: 662-325-8573, E-mail: rajala@bagley.msstate.edu. *Application contact:* Rita Burrell, Manager, Graduate and Distance Education, 662-325-5923, Fax: 662-325-8573, E-mail: rburrell@bagley.msstate.edu. Web site: http://www.engr.msstate.edu/.

Missouri University of Science and Technology, Graduate School, School of Engineering, Rolla, MO 65409. Offers M Eng, MS, DE, PhD. Part-time and evening/weekend programs available. Electronic applications accepted.

Missouri Western State University, Program in Applied Science, St. Joseph, MO 64507-2294. Offers chemistry (MAS); engineering technology management (MAS); human factors and usability testing (MAS); information technology management (MAS). Part-time programs available. *Application deadline:* For fall admission, 7/15 for domestic and international students; for spring admission, 10/1 for domestic and international students. Electronic applications accepted. *Expenses:* Tuition, state resident: full-time $4697; part-time $261 per credit hour. Tuition, nonresident: full-time $9355; part-time $520 per credit hour. *Required fees:* $343; $19.10 per credit hour. $30 per semester. Tuition and fees vary according to course load. *Application contact:* Dr. Brian C. Cronk, Dean of the Graduate School, 816-271-4394, E-mail: graduate@missouriwestern.edu.

Montana State University, College of Graduate Studies, College of Engineering, Department of Chemical and Biological Engineering, Bozeman, MT 59717. Offers chemical engineering (MS); engineering (PhD), including chemical engineering option, environmental engineering option; environmental engineering (MS). Part-time programs available. *Degree requirements:* For master's, comprehensive exam, thesis (for some programs); for doctorate, comprehensive exam, thesis/dissertation. *Entrance requirements:* For master's and doctorate, GRE General Test. Additional exam requirements/recommendations for international students: Required—TOEFL (minimum score 550 paper-based; 213 computer-based). Electronic applications accepted. *Faculty research:* Biofuels, extremophilic bioprocessing, and situ biocatalyzed heavy metal transformations; metabolic network analysis and engineering; magnetic resonance microscopy; modeling of biological systems; the development of protective coatings on planar solid oxide fuel cell (SOFC) metallic interconnects; characterizing corrosion mechanisms of materials in precisely-controlled exposures; testing materials in poly-crystalline silicon production environments; environmental biotechnology and bioremediation.

Montana State University, College of Graduate Studies, College of Engineering, Department of Civil Engineering, Bozeman, MT 59717. Offers civil engineering (MS); construction engineering management (MCEM); engineering (PhD), including applied mechanics option, civil engineering option. Part-time programs available. *Degree requirements:* For master's, comprehensive exam, thesis (for some programs); for doctorate, comprehensive exam, thesis/dissertation. *Entrance requirements:* For master's and doctorate, GRE General Test. Additional exam requirements/recommendations for international students: Required—TOEFL (minimum score 550 paper-based; 213 computer-based). Electronic applications accepted. *Faculty research:* Snow and ice mechanics, biofilm engineering, transportation, structural and geo materials, water resources.

Montana State University, College of Graduate Studies, College of Engineering, Department of Mechanical and Industrial Engineering, Bozeman, MT 59717. Offers engineering (PhD), including industrial engineering, mechanical engineering; industrial and management engineering (MS); mechanical engineering (MS). Part-time programs available. *Degree requirements:* For master's, comprehensive exam, thesis, oral exams; for doctorate, comprehensive exam, thesis/dissertation, qualifying exam. *Entrance requirements:* For master's, GRE, official transcript, minimum GPA of 3.0, demonstrated potential for success, statement of goals, three letters of recommendation, proof of funds affidavit; for doctorate, minimum undergraduate GPA of 3.0, 3.2 graduate; three letters of recommendation; statement of objectives. Additional exam requirements/recommendations for international students: Required—TOEFL or IELTS. Electronic applications accepted. *Faculty research:* Human factors engineering, energy, design and manufacture, systems modeling, materials and structures, measurement systems.

Montana Tech of The University of Montana, Graduate School, Department of General Engineering, Butte, MT 59701-8997. Offers MS. Part-time programs available. *Faculty:* 7 full-time (0 women), 4 part-time/adjunct (0 women). *Students:* 11 full-time (1 woman), 1 part-time (0 women); includes 1 minority (Hispanic/Latino), 2 international. 12 applicants, 42% accepted, 5 enrolled. In 2011, 2 master's awarded. *Degree requirements:* For master's, comprehensive exam (for some programs), thesis optional. *Entrance requirements:* For master's, minimum GPA of 3.0. Additional exam requirements/recommendations for international students: Required—TOEFL (minimum score 525 paper-based; 195 computer-based; 71 iBT). *Application deadline:* For fall admission, 4/1 priority date for domestic students, 3/1 for international students; for spring admission, 10/1 priority date for domestic students, 7/1 for international students. Applications are processed on a rolling basis. Application fee: $30. Electronic applications accepted. *Financial support:* In 2011–12, 9 students received support, including 11 teaching assistantships with partial tuition reimbursements available (averaging $3,500 per year); research assistantships with partial tuition reimbursements available, career-related internships or fieldwork, tuition waivers (full and partial), and unspecified assistantships also available. Financial award application deadline: 4/1; financial award applicants required to submit FAFSA. *Faculty research:* Wind energy and power controls, robotics, concurrent engineering, remotely piloted aircraft, composite materials. *Unit head:* Dr. Bruce Madigan, Department Head, 406-496-4109, Fax: 406-496-4650, E-mail: bmadigan@mtech.edu. *Application contact:* Fred Sullivan, Administrator, Graduate School, 406-496-4304, Fax: 406-496-4710, E-mail: fsullivan@mtech.edu.

Morgan State University, School of Graduate Studies, Clarence M. Mitchell, Jr. School of Engineering, Baltimore, MD 21251. Offers civil engineering (M Eng, D Eng); electrical engineering (M Eng, D Eng); industrial engineering (M Eng, D Eng); transportation (MS). Part-time and evening/weekend programs available. *Degree requirements:* For master's, thesis, comprehensive exam or equivalent; for doctorate, thesis/dissertation, comprehensive exam or equivalent. *Entrance requirements:* For master's, GRE, minimum undergraduate GPA of 2.5; for doctorate, GRE, minimum GPA of 3.0. Additional exam requirements/recommendations for international students: Required—TOEFL (minimum score 550 paper-based; 213 computer-based).

National University, Academic Affairs, School of Engineering, Technology and Media, Department of Applied Engineering, La Jolla, CA 92037-1011. Offers engineering management (MS); environmental engineering (MS); homeland security and safety engineering (MS); project management (Certificate); security and safety engineering (Certificate); sustainability management (MS); wireless communications (MS). Part-time and evening/weekend programs available. Postbaccalaureate distance learning degree programs offered (no on-campus study). *Degree requirements:* For master's, thesis. *Entrance requirements:* For master's, interview, minimum GPA of 2.5. Additional exam requirements/recommendations for international students: Required—TOEFL (minimum score 550 paper-based; 213 computer-based; 79 iBT), IELTS (minimum score 6). *Application deadline:* Applications are processed on a rolling basis. Application fee: $60 ($65 for international students). Electronic applications accepted. *Financial support:* Career-related internships or fieldwork, institutionally sponsored loans, scholarships/grants, and tuition waivers (partial) available. Support available to part-time students. Financial award application deadline: 6/30; financial award applicants required to submit FAFSA. *Unit head:* Dr. Shekar Viswanathan, Chair and Associate Professor, 858-309-3416, Fax: 858-309-3420, E-mail: sviswana@nu.edu. *Application contact:* Dominick Giovanniello, Associate Regional Dean, 800-NAT-UNIV, Fax: 858-541-7792, E-mail: dgiovann@nu.edu. Web site: http://www.nu.edu/OurPrograms/SchoolOfEngineeringAndTechnology/AppliedEngineering.html.

New Jersey Institute of Technology, Office of Graduate Studies, Newark, NJ 07102. Offers M Arch, MA, MAT, MBA, MIP, MS, MS Arch, PhD, M Arch/MIP, M Arch/MS. Part-time and evening/weekend programs available. *Faculty:* 399 full-time (72 women), 245 part-time/adjunct (62 women). *Students:* 1,573 full-time (542 women), 1,245 part-time (358 women); includes 885 minority (221 Black or African American, non-Hispanic/Latino; 3 American Indian or Alaska Native, non-Hispanic/Latino; 388 Asian, non-Hispanic/Latino; 260 Hispanic/Latino; 2 Native Hawaiian or other Pacific Islander, non-Hispanic/Latino; 11 Two or more races, non-Hispanic/Latino), 1,221 international. Average age 30. 5,755 applicants, 65% accepted, 1242 enrolled. In 2011, 921 master's, 65 doctorates awarded. Terminal master's awarded for partial completion of doctoral program. *Degree requirements:* For master's, thesis optional; for doctorate, thesis/dissertation. *Entrance requirements:* For master's, GRE General Test, official transcripts and proof of degree completion from all colleges and universities attended; one letter of recommendation in sealed envelope; for doctorate, GRE General Test, official transcripts and proof of degree completion from all colleges and universities attended; three letters of recommendation in sealed envelopes; statement of purpose. Additional exam requirements/recommendations for international students: Required—TOEFL (minimum score 550 paper-based; 213 computer-based; 79 iBT). *Application deadline:* For fall admission, 6/1 priority date for domestic students, 5/1 for international students; for spring admission, 11/15 priority date for domestic students, 11/15 for international students. Applications are processed on a rolling basis. Application fee: $65. Electronic applications accepted. *Expenses:* Tuition, state resident: full-time $7980; part-time $867 per credit. Tuition, nonresident: full-time $11,336; part-time $1196 per credit. *Required fees:* $230 per credit. *Financial support:* Fellowships with full and partial tuition reimbursements, research assistantships with full and partial tuition reimbursements, teaching assistantships with full and partial tuition reimbursements, career-related internships or fieldwork, Federal Work-Study, institutionally sponsored loans, and unspecified assistantships available. Financial award application deadline: 1/15. *Faculty research:* Toxic and hazardous waste management, transportation, biomedical engineering, computer-integrated manufacturing, management of technology. *Unit head:* Dr. Marino Xanthos, Associate Provost, 973-596-3462, E-mail: marinos.xanthos@njit.edu. *Application contact:* Kathryn Kelly, Director of Admissions, 973-596-3300, Fax: 973-596-3461, E-mail: admissions@njit.edu. Web site: http://www.njit.edu/graduatestudies/.

New Jersey Institute of Technology, Office of Graduate Studies, Newark College of Engineering, Interdisciplinary Program in Engineering Science, Newark, NJ 07102. Offers MS. Part-time and evening/weekend programs available. *Students:* 1 applicant, 0% accepted, 0 enrolled. In 2011, 1 master's awarded. *Entrance requirements:* For master's, GRE General Test. Additional exam requirements/recommendations for international students: Required—TOEFL (minimum score 550 paper-based; 213 computer-based; 79 iBT). *Application deadline:* For fall admission, 6/1 priority date for domestic students, 5/1 for international students; for spring admission, 11/15 priority date for domestic students, 11/15 for international students. Applications are processed on a rolling basis. Application fee: $65. Electronic applications accepted. *Expenses:* Tuition, state resident: full-time $7980; part-time $867 per credit. Tuition, nonresident: full-time $11,336; part-time $1196 per credit. *Required fees:* $230 per credit. *Financial support:* Fellowships with full and partial tuition reimbursements, research assistantships with full and partial tuition reimbursements, teaching assistantships with full and partial tuition reimbursements, career-related internships or fieldwork, Federal Work-Study, institutionally sponsored loans, and unspecified assistantships available. Financial award application deadline: 3/15. *Unit head:* Dr. Sunil Saigal, Program Director, 973-596-5443, E-mail: sunil.saigal@njit.edu. *Application contact:* Kathryn Kelly, Director of Admissions, 973-596-3300, Fax: 973-596-3461, E-mail: admissions@njit.edu.

New Mexico State University, Graduate School, College of Engineering, Las Cruces, NM 88003-8001. Offers MS Ch E, MS Env E, MSCE, MSEE, MSIE, MSME, PhD, Graduate Certificate. Part-time programs available. *Faculty:* 63 full-time (10 women), 2 part-time/adjunct (0 women). *Students:* 259 full-time (58 women), 160 part-time (34 women); includes 105 minority (8 Black or African American, non-Hispanic/Latino; 6 American Indian or Alaska Native, non-Hispanic/Latino; 3 Asian, non-Hispanic/Latino; 84 Hispanic/Latino; 4 Two or more races, non-Hispanic/Latino), 168 international. Average age 30. 189 applicants, 70% accepted, 76 enrolled. In 2011, 110 master's, 9 doctorates awarded. *Degree requirements:* For doctorate, thesis/dissertation. *Entrance requirements:* Additional exam requirements/recommendations for international students: Required—TOEFL (minimum score 550 paper-based; 79 iBT), IELTS (minimum score 6.5). *Application deadline:* For fall admission, 7/1 priority date for domestic students; for spring admission, 11/1 for domestic students. Applications are processed on a rolling basis. Application fee: $40 ($50 for international students). Electronic applications accepted. *Expenses:* Tuition, state resident: full-time $5004; part-time $208.50 per credit. Tuition, nonresident: full-time $17,446; part-time $726.90 per credit. *Financial support:* In 2011–12, 45 students received support, including 20 fellowships (averaging $8,320 per year), 93 research assistantships (averaging $19,498 per year), 88 teaching assistantships (averaging $19,995 per year); career-related internships or fieldwork, Federal Work-Study, scholarships/grants, traineeships, health care benefits, and unspecified assistantships also available. Support available to part-time students. Financial award application deadline: 3/1. *Faculty research:* Structures and nondestructive testing, environmental science and engineering, telecommunication theory and systems, manufacturing methods and systems, high performance computing and software engineering. *Unit head:* Dr. Ricardo Jacquez, Dean, 575-646-7234, Fax: 575-646-3549, E-mail: rjaquez@nmsu.edu. *Application contact:* Coordinator, 575-646-2736, Fax: 575-646-7721, E-mail: gradinfo@nmsu.edu. Web site: http://engr.nmsu.edu/.

New York Institute of Technology, Graduate Division, School of Engineering and Computing Sciences, Old Westbury, NY 11568-8000. Offers MS, Advanced Certificate. Part-time and evening/weekend programs available. Postbaccalaureate distance learning degree programs offered. *Students:* 288 full-time (57 women), 273 part-time (46 women); includes 108 minority (32 Black or African American, non-Hispanic/Latino; 2 American Indian or Alaska Native, non-Hispanic/Latino; 37 Asian, non-Hispanic/Latino; 32 Hispanic/Latino; 5 Two or more races, non-Hispanic/Latino), 261 international. Average age 29. In 2011, 234 master's, 28 other advanced degrees awarded. *Entrance requirements:* Additional exam requirements/recommendations for international students: Required—TOEFL (minimum score 550 paper-based; 213 computer-based). *Application deadline:* For fall admission, 7/1 priority date for domestic students; for spring admission, 12/1 priority date for domestic students. Applications are processed on a rolling basis. Application fee: $50. Electronic applications accepted. *Expenses: Tuition:* Part-time $930 per credit hour. *Financial support:* Fellowships, research assistantships with partial tuition reimbursements, career-related internships or fieldwork, institutionally sponsored loans, tuition waivers (full and partial), and unspecified assistantships available. Support available to part-time students. Financial award applicants required to submit FAFSA. *Faculty research:* Hybrid vehicle development, system design of photovoltaic cells, prototype module of DTV application environment, adaptive target detection in nonhomogeneous environment. *Unit head:* Dr. Nada Anid, Dean, 516-686-7931, Fax: 516-625-7933, E-mail: nanid@nyit.edu. *Application contact:* Dr. Jacquelyn Nealon, Vice President for Enrollment Services, 516-686-7925, Fax: 516-686-7597, E-mail: jnealon@nyit.edu.

North Carolina Agricultural and Technical State University, School of Graduate Studies, College of Engineering, Greensboro, NC 27411. Offers MS, MSCE, MSCS, MSE, MSEE, MSIE, MSME, PhD. Part-time programs available.

North Carolina State University, Graduate School, College of Engineering, Raleigh, NC 27695. Offers M Ch E, M Eng, MC Sc, MCE, MIE, MIMS, MMSE, MNE, MOR, MS, PhD. Part-time programs available. Terminal master's awarded for partial completion of doctoral program. *Degree requirements:* For doctorate, thesis/dissertation. Electronic applications accepted.

See Display on next page and Close-Up on page 79.

North Dakota State University, College of Graduate and Interdisciplinary Studies, College of Engineering and Architecture, Fargo, ND 58108. Offers M Arch, MS, PhD. Part-time programs available. *Faculty:* 71 full-time (9 women), 8 part-time/adjunct (2 women). *Students:* 215 full-time (51 women), 100 part-time (20 women); includes 15 minority (1 Black or African American, non-Hispanic/Latino; 1 American Indian or Alaska Native, non-Hispanic/Latino; 5 Asian, non-Hispanic/Latino; 2 Hispanic/Latino; 1 Native Hawaiian or other Pacific Islander, non-Hispanic/Latino; 5 Two or more races, non-Hispanic/Latino), 146 international. Average age 27. 248 applicants, 49% accepted, 58 enrolled. In 2011, 96 master's, 4 doctorates awarded. Terminal master's awarded for partial completion of doctoral program. *Degree requirements:* For master's, thesis; for doctorate, comprehensive exam, thesis/dissertation. *Entrance requirements:* For master's and doctorate, minimum GPA of 3.0. Additional exam requirements/recommendations for international students: Required—TOEFL. *Application deadline:* For fall admission, 4/1 priority date for domestic students, 5/1 for international students; for spring admission, 10/1 priority date for domestic students, 8/1 for international students. Applications are processed on a rolling basis. Application fee: $35. Electronic applications accepted. *Expenses:* Contact institution. *Financial support:* In 2011–12, 150 students received support, including fellowships with full tuition reimbursements available (averaging $15,000 per year), research assistantships with full tuition reimbursements available (averaging $9,000 per year), teaching assistantships with full tuition reimbursements available (averaging $8,000 per year); career-related internships or fieldwork, Federal Work-Study, institutionally sponsored loans, scholarships/grants, and tuition waivers (full) also available. Support available to part-time students. Financial award application deadline: 4/15. *Faculty research:* Theoretical mechanics, robotics, automation, environmental engineering, man-made materials. *Unit head:* Dr. Gary R. Smith, Dean, 701-231-7494, Fax: 701-231-8957, E-mail: gary.smith@ndsu.edu. *Application contact:* Dr. David A. Wittrock, Dean, 701-231-7033, Fax: 701-231-6524.

Northeastern University, College of Engineering, Boston, MA 02115-5096. Offers MS, PhD, Certificate. Part-time programs available. *Faculty:* 120 full-time, 25 part-time/adjunct. *Students:* 1,069 full-time (289 women), 298 part-time (51 women). 2,648 applicants, 62% accepted, 496 enrolled. In 2011, 360 master's, 27 doctorates awarded. *Entrance requirements:* For master's and doctorate, GRE General Test. Additional exam requirements/recommendations for international students: Required—TOEFL. *Application deadline:* For fall admission, 1/15 priority date for domestic students, 1/15 for international students. Applications are processed on a rolling basis. Application fee: $50. Electronic applications accepted. *Expenses:* Contact institution. *Financial support:* In 2011–12, 268 students received support, including 4 fellowships with full tuition reimbursements available, 146 research assistantships with full tuition reimbursements available (averaging $18,320 per year), 117 teaching assistantships with full tuition reimbursements available (averaging $18,320 per year); career-related internships or fieldwork, Federal Work-Study, scholarships/grants, tuition waivers (full), and unspecified assistantships also available. Support available to part-time students. Financial award application deadline: 1/15; financial award applicants required to submit FAFSA. *Unit head:* Dr. Yaman Yener, Associate Dean of Engineering for Research and Graduate Studies, 617-373-2711, Fax: 617-373-2501. *Application contact:* Jeffery Hengel, Admissions Specialist, 617-373-2711, Fax: 617-373-2501, E-mail: grad-eng@coe.neu.edu. Web site: http://www.coe.neu.edu/.

Northern Arizona University, Graduate College, College of Engineering, Forestry and Natural Sciences, Flagstaff, AZ 86011. Offers M Ed, M Eng, MAST, MAT, MF, MS, MSE, MSF, PhD, Certificate. *Faculty:* 210 full-time (72 women). *Students:* 274 full-time (137 women), 80 part-time (37 women); includes 44 minority (2 Black or African American, non-Hispanic/Latino; 9 American Indian or Alaska Native, non-Hispanic/Latino; 6 Asian, non-Hispanic/Latino; 22 Hispanic/Latino; 5 Two or more races, non-Hispanic/Latino), 21 international. 336 applicants, 35% accepted, 89 enrolled. In 2011, 103 master's, 14 doctorates, 10 other advanced degrees awarded. *Entrance requirements:* For master's, minimum GPA of 3.0 in final 60 hours of undergraduate course work. Application fee: $65. *Expenses:* Tuition, state resident: full-time $7190; part-time $355 per credit hour. Tuition, nonresident: full-time $18,092; part-time $1005 per credit hour. *Required fees:* $818; $328 per semester. *Financial support:* In 2011–12, 32 students received support, including 23 fellowships, 62 research assistantships, 113 teaching assistantships. Financial award applicants required to submit FAFSA. *Unit head:* Paul W. Jagodzinski, Dean, 928-523-2701, Fax: 928-523-2300, E-mail: paul.jagodzinski@nau.edu. *Application contact:* April Sandoval, Coordinator, 928-523-4348, Fax: 928-523-8950, E-mail: april.sandoval@nau.edu. Web site: http://nau.edu/cefns/.

Northern Illinois University, Graduate School, College of Engineering and Engineering Technology, De Kalb, IL 60115-2854. Offers MS. Part-time and evening/weekend programs available. *Faculty:* 36 full-time (2 women), 2 part-time/adjunct (0 women). *Students:* 76 full-time (13 women), 107 part-time (21 women); includes 26 minority (8 Black or African American, non-Hispanic/Latino; 10 Asian, non-Hispanic/Latino; 4 Hispanic/Latino; 4 Two or more races, non-Hispanic/Latino), 160 international. Average age 26. 302 applicants, 39% accepted, 43 enrolled. In 2011, 133 master's awarded. *Degree requirements:* For master's, comprehensive exam, thesis optional. *Entrance requirements:* For master's, GRE General Test, minimum GPA of 2.75. Additional exam requirements/recommendations for international students: Required—TOEFL (minimum score 550 paper-based; 213 computer-based). *Application deadline:* For fall admission, 6/1 for domestic students, 5/1 for international students; for spring admission, 11/1 for domestic students, 10/1 for international students. Applications are processed on a rolling basis. Application fee: $40. Electronic applications accepted. *Financial support:* In 2011–12, 11 research assistantships with full tuition reimbursements, 2 teaching assistantships with full tuition reimbursements were awarded; fellowships with full tuition reimbursements, career-related internships or fieldwork, Federal Work-Study, scholarships/grants, tuition waivers (full), and unspecified assistantships also available. Support available to part-time students. Financial award applicants required to submit FAFSA. *Unit head:* Dr. Promod Vohra, Dean, 815-753-1281, Fax: 815-753-1310, E-mail: pvohra@niu.edu. *Application contact:* Graduate School Office, 815-753-0395, E-mail: gradsch@niu.edu. Web site: http://www.niu.edu/CEET/.

Northwestern Polytechnic University, School of Engineering, Fremont, CA 94539-7482. Offers computer science (MS); computer systems engineering (MS); electrical engineering (MS). Part-time and evening/weekend programs available. *Degree requirements:* For master's, thesis optional. *Entrance requirements:* For master's, minimum GPA of 3.0. Additional exam requirements/recommendations for international students: Required—TOEFL (minimum score 550 paper-based; 213 computer-based; 79 iBT). *Faculty research:* Computer networking, database design, Internet technology, software engineering, digital signal processing.

Northwestern University, McCormick School of Engineering and Applied Science, Evanston, IL 60208. Offers MEM, MIT, MME, MMM, MPD, MS, PhD, Certificate, MBA/MEM. MS and PhD admissions and degrees offered through The Graduate School. Part-time and evening/weekend programs available. *Faculty:* 188 full-time (38 women). *Students:* 1,298 full-time (385 women), 233 part-time (61 women); includes 296 minority (40 Black or African American, non-Hispanic/Latino; 1 American Indian or Alaska Native, non-Hispanic/Latino; 161 Asian, non-Hispanic/Latino; 69 Hispanic/Latino; 3 Native Hawaiian or other Pacific Islander, non-Hispanic/Latino; 22 Two or more races, non-Hispanic/Latino), 629 international. Average age 26. 4,618 applicants, 22% accepted, 498 enrolled. In 2011, 392 master's, 108 doctorates awarded. Terminal master's awarded for partial completion of doctoral program. *Degree requirements:* For master's, comprehensive exam (for some programs), thesis (for some programs); for doctorate, comprehensive exam, thesis/dissertation. *Entrance requirements:* For master's and doctorate, GRE General Test. Additional exam requirements/recommendations for international students: Required—TOEFL (minimum score 577 paper-based, 233 computer-based, 90 iBT) or IELTS (minimum score 7). *Application deadline:* For fall admission, 12/31 for domestic and international students; for winter admission, 11/15 for domestic students, 11/1 for international students; for spring admission, 2/1 for international students. Application fee: $75. Electronic applications accepted. *Financial support:* In 2011–12, 75 students received support. Fellowships with tuition reimbursements available, research assistantships with tuition reimbursements available, teaching assistantships with tuition reimbursements available, career-related internships or fieldwork, Federal Work-Study, institutionally sponsored loans, traineeships, health care benefits, and unspecified assistantships available. Financial award application deadline: 1/15; financial award applicants required to submit FAFSA. *Total annual research expenditures:* $117 million. *Unit head:* Dr. Julio Ottino, Dean, 847-491-3558, Fax: 847-491-5220, E-mail: jm-ottino@northwestern.edu. *Application contact:* Dr. Bruce Alan Lindvall, Assistant Dean for Graduate Studies, 847-491-4547, Fax: 847-491-5341, E-mail: b-lindvall@northwestern.edu. Web site: http://www.tech.northwestern.edu/.

Oakland University, Graduate Study and Lifelong Learning, School of Engineering and Computer Science, Rochester, MI 48309-4401. Offers MS, PhD. Part-time and evening/weekend programs available. *Degree requirements:* For doctorate, thesis/dissertation. *Entrance requirements:* For master's and doctorate, minimum GPA of 3.0 for unconditional admission. Additional exam requirements/recommendations for international students: Required—TOEFL (minimum score 550 paper-based; 213 computer-based). Electronic applications accepted. *Expenses:* Contact institution. *Faculty research:* Acquisition of automotive antenna measurements instrumentation, high fidelity antenna model, development for LAAS Cat-1 siting criteria, cyber security, 3D imaging of neurochemical in rat brains.

The Ohio State University, Graduate School, College of Engineering, Columbus, OH 43210. Offers M Arch, M Land Arch, MCRP, MS, MWE, PhD. Part-time and evening/weekend programs available. *Faculty:* 280. *Students:* 1,403 full-time (312 women), 472 part-time (80 women); includes 121 minority (25 Black or African American, non-Hispanic/Latino; 1 American Indian or Alaska Native, non-Hispanic/Latino; 51 Asian, non-Hispanic/Latino; 34 Hispanic/Latino; 10 Two or more races, non-Hispanic/Latino), 984 international. Average age 27. In 2011, 230 master's, 98 doctorates awarded. *Degree requirements:* For doctorate, thesis/dissertation. *Entrance requirements:* Additional exam requirements/recommendations for international students: Required—Michigan English Language Assessment Battery (minimum score 82); Recommended—TOEFL (minimum score 600 paper-based; 250 computer-based; 79 iBT). *Application deadline:* For fall admission, 8/15 priority date for domestic students, 7/1 for international students; for winter admission, 12/1 priority date for domestic students, 11/1 for international students; for spring admission, 3/1 priority date for domestic students, 2/1 for international students. Applications are processed on a rolling basis. Application fee: $40 ($50 for international students). Electronic applications accepted. *Expenses:* Tuition, state resident: full-time $11,400. Tuition, nonresident: full-time $28,125. Tuition and fees vary according to course load, degree level, campus/location and program. *Financial support:* Fellowships, research assistantships, teaching assistantships, career-related internships or fieldwork, Federal Work-Study, institutionally sponsored loans, and unspecified assistantships available. Support available to part-time students. *Unit head:* Dr. David B. Williams, Dean, 614-292-2836, Fax: 614-292-9615, E-mail: williams.4219@osu.edu. *Application contact:* Graduate Admissions, 614-292-6031, Fax: 614-292-3656, E-mail: gradadmissions@osu.edu. Web site: http://engineering.osu.edu/.

Ohio University, Graduate College, Russ College of Engineering and Technology, Athens, OH 45701-2979. Offers M Eng Mgt, MS, PhD. Part-time programs available. *Faculty:* 84 full-time (9 women), 14 part-time/adjunct (1 woman). *Students:* 250 full-time (65 women), 77 part-time (17 women); includes 15 minority (4 Black or African American, non-Hispanic/Latino; 1 Asian, non-Hispanic/Latino; 6 Hispanic/Latino; 4 Two or more races, non-Hispanic/Latino), 168 international. 420 applicants, 37% accepted, 80 enrolled. In 2011, 73 master's, 10 doctorates awarded. *Degree requirements:* For master's, comprehensive exam (for some programs), thesis (for some programs); for doctorate, comprehensive exam, thesis/dissertation. *Entrance requirements:* For master's, GRE General Test, BS in engineering or related field; for doctorate, GRE General Test, MS in engineering or related field. Additional exam requirements/recommendations for international students: Required—TOEFL or IELTS. *Application deadline:* Applications are processed on a rolling basis. Application fee: $50 ($55 for international students). Electronic applications accepted. *Expenses:* Contact institution. *Financial support:* Fellowships with full tuition reimbursements, research assistantships with full tuition reimbursements, teaching assistantships with full tuition reimbursements, career-related internships or fieldwork, Federal Work-Study, institutionally sponsored loans, and unspecified assistantships available. Financial award application deadline: 3/15. *Faculty research:* Avionics engineering, coal research, transportation engineering, software systems integration, materials processing. *Total annual research expenditures:* $14.7 million. *Unit head:* Dr. Dennis Irwin, Dean, 740-593-1482, Fax: 740-593-0659, E-mail: irwind@ohio.edu. *Application contact:* Dr. Shawn Ostermann, Associate Dean, 740-593-1482, Fax: 740-593-0659, E-mail: ostermann@ohio.edu. Web site: http://www.ohio.edu/engineering/.

Oklahoma State University, College of Engineering, Architecture and Technology, Stillwater, OK 74078. Offers MS, PhD. Postbaccalaureate distance learning degree programs offered. *Faculty:* 112 full-time (11 women), 10 part-time/adjunct (2 women). *Students:* 326 full-time (69 women), 433 part-time (76 women); includes 82 minority (22 Black or African American, non-Hispanic/Latino; 13 American Indian or Alaska Native, non-Hispanic/Latino; 18 Asian, non-Hispanic/Latino; 16 Hispanic/Latino; 13 Two or more races, non-Hispanic/Latino), 440 international. Average age 29. 1,167 applicants, 32% accepted, 159 enrolled. In 2011, 247 master's, 15 doctorates awarded. *Degree requirements:* For master's, thesis (for some programs); for doctorate, comprehensive exam, thesis/dissertation. *Entrance requirements:* For master's and doctorate, GRE or GMAT. Additional exam requirements/recommendations for international students: Required—TOEFL (minimum score 550 paper-based; 79 iBT). *Application deadline:* For fall admission, 3/1 for international students; for spring admission, 8/1 for international students. Applications are processed on a rolling basis. Application fee: $40 ($75 for international students). Electronic applications accepted. *Expenses:* Tuition, state resident: full-time $4044; part-time $168.50 per credit hour. Tuition, nonresident: full-time $16,008; part-time $667 per credit hour. *Required fees:* $2122; $88.45 per credit hour. One-time fee: $50. Tuition and fees vary according to course load and campus/location. *Financial support:* In 2011–12, 246 research assistantships (averaging $12,070 per year), 148 teaching assistantships (averaging $8,262 per year) were awarded; career-related internships or fieldwork, Federal Work-Study, scholarships/grants, health care benefits, tuition waivers (partial), and unspecified assistantships also available. Support available to part-time students. Financial award application deadline: 3/1; financial award applicants required to submit FAFSA. *Unit head:* Dr. Karl N. Reid, Dean, 405-744-5140. *Application contact:* Dr. Sheryl Tucker, Dean, 405-744-7099, Fax: 405-744-0355, E-mail: grad-i@okstate.edu. Web site: http://www.ceat.okstate.edu.
See Display below and Close-Up on page 81.

Old Dominion University, Frank Batten College of Engineering and Technology, Norfolk, VA 23529. Offers ME, MEM, MS, D Eng, PhD. Part-time and evening/weekend programs available. Postbaccalaureate distance learning degree programs offered. *Faculty:* 93 full-time (12 women), 32 part-time/adjunct (5 women). *Students:* 241 full-time (50 women), 567 part-time (114 women); includes 141 minority (65 Black or African American, non-Hispanic/Latino; 1 American Indian or Alaska Native, non-Hispanic/Latino; 29 Asian, non-Hispanic/Latino; 32 Hispanic/Latino; 4 Native Hawaiian or other Pacific Islander, non-Hispanic/Latino; 10 Two or more races, non-Hispanic/Latino), 184 international. Average age 32. 558 applicants, 63% accepted, 144 enrolled. In 2011, 179 master's, 38 doctorates awarded. *Degree requirements:* For master's, comprehensive exam, thesis (for some programs); for doctorate, thesis/dissertation, candidacy exam. *Entrance requirements:* For master's, GRE, minimum GPA of 3.0; for doctorate, GRE, minimum GPA of 3.5. Additional exam requirements/recommendations for international students: Required—TOEFL (minimum score 550 paper-based). *Application deadline:* For fall admission, 6/1 for domestic students, 2/15 for international students; for spring admission, 11/1 for domestic students, 10/1 for international students. Applications are processed on a rolling basis. Application fee: $50. Electronic applications accepted. *Expenses:* Tuition, state resident: full-time $9096; part-time $379 per credit. Tuition, nonresident: full-time $23,064; part-time $961 per credit. *Required fees:* $127 per semester. One-time fee: $50. *Financial support:* In 2011–12, 168 students received support, including 8 fellowships with full and partial tuition reimbursements available (averaging $15,000 per year), 92 research assistantships with full and partial tuition reimbursements available (averaging $15,000 per year), 68 teaching assistantships with full and partial tuition reimbursements available (averaging $15,000 per year); career-related internships or fieldwork, Federal Work-Study, institutionally sponsored loans, scholarships/grants, and unspecified assistantships also available. Support available to part-time students. Financial award applicants required to submit FAFSA. *Faculty research:* Physical electronics, computational applied mechanics, structural dynamics, computational fluid dynamics, coastal engineering of water resources, modeling and simulation. *Total annual research expenditures:* $32.4 million. *Unit head:* Dr. Oktay Baysal, Dean, 757-683-3789, Fax: 757-683-4898, E-mail: obaysal@odu.edu. *Application contact:* Dr. Linda Vahala, Associate Dean, 757-683-3789, Fax: 757-683-4898, E-mail: lvahala@odu.edu. Web site: http://www.eng.odu.edu/index.php.

Oregon State University, Graduate School, College of Engineering, Corvallis, OR 97331. Offers M Eng, M Engr, M Oc E, MA, MAIS, MBE, MHP, MS, PhD. Part-time programs available. Terminal master's awarded for partial completion of doctoral program. *Degree requirements:* For doctorate, thesis/dissertation. *Entrance requirements:* For master's and doctorate, minimum GPA of 3.0 in last 90 hours. Additional exam requirements/recommendations for international students: Required—TOEFL (minimum score 550 paper-based; 213 computer-based). *Faculty research:* Molecular beam epitaxy, wave-structure interaction, pavement materials, toxic wastes, mechanical design methodology.

Penn State Erie, The Behrend College, Graduate School, Erie, PA 16563-0001. Offers business administration (MBA); project management (MPM). *Accreditation:* AACSB. Part-time programs available. *Students:* 34 full-time (8 women), 57 part-time (14 women). Average age 28. 46 applicants, 63% accepted, 22 enrolled. In 2011, 86 master's awarded. *Entrance requirements:* Additional exam requirements/recommendations for international students: Required—TOEFL (minimum score 550 paper-based; 213 computer-based; 80 iBT). *Application deadline:* Applications are processed on a rolling basis. Application fee: $65. Electronic applications accepted. *Financial support:* Federal Work-Study available. Financial award application deadline: 2/15; financial award applicants required to submit FAFSA. *Unit head:* Dr. Donald L. Birx, Chancellor, 814-898-6160, Fax: 814-898-6461, E-mail: dlb69@psu.edu.

Application contact: Ann M. Burbules, Graduate Admissions Counselor, 814-898-7255, Fax: 814-898-6044, E-mail: amb29@psu.edu. Web site: http://psbehrend.psu.edu/.

Penn State Great Valley, Graduate Studies, Engineering Division, Malvern, PA 19355-1488. Offers engineering management (MEM); information science (MS); software engineering (MSE); systems engineering (M Eng). Postbaccalaureate distance learning degree programs offered (no on-campus study). *Unit head:* Dr. James A. Nemes, Interim Director, Academic Affairs, 610-648-3335 Ext. 610, Fax: 648-648-3377, E-mail: jan16@psu.edu. *Application contact:* 610-648-3242, Fax: 610-889-1334. Web site: http://www.sgps.psu.edu/Level3.aspx?id=662.

Penn State Harrisburg, Graduate School, School of Science, Engineering and Technology, Middletown, PA 17057-4898. Offers computer science (MS); electrical engineering (M Eng, MS); engineering management (MPS); engineering science (M Eng); environmental engineering (M Eng); environmental pollution control (MEPC, MS). Part-time and evening/weekend programs available. *Unit head:* Dr. Jerry F. Shoup, Interim Director, 717-948-6352, E-mail: jfs1@psu.edu. *Application contact:* Robert Coffman, Director of Admissions, 717-948-6250, Fax: 717-948-6325, E-mail: ric1@psu.edu. Web site: http://harrisburg.psu.edu/science-engineering-technology.

Penn State University Park, Graduate School, College of Engineering, State College, University Park, PA 16802-1503. Offers M Eng, MAE, MS, PhD. *Students:* 1,194 full-time (252 women), 161 part-time (14 women). Average age 27. 4,205 applicants, 25% accepted, 390 enrolled. In 2011, 296 master's, 145 doctorates awarded. *Entrance requirements:* Additional exam requirements/recommendations for international students: Required—TOEFL (minimum score 550 paper-based; 213 computer-based; 80 iBT). *Application deadline:* Applications are processed on a rolling basis. Application fee: $65. Electronic applications accepted. *Financial support:* Fellowships, research assistantships, and teaching assistantships available. Financial award applicants required to submit FAFSA. *Unit head:* Dr. David N. Wormley, Dean, 814-865-7537, Fax: 814-865-8767, E-mail: dnw2@engr.psu.edu. *Application contact:* Cynthia E. Nicosia, Director, Graduate Enrollment Services, 814-865-1834, E-mail: cey1@psu.edu. Web site: http://www.engr.psu.edu/.

Pittsburg State University, Graduate School, College of Technology, Department of Engineering Technology, Pittsburg, KS 66762. Offers MET. *Degree requirements:* For master's, thesis or alternative.

Pontificia Universidad Catolica Madre y Maestra, Graduate School, Faculty of Engineering Sciences, Santiago, Dominican Republic. Offers earthquake engineering (ME); logistics management (ME).

Portland State University, Graduate Studies, Maseeh College of Engineering and Computer Science, Portland, OR 97207-0751. Offers M Eng, ME, MS, MSE, PhD, Certificate, MS/MBA, MS/MS. Part-time and evening/weekend programs available. *Degree requirements:* For doctorate, one foreign language, thesis/dissertation, oral and written exams. *Entrance requirements:* For master's, minimum GPA of 3.0 in upper-division course work or 2.75 overall; for doctorate, GRE General Test, GRE Subject Test, minimum GPA of 3.0 in upper-division course work. Additional exam requirements/recommendations for international students: Required—TOEFL (minimum score 550 paper-based; 213 computer-based).

Prairie View A&M University, College of Engineering, Prairie View, TX 77446-0519. Offers computer information systems (MSCIS); computer science (MSCS); electrical engineering (MSEE, PhDEE); engineering (MS Engr). Part-time and evening/weekend programs available. *Degree requirements:* For master's, thesis (for some programs); for doctorate, comprehensive exam, thesis/dissertation. *Entrance requirements:* For master's, GRE General Test, bachelor's degree in engineering from an ABET accredited institution; for doctorate, GRE. Additional exam requirements/recommendations for international students: Required—TOEFL (minimum score 550 paper-based). Electronic applications accepted. *Faculty research:* Applied radiation research, thermal science, computational fluid dynamics, analog mixed signal, aerial space battlefield.

Princeton University, Graduate School, School of Engineering and Applied Science, Princeton, NJ 08544-1019. Offers M Eng, MSE, PhD. Terminal master's awarded for partial completion of doctoral program. *Degree requirements:* For master's, thesis (for some programs); for doctorate, thesis/dissertation, research, teaching, general exam. *Entrance requirements:* For master's and doctorate, GRE General Test, official transcript(s), 3 letters of recommendation, personal statement. Additional exam requirements/recommendations for international students: Required—TOEFL. Electronic applications accepted.

Purdue University, College of Engineering, West Lafayette, IN 47907-2045. Offers MS, MSAAE, MSABE, MSBME, MSCE, MSChE, MSE, MSECE, MSIE, MSME, MSMSE, MSNE, PhD, Certificate, MD/PhD. *Accreditation:* ABET. Part-time programs available. Postbaccalaureate distance learning degree programs offered (no on-campus study). Terminal master's awarded for partial completion of doctoral program. *Degree requirements:* For master's, thesis (for some programs); for doctorate, comprehensive exam, thesis/dissertation. *Entrance requirements:* Additional exam requirements/recommendations for international students: Required—TOEFL (minimum score 550 paper-based; 213 computer-based) or IELTS (minimum score 6.5); Recommended—TWE. Electronic applications accepted. *Expenses:* Contact institution. *Faculty research:* Nanotechnology, advanced materials manufacturing, tissue and cell engineering, intelligent infrastructures, global sustainable industrial systems.

Purdue University Calumet, Graduate Studies Office, School of Engineering, Mathematics, and Science, Department of Engineering, Hammond, IN 46323-2094. Offers computer engineering (MSE); electrical engineering (MSE); engineering (MS); mechanical engineering (MSE). Evening/weekend programs available. *Entrance requirements:* Additional exam requirements/recommendations for international students: Required—TOEFL.

Purdue University Calumet, Graduate Studies Office, School of Technology, Hammond, IN 46323-2094. Offers MS.

Queen's University at Kingston, School of Graduate Studies and Research, Faculty of Applied Science, Kingston, ON K7L 3N6, Canada. Offers M Eng, M Sc, M Sc Eng, PhD. Part-time programs available. *Degree requirements:* For doctorate, comprehensive exam, thesis/dissertation. *Entrance requirements:* Additional exam requirements/recommendations for international students: Required—TOEFL. Electronic applications accepted.

Rensselaer at Hartford, Department of Engineering, Hartford, CT 06120-2991. Offers ME, MS. Part-time and evening/weekend programs available. *Entrance requirements:* For master's, GRE. Additional exam requirements/recommendations for international students: Required—TOEFL (minimum score 600 paper-based; 250 computer-based; 100 iBT). Electronic applications accepted.

Rensselaer Polytechnic Institute, Graduate School, School of Engineering, Troy, NY 12180-3590. Offers M Eng, MS, D Eng, PhD. Part-time and evening/weekend programs available. Postbaccalaureate distance learning degree programs offered (no on-campus

study). Terminal master's awarded for partial completion of doctoral program. *Degree requirements:* For master's, comprehensive exam (for some programs), thesis (for some programs); for doctorate, comprehensive exam (for some programs), thesis/dissertation. *Entrance requirements:* For master's and doctorate, GRE. Additional exam requirements/recommendations for international students: Required—TOEFL (minimum score 570 paper-based; 230 computer-based; 89 iBT), IELTS (minimum score 6.5). Electronic applications accepted. *Faculty research:* Computer networking, materials, computational mechanics and modeling, microelectronic technology, data mining.

Rice University, Graduate Programs, George R. Brown School of Engineering, Houston, TX 77251-1892. Offers M Ch E, M Stat, MA, MBE, MCAM, MCE, MCS, MEE, MEE, MES, MME, MMS, MS, PhD, MBA/M Stat, MBA/ME, MBA/MEE, MD/PhD. MD/PhD offered jointly with Baylor College of Medicine, The University of Texas Health Science Center at Houston. Part-time programs available. Terminal master's awarded for partial completion of doctoral program. *Degree requirements:* For master's, comprehensive exam (for some programs), thesis (for some programs); for doctorate, comprehensive exam (for some programs), thesis/dissertation. *Entrance requirements:* For master's and doctorate, GRE General Test. Additional exam requirements/recommendations for international students: Required—TOEFL (minimum score 600 paper-based; 250 computer-based). Electronic applications accepted. *Faculty research:* Digital signal processing, tissue engineering, groundwater remediation, computational engineering and high performance computing, nanoscale science and technology.

Robert Morris University, Graduate Studies, School of Engineering, Mathematics and Science, Moon Township, PA 15108-1189. Offers engineering management (MS). Part-time and evening/weekend programs available. *Faculty:* 3 full-time (0 women). *Students:* 30 part-time (0 women); includes 2 minority (1 Black or African American, non-Hispanic/Latino; 1 American Indian or Alaska Native, non-Hispanic/Latino), 9 international. *Entrance requirements:* For master's, letters of recommendation. Additional exam requirements/recommendations for international students: Required—TOEFL (minimum score 550 paper-based; 213 computer-based; 79 iBT). *Application deadline:* For fall admission, 7/1 priority date for domestic students, 7/1 for international students; for spring admission, 11/1 priority date for domestic students, 11/1 for international students. Applications are processed on a rolling basis. Application fee: $35. Electronic applications accepted. *Expenses:* Contact institution. *Financial support:* Federal Work-Study, institutionally sponsored loans, and unspecified assistantships available. Financial award application deadline: 5/1; financial award applicants required to submit FAFSA. *Unit head:* Dr. Maria V. Kalevitch, Dean, 412-397-4020, Fax: 412-397-2472, E-mail: kalevitch@rmu.edu. *Application contact:* Deborah Roach, Assistant Dean, Graduate Admissions, 412-397-5200, Fax: 412-397-2425, E-mail: graduateadmissions@rmu.edu. Web site: http://www.rmu.edu/web/cms/schools/sems/.

Rochester Institute of Technology, Graduate Enrollment Services, College of Applied Science and Technology, School of Engineering Technology, Department of Electrical, Computer and Telecommunications Engineering Technology, Rochester, NY 14623-5603. Offers facility management (MS); manufacturing and mechanical systems integration (MS); telecommunications engineering technology (MS). Part-time and evening/weekend programs available. Postbaccalaureate distance learning degree programs offered (no on-campus study). *Students:* 54 full-time (13 women), 34 part-time (6 women); includes 7 minority (4 Black or African American, non-Hispanic/Latino; 1 Asian, non-Hispanic/Latino; 1 Hispanic/Latino; 1 Two or more races, non-Hispanic/Latino), 70 international. Average age 26. 154 applicants, 55% accepted, 32 enrolled. In 2011, 24 master's awarded. *Degree requirements:* For master's, thesis. *Entrance requirements:* For master's, GRE, minimum GPA of 3.0. Additional exam requirements/recommendations for international students: Required—TOEFL (minimum score 550 paper-based; 213 computer-based; 79 iBT) or IELTS (minimum score 6.5). *Application deadline:* For fall admission, 2/15 priority date for domestic students, 2/15 for international students; for winter admission, 11/1 for domestic and international students; for spring admission, 2/1 for domestic and international students. Applications are processed on a rolling basis. Application fee: $50. Electronic applications accepted. *Expenses: Tuition:* Full-time $34,659; part-time $963 per credit hour. *Required fees:* $228; $76 per quarter. *Financial support:* Research assistantships with partial tuition reimbursements, teaching assistantships with partial tuition reimbursements, career-related internships or fieldwork, and unspecified assistantships available. Support available to part-time students. Financial award application deadline: 2/15; financial award applicants required to submit FAFSA. *Faculty research:* Fiber optic networks, next generation networks, project management. *Unit head:* Michael Eastman, Department Chair, 585-475-7787, Fax: 585-475-2178, E-mail: mgeiee@rit.edu. *Application contact:* Diane Ellison, Assistant Vice President, Graduate Enrollment Services, 585-475-2229, Fax: 585-475-7164, E-mail: gradinfo@rit.edu. Web site: http://www.rit.edu/cast/ectet/.

Rochester Institute of Technology, Graduate Enrollment Services, Kate Gleason College of Engineering, Rochester, NY 14623-5603. Offers ME, MS, MSEE, PhD, AC. Part-time and evening/weekend programs available. Postbaccalaureate distance learning degree programs offered (no on-campus study). *Students:* 314 full-time (57 women), 296 part-time (53 women); includes 43 minority (8 Black or African American, non-Hispanic/Latino; 2 American Indian or Alaska Native, non-Hispanic/Latino; 22 Asian, non-Hispanic/Latino; 11 Hispanic/Latino), 252 international. Average age 28. 1,010 applicants, 56% accepted, 185 enrolled. In 2011, 185 master's, 11 doctorates, 5 other advanced degrees awarded. Terminal master's awarded for partial completion of doctoral program. *Entrance requirements:* For master's, minimum GPA of 3.0. Additional exam requirements/recommendations for international students: Required—TOEFL (minimum score 570 paper-based; 230 computer-based; 88 iBT) or IELTS (minimum score 6.5). *Application deadline:* For fall admission, 2/15 priority date for domestic students, 2/15 for international students. Applications are processed on a rolling basis. Application fee: $50. Electronic applications accepted. *Expenses: Tuition:* Full-time $34,659; part-time $963 per credit hour. *Required fees:* $228; $76 per quarter. *Financial support:* Fellowships with partial tuition reimbursements, research assistantships with partial tuition reimbursements, teaching assistantships with partial tuition reimbursements, career-related internships or fieldwork, institutionally sponsored loans, scholarships/grants, tuition waivers (partial), and unspecified assistantships available. Support available to part-time students. Financial award applicants required to submit FAFSA. *Faculty research:* Computer-integrated manufacturing, industrial ergonomics, optics and photonics, micromachines, electrochemical heating, signal and image processing, cardiovascular biomechanics, robotics and control, VLSI design, electron beam lithography, computer architecture, multimedia information systems, object-oriented software development. *Unit head:* Dr. Harvey Palmer, Dean, 585-475-2145, Fax: 585-475-6879, E-mail: coe@rit.edu. *Application contact:* Diane Ellison, Assistant Vice President, Graduate Enrollment Services, 585-475-2229, Fax: 585-475-7164, E-mail: gradinfo@rit.edu. Web site: http://www.rit.edu/kgcoe/.

Rose-Hulman Institute of Technology, Faculty of Engineering and Applied Sciences, Terre Haute, IN 47803-3999. Offers M Eng, MS, MD/MS. Part-time and evening/weekend programs available. Postbaccalaureate distance learning degree programs offered (minimal on-campus study). *Faculty:* 91 full-time (19 women), 8 part-time/adjunct (1 woman). *Students:* 49 full-time (11 women), 36 part-time (6 women); includes 4 minority (1 Black or African American, non-Hispanic/Latino; 3 Asian, non-Hispanic/Latino), 22 international. Average age 24. 59 applicants, 95% accepted, 41 enrolled. In 2011, 57 master's awarded. *Degree requirements:* For master's, thesis (for some programs). *Entrance requirements:* For master's, GRE, minimum GPA of 3.0. Additional exam requirements/recommendations for international students: Required—TOEFL (minimum score 580 paper-based; 237 computer-based; 92 iBT). *Application deadline:* For fall admission, 2/1 priority date for domestic students. Applications are processed on a rolling basis. Application fee: $0. *Expenses:* Tuition: Full-time $37,197; part-time $1085 per credit hour. *Financial support:* In 2011–12, 46 students received support. Fellowships with full and partial tuition reimbursements available, research assistantships with full and partial tuition reimbursements available, institutionally sponsored loans, scholarships/grants, and tuition waivers (full and partial) available. *Faculty research:* Optical instrument design and prototypes, biomaterials, adsorption and adsorption-based separations, image and speech processing, groundwater, solid and hazardous waste. *Total annual research expenditures:* $830,412. *Unit head:* Dr. Daniel J. Moore, Associate Dean of the Faculty, 812-877-8110, Fax: 812-877-8061, E-mail: daniel.j.moore@rose-hulman.edu. *Application contact:* Dr. Daniel J. Moore, Associate Dean of the Faculty, 812-877-8110, Fax: 812-877-8061, E-mail: daniel.j.moore@rose-hulman.edu. Web site: http://www.rose-hulman.edu.

Rowan University, Graduate School, College of Engineering, Program in Engineering, Glassboro, NJ 08028-1701. Offers MS. Part-time and evening/weekend programs available. *Degree requirements:* For master's, thesis (for some programs). *Entrance requirements:* For master's, GRE General Test. Additional exam requirements/recommendations for international students: Required—TOEFL. Electronic applications accepted.

Royal Military College of Canada, Division of Graduate Studies and Research, Engineering Division, Kingston, ON K7K 7B4, Canada. Offers M Eng, M Sc, MA Sc, PhD. *Degree requirements:* For master's, thesis; for doctorate, comprehensive exam, thesis/dissertation. *Entrance requirements:* For master's, honours degree with second-class standing; for doctorate, master's degree. Electronic applications accepted.

St. Cloud State University, School of Graduate Studies, College of Science and Engineering, St. Cloud, MN 56301-4498. Offers MA, MEM, MS. *Degree requirements:* For master's, thesis or alternative. *Entrance requirements:* For master's, GRE General Test, minimum GPA of 2.75. Additional exam requirements/recommendations for international students: Required—TOEFL (minimum score 550 paper-based; 213 computer-based). Electronic applications accepted.

St. Mary's University, Graduate School, Department of Engineering, San Antonio, TX 78228-8507. Offers electrical engineering (MS), including electrical engineering, electrical/computer engineering; engineering administration (MS); engineering systems management (MS); industrial engineering (MS), including engineering computer applications, engineering management, industrial engineering, operations research; software engineering (MS); JD/MS. Part-time programs available. *Degree requirements:* For master's, comprehensive exam. *Entrance requirements:* For master's, GRE General Test. Additional exam requirements/recommendations for international students: Required—TOEFL (minimum score 550 paper-based; 213 computer-based). Electronic applications accepted. *Faculty research:* Image processing, control, communication, artificial intelligence, robotics.

San Diego State University, Graduate and Research Affairs, College of Engineering, San Diego, CA 92182. Offers MS, PhD. Part-time and evening/weekend programs available. Terminal master's awarded for partial completion of doctoral program. *Degree requirements:* For master's, thesis optional; for doctorate, thesis/dissertation. *Entrance requirements:* For master's, GRE General Test; for doctorate, GRE, 3 letters of recommendation. Additional exam requirements/recommendations for international students: Required—TOEFL. Electronic applications accepted.

San Francisco State University, Division of Graduate Studies, College of Science and Engineering, School of Engineering, San Francisco, CA 94132-1722. Offers embedded electrical and computer systems (MS); structural/earthquake engineering (MS). Part-time programs available. *Application deadline:* Applications are processed on a rolling basis. Electronic applications accepted. *Unit head:* Dr. Wenshen Pong, Director, 415-338-1174, E-mail: engineer@sfsu.edu. *Application contact:* Dr. Hamid Shahnasser, Graduate Coordinator, 415-338-2124, E-mail: hamid@sfsu.edu. Web site: http://engineering.sfsu.edu/.

San Jose State University, Graduate Studies and Research, Charles W. Davidson College of Engineering, Department of General Engineering, San Jose, CA 95192-0001. Offers MS. Electronic applications accepted.

Santa Clara University, School of Engineering, Santa Clara, CA 95053. Offers MS, PhD, Certificate, Engineer. Part-time and evening/weekend programs available. *Faculty:* 49 full-time (14 women), 62 part-time/adjunct (8 women). *Students:* 316 full-time (99 women), 464 part-time (102 women); includes 250 minority (10 Black or African American, non-Hispanic/Latino; 206 Asian, non-Hispanic/Latino; 26 Hispanic/Latino; 4 Native Hawaiian or other Pacific Islander, non-Hispanic/Latino; 4 Two or more races, non-Hispanic/Latino), 297 international. Average age 29. 688 applicants, 53% accepted, 211 enrolled. In 2011, 304 master's, 6 doctorates, 8 other advanced degrees awarded. *Degree requirements:* For master's, thesis (for some programs); for doctorate, thesis/dissertation; for other advanced degree, thesis. *Entrance requirements:* For master's, GRE, transcript; for doctorate, GRE, master's degree or equivalent; for other advanced degree, master's degree, published paper. Additional exam requirements/recommendations for international students: Required—TOEFL (minimum score 550 paper-based; 213 computer-based; 79 iBT). *Application deadline:* For fall admission, 8/1 for domestic students, 7/15 for international students; for winter admission, 10/28 for domestic students, 9/23 for international students; for spring admission, 2/25 for domestic students, 1/21 for international students. Applications are processed on a rolling basis. Application fee: $60. Electronic applications accepted. *Expenses:* Contact institution. *Financial support:* Research assistantships and teaching assistantships available. Financial award application deadline: 3/2; financial award applicants required to submit FAFSA. *Faculty research:* Development of small satellite design, tests and operations technology, Thermal and Electrical Nanoscale Transport (TENT). *Unit head:* Dr. Alex Zecevic, Associate Dean for Graduate Studies, 408-554-2394, E-mail: azecevic@scu.edu. *Application contact:* Stacey Tinker, Director of Enrollment Management, 408-554-4748, Fax: 408-554-4323, E-mail: stinker@scu.edu. Web site: http://www.scu.edu/engineering/graduate/.

Seattle University, College of Science and Engineering, Seattle, WA 98122-1090. Offers MSE. Part-time and evening/weekend programs available. *Faculty:* 10 full-time (4 women), 1 (woman) part-time/adjunct. *Students:* 16 full-time (7 women), 30 part-time (8 women); includes 13 minority (1 Black or African American, non-Hispanic/Latino; 10 Asian, non-Hispanic/Latino; 2 Hispanic/Latino), 15 international. Average age 30. 45

applicants, 49% accepted, 10 enrolled. In 2011, 17 master's awarded. *Degree requirements:* For master's, thesis. *Entrance requirements:* For master's, GRE General Test, 2 years of related work experience. *Application deadline:* For fall admission, 7/1 for domestic students. Application fee: $55. *Expenses:* Contact institution. *Financial support:* Career-related internships or fieldwork and Federal Work-Study available. Support available to part-time students. Financial award applicants required to submit FAFSA. *Unit head:* Dr. Michael Quinn, Dean, 206-296-5500, Fax: 206-296-2071. *Application contact:* Janet Shandley, Associate Dean of Graduate Admissions, 206-296-5900, Fax: 206-298-5656, E-mail: grad_admissions@seattleu.edu. Web site: http://www.seattleu.edu/.

Simon Fraser University, Graduate Studies, Faculty of Applied Sciences, School of Engineering Science, Burnaby, BC V5A 1S6, Canada. Offers M Eng, MA Sc, PhD. *Degree requirements:* For master's, thesis (for some programs); for doctorate, thesis/dissertation, qualifying exam. *Entrance requirements:* For master's, GRE, minimum GPA of 3.0; for doctorate, GRE, minimum GPA of 3.5. Additional exam requirements/recommendations for international students: Required—TOEFL or IELTS. *Faculty research:* Signal processing, electronics, communications, systems and control.

South Dakota School of Mines and Technology, Graduate Division, College of Engineering, Rapid City, SD 57701-3995. Offers MS, PhD. Part-time programs available. *Degree requirements:* For doctorate, thesis/dissertation. *Entrance requirements:* For doctorate, minimum graduate GPA of 3.0. Additional exam requirements/recommendations for international students: Required—TOEFL, TWE. Electronic applications accepted.

South Dakota State University, Graduate School, College of Engineering, Brookings, SD 57007. Offers MS, PhD. Part-time programs available. *Degree requirements:* For master's, thesis, oral exam; for doctorate, thesis/dissertation, preliminary oral and written exams. *Entrance requirements:* Additional exam requirements/recommendations for international students: Required—TOEFL. *Faculty research:* Process control and management, ground source heat pumps, water quality, heat transfer, power systems.

Southern Illinois University Carbondale, Graduate School, College of Engineering, Carbondale, IL 62901-4701. Offers ME, MS, PhD. *Faculty:* 55 full-time (3 women), 3 part-time/adjunct (0 women). *Students:* 239 full-time (48 women), 154 part-time (24 women); includes 22 minority (15 Black or African American, non-Hispanic/Latino; 4 Asian, non-Hispanic/Latino; 3 Hispanic/Latino), 300 international. 497 applicants, 77% accepted, 89 enrolled. In 2011, 132 master's, 10 doctorates awarded. *Degree requirements:* For master's, comprehensive exam; for doctorate, thesis/dissertation. *Entrance requirements:* For master's, minimum GPA of 2.7; for doctorate, GRE General Test, minimum GPA of 3.5. Additional exam requirements/recommendations for international students: Required—TOEFL. *Application deadline:* Applications are processed on a rolling basis. Application fee: $20. *Financial support:* In 2011–12, 1 fellowship, 58 research assistantships, 95 teaching assistantships were awarded; Federal Work-Study, institutionally sponsored loans, and tuition waivers (full) also available. Support available to part-time students. *Faculty research:* Electrical systems, all facets of fossil energy, mechanics. *Unit head:* R. Viswanathan, Interim Dean, 618-453-4321. *Application contact:* Anna Maria Alms, Student Contact, 618-453-4321, Fax: 618-453-4235, E-mail: amalms@siu.edu.

Southern Illinois University Edwardsville, Graduate School, School of Engineering, Edwardsville, IL 62026-0001. Offers MS. Part-time programs available. *Faculty:* 45 full-time (2 women). *Students:* 93 full-time (16 women), 127 part-time (29 women); includes 19 minority (13 Black or African American, non-Hispanic/Latino; 3 Asian, non-Hispanic/Latino; 1 Hispanic/Latino; 2 Two or more races, non-Hispanic/Latino), 112 international. 410 applicants, 44% accepted. In 2011, 79 master's awarded. *Degree requirements:* For master's, thesis (for some programs), research paper, final exam. *Entrance requirements:* Additional exam requirements/recommendations for international students: Required—TOEFL (minimum score 550 paper-based; 213 computer-based; 79 iBT), IELTS (minimum score 6.5). *Application deadline:* For fall admission, 7/22 for domestic students, 6/1 for international students; for spring admission, 12/9 for domestic students, 10/1 for international students. Applications are processed on a rolling basis. Application fee: $30. Electronic applications accepted. Tuition and fees vary according to course load and program. *Financial support:* In 2011–12, 2 fellowships with full tuition reimbursements (averaging $8,370 per year), 29 research assistantships with full tuition reimbursements (averaging $9,927 per year), 65 teaching assistantships with full tuition reimbursements (averaging $9,927 per year) were awarded; institutionally sponsored loans, scholarships/grants, and unspecified assistantships also available. Financial award application deadline: 3/1; financial award applicants required to submit FAFSA. *Unit head:* Dr. Hasan Sevim, Dean, 618-650-2541, E-mail: hsevim@siue.edu. *Application contact:* Michelle Robinson, Coordinator of Graduate Recruitment, 618-650-2811, Fax: 618-650-3523, E-mail: michero@siue.edu. Web site: http://www.siue.edu/engineering.

Southern Methodist University, Bobby B. Lyle School of Engineering, Dallas, TX 75275. Offers MS, MS Cp E, MSEE, MSEM, MSIEM, MSME, DE, PhD. Part-time and evening/weekend programs available. Postbaccalaureate distance learning degree programs offered (no on-campus study). Terminal master's awarded for partial completion of doctoral program. *Degree requirements:* For master's, thesis optional; for doctorate, thesis/dissertation, oral and written qualifying exams. *Entrance requirements:* For master's, GRE General Test, minimum GPA of 3.0 in last 2 years; bachelor's degree in engineering, mathematics, or sciences; for doctorate, bachelor's degree in related field. Additional exam requirements/recommendations for international students: Required—TOEFL (minimum score 550 paper-based; 213 computer-based). *Expenses:* Contact institution. *Faculty research:* Mobile and fault-tolerant computing, manufacturing systems, telecommunications, solid state devices and materials, fluid and thermal sciences.

Southern Polytechnic State University, School of Engineering, Marietta, GA 30060-2896. Offers MS, Advanced Certificate, Graduate Certificate. Part-time and evening/weekend programs available. Postbaccalaureate distance learning degree programs offered (no on-campus study). *Faculty:* 3 full-time (1 woman), 2 part-time/adjunct (0 women). *Students:* 3 full-time (0 women), 49 part-time (9 women); includes 17 minority (10 Black or African American, non-Hispanic/Latino; 4 Asian, non-Hispanic/Latino; 2 Hispanic/Latino; 1 Two or more races, non-Hispanic/Latino), 3 international. Average age 39. 19 applicants, 84% accepted, 12 enrolled. In 2011, 13 master's awarded. *Degree requirements:* For master's, thesis optional. *Entrance requirements:* For master's, GRE. Additional exam requirements/recommendations for international students: Required—TOEFL (minimum score 550 paper-based; 213 computer-based; 79 iBT), IELTS (minimum score 6.5). *Application deadline:* For fall admission, 7/1 priority date for domestic students, 5/1 for international students; for spring admission, 11/1 priority date for domestic students, 9/1 for international students. Applications are processed on a rolling basis. Application fee: $50. Electronic applications accepted. *Expenses:* Tuition, state resident: full-time $2592; part-time $216 per semester hour.

Engineering and Applied Sciences—General

Tuition, nonresident: full-time $9408; part-time $784 per semester hour. *Required fees:* $698 per term. *Faculty research:* Supply chain and logistics reliability, maintainability system analysis, design optimization, engineering education. *Unit head:* Dr. Thomas Currin, Dean, 678-915-7482, Fax: 678-915-5527, E-mail: tcurrin@spsu.edu. *Application contact:* Nikki Palamiotis, Director of Graduate Studies, 678-915-4276, Fax: 678-915-7292, E-mail: npalamio@spsu.edu. Web site: http://www.spsu.edu/engineering/index.htm.

Southern Polytechnic State University, School of Engineering Technology and Management, Marietta, GA 30060-2896. Offers MBA, MS, MSA, Graduate Certificate, Graduate Transition Certificate. Part-time and evening/weekend programs available. Postbaccalaureate distance learning degree programs offered. *Faculty:* 24 full-time (7 women), 16 part-time/adjunct (7 women). *Students:* 115 full-time (54 women), 209 part-time (99 women); includes 160 minority (117 Black or African American, non-Hispanic/Latino; 1 American Indian or Alaska Native, non-Hispanic/Latino; 25 Asian, non-Hispanic/Latino; 13 Hispanic/Latino; 4 Two or more races, non-Hispanic/Latino), 50 international. Average age 34. 148 applicants, 88% accepted, 92 enrolled. In 2011, 103 master's, 1 other advanced degree awarded. *Entrance requirements:* Additional exam requirements/recommendations for international students: Required—TOEFL (minimum score 550 paper-based; 213 computer-based; 79 iBT), IELTS (minimum score 6.5). *Application deadline:* For fall admission, 7/1 priority date for domestic students, 5/1 for international students; for spring admission, 11/1 priority date for domestic students, 9/1 for international students. Applications are processed on a rolling basis. Application fee: $50. Electronic applications accepted. *Expenses:* Tuition, state resident: full-time $2592; part-time $216 per semester hour. Tuition, nonresident: full-time $9408; part-time $784 per semester hour. *Required fees:* $698 per term. *Financial support:* Research assistantships with tuition reimbursements, teaching assistantships with tuition reimbursements, career-related internships or fieldwork, scholarships/grants, and unspecified assistantships available. Support available to part-time students. Financial award application deadline: 5/1; financial award applicants required to submit FAFSA. *Faculty research:* Ethics, virtual reality, sustainability, management of technology, quality management, capacity planning, human-computer interaction/interface, enterprise integration planning, economic impact of educational institutions, behavioral accounting, accounting ethics, taxation, information security, visualizational simulation, human-computer interaction, analog and digital communications, computer networking, analog and low power electronics design, control systems and digital signal processing. *Unit head:* Dr. Jeff Ray, Dean, 678-915-7205, Fax: 678-915-7134, E-mail: jray@spsu.edu. *Application contact:* Nikki Palamiotis, Director of Graduate Studies, 678-915-4276, Fax: 678-915-7292, E-mail: npalamio@spsu.edu. Web site: http://www.spsu.edu/schoolofetandm/.

Southern University and Agricultural and Mechanical College, Graduate School, College of Engineering, Baton Rouge, LA 70813. Offers ME. *Degree requirements:* For master's, thesis. *Entrance requirements:* For master's, GRE General Test. Additional exam requirements/recommendations for international students: Required—TOEFL (minimum score 525 paper-based; 193 computer-based).

Stanford University, School of Engineering, Stanford, CA 94305-9991. Offers MS, PhD, Eng. *Degree requirements:* For doctorate, thesis/dissertation; for Eng, thesis. *Entrance requirements:* For master's, doctorate, and Eng, GRE General Test. Additional exam requirements/recommendations for international students: Required—TOEFL. Electronic applications accepted. *Expenses:* Contact institution.

State University of New York at Binghamton, Graduate School, Thomas J. Watson School of Engineering and Applied Science, Binghamton, NY 13902-6000. Offers M Eng, MS, MSAT, PhD. Part-time and evening/weekend programs available. *Faculty:* 76 full-time (10 women), 25 part-time/adjunct (6 women). *Students:* 371 full-time (79 women), 337 part-time (55 women); includes 62 minority (9 Black or African American, non-Hispanic/Latino; 2 American Indian or Alaska Native, non-Hispanic/Latino; 19 Asian, non-Hispanic/Latino; 10 Hispanic/Latino; 22 Native Hawaiian or other Pacific Islander, non-Hispanic/Latino), 427 international. Average age 28. 896 applicants, 63% accepted, 117 enrolled. In 2011, 214 master's, 29 doctorates awarded. Terminal master's awarded for partial completion of doctoral program. *Degree requirements:* For doctorate, thesis/dissertation. *Entrance requirements:* For master's and doctorate, GRE General Test, GRE Subject Test. Additional exam requirements/recommendations for international students: Required—TOEFL (minimum score 550 paper-based; 213 computer-based; 80 iBT). *Application deadline:* Applications are processed on a rolling basis. Application fee: $60. Electronic applications accepted. *Financial support:* In 2011–12, 253 students received support, including 4 fellowships with full tuition reimbursements available (averaging $16,500 per year), 140 research assistantships with full tuition reimbursements available (averaging $16,500 per year), 83 teaching assistantships with full tuition reimbursements available (averaging $16,500 per year); career-related internships or fieldwork, Federal Work-Study, institutionally sponsored loans, scholarships/grants, health care benefits, tuition waivers (full and partial), and unspecified assistantships also available. Financial award application deadline: 2/15; financial award applicants required to submit FAFSA. *Unit head:* Dr. Hari Srihari, Dean, 607-777-2871, E-mail: hsrihari@binghamton.edu. *Application contact:* Catherine Smith, Recruiting and Admissions Coordinator, 607-777-2151, Fax: 607-777-2501, E-mail: cmsmith@binghamton.edu. Web site: http://watson.binghamton.edu.

Stevens Institute of Technology, Graduate School, Charles V. Schaefer Jr. School of Engineering, Hoboken, NJ 07030. Offers M Eng, MS, PhD, Certificate, Engr. Part-time and evening/weekend programs available. Postbaccalaureate distance learning degree programs offered. Terminal master's awarded for partial completion of doctoral program. *Degree requirements:* For doctorate, thesis/dissertation. *Entrance requirements:* Additional exam requirements/recommendations for international students: Required—TOEFL. Electronic applications accepted.

Stony Brook University, State University of New York, Graduate School, College of Engineering and Applied Sciences, Stony Brook, NY 11794. Offers MS, PhD, Advanced Certificate, Certificate. Part-time and evening/weekend programs available. *Degree requirements:* For doctorate, comprehensive exam, thesis/dissertation. *Entrance requirements:* For doctorate, GRE General Test. Additional exam requirements/recommendations for international students: Required—TOEFL.

Syracuse University, L. C. Smith College of Engineering and Computer Science, Syracuse, NY 13244. Offers MS, PhD, CAS, CE, EE. Part-time and evening/weekend programs available. *Faculty:* 75 full-time (10 women), 27 part-time/adjunct (6 women). *Students:* 720 full-time (191 women), 121 part-time (16 women); includes 39 minority (8 Black or African American, non-Hispanic/Latino; 1 American Indian or Alaska Native, non-Hispanic/Latino; 21 Asian, non-Hispanic/Latino; 8 Hispanic/Latino; 1 Two or more races, non-Hispanic/Latino), 652 international. Average age 26. 2,431 applicants, 36% accepted, 298 enrolled. In 2011, 250 master's, 23 doctorates, 1 other advanced degree awarded. *Degree requirements:* For doctorate, thesis/dissertation. *Entrance requirements:* For master's and doctorate, GRE General Test. Additional exam requirements/recommendations for international students: Required—TOEFL (minimum

score 100 iBT). *Application deadline:* For fall admission, 7/1 priority date for domestic students, 6/1 for international students. Applications are processed on a rolling basis. Application fee: $75. Electronic applications accepted. *Expenses: Tuition:* Part-time $1206 per credit. *Financial support:* Fellowships with full tuition reimbursements, research assistantships with full and partial tuition reimbursements, teaching assistantships with full and partial tuition reimbursements, scholarships/grants, and tuition waivers (partial) available. Financial award application deadline: 1/1; financial award applicants required to submit FAFSA. *Faculty research:* Environmental systems, information assurance, biomechanics, solid mechanics and materials, software engineering. *Unit head:* Dr. Laura J. Steinberg, Dean, 315-443-2545, E-mail: ljs@syr.edu. *Application contact:* Kathleen Joyce, Assistant Dean, 314-443-2219, E-mail: topgrads@syr.edu. Web site: http://lcs.syr.edu/.

Temple University, College of Engineering, Philadelphia, PA 19122-6096. Offers MS, MSE, PhD. Part-time programs available. *Faculty:* 29 full-time (5 women). *Students:* 80 full-time (27 women), 36 part-time (10 women); includes 20 minority (5 Black or African American, non-Hispanic/Latino; 2 American Indian or Alaska Native, non-Hispanic/Latino; 12 Asian, non-Hispanic/Latino; 1 Hispanic/Latino), 59 international. Average age 28. 111 applicants, 75% accepted, 34 enrolled. In 2011, 46 master's, 6 doctorates awarded. *Degree requirements:* For master's, thesis optional; for doctorate, comprehensive exam, thesis/dissertation, 2 published papers. *Entrance requirements:* For master's, GRE General Test, minimum undergraduate GPA of 3.0; for doctorate, GRE General Test, minimum graduate GPA of 3.5, MS. Additional exam requirements/recommendations for international students: Required—TOEFL (minimum score 550 paper-based; 213 computer-based; 79 iBT). *Application deadline:* For fall admission, 7/1 priority date for domestic students, 12/15 for international students; for spring admission, 11/1 priority date for domestic students, 8/1 for international students. Applications are processed on a rolling basis. Application fee: $50. Electronic applications accepted. *Expenses:* Tuition, state resident: full-time $12,366; part-time $687 per credit hour. Tuition, nonresident: full-time $17,298; part-time $961 per credit hour. *Required fees:* $590; $213 per year. *Financial support:* Fellowships with full tuition reimbursements, research assistantships with full tuition reimbursements, teaching assistantships with full tuition reimbursements, career-related internships or fieldwork, Federal Work-Study, and institutionally sponsored loans available. Financial award application deadline: 1/15. *Faculty research:* Computer engineering, digital systems, bioengineering, transportation, materials. *Unit head:* Dr. Keyanoush Sadeghipour, Dean, 215-204-5285, Fax: 215-204-6936, E-mail: keya@temple.edu. *Application contact:* Tara Schumacher, Coordinator of Outreach, 215-204-6575, Fax: 215-204-8781, E-mail: tara.schumacher@temple.edu. Web site: http://www.temple.edu/engineering/.

Tennessee State University, The School of Graduate Studies and Research, College of Engineering, Technology, and Computer Science, Nashville, TN 37209-1561. Offers computer and information systems engineering (MS, PhD); engineering (ME). Part-time and evening/weekend programs available. *Degree requirements:* For master's, project; for doctorate, comprehensive exam, thesis/dissertation. *Entrance requirements:* For doctorate, minimum GPA of 3.3. *Faculty research:* Robotics, intelligent systems, human-computer interaction software systems, biomedical engineering, signal/image processing, probabilistic design, intelligent manufacturing, cooperative mobile robots, condition based maintenance, sensor fusion.

Tennessee Technological University, Graduate School, College of Engineering, Cookeville, TN 38505. Offers MS, PhD. Part-time programs available. *Faculty:* 76 full-time (2 women). *Students:* 77 full-time (12 women), 74 part-time (6 women); includes 13 minority (6 Black or African American, non-Hispanic/Latino; 1 American Indian or Alaska Native, non-Hispanic/Latino; 5 Asian, non-Hispanic/Latino; 1 Hispanic/Latino), 68 international. Average age 28. 231 applicants, 58% accepted, 35 enrolled. In 2011, 39 master's, 10 doctorates awarded. *Degree requirements:* For master's, comprehensive exam, thesis; for doctorate, comprehensive exam, thesis/dissertation. *Entrance requirements:* For master's, GRE General Test; for doctorate, GRE, minimum GPA of 3.5. Additional exam requirements/recommendations for international students: Required—TOEFL (minimum score 550 paper-based; 79 iBT), IELTS (minimum score 5.5), PTE Academic. *Application deadline:* For fall admission, 8/1 for domestic students, 5/1 for international students; for spring admission, 12/1 for domestic students, 10/1 for international students. Application fee: $25 ($30 for international students). Electronic applications accepted. *Expenses:* Tuition, state resident: full-time $8094; part-time $422 per credit hour. Tuition, nonresident: full-time $20,574; part-time $1046 per credit hour. *Financial support:* In 2011–12, 3 fellowships (averaging $8,000 per year), 71 research assistantships (averaging $9,293 per year), 41 teaching assistantships (averaging $7,223 per year) were awarded; career-related internships or fieldwork also available. Support available to part-time students. Financial award application deadline: 4/1. *Unit head:* Dr. Joseph Rencis, Dean, 931-372-3172, Fax: 931-372-6172, E-mail: jjrencis@tntech.edu. *Application contact:* Shelia K. Kendrick, Coordinator of Graduate Admissions, 931-372-3808, Fax: 931-372-3497, E-mail: skendrick@tntech.edu.

Texas A&M University, College of Engineering, College Station, TX 77843. Offers M En, M Eng, MCS, MID, MS, D Eng, PhD. Part-time programs available. Postbaccalaureate distance learning degree programs offered (minimal on-campus study). *Faculty:* 368. *Students:* 2,439 full-time (518 women), 411 part-time (63 women); includes 332 minority (55 Black or African American, non-Hispanic/Latino; 2 American Indian or Alaska Native, non-Hispanic/Latino; 110 Asian, non-Hispanic/Latino; 142 Hispanic/Latino; 1 Native Hawaiian or other Pacific Islander, non-Hispanic/Latino; 22 Two or more races, non-Hispanic/Latino), 1,806 international. In 2011, 668 master's, 192 doctorates awarded. Terminal master's awarded for partial completion of doctoral program. *Entrance requirements:* For master's and doctorate, GRE General Test. Additional exam requirements/recommendations for international students: Required—TOEFL. Application fee: $50 ($75 for international students). Electronic applications accepted. *Expenses:* Tuition, state resident: full-time $5437; part-time $226.55 per credit hour. Tuition, nonresident: full-time $12,949; part-time $539.55 per credit hour. *Required fees:* $2741. *Financial support:* Fellowships, research assistantships, teaching assistantships, career-related internships or fieldwork, institutionally sponsored loans, scholarships/grants, and unspecified assistantships available. Financial award applicants required to submit FAFSA. *Unit head:* Dr. M. Katherine Banks, Dean and Vice Chancellor, 979-845-7203, Fax: 979-845-8986, E-mail: k-banks@tamu.edu. *Application contact:* Graduate Admissions, 979-458-0427, E-mail: admissions@tamu.edu. Web site: http://engineering.tamu.edu/.

Texas A&M University–Kingsville, College of Graduate Studies, College of Engineering, Kingsville, TX 78363. Offers ME, MS, PhD. Part-time and evening/weekend programs available. *Degree requirements:* For master's, comprehensive exam. *Entrance requirements:* For master's, GRE General Test. Additional exam requirements/recommendations for international students: Required—TOEFL.

Texas Tech University, Graduate School, Edward E. Whitacre Jr. College of Engineering, Lubbock, TX 79409. Offers M Engr, MENVEGR, MS, MS Ch E, MSCE, MSEE, MSIE, MSME, MSPE, MSSEM, PhD. Part-time programs available. *Faculty:* 130

full-time (18 women), 8 part-time/adjunct (2 women). *Students:* 571 full-time (106 women), 181 part-time (24 women); includes 71 minority (9 Black or African American, non-Hispanic/Latino; 16 Asian, non-Hispanic/Latino; 38 Hispanic/Latino; 8 Two or more races, non-Hispanic/Latino), 466 international. Average age 27. 1,584 applicants, 37% accepted, 169 enrolled. In 2011, 186 master's, 31 doctorates awarded. *Degree requirements:* For master's, thesis (for some programs); for doctorate, thesis/dissertation. *Entrance requirements:* For master's and doctorate, GRE General Test, minimum GPA of 3.0. Additional exam requirements/recommendations for international students: Required—TOEFL (minimum score 550 paper-based; 213 computer-based; 79 iBT). *Application deadline:* For fall admission, 6/1 priority date for domestic students, 1/15 for international students; for spring admission, 9/1 priority date for domestic students, 6/15 for international students. Applications are processed on a rolling basis. Application fee: $50 ($75 for international students). Electronic applications accepted. *Expenses:* Contact institution. *Financial support:* In 2011–12, 346 students received support. Career-related internships or fieldwork, Federal Work-Study, institutionally sponsored loans, scholarships/grants, traineeships, health care benefits, and unspecified assistantships available. Support available to part-time students. Financial award application deadline: 4/15; financial award applicants required to submit FAFSA. *Faculty research:* Energy (wind, petroleum), water resources, nanophotonics and nanotechnology, pulsed power and power electronics, polymer and energetic materials. *Total annual research expenditures:* $23.1 million. *Unit head:* Dr. Albert Sacco, Jr., Dean, 806-742-3451, Fax: 806-742-3493, E-mail: al.sacco-jr@ttu.edu. *Application contact:* Dr. John E. Kobza, Senior Associate Dean, 806-742-3451, Fax: 806-742-3493, E-mail: john.kobza@ttu.edu. Web site: http://www.depts.ttu.edu/coe/.

Trine University, Allen School of Engineering and Technology, Angola, IN 46703-1764. Offers civil engineering (ME); mechanical engineering (ME). Part-time and evening/weekend programs available. *Degree requirements:* For master's, comprehensive exam, thesis. *Faculty research:* CAD, computer aided MFG, computer numerical control, parametric modeling, megatronics.

Tufts University, School of Engineering, Medford, MA 02155. Offers ME, MS, MSEM, PhD. Part-time programs available. *Faculty:* 74 full-time, 22 part-time/adjunct. *Students:* 622 (198 women); includes 89 minority (11 Black or African American, non-Hispanic/Latino; 4 American Indian or Alaska Native, non-Hispanic/Latino; 63 Asian, non-Hispanic/Latino; 11 Hispanic/Latino), 142 international. 991 applicants, 44% accepted, 209 enrolled. In 2011, 117 master's, 25 doctorates awarded. Terminal master's awarded for partial completion of doctoral program. *Degree requirements:* For master's, thesis (for some programs); for doctorate, thesis/dissertation. *Entrance requirements:* For master's and doctorate, GRE General Test. Additional exam requirements/recommendations for international students: Required—TOEFL (minimum score 550 paper-based; 213 computer-based; 80 iBT). *Application deadline:* For fall admission, 1/15 priority date for domestic students, 12/15 for international students; for spring admission, 10/15 for domestic students, 9/15 for international students. Applications are processed on a rolling basis. Application fee: $75. Electronic applications accepted. *Expenses:* Tuition: Full-time $41,208; part-time $1030 per credit hour. Full-time tuition and fees vary according to degree level, program and student level. Part-time tuition and fees vary according to course load. *Financial support:* Fellowships with full tuition reimbursements, research assistantships with full and partial tuition reimbursements, teaching assistantships with full and partial tuition reimbursements, Federal Work-Study, scholarships/grants, tuition waivers (partial), and unspecified assistantships available. Financial award application deadline: 1/15; financial award applicants required to submit FAFSA. *Unit head:* Linda Abriola, Dean, 617-627-3237, Fax: 617-627-3819. *Application contact:* Information Contact, 617-628-5000. Web site: http://www.ase.tufts.edu/engineering/.

Tuskegee University, Graduate Programs, College of Engineering, Architecture and Physical Sciences, Tuskegee, AL 36088. Offers MSEE, MSME, PhD. *Faculty:* 19 full-time (0 women). *Students:* 45 full-time (19 women), 5 part-time (1 woman); includes 24 minority (all Black or African American, non-Hispanic/Latino), 21 international. Average age 28. 104 applicants, 59% accepted. In 2011, 56 master's, 2 doctorates awarded. *Degree requirements:* For master's, thesis or alternative. *Entrance requirements:* For master's, GRE General Test, GRE Subject Test. Additional exam requirements/recommendations for international students: Required—TOEFL (minimum score 500 paper-based; 69 computer-based). *Application deadline:* For fall admission, 7/15 for domestic students. Applications are processed on a rolling basis. Application fee: $25 ($35 for international students). *Expenses:* Tuition: Full-time $17,070; part-time $705 per credit hour. *Financial support:* Fellowships, research assistantships, teaching assistantships, career-related internships or fieldwork, Federal Work-Study, and institutionally sponsored loans available. Support available to part-time students. Financial award application deadline: 4/15. *Unit head:* Dr. Legand L. Burge, Acting Dean, 334-727-8356. *Application contact:* Dr. Robert L. Laney, Jr., Vice President/ Director of Admissions and Enrollment Management, 334-727-8580, Fax: 334-727-5750, E-mail: planey@tuskegee.edu.

Union Graduate College, School of Engineering and Computer Science, Schenectady, NY 12308-3107. Offers computer science (MS); electrical engineering (MS); engineering and management systems (MS); mechanical engineering (MS). Part-time and evening/weekend programs available. *Faculty:* 3 full-time (0 women), 20 part-time/adjunct (2 women). *Students:* 13 full-time (1 woman), 103 part-time (13 women); includes 15 minority (2 Black or African American, non-Hispanic/Latino; 6 Asian, non-Hispanic/Latino; 6 Hispanic/Latino; 1 Two or more races, non-Hispanic/Latino), 3 international. Average age 28. 62 applicants, 69% accepted, 38 enrolled. In 2011, 29 master's awarded. *Degree requirements:* For master's, capstone course. *Entrance requirements:* For master's, minimum GPA of 3.0, letters of recommendation. Additional exam requirements/recommendations for international students: Required—TOEFL (minimum score 550 paper-based; 213 computer-based). *Application deadline:* Applications are processed on a rolling basis. Application fee: $60. Electronic applications accepted. *Expenses:* Contact institution. *Financial support:* In 2011–12, 2 students received support. Research assistantships, Federal Work-Study, scholarships/grants, health care benefits, and tuition waivers (full and partial) available. Support available to part-time students. Financial award applicants required to submit FAFSA. *Unit head:* Robert Kozik, Dean, 515-631-9881, Fax: 518-631-9902, E-mail: kozikr@union.edu. *Application contact:* Diane Trzaskos, Coordinator, Admissions, 518-631-9837, Fax: 518-631-9901, E-mail: trzaskod@uniongraduatecollege.edu.

Universidad de las Américas–Puebla, Division of Graduate Studies, School of Engineering, Puebla, Mexico. Offers M Adm, MS, PhD. Part-time and evening/weekend programs available. *Degree requirements:* For master's, one foreign language, thesis. *Faculty research:* Artificial intelligence, food technology, construction, telecommunications, computers in education, operations research.

Université de Moncton, Faculty of Engineering, Moncton, NB E1A 3E9, Canada. Offers civil engineering (M Sc A); electrical engineering (M Sc A); industrial engineering (M Sc A); mechanical engineering (M Sc A). *Degree requirements:* For master's, thesis,

proficiency in French. *Faculty research:* Structures, energy, composite materials, quality control, geo-environment, telecommunications, instrumentation, analog and digital electronics.

Université de Sherbrooke, Faculty of Engineering, Sherbrooke, QC J1K 2R1, Canada. Offers M Eng, M Env, M Sc A, PhD, Diploma. Part-time programs available. *Degree requirements:* For master's, one foreign language, thesis; for doctorate, comprehensive exam, thesis/dissertation. *Entrance requirements:* For master's, bachelor's degree in engineering or equivalent. Electronic applications accepted.

Université du Québec à Chicoutimi, Graduate Programs, Program in Engineering, Chicoutimi, QC G7H 2B1, Canada. Offers M Sc A, PhD. Part-time programs available. *Degree requirements:* For master's, thesis; for doctorate, thesis/dissertation. *Entrance requirements:* For master's, appropriate bachelor's degree, proficiency in French.

Université du Québec à Rimouski, Graduate Programs, Program in Engineering, Rimouski, QC G5L 3A1, Canada. Offers M Sc A. Program offered jointly with Université du Québec à Chicoutimi.

Université du Québec, École de technologie supérieure, Graduate Programs, Montréal, QC H3C 1K3, Canada. Offers M Eng, PhD, Diploma. Postbaccalaureate distance learning degree programs offered (minimal on-campus study). *Entrance requirements:* For master's and Diploma, appropriate bachelor's degree, proficiency in French; for doctorate, appropriate master's degree, proficiency in French.

Université du Québec en Abitibi-Témiscamingue, Graduate Programs, Program in Engineering, Rouyn-Noranda, QC J9X 5E4, Canada. Offers engineering (ME); mineral engineering (ME); mining engineering (DESS).

Université Laval, Faculty of Sciences and Engineering, Québec, QC G1K 7P4, Canada. Offers M Sc, PhD, Diploma. Part-time programs available. *Degree requirements:* For doctorate, thesis/dissertation. Electronic applications accepted.

University at Buffalo, the State University of New York, Graduate School, School of Engineering and Applied Sciences, Buffalo, NY 14260. Offers ME, MS, PhD, Certificate. Part-time and evening/weekend programs available. Postbaccalaureate distance learning degree programs offered (minimal on-campus study). *Faculty:* 152 full-time (17 women), 27 part-time/adjunct (2 women). *Students:* 1,133 full-time (234 women), 105 part-time (11 women); includes 40 minority (11 Black or African American, non-Hispanic/Latino; 3 American Indian or Alaska Native, non-Hispanic/Latino; 15 Asian, non-Hispanic/Latino; 11 Hispanic/Latino), 955 international. Average age 26. 5,117 applicants, 21% accepted, 460 enrolled. In 2011, 460 master's, 66 doctorates awarded. Terminal master's awarded for partial completion of doctoral program. *Degree requirements:* For doctorate, thesis/dissertation. *Entrance requirements:* For master's and doctorate, GRE General Test. Additional exam requirements/recommendations for international students: Required—TOEFL (minimum score 550 paper-based; 217 computer-based; 79 iBT). *Application deadline:* Applications are processed on a rolling basis. Application fee: $75. Electronic applications accepted. *Financial support:* In 2011–12, 446 students received support, including 32 fellowships with full tuition reimbursements available (averaging $28,908 per year), 219 research assistantships with full and partial tuition reimbursements available (averaging $27,600 per year), 148 teaching assistantships with full tuition reimbursements available (averaging $20,900 per year); career-related internships or fieldwork, Federal Work-Study, institutionally sponsored loans, scholarships/grants, tuition waivers (full and partial), and unspecified assistantships also available. Support available to part-time students. Financial award applicants required to submit FAFSA. *Faculty research:* Bioengineering, infrastructure and environmental engineering, electronic and photonic materials, simulation and visualization, information technology and computing. *Total annual research expenditures:* $55.7 million. *Unit head:* Dr. Rajan Batta, Interim Dean, 716-645-2771, Fax: 716-645-2495, E-mail: dean@.buffalo.edu. *Application contact:* Dr. Paschalis Alexandridis, Acting Associate Dean for Graduate Education and Research, 716-645-1183, Fax: 716-645-2495, E-mail: palexand@buffalo.edu. Web site: http://www.eng.buffalo.edu/.

See Display on next page and Close-Up on page 83.

The University of Akron, Graduate School, College of Engineering, Akron, OH 44325. Offers MS, PhD, MD/PhD. Part-time and evening/weekend programs available. *Faculty:* 77 full-time (12 women), 21 part-time/adjunct (2 women). *Students:* 270 full-time (59 women), 96 part-time (20 women); includes 16 minority (13 Asian, non-Hispanic/Latino; 1 Hispanic/Latino; 1 Native Hawaiian or other Pacific Islander, non-Hispanic/Latino; 1 Two or more races, non-Hispanic/Latino), 223 international. Average age 28. 411 applicants, 55% accepted, 63 enrolled. In 2011, 33 master's, 15 doctorates awarded. Terminal master's awarded for partial completion of doctoral program. *Degree requirements:* For master's, thesis optional; for doctorate, one foreign language, thesis/dissertation, candidacy exam, qualifying exam. *Entrance requirements:* For master's, GRE, minimum GPA of 2.75, letters of recommendation, statement of purpose, resume; for doctorate, GRE, minimum GPA of 3.0 with bachelor's degree, 3.5 with master's degree; letters of recommendation; statement of purpose, resume. Additional exam requirements/recommendations for international students: Required—TOEFL (minimum score 550 paper-based; 213 computer-based; 79 iBT). *Application deadline:* Applications are processed on a rolling basis. Application fee: $30 ($40 for international students). Electronic applications accepted. *Expenses:* Tuition, state resident: full-time $7038; part-time $391 per credit hour. Tuition, nonresident: full-time $12,051; part-time $670 per credit hour. Required fees: $1274; $34 per credit hour. *Financial support:* In 2011–12, 98 research assistantships with full tuition reimbursements, 143 teaching assistantships with full tuition reimbursements were awarded; career-related internships or fieldwork and Federal Work-Study also available. *Faculty research:* Engineering materials, energy research, NEMS and MEMS, bio-engineering, computational methods. *Total annual research expenditures:* $6.5 million. *Unit head:* Dr. George Haritos, Dean, 330-972-6978, E-mail: haritos@uakron.edu. *Application contact:* Dr. Craig Menzemer, Associate Dean, 330-972-5536, E-mail: ccmenze@uakron.edu. Web site: http://www.uakron.edu/engineering/.

The University of Alabama, Graduate School, College of Engineering, Tuscaloosa, AL 35487. Offers MAE, MES, MS, MS Ch E, MS Met E, MSCE, PhD. Part-time programs available. Postbaccalaureate distance learning degree programs offered (no on-campus study). *Faculty:* 105 full-time (15 women), 1 part-time/adjunct (0 women). *Students:* 275 full-time (44 women), 78 part-time (18 women); includes 33 minority (19 Black or African American, non-Hispanic/Latino; 5 Asian, non-Hispanic/Latino; 7 Hispanic/Latino; 2 Two or more races, non-Hispanic/Latino), 132 international. Average age 27. 439 applicants, 42% accepted, 83 enrolled. In 2011, 101 master's, 16 doctorates awarded. Terminal master's awarded for partial completion of doctoral program. *Median time to degree:* Of those who began their doctoral program in fall 2003, 58% received their degree in 8 years or less. *Degree requirements:* For master's, comprehensive exam; for doctorate, thesis/dissertation. *Entrance requirements:* For master's and doctorate, minimum GPA of 3.0. Additional exam requirements/recommendations for international students: Required—TOEFL (minimum score 550 paper-based; 213 computer-based). *Application* *deadline:* For fall admission, 7/1 for domestic students, 4/15 for international students; for spring admission, 11/15 for domestic students, 9/1 for international students. Applications are processed on a rolling basis. Application fee: $50 ($60 for international students). Electronic applications accepted. *Expenses:* Tuition, state resident: full-time $8600. Tuition, nonresident: full-time $21,900. *Financial support:* In 2011–12, 188 students received support, including 23 fellowships with full tuition reimbursements available (averaging $16,022 per year), 85 research assistantships with full tuition reimbursements available (averaging $16,022 per year), 73 teaching assistantships with full tuition reimbursements available (averaging $16,022 per year); career-related internships or fieldwork, Federal Work-Study, and institutionally sponsored loans also available. Financial award application deadline: 2/15. *Faculty research:* Materials and biomaterials networks and sensors, transportation, energy. *Total annual research expenditures:* $20.9 million. *Unit head:* Dr. Charles Karr, Dean, 205-348-6405, Fax: 205-348-8573. *Application contact:* Dr. David A. Francko, Dean, 205-348-8280, Fax: 205-348-0400, E-mail: dfrancko@ua.edu. Web site: http://coeweb.eng.ua.edu/.

The University of Alabama at Birmingham, School of Engineering, Birmingham, AL 35294. Offers M Eng, MS Mt E, MSBME, MSCE, MSEE, MSME, PhD. Evening/weekend programs available. *Degree requirements:* For doctorate, thesis/dissertation. *Entrance requirements:* For master's, GRE General Test. *Application deadline:* Applications are processed on a rolling basis. Electronic applications accepted. *Expenses:* Tuition, state resident: full-time $5922; part-time $309 per hour. Tuition, nonresident: full-time $13,428; part-time $726 per hour. Tuition and fees vary according to program. *Financial support:* Fellowships with full tuition reimbursements, research assistantships with full tuition reimbursements, career-related internships or fieldwork, Federal Work-Study, institutionally sponsored loans, and tuition waivers (full and partial) available. Support available to part-time students. *Unit head:* Dr. Melinda Lalor, Dean, 205-934-8410, Fax: 205-934-8437, E-mail: mlalor@uab.edu. Web site: http://www.eng.uab.edu/.

The University of Alabama in Huntsville, School of Graduate Studies, College of Engineering, Huntsville, AL 35899. Offers MS, MSE, MSOR, MSSE, PhD. Part-time and evening/weekend programs available. Postbaccalaureate distance learning degree programs offered (minimal on-campus study). *Faculty:* 61 full-time (6 women), 14 part-time/adjunct (1 woman). *Students:* 155 full-time (35 women), 422 part-time (87 women); includes 66 minority (28 Black or African American, non-Hispanic/Latino; 6 American Indian or Alaska Native, non-Hispanic/Latino; 20 Asian, non-Hispanic/Latino; 9 Hispanic/Latino; 3 Two or more races, non-Hispanic/Latino; 75 international. Average age 31. 416 applicants, 62% accepted, 143 enrolled. In 2011, 97 master's, 14 doctorates awarded. *Degree requirements:* For master's, comprehensive exam, thesis or alternative, oral and written exams; for doctorate, comprehensive exam, thesis/dissertation, oral and written exams. *Entrance requirements:* For master's and doctorate, GRE General Test, minimum GPA of 3.0. Additional exam requirements/recommendations for international students: Required—TOEFL (minimum score 500 paper-based; 173 computer-based; 62 iBT). *Application deadline:* For fall admission, 7/15 for domestic students, 4/1 for international students; for spring admission, 11/30 for domestic students, 9/1 for international students. Applications are processed on a rolling basis. Application fee: $40 ($50 for international students). Electronic applications accepted. *Expenses:* Tuition, state resident: full-time $7830; part-time $473.50 per credit. Tuition, nonresident: full-time $18,748; part-time $1128.33 per credit. Tuition and fees vary according to course load and program. *Financial support:* In 2011–12, 106 students received support, including 2 fellowships with full and partial tuition

reimbursements available (averaging $11,154 per year), 54 research assistantships with full and partial tuition reimbursements available (averaging $12,159 per year), 53 teaching assistantships with full and partial tuition reimbursements available (averaging $11,495 per year); career-related internships or fieldwork, Federal Work-Study, institutionally sponsored loans, scholarships/grants, health care benefits, tuition waivers, and unspecified assistantships also available. Support available to part-time students. Financial award application deadline: 4/1; financial award applicants required to submit FAFSA. *Faculty research:* Propulsion, missile systems, automation, robotics, plasma. *Total annual research expenditures:* $46.1 million. *Unit head:* Dr. Shankar Mahalingam, Dean, 256-824-6474, Fax: 256-824-6843, E-mail: shankar.mahalingam@uah.edu. *Application contact:* Kim Gray, Graduate Studies Admissions Coordinator, 256-824-6002, Fax: 256-824-6405, E-mail: deangrad@uah.edu. Web site: http://uahweb.uah.edu/eng/welcome.

University of Alaska Anchorage, School of Engineering, Anchorage, AK 99508. Offers M AEST, MCE, MS, Certificate. Part-time and evening/weekend programs available. *Degree requirements:* For master's, comprehensive exam (for some programs), thesis (for some programs). *Entrance requirements:* For master's, GRE General Test. Additional exam requirements/recommendations for international students: Required—TOEFL (minimum score 550 paper-based; 213 computer-based).

University of Alaska Fairbanks, College of Engineering and Mines, Department of Civil and Environmental Engineering, Program in Environmental Engineering, Fairbanks, AK 99775-5900. Offers engineering (PhD), including environmental engineering; environmental engineering (MS), including environmental contaminants, environmental science and management, water supply and waste treatment. Part-time programs available. *Students:* 3 full-time (0 women), 1 (woman) part-time. Average age 26. 5 applicants, 60% accepted, 1 enrolled. In 2011, 2 degrees awarded. *Degree requirements:* For master's, comprehensive exam, thesis or alternative; for doctorate, comprehensive exam, thesis/dissertation, oral exam, oral defense. *Entrance requirements:* For master's, basic computer techniques; for doctorate, GRE General Test. Additional exam requirements/recommendations for international students: Required—TOEFL (minimum score 575 paper-based; 213 computer-based). *Application deadline:* For fall admission, 6/1 for domestic students, 3/1 for international students; for spring admission, 10/15 for domestic students, 9/1 for international students. Applications are processed on a rolling basis. Application fee: $60. Electronic applications accepted. *Expenses:* Tuition, state resident: full-time $6696; part-time $372 per credit. Tuition, nonresident: full-time $13,680; part-time $760 per credit. Tuition and fees vary according to course load and reciprocity agreements. *Financial support:* In 2011–12, 1 research assistantship (averaging $16,834 per year), 2 teaching assistantships (averaging $6,390 per year) were awarded; fellowships, career-related internships or fieldwork, Federal Work-Study, scholarships/grants, health care benefits, and unspecified assistantships also available. Support available to part-time students. Financial award application deadline: 7/1; financial award applicants required to submit FAFSA. *Unit head:* Dr. David Barnes, Department Chair, 907-474-7241, Fax: 907-474-6087, E-mail: fyeqe@uaf.edu. *Application contact:* Mike Earnest, Director of Admissions, 907-474-7500, Fax: 907-474-5379, E-mail: admissions@uaf.edu. Web site: http://www.alaska.edu/uaf/cem/cee/env/.

University of Alaska Fairbanks, College of Engineering and Mines, Department of Electrical and Computer Engineering, Fairbanks, AK 99775-5915. Offers electrical engineering (MEE, MS, PhD); engineering (PhD). Part-time programs available. *Faculty:* 9 full-time (2 women). *Students:* 17 full-time (4 women), 8 international. Average age 24.

21 applicants, 29% accepted, 5 enrolled. In 2011, 4 master's awarded. Terminal master's awarded for partial completion of doctoral program. *Degree requirements:* For master's, comprehensive exam, thesis or alternative; for doctorate, comprehensive exam, thesis/dissertation, oral exam, oral defense. *Entrance requirements:* For master's and doctorate, GRE General Test. Additional exam requirements/recommendations for international students: Required—TOEFL (minimum score 550 paper-based; 213 computer-based; 80 iBT). *Application deadline:* For fall admission, 6/1 for domestic students, 3/1 for international students; for spring admission, 10/15 for domestic students, 9/1 for international students. Applications are processed on a rolling basis. Application fee: $60. Electronic applications accepted. *Expenses:* Tuition, state resident: full-time $6696; part-time $372 per credit. Tuition, nonresident: full-time $13,680; part-time $760 per credit. Tuition and fees vary according to course load and reciprocity agreements. *Financial support:* In 2011–12, 11 research assistantships with tuition reimbursements (averaging $12,733 per year), 7 teaching assistantships with tuition reimbursements (averaging $5,216 per year) were awarded; fellowships with tuition reimbursements, career-related internships or fieldwork, Federal Work-Study, scholarships/grants, health care benefits, and unspecified assistantships also available. Support available to part-time students. Financial award application deadline: 7/1; financial award applicants required to submit FAFSA. *Faculty research:* Geomagnetically-induced currents in power lines, electromagnetic wave propagation, laser radar systems, bioinformatics, distributed sensor networks. *Unit head:* Dr. Charles Mayer, Chair, 907-474-7137, Fax: 907-474-5135, E-mail: fyee@uaf.edu. *Application contact:* Mike Earnest, Director of Admissions, 907-474-7500, Fax: 907-474-5379, E-mail: admissions@uaf.edu. Web site: http://cem.uaf.edu/ece/.

University of Alaska Fairbanks, College of Engineering and Mines, Department of Mechanical Engineering, Fairbanks, AK 99775-5905. Offers engineering (PhD); mechanical engineering (MS). Part-time programs available. *Faculty:* 7 full-time (0 women). *Students:* 14 full-time (4 women), 4 part-time (1 woman); includes 4 minority (1 Black or African American, non-Hispanic/Latino; 2 Asian, non-Hispanic/Latino; 1 Two or more races, non-Hispanic/Latino), 6 international. Average age 28. 16 applicants, 19% accepted, 3 enrolled. In 2011, 6 degrees awarded. Terminal master's awarded for partial completion of doctoral program. *Degree requirements:* For master's, comprehensive exam, thesis or alternative; for doctorate, comprehensive exam, thesis/dissertation, oral exam, oral defense. *Entrance requirements:* For master's and doctorate, GRE General Test. Additional exam requirements/recommendations for international students: Required—TOEFL (minimum score 550 paper-based; 213 computer-based; 80 iBT). *Application deadline:* For fall admission, 6/1 for domestic students, 3/1 for international students; for spring admission, 10/15 for domestic students, 9/1 for international students. Applications are processed on a rolling basis. Application fee: $60. Electronic applications accepted. *Expenses:* Tuition, state resident: full-time $6696; part-time $372 per credit. Tuition, nonresident: full-time $13,680; part-time $760 per credit. Tuition and fees vary according to course load and reciprocity agreements. *Financial support:* In 2011–12, 6 research assistantships with tuition reimbursements (averaging $14,327 per year), 5 teaching assistantships with tuition reimbursements (averaging $7,302 per year) were awarded; fellowships with tuition reimbursements, career-related internships or fieldwork, Federal Work-Study, scholarships/grants, health care benefits, and unspecified assistantships also available. Support available to part-time students. Financial award application deadline: 7/1; financial award applicants required to submit FAFSA. *Faculty research:* Cold regions engineering, fluid mechanics, heat transfer, energy systems, indoor air quality. *Unit head:* Dr. Jonah Lee, Department Chair, 907-474-7136, Fax: 907-474-6141, E-mail: fymech@uaf.edu. *Application contact:* Mike Earnest, Director of Admissions, 907-474-7500, Fax: 907-474-5379, E-mail: admissions@uaf.edu. Web site: http://cem.uaf.edu/me/.

The University of Arizona, College of Engineering, Tucson, AZ 85721. Offers M Eng, ME, MS, PhD, Certificate. Part-time programs available. Postbaccalaureate distance learning degree programs offered (no on-campus study). *Faculty:* 92 full-time (8 women), 15 part-time/adjunct (5 women). *Students:* 426 full-time (89 women), 126 part-time (17 women); includes 86 minority (9 Black or African American, non-Hispanic/Latino; 13 Asian, non-Hispanic/Latino; 36 Hispanic/Latino; 28 Two or more races, non-Hispanic/Latino), 288 international. Average age 30. 1,110 applicants, 36% accepted, 109 enrolled. In 2011, 110 master's, 48 doctorates awarded. *Degree requirements:* For doctorate, thesis/dissertation. *Entrance requirements:* Additional exam requirements/recommendations for international students: Required—TOEFL (minimum score 550 paper-based; 213 computer-based; 79 iBT). Application fee: $75. *Expenses:* Tuition, state resident: full-time $10,840. Tuition, nonresident: full-time $25,802. *Financial support:* In 2011–12, 238 research assistantships with full tuition reimbursements (averaging $23,836 per year), 69 teaching assistantships with full tuition reimbursements (averaging $23,586 per year) were awarded; institutionally sponsored loans, scholarships/grants, health care benefits, and unspecified assistantships also available. *Total annual research expenditures:* $26.7 million. *Unit head:* Dr. Jeff Goldberg, Dean, 520-621-6594, Fax: 520-621-2232, E-mail: twp@engr.arizona.edu. *Application contact:* General Information Contact, 520-621-3471, Fax: 520-621-7112, E-mail: gradadm@grad.arizona.edu. Web site: http://www.engineering.arizona.edu/.

University of Arkansas, Graduate School, College of Engineering, Fayetteville, AR 72701-1201. Offers MS, MS Cmp E, MS Ch E, MS En E, MS Tc E, MSBE, MSBME, MSCE, MSE, MSEE, MSIE, MSME, MSOR, MSTE, PhD. *Students:* 154 full-time (41 women), 657 part-time (144 women); includes 128 minority (71 Black or African American, non-Hispanic/Latino; 8 American Indian or Alaska Native, non-Hispanic/Latino; 17 Asian, non-Hispanic/Latino; 18 Hispanic/Latino; 1 Native Hawaiian or other Pacific Islander, non-Hispanic/Latino; 13 Two or more races, non-Hispanic/Latino), 181 international. In 2011, 251 master's, 10 doctorates awarded. *Degree requirements:* For doctorate, one foreign language, thesis/dissertation. *Application deadline:* For fall admission, 4/1 for international students; for spring admission, 10/1 for international students. Applications are processed on a rolling basis. Application fee: $40 ($50 for international students). Electronic applications accepted. *Financial support:* In 2011–12, 198 research assistantships, 21 teaching assistantships were awarded; fellowships with tuition reimbursements, career-related internships or fieldwork, and Federal Work-Study also available. Support available to part-time students. Financial award application deadline: 4/1; financial award applicants required to submit FAFSA. *Unit head:* Ashok Saxena, Dean, 479-575-4153, Fax: 479-575-4346, E-mail: asaxena@uark.edu. *Application contact:* Dr. Terry Martin, Associate Dean for Academic Affairs, 479-575-3052, E-mail: tmartin@uark.edu. Web site: http://www.engr.uark.edu/.

University of Bridgeport, School of Engineering, Bridgeport, CT 06604. Offers MS, PhD. Part-time and evening/weekend programs available. Postbaccalaureate distance learning degree programs offered (no on-campus study). *Faculty:* 19 full-time (5 women), 26 part-time/adjunct (2 women). *Students:* 437 full-time (111 women), 233 part-time (44 women); includes 36 minority (7 Black or African American, non-Hispanic/Latino; 16 Asian, non-Hispanic/Latino; 7 Hispanic/Latino; 6 Two or more races, non-Hispanic/Latino), 604 international. Average age 27. 1,612 applicants, 67% accepted, 102 enrolled. In 2011, 393 master's, 1 doctorate awarded. *Degree requirements:* For

master's, thesis optional; for doctorate, thesis/dissertation. *Entrance requirements:* Additional exam requirements/recommendations for international students: Recommended—TOEFL (minimum score 550 paper-based; 213 computer-based; 80 iBT), IELTS (minimum score 6.5). *Application deadline:* For fall admission, 8/1 priority date for domestic students, 8/1 for international students; for spring admission, 12/1 priority date for domestic students, 12/1 for international students. Applications are processed on a rolling basis. Application fee: $50. Electronic applications accepted. *Expenses:* Contact institution. *Financial support:* In 2011–12, 106 students received support. Fellowships, research assistantships, teaching assistantships, career-related internships or fieldwork, Federal Work-Study, institutionally sponsored loans, and tuition waivers (partial) available. Support available to part-time students. Financial award application deadline: 6/1; financial award applicants required to submit FAFSA. *Faculty research:* Atmospheric chemistry, minicomputers, heat transfer. *Unit head:* Dr. Tarek M. Sobh, Vice President for Graduate Studies and Research/Dean, School of Engineering, 203-576-4111, Fax: 203-576-4766, E-mail: sobh@bridgeport.edu. *Application contact:* Karissa Peckham, Vice President of Enrollment Management, 203-576-4552, Fax: 203-576-4941, E-mail: admit@bridgeport.edu.

The University of British Columbia, Faculty of Applied Science, Vancouver, BC V6T 1Z1, Canada. Offers M Arch, M Eng, M Sc, MA Sc, MASA, MASLA, MLA, MSN, MSS, PhD. Part-time programs available. *Degree requirements:* For master's, comprehensive exam (for some programs), thesis (for some programs); for doctorate, comprehensive exam, thesis/dissertation. *Entrance requirements:* Additional exam requirements/recommendations for international students: Required—TOEFL (minimum score 550 paper-based; 213 computer-based). Electronic applications accepted. *Faculty research:* Architecture, nursing, engineering, landscape architecture.

University of Calgary, Faculty of Graduate Studies, Schulich School of Engineering, Calgary, AB T2N 1N4, Canada. Offers M Eng, M Sc, MPM, PhD. Part-time and evening/weekend programs available. *Degree requirements:* For doctorate, comprehensive exam, thesis/dissertation, candidacy exam. *Entrance requirements:* For master's, minimum GPA of 3.0; for doctorate, minimum GPA of 3.5. Additional exam requirements/recommendations for international students: Required—TOEFL, IELTS. *Faculty research:* Chemical and petroleum engineering, civil engineering, electrical and computer engineering, geomatics engineering, mechanical engineering and computer-integrated manufacturing.

University of California, Berkeley, Graduate Division, College of Engineering, Berkeley, CA 94720-1500. Offers M Eng, MS, D Eng, PhD, M Arch/MS, MCP/MS, MPP/MS. *Degree requirements:* For doctorate, thesis/dissertation, exam. *Entrance requirements:* For master's and doctorate, GRE General Test, minimum GPA of 3.0, 3 letters of recommendation.

University of California, Berkeley, UC Berkeley Extension, Certificate Programs in Engineering, Construction and Facilities Management, Berkeley, CA 94720-1500. Offers construction management (Certificate); HVAC (Certificate); integrated circuit design and techniques (online) (Certificate). Postbaccalaureate distance learning degree programs offered.

University of California, Davis, College of Engineering, Davis, CA 95616. Offers M Engr, MS, D Engr, PhD, Certificate, M Engr/MBA. Part-time programs available. Terminal master's awarded for partial completion of doctoral program. *Degree requirements:* For master's, comprehensive exam (for some programs), thesis (for some programs); for doctorate, comprehensive exam, thesis/dissertation. *Entrance requirements:* For doctorate, GRE. Additional exam requirements/recommendations for international students: Required—TOEFL (minimum score 550 paper-based; 213 computer-based). Electronic applications accepted.

University of California, Irvine, School of Engineering, Irvine, CA 92697. Offers MS, PhD. Part-time programs available. *Students:* 740 full-time (173 women), 59 part-time (13 women); includes 179 minority (2 Black or African American, non-Hispanic/Latino; 3 American Indian or Alaska Native, non-Hispanic/Latino; 140 Asian, non-Hispanic/Latino; 25 Hispanic/Latino; 1 Native Hawaiian or other Pacific Islander, non-Hispanic/Latino; 8 Two or more races, non-Hispanic/Latino), 434 international. Average age 27. 2,849 applicants, 24% accepted, 267 enrolled. In 2011, 153 master's, 80 doctorates awarded. Terminal master's awarded for partial completion of doctoral program. *Degree requirements:* For doctorate, thesis/dissertation. *Entrance requirements:* For master's and doctorate, GRE General Test, minimum GPA of 3.0, 3 letters of recommendation. Additional exam requirements/recommendations for international students: Required—TOEFL (minimum score 550 paper-based; 213 computer-based). *Application deadline:* For fall admission, 1/15 priority date for domestic students, 1/15 for international students. Applications are processed on a rolling basis. Application fee: $80 ($100 for international students). Electronic applications accepted. *Financial support:* Fellowships with tuition reimbursements, research assistantships with full tuition reimbursements, teaching assistantships with tuition reimbursements, institutionally sponsored loans, traineeships, health care benefits, and unspecified assistantships available. Financial award application deadline: 3/1; financial award applicants required to submit FAFSA. *Faculty research:* Biomedical, chemical and biochemical, civil and environmental, electrical and computer, and mechanical and aerospace engineering. *Unit head:* Dr. Gregory Washington, Dean, 949-824-6002, Fax: 949-824-8200, E-mail: engineeringdean@uci.edu. *Application contact:* Prof. John C. LaRue, Associate Dean, 949-824-6737, Fax: 949-824-8585, E-mail: jclarue@uci.edu. Web site: http://www.eng.uci.edu/.

University of California, Los Angeles, Graduate Division, Henry Samueli School of Engineering and Applied Science, Los Angeles, CA 90095-1601. Offers MS, PhD, MBA/MS. Evening/weekend programs available. Postbaccalaureate distance learning degree programs offered (no on-campus study). *Faculty:* 154 full-time (21 women), 24 part-time/adjunct (0 women). *Students:* 1,845 full-time (368 women); includes 560 minority (27 Black or African American, non-Hispanic/Latino; 1 American Indian or Alaska Native, non-Hispanic/Latino; 423 Asian, non-Hispanic/Latino; 86 Hispanic/Latino; 2 Native Hawaiian or other Pacific Islander, non-Hispanic/Latino; 21 Two or more races, non-Hispanic/Latino), 799 international. 4,756 applicants, 31% accepted, 649 enrolled. In 2011, 441 master's, 134 doctorates awarded. Terminal master's awarded for partial completion of doctoral program. *Degree requirements:* For master's, comprehensive exam or thesis; for doctorate, thesis/dissertation, qualifying exams. *Entrance requirements:* For master's, GRE General Test, minimum GPA of 3.0; for doctorate, GRE General Test, minimum GPA of 3.25. Additional exam requirements/recommendations for international students: Required—TOEFL (minimum score 560 paper-based; 220 computer-based; 87 iBT). *Application deadline:* For fall admission, 12/1 for domestic and international students. Application fee: $80 ($100 for international students). Electronic applications accepted. *Financial support:* In 2011–12, 546 fellowships, 1,954 research assistantships, 504 teaching assistantships were awarded; career-related internships or fieldwork, Federal Work-Study, institutionally sponsored loans, and tuition waivers (full and partial) also available. Financial award application deadline: 3/2; financial award applicants required to submit FAFSA. *Total annual* *research expenditures:* $100.5 million. *Unit head:* Dr. Richard D. Wesel, Associate Dean, Academic and Student Affairs, 310-825-2942. *Application contact:* Jan LaBuda, Director, Office of Academic and Student Affairs, 310-825-2514, Fax: 310-825-2473, E-mail: jan@ea.ucla.edu. Web site: http://www.engineer.ucla.edu/.

University of California, Merced, Division of Graduate Studies, School of Engineering, Merced, CA 95343. Offers electrical engineering and computer science (MS, PhD). *Unit head:* Dr. Samuel J. Traina, Dean, 209-228-4723, Fax: 209-228-6906, E-mail: grad.dean@ucmerced.edu. *Application contact:* Tsu Ya, Graduate Admissions and Academic Services Manager, 209-228-4723, Fax: 209-228-6906, E-mail: tya@ucmerced.edu.

University of California, Santa Barbara, Graduate Division, College of Engineering, Santa Barbara, CA 93106-5130. Offers MS, PhD, MS/PhD. *Faculty:* 144 full-time (15 women), 20 part-time/adjunct (3 women). *Students:* 715 full-time (142 women); includes 93 minority (3 Black or African American, non-Hispanic/Latino; 3 American Indian or Alaska Native, non-Hispanic/Latino; 66 Asian, non-Hispanic/Latino; 17 Hispanic/Latino; 1 Native Hawaiian or other Pacific Islander, non-Hispanic/Latino; 3 Two or more races, non-Hispanic/Latino), 330 international. Average age 26. 2,816 applicants, 23% accepted, 210 enrolled. In 2011, 89 master's, 70 doctorates awarded. Terminal master's awarded for partial completion of doctoral program. *Degree requirements:* For doctorate, thesis/dissertation. *Entrance requirements:* For master's, GRE, 3 letters of recommendation, resume/curriculum vitae; for doctorate, GRE, 3 letters of recommendation, statement of purpose, personal achievements/contributions statement, resume/curriculum vitae, transcripts for post-secondary institutions attended. Additional exam requirements/recommendations for international students: Required—TOEFL, IELTS. Application fee: $80 ($100 for international students). Electronic applications accepted. *Expenses:* Tuition, state resident: full-time $12,192. Tuition, nonresident: full-time $27,294. *Required fees:* $764.13. *Financial support:* In 2011–12, 469 students received support, including 199 fellowships with full and partial tuition reimbursements available (averaging $13,763 per year), 384 research assistantships with full and partial tuition reimbursements available (averaging $18,431 per year), 183 teaching assistantships with partial tuition reimbursements available (averaging $10,262 per year); career-related internships or fieldwork, Federal Work-Study, institutionally sponsored loans, scholarships/grants, traineeships, health care benefits, tuition waivers (full and partial), and unspecified assistantships also available. Financial award applicants required to submit FAFSA. *Unit head:* Dr. Rod C. Alferness, Dean, 805-893-3141, E-mail: alferness@engineering.ucsb.edu. *Application contact:* 805-893-3207, E-mail: engrdean@engineering.ucsb.edu. Web site: http://www.engineering.ucsb.edu/.

University of California, Santa Cruz, Division of Graduate Studies, Jack Baskin School of Engineering, Santa Cruz, CA 95064. Offers MS, PhD. *Entrance requirements:* For master's and doctorate, GRE General Test. Additional exam requirements/recommendations for international students: Required—TOEFL (minimum score 570 paper-based; 230 computer-based; 89 iBT); Recommended—IELTS (minimum score 8). Electronic applications accepted.

University of Central Florida, College of Engineering and Computer Science, Orlando, FL 32816. Offers MS, MS Cp E, MS Env E, MSAE, MSCE, MSEE, MSIE, MSME, MSMSE, PSM, PhD, Certificate. Part-time and evening/weekend programs available. *Faculty:* 121 full-time (15 women), 35 part-time/adjunct (4 women). *Students:* 691 full-time (147 women), 635 part-time (132 women); includes 293 minority (63 Black or African American, non-Hispanic/Latino; 2 American Indian or Alaska Native, non-Hispanic/Latino; 70 Asian, non-Hispanic/Latino; 140 Hispanic/Latino; 1 Native Hawaiian or other Pacific Islander, non-Hispanic/Latino; 17 Two or more races, non-Hispanic/Latino), 392 international. Average age 30. 1,259 applicants, 74% accepted, 374 enrolled. In 2011, 326 master's, 60 doctorates, 40 other advanced degrees awarded. *Degree requirements:* For doctorate, thesis/dissertation, candidacy exam, departmental qualifying exam. *Entrance requirements:* For master's, GRE General Test, minimum GPA of 3.0 in last 60 hours; for doctorate, minimum GPA of 3.5 in last 60 hours, resume. Additional exam requirements/recommendations for international students: Required—TOEFL. *Application deadline:* For fall admission, 7/15 for domestic students; for spring admission, 12/1 for domestic students. Application fee: $30. Electronic applications accepted. *Expenses:* Tuition, state resident: part-time $277.08 per credit hour. Tuition, nonresident: part-time $277.08 per credit hour. Part-time tuition and fees vary according to degree level and program. *Financial support:* In 2011–12, 319 students received support, including 92 fellowships with partial tuition reimbursements available (averaging $6,100 per year), 202 research assistantships with partial tuition reimbursements available (averaging $10,200 per year), 130 teaching assistantships with partial tuition reimbursements available (averaging $9,800 per year); career-related internships or fieldwork, Federal Work-Study, institutionally sponsored loans, tuition waivers (partial), and unspecified assistantships also available. Financial award application deadline: 3/1; financial award applicants required to submit FAFSA. *Faculty research:* Electro-optics, lasers, materials, simulation, microelectronics. *Unit head:* Dr. Marwan Simaan, Dean, 407-823-2156, E-mail: simaan@eecs.ucf.edu. *Application contact:* Barbara Rodriguez, Director, Admissions and Registration, 407-823-2766, Fax: 407-823-6442, E-mail: gradadmissions@ucf.edu. Web site: http://www.cecs.ucf.edu/.

University of Central Oklahoma, College of Graduate Studies and Research, College of Mathematics and Science, Department of Engineering and Physics, Edmond, OK 73034-5209. Offers MS. Part-time programs available. *Faculty:* 6 full-time (0 women), 3 part-time/adjunct (0 women). *Students:* 5 full-time (0 women), 9 part-time (3 women); includes 2 minority (1 American Indian or Alaska Native, non-Hispanic/Latino; 1 Asian, non-Hispanic/Latino), 7 international. Average age 27. In 2011, 4 master's awarded. *Degree requirements:* For master's, thesis optional. *Entrance requirements:* For master's, GRE, 24 hours of course work in physics, minimum GPA of 2.75 overall and 3.0 in last 60 hours attempted. Additional exam requirements/recommendations for international students: Required—TOEFL (minimum score 550 paper-based; 213 computer-based). *Application deadline:* Applications are processed on a rolling basis. Application fee: $50. Electronic applications accepted. *Expenses:* Tuition, state resident: full-time $3901; part-time $218.30 per credit hour. Tuition, nonresident: full-time $9198; part-time $511.20 per credit hour. Tuition and fees vary according to program. *Financial support:* Unspecified assistantships available. Financial award application deadline: 3/31; financial award applicants required to submit FAFSA. *Faculty research:* Laser tissue interactions for soft and hard tissues, microfluidics, quantum optics, design of scaffold for tissue engineering applications, micro and nano devices and sensors. *Unit head:* Dr. Baha Jassemnejad, Chairperson, 405-974-5461, Fax: 405-974-3812, E-mail: bjassemnejad@uco.edu. *Application contact:* Dr. Richard Bernard, Dean, Graduate College, 405-974-3493, Fax: 405-974-3852, E-mail: gradcoll@uco.edu. Web site: http://www.uco.edu/cms/engineering/Graduate%20Programs/index.asp.

University of Cincinnati, Graduate School, College of Engineering and Applied Science, Cincinnati, OH 45221. Offers MS, PhD, MBA/MS. *Accreditation:* ABET (one or more programs are accredited). Part-time and evening/weekend programs available. Terminal master's awarded for partial completion of doctoral program. *Degree requirements:* For master's, thesis or alternative; for doctorate, comprehensive exam, thesis/dissertation. *Entrance requirements:* For master's and doctorate, GRE General Test. Additional exam requirements/recommendations for international students: Required—TOEFL (minimum score 520 paper-based; 190 computer-based).

University of Colorado at Colorado Springs, College of Engineering and Applied Science, Colorado Springs, CO 80933-7150. Offers ME, MS, PhD. Part-time and evening/weekend programs available. *Faculty:* 29 full-time (5 women), 1 part-time/adjunct (0 women). *Students:* 180 full-time (33 women), 93 part-time (12 women); includes 38 minority (6 Black or African American, non-Hispanic/Latino; 14 Asian, non-Hispanic/Latino; 15 Hispanic/Latino; 3 Two or more races, non-Hispanic/Latino), 41 international. Average age 33. 159 applicants, 67% accepted, 55 enrolled. In 2011, 30 master's, 3 doctorates awarded. *Degree requirements:* For doctorate, comprehensive exam, thesis/dissertation. *Entrance requirements:* For master's, GRE General Test, minimum GPA of 3.0; for doctorate, GRE General Test, minimum GPA of 3.3. Additional exam requirements/recommendations for international students: Required—TOEFL (minimum score 550 paper-based; 213 computer-based). *Application deadline:* For fall admission, 6/15 for domestic students, 4/1 for international students; for spring admission, 10/1 for domestic and international students. Applications are processed on a rolling basis. Application fee: $60 ($75 for international students). *Expenses:* Contact institution. *Financial support:* In 2011–12, 14 students received support. Fellowships, research assistantships, teaching assistantships, career-related internships or fieldwork, Federal Work-Study, and scholarships/grants available. Support available to part-time students. Financial award application deadline: 3/1; financial award applicants required to submit FAFSA. *Faculty research:* Ferroelectronics, electronics communication, computer-aided design, electromagnetics. *Total annual research expenditures:* $1.6 million. *Unit head:* Dr. Ramaswami Dandapani, Dean, 719-255-3543, Fax: 719-255-3542, E-mail: rdan@cas.uccs.edu. *Application contact:* Tina Moore, Director, Office of Student Support, 719-255-3347, E-mail: tmoore@uccs.edu. Web site: http://eas.uccs.edu/.

University of Colorado Boulder, Graduate School, College of Engineering and Applied Science, Boulder, CO 80309. Offers ME, MS, PhD, JD/MS, MBA/MS. *Faculty:* 169 full-time (33 women). *Students:* 1,207 full-time (278 women), 422 part-time (101 women); includes 161 minority (14 Black or African American, non-Hispanic/Latino; 9 American Indian or Alaska Native, non-Hispanic/Latino; 75 Asian, non-Hispanic/Latino; 52 Hispanic/Latino; 11 Two or more races, non-Hispanic/Latino), 464 international. Average age 28. 2,707 applicants, 43% accepted, 373 enrolled. In 2011, 451 master's, 86 doctorates awarded. *Degree requirements:* For doctorate, thesis/dissertation. *Entrance requirements:* For master's, minimum undergraduate GPA of 2.75. Application fee: $50 ($60 for international students). Electronic applications accepted. *Expenses:* Contact institution. *Financial support:* In 2011–12, 923 students received support, including 427 fellowships (averaging $10,159 per year), 390 research assistantships with full and partial tuition reimbursements available (averaging $22,732 per year), 124 teaching assistantships with full and partial tuition reimbursements available (averaging $17,066 per year); institutionally sponsored loans, scholarships/grants, health care benefits, and unspecified assistantships also available. Financial award applicants required to submit FAFSA. *Total annual research expenditures:* $61.3 million. *Application contact:* E-mail: gradinfo@colorado.edu. Web site: http://www.colorado.edu/engineering/.

University of Colorado Denver, College of Engineering and Applied Science, Denver, CO 80217. Offers M Eng, MS, EASPh D, PhD. Part-time and evening/weekend programs available. *Faculty:* 44 full-time (5 women), 13 part-time/adjunct (3 women). *Students:* 272 full-time (71 women), 167 part-time (38 women); includes 71 minority (24 Black or African American, non-Hispanic/Latino; 25 Asian, non-Hispanic/Latino; 19 Hispanic/Latino; 3 Two or more races, non-Hispanic/Latino), 136 international. Average age 32. 347 applicants, 63% accepted, 108 enrolled. In 2011, 110 master's, 2 doctorates awarded. *Degree requirements:* For doctorate, comprehensive exam, thesis/dissertation. *Entrance requirements:* For master's, GRE, minimum undergraduate GPA of 2.75; for doctorate, GRE, minimum cumulative GPA of 3.0. Additional exam requirements/recommendations for international students: Required—TOEFL (minimum score 550 paper-based; 213 computer-based; 79 iBT). Application fee: $50 ($75 for international students). Electronic applications accepted. *Expenses:* Contact institution. *Financial support:* In 2011–12, 41 students received support. Research assistantships, teaching assistantships, Federal Work-Study, and scholarships/grants available. Financial award application deadline: 4/1; financial award applicants required to submit FAFSA. *Faculty research:* Civil engineering, bioengineering, mechanical engineering, electrical engineering, computer science. *Total annual research expenditures:* $2.3 million. *Unit head:* Dr. Paul Rakowski, Assistant Dean of Student Affairs, 303-556-6771, Fax: 303-556-2511, E-mail: paul.rakowski@ucdenver.edu. *Application contact:* Graduate School Admissions, 303-556-2704, E-mail: admissions@ucdenver.edu. Web site: http://www.ucdenver.edu/academics/colleges/Engineering/Pages/EngineeringAppliedScience.aspx.

University of Connecticut, Graduate School, School of Engineering, Storrs, CT 06269. Offers M Eng, MS, PhD. Terminal master's awarded for partial completion of doctoral program. *Degree requirements:* For master's, comprehensive exam; for doctorate, thesis/dissertation. *Entrance requirements:* For master's and doctorate, GRE General Test. Additional exam requirements/recommendations for international students: Required—TOEFL (minimum score 550 paper-based; 213 computer-based). Electronic applications accepted.

University of Delaware, College of Engineering, Newark, DE 19716. Offers M Ch E, MAS, MCE, MEM, MMSE, MS, MSECE, MSME, PhD. Part-time and evening/weekend programs available. Postbaccalaureate distance learning degree programs offered (minimal on-campus study). Terminal master's awarded for partial completion of doctoral program. *Degree requirements:* For master's, thesis (for some programs); for doctorate, thesis/dissertation. *Entrance requirements:* For master's and doctorate, GRE General Test. Additional exam requirements/recommendations for international students: Required—TOEFL (minimum score 550 paper-based; 213 computer-based). Electronic applications accepted. *Faculty research:* Biotechnology, photonics, transportation, composite materials, materials science.

University of Denver, School of Engineering and Computer Science, Denver, CO 80208. Offers MS, PhD. *Faculty:* 31 full-time (4 women), 10 part-time/adjunct (3 women). *Students:* 8 full-time (3 women), 213 part-time (36 women); includes 25 minority (1 Black or African American, non-Hispanic/Latino; 11 Asian, non-Hispanic/Latino; 11 Hispanic/Latino; 2 Two or more races, non-Hispanic/Latino), 56 international. Average age 30. 282 applicants, 73% accepted, 69 enrolled. In 2011, 71 master's, 5 doctorates awarded. *Median time to degree:* Of those who began their doctoral program in fall 2003, 100% received their degree in 8 years or less. *Degree requirements:* For master's, thesis (for some programs); for doctorate, variable foreign language requirement, comprehensive exam, thesis/dissertation. *Entrance requirements:* For master's and doctorate, GRE General Test, three letters of recommendation, essay/personal statement. Additional exam requirements/recommendations for international students: Required—TOEFL (minimum score 550 paper-based; 80 iBT). *Application deadline:* Applications are processed on a rolling basis. Application fee: $60. Electronic applications accepted. *Financial support:* In 2011–12, 113 students received support, including 23 research assistantships with full and partial tuition reimbursements available (averaging $16,323 per year), 26 teaching assistantships with full and partial tuition reimbursements available (averaging $15,014 per year); Federal Work-Study, health care benefits, and unspecified assistantships also available. Financial award application deadline: 2/5; financial award applicants required to submit FAFSA. *Unit head:* Dr. Michael Keables, Interim Dean, 303-871-2621, Fax: 303-871-2716, E-mail: mkeables@du.edu. *Application contact:* Information Request, 303-871-2716, E-mail: secs@du.edu. Web site: http://secs.du.edu.

University of Detroit Mercy, College of Engineering and Science, Detroit, MI 48221. Offers M Eng Mgt, MATM, ME, MS, MSCS, DE. Part-time and evening/weekend programs available. *Degree requirements:* For doctorate, thesis/dissertation. *Expenses:* Contact institution.

University of Evansville, College of Engineering and Computer Science, Evansville, IN 47722. Offers MS. Part-time programs available. *Degree requirements:* For master's, thesis. *Entrance requirements:* For master's, GRE, minimum undergraduate GPA of 2.8, 2 letters of recommendation, BS in electrical engineering or computer science. Additional exam requirements/recommendations for international students: Required—TOEFL (minimum score 550 paper-based; 79 iBT), IELTS (minimum score 6.5). *Expenses:* Contact institution.

University of Florida, Graduate School, College of Engineering, Gainesville, FL 32611. Offers MCE, ME, MS, PhD, Certificate, Engr, JD/MS, MD/PhD. *Accreditation:* ABET (one or more programs are accredited). Part-time programs available. Postbaccalaureate distance learning degree programs offered (no on-campus study). *Faculty:* 235 full-time (25 women), 12 part-time/adjunct (3 women). *Students:* 2,499 full-time (547 women), 633 part-time (152 women); includes 395 minority (73 Black or African American, non-Hispanic/Latino; 7 American Indian or Alaska Native, non-Hispanic/Latino; 142 Asian, non-Hispanic/Latino; 173 Hispanic/Latino), 1,816 international. Average age 27. 6,477 applicants, 41% accepted, 871 enrolled. In 2011, 876 master's, 213 doctorates awarded. *Entrance requirements:* For master's and doctorate, GRE General Test, minimum GPA of 3.0; for other advanced degree, GRE General Test. Additional exam requirements/recommendations for international students: Required—TOEFL (minimum score 550 paper-based; 213 computer-based; 80 iBT), IELTS (minimum score 6). *Application deadline:* Applications are processed on a rolling basis. Application fee: $30. Electronic applications accepted. *Financial support:* In 2011–12, 880 students received support, including 39 fellowships with full tuition reimbursements available, 653 research assistantships with full tuition reimbursements available, 188 teaching assistantships with full tuition reimbursements available; career-related internships or fieldwork, Federal Work-Study, institutionally sponsored loans, and unspecified assistantships also available. Support available to part-time students. Financial award applicants required to submit FAFSA. *Total annual research expenditures:* $104 million. *Unit head:* Dr. Cammy R. Abernathy, Dean, 352-392-6000, E-mail: info@eng.ufl.edu. *Application contact:* Dr. David Norton, Associate Dean for Research and Graduate Programs, 352-392-0946, E-mail: dnort@eng.ufl.edu. Web site: http://www.eng.ufl.edu/.

University of Guelph, Graduate Studies, College of Physical and Engineering Science, School of Engineering, Guelph, ON N1G 2W1, Canada. Offers biological engineering (M Eng, M Sc, MA Sc, PhD); engineering systems and computing (M Eng, M Sc, MA Sc, PhD); environmental engineering (M Eng, M Sc, MA Sc, PhD); water resources engineering (M Eng, M Sc, MA Sc, PhD). Part-time programs available. *Degree requirements:* For master's, thesis (for some programs); for doctorate, comprehensive exam, thesis/dissertation. *Entrance requirements:* For master's, minimum B- average during previous 2 years of course work; for doctorate, minimum B average. Additional exam requirements/recommendations for international students: Required—TOEFL (minimum score 550 paper-based; 213 computer-based; 89 iBT), IELTS (minimum score 6.5). Electronic applications accepted. *Faculty research:* Water and food safety, environmental contaminant fates and mechanisms, computer systems, robotics and mechatronics, waste treatment.

University of Hartford, College of Engineering, Technology and Architecture, Program in Engineering, West Hartford, CT 06117-1599. Offers M Eng. *Entrance requirements:* Additional exam requirements/recommendations for international students: Required—TOEFL.

University of Hawaii at Manoa, Graduate Division, College of Engineering, Honolulu, HI 96822. Offers MS, PhD. *Accreditation:* ABET (one or more programs are accredited). Part-time programs available. *Entrance requirements:* Additional exam requirements/recommendations for international students: Required—TOEFL or IELTS.

University of Houston, Cullen College of Engineering, Houston, TX 77204. Offers M Pet E, MCE, MCHE, MEE, MIE, MME, MSEE, MSME, PhD. Part-time programs available. Terminal master's awarded for partial completion of doctoral program. *Degree requirements:* For master's, thesis (for some programs); for doctorate, thesis/dissertation, departmental qualifying exam. *Entrance requirements:* For master's and doctorate, GRE General Test. *Faculty research:* Superconducting materials, microantennas for space packs, direct numerical simulation of pairing vortices.

University of Idaho, College of Graduate Studies, College of Engineering, Moscow, ID 83844-1011. Offers M Engr, MS, PhD. *Faculty:* 75 full-time, 5 part-time/adjunct. *Students:* 168 full-time (19 women), 294 part-time (42 women). Average age 34. In 2011, 181 master's, 4 doctorates awarded. *Degree requirements:* For doctorate, thesis/dissertation. *Entrance requirements:* For doctorate, minimum undergraduate GPA of 2.8, graduate 3.0. *Application deadline:* For fall admission, 8/1 for domestic students; for spring admission, 12/15 for domestic students. Applications are processed on a rolling basis. Application fee: $60. Electronic applications accepted. *Expenses:* Tuition, state resident: full-time $3874; part-time $334 per credit hour. Tuition, nonresident: full-time $16,394; part-time $861 per credit hour. *Required fees:* $2808; $99 per credit hour. Tuition and fees vary according to program. *Financial support:* Fellowships, research assistantships, teaching assistantships, career-related internships or fieldwork, and Federal Work-Study available. Support available to part-time students. Financial award applicants required to submit FAFSA. *Faculty research:* Robotics, micro-electronic packaging, water resources engineering and science, oscillating flows in macro- and micro-scale methods of mechanical separation, nuclear energy. *Unit head:* Dr. Larry Stauffer, Interim Dean, 208-885-6479, E-mail: deanengr@uidaho.edu. *Application contact:* Erick Larson, Director of Graduate Admissions, 208-885-4723, E-mail: gadms@uidaho.edu. Web site: http://www.uidaho.edu/engr/.

University of Illinois at Chicago, Graduate College, College of Engineering, Chicago, IL 60607-7128. Offers M Eng, MEE, MS, PhD. Part-time and evening/weekend programs available. Terminal master's awarded for partial completion of doctoral program. *Degree requirements:* For doctorate, thesis/dissertation. *Entrance requirements:* For doctorate, GRE. Additional exam requirements/recommendations for international students: Required—TOEFL. Electronic applications accepted. *Expenses:* Contact institution.

University of Illinois at Urbana–Champaign, Graduate College, College of Engineering, Champaign, IL 61820. Offers MCS, MS, PhD, M Arch/MS, MBA/MS, MCS/JD, MCS/M Arch, MCS/MBA, MS/MBA, PhD/MBA. *Faculty:* 354 full-time (40 women), 17 part-time/adjunct (0 women). *Students:* 1,920 full-time (378 women), 296 part-time (59 women); includes 254 minority (13 Black or African American, non-Hispanic/Latino; 2 American Indian or Alaska Native, non-Hispanic/Latino; 155 Asian, non-Hispanic/Latino; 57 Hispanic/Latino; 27 Two or more races, non-Hispanic/Latino), 1,245 international. 5,885 applicants, 25% accepted, 558 enrolled. In 2011, 438 master's, 224 doctorates awarded. *Application deadline:* Applications are processed on a rolling basis. Application fee: $75 ($90 for international students). Electronic applications accepted. *Expenses:* Contact institution. *Financial support:* In 2011–12, 285 fellowships, 1,635 research assistantships, 764 teaching assistantships were awarded; tuition waivers (full and partial) also available. *Unit head:* Dr. Ilesanmi Adesida, Dean, 217-333-2150, Fax: 217-244-7705, E-mail: iadesida@illinois.edu. *Application contact:* Gregory S. Harman, Admissions Support Staff, 217-244-4637. Web site: http://engineering.illinois.edu/.

The University of Iowa, Graduate College, College of Engineering, Iowa City, IA 52242-1527. Offers MS, PhD. *Faculty:* 85 full-time (11 women), 6 part-time/adjunct (2 women). *Students:* 370 full-time (96 women); includes 26 minority (10 Black or African American, non-Hispanic/Latino; 9 Asian, non-Hispanic/Latino; 7 Hispanic/Latino), 191 international. Average age 27. 672 applicants, 24% accepted, 77 enrolled. In 2011, 83 master's, 35 doctorates awarded. *Degree requirements:* For master's, comprehensive exam (for some programs), thesis optional, oral exam and/or thesis; for doctorate, comprehensive exam, thesis/dissertation. *Entrance requirements:* For master's and doctorate, GRE, official academic records/transcripts, 3 letters of recommendation, resume, statement of purpose. Additional exam requirements/recommendations for international students: Required—TOEFL. *Application deadline:* For fall admission, 2/1 priority date for domestic students, 2/1 for international students; for spring admission, 8/1 priority date for domestic students, 8/1 for international students. Applications are processed on a rolling basis. Application fee: $60 ($100 for international students). Electronic applications accepted. *Financial support:* In 2011–12, 32 fellowships with full and partial tuition reimbursements (averaging $23,262 per year), 266 research assistantships with full and partial tuition reimbursements (averaging $22,378 per year), 84 teaching assistantships with full and partial tuition reimbursements (averaging $17,174 per year) were awarded; career-related internships or fieldwork, Federal Work-Study, scholarships/grants, traineeships, health care benefits, and unspecified assistantships also available. Financial award application deadline: 2/1; financial award applicants required to submit FAFSA. *Total annual research expenditures:* $48.9 million. *Unit head:* Dr. Alec Scranton, Interim Dean, 319-335-5766, Fax: 319-335-6086, E-mail: alec-scranton@uiowa.edu. *Application contact:* Michael Barron, Director of Admissions, 319-335-1525, Fax: 319-335-1535, E-mail: admissions@uiowa.edu. Web site: http://www.engineering.uiowa.edu/.

See Display on next page and Close-Up on page 85.

The University of Kansas, Graduate Studies, School of Engineering, Lawrence, KS 66045. Offers MCE, MCM, ME, MS, DE, PhD. Part-time and evening/weekend programs available. Postbaccalaureate distance learning degree programs offered (no on-campus study). *Students:* 342 full-time (100 women), 275 part-time (52 women); includes 68 minority (13 Black or African American, non-Hispanic/Latino; 3 American Indian or Alaska Native, non-Hispanic/Latino; 30 Asian, non-Hispanic/Latino; 18 Hispanic/Latino; 1 Native Hawaiian or other Pacific Islander, non-Hispanic/Latino; 3 Two or more races, non-Hispanic/Latino), 212 international. Average age 29. 645 applicants, 49% accepted, 128 enrolled. In 2011, 131 master's, 27 doctorates awarded. Terminal master's awarded for partial completion of doctoral program. *Degree requirements:* For doctorate, comprehensive exam, thesis/dissertation. *Entrance requirements:* For master's, GRE, minimum GPA of 3.0; for doctorate, GRE, minimum GPA of 3.5. Additional exam requirements/recommendations for international students: Required—TOEFL. *Application deadline:* Applications are processed on a rolling basis. Application fee: $55 ($65 for international students). Electronic applications accepted. *Expenses:* Contact institution. *Financial support:* Fellowships, research assistantships with full and partial tuition reimbursements, teaching assistantships with full and partial tuition reimbursements, career-related internships or fieldwork, Federal Work-Study, scholarships/grants, and unspecified assistantships available. *Faculty research:* Telecommunications, oil recovery, airplane design, structured materials, robotics. *Unit head:* Dr. Stuart R. Bell, Dean, 785-864-3881, E-mail: kuengr@ku.edu. *Application contact:* Dr. Glen Marotz, Associate Dean, 785-864-2980, Fax: 785-864-5445, E-mail: gama@ku.edu. Web site: http://www.engr.ku.edu/.

University of Kentucky, Graduate School, College of Engineering, Lexington, KY 40506-0032. Offers M Eng, MCE, MME, MS, MS Ch E, MS Min, MSCE, MSEE, MSEM, MSMAE, MSME, MSMSE, PhD. Part-time programs available. *Degree requirements:* For master's, comprehensive exam; for doctorate, comprehensive exam, thesis/dissertation. *Entrance requirements:* For master's, GRE General Test, minimum undergraduate GPA of 2.75; for doctorate, GRE General Test, minimum undergraduate GPA of 3.0. Additional exam requirements/recommendations for international students: Required—TOEFL (minimum score 550 paper-based; 213 computer-based). Electronic applications accepted.

University of Louisville, J. B. Speed School of Engineering, Louisville, KY 40292-0001. Offers M Eng, MS, PhD, Certificate, M Eng/MBA. *Accreditation:* ABET (one or more programs are accredited). Part-time programs available. Postbaccalaureate distance learning degree programs offered (no on-campus study). *Faculty:* 74 full-time (9 women). *Students:* 344 full-time (64 women), 130 part-time (26 women); includes 41 minority (14 Black or African American, non-Hispanic/Latino; 3 American Indian or Alaska Native, non-Hispanic/Latino; 15 Asian, non-Hispanic/Latino; 6 Hispanic/Latino; 3 Two or more races, non-Hispanic/Latino), 136 international. Average age 28. 219 applicants, 43% accepted, 47 enrolled. In 2011, 235 master's, 24 doctorates awarded. Terminal master's awarded for partial completion of doctoral program. *Degree requirements:* For master's, comprehensive exam (for some programs), thesis or alternative; for doctorate, comprehensive exam, thesis/dissertation, minimum GPA of 3.0. *Entrance requirements:* For master's, doctorate, and Certificate, GRE General Test. Additional exam requirements/recommendations for international students: Required—TOEFL (minimum score 550 paper-based; 213 computer-based; 80 iBT), IELTS (minimum score 6.5). *Application deadline:* For fall admission, 5/1 priority date for domestic students, 5/1 for international students; for spring admission, 11/1 priority date for domestic students, 11/1 for international students. Applications are processed on a rolling basis. Application fee: $50. Electronic applications accepted. *Expenses:* Tuition, state resident: full-time $9692; part-time $539 per credit hour. Tuition, nonresident: full-time $20,168; part-time $1121 per credit hour. Tuition and fees vary according to program and reciprocity agreements. *Financial support:* In 2011–12, 87 students

Engineering and Applied Sciences—General

received support, including 17 fellowships with full tuition reimbursements available (averaging $20,000 per year), 29 research assistantships with full tuition reimbursements available (averaging $20,000 per year), 41 teaching assistantships with full tuition reimbursements available (averaging $20,000 per year); scholarships/grants also available. Financial award applicants required to submit FAFSA. *Faculty research:* Bioengineering, civil infrastructure, computer engineering and computer science, logistics and distribution, materials management. *Total annual research expenditures:* $14.8 million. *Unit head:* Dr. Mickey R. Wilhelm, Dean, 502-852-6281, Fax: 502-852-7033, E-mail: wilhelm@louisville.edu. *Application contact:* Dr. Michael Day, Associate Dean, 502-852-6195, Fax: 502-852-7294, E-mail: day@louisville.edu.

University of Maine, Graduate School, College of Engineering, Orono, ME 04469. Offers ME, MS, PhD. Part-time programs available. *Faculty:* 49 full-time (4 women), 7 part-time/adjunct (1 woman). *Students:* 93 full-time (22 women), 50 part-time (10 women); includes 8 minority (1 Black or African American, non-Hispanic/Latino; 2 American Indian or Alaska Native, non-Hispanic/Latino; 4 Asian, non-Hispanic/Latino; 1 Hispanic/Latino), 47 international. Average age 28. 137 applicants, 50% accepted, 53 enrolled. In 2011, 28 master's, 10 doctorates awarded. Terminal master's awarded for partial completion of doctoral program. *Degree requirements:* For doctorate, thesis/dissertation. *Entrance requirements:* For master's and doctorate, GRE General Test. Additional exam requirements/recommendations for international students: Required—TOEFL. *Application deadline:* For fall admission, 2/1 priority date for domestic students. Applications are processed on a rolling basis. Application fee: $65. Electronic applications accepted. *Expenses:* Tuition, state resident: full-time $5016. Tuition, nonresident: full-time $14,424. *Financial support:* In 2011–12, 1 teaching assistantship (averaging $13,600 per year) was awarded; Federal Work-Study, institutionally sponsored loans, scholarships/grants, and tuition waivers (full and partial) also available. Financial award application deadline: 3/1. *Unit head:* Dr. Dana Humphrey, Interim Dean, 207-581-2216, Fax: 207-581-2220. *Application contact:* Scott G. Delcourt, Associate Dean of the Graduate School, 207-581-3291, Fax: 207-581-3232, E-mail: graduate@maine.edu. Web site: http://www2.umaine.edu/graduate/.

University of Manitoba, Faculty of Graduate Studies, Faculty of Engineering, Winnipeg, MB R3T 2N2, Canada. Offers M Eng, M Sc, PhD.

University of Maryland, Baltimore County, Graduate School, College of Engineering and Information Technology, Baltimore, MD 21250. Offers MS, PhD, Postbaccalaureate Certificate. Part-time and evening/weekend programs available. Postbaccalaureate distance learning degree programs offered (no on-campus study). *Faculty:* 89 full-time (25 women), 44 part-time/adjunct (7 women). *Students:* 374 full-time (115 women), 543 part-time (133 women); includes 229 minority (107 Black or African American, non-Hispanic/Latino; 3 American Indian or Alaska Native, non-Hispanic/Latino; 79 Asian, non-Hispanic/Latino; 25 Hispanic/Latino; 3 Native Hawaiian or other Pacific Islander, non-Hispanic/Latino; 12 Two or more races, non-Hispanic/Latino), 250 international. Average age 33. 1,066 applicants, 51% accepted, 252 enrolled. In 2011, 210 master's, 34 doctorates, 33 other advanced degrees awarded. *Degree requirements:* For master's, comprehensive exam (for some programs), thesis (for some programs); for doctorate, comprehensive exam, thesis/dissertation. *Entrance requirements:* For master's and doctorate, GRE General Test, minimum GPA of 3.0. Additional exam requirements/recommendations for international students: Required—TOEFL (minimum score 550 paper-based; 213 computer-based; 80 iBT). *Application deadline:* For fall

admission, 6/1 for domestic students, 1/1 for international students; for spring admission, 11/1 for domestic students, 6/1 for international students. Applications are processed on a rolling basis. Application fee: $70. Electronic applications accepted. *Financial support:* In 2011–12, 14 fellowships with full tuition reimbursements (averaging $25,000 per year), 85 research assistantships with full tuition reimbursements (averaging $22,000 per year), 79 teaching assistantships with full tuition reimbursements (averaging $17,000 per year) were awarded; career-related internships or fieldwork, Federal Work-Study, scholarships/grants, health care benefits, tuition waivers (partial), and unspecified assistantships also available. Support available to part-time students. Financial award application deadline: 6/30; financial award applicants required to submit FAFSA. *Faculty research:* Biomaterials engineering, water resources engineering, security and information assurance, human-centered computing, design and manufacturing. *Total annual research expenditures:* $11.6 million. *Unit head:* Dr. Warren R. DeVries, Dean, 410-455-3270, Fax: 410-455-3559, E-mail: wdevries@umbc.edu. *Application contact:* Graduate School, 410-455-2537, E-mail: umbcgrad@umbc.edu. Web site: http://www.coeit.umbc.edu.

University of Maryland, College Park, Academic Affairs, A. James Clark School of Engineering and School of Public Policy, Program in Engineering and Public Policy, College Park, MD 20742. Offers MS. *Students:* 11 full-time (4 women), 8 part-time (2 women); includes 1 minority (Asian, non-Hispanic/Latino), 1 international. 34 applicants, 59% accepted, 5 enrolled. In 2011, 2 master's awarded. *Application deadline:* For fall admission, 4/1 for domestic students, 2/1 for international students; for spring admission, 10/15 for domestic students, 6/1 for international students. Application fee: $75. *Expenses: Tuition, area resident:* Part-time $525 per credit hour. Tuition, state resident: part-time $525 per credit hour. Tuition, nonresident: part-time $1131 per credit hour. *Required fees:* $386.31 per term. Tuition and fees vary according to program. *Financial support:* In 2011–12, 1 teaching assistantship (averaging $18,000 per year) was awarded. *Unit head:* Dr. Steven Gabriel, Co-Director, 301-405-3242, E-mail: sgabriel@umd.edu. *Application contact:* Dean of the Graduate School, 301-405-0358, Fax: 301-314-9305, E-mail: ccaramel@umd.edu.

University of Massachusetts Amherst, Graduate School, College of Engineering, Amherst, MA 01003. Offers MS, MSCE, MSChE, MSECE, MSME, PhD. *Accreditation:* ABET (one or more programs are accredited). Part-time programs available. *Faculty:* 127 full-time (15 women). *Students:* 456 full-time (113 women), 55 part-time (16 women); includes 41 minority (8 Black or African American, non-Hispanic/Latino; 16 Asian, non-Hispanic/Latino; 12 Hispanic/Latino; 1 Native Hawaiian or other Pacific Islander, non-Hispanic/Latino; 4 Two or more races, non-Hispanic/Latino), 306 international. Average age 26. 1,705 applicants, 31% accepted, 154 enrolled. In 2011, 108 master's, 27 doctorates awarded. Terminal master's awarded for partial completion of doctoral program. *Degree requirements:* For master's, thesis (for some programs); for doctorate, comprehensive exam, thesis/dissertation. *Entrance requirements:* For master's and doctorate, GRE General Test. Additional exam requirements/recommendations for international students: Required—TOEFL (minimum score 550 paper-based; 213 computer-based; 80 iBT), IELTS (minimum score 6.5). *Application deadline:* For fall admission, 1/15 for domestic and international students; for spring admission, 10/1 for domestic and international students. Applications are processed on a rolling basis. Application fee: $50 ($65 for international students). Electronic applications accepted. Tuition and fees vary according to course load, campus/location and program. *Financial support:* Fellowships with full and partial tuition reimbursements, research assistantships with full and partial tuition reimbursements, teaching

assistantships with full and partial tuition reimbursements, career-related internships or fieldwork, Federal Work-Study, scholarships/grants, traineeships, health care benefits, tuition waivers (full and partial), and unspecified assistantships available. Support available to part-time students. Financial award application deadline: 1/15. *Unit head:* Dr. Theodore Djaferis, Dean, 413-545-0300, Fax: 413-545-0300. *Application contact:* Lindsay DeSantis, Interim Supervisor of Admissions, 413-545-0722, Fax: 413-577-0010, E-mail: gradadm@grad.umass.edu. Web site: http://www.engineering.umass.edu/.

University of Massachusetts Dartmouth, Graduate School, College of Engineering, North Dartmouth, MA 02747-2300. Offers MS, PhD, Postbaccalaureate Certificate. Part-time programs available. *Faculty:* 57 full-time (9 women), 11 part-time/adjunct (2 women). *Students:* 111 full-time (14 women), 110 part-time (19 women); includes 16 minority (4 Black or African American, non-Hispanic/Latino; 3 Asian, non-Hispanic/Latino; 4 Hispanic/Latino; 5 Two or more races, non-Hispanic/Latino), 113 international. Average age 27. 266 applicants, 87% accepted, 75 enrolled. In 2011, 64 master's, 3 doctorates awarded. *Degree requirements:* For master's, thesis or alternative; for doctorate, comprehensive exam, thesis/dissertation. *Entrance requirements:* For master's and doctorate, GRE, 3 letters of recommendation, resume, statement of intent; for Postbaccalaureate Certificate, 3 letters of recommendation, resume, statement of intent. Additional exam requirements/recommendations for international students: Required—TOEFL (minimum score 533 paper-based; 200 computer-based; 72 iBT). *Application deadline:* Applications are processed on a rolling basis. Application fee: $40 ($60 for international students). Electronic applications accepted. *Expenses:* Tuition, state resident: full-time $2071; part-time $86.29 per credit. Tuition, nonresident: full-time $8099; part-time $337.46 per credit. *Required fees:* $438.58 per credit. Part-time tuition and fees vary according to class time, course load, degree level and reciprocity agreements. *Financial support:* In 2011–12, 32 research assistantships with full tuition reimbursements (averaging $11,342 per year), 47 teaching assistantships with full tuition reimbursements (averaging $8,435 per year) were awarded; fellowships, Federal Work-Study, and unspecified assistantships also available. Support available to part-time students. Financial award application deadline: 3/1; financial award applicants required to submit FAFSA. *Faculty research:* Soil-geosynthetic systems, signals and systems, heat exchanger optimization, tracking of mesoscale features, blue light cures. *Total annual research expenditures:* $3.1 million. *Unit head:* Dr. Robert Peck, Dean, 508-999-8539, Fax: 508-999-9137, E-mail: rpeck@umassd.edu. *Application contact:* Elan Turcotte-Shamski, Graduate Admissions Officer, 508-999-8604, Fax: 508-999-8183, E-mail: graduate@umassd.edu. Web site: http://www.umassd.edu/engineering/.

University of Massachusetts Lowell, College of Engineering, Lowell, MA 01854-2881. Offers MS Eng, MSES, D Eng, PhD, Certificate, Graduate Certificate. Part-time and evening/weekend programs available. Terminal master's awarded for partial completion of doctoral program. *Degree requirements:* For doctorate, thesis/dissertation. *Entrance requirements:* For master's and doctorate, GRE General Test.

University of Memphis, Graduate School, Herff College of Engineering, Memphis, TN 38152. Offers MS, PhD. Part-time programs available. *Degree requirements:* For master's, comprehensive exam, thesis optional, 30-36 hours of course work, completion of course work within 6 years, continuous enrollment; for doctorate, comprehensive exam, thesis/dissertation, completion of degree within 12 years, residency, continuous enrollment. *Entrance requirements:* For master's, GRE, MAT, GMAT or PRAXIS; for doctorate, GRE, MAT, GMAT. Additional exam requirements/recommendations for international students: Required—TOEFL (minimum score 550 paper-based; 210 computer-based; 79 iBT). Electronic applications accepted. *Faculty research:* Medical and biological applications of engineering; infrastructure, including transportation, ground water and GPS studies; computational intelligence and modeling; sensors.

University of Miami, Graduate School, College of Engineering, Coral Gables, FL 33124. Offers MS, MSAE, MSBE, MSCE, MSECE, MSEVH, MSIE, MSME, MSOES, PhD, MBA/MSIE. Part-time and evening/weekend programs available. *Degree requirements:* For master's, thesis (for some programs); for doctorate, comprehensive exam, thesis/dissertation. *Entrance requirements:* For master's and doctorate, GRE General Test, minimum GPA of 3.0. Additional exam requirements/recommendations for international students: Required—TOEFL (minimum score 550 paper-based; 213 computer-based; 59 iBT). Electronic applications accepted.

University of Michigan, College of Engineering, Ann Arbor, MI 48109. Offers M Eng, MS, MSE, D Eng, PhD, CE, Certificate, Ch E, Mar Eng, Nav Arch, Nuc E, M Arch/M Eng, M Arch/MSE, MBA/M Eng, MBA/MS, MBA/MSE, MSE/MS. Part-time programs available. Postbaccalaureate distance learning degree programs offered (no on-campus study). *Faculty:* 362 full-time (59 women). *Students:* 2,935 full-time (647 women), 298 part-time (40 women). 8,175 applicants, 29% accepted, 1101 enrolled. In 2011, 845 master's, 212 doctorates awarded. *Application deadline:* Applications are processed on a rolling basis. Application fee: $65 ($75 for international students). Electronic applications accepted. *Expenses:* Contact institution. *Financial support:* Fellowships, research assistantships, teaching assistantships, career-related internships or fieldwork, Federal Work-Study, institutionally sponsored loans, scholarships/grants, traineeships, health care benefits, tuition waivers (full and partial), and unspecified assistantships available. Support available to part-time students. Financial award applicants required to submit FAFSA. *Total annual research expenditures:* $188.5 million. *Unit head:* Prof. David C. Munson, Chair, 734-647-7008, Fax: 734-647-7009, E-mail: munson@umich.edu. *Application contact:* Mike Nazareth, Recruiting Contact, 734-647-7030, Fax: 734-647-7045, E-mail: mikenaz@umich.edu. Web site: http://www.engin.umich.edu/.

University of Michigan–Dearborn, College of Engineering and Computer Science, Dearborn, MI 48128-1491. Offers MS, MSE, PhD, MBA/MSE. Part-time and evening/weekend programs available. *Faculty:* 66 full-time (5 women), 25 part-time/adjunct (3 women). *Students:* 103 full-time (18 women), 414 part-time (69 women); includes 130 minority (23 Black or African American, non-Hispanic/Latino; 1 American Indian or Alaska Native, non-Hispanic/Latino; 86 Asian, non-Hispanic/Latino; 17 Hispanic/Latino; 3 Two or more races, non-Hispanic/Latino), 85 international. Average age 27. 350 applicants, 55% accepted, 129 enrolled. In 2011, 130 master's awarded. *Degree requirements:* For master's, thesis optional; for doctorate, thesis/dissertation. *Entrance requirements:* Additional exam requirements/recommendations for international students: Required—TOEFL (minimum score 560 paper-based; 220 computer-based; 84 iBT). *Application deadline:* For fall admission, 6/15 for domestic students, 4/1 for international students; for winter admission, 12/1 for domestic students, 10/15 for international students; for spring admission, 2/15 for domestic and international students. Applications are processed on a rolling basis. Application fee: $60. Electronic applications accepted. *Financial support:* In 2011–12, 12 students received support, including 18 research assistantships with full tuition reimbursements available (averaging $60,476 per year), 4 teaching assistantships (averaging $12,251 per year); fellowships, career-related internships or fieldwork, and Federal Work-Study also available. Financial award application deadline: 4/1; financial award applicants required to submit FAFSA. *Faculty research:* CAD/CAM, expert systems, acoustics, vehicle electronics, engines and fuels. *Unit head:* Dr. Subrata Sengupta, Dean, 313-593-5290,

Fax: 313-593-9967, E-mail: razal@engin.umd.umich.edu. *Application contact:* Dr. Keshav Varde, Associate Dean, 313-593-5117, Fax: 313-593-9967, E-mail: varde@engin.umd.umich.edu. Web site: http://www.engin.umd.umich.edu/.

University of Minnesota, Twin Cities Campus, College of Science and Engineering, Minneapolis, MN 55455. Offers M Aero E, M Ch E, M Geo E, M Mat SE, MA, MCE, MCS, MFM, MS, MS Ch E, MS Mat SE, MSEE, MSISE, MSME, MSMOT, MSSE, MSST, PhD, Certificate, MD/PhD. Part-time and evening/weekend programs available. Postbaccalaureate distance learning degree programs offered (minimal on-campus study). *Faculty:* 392 full-time (42 women). *Students:* 2,102 full-time (480 women), 596 part-time (114 women); includes 214 minority (34 Black or African American, non-Hispanic/Latino; 5 American Indian or Alaska Native, non-Hispanic/Latino; 121 Asian, non-Hispanic/Latino; 34 Hispanic/Latino; 1 Native Hawaiian or other Pacific Islander, non-Hispanic/Latino; 19 Two or more races, non-Hispanic/Latino), 1,205 international. Average age 30. 5,266 applicants, 616 enrolled. In 2011, 518 master's, 226 doctorates awarded. *Degree requirements:* For doctorate, thesis/dissertation. *Entrance requirements:* Additional exam requirements/recommendations for international students: Required—TOEFL (minimum score 550 paper-based; 79 iBT). *Application deadline:* Applications are processed on a rolling basis. Application fee: $75 ($95 for international students). Electronic applications accepted. *Financial support:* Fellowships, research assistantships, teaching assistantships, and unspecified assistantships available. Financial award applicants required to submit FAFSA. *Total annual research expenditures:* $149.4 million. *Unit head:* Steven L. Crouch, Dean, 612-624-2006, Fax: 612-624-2841, E-mail: crouch@umn.edu. *Application contact:* Graduate Admissions Office, 612-625-3014. Web site: http://cse.umn.edu/.

University of Mississippi, Graduate School, School of Engineering, Oxford, University, MS 38677. Offers engineering science (MS, PhD). *Students:* 121 full-time (31 women), 33 part-time (7 women); includes 18 minority (11 Black or African American, non-Hispanic/Latino; 4 Asian, non-Hispanic/Latino; 2 Hispanic/Latino; 1 Two or more races, non-Hispanic/Latino), 79 international. *Degree requirements:* For master's, thesis (for some programs); for doctorate, thesis/dissertation. *Entrance requirements:* For master's, GRE General Test, minimum GPA of 3.0; for doctorate, GRE General Test. Additional exam requirements/recommendations for international students: Required—TOEFL. *Application deadline:* For fall admission, 4/1 for domestic students; for spring admission, 10/1 for domestic students. Applications are processed on a rolling basis. Application fee: $25. Electronic applications accepted. *Financial support:* Scholarships/grants available. Financial award application deadline: 3/1; financial award applicants required to submit FAFSA. *Unit head:* Dr. Alexander Cheng, 662-915-7407, Fax: 662-915-1287, E-mail: engineer@olemiss.edu. *Application contact:* Dr. Christy M. Wyandt, Associate Dean, 662-915-7474, Fax: 662-915-7577, E-mail: cwyandt@olemiss.edu.

University of Missouri, Graduate School, College of Engineering, Columbia, MO 65211. Offers ME, MS, PhD. Part-time programs available. *Faculty:* 111 full-time (10 women), 10 part-time/adjunct (0 women). *Students:* 299 full-time (54 women), 221 part-time (45 women); includes 27 minority (8 Black or African American, non-Hispanic/Latino; 12 Asian, non-Hispanic/Latino; 3 Hispanic/Latino; 4 Two or more races, non-Hispanic/Latino), 324 international. Average age 27. 682 applicants, 36% accepted, 111 enrolled. In 2011, 109 master's, 44 doctorates awarded. *Degree requirements:* For doctorate, thesis/dissertation. *Entrance requirements:* For master's and doctorate, GRE General Test. Additional exam requirements/recommendations for international students: Required—TOEFL. *Application deadline:* Applications are processed on a rolling basis. Application fee: $55 ($75 for international students). *Expenses:* Tuition, state resident: full-time $5881. Tuition, nonresident: full-time $15,183. *Required fees:* $952. Tuition and fees vary according to campus/location and program. *Financial support:* Fellowships, research assistantships, teaching assistantships, and institutionally sponsored loans available. *Unit head:* Dr. James E. Thompson, Dean, 573-882-4378, E-mail: thompsonje@missouri.edu. *Application contact:* Dr. Lex Akers, Associate Dean for Academic Programs/Professor of Electrical and Computer Engineering, 573-882-4765, E-mail: akersl@missouri.edu. Web site: http://engineering.missouri.edu/.

University of Missouri–Kansas City, School of Computing and Engineering, Kansas City, MO 64110-2499. Offers civil engineering (MS); computer and electrical engineering (PhD); computer science (MS), including bioinformatics, software engineering, telecommunications networking; computer science and informatics (PhD); computing (PhD); electrical engineering (MS); engineering (PhD); mechanical engineering (MS); telecommunications (PhD). PhD (interdisciplinary) offered through the School of Graduate Studies. Part-time programs available. *Faculty:* 36 full-time (6 women), 27 part-time/adjunct (3 women). *Students:* 155 full-time (44 women), 136 part-time (24 women); includes 19 minority (4 Black or African American, non-Hispanic/Latino; 7 Asian, non-Hispanic/Latino; 6 Hispanic/Latino; 2 Two or more races, non-Hispanic/Latino), 201 international. Average age 26. 455 applicants, 46% accepted, 96 enrolled. In 2011, 194 degrees awarded. *Degree requirements:* For doctorate, thesis/dissertation. *Entrance requirements:* For master's, GRE General Test, minimum GPA of 3.0, 3 letters of recommendation from professors; for doctorate, GRE General Test, minimum GPA of 3.5. Additional exam requirements/recommendations for international students: Required—TOEFL (minimum score 550 paper-based; 213 computer-based; 80 iBT). *Application deadline:* For fall admission, 1/15 priority date for domestic students, 1/15 for international students. Applications are processed on a rolling basis. Application fee: $45 ($50 for international students). *Expenses:* Tuition, state resident: full-time $5798; part-time $322.10 per credit hour. Tuition, nonresident: full-time $14,969; part-time $831.60 per credit hour. *Required fees:* $93.51 per credit hour. *Financial support:* In 2011–12, 47 research assistantships with partial tuition reimbursements (averaging $13,190 per year), 10 teaching assistantships with partial tuition reimbursements (averaging $9,815 per year) were awarded; career-related internships or fieldwork, Federal Work-Study, scholarships/grants, tuition waivers (partial), and unspecified assistantships also available. Support available to part-time students. Financial award application deadline: 3/1; financial award applicants required to submit FAFSA. *Faculty research:* Algorithms, bioinformatics and medical informatics, biomechanics/biomaterials, civil engineering materials, networking and telecommunications, thermal science. *Unit head:* Dr. Kevin Z. Truman, Dean, 816-235-2399, Fax: 816-235-5159. *Application contact:* 816-235-2399, Fax: 816-235-5159. Web site: http://sce.umkc.edu/.

University of Nebraska–Lincoln, Graduate College, College of Engineering, Lincoln, NE 68588. Offers M Eng, MAE, MEE, MS, PhD. *Degree requirements:* For doctorate, comprehensive exam, thesis/dissertation. *Entrance requirements:* For master's and doctorate, GRE General Test. Additional exam requirements/recommendations for international students: Required—TOEFL. Electronic applications accepted.

University of Nevada, Las Vegas, Graduate College, Howard R. Hughes College of Engineering, Las Vegas, NV 89154-4005. Offers MS, MSE, PhD. Part-time programs available. *Faculty:* 70 full-time (11 women), 40 part-time/adjunct (3 women). *Students:* 56 full-time (9 women), 157 part-time (31 women); includes 40 minority (4 Black or African American, non-Hispanic/Latino; 2 American Indian or Alaska Native, non-

Hispanic/Latino; 8 Asian, non-Hispanic/Latino; 15 Hispanic/Latino; 1 Native Hawaiian or other Pacific Islander, non-Hispanic/Latino; 10 Two or more races, non-Hispanic/Latino), 86 international. Average age 30. 136 applicants, 74% accepted, 45 enrolled. In 2011, 64 master's, 13 doctorates awarded. *Degree requirements:* For master's, comprehensive exam (for some programs), thesis (for some programs), final project; for doctorate, comprehensive exam, thesis/dissertation. *Entrance requirements:* Additional exam requirements/recommendations for international students: Required—TOEFL (minimum score 550 paper-based; 213 computer-based; 80 iBT), IELTS (minimum score 7). *Application deadline:* For fall admission, 5/1 for international students; for spring admission, 10/1 for international students. Application fee: $60 ($95 for international students). Electronic applications accepted. *Financial support:* In 2011–12, 134 students received support, including 57 research assistantships with partial tuition reimbursements available (averaging $9,143 per year), 77 teaching assistantships with partial tuition reimbursements available (averaging $9,182 per year); institutionally sponsored loans, scholarships/grants, health care benefits, and unspecified assistantships also available. Financial award application deadline: 3/1. *Total annual research expenditures:* $4.9 million. *Unit head:* Dr. Rama Venkat, Interim Dean, 702-895-1094, Fax: 702-895-4059, E-mail: venkat@ee.unlv.edu. *Application contact:* Graduate College Admissions Evaluator, 702-895-3320, Fax: 702-895-4180, E-mail: gradcollege@unlv.edu. Web site: http://engineering.unlv.edu/.

University of Nevada, Reno, Graduate School, College of Engineering, Reno, NV 89557. Offers MS, PhD. Terminal master's awarded for partial completion of doctoral program. *Degree requirements:* For master's, thesis optional; for doctorate, thesis/dissertation. *Entrance requirements:* For master's, GRE General Test, minimum GPA of 2.75; for doctorate, GRE General Test, minimum GPA of 3.0. Additional exam requirements/recommendations for international students: Required—TOEFL (minimum score 500 paper-based; 173 computer-based; 61 iBT), IELTS (minimum score 6). Electronic applications accepted. *Faculty research:* Fabrication, development of new materials, structural and earthquake engineering, computer vision/virtual reality, acoustics, smart materials.

University of New Brunswick Fredericton, School of Graduate Studies, Faculty of Engineering, Fredericton, NB E3B 5A3, Canada. Offers M Eng, M Sc E, PhD, Certificate, Diploma. Part-time programs available. *Faculty:* 68 full-time (10 women), 17 part-time/adjunct (1 woman). *Students:* 247 full-time (48 women), 42 part-time (5 women). In 2011, 51 master's, 6 doctorates awarded. *Degree requirements:* For master's, thesis; for doctorate, comprehensive exam, thesis/dissertation, qualifying exam. *Entrance requirements:* For master's, minimum GPA of 3.0. Additional exam requirements/recommendations for international students: Required—TOEFL, TWE. *Application deadline:* For fall admission, 3/1 priority date for domestic students. Applications are processed on a rolling basis. Application fee: $50 Canadian dollars. *Financial support:* In 2011–12, 284 research assistantships, 209 teaching assistantships were awarded; fellowships and career-related internships or fieldwork also available. *Unit head:* Dr. David Coleman, Dean, 506-453-4570, Fax: 506-453-4569, E-mail: dcoleman@unb.ca. *Application contact:* Dr. Edmund Biden, Dean of Graduate Studies, 506-458-7154, Fax: 506-453-4817, E-mail: biden@unb.ca. Web site: http://www.unbf.ca/eng/.

University of New Haven, Graduate School, Tagliatela College of Engineering, West Haven, CT 06516-1916. Offers EMS, MS, MSIE, Certificate. Part-time and evening/weekend programs available. *Faculty:* 37 full-time (10 women), 15 part-time/adjunct (3 women). *Students:* 174 full-time (43 women), 144 part-time (18 women); includes 28 minority (10 Black or African American, non-Hispanic/Latino; 14 Asian, non-Hispanic/Latino; 4 Hispanic/Latino), 204 international. 364 applicants, 99% accepted, 87 enrolled. In 2011, 85 master's, 7 other advanced degrees awarded. *Degree requirements:* For master's, thesis or alternative. *Entrance requirements:* Additional exam requirements/recommendations for international students: Required—TOEFL (minimum score 520 paper-based; 190 computer-based; 70 iBT); Recommended—IELTS (minimum score 5.5). *Application deadline:* For fall admission, 5/30 for international students; for winter admission, 10/15 for international students; for spring admission, 1/15 for international students. Applications are processed on a rolling basis. Application fee: $50. Electronic applications accepted. *Expenses: Tuition:* Part-time $750 per credit. *Financial support:* Research assistantships with partial tuition reimbursements, teaching assistantships with partial tuition reimbursements, career-related internships or fieldwork, Federal Work-Study, scholarships/grants, tuition waivers, and unspecified assistantships available. Support available to part-time students. Financial award applicants required to submit FAFSA. *Unit head:* Dr. Ronald Harichandran, Dean, 203-932-7167. *Application contact:* Eloise Gormley, Director of Graduate Admissions, 203-932-7449, Fax: 203-932-7137, E-mail: gradinfo@newhaven.edu. Web site: http://www.newhaven.edu/8/.

University of New Mexico, Graduate School, School of Engineering, Albuquerque, NM 87131. Offers M Eng, MCM, MEME, MS, MSCE, PhD, Post-Doctoral Certificate, MBA/MEME. Part-time programs available. *Faculty:* 97 full-time (9 women), 20 part-time/adjunct (2 women). *Students:* 361 full-time (75 women), 334 part-time (68 women); includes 143 minority (8 Black or African American, non-Hispanic/Latino; 8 American Indian or Alaska Native, non-Hispanic/Latino; 19 Asian, non-Hispanic/Latino; 98 Hispanic/Latino; 1 Native Hawaiian or other Pacific Islander, non-Hispanic/Latino; 9 Two or more races, non-Hispanic/Latino), 242 international. Average age 33. 1,246 applicants, 40% accepted, 325 enrolled. In 2011, 123 master's, 38 doctorates, 1 other advanced degree awarded. Terminal master's awarded for partial completion of doctoral program. *Degree requirements:* For master's, comprehensive exam, thesis or alternative; for doctorate, comprehensive exam, thesis/dissertation. *Entrance requirements:* For master's, GRE, GMAT, letters of recommendation; letter of intent; for doctorate, GRE, letters of recommendation; letter of intent. Additional exam requirements/recommendations for international students: Required—TOEFL (minimum score 550 paper-based; 213 computer-based). *Application deadline:* For fall admission, 1/15 priority date for domestic students, 1/15 for international students; for spring admission, 7/14 priority date for domestic students, 7/14 for international students. Applications are processed on a rolling basis. Application fee: $50. Electronic applications accepted. *Financial support:* In 2011–12, 14 students received support, including 36 fellowships (averaging $18,310 per year), 246 research assistantships (averaging $16,933 per year), 22 teaching assistantships (averaging $13,598 per year); Federal Work-Study, scholarships/grants, health care benefits, unspecified assistantships, and graduate and project assistantships, (43 awarded, $11,420 average yearly) also available. Financial award application deadline: 3/1; financial award applicants required to submit FAFSA. *Faculty research:* Emerging energy technologies, biomedical engineering and biocomputing, water resources and environmental engineering, optical engineering and optoelectronic materials, graphics and digital imaging. *Total annual research expenditures:* $31.2 million. *Unit head:* Prof. Gruia-Catalin Roman, Dean, 505-277-5522, Fax: 505-277-1422, E-mail: gcroman@unm.edu. *Application contact:* Deborah Kieltyka, Associate Director, Admissions, 505-277-3140, Fax: 505-277-6686, E-mail: deborahk@unm.edu. Web site: http://soe.unm.edu/.

University of New Orleans, Graduate School, College of Engineering, New Orleans, LA 70148. Offers MS, PhD, Certificate. Part-time programs available. Terminal master's awarded for partial completion of doctoral program. *Degree requirements:* For master's, comprehensive exam, thesis optional; for doctorate, comprehensive exam, thesis/dissertation. *Entrance requirements:* For master's, GRE General Test, minimum GPA of 3.0; for doctorate, GRE General Test. Additional exam requirements/recommendations for international students: Required—TOEFL (minimum score 550 paper-based; 213 computer-based; 79 iBT). Electronic applications accepted. *Faculty research:* Electrical, civil, environmental, mechanical, naval architecture, and marine engineering.

The University of North Carolina at Charlotte, Graduate School, The William States Lee College of Engineering, Charlotte, NC 28223-0001. Offers MS, MSCE, MSE, MSEE, MSME, PhD. Part-time and evening/weekend programs available. *Faculty:* 115 full-time (14 women), 1 (woman) part-time/adjunct. *Students:* 239 full-time (51 women), 172 part-time (29 women); includes 42 minority (15 Black or African American, non-Hispanic/Latino; 3 American Indian or Alaska Native, non-Hispanic/Latino; 13 Asian, non-Hispanic/Latino; 10 Hispanic/Latino; 1 Two or more races, non-Hispanic/Latino), 198 international. Average age 28. 539 applicants, 65% accepted, 114 enrolled. In 2011, 104 master's, 8 doctorates awarded. Terminal master's awarded for partial completion of doctoral program. *Median time to degree:* Of those who began their doctoral program in fall 2003, 33% received their degree in 8 years or less. *Degree requirements:* For master's, thesis or alternative, project; for doctorate, thesis/dissertation. *Entrance requirements:* For master's, GRE General Test. Additional exam requirements/recommendations for international students: Required—TOEFL (minimum score 557 paper-based; 220 computer-based; 83 iBT). *Application deadline:* For fall admission, 7/1 for domestic students, 5/1 for international students; for spring admission, 11/1 for domestic students, 10/1 for international students. Applications are processed on a rolling basis. Application fee: $65 ($75 for international students). Electronic applications accepted. *Expenses:* Tuition, state resident: full-time $3689. Tuition, nonresident: full-time $15,226. *Required fees:* $2198. Tuition and fees vary according to course load and program. *Financial support:* In 2011–12, 164 students received support, including 6 fellowships (averaging $37,891 per year), 98 research assistantships (averaging $8,754 per year), 60 teaching assistantships (averaging $7,496 per year); career-related internships or fieldwork, institutionally sponsored loans, scholarships/grants, and administrative assistantship also available. Support available to part-time students. Financial award application deadline: 4/1; financial award applicants required to submit FAFSA. *Faculty research:* Environmental engineering, structures and geotechnical engineering, precision engineering and precision metrology, optoelectronics and microelectronics, communications. *Total annual research expenditures:* $5.7 million. *Unit head:* Dr. Robert E. Johnson, Dean, 704-687-8242, Fax: 704-687-2352, E-mail: robejohn@.uncc.edu. *Application contact:* Kathy B. Giddings, Director of Graduate Admissions, 704-687-5503, Fax: 704-687-3279, E-mail: gradadm@uncc.edu. Web site: http://www.coe.uncc.edu/.

University of North Dakota, Graduate School, School of Engineering and Mines, Program in Engineering, Grand Forks, ND 58202. Offers PhD. *Degree requirements:* For doctorate, comprehensive exam, thesis/dissertation, final exam. *Entrance requirements:* For doctorate, minimum GPA of 3.0. Additional exam requirements/recommendations for international students: Required—TOEFL (minimum score 550 paper-based; 213 computer-based; 79 iBT), IELTS (minimum score 6.5). Electronic applications accepted. *Faculty research:* Combustion science, energy conversion, power transmission, environmental engineering.

University of North Texas, Toulouse Graduate School, College of Engineering, Department of Engineering Technology, Denton, TX 76203-5017. Offers MS. Part-time programs available. *Degree requirements:* For master's, comprehensive exam (for some programs), project or thesis. *Entrance requirements:* For master's, GRE General Test, BS in related field. Additional exam requirements/recommendations for international students: Recommended—TOEFL (minimum score 550 paper-based; 213 computer-based; 79 iBT), IELTS (minimum score 6.5). Electronic applications accepted. *Expenses:* Tuition, state resident: part-time $100 per credit hour. Tuition, nonresident: part-time $413 per credit hour. *Faculty research:* Green design, steel structures, Piezoelectric system modeling, biophotonics, concrete pavement cracking.

University of Notre Dame, Graduate School, College of Engineering, Notre Dame, IN 46556. Offers M Eng, MEME, MS, MS Aero E, MS Bio E, MS Ch E, MS Env E, MSCE, MSCSE, MSEE, MSME, PhD. Terminal master's awarded for partial completion of doctoral program. *Degree requirements:* For master's, comprehensive exam; for doctorate, thesis/dissertation. *Entrance requirements:* For master's and doctorate, GRE General Test. Additional exam requirements/recommendations for international students: Required—TOEFL. Electronic applications accepted.

University of Oklahoma, College of Engineering, Program in Engineering, Norman, OK 73019. Offers MS, PhD. Part-time programs available. *Faculty:* 1 (woman) full-time. *Students:* 8 full-time (2 women), 8 part-time (1 woman); includes 2 minority (1 Black or African American, non-Hispanic/Latino; 1 American Indian or Alaska Native, non-Hispanic/Latino), 3 international. Average age 35. 3 applicants, 100% accepted, 0 enrolled. *Degree requirements:* For doctorate, comprehensive exam, thesis/dissertation, oral and qualifying exams. *Entrance requirements:* For doctorate, GRE. Additional exam requirements/recommendations for international students: Required—TOEFL (minimum score 550 paper-based; 79 iBT). *Application deadline:* For fall admission, 6/1 for domestic students, 3/1 for international students; for spring admission, 11/1 for domestic students, 9/1 for international students. Applications are processed on a rolling basis. Application fee: $40 ($90 for international students). Electronic applications accepted. *Expenses:* Tuition, state resident: full-time $4087; part-time $170.30 per credit hour. Tuition, nonresident: full-time $14,875; part-time $619.80 per credit hour. *Required fees:* $2659; $100.25 per credit hour. Tuition and fees vary according to course load and degree level. *Financial support:* In 2011–12, 13 students received support. Federal Work-Study, scholarships/grants, health care benefits, and unspecified assistantships available. Support available to part-time students. Financial award applicants required to submit FAFSA. *Faculty research:* Bioengineering, energy, engineering education, infrastructure environment, nanotechnology and weather technology. *Unit head:* Dr. Thomas Landers, Dean, 405-325-2621, Fax: 405-325-7508, E-mail: landers@ou.edu. *Application contact:* Miranda Sowell, Coordinator of Graduate Admissions, 405-325-3811, Fax: 405-325-5346, E-mail: mgsowell@ou.edu. Web site: http://www.coe.ou.edu.

University of Ottawa, Faculty of Graduate and Postdoctoral Studies, Faculty of Engineering, Ottawa, ON K1N 6N5, Canada. Offers M Eng, MA Sc, MCS, PhD, Certificate. *Degree requirements:* For master's, thesis or alternative; for doctorate, thesis/dissertation. *Entrance requirements:* For master's, honors degree or equivalent, minimum B average. Electronic applications accepted.

University of Pennsylvania, School of Engineering and Applied Science, Philadelphia, PA 19104. Offers EMBA, MCIT, MS, MSE, PhD, AC, M Arch/MSE, MD/PhD, MSE/MBA, MSE/MCP, VMD/PhD. Part-time and evening/weekend programs available. *Faculty:* 106 full-time (13 women), 20 part-time/adjunct (1 woman). *Students:* 1,220 full-time (357

women), 286 part-time (71 women); includes 187 minority (23 Black or African American, non-Hispanic/Latino; 1 American Indian or Alaska Native, non-Hispanic/Latino; 134 Asian, non-Hispanic/Latino; 24 Hispanic/Latino; 1 Native Hawaiian or other Pacific Islander, non-Hispanic/Latino; 4 Two or more races, non-Hispanic/Latino), 900 international. 4,999 applicants, 30% accepted, 722 enrolled. In 2011, 389 master's, 63 doctorates awarded. *Degree requirements:* For doctorate, thesis/dissertation. *Entrance requirements:* Additional exam requirements/recommendations for international students: Required—TOEFL. *Application deadline:* For fall admission, 6/1 priority date for domestic students, 5/1 for international students; for spring admission, 11/1 priority date for domestic students, 10/1 for international students. Applications are processed on a rolling basis. Application fee: $70. Electronic applications accepted. *Expenses: Tuition:* Full-time $26,660; part-time $4944 per course. *Required fees:* $2318; $291 per course. Tuition and fees vary according to course load, degree level and program. *Financial support:* In 2011–12, 393 students received support. Fellowships, research assistantships, teaching assistantships, institutionally sponsored loans, scholarships/grants, traineeships, health care benefits, and unspecified assistantships available. Financial award application deadline: 12/15. *Unit head:* Eduardo D. Glandt, Dean, 215-898-7244, Fax: 215-573-2018, E-mail: seasdean@seas.upenn.edu. *Application contact:* Academic Programs Office, 215-898-4542, Fax: 215-573-5577, E-mail: engstats@seas.upenn.edu. Web site: http://www.seas.upenn.edu/.
See Display on this page and Close-Up on page 87.

University of Pittsburgh, Katz Graduate School of Business, MBA/Master of Science in Engineering Joint Degree Program, Pittsburgh, PA 15260. Offers MBA/MSE. *Accreditation:* AACSB. Part-time and evening/weekend programs available. *Faculty:* 62 full-time (17 women), 21 part-time/adjunct (4 women). *Students:* 11 full-time (1 woman), 33 part-time (7 women); includes 6 minority (2 Black or African American, non-Hispanic/Latino; 3 Asian, non-Hispanic/Latino; 1 Hispanic/Latino), 2 international. Average age 28. 13 applicants, 69% accepted, 4 enrolled. *Entrance requirements:* Additional exam requirements/recommendations for international students: Required—TOEFL (minimum score 600 paper, 250 computer, 100 iBT) or IELTS. *Application deadline:* For fall admission, 4/1 for domestic students, 2/1 for international students. Application fee: $50. Electronic applications accepted. *Expenses:* Tuition, state resident: full-time $18,774; part-time $760 per credit. Tuition, nonresident: full-time $30,736; part-time $1258 per credit. *Required fees:* $740; $200 per term. Tuition and fees vary according to program. *Financial support:* In 2011–12, 4 students received support. Career-related internships or fieldwork and scholarships/grants available. Financial award application deadline: 3/1; financial award applicants required to submit FAFSA. *Faculty research:* Accounting statements and reporting, corporate finance, information systems processes, structures and decision-making, consumer behavior and marketing models. *Unit head:* William T. Valenta, Assistant Dean/Director, 412-648-1610, Fax: 412-648-1659, E-mail: wtvalenta@katz.pitt.edu. *Application contact:* Thomas Keller, Director of MBA Admissions, 412-648-1700, Fax: 412-648-1659, E-mail: mba@katz.pitt.edu. Web site: http://www.business.pitt.edu/katz/mba/academics/programs/mba-msengineering.php.

University of Pittsburgh, Swanson School of Engineering, Pittsburgh, PA 15260. Offers MS, MS Ch E, MSBENG, MSCEE, MSEE, MSIE, MSME, MSPE, PhD, MD/PhD, MS Ch E/MSPE. Part-time programs available. *Faculty:* 111 full-time (16 women), 181 part-time/adjunct (22 women). *Students:* 533 full-time (127 women), 298 part-time (61 women); includes 73 minority (19 Black or African American, non-Hispanic/Latino; 2 American Indian or Alaska Native, non-Hispanic/Latino; 42 Asian, non-Hispanic/Latino; 9 Hispanic/Latino; 1 Native Hawaiian or other Pacific Islander, non-Hispanic/Latino), 312 international. 2,443 applicants, 33% accepted, 230 enrolled. In 2011, 165 master's, 57 doctorates awarded. Terminal master's awarded for partial completion of doctoral program. *Degree requirements:* For doctorate, comprehensive exam, thesis/dissertation, final oral exams. *Entrance requirements:* Additional exam requirements/recommendations for international students: Required—TOEFL (minimum score 550 paper-based; 213 computer-based; 80 iBT). *Application deadline:* For fall admission, 3/1 priority date for domestic students; for spring admission, 7/1 priority date for domestic students. Applications are processed on a rolling basis. Application fee: $50. Electronic applications accepted. *Financial support:* Contact institution. *Financial support:* In 2011–12, 351 students received support, including 47 fellowships with full tuition reimbursements available (averaging $20,772 per year), 206 research assistantships with full tuition reimbursements available (averaging $22,000 per year), 98 teaching assistantships with full tuition reimbursements available (averaging $21,000 per year); scholarships/grants, traineeships, and tuition waivers (full and partial) also available. Financial award application deadline: 4/15. *Faculty research:* Artificial organs, biotechnology, signal processing, construction management, fluid dynamics. *Total annual research expenditures:* $80.8 million. *Unit head:* Dr. Gerald D. Holder, Dean, 412-624-9811, Fax: 412-624-0412, E-mail: holder@engrng.pitt.edu. *Application contact:* 412-624-9800, Fax: 412-624-9808, E-mail: admin@engrng.pitt.edu. Web site: http://www.engineering.pitt.edu/.

University of Portland, School of Engineering, Portland, OR 97203-5798. Offers ME. Part-time and evening/weekend programs available. *Faculty:* 2 full-time (0 women). *Students:* 1 full-time (0 women), all international. Average age 23. *Entrance requirements:* For master's, GRE General Test, minimum GPA of 3.0, 3 letters of recommendation, resume, statement of goals, official transcripts. Additional exam requirements/recommendations for international students: Required—TOEFL (minimum score 550 paper-based; 80 iBT), IELTS (minimum score 7). *Application deadline:* For fall admission, 7/15 priority date for domestic students, 7/15 for international students; for spring admission, 12/15 priority date for domestic students, 12/15 for international students. Applications are processed on a rolling basis. Application fee: $50. *Expenses:* Contact institution. *Financial support:* Teaching assistantships, career-related internships or fieldwork, Federal Work-Study, and scholarships/grants available. Support available to part-time students. Financial award application deadline: 3/1; financial award applicants required to submit FAFSA. *Unit head:* Dr. Sharon Jones, Dean, 503-943-8169, E-mail: joness@up.edu. *Application contact:* Dr. Khalid Khan, Director, 503-943-7276, E-mail: khan@up.edu.

University of Puerto Rico, Mayagüez Campus, Graduate Studies, College of Engineering, Mayagüez, PR 00681-9000. Offers ME, MS, PhD. Part-time programs available. *Students:* 334 full-time (117 women), 42 part-time (8 women); includes 278 minority (all Hispanic/Latino), 98 international. 147 applicants, 65% accepted, 67 enrolled. In 2011, 55 master's, 3 doctorates awarded. *Degree requirements:* For master's, comprehensive exam, thesis; for doctorate, one foreign language, thesis/dissertation. *Entrance requirements:* For doctorate, GRE. Additional exam requirements/recommendations for international students: Required—TOEFL or IELTS. *Application deadline:* For fall admission, 2/15 for domestic and international students; for spring admission, 9/15 for domestic and international students. Applications are processed on a rolling basis. Application fee: $25. Tuition and fees vary according to course level and course load. *Financial support:* In 2011–12, 204 students received support, including 124 research assistantships (averaging $15,000 per year), 80

teaching assistantships (averaging $8,500 per year); Federal Work-Study and institutionally sponsored loans also available. *Total annual research expenditures:* $10.7 million. *Unit head:* Dr. Jaime Seguel, Dean, 787-265-3823, Fax: 787-833-1190, E-mail: jaime.seguel@upr.edu. *Application contact:* Dr. Agustin Rullan, Graduate Affairs Officer, 787-265-3823, Fax: 787 833-0905, E-mail: agustin.rullan@upr.edu. Web site: http://ing.uprm.edu/.

University of Regina, Faculty of Graduate Studies and Research, Faculty of Engineering and Applied Science, Regina, SK S4S 0A2, Canada. Offers M Eng, MA Sc, PhD. Part-time programs available. *Faculty:* 37 full-time (7 women), 2 part-time/adjunct (0 women). *Students:* 206 full-time (49 women), 32 part-time (6 women). 450 applicants, 25% accepted. In 2011, 42 master's, 10 doctorates awarded. *Degree requirements:* For master's, thesis (for some programs), project or thesis; for doctorate, comprehensive exam, thesis/dissertation. *Entrance requirements:* Additional exam requirements/recommendations for international students: Required—TOEFL (minimum score 550 paper-based; 80 iBT), IELTS (minimum score 6.5). *Application deadline:* For fall admission, 3/31 for domestic and international students; for winter admission, 7/31 for domestic and international students; for spring admission, 11/30 for domestic and international students. Application fee: $100. Electronic applications accepted. *Expenses:* Contact institution. *Financial support:* In 2011–12, 34 fellowships (averaging $6,500 per year), 1 research assistantship (averaging $5,500 per year), 45 teaching assistantships (averaging $2,298 per year) were awarded; career-related internships or fieldwork and scholarships/grants also available. Financial award application deadline: 6/15. *Unit head:* Dr. Paitoon Tontiwachwuthikul, Dean, 306-585-4160, Fax: 306-585-4855, E-mail: paitoon.tontiwachwuthikul@uregina.ca. *Application contact:* Melissa Dyck, Administrative Contact, 306-337-2603, Fax: 306-585-4855, E-mail: melissa.dyck@uregina.ca.

University of Rhode Island, Graduate School, College of Engineering, Kingston, RI 02881. Offers MS, PhD, Graduate Certificate. *Accreditation:* ABET (one or more programs are accredited). Part-time programs available. *Faculty:* 65 full-time (12 women), 5 part-time/adjunct (1 woman). *Students:* 146 full-time (27 women), 84 part-time (12 women); includes 17 minority (2 Black or African American, non-Hispanic/Latino; 9 Asian, non-Hispanic/Latino; 5 Hispanic/Latino; 1 Two or more races, non-Hispanic/Latino), 54 international. In 2011, 52 master's, 10 doctorates awarded. *Entrance requirements:* Additional exam requirements/recommendations for international students: Required—TOEFL (minimum score 550 paper-based; 213 computer-based). Application fee: $65. Electronic applications accepted. *Expenses:* Tuition, state resident: full-time $10,432; part-time $580 per credit hour. Tuition, nonresident: full-time $23,130; part-time $1285 per credit hour. *Required fees:* $1362; $36 per credit hour. $35 per semester. One-time fee: $130. *Financial support:* In 2011–12, 30 research assistantships with full and partial tuition reimbursements (averaging $8,510 per year), 19 teaching assistantships with full and partial tuition reimbursements (averaging $8,510 per year) were awarded. Financial award applicants required to submit FAFSA. *Unit head:* Dr. Raymond Wright, Dean, 401-874-2186, Fax: 401-782-1066, E-mail: dean@egr.uri.edu. *Application contact:* Nasser H. Zawia, Dean of the Graduate School, 401-874-5909, Fax: 401-874-5787, E-mail: nzawia@uri.edu. Web site: http://www.egr.uri.edu/.

University of Rochester, Hajim School of Engineering and Applied Sciences, Rochester, NY 14627. Offers MS, PhD. Part-time programs available. *Faculty:* 87 full-time (11 women). *Students:* 424 full-time (103 women), 25 part-time (8 women); includes 34 minority (4 Black or African American, non-Hispanic/Latino; 22 Asian, non-Hispanic/Latino; 6 Hispanic/Latino; 2 Two or more races, non-Hispanic/Latino), 236 international. 1,545 applicants, 30% accepted, 195 enrolled. In 2011, 97 master's, 46 doctorates awarded. Terminal master's awarded for partial completion of doctoral program. *Degree requirements:* For master's, comprehensive exam, thesis optional; for doctorate, thesis/dissertation, preliminary and oral exams. *Entrance requirements:* For master's and doctorate, GRE. Additional exam requirements/recommendations for international students: Required—TOEFL. *Application deadline:* For fall admission, 1/1 priority date for domestic students. Application fee: $60. *Expenses:* Tuition: Full-time $41,040. *Financial support:* Fellowships, research assistantships, teaching assistantships, and tuition waivers (full and partial) available. Financial award application deadline: 2/1. *Unit head:* Rob Clark, Dean, 585-275-4151. *Application contact:* Dr. Margaret Kearney, Dean of Graduate Studies, 585-275-3540. Web site: http://www.hajim.rochester.edu/.

University of St. Thomas, Graduate Studies, School of Engineering, St. Paul, MN 55105-1096. Offers manufacturing engineering and operations (MS); mechanical engineering (MS); medical device development (Certificate); regulatory science (MS); software engineering (MS); software management (MS); software systems (MSS); systems engineering (MS); technology management (MS). *Accreditation:* ABET (one or more programs are accredited). *Students:* 8 full-time, 210 part-time (38 women); includes 47 minority (22 Black or African American, non-Hispanic/Latino; 4 Asian, non-Hispanic/Latino; 6 Hispanic/Latino; 1 Native Hawaiian or other Pacific Islander, non-Hispanic/Latino; 14 Two or more races, non-Hispanic/Latino), 14 international. Average age 33. *Entrance requirements:* For master's, resume, official transcripts. Additional exam requirements/recommendations for international students: Required—TOEFL (minimum score 550 paper-based). *Application deadline:* For fall admission, 8/1 priority date for domestic students; for spring admission, 1/1 priority date for domestic students. Applications are processed on a rolling basis. Application fee: $30. Electronic applications accepted. *Expenses:* Contact institution. *Financial support:* Fellowships, research assistantships, institutionally sponsored loans, and scholarships/grants available. Support available to part-time students. Financial award application deadline: 4/1; financial award applicants required to submit FAFSA. *Unit head:* Don Weinkauf, Dean, 651-962-5760, Fax: 651-962-6419, E-mail: dhweinkauf@stthomas.edu. *Application contact:* Joyce A. Taylor, Graduate Programs Coordinator, 651-962-5756, Fax: 651-962-6419, E-mail: jataylor1@stthomas.edu.

University of Saskatchewan, College of Graduate Studies and Research, College of Engineering, Saskatoon, SK S7N 5A2, Canada. Offers M Eng, M Sc, PhD, Diploma. *Degree requirements:* For doctorate, thesis/dissertation. *Entrance requirements:* For master's and doctorate, GRE. Additional exam requirements/recommendations for international students: Required—TOEFL.

University of South Africa, College of Science, Engineering and Technology, Pretoria, South Africa. Offers chemical engineering (M Tech); information technology (M Tech).

University of South Alabama, Graduate School, College of Engineering, Mobile, AL 36688. Offers MS Ch E, MSCE, MSEE, MSME. Part-time programs available. *Faculty:* 26 full-time (2 women). *Students:* 78 full-time (15 women), 21 part-time (5 women); includes 8 minority (1 Black or African American, non-Hispanic/Latino; 3 Asian, non-Hispanic/Latino; 4 Hispanic/Latino), 55 international. 129 applicants, 64% accepted, 31 enrolled. In 2011, 89 master's awarded. *Degree requirements:* For master's, project or thesis. *Entrance requirements:* For master's, GRE General Test, BS in engineering, minimum GPA of 3.0. *Application deadline:* For fall admission, 7/15 priority date for

domestic students, 6/15 for international students; for spring admission, 12/1 for domestic students, 11/1 for international students. Applications are processed on a rolling basis. Application fee: $35. *Expenses:* Tuition, state resident: full-time $7968; part-time $332 per credit hour. Tuition, nonresident: full-time $15,936; part-time $664 per credit hour. *Financial support:* Research assistantships, career-related internships or fieldwork, and institutionally sponsored loans available. Support available to part-time students. Financial award application deadline: 4/1. *Unit head:* Dr. Thomas G. Thomas, Director of Graduate Studies, 251-460-6140. *Application contact:* Dr. B. Keith Harrison, Director of Graduate Studies, 251-460-6160. Web site: http://www.southalabama.edu/engineering.

University of South Carolina, The Graduate School, College of Engineering and Computing, Columbia, SC 29208. Offers ME, MS, PhD. Part-time and evening/weekend programs available. Postbaccalaureate distance learning degree programs offered (minimal on-campus study). *Degree requirements:* For master's, thesis (for some programs); for doctorate, thesis/dissertation. *Entrance requirements:* For master's and doctorate, GRE General Test. Additional exam requirements/recommendations for international students: Required—TOEFL. Electronic applications accepted. *Faculty research:* Electrochemical engineering/fuel cell technology, fracture mechanics and nondestructive evaluation, virtual prototyping for electric power systems, wideband-gap electronics materials behavior/composites and smart materials.

University of Southern California, Graduate School, Viterbi School of Engineering, Los Angeles, CA 90089. Offers MCM, ME, MS, PhD, Engr, Graduate Certificate, MS/MBA. Part-time programs available. Postbaccalaureate distance learning degree programs offered (no on-campus study). Terminal master's awarded for partial completion of doctoral program. *Degree requirements:* For doctorate, comprehensive exam, thesis/dissertation. *Entrance requirements:* For master's and doctorate, GRE. Additional exam requirements/recommendations for international students: Recommended—TOEFL. Electronic applications accepted. *Expenses:* Contact institution. *Faculty research:* Mechanics and materials, aerodynamics of air/ground vehicles, gas dynamics, aerosols, astronautics and space science, geophysical and microgravity flows, planetary physics, power MEMs and MEMS vacuum pumps, heat transfer and combustion, health systems, transportation and logistics, manufacturing and automation, engineering systems design, risk and economic analysis, electromagnetic devices circuits and VLSI, MEMS and nanotechnology, electromagnetics and plasmas.

University of Southern Indiana, Graduate Studies, College of Science, Engineering, and Education, Evansville, IN 47712-3590. Offers MS, MSE. Part-time and evening/weekend programs available. *Faculty:* 19 full-time (8 women), 2 part-time/adjunct (1 woman). *Students:* 1 (woman) full-time, 144 part-time (102 women); includes 7 minority (5 Black or African American, non-Hispanic/Latino; 1 Asian, non-Hispanic/Latino; 1 Hispanic/Latino), 2 international. Average age 32. 77 applicants, 99% accepted, 55 enrolled. In 2011, 36 master's awarded. *Degree requirements:* For master's, project. *Entrance requirements:* For master's, GRE General Test, NTE, PRAXIS I, minimum GPA of 2.5 and BS in engineering or engineering technology (MSIM); minimum GPA of 3.0 and teaching license (MSE). Additional exam requirements/recommendations for international students: Required—TOEFL (minimum score 550 paper-based; 213 computer-based; 79 iBT), IELTS (minimum score 6). *Application deadline:* For fall admission, 8/15 priority date for domestic students, 3/1 for international students. Applications are processed on a rolling basis. Application fee: $35. Electronic applications accepted. *Expenses:* Tuition, state resident: full-time $5044; part-time $280.21 per credit hour. Tuition, nonresident: full-time $9949; part-time $552.71 per credit hour. *Required fees:* $240; $22.75 per term. Tuition and fees vary according to course load and reciprocity agreements. *Financial support:* In 2011–12, 4 students received support. Federal Work-Study, scholarships/grants, tuition waivers (full and partial), and unspecified assistantships available. Financial award application deadline: 3/1; financial award applicants required to submit FAFSA. *Unit head:* Dr. Scott A. Gordon, Dean, 812-465-7137, E-mail: sgordon@usi.edu. *Application contact:* Dr. Wes Durham, Interim Director, Graduate Studies, 812-465-7015, Fax: 812-464-1956, E-mail: wdurham@usi.edu. Web site: http://www.usi.edu/science/.

University of South Florida, Graduate School, College of Engineering, Tampa, FL 33620-9951. Offers MCE, MCH, ME, MEVE, MIE, MME, MSBE, MSBE, MSCE, MSCH, MSCP, MSCS, MSEE, MSEM, MSES, MSEV, MSIE, MSME, PhD. Part-time and evening/weekend programs available. *Faculty:* 113 full-time (16 women), 28 part-time/adjunct (4 women). *Students:* 531 full-time (137 women), 266 part-time (58 women); includes 181 minority (48 Black or African American, non-Hispanic/Latino; 42 Asian, non-Hispanic/Latino; 83 Hispanic/Latino; 1 Native Hawaiian or other Pacific Islander, non-Hispanic/Latino; 7 Two or more races, non-Hispanic/Latino), 312 international. Average age 30. 925 applicants, 47% accepted, 178 enrolled. In 2011, 239 master's, 40 doctorates awarded. Terminal master's awarded for partial completion of doctoral program. *Degree requirements:* For master's, comprehensive exam, thesis; for doctorate, comprehensive exam, thesis/dissertation. *Entrance requirements:* For master's, GRE General Test, minimum GPA of 3.0 in last 60 hours of coursework; for doctorate, GRE General Test, minimum GPA of 3.3 in last 60 hours of coursework. Additional exam requirements/recommendations for international students: Required—TOEFL (minimum score 550 paper-based; 213 computer-based). *Application deadline:* For fall admission, 2/15 for domestic students, 1/2 for international students; for spring admission, 10/15 for domestic students, 6/1 for international students. Applications are processed on a rolling basis. Application fee: $30. Electronic applications accepted. *Financial support:* Career-related internships or fieldwork, Federal Work-Study, scholarships/grants, health care benefits, and unspecified assistantships available. Financial award application deadline: 3/1. *Total annual research expenditures:* $50,679. *Unit head:* Dr. John Wieneck, Dean, 813-974-2530, Fax: 813-974-5094, E-mail: wieneck@eng.usf.edu. *Application contact:* Marsha L. Brett, Administrative Assistant, 813-974-3782, Fax: 813-974-5094, E-mail: brett@eng.usf.edu. Web site: http://www2.eng.usf.edu/.

The University of Tennessee, Graduate School, College of Engineering, Knoxville, TN 37996. Offers MS, PhD, MS/MBA, MS/PhD. Part-time programs available. Postbaccalaureate distance learning degree programs offered (minimal on-campus study). *Faculty:* 171 full-time (17 women), 77 part-time/adjunct (9 women). *Students:* 643 full-time (115 women), 242 part-time (39 women); includes 76 minority (30 Black or African American, non-Hispanic/Latino; 4 American Indian or Alaska Native, non-Hispanic/Latino; 30 Asian, non-Hispanic/Latino; 11 Hispanic/Latino; 1 Native Hawaiian or other Pacific Islander, non-Hispanic/Latino), 310 international. Average age 28. 1,731 applicants, 26% accepted, 255 enrolled. In 2011, 158 master's, 43 doctorates awarded. *Degree requirements:* For master's, thesis or alternative; for doctorate, comprehensive exam, thesis/dissertation. *Entrance requirements:* For master's, GRE General Test (for MS students pursuing research thesis), minimum GPA of 2.7 (for U.S. degree holders), 3.0 (for international degree holders); 3 references; statement of purpose; for doctorate, GRE General Test, minimum GPA of 3.0 on previous graduate course work; 3 references; statement of purpose. Additional exam requirements/recommendations for international students: Required—TOEFL (minimum score 550 paper-based; 213 computer-based). *Application deadline:* For fall admission, 2/1 priority date for domestic students, 2/1 for international students; for spring admission, 6/15 for domestic and international students. Applications are processed on a rolling basis. Application fee: $35. Electronic applications accepted. *Expenses:* Tuition, state resident: full-time $8332; part-time $464 per credit hour. Tuition, nonresident: full-time $25,174; part-time $1400 per credit hour. *Required fees:* $1162; $56 per credit hour. Tuition and fees vary according to program. *Financial support:* In 2011–12, 565 students received support, including 40 fellowships with full tuition reimbursements available (averaging $20,348 per year), 308 research assistantships with full tuition reimbursements available (averaging $21,936 per year), 175 teaching assistantships with full tuition reimbursements available (averaging $17,835 per year); career-related internships or fieldwork, Federal Work-Study, institutionally sponsored loans, health care benefits, and unspecified assistantships also available. Financial award application deadline: 2/1; financial award applicants required to submit FAFSA. *Faculty research:* Chemical and biomolecular engineering; civil and environmental engineering; electrical engineering and computer science; nuclear engineering; materials science and engineering; mechanical, aerospace, and biomedical engineering; industrial and information engineering. *Total annual research expenditures:* $52.7 million. *Unit head:* Dr. Wayne T. Davis, Dean, 865-974-5321, Fax: 865-974-8890, E-mail: wtdavis@utk.edu. *Application contact:* Dr. Masood Parang, Associate Dean of Student Affairs, 865-974-2454, Fax: 865-974-9871, E-mail: mparang@utk.edu. Web site: http://www.engr.utk.edu/.

The University of Tennessee at Chattanooga, Graduate School, College of Engineering and Computer Science, Chattanooga, TN 37403. Offers MS, MS Engr, PhD, Graduate Certificate. Part-time and evening/weekend programs available. Postbaccalaureate distance learning degree programs offered (no on-campus study). *Faculty:* 38 full-time (7 women), 4 part-time/adjunct (1 woman). *Students:* 74 full-time (11 women), 137 part-time (27 women); includes 42 minority (24 Black or African American, non-Hispanic/Latino; 1 American Indian or Alaska Native, non-Hispanic/Latino; 10 Asian, non-Hispanic/Latino; 5 Hispanic/Latino; 2 Two or more races, non-Hispanic/Latino), 38 international. Average age 30. 209 applicants, 93% accepted, 60 enrolled. In 2011, 52 master's, 3 doctorates, 4 other advanced degrees awarded. *Degree requirements:* For master's, comprehensive exam, thesis or alternative, capstone project; for doctorate, comprehensive exam, thesis/dissertation. *Entrance requirements:* For master's, GRE. Additional exam requirements/recommendations for international students: Required—TOEFL (minimum score 550 paper-based; 213 computer-based; 79 iBT), IELTS (minimum score 6). *Application deadline:* For fall admission, 8/1 priority date for domestic students, 6/1 for international students; for spring admission, 12/1 priority date for domestic students, 10/1 for international students. Applications are processed on a rolling basis. Application fee: $35. Electronic applications accepted. *Expenses:* Tuition, state resident: full-time $6472; part-time $359 per credit hour. Tuition, nonresident: full-time $20,006; part-time $1111 per credit hour. *Required fees:* $1320; $160 per credit hour. *Financial support:* Career-related internships or fieldwork, scholarships/grants, and unspecified assistantships available. Support available to part-time students. Financial award applicants required to submit FAFSA. *Faculty research:* Quality control and project management, aerodynamics, artificial intelligence, computational design, network security. *Total annual research expenditures:* $4.1 million. *Unit head:* Dr. William Sutton, Dean, 423-425-2256, Fax: 423-425-5229, E-mail: will-sutton@utc.edu. *Application contact:* Dr. Jerald Ainsworth, Dean of Graduate Studies, 423-425-4478, Fax: 423-425-5223, E-mail: jerald-ainsworth@utc.edu. Web site: http://www.utc.edu/Academic/EngineeringAndComputerScience/.

The University of Tennessee Space Institute, Graduate Programs, Tullahoma, TN 37388-9700. Offers MS, PhD. Part-time programs available. Postbaccalaureate distance learning degree programs offered. *Faculty:* 21 full-time (2 women), 13 part-time/adjunct (1 woman). *Students:* 61 full-time (8 women), 95 part-time (20 women); includes 21 minority (11 Black or African American, non-Hispanic/Latino; 1 American Indian or Alaska Native, non-Hispanic/Latino; 6 Asian, non-Hispanic/Latino; 2 Hispanic/Latino; 1 Two or more races, non-Hispanic/Latino), 13 international. 103 applicants, 54% accepted, 45 enrolled. In 2011, 39 master's, 2 doctorates awarded. Terminal master's awarded for partial completion of doctoral program. *Degree requirements:* For doctorate, one foreign language, thesis/dissertation. *Entrance requirements:* Additional exam requirements/recommendations for international students: Required—TOEFL (minimum score 550 paper-based; 213 computer-based; 80 iBT), IELTS (minimum score 6.5). *Application deadline:* For fall admission, 2/1 for international students; for spring admission, 6/15 for international students. Applications are processed on a rolling basis. Application fee: $35. Electronic applications accepted. *Financial support:* In 2011–12, 7 fellowships with full and partial tuition reimbursements (averaging $1,671 per year), 36 research assistantships with full tuition reimbursements (averaging $17,791 per year) were awarded; career-related internships or fieldwork, Federal Work-Study, institutionally sponsored loans, health care benefits, tuition waivers (full and partial), and unspecified assistantships also available. *Faculty research:* Materials processing, computational fluid dynamics, aerodynamics, laser applications. *Unit head:* Dr. Charles Johnson, Associate Executive Director, 931-393-7318, Fax: 931-393-7211, E-mail: cjohnson@utsi.edu. *Application contact:* Dee Merriman, Coordinator III, 931-393-7213, Fax: 931-393-7211, E-mail: dmerrima@utsi.edu. Web site: http://www.utsi.edu/futurestudents/graduate.htm.

The University of Texas at Arlington, Graduate School, College of Engineering, Arlington, TX 76019. Offers M Engr, MS, PhD. Part-time and evening/weekend programs available. Postbaccalaureate distance learning degree programs offered (minimal on-campus study). *Faculty:* 135 full-time (13 women), 4 part-time/adjunct (0 women). *Students:* 985 full-time (222 women), 569 part-time (119 women); includes 180 minority (43 Black or African American, non-Hispanic/Latino; 77 Asian, non-Hispanic/Latino; 51 Hispanic/Latino; 1 Native Hawaiian or other Pacific Islander, non-Hispanic/Latino; 8 Two or more races, non-Hispanic/Latino), 1,081 international. Average age 27. 5,615 applicants, 61% accepted, 1554 enrolled. In 2011, 2,417 master's, 127 doctorates awarded. Terminal master's awarded for partial completion of doctoral program. *Degree requirements:* For master's, thesis optional; for doctorate, thesis/dissertation. *Entrance requirements:* For master's, GRE General Test, minimum GPA of 3.0 in last 60 hours of coursework; for doctorate, GRE General Test. Additional exam requirements/recommendations for international students: Required—TOEFL (minimum score 550 paper-based; 213 computer-based). *Application deadline:* For fall admission, 6/6 for domestic students, 4/4 for international students; for spring admission, 10/15 for domestic students, 9/5 for international students. Applications are processed on a rolling basis. Application fee: $35 ($50 for international students). *Financial support:* Fellowships, research assistantships, teaching assistantships, career-related internships or fieldwork, Federal Work-Study, institutionally sponsored loans, scholarships/grants, and tuition waivers (partial) available. Financial award application deadline: 6/1; financial award applicants required to submit FAFSA. *Faculty research:* Nanotechnology, mobile pervasive computing, bioinformatics intelligent systems. *Unit head:* Dr. Jean-Pierre Bardet, Dean, 817-272-2571, Fax: 817-272-5110, E-mail: bardet@uta.edu. *Application contact:* Dr. Lynn L. Peterson, Associate Dean for Academic Affairs, 817-272-2571, Fax: 817-272-2548, E-mail: peterson@uta.edu. Web site: http://www.uta.edu/engineering/.

The University of Texas at Austin, Graduate School, Cockrell School of Engineering, Austin, TX 78712-1111. Offers MA, MS, MSE, PhD, MBA/MSE, MD/PhD, MP Aff/MSE. *Accreditation:* ABET (one or more programs are accredited). Part-time and evening/weekend programs available. *Entrance requirements:* For master's and doctorate, GRE General Test. Additional exam requirements/recommendations for international students: Required—TOEFL (minimum score 550 paper-based; 213 computer-based). Application fee: $50 ($75 for international students). Electronic applications accepted. *Financial support:* Fellowships with partial tuition reimbursements, research assistantships with full tuition reimbursements, teaching assistantships with partial tuition reimbursements, career-related internships or fieldwork, Federal Work-Study, institutionally sponsored loans, scholarships/grants, tuition waivers (partial), unspecified assistantships, and academic assistantships, tutorships available. Support available to part-time students. Financial award applicants required to submit FAFSA. *Unit head:* Dr. Gregory L. Fenves, Dean, 512-471-1166, Fax: 512-475-7072, E-mail: fenves@mail.utexas.edu. *Application contact:* Tina Woods, Graduate Program Coordinator II, 521-471-7595, E-mail: twoods@mail.utexas.edu. Web site: http://www.engr.utexas.edu/.

The University of Texas at Dallas, Erik Jonsson School of Engineering and Computer Science, Richardson, TX 75080. Offers MS, MSEE, MSME, MSTE, PhD. Part-time and evening/weekend programs available. *Faculty:* 112 full-time (14 women), 6 part-time/adjunct (0 women). *Students:* 1,088 full-time (245 women), 430 part-time (84 women); includes 160 minority (21 Black or African American, non-Hispanic/Latino; 91 Asian, non-Hispanic/Latino; 41 Hispanic/Latino; 7 Two or more races, non-Hispanic/Latino), 1,117 international. Average age 27. 3,652 applicants, 49% accepted, 548 enrolled. In 2011, 354 master's, 58 doctorates awarded. *Degree requirements:* For master's, thesis optional; for doctorate, thesis/dissertation. *Entrance requirements:* For master's, GRE General Test, minimum GPA of 3.0 in related bachelor's course work; for doctorate, GRE General Test, minimum GPA of 3.5. Additional exam requirements/recommendations for international students: Required—TOEFL (minimum score 550 paper-based; 215 computer-based). *Application deadline:* For fall admission, 7/15 for domestic students, 5/1 for international students; for spring admission, 11/15 for domestic students, 9/1 for international students. Applications are processed on a rolling basis. Application fee: $50 ($100 for international students). Electronic applications accepted. *Expenses:* Tuition, state resident: full-time $11,170; part-time $620.56 per credit hour. Tuition, nonresident: full-time $20,212; part-time $1122.89 per credit hour. *Financial support:* In 2011–12, 448 students received support, including 6 fellowships with partial tuition reimbursements available (averaging $11,572 per year), 253 research assistantships with partial tuition reimbursements available (averaging $21,912 per year), 95 teaching assistantships with partial tuition reimbursements available (averaging $15,905 per year); career-related internships or fieldwork, Federal Work-Study, institutionally sponsored loans, scholarships/grants, and unspecified assistantships also available. Support available to part-time students. Financial award application deadline: 4/30; financial award applicants required to submit FAFSA. *Faculty research:* Semiconducting materials, nano-fabrication and bio-nanotechnology, biomedical devices and organic electronics, signal processing and language technology, cloud computing and IT security. *Total annual research expenditures:* $30.8 million. *Unit head:* Dr. Mark W. Spong, Dean, 972-883-2974, Fax: 972-883-2813, E-mail: ecsdean@utdallas.edu. *Application contact:* Dr. Cy Cantrell, Senior Associate Dean, 972-883-6234, Fax: 972-883-2813, E-mail: gradecs@utdallas.edu. Web site: http://ecs.utdallas.edu/.

The University of Texas at El Paso, Graduate School, College of Engineering, El Paso, TX 79968-0001. Offers MEENE, MS, MSENE, MSIT, PhD, Certificate. Part-time and evening/weekend programs available. *Students:* 513 (106 women); includes 263 minority (3 Black or African American, non-Hispanic/Latino; 9 Asian, non-Hispanic/Latino; 251 Hispanic/Latino), 219 international. Average age 28. 264 applicants, 79% accepted, 141 enrolled. In 2011, 80 master's, 3 doctorates awarded. *Degree requirements:* For master's, thesis optional; for doctorate, thesis/dissertation. *Entrance requirements:* For master's, GRE, minimum GPA of 3.0, letters of reference; for doctorate, GRE, statement of purpose, letters of reference. Additional exam requirements/recommendations for international students: Required—TOEFL; Recommended—IELTS. *Application deadline:* For fall admission, 8/1 priority date for domestic students, 3/1 for international students; for spring admission, 11/1 priority date for domestic students, 9/1 for international students. Applications are processed on a rolling basis. Application fee: $45 ($80 for international students). Electronic applications accepted. *Expenses:* Contact institution. *Financial support:* In 2011–12, research assistantships with partial tuition reimbursements (averaging $21,125 per year), teaching assistantships with partial tuition reimbursements (averaging $16,900 per year) were awarded; fellowships with partial tuition reimbursements, institutionally sponsored loans, scholarships/grants, health care benefits, tuition waivers (partial), and unspecified assistantships also available. Support available to part-time students. Financial award application deadline: 3/15; financial award applicants required to submit FAFSA. *Unit head:* Dr. Richard Schoephoerster, Dean, 915-747-6444, Fax: 915-747-5437, E-mail: schoephoerster@utep.edu. *Application contact:* Dr. Benjamin Flores, Interim Dean of the Graduate School, 915-747-5491, Fax: 915-747-5788, E-mail: bflores@utep.edu. Web site: http://www.utep.edu/engineer/.

The University of Texas at San Antonio, College of Engineering, San Antonio, TX 78249-0617. Offers MCE, MS, MSCE, MSEE, MSME, PhD. *Faculty:* 85 full-time (9 women), 37 part-time/adjunct (1 woman). *Students:* 253 full-time (73 women), 127 part-time (18 women); includes 109 minority (13 Black or African American, non-Hispanic/Latino; 27 Asian, non-Hispanic/Latino; 63 Hispanic/Latino; 6 Two or more races, non-Hispanic/Latino), 182 international. 467 applicants, 62% accepted, 117 enrolled. In 2011, 84 master's, 10 doctorates awarded. *Entrance requirements:* Additional exam requirements/recommendations for international students: Required—TOEFL (minimum score 500 paper-based). *Application deadline:* For fall admission, 7/1 for domestic students, 4/1 for international students; for spring admission, 11/1 for domestic students, 9/1 for international students. Application fee: $45 ($85 for international students). *Expenses:* Tuition, state resident: full-time $3148; part-time $2176 per semester. Tuition, nonresident: full-time $8782; part-time $5932 per semester. *Required fees:* $719 per semester. *Unit head:* Dr. C. Mauli Agarwal, Dean, 210-458-4490, Fax: 210-458-5556, E-mail: mauli.agarwal@utsa.edu.

University of the District of Columbia, School of Engineering and Applied Science, Washington, DC 20008-1175. Offers MS. *Expenses: Tuition, area resident:* Full-time $7580; part-time $421 per credit hour. Tuition, state resident: full-time $8580; part-time $477 per credit hour. Tuition, nonresident: full-time $14,580; part-time $810 per credit hour. *Required fees:* $620; $30 per credit hour. $310 per semester.

Engineering and Applied Sciences—General

The University of Toledo, College of Graduate Studies, College of Engineering, Program in Engineering, Toledo, OH 43606-3390. Offers general engineering (MS). *Entrance requirements:* For master's, GRE General Test, minimum GPA of 2.7, industrial experience.

University of Toronto, School of Graduate Studies, Faculty of Applied Science and Engineering, Toronto, ON M5S 1A1, Canada. Offers M Eng, MA Sc, MH Sc, PhD. Part-time programs available. *Degree requirements:* For doctorate, thesis/dissertation. *Expenses:* Contact institution.

University of Tulsa, Graduate School, College of Engineering and Natural Sciences, Tulsa, OK 74104-3189. Offers ME, MS, MSE, MTA, PhD, JD/MS, MBA/MS, MSF/MSAM. Part-time programs available. *Faculty:* 102 full-time (11 women), 2 part-time/adjunct (1 woman). *Students:* 241 full-time (65 women), 83 part-time (24 women); includes 19 minority (4 Black or African American, non-Hispanic/Latino; 8 American Indian or Alaska Native, non-Hispanic/Latino; 4 Asian, non-Hispanic/Latino; 3 Hispanic/Latino), 176 international. Average age 26. 608 applicants, 31% accepted, 98 enrolled. In 2011, 90 master's, 15 doctorates awarded. Terminal master's awarded for partial completion of doctoral program. *Degree requirements:* For master's, thesis (for some programs); for doctorate, comprehensive exam, thesis/dissertation. *Entrance requirements:* For master's and doctorate, GRE General Test. Additional exam requirements/recommendations for international students: Required—TOEFL (minimum score 550 paper-based; 213 computer-based), IELTS (minimum score 6). *Application deadline:* Applications are processed on a rolling basis. Application fee: $40. Electronic applications accepted. *Expenses: Tuition:* Full-time $17,748; part-time $986 per hour. *Required fees:* $5 per contact hour. $75 per semester. Tuition and fees vary according to program. *Financial support:* In 2011–12, 235 students received support, including 36 fellowships with full and partial tuition reimbursements available (averaging $5,528 per year), 172 research assistantships with full and partial tuition reimbursements available (averaging $11,680 per year), 98 teaching assistantships with full and partial tuition reimbursements available (averaging $10,048 per year); career-related internships or fieldwork, Federal Work-Study, scholarships/grants, health care benefits, tuition waivers (full and partial), and unspecified assistantships also available. Support available to part-time students. Financial award application deadline: 2/1; financial award applicants required to submit FAFSA. *Total annual research expenditures:* $16.2 million. *Unit head:* Dr. James Sorem, Interim Dean, 918-631-2288, E-mail: james-sorem@utulsa.edu. *Application contact:* Graduate School, 918-631-2336, Fax: 918-631-2156, E-mail: grad@utulsa.edu. Web site: http://www.ens.utulsa.edu/.

University of Utah, Graduate School, College of Engineering, Salt Lake City, UT 84112. Offers M Phil, ME, MS, PhD. *Accreditation:* ABET. *Faculty:* 161 full-time (21 women), 14 part-time/adjunct (1 woman). *Students:* 696 full-time (106 women), 272 part-time (30 women); includes 61 minority (3 Black or African American, non-Hispanic/Latino; 2 American Indian or Alaska Native, non-Hispanic/Latino; 40 Asian, non-Hispanic/Latino; 12 Hispanic/Latino; 4 Two or more races, non-Hispanic/Latino), 381 international. Average age 29. 1,658 applicants, 32% accepted, 261 enrolled. In 2011, 222 master's, 66 doctorates awarded. *Application deadline:* Applications are processed on a rolling basis. Application fee: $55 ($65 for international students). *Expenses:* Contact institution. *Financial support:* Applicants required to submit FAFSA. *Faculty research:* Biomaterials, wastewater treatment, computer-aided graphics design, semiconductors, polymers. *Total annual research expenditures:* $69.8 million. *Unit head:* Dr. Richard B. Brown, Dean, 801-581-6912, E-mail: brown@coe.utah.edu. *Application contact:* Dianne Leonard, Coordinator, Administrative Program, 801-585-7769, Fax: 801-581-8692, E-mail: dleonard@coe.utah.edu. Web site: http://www.coe.utah.edu/.

University of Vermont, Graduate College, College of Engineering and Mathematics, Burlington, VT 05405. Offers MS, MST, PhD. Part-time programs available. *Students:* 185 (48 women); includes 10 minority (4 Black or African American, non-Hispanic/Latino; 5 Asian, non-Hispanic/Latino; 1 Hispanic/Latino), 51 international. 320 applicants, 51% accepted, 43 enrolled. In 2011, 25 master's, 7 doctorates awarded. *Degree requirements:* For doctorate, thesis/dissertation. *Entrance requirements:* Additional exam requirements/recommendations for international students: Required—TOEFL (minimum score 550 paper-based; 213 computer-based; 80 iBT). *Application deadline:* For fall admission, 4/1 priority date for domestic students. Applications are processed on a rolling basis. Application fee: $40. Electronic applications accepted. *Financial support:* Fellowships, research assistantships, teaching assistantships, and Federal Work-Study available. Financial award application deadline: 3/1. *Unit head:* Bernard Cole, Interim Dean, 802-656-3333.

University of Victoria, Faculty of Graduate Studies, Faculty of Engineering, Victoria, BC V8W 2Y2, Canada. Offers M Eng, M Sc, MA Sc, PhD.

University of Virginia, School of Engineering and Applied Science, Charlottesville, VA 22903. Offers MCS, ME, MEP, MMSE, MS, PhD, ME/MBA. Part-time programs available. Postbaccalaureate distance learning degree programs offered (no on-campus study). *Faculty:* 142 full-time (13 women), 5 part-time/adjunct (2 women). *Students:* 587 full-time (136 women), 37 part-time (6 women); includes 73 minority (21 Black or African American, non-Hispanic/Latino; 39 Asian, non-Hispanic/Latino; 8 Hispanic/Latino; 5 Two or more races, non-Hispanic/Latino), 246 international. Average age 27. 1,595 applicants, 17% accepted, 139 enrolled. In 2011, 133 master's, 90 doctorates awarded. Terminal master's awarded for partial completion of doctoral program. *Degree requirements:* For doctorate, comprehensive exam, thesis/dissertation. *Entrance requirements:* For master's, GRE General Test, 3 letters of recommendation; for doctorate, GRE General Test, 3 letters of recommendation, essay. Additional exam requirements/recommendations for international students: Required—TOEFL (minimum score 600 paper-based; 250 computer-based; 90 iBT), IELTS (minimum score 7). *Application deadline:* For fall admission, 8/1 for domestic students, 4/1 for international students; for winter admission, 12/1 for domestic students, 8/1 for international students; for spring admission, 5/1 for domestic students, 1/1 for international students. Applications are processed on a rolling basis. Application fee: $60. Electronic applications accepted. *Financial support:* Fellowships with full tuition reimbursements, research assistantships with full tuition reimbursements, teaching assistantships with full tuition reimbursements, and career-related internships or fieldwork available. Financial award application deadline: 1/15; financial award applicants required to submit FAFSA. *Unit head:* James H. Aylor, Dean, 434-924-3072, Fax: 434-243-2083. *Application contact:* Kathryn C. Thornton, Associate Dean for Graduate Programs, 434-924-3897, Fax: 434-982-3044, E-mail: seas-grad-admission@virginia.edu. Web site: http://www.seas.virginia.edu/.

University of Washington, Graduate School, College of Engineering, Seattle, WA 98195-2180. Offers MAE, MME, MS, MSCE, MSE, MSME, PMS, PhD. Part-time programs available. Postbaccalaureate distance learning degree programs offered (no on-campus study). *Faculty:* 332 full-time (67 women), 80 part-time/adjunct (18 women). *Students:* 1,062 full-time (297 women), 725 part-time (152 women); includes 345 minority (32 Black or African American, non-Hispanic/Latino; 7 American Indian or Alaska Native, non-Hispanic/Latino; 240 Asian, non-Hispanic/Latino; 66 Hispanic/Latino), 478 international. Average age 28. 5,187 applicants, 27% accepted, 514 enrolled. In 2011, 408 master's, 110 doctorates awarded. *Degree requirements:* For master's, comprehensive exam (for some programs), thesis optional, teaching assistantship for 1 quarter, research project, final exam; for doctorate, comprehensive exam, thesis/dissertation, qualifying, general and final exams; thesis defense; research/independent project; completion of all work towards degree within 10 years. *Entrance requirements:* For master's and doctorate, GRE General Test, minimum GPA of 3.0. Additional exam requirements/recommendations for international students: Required—TOEFL (minimum score 580 paper-based; 237 computer-based; 92 iBT); Recommended—IELTS (minimum score 7). *Application deadline:* For fall admission, 12/15 for domestic students, 11/15 for international students. Applications are processed on a rolling basis. Application fee: $75. Electronic applications accepted. *Expenses:* Contact institution. *Financial support:* In 2011–12, 1,002 students received support, including 145 fellowships with full tuition reimbursements available (averaging $17,899 per year), 642 research assistantships with full tuition reimbursements available (averaging $17,365 per year), 174 teaching assistantships with full tuition reimbursements available (averaging $16,263 per year); career-related internships or fieldwork, Federal Work-Study, institutionally sponsored loans, scholarships/grants, traineeships, health care benefits, tuition waivers (full), unspecified assistantships, and stipend supplements also available. Financial award application deadline: 2/28; financial award applicants required to submit FAFSA. *Faculty research:* Biomaterials and tissue engineering, molecular energy processes, human-computer interaction, artificial intelligence, environmentally-sensitive energy conversion. *Total annual research expenditures:* $113 million. *Unit head:* Dr. Matthew O'Donnell, Dean, 206-543-0340, Fax: 206-685-0666, E-mail: odonnel@uw.edu. *Application contact:* Dr. Eve Riskin, Associate Dean, Academic Affairs, 206-685-2313, Fax: 206-685-0666, E-mail: riskin@u.washington.edu. Web site: http://www.engr.washington.edu/.

University of Waterloo, Graduate Studies, Faculty of Engineering, Waterloo, ON N2L 3G1, Canada. Offers M Arch, M Eng, MA Sc, MBET, MMS, PhD. Part-time and evening/weekend programs available. Postbaccalaureate distance learning degree programs offered (no on-campus study). *Degree requirements:* For master's, research paper or thesis; for doctorate, comprehensive exam, thesis/dissertation. *Entrance requirements:* For master's, honors degree; for doctorate, master's degree, minimum A- average. Additional exam requirements/recommendations for international students: Required—TOEFL, TWE. Electronic applications accepted.

The University of Western Ontario, Faculty of Graduate Studies, Physical Sciences Division, Faculty of Engineering, London, ON N6A 5B8, Canada. Offers chemical and biochemical engineering (ME Sc, PhD); civil and environmental engineering (M Eng, ME Sc, PhD); electrical and computer engineering (M Eng, ME Sc, PhD); mechanical and materials engineering (M Eng, ME Sc, PhD). Part-time programs available. Terminal master's awarded for partial completion of doctoral program. *Degree requirements:* For master's, thesis; for doctorate, thesis/dissertation. *Entrance requirements:* For master's, minimum B average; for doctorate, minimum B+ average. *Faculty research:* Wind, geotechnical, chemical reactor engineering, applied electrostatics, biochemical engineering.

University of Windsor, Faculty of Graduate Studies, Faculty of Engineering, Windsor, ON N9B 3P4, Canada. Offers M Eng, MA Sc, PhD. Part-time programs available. *Degree requirements:* For doctorate, comprehensive exam, thesis/dissertation. *Entrance requirements:* For master's, minimum B average; for doctorate, master's degree. Additional exam requirements/recommendations for international students: Required—TOEFL. Electronic applications accepted.

University of Wisconsin–Madison, Graduate School, College of Engineering, Madison, WI 53706-1380. Offers ME, MS, PhD. Part-time programs available. Postbaccalaureate distance learning degree programs offered (minimal on-campus study). *Degree requirements:* For doctorate, thesis/dissertation. Electronic applications accepted. *Expenses:* Tuition, state resident: full-time $10,296; part-time $643.51 per credit. Tuition, nonresident: full-time $24,054; part-time $1503.40 per credit. *Required fees:* $70.06 per credit. Tuition and fees vary according to course load, campus/location, program and reciprocity agreements.

University of Wisconsin–Milwaukee, Graduate School, College of Engineering and Applied Science, Milwaukee, WI 53201. Offers MS, PhD, Certificate, MUP/MS. Part-time programs available. *Faculty:* 65 full-time (9 women), 2 part-time/adjunct (0 women). *Students:* 204 full-time (44 women), 141 part-time (28 women); includes 40 minority (7 Black or African American, non-Hispanic/Latino; 23 Asian, non-Hispanic/Latino; 2 Hispanic/Latino; 8 Two or more races, non-Hispanic/Latino), 185 international. Average age 30. 342 applicants, 56% accepted, 64 enrolled. In 2011, 63 master's, 12 doctorates awarded. *Degree requirements:* For master's, comprehensive exam (for some programs), thesis or alternative; for doctorate, thesis/dissertation, internship. *Entrance requirements:* For master's, GRE, minimum GPA of 2.75; for doctorate, GRE, minimum GPA of 3.5. Additional exam requirements/recommendations for international students: Required—TOEFL (minimum score 550 paper-based; 79 iBT), IELTS (minimum score 6.5). *Application deadline:* For fall admission, 1/1 priority date for domestic students; for spring admission, 9/1 for domestic students. Applications are processed on a rolling basis. Application fee: $56. Electronic applications accepted. One-time fee: $506.10 full-time. Tuition and fees vary according to course load and reciprocity agreements. *Financial support:* In 2011–12, 31 research assistantships, 82 teaching assistantships were awarded; fellowships, career-related internships or fieldwork, Federal Work-Study, and unspecified assistantships also available. Support available to part-time students. Financial award application deadline: 4/15. *Total annual research expenditures:* $13.5 million. *Unit head:* Dr. Tien-Chen Jen, Interim Dean, 414-229-4126, E-mail: jent@uwm.edu. *Application contact:* Betty Warras, General Information Contact, 414-229-6169, Fax: 414-229-6958, E-mail: ceas-graduate@uwm.edu. Web site: http://www.uwm.edu/CEAS/.

University of Wisconsin–Platteville, School of Graduate Studies, Distance Learning Center, Online Master of Science in Engineering Program, Platteville, WI 53818-3099. Offers MS. Part-time and evening/weekend programs available. Postbaccalaureate distance learning degree programs offered (no on-campus study). *Students:* 3 full-time (2 women), 125 part-time (22 women); includes 6 minority (4 Black or African American, non-Hispanic/Latino; 1 Hispanic/Latino; 1 Native Hawaiian or other Pacific Islander, non-Hispanic/Latino), 18 international. 42 applicants, 83% accepted, 23 enrolled. In 2011, 29 master's awarded. *Degree requirements:* For master's, thesis or alternative. *Entrance requirements:* Additional exam requirements/recommendations for international students: Required—TOEFL (minimum score 500 paper-based; 61 iBT), IELTS (minimum score 6). *Application deadline:* For fall admission, 7/1 priority date for domestic students; for spring admission, 11/1 priority date for domestic students. Applications are processed on a rolling basis. Application fee: $56. Electronic applications accepted. *Expenses:* Contact institution. *Financial support:* Scholarships/grants available. Support available to part-time students. *Unit head:* Jill Clough,

Coordinator, 608-342-1665, Fax: 608-342-1071, E-mail: clough@uwplatt.edu. *Application contact:* Jill Clough, Coordinator, 608-342-1665, Fax: 608-342-1071, E-mail: disted@uwplatt.edu.

University of Wyoming, College of Engineering and Applied Sciences, Laramie, WY 82070. Offers MS, PhD. Part-time programs available. *Entrance requirements:* For master's and doctorate, GRE General Test, minimum GPA of 3.0. Additional exam requirements/recommendations for international students: Required—TOEFL. Electronic applications accepted.

Utah State University, School of Graduate Studies, College of Engineering, Logan, UT 84322. Offers ME, MS, PhD, CE. Part-time and evening/weekend programs available. Terminal master's awarded for partial completion of doctoral program. *Degree requirements:* For master's, thesis (for some programs); for doctorate, thesis/dissertation. *Entrance requirements:* For master's and doctorate, GRE General Test, minimum GPA of 3.0. Additional exam requirements/recommendations for international students: Required—TOEFL. Electronic applications accepted. *Faculty research:* Crop-yield modeling, earthquake engineering, digital signal processing, technology and the public school, cryogenic cooling.

Vanderbilt University, School of Engineering, Nashville, TN 37235. Offers M Eng, MS, PhD, MD/PhD. MS and PhD offered through the Graduate School. Part-time programs available. *Faculty:* 121 full-time (22 women), 25 part-time/adjunct (2 women). *Students:* 450 full-time (132 women); includes 61 minority (18 Black or African American, non-Hispanic/Latino; 10 Asian, non-Hispanic/Latino; 11 Hispanic/Latino; 22 Two or more races, non-Hispanic/Latino), 170 international. Average age 26. 1,358 applicants, 16% accepted, 120 enrolled. In 2011, 79 master's, 56 doctorates awarded. Terminal master's awarded for partial completion of doctoral program. *Degree requirements:* For master's, comprehensive exam (for some programs), thesis (for some programs); for doctorate, comprehensive exam (for some programs), thesis/dissertation. *Entrance requirements:* For master's and doctorate, GRE General Test. Additional exam requirements/recommendations for international students: Required—TOEFL. *Application deadline:* For fall admission, 1/15 for domestic and international students; for spring admission, 11/1 for domestic and international students. Application fee: $0. Electronic applications accepted. *Financial support:* Fellowships with full tuition reimbursements, research assistantships with full tuition reimbursements, teaching assistantships with full tuition reimbursements, career-related internships or fieldwork, Federal Work-Study, institutionally sponsored loans, scholarships/grants, traineeships, health care benefits, and tuition waivers (full and partial) available. Support available to part-time students. Financial award application deadline: 1/15; financial award applicants required to submit CSS PROFILE or FAFSA. *Faculty research:* Robotics, microelectronics, reliability in design, software engineering, medical imaging. *Total annual research expenditures:* $54.6 million. *Unit head:* Kenneth F. Galloway, Dean, 615-322-0720, Fax: 615-343-8006, E-mail: kenneth.f.galloway@vanderbilt.edu. *Application contact:* Dr. George E. Cook, Associate Dean for Research and Graduate Studies, 615-343-5032, Fax: 615-343-8006, E-mail: george.e.cook@vanderbilt.edu. Web site: http://www.vanderbilt.edu.

Villanova University, College of Engineering, Villanova, PA 19085-1699. Offers MSCPE, MSChE, MSEE, MSME, MSWREE, PhD, Certificate. Part-time and evening/weekend programs available. Postbaccalaureate distance learning degree programs offered (minimal on-campus study). Terminal master's awarded for partial completion of doctoral program. *Degree requirements:* For master's, thesis optional; for doctorate, thesis/dissertation. *Entrance requirements:* For master's, GRE General Test (for applicants with degrees from foreign universities), minimum GPA of 3.0; for doctorate, GRE General Test. Additional exam requirements/recommendations for international students: Required—TOEFL (minimum score 600 paper-based; 250 computer-based; 100 iBT). Electronic applications accepted. *Expenses:* Contact institution. *Faculty research:* Composite materials, economy and risk, heat transfer, signal detection.

Virginia Commonwealth University, Graduate School, School of Engineering, Richmond, VA 23284-9005. Offers MS, PhD, MD/PhD. *Degree requirements:* For doctorate, thesis/dissertation, comprehensive oral and written exams. *Entrance requirements:* For master's and doctorate, GRE General Test. Additional exam requirements/recommendations for international students: Required—TOEFL (minimum score 600 paper-based; 250 computer-based; 100 iBT). Electronic applications accepted. *Expenses:* Tuition, state resident: full-time $9133; part-time $507 per credit. Tuition, nonresident: full-time $18,777; part-time $1043 per credit. *Required fees:* $77 per credit. Tuition and fees vary according to degree level, campus/location, program and student level. *Faculty research:* Artificial hearts, orthopedic implants, medical imaging, medical instrumentation and sensors, cardiac monitoring.

Virginia Polytechnic Institute and State University, Graduate School, College of Engineering, Blacksburg, VA 24061. Offers M Eng, MEA, MS, PhD, Certificate. *Accreditation:* ABET (one or more programs are accredited). *Faculty:* 346 full-time (54 women), 1 part-time/adjunct (0 women). *Students:* 1,693 full-time (363 women), 385 part-time (81 women); includes 202 minority (41 Black or African American, non-Hispanic/Latino; 1 American Indian or Alaska Native, non-Hispanic/Latino; 98 Asian, non-Hispanic/Latino; 43 Hispanic/Latino; 19 Two or more races, non-Hispanic/Latino), 944 international. Average age 28. 4,550 applicants, 20% accepted, 486 enrolled. In 2011, 455 master's, 154 doctorates awarded. *Degree requirements:* For master's, comprehensive exam (for some programs), thesis (for some programs); for doctorate, comprehensive exam (for some programs), thesis/dissertation (for some programs). *Entrance requirements:* For master's and doctorate, GRE. Additional exam requirements/recommendations for international students: Required—TOEFL (minimum score 550 paper-based; 213 computer-based). *Application deadline:* For fall admission, 7/1 for domestic students, 4/1 for international students; for spring admission, 12/1 for domestic students, 9/1 for international students. Applications are processed on a rolling basis. Application fee: $65. Electronic applications accepted. *Expenses:* Tuition, state resident: full-time $10,048; part-time $558.25 per credit hour. Tuition, nonresident: full-time $19,497; part-time $1083.25 per credit hour. *Required fees:* $405 per semester. Tuition and fees vary according to course load, campus/location and program. *Financial support:* In 2011–12, 145 fellowships with full tuition reimbursements (averaging $6,262 per year), 841 research assistantships with full tuition reimbursements (averaging $21,164 per year), 257 teaching assistantships with full tuition reimbursements (averaging $18,268 per year) were awarded. Financial award application deadline: 3/1. *Total annual research expenditures:* $85.2 million. *Unit head:* Dr. Richard C. Benson, Dean, 540-231-9752, Fax: 540-231-3031, E-mail: deaneng@vt.edu. *Application contact:* Linda Perkins, Information Contact, 540-231-9752, Fax: 540-231-3031, E-mail: lperkins@vt.edu. Web site: http://www.eng.vt.edu/.

Washington State University, Graduate School, College of Engineering and Architecture, Pullman, WA 99164. Offers M Arch, MS, PhD. *Faculty:* 106. *Students:* 501 full-time (137 women), 108 part-time (28 women); includes 53 minority (9 Black or African American, non-Hispanic/Latino; 2 American Indian or Alaska Native, non-Hispanic/Latino; 20 Asian, non-Hispanic/Latino; 18 Hispanic/Latino; 4 Two or more races, non-Hispanic/Latino), 310 international. Average age 28. 1,244 applicants, 23%

accepted, 177 enrolled. In 2011, 99 master's, 37 doctorates awarded. Terminal master's awarded for partial completion of doctoral program. *Degree requirements:* For master's, comprehensive exam (for some programs), thesis (for some programs), oral exam; for doctorate, comprehensive exam, thesis/dissertation, oral exam. *Entrance requirements:* For master's, GRE, minimum GPA of 3.0, 3 letters of recommendation; for doctorate, GRE, minimum GPA of 3.4, 3 letters of recommendation. Additional exam requirements/recommendations for international students: Required—TOEFL (minimum score 520 paper-based; 190 computer-based). *Application deadline:* For fall admission, 3/1 priority date for domestic students, 3/1 for international students; for spring admission, 7/1 priority date for domestic students, 7/1 for international students. Applications are processed on a rolling basis. Application fee: $75. *Financial support:* In 2011–12, 141 research assistantships with full and partial tuition reimbursements (averaging $18,204 per year), 92 teaching assistantships with full and partial tuition reimbursements (averaging $18,204 per year) were awarded; career-related internships or fieldwork, Federal Work-Study, institutionally sponsored loans, tuition waivers (partial), and teaching associateships also available. Financial award application deadline: 4/1; financial award applicants required to submit FAFSA. *Total annual research expenditures:* $14.6 million. *Unit head:* Dr. Candis Claiborn, Dean, 509-335-5593, Fax: 509-335-7632, E-mail: claiborn@wsu.edu. *Application contact:* Graduate School Admissions, 800-GRADWSU, Fax: 509-335-1949, E-mail: gradsch@wsu.edu. Web site: http://www.cea.wsu.edu/.

Washington State University Tri-Cities, Graduate Programs, College of Engineering and Architecture, Richland, WA 99352-1671. Offers computer science (MS, PhD); electrical engineering (MS, PhD); mechanical engineering (MS, PhD). Part-time programs available. *Faculty:* 28. *Students:* 20 full-time (5 women), 37 part-time (10 women); includes 6 minority (1 Black or African American, non-Hispanic/Latino; 2 Asian, non-Hispanic/Latino; 1 Hispanic/Latino; 2 Two or more races, non-Hispanic/Latino), 4 international. Average age 27. 27 applicants, 33% accepted, 6 enrolled. *Degree requirements:* For master's, comprehensive exam, thesis (for some programs); for doctorate, comprehensive exam, thesis/dissertation, oral exam. *Entrance requirements:* For master's and doctorate, GRE, minimum GPA of 3.0, 3 letters of recommendation. Additional exam requirements/recommendations for international students: Required—TOEFL (minimum score 550 paper-based; 213 computer-based). *Application deadline:* For fall admission, 1/10 priority date for domestic students, 1/10 for international students; for spring admission, 7/1 priority date for domestic students, 7/1 for international students. Application fee: $75. *Financial support:* Application deadline: 3/1. *Faculty research:* Positive ion track structure, biological systems computer simulations. *Unit head:* Dr. Ali Saberi, Chair, 509-372-7178, E-mail: sidra@eecs.wsu.edu. *Application contact:* Dr. Scott Hudson, Associate Director, 509-372-7254, Fax: 509-335-1949, E-mail: hudson@tricity.wsu.edu. Web site: http://cea.tricity.wsu.edu/.

Washington State University Vancouver, Graduate Programs, School of Engineering and Computer Science, Vancouver, WA 98686. Offers computer science (MS); mechanical engineering (MS). Part-time programs available. *Faculty:* 9. *Students:* 22 full-time (2 women), 5 part-time (1 woman); includes 2 minority (both Asian, non-Hispanic/Latino), 10 international. Average age 29. 48 applicants, 33% accepted, 13 enrolled. *Degree requirements:* For master's, comprehensive exam (for some programs), thesis, research project. *Entrance requirements:* For master's, minimum GPA of 3.0, 3 letters of recommendation with evaluation forms, resume. Additional exam requirements/recommendations for international students: Required—TOEFL (minimum score 550 paper-based). *Application deadline:* For fall admission, 1/10 priority date for domestic students, 1/10 for international students; for spring admission, 7/1 priority date for domestic students, 7/1 for international students. Applications are processed on a rolling basis. Application fee: $75. *Financial support:* In 2011–12, research assistantships with full tuition reimbursements (averaging $14,634 per year), teaching assistantships with full tuition reimbursements (averaging $13,383 per year) were awarded; health care benefits and unspecified assistantships also available. Financial award application deadline: 2/15. *Faculty research:* Software design, artificial intelligence, sensor networks, robotics, nanotechnology. *Total annual research expenditures:* $3.4 million. *Unit head:* Dr. Hakan Gurocak, Director, 360-546-9637, Fax: 360-546-9438, E-mail: hgurocak@vancouver.wsu.edu. *Application contact:* Peggy Moore, Academic Coordinator, 360-546-9638, Fax: 360-546-9438, E-mail: moorep@vancouver.wsu.edu. Web site: http://ecs.vancouver.wsu.edu/.

Washington University in St. Louis, School of Engineering and Applied Science, Saint Louis, MO 63130-4899. Offers M Eng, MCE, MCM, MEM, MIM, MPM, MS, MSEE, MSEE, MSI, D Sc, PhD. Part-time and evening/weekend programs available. *Faculty:* 76 full-time, 68 part-time/adjunct. *Students:* 423 full-time (107 women), 278 part-time (64 women); includes 86 minority (17 Black or African American, non-Hispanic/Latino; 2 American Indian or Alaska Native, non-Hispanic/Latino; 45 Asian, non-Hispanic/Latino; 11 Hispanic/Latino; 1 Native Hawaiian or other Pacific Islander, non-Hispanic/Latino; 10 Two or more races, non-Hispanic/Latino), 232 international. 1,560 applicants, 36% accepted, 216 enrolled. In 2011, 202 master's, 35 doctorates awarded. Terminal master's awarded for partial completion of doctoral program. *Degree requirements:* For master's, comprehensive exam (for some programs), thesis (for some programs); for doctorate, comprehensive exam, thesis/dissertation. *Entrance requirements:* For master's and doctorate, GRE. Additional exam requirements/recommendations for international students: Required—TOEFL (minimum score 550 paper-based; 213 computer-based; 90 iBT), IELTS (minimum score 6.5) or TWE. *Application deadline:* For fall admission, 1/15 for domestic and international students. Applications are processed on a rolling basis. Application fee: $60. Electronic applications accepted. *Financial support:* In 2011–12, 301 students received support, including 34 fellowships with full tuition reimbursements available, 257 research assistantships with full tuition reimbursements available, 10 teaching assistantships with full tuition reimbursements available; career-related internships or fieldwork, Federal Work-Study, institutionally sponsored loans, scholarships/grants, health care benefits, tuition waivers (full and partial), and unspecified assistantships also available. Financial award applicants required to submit FAFSA. *Total annual research expenditures:* $23.2 million. *Unit head:* Dr. Ralph S. Quatrano, Dean, 314-935-6350, E-mail: rsq@wustl.edu. *Application contact:* Beth Schnettler, Director of Graduate Admissions, 314-935-7974, Fax: 314-719-4703, E-mail: bethschnettler@seas.wustl.edu. Web site: http://engineering.wustl.edu/GraduateProgram.aspx.

Wayne State University, College of Engineering, Detroit, MI 48202. Offers MS, PhD, Certificate, Graduate Certificate. Part-time programs available. *Students:* 505 full-time (118 women), 349 part-time (78 women); includes 152 minority (40 Black or African American, non-Hispanic/Latino; 1 American Indian or Alaska Native, non-Hispanic/Latino; 91 Asian, non-Hispanic/Latino; 14 Hispanic/Latino; 1 Native Hawaiian or other Pacific Islander, non-Hispanic/Latino; 5 Two or more races, non-Hispanic/Latino), 375 international. Average age 31. 1,041 applicants, 50% accepted, 208 enrolled. In 2011, 254 master's, 27 doctorates, 7 other advanced degrees awarded. Terminal master's awarded for partial completion of doctoral program. *Degree requirements:* For master's, thesis optional; for doctorate, thesis/dissertation. *Entrance requirements:* For master's, minimum GPA of 2.8 from ABET-accredited institution and in all upper-division courses; for doctorate, minimum overall GPA of 3.2, 3.5 in last two years as undergraduate student if being admitted directly from a bachelor's program. Additional exam requirements/recommendations for international students: Required—TOEFL (minimum score 550 paper-based; 213 computer-based); Recommended—TWE (minimum score 5.5). *Application deadline:* For fall admission, 6/1 priority date for domestic students, 5/1 for international students; for winter admission, 10/1 priority date for domestic students, 9/1 for international students; for spring admission, 2/1 priority date for domestic students, 1/1 for international students. Applications are processed on a rolling basis. Application fee: $50. Electronic applications accepted. *Expenses:* Tuition, state resident: part-time $512.85 per credit. Tuition, nonresident: part-time $1132.65 per credit. *Required fees:* $26.60 per credit. $199.65 per semester. Tuition and fees vary according to course load and program. *Financial support:* In 2011–12, 233 students received support, including 27 fellowships with tuition reimbursements available (averaging $18,667 per year), 91 research assistantships with tuition reimbursements available (averaging $18,148 per year), 81 teaching assistantships with tuition reimbursements available (averaging $17,455 per year); career-related internships or fieldwork, Federal Work-Study, institutionally sponsored loans, scholarships/grants, health care benefits, tuition waivers (full and partial), and unspecified assistantships also available. Support available to part-time students. *Faculty research:* Smart sensors and integrated micro systems, biomedical engineering, civil infrastructures, nanotechnology, manufacturing and automotive engineering. *Total annual research expenditures:* $14.2 million. *Unit head:* Dr. Farshad Fotouhi, Dean, 313-577-3776, E-mail: fotouhi@wayne.edu. Web site: http://engineering.wayne.edu/.

Western Michigan University, Graduate College, College of Engineering and Applied Sciences, Kalamazoo, MI 49008. Offers MS, MSE, PhD. Part-time programs available. *Degree requirements:* For doctorate, thesis/dissertation, oral exam. *Entrance requirements:* For master's, minimum GPA of 3.0; for doctorate, GRE General Test, minimum GPA of 3.0.

Western New England University, College of Engineering, Springfield, MA 01119. Offers MSE, MSEE, MSEM, PhD. Part-time and evening/weekend programs available. *Students:* 59 part-time (9 women); includes 10 minority (2 Black or African American, non-Hispanic/Latino; 2 Asian, non-Hispanic/Latino; 6 Hispanic/Latino), 4 international. *Degree requirements:* For master's, comprehensive exam, thesis optional. *Entrance requirements:* For master's, GRE, bachelor's degree in engineering or related field, letters of recommendation, resume. *Application deadline:* Applications are processed on a rolling basis. Application fee: $30. *Financial support:* Available to part-time students. Applicants required to submit FAFSA. *Faculty research:* Fluid mechanics, control systems. *Unit head:* Dr. S. Hossein Cheraghi, Dean, 413-782-1272, E-mail: cheraghi@wne.edu. *Application contact:* Matt Fox, Director of Recruiting and Marketing for Adult Learners, 413-782-1517, Fax: 413-782-1777, E-mail: learn@wne.edu. Web site: http://www1.wne.edu/adultlearning/index.cfm?selection-doc.6281.

West Texas A&M University, College of Agriculture, Nursing, and Natural Sciences, Department of Mathematics, Physical Sciences and Engineering Technology, Program in Engineering Technology, Canyon, TX 79016-0001. Offers MS. Part-time programs available. *Degree requirements:* For master's, comprehensive exam, thesis optional. *Entrance requirements:* For master's, GRE General Test. Additional exam requirements/recommendations for international students: Required—TOEFL (minimum score 550 paper-based). Electronic applications accepted. *Faculty research:* Composites, firearms technology, small arms research and development.

West Virginia University, College of Engineering and Mineral Resources, Morgantown, WV 26506. Offers MS, MS Ch E, MS Min E, MSAE, MSCE, MSCS, MSE, MSEE, MSIE, MSME, MSPNGE, MSSE, PhD, Graduate Certificate. *Accreditation:* ABET (one or more programs are accredited). Part-time programs available. Terminal master's awarded for partial completion of doctoral program. *Degree requirements:* For master's, thesis optional; for doctorate, comprehensive exam, thesis/dissertation. *Entrance requirements:* Additional exam requirements/recommendations for international students: Required—TOEFL (minimum score 550 paper-based; 213 computer-based). *Expenses:* Contact institution. *Faculty research:* Composite materials, software engineering, information systems, aerodynamics, vehicle propulsion and emission.

Wichita State University, Graduate School, College of Engineering, Wichita, KS 67260. Offers MEM, MS, PhD. Part-time and evening/weekend programs available. *Expenses:* Tuition, state resident: full-time $4746; part-time $263.65 per credit. Tuition, nonresident: full-time $11,669; part-time $648.30 per credit. *Unit head:* Dr. Zulma Toro-Ramos, Dean, 316-978-3400, Fax: 316-978-3853, E-mail: zulma.toro-ramos@wichita.edu. *Application contact:* Carrie C. Henderson, Admissions Coordinator, 316-978-3095, Fax: 316-978-3253, E-mail: carrie.henderson@wichita.edu. Web site: http://www.wichita.edu/.

Widener University, Graduate Programs in Engineering, Chester, PA 19013-5792. Offers chemical engineering (M Eng); civil engineering (M Eng); computer and software engineering (M Eng); engineering management (M Eng); management and technology (MSMT); mechanical engineering (M Eng); telecommunications engineering (M Eng); ME/MBA. Part-time and evening/weekend programs available. *Degree requirements:* For master's, thesis optional. *Entrance requirements:* Additional exam requirements/recommendations for international students: Required—TOEFL (minimum score 550 paper-based; 213 computer-based). *Expenses:* Contact institution. *Faculty research:* Collagen, geosynthetics, mobile computing, image and signal processing.

Wilkes University, College of Graduate and Professional Studies, College of Science and Engineering, Wilkes-Barre, PA 18766-0002. Offers MS, MS Ed, MSEE. Part-time programs available. *Students:* 27 full-time (2 women), 33 part-time (6 women); includes 2 minority (both Asian, non-Hispanic/Latino), 19 international. Average age 30. In 2011, 12 master's awarded. *Entrance requirements:* Additional exam requirements/recommendations for international students: Required—TOEFL (minimum score 550 paper-based; 213 computer-based; 79 iBT). *Application deadline:* Applications are processed on a rolling basis. Application fee: $45 ($65 for international students). Electronic applications accepted. *Financial support:* Federal Work-Study and unspecified assistantships available. Financial award application deadline: 3/1; financial award applicants required to submit FAFSA. *Unit head:* Dr. Dale Bruns, Dean, 570-408-4600, Fax: 570-408-7860, E-mail: dale.bruns@wilkes.edu. *Application contact:* Erin Sutzko, Director of Extended Learning, 570-408-4253, Fax: 570-408-7846, E-mail: erin.sutzko@wilkes.edu. Web site: http://www.wilkes.edu/pages/372.asp.

Worcester Polytechnic Institute, Graduate Studies and Research, Worcester, MA 01609-2280. Offers M Eng, MBA, ME, MME, MS, PhD, Advanced Certificate, Graduate Certificate. Part-time and evening/weekend programs available. Postbaccalaureate distance learning degree programs offered (no on-campus study). *Faculty:* 152 full-time (28 women), 44 part-time/adjunct (7 women). *Students:* 613 full-time (207 women), 944 part-time (207 women); includes 149 minority (18 Black or African American, non-Hispanic/Latino; 1 American Indian or Alaska Native, non-Hispanic/Latino; 76 Asian, non-Hispanic/Latino; 35 Hispanic/Latino; 19 Two or more races, non-Hispanic/Latino), 549 international. Average age 29. 2,612 applicants, 58% accepted, 566 enrolled. In 2011, 446 master's, 21 doctorates awarded. Terminal master's awarded for partial completion of doctoral program. *Degree requirements:* For master's, thesis (for some programs); for doctorate, thesis/dissertation. *Entrance requirements:* For master's and doctorate, 3 letters of recommendation. Additional exam requirements/recommendations for international students: Required—TOEFL (minimum score 563 paper-based; 223 computer-based; 84 iBT), IELTS (minimum score 7). *Application deadline:* For fall admission, 1/1 priority date for domestic students, 1/1 for international students; for spring admission, 10/1 priority date for domestic students, 10/1 for international students. Applications are processed on a rolling basis. Application fee: $70. Electronic applications accepted. *Financial support:* Research assistantships, teaching assistantships, institutionally sponsored loans, scholarships/grants, tuition waivers, and unspecified assistantships available. Financial award application deadline: 1/1; financial award applicants required to submit FAFSA. *Unit head:* Richard Sisson, Dean, 508-831-5633, Fax: 508-831-5178, E-mail: grad@wpi.edu. *Application contact:* Lynne Dougherty, Administrative Assistant, 508-831-5301, Fax: 508-831-5717, E-mail: grad@wpi.edu. Web site: http://grad.wpi.edu/.

Wright State University, School of Graduate Studies, College of Engineering and Computer Science, Dayton, OH 45435. Offers MS, MSCE, MSE, PhD. Part-time and evening/weekend programs available. *Degree requirements:* For master's, thesis optional; for doctorate, thesis/dissertation, candidacy and general exams. *Entrance requirements:* For doctorate, GRE General Test, minimum GPA of 3.3. Additional exam requirements/recommendations for international students: Required—TOEFL. *Faculty research:* Robotics, heat transfer, fluid dynamics, microprocessors, mechanical vibrations.

Yale University, Graduate School of Arts and Sciences, School of Engineering and Applied Science, New Haven, CT 06520. Offers MS, PhD. Part-time programs available. Terminal master's awarded for partial completion of doctoral program. *Degree requirements:* For doctorate, thesis/dissertation, exam. *Entrance requirements:* For master's and doctorate, GRE General Test. Additional exam requirements/recommendations for international students: Required—TOEFL.

See Display on next page and Close-Up on page 89.

Youngstown State University, Graduate School, College of Science, Technology, Engineering and Mathematics, Youngstown, OH 44555-0001. Offers MCIS, MSE. Part-time and evening/weekend programs available. *Degree requirements:* For master's, thesis optional. *Entrance requirements:* For master's, minimum GPA of 2.75 in field. Additional exam requirements/recommendations for international students: Required—TOEFL. *Faculty research:* Structural mechanics, water quality, wetlands engineering, control systems, power systems, heat transfer, kinematics and dynamics.

Applied Science and Technology

American University, College of Arts and Sciences, Department of Biology, Washington, DC 20016-8007. Offers applied science (MS), including biotechnology, environmental science assessment; biology (MA, MS). Part-time programs available. *Faculty:* 10 full-time (4 women), 3 part-time/adjunct (2 women). *Students:* 8 full-time (2 women), 4 part-time (1 woman); includes 4 minority (1 Black or African American, non-Hispanic/Latino; 3 Asian, non-Hispanic/Latino), 1 international. Average age 25. 15 applicants, 60% accepted, 6 enrolled. In 2011, 9 master's awarded. *Degree requirements:* For master's, comprehensive exam, thesis (for some programs). *Entrance requirements:* For master's, GRE General Test, GRE Subject Test. Additional exam requirements/recommendations for international students: Required—TOEFL. *Application deadline:* For fall admission, 2/1 for domestic students; for spring admission, 10/1 for domestic students. Application fee: $80. *Expenses: Tuition:* Full-time $24,264; part-time $1348 per credit hour. *Required fees:* $430. Tuition and fees vary according to course load and program. *Financial support:* Fellowships, research assistantships with tuition reimbursements, teaching assistantships with tuition reimbursements, career-related internships or fieldwork, Federal Work-Study, and institutionally sponsored loans available. Financial award application deadline: 2/1. *Faculty research:* Neurobiology, cave biology, population genetics, vertebrate physiology. *Unit head:* Dr. David Carlini, Chair, 202-885-2194, Fax: 202-885-2182, E-mail: carlini@american.edu. *Application contact:* Kathleen Clowery, Director, Graduate Admissions, 202-885-3621, Fax: 202-885-1505, E-mail: clowery@american.edu. Web site: http://www.american.edu/cas/biology/.

American University, College of Arts and Sciences, Program in Computer Science, Washington, DC 20016-8058. Offers applied science (MS); computer science (MS, Certificate). Part-time and evening/weekend programs available. *Faculty:* 3 full-time (0 women), 1 part-time/adjunct (0 women). *Students:* 1 (woman) part-time; minority (Black or African American, non-Hispanic/Latino). Average age 53. 13 applicants, 54% accepted, 0 enrolled. In 2011, 1 master's awarded. *Degree requirements:* For master's, comprehensive exam, thesis or alternative. *Entrance requirements:* For master's, GRE, minimum GPA of 3.0; for Certificate, bachelor's degree. Additional exam requirements/recommendations for international students: Required—TOEFL. *Application deadline:* For fall admission, 2/1 priority date for domestic students; for spring admission, 10/1 for domestic students. Applications are processed on a rolling basis. Application fee: $80. *Expenses: Tuition:* Full-time $24,264; part-time $1348 per credit hour. *Required fees:* $430. Tuition and fees vary according to course load and program. *Financial support:* Fellowships with full tuition reimbursements, career-related internships or fieldwork, Federal Work-Study, institutionally sponsored loans, tuition waivers (full and partial), and unspecified assistantships available. Financial award application deadline: 2/1. *Faculty research:* Artificial intelligence, database systems, software engineering, expert systems. *Unit head:* Dr. Ulysses J. Sofia, Chair, 202-885-2728, Fax: 202-885-2429, E-mail: sofia@american.edu. *Application contact:* Kathleen Clowery, Director, Graduate

Admissions, 202-885-3621, Fax: 202-885-1505, E-mail: clowery@american.edu. Web site: http://www.american.edu/cas/cs.

The College of William and Mary, Faculty of Arts and Sciences, Department of Applied Science, Williamsburg, VA 23187-8795. Offers MS, PhD. *Faculty:* 11 full-time (2 women). *Students:* 34 full-time (14 women); includes 2 minority (1 Black or African American, non-Hispanic/Latino; 1 Asian, non-Hispanic/Latino), 23 international. Average age 27. 33 applicants, 30% accepted, 7 enrolled. In 2011, 2 master's, 4 doctorates awarded. *Degree requirements:* For master's, comprehensive exam, thesis; for doctorate, comprehensive exam, thesis/dissertation, 4 core courses. *Entrance requirements:* For master's and doctorate, GRE General Test, GRE Subject Test. Additional exam requirements/recommendations for international students: Required—TOEFL, TWE. *Application deadline:* For fall admission, 2/3 priority date for domestic students, 2/3 for international students; for spring admission, 10/15 priority date for domestic students, 10/14 for international students. Applications are processed on a rolling basis. Application fee: $45. Electronic applications accepted. *Expenses:* Tuition, state resident: full-time $6400; part-time $365 per credit hour. Tuition, nonresident: full-time $19,720; part-time $985 per credit hour. *Required fees:* $4562. *Financial support:* Fellowships, research assistantships, teaching assistantships, Federal Work-Study, health care benefits, tuition waivers (full), and unspecified assistantships available. Financial award application deadline: 4/15; financial award applicants required to submit FAFSA. *Faculty research:* Computational biology, non-destructive evaluation, neurophysiology, lasers 8 optics, solid state FTNMR. *Total annual research expenditures:* $2.3 million. *Unit head:* Dr. Mark Hinders, Chair, 757-221-1519, Fax: 757-221-2050, E-mail: hinders@as.wm.edu. *Application contact:* Rosario Fox, Education Support Specialist, 757-221-2563, Fax: 757-221-2050, E-mail: rxfoxx@wm.edu. Web site: http://www.wm.edu/as/appliedscience.

Colorado State University–Pueblo, College of Science and Mathematics, Pueblo, CO 81001-4901. Offers applied natural science (MS), including biochemistry, biology, chemistry. Part-time and evening/weekend programs available. *Degree requirements:* For master's, comprehensive exam (for some programs), thesis (for some programs), internship report (if non-thesis). *Entrance requirements:* For master's, GRE General Test (minimum score 1000), 2 letters of reference, minimum GPA of 3.0. Additional exam requirements/recommendations for international students: Required—TOEFL (minimum score 500 paper-based; 173 computer-based), IELTS (minimum score 5). *Faculty research:* Fungal cell walls, molecular biology, bioactive materials synthesis, atomic force microscopy-surface chemistry, nanoscience.

Harvard University, Extension School, Cambridge, MA 02138-3722. Offers applied sciences (CAS); biotechnology (ALM); educational technologies (ALM); educational technology (CET); English for graduate and professional studies (DGP); environmental management (ALM, CEM); information technology (ALM); journalism (ALM); liberal arts (ALM); management (ALM, CM); mathematics for teaching (ALM); museum studies (ALM); premedical studies (Diploma); publication and communication (CPC). Part-time and evening/weekend programs available. *Degree requirements:* For master's, thesis. *Entrance requirements:* For master's, 3 completed graduate courses with grade of B or higher. Additional exam requirements/recommendations for international students: Required—TOEFL (minimum score 600 paper-based; 250 computer-based), TWE (minimum score 5). *Expenses:* Contact institution.

James Madison University, The Graduate School, College of Integrated Science and Technology, Department of Integrated Science and Technology, Harrisonburg, VA 22807. Offers MS. *Faculty:* 14 full-time (3 women), 1 part-time/adjunct (0 women).

Students: 26 full-time (10 women), 20 part-time (7 women); includes 1 minority (Hispanic/Latino), 19 international. Average age 27. In 2011, 26 master's awarded. *Degree requirements:* For master's, thesis or alternative. *Entrance requirements:* For master's, GRE General Test. Additional exam requirements/recommendations for international students: Required—TOEFL. *Application deadline:* For fall admission, 5/1 priority date for domestic students; for spring admission, 9/1 priority date for domestic students. Applications are processed on a rolling basis. Application fee: $55. Electronic applications accepted. *Expenses:* Tuition, state resident: full-time $8016; part-time $334 per credit hour. Tuition, nonresident: full-time $22,656; part-time $944 per credit hour. *Financial support:* In 2011–12, 7 students received support. Federal Work-Study and 7 graduate assistantships ($7382) available. Financial award application deadline: 3/1; financial award applicants required to submit FAFSA. *Unit head:* Dr. Eric H. Maslen, Interim Academic Unit Head, 540-568-2740, E-mail: masleneh@jmu.edu. *Application contact:* Lynette M. Bible, Director of Graduate Admissions, 540-568-6395, Fax: 540-568-7860, E-mail: biblelm@jmu.edu.

Louisiana State University and Agricultural and Mechanical College, Graduate School, College of Science, Master of Natural Sciences Program, Baton Rouge, LA 70803. Offers MNS. Part-time programs available. *Students:* 8 full-time (6 women), 4 part-time (2 women); includes 3 minority (2 Black or African American, non-Hispanic/Latino; 1 Asian, non-Hispanic/Latino), 1 international. Average age 30. 3 applicants, 67% accepted, 1 enrolled. In 2011, 22 master's awarded. *Degree requirements:* For master's, comprehensive exam. *Entrance requirements:* For master's, GRE General Test, minimum GPA of 3.0. Additional exam requirements/recommendations for international students: Required—TOEFL (minimum score 550 paper-based; 213 computer-based; 79 iBT) or IELTS (minimum score 6.5). *Application deadline:* For fall admission, 5/15 priority date for domestic students, 5/15 for international students; for spring admission, 10/15 for international students. Applications are processed on a rolling basis. Application fee: $50 ($70 for international students). Electronic applications accepted. *Financial support:* In 2011–12, 15 research assistantships (averaging $31,667 per year) were awarded; fellowships, teaching assistantships with partial tuition reimbursements, Federal Work-Study, institutionally sponsored loans, and health care benefits also available. Financial award applicants required to submit FAFSA. *Total annual research expenditures:* $28,121. *Unit head:* Dr. Frank Neubrander, Director, E-mail: fneubr1@campus.lsu.edu. *Application contact:* Dr. Frank Neubrander, Director, E-mail: fneubr1@campus.lsu.edu. Web site: http://science.lsu.edu/Student-Resources/Degree-Program-Choices/MNS/item39871.html.

Missouri State University, Graduate College, College of Natural and Applied Sciences, Department of Biology, Springfield, MO 65897. Offers biology (MS); natural and applied science (MNAS), including biology (MNAS, MS Ed); secondary education (MS Ed), including biology (MNAS, MS Ed). *Faculty:* 19 full-time (4 women), 6 part-time/adjunct (1 woman). *Students:* 21 full-time (9 women), 37 part-time (18 women); includes 3 minority (all Two or more races, non-Hispanic/Latino), 2 international. Average age 28. 18 applicants, 94% accepted, 15 enrolled. In 2011, 14 master's awarded. *Degree requirements:* For master's, comprehensive exam, thesis or alternative. *Entrance requirements:* For master's, GRE (MS, MNAS), 24 hours of course work in biology (MS); minimum GPA of 3.0 (MS, MNAS), 9-12 teacher certification (MS Ed). Additional exam requirements/recommendations for international students: Required—TOEFL (minimum score 550 paper-based; 213 computer-based; 79 iBT). *Application deadline:* For fall admission, 7/20 priority date for domestic students, 5/1 for international students; for spring admission, 12/20 priority date for domestic students, 9/1 for international students. Applications are processed on a rolling basis. Application fee: $35 ($50 for international students). Electronic applications accepted. *Expenses:* Tuition, state resident: full-time $4086; part-time $227 per credit hour. Tuition, nonresident: full-time $8172; part-time $454 per credit hour. *Required fees:* $275 per semester. Tuition and fees vary according to course load, campus/location and program. *Financial support:* In 2011–12, 3 research assistantships with full tuition reimbursements (averaging $8,865 per year), 12 teaching assistantships with full tuition reimbursements (averaging $9,730 per year) were awarded; Federal Work-Study, institutionally sponsored loans, scholarships/grants, and unspecified assistantships also available. Financial award application deadline: 3/31; financial award applicants required to submit FAFSA. *Faculty research:* Hibernation physiology of bats, behavioral ecology of salamanders, mussel conservation, plant evolution and systematics, cellular/molecular mechanisms involved in migraine pathology. *Unit head:* Dr. S. Alicia Mathis, Head, 417-836-5126, Fax: 417-836-6934, E-mail: biology@missouristate.edu. *Application contact:* Misty Stewart, Coordinator of Graduate Recruitment, 417-836-6079, Fax: 417-836-6200, E-mail: mistystewart@missouristate.edu. Web site: http://biology.missouristate.edu/.

Missouri State University, Graduate College, College of Natural and Applied Sciences, Department of Chemistry, Springfield, MO 65897. Offers chemistry (MS); natural and applied science (MNAS), including chemistry (MNAS, MS Ed); secondary education (MS Ed), including chemistry (MNAS, MS Ed). Part-time programs available. *Faculty:* 15 full-time (2 women). *Students:* 18 full-time (6 women), 7 part-time (3 women); includes 1 minority (Black or African American, non-Hispanic/Latino), 6 international. Average age 31. 16 applicants, 38% accepted, 4 enrolled. In 2011, 5 master's awarded. *Degree requirements:* For master's, comprehensive exam, thesis. *Entrance requirements:* For master's, GRE General Test (MS, MNAS), minimum undergraduate GPA of 3.0 (MS and MNAS), 9-12 teacher certification (MS Ed). Additional exam requirements/recommendations for international students: Required—TOEFL (minimum score 550 paper-based; 213 computer-based; 79 iBT). *Application deadline:* For fall admission, 7/20 priority date for domestic students, 5/1 for international students; for spring admission, 12/20 priority date for domestic students, 9/1 for international students. Applications are processed on a rolling basis. Application fee: $35 ($50 for international students). Electronic applications accepted. *Expenses:* Tuition, state resident: full-time $4086; part-time $227 per credit hour. Tuition, nonresident: full-time $8172; part-time $454 per credit hour. *Required fees:* $275 per semester. Tuition and fees vary according to course load, campus/location and program. *Financial support:* In 2011–12, 1 research assistantship with full tuition reimbursement (averaging $8,865 per year), 4 teaching assistantships with full tuition reimbursements (averaging $9,730 per year) were awarded; Federal Work-Study, institutionally sponsored loans, scholarships/grants, and unspecified assistantships also available. Financial award application deadline: 3/31; financial award applicants required to submit FAFSA. *Faculty research:* Polyethylene glycol derivatives, electrochemiluminescence of environmental systems, enzymology, environmental organic pollutants, DNA repair via NMR. *Unit head:* Dr. Alan Schick, Department Head, 417-836-5506, Fax: 417-836-5507, E-mail: chemistry@missouristate.edu. *Application contact:* Misty Stewart, Coordinator of Graduate Recruitment, 417-836-6079, Fax: 417-836-6200, E-mail: mistystewart@missouristate.edu. Web site: http://chemistry.missouristate.edu/.

Missouri State University, Graduate College, College of Natural and Applied Sciences, Department of Geography, Geology, and Planning, Springfield, MO 65897. Offers geospatial sciences (MS, MS Ed), including earth science (MS Ed), geology (MS), human geography and planning (MS), physical geography (MS Ed); natural and applied science (MNAS), including geography, geology and planning; secondary education (MS Ed), including geography. Part-time and evening/weekend programs available. *Faculty:* 19 full-time (4 women). *Students:* 19 full-time (9 women), 12 part-time (7 women), 2 international. Average age 31. 20 applicants, 80% accepted, 11 enrolled. In 2011, 15 master's awarded. *Degree requirements:* For master's, comprehensive exam, thesis (for some programs). *Entrance requirements:* For master's, GRE General Test (MS, MNAS), minimum undergraduate GPA of 3.0 (MS, MNAS), 9-12 teacher certification (MS Ed). Additional exam requirements/recommendations for international students: Required—TOEFL (minimum score 550 paper-based; 213 computer-based; 79 iBT). *Application deadline:* For fall admission, 7/20 priority date for domestic students, 5/1 for international students; for spring admission, 12/20 priority date for domestic students, 9/1 for international students. Applications are processed on a rolling basis. Application fee: $35 ($50 for international students). Electronic applications accepted. *Expenses:* Tuition, state resident: full-time $4086; part-time $227 per credit hour. Tuition, nonresident: full-time $8172; part-time $454 per credit hour. *Required fees:* $275 per semester. Tuition and fees vary according to course load, campus/location and program. *Financial support:* In 2011–12, 3 research assistantships with full tuition reimbursements (averaging $8,000 per year), 9 teaching assistantships with full tuition reimbursements (averaging $8,000 per year) were awarded; career-related internships or fieldwork, Federal Work-Study, institutionally sponsored loans, scholarships/grants, and unspecified assistantships also available. Financial award application deadline: 3/31; financial award applicants required to submit FAFSA. *Faculty research:* Stratigraphy and ancient meteorite impacts, environmental geochemistry of karst, hyperspectral image processing, water quality, small town planning. *Unit head:* Dr. Thomas Plymate, Head, 417-836-5800, Fax: 417-836-6934, E-mail: tomplymate@missouristate.edu. *Application contact:* Misty Stewart, Coordinator of Graduate Recruitment, 417-836-6079, Fax: 417-836-6200, E-mail: mistystewart@missouristate.edu. Web site: http://geosciences.missouristate.edu/.

Missouri State University, Graduate College, College of Natural and Applied Sciences, Department of Mathematics, Springfield, MO 65897. Offers mathematics (MS); natural and applied science (MNAS), including mathematics (MNAS, MS Ed); secondary education (MS Ed), including mathematics (MNAS, MS Ed). Part-time programs available. *Faculty:* 21 full-time (6 women). *Students:* 18 full-time (8 women), 7 part-time (3 women); includes 2 minority (1 Black or African American, non-Hispanic/Latino; 1 Hispanic/Latino), 4 international. Average age 27. 11 applicants, 100% accepted, 8 enrolled. In 2011, 4 master's awarded. *Degree requirements:* For master's, comprehensive exam, thesis or alternative. *Entrance requirements:* For master's, GRE (MS, MNAS), minimum undergraduate GPA of 3.0 (MS, MNAS), 9-12 teacher certification (MS Ed). Additional exam requirements/recommendations for international students: Required—TOEFL (minimum score 550 paper-based; 213 computer-based; 79 iBT). *Application deadline:* For fall admission, 7/20 priority date for domestic students, 5/1 for international students; for spring admission, 12/20 priority date for domestic students, 9/1 for international students. Applications are processed on a rolling basis. Application fee: $35 ($50 for international students). Electronic applications accepted. *Expenses:* Tuition, state resident: full-time $4086; part-time $227 per credit hour. Tuition, nonresident: full-time $8172; part-time $454 per credit hour. *Required fees:* $275 per semester. Tuition and fees vary according to course load, campus/location and program. *Financial support:* In 2011–12, 4 teaching assistantships with full tuition reimbursements (averaging $9,730 per year) were awarded; Federal Work-Study, institutionally sponsored loans, scholarships/grants, and unspecified assistantships also

available. Financial award application deadline: 3/31; financial award applicants required to submit FAFSA. *Faculty research:* Harmonic analysis, commutative algebra, number theory, K-theory, probability. *Unit head:* Dr. Kenneth Vollmar, Interim Head, 417-836-5112, Fax: 417-836-6966, E-mail: mathematics@missouristate.edu. *Application contact:* Misty Stewart, Coordinator of Graduate Recruitment, 417-836-6079, Fax: 417-836-6200, E-mail: mistystewart@missouristate.edu. Web site: http://math.missouristate.edu/

Naval Postgraduate School, Departments and Academic Groups, Department of Operations Research, Monterey, CA 93943. Offers applied science (MS), including operations research; cost estimating analysis (MS); human systems integration (MS); operations research (MS, PhD); systems analysis (MS). Program only open to commissioned officers of the United States and friendly nations and selected United States federal civilian employees. Part-time programs available. *Faculty:* 38 full-time (11 women), 12 part-time/adjunct (3 women). *Students:* 142 full-time (21 women), 137 part-time (30 women); includes 66 minority (19 Black or African American, non-Hispanic/Latino; 3 American Indian or Alaska Native, non-Hispanic/Latino; 27 Asian, non-Hispanic/Latino; 17 Hispanic/Latino), 18 international. Average age 41. In 2011, 97 master's, 2 doctorates awarded. *Degree requirements:* For master's, thesis (for some programs); for doctorate, thesis/dissertation. *Faculty research:* Next generation network science, performance analysis of ground solider mobile ad-hoc networks, irregular warfare methods and tools, human social cultural behavior modeling, large-scale optimization. *Total annual research expenditures:* $6.7 million. *Unit head:* Prof. Robert Dell, Chairman, 831-656-2853, E-mail: dell@nps.edu. Web site: http://nps.edu/Academics/Schools/GSOIS/Departments/OR/index.html.

Naval Postgraduate School, Departments and Academic Groups, Undersea Warfare Academic Group, Monterey, CA 93943. Offers applied mathematics (MS); applied physics (MS); applied science (MS), including acoustics, operations research, physical oceanography, signal processing; electrical engineering (MS); engineering acoustics (MS, PhD); engineering science (MS), including electrical engineering, mechanical engineering; mechanical engineer (ME); mechanical engineering (MS, MSME); meteorology (MS); operations research (MS); physical oceanography (MS). Program only open to commissioned officers of the United States and friendly nations and selected United States federal civilian employees. Part-time programs available. *Students:* 2 full-time, both international. Average age 36. *Degree requirements:* For master's, thesis. *Faculty research:* Unmanned/autonomous vehicles, sea mines and countermeasures, submarine warfare in the twentieth and twenty-first centuries. *Unit head:* Dr. Clyde Scandrett, Academic Group Chairman, 831-656-2027. Web site: http://www.nps.edu/Academics/Schools/GSEAS/Departments/USW/USW-Index.html.

Oklahoma State University, Graduate College, Stillwater, OK 74078. Offers aerospace security (Graduate Certificate); biobased products and bioenergy (Graduate Certificate); bioinformatics (Graduate Certificate); business data mining (Graduate Certificate); engineering and technology management (Graduate Certificate); environmental science (MS); global issues (Graduate Certificate); information assurance (Graduate Certificate); international studies (MS); natural and applied science (MS); photonics (PhD); plant science (PhD); teaching English to speakers of other languages (Graduate Certificate). Programs are interdisciplinary. *Faculty:* 2 full-time (both women), 3 part-time/adjunct (0 women). *Students:* 86 full-time (50 women), 149 part-time (76 women); includes 55 minority (14 Black or African American, non-Hispanic/Latino; 11 American Indian or Alaska Native, non-Hispanic/Latino; 8 Asian, non-Hispanic/Latino; 7 Hispanic/Latino; 1 Native Hawaiian or other Pacific Islander, non-Hispanic/Latino; 14 Two or more races, non-Hispanic/Latino), 57 international. Average age 31. 597 applicants, 68% accepted, 78 enrolled. In 2011, 98 master's, 8 doctorates awarded. *Degree requirements:* For master's, thesis (for some programs); for doctorate, comprehensive exam, thesis/dissertation. *Entrance requirements:* For master's and doctorate, GRE or GMAT. Additional exam requirements/recommendations for international students: Required—TOEFL (minimum score 550 paper-based; 79 iBT). *Application deadline:* For fall admission, 3/1 for international students; for spring admission, 8/1 for international students. Applications are processed on a rolling basis. Application fee: $40 ($75 for international students). Electronic applications accepted. *Expenses:* Tuition, state resident: full-time $4044; part-time $168.50 per credit hour. Tuition, nonresident: full-time $16,008; part-time $667 per credit hour. *Required fees:* $2122; $88.45 per credit hour. One-time fee: $50. Tuition and fees vary according to course load and campus/location. *Financial support:* In 2011–12, 2 research assistantships (averaging $10,302 per year) were awarded; career-related internships or fieldwork, Federal Work-Study, scholarships/grants, health care benefits, tuition waivers (partial), and unspecified assistantships also available. Support available to part-time students. Financial award application deadline: 3/1; financial award applicants required to submit FAFSA. *Unit head:* Dr. Sheryl Tucker, Dean, 405-744-7099, Fax: 405-744-0355, E-mail: grad-i@okstate.edu. *Application contact:* Dr. Susan Mathew, Coordinator of Admissions, 405-744-6368, Fax: 405-744-0355, E-mail: grad-i@okstate.edu. Web site: http://gradcollege.okstate.edu/.

Saint Mary's University, Faculty of Science, Interdisciplinary Program in Applied Science, Halifax, NS B3H 3C3, Canada. Offers M Sc.

Southeastern Louisiana University, College of Science and Technology, Program in Integrated Science and Technology, Hammond, LA 70402. Offers MS. Part-time and evening/weekend programs available. *Faculty:* 18 full-time (3 women). *Students:* 12 full-time (7 women), 15 part-time (3 women); includes 2 minority (1 Black or African American, non-Hispanic/Latino; 1 Hispanic/Latino), 8 international. Average age 32. 8 applicants, 100% accepted, 7 enrolled. In 2011, 10 master's awarded. *Degree requirements:* For master's, thesis (for some programs), 33-36 hours. *Entrance requirements:* For master's, GRE (minimum combined score 850), undergraduate degree; minimum GPA of 2.75; 30 semester hours in any combination of chemistry, computer science, industrial technology, mathematics, or physics; two letters of recommendation; transcripts of previous undergraduate or graduate work. Additional exam requirements/recommendations for international students: Required—TOEFL (minimum score 500 paper-based; 173 computer-based; 61 iBT). *Application deadline:* For fall admission, 7/15 priority date for domestic students, 6/1 for international students; for spring admission, 12/1 priority date for domestic students, 10/1 for international students. Applications are processed on a rolling basis. Application fee: $20 ($30 for international students). Electronic applications accepted. *Expenses:* Tuition, state resident: full-time $3977; part-time $283 per semester hour. Tuition, nonresident: full-time $13,482; part-time $811 per semester hour. *Financial support:* In 2011–12, 5 research assistantships (averaging $10,100 per year), 2 teaching assistantships (averaging $10,100 per year) were awarded; career-related internships or fieldwork, Federal Work-Study, institutionally sponsored loans, scholarships/grants, and unspecified assistantships also available. Support available to part-time students. Financial award application deadline: 5/1; financial award applicants required to submit FAFSA. *Faculty research:* Remote sensing of magnetospheic dynamics, molecular modeling, CAD solid modeling, statistical computational methods, artificial intelligence. *Unit head:* Dr. Ken Li, Coordinator, 985-549-3822, E-mail: kli@selu.edu. *Application* *contact:* Sandra Meyers, Graduate Admissions Analyst, 985-549-5620, Fax: 985-549-5632, E-mail: admissions@selu.edu. Web site: http://www.selu.edu/future_students/degree_prog/degrees/coll_science_tech/ms_isat.html.

Southern Methodist University, Bobby B. Lyle School of Engineering, Department of Engineering Management, Information, and Systems, Dallas, TX 75275. Offers applied science (MS); engineering management (MSEM, DE); information engineering and management (MSIEM); operations research (MS, PhD); systems engineering (MS, PhD). Part-time and evening/weekend programs available. Postbaccalaureate distance learning degree programs offered. Terminal master's awarded for partial completion of doctoral program. *Degree requirements:* For master's, thesis optional; for doctorate, thesis/dissertation, oral and written qualifying exams. *Entrance requirements:* For master's, minimum GPA of 3.0 in last 2 years; bachelor's degree in engineering, mathematics, sciences, or technical area; for doctorate, GRE General Test (operations research, engineering management), bachelor's degree in related field. Additional exam requirements/recommendations for international students: Required—TOEFL. *Faculty research:* Telecommunications, decision systems, information engineering, operations research, software.

Southern Methodist University, Bobby B. Lyle School of Engineering, Department of Environmental and Civil Engineering, Dallas, TX 75275-0340. Offers applied science (MS, PhD); civil and environmental engineering (PhD); civil engineering (MS); environmental engineering (MS); environmental science (MS), including environmental systems management. Part-time and evening/weekend programs available. Postbaccalaureate distance learning degree programs offered (no on-campus study). Terminal master's awarded for partial completion of doctoral program. *Degree requirements:* For master's, thesis optional; for doctorate, thesis/dissertation, oral and written qualifying exams. *Entrance requirements:* For master's, GRE General Test, minimum GPA of 3.0 in last 2 years; bachelor's degree in engineering, mathematics, or sciences; for doctorate, GRE, BS and MS in related field, minimum GPA of 3.3. Additional exam requirements/recommendations for international students: Required—TOEFL. Electronic applications accepted. *Faculty research:* Human and environmental health effects of endocrine disrupters, development of air pollution control systems for diesel engines, structural analysis and design, modeling and design of waste treatment systems.

Thomas Edison State College, School of Applied Science and Technology, Trenton, NJ 08608-1176. Offers Graduate Certificate. Part-time programs available. Postbaccalaureate distance learning degree programs offered (no on-campus study). *Students:* 36 part-time (17 women); includes 13 minority (5 Black or African American, non-Hispanic/Latino; 3 Asian, non-Hispanic/Latino; 5 Hispanic/Latino). Average age 41. In 2011, 6 Graduate Certificates awarded. *Entrance requirements:* Additional exam requirements/recommendations for international students: Required—TOEFL (minimum score 550 paper-based; 213 computer-based; 79 iBT). *Application deadline:* For fall admission, 8/15 priority date for domestic students, 8/15 for international students; for winter admission, 11/15 priority date for domestic students, 11/15 for international students; for spring admission, 2/15 priority date for domestic students, 1/15 for international students. Applications are processed on a rolling basis. Application fee: $75. Electronic applications accepted. *Financial support:* Applicants required to submit FAFSA. *Unit head:* Dr. Marcus Tillery, Dean, School of Applied Science and Technology, 609-984-1130, Fax: 609-984-3898, E-mail: info@tesc.edu. *Application contact:* David Hoftiezer, Director of Admissions, 888-442-8372, Fax: 609-984-8447, E-mail: admissions@tesc.edu. Web site: http://www.tesc.edu/758.php.

University of Arkansas at Little Rock, Graduate School, George W. Donughey College of Engineering and Information Technology, Department of Applied Science, Little Rock, AR 72204-1099. Offers MS, PhD. Part-time programs available. *Degree requirements:* For master's, comprehensive exam, thesis optional; for doctorate, thesis/dissertation, 2 semesters of residency, candidacy exams. *Entrance requirements:* For master's, GRE General Test, interview, minimum GPA of 3.0; for doctorate, GRE General Test, interview, minimum graduate GPA of 3.5. Additional exam requirements/recommendations for international students: Required—TOEFL. *Faculty research:* Particle and powder science and technology, optical sensors, process control and automation, signal and image processing, biomedical measurement systems.

University of California, Berkeley, Graduate Division, College of Engineering, Group in Applied Science and Technology, Berkeley, CA 94720-1500. Offers PhD. *Degree requirements:* For doctorate, thesis/dissertation, preliminary exam, qualifying exam. *Entrance requirements:* For doctorate, GRE General Test, BA or BS in engineering, physics, mathematics, chemistry, or related field; minimum GPA of 3.0, 3 letters of recommendation.

University of California, Davis, College of Engineering, Program in Applied Science, Davis, CA 95616. Offers MS, PhD. Terminal master's awarded for partial completion of doctoral program. *Degree requirements:* For master's, comprehensive exam (for some programs), thesis (for some programs); for doctorate, thesis/dissertation. *Entrance requirements:* For master's and doctorate, GRE General Test, minimum GPA of 3.3. Additional exam requirements/recommendations for international students: Required—TOEFL (minimum score 550 paper-based; 213 computer-based). Electronic applications accepted. *Faculty research:* Plasma physics, scientific computing, fusion technology, laser physics and nonlinear optics.

University of Colorado at Colorado Springs, College of Letters, Arts and Sciences, Department of Mathematics, Colorado Springs, CO 80933-7150. Offers applied mathematics (MS); applied science (PhD); mathematics (M Sc). Part-time and evening/weekend programs available. *Faculty:* 10 full-time (1 woman), 1 (woman) part-time/adjunct. *Students:* 9 full-time (2 women), 8 part-time (3 women); includes 1 minority (Black or African American, non-Hispanic/Latino), 1 international. Average age 34. 2 applicants, 100% accepted, 1 enrolled. In 2011, 4 master's awarded. *Degree requirements:* For master's, thesis, qualifying exam. *Entrance requirements:* For master's, GRE General Test, minimum GPA of 3.0. Additional exam requirements/recommendations for international students: Required—TOEFL (minimum score 550 paper-based; 213 computer-based). *Application deadline:* For fall admission, 6/1 for domestic and international students; for spring admission, 11/1 for domestic and international students. Applications are processed on a rolling basis. Application fee: $60 ($75 for international students). Electronic applications accepted. *Expenses:* Tuition, state resident: part-time $660 per credit hour. Tuition, nonresident: part-time $1133 per credit hour. Tuition and fees vary according to degree level, program and student level. *Financial support:* In 2011–12, 3 students received support. Teaching assistantships, Federal Work-Study, and scholarships/grants available. Support available to part-time students. Financial award application deadline: 3/1; financial award applicants required to submit FAFSA. *Faculty research:* Abelian groups and noncommutative rings, hormone analysis and computer vision, probability and mathematical physics, stochastic dynamics, probability models. *Total annual research expenditures:* $110,911. *Unit head:* Dr. Sarbarish Chakravarty, Chair, 719-255-3549, Fax: 719-255-3605, E-mail: schakrav@uccs.edu. *Application contact:* Josh Goldman, Graduate Assistant, 719-255-3554, Fax: 719-255-3605, E-mail: jgoldman@uccs.edu. Web site: http://www.uccs.edu/math.

University of Colorado Denver, College of Liberal Arts and Sciences, Program in Integrated Sciences, Denver, CO 80217. Offers applied science (MIS); computer science (MIS); mathematics (MIS). Part-time and evening/weekend programs available. *Students:* 5 full-time (3 women), 2 part-time; includes 3 minority (2 Hispanic/Latino; 1 Two or more races, non-Hispanic/Latino). Average age 38. 4 applicants, 25% accepted, 1 enrolled. In 2011, 1 master's awarded. *Degree requirements:* For master's, thesis or alternative, 30 credit hours; thesis or project. *Entrance requirements:* For master's, GRE if undergraduate GPA is 3.0 or less, minimum of 40 semester hours in mathematics, computer science, physics, biology, chemistry and/or geology; essay; three letters of recommendation. Additional exam requirements/recommendations for international students: Required—TOEFL (minimum score 525 paper-based; 197 computer-based; 71 iBT). *Application deadline:* For fall admission, 4/15 for domestic and international students; for spring admission, 10/15 for domestic and international students. Application fee: $50 ($75 for international students). Electronic applications accepted. *Financial support:* Application deadline: 4/1; applicants required to submit FAFSA. *Faculty research:* Computer science, applied science, mathematics. *Unit head:* Dr. Daniel Howard, Professor and Dean, 303-556-2624, Fax: 303-556-4861, E-mail: dan.howard@ucdenver.edu. *Application contact:* 303-556-2557, Fax: 303-556-4861, E-mail: clas@ucdenver.edu. Web site: http://thunder1.cudenver.edu/clas/mis/index.html.

University of Mississippi, Graduate School, School of Applied Sciences, Oxford, University, MS 38677. Offers MA, MS, MSW, PhD. *Students:* 150 full-time (118 women), 55 part-time (31 women); includes 37 minority (35 Black or African American, non-Hispanic/Latino; 2 Two or more races, non-Hispanic/Latino), 11 international. In 2011, 34 master's, 1 doctorate awarded. *Entrance requirements:* For master's, GRE General Test, minimum GPA of 3.0. Additional exam requirements/recommendations for international students: Required—TOEFL. *Application deadline:* For fall admission, 4/1 for domestic students; for spring admission, 10/1 for domestic students. Applications are processed on a rolling basis. Application fee: $25. Electronic applications accepted. *Financial support:* Scholarships/grants available. Financial award application deadline: 3/1; financial award applicants required to submit FAFSA. *Unit head:* Dr. Carol Minor Boyd, Interim Dean, 662-915-1081, Fax: 662-915-5717, E-mail: cboyd@olemiss.edu.

CLARKSON UNIVERSITY
Coulter School of Engineering

Programs of Study

The Coulter School of Engineering, comprising departments of chemical and biomolecular, civil and environmental, electrical and computer, and mechanical and aeronautical engineering, offers programs of study leading to the Doctor of Philosophy (Ph.D.), Master of Science (M.S.), and Master of Engineering (M.E.) degrees. Interdisciplinary programs allow the student to specialize in such areas as materials processing, information technology, computer science, and environmental science and engineering. Descriptions of these programs can be found at http://www.clarkson.edu/engineering/graduate.

The Master of Science degree is awarded upon completion of 30 credit hours of graduate work, including a thesis. The Master of Engineering degree can be obtained in one calendar year; it includes the completion of a design-oriented project. In addition, Clarkson has initiated a two-year, two-degree program whereby students may obtain an M.E. degree in one year and continue on for an additional year to obtain an M.B.A.

The Ph.D. is awarded upon completion of a minimum of 90 credit hours of graduate work, corresponding to a minimum of three academic years of full-time study beyond the bachelor's degree. The candidacy procedure for the Ph.D. requires the presentation and defense of a proposal for the Ph.D. research. Candidates for the Ph.D. are required to prepare an original dissertation in an advanced research area and defend it in an oral examination.

The academic year consists of two semesters of fifteen weeks each. There is no formal summer session for graduate classes; graduate students and faculty members devote the summer entirely to research.

Research Facilities

The Department of Chemical and Biomolecular Engineering houses research labs for chemical-mechanical planarization (CMP); bioengineering; nucleation; chemical metallurgy; chemical kinetics; process design; electrochemistry and electrochemical engineering; materials synthesis and characterization; experimental and computational fluid mechanics, including two research-grade wind tunnels; heat and mass transfer; and interfacial fluid mechanics, including a bubble column equipped with a motorized camera platform. The Department has facilities for conducting research on thin films and coatings, alternative energy sources, nonthermal plasma; and access to a 150 kW high-efficiency, low-emissions word pellet boiler. In addition, excellent facilities are available for aerosol generation, chamber studies, and ambient and indoor air pollution sampling and chemical analysis, as well as tools for advanced data analysis.

The Department of Civil and Environmental Engineering has well-equipped environmental engineering laboratories with pilot plant facilities, walk-in constant-temperature rooms, and modern research instrumentation for organic and inorganic analyses; a hydraulics laboratory with a large automated tilting flume; temperature-controlled cold rooms and ice mechanics laboratories; a geomechanics laboratory with a wide array of laboratory and field testing equipment for geotechnical problems, including a number of specialized sensors, and a variety of loading systems, such as 200-kip closed-loop controlled stepping motor system and a 20-kip hydraulic closed-loop controlled servo-valve controlled axial-torsional system; structural and materials testing laboratories, including a unique strong floor and strong wall testing facility and an Instron 220-kip UTM; and soil mechanics and materials laboratories.

The Department of Electrical and Computer Engineering has laboratories for distributed computing networks, intelligent information processing, microelectronics, motion control, robotics, software engineering, power electronics, microwave photonics, electric machines and drives, embedded systems, liquid dielectric breakdown, biomedical signal and image processing, advanced visualization and networked multimedia and networked systems, and a 1-million-volt high-voltage measurement laboratory.

The Department of Mechanical and Aeronautical Engineering houses three wind tunnels, a clean room for microcontamination and nanotechnology research, and labs for fluid mechanics, heat transfer, aerosol and multiphase flow, CAD, image processing, energy conversion, vibrations, combustion, materials processing, manufacturing, and welding.

Much of the research work is conducted in conjunction with the University's interdisciplinary research centers: the New York State Center for Advanced Materials Processing (CAMP), Institute for the Sustainable Environment (ISE), Center for Sustainable Energy Systems (CRES), Center for Rehabilitation Engineering Science and Technology (CREST), and Center for Air Resources Engineering and Science (CARES). Computing facilities within the School of Engineering include an IBM series and a variety of Sun and IBM workstations, all interconnected to each office and laboratory by a high-speed wide-band network. Clarkson's Campus Information Services houses modern information storage and retrieval facilities, the computing center, and the library.

Financial Aid

Several forms of financial assistance are available, which permit a full-time program of study and provide a stipend plus tuition. Instructional assistantships involve an obligation of 12 hours per week of assistance in courses or laboratories. Research assistantships require research activity that is also used to satisfy thesis requirements. Partial-tuition scholarships are available for all degree programs.

Cost of Study

Tuition for graduate work is $1259 per credit hour in 2012–13. Fees are about $590 per year.

Living and Housing Costs

Graduate students can find rooms or apartments near the campus. The University maintains single and married student housing units. Off-campus apartments for 2 students rent for approximately $400 per month and up.

Student Group

There are approximately 200 students on campus pursuing graduate work in engineering. The total Graduate School enrollment is 400, and the undergraduate enrollment is 2,600.

Location

Potsdam, New York, is an attractive village located along the banks of the Raquette River on a rolling plain between the Adirondack Mountains and the St. Lawrence River. Three other colleges (one in Potsdam) provide a total college student body of 11,000 within a 12-mile radius. Potsdam is 100 miles from Montreal, 80 miles from Ottawa and Lake Placid, and 140 miles from Syracuse. The St. Lawrence Seaway, the Thousand Islands, and Adirondack resort areas are within a short drive. Opportunities for fishing, hiking, boating, golfing, camping, swimming, and skiing abound throughout the area.

The University

Clarkson University is a privately endowed school of science, engineering, and business. Master's degrees are offered in the engineering departments and in business administration, chemistry, computer science, mathematics, management systems, and physics; Ph.D. degrees are offered in chemical engineering, chemistry, civil and environmental engineering, electrical and computer engineering, engineering science, environmental science and engineering, materials science and engineering, mathematics, mechanical engineering, and physics.

Applying

It is recommended that applications be submitted by January 30 for the fall semester and September 15 for the spring semester to allow for full financial aid consideration. Study may begin in August, January, or June. Scores on the General Test of the GRE are required for all applications except those of Clarkson students. TOEFL scores of at least 550 (paper-based test), 213 (computer-based test), or 80 (Internet-based test) are required for all international applications.

Correspondence and Information

Wallace H. Coulter School of Engineering
Graduate Studies Office
Box 5700
Clarkson University
Potsdam, New York 13699-5700
Phone: 315-268-7929
Fax: 315-268-4494
E-mail: enggrad@clarkson.edu
Web site: http://www.clarkson.edu/engineering/graduate

THE FACULTY AND THEIR RESEARCH

Department of Chemical and Biomolecular Engineering

S. V. Babu, Professor; Ph.D., SUNY at Stony Brook. Chemical-mechanical planarization of metal and dielectric films and thin films for photovoltaic applications.

Ruth E. Baltus, Professor; Ph.D., Carnegie Mellon. Transport in porous media, membrane separations, membrane characterization, room temperature ionic liquids and biosensors.

Sandra L. Harris, Associate Professor; Ph.D., California, Santa Barbara. Adaptive control, process control, and process identification; periodic processing; the control of systems having varying dead-times; the generation of input signals for efficient process identification.

Philip K. Hopke, Professor; Ph.D., Princeton. Multivariate statistical methods for data analysis; characterization of source/receptor relationships for ambient air pollutants; sampling, chemical, and physical characterization of airborne particles; experimental studies of homogeneous, heterogeneous, and ion-induced nucleation; indoor air quality; exposure and risk assessment.

R. J. J. Jachuck, Research Associate Professor; Ph.D., Newcastle Upon Tyne. Process intensification and miniaturization, intensified heat and mass transfer, polymerization.

Sitaraman Krishnan, Assistant Professor; Ph.D., Lehigh. Antifouling and biocompatible polymers, biomaterials, responsive materials, nanostructured material design using self-assembly, X-ray techniques for nanoscale materials characterization, multiphase polymerization kinetics.

Richard J. McCluskey, Associate Professor; Ph.D., Minnesota. Reaction kinetics and thermodynamics.

John B. McLaughlin, Professor; Ph.D., Harvard. Fluid mechanics, modeling of protective textiles, self-healing composite materials and the flow of air and suspended particles, electrostatic precipitator.

Don H. Rasmussen, Professor; Ph.D., Wisconsin–Madison. Nucleation and phase transformations, metal reduction, colloidal and interfacial phenomena.

R. Shankar Subramanian, Professor; Ph.D., Clarkson. Transport phenomena, colloidal and interfacial phenomena.

Ian Ivar Suni, Professor; Ph.D., Harvard. Electrochemical and electrochemical engineering with applications to biosensors, thin film growth and nanotechnology.

Ross Taylor, Professor; Ph.D., Manchester. Multicomponent mass transfer, separation process simulation, engineering applications of computer algebra.

Clarkson University

Selma Mededovic Thagard, Assistant Professor; Ph.D., Florida State. Nonthermal plasma for air and wastewater treatment, plasma-assisted material synthesis, plasma chemistry, mathematical modeling of electrical discharges in gases and liquids.

William R. Wilcox, Professor and Co-Director, International Center for Gravity Materials Science and Applications; Ph.D., Berkeley. Materials processing, crystal growth.

Department of Civil and Environmental Engineering

Norbert L. Ackermann, Professor Emeritus; Ph.D., Carnegie Tech. Mechanics of granular flow, river hydraulics.

Christopher Bellona, Assistant Professor; Ph.D., Colorado School of Mines. Research and development of novel water treatment processes and systems.

James S. Bonner, Professor and Shipley Center for Innovation Fellow; Ph.D., Clarkson. Water quality and spill monitoring.

John P. Dempsey, Professor and Shipley Center for Innovation Fellow; Ph.D., Auckland (New Zealand). Fracture mechanics, tribology, ice-structure interaction.

Andrea Ferro, Associate Professor; Ph.D., Stanford. Air pollution, indoor air quality.

Stefan J. Grimberg, Professor and Chair; Ph.D., North Carolina at Chapel Hill. Bioremediation, bioavailability of organic environmental pollutants.

Thomas M. Holsen, Professor; Ph.D., Berkeley. Fate and transport of chemicals in the environment.

Kerop Janoyan, Associate Professor and Executive Officer; Ph.D., UCLA. Geotechnical and structural engineering, soil-structural interactions, structural health monitoring.

Feng-Bor Lin, Professor; Ph.D., Carnegie Mellon. Modeling traffic operations, systems analysis.

Levon Minnetyan, Professor; Ph.D., Duke. Structural analysis and design.

Sulapha Peethamparan, Assistant Professor; Ph.D, Purdue. Characterization and control of cement and concrete materials.

Susan E. Powers, Professor and Associate Director for Sustainability; Ph.D., Michigan. Multiphase fluid flow; hazardous-waste management.

Shane Rogers, Assistant Professor; Ph.D., Iowa State. Fate and transport of etiological agents and anthropogenic compounds.

Hayley H. Shen, Professor; Ph.D., Clarkson; Ph.D., Iowa. Granular flow, sea ice processes.

Hung Tao Shen, Professor and Associate Dean for Research and Graduate Studies; Ph.D., Iowa. River hydraulics, river ice processes, mathematical modeling.

Tyler J. Smith, Assistant Professor; Ph.D., Montana State. Water resources, water quality.

Khiem Tran, Assistant Professor, Ph.D., Florida. Nondestructive Testing and evaluation, foundation design, and capacity verification.

Lifeng Wang, Assistant Professor; Ph.D., Tsinghua (China). Mechanical properties of carbon nanotubes and related nanostructures.

Poojitha Yapa, Professor; Ph.D., Clarkson. Mathematical modeling of oil spills.

Department of Electrical and Computer Engineering

James J. Carroll, Associate Professor; Ph.D., Clemson. High-performance motion control, nonlinear control, control strategies.

Ming-Cheng Cheng, Associate Professor; Ph.D., Polytechnic. Device physics and modeling and simulation of electronic and thermal characteristics for advanced solid state devices.

Susan E. Conry, Associate Professor; Ph.D., Rice. Multiagent systems, distributed problem solving, design of coordination strategies.

Daqing Hou, Assistant Professor; Ph.D., Alberta. Software design, program analysis, semantics of programming languages, software development environments and tools, software reuse, documentation, software evolution, formal methods.

William Jemison, Professor and Chair; Ph.D. Drexel. Microwave photonic systems and substations, microwave/mm-wave antenna design and measurement, radar systems, wireless and optical communications systems, lidar systems, biological applications of microwaves and photonics.

Abul N. Khondker, Associate Professor; Ph.D., Rice. Solid-state materials and device theory, modeling and characterization of semiconductor devices.

Jack Koplowitz, Associate Professor; Ph.D., Colorado. Image and signal processing, computer vision, pattern recognition.

Chen Liu, Assistant Professor, Ph.D., California, Irvine. Embedded systems, processor architectures, power-aware many-core computing, interaction between operating systems and micro-architectures.

Paul B. McGrath, Professor; Ph.D., London. Dielectric materials and high-voltage engineering, insulation problems.

Robert A. Meyer, Associate Professor; Ph.D., Rice. Artificial intelligence and distributed problem solving, verification of hardware designs, software engineering.

Thomas H. Ortmeyer, Professor; Ph.D., Iowa State. Power electronics, power quality, power system operation.

Vladimir Privman, Professor; D.Sci., Technion (Israel). Quantum devices: quantum computing, spintronics, nanoscale electronics; colloids and nanoparticles; synthesis and properties.

Liya L. Regel, Research Professor and Director, International Center for Gravity Materials Science and Applications; Ph.D., Irkutsk State (Russia); Doctorat, Ioffe Institute (Russia). Materials science and its influence on properties and device performance.

Jeremiah Remus, Assistant Professor; Ph.D., Duke. Statistical signal processing, model inversion and optimization, pattern recognition.

Charles J. Robinson, Founding Director, Center for Rehabilitation Engineering, Science, and Technology (CREST), and Herman L. Shulman Chair Professor; D.Sc., Washington (St. Louis). Combining the development of microdevices and nanodevices capable of measuring stroke sequences with fundamental research that characterizes the behavior of the nervous system, quantification of tremor through signal processing analysis of graphical drawings, and determining and describing the control systems employed in health and disease to permit upright standing in humans.

Edward Sazonov, Research Associate Professor; Ph.D., West Virginia. Computational intelligence, biomedical engineering, nondestructive testing.

Robert J. Schilling, Professor; Ph.D., Berkeley. Control, nonlinear systems, robotics, active control of acoustic noise, motion planning.

Stephanie Schuckers, Associate Professor; Ph.D., Michigan. Biomedical signal processing, medical devices, pattern recognition, large datasets.

James A. Svoboda, Associate Professor and Associate Chair; Ph.D., Wisconsin. Circuit theory, system theory, electronics, digital signal processing.

Lei Wu, Assistant Professor, Ph.D., IIT. Stochastic modeling and optimization of large-scale power systems, smart grid, high-penetration renewable energy applications, power systems reliability and economics, market power analysis and risk management.

Department of Mechanical and Aeronautical Engineering

Goodarz Ahmadi, Clarkson Distinguished Professor, Robert R. Hill '48 Professor, and Dean, Coulter School of Engineering; Ph.D., Purdue. Fluid mechanics, solid mechanics, multiphase flows, aerosols, microcontamination, surface cleaning.

Ajit Achuthan, Assistant Professor; Ph.D., Purdue. Solid mechanics, ferroelectrics, nanomechanics and smart structures and materials, fiber optic sensors.

Daryush Aidun, Professor and Chair; Ph.D., Rensselaer. Welding metallurgy and automation, corrosion, materials processing and solidification, reliability analysis of engineering components/systems.

Douglas Bohl, Associate Professor; Ph.D., Michigan State. Experimental fluid mechanics and thermal science.

Frederick Carlson, Associate Professor; Ph.D., Connecticut. Heat transfer, crystal growth.

Cetin Cetinkaya, Professor; Ph.D., Illinois at Urbana-Champaign. Solid mechanics, stress wave propagation, surface cleaning and nanotechnology.

Suresh Dhaniyala, Associate Professor; Ph.D., Minnesota. Aerosols, nanoparticles, particle instrumentation, atmospheric aerosols, aircraft and ground-based sampling, fluid mechanics.

Bryon Erath, Assistant Professor; Ph.D., Purdue. Fluid mechanics, focus on laryngeal aerodynamics of voiced speech, experimental investigations and computational modeling of the speech process.

Kevin Fite, Assistant Professor; Ph.D., Vanderbilt. Dynamic systems and controls, robotics and mechatronics.

Brian Helenbrook, Associate Professor; Ph.D., Princeton. Computational fluid dynamics and combustion.

Kathleen Issen, Associate Professor; Ph.D., Northwestern. Solid mechanics, inelastic behavior and failure of geomaterials.

Ratneshwar Jha, Associate Professor; Ph.D., Arizona State. Solid mechanics, optimization, smart materials.

James Kane, Associate Professor; Ph.D., Connecticut. Solid mechanics, boundary-element methods.

Laurel Kuxhaus, Assistant Professor; Ph.D., Pittsburgh. Biomechanics; mechanics and control of the upper extremity, especially the elbow; elbow joint stiffness and its application to arthritis; prosthetic upper limb control and the diagnosis of Parkinson's disease; mathematical modeling of ligaments; mechanical properties of vertebral bone.

Ronald LaFleur, Associate Professor; Ph.D., Connecticut. Fluid mechanics, thermofluid design.

Sung P. Lin, Professor Emeritus; Ph.D., Michigan. Fluid mechanics, fluid dynamic stability.

Pier Marzocca, Associate Professor; Ph.D., Virginia Tech. Solid mechanics, nonlinear systems control.

Parisa Mirbod, Assistant Professor; Ph.D., CUNY, City College. Fluid and solid mechanics, flow through porous media, non-Newtonian fluid mechanics, suspensions and technology development.

John Moosbrugger, Professor and Associate Dean; Ph.D., Georgia Tech. Solid mechanics, plasticity.

David Morrison, Associate Professor; Ph.D., Michigan. Materials science, fracture mechanics.

Eric Thacher, Professor Emeritus and Senior Research Professor; Ph.D., New Mexico State. Thermal sciences, solar energy.

Daniel Valentine, Associate Professor and Executive Officer; Ph.D., Catholic University. Fluid mechanics, hydrodynamics.

Kenneth Visser, Associate Professor; Ph.D., Notre Dame. Experimental aerodynamics.

Kenneth Willmert, Professor; Ph.D., Case Western Reserve. Solid mechanics, optimal design.

Steven W. Yurgartis, Associate Professor; Ph.D., Rensselaer. Solid mechanics, composite materials.

Philip A. Yuya, Assistant Professor; Ph.D., Nebraska-Lincoln. Constitutive modeling and experimental mechanics of materials with special emphasis on biomaterials, nanofibers and polymers.

Materials Science and Engineering Ph.D. program

Director, Ian Ivar Suni, Ph.D., Harvard. Electrochemical and electrochemical engineering with applications to biosensors, thin film growth, and nanotechnology.

About 30 Clarkson faculty members participate in the interdisciplinary Ph.D. program in Materials Science and Engineering, with a goal of understanding the properties, synthesis, and processing of advanced materials. This multidisciplinary approach is required given the complex nature of advanced materials. Applications of advanced materials to the fields of alternative energy, biotechnology, microelectronic devices, and the environment are at the forefront of current materials research. Further information is available online at http://www.clarkson.edu/engineering/graduate/mat_sci_eng_phd/index.html.

Topics covered in the program include:
- Advanced materials for alternative energy:
- Polymers that absorb visible light and form anti-reflective coatings on photovoltaic cells.
- Colloidal methods for creating electrical contacts to photovoltaic cells.
- Phase change materials for solar thermal applications.
- Thin film deposition of semiconductor materials that absorb visible light.
- Biomaterials:
- Materials for enzymatic biosensors, antibody biosensors, and enzymatic biocomputing.
- Biopolymers and stimuli-responsive polymers.
- Fluid mechanics of inhalable drugs.
- New polymer materials for protein immobilization, and to prevent biofouling.
- Acoustic methods for monitoring drug tablets.
- Colloid science and technology:
- Colloidal methods for creating electrical contacts to photovoltaic cells, microelectronic devices, fuel cells, and other electrical devices.
- Creation of catalyst materials for fuel cells, reduction of environmentally harmful emissions, and other applications.
- Mechanical properties of metals with nano-sized grains.
- Particle removal using acoustic methods.
- Materials processing for microelectronic devices:
- Chemical mechanical planarization (CMP)
- Fluid mechanics and particle mechanics during CMP.
- Nanoparticle removal using laser-induced plasmas.
- Thin film deposition using colloidal methods and electrochemical methods.
- Materials of construction:
- Metallurgy
- Concrete
- Fatigue and fracture of construction materials.

FLORIDA INTERNATIONAL UNIVERSITY
College of Engineering and Computing

Programs of Study

The College of Engineering and Computing is committed to educating professionals who can serve industry and the community at large in a wide variety of fields, as well as conduct innovative basic and applied research that meets the technical needs of industry and government, improves the quality of life, and contributes to the economic viability of Florida, the nation, and the world.

The College of Engineering and Computing consists of the School of Computing and Information Sciences and five academic departments: biomedical engineering, civil and environmental engineering, construction management, electrical and computer engineering, and mechanical and materials engineering. These academic departments offer programs leading to the Bachelor of Science (B.S.), the Master of Science (M.S.), and the Doctor of Philosophy (Ph.D.) degrees.

The College offers the Ph.D. in biomedical engineering, civil engineering electrical engineering, computer science, and mechanical engineering. The Master of Science is available in biomedical engineering, civil engineering, computer engineering, computer science, construction management, electrical engineering, engineering management, environmental engineering, information technology, materials science and engineering, mechanical engineering, and telecommunications and networking.

Research Facilities

The College of Engineering and Computing has numerous research institutes, centers, and laboratories that support its academic and research programs. The institutes include the Advanced Materials Research Institute (AMERI) and the Telecommunications and Information Technology Institute (IT2).

The research centers include the Applied Research Center (ARC), the Center for Advanced Distributed System Engineering (CADSE), the Center for Advanced Technology and Education (CATE), the Center for the Study of Matter at Extreme Conditions (CeSMEC), the Center for Energy and Technology of the Americas (CETA), the Center of Emerging Technologies for Advanced Information and High-Confidence Systems (CREST), the Engineering Information Center (EIC), the Engineering Manufacturing Center (EMC), the High Performance Database Research Center (HPDRC), the Lehman Center for Transportation Research (LCTR), the IBM Latin American Supercomputing Consortium (LA GRID), the Center for NanoMedicine, the Plasma Spray Forming Lab, the High Temperature Tribology Lab, the Nanomechanics and Nanotribology Lab, the Spark Plasma Sintering Lab, the Optical Metrology Lab (OML), the Microstructure FEA (MFEA) Lab, and the Splat Simulation Lab.

Research laboratories include the Accelerated Bridge Construction (ABC) Center; the Construction and Structures Research and Testing Laboratory; the Distributed Multimedia Information System Laboratory (DMIS); the Digital Signal Processing Laboratory (DSP); the Enterprise Information Systems Research Laboratory; the Enterprise Systems Engineering Laboratory (ESE); the Graphic Simulation Laboratory (GSL), the Human Factors and Ergonomics Laboratory; the Information Systems Research Laboratory; the Laboratory for Wind Engineering Research (LWER), the Multidisciplinary Analysis; Inverse Design; Robust Optimal Control Laboratory (MAIDROC); the Optical Imaging and Tomography Laboratory; the Plasma Forming Laboratory (PFL); Bioinformatics Research Group (BioRG); the Photonics Research Laboratory; the Systems Research Laboratory (SyLab); the Knowledge Discovery Research Group (KDRG); the Modeling and Networking Systems Research Group (MNSRG); the Laboratory for Virtualized Infrastructure, Systems, and Applications (VISA); the Discovery Lab; the Energy Systems Research Lab; the Integrated Nanosystems Research Lab (INSYST); and the Adaptive Neural Systems Laboratory.

Affiliated Centers and Programs include the AMPATH International Exchange Point in Miami, CHEPREO: Center for High Energy Physics Research and Education Outreach, CIARA: Center for Internet Augmented Research and Assessment, CyberBridges, GEC: The Eugenio Pino and Family Global Entrepreneurship Center, IHRC: the International Hurricane Research Center, MOTOROLA Women in Engineering (MWIE), NASA All-Star Project, and Ware Foundation Neuro-Engineering and Brain Research Laboratory at Miami Children's Hospital.

Financial Aid

The College of Engineering and Computing offers a variety of merit-based fellowships, assistantships, and scholarships to qualified domestic and international students. These awards are highly competitive, and the amounts vary depending on the type of the award. Additional financial aid information is available from the Financial Aid Office at http://www.finaid.fiu.edu.

Cost of Study

For the 2012–13 academic year, tuition is $422.16 per credit for Florida residents and $926.24 per credit for out-of-state and international students. An additional $193 per semester is charged for student activity fees, a health fee, a photo ID, and parking. Books and supplies are estimated at $1545 per semester, and health insurance costs $1910 for two semesters.

Living and Housing Costs

Graduate student housing is available at University Park (305-348-4190) and the Biscayne Bay Campus (305-919-5587). On-campus housing ranges between $4900 and $6600 per semester, depending on the type of accommodation and meal plan selected. Additional information about on- and off-campus housing can be found through the Office of Housing and Residential Life Web site at http://www.housing.fiu.edu.

Student Group

The College of Engineering and Computing has 828 graduate students, of whom 481 are full-time, 192 are women, and 388 are international students.

Location

Greater Miami is noted for its cultural diversity. Greater Miami has extensive cultural amenities, such as the New World Symphony, the Florida Grand Opera, and the Miami City Ballet, in addition to a tropical climate. The area has franchises in all major sports, and the University has inaugurated intercollegiate football to round out its extensive sports offerings. Miami is a major transportation hub with easy air and sea connections throughout the Americas and Europe.

The University and The College

Florida International University (FIU) is Miami's first public four-year university. With more than 39,000 students, almost 1100 full-time faculty members, and 124,000 alumni, FIU is the largest university in South Florida and one of the most dynamic institutions in the United States. The University's growth in enrollment and stature in the academic community are remarkable. In four decades, FIU has become nationally renowned as a doctoral-granting institution, with more than 200 degree programs. For the past five years, FIU was ranked among the top 100 public universities in *U.S. News & World Report*'s "America's Best Colleges," and it is also ranked as a Research University in the High Research Activity category of the Carnegie Foundation's prestigious classification system. FIU recently graduated its first law class, and opened a medical school, attesting to the University's growth and recognition.

The College of Engineering and Computing is South Florida's leading engineering education resource. The College offers a full range of bachelor's, master's, and doctoral degree programs in engineering, construction, management, and computer sciences. Research is an integral part of the College's mission and its success, with more than $90 million in external research funding over the last five years from a variety of governmental and corporate sources.

Applying

In general, applicants must submit the completed application, the application fee, official transcripts, proof of degree, and GRE scores. In addition, some doctoral-program applicants must submit three letters of recommendation and a resume or curriculum vitae. International students must send in their TOEFL scores and have their transcripts evaluated. More information, including specific deadlines, is available from the College of Engineering and Computing.

Correspondence and Information

College of Engineering and Computing
Florida International University
10555 West Flagler Street, EC2430
Miami, Florida 33174-1630
Phone: 305-348-1890
Fax: 305-348-6142
E-mail: grad_eng@fiu.edu
Web site: http://cec.fiu.edu

Florida International University

THE FACULTY

School of Computing and Information Sciences
Walid Akache, Instructor; M.S., Miami (Florida).
Toby S. Berk, Professor Emeritus; Ph.D., Purdue.
Shu-Ching Chen, Associate Professor; Ph.D., Purdue.
Radu Jianu, Assistant Professor; Ph.D., Brown.
Shaoli Ren, Assistant Professor; Ph.D., UCLA.
Ning Xie, Assistant Professor; Ph.D., MIT.
Xin Sun, Assistant Professor; Ph.D., Purdue.
Wei Zeng, Assistant Professor; Ph.D., Stony Brook, SUNY.
Peter J. Clarke, Associate Professor; Ph.D., Clemson.
Tim Downey, Instructor; M.S., SUNY at Albany.
Xudong He, Professor; Ph.D., Virginia Tech.
Vagelis Hristidis, Assistant Professor; Ph.D., California, San Diego.
Kip Irvine, Instructor; M.S., Miami (Florida).
Sitharama Iyengar, Professor and Director; Ph.D., Mississippi State.
Tao Li, Assistant Professor; Ph.D., Rochester.
Christine Lisetti, Associate Professor; Ph.D., Florida International.
Masoud Milani, Associate Professor; Ph.D., Central Florida.
Giri Narasimhan, Professor; Ph.D., Wisconsin–Madison.
Jainendra K. Navlakha, Professor; Ph.D., Case Western Reserve.
Deng Pan, Assistant Professor; Ph.D., SUNY at Stony Brook.
Alex Pelin, Associate Professor; Ph.D., Pennsylvania.
Norman D. Pestaina, Instructor; M.S., Penn State.
Niki Pissinou, Professor; Ph.D., USC.
Nagarajan Prabakar, Associate Professor; Ph.D., Queensland (Australia).
Raju Rangaswami, Assistant Professor; Ph.D., California, Santa Barbara.
Naphtali Rishe, Professor; Ph.D., Tel Aviv.
S. Masoud Sadjadi, Assistant Professor; Ph.D., Michigan State.
Greg Shaw, Instructor; M.S., Barry.
Geoffrey Smith, Associate Professor; Ph.D., Cornell.
Joslyn Smith, Instructor; M.S., New Brunswick (Canada).
Jinpeng Wei, Assistant Professor; Ph.D., Georgia Tech.
Jill Weiss, Instructor; M.S., Barry.
Mark Allen Weiss, Professor and Associate Director; Ph.D., Princeton.
Ming Zhao, Assistant Professor; Ph.D., Florida.

Department of Biomedical Engineering
Michael Brown, Instructor; M.D./Ph.D., Miami (Florida).
James D. Byrne, Laboratory Instructor, Ph.D., Florida.
Michael Christie, Instructor and Undergraduate Adviser; Ph.D., Rutgers.
Shuliang Jiao, Associate Professor; Ph.D., Texas A&M.
Anuradha Godavarty, Assistant Professor; Ph.D., Texas A&M.
Yen-Chi Huang, Assistant Professor; Ph.D., Michigan.
Ranu Jung, Chair; Ph.D., Case Western Reserve.
Chenzhong Li, Assistant Professor; Ph.D., Kumamoto (Japan).
Wei-Chiang Lin, Assistant Professor; Ph.D., Texas at Austin.
Anthony J. McGoron, Associate Professor; Ph.D., Louisiana Tech.
Sharan Ramaswamy, Assistant Professor; Ph.D., Iowa.
Nikolaos Tsoukias, Assistant Professor; Ph.D., California, Irvine.

Department of Civil and Environmental Engineering
Atorod Azizinamini, Chair; Ph.D., South Carolina.
Arindam Gan Chowdhury, Assistant Professor; Ph.D., Iowa State.
Hector R. Fuentes, Professor; Ph.D., Vanderbilt; PE, DEE.
Ioanis Zisis, Assistant Professor; Ph.D., Concordia.
Ralf Arndt, Assistant Professor; Ph.D., Berlin.
Kingsley Lau, Assistant Professor; Ph.D., Florida.
Albert Gan, Associate Professor; Ph.D., Florida.
Mohammed Hadi, Assistant Professor; Ph.D., Florida; PE.
Sylvan C. Jolibois Jr., Associate Professor; Ph.D., Berkeley.
Shonali Laha, Associate Professor; Ph.D., Carnegie Mellon; PE.
Amir Mirmiran, Professor and Dean; Ph.D., Maryland; PE.
Caesar Abi Shdid, Director of External Programs; Ph.D., Florida.
L. David Shen, Professor, Graduate Program Director and Director, Lehman Center for Transportation Research; Ph.D., Clemson; PE, TE.
Nakin Suksawang, Assistant Professor; Ph.D., Rutgers.
Walter Z. Tang, Associate Professor; Ph.D., Delaware; PE.
Berrin Tansel, Professor; Ph.D., Wisconsin–Madison, 1985; PE.
Ton-Lo Wang, Professor and Associate Chair; Ph.D., IIT.

Department of Construction Management
Irtishad U. Ahmad, Associate Professor and Chairman; Ph.D., Cincinnati; PE.
Ronald A. Baier, Instructor and Undergraduate Advisor; M.E., Florida; PE.
Mehmet Emre Bayraktar, Assistant Professor; Ph.D., Purdue.
José A. Faria, Assistant Professor; Ph.D., Maryland.
Eugene D. Farmer, Associate Professor and Undergraduate Program Director; M.Arch., Illinois; RA, AIA.
Jose D. Mitrani, Associate Professor; M.E., Florida; PE, CPC, CGC.
Yimin Zhu, Assistant Professor and Graduate Program Director; Ph.D., Florida; CCE.

Department of Electrical and Computer Engineering
Malek Adjouadi, Professor and Director, CATE Center; Ph.D., Florida.
Jean Andrian, Associate Professor; Ph.D., Florida.
Armando Barreto, Professor, Graduate Program Director, and Director, Digital Signals Processing Lab; Ph.D., Florida.
Shekhar Bhansali, Alcatel-Lucent Professor and Chairperson; Ph.D., Royal Melbourne.
Hai Deng, Assistant Professor; Ph.D., Texas at Austin.
Jeffrey Fan, Assistant Professor; Ph.D., California, Riverside.
Stravos V. Georgakopoulos, Assistant Professor; Ph.D., Arizona State.
Grover L. Larkins, Professor; Ph.D., Case Western Reserve.
Osama Mohammed, Professor; Ph.D., Virginia Tech.
Mercedes Cabrerizo, Assistant Professor; Ph.D., Florida.
Irene Calizo, Assistant Professor; Ph.D., Riverside, California.
Nasir Ghani, Associate Professor; Ph.D., Waterloo.
Arif Islam, Assistant Professor; Ph.D., Florida.
Ismail Guvenc, Assistant Professor; Ph.D., Florida.
Nezih Pala, Assistant Professor; Ph.D., Rensselaer.
Roberto R. Panepucci, Assistant Professor; Ph.D., Illinois at Urbana-Champaign.
Gang Quan, Associate Professor; Ph.D., Notre Dame.
Gustavo Roig, Professor; Ph.D., Florida.
Frank K. Urban, Associate Professor; Ph.D., Florida.
Kang K. Yen, Professor and Director of International Program Development; Ph.D., Vanderbilt.

Department of Mechanical and Materials Engineering
Arvind Agarwal, Assistant Professor; Ph.D., Tennessee.
Yiding Cao, Professor, and Co-Graduate Program Director; Ph.D., Dayton.
Jiuhua Chen, Professor; Ph.D., Tennessee.
Won-Bong Choi, Associate Professor; Ph.D., North Carolina State.
George S. Dulikravich, Professor; Ph.D., Cornell.
Ali Ebadian, Professor; Ph.D., LSU.
Dennis Fan, Assistant Professor; Ph.D., SUNY at Stony Brook.
Gordon Hopkins, Professor; Ph.D., Alabama.
W. Kinzy Jones, Professor and Director, AMERI; Ph.D., MIT.
Cesar Levy, Professor, Chair, and Co-Graduate Program Director; Ph.D., Stanford.
Norman D. H. Munroe, Associate Professor and Associate Dean for Undergraduate Studies; Eng.Sc.D., Columbia.
Surendra K. Saxena, Professor; Ph.D., Uppsala (Sweden).
Carmen Schenck, Instructor/Counselor; M.S., Florida International.
Yong X. Tao, Professor and Undergraduate Program Director; Ph.D., Michigan.
Ibrahim Nur Tansel, Associate Professor; Ph.D., Wisconsin–Madison.
Sabri Tosunoglu, Associate Professor; Ph.D., Florida at Gainesville.
Igor Tsukanov, Assistant Professor; Ph.D., Northwestern.
Chunlei (Peggy) Wang, Assistant Professor; Ph.D., Jilin (China).
Kuang-Hsi Wu, Professor; Ph.D., Illinois at Urbana-Champaign.

KANSAS STATE UNIVERSITY
College of Engineering

Programs of Study

The College of Engineering's eight academic departments offer eight Ph.D. programs and eleven master's level programs. The M.S. and Ph.D. programs include: biological and agricultural engineering, chemical engineering, civil engineering, computing and information sciences, electrical engineering, industrial engineering, mechanical engineering, and nuclear engineering. Additional programs include the M.S. in architectural engineering, M.S. in operations research, Master of Software Engineering, and Master of Engineering Management.

Candidates for the M.S. degree are normally required to spend one academic year in residence; however, some M.S. degree programs are available partially or fully by distance. Subject to the approval of the major department, the candidate may choose one of the following options: (1) a minimum of 30 semester hours of graduate credit, including a master's thesis of 6 to 8 semester hours; (2) a minimum of 30 semester hours of graduate credit, including a written report of 2 semester hours, either of research or of problem work on a topic in the major field; or (3) a minimum of 30 semester hours of graduate credit in course work only, but including evidence of scholarly effort such as term papers and production of creative work, as determined by the student's supervisory committee.

Candidates for the Ph.D. degree normally devote at least three years of two semesters each to graduate study, or about 90 semester hours beyond the bachelor's degree. A dissertation is required. Ph.D. candidates must complete a year of full-time study in residence at Kansas State University. Furthermore, a minimum registration of 30 hours in research is required, not including work done toward a master's degree. Each candidate also must have completed at least 24 hours of course work at the University. The foreign language requirement is determined as a matter of policy by the graduate faculty in each department.

Research Facilities

Each of the eight departments in the College of Engineering has modern and fully equipped teaching and research laboratories. In addition, the College has several centers and institutes, including the Civil Infrastructure Systems Laboratory, the Advanced Manufacturing Institute, the Center for Sustainable Energy, the Center for Hazardous Substance Research, the Pollution Prevention Institute, the Institute for Environmental Research, and the National Gas Machinery Laboratory.

Financial Aid

The College of Engineering offers approximately 300 fellowships, traineeships, and assistantships each year. These awards are administered by individual departments.

Cost of Study

Fees for 2012–13 are $327 per credit hour for residents and $738 per credit hour for nonresidents. In addition, an $85 campus fee is charged for the first credit hour, with $25 charged for each additional credit hour, up to a maximum fee of $365 per semester. Students enrolled in the College of Engineering are assessed an engineering equipment fee of $19 per credit hour and a tuition surcharge of $20 per credit hour for engineering courses. Students with graduate assistantships may qualify for resident fees.

Living and Housing Costs

Residence hall rates for room and board for a double room with a fifteen-meal plan are $3878 per semester per student in 2012–13. A variety of apartments is also available at the Jardine complex, with monthly rent for one-bedroom apartments ranging from $400 to $580. In addition, there are scholarship housing units available that function as cooperatives in which students provide their own services. Complete information for Housing and Dining Services is available at http://housing.k-state.edu/. There are numerous privately owned apartments with a wide range of rental rates in the community.

Student Group

Kansas State University enrolls more than 23,000 students. The College of Engineering has approximately 3,000 undergraduate and 500 graduate students.

Location

The University's 664-acre campus is located in Manhattan, Kansas, a community of about 50,000 residents located in the scenic Flint Hills of northeast Kansas.

The University

Kansas State University was established in 1863 as the first land-grant institution under the Morrill Act. The University is composed of the Graduate School and the Colleges of Agriculture, Architecture and Design, Arts and Sciences, Business Administration, Education, Engineering, Human Ecology, Technology, and Veterinary Medicine. The College of Technology is located at Kansas State in Salina.

There are numerous cultural and entertainment activities associated with the University and the community. One of the most noteworthy is the Alfred M. Landon Lecture Series on Public Issues, which regularly brings outstanding speakers to the campus. The list of notables has included Tom Brokaw, George H. W. Bush, George W. Bush, Jimmy Carter, Bill Clinton, Bob Dole, Elizabeth Dole, Gerald Ford, Robert M. Gates, Mikhail Gorbachev, Billy Graham, Nancy Landon Kassebaum, Robert Kennedy, General Richard Myers, Richard Nixon, Sandra Day O'Connor, General David Petraeus, General Colin Powell, Dan Rather, Ronald Reagan, Sonia Sotomayor, Sheikh Yamani, and many others.

The University is a member of the Big Twelve Conference and provides numerous facilities for athletic activities.

Applying

The Graduate School has a nonrefundable application fee of $50 for domestic students and $75 for international students. Requirements vary according to department. Students interested in graduate study in the College of Engineering are invited to write to the Dean of Engineering, stating their area of interest.

Correspondence and Information

John R. English, Dean of Engineering
1046 Rathbone Hall
Kansas State University
Manhattan, Kansas 66506-5201
Phone: 785-532-5590
E-mail: ees@ksu.edu
Web site: http://www.ksu.edu

FACULTY HEADS AND AREAS OF RESEARCH

Architectural Engineering/Construction Science. David R. Fritchen, Head; M.S., Washington (Seattle). (17 faculty members) Structural, mechanical, and electrical systems design for buildings: domestic water-supply and sanitation systems, fire protection, heating and air-conditioning systems, lighting and electrical systems, environmental control systems in buildings, communication and energy management systems for buildings. Building design and construction: integration of structural, mechanical, and electrical systems in buildings.

Biological and Agricultural Engineering. Joseph P. Harner, Head; Ph.D., Virginia Tech. (15 faculty members) Grain processing, handling, drying, and storage. Water and soil resources: irrigation systems, movement of pesticides and other chemicals in surface water and groundwater, improved water management techniques, erosion and sedimentation control, water quality and nonpoint pollution control, animal waste management. Off-highway vehicle systems: chemical application systems, site-specific and precision agriculture. Energy use in agriculture: efficient internal-combustion engine operation. Control systems: instrumentation and controls, sensor development, image processing, chemical spray metering and control. Animal environment: air quality, environmental modification, ventilation-fan performance. Process engineering: process design, cereal-based product development, properties of biological products, biobased fuels. Environmental engineering: constructed wetlands, vegetative filters, watershed modeling, bioremediation.

Chemical Engineering. James H. Edgar, Head; Ph.D., Florida. (10 faculty members) Bioconversion and bioprocessing: enzyme manipulation and reactor design, biomass conversion, biobased industrial products, separation and purification of biological systems, environmental engineering. Sensors and advanced materials: microelectronic materials, polymer science, adsorbents, catalysts, graphene technologies, bionanotechnology, and nanoelectronics. Alternative energy: catalysts and reactor design for hydrogen production, process synthesis, hydrogen and natural gas storage, artificial membranes for separation and purification.

Civil Engineering. Alok Bhandari, Head; Ph.D., Virginia Tech. (15 faculty members) Hydrology and hydraulic engineering: hydraulic and hydrologic modeling, overland flow hydraulics. Environmental engineering: physical,

Kansas State University

chemical, and biological processes for water, wastewater, and hazardous-waste treatment. Soil mechanics and foundation engineering: physical and mechanical properties of soil, soil stabilization, earth pressures and reactions, environmental geotechnology. Structural engineering: behavior and load-carrying capacity of steel and reinforced concrete members, fracture mechanics of concrete, finite-element methods, optimization applied to civil engineering structures, structural dynamics and earthquake engineering. Transportation engineering: urban transportation planning, transportation systems, analysis and simulation, geometric design of highways, highway safety, pavements and highway materials.

Computing and Information Sciences. Gurdip Singh, Head; Ph.D., SUNY at Stony Brook. (17 faculty members) Languages and software: high assurance software, software verification and certification, programming language and programming environment design. Cyber-security: language-based security, information assurance, enterprise systems security. Parallel and distributed computing systems: distributed mutual exclusion, real-time embedded systems, cluster computing, synchronization and concurrency, construction, distributed algorithms and protocols, operating systems, parallel programming languages and systems. Database systems: database design, object-oriented databases, artificial intelligence, data mining, bioinformatics. Software engineering: software life cycle, software environments and tools, software metrics, software specification, software testing, large software systems, computational science and engineering, agent-oriented software engineering.

Electrical and Computer Engineering. Don M. Gruenbacher, Head; Ph.D., Kansas State. (19 faculty members) Bioengineering: biomedicine, light-based bioinstrumentation, telemedicine. Communication systems: detection and estimation, analog/digital/RF circuits and systems, wireless telecommunications. Computer systems: computer vision, testing of digital systems, neural networks, computer architecture, noncontact sensing. Electromagnetics: device modeling and simulation, bioelectromagnetics. Instrumentation: computer-based instrumentation, sensors, intelligent instrumentation, microcontroller applications. Power systems: renewable energy, power system and stability, nonlinear dynamic systems, load management, distribution automation, power electronics, power devices, high-voltage circuits. Signal processing: adaptive signal processing, image processing. Solid-state electronics: sensors, device and process modeling, analog and digital integrated circuit design, infrared emitters and detectors, wide-bandgap semiconductors.

Industrial and Manufacturing Systems Engineering. Bradley A. Kramer, Head; Ph.D., Kansas State. (14 faculty members) Operations research: network optimization, graph theory, mathematical programming, health systems modeling and control, disaster recovery logistics, stochastic processes and queuing, fuzzy and uncertainty reasoning. Manufacturing systems engineering: advanced manufacturing processes, machining difficult materials, energy manufacturing, quality control. Ergonomics: highway safety, work environments. Engineering management: project management, management decision making.

Mechanical and Nuclear Engineering. Donald L. Fenton, Head; Ph.D., Illinois at Urbana-Champaign. (22 faculty members) Heat and mass transfer: fluid mechanics, room air diffusion. Machine design and materials science: acoustics, composite materials, dynamics, kinematics, rock mechanics, stress analysis, vibrations. Control systems: dynamic system modeling, stability, robust control, instrumentation and measurements, simulation and control, aircraft navigation and control. Heating, air conditioning, human comfort. Computer-assisted design and graphics. Nuclear reactor physics and engineering: radiation transport theory, neutron spectroscopy. Radiation detection and measurement: neutron activation analysis, X-ray and gamma-ray spectroscopy, nondestructive assay of fissile materials. Radiation protection: radiation shielding, environmental monitoring. Controlled thermonuclear power: radiation damage and materials problems.

Advanced Manufacturing Institute. Bradley A. Kramer, Director; Ph.D., Kansas State. The Advanced Manufacturing Institute (AMI) is dedicated to providing innovative and cost-effective engineering and business solutions. AMI offers a full spectrum of capabilities that integrate business and creative insight with design and engineering expertise. AMI works with entrepreneurs and businesses of all sizes—from startups to Fortune 500 companies—in every market imaginable, including manufacturing, transportation, aerospace, consumer products, agriculture, food, chemicals, plastics, bioprocessing, equipment, and machinery. AMI also manages a highly successful intern program that allows undergraduate and graduate students to gain real work experience in the company of experienced professionals. The program helps students increase their skills and knowledge and be more productive in the workplace upon graduation.

Center for Sustainable Energy. Mary Rezac, Co-director; Ph.D., Texas at Austin. The center is focused on efforts related to assessment, conversion, and/or utilization of sustainable energy resources such as biomass, wind, and solar. Faculty from the Colleges of Engineering, Agriculture, Arts and Sciences, and Business are involved in research and educational outreach efforts with biomass resource assessment, plant genetics for efficient biofuel production, and conversion and utilization of renewable resources to fuels for transportation and electricity.

Center for Hazardous Substance Research. Larry E. Erickson, Director; Ph.D., Kansas State. Handling and processing hazardous waste/materials; protection of water supplies: resource recovery, treatment, disposal, and storage of hazardous materials.

Health Care Operations Resource Center. David H. Ben Arieh, Director; Ph.D., Purdue. The Health Care Operations Resource Center conducts research and develops new technology and applied solutions to resolve operational issues that face the medical community. The center seeks to improve service quality, reduce costs, and improve patient care and is engaged in improving health-care operations at all levels of care from small rural clinics to large urban hospitals. The center engages both graduate and undergraduate students to work on these client projects and also involves students in research projects. The center emphasizes the use of operations research, analytical models, and information systems in its work.

Pollution Prevention Institute. Nancy Larson, Director; B.S., Montana State. Provides technical assistance and training in source reduction and environmental compliance to businesses, institutions, technical assistance groups, and private citizens throughout the Midwest. The institute also supports engineering interns, hosts an environmental management system (EMS) peer center, and serves as a meeting ground for KSU faculty members involved in pollution prevention and other related activities.

Institute for Environmental Research. Steven Eckels, Director; Ph.D., Iowa State. This internationally known lab studies the interaction between people and their thermal environment. With eight environmental chambers and special equipment such as sweating mannequins, IER focuses on factors affecting thermal comfort and thermal stress including environmental factors and HVAC systems; protective materials, clothing systems, and sleeping bags; and physical activity. Projects also deal with biothermal modeling, automobile environmental systems, and aircraft cabin environmental quality.

National Gas Machinery Laboratory. Byron W. Jones, Acting Director; Ph.D., Oklahoma State. This laboratory provides the natural gas industry with independent testing and research capabilities, knowledge databases, and educational programs. A premier turbocharger test and research facility has been developed through acquisition of gas turbine engines, instrumentation, and a laboratory building.

Civil Infrastructure Systems Laboratory. Alok Bhandari, Supervisor; Ph.D., Virginia Tech. The testing facility includes a pavement accelerated testing lab, a falling weight deflectometer state calibration station, and facilities for structural testing of bridge components and prestressed concrete girders. The facility is a center for cooperation between academia, industry, and state departments of transportation. The pavement research and testing activity is sponsored by a consortium called the Midwest States Accelerated Testing Pooled Funds Program that fulfills the needs of the surrounding states for full-scale testing and addresses research topics of national and international importance.

University Transportation Center. Robert W. Stokes, Director; Ph.D., Texas A&M. The University Transportation Center (UTC) coordinates interdisciplinary transportation education, research, training, and outreach efforts at K-State. The UTC's theme, "The sustainability and safety of rural transportation systems and infrastructure," emphasizes the unique needs of rural transportation systems. The UTC conducts research concerning local, state, regional, national, and international transportation problems through a coordinated effort between K-State, the Kansas Department of Transportation (KDOT), and the Research and Innovative Technology Administration (RITA) of the US Department of Transportation (USDOT). Dissemination of research information is achieved through the Center's Web site (http://transport.ksu.edu/), publication of reports, and through seminars for members of industry, government, and academia. Continuing education is also provided on transportation-related issues for licensed professional engineers. Training includes the development of short courses, handbooks, manuals, and other training materials developed under the Traffic Assistance Services for Kansas (TASK) Program and the American Concrete Institute (ACI) and Superpave certification training programs for personnel engaged in the construction of Kansas's highways. The Center also sponsors the annual Kansas Transportation Engineering Conference.

NORTH CAROLINA STATE UNIVERSITY
College of Engineering

Programs of Study

The College of Engineering comprises eleven degree-granting departments which are authorized to award the Master of Science, the Master of Engineering in a designated field, and the Doctor of Philosophy. Programs of graduate study leading to the M.S. and Ph.D. are aerospace engineering, biological and agricultural engineering, biomedical engineering (jointly with School of Medicine at the University of North Carolina at Chapel Hill), chemical engineering, civil engineering, computer science, electrical and computer engineering, industrial and systems engineering, materials science and engineering, mechanical engineering, and nuclear engineering; textile engineering offers the M.S. degree. Nonthesis master's degrees are also offered in most of the discipline areas and in the interdisciplinary program of integrated manufacturing systems engineering. Most nonthesis degrees require project or research work and a written technical report. The M.S. and Ph.D. degrees as well as the nonthesis master's degree are offered in the interdisciplinary program of operations research. Master's degrees are offered via distance learning through Engineering Online in aerospace engineering, chemical engineering, civil engineering, computer engineering, computer science, electrical engineering, industrial and systems engineering, integrated manufacturing systems engineering, materials science and engineering, mechanical engineering, and nuclear engineering. The Master of Engineering degree can be earned via distance education as well.

In most departments, the Master of Science degree is awarded for completing 30 credits of work, including a thesis. The Master of Engineering in a designated field is awarded for completing 30–36 course credits. A Ph.D. degree is awarded for completing a program of work, passing the oral preliminary examination, completing a research dissertation, and passing a final examination on the dissertation.

Research Facilities

Special research facilities and equipment include RAMAN and FIIR facilities; transmission electron microscopes; computerized SEM with full X-ray and image analysis capabilities; electron beam–induced current and cathodoluminescence microscopy equipment; a scanning laser microscope; laser MBE and pulsed laser depositions systems with full diagnostics; field emission electron beam lithography equipment; an imaging ion microscope for SIMS and 3-D ion imaging; a scanning Auger microprobe; an electron microprobe; complete X-ray analysis facilities including equipment for diffraction, topography, and radiography; a photoluminescence laboratory; MBE systems with in situ surface analysis; focused ion beam micromachinery; atomic resolution scanning tunneling microscopes; a precision engineering laboratory including diamond turning, ductile regime grinding, and surface metrology capabilities; a nuclear reactor with radiographic and neutron activation analysis; an applied energy laboratory; a plasma studies laboratory; a Freon simulator of a PWR fission reactor; a synthesis laboratory for III-V semiconductor materials; an organometallic chemical vapor deposition system; a semiconductor device fabrication laboratory; a deep UV mask aligner, and oxidation diffusion furnaces; a plasma and chemical etching and vapor deposition facility; computer systems for research in communications and signal processing and in microelectronics; a commercial computer design system for large integrated circuits; an EPA automated pollution and combustion gas facility; anechoic and reverberation chambers; a computer-controlled gas chromatograph–mass spectrometer; a robotics and automation laboratory; state-of-the-art multimedia, voice I/O, and software engineering labs; UNIX, Linux, and Windows workstations linked through Ethernet; a large structures-testing system; pavement wheel-track testing; superpave asphalt testing; a shake table; geotechnical test pits; plasmas for fusion; plasma propulsion; and laser-ablated plasmas for thin-film deposition. An engineering graduate research center features more than 120,000 square feet of dedicated laboratory facilities, including a class-10 clean room for processing.

Financial Aid

Approximately half of the engineering graduate students are provided assistantships with full support for studies, including tuition and health insurance.

Cost of Study

Tuition and fees for full-time study in 2012–13 are $4511 per semester for North Carolina residents and $10,535 per semester for nonresidents. Students taking fewer than 9 credits pay reduced amounts. Most students appointed as teaching or research assistants qualify for tuition and health insurance support.

Living and Housing Costs

On-campus dormitory facilities are provided for unmarried graduate students. In 2012–13, the rent for double rooms starts at $2600 per semester. Apartments for married students in King Village rent for $580 per month for a studio, $640 for a one-bedroom apartment, and $725 for a two-bedroom apartment.

Student Group

The College of Engineering had an enrollment of 6,311 undergraduate students and 2,899 graduate students in 2011–12. Most graduate students find full- or part-time support through fellowships, assistantships, and special duties with research organizations in the area. During the 2011–12 academic year, the College conferred 142 doctoral degrees, 641 master's degrees, and 1,112 Bachelor of Science degrees.

Location

Raleigh, the state capital of North Carolina, has a metropolitan population of over 500,000 and is ranked among the best places to live and work. Nearby is Research Triangle Park, one of the largest and fastest-growing research parks in the nation. The area offers numerous opportunities for recreation, sports, the arts, and other entertainment.

The University and The College

North Carolina State University is the principal technological institution of the University of North Carolina system. It is the home of the nationally acclaimed Centennial Campus, a model industry–government–university research park where students and professors work alongside industry leaders. The University's largest schools are the Colleges of Engineering, Agriculture and Life Sciences, Physical and Mathematical Sciences, and Humanities and Social Sciences. Total enrollment is more than 32,000. A cooperative relationship with Duke University and the University of North Carolina at Chapel Hill contributes to a rich academic and research atmosphere, as does the University's association with the Research Triangle Park and the Oak Ridge National Lab. The College has 300 faculty members with professorial rank.

Applying

Applications may be submitted at any time. Although the GRE General Test is not always required, it is helpful in making decisions concerning financial aid. An applicant desiring to visit the campus may request information concerning travel allowances by writing to the graduate administrator of the preferred program of study. Students may apply for fellowships or assistantships in their application for admission. Applications for all students are accepted online at http://www2.acs.ncsu.edu/grad/applygrad.htm.

Correspondence and Information

Dean of the Graduate School
North Carolina State University
P.O. Box 7102
Raleigh, North Carolina 27695-7102
Phone: 919-515-2872
Web site: https://www.ncsu.edu

THE FACULTY AND THEIR RESEARCH

BIOLOGICAL AND AGRICULTURAL ENGINEERING: R. Evans, Department Head. **Faculty:** D. Beasley, F. Birgand, M. Boyette, M. Burchell, L. Cartee, J. Cheng, G. Chescheir, M. Chinn, J. Classen, C. Daubert, B. Farkas, G. Grabow, S. Hale, R. Huffman, W. Hunt, G. Jennings, P. Kolar, T. Losordo, P. Mente, G. Roberson, S. Roe, K. Sandeep, S. Shah, R. Sharma, R. Skaggs, O. Simmons, J. Spooner, L. Stikeleather, K. Swartzel, M. Veal, L. Wang, P. Westerman, T. Whitaker, D. Willits, M. Youssef. **Research areas:** Bioinstrumentation, bioprocessing, materials handling, energy conservation and alternative fuels, environmental control, machine systems, microprocessor applications, water and waste management, hydrology, ecological and environmental engineering.

BIOMEDICAL ENGINEERING: N. Allbritton, Department Head. **Faculty:** A. Banes, T. Bateman, L. Cartee, P. Dayton, R. Dennis, O. Favorov, C. Finley, G. Forest, C. Gallippi, M. Gamcsik, M. Giddings, R. Goldberg, S. Gomez, E. Grant, D. Lalush, W. Lin, E. Loboa, J. Macdonald, T. Magnuson, G. McCarty, M. McCord, P. Mente, H. Troy Nagle, R. Narayan, H. Ozturk, H. Pillsbury, J. Ramsey, B. Steele, M. Tommerdahl, A. Veleva, G. Walker, P. Weinhold. **Affiliated Faculty:** A. Aleksandrov, N. Allen, D. Bitzer, M. Bourham, J. Brickley Jr., G. Buckner, B. Button, J. Cavanagh, E. Chaney, M. Chow, L. Clarke, S. Cooper, D. Cormier, S. Franzen, H. Fuchs, R. Gardner, R. Gorga, R. Grossfeld, Z. Gu, M. Haider, A. Hale, O. Harrysson, A. Hickey, W. Holton, T. Johnson, J. Kimbell, C. Kleinstreuer, K. Kocis, H. Krim, A. Kuznetsov, G. Lazzi, S. Lubkin, N. Monteiro-Riviere, J. Muth, B. Oberhardt, T. O'Connell, A. Oldenburg, M. Olufsen, D. Padua, S. Pizer, B. Pourdeyhimi, J. Qi, A. Rabiei, M. Ramasubramanian, L. Reid, S. Roe, J. Rubin, M. Schoenfisch, S. Seelecke, D. Shen, C. Smith, W. Snyder, A. Spagnoli, L. Stikeleather, A. Stomp, M. Stoskopf, R. Superfine, A. Taylor, J. Thompson, D. Thrall, A. Tonelli, A. Tropsha, B. Vaughn, M. Vouk, S. Washburn, D. Woodward, B. Yu. **Research areas:** Biomedical imaging, micro- and nano-systems engineering, rehabilitation engineering, pharmacoengineering.

CHEMICAL AND BIOMOLECULAR ENGINEERING: P. Fedkiw, Department Head. **Faculty:** C. Beisel, R. Carbonell, J. DeSimone, M. Dickey, J. Genzer, C. Grant, K. Gubbins, C. Hall, J. Haugh, W. Henderson, R. Kelly, S. Khan, H. Lamb, F. Li, P. Lim, D. Ollis, G. Parsons, S. Peretti, B. Rao, G. Reeves, E. Santiso, R.

Spontak, O. Velev, P. Westmoreland. **Research areas:** Biomolecular engineering and biotechnology; biofuels and biomass conversion; catalysis, kinetics, and electrochemical engineering; electronic materials; energy; green chemistry and engineering; innovative textiles; computational nanoscience and biology; nanotechnology and microfluidics; polymers science.

CIVIL ENGINEERING: M. Barlaz, Department Head. V. Matzen, Director of Graduate Programs. **Faculty:** S. Arumugam, J. Baugh, C. Bobko, R. C. Borden, R. H. Borden, E. Downey Brill Jr., J. DeCarolis, F. de los Reyes, J. Ducoste, B. Edge, C. Frey, M. Gabr, A. Grieshop, M. Guddati, A. Gupta, T. Hassan, C. Hintz, E. Jaselskis, N. Khosla, Y. Kim, D. Knappe, M. Kowalsky, M. Leming, G. List, M. Liu, G. Mahinthakumar, B. Montoya, J. Nau, M. Overton, M. Pour-Ghaz, S. Rahman, S. Ranjithan, W. Rasdorf, S. Rizkalla, N. Rouphail, R. Seracino, J. Stone, A. Tayebali, B. Williams, J. Yu, E. Zechman. **Research areas:** Computing and systems, construction engineering and management, construction materials, energy modeling, environmental engineering, geotechnical and geoenvironmental engineering, transportation systems and materials, solid mechanics, structural engineering, water resources and coastal engineering.

COMPUTER SCIENCE: M. Vouk, Department Head. **Faculty:** A. Anton, K. Anyanwu, R. Avent, D. Bahler, T. Barnes, L. Battestilli, D. Bitzer, K. Boyer, R. Chirkova, J. Doyle, R. Dutta, W. Enck, R. Fornaro, V. Freeh, E. Gehringer, X. Gu, K. Harfoush, C. Healey, S. Heber, S. Heckman, X. Jiang, J. Lester, X. Ma, F. Mueller, E. Murphy-Hill, P. Ning, H. Perros, M. Rappa, D. Reeves, I. Rhee, D. Roberts, R. Rodman, G. Rouskas, N. Samatova, R. St. Amant, C. Savage, M. Singh, M. Stallmann, W. Stewart, D. Sturgill, D. Thuente, B. Watson, L. Williams, T. Xie, R. Young, T. Yu. **Research areas:** Theory (algorithms, theory of computation), systems (computer architectures and operating systems, embedded and real-time systems, parallel and distributed systems, scientific and high performance computing), artificial intelligence (intelligent agents; data-mining, information and knowledge discovery, engineering and management; ecommerce technologies; information visualization, graphics and human-computer interaction), networks (networking and performance evaluation), security (software and network systems security, information assurance, privacy), software engineering (requirements, formal methods, reliability engineering, process and methods, programming languages), advanced learning technologies, analytics, computer games, information and knowledge management.

ELECTRICAL AND COMPUTER ENGINEERING: D. Stancil, Department Head. **Faculty:** T. Alexander, W. Alexander, J. Baliga, M. Baran, D. Baron, S. Bedair, S. Bhattacharya, G. Bilbro, A. Bozkurt, G. Byrd, A. Chakrabortty, M. Chow, H. Dai, R. Davis, A. Dean, M. Devetsikiotis, A. Duel-Hallen, M. Escuti, D. Eun, B. Floyd, T. Franzon, E. Grant, D. Hopkins, A. Huang, B. Hughes, I. Husain, K. Kim, R. Kolbas, H. Krim, M. Kudenov, E. Lobaton, N. Lu, D. Lubkeman, S. Lukic, L. Lunardi, T. Miller, V. Misra, J. Muth, T. Nagle, A. Nilsson, O. Oralkan, H. Ozturk, M. Ozturk, T. Paskova, D. Ricketts, E. Rotenberg, M. Sichitiu, W. Snyder, Y. Solihin, D. Stancil, M. Steer, C. Townsend, K. Townsend, R. Trew, J. Trussell, J. Tuck, I. Viniotis, W. Wang, C. Williams, G. Yu, H. Zhou. **Research areas:** Bioelectronics engineering; communications and digital signal processing; computer architecture and systems; control, robotics, and mechatronics; electronic circuits and systems; nanoelectronics and photonics; networking; power electronics and power systems.

INDUSTRIAL AND SYSTEMS ENGINEERING: P. Cohen, Department Head. **Faculty:** R. Bernhard, T. Culbreth, B. Denton, J. Dong, S. Elmaghraby, S.-C. Fang, Y. Fathi, O. Harrysson, T. Hodgson, J. Ivy, D. Kaber, M. Kay, R. King, Y.-S. Lee, Y. Liu, C. Nam, S. Roberts, E. Sanii, R. Shirwaiker, R. Uzsoy, A. Vila-Parrish, J. Wilson, R. Young. **Research areas:** Medical device manufacturing; health systems; investment science; ergonomics; occupational safety; facilities design; production planning, scheduling, and control; logistics systems; supply chain design and management; material handling; concurrent engineering; manufacturing processes; rapid prototyping; optimization; soft computing; stochastic processes and simulation.

INTEGRATED MANUFACTURING SYSTEMS ENGINEERING: S. D. Jackson, Director. **Associate Faculty:** D. R. Bahler, P. Banks-Lee, R. L. Barker, K. Barletta, M. D. Boyette, C. Bozarth, M. Brandford, G. D. Buckner, T. Clapp, Y. Fathi, T. K. Ghosh, E. Grant, R. Handfield, O. L. A. Harrysson, G. L. Hodge, T. J. Hodgson, J. Ivy, J. Joines, M. G. Kay, R. E. King, J. P. Lavelle, J. W. Leach, Y.-S. Lee, R. L. Lemaster, K. Mitchell, M. Montoya-Weiss, W. J. Rasdorf, P. Ro, S. Roberts, R. Rodman, C. Rossetti, D. Saloni, E. T. Sanii, L. M. Silverberg, D. Warsing, J. R. Wilson, R. E. Young, C. F. Zorowski. **Adjunct Faculty:** J. A. Janet, J. Taheri. The Integrated Manufacturing Systems Engineering (IMSE) Institute was established in 1984. IMSE provides multidisciplinary graduate-level education and practical training opportunities in the theory and practice of integrated manufacturing systems engineering at the master's level. IMSE focuses on providing a manufacturing presence and a program environment in the College of Engineering where faculty, graduate students, and industry can engage cooperatively in multidisciplinary graduate education, basic and applied research, and technology transfer in areas of common interest related to modern manufacturing systems technology. The objective of the IMSE program is to offer students with traditional discipline backgrounds in engineering and the physical sciences an opportunity to broaden their understanding of the multidisciplinary area of manufacturing systems. Core areas of concentration are offered in manufacturing systems, logistics, mechatronics, and biomanufacturing. **Research areas:** Automation, CAD, CAM, CIM and advanced information technology, logistics, manufacturing system simulations, material handling, mechatronics, part fabrication, quality assurance and testing, process and facilities planning, product assembly, product design, robotics, scheduling and operations management, supply chain management.

MATERIALS SCIENCE AND ENGINEERING: J. Schwartz, Department Head. **Faculty:** C. M. Balik, D. Brenner, L. Cao, R. Callazo, J. Cuomo, E. C. Dickey, N. El-Masry, D. Irving, A. Ivanisevic, M. Johnson, J. Kasichainula, C. Koch, T. LaBean, J. LeBeau, E. Laboa, J. P. Maria, A. Melechko, K. L. Murty, J. Narayan, T. Rawanowicz, C. L. Reynolds, J. M. Rigsbee, G. Rozgonyi, R. Scattergood, Z. Sitar, R. Spontak, J. Tracy, Y. Yingling, Y. Zhu. **Emeritus Faculty:** K. Bachman, R. Benson Jr., H. Conrad, R. F. Davis, A. Fahmy, K. Havner, J. Hren, H. Palmour III, J. Russ. **Research areas:** Aberration-corrected electron microscopy, advanced materials and processing methods, biomaterials, composite materials, computer simulation techniques, dielectric materials, electronic materials, electrical and mechanical properties, magnetic materials, metals, nanostructured materials, nonequilibrium processing, nuclear materials, polymers, structure-property relations, surface phenomena, thin-film processing and characterization.

MECHANICAL AND AEROSPACE ENGINEERING: R. Gould, Department Head. **Faculty:** G. Buckner, F. DeJarnette, T. Dow, T. Echekki, H. Eckerlin, J. Edwards Jr., J. Eischen, T. Fang, S. Ferguson, A. Gopalarathnam, C. Hall Jr., H. Hassan, H. Y. Huang, X. Jiang, Y. Jing, R. Keltie, E. Klang, C. Kleinstreuer, A. Kuznetsov, H. Luo, K. Lyons, A. Mazzoleni, R. Nagel, G. Ngaile, B. O'Conner, K. Peters, A. Rabiei, P. Ro, W. Roberts, A. Saveliev, L. Silverberg, J. Strenkowski, R. Tolson, J. Tu, F. Wu, F. Yuan, Y. Zhu, M. Zikry. **Research areas:** Aerothermodynamics, autoadaptive systems, biofluid dynamics, biomechanics, combustion, composite structures, computational fluid dynamics, control systems, electromechanics, energy conversion, environmental engineering, flight dynamics and aircraft design, fluid/aero dynamics, fluid mechanics and two-phase flow, fracture mechanics, heat transfer, hypersonics, manufacturing, materials processing, mechanical and random vibrations, mechatronics, micro/nano mechanical and electrical systems, nano thermosystems, precision engineering, probabilistic mechanics, propulsion, risk and reliability, robotics, solid mechanics, space systems and dynamics, structural health monitoring, thermal management, theoretical and structural acoustics.

NUCLEAR ENGINEERING: Y. Y. Azmy, Department Head. **Faculty:** H. S. Abdel-Khalik, D. Anistratov, I. Bolotnov, M. A. Bourham, J. M. Doster, J. Eapen, R. P. Gardner, J. G. Gilligan, A. I. Hawari, J. Mattingly, K. L. Murty, S. C. Shannon, P. J. Turinsky. **Research areas:** Computational reactor physics; fuel management; plasma engineering; radiation effects in nuclear materials; nuclear power systems modeling; plasma-surface interactions; radiation transport; reactor dynamics, control, and safety; computational thermal hydraulics; nuclear waste management; radiological engineering; industrial radiation applications; medical radiation physics; plasmas for fusion; plasma propulsion; laser-ablated plasmas for thin-film deposition; nuclear environmental risk analysis; radiation measurements; neutron scattering and imaging; advanced nuclear fuel cycles; multiscale and multiphysics modeling.

OPERATIONS RESEARCH: T. J. Hodgson, Co-Director; N. Medhin, Co-Director. **Faculty:** J. Baugh, R. Bernhard, B. Bhattacharyya, J. Bishir, P. Bloomfield, E. Brill Jr., R. Buche, S. Campbell, R. Chirkova, W. Chou, B. Denton, M. Devetsikiotis, J. Dunn, B. Edge, S. Elmaghraby, S. Fang, Y. Fathi, S. Ghosal, H. Gold, R. Handfield, R. Hartwig, P. Hersh, T. Hodgson, D. Holthausen, T. Honeycutt, I. Ipsen, K. Ito, J. Ivy, J. Joines, M. Kang, M. Kay, C. Kelley, R. King, J. Lavery, Z. Li, M. Liu, Y. Liu, G. List, D. McAllister, C. Meyer Jr., A. Nilsson, H. Nuttle, T. Pang, H. Perros, K. Pollock, S. Ranjithan, M. Rappa, T. Reiland, S. Roberts, J. Roise, G. Rouskas, C. Savage, J. Scroggs, M. Singh, C. Smith, R. Smith, M. Stallmann, J. Stape, M. Steer, W. Stewart, J. Stone, M. Suh, W. Sun, J. Taheri, K. Thoney-Barletta, H. Tran, R. Uzsoy, I. Viniotis, M. Vouk, W. Wang, D. Warsing, J. Wilson, F. Wu, R. Young, T. Yu, Z. Zeng, D. Zenkov. **Research areas:** Mathematical programming, fuzzy optimization and decision making, networks, queuing, production planning, scheduling, project management, routing, simulation, stochastic processes and modeling, systems theory and optimal control, facilities layout and planning, logistics, inventory theory, supply chain management, financial engineering, health systems.

TEXTILE ENGINEERING: J. Rust, Department Head. H. Hamouda, Program Director. **Faculty:** R. Barker, K. Beck, T. Clapp, R. Gorga, B. Gupta, J. Hinestroza, W. Jasper, J. Joines, W. Krause, M. McCord, G. Mock, J. Rust. **Research areas:** Electromechanical design, real-time monitoring and control, studies in thermal and fluid sciences, polymer and fiber science, biomedical application of textiles, design and fabrication, process optimization, product/machine/system design, nanocomposites, nanolayer electrostatic self-assembles, mathematical modeling of transport phenomena, rheology, polyelectrolytes, semi-crystalline polymers, carbon nanotube composite extrusion for enhanced mechanical/thermal/electrical properties, barrier fabrics, biopolymers, structure-property relationships.

OKLAHOMA STATE UNIVERSITY
College of Engineering, Architecture and Technology

Programs of Study

The College of Engineering, Architecture and Technology offers Master of Science and Doctor of Philosophy degree programs in biosystems, chemical, civil, computer, electrical, and mechanical engineering and industrial engineering and management. Master of Science degrees are also offered in engineering and technology management, and environmental engineering.

The master's degree may consist of 24 credit hours of course work plus 6 credit hours of thesis or 32 credit hours (35 credit hours for the Master of Science in mechanical engineering), including a creative component (independent study) of at least 2 hours.

The Doctor of Philosophy degree requires 90 credit hours beyond the B.S. or 60 beyond the master's, including 18 to 30 thesis credits. Preliminary, qualifying, and final examinations are required.

The master's degrees can be completed in twelve months but usually require more time. The Ph.D. requires from two to three years beyond the master's. The University offers two 16-week semesters plus an eight-week summer session each year.

Research Facilities

The College of Engineering's annual research budget is approximately $25 million. A wide variety of computer equipment and numerous minicomputers, microcomputers, and microprocessors, with interactive graphics capability, are available within the College. Extensive laboratory space and research equipment are available for use by students. The College's Office of Engineering Research provides administrative support services for more than 200 active research projects. These services include budget preparation, assistance with compliance issues, and production and fiscal reporting on contracts and grants. The University has a large central research library covering more than 6 acres of floor space, with a substantial amount devoted to engineering and physical science volumes. Research laboratories are located in the engineering schools in the Advanced Technology Research Center and in the Helmerich ATRC in Tulsa.

Financial Aid

Financial aid for graduate students includes fellowships, scholarships, and teaching and research assistantships. Stipends for half-time assistantships ranged from $900 to $2400 per month for master's students and from $975 to $2800 per month for Ph.D. students. Nonresident tuition is waived for graduate assistants. Depending on the appointments, the resident tuition for up to 6 credits per semester may also be waived. The fellowship and scholarship application deadline is February 1 for the following academic year, but early application is encouraged. All amounts are estimates and subject to change for the next year.

Cost of Study

Tuition for graduate-level credit was $154.85 per credit hour for Oklahoma residents and $620.50 for nonresidents. Other miscellaneous per-credit-hour fees totaled approximately $1359.20 per semester. All engineering students pay a technology fee of $21.50 per credit hour to support high-end desktop computers available to students. These are estimated costs and subject to change.

Living and Housing Costs

Residential hall single rooms were available for approximately $590 to $755 per month last year. Deluxe suites with private bedrooms and baths were available for approximately $715 per month. Apartments with private bedrooms and baths and shared kitchens and living rooms were available for approximately $735 per month. All rooms assume a twelve-month contract and include furnishings, basic utilities, cable television, and connection to the Internet. Family housing is also available. Meal plans were available for approximately $800 to $2000 per semester, depending on the number of meals requested. A single resident student should expect to spend approximately $8000 per semester for room, food, books, and miscellaneous expenses. These totals are close to estimated costs for the coming academic year.

Student Group

The OSU enrollment is nearly 25,000 full-time on-campus students; approximately 5,000 of these are graduate students. Men constitute approximately 52 percent and women, 48 percent of the student body. The College of Engineering, Architecture, and Technology has nearly 4,000 students, including over 800 graduate students in engineering.

Student Outcomes

While students receiving graduate degrees in engineering at Oklahoma State University are recruited in the national marketplace, increasing numbers of employment opportunities are available within the geographical area. Companies include Delphi in Wichita Falls, Texas; Koch Industries in Wichita, Kansas; Raytheon in the Dallas area; American Airlines, The Williams Companies, and the Corps of Engineers in Tulsa; and AT&T and Xerox in Oklahoma City.

Location

Stillwater, located 65 miles from both Tulsa and Oklahoma City, has a population of 45,000 and is essentially a university town. There are a number of lakes and recreational areas nearby that are usually not crowded. The climate is mild and pleasant, typical of the Sun Belt area.

The University

Founded in 1890, Oklahoma State University is a land-grant institution with eight colleges: Agricultural Sciences and Natural Resources; Arts and Sciences; Spears School of Business Administration; Education; Engineering, Architecture and Technology; Graduate Studies; Human Sciences; and Veterinary Medicine. The Stillwater campus has more than 100 buildings situated on 415 acres, plus the nearby Lake Carl Blackwell area of 19,364 acres. Cultural and recreational facilities are provided by the Seretean Center for the Performing Arts, the Valerie Colvin Physical Education Center, and the award-winning Student Union. The University participates in all major intercollegiate sports and ranks third nationally in the number of NCAA championships in varsity sports. OSU is a member of the Big Twelve Conference.

Applying

Application forms are available from the Graduate College or at https://app.it.okstate.edu/gradcollege/ and may be submitted online. Requests for financial aid should be made directly to the school of interest by February 1 for summer or fall admission and by October 1 for spring admission.

Correspondence and Information

Graduate Adviser
School of (specify)
Oklahoma State University
Stillwater, Oklahoma 74078
Web site: http://www.ceat.okstate.edu/

Dean of the Graduate College
202 Whitehurst Hall
Oklahoma State University
Stillwater, Oklahoma 74078

Oklahoma State University

FACULTY HEADS AND RESEARCH AREAS

Dean, College of Engineering, Architecture and Technology: Paul Tikalsky.

Associate Deans: David R. Thompson, Academics; D. Alan Tree, Research.

Biosystems Engineering. Professor Daniel Thomas, Head. Areas of emphasis include soil erosion, sediment control, nonpoint-source pollution, hydrology, stream processes, water quality, crop processing, bioconversion processes, renewable energy, animal-waste management, grain storage, food processing, physical properties of biological materials, sensors and control technology, mechatronics, machine vision, image processing, biosensors, energy conservation, equipment design, and precision agriculture. More information can be found at http://biosystems.okstate.edu.

Chemical Engineering. Professor Khaled Gasem, Interim Head. The School of Chemical Engineering is involved in a variety of industrially relevant and fundamental research projects. Students have the opportunity to pursue traditional areas of chemical engineering, including vapor-liquid equilibrium thermodynamics, adsorption thermodynamics, and rheology. In addition, graduate research is available in areas such as computer-assisted process design, CPD methods for reactor design, ultrapure water processing, industrial ion exchange, artificial intelligence applied to process control and monitoring, biomedical applications, bioproduction of fuels, and development of design strategies for environmentally benign processes.

Civil and Environmental Engineering. Professor John Veenstra, Head. Research interests include structural analysis and design; expansive soils; dynamic compaction; biological and chemical treatment of industrial, domestic, and hazardous wastes; air and water pollution; groundwater pollution; aquifer restoration; geosynthetics; flexible and rigid pavements; "smart" bridges; construction material; offshore structures; computational mechanics; composites; lightweight concrete; construction scheduling and estimating; and alternate disputes resolution. The Oklahoma Transportation Center is a major research entity of the school.

Electrical and Computer Engineering. Professor Keith A. Teague, Head. The School of Electrical and Computer Engineering offers degrees and areas of study across the disciplines of electrical engineering and computer engineering. Graduate and research fields of specialization include control systems, system identification, optimization, neural networks, intelligent systems and fuzzy logic, telecommunication systems and networks, security and information assurance, communication theory, wireless communication systems and networking, error control coding, intelligent sensor networks, robotics, embedded systems, computer architecture, programmable and reconfigurable digital systems, high-speed computer arithmetic, compiler optimization for computer architecture, system-on-a-chip architectures, digital computer design, VLSI and mixed-signal VLSI, analog CMOS electronics, high-temperature VLSI, energy/power/renewable-energy systems, power economics, power electronics, statistical signal processing, image processing and machine vision, image coding, biomedical image processing and bioimaging, biosensors, speech coding and compression, digital signal processing, engineering reliability, estimation theory, electromagnetics/antennas/radar, numerical electromagnetics, electromagnetic compatibility, optical engineering, photonics and electrooptics, terahertz optoelectronics, MEMS, nanodevices and nanotechnology, thermoelectric devices, advanced electronic materials, microfabrication, ultrafast optics, fiber optics, and laser systems. Excellent research laboratories and facilities are available in photonics and terahertz optoelectronics, communications and signal processing, wireless communications and networks, image processing and machine vision, bioimaging and instrumentation, mixed-signal VLSI and high-temperature semiconductors, MEMS, nanodevices and nanofabrication, intelligent sensor networks, embedded systems and robotics, high-speed computer arithmetic, computer architecture, electromagnetic compatibility, numerical electromagnetics, intelligent control, and power and energy systems. Modern computer and laboratory facilities are readily available for use by graduate students and faculty members. More information can be found at http://www.ece.okstate.edu.

Engineering and Technology Management. Professor Camille DeYong, Ph.D., PE, Director. The Engineering and Technology Management program provides experienced engineers, scientists, and technical managers with career-enhancing management skills. This program is offered through distance learning and is not designed for full-time on-campus students. Objectives of the program are to improve the participants' ability to identify and act on strategic issues; strategically manage technologies; integrate company functions; implement management skills, knowledge, and tools; and manage an organization's intellectual capabilities and properties. Core topics include technology strategy development, forecasting, and integration; project management; change management; benchmarking and competitive analysis; technical employee leadership and motivation; organization systems; new product planning, development, and management; technology sourcing and transfer; team approaches; integrating product and process design; and global marketing and manufacturing. More information can be found on the program's Web site at http://etm.okstate.edu.

Industrial Engineering and Management. Professor William J. Kolarik, Head, and Professor Manjunath Kamath, Graduate Program Director. The Computer Integrated Manufacturing Center, the Center for Engineering Logistics and Distribution, the Oklahoma Industrial Assessment Center, and the Sensor Networks and Complex Manufacturing Systems Lab are among the school's research facilities. Focus areas of research and instruction include manufacturing systems, enterprise modeling and supply chains, quality and reliability, operations research, facilities and energy management, and management and organizational behavior. Sub-area specialization is available within each of the focus areas. Further details are available at the Web site: http://www.okstate.edu/ceat/iem. For further information, students may contact the program at IEM-GRAD@okstate.edu.

Mechanical and Aerospace Engineering. Professor Larry L. Hoberock, Head. The School of Mechanical and Aerospace Engineering is a major participant in the interdisciplinary Web Handling Research Center and houses research labs for manufacturing process materials, nanotechnology, solid mechanics, fluid mechanics, aerodynamics, composite materials controls, ultraprecision surfaces, robotics, indoor environmental research psychometrics, and biomedical engineering. Students without B.S.M.E. degrees may need prerequisite work at the undergraduate level. The research program covers a wide variety of topics. The research for manufacturing processes and materials includes ultraprecision machining and grinding, nontraditional machining, synthesis of diamond films and coatings, advanced ceramic finishing and processing, surface and subsurface characterization and metrology, and molecular dynamics modeling. For web handling, the research involves nip mechanics, roll defects, roll structure analysis and measurement, constituent properties of web stacks, winding mechanics, air entrainment, roll buckling and wrinkling, viscoelastic and hygroscopic material effects, online tension measurement and control, traction, web flutter, and lateral dynamics and control. The research for fluid mechanics, aerodynamics, and propulsion focuses on computational fluid dynamics, aeroservoelasticity, numerical modeling of airfoil performance, two-phase flow, filtration flows, slurry flows, micro-UAV propulsion, and unmanned aerospace vehicles and systems. The thrust areas for heat transfer, thermal, and environmental systems involve thermal system simulation and optimization, building simulation and load calculation, ground-source heat pumps, bridge de-icing, heat transfer in machining and grinding, refrigeration, psychometrics, numerical modeling of thermal reactors, and micro heat exchangers. The research topics for solid mechanics and materials are material characterization, nondestructive evaluation, viscoelastic material characterization, aerogel synthesis, high-speed slitting, nanoscale sensors, and composite materials. For dynamics and control, the thrust areas involve control of nonlinear uncertain systems, system identification and parameter estimation, robotic systems control, control of large interconnected systems, machine vision, target tracking, applied automation, web tension control, and lateral web guidance. For biomedical engineering, the thrust areas are artificial tissues, tissue scaffolding, blood-flow simulation, and endolithial blood-cell behavior.

UNIVERSITY AT BUFFALO, THE STATE UNIVERSITY OF NEW YORK

School of Engineering and Applied Sciences

Programs of Study

The University at Buffalo offers degrees in all major fields of engineering through the School of Engineering and Applied Sciences (SEAS). Students may pursue master's and doctoral degrees in the departments of biomedical engineering; chemical and biological engineering; civil, structural, and environmental engineering; computer science and engineering; electrical engineering; industrial and systems engineering; and mechanical and aerospace engineering. In the top 15 percent of the nation's 300 engineering schools, the School of Engineering and Applied Sciences offers a wide variety of excellent instruction, research opportunities, resources, and facilities to its students.

SEAS faculty members participate in many research activities, including extensive involvement in two major Integrative Graduate Education Research and Traineeship (IGERT) grants funded by the National Science Foundation.

Research Facilities

Research facilities are supported by the School of Engineering and Applied Sciences to give students the opportunity to conduct research specific to their area of study. The Center for Biomedical Engineering coordinates research in biomedical engineering through cooperation among engineering departments and other schools, especially medicine and pharmacy. Research at the Center of Excellence for Document Analysis and Recognition focuses on the theory and applications of pattern recognition, machine learning, and information retrieval. The Center for Excellence in Global Enterprise Management was established in 1998 to deliver leading-edge research driven by industrial need with results that have immediate practical impact. The Center for Unified Biometrics is focused on advancing the fundamental science of biometrics and providing key enabling technologies to build engineered systems. The goals of the Center for Excellence in Information Systems Assurance Research and Education are graduate education and coordinated research in computer security and information assurance by faculty members from several schools and departments at the University at Buffalo. Founded in 1987 as the New York State Center for Hazardous Waste Management, the Center for Integrated Waste Management was established by the New York State Legislation to initiate and coordinate research and technology development in the areas of toxic substances and hazardous wastes. The Center for Multisource Information Fusion serves as one focal point for the conduct of research and development in information fusion and as an incubation center for small businesses and professorial and individual entrepreneurial activities. The research focus of the Energy Systems Institute is the development of mechanisms to predict failure in electronic systems.

The mission of the Great Lakes Program is to develop, evaluate, and synthesize scientific and technical knowledge on the Great Lakes Ecosystem in support of public education and policy formation. The Multidisciplinary Center for Earthquake Engineering Research's overall goal is to enhance the seismic resiliency of communities through improved engineering and management tools for critical infrastructure systems (water supply, electric power, hospitals, and transportation systems). The New York State Center for Engineering Design and Industrial Innovation carries out research to develop state-of-the-art simulation techniques and tools for the design of products, complex systems, and scientific applications. The Center for Industrial Effectiveness forges a link between the University at Buffalo's technical resources and the business community.

Financial Aid

For highly qualified applicants, a variety of research appointments are available, as are University-supported assistantships and fellowships.

Tuition scholarships are also available. Summer support is available for most research appointments. Work done as a research assistant is generally applicable to the student's thesis or dissertation.

Cost of Study

Tuition and fees for in-state residents total $11,231 per academic year for full-time study. Out-of-state tuition and fees total $18,541 per academic year.

Living and Housing Costs

The University at Buffalo offers students residence hall accommodations as well as apartments at several complexes surrounding the campus. Housing costs vary, depending upon location.

Student Group

More than 1,200 graduate students are enrolled in degree programs through the School of Engineering and Applied Sciences. Approximately 450 students are enrolled in doctoral programs, while the remaining students are enrolled as master's degree candidates.

Location

The city of Buffalo, New York, is located on the banks of Lake Erie, within an hour's drive of Lake Ontario and just minutes from the majestic scenery of Niagara Falls. It is within easy driving distance of Toronto and lies directly in the middle of the Northeastern trade corridor that runs from Chicago to Boston. With more than 9 million residents, it is the third-largest trade market in North America and is home to several professional sports franchises, museums, art galleries, and numerous areas for outdoor recreation throughout the year.

The University and The School

The School of Engineering and Applied Sciences is part of the University at Buffalo, the largest comprehensive public university in the state of New York, and is located on the North Campus in Amherst, New York.

Applying

To apply, interested students should visit their department of interest at http://www.eng.buffalo.edu/academics/depts/. The deadline for application materials varies by each department. The academic year begins in August. Applicants must hold a bachelor's degree in a science or engineering-related field. All international applicants must be able to document their ability to meet all educational and living expenses for their entire length of study.

Additional admissions information may be obtained via e-mail: seasgrad@buffalo.edu.

Correspondence and Information

University at Buffalo (SUNY)
School of Engineering and Applied Sciences
412 Bonner Hall
Buffalo, New York 14260-1900
Phone: 716-645-0956
E-mail: seasgrad@buffalo.edu
Web site: http://www.eng.buffalo.edu

University at Buffalo, The State University of New York

FACULTY HEADS AND AREAS OF RESEARCH

Biomedical Engineering
Dr. Debanjan Sarkar, Director of Graduate Study.

The Department of Biomedical Engineering combines expertise from the School of Engineering and the School of Medicine and Biomedical Sciences to engage in cutting-edge research for improvement of overall quality of life. Examples of research include photoacoustic imaging, nanomedicine, regenerative therapeutics, orthopedic prostheses, sensors, and imaging. Funding for this research comes from federal agencies such as the National Science Foundation, the National Institutes of Health, and the Department of Defense as well as from industry. (Web site: http://www.bme.buffalo.edu)

Chemical and Biological Engineering
Dr. Mark Swihart, Director of Graduate Study.

The Department of Chemical and Biological Engineering has attained international recognition for its excellence in research and teaching. Cutting-edge research projects span the areas of advanced materials and nanotechnology; molecular and multiscale modeling and simulation; and biochemical, biomolecular, and biomedical engineering. These projects are supported by federal agencies such as the National Science Foundation and the National Institutes of Health, and by industry. (Web site: http://www.cbe.buffalo.edu)

Civil, Structural, and Environmental Engineering
Dr. Adel Sadek, Director of Graduate Study.

Current research in the Department of Civil, Structural, and Environmental Engineering focuses on five key areas including computational mechanics; environmental and hydrosystems engineering (biological process analysis, bioremediation, drinking water, ecosystem restoration, groundwater, toxic substances fate, volatile organics, and wastewater treatment); geomechanics and geotechnical engineering (soil dynamics); structural and earthquake engineering (active and passive control of structures, blast-resistant design, bridge engineering, fiber-reinforced polymeric structures, nuclear structures, nonstructural systems, and steel and reinforced concrete structures); and transportation systems engineering (artificial intelligence applications, dynamic network modeling and control, freight modeling, integrated transportation and land-use modeling, intelligent transportation systems, traffic simulation, and traveler behavior modeling). The department is home to the Multidisciplinary Center for Earthquake Engineering Research (MCEER), the Great Lakes Program, and the Structural Engineering and Earthquake Simulation Laboratory, among others. (Web site: http://www.csee.buffalo.edu/)

Computer Science and Engineering
Dr. Hung Ngo, Director of Graduate Study.

The Department of Computer Science and Engineering conducts research in algorithms and theory of computing, augmentative technology for the handicapped, bioinformatics and computational biology, biometrics, computational linguistics and cognitive science, computer networks and distributed systems, computer science education, computer security and information assurance, computer vision, cyberinfrastructure and computational science, databases, data fusion, data mining, data-intensive computing, embedded systems and computer architecture, high-performance computing, grid and cloud computing, information visualization, knowledge representation and reasoning, medical image processing and applications, multimedia databases and information retrieval, pattern recognition and machine learning, pervasive computing, programming languages and software systems, VLSI circuits and systems, and wireless and sensor networks. (Web site: http://www.cse.buffalo.edu/)

Electrical Engineering
Dr. Leslie Ying, Director of Graduate Study.

The Department of Electrical Engineering conducts research in the following areas:

• signal processing, communications, and networking (adaptive signal processing, detection and estimation, coding and sequences, radar systems, communication theory and systems, secure communications, multimedia systems and video communications, digital data hiding, MIMO communications, cooperative communications, wireless networks, cognitive cross-layer networking, underwater communications, and networks);

• electronics, optics, and photonics (bio-MEMS, computational and applied magnetics, computational electromagnetics/photonics, computational fluid dynamics, electromagnetic compatibility, MEMS, metamaterials, microfluidics, micromachined microwave systems, MIR and THz devices, molecular beam epitaxy, nanotechnology, optoelectronics, photonics, photovoltaics, plasmonics, superconductivity, and TFTs); and

• energy systems (batteries, clean and renewable energy, electrochemical power, energy distribution and generation, energy storage, power electronics, power packaging, plasma processing, and smart grid power systems). (Web site: http://www.ee.buffalo.edu).

Industrial and Systems Engineering
Dr. Li Lin, Director of Graduate Study.

The Department of Industrial and Systems Engineering offers three areas of specialization for the Ph.D.: human factors (applications of engineering, psychology, computer science, and physical ergonomics to the modeling, analysis, and design of various environments and other systems), operations research (applies math and engineering principles to formulate models and solve problems in long range planning, energy and urban systems, and manufacturing), and production systems (focuses on production planning and scheduling, computer-integrated manufacturing, quality assurance, and related topics). In addition to the three areas of specialization mentioned above, there are two other programs (for a total of five) at the master's level: service systems engineering (applies industrial engineering principles to the growing service sector) and engineering management (focuses on leadership practices for a variety of engineering areas). (Web site: http://www.ise.buffalo.edu/index.shtml.)

Mechanical and Aerospace Engineering
Dr. John Crassidis, Director of Graduate Study.

Faculty members and students in the Department of Mechanical and Aerospace Engineering are involved in a wide range of research activities in the fluid and thermal sciences, dynamic systems and control, design, materials engineering, biomedical engineering, and applied mechanics. Faculty interests include computer and mathematical modeling as well as laboratory and experimental efforts in both basic and applied research. (Web site: http://www.mae.buffalo.edu/)

THE UNIVERSITY OF IOWA

College of Engineering

THE UNIVERSITY OF IOWA
College of Engineering

Programs of Study

The College of Engineering (http://www.engineering.uiowa.edu) at the University of Iowa (http://www.uiowa.edu) offers M.S. and Ph.D. programs in biomedical engineering, chemical and biochemical engineering, civil and environmental engineering, electrical and computer engineering, industrial engineering, and mechanical engineering. The College excels nationally and internationally in several specialty and interdisciplinary research areas, including computer-aided design and simulation, human factors, environmental health solutions, biotechnology, bioinformatics, medical imaging, photopolymerization, hydraulics and water/air resources, and nanotechnology. Master's candidates must maintain at least a 3.0 grade point average and may choose either a thesis or nonthesis program. Students must also successfully complete a minimum of 30 semester hours, 24 of which must be taken at the University of Iowa. Doctoral candidates must complete three years beyond the bachelor's degree, with a minimum of 72 semester hours. One academic year must be in residence. Research tools may be required as specified by the individual program. Those interested should contact the specific department for additional requirements. Graduate students often do interdisciplinary research work in a variety of programs and facilities noted in this description.

Research Facilities

The College of Engineering has twenty research locations in eastern Iowa, covering its six academic programs, four research centers reporting to the College, and interdisciplinary research efforts. IIHR–Hydroscience & Engineering (http://www.iihr.uiowa.edu) is unique for its state-of-the-art in-house capabilities in both computational simulations and laboratory modeling and for field observational research. Today IIHR pioneers high-speed computational analysis and simulation of complex flow phenomena while maintaining exceptional experimental laboratory capabilities and facilities. Observational facilities include a Mississippi River environmental research station (http://www.iihr.uiowa.edu/lacmrers) and a wide range of remote sensing equipment. Experimental facilities include hydraulic flumes, a hydraulic wave basin, air- and water-flow units, sediment labs, and advanced instruments for laboratory and field measurements. Engineers in IIHR's mechanical and electronic shops provide in-house expertise for construction of models and instruments. Active academic and research programs at IIHR are supported by a diverse set of computing resources and facilities. For high-performance computing (HPC) IIHR operates a parallel, distributed-memory computer cluster comprised of more than 3,500 2.66 GHz Intel Xeon X5650 cores, 9.5 TB memory, and 1.5 PB of scratch space running Linux, MPI, OpenMP, and the Intel and GNU compiler and tool suites. The computing nodes feature an InfiniBand quad data rate (fully unblocked at DDR) interconnect for high-speed, low-latency message passing. Three log-in nodes provide access to the cluster for compiling and launching jobs.

Other engineering research-related facilities include the Engineering Research Facility, Iowa Advanced Technology Laboratories, Iowa Injury Prevention Research Center (http://www.public-health.uiowa.edu/IPRC), University of Iowa Hospitals and Clinics (http://www.uihealthcare.com/uihospitalsandclinics/index.html), National Advanced Driving Simulator (http://www.nads-sc.uiowa.edu), Center for Biocatalysis and Bioprocessing (http:/www.uiowa.edu/~biocat), and Chemistry Building, which support laboratories devoted to such areas as biomechanics, biotechnology, molecular and computational biology, bioinformatics, environmental contamination, and remote sensing.

The Center for Computer-Aided Design (http://www.ccad.uiowa.edu) is housed in the Engineering Research Facility and in two buildings located off site, at the Iowa City Regional Airport and the University of Iowa Research Park. The Engineering Research Facility has 7,500 square feet of office space for staff researchers, student assistants, and program administration. Eight on-site laboratories house research facilities for two state-of-the-art motion capture research laboratories, one of which includes a 6-DOF shaker table motion platform, a fully immersive virtual reality environment, robotic systems, materials testing fixtures, and equipment for individual student research in various engineering disciplines. The off-site facility at the Iowa City Regional Airport that includes three flight simulation capabilities (a high-performance, functional Boeing 737-800 mockup for high-workload simulation and analysis as well as functional Boeing 777 and F-15 mock-ups). CCAD's Iowa City airport facility also houses six dedicated research aircraft, including a single-engine Beechcraft A-36 Bonanza aircraft, outfitted to create the CCAD Computerized Airborne Research Platform (CARP) in support of airborne human factors research for advanced flight deck technology; two single-engine tandem seat L-29 jet trainer aircraft, to provide flight testing for additional avionics systems research programs; two Czechoslovakian L-29s; and an MI-2 helicopter. The Iowa City Airport facility also houses a fully instrumented automotive test platform and a recently acquired HMMWV vehicle platform supporting cognitive assessment testing related to ground vehicle human-machine interaction and operation activities at the Operator Performance Laboratory. The center's computer infrastructure incorporates high-performance workstations, servers, and PC network in support of intensive computation, geometric modeling and analysis, software development, and visualization and simulation. The National Advanced Driving Simulator (NADS) is located at the University of Iowa Research Park (http://enterprise.uiowa.edu/researchpark). The NADS conducts groundbreaking research and development in the field of driving simulation. Utilizing one of the world's most advanced driving simulator capabilities, researchers at the University have defined the state-of-the-art in driving simulation, vehicle performance, and cognitive systems engineering. The NADS houses the NADS-1 driving simulator as well as several lower-fidelity driving simulators primarily used to support development, testing, and refinement of experimental procedures at lower cost to the client. These include the NADS-2, a static-base simulator with a limited field of view, and several portable PC-based mini-simulators. All simulation platforms at the center share a common software architecture with the NADS-1, ensuring compatibility of scenarios and data across all NADS simulators.

Engineering Computer Systems Support (http://css.engineering.uiowa.edu) provides the curricular and research computing needs of the College through state-of-the-art hardware, the same commercial software used by engineers in the industry, and a dedicated professional support staff. All engineering students receive computer accounts and maintain those accounts throughout their college careers. Full Internet and Web access complement local educational resources, which include enhanced classroom instruction, online classes, engineering design and simulation packages, programming languages, and productivity software. There are twenty-eight Linux and approximately 300 Windows workstations, supported by more than $10-million worth of professional software dedicated for student use 24 hours a day. The H. William Lichtenberger Engineering Library provides Internet access to indexes and abstracts, more than 125,000 volumes, ANSI standards, and electronic access to thousands of engineering and science journals.

Financial Aid

Financial aid is available to graduate students in the form of research and teaching assistantships as well as fellowships from federal agencies and industry. Support includes a competitive stipend reduction in tuition and partial payment of tuition. Specific information is available from individual departments.

Cost of Study

For 2012–13, tuition per semester is $3950 for Iowa residents and $12,032 for nonresidents. There is a technology fee of $337 per semester, which allows students the use of Computer Systems Support. In addition there are, per semester, a mandatory student health fee of $118.50, a student activities fee of $34.50, a student services fee of $37, a student union fee of $60, a building fee of $61.50, an arts and cultural events fee of $12, recreation fee of $121.50, and a professional enhancement fee of $30.

Living and Housing Costs

Housing is available in apartments or private homes within walking distance of the campus.

Student Group

Total enrollment at the University for fall 2011 was 30,893 students. Students come from all fifty states, three U.S. possessions, and ninety-seven other countries. Engineering enrollment for fall 2011 was 1,667 undergraduate students and 370 graduate students.

Student Outcomes

Nearly half of the graduates accept positions in Iowa and Illinois, though companies and academic institutions from across the country present offers. Recent graduates have taken positions with companies such as 3M, Accenture, Cargill, Caterpillar, Deere & Company, General Mills, Hewlett-Packard, HNI, Monsanto, Motorola, Pella, and Rockwell Collins.

Location

The University is located in Iowa City, known as the "Athens of the Midwest" because of the many cultural, intellectual, and diverse opportunities available. The Iowa City metropolitan area is a community of 139,600 people, approximately 25 miles from Cedar Rapids, Iowa's second-largest city, with nearly 246,400 people.

The University

The University of Iowa, established in 1847, comprises eleven colleges. The University was the first state university to admit women on an equal basis with men. The University founded the first law school west of the Mississippi River, established one of the first university-based medical centers in the Midwest, and was the first state university in the nation to establish an interfaith school of religion. It was an innovator in accepting creative work—fine art, musical compositions, poetry, drama, and fiction—for academic credit. The University established Iowa City as a national college-prospect testing center. It was a leader in the development of actuarial science as an essential tool of business administration. As a pioneering participant in space exploration, it has become a center for education and research in astrophysical science.

Applying

The application fee is $60 ($100 for international students). Admission requirements differ in each department; students should contact the department in which they are interested for additional requirements.

Correspondence and Information

Admissions
107 Calvin Hall
The University of Iowa
Iowa City, Iowa 52242
Web site: http://www.grad.uiowa.edu/ (Graduate College)
http://www.engineering.uiowa.edu/research (College of Engineering)
http://www.engineering.uiowa.edu/future-students.html (College of Engineering)

DEPARTMENTS, CHAIRS, AND AREAS OF FACULTY RESEARCH

STUDIES BY ENGINEERING DISCIPLINE

Biomedical Engineering (http://www.bme.engineering.uiowa.edu).
Joseph M. Reinhardt, Departmental Executive Officer. Biomechanics of the spine, low back pain and scoliosis, upper-extremity biomechanics, articular joint contact mechanics, total joint replacement, computational simulation of artificial heart valve dynamics, hemodynamics of arterial disease, mechanical properties of diseased arteries, biomechanics and rupture predication of abdominal aorta aneurysms, solution-perfused tubes for preventing blood-materials interaction, control and coordination of the cardiovascular and respiratory systems, controlled drug delivery, medical image acquisition, processing and quantitative analysis, wire coil–reinforced bone cement, models of cellular processes based on nonequilibrium thermodynamics, tissue engineered vascular grafts, bioinformatics and computational biology, drug/target discovery, gene therapy, development of genomic resources.

Chemical and Biochemical Engineering (http://www.cbe.engineering.uiowa.edu).
Allan Guymon, Departmental Executive Officer. Air pollution engineering, atmospheric aerosol particles, atmospheric chemistry, biocatalysis, biochemical engineering, biofilms, biofuels, biomaterials, biotechnological applications of extremophiles, controlled release, drug delivery, engineering education, fermentation, high-speed computing, insect and mammalian cell culture, medical aerosols, microlithography, nanotechnology, oxidative stress in cell culture, photopolymerization, polymer reaction engineering, polymer science, polymer/liquid crystal composites, process scale protein purification, protein crystallography, reversible emulsifiers, spectroscopy, supercritical fluids, surface science, vaccines, virus infection, chemicals from biomass, green chemistry, and sustainable energy.

Civil and Environmental Engineering (http://www.cee.engineering.uiowa.edu).
Michelle M. Scherer, Departmental Executive Officer. Water sustainability, water quality, flood prediction and mitigation, environmental remediation, air pollution, drinking water quality, bioremediation, biogeochemistry, computational solid mechanics, digital human modeling, design of hydraulics structures, design simulation, hydropower, optimal control of nonlinear systems, optimal design of nonlinear structures, diverse aspects of water resources engineering, rainfall and flood forecasting, thermal pollution/power plant operation, transportation-infrastructure modeling, highway pavements, winter highway maintenance.

The University of Iowa

Electrical and Computer Engineering (http://www.ece.engineering.uiowa.edu). Milan Sonka, Departmental Executive Officer. Sustainable energy, quantitative medical image processing, communication systems and computer networks, sensors and sensor networks, wireless communication, controls, signal processing, parallel and distributed computing systems, large-scale intelligent systems, bioinformatics, photonics, plasma waves, software engineering, design and testing of very-large-scale integrated circuits, nanotechnology, materials, and devices.

Industrial Engineering (http://www.mie.engineering.uiowa.edu/IEProgram/IEMain.php). Andrew Kusiak, Departmental Executive Officer. Biomanufacturing, computational intelligence, data analytics, informatics, engineering economics, engineering management, financial engineering, health-care systems, human factors and ergonomics, human-computer interfaces, flight simulation, driver behavior, manufacturing processes control and operations, operations research and applied statistics, optimization of energy systems, reliability, telerobotics, quality control, and wind energy.

Mechanical Engineering (http://www.mie.engineering.uiowa.edu/MEProgram/MEMain.php). Andrew Kusiak, Departmental Executive Officer. Biomechanics and biofluids, biology-based design, biorenewable and alternative fuels, bioengineering, casting and solidification, cloud computation, combustion, chemically reactive flows, computational mechanics, computer-aided analysis and design, dynamics, fatigue and fracture mechanics, fluid mechanics and ship hydrodynamics, fluid mechanics, human organ modeling, heat transfer, manufacturing, materials processing and behavior, multiscale modeling and simulation, reliability-based design, robotics, composite materials, nanotechnology, renewable energy, structural mechanics, system simulation, thermal systems, vehicle dynamics and simulation, virtual prototyping, and wind energy.

COLLEGE RESEARCH CENTERS, INSTITUTES, AND LABORATORIES

Center for Bioinformatics and Computational Biology (http://genome.uiowa.edu). Thomas L. Casavant, Director. A multidisciplinary research center dedicated to applying high-performance networking and computing to basic life science and applied biomedical research.

Center for Computer-Aided Design (http://www.ccad.uiowa.edu). Karim Abdel-Malek, Director. Virtual Soldier Research (musculoskeletal model, whole body vibration, validation, motion capture, intuitive interface, immersive virtual reality, physiology, standard ergonomic assessments, zone differentiation, posture and motion prediction, hand model, spine modeling, gait: walking and running, predictive dynamics, dynamic strength and fatigue, modeling of clothing, human performance, armor and soldier performance); Operator Performance Laboratory (optimal aircraft instrumentation configuration, rotorcraft, flight simulation supporting aircraft operation task analysis, warning-system effectiveness, roadway markings and illumination analysis, driver performance measurement, cognitive processing burden assessment/sensory and data input cognitive impact, human-vehicle interaction optimization for operational control and safety); Reliability and Sensor Prognostic Systems (mesh-free methods for structural analysis and design-sensitivity analysis, composite materials, probabilistic mechanics and reliability, reliability-based design optimization, topology optimization, multidisciplinary design optimization, sensor technologies, sensor-based process monitoring optimization); National Advanced Driving Simulator (highway safety and transportation efficiency, equipment product development effectiveness enhancement via virtual prototyping, vehicle dynamics and simulation, simulator technology and virtual reality environment and human factors); Musculoskeletal Imaging Modeling and Experimentation Program (computational modeling of anatomic structures, with emphasis on finite modeling); Biomechanics of Soft Tissue (soft tissue mechanics, biomechanics of the heart, cardiovascular system, aneurysm formation, CFD, nonlinear FEA).

IIHR–Hydroscience and Engineering (http://www.iihr.uiowa.edu). Larry J. Weber, Director. A leading institute in fluids-related fundamental and applied research. Cutting-edge research activities incorporate computational fluid dynamics with laboratory modeling and field observational studies. Research includes: fluid dynamics (ship hydrodynamics, turbulent flows, biological fluid flow); environmental hydraulics (structures, river and dam hydraulics, fish passage at dams, sediment management, heat dispersal in water bodies and power production, water-quality monitoring, air-water exchange processes); and water and air resources (atmospheric boundary layer, air pollution, hydrogeology, hydrology, hydrometeorology, remote sensing).

Iowa Institute for Biomedical Imaging (http://www.biomed-imaging.uiowa.edu). Milan Sonka, Director. Medical image acquisition (MR, CT, ultrasound, X-ray, OCT, and MR spectroscopy). Knowledge-based analysis of biomedical images from a variety of imaging modalities (e.g., CT, MR, OCT, and ultrasound). Current focus areas include development of computer-aided and automated techniques for quantitative analysis of human, animal, and cellular image data with applications to translational applications in radiology, radiation oncology, cardiology, pulmonology, ophthalmology, and orthopedics, as well as in clinical and epidemiologic trials.

INTERDISCIPLINARY RESEARCH CENTERS AND INSTITUTES

Medicine and Bioengineering

The Center for Biocatalysis and Bioprocessing (http://www.uiowa.edu/~biocat). Mani Subramanian, Director. Biocatalystic mechanisms, bioremediation, bioprocessing, new biocatalyst discovery, novel biocatalyst applications for chemicals and fuels, biosensing technology, and gene/protein expression and production, including for Phase I human trials.

Center for International Rural and Environmental Health (http://www.public-health.uiowa.edu/cireh). Tom Cook, Director. Rural and environmental health, with special emphasis on adverse health effects that threaten agricultural and other rural populations; promotes greater understanding and awareness of the causes, consequences, and prevention of communicable, chronic, environmental, and occupational diseases in all regions of the globe, focusing on nations with substantial agrarian economies.

Iowa Injury Prevention Research Center (http://www.public-health.uiowa.edu/IPRC). John Lundell, Director. Established in 1990, the University of Iowa Injury Prevention Center (IPRC) aims to use interdisciplinary research to control and prevent injuries, especially in rural communities. The center's activities constitute a broad multidisciplinary and collaborative program in research, training, and outreach. The IPRC has grown to include 66 researchers from twenty-three departments in five colleges, as well as a wide network of community and government collaborators. Six expert research teams are organized around priority research topics: road traffic safety; interpersonal violence; intervention and translation science; rural acute care; global injury and violence, and sports and recreational injury prevention. Teams promote the growth of research within their topic areas by linking researchers to IPRC core services, mentoring students and junior faculty, and engaging with community partners.

Orthopaedic Biomechanics Laboratory (http://poppy.obrl.uiowa.edu). Thomas D. Brown, Director. Application of advanced innovative computational formulations and novel experimental approaches to clinically-oriented problems across the diverse spectrum of musculoskeletal biomechanical research; total joint replacement (hip, spine, knee, ankle), posttraumatic arthritis, osteonecrosis of the hip, high-energy limb trauma, carpal tunnel syndrome, and articular contact stresses as they relate to joint degeneration.

Environmental and Hydroscience

NSF Center for Environmentally Beneficial Catalysis (http://www.erc-assoc.org/factsheets/09/09-Fact%20Sheet%202005.htm). Mani Subramanian, Director. A multidisciplinary, multi-university research center. Catalyst design, synthesis, and characterization; biocatalyst preparation and characterization; synthesis of catalyst supports with controlled pore structure; benign media, including carbon dioxide–based solvents and ionic liquids; probing reaction mechanisms with advanced analytical tools; advanced molecular modeling of chemical, physical, and thermodynamic properties involving reactions and media; multiphase reactor design and analysis; economic and environmental impact analysis; computational fluid dynamics.

Center for Global and Regional Environmental Research (http://www.cgrer.uiowa.edu). Gregory R. Carmichael and Jerald L. Schnoor, Co-directors. Multiple aspects of global environmental change, including the regional effects on natural ecosystems, environments, and resources and on human health, culture, and social systems.

Center for Health Effects of Environmental Contamination (http://www.cheec.uiowa.edu). Gene F. Parkin, Director. Conducts and supports research on the identification and measurement of environmental toxins, particularly water contaminants, and possible associations between exposure to environmental contaminants and adverse health effects. Provides environmental database design and development and systems support for environmental health research.

Environmental Health Sciences Research Center (http://www.ehsrc.uiowa.edu). Peter S. Thorne, Director. Agricultural and rural environmental exposures and health effects, agricultural chemical exposures and health effects.

Science and Technology

Iowa Alliance for Wind Innovation and Novel Development (http://www.iawind.org). P. Barry Butler, Principal Investigator. The Iowa Alliance for Wind Innovation and Novel Development (IAWIND) is a partnership with state and local governments, community colleges, Regents Universities, independent Iowa colleges, the private sector, and the federal government. It is designed to serve as a catalyst for the growth of wind energy and to support and to facilitate the research and training needs of wind energy companies.

Nanoscience and Nanotechnology Institute (http://research.uiowa.edu/nniui). Vicki Grassian, Director. Environment and health (air quality, natural environment, workplace environment, human and animal toxicity, environmental health, drug delivery, disease detection, imaging, bioanalytical assays, environmental remediation and decontamination, green chemistry, fuel cells, energy, sustainability, sensors); nanomaterials (quantum theory, understanding condensed-phase matter at the nanoscale, synthesis and characterization of nanomaterials, defense-related applications).

Optical Science and Technology Center (http://www.ostc.uiowa.edu). Michael Flatté, Director. Laser spectroscopy and photochemistry, photonics and optoelectronics, ultrafast laser development, condensed-matter physics, materials growth techniques, device physics/engineering, surface chemistry, chemical sensors, environmental chemistry, polymer science, plasma physics, nonlinear optics.

NSF IUCRC Photopolymerization Center (http://css.engineering.uiowa.edu/~cfap). Alec Scranton, Director. Kinetics and mechanisms of photopolymerizations and their impact on the structure and properties of photopolymerized materials.

Public Policy Center (http://ppc.uiowa.edu). Peter C. Damiano, Director. Transportation, environmental quality, health care, economic growth and development.

Water Sustainability Initiative (http://watersustainability.uiowa.edu). Jerald Schnoor, Chair, Steering Committee. The University of Iowa has expanded its existing strength in interdisciplinary research on water including its availability, quality, reuse, health impact, and its relationship to a changing climate. Economics, policy, and law, as well as the natural sciences and engineering, are all engaged to solve the problems of water. The faculty alliance on water sustainability encompasses the Colleges of Liberal Arts and Sciences, Public Health, Law, Engineering, the Graduate College, and the Public Policy Center. Among the various resources already developed to advance the initiative are the new Iowa Flood Center and the University of Iowa Office of Sustainability.

Engineering graduate students at the University of Iowa work very closely with faculty members on computer simulation, human factors, environmental health solutions, biotechnology, medical imaging, hydraulics and water/air resources, photopolymerization, sustainability, and many other areas.

UNIVERSITY OF PENNSYLVANIA
School of Engineering and Applied Science

Programs of Study

Research and education form the creative graduate mission of Penn Engineering. The excitement and discovery of research is open to all students and is the keystone of the School's world-renowned Ph.D. programs. These programs are augmented by a diverse array of master's degree offerings.

Penn Engineering's collaborative research and learning environment truly distinguish the School from its peers. Students work with and learn from faculty mentors within the core disciplinary programs as well as through scholarly interactions involving the School of Medicine, the School of Arts and Sciences, and the Wharton School, to note a few. This environment is further enriched by Penn's many institutes, centers, and laboratories. For more than 100 years, Penn Engineering has been at the forefront of innovation, just like the University's founder: America's first scientist and engineer—Benjamin Franklin.

The six Doctor of Philosophy (Ph.D.) programs are research-oriented degree programs for students of superior caliber who will make original contributions to theory and practice in their fields of interest. The programs prepare them for a research career in academe, government, or industry. Curricula are purposely designed to develop the intellectual skills essential for the rapidly changing character of research.

Penn Engineering's fifteen master's programs serve a wide range of highly qualified students such as working professionals seeking greater expertise to advance their careers and students expanding on their undergraduate training for professional engineering practice, preparing for doctoral studies, or pursuing an entirely new field of interest. The School's constantly evolving curricula, grounded in up-to-the-minute research findings and industrial priorities, and focused on practical applications of knowledge, are designed to be responsive to career and professional interests, as well as to the needs of today's high-tech society and economy.

Research Facilities

Shared research laboratories and facilities are an integral part of research and education at Penn Engineering. From nanotechnology to fluid mechanics to robotics to entrepreneurship, dedicated space exists for all forms of research in which students and faculty engage. The School's collection of labs and facilities include the Mechanical Engineering and Applied Mechanics Design and Prototyping Laboratories, SIG Center for Computer Graphics, Nano Probe Innovation Facility, Penn Regional Nanotechnology Facility, the Weiss Tech House, and Wolf Nanofabrication Facility.

Interdisciplinary research centers and institutes span all departments within Penn Engineering and foster collaborations across different schools throughout the University. The physical connectivity of engineering buildings and the proximity to each of the other schools enables exciting collaborations with faculty, students, and postdoctoral scholars across Penn. From biotechnology and robotics to computer animation and nanotechnology, Penn Engineering's centers and institutes are at the forefront of research on each scientific and technological frontier. (http://www.seas.upenn.edu/research/centers-institutes.php)

Financial Aid

A number of fellowships, assistantships, and scholarships are available on a yearly competitive basis, mainly for doctoral candidates. Provisions of these awards vary; the maximum benefits include payment of tuition and the general and technology fees plus a stipend and health insurance.

Cost of Study

Tuition for four courses in the academic year 2011–12 was $19,960, and there was a general fee of $1159 and a technology fee of $334 for full-time study. For part-time study the tuition was $4990 per course unit (one course), the general fee was $291, and the technology fee was $84.

Living and Housing Costs

On-campus housing is available for both single and married students. Students who choose to live on campus can expect to pay $746 to $1464 per month. There are numerous privately-owned apartments for rent in the immediate area.

Student Group

There are approximately 21,000 students at the University, around 11,000 of whom are enrolled in graduate and professional schools. Of these, approximately 1,500 are in graduate engineering programs.

Location

The University of Pennsylvania is located in West Philadelphia, just a few blocks from the heart of the city. Philadelphia is a twenty-first-century city with seventeenth-century origins. Renowned museums, concert halls, theaters, and sports arenas provide cultural and recreational outlets for students. Fairmount Park extends through large sections of Philadelphia, occupying both banks of the Schuylkill River. Not far away are the Jersey shore to the east, Pennsylvania Dutch country to the west, and the Pocono Mountains to the north. Less than a 3-hour drive from New York City and Washington, D.C., the city of Philadelphia is a patchwork of distinctive neighborhoods ranging from colonial Society Hill to Chinatown.

The School

The School of Engineering and Applied Science has a distinguished reputation for the quality of its programs. Its alumni have achieved international distinction in research, higher education, management, entrepreneurship and industrial development, and government service. Its faculty leads a research program that is at the forefront of modern technology and has made major contributions in a wide variety of fields.

The University of Pennsylvania was founded in 1740 by Benjamin Franklin. A member of the Ivy League and one of the world's leading universities, Penn is renowned for its graduate schools, faculty, research centers, and institutes. Conveniently situated on a compact and attractive campus, Penn offers an abundance of multidisciplinary and cross-school educational programs with exceptional opportunities for individually tailored graduate education. It also offers students all the amenities of a 21,000-student university.

Applying

Candidates may apply directly to the School of Engineering through an online application system. Applicants should visit http://www.seas.upenn.edu/prospective-students/graduate/admissions.php for detailed application requirements and access to the online application system. Ph.D. applications for fall admission must be received by December 15, January 2, or January 15 (varies by program) to ensure consideration for financial aid. Master's applications must be received by November 15, March 15, or May 15. Admission is based on the student's past record as well as on letters of recommendation. Scores on the Graduate Record Examinations (GRE) are required. All students whose native language is not English must arrange to take either the Test of English as a Foreign Language (TOEFL) or International English Language Testing System (IELTS) test prior to the application process.

Correspondence and Information

Graduate Admissions
School of Engineering and Applied Science
111 Towne Building
220 South 33rd Street
University of Pennsylvania
Philadelphia, Pennsylvania 19104-6391
Phone: 215-898-7246
E-mail: gradstudies@seas.upenn.edu
Web site: http://www.seas.upenn.edu

AREAS OF RESEARCH

Bioengineering: The nation's first Ph.D. in bioengineering was granted at the University of Pennsylvania, and today the department consists of 16 primary faculty members and more than 80 secondary and associated faculty members. The bioengineering Ph.D. program is designed to train individuals for academic, government, or industrial research careers. Research interests include cellular biomechanics, bioactive biomaterials, cell and tissue engineering, neuroengineering, orthopedic bioengineering, neurorehabilitation, respiratory mechanics and transport, molecular and cellular aspects of bioengineering, and biomedical imaging. Penn's interdisciplinary research training laboratories are in the Department of Bioengineering, the School of Engineering and Applied Science, and the Institute for Medicine and Engineering; the University's medical, dental, and veterinary schools; and four research-oriented hospitals, all of which are located on campus. Students are exposed to clinical applications of bioengineering. The department also offers an M.S.E. in bioengineering and a professional master's program as a medical engineering track in the master of biotechnology program. (http://www.be.seas.upenn.edu/)

Biotechnology: The Master of biotechnology program draws its faculty and courses from the School of Arts and Sciences and the School of Engineering and Applied Science. This interdisciplinary program prepares both full- and part-time students for productive and creative careers in the biotechnology and pharmaceutical industries. Students can specialize in one of the following tracks: bioinformatics/computational biology, biopharmaceutical/engineering biotechnology, biomedical technologies, or molecular biotechnology. These tracks, in combination with core courses, ensure that the students get a uniquely broad exposure to the entire field of biotechnology. (http://www.upenn.edu/biotech/)

Chemical and Biomolecular Engineering: The department was one of the first in the United States to offer a degree in chemical engineering. Courses and research programs are offered in applied mathematics, adsorption, biochemical and biomedical engineering, computer-aided design, transport and interfacial phenomena, thermodynamics, polymer engineering, semiconductor and ceramic materials processing, reaction kinetics, catalysis, artificial intelligence, and process control. Many research projects are collaborative and take advantage of other strong programs in the University. Ongoing research includes joint projects with faculty members from the School of Medicine and Wistar Institute, the Department of Biology, the Department of Chemistry, Computer Science and Engineering, and Materials Science and Engineering. (http://www.seas.upenn.edu/cbe/)

Computer and Information Science: The program is intended for students from many disciplines and backgrounds who have had substantial course work in mathematics and computer science. Research and teaching covers a wide range of topics in theory and applications, including algorithms, architecture, programming languages, operating systems, logic and computation, software engineering, databases, parallel and distributed systems, real-time systems, high-speed networks, graphics, computational biology, artificial intelligence, natural language processing, machine learning, data-mining, vision, and robotics. Much of this research involves multidisciplinary collaborations with other graduate programs in the School of Engineering, as well as the Mathematics, Linguistics, Philosophy, Psychology, Biology, and Neuroscience departments. The department also has a number of ongoing research collaborations with national and international organizations and laboratories. The CIS faculty seeks students who, whether pursuing a master's degree or doctoral studies, will be actively involved at the leading edge of computer science research. (http://www.cis.upenn.edu)

Computer and Information Technology: The program is designed for candidates who have a strong academic background in areas other than computer science but who have a need for graduate education in computer science. Completion of the MCIT program gives the graduate a solid foundation in computer science, providing the advanced expertise needed to meet the demands of a fast-paced, high-tech global society. The program is also suitable for IT professionals who wish to augment their practical skills with an understanding of the foundations of computing. (http://www.cis.upenn.edu/mcit/index.shtml)

Computer Graphics and Game Technology: The goal of the program is to expose recent graduates, as well as students returning from industry, to state-of-the-art graphics and animation technologies, interactive media design principles, product development methodologies, and engineering entrepreneurship. This degree program prepares students for those positions that require multi-disciplinary skills, such as designers, technical animators, directors, and game programmers. Opportunities for specialization are provided in such core areas as art and animation, creative design, animation and simulation technology, human/computer interfaces, and production management. (http://www.cis.upenn.edu/grad/cggt/cggt-overview.shtml)

Electrical and Systems Engineering: The graduate group in electrical and systems engineering offers the following programs: Ph.D. in electrical and systems engineering (ESE), M.S.E. in electrical engineering (EE), and an M.S.E. in systems engineering (SE). The department is a leader in the areas of electroscience, systems science, network systems, and telecommunications. Electroscience includes electromagnetics and photonics, sensors and MEMS, LSI, and nanotechnology. Systems science covers signal processing, optimization, simulation, control and cybernetics, complex adaptive systems, stochastic processes, and decision sciences. Most of the research activities are interdisciplinary in nature and electrical and systems engineering faculty members and students typically interact or collaborate with professors and students from other departments within the School of Engineering and Applied Science, the School of Arts and Sciences, and the Wharton School. (http://www.ese.upenn.edu/about-ese/index.php)

Embedded Systems: The Master of Science in Engineering in Embedded Systems (EMBS) program spans the core topics of embedded control, real-time operating systems, model-based design and verification, and implementation of embedded systems. This innovative and unique degree program is offered jointly by the departments of Computer and Information Science and Electrical and Systems Engineering and is integrated with the PRECISE Center for Research in Embedded Systems. The program is ideally suited for students with either computer science or electrical engineering academic backgrounds who wish to pursue industrial jobs within automotive, aerospace, defense, and consumer electronics, as well as for practicing engineers in the embedded systems industry who want to gain knowledge of state-of-the-art tools and theories. (http://www.cis.upenn.edu/grad/embedded.shtml)

Integrated Product Design: The IPD program is intended to cultivate design professionals who possess both a breadth of knowledge and a depth of expertise in a specialty to bridge the domains of technology, manufacturing, business, aesthetics, and human-product interaction. The guiding philosophy of the program is not only to teach students to create products but to understand and address the social, environmental, and experiential contexts of those products, so that product design can be harnessed as a force for the greater good. The program builds the skills to investigate, imagine, conceptualize, and model a wide range of products and their complementary business models. The program draws on the strengths of three internationally recognized schools within the University: the School of Engineering and Applied Science, the Wharton School, and the School of Design. The graduate courses that make up the program create an interdisciplinary point of view and are taught by professors from all three schools. Studio classes accompany classroom studies, providing creative and analytical approaches and shifting students between rigorous technical and explorative processes in the development of both experiential and theoretical knowledge. Collaborative team projects and student-driven independent projects complement the core courses to give students both a solid grasp of the fundamentals and a deep understanding of the nuances of these fields. (http://www.me.upenn.edu/ipd/)

Materials Science and Engineering. The department conducts an extensive program of graduate education and research aimed at understanding the physical origins of the behavior of ceramics, polymers, metals, and alloys in electronic, structural, magnetic, and interfacial applications. Students have access to a broad range of state-of-the-art instrumentation in the department and the Laboratory for Research on the Structure of Matter (LRSM), which is housed in the same building. The LRSM is one of the largest NSF-supported materials research science and engineering centers in the country and includes central facilities for surface studies, ion scattering, electron microscopy, X-ray diffraction, computer simulation, mechanical testing, and materials synthesis and processing. Access to synchrotron radiation (X-ray and UV) and neutron-scattering facilities is also available at nearby national labs. Research within the department can be grouped under four general headings: surfaces and interfaces (polymer-polymer, metal-ceramic, and grain boundaries in metallic materials), complex materials (carbon-based nanotubes, copolymers, intermetallic alloys, and nanomaterials), failure mechanisms (plastic deformation, fatigue, embrittlement, corrosion, and predictive modeling), and novel electronic ceramics (ferroelectrics, microwave materials, batteries and fuel cells, superconductors, and catalysts). (http://www.seas.upenn.edu/mse/)

Mechanical Engineering and Applied Mechanics: The research in the department combines theory, computation, and experiments with applications. It is often interdisciplinary in nature and is done in collaboration with material sciences, computer sciences, electrical and systems engineering, chemical and biomolecular engineering, and the School of Medicine. The areas of focus are thermal and fluid sciences, mechanics of materials, computational science and engineering, mechanical systems and robotics, and biomechanics. Research in thermal fluids focuses on energy conversion, advanced power generation, second-law (energy) analysis, combustion, water desalination, microelectronic device fabrication and cooling, inorganic and organic (macromolecular) crystal growth, active control of flow patterns, transport processes associated with mesodevices and microdevices and with sensors, material processing, multiphase flows, computational fluid dynamics, and micro- and nano-scale thermofluid transport. The research in mechanics of materials focuses on crystal plasticity, effective properties of nonlinear composites, intermetallic compounds, localization studies, metal-forming processes, interfacial fracture, fatigue and high-temperature fracture, soft material, phase transitions in thermoelastic solids, nano-scale mechanics and tribology (friction, adhesion, and wear), and cell mechanics. Research in computational science and engineering focuses on parallel algorithms for the solution of differential and integral equations, inverse problems in nonlinear transport and wave propagation, and numerical study of systems with coupled multiple physics domains and multiple scales. Research in mechanical systems focuses on robotics, computational design, compliant mechanisms, optimization, computer vision, hybrid systems, dynamics, controls, virtual and rapid prototyping, and microelectromechanical systems (MEMS). Robotics research addresses control of multi-robot systems, active sensor networks, micromanipulation, and distributed control and sensing, flying robots, modular reconfigurable robots, robotic locomotion, haptic interfaces, teleoperation, and medical robotics. Biomechanics research spans scales from the tissue level through the molecular, with major efforts in cell mechanics, tendon and ligament properties, biomolecular network simulation, and gravity effects on cells and tissues. (http://www.me.upenn.edu)

Nanotechnology: The Master of Science in Engineering degree in nanotechnology prepares students for this profession with a solid foundation in the three technical core areas: nanofabrication, devices and fundamental properties, and biotechnology, as well as commercialization and societal impacts of technology. Courses are offered by the School of Engineering and Applied Science, the School of Arts and Sciences, and the Wharton School. (http://www.masters.nano.upenn.edu/)

Robotics: This new and unique program educates students in the interdisciplinary aspects of the science and technology of robotic and intelligent machines. The modern expert in robotics and intelligent systems must be proficient in artificial intelligence, computer vision, controls systems, dynamics, and machine learning as well as in design, programming, and prototyping of robotic systems. This multidepartmental, multidisciplinary program provides an ideal foundation for industrial jobs in robotics, defense, aerospace, and automotive industries and various government agencies. (https://www.grasp.upenn.edu/education/masters)

Telecommunications and Networking: This interdisciplinary program draws its faculty members and courses from two School of Engineering and Applied Science departments—electrical and systems engineering and computer and information science—from the Wharton School. Two required courses cover the theory and practice of modern data and voice networking as well as future broadband-integrated networking; five telecommunications electives provide breadth and depth in the field. Three additional free electives allow students to further deepen their technical proficiency or address the increasingly complex managerial and business demands placed on telecommunications professionals. The program's interdisciplinary nature offers full- and part-time students the flexibility to tailor the curriculum to their specific interests, backgrounds, and career goals. (http://www.seas.upenn.edu/profprog/tcom/index.html)

YALE UNIVERSITY
School of Engineering & Applied Science

Programs of Study

All research and instructional programs in engineering and applied science are coordinated by the School of Engineering & Applied Science, which consists of the Departments of Biomedical Engineering, Chemical & Environmental Engineering, Electrical Engineering, and Mechanical Engineering & Materials Science. These four units have autonomous faculty appointments and instructional programs, and students may obtain degrees designated according to different disciplines. A Director of Graduate Studies in each department oversees all graduate student matters. Students have considerable freedom in selecting programs to suit their interests and may choose programs of study that draw upon the resources of departments that are not within the School of Engineering & Applied Science, including the Departments of Applied Physics, Physics, Chemistry, Mathematics, Statistics, Astronomy, Geology and Geophysics, Molecular Biophysics and Biochemistry, and Computer Science, and departments of the School of Medicine and the School of Management.

The student plans his or her course of study in consultation with faculty advisers (the student's advisory committee). A minimum of ten term courses is required and they must be completed in the first two years. Mastery of the topics is expected, and the core courses, as identified by each department/program, should be taken in the first year. No more than two courses should be Special Investigations, and at least two should be outside the area of the dissertation. Periodically, the faculty reviews the overall performance of the student to determine whether he or she may continue working toward the Ph.D. degree. At the end of the first year, a faculty member typically agrees to accept the student as a research assistant. By December 5 of the third year, an area examination must be passed and a written prospectus submitted before dissertation research is begun. These events result in the student's admission to candidacy. Subsequently, students report orally each year to the full advisory committee on their progress. When the research is nearing completion, but before the thesis writing has commenced, the full advisory committee advises the student on the thesis plan. A final oral presentation of the dissertation research is required during term time. There is no foreign language requirement.

M.S. degrees are offered and require the successful completion of at least eight term courses, two of which may be special projects. Although this program can normally be completed in one year of full-time study, a part-time M.S. program is available for practicing engineers and others. Its requirements are the successful completion of eight term courses in a time period not to exceed four calendar years.

Research Facilities

Department facilities are equipped with state-of-the-art experimental and computational equipment in support of the research activity described above. They are centrally located on campus in Mason, Dunham, and Becton Laboratories and in the Malone Engineering Center, adjacent to the Departments of Mathematics and Computer Science and near the complex of facilities for physics, chemistry, and the biological sciences. The School of Engineering & Applied Science has a rich computing environment, including servers, UNIX workstations, and Macintosh and Microsoft Windows personal computers. High-speed data wired and wireless networks interconnect engineering and extends to the campus network. Yale has long been connected to the Internet and is now participating in vBNS and the emerging Internet2. In addition, advanced instrumentation, computing, and networking are combined in a number of laboratories.

Financial Aid

Almost all first-year Ph.D. students receive a University fellowship paying full tuition and an adjusted stipend. Support thereafter is generally provided by research assistantships, which pay $30,450 plus full tuition in 2012–13. Prize fellowships are available to exceptional students. Fellowship support is not available for master's degree students.

Cost of Study

Tuition is $35,500 for the 2012–13 academic year.

Living and Housing Costs

On-campus graduate dormitory housing units range from $4412 to $7518 per academic year. Graduate apartment units range from $834 to $1256 per month. Additional housing details can be found at http://www.yale.edu/gradhousing.

Student Group

Yale has 11,600 students—5,300 are undergraduates and the remainder are graduate and professional students. About 250 graduate students are in engineering, most of them working toward the Ph.D.

Location

Situated on Long Island Sound, among the scenic attractions of southern New England, New Haven provides outstanding cultural and recreational opportunities. The greater New Haven area has a population of more than 350,000 and is only 1½ hours from New York by train or car.

The University

Yale is the third-oldest university in the United States, and its engineering program is also one of the oldest. All programs at the University, including those in the School of Engineering & Applied Science, are structured to give students a high degree of flexibility in arranging their programs, with close interaction between individual students and faculty members.

Applying

Students with a bachelor's degree in any field of engineering or in mathematics, physics, or chemistry may apply for admission to graduate study, as may other students prepared to do graduate-level work in any of the study areas of the chosen department, regardless of their specific undergraduate field. Students are admitted only for the beginning of the fall term. Application should be initiated about a year in advance of desired admission, and the application should be submitted before December 25; the file, including letters of reference, should be completed before January 2. Notifications of admission and award of financial aid are sent by April 1. Applicants must take the General Test of the Graduate Record Examinations; the exam should be taken in October. International applicants must submit scores on the TOEFL unless the undergraduate degree is from an institution in which English is the primary language of instruction.

Yale University

Correspondence and Information

Office of Graduate Studies
School of Engineering & Applied Science
Yale University
P.O. Box 208267
New Haven, Connecticut 06520-8267
United States
Phone: 203-432-4250
Fax: 203-432-7736
Web site: http://www.seas.yale.edu/

THE FACULTY AND AREAS OF RESEARCH

APPLIED MECHANICS/MECHANICAL ENGINEERING/MATERIALS SCIENCE. A. Dollar, E. Dufresne, J. Fernández de la Mora, A. Gomez, M. B Long, J. Morrell, C. S. O'Hern, N. Ouellette, A. G. Ramirez, J. Schroers, U. D. Schwarz, M. D. Smooke, H. Tang. Joint appointments (with primary appointment in another department): C. Ahn, D. Bercovici, S.-I. Karato, D. E. Rosner, R. B. Smith. Adjunct faculty: A. Liñan-Martinez, F. A. Williams. Emeritus faculty: I. B. Bernstein.

Mechanics of Fluids. Dynamics and stability of drops and bubbles; dynamics of thin liquid films; macroscopic and particle-scale dynamics of emulsions, foams, and colloidal suspensions; electrospray theory and applications; electrical propulsion applications; combustion and flames; computational methods for fluid dynamics and reacting flows; turbulence; particle tracking in fluid mechanics; laser diagnostics of reacting and nonreacting flows.

Mechanics of Solids/Material Science/Soft Matter. Characterization of crystallization and other phase transformations; studies of thin films, MEMS, smart materials such as shape memory alloys, amorphous metals, and nanomaterials including nanocomposites; jamming and slow dynamics in glasses and granular materials; mechanical properties of soft and biological materials; self assembly; dynamics of macromolecules; NEMS; nano-imprinting; classical and quantum optomechanics; atomic-scale investigations of surface interactions and properties; classical and quantum nanomechanics; and nanotribology.

Robotics/Mechatronics. Machine and mechanism design; dynamics and control; robotic grasping and manipulation; human-machine interface; rehabilitation robotics; haptics; electromechanical energy conversion; biomechanics of human movement; human powered vehicles.

BIOMEDICAL ENGINEERING. R. E. Carson, R. T. Constable, J. Duncan, T. Fahmy, R. Fan, A. Gonzalez, J. Humphrey, F. Hyder, T. Kyriakides, M. Levene, K. Miller-Jensen, D. Rothman, M. Saltzman, L. Staib, S. Zucker. Joint appointments (with primary appointment in another department): J. Bewersdorf, R. de Graaf, E. Morris, L. Niklason, X. Papademetris, S. Sampath, E. Shapiro, F. Sigworth, H. Tagare.

Biomedical Imaging and Biosignals. Formation of anatomical and functional medical images; magnetic resonance spectroscopy; analysis and processing of medical image data, including functional MRI (fMRI); diffusion tensor imaging; imaging of brain biochemical processes; image-guided neurosurgery; using biomechanical models to guide recovery of left ventricular strain from medical images; biomedical signal processing; relating EEG and fMRI information.

Biomechanics. Simulation and loading of the lumbar spine in regard to tissue loads during heavy lifting, low-back pain and mechanical instability of the spine, muscle mechanics and electromyography, mechanical performance of implants, microcirculation in skeletal muscle, mechanisms of blood-flow control, cell-to-cell communication in vascular resistance networks.

Biomolecular Engineering and Biotechnology. Drug delivery and tissue engineering, drug delivery systems, polymers as biomaterials, tissue engineering, spinal cord regeneration, drug delivery and repair in retina and optic nerve, new biomaterials for drug delivery and tissue engineering, bioseparations, chromatography and electrophoresis, electrical recording (patch clamp) and signal processing of ion channel currents, studies of structure and function of ion channel proteins, cryoelectron microscopy methods for macromolecular structure determination.

CHEMICAL & ENVIRONMENTAL ENGINEERING. E. I. Altman, M. Elimelech, G. L. Haller, M. Loewenberg, W. Mitch, C. Osuji, J. Peccia, L. D Pfefferle, D. E. Rosner, M. Saltzman, A. D. Taylor, P. Van Tassel, T. K Vanderlick, C. Wilson, J. Zimmerman. Adjunct faculty: A. Firoozabadi, Y. Khalil, R. McGraw, J. Pignatello. Joint appointments (with primary appointment in another department): M. Bell, G. Benoit, R. Blake, E. Dufresne, T. Fahmy, T. E. Graedel, E. Kaplan, J. Saiers, U. D. Schwarz, K. W. Zilm.

Nanomaterials. Carbon and inorganic nanotubes, nanoscale polymer films, nanoscale devices, nanomaterials and biomolecules in engineered and natural aquatic systems.

Soft Matter and Interfacial Phenomena. Colloidal and interfacial phenomena, surface science, physics of synthetic and biological macromolecules, microfluidic biosensors, self-assembled soft materials for biomedical applications.

Biomolecular Engineering. Biomolecules at interfaces, nanofilm biomaterials, bioaerosol detection and source tracking, microarrays and other high throughput measurements, production of functional binding biomolecules, biological production of sustainable fuels, transport and fate of microbial pathogens in aquatic environments, membrane separations for desalination and water quality control.

Energy. Biofuels, energy extraction from waste materials, efficient water treatment and delivery, integration of science and engineering with economics and policy.

Water. Sustainable and culturally appropriate technologies for low-quality-source water reclamation in the developing world.

Sustainability. Green solvents, bio-based materials, safer nanotechnology and systems optimization for reduced environmental impact and enhanced economic competitiveness.

ELECTRICAL ENGINEERING. E. Culurciello, J. Han, R. Kuc, M. Lee, T. P. Ma, A. S. Morse, K. S. Narendra, M. A. Reed, A. Savvides, H. Tang, S. Tatikonda, J. R. Vaisnys. Joint appointments (with primary appointment in another department): J. Duncan, L. Staib, H. D. Tagare, R. Yang. Adjunct faculty: P. J. Kindlmann, Y. Makris, R. Lethin. Emeritus faculty: R. C Barker, P. M. Schultheiss.

Signal Processing, Control, and Communications. Linear system models, automatic control systems, representation of information in signals, transmission and storage of information, processing information by computers, networking and communication theory. Applications include bioengineering, digital signal processing, image processing, neural networks, robotics, sensors, and telecommunication systems.

Computer Engineering, Sensor Networks, Circuits and Systems. Study and design of digital circuits and computer systems; computer architecture; sensor networks; very-large-scale integrated (VLSI) circuit design, implementation, and testing. Applications include computing networks, computer design, biomedical instrumentation, bio-inspired circuits and systems.

Electronics, Photonics, and Nanodevices. Design, fabrication, and characterization of novel electronic, photonic, and nano devices; study of structure-property relationships in electronic and photonic materials. Applications include chem/bio-sensing, solid-state lighting, solar cells, micro/nano-electromechanical systems, non-volatile memory, and ultrafast devices.

Section 2
Aerospace/Aeronautical Engineering

This section contains a directory of institutions offering graduate work in aerospace/aeronautical engineering. Additional information about programs listed in the directory but not augmented by an in-depth entry may be obtained by writing directly to the dean of a graduate school or chair of a department at the address given in the directory.

For programs offering related work, see also in this book *Engineering and Applied Sciences* and *Mechanical Engineering and Mechanics.* In another guide in this series:

Graduate Programs in the Physical Sciences, Mathematics, Agricultural Sciences, the Environment & Natural Resources

See *Geosciences* and *Physics*

CONTENTS

Program Directories

Aerospace/Aeronautical Engineering

Air Force Institute of Technology, Graduate School of Engineering and Management, Department of Aeronautics and Astronautics, Dayton, OH 45433-7765. Offers aeronautical engineering (MS, PhD); astronautical engineering (MS, PhD); materials science (MS, PhD); space operations (MS); systems engineering (MS, PhD). *Accreditation:* ABET (one or more programs are accredited). Part-time programs available. *Degree requirements:* For master's, thesis; for doctorate, thesis/dissertation. *Entrance requirements:* For master's and doctorate, GRE General Test, minimum GPA of 3.0, U.S. citizenship. *Faculty research:* Computational fluid dynamics, experimental aerodynamics, computational structural mechanics, experimental structural mechanics, aircraft and spacecraft stability and control.

American Public University System, AMU/APU Graduate Programs, Charles Town, WV 25414. Offers accounting (MBA, MS); administration and supervision (M Ed); criminal justice (MA); emergency and disaster management (MA); entrepreneurship (MBA); environmental policy and management (MS), including environmental planning, environmental sustainability, fish and wildlife management, general (MA, MS), global environmental management; finance (MBA); general (MBA); global business management (MBA); guidance and counseling (M Ed); history (MA), including American history, ancient and classical history, European history, global history, military and diplomatic history, public history; homeland security (MA); homeland security resource allocation (MBA); humanities (MA); information technology (MS), including digital forensics, enterprise software development, information assurance and security, IT project management; information technology management (MBA); intelligence studies (MA), including criminal intelligence, general (MA, MS), homeland security, intelligence analysis, intelligence collection, intelligence operations, terrorism studies; international relations and conflict resolution (MA), including comparative and security issues, conflict resolution, international and transnational security issues, peacekeeping; legal studies (MA); management (MA), including defense management, general (MA, MS); human resource management, organizational leadership, public administration, reverse logistics, strategic consulting; marketing (MBA); military history (MA), including American military history, American revolution, civil war, war since 1946, World War II; military studies (MA), including air warfare, asymmetrical warfare, joint warfare, land warfare, naval warfare, strategic leadership; national security studies (MA), including general (MA, MS), homeland security, regional security studies, security and intelligence analysis, terrorism studies; nonprofit management (MBA); political science (MA), including American politics and government, comparative government and development, public policy; psychology (MA); public administration (MA, MPA), including disaster management (MPA), environmental policy (MA), health policy (MPA), human resources (MPA), national security (MPA), organizational management (MPA), security management (MPA); public health (MA, MPH), including emergency management (MPH), environmental health (MPH), public administration (MA); reverse logistics management (MA); security management (MA); space studies (MS), including aerospace science, planetary science; sports and health sciences (MS); sports management (MS), including coaching theory and strategy, sports administration; teaching (M Ed), including curriculum and instruction for elementary teachers, elementary, elementary reading, English language learners, instructional leadership, online learning, secondary social sciences, special education; transportation and logistics management (MA), including maritime engineering management. Programs offered via distance learning only. Part-time and evening/weekend programs available. Postbaccalaureate distance learning degree programs offered (no on-campus study). *Faculty:* 445 full-time (241 women), 1,360 part-time/adjunct (617 women). *Students:* 688 full-time (338 women), 10,168 part-time (3,706 women); includes 3,130 minority (1,007 Black or African American, non-Hispanic/Latino; 103 American Indian or Alaska Native, non-Hispanic/Latino; 825 Asian, non-Hispanic/Latino; 810 Hispanic/Latino; 51 Native Hawaiian or other Pacific Islander, non-Hispanic/Latino; 334 Two or more races, non-Hispanic/Latino), 134 international. Average age 35. In 2011, 2,386 master's awarded. *Degree requirements:* For master's, comprehensive exam or practicum. *Entrance requirements:* For master's, official transcript showing earned bachelor's degree from institution accredited by recognized accrediting body. Additional exam requirements/recommendations for international students: Required—TOEFL (minimum score 550 paper-based; 213 computer-based), IELTS (minimum score 6.5). *Application deadline:* Applications are processed on a rolling basis. Application fee: $0. Electronic applications accepted. *Expenses: Tuition:* Part-time $325 per credit hour. *Financial support:* Applicants required to submit FAFSA. *Faculty research:* Military history, criminal justice, management performance, national security. *Unit head:* Dr. Karan Powell, Executive Vice President and Provost, 877-468-6268, Fax: 304-724-3780. *Application contact:* Terry Grant, Vice President of Enrollment Management, 877-468-6268, Fax: 304-724-3780, E-mail: info@apus.edu. Web site: http://www.apus.edu.

Arizona State University, Ira A. Fulton School of Engineering, Department of Mechanical and Aerospace Engineering, Tempe, AZ 85281. Offers aerospace engineering (MS, MSE, PhD); chemical engineering (MS, MSE, PhD); materials science and engineering (MS, PhD); mechanical engineering (MS, MSE, PhD). Part-time and evening/weekend programs available. Postbaccalaureate distance learning degree programs offered (minimal on-campus study). Terminal master's awarded for partial completion of doctoral program. *Degree requirements:* For master's, thesis and oral defense (MS); applied project or comprehensive exam (MSE); interactive Program of Study (iPOS) submitted before completing 50 percent of required credit hours; for doctorate, comprehensive exam, thesis/dissertation, interactive Program of Study (iPOS) submitted before completing 50 percent of required credit hours. *Entrance requirements:* For master's, GRE, minimum GPA of 3.0 or equivalent in last 2 years of work leading to bachelor's degree; for doctorate, GRE, minimum GPA of 3.0 in last 2 years of work leading to bachelor's degree. Additional exam requirements/recommendations for international students: Required—TOEFL (minimum score 80 iBT), TOEFL, IELTS, or Pearson Test of English. Electronic applications accepted. *Expenses:* Contact institution. *Faculty research:* Electronic materials and packaging, materials for energy (batteries), adaptive/intelligent materials and structures, multiscale fluid mechanics, membranes, therapeutics and bioseparations, flexible structures, nanostructured materials, and micro/nano transport.

Auburn University, Graduate School, Ginn College of Engineering, Department of Aerospace Engineering, Auburn University, AL 36849. Offers MAE, MS, PhD. Part-time programs available. *Faculty:* 9 full-time (0 women), 3 part-time/adjunct (0 women). *Students:* 19 full-time (3 women), 29 part-time (7 women); includes 4 minority (1 Asian, non-Hispanic/Latino; 3 Hispanic/Latino), 8 international. Average age 26. 38 applicants, 66% accepted, 14 enrolled. In 2011, 12 master's awarded. *Degree requirements:* For master's, thesis (MS), exam; for doctorate, thesis/dissertation, exams. *Entrance requirements:* For master's and doctorate, GRE General Test. *Application deadline:* For fall admission, 7/7 for domestic students; for spring admission, 11/24 for domestic students. Applications are processed on a rolling basis. Application fee: $50 ($60 for international students). Electronic applications accepted. *Expenses: Tuition,* state resident: full-time $7290; part-time $405 per credit hour. Tuition, nonresident: full-time

$21,870; part-time $1215 per credit hour. *International tuition:* $22,000 full-time. *Required fees:* $1402. *Financial support:* Fellowships, research assistantships, teaching assistantships, and Federal Work-Study available. Support available to part-time students. Financial award application deadline: 3/15; financial award applicants required to submit FAFSA. *Faculty research:* Aerodynamics, flight dynamics and simulation, propulsion, structures and aeroelasticity, aerospace smart structures. *Unit head:* Dr. John E. Cochran, Jr., Head, 334-844-6800. *Application contact:* Dr. George Flowers, Dean of the Graduate School, 334-844-2125. Web site: http://www.eng.auburn.edu/department/ae/.

California Institute of Technology, Division of Engineering and Applied Science, Option in Aeronautics, Pasadena, CA 91125-0001. Offers MS, PhD, Engr. Terminal master's awarded for partial completion of doctoral program. *Degree requirements:* For doctorate, thesis/dissertation. *Faculty research:* Computational fluid dynamics, technical fluid dynamics, structural mechanics, mechanics of fracture, aeronautical engineering and propulsion.

California Polytechnic State University, San Luis Obispo, College of Engineering, Department of Aerospace Engineering, San Luis Obispo, CA 93407. Offers MS. Part-time programs available. *Faculty:* 1 full-time (0 women). *Students:* 29 full-time (3 women), 19 part-time (2 women); includes 12 minority (1 American Indian or Alaska Native, non-Hispanic/Latino; 7 Asian, non-Hispanic/Latino; 4 Hispanic/Latino). Average age 25. 60 applicants, 58% accepted, 24 enrolled. In 2011, 19 master's awarded. *Degree requirements:* For master's, thesis. *Entrance requirements:* For master's, GRE General Test, minimum GPA of 3.0 in last 90 quarter units. Additional exam requirements/recommendations for international students: Required—TOEFL (minimum score 550 paper-based; 213 computer-based) or IELTS (minimum score 6). *Application deadline:* For fall admission, 7/1 for domestic students, 11/30 for international students; for winter admission, 11/1 for domestic students, 6/30 for international students; for spring admission, 2/1 for domestic students. Applications are processed on a rolling basis. Application fee: $55. Electronic applications accepted. *Expenses:* Tuition, state resident: full-time $6738. Tuition, nonresident: full-time $17,898. *Required fees:* $2449. *Financial support:* Fellowships, research assistantships, teaching assistantships, career-related internships or fieldwork, Federal Work-Study, scholarships/grants, and unspecified assistantships available. Support available to part-time students. Financial award application deadline: 3/2; financial award applicants required to submit FAFSA. *Faculty research:* Space systems engineering, space vehicle design, aerodynamics, aerospace propulsion, dynamics and control. *Unit head:* Dr. Jin Tso, Graduate Coordinator/Department Chair, 805-756-1391, Fax: 805-756-2376, E-mail: jtso@calpoly.edu. *Application contact:* Dr. James Maraviglia, Associate Vice Provost for Marketing and Enrollment Development, 805-756-2311, Fax: 805-756-5400, E-mail: admissions@calpoly.edu. Web site: http://aero.calpoly.edu.

California State Polytechnic University, Pomona, Academic Affairs, College of Engineering, Program in Engineering, Pomona, CA 91768-2557. Offers aerospace engineering (MSE). *Students:* 10 part-time (2 women); includes 4 minority (1 Black or African American, non-Hispanic/Latino; 1 Asian, non-Hispanic/Latino; 1 Hispanic/Latino; 1 Two or more races, non-Hispanic/Latino). 10 applicants, 30% accepted, 2 enrolled. In 2011, 9 master's awarded. *Application deadline:* Applications are processed on a rolling basis. Application fee: $55. Electronic applications accepted. *Expenses:* Tuition, state resident: full-time $6738. Tuition, nonresident: full-time $12,300. *Required fees:* $657. Tuition and fees vary according to course load and program. *Unit head:* Dr. Ali R. Ahmadi, Department Chair, 909-869-2470, E-mail: arahmadi@csupomona.edu. *Application contact:* Deborah L. Brandon, Executive Director, Admissions and Outreach, 909-869-3427, Fax: 909-869-5315, E-mail: dlbrandon@csupomona.edu. Web site: http://www.csupomona.edu/~aro.

California State University, Long Beach, Graduate Studies, College of Engineering, Department of Mechanical and Aerospace Engineering, Program in Aerospace Engineering, Long Beach, CA 90840. Offers MSAE. Part-time programs available. *Students:* 17 full-time (2 women), 23 part-time (1 woman); includes 20 minority (1 Black or African American, non-Hispanic/Latino; 1 American Indian or Alaska Native, non-Hispanic/Latino; 10 Asian, non-Hispanic/Latino; 7 Hispanic/Latino; 1 Two or more races, non-Hispanic/Latino), 5 international. Average age 28. 45 applicants, 62% accepted, 10 enrolled. In 2011, 13 master's awarded. *Degree requirements:* For master's, thesis or alternative. *Entrance requirements:* Additional exam requirements/recommendations for international students: Required—TOEFL. *Application deadline:* For fall admission, 7/1 for domestic students. Application fee: $55. Electronic applications accepted. *Financial support:* Career-related internships or fieldwork, Federal Work-Study, institutionally sponsored loans, scholarships/grants, and unspecified assistantships available. Financial award application deadline: 3/2. *Faculty research:* Aerodynamic flows, ice accretion, stability and transition. *Unit head:* Dr. Hamid Hefazi, Chairman, 562-985-1563, Fax: 562-985-4408, E-mail: hefazi@csulb.edu. *Application contact:* Dr. Hsin-Piao Chen, Graduate Advisor, 562-985-1563.

Carleton University, Faculty of Graduate Studies, Faculty of Engineering and Design, Department of Mechanical and Aerospace Engineering, Ottawa, ON K1S 5B6, Canada. Offers aerospace engineering (M Eng, MA Sc, PhD); materials engineering (M Eng, MA Sc); mechanical engineering (M Eng, MA Sc, PhD). *Degree requirements:* For master's, thesis optional; for doctorate, thesis/dissertation. *Entrance requirements:* For master's, honors degree; for doctorate, MA Sc or M Eng. Additional exam requirements/recommendations for international students: Required—TOEFL. *Faculty research:* Thermal fluids engineering, heat transfer, vehicle engineering.

Case Western Reserve University, School of Graduate Studies, Case School of Engineering, Department of Mechanical and Aerospace Engineering, Cleveland, OH 44106. Offers MS, PhD, MD/PhD. Part-time programs available. Postbaccalaureate distance learning degree programs offered (no on-campus study). *Faculty:* 13 full-time (3 women). *Students:* 58 full-time (4 women), 16 part-time (4 women); includes 12 minority (4 Black or African American, non-Hispanic/Latino; 6 Asian, non-Hispanic/Latino; 2 Two or more races, non-Hispanic/Latino), 29 international. In 2011, 13 master's, 8 doctorates awarded. *Degree requirements:* For master's, thesis (for some programs); for doctorate, thesis/dissertation, qualifying exam, teaching experience. *Entrance requirements:* For master's and doctorate, GRE General Test. Additional exam requirements/recommendations for international students: Required—TOEFL. *Application deadline:* For fall admission, 7/1 priority date for domestic students. Applications are processed on a rolling basis. Application fee: $50. *Financial support:* Fellowships with full and partial tuition reimbursements, research assistantships with full and partial tuition reimbursements, teaching assistantships, institutionally sponsored loans, and tuition waivers (full and partial) available. Financial award application deadline: 3/1; financial award applicants required to submit FAFSA. *Faculty research:* Musculoskeletal biomechanics, combustion diagnostics and computation, mechanical behavior of advanced materials and nanostructures, biorobotics. *Total annual research expenditures:* $6.2 million. *Unit head:* Dr. Iwan Alexander, Department Chair, 216-368-

6045, Fax: 216-368-6445, E-mail: ida2@case.edu. *Application contact:* Carla Wilson, Student Affairs Coordinator, 216-368-4580, Fax: 216-368-3007, E-mail: cxw75@case.edu. Web site: http://www.engineering.case.edu/emae.

Concordia University, School of Graduate Studies, Faculty of Engineering and Computer Science, Program in Aerospace Engineering, Montréal, QC H3G 1M8, Canada. Offers M Eng. Program offered jointly with École Polytechnique de Montréal and McGill University. *Degree requirements:* For master's, thesis or alternative. *Faculty research:* Aeronautics and propulsion avionics and control, structures and materials, space engineering.

Cornell University, Graduate School, Graduate Fields of Engineering, Field of Aerospace Engineering, Ithaca, NY 14853-0001. Offers M Eng, MS, PhD. *Faculty:* 34 full-time (5 women). *Students:* 42 full-time (7 women); includes 8 minority (4 Asian, non-Hispanic/Latino; 4 Hispanic/Latino), 7 international. Average age 24. 139 applicants, 29% accepted, 26 enrolled. In 2011, 26 master's, 3 doctorates awarded. Terminal master's awarded for partial completion of doctoral program. *Degree requirements:* For master's, thesis (MS); for doctorate, one foreign language, comprehensive exam, thesis/dissertation. *Entrance requirements:* For master's and doctorate, GRE General Test, 3 letters of recommendation. Additional exam requirements/recommendations for international students: Required—TOEFL (minimum score 550 paper-based; 213 computer-based; 77 iBT). *Application deadline:* For fall admission, 1/15 for domestic students; for spring admission, 11/1 for domestic students. Application fee: $95. Electronic applications accepted. *Financial support:* In 2011–12, 22 students received support, including 8 fellowships with full tuition reimbursements available, 10 research assistantships with full tuition reimbursements available, 3 teaching assistantships with full tuition reimbursements available; institutionally sponsored loans, scholarships/grants, health care benefits, tuition waivers (full and partial), and unspecified assistantships also available. Financial award applicants required to submit FAFSA. *Faculty research:* Aerodynamics, fluid mechanics, turbulence, combustion/propulsion, aeroacoustics. *Unit head:* Director of Graduate Studies, 607-255-5250. *Application contact:* Graduate Field Assistant, 607-255-5250, E-mail: maegrad@cornell.edu. Web site: http://www.gradschool.cornell.edu/fields.php?id-20&a-2.

École Polytechnique de Montréal, Graduate Programs, Department of Mechanical Engineering, Montréal, QC H3C 3A7, Canada. Offers aerothermics (M Eng, M Sc A, PhD); applied mechanics (M Eng, M Sc A, PhD); tool design (M Eng, M Sc A, PhD). Part-time and evening/weekend programs available. *Degree requirements:* For master's, one foreign language, thesis; for doctorate, one foreign language, thesis/dissertation. *Entrance requirements:* For master's, minimum GPA of 2.75; for doctorate, minimum GPA of 3.0. *Faculty research:* Noise control and vibration, fatigue and creep, aerodynamics, composite materials, biomechanics, robotics.

Embry-Riddle Aeronautical University–Daytona, Daytona Beach Campus Graduate Program, Department of Aerospace Engineering, Daytona Beach, FL 32114-3900. Offers MAE, MSAE. Part-time programs available. *Faculty:* 10 full-time (0 women). *Students:* 92 full-time (19 women), 8 part-time (2 women); includes 12 minority (1 Black or African American, non-Hispanic/Latino; 5 Asian, non-Hispanic/Latino; 5 Hispanic/Latino; 1 Two or more races, non-Hispanic/Latino), 45 international. Average age 24. 132 applicants, 59% accepted, 30 enrolled. In 2011, 31 master's awarded. *Degree requirements:* For master's, thesis. *Entrance requirements:* For master's, BS in aeronautical engineering or equivalent; minimum GPA of 3.0 in last 2 undergraduate years, 2.5 overall. Additional exam requirements/recommendations for international students: Required—TOEFL (minimum score 550 paper-based; 213 computer-based; 79 iBT). *Application deadline:* For fall admission, 6/1 priority date for domestic students, 5/1 for international students; for spring admission, 11/1 priority date for domestic students, 10/1 for international students. Applications are processed on a rolling basis. Application fee: $50. Electronic applications accepted. *Expenses: Tuition:* Full-time $14,340; part-time $1195 per credit hour. *Financial support:* In 2011–12, 59 students received support, including 6 research assistantships with full and partial tuition reimbursements available (averaging $6,092 per year), 15 teaching assistantships with full and partial tuition reimbursements available (averaging $6,092 per year); career-related internships or fieldwork, Federal Work-Study, and unspecified assistantships also available. Support available to part-time students. Financial award application deadline: 4/15; financial award applicants required to submit FAFSA. *Faculty research:* Pitch motionstability in elliptic orbits, the use of integral techniques in computational aeroacoustics, aircraft jet and fan noise for supersonic business jet engines, next-generation aeronautics, aluminum droplet combustion. *Total annual research expenditures:* $501,313. *Unit head:* Dr. Yi Zhao, Graduate Program Coordinator, 386-226-6746, Fax: 386-226-6747, E-mail: yi.zhao@erau.edu. *Application contact:* Flavia Carreiro, Assistant Director, International and Graduate Admissions, 800-388-3728, Fax: 386-226-7070, E-mail: graduate.admissions@erau.edu.

Embry-Riddle Aeronautical University–Daytona, Daytona Beach Campus Graduate Program, Department of Applied Aviation Sciences, Daytona Beach, FL 32114-3900. Offers MSA. Part-time and evening/weekend programs available. *Faculty:* 18 full-time (1 woman), 17 part-time/adjunct (1 woman). *Students:* 138 full-time (34 women), 43 part-time (10 women); includes 41 minority (20 Black or African American, non-Hispanic/Latino; 9 Asian, non-Hispanic/Latino; 10 Hispanic/Latino; 2 Two or more races, non-Hispanic/Latino), 44 international. Average age 27. 124 applicants, 76% accepted, 63 enrolled. In 2011, 38 master's awarded. *Degree requirements:* For master's, thesis optional. *Entrance requirements:* For master's, minimum GPA of 2.5. Additional exam requirements/recommendations for international students: Required—TOEFL (minimum score 550 paper-based; 213 computer-based; 79 iBT). *Application deadline:* For fall admission, 6/1 priority date for domestic students, 6/1 for international students; for spring admission, 11/1 priority date for domestic students, 10/1 for international students. Applications are processed on a rolling basis. Application fee: $50. Electronic applications accepted. *Expenses: Tuition:* Full-time $14,340; part-time $1195 per credit hour. *Financial support:* In 2011–12, 24 students received support, including 8 research assistantships with full and partial tuition reimbursements available (averaging $3,338 per year); teaching assistantships with full and partial tuition reimbursements available, career-related internships or fieldwork, Federal Work-Study, and unspecified assistantships also available. Support available to part-time students. Financial award application deadline: 4/15; financial award applicants required to submit FAFSA. *Faculty research:* 4D flight management system trajectory-based operation, next-generation air transportation system, weather research, agriculture in a changing climate, weather technology in the cockpit, pilot training requirements, environmental security research. *Unit head:* Dr. Marvin Smith, Program Coordinator, 386-226-6448, E-mail: smithm@erau.edu. *Application contact:* Flavia Carreiro, Assistant Director, International and Graduate Admissions, 800-388-3728, Fax: 386-226-7070, E-mail: graduate.admissions@erau.edu. Web site: http://daytonabeach.erau.edu/degrees/graduate/aeronautics/index.html.

Embry-Riddle Aeronautical University–Worldwide, Worldwide Headquarters - Graduate Degrees and Programs, Program in Aeronautics, Daytona Beach, FL 32114-3900. Offers aeronautical science (MAS); air transportation management (Graduate Certificate); airport planning design and development (Graduate Certificate); aviation/aerospace industrial management (Graduate Certificate); aviation/aerospace safety (Graduate Certificate); instructional system design (Graduate Certificate). Part-time and evening/weekend programs available. Postbaccalaureate distance learning degree programs offered (minimal on-campus study). *Faculty:* 24 full-time (2 women), 177 part-time/adjunct (20 women). *Students:* 1,684 full-time (248 women), 1,771 part-time (239 women); includes 497 minority (154 Black or African American, non-Hispanic/Latino; 20 American Indian or Alaska Native, non-Hispanic/Latino; 58 Asian, non-Hispanic/Latino; 251 Hispanic/Latino; 3 Native Hawaiian or other Pacific Islander, non-Hispanic/Latino; 11 Two or more races, non-Hispanic/Latino), 32 international. Average age 36. 913 applicants, 77% accepted, 330 enrolled. In 2011, 1032 degrees awarded. *Degree requirements:* For master's, comprehensive exam (for some programs), thesis optional. *Entrance requirements:* Additional exam requirements/recommendations for international students: Recommended—TOEFL (minimum score 550 paper-based; 213 computer-based; 79 iBT). *Application deadline:* Applications are processed on a rolling basis. Application fee: $50. Electronic applications accepted. *Expenses: Tuition:* Part-time $395 per credit hour. Tuition and fees vary according to degree level and program. *Financial support:* In 2011–12, 570 students received support. Available to part-time students. Applicants required to submit FAFSA. *Faculty research:* Unmanned aircraft system (UAS) operations, human factors, crash investigation, reliability and hazard analysis, aviation security. *Unit head:* Dr. Katherine A. Moran, Department Chair, 360-597-4560, E-mail: morank@erau.edu. *Application contact:* Linda Dammer, Director of Admissions, 386-226-6396 Ext. 1, Fax: 386-226-6984, E-mail: worldwide@erau.edu.

Florida Institute of Technology, Graduate Programs, College of Aeronautics, Melbourne, FL 32901-6975. Offers airport development and management (MSA); applied aviation safety option (MSA); aviation human factors (MS); human factors in aeronautics (MS). Part-time and evening/weekend programs available. *Faculty:* 5 full-time (0 women), 2 part-time/adjunct (0 women). *Students:* 27 full-time (6 women), 18 part-time (7 women); includes 6 minority (4 Black or African American, non-Hispanic/Latino; 1 Asian, non-Hispanic/Latino; 1 Hispanic/Latino), 12 international. Average age 26. 70 applicants, 76% accepted, 29 enrolled. In 2011, 14 master's awarded. *Degree requirements:* For master's, thesis (for some programs). *Entrance requirements:* For master's, GRE, minimum GPA of 3.0, 3 letters of recommendation, resume, statement of objectives. Additional exam requirements/recommendations for international students: Required—TOEFL (minimum score 550 paper-based; 213 computer-based; 79 iBT). *Application deadline:* For fall admission, 4/1 for international students; for spring admission, 9/30 for international students. Applications are processed on a rolling basis. Electronic applications accepted. *Expenses: Tuition:* Full-time $19,620; part-time $1090 per credit hour. Tuition and fees vary according to campus/location. *Financial support:* In 2011–12, 1 research assistantship with full and partial tuition reimbursement (averaging $2,000 per year) was awarded; career-related internships or fieldwork, institutionally sponsored loans, tuition waivers (partial), and tuition remissions also available. Support available to part-time students. Financial award application deadline: 3/1; financial award applicants required to submit FAFSA. *Faculty research:* Aircraft cockpit design, medical human factors, operating room human factors, hypobaric chamber operations and effects, aviation professional education. *Total annual research expenditures:* $4.5 million. *Unit head:* Dr. Kenneth P. Stackpoole, Dean, 321-674-8971, Fax: 321-674-7368, E-mail: kenStackpoole@fit.edu. *Application contact:* Cheryl A. Brown, Associate Director of Graduate Admissions, 321-674-7581, Fax: 321-723-9468, E-mail: cbrown@fit.edu. Web site: http://coa.fit.edu.

Florida Institute of Technology, Graduate Programs, College of Engineering, Mechanical and Aerospace Engineering Department, Melbourne, FL 32901-6975. Offers aerospace engineering (MS, PhD); mechanical engineering (MS, PhD). Part-time programs available. *Faculty:* 9 full-time (0 women). *Students:* 59 full-time (8 women), 36 part-time (4 women); includes 7 minority (1 Black or African American, non-Hispanic/Latino; 2 Asian, non-Hispanic/Latino; 4 Hispanic/Latino), 50 international. Average age 27. 259 applicants, 61% accepted, 44 enrolled. In 2011, 27 master's, 1 doctorate awarded. Terminal master's awarded for partial completion of doctoral program. *Degree requirements:* For master's, comprehensive exam (for some programs), thesis optional; for doctorate, comprehensive exam, thesis/dissertation, oral section of written exam, complete program of significant original research. *Entrance requirements:* For master's, GRE General Test, minimum GPA of 3.0, bachelor's degree from an ABET-accredited program, transcripts; for doctorate, GRE General Test, 3 letters of recommendation, minimum GPA of 3.2, resume, statement of objectives. Additional exam requirements/recommendations for international students: Required—TOEFL (minimum score 550 paper-based; 213 computer-based; 79 iBT). *Application deadline:* For fall admission, 4/1 for international students; for spring admission, 9/30 for international students. Applications are processed on a rolling basis. Application fee: $0. Electronic applications accepted. *Expenses: Tuition:* Full-time $19,620; part-time $1090 per credit hour. Tuition and fees vary according to campus/location. *Financial support:* In 2011–12, 6 research assistantships with full and partial tuition reimbursements (averaging $4,472 per year), 12 teaching assistantships with full and partial tuition reimbursements (averaging $3,893 per year) were awarded; career-related internships or fieldwork, institutionally sponsored loans, tuition waivers (partial), unspecified assistantships, and tuition remissions also available. Support available to part-time students. Financial award application deadline: 3/1; financial award applicants required to submit FAFSA. *Faculty research:* Dynamic systems, robotics, and controls; structures, solid mechanics, and materials; thermal-fluid sciences, optical tomography, composite/recycled materials. *Total annual research expenditures:* $733,898. *Unit head:* Dr. Pei-feng Hsu, Department Head, 321-674-8092, Fax: 321-674-8813, E-mail: phsu@fit.edu. *Application contact:* Cheryl A. Brown, Associate Director of Graduate Admissions, 321-674-7581, Fax: 321-723-9468, E-mail: cbrown@fit.edu. Web site: http://coe.fit.edu/mae/.

Florida Institute of Technology, Graduate Programs, Extended Studies Division, Melbourne, FL 32901-6975. Offers acquisition and contract management (MS); aerospace engineering (MS); business administration (MBA); computer information systems (MS); computer science (MS); electrical engineering (MS); engineering management (MS); human resources management (MS); logistics management (MS), including humanitarian and disaster relief logistics; management (MS), including acquisition and contract management, e-business, human resources management, information systems, logistics management, management, transportation management; material acquisition management (MS); mechanical engineering (MS); operations research (MS); project management (MS), including information systems, operations research; public administration (MPA); quality management (MS); software engineering (MS); space systems (MS); space systems management (MS); supply chain management (MS); systems management (MS), including information systems, operations research. Part-time and evening/weekend programs available. Postbaccalaureate distance learning degree programs offered (no on-campus study). *Faculty:* 9 full-time (2 women), 105 part-time/adjunct (24 women). *Students:* 113 full-time (52 women), 1,150 part-time (484 women); includes 496 minority (332 Black or African

American, non-Hispanic/Latino; 11 American Indian or Alaska Native, non-Hispanic/Latino; 42 Asian, non-Hispanic/Latino; 71 Hispanic/Latino; 2 Native Hawaiian or other Pacific Islander, non-Hispanic/Latino; 38 Two or more races, non-Hispanic/Latino), 11 international. Average age 35. 568 applicants, 56% accepted, 296 enrolled. In 2011, 471 master's awarded. *Degree requirements:* For master's, comprehensive exam (for some programs), capstone course. *Entrance requirements:* For master's, GMAT or resume showing 8 years of supervised experience, minimum GPA of 3.0, 2 letters of recommendation, resume. Additional exam requirements/recommendations for international students: Required—TOEFL (minimum score 550 paper-based; 213 computer-based; 79 iBT). *Application deadline:* For fall admission, 4/1 for international students; for spring admission, 9/30 for international students. Applications are processed on a rolling basis. Application fee: $0. Electronic applications accepted. *Expenses:* Contact institution. *Financial support:* Application deadline: 3/1; applicants required to submit FAFSA. *Unit head:* Dr. Theodore R. Richardson, III, Senior Associate Dean, 321-674-8123, Fax: 321-674-7597, E-mail: trichardson@fit.edu. *Application contact:* Carolyn Farrior, Director of Graduate Admissions, Online Learning and Off-Campus Programs, 321-674-7118, Fax: 321-674-8216, E-mail: cfarrior@fit.edu. Web site: http://es.fit.edu.

The George Washington University, School of Engineering and Applied Science, Department of Mechanical and Aerospace Engineering, Washington, DC 20052. Offers MS, D Sc, App Sc, Engr, Graduate Certificate. Part-time and evening/weekend programs available. *Faculty:* 17 full-time (1 woman), 13 part-time/adjunct (2 women). *Students:* 51 full-time (13 women), 37 part-time (5 women); includes 17 minority (7 Black or African American, non-Hispanic/Latino; 1 American Indian or Alaska Native, non-Hispanic/Latino; 4 Asian, non-Hispanic/Latino; 4 Hispanic/Latino; 1 Two or more races, non-Hispanic/Latino), 28 international. Average age 29. 123 applicants, 77% accepted, 25 enrolled. In 2011, 16 master's, 6 doctorates, 1 other advanced degree awarded. *Degree requirements:* For master's, thesis optional; for doctorate, thesis/dissertation, final and qualifying exams. *Entrance requirements:* For master's, appropriate bachelor's degree, minimum GPA of 3.0; for doctorate, GRE (if highest earned degree is BS), appropriate bachelor's or master's degree, minimum GPA of 3.4; for other advanced degree, appropriate master's degree, minimum GPA of 3.0. Additional exam requirements/recommendations for international students: Required—TOEFL or The George Washington University English as a Foreign Language Test. *Application deadline:* For fall admission, 3/1 priority date for domestic students; for spring admission, 10/1 for domestic students. Applications are processed on a rolling basis. Application fee: $75. *Financial support:* In 2011–12, 51 students received support. Fellowships with tuition reimbursements available, research assistantships, teaching assistantships with tuition reimbursements available, career-related internships or fieldwork, and institutionally sponsored loans available. Financial award application deadline: 3/1; financial award applicants required to submit FAFSA. *Unit head:* Dr. Michael Plesniak, Chairman, 202-994-6749, E-mail: maeng@gwu.edu. *Application contact:* Adina Lav, Marketing, Recruiting and Admissions, 202-994-5827, Fax: 202-994-0909, E-mail: engineering@gwu.edu. Web site: http://www.mae.gwu.edu/.

Georgia Institute of Technology, Graduate Studies and Research, College of Engineering, School of Aerospace Engineering, Atlanta, GA 30332-0001. Offers MS, MSAE, PhD. Part-time programs available. Terminal master's awarded for partial completion of doctoral program. *Degree requirements:* For master's, thesis optional; for doctorate, thesis/dissertation. *Entrance requirements:* For master's, GRE, minimum GPA of 3.0; for doctorate, GRE, minimum GPA of 3.25. Additional exam requirements/recommendations for international students: Required—TOEFL. *Faculty research:* Structural mechanics and dynamics, fluid mechanics, flight mechanics and controls, combustion and propulsion, system design and optimization.

Illinois Institute of Technology, Graduate College, Armour College of Engineering, Department of Mechanical, Materials and Aerospace Engineering, Chicago, IL 60616-3793. Offers manufacturing engineering (MME, MS); materials science and engineering (MMME, MS, PhD); mechanical and aerospace engineering (MMAE, MS, PhD), including economics (MS), energy (MS), environment (MS). Part-time and evening/weekend programs available. Postbaccalaureate distance learning degree programs offered (minimal on-campus study). Terminal master's awarded for partial completion of doctoral program. *Degree requirements:* For master's, comprehensive exam (for some programs), thesis (for some programs); for doctorate, comprehensive exam, thesis/dissertation. *Entrance requirements:* For master's and doctorate, GRE General Test (minimum score 1000 Quantitative and Verbal, 3.0 Analytical Writing), minimum undergraduate GPA of 3.0. Additional exam requirements/recommendations for international students: Required—TOEFL (minimum score 523 paper-based; 70 iBT); Recommended—IELTS (minimum score 5.5). Electronic applications accepted. *Faculty research:* Fluid dynamics, metallurgical and materials engineering, solids and structures, computational mechanics, theoretical mechanics.

Iowa State University of Science and Technology, Department of Aerospace Engineering and Engineering Mechanics, Ames, IA 50011-2271. Offers aerospace engineering (M Eng, MS, PhD); engineering mechanics (M Eng, MS, PhD). *Degree requirements:* For master's, thesis (for some programs); for doctorate, thesis/dissertation. *Entrance requirements:* For master's and doctorate, GRE General Test, resume. Additional exam requirements/recommendations for international students: Required—TOEFL (minimum score 550 paper-based; 80 iBT), IELTS (minimum score 6.5). *Application deadline:* For fall admission, 1/1 priority date for domestic students, 1/1 for international students; for spring admission, 9/1 priority date for domestic students, 9/1 for international students. Application fee: $40 ($90 for international students). Electronic applications accepted. *Unit head:* Dr. Zhi Wang, Director of Graduate Education, 515-294-9669, Fax: 515-294-3262, E-mail: aero-info@iastate.edu. *Application contact:* Gayle Fay, Director of Graduate Education, 515-294-9669, Fax: 515-294-3262, E-mail: aere-info@iastate.edu. Web site: http://www.aere.iastate.edu/.

Massachusetts Institute of Technology, School of Engineering, Department of Aeronautics and Astronautics, Cambridge, MA 02139. Offers aeronautics and astronautics (SM, PhD, Sc D, EAA); aerospace computational engineering (PhD, Sc D); air transportation systems (PhD, Sc D); air-breathing propulsion (PhD, Sc D); aircraft systems engineering (PhD, Sc D); autonomous systems (PhD, Sc D); communications and networks (PhD, Sc D); controls (PhD, Sc D); humans in aerospace (PhD, Sc D); materials and structures (PhD, Sc D); space propulsion (PhD, Sc D); space systems (PhD, Sc D); SM/MBA. *Faculty:* 35 full-time (9 women). *Students:* 227 full-time (37 women), 2 part-time (0 women); includes 36 minority (1 Black or African American, non-Hispanic/Latino; 18 Asian, non-Hispanic/Latino; 13 Hispanic/Latino; 4 Two or more races, non-Hispanic/Latino), 76 international. Average age 26. 492 applicants, 20% accepted, 74 enrolled. In 2011, 62 master's, 16 doctorates awarded. *Degree requirements:* For master's and EAA, thesis; for doctorate, comprehensive exam, thesis/dissertation. *Entrance requirements:* For master's and doctorate, GRE General Test. Additional exam requirements/recommendations for international students: Required—TOEFL (minimum score 600 paper-based; 250 computer-based; 100 iBT), IELTS (minimum score 7). *Application deadline:* For fall admission, 12/15 for domestic and international students. Application fee: $75. Electronic applications accepted. *Expenses: Tuition:* Full-time $40,460; part-time $630 per credit hour. *Required fees:* $272. *Financial support:* In 2011–12, 214 students received support, including 58 fellowships (averaging $31,700 per year), 145 research assistantships (averaging $29,200 per year), 14 teaching assistantships (averaging $33,000 per year); Federal Work-Study, institutionally sponsored loans, scholarships/grants, health care benefits, and unspecified assistantships also available. *Faculty research:* Aerospace information engineering, aerospace systems engineering, aerospace vehicles engineering. *Total annual research expenditures:* $27.7 million. *Unit head:* Prof. Jaime Peraire, Head, 617-258-7537, Fax: 617-258-7566. *Application contact:* Graduate Administrator, 617-253-0043, Fax: 617-253-0823, E-mail: aa-studentservices@mit.edu. Web site: http://aeroastro.mit.edu/.

McGill University, Faculty of Graduate and Postdoctoral Studies, Faculty of Engineering, Department of Mechanical Engineering, Montréal, QC H3A 2T5, Canada. Offers aerospace (M Eng); manufacturing management (MMM); mechanical engineering (M Eng, M Sc, PhD).

Middle Tennessee State University, College of Graduate Studies, College of Basic and Applied Sciences, Department of Aerospace, Murfreesboro, TN 37132. Offers aerospace education (M Ed); aviation administration (MS). Part-time and evening/weekend programs available. Postbaccalaureate distance learning degree programs offered. *Faculty:* 4 full-time (1 woman). *Students:* 10 full-time (2 women), 24 part-time (4 women); includes 6 minority (5 Black or African American, non-Hispanic/Latino; 1 Hispanic/Latino). Average age 30. 34 applicants, 71% accepted. In 2011, 12 master's awarded. *Degree requirements:* For master's, comprehensive exam, thesis optional. *Entrance requirements:* For master's, GRE General Test or MAT. Additional exam requirements/recommendations for international students: Required—TOEFL (minimum score 525 paper-based; 195 computer-based; 71 iBT) or IELTS (minimum score 6). *Application deadline:* For fall admission, 6/1 for domestic and international students. Applications are processed on a rolling basis. Application fee: $25 ($30 for international students). Electronic applications accepted. *Expenses:* Tuition, state resident: full-time $10,008. Tuition, nonresident: full-time $25,056. *Financial support:* In 2011–12, 4 students received support. Tuition waivers available. Support available to part-time students. Financial award application deadline: 5/1. *Faculty research:* Unmanned vehicles, air traffic control. *Unit head:* Dr. Ron Ferrara, Interim Chair, 615-898-2788, Fax: 615-904-8273, E-mail: ron.ferrara@mtsu.edu. *Application contact:* Dr. Michael D. Allen, Dean and Vice Provost for Research, 615-898-2840, Fax: 615-904-8020, E-mail: michael.allen@mtsu.edu.

Mississippi State University, Bagley College of Engineering, Department of Aerospace Engineering, Mississippi State, MS 39762. Offers aerospace engineering (MS); engineering (PhD), including aerospace engineering. Part-time programs available. *Faculty:* 13 full-time (2 women), 4 part-time/adjunct (0 women). *Students:* 26 full-time (3 women), 8 part-time (0 women); includes 3 minority (2 Black or African American, non-Hispanic/Latino; 1 Asian, non-Hispanic/Latino), 13 international. Average age 26. 34 applicants, 47% accepted, 10 enrolled. In 2011, 8 master's, 4 doctorates awarded. *Degree requirements:* For master's, comprehensive exam, thesis; for doctorate, comprehensive exam, thesis/dissertation. *Entrance requirements:* For master's, GRE, bachelor's degree in engineering; for doctorate, GRE, bachelor's or master's degree in engineering. Additional exam requirements/recommendations for international students: Required—TOEFL (minimum score 550 paper-based; 213 computer-based; 79 iBT); Recommended—IELTS (minimum score 6.5). *Application deadline:* For fall admission, 7/1 for domestic students, 5/1 for international students; for spring admission, 11/1 for domestic students, 9/1 for international students. Applications are processed on a rolling basis. Application fee: $40. Electronic applications accepted. *Expenses:* Tuition, state resident: full-time $5805; part-time $322.50 per credit hour. Tuition, nonresident: full-time $14,670; part-time $815 per credit hour. *Financial support:* In 2011–12, 8 research assistantships with partial tuition reimbursements (averaging $14,724 per year), 4 teaching assistantships with partial tuition reimbursements (averaging $14,356 per year) were awarded; Federal Work-Study, institutionally sponsored loans, and unspecified assistantships also available. Financial award application deadline: 4/1; financial award applicants required to submit FAFSA. *Faculty research:* Computational fluid dynamics, flight mechanics, aerodynamics, composite structures, prototype development. *Total annual research expenditures:* $3.7 million. *Unit head:* Dr. Pasquale J. Cinnella, Department Head, 662-325-3623, Fax: 662-325-7730, E-mail: cinnella@ae.msstate.edu. *Application contact:* Dr. Mark Janus, Professor and Graduate Coordinator, 662-325-2463, Fax: 662-325-7730, E-mail: mark@hpc.msstate.edu. Web site: http://www.ae.msstate.edu/.

Missouri University of Science and Technology, Graduate School, Department of Mechanical and Aerospace Engineering, Rolla, MO 65409. Offers aerospace engineering (MS, PhD); mechanical engineering (MS, DE, PhD). Part-time and evening/weekend programs available. Terminal master's awarded for partial completion of doctoral program. *Degree requirements:* For master's, thesis optional; for doctorate, comprehensive exam, thesis/dissertation. *Entrance requirements:* For master's, GRE General Test (minimum score 1100 verbal and quantitative, writing 3.5), minimum GPA of 3.0; for doctorate, GRE General Test (minimum score: verbal and quantitative 1100, writing 3.5), minimum GPA of 3.5. Additional exam requirements/recommendations for international students: Required—TOEFL. Electronic applications accepted. *Faculty research:* Dynamics and controls, acoustics, computational fluid dynamics, space mechanics, hypersonics.

Naval Postgraduate School, Departments and Academic Groups, Department of Defense Analysis, Monterey, CA 93943. Offers command and control (MS); communications (MS); defense analysis (MS), including astronautics; financial management (MS); information operations (MS); irregular warfare (MS); national security affairs (MS); operations analysis (MS); special operations (MA, MS), including command and control (MS), communications (MS), financial management (MS), information operations (MS), irregular warfare (MS), national security affairs, operations analysis (MS), tactile missiles (MS), terrorist operations and financing (MS); tactile missiles (MS); terrorist operations and financing (MS). Program only open to commissioned officers of the United States and friendly nations and selected United States federal civilian employees. Part-time programs available. *Faculty:* 26 full-time (10 women), 2 part-time/adjunct (both women). *Students:* 182 full-time (5 women); includes 18 minority (5 Black or African American, non-Hispanic/Latino; 1 American Indian or Alaska Native, non-Hispanic/Latino; 5 Asian, non-Hispanic/Latino; 7 Hispanic/Latino), 36 international. Average age 38. In 2011, 98 master's awarded. *Degree requirements:* For master's, thesis. *Faculty research:* CTF Global Ecco Project, long-term strategy seminar: SOF 2030, Afghanistan endgames, core lab Philippines project, DMDC data vulnerability. *Total annual research expenditures:* $3.4 million. *Unit head:* Prof. John Arquilla, Department Chair, 831-656-3540, E-mail: jarquilla@nps.edu. Web site: http://nps.edu/Academics/Schools/GSOIS/Departments/DA/index.html.

Naval Postgraduate School, Departments and Academic Groups, Department of Mechanical and Aerospace Engineering, Monterey, CA 93943. Offers astronautical engineer (AstE); astronautical engineering (MS); engineering science (MS), including astronautical engineering, mechanical engineering; mechanical and aerospace engineering (PhD); mechanical engineering (MS). Program only open to commissioned officers of the United States and friendly nations and selected United States federal civilian employees. *Accreditation:* ABET (one or more programs are accredited). Part-time programs available. Postbaccalaureate distance learning degree programs offered. *Faculty:* 30 full-time (3 women), 2 part-time/adjunct (1 woman). *Students:* 81 full-time (10 women), 88 part-time (3 women); includes 16 minority (5 Black or African American, non-Hispanic/Latino; 1 American Indian or Alaska Native, non-Hispanic/Latino; 3 Asian, non-Hispanic/Latino; 7 Hispanic/Latino), 14 international. Average age 35. In 2011, 29 master's, 7 other advanced degrees awarded. *Degree requirements:* For master's, thesis (for some programs), capstone or research/dissertation paper (for some programs); for doctorate, thesis/dissertation; for AstE, thesis. *Faculty research:* Sensors and actuators, new materials and methods, mechanics of materials, laser and material interaction, energy harvesting and storage. *Total annual research expenditures:* $8.2 million. *Unit head:* Prof. Knox Millsaps, Department Chairman, 831-656-3382, E-mail: millsaps@nps.edu. Web site: http://www.nps.edu/Academics/GSEAS/MAE/Index.asp.

Naval Postgraduate School, Departments and Academic Groups, Space Systems Academic Group, Monterey, CA 93943. Offers applied physics (MS); astronautical engineering (MS); computer science (MS); electrical engineering (MS); mechanical engineering (MS); space systems (Engr); space systems operations (MS). Program only open to commissioned officers of the United States and friendly nations and selected United States federal civilian employees. Part-time programs available. *Faculty:* 5 full-time, 5 part-time/adjunct (2 women). *Students:* 37 full-time (2 women), 14 part-time; includes 11 minority (5 Black or African American, non-Hispanic/Latino; 2 Asian, non-Hispanic/Latino; 4 Hispanic/Latino), 1 international. Average age 33. In 2011, 20 master's awarded. *Degree requirements:* For master's and Engr, thesis; for doctorate, thesis/dissertation. *Faculty research:* Militaryapplications for space; space reconnaissance and remote sensing; radiation-hardened electronics for space; design, construction and operations of small satellites; satellite communications systems. *Total annual research expenditures:* $2 million. *Unit head:* Dr. Rudy Panholzer, Chairman, 831-656-2154. Web site: http://www.nps.edu/Academics/Schools/GSEAS/Departments/SpaceSystems/.

North Carolina State University, Graduate School, College of Engineering, Department of Mechanical and Aerospace Engineering, Program in Aerospace Engineering, Raleigh, NC 27695. Offers MS, PhD. Postbaccalaureate distance learning degree programs offered (no on-campus study). *Degree requirements:* For master's, thesis (for some programs), oral exam; for doctorate, thesis/dissertation, oral and preliminary exams. *Entrance requirements:* For master's and doctorate, GRE General Test. Additional exam requirements/recommendations for international students: Required—TOEFL (minimum score 550 paper-based; 213 computer-based). Electronic applications accepted. *Faculty research:* Aerodynamics, computational fluid dynamics, flight research, smart structures, propulsion.

Old Dominion University, Frank Batten College of Engineering and Technology, Programs in Aerospace Engineering, Norfolk, VA 23529. Offers ME, MS, D Eng, PhD. Part-time and evening/weekend programs available. Postbaccalaureate distance learning degree programs offered (no on-campus study). *Faculty:* 22 full-time (0 women). *Students:* 35 full-time (4 women), 34 part-time (2 women); includes 7 minority (1 Black or African American, non-Hispanic/Latino; 3 Asian, non-Hispanic/Latino; 2 Hispanic/Latino; 1 Two or more races, non-Hispanic/Latino), 25 international. Average age 28. 50 applicants, 60% accepted, 10 enrolled. In 2011, 11 master's, 8 doctorates awarded. *Degree requirements:* For master's, comprehensive exam, thesis (MS), exam/project (ME); for doctorate, thesis/dissertation, candidacy exam, proposal, exam. *Entrance requirements:* For master's, GRE, minimum GPA of 3.0; for doctorate, GRE, minimum GPA of 3.5. Additional exam requirements/recommendations for international students: Required—TOEFL (minimum score 550 paper-based; 230 computer-based; 79 iBT). *Application deadline:* For fall admission, 7/1 priority date for domestic students, 5/1 for international students; for spring admission, 10/1 priority date for domestic students, 9/1 for international students. Applications are processed on a rolling basis. Application fee: $50. Electronic applications accepted. *Expenses:* Tuition, state resident: full-time $9096; part-time $379 per credit. Tuition, nonresident: full-time $23,064; part-time $961 per credit. *Required fees:* $127 per semester. One-time fee: $50. *Financial support:* In 2011–12, 4 students received support, including 3 fellowships with full and partial tuition reimbursements available (averaging $16,000 per year), 30 research assistantships with full and partial tuition reimbursements available (averaging $16,000 per year); career-related internships or fieldwork, scholarships/grants, and unspecified assistantships also available. Financial award application deadline: 2/15; financial award applicants required to submit FAFSA. *Faculty research:* Computational fluid dynamics, experimental fluid dynamics, structural mechanics, dynamics and control, maglev, microfluidics. *Total annual research expenditures:* $1.6 million. *Unit head:* Dr. Colin Britcher, Chair, 757-683-4916, Fax: 757-683-3200, E-mail: britcher@aero.odu.edu. *Application contact:* Dr. Colin Britcher, Graduate Program Director, 757-683-4916, Fax: 757-683-3200, E-mail: britcher@aero.odu.edu. Web site: http://www.eng.odu.edu/mae.

Penn State University Park, Graduate School, College of Engineering, Department of Aerospace Engineering, State College, University Park, PA 16802-1503. Offers M Eng, MS, PhD. *Unit head:* Dr. David N. Wormley, Dean, 814-865-7537, Fax: 814-865-8767, E-mail: dnw2@engr.psu.edu. *Application contact:* Cynthia E. Nicosia, Director, Graduate Enrollment Services, 814-865-1834, E-mail: cey1@psu.edu. Web site: http://www.engr.psu.edu/e3i/a_aerospace.htm.

Polytechnic Institute of NYU, Long Island Graduate Center, Graduate Programs, Department of Mechanical and Aerospace Engineering, Melville, NY 11747. Offers aeronautics and astronautics (MS); industrial engineering (MS); manufacturing engineering (MS); mechanical engineering (MS). Part-time and evening/weekend programs available. *Students:* 1 full-time (0 women). Average age 28. In 2011, 2 master's awarded. *Degree requirements:* For master's, comprehensive exam (for some programs), thesis (for some programs). *Entrance requirements:* Additional exam requirements/recommendations for international students: Required—TOEFL (minimum score 550 paper-based; 213 computer-based; 80 iBT); Recommended—IELTS (minimum score 6.5). *Application deadline:* For fall admission, 7/31 priority date for domestic students, 4/30 for international students; for spring admission, 12/31 priority date for domestic students, 11/30 for international students. Applications are processed on a rolling basis. Application fee: $75. Electronic applications accepted. *Financial support:* In 2011–12, 16 fellowships with tuition reimbursements (averaging $1,394 per year) were awarded; research assistantships with tuition reimbursements, institutionally sponsored loans, scholarships/grants, and unspecified assistantships also available. Support available to part-time students. Financial award applicants required to submit FAFSA. *Faculty research:* UV filter, fuel efficient hydrodynamic containment for gas core fission, turbulent boundary layer research. *Unit head:* Dr. George Vradis, Department Head, 718-260-3875, E-mail: gvradis@duke.poly.edu. *Application contact:* JeanCarlo Bonilla, Director of Graduate Enrollment Management, 718-260-3182, Fax: 718-260-3624, E-mail: gradinfo@poly.edu.

Princeton University, Graduate School, School of Engineering and Applied Science, Department of Mechanical and Aerospace Engineering, Princeton, NJ 08544. Offers M Eng, MSE, PhD. Terminal master's awarded for partial completion of doctoral program. *Degree requirements:* For master's, thesis (MSE); for doctorate, thesis/dissertation, general exam. *Entrance requirements:* For master's, GRE General Test, 3 letters of recommendation; for doctorate, GRE General Test, official transcript(s), 3 letters of recommendation, personal statement. Additional exam requirements/recommendations for international students: Required—TOEFL. Electronic applications accepted. *Faculty research:* Bioengineering and bio-mechanics; combustion, energy conversion, and climate; fluid mechanics, dynamics, and control systems; lasers and applied physics; materials and mechanical systems.

Purdue University, College of Engineering, School of Aeronautics and Astronautics Engineering, West Lafayette, IN 47907. Offers MS, MSAAE, MSE, PhD. Part-time programs available. Postbaccalaureate distance learning degree programs offered (no on-campus study). Terminal master's awarded for partial completion of doctoral program. *Entrance requirements:* For master's, GRE General Test, minimum GPA of 3.2; for doctorate, GRE General Test, minimum GPA of 3.5. Additional exam requirements/recommendations for international students: Required—TOEFL (minimum score 550 paper-based; 213 computer-based; 77 iBT), IELTS (minimum score 6.5); Recommended—TWE. Electronic applications accepted. *Faculty research:* Structures and materials, propulsion, aerodynamics, dynamics and control.

Rensselaer Polytechnic Institute, Graduate School, School of Engineering, Program in Aerospace Engineering, Troy, NY 12180-3590. Offers M Eng, MS, PhD. Part-time programs available. *Degree requirements:* For master's, thesis (for some programs); for doctorate, thesis/dissertation. *Entrance requirements:* For master's and doctorate, GRE. Additional exam requirements/recommendations for international students: Required—TOEFL (minimum score 600 paper-based; 250 computer-based; 100 iBT); Recommended—IELTS. Electronic applications accepted. *Faculty research:* Vehicular performance and flight mechanics, gas dynamics, aerodynamics, structural dynamics, advanced propulsion, fluids.

Rutgers, The State University of New Jersey, New Brunswick, Graduate School-New Brunswick, Program in Mechanical and Aerospace Engineering, Piscataway, NJ 08854-8097. Offers design and control (MS, PhD); fluid mechanics (MS, PhD); solid mechanics (MS, PhD); thermal sciences (MS, PhD). Part-time and evening/weekend programs available. *Degree requirements:* For master's, thesis (for some programs); for doctorate, thesis/dissertation. *Entrance requirements:* For master's, GRE General Test, BS in mechanical/aerospace engineering or related field; for doctorate, GRE General Test, MS in mechanical/aerospace engineering or related field. Additional exam requirements/recommendations for international students: Required—TOEFL. Electronic applications accepted. *Faculty research:* Combustion, propulsion, thermal transport, crystal plasticity, optimization, fabrication, nanoidentation.

San Diego State University, Graduate and Research Affairs, College of Engineering, Department of Aerospace Engineering and Engineering Mechanics, San Diego, CA 92182. Offers aerospace engineering (MS); engineering mechanics (MS); engineering sciences and applied mechanics (PhD); flight dynamics (MS); fluid dynamics (MS). PhD offered jointly with University of California, San Diego and Department of Mechanical Engineering. Terminal master's awarded for partial completion of doctoral program. *Degree requirements:* For master's, comprehensive exam (for some programs), thesis (for some programs); for doctorate, thesis/dissertation. *Entrance requirements:* For master's, GRE General Test; for doctorate, GRE, 3 letters of recommendation. Additional exam requirements/recommendations for international students: Required—TOEFL. Electronic applications accepted. *Faculty research:* Organized structures in post-stall flow over wings/three dimensional separated flow, airfoil growth effect, probabilities, structural mechanics.

San Jose State University, Graduate Studies and Research, Charles W. Davidson College of Engineering, Department of Mechanical and Aerospace Engineering, Program in Aerospace Engineering, San Jose, CA 95192-0001. Offers MS. *Entrance requirements:* For master's, GRE. Electronic applications accepted.

Stanford University, School of Engineering, Department of Aeronautics and Astronautics, Stanford, CA 94305-9991. Offers MS, PhD, Eng. Terminal master's awarded for partial completion of doctoral program. *Degree requirements:* For doctorate, thesis/dissertation; for Eng, thesis. *Entrance requirements:* For master's and Eng, GRE General Test, GRE Subject Test; for doctorate, GRE General Test, GRE Engineering Subject Test. Additional exam requirements/recommendations for international students: Required—TOEFL. Electronic applications accepted. *Expenses: Tuition:* Full-time $40,050; part-time $890 per credit.

Stevens Institute of Technology, Graduate School, School of Systems and Enterprises, Program in Space Systems Engineering, Hoboken, NJ 07030. Offers M Eng, Certificate.

Syracuse University, L. C. Smith College of Engineering and Computer Science, Program in Mechanical and Aerospace Engineering, Syracuse, NY 13244. Offers MS, PhD. *Students:* 112 full-time (19 women), 12 part-time (1 woman); includes 4 minority (1 Black or African American, non-Hispanic/Latino; 2 Asian, non-Hispanic/Latino; 1 Hispanic/Latino), 100 international. Average age 25. 213 applicants, 46% accepted, 49 enrolled. In 2011, 28 master's, 7 doctorates awarded. *Degree requirements:* For master's, project or thesis; for doctorate, thesis/dissertation. *Entrance requirements:* For master's and doctorate, GRE General Test. Additional exam requirements/recommendations for international students: Required—TOEFL (minimum score 100 iBT). *Application deadline:* For fall admission, 7/1 priority date for domestic students, 6/1 for international students. Applications are processed on a rolling basis. Application fee: $75. Electronic applications accepted. *Expenses: Tuition:* Part-time $1206 per credit. *Financial support:* Fellowships with full tuition reimbursements, research assistantships with full and partial tuition reimbursements, teaching assistantships with full and partial tuition reimbursements, scholarships/grants, and tuition waivers (partial) available. Financial award application deadline: 1/1. *Faculty research:* Solid mechanics and materials, fluid mechanics, thermal sciences, controls and robotics. *Unit head:* Dr. Achille Messac, Chair, 315-443-2341, Fax: 315-443-9099, E-mail: messac@syr.edu. *Application contact:* Kathy Datthyn-Madigan, Information Contact, 315-443-4367, E-mail: kjdatthy@syr.edu. Web site: http://www.ecs.syr.edu/academic/mechaero_engineering/.

Texas A&M University, College of Engineering, Department of Aerospace Engineering, College Station, TX 77843. Offers M Eng, MS, PhD. *Faculty:* 27. *Students:* 125 full-time (16 women), 10 part-time (2 women); includes 11 minority (1 Black or African American, non-Hispanic/Latino; 2 Asian, non-Hispanic/Latino; 6 Hispanic/Latino; 2 Two or more races, non-Hispanic/Latino), 47 international. Average age 27. In 2011, 20 master's, 13 doctorates awarded. *Degree requirements:* For master's, thesis (MS); for doctorate, thesis/dissertation. *Entrance requirements:* For master's and doctorate, GRE General Test. Additional exam requirements/recommendations for international students: Required—TOEFL. *Application deadline:* For fall admission, 1/15 priority date for domestic students; for spring admission, 9/15 for domestic students. Applications are processed on a rolling basis. Application fee: $50 ($75 for international students). Electronic applications accepted. *Expenses:* Tuition, state resident: full-time $5437; part-time $226.55 per credit hour. Tuition, nonresident: full-time $12,949; part-time $539.55 per credit hour. *Required fees:* $2741. *Financial support:* Fellowships, research assistantships, and teaching assistantships available. Financial award application deadline: 3/1; financial award applicants required to submit FAFSA. *Faculty research:* Materials and structures, aerodynamics and CFD, flight dynamics and control. *Unit head:* Dr. Walter Haisler, Head, 979-854-1640, E-mail: haisler@tamu.edu. *Application contact:* Karen Knabe, Administrative Coordinator, Graduate Programs, 979-845-5520, Fax: 979-845-6051, E-mail: gradadvising@aero.tamu.edu. Web site: http://aero.tamu.edu.

Université Laval, Faculty of Sciences and Engineering, Department of Mechanical Engineering, Program in Aerospace Engineering, Québec, QC G1K 7P4, Canada. Offers M Sc. Program offered jointly with Concordia University, École Polytechnique de Montréal, McGill University, and Université de Sherbrooke. Part-time programs available. *Entrance requirements:* For master's, knowledge of French and English. Electronic applications accepted.

University at Buffalo, the State University of New York, Graduate School, School of Engineering and Applied Sciences, Department of Mechanical and Aerospace Engineering, Buffalo, NY 14260. Offers aerospace engineering (MS, PhD); mechanical engineering (MS, PhD). Part-time programs available. *Faculty:* 28 full-time (4 women), 8 part-time/adjunct (0 women). *Students:* 164 full-time (16 women), 53 part-time (4 women); includes 10 minority (3 Black or African American, non-Hispanic/Latino; 1 American Indian or Alaska Native, non-Hispanic/Latino; 3 Asian, non-Hispanic/Latino; 3 Hispanic/Latino), 114 international. Average age 26. 842 applicants, 8% accepted, 63 enrolled. In 2011, 92 master's, 7 doctorates awarded. Terminal master's awarded for partial completion of doctoral program. *Degree requirements:* For master's, comprehensive exam, project or thesis; for doctorate, thesis/dissertation. *Entrance requirements:* For master's and doctorate, GRE General Test, GRE Subject Test. Additional exam requirements/recommendations for international students: Required—TOEFL (minimum score 79 iBT). *Application deadline:* For fall admission, 1/15 for domestic and international students; for spring admission, 9/15 for domestic and international students. Applications are processed on a rolling basis. Application fee: $75. *Financial support:* In 2011–12, 73 students received support, including 3 fellowships with full tuition reimbursements available (averaging $28,900 per year), 24 research assistantships with full tuition reimbursements available (averaging $26,000 per year), 31 teaching assistantships with full tuition reimbursements available (averaging $20,900 per year); Federal Work-Study, institutionally sponsored loans, tuition waivers (partial), and unspecified assistantships also available. Financial award application deadline: 1/15; financial award applicants required to submit FAFSA. *Faculty research:* Fluid and thermal sciences, systems and design, mechanics and materials. *Total annual research expenditures:* $4.6 million. *Unit head:* Dr. Gary Dargush, Chair, 716-645-2593, Fax: 716-645-2883, E-mail: gdargush@buffalo.edu. *Application contact:* Dr. John Crassidis, Director of Graduate Studies, 716-645-1426, Fax: 716-645-3875, E-mail: johnc@.buffalo.edu. Web site: http://www.mae.buffalo.edu/.

The University of Alabama, Graduate School, College of Engineering, Department of Aerospace Engineering and Mechanics, Tuscaloosa, AL 35487. Offers aerospace engineering (MAE); engineering science and mechanics (MES, PhD). Part-time programs available. Postbaccalaureate distance learning degree programs offered (no on-campus study). *Faculty:* 14 full-time (1 woman). *Students:* 22 full-time (4 women), 33 part-time (7 women); includes 3 minority (all Hispanic/Latino), 13 international. Average age 29. 41 applicants, 73% accepted, 15 enrolled. In 2011, 14 degrees awarded. Terminal master's awarded for partial completion of doctoral program. *Degree requirements:* For master's, comprehensive exam (for some programs), thesis (for some programs); for doctorate, comprehensive exam, thesis/dissertation, 1-year residency. *Entrance requirements:* For master's and doctorate, GRE, minimum undergraduate GPA of 3.0. Additional exam requirements/recommendations for international students: Required—TOEFL (minimum score 550 paper-based). *Application deadline:* For fall admission, 7/1 priority date for domestic students, 1/15 for international students; for spring admission, 11/1 priority date for domestic students, 6/1 for international students. Applications are processed on a rolling basis. Application fee: $50 ($60 for international students). Electronic applications accepted. *Expenses:* Tuition, state resident: full-time $8600. Tuition, nonresident: full-time $21,900. *Financial support:* In 2011–12, 18 students received support, including fellowships with full tuition reimbursements available (averaging $20,000 per year), research assistantships with full tuition reimbursements available (averaging $18,375 per year), teaching assistantships with full tuition reimbursements available (averaging $18,375 per year); Federal Work-Study, institutionally sponsored loans, scholarships/grants, health care benefits, and unspecified assistantships also available. Financial award application deadline: 2/15. *Faculty research:* Intelligent computer systems, genetic algorithms, neural networks, impact and penetration mechanics, spacecraft dynamics and controls. *Total annual research expenditures:* $1.5 million. *Unit head:* Dr. Stanley E. Jones, Interim Head/Professor, 205-348-7242, Fax: 205-348-7240, E-mail: sejones@eng.ua.edu. *Application contact:* Dr. John E. Jackson, Professor, 205-348-7306, Fax: 208-348-7240, E-mail: johnjackson@eng.ua.edu. Web site: http://aem.eng.ua.edu/.

The University of Alabama in Huntsville, School of Graduate Studies, College of Engineering, Department of Mechanical and Aerospace Engineering, Huntsville, AL 35899. Offers aerospace engineering (MSE), including aerospace engineering, missile systems engineering, rotorcraft systems engineering; aerospace systems engineering (MS, PhD); mechanical engineering (MSE, PhD). Part-time and evening/weekend programs available. *Faculty:* 19 full-time (0 women), 6 part-time/adjunct (0 women). *Students:* 62 full-time (10 women), 120 part-time (18 women); includes 17 minority (6 Black or African American, non-Hispanic/Latino; 1 American Indian or Alaska Native, non-Hispanic/Latino; 6 Asian, non-Hispanic/Latino; 4 Hispanic/Latino), 16 international. Average age 30. 124 applicants, 62% accepted, 52 enrolled. In 2011, 41 master's, 2 doctorates awarded. *Degree requirements:* For master's, comprehensive exam, thesis or alternative, oral and written exams; for doctorate, comprehensive exam, thesis/dissertation, oral and written exams. *Entrance requirements:* For master's, GRE General Test, BSE, minimum GPA of 3.0; for doctorate, GRE General Test, minimum GPA of 3.0. Additional exam requirements/recommendations for international students: Required—TOEFL (minimum score 500 paper-based; 173 computer-based; 62 iBT). *Application deadline:* For fall admission, 7/15 for domestic students, 4/1 for international students; for spring admission, 1/30 for domestic students, 9/1 for international students. Applications are processed on a rolling basis. Application fee: $40 ($50 for international students). Electronic applications accepted. *Expenses:* Tuition, state resident: full-time $7830; part-time $473.50 per credit. Tuition, nonresident: full-time $18,748; part-time $1128.33 per credit. Tuition and fees vary according to course load and program. *Financial support:* In 2011–12, 46 students received support, including 29 research assistantships with full tuition reimbursements available (averaging $12,881 per year), 17 teaching assistantships with full tuition reimbursements available (averaging $11,141 per year); career-related internships or fieldwork, Federal Work-Study, institutionally sponsored loans, scholarships/grants, health care benefits, and unspecified assistantships also available. Support available to part-time students. Financial award application deadline: 4/1; financial award applicants required to submit FAFSA. *Faculty research:* Combustion, fluid dynamics, materials and structures, propulsion, laser diagnostics. *Total annual research expenditures:* $19.7 million. *Unit head:* Dr. Keith Hollingsworth, Chair, 256-824-6154, Fax: 256-824-6758, E-mail: keith.hollingsworth@uah.edu. *Application contact:* Kim Gray, Graduate Studies Admissions Coordinator, 256-824-6002, Fax: 256-824-6405, E-mail: deangrad@uah.edu. Web site: http://www.mae.uah.edu/graduate.shtml.

The University of Arizona, College of Engineering, Department of Aerospace and Mechanical Engineering, Program in Aerospace Engineering, Tucson, AZ 85721. Offers MS, PhD. Part-time programs available. *Faculty:* 20 full-time (0 women), 2 part-time/adjunct (0 women). *Students:* 27 full-time (3 women), 6 part-time (0 women); includes 2 minority (both Two or more races, non-Hispanic/Latino), 15 international. Average age 27. 37 applicants, 68% accepted, 17 enrolled. In 2011, 8 master's, 4 doctorates awarded. *Degree requirements:* For master's, thesis or alternative; for doctorate, thesis/dissertation. *Entrance requirements:* For master's and doctorate, GRE General Test, minimum GPA of 3.25. Additional exam requirements/recommendations for international students: Required—TOEFL (minimum score 550 paper-based; 213 computer-based; 79 iBT). *Application deadline:* For fall admission, 6/1 for domestic students, 12/1 for international students; for spring admission, 10/1 for domestic students, 6/1 for international students. Applications are processed on a rolling basis. Application fee: $75. Electronic applications accepted. *Expenses:* Tuition, state resident: full-time $10,840. Tuition, nonresident: full-time $25,802. *Financial support:* Research assistantships, teaching assistantships, and unspecified assistantships available. *Faculty research:* Fluid mechanics, structures, computer-aided design, stability and control, combustion. *Unit head:* Dr. Ara Arabyan, Interim Department Head, 520-621-2116, Fax: 520-621-8191, E-mail: arabyan@email.arizona.edu. *Application contact:* Barbara Heefner, Graduate Secretary, 520-621-4692, Fax: 520-621-8191, E-mail: heefner@email.arizona.edu. Web site: http://www.ame.arizona.edu/graduates/.

University of California, Davis, College of Engineering, Program in Mechanical and Aeronautical Engineering, Davis, CA 95616. Offers aeronautical engineering (M Engr, MS, D Engr, PhD, Certificate); mechanical engineering (M Engr, MS, D Engr, PhD, Certificate); M Engr/MBA. *Degree requirements:* For master's, comprehensive exam (for some programs), thesis (for some programs); for doctorate, thesis/dissertation. *Entrance requirements:* For master's and doctorate, GRE General Test, minimum GPA of 3.0. Additional exam requirements/recommendations for international students: Required—TOEFL (minimum score 550 paper-based; 213 computer-based). Electronic applications accepted.

University of California, Irvine, School of Engineering, Department of Mechanical and Aerospace Engineering, Irvine, CA 92697. Offers MS, PhD. Part-time programs available. *Students:* 111 full-time (16 women), 6 part-time (0 women); includes 31 minority (18 Asian, non-Hispanic/Latino; 11 Hispanic/Latino; 2 Two or more races, non-Hispanic/Latino), 49 international. Average age 27. 448 applicants, 25% accepted, 30 enrolled. In 2011, 36 master's, 14 doctorates awarded. Terminal master's awarded for partial completion of doctoral program. *Degree requirements:* For doctorate, thesis/dissertation. *Entrance requirements:* For master's and doctorate, GRE General Test, minimum GPA of 3.0, 3 letters of recommendation. Additional exam requirements/recommendations for international students: Required—TOEFL (minimum score 550 paper-based; 213 computer-based). *Application deadline:* For fall admission, 1/15 priority date for domestic students, 1/15 for international students. Applications are processed on a rolling basis. Application fee: $80 ($100 for international students). Electronic applications accepted. *Financial support:* Fellowships with tuition reimbursements, research assistantships with full tuition reimbursements, teaching assistantships with tuition reimbursements, institutionally sponsored loans, traineeships, health care benefits, and unspecified assistantships available. Financial award application deadline: 3/1; financial award applicants required to submit FAFSA. *Faculty research:* Thermal and fluid sciences, combustion and propulsion, control systems, robotics, lightweight structures. *Unit head:* Prof. Derek Dunn-Rankin, Chair, 949-824-8745, Fax: 949-824-8585, E-mail: ddunnran@uci.edu. *Application contact:* Lousie Yeager, Graduate Coordinator, 949-824-7984, Fax: 949-824-8585, E-mail: lyeager@uci.edu. Web site: http://mae.eng.uci.edu/.

University of California, Los Angeles, Graduate Division, Henry Samueli School of Engineering and Applied Science, Department of Mechanical and Aerospace Engineering, Program in Aerospace Engineering, Los Angeles, CA 90095-1597. Offers MS, PhD. *Faculty:* 29 full-time (2 women), 6 part-time/adjunct. *Students:* 67 full-time (8 women); includes 31 minority (2 Black or African American, non-Hispanic/Latino; 19 Asian, non-Hispanic/Latino; 8 Hispanic/Latino; 1 Native Hawaiian or other Pacific Islander, non-Hispanic/Latino; 1 Two or more races, non-Hispanic/Latino), 5 international. 127 applicants, 55% accepted, 27 enrolled. In 2011, 17 master's, 4 doctorates awarded. *Degree requirements:* For master's, comprehensive exam or thesis; for doctorate, thesis/dissertation, qualifying exams. *Entrance requirements:* For master's, GRE General Test, minimum GPA of 3.0; for doctorate, GRE General Test, minimum GPA of 3.25. Additional exam requirements/recommendations for international students: Required—TOEFL (minimum score 560 paper-based; 87 iBT). *Application deadline:* For fall admission, 12/15 for domestic and international students; for winter admission, 10/1 for domestic students; for spring admission, 12/31 for domestic students. Application fee: $80 ($100 for international students). Electronic applications accepted. *Financial support:* In 2011–12, 126 fellowships, 273 research assistantships, 93 teaching assistantships were awarded; Federal Work-Study, institutionally sponsored loans, and tuition waivers (full and partial) also available. Financial award application deadline: 12/15; financial award applicants required to submit FAFSA. *Faculty research:* Dynamics fluid mechanics, heat and mass transfer, manufacturing and design, nanoelectromechanical/microelectromechanical systems (NEMS/MEMS), structural and solid mechanics, systems and control. *Total annual research expenditures:* $15 million. *Unit head:* Dr. Tsu-Chin Tsao, Chair, 310-206-2819, E-mail: ttsao@seas.ucla.edu. *Application contact:* Angie Castillo, Student Affairs Officer, 310-825-7793, Fax: 310-206-4830, E-mail: angie@ea.ucla.edu. Web site: http://www.mae.ucla.edu/.

University of California, San Diego, Office of Graduate Studies, Department of Mechanical and Aerospace Engineering, Program in Aerospace Engineering, La Jolla, CA 92093. Offers MS, PhD. Part-time programs available. *Degree requirements:* For master's, comprehensive exam or thesis; for doctorate, thesis/dissertation, qualifying exam. *Entrance requirements:* For master's and doctorate, GRE General Test, minimum

GPA of 3.0. Additional exam requirements/recommendations for international students: Required—TOEFL. *Faculty research:* Aerospace structures, turbulence, gas dynamics and combustion.

University of Central Florida, College of Engineering and Computer Science, Department of Mechanical, Materials, and Aerospace Engineering, Program in Aerospace Engineering, Orlando, FL 32816. Offers MSAE. *Students:* 21 full-time (3 women), 13 part-time (1 woman); includes 7 minority (1 Black or African American, non-Hispanic/Latino; 5 Hispanic/Latino; 1 Two or more races, non-Hispanic/Latino), 2 international. Average age 25. 39 applicants, 82% accepted, 17 enrolled. In 2011, 8 master's awarded. *Degree requirements:* For master's, thesis or alternative. *Application deadline:* For fall admission, 7/15 priority date for domestic students; for spring admission, 12/1 priority date for domestic students. Application fee: $30. Electronic applications accepted. *Expenses:* Tuition, state resident: part-time $277.08 per credit hour. Tuition, nonresident: part-time $277.08 per credit hour. Part-time tuition and fees vary according to degree level and program. *Financial support:* In 2011–12, 7 students received support, including 8 research assistantships (averaging $7,100 per year), 2 teaching assistantships (averaging $11,000 per year); career-related internships or fieldwork, institutionally sponsored loans, scholarships/grants, tuition waivers (partial), and unspecified assistantships also available. *Unit head:* Dr. Suhada Jayasuriya, Chair, 407-823-5792, Fax: 407-823-0208, E-mail: suhada@ucf.edu. *Application contact:* Barbara Rodriguez, Director, Admissions and Registration, 407-823-2766, Fax: 407-823-6442, E-mail: gradadmissions@ucf.edu. Web site: http://mmae.ucf.edu/.

University of Central Missouri, The Graduate School, College of Science and Technology, Warrensburg, MO 64093. Offers applied mathematics (MS); aviation safety (MS); biology (MS); computer science (MS); environmental studies (MA); industrial management (MS); mathematics (MS); technology (MS); technology management (PhD). PhD is offered jointly with Indiana State University. Part-time programs available. Postbaccalaureate distance learning degree programs offered. *Entrance requirements:* Additional exam requirements/recommendations for international students: Required—TOEFL (minimum score 550 paper-based; 79 computer-based). Electronic applications accepted.

University of Cincinnati, Graduate School, College of Engineering and Applied Science, Department of Aerospace Engineering and Engineering Mechanics, Cincinnati, OH 45221. Offers MS, PhD. Part-time programs available. Terminal master's awarded for partial completion of doctoral program. *Degree requirements:* For master's, project or thesis; for doctorate, thesis/dissertation. *Entrance requirements:* For master's and doctorate, GRE General Test. Additional exam requirements/recommendations for international students: Required—TOEFL (minimum score 550 paper-based; 213 computer-based). Electronic applications accepted. *Faculty research:* Computational fluid mechanics/propulsion, large space structures, dynamics and guidance of VTOL vehicles.

University of Colorado at Colorado Springs, College of Engineering and Applied Science, Department of Mechanical and Aerospace Engineering, Colorado Springs, CO 80933-7150. Offers engineering management (ME); information operations (ME); manufacturing (ME); mechanical engineering (MS); software engineering (ME); space operations (ME); space systems (MS). Part-time and evening/weekend programs available. *Faculty:* 11 full-time (2 women). *Students:* 48 full-time (14 women), 44 part-time (11 women); includes 15 minority (3 Black or African American, non-Hispanic/Latino; 6 Asian, non-Hispanic/Latino; 5 Hispanic/Latino; 1 Two or more races, non-Hispanic/Latino), 3 international. Average age 33. 40 applicants, 60% accepted, 13 enrolled. In 2011, 31 degrees awarded. *Degree requirements:* For master's, thesis optional. *Entrance requirements:* For master's, GRE General Test, bachelor's degree in engineering or related degree, minimum GPA of 3.0. Additional exam requirements/recommendations for international students: Required—TOEFL (minimum score 550 paper-based; 213 computer-based; 79 iBT). *Application deadline:* For fall admission, 3/1 for domestic and international students; for spring admission, 10/1 for domestic and international students. Applications are processed on a rolling basis. Application fee: $60 ($75 for international students). *Expenses:* Tuition, state resident: part-time $660 per credit hour. Tuition, nonresident: part-time $1133 per credit hour. Tuition and fees vary according to degree level, program and student level. *Financial support:* In 2011–12, 5 students received support. Federal Work-Study and scholarships/grants available. Support available to part-time students. Financial award application deadline: 3/1; financial award applicants required to submit FAFSA. *Faculty research:* Neural networks, artificial intelligence, robust control, space operations, space propulsion. *Total annual research expenditures:* $163,405. *Unit head:* Rebecca Webb, Director, 719-255-3581, Fax: 719-255-3674, E-mail: rwebb@uccs.edu. *Application contact:* Siew Nylund, Academic Adviser, 719-255-3243, Fax: 719-255-3589, E-mail: snylund@eas.uccs.edu. Web site: http://eas.uccs.edu/mae/.

University of Colorado Boulder, Graduate School, College of Engineering and Applied Science, Department of Aerospace Engineering Sciences, Boulder, CO 80309. Offers MS, PhD. *Faculty:* 26 full-time (3 women). *Students:* 193 full-time (32 women), 40 part-time (6 women); includes 17 minority (2 Black or African American, non-Hispanic/Latino; 1 American Indian or Alaska Native, non-Hispanic/Latino; 5 Asian, non-Hispanic/Latino; 6 Hispanic/Latino; 3 Two or more races, non-Hispanic/Latino), 37 international. Average age 27. 197 applicants, 61% accepted, 48 enrolled. In 2011, 75 master's, 14 doctorates awarded. Terminal master's awarded for partial completion of doctoral program. *Median time to degree:* Of those who began their doctoral program in fall 2003, 57% received their degree in 8 years or less. *Degree requirements:* For master's, comprehensive exam, thesis or alternative; for doctorate, comprehensive exam, thesis/dissertation. *Entrance requirements:* For master's, GRE General Test, minimum undergraduate GPA of 3.0; for doctorate, minimum undergraduate GPA of 3.25. *Application deadline:* For fall admission, 2/1 for domestic students, 12/1 for international students; for spring admission, 10/1 for domestic students, 8/1 for international students. Applications are processed on a rolling basis. Application fee: $50 ($60 for international students). Electronic applications accepted. *Financial support:* In 2011–12, 138 students received support, including 73 fellowships (averaging $13,455 per year), 61 research assistantships with full and partial tuition reimbursements available (averaging $22,938 per year), 13 teaching assistantships with full and partial tuition reimbursements available (averaging $21,323 per year); institutionally sponsored loans, scholarships/grants, health care benefits, and unspecified assistantships also available. Financial award application deadline: 2/1; financial award applicants required to submit FAFSA. *Faculty research:* Aerodynamics, gas dynamics and fluid mechanics; astrodynamics; atmospheric and oceanic sciences; bioengineering; computational fluid dynamics; global positioning; guidance and control. *Total annual research expenditures:* $13.7 million. *Application contact:* E-mail: aerograd@colorado.edu. Web site: http://colorado.edu/aerospace/.

University of Dayton, Department of Mechanical and Aerospace Engineering, Dayton, OH 45469-1300. Offers aerospace engineering (MSAE, DE, PhD); mechanical engineering (MSME, DE, PhD); renewable and clean energy (MS). Part-time programs available. Postbaccalaureate distance learning degree programs offered (no on-campus study). *Faculty:* 16 full-time (2 women), 11 part-time/adjunct (1 woman). *Students:* 150 full-time (22 women), 28 part-time (6 women); includes 15 minority (7 Black or African American, non-Hispanic/Latino; 3 Asian, non-Hispanic/Latino; 5 Hispanic/Latino), 77 international. Average age 27. 177 applicants, 63% accepted, 55 enrolled. In 2011, 66 master's, 4 doctorates awarded. Terminal master's awarded for partial completion of doctoral program. *Degree requirements:* For master's, thesis optional; for doctorate, variable foreign language requirement, thesis/dissertation, departmental qualifying exam. *Entrance requirements:* Additional exam requirements/recommendations for international students: Required—TOEFL (minimum score 550 paper-based; 213 computer-based; 80 iBT). *Application deadline:* For fall admission, 8/1 priority date for domestic students, 6/1 for international students; for winter admission, 9/1 for international students; for spring admission, 3/1 for international students. Applications are processed on a rolling basis. Application fee: $0. Electronic applications accepted. *Expenses: Tuition:* Full-time $8400; part-time $700 per credit hour. *Required fees:* $25 per semester. Tuition and fees vary according to degree level. *Financial support:* In 2011–12, 25 students received support, including 29 research assistantships with full tuition reimbursements available (averaging $11,000 per year), 7 teaching assistantships with full tuition reimbursements available (averaging $9,100 per year). Financial award applicants required to submit FAFSA. *Faculty research:* Jet engine combustion, surface coating friction and wear, aircraft thermal management, aerospace fuels, energy efficient buildings, energy efficient manufacturing, renewable energy. *Total annual research expenditures:* $1.2 million. *Unit head:* Dr. Kelly Kissock, Chair, 937-229-2999, Fax: 937-229-4766, E-mail: kelly.kissock@udayton.edu. *Application contact:* Dr. Vinod Jain, Graduate Program Director, 937-229-2992, Fax: 937-229-4766, E-mail: vinod.jain@notes.udayton.edu. Web site: http://www.udayton.edu/engineering/mechanical_and_aerospace/.

University of Florida, Graduate School, College of Engineering, Department of Mechanical and Aerospace Engineering, Gainesville, FL 32611. Offers aerospace engineering (ME, MS, PhD, Engr); mechanical engineering (ME, MS, PhD, Engr). Part-time programs available. *Degree requirements:* For master's, thesis (for some programs); for doctorate, comprehensive exam, thesis/dissertation; for Engr, thesis. *Entrance requirements:* For master's and doctorate, GRE General Test, minimum GPA of 3.0; for Engr, GRE General Test. Additional exam requirements/recommendations for international students: Required—TOEFL (minimum score 550 paper-based; 213 computer-based; 80 iBT), IELTS (minimum score 6). Electronic applications accepted. *Faculty research:* Thermal sciences, design, controls and robotics, manufacturing, energy transport and utilization.

University of Illinois at Urbana–Champaign, Graduate College, College of Engineering, Department of Aerospace Engineering, Champaign, IL 61820. Offers MS, PhD. *Faculty:* 18 full-time (2 women), 1 part-time/adjunct (0 women). *Students:* 110 full-time (16 women), 28 part-time (4 women); includes 17 minority (12 Asian, non-Hispanic/Latino; 3 Hispanic/Latino; 2 Two or more races, non-Hispanic/Latino), 69 international. 244 applicants, 59% accepted, 26 enrolled. In 2011, 33 master's, 5 doctorates awarded. *Entrance requirements:* For master's and doctorate, GRE General Test. Additional exam requirements/recommendations for international students: Required—TOEFL (minimum score 613 paper-based; 257 computer-based; 103 iBT) or IELTS (minimum score 7). *Application deadline:* Applications are processed on a rolling basis. Application fee: $75 ($90 for international students). Electronic applications accepted. *Financial support:* In 2011–12, 20 fellowships, 74 research assistantships, 51 teaching assistantships were awarded; tuition waivers (full and partial) also available. *Unit head:* Dr. Philippe H. Geubelle, Head, 217-244-7648, Fax: 217-244-0720, E-mail: geubelle@illinois.edu. *Application contact:* Staci L. Tankersley, Program Coordinator, 217-333-3674, Fax: 217-244-0720, E-mail: tank@illinois.edu. Web site: http://www.ae.illinois.edu/.

The University of Kansas, Graduate Studies, School of Engineering, Program in Aerospace Engineering, Lawrence, KS 66045. Offers ME, MS, DE, PhD. *Faculty:* 8 full-time (0 women), 1 part-time/adjunct (0 women). *Students:* 29 full-time (5 women), 8 part-time (0 women); includes 5 minority (1 Black or African American, non-Hispanic/Latino; 1 American Indian or Alaska Native, non-Hispanic/Latino; 2 Asian, non-Hispanic/Latino; 1 Hispanic/Latino), 12 international. Average age 28. 28 applicants, 61% accepted, 7 enrolled. In 2011, 9 degrees awarded. *Degree requirements:* For master's, comprehensive exam, thesis; for doctorate, comprehensive exam, thesis/dissertation, research and responsible scholarship skills, qualifying exam. *Entrance requirements:* For master's, GRE, minimum GPA of 3.0; for doctorate, GRE, minimum GPA of 3.5. Additional exam requirements/recommendations for international students: Required—TOEFL (minimum score 570 paper-based; 80 computer-based; 80 iBT). *Application deadline:* For fall admission, 3/1 for domestic and international students; for spring admission, 12/1 priority date for domestic students, 12/1 for international students. Applications are processed on a rolling basis. Application fee: $55 ($65 for international students). Electronic applications accepted. Tuition and fees vary according to course load, campus/location, program and reciprocity agreements. *Financial support:* Fellowships with full and partial tuition reimbursements, research assistantships with full and partial tuition reimbursements, teaching assistantships with full and partial tuition reimbursements, career-related internships or fieldwork, scholarships/grants, tuition waivers (full and partial), and unspecified assistantships available. Financial award application deadline: 1/1. *Faculty research:* Aerodynamics, propulsion, astronautics, fluid mechanics, flight dynamics and control, structures, flight vehicle design, flight testing, orbital mechanics, spacecraft attitude determination and control. *Unit head:* Dr. Mark Ewing, Chair and Associate Professor, 785-864-4267, Fax: 785-864-3597, E-mail: aerohawk@ku.edu. *Application contact:* Amy Borton, Graduate Secretary, 785-864-4267, Fax: 785-864-3597, E-mail: aerohawk@ku.edu. Web site: http://www.ae.engr.ku.edu/.

The University of Manchester, School of Materials, Manchester, United Kingdom. Offers advanced aerospace materials engineering (M Sc); advanced metallic systems (PhD); biomedical materials (M Phil, M Sc, PhD); ceramics and glass (M Phil, M Sc, PhD); composite materials (M Sc, PhD); corrosion and protection (M Phil, M Sc, PhD); materials (M Phil, PhD); metallic materials (M Phil, M Sc, PhD); nanostructural materials (M Phil, M Sc, PhD); paper science (M Phil, M Sc, PhD); polymer science and engineering (M Phil, M Sc, PhD); technical textiles (M Sc); textile design, fashion and management (M Phil, M Sc, PhD); textile science and technology (M Phil, M Sc, PhD); textiles (M Phil, PhD); textiles and fashion (M Ent).

The University of Manchester, School of Mechanical, Aerospace and Civil Engineering, Manchester, United Kingdom. Offers advanced manufacturing technology (M Ent); aerospace engineering (M Phil, M Sc, PhD); civil engineering (M Phil, M Sc, PhD); environmental engineering (M Phil, PhD); management of projects (M Phil, M Sc, PhD); mechanical engineering (M Phil, M Sc, PhD); mechanical engineering design (M Ent); nuclear engineering (M Phil, D Eng, PhD).

University of Maryland, College Park, Academic Affairs, A. James Clark School of Engineering, Department of Aerospace Engineering, College Park, MD 20742. Offers

M Eng, MS, PhD. Part-time and evening/weekend programs available. Postbaccalaureate distance learning degree programs offered. *Faculty:* 37 full-time (3 women), 10 part-time/adjunct (0 women). *Students:* 126 full-time (23 women), 66 part-time (13 women); includes 32 minority (6 Black or African American, non-Hispanic/Latino; 19 Asian, non-Hispanic/Latino; 6 Hispanic/Latino; 1 Two or more races, non-Hispanic/Latino), 38 international. 320 applicants, 33% accepted, 40 enrolled. In 2011, 34 master's, 11 doctorates awarded. *Degree requirements:* For master's, thesis optional; for doctorate, thesis/dissertation. *Entrance requirements:* For master's and doctorate, GRE General Test (recommended), 3 letters of recommendation. *Application deadline:* For fall admission, 5/15 for domestic students, 2/1 for international students; for spring admission, 10/31 for domestic students, 6/1 for international students. Applications are processed on a rolling basis. Application fee: $75. Electronic applications accepted. *Expenses: Tuition, area resident:* Part-time $525 per credit hour. Tuition, state resident: part-time $525 per credit hour. Tuition, nonresident: part-time $1131 per credit hour. *Required fees:* $386.31 per term. Tuition and fees vary according to program. *Financial support:* In 2011–12, 17 fellowships with full and partial tuition reimbursements (averaging $16,171 per year), 104 research assistantships with tuition reimbursements (averaging $23,524 per year), 11 teaching assistantships with tuition reimbursements (averaging $18,652 per year) were awarded; Federal Work-Study and scholarships/grants also available. Support available to part-time students. Financial award applicants required to submit FAFSA. *Faculty research:* Aerodynamics and propulsion, structural mechanics, flight dynamics, rotor craft, space robotics. *Total annual research expenditures:* $14.4 million. *Unit head:* Mark Lewis, Chair, 301-405-0263, E-mail: lewis@umd.edu. *Application contact:* Dr. Charles A. Caramello, Dean of Graduate School, 301-405-0358, Fax: 301-314-9305.

University of Maryland, College Park, Academic Affairs, A. James Clark School of Engineering, Department of Continuing and Distance Learning in Engineering, College Park, MD 20742. Offers engineering (M Eng), including aerospace engineering, chemical engineering, civil engineering, electrical engineering, engineering, fire protection engineering, materials science and engineering, mechanical engineering, reliability engineering, systems engineering. *Faculty:* 3 full-time (0 women), 8 part-time/adjunct (0 women). *Students:* 75 full-time (24 women), 418 part-time (81 women); includes 154 minority (62 Black or African American, non-Hispanic/Latino; 64 Asian, non-Hispanic/Latino; 23 Hispanic/Latino; 5 Two or more races, non-Hispanic/Latino; 67 international. 447 applicants, 52% accepted, 154 enrolled. In 2011, 155 master's awarded. *Application deadline:* For fall admission, 8/15 for domestic students, 2/1 for international students; for spring admission, 1/10 for domestic students, 8/1 for international students. Applications are processed on a rolling basis. Application fee: $75. Electronic applications accepted. *Expenses: Tuition, area resident:* Part-time $525 per credit hour. Tuition, state resident: part-time $525 per credit hour. Tuition, nonresident: part-time $1131 per credit hour. *Required fees:* $386.31 per term. Tuition and fees vary according to program. *Financial support:* In 2011–12, 3 research assistantships (averaging $21,498 per year), 13 teaching assistantships (averaging $16,889 per year) were awarded. *Unit head:* Dr. Darryll Pines, Dean, 301-405-8539, E-mail: pines@umd.edu. *Application contact:* Dr. Charles A. Caramello, Dean of the Graduate School, 301-405-0358, Fax: 301-314-9305.

University of Miami, Graduate School, College of Engineering, Department of Mechanical and Aerospace Engineering, Coral Gables, FL 33124. Offers MSME, PhD. Part-time programs available. *Degree requirements:* For master's, thesis (for some programs); for doctorate, comprehensive exam, thesis/dissertation. *Entrance requirements:* For master's and doctorate, GRE General Test, minimum GPA of 3.0. Additional exam requirements/recommendations for international students: Required—TOEFL (minimum score 550 paper-based; 213 computer-based). Electronic applications accepted. *Faculty research:* Internal combustion engines, heat transfer, hydrogen energy, controls, fuel cells.

University of Michigan, College of Engineering, Department of Aerospace Engineering, Ann Arbor, MI 48109. Offers M Eng, MS, MSE, PhD. Part-time programs available. *Students:* 210 full-time (28 women), 1 part-time (0 women). 456 applicants, 46% accepted, 85 enrolled. In 2011, 72 master's, 13 doctorates awarded. *Degree requirements:* For doctorate, thesis/dissertation, oral defense of dissertation, preliminary exams. *Entrance requirements:* For master's, GRE General Test; for doctorate, GRE General Test, master's degree. *Application deadline:* Applications are processed on a rolling basis. Application fee: $65 ($75 for international students). Electronic applications accepted. *Financial support:* Fellowships, research assistantships, teaching assistantships, Federal Work-Study, and tuition waivers (full and partial) available. *Faculty research:* Turbulent flows and combustion, advanced spacecraft control, helicopter aeroelasticity, experimental fluid dynamics, space propulsion, optimal structural design, interactive materials, computational fluid and solid dynamics. *Unit head:* Dr. Daniel Inman, Department Chair, 734-647-4701, Fax: 734-763-0578, E-mail: daninman@umich.edu. *Application contact:* Denise Phelps, Graduate Admissions Coordinator, 734-615-4406, Fax: 734-763-0578, E-mail: dphelps@umich.edu. Web site: http://www.engin.umich.edu/dept/aero/.

University of Michigan, College of Engineering, Department of Atmospheric, Oceanic, and Space Sciences, Ann Arbor, MI 48109. Offers atmospheric and space sciences (MS, PhD); geoscience and remote sensing (PhD); space and planetary sciences (PhD); space engineering (M Eng). Part-time programs available. *Students:* 104 full-time (35 women), 1 part-time (0 women). 122 applicants, 57% accepted, 37 enrolled. In 2011, 28 master's, 7 doctorates awarded. Terminal master's awarded for partial completion of doctoral program. *Degree requirements:* For master's, thesis (for some programs); for doctorate, thesis/dissertation, oral defense of dissertation, preliminary exams. *Entrance requirements:* For master's and doctorate, GRE General Test. Additional exam requirements/recommendations for international students: Required—TOEFL. *Application deadline:* Applications are processed on a rolling basis. Application fee: $65 ($75 for international students). Electronic applications accepted. *Financial support:* Fellowships, research assistantships, teaching assistantships, career-related internships or fieldwork, Federal Work-Study, institutionally sponsored loans, and health care benefits available. Support available to part-time students. Financial award applicants required to submit FAFSA. *Faculty research:* Planetary environments, space instrumentation, air pollution meteorology, global climate change, sun-earth connection, space weather. *Unit head:* Dr. James Slavin, Chair, 734-764-7221, Fax: 734-615-4645, E-mail: jaslavin@umich.edu. *Application contact:* Margaret Reid, Student Services Associate, 734-936-0482, Fax: 734-763-0437, E-mail: aoss.um@umich.edu. Web site: http://aoss.engin.umich.edu/.

University of Minnesota, Twin Cities Campus, College of Science and Engineering, Department of Aerospace Engineering and Mechanics, Minneapolis, MN 55455-0213. Offers aerospace engineering (M Aero E); aerospace engineering and mechanics (MS, PhD). Part-time programs available. *Degree requirements:* For doctorate, thesis/dissertation. *Entrance requirements:* Additional exam requirements/recommendations for international students: Required—TOEFL (minimum score 550 paper-based; 213

computer-based). Electronic applications accepted. *Faculty research:* Fluid mechanics, solid and continuum fluid mechanics, computational mechanics, aerospace systems.

University of Missouri, Graduate School, College of Engineering, Department of Mechanical and Aerospace Engineering, Columbia, MO 65211. Offers MS, PhD. *Faculty:* 22 full-time (0 women), 1 part-time/adjunct (0 women). *Students:* 60 full-time (3 women), 27 part-time (4 women); includes 5 minority (1 Black or African American, non-Hispanic/Latino; 1 Asian, non-Hispanic/Latino; 1 Hispanic/Latino; 2 Two or more races, non-Hispanic/Latino), 42 international. Average age 26. 125 applicants, 42% accepted, 23 enrolled. In 2011, 11 master's, 7 doctorates awarded. *Degree requirements:* For master's, thesis; for doctorate, one foreign language, thesis/dissertation. *Entrance requirements:* For master's and doctorate, GRE General Test, minimum GPA of 3.0. Additional exam requirements/recommendations for international students: Required—TOEFL (minimum score 500 paper-based; 173 computer-based; 61 iBT). *Application deadline:* Applications are processed on a rolling basis. Application fee: $55 ($75 for international students). *Expenses:* Tuition, state resident: full-time $5881. Tuition, nonresident: full-time $15,183. *Required fees:* $952. Tuition and fees vary according to campus/location and program. *Financial support:* Fellowships, research assistantships, teaching assistantships, and institutionally sponsored loans available. *Faculty research:* Dynamics and Control, design and manufacturing, materials and solids and thermal and fluid science engineering. *Unit head:* Dr. Roberta Tzou, Department Chair, E-mail: tzour@missouri.edu. *Application contact:* Melanie Gerlach, 573-882-2085, E-mail: gerlachm@missouri.edu. Web site: http://engineering.missouri.edu/mae/.

University of Nevada, Las Vegas, Graduate College, Howard R. Hughes College of Engineering, Department of Mechanical Engineering, Las Vegas, NV 89154-4027. Offers aerospace engineering (MS); biomedical engineering (MS); materials and nuclear engineering (MS); mechanical engineering (MSE, PhD). Part-time programs available. *Faculty:* 14 full-time (0 women), 19 part-time/adjunct (1 woman). *Students:* 14 full-time (2 women), 40 part-time (8 women); includes 12 minority (1 Black or African American, non-Hispanic/Latino; 4 Asian, non-Hispanic/Latino; 3 Hispanic/Latino; 1 Native Hawaiian or other Pacific Islander, non-Hispanic/Latino; 3 Two or more races, non-Hispanic/Latino), 13 international. Average age 31. 31 applicants, 74% accepted, 8 enrolled. In 2011, 18 master's, 3 doctorates awarded. *Degree requirements:* For master's, comprehensive exam, thesis (for some programs), project; for doctorate, comprehensive exam, thesis/dissertation. *Entrance requirements:* For master's and doctorate, GRE General Test. Additional exam requirements/recommendations for international students: Required—TOEFL (minimum score 550 paper-based; 213 computer-based; 80 iBT), IELTS (minimum score 7). *Application deadline:* For fall admission, 8/1 priority date for domestic students, 5/1 for international students; for spring admission, 12/1 priority date for domestic students, 10/1 for international students. Applications are processed on a rolling basis. Application fee: $60 ($95 for international students). Electronic applications accepted. *Financial support:* In 2011–12, 29 students received support, including 14 research assistantships with partial tuition reimbursements available (averaging $9,415 per year), 15 teaching assistantships with partial tuition reimbursements available (averaging $10,934 per year); institutionally sponsored loans, scholarships/grants, health care benefits, and unspecified assistantships also available. Financial award application deadline: 3/1. *Faculty research:* Dynamics and control systems; energy systems including renewable and nuclear; computational fluid and solid mechanics; structures, materials and manufacturing; vibrations and acoustics. *Total annual research expenditures:* $2.9 million. *Unit head:* Dr. Woosoon Yim, Chair/Professor, 702-895-0956, Fax: 702-895-3936, E-mail: wy@me.unlv.edu. *Application contact:* Graduate College Admissions Evaluator, 702-895-3320, Fax: 702-895-4180, E-mail: gradcollege@unlv.edu. Web site: http://www.me.unlv.edu/.

University of Notre Dame, Graduate School, College of Engineering, Department of Aerospace and Mechanical Engineering, Notre Dame, IN 46556. Offers aerospace and mechanical engineering (M Eng, PhD); aerospace engineering (MS Aero E); mechanical engineering (MEME, MSME). Terminal master's awarded for partial completion of doctoral program. *Degree requirements:* For master's, comprehensive exam, thesis or alternative; for doctorate, thesis/dissertation, candidacy exam. *Entrance requirements:* For master's and doctorate, GRE General Test. Additional exam requirements/recommendations for international students: Required—TOEFL (minimum score 600 paper-based; 250 computer-based; 80 iBT). Electronic applications accepted. *Faculty research:* Aerodynamics/fluid dynamics, design and manufacturing, controls/robotics, solid mechanics or biomechanics/biomaterials.

University of Oklahoma, College of Engineering, School of Aerospace and Mechanical Engineering, Program in Aerospace Engineering, Norman, OK 73019. Offers aerospace engineering (MS, PhD), including aerodynamics, composites, fluid mechanics, general, structures. Part-time programs available. *Students:* 12 full-time (2 women), 11 part-time (0 women); includes 5 minority (1 Black or African American, non-Hispanic/Latino; 1 American Indian or Alaska Native, non-Hispanic/Latino; 2 Asian, non-Hispanic/Latino; 1 Hispanic/Latino), 4 international. Average age 29. 11 applicants, 45% accepted, 4 enrolled. In 2011, 3 degrees awarded. *Degree requirements:* For master's, comprehensive exam, thesis or alternative; for doctorate, comprehensive exam, thesis/dissertation, combined general and qualifying exam. *Entrance requirements:* For master's, GRE General Test, BS in engineering or physical sciences; for doctorate, GRE General Test, MS in aerospace engineering or equivalent. Additional exam requirements/recommendations for international students: Required—TOEFL (minimum score 600 paper-based; 100 iBT). *Application deadline:* For fall admission, 6/1 priority date for domestic students, 3/1 for international students; for spring admission, 11/1 for domestic students, 9/1 for international students. Applications are processed on a rolling basis. Application fee: $40 ($90 for international students). Electronic applications accepted. *Expenses:* Tuition, state resident: full-time $4087; part-time $170.30 per credit hour. Tuition, nonresident: full-time $14,875; part-time $619.80 per credit hour. *Required fees:* $2659; $100.25 per credit hour. Tuition and fees vary according to course load and degree level. *Financial support:* In 2011–12, 9 students received support. Unspecified assistantships available. Financial award applicants required to submit FAFSA. *Faculty research:* Composite materials, computational methods development, robotics/intelligent systems, combustion and propulsion, unmanned systems. *Unit head:* Farrokh Mistree, Director, 405-325-5011, Fax: 405-325-1088, E-mail: farrokh.mistree@ou.edu. *Application contact:* Dr. Peter Attar, Graduate Liaison, Fax: 405-325-1088, E-mail: peter.attar@ou.edu. Web site: http://www.ame.ou.edu.

University of Ottawa, Faculty of Graduate and Postdoctoral Studies, Faculty of Engineering, Ottawa-Carleton Institute for Mechanical and Aerospace Engineering, Ottawa, ON K1N 6N5, Canada. Offers M Eng, MA Sc, PhD. MA Sc, M Eng, PhD offered jointly with Carleton University. *Degree requirements:* For master's, thesis or alternative; for doctorate, thesis/dissertation, seminar series, qualifying exam. *Entrance requirements:* For master's, honors degree or equivalent, minimum B average; for doctorate, master's degree, minimum B+ average. Electronic applications accepted. *Faculty research:* Fluid mechanics-heat transfer, solid mechanics, design, manufacturing and control.

University of Southern California, Graduate School, Viterbi School of Engineering, Department of Aerospace and Mechanical Engineering, Los Angeles, CA 90089. Offers aerospace and mechanical engineering: computational fluid and solid mechanics (MS); aerospace and mechanical engineering: dynamics and control (MS); aerospace engineering (MS, PhD, Engr), including aerospace engineering (PhD, Engr); green technologies (MS); mechanical engineering (MS, PhD, Engr), including mechanical engineering (PhD, Engr); product development engineering (MS). Part-time and evening/weekend programs available. Postbaccalaureate distance learning degree programs offered (no on-campus study). Terminal master's awarded for partial completion of doctoral program. *Degree requirements:* For master's, thesis optional; for doctorate, thesis/dissertation. *Entrance requirements:* For master's, doctorate, and Engr, GRE General Test. Additional exam requirements/recommendations for international students: Recommended—TOEFL. Electronic applications accepted. *Faculty research:* Mechanics and materials, aerodynamics of air/ground vehicles, gas dynamics, aerosols, astronautics and space science, geophysical and microgravity flows, planetary physics, power MEMs and MEMS vacuum pumps, heat transfer and combustion.

University of Southern California, Graduate School, Viterbi School of Engineering, Division of Astronautics and Space Technology, Los Angeles, CA 90089. Offers astronautical engineering (MS, PhD, Engr, Graduate Certificate). Part-time and evening/weekend programs available. Postbaccalaureate distance learning degree programs offered (no on-campus study). Terminal master's awarded for partial completion of doctoral program. *Degree requirements:* For master's, thesis optional; for doctorate, thesis/dissertation; for other advanced degree, comprehensive exam (for some programs). *Entrance requirements:* For master's, doctorate, and other advanced degree, GRE General Test. Additional exam requirements/recommendations for international students: Recommended—TOEFL. Electronic applications accepted. *Faculty research:* Space technology, space science and applications, space instrumentation, advanced propulsion, fundamental processes in gases and plasmas.

The University of Tennessee, Graduate School, College of Engineering, Department of Mechanical, Aerospace and Biomedical Engineering, Program in Aerospace Engineering, Knoxville, TN 37996. Offers MS, PhD, MS/MBA. Part-time programs available. Postbaccalaureate distance learning degree programs offered (minimal on-campus study). *Faculty:* 5 full-time (0 women). *Students:* 21 full-time (2 women), 9 part-time (0 women); includes 2 minority (1 Black or African American, non-Hispanic/Latino; 1 Hispanic/Latino), 5 international. Average age 26. 22 applicants, 41% accepted, 2 enrolled. In 2011, 7 master's, 2 doctorates awarded. *Degree requirements:* For master's, thesis or alternative; for doctorate, comprehensive exam, thesis/dissertation. *Entrance requirements:* For master's, GRE General Test (for MS students pursuing research thesis), minimum GPA of 2.7 (for U.S. degree holders), 3.0 (for international degree holders); 3 references; statement of purpose; for doctorate, College requires GRE General Test for all PhD candidates, minimum GPA of 3.0 on previous graduate course work; 3 references; statement of purpose. Additional exam requirements/recommendations for international students: Required—TOEFL (minimum score 550 paper-based; 213 computer-based). *Application deadline:* For fall admission, 2/1 priority date for domestic students, 2/1 for international students; for spring admission, 6/15 for domestic and international students. Applications are processed on a rolling basis. Application fee: $35. Electronic applications accepted. *Expenses:* Tuition, state resident: full-time $8332; part-time $464 per credit hour. Tuition, nonresident: full-time $25,174; part-time $1400 per credit hour. *Required fees:* $1162; $56 per credit hour. Tuition and fees vary according to program. *Financial support:* In 2011–12, 6 students received support, including 2 research assistantships with full tuition reimbursements available (averaging $17,725 per year), 2 teaching assistantships with full tuition reimbursements available (averaging $15,900 per year); fellowships with full tuition reimbursements available, career-related internships or fieldwork, Federal Work-Study, institutionally sponsored loans, health care benefits, and unspecified assistantships also available. Financial award application deadline: 2/1; financial award applicants required to submit FAFSA. *Faculty research:* Atmospheric re-entry mechanics, hybrid rocket propulsion, laser-induced plasma spectroscopy, unsteady aerodynamics and aeroelasticity. *Unit head:* Dr. William Hamel, Head, 865-974-5115, Fax: 865-974-5274, E-mail: whamel@utk.edu. *Application contact:* Dr. Gary V. Smith, Associate Head, 865-974-5271, Fax: 865-974-5274, E-mail: gvsmith@utk.edu. Web site: http://www.engr.utk.edu/mabe/.

The University of Tennessee Space Institute, Graduate Programs, Program in Aerospace Engineering, Tullahoma, TN 37388-9700. Offers MS, PhD. Part-time programs available. *Faculty:* 8 full-time (1 woman), 8 part-time/adjunct (0 women). *Students:* 14 full-time (1 woman), 9 part-time (0 women); includes 2 minority (1 Black or African American, non-Hispanic/Latino; 1 Hispanic/Latino), 3 international. 8 applicants, 63% accepted, 3 enrolled. In 2011, 7 master's, 2 doctorates awarded. *Degree requirements:* For master's, thesis (for some programs); for doctorate, one foreign language, thesis/dissertation. *Entrance requirements:* For master's and doctorate, GRE General Test. Additional exam requirements/recommendations for international students: Required—TOEFL (minimum score 550 paper-based; 213 computer-based), IELTS (minimum score 6.5). *Application deadline:* For fall admission, 2/1 for international students; for spring admission, 6/15 for international students. Applications are processed on a rolling basis. Application fee: $35. Electronic applications accepted. *Financial support:* In 2011–12, 2 fellowships (averaging $2,500 per year), 12 research assistantships with full tuition reimbursements (averaging $17,791 per year) were awarded; career-related internships or fieldwork, Federal Work-Study, institutionally sponsored loans, health care benefits, tuition waivers (full and partial), and unspecified assistantships also available. Financial award applicants required to submit FAFSA. *Faculty research:* Air and space vehicles, flight mechanics, propulsion, fluid mechanics, gas dynamics, energy conversion, structure. *Unit head:* Dr. Trevor Moeller, Degree Program Chairman, 931-393-7351, Fax: 931-393-7437, E-mail: tmoeller@utsi.edu. *Application contact:* Dee Merriman, Coordinator III, 931-393-7213, Fax: 931-393-7211, E-mail: dmerrima@utsi.edu. Web site: http://www.utsi.edu/academics/MABE/.

The University of Texas at Arlington, Graduate School, College of Engineering, Department of Mechanical and Aerospace Engineering, Program in Aerospace Engineering, Arlington, TX 76019. Offers M Engr, MS, PhD. Part-time and evening/weekend programs available. Postbaccalaureate distance learning degree programs offered (minimal on-campus study). *Students:* 68 full-time (11 women), 49 part-time (5 women); includes 26 minority (5 Black or African American, non-Hispanic/Latino; 13 Asian, non-Hispanic/Latino; 8 Hispanic/Latino), 53 international. 72 applicants, 82% accepted, 33 enrolled. In 2011, 22 degrees awarded. Terminal master's awarded for partial completion of doctoral program. *Degree requirements:* For master's, thesis optional; for doctorate, comprehensive exam, thesis/dissertation. *Entrance requirements:* For master's and doctorate, GRE General Test, minimum GPA of 3.0. Additional exam requirements/recommendations for international students: Required—TOEFL (minimum score 550 paper-based; 213 computer-based). *Application deadline:* For fall admission, 6/1 for domestic students, 4/1 for international students; for spring

admission, 10/15 for domestic students, 9/15 for international students. Applications are processed on a rolling basis. Application fee: $50 ($70 for international students). *Financial support:* In 2011–12, 7 fellowships with partial tuition reimbursements (averaging $1,000 per year), 6 research assistantships with partial tuition reimbursements (averaging $1,800 per year), 21 teaching assistantships with partial tuition reimbursements (averaging $1,920 per year) were awarded; institutionally sponsored loans, scholarships/grants, health care benefits, and unspecified assistantships also available. Financial award application deadline: 6/1; financial award applicants required to submit FAFSA. *Unit head:* Dr. Erian Armanios, Chair, 817-272-2603, Fax: 817-272-5010, E-mail: armanios@uta.edu. *Application contact:* Dr. Kamesh Subbarao, Graduate Advisor, 817-272-7467, Fax: 817-272-2952, E-mail: subbarao@uta.edu. Web site: http://www.mae.uta.edu/.

The University of Texas at Austin, Graduate School, Cockrell School of Engineering, Department of Aerospace Engineering and Engineering Mechanics, Program in Aerospace Engineering, Austin, TX 78712-1111. Offers MSE, PhD. *Entrance requirements:* For master's and doctorate, GRE General Test. *Application deadline:* For fall admission, 1/15 priority date for domestic students; for spring admission, 10/1 priority date for domestic students. Applications are processed on a rolling basis. Application fee: $50 ($75 for international students). Electronic applications accepted. *Financial support:* Fellowships with tuition reimbursements, research assistantships with full tuition reimbursements, and teaching assistantships with tuition reimbursements available. Financial award application deadline: 1/15. *Unit head:* Prof. Glenn Lightsey, Graduate Advisor, 512-471-5322, E-mail: ase.grad@mail.ae.utexas.edu. *Application contact:* Tina K. Woods, Graduate Coordinator, 512-471-7595, Fax: 512-471-3788, E-mail: twoods@mail.utexas. Web site: http://www.ae.utexas.edu/graduate-programs/ase.

University of Toronto, School of Graduate Studies, Faculty of Applied Science and Engineering, Institute for Aerospace Studies, Toronto, ON M5S 1A1, Canada. Offers M Eng, MA Sc, PhD. Part-time programs available. *Degree requirements:* For master's, thesis (for some programs); for doctorate, thesis/dissertation, formal manuscript for publication. *Entrance requirements:* For master's, BA Sc or equivalent in engineering (M Eng); bachelor's degree in physics, mathematics, engineering or chemistry (MA Sc); 2 letters of reference; for doctorate, master's degree in applied science, engineering, mathematics, physics, or chemistry; demonstrated ability to perform advanced research, 2 letters of reference. Additional exam requirements/recommendations for international students: Required—TOEFL (minimum score 580 paper-based; 237 computer-based), TWE (minimum score 5). Electronic applications accepted.

University of Virginia, School of Engineering and Applied Science, Department of Mechanical and Aerospace Engineering, Charlottesville, VA 22903. Offers ME, MS, PhD. Postbaccalaureate distance learning degree programs offered (no on-campus study). *Faculty:* 20 full-time (2 women), 2 part-time/adjunct (1 woman). *Students:* 77 full-time (9 women), 8 part-time (1 woman); includes 4 minority (all Asian, non-Hispanic/Latino), 24 international. Average age 27. 191 applicants, 18% accepted, 21 enrolled. In 2011, 19 master's, 12 doctorates awarded. *Degree requirements:* For master's, thesis (MS); for doctorate, comprehensive exam, thesis/dissertation. *Entrance requirements:* For master's and doctorate, GRE General Test, 3 letters of recommendation. Additional exam requirements/recommendations for international students: Required—TOEFL (minimum score 650 paper-based; 250 computer-based; 90 iBT), IELTS (minimum score 7). *Application deadline:* For fall admission, 8/1 for domestic students, 4/1 for international students; for winter admission, 12/1 for domestic students, 8/1 for international students; for spring admission, 5/1 for domestic students, 1/1 for international students. Applications are processed on a rolling basis. Application fee: $60. Electronic applications accepted. *Financial support:* Fellowships, research assistantships, and teaching assistantships available. Financial award application deadline: 1/15; financial award applicants required to submit FAFSA. *Faculty research:* Solid mechanics, dynamical systems and control, thermofluids. *Unit head:* Hossein Haj-Hariri, Chair, 434-924-7424, Fax: 434-982-2037, E-mail: mae-adm@virginia.edu. *Application contact:* Graduate Secretary, 434-924-7425, Fax: 434-982-2037, E-mail: mae-adm@virginia.edu. Web site: http://www.mae.virginia.edu/.

University of Washington, Graduate School, College of Engineering, Department of Aeronautics and Astronautics, Seattle, WA 98195-2400. Offers aeronautics and astronautics (MS, PhD); aerospace engineering (MAE), including composite materials and structures; global trade, transportation and logistics (MS). Part-time programs available. Postbaccalaureate distance learning degree programs offered (no on-campus study). *Faculty:* 24 full-time (1 woman), 9 part-time/adjunct (1 woman). *Students:* 76 full-time (16 women), 115 part-time (17 women); includes 43 minority (5 Black or African American, non-Hispanic/Latino; 1 American Indian or Alaska Native, non-Hispanic/Latino; 21 Asian, non-Hispanic/Latino; 16 Hispanic/Latino), 28 international. Average age 27. 297 applicants, 52% accepted, 74 enrolled. In 2011, 24 master's, 5 doctorates awarded. *Degree requirements:* For master's, thesis optional; for doctorate, comprehensive exam, thesis/dissertation, qualifying, general and final exams; completion of all work toward degree within 10 years. *Entrance requirements:* For master's and doctorate, GRE General Test, minimum GPA of 3.0, letters of recommendation, statement of objectives, undergraduate degree in aerospace or mechanical engineering. Additional exam requirements/recommendations for international students: Required—TOEFL (minimum score 580 paper-based; 237 computer-based; 92 iBT); Recommended—IELTS (minimum score 7). *Application deadline:* For fall admission, 1/15 priority date for domestic students, 1/15 for international students. Applications are processed on a rolling basis. Application fee: $75. Electronic applications accepted. *Expenses:* Contact institution. *Financial support:* In 2011–12, 57 students received support, including 15 fellowships (averaging $9,540 per year), 26 research assistantships with full tuition reimbursements available (averaging $17,172 per year), 11 teaching assistantships with full tuition reimbursements available (averaging $13,725 per year); career-related internships or fieldwork, Federal Work-Study, health care benefits, tuition waivers (full), and unspecified assistantships also available. Financial award application deadline: 1/15; financial award applicants required to submit FAFSA. *Faculty research:* Space systems, aircraft systems, energy systems, composites/structures, fluid dynamics, controls. *Total annual research expenditures:* $7.8 million. *Unit head:* Dr. James Hermanson, Professor and Chair, 206-543-1950, Fax: 206-543-0217, E-mail: jherm@aa.washington.edu. *Application contact:* Wanda Frederick, Manager of Graduate Programs and External Relations, 206-616-1113, Fax: 206-543-0217, E-mail: wanda@aa.washington.edu. Web site: http://www.aa.washington.edu/.

Utah State University, School of Graduate Studies, College of Engineering, Department of Mechanical and Aerospace Engineering, Logan, UT 84322. Offers aerospace engineering (MS, PhD); mechanical engineering (ME, MS, PhD). Terminal master's awarded for partial completion of doctoral program. *Degree requirements:* For master's, thesis (for some programs); for doctorate, thesis/dissertation. *Entrance requirements:* For master's, GRE General Test, minimum GPA of 3.0; for doctorate, GRE General Test, minimum GPA of 3.3. Additional exam requirements/

recommendations for international students: Required—TOEFL. *Faculty research:* In-space instruments, cryogenic cooling, thermal science, space structures, composite materials.

Virginia Polytechnic Institute and State University, Graduate School, College of Engineering, Department of Aerospace and Ocean Engineering, Blacksburg, VA 24061. Offers aerospace engineering (M Eng, MS, PhD); naval engineering (Certificate); ocean engineering (MS). *Degree requirements:* For master's, comprehensive exam (for some programs), thesis (for some programs); for doctorate, comprehensive exam (for some programs), thesis/dissertation (for some programs). *Entrance requirements:* For master's and doctorate, GRE. Additional exam requirements/recommendations for international students: Required—TOEFL (minimum score 550 paper-based; 213 computer-based). *Application deadline:* For fall admission, 7/1 for domestic and international students; for spring admission, 12/1 for domestic and international students. Applications are processed on a rolling basis. Application fee: $65. Electronic applications accepted. *Expenses:* Tuition, state resident: full-time $10,048; part-time $558.25 per credit hour. Tuition, nonresident: full-time $19,497; part-time $1083.25 per credit hour. *Required fees:* $405 per semester. Tuition and fees vary according to course load, campus/location and program. *Financial support:* Fellowships with full tuition reimbursements, research assistantships with full tuition reimbursements, teaching assistantships with full tuition reimbursements, career-related internships or fieldwork, Federal Work-Study, scholarships/grants, health care benefits, and unspecified assistantships available. Financial award application deadline: 1/15. *Faculty research:* Aerodynamics, flight mechanics, vehicle structures, space mechanics and design. *Unit head:* Dr. Rachel M. Hall Smith, Unit Head, 540-231-6612, Fax: 540-231-9632, E-mail: rahall@vt.edu. *Application contact:* Craig Woolsey, Information Contact, 540-231-8117, Fax: 540-231-9632, E-mail: cwoolsey@vt.edu. Web site: http://www.aoe.vt.edu/.

Virginia Polytechnic Institute and State University, VT Online, Blacksburg, VA 24061. Offers advanced transportation systems (Certificate); aerospace engineering (MS); agricultural and life sciences (MSLFS); business information systems (Graduate Certificate); career and technical education (MS); civil engineering (MS); computer engineering (M Eng, MS); decision support systems (Graduate Certificate); eLearning leadership (MA); electrical engineering (M Eng, MS); engineering administration (MEA); environmental engineering (Certificate); environmental politics and policy (Graduate Certificate); environmental sciences and engineering (MS); foundations of political analysis (Graduate Certificate); health product risk management (Graduate Certificate); industrial and systems engineering (MS); information policy and society (Graduate Certificate); information security (Graduate Certificate); information technology (MIT); instructional technology (MA); integrative STEM education (MA Ed); liberal arts (Graduate Certificate); life sciences: health product risk management (MS); natural resources (MNR, Graduate Certificate); networking (Graduate Certificate); nonprofit and nongovernmental organization management (Graduate Certificate); ocean engineering (MS); political science (MA); security studies (Graduate Certificate); software development (Graduate Certificate). *Expenses:* Tuition, state resident: full-time $10,048; part-time $558.25 per credit hour. Tuition, nonresident: full-time $19,497; part-time $1083.25 per credit hour. *Required fees:* $405 per semester. Tuition and fees vary according to course load, campus/location and program. *Application contact:* Graduate School Applications General Assistance, 540-231-8636, Fax: 540-231-2039, E-mail: gradappl@vt.edu. Web site: http://www.vto.vt.edu/.

Washington University in St. Louis, School of Engineering and Applied Science, Department of Mechanical, Aerospace and Structural Engineering, St. Louis, MO 63130-4899. Offers MS, D Sc, PhD. Part-time programs available. Terminal master's awarded for partial completion of doctoral program. *Degree requirements:* For master's, thesis optional; for doctorate, thesis/dissertation optional. *Entrance requirements:* For master's, GRE; for doctorate, GRE General Test, departmental qualifying exam. *Faculty research:* Aerosols science and technology, applied mechanics, biomechanics and biomedical engineering, design, dynamic systems, combustion science, composite materials, materials science.

Webster University, George Herbert Walker School of Business and Technology, Department of Management, St. Louis, MO 63119-3194. Offers business and organizational security management (MA); computer resources and information management (MA); environmental management (MS); government contracting (Certificate); health care management (MA); health services management (MA); human resources development (MA); human resources management (MA); management (DM); management and leadership (MA); marketing (MA); nonprofit management (Certificate); procurement and acquisitions management (MA); public administration (MA); quality management (MA); space systems operations management (MS); telecommunications management (MA). *Accreditation:* ACBSP. Part-time and evening/weekend programs available. Postbaccalaureate distance learning degree programs offered (no on-campus study). *Degree requirements:* For master's, thesis (for some programs); for doctorate, thesis/dissertation, written exam. *Entrance requirements:* For doctorate, GMAT, 3 years of work experience, MBA. Additional exam requirements/recommendations for international students: Required—TOEFL. *Expenses: Tuition:* Full-time $10,890; part-time $605 per credit hour. Tuition and fees vary according to campus/location and program.

West Virginia University, College of Engineering and Mineral Resources, Department of Mechanical and Aerospace Engineering, Program in Aerospace Engineering, Morgantown, WV 26506. Offers MSAE, PhD. Part-time programs available. Terminal master's awarded for partial completion of doctoral program. *Degree requirements:* For master's, thesis; for doctorate, comprehensive exam, thesis/dissertation, qualifying exams, proposal defense. *Entrance requirements:* For master's and doctorate, GRE General Test, minimum GPA of 3.0, 3 reference letters. Additional exam requirements/recommendations for international students: Required—TOEFL (minimum score 550 paper-based; 213 computer-based; 79 iBT). *Faculty research:* Transonic flight controls and simulations, thermal science, composite materials, aerospace design.

Wichita State University, Graduate School, College of Engineering, Department of Aerospace Engineering, Wichita, KS 67260. Offers MS, PhD. Part-time programs available. *Expenses:* Tuition, state resident: full-time $4746; part-time $263.65 per credit. Tuition, nonresident: full-time $11,669; part-time $648.30 per credit. *Unit head:* Dr. L. Scott Miller, Chairperson, 316-978-3410, E-mail: scott.miller@wichita.edu. *Application contact:* Dr. Kamran Rokhsaz, Graduate Coordinator for MS Program, 316-978-3410, E-mail: kamran.rokhsaz@wichita.edu. Web site: http://www.wichita.edu/.

Aviation

Embry-Riddle Aeronautical University–Worldwide, Worldwide Headquarters - Graduate Degrees and Programs, Program in Aviation, Daytona Beach, FL 32114-3900. Offers PhD. *Faculty:* 2 full-time (0 women), 3 part-time/adjunct (1 woman). *Students:* 10 full-time (1 woman), 13 part-time (2 women); includes 3 minority (1 Asian, non-Hispanic/Latino; 1 Hispanic/Latino; 1 Two or more races, non-Hispanic/Latino), 3 international. Average age 39. 55 applicants, 15% accepted, 7 enrolled. *Entrance requirements:* For doctorate, GRE. Additional exam requirements/recommendations for international students: Required—TOEFL (minimum score 600 paper-based; 250 computer-based; 105 iBT). *Application deadline:* For fall admission, 2/1 for domestic students. Applications are processed on a rolling basis. Application fee: $50. Electronic applications accepted. *Expenses: Tuition:* Part-time $395 per credit hour. Tuition and fees vary according to degree level and program. *Financial support:* In 2011–12, 1 student received support. Applicants required to submit FAFSA. *Faculty research:* Aviation safety, safety management systems, human factors, aviation history, flight data monitoring, aviation safety information analysis and sharing. *Total annual research expenditures:* $468,634. *Unit head:* Dr. Tim Brady, Dean, College of Aviation, 386-226-6849, E-mail: tim.brady@erau.edu. *Application contact:* Linda Dammer, Director of Admissions, 386-226-6386 Ext. 1, Fax: 386-226-6984, E-mail: worldwide@erau.edu. Web site: http://aviationphd.erau.edu/.

Everglades University, Graduate Programs, Program in Aviation Science, Boca Raton, FL 33431. Offers MSA. *Entrance requirements:* Additional exam requirements/recommendations for international students: Recommended—TOEFL (minimum score 500 paper-based; 173 computer-based). Electronic applications accepted.

Lewis University, College of Arts and Sciences, Program in Aviation and Transportation, Romeoville, IL 60446. Offers administration (MS); safety and security (MS). Part-time and evening/weekend programs available. Postbaccalaureate distance learning degree programs offered (no on-campus study). *Faculty:* 2 full-time (0 women), 1 part-time/adjunct (0 women). *Students:* 10 full-time (2 women), 14 part-time (4 women); includes 12 minority (4 Black or African American, non-Hispanic/Latino; 6 Hispanic/Latino; 2 Two or more races, non-Hispanic/Latino). Average age 37. In 2011, 4 master's awarded. *Entrance requirements:* For master's, bachelor's degree, minimum GPA of 3.0, personal statement, 3 letters of recommendation. Additional exam requirements/recommendations for international students: Required—TOEFL (minimum score 550 paper-based; 213 computer-based; 80 iBT). *Application deadline:* For fall admission, 5/1 for international students; for spring admission, 11/15 for international students. Applications are processed on a rolling basis. Application fee: $40. Electronic applications accepted. *Financial support:* Application deadline: 5/1; applicants required to submit FAFSA. *Unit head:* Dr. Randal DeMik, Program Chair, 815-838-0500 Ext. 5559, E-mail: demikra@lewisu.edu. *Application contact:* Julie Branchaw, Assistant Director, Graduate and Adult Admission, 815-836-5574, E-mail: branchju@lewisu.edu.

Southeastern Oklahoma State University, Department of Aviation Science, Durant, OK 74701-0609. Offers aerospace administration and logistics (MS). Part-time and evening/weekend programs available. *Students:* 57 full-time (10 women), 68 part-time (11 women); includes 28 minority (10 Black or African American, non-Hispanic/Latino; 4 American Indian or Alaska Native, non-Hispanic/Latino; 7 Asian, non-Hispanic/Latino; 7 Hispanic/Latino), 1 international. Average age 30. 23 applicants, 96% accepted, 22 enrolled. *Entrance requirements:* For master's, minimum GPA of 3.0 in last 60 hours or 2.75 overall. Additional exam requirements/recommendations for international students: Required—TOEFL (minimum score 550 paper-based; 213 computer-based; 79 iBT). *Application deadline:* For fall admission, 8/1 for domestic students, 6/1 for international students; for spring admission, 1/5 for domestic students, 11/1 for international students. Application fee: $20 ($55 for international students). Electronic applications accepted. *Expenses:* Tuition, state resident: full-time $3537; part-time $173.95 per credit hour. Tuition, nonresident: full-time $8673; part-time $459.30 per credit hour. *Required fees:* $22.55 per credit hour. *Financial support:* Federal Work-Study and institutionally sponsored loans available. Support available to part-time students. Financial award application deadline: 6/15. *Unit head:* Dr. David Conway, Director, 580-745-3240, Fax: 580-924-0741, E-mail: dconway@se.edu. *Application contact:* Carrie Williamson, Administrative Assistant, Graduate Office, 580-745-2220, Fax: 580-745-7474, E-mail: cwilliamson@se.edu. Web site: http://aviation.se.edu/.

University of Illinois at Urbana–Champaign, Institute of Aviation, Champaign, IL 61820. Offers human factors (MS). *Students:* 1 full-time (0 women). 10 applicants, 0% accepted, 0 enrolled. In 2011, 5 master's awarded. *Entrance requirements:* For master's, GRE, minimum undergraduate GPA of 3.0 for last 60 hours. Additional exam requirements/recommendations for international students: Required—TOEFL. *Application deadline:* Applications are processed on a rolling basis. Application fee: $75 ($90 for international students). Electronic applications accepted. *Financial support:* Fellowships, research assistantships, teaching assistantships, and tuition waivers (full and partial) available. *Unit head:* Tom Emanuel, Acting Head, 217-244-8972, E-mail: emanuel@illinois.edu. *Application contact:* Peter Vlach, Information Systems Specialist, 217-265-9456, E-mail: pvlach@illinois.edu. Web site: http://www.aviation.illinois.edu.

University of North Dakota, Graduate School, John D. Odegard School of Aerospace Sciences, Department of Aviation, Grand Forks, ND 58202. Offers MS. Part-time programs available. Postbaccalaureate distance learning degree programs offered (minimal on-campus study). *Degree requirements:* For master's, comprehensive exam. *Entrance requirements:* For master's, GRE General Test, FAA private pilot certificate or foreign equivalent. Additional exam requirements/recommendations for international students: Required—TOEFL (minimum score 550 paper-based; 213 computer-based; 79 iBT), IELTS (minimum score 6.5). Electronic applications accepted.

The University of Tennessee, Graduate School, Intercollegiate Programs, Program in Aviation Systems, Knoxville, TN 37996. Offers MS. Part-time programs available. Postbaccalaureate distance learning degree programs offered (no on-campus study). *Degree requirements:* For master's, thesis optional. *Entrance requirements:* For master's, minimum GPA of 2.7. Additional exam requirements/recommendations for international students: Required—TOEFL. Electronic applications accepted. *Expenses:* Tuition, state resident: full-time $8332; part-time $464 per credit hour. Tuition, nonresident: full-time $25,174; part-time $1400 per credit hour. *Required fees:* $1162; $56 per credit hour. Tuition and fees vary according to program.

The University of Tennessee Space Institute, Graduate Programs, Program in Aviation Systems, Tullahoma, TN 37388-9700. Offers MS. *Faculty:* 3 full-time (0 women), 1 part-time/adjunct (0 women). *Students:* 9 full-time (2 women), 10 part-time (1 woman), 6 international. 7 applicants, 86% accepted, 5 enrolled. In 2011, 10 degrees awarded. *Degree requirements:* For master's, thesis (for some programs). *Entrance requirements:* Additional exam requirements/recommendations for international students: Required—TOEFL (minimum score 550 paper-based; 213 computer-based), IELTS (minimum score 6.5). *Application deadline:* For fall admission, 2/1 for international students; for spring admission, 6/15 for international students. Applications are processed on a rolling basis. Application fee: $35. Electronic applications accepted. *Financial support:* In 2011–12, 2 fellowships (averaging $1,500 per year), 6 research assistantships with full tuition reimbursements (averaging $17,791 per year) were awarded; career-related internships or fieldwork, Federal Work-Study, institutionally sponsored loans, health care benefits, tuition waivers (full and partial), and unspecified assistantships also available. Financial award applicants required to submit FAFSA. *Faculty research:* Aircraft performance and flying qualities, atmospheric and earth/ocean science, flight systems and human factors, aircraft design, advanced flight test instrumentation. *Unit head:* Dr. Stephen Corda, Chairman, 931-393-7413, Fax: 931-393-7533, E-mail: scorda@utsi.edu. *Application contact:* Dee Merriman, Coordinator III, 931-393-7213, Fax: 931-393-7211, E-mail: dmerrima@utsi.edu. Web site: http://www.utsi.edu/academics/AvSys/.

Section 3
Agricultural Engineering and Bioengineering

This section contains a directory of institutions offering graduate work in agricultural engineering and bioengineering, followed by an in-depth entry submitted by an institution that chose to prepare a detailed program description. Additional information about programs listed in the directory but not augmented by an in-depth entry may be obtained by writing directly to the dean of a graduate school or chair of a department at the address given in the directory.

For programs offering related work, see also in this book *Biomedical Engineering and Biotechnology; Civil and Environmental Engineering; Engineering and Applied Sciences;* and *Management of Engineering and Technology.* In the other guides in this series:

Graduate Programs in the Biological/Biomedical Sciences & Health-Related Medical Professions

See *Biological and Biomedical Sciences; Ecology, Environmental Biology, and Evolutionary Biology; Marine Biology; Nutrition;* and *Zoology*

Graduate Programs in the Physical Sciences, Mathematics, Agricultural Sciences, the Environment & Natural Resources

See *Agricultural and Food Sciences* and *Natural Resources*

CONTENTS

Program Directories

Display and Close-Up

Agricultural Engineering

Cornell University, Graduate School, Graduate Fields of Agriculture and Life Sciences and Graduate Fields of Engineering, Field of Biological and Environmental Engineering, Ithaca, NY 14853-0001. Offers biological engineering (M Eng, MPS, MS, PhD); energy (M Eng, MPS, MS, PhD); environmental engineering (M Eng, MPS, MS, PhD); environmental management (MPS); food processing engineering (M Eng, MPS, MS, PhD); international agriculture (M Eng, MPS, MS, PhD); local roads (M Eng, MPS, MS, PhD); machine systems (M Eng, MPS, MS, PhD); soil and water engineering (M Eng, MPS, MS, PhD); structures and environment (M Eng, MPS, MS, PhD). *Faculty:* 32 full-time (6 women). *Students:* 70 full-time (32 women); includes 11 minority (3 Black or African American, non-Hispanic/Latino; 4 Asian, non-Hispanic/Latino; 4 Hispanic/Latino), 26 international. Average age 28. 115 applicants, 25% accepted, 18 enrolled. In 2011, 18 master's, 6 doctorates awarded. Terminal master's awarded for partial completion of doctoral program. *Degree requirements:* For master's, thesis (MS); for doctorate, comprehensive exam, thesis/dissertation. *Entrance requirements:* For master's, letters of recommendation (3 for MS, 2 for M Eng and MPS); for doctorate, GRE General Test, 3 letters of recommendation. Additional exam requirements/recommendations for international students: Required—TOEFL (minimum score 550 paper-based; 213 computer-based; 77 iBT). *Application deadline:* For fall admission, 1/15 priority date for domestic students; for spring admission, 10/1 for domestic students. Applications are processed on a rolling basis. Application fee: $95. Electronic applications accepted. *Financial support:* In 2011–12, 11 fellowships with full tuition reimbursements, 32 research assistantships with full tuition reimbursements, 7 teaching assistantships with full tuition reimbursements were awarded; institutionally sponsored loans, scholarships/grants, health care benefits, tuition waivers (full and partial), and unspecified assistantships also available. Financial award applicants required to submit FAFSA. *Faculty research:* Biological and food engineering, environmental, soil and water engineering, international agricultural engineering, structures and controlled environments, machine systems and energy. *Unit head:* Director of Graduate Studies, 607-255-2173, Fax: 607-255-4080, E-mail: abengradfield@cornell.edu. *Application contact:* Graduate Field Assistant, 607-255-2173, Fax: 607-255-4080, E-mail: abengradfield@cornell.edu. Web site: http://www.gradschool.cornell.edu/fields.php?id-21&a-2.

Dalhousie University, Faculty of Engineering, Department of Biological Engineering, Halifax, NS B3J 2X4, Canada. Offers M Eng, MA Sc, PhD. *Degree requirements:* For master's, thesis; for doctorate, thesis/dissertation. *Entrance requirements:* Additional exam requirements/recommendations for international students: Required—TOEFL, IELTS, CANTEST, CAEL, or Michigan English Language Assessment Battery. *Faculty research:* Waste management, energy and environment, bio-machinery and robotics, soil and water, aquacultural and food engineering.

Illinois Institute of Technology, Graduate College, Armour College of Engineering, Department of Chemical and Biological Engineering, Chicago, IL 60616-3793. Offers biological engineering (MBE); chemical engineering (M Ch E, MS, PhD); food process engineering (MFPE, MS). Part-time and evening/weekend programs available. Postbaccalaureate distance learning degree programs offered (minimal on-campus study). Terminal master's awarded for partial completion of doctoral program. *Degree requirements:* For master's, comprehensive exam (for some programs), thesis (for some programs); for doctorate, comprehensive exam, thesis/dissertation. *Entrance requirements:* For master's, GRE General Test (minimum score 900 Quantitative and Verbal, 2.5 Analytical Writing), minimum undergraduate GPA of 3.0; for doctorate, GRE General Test (minimum score 1000 Quantitative and Verbal, 3.0 Analytical Writing), minimum undergraduate GPA of 3.0. Additional exam requirements/recommendations for international students: Required—TOEFL (minimum score 523 paper-based; 70 iBT); Recommended—IELTS (minimum score 5.5). Electronic applications accepted. *Faculty research:* Energy and sustainability, biological engineering, advanced materials, systems engineering.

Instituto Tecnológico y de Estudios Superiores de Monterrey, Campus Monterrey, Graduate and Research Division, Program in Agriculture, Monterrey, Mexico. Offers agricultural parasitology (PhD); agricultural sciences (MS); farming productivity (MS); food processing engineering (MS); phytopathology (MS). Part-time programs available. *Degree requirements:* For master's, one foreign language, thesis; for doctorate, one foreign language, thesis/dissertation. *Entrance requirements:* For master's, EXADEP; for doctorate, GMAT or GRE, master's degree in related field. Additional exam requirements/recommendations for international students: Required—TOEFL. *Faculty research:* Animal embryos and reproduction, crop entomology, tropical agriculture, agricultural productivity, induced mutation in oleaginous plants.

Iowa State University of Science and Technology, Program in Agricultural and Biosystems Engineering, Ames, IA 50011-3130. Offers M En, MS, PhD. *Faculty:* 30 full-time (2 women), 3 part-time/adjunct (0 women). *Students:* 55 full-time (21 women), 21 part-time (7 women); includes 7 minority (3 Black or African American, non-Hispanic/Latino; 1 American Indian or Alaska Native, non-Hispanic/Latino; 2 Asian, non-Hispanic/Latino; 1 Hispanic/Latino), 29 international. 52 applicants, 31% accepted, 13 enrolled. In 2011, 9 master's, 5 doctorates awarded. *Degree requirements:* For master's, thesis (for some programs); for doctorate, thesis/dissertation. *Entrance requirements:* For master's and doctorate, GRE. Additional exam requirements/recommendations for international students: Required—TOEFL (minimum score 550 paper-based; 79 iBT), IELTS (minimum score 6.5). *Application deadline:* For fall admission, 2/15 priority date for domestic students, 2/1 for international students; for spring admission, 7/1 priority date for domestic students, 7/1 for international students. Application fee: $40 ($90 for international students). Electronic applications accepted. *Financial support:* In 2011–12, 51 research assistantships with full and partial tuition reimbursements (averaging $15,435 per year), 1 teaching assistantship with full and partial tuition reimbursement (averaging $9,613 per year) were awarded; fellowships, scholarships/grants, health care benefits, and unspecified assistantships also available. *Faculty research:* Grain processing and quality, tillage systems, simulation and controls, water management, environmental quality. *Unit head:* Dr. Steve Hoff, Director of Graduate Education, 515-294-1033. *Application contact:* Kris Bell, Graduate Secretary, 515-294-1033, E-mail: kabell@iastate.edu. Web site: http://www.abe.iastate.edu.

Kansas State University, Graduate School, College of Agriculture, Department of Grain Science and Industry, Manhattan, KS 66506. Offers MS, PhD. Part-time programs available. *Faculty:* 12 full-time (3 women), 8 part-time/adjunct (2 women). *Students:* 38 full-time (19 women), 10 part-time (2 women); includes 4 minority (2 Black or African American, non-Hispanic/Latino; 1 Asian, non-Hispanic/Latino; 1 Hispanic/Latino), 25 international. Average age 29. 26 applicants, 54% accepted, 13 enrolled. In 2011, 11 master's, 5 doctorates awarded. Terminal master's awarded for partial completion of doctoral program. *Degree requirements:* For master's, thesis, oral exam; for doctorate, thesis/dissertation, preliminary exam. *Entrance requirements:* For master's and doctorate, GRE General Test, minimum undergraduate GPA of 3.0. Additional exam requirements/recommendations for international students: Required—TOEFL (minimum score 550 paper-based; 213 computer-based; 79 iBT), IELTS (minimum score 7). *Application deadline:* For fall admission, 5/1 priority date for domestic students, 2/1 for international students; for spring admission, 10/1 priority date for domestic students, 8/1 for international students. Applications are processed on a rolling basis. Application fee: $40 ($55 for international students). Electronic applications accepted. *Financial support:* In 2011–12, 3 fellowships (averaging $25,000 per year), 29 research assistantships (averaging $23,393 per year), 3 teaching assistantships with partial tuition reimbursements (averaging $24,500 per year) were awarded; Federal Work-Study, institutionally sponsored loans, and scholarships/grants also available. Support available to part-time students. Financial award application deadline: 3/1; financial award applicants required to submit FAFSA. *Faculty research:* Particle management, grain and cereal product research, industrial value added products from cereals and legumes, grain stored wheat and pest management, biosecurity and global tracing. *Total annual research expenditures:* $2.3 million. *Unit head:* Dirk Maier, Head, 785-532-6161, Fax: 785-532-7010, E-mail: dmaier@ksu.edu. *Application contact:* Jon Faubion, Chair, Graduate Program, 785-532-5320, Fax: 785-532-7010, E-mail: jfaubion@ksu.edu. Web site: http://www.grains.k-state.edu/DesktopDefault.aspx.

Kansas State University, Graduate School, College of Engineering, Department of Biological and Agricultural Engineering, Manhattan, KS 66506. Offers MS, PhD. *Faculty:* 13 full-time (1 woman), 6 part-time/adjunct (0 women). *Students:* 26 full-time (12 women), 7 part-time (2 women); includes 1 minority (Black or African American, non-Hispanic/Latino), 19 international. Average age 28. 26 applicants, 38% accepted, 7 enrolled. In 2011, 7 master's, 1 doctorate awarded. Terminal master's awarded for partial completion of doctoral program. *Degree requirements:* For master's, thesis; for doctorate, thesis/dissertation. *Entrance requirements:* For master's, GRE (recommended), bachelor's degree in agricultural engineering; for doctorate, GRE (recommended). Additional exam requirements/recommendations for international students: Required—TOEFL (minimum score 600 paper-based; 250 computer-based). *Application deadline:* For fall admission, 2/1 priority date for domestic students, 2/1 for international students; for spring admission, 8/1 priority date for domestic students, 8/1 for international students. Applications are processed on a rolling basis. Application fee: $40 ($55 for international students). Electronic applications accepted. *Financial support:* In 2011–12, 22 research assistantships (averaging $21,509 per year) were awarded; fellowships, teaching assistantships, Federal Work-Study, institutionally sponsored loans, and scholarships/grants also available. Support available to part-time students. Financial award application deadline: 3/1; financial award applicants required to submit FAFSA. *Faculty research:* Ecological engineering, watershed modeling, air quality, bioprocessing, bio-fuel, sensors and controls. *Total annual research expenditures:* $1.7 million. *Unit head:* Joseph Harner, Head, 785-532-5580, Fax: 785-532-5825, E-mail: jharner@ksu.edu. *Application contact:* Naiqian Zhang, Graduate Coordinator, 785-532-2910, Fax: 785-532-5825, E-mail: zhangn@ksu.edu. Web site: http://www.bae.ksu.edu/.

Louisiana State University and Agricultural and Mechanical College, Graduate School, College of Agriculture, Department of Biological and Agricultural Engineering, Baton Rouge, LA 70803. Offers biological and agricultural engineering (MSBAE); engineering science (MS, PhD). Part-time programs available. *Faculty:* 11 full-time (2 women). *Students:* 16 full-time (4 women), 2 part-time (1 woman); includes 7 minority (3 Black or African American, non-Hispanic/Latino; 3 Asian, non-Hispanic/Latino; 1 Hispanic/Latino), 6 international. Average age 26. 9 applicants, 56% accepted, 2 enrolled. In 2011, 7 master's awarded. Terminal master's awarded for partial completion of doctoral program. *Degree requirements:* For master's, thesis; for doctorate, thesis/dissertation. *Entrance requirements:* For master's and doctorate, GRE General Test, minimum GPA of 3.0. Additional exam requirements/recommendations for international students: Required—TOEFL (minimum score 550 paper-based; 213 computer-based; 79 iBT) or IELTS (minimum score 6.5). *Application deadline:* For fall admission, 1/25 priority date for domestic students, 5/15 for international students; for spring admission, 10/15 for international students. Applications are processed on a rolling basis. Application fee: $50 ($70 for international students). Electronic applications accepted. *Financial support:* In 2011–12, 16 students received support, including 1 fellowship (averaging $6,300 per year), 14 research assistantships with partial tuition reimbursements available (averaging $17,956 per year); teaching assistantships with partial tuition reimbursements available, career-related internships or fieldwork, Federal Work-Study, institutionally sponsored loans, scholarships/grants, health care benefits, and unspecified assistantships also available. Financial award application deadline: 7/1; financial award applicants required to submit FAFSA. *Faculty research:* Bioenergy, bioprocess engineering, cellular and molecular engineering, drug delivery using nanotechnology, environmental engineering. *Total annual research expenditures:* $87,691. *Unit head:* Dr. Dan Thomas, Head, 225-578-3153, Fax: 225-578-3492, E-mail: dthomas@agcenter.lsu.edu. *Application contact:* Dr. Steven Hall, Graduate Coordinator, 225-578-1058, Fax: 225-578-3492, E-mail: sghall@agcenter.lsu.edu. Web site: http://www.bae.lsu.edu/.

McGill University, Faculty of Graduate and Postdoctoral Studies, Faculty of Agricultural and Environmental Sciences, Department of Bioresource Engineering, Montréal, QC H3A 2T5, Canada. Offers computer applications (M Sc, M Sc A, PhD); food engineering (M Sc, M Sc A, PhD); grain drying (M Sc, M Sc A, PhD); irrigation and drainage (M Sc, M Sc A, PhD); machinery (M Sc, M Sc A, PhD); pollution control (M Sc, M Sc A, PhD); post-harvest technology (M Sc, M Sc A, PhD); soil dynamics (M Sc, M Sc A, PhD); structure and environment (M Sc, M Sc A, PhD); vegetable and fruit storage (M Sc, M Sc A, PhD).

New York University, Graduate School of Arts and Science, Department of Environmental Medicine, New York, NY 10012-1019. Offers environmental health sciences (MS, PhD), including biostatistics (PhD), environmental hygiene (MS); epidemiology (PhD), ergonomics and biomechanics (PhD), exposure assessment and health effects (PhD), molecular toxicology/carcinogenesis (PhD), toxicology. Part-time programs available. *Faculty:* 26 full-time (7 women). *Students:* 62 full-time (43 women), 9 part-time (4 women); includes 12 minority (2 Black or African American, non-Hispanic/Latino; 3 Asian, non-Hispanic/Latino; 7 Hispanic/Latino), 27 international. Average age 30. 70 applicants, 56% accepted, 26 enrolled. In 2011, 9 master's, 8 doctorates awarded. Terminal master's awarded for partial completion of doctoral program. *Degree requirements:* For master's, thesis or alternative; for doctorate, one foreign language, thesis/dissertation, oral and written exams. *Entrance requirements:* For master's and doctorate, GRE General Test, GRE Subject Test, minimum GPA of 3.0; bachelor's degree in biological, physical, or engineering science. Additional exam requirements/recommendations for international students: Required—TOEFL. *Application deadline:* For fall admission, 12/12 for domestic and international students. Application fee: $90. *Financial support:* Fellowships with tuition reimbursements, teaching assistantships with tuition reimbursements, career-related internships or fieldwork, Federal Work-Study, institutionally sponsored loans, and health care benefits available. Financial award application deadline: 12/12; financial award applicants required to submit FAFSA. *Unit head:* Dr. Max Costa, Chair, 845-731-3661, Fax: 845-351-4510, E-mail: ehs@env.med.nyu.edu. *Application contact:* Dr. Jerome J. Solomon, Director of Graduate Studies, 845-731-3661, Fax: 845-351-4510, E-mail: ehs@env.med.nyu.edu. Web site: http://environmental-medicine.med.nyu.edu/.

North Carolina State University, Graduate School, College of Agriculture and Life Sciences, Department of Biological and Agricultural Engineering, Raleigh, NC 27695. Offers MBAE, MS, PhD, Certificate. Part-time programs available. Postbaccalaureate distance learning degree programs offered. *Degree requirements:* For master's, thesis (for some programs); for doctorate, thesis/dissertation. *Entrance requirements:* For master's and doctorate, GRE. Additional exam requirements/recommendations for international students: Required—TOEFL. Electronic applications accepted. *Faculty research:* Bioinstrumentation, animal waste management, water quality engineering, machine systems, controlled environment agriculture.

North Dakota State University, College of Graduate and Interdisciplinary Studies, College of Engineering and Architecture, Department of Agricultural and Biosystems Engineering, Fargo, ND 58108. Offers agricultural and biosystems engineering (MS, PhD); engineering (PhD); natural resource management (MS); natural resources management (PhD). Part-time programs available. *Faculty:* 6 full-time (0 women). *Students:* 7 full-time (3 women), 2 part-time (0 women), all international. Average age 28. 12 applicants, 8% accepted, 0 enrolled. In 2011, 4 degrees awarded. *Degree requirements:* For master's, thesis; for doctorate, thesis/dissertation. *Entrance requirements:* For master's and doctorate, BS in engineering or the equivalent, minimum undergraduate GPA of 3.0. Additional exam requirements/recommendations for international students: Required—TOEFL (minimum score 550 paper-based; 213 computer-based; 79 iBT). *Application deadline:* For fall admission, 5/1 for international students; for spring admission, 8/1 for international students. Applications are processed on a rolling basis. Application fee: $35. Electronic applications accepted. *Financial support:* In 2011–12, 9 research assistantships with full tuition reimbursements (averaging $15,000 per year) were awarded; career-related internships or fieldwork, Federal Work-Study, institutionally sponsored loans, and unspecified assistantships also available. Support available to part-time students. Financial award application deadline: 4/15. *Faculty research:* Irrigation, crop processing, food engineering, environmental resources, sensors and instrumentation. *Unit head:* Dr. James Venette, Chair, 701-231-7261, Fax: 701-231-1008, E-mail: james.venette@ndsu.edu. *Application contact:* Dr. David A. Wittrock, Dean, 701-231-7033, Fax: 701-231-6524. Web site: http://www.ageng.ndsu.nodak.edu/.

The Ohio State University, Graduate School, College of Food, Agricultural, and Environmental Sciences, Department of Food, Agricultural, and Biological Engineering, Columbus, OH 43210. Offers MS, PhD. *Faculty:* 18. *Students:* 36 full-time (13 women), 7 part-time (2 women); includes 5 minority (2 Black or African American, non-Hispanic/Latino; 1 Asian, non-Hispanic/Latino; 2 Hispanic/Latino), 17 international. Average age 28. In 2011, 4 master's, 4 doctorates awarded. *Degree requirements:* For master's, thesis optional; for doctorate, thesis/dissertation. *Entrance requirements:* For master's and doctorate, GRE General Test, GRE Subject Test in engineering (recommended). Additional exam requirements/recommendations for international students: Required—TOEFL (minimum score 550 paper-based; 213 computer-based), IELTS (minimum score 6.5), or Michigan English Language Assessment Battery (minimum score 82). *Application deadline:* For fall admission, 8/15 priority date for domestic students, 7/1 for international students; for winter admission, 12/1 priority date for domestic students, 11/1 for international students; for spring admission, 3/1 priority date for domestic students, 2/1 for international students. Applications are processed on a rolling basis. Application fee: $40 ($50 for international students). Electronic applications accepted. *Expenses:* Tuition, state resident: full-time $11,400. Tuition, nonresident: full-time $28,125. Tuition and fees vary according to course load, degree level, campus/location and program. *Financial support:* Fellowships, research assistantships, teaching assistantships, career-related internships or fieldwork, Federal Work-Study, and institutionally sponsored loans available. Support available to part-time students. *Unit head:* Scott Shearer, Chair, 614-292-7284, E-mail: shearer.95@osu.edu. *Application contact:* Graduate Admissions, 614-292-6031, Fax: 614-292-3656, E-mail: gradadmissions@osu.edu. Web site: http://fabe.osu.edu/.

Oklahoma State University, College of Agricultural Science and Natural Resources, Department of Biosystems and Agricultural Engineering, Stillwater, OK 74078. Offers biosystems engineering (MS, PhD); environmental and natural resources (MS, PhD). *Faculty:* 22 full-time (3 women), 3 part-time/adjunct (0 women). *Students:* 18 full-time (6 women), 50 part-time (21 women); includes 7 minority (1 Black or African American, non-Hispanic/Latino; 1 American Indian or Alaska Native, non-Hispanic/Latino; 1 Asian, non-Hispanic/Latino; 2 Hispanic/Latino; 2 Two or more races, non-Hispanic/Latino), 35 international. Average age 31. 57 applicants, 23% accepted, 3 enrolled. In 2011, 6 master's, 4 doctorates awarded. *Degree requirements:* For master's, thesis; for doctorate, comprehensive exam, thesis/dissertation. *Entrance requirements:* For master's and doctorate, GRE or GMAT. Additional exam requirements/recommendations for international students: Required—TOEFL (minimum score 550 paper-based; 79 iBT). *Application deadline:* For fall admission, 3/1 for international students; for spring admission, 8/1 for international students. Applications are processed on a rolling basis. Application fee: $40 ($75 for international students). Electronic applications accepted. *Expenses:* Tuition, state resident: full-time $4044; part-time $168.50 per credit hour. Tuition, nonresident: full-time $16,008; part-time $667 per credit hour. *Required fees:* $2122; $88.45 per credit hour. One-time fee: $50. Tuition and fees vary according to course load and campus/location. *Financial support:* In 2011–12, 43 research assistantships (averaging $17,505 per year) were awarded; teaching assistantships, career-related internships or fieldwork, Federal Work-Study, scholarships/grants, health care benefits, tuition waivers (partial), and unspecified assistantships also available. Support available to part-time students. Financial award application deadline: 3/1; financial award applicants required to submit FAFSA. *Unit head:* Dr. Daniel Thomas, Head, 405-744-5431, Fax: 405-744-6059. *Application contact:* Dr. Sheryl Tucker, Dean, 405-744-7099, Fax: 405-744-0355, E-mail: grad-i@okstate.edu. Web site: http://bioen.okstate.edu/.

Penn State University Park, Graduate School, College of Agricultural Sciences, Department of Agricultural and Biological Engineering, State College, University Park, PA 16802-1503. Offers MS, PhD. *Unit head:* Dr. Bruce A. McPheron, Dean, 814-865-2541, Fax: 814-865-3103, E-mail: bam10@psu.edu. *Application contact:* Cynthia E. Nicosia, Director of Graduate Enrollment Services, 814-865-1834, E-mail: cey1@psu.edu. Web site: http://www.abe.psu.edu.

Purdue University, College of Engineering, Department of Agricultural and Biological Engineering, West Lafayette, IN 47907-2093. Offers MS, MSABE, MSE, PhD. Part-time programs available. Terminal master's awarded for partial completion of doctoral program. *Degree requirements:* For master's, thesis (for some programs); for doctorate, thesis/dissertation. *Entrance requirements:* For master's and doctorate, GRE General Test. Additional exam requirements/recommendations for international students: Required—TOEFL (minimum score 550 paper-based; 213 computer-based; 77 iBT). Electronic applications accepted. *Faculty research:* Food and biological engineering, environmental engineering, machine systems, biotechnology, machine intelligence.

South Dakota State University, Graduate School, College of Engineering, Department of Agricultural and Biosystems Engineering, Brookings, SD 57007. Offers biological sciences (MS, PhD); engineering (MS). PhD offered jointly with Iowa State University of Science and Technology. Part-time programs available. *Degree requirements:* For master's, thesis (for some programs), oral exam; for doctorate, thesis/dissertation, preliminary oral and written exams. *Entrance requirements:* For master's and doctorate, engineering degree. Additional exam requirements/recommendations for international students: Required—TOEFL (minimum score 550 paper-based; 213 computer-based; 79 iBT). *Faculty research:* Water resources, food engineering, natural resources engineering, machine design, bioprocess engineering.

Texas A&M University, College of Agriculture and Life Sciences and College of Engineering, Department of Biological and Agricultural Engineering, College Station, TX 77843. Offers M Agr, M Eng, MS, DE, PhD. Part-time programs available. *Faculty:* 18. *Students:* 16 full-time (5 women), 68 part-time (25 women); includes 9 minority (4 Black or African American, non-Hispanic/Latino; 2 Asian, non-Hispanic/Latino; 3 Hispanic/Latino), 51 international. Average age 29. In 2011, 7 master's, 2 doctorates awarded. *Degree requirements:* For master's, thesis (MS), preliminary and final exams; for doctorate, thesis/dissertation, preliminary and final exams. *Entrance requirements:* For master's and doctorate, GRE General Test. Additional exam requirements/recommendations for international students: Required—TOEFL (minimum score 550 paper-based; 213 computer-based). *Application deadline:* For fall admission, 2/1 priority date for domestic students; for spring admission, 10/1 for domestic students. Applications are processed on a rolling basis. Application fee: $50 ($75 for international students). Electronic applications accepted. *Expenses:* Tuition, state resident: full-time $5437; part-time $226.55 per credit hour. Tuition, nonresident: full-time $12,949; part-time $539.55 per credit hour. *Required fees:* $2741. *Financial support:* In 2011–12, 3 fellowships with full and partial tuition reimbursements (averaging $15,000 per year), 17 research assistantships with full and partial tuition reimbursements (averaging $18,150 per year), 12 teaching assistantships with partial tuition reimbursements (averaging $19,590 per year) were awarded; career-related internships or fieldwork, institutionally sponsored loans, scholarships/grants, tuition waivers, and unspecified assistantships also available. Financial award application deadline: 3/1; financial award applicants required to submit FAFSA. *Faculty research:* Water quality and quantity; air quality; biological, food, ecological engineering; off-road equipment; mechatronics. *Unit head:* Dr. Steve Searcy, Interim Head, 979-845-3668, Fax: 979-862-3442, E-mail: s-searcy@tamu.edu. *Application contact:* Graduate Admissions, 979-845-1044, E-mail: admissions@tamu.edu. Web site: http://baen.tamu.edu.

Université Laval, Faculty of Agricultural and Food Sciences, Department of Soils and Agricultural Engineering, Programs in Agri-Food Engineering, Québec, QC G1K 7P4, Canada. Offers agri-food engineering (M Sc); environmental technology (M Sc). *Degree requirements:* For master's, thesis (for some programs). *Entrance requirements:* For master's, knowledge of French. Electronic applications accepted.

The University of Arizona, College of Agriculture and Life Sciences, Department of Agricultural and Biosystems Engineering, Tucson, AZ 85721. Offers MS, PhD. *Faculty:* 10 full-time (1 woman). *Students:* 25 full-time (12 women), 5 part-time (0 women); includes 4 minority (2 Asian, non-Hispanic/Latino; 1 Hispanic/Latino; 1 Two or more races, non-Hispanic/Latino), 17 international. Average age 32. 19 applicants, 74% accepted, 6 enrolled. In 2011, 4 master's, 7 doctorates awarded. Terminal master's awarded for partial completion of doctoral program. *Degree requirements:* For master's, thesis; for doctorate, thesis/dissertation. *Entrance requirements:* For master's, minimum GPA of 3.0 in last 2 years of undergraduate study, 3 letters of recommendation; for doctorate, minimum GPA of 3.0 in last 2 years of undergraduate study, 3 letters of recommendation, statement of purpose. Additional exam requirements/recommendations for international students: Required—TOEFL (minimum score 213 computer-based). *Application deadline:* For fall admission, 6/1 for domestic students, 2/1 for international students; for spring admission, 9/1 for domestic students, 8/1 for international students. Applications are processed on a rolling basis. Application fee: $75. Electronic applications accepted. *Expenses:* Tuition, state resident: full-time $10,840. Tuition, nonresident: full-time $25,802. *Financial support:* In 2011–12, 9 research assistantships with full and partial tuition reimbursements (averaging $24,985 per year), 1 teaching assistantship with full and partial tuition reimbursement (averaging $24,435 per year) were awarded; fellowships, career-related internships or fieldwork, Federal Work-Study, institutionally sponsored loans, scholarships/grants, traineeships, health care benefits, tuition waivers (full and partial), and unspecified assistantships also available. Financial award application deadline: 5/1. *Faculty research:* Irrigation system design, energy-use management, equipment for alternative crops, food properties enhancement. *Total annual research expenditures:* $2 million. *Unit head:* Mark R. Riley, Head, 520-626-9120, Fax: 520-621-3963, E-mail: riley@ag.arizona.edu. *Application contact:* Daniela Ibarra, Senior Office Specialist, 520-621-1753, Fax: 520-621-3963, E-mail: dcastro@email.arizona.edu. Web site: http://ag.arizona.edu/abe.

University of Arkansas, Graduate School, College of Engineering, Department of Biological and Agricultural Engineering, Fayetteville, AR 72701-1201. Offers biological and agricultural engineering (MSE, PhD); biological engineering (MSBE); biomedical engineering (MSBME). *Students:* 9 full-time (3 women), 15 part-time (3 women), 11 international. In 2011, 4 master's awarded. *Degree requirements:* For master's, thesis; for doctorate, one foreign language, thesis/dissertation. *Application deadline:* For fall admission, 4/1 for international students; for spring admission, 10/1 for international students. Applications are processed on a rolling basis. Application fee: $40 ($50 for international students). Electronic applications accepted. *Financial support:* In 2011–12, 21 research assistantships, 3 teaching assistantships were awarded; fellowships with tuition reimbursements, career-related internships or fieldwork, and Federal Work-Study also available. Support available to part-time students. Financial award application deadline: 4/1; financial award applicants required to submit FAFSA. *Unit head:* Dr. Lalit Verma, Department Head, 479-575-2351, Fax: 479-575-2846, E-mail: lverma@uark.edu. *Application contact:* Dr. Jin-Woo Kim, Program Coordinator, 479-575-2351, Fax: 479-575-2846, E-mail: jwkim@uark.edu. Web site: http://www.baeg.uark.edu/.

University of Dayton, Department of Civil and Environmental Engineering and Engineering Mechanics, Dayton, OH 45469-1300. Offers engineering mechanics

(MSEM); environmental engineering (MSCE); geotechnical engineering (MSCE); structural engineering (MSCE); transportation engineering (MSCE); water resources engineering (MSCE). Part-time programs available. *Faculty:* 7 full-time (2 women), 2 part-time/adjunct (0 women). *Students:* 16 full-time (4 women), 9 part-time (4 women); includes 1 minority (Asian, non-Hispanic/Latino), 13 international. Average age 27. 53 applicants, 38% accepted, 5 enrolled. In 2011, 7 degrees awarded. *Degree requirements:* For master's, thesis optional. *Entrance requirements:* For master's, minimum GPA of 3.0 in undergraduate work. Additional exam requirements/ recommendations for international students: Required—TOEFL (minimum score 550 paper-based; 213 computer-based; 80 iBT). *Application deadline:* For fall admission, 8/1 for domestic students, 3/1 for international students; for winter admission, 7/1 for international students; for spring admission, 1/1 for international students. Applications are processed on a rolling basis. Application fee: $0 ($50 for international students). Electronic applications accepted. *Expenses: Tuition:* Full-time $8400; part-time $700 per credit hour. *Required fees:* $25 per semester. Tuition and fees vary according to degree level. *Financial support:* Research assistantships available. Financial award applicants required to submit FAFSA. *Faculty research:* Physical modeling of hydraulic systems, finite element methods, mechanics of composite materials, transportation systems safety, biological treatment processes. *Total annual research expenditures:* $200,000. *Unit head:* Dr. Donald V. Chase, Chair, 937-229-3847, Fax: 937-229-3491, E-mail: dchase1@udayton.edu. *Application contact:* Dr. Donald Chase, Chair, 937-229-3847, Fax: 937-229-3491, E-mail: dchase1@udayton.edu. Web site: http://www.udayton.edu/ engineering/civil.

University of Florida, Graduate School, College of Engineering and College of Agricultural and Life Sciences, Department of Agricultural and Biological Engineering, Gainesville, FL 32611. Offers ME, MS, PhD, Engr. Part-time programs available. Terminal master's awarded for partial completion of doctoral program. *Degree requirements:* For master's, comprehensive exam, thesis (for some programs); for doctorate, comprehensive exam, thesis/dissertation. *Entrance requirements:* For master's and doctorate, GRE General Test, minimum GPA of 3.0; for Engr, GRE General Test. Additional exam requirements/recommendations for international students: Required—TOEFL (minimum score 550 paper-based; 213 computer-based; 80 iBT), IELTS (minimum score 6). Electronic applications accepted. *Faculty research:* Biological processing, crop and climate modeling, land and water resources, robotic harvesting, food and packaging.

University of Georgia, College of Agricultural and Environmental Sciences, Department of Biological and Agricultural Engineering, Athens, GA 30602. Offers agricultural engineering (MS); biological and agricultural engineering (PhD); biological engineering (MS). *Faculty:* 36 full-time (13 women), 6 part-time/adjunct (0 women). *Students:* 36 full-time (13 women), 6 part-time (0 women); includes 4 minority (all Black or African American, non-Hispanic/Latino), 23 international. Average age 30. 49 applicants, 43% accepted, 7 enrolled. In 2011, 11 master's, 5 doctorates awarded. *Degree requirements:* For master's, thesis; for doctorate, one foreign language, thesis/ dissertation. *Entrance requirements:* For master's and doctorate, GRE General Test. *Application deadline:* For fall admission, 7/1 priority date for domestic students; for spring admission, 11/15 for domestic students. Application fee: $50. Electronic applications accepted. *Financial support:* Fellowships, research assistantships, teaching assistantships, and unspecified assistantships available. *Unit head:* Dr. E. Dale Threadgill, Head, 706-542-1653, Fax: 706-542-8806, E-mail: tgill@engr.uga.edu. *Application contact:* Dr. William Tollner, Graduate Coordinator, 706-542-3047, Fax: 706-542-8806, E-mail: btollner@engr.uga.edu. Web site: http://www.engr.uga.edu.

University of Idaho, College of Graduate Studies, College of Engineering, Department of Biological and Agricultural Engineering, Moscow, ID 83844-0904. Offers M Engr, MS, PhD. Program offered jointly with College of Agricultural and Life Sciences. *Faculty:* 6 full-time. *Students:* 7 full-time, 3 part-time. Average age 37. In 2011, 1 master's, 1 doctorate awarded. *Degree requirements:* For master's, thesis or alternative; for doctorate, one foreign language, thesis/dissertation. *Entrance requirements:* For master's, minimum GPA of 2.8; for doctorate, minimum undergraduate GPA of 2.8, 3.0 graduate. *Application deadline:* For fall admission, 8/1 for domestic students; for spring admission, 12/15 for domestic students. Applications are processed on a rolling basis. Application fee: $60. Electronic applications accepted. *Expenses:* Tuition, state resident: full-time $3874; part-time $334 per credit hour. Tuition, nonresident: full-time $16,394; part-time $861 per credit hour. *Required fees:* $2808; $99 per credit hour. Tuition and fees vary according to program. *Financial support:* Research assistantships, teaching assistantships, and career-related internships or fieldwork available. Financial award applicants required to submit FAFSA. *Faculty research:* Water and environmental research, alternative fuels/biodiesel, agricultural safety health, biological processes for agricultural/food waste. *Unit head:* Dr. Jon Harlan Van Gerpen, Department Head, 208-885-7891, E-mail: baengr@uidaho.edu. *Application contact:* Erick Larson, Director of Graduate Admissions, 208-885-4723, E-mail: gadms@uidaho.edu. Web site: http:// www.uidaho.edu/cals/bae/.

University of Illinois at Urbana–Champaign, Graduate College, College of Agricultural, Consumer and Environmental Sciences, Department of Agricultural and Biological Engineering, Champaign, IL 61820. Offers agricultural and biological engineering (MS, PhD); technical systems management (MS, PSM). *Faculty:* 19 full-time (2 women). *Students:* 59 full-time (15 women), 9 part-time (3 women); includes 7 minority (1 Black or African American, non-Hispanic/Latino; 1 Asian, non-Hispanic/ Latino; 2 Hispanic/Latino; 3 Two or more races, non-Hispanic/Latino), 47 international. 66 applicants, 41% accepted, 22 enrolled. In 2011, 10 master's, 5 doctorates awarded. *Entrance requirements:* For master's and doctorate, minimum GPA of 3.0. Additional exam requirements/recommendations for international students: Required—TOEFL (minimum score 570 paper-based; 230 computer-based; 88 iBT) or IELTS (minimum score 6.5). *Application deadline:* Applications are processed on a rolling basis. Application fee: $75 ($90 for international students). Electronic applications accepted. *Financial support:* In 2011–12, 16 fellowships, 47 research assistantships, 19 teaching assistantships were awarded; tuition waivers (full and partial) also available. *Unit head:* Kuan Chong Ting, Head, 217-333-3570, Fax: 217-244-0323, E-mail: kcting@illinois.edu. *Application contact:* Mary Schultze, Office Manager, 217-333-5423, Fax: 217-244-0323, E-mail: mlschltz@illinois.edu. Web site: http://abe.illinois.edu.

University of Kentucky, Graduate School, College of Agriculture, Program in Biosystems and Agricultural Engineering, Lexington, KY 40506-0032. Offers MS, PhD. Part-time programs available. *Degree requirements:* For master's, comprehensive exam, thesis optional; for doctorate, comprehensive exam, thesis/dissertation. *Entrance requirements:* For master's, GRE General Test, minimum undergraduate GPA of 2.75; for doctorate, GRE General Test, minimum graduate GPA of 3.0. Additional exam requirements/recommendations for international students: Required—TOEFL (minimum score 550 paper-based; 213 computer-based). Electronic applications accepted. *Faculty research:* Machine systems, food engineering, fermentation, hydrology, water quality.

University of Missouri, Graduate School, College of Engineering, Department of Biological Engineering, Columbia, MO 65211. Offers agricultural engineering (MS); biological engineering (MS, PhD). *Faculty:* 20 full-time (2 women). *Students:* 35 full-time (11 women), 16 part-time (6 women); includes 4 minority (1 Black or African American, non-Hispanic/Latino; 2 Asian, non-Hispanic/Latino; 1 Hispanic/Latino), 26 international. Average age 26. 38 applicants, 47% accepted, 10 enrolled. In 2011, 9 master's, 9 doctorates awarded. *Degree requirements:* For master's, thesis; for doctorate, thesis/ dissertation. *Entrance requirements:* For master's and doctorate, GRE General Test, minimum GPA of 3.0. Additional exam requirements/recommendations for international students: Required—TOEFL (minimum score 550 paper-based; 213 computer-based; 80 iBT). *Application deadline:* For fall admission, 4/1 priority date for domestic students. Applications are processed on a rolling basis. Application fee: $55 ($75 for international students). *Expenses:* Tuition, state resident: full-time $5881. Tuition, nonresident: full-time $15,183. *Required fees:* $952. Tuition and fees vary according to campus/location and program. *Financial support:* Fellowships, research assistantships, teaching assistantships, and institutionally sponsored loans available. *Unit head:* Dr. Jinglu Tan, Department Chair, E-mail: tanj@missouri.edu. *Application contact:* JoAnn Lewis, 573-882-4113, E-mail: lewisj@missouri.edu. Web site: http://bioengineering.missouri.edu/ graduate/.

University of Nebraska–Lincoln, Graduate College, College of Engineering, Department of Biological Systems Engineering, Interdepartmental Area of Agricultural and Biological Systems Engineering, Lincoln, NE 68588. Offers MS, PhD. *Degree requirements:* For master's, thesis optional. *Entrance requirements:* Additional exam requirements/recommendations for international students: Required—TOEFL (minimum score 550 paper-based; 213 computer-based). Electronic applications accepted. *Faculty research:* Hydrological engineering, tractive performance, biomedical engineering, irrigation systems.

University of Saskatchewan, College of Graduate Studies and Research, College of Engineering, Department of Agricultural and Bioresource Engineering, Saskatoon, SK S7N 5A2, Canada. Offers M Eng, M Sc, PhD. *Degree requirements:* For master's, thesis (for some programs); for doctorate, thesis/dissertation. *Entrance requirements:* For master's and doctorate, GRE. Additional exam requirements/recommendations for international students: Required—TOEFL.

The University of Tennessee, Graduate School, College of Agricultural Sciences and Natural Resources, Department of Biosystems Engineering and Environmental Science, Program in Biosystems Engineering Technology, Knoxville, TN 37996. Offers MS. *Degree requirements:* For master's, thesis or alternative. *Entrance requirements:* For master's, GRE General Test, minimum GPA of 2.7. Additional exam requirements/ recommendations for international students: Required—TOEFL. Electronic applications accepted. *Expenses:* Tuition, state resident: full-time $8332; part-time $464 per credit hour. Tuition, nonresident: full-time $25,174; part-time $1400 per credit hour. *Required fees:* $1162; $56 per credit hour. Tuition and fees vary according to program.

University of Wisconsin–Madison, Graduate School, College of Agricultural and Life Sciences, Department of Biological Systems Engineering, Madison, WI 53706. Offers MS, PhD. Part-time programs available. Terminal master's awarded for partial completion of doctoral program. *Degree requirements:* For master's, thesis; for doctorate, thesis/dissertation. *Entrance requirements:* Additional exam requirements/ recommendations for international students: Required—TOEFL. Electronic applications accepted. *Expenses:* Tuition, state resident: full-time $10,296; part-time $643.51 per credit. Tuition, nonresident: full-time $24,054; part-time $1503.40 per credit. *Required fees:* $70.06 per credit. Tuition and fees vary according to course load, campus/location, program and reciprocity agreements. *Faculty research:* Biomaterials, biosensors, food safety, food engineering, bioprocessing, machinery systems, natural resources and environment, structures engineering.

Utah State University, School of Graduate Studies, College of Engineering, Department of Biological and Irrigation Engineering, Logan, UT 84322. Offers biological and agricultural engineering (MS, PhD); irrigation engineering (MS, PhD). Part-time programs available. Terminal master's awarded for partial completion of doctoral program. *Degree requirements:* For master's, thesis (for some programs); for doctorate, thesis/dissertation. *Entrance requirements:* For master's and doctorate, GRE General Test, minimum GPA of 3.0. Additional exam requirements/recommendations for international students: Required—TOEFL. *Faculty research:* On-farm water management, crop-water yield modeling, irrigation, biosensors, biological engineering.

Virginia Polytechnic Institute and State University, Graduate School, College of Engineering, Department of Biological Systems Engineering, Blacksburg, VA 24061. Offers M Eng, MS, PhD. *Degree requirements:* For master's, comprehensive exam (for some programs), thesis (for some programs); for doctorate, comprehensive exam (for some programs), thesis/dissertation (for some programs). *Entrance requirements:* For master's and doctorate, GRE. Additional exam requirements/recommendations for international students: Required—TOEFL (minimum score 550 paper-based; 213 computer-based). *Application deadline:* For fall admission, 7/1 for domestic and international students; for spring admission, 12/1 for domestic and international students. Applications are processed on a rolling basis. Application fee: $65. Electronic applications accepted. *Expenses:* Tuition, state resident: full-time $10,048; part-time $558.25 per credit hour. Tuition, nonresident: full-time $19,497; part-time $1083.25 per credit hour. *Required fees:* $405 per semester. Tuition and fees vary according to course load, campus/location and program. *Financial support:* Fellowships with full tuition reimbursements, research assistantships with full tuition reimbursements, teaching assistantships with full tuition reimbursements, career-related internships or fieldwork, Federal Work-Study, scholarships/grants, health care benefits, and unspecified assistantships available. Financial award application deadline: 1/15. *Faculty research:* Soil and water engineering, alternative energy sources for agriculture and agricultural mechanization. *Unit head:* Dr. Mary Leigh Wolfe, Unit Head, 540-231-6092, Fax: 540-231-3199, E-mail: mlwolfe@vt.edu. *Application contact:* Cully Hession, Graduate Program Director, 540-231-9480, Fax: 540-231-3199, E-mail: chession@ vt.edu. Web site: http://www.bse.vt.edu/.

Washington State University, Graduate School, College of Engineering and Architecture, Department of Biological Systems Engineering, Pullman, WA 99164. Offers biological and agricultural engineering (MS, PhD). *Faculty:* 10. *Students:* 61 full-time (16 women), 3 part-time (1 woman); includes 1 minority (Asian, non-Hispanic/ Latino), 53 international. Average age 29. 72 applicants, 43% accepted, 15 enrolled. In 2011, 4 master's, 3 doctorates awarded. *Degree requirements:* For master's, comprehensive exam, thesis (for some programs), written and oral exam; for doctorate, comprehensive exam, thesis/dissertation, written and oral exam. *Entrance requirements:* For master's, GRE General Test, GRE Subject Test, minimum GPA of 3.0, bachelor's degree in engineering or closely related subject; for doctorate, minimum GPA of 3.0, bachelor's degree in engineering or closely related subject. Additional exam requirements/recommendations for international students: Required—TOEFL. *Application deadline:* For fall admission, 2/1 priority date for domestic students, 3/1 for international students; for spring admission, 9/1 for domestic students, 7/1 for international students. Applications are processed on a rolling basis. Application fee: $75. *Financial support:* In 2011–12, 20 research assistantships (averaging $18,204 per year), 17 teaching assistantships (averaging $18,204 per year) were awarded. *Faculty*

research: Social issues and engineering education, electronic instrument design, prediction, technology for dust from agricultural lands. *Total annual research expenditures:* $3.1 million. *Unit head:* Dr. Claudio Stockle, Chair, 509-335-1578, Fax: 509-335-2722, E-mail: stockle@wsu.edu. *Application contact:* Graduate School Admissions, 800-GRADWSU, Fax: 509-335-1949, E-mail: gradsch@wsu.edu. Web site: http://www.bsyse.wsu.edu.

Bioengineering

Alfred University, Graduate School, New York State College of Ceramics, School of Engineering, Alfred, NY 14802-1205. Offers biomedical materials engineering science (MS); ceramic engineering (MS); ceramics (PhD); electrical engineering (MS); glass science (MS, PhD); materials science and engineering (MS, PhD); mechanical engineering (MS). *Degree requirements:* For master's, thesis; for doctorate, thesis/dissertation. *Entrance requirements:* Additional exam requirements/recommendations for international students: Required—TOEFL (minimum score 590 paper-based; 243 computer-based). Electronic applications accepted. *Expenses:* Contact institution. *Faculty research:* Fine-particle technology, x-ray diffraction, superconductivity, electronic materials.

Baylor College of Medicine, Graduate School of Biomedical Sciences, Program in Translational Biology and Molecular Medicine, Houston, TX 77030-3498. Offers PhD. *Faculty:* 192 full-time (56 women). *Students:* 63 full-time (35 women); includes 24 minority (10 Black or African American, non-Hispanic/Latino; 9 Asian, non-Hispanic/Latino; 5 Hispanic/Latino), 17 international. Average age 27. 133 applicants, 17% accepted, 12 enrolled. In 2011, 1 doctorate awarded. *Degree requirements:* For doctorate, thesis/dissertation, public defense. *Entrance requirements:* For doctorate, GRE, minimum GPA of 3.0. Additional exam requirements/recommendations for international students: Required—TOEFL. *Application deadline:* For fall admission, 1/1 for domestic students. Application fee: $0. Electronic applications accepted. *Financial support:* In 2011–12, 63 students received support, including 36 fellowships with full tuition reimbursements available (averaging $29,000 per year), 27 research assistantships with full tuition reimbursements available (averaging $29,000 per year); career-related internships or fieldwork, Federal Work-Study, health care benefits, and scholarships (to all students unless there are grant funds available to pay tuition) also available. Financial award applicants required to submit FAFSA. *Faculty research:* Molecular medicine, translational biology, human disease biology and therapy. *Unit head:* Dr. Mary Estes, Director, 713-798-3585, Fax: 713-798-3586, E-mail: tbmm@bcm.edu. *Application contact:* Wanda Waguespack, Graduate Program Administrator, 713-798-1077, Fax: 713-798-3586, E-mail: wandaw@bcm.edu. Web site: http://www.bcm.edu/tbmm.

California Institute of Technology, Division of Engineering and Applied Science, Option in Bioengineering, Pasadena, CA 91125-0001. Offers MS, PhD. *Degree requirements:* For master's, thesis; for doctorate, thesis/dissertation. *Faculty research:* Biosynthesis and analysis, biometrics.

Carnegie Mellon University, Carnegie Institute of Technology, Biomedical and Health Engineering Program, Pittsburgh, PA 15213-3891. Offers bioengineering (MS, PhD); MD/PhD. *Degree requirements:* For master's, thesis; for doctorate, thesis/dissertation, qualifying exam. *Entrance requirements:* For master's and doctorate, GRE General Test. Additional exam requirements/recommendations for international students: Required—TOEFL. Electronic applications accepted. *Faculty research:* Cellular and molecular systematics, signal and image processing, materials and mechanics.

Clemson University, Graduate School, College of Engineering and Science, Department of Bioengineering, Clemson, SC 29634. Offers MS, PhD. Part-time programs available. *Faculty:* 18 full-time (5 women), 4 part-time/adjunct (3 women). *Students:* 113 full-time (32 women), 16 part-time (2 women); includes 16 minority (3 Black or African American, non-Hispanic/Latino; 1 American Indian or Alaska Native, non-Hispanic/Latino; 9 Asian, non-Hispanic/Latino; 1 Hispanic/Latino; 2 Two or more races, non-Hispanic/Latino), 43 international. Average age 27. 164 applicants, 61% accepted, 39 enrolled. In 2011, 16 master's, 9 doctorates awarded. *Degree requirements:* For master's, thesis optional; for doctorate, thesis/dissertation. *Entrance requirements:* For master's and doctorate, GRE General Test. Additional exam requirements/recommendations for international students: Required—TOEFL. *Application deadline:* For fall admission, 6/1 for domestic students, 4/15 for international students; for spring admission, 11/1 for domestic students, 9/15 for international students. Applications are processed on a rolling basis. Application fee: $70 ($80 for international students). Electronic applications accepted. *Financial support:* In 2011–12, 96 students received support, including 3 fellowships with full and partial tuition reimbursements available (averaging $18,133 per year), 73 research assistantships with partial tuition reimbursements available (averaging $16,830 per year), 25 teaching assistantships with partial tuition reimbursements available (averaging $14,316 per year); career-related internships or fieldwork, institutionally sponsored loans, scholarships/grants, health care benefits, and unspecified assistantships also available. Support available to part-time students. Financial award application deadline: 2/15; financial award applicants required to submit FAFSA. *Faculty research:* Biomaterials, biomechanics, bioimaging, tissue engineering. *Total annual research expenditures:* $7.1 million. *Unit head:* Dr. Martine LaBerge, Interim Chair, 864-656-5556, Fax: 864-656-4466, E-mail: laberge@eng.clemson.edu. *Application contact:* Dr. Jiro Nagatomi, Graduate Student Coordinator, 864-656-5193, Fax: 864-656-4466, E-mail: jnagato@clemson.edu. Web site: http://www.clemson.edu/ces/departments/bioe/.

Colorado School of Mines, Graduate School, Department of Chemical Engineering, Golden, CO 80401-1887. Offers MS, PhD. Part-time programs available. *Faculty:* 38 full-time (8 women), 9 part-time/adjunct (3 women). *Students:* 63 full-time (15 women), 3 part-time (1 woman); includes 4 minority (2 Asian, non-Hispanic/Latino; 1 Native Hawaiian or other Pacific Islander, non-Hispanic/Latino; 1 Two or more races, non-Hispanic/Latino), 29 international. Average age 28. 131 applicants, 34% accepted, 20 enrolled. In 2011, 10 master's, 4 doctorates awarded. *Degree requirements:* For master's, thesis (for some programs); for doctorate, comprehensive exam, thesis/dissertation. *Entrance requirements:* For master's and doctorate, GRE General Test. Additional exam requirements/recommendations for international students: Required—TOEFL (minimum score 550 paper-based; 213 computer-based; 80 iBT). *Application deadline:* For fall admission, 1/15 for domestic and international students; for spring admission, 10/15 for domestic and international students. Application fee: $50 ($70 for international students). Electronic applications accepted. *Expenses:* Tuition, state

resident: full-time $12,585; part-time $699 per credit. Tuition, nonresident: full-time $27,270; part-time $1516 per credit. *Required fees:* $1864.20; $670 per semester. *Financial support:* In 2011–12, 65 students received support, including 1 fellowship with full tuition reimbursement available (averaging $20,000 per year), 53 research assistantships with full tuition reimbursements available (averaging $20,000 per year), 11 teaching assistantships with full tuition reimbursements available (averaging $20,000 per year); scholarships/grants, health care benefits, and unspecified assistantships also available. Financial award application deadline: 1/15; financial award applicants required to submit FAFSA. *Faculty research:* Liquid fuels for the future, responsible management of hazardous substances, surface and interfacial engineering, advanced computational methods and process control, gas hydrates. *Total annual research expenditures:* $4.4 million. *Unit head:* Dr. David Marr, Head, 303-273-3008, E-mail: dmarr@mines.edu. *Application contact:* Dr. Amadeu Sum, Professor, 303-273-3873, Fax: 303-273-3730, E-mail: asum@mines.edu. Web site: http://chemeng.mines.edu/.

Cornell University, Graduate School, Graduate Fields of Agriculture and Life Sciences and Graduate Fields of Engineering, Field of Biological and Environmental Engineering, Ithaca, NY 14853-0001. Offers biological engineering (M Eng, MPS, MS, PhD); energy (M Eng, MPS, MS, PhD); environmental engineering (M Eng, MPS, MS, PhD); environmental management (MPS); food processing engineering (M Eng, MPS, MS, PhD); international agriculture (M Eng, MPS, MS, PhD); local roads (M Eng, MPS, MS, PhD); machine systems (M Eng, MPS, MS, PhD); soil and water engineering (M Eng, MPS, MS, PhD); structures and environment (M Eng, MPS, MS, PhD). *Faculty:* 32 full-time (6 women). *Students:* 70 full-time (32 women); includes 11 minority (3 Black or African American, non-Hispanic/Latino; 4 Asian, non-Hispanic/Latino; 4 Hispanic/Latino), 26 international. Average age 28. 115 applicants, 25% accepted, 18 enrolled. In 2011, 18 master's, 6 doctorates awarded. Terminal master's awarded for partial completion of doctoral program. *Degree requirements:* For master's, thesis (MS); for doctorate, comprehensive exam, thesis/dissertation. *Entrance requirements:* For master's, letters of recommendation (3 for MS, 2 for M Eng and MPS); for doctorate, GRE General Test, 3 letters of recommendation. Additional exam requirements/recommendations for international students: Required—TOEFL (minimum score 550 paper-based; 213 computer-based; 77 iBT). *Application deadline:* For fall admission, 1/15 priority date for domestic students; for spring admission, 10/1 for domestic students. Applications are processed on a rolling basis. Application fee: $95. Electronic applications accepted. *Financial support:* In 2011–12, 11 fellowships with full tuition reimbursements, 32 research assistantships with full tuition reimbursements, 7 teaching assistantships with full tuition reimbursements were awarded; institutionally sponsored loans, scholarships/grants, health care benefits, tuition waivers (full and partial), and unspecified assistantships also available. Financial award applicants required to submit FAFSA. *Faculty research:* Biological and food engineering, environmental, soil and water engineering, international agricultural engineering, structures and controlled environments, machine systems and energy. *Unit head:* Director of Graduate Studies, 607-255-2173, Fax: 607-255-4080, E-mail: abengradfield@cornell.edu. *Application contact:* Graduate Field Assistant, 607-255-2173, Fax: 607-255-4080, E-mail: abengradfield@cornell.edu. Web site: http://www.gradschool.cornell.edu/fields.php?id-21&a-2.

Dalhousie University, Faculty of Engineering, Department of Biological Engineering, Halifax, NS B3J 2X4, Canada. Offers M Eng, MA Sc, PhD. *Degree requirements:* For master's, thesis; for doctorate, thesis/dissertation. *Entrance requirements:* Additional exam requirements/recommendations for international students: Required—TOEFL, IELTS, CANTEST, CAEL, or Michigan English Language Assessment Battery. *Faculty research:* Waste management, energy and environment, bio-machinery and robotics, soil and water, aquacultural and food engineering.

Georgia Institute of Technology, Graduate Studies and Research, College of Engineering, School of Chemical and Biomolecular Engineering, Atlanta, GA 30332-0001. Offers bioengineering (MS Bio E, PhD); chemical engineering (MS Ch E, PhD); paper science and engineering (MS, PhD); polymers (MS Poly). *Degree requirements:* For master's, thesis; for doctorate, comprehensive exam, thesis/dissertation. *Entrance requirements:* For master's and doctorate, GRE, minimum GPA of 3.0. Additional exam requirements/recommendations for international students: Required—TOEFL (minimum score 550 paper-based; 213 computer-based). Electronic applications accepted. *Faculty research:* Biochemical engineering; process modeling, synthesis, and control; polymer science and engineering; thermodynamics and separations; surface and particle science.

Georgia Institute of Technology, Graduate Studies and Research, College of Engineering, The Wallace H. Coulter Department of Biomedical Engineering at Georgia Tech and Emory University, Atlanta, GA 30332-0001. Offers bioengineering (PhD); bioinformatics (PhD); biomedical engineering (PhD); MD/PhD. PhD in biomedical engineering program jointly offered with Emory University (Georgia) and Peking University (China). Terminal master's awarded for partial completion of doctoral program. *Degree requirements:* For doctorate, thesis/dissertation. *Entrance requirements:* Additional exam requirements/recommendations for international students: Required—TOEFL. *Faculty research:* Biomechanics and tissue engineering, bioinstrumentation and medical imaging.

Illinois Institute of Technology, Graduate College, Armour College of Engineering, Department of Chemical and Biological Engineering, Chicago, IL 60616-3793. Offers biological engineering (MBE); chemical engineering (M Ch E, MS, PhD); food process engineering (MFPE, MS). Part-time and evening/weekend programs available. Postbaccalaureate distance learning degree programs offered (minimal on-campus study). Terminal master's awarded for partial completion of doctoral program. *Degree requirements:* For master's, comprehensive exam (for some programs), thesis (for some programs); for doctorate, comprehensive exam, thesis/dissertation. *Entrance requirements:* For master's, GRE General Test (minimum score 900 Quantitative and Verbal, 2.5 Analytical Writing), minimum undergraduate GPA of 3.0; for doctorate, GRE

General Test (minimum score 1000 Quantitative and Verbal, 3.0 Analytical Writing), minimum undergraduate GPA of 3.0. Additional exam requirements/recommendations for international students: Required—TOEFL (minimum score 523 paper-based; 70 iBT); Recommended—IELTS (minimum score 5.5). Electronic applications accepted. *Faculty research:* Energy and sustainability, biological engineering, advanced materials, systems engineering.

The Johns Hopkins University, Whiting School of Engineering and School of Medicine, Department of Biomedical Engineering, Baltimore, MD 21205. Offers bioengineering innovation and design (MSE); biomedical engineering (MSE, PhD). Terminal master's awarded for partial completion of doctoral program. *Degree requirements:* For master's, thesis; for doctorate, comprehensive exam, thesis/dissertation, oral exam. *Entrance requirements:* For master's and doctorate, GRE General Test. Additional exam requirements/recommendations for international students: Required—TOEFL or IELTS. Electronic applications accepted. *Faculty research:* Cell and tissue engineering, systems neuroscience, imaging, cardiovascular systems physiology, theoretical and computational biology.

The Johns Hopkins University, Whiting School of Engineering, Department of Chemical and Biomolecular Engineering, Baltimore, MD 21218. Offers MSE, PhD. Part-time programs available. *Degree requirements:* For doctorate, thesis/dissertation, oral exam. *Entrance requirements:* For doctorate, GRE General Test. Additional exam requirements/recommendations for international students: Required—TOEFL (minimum score 600 paper-based; 250 computer-based; 100 iBT). Electronic applications accepted. *Faculty research:* Polymers and complex fluids, nucleation, bioengineering and biotechnology, computational biology and genomics, cell and molecular biotechnology.

Kansas State University, Graduate School, College of Engineering, Department of Biological and Agricultural Engineering, Manhattan, KS 66506. Offers MS, PhD. *Faculty:* 13 full-time (1 woman), 6 part-time/adjunct (0 women). *Students:* 26 full-time (12 women), 7 part-time (2 women); includes 1 minority (Black or African American, non-Hispanic/Latino), 19 international. Average age 28. 26 applicants, 38% accepted, 7 enrolled. In 2011, 7 master's, 1 doctorate awarded. Terminal master's awarded for partial completion of doctoral program. *Degree requirements:* For master's, thesis; for doctorate, thesis/dissertation. *Entrance requirements:* For master's, GRE (recommended), bachelor's degree in agricultural engineering; for doctorate, GRE (recommended). Additional exam requirements/recommendations for international students: Required—TOEFL (minimum score 600 paper-based; 250 computer-based). *Application deadline:* For fall admission, 2/1 priority date for domestic students, 2/1 for international students; for spring admission, 8/1 priority date for domestic students, 8/1 for international students. Applications are processed on a rolling basis. Application fee: $40 ($55 for international students). Electronic applications accepted. *Financial support:* In 2011–12, 22 research assistantships (averaging $21,509 per year) were awarded; fellowships, teaching assistantships, Federal Work-Study, institutionally sponsored loans, and scholarships/grants also available. Support available to part-time students. Financial award application deadline: 3/1; financial award applicants required to submit FAFSA. *Faculty research:* Ecological engineering, watershed modeling, air quality, bioprocessing, bio-fuel, sensors and controls. *Total annual research expenditures:* $1.7 million. *Unit head:* Joseph Harner, Head, 785-532-5580, Fax: 785-532-5825, E-mail: jharner@ksu.edu. *Application contact:* Naiqian Zhang, Graduate Coordinator, 785-532-2910, Fax: 785-532-5825, E-mail: zhangn@ksu.edu. Web site: http://www.bae.ksu.edu/

Lehigh University, P.C. Rossin College of Engineering and Applied Science, Department of Chemical Engineering, Bethlehem, PA 18015. Offers biological chemical engineering (M Eng); chemical engineering (M Eng, MS, PhD); MBA/E. Part-time programs available. Postbaccalaureate distance learning degree programs offered (no on-campus study). *Faculty:* 16 full-time (2 women), 2 part-time/adjunct (0 women). *Students:* 38 full-time (7 women), 40 part-time (18 women); includes 11 minority (2 Black or African American, non-Hispanic/Latino; 6 Asian, non-Hispanic/Latino; 3 Hispanic/Latino), 28 international. Average age 28. 184 applicants, 6% accepted, 11 enrolled. In 2011, 4 master's, 7 doctorates awarded. Terminal master's awarded for partial completion of doctoral program. *Degree requirements:* For master's, thesis (for some programs); for doctorate, comprehensive exam, thesis/dissertation. *Entrance requirements:* For master's and doctorate, GRE General Test. Additional exam requirements/recommendations for international students: Required—TOEFL (minimum score 570 paper-based; 230 computer-based; 79 iBT). *Application deadline:* For fall admission, 7/15 for domestic students, 1/15 for international students; for spring admission, 12/1 for domestic and international students. Applications are processed on a rolling basis. Application fee: $75. Electronic applications accepted. *Financial support:* In 2011–12, 36 students received support, including 4 fellowships with full tuition reimbursements available (averaging $24,500 per year), 27 research assistantships with full tuition reimbursements available (averaging $24,500 per year), 5 teaching assistantships with full tuition reimbursements available (averaging $24,500 per year); career-related internships or fieldwork, institutionally sponsored loans, scholarships/grants, health care benefits, and unspecified assistantships also available. Financial award application deadline: 1/15. *Faculty research:* Emulsion polymers, process control, energy, biotechnology, catalysis. *Total annual research expenditures:* $2.9 million. *Unit head:* Dr. Anthony J. McHugh, Chairman, 610-758-4260, Fax: 610-758-5057, E-mail: ajm8@lehigh.edu. *Application contact:* Barbara A. Kessler, Graduate Coordinator, 610-758-4261, Fax: 610-758-5057, E-mail: inchegs@mail.lehigh.edu. Web site: http://www.che.lehigh.edu/

Lehigh University, P.C. Rossin College of Engineering and Applied Science, Program in Bioengineering, Bethlehem, PA 18015-3094. Offers MS, PhD. *Students:* 11 full-time (4 women); includes 1 minority (Asian, non-Hispanic/Latino), 6 international. Average age 24. 23 applicants, 26% accepted, 5 enrolled. Terminal master's awarded for partial completion of doctoral program. *Degree requirements:* For master's, thesis; for doctorate, comprehensive exam, thesis/dissertation. *Entrance requirements:* For master's and doctorate, GRE. Additional exam requirements/recommendations for international students: Required—TOEFL (minimum score 79 iBT). *Application deadline:* For fall admission, 7/15 for domestic and international students. Applications are processed on a rolling basis. Application fee: $75. Electronic applications accepted. *Financial support:* In 2011–12, 8 research assistantships (averaging $24,500 per year), 4 teaching assistantships (averaging $19,000 per year) were awarded; health care benefits also available. Financial award application deadline: 1/15. *Faculty research:* Biomaterials, biomechanics (biomolecular, cellular, fluid and solid mechanics), BioMEMS/biosensors, bioelectronics/biophotonics, biopharmaceutical engineering. *Unit head:* Dr. Susan Perry, Faculty Graduate Coordinator in Bioengineering, 610-758-4330, E-mail: sup3@lehigh.edu. *Application contact:* Brianne Lisk, Administrative Coordinator of Graduate Studies and Research, 610-758-6310, Fax: 610-758-5623, E-mail: brc3@lehigh.edu. Web site: http://www.lehigh.edu/bioe/grad.html.

Louisiana State University and Agricultural and Mechanical College, Graduate School, College of Agriculture, Department of Biological and Agricultural Engineering, Baton Rouge, LA 70803. Offers biological and agricultural engineering (MSBAE); engineering science (MS, PhD). Part-time programs available. *Faculty:* 11 full-time (2 women). *Students:* 16 full time (4 women), 2 part-time (1 woman); includes 7 minority (3 Black or African American, non-Hispanic/Latino; 3 Asian, non-Hispanic/Latino; 1 Hispanic/Latino), 6 international. Average age 26. 9 applicants, 56% accepted, 2 enrolled. In 2011, 7 master's awarded. Terminal master's awarded for partial completion of doctoral program. *Degree requirements:* For master's, thesis; for doctorate, thesis/dissertation. *Entrance requirements:* For master's and doctorate, GRE General Test, minimum GPA of 3.0. Additional exam requirements/recommendations for international students: Required—TOEFL (minimum score 550 paper-based; 213 computer-based; 79 iBT) or IELTS (minimum score 6.5). *Application deadline:* For fall admission, 1/25 priority date for domestic students, 5/15 for international students; for spring admission, 10/15 for international students. Applications are processed on a rolling basis. Application fee: $50 ($70 for international students). Electronic applications accepted. *Financial support:* In 2011–12, 16 students received support, including 1 fellowship (averaging $6,300 per year), 14 research assistantships with partial tuition reimbursements available (averaging $17,956 per year); teaching assistantships with partial tuition reimbursements available, career-related internships or fieldwork, Federal Work-Study, institutionally sponsored loans, scholarships/grants, health care benefits, and unspecified assistantships also available. Financial award application deadline: 7/1; financial award applicants required to submit FAFSA. *Faculty research:* Bioenergy, bioprocess engineering, cellular and molecular engineering, drug delivery using nanotechnology, environmental engineering. *Total annual research expenditures:* $87,691. *Unit head:* Dr. Dan Thomas, Head, 225-578-3153, Fax: 225-578-3492, E-mail: dthomas@agcenter.lsu.edu. *Application contact:* Dr. Steven Hall, Graduate Coordinator, 225-578-1058, Fax: 225-578-3492, E-mail: sghall@agcenter.lsu.edu. Web site: http://www.bae.lsu.edu/

Massachusetts Institute of Technology, School of Engineering, Department of Biological Engineering, Cambridge, MA 02139. Offers applied biosciences (PhD, Sc D); bioengineering (PhD, Sc D); biological engineering (PhD, Sc D); biomedical engineering (M Eng); toxicology (SM); SM/MBA. *Faculty:* 33 full-time (7 women). *Students:* 124 full-time (55 women); includes 36 minority (3 Black or African American, non-Hispanic/Latino; 22 Asian, non-Hispanic/Latino; 7 Hispanic/Latino; 4 Two or more races, non-Hispanic/Latino), 38 international. Average age 26. 483 applicants, 10% accepted, 30 enrolled. In 2011, 3 master's, 13 doctorates awarded. Terminal master's awarded for partial completion of doctoral program. *Degree requirements:* For master's, thesis; for doctorate, comprehensive exam, thesis/dissertation. *Entrance requirements:* For master's and doctorate, GRE General Test. Additional exam requirements/recommendations for international students: Required—IELTS (minimum score 7). *Application deadline:* For fall admission, 12/15 for domestic and international students. Application fee: $75. Electronic applications accepted. *Expenses: Tuition:* Full-time $40,460; part-time $630 per credit hour. *Required fees:* $272. *Financial support:* In 2011–12, 113 students received support, including 67 fellowships (averaging $36,300 per year), 53 research assistantships (averaging $34,000 per year), 1 teaching assistantship (averaging $33,100 per year); Federal Work-Study, institutionally sponsored loans, scholarships/grants, traineeships, health care benefits, and unspecified assistantships also available. *Faculty research:* Bioinformatics, computational, systems, and synthetic biology; biological materials, imaging, and transport phenomena; biomolecular and cell engineering; cancer initiation, progression, and therapeutics; genomics, proteomics, and glycomics; nanoscale engineering of biological systems; neurobiological systems; systems biology; macromolecular biochemistry and biophysics. *Total annual research expenditures:* $36.7 million. *Unit head:* Prof. Douglas A. Lauffenburger, Head, 617-253-1712, E-mail: be-acad@mit.edu. Web site: http://web.mit.edu/be/

McGill University, Faculty of Graduate and Postdoctoral Studies, Faculty of Agricultural and Environmental Sciences, Department of Bioresource Engineering, Montréal, QC H3A 2T5, Canada. Offers computer applications (M Sc, M Sc A, PhD); food engineering (M Sc, M Sc A, PhD); grain drying (M Sc, M Sc A, PhD); irrigation and drainage (M Sc, M Sc A, PhD); machinery (M Sc, M Sc A, PhD); pollution control (M Sc, M Sc A, PhD); post-harvest technology (M Sc, M Sc A, PhD); soil dynamics (M Sc, M Sc A, PhD); structure and environment (M Sc, M Sc A, PhD); vegetable and fruit storage (M Sc, M Sc A, PhD).

Mississippi State University, College of Agriculture and Life Sciences, Department of Agricultural and Biological Engineering, Mississippi State, MS 39762. Offers agricultural sciences (PhD), including engineering technology (MS, PhD); agriculture (MS), including engineering technology (MS, PhD); biological engineering (MS); biomedical engineering (MS, PhD). PhD in agricultural sciences and MS in agriculture are interdisciplinary. *Faculty:* 12 full-time (1 woman). *Students:* 41 full-time (16 women), 5 part-time (2 women); includes 10 minority (6 Black or African American, non-Hispanic/Latino; 2 Asian, non-Hispanic/Latino; 1 Native Hawaiian or other Pacific Islander, non-Hispanic/Latino; 1 Two or more races, non-Hispanic/Latino), 12 international. Average age 28. 43 applicants, 30% accepted, 11 enrolled. In 2011, 8 master's awarded. *Degree requirements:* For master's, thesis; for doctorate, thesis/dissertation, preliminary exam. *Entrance requirements:* For master's, GRE General Test, minimum undergraduate GPA of 2.75 (3.0 for biomedical engineering); for doctorate, GRE General Test, minimum GPA of 3.0 (biomedical engineering). Additional exam requirements/recommendations for international students: Required—TOEFL (minimum score 550 paper-based; 213 computer-based; 79 iBT). Recommended—IELTS (minimum score 6.5). *Application deadline:* For fall admission, 7/1 for domestic students, 5/1 for international students; for spring admission, 11/1 for domestic students, 9/1 for international students. Applications are processed on a rolling basis. Application fee: $40. Electronic applications accepted. *Expenses:* Tuition, state resident: full-time $5805; part-time $322.50 per credit hour. Tuition, nonresident: full-time $14,670; part-time $815 per credit hour. *Financial support:* In 2011–12, 32 research assistantships with partial tuition reimbursements (averaging $15,291 per year) were awarded; Federal Work-Study, institutionally sponsored loans, and unspecified assistantships also available. Financial award application deadline: 4/1; financial award applicants required to submit FAFSA. *Faculty research:* Bioenvironmental engineering, bioinstrumentation, biomechanics/biomaterials, precision agriculture, tissue engineering, ergonomics human factors, biosimulation and modeling. *Total annual research expenditures:* $496,000. *Unit head:* Dr. Jonathan Pote, Interim Department Head and Professor, 662-325-3280, Fax: 662-325-3853, E-mail: jpote@mafes.msstate.edu. *Application contact:* Dr. Steven Elder, Professor and Graduate Coordinator, 662-325-9107, Fax: 662-325-3853, E-mail: selder@abe.msstate.edu. Web site: http://www.abe.msstate.edu/

North Carolina Agricultural and Technical State University, School of Graduate Studies, College of Engineering, Department of Chemical and Bioengineering,

Greensboro, NC 27411. Offers bioengineering (MS); biological engineering (MS); chemical engineering (MS).

North Carolina State University, Graduate School, College of Agriculture and Life Sciences, Department of Biological and Agricultural Engineering, Raleigh, NC 27695. Offers MBAE, MS, PhD, Certificate. Part-time programs available. Postbaccalaureate distance learning degree programs offered. *Degree requirements:* For master's, thesis (for some programs); for doctorate, thesis/dissertation. *Entrance requirements:* For master's and doctorate, GRE. Additional exam requirements/recommendations for international students: Required—TOEFL. Electronic applications accepted. *Faculty research:* Bioinstrumentation, animal waste management, water quality engineering, machine systems, controlled environment agriculture.

The Ohio State University, Graduate School, College of Food, Agricultural, and Environmental Sciences, Department of Food, Agricultural, and Biological Engineering, Columbus, OH 43210. Offers MS, PhD. *Faculty:* 18. *Students:* 36 full-time (13 women), 7 part-time (2 women); includes 5 minority (2 Black or African American, non-Hispanic/Latino; 1 Asian, non-Hispanic/Latino; 2 Hispanic/Latino), 17 international. Average age 28. In 2011, 4 master's, 4 doctorates awarded. *Degree requirements:* For master's, thesis optional; for doctorate, thesis/dissertation. *Entrance requirements:* For master's and doctorate, GRE General Test, GRE Subject Test in engineering (recommended). Additional exam requirements/recommendations for international students: Required—TOEFL (minimum score 550 paper-based; 213 computer-based), IELTS (minimum score 6.5), or Michigan English Language Assessment Battery (minimum score 82). *Application deadline:* For fall admission, 8/15 priority date for domestic students, 7/1 for international students; for winter admission, 12/1 priority date for domestic students, 11/1 for international students; for spring admission, 3/1 priority date for domestic students, 2/1 for international students. Applications are processed on a rolling basis. Application fee: $40 ($50 for international students). Electronic applications accepted. *Expenses:* Tuition, state resident: full-time $11,400. Tuition, nonresident: full-time $28,125. Tuition and fees vary according to course load, degree level, campus/location and program. *Financial support:* Fellowships, research assistantships, teaching assistantships, career-related internships or fieldwork, Federal Work-Study, and institutionally sponsored loans available. Support available to part-time students. *Unit head:* Scott Shearer, Chair, 614-292-7284, E-mail: shearer.95@osu.edu. *Application contact:* Graduate Admissions, 614-292-6031, Fax: 614-292-3656, E-mail: gradadmissions@osu.edu. Web site: http://fabe.osu.edu/.

Oklahoma State University, College of Agricultural Science and Natural Resources, Department of Biosystems and Agricultural Engineering, Stillwater, OK 74078. Offers biosystems engineering (MS, PhD); environmental and natural resources (MS, PhD). *Faculty:* 22 full-time (3 women), 3 part-time/adjunct (0 women). *Students:* 18 full-time (6 women), 50 part-time (21 women); includes 7 minority (1 Black or African American, non-Hispanic/Latino; 1 American Indian or Alaska Native, non-Hispanic/Latino; 1 Asian, non-Hispanic/Latino; 2 Hispanic/Latino; 2 Two or more races, non-Hispanic/Latino), 35 international. Average age 31. 57 applicants, 23% accepted, 3 enrolled. In 2011, 6 master's, 4 doctorates awarded. *Degree requirements:* For master's, thesis; for doctorate, comprehensive exam, thesis/dissertation. *Entrance requirements:* For master's and doctorate, GRE or GMAT. Additional exam requirements/recommendations for international students: Required—TOEFL (minimum score 550 paper-based; 79 iBT). *Application deadline:* For fall admission, 3/1 for international students; for spring admission, 8/1 for international students. Applications are processed on a rolling basis. Application fee: $40 ($75 for international students). Electronic applications accepted. *Expenses:* Tuition, state resident: full-time $4044; part-time $168.50 per credit hour. Tuition, nonresident: full-time $16,008; part-time $667 per credit hour. *Required fees:* $2122; $88.45 per credit hour. One-time fee: $50. Tuition and fees vary according to course load and campus/location. *Financial support:* In 2011–12, 43 research assistantships (averaging $17,505 per year) were awarded; teaching assistantships, career-related internships or fieldwork, Federal Work-Study, scholarships/grants, health care benefits, tuition waivers (partial), and unspecified assistantships also available. Support available to part-time students. Financial award application deadline: 3/1; financial award applicants required to submit FAFSA. *Unit head:* Dr. Daniel Thomas, Head, 405-744-5431, Fax: 405-744-6059. *Application contact:* Dr. Sheryl Tucker, Dean, 405-744-7099, Fax: 405-744-0355, E-mail: grad-i@okstate.edu. Web site: http://bioen.okstate.edu/.

Oregon State University, Graduate School, College of Engineering, Department of Biological and Ecological Engineering, Corvallis, OR 97331. Offers M Eng, MS, PhD. Terminal master's awarded for partial completion of doctoral program. *Degree requirements:* For master's, thesis or alternative; for doctorate, thesis/dissertation. *Entrance requirements:* For master's and doctorate, minimum GPA of 3.0 in last 90 hours. Additional exam requirements/recommendations for international students: Required—TOEFL (minimum score 550 paper-based; 213 computer-based). *Expenses:* Contact institution. *Faculty research:* Bioengineering, water resources engineering, food engineering, cell culture and fermentation, vadose zone transport.

Oregon State University, Graduate School, College of Engineering, School of Mechanical, Industrial, and Manufacturing Engineering, Corvallis, OR 97331. Offers human systems engineering (MS, PhD); industrial engineering (MS, PhD); information systems engineering (MS, PhD); manufacturing engineering (M Engr); manufacturing systems engineering (MS, PhD); materials science (MAIS, MS, PhD); mechanical engineering (MS, PhD); nano/micro fabrication (MS, PhD). Part-time programs available. Postbaccalaureate distance learning degree programs offered (minimal on-campus study). *Degree requirements:* For master's, thesis or alternative; for doctorate, thesis/dissertation. *Entrance requirements:* For master's, placement exam, minimum GPA of 3.0 in last 90 hours of course work; for doctorate, GRE, placement exam, minimum GPA of 3.0 in last 90 hours of course work. Additional exam requirements/recommendations for international students: Required—TOEFL (minimum score 550 paper-based; 213 computer-based). *Faculty research:* Computer-integrated manufacturing, human factors, robotics, decision support systems, simulation modeling and analysis.

Penn State University Park, Graduate School, College of Agricultural Sciences, Department of Agricultural and Biological Engineering, State College, University Park, PA 16802-1503. Offers MS, PhD. *Unit head:* Dr. Bruce A. McPheron, Dean, 814-865-2541, Fax: 814-865-3103, E-mail: bam10@psu.edu. *Application contact:* Cynthia E. Nicosia, Director of Graduate Enrollment Services, 814-865-1834, E-mail: cey1@psu.edu. Web site: http://www.abe.psu.edu.

Penn State University Park, Graduate School, Intercollege Graduate Programs, Intercollege Graduate Program in Bioengineering, State College, University Park, PA 16802-1503. Offers MS, PhD. *Unit head:* Dr. Herbert H. Lipowsky, Head, 814-865-1407, Fax: 814-863-0490, E-mail: hhlbio@engr.psu.edu. *Application contact:* Cynthia E.

Nicosia, Director, Graduate Enrollment Services, 814-865-1795, Fax: 814-865-4627, E-mail: cey1@psu.edu.

Rensselaer Polytechnic Institute, Graduate School, School of Engineering, Program in Chemical Engineering, Troy, NY 12180-3590. Offers M Eng, MS, PhD. Part-time programs available. Terminal master's awarded for partial completion of doctoral program. *Entrance requirements:* For master's, GRE (minimum score 550 verbal); for doctorate, GRE (Verbal minimum score of 550). Additional exam requirements/recommendations for international students: Required—TOEFL (minimum score 570 paper-based). Electronic applications accepted. *Faculty research:* Biocatalysis, bioseparations, biotechnology, molecular modeling and simulation, advanced materials, interfacial phenomena, systems biology.

Rice University, Graduate Programs, George R. Brown School of Engineering, Department of Bioengineering, Houston, TX 77251-1892. Offers MBE, MS, PhD, MD/PhD. Terminal master's awarded for partial completion of doctoral program. *Degree requirements:* For master's, thesis; for doctorate, thesis/dissertation, qualifying exam, internship. *Entrance requirements:* For master's and doctorate, GRE General Test. Additional exam requirements/recommendations for international students: Required—TOEFL (minimum score 600 paper-based; 250 computer-based; 90 iBT). Electronic applications accepted. *Faculty research:* Biomaterials, tissue engineering, laser-tissue interactions, biochemical engineering, gene therapy.

Rice University, Graduate Programs, George R. Brown School of Engineering, Department of Electrical and Computer Engineering, Houston, TX 77251-1892. Offers bioengineering (MS, PhD); circuits, controls, and communication systems (MS, PhD); computer science and engineering (MS, PhD); electrical engineering (MEE); lasers, microwaves, and solid-state electronics (MS, PhD); MBA/MEE. Part-time programs available. *Degree requirements:* For master's, thesis (for some programs); for doctorate, thesis/dissertation. *Entrance requirements:* For master's and doctorate, GRE General Test, GRE Subject Test, minimum GPA of 3.0. Additional exam requirements/recommendations for international students: Required—TOEFL (minimum score 600 paper-based; 250 computer-based; 90 iBT). Electronic applications accepted. *Faculty research:* Physical electronics, systems, computer engineering, bioengineering.

South Dakota School of Mines and Technology, Graduate Division, Program in Chemical and Biological Engineering, Rapid City, SD 57701-3995. Offers PhD.

Stanford University, School of Medicine, Department of Bioengineering, Stanford, CA 94305-9991. Offers MS, PhD. *Degree requirements:* For master's, thesis optional; for doctorate, comprehensive exam, thesis/dissertation. *Entrance requirements:* For master's and doctorate, GRE General Test. Additional exam requirements/recommendations for international students: Required—TOEFL. Electronic applications accepted. *Expenses: Tuition:* Full-time $40,050; part-time $890 per credit. *Faculty research:* Biomedical computation, regenerative medicine/tissue engineering, molecular and cell bioengineering, biomedical imaging, biomedical devices.

Syracuse University, L. C. Smith College of Engineering and Computer Science, Program in Bioengineering, Syracuse, NY 13244. Offers MS, PhD. Part-time programs available. *Students:* 43 full-time (22 women), 6 part-time (0 women); includes 5 minority (1 Black or African American, non-Hispanic/Latino; 2 Asian, non-Hispanic/Latino; 2 Hispanic/Latino), 26 international. Average age 26. 67 applicants, 34% accepted, 13 enrolled. In 2011, 3 master's, 3 doctorates awarded. *Entrance requirements:* For master's and doctorate, GRE General Test. Additional exam requirements/recommendations for international students: Required—TOEFL (minimum score 100 iBT). *Application deadline:* For fall admission, 7/1 priority date for domestic students, 6/1 for international students. Applications are processed on a rolling basis. Application fee: $75. Electronic applications accepted. *Expenses: Tuition:* Part-time $1206 per credit. *Financial support:* Fellowships with full tuition reimbursements, research assistantships with full and partial tuition reimbursements, teaching assistantships with full and partial tuition reimbursements, and tuition waivers (partial) available. Financial award application deadline: 1/1; financial award applicants required to submit FAFSA. *Unit head:* Dr. Radhakrishna Sureshkumar, Chair, 315-443-3194, Fax: 315-443-9175, E-mail: rsureshk@syr.edu. *Application contact:* Kathleen Joyce, Assistant Dean, 314-443-2219, E-mail: topgrads@syr.edu. Web site: http://lcs.syr.edu/.

Texas A&M University, College of Agriculture and Life Sciences and College of Engineering, Department of Biological and Agricultural Engineering, College Station, TX 77843. Offers M Agr, M Eng, MS, DE, PhD. Part-time programs available. *Faculty:* 18. *Students:* 16 full-time (5 women), 68 part-time (25 women); includes 9 minority (4 Black or African American, non-Hispanic/Latino; 2 Asian, non-Hispanic/Latino; 3 Hispanic/Latino), 51 international. Average age 29. In 2011, 7 master's, 2 doctorates awarded. *Degree requirements:* For master's, thesis (MS), preliminary and final exams; for doctorate, thesis/dissertation, preliminary and final exams. *Entrance requirements:* For master's and doctorate, GRE General Test. Additional exam requirements/recommendations for international students: Required—TOEFL (minimum score 550 paper-based; 213 computer-based). *Application deadline:* For fall admission, 2/1 priority date for domestic students; for spring admission, 10/1 for domestic students. Applications are processed on a rolling basis. Application fee: $50 ($75 for international students). Electronic applications accepted. *Expenses:* Tuition, state resident: full-time $5437; part-time $226.55 per credit hour. Tuition, nonresident: full-time $12,949; part-time $539.55 per credit hour. *Required fees:* $2741. *Financial support:* In 2011–12, 3 fellowships with full and partial tuition reimbursements (averaging $15,000 per year), 17 research assistantships with full and partial tuition reimbursements (averaging $18,150 per year), 12 teaching assistantships with partial tuition reimbursements (averaging $19,590 per year) were awarded; career-related internships or fieldwork, institutionally sponsored loans, scholarships/grants, tuition waivers, and unspecified assistantships also available. Financial award application deadline: 3/1; financial award applicants required to submit FAFSA. *Faculty research:* Water quality and quantity; air quality; biological, food, ecological engineering; off-road equipment; mechatronics. *Unit head:* Dr. Steve Searcy, Interim Head, 979-845-3668, Fax: 979-862-3442, E-mail: s-searcy@tamu.edu. *Application contact:* Graduate Admissions, 979-845-1044, E-mail: admissions@tamu.edu. Web site: http://baen.tamu.edu.

Tufts University, Graduate School of Arts and Sciences, Graduate Certificate Programs, Program in Bioengineering, Medford, MA 02155. Offers Certificate. Part-time and evening/weekend programs available. Electronic applications accepted. *Expenses: Tuition:* Full-time $41,208; part-time $1030 per credit hour. Full-time tuition and fees vary according to degree level, program and student level. Part-time tuition and fees vary according to course load.

Tufts University, School of Engineering, Department of Biomedical Engineering, Medford, MA 02155. Offers bioengineering (ME, MS), including biomaterials; biomedical engineering (PhD). Part-time programs available. *Faculty:* 7 full-time, 4 part-time/adjunct. *Students:* 74 (34 women); includes 15 minority (1 Black or African American, non-Hispanic/Latino; 12 Asian, non-Hispanic/Latino; 2 Hispanic/Latino), 17 international. 150 applicants, 38% accepted, 29 enrolled. In 2011, 13 master's, 7 doctorates awarded. Terminal master's awarded for partial completion of doctoral program. *Degree requirements:* For master's, thesis (for some programs); for doctorate, thesis/dissertation. *Entrance requirements:* For master's and doctorate, GRE General Test. Additional exam requirements/recommendations for international students: Required—TOEFL (minimum score 550 paper-based; 213 computer-based; 80 iBT). *Application deadline:* For fall admission, 1/15 priority date for domestic students, 12/15 for international students; for spring admission, 10/15 for domestic students, 9/15 for international students. Applications are processed on a rolling basis. Application fee: $75. Electronic applications accepted. *Expenses: Tuition:* Full-time $41,208; part-time $1030 per credit hour. Full-time tuition and fees vary according to degree level, program and student level. Part-time tuition and fees vary according to course load. *Financial support:* Fellowships with full tuition reimbursements, research assistantships with full and partial tuition reimbursements, teaching assistantships with full and partial tuition reimbursements, Federal Work-Study, scholarships/grants, tuition waivers (partial), and unspecified assistantships available. Financial award application deadline: 1/15; financial award applicants required to submit FAFSA. *Faculty research:* Regenerative medicine with biomaterials and tissue engineering, diffuse optical Imaging and spectroscopy, optics in the development of biomedical devices, ultrafast nonlinear optics and biophotonics, optical diagnostics for diseased and engineered tissues. *Unit head:* Dr. David Kaplan, Chair, 617-627-2580. *Application contact:* Vilva Ricci, Information Contact, 617-627-2580, E-mail: bme@tufts.edu. Web site: http://engineering.tufts.edu/bme.

Tufts University, School of Engineering, Department of Chemical and Biological Engineering, Medford, MA 02155. Offers bioengineering (ME, MS), including cell and bioprocess engineering; biotechnology engineering (ME, MS, PhD). Part-time programs available. *Faculty:* 8 full-time, 2 part-time/adjunct. *Students:* 34 full-time (16 women); includes 8 minority (1 Black or African American, non-Hispanic/Latino; 7 Asian, non-Hispanic/Latino), 13 international. Average age 27. 79 applicants, 30% accepted, 10 enrolled. In 2011, 8 master's, 6 doctorates awarded. Terminal master's awarded for partial completion of doctoral program. *Degree requirements:* For master's, thesis (for some programs); for doctorate, thesis/dissertation. *Entrance requirements:* For master's and doctorate, GRE General Test. Additional exam requirements/recommendations for international students: Required—TOEFL (minimum score 550 paper-based; 213 computer-based; 80 iBT). *Application deadline:* For fall admission, 1/15 priority date for domestic students, 12/15 for international students; for spring admission, 10/15 for domestic students, 9/15 for international students. Applications are processed on a rolling basis. Application fee: $75. Electronic applications accepted. *Expenses: Tuition:* Full-time $41,208; part-time $1030 per credit hour. Full-time tuition and fees vary according to degree level, program and student level. Part-time tuition and fees vary according to course load. *Financial support:* Fellowships with full tuition reimbursements, research assistantships with full and partial tuition reimbursements, teaching assistantships with full and partial tuition reimbursements, Federal Work-Study, scholarships/grants, tuition waivers (partial), and unspecified assistantships available. Financial award application deadline: 1/15; financial award applicants required to submit FAFSA. *Faculty research:* Clean energy with materials, biomaterials, colloids; metabolic engineering, biotechnology; process control; reaction kinetics, catalysis; transport phenomena. *Unit head:* Dr. Kyongbum Lee, Chair, 617-627-3900. *Application contact:* Beth Frasso, Staff, 617-627-3900, E-mail: chbe@tufts.edu. Web site: http://engineering.tufts.edu/chbe/.

Tufts University, School of Engineering, Department of Civil and Environmental Engineering, Medford, MA 02155. Offers bioengineering (ME, MS), including environmental technology; civil engineering (ME, MS, PhD), including geotechnical engineering, structural engineering, water diplomacy (PhD); environmental engineering (ME, MS, PhD), including environmental engineering and environmental sciences, environmental geotechnology, environmental health, environmental science and management, hazardous materials management, water diplomacy (PhD), water resources engineering. Part-time programs available. *Faculty:* 18 full-time, 5 part-time/adjunct. *Students:* 102 full-time (50 women); includes 8 minority (1 Black or African American, non-Hispanic/Latino; 6 Asian, non-Hispanic/Latino; 1 Hispanic/Latino), 37 international. Average age 27. 162 applicants, 59% accepted, 37 enrolled. In 2011, 18 degrees awarded. Terminal master's awarded for partial completion of doctoral program. *Degree requirements:* For master's, thesis or alternative; for doctorate, thesis/dissertation. *Entrance requirements:* For master's and doctorate, GRE General Test. Additional exam requirements/recommendations for international students: Required—TOEFL (minimum score 550 paper-based; 213 computer-based; 80 iBT). *Application deadline:* For fall admission, 1/15 priority date for domestic students, 12/15 for international students; for spring admission, 10/15 for domestic students, 9/15 for international students. Applications are processed on a rolling basis. Application fee: $75. Electronic applications accepted. *Expenses: Tuition:* Full-time $41,208; part-time $1030 per credit hour. Full-time tuition and fees vary according to degree level, program and student level. Part-time tuition and fees vary according to course load. *Financial support:* Fellowships with full tuition reimbursements, research assistantships with full and partial tuition reimbursements, teaching assistantships with full and partial tuition reimbursements, Federal Work-Study, scholarships/grants, tuition waivers (partial), and unspecified assistantships available. Financial award application deadline: 1/15; financial award applicants required to submit FAFSA. *Faculty research:* Environmental and water resources engineering, environmental health, geotechnical and geoenvironmental engineering, structural engineering and mechanics, water diplomacy. *Unit head:* Dr. Kurt Penell, Chair, 617-627-3211, Fax: 617-627-3994. *Application contact:* Laura Sacco, Information Contact, 617-627-3211, E-mail: ceeinfo@tufts.edu. Web site: http://www.ase.tufts.edu/cee/.

Tufts University, School of Engineering, Department of Computer Science, Medford, MA 02155. Offers bioengineering (MS), including bioinformatics; computer science (PhD), including cognitive science. Part-time programs available. *Faculty:* 16 full-time, 1 part-time/adjunct. *Students:* 62 (16 women); includes 10 minority (all Asian, non-Hispanic/Latino), 19 international. Average age 27. 169 applicants, 34% accepted, 23 enrolled. In 2011, 13 master's, 9 doctorates awarded. Terminal master's awarded for partial completion of doctoral program. *Degree requirements:* For master's, thesis (for some programs); for doctorate, thesis/dissertation. *Entrance requirements:* For master's and doctorate, GRE. Additional exam requirements/recommendations for international students: Required—TOEFL (minimum score 550 paper-based; 213 computer-based; 80 iBT). *Application deadline:* For fall admission, 1/15 for domestic students, 12/15 for international students; for spring admission, 9/15 for domestic and international students. Applications are processed on a rolling basis. Application fee: $75. Electronic applications accepted. *Expenses: Tuition:* Full-time $41,208; part-time $1030 per credit hour. Full-time tuition and fees vary according to degree level, program and student level. Part-time tuition and fees vary according to course load. *Financial support:* Fellowships with full tuition reimbursements, research assistantships with full and partial tuition reimbursements, teaching assistantships with full and partial tuition reimbursements, Federal Work-Study, scholarships/grants, tuition waivers (partial), and unspecified assistantships available. Financial award application deadline: 1/15; financial award applicants required to submit FAFSA. *Faculty research:* Computational biology, computational geometry, and computational systems biology; cognitive sciences, human-computer interaction, and human robotic interaction; visualization and graphics, educational technologies; machine learning and data mining; programming languages and systems. *Unit head:* Dr. Carla Brodley, Chair, 617-627-2225, Fax: 617-627-2227. *Application contact:* Dr. Lenore Cowen, Information Contact, 617-623-3217, Fax: 617-627-3220, E-mail: csadmin@cs.tufts.edu. Web site: http://www.cs.tufts.edu/.

Tufts University, School of Engineering, Department of Electrical and Computer Engineering, Medford, MA 02155. Offers bioengineering (MS), including signals and systems; electrical engineering (MS, PhD). Part-time programs available. *Faculty:* 12 full-time, 3 part-time/adjunct. *Students:* 70 full-time (13 women); includes 10 minority (2 Black or African American, non-Hispanic/Latino; 6 Asian, non-Hispanic/Latino; 2 Hispanic/Latino), 31 international. Average age 27. 157 applicants, 28% accepted, 16 enrolled. In 2011, 10 master's, 3 doctorates awarded. Terminal master's awarded for partial completion of doctoral program. *Degree requirements:* For master's, thesis or alternative; for doctorate, thesis/dissertation. *Entrance requirements:* For master's and doctorate, GRE General Test. Additional exam requirements/recommendations for international students: Required—TOEFL (minimum score 550 paper-based; 213 computer-based; 80 iBT). *Application deadline:* For fall admission, 1/15 priority date for domestic students, 12/15 for international students; for spring admission, 10/15 for domestic students, 9/15 for international students. Applications are processed on a rolling basis. Application fee: $75. Electronic applications accepted. *Expenses: Tuition:* Full-time $41,208; part-time $1030 per credit hour. Full-time tuition and fees vary according to degree level, program and student level. Part-time tuition and fees vary according to course load. *Financial support:* Fellowships with full tuition reimbursements, research assistantships with full and partial tuition reimbursements, teaching assistantships with full and partial tuition reimbursements, Federal Work-Study, scholarships/grants, tuition waivers (partial), and unspecified assistantships available. Financial award application deadline: 2/1; financial award applicants required to submit FAFSA. *Faculty research:* Communication theory, networks, protocol, and transmission technology; simulation and modeling; digital processing technology; image and signal processing for security and medical applications; integrated circuits and VLSI. *Unit head:* Dr. Jeffrey Hopwood, Chair, 617-627-3217, Fax: 617-627-3220. *Application contact:* Dr. Eric Miller, Graduate Advisor, 617-627-3217, E-mail: eceadmin@ece.tufts.edu. Web site: http://www.ece.tufts.edu/.

Tufts University, School of Engineering, Department of Mechanical Engineering, Medford, MA 02155. Offers bioengineering (ME, MS), including bioinformatics (ME), biomechanical systems and devices, signals and systems (ME); human factors (MS); mechanical engineering (ME, MS, PhD). Part-time programs available. *Faculty:* 13 full-time, 5 part-time/adjunct. *Students:* 83 full-time (22 women); includes 13 minority (2 Black or African American, non-Hispanic/Latino; 2 American Indian or Alaska Native, non-Hispanic/Latino; 7 Asian, non-Hispanic/Latino; 2 Hispanic/Latino), 14 international. Average age 27. 126 applicants, 46% accepted, 28 enrolled. In 2011, 21 degrees awarded. Terminal master's awarded for partial completion of doctoral program. *Degree requirements:* For master's, thesis; for doctorate, thesis/dissertation. *Entrance requirements:* For master's and doctorate, GRE General Test. Additional exam requirements/recommendations for international students: Required—TOEFL (minimum score 550 paper-based; 213 computer-based; 80 iBT). *Application deadline:* For fall admission, 1/15 priority date for domestic students, 12/15 for international students; for spring admission, 10/15 for domestic students, 9/15 for international students. Applications are processed on a rolling basis. Application fee: $75. Electronic applications accepted. *Expenses: Tuition:* Full-time $41,208; part-time $1030 per credit hour. Full-time tuition and fees vary according to degree level, program and student level. Part-time tuition and fees vary according to course load. *Financial support:* Fellowships with full tuition reimbursements, research assistantships with full and partial tuition reimbursements, teaching assistantships with full and partial tuition reimbursements, Federal Work-Study, scholarships/grants, tuition waivers (partial), and unspecified assistantships available. Financial award application deadline: 1/15; financial award applicants required to submit FAFSA. *Faculty research:* Applied mechanics, biomaterials, controls/robotics, design/systems, human factors. *Unit head:* Dr. Robert Hannemann, Acting Department Chair, 617-627-3239, Fax: 617-627-3058. *Application contact:* Lorin Polidora, Department Administrator, 617-627-3239, E-mail: meinfo@tufts.edu. Web site: http://engineering.tufts.edu/me.

University at Buffalo, the State University of New York, Graduate School, School of Engineering and Applied Sciences, Department of Chemical and Biological Engineering, Buffalo, NY 14260. Offers ME, MS, PhD. Part-time programs available. *Faculty:* 18 full-time (1 woman), 5 part-time/adjunct (1 woman). *Students:* 111 full-time (40 women), 5 part-time (1 woman); includes 3 minority (1 Black or African American, non-Hispanic/Latino; 2 Asian, non-Hispanic/Latino), 93 international. Average age 25. 401 applicants, 11% accepted, 36 enrolled. In 2011, 21 master's, 10 doctorates awarded. *Degree requirements:* For master's, thesis (for some programs); for doctorate, comprehensive exam, thesis/dissertation. *Entrance requirements:* For master's and doctorate, GRE General Test. Additional exam requirements/recommendations for international students: Required—TOEFL (minimum score 550 paper-based; 213 computer-based; 79 iBT). *Application deadline:* For fall admission, 2/1 priority date for domestic students, 2/1 for international students; for spring admission, 10/1 priority date for domestic students, 10/1 for international students. Applications are processed on a rolling basis. Application fee: $75. Electronic applications accepted. *Financial support:* In 2011–12, 60 students received support, including 2 fellowships (averaging $28,900 per year), 31 research assistantships with full tuition reimbursements available (averaging $28,300 per year), 5 teaching assistantships with full tuition reimbursements available (averaging $20,900 per year); institutionally sponsored loans, scholarships/grants, health care benefits, tuition waivers (partial), and unspecified assistantships also available. Support available to part-time students. Financial award application deadline: 2/28; financial award applicants required to submit FAFSA. *Faculty research:* Transport, polymers, nanomaterials, biochemical engineering, catalysis. *Total annual research expenditures:* $8.4 million. *Unit head:* Dr. David A. Kofke, Chairman, 716-645-2911, Fax: 716-645-3822, E-mail: kofke@buffalo.edu. *Application contact:* Dr. Mark Swihart, Director of Graduate Studies, 716-645-1181, Fax: 716-645-3822, E-mail: swihart@buffalo.edu. Web site: http://www.cbe.buffalo.edu/.

University of Arkansas, Graduate School, College of Engineering, Department of Biological and Agricultural Engineering, Program in Biological Engineering, Fayetteville, AR 72701-1201. Offers MSBE. *Accreditation:* ABET. *Students:* 7 full-time (2 women), 11 part-time (2 women), 9 international. In 2011, 2 degrees awarded. *Application deadline:* For fall admission, 4/1 for international students; for spring admission, 10/1 for international students. Applications are processed on a rolling basis. Application fee: $40 ($50 for international students). Electronic applications accepted. *Financial support:* In 2011–12, 17 research assistantships, 1 teaching assistantship were awarded; fellowships also available. *Unit head:* Dr. Lalit Verma, Department Head, 479-575-2351, Fax: 479-575-2846, E-mail: lverma@uark.edu. *Application contact:* Dr. Jin-Woo Kim, Program Coordinator, 479-575-2351, Fax: 479-575-2846, E-mail: jwkim@uark.edu. Web site: http://www.baeg.uark.edu/.

University of California, Berkeley, Graduate Division, Bioengineering Graduate Program Berkeley/UCSF, Berkeley, CA 94720-1762. Offers PhD. Program offered jointly with University of California, San Francisco. *Degree requirements:* For doctorate, comprehensive exam, thesis/dissertation. *Entrance requirements:* For doctorate, GRE General Test, minimum GPA of 3.0. Additional exam requirements/recommendations for international students. Required—TOEFL (minimum score 570 paper-based; 230 computer-based; 68 iBT). Electronic applications accepted. *Faculty research:* Biomaterials, biomechanics, biomedical imaging and instrumentation, computational biology, drug delivery systems and pharmacogenomics, neural systems engineering and vision science, systems and synthetic biology, tissue engineering and regenerative medicine.

University of California, Davis, College of Engineering, Program in Biological Systems Engineering, Davis, CA 95616. Offers M Engr, MS, D Engr, PhD, M Engr/MBA. Terminal master's awarded for partial completion of doctoral program. *Degree requirements:* For master's, thesis; for doctorate, thesis/dissertation. *Entrance requirements:* For master's, minimum GPA of 3.0; for doctorate, GRE, minimum graduate GPA of 3.25. Additional exam requirements/recommendations for international students: Required—TOEFL (minimum score 550 paper-based; 213 computer-based). Electronic applications accepted. *Faculty research:* Forestry, irrigation and drainage, power and machinery, structures and environment, information and energy technologies.

University of California, Merced, Division of Graduate Studies, School of Natural Sciences, Merced, CA 95343. Offers applied mathematics (MS, PhD); biological engineering and small-scale technologies (MS, PhD); environmental systems (MS, PhD); mechanical engineering and applied mechanics (MS, PhD); physics and chemistry (PhD); quantitative and systems biology (MS, PhD). *Unit head:* Dr. Samuel J. Traina, Dean, 209-228-4723, Fax: 209-228-6906, E-mail: grad.dean@ucmerced.edu. *Application contact:* Tsu Ya, Graduate Admissions and Academic Services Manager, 209-228-4723, Fax: 209-228-6906, E-mail: tya@ucmerced.edu.

University of California, Riverside, Graduate Division, Department of Bioengineering, Riverside, CA 92521-0102. Offers MS, PhD. Part-time programs available. *Degree requirements:* For doctorate, thesis/dissertation, qualifying exams. *Entrance requirements:* Additional exam requirements/recommendations for international students: Required—TOEFL (minimum score 550 paper-based; 213 computer-based; 80 iBT).

University of California, San Diego, Office of Graduate Studies, Department of Bioengineering, La Jolla, CA 92093. Offers M Eng, MS, PhD. *Entrance requirements:* For master's, GRE General Test, minimum GPA of 3.0 (for M Eng), 3.4 (for MS); for doctorate, GRE General Test, minimum GPA of 3.4. Additional exam requirements/recommendations for international students: Required—TOEFL. Electronic applications accepted.

University of California, San Francisco, Graduate Division, Program in Bioengineering, Berkeley, CA 94720-1762. Offers PhD. Program offered jointly with University of California, Berkeley. *Degree requirements:* For doctorate, thesis/dissertation, qualifying exam. *Entrance requirements:* For doctorate, GRE General Test, minimum GPA of 3.0. Additional exam requirements/recommendations for international students: Required—TOEFL (minimum score 570 paper-based). Electronic applications accepted. *Faculty research:* Bioengineering, biomaterials, biomedical imaging and instrumentation, biomechanics, microfluidics, computational biology, systems biology, drug delivery systems and pharmacogenomics, neural systems engineering and vision science, synthetic biology, tissue engineering, regenerative medicine.

University of California, Santa Barbara, Graduate Division, College of Letters and Sciences, Division of Mathematics, Life, and Physical Sciences, Interdepartmental Graduate Program in Biomolecular Science and Engineering, Santa Barbara, CA 93106-2014. Offers biochemistry and molecular biology (PhD), including biochemistry and molecular biology, biophysics and bioengineering. *Faculty:* 38 full-time (5 women), 1 (woman) part-time/adjunct. *Students:* 29 full-time (14 women); includes 3 minority (2 Asian, non-Hispanic/Latino; 1 Two or more races, non-Hispanic/Latino), 3 international. Average age 28. 83 applicants, 20% accepted, 4 enrolled. In 2011, 4 degrees awarded. Terminal master's awarded for partial completion of doctoral program. *Median time to degree:* Of those who began their doctoral program in fall 2003, 100% received their degree in 8 years or less. *Degree requirements:* For doctorate, thesis/dissertation. *Entrance requirements:* For doctorate, GRE General Test. Additional exam requirements/recommendations for international students: Required—TOEFL (minimum score 630 paper-based; 109 iBT), IELTS (minimum score 7). *Application deadline:* For fall admission, 12/15 for domestic and international students. Application fee: $80 ($100 for international students). Electronic applications accepted. *Expenses:* Tuition, state resident: full-time $12,192. Tuition, nonresident: full-time $27,294. *Required fees:* $764.13. *Financial support:* In 2011–12, 29 students received support, including 16 fellowships with full and partial tuition reimbursements available (averaging $11,321 per year), 31 research assistantships with full and partial tuition reimbursements available (averaging $14,777 per year), 16 teaching assistantships with full and partial tuition reimbursements available (averaging $6,307 per year); Federal Work-Study, traineeships, health care benefits, tuition waivers (full and partial), and unspecified assistantships also available. Financial award application deadline: 12/15; financial award applicants required to submit FAFSA. *Faculty research:* Biochemistry and molecular biology, biophysics, biomaterials, bioengineering, systems biology. *Unit head:* Prof. Philip A. Pincus, Director/Professor, 805-893-4685, E-mail: fyl@mrl.ucsb.edu. *Application contact:* Graduate Admissions Coordinator, 805-893-2278, Fax: 805-893-8259, E-mail: gradadmissions@graddiv.ucsb.edu. Web site: http://www.bmse.ucsb.edu/.

University of Colorado Denver, College of Engineering and Applied Science, Department of Bioengineering, Aurora, CO 80045-2560. Offers bioengineering (PhD); clinical application (PhD); clinical imaging (MS); commercialization of medical technologies (MS, PhD); device design and entrepreneurship (MS); research (MS). Part-time programs available. *Faculty:* 3 full-time (1 woman). *Students:* 38 full-time (13 women), 1 part-time; includes 7 minority (3 Black or African American, non-Hispanic/Latino; 2 Asian, non-Hispanic/Latino; 1 Hispanic/Latino; 1 Two or more races, non-Hispanic/Latino), 2 international. Average age 27. 56 applicants, 48% accepted, 24 enrolled. Terminal master's awarded for partial completion of doctoral program. *Degree*

requirements: For master's, thesis or alternative, 30 credit hours; for doctorate, comprehensive exam, thesis/dissertation, 36 credit hours of classwork (18 core, 18 elective), additional 30 hours of thesis work, three formal examinations, approval of dissertations. *Entrance requirements:* For master's and doctorate, GRE, transcripts, three letters of recommendation, resume, statement of purpose. Additional exam requirements/recommendations for international students: Required—TOEFL (minimum score 550 paper-based; 213 computer-based; 79 iBT), TOEFL (minimum score 600 paper-based; 250 computer-based; 100 iBT) for Ph D. *Application deadline:* For fall admission, 2/15 for domestic students. Application fee: $50. Electronic applications accepted. *Expenses:* Contact institution. *Financial support:* Fellowships, research assistantships, teaching assistantships, and Federal Work-Study available. Financial award application deadline: 4/1; financial award applicants required to submit FAFSA. *Faculty research:* Imaging and biophotonics, cardiovascular biomechanics and hemodynamics, orthopedic biomechanics, ophthalmology, neuroscience engineering, diabetes, surgery and urological sciences. *Unit head:* Dr. Robin Shandas, Chair, 303-724-4196, E-mail: robin.shandas@ucdenver.edu. *Application contact:* Graduate School Admissions, 303-556-2704, E-mail: admissions@ucdenver.edu. Web site: http://bioengineering.ucdenver.edu/.

University of Dayton, Department of Chemical Engineering, Dayton, OH 45469-1300. Offers bioengineering instrumentation (MS); bioprocess engineering (MS); biosystems engineering (MS). Part-time and evening/weekend programs available. *Faculty:* 11 full-time (1 woman), 4 part-time/adjunct (0 women). *Students:* 37 full-time (9 women), 13 part-time (1 woman); includes 3 minority (2 Black or African American, non-Hispanic/Latino; 1 Asian, non-Hispanic/Latino), 29 international. Average age 26. 80 applicants, 70% accepted, 24 enrolled. In 2011, 10 degrees awarded. *Degree requirements:* For master's, thesis optional. *Entrance requirements:* Additional exam requirements/recommendations for international students: Required—TOEFL (minimum score 550 paper-based; 213 computer-based; 80 iBT). *Application deadline:* For fall admission, 8/1 priority date for domestic students. Applications are processed on a rolling basis. Application fee: $0 ($50 for international students). Electronic applications accepted. *Expenses:* Tuition: Full-time $8400; part-time $700 per credit hour. *Required fees:* $25 per semester. Tuition and fees vary according to degree level. *Financial support:* In 2011–12, 13 research assistantships with full tuition reimbursements (averaging $11,400 per year) were awarded; institutionally sponsored loans, health care benefits, and unspecified assistantships also available. Financial award applicants required to submit FAFSA. *Faculty research:* Vertically-aligned carbon nanotubes infiltrated with temperature-responsive polymers: smart nanocomposite films for self-cleaning and controlled release, bilayer and bulk heterojunction solar cells using liquid crystalline porphyrins as donors by solution processing, DNA damage induced by multiwalled carbon nanotubes in mouse embryonic stem cells. Total annual research expenditures: $1.5 million. *Unit head:* Dr. Robert Wilkens, Chair, 937-229-2627, E-mail: rwilkens1@udayton.edu. *Application contact:* Dr. Robert Wilkens, Chair, 937-229-2627, E-mail: rwilkens1@udayton.edu.

University of Denver, School of Engineering and Computer Science, Department of Mechanical and Materials Engineering, Denver, CO 80208. Offers bioengineering (MS); engineering (MS, PhD); engineering/management (MS); interdisciplinary engineering (PhD); materials science (MS, PhD); mechanical engineering (MS, PhD); nanoscale science and engineering (MS, PhD). Part-time programs available. *Faculty:* 10 full-time (2 women), 1 part-time/adjunct (0 women). *Students:* 1 (woman) full-time, 25 part-time (5 women); includes 1 minority (Asian, non-Hispanic/Latino), 9 international. Average age 30. 69 applicants, 67% accepted, 11 enrolled. In 2011, 6 degrees awarded. Terminal master's awarded for partial completion of doctoral program. *Degree requirements:* For master's, thesis or alternative; for doctorate, comprehensive exam, thesis/dissertation. *Entrance requirements:* For master's, GRE General Test, essay/personal statement, three letters of recommendation; for doctorate, GRE General Test, essay/personal statement, three letters of recommendation, curriculum vitae. Additional exam requirements/recommendations for international students: Required—TOEFL (minimum score 550 paper-based; 80 iBT). *Application deadline:* Applications are processed on a rolling basis. Application fee: $60. Electronic applications accepted. *Financial support:* In 2011–12, 14 students received support, including 8 research assistantships with full and partial tuition reimbursements available (averaging $15,631 per year), 7 teaching assistantships with full and partial tuition reimbursements available (averaging $13,943 per year); Federal Work-Study, health care benefits, and unspecified assistantships also available. Financial award application deadline: 2/15; financial award applicants required to submit FAFSA. *Faculty research:* Aerosols, biomechanics, composite materials, photo optics, drug delivery. Total annual research expenditures: $818,288. *Unit head:* Dr. Matt Gordon, Chair, 303-871-3580, Fax: 303-871-4450, E-mail: matthew.gordon@du.edu. *Application contact:* Renee Carvalho, Assistant to the Chair, 303-871-2107, Fax: 303-871-4450, E-mail: renee.carvalho@du.edu. Web site: http://www.mme.du.edu.

University of Florida, Graduate School, College of Engineering and College of Agricultural and Life Sciences, Department of Agricultural and Biological Engineering, Gainesville, FL 32611. Offers ME, MS, PhD, Engr. Part-time programs available. Terminal master's awarded for partial completion of doctoral program. *Degree requirements:* For master's, comprehensive exam, thesis (for some programs); for doctorate, comprehensive exam, thesis/dissertation. *Entrance requirements:* For master's and doctorate, GRE General Test, minimum GPA of 3.0; for Engr, GRE General Test. Additional exam requirements/recommendations for international students: Required—TOEFL (minimum score 550 paper-based; 213 computer-based; 80 iBT), IELTS (minimum score 6). Electronic applications accepted. *Faculty research:* Biological processing, crop and climate modeling, land and water resources, robotic harvesting, food and packaging.

University of Georgia, College of Agricultural and Environmental Sciences, Department of Biological and Agricultural Engineering, Athens, GA 30602. Offers agricultural engineering (MS); biological and agricultural engineering (PhD); biological engineering (MS). *Faculty:* 36 full-time (13 women), 6 part-time/adjunct (0 women). *Students:* 36 full-time (13 women), 6 part-time (0 women); includes 4 minority (all Black or African American, non-Hispanic/Latino), 23 international. Average age 30. 49 applicants, 43% accepted, 7 enrolled. In 2011, 11 master's, 5 doctorates awarded. *Degree requirements:* For master's, thesis; for doctorate, one foreign language, thesis/dissertation. *Entrance requirements:* For master's and doctorate, GRE General Test. *Application deadline:* For fall admission, 7/1 priority date for domestic students; for spring admission, 11/15 for domestic students. Application fee: $50. Electronic applications accepted. *Financial support:* Fellowships, research assistantships, teaching assistantships and unspecified assistantships available. *Unit head:* Dr. E. Dale Threadgill, Head, 706-542-1653, Fax: 706-542-8806, E-mail: tgill@engr.uga.edu. *Application contact:* Dr. William Tollner, Graduate Coordinator, 706-542-3047, Fax: 706-542-8806, E-mail: btollner@engr.uga.edu. Web site: http://www.engr.uga.edu.

Bioengineering

University of Guelph, Graduate Studies, College of Physical and Engineering Science, School of Engineering, Guelph, ON N1G 2W1, Canada. Offers biological engineering (M Eng, M Sc, MA Sc, PhD); engineering systems and computing (M Eng, M Sc, MA Sc, PhD); environmental engineering (M Eng, M Sc, MA Sc, PhD); water resources engineering (M Eng, M Sc, MA Sc, PhD). Part-time programs available. *Degree requirements:* For master's, thesis (for some programs); for doctorate, comprehensive exam, thesis/dissertation. *Entrance requirements:* For master's, minimum B- average during previous 2 years of course work; for doctorate, minimum B average. Additional exam requirements/recommendations for international students: Required—TOEFL (minimum score 550 paper-based; 213 computer-based; 89 iBT), IELTS (minimum score 6.5). Electronic applications accepted. *Faculty research:* Water and food safety, environmental contaminant fates and mechanisms, computer systems, robotics and mechatronics, waste treatment.

University of Hawaii at Manoa, Graduate Division, College of Tropical Agriculture and Human Resources, Department of Molecular Biosciences and Bioengineering, Program in Bioengineering, Honolulu, HI 96822. Offers MS. Part-time programs available. *Degree requirements:* For master's, thesis optional. *Entrance requirements:* For master's, GRE General Test. Additional exam requirements/recommendations for international students: Required—TOEFL (minimum score 500 paper-based; 173 computer-based; 61 iBT), IELTS (minimum score 5).

University of Idaho, College of Graduate Studies, College of Engineering, Department of Biological and Agricultural Engineering, Moscow, ID 83844-0904. Offers M Engr, MS, PhD. Program offered jointly with College of Agricultural and Life Sciences. *Faculty:* 6 full-time. *Students:* 7 full-time, 3 part-time. Average age 37. In 2011, 1 master's, 1 doctorate awarded. *Degree requirements:* For master's, thesis or alternative; for doctorate, one foreign language, thesis/dissertation. *Entrance requirements:* For master's, minimum GPA of 2.8; for doctorate, minimum undergraduate GPA of 2.8, 3.0 graduate. *Application deadline:* For fall admission, 8/1 for domestic students; for spring admission, 12/15 for domestic students. Applications are processed on a rolling basis. Application fee: $60. Electronic applications accepted. *Expenses:* Tuition, state resident: full-time $3874; part-time $334 per credit hour. Tuition, nonresident: full-time $16,394; part-time $861 per credit hour. *Required fees:* $2808; $99 per credit hour. Tuition and fees vary according to program. *Financial support:* Research assistantships, teaching assistantships, and career-related internships or fieldwork available. Financial award applicants required to submit FAFSA. *Faculty research:* Water and environmental research, alternative fuels/biodiesel, agricultural safety health, biological processes for agricultural/food waste. *Unit head:* Dr. Jon Harlan Van Gerpen, Department Head, 208-885-7891, E-mail: baengr@uidaho.edu. *Application contact:* Erick Larson, Director of Graduate Admissions, 208-885-4723, E-mail: gadms@uidaho.edu. Web site: http://www.uidaho.edu/cals/bae/.

University of Illinois at Chicago, Graduate College, College of Engineering, Department of Bioengineering, Chicago, IL 60607-7128. Offers MS, PhD. Terminal master's awarded for partial completion of doctoral program. *Degree requirements:* For master's, thesis; for doctorate, thesis/dissertation. *Entrance requirements:* For master's and doctorate, GRE Subject Test, minimum GPA of 3.0. Additional exam requirements/recommendations for international students: Required—TOEFL. Electronic applications accepted. *Faculty research:* Imaging systems, bioinstrumentation, electrophysiology, biological control, laser scattering.

University of Illinois at Urbana–Champaign, Graduate College, College of Agricultural, Consumer and Environmental Sciences, Department of Agricultural and Biological Engineering, Champaign, IL 61820. Offers agricultural and biological engineering (MS, PhD); technical systems management (MS, PSM). *Faculty:* 19 full-time (2 women). *Students:* 59 full-time (15 women), 9 part-time (3 women); includes 7 minority (1 Black or African American, non-Hispanic/Latino; 1 Asian, non-Hispanic/Latino; 2 Hispanic/Latino; 3 Two or more races, non-Hispanic/Latino), 47 international. 66 applicants, 41% accepted, 22 enrolled. In 2011, 10 master's, 5 doctorates awarded. *Entrance requirements:* For master's and doctorate, minimum GPA of 3.0. Additional exam requirements/recommendations for international students: Required—TOEFL (minimum score 570 paper-based; 230 computer-based; 88 iBT) or IELTS (minimum score 6.5). *Application deadline:* Applications are processed on a rolling basis. Application fee: $75 ($90 for international students). Electronic applications accepted. *Financial support:* In 2011–12, 16 fellowships, 47 research assistantships, 19 teaching assistantships were awarded; tuition waivers (full and partial) also available. *Unit head:* Kuan Chong Ting, Head, 217-333-3570, Fax: 217-244-0323, E-mail: kcting@illinois.edu. *Application contact:* Mary Schultze, Office Manager, 217-333-5423, Fax: 217-244-0323, E-mail: mlschltz@illinois.edu. Web site: http://abe.illinois.edu.

University of Illinois at Urbana–Champaign, Graduate College, College of Engineering, Department of Bioengineering, Champaign, IL 61820. Offers MS, PhD. *Faculty:* 8 full-time (1 woman). *Students:* 57 full-time (24 women); includes 17 minority (1 Black or African American, non-Hispanic/Latino; 11 Asian, non-Hispanic/Latino; 4 Hispanic/Latino; 1 Two or more races, non-Hispanic/Latino), 21 international. 132 applicants, 17% accepted, 21 enrolled. In 2011, 10 master's, 2 doctorates awarded. *Entrance requirements:* For doctorate, GRE. Additional exam requirements/recommendations for international students: Required—TOEFL (minimum score 590 paper-based; 243 computer-based; 96 iBT) or IELTS (minimum score 6.5). *Application deadline:* Applications are processed on a rolling basis. Application fee: $75 ($90 for international students). Electronic applications accepted. *Financial support:* In 2011–12, 18 fellowships, 30 research assistantships, 9 teaching assistantships were awarded; tuition waivers (full and partial) also available. *Unit head:* Michael Insana, Interim Head, 217-244-0739, Fax: 217-265-0246, E-mail: mfi@illinois.edu. *Application contact:* Wendy Evans, Academic Programs Specialist, 217-333-1978, Fax: 217-265-0246, E-mail: wevans@illinois.edu. Web site: http://www.bioen.illinois.edu/.

University of Illinois at Urbana–Champaign, Graduate College, College of Liberal Arts and Sciences, School of Chemical Sciences, Department of Chemical and Biomolecular Engineering, Champaign, IL 61820. Offers bioinformatics: chemical and biomolecular engineering (MS); chemical engineering (MS, PhD). *Faculty:* 13 full-time (2 women), 1 (woman) part-time/adjunct. *Students:* 103 full-time (37 women); includes 12 minority (9 Asian, non-Hispanic/Latino; 2 Hispanic/Latino; 1 Two or more races, non-Hispanic/Latino), 49 international. 377 applicants, 5% accepted, 19 enrolled. In 2011, 25 master's, 9 doctorates awarded. *Entrance requirements:* For master's and doctorate, GRE, minimum GPA of 3.0. Additional exam requirements/recommendations for international students: Required—TOEFL (minimum score 610 paper-based; 257 computer-based). *Application deadline:* Applications are processed on a rolling basis. Application fee: $75 ($90 for international students). Electronic applications accepted. *Financial support:* In 2011–12, 32 fellowships, 85 research assistantships, 34 teaching assistantships were awarded; tuition waivers (full and partial) also available. *Unit head:* Paul Kenis, Head, 217-244-9214, Fax: 217-333-5052, E-mail: kenis@illinois.edu. *Application contact:* Cathy Paceley, Office Manager, 217-333-3640, Fax: 217-333-5052, E-mail: paceley@illinois.edu. Web site: http://www.chbe.illinois.edu/.

The University of Kansas, Graduate Studies, School of Engineering, Program in Bioengineering, Lawrence, KS 66045. Offers MS, PhD. *Faculty:* 7. *Students:* 44 full-time (17 women), 7 part-time (5 women); includes 3 minority (1 American Indian or Alaska Native, non-Hispanic/Latino; 1 Asian, non-Hispanic/Latino; 1 Hispanic/Latino), 18 international. Average age 26. 29 applicants, 59% accepted, 9 enrolled. In 2011, 3 master's, 2 doctorates awarded. Terminal master's awarded for partial completion of doctoral program. *Degree requirements:* For master's, thesis; for doctorate, comprehensive exam, thesis/dissertation. *Entrance requirements:* For master's and doctorate, GRE. Additional exam requirements/recommendations for international students: Required—TOEFL. *Application deadline:* For fall admission, 12/14 for domestic and international students; for spring admission, 10/31 for domestic students, 9/28 for international students. Application fee: $55 ($65 for international students). Electronic applications accepted. Tuition and fees vary according to course load, campus/location, program and reciprocity agreements. *Financial support:* Fellowships, research assistantships with full and partial tuition reimbursements, and teaching assistantships available. Financial award application deadline: 12/15. *Faculty research:* Bioimaging, bioinformatics, biomaterials and tissue engineering, biomechanics and neural engineering, biomedical product design and development, biomolecular engineering. *Unit head:* Dr. Sara E. Wilson, Academic Director, 785-864-2103, Fax: 785-864-5445, E-mail: sewilson@ku.edu. *Application contact:* Destiny Poole, Program Assistant, 785-864-5258, Fax: 785-864-5445, E-mail: bioe@ku.edu. Web site: http://bio.engr.ku.edu/.

University of Maine, Graduate School, College of Engineering, Department of Chemical and Biological Engineering, Orono, ME 04469. Offers biological engineering (ME, MS); chemical engineering (MS, PhD). Part-time programs available. *Students:* 11 full-time (2 women), 7 part-time (0 women); includes 1 minority (Black or African American, non-Hispanic/Latino), 9 international. Average age 29. 29 applicants, 24% accepted, 5 enrolled. In 2011, 2 master's, 4 doctorates awarded. *Degree requirements:* For doctorate, thesis/dissertation. *Entrance requirements:* For master's and doctorate, GRE General Test. Additional exam requirements/recommendations for international students: Required—TOEFL. *Application deadline:* For fall admission, 2/1 priority date for domestic students. Applications are processed on a rolling basis. Application fee: $65. Electronic applications accepted. *Expenses:* Tuition, state resident: full-time $5016. Tuition, nonresident: full-time $14,424. *Financial support:* In 2011–12, 1 fellowship with full tuition reimbursement (averaging $18,000 per year), 19 research assistantships with full tuition reimbursements (averaging $18,760 per year) were awarded; Federal Work-Study and tuition waivers (full and partial) also available. Financial award application deadline: 3/1. *Faculty research:* Transport phenomena, process modeling, polymer science and engineering, material characterization, unit operations in pulp and paper. *Total annual research expenditures:* $301,883. *Unit head:* Dr. Hemant Pendse, Chair, 207-581-2277, Fax: 207-581-2323. *Application contact:* Scott G. Delcourt, Associate Dean of the Graduate School, 207-581-3291, Fax: 207-581-3232, E-mail: graduate@maine.edu. Web site: http://www2.umaine.edu/graduate/.

University of Maryland, College Park, Academic Affairs, A. James Clark School of Engineering, Department of Chemical and Biomolecular Engineering, College Park, MD 20742. Offers bioengineering (MS, PhD); chemical engineering (M Eng, MS, PhD). Part-time and evening/weekend programs available. *Faculty:* 27 full-time (2 women). *Students:* 48 full-time (16 women), 6 part-time (2 women); includes 7 minority (1 Black or African American, non-Hispanic/Latino; 6 Asian, non-Hispanic/Latino), 31 international. 184 applicants, 18% accepted, 15 enrolled. In 2011, 3 master's, 6 doctorates awarded. *Degree requirements:* For master's, thesis optional; for doctorate, variable foreign language requirement, thesis/dissertation, exam, oral presentation. *Entrance requirements:* For master's and doctorate, GRE General Test, 3 letters of recommendation. Additional exam requirements/recommendations for international students: Required—TOEFL. *Application deadline:* For fall admission, 1/15 for domestic students, 2/1 for international students; for spring admission, 6/1 for domestic and international students. Applications are processed on a rolling basis. Application fee: $75. Electronic applications accepted. *Expenses: Tuition, area resident:* Part-time $525 per credit hour. Tuition, state resident: part-time $525 per credit hour. Tuition, nonresident: part-time $1131 per credit hour. *Required fees:* $386.31 per term. Tuition and fees vary according to program. *Financial support:* In 2011–12, 3 fellowships with full and partial tuition reimbursements (averaging $15,000 per year), 31 research assistantships with tuition reimbursements (averaging $23,851 per year), 13 teaching assistantships with tuition reimbursements (averaging $21,104 per year) were awarded; Federal Work-Study and scholarships/grants also available. Support available to part-time students. Financial award applicants required to submit FAFSA. *Faculty research:* Applied polymer science, biochemical engineering, thermal properties, bioprocess monitoring. *Total annual research expenditures:* $1.8 million. *Unit head:* Sheryl Ehrman, Chair, 301-405-1074, E-mail: sehrman@umd.edu. *Application contact:* Dr. Charles A. Caramello, Dean of Graduate School, 301-405-0358, Fax: 301-314-9305, E-mail: ccaramel@umd.edu.

University of Maryland, College Park, Academic Affairs, A. James Clark School of Engineering, Fischell Department of Bioengineering, College Park, MD 20742. Offers MS, PhD. *Faculty:* 82 full-time (16 women), 2 part-time/adjunct (0 women). *Students:* 56 full-time (26 women), 5 part-time (2 women); includes 11 minority (1 Black or African American, non-Hispanic/Latino; 7 Asian, non-Hispanic/Latino; 3 Two or more races, non-Hispanic/Latino), 11 international. 149 applicants, 15% accepted, 11 enrolled. In 2011, 1 master's, 10 doctorates awarded. *Degree requirements:* For master's, thesis optional; for doctorate, thesis/dissertation. *Entrance requirements:* For master's, GRE General Test, minimum GPA of 3.0, 3 letters of recommendation. *Application deadline:* For fall admission, 12/1 for domestic and international students. Applications are processed on a rolling basis. Application fee: $75. Electronic applications accepted. *Expenses: Tuition, area resident:* Part-time $525 per credit hour. Tuition, state resident: part-time $525 per credit hour. Tuition, nonresident: part-time $1131 per credit hour. *Required fees:* $386.31 per term. Tuition and fees vary according to program. *Financial support:* In 2011–12, 10 fellowships with full and partial tuition reimbursements (averaging $24,715 per year), 47 research assistantships (averaging $23,937 per year), 1 teaching assistantship (averaging $19,064 per year) were awarded; career-related internships or fieldwork also available. Financial award applicants required to submit FAFSA. *Faculty research:* Bioengineering, bioenvironmental and water resources engineering, natural resources management. *Total annual research expenditures:* $3.1 million. *Unit head:* Dr. William Bentley, Chair, 301-405-4321, Fax: 301-405-9023, E-mail: bentley@umd.edu. *Application contact:* Dean of Graduate School, 301-405-0358, Fax: 301-314-9305.

University of Missouri, Graduate School, College of Engineering, Department of Biological Engineering, Columbia, MO 65211. Offers agricultural engineering (MS);

biological engineering (MS, PhD). *Faculty:* 20 full-time (2 women). *Students:* 35 full-time (11 women), 16 part-time (6 women); includes 4 minority (1 Black or African American, non-Hispanic/Latino; 2 Asian, non-Hispanic/Latino; 1 Hispanic/Latino), 26 international. Average age 26. 38 applicants, 47% accepted, 10 enrolled. In 2011, 9 master's, 9 doctorates awarded. *Degree requirements:* For master's, thesis; for doctorate, thesis/dissertation. *Entrance requirements:* For master's and doctorate, GRE General Test, minimum GPA of 3.0. Additional exam requirements/recommendations for international students: Required—TOEFL (minimum score 550 paper-based; 213 computer-based; 80 iBT). *Application deadline:* For fall admission, 4/1 priority date for domestic students. Applications are processed on a rolling basis. Application fee: $55 ($75 for international students). *Expenses:* Tuition, state resident: full-time $5881. Tuition, nonresident: full-time $15,183. *Required fees:* $952. Tuition and fees vary according to campus/location and program. *Financial support:* Fellowships, research assistantships, teaching assistantships, and institutionally sponsored loans available. *Unit head:* Dr. Jinglu Tan, Department Chair, E-mail: tanj@missouri.edu. *Application contact:* JoAnn Lewis, 573-882-4113, E-mail: lewisj@missouri.edu. Web site: http://bioengineering.missouri.edu/graduate/.

University of Nebraska–Lincoln, Graduate College, College of Engineering, Department of Biological Systems Engineering, Interdepartmental Area of Agricultural and Biological Systems Engineering, Lincoln, NE 68588. Offers MS, PhD. *Degree requirements:* For master's, thesis optional. *Entrance requirements:* Additional exam requirements/recommendations for international students: Required—TOEFL (minimum score 550 paper-based; 213 computer-based). Electronic applications accepted. *Faculty research:* Hydrological engineering, tractive performance, biomedical engineering, irrigation systems.

University of Nebraska–Lincoln, Graduate College, College of Engineering, Department of Chemical and Biomolecular Engineering, Lincoln, NE 68588. Offers MS, PhD. *Degree requirements:* For master's, thesis; for doctorate, comprehensive exam, thesis/dissertation. *Entrance requirements:* For master's and doctorate, GRE. Additional exam requirements/recommendations for international students: Required—TOEFL (minimum score 550 paper-based; 213 computer-based). Electronic applications accepted. *Faculty research:* Fermentation, radioactive waste remediation, chemical fuels from renewable feedstocks.

University of Notre Dame, Graduate School, College of Engineering, Department of Civil Engineering and Geological Sciences, Notre Dame, IN 46556. Offers bioengineering (MS Bio E); civil engineering (MSCE); civil engineering and geological sciences (PhD); environmental engineering (MS Env E); geological sciences (MS). Terminal master's awarded for partial completion of doctoral program. *Degree requirements:* For master's, comprehensive exam; for doctorate, thesis/dissertation, candidacy exam. *Entrance requirements:* For master's and doctorate, GRE General Test. Additional exam requirements/recommendations for international students: Required—TOEFL (minimum score 600 paper-based; 250 computer-based; 80 iBT). Electronic applications accepted. *Faculty research:* Environmental modeling, biological-waste treatment, petrology, environmental geology, geochemistry.

University of Oklahoma, College of Engineering, Center for Bioengineering, Norman, OK 73019. Offers MS, PhD. *Students:* 13 full-time (4 women), 16 part-time (4 women); includes 2 minority (1 Black or African American, non-Hispanic/Latino; 1 Asian, non-Hispanic/Latino), 13 international. Average age 27. 6 applicants, 33% accepted, 2 enrolled. In 2011, 2 degrees awarded. Terminal master's awarded for partial completion of doctoral program. *Degree requirements:* For master's, thesis; for doctorate, thesis/dissertation, oral exam. *Entrance requirements:* For master's and doctorate, minimum GPA of 3.0. Additional exam requirements/recommendations for international students: Required—TOEFL (minimum score 600 paper-based; 100 iBT). *Application deadline:* For fall admission, 4/1 for domestic students, 3/1 for international students; for spring admission, 11/1 priority date for domestic students, 9/1 for international students. Application fee: $40 ($90 for international students). Electronic applications accepted. *Expenses:* Tuition, state resident: full-time $4087; part-time $170.30 per credit hour. Tuition, nonresident: full-time $14,875; part-time $619.80 per credit hour. *Required fees:* $2659; $100.25 per credit hour. Tuition and fees vary according to course load and degree level. *Financial support:* In 2011–12, 29 students received support, including 1 fellowship with full tuition reimbursement available (averaging $2,500 per year); unspecified assistantships also available. Financial award applicants required to submit FAFSA. *Faculty research:* Bioengineering, biomaterials, biomchanics, biomedical nanomaterials, biosensors, cell adhesion, drug delivery/targeted therapeutics, medical implants, microfluidics, and tissue engineering. *Unit head:* Dr. David Schmidtke, Director. *Application contact:* Dr. Ulli Nollert, Graduate Program Coordinator and Associate Professor, 405-325-4366, Fax: 405-325-5813, E-mail: nollert@ou.edu. Web site: http://www.ou.edu/coe/oubc.

University of Ottawa, Faculty of Graduate and Postdoctoral Studies, Faculty of Engineering, Department of Chemical and Biological Engineering, Ottawa, ON K1N 6N5, Canada. Offers M Eng, MA Sc, PhD. *Degree requirements:* For master's, thesis or alternative; for doctorate, comprehensive exam, thesis/dissertation. *Entrance requirements:* For master's, honors degree or equivalent, minimum B average; for doctorate, master's degree, minimum B+ average. Electronic applications accepted. *Faculty research:* Material development, process engineering, clean technologies.

University of Pennsylvania, School of Engineering and Applied Science, Department of Bioengineering, Philadelphia, PA 19104. Offers MSE, PhD, MD/PhD, VMD/PhD. *Faculty:* 45 full-time (5 women), 13 part-time/adjunct (0 women). *Students:* 134 full-time (57 women), 19 part-time (9 women); includes 40 minority (3 Black or African American, non-Hispanic/Latino; 1 American Indian or Alaska Native, non-Hispanic/Latino; 29 Asian, non-Hispanic/Latino; 7 Hispanic/Latino), 34 international. 469 applicants, 25% accepted, 48 enrolled. In 2011, 26 master's, 23 doctorates awarded. Terminal master's awarded for partial completion of doctoral program. *Degree requirements:* For master's, thesis optional; for doctorate, thesis/dissertation. *Entrance requirements:* For master's and doctorate, GRE General Test. Additional exam requirements/recommendations for international students: Required—TOEFL. *Application deadline:* For fall admission, 6/1 priority date for domestic students, 5/1 for international students. Applications are processed on a rolling basis. Application fee: $70. Electronic applications accepted. *Expenses: Tuition:* Full-time $26,660; part-time $4944 per course. *Required fees:* $2318; $291 per course. Tuition and fees vary according to course load, degree level and program. *Financial support:* Fellowships, research assistantships, teaching assistantships, institutionally sponsored loans, scholarships/grants, traineeships, health care benefits, and unspecified assistantships available. *Faculty research:* Biomaterials and biomechanics, biofluid mechanics and transport, bioelectric phenomena, computational neuroscience. *Unit head:* Eduardo D. Glandt, Dean, 215-898-7244, Fax: 215-573-2018, E-mail: seasdean@seas.upenn.edu. *Application contact:* Kathleen Venit,

Graduate Coordinator, 215-746-8604, E-mail: kvenit@seas.upenn.edu. Web site: http://www.seas.upenn.edu/be/index.html.

University of Pittsburgh, Swanson School of Engineering, Department of Bioengineering, Pittsburgh, PA 15260. Offers MSBENG, PhD, MD/PhD. Part-time programs available. *Faculty:* 20 full-time (2 women), 72 part-time/adjunct (9 women). *Students:* 134 full-time (44 women), 11 part-time (2 women); includes 29 minority (3 Black or African American, non-Hispanic/Latino; 1 American Indian or Alaska Native, non-Hispanic/Latino; 20 Asian, non-Hispanic/Latino; 5 Hispanic/Latino), 27 international. Average age 23. 280 applicants, 19% accepted, 29 enrolled. In 2011, 17 master's, 23 doctorates awarded. Terminal master's awarded for partial completion of doctoral program. *Degree requirements:* For master's, thesis; for doctorate, comprehensive exam, thesis/dissertation, final oral exams. *Entrance requirements:* For master's and doctorate, GRE General Test, minimum QPA of 3.0. Additional exam requirements/recommendations for international students: Required—TOEFL (minimum score 550 paper-based; 213 computer-based; 80 iBT). *Application deadline:* For fall admission, 3/1 priority date for domestic students; for spring admission, 7/1 for domestic students. Applications are processed on a rolling basis. Application fee: $50. Electronic applications accepted. *Expenses:* Tuition, state resident: full-time $18,774; part-time $760 per credit. Tuition, nonresident: full-time $30,736; part-time $1258 per credit. *Required fees:* $740; $200 per term. Tuition and fees vary according to program. *Financial support:* In 2011–12, 108 students received support, including 25 fellowships with full tuition reimbursements available (averaging $28,500 per year), 59 research assistantships with full tuition reimbursements available (averaging $25,296 per year), 24 teaching assistantships with full tuition reimbursements available (averaging $25,500 per year); scholarships/grants and traineeships also available. Financial award application deadline: 4/15. *Faculty research:* Artificial organs, biomechanics, biomaterials, signal processing, biotechnology. *Total annual research expenditures:* $48.2 million. *Unit head:* Harvey S. Borovetz, Chairman, 412-383-9713, Fax: 412-383-8788, E-mail: borovetzhs@msx.upmc.edu. *Application contact:* 412-624-9800, Fax: 412-624-9808, E-mail: admin@engrng.pitt.edu. Web site: http://www.engineering.pitt.edu/Bioengineering/.

The University of Texas at Arlington, Graduate School, College of Engineering, Bioengineering Department, Arlington, TX 76019. Offers MS, PhD. Programs offered jointly with The University of Texas Southwestern Medical Center at Dallas. Part-time programs available. *Faculty:* 11 full-time (2 women). *Students:* 103 full-time (49 women), 54 part-time (21 women); includes 21 minority (3 Black or African American, non-Hispanic/Latino; 13 Asian, non-Hispanic/Latino; 3 Hispanic/Latino; 2 Two or more races, non-Hispanic/Latino), 102 international. 127 applicants, 69% accepted, 38 enrolled. In 2011, 46 master's, 5 doctorates awarded. Terminal master's awarded for partial completion of doctoral program. *Degree requirements:* For master's, comprehensive exam (for some programs), thesis (for some programs); for doctorate, comprehensive exam, thesis/dissertation, qualifying exam. *Entrance requirements:* For master's, GRE General Test (minimum total of 1100 with minimum verbal score of 400), minimum GPA of 3.0 in last 60 hours of course work, 3 letters of recommendation; for doctorate, GRE General Test (minimum total of 1175 with minimum verbal score of 400), minimum GPA of 3.4 in last 60 hours of course work, 3 letters of recommendation. Additional exam requirements/recommendations for international students: Required—TOEFL. *Application deadline:* For fall admission, 6/6 for domestic students, 4/4 for international students; for spring admission, 10/15 for domestic students, 9/5 for international students. Applications are processed on a rolling basis. Application fee: $35 ($50 for international students). *Financial support:* In 2011–12, 1 student received support, including 4 fellowships (averaging $1,000 per year), 5 research assistantships (averaging $10,000 per year), 9 teaching assistantships (averaging $18,000 per year); career-related internships or fieldwork, Federal Work-Study, institutionally sponsored loans, scholarships/grants, and tuition waivers (partial) also available. Financial award application deadline: 6/1; financial award applicants required to submit FAFSA. *Faculty research:* Instrumentation, mechanics, materials. *Unit head:* Dr. Khosrow Behbehani, Chair, 817-272-2249, Fax: 817-272-2251, E-mail: kb@uta.edu. *Application contact:* Amanda Kerby, Academic Advisor, 817-272-0783, Fax: 817-272-5388, E-mail: akerby@uta.edu.

The University of Toledo, College of Graduate Studies, College of Engineering, Department of Bioengineering, Toledo, OH 43606-3390. Offers MS, PhD. Terminal master's awarded for partial completion of doctoral program. *Degree requirements:* For master's, thesis optional; for doctorate, thesis/dissertation, qualifying exam. *Entrance requirements:* For master's, GRE General Test, minimum GPA of 3.0; for doctorate, GRE General Test, minimum GPA of 3.3. Additional exam requirements/recommendations for international students: Required—TOEFL (minimum score 550 paper-based; 213 computer-based; 80 iBT). Electronic applications accepted. *Faculty research:* Artificial organs, biochemical engineering, bioelectrical systems, biomechanics, cellular engineering.

University of Utah, Graduate School, College of Engineering, Department of Bioengineering, Salt Lake City, UT 84112-9202. Offers MS, PhD. *Faculty:* 20 full-time (2 women), 1 part-time/adjunct (0 women). *Students:* 115 full-time (24 women), 27 part-time (7 women); includes 8 minority (all Asian, non-Hispanic/Latino), 26 international. Average age 28. 265 applicants, 30% accepted, 29 enrolled. In 2011, 13 master's, 18 doctorates awarded. Terminal master's awarded for partial completion of doctoral program. *Median time to degree:* Of those who began their doctoral program in fall 2003, 100% received their degree in 8 years or less. *Degree requirements:* For master's, comprehensive exam, thesis, written project, oral presentation; for doctorate, thesis/dissertation. *Entrance requirements:* For master's and doctorate, GRE General Test, minimum GPA of 3.0. Additional exam requirements/recommendations for international students: Required—TOEFL (minimum score 500 paper-based; 173 computer-based; 61 iBT), IELTS. *Application deadline:* For fall admission, 4/1 for domestic and international students. Application fee: $55 ($65 for international students). Electronic applications accepted. *Expenses:* Contact institution. *Financial support:* In 2011–12, 8 fellowships with full tuition reimbursements (averaging $20,000 per year), 106 research assistantships with full tuition reimbursements (averaging $23,000 per year), 10 teaching assistantships with full tuition reimbursements (averaging $23,000 per year) were awarded; traineeships, health care benefits, tuition waivers (full), and unspecified assistantships also available. Financial award application deadline: 3/2; financial award applicants required to submit FAFSA. *Faculty research:* Ultrasonic bioinstrumentation, medical imaging, neuroprosthesis, biomaterials and tissue engineering, biomechanic biomedical computing/modeling. *Total annual research expenditures:* $6.8 million. *Unit head:* Dr. Patrick A. Tresco, Chair, 801-587-9263, Fax: 801-585-5151, E-mail: patrick.tresco@utah.edu. *Application contact:* Karen Lynn Terry, Graduate Program

Bioengineering

Advisor and Coordinator, 801-581-8559, Fax: 801-585-5151, E-mail: karen.terry@utah.edu. Web site: http://www.bioen.utah.edu/.

See Display below and Close-Up on page 117.

University of Washington, Graduate School, College of Engineering and School of Medicine, Department of Bioengineering, Seattle, WA 98195-5061. Offers bioengineering (MS, PhD); bioengineering and nanotechnology (PhD); medical engineering (MME); pharmaceutical bioengineering (MS). Evening/weekend programs available. Postbaccalaureate distance learning degree programs offered (no on-campus study). *Faculty:* 35 full-time (10 women), 11 part-time/adjunct (2 women). *Students:* 116 full-time (46 women), 63 part-time (27 women); includes 48 minority (2 Black or African American, non-Hispanic/Latino; 1 American Indian or Alaska Native, non-Hispanic/Latino; 42 Asian, non-Hispanic/Latino; 3 Hispanic/Latino), 30 international. Average age 26. 495 applicants, 18% accepted, 35 enrolled. In 2011, 14 master's, 12 doctorates awarded. *Degree requirements:* For master's, comprehensive exam, thesis; for doctorate, comprehensive exam, thesis/dissertation, qualifying exam, general exam, thesis defense. *Entrance requirements:* For master's and doctorate, GRE General Test, minimum GPA of 3.0, transcripts, statement of purpose, letters of recommendation. Additional exam requirements/recommendations for international students: Required—TOEFL (minimum score 580 paper-based; 237 computer-based; 92 iBT); Recommended—IELTS (minimum score 7). *Application deadline:* For fall admission, 12/15 priority date for domestic students, 12/1 for international students. Applications are processed on a rolling basis. Application fee: $75. Electronic applications accepted. *Expenses:* Contact institution. *Financial support:* In 2011–12, 177 students received support, including 18 fellowships with full tuition reimbursements available (averaging $21,330 per year), 125 research assistantships with full tuition reimbursements available (averaging $19,224 per year), 22 teaching assistantships with full tuition reimbursements available (averaging $19,224 per year); Federal Work-Study, institutionally sponsored loans, traineeships, health care benefits, and tuition waivers (full) also available. Support available to part-time students. Financial award application deadline: 12/15; financial award applicants required to submit FAFSA. *Faculty research:* Biomaterials and tissue engineering; global health, distributed diagnosis and home healthcare; bioinstrumentation; molecular bioengineering; imaging and image-guided therapy. *Total annual research expenditures:* $22.6 million. *Unit head:* Dr. Paul Yager, Professor/Chair, 206-685-2000, Fax: 206-685-3300, E-mail: yagerp@u.washington.edu. *Application contact:* Dorian Varga, Senior Academic Counselor, 206-685-3494, Fax: 206-685-3300, E-mail: dst@u.washington.edu. Web site: http://depts.washington.edu.bioe.

University of Wisconsin–Madison, Graduate School, College of Engineering, Department of Chemical and Biological Engineering, Madison, WI 53706-0607. Offers chemical engineering (MS, PhD). *Faculty:* 19 full-time (2 women), 1 part-time/adjunct (0 women). *Students:* 131 full-time (38 women); includes 17 minority (1 American Indian or Alaska Native, non-Hispanic/Latino; 9 Asian, non-Hispanic/Latino; 7 Hispanic/Latino), 51 international. Average age 25. 428 applicants, 21% accepted, 28 enrolled. In 2011, 3 master's, 15 doctorates awarded. Terminal master's awarded for partial completion of doctoral program. *Degree requirements:* For master's, thesis or alternative; for doctorate, thesis/dissertation, 2 semesters of teaching assistantship. *Entrance requirements:* For master's and doctorate, GRE General Test. Additional exam requirements/recommendations for international students: Required—TOEFL (minimum score 550 paper-based; 213 computer-based; 80 iBT). *Application deadline:* For fall admission, 1/1 for domestic and international students; for spring admission, 10/15 for domestic and international students. Application fee: $56. Electronic applications accepted. *Expenses:* Tuition, state resident: full-time $10,296; part-time $643.51 per credit. Tuition, nonresident: full-time $24,054; part-time $1503.40 per credit. *Required fees:* $70.06 per credit. Tuition and fees vary according to course load, campus/location, program and reciprocity agreements. *Financial support:* In 2011–12, 122 students received support, including 21 fellowships with full tuition reimbursements available (averaging $28,752 per year), 66 research assistantships with full tuition reimbursements available (averaging $24,000 per year), 45 teaching assistantships with full tuition reimbursements available (averaging $25,167 per year); traineeships and health care benefits also available. Financial award application deadline: 1/15. *Faculty research:* Biotechnology, nanotechnology, complex fluids, molecular and systems modeling, renewable energy and chemicals: materials and processes. *Total annual research expenditures:* $17.7 million. *Unit head:* Prof. Thomas F. Kuech, Chair, 608-263-2922, Fax: 608-262-5434, E-mail: kuech@engr.wisc.edu. *Application contact:* Graduate Coordinator, Graduate Coordinator, 608-263-3138, Fax: 608-262-5434, E-mail: gradoffice@che.wisc.edu. Web site: http://www.engr.wisc.edu/che/.

Virginia Commonwealth University, Graduate School, School of Engineering, Department of Chemical and Life Science Engineering, Richmond, VA 23284-9005. Offers MS, PhD. *Entrance requirements:* For master's and doctorate, GRE. Additional exam requirements/recommendations for international students: Required—TOEFL (minimum score 600 paper-based; 250 computer-based; 100 iBT). Electronic applications accepted. *Expenses:* Tuition, state resident: full-time $9133; part-time $507 per credit. Tuition, nonresident: full-time $18,777; part-time $1043 per credit. *Required fees:* $77 per credit. Tuition and fees vary according to degree level, campus/location, program and student level. *Faculty research:* Advanced polymers, including biopolymers and polymers in medicine; chemical and biochemical reactor analysis; the study of supercritical fluids for environmentally favorable processes; systems biological engineering; stem cell engineering; biosensors and biochips; computational bioinformatics and rational drug design.

Virginia Polytechnic Institute and State University, Graduate School, College of Engineering, Department of Biological Systems Engineering, Blacksburg, VA 24061. Offers M Eng, MS, PhD. *Degree requirements:* For master's, comprehensive exam (for some programs), thesis (for some programs); for doctorate, comprehensive exam (for some programs), thesis/dissertation (for some programs). *Entrance requirements:* For master's and doctorate, GRE. Additional exam requirements/recommendations for international students: Required—TOEFL (minimum score 550 paper-based; 213 computer-based). *Application deadline:* For fall admission, 7/1 for domestic and international students; for spring admission, 12/1 for domestic and international students. Applications are processed on a rolling basis. Application fee: $65. Electronic applications accepted. *Expenses:* Tuition, state resident: full-time $10,048; part-time $558.25 per credit hour. Tuition, nonresident: full-time $19,497; part-time $1083.25 per credit hour. *Required fees:* $405 per semester. Tuition and fees vary according to course load, campus/location and program. *Financial support:* Fellowships with full tuition reimbursements, research assistantships with full tuition reimbursements, teaching assistantships with full tuition reimbursements, career-related internships or fieldwork, Federal Work-Study, scholarships/grants, health care benefits, and unspecified assistantships available. Financial award application deadline: 1/15. *Faculty*

research: Soil and water engineering, alternative energy sources for agriculture and agricultural mechanization. *Unit head:* Dr. Mary Leigh Wolfe, Unit Head, 540-231-6092, Fax: 540-231-3199, E-mail: mlwolfe@vt.edu. *Application contact:* Cully Hession, Graduate Program Director, 540-231-9480, Fax: 540-231-3199, E-mail: chession@vt.edu. Web site: http://www.bse.vt.edu/.

Washington State University, Graduate School, College of Engineering and Architecture, Department of Biological Systems Engineering, Pullman, WA 99164. Offers biological and agricultural engineering (MS, PhD). *Faculty:* 10. *Students:* 61 full-time (16 women), 3 part-time (1 woman); includes 1 minority (Asian, non-Hispanic/Latino), 53 international. Average age 29. 72 applicants, 43% accepted, 15 enrolled. In 2011, 4 master's, 3 doctorates awarded. *Degree requirements:* For master's, comprehensive exam, thesis (for some programs), written and oral exam; for doctorate, comprehensive exam, thesis/dissertation, written and oral exam. *Entrance requirements:* For master's, GRE General Test, GRE Subject Test, minimum GPA of 3.0, bachelor's degree in engineering or closely related subject; for doctorate, minimum GPA of 3.0, bachelor's degree in engineering or closely related subject. Additional exam requirements/recommendations for international students: Required—TOEFL. *Application deadline:* For fall admission, 2/1 priority date for domestic students, 3/1 for international students; for spring admission, 9/1 for domestic students, 7/1 for international students. Applications are processed on a rolling basis. Application fee: $75. *Financial support:* In 2011–12, 20 research assistantships (averaging $18,204 per year), 17 teaching assistantships (averaging $18,204 per year) were awarded. *Faculty research:* Social issues and engineering education, electronic instrument design, prediction, technology for dust from agricultural lands. *Total annual research expenditures:* $3.1 million. *Unit head:* Dr. Claudio Stockle, Chair, 509-335-1578, Fax: 509-335-2722, E-mail: stockle@wsu.edu. *Application contact:* Graduate School Admissions, 800-GRADWSU, Fax: 509-335-1949, E-mail: gradsch@wsu.edu. Web site: http://www.bsyse.wsu.edu.

Biosystems Engineering

Auburn University, Graduate School, Ginn College of Engineering, Department of Biosystems Engineering, Auburn University, AL 36849. Offers MS, PhD. *Faculty:* 11 full-time. *Students:* 14 full-time (6 women), 4 part-time (1 woman), 16 international. Average age 26. 24 applicants, 54% accepted, 8 enrolled. In 2011, 1 doctorate awarded. *Expenses:* Tuition, state resident: full-time $7290; part-time $405 per credit hour. Tuition, nonresident: full-time $21,870; part-time $1215 per credit hour. International tuition: $22,000 full-time. *Required fees:* $1402. *Unit head:* Steven Taylor, Head, 334-844-4180. *Application contact:* Dr. George Flowers, Dean of the Graduate School, 334-844-2125. Web site: http://www.eng.auburn.edu/programs/bsen/programs/graduate/index.html.

Clemson University, Graduate School, College of Engineering and Science, Department of Environmental Engineering and Earth Sciences and College of Engineering and Science, Program in Biosystems Engineering, Clemson, SC 29634. Offers MS, PhD. Part-time programs available. *Students:* 19 full-time (6 women), 4 part-time (0 women); includes 1 minority (Black or African American, non-Hispanic/Latino), 12 international. Average age 28. 31 applicants, 58% accepted, 9 enrolled. In 2011, 4 master's, 2 doctorates awarded. *Degree requirements:* For master's, thesis; for doctorate, comprehensive exam, thesis/dissertation. *Entrance requirements:* For master's and doctorate, GRE General Test, minimum GPA of 3.0. Additional exam requirements/recommendations for international students: Required—TOEFL. *Application deadline:* For fall admission, 6/1 for domestic students, 4/15 for international students; for spring admission, 9/15 for international students. Applications are processed on a rolling basis. Application fee: $70 ($80 for international students). Electronic applications accepted. *Financial support:* In 2011–12, 18 students received support, including 17 research assistantships with partial tuition reimbursements available (averaging $10,218 per year), 3 teaching assistantships with partial tuition reimbursements available (averaging $10,062 per year); fellowships with full and partial tuition reimbursements available, career-related internships or fieldwork, institutionally sponsored loans, scholarships/grants, health care benefits, and unspecified assistantships also available. Support available to part-time students. Financial award application deadline: 2/15. *Faculty research:* Sustainable bioprocessing, biofuels and bioenergy, ecological engineering. *Unit head:* Dr. Tanju Karanfil, Chair, 864-653-3278, Fax: 864-656-0672, E-mail: tkaranf@clemson.edu. *Application contact:* Dr. Terry Walker, Graduate Coordinator, 864-656-0351, Fax: 864-656-0672, E-mail: walker4@clemson.edu. Web site: http://www.clemson.edu/cafls/departments/agbioeng/be/.

Michigan State University, The Graduate School, College of Agriculture and Natural Resources and College of Engineering, Department of Biosystems and Agricultural Engineering, East Lansing, MI 48824. Offers biosystems engineering (MS, PhD). *Entrance requirements:* Additional exam requirements/recommendations for international students: Required—TOEFL. Electronic applications accepted.

North Dakota State University, College of Graduate and Interdisciplinary Studies, College of Engineering and Architecture, Department of Agricultural and Biosystems Engineering, Fargo, ND 58108. Offers agricultural and biosystems engineering (MS, PhD); engineering (PhD); natural resource management (MS); natural resources management (PhD). Part-time programs available. *Faculty:* 6 full-time (0 women). *Students:* 7 full-time (3 women), 2 part-time (0 women), all international. Average age 28. 12 applicants, 8% accepted, 0 enrolled. In 2011, 4 degrees awarded. *Degree requirements:* For master's, thesis; for doctorate, thesis/dissertation. *Entrance requirements:* For master's and doctorate, BS in engineering or the equivalent, minimum undergraduate GPA of 3.0. Additional exam requirements/recommendations for international students: Required—TOEFL (minimum score 550 paper-based; 213 computer-based; 79 iBT). *Application deadline:* For fall admission, 5/1 for international students; for spring admission, 8/1 for international students. Applications are processed on a rolling basis. Application fee: $35. Electronic applications accepted. *Financial support:* In 2011–12, 9 research assistantships with full tuition reimbursements (averaging $15,000 per year) were awarded; career-related internships or fieldwork, Federal Work-Study, institutionally sponsored loans, and unspecified assistantships also available. Support available to part-time students. Financial award application deadline: 4/15. *Faculty research:* Irrigation, crop processing, food engineering, environmental resources, sensors and instrumentation. *Unit head:* Dr. James Venette, Chair, 701-231-7261, Fax: 701-231-1008, E-mail: james.venette@ndsu.edu. *Application contact:* Dr. David A. Wittrock, Dean, 701-231-7033, Fax: 701-231-6524. Web site: http://www.ageng.ndsu.nodak.edu/.

South Dakota State University, Graduate School, College of Agriculture and Biological Sciences, Department of Agricultural and Biosystems Engineering, Brookings, SD 57007. Offers MS, PhD. Part-time programs available. *Degree requirements:* For master's, thesis; for doctorate, comprehensive exam, thesis/dissertation, preliminary oral and written exams. *Entrance requirements:* Additional exam requirements/recommendations for international students: Required—TOEFL (minimum score 525 paper-based; 197 computer-based; 71 iBT).

South Dakota State University, Graduate School, College of Engineering, Department of Agricultural and Biosystems Engineering, Brookings, SD 57007. Offers biological sciences (MS, PhD); engineering (MS). PhD offered jointly with Iowa State University of Science and Technology. Part-time programs available. *Degree requirements:* For master's, thesis (for some programs), oral exam; for doctorate, thesis/dissertation, preliminary oral and written exams. *Entrance requirements:* For master's and doctorate, engineering degree. Additional exam requirements/recommendations for international students: Required—TOEFL (minimum score 550 paper-based; 213 computer-based; 79 iBT). *Faculty research:* Water resources, food engineering, natural resources engineering, machine design, bioprocess engineering.

The University of Arizona, College of Agriculture and Life Sciences, Department of Agricultural and Biosystems Engineering, Tucson, AZ 85721. Offers MS, PhD. *Faculty:* 10 full-time (1 woman). *Students:* 25 full-time (12 women), 5 part-time (0 women); includes 4 minority (2 Asian, non-Hispanic/Latino; 1 Hispanic/Latino; 1 Two or more races, non-Hispanic/Latino), 17 international. Average age 32. 19 applicants, 74% accepted, 6 enrolled. In 2011, 4 master's, 7 doctorates awarded. Terminal master's awarded for partial completion of doctoral program. *Degree requirements:* For master's, thesis; for doctorate, thesis/dissertation. *Entrance requirements:* For master's, minimum GPA of 3.0 in last 2 years of undergraduate study, 3 letters of recommendation; for doctorate, minimum GPA of 3.0 in last 2 years of undergraduate study, 3 letters of recommendation, statement of purpose. Additional exam requirements/recommendations for international students: Required—TOEFL (minimum score 213 computer-based). *Application deadline:* For fall admission, 6/1 for domestic students, 2/1 for international students; for spring admission, 9/1 for domestic students, 8/1 for international students. Applications are processed on a rolling basis. Application fee: $75. Electronic applications accepted. *Expenses:* Tuition, state resident: full-time $10,840. Tuition, nonresident: full-time $25,802. *Financial support:* In 2011–12, 9 research assistantships with full and partial tuition reimbursements (averaging $24,985 per year), 1 teaching assistantship with full and partial tuition reimbursement (averaging $24,435 per year) were awarded; fellowships, career-related internships or fieldwork, Federal Work-Study, institutionally sponsored loans, scholarships/grants, traineeships, health care benefits, tuition waivers (full and partial), and unspecified assistantships also available. Financial award application deadline: 5/1. *Faculty research:* Irrigation system design, energy-use management, equipment for alternative crops, food properties enhancement. *Total annual research expenditures:* $2 million. *Unit head:* Mark R. Riley, Head, 520-626-9120, Fax: 520-621-3963, E-mail: riley@ag.arizona.edu. *Application contact:* Daniela Ibarra, Senior Office Specialist, 520-621-1753, Fax: 520-621-3963, E-mail: dcastro@email.arizona.edu. Web site: http://ag.arizona.edu/abe.

University of Dayton, Department of Chemical Engineering, Dayton, OH 45469-1300. Offers bioengineering instrumentation (MS); bioprocess engineering (MS); biosystems engineering (MS). Part-time and evening/weekend programs available. *Faculty:* 11 full-time (1 woman), 4 part-time/adjunct (0 women). *Students:* 37 full-time (9 women), 13 part-time (1 woman); includes 3 minority (2 Black or African American, non-Hispanic/Latino; 1 Asian, non-Hispanic/Latino), 29 international. Average age 26. 80 applicants, 70% accepted, 24 enrolled. In 2011, 10 degrees awarded. *Degree requirements:* For master's, thesis optional. *Entrance requirements:* Additional exam requirements/recommendations for international students: Required—TOEFL (minimum score 550 paper-based; 213 computer-based; 80 iBT). *Application deadline:* For fall admission, 8/1 priority date for domestic students. Applications are processed on a rolling basis. Application fee: $0 ($50 for international students). Electronic applications accepted. *Expenses:* Tuition: Full-time $8400; part-time $700 per credit hour. *Required fees:* $25 per semester. Tuition and fees vary according to degree level. *Financial support:* In 2011–12, 13 research assistantships with full tuition reimbursements (averaging $11,400 per year) were awarded; institutionally sponsored loans, health care benefits, and unspecified assistantships also available. Financial award applicants required to submit FAFSA. *Faculty research:* Vertically-aligned carbon nanotubes infiltrated with temperature-responsive polymers: smart nanocomposite films for self-cleaning and controlled release, bilayer and bulk heterojunction solar cells using liquid crystalline porphyrins as donors by solution processing, DNA damage induced by multiwalled carbon nanotubes in mouse embryonic stem cells. *Total annual research expenditures:* $1.5 million. *Unit head:* Dr. Robert Wilkens, Chair, 937-229-2627, E-mail: rwilkens1@udayton.edu. *Application contact:* Dr. Robert Wilkens, Chair, 937-229-2627, E-mail: rwilkens1@udayton.edu.

University of Manitoba, Faculty of Graduate Studies, Faculty of Engineering, Department of Biosystems Engineering, Winnipeg, MB R3T 2N2, Canada. Offers M Eng, M Sc, PhD.

University of Minnesota, Twin Cities Campus, Graduate School, College of Food, Agricultural and Natural Resource Sciences, Bioproducts and Biosystems Science, Engineering and Management Graduate Program, Saint Paul, MN 55108. Offers MS, PhD. Part-time programs available. *Faculty:* 42 full-time (3 women). *Students:* 33 full-time (15 women), 2 part-time (1 woman); includes 1 minority (Native Hawaiian or other Pacific Islander, non-Hispanic/Latino), 21 international. Average age 30. 50 applicants, 44% accepted, 9 enrolled. In 2011, 3 master's, 2 doctorates awarded. Terminal master's awarded for partial completion of doctoral program. *Degree requirements:* For master's, comprehensive exam, thesis; for doctorate, comprehensive exam, thesis/dissertation. *Entrance requirements:* For master's and doctorate, GRE, BS in engineering, mathematics, physical or biological sciences, or related field. Additional exam requirements/recommendations for international students: Required—TOEFL (minimum score 550 paper-based; 213 computer-based; 79 iBT), IELTS (minimum score 6.5), TOEFL preferred. *Application deadline:* For fall admission, 12/15 for domestic and international students; for spring admission, 10/15 for domestic and international

Biosystems Engineering

students. Applications are processed on a rolling basis. Application fee: $75 ($95 for international students). Electronic applications accepted. *Financial support:* In 2011–12, fellowships with full tuition reimbursements (averaging $23,500 per year), research assistantships with full and partial tuition reimbursements (averaging $20,280 per year), teaching assistantships with full and partial tuition reimbursements (averaging $20,280 per year) were awarded; scholarships/grants, health care benefits, and unspecified assistantships also available. Support available to part-time students. Financial award application deadline: 12/15. *Faculty research:* Water quality, bioprocessing, food engineering, terramechanics, process and machine control. *Total annual research expenditures:* $6.2 million. *Unit head:* Dr. Gary Sands, Director of Graduate Studies, 612-625-4756, Fax: 612-624-3005, E-mail: grsands@umn.edu. *Application contact:* Sue Olsen, Graduate Coordinator, 612-625-7733, Fax: 612-624-3005, E-mail: olsen005@umn.edu. Web site: http://www.bbe.umn.edu/.

The University of Tennessee, Graduate School, College of Agricultural Sciences and Natural Resources, Department of Biosystems Engineering and Environmental Science, Program in Biosystems Engineering, Knoxville, TN 37996. Offers MS, PhD. *Degree requirements:* For master's, thesis; for doctorate, thesis/dissertation. *Entrance requirements:* For master's and doctorate, GRE General Test, minimum GPA of 2.7. Additional exam requirements/recommendations for international students: Required—TOEFL. Electronic applications accepted. *Expenses:* Tuition, state resident: full-time $8332; part-time $464 per credit hour. Tuition, nonresident: full-time $25,174; part-time $1400 per credit hour. *Required fees:* $1162; $56 per credit hour. Tuition and fees vary according to program.

The University of Tennessee, Graduate School, College of Agricultural Sciences and Natural Resources, Department of Biosystems Engineering and Environmental Science, Program in Biosystems Engineering Technology, Knoxville, TN 37996. Offers MS. *Degree requirements:* For master's, thesis or alternative. *Entrance requirements:* For master's, GRE General Test, minimum GPA of 2.7. Additional exam requirements/recommendations for international students: Required—TOEFL. Electronic applications accepted. *Expenses:* Tuition, state resident: full-time $8332; part-time $464 per credit hour. Tuition, nonresident: full-time $25,174; part-time $1400 per credit hour. *Required fees:* $1162; $56 per credit hour. Tuition and fees vary according to program.

UNIVERSITY OF UTAH
Department of Bioengineering

Programs of Study

The Department of Bioengineering at the University of Utah prepares graduates to be leaders in the integration of engineering, biology, and medicine to detect and treat human disease and disability. The Department's programs are consistently ranked among the highest in the United States. The students are among the highest achieving students entering any interdepartmental program on campus. Graduate instruction leads to the Master of Science (M.S.) (Defense and Course Option) and Doctor of Philosophy (Ph.D.) degrees. Research programs include biomechanics, biomaterials, biosensors, computation and modeling, drug and gene delivery, medical imaging, neural interfaces, tissue engineering, and other specialty areas. The graduate program draws more than 95 faculty members from over thirty departments across four colleges.

Students in the M.S. program must complete the master's-level core curriculum and elective courses in one of the following areas: bioInnovate, biomaterials, bioinstrumentation, biomechanics, cardiac electrophysiology, neural interfaces or imaging. In addition, all M.S. students are required to defend their thesis in a public forum. The Department also offers an M.S./Course Option program.

Students may be admitted directly to the Ph.D. program at the time of admission, depending upon the decision of the Graduate Admissions Committee. Ph.D. students must successfully complete the bioengineering graduate core curriculum or its equivalent and take additional advanced graduate courses. Students must also pass a written qualifying exam, write a research proposal on their dissertation topic, and publicly defend their dissertation.

The Ph.D. degree program typically takes a minimum of five years to complete. It is strongly recommended that all graduate students select a research direction and begin thesis research as soon as they begin their studies. In addition, the program is individually tailored to meet the specific objectives of each candidate and may involve collaboration with faculty members in other departments.

Research Facilities

The Department of Bioengineering at the University of Utah is an internationally renowned center of interdisciplinary basic and applied medically related research. It has a rich history in artificial organs, biomaterials, and drug delivery. Research laboratories and offices are located on the Heath Sciences Campus with the University Hospital, Huntsman Cancer, Primary Children's and Orthopedic Specialty Hospitals, the School of Medicine, and the College of Pharmacy. Centers and institutes include the Institute for Biomedical Engineering; Brain Institute; Scientific Computing and Imaging Institute (SCI); Cardiovascular Research and Training Institute (CVRTI); Huntsman Cancer Institute (HCI); Utah Center for Advanced Imaging Research (UCAIR); NIH Center for Bioelectric Field Modeling, Simulation, and Visualization; Center for Controlled Chemical Delivery (CCCD); Keck Center for Tissue Engineering (KCTE); Center for Neural Interfaces; Center for Biopolymers at Interfaces; and Utah State Center of Excellence for Biomedical Microfluidics.

The University has excellent libraries and state-of-the-art computing centers.

Financial Aid

Students making satisfactory progress in the Department typically receive stipend support and tuition waivers throughout their graduate studies, typically through their graduate adviser. A limited number of University and Department fellowships are offered on a competitive basis to exceptionally well-qualified applicants.

Cost of Study

Virtually all bioengineering graduate students receive full-time scholarships, fellowships, or assistantships. In addition, graduate students receiving financial support through the University of Utah are given full tuition waivers. Tuition and fees for 2011–12 for 11 credit hours were $4048 for state residents and $11,418 for nonresidents per semester.

Living and Housing Costs

On-campus housing for unmarried graduate students begins at approximately $539 per month. Unfurnished apartments for married students range from $468 to $828 per month at University Village and from $788 to $1041 per month at Shoreline Ridge. Medical Plaza housing costs for both married and single students range from approximately $611 to $1057 per month. Off-campus housing near the University is also available. For more specific information, students should visit http://www.apartments.utah.edu or http://www.orl.utah.edu.

Student Group

The University of Utah has a student population of 30,000, representing all fifty states and fifty other countries. The Department of Bioengineering welcomes approximately 35 to 40 new students each year and maintains an average total graduate enrollment of more than 130. Graduates are successful in industry, academics, medicine, government, and entrepreneurial pursuits.

Location

Salt Lake City is the center of a metropolitan area of nearly a million people. It lies in a valley with an elevation varying between 4,200 and 5,500 feet and is surrounded by mountain peaks reaching nearly 12,000 feet in elevation. The city is the cultural center of the intermountain area, with world-class ballet and modern dance companies, theater and opera companies, and a symphony orchestra. It also supports professional basketball, hockey, soccer, arena football, and baseball. Salt Lake City was the proud host of the 2002 Winter Olympics and is within 30 minutes of several world-class ski resorts. A major wilderness area is less than 2 hours away, and ten national parks are within a short drive of the city.

The University

The 1,500-acre University campus is nestled in the foothills of the Wasatch Mountains and is characterized by its modern buildings and attractive landscaping. Within a few minutes' walk of the University is Red Butte Gardens, which is a large, established garden and ecological center with an area of more than 400 miles, with display gardens and hiking trails. An international faculty of 3,600 members provides comprehensive instruction and research in disciplines ranging from medicine and law to fine arts and business.

Applying

Instructions for applying to the program can be obtained by writing to the Department of Bioengineering or from the Department's home page at http://www.bioen.utah.edu. In addition to the application form and fee, students must submit three letters of recommendation, scores on the General Test of the Graduate Record Examinations, university transcripts, and a written statement of interests and goals.

Detailed information on the various aspects of the Department of Bioengineering at the University of Utah can be obtained by accessing the Department's home page.

Correspondence and Information

Chair, Graduate Admissions Committee
Department of Bioengineering
University of Utah
20 South 2030 East, 108 BPRB
Salt Lake City, Utah 84112-9458
United States
Web site: http://www.bioen.utah.edu

THE FACULTY AND THEIR RESEARCH

Orly Alter, Ph.D., Stanford. Genomic signal processing and systems biology.
*B. Ambati, Ph.D., Medical College of Georgia. Computational biomechanics, biochemical analysis/molecular marker, characterization of hip osteoarthritis.
J. D. Andrade, Ph.D., Denver. Interfacial biochemistry, biochemical sensors, proteins engineering, integrated science education, bioluminescence.
*A. Angelucci, M.D., Rome (Italy); Ph.D., MIT. Mammalian visual system.
K. N. Bachus, Ph.D., Utah. Bone biomechanics, fracture analysis, implant failure mechanisms.
*You Han Bae, Ph.D., Korea. Pharmaceutical chemistry.
*K. Balagurunathan, Ph.D., Iowa. Biomaterials, chemical biology.
*Stacy Bamberg, Ph.D., Harvard-MIT. Bioinstrumentation, gait analysis, aging.
*D. Bearss, Ph.D., Texas at San Antonio. Pharmaceutics and drug/gene delivery.
*S. M. Blair, Ph.D., Colorado. Integrated-optics resonance biosensors.
R. D. Bloebaum, Ph.D., Western Australia. Orthopedic implants.
*D. Bloswick, Ph.D., Michigan. Biomechanics, ergonomics.
S. C. Bock, Ph.D., California, Irvine. Antithrombin III heparin cofactor, medically useful serpins, glycoprotein N-glycosylation.
*D. W. Britt, Ph.D., Utah. High-resolution microscopy, thin films, protein-surface interactions.
K. Broadhead, Ph.D., Utah. Tissue engineering.
*M. B. Bromberg, Ph.D., Vermont; M.D., Michigan. Bioelectric signals from nerve/muscle, neurophysiology.

SECTION 3: AGRICULTURAL ENGINEERING AND BIOENGINEERING

University of Utah

*R. B. Brown, Ph.D., Utah. Medical applications for sensors, bioinstrumentation, implantable electronics.

*J. B. Bunnell, Sc.D., MIT. Medical device development.

*G. Burns, D.V.M., Colorado State; Ph.D., Washington State. Biomaterial implant pathology and immune response, artificial heart.

*K. D. Caldwell, Ph.D., Uppsala (Sweden). Separation and characterization of biopolymers, subcellular particles, and cells.

*T. E. Cheatham, Ph.D., California, San Francisco. Computer simulation of biological macromolecules.

*Elena Cherkaev, Ph.D., St. Petersburg (Russia). Mathematics.

D. A. Christensen, Ph.D., Utah. Optical/ultrasonic bioinstrumentation.

G. A. Clark, Ph.D., California, Irvine. Neurobiology, basis of behavior, cell neurophysiology and learning mechanisms, computational neuroscience.

Brittany Coats, Ph.D., Pennsylvania. Head and eye injury biomechanics.

*E. V. R. DiBella, Ph.D., Georgia Tech. Medical imaging, dynamic cardiac SPECT.

A. D. Dorval, Ph.D. Boston. Neural engineering and interfaces.

*Derek Dosdall, Ph.D., Arizona State. Cardiac mapping and electrophyusiology.

*R. O. Dull, Ph.D., Penn State; M.D., Illinois at Chicago. Microvascular endothelial cells, tissue/cell engineering.

*K. Dusek, Ph.D., Czechoslovak Academy of Sciences. Formation-structure-properties relations of polymers.

*Talmage D. Egan, M.D., Utah. Anesthesiology.

*Colleen Farmer, Ph.D. Brown, Pulmonary fluid dynamics.

Peter Fitzgerald, Ph.D. Tissue remodeling.

*A. L. Fogelson, Ph.D., NYU. Physiological systems modeling.

*Darin Furgeson, Ph.D., Utah. Pharmaeutical chemistry.

*B. K. Gale, Ph.D., Utah. MEMS devices and their applications to biology and medicine.

*Guido Gerig, Ph.D., ETH Zurich. Medical imaging analysis.

*J. M. Gerton, Ph.D., Rice. Bioimaging techniques, biophysics.

H. Ghandehari, Ph.D., Utah. Pharmaceutics, drug/gene delivery.

D. W. Grainger, Ph.D., Utah. Biomaterials, drug delivery, biotechnology, fluorinated surface chemistry.

B. E. Greger, Ph.D., Washington (St. Louis). Neuroprosthetic technology, neural systems, sensory-motor processing/plasticity.

*J. M. Harris, Ph.D., Purdue. Laser-based bioinstrumentation, interfacial spectroscopy.

*T. G. Henderson, Ph.D., Texas at Austin. Artificial intelligence, computer vision, robotics.

*Heath B. Henninger, Ph.D., Utah, Orthopaedics.

J. N. Herron, Ph.D., Illinois. Protein engineering, molecular graphics, biosensors.

*R. W. Hitchcock, Ph.D., Utah. Medical product development.

V. Hlady, Ph.D., Zagreb (Croatia). Biochemistry/biophysics at interfaces, solid-liquid interface of biomaterials, proteins as engineering.

*Holly A. Holman, Ph.D., Glasgow. Sensor biophysics.

K. W. Horch, D.Sc., Yale. Neuroprostheses, biomedical instrumentation, information processing in the somatosensory system, tactile aids.

*Harriet Hopf, Ph.D., Dartmouth. Genetics of health-care associated infection.

Eric Hunter, Ph.D., Iowa. Vibration, exposure, acoustics.

E. W. Hsu, Ph.D., Johns Hopkins. Magnetic resonance imaging and applications to bioengineering.

*D. T. Hutchinson, M.D., Jefferson Medical. Orthopedics implants for the hand.

S. C. Jacobsen, Ph.D., MIT. Prosthesis design, microelectromechanical systems, control theory, robotics.

C. R. Johnson, Ph.D., Utah. Theoretical/computational electrophysiology, inverse electrocardiography, dynamical systems theory.

Kenward Johnson, M.D., Tulane. Anesthesiology.

*E. M. Jorgensen, Ph.D., Washington (Seattle). Molecular biology, genetics, cellular neurophysiology.

S. C. Joshi, D.Sc., Washington (St. Louis). Computational anatomy, statistical shape analysis in medical imaging.

*D. J. Kadrmas, Ph.D., North Carolina. Molecular imaging, positron emission tomography (PET) of cancerous tissues.

*J. P. Keener, Ph.D., Caltech. Applied mathematics, nonlinear differential equations, chemical/biological dynamics.

S. E. Kern, Ph.D., Utah. Pharmacokinetics and pharmacodynamics modeling and control.

P. S. Khanwilkar, Ph.D., Utah. Artificial heart/assist devices, design, control, surgical implantation/physiologic interfaces.

*Hanseup Kim, Ph.D., Michigan. Bionano-micro systems in moving fluids.

S. W. Kim, Ph.D., Utah. Blood compatibility, drug-delivery systems.

Richard Daniel King, Ph.D., Harvard. Alzheimer's image analysis.

*Mike Kirby, Ph.D., Brown. Large-scale scientific computation and visualization.

P. F. Kiser, Ph.D., Duke. Drug-delivery systems, biomimetic materials engineering, combinatorial materials engineering.

J. Kopecek, Ph.D., Czechoslovak Academy of Sciences. Biomaterials, chemistry/biochemistry of macromolecules, drug-delivery systems.

*Erik Kubiak, M.D., Washington (Seattle). Scientific computing and visualization, modeling, stimulation of ECG drug diffusion.

*John T. Langell, M.D., Ph.D., Drexel. Surgery.

*Paul LaStayo, Ph.D. Northern Arizona. Physical therapy

*Gianluca Lazzi, Ph.D., Utah. Computation, electromagnetics.

*Stephen Lessnick, M.D., Ph.D., UCLA. Pediatric hematology.

R. S. MacLeod, Ph.D., Dalhousie. Cardiac bioelectric modeling, body surface potential mapping, cardiac electrophysiology, scientific visualization.

*B. A. MacWilliams, Ph.D., Worcester Polytechnic. Vascular fluid dynamics, kinematic/kinetic biomechanics.

B. Mann, Ph.D., Iowa State. Tissue engineering.

*Carlos Mastrangelo, Ph.D., Berekley. Microfabricated systems, bioMEMS.

*E. M. Maynard, Ph.D., Utah. Application of microelectrode arrays restoring vision.

*James P. (Pat) McAllister, Ph.D., Purdue. Pathophysiology of hydrocephalus and brain injury, neural prosthesis, biocompatibility.

*Tyler McCabe, Ph.D., Utah. Research Scientist.

*J. C. McRea, Ph.D., Utah. Medical device development.

*S. G. Meek, Ph.D., Utah. Prosthetic design and control, EMG signal processing, biomechanics.

*Ken Monson, Ph.D., Berkeley, Traumatic brain injury, biomechanics.

Alonso P. Moreno, Ph.D., IPN (Mexico). Molecular and biophysical properties of gap junctions, intercellular heterologous communication.

*C. J. Myers, Ph.D., Stanford. Modeling/analysis of biological networks.

*J. R. Nelson, Ph.D., Utah. Microbiology, immunology.

*F. Noo, Ph.D., Liege (Belgium). 3-D tomographic reconstruction.

R. A. Normann, Ph.D., Berkeley. Cell physiology, bioinstrumentation, neuroprosthetics.

D. B. Olsen, D.V.M., Colorado State. Artificial heart/assist devices, design, control, surgical implantation/physiologic interfaces.

*Agnes E. Ostafin, Ph.D., Minnesota. Nanobiotechnology.

*Huaizhong Pan, Ph.D. Molecular bioengineering.

*D. L. Parker, Ph.D., Utah. Medical imaging, applications of physics in medicine.

*T. J. Petelenz, Ph.D., Utah. Medical instrumentation.

*W. G. Pitt, Ph.D., Wisconsin–Madison. Polymers and composite materials for biomedical applications, surface chemistry.

S. Poelzing, Ph.D., Case Western Reserve. Cardioelectrophysiology.

*Mark Porter, Ph.D., Ohio State. Discovery, rapid screening therapeutic compounds.

*G. D. Prestwich, Ph.D., Stanford. Bioorganic chemistry.

*A. Pungor, Ph.D., Technical University (Hungary). Scanning-force microscopy, near-field optical microscopy, bioinstrumentation.

*B. B. Punske, Ph.D., North Carolina. Cardiovascular biomechanics.

R. D. Rabbitt, Ph.D., Rensselaer. Biomechanics, hearing/vestibular mechanisms, computational mechanics, computational neuroscience.

*Ravi Ranjan, Ph.D., John's Hopkins. Cardiac electrophysiology.

N. Rapoport, Ph.D., Moscow State; D.Sc., Academy of Sciences (USSR). Polymeric materials, biological magnetic resonance.

*R. B. Roemer, Ph.D., Stanford. Heat transfer, thermodynamics, design, optimization to biomedical problems.

F. B. Sachse, Dr.-Ing., Karlsruhe (Germany). Computational cardiac electrophysiology, cardiac electromechanics.

*Charles Saltzman, Ph.D., North Carolina. Orthopaedics.

*C. Shelton, M.D., Texas Southwestern Medical Center at Dallas. Hearing systems physiology.

Y.-T. Shiu, Ph.D., Rice. Cellular/tissue engineering of the cardiovascular system, biofluid dynamics, blood-material interactions.

*M. E. Smith, M.D., Illinois. Otolaryngology, neural interfaces.

*F. Solzbacher, Ph.D., Technical University (Germany). MEMS, micromachining.

*K. W. Spitzer, Ph.D., Buffalo, SUNY. Cardiac cellular electrophysiology, intracellular pH regulation.

R. J. Stewart, Ph.D., California, Santa Barbara. Protein engineering, energy transduction, protein structure-activities, molecular motors.

*Masood Tabib-Azar, Ph.D., Rensselaer. Advanced metrology and nano-device applications.

P. A. Tresco, Ph.D., Brown. Molecular delivery systems, synthetic membrane fabrication, neurodegenerative/neuroendocrine/endocrine disorders.

*P. Triolo, Ph.D., Utah. Development/regulatory approval of biomaterials/ diagnostic devices, tissue-engineered products.

J. A. Weiss, Ph.D., Utah. Biomechanics, mechanics of normal/healing soft tissues, evaluation of injury mechanics/treatment regimens.

D. R. Westenskow, Ph.D., Utah. Bioinstrumentation, microprocessor applications in medicine.

*Ross Whitaker, Ph.D., North Carolina. Image processing, computer vision, visualization.

J. White, Ph.D., Johns Hopkins. Neural engineering and interfaces.

*J. W. Wiskin, Ph.D., Utah. Mathematical modeling/numerical techniques, inverse scattering.

*Carl Thomas Wittwer, Ph.D., Michigan. Real-time PCR and DNA analysis.

*M. Yoshigi, M.D., Kyoto (Japan); Ph.D., Tokyo Women's Medical College. Cardiovascular physiology and embryology.

*Darrin Young, Ph.D., Berkeley. Wireless micro-nano-system.

A. V. Zaitsev, Ph.D., Moscow State (Russia). Cardioelectrophysiology.

*G. L. Zeng, Ph.D., New Mexico. Biomedical imaging.

* *Adjunct faculty*

Section 4
Architectural Engineering

This section contains a directory of institutions offering graduate work in architectural engineering. Additional information about programs listed in the directory but not augmented by an in-depth entry may be obtained by writing directly to the dean of a graduate school or chair of a department at the address given in the directory.

For programs offering related work, see also in this book *Engineering and Applied Sciences* and *Management of Engineering and Technology*. In the other guides in this series:

Graduate Programs in the Humanities, Arts & Social Sciences
See *Applied Arts and Design (Industrial Design and Interior Design), Architecture (Environmental Design), Political Science and International Affairs,* and *Public, Regional, and Industrial Affairs (Urban and Regional Planning and Urban Studies)*

Graduate Programs in the Physical Sciences, Mathematics, Agricultural Sciences, the Environment & Natural Resources
See *Environmental Sciences and Management*

CONTENTS

Program Directory

Architectural Engineering

Carnegie Mellon University, College of Fine Arts, School of Architecture, Pittsburgh, PA 15213-3891. Offers architectural engineering construction management (M Sc); architecture (MSA); architecture, engineering, and construction management (PhD); building performance and diagnostics (M Sc, PhD); computational design (M Sc, PhD); sustainable design (M Sc); urban design (M Sc). Terminal master's awarded for partial completion of doctoral program. *Degree requirements:* For doctorate, thesis/dissertation. *Entrance requirements:* For master's and doctorate, GRE General Test. Additional exam requirements/recommendations for international students: Required—TOEFL.

Drexel University, College of Engineering, Department of Civil, Architectural, and Environmental Engineering, Philadelphia, PA 19104-2875. Offers architectural / building systems engineering (PhD); architectural/building systems engineering (MS); civil engineering (MS, PhD); environmental engineering (MS, PhD); geotechnical, geoenvironmental and geosynthetics engineering (MS, PhD); hydraulics, hydrology and water resources engineering (MS, PhD); structures (MS). Part-time and evening/weekend programs available. *Degree requirements:* For master's, thesis optional; for doctorate, thesis/dissertation. *Entrance requirements:* For master's, minimum GPA of 3.0; for doctorate, minimum GPA of 3.5, MS in civil engineering. Additional exam requirements/recommendations for international students: Required—TOEFL. Electronic applications accepted. *Faculty research:* Structural dynamics, hazardous wastes, water resources, pavement materials, groundwater.

Illinois Institute of Technology, Graduate College, Armour College of Engineering, Department of Civil, Architectural and Environmental Engineering, Chicago, IL 60616-3793. Offers architectural engineering (M Arch E); civil engineering (MS, PhD), including architectural engineeering (MS), construction engineering and management (MS), geoenvironmental engineering (MS), geotechnical engineering (MS), structural engineering (MS), transportation engineering (MS); construction engineering and management (MCEM); environmental engineering (M Env E, PhD); geoenvironmental engineering (M Geoenv E); geotechnical engineering (MGE); public works (MPW); structural engineering (MSE); transportation engineering (M Trans E). Part-time and evening/weekend programs available. Postbaccalaureate distance learning degree programs offered (minimal on-campus study). Terminal master's awarded for partial completion of doctoral program. *Degree requirements:* For master's, thesis (for some programs); for doctorate, comprehensive exam, thesis/dissertation. *Entrance requirements:* For master's, GRE General Test (minimum score 900 Quantitative and Verbal, 2.5 Analytical Writing), minimum undergraduate GPA of 3.0; for doctorate, GRE General Test (minimum score 1000 Quantitative and Verbal, 3.0 Analytical Writing), minimum undergraduate GPA of 3.0. Additional exam requirements/recommendations for international students: Required—TOEFL (minimum score 523 paper-based; 70 iBT); Recommended—IELTS (minimum score 5.5). Electronic applications accepted. *Faculty research:* Structural, architectural, geotechnical and geoenvironmental engineering; construction engineering and management; transportation engineering; environmental engineering and public works.

Kansas State University, Graduate School, College of Engineering, Department of Architectural Engineering and Construction Science, Manhattan, KS 66506. Offers architectural engineering (MS). *Faculty:* 10 full-time (2 women). *Students:* 10 full-time (4 women), 1 part-time (0 women). Average age 23. 20 applicants, 40% accepted, 1 enrolled. In 2011, 10 master's awarded. *Degree requirements:* For master's, thesis or alternative. *Entrance requirements:* For master's, GRE, minimum GPA of 3.25. Additional exam requirements/recommendations for international students: Required—TOEFL. *Application deadline:* For fall admission, 2/1 priority date for domestic students, 2/1 for international students; for spring admission, 8/1 priority date for domestic students, 8/1 for international students. Applications are processed on a rolling basis. Application fee: $40 ($55 for international students). Electronic applications accepted. *Financial support:* Fellowships, research assistantships, teaching assistantships, career-related internships or fieldwork, institutionally sponsored loans, and scholarships/grants available. Support available to part-time students. Financial award application deadline: 3/1; financial award applicants required to submit FAFSA. *Faculty research:* Structural systems design and analysis, building electrical and lighting systems, building HVAC and plumbing systems, sustainable engineering. *Unit head:* David Fritchen, Head, 785-532-5964, Fax: 785-532-3556, E-mail: dfritch@ksu.edu. *Application contact:* Kimberly Kramer, Director, 785-532-5964, Fax: 785-532-3556, E-mail: kramer@ksu.edu. Web site: http://www.k-state.edu/are-cns/.

Lawrence Technological University, College of Engineering, Southfield, MI 48075-1058. Offers architectural engineering (MS); automotive engineering (MS); civil engineering (MA, MS); construction engineering management (MA); electrical and computer engineering (MS); engineering management (MEM); industrial engineering (MS); manufacturing systems (ME, DE); mechanical engineering (MS, DE); mechatronic systems engineering (MS). Part-time and evening/weekend programs available. *Faculty:* 25 full-time (4 women), 20 part-time/adjunct (1 woman). *Students:* 8 full-time (0 women), 332 part-time (52 women); includes 58 minority (21 Black or African American, non-Hispanic/Latino; 1 American Indian or Alaska Native, non-Hispanic/Latino; 32 Asian, non-Hispanic/Latino; 2 Hispanic/Latino; 2 Two or more races, non-Hispanic/Latino), 84 international. Average age 32. 652 applicants, 44% accepted, 70 enrolled. In 2011, 127 master's, 2 doctorates awarded. *Degree requirements:* For master's, thesis (for some programs). *Entrance requirements:* Additional exam requirements/recommendations for international students: Required—TOEFL (minimum score 550 paper-based; 213 computer-based; 79 iBT). *Application deadline:* For fall admission, 7/27 priority date for domestic students, 5/23 for international students; for spring admission, 11/15 priority date for domestic students, 11/15 for international students. Applications are processed on a rolling basis. Application fee: $50. Electronic applications accepted. *Financial support:* In 2011–12, 68 students received support, including 6 research assistantships (averaging $8,078 per year); Federal Work-Study and institutionally sponsored loans also available. Support available to part-time students. Financial award application deadline: 4/1; financial award applicants required to submit FAFSA. *Faculty research:* Advanced composite materials in bridges, strengthening existing bridges with carbon and glass fiber sheets, development of drive shafts using composite materials. *Unit head:* Dr. Nabil Grace, Dean, 248-204-2500, Fax: 248-204-2509, E-mail: engrdean@ltu.edu. *Application contact:* Jane Rohrback, Director of Admissions, 248-204-3160, Fax: 248-204-2228, E-mail: admissions@ltu.edu. Web site: http://www.ltu.edu/engineering/index.asp.

Penn State University Park, Graduate School, College of Engineering, Department of Architectural Engineering, State College, University Park, PA 16802-1503. Offers M Eng, MAE, MS, PhD. *Unit head:* Dr. David N. Wormley, Dean, 814-865-7537, Fax: 814-865-8767, E-mail: dnw2@engr.psu.edu. *Application contact:* Cynthia E. Nicosia, Director, Graduate Enrollment Services, 814-865-1834, E-mail: cey1@psu.edu. Web site: http://www.engr.psu.edu/ae.

University of Colorado Boulder, Graduate School, College of Engineering and Applied Science, Department of Civil, Environmental, and Architectural Engineering, Boulder, CO 80309. Offers building systems (MS, PhD); construction engineering management (MS, PhD); environmental engineering (MS, PhD); geotechnical engineering and geomechanics (MS, PhD); hydrology, water resources and environmental fluid mechanics (MS, PhD); structural engineering and structural mechanics (MS, PhD). *Faculty:* 37 full-time (8 women). *Students:* 245 full-time (90 women), 53 part-time (15 women); includes 37 minority (1 Black or African American, non-Hispanic/Latino; 2 American Indian or Alaska Native, non-Hispanic/Latino; 15 Asian, non-Hispanic/Latino; 17 Hispanic/Latino; 2 Two or more races, non-Hispanic/Latino), 56 international. Average age 27. 483 applicants, 58% accepted, 83 enrolled. In 2011, 84 master's, 15 doctorates awarded. Terminal master's awarded for partial completion of doctoral program. *Degree requirements:* For master's, comprehensive exam, thesis or alternative; for doctorate, thesis/dissertation. *Entrance requirements:* For master's, GRE General Test, minimum undergraduate GPA of 3.0. *Application deadline:* For fall admission, 3/1 for domestic students, 12/1 for international students; for spring admission, 10/31 for domestic students, 10/1 for international students. Application fee: $50 ($60 for international students). Electronic applications accepted. *Financial support:* In 2011–12, 167 students received support, including 69 fellowships (averaging $12,440 per year), 62 research assistantships with full and partial tuition reimbursements available (averaging $21,979 per year), 20 teaching assistantships with full and partial tuition reimbursements available (averaging $19,877 per year); institutionally sponsored loans, scholarships/grants, health care benefits, and unspecified assistantships also available. Financial award application deadline: 1/15; financial award applicants required to submit FAFSA. *Faculty research:* Building systems engineering, construction engineering and management, environmental engineering, geoenvironmental engineering, geotechnical engineering, materials and mechanics, structural engineering, water resources engineering, life-cycle engineering. *Total annual research expenditures:* $10.9 million. *Application contact:* E-mail: cvengrad@colorado.edu. Web site: http://ceae.colorado.edu/new/.

University of Detroit Mercy, School of Architecture, Detroit, MI 48221. Offers M Arch. *Entrance requirements:* For master's, BS in architecture, minimum GPA of 3.0, portfolio.

The University of Kansas, Graduate Studies, School of Engineering, Program in Architectural Engineering, Lawrence, KS 66045. Offers MS. Part-time programs available. *Faculty:* 11 full-time (2 women). *Students:* 5 full-time (1 woman), 6 part-time (2 women); includes 1 minority (Black or African American, non-Hispanic/Latino), 2 international. Average age 27. 17 applicants, 65% accepted, 3 enrolled. In 2011, 1 master's awarded. *Degree requirements:* For master's, thesis or alternative, exam. *Entrance requirements:* For master's, GRE, BS in engineering. Additional exam requirements/recommendations for international students: Required—TOEFL. *Application deadline:* For fall admission, 7/1 priority date for domestic students, 3/1 for international students; for spring admission, 12/1 priority date for domestic students, 8/15 for international students. Applications are processed on a rolling basis. Application fee: $55 ($65 for international students). Electronic applications accepted. Tuition and fees vary according to course load, campus/location, program and reciprocity agreements. *Financial support:* Fellowships with full tuition reimbursements, research assistantships with full tuition reimbursements, teaching assistantships with full tuition reimbursements, and career-related internships or fieldwork available. Financial award application deadline: 2/7. *Faculty research:* Structural engineering, construction engineering, building mechanical systems, energy management. *Unit head:* Craig D. Adams, Chair, 785-864-2700, Fax: 785-864-5631, E-mail: adamscd@ku.edu. *Application contact:* Bruce M. McEnroe, Graduate Advisor, 785-864-2925, Fax: 785-864-2925, E-mail: mcenroe@ku.edu. Web site: http://www.ceae.ku.edu/.

University of Louisiana at Lafayette, College of the Arts, School of Architecture, Lafayette, LA 70504. Offers M Arch. *Degree requirements:* For master's, thesis. *Entrance requirements:* For master's, GRE General Test. Additional exam requirements/recommendations for international students: Required—TOEFL (minimum score 550 paper-based; 213 computer-based). Electronic applications accepted.

University of Massachusetts Amherst, Graduate School, College of Natural Sciences, Department of Environmental Conservation, Amherst, MA 01003. Offers building systems (MS, PhD); environmental policy and human dimensions (MS, PhD); forest resources (MS, PhD); sustainability science (MS); water, wetlands and watersheds (MS, PhD); wildlife and fisheries conservation (MS, PhD). Part-time programs available. *Faculty:* 57 full-time (10 women). *Students:* 61 full-time (26 women), 34 part-time (13 women); includes 4 minority (1 Black or African American, non-Hispanic/Latino; 2 Hispanic/Latino; 1 Two or more races, non-Hispanic/Latino), 12 international. Average age 32. 84 applicants, 40% accepted, 22 enrolled. In 2011, 1 master's, 2 doctorates awarded. Terminal master's awarded for partial completion of doctoral program. *Degree requirements:* For master's, thesis or alternative; for doctorate, comprehensive exam, thesis/dissertation. *Entrance requirements:* For master's and doctorate, GRE General Test. Additional exam requirements/recommendations for international students: Required—TOEFL (minimum score 550 paper-based; 213 computer-based; 80 iBT), IELTS (minimum score 6.5). *Application deadline:* For fall admission, 2/1 for domestic and international students; for spring admission, 10/1 for domestic and international students. Applications are processed on a rolling basis. Application fee: $50 ($65 for international students). Electronic applications accepted. Tuition and fees vary according to course load, campus/location and program. *Financial support:* Fellowships with full and partial tuition reimbursements, research assistantships with full and partial tuition reimbursements, teaching assistantships with full and partial tuition reimbursements, career-related internships or fieldwork, Federal Work-Study, scholarships/grants, traineeships, health care benefits, tuition waivers (full and partial), and unspecified assistantships available. Support available to part-time students. Financial award application deadline: 2/1. *Unit head:* Dr. Kevin McGarigal, Graduate Program Director, 413-545-2257, Fax: 413-545-4358. *Application contact:* Lindsay DeSantis, Interim Supervisor of Admissions, 413-545-0721, Fax: 413-577-0100, E-mail: gradadm@grad.umass.edu. Web site: http://eco.umass.edu/.

University of Miami, Graduate School, College of Engineering, Department of Civil, Architectural, and Environmental Engineering, Coral Gables, FL 33124. Offers architectural engineering (MSAE); civil engineering (MSCE, PhD). Part-time programs available. Terminal master's awarded for partial completion of doctoral program. *Degree requirements:* For master's, thesis (for some programs); for doctorate, comprehensive exam, thesis/dissertation. *Entrance requirements:* For master's, GRE General Test (minimum score 1000 verbal and quantitative), minimum GPA of 3.0; for doctorate, GRE General Test, minimum GPA of 3.5 in preceding degree. Additional exam requirements/recommendations for international students: Required—TOEFL (minimum score 550 paper-based; 213 computer-based). Electronic applications accepted. *Faculty research:* Structural assessment and wind engineering, sustainable construction and materials, moisture transport and management, wastewater and waste engineering, water management and risk analysis.

University of Nebraska–Lincoln, Graduate College, College of Engineering, Program in Architectural Engineering, Lincoln, NE 68588. Offers M Eng, MAE, MS, PhD. *Accreditation:* ABET. *Entrance requirements:* Additional exam requirements/recommendations for international students: Required—TOEFL (minimum score 550 paper-based; 213 computer-based).

The University of Texas at Austin, Graduate School, Cockrell School of Engineering, Department of Civil, Architectural and Environmental Engineering, Program in Architectural Engineering, Austin, TX 78712-1111. Offers MSE. Part-time programs available. *Degree requirements:* For master's, thesis. *Entrance requirements:* For master's, GRE General Test. Additional exam requirements/recommendations for international students: Required—TOEFL. *Application deadline:* For fall admission, 1/15 priority date for domestic students, 1/15 for international students; for spring admission, 9/1 priority date for domestic students, 9/1 for international students. Applications are processed on a rolling basis. Application fee: $50 ($75 for international students). Electronic applications accepted. *Financial support:* Fellowships, research assistantships, teaching assistantships, and career-related internships or fieldwork available. Support available to part-time students. Financial award application deadline: 2/1. *Faculty research:* Materials engineering, structural engineering, construction engineering, project management. *Unit head:* Dr. Sharon L. Wood, Chair, 512-471-4558, Fax: 512-471-1944, E-mail: swood@mail.utexas.edu. *Application contact:* Dr. Howard M. Liljestrand, Graduate Advisor, 512-471-4604, Fax: 512-471-5870, E-mail: liljestrand@mail.utexas.edu. Web site: http://www.caee.utexas.edu/dept/area/arch/.

Section 5
Biomedical Engineering and Biotechnology

This section contains a directory of institutions offering graduate work in bio-medical engineering and biotechnology, followed by an in-depth entry submitted by an institution that chose to prepare a detailed program description. Additional information about programs listed in the directory but not augmented by an in-depth entry may be obtained by writing directly to the dean of a graduate school or chair of a department at the address given in the directory.

For programs offering related work, see also in this book *Aerospace/Aeronautical Engineering, Engineering and Applied Sciences, Engineering Design, Engineering Physics, Management of Engineering and Technology,* and *Mechanical Engineering and Mechanics.* In the other guides in this series:

Graduate Programs in the Biological/Biomedical Sciences & Health-Related Medical Professions
See *Allied Health, Biological and Biomedical Sciences,* and *Physiology*
Graduate Programs in the Physical Sciences, Mathematics, Agricultural Sciences, the Environment & Natural Resources
See *Mathematical Sciences (Biometrics and Biostatistics)*

CONTENTS

Program Directories

Display and Close-Up

Biomedical Engineering

Arizona State University, Ira A. Fulton School of Engineering, School of Biological and Health Systems Engineering, Tempe, AZ 85287-9709. Offers biomedical engineering (MS, PhD). Part-time and evening/weekend programs available. Terminal master's awarded for partial completion of doctoral program. *Degree requirements:* For master's, thesis and oral defense or applied project; interactive Program of Study (iPOS) submitted before completing 50 percent of required credit hours; for doctorate, comprehensive exam, thesis/dissertation, interactive Program of Study (iPOS) submitted before completing 50 percent of required credit hours. *Entrance requirements:* For master's and doctorate, GRE General Test, minimum GPA of 3.0 or equivalent in last 2 years of work leading to bachelor's degree, 3 letters of recommendation, one-page personal statement. Additional exam requirements/recommendations for international students: Required—TOEFL (minimum score 580 paper-based; 92 iBT). Electronic applications accepted. *Expenses:* Contact institution. *Faculty research:* Cardiovascular engineering; synthetic/computational biology; medical devices and diagnostics; neuroengineering; rehabilitation; regenerative medicine; imaging; molecular, cellular and tissue engineering; and virtual reality healthcare delivery systems.

Baylor College of Medicine, Graduate School of Biomedical Sciences, Program in Translational Biology and Molecular Medicine, Houston, TX 77030-3498. Offers PhD. *Faculty:* 192 full-time (56 women). *Students:* 63 full-time (35 women); includes 24 minority (10 Black or African American, non-Hispanic/Latino; 9 Asian, non-Hispanic/Latino; 5 Hispanic/Latino), 17 international. Average age 27. 133 applicants, 17% accepted, 12 enrolled. In 2011, 1 doctorate awarded. *Degree requirements:* For doctorate, thesis/dissertation, public defense. *Entrance requirements:* For doctorate, GRE, minimum GPA of 3.0. Additional exam requirements/recommendations for international students: Required—TOEFL. *Application deadline:* For fall admission, 1/1 for domestic students. Application fee: $0. Electronic applications accepted. *Financial support:* In 2011–12, 63 students received support, including 36 fellowships with full tuition reimbursements available (averaging $29,000 per year), 27 research assistantships with full tuition reimbursements available (averaging $29,000 per year); career-related internships or fieldwork, Federal Work-Study, health care benefits, and scholarships (to all students unless there are grant funds available to pay tuition) also available. Financial award applicants required to submit FAFSA. *Faculty research:* Molecular medicine, translational biology, human disease biology and therapy. *Unit head:* Dr. Mary Estes, Director, 713-798-3585, Fax: 713-798-3586, E-mail: tbmm@bcm.edu. *Application contact:* Wanda Waguespack, Graduate Program Administrator, 713-798-1077, Fax: 713-798-3586, E-mail: wandaw@bcm.edu. Web site: http://www.bcm.edu/tbmm.

Baylor University, Graduate School, School of Engineering and Computer Science, Department of Engineering, Waco, TX 76798. Offers biomedical engineering (MSBE); electrical and computer engineering (MSECE, PhD); engineering (ME); mechanical engineering (MSME). *Faculty:* 14 full-time (1 woman). *Students:* 25 full-time (2 women), 7 part-time (1 woman); includes 6 minority (2 Black or African American, non-Hispanic/Latino; 1 Asian, non-Hispanic/Latino; 1 Hispanic/Latino; 2 Two or more races, non-Hispanic/Latino), 6 international. In 2011, 19 master's awarded. *Unit head:* Dr. Mike Thompson, Graduate Director, 254-710-4188. *Application contact:* Linda Keer, Administrative Assistant, 254-710-4188, Fax: 254-710-3870, E-mail: linda_kerr@baylor.edu. Web site: http://www.ecs.baylor.edu/engineering.

Boston University, College of Engineering, Department of Biomedical Engineering, Boston, MA 02215. Offers M Eng, MS, PhD, MD/PhD. Part-time programs available. *Faculty:* 34 full-time (4 women), 3 part-time/adjunct (1 woman). *Students:* 154 full-time (42 women), 5 part-time (2 women); includes 43 minority (33 Asian, non-Hispanic/Latino; 8 Hispanic/Latino; 2 Two or more races, non-Hispanic/Latino), 36 international. Average age 25. 550 applicants, 24% accepted, 50 enrolled. In 2011, 37 master's, 23 doctorates awarded. Terminal master's awarded for partial completion of doctoral program. *Degree requirements:* For master's, thesis (for some programs); for doctorate, comprehensive exam, thesis/dissertation. *Entrance requirements:* For master's and doctorate, GRE General Test. Additional exam requirements/recommendations for international students: Required—TOEFL (minimum score 550 paper-based; 213 computer-based; 84 iBT), IELTS (minimum score 6.5). *Application deadline:* For fall admission, 1/15 for domestic and international students; for spring admission, 10/1 for domestic and international students. Applications are processed on a rolling basis. Application fee: $70. Electronic applications accepted. *Expenses: Tuition:* Full-time $40,848; part-time $1276 per credit hour. *Required fees:* $572; $286 per semester. *Financial support:* In 2011–12, 158 students received support, including 40 fellowships with full tuition reimbursements available (averaging $28,950 per year), 86 research assistantships with full tuition reimbursements available (averaging $19,300 per year), 18 teaching assistantships with full tuition reimbursements available (averaging $19,300 per year); career-related internships or fieldwork, Federal Work-Study, institutionally sponsored loans, scholarships/grants, traineeships, and health care benefits also available. Financial award application deadline: 1/15; financial award applicants required to submit FAFSA. *Faculty research:* Biomaterials, tissue engineering and drug delivery; modeling of biological systems; molecular bioengineering and biophysics; neuroscience and neural disease; synthetic biology and systems biology. *Total annual research expenditures:* $18.7 million. *Unit head:* Dr. Solomon Eisenberg, Chairman, 617-353-2805, Fax: 617-353-6766, E-mail: sre@bu.edu. *Application contact:* Stephen Doherty, Director of Graduate Programs, 617-353-9760, Fax: 617-353-0259, E-mail: enggrad@bu.edu. Web site: http://www.bu.edu/bme/.

Brown University, Graduate School, Division of Biology and Medicine, Program in Artificial Organs, Biomaterials, and Cell Technology, Providence, RI 02912. Offers MA, Sc M, PhD. Terminal master's awarded for partial completion of doctoral program. *Degree requirements:* For doctorate, thesis/dissertation, preliminary exam. *Entrance requirements:* For master's and doctorate, GRE General Test, GRE Subject Test. Additional exam requirements/recommendations for international students: Required—TOEFL. Electronic applications accepted.

Brown University, Graduate School, Division of Biology and Medicine and Division of Engineering, Program in Biomedical Engineering, Providence, RI 02912. Offers MS, PhD. *Entrance requirements:* For master's and doctorate, GRE General Test, interview. Additional exam requirements/recommendations for international students: Required—TOEFL.

Brown University, Graduate School, Division of Engineering and Division of Biology and Medicine, Center for Biomedical Engineering, Providence, RI 02912. Offers Sc M, PhD. *Degree requirements:* For master's, thesis.

Carleton University, Faculty of Graduate Studies, Faculty of Engineering and Design, Ottawa-Carleton Institute for Biomedical Engineering, Ottawa, ON K1S 5B6, Canada. Offers MA Sc. *Degree requirements:* For master's, thesis optional. *Entrance requirements:* For master's, honours degree. Additional exam requirements/recommendations for international students: Required—TOEFL.

Carnegie Mellon University, Carnegie Institute of Technology, Biomedical and Health Engineering Program, Pittsburgh, PA 15213-3891. Offers bioengineering (MS, PhD); MD/PhD. *Degree requirements:* For master's, thesis; for doctorate, thesis/dissertation, qualifying exam. *Entrance requirements:* For master's and doctorate, GRE General Test. Additional exam requirements/recommendations for international students: Required—TOEFL. Electronic applications accepted. *Faculty research:* Cellular and molecular systematics, signal and image processing, materials and mechanics.

Case Western Reserve University, School of Graduate Studies, Case School of Engineering, Department of Biomedical Engineering, Cleveland, OH 44106. Offers MS, PhD, MD/MS, MD/PhD. *Faculty:* 21 full-time (4 women). *Students:* 117 full-time (42 women), 14 part-time (2 women); includes 34 minority (4 Black or African American, non-Hispanic/Latino; 1 American Indian or Alaska Native, non-Hispanic/Latino; 23 Asian, non-Hispanic/Latino; 6 Hispanic/Latino), 36 international. In 2011, 12 master's, 19 doctorates awarded. Terminal master's awarded for partial completion of doctoral program. *Degree requirements:* For master's, thesis (for some programs); for doctorate, thesis/dissertation, qualifying exam, teaching experience. *Entrance requirements:* For master's and doctorate, GRE General Test. Additional exam requirements/recommendations for international students: Required—TOEFL. *Application deadline:* For fall admission, 4/1 priority date for domestic students; for spring admission, 10/1 priority date for domestic students. Applications are processed on a rolling basis. Application fee: $50. *Financial support:* Fellowships with full tuition reimbursements, research assistantships with full and partial tuition reimbursements, and traineeships available. Financial award application deadline: 2/15; financial award applicants required to submit FAFSA. *Faculty research:* Neuroengineering, biomaterials/tissue engineering, biomedical imaging, biomedical sensors/systems. *Total annual research expenditures:* $12.7 million. *Unit head:* Dr. Robert Kirsch, Interim Department Chair, 216-368-3158, Fax: 216-368-4969, E-mail: robert.kirsch@case.edu. *Application contact:* Carol Adrine, Academic Operations Coordinator, 216-368-4094, Fax: 216-368-4969, E-mail: caa7@case.edu. Web site: http://bme.case.edu.

See Display on next page and Close-Up on page 145.

The Catholic University of America, School of Engineering, Department of Biomedical Engineering, Washington, DC 20064. Offers MBE, PhD. Part-time programs available. *Faculty:* 6 full-time (1 woman), 1 part-time/adjunct (0 women). *Students:* 7 full-time (3 women), 12 part-time (6 women); includes 6 minority (3 Black or African American, non-Hispanic/Latino; 1 Asian, non-Hispanic/Latino; 2 Hispanic/Latino), 6 international. Average age 31. 17 applicants, 59% accepted, 5 enrolled. In 2011, 6 degrees awarded. *Degree requirements:* For master's, thesis or alternative; for doctorate, comprehensive exam, thesis/dissertation, oral exams. *Entrance requirements:* For master's, GRE (minimum score: 1250), minimum GPA of 3.0, statement of purpose, official copies of academic transcripts, three letters of recommendation; for doctorate, GRE (minimum score: 1300), minimum GPA of 3.4, statement of purpose, official copies of academic transcripts, three letters of recommendation. Additional exam requirements/recommendations for international students: Required—TOEFL (minimum score 580 paper-based; 237 computer-based). *Application deadline:* For fall admission, 8/1 priority date for domestic students, 7/15 for international students; for spring admission, 12/1 priority date for domestic students, 10/15 for international students. Applications are processed on a rolling basis. Application fee: $55. Electronic applications accepted. *Expenses:* Contact institution. *Financial support:* Fellowships, research assistantships, teaching assistantships, Federal Work-Study, scholarships/grants, tuition waivers (full and partial), and unspecified assistantships available. Financial award application deadline: 2/1; financial award applicants required to submit FAFSA. *Faculty research:* Cardiopulmonary biomechanics, robotics and human motor control, cell and tissue engineering, biomechanics, rehabilitation engineering. *Total annual research expenditures:* $671,668. *Unit head:* Dr. Binh Q. Tran, Chair, 202-319-5181, Fax: 202-319-4287, E-mail: tran@cua.edu. *Application contact:* Andrew Woodall, Director of Graduate Admissions, 202-319-5057, Fax: 202-319-6533, E-mail: cua-admissions@cua.edu. Web site: http://biomedical.cua.edu/.

City College of the City University of New York, Graduate School, Grove School of Engineering, Department of Biomedical Engineering, New York, NY 10031-9198. Offers ME, PhD. *Entrance requirements:* For master's, GRE. Additional exam requirements/recommendations for international students: Required—TOEFL (minimum score 550 paper-based; 213 computer-based).

Cleveland State University, College of Graduate Studies, Fenn College of Engineering, Department of Chemical and Biomedical Engineering, Program in Applied Biomedical Engineering, Cleveland, OH 44115. Offers D Eng. Part-time and evening/weekend programs available. *Faculty:* 8 full-time (1 woman), 1 part-time/adjunct (0 women). *Students:* 9 full-time (4 women), 11 part-time (4 women); includes 1 minority (Black or African American, non-Hispanic/Latino), 12 international. Average age 27. 21 applicants, 62% accepted, 6 enrolled. In 2011, 6 doctorates awarded. *Degree requirements:* For doctorate, thesis/dissertation. *Entrance requirements:* For doctorate, GRE, minimum undergraduate GPA of 2.75, MS or MD 3.25; 1 degree in engineering. Additional exam requirements/recommendations for international students: Required—TOEFL (minimum score 525 paper-based; 197 computer-based). *Application deadline:* For fall admission, 4/15 for domestic and international students; for spring admission, 11/15 for domestic and international students. Applications are processed on a rolling basis. Application fee: $30. *Expenses:* Tuition, state resident: full-time $6416; part-time $494 per credit hour. Tuition, nonresident: full-time $12,074; part-time $929 per credit hour. *Financial support:* In 2011–12, research assistantships with full and partial tuition reimbursements (averaging $5,696 per year) were awarded; career-related internships or fieldwork, scholarships/grants, and tuition waivers (full) also available. Financial award application deadline: 3/30. *Faculty research:* Biomechanics, drug delivery systems, medical imaging, tissue engineering, artificial heart valves. *Unit head:* Dr. Dhananjai B. Shah, Director, 216-687-3569, Fax: 216-687-9220, E-mail: d.shah@csuohio.edu. *Application contact:* Becky Laird, Administrative Coordinator, 216-687-2571, Fax: 216-687-9220, E-mail: b.laird@csuohio.edu. Web site: http://www.csuohio.edu/chemical_engineering/ABE/.

Colorado State University, Graduate School, School of Biomedical Engineering, Fort Collins, CO 80523-1376. Offers ME, MS, PhD. Part-time and evening/weekend programs available. *Students:* 23 full-time (11 women), 11 part-time (3 women); includes 5 minority (3 Hispanic/Latino; 2 Two or more races, non-Hispanic/Latino). Average age 27. 63 applicants, 29% accepted, 7 enrolled. In 2011, 4 master's, 3 doctorates awarded. *Degree requirements:* For master's, thesis; for doctorate, comprehensive exam, thesis/dissertation. *Entrance requirements:* For master's, GRE General Test, minimum GPA of 3.0, 3 letters of recommendation, resume; for doctorate, GRE General Test, minimum

GPA of 3.0, 3 letters of recommendation, resume, official transcripts, statement of purpose. Additional exam requirements/recommendations for international students: Required—TOEFL (minimum score 550 paper-based; 213 computer-based; 95 iBT). *Application deadline:* For fall admission, 1/15 priority date for domestic students, 1/15 for international students; for spring admission, 9/1 priority date for domestic students, 8/1 for international students. Applications are processed on a rolling basis. Application fee: $50. Electronic applications accepted. *Expenses:* Tuition, state resident: full-time $7992. Tuition, nonresident: full-time $19,592. *Required fees:* $1735; $58 per credit. *Financial support:* In 2011–12, 19 students received support, including 17 research assistantships with full tuition reimbursements available (averaging $14,047 per year), 2 teaching assistantships with full tuition reimbursements available (averaging $32,083 per year); fellowships and unspecified assistantships also available. Financial award application deadline: 2/15; financial award applicants required to submit FAFSA. *Faculty research:* Biomechanics and biomaterials; molecular, cellular and tissues engineering; medical diagnostics, devices and imaging. *Total annual research expenditures:* $2,141. *Unit head:* Dr. Stuart Tobet, Director, 970-491-1672, Fax: 970-491-3827, E-mail: stuart.tobet@colostate.edu. *Application contact:* Sara Neys, Academic Advisor, 970-491-7157, E-mail: sara.neys@colostate.edu. Web site: http://www.engr.colostate.edu/sbme/.

Columbia University, The Fu Foundation School of Engineering and Applied Science, Department of Biomedical Engineering, New York, NY 10027. Offers MS, Eng Sc D, PhD. Part-time programs available. Postbaccalaureate distance learning degree programs offered (no on-campus study). *Faculty:* 21 full-time (5 women), 4 part-time/adjunct (0 women). *Students:* 102 full-time (39 women), 20 part-time (11 women); includes 28 minority (22 Asian, non-Hispanic/Latino; 1 Hispanic/Latino; 5 Two or more races, non-Hispanic/Latino), 42 international. Average age 27. 349 applicants, 20% accepted, 31 enrolled. In 2011, 31 master's, 9 doctorates awarded. *Degree requirements:* For doctorate, thesis/dissertation, qualifying exam. *Entrance requirements:* For master's and doctorate, GRE General Test. Additional exam requirements/recommendations for international students: Required—TOEFL, IELTS. *Application deadline:* For fall admission, 12/1 priority date for domestic students, 12/1 for international students; for spring admission, 10/1 priority date for domestic students, 10/1 for international students. Application fee: $95. Electronic applications accepted. *Financial support:* In 2011–12, 75 students received support, including 17 fellowships with full tuition reimbursements available (averaging $34,166 per year), 47 research assistantships with full tuition reimbursements available (averaging $31,333 per year), 11 teaching assistantships with full tuition reimbursements available (averaging $31,333 per year); traineeships and health care benefits also available. Financial award application deadline: 12/1; financial award applicants required to submit FAFSA. *Faculty research:* Biomechanics, biosignal and biomedical imaging, cellular and tissue engineering. *Unit head:* Dr. Andreas H. Hielscher, Professor of Biomedical Engineering and Radiology/Interim Chairman, 212-854-5080, E-mail: ahh2004@columbia.edu. *Application contact:* Jarmaine Lomax, Administrative Assistant for Student Affairs, 212-854-4418, Fax: 212-854-8725, E-mail: jl432@columbia.edu. Web site: http://www.bme.columbia.edu.

Cornell University, Graduate School, Graduate Fields of Engineering, Field of Biomedical Engineering, Ithaca, NY 14853-0001. Offers M Eng, MS, PhD. *Faculty:* 53 full-time (12 women). *Students:* 182 full-time (75 women); includes 64 minority (15 Black or African American, non-Hispanic/Latino; 40 Asian, non-Hispanic/Latino; 9 Hispanic/Latino), 45 international. Average age 24. 425 applicants, 50% accepted, 111 enrolled. In 2011, 77 master's, 12 doctorates awarded. *Degree requirements:* For master's, thesis; for doctorate, comprehensive exam, thesis/dissertation. *Entrance requirements:* For master's and doctorate, GRE General Test, GRE Subject Test (engineering), 3 letters of recommendation. Additional exam requirements/recommendations for international students: Required—TOEFL (minimum score 77 iBT). *Application deadline:* For fall admission, 1/15 priority date for domestic students. Application fee: $70. Electronic applications accepted. *Financial support:* In 2011–12, 57 students received support, including 29 fellowships with full tuition reimbursements available, 39 research assistantships with full tuition reimbursements available, 9 teaching assistantships; institutionally sponsored loans, scholarships/grants, health care benefits, tuition waivers (full and partial), and unspecified assistantships also available. *Faculty research:* Biomaterials; biomedical instrumentation and diagnostics; biomedical mechanics; drug delivery, design, and metabolism. *Unit head:* Director of Graduate Studies, 607-255-1003, Fax: 607-255-1136. *Application contact:* Graduate Field Assistant, 607-255-2573, Fax: 607-255-1136, E-mail: biomedgrad@cornell.edu. Web site: http://www.gradschool.cornell.edu/fields.php?id-38&a-2.

Dalhousie University, Faculty of Engineering and Faculty of Medicine, Department of Biomedical Engineering, Halifax, NS B3H3J5, Canada. Offers MA Sc, PhD. *Entrance requirements:* Additional exam requirements/recommendations for international students: Required—TOEFL, IELTS, CANTEST, CAEL, or Michigan English Language Assessment Battery. Electronic applications accepted.

Dartmouth College, Thayer School of Engineering, Program in Biomedical Engineering, Hanover, NH 03755. Offers MS, PhD. *Faculty research:* Imaging, physiological modeling, cancer hyperthermia and radiation therapy, bioelectromagnetics, biomedical optics and lasers. *Total annual research expenditures:* $6.3 million. *Unit head:* Dr. Joseph J. Helbie, Dean, 603-646-2238, Fax: 603-646-2580, E-mail: joseph.j.helbie@dartmouth.edu. *Application contact:* Candace S. Potter, Graduate Admissions Administrator, 603-646-3844, Fax: 603-646-1620, E-mail: candace.potter@dartmouth.edu.

Drexel University, School of Biomedical Engineering, Science and Health Systems, Program in Biomedical Engineering, Philadelphia, PA 19104-2875. Offers MS, PhD. *Degree requirements:* For master's, thesis (for some programs); for doctorate, thesis/dissertation. Electronic applications accepted.

Duke University, Graduate School, Pratt School of Engineering, Department of Biomedical Engineering, Durham, NC 27708. Offers MS, PhD. *Degree requirements:* For doctorate, thesis/dissertation. *Entrance requirements:* For master's and doctorate, GRE General Test. Additional exam requirements/recommendations for international students: Required—TOEFL (minimum score 550 paper-based; 213 computer-based; 83 iBT), IELTS (minimum score 7). *Expenses: Tuition:* Full-time $40,720. *Required fees:* $3107.

Duke University, Graduate School, Pratt School of Engineering, Master of Engineering Program, Durham, NC 27708-0271. Offers biomedical engineering (M Eng); civil engineering (M Eng); electrical and computer engineering (M Eng); environmental engineering (M Eng); materials science and engineering (M Eng); mechanical engineering (M Eng); photonics and optical sciences (M Eng). Part-time programs available. *Entrance requirements:* For master's, GRE General Test, resume, 3 letters of recommendation, statement of purpose. Additional exam requirements/recommendations for international students: Required—TOEFL. *Expenses: Tuition:* Full-time $40,720. *Required fees:* $3107.

Biomedical Engineering

École Polytechnique de Montréal, Graduate Programs, Institute of Biomedical Engineering, Montréal, QC H3C 3A7, Canada. Offers M Sc A, PhD, DESS. M Sc A and PhD programs offered jointly with Université de Montréal. Part-time programs available. *Degree requirements:* For master's, one foreign language, thesis; for doctorate, one foreign language, thesis/dissertation. *Entrance requirements:* For master's, minimum GPA of 2.75; for doctorate, minimum GPA of 3.0. *Faculty research:* Cardiac electrophysiology, biomedical instrumentation, biomechanics, biomaterials, medical imagery.

Florida Agricultural and Mechanical University, Division of Graduate Studies, Research, and Continuing Education, FAMU-FSU College of Engineering, Department of Biomedical Engineering, Tallahassee, FL 32307-3200. Offers MS, PhD. *Degree requirements:* For master's, thesis optional; for doctorate, thesis/dissertation, paper presentation at professional meeting. *Entrance requirements:* For master's, GRE General Test, minimum GPA of 3.3, letters of recommendation (3); for doctorate, minimum GPA of 3.3. Additional exam requirements/recommendations for international students: Required—TOEFL (minimum score 550 paper-based; 213 computer-based). *Faculty research:* Cellular signaling, cancer therapy, drug delivery, cellular and tissue engineering, brain physiology.

Florida Institute of Technology, Graduate Programs, College of Engineering, Biomedical Engineering Department, Melbourne, FL 32901-6975. Offers MS, PhD. *Expenses: Tuition:* Full-time $19,620; part-time $1090 per credit hour. Tuition and fees vary according to campus/location. *Unit head:* Dr. Kunal Mitra, Chair, 321-674-8068, Fax: 321-674-7565. *Application contact:* Cheryl A. Brown, Associate Director of Graduate Admissions, 321-674-7581, Fax: 321-723-9468, E-mail: cbrown@fit.edu. Web site: http://coe.fit.edu/biomedical-engineering/.

Florida International University, College of Engineering and Computing, Department of Biomedical Engineering, Miami, FL 33175. Offers MS, PhD. Part-time and evening/weekend programs available. *Degree requirements:* For master's, thesis; for doctorate, comprehensive exam, thesis/dissertation. *Entrance requirements:* For master's, GRE General Test (minimum combined score 1000, verbal 350, quantitative 650), minimum GPA of 3.0; for doctorate, GRE General Test (minimum combined score 1150, verbal 450, quantitative 700), minimum GPA of 3.0, letter of intent, letters of recommendation. Additional exam requirements/recommendations for international students: Required—TOEFL (minimum score 550 paper-based; 80 iBT). Electronic applications accepted. *Faculty research:* Bio-imaging and bio-signal processing, bio-instrumentation, devices and sensors, biomaterials and bio-nano technology, cellular and tissue engineering.

Florida State University, The Graduate School, FAMU-FSU College of Engineering, Department of Chemical and Biomedical Engineering, Tallahassee, FL 32310-6046. Offers biomedical engineering (MS, PhD); chemical engineering (MS, PhD). Part-time programs available. *Faculty:* 13 full-time (2 women). *Students:* 34 full-time (14 women); includes 22 minority (4 Black or African American, non-Hispanic/Latino; 16 Asian, non-Hispanic/Latino; 2 Hispanic/Latino), 19 international. Average age 25. 91 applicants, 10% accepted, 9 enrolled. In 2011, 7 master's, 3 doctorates awarded. Terminal master's awarded for partial completion of doctoral program. *Degree requirements:* For master's, thesis (for some programs); for doctorate, comprehensive exam, thesis/dissertation, qualifying exam. *Entrance requirements:* For master's, GRE General Test (minimum score 1200), BS in chemical engineering or other physical science/engineering, minimum GPA of 3.0; for doctorate, GRE General Test (minimum score: 1200), BS in chemical engineering or other physical science/engineering, minimum GPA of 3.0, or MS in chemical or biomedical engineering. Additional exam requirements/recommendations for international students: Required—TOEFL (minimum score 550 paper-based; 80 iBT), Michigan English Language Assessment Battery (minimum score 77); Recommended—IELTS (minimum score 6.5). *Application deadline:* For fall admission, 3/1 priority date for domestic students, 3/1 for international students; for spring admission, 11/1 for domestic and international students. Applications are processed on a rolling basis. Application fee: $30. *Expenses:* Contact institution. *Financial support:* In 2011–12, 31 students received support, including 6 fellowships with full tuition reimbursements available (averaging $20,880 per year), 17 research assistantships with full tuition reimbursements available (averaging $20,880 per year), 8 teaching assistantships with full tuition reimbursements available (averaging $20,880 per year). Financial award application deadline: 3/1. *Faculty research:* Macromolecular transport and reaction; polymer characterization and processing; biomass conversion; solid NMR-MRI for solid state spectroscopy and cell microscopy; protein, cell, and tissue engineering. *Total annual research expenditures:* $1.2 million. *Unit head:* Dr. Bruce R. Locke, Chair and Professor, 850-410-6149, Fax: 850-410-6150, E-mail: locke@eng.fsu.edu. *Application contact:* Lisa Fowler, Office Administrator, 850-410-6151, Fax: 850-410-6150, E-mail: lfowler@fsu.edu. Web site: http://www.eng.fsu.edu/cbe.

Georgia Institute of Technology, Graduate Studies and Research, College of Engineering, The Wallace H. Coulter Department of Biomedical Engineering at Georgia Tech and Emory University, Atlanta, GA 30332-0001. Offers bioengineering (PhD); bioinformatics (PhD); biomedical engineering (PhD); MD/PhD. PhD in biomedical engineering program jointly offered with Emory University (Georgia) and Peking University (China). Terminal master's awarded for partial completion of doctoral program. *Degree requirements:* For doctorate, thesis/dissertation. *Entrance requirements:* Additional exam requirements/recommendations for international students: Required—TOEFL. *Faculty research:* Biomechanics and tissue engineering, bioinstrumentation and medical imaging.

Graduate School and University Center of the City University of New York, Graduate Studies, Program in Engineering, New York, NY 10016-4039. Offers biomedical engineering (PhD); chemical engineering (PhD); civil engineering (PhD); electrical engineering (PhD); mechanical engineering (PhD). *Degree requirements:* For doctorate, thesis/dissertation. *Entrance requirements:* For doctorate, GRE General Test. Additional exam requirements/recommendations for international students: Required—TOEFL. Electronic applications accepted.

Harvard University, Graduate School of Arts and Sciences, Department of Physics, Cambridge, MA 02138. Offers experimental physics (PhD); medical engineering/medical physics (PhD), including applied physics, engineering sciences, physics; theoretical physics (PhD). *Degree requirements:* For doctorate, thesis/dissertation, final exams, laboratory experience. *Entrance requirements:* For doctorate, GRE General Test, GRE Subject Test. Additional exam requirements/recommendations for international students: Required—TOEFL. *Expenses: Tuition:* Full-time $36,304. *Required fees:* $1186. Full-time tuition and fees vary according to program. *Faculty research:* Particle physics, condensed matter physics, atomic physics.

Harvard University, Harvard Medical School and Graduate School of Arts and Sciences, Division of Health Sciences and Technology and Department of Physics and School of Engineering and Applied Sciences, Program in Medical Engineering/Medical Physics, Cambridge, MA 02138. Offers medical engineering (PhD); medical engineering/medical physics (Sc D); medical physics (PhD). Programs offered jointly with Massachusetts Institute of Technology. *Students:* 112 full-time (38 women); includes 33 minority (2 Black or African American, non-Hispanic/Latino; 22 Asian, non-Hispanic/Latino; 6 Hispanic/Latino; 3 Two or more races, non-Hispanic/Latino), 38 international. Average age 26. 222 applicants, 13% accepted, 18 enrolled. In 2011, 14 doctorates awarded. *Degree requirements:* For doctorate, comprehensive exam, thesis/dissertation, oral and written qualifying exams. *Entrance requirements:* For doctorate, GRE, bachelor's degree in engineering or science. Additional exam requirements/recommendations for international students: Required—TOEFL; Recommended—IELTS. *Application deadline:* For fall admission, 12/15 for domestic and international students. Application fee: $75. Electronic applications accepted. *Expenses:* Contact institution. *Financial support:* In 2011–12, 94 students received support, including 70 fellowships with full and partial tuition reimbursements available (averaging $55,371 per year), 45 research assistantships with full and partial tuition reimbursements available (averaging $43,229 per year), 9 teaching assistantships with full and partial tuition reimbursements available (averaging $5,603 per year); career-related internships or fieldwork, institutionally sponsored loans, traineeships, health care benefits, and unspecified assistantships also available. Financial award application deadline: 12/15; financial award applicants required to submit FAFSA. *Faculty research:* Regenerative biomedical technologies, biomedical imaging and optics, biophysics, systems physiology, bioinstrumentation, biomedical informatics/integrative genomics. *Unit head:* Director, 617-253 Ext. 4418. *Application contact:* Laurie Ward, Administrator, 617-253-3609, Fax: 617-253-6692, E-mail: laurie@mit.edu.

Illinois Institute of Technology, Graduate College, Armour College of Engineering, Department of Biomedical Engineering, Chicago, IL 60616-3793. Offers PhD. Part-time programs available. *Degree requirements:* For doctorate, comprehensive exam, thesis/dissertation. *Entrance requirements:* For doctorate, GRE General Test (minimum score of 1200 Quantitative plus Verbal and 3.0 Analytical Writing), minimum cumulative undergraduate GPA of 3.2. Additional exam requirements/recommendations for international students: Required—TOEFL (minimum score 523 paper-based; 70 iBT); Recommended—IELTS (minimum score 5.5). Electronic applications accepted. *Faculty research:* Medical imaging, cell and tissue engineering, neural engineering, diabetes research, bioinformatics.

Indiana University–Purdue University Indianapolis, School of Engineering and Technology, Department of Electrical Engineering, Indianapolis, IN 46202-2896. Offers biomedical engineering (MS, PhD); electrical and computer engineering (MS, MSECE, PhD), including biomedical engineering (MSECE), control and automation (MSECE), signal processing (MSECE); engineering (interdisciplinary) (MSE). *Students:* 49 full-time (15 women), 48 part-time (5 women); includes 8 minority (2 Black or African American, non-Hispanic/Latino; 2 Asian, non-Hispanic/Latino; 2 Hispanic/Latino; 2 Two or more races, non-Hispanic/Latino), 56 international. Average age 27. 150 applicants, 49% accepted, 45 enrolled. In 2011, 29 degrees awarded. Application fee: $55 ($65 for international students). *Unit head:* Yaobin Chen, Unit Head, 317-274-4032, Fax: 317-274-4493. *Application contact:* Valerie Diemer, Graduate Program, 317-278-4960, Fax: 317-278-1671, E-mail: grad@engr.iupui.edu.

Indiana University–Purdue University Indianapolis, School of Engineering and Technology, Department of Mechanical Engineering, Indianapolis, IN 46202-2896. Offers biomedical engineering (MS Bm E); computer-aided mechanical engineering (Certificate); mechanical engineering (MSME, PhD). Part-time programs available. *Students:* 25 full-time (2 women), 49 part-time (7 women); includes 5 minority (1 Black or African American, non-Hispanic/Latino; 2 Asian, non-Hispanic/Latino; 2 Hispanic/Latino), 32 international. Average age 28. 84 applicants, 55% accepted, 25 enrolled. In 2011, 19 master's, 1 other advanced degree awarded. *Degree requirements:* For master's, thesis optional. *Entrance requirements:* For master's, GRE. Additional exam requirements/recommendations for international students: Required—TOEFL. *Application deadline:* For fall admission, 7/1 for domestic students. Application fee: $55 ($65 for international students). *Financial support:* Fellowships with tuition reimbursements, research assistantships with full and partial tuition reimbursements, and tuition waivers (full and partial) available. Financial award application deadline: 3/1. *Faculty research:* Computational fluid dynamics, heat transfer, finite-element methods, composites, biomechanics. *Unit head:* Dr. Hasan Akay, Chairman, 317-274-9717, Fax: 317-274-9744. *Application contact:* Valerie Diemer, Graduate Program, 317-278-4960, Fax: 317-278-1671, E-mail: grad@engr.iupui.edu. Web site: http://www.engr.iupui.edu/me/.

The Johns Hopkins University, Engineering Program for Professionals, Part-time Program in Applied Biomedical Engineering, Baltimore, MD 21218-2699. Offers MS, Post-Master's Certificate. Part-time and evening/weekend programs available. Electronic applications accepted.

The Johns Hopkins University, Whiting School of Engineering and School of Medicine, Department of Biomedical Engineering, Baltimore, MD 21205. Offers bioengineering innovation and design (MSE); biomedical engineering (MSE, PhD). Terminal master's awarded for partial completion of doctoral program. *Degree requirements:* For master's, thesis; for doctorate, comprehensive exam, thesis/dissertation, oral exam. *Entrance requirements:* For master's and doctorate, GRE General Test. Additional exam requirements/recommendations for international students: Required—TOEFL or IELTS. Electronic applications accepted. *Faculty research:* Cell and tissue engineering, systems neuroscience, imaging, cardiovascular systems physiology, theoretical and computational biology.

Louisiana Tech University, Graduate School, College of Engineering and Science, Department of Biomedical Engineering, Ruston, LA 71272. Offers MS, PhD. Part-time programs available. Terminal master's awarded for partial completion of doctoral program. *Degree requirements:* For master's, thesis; for doctorate, thesis/dissertation. *Entrance requirements:* For master's, GRE General Test, minimum GPA of 3.0 in last 60 hours; for doctorate, minimum graduate GPA of 3.25 (MS) or GRE General Test. Additional exam requirements/recommendations for international students: Required—TOEFL. *Faculty research:* Microbiosensors and microcirculatory transport, speech recognition, artificial intelligence, rehabilitation engineering, bioelectromagnetics.

Marquette University, Graduate School, College of Engineering, Department of Biomedical Engineering, Milwaukee, WI 53201-1881. Offers biocomputing (ME); bioimaging (ME); bioinstrumentation (ME); bioinstrumentation/computers (MS, PhD); biomechanics (ME); biomechanics/biomaterials (MS, PhD); biorehabilitation (ME); functional imaging (PhD); healthcare technologies management (MS); rehabilitation bioengineering (PhD); systems physiology (MS, PhD). Part-time and evening/weekend programs available. *Faculty:* 15 full-time (5 women), 5 part-time/adjunct (2 women). *Students:* 39 full-time (13 women), 24 part-time (7 women); includes 8 minority (5 Asian, non-Hispanic/Latino; 1 Hispanic/Latino; 1 Native Hawaiian or other Pacific Islander, non-

Hispanic/Latino; 1 Two or more races, non-Hispanic/Latino), 13 international. Average age 28. 86 applicants, 35% accepted, 14 enrolled. In 2011, 19 master's, 5 doctorates awarded. Terminal master's awarded for partial completion of doctoral program. *Degree requirements:* For master's, comprehensive exam, thesis; for doctorate, comprehensive exam, thesis/dissertation, dissertation defense, qualifying exam. *Entrance requirements:* For master's, GRE General Test, minimum GPA of 3.0, official transcripts from all current and previous colleges/universities except Marquette, three letters of recommendation, brief statement of purpose that includes proposed area of research specialization, interview with program director (for ME), one year of post-baccalaureate professional work experience; for doctorate, GRE General Test, minimum GPA of 3.0, official transcripts from all current and previous colleges/universities except Marquette, three letters of recommendation, brief statement of purpose that includes proposed area of research specialization. Additional exam requirements/recommendations for international students: Required—TOEFL (minimum score 530 paper-based; 78 computer-based). *Application deadline:* For fall admission, 2/15 priority date for domestic students; for spring admission, 11/15 priority date for domestic students. Applications are processed on a rolling basis. Application fee: $50. Electronic applications accepted. *Expenses: Tuition:* Full-time $17,010; part-time $945 per credit hour. Tuition and fees vary according to program. *Financial support:* In 2011–12, 8 students received support, including 2 research assistantships with full tuition reimbursements available (averaging $20,134 per year), 6 teaching assistantships with full tuition reimbursements available; fellowships, scholarships/grants, health care benefits, tuition waivers (partial), and unspecified assistantships also available. Support available to part-time students. Financial award application deadline: 2/15. *Faculty research:* Cell and organ physiology, signal processing, gait analysis, orthopedic rehabilitation engineering, telemedicine. *Total annual research expenditures:* $2 million. *Unit head:* Dr. Kristina Ropella, Chair, 414-288-3375, Fax: 414-288-7938, E-mail: kristina.ropella@marquette.edu. *Application contact:* Craig Pierce, Assistant Dean of the Graduate School, 414-288-5740, Fax: 414-288-1902, E-mail: craig.pierce@marquette.edu. Web site: http://www.marquette.edu/engineering/biomedical/.

Massachusetts Institute of Technology, Harvard-MIT Division of Health Sciences and Technology, Medical Engineering/Medical Physics Program, Cambridge, MA 02139-4307. Offers medical engineering (PhD); medical engineering and medical physics (Sc D); medical physics (PhD). PhD and Sc D offered jointly with Harvard University. *Students:* 112 full-time (38 women); includes 33 minority (2 Black or African American, non-Hispanic/Latino; 22 Asian, non-Hispanic/Latino; 6 Hispanic/Latino; 3 Two or more races, non-Hispanic/Latino), 38 international. Average age 26. 222 applicants, 13% accepted, 18 enrolled. In 2011, 14 doctorates awarded. *Degree requirements:* For doctorate, comprehensive exam, thesis/dissertation, oral and written departmental qualifying exams. *Entrance requirements:* For doctorate, GRE, bachelor's degree in engineering or science. Additional exam requirements/recommendations for international students: Required—TOEFL; Recommended—IELTS. *Application deadline:* For fall admission, 12/15 for domestic and international students. Application fee: $75. Electronic applications accepted. *Expenses: Tuition:* Full-time $40,460; part-time $630 per credit hour. *Required fees:* $272. *Financial support:* In 2011–12, 94 students received support, including 70 fellowships with full and partial tuition reimbursements available (averaging $55,371 per year), 45 research assistantships with full and partial tuition reimbursements available (averaging $43,229 per year), 9 teaching assistantships with full and partial tuition reimbursements available (averaging $5,603 per year); career-related internships or fieldwork, institutionally sponsored loans, traineeships, health care benefits, and unspecified assistantships also available. Financial award application deadline: 12/15; financial award applicants required to submit FAFSA. *Faculty research:* Regenerative biomedical technologies, biomedical imaging and optics, biophysics, systems physiology, bioinstrumentation, biomedical informatics/integrative genomics. *Unit head:* Director. *Application contact:* Laurie Ward, Graduate Administrator, 617-253-3609, Fax: 617-253-6692, E-mail: laurie@mit.edu. Web site: http://hst.mit.edu/.

Massachusetts Institute of Technology, School of Engineering, Department of Biological Engineering, Cambridge, MA 02139. Offers applied biosciences (PhD, Sc D); bioengineering (PhD, Sc D); biological engineering (PhD, Sc D); biomedical engineering (M Eng); toxicology (SM); SM/MBA. *Faculty:* 33 full-time (7 women). *Students:* 124 full-time (55 women); includes 36 minority (3 Black or African American, non-Hispanic/Latino; 22 Asian, non-Hispanic/Latino; 7 Hispanic/Latino; 4 Two or more races, non-Hispanic/Latino), 38 international. Average age 26. 483 applicants, 10% accepted, 30 enrolled. In 2011, 3 master's, 13 doctorates awarded. Terminal master's awarded for partial completion of doctoral program. *Degree requirements:* For master's, thesis; for doctorate, comprehensive exam, thesis/dissertation. *Entrance requirements:* For master's and doctorate, GRE General Test. Additional exam requirements/recommendations for international students: Required—IELTS (minimum score 7). *Application deadline:* For fall admission, 12/15 for domestic and international students. Application fee: $75. Electronic applications accepted. *Expenses: Tuition:* Full-time $40,460; part-time $630 per credit hour. *Required fees:* $272. *Financial support:* In 2011–12, 113 students received support, including 67 fellowships (averaging $36,300 per year), 53 research assistantships (averaging $34,000 per year), 1 teaching assistantship (averaging $33,100 per year); Federal Work-Study, institutionally sponsored loans, scholarships/grants, traineeships, health care benefits, and unspecified assistantships also available. *Faculty research:* Bioinformatics, computational, systems, and synthetic biology; biological materials, imaging, and transport phenomena; biomolecular and cell engineering; cancer initiation, progression, and therapeutics; genomics, proteomics, and glycomics; nanoscale engineering of biological systems; neurobiological systems; systems biology; macromolecular biochemistry and biophysics. *Total annual research expenditures:* $36.7 million. *Unit head:* Prof. Douglas A. Lauffenburger, Head, 617-253-1712, E-mail: be-acad@mit.edu. Web site: http://web.mit.edu/be/.

Mayo Graduate School, Graduate Programs in Biomedical Sciences, Program in Biomedical Engineering, Rochester, MN 55905. Offers PhD. *Degree requirements:* For doctorate, oral defense of dissertation, qualifying oral and written exam. *Entrance requirements:* For doctorate, GRE, 1 year of chemistry, biology, calculus, and physics. Additional exam requirements/recommendations for international students: Required—TOEFL. Electronic applications accepted.

McGill University, Faculty of Graduate and Postdoctoral Studies, Faculty of Medicine, Department of Biomedical Engineering, Montréal, QC H3A 2T5, Canada. Offers M Eng, PhD.

Mercer University, Graduate Studies, Macon Campus, School of Engineering, Macon, GA 31207-0003. Offers biomedical engineering (MSE); computer engineering (MSE); electrical engineering (MSE); engineering management (MSE); environmental engineering (MSE); environmental systems (MS); mechanical engineering (MSE); software engineering (MSE); software systems (MS); technical communications management (MS); technical management (MS). Part-time and evening/weekend programs available. Postbaccalaureate distance learning degree programs offered (no on-campus study). *Faculty:* 17 full-time (3 women), 1 part-time/adjunct (0 women). *Students:* 12 full-time (3 women), 113 part-time (28 women); includes 23 minority (13 Black or African American, non-Hispanic/Latino; 9 Asian, non-Hispanic/Latino; 1 Hispanic/Latino). Average age 31. In 2011, 44 master's awarded. *Degree requirements:* For master's, thesis or alternative. *Entrance requirements:* For master's, minimum undergraduate GPA of 3.0. Additional exam requirements/recommendations for international students: Required—TOEFL. *Application deadline:* For fall admission, 7/1 for domestic students; for spring admission, 11/15 for domestic students. Applications are processed on a rolling basis. Application fee: $35 ($50 for international students). Electronic applications accepted. *Expenses:* Contact institution. *Financial support:* Federal Work-Study available. *Unit head:* Dr. Wade H. Shaw, Dean, 478-301-2459, Fax: 478-301-5593, E-mail: shaw_wh@mercer.edu. *Application contact:* Greg Lofton, Graduate Program Coordinator, 478-301-5480, Fax: 478-301-5434, E-mail: lofton_g@mercer.edu. Web site: http://engineering.mercer.edu/.

Michigan Technological University, Graduate School, College of Engineering, Department of Biomedical Engineering, Houghton, MI 49931. Offers PhD. Part-time programs available. *Faculty:* 12 full-time (2 women), 2 part-time/adjunct (0 women). *Students:* 10 full-time (4 women), 3 international. Average age 26. 49 applicants, 6% accepted, 1 enrolled. In 2011, 4 doctorates awarded. *Degree requirements:* For doctorate, comprehensive exam, thesis/dissertation. *Entrance requirements:* For doctorate, GRE, statement of purpose, official transcripts, 3 letters of recommendation. Additional exam requirements/recommendations for international students: Required—TOEFL (minimum score 100 iBT) or IELTS. *Application deadline:* Applications are processed on a rolling basis. Electronic applications accepted. *Expenses:* Contact institution. *Financial support:* In 2011–12, 10 students received support, including 1 fellowship with full tuition reimbursement available (averaging $6,065 per year), 7 research assistantships with full tuition reimbursements available (averaging $6,065 per year), 1 teaching assistantship with full tuition reimbursement available (averaging $6,065 per year); career-related internships or fieldwork, Federal Work-Study, scholarships/grants, health care benefits, tuition waivers (partial), unspecified assistantships, and cooperative program also available. Financial award applicants required to submit FAFSA. *Faculty research:* Biomaterials/tissue engineering, physiology measurement, biomechanics, mechanotransduction, bone metabolism. *Total annual research expenditures:* $1.2 million. *Unit head:* Dr. Sean J. Kirkpatrick, Chair, 906-487-2772, Fax: 906-487-1717, E-mail: sjkirkpa@mtu.edu. *Application contact:* Judy L. Schaefer, Senior Staff Assistant, 906-487-2772, Fax: 906-487-1717, E-mail: jlschaef@mtu.edu. Web site: http://www.mtu.edu/biomedical/.

Mississippi State University, College of Agriculture and Life Sciences, Department of Agricultural and Biological Engineering, Mississippi State, MS 39762. Offers agricultural sciences (PhD), including engineering technology (MS, PhD); agriculture (MS), including engineering technology (MS, PhD); biological engineering (MS); biomedical engineering (MS, PhD). PhD in agricultural sciences and MS in agriculture are interdisciplinary. *Faculty:* 12 full-time (1 woman). *Students:* 41 full-time (16 women), 5 part-time (2 women); includes 10 minority (6 Black or African American, non-Hispanic/Latino; 2 Asian, non-Hispanic/Latino; 1 Native Hawaiian or other Pacific Islander, non-Hispanic/Latino; 1 Two or more races, non-Hispanic/Latino), 12 international. Average age 28. 43 applicants, 30% accepted, 11 enrolled. In 2011, 8 master's awarded. *Degree requirements:* For master's, thesis; for doctorate, thesis/dissertation, preliminary exam. *Entrance requirements:* For master's, GRE General Test, minimum undergraduate GPA of 2.75 (3.0 for biomedical engineering); for doctorate, GRE General Test, minimum GPA of 3.0 (biomedical engineering). Additional exam requirements/recommendations for international students: Required—TOEFL (minimum score 550 paper-based; 213 computer-based; 79 iBT); Recommended—IELTS (minimum score 6.5). *Application deadline:* For fall admission, 7/1 for domestic students, 5/1 for international students; for spring admission, 11/1 for domestic students, 9/1 for international students. Applications are processed on a rolling basis. Application fee: $40. Electronic applications accepted. *Expenses:* Tuition, state resident: full-time $5805; part-time $322.50 per credit hour. Tuition, nonresident: full-time $14,670; part-time $815 per credit hour. *Financial support:* In 2011–12, 32 research assistantships with partial tuition reimbursements (averaging $15,291 per year) were awarded; Federal Work-Study, institutionally sponsored loans, and unspecified assistantships also available. Financial award application deadline: 4/1; financial award applicants required to submit FAFSA. *Faculty research:* Bioenvironmental engineering, bioinstrumentation, biomechanics/biomaterials, precision agriculture, tissue engineering, ergonomics human factors, biosimulation and modeling. *Total annual research expenditures:* $496,000. *Unit head:* Dr. Jonathan Pote, Interim Department Head and Professor, 662-325-3280, Fax: 662-325-3853, E-mail: jpote@mafes.msstate.edu. *Application contact:* Dr. Steven Elder, Professor and Graduate Coordinator, 662-325-9107, Fax: 662-325-3853, E-mail: selder@abe.msstate.edu. Web site: http://www.abe.msstate.edu/.

New Jersey Institute of Technology, Office of Graduate Studies, Newark College of Engineering, Department of Biomedical Engineering, Newark, NJ 07102. Offers MS, PhD. Part-time and evening/weekend programs available. *Faculty:* 17 full-time (4 women), 2 part-time/adjunct (both women). *Students:* 126 full-time (55 women), 42 part-time (16 women); includes 61 minority (6 Black or African American, non-Hispanic/Latino; 43 Asian, non-Hispanic/Latino; 12 Hispanic/Latino), 68 international. Average age 27. 257 applicants, 67% accepted, 70 enrolled. In 2011, 59 master's, 5 doctorates awarded. Terminal master's awarded for partial completion of doctoral program. *Degree requirements:* For master's, thesis optional; for doctorate, thesis/dissertation. *Entrance requirements:* For master's and doctorate, GRE General Test. Additional exam requirements/recommendations for international students: Required—TOEFL (minimum score 550 paper-based; 213 computer-based; 79 iBT). *Application deadline:* For fall admission, 6/1 priority date for domestic students, 5/1 for international students; for spring admission, 11/15 priority date for domestic students, 11/15 for international students. Applications are processed on a rolling basis. Application fee: $65. Electronic applications accepted. *Expenses:* Tuition, state resident: full-time $7980; part-time $867 per credit. Tuition, nonresident: full-time $11,336; part-time $1196 per credit. *Required fees:* $230 per credit. *Financial support:* Fellowships with full and partial tuition reimbursements, research assistantships with full and partial tuition reimbursements, teaching assistantships with full and partial tuition reimbursements, career-related internships or fieldwork, Federal Work-Study, institutionally sponsored loans, and unspecified assistantships available. Financial award application deadline: 1/15. *Total annual research expenditures:* $2.7 million. *Unit head:* Dr. William C. Van Buskirk, Chair, 973-596-8380, E-mail: vanb@njit.edu. *Application contact:* Kathryn Kelly, Director of Admissions, 973-596-3300, Fax: 973-596-3461, E-mail: admissions@njit.edu. Web site: http://biomedical.njit.edu/.

North Carolina State University, Graduate School, College of Engineering, Joint Department of Biomedical Engineering UNC-Chapel Hill and NC State, Raleigh, NC

27695. Offers MS, PhD. Programs offered jointly with the University of North Carolina at Chapel Hill. Terminal master's awarded for partial completion of doctoral program. *Degree requirements:* For master's, comprehensive exam, thesis, research laboratory experience; for doctorate, one foreign language, comprehensive exam, thesis/dissertation, written and oral examinations, dissertation defense, teaching experience, research laboratory experience. *Entrance requirements:* For master's and doctorate, GRE General Test. Additional exam requirements/recommendations for international students: Required—TOEFL. Electronic applications accepted.

Northwestern University, McCormick School of Engineering and Applied Science, Department of Biomedical Engineering, Evanston, IL 60208. Offers MS, PhD. Admissions and degrees offered through The Graduate School. Part-time programs available. *Faculty:* 20 full-time (5 women). *Students:* 152 full-time (64 women), 8 part-time (4 women); includes 42 minority (6 Black or African American, non-Hispanic/Latino; 24 Asian, non-Hispanic/Latino; 9 Hispanic/Latino; 3 Two or more races, non-Hispanic/Latino), 43 international. Average age 26. 442 applicants, 19% accepted, 32 enrolled. In 2011, 37 master's, 8 doctorates awarded. Terminal master's awarded for partial completion of doctoral program. *Degree requirements:* For master's, comprehensive exam, thesis (for some programs); for doctorate, comprehensive exam, thesis/dissertation. *Entrance requirements:* For master's and doctorate, GRE General Test. Additional exam requirements/recommendations for international students: Required—TOEFL (minimum score 577 paper-based; 233 computer-based; 90 iBT), IELTS (minimum score 7). *Application deadline:* For fall admission, 12/31 for domestic and international students; for winter admission, 11/15 for domestic students, 11/1 for international students; for spring admission, 2/15 for domestic students, 2/1 for international students. Application fee: $75. Electronic applications accepted. *Financial support:* Fellowships with full tuition reimbursements, research assistantships with full tuition reimbursements, teaching assistantships with full tuition reimbursements, career-related internships or fieldwork, institutionally sponsored loans, traineeships, health care benefits, and unspecified assistantships available. Support available to part-time students. Financial award application deadline: 1/15; financial award applicants required to submit FAFSA. *Faculty research:* Neural engineering and rehabilitation; cardiovascular engineering; materials, cells, and tissues; imaging and biophotonics; vision research. *Total annual research expenditures:* $32.3 million. *Unit head:* Dr. John B. Troy, Chair, 847-491-3822, Fax: 847-491-4928, E-mail: j-troy@northwestern.edu. *Application contact:* Dr. Phillip Messersmith, Director of Graduate Admissions, 847-467-5273, Fax: 847-491-4928, E-mail: philm@northwestern.edu. Web site: http://www.bme.northwestern.edu/.

The Ohio State University, Graduate School, College of Engineering, Program in Biomedical Engineering, Columbus, OH 43210. Offers MS, PhD. Evening/weekend programs available. *Faculty:* 14. *Students:* 47 full-time (15 women), 19 part-time (7 women); includes 12 minority (2 Black or African American, non-Hispanic/Latino; 7 Asian, non-Hispanic/Latino; 3 Hispanic/Latino), 14 international. Average age 25. In 2011, 7 master's, 6 doctorates awarded. *Degree requirements:* For master's, thesis optional; for doctorate, thesis/dissertation. *Entrance requirements:* For master's and doctorate, GRE General Test. Additional exam requirements/recommendations for international students: Required—Michigan English Language Assessment Battery (minimum score 82); Recommended—TOEFL (minimum score 600 paper-based; 250 computer-based; 79 iBT). *Application deadline:* For fall admission, 8/15 priority date for domestic students, 7/1 for international students; for winter admission, 12/1 priority date for domestic students, 11/1 for international students; for spring admission, 3/1 priority date for domestic students, 2/1 for international students. Applications are processed on a rolling basis. Application fee: $40 ($50 for international students). Electronic applications accepted. *Expenses:* Tuition, state resident: full-time $11,400. Tuition, nonresident: full-time $28,125. Tuition and fees vary according to course load, degree level, campus/location and program. *Financial support:* Fellowships, research assistantships, career-related internships or fieldwork, Federal Work-Study, and institutionally sponsored loans available. Support available to part-time students. *Unit head:* Richard T. Hart, Chair, 614-292-1285, E-mail: hart.322@osu.edu. *Application contact:* Dr. Samir Ghadiali, Graduate Studies Committee Chair, 614-292-7742, Fax: 614-292-3656, E-mail: ghadiali.1@osu.edu. Web site: http://bme.osu.edu.

Ohio University, Graduate College, Russ College of Engineering and Technology, Department of Chemical and Biomolecular Engineering, Program in Biomedical Engineering, Athens, OH 45701-2979. Offers MS. Part-time programs available. *Students:* 13 full-time (8 women), 8 international. 14 applicants, 43% accepted, 6 enrolled. In 2011, 1 master's awarded. *Degree requirements:* For master's, thesis. *Entrance requirements:* For master's, GRE General Test. Additional exam requirements/recommendations for international students: Required—TOEFL (minimum score 590 paper-based; 243 computer-based; 96 iBT), IELTS (minimum score 7). *Application deadline:* For fall admission, 2/1 priority date for domestic students, 2/1 for international students. Applications are processed on a rolling basis. Application fee: $50 ($55 for international students). Electronic applications accepted. *Financial support:* In 2011–12, 1 fellowship with full tuition reimbursement (averaging $18,000 per year), 2 research assistantships with full tuition reimbursements (averaging $18,000 per year) were awarded; institutionally sponsored loans also available. Financial award application deadline: 2/1. *Faculty research:* Molecular mechanisms of human disease, molecular therapeutics, biomedical information analysis and management, image analysis, biomechanics. *Total annual research expenditures:* $1.5 million. *Unit head:* Dr. Douglas J. Goetz, Director, 740-593-1000. *Application contact:* Tom Riggs, Biomedical Engineering Assistant, 740-597-2797, Fax: 740-593-0873, E-mail: biomed@ohio.edu. Web site: http://www.ohio.edu/engineering/biomedical.

Ohio University, Graduate College, Russ College of Engineering and Technology, Department of Mechanical Engineering, Athens, OH 45701-2979. Offers biomedical engineering (MS); mechanical engineering (MS), including CAD/CAM, design, energy, manufacturing, materials, robotics, thermofluids. Part-time programs available. *Students:* 23 full-time (2 women), 4 part-time (0 women); includes 2 minority (1 Black or African American, non-Hispanic/Latino; 1 Two or more races, non-Hispanic/Latino), 10 international. 52 applicants, 23% accepted, 7 enrolled. In 2011, 8 master's awarded. *Degree requirements:* For master's, comprehensive exam (for some programs), thesis. *Entrance requirements:* For master's, GRE, BS in engineering or science, minimum GPA of 2.8. Additional exam requirements/recommendations for international students: Required—TOEFL (minimum score 550 paper-based; 80 iBT) or IELTS (minimum score 6.5). *Application deadline:* For fall admission, 2/15 priority date for domestic students, 2/15 for international students. Applications are processed on a rolling basis. Application fee: $50 ($55 for international students). Electronic applications accepted. *Financial support:* In 2011–12, research assistantships with tuition reimbursements (averaging $14,000 per year), teaching assistantships with tuition reimbursements (averaging $14,000 per year) were awarded; career-related internships or fieldwork, Federal Work-Study, institutionally sponsored loans, tuition waivers (full and partial), and unspecified assistantships also available. Financial award application deadline: 2/15; financial award applicants required to submit FAFSA. *Faculty research:* Biomedical, energy and the environment, materials and manufacturing, bioengineering. *Unit head:* Dr. Greg Kremer, Chairman, 740-593-1561, Fax: 740-593-0476, E-mail: kremer@bobcat.ent.ohiou.edu. *Application contact:* Dr. Frank F. Kraft, Graduate Chairman, 740-597-1478, Fax: 740-593-0476, E-mail: kraft@ohio.edu. Web site: http://www.ohio.edu/mechanical.

Old Dominion University, Frank Batten College of Engineering and Technology, Program in Biomedical Engineering, Norfolk, VA 23529. Offers PhD. Part-time and evening/weekend programs available. *Faculty:* 3 full-time. *Students:* 2 full-time. 4 applicants, 50% accepted, 2 enrolled. *Degree requirements:* For doctorate, thesis/dissertation, candidacy exam. *Entrance requirements:* For doctorate, GRE, master's degree, minimum graduate GPA of 3.5, three letters of recommendation, statement of purpose. Additional exam requirements/recommendations for international students: Required—TOEFL (minimum score 550 paper-based; 213 computer-based). *Application deadline:* For fall admission, 6/1 for domestic students, 2/15 for international students; for spring admission, 11/1 for domestic students, 10/1 for international students. Applications are processed on a rolling basis. Application fee: $50. Electronic applications accepted. *Expenses:* Tuition, state resident: full-time $9096; part-time $379 per credit. Tuition, nonresident: full-time $23,064; part-time $961 per credit. *Required fees:* $127 per semester. One-time fee: $50. *Financial support:* In 2011–12, 2 students received support. Applicants required to submit FAFSA. *Faculty research:* Brain-computer interface, cardiac electrophysiology, medical devices. *Unit head:* Dr. Stephen Knisley, Director, 757-683-3549, Fax: 757-683-5344, E-mail: sknisley@odu.edu. *Application contact:* Dr. Linda Vahala, Associate Dean, 757-683-3789, Fax: 757-683-4898, E-mail: lvahala@odu.edu. Web site: http://www.eng.odu.edu/bme/academics/PhD.shtml.

Oregon Health & Science University, School of Medicine, Graduate Programs in Medicine, Department of Biomedical Engineering, Portland, OR 97239-3098. Offers biomedical engineering (MS, PhD); computer science and electrical engineering (PhD). Part-time programs available. *Faculty:* 20 full-time (8 women), 3 part-time/adjunct (1 woman). *Students:* 16 full-time (4 women), 3 part-time (1 woman); includes 1 minority (Hispanic/Latino), 4 international. Average age 29. 28 applicants, 25% accepted, 5 enrolled. In 2011, 1 master's, 4 doctorates awarded. Terminal master's awarded for partial completion of doctoral program. *Degree requirements:* For master's, thesis optional, thesis or capstone project; for doctorate, comprehensive exam, thesis/dissertation, qualifying exam. *Entrance requirements:* For master's and doctorate, GRE General Test (minimum scores: 153 Verbal/148 Quantitative/4.5 Analytical). Additional exam requirements/recommendations for international students: Required—TOEFL. *Application deadline:* For fall admission, 7/15 for domestic students, 5/15 for international students; for winter admission, 10/15 for domestic students, 9/15 for international students; for spring admission, 1/15 for domestic students, 12/15 for international students. Applications are processed on a rolling basis. Application fee: $70. Electronic applications accepted. *Financial support:* Health care benefits, tuition waivers, and full tuition and stipends for PhD students available. *Faculty research:* Blood cells in cancer and cancer biology, smart homes and machine learning, computational mechanics and multiscale modeling, tissue optics and biophotonics, nanomedicine and nanobiotechnology. *Unit head:* Dr. Peter Heeman, Program Director, 503-418-9316, E-mail: info@bme.ogi.edu. *Application contact:* Janet Itami, Administrative Coordinator, 503-418-9304, E-mail: itamij@ohsu.edu.

Polytechnic Institute of New York University, Department of Chemical and Biological Sciences, Major in Biomedical Engineering, Brooklyn, NY 11201-2990. Offers MS, PhD. *Students:* 40 full-time (14 women), 25 part-time (12 women); includes 19 minority (2 Black or African American, non-Hispanic/Latino; 13 Asian, non-Hispanic/Latino; 4 Hispanic/Latino), 29 international. Average age 25. 133 applicants; 48% accepted, 22 enrolled. In 2011, 25 master's, 3 doctorates awarded. *Degree requirements:* For master's, comprehensive exam (for some programs), thesis (for some programs); for doctorate, comprehensive exam, thesis/dissertation. *Entrance requirements:* Additional exam requirements/recommendations for international students: Required—TOEFL (minimum score 550 paper-based; 213 computer-based; 80 iBT); Recommended—IELTS (minimum score 6.5). *Application deadline:* For fall admission, 7/31 priority date for domestic students, 4/30 for international students; for spring admission, 12/31 priority date for domestic students, 10/30 for international students. Applications are processed on a rolling basis. Application fee: $75. Electronic applications accepted. *Expenses:* *Tuition:* Full-time $22,464; part-time $1248 per credit. *Required fees:* $501 per semester. *Unit head:* Dr. Bruce Garetz, Department Head, 718-260-3287, E-mail: bgaretz@poly.edu. *Application contact:* JeanCarlo Bonilla, Director, Graduate Enrollment Management, 718-260-3182, Fax: 718-260-3624, E-mail: gradinfo@poly.edu.

Purdue University, College of Engineering, Weldon School of Biomedical Engineering, West Lafayette, IN 47907-2032. Offers MSBME, PhD, MD/PhD. Degree programs offered jointly with School of Mechanical Engineering, School of Electrical and Computer Engineering, and School of Chemical Engineering. *Entrance requirements:* For master's and doctorate, GRE General Test, minimum GPA of 3.25. Additional exam requirements/recommendations for international students: Required—TOEFL (minimum score 550 paper-based; 213 computer-based; 77 iBT); Recommended—TWE. Electronic applications accepted. *Faculty research:* Biomaterials, biomechanics, medical image and signal processing, medical instrumentation, tissue engineering.

Rensselaer Polytechnic Institute, Graduate School, School of Engineering, Program in Biomedical Engineering, Troy, NY 12180-3590. Offers MS, D Eng, PhD. Terminal master's awarded for partial completion of doctoral program. *Degree requirements:* For master's, thesis optional; for doctorate, thesis/dissertation. *Entrance requirements:* For master's and doctorate, GRE, minimum GPA of 3.0. Additional exam requirements/recommendations for international students: Required—TOEFL (minimum score 620 paper-based; 260 computer-based; 106 iBT). Electronic applications accepted. *Faculty research:* Computational biomechanics, cellular and tissue bioengineering, biofluids and cellular bioengineering, functional tissue engineering, orthopedic biomechanics.

Rice University, Graduate Programs, George R. Brown School of Engineering, Department of Chemical and Biomolecular Engineering, Houston, TX 77251-1892. Offers chemical and biomolecular engineering (MS, PhD); chemical engineering (M Ch E). Part-time programs available. *Degree requirements:* For master's, thesis (for some programs); for doctorate, thesis/dissertation. *Entrance requirements:* For master's and doctorate, GRE General Test, minimum GPA of 3.0. Additional exam requirements/recommendations for international students: Required—TOEFL (minimum score 600 paper-based; 250 computer-based; 90 iBT). Electronic applications accepted. *Faculty research:* Thermodynamics, phase equilibria, rheology, fluid mechanics, polymers, biomedical engineering, interfacial phenomena, process control, petroleum engineering, reaction engineering and catalysis, biomaterials, metabolic engineering.

Rose-Hulman Institute of Technology, Faculty of Engineering and Applied Sciences, Department of Applied Biology and Biomedical Engineering, Terre Haute, IN 47803-3999. Offers biomedical engineering (MD/MS); MD/MS. Part-time programs available. *Faculty:* 14 full-time (6 women), 1 part-time/adjunct (0 women). *Students:* 7 full-time (3 women), 2 part-time (1 woman); includes 1 minority (Asian, non-Hispanic/Latino), 1 international. Average age 23. 6 applicants, 100% accepted, 4 enrolled. *Degree requirements:* For master's, thesis. *Entrance requirements:* For master's, GRE, minimum GPA of 3.0. Additional exam requirements/recommendations for international students: Required—TOEFL (minimum score 580 paper-based; 237 computer-based; 92 iBT). *Application deadline:* For fall admission, 2/1 priority date for domestic students. Applications are processed on a rolling basis. Application fee: $0. *Expenses: Tuition:* Full-time $37,197; part-time $1085 per credit hour. *Financial support:* In 2011–12, 7 students received support. Fellowships with full and partial tuition reimbursements available, research assistantships with full and partial tuition reimbursements available, institutionally sponsored loans, scholarships/grants, and tuition waivers (full and partial) available. *Faculty research:* Soft tissue biomechanics, tissue-biomaterial interaction, biomaterials, biomedical instrumentation, biomedical fluid mechanics. *Total annual research expenditures:* $31,715. *Unit head:* Dr. Jameel Ahmed, Interim Chairman, 812-872-6033, Fax: 812-877-8545, E-mail: jameel.ahmed@rose-hulman.edu. *Application contact:* Dr. Daniel J. Moore, Associate Dean of the Faculty, 812-877-8110, Fax: 812-877-8061, E-mail: daniel.j.moore@rose-hulman.edu. Web site: http://www.rose-hulman.edu/abbe/.

Rutgers, The State University of New Jersey, New Brunswick, Graduate School-New Brunswick, Program in Biomedical Engineering, Piscataway, NJ 08854-8097. Offers MS, PhD. MS, PhD offered jointly with University of Medicine and Dentistry of New Jersey. Part-time programs available. Terminal master's awarded for partial completion of doctoral program. *Degree requirements:* For master's, thesis optional; for doctorate, comprehensive exam, thesis/dissertation. *Entrance requirements:* For master's and doctorate, GRE General Test, minimum GPA of 3.0. Additional exam requirements/recommendations for international students: Required—TOEFL. Electronic applications accepted. *Faculty research:* Molecular, cellular and nanosystems bioengineering; biomaterials and tissue engineering; biomechanics and rehabilitation engineering; integrative systems physiology and biomedical instrumentation; computational bioengineering and biomedical imaging.

St. Cloud State University, School of Graduate Studies, College of Science and Engineering, Academic Center for Regulatory Affairs and Services, St. Cloud, MN 56301-4498. Offers MS. Part-time programs available. *Degree requirements:* For master's, final paper. *Entrance requirements:* For master's, GRE General Test, minimum GPA of 2.75. *Expenses:* Contact institution.

Saint Louis University, Graduate Education, Parks College of Engineering, Aviation, and Technology and Graduate Education, Department of Biomedical Engineering, St. Louis, MO 63103-2097. Offers MS, MS-R, PhD. *Degree requirements:* For master's, thesis optional; for doctorate, thesis/dissertation. *Entrance requirements:* For master's, GRE General Test, letters of recommendation, resume, interview; for doctorate, GRE General Test, letters of recommendation, resumé, interview, transcripts, goal statement. Additional exam requirements/recommendations for international students: Required—TOEFL (minimum score 525 paper-based; 194 computer-based). *Faculty research:* Tissue engineering and biomaterialsneural cardiovascular and orthopedic tissue engineering; tissue engineeringairway remodeling, vasculopathy, and elastic, biodegradable scaffolds; biomechanicsorthopedics, trauma biomechanics and biomechanical modeling; biosignalselectrophysiology, signal processing, and biomechanical instrumentation.

South Dakota School of Mines and Technology, Graduate Division, Program in Biomedical Engineering, Rapid City, SD 57701-3995. Offers MS, PhD. *Entrance requirements:* For doctorate, GRE General Test, 3 letters of recommendation, minimum GPA of 3.0. Additional exam requirements/recommendations for international students: Required—TOEFL.

Southern Illinois University Carbondale, Graduate School, College of Engineering, Program in Biomedical Engineering, Carbondale, IL 62901-4701. Offers ME, MS. *Students:* 18 full-time (9 women), 14 part-time (7 women); includes 4 minority (3 Black or African American, non-Hispanic/Latino; 1 Asian, non-Hispanic/Latino), 21 international. 29 applicants, 45% accepted, 2 enrolled. In 2011, 5 master's awarded. *Entrance requirements:* Additional exam requirements/recommendations for international students: Required—TOEFL. *Unit head:* R. Viswanathan, Interim Dean, 618-453-4321. *Application contact:* Anna Maria Alms, Student Contact, 618-453-4321, Fax: 618-453-4235, E-mail: amalms@siu.edu.

Stanford University, School of Engineering, Department of Mechanical Engineering, Program in Biomechanical Engineering, Stanford, CA 94305-9991. Offers MS. *Entrance requirements:* For master's, GRE General Test, undergraduate degree in engineering, math or sciences. Additional exam requirements/recommendations for international students: Required—TOEFL. *Expenses: Tuition:* Full-time $40,050; part-time $890 per credit.

State University of New York at Binghamton, Graduate School, Thomas J. Watson School of Engineering and Applied Science, Department of Bioengineering, Binghamton, NY 13902-6000. Offers biomedical engineering (MS, PhD). *Faculty:* 8 full-time (2 women), 5 part-time/adjunct (1 woman). *Students:* 14 full-time (7 women), 8 part-time (4 women); includes 2 minority (1 Black or African American, non-Hispanic/Latino; 1 Asian, non-Hispanic/Latino), 11 international. Average age 25. 29 applicants, 59% accepted, 8 enrolled. In 2011, 6 master's awarded. *Financial support:* In 2011–12, 8 students received support, including 2 fellowships with full tuition reimbursements available (averaging $16,500 per year), 5 teaching assistantships with full tuition reimbursements available (averaging $16,500 per year); career-related internships or fieldwork, Federal Work-Study, institutionally sponsored loans, scholarships/grants, health care benefits, tuition waivers (full and partial), and unspecified assistantships also available. Financial award application deadline: 2/15; financial award applicants required to submit FAFSA. *Unit head:* Dr. John A. Fillo, Director, 607-777-5779, Fax: 607-777-5780, E-mail: jfillo@binghamton.edu. *Application contact:* Catherine Smith, Recruiting and Admissions Coordinator, 607-777-2151, Fax: 607-777-2501, E-mail: cmsmith@binghamton.edu. Web site: http://www2.binghamton.edu/watson/programs/academic-departments/bioengineering/.

State University of New York Downstate Medical Center, School of Graduate Studies, Program in Biomedical Engineering, Brooklyn, NY 11203-2098. Offers bioimaging and neuroengineering (PhD); biomedical engineering (MS); MD/PhD. *Degree requirements:* For doctorate, comprehensive exam, thesis/dissertation.

Stevens Institute of Technology, Graduate School, Charles V. Schaefer Jr. School of Engineering, Department of Chemistry, Chemical Biology and Biomedical Engineering, Program in Biomedical Engineering, Hoboken, NJ 07030. Offers M Eng, Certificate.

Stony Brook University, State University of New York, Graduate School, College of Engineering and Applied Sciences, Department of Biomedical Engineering, Stony Brook, NY 11794. Offers biomedical engineering (MS, PhD, Certificate); medical physics (MS, PhD). *Degree requirements:* For doctorate, thesis/dissertation, qualifying exams. *Entrance requirements:* For master's and doctorate, GRE General Test. Additional exam requirements/recommendations for international students: Required—TOEFL.

Texas A&M University, College of Engineering, Department of Biomedical Engineering, College Station, TX 77843. Offers M Eng, MS, D Eng, PhD. Part-time programs available. *Faculty:* 18. *Students:* 95 full-time (38 women), 9 part-time (3 women); includes 23 minority (3 Black or African American, non-Hispanic/Latino; 11 Asian, non-Hispanic/Latino; 8 Hispanic/Latino; 1 Two or more races, non-Hispanic/Latino), 35 international. Average age 27. In 2011, 7 master's, 7 doctorates awarded. *Degree requirements:* For master's, thesis (MS); for doctorate, dissertation (PhD). *Entrance requirements:* For master's and doctorate, GRE General Test, leveling courses if non-engineering undergraduate major. Additional exam requirements/recommendations for international students: Required—TOEFL. *Application deadline:* For fall admission, 7/1 priority date for domestic students, 6/1 for international students; for winter admission, 11/1 priority date for domestic students, 3/1 for international students; for spring admission, 4/1 priority date for domestic students, 10/1 for international students. Applications are processed on a rolling basis. Application fee: $50 ($75 for international students). Electronic applications accepted. *Expenses:* Tuition, state resident: full-time $5437; part-time $226.55 per credit hour. Tuition, nonresident: full-time $12,949; part-time $539.55 per credit hour. *Required fees:* $2741. *Financial support:* In 2011–12, research assistantships with partial tuition reimbursements (averaging $12,600 per year), teaching assistantships (averaging $11,400 per year) were awarded; fellowships with partial tuition reimbursements, career-related internships or fieldwork, scholarships/grants, and unspecified assistantships also available. Financial award application deadline: 4/15; financial award applicants required to submit FAFSA. *Faculty research:* Medical lasers, optical biosensors, medical instrumentation, cardiovascular mechanics, orthopedic mechanics. *Unit head:* Gerard L. Cote, Head, 979-845-4196, Fax: 979-845-4450, E-mail: bmen@tamu.edu. *Application contact:* Dr. Fidel Fernandez, Academic Advisor, 979-845-5532, Fax: 979-845-4450, E-mail: fidel@tamu.edu. Web site: http://biomed.tamu.edu/.

Thomas Jefferson University, Jefferson College of Graduate Studies, PhD Program in Tissue Engineering and Regenerative Medicine, Philadelphia, PA 19107. Offers PhD. *Faculty:* 18 full-time (6 women). *Students:* 4 full-time (3 women); includes 1 minority (Asian, non-Hispanic/Latino). 3 applicants, 0% accepted. In 2011, 2 doctorates awarded. *Degree requirements:* For doctorate, comprehensive exam, thesis/dissertation. *Entrance requirements:* For doctorate, GRE General Test, minimum GPA of 3.2. Additional exam requirements/recommendations for international students: Required—TOEFL (minimum score 250 computer-based; 100 iBT) or IELTS. *Application deadline:* For fall admission, 1/15 priority date for domestic students, 1/15 for international students. Applications are processed on a rolling basis. Application fee: $50. Electronic applications accepted. *Financial support:* In 2011–12, 4 students received support, including 4 fellowships with full tuition reimbursements available (averaging $52,883 per year); Federal Work-Study, institutionally sponsored loans, traineeships, and stipend also available. Financial award application deadline: 5/1; financial award applicants required to submit FAFSA. *Faculty research:* Skeletal development, biomaterials, bone implant interaction, tissue engineering, high resolution imaging. *Total annual research expenditures:* $8 million. *Unit head:* Dr. Irving Shapiro, Program Director, 215-955-7217, Fax: 215-955-9159, E-mail: irving.shapiro@jefferson.edu. *Application contact:* Marc E. Stearns, Director of Admissions, 215-503-0155, Fax: 215-503-9920, E-mail: jcgs-info@jefferson.edu. Web site: http://www.jefferson.edu/jcgs/phd/term/.

Tufts University, School of Engineering, Department of Biomedical Engineering, Medford, MA 02155. Offers bioengineering (ME, MS), including biomaterials; biomedical engineering (PhD). Part-time programs available. *Faculty:* 7 full-time, 4 part-time/adjunct. *Students:* 74 (34 women); includes 15 minority (1 Black or African American, non-Hispanic/Latino; 12 Asian, non-Hispanic/Latino; 2 Hispanic/Latino), 17 international. 150 applicants, 38% accepted, 29 enrolled. In 2011, 13 master's, 7 doctorates awarded. Terminal master's awarded for partial completion of doctoral program. *Degree requirements:* For master's, thesis (for some programs); for doctorate, thesis/dissertation. *Entrance requirements:* For master's and doctorate, GRE General Test. Additional exam requirements/recommendations for international students: Required—TOEFL (minimum score 550 paper-based; 213 computer-based; 80 iBT). *Application deadline:* For fall admission, 1/15 priority date for domestic students, 12/15 for international students; for spring admission, 10/15 for domestic students, 9/15 for international students. Applications are processed on a rolling basis. Application fee: $75. Electronic applications accepted. *Expenses: Tuition:* Full-time $41,208; part-time $1030 per credit hour. Full-time tuition and fees vary according to degree level, program and student level. Part-time tuition and fees vary according to course load. *Financial support:* Fellowships with full tuition reimbursements, research assistantships with full and partial tuition reimbursements, teaching assistantships with full and partial tuition reimbursements, Federal Work-Study, scholarships/grants, tuition waivers (partial), and unspecified assistantships available. Financial award application deadline: 1/15; financial award applicants required to submit FAFSA. *Faculty research:* Regenerative medicine with biomaterials and tissue engineering, diffuse optical imaging and spectroscopy, optics in the development of biomedical devices, ultrafast nonlinear optics and biophotonics, optical diagnostics for diseased and engineered tissues. *Unit head:* Dr. David Kaplan, Chair, 617-627-2580. *Application contact:* Vilva Ricci, Information Contact, 617-627-2580, E-mail: bme@tufts.edu. Web site: http://engineering.tufts.edu/bme.

Tulane University, School of Science and Engineering, Department of Biomedical Engineering, New Orleans, LA 70118-5669. Offers MS, PhD. MS and PhD offered through the Graduate School. Part-time programs available. Terminal master's awarded for partial completion of doctoral program. *Degree requirements:* For master's, thesis (for some programs); for doctorate, thesis/dissertation. *Entrance requirements:* For master's and doctorate, GRE General Test, minimum B average in undergraduate course work. Additional exam requirements/recommendations for international students: Required—TOEFL. Electronic applications accepted. *Faculty research:* Pulmonary and biofluid mechanics and biomechanics of bone, biomaterials science, finite element analysis, electric fields of the brain.

Université de Montréal, Faculty of Medicine, Institute of Biomedical Engineering, Montréal, QC H3C 3J7, Canada. Offers M Sc A, PhD, DESS. M Sc A and PhD programs offered jointly with École Polytechnique de Montréal. *Degree requirements:* For master's, thesis; for doctorate, thesis/dissertation, general exam. *Entrance requirements:* For master's and doctorate, proficiency in French, knowledge of English. Electronic applications accepted. *Faculty research:* Electrophysiology, biomechanics, instrumentation, imaging, simulation.

The University of Akron, Graduate School, College of Engineering, Department of Biomedical Engineering, Akron, OH 44325. Offers MS, PhD. Part-time and evening/weekend programs available. *Faculty:* 9 full-time (4 women), 3 part-time/adjunct (1 woman). *Students:* 25 full-time (9 women), 5 part-time (3 women); includes 3 minority (all Asian, non-Hispanic/Latino), 15 international. Average age 27. 48 applicants, 69% accepted, 8 enrolled. In 2011, 6 master's, 1 doctorate awarded. *Degree requirements:* For master's, thesis; for doctorate, one foreign language, thesis/dissertation, candidacy exam, qualifying exam. *Entrance requirements:* For master's, GRE, minimum GPA of 2.75, three letters of recommendation, statement of purpose, resume; for doctorate, GRE, minimum GPA of 3.0 with bachelor's degree, 3.5 with master's degree; three letters of recommendation; personal statement, resume. Additional exam requirements/recommendations for international students: Required—TOEFL (minimum score 590 paper-based; 243 computer-based; 96 iBT). *Application deadline:* Applications are processed on a rolling basis. Application fee: $30 ($40 for international students). Electronic applications accepted. *Expenses:* Tuition, state resident: full-time $7038; part-time $391 per credit hour. Tuition, nonresident: full-time $12,051; part-time $670 per credit hour. *Required fees:* $1274; $34 per credit hour. *Financial support:* In 2011–12, 14 research assistantships with full tuition reimbursements, 8 teaching assistantships with full tuition reimbursements were awarded; career-related internships or fieldwork, Federal Work-Study, and scholarships/grants also available. *Faculty research:* Signal and image processing, physiological controls and instrumentation, biomechanics - orthopaedic and hemodynamic, biomaterials for gene and drug delivery systems, telemedicine. *Total annual research expenditures:* $159,545. *Unit head:* Dr. Daniel Sheffer, Chair, 330-972-6977, E-mail: dsheffer@uakron.edu. *Application contact:* Dr. Craig Menzemer, Associate Dean, 330-972-5536, E-mail: ccmenze@uakron.edu. Web site: http://www.uakron.edu/engineering/BME/.

The University of Akron, Graduate School, College of Engineering, Program in Engineering (Biomedical Engineering Specialization), Akron, OH 44325. Offers MS. *Students:* 2 applicants, 0% accepted, 0 enrolled. *Entrance requirements:* For master's, GRE, minimum GPA of 2.75, three letters of recommendation, statement of purpose, resume. Additional exam requirements/recommendations for international students: Required—TOEFL (minimum score 590 paper-based; 243 computer-based; 96 iBT). *Application deadline:* Applications are processed on a rolling basis. Application fee: $30 ($40 for international students). Electronic applications accepted. *Expenses:* Tuition, state resident: full-time $7038; part-time $391 per credit hour. Tuition, nonresident: full-time $12,051; part-time $670 per credit hour. *Required fees:* $1274; $34 per credit hour. *Unit head:* Dr. Daniel Sheffer, Chair, 330-972-6977, E-mail: sheffer@uakron.edu. *Application contact:* Director of Graduate Studies. Web site: http://www.uakron.edu/engineering/BME/graduate-program/.

The University of Alabama at Birmingham, School of Engineering, Program in Biomedical Engineering, Birmingham, AL 35294. Offers MSBME, PhD. *Degree requirements:* For master's, thesis or alternative, oral exam; for doctorate, comprehensive exam, thesis/dissertation. *Entrance requirements:* For master's and doctorate, GRE General Test. Additional exam requirements/recommendations for international students: Required—TOEFL. *Expenses:* Tuition, state resident: full-time $5922; part-time $309 per hour. Tuition, nonresident: full-time $13,428; part-time $726 per hour. Tuition and fees vary according to program. *Financial support:* Fellowships with full tuition reimbursements, research assistantships, career-related internships or fieldwork, Federal Work-Study, and institutionally sponsored loans available. *Unit head:* Dr. Timothy M. Wick, Chair, 205-934-8420, E-mail: macsmith@uab.edu. Web site: http://www.eng.uab.edu/BME/.

University of Alberta, Faculty of Medicine and Dentistry and Faculty of Graduate Studies and Research, Graduate Programs in Medicine, Department of Biomedical Engineering, Edmonton, AB T6G 2E1, Canada. Offers biomedical engineering (M Sc); medical sciences (PhD). *Degree requirements:* For master's, thesis; for doctorate, thesis/dissertation. Electronic applications accepted. *Faculty research:* Medical imaging, rehabilitation engineering, biomaterials and tissue engineering, biomechanics, cryobiology.

The University of Arizona, Graduate Interdisciplinary Programs, Graduate Interdisciplinary Program in Biomedical Engineering, Tucson, AZ 85721. Offers MS, PhD. *Faculty:* 6 full-time (1 woman). *Students:* 37 full-time (21 women), 3 part-time (0 women); includes 17 minority (2 Black or African American, non-Hispanic/Latino; 1 Asian, non-Hispanic/Latino; 2 Hispanic/Latino; 12 Two or more races, non-Hispanic/Latino). Average age 26. 46 applicants, 20% accepted, 7 enrolled. In 2011, 13 master's, 2 doctorates awarded. *Entrance requirements:* For master's, GRE, 3 letters of recommendation; for doctorate, GRE, 3 letters of recommendation, statement of purpose. Additional exam requirements/recommendations for international students: Required—TOEFL (minimum score 600 paper-based; 250 computer-based). *Application deadline:* For fall admission, 2/1 for domestic students, 12/1 for international students. Application fee: $75. Electronic applications accepted. *Expenses:* Tuition, state resident: full-time $10,840. Tuition, nonresident: full-time $25,802. *Financial support:* In 2011–12, 6 research assistantships with full tuition reimbursements (averaging $18,773 per year) were awarded; institutionally sponsored loans, scholarships/grants, traineeships, health care benefits, tuition waivers (full), and unspecified assistantships also available. *Unit head:* Dr. John Szivek, Chair, 520-626-8726, E-mail: szivek@email.arizona.edu. *Application contact:* Debbi Howard, Program Coordinator, 520-626-8726, Fax: 520-626-9134, E-mail: dhoward@u.arizona.edu. Web site: http://www.bme.arizona.edu/.

University of Arkansas, Graduate School, College of Engineering, Department of Biological and Agricultural Engineering, Program in Biomedical Engineering, Fayetteville, AR 72701-1201. Offers MSBME. *Students:* 2 full-time (1 woman), 4 part-time (1 woman), 2 international. In 2011, 2 master's awarded. *Application deadline:* For fall admission, 4/1 for international students; for spring admission, 10/1 for international students. Applications are processed on a rolling basis. Application fee: $40 ($50 for international students). Electronic applications accepted. *Financial support:* In 2011–12, 4 research assistantships, 2 teaching assistantships were awarded; fellowships also available. *Unit head:* Dr. Lalit Verma, Department Head, 479-575-2351, Fax: 479-575-2846, E-mail: lverma@uark.edu. *Application contact:* Dr. Jin-Woo Kim, Program Coordinator, 479-575-2351, Fax: 479-575-2846, E-mail: jwkim@uark.edu. Web site: http://www.baeg.uark.edu/.

University of Bridgeport, School of Engineering, Department of Biomedical Engineering, Bridgeport, CT 06604. Offers MS. Part-time and evening/weekend programs available. *Faculty:* 3 full-time (1 woman), 5 part-time/adjunct (2 women). *Students:* 69 full-time (30 women), 18 part-time (7 women); includes 6 minority (1 Black or African American, non-Hispanic/Latino; 2 Asian, non-Hispanic/Latino; 3 Hispanic/Latino), 78 international. Average age 26. 200 applicants, 76% accepted, 20 enrolled. In 2011, 7 master's awarded. *Degree requirements:* For master's, thesis optional. *Entrance requirements:* Additional exam requirements/recommendations for international students: Recommended—TOEFL (minimum score 550 paper-based; 213 computer-based; 80 iBT), IELTS (minimum score 6.5). *Application deadline:* For fall admission, 8/1 priority date for domestic students, 8/1 for international students; for spring admission, 12/1 priority date for domestic students, 12/1 for international students. Application fee: $50. *Expenses: Tuition:* Full-time $22,880; part-time $700 per credit. *Required fees:* $1870; $95 per semester. Tuition and fees vary according to course load and program. *Financial support:* In 2011–12, 25 students received support. Fellowships, research assistantships, career-related internships or fieldwork, scholarships/grants, and unspecified assistantships available. Support available to part-time students. Financial award application deadline: 8/1; financial award applicants required to submit FAFSA. *Unit head:* Dr. Prabir K. Patra, Director, 203-576-4165, Fax: 203-576-4750, E-mail: ppatra@bridgeport.edu. *Application contact:* Karissa Peckham, Dean of Admissions, 203-576-4552, Fax: 203-576-4941, E-mail: admit@bridgeport.edu.

University of Calgary, Faculty of Graduate Studies, Faculty of Kinesiology, Calgary, AB T2N 1N4, Canada. Offers biomedical engineering (M Sc, PhD); kinesiology (M Kin, M Sc, PhD), including biomechanics (PhD), health and exercise physiology (PhD). *Degree requirements:* For master's, thesis (M Sc); for doctorate, thesis/dissertation. *Entrance requirements:* Additional exam requirements/recommendations for international students: Required—TOEFL. Electronic applications accepted. *Faculty research:* Load acting on the human body, muscle mechanics and physiology, optimizing high performance athlete performance, eye movement in sports, analysis of body composition.

University of Calgary, Faculty of Graduate Studies, Schulich School of Engineering, Graduate Program in Biomedical Engineering, Calgary, AB T2N 1N4, Canada. Offers M Eng, M Sc, PhD. *Degree requirements:* For master's, thesis; for doctorate, comprehensive exam, thesis/dissertation. *Faculty research:* Bioinstrumentation and imaging, clinical engineering, biomechanics, biomaterials, systems physiology.

University of California, Davis, College of Engineering, Graduate Group in Biomedical Engineering, Davis, CA 95616. Offers MS, PhD. *Degree requirements:* For master's, thesis; for doctorate, thesis/dissertation. *Entrance requirements:* For master's and doctorate, GRE General Test, minimum GPA of 3.25. Additional exam requirements/recommendations for international students: Required—TOEFL (minimum score 550 paper-based; 213 computer-based), IELTS (minimum score 7). Electronic applications accepted. *Faculty research:* Orthopedic biomechanics, cell/molecular biomechanics and transport, biosensors and instrumentation, human movement, biomedical image analysis, spectroscopy.

University of California, Irvine, School of Engineering, Department of Biomedical Engineering, Irvine, CA 92697. Offers MS, PhD. Part-time programs available. *Students:* 126 full-time (38 women), 14 part-time (4 women); includes 57 minority (1 Black or African American, non-Hispanic/Latino; 1 American Indian or Alaska Native, non-Hispanic/Latino; 48 Asian, non-Hispanic/Latino; 5 Hispanic/Latino; 2 Two or more races, non-Hispanic/Latino), 37 international. Average age 26. 312 applicants, 31% accepted, 39 enrolled. In 2011, 21 master's, 16 doctorates awarded. Terminal master's awarded for partial completion of doctoral program. *Degree requirements:* For doctorate, thesis/dissertation. *Entrance requirements:* For master's and doctorate, GRE General Test, minimum GPA of 3.0, 3 letters of recommendation. Additional exam requirements/recommendations for international students: Required—TOEFL (minimum score 550 paper-based; 213 computer-based). *Application deadline:* For fall admission, 1/15 priority date for domestic students, 1/15 for international students. Applications are processed on a rolling basis. Application fee: $80 ($100 for international students). Electronic applications accepted. *Financial support:* Fellowships, research assistantships with full tuition reimbursements, teaching assistantships, institutionally sponsored loans, traineeships, health care benefits, and unspecified assistantships available. Financial award application deadline: 3/1; financial award applicants required to submit FAFSA. *Faculty research:* Biomedical photonics, biomedical imaging, biomedical nano- and micro-scale systems, biomedical computation/modeling, neuroengineering, tissue engineering. *Unit head:* Prof. Abraham P. Lee, Chair, 949-824-8155, Fax: 949-824-1727, E-mail: aplee@uci.edu. *Application contact:* Karen Stephens, Graduate Academic Counselor, 949-824-3494, Fax: 949-824-1727, E-mail: aplee@uci.edu. Web site: http://www.eng.uci.edu/dept/bme.

University of California, Los Angeles, Graduate Division, Henry Samueli School of Engineering and Applied Science, Interdepartmental Graduate Program in Biomedical Engineering, Los Angeles, CA 90095-1600. Offers MS, PhD. *Faculty:* 8 full-time (1 woman), 1 part-time/adjunct (0 women). *Students:* 172 full-time (58 women); includes 69 minority (2 Black or African American, non-Hispanic/Latino; 60 Asian, non-Hispanic/Latino; 6 Hispanic/Latino; 1 Two or more races, non-Hispanic/Latino), 49 international. 335 applicants, 36% accepted, 42 enrolled. In 2011, 31 master's, 13 doctorates awarded. *Degree requirements:* For master's, comprehensive exam or thesis; for doctorate, thesis/dissertation, qualifying exams. *Entrance requirements:* For master's, GRE General Test, minimum GPA of 3.0; for doctorate, GRE General Test, minimum GPA of 3.25. Additional exam requirements/recommendations for international students: Required—TOEFL (minimum score 560 paper-based; 220 computer-based; 87 iBT). *Application deadline:* For fall admission, 12/15 for domestic and international students. Application fee: $80 ($100 for international students). Electronic applications accepted. *Financial support:* In 2011–12, 54 fellowships, 106 research assistantships, 46 teaching assistantships were awarded; career-related internships or fieldwork, Federal Work-Study, institutionally sponsored loans, and tuition waivers (full and partial) also available. Financial award application deadline: 1/15; financial award applicants required to submit FAFSA. *Faculty research:* Biomaterials, tissue engineering, and biomechanics, biomedical instrumentation, biomedical signal and image processing, biosystem science and engineering, medical imaging informatics, molecular and cellular bioengineering, neuroengineering. *Total annual research expenditures:* $4 million. *Unit head:* Dr. James Dunn, Chair, 310-794-5945. *Application contact:* Larry Nadeau, Student Affairs Officer, 310-794-5945, Fax: 310-794-5956, E-mail: nadeau@ea.ucla.edu. Web site: http://www.bme.ucla.edu/.

University of Cincinnati, Graduate School, College of Engineering and Applied Science, Department of Biomedical Engineering, Cincinnati, OH 45221. Offers bioinformatics (PhD); biomechanics (PhD); medical imaging (PhD); tissue engineering (PhD). Part-time programs available. *Degree requirements:* For doctorate, one foreign language, thesis/dissertation. *Entrance requirements:* For doctorate, GRE General Test.

Additional exam requirements/recommendations for international students: Required—TOEFL (minimum score 600 paper-based; 250 computer-based).

University of Connecticut, Graduate School, School of Engineering, Department of Electrical and Computer Engineering, Field of Biomedical Engineering, Storrs, CT 06269. Offers MS, PhD. Terminal master's awarded for partial completion of doctoral program. *Degree requirements:* For master's, comprehensive exam, thesis or alternative; for doctorate, thesis/dissertation. *Entrance requirements:* For master's and doctorate, GRE General Test. Additional exam requirements/recommendations for international students: Required—TOEFL (minimum score 550 paper-based; 213 computer-based). Electronic applications accepted.

University of Florida, Graduate School, College of Engineering, Department of Biomedical Engineering, Gainesville, FL 32611. Offers ME, MS, PhD, Certificate. Terminal master's awarded for partial completion of doctoral program. *Degree requirements:* For master's, comprehensive exam (for some programs), thesis (for some programs); for doctorate, comprehensive exam (for some programs), thesis/dissertation (for some programs). *Entrance requirements:* For master's, GRE General Test, minimum GPA of 3.1; for doctorate, GRE General Test, minimum GPA of 3.3. Additional exam requirements/recommendations for international students: Required—TOEFL (minimum score 550 paper-based; 213 computer-based; 80 iBT), IELTS (minimum score 6). Electronic applications accepted. *Faculty research:* Neural engineering, tissue engineering, biomedical imaging.

University of Houston, Cullen College of Engineering, Department of Biomedical Engineering, Houston, TX 77204. Offers PhD. Part-time programs available. *Degree requirements:* For doctorate, seminar. *Entrance requirements:* For doctorate, GRE, BS or MS in biomedical engineering or related field, minimum GPA of 3.3 on last 60 hours. Additional exam requirements/recommendations for international students: Required—TOEFL (minimum score 580 paper-based; 237 computer-based; 92 iBT), IELTS (minimum score 6). Electronic applications accepted.

The University of Iowa, Graduate College, College of Engineering, Department of Biomedical Engineering, Iowa City, IA 52242-1316. Offers MS, PhD. Part-time programs available. *Faculty:* 14 full-time (2 women), 1 (woman) part-time/adjunct. *Students:* 88 full-time (31 women); includes 7 minority (5 Asian, non-Hispanic/Latino; 2 Hispanic/Latino), 40 international. Average age 26. 106 applicants, 35% accepted, 13 enrolled. In 2011, 15 master's, 5 doctorates awarded. *Degree requirements:* For master's, thesis (for some programs), written and oral exam; for doctorate, comprehensive exam, thesis/dissertation, written and oral exam. *Entrance requirements:* For master's, GRE, minimum undergraduate GPA of 3.0; for doctorate, GRE. Additional exam requirements/recommendations for international students: Required—TOEFL (minimum score 600 paper-based; 250 computer-based; 100 iBT), IELTS (minimum score 7). *Application deadline:* For fall admission, 3/1 for domestic and international students; for spring admission, 8/1 for domestic and international students. Applications are processed on a rolling basis. Application fee: $60 ($100 for international students). Electronic applications accepted. *Financial support:* In 2011–12, 3 fellowships with partial tuition reimbursements (averaging $17,236 per year), 67 research assistantships with partial tuition reimbursements (averaging $23,776 per year), 14 teaching assistantships with partial tuition reimbursements (averaging $16,635 per year) were awarded; scholarships/grants, health care benefits, and unspecified assistantships also available. Support available to part-time students. Financial award application deadline: 3/1. *Faculty research:* Biomaterials, tissue engineering and cellular mechanics; cell motion analysis and modeling; spinal and joint biomechanics, digital human modeling, and biomedical imaging; bioinformatics and computational biology; fluid and cardiovascular biomechanics. *Total annual research expenditures:* $8.4 million. *Unit head:* Dr. Joseph M. Reinhardt, Departmental Executive Officer, 319-335-5634, Fax: 319-335-5631, E-mail: joe-reinhardt@uiowa.edu. *Application contact:* Angie Dickey, Academic Program Specialist, 319-384-0671, Fax: 319-335-5631, E-mail: bme@engineering.uiowa.edu. Web site: http://www.bme.engineering.uiowa.edu/.

The University of Iowa, Roy J. and Lucille A. Carver College of Medicine and Graduate College, Biosciences Program, Iowa City, IA 52242-1316. Offers anatomy and biology (PhD); biochemistry (PhD); biology (PhD); biomedical engineering (PhD); chemistry (PhD); free radical and radiation biology (PhD); genetics (PhD); human toxicology (PhD); immunology (PhD); microbiology (PhD); molecular and cellular biology (PhD); molecular physiology and biophysics (PhD); neuroscience (PhD); pharmacology (PhD); physical therapy and rehabilitation science (PhD); speech and hearing (PhD). *Faculty:* 310 full-time. *Students:* 9 full-time (5 women); includes 4 minority (1 Black or African American, non-Hispanic/Latino; 2 Asian, non-Hispanic/Latino; 1 Hispanic/Latino). 225 applicants. *Degree requirements:* For doctorate, thesis/dissertation. *Entrance requirements:* For doctorate, GRE General Test, minimum GPA of 3.0. Additional exam requirements/recommendations for international students: Required—TOEFL (minimum score 600 paper-based; 250 computer-based; 100 iBT). *Application deadline:* For fall admission, 1/15 priority date for domestic students, 1/15 for international students. Applications are processed on a rolling basis. Application fee: $60 ($100 for international students). Electronic applications accepted. *Expenses:* Contact institution. *Financial support:* In 2011–12, 9 students received support, including 9 research assistantships with full tuition reimbursements available (averaging $25,000 per year); fellowships, teaching assistantships, and health care benefits also available. *Unit head:* Dr. Douglas Spitz, Director, 319-335-8001, Fax: 319-335-7656, E-mail: andrew-russo@uiowa.edu. *Application contact:* Jodi M. Graff, Program Associate, 319-335-8305, Fax: 319-335-7656, E-mail: biosciences-admissions@uiowa.edu. Web site: http://www.biology.uiowa.edu/graduate.php.

University of Kentucky, Graduate School, Program in Biomedical Engineering, Lexington, KY 40506-0032. Offers MSBE, PBME, PhD. *Degree requirements:* For master's, comprehensive exam, thesis optional; for doctorate, comprehensive exam, thesis/dissertation. *Entrance requirements:* For master's, GRE General Test, minimum undergraduate GPA of 2.75; for doctorate, GRE General Test, minimum graduate GPA of 3.0. Additional exam requirements/recommendations for international students: Required—TOEFL (minimum score 550 paper-based; 213 computer-based). Electronic applications accepted. *Faculty research:* Signal processing and dynamical systems, cardiopulmonary mechanics and systems, bioelectromagnetics, neuromotor control and electrical stimulation, biomaterials and musculoskeletal biomechanics.

University of Maine, Graduate School, Program in Biomedical Sciences, Orono, ME 04469. Offers biomedical engineering (PhD); cell and molecular biology (PhD); neuroscience (PhD); toxicology (PhD). *Students:* 11 full-time (7 women), 19 part-time (11 women); includes 1 minority (American Indian or Alaska Native, non-Hispanic/Latino), 8 international. Average age 29. 32 applicants, 31% accepted, 8 enrolled. In 2011, 3 degrees awarded. Application fee: $65. *Expenses:* Tuition, state resident: full-time $5016. Tuition, nonresident: full-time $14,424. *Financial support:* In 2011–12, 2 fellowships with full tuition reimbursements (averaging $18,000 per year), 8 research

assistantships with full tuition reimbursements (averaging $23,000 per year) were awarded. *Unit head:* Dr. Carol Kim, Unit Head, 207-581-2803. *Application contact:* Scott G. Delcourt, Associate Dean of the Graduate School, 207-581-3291, Fax: 207-581-3232, E-mail: graduate@maine.edu. Web site: http://www2.umaine.edu/graduate.

University of Massachusetts Dartmouth, Graduate School, Program in Biomedical Engineering and Biotechnology, North Dartmouth, MA 02747-2300. Offers MS, PhD. Part-time programs available. *Students:* 20 full-time (12 women), 13 part-time (6 women); includes 1 minority (Asian, non-Hispanic/Latino), 17 international. Average age 29. 21 applicants, 52% accepted, 4 enrolled. In 2011, 2 degrees awarded. *Median time to degree:* Of those who began their doctoral program in fall 2003, 33% received their degree in 8 years or less. *Degree requirements:* For doctorate, comprehensive exam, thesis/dissertation. *Entrance requirements:* For master's and doctorate, GRE, minimum GPA of 3.0, 3 letters of recommendation, resume, statement of intent. Additional exam requirements/recommendations for international students: Required—TOEFL (minimum score 533 paper-based; 200 computer-based; 72 iBT). *Application deadline:* For fall admission, 2/15 for domestic students, 1/15 for international students; for spring admission, 11/15 for domestic students, 10/15 for international students. Application fee: $40 ($60 for international students). Electronic applications accepted. *Expenses:* Tuition, state resident: full-time $2071; part-time $86.29 per credit. Tuition, nonresident: full-time $8099; part-time $337.46 per credit. *Required fees:* $438.58 per credit. Part-time tuition and fees vary according to class time, course load, degree level and reciprocity agreements. *Financial support:* In 2011–12, 2 fellowships with full tuition reimbursements (averaging $20,000 per year), 11 research assistantships with full tuition reimbursements (averaging $11,277 per year), 2 teaching assistantships with full tuition reimbursements (averaging $11,250 per year) were awarded; unspecified assistantships also available. Financial award application deadline: 3/1; financial award applicants required to submit FAFSA. *Faculty research:* Tetracycline-encapsulated chitosan microspheres, artificial tissues, sensor arrays for orthopedic rehab, blue light cures, healing bandages. *Total annual research expenditures:* $197,000. *Unit head:* Sanka Bhowmick, Graduate Program Director for Engineering Options, 508-999-8619, Fax: 508-999-8881, E-mail: sbhowmick@umassd.edu. *Application contact:* Elan Turcotte-Shamski, Graduate Admissions Officer, 508-999-8604, Fax: 508-999-8183, E-mail: graduate@umassd.edu.

University of Medicine and Dentistry of New Jersey, Graduate School of Biomedical Sciences, Graduate Programs in Biomedical Sciences–Newark, Department of Biomedical Engineering, Newark, NJ 07107. Offers Certificate. *Entrance requirements:* Additional exam requirements/recommendations for international students: Required—TOEFL. Electronic applications accepted.

University of Medicine and Dentistry of New Jersey, Graduate School of Biomedical Sciences, Graduate Programs in Biomedical Sciences–Piscataway, Program in Biomedical Engineering, Piscataway, NJ 08854-5635. Offers MS, PhD, MD/PhD. MS, PhD offered jointly with Rutgers, The State University of New Jersey, New Brunswick. *Degree requirements:* For master's, thesis, qualifying exam; for doctorate, thesis/dissertation, qualifying exam. *Entrance requirements:* For master's and doctorate, GRE General Test. Additional exam requirements/recommendations for international students: Required—TOEFL. Electronic applications accepted.

University of Memphis, Graduate School, Herff College of Engineering, Program in Biomedical Engineering, Memphis, TN 38152. Offers MS, PhD. *Degree requirements:* For master's, thesis or alternative, oral exam; for doctorate, thesis/dissertation, exams. *Entrance requirements:* For master's, GRE General Test or MAT, minimum undergraduate GPA of 3.0; for doctorate, GRE General Test, minimum undergraduate GPA of 3.25 or master's degree in biomedical engineering. Electronic applications accepted. *Faculty research:* Biomaterials and cell/tissue engineering, especially for orthopedic applications; biosensors; biomechanics (hemodynamics, soft tissue, lung, gait); electrophysiology; novel medical image-acquisition devices.

University of Miami, Graduate School, College of Engineering, Department of Biomedical Engineering, Coral Gables, FL 33124. Offers MSBE, PhD. Part-time programs available. *Degree requirements:* For master's, thesis (for some programs); for doctorate, comprehensive exam, thesis/dissertation. *Entrance requirements:* For master's and doctorate, GRE General Test, minimum GPA of 3.0. Additional exam requirements/recommendations for international students: Required—TOEFL (minimum score 550 paper-based; 213 computer-based). Electronic applications accepted. *Faculty research:* Biomedical signal processing and instrumentation, cardiovascular engineering, optics and lasers, rehabilitation engineering, tissue mechanics.

University of Michigan, College of Engineering, Department of Biomedical Engineering, Ann Arbor, MI 48109. Offers MS, MSE, PhD. Part-time programs available. *Students:* 218 full-time (87 women). 542 applicants, 34% accepted, 84 enrolled. In 2011, 80 master's, 20 doctorates awarded. *Degree requirements:* For master's, thesis optional; for doctorate, comprehensive exam, oral defense of dissertation. *Entrance requirements:* For master's, GRE General Test; for doctorate, GRE General Test, master's degree. Additional exam requirements/recommendations for international students: Required—TOEFL. *Application deadline:* Applications are processed on a rolling basis. Application fee: $65 ($75 for international students). Electronic applications accepted. *Financial support:* Fellowships, research assistantships, teaching assistantships, Federal Work-Study, scholarships/grants, traineeships, and tuition waivers (partial) available. Financial award applicants required to submit FAFSA. *Faculty research:* Cellular and tissue engineering, biotechnology, biomedical materials, biomechanics, biomedical imaging, rehabilitation engineering. *Unit head:* Douglas Noll, Chair, 734-647-1091, Fax: 734-936-1905, E-mail: biomede@umich.edu. *Application contact:* Maria E. Steele, Senior Student Administration Assistant, 734-647-1091, Fax: 734-936-1905, E-mail: msteele@umich.edu. Web site: http://www.bme.umich.edu/.

University of Minnesota, Twin Cities Campus, College of Science and Engineering and Medical School, Department of Biomedical Engineering, Minneapolis, MN 55455-0213. Offers MS, PhD, MD/PhD. Part-time programs available. *Faculty:* 14 full-time (2 women). *Students:* 136 (49 women); includes 23 minority (3 Black or African American, non-Hispanic/Latino; 19 Asian, non-Hispanic/Latino; 1 Hispanic/Latino), 34 international. Terminal master's awarded for partial completion of doctoral program. *Degree requirements:* For master's, thesis optional; for doctorate, thesis/dissertation. *Entrance requirements:* For master's and doctorate, GRE General Test. Additional exam requirements/recommendations for international students: Required—TOEFL. *Application deadline:* For fall admission, 1/10 priority date for domestic students, 1/10 for international students. Applications are processed on a rolling basis. Application fee: $75 ($95 for international students). Electronic applications accepted. *Financial support:* Fellowships with tuition reimbursements, research assistantships with tuition reimbursements, and teaching assistantships with tuition reimbursements available. *Faculty research:* bioinstrumentation and medical devices; biomaterials; biomechanics; biomedical optics and imaging; biomolecular, cellular, and tissue engineering;

cardiovascular engineering; neural engineering. *Application contact:* Biomedical Engineering Graduate Program, E-mail: bmengp@umn.edu. Web site: http://www.bme.umn.edu.

University of Nevada, Las Vegas, Graduate College, Howard R. Hughes College of Engineering, Department of Mechanical Engineering, Las Vegas, NV 89154-4027. Offers aerospace engineering (MS); biomedical engineering (MS); materials and nuclear engineering (MS); mechanical engineering (MSE, PhD). Part-time programs available. *Faculty:* 14 full-time (0 women), 19 part-time/adjunct (1 woman). *Students:* 14 full-time (2 women), 40 part-time (8 women); includes 12 minority (1 Black or African American, non-Hispanic/Latino; 4 Asian, non-Hispanic/Latino; 3 Hispanic/Latino; 1 Native Hawaiian or other Pacific Islander, non-Hispanic/Latino; 3 Two or more races, non-Hispanic/Latino), 13 international. Average age 31. 31 applicants, 74% accepted, 8 enrolled. In 2011, 18 master's, 3 doctorates awarded. *Degree requirements:* For master's, comprehensive exam, thesis (for some programs), project; for doctorate, comprehensive exam, thesis/dissertation. *Entrance requirements:* For master's and doctorate, GRE General Test. Additional exam requirements/recommendations for international students: Required—TOEFL (minimum score 550 paper-based; 213 computer-based; 80 iBT), IELTS (minimum score 7). *Application deadline:* For fall admission, 8/1 priority date for domestic students, 5/1 for international students; for spring admission, 12/1 priority date for domestic students, 10/1 for international students. Applications are processed on a rolling basis. Application fee: $60 ($95 for international students). Electronic applications accepted. *Financial support:* In 2011–12, 29 students received support, including 14 research assistantships with partial tuition reimbursements available (averaging $9,415 per year), 15 teaching assistantships with partial tuition reimbursements available (averaging $10,934 per year); institutionally sponsored loans, scholarships/grants, health care benefits, and unspecified assistantships also available. Financial award application deadline: 3/1. *Faculty research:* Dynamics and control systems; energy systems including renewable and nuclear; computational fluid and solid mechanics; structures, materials and manufacturing; vibrations and acoustics. *Total annual research expenditures:* $2.9 million. *Unit head:* Dr. Woosoon Yim, Chair/Professor, 702-895-0956, Fax: 702-895-3936, E-mail: wy@me.unlv.edu. *Application contact:* Graduate College Admissions Evaluator, 702-895-3320, Fax: 702-895-4180, E-mail: gradcollege@unlv.edu. Web site: http://www.me.unlv.edu/.

University of Nevada, Reno, Graduate School, Interdisciplinary Program in Biomedical Engineering, Reno, NV 89557. Offers MS, PhD. Terminal master's awarded for partial completion of doctoral program. *Degree requirements:* For master's, thesis optional; for doctorate, thesis/dissertation. *Entrance requirements:* For master's, GRE General Test (recommended), minimum GPA of 2.75; for doctorate, GRE General Test (recommended), minimum GPA of 3.0. Additional exam requirements/recommendations for international students: Required—TOEFL (minimum score 500 paper-based; 173 computer-based; 61 iBT), IELTS (minimum score 6). Electronic applications accepted. *Faculty research:* Bioengineering, biophysics, biomedical instrumentation, biosensors.

University of New Mexico, Graduate School, School of Engineering, Program in Biomedical Engineering, Albuquerque, NM 87131-2039. Offers PhD. *Students:* 4 full-time (2 women), 4 part-time (3 women); includes 2 minority (both Hispanic/Latino), 3 international. Average age 30. 6 applicants, 67% accepted, 3 enrolled. In 2011, 14 doctorates awarded. Application fee: $50. *Unit head:* Dr. Steven Graves, Program Director, 505-277-5521. *Application contact:* Deborah Kieltyka, Associate Director, Admissions, 505-277-3140, Fax: 505-277-6686, E-mail: deborahk@unm.edu.

The University of North Carolina at Chapel Hill, School of Medicine and Graduate School, Graduate Programs in Medicine, Joint Department of Biomedical Engineering UNC-Chapel Hill and NC State, Chapel Hill, NC 27599. Offers MS, PhD. Terminal master's awarded for partial completion of doctoral program. *Degree requirements:* For master's, comprehensive exam, thesis, ethics seminar; for doctorate, comprehensive exam, thesis/dissertation, qualifying exam, teaching and ethics seminar. *Entrance requirements:* For master's, GRE General Test, minimum GPA of 3.0; for doctorate, GRE General Test, minimum GPA of 3.3. Additional exam requirements/recommendations for international students: Required—TOEFL. Electronic applications accepted. *Faculty research:* Biomedical imaging, rehabilitation engineering, microsystems engineering.

University of Ottawa, Faculty of Graduate and Postdoctoral Studies, Ottawa—Carlton Joint Program in Biomedical Engineering, Ottawa, ON K1N 6N5, Canada. Offers MA Sc. *Degree requirements:* For master's, thesis or alternative. *Entrance requirements:* For master's, honors degree or equivalent, minimum B average.

University of Rhode Island, Graduate School, College of Engineering, Department of Electrical, Computer and Biomedical Engineering, Kingston, RI 02881. Offers MS, PhD, Graduate Certificate. Part-time programs available. *Faculty:* 18 full-time (3 women), 2 part-time/adjunct (1 woman). *Students:* 32 full-time (6 women), 25 part-time (1 woman); includes 8 minority (5 Asian, non-Hispanic/Latino; 3 Hispanic/Latino), 14 international. In 2011, 4 master's, 2 doctorates awarded. *Degree requirements:* For master's, comprehensive exam (for some programs), thesis optional; for doctorate, comprehensive exam, thesis/dissertation. *Entrance requirements:* For master's and doctorate, 2 letters of recommendation. Additional exam requirements/recommendations for international students: Required—TOEFL (minimum score 550 paper-based; 213 computer-based). *Application deadline:* For fall admission, 7/15 for domestic students, 2/1 for international students; for spring admission, 11/15 for domestic students, 7/15 for international students. Application fee: $65. Electronic applications accepted. *Expenses:* Tuition, state resident: full-time $10,432; part-time $580 per credit hour. Tuition, nonresident: full-time $23,130; part-time $1285 per credit hour. *Required fees:* $1362; $36 per credit hour. $35 per semester. One-time fee: $130. *Financial support:* In 2011–12, 9 research assistantships with full and partial tuition reimbursements (averaging $9,465 per year), 5 teaching assistantships with full and partial tuition reimbursements (averaging $8,520 per year) were awarded. Financial award application deadline: 7/15; financial award applicants required to submit FAFSA. *Faculty research:* Biomedical Instrumentation, cardiac physiology and computational modeling, analog/digital CMOS circuits, neural-machine interface, digital circuit design and VLSI testing. *Total annual research expenditures:* $985,856. *Unit head:* Dr. Godi Fischer, Chair, 401-874-5879, Fax: 401-782-6422, E-mail: fischer@ele.uri.edu. *Application contact:* Dr. Godi Fischer, Director of Graduate Studies, 401-874-5879, Fax: 401-782-6422, E-mail: fischer@ele.uri.edu. Web site: http://www.ele.uri.edu/.

University of Rochester, Hajim School of Engineering and Applied Sciences, Center for Entrepreneurship, Rochester, NY 14627-0360. Offers technical entrepreneurship and management (TEAM) (MS), including biomedical engineering, chemical engineering, computer science, electrical and computer engineering, energy and the environment, materials science, mechanical engineering, optics. *Faculty:* 61 full-time (8 women), 5 part-time/adjunct (1 woman). *Students:* 18 full-time (5 women), 3 part-time (1 woman); includes 4 minority (1 Asian, non-Hispanic/Latino; 3 Hispanic/Latino), 12 international. Average age 23. 134 applicants, 48% accepted, 21 enrolled. *Degree requirements:* For master's, comprehensive exam. *Entrance requirements:* For master's, GRE or GMAT, technical concentration of interest, 3 letters of recommendation, personal statement, official transcript. Additional exam requirements/recommendations for international students: Required—TOEFL or IELTS. *Application deadline:* For fall admission, 2/1 for domestic and international students. Applications are processed on a rolling basis. Application fee: $60. Electronic applications accepted. *Expenses: Tuition:* Full-time $41,040. *Financial support:* Career-related internships or fieldwork and scholarships/grants available. Financial award application deadline: 2/1. *Faculty research:* High efficiency solar cells, macromolecular self-assembly, digital signal processing, memory hierarchy management, molecular and physical mechanisms in cell migration. *Unit head:* Duncan T. Moore, Vice Provost for Entrepreneurship, 585-275-5248, Fax: 585-473-6745, E-mail: moore@optics.rochester.edu. *Application contact:* Andrea M. Galati, Executive Director, 585-276-3407, Fax: 585-276-2357, E-mail: andrea.galati@rochester.edu. Web site: http://www.rochester.edu/team.

University of Rochester, Hajim School of Engineering and Applied Sciences, Department of Biomedical Engineering, Rochester, NY 14627. Offers MS, PhD. Part-time programs available. *Faculty:* 3 full-time (1 woman). *Students:* 52 full-time (18 women), 3 part-time; includes 7 minority (5 Asian, non-Hispanic/Latino; 1 Hispanic/Latino; 1 Two or more races, non-Hispanic/Latino), 11 international. 144 applicants, 24% accepted, 12 enrolled. In 2011, 13 master's, 6 doctorates awarded. Terminal master's awarded for partial completion of doctoral program. *Degree requirements:* For master's, comprehensive exam; for doctorate, thesis/dissertation, qualifying exam. *Entrance requirements:* For master's and doctorate, GRE General Test. Additional exam requirements/recommendations for international students: Required—TOEFL. *Application deadline:* For fall admission, 1/1 for domestic students. Application fee: $60. Electronic applications accepted. *Expenses: Tuition:* Full-time $41,040. *Financial support:* Fellowships, research assistantships, teaching assistantships, and tuition waivers (full and partial) available. Financial award application deadline: 1/1. *Faculty research:* Biomechanics, biomedical optics, cell and tissue engineering, medical imaging, neuroengineering. *Unit head:* Dr. Richard Waugh, Chair, 585-275-3768. *Application contact:* Donna Porcelli, Graduate Program Coordinator, 585-275-3891. Web site: http://www.urmc.rochester.edu/bme/graduate/.

University of Saskatchewan, College of Graduate Studies and Research, College of Engineering, Division of Biomedical Engineering, Saskatoon, SK S7N 5A2, Canada. Offers M Eng, M Sc, PhD. *Degree requirements:* For master's, thesis (for some programs); for doctorate, thesis/dissertation. *Entrance requirements:* For master's and doctorate, GRE. Additional exam requirements/recommendations for international students: Required—TOEFL.

University of Southern California, Graduate School, Viterbi School of Engineering, Department of Biomedical Engineering, Los Angeles, CA 90089. Offers biomedical engineering (PhD); medical device and diagnostic engineering (MS); medical imaging and imaging informatics (MS). Postbaccalaureate distance learning degree programs offered (minimal on-campus study). Terminal master's awarded for partial completion of doctoral program. *Degree requirements:* For master's, thesis optional; for doctorate, thesis/dissertation. *Entrance requirements:* For master's and doctorate, GRE General Test. Additional exam requirements/recommendations for international students: Recommended—TOEFL. Electronic applications accepted. *Faculty research:* Medical ultrasound, BioMEMS, neural prosthetics, computational bioengineering, bioengineering of vision, medical devices.

University of South Florida, Graduate School, College of Engineering, Department of Chemical and Biomedical Engineering, Tampa, FL 33620. Offers biomedical engineering (MSBE, MSES, PhD); chemical engineering (MCH, ME, MSCH, MSES, PhD). Part-time programs available. *Faculty:* 14 full-time (2 women), 6 part-time/adjunct (1 woman). *Students:* 70 full-time (11 women), 18 part-time (0 women); includes 25 minority (10 Black or African American, non-Hispanic/Latino; 4 Asian, non-Hispanic/Latino; 11 Hispanic/Latino), 29 international. Average age 30. 87 applicants, 46% accepted, 20 enrolled. In 2011, 18 master's, 5 doctorates awarded. Terminal master's awarded for partial completion of doctoral program. *Degree requirements:* For master's, comprehensive exam, thesis (for some programs); for doctorate, comprehensive exam, thesis/dissertation. *Entrance requirements:* For master's and doctorate, GRE, minimum GPA of 3.0 in last 60 hours of course work, at least two letters of recommendation, bachelor's degree in engineering or science. Additional exam requirements/recommendations for international students: Required—TOEFL (minimum score 550 paper-based; 213 computer-based; 79 iBT) or IELTS (minimum score 6.5). *Application deadline:* For fall admission, 2/15 for domestic students, 1/2 for international students; for spring admission, 10/15 for domestic students, 6/1 for international students. Application fee: $30. Electronic applications accepted. *Financial support:* In 2011–12, 41 students received support, including 29 research assistantships with tuition reimbursements available (averaging $13,171 per year), 12 teaching assistantships with tuition reimbursements available (averaging $14,017 per year); unspecified assistantships also available. Financial award applicants required to submit FAFSA. *Faculty research:* Biomedical engineering, supercritical fluid technology, advanced materials, surface and interfacial science, alternative and renewable energy. *Total annual research expenditures:* $1.2 million. *Unit head:* Dr. Venkat R. Bhethanabotla, Chair, 813-974-3997, E-mail: bhethana@usf.edu. *Application contact:* Dr. Vinay Gupta, Graduate Admissions Coordinator for Chemical Engineering, 813-974-0851, Fax: 813-974-3651, E-mail: vkgupta@usf.edu. Web site: http://che.eng.usf.edu/.

The University of Tennessee, Graduate School, College of Engineering, Department of Mechanical, Aerospace and Biomedical Engineering, Program in Biomedical Engineering, Knoxville, TN 37996. Offers MS, PhD, MS/PhD. Part-time programs available. Postbaccalaureate distance learning degree programs offered (minimal on-campus study). *Faculty:* 7 full-time (1 woman). *Students:* 34 full-time (8 women), 6 part-time (1 woman); includes 5 minority (3 Black or African American, non-Hispanic/Latino; 2 Asian, non-Hispanic/Latino), 13 international. Average age 28. 75 applicants, 27% accepted, 12 enrolled. In 2011, 5 master's, 1 doctorate awarded. *Degree requirements:* For master's, thesis or alternative; for doctorate, comprehensive exam, thesis/dissertation. *Entrance requirements:* For master's, GRE General Test (for MS students pursuing research thesis), minimum GPA of 2.7 (for U.S. degree holders), 3.0 (for international degree holders); 3 references; statement of purpose; for doctorate, College requires GRE General Test for all PhD candidates, minimum GPA of 3.0 on previous graduate course work; 3 references; statement of purpose. Additional exam requirements/recommendations for international students: Required—TOEFL (minimum score 550 paper-based; 213 computer-based). *Application deadline:* For fall admission, 2/1 priority date for domestic students, 2/1 for international students; for spring admission, 6/15 for domestic and international students. Applications are processed on a rolling basis. Application fee: $35. Electronic applications accepted. *Expenses:* Tuition, state resident: full-time $8332; part-time $464 per credit hour. Tuition, nonresident: full-time $25,174; part-time $1400 per credit hour. *Required fees:* $1162; $56 per credit hour. Tuition and fees vary according to program. *Financial support:* In 2011–12, 26 students received support, including 16 research assistantships with full tuition reimbursements available (averaging $21,377 per year), 8 teaching assistantships with full tuition reimbursements available (averaging $17,888 per year); fellowships with full tuition reimbursements available, career-related internships or fieldwork, Federal Work-Study, institutionally sponsored loans, health care benefits, and unspecified assistantships also available. Financial award application deadline: 2/1; financial award applicants required to submit FAFSA. *Faculty research:* Bioimaging, biomechanics, biorobotics, biosensors, biomaterials. *Unit head:* Dr. William Hamel, Head, 865-974-5115, Fax: 865-974-5274, E-mail: whamel@utk.edu. *Application contact:* Dr. Gary V. Smith, Associate Head, 865-974-5271, Fax: 865-974-5274, E-mail: gvsmith@utk.edu. Web site: http://www.engr.utk.edu/mabe.

The University of Texas at Austin, Graduate School, Cockrell School of Engineering, Department of Biomedical Engineering, Austin, TX 78712-1111. Offers MS, PhD, MD/PhD. MD/PhD offered jointly with The University of Texas Medical Branch. Part-time programs available. *Degree requirements:* For master's, thesis optional; for doctorate, comprehensive exam, thesis/dissertation. *Entrance requirements:* For master's and doctorate, GRE General Test. Additional exam requirements/recommendations for international students: Required—TOEFL (minimum score 550 paper-based; 213 computer-based). *Application deadline:* For fall admission, 12/15 for domestic and international students; for spring admission, 10/1 for domestic and international students. Application fee: $50 ($75 for international students). Electronic applications accepted. *Financial support:* Fellowships with full and partial tuition reimbursements, research assistantships with full and partial tuition reimbursements, teaching assistantships with full and partial tuition reimbursements, Federal Work-Study, institutionally sponsored loans, scholarships/grants, health care benefits, and unspecified assistantships available. Financial award application deadline: 12/15. *Faculty research:* Biomechanics, bioengineering, tissue engineering, tissue optics, biothermal studies. *Unit head:* Dr. Nicholas A. Peppas, Chair, 512-471-6644. *Application contact:* Krystal Peralez, Graduate Coordinator, 512-475-8500, E-mail: krystal.peralez@austin.utexas.edu. Web site: http://www.bme.utexas.edu.

The University of Texas at Dallas, Erik Jonsson School of Engineering and Computer Science, Department of Bioengineering, Richardson, TX 75080. Offers biomedical engineering (MS, PhD). *Faculty:* 5 full-time (2 women). *Students:* 33 full-time (15 women), 2 part-time (1 woman); includes 4 minority (3 Asian, non-Hispanic/Latino; 1 Two or more races, non-Hispanic/Latino), 24 international. Average age 26. 69 applicants, 39% accepted, 19 enrolled. In 2011, 1 degree awarded. *Degree requirements:* For master's, thesis (for some programs); for doctorate, comprehensive exam, thesis/dissertation. *Entrance requirements:* For master's, GRE (minimum scores of 500 in verbal, 700 in quantitative and 4 in analytical writing), minimum GPA of 3.0 in upper-division quantitative course work; for doctorate, GRE (minimum scores of 500 in verbal, 700 in quantitative and 4 in analytical writing), minimum GPA of 3.5 in upper-division quantitative course work. Additional exam requirements/recommendations for international students: Required—TOEFL (minimum score 550 paper-based; 215 computer-based). *Application deadline:* For fall admission, 7/15 for domestic students, 5/1 for international students; for spring admission, 11/15 for domestic students, 9/1 for international students. Applications are processed on a rolling basis. Application fee: $50 ($100 for international students). Electronic applications accepted. *Expenses:* Tuition, state resident: full-time $11,170; part-time $620.56 per credit hour. Tuition, nonresident: full-time $20,212; part-time $1122.89 per credit hour. *Financial support:* In 2011–12, 19 students received support, including 3 fellowships (averaging $5,000 per year), 13 research assistantships with partial tuition reimbursements available (averaging $19,419 per year); career-related internships or fieldwork, Federal Work-Study, institutionally sponsored loans, scholarships/grants, and unspecified assistantships also available. Support available to part-time students. Financial award application deadline: 4/30; financial award applicants required to submit FAFSA. *Faculty research:* Bio-nanotechnology, organic electronics, system-level design for medical devices, computational geometry and biomedical computing. *Unit head:* Dr. Mathukumalli Vidyasagar, Head, 972-883-4679, E-mail: m.vidyasagar@utdallas.edu. *Application contact:* Laranda D. Eakin, Administrative Services Officer, 972-883-4657, E-mail: laranda.eakin@utdallas.edu. Web site: http://be.utdallas.edu/.

The University of Texas at San Antonio, College of Engineering, UTSA/UTHSCSA Joint Graduate Program in Biomedical Engineering, San Antonio, TX 78249. Offers MS, PhD. Part-time programs available. *Faculty:* 37 full-time (3 women), 26 part-time/adjunct (1 woman). *Students:* 57 full-time (22 women), 8 part-time (1 woman); includes 29 minority (2 Black or African American, non-Hispanic/Latino; 16 Asian, non-Hispanic/Latino; 11 Hispanic/Latino), 17 international. Average age 29. 83 applicants, 36% accepted, 18 enrolled. In 2011, 6 master's, 4 doctorates awarded. Terminal master's awarded for partial completion of doctoral program. *Degree requirements:* For master's, comprehensive exam, thesis; for doctorate, comprehensive exam, thesis/dissertation. *Entrance requirements:* For master's, GRE, three letters of recommendation, statement of purpose; for doctorate, GRE, resume, three letters of recommendation, statement of purpose. Additional exam requirements/recommendations for international students: Required—TOEFL (minimum score 550 paper-based; 79 iBT), IELTS (minimum score 6.5). *Application deadline:* For fall admission, 2/1 for domestic and international students; for spring admission, 10/1 for domestic and international students. Applications are processed on a rolling basis. Application fee: $45 ($85 for international students). Electronic applications accepted. *Expenses:* Tuition, state resident: full-time $3148; part-time $2176 per semester. Tuition, nonresident: full-time $8782; part-time $5932 per semester. *Required fees:* $719 per semester. *Financial support:* In 2011–12, 37 students received support, including 21 fellowships with full tuition reimbursements available (averaging $21,000 per year), 16 research assistantships with full tuition reimbursements available (averaging $21,000 per year), 1 teaching assistantship (averaging $5,000 per year); scholarships/grants, health care benefits, unspecified assistantships, and student health insurance premiums also available. *Faculty research:* Biomaterials, biomaterial-cell/tissue interactions; cardiovascular, orthopaedic and ocular biomechanics; drug delivery methods and devices; computational intelligence and neural networks; failure/fatigue analysis of materials; medical devices and implants; methods, devices and biosensors; medical imaging and biophotonics; nano-manipulation of materials and tissues; neuroscience; signal and digital image processing; tissue engineering and cellular engineering. *Total annual research expenditures:* $3.4 million. *Unit head:* Dr. Joo L. Ong, Department Chair, 210-458-7084, Fax: 210-458-7007, E-mail: anson.ong@utsa.edu. *Application contact:* Dr. Mark Appleford, Graduate Advisor of Record, 210-458-6840, Fax: 210-458-7007, E-mail: mark.appleford@utsa.edu. Web site: http://engineering.utsa.edu/BME/BME_Program.

The University of Texas Southwestern Medical Center, Southwestern Graduate School of Biomedical Sciences, Division of Basic Science, Biomedical Engineering Program, Dallas, TX 75390. Offers MS, PhD. Programs offered jointly with The University of Texas at Arlington. *Degree requirements:* For master's, comprehensive exam or thesis; for doctorate, comprehensive exam, thesis/dissertation. *Entrance requirements:* For master's, GRE General Test, minimum GPA of 3.0; for doctorate, GRE General Test, minimum GPA of 3.4. Additional exam requirements/recommendations for international students: Required—TOEFL. Electronic applications accepted. *Faculty research:* Noninvasive image analysis, biomaterials development, rehabilitation engineering, biomechanics, bioinstrumentation.

The University of Toledo, College of Graduate Studies, College of Engineering and College of Medicine and Life Sciences, PhD Program in Biomedical Engineering, Toledo, OH 43606-3390. Offers PhD. *Degree requirements:* For doctorate, thesis/dissertation, qualifying exam. *Entrance requirements:* For doctorate, GRE General Test, minimum GPA of 3.3. Additional exam requirements/recommendations for international students: Required—TOEFL (minimum score 550 paper-based; 213 computer-based; 80 iBT). Electronic applications accepted. *Faculty research:* Biomechanics, biomaterials, tissue engineering, artificial organs, biosensors.

University of Toronto, School of Graduate Studies, Faculty of Applied Science and Engineering, Institute of Biomaterials and Biomedical Engineering, Toronto, ON M5S 1A1, Canada. Offers biomedical engineering (MA Sc, PhD); clinical engineering (MH Sc, PhD). Part-time programs available. *Degree requirements:* For master's, thesis (for some programs), research project (MH Sc), oral presentation (MA Sc); for doctorate, thesis/dissertation, qualifying exam. *Entrance requirements:* For master's, minimum A-average; bachelor's degree or equivalent in engineering, physical or biological science (for MA Sc), applied science or engineering (for MH Sc); for doctorate, master's degree in engineering, engineering science, medicine, dentistry, or a physical or biological science. Additional exam requirements/recommendations for international students: Required—TOEFL (minimum score 600 paper-based; 260 computer-based), TWE (minimum score 4), IELTS, Michigan English Language Assessment Battery, or COPE. Electronic applications accepted.

University of Vermont, Graduate College, College of Engineering and Mathematics, Program in Biomedical Engineering, Burlington, VT 05405. Offers MS. *Students:* 5 (3 women), 1 international. 22 applicants, 23% accepted, 1 enrolled. In 2011, 1 master's awarded. *Degree requirements:* For master's, thesis. *Entrance requirements:* For master's, GRE General Test. Additional exam requirements/recommendations for international students: Required—TOEFL (minimum score 550 paper-based; 213 computer-based; 80 iBT). *Application deadline:* Applications are processed on a rolling basis. Electronic applications accepted. *Financial support:* Fellowships, research assistantships, and teaching assistantships available. Financial award application deadline: 3/1.

University of Virginia, School of Engineering and Applied Science, Department of Biomedical Engineering, Charlottesville, VA 22903. Offers ME, MS, PhD. *Faculty:* 7 full-time (0 women). *Students:* 70 full-time (24 women), 3 part-time (1 woman); includes 9 minority (1 Black or African American, non-Hispanic/Latino; 7 Asian, non-Hispanic/Latino; 1 Two or more races, non-Hispanic/Latino), 13 international. Average age 26. 235 applicants, 18% accepted, 11 enrolled. In 2011, 1 master's, 17 doctorates awarded. *Degree requirements:* For master's, project or thesis; for doctorate, thesis/dissertation. *Entrance requirements:* For master's, GRE General Test, 3 letters of recommendation; for doctorate, GRE General Test, 3 letters of recommendation, essay. Additional exam requirements/recommendations for international students: Required—TOEFL (minimum score 600 paper-based; 250 computer-based; 90 iBT), IELTS (minimum score 7). *Application deadline:* For fall admission, 8/1 for domestic students, 4/1 for international students; for winter admission, 12/1 for domestic students, 8/1 for international students; for spring admission, 5/1 for domestic students, 1/1 for international students. Applications are processed on a rolling basis. Application fee: $60. Electronic applications accepted. *Financial support:* Fellowships, research assistantships, and teaching assistantships available. Financial award application deadline: 1/15; financial award applicants required to submit FAFSA. *Faculty research:* Cardiopulmonary and neural engineering, cellular engineering, image processing, orthopedics and rehabilitation engineering. *Unit head:* Frederick Epstein, Chair, 434-924-5101, Fax: 434-982-3870, E-mail: bme-dept@virginia.edu. *Application contact:* Jeffrey Holmes, Director of Graduate Programs, 434-243-6906, Fax: 434-982-3870, E-mail: bmegrad@virginia.edu. Web site: http://bme.virginia.edu/grad/.

University of Washington, Graduate School, College of Engineering and School of Medicine, Department of Bioengineering, Seattle, WA 98195-5061. Offers bioengineering (MS, PhD); bioengineering and nanotechnology (PhD); medical engineering (MME); pharmaceutical bioengineering (MS). Evening/weekend programs available. Postbaccalaureate distance learning degree programs offered (no on-campus study). *Faculty:* 35 full-time (10 women), 11 part-time/adjunct (2 women). *Students:* 116 full-time (46 women), 63 part-time (27 women); includes 48 minority (2 Black or African American, non-Hispanic/Latino; 1 American Indian or Alaska Native, non-Hispanic/Latino; 42 Asian, non-Hispanic/Latino; 3 Hispanic/Latino), 30 international. Average age 26. 495 applicants, 18% accepted, 35 enrolled. In 2011, 14 master's, 12 doctorates awarded. *Degree requirements:* For master's, comprehensive exam, thesis; for doctorate, comprehensive exam, thesis/dissertation, qualifying exam, general exam, thesis defense. *Entrance requirements:* For master's and doctorate, GRE General Test, minimum GPA of 3.0, transcripts, statement of purpose, letters of recommendation. Additional exam requirements/recommendations for international students: Required—TOEFL (minimum score 580 paper-based; 237 computer-based; 92 iBT); Recommended—IELTS (minimum score 7). *Application deadline:* For fall admission, 12/15 priority date for domestic students, 12/1 for international students. Applications are processed on a rolling basis. Application fee: $75. Electronic applications accepted. *Expenses:* Contact institution. *Financial support:* In 2011–12, 177 students received support, including 18 fellowships with full tuition reimbursements available (averaging $21,330 per year), 125 research assistantships with full tuition reimbursements available (averaging $19,224 per year), 22 teaching assistantships with full tuition reimbursements available (averaging $19,224 per year); Federal Work-Study, institutionally sponsored loans, traineeships, health care benefits, and tuition waivers (full) also available. Support available to part-time students. Financial award application deadline: 12/15; financial award applicants required to submit FAFSA. *Faculty research:* Biomaterials and tissue engineering; global health, distributed diagnosis and home healthcare; bioinstrumentation; molecular bioengineering; imaging and image-guided therapy. *Total annual research expenditures:* $22.6 million. *Unit head:* Dr. Paul Yager, Professor/Chair, 206-685-2000, Fax: 206-685-3300, E-mail: yagerp@u.washington.edu. *Application contact:* Dorian Varga, Senior Academic Counselor, 206-685-3494, Fax: 206-685-3300, E-mail: dst@u.washington.edu. Web site: http://depts.washington.edu.bioe.

University of Wisconsin–Madison, Graduate School, College of Engineering, Department of Biomedical Engineering, Madison, WI 53706. Offers MS, PhD. Part-time programs available. *Faculty:* 23 full-time (7 women), 67 part-time/adjunct (14 women). *Students:* 82 full-time (33 women), 11 part-time (1 woman); includes 19 minority (2 Black or African American, non-Hispanic/Latino; 10 Asian, non-Hispanic/Latino; 7 Hispanic/Latino), 16 international. Average age 25. 410 applicants, 14% accepted, 22 enrolled. In 2011, 23 master's, 10 doctorates awarded. Terminal master's awarded for partial completion of doctoral program. *Degree requirements:* For master's, thesis optional; for doctorate, comprehensive exam, thesis/dissertation, 32 credits of coursework. *Entrance requirements:* For master's and doctorate, GRE, bachelor's degree in engineering or a physical science (chemistry or physics). Additional exam requirements/recommendations for international students: Recommended—TOEFL (minimum score 550 paper-based; 213 computer-based; 80 iBT), IELTS (minimum score 6). *Application deadline:* For fall admission, 12/31 for domestic and international students; for spring admission, 10/1 for domestic and international students. Application fee: $56. Electronic applications accepted. *Expenses:* Tuition, state resident: full-time $10,296; part-time $643.51 per credit. Tuition, nonresident: full-time $24,054; part-time $1503.40 per credit. *Required fees:* $70.06 per credit. Tuition and fees vary according to course load, campus/location, program and reciprocity agreements. *Financial support:* In 2011–12, 77 students received support, including 2 fellowships with full tuition reimbursements available (averaging $22,260 per year), 48 research assistantships with full tuition reimbursements available (averaging $40,800 per year), 7 teaching assistantships with full tuition reimbursements available (averaging $28,175 per year); career-related internships or fieldwork, Federal Work-Study, scholarships/grants, traineeships, and health care benefits also available. *Faculty research:* Biomaterials; bioinstrumentation; cellular scale; biomechanics; biomedical imaging; ergonomics; design, fabrication, and testing of novel micro fabrication techniques; magnetic resonance; tissue engineering; biomedical optics. *Total annual research expenditures:* $10.2 million. *Unit head:* Dr. Elizabeth Meyerand, Professor and Chair, 608-263-1685, Fax: 608-263-1352, E-mail: bme@engr.wisc.edu. *Application contact:* Staci Rubenzer, Graduate Admissions Coordinator, 608-890-2248, Fax: 608-890-2204, E-mail: srubenzer@engr.wisc.edu. Web site: http://www.engr.wisc.edu/bme.html.

Vanderbilt University, School of Engineering and Graduate School, Department of Biomedical Engineering, Nashville, TN 37240-1001. Offers M Eng, MS, PhD, MD/PhD. *Faculty:* 16 full-time (1 woman), 10 part-time/adjunct (0 women). *Students:* 67 full-time (24 women); includes 11 minority (2 Black or African American, non-Hispanic/Latino; 4 Asian, non-Hispanic/Latino; 2 Hispanic/Latino; 3 Two or more races, non-Hispanic/Latino), 11 international. Average age 26. 186 applicants, 13% accepted, 11 enrolled. In 2011, 8 master's, 4 doctorates awarded. *Degree requirements:* For master's, thesis (for some programs); for doctorate, thesis/dissertation. *Entrance requirements:* For master's, GRE General Test (for all except M Eng); for doctorate, GRE General Test. Additional exam requirements/recommendations for international students: Required—TOEFL. *Application deadline:* For fall admission, 1/15 for domestic and international students; for spring admission, 11/1 for domestic and international students. Application fee: $0. Electronic applications accepted. *Financial support:* In 2011–12, 2 fellowships with full tuition reimbursements (averaging $30,000 per year), 31 research assistantships with full tuition reimbursements (averaging $27,252 per year), 11 teaching assistantships with full tuition reimbursements (averaging $26,256 per year) were awarded; institutionally sponsored loans, scholarships/grants, traineeships, and tuition waivers (partial) also available. Support available to part-time students. Financial award application deadline: 1/15. *Faculty research:* Bio-medical imaging, cell bioengineering, biomedical optics, technology-guided therapy, laser-tissue interaction and spectroscopy. *Total annual research expenditures:* $10.5 million. *Unit head:* Dr. Todd D. Giorgio, Chair, 615-322-3756, Fax: 615-343-7919, E-mail: todd.d.giorgio@vanderbilt.edu. *Application contact:* Dr. E. Duco Jansen, Director of Graduate Studies, 615-343-1911, Fax: 615-343-7919, E-mail: duco.jansen@vanderbilt.edu. Web site: http://www.bme.vanderbilt.edu/.

Virginia Commonwealth University, Graduate School, School of Engineering, Department of Biomedical Engineering, Richmond, VA 23284-9005. Offers MS, PhD, MD/PhD. *Degree requirements:* For master's, thesis; for doctorate, thesis/dissertation, comprehensive oral and written exams. *Entrance requirements:* For master's and doctorate, GRE General Test. Additional exam requirements/recommendations for international students: Required—TOEFL (minimum score 600 paper-based; 250 computer-based; 100 iBT). Electronic applications accepted. *Expenses:* Tuition, state resident: full-time $9133; part-time $507 per credit. Tuition, nonresident: full-time $18,777; part-time $1043 per credit. *Required fees:* $77 per credit. Tuition and fees vary according to degree level, campus/location, program and student level. *Faculty research:* Clinical instrumentation, mathematical modeling, neurosciences, radiation physics and rehabilitation.

Virginia Polytechnic Institute and State University, Graduate School, College of Engineering, Virginia Tech-Wake Forest University School of Biomedical Engineering and Sciences, Blacksburg, VA 24061. Offers MS, PhD. Terminal master's awarded for partial completion of doctoral program. *Degree requirements:* For master's, comprehensive exam (for some programs), thesis (for some programs); for doctorate, comprehensive exam (for some programs), thesis/dissertation (for some programs), clinical rotation. *Entrance requirements:* For master's and doctorate, GRE. Additional exam requirements/recommendations for international students: Required—TOEFL (minimum score 550 paper-based; 213 computer-based). *Application deadline:* For fall admission, 7/1 for domestic and international students; for spring admission, 12/1 for domestic and international students. Applications are processed on a rolling basis. Application fee: $65. Electronic applications accepted. *Expenses:* Tuition, state resident: full-time $10,048; part-time $558.25 per credit hour. Tuition, nonresident: full-time $19,497; part-time $1083.25 per credit hour. *Required fees:* $405 per semester. Tuition and fees vary according to course load, campus/location and program. *Financial support:* Fellowships with full tuition reimbursements, research assistantships with full tuition reimbursements, teaching assistantships with full tuition reimbursements, career-related internships or fieldwork, Federal Work-Study, scholarships/grants, health care benefits, and unspecified assistantships available. Financial award application deadline: 7/1. *Faculty research:* Biomechanics, cell and tissue engineering, imaging and signal analysis. *Unit head:* Dr. Stefan M. Duma, Unit Head, 540-231-8191, Fax: 540-231-9100, E-mail: duma@vt.edu. *Application contact:* Clay Gabler, Application Contact, 540-231-

7190, Fax: 540-231-9100, E-mail: gabler@vt.edu. Web site: http://www.me.vt.edu/overview/sbes.pdf.

Wake Forest University, Virginia Tech-Wake Forest University School of Biomedical Engineering and Sciences, Winston-Salem, NC 27109. Offers biomedical engineering (MS, PhD); DVM/PhD; MD/PhD. Terminal master's awarded for partial completion of doctoral program. *Degree requirements:* For master's, comprehensive exam, thesis; for doctorate, comprehensive exam, thesis/dissertation. *Entrance requirements:* For master's and doctorate, GRE, 3 letters of recommendation. Additional exam requirements/recommendations for international students: Required—TOEFL (minimum score 603 paper-based; 250 computer-based). Electronic applications accepted. *Faculty research:* Biomechanics, cell and tissue engineering, medical imaging, medical physics.

Washington University in St. Louis, School of Engineering and Applied Science, Department of Biomedical Engineering, St. Louis, MO 63130-4899. Offers MS, D Sc, PhD. Terminal master's awarded for partial completion of doctoral program. *Degree requirements:* For master's, thesis optional; for doctorate, thesis/dissertation. *Entrance requirements:* For master's, GRE, minimum GPA of 3.0; for doctorate, GRE General Test, minimum GPA of 3.5. Additional exam requirements/recommendations for international students: Required—TOEFL. Electronic applications accepted. *Faculty research:* Cell and tissue engineering, molecular engineering, neural engineering.

Wayne State University, College of Engineering, Department of Biomedical Engineering, Detroit, MI 48202. Offers MS, PhD. *Students:* 95 full-time (37 women), 51 part-time (21 women); includes 18 minority (1 Black or African American, non-Hispanic/Latino; 14 Asian, non-Hispanic/Latino; 1 Hispanic/Latino; 2 Two or more races, non-Hispanic/Latino), 48 international. Average age 28. 168 applicants, 57% accepted, 32 enrolled. In 2011, 57 master's, 5 doctorates awarded. *Degree requirements:* For master's, thesis optional; for doctorate, thesis/dissertation. *Entrance requirements:* For master's, GRE (recommended), minimum undergraduate GPA of 3.0, one-page statement of purpose, completion of prerequisite coursework in calculus and engineering physics; for doctorate, GRE, personal statement, minimum undergraduate GPA of 3.5, undergraduate major or substantial specialized work in proposed doctoral major field. Additional exam requirements/recommendations for international students: Required—TOEFL (minimum score 550 paper-based; 213 computer-based); Recommended—TWE (minimum score 5.5). *Application deadline:* For fall admission, 6/1 priority date for domestic students, 5/1 for international students; for winter admission, 10/1 priority date for domestic students, 9/1 for international students; for spring admission, 2/1 priority date for domestic students, 1/1 for international students. Applications are processed on a rolling basis. Application fee: $50. Electronic applications accepted. *Expenses:* Tuition, state resident: part-time $512.85 per credit. Tuition, nonresident: part-time $1132.65 per credit. *Required fees:* $26.60 per credit. $199.65 per semester. Tuition and fees vary according to course load and program. *Financial support:* In 2011–12, 31 students received support, including 3 fellowships with tuition reimbursements available (averaging $17,250 per year), 5 research assistantships with tuition reimbursements available (averaging $16,929 per year), 6 teaching assistantships with tuition reimbursements available (averaging $17,492 per year); scholarships/grants, health care benefits, and unspecified assistantships also available. Support available to part-time students. *Faculty research:* Injury and orthopedic biomechanics, neurophysiology of pain, smart sensors, biomaterials and imaging. *Total annual research expenditures:* $2.7 million. *Unit head:* Dr. Albert King, Chair, 313-577-1347, Fax: 313-577-8333, E-mail: king@rrb.eng.wayne.edu. *Application contact:* 313-577-1345, Fax: 313-577-8333, E-mail: bme@rrb.eng.wayne.edu. Web site: http://www.eng.wayne.edu/page.php?id=12.

Worcester Polytechnic Institute, Graduate Studies and Research, Department of Biomedical Engineering, Worcester, MA 01609-2280. Offers biomedical engineering (M Eng, MS, PhD, Graduate Certificate). Part-time and evening/weekend programs available. *Faculty:* 9 full-time (2 women), 3 part-time/adjunct (0 women). *Students:* 34 full-time (8 women), 22 part-time (5 women); includes 7 minority (1 Black or African American, non-Hispanic/Latino; 6 Asian, non-Hispanic/Latino), 12 international. 117 applicants, 57% accepted, 30 enrolled. In 2011, 14 master's, 4 doctorates awarded. Terminal master's awarded for partial completion of doctoral program. *Degree requirements:* For master's, thesis optional; for doctorate, comprehensive exam, thesis/dissertation. *Entrance requirements:* For master's and doctorate, GRE General Test, 3 letters of recommendation, statement of purpose. Additional exam requirements/recommendations for international students: Required—TOEFL (minimum score 563 paper-based; 223 computer-based; 84 iBT), IELTS (minimum score 7). *Application deadline:* For fall admission, 1/1 priority date for domestic students, 1/1 for international students. Application fee: $70. Electronic applications accepted. *Financial support:* Research assistantships, teaching assistantships, career-related internships or fieldwork, institutionally sponsored loans, scholarships/grants, and unspecified assistantships available. Financial award application deadline: 1/1; financial award applicants required to submit FAFSA. *Faculty research:* Biomedical sensors and instrumentation, biomechanics, nuclear magnetic resonance image and spectroscopy, medical imaging, biomaterial/tissue interactions, engineering and regenerative medicine, biosignal processing. *Unit head:* Dr. Ki H Chon, Head, 508-831-5447, Fax: 508-831-5541, E-mail: kichon@wpi.edu. *Application contact:* Dr. Marsha Rolle, Graduate Coordinator, 508-831-5447, Fax: 508-831-5447, E-mail: mrolle@wpi.edu. Web site: http://www.wpi.edu/Academics/Depts/BME/.

Wright State University, School of Graduate Studies, College of Engineering and Computer Science, Programs in Engineering, Program in Biomedical and Human Factors Engineering, Dayton, OH 45435. Offers biomedical engineering (MSE); human factors engineering (MSE). Part-time programs available. *Degree requirements:* For master's, thesis or course option alternative. *Entrance requirements:* Additional exam requirements/recommendations for international students: Required—TOEFL. *Faculty research:* Medical imaging, functional electrical stimulation, implantable aids, man-machine interfaces, expert systems.

Yale University, Graduate School of Arts and Sciences, School of Engineering and Applied Science, Department of Biomedical Engineering, New Haven, CT 06520. Offers MS, PhD. *Faculty research:* Biomedical imaging and biosignals; biomechanics; biomolecular engineering and biotechnology.

Biotechnology

Albany College of Pharmacy and Health Sciences, School of Health Sciences, Albany, NY 12208. Offers biotechnology (MS); cytotechnology and molecular cytology (MS); health outcomes research (MS). *Faculty:* 8 full-time (3 women), 6 part-time/adjunct (5 women). *Students:* 47 full-time (22 women), 2 part-time (both women); includes 1 minority (Asian, non-Hispanic/Latino), 29 international. 49 applicants, 94% accepted, 32 enrolled. *Degree requirements:* For master's, thesis. *Entrance requirements:* For master's, GRE, minimum GPA of 3.0. Additional exam requirements/recommendations for international students: Required—TOEFL (minimum score 474 paper-based; 84 iBT). *Application deadline:* For fall admission, 3/1 for domestic and international students. Applications are processed on a rolling basis. Application fee: $75. Electronic applications accepted. *Expenses: Tuition:* Full-time $29,100; part-time $855 per credit hour. *Required fees:* $1230; $680. Tuition and fees vary according to degree level. *Financial support:* Federal Work-Study and scholarships/grants available. Support available to part-time students. Financial award application deadline: 3/1; financial award applicants required to submit FAFSA. *Unit head:* Dr. Hassan El-Fawal, Dean, 888-203-8010. *Application contact:* Donna Myers, Director of Pharmacy and Graduate Admissions, 518-694-7186, Fax: 518-694-7929, E-mail: graduate@acphs.edu.

American University, College of Arts and Sciences, Department of Biology, Washington, DC 20016-8007. Offers applied science (MS), including biotechnology, environmental science assessment; biology (MA, MS). Part-time programs available. *Faculty:* 10 full-time (4 women), 3 part-time/adjunct (2 women). *Students:* 8 full-time (2 women), 4 part-time (1 woman); includes 4 minority (1 Black or African American, non-Hispanic/Latino; 3 Asian, non-Hispanic/Latino), 1 international. Average age 25. 15 applicants, 60% accepted, 6 enrolled. In 2011, 9 master's awarded. *Degree requirements:* For master's, comprehensive exam, thesis (for some programs). *Entrance requirements:* For master's, GRE General Test, GRE Subject Test. Additional exam requirements/recommendations for international students: Required—TOEFL. *Application deadline:* For fall admission, 2/1 for domestic students; for spring admission, 10/1 for domestic students. Application fee: $80. *Expenses: Tuition:* Full-time $24,264; part-time $1348 per credit hour. *Required fees:* $430. Tuition and fees vary according to course load and program. *Financial support:* Fellowships, research assistantships with tuition reimbursements, teaching assistantships with tuition reimbursements, career-related internships or fieldwork, Federal Work-Study, and institutionally sponsored loans available. Financial award application deadline: 2/1. *Faculty research:* Neurobiology, cave biology, population genetics, vertebrate physiology. *Unit head:* Dr. David Carlini, Chair, 202-885-2194, Fax: 202-885-2182, E-mail: carlini@american.edu. *Application contact:* Kathleen Clowery, Director, Graduate Admissions, 202-885-3621, Fax: 202-885-1505, E-mail: clowery@american.edu. Web site: http://www.american.edu/cas/biology/.

Arizona State University, Sandra Day O'Connor College of Law, Tempe, AZ 85287-7906. Offers biotechnology and genomics (LL M); global legal studies (LL M); law (JD); law (customized) (LL M); legal studies (MLS); tribal policy, law and government (LL M); JD/MBA; JD/MD; JD/PhD. JD/MD offered jointly with Mayo Medical School. *Accreditation:* ABA. *Faculty:* 62 full-time (23 women), 68 part-time/adjunct (18 women). *Students:* 615 full-time (247 women), 32 part-time (17 women); includes 148 minority (11 Black or African American, non-Hispanic/Latino; 31 American Indian or Alaska Native, non-Hispanic/Latino; 22 Asian, non-Hispanic/Latino; 67 Hispanic/Latino; 17 Two or more races, non-Hispanic/Latino), 11 international. Average age 28. 2,334 applicants, 28% accepted, 168 enrolled. In 2011, 19 master's, 200 doctorates awarded. *Degree requirements:* For doctorate, papers. *Entrance requirements:* For master's, bachelor's degree and JD (for LL M); for doctorate, LSAT, bachelor's degree. Additional exam requirements/recommendations for international students: Required—TOEFL (minimum score 550 paper-based; 80 iBT). *Application deadline:* For fall admission, 2/1 priority date for domestic students, 2/1 for international students. Applications are processed on a rolling basis. Application fee: $60. Electronic applications accepted. *Expenses:* Contact institution. *Financial support:* In 2011–12, 322 students received support. Research assistantships, teaching assistantships, career-related internships or fieldwork, Federal Work-Study, institutionally sponsored loans, scholarships/grants, tuition waivers (full and partial), and unspecified assistantships available. Financial award application deadline: 3/15; financial award applicants required to submit FAFSA. *Faculty research:* Emerging technologies and the law, Indian law, law and philosophy, international law, intellectual property. *Total annual research expenditures:* $925,469. *Unit head:* Douglas Sylvester, Dean/Professor, 480-965-6188, Fax: 480-965-6521, E-mail: douglas.sylvester@asu.edu. *Application contact:* Chitra Damania, Director of Operations, 480-965-1474, Fax: 480-727-7930, E-mail: law.admissions@asu.edu. Web site: http://www.law.asu.edu/.

Arkansas State University, Graduate School, College of Sciences and Mathematics, Department of Biological Sciences, Jonesboro, State University, AR 72467. Offers biological sciences (MA); biology (MS); biology education (MSE, SCCT); biotechnology (PSM). Part-time programs available. *Faculty:* 22 full-time (7 women). *Students:* 13 full-time (8 women), 22 part-time (14 women); includes 2 minority (1 Black or African American, non-Hispanic/Latino; 1 American Indian or Alaska Native, non-Hispanic/Latino), 9 international. Average age 27. 31 applicants, 71% accepted, 13 enrolled. In 2011, 14 master's awarded. *Degree requirements:* For master's, comprehensive exam, thesis (for some programs); for SCCT, comprehensive exam. *Entrance requirements:* For master's, GRE General Test, appropriate bachelor's degree, letters of reference, interview, official transcripts, immunization records, statement of educational objectives and career goals, teaching certificate (MSE); for SCCT, GRE General Test or MAT, interview, master's degree, letters of reference, official transcript, personal statement, immunization records. Additional exam requirements/recommendations for international students: Required—TOEFL (minimum score 550 paper-based; 213 computer-based; 79 iBT), IELTS (minimum score 6), PTE: Pearson Test of English Academic (minimum score 56). *Application deadline:* For fall admission, 7/1 for domestic and international students; for spring admission, 11/15 for domestic students, 11/14 for international students. Applications are processed on a rolling basis. Application fee: $30 ($40 for international students). Electronic applications accepted. *Expenses:* Tuition, state resident: full-time $4044; part-time $225 per credit hour. Tuition, nonresident: full-time $8087; part-time $449 per credit hour. *Required fees:* $936; $52 per credit hour. $25 per term. One-time fee: $30. Tuition and fees vary according to course load and program. *Financial support:* In 2011–12, 17 students received support. Research assistantships, career-related internships or fieldwork, scholarships/grants, and unspecified assistantships available. Financial award application deadline: 7/1; financial award applicants required to submit FAFSA. *Unit head:* Dr. Thomas Risch, Chair, 870-972-3082, Fax: 870-972-2638, E-mail: trisch@astate.edu. *Application contact:* Dr. Andrew Sustich, Dean of the Graduate School, 870-972-3029, Fax: 870-972-3857, E-mail: sustich@astate.edu. Web site: http://www.astate.edu/a/scimath/biology/.

Brandeis University, Graduate School of Arts and Sciences, Program in Biotechnology, Waltham, MA 02454-9110. Offers MS. *Degree requirements:* For master's, poster presentation. *Entrance requirements:* For master's, GRE, official transcript(s), 3 recommendation letters, curriculum vitae or resume, statement of purpose. Additional exam requirements/recommendations for international students: Required—TOEFL (minimum score 600 paper-based; 250 computer-based; 100 iBT); Recommended—IELTS (minimum score 7). Electronic applications accepted. *Faculty research:* Biosciences, business and biology, biotechnology, pharmaceutics.

Brigham Young University, Graduate Studies, College of Life Sciences, Department of Plant and Wildlife Sciences, Provo, UT 84602-1001. Offers environmental science (MS); genetics and biotechnology (MS); wildlife and wildlands conservation (MS, PhD). *Faculty:* 26 full-time (1 woman), 1 (woman) part-time/adjunct. *Students:* 50 full-time (18 women); includes 8 minority (2 Asian, non-Hispanic/Latino; 4 Hispanic/Latino; 2 Native Hawaiian or other Pacific Islander, non-Hispanic/Latino), 4 international. Average age 25. 29 applicants, 41% accepted, 9 enrolled. In 2011, 18 master's, 1 doctorate awarded. *Degree requirements:* For master's, thesis; for doctorate, comprehensive exam, thesis/dissertation, minimum GPA of 3.2, 54 hours (18 dissertation, 36 coursework). *Entrance requirements:* For master's, GRE General Test, minimum GPA of 3.2 during last 60 hours of course work; for doctorate, GRE, minimum GPA of 3.2. Additional exam requirements/recommendations for international students: Required—TOEFL (minimum score 580 paper-based; 237 computer-based; 85 iBT). *Application deadline:* 2/1 for domestic and international students. Applications are processed on a rolling basis. Electronic applications accepted. *Expenses: Tuition:* Full-time $5760; part-time $320 per credit. Tuition and fees vary according to student's religious affiliation. *Financial support:* In 2011–12, 2 research assistantships with partial tuition reimbursements (averaging $16,650 per year), 37 teaching assistantships with partial tuition reimbursements (averaging $16,650 per year) were awarded; scholarships/grants and tuition waivers (partial) also available. Financial award application deadline: 2/1. *Faculty research:* Environmental science, plant genetics, plant ecology, plant nutrition and pathology, wildlife and wildlands conservation. *Total annual research expenditures:* $2.1 million. *Unit head:* Dr. Val J. Anderson, Chair, 801-422-3527, Fax: 801-422-0008, E-mail: val_anderson@byu.edu. *Application contact:* Dr. Loreen Allphin, Graduate Coordinator, 801-422-5603, Fax: 801-422-0008, E-mail: loreen_allphin@byu.edu. Web site: http://pws.byu.edu/home/.

Brock University, Faculty of Graduate Studies, Faculty of Mathematics and Science, Program in Biotechnology, St. Catharines, ON L2S 3A1, Canada. Offers M Sc, PhD. Part-time programs available. *Degree requirements:* For master's, thesis; for doctorate, thesis/dissertation. *Entrance requirements:* For master's, honors B Sc; for doctorate, M Sc. Additional exam requirements/recommendations for international students: Required—TOEFL (minimum score 550 paper-based; 213 computer-based; 80 iBT), IELTS (minimum score 6.5), TWE (minimum score 4). Electronic applications accepted. *Faculty research:* Bioorganic chemistry, structural chemistry, electrochemistry, cell and molecular biology, plant sciences, oenology, and viticulture.

Brown University, Graduate School, Division of Biology and Medicine, Program in Artificial Organs, Biomaterials, and Cell Technology, Providence, RI 02912. Offers MA, Sc M, PhD. Terminal master's awarded for partial completion of doctoral program. *Degree requirements:* For doctorate, thesis/dissertation, preliminary exam. *Entrance requirements:* For master's and doctorate, GRE General Test, GRE Subject Test. Additional exam requirements/recommendations for international students: Required—TOEFL. Electronic applications accepted.

California State Polytechnic University, Pomona, Academic Affairs, College of Science, Program in Applied Biotechnology, Pomona, CA 91768-2557. Offers MBT. *Students:* 12 part-time (6 women); includes 1 minority (Asian, non-Hispanic/Latino), 2 international. Average age 31. 20 applicants, 70% accepted, 1 enrolled. *Application deadline:* Applications are processed on a rolling basis. Application fee: $55. Electronic applications accepted. *Expenses:* Tuition, state resident: full-time $6738. Tuition, nonresident: full-time $12,300. *Required fees:* $657. Tuition and fees vary according to course load and program. *Unit head:* Dr. Jill Adler-Moore, Liaison, 909-869-4047, E-mail: jadler@csupomona.edu. *Application contact:* Deborah L. Brandon, Executive Director, Admissions and Outreach, 909-869-3427, Fax: 909-869-5315, E-mail: dlbrandon@csupomona.edu. Web site: http://www.csupomona.edu/~biology/gradprog/.

California State University Channel Islands, Extended Education, Programs in Biotechnology, Camarillo, CA 93012. Offers biotechnology and bioinformatics (MS); MS/MBA. *Entrance requirements:* Additional exam requirements/recommendations for international students: Required—TOEFL (minimum score 550 paper-based).

Carnegie Mellon University, Heinz College, School of Public Policy and Management, Master of Science Program in Biotechnology and Management, Pittsburgh, PA 15213-3891. Offers MS. *Accreditation:* AACSB. *Entrance requirements:* For master's, GRE or GMAT, college-level course in advanced algebra/pre-calculus; college-level courses in economics and statistics (recommended). Additional exam requirements/recommendations for international students: Required—TOEFL or IELTS.

Carnegie Mellon University, Mellon College of Science, Department of Chemistry, Pittsburgh, PA 15213-3891. Offers biotechnology and management (MS); chemistry (PhD), including bioinorganic, bioorganic, organic and materials, biophysics and spectroscopy, computational and theoretical, polymer; colloids, polymers and surfaces (MS). Part-time programs available. Terminal master's awarded for partial completion of doctoral program. *Degree requirements:* For doctorate, thesis/dissertation, departmental qualifying and oral exams, teaching experience. *Entrance requirements:* For master's, GRE General Test; for doctorate, GRE General Test, GRE Subject Test. Additional exam requirements/recommendations for international students: Required—TOEFL. Electronic applications accepted. *Faculty research:* Physical and theoretical chemistry, chemical synthesis, biophysical/bioinorganic chemistry.

Claflin University, Graduate Programs, Orangeburg, SC 29115. Offers biotechnology (MS); business administration (MBA). Part-time programs available. *Students:* 43 full-time (30 women), 25 part-time (19 women); includes 59 minority (56 Black or African American, non-Hispanic/Latino; 2 Asian, non-Hispanic/Latino; 1 Two or more races, non-Hispanic/Latino), 7 international. *Entrance requirements:* For master's, GRE,

GMAT, baccalaureate degree, 3 letters of recommendation. Additional exam requirements/recommendations for international students: Recommended—TOEFL (minimum score 550 paper-based; 213 computer-based). *Application deadline:* For fall admission, 8/1 for domestic students; for spring admission, 12/1 for domestic students. Application fee: $45 ($70 for international students). *Expenses: Tuition:* Full-time $9400; part-time $395 per credit hour. *Required fees:* $310. One-time fee: $20 full-time. *Financial support:* Research assistantships and teaching assistantships available. Financial award application deadline: 4/15; financial award applicants required to submit FAFSA. *Unit head:* Michael Zeigler, Director of Admissions, 803-5355340, Fax: 803-5355385, E-mail: mike.zeigler@claflin.edu. Web site: http://www.claflin.edu.

Clarkson University, Graduate School, School of Arts and Sciences, Program in Interdisciplinary Bioscience and Biotechnology, Potsdam, NY 13699. Offers PhD. Part-time programs available. *Degree requirements:* For doctorate, thesis/dissertation, departmental qualifying exam. *Entrance requirements:* For doctorate, GRE, transcripts of all college coursework, three letters of recommendation; resume and personal statement (recommended). Additional exam requirements/recommendations for international students: Required—TOEFL, TSE recommended. *Application deadline:* For fall admission, 1/30 priority date for domestic students, 1/30 for international students; for spring admission, 9/1 priority date for domestic students, 9/1 for international students. Applications are processed on a rolling basis. Application fee: $25 ($35 for international students). Electronic applications accepted. *Expenses: Tuition:* Full-time $14,376; part-time $1198 per credit hour. *Required fees:* $295 per semester. *Financial support:* In 2011–12, fellowships with full tuition reimbursements (averaging $21,999 per year), research assistantships with full tuition reimbursements (averaging $21,999 per year), teaching assistantships with full tuition reimbursements (averaging $21,999 per year) were awarded; scholarships/grants, tuition waivers (partial), and unspecified assistantships also available. *Unit head:* Dr. James A. Schulte, II, Director, 315-268-4401, Fax: 315-268-7118, E-mail: jschulte@clarkson.edu. *Application contact:* Jennifer Reed, Graduate School Coordinator, School of Arts and Sciences, 315-268-3802, Fax: 315-268-3989, E-mail: sciencegrad@clarkson.edu. Web site: http://www.clarkson.edu/biology/graduate/.

Concordia University, School of Graduate Studies, Faculty of Arts and Science, Department of Biology, Montréal, QC H3G 1M8, Canada. Offers biology (M Sc, PhD); biotechnology and genomics (Diploma). *Degree requirements:* For master's, thesis; for doctorate, thesis/dissertation, pedagogical training. *Entrance requirements:* For master's, honors degree in biology; for doctorate, M Sc in life science. *Faculty research:* Cell biology, animal physiology, ecology, microbiology/molecular biology, plant physiology/biochemistry and biotechnology.

Dartmouth College, Thayer School of Engineering, Program in Biotechnology and Biochemical Engineering, Hanover, NH 03755. Offers MS, PhD. *Degree requirements:* For master's, thesis; for doctorate, thesis/dissertation, candidacy oral exam. *Entrance requirements:* For master's and doctorate, GRE General Test. *Application deadline:* For fall admission, 1/1 priority date for domestic students. Application fee: $45. *Financial support:* Fellowships, research assistantships, teaching assistantships, career-related internships or fieldwork, Federal Work-Study, institutionally sponsored loans, and tuition waivers (full and partial) available. Financial award application deadline: 1/15. *Faculty research:* Biomass processing, metabolic engineering, kinetics and reactor design, applied microbiology, resource and environmental analysis. *Total annual research expenditures:* $3 million. *Unit head:* Dr. Joseph J. Helbie, Dean, 603-646-2238, Fax: 603-646-2580, E-mail: joseph.j.helbie@dartmouth.edu. *Application contact:* Candace S. Potter, Graduate Admissions Administrator, 603-646-3844, Fax: 603-646-1620, E-mail: candace.potter@dartmouth.edu. Web site: http://engineering.dartmouth.edu/.

Duquesne University, Bayer School of Natural and Environmental Sciences, Program in Biotechnology, Pittsburgh, PA 15282-0001. Offers MS. Part-time programs available. *Faculty:* 1 full-time (0 women). *Students:* 12 full-time (5 women), 5 part-time (1 woman), 8 international. Average age 23. 30 applicants, 70% accepted, 10 enrolled. In 2011, 10 master's awarded. *Entrance requirements:* For master's, GRE General Test, statement of purpose, 3 letters of recommendation, official transcripts. Additional exam requirements/recommendations for international students: Required—TOEFL (minimum score 80 iBT). *Application deadline:* For fall admission, 5/1 priority date for domestic students, 5/1 for international students; for spring admission, 10/1 priority date for domestic students, 10/1 for international students. Applications are processed on a rolling basis. Application fee: $0 ($40 for international students). Electronic applications accepted. *Expenses: Tuition:* Full-time $16,596; part-time $922 per credit. *Required fees:* $1584; $88 per credit. Tuition and fees vary according to program. *Financial support:* In 2011–12, 6 students received support. Career-related internships or fieldwork and tuition waivers (partial) available. *Unit head:* Dr. Alan W. Seadler, Director, 412-396-1568, E-mail: seadlera@duq.edu. *Application contact:* Heather Costello, Graduate Academic Advisor, 412-396-6339, Fax: 412-396-4881, E-mail: costelloh@duq.edu.

East Carolina University, Graduate School, Thomas Harriot College of Arts and Sciences, Department of Biology, Greenville, NC 27858-4353. Offers biology (MS); molecular biology/biotechnology (MS). Part-time programs available. *Degree requirements:* For master's, one foreign language, comprehensive exam, thesis. *Entrance requirements:* For master's, GRE General Test, GRE Subject Test. Additional exam requirements/recommendations for international students: Required—TOEFL. *Application deadline:* For fall admission, 6/1 priority date for domestic students; for spring admission, 10/15 for domestic students. Applications are processed on a rolling basis. Application fee: $50. *Expenses:* Tuition, state resident: full-time $3557; part-time $444.63 per semester hour. Tuition, nonresident: full-time $14,351; part-time $1793.88 per semester hour. *Required fees:* $2016; $252 per semester hour. Part-time tuition and fees vary according to course load, campus/location and program. *Financial support:* Fellowships with partial tuition reimbursements, research assistantships with partial tuition reimbursements, teaching assistantships with partial tuition reimbursements, career-related internships or fieldwork, Federal Work-Study, scholarships/grants, and unspecified assistantships available. Support available to part-time students. Financial award application deadline: 6/1. *Faculty research:* Biochemistry, microbiology, cell biology. *Application contact:* Interim Dean of Graduate School, 252-328-6012, Fax: 252-328-6071, E-mail: gradschool@ecu.edu. Web site: http://www.ecu.edu/cs-cas/biology/graduate.cfm.

Florida Institute of Technology, Graduate Programs, College of Science, Department of Biological Sciences, Melbourne, FL 32901-6975. Offers biological science (PhD); biotechnology (MS); cell and molecular biology option (MS); conservation technology (MS); ecology and marine biology (MS), including ecology, marine biology. Part-time programs available. *Faculty:* 16 full-time (2 women). *Students:* 84 full-time (52 women), 12 part-time (6 women); includes 6 minority (1 Asian, non-Hispanic/Latino; 3 Hispanic/Latino; 2 Two or more races, non-Hispanic/Latino), 50 international. Average age 26. 241 applicants, 35% accepted, 29 enrolled. In 2011, 21 master's, 3 doctorates awarded. *Degree requirements:* For master's, thesis (for some programs), research, seminar, internship, or summer lab; for doctorate, comprehensive exam, thesis/dissertation, dissertations seminar, publications. *Entrance requirements:* For master's, GRE General Test, 3 letters of recommendation, minimum GPA of 3.0, resume, statement of objectives; for doctorate, GRE General Test, resume, 3 letters of recommendation, minimum GPA of 3.2, statement of objectives. Additional exam requirements/recommendations for international students: Required—TOEFL (minimum score 550 paper-based; 213 computer-based; 79 iBT). *Application deadline:* For fall admission, 3/1 for domestic students, 4/1 for international students; for spring admission, 9/1 for domestic and international students. Applications are processed on a rolling basis. Electronic applications accepted. *Expenses: Tuition:* Full-time $19,620; part-time $1090 per credit hour. Tuition and fees vary according to campus/location. *Financial support:* In 2011–12, 6 fellowships (averaging $20,737 per year), 18 research assistantships with full and partial tuition reimbursements (averaging $10,742 per year), 20 teaching assistantships with full and partial tuition reimbursements (averaging $13,883 per year) were awarded; career-related internships or fieldwork, institutionally sponsored loans, tuition waivers (partial), unspecified assistantships, and tuition remissions also available. Support available to part-time students. Financial award application deadline: 3/1; financial award applicants required to submit FAFSA. *Faculty research:* Initiation of protein synthesis in eukaryotic cells, fixation of radioactive carbon, changes in DNA molecule, endangered or threatened avian and mammalian species, hydroacoustics and feeding preference of the West Indian manatee. *Total annual research expenditures:* $1.9 million. *Unit head:* Dr. Richard B. Aronson, Department Head, 321-674-8034, Fax: 321-674-7238, E-mail: raronson@fit.edu. *Application contact:* Cheryl A. Brown, Associate Director of Graduate Admissions, 321-674-7581, Fax: 321-723-9468, E-mail: cbrown@fit.edu. Web site: http://cos.fit.edu/biology/.

The George Washington University, College of Professional Studies, Program in Molecular Biotechnology, Washington, DC 20052. Offers MPS. *Students:* 4 full-time (3 women), 1 (woman) part-time; includes 3 minority (all Hispanic/Latino), 1 international. Average age 28. 22 applicants, 73% accepted, 2 enrolled. In 2011, 4 master's awarded. *Application deadline:* For fall admission, 4/1 for domestic and international students. Application fee: $25. Electronic applications accepted. *Financial support:* In 2011–12, 8 students received support. Tuition waivers available. *Unit head:* Dr. Mark Reeves, Director, 202-994-6279, Fax: 202-994-3001, E-mail: reevesme@gwu.edu. *Application contact:* Kristin Williams, Assistant Vice President for Graduate and Special Enrollment Management, 202-994-0467, Fax: 202-994-0371, E-mail: ksw@gwu.edu. Web site: http://cps.gwu.edu/mmb/index.html.

Harvard University, Extension School, Cambridge, MA 02138-3722. Offers applied sciences (CAS); biotechnology (ALM); educational technologies (ALM); educational technology (CET); English for graduate and professional studies (DGP); environmental management (ALM, CEM); information technology (ALM); journalism (ALM); liberal arts (ALM); management (ALM, CM); mathematics for teaching (ALM); museum studies (ALM); premedical studies (Diploma); publication and communication (CPC). Part-time and evening/weekend programs available. *Degree requirements:* For master's, thesis. *Entrance requirements:* For master's, 3 completed graduate courses with grade of B or higher. Additional exam requirements/recommendations for international students: Required—TOEFL (minimum score 600 paper-based; 250 computer-based), TWE (minimum score 5). *Expenses:* Contact institution.

Hood College, Graduate School, Program in Biomedical Science, Frederick, MD 21701-8575. Offers biomedical science (MS), including biotechnology/molecular biology, microbiology/immunology/virology, regulatory compliance; regulatory compliance (Certificate). Part-time and evening/weekend programs available. *Degree requirements:* For master's, comprehensive exam, thesis or alternative. *Entrance requirements:* For master's, bachelor's degree in biology; minimum GPA of 2.75; undergraduate course work in cell biology, chemistry, organic chemistry, and genetics. Additional exam requirements/recommendations for international students: Required—TOEFL (minimum score 575 paper-based; 231 computer-based; 89 iBT). Electronic applications accepted.

Howard University, College of Medicine, Department of Biochemistry and Molecular Biology, Washington, DC 20059-0002. Offers biochemistry and molecular biology (PhD); biotechnology (MS); MD/PhD. Part-time programs available. *Degree requirements:* For master's, externship; for doctorate, comprehensive exam, thesis/dissertation. *Entrance requirements:* For master's and doctorate, GRE General Test, minimum GPA of 3.0. *Faculty research:* Cellular and molecular biology of olfaction, gene regulation and expression, enzymology, NMR spectroscopy of molecular structure, hormone regulation/metabolism.

Illinois Institute of Technology, Graduate College, College of Science and Letters, Department of Biological, Chemical and Physical Sciences, Biology Division, Chicago, IL 60616. Offers biochemistry (MBS, MS); biology (PhD); biotechnology (MBS, MS); cell and molecular biology (MBS, MS); microbiology (MB, MS); molecular biochemistry and biophysics (PhD); molecular biology and biophysics (MS). Part-time and evening/weekend programs available. Postbaccalaureate distance learning degree programs offered (minimal on-campus study). Terminal master's awarded for partial completion of doctoral program. *Degree requirements:* For master's, comprehensive exam, thesis (for some programs); for doctorate, comprehensive exam, thesis/dissertation. *Entrance requirements:* For master's, GRE General Test (minimum score 1000 Quantitative and Verbal, 2.5 Analytical Writing), minimum undergraduate GPA of 3.0; for doctorate, GRE General Test (minimum score 1200 Quantitative and Verbal, 3.0 Analytical Writing), minimum undergraduate GPA of 3.0. Additional exam requirements/recommendations for international students: Required—TOEFL (minimum score 523 paper-based; 213 computer-based; 70 iBT); Recommended—IELTS (minimum score 5.5). Electronic applications accepted. *Faculty research:* Structure and biophysics of macromolecular systems; efficacy and mechanism of action of chemopreventive agents in experimental carcinogenesis of breast, colon, lung and prostate; study of fundamental structural biochemistry problems that have direct links to the understanding and treatment of disease; spectroscopic techniques for the study of multi-domain proteins; molecular mechanisms of cancer and cancer gene therapy.

Illinois State University, Graduate School, College of Arts and Sciences, Department of Biological Sciences, Program in Biotechnology, Normal, IL 61790-2200. Offers MS. *Degree requirements:* For master's, thesis or alternative. *Entrance requirements:* For master's, GRE General Test, minimum GPA of 2.6 in last 60 hours of course work.

Indiana University Bloomington, University Graduate School, College of Arts and Sciences, Department of Biology, Bloomington, IN 47405. Offers biology teaching (MAT); biotechnology (MA); evolution, ecology, and behavior (MA, PhD); genetics (PhD); microbiology (MA, PhD); molecular, cellular, and developmental biology (PhD); plant sciences (MA, PhD); zoology (MA, PhD). *Faculty:* 58 full-time (15 women), 21 part-time/adjunct (6 women). *Students:* 175 full-time (100 women), 3 part-time (all women); includes 20 minority (5 Black or African American, non-Hispanic/Latino; 8 Asian, non-Hispanic/Latino; 7 Hispanic/Latino), 55 international. Average age 27. 316 applicants, 22% accepted, 31 enrolled. In 2011, 8 master's, 20 doctorates awarded. Terminal master's awarded for partial completion of doctoral program. *Degree requirements:* For master's, thesis, oral defense; for doctorate, thesis/dissertation, oral defense. *Entrance requirements:* For master's and doctorate, GRE General Test. Additional exam requirements/recommendations for international students: Required—TOEFL (minimum score 100 iBT). *Application deadline:* For fall admission, 1/5 priority date for domestic students, 12/1 for international students. Application fee: $55 ($65 for international students). Electronic applications accepted. *Financial support:* In 2011–12, fellowships with tuition reimbursements (averaging $19,484 per year), research assistantships with tuition reimbursements (averaging $20,300 per year), teaching assistantships with tuition reimbursements (averaging $20,521 per year) were awarded; scholarships/grants, traineeships, health care benefits, and unspecified assistantships also available. Financial award application deadline: 1/5. *Faculty research:* Evolution, ecology and behavior; microbiology; molecular biology and genetics; plant biology. *Unit head:* Dr. Roger Innes, Chair, 812-855-2219, Fax: 812-855-6082, E-mail: rinnes@indiana.edu. *Application contact:* Tracey D. Stohr, Graduate Student Recruitment Coordinator, 812-856-6303, Fax: 812-855-6082, E-mail: gradbio@indiana.edu. Web site: http://www.bio.indiana.edu/.

Instituto Tecnológico y de Estudios Superiores de Monterrey, Campus Monterrey, Graduate and Research Division, Program in Natural and Social Sciences, Monterrey, Mexico. Offers biotechnology (MS); chemistry (MS, PhD); communications (MS); education (MA). Part-time programs available. *Degree requirements:* For master's, one foreign language, thesis; for doctorate, one foreign language, thesis/dissertation. *Entrance requirements:* For master's, EXADEP; for doctorate, EXADEP, master's degree in related field. Additional exam requirements/recommendations for international students: Required—TOEFL. *Faculty research:* Cultural industries, mineral substances, bioremediation, food processing, CQ in industrial chemical processing.

Inter American University of Puerto Rico, Bayamón Campus, Graduate School, Bayamón, PR 00957. Offers biology (MS), including environmental sciences and ecology, molecular biotechnology; human resources (MBA). Part-time and evening/weekend programs available. *Faculty:* 6 full-time (2 women), 2 part-time/adjunct (1 woman). *Students:* 7 full-time (6 women), 120 part-time (83 women); all minorities (1 Asian, non-Hispanic/Latino; 120 Hispanic/Latino; 6 Two or more races, non-Hispanic/Latino). Average age 29. *Degree requirements:* For master's, comprehensive exam, research project. *Entrance requirements:* For master's, EXADEP, GRE General Test, letters of recommendation. *Application deadline:* For fall admission, 7/1 for domestic students, 5/1 for international students; for winter admission, 11/15 priority date for domestic students, 11/15 for international students; for spring admission, 2/15 priority date for domestic students, 2/15 for international students. Application fee: $31. *Unit head:* Prof. Juan F. Martinez, Chancellor, 787-279-1200 Ext. 2295, Fax: 787-279-2205, E-mail: jmartinez@bayamon.inter.edu. *Application contact:* Carlos Alicea, Director of Admission, 787-279-1200 Ext. 2017, Fax: 787-279-2205, E-mail: calicea@bayamon.inter.edu.

The Johns Hopkins University, Whiting School of Engineering, Program in Engineering Management, Baltimore, MD 21218-2699. Offers biomaterials (MSEM); communications science (MSEM); computer science (MSEM); fluid mechanics (MSEM); materials science and engineering (MSEM); mechanical engineering (MSEM); mechanics and materials (MSEM); nano-biotechnology (MSEM); nanomaterials and nanotechnology (MSEM); probability and statistics (MSEM); smart product and device design (MSEM); systems analysis, management and environmental policy (MSEM). *Entrance requirements:* For master's, GRE, 3 letters of recommendation, resume. Additional exam requirements/recommendations for international students: Required—TOEFL (minimum score 600 paper-based; 250 computer-based; 100 iBT) or IELTS (minimum score 7). Electronic applications accepted.

The Johns Hopkins University, Zanvyl Krieger School of Arts and Sciences, Advanced Academic Programs, Program in Biotechnology, Baltimore, MD 21218-2699. Offers MS, MS/MBA. Part-time and evening/weekend programs available. Postbaccalaureate distance learning degree programs offered (minimal on-campus study). *Degree requirements:* For master's, thesis (for some programs). *Entrance requirements:* For master's, minimum GPA of 3.0; coursework in biology and chemistry. Additional exam requirements/recommendations for international students: Required—TOEFL (minimum score 250 computer-based; 100 iBT). Electronic applications accepted.

The Johns Hopkins University, Zanvyl Krieger School of Arts and Sciences, Advanced Academic Programs, Program in Biotechnology Enterprise and Entrepreneurship, Baltimore, MD 21218-2699. Offers MBEE. *Degree requirements:* For master's, practicum.

Kean University, New Jersey Center for Science, Technology and Mathematics, Program in Biotechnology, Union, NJ 07083. Offers MS. *Faculty:* 8 full-time (4 women). *Students:* 24 full-time (15 women), 14 part-time (11 women); includes 22 minority (1 Black or African American, non-Hispanic/Latino; 15 Asian, non-Hispanic/Latino; 6 Hispanic/Latino), 7 international. Average age 26. 24 applicants, 96% accepted, 17 enrolled. In 2011, 5 master's awarded. *Degree requirements:* For master's, written research project paper, presentation of research. *Entrance requirements:* For master's, GRE General Test, minimum GPA of 3.0 overall and in all science and math courses, 3 letters of recommendation, interview, resume, personal statement. Additional exam requirements/recommendations for international students: Required—TOEFL (minimum score 79 iBT). *Application deadline:* For fall admission, 6/1 for domestic and international students; for spring admission, 12/1 for domestic and international students. Applications are processed on a rolling basis. Application fee: $75 ($150 for international students). Electronic applications accepted. *Expenses:* Tuition, state resident: full-time $11,302; part-time $550 per credit. Tuition, nonresident: full-time $15,318; part-time $674 per credit. *Required fees:* $2849; $130 per credit. Tuition and fees vary according to degree level. *Financial support:* In 2011–12, 5 research assistantships with full tuition reimbursements (averaging $3,263 per year) were awarded; unspecified assistantships also available. Financial award applicants required to submit FAFSA. *Unit head:* Dr. Dil Ramanathan, Program Coordinator, 908-737-3426, E-mail: ramanatd@kean.edu. *Application contact:* Reenat Hasan, Pre-Admissions Coordinator, 908-737-5923, Fax: 908-737-5925, E-mail: rhasan@exchange.kean.edu. Web site: http://www.kean.edu/KU/Biotechnology.

Marywood University, Academic Affairs, College of Liberal Arts and Sciences, Science Department, Program in Biotechnology, Scranton, PA 18509-1598. Offers MS. *Entrance requirements:* Additional exam requirements/recommendations for international students: Required—TOEFL (minimum score 550 paper-based; 213 computer-based; 79 iBT). *Application deadline:* For fall admission, 1/9 priority date for domestic students,

1/9 for international students. Application fee: $35. Electronic applications accepted. *Financial support:* Career-related internships or fieldwork, scholarships/grants, and unspecified assistantships available. Support available to part-time students. Financial award application deadline: 6/30; financial award applicants required to submit FAFSA. *Faculty research:* Microbiology, molecular biology, genetics. *Unit head:* Dr. Michael Kiel, Interim Chair, 570-348-6211 Ext. 2478, E-mail: mkiel@marywood.edu. *Application contact:* Tammy Manka, Assistant Director of Graduate Admissions, 570-348-6211 Ext. 2322, E-mail: tmanka@marywood.edu. Web site: http://www.marywood.edu/science/graduate/.

McGill University, Faculty of Graduate and Postdoctoral Studies, Faculty of Agricultural and Environmental Sciences, Institute of Parasitology, Montréal, QC H3A 2T5, Canada. Offers biotechnology (M Sc A, Certificate); parasitology (M Sc, PhD).

New Mexico State University, Graduate School, College of Arts and Sciences, Department of Biology, Las Cruces, NM 88003-8001. Offers biology (MS, PhD); biotechnology and business (MS). Part-time programs available. *Faculty:* 21 full-time (9 women). *Students:* 71 full-time (42 women), 15 part-time (12 women); includes 26 minority (3 Black or African American, non-Hispanic/Latino; 3 American Indian or Alaska Native, non-Hispanic/Latino; 1 Asian, non-Hispanic/Latino; 18 Hispanic/Latino; 1 Two or more races, non-Hispanic/Latino), 22 international. Average age 30. 41 applicants, 44% accepted, 12 enrolled. In 2011, 11 master's, 7 doctorates awarded. *Degree requirements:* For master's, thesis (for some programs), defense or oral exam; for doctorate, comprehensive exam, thesis/dissertation, qualifying exam, defense. *Entrance requirements:* Additional exam requirements/recommendations for international students: Required—TOEFL (minimum score 550 paper-based; 0 computer-based; 79 iBT), IELTS (minimum score 6.5). *Application deadline:* For fall admission, 1/15 priority date for domestic students, 1/15 for international students; for spring admission, 10/4 priority date for domestic students, 10/4 for international students. Applications are processed on a rolling basis. Application fee: $40 ($50 for international students). Electronic applications accepted. *Expenses:* Tuition, state resident: full-time $5004; part-time $208.50 per credit. Tuition, nonresident: full-time $17,446; part-time $726.90 per credit. *Financial support:* In 2011–12, 12 fellowships (averaging $9,914 per year), 30 research assistantships (averaging $22,031 per year), 28 teaching assistantships (averaging $22,625 per year) were awarded; Federal Work-Study and health care benefits also available. Support available to part-time students. Financial award application deadline: 1/15. *Faculty research:* Microbiology, cell and organismal physiology, ecology and ethology, evolution, genetics, developmental biology. *Total annual research expenditures:* $4.4 million. *Unit head:* Dr. John Gustafson, Head, 575-646-3611, Fax: 575-646-5665, E-mail: jgustafs@nmsu.edu. *Application contact:* Gloria Valencia, Administration Assistant, 575-646-3611, Fax: 575-646-5665, E-mail: gvalenci@nmsu.edu. Web site: http://biology-web.nmsu.edu/.

North Carolina State University, Graduate School, College of Agriculture and Life Sciences, Department of Microbiology, Program in Microbial Biotechnology, Raleigh, NC 27695. Offers MMB. *Entrance requirements:* For master's, GRE. Electronic applications accepted.

Northeastern University, College of Science, Department of Biology and College of Arts and Sciences and College of Engineering, Program in Biotechnology, Boston, MA 02115-5096. Offers MS, PSM. Part-time and evening/weekend programs available. *Students:* 72 full-time (42 women), 28 part-time (14 women). 150 applicants, 73% accepted, 36 enrolled. In 2011, 21 master's awarded. *Entrance requirements:* For master's, GRE. Additional exam requirements/recommendations for international students: Required—TOEFL (minimum score 600 paper-based; 250 computer-based; 100 iBT). *Application deadline:* For fall admission, 4/1 for domestic students. Application fee: $50. Electronic applications accepted. *Expenses:* Contact institution. *Financial support:* Teaching assistantships and scholarships/grants available. *Faculty research:* Genomics, proteomics, gene expression analysis (molecular biotechnology), drug discovery, development, delivery (pharmaceutical biotechnology), bioprocess development and optimization (process development). *Unit head:* Prof. Thomas Gilbert, Professor, 617-373-4505, E-mail: t.gilbert@neu.edu. *Application contact:* Cynthia Bainton, Administrative Manager, 617-373-2627, Fax: 617-373-8795, E-mail: c.bainton@neu.edu. Web site: http://www.biotechms.neu.edu/.

Northwestern University, The Graduate School, Interdepartmental Biological Sciences Program (IBiS), Evanston, IL 60208. Offers biochemistry, molecular biology, and cell biology (PhD), including biochemistry, cell and molecular biology, molecular biophysics, structural biology; biotechnology (PhD); cell and molecular biology (PhD); developmental biology and genetics (PhD); hormone action and signal transduction (PhD); neuroscience (PhD); structural biology, biochemistry, and biophysics (PhD). Program participants include the Departments of Biochemistry, Molecular Biology, and Cell Biology; Chemistry; Neurobiology and Physiology; Chemical Engineering; Civil Engineering; and Evanston Hospital. *Degree requirements:* For doctorate, thesis/dissertation, qualifying exam. *Entrance requirements:* For doctorate, GRE General Test. Additional exam requirements/recommendations for international students: Required—TOEFL (minimum score 600 paper-based). Electronic applications accepted. *Faculty research:* Developmental genetics, gene regulation, DNA-protein interactions, biological clocks, bioremediation.

Northwestern University, McCormick School of Engineering and Applied Science, MS in Biotechnology Program, Evanston, IL 60208. Offers MS. *Students:* 76 full-time (41 women); includes 10 minority (1 Black or African American, non-Hispanic/Latino; 7 Asian, non-Hispanic/Latino; 2 Hispanic/Latino), 38 international. 136 applicants, 57% accepted, 34 enrolled. In 2011, 18 master's awarded. *Entrance requirements:* Additional exam requirements/recommendations for international students: Required—TOEFL, IELTS. *Application deadline:* For fall admission, 5/31 for domestic and international students. Application fee: $50. Electronic applications accepted. *Financial support:* Career-related internships or fieldwork, institutionally sponsored loans, and health care benefits available. Financial award application deadline: 1/15; financial award applicants required to submit FAFSA. *Unit head:* Dr. William M. Miller, Director, 847-491-7399. *Application contact:* Joshua Lobb, Program Assistant, 847-491-7399, E-mail: j-lobb@northwestern.edu. Web site: http://www.mbp.northwestern.edu/.

Penn State University Park, Graduate School, Eberly College of Science, Department of Biochemistry and Molecular Biology, State College, University Park, PA 16802-1503. Offers biochemistry, microbiology, and molecular biology (MS, PhD); biotechnology (MBIOT). *Unit head:* Dr. Richard J. Frisque, Head, 814-863-1851, E-mail: rjf6@psu.edu. *Application contact:* Dr. Ronald Porter, Director of Graduate Studies, 814-863-4903, E-mail: rdp1@psu.edu. Web site: http://bmb.psu.edu.

Polytechnic Institute of New York University, Department of Chemical and Biological Sciences, Major in Biotechnology, Brooklyn, NY 11201-2990. Offers MS. *Students:* 53 full-time (35 women), 10 part-time (6 women); includes 7 minority (all Asian, non-

Hispanic/Latino), 52 international. 152 applicants, 46% accepted, 22 enrolled. In 2011, 46 degrees awarded. *Entrance requirements:* Additional exam requirements/recommendations for international students: Required—TOEFL (minimum score 550 paper-based; 213 computer-based; 80 iBT); Recommended—IELTS (minimum score 6.5). *Application deadline:* For fall admission, 7/31 priority date for domestic students, 4/30 for international students; for spring admission, 12/31 priority date for domestic students, 10/30 for international students. Applications are processed on a rolling basis. Application fee: $75. Electronic applications accepted. *Expenses: Tuition:* Full-time $22,464; part-time $1248 per credit. *Required fees:* $501 per semester. *Unit head:* Dr. Bruce Garetz, Department Head, 718-260-3287, E-mail: bgaretz@poly.edu. *Application contact:* JeanCarlo Bonilla, Director, Graduate Enrollment Management, 718-260-3182, Fax: 718-260-3624, E-mail: gradinfo@poly.edu.

Polytechnic Institute of New York University, Department of Chemical and Biological Sciences, Major in Biotechnology and Entrepreneurship, Brooklyn, NY 11201-2990. Offers MS. *Students:* 17 full-time (11 women), 8 part-time (1 woman); includes 1 minority (Asian, non-Hispanic/Latino), 18 international. Average age 24. 62 applicants, 48% accepted, 22 enrolled. In 2011, 10 degrees awarded. *Entrance requirements:* Additional exam requirements/recommendations for international students: Required—TOEFL (minimum score 550 paper-based; 213 computer-based; 80 iBT); Recommended—IELTS (minimum score 6.5). *Application deadline:* For fall admission, 7/31 priority date for domestic students, 4/30 for international students; for spring admission, 12/31 priority date for domestic students, 10/30 for international students. Applications are processed on a rolling basis. Application fee: $75. Electronic applications accepted. *Expenses: Tuition:* Full-time $22,464; part-time $1248 per credit. *Required fees:* $501 per semester. *Financial support:* Institutionally sponsored loans, scholarships/grants, and unspecified assistantships available. Support available to part-time students. *Unit head:* Dr. Bruce Garetz, Department Head, 718-260-3287, E-mail: bgaretz@poly.edu. *Application contact:* JeanCarlo Bonilla, Director, Graduate Enrollment Management, 718-260-3182, Fax: 718-260-3624, E-mail: gradinfo@poly.edu.

Purdue University, Graduate School, PULSe - Purdue University Life Sciences Program, West Lafayette, IN 47907. Offers biomolecular structure and biophysics (PhD); biotechnology (PhD); chemical biology (PhD); chromatin and regulation of gene expression (PhD); integrative neuroscience (PhD); integrative plant sciences (PhD); membrane biology (PhD); microbiology (PhD); molecular evolutionary and cancer biology (PhD); molecular evolutionary genetics (PhD); molecular virology (PhD). *Students:* 90 full-time (45 women); includes 7 minority (3 Black or African American, non-Hispanic/Latino; 1 Asian, non-Hispanic/Latino; 2 Hispanic/Latino; 1 Two or more races, non-Hispanic/Latino), 40 international. Average age 26. 427 applicants, 24% accepted, 35 enrolled. *Entrance requirements:* For doctorate, GRE test required, minimum undergraduate GPA of 3.0. Additional exam requirements/recommendations for international students: Required—TOEFL (minimum score 550 paper-based; 77 iBT). *Application deadline:* For fall admission, 1/15 priority date for domestic students, 1/15 for international students. Applications are processed on a rolling basis. Application fee: $60 ($75 for international students). Electronic applications accepted. *Financial support:* In 2011–12, research assistantships with tuition reimbursements (averaging $22,500 per year), teaching assistantships with tuition reimbursements (averaging $22,500 per year) were awarded. *Unit head:* Dr. Christine A. Hrycyna, Head, 765-494-7322, E-mail: hrycyna@purdue.edu. *Application contact:* Emily E. Bramson, Graduate Contact, 765-494-5865, E-mail: bramson@purdue.edu. Web site: http://www.gradschool.purdue.edu/pulse.

Purdue University Calumet, Graduate Studies Office, School of Engineering, Mathematics, and Science, Department of Biological Sciences, Program in Biotechnology, Hammond, IN 46323-2094. Offers MS. *Degree requirements:* For master's, thesis (for some programs). *Entrance requirements:* For master's, GRE General Test, 3 letters of recommendation.

Regis College, Program in Regulatory and Clinical Research Management, Weston, MA 02493. Offers MS. Part-time and evening/weekend programs available. *Degree requirements:* For master's, thesis optional, internship. *Entrance requirements:* For master's, GRE or MAT. Additional exam requirements/recommendations for international students: Required—TOEFL (minimum score 550 paper-based; 213 computer-based). *Expenses:* Contact institution. *Faculty research:* FDA regulatory affairs medical device.

Roosevelt University, Graduate Division, College of Arts and Sciences, Department of Biological, Chemical, and Physical Sciences, Chicago, IL 60605. Offers biotechnology and chemical science (MS). Part-time and evening/weekend programs available. *Degree requirements:* For master's, thesis optional. *Entrance requirements:* For master's, minimum GPA of 2.7, undergraduate course work in science and mathematics. *Faculty research:* Phase-transfer catalysts, bioinorganic chemistry, long chain dicarboxylic acids, organosilicon compounds, spectroscopic studies.

St. John's University, Institute for Biotechnology, Queens, NY 11439. Offers biological/pharmaceutical biotechnology (MS). *Students:* 12 full-time (7 women), 8 part-time (6 women); includes 5 minority (1 Black or African American, non-Hispanic/Latino; 4 Asian, non-Hispanic/Latino), 7 international. Average age 27. 58 applicants, 40% accepted, 6 enrolled. In 2011, 7 master's awarded. *Degree requirements:* For master's, comprehensive exam, thesis optional. *Entrance requirements:* For master's, GRE General Test, minimum GPA of 3.0, 2 letters of recommendation, 1-page essay. Additional exam requirements/recommendations for international students: Required—TOEFL (minimum score 600 paper-based; 250 computer-based; 100 iBT), IELTS (minimum score 5.5). *Application deadline:* For fall admission, 5/1 priority date for domestic students, 5/1 for international students; for spring admission, 11/1 priority date for domestic students, 11/1 for international students. Applications are processed on a rolling basis. Application fee: $70. Electronic applications accepted. *Expenses:* Contact institution. *Financial support:* In 2011–12, 1 teaching assistantship with full tuition reimbursement (averaging $15,975 per year) was awarded. Financial award application deadline: 3/1; financial award applicants required to submit FAFSA. *Unit head:* Dr. Vijaya L. Korlipara, Director, 718-990-5369, E-mail: korlipav@stjohns.edu. *Application contact:* Robert Medrano, Director of Graduate Admission, 718-990-1601, E-mail: gradhelp@stjohns.edu. Web site: http://www.stjohns.edu/academics/centers/ifb.

San Francisco State University, Division of Graduate Studies, College of Science and Engineering, Department of Biology, Professional Science Master's Program, San Francisco, CA 94132-1722. Offers biotechnology (PSM); stem cell science (PSM). *Unit head:* Dr. Lily Chen, Director, 415-338-6763, E-mail: lilychen@sfsu.edu. *Application contact:* Dr. Linda H. Chen, Program Coordinator, 415-338-1696, E-mail: psm@sfsu.edu. Web site: http://www.sfsu.edu/~psm/.

Simon Fraser University, Graduate Studies, Faculty of Business Administration, Burnaby, BC V5A 1S6, Canada. Offers business administration (EMBA, PhD); financial management (MA); general business (MBA); global asset and wealth management (MBA); management of technology/biotechnology (MBA); MBA/MRM. *Accreditation:* AACSB. Postbaccalaureate distance learning degree programs offered. *Degree requirements:* For master's, thesis or written project. *Entrance requirements:* For master's, minimum GPA of 3.0. Additional exam requirements/recommendations for international students: Required—TOEFL. *Expenses:* Contact institution. *Faculty research:* Leadership, marketing and technology, wealth management.

Southeastern Oklahoma State University, School of Arts and Sciences, Durant, OK 74701-0609. Offers biology (MT); computer information systems (MT); occupational safety and health (MT). Part-time and evening/weekend programs available. *Faculty:* 12 full-time (4 women), 1 part-time/adjunct (0 women). *Students:* 17 full-time (6 women), 45 part-time (8 women); includes 18 minority (1 Black or African American, non-Hispanic/Latino; 15 American Indian or Alaska Native, non-Hispanic/Latino; 2 Hispanic/Latino), 2 international. Average age 28. 19 applicants, 95% accepted, 18 enrolled. *Degree requirements:* For master's, thesis optional. *Entrance requirements:* For master's, minimum GPA of 3.0 in last 60 hours or 2.75 overall. Additional exam requirements/recommendations for international students: Required—TOEFL (minimum score 550 paper-based; 213 computer-based; 79 iBT). *Application deadline:* For fall admission, 8/1 for domestic students, 6/1 for international students; for spring admission, 1/5 for domestic students, 11/1 for international students. Application fee: $20 ($55 for international students). Electronic applications accepted. *Expenses:* Tuition, state resident: full-time $3537; part-time $173.95 per credit hour. Tuition, nonresident: full-time $8673; part-time $459.30 per credit hour. *Required fees:* $22.55 per credit hour. *Financial support:* In 2011–12, 8 students received support. Fellowships, research assistantships, teaching assistantships, Federal Work-Study, and institutionally sponsored loans available. Support available to part-time students. Financial award application deadline: 6/15; financial award applicants required to submit FAFSA. *Unit head:* Dr. Teresa Golden, Graduate Coordinator, 580-745-2286, E-mail: tgolden@se.edu. *Application contact:* Carrie Williamson, Graduate Secretary, 580-745-2220, Fax: 580-745-7474, E-mail: cwilliamson@se.edu. Web site: http://www.se.edu/arts-and-sciences/.

Southern Illinois University Edwardsville, Graduate School, College of Arts and Sciences, Department of Biological Sciences, Program in Biotechnology Management, Edwardsville, IL 62026-0001. Offers MS. Part-time programs available. *Students:* 2 full-time (both women), 4 part-time (1 woman); includes 1 minority (Black or African American, non-Hispanic/Latino), 2 international. 39 applicants, 33% accepted. In 2011, 3 master's awarded. *Degree requirements:* For master's, thesis or alternative, internship, research paper. *Entrance requirements:* For master's, GRE. Additional exam requirements/recommendations for international students: Required—TOEFL (minimum score 550 paper-based; 213 computer-based; 79 iBT), IELTS (minimum score 6.5). *Application deadline:* For fall admission, 2/28 for domestic and international students. Application fee: $30. Electronic applications accepted. Tuition and fees vary according to course load and program. *Financial support:* Fellowships with full tuition reimbursements, research assistantships with full tuition reimbursements, teaching assistantships with full tuition reimbursements, institutionally sponsored loans, scholarships/grants, and unspecified assistantships available. Financial award application deadline: 3/1; financial award applicants required to submit FAFSA. *Unit head:* Dr. Vance McCracken, Director, 618-650-5246, E-mail: vmccrac@siue.edu. *Application contact:* Michelle Robinson, Coordinator of Graduate Recruitment, 618-650-2811, Fax: 618-650-3523, E-mail: michero@siue.edu. Web site: http://www.siue.edu/BIOLOGY/PSM/index.html.

Stephen F. Austin State University, Graduate School, College of Sciences and Mathematics, Division of Biotechnology, Nacogdoches, TX 75962. Offers MS. *Degree requirements:* For master's, comprehensive exam, thesis. *Entrance requirements:* For master's, GRE General Test, minimum GPA of 2.8 in last 60 hours, 2.5 overall. Additional exam requirements/recommendations for international students: Required—TOEFL.

Texas Tech University, Graduate School, Center for Biotechnology and Genomics, Lubbock, TX 79409. Offers biotechnology (MS); JD/MS. Part-time programs available. *Students:* 17 full-time (10 women), 6 part-time (4 women); includes 1 minority (Asian, non-Hispanic/Latino), 17 international. Average age 24. 69 applicants, 55% accepted, 13 enrolled. In 2011, 16 master's awarded. *Degree requirements:* For master's, thesis or alternative. *Entrance requirements:* For master's, GRE General Test. Additional exam requirements/recommendations for international students: Required—TOEFL (minimum score 550 paper-based; 213 computer-based; 79 iBT). *Application deadline:* For fall admission, 6/1 priority date for domestic students, 1/15 for international students; for spring admission, 9/1 priority date for domestic students, 6/15 for international students. Applications are processed on a rolling basis. Application fee: $50 ($75 for international students). Electronic applications accepted. *Expenses:* Tuition, state resident: full-time $5899; part-time $245.80 per credit hour. Tuition, nonresident: full-time $13,411; part-time $558.80 per credit hour. *Required fees:* $2680.60; $86.50 per credit hour. $920.30 per semester. *Financial support:* In 2011–12, 3 students received support. Application deadline: 4/15; applicants required to submit FAFSA. *Faculty research:* Biotechnology and applied science. *Unit head:* Dr. David B. Knaff, Advisor, 806-742-0288, Fax: 806-742-1289, E-mail: david.knaff@ttu.edu. *Application contact:* Jatindra Tripathy, Senior Research Associate, 806-742-3722 Ext. 229, Fax: 806-742-3788, E-mail: jatindra.tripathy@ttu.edu. Web site: http://www.orgs.ttu.edu/biotechnologyandgenomics/.

Texas Tech University Health Sciences Center, Graduate School of Biomedical Sciences, Department of Cell Biology and Biochemistry, Program in Biotechnology, Lubbock, TX 79430. Offers MS. *Entrance requirements:* For master's, GRE General Test, minimum GPA of 3.0. Additional exam requirements/recommendations for international students: Required—TOEFL. *Faculty research:* Reproductive endocrinology, immunology, molecular biology and developmental biochemistry, biology of developing systems.

Thomas Jefferson University, Jefferson College of Graduate Studies, PhD Program in Tissue Engineering and Regenerative Medicine, Philadelphia, PA 19107. Offers PhD. *Faculty:* 18 full-time (6 women). *Students:* 4 full-time (3 women); includes 1 minority (Asian, non-Hispanic/Latino). 3 applicants, 0% accepted. In 2011, 2 doctorates awarded. *Degree requirements:* For doctorate, comprehensive exam, thesis/dissertation. *Entrance requirements:* For doctorate, GRE General Test, minimum GPA of 3.2. Additional exam requirements/recommendations for international students: Required—TOEFL (minimum score 250 computer-based; 100 iBT) or IELTS. *Application deadline:* For fall admission, 1/15 priority date for domestic students, 1/15 for international students. Applications are processed on a rolling basis. Application fee: $50. Electronic applications accepted. *Financial support:* In 2011–12, 4 students received support, including 4 fellowships with full tuition reimbursements available (averaging $52,883 per year); Federal Work-Study, institutionally sponsored loans, traineeships, and stipend also available. Financial award application deadline: 5/1; financial award applicants required to submit FAFSA. *Faculty research:* Skeletal development, biomaterials, bone implant interaction, tissue engineering, high resolution imaging. *Total annual research expenditures:* $8 million. *Unit head:* Dr. Irving Shapiro, Program Director, 215-955-7217, Fax: 215-955-9159, E-mail: irving.shapiro@jefferson.edu. *Application contact:* Marc E. Stearns, Director of Admissions, 215-503-0155, Fax: 215-503-9920, E-mail: jcgs-info@jefferson.edu. Web site: http://www.jefferson.edu/jcgs/phd/term/.

Tufts University, Graduate School of Arts and Sciences, Graduate Certificate Programs, Biotechnology Engineering Program, Medford, MA 02155. Offers Certificate. Part-time and evening/weekend programs available. Electronic applications accepted. *Expenses: Tuition:* Full-time $41,208; part-time $1030 per credit hour. Full-time tuition and fees vary according to degree level, program and student level. Part-time tuition and fees vary according to course load.

Tufts University, Graduate School of Arts and Sciences, Graduate Certificate Programs, Biotechnology Program, Medford, MA 02155. Offers Certificate. Part-time and evening/weekend programs available. Electronic applications accepted. *Expenses: Tuition:* Full-time $41,208; part-time $1030 per credit hour. Full-time tuition and fees vary according to degree level, program and student level. Part-time tuition and fees vary according to course load.

Tufts University, School of Engineering, Department of Chemical and Biological Engineering, Medford, MA 02155. Offers bioengineering (ME, MS), including cell and bioprocess engineering; biotechnology engineering (ME, MS, PhD). Part-time programs available. *Faculty:* 8 full-time, 2 part-time/adjunct. *Students:* 34 full-time (16 women); includes 8 minority (1 Black or African American, non-Hispanic/Latino; 7 Asian, non-Hispanic/Latino), 13 international. Average age 27. 79 applicants, 30% accepted, 10 enrolled. In 2011, 8 master's, 6 doctorates awarded. Terminal master's awarded for partial completion of doctoral program. *Degree requirements:* For master's, thesis (for some programs); for doctorate, thesis/dissertation. *Entrance requirements:* For master's and doctorate, GRE General Test. Additional exam requirements/recommendations for international students: Required—TOEFL (minimum score 550 paper-based; 213 computer-based; 80 iBT). *Application deadline:* For fall admission, 1/15 priority date for domestic students, 12/15 for international students; for spring admission, 10/15 for domestic students, 9/15 for international students. Applications are processed on a rolling basis. Application fee: $75. Electronic applications accepted. *Expenses: Tuition:* Full-time $41,208; part-time $1030 per credit hour. Full-time tuition and fees vary according to degree level, program and student level. Part-time tuition and fees vary according to course load. *Financial support:* Fellowships with full tuition reimbursements, research assistantships with full and partial tuition reimbursements, teaching assistantships with full and partial tuition reimbursements, Federal Work-Study, scholarships/grants, tuition waivers (partial), and unspecified assistantships available. Financial award application deadline: 1/15; financial award applicants required to submit FAFSA. *Faculty research:* Clean energy with materials, biomaterials, colloids; metabolic engineering, biotechnology; process control; reaction kinetics, catalysis; transport phenomena. *Unit head:* Dr. Kyongbum Lee, Chair, 617-627-3900. *Application contact:* Beth Frasso, Staff, 617-627-3900, E-mail: chbe@tufts.edu. Web site: http://engineering.tufts.edu/chbe/.

Universidad de las Américas–Puebla, Division of Graduate Studies, School of Sciences, Program in Biotechnology, Puebla, Mexico. Offers MS. *Degree requirements:* For master's, one foreign language, thesis.

University at Buffalo, the State University of New York, Graduate School, School of Medicine and Biomedical Sciences, Graduate Programs in Medicine and Biomedical Sciences, Department of Biotechnical and Clinical Laboratory Sciences, Buffalo, NY 14214. Offers biotechnology (MS). *Accreditation:* NAACLS. Part-time programs available. *Faculty:* 8 full-time (3 women). *Students:* 15 full-time (9 women), 1 (woman) part-time; includes 1 minority (Asian, non-Hispanic/Latino), 11 international. 128 applicants, 9% accepted, 11 enrolled. In 2011, 9 master's awarded. *Degree requirements:* For master's, thesis. *Entrance requirements:* For master's, GRE General Test, minimum GPA of 3.0 or equivalent, 4-year U.S. bachelor's degree or equivalent. Additional exam requirements/recommendations for international students: Required—TOEFL (minimum score 213 computer-based; 79 iBT), IELTS (minimum score 6). *Application deadline:* For fall admission, 3/1 priority date for domestic students, 2/1 for international students. Applications are processed on a rolling basis. Application fee: $50. Electronic applications accepted. *Financial support:* In 2011–12, 5 teaching assistantships with full tuition reimbursements (averaging $9,000 per year) were awarded; health care benefits and unspecified assistantships also available. *Faculty research:* Tumor immunology, oxidative stress, breast cancer, erythropoiesis, toxicology. *Total annual research expenditures:* $756,762. *Unit head:* Dr. Stephen Thomas Koury, Director of Graduate Studies, 716-829-5188, Fax: 716-829-3601, E-mail: stvkoury@buffalo.edu. *Application contact:* Elizabeth A. White, Administrative Director, 716-829-3399, Fax: 716-829-2437, E-mail: bethw@buffalo.edu. Web site: http://www.smbs.buffalo.edu/cls/biotech-ms.html.

The University of Alabama in Huntsville, School of Graduate Studies, Interdisciplinary Studies, Interdisciplinary Program in Biotechnology Science and Engineering, Huntsville, AL 35899. Offers PhD. Part-time and evening/weekend programs available. *Faculty:* 19 full-time (3 women), 1 (woman) part-time/adjunct. *Students:* 25 full-time (14 women), 5 part-time (3 women); includes 5 minority (4 Black or African American, non-Hispanic/Latino; 1 American Indian or Alaska Native, non-Hispanic/Latino), 13 international. Average age 30. 17 applicants, 65% accepted, 5 enrolled. In 2011, 2 doctorates awarded. *Degree requirements:* For doctorate, comprehensive exam, thesis/dissertation, oral and written exams. *Entrance requirements:* For doctorate, GRE General Test, bachelor's degree in science or engineering, minimum GPA of 3.0. Additional exam requirements/recommendations for international students: Required—TOEFL (minimum score 550 paper-based; 213 computer-based; 62 iBT). *Application deadline:* For fall admission, 7/15 for domestic students, 4/1 for international students; for spring admission, 11/30 for domestic students, 9/1 for international students. Applications are processed on a rolling basis. Application fee: $40 ($50 for international students). Electronic applications accepted. *Expenses:* Tuition, state resident: full-time $7830; part-time $473.50 per credit. Tuition, nonresident: full-time $18,748; part-time $1128.33 per credit. Tuition and fees vary according to course load and program. *Financial support:* In 2011–12, 25 students received support, including 1 fellowship with full tuition reimbursement available (averaging $22,500 per year), 8 research assistantships with full tuition reimbursements available (averaging $13,222 per year), 14 teaching assistantships with full tuition reimbursements available (averaging $11,021 per year); career-related internships or fieldwork, Federal Work-Study, institutionally sponsored loans, scholarships/grants, health care benefits, tuition waivers (full), and unspecified assistantships also available. Support available to part-time students. Financial award application deadline: 4/1; financial award applicants required to submit FAFSA. *Faculty research:* Protein structure and function, drug discovery, NMR spectroscopy, gene function and expression, molecular patterning. *Unit head:* Dr. Joseph Ng, Coordinator, 256-824-2711, Fax: 256-824-6349, E-mail: uahbiotechnology@gmail.com. *Application contact:* Kim Gray, Graduate Studies Admissions Coordinator, 256-824-6002, Fax: 256-824-6405, E-mail: deangrad@uah.edu. Web site: http://biotech.uah.edu.

University of Alberta, Faculty of Graduate Studies and Research, Department of Biological Sciences, Edmonton, AB T6G 2E1, Canada. Offers environmental biology and ecology (M Sc, PhD); microbiology and biotechnology (M Sc, PhD); molecular biology and genetics (M Sc, PhD); physiology and cell biology (M Sc, PhD); plant biology (M Sc, PhD); systematics and evolution (M Sc, PhD). Terminal master's awarded for partial completion of doctoral program. *Degree requirements:* For master's, thesis; for doctorate, thesis/dissertation. *Entrance requirements:* Additional exam requirements/recommendations for international students: Required—TOEFL.

University of Calgary, Faculty of Medicine and Faculty of Graduate Studies, Program in Biomedical Technology, Calgary, AB T2N 1N4, Canada. Offers MBT. Part-time programs available. *Degree requirements:* For master's, comprehensive exam, practicum. *Entrance requirements:* For master's, minimum GPA of 3.2 in last 2 years, B Sc in biological science. Additional exam requirements/recommendations for international students: Required—TOEFL (minimum score 600 paper-based; 250 computer-based). Electronic applications accepted. *Expenses:* Contact institution. *Faculty research:* Patent law, intellectual proprietorship.

University of California, Irvine, School of Biological Sciences, Department of Molecular Biology and Biochemistry, Program in Biotechnology, Irvine, CA 92697. Offers MS. *Students:* 33 full-time (18 women); includes 14 minority (10 Asian, non-Hispanic/Latino; 4 Two or more races, non-Hispanic/Latino), 11 international. Average age 25. 147 applicants, 19% accepted, 16 enrolled. In 2011, 14 master's awarded. *Entrance requirements:* For master's, GRE General Test, GRE Subject Test, minimum GPA of 3.0. *Application deadline:* For fall admission, 3/1 priority date for domestic students, 3/1 for international students. Applications are processed on a rolling basis. Application fee: $80 ($100 for international students). Electronic applications accepted. *Financial support:* Application deadline: 3/1; applicants required to submit FAFSA. *Unit head:* Renee Meria Frigo, Program Manager, 949-824-8145, Fax: 949-824-1965, E-mail: rfrigo@uci.edu. *Application contact:* Cathy A. Temple, Student Affairs Officer I, 949-824-6034, Fax: 949-824-8551, E-mail: catemple@uci.edu.

University of Central Florida, College of Medicine, Burnett School of Biomedical Sciences, Orlando, FL 32816. Offers biomedical sciences (MS, PhD); biotechnology (MS). *Faculty:* 41 full-time (13 women), 6 part-time/adjunct (3 women). *Students:* 105 full-time (62 women), 16 part-time (11 women); includes 20 minority (3 Black or African American, non-Hispanic/Latino; 10 Asian, non-Hispanic/Latino; 7 Hispanic/Latino), 54 international. Average age 27. 208 applicants, 35% accepted, 40 enrolled. In 2011, 38 master's, 9 doctorates awarded. *Expenses:* Tuition, state resident: part-time $277.08 per credit hour. Tuition, nonresident: part-time $277.08 per credit hour. Part-time tuition and fees vary according to degree level and program. *Financial support:* In 2011–12, 85 students received support, including 10 fellowships (averaging $10,800 per year), 55 research assistantships (averaging $10,000 per year), 51 teaching assistantships (averaging $8,500 per year). *Unit head:* Dr. Pappachan E. Kolattukudy, Director, 407-823-2357, Fax: 407-823-0956, E-mail: pk@ucf.edu. *Application contact:* Barbara Rodriguez, Director, Admissions and Registration, 407-823-2766, Fax: 407-823-6442, E-mail: gradadmissions@ucf.edu. Web site: http://www.biomed.ucf.edu/.

University of Delaware, College of Arts and Sciences, Department of Biological Sciences, Newark, DE 19716. Offers biotechnology (MS); cancer biology (MS, PhD); cell and extracellular matrix biology (MS, PhD); cell and systems physiology (MS, PhD); developmental biology (MS, PhD); ecology and evolution (MS, PhD); microbiology (MS, PhD); molecular biology and genetics (MS, PhD). Terminal master's awarded for partial completion of doctoral program. *Degree requirements:* For master's, thesis, preliminary exam; for doctorate, comprehensive exam, thesis/dissertation, preliminary exam. *Entrance requirements:* For master's and doctorate, GRE General Test. Additional exam requirements/recommendations for international students: Required—TOEFL (minimum score 600 paper-based; 250 computer-based); Recommended—TWE. Electronic applications accepted. *Faculty research:* Microorganisms, bone, cancer metastasis, developmental biology, cell biology, DNA.

University of Guelph, Graduate Studies, Ontario Agricultural College, Department of Environmental Biology, Guelph, ON N1G 2W1, Canada. Offers entomology (M Sc, PhD); environmental microbiology and biotechnology (M Sc, PhD); environmental toxicology (M Sc, PhD); plant and forest systems (M Sc, PhD); plant pathology (M Sc, PhD). Part-time programs available. *Degree requirements:* For master's, thesis; for doctorate, comprehensive exam, thesis/dissertation. *Entrance requirements:* For master's, minimum 75% average during previous 2 years of course work; for doctorate, minimum 75% average. Additional exam requirements/recommendations for international students: Required—TOEFL or IELTS. Electronic applications accepted. *Faculty research:* Entomology, environmental microbiology and biotechnology, environmental toxicology, forest ecology, plant pathology.

University of Houston–Clear Lake, School of Science and Computer Engineering, Program in Biotechnology, Houston, TX 77058-1098. Offers MS.

University of Illinois at Chicago, College of Pharmacy, Center for Pharmaceutical Biotechnology, Chicago, IL 60607-7173. Offers PhD.

The University of Kansas, University of Kansas Medical Center, School of Health Professions, Program in Molecular Biotechnology, Lawrence, KS 66045. Offers MS. *Faculty:* 4. *Students:* 5 full-time (4 women), 2 part-time (0 women); includes 1 minority (American Indian or Alaska Native, non-Hispanic/Latino), 4 international. Average age 25. 13 applicants, 54% accepted, 5 enrolled. *Degree requirements:* For master's, comprehensive exam. *Entrance requirements:* For master's, GRE General Test. Additional exam requirements/recommendations for international students: Required—TOEFL. *Application deadline:* For fall admission, 2/1 priority date for domestic students, 2/1 for international students. Application fee: $60. Electronic applications accepted. Tuition and fees vary according to course load, campus/location, program and reciprocity agreements. *Financial support:* Career-related internships or fieldwork available. Financial award application deadline: 2/14; financial award applicants required to submit FAFSA. *Faculty research:* Diabetes, obesity, polycystic kidney disease, protein structure and function, cell signaling pathways. *Total annual research expenditures:* $85,936. *Unit head:* Dr. Eric Elsinghorst, Director of Graduate Studies, 913-588-1089, E-mail: eelsinghorst@kumc.edu. *Application contact:* Moffett Ferguson,

Student Affairs Coordinator, 913-588-5275, Fax: 913-588-5254, E-mail: mfergus1@kumc.edu. Web site: http://mb.kumc.edu.

The University of Manchester, Faculty of Life Sciences, Manchester, United Kingdom. Offers adaptive organismal biology (M Phil, PhD); animal biology (M Phil, PhD); biochemistry (M Phil, PhD); bioinformatics (M Phil, PhD); biomolecular sciences (M Phil, PhD); biotechnology (M Phil, PhD); cell biology (M Phil, PhD); cell matrix research (M Phil, PhD); channels and transporters (M Phil, PhD); developmental biology (M Phil, PhD); Egyptology (M Phil, PhD); environmental biology (M Phil, PhD); evolutionary biology (M Phil, PhD); gene expression (M Phil, PhD); genetics (M Phil, PhD); history of science, technology and medicine (M Phil, PhD); immunology (M Phil, PhD); integrative neurobiology and behavior (M Phil, PhD); membrane trafficking (M Phil, PhD); microbiology (M Phil, PhD); molecular and cellular neuroscience (M Phil, PhD); molecular biology (M Phil, PhD); molecular cancer studies (M Phil, PhD); neuroscience (M Phil, PhD); ophthalmology (M Phil, PhD); optometry (M Phil, PhD); organelle function (M Phil, PhD); pharmacology (M Phil, PhD); physiology (M Phil, PhD); plant sciences (M Phil, PhD); stem cell research (M Phil, PhD); structural biology (M Phil, PhD); systems neuroscience (M Phil, PhD); toxicology (M Phil, PhD).

University of Maryland, Baltimore County, Graduate School, College of Natural and Mathematical Sciences, Department of Biological Sciences, Program in Biotechnology Management, Baltimore, MD 21250. Offers MPS, Graduate Certificate. Part-time and evening/weekend programs available. *Faculty:* 10 part-time/adjunct (5 women). *Students:* 8 full-time (4 women), 25 part-time (13 women); includes 15 minority (6 Black or African American, non-Hispanic/Latino; 8 Asian, non-Hispanic/Latino; 1 Hispanic/Latino), 4 international. Average age 28. 43 applicants, 60% accepted, 17 enrolled. In 2011, 17 master's, 2 other advanced degrees awarded. *Entrance requirements:* Additional exam requirements/recommendations for international students: Required—TOEFL (minimum score 597 paper-based; 247 computer-based; 99 iBT). *Application deadline:* For fall admission, 8/15 for domestic students, 1/1 for international students; for spring admission, 12/15 for domestic students. Electronic applications accepted. *Financial support:* Career-related internships or fieldwork available. Financial award applicants required to submit FAFSA. *Unit head:* Sonya Crosby, Director, Professional Studies, 410-455-3899, E-mail: scrosby@umbc.edu. *Application contact:* Nancy Clements, Program Specialist, 410-455-5536, E-mail: nancyc@umbc.edu. Web site: http://www.umbc.edu/biotech/.

University of Maryland University College, Graduate School of Management and Technology, Program in Biotechnology Studies, Adelphi, MD 20783. Offers MS, Certificate. Part-time and evening/weekend programs available. Postbaccalaureate distance learning degree programs offered (no on-campus study). *Students:* 13 full-time (9 women), 472 part-time (281 women); includes 228 minority (129 Black or African American, non-Hispanic/Latino; 2 American Indian or Alaska Native, non-Hispanic/Latino; 54 Asian, non-Hispanic/Latino; 35 Hispanic/Latino; 2 Native Hawaiian or other Pacific Islander, non-Hispanic/Latino; 6 Two or more races, non-Hispanic/Latino), 14 international. Average age 33. 134 applicants, 100% accepted, 89 enrolled. In 2011, 65 master's, 17 other advanced degrees awarded. *Degree requirements:* For master's, thesis or alternative, capstone course. *Application deadline:* Applications are processed on a rolling basis. Application fee: $50. Electronic applications accepted. *Financial support:* Federal Work-Study and scholarships/grants available. Support available to part-time students. Financial award application deadline: 6/1; financial award applicants required to submit FAFSA. *Unit head:* Dr. Rana Khan, Director, 240-684-2400, Fax: 240-684-2401, E-mail: rkhan@umuc.edu. *Application contact:* Coordinator, Graduate Admissions, 800-888-8682, Fax: 240-684-2151, E-mail: newgrad@umuc.edu. Web site: http://www.umuc.edu/grad/msbt.shtml.

University of Massachusetts Amherst, Graduate School, College of Natural Sciences, Department of Animal Biotechnology and Biomedical Sciences, Amherst, MA 01003. Offers MS, PhD. Part-time programs available. *Faculty:* 23 full-time (10 women). *Students:* 27 full-time (16 women), 9 international. Average age 30. 51 applicants, 18% accepted, 6 enrolled. In 2011, 6 master's, 2 doctorates awarded. Terminal master's awarded for partial completion of doctoral program. *Degree requirements:* For master's, thesis or alternative; for doctorate, comprehensive exam, thesis/dissertation. *Entrance requirements:* For master's and doctorate, GRE General Test. Additional exam requirements/recommendations for international students: Required—TOEFL (minimum score 550 paper-based; 213 computer-based; 80 iBT), IELTS (minimum score 6.5). *Application deadline:* For fall admission, 2/1 for domestic and international students; for spring admission, 10/1 for domestic and international students. Applications are processed on a rolling basis. Application fee: $50 ($65 for international students). Electronic applications accepted. Tuition and fees vary according to course load, campus/location and program. *Financial support:* Fellowships with full and partial tuition reimbursements, research assistantships with full and partial tuition reimbursements, teaching assistantships with full and partial tuition reimbursements, career-related internships or fieldwork, Federal Work-Study, scholarships/grants, traineeships, health care benefits, tuition waivers (full and partial), and unspecified assistantships available. Support available to part-time students. Financial award application deadline: 2/1. *Unit head:* Dr. Lisa Minter, Graduate Program Director, 413-577-1193, Fax: 413-577-1150. *Application contact:* Lindsay DeSantis, Interim Supervisor of Admissions, 413-545-0722, Fax: 413-577-0010, E-mail: gradadm@grad.umass.edu. Web site: http://www.vasci.umass.edu/graduate-program-overview.

University of Massachusetts Boston, Office of Graduate Studies, College of Science and Mathematics, Program in Biotechnology and Biomedical Science, Boston, MA 02125-3393. Offers MS. Part-time and evening/weekend programs available. *Degree requirements:* For master's, comprehensive exam, thesis optional, oral exams. *Entrance requirements:* For master's, GRE General Test, GRE Subject Test, minimum GPA of 2.75, 3.0 in science and math. *Faculty research:* Evolutionary and molecular immunology, molecular genetics, tissue culture, computerized laboratory technology.

University of Massachusetts Dartmouth, Graduate School, Program in Biomedical Engineering and Biotechnology, North Dartmouth, MA 02747-2300. Offers MS, PhD. Part-time programs available. *Students:* 20 full-time (12 women), 13 part-time (6 women); includes 1 minority (Asian, non-Hispanic/Latino), 17 international. Average age 29. 21 applicants, 52% accepted, 4 enrolled. In 2011, 2 degrees awarded. *Median time to degree:* Of those who began their doctoral program in fall 2003, 33% received their degree in 8 years or less. *Degree requirements:* For doctorate, comprehensive exam, thesis/dissertation. *Entrance requirements:* For master's and doctorate, GRE, minimum GPA of 3.0, 3 letters of recommendation, resume, statement of intent. Additional exam requirements/recommendations for international students: Required—TOEFL (minimum score 533 paper-based; 200 computer-based; 72 iBT). *Application deadline:* For fall admission, 2/15 for domestic students, 1/15 for international students; for spring admission, 11/15 for domestic students, 10/15 for international students. Application fee: $40 ($60 for international students). Electronic applications accepted. *Expenses:* Tuition, state resident: full-time $2071; part-time $86.29 per credit. Tuition, nonresident: full-time $8099; part-time $337.46 per credit. *Required fees:* $438.58 per credit. Part-time tuition and fees vary according to class time, course load, degree level and reciprocity agreements. *Financial support:* In 2011–12, 2 fellowships with full tuition reimbursements (averaging $20,000 per year), 11 research assistantships with full tuition reimbursements (averaging $11,277 per year), 2 teaching assistantships with full tuition reimbursements (averaging $11,250 per year) were awarded; unspecified assistantships also available. Financial award application deadline: 3/1; financial award applicants required to submit FAFSA. *Faculty research:* Tetracycline-encapsulated chitosan microspheres, artificial tissues, sensor arrays for orthopedic rehab, blue light cures, healing bandages. *Total annual research expenditures:* $197,000. *Unit head:* Sanka Bhowmick, Graduate Program Director for Engineering Options, 508-999-8619, Fax: 508-999-8881, E-mail: sbhowmick@umassd.edu. *Application contact:* Elan Turcotte-Shamski, Graduate Admissions Officer, 508-999-8604, Fax: 508-999-8183, E-mail: graduate@umassd.edu.

University of Massachusetts Lowell, College of Sciences, Department of Biological Sciences, Lowell, MA 01854-2881. Offers biochemistry (PhD); biological sciences (MS); biotechnology (MS). Part-time programs available. *Degree requirements:* For master's, thesis; for doctorate, thesis/dissertation. *Entrance requirements:* For master's and doctorate, GRE General Test. Electronic applications accepted.

University of Minnesota, Twin Cities Campus, Graduate School, Program in Microbial Engineering, Minneapolis, MN 55455-0213. Offers MS. Part-time programs available. *Degree requirements:* For master's, thesis. *Entrance requirements:* For master's, GRE General Test. Additional exam requirements/recommendations for international students: Required—TOEFL. *Faculty research:* Microbial genetics, oncogenesis, gene transfer, fermentation, bioreactors, genetics of antibiotic biosynthesis.

University of Missouri–St. Louis, College of Arts and Sciences, Department of Biology, St. Louis, MO 63121. Offers biotechnology (Certificate); cell and molecular biology (MS, PhD); ecology, evolution and systematics (MS, PhD); tropical biology and conservation (Certificate). Part-time programs available. *Faculty:* 43 full-time (13 women), 4 part-time/adjunct (1 woman). *Students:* 68 full-time (33 women), 64 part-time (28 women); includes 20 minority (9 Black or African American, non-Hispanic/Latino; 7 Asian, non-Hispanic/Latino; 3 Hispanic/Latino; 1 Two or more races, non-Hispanic/Latino), 43 international. Average age 28. 122 applicants, 48% accepted, 36 enrolled. In 2011, 20 master's, 3 doctorates, 11 other advanced degrees awarded. *Degree requirements:* For master's, thesis or alternative; for doctorate, thesis/dissertation, 1 semester of teaching experience. *Entrance requirements:* For master's, 3 letters of recommendation; for doctorate, GRE General Test, 3 letters of recommendation. Additional exam requirements/recommendations for international students: Required—TOEFL. *Application deadline:* For fall admission, 12/15 priority date for domestic students, 12/15 for international students; for spring admission, 12/1 priority date for domestic students, 12/1 for international students. Applications are processed on a rolling basis. Application fee: $35 ($40 for international students). Electronic applications accepted. *Expenses:* Tuition, state resident: full-time $6273; part-time $3866 per year. Tuition, nonresident: full-time $14,969; part-time $9980 per year. *Required fees:* $315 per year. *Financial support:* In 2011–12, 13 research assistantships with full and partial tuition reimbursements (averaging $15,300 per year), 27 teaching assistantships with full and partial tuition reimbursements (averaging $15,300 per year) were awarded; fellowships with full tuition reimbursements, career-related internships or fieldwork, and Federal Work-Study also available. Support available to part-time students. Financial award application deadline: 2/1. *Faculty research:* Molecular biology, microbial genetics, animal behavior, tropical ecology, plant systematics. *Unit head:* Dr. Wendy Olivas, Director of Graduate Studies, 314-516-6200, Fax: 314-516-6233, E-mail: olivasw@umsl.edu. *Application contact:* 314-516-5458, Fax: 314-516-6996, E-mail: gradadm@umsl.edu. Web site: http://www.umsl.edu/divisions/artscience/biology/.

University of Nevada, Reno, Graduate School, College of Agriculture, Biotechnology and Natural Resources, Program in Biotechnology, Reno, NV 89557. Offers MS. 5 year degree; students are admitted to as undergraduates. *Degree requirements:* For master's, thesis. *Entrance requirements:* For master's, GRE, minimum GPA of 2.75. Additional exam requirements/recommendations for international students: Required—TOEFL (minimum score 500 paper-based; 173 computer-based; 61 iBT), IELTS (minimum score 6). Electronic applications accepted. *Faculty research:* Cancer biology, plant virology.

University of Northern Iowa, Graduate College, College of Humanities, Arts and Sciences, Department of Biology, Cedar Falls, IA 50614. Offers biology (MA, MS); biotechnology (PSM); ecosystem management (PSM). Part-time programs available. *Students:* 30 full-time (11 women), 4 part-time (2 women); includes 1 minority (Asian, non-Hispanic/Latino), 4 international. 57 applicants, 60% accepted, 23 enrolled. In 2011, 19 master's awarded. *Degree requirements:* For master's, comprehensive exam (for some programs), thesis or alternative. *Entrance requirements:* For master's, minimum GPA of 3.0; 3 letters of recommendation. Additional exam requirements/recommendations for international students: Required—TOEFL (minimum score 500 paper-based; 180 computer-based; 61 iBT). *Application deadline:* For fall admission, 8/1 priority date for domestic students. Applications are processed on a rolling basis. Application fee: $50 ($70 for international students). Electronic applications accepted. *Expenses:* Tuition, state resident: full-time $7476. Tuition, nonresident: full-time $16,410. *Required fees:* $942. *Financial support:* Scholarships/grants available. Financial award application deadline: 2/1. *Unit head:* Dr. David Saunders, Head, 319-273-2456, Fax: 319-273-7125, E-mail: david.saunders@uni.edu. *Application contact:* Laurie S. Russell, Record Analyst, 319-273-2623, Fax: 319-273-2885, E-mail: laurie.russell@uni.edu. Web site: http://www.biology.uni.edu/.

University of North Texas Health Science Center at Fort Worth, Graduate School of Biomedical Sciences, Fort Worth, TX 76107-2699. Offers anatomy and cell biology (MS, PhD); biochemistry and molecular biology (MS, PhD); biomedical sciences (MS, PhD); biotechnology (MS); forensic genetics (MS); integrative physiology (MS, PhD); medical science (MS); microbiology and immunology (MS, PhD); pharmacology (MS, PhD); science education (MS); DO/MS; DO/PhD. Terminal master's awarded for partial completion of doctoral program. *Degree requirements:* For master's, thesis; for doctorate, thesis/dissertation. *Entrance requirements:* For master's and doctorate, GRE General Test. Additional exam requirements/recommendations for international students: Required—TOEFL. *Expenses:* Contact institution. *Faculty research:* Alzheimer's disease, aging, eye diseases, cancer, cardiovascular disease.

University of Pennsylvania, School of Engineering and Applied Science, Program in Biotechnology, Philadelphia, PA 19104. Offers MS. Part-time programs available. *Students:* 95 full-time (54 women), 28 part-time (17 women); includes 20 minority (1 Black or African American, non-Hispanic/Latino; 14 Asian, non-Hispanic/Latino; 3

Hispanic/Latino; 2 Two or more races, non-Hispanic/Latino), 76 international. 211 applicants, 44% accepted, 72 enrolled. In 2011, 56 master's awarded. *Entrance requirements:* For master's, GRE General Test, bachelor's degree in science or undergraduate course work in molecular biology. Additional exam requirements/ recommendations for international students: Required—TOEFL. *Application deadline:* For fall admission, 6/1 priority date for domestic students, 5/1 for international students. Applications are processed on a rolling basis. Application fee: $70. Electronic applications accepted. *Expenses: Tuition:* Full-time $26,660; part-time $4944 per course. *Required fees:* $2318; $291 per course. Tuition and fees vary according to course load, degree level and program. *Unit head:* Eduardo D. Glandt, Dean, 215-898-7244, Fax: 215-573-2018, E-mail: seasdean@seas.upenn.edu. *Application contact:* 215-898-0221, E-mail: biotech@seas.upenn.edu. Web site: http://www.seas.upenn.edu.

University of Rhode Island, Graduate School, College of the Environment and Life Sciences, Department of Cell and Molecular Biology, Kingston, RI 02881. Offers biochemistry (MS, PhD); clinical laboratory sciences (MS), including biotechnology, clinical laboratory science, cytopathology; microbiology (MS, PhD); molecular genetics (MS, PhD). Part-time programs available. *Faculty:* 14 full-time (5 women), 3 part-time/ adjunct (2 women). *Students:* 32 full-time (15 women), 37 part-time (23 women); includes 2 minority (1 Asian, non-Hispanic/Latino; 1 Hispanic/Latino), 1 international. In 2011, 2 master's, 2 doctorates awarded. *Degree requirements:* For master's, comprehensive exam (for some programs); for doctorate, comprehensive exam. *Entrance requirements:* For master's and doctorate, GRE, 2 letters of recommendation. Additional exam requirements/recommendations for international students: Required—TOEFL (minimum score 550 paper-based; 213 computer-based). *Application deadline:* For fall admission, 7/15 for domestic students, 2/1 for international students; for spring admission, 11/15 for domestic students, 7/15 for international students. Application fee: $65. Electronic applications accepted. *Expenses:* Tuition, state resident: full-time $10,432; part-time $580 per credit hour. Tuition, nonresident: full-time $23,130; part-time $1285 per credit hour. *Required fees:* $1362; $36 per credit hour. $35 per semester. One-time fee: $130. *Financial support:* In 2011–12, 2 research assistantships with full and partial tuition reimbursements (averaging $13,894 per year), 6 teaching assistantships with full and partial tuition reimbursements (averaging $12,850 per year) were awarded. Financial award application deadline: 7/15; financial award applicants required to submit FAFSA. *Faculty research:* Genomics and Sequencing Center: an interdisciplinary genomics research and undergraduate and graduate student training program which provides researchers access to cutting-edge technologies in the field of genomics. *Unit head:* Dr. Jay Sperry, Chairperson, 401-874-2201, Fax: 401-874-2202, E-mail: jsperry@mail.uri.edu. *Application contact:* Nasser H. Zawia, Dean of the Graduate School, 401-874-5909, Fax: 401-874-5787, E-mail: nzawia@uri.edu. Web site: http://cels.uri.edu/cmb/.

University of San Francisco, College of Arts and Sciences, Biotechnology Program, San Francisco, CA 94117-1080. Offers PSM. *Expenses: Tuition:* Full-time $20,070; part-time $1115 per unit. Tuition and fees vary according to course load, campus/location and program. *Unit head:* Dr. Jennifer Dever, Director, 415-422-6755, E-mail: dever@usfca.edu. *Application contact:* Information Contact, 415-422-5135, Fax: 415-422-2217, E-mail: asgraduate@usfca.edu. Web site: http://www.usfca.edu/biotech/.

University of Saskatchewan, College of Graduate Studies and Research, Edwards School of Business, Program in Business Administration, Saskatoon, SK S7N 5A2, Canada. Offers agribusiness management (MBA); biotechnology management (MBA); health services management (MBA); indigenous management (MBA); international business management (MBA).

University of South Florida, Graduate School, College of Medicine and Graduate School, Graduate Programs in Medical Sciences, Tampa, FL 33620-9951. Offers bioethics and medical humanities (MABMH); bioinformatics and computational biology (MSBCB); biotechnology (MSB); medical sciences (MSMS, PhD). *Students:* 439 full-time (235 women), 111 part-time (65 women); includes 258 minority (82 Black or African American, non-Hispanic/Latino; 2 American Indian or Alaska Native, non-Hispanic/ Latino; 85 Asian, non-Hispanic/Latino; 77 Hispanic/Latino; 12 Two or more races, non-Hispanic/Latino), 24 international. Average age 27. 1,032 applicants, 53% accepted, 364 enrolled. In 2011, 167 master's, 14 doctorates awarded. Terminal master's awarded for partial completion of doctoral program. *Degree requirements:* For master's, comprehensive exam, thesis; for doctorate, comprehensive exam, thesis/dissertation. *Entrance requirements:* For master's, GRE, MCAT, or GMAT, minimum GPA of 3.0 in last 60 hours of coursework; for doctorate, GRE, minimum GPA of 3.0 in last 60 hours of coursework, three letters of recommendation, personal statement, interview. Additional exam requirements/recommendations for international students: Required—TOEFL (minimum score 550 paper-based; 213 computer-based; 79 iBT) or IELTS (minimum score 6.5). *Application deadline:* For fall admission, 2/15 for domestic students, 1/2 for international students. Application fee: $30. *Expenses:* Contact institution. *Unit head:* Dr. Michael Barber, Program Director, 813-974-9702, Fax: 813-974-4317, E-mail: mbarber@health.usf.edu. *Application contact:* Francisco Vera, Assistant Director for Admissions, 813-974-8800, E-mail: fvera@usf.edu. Web site: http://health.usf.edu/ medicine/graduatestudies.

The University of Texas at Dallas, School of Natural Sciences and Mathematics, Department of Biology, Richardson, TX 75080. Offers bioinformatics and computational biology (MS); biotechnology (MS); molecular and cell biology (MS, PhD). Part-time and evening/weekend programs available. *Faculty:* 18 full-time (2 women), 1 part-time/ adjunct (0 women). *Students:* 111 full-time (59 women), 13 part-time (6 women); includes 19 minority (2 Black or African American, non-Hispanic/Latino; 14 Asian, non-Hispanic/Latino; 3 Hispanic/Latino), 86 international. Average age 27. 483 applicants, 31% accepted, 67 enrolled. In 2011, 39 master's, 7 doctorates awarded. *Degree requirements:* For master's, thesis optional; for doctorate, thesis/dissertation, publishable paper. *Entrance requirements:* For master's and doctorate, GRE (minimum combined score of 1000 on verbal and quantitative). Additional exam requirements/ recommendations for international students: Required—TOEFL (minimum score 550 paper-based; 215 computer-based; 80 iBT). *Application deadline:* For fall admission, 7/ 15 for domestic students, 5/1 for international students; for spring admission, 11/15 for domestic students, 9/1 for international students. Applications are processed on a rolling basis. Application fee: $50 ($100 for international students). Electronic applications accepted. *Expenses:* Tuition, state resident: full-time $11,170; part-time $620.56 per credit hour. Tuition, nonresident: full-time $20,212; part-time $1122.89 per credit hour. *Financial support:* In 2011–12, 49 students received support, including 18 research assistantships with partial tuition reimbursements available (averaging $20,911 per year), 36 teaching assistantships with partial tuition reimbursements available (averaging $15,300 per year); career-related internships or fieldwork, Federal Work-Study, institutionally sponsored loans, scholarships/grants, and unspecified assistantships also available. Support available to part-time students. Financial award application deadline: 4/30; financial award applicants required to submit FAFSA. *Faculty research:* Role of mitochondria in neurodegenerative diseases, protein-DNA interactions in site-specific recombination, eukaryotic gene expression, bio-nanotechnology, sickle cell research. *Unit head:* Dr. Stephen Spiro, Department Head, 972-883-6032, Fax: 972-883-2502, E-mail: stephen.spiro@utdallas.edu. *Application contact:* Dr. Lawrence Reitzer, Graduate Advisor, 972-883-2502, Fax: 972-883-2402, E-mail: reitzer@utdallas.edu. Web site: http://www.utdallas.edu/biology/.

The University of Texas at San Antonio, College of Sciences, Department of Biology, San Antonio, TX 78249-0617. Offers biology (MS); biotechnology (MS), including bioprocessing technician, biotechnology; cell and molecular biology (PhD); environmental science (MS); neurobiology (PhD). *Faculty:* 34 full-time (6 women), 7 part-time/adjunct (1 woman). *Students:* 117 full-time (62 women), 64 part-time (35 women); includes 63 minority (10 Black or African American, non-Hispanic/Latino; 10 Asian, non-Hispanic/Latino; 36 Hispanic/Latino; 7 Two or more races, non-Hispanic/ Latino), 54 international. Average age 27. 239 applicants, 45% accepted, 50 enrolled. In 2011, 62 master's, 3 doctorates awarded. Terminal master's awarded for partial completion of doctoral program. *Degree requirements:* For master's, comprehensive exam, thesis or alternative; for doctorate, thesis/dissertation. *Entrance requirements:* For master's, GRE General Test, bachelor's degree with 18 credit hours in field of study or in another appropriate field of study; for doctorate, GRE General Test, 3 letters of recommendation, statement of purpose, resume. Additional exam requirements/ recommendations for international students: Required—TOEFL (minimum score 500 paper-based; 100 iBT), IELTS (minimum score 5). *Application deadline:* For fall admission, 7/1 for domestic students, 4/1 for international students; for spring admission, 11/1 for domestic students, 9/1 for international students. Application fee: $45 ($85 for international students). *Expenses:* Tuition, state resident: full-time $3148; part-time $2176 per semester. Tuition, nonresident: full-time $8782; part-time $5932 per semester. *Required fees:* $719 per semester. *Financial support:* In 2011–12, 66 students received support, including 4 fellowships (averaging $22,350 per year), 34 research assistantships (averaging $22,350 per year), 8 teaching assistantships (averaging $22,350 per year). *Faculty research:* Development of human and veterinary vaccines against a fungal disease, mammalian germ cells and stem cells, dopamine neuron physiology and addiction, plant biochemistry, dendritic computation and synaptic plasticity. *Total annual research expenditures:* $2.8 million. *Unit head:* Dr. Edwin J. Barea-Rodriguez, Chair, 210-458-4511, Fax: 210-458-5658, E-mail: edwin.barea@utsa.edu. *Application contact:* Rene Munguia, Program Coordinator, 210-458-4642, Fax: 210-458-5658, E-mail: rene.munguia@utsa.edu.

University of the Sciences in Philadelphia, College of Graduate Studies, Program in Cell Biology and Biotechnology, Philadelphia, PA 19104-4495. Offers cell and molecular biology (PhD); cell biology (MS). Part-time and evening/weekend programs available. *Degree requirements:* For master's, thesis (for some programs). *Entrance requirements:* For master's, GRE General Test. Additional exam requirements/recommendations for international students: Required—TOEFL, TWE. *Expenses:* Contact institution. *Faculty research:* Invertebrate cell adhesion, plant-microbe interactions, natural product mechanisms, cell signal transduction, gene regulation and organization.

University of Toronto, School of Graduate Studies, Program in Biotechnology, Toronto, ON M5S 1A1, Canada. Offers MBiotech. *Entrance requirements:* For master's, minimum B+ average in the last two years of study and/or GRE. Additional exam requirements/recommendations for international students: Required—TOEFL (minimum score 580 paper-based; 93 iBT), TWE (minimum score 5). Electronic applications accepted.

University of Utah, Graduate School, Professional Master of Science and Technology Program, Salt Lake City, UT 84112-1107. Offers biotechnology (PSM); computational science (PSM); environmental science (PSM); science instrumentation (PSM). Part-time programs available. *Students:* 15 full-time (10 women), 42 part-time (12 women); includes 7 minority (2 Black or African American, non-Hispanic/Latino; 2 Asian, non-Hispanic/Latino; 2 Hispanic/Latino; 1 Native Hawaiian or other Pacific Islander, non-Hispanic/Latino), 2 international. Average age 33. 66 applicants, 48% accepted, 16 enrolled. In 2011, 18 master's awarded. *Degree requirements:* For master's, internship. *Entrance requirements:* For master's, GRE (recommended), minimum undergraduate GPA of 3.0, bachelor's degree from accredited university or college. Additional exam requirements/recommendations for international students: Required—TOEFL (minimum score 500 paper-based; 173 computer-based; 61 iBT), IELTS (minimum score 6). *Application deadline:* For fall admission, 3/1 for domestic and international students. Application fee: $55 ($65 for international students). Electronic applications accepted. *Financial support:* In 2011–12, 8 students received support, including 5 fellowships with full and partial tuition reimbursements available (averaging $16,800 per year), 2 research assistantships (averaging $6,200 per year); unspecified assistantships also available. Financial award applicants required to submit FAFSA. *Faculty research:* Drug delivery systems, in vitro erythroid expansion and HRE (Hypoxia responsive element). *Unit head:* Jennifer Schmidt, Program Director, 801-585-5630, E-mail: jennifer.schmidt@gradschool.utah.edu. *Application contact:* Amy Kimball, Project Coordinator, 801-585-3650, Fax: 801-585-6749, E-mail: amy.kimball@gradschool.utah.edu. Web site: http://www.utah.edu/pmst/.

University of Washington, Graduate School, School of Medicine, Graduate Programs in Medicine, Department of Genome Sciences, Seattle, WA 98195. Offers PhD. *Degree requirements:* For doctorate, thesis/dissertation, general exam. *Entrance requirements:* For doctorate, GRE General Test, minimum GPA of 3.0. Additional exam requirements/ recommendations for international students: Required—TOEFL. Electronic applications accepted. *Faculty research:* Model organism genetics, human and medical genetics, genomics and proteomics, computational biology.

University of West Florida, College of Arts and Sciences: Sciences, School of Allied Health and Life Sciences, Department of Biology, Pensacola, FL 32514-5750. Offers biological chemistry (MS); biology (MS); biology education (MST); biotechnology (MS); coastal zone studies (MS); environmental biology (MS). *Faculty:* 12 full-time (3 women), 1 part-time/adjunct (0 women). *Students:* 9 full-time (7 women), 30 part-time (16 women); includes 2 minority (both Hispanic/Latino), 3 international. Average age 29. 21 applicants, 48% accepted, 5 enrolled. In 2011, 4 master's awarded. *Degree requirements:* For master's, thesis. *Entrance requirements:* For master's, GRE (minimum score: verbal 450, quantitative 550), official transcripts; BS in biology or related field; letter of interest; relevant past experience; three letters of recommendation from individuals who can evaluate applicant's academic ability. Additional exam requirements/recommendations for international students: Required—TOEFL (minimum score 550 paper-based; 213 computer-based). *Application deadline:* For fall admission, 6/1 for domestic and international students; for spring admission, 10/1 for domestic and international students. Applications are processed on a rolling basis. Application fee: $30. *Expenses:* Tuition, state resident: full-time $5729; part-time $302 per credit hour.

Tuition, nonresident: full-time $20,059; part-time $961 per credit hour. *Required fees:* $1509; $63 per credit hour. *Financial support:* In 2011–12, 18 fellowships with partial tuition reimbursements (averaging $126 per year), 14 research assistantships with partial tuition reimbursements (averaging $5,980 per year), 4 teaching assistantships with partial tuition reimbursements (averaging $7,858 per year) were awarded; unspecified assistantships also available. Financial award application deadline: 4/15; financial award applicants required to submit FAFSA. *Unit head:* Dr. George L. Stewart, Chairperson, 850-474-2748. *Application contact:* Terry McCray, Assistant Director of Graduate Admissions, 850-473-7718, Fax: 850-473-7714, E-mail: gradadmissions@uwf.edu.

University of Wyoming, Graduate Program in Molecular and Cellular Life Sciences, Laramie, WY 82070. Offers PhD. *Degree requirements:* For doctorate, thesis/dissertation, four eight-week laboratory rotations, comprehensive basic practical exam, two-part qualifying exam, seminars, symposium.

Virginia Polytechnic Institute and State University, Graduate School, College of Science, Program in Biomedical Technology Development and Management, Blacksburg, VA 24061. Offers MS. *Degree requirements:* For master's, comprehensive exam (for some programs), thesis (for some programs). *Entrance requirements:* For master's, GRE. Additional exam requirements/recommendations for international students: Required—TOEFL (minimum score 550 paper-based; 213 computer-based). *Application deadline:* For fall admission, 7/1 for domestic and international students; for spring admission, 12/1 for domestic and international students. Applications are processed on a rolling basis. Application fee: $65. Electronic applications accepted. *Expenses:* Tuition, state resident: full-time $10,048; part-time $558.25 per credit hour. Tuition, nonresident: full-time $19,497; part-time $1083.25 per credit hour. *Required fees:* $405 per semester. Tuition and fees vary according to course load, campus/location and program. *Financial support:* Career-related internships or fieldwork, Federal Work-Study, scholarships/grants, health care benefits, and unspecified assistantships available. *Unit head:* Dr. Kenneth H. Wong, Unit Head, 571-858-3203, Fax: 540-231-7511, E-mail: khwong@vt.edu. *Application contact:* Jennifer LeFurgy, Information Contact, 571-858-3200, Fax: 540-231-7511, E-mail: jlefurgy@vt.edu.

West Virginia State University, Graduate Programs, Institute, WV 25112-1000. Offers biotechnology (MA, MS); media studies (MA). *Entrance requirements:* For master's, GRE General Test, minimum GPA of 3.0, 3 letters of recommendation. Additional exam requirements/recommendations for international students: Required—TOEFL (minimum score 550 paper-based).

William Paterson University of New Jersey, College of Science and Health, Wayne, NJ 07470-8420. Offers biotechnology (MS); communication disorders (MS); general biology (MS); nursing (MSN). Part-time and evening/weekend programs available. *Entrance requirements:* For master's, GRE General Test, minimum GPA of 2.75. Electronic applications accepted. *Faculty research:* Plant tissue culture, DNA cloning, cellular structure, language development, speech and hearing science.

Worcester Polytechnic Institute, Graduate Studies and Research, Department of Biology and Biotechnology, Worcester, MA 01609-2280. Offers biology and biotechnology (MS); biotechnology (PhD). *Faculty:* 20 full-time (9 women). *Students:* 13 full-time (9 women); includes 1 minority (Asian, non-Hispanic/Latino), 5 international. 86 applicants, 8% accepted, 4 enrolled. In 2011, 3 degrees awarded. Terminal master's awarded for partial completion of doctoral program. *Degree requirements:* For master's, thesis; for doctorate, comprehensive exam, thesis/dissertation, qualifying exam. *Entrance requirements:* For master's and doctorate, GRE General Test, 3 letters of recommendation, statement of purpose. Additional exam requirements/recommendations for international students: Required—TOEFL (minimum score 563 paper-based; 223 computer-based; 84 iBT), IELTS (minimum score 7). *Application deadline:* For fall admission, 1/1 priority date for domestic students, 1/1 for international students. Application fee: $70. Electronic applications accepted. *Financial support:* Research assistantships, teaching assistantships, career-related internships or fieldwork, institutionally sponsored loans, scholarships/grants, and unspecified assistantships available. Financial award application deadline: 1/1; financial award applicants required to submit FAFSA. *Faculty research:* Cellular, developmental and molecular biology; neuro and regenerative biology; behavioral and environmental biology; plant biology; immunology and microbiology. *Unit head:* Dr. Joseph Duffy, Head, 508-831-4111, Fax: 508-831-5936, E-mail: jduffy@wpi.edu. *Application contact:* Dr. Reeta Rao, Graduate Coordinator, 508-831-4111, Fax: 508-831-5936, E-mail: rpr@wpi.edu. Web site: http://www.wpi.edu/Academics/Depts/BBT/.

Worcester State University, Graduate Studies, Program in Biotechnology, Worcester, MA 01602-2597. Offers MS. Part-time and evening/weekend programs available. *Faculty:* 6 full-time (2 women). *Students:* 23 part-time (16 women); includes 6 minority (1 Black or African American, non-Hispanic/Latino; 3 Asian, non-Hispanic/Latino; 1 Hispanic/Latino; 1 Two or more races, non-Hispanic/Latino). Average age 30. 27 applicants, 56% accepted, 6 enrolled. In 2011, 8 master's awarded. *Degree requirements:* For master's, comprehensive exam, thesis. *Entrance requirements:* For master's, GRE General Test or MAT, minimum undergraduate GPA of 3.0 in biology. Additional exam requirements/recommendations for international students: Required—TOEFL (minimum score 500 paper-based; 61 iBT). *Application deadline:* For fall admission, 6/15 for domestic and international students; for spring admission, 4/1 for domestic and international students. Applications are processed on a rolling basis. Application fee: $40. Electronic applications accepted. *Expenses:* Tuition, state resident: full-time $2700; part-time $150 per credit. Tuition, nonresident: full-time $2700; part-time $150 per credit. *Required fees:* $2016; $112 per credit. *Financial support:* Application deadline: 3/1; applicants required to submit FAFSA. *Faculty research:* Effects of insulin in invertebrates, ecology of freshwater turtles, symbiotic relations of plants and animals. *Unit head:* Dr. Peter Bradley, Coordinator, 508-929-8571, Fax: 508-929-8171, E-mail: pbradley@worcester.edu. *Application contact:* Sara Grady, Assistant Dean of Graduate and Continuing Education, 508-929-8787, Fax: 508-929-8100, E-mail: sara.grady@worcester.edu.

Nanotechnology

Arizona State University, College of Liberal Arts and Sciences, Department of Chemistry and Biochemistry, Tempe, AZ 85287-1604. Offers biochemistry (MS, PhD); chemistry (MS, PhD); nanoscience (PSM). Terminal master's awarded for partial completion of doctoral program. *Degree requirements:* For master's, thesis, interactive Program of Study (iPOS) submitted before completing 50 percent of required credit hours; for doctorate, comprehensive exam, thesis/dissertation, interactive Program of Study (iPOS) submitted before completing 50 percent of required credit hours. *Entrance requirements:* For master's and doctorate, GRE, minimum GPA of 3.0 or equivalent in last 2 years of work leading to bachelor's degree. Additional exam requirements/recommendations for international students: Required—TOEFL (minimum score 80 iBT), TOEFL, IELTS, or Pearson Test of English. Electronic applications accepted.

Arizona State University, College of Liberal Arts and Sciences, Department of Physics, Tempe, AZ 85287-1504. Offers nanoscience (PSM); physics (MNS, PhD). Part-time programs available. Terminal master's awarded for partial completion of doctoral program. *Degree requirements:* For master's, comprehensive exam, thesis or alternative, interactive Program of Study (iPOS) submitted before completing 50 percent of required credit hours; for doctorate, comprehensive exam, thesis/dissertation, interactive Program of Study (iPOS) submitted before completing 50 percent of required credit hours. *Entrance requirements:* For master's and doctorate, GRE, minimum GPA of 3.0 or equivalent in last 2 years of work leading to bachelor's degree. Additional exam requirements/recommendations for international students: Required—TOEFL (minimum score 80 iBT), TOEFL, IELTS, or Pearson Test of English. Electronic applications accepted. *Expenses:* Contact institution.

The Johns Hopkins University, Whiting School of Engineering, Program in Engineering Management, Baltimore, MD 21218-2699. Offers biomaterials (MSEM); communications science (MSEM); computer science (MSEM); fluid mechanics (MSEM); materials science and engineering (MSEM); mechanical engineering (MSEM); mechanics and materials (MSEM); nano-biotechnology (MSEM); nanomaterials and nanotechnology (MSEM); probability and statistics (MSEM); smart product and device design (MSEM); systems analysis, management and environmental policy (MSEM). *Entrance requirements:* For master's, GRE, 3 letters of recommendation, resume. Additional exam requirements/recommendations for international students: Required—TOEFL (minimum score 600 paper-based; 250 computer-based; 100 iBT) or IELTS (minimum score 7). Electronic applications accepted.

North Dakota State University, College of Graduate and Interdisciplinary Studies, Interdisciplinary Program in Materials and Nanotechnology, Fargo, ND 58108. Offers PhD. *Students:* 13 full-time (2 women), 3 part-time (0 women), 12 international. 12 applicants, 42% accepted, 3 enrolled. *Entrance requirements:* For doctorate, GRE General Test. Additional exam requirements/recommendations for international students: Required—TOEFL (minimum score 525 paper-based; 197 computer-based; 71 iBT). *Application deadline:* For fall admission, 5/1 for international students; for spring admission, 8/1 for international students. Application fee: $35. *Unit head:* Dr. Erik Hobbe, Director, 701-231-7049, E-mail: erik.hobbie@ndsu.edu. *Application contact:* Sonya Goergen, Marketing, Recruitment, and Public Relations Coordinator, 701-231-7033, Fax: 701-231-6524.

Oregon State University, Graduate School, College of Engineering, School of Mechanical, Industrial, and Manufacturing Engineering, Corvallis, OR 97331. Offers human systems engineering (MS, PhD); industrial engineering (MS, PhD); information systems engineering (MS, PhD); manufacturing engineering (M Engr); manufacturing systems engineering (MS, PhD); materials science (MAIS, MS, PhD); mechanical engineering (MS, PhD); nano/micro fabrication (MS, PhD). Part-time programs available. Postbaccalaureate distance learning degree programs offered (minimal on-campus study). *Degree requirements:* For master's, thesis or alternative; for doctorate, thesis/dissertation. *Entrance requirements:* For master's, placement exam, minimum GPA of 3.0 in last 90 hours of course work; for doctorate, GRE, placement exam, minimum GPA of 3.0 in last 90 hours of course work. Additional exam requirements/recommendations for international students: Required—TOEFL (minimum score 550 paper-based; 213 computer-based). *Faculty research:* Computer-integrated manufacturing, human factors, robotics, decision support systems, simulation modeling and analysis.

South Dakota School of Mines and Technology, Graduate Division, Program in Nanoscience and Nanoengineering, Rapid City, SD 57701-3995. Offers PhD.

University at Albany, State University of New York, College of Nanoscale Science and Engineering, Albany, NY 12222-0001. Offers MS, PhD. *Entrance requirements:* Additional exam requirements/recommendations for international students: Required—TOEFL (minimum score 550 paper-based; 213 computer-based). *Faculty research:* Thin film material structures, optoelectronic materials, design and fabrication of nano-mechanical systems, materials characterization.

University of Alberta, Faculty of Graduate Studies and Research, Department of Electrical and Computer Engineering, Edmonton, AB T6G 2E1, Canada. Offers communications (M Eng, M Sc, PhD); computer engineering (M Eng, M Sc, PhD); electromagnetics (M Eng, M Sc, PhD); nanotechnology and microdevices (M Eng, M Sc, PhD); power/power electronics (M Eng, M Sc, PhD); systems (M Eng, M Sc, PhD). Terminal master's awarded for partial completion of doctoral program. *Degree requirements:* For master's, thesis; for doctorate, thesis/dissertation. *Entrance requirements:* Additional exam requirements/recommendations for international students: Required—TOEFL. Electronic applications accepted. *Faculty research:* Controls, communications, microelectronics, electromagnetics.

University of California, Riverside, Graduate Division, Graduate Materials Science and Engineering Program, Riverside, CA 92521. Offers MS, PhD. *Entrance requirements:* For master's and doctorate, GRE. Additional exam requirements/recommendations for international students: Required—TOEFL (minimum score 550 paper-based; 213 computer-based; 80 iBT). Electronic applications accepted.

University of New Mexico, Graduate School, School of Engineering, Program in Nanoscience and Microsystems, Albuquerque, NM 87131-2039. Offers MS, PhD. Part-time programs available. *Faculty:* 2 full-time (both women). *Students:* 32 full-time (11 women), 16 part-time (5 women); includes 17 minority (2 Black or African American, non-Hispanic/Latino; 1 American Indian or Alaska Native, non-Hispanic/Latino; 4 Asian, non-Hispanic/Latino; 9 Hispanic/Latino; 1 Two or more races, non-Hispanic/Latino), 2 international. Average age 31. 20 applicants, 40% accepted, 7 enrolled. In 2011, 11 degrees awarded. *Degree requirements:* For master's, comprehensive exam, thesis; for doctorate, comprehensive exam, thesis/dissertation. *Entrance requirements:* For master's and doctorate, GRE. Additional exam requirements/recommendations for international students: Required—TOEFL. *Application deadline:* For fall admission, 7/30 for domestic students, 2/1 for international students; for spring admission, 11/30 for domestic students, 6/1 for international students. Application fee: $50. Electronic applications accepted. *Financial support:* In 2011–12, 31 students received support, including 30 research assistantships (averaging $17,556 per year), 7 teaching assistantships (averaging $7,505 per year). *Unit head:* Dr. Abhaya Datye, Professor, 505-277-0477, Fax: 505-277-1024, E-mail: datye@unm.edu. *Application contact:* Heather Elizabeth Armstrong, Program Specialist, 505-277-6824, Fax: 505-277-1024, E-mail: heathera@unm.edu. Web site: http://www.unm.edu/~nsms.

University of Washington, Graduate School, College of Engineering and School of Medicine, Department of Bioengineering, Seattle, WA 98195-5061. Offers bioengineering (MS, PhD); bioengineering and nanotechnology (PhD); medical engineering (MME); pharmaceutical bioengineering (MS). Evening/weekend programs available. Postbaccalaureate distance learning degree programs offered (no on-campus study). *Faculty:* 35 full-time (10 women), 11 part-time/adjunct (2 women). *Students:* 116 full-time (46 women), 63 part-time (27 women); includes 48 minority (2 Black or African American, non-Hispanic/Latino; 1 American Indian or Alaska Native, non-Hispanic/Latino; 42 Asian, non-Hispanic/Latino; 3 Hispanic/Latino), 30 international. Average age 26. 495 applicants, 18% accepted, 35 enrolled. In 2011, 14 master's, 12 doctorates awarded. *Degree requirements:* For master's, comprehensive exam, thesis; for doctorate, comprehensive exam, thesis/dissertation, qualifying exam, general exam, thesis defense. *Entrance requirements:* For master's and doctorate, GRE General Test, minimum GPA of 3.0, transcripts, statement of purpose, letters of recommendation. Additional exam requirements/recommendations for international students: Required—TOEFL (minimum score 580 paper-based; 237 computer-based; 92 iBT); Recommended—IELTS (minimum score 7). *Application deadline:* For fall admission, 12/15 priority date for domestic students, 12/1 for international students. Applications are processed on a rolling basis. Application fee: $75. Electronic applications accepted. *Expenses:* Contact institution. *Financial support:* In 2011–12, 177 students received support, including 18 fellowships with full tuition reimbursements available (averaging $21,330 per year), 125 research assistantships with full tuition reimbursements available (averaging $19,224 per year), 22 teaching assistantships with full tuition reimbursements available (averaging $19,224 per year); Federal Work-Study, institutionally sponsored loans, traineeships, health care benefits, and tuition waivers (full) also available. Support available to part-time students. Financial award application deadline: 12/15; financial award applicants required to submit FAFSA. *Faculty research:* Biomaterials and tissue engineering; global health, distributed diagnosis and home healthcare; bioinstrumentation; molecular bioengineering; imaging and image-guided therapy. *Total annual research expenditures:* $22.6 million. *Unit head:* Dr. Paul Yager, Professor/Chair, 206-685-2000, Fax: 206-685-3300, E-mail: yagerp@u.washington.edu. *Application contact:* Dorian Varga, Senior Academic Counselor, 206-685-3494, Fax: 206-685-3300, E-mail: dst@u.washington.edu.
Web site: http://depts.washington.edu.bioe.

University of Washington, Graduate School, College of Engineering, Department of Chemical Engineering, Seattle, WA 98195-1750. Offers chemical engineering (MS, MSE, PhD); chemical engineering and nanotechnology (PhD). *Faculty:* 20 full-time (3 women), 5 part-time/adjunct (2 women). *Students:* 75 full-time (20 women), 2 part-time (0 women); includes 17 minority (1 Black or African American, non-Hispanic/Latino; 1 American Indian or Alaska Native, non-Hispanic/Latino; 11 Asian, non-Hispanic/Latino; 4 Hispanic/Latino), 19 international. Average age 25. 250 applicants, 18% accepted, 17 enrolled. In 2011, 17 master's, 7 doctorates awarded. Terminal master's awarded for partial completion of doctoral program. *Degree requirements:* For master's, thesis, final exam, teaching assistantship for 1 quarter, research project; for doctorate, thesis/dissertation, general and final exams, research project, completion of all work for degree within 10 years. *Entrance requirements:* For master's and doctorate, GRE General Test (minimum Quantitative score of 750), minimum GPA of 3.0, official transcripts, personal statement, confidential evaluations by 3 professors or other technical professional, high rank (top 5%) in respected chemical engineering program. Additional exam requirements/recommendations for international students: Required—TOEFL (minimum score 580 paper-based; 237 computer-based; 92 iBT); Recommended—IELTS (minimum score 7). *Application deadline:* For fall admission, 1/15 priority date for domestic students, 12/15 for international students. Applications are processed on a rolling basis. Application fee: $75. Electronic applications accepted. *Expenses:* Contact institution. *Financial support:* In 2011–12, 102 students received support, including 16 fellowships with full tuition reimbursements available (averaging $19,035 per year), 73 research assistantships with full tuition reimbursements available (averaging $19,035 per year), 12 teaching assistantships with full tuition reimbursements available (averaging $19,035 per year); career-related internships or fieldwork, Federal Work-Study, health care benefits, and unspecified assistantships also available. Financial award application deadline: 1/15; financial award applicants required to submit FAFSA. *Faculty research:* Molecular energy processes, living systems and biomolecular processes, molecular aspects of materials and interfaces, molecular/organic electronics. *Total annual research expenditures:* $8.9 million. *Unit head:* Dr. Daniel T. Schwartz, Professor/Chair, 206-543-2250, Fax: 206-543-3778, E-mail: dts@uw.edu. *Application contact:* Dave Drischell, Lead Academic Counselor, 206-543-2252, Fax: 206-543-3778, E-mail: rdd@u.washington.edu. Web site: http://www.cheme.washington.edu/.

University of Washington, Graduate School, College of Engineering, Department of Electrical Engineering, Seattle, WA 98195-2500. Offers electrical engineering (MS, PhD); electrical engineering and nanotechnology (PhD). Postbaccalaureate distance learning degree programs offered (no on-campus study). *Faculty:* 58 full-time (9 women), 14 part-time/adjunct (3 women). *Students:* 199 full-time (39 women), 135 part-time (19 women); includes 72 minority (10 Black or African American, non-Hispanic/Latino; 1 American Indian or Alaska Native, non-Hispanic/Latino; 51 Asian, non-Hispanic/Latino; 10 Hispanic/Latino), 130 international. 1,061 applicants, 21% accepted, 94 enrolled. In 2011, 60 master's, 32 doctorates awarded. *Degree requirements:* For master's, thesis optional; for doctorate, thesis/dissertation, qualifying, general, and final exams. *Entrance requirements:* For master's and doctorate, GRE General Test (recommended minimum scores: Verbal 500, Quantitative 720, Analytical 600), minimum GPA of 3.2, resume or curriculum vitae, statement of purpose, 3 letters of recommendation, undergraduate and graduate transcripts. Additional exam requirements/recommendations for international students: Required—TOEFL (minimum score 600 paper-based; 250 computer-based; 92 iBT); Recommended—IELTS (minimum score 7). *Application deadline:* For fall admission, 1/1 priority date for domestic students, 12/15 for international students. Applications are processed on a rolling basis. Application fee: $75. Electronic applications accepted. *Expenses:* Contact institution. *Financial support:* In 2011–12, 143 students received support, including 5 fellowships with full tuition reimbursements available (averaging $19,485 per year), 98 research assistantships with partial tuition reimbursements available (averaging $19,485 per year), 34 teaching assistantships with partial tuition reimbursements available (averaging $14,751 per year); career-related internships or fieldwork, Federal Work-Study, and institutionally sponsored loans also available. Financial award application deadline: 1/1; financial award applicants required to submit FAFSA. *Faculty research:* Controls and robotics, communications and signal processing, electromagnetics, optics and acoustics, electronic devices and photonics. *Total annual research expenditures:* $15.7 million. *Unit head:* Dr. Vikram Jandhyala, Professor/Chair, 206-616-0959, Fax: 206-543-3842, E-mail: vj@uw.edu. *Application contact:* Scott Latiolais, Lead Graduate Program Academic Counselor, 206-221-7913, Fax: 206-543-3842, E-mail: latiolais@ee.washington.edu. Web site: http://www.ee.washington.edu/.

University of Washington, Graduate School, College of Engineering, Department of Materials Science and Engineering, Seattle, WA 98195-2120. Offers ceramic engineering (PhD); materials science and engineering (MS, MSE, PhD); materials science and engineering and nanotechnology (PhD). Part-time programs available. *Faculty:* 23 full-time (5 women), 1 part-time/adjunct (0 women). *Students:* 53 full-time (16 women), 9 part-time (2 women); includes 11 minority (1 Black or African American, non-Hispanic/Latino; 1 American Indian or Alaska Native, non-Hispanic/Latino; 6 Asian, non-Hispanic/Latino; 3 Hispanic/Latino), 20 international. Average age 30. 291 applicants, 9% accepted, 9 enrolled. In 2011, 4 master's, 8 doctorates awarded. *Degree requirements:* For master's, comprehensive exam, thesis optional; for doctorate, comprehensive exam, thesis/dissertation, qualifying evaluation, general and final exams. *Entrance requirements:* For master's and doctorate, GRE General Test, minimum GPA of 3.0. Additional exam requirements/recommendations for international students: Required—TOEFL (minimum score 580 paper-based; 237 computer-based; 92 iBT); Recommended—IELTS (minimum score 7). *Application deadline:* For fall admission, 1/15 priority date for domestic students, 12/15 for international students. Applications are processed on a rolling basis. Application fee: $75. Electronic applications accepted. *Expenses:* Contact institution. *Financial support:* In 2011–12, 51 students received support, including 4 fellowships with full tuition reimbursements available (averaging $16,200 per year), 36 research assistantships with full tuition reimbursements available (averaging $16,416 per year), 8 teaching assistantships with full tuition reimbursements available (averaging $16,416 per year); career-related internships or fieldwork, Federal Work-Study, institutionally sponsored loans, scholarships/grants, health care benefits, unspecified assistantships, and stipend supplements also available. Financial award application deadline: 1/15; financial award applicants required to submit FAFSA. *Faculty research:* Biomimetics and biomaterials; electronic, optical and magnetic materials; eco-materials and materials for energy applications; ceramics, metals, composites, and polymers. *Total annual research expenditures:* $7.4 million. *Unit head:* Dr. Alex Jen, Professor/Chair, 206-543-2600, Fax: 206-543-3100, E-mail: ajen@uw.edu. *Application contact:* Kathleen A. Elkins, Academic Counselor, 206-616-6581, Fax: 206-543-3100, E-mail: kelkins@uw.edu. Web site: http://depts.washington.edu/mse/.

Virginia Commonwealth University, Graduate School, College of Humanities and Sciences, Department of Physics, Richmond, VA 23284-9005. Offers medical physics (MS, PhD); nanoscience and nanotechnology (PhD); physics and applied physics (MS). Part-time programs available. *Students:* 51 full-time (13 women), 4 part-time (2 women); includes 6 minority (2 Black or African American, non-Hispanic/Latino; 1 American Indian or Alaska Native, non-Hispanic/Latino; 1 Asian, non-Hispanic/Latino; 2 Hispanic/Latino), 20 international. 104 applicants, 32% accepted, 18 enrolled. In 2011, 5 master's, 4 doctorates awarded. *Degree requirements:* For master's, comprehensive exam, thesis optional. *Entrance requirements:* For master's, GRE. Additional exam requirements/recommendations for international students: Required—TOEFL (minimum score 600 paper-based; 250 computer-based; 100 iBT); Recommended—IELTS (minimum score 6.5). *Application deadline:* For fall admission, 3/15 for domestic students; for spring admission, 11/15 for domestic students. Applications are processed on a rolling basis. Application fee: $50. Electronic applications accepted. *Expenses:* Tuition, state resident: full-time $9133; part-time $507 per credit. Tuition, nonresident: full-time $18,777; part-time $1043 per credit. *Required fees:* $77 per credit. Tuition and fees vary according to degree level, campus/location, program and student level. *Financial support:* Fellowships, teaching assistantships, Federal Work-Study, institutionally sponsored loans, and tuition waivers (full and partial) available. Support available to part-time students. *Faculty research:* Condensed-matter theory and experimentation, electronic instrumentation, relativity. *Unit head:* Dr. Alison A. Baski, Chair, 804-828-8295, Fax: 804-828-7073, E-mail: aabaski@vcu.edu. *Application contact:* Dr. Shiv Khanna, Graduate Program Director, 804-828-1820, Fax: 804-828-7073, E-mail: snkhanna@vcu.edu. Web site: http://www.has.vcu.edu/phy/physic.html.

Virginia Commonwealth University, Graduate School, College of Humanities and Sciences, Program in Nanosciences, Richmond, VA 23284-9005. Offers PhD. *Students:* 12 full-time (3 women); includes 1 minority (American Indian or Alaska Native, non-Hispanic/Latino), 7 international. 15 applicants, 40% accepted, 5 enrolled. *Entrance requirements:* For doctorate, GRE General Test. Additional exam requirements/recommendations for international students: Required—TOEFL (minimum score 600 paper-based; 250 computer-based; 100 iBT); Recommended—IELTS (minimum score 6.5). *Application deadline:* For fall admission, 3/15 for domestic students; for spring admission, 11/15 for domestic students. Application fee: $50. Electronic applications accepted. *Expenses:* Tuition, state resident: full-time $9133; part-time $507 per credit. Tuition, nonresident: full-time $18,777; part-time $1043 per credit. *Required fees:* $77 per credit. Tuition and fees vary according to degree level, campus/location, program and student level. *Faculty research:* Nanotechnology, nanoscience. *Unit head:* Dr. Everett E. Carpenter, Program Director, 804-828-7508, E-mail: ecarpenter2@vcu.edu. *Application contact:* Dr. Everett E. Carpenter, Program Director, 804-828-7508, E-mail: ecarpenter2@vcu.edu. Web site: http://www.nano.vcu.edu/.

CASE WESTERN RESERVE UNIVERSITY
Department of Biomedical Engineering

Programs of Study

The Department offers many exceptional and innovative educational programs leading to career opportunities in biomedical engineering (BME) research, development, and design in industry, medical centers, and academic institutions. Graduate degrees offered include the M.S. and Ph.D. in BME, a combined M.D./M.S. degree offered to students admitted to the School of Medicine, and combined M.D./Ph.D. degrees in BME offered through the Physician Engineer Training Program or the Medical Scientist Training Program. Individualized BME programs of study allow students to develop strength in an engineering specialty and apply this expertise to an important biomedical problem under the supervision of a Faculty Guidance Committee. Students can choose from more than forty-three courses regularly taught in BME, as well as many courses in other departments. Typically, an M.S. program consists of seven to nine courses, and a Ph.D. program consists of about thirteen courses beyond the B.S. Students can select research projects from among the many strengths of the Department, including neural engineering and neural prostheses, biomaterials, tissue engineering, drug and gene delivery, biomedical imaging, sensors, optical imaging and diagnostics, the cardiovascular system, biomechanics, mass and heat transport, and metabolic systems. Collaborative research and training in basic biomedical sciences, as well as clinical and translational research, are available through primary faculty members, associated faculty members, and researchers in the nearby major medical centers.

Research Facilities

The primary faculty members have laboratories focusing on cardiovascular and skeletal biomaterials; cardiovascular, orthopaedic, and neural tissue engineering; materials and nanoparticles for drug and gene delivery, biomedical image processing, biomedical imaging in several modalities, cellular and tissue cardiac bioelectricity, ion channel function, electrochemical and fiber-optic sensors, neural engineering and brain electrophysiology, and neural prostheses. BME faculty members and students also make extensive use of campus research centers for special purposes such as microelectronic fabrication, biomedical imaging, and material analyses. Associated faculty members have labs devoted to eye movement control, gait analysis, implantable sensors/actuators, biomedical imaging, metabolism, and tissue pathology. These are located at four major medical centers and teaching hospitals that (with one exception) are within walking distance.

Financial Aid

Graduate students pursuing the Ph.D. may receive financial support from faculty members as research assistants, from training grants (NIH, NSF, DoE GAANN), or from the School of Medicine (M.D./Ph.D. only). These positions are awarded on a competitive basis. There are also opportunities for research assistantships in order to pursue the M.S.

Cost of Study

Tuition at Case in 20012–13 for graduate students is $1546 per credit hour. A full load for graduate students is a minimum of 9 credits per semester. Fees for health insurance and activities are estimated at $500 per semester.

Living and Housing Costs

Within a 2-mile radius of the campus, numerous apartments are available for married and single graduate students, with rent ranging from $450 to $900 per month.

Student Group

The Department of Biomedical Engineering has 140 graduate students, of whom about 85 percent are advancing toward the Ph.D. At Case Western Reserve University, approximately 3,681 students are enrolled as undergraduates, 2,767 in graduate studies, and 1,823 in the professional schools.

Location

Case is located on the eastern boundary of Cleveland in University Circle, which is the city's cultural center. The area includes Severance Hall (home of the Cleveland Orchestra), the Museum of Art, the Museum of Natural History, the Garden Center, the Institute of Art, the Institute of Music, the Western Reserve Historical Society, and the Crawford Auto-Aviation Museum. Metropolitan Cleveland has a population of almost 2 million. The Cleveland Hopkins International Airport is 30 minutes away by rail transit. A network of parks encircles the greater Cleveland area. Opportunities are available for sailing on Lake Erie and for hiking and skiing nearby in Ohio, Pennsylvania, and New York. Major-league sports, theater, and all types of music provide a full range of entertainment.

The University and The Department

The Department of Biomedical Engineering at Case Western Reserve University is part of both the Case School of Engineering and the School of Medicine, which are located on the same campus. Established in 1967, the Department is one of the pioneers in biomedical engineering education and is currently among the nation's largest and highest rated (according to *U.S. News & World Report*). Case Western Reserve University was formed in 1967 by a federation of Western Reserve College and Case Institute of Technology. Numerous interdisciplinary programs exist with the professional Schools of Medicine, Dentistry, Nursing, Law, Social Work, and Management.

Applying

Applications that request financial aid should be submitted before February 1. The completed application requires official transcripts, scores on the GRE General Test, and three letters of reference. Application forms are available from the BME Admissions Coordinator or can be downloaded from the Case Web site (http://www.case.edu). Applicants for the M.D./M.S. and M.D./Ph.D. programs can apply through the School of Medicine.

Correspondence and Information

Admissions Coordinator
Department of Biomedical Engineering
Wickenden Building 310
Case Western Reserve University
10900 Euclid Avenue
Cleveland, Ohio 44106-7207
Phone: 216-368-4094
Fax: 216-368-4969
Web site: http://bme.case.edu

THE FACULTY AND THEIR RESEARCH

Primary Faculty

A. Bolu Ajiboye, Ph.D., Assistant Professor. Development and control of brain-computer-interface (BCI) technologies for restoring function to individuals with nervous system injuries.

Eben Alsberg, Ph.D., Associate Professor. Biomimetic tissue engineering, innovative biomaterials and drug delivery vehicles for functional tissue regeneration and cancer therapy, control of stem cell differentiation, mechanotransduction and the influence of mechanics on cell and tissue function, cell-cell interactions.

James P. Basilion, Ph.D., Associate Professor of BME and Radiology. Molecular imaging, biomarkers, diagnosis and treatment of cancer.

Harihara Baskaran, Ph.D., Assistant Professor of BME and Chemical Engineering. Tissue engineering; cell/cellular transport processes in inflammation, wound healing, and cancer metastasis.

Patrick E. Crago, Ph.D., Professor. Control of neuroprostheses for motor function, neuromuscular control systems.

Jeffrey L. Duerk, Ph.D., Dean and Professor. Radiology, MRI, fast MRI pulse sequence design, interventional MRI, MRI reconstruction.

Dominique M. Durand, Ph.D., Professor. Neural engineering, neuroprostheses, neural dynamics, magnetic and electric stimulation of the nervous system, neural interfaces with electronic devices, analysis and control of epilepsy.

Steven J. Eppell, Ph.D., Associate Professor. Nanoscale instrumentation for biomaterials, bone and cartilage structure and function.

Miklos Gratzl, Ph.D., Associate Professor. Fine chemical manipulation of microdroplets and single cells, cancer research and neurochemistry at the single-cell level, cost-effective biochemical diagnostics in microliter body fluids.

Kenneth Gustafson, Ph.D., Assistant Professor. Neural engineering, neural prostheses, neurophysiology and neural control of genitourinary function, devices to restore genitourinary function, functional neuromuscular stimulation.

Efstathios Karathanasis, Ph.D., Assistant Professor. Fabricating multifunctional agents that facilitate diagnosing, treating, and monitoring of therapies in a patient-specific manner.

J. Lawrence Katz, Ph.D., Professor Emeritus. Structure-property relationships in bone, osteophilic biomaterials, ultrasonic studies of tissue anisotropy, scanning acoustic microscopy.

Robert Kirsch, Ph.D., Professor and Interim Chair, Executive Director, FES Center. Functional neuromuscular stimulation, biomechanics and neural control of human movement, modeling and simulation of musculoskeletal systems, identification of physiological systems.

Melissa Knothe-Tate, Ph.D., Professor of BME and Mechanical and Aerospace Engineering. Etiology and innovative treatment modalities for osteoporosis, fracture healing, osteolysis, and osteonecrosis.

Erin Lavik, Sc.D., Associate Professor. Biomaterials and synthesis of new degradable polymers, tissue engineering, spinal cord repair, retinal regeneration, drug delivery for optic nerve preservation and repair.

Case Western Reserve University

Zheng-Rong Lu, Ph.D., Professor. Molecular imaging and drug delivery using novel nanotechnology.

Roger E. Marchant, Ph.D., Professor and Director of the Center for Cardiovascular Biomaterials. Surface modification of cardiovascular devices, molecular-level structure and function of plasma proteins, liposome drug delivery systems, mechanisms of bacterial adhesion to biomaterials.

J. Thomas Mortimer, Ph.D., Professor Emeritus. Neural prostheses, electrical activation of the nervous system, bowel and bladder assist device, respiratory assist device, selective stimulation and electrode development, electrochemical aspects of electrical stimulation.

P. Hunter Peckham, Ph.D., Professor. Neural prostheses, implantable stimulation and control of movement, rehabilitation engineering.

Andrew M. Rollins, Ph.D., Associate Professor. Biomedical diagnosis; novel optical methods for high-resolution, minimally invasive imaging; tissue characterization and analyte sensing; real-time microstructural and functional imaging using coherence tomography; endoscopy.

Gerald M. Saidel, Ph.D., Professor and Director of the Center for Modeling Integrated Metabolic Systems. Mass and heat transport and metabolic analysis in cells, tissues, and organs; mathematical modeling, simulation, and parameter estimation; optimal experimental design; metabolic dynamics; minimally invasive thermal tumor ablation; slow-release drug delivery.

Nicole Seiberlich, Ph.D., Assistant Professor. Advanced signal processing and data acquisition techniques for rapid Magnetic Resonance Imaging (MRI).

Anirban Sen Gupta, Ph.D., Assistant Professor. Targeted drug delivery, targeted molecular imaging, image-guided therapy, platelet substitutes, novel polymeric biomaterials for tissue engineering scaffolds.

Nicole F. Steinmetz, Ph.D., Assistant Professor. Engineering of viral nanoparticles as smart devices for applications in medicine: tissue-specific imaging, drug-delivery, and tissue engineering.

Dustin Tyler, Ph.D., Associate Professor. Neuromimetic neuroprostheses, laryngeal neuroprostheses, clinical implementation of nerve electrodes, cortical neuroprostheses, minimally invasive implantation techniques, modeling of neural stimulation and neuroprostheses.

Horst von Recum, Ph.D., Associate Professor. Tissue-engineered epithelia, prevascularized polymer scaffolds, directed stem cell differentiation, novel stimuli-responsive biomaterials for gene and drug delivery, systems biology approaches to the identification of angiogenic factors.

David L. Wilson, Ph.D., Professor. In vivo microscopic and molecular imaging; medical image processing; image segmentation, registration, and analysis; quantitative image quality of X-ray fluoroscopy and fast MRI; interventional MRI treatment of cancer.

Xin Yu, Sc.D., Associate Professor. Cardiovascular physiology, magnetic resonance imaging and spectroscopy, characterization of the structure-function and energy-function relationships in normal and diseased hearts, small-animal imaging and spectroscopy.

Associated Faculty (partial list)

Jay Alberts, Ph.D., Assistant Professor (BME, Cleveland Clinic Foundation). Neural basis of upper-extremity motor function and deep-brain stimulation in Parkinson's disease.

James M. Anderson, M.D./Ph.D., Professor (Pathology, University Hospitals). Biocompatibility of implants, human vascular grafts.

Richard C. Burgess, M.D./Ph.D., Adjunct Professor (Staff Physician, Neurology, Cleveland Clinic Foundation). Electrophysiological monitoring, EEG processing.

Arnold Caplan, Ph.D., Professor of Biology. Tissue engineering.

Ronald L. Cechner, Clinical Ph.D. (Anesthesiology) Associate Professor. Technical Director, Anesthesia Simulation Laboratory, University Hospitals-Cas Medical Center. Simulation in medical education.

John Chae, M.D., Associate Professor (Neural Rehabilitation, MetroHealth Medical Center). Application of neuroprostheses in hemiplegia.

Hillel J. Chiel, Ph.D., Professor. Biomechanical and neural basis of feeding behavior in *Aplysia californica*, neuromechanical system modeling.

Guy Chisolm, Ph.D., Adjunct Professor (Vice Chairman, Lerner Research Institute, and Staff, Cell Biology, Cleveland Clinic Foundation). Cell and molecular mechanisms in vascular disease and vascular biology; role of lipoprotein oxidation in atherosclerosis; lipoprotein transport into, accumulation in, and injury to arterial tissue.

Margot Damaser, Ph.D., Assistant Professor of Molecular Medicine (BME, Cleveland Clinic Foundation). Biomechanics as it relates to function and dysfunction of the lower urinary tract.

Brian Davis, Ph.D., Adjunct Associate Professor (BME, Cleveland Clinic Foundation). Human locomotion, diabetic foot pathology, space flight–induced osteoporosis, biomedical instrumentation.

David Dean, Ph.D., Assistant Professor (Neurological Surgery, University Hospitals). 3-D medical imaging and morphometrics; skull, brain, soft tissue face.

Louis F. Dell'Osso, Ph.D., Professor (Neurology, VA Medical Center). Neurophysiological control, ocular motor control and oscillations.

Kathleen Derwin, Ph.D., Assistant Professor (BME, Cleveland Clinic Foundation). Tendon mechanobiology and tissue engineering.

Isabelle Deschenes, Ph.D., Assistant Professor (Cardiology, MetroHealth Medical Center). Molecular imaging, ion channel structure and function, genetic regulation of ion channels, cellular and molecular mechanisms of cardiac arrhythmias.

Claire M. Doerschuk, M.D., Associate Professor (Pediatrics, RB&C, University Hospitals). Regulation of the inflammatory response in the lungs.

Agata Exner, Ph.D., Assistant Professor (Radiology, University Hospitals). Image-guided drug delivery, polymers for interventional radiology, models of cancer.

Baowei Fei, Ph.D., Assistant Professor (Radiology, University Hospitals). Quantitative image analysis, multimodality image registration, fusion visualization, image-guided minimally invasive therapy, prostate cancer, photodynamic therapy.

Elizabeth Fisher, Ph.D., Assistant Staff (BME, Cleveland Clinic Foundation). Quantitative image analysis for monitoring multiple sclerosis.

Mark Griswold, Ph.D., Professor (Radiology, University Hospitals). Rapid magnetic resonance imaging, image reconstruction and processing, MRI hardware/instrumentation.

Elizabeth C. Hardin, Ph.D., Adjunct Assistant Professor (Rehabilitation Research and Development, VA Medical Center). Neural prostheses and gait mechanics, improving gait performance with neural prostheses using strategies developed in conjunction with forward dynamics musculoskeletal models.

Michael W. Keith, M.D., Professor (Orthopaedics, MetroHealth Medical Center). Restoration of motor function in hands.

Kevin Kilgore, Ph.D., Adjunct Assistant Professor (MetroHealth Medical Center). Functional electrical stimulation, restoration of hand function.

Kandice Kottke-Marchant, M.D./Ph.D., Adjunct Associate Professor (Staff, Clinical Pathology, Cleveland Clinic Foundation). Interaction of blood and materials, endothelial cell function on biomaterials.

Kenneth R. Laurita, Ph.D., Assistant Professor (Heart and Vascular Research Center, MetroHealth Medical Center). Cardiac electrophysiology, arrhythmia mechanisms, intracellular calcium homeostasis, fluorescence imaging, instrumentation and software for potential mapping.

Zhenghong Lee, Ph.D., Assistant Professor (Radiology, University Hospitals). Quantitative PET and SPECT imaging, multimodal image registration, 3-D visualization, molecular imaging, small-animal imaging systems.

R. John Leigh, M.D., Professor (Neurology, VA Medical Center). Normal and abnormal motor control, eye movements.

Cameron McIntyre, Ph.D., Adjunct Assistant Professor (BME, Cleveland Clinic Foundation). Electric field modeling in the nervous system, deep brain stimulation.

George Muschler, M.D., Professor (Staff, BME, Cleveland Clinic Foundation). Musculoskeletal oncology, adult reconstructive orthopaedic surgery, fracture nonunion, research in bone healing and bone-grafting materials.

Raymond Muzic, Ph.D., Assistant Professor (Radiology, University Hospitals). Modeling and experiment design for PET, image reconstruction.

Sherif G. Nour, M.D., Assistant Professor (Radiology, University Hospitals). Interventional MRI.

Marc Penn, M.D., Ph.D., Adjunct Assistant Professor (Assistant Staff, Cardiology and Cell Biology, Cleveland Clinic Foundation). Myocardial ischemia, remodeling, gene regulation and therapy.

Clare Rimnac, Ph.D., Associate Professor and Director of the Musculoskeletal Mechanics and Materials Laboratories, Mechanical and Aerospace Engineering. Orthopaedic implant performance and design, mechanical behavior of hand tissues.

David S. Rosenbaum, M.D., Associate Professor (Director, Heart and Vascular Research Center, MetroHealth Medical Center). High-resolution cardiac optical mapping, arrhythmia mechanisms, ECG signal processing.

Mark S. Rzeszotarski, Ph.D., Assistant Professor (Radiology, MetroHealth Medical Center). Computers in radiology: MRI/CT/nuclear medicine, ultrasound.

Dawn Taylor, Ph.D., Assistant Professor (BME, Cleveland Clinic Foundation). Brain-computer interfaces for control of computers, neural prostheses, and robotic devices; invasive and noninvasive brain signal acquisition; adaptive decoding algorithms for retraining the brain to control alternative devices after paralysis.

Ronald Triolo, Ph.D., Associate Professor (Orthopaedics, VA Medical Center). Rehabilitation engineering, neuroprostheses, orthopaedic biomechanics.

Antonie J. van den Bogert, Ph.D., Adjunct Assistant Professor (Assistant Staff, BME, Cleveland Clinic Foundation). Biomechanics of human movement.

D. Geoffrey Vince, Ph.D., Adjunct Assistant Professor (Assistant Staff, BME, Cleveland Clinic Foundation). Image and signal processing of intravascular ultrasound images, coronary plaque rupture, cellular aspects of atherosclerosis.

Albert L. Waldo, M.D., Professor (Medicine, University Hospitals). Cardiac electrophysiology, cardiac excitation mapping, mechanisms of cardiac arrhythmias and conduction.

Barry W. Wessels, Ph.D., Professor (Radiation Oncology, University Hospitals). Radio-labeled antibody therapy (dosimeter and clinical trials); image-guided radiotherapy; intensity-modulated radiation therapy; image fusion of CT, MR, SPECT, and PET for adaptive radiation therapy treatment planning.

Guang H. Yue, Ph.D., Adjunct Assistant Professor (Assistant Staff, BME, Cleveland Clinic Foundation). Neural control of movement, electrophysiology, MRI.

Marcie Zborowski, Ph.D., Adjunct Assistant Professor (Assistant Staff, BME, Cleveland Clinic Foundation). High-speed magnetic cell sorting.

Nicholas P. Ziats, Ph.D., Assistant Professor (Pathology, University Hospitals). Vascular grafts, cell-material interactions, extracellular matrix, tissue engineering, blood compatibility.

Section 6
Chemical Engineering

This section contains a directory of institutions offering graduate work in chemical engineering, followed by an in-depth entry submitted by an institution that chose to prepare a detailed program description. Additional information about programs listed in the directory but not augmented by an in-depth entry may be obtained by writing directly to the dean of a graduate school or chair of a department at the address given in the directory.

For programs offering related work, see also in this book *Engineering and Applied Sciences; Geological, Mineral/Mining, and Petroleum Engineering; Management of Engineering and Technology;* and *Materials Sciences and Engineering.* In the other guides in this series:

Graduate Programs in the Humanities, Arts & Social Sciences
See *Family and Consumer Sciences (Clothing and Textiles)*
Graduate Programs in the Biological/Biomedical Sciences & Health-Related Medical Professions
See *Biochemistry*

Graduate Programs in the Physical Sciences, Mathematics, Agricultural Sciences, the Environment & Natural Resources
See *Chemistry* and *Geosciences (Geochemistry* and *Geology)*

CONTENTS

Program Directories

Display and Close-Up

Biochemical Engineering

Cornell University, Graduate School, Graduate Fields of Engineering, Field of Chemical Engineering, Ithaca, NY 14853-0001. Offers advanced materials processing (M Eng, MS, PhD); applied mathematics and computational methods (M Eng, MS, PhD); biochemical engineering (M Eng, MS, PhD); chemical reaction engineering (M Eng, MS, PhD); classical and statistical thermodynamics (M Eng, MS, PhD); fluid dynamics, rheology and biorheology (M Eng, MS, PhD); heat and mass transfer (M Eng, MS, PhD); kinetics and catalysis (M Eng, MS, PhD); polymers (M Eng, MS, PhD); surface science (M Eng, MS, PhD). *Faculty:* 29 full-time (2 women). *Students:* 106 full-time (30 women); includes 21 minority (3 Black or African American, non-Hispanic/Latino; 14 Asian, non-Hispanic/Latino; 4 Hispanic/Latino), 46 international. Average age 25. 379 applicants, 35% accepted, 53 enrolled. In 2011, 50 master's, 8 doctorates awarded. *Degree requirements:* For master's, thesis (MS); for doctorate, comprehensive exam, thesis/dissertation. *Entrance requirements:* For master's and doctorate, GRE General Test, 2 letters of recommendation. Additional exam requirements/recommendations for international students: Required—TOEFL (minimum score 600 paper-based; 237 computer-based; 77 iBT). *Application deadline:* For fall admission, 1/15 priority date for domestic students. Application fee: $95. Electronic applications accepted. *Financial support:* In 2011–12, 67 students received support, including 24 fellowships with full tuition reimbursements available, 44 research assistantships with full tuition reimbursements available, 5 teaching assistantships with full tuition reimbursements available; institutionally sponsored loans, scholarships/grants, health care benefits, tuition waivers (full and partial), and unspecified assistantships also available. Financial award applicants required to submit FAFSA. *Faculty research:* Biochemical, biomedical and metabolic engineering; fluid and polymer dynamics; surface science and chemical kinetics; electronics materials; microchemical systems and nanotechnology. *Unit head:* Director of Graduate Studies, 607-255-4550. *Application contact:* Graduate Field Assistant, 607-255-4550, E-mail: dgs@cheme.cornell.edu. Web site: http://www.gradschool.cornell.edu/fields.php?id-25&a-2.

Dartmouth College, Thayer School of Engineering, Program in Biotechnology and Biochemical Engineering, Hanover, NH 03755. Offers MS, PhD. *Degree requirements:* For master's, thesis; for doctorate, thesis/dissertation, candidacy oral exam. *Entrance requirements:* For master's and doctorate, GRE General Test. *Application deadline:* For fall admission, 1/1 priority date for domestic students. Application fee: $45. *Financial support:* Fellowships, research assistantships, teaching assistantships, career-related internships or fieldwork, Federal Work-Study, institutionally sponsored loans, and tuition waivers (full and partial) available. Financial award application deadline: 1/15. *Faculty research:* Biomass processing, metabolic engineering, kinetics and reactor design, applied microbiology, resource and environmental analysis. *Total annual research expenditures:* $3 million. *Unit head:* Dr. Joseph J. Helbie, Dean, 603-646-2238, Fax: 603-646-2580, E-mail: joseph.j.helbie@dartmouth.edu. *Application contact:* Candace S. Potter, Graduate Admissions Administrator, 603-646-3844, Fax: 603-646-1620, E-mail: candace.potter@dartmouth.edu. Web site: http://engineering.dartmouth.edu/.

Drexel University, College of Engineering, Department of Chemical and Biological Engineering, Program in Biochemical Engineering, Philadelphia, PA 19104-2875. Offers MS. Part-time and evening/weekend programs available. *Degree requirements:* For master's, thesis. *Entrance requirements:* For master's, minimum GPA of 3.0 in chemical engineering or biological sciences. Additional exam requirements/recommendations for international students: Required—TOEFL. Electronic applications accepted. *Faculty research:* Monitoring and control of bioreactors, sensors for bioreactors, large-scale production of monoclonal antibodies.

Rutgers, The State University of New Jersey, New Brunswick, Graduate School-New Brunswick, Program in Chemical and Biochemical Engineering, Piscataway, NJ 08854-8097. Offers MS, PhD. Part-time and evening/weekend programs available. Terminal master's awarded for partial completion of doctoral program. *Degree requirements:* For master's, thesis or alternative; for doctorate, thesis/dissertation. *Entrance requirements:* For master's and doctorate, GRE General Test. Additional exam requirements/recommendations for international students: Required—TOEFL. *Faculty research:* Biotechnology, pharmaceutical engineering, nanotechnology, process system engineering, materials and polymer science, chemical engineering sciences.

University of California, Irvine, School of Engineering, Department of Chemical Engineering and Materials Science, Irvine, CA 92697. Offers chemical and biochemical engineering (MS, PhD); materials science and engineering (MS, PhD). Part-time programs available. *Students:* 84 full-time (29 women), 2 part-time (0 women); includes 23 minority (1 American Indian or Alaska Native, non-Hispanic/Latino; 19 Asian, non-Hispanic/Latino; 2 Hispanic/Latino; 1 Native Hawaiian or other Pacific Islander, non-Hispanic/Latino), 37 international. Average age 27. 343 applicants, 22% accepted, 22 enrolled. In 2011, 17 master's, 4 doctorates awarded. Terminal master's awarded for partial completion of doctoral program. *Degree requirements:* For doctorate, thesis/dissertation. *Entrance requirements:* For master's and doctorate, GRE General Test, minimum GPA of 3.0, 3 letters of recommendation. Additional exam requirements/recommendations for international students: Required—TOEFL (minimum score 550 paper-based; 213 computer-based). *Application deadline:* For fall admission, 1/15 priority date for domestic students, 1/15 for international students. Applications are processed on a rolling basis. Application fee: $80 ($100 for international students). Electronic applications accepted. *Financial support:* Fellowships with tuition reimbursements, research assistantships with full tuition reimbursements, teaching assistantships with tuition reimbursements, institutionally sponsored loans, traineeships, health care benefits, and unspecified assistantships available. Financial award application deadline: 3/1; financial award applicants required to submit FAFSA. *Faculty research:* Molecular biotechnology, nano-bio-materials, biophotonics, synthesis, superplasticity and mechanical behavior, characterization of advanced and nanostructural materials. *Unit head:* Prof. Albert Yee, Chair, 949-824-7320, Fax: 949-824-2541, E-mail: albert.yee@uci.edu. *Application contact:* Grace Hai-Chin Chau, Academic Program and Graduate Admission Coordinator, 949-824-3887, Fax: 949-824-2541, E-mail: chaug@uci.edu. Web site: http://www.eng.uci.edu/dept/chems.

University of Georgia, Faculty of Engineering, Athens, GA 30602. Offers MS. *Students:* 13 full-time (4 women), 1 part-time (0 women); includes 3 minority (1 Asian, non-Hispanic/Latino; 1 Hispanic/Latino; 1 Two or more races, non-Hispanic/Latino), 5 international. Average age 27. 15 applicants, 33% accepted, 3 enrolled. In 2011, 5 master's awarded. *Unit head:* Dr. E. Dale Threadgill. *Application contact:* Dr. Melissa Barry, Assistant Dean of The Graduate School, 706-425-2934, Fax: 706-425-3093, E-mail: mjb14@uga.edu. Web site: http://www.engineering.uga.edu/.

The University of Iowa, Graduate College, College of Engineering, Department of Chemical and Biochemical Engineering, Iowa City, IA 52242-1316. Offers MS, PhD.

Part-time programs available. *Faculty:* 11 full-time (3 women), 1 (woman) part-time/adjunct. *Students:* 38 full-time (11 women); includes 6 minority (5 Black or African American, non-Hispanic/Latino; 1 Hispanic/Latino), 16 international. Average age 28. 47 applicants, 30% accepted, 11 enrolled. In 2011, 14 master's, 3 doctorates awarded. *Degree requirements:* For master's, comprehensive exam (for some programs), thesis (for some programs); for doctorate, comprehensive exam, thesis/dissertation. *Entrance requirements:* For master's and doctorate, GRE, minimum undergraduate GPA of 3.0. Additional exam requirements/recommendations for international students: Required—TOEFL (minimum score 550 paper-based; 213 computer-based). *Application deadline:* For fall admission, 2/1 for domestic and international students; for spring admission, 10/1 for domestic and international students. Applications are processed on a rolling basis. Application fee: $60 ($100 for international students). Electronic applications accepted. *Financial support:* In 2011–12, 11 fellowships with full tuition reimbursements (averaging $26,000 per year), 19 research assistantships with partial tuition reimbursements (averaging $24,500 per year), 10 teaching assistantships with partial tuition reimbursements (averaging $10,022 per year) were awarded; unspecified assistantships also available. Financial award applicants required to submit FAFSA. *Faculty research:* Polymeric materials, photopolymerization, atmospheric chemistry and air pollution, biochemical engineering, bioprocessing and biomedical engineering. *Total annual research expenditures:* $5.5 million. *Unit head:* Dr. David W. Murhammer, Department Executive Officer, 319-335-1228, Fax: 319-335-1415, E-mail: david-murhammer@uiowa.edu. *Application contact:* Natalie Potter, Academic Program Specialist, 319-335-1215, Fax: 319-335-1415, E-mail: chemeng@engineering.uiowa.edu. Web site: http://www.cbe.engineering.uiowa.edu/.

The University of Manchester, School of Chemical Engineering and Analytical Science, Manchester, United Kingdom. Offers biocatalysis (M Phil, PhD); chemical engineering (M Phil, PhD); chemical engineering and analytical science (M Phil, D Eng, PhD); colloids, crystals, interfaces and materials (M Phil, PhD); environment and sustainable technology (M Phil, PhD); instrumentation (M Phil, PhD); multi-scale modeling (M Phil, PhD); process integration (M Phil, PhD); systems biology (M Phil, PhD).

University of Maryland, Baltimore County, Graduate School, College of Engineering and Information Technology, Department of Chemical, Biochemical, and Environmental Engineering, Post Baccalaureate Certificate Program in Biochemical Regulatory Engineering, Baltimore, MD 21250. Offers Postbaccalaureate Certificate. Part-time programs available. *Students:* 2 part-time (both women); both minorities (both Asian, non-Hispanic/Latino). Average age 37. 2 applicants, 0% accepted, 0 enrolled. In 2011, 7 Postbaccalaureate Certificates awarded. *Application deadline:* For fall admission, 7/1 for domestic and international students; for spring admission, 2/1 for domestic students, 12/1 for international students. Applications are processed on a rolling basis. Application fee: $70. Electronic applications accepted. *Unit head:* Dr. Antonio Moreira, Vice Provost for Academic Affairs, 410-455-6576, E-mail: moreira@umbc.edu. *Application contact:* 410-455-3400, Fax: 410-455-1049. Web site: http://umbc.edu/cbe/grad/certificate.php.

University of Maryland, Baltimore County, Graduate School, College of Engineering and Information Technology, Department of Chemical, Biochemical, and Environmental Engineering, Program in Chemical and Biochemical Engineering, Baltimore, MD 21250. Offers MS, PhD. Part-time programs available. *Students:* 31 full-time (15 women), 6 part-time (2 women); includes 6 minority (3 Black or African American, non-Hispanic/Latino; 2 Asian, non-Hispanic/Latino; 1 Two or more races, non-Hispanic/Latino), 21 international. Average age 26. 49 applicants, 45% accepted, 13 enrolled. In 2011, 6 master's, 4 doctorates awarded. *Degree requirements:* For master's, comprehensive exam (for some programs), thesis (for some programs); for doctorate, comprehensive exam, thesis/dissertation. *Entrance requirements:* For master's, GRE General Test, minimum GPA of 3.0; for doctorate, GRE General Test (within last 5 years), GRE Subject Test, minimum GPA of 3.0. Additional exam requirements/recommendations for international students: Required—TOEFL (minimum score 550 paper-based; 213 computer-based; 80 iBT). *Application deadline:* For fall admission, 6/1 for domestic students, 1/1 for international students; for spring admission, 11/1 for domestic students, 6/1 for international students. Applications are processed on a rolling basis. Application fee: $70. Electronic applications accepted. *Financial support:* In 2011–12, 3 students received support, including 14 research assistantships with full tuition reimbursements available (averaging $22,000 per year), 7 teaching assistantships with full tuition reimbursements available (averaging $17,000 per year); career-related internships or fieldwork, Federal Work-Study, scholarships/grants, health care benefits, tuition waivers (partial), and unspecified assistantships also available. Support available to part-time students. Financial award application deadline: 6/30; financial award applicants required to submit FAFSA. *Faculty research:* Biomaterials engineering, bioprocess engineering, cellular engineering, education education and outreach, sensors and monitoring, systems biology and functional genomics. *Unit head:* Dr. Julia M. Ross, Professor and Chair. *Application contact:* Dr. Doug Frey, Professor and Graduate Program Director, 410-455-3418, Fax: 410-455-1049, E-mail: dfrey1@umbc.edu. Web site: http://www.wmbc.edu/engineering/cbe/.

The University of Western Ontario, Faculty of Graduate Studies, Physical Sciences Division, Faculty of Engineering, London, ON N6A 5B8, Canada. Offers chemical and biochemical engineering (ME Sc, PhD); civil and environmental engineering (M Eng, ME Sc, PhD); electrical and computer engineering (M Eng, ME Sc, PhD); mechanical and materials engineering (M Eng, ME Sc, PhD). Part-time programs available. Terminal master's awarded for partial completion of doctoral program. *Degree requirements:* For master's, thesis; for doctorate, thesis/dissertation. *Entrance requirements:* For master's, minimum B average; for doctorate, minimum B+ average. *Faculty research:* Wind, geotechnical, chemical reactor engineering, applied electrostatics, biochemical engineering.

Villanova University, College of Engineering, Department of Chemical Engineering, Villanova, PA 19085-1699. Offers biochemical engineering (Certificate); chemical engineering (MSChE); environmental protection in the chemical process industries (Certificate). Part-time and evening/weekend programs available. *Degree requirements:* For master's, comprehensive exam, thesis optional. *Entrance requirements:* For master's, GRE General Test (for applicants with degrees from foreign universities), B Ch E, minimum GPA of 3.0. Additional exam requirements/recommendations for international students: Required—TOEFL (minimum score 600 paper-based; 250 computer-based; 100 iBT). *Expenses: Tuition:* Part-time $675 per credit. Part-time tuition and fees vary according to degree level and program. *Faculty research:* Heat transfer, advanced materials, chemical vapor deposition, pyrolysis and combustion chemistry, industrial waste treatment.

Chemical Engineering

American University of Sharjah, Graduate Programs, Sharjah, United Arab Emirates. Offers business (EMBA, GEMPA, MBA); chemical engineering (MS Ch E); civil engineering (MSCE); computer engineering (MS); electrical engineering (MSEE); mechanical engineering (MSME); mechatronics engineering (MS); public administration (MPA); teaching English to speakers of other languages (MA); translation and interpreting (MA); urban planning (MUP). Part-time and evening/weekend programs available. *Entrance requirements:* For master's, GMAT (MBA). Additional exam requirements/recommendations for international students: Required—TOEFL (minimum score 550 paper-based; 213 computer-based; 80 iBT), TWE (minimum score 5). Electronic applications accepted. *Faculty research:* Chemical engineering, civil engineering, computer engineering, electrical engineering, linguistics, translation.

Arizona State University, Ira A. Fulton School of Engineering, Department of Mechanical and Aerospace Engineering, Tempe, AZ 85281. Offers aerospace engineering (MS, MSE, PhD); chemical engineering (MS, MSE, PhD); materials science and engineering (MS, PhD); mechanical engineering (MS, MSE, PhD). Part-time and evening/weekend programs available. Postbaccalaureate distance learning degree programs offered (minimal on-campus study). Terminal master's awarded for partial completion of doctoral program. *Degree requirements:* For master's, thesis and oral defense (MS); applied project or comprehensive exam (MSE); interactive Program of Study (iPOS) submitted before completing 50 percent of required credit hours; for doctorate, comprehensive exam, thesis/dissertation, interactive Program of Study (iPOS) submitted before completing 50 percent of required credit hours. *Entrance requirements:* For master's, GRE, minimum GPA of 3.0 or equivalent in last 2 years of work leading to bachelor's degree; for doctorate, GRE, minimum GPA of 3.0 in last 2 years of work leading to bachelor's degree. Additional exam requirements/ recommendations for international students: Required—TOEFL (minimum score 80 iBT), TOEFL, IELTS, or Pearson Test of English. Electronic applications accepted. *Expenses:* Contact institution. *Faculty research:* Electronic materials and packaging, materials for energy (batteries), adaptive/intelligent materials and structures, multiscale fluid mechanics, membranes, therapeutics and bioseparations, flexible structures, nanostructured materials, and micro/nano transport.

Auburn University, Graduate School, Ginn College of Engineering, Department of Chemical Engineering, Auburn University, AL 36849. Offers M Ch E, MS, PhD. Part-time programs available. *Faculty:* 17 full-time (3 women), 1 part-time/adjunct (0 women). *Students:* 38 full-time (10 women), 43 part-time (15 women); includes 4 minority (1 Black or African American, non-Hispanic/Latino; 3 Asian, non-Hispanic/Latino), 53 international. Average age 26. 156 applicants, 20% accepted, 14 enrolled. In 2011, 6 master's, 11 doctorates awarded. *Degree requirements:* For master's, thesis (for some programs); for doctorate, comprehensive exam, thesis/dissertation. *Entrance requirements:* For master's and doctorate, GRE General Test. *Application deadline:* For fall admission, 7/7 for domestic students; for spring admission, 11/24 for domestic students. Applications are processed on a rolling basis. Application fee: $50 ($60 for international students). Electronic applications accepted. *Expenses:* Tuition, state resident: full-time $7290; part-time $405 per credit hour. Tuition, nonresident: full-time $21,870; part-time $1215 per credit hour. *International tuition:* $22,000 full-time. *Required fees:* $1402. *Financial support:* Fellowships, research assistantships, teaching assistantships, and Federal Work-Study available. Support available to part-time students. Financial award application deadline: 3/15; financial award applicants required to submit FAFSA. *Faculty research:* Coal liquefaction, asphalt research, pulp and paper engineering, surface science, biochemical engineering. *Unit head:* Dr. Christopher Roberts, Chair, 334-844-2036. *Application contact:* Dr. George Flowers, Dean of the Graduate School, 334-844-2125. Web site: http://www.eng.auburn.edu/ department/che/.

Brigham Young University, Graduate Studies, Ira A. Fulton College of Engineering and Technology, Department of Chemical Engineering, Provo, UT 84602. Offers MS, PhD. *Faculty:* 13 full-time (0 women), 10 part-time/adjunct (0 women). *Students:* 55 full-time (10 women); includes 24 minority (23 Asian, non-Hispanic/Latino; 1 Hispanic/ Latino). Average age 25. 32 applicants, 41% accepted, 8 enrolled. In 2011, 3 master's, 8 doctorates awarded. *Degree requirements:* For master's, comprehensive exam, thesis; for doctorate, comprehensive exam, thesis/dissertation. *Entrance requirements:* For master's, GRE, minimum GPA of 3.0 in upper-division course work in major; for doctorate, GRE, minimum GPA of 3.3. Additional exam requirements/recommendations for international students: Required—TOEFL (minimum score 580 paper-based; 85 iBT), IELTS (minimum score 7). *Application deadline:* For fall admission, 2/15 for domestic and international students; for winter admission, 6/15 for domestic and international students; for spring admission, 10/15 for domestic and international students. Application fee: $50. Electronic applications accepted. *Expenses: Tuition:* Full-time $5760; part-time $320 per credit. Tuition and fees vary according to student's religious affiliation. *Financial support:* In 2011–12, 47 students received support, including 42 research assistantships with partial tuition reimbursements available (averaging $23,000 per year), 10 teaching assistantships with full and partial tuition reimbursements available (averaging $11,500 per year); fellowships, career-related internships or fieldwork, and tuition scholarships for students receiving teaching or research assistantships also available. Financial award application deadline: 6/30. *Faculty research:* Biomedical engineering, oil reservoir simulation, electrochemical engineering, energy and combustion, molecular modeling, thermodynamics. *Total annual research expenditures:* $2.1 million. *Unit head:* Dr. Randy S. Lewis, Chair, 801-422-2586, Fax: 801-422-0151, E-mail: cheme@byu.edu. *Application contact:* Dr. Dean R. Wheeler, Graduate Coordinator, 801-422-2588, Fax: 801-422-0151, E-mail: dean_wheeler@ byu.edu. Web site: http://www.chemicalengineering.byu.edu.

Brown University, Graduate School, Division of Engineering, Program in Fluid, Thermal and Chemical Processes, Providence, RI 02912. Offers Sc M, PhD. *Degree requirements:* For doctorate, thesis/dissertation, preliminary exam.

Bucknell University, Graduate Studies, College of Engineering, Department of Chemical Engineering, Lewisburg, PA 17837. Offers MS Ch E. *Faculty:* 12 full-time (2 women). *Students:* 2 full-time (1 woman). 5 applicants, 20% accepted, 1 enrolled. In 2011, 7 master's awarded. *Degree requirements:* For master's, thesis. *Entrance requirements:* For master's, GRE General Test, minimum GPA of 3.0. Additional exam requirements/recommendations for international students: Required—TOEFL (minimum score 600 paper-based). *Application deadline:* For fall admission, 2/1 priority date for domestic students, 1/1 for international students. Application fee: $25. *Financial support:* In 2011–12, 2 students received support, including 2 research assistantships with full tuition reimbursements available (averaging $28,000 per year); unspecified

assistantships also available. Financial award application deadline: 2/1. *Faculty research:* Computer-aided design, software engineering, applied mathematics and modeling, polymer science, digital process control. *Unit head:* Dr. Kat Wakabayashi, Chairman, 570-577-1114. *Application contact:* Gretchen H. Fegley, Coordinator, 570-577-3655, Fax: 570-577-3760, E-mail: gfegley@bucknell.edu. Web site: http:// www.bucknell.edu/chemicalengineering.

California Institute of Technology, Division of Chemistry and Chemical Engineering, Program in Chemical Engineering, Pasadena, CA 91125-0001. Offers MS, PhD. *Faculty:* 11 full-time (3 women). *Students:* 53 full-time (18 women); includes 2 minority (1 Black or African American, non-Hispanic/Latino; 1 Hispanic/Latino). Average age 25. 222 applicants, 5% accepted, 10 enrolled. In 2011, 6 master's, 11 doctorates awarded. Terminal master's awarded for partial completion of doctoral program. *Degree requirements:* For master's, thesis; for doctorate, thesis/dissertation. *Entrance requirements:* For doctorate, GRE, BS. Additional exam requirements/recommendations for international students: Required—TOEFL; Recommended—IELTS, TWE. *Application deadline:* For fall admission, 1/15 for domestic and international students. Application fee: $80. Electronic applications accepted. *Financial support:* Fellowships, research assistantships, teaching assistantships, institutionally sponsored loans, scholarships/grants, traineeships, health care benefits, and unspecified assistantships available. Financial award application deadline: 1/15. *Faculty research:* Fluids, biomolecular engineering, atmospheric chemistry, polymers/materials, catalysis. *Unit head:* Prof. Jacqueline K. Barton, Chair, Chemistry and Chemical Engineering, 626-395-3646, Fax: 626-568-8824, E-mail: jkbarton@caltech.edu. *Application contact:* Kathy J. Bubash, Graduate Option Secretary, 626-395-4193, E-mail: kathy@cheme.caltech.edu. Web site: http://www.che.caltech.edu/.

California State University, Long Beach, Graduate Studies, College of Engineering, Department of Chemical Engineering, Long Beach, CA 90840. Offers MS. *Faculty:* 4 full-time (1 woman), 2 part-time/adjunct (0 women). *Unit head:* Dr. Larry Jang, Chair/ Graduate Advisor, 562-985-7533, E-mail: jang@csulb.edu. *Application contact:* Dr. Sandra Cynar, Associate Dean for Instruction, 562-985-1512, Fax: 562-985-7561, E-mail: cynar@csulb.edu. Web site: http://www.csulb.edu/colleges/coe/che/.

Carnegie Mellon University, Carnegie Institute of Technology, Department of Chemical Engineering, Pittsburgh, PA 15213-3891. Offers chemical engineering (M Ch E, MS, PhD); colloids, polymers and surfaces (MS). Part-time and evening/ weekend programs available. Terminal master's awarded for partial completion of doctoral program. *Degree requirements:* For doctorate, thesis/dissertation, qualifying exam. *Entrance requirements:* For master's and doctorate, GRE General Test, GRE Subject Test. Additional exam requirements/recommendations for international students: Required—TOEFL. *Faculty research:* Computer-aided design in process engineering, biomedical engineering, biotechnology, complex fluids.

Case Western Reserve University, School of Graduate Studies, Case School of Engineering, Department of Chemical Engineering, Cleveland, OH 44106. Offers MS, PhD. Part-time and evening/weekend programs available. Postbaccalaureate distance learning degree programs offered. *Faculty:* 10 full-time (1 woman). *Students:* 36 full-time (11 women), 1 (woman) part-time; includes 4 minority (all Asian, non-Hispanic/Latino), 22 international. In 2011, 2 master's, 5 doctorates awarded. Terminal master's awarded for partial completion of doctoral program. *Degree requirements:* For master's, thesis (for some programs); for doctorate, thesis/dissertation, qualifying exam, research proposal, teaching experience. *Entrance requirements:* For master's and doctorate, GRE General Test. Additional exam requirements/recommendations for international students: Required—TOEFL. *Application deadline:* For fall admission, 2/15 priority date for domestic students; for spring admission, 11/1 for domestic students. Applications are processed on a rolling basis. Application fee: $50. *Financial support:* Fellowships with full and partial tuition reimbursements, research assistantships with full and partial tuition reimbursements, teaching assistantships, Federal Work-Study, and institutionally sponsored loans available. Financial award application deadline: 3/1; financial award applicants required to submit FAFSA. *Faculty research:* Biotransport and bioprocessing, electrochemical engineering, materials engineering, energy storage and fuel cells. *Total annual research expenditures:* $2.5 million. *Unit head:* Uziel Landau, Department Chair, 216-368-4132, Fax: 216-368-3016, E-mail: uziel.landau@case.edu. *Application contact:* Theresa Claytor, Student Affairs Coordinator, 216-368-8555, Fax: 216-368-8555, E-mail: theresa.claytor@case.edu. Web site: http://www.case.edu/cse/eche.

City College of the City University of New York, Graduate School, Grove School of Engineering, Department of Chemical Engineering, New York, NY 10031-9198. Offers ME, MS, PhD. PhD program offered jointly with Graduate School and University Center of the City University of New York. Part-time programs available. *Degree requirements:* For master's, thesis optional; for doctorate, one foreign language, comprehensive exam, thesis/dissertation. *Entrance requirements:* For master's and doctorate, GRE General Test. Additional exam requirements/recommendations for international students: Required—TOEFL (minimum score 500 paper-based; 173 computer-based; 61 iBT). *Faculty research:* Theoretical turbulences, bio-fluid dynamics, polymers, fluidization, transport phenomena.

Clarkson University, Graduate School, Wallace H. Coulter School of Engineering, Department of Chemical and Biomolecular Engineering, Potsdam, NY 13699. Offers chemical engineering (ME, MS, PhD). Part-time programs available. *Faculty:* 15 full-time (3 women), 1 (woman) part-time/adjunct. *Students:* 23 full-time (4 women), 19 international. Average age 26. 48 applicants, 71% accepted, 3 enrolled. In 2011, 6 master's, 2 doctorates awarded. Terminal master's awarded for partial completion of doctoral program. *Degree requirements:* For master's, thesis; for doctorate, comprehensive exam, thesis/dissertation, departmental qualifying exam. *Entrance requirements:* For master's and doctorate, GRE, transcripts of all college coursework, resume, personal statement, three letters of recommendation. Additional exam requirements/recommendations for international students: Required—TOEFL (minimum score 550 paper-based; 213 computer-based; 80 iBT), IELTS (minimum score 6.5). *Application deadline:* For fall admission, 1/30 priority date for domestic students, 1/30 for international students; for spring admission, 9/1 priority date for domestic students, 9/1 for international students. Applications are processed on a rolling basis. Application fee: $25 ($35 for international students). Electronic applications accepted. *Expenses: Tuition:* Full-time $14,376; part-time $1198 per credit hour. *Required fees:* $295 per semester. *Financial support:* In 2011–12, 22 students received support, including 1 fellowship with full tuition reimbursement available (averaging $21,999 per year), 12 research assistantships with full tuition reimbursements available (averaging $21,999 per year), 7 teaching assistantships with full tuition reimbursements available (averaging $21,999 per year); scholarships/grants, tuition waivers (partial), and unspecified assistantships also available. *Faculty research:* Intelligent systems, tubular PEM fuel cells, solar rectenna, atmospheric species . *Total annual research expenditures:* $645,946. *Unit head:* Dr. John McLaughlin, Chair, 315-268-6650, Fax: 315-268-6654, E-mail: jmclau@clarkson.edu. *Application contact:* Kelly Sharlow, Assistant to the Dean, 315-268-7929, Fax: 315-268-4494, E-mail: ksharlow@clarkson.edu. Web site: http://www.clarkson.edu/chemeng/.

Clemson University, Graduate School, College of Engineering and Science, Department of Chemical and Biomolecular Engineering, Clemson, SC 29634. Offers MS, PhD. *Faculty:* 12 full-time (2 women). *Students:* 29 full-time (15 women), 3 part-time (0 women); includes 1 minority (Black or African American, non-Hispanic/Latino), 24 international. Average age 28. 114 applicants, 14% accepted, 7 enrolled. In 2011, 5 degrees awarded. *Median time to degree:* Of those who began their doctoral program in fall 2003, 50% received their degree in 8 years or less. *Degree requirements:* For master's, thesis; for doctorate, thesis/dissertation. *Entrance requirements:* For master's and doctorate, GRE General Test. Additional exam requirements/recommendations for international students: Required—TOEFL. *Application deadline:* For fall admission, 6/1 for domestic students, 4/15 for international students; for spring admission, 10/1 for domestic students, 9/15 for international students. Applications are processed on a rolling basis. Application fee: $70 ($80 for international students). Electronic applications accepted. *Financial support:* In 2011–12, 27 students received support, including 2 fellowships with full and partial tuition reimbursements available (averaging $19,000 per year), 17 research assistantships with partial tuition reimbursements available (averaging $24,000 per year), 8 teaching assistantships with partial tuition reimbursements available (averaging $24,000 per year); career-related internships or fieldwork, institutionally sponsored loans, scholarships/grants, health care benefits, and unspecified assistantships also available. Support available to part-time students. Financial award applicants required to submit FAFSA. *Faculty research:* Advanced materials, biotechnology, energy, molecular simulation, chemical and biochemical processing. *Total annual research expenditures:* $1.3 million. *Unit head:* Dr. Douglas E. Hirt, Chair, 864-656-0822, Fax: 864-656-0784, E-mail: hirtd@clemson.edu. *Application contact:* Dr. Scott M. Husson, Coordinator, 864-656-4502, Fax: 864-656-0784, E-mail: shusson@clemson.edu. Web site: http://www.clemson.edu/ces/chbe/.

Cleveland State University, College of Graduate Studies, Fenn College of Engineering, Department of Chemical and Biomedical Engineering, Cleveland, OH 44115. Offers applied biomedical engineering (D Eng); chemical engineering (MS, D Eng). Part-time and evening/weekend programs available. *Faculty:* 8 full-time (1 woman), 1 part-time/adjunct (0 women). *Students:* 36 full-time (16 women), 56 part-time (19 women); includes 11 minority (2 Black or African American, non-Hispanic/Latino; 1 American Indian or Alaska Native, non-Hispanic/Latino; 6 Asian, non-Hispanic/Latino; 1 Hispanic/Latino; 1 Native Hawaiian or other Pacific Islander, non-Hispanic/Latino), 42 international. Average age 26. 102 applicants, 63% accepted, 24 enrolled. In 2011, 12 master's, 6 doctorates awarded. *Degree requirements:* For master's, project or thesis; for doctorate, thesis/dissertation, candidacy and qualifying exams. *Entrance requirements:* For master's, GRE General Test, minimum GPA of 2.75; for doctorate, GRE General Test, minimum GPA of 3.25. Additional exam requirements/recommendations for international students: Required—TOEFL (minimum score 550 paper-based; 213 computer-based; 78 iBT). *Application deadline:* For fall admission, 4/15 for domestic and international students; for spring admission, 10/15 for domestic and international students. Applications are processed on a rolling basis. Application fee: $30. *Expenses:* Tuition, state resident: full-time $6416; part-time $494 per credit hour. Tuition, nonresident: full-time $12,074; part-time $929 per credit hour. *Financial support:* In 2011–12, 19 research assistantships with full and partial tuition reimbursements (averaging $15,750 per year), 7 teaching assistantships with full and partial tuition reimbursements (averaging $15,000 per year) were awarded; fellowships, career-related internships or fieldwork, Federal Work-Study, institutionally sponsored loans, scholarships/grants, tuition waivers (full), and unspecified assistantships also available. Financial award application deadline: 3/30. *Faculty research:* Absorption equilibrium and dynamics, advanced materials processing, biomaterials surface characterization, bioprocessing, cardiovascular mechanics, magnetic resonance imaging, mechanics of biomolecules, metabolic modeling, molecular simulation, process systems engineering, statistical mechanics. *Unit head:* Dr. Dhananjai B. Shah, Chairperson, 216-687-3569, Fax: 216-687-9220, E-mail: d.shah@csuohio.edu. *Application contact:* Becky Laird, Administrative Coordinator, 216-687-2571, Fax: 216-687-9220, E-mail: b.laird@csuohio.edu. Web site: http://www.csuohio.edu/chemical_engineering/.

Colorado School of Mines, Graduate School, Department of Chemical Engineering, Golden, CO 80401-1887. Offers MS, PhD. Part-time programs available. *Faculty:* 38 full-time (8 women), 9 part-time/adjunct (3 women). *Students:* 63 full-time (15 women), 3 part-time (1 woman); includes 4 minority (2 Asian, non-Hispanic/Latino; 1 Native Hawaiian or other Pacific Islander, non-Hispanic/Latino; 1 Two or more races, non-Hispanic/Latino), 29 international. Average age 28. 131 applicants, 34% accepted, 20 enrolled. In 2011, 10 master's, 4 doctorates awarded. *Degree requirements:* For master's, thesis (for some programs); for doctorate, comprehensive exam, thesis/dissertation. *Entrance requirements:* For master's and doctorate, GRE General Test. Additional exam requirements/recommendations for international students: Required—TOEFL (minimum score 550 paper-based; 213 computer-based; 80 iBT). *Application deadline:* For fall admission, 1/15 for domestic and international students; for spring admission, 10/15 for domestic and international students. Application fee: $50 ($70 for international students). Electronic applications accepted. *Expenses:* Tuition, state resident: full-time $12,585; part-time $699 per credit. Tuition, nonresident: full-time $27,270; part-time $1516 per credit. *Required fees:* $1864.20; $670 per semester. *Financial support:* In 2011–12, 65 students received support, including 1 fellowship with full tuition reimbursement available (averaging $20,000 per year), 53 research assistantships with full tuition reimbursements available (averaging $20,000 per year), 11 teaching assistantships with full tuition reimbursements available (averaging $20,000 per year); scholarships/grants, health care benefits, and unspecified assistantships also available. Financial award application deadline: 1/15; financial award applicants required to submit FAFSA. *Faculty research:* Liquid fuels for the future, responsible management of hazardous substances, surface and interfacial engineering, advanced computational methods and process control, gas hydrates. *Total annual research expenditures:* $4.4 million. *Unit head:* Dr. David Marr, Head, 303-273-3008, E-mail: dmarr@mines.edu. *Application contact:* Dr. Amadeu Sum, Professor, 303-273-3873, Fax: 303-273-3730, E-mail: asum@mines.edu. Web site: http://chemeng.mines.edu/.

Colorado State University, Graduate School, College of Engineering, Department of Chemical and Biological Engineering, Fort Collins, CO 80523-1370. Offers chemical engineering (MS, PhD); engineering (ME). *Faculty:* 11 full-time (1 woman). *Students:* 12 full-time (2 women), 11 part-time (5 women); includes 1 minority (Asian, non-Hispanic/Latino), 11 international. Average age 27. 91 applicants, 5% accepted, 5 enrolled. In 2011, 3 degrees awarded. Terminal master's awarded for partial completion of doctoral program. *Degree requirements:* For master's, comprehensive exam, thesis (for some programs), preliminary exam (first-year); for doctorate, comprehensive exam, thesis/dissertation, exams. *Entrance requirements:* For master's and doctorate, GRE General Test, minimum GPA of 3.0. Additional exam requirements/recommendations for international students: Required—TOEFL (minimum score 550 paper-based; 213 computer-based; 80 iBT). *Application deadline:* For fall admission, 1/15 priority date for domestic students, 1/15 for international students; for spring admission, 9/15 priority date for domestic students, 9/15 for international students. Applications are processed on a rolling basis. Application fee: $50. Electronic applications accepted. *Expenses:* Tuition, state resident: full-time $7992. Tuition, nonresident: full-time $19,592. *Required fees:* $1735; $58 per credit. *Financial support:* In 2011–12, 15 students received support, including 3 fellowships (averaging $40,841 per year), 7 research assistantships with full tuition reimbursements available (averaging $22,602 per year), 5 teaching assistantships with full tuition reimbursements available (averaging $6,122 per year); scholarships/grants and unspecified assistantships also available. Financial award application deadline: 2/15; financial award applicants required to submit FAFSA. *Faculty research:* Biochemical and biomedical engineering, nanostructured materials, polymer science, transport phenomena, mathematical modeling . *Total annual research expenditures:* $2.9 million. *Unit head:* Dr. David S. Dandy, Department Head, 970-491-7437, Fax: 970-491-7369, E-mail: david.dandy@colostate.edu. *Application contact:* Marilyn Gross, Graduate Contact, 970-491-5252, Fax: 970-491-7369, E-mail: marilyn.gross@colostate.edu. Web site: http://www.engr.colostate.edu/cheme/.

Columbia University, The Fu Foundation School of Engineering and Applied Science, Department of Chemical Engineering, New York, NY 10027. Offers MS, Eng Sc D, PhD. PhD offered through the Graduate School of Arts and Sciences. Part-time programs available. Postbaccalaureate distance learning degree programs offered (no on-campus study). *Faculty:* 14 full-time (3 women), 5 part-time/adjunct (1 woman). *Students:* 50 full-time (18 women), 19 part-time (7 women); includes 11 minority (all Asian, non-Hispanic/Latino), 34 international. Average age 26. 185 applicants, 32% accepted, 21 enrolled. In 2011, 20 master's, 8 doctorates awarded. *Degree requirements:* For doctorate, thesis/dissertation, qualifying exam. *Entrance requirements:* For master's and doctorate, GRE General Test. Additional exam requirements/recommendations for international students: Required—TOEFL, IELTS. *Application deadline:* For fall admission, 12/1 priority date for domestic students, 12/1 for international students; for spring admission, 10/1 priority date for domestic students, 10/1 for international students. Application fee: $95. Electronic applications accepted. *Financial support:* In 2011–12, 35 students received support, including 23 research assistantships with full tuition reimbursements available (averaging $30,000 per year), 12 teaching assistantships with full tuition reimbursements available (averaging $23,350 per year); health care benefits and tuition waivers also available. Financial award application deadline: 12/1; financial award applicants required to submit FAFSA. *Faculty research:* Molecular design and modification of material surfaces, biophysics and soft matter physics, genomics engineering, interfacial engineering and electrochemistry, protein and metabolic engineering. *Unit head:* Dr. Sanat K. Kumar, Professor/Chairman, 212-854-2193, Fax: 212-854-3054, E-mail: sk2794@columbia.edu. *Application contact:* Teresa Colaizzo, Departmental Administrator, 212-854-4415, Fax: 212-854-3054, E-mail: tc16@columbia.edu. Web site: http://www.cheme.columbia.edu/.

Cooper Union for the Advancement of Science and Art, Albert Nerken School of Engineering, New York, NY 10003-7120. Offers chemical engineering (ME); civil engineering (ME); electrical engineering (ME); mechanical engineering (ME). Part-time programs available. *Faculty:* 27 full-time (1 woman), 15 part-time/adjunct (2 women). *Students:* 39 full-time (10 women), 17 part-time (3 women); includes 18 minority (1 Black or African American, non-Hispanic/Latino; 1 American Indian or Alaska Native, non-Hispanic/Latino; 15 Asian, non-Hispanic/Latino; 1 Hispanic/Latino), 11 international. *Degree requirements:* For master's, thesis. *Entrance requirements:* For master's, GRE, BE, minimum GPA of 3.5. Additional exam requirements/recommendations for international students: Required—TOEFL (minimum score 600 paper-based; 250 computer-based; 100 iBT). *Application deadline:* For fall admission, 2/15 for domestic and international students. Application fee: $65. *Expenses: Tuition:* Full-time $37,500. *Required fees:* $825 per semester. *Financial support:* Fellowships with full tuition reimbursements, career-related internships or fieldwork, Federal Work-Study, tuition waivers (full), and full-tuition scholarships for all admitted students available. Support available to part-time students. Financial award application deadline: 5/1; financial award applicants required to submit CSS PROFILE or FAFSA. *Faculty research:* Civil infrastructure, imaging and sensing technology, biomedical engineering, encryption technology, process engineering. *Unit head:* Dr. Simon Ben-Avi, Acting Dean, 212-353-4286, E-mail: benavi@cooper.edu. *Application contact:* Student Contact, 212-353-4120, E-mail: admissions@cooper.edu. Web site: http://cooper.edu/engineering.

Cornell University, Graduate School, Graduate Fields of Engineering, Field of Chemical Engineering, Ithaca, NY 14853-0001. Offers advanced materials processing (M Eng, MS, PhD); applied mathematics and computational methods (M Eng, MS, PhD); biochemical engineering (M Eng, MS, PhD); chemical reaction engineering (M Eng, MS, PhD); classical and statistical thermodynamics (M Eng, MS, PhD); fluid dynamics, rheology and biorheology (M Eng, MS, PhD); heat and mass transfer (M Eng, MS, PhD); kinetics and catalysis (M Eng, MS, PhD); polymers (M Eng, MS, PhD); surface science (M Eng, MS, PhD). *Faculty:* 29 full-time (2 women). *Students:* 106 full-time (30 women); includes 21 minority (3 Black or African American, non-Hispanic/Latino; 14 Asian, non-Hispanic/Latino; 4 Hispanic/Latino), 46 international. Average age 25. 379 applicants, 35% accepted, 53 enrolled. In 2011, 50 master's, 8 doctorates awarded. *Degree requirements:* For master's, thesis (MS); for doctorate, comprehensive exam, thesis/dissertation. *Entrance requirements:* For master's and doctorate, GRE General Test, 2 letters of recommendation. Additional exam requirements/recommendations for international students: Required—TOEFL (minimum score 600 paper-based; 237 computer-based; 77 iBT). *Application deadline:* For fall admission, 1/15 priority date for domestic students. Application fee: $95. Electronic applications accepted. *Financial support:* In 2011–12, 67 students received support, including 24 fellowships with full tuition reimbursements available, 44 research assistantships with full tuition reimbursements available, 5 teaching assistantships with full tuition reimbursements available; institutionally sponsored loans, scholarships/grants, health care benefits, tuition waivers (full and partial), and unspecified assistantships also available. Financial award applicants required to submit FAFSA. *Faculty research:* Biochemical, biomedical and metabolic engineering; fluid and polymer dynamics; surface science and chemical kinetics; electronics materials; microchemical systems and nanotechnology. *Unit head:* Director of Graduate Studies, 607-255-4550. *Application contact:* Graduate Field Assistant, 607-255-4550, E-mail: dgs@cheme.cornell.edu. Web site: http://www.gradschool.cornell.edu/fields.php?id-25&a-2.

Dalhousie University, Faculty of Engineering, Department of Chemical Engineering, Halifax, NS B3J 1Z1, Canada. Offers M Eng, MA Sc, PhD. *Degree requirements:* For master's, thesis; for doctorate, thesis/dissertation. *Entrance requirements:* Additional exam requirements/recommendations for international students: Required—TOEFL, IELTS, CANTEST, CAEL, or Michigan English Language Assessment Battery. Electronic applications accepted. *Faculty research:* Explosions, process optimization, combustion synthesis of materials, waste minimization, treatment of industrial wastewater.

Drexel University, College of Engineering, Department of Chemical and Biological Engineering, Program in Chemical Engineering, Philadelphia, PA 19104-2875. Offers MS, PhD. *Degree requirements:* For doctorate, thesis/dissertation. *Entrance requirements:* For master's, minimum GPA of 3.0; for doctorate, minimum GPA of 3.5, MS in chemical engineering. Additional exam requirements/recommendations for international students: Required—TOEFL. Electronic applications accepted.

École Polytechnique de Montréal, Graduate Programs, Department of Chemical Engineering, Montréal, QC H3C 3A7, Canada. Offers M Eng, M Sc A, PhD, DESS. Part-time and evening/weekend programs available. Terminal master's awarded for partial completion of doctoral program. *Degree requirements:* For master's, one foreign language, thesis; for doctorate, one foreign language, thesis/dissertation. *Entrance requirements:* For master's, minimum GPA of 2.75; for doctorate, minimum GPA of 3.0. Electronic applications accepted. *Faculty research:* Polymer engineering, biochemical and food engineering, reactor engineering and industrial processes pollution control engineering, gas technology.

Fairleigh Dickinson University, College at Florham, Silberman College of Business, Program in Pharmaceutical Studies, Madison, NJ 07940-1099. Offers MBA, Certificate.

Florida Agricultural and Mechanical University, Division of Graduate Studies, Research, and Continuing Education, FAMU-FSU College of Engineering, Department of Chemical Engineering, Tallahassee, FL 32310-6046. Offers MS, PhD. *Degree requirements:* For master's, thesis (for some programs); for doctorate, thesis/dissertation, presentation of research topic at professional meeting. *Entrance requirements:* For master's, GRE General Test, minimum GPA of 3.0; for doctorate, GRE General Test, minimum GPA of 3.3. Additional exam requirements/recommendations for international students: Required—TOEFL (minimum score 550 paper-based; 213 computer-based). *Expenses:* Contact institution. *Faculty research:* Macromolecular transport, polymer processing, biochemical engineering, process control, environmental engineering.

Florida Institute of Technology, Graduate Programs, College of Engineering, Chemical Engineering Department, Melbourne, FL 32901-6975. Offers MS, PhD. Part-time programs available. *Faculty:* 5 full-time (1 woman). *Students:* 19 full-time (7 women), 5 part-time (0 women), 15 international. Average age 27. 43 applicants, 40% accepted, 1 enrolled. In 2011, 4 degrees awarded. Terminal master's awarded for partial completion of doctoral program. *Degree requirements:* For master's, thesis, seminar, independent research project; for doctorate, comprehensive exam, thesis/dissertation, oral exam, original research project, written exam. *Entrance requirements:* For master's, minimum GPA of 3.0; for doctorate, GRE General Test, GRE Subject Test, minimum GPA of 3.5, resume, 3 letters of recommendation, statement of objectives. Additional exam requirements/recommendations for international students: Required—TOEFL (minimum score 550 paper-based; 213 computer-based; 79 iBT). *Application deadline:* For fall admission, 4/1 for international students; for spring admission, 9/30 for international students. Applications are processed on a rolling basis. Electronic applications accepted. *Expenses: Tuition:* Full-time $19,620; part-time $1090 per credit hour. Tuition and fees vary according to campus/location. *Financial support:* In 2011–12, 3 teaching assistantships with full and partial tuition reimbursements (averaging $7,878 per year) were awarded; research assistantships with full and partial tuition reimbursements, career-related internships or fieldwork, institutionally sponsored loans, tuition waivers (partial), unspecified assistantships, and tuition remissions also available. Support available to part-time students. Financial award application deadline: 3/1; financial award applicants required to submit FAFSA. *Faculty research:* Space technology, biotechnology, materials synthesis and processing, supercritical fluids, water treatment, process control. *Total annual research expenditures:* $121,345. *Unit head:* Dr. Manolis M. Tomadakis, Interim Head, 321-674-7243, Fax: 321-674-7565, E-mail: tomadaki@fit.edu. *Application contact:* Cheryl A. Brown, Associate Director of Graduate Admissions, 321-674-7581, Fax: 321-723-9468, E-mail: cbrown@fit.edu. Web site: http://coe.fit.edu/chemical/.

Florida State University, The Graduate School, FAMU-FSU College of Engineering, Department of Chemical and Biomedical Engineering, Tallahassee, FL 32310-6046. Offers biomedical engineering (MS, PhD); chemical engineering (MS, PhD). Part-time programs available. *Faculty:* 13 full-time (2 women). *Students:* 34 full-time (14 women); includes 22 minority (4 Black or African American, non-Hispanic/Latino; 16 Asian, non-Hispanic/Latino; 2 Hispanic/Latino), 19 international. Average age 25. 91 applicants, 10% accepted, 9 enrolled. In 2011, 7 master's, 3 doctorates awarded. Terminal master's awarded for partial completion of doctoral program. *Degree requirements:* For master's, thesis (for some programs); for doctorate, comprehensive exam, thesis/dissertation, qualifying exam. *Entrance requirements:* For master's, GRE General Test (minimum score 1200), BS in chemical engineering or other physical science/engineering, minimum GPA of 3.0; for doctorate, GRE General Test (minimum score: 1200), BS in chemical engineering or other physical science/engineering, minimum GPA of 3.0, or MS in chemical or biomedical engineering. Additional exam requirements/recommendations for international students: Required—TOEFL (minimum score 550 paper-based; 80 iBT), Michigan English Language Assessment Battery (minimum score 77); Recommended—IELTS (minimum score 6.5). *Application deadline:* For fall admission, 3/1 priority date for domestic students, 3/1 for international students; for spring admission, 11/1 for domestic and international students. Applications are processed on a rolling basis. Application fee: $30. *Expenses:* Contact institution. *Financial support:* In 2011–12, 31 students received support, including 6 fellowships with full tuition reimbursements available (averaging $20,880 per year), 17 research assistantships with full tuition reimbursements available (averaging $20,880 per year), 8 teaching assistantships with full tuition reimbursements available (averaging $20,880 per year). Financial award application deadline: 3/1. *Faculty research:* Macromolecular transport and reaction; polymer characterization and processing; biomass conversion; solid NMR-MRI for solid state spectroscopy and cell microscopy; protein, cell, and tissue engineering. *Total annual research expenditures:* $1.2 million. *Unit head:* Dr. Bruce R. Locke, Chair and Professor, 850-410-6149, Fax: 850-410-6150, E-mail: locke@eng.fsu.edu. *Application contact:* Lisa Fowler, Office Administrator, 850-410-6151, Fax: 850-410-6150, E-mail: lfowler@fsu.edu. Web site: http://www.eng.fsu.edu/cbe.

Georgia Institute of Technology, Graduate Studies and Research, College of Engineering, School of Chemical and Biomolecular Engineering, Atlanta, GA 30332-0001. Offers bioengineering (MS Bio E, PhD); chemical engineering (MS Ch E, PhD); paper science and engineering (MS, PhD); polymers (MS Poly). *Degree requirements:*

For master's, thesis; for doctorate, comprehensive exam, thesis/dissertation. *Entrance requirements:* For master's and doctorate, GRE, minimum GPA of 3.0. Additional exam requirements/recommendations for international students: Required—TOEFL (minimum score 550 paper-based; 213 computer-based). Electronic applications accepted. *Faculty research:* Biochemical engineering; process modeling, synthesis, and control; polymer science and engineering; thermodynamics and separations; surface and particle science.

Graduate School and University Center of the City University of New York, Graduate Studies, Program in Engineering, New York, NY 10016-4039. Offers biomedical engineering (PhD); chemical engineering (PhD); civil engineering (PhD); electrical engineering (PhD); mechanical engineering (PhD). *Degree requirements:* For doctorate, thesis/dissertation. *Entrance requirements:* For doctorate, GRE General Test. Additional exam requirements/recommendations for international students: Required—TOEFL. Electronic applications accepted.

Howard University, College of Engineering, Architecture, and Computer Sciences, School of Engineering and Computer Science, Department of Chemical Engineering, Washington, DC 20059-0002. Offers MS. Offered through the Graduate School of Arts and Sciences. Part-time programs available. *Degree requirements:* For master's, thesis. *Entrance requirements:* For master's, GRE General Test, minimum GPA of 2.75. Additional exam requirements/recommendations for international students: Required—TOEFL. *Faculty research:* Bioengineering, reactor modeling, environmental engineering, nanotechnology, fuel cells.

Illinois Institute of Technology, Graduate College, Armour College of Engineering, Department of Chemical and Biological Engineering, Chicago, IL 60616-3793. Offers biological engineering (MBE); chemical engineering (M Ch E, MS, PhD); food process engineering (MFPE, MS). Part-time and evening/weekend programs available. Postbaccalaureate distance learning degree programs offered (minimal on-campus study). Terminal master's awarded for partial completion of doctoral program. *Degree requirements:* For master's, comprehensive exam (for some programs), thesis (for some programs); for doctorate, comprehensive exam, thesis/dissertation. *Entrance requirements:* For master's, GRE General Test (minimum score 900 Quantitative and Verbal, 2.5 Analytical Writing), minimum undergraduate GPA of 3.0; for doctorate, GRE General Test (minimum score 1000 Quantitative and Verbal, 3.0 Analytical Writing), minimum undergraduate GPA of 3.0. Additional exam requirements/recommendations for international students: Required—TOEFL (minimum score 523 paper-based; 70 iBT); Recommended—IELTS (minimum score 5.5). Electronic applications accepted. *Faculty research:* Energy and sustainability, biological engineering, advanced materials, systems engineering.

Instituto Tecnológico y de Estudios Superiores de Monterrey, Campus Monterrey, Graduate and Research Division, Programs in Engineering, Monterrey, Mexico. Offers applied statistics (M Eng); artificial intelligence (PhD); automation engineering (M Eng); chemical engineering (M Eng); civil engineering (M Eng); electrical engineering (M Eng); electronic engineering (M Eng); environmental engineering (M Eng); industrial engineering (M Eng, PhD); manufacturing engineering (M Eng); mechanical engineering (M Eng); systems and quality engineering (M Eng). M Eng program offered jointly with University of Waterloo; PhD in industrial engineering with Texas A&M University. Part-time and evening/weekend programs available. Terminal master's awarded for partial completion of doctoral program. *Degree requirements:* For master's, one foreign language, thesis; for doctorate, one foreign language, thesis/dissertation. *Entrance requirements:* For master's, EXADEP; for doctorate, GRE, master's degree in related field. Additional exam requirements/recommendations for international students: Required—TOEFL. *Faculty research:* Flexible manufacturing cells, materials, statistical methods, environmental prevention, control and evaluation.

Iowa State University of Science and Technology, Department of Chemical and Biological Engineering, Ames, IA 50011-2230. Offers M Eng, MS, PhD. *Degree requirements:* For master's, thesis (for some programs); for doctorate, thesis/dissertation. *Entrance requirements:* For master's and doctorate, GRE General Test. Additional exam requirements/recommendations for international students: Recommended—TOEFL (minimum score 587 paper-based; 94 iBT), IELTS (minimum score 7). *Application deadline:* For fall admission, 1/15 priority date for domestic students, 1/15 for international students; for spring admission, 10/1 for domestic and international students. Application fee: $40 ($90 for international students). Electronic applications accepted. *Unit head:* Dr. Monica Lamm, Director of Graduate Education, 515-294-7643, Fax: 515-294-2689, E-mail: chemengr@iastate.edu. *Application contact:* Christi Patterson, Application Contact, 515-294-7643, Fax: 515-294-2689, E-mail: christip@iastate.edu. Web site: http://www.cbe.iastate.edu.

The Johns Hopkins University, Engineering Program for Professionals, Part-time Program in Chemical and Biomolecular Engineering, Baltimore, MD 21218-2699. Offers M Ch E. Part-time and evening/weekend programs available. Electronic applications accepted.

The Johns Hopkins University, Whiting School of Engineering, Department of Chemical and Biomolecular Engineering, Baltimore, MD 21218. Offers MSE, PhD. Part-time programs available. *Degree requirements:* For doctorate, thesis/dissertation, oral exam. *Entrance requirements:* For doctorate, GRE General Test. Additional exam requirements/recommendations for international students: Required—TOEFL (minimum score 600 paper-based; 250 computer-based; 100 iBT). Electronic applications accepted. *Faculty research:* Polymers and complex fluids, nucleation, bioengineering and biotechnology, computational biology and genomics, cell and molecular biotechnology.

Kansas State University, Graduate School, College of Engineering, Department of Chemical Engineering, Manhattan, KS 66506. Offers MS, PhD. Postbaccalaureate distance learning degree programs offered (minimal on-campus study). *Faculty:* 9 full-time (2 women), 3 part-time/adjunct (0 women). *Students:* 22 full-time (6 women), 11 part-time (3 women); includes 4 minority (1 Black or African American, non-Hispanic/Latino; 1 Asian, non-Hispanic/Latino; 1 Hispanic/Latino; 1 Two or more races, non-Hispanic/Latino), 14 international. Average age 29. 68 applicants, 25% accepted, 9 enrolled. In 2011, 2 master's, 7 doctorates awarded. Terminal master's awarded for partial completion of doctoral program. *Degree requirements:* For master's, 24 hours of coursework; 6 hours of thesis; for doctorate, thesis/dissertation, 90 hours of credit. *Entrance requirements:* For doctorate, GRE. Additional exam requirements/recommendations for international students: Required—TOEFL. *Application deadline:* For fall admission, 2/1 priority date for domestic students, 2/1 for international students; for spring admission, 8/1 priority date for domestic students, 8/1 for international students. Applications are processed on a rolling basis. Application fee: $40 ($55 for international students). Electronic applications accepted. *Financial support:* In 2011–12, 22 students received support, including 22 research assistantships with full tuition reimbursements available (averaging $27,500 per year), 2 teaching assistantships with partial tuition reimbursements available (averaging $27,500 per year); fellowships with partial tuition reimbursements available, scholarships/grants, and tuition waivers (full) also available. Financial award application deadline: 3/1; financial award applicants required to submit FAFSA. *Faculty research:* Renewable sustainable energy, molecular engineering, advanced materials. *Total annual research expenditures:* $2.2 million. *Unit head:* James Edgar, Head, 785-532-4320, Fax: 785-532-7372, E-mail: edgarjh@ksu.edu. Web site: http://www.che.ksu.edu/.

Lamar University, College of Graduate Studies, College of Engineering, Dan F. Smith Department of Chemical Engineering, Beaumont, TX 77710. Offers ME, MES, DE, PhD. *Faculty:* 13 full-time (1 woman), 1 (woman) part-time/adjunct. *Students:* 56 full-time (16 women), 27 part-time (4 women); includes 5 minority (1 Black or African American, non-Hispanic/Latino; 3 Asian, non-Hispanic/Latino; 1 Hispanic/Latino), 72 international. Average age 27. 54 applicants, 76% accepted, 13 enrolled. In 2011, 53 master's, 4 doctorates awarded. *Degree requirements:* For master's, comprehensive exam (for some programs), thesis (for some programs); for doctorate, comprehensive exam, thesis/dissertation. *Entrance requirements:* For master's and doctorate, GRE General Test. Additional exam requirements/recommendations for international students: Required—TOEFL. *Application deadline:* For fall admission, 5/15 priority date for domestic students; for spring admission, 10/1 priority date for domestic students. Applications are processed on a rolling basis. Application fee: $25 ($50 for international students). *Expenses:* Tuition, state resident: full-time $5430; part-time $272 per credit hour. Tuition, nonresident: full-time $11,540; part-time $577 per credit hour. *Required fees:* $1916. *Financial support:* In 2011–12, 49 fellowships with partial tuition reimbursements (averaging $1,000 per year), 15 research assistantships with partial tuition reimbursements (averaging $6,000 per year), 8 teaching assistantships with partial tuition reimbursements (averaging $12,600 per year) were awarded; tuition waivers (full and partial) also available. Financial award application deadline: 4/1. *Faculty research:* Flare minimization, process optimization, process integration. *Unit head:* Dr. Kuyen Li, Chair, 409-880-8784, Fax: 409-880-2197, E-mail: che_dept@hal.lamar.edu. *Application contact:* Sandy Drane, Coordinator of Graduate Admissions, 409-880-8356, Fax: 409-880-8414, E-mail: gradmissions@hal.lamar.edu. Web site: http://dept.lamar.edu/chemicalengineering/.

Lehigh University, P.C. Rossin College of Engineering and Applied Science, Department of Chemical Engineering, Bethlehem, PA 18015. Offers biological chemical engineering (M Eng); chemical engineering (M Eng, MS, PhD); MBA/E. Part-time programs available. Postbaccalaureate distance learning degree programs offered (no on-campus study). *Faculty:* 16 full-time (2 women), 2 part-time/adjunct (0 women). *Students:* 38 full-time (7 women), 40 part-time (18 women); includes 11 minority (2 Black or African American, non-Hispanic/Latino; 6 Asian, non-Hispanic/Latino; 3 Hispanic/Latino), 28 international. Average age 28. 184 applicants, 6% accepted, 11 enrolled. In 2011, 4 master's, 7 doctorates awarded. Terminal master's awarded for partial completion of doctoral program. *Degree requirements:* For master's, thesis (for some programs); for doctorate, comprehensive exam, thesis/dissertation. *Entrance requirements:* For master's and doctorate, GRE General Test. Additional exam requirements/recommendations for international students: Required—TOEFL (minimum score 570 paper-based; 230 computer-based; 79 iBT). *Application deadline:* For fall admission, 7/15 for domestic students, 1/15 for international students; for spring admission, 12/1 for domestic and international students. Applications are processed on a rolling basis. Application fee: $75. Electronic applications accepted. *Financial support:* In 2011–12, 36 students received support, including 4 fellowships with full tuition reimbursements available (averaging $24,500 per year), 27 research assistantships with full tuition reimbursements available (averaging $24,500 per year), 5 teaching assistantships with full tuition reimbursements available (averaging $24,500 per year); career-related internships or fieldwork, institutionally sponsored loans, scholarships/grants, health care benefits, and unspecified assistantships also available. Financial award application deadline: 1/15. *Faculty research:* Emulsion polymers, process control, energy, biotechnology, catalysis. *Total annual research expenditures:* $2.9 million. *Unit head:* Dr. Anthony J. McHugh, Chairman, 610-758-4260, Fax: 610-758-5057, E-mail: ajm8@lehigh.edu. *Application contact:* Barbara A. Kessler, Graduate Coordinator, 610-758-4261, Fax: 610-758-5057, E-mail: inchegs@mail.lehigh.edu. Web site: http://www.che.lehigh.edu/.

Louisiana State University and Agricultural and Mechanical College, Graduate School, College of Engineering, Cain Department of Chemical Engineering, Baton Rouge, LA 70803. Offers MS Ch E, PhD. Part-time and evening/weekend programs available. *Faculty:* 14 full-time (1 woman). *Students:* 56 full-time (13 women), 5 part-time (1 woman); includes 2 minority (1 Asian, non-Hispanic/Latino; 1 Hispanic/Latino), 37 international. Average age 27. 162 applicants, 15% accepted, 7 enrolled. In 2011, 15 master's, 6 doctorates awarded. Terminal master's awarded for partial completion of doctoral program. *Degree requirements:* For master's, comprehensive exam or thesis; for doctorate, thesis/dissertation, general exam, qualifying exam. *Entrance requirements:* For master's and doctorate, GRE General Test, minimum GPA of 3.0. Additional exam requirements/recommendations for international students: Required—TOEFL (minimum score 550 paper-based; 213 computer-based; 79 iBT) or IELTS (minimum score 6.5). *Application deadline:* For fall admission, 1/25 priority date for domestic students, 5/15 for international students; for spring admission, 10/15 for international students. Applications are processed on a rolling basis. Application fee: $50 ($70 for international students). Electronic applications accepted. *Financial support:* In 2011–12, 56 students received support, including 3 fellowships (averaging $23,473 per year), 49 research assistantships with full and partial tuition reimbursements available (averaging $23,257 per year); teaching assistantships, Federal Work-Study, health care benefits, and tuition waivers (full and partial) also available. Financial award application deadline: 4/15; financial award applicants required to submit FAFSA. *Faculty research:* Reaction engineering, control, thermodynamic and transport phenomena, polymer processing and properties, biochemical engineering. *Total annual research expenditures:* $4.7 million. *Unit head:* Dr. Mary Julia Wornat, Chair, 225-578-7509, Fax: 225-578-1476, E-mail: mjwornat@lsu.edu. *Application contact:* Dr. John Flake, Director of Graduate Instruction, 225-578 3060, Fax: 225-578-1476, E-mail: johnflake@lsu.edu. Web site: http://www.che.lsu.edu/.

Louisiana Tech University, Graduate School, College of Engineering and Science, Department of Chemical Engineering, Ruston, LA 71272. Offers MS, PhD. Part-time programs available. Terminal master's awarded for partial completion of doctoral program. *Degree requirements:* For master's, thesis; for doctorate, thesis/dissertation. *Entrance requirements:* For master's, GRE General Test, minimum GPA of 3.0 in last 60 hours; for doctorate, minimum graduate GPA of 3.25 (with MS) or GRE General Test. Additional exam requirements/recommendations for international students: Required—TOEFL. *Faculty research:* Artificial intelligence, biotechnology, hazardous waste process safety.

Manhattan College, Graduate Division, School of Engineering, Program in Chemical Engineering, Riverdale, NY 10471. Offers chemical engineering (MS); cosmetic engineering (MS). Part-time programs available. *Faculty:* 6 full-time (1 woman), 2 part-time/adjunct (0 women). *Students:* 15 full-time (4 women), 3 part-time (2 women); includes 10 minority (2 Black or African American, non-Hispanic/Latino; 4 Asian, non-Hispanic/Latino; 4 Hispanic/Latino). Average age 22. 20 applicants, 80% accepted, 16 enrolled. In 2011, 11 master's awarded. *Degree requirements:* For master's, thesis or alternative. *Entrance requirements:* For master's, GRE (recommended), minimum GPA of 3.0. Additional exam requirements/recommendations for international students: Required—TOEFL (minimum score 550 paper-based; 213 computer-based; 80 iBT), IELTS (minimum score 6). *Application deadline:* For fall admission, 8/10 priority date for domestic students, 8/10 for international students; for spring admission, 1/7 for domestic and international students. Applications are processed on a rolling basis. Application fee: $50. *Expenses: Tuition:* Full-time $14,850; part-time $825 per credit. *Required fees:* $390; $150. *Financial support:* In 2011–12, 7 students received support, including 8 teaching assistantships with partial tuition reimbursements available; career-related internships or fieldwork, Federal Work-Study, scholarships/grants, and tuition waivers (partial) also available. Support available to part-time students. Financial award application deadline: 2/1. *Faculty research:* Advanced separation processes, environmental management, combustion, pollution prevention. *Unit head:* Dr. Ann Marie Flynn, Chairperson, 718-862-7420, Fax: 718-862-7819, E-mail: chmldept@manhattan.edu. *Application contact:* Kathy Ciarletta, Information Contact, 718-862-7185, Fax: 718-863-7819, E-mail: chmldept@manhattan.edu.

Massachusetts Institute of Technology, School of Engineering, Department of Chemical Engineering, Cambridge, MA 02139. Offers chemical engineering (SM, PhD, Sc D); chemical engineering practice (SM, PhD); SM/MBA. *Faculty:* 31 full-time (4 women). *Students:* 239 full-time (75 women), 1 (woman) part-time; includes 35 minority (1 Black or African American, non-Hispanic/Latino; 28 Asian, non-Hispanic/Latino; 4 Hispanic/Latino; 2 Two or more races, non-Hispanic/Latino), 88 international. Average age 25. 508 applicants, 16% accepted, 60 enrolled. In 2011, 43 master's, 38 doctorates awarded. Terminal master's awarded for partial completion of doctoral program. *Degree requirements:* For master's, thesis (for some programs), one semester of the Practice School (for SM in chemical engineering practice); for doctorate, comprehensive exam, thesis/dissertation. *Entrance requirements:* For master's and doctorate, GRE General Test. Additional exam requirements/recommendations for international students: Required—TOEFL (minimum score 600 paper-based; 250 computer-based; 100 iBT), IELTS (minimum score 7). *Application deadline:* For fall admission, 12/15 for domestic and international students. Application fee: $75. Electronic applications accepted. *Expenses: Tuition:* Full-time $40,460; part-time $630 per credit hour. *Required fees:* $272. *Financial support:* In 2011–12, 209 students received support, including 101 fellowships (averaging $32,600 per year), 119 research assistantships (averaging $32,000 per year), 13 teaching assistantships (averaging $34,700 per year); career-related internships or fieldwork, Federal Work-Study, institutionally sponsored loans, scholarships/grants, traineeships, health care benefits, and unspecified assistantships also available. *Faculty research:* Catalysis and reaction engineering; biological engineering; materials and polymers; surfaces and nanostructures; thermodynamics and molecular computation. *Total annual research expenditures:* $46 million. *Unit head:* Prof. Klavs F. Jensen, Head, 617-253-4561, Fax: 617-258-8992. *Application contact:* Graduate Admissions, 617-253-4577, Fax: 617-253-9695, E-mail: chemegrad@mit.edu. Web site: http://web.mit.edu/cheme/.

McGill University, Faculty of Graduate and Postdoctoral Studies, Faculty of Engineering, Department of Chemical Engineering, Montréal, QC H3A 2T5, Canada. Offers chemical engineering (M Eng, PhD); environmental engineering (M Eng).

McMaster University, School of Graduate Studies, Faculty of Engineering, Department of Chemical Engineering, Hamilton, ON L8S 4M2, Canada. Offers M Eng, MA Sc, PhD. *Degree requirements:* For master's, thesis; for doctorate, comprehensive exam, thesis/dissertation. *Entrance requirements:* For master's, minimum B average in the last two years. Additional exam requirements/recommendations for international students: Required—TOEFL (minimum score 550 paper-based; 213 computer-based). *Faculty research:* Biomaterials, computer process control, polymer processing, environmental biotechnology, reverse osmosis.

McNeese State University, Doré School of Graduate Studies, College of Engineering and Engineering Technology, Lake Charles, LA 70609. Offers chemical engineering (M Eng); civil engineering (M Eng); electrical engineering (M Eng); engineering management (M Eng); mechanical engineering (M Eng); pump reliability engineering (Postbaccalaureate Certificate). Part-time and evening/weekend programs available. *Faculty:* 13 full-time (1 woman). *Students:* 21 full-time (4 women), 18 part-time (5 women); includes 5 minority (4 Black or African American, non-Hispanic/Latino; 1 American Indian or Alaska Native, non-Hispanic/Latino), 23 international. In 2011, 28 master's awarded. *Degree requirements:* For master's, thesis or alternative. *Entrance requirements:* For master's, GRE, minimum undergraduate GPA of 3.0. Additional exam requirements/recommendations for international students: Required—TOEFL (minimum score 560 paper-based; 220 computer-based; 83 iBT). *Application deadline:* For fall admission, 5/15 priority date for domestic students, 5/15 for international students; for spring admission, 10/15 priority date for domestic students, 10/15 for international students. Applications are processed on a rolling basis. Application fee: $20 ($30 for international students). *Expenses:* Tuition, state resident: part-time $519 per credit hour. Tuition and fees vary according to course load. *Financial support:* Federal Work-Study available. Support available to part-time students. Financial award application deadline: 5/1. *Unit head:* Dr. Nikos Kiritsis, Dean, 337-475-5875, Fax: 337-475-5237, E-mail: nikosk@mcneese.edu. *Application contact:* Dr. George F. Mead, Jr., Interim Dean of Dore' School of Graduate Studies, 337-475-5396, Fax: 337-475-5397, E-mail: admissions@mcneese.edu.

Michigan State University, The Graduate School, College of Engineering, Department of Chemical Engineering and Materials Science, East Lansing, MI 48824. Offers chemical engineering (MS, PhD); materials science and engineering (MS, PhD). *Entrance requirements:* Additional exam requirements/recommendations for international students: Required—TOEFL. Electronic applications accepted.

Michigan Technological University, Graduate School, College of Engineering, Department of Chemical Engineering, Houghton, MI 49931. Offers MS, PhD. Part-time programs available. *Faculty:* 22 full-time (4 women), 1 part-time/adjunct (0 women). *Students:* 51 full-time (16 women), 6 part-time (3 women); includes 5 minority (4 Black or African American, non-Hispanic/Latino; 1 Hispanic/Latino), 35 international. Average age 26. 137 applicants, 53% accepted, 17 enrolled. In 2011, 10 master's, 4 doctorates awarded. Terminal master's awarded for partial completion of doctoral program. *Degree requirements:* For master's, comprehensive exam (for some programs), thesis (for some programs); for doctorate, comprehensive exam, thesis/dissertation. *Entrance* *requirements:* For master's and doctorate, GRE, statement of purpose, official transcripts, 3 letters of recommendation. Additional exam requirements/recommendations for international students: Required—TOEFL (minimum score 100 iBT) or IELTS. *Application deadline:* For fall admission, 1/15 for domestic and international students. Applications are processed on a rolling basis. Electronic applications accepted. *Expenses:* Contact institution. *Financial support:* In 2011–12, 43 students received support, including 9 fellowships with full tuition reimbursements available (averaging $6,065 per year), 17 research assistantships with full tuition reimbursements available (averaging $6,065 per year), 8 teaching assistantships with full tuition reimbursements available (averaging $6,065 per year); career-related internships or fieldwork, Federal Work-Study, scholarships/grants, health care benefits, unspecified assistantships, and cooperative program also available. Financial award applicants required to submit FAFSA. *Faculty research:* Polymer engineering, thermodynamics, chemical process safety, surface science/catalysis, environmental chemical engineering. *Total annual research expenditures:* $1.2 million. *Unit head:* Dr. Komar Kawatra, Chair, 906-487-3132, Fax: 906-487-3213, E-mail: skkawatr@mtu.edu. *Application contact:* Alexis E. Snell, Secretary 3, 906-487-3132, Fax: 906-487-3213, E-mail: aesnell@mtu.edu. Web site: http://www.chem.mtu.edu/chem_eng/.

Mississippi State University, Bagley College of Engineering, David C. Swalm School of Chemical Engineering, Mississippi State, MS 39762. Offers chemical engineering (MS); engineering (PhD), including chemical engineering. *Faculty:* 9 full-time (3 women), 2 part-time/adjunct (0 women). *Students:* 10 full-time (4 women), 8 part-time (2 women); includes 1 minority (Black or African American, non-Hispanic/Latino), 7 international. Average age 29. 22 applicants, 9% accepted, 2 enrolled. In 2011, 2 master's, 6 doctorates awarded. *Degree requirements:* For master's, thesis optional, comprehensive oral or written exam; for doctorate, comprehensive exam, thesis/dissertation. *Entrance requirements:* For master's and doctorate, GRE, minimum GPA of 3.0. Additional exam requirements/recommendations for international students: Required—TOEFL (minimum score 550 paper-based; 213 computer-based; 79 iBT); Recommended—IELTS (minimum score 6.5). *Application deadline:* For fall admission, 4/1 priority date for domestic students, 5/1 for international students; for spring admission, 8/1 priority date for domestic students, 9/1 for international students. Applications are processed on a rolling basis. Application fee: $40. Electronic applications accepted. *Expenses:* Tuition, state resident: full-time $5805; part-time $322.50 per credit hour. Tuition, nonresident: full-time $14,670; part-time $815 per credit hour. *Financial support:* In 2011–12, 7 research assistantships with full tuition reimbursements (averaging $15,974 per year), 1 teaching assistantship with full tuition reimbursement (averaging $11,025 per year) were awarded; Federal Work-Study, institutionally sponsored loans, and unspecified assistantships also available. Financial award application deadline: 4/1; financial award applicants required to submit FAFSA. *Faculty research:* Thermodynamics, composite materials, catalysis, surface science, environmental engineering. *Total annual research expenditures:* $5 million. *Unit head:* Dr. Bill Elmore, Interim Director and Associate Professor, 662-325-7206, Fax: 662-325-2482, E-mail: elmore@che.msstate.edu. *Application contact:* Dr. Rafael Hernandez, Associate Professor and Graduate Coordinator, 662-325-0790, Fax: 662-325-2482, E-mail: rhernandez@che.msstate.edu. Web site: http://www.che.msstate.edu/.

Missouri University of Science and Technology, Graduate School, Department of Chemical and Biological Engineering, Rolla, MO 65409. Offers chemical engineering (MS, DE, PhD). *Degree requirements:* For master's, thesis optional; for doctorate, comprehensive exam. *Entrance requirements:* For master's, GRE (minimum score 1100 verbal and quantitative, 4 writing); for doctorate, GRE (minimum score: verbal and quantitative 1200, writing 4). Additional exam requirements/recommendations for international students: Required—TOEFL (minimum score 550 paper-based; 213 computer-based). *Faculty research:* Mixing, fluid mechanics, bioengineering, freeze-drying, extraction.

Montana State University, College of Graduate Studies, College of Engineering, Department of Chemical and Biological Engineering, Bozeman, MT 59717. Offers chemical engineering (MS); engineering (PhD), including chemical engineering option, environmental engineering option; environmental engineering (MS). Part-time programs available. *Degree requirements:* For master's, comprehensive exam, thesis (for some programs); for doctorate, comprehensive exam, thesis/dissertation. *Entrance requirements:* For master's and doctorate, GRE General Test. Additional exam requirements/recommendations for international students: Required—TOEFL (minimum score 550 paper-based; 213 computer-based). Electronic applications accepted. *Faculty research:* Biofuels, extremophilic bioprocessing, and situ biocatalyzed heavy metal transformations; metabolic network analysis and engineering; magnetic resonance microscopy; modeling of biological systems; the development of protective coatings on planar solid oxide fuel cell (SOFC) metallic interconnects; characterizing corrosion mechanisms of materials in precisely-controlled exposures; testing materials in polycrystalline silicon production environments; environmental biotechnology and bioremediation.

New Jersey Institute of Technology, Office of Graduate Studies, Newark College of Engineering, Department of Chemical Engineering, Program in Chemical Engineering, Newark, NJ 07102. Offers MS, PhD. Part-time and evening/weekend programs available. *Students:* 55 full-time (23 women), 21 part-time (7 women); includes 20 minority (5 Black or African American, non-Hispanic/Latino; 11 Asian, non-Hispanic/Latino; 4 Hispanic/Latino), 40 international. Average age 30. 156 applicants, 47% accepted, 26 enrolled. In 2011, 19 master's, 9 doctorates awarded. Terminal master's awarded for partial completion of doctoral program. *Degree requirements:* For master's, thesis optional; for doctorate, thesis/dissertation, residency. *Entrance requirements:* For master's, GRE General Test; for doctorate, GRE General Test, minimum graduate GPA of 3.5. Additional exam requirements/recommendations for international students: Required—TOEFL (minimum score 550 paper-based; 213 computer-based; 79 iBT). *Application deadline:* For fall admission, 6/1 priority date for domestic students, 5/1 for international students; for spring admission, 11/15 for domestic and international students. Applications are processed on a rolling basis. Application fee: $65. Electronic applications accepted. *Expenses:* Tuition, state resident: full-time $7980; part-time $867 per credit. Tuition, nonresident: full-time $11,336; part-time $1196 per credit. *Required fees:* $230 per credit. *Financial support:* Fellowships with full and partial tuition reimbursements, research assistantships with full and partial tuition reimbursements, teaching assistantships with full and partial tuition reimbursements, career-related internships or fieldwork, Federal Work-Study, institutionally sponsored loans, and unspecified assistantships available. Financial award application deadline: 1/15. *Unit head:* Dr. Norman Loney, Chair, 973-596-6598, E-mail: norman.loney@njit.edu. *Application contact:* Kathryn Kelly, Director of Admissions, 973-596-3300, Fax: 973-596-3461, E-mail: admissions@njit.edu.

New Mexico State University, Graduate School, College of Engineering, Department of Chemical Engineering, Las Cruces, NM 88003-8001. Offers MS Ch E, PhD. Part-time

programs available. *Faculty:* 7 full-time (3 women). *Students:* 23 full-time (7 women), 5 part-time (0 women); includes 3 minority (1 Black or African American, non-Hispanic/Latino; 2 Hispanic/Latino), 19 international. Average age 29. 24 applicants, 83% accepted, 8 enrolled. In 2011, 7 degrees awarded. Terminal master's awarded for partial completion of doctoral program. *Degree requirements:* For master's, thesis (for some programs); for doctorate, comprehensive exam, thesis/dissertation. *Entrance requirements:* For master's and doctorate, GRE General Test. Additional exam requirements/recommendations for international students: Required—TOEFL (minimum score 550 paper-based; 79 iBT), IELTS (minimum score 6.5). *Application deadline:* For fall admission, 3/1 priority date for domestic students, 3/1 for international students; for spring admission, 11/1 priority date for domestic students, 11/1 for international students. Applications are processed on a rolling basis. Application fee: $40 ($50 for international students). Electronic applications accepted. *Expenses:* Tuition, state resident: full-time $5004; part-time $208.50 per credit. Tuition, nonresident: full-time $17,446; part-time $726.90 per credit. *Financial support:* In 2011–12, 1 fellowship with full tuition reimbursement (averaging $5,612 per year), 14 research assistantships with full and partial tuition reimbursements (averaging $22,791 per year), 9 teaching assistantships with full and partial tuition reimbursements (averaging $23,607 per year) were awarded; career-related internships or fieldwork, Federal Work-Study, scholarships/grants, health care benefits, and unspecified assistantships also available. Support available to part-time students. Financial award application deadline: 3/1. *Faculty research:* Advanced materials separations, environmental engineering, computer-aided design, bioengineering, biofuels, biomedical engineering. *Unit head:* Dr. Martha C. Mitchell, Head, 575-646-2093, Fax: 575-646-7706, E-mail: martmitc@nmsu.edu. *Application contact:* Dr. David A. Rockstraw, Professor, 575-646-7705, Fax: 575-646-7706, E-mail: drockstr@nmsu.edu. Web site: http://chemeng.nmsu.edu/.

North Carolina Agricultural and Technical State University, School of Graduate Studies, College of Engineering, Department of Chemical and Bioengineering, Greensboro, NC 27411. Offers bioengineering (MS); biological engineering (MS); chemical engineering (MS).

North Carolina State University, Graduate School, College of Engineering, Department of Chemical and Biomolecular Engineering, Raleigh, NC 27695. Offers chemical engineering (M Ch E, MS, PhD). Part-time programs available. Terminal master's awarded for partial completion of doctoral program. *Degree requirements:* For master's, thesis optional; for doctorate, thesis/dissertation. *Entrance requirements:* For master's and doctorate, GRE General Test. Additional exam requirements/recommendations for international students: Required—TOEFL. Electronic applications accepted. *Faculty research:* Molecular thermodynamics and computer simulation, catalysis, kinetics, electrochemical reaction engineering, biochemical engineering.

Northeastern University, College of Engineering, Department of Chemical Engineering, Boston, MA 02115-5096. Offers MS, PhD. Part-time programs available. *Faculty:* 8 full-time. *Students:* 40 full-time, 6 part-time. 111 applicants, 15% accepted, 11 enrolled. In 2011, 2 master's, 4 doctorates awarded. *Degree requirements:* For master's, thesis optional; for doctorate, thesis/dissertation, departmental qualifying exam. *Entrance requirements:* For master's and doctorate, GRE General Test. Additional exam requirements/recommendations for international students: Required—TOEFL (minimum score 550 paper-based; 213 computer-based; 80 iBT). *Application deadline:* For fall admission, 1/15 priority date for domestic students, 1/15 for international students. Applications are processed on a rolling basis. Application fee: $50. Electronic applications accepted. *Financial support:* In 2011–12, 21 students received support, including 1 fellowship with full tuition reimbursement available, 13 research assistantships with full tuition reimbursements available, 17 teaching assistantships with full tuition reimbursements available (averaging $18,320 per year); career-related internships or fieldwork, Federal Work-Study, scholarships/grants, tuition waivers (full), and unspecified assistantships also available. Support available to part-time students. Financial award application deadline: 1/15; financial award applicants required to submit FAFSA. *Faculty research:* Aerogel, catalysts, advanced microgravity materials processing, biomaterials, catalyst development, biochemical reactions. *Unit head:* Dr. Laura H. Lewis, Chair, 617-373-2989, Fax: 617-373-8504. *Application contact:* Jeffery Hengel, Admissions Specialist, 617-373-2711, Fax: 617-373-2501, E-mail: grad-eng@coe.neu.edu. Web site: http://www.coe.neu.edu/.

Northwestern University, McCormick School of Engineering and Applied Science, Department of Chemical and Biological Engineering, Evanston, IL 60208. Offers chemical engineering (MS, PhD). Admissions and degrees offered through The Graduate School. Part-time programs available. *Faculty:* 15 full-time (1 woman). *Students:* 96 full-time (45 women); includes 32 minority (2 Black or African American, non-Hispanic/Latino; 15 Asian, non-Hispanic/Latino; 13 Hispanic/Latino; 2 Two or more races, non-Hispanic/Latino), 21 international. Average age 26. 351 applicants, 19% accepted, 22 enrolled. In 2011, 16 master's, 16 doctorates awarded. Terminal master's awarded for partial completion of doctoral program. *Degree requirements:* For master's, comprehensive exam (for some programs), thesis optional; for doctorate, comprehensive exam, thesis/dissertation. *Entrance requirements:* For master's and doctorate, GRE General Test. Additional exam requirements/recommendations for international students: Required—TOEFL (minimum score 577 paper-based; 233 computer-based; 90 iBT), IELTS (minimum score 7). *Application deadline:* For fall admission, 12/31 for domestic and international students. Application fee: $75. Electronic applications accepted. *Financial support:* Fellowships with full tuition reimbursements, research assistantships with full tuition reimbursements, teaching assistantships with full tuition reimbursements, career-related internships or fieldwork, institutionally sponsored loans, traineeships, health care benefits, and unspecified assistantships available. Financial award application deadline: 1/15; financial award applicants required to submit FAFSA. *Faculty research:* Biotechnology and bioengineering; complex systems; environmental catalysis, kinetics and reaction engineering; modeling, theory, and simulation; polymer science and engineering; transport processes. *Total annual research expenditures:* $10.8 million. *Unit head:* Dr. Linda Broadbelt, Chair, 847-491-2890, Fax: 847-491-3728, E-mail: broadbelt@northwestern.edu. *Application contact:* Dr. Luis Amaral, Admissions Officer, 847-491-7850, Fax: 847-491-3728, E-mail: amaral@northwestern.edu. Web site: http://www.chem-biol-eng.northwestern.edu/.

The Ohio State University, Graduate School, College of Engineering, Department of Chemical and Biomolecular Engineering, Columbus, OH 43210. Offers chemical engineering (MS, PhD). *Faculty:* 20. *Students:* 66 full-time (19 women), 23 part-time (6 women); includes 8 minority (4 Asian, non-Hispanic/Latino; 3 Hispanic/Latino; 1 Two or more races, non-Hispanic/Latino), 61 international. Average age 26. In 2011, 11 master's, 13 doctorates awarded. *Degree requirements:* For master's, thesis; for doctorate, thesis/dissertation. *Entrance requirements:* For master's and doctorate, GRE General Test. Additional exam requirements/recommendations for international students: Required—Michigan English Language Assessment Battery (minimum score

82); Recommended—TOEFL (minimum score 600 paper-based; 250 computer-based). *Application deadline:* For fall admission, 8/15 priority date for domestic students, 7/1 for international students; for winter admission, 12/1 priority date for domestic students, 11/1 for international students; for spring admission, 3/1 priority date for domestic students, 2/1 for international students. Applications are processed on a rolling basis. Application fee: $40 ($50 for international students). Electronic applications accepted. *Expenses:* Tuition, state resident: full-time $11,400. Tuition, nonresident: full-time $28,125. Tuition and fees vary according to course load, degree level, campus/location and program. *Financial support:* Fellowships, research assistantships, teaching assistantships, career-related internships or fieldwork, Federal Work-Study, institutionally sponsored loans, and unspecified assistantships available. Support available to part-time students. *Unit head:* Stuart L. Cooper, Chair, 614-247-8015, E-mail: coopers@chbmeng.ohio-state.edu. *Application contact:* Graduate Admissions, 614-292-6031, Fax: 614-292-3656, E-mail: gradadmissions@osu.edu. Web site: http://www.chbmeng.ohio-state.edu.

Ohio University, Graduate College, Russ College of Engineering and Technology, Department of Chemical and Biomolecular Engineering, Athens, OH 45701-2979. Offers biomedical engineering (MS); chemical engineering (MS, PhD). Part-time programs available. *Students:* 53 full-time (25 women), 10 part-time (4 women), 51 international. 59 applicants, 25% accepted, 14 enrolled. In 2011, 3 master's, 5 doctorates awarded. *Degree requirements:* For master's, comprehensive exam (for some programs), thesis; for doctorate, comprehensive exam, thesis/dissertation, qualifying exams. *Entrance requirements:* For master's and doctorate, GRE General Test. Additional exam requirements/recommendations for international students: Required—TOEFL (minimum score 590 paper-based; 96 iBT) or IELTS (minimum score 7). *Application deadline:* For fall admission, 3/1 priority date for domestic students, 3/1 for international students. Applications are processed on a rolling basis. Application fee: $50 ($55 for international students). Electronic applications accepted. *Financial support:* In 2011–12, fellowships with full tuition reimbursements (averaging $19,000 per year), research assistantships with full tuition reimbursements (averaging $17,000 per year), teaching assistantships with full tuition reimbursements (averaging $15,000 per year) were awarded; Federal Work-Study, institutionally sponsored loans, and unspecified assistantships also available. Financial award application deadline: 3/1; financial award applicants required to submit FAFSA. *Faculty research:* Corrosion and multiphase flow, biochemical engineering, thin film materials, air pollution modeling and control, biomedical engineering. *Total annual research expenditures:* $1.8 million. *Unit head:* Dr. Valerie L. Young, Chair, 740-593-1496, Fax: 740-593-0873, E-mail: youngv@ohio.edu. *Application contact:* Dr. Daniel A. Gulino, Assistant Chair for Graduate Studies, 740-593-1495, Fax: 740-593-0873, E-mail: gulino@ohio.edu. Web site: http://www.ohio.edu/chemical/.

Oklahoma State University, College of Engineering, Architecture and Technology, School of Chemical Engineering, Stillwater, OK 74078. Offers MS, PhD. *Faculty:* 13 full-time (2 women), 1 part-time/adjunct (0 women). *Students:* 29 full-time (10 women), 22 part-time (7 women); includes 3 minority (2 American Indian or Alaska Native, non-Hispanic/Latino; 1 Asian, non-Hispanic/Latino), 43 international. Average age 27. 104 applicants, 22% accepted, 12 enrolled. In 2011, 16 master's, 1 doctorate awarded. *Degree requirements:* For master's, thesis or alternative; for doctorate, comprehensive exam, thesis/dissertation. *Entrance requirements:* For master's and doctorate, GRE or GMAT. Additional exam requirements/recommendations for international students: Required—TOEFL (minimum score 550 paper-based; 79 iBT). *Application deadline:* For fall admission, 3/1 for international students; for spring admission, 8/1 for international students. Applications are processed on a rolling basis. Application fee: $40 ($75 for international students). Electronic applications accepted. *Expenses:* Tuition, state resident: full-time $4044; part-time $168.50 per credit hour. Tuition, nonresident: full-time $16,008; part-time $667 per credit hour. *Required fees:* $2122; $88.45 per credit hour. One-time fee: $50. Tuition and fees vary according to course load and campus/location. *Financial support:* In 2011–12, 26 research assistantships (averaging $13,408 per year), 28 teaching assistantships (averaging $8,177 per year) were awarded; fellowships, career-related internships or fieldwork, Federal Work-Study, scholarships/grants, health care benefits, tuition waivers (partial), and unspecified assistantships also available. Support available to part-time students. Financial award application deadline: 3/1; financial award applicants required to submit FAFSA. *Unit head:* Dr. Khaled Gasem, Head, 405-744-5280, Fax: 405-744-6338. *Application contact:* Dr. Sheryl Tucker, Dean, 405-744-7099, Fax: 405-744-0355, E-mail: grad-i@okstate.edu. Web site: http://www.cheng.okstate.edu.

Oregon State University, Graduate School, College of Engineering, School of Chemical, Biological and Environmental Engineering, Department of Chemical Engineering, Corvallis, OR 97331. Offers M Eng, MS, PhD.

Penn State University Park, Graduate School, College of Engineering, Department of Chemical Engineering, State College, University Park, PA 16802-1503. Offers MS, PhD. *Unit head:* Dr. David N. Wormley, Dean, 814-865-7537, Fax: 814-865-8767, E-mail: dnw2@engr.psu.edu. *Application contact:* Cynthia E. Nicosia, Director, Graduate Enrollment Services, 814-865-1834, E-mail: cey1@psu.edu. Web site: http://fenske.che.psu.edu/.

Polytechnic Institute of New York University, Department of Chemical and Biological Engineering, Major in Chemical Engineering, Brooklyn, NY 11201-2990. Offers MS, PhD. Part-time and evening/weekend programs available. *Students:* 25 full-time (10 women), 17 part-time (7 women); includes 12 minority (6 Black or African American, non-Hispanic/Latino; 5 Asian, non-Hispanic/Latino; 1 Hispanic/Latino), 23 international. Average age 26. 154 applicants, 42% accepted, 12 enrolled. In 2011, 10 master's, 1 doctorate awarded. *Degree requirements:* For master's, comprehensive exam (for some programs), thesis (for some programs); for doctorate, comprehensive exam, thesis/dissertation. *Entrance requirements:* For master's, GRE General Test, BS in chemical engineering; for doctorate, GRE General Test. Additional exam requirements/recommendations for international students: Required—TOEFL (minimum score 550 paper-based; 213 computer-based; 80 iBT); Recommended—IELTS (minimum score 6.5). *Application deadline:* For fall admission, 7/31 priority date for domestic students, 4/30 for international students; for spring admission, 12/31 priority date for domestic students, 11/30 for international students. Applications are processed on a rolling basis. Application fee: $75. Electronic applications accepted. *Expenses: Tuition:* Full-time $22,464; part-time $1248 per credit. *Required fees:* $501 per semester. *Financial support:* Fellowships, research assistantships, teaching assistantships, institutionally sponsored loans, scholarships/grants, and unspecified assistantships available. Support available to part-time students. Financial award applicants required to submit FAFSA. *Faculty research:* Plasma polymerization, crystallization of organic compounds, dipolar relaxations in reactive polymers. *Unit head:* Dr. Walter Zurawsky, Head, 718-260-3725, Fax: 718-260-3125, E-mail: zurawsky@poly.edu. *Application contact:* JeanCarlo Bonilla, Director, Graduate Enrollment Management, 718-260-3182, Fax: 718-260-3624, E-mail: gradinfo@poly.edu.

Polytechnic Institute of NYU, Long Island Graduate Center, Graduate Programs, Department of Chemical and Biological Engineering, Major in Chemical Engineering, Melville, NY 11747. Offers MS. *Students:* 2 applicants, 100% accepted, 0 enrolled. *Degree requirements:* For master's, comprehensive exam (for some programs), thesis (for some programs). *Entrance requirements:* Additional exam requirements/recommendations for international students: Required—TOEFL (minimum score 550 paper-based; 213 computer-based; 80 iBT); Recommended—IELTS (minimum score 6.5). *Application deadline:* For fall admission, 7/31 priority date for domestic students, 4/30 for international students; for spring admission, 12/31 priority date for domestic students, 11/30 for international students. Applications are processed on a rolling basis. Application fee: $75. Electronic applications accepted. *Financial support:* Institutionally sponsored loans, scholarships/grants, and unspecified assistantships available. Support available to part-time students. *Unit head:* Dr. Walter Zurawsky, Department Head, 718-260-3725, E-mail: zurawsky@poly.edu. *Application contact:* JeanCarlo Bonilla, Director of Graduate Enrollment Management, 718-260-3182, Fax: 718-260-3624, E-mail: gradinfo@poly.edu.

Princeton University, Graduate School, School of Engineering and Applied Science, Department of Chemical Engineering, Princeton, NJ 08544-1019. Offers M Eng, MSE, PhD. Terminal master's awarded for partial completion of doctoral program. *Degree requirements:* For master's, thesis (MSE); for doctorate, thesis/dissertation, general exam. *Entrance requirements:* For master's, GRE General Test, 3 letters of recommendation; for doctorate, GRE General Test, official transcript(s), 3 letters of recommendation, personal statement. Additional exam requirements/recommendations for international students: Required—TOEFL. Electronic applications accepted. *Faculty research:* Applied and computational mathematics, bioengineering, environmental and energy science and technology, fluid mechanics and transport phenomena, materials science.

Purdue University, College of Engineering, School of Chemical Engineering, West Lafayette, IN 47907-2050. Offers MSChE, PhD. Terminal master's awarded for partial completion of doctoral program. *Entrance requirements:* For master's and doctorate, GRE, minimum GPA of 3.0. Additional exam requirements/recommendations for international students: Required—TOEFL (minimum score 550 paper-based; 213 computer-based); Recommended—TWE. Electronic applications accepted. *Faculty research:* Biochemical and biomedical processes, polymer materials, interfacial and surface phenomena, applied thermodynamics, process systems engineering.

Queen's University at Kingston, School of Graduate Studies and Research, Faculty of Applied Science, Department of Chemical Engineering, Kingston, ON K7L 3N6, Canada. Offers M Sc, PhD. Part-time programs available. *Degree requirements:* For master's, thesis or alternative; for doctorate, comprehensive exam, thesis/dissertation. *Entrance requirements:* Additional exam requirements/recommendations for international students: Required—TOEFL (minimum score 580 paper-based; 237 computer-based). Electronic applications accepted. *Faculty research:* Polymers and reaction engineering, process control and applied statistics, combustion, fermentation and bioremediation, biomaterials.

Rensselaer Polytechnic Institute, Graduate School, School of Engineering, Program in Chemical Engineering, Troy, NY 12180-3590. Offers M Eng, MS, PhD. Part-time programs available. Terminal master's awarded for partial completion of doctoral program. *Entrance requirements:* For master's, GRE (minimum score 550 verbal); for doctorate, GRE (Verbal minimum score of 550). Additional exam requirements/recommendations for international students: Required—TOEFL (minimum score 570 paper-based). Electronic applications accepted. *Faculty research:* Biocatalysis, bioseparations, biotechnology, molecular modeling and simulation, advanced materials, interfacial phenomena, systems biology.

Rice University, Graduate Programs, George R. Brown School of Engineering, Department of Chemical and Biomolecular Engineering, Houston, TX 77251-1892. Offers chemical and biomolecular engineering (MS, PhD); chemical engineering (M Ch E). Part-time programs available. *Degree requirements:* For master's, thesis (for some programs); for doctorate, thesis/dissertation. *Entrance requirements:* For master's and doctorate, GRE General Test, minimum GPA of 3.0. Additional exam requirements/recommendations for international students: Required—TOEFL (minimum score 600 paper-based; 250 computer-based; 90 iBT). Electronic applications accepted. *Faculty research:* Thermodynamics, phase equilibria, rheology, fluid mechanics, polymers, biomedical engineering, interfacial phenomena, process control, petroleum engineering, reaction engineering and catalysis, biomaterials, metabolic engineering.

Rose-Hulman Institute of Technology, Faculty of Engineering and Applied Sciences, Department of Chemical Engineering, Terre Haute, IN 47803-3999. Offers MS. Part-time programs available. *Faculty:* 9 full-time (2 women). *Students:* 2 full-time (0 women), 2 part-time (0 women). Average age 25. 3 applicants, 100% accepted, 1 enrolled. *Degree requirements:* For master's, thesis. *Entrance requirements:* For master's, GRE, minimum GPA of 3.0. Additional exam requirements/recommendations for international students: Required—TOEFL (minimum score 580 paper-based; 237 computer-based; 92 iBT). *Application deadline:* For fall admission, 2/1 priority date for domestic students. Applications are processed on a rolling basis. Application fee: $0. *Expenses: Tuition:* Full-time $37,197; part-time $1085 per credit hour. *Financial support:* In 2011–12, 3 students received support. Fellowships with full and partial tuition reimbursements available, research assistantships with full and partial tuition reimbursements available, institutionally sponsored loans, scholarships/grants, and tuition waivers (full and partial) available. *Faculty research:* Emulsification and emulsion stability, fermentation technology, adsorption and adsorption-based separations, process control. *Total annual research expenditures:* $10,562. *Unit head:* Dr. Mark Anklam, Chairman, 812-877-8098, Fax: 812-877-8992, E-mail: mark.r.anklam@rose-hulman.edu. *Application contact:* Dr. Daniel J. Moore, Associate Dean of the Faculty, 812-877-8110, Fax: 812-877-8061, E-mail: daniel.j.moore@rose-hulman.edu. Web site: http://www.rose-hulman.edu/che/.

Rowan University, Graduate School, College of Engineering, Department of Chemical Engineering, Glassboro, NJ 08028-1701. Offers MS. Part-time and evening/weekend programs available. *Degree requirements:* For master's, thesis optional. *Entrance requirements:* For master's, GRE General Test. Additional exam requirements/recommendations for international students: Required—TOEFL. Electronic applications accepted.

Royal Military College of Canada, Division of Graduate Studies and Research, Science Division, Department of Chemistry and Chemical and Materials Engineering, Kingston, ON K7K 7B4, Canada. Offers chemical engineering (M Eng, MA Sc, PhD); chemistry (M Sc, PhD). *Degree requirements:* For master's, thesis; for doctorate, comprehensive exam, thesis/dissertation. *Entrance requirements:* For master's, honour's degree with second-class standing; for doctorate, master's degree. Electronic applications accepted.

Rutgers, The State University of New Jersey, New Brunswick, Graduate School-New Brunswick, Program in Chemical and Biochemical Engineering, Piscataway, NJ 08854-8097. Offers MS, PhD. Part-time and evening/weekend programs available. Terminal master's awarded for partial completion of doctoral program. *Degree requirements:* For master's, thesis or alternative; for doctorate, thesis/dissertation. *Entrance requirements:* For master's and doctorate, GRE General Test. Additional exam requirements/recommendations for international students: Required—TOEFL. *Faculty research:* Biotechnology, pharmaceutical engineering, nanotechnology, process system engineering, materials and polymer science, chemical engineering sciences.

San Jose State University, Graduate Studies and Research, Charles W. Davidson College of Engineering, Department of Chemical and Materials Engineering, Program in Chemical Engineering, San Jose, CA 95192-0001. Offers MS. *Degree requirements:* For master's, thesis or alternative. Electronic applications accepted.

South Dakota School of Mines and Technology, Graduate Division, Program in Chemical and Biological Engineering, Rapid City, SD 57701-3995. Offers PhD.

South Dakota School of Mines and Technology, Graduate Division, Program in Chemical Engineering, Rapid City, SD 57701-3995. Offers MS. Part-time programs available. *Degree requirements:* For master's, thesis. *Entrance requirements:* For master's, GRE General Test. Additional exam requirements/recommendations for international students: Required—TOEFL, TWE. Electronic applications accepted. *Faculty research:* Incineration chemistry, environmental chemistry, polymer surface chemistry.

Stanford University, School of Engineering, Department of Chemical Engineering, Stanford, CA 94305-9991. Offers MS, PhD, Eng. Terminal master's awarded for partial completion of doctoral program. *Degree requirements:* For doctorate, thesis/dissertation; for Eng, thesis. *Entrance requirements:* For master's, doctorate, and Eng, GRE General Test. Additional exam requirements/recommendations for international students: Required—TOEFL. Electronic applications accepted. *Expenses: Tuition:* Full-time $40,050; part-time $890 per credit.

Stevens Institute of Technology, Graduate School, Charles V. Schaefer Jr. School of Engineering, Department of Chemical Engineering and Materials Science, Program in Chemical Engineering, Hoboken, NJ 07030. Offers M Eng, PhD, Engr.

Syracuse University, L. C. Smith College of Engineering and Computer Science, Program in Chemical Engineering, Syracuse, NY 13244. Offers MS, PhD. Part-time programs available. *Students:* 34 full-time (16 women), 6 part-time (4 women); includes 4 minority (2 Black or African American, non-Hispanic/Latino; 2 Asian, non-Hispanic/Latino), 30 international. Average age 26. 103 applicants, 30% accepted, 13 enrolled. In 2011, 2 master's, 2 doctorates awarded. *Entrance requirements:* For master's, GRE General Test. Additional exam requirements/recommendations for international students: Required—TOEFL (minimum score 100 iBT). *Application deadline:* For fall admission, 7/1 priority date for domestic students, 6/1 for international students. Applications are processed on a rolling basis. Application fee: $75. Electronic applications accepted. *Expenses: Tuition:* Part-time $1206 per credit. *Financial support:* Fellowships with full tuition reimbursements, research assistantships with full and partial tuition reimbursements, teaching assistantships with full and partial tuition reimbursements, and tuition waivers (partial) available. Financial award application deadline: 1/1. *Unit head:* Dr. Radhakrishna Sureshkumar, Interim Dean, 315-443-1931. *Application contact:* Kathleen Joyce, Assistant Dean, 314-443-2219, E-mail: topgrads@syr.edu. Web site: http://lcs.syr.edu/.

Tennessee Technological University, Graduate School, College of Engineering, Department of Chemical Engineering, Cookeville, TN 38505. Offers MS. Part-time programs available. *Faculty:* 8 full-time (0 women). *Students:* 3 full-time (0 women), 2 part-time (0 women); includes 2 minority (1 Black or African American, non-Hispanic/Latino; 1 Asian, non-Hispanic/Latino), 2 international. Average age 26. 16 applicants, 50% accepted, 2 enrolled. In 2011, 4 master's awarded. *Degree requirements:* For master's, thesis. *Entrance requirements:* For master's, GRE General Test. Additional exam requirements/recommendations for international students: Required—TOEFL (minimum score 550 paper-based; 79 iBT), IELTS (minimum score 5.5), PTE Academic. *Application deadline:* For fall admission, 8/1 for domestic students, 5/1 for international students; for spring admission, 12/1 for domestic students, 10/1 for international students. Application fee: $25 ($30 for international students). Electronic applications accepted. *Expenses:* Tuition, state resident: full-time $8094; part-time $422 per credit hour. Tuition, nonresident: full-time $20,574; part-time $1046 per credit hour. *Financial support:* In 2011–12, fellowships (averaging $8,000 per year), 7 research assistantships (averaging $7,000 per year), 5 teaching assistantships (averaging $5,433 per year) were awarded; career-related internships or fieldwork also available. Financial award application deadline: 4/1. *Faculty research:* Biochemical conversion, insulation, fuel reprocessing. *Unit head:* Dr. Pedro Arce, Chairperson, 931-372-3297, Fax: 931-372-6372, E-mail: parce@tntech.edu. *Application contact:* Shelia K. Kendrick, Coordinator of Graduate Admissions, 931-372-3808, Fax: 931-372-3497, E-mail: skendrick@tntech.edu.

Texas A&M University, College of Engineering, Artie McFerrin Department of Chemical Engineering, College Station, TX 77843. Offers M Eng, MS, PhD. *Faculty:* 32. *Students:* 143 full-time (50 women), 11 part-time (2 women); includes 19 minority (5 Black or African American, non-Hispanic/Latino; 5 Asian, non-Hispanic/Latino; 7 Hispanic/Latino; 2 Two or more races, non-Hispanic/Latino), 113 international. Average age 27. In 2011, 11 master's, 28 doctorates awarded. Terminal master's awarded for partial completion of doctoral program. *Degree requirements:* For master's, thesis (MS); for doctorate, thesis/dissertation. *Entrance requirements:* For master's and doctorate, GRE General Test. Additional exam requirements/recommendations for international students: Required—TOEFL. *Application deadline:* For fall admission, 3/1 priority date for domestic students, 3/1 for international students; for spring admission, 10/1 priority date for domestic students, 10/1 for international students. Applications are processed on a rolling basis. Application fee: $50 ($75 for international students). Electronic applications accepted. *Expenses:* Tuition, state resident: full-time $5437; part-time $226.55 per credit hour. Tuition, nonresident: full-time $12,949; part-time $539.55 per credit hour. *Required fees:* $2741. *Financial support:* In 2011–12, fellowships with full tuition reimbursements (averaging $18,240 per year), research assistantships with full tuition reimbursements (averaging $17,000 per year), teaching assistantships with full tuition reimbursements (averaging $17,132 per year) were awarded; career-related internships or fieldwork, scholarships/grants, and tuition waivers (full) also available. Financial award application deadline: 3/31; financial award applicants required to submit FAFSA. *Faculty research:* Reaction engineering, interface phenomena, environmental applications, biochemical engineering, polymers. *Unit head:* Dr. Charles Glover, Head, 979-845-4613, Fax: 979-862-3266, E-mail: c-glover@tamu.edu. *Application contact:* Towanna H. Arnold, Program Coordinator, 979-845-3364, Fax: 979-845-6446, E-mail: towanna@tamu.edu. Web site: http://www.che.tamu.edu/.

Texas A&M University–Kingsville, College of Graduate Studies, College of Engineering, Department of Chemical Engineering and Natural Gas Engineering, Program in Chemical Engineering, Kingsville, TX 78363. Offers ME, MS. Part-time and evening/weekend programs available. *Degree requirements:* For master's, comprehensive exam, thesis or alternative. *Entrance requirements:* For master's, GRE General Test, minimum GPA of 3.0. Additional exam requirements/recommendations for international students: Required—TOEFL. *Faculty research:* Process control, error detection and reconciliation, fluid mechanics, handling of solids.

Texas Tech University, Graduate School, Edward E. Whitacre Jr. College of Engineering, Department of Chemical Engineering, Lubbock, TX 79409. Offers MS Ch E, PhD. Part-time programs available. *Faculty:* 13 full-time (2 women), 1 part-time/adjunct (0 women). *Students:* 52 full-time (26 women), 2 part-time (0 women); includes 3 minority (1 Asian, non-Hispanic/Latino; 2 Hispanic/Latino), 47 international. Average age 26. 113 applicants, 14% accepted, 6 enrolled. In 2011, 2 master's, 8 doctorates awarded. *Degree requirements:* For master's, thesis or alternative; for doctorate, thesis/dissertation. *Entrance requirements:* For master's and doctorate, GRE General Test, minimum GPA of 3.0. Additional exam requirements/recommendations for international students: Required—TOEFL (minimum score 550 paper-based; 213 computer-based; 79 iBT). *Application deadline:* For fall admission, 6/1 priority date for domestic students, 1/15 for international students; for spring admission, 9/1 priority date for domestic students, 6/15 for international students. Applications are processed on a rolling basis. Application fee: $50 ($75 for international students). Electronic applications accepted. *Expenses:* Tuition, state resident: full-time $5899; part-time $245.80 per credit hour. Tuition, nonresident: full-time $13,411; part-time $558.80 per credit hour. *Required fees:* $2680.60; $86.50 per credit hour. $920.30 per semester. *Financial support:* In 2011–12, 22 students received support. Application deadline: 4/15; applicants required to submit FAFSA. *Faculty research:* Chemical process control, polymers and materials science, computational methods, bioengineering, renewable resources. *Total annual research expenditures:* $2.5 million. *Unit head:* Dr. M. Nazmul Karim, Chair, 806-742-3553, Fax: 806-742-3552, E-mail: naz.karim@ttu.edu. *Application contact:* Dr. John E. Kobza, Senior Associate Dean, 806-742-3451, Fax: 806-742-3493, E-mail: john.kobza@ttu.edu. Web site: http://www.che.ttu.edu/.

Tufts University, School of Engineering, Department of Chemical and Biological Engineering, Medford, MA 02155. Offers bioengineering (ME, MS), including cell and bioprocess engineering; biotechnology engineering (ME, MS, PhD). Part-time programs available. *Faculty:* 8 full-time, 2 part-time/adjunct. *Students:* 34 full-time (16 women); includes 8 minority (1 Black or African American, non-Hispanic/Latino; 7 Asian, non-Hispanic/Latino), 13 international. Average age 27. 79 applicants, 30% accepted, 10 enrolled. In 2011, 8 master's, 6 doctorates awarded. Terminal master's awarded for partial completion of doctoral program. *Degree requirements:* For master's, thesis (for some programs); for doctorate, thesis/dissertation. *Entrance requirements:* For master's and doctorate, GRE General Test. Additional exam requirements/recommendations for international students: Required—TOEFL (minimum score 550 paper-based; 213 computer-based; 80 iBT). *Application deadline:* For fall admission, 1/15 priority date for domestic students, 12/15 for international students; for spring admission, 10/15 for domestic students, 9/15 for international students. Applications are processed on a rolling basis. Application fee: $75. Electronic applications accepted. *Expenses: Tuition:* Full-time $41,208; part-time $1030 per credit hour. Full-time tuition and fees vary according to degree level, program and student level. Part-time tuition and fees vary according to course load. *Financial support:* Fellowships with full tuition reimbursements, research assistantships with full and partial tuition reimbursements, teaching assistantships with full and partial tuition reimbursements, Federal Work-Study, scholarships/grants, tuition waivers (partial), and unspecified assistantships available. Financial award application deadline: 1/15; financial award applicants required to submit FAFSA. *Faculty research:* Clean energy with materials, biomaterials, colloids; metabolic engineering, biotechnology; process control; reaction kinetics, catalysis; transport phenomena. *Unit head:* Dr. Kyongbum Lee, Chair, 617-627-3900. *Application contact:* Beth Frasso, Staff, 617-627-3900, E-mail: chbe@tufts.edu. Web site: http://engineering.tufts.edu/chbe/.

Tulane University, School of Science and Engineering, Department of Chemical and Biomolecular Engineering, New Orleans, LA 70118-5669. Offers PhD. Part-time programs available. Terminal master's awarded for partial completion of doctoral program. *Degree requirements:* For doctorate, thesis/dissertation. *Entrance requirements:* For doctorate, GRE General Test, minimum B average in undergraduate course work. Additional exam requirements/recommendations for international students: Required—TOEFL. Electronic applications accepted. *Faculty research:* Interfacial phenomena catalysis, electrochemical engineering, environmental science.

Universidad de las Américas–Puebla, Division of Graduate Studies, School of Engineering, Program in Chemical Engineering, Puebla, Mexico. Offers chemical engineering (MS); food technology (MS). Part-time and evening/weekend programs available. *Degree requirements:* For master's, one foreign language, thesis. *Faculty research:* Food science, reactors, oil industry, biotechnology.

Université de Sherbrooke, Faculty of Engineering, Department of Chemical Engineering, Sherbrooke, QC J1K 2R1, Canada. Offers M Sc A, PhD. *Degree requirements:* For master's, one foreign language, thesis; for doctorate, comprehensive exam, thesis/dissertation. *Entrance requirements:* For doctorate, master's degree in engineering or equivalent. Electronic applications accepted. *Faculty research:* Conversion processes, high-temperature plasma technologies, system engineering, environmental engineering, textile technologies.

Université Laval, Faculty of Sciences and Engineering, Department of Chemical Engineering, Programs in Chemical Engineering, Québec, QC G1K 7P4, Canada. Offers M Sc, PhD. Terminal master's awarded for partial completion of doctoral program. *Degree requirements:* For master's, thesis (for some programs); for doctorate, comprehensive exam, thesis/dissertation. *Entrance requirements:* Additional exam requirements/recommendations for international students: Required—TOEFL (minimum score 500 paper-based). Electronic applications accepted.

University at Buffalo, the State University of New York, Graduate School, School of Engineering and Applied Sciences, Department of Chemical and Biological Engineering, Buffalo, NY 14260. Offers ME, MS, PhD. Part-time programs available. *Faculty:* 18 full-time (1 woman), 5 part-time/adjunct (1 woman). *Students:* 111 full-time (40 women), 5 part-time (1 woman); includes 3 minority (1 Black or African American, non-Hispanic/Latino; 2 Asian, non-Hispanic/Latino), 93 international. Average age 25. 401 applicants, 11% accepted, 36 enrolled. In 2011, 21 master's, 10 doctorates awarded. *Degree requirements:* For master's, thesis (for some programs); for doctorate, comprehensive exam, thesis/dissertation. *Entrance requirements:* For master's and doctorate, GRE General Test. Additional exam requirements/recommendations for international students: Required—TOEFL (minimum score 550 paper-based; 213 computer-based; 79 iBT). *Application deadline:* For fall admission, 2/1 priority date for domestic students, 2/1 for international students; for spring admission, 10/1 priority date for domestic students, 10/1 for international students. Applications are processed on a rolling basis. Application fee: $75. Electronic applications accepted. *Financial support:* In 2011–12, 60 students received support, including 2 fellowships (averaging $28,900 per year), 31 research assistantships with full tuition reimbursements available (averaging $28,300 per year), 5 teaching assistantships with full tuition reimbursements available (averaging $20,900 per year); institutionally sponsored loans, scholarships/grants, health care benefits, tuition waivers (partial), and unspecified assistantships also available. Support available to part-time students. Financial award application deadline: 2/28; financial award applicants required to submit FAFSA. *Faculty research:* Transport, polymers, nanomaterials, biochemical engineering, catalysis. *Total annual research expenditures:* $8.4 million. *Unit head:* Dr. David A. Kofke, Chairman, 716-645-2911, Fax: 716-645-3822, E-mail: kofke@buffalo.edu. *Application contact:* Dr. Mark Swihart, Director of Graduate Studies, 716-645-1181, Fax: 716-645-3822, E-mail: swihart@buffalo.edu. Web site: http://www.cbe.buffalo.edu/.

The University of Akron, Graduate School, College of Engineering, Department of Chemical and Biomolecular Engineering, Akron, OH 44325. Offers MS, PhD. Part-time and evening/weekend programs available. *Faculty:* 16 full-time (4 women), 1 part-time/adjunct (0 women). *Students:* 63 full-time (16 women), 8 part-time (2 women); includes 5 minority (4 Asian, non-Hispanic/Latino; 1 Hispanic/Latino), 49 international. Average age 28. 71 applicants, 70% accepted, 12 enrolled. In 2011, 5 master's, 3 doctorates awarded. *Degree requirements:* For master's, thesis optional; for doctorate, one foreign language, thesis/dissertation, candidacy exam, qualifying exam. *Entrance requirements:* For master's, GRE, minimum GPA of 2.75, letter of recommendation; for doctorate, GRE, minimum GPA of 3.0 with bachelor's degree, 3.5 with master's degree; letters of recommendation; personal statement. Additional exam requirements/recommendations for international students: Required—TOEFL (minimum score 550 paper-based; 213 computer-based; 79 iBT). *Application deadline:* For fall admission, 5/1 for domestic and international students; for spring admission, 10/31 for domestic and international students. Application fee: $30 ($40 for international students). Electronic applications accepted. *Expenses:* Tuition, state resident: full-time $7038; part-time $391 per credit hour. Tuition, nonresident: full-time $12,051; part-time $670 per credit hour. *Required fees:* $1274; $34 per credit hour. *Financial support:* In 2011–12, 23 research assistantships with full tuition reimbursements, 33 teaching assistantships with full tuition reimbursements were awarded; career-related internships or fieldwork and scholarships/grants also available. *Faculty research:* Renewable energy, fuel cell and CO12 sequestration, nanofiber synthesis and applications, materials for biomedical applications, engineering, surface characterization and modification. *Total annual research expenditures:* $1.9 million. *Unit head:* Dr. Lu-Kwang Ju, Chair, 330-972-7252, E-mail: lukeju@uakron.edu. *Application contact:* Dr. Craig Menzemer, Associate Dean, 330-972-5536, E-mail: ccmenze@uakron.edu. Web site: http://www.uakron.edu/engineering/CBE/.

The University of Alabama, Graduate School, College of Engineering, Department of Chemical and Biological Engineering, Tuscaloosa, AL 35487. Offers MS Ch E, PhD. *Faculty:* 12 full-time (2 women). *Students:* 25 full-time (5 women), 4 part-time (1 woman); includes 3 minority (1 Black or African American, non-Hispanic/Latino; 1 Asian, non-Hispanic/Latino; 1 Hispanic/Latino), 15 international. Average age 27. 70 applicants, 17% accepted, 9 enrolled. In 2011, 4 master's, 1 doctorate awarded. Terminal master's awarded for partial completion of doctoral program. *Median time to degree:* Of those who began their doctoral program in fall 2003, 100% received their degree in 8 years or less. *Degree requirements:* For master's, comprehensive exam, thesis; for doctorate, comprehensive exam, thesis/dissertation. *Entrance requirements:* For master's, GRE, minimum GPA of 3.0 overall; for doctorate, GRE General Test or minimum GPA of 3.0. Additional exam requirements/recommendations for international students: Required—TOEFL (minimum score 550 paper-based; 213 computer-based); Recommended—IELTS (minimum score 6.5). *Application deadline:* Applications are processed on a rolling basis. Application fee: $50 ($60 for international students). Electronic applications accepted. *Expenses:* Tuition, state resident: full-time $8600. Tuition, nonresident: full-time $21,900. *Financial support:* In 2011–12, 2 fellowships with full tuition reimbursements (averaging $22,000 per year), 14 research assistantships with · full tuition reimbursements, 4 teaching assistantships with full tuition reimbursements were awarded; Federal Work-Study also available. *Faculty research:* Nanostructured materials, catalysis, alternative energy. *Total annual research expenditures:* $4.9 million. *Unit head:* Dr. Viola L. Acoff, Interim Head, 205-348-2080, Fax: 205-348-6579, E-mail: vacoff@eng.ua.edu. *Application contact:* Dr. Stephen M. C. Ritchie, Associate Professor, 205-348-2712, Fax: 205-348-6579, E-mail: sritchie@eng.ua.edu. Web site: http://www.eng.ua.edu/~chedept/.

The University of Alabama in Huntsville, School of Graduate Studies, College of Engineering, Department of Chemical and Materials Engineering, Huntsville, AL 35899. Offers chemical engineering (MSE). Part-time and evening/weekend programs available. *Faculty:* 6 full-time (0 women). *Students:* 8 full-time (2 women), 5 part-time (2 women); includes 3 minority (2 Asian, non-Hispanic/Latino; 1 Two or more races, non-Hispanic/Latino), 3 international. Average age 30. 11 applicants, 64% accepted, 5 enrolled. In 2011, 4 master's awarded. *Degree requirements:* For master's, comprehensive exam, thesis or alternative, oral and written exams. *Entrance requirements:* For master's, GRE General Test, appropriate bachelor's degree, minimum GPA of 3.0. Additional exam requirements/recommendations for international students: Required—TOEFL (minimum score 500 paper-based; 173 computer-based; 62 iBT). *Application deadline:* For fall admission, 7/15 for domestic students, 4/1 for international students; for spring admission, 11/30 for domestic students, 9/1 for international students. Applications are processed on a rolling basis. Application fee: $40 ($50 for international students). Electronic applications accepted. *Expenses:* Tuition, state resident: full-time $7830; part-time $473.50 per credit. Tuition, nonresident: full-time $18,748; part-time $1128.33 per credit. Tuition and fees vary according to course load and program. *Financial support:* In 2011–12, 7 students received support, including 4 research assistantships with full and partial tuition reimbursements available (averaging $12,007 per year), 5 teaching assistantships with full and partial tuition reimbursements available (averaging $11,605 per year); career-related internships or fieldwork, Federal Work-Study, institutionally sponsored loans, scholarships/grants, health care benefits, and unspecified assistantships also available. Support available to part-time students. Financial award application deadline: 4/1; financial award applicants required to submit FAFSA. *Faculty research:* Ultrathin films for optical, sensor and biological applications; materials processing including low gravity; hypergolic reactants; computational fluid dynamics; biofuels and renewable resources. *Total annual research expenditures:* $441,120. *Unit head:* Dr. Chien Pin Chen, Jr.,

Chair, 256-824-7313, Fax: 256-824-6839, E-mail: chien-pin.chen@uah.edu. *Application contact:* Kim Gray, Graduate Studies Admissions Coordinator, 256-824-6002, Fax: 256-824-6405, E-mail: deangrad@uah.edu. Web site: http://www.che.uah.edu/.

University of Alberta, Faculty of Graduate Studies and Research, Department of Chemical and Materials Engineering, Edmonton, AB T6G 2E1, Canada. Offers chemical engineering (M Eng, M Sc, PhD); materials engineering (M Eng, M Sc, PhD); process control (M Eng, M Sc, PhD); welding (M Eng). Part-time programs available. Postbaccalaureate distance learning degree programs offered (minimal on-campus study). Terminal master's awarded for partial completion of doctoral program. *Degree requirements:* For master's, thesis; for doctorate, thesis/dissertation. *Faculty research:* Advanced materials and polymers, catalytic and reaction engineering, mineral processing, physical metallurgy, fluid mechanics.

The University of Arizona, College of Engineering, Department of Chemical and Environmental Engineering, Program in Chemical Engineering, Tucson, AZ 85721. Offers MS, PhD. *Faculty:* 13 full-time (1 woman), 1 (woman) part-time/adjunct. *Students:* 30 full-time (10 women), 2 part-time (0 women); includes 6 minority (1 Black or African American, non-Hispanic/Latino; 2 Hispanic/Latino; 3 Two or more races, non-Hispanic/Latino), 16 international. Average age 28. 72 applicants, 15% accepted, 8 enrolled. In 2011, 5 master's, 4 doctorates awarded. *Entrance requirements:* For master's and doctorate, GRE, 3 letters of recommendation, resume, statement of purpose. Additional exam requirements/recommendations for international students: Required—TOEFL (minimum score 550 paper-based; 213 computer-based; 79 iBT). *Application deadline:* Applications are processed on a rolling basis. Application fee: $75. Electronic applications accepted. *Expenses:* Tuition, state resident: full-time $10,840. Tuition, nonresident: full-time $25,802. *Financial support:* Unspecified assistantships available. *Unit head:* Dr. Jim Field, Department Head, 520-621-2591, Fax: 520-621-6048, E-mail: jimfield@email.arizona.edu. *Application contact:* Jo Leeming, Program Coordinator, 520-621-6044, Fax: 520-621-6048, E-mail: leeming@email.arizona.edu. Web site: http://www.chee.arizona.edu/.

University of Arkansas, Graduate School, College of Engineering, Department of Chemical Engineering, Fayetteville, AR 72701-1201. Offers MS Ch E, MSE, PhD. Part-time programs available. *Students:* 10 full-time (1 woman), 17 part-time (7 women); includes 4 minority (1 American Indian or Alaska Native, non-Hispanic/Latino; 1 Hispanic/Latino; 2 Two or more races, non-Hispanic/Latino), 13 international. In 2011, 5 master's awarded. *Degree requirements:* For master's, thesis optional; for doctorate, one foreign language, thesis/dissertation. *Entrance requirements:* For master's and doctorate, GRE General Test. *Application deadline:* For fall admission, 4/1 for international students; for spring admission, 10/1 for international students. Applications are processed on a rolling basis. Application fee: $40 ($50 for international students). Electronic applications accepted. *Financial support:* In 2011–12, 18 research assistantships were awarded; fellowships with tuition reimbursements, teaching assistantships, career-related internships or fieldwork, and Federal Work-Study also available. Support available to part-time students. Financial award application deadline: 4/1; financial award applicants required to submit FAFSA. *Unit head:* Dr. Tom Spicer, Department Chair, 479-575-4951, E-mail: tos@uark.edu. *Application contact:* Dr. Keith Roper, Graduate Coordinator, 479-575-5645, E-mail: dkroper@uark.edu. Web site: http://www.cheg.uark.edu.

The University of British Columbia, Faculty of Applied Science, Program in Chemical and Biological Engineering, Vancouver, BC V6T 1Z1, Canada. Offers chemical engineering (M Eng, M Sc, MA Sc, PhD). Part-time and evening/weekend programs available. *Degree requirements:* For master's, thesis (for some programs); for doctorate, thesis/dissertation. *Entrance requirements:* Additional exam requirements/recommendations for international students: Required—TOEFL, IELTS. Electronic applications accepted. *Faculty research:* Biotechnology, catalysis, polymers, fluidization, pulp and paper.

University of Calgary, Faculty of Graduate Studies, Schulich School of Engineering, Department of Chemical and Petroleum Engineering, Calgary, AB T2N 1N4, Canada. Offers M Eng, M Sc, PhD. Part-time programs available. *Degree requirements:* For master's, thesis (for some programs); for doctorate, comprehensive exam, thesis/dissertation, candidacy exam. *Entrance requirements:* For master's, minimum GPA of 3.0; for doctorate, minimum GPA of 3.5. Additional exam requirements/recommendations for international students: Required—TOEFL (minimum score 550 paper-based; 213 computer-based; 80 iBT), IELTS (minimum score 7). Electronic applications accepted. *Faculty research:* Environmental engineering, biomedical engineering modeling, simulation and control, petroleum recovery and reservoir engineering, phase equilibria and transport properties.

University of California, Berkeley, Graduate Division, College of Chemistry, Department of Chemical Engineering, Berkeley, CA 94720-1500. Offers MS, PhD. *Degree requirements:* For master's, thesis; for doctorate, thesis/dissertation, qualifying exam. *Entrance requirements:* For master's and doctorate, GRE General Test, minimum GPA of 3.0, 3 letters of recommendation. Additional exam requirements/recommendations for international students: Required—TOEFL. *Faculty research:* Biochemical engineering, electrochemical engineering, electronic materials, heterogeneous catalysis and reaction engineering, complex fluids.

University of California, Davis, College of Engineering, Program in Chemical Engineering, Davis, CA 95616. Offers MS, PhD. Terminal master's awarded for partial completion of doctoral program. *Degree requirements:* For master's, comprehensive exam (for some programs), thesis (for some programs); for doctorate, thesis/dissertation. *Entrance requirements:* For master's and doctorate, GRE General Test, minimum GPA of 3.0. Additional exam requirements/recommendations for international students: Required—TOEFL (minimum score 550 paper-based; 213 computer-based). Electronic applications accepted. *Faculty research:* Transport phenomena, colloid science, catalysis, biotechnology, materials.

University of California, Irvine, School of Engineering, Department of Chemical Engineering and Materials Science, Irvine, CA 92697. Offers chemical and biochemical engineering (MS, PhD); materials science and engineering (MS, PhD). Part-time programs available. *Students:* 84 full-time (29 women), 2 part-time (0 women); includes 23 minority (1 American Indian or Alaska Native, non-Hispanic/Latino; 19 Asian, non-Hispanic/Latino; 2 Hispanic/Latino; 1 Native Hawaiian or other Pacific Islander, non-Hispanic/Latino), 37 international. Average age 27. 343 applicants, 22% accepted, 22 enrolled. In 2011, 17 master's, 4 doctorates awarded. Terminal master's awarded for partial completion of doctoral program. *Degree requirements:* For doctorate, thesis/dissertation. *Entrance requirements:* For master's and doctorate, GRE General Test, minimum GPA of 3.0, 3 letters of recommendation. Additional exam requirements/recommendations for international students: Required—TOEFL (minimum score 550 paper-based; 213 computer-based). *Application deadline:* For fall admission, 1/15 priority date for domestic students, 1/15 for international students. Applications are processed on a rolling basis. Application fee: $80 ($100 for international students). Electronic applications accepted. *Financial support:* Fellowships with tuition reimbursements, research assistantships with full tuition reimbursements, teaching assistantships with tuition reimbursements, institutionally sponsored loans, traineeships, health care benefits, and unspecified assistantships available. Financial award application deadline: 3/1; financial award applicants required to submit FAFSA. *Faculty research:* Molecular biotechnology, nano-bio-materials, biophotonics, synthesis, superplasticity and mechanical behavior, characterization of advanced and nanostructural materials. *Unit head:* Prof. Albert Yee, Chair, 949-824-7320, Fax: 949-824-2541, E-mail: albert.yee@uci.edu. *Application contact:* Grace Hai-Chin Chau, Academic Program and Graduate Admission Coordinator, 949-824-3887, Fax: 949-824-2541, E-mail: chaug@uci.edu. Web site: http://www.eng.uci.edu/dept/chems.

University of California, Los Angeles, Graduate Division, Henry Samueli School of Engineering and Applied Science, Department of Chemical and Biomolecular Engineering, Los Angeles, CA 90095-1592. Offers MS, PhD. *Faculty:* 13 full-time (3 women), 2 part-time/adjunct (0 women). *Students:* 79 full-time (30 women); includes 26 minority (1 Black or African American, non-Hispanic/Latino; 20 Asian, non-Hispanic/Latino; 5 Hispanic/Latino), 36 international. 341 applicants, 9% accepted, 15 enrolled. In 2011, 6 master's, 11 doctorates awarded. *Degree requirements:* For master's, comprehensive exam (for some programs), thesis (for some programs); for doctorate, thesis/dissertation, qualifying exams. *Entrance requirements:* For master's, GRE General Test, minimum GPA of 3.0; for doctorate, GRE General Test, minimum GPA of 3.25. Additional exam requirements/recommendations for international students: Required—TOEFL (minimum score 560 paper-based; 220 computer-based; 87 iBT). *Application deadline:* For fall admission, 1/15 for domestic and international students; for winter admission, 10/1 for domestic and international students; for spring admission, 12/31 for domestic and international students. Application fee: $80 ($100 for international students). Electronic applications accepted. *Financial support:* In 2011–12, 27 fellowships, 173 research assistantships, 51 teaching assistantships were awarded; Federal Work-Study, institutionally sponsored loans, and tuition waivers (full and partial) also available. Financial award application deadline: 1/15; financial award applicants required to submit FAFSA. *Faculty research:* Biomolecular engineering, renewable energy, water technology, advanced materials processing, process systems engineering. *Total annual research expenditures:* $6.2 million. *Unit head:* Dr. Harold G. Monbouquette, Chair, 310-825-8946. *Application contact:* John Berger, Student Affairs Officer, 310-825-9063, Fax: 310-206-4107, E-mail: jpberger@ea.ucla.edu. Web site: http://www.chemeng.ucla.edu/.

University of California, Riverside, Graduate Division, Department of Chemical and Environmental Engineering, Riverside, CA 92521-0102. Offers MS, PhD. Part-time programs available. Terminal master's awarded for partial completion of doctoral program. *Degree requirements:* For master's, thesis (for some programs); for doctorate, comprehensive exam, thesis/dissertation. *Entrance requirements:* For master's and doctorate, GRE General Test, minimum GPA of 3.0. Additional exam requirements/recommendations for international students: Required—TOEFL (minimum score 550 paper-based; 213 computer-based; 80 iBT). Electronic applications accepted. *Faculty research:* Air quality systems, water quality systems, advanced materials and nanotechnology, energy systems/alternative fuels, theory and molecular modeling.

University of California, San Diego, Office of Graduate Studies, Chemical Engineering Program, La Jolla, CA 92093. Offers MS, PhD. Part-time programs available. *Degree requirements:* For master's, thesis; for doctorate, thesis/dissertation. *Entrance requirements:* For master's and doctorate, GRE General Test. Additional exam requirements/recommendations for international students: Required—TOEFL (minimum score 550 paper-based). Electronic applications accepted. *Faculty research:* Semiconductor and composite materials processing, biochemical processing, electrochemistry and catalysis.

University of California, Santa Barbara, Graduate Division, College of Engineering, Department of Chemical Engineering, Santa Barbara, CA 93106-5080. Offers MS, PhD. *Faculty:* 20 full-time (1 woman). *Students:* 81 full-time (17 women); includes 17 minority (1 Black or African American, non-Hispanic/Latino; 9 Asian, non-Hispanic/Latino; 6 Hispanic/Latino; 1 Two or more races, non-Hispanic/Latino), 18 international. Average age 26. 329 applicants, 19% accepted, 13 enrolled. In 2011, 9 degrees awarded. *Median time to degree:* Of those who began their doctoral program in fall 2003, 100% received their degree in 8 years or less. *Degree requirements:* For master's, thesis or comprehensive exam; for doctorate, thesis/dissertation, candidacy exam, thesis defense, seminar. *Entrance requirements:* For master's and doctorate, GRE. Additional exam requirements/recommendations for international students: Required—TOEFL (minimum score 560 paper-based; 83 iBT), IELTS (minimum score 7). *Application deadline:* For fall admission, 1/3 priority date for domestic students, 1/3 for international students. Application fee: $80 ($100 for international students). Electronic applications accepted. *Expenses:* Tuition, state resident: full-time $12,192. Tuition, nonresident: full-time $27,294. *Required fees:* $764.13. *Financial support:* In 2011–12, 73 students received support, including 41 fellowships with full and partial tuition reimbursements available (averaging $7,652 per year), 69 research assistantships with full and partial tuition reimbursements available (averaging $14,947 per year), 37 teaching assistantships with full and partial tuition reimbursements available (averaging $3,897 per year); tuition waivers (full and partial) also available. Financial award application deadline: 1/3; financial award applicants required to submit FAFSA. *Faculty research:* Fluid transport, complex fluid and polymers, biomaterials/bioengineering, catalysis and reaction engineering, systems process design and control. *Total annual research expenditures:* $7.4 million. *Unit head:* Prof. Michael Doherty, Chair, 805-893-5309, Fax: 805-893-4731, E-mail: mfd@engineering.ucsb.edu. *Application contact:* Laura Crownover, Student Affairs Officer, 805-893-8671, Fax: 805-893-4731, E-mail: laura@engineering.ucsb.edu. Web site: http://www.chemengr.ucsb.edu/.

University of Cincinnati, Graduate School, College of Engineering and Applied Science, Department of Chemical and Materials Engineering, Program in Chemical Engineering, Cincinnati, OH 45221. Offers MS, PhD. Part-time and evening/weekend programs available. Terminal master's awarded for partial completion of doctoral program. *Degree requirements:* For master's, thesis; for doctorate, thesis/dissertation. *Entrance requirements:* For master's and doctorate, GRE General Test. Additional exam requirements/recommendations for international students: Required—TOEFL (minimum score 600 paper-based; 250 computer-based).

University of Colorado Boulder, Graduate School, College of Engineering and Applied Science, Department of Chemical and Biological Engineering, Boulder, CO 80309. Offers ME, MS, PhD. *Faculty:* 20 full-time (4 women). *Students:* 54 full-time (22 women), 66 part-time (28 women); includes 12 minority (1 Black or African American, non-Hispanic/Latino; 1 American Indian or Alaska Native, non-Hispanic/Latino; 5 Asian, non-

Hispanic/Latino; 5 Hispanic/Latino), 16 international. Average age 26. 425 applicants, 14% accepted, 21 enrolled. In 2011, 12 master's, 17 doctorates awarded. Terminal master's awarded for partial completion of doctoral program. *Degree requirements:* For master's, comprehensive exam, thesis; for doctorate, thesis/dissertation. *Entrance requirements:* For master's, minimum undergraduate GPA of 3.0. *Application deadline:* Applications are processed on a rolling basis. Application fee: $50 ($60 for international students). Electronic applications accepted. *Financial support:* In 2011–12, 129 students received support, including 46 fellowships (averaging $14,805 per year), 82 research assistantships with full and partial tuition reimbursements available (averaging $22,486 per year), 27 teaching assistantships with full and partial tuition reimbursements available (averaging $11,631 per year); institutionally sponsored loans, scholarships/grants, health care benefits, and unspecified assistantships also available. Financial award applicants required to submit FAFSA. *Faculty research:* Bioengineering and biotechnology, ceramic materials, fluid dynamics and fluid-article technology, heterogeneous catalysis, interfacial and surface phenomena, low-gravity fluid mechanics and materials. *Total annual research expenditures:* $13.1 million. *Application contact:* E-mail: chbegrad@colorado.edu. Web site: http://www.colorado.edu/che/.

University of Connecticut, Graduate School, School of Engineering, Department of Chemical, Materials and Biomolecular Engineering, Field of Chemical Engineering, Storrs, CT 06269. Offers MS, PhD. Terminal master's awarded for partial completion of doctoral program. *Degree requirements:* For master's, comprehensive exam, thesis or alternative; for doctorate, thesis/dissertation. *Entrance requirements:* For master's and doctorate, GRE General Test. Additional exam requirements/recommendations for international students: Required—TOEFL (minimum score 550 paper-based; 213 computer-based). Electronic applications accepted.

University of Dayton, Department of Chemical Engineering, Dayton, OH 45469-1300. Offers bioengineering instrumentation (MS); bioprocess engineering (MS); biosystems engineering (MS). Part-time and evening/weekend programs available. *Faculty:* 11 full-time (1 woman), 4 part-time/adjunct (0 women). *Students:* 37 full-time (9 women), 13 part-time (1 woman); includes 3 minority (2 Black or African American, non-Hispanic/Latino; 1 Asian, non-Hispanic/Latino), 29 international. Average age 26. 80 applicants, 70% accepted, 24 enrolled. In 2011, 10 degrees awarded. *Degree requirements:* For master's, thesis optional. *Entrance requirements:* Additional exam requirements/recommendations for international students: Required—TOEFL (minimum score 550 paper-based; 213 computer-based; 80 iBT). *Application deadline:* For fall admission, 8/1 priority date for domestic students. Applications are processed on a rolling basis. Application fee: $0 ($50 for international students). Electronic applications accepted. *Expenses:* Tuition: Full-time $8400; part-time $700 per credit hour. *Required fees:* $25 per semester. Tuition and fees vary according to degree level. *Financial support:* In 2011–12, 13 research assistantships with full tuition reimbursements (averaging $11,400 per year) were awarded; institutionally sponsored loans, health care benefits, and unspecified assistantships also available. Financial award applicants required to submit FAFSA. *Faculty research:* Vertically-aligned carbon nanotubes infiltrated with temperature-responsive polymers: smart nanocomposite films for self-cleaning and controlled release, bilayer and bulk heterojunction solar cells using liquid crystalline porphyrins as donors by solution processing, DNA damage induced by multiwalled carbon nanotubes in mouse embryonic stem cells. *Total annual research expenditures:* $1.5 million. *Unit head:* Dr. Robert Wilkens, Chair, 937-229-2627, E-mail: rwilkens1@udayton.edu. *Application contact:* Dr. Robert Wilkens, Chair, 937-229-2627, E-mail: rwilkens1@udayton.edu.

University of Delaware, College of Engineering, Department of Chemical Engineering, Newark, DE 19716. Offers M Ch E, PhD. Part-time and evening/weekend programs available. Postbaccalaureate distance learning degree programs offered (minimal on-campus study). Terminal master's awarded for partial completion of doctoral program. *Degree requirements:* For master's, thesis (for some programs); for doctorate, thesis/dissertation. *Entrance requirements:* For master's and doctorate, GRE General Test. Additional exam requirements/recommendations for international students: Required—TOEFL. Electronic applications accepted. *Faculty research:* Biochemical/biomedical engineer, thermodynamics, polymers/composites, materials, catalysis/reactions, colloid/interfaces, expert systems/process control.

University of Florida, Graduate School, College of Engineering, Department of Chemical Engineering, Gainesville, FL 32611. Offers ME, MS, PhD. Part-time programs available. Terminal master's awarded for partial completion of doctoral program. *Degree requirements:* For master's, thesis or final report; for doctorate, comprehensive exam, thesis/dissertation. *Entrance requirements:* For master's and doctorate, GRE General Test, minimum GPA of 3.0. Additional exam requirements/recommendations for international students: Required—TOEFL (minimum score 550 paper-based; 213 computer-based; 80 iBT), IELTS (minimum score 6). Electronic applications accepted. *Faculty research:* Biomedical and microelectronic materials, complex fluids, interfacial and colloidal phenomena, electrochemistry, nanotechnology.

University of Houston, Cullen College of Engineering, Department of Chemical and Biomolecular Engineering, Houston, TX 77204. Offers chemical engineering (MCHE, PhD); petroleum engineering (M Pet E). Part-time programs available. Terminal master's awarded for partial completion of doctoral program. *Entrance requirements:* For master's and doctorate, GRE General Test. Additional exam requirements/recommendations for international students: Required—TOEFL (minimum score 550 paper-based; 79 iBT), IELTS (minimum score 6.5). *Faculty research:* Chemical engineering.

University of Idaho, College of Graduate Studies, College of Engineering, Department of Chemical and Materials Engineering, Moscow, ID 83844-3024. Offers chemical engineering (MS, PhD); materials science and engineering (MS, PhD), including materials science and engineering, metallurgical engineering (MS); metallurgy (MS). *Faculty:* 10 full-time. *Students:* 16 full-time, 10 part-time. Average age 33. In 2011, 6 master's awarded. *Degree requirements:* For master's, thesis; for doctorate, one foreign language, thesis/dissertation. *Entrance requirements:* For master's, GRE, minimum GPA of 2.8; for doctorate, GRE, minimum undergraduate GPA of 2.8, 3.0 graduate. *Application deadline:* For fall admission, 8/1 for domestic students; for spring admission, 12/15 for domestic students. Applications are processed on a rolling basis. Application fee: $60. Electronic applications accepted. *Expenses:* Tuition, state resident: full-time $3874; part-time $334 per credit hour. Tuition, nonresident: full-time $16,394; part-time $861 per credit hour. *Required fees:* $2808; $99 per credit hour. Tuition and fees vary according to program. *Financial support:* Fellowships, research assistantships, and teaching assistantships available. Financial award applicants required to submit FAFSA. *Faculty research:* Geothermal energy utilization, alcohol production from agriculture waste material, energy conservation in pulp and paper mills. *Unit head:* Dr. Wudneh Admassu, 208-885-7572, E-mail: gailb@uidaho.edu. *Application contact:* Erick Larson,

Chemical Engineering

Director of Graduate Admissions, 208-885-4723, E-mail: gadms@uidaho.edu. Web site: http://www.uidaho.edu/engr/cme/about/materials.

University of Illinois at Chicago, Graduate College, College of Engineering, Department of Chemical Engineering, Chicago, IL 60607-7128. Offers MS, PhD. Part-time programs available. *Degree requirements:* For master's, thesis or project; for doctorate, thesis/dissertation, departmental qualifying exam. *Entrance requirements:* For master's and doctorate, GRE General Test, minimum GPA of 2.75. Additional exam requirements/recommendations for international students: Required—TOEFL. *Faculty research:* Multiphase flows, interfacial transport, heterogeneous catalysis, coal technology, molecular and static thermodynamics.

University of Illinois at Urbana–Champaign, Graduate College, College of Liberal Arts and Sciences, School of Chemical Sciences, Department of Chemical and Biomolecular Engineering, Champaign, IL 61820. Offers bioinformatics: chemical and biomolecular engineering (MS); chemical engineering (MS, PhD). *Faculty:* 13 full-time (2 women), 1 (woman) part-time/adjunct. *Students:* 103 full-time (37 women); includes 12 minority (9 Asian, non-Hispanic/Latino; 2 Hispanic/Latino; 1 Two or more races, non-Hispanic/Latino), 49 international. 377 applicants, 5% accepted, 19 enrolled. In 2011, 25 master's, 9 doctorates awarded. *Entrance requirements:* For master's and doctorate, GRE, minimum GPA of 3.0. Additional exam requirements/recommendations for international students: Required—TOEFL (minimum score 610 paper-based; 257 computer-based). *Application deadline:* Applications are processed on a rolling basis. Application fee: $75 ($90 for international students). Electronic applications accepted. *Financial support:* In 2011–12, 32 fellowships, 85 research assistantships, 34 teaching assistantships were awarded; tuition waivers (full and partial) also available. *Unit head:* Paul Kenis, Head, 217-244-9214, Fax: 217-333-5052, E-mail: kenis@illinois.edu. *Application contact:* Cathy Paceley, Office Manager, 217-333-3640, Fax: 217-333-5052, E-mail: paceley@illinois.edu. Web site: http://www.chbe.illinois.edu/.

The University of Iowa, Graduate College, College of Engineering, Department of Chemical and Biochemical Engineering, Iowa City, IA 52242-1316. Offers MS, PhD. Part-time programs available. *Faculty:* 11 full-time (3 women), 1 (woman) part-time/adjunct. *Students:* 38 full-time (11 women); includes 6 minority (5 Black or African American, non-Hispanic/Latino; 1 Hispanic/Latino), 16 international. Average age 28. 47 applicants, 30% accepted, 11 enrolled. In 2011, 14 master's, 3 doctorates awarded. *Degree requirements:* For master's, comprehensive exam (for some programs), thesis (for some programs); for doctorate, comprehensive exam, thesis/dissertation. *Entrance requirements:* For master's and doctorate, GRE, minimum undergraduate GPA of 3.0. Additional exam requirements/recommendations for international students: Required—TOEFL (minimum score 550 paper-based; 213 computer-based). *Application deadline:* For fall admission, 2/1 for domestic and international students; for spring admission, 10/1 for domestic and international students. Applications are processed on a rolling basis. Application fee: $60 ($100 for international students). Electronic applications accepted. *Financial support:* In 2011–12, 11 fellowships with full tuition reimbursements (averaging $26,000 per year), 19 research assistantships with partial tuition reimbursements (averaging $24,500 per year), 10 teaching assistantships with partial tuition reimbursements (averaging $10,022 per year) were awarded; unspecified assistantships also available. Financial award applicants required to submit FAFSA. *Faculty research:* Polymeric materials, photopolymerization, atmospheric chemistry and air pollution, biochemical engineering, bioprocessing and biomedical engineering. *Total annual research expenditures:* $5.5 million. *Unit head:* Dr. David W. Murhammer, Department Executive Officer, 319-335-1228, Fax: 319-335-1415, E-mail: david-murhammer@uiowa.edu. *Application contact:* Natalie Potter, Academic Program Specialist, 319-335-1215, Fax: 319-335-1415, E-mail: chemeng@engineering.uiowa.edu. Web site: http://www.cbe.engineering.uiowa.edu/.

The University of Kansas, Graduate Studies, School of Engineering, Program in Chemical and Petroleum Engineering, Lawrence, KS 66045. Offers MS, PhD. *Faculty:* 14 full-time (4 women). *Students:* 32 full-time (14 women), 5 part-time (3 women); includes 3 minority (1 American Indian or Alaska Native, non-Hispanic/Latino; 2 Asian, non-Hispanic/Latino), 25 international. Average age 27. 101 applicants, 13% accepted, 1 enrolled. In 2011, 6 master's, 7 doctorates awarded. *Degree requirements:* For master's, thesis (for some programs), exam; for doctorate, comprehensive exam, thesis/dissertation, qualifying exams. *Entrance requirements:* For master's, GRE General Test, minimum GPA of 3.0; for doctorate, GRE General Test, minimum GPA of 3.5. Additional exam requirements/recommendations for international students: Required—TOEFL. *Application deadline:* For fall admission, 1/10 priority date for domestic students, 1/10 for international students; for spring admission, 6/10 priority date for domestic students, 6/10 for international students. Applications are processed on a rolling basis. Application fee: $55 ($65 for international students). Electronic applications accepted. Tuition and fees vary according to course load, campus/location, program and reciprocity agreements. *Financial support:* Fellowships, research assistantships with full and partial tuition reimbursements, teaching assistantships with full and partial tuition reimbursements, career-related internships or fieldwork, Federal Work-Study, scholarships/grants, traineeships, and unspecified assistantships available. Financial award application deadline: 4/1; financial award applicants required to submit FAFSA. *Faculty research:* Enhanced oil recovery, catalysis and kinetics, electrochemical engineering, biomedical engineering, semiconductor materials processing. *Unit head:* Prof. Laurence Weatherley, Chairperson, 785-864-4965, Fax: 785-864-4967, E-mail: lweather@ku.edu. *Application contact:* Prof. Marylee Southard, Graduate Recruiting Officer, 785-864-4965, Fax: 785-864-4967, E-mail: marylee@ku.edu. Web site: http://www.cpe.engr.ku.edu.

The University of Kansas, Graduate Studies, School of Engineering, Program in Chemical Engineering, Lawrence, KS 66045. Offers MS. Tuition and fees vary according to course load, campus/location, program and reciprocity agreements. *Unit head:* Dr. Stuart R. Bell, Dean, 785-864-3881, E-mail: kuengr@ku.edu. *Application contact:* Dr. Glen Marotz, Associate Dean, 785-864-2980, Fax: 785-864-5445, E-mail: gama@ku.edu.

University of Kentucky, Graduate School, College of Engineering, Program in Chemical Engineering, Lexington, KY 40506-0032. Offers MS, PhD. *Degree requirements:* For master's, comprehensive exam, thesis optional; for doctorate, comprehensive exam, thesis/dissertation. *Entrance requirements:* For master's, GRE General Test, minimum undergraduate GPA of 2.75; for doctorate, GRE General Test, minimum undergraduate GPA of 3.0. Additional exam requirements/recommendations for international students: Required—TOEFL (minimum score 550 paper-based; 213 computer-based). Electronic applications accepted. *Faculty research:* Aerosol physics and chemistry, biocellular engineering fuel science, poly and membrane science.

University of Louisiana at Lafayette, College of Engineering, Department of Chemical Engineering, Lafayette, LA 70504. Offers MSE. Evening/weekend programs available. *Degree requirements:* For master's, comprehensive exam, thesis or alternative.

Entrance requirements: For master's, GRE General Test, BS in chemical engineering, minimum GPA of 2.85. Additional exam requirements/recommendations for international students: Required—TOEFL (minimum score 550 paper-based; 213 computer-based). Electronic applications accepted. *Faculty research:* Corrosion, transport phenomena and thermodynamics in the oil and gas industry.

University of Louisville, J. B. Speed School of Engineering, Department of Chemical Engineering, Louisville, KY 40292-0001. Offers M Eng, MS, PhD. *Accreditation:* ABET (one or more programs are accredited). Part-time programs available. *Faculty:* 9 full-time (2 women). *Students:* 40 full-time (13 women), 10 part-time (3 women); includes 3 minority (1 Black or African American, non-Hispanic/Latino; 2 Asian, non-Hispanic/Latino), 15 international. Average age 27. 25 applicants, 48% accepted, 5 enrolled. In 2011, 26 master's, 6 doctorates awarded. Terminal master's awarded for partial completion of doctoral program. *Degree requirements:* For master's, comprehensive exam (for some programs), thesis or alternative; for doctorate, comprehensive exam, thesis/dissertation, minimum GPA of 3.0. *Entrance requirements:* For master's and doctorate, GRE General Test. Additional exam requirements/recommendations for international students: Required—TOEFL (minimum score 550 paper-based; 213 computer-based; 80 iBT), IELTS (minimum score 6.5). *Application deadline:* For fall admission, 5/1 priority date for domestic students, 5/1 for international students; for spring admission, 11/1 priority date for domestic students, 11/1 for international students. Applications are processed on a rolling basis. Application fee: $50. Electronic applications accepted. *Expenses:* Tuition, state resident: full-time $9692; part-time $539 per credit hour. Tuition, nonresident: full-time $20,168; part-time $1121 per credit hour. Tuition and fees vary according to program and reciprocity agreements. *Financial support:* In 2011–12, 11 students received support, including 3 fellowships with full tuition reimbursements available (averaging $20,000 per year), 3 research assistantships with full tuition reimbursements available (averaging $20,000 per year), 5 teaching assistantships with full tuition reimbursements available (averaging $20,000 per year). Financial award application deadline: 1/25; financial award applicants required to submit FAFSA. *Faculty research:* Mixing in chemical and biochemical systems; nanomaterials processing; nanoparticles; surface science; materials including polymers, thin films, and rapid prototyping. *Total annual research expenditures:* $1.4 million. *Unit head:* Dr. James C. Waters, Chair, 502-852-6347, Fax: 502-852-6355, E-mail: jcwatt01@louisville.edu. *Application contact:* Dr. Michael Day, Associate Dean, 502-852-6195, Fax: 502-852-7294, E-mail: day@louisville.edu. Web site: http://www.louisville.edu/speed/chemical/.

University of Maine, Graduate School, College of Engineering, Department of Chemical and Biological Engineering, Orono, ME 04469. Offers biological engineering (ME, MS); chemical engineering (MS, PhD). Part-time programs available. *Students:* 11 full-time (2 women), 7 part-time (0 women); includes 1 minority (Black or African American, non-Hispanic/Latino), 9 international. Average age 29. 29 applicants, 24% accepted, 5 enrolled. In 2011, 2 master's, 4 doctorates awarded. *Degree requirements:* For doctorate, thesis/dissertation. *Entrance requirements:* For master's and doctorate, GRE General Test. Additional exam requirements/recommendations for international students: Required—TOEFL. *Application deadline:* For fall admission, 2/1 priority date for domestic students. Applications are processed on a rolling basis. Application fee: $65. Electronic applications accepted. *Expenses:* Tuition, state resident: full-time $5016. Tuition, nonresident: full-time $14,424. *Financial support:* In 2011–12, 1 fellowship with full tuition reimbursement (averaging $18,000 per year), 19 research assistantships with full tuition reimbursements (averaging $18,760 per year) were awarded; Federal Work-Study and tuition waivers (full and partial) also available. Financial award application deadline: 3/1. *Faculty research:* Transport phenomena, process modeling, polymer science and engineering, material characterization, unit operations in pulp and paper. *Total annual research expenditures:* $301,883. *Unit head:* Dr. Hemant Pendse, Chair, 207-581-2277, Fax: 207-581-2323. *Application contact:* Scott G. Delcourt, Associate Dean of the Graduate School, 207-581-3291, Fax: 207-581-3232, E-mail: graduate@maine.edu. Web site: http://www2.umaine.edu/graduate/.

The University of Manchester, School of Chemical Engineering and Analytical Science, Manchester, United Kingdom. Offers biocatalysis (M Phil, PhD); chemical engineering (M Phil, PhD); chemical engineering and analytical science (M Phil, D Eng, PhD); colloids, crystals, interfaces and materials (M Phil, PhD); environment and sustainable technology (M Phil, PhD); instrumentation (M Phil, PhD); multi-scale modeling (M Phil, PhD); process integration (M Phil, PhD); systems biology (M Phil, PhD).

University of Maryland, Baltimore County, Graduate School, College of Engineering and Information Technology, Department of Chemical, Biochemical, and Environmental Engineering, Program in Chemical and Biochemical Engineering, Baltimore, MD 21250. Offers MS, PhD. Part-time programs available. *Students:* 31 full-time (15 women), 6 part-time (2 women); includes 6 minority (3 Black or African American, non-Hispanic/Latino; 2 Asian, non-Hispanic/Latino; 1 Two or more races, non-Hispanic/Latino), 21 international. Average age 26. 49 applicants, 45% accepted, 13 enrolled. In 2011, 6 master's, 4 doctorates awarded. *Degree requirements:* For master's, comprehensive exam (for some programs), thesis (for some programs); for doctorate, comprehensive exam, thesis/dissertation. *Entrance requirements:* For master's, GRE General Test, minimum GPA of 3.0; for doctorate, GRE General Test (within last 5 years), GRE Subject Test, minimum GPA of 3.0. Additional exam requirements/recommendations for international students: Required—TOEFL (minimum score 550 paper-based; 213 computer-based; 80 iBT). *Application deadline:* For fall admission, 6/1 for domestic students, 1/1 for international students; for spring admission, 11/1 for domestic students, 6/1 for international students. Applications are processed on a rolling basis. Application fee: $70. Electronic applications accepted. *Financial support:* In 2011–12, 3 students received support, including 14 research assistantships with full tuition reimbursements available (averaging $22,000 per year), 7 teaching assistantships with full tuition reimbursements available (averaging $17,000 per year); career-related internships or fieldwork, Federal Work-Study, scholarships/grants, health care benefits, tuition waivers (partial), and unspecified assistantships also available. Support available to part-time students. Financial award application deadline: 6/30; financial award applicants required to submit FAFSA. *Faculty research:* Biomaterials engineering, bioprocess engineering, cellular engineering, education education and outreach, sensors and monitoring, systems biology and functional genomics. *Unit head:* Dr. Julia M. Ross, Professor and Chair. *Application contact:* Dr. Doug Frey, Professor and Graduate Program Director, 410-455-3418, Fax: 410-455-1049, E-mail: dfrey1@umbc.edu. Web site: http://www.wmbc.edu/engineering/cbe/.

University of Maryland, College Park, Academic Affairs, A. James Clark School of Engineering, Department of Chemical and Biomolecular Engineering, College Park, MD 20742. Offers bioengineering (MS, PhD); chemical engineering (M Eng, MS, PhD). Part-time and evening/weekend programs available. *Faculty:* 27 full-time (2 women). *Students:* 48 full-time (16 women), 6 part-time (2 women); includes 7 minority (1 Black or

African American, non-Hispanic/Latino; 6 Asian, non-Hispanic/Latino), 31 international. 184 applicants, 18% accepted, 15 enrolled. In 2011, 3 master's, 6 doctorates awarded. *Degree requirements:* For master's, thesis optional; for doctorate, variable foreign language requirement, thesis/dissertation, exam, oral presentation. *Entrance requirements:* For master's and doctorate, GRE General Test, 3 letters of recommendation. Additional exam requirements/recommendations for international students: Required—TOEFL. *Application deadline:* For fall admission, 1/15 for domestic students, 2/1 for international students; for spring admission, 6/1 for domestic and international students. Applications are processed on a rolling basis. Application fee: $75. Electronic applications accepted. *Expenses: Tuition, area resident:* Part-time $525 per credit hour. Tuition, state resident: part-time $525 per credit hour. Tuition, nonresident: part-time $1131 per credit hour. *Required fees:* $386.31 per term. Tuition and fees vary according to program. *Financial support:* In 2011–12, 3 fellowships with full and partial tuition reimbursements (averaging $15,000 per year), 31 research assistantships with tuition reimbursements (averaging $23,851 per year), 13 teaching assistantships with tuition reimbursements (averaging $21,104 per year) were awarded; Federal Work-Study and scholarships/grants also available. Support available to part-time students. Financial award applicants required to submit FAFSA. *Faculty research:* Applied polymer science, biochemical engineering, thermal properties, bioprocess monitoring. *Total annual research expenditures:* $1.8 million. *Unit head:* Sheryl Ehrman, Chair, 301-405-1074, E-mail: sehrman@umd.edu. *Application contact:* Dr. Charles A. Caramello, Dean of Graduate School, 301-405-0358, Fax: 301-314-9305, E-mail: ccaramel@umd.edu.

University of Maryland, College Park, Academic Affairs, A. James Clark School of Engineering, Department of Continuing and Distance Learning in Engineering, College Park, MD 20742. Offers engineering (M Eng), including aerospace engineering, chemical engineering, civil engineering, electrical engineering, engineering, fire protection engineering, materials science and engineering, mechanical engineering, reliability engineering, systems engineering. *Faculty:* 3 full-time (0 women), 8 part-time/adjunct (0 women). *Students:* 75 full-time (24 women), 418 part-time (81 women); includes 154 minority (62 Black or African American, non-Hispanic/Latino; 64 Asian, non-Hispanic/Latino; 23 Hispanic/Latino; 5 Two or more races, non-Hispanic/Latino), 67 international. 447 applicants, 52% accepted, 154 enrolled. In 2011, 155 master's awarded. *Application deadline:* For fall admission, 8/15 for domestic students, 2/1 for international students; for spring admission, 1/10 for domestic students, 8/1 for international students. Applications are processed on a rolling basis. Application fee: $75. Electronic applications accepted. *Expenses: Tuition, area resident:* Part-time $525 per credit hour. Tuition, state resident: part-time $525 per credit hour. Tuition, nonresident: part-time $1131 per credit hour. *Required fees:* $386.31 per term. Tuition and fees vary according to program. *Financial support:* In 2011–12, 3 research assistantships (averaging $21,498 per year), 13 teaching assistantships (averaging $16,889 per year) were awarded. *Unit head:* Dr. Darryll Pines, Dean, 301-405-8539, E-mail: pines@umd.edu. *Application contact:* Dr. Charles A. Caramello, Dean of the Graduate School, 301-405-0358, Fax: 301-314-9305.

University of Massachusetts Amherst, Graduate School, College of Engineering, Department of Chemical Engineering, Amherst, MA 01003. Offers MSChE, PhD. Part-time programs available. *Faculty:* 22 full-time (3 women). *Students:* 66 full-time (19 women), 7 part-time (2 women); includes 5 minority (1 Asian, non-Hispanic/Latino; 1 Hispanic/Latino; 3 Two or more races, non-Hispanic/Latino), 42 international. Average age 26. 286 applicants, 15% accepted, 14 enrolled. In 2011, 1 master's, 13 doctorates awarded. Terminal master's awarded for partial completion of doctoral program. *Degree requirements:* For master's, thesis; for doctorate, comprehensive exam, thesis/dissertation. *Entrance requirements:* For master's and doctorate, GRE General Test. Additional exam requirements/recommendations for international students: Required—TOEFL (minimum score 550 paper-based; 213 computer-based; 80 iBT), IELTS (minimum score 6.5). *Application deadline:* For fall admission, 1/15 for domestic and international students. Applications are processed on a rolling basis. Application fee: $50 ($65 for international students). Electronic applications accepted. Tuition and fees vary according to course load, campus/location and program. *Financial support:* Fellowships with full and partial tuition reimbursements, research assistantships with full and partial tuition reimbursements, teaching assistantships with full and partial tuition reimbursements, career-related internships or fieldwork, Federal Work-Study, scholarships/grants, traineeships, health care benefits, tuition waivers (full and partial), and unspecified assistantships available. Support available to part-time students. Financial award application deadline: 1/15. *Unit head:* Dr. David Ford, Graduate Program Director, 413-577-6164, Fax: 413-545-1647. *Application contact:* Lindsay DeSantis, Interim Supervisor of Admissions, 413-545-0722, Fax: 413-577-0010, E-mail: gradadm@grad.umass.edu. Web site: http://che.umass.edu/.

University of Massachusetts Lowell, College of Engineering, Department of Chemical Engineering, Lowell, MA 01854-2881. Offers MS Eng, D Eng, PhD. Part-time programs available. *Degree requirements:* For master's, thesis; for doctorate, thesis/dissertation, seminar, qualifying examination. *Entrance requirements:* For master's, GRE General Test. Electronic applications accepted. *Faculty research:* Biotechnology/bioprocessing, nanomaterials, ceramic materials, materials characterization.

University of Michigan, College of Engineering, Department of Chemical Engineering, Ann Arbor, MI 48109. Offers MSE, PhD, Ch E. Part-time programs available. Postbaccalaureate distance learning degree programs offered (no on-campus study). *Students:* 102 full-time (34 women), 1 part-time (0 women). 303 applicants, 27% accepted, 22 enrolled. In 2011, 21 master's, 18 doctorates awarded. Terminal master's awarded for partial completion of doctoral program. *Degree requirements:* For doctorate, thesis/dissertation, oral defense of dissertation, preliminary exams. *Entrance requirements:* For master's and doctorate, GRE General Test. Additional exam requirements/recommendations for international students: Required—TOEFL (minimum score 600 paper-based; 250 computer-based). *Application deadline:* Applications are processed on a rolling basis. Application fee: $65 ($75 for international students). Electronic applications accepted. *Financial support:* Fellowships, research assistantships, teaching assistantships, scholarships/grants, traineeships, health care benefits, tuition waivers (partial), and unspecified assistantships available. Financial award applicants required to submit FAFSA. *Faculty research:* Life sciences and biotechnology, energy and environment, complex fluids and nanostructured materials. *Unit head:* Mark Burns, Department Chair, 734-764-1516, E-mail: maburns@umich.edu. *Application contact:* Sue Hamlin, Department Office, 734-763-1148, Fax: 734-764-7453, E-mail: hamlins@umich.edu. Web site: http://che.engin.umich.edu/.

University of Minnesota, Twin Cities Campus, College of Science and Engineering, Department of Chemical Engineering and Materials Science, Program in Chemical Engineering, Minneapolis, MN 55455-0132. Offers M Ch E, MS Ch E, PhD. Part-time programs available. *Students:* 115 (34 women); includes 9 minority (7 Asian, non-Hispanic/Latino; 2 Hispanic/Latino), 54 international. Terminal master's awarded for partial completion of doctoral program. *Degree requirements:* For master's, thesis; for doctorate, thesis/dissertation. *Entrance requirements:* For master's and doctorate, GRE General Test. Additional exam requirements/recommendations for international students: Required—TOEFL. *Application deadline:* For fall admission, 1/1 for domestic and international students. Applications are processed on a rolling basis. Application fee: $75 ($95 for international students). Electronic applications accepted. *Financial support:* Fellowships, research assistantships, and teaching assistantships available. *Faculty research:* Biotechnology and bioengineering, chemical kinetics, reaction engineering and chemical process synthesis. *Application contact:* Graduate Programs in Chemical Engineering and Materials Science, E-mail: cemsgrad@umn.edu. Web site: http://www.cems.umn.edu/.

University of Missouri, Graduate School, College of Engineering, Department of Chemical Engineering, Columbia, MO 65211. Offers MS, PhD. *Faculty:* 9 full-time (1 woman), 1 part-time/adjunct (0 women). *Students:* 20 full-time (1 woman), 2 part-time (1 woman); includes 3 minority (1 Black or African American, non-Hispanic/Latino; 2 Asian, non-Hispanic/Latino), 5 international. Average age 25. 61 applicants, 15% accepted, 6 enrolled. In 2011, 5 master's, 3 doctorates awarded. *Degree requirements:* For master's, thesis; for doctorate, thesis/dissertation. *Entrance requirements:* For master's and doctorate, GRE General Test, minimum GPA of 3.0. Additional exam requirements/recommendations for international students: Required—TOEFL (minimum score 550 paper-based; 213 computer-based; 80 iBT). *Application deadline:* Applications are processed on a rolling basis. Application fee: $55 ($75 for international students). *Expenses:* Tuition, state resident: full-time $5881. Tuition, nonresident: full-time $15,183. *Required fees:* $952. Tuition and fees vary according to campus/location and program. *Financial support:* Fellowships, research assistantships, teaching assistantships, and institutionally sponsored loans available. *Faculty research:* Batteries, biochemical engineering, biomaterials, carbon, ceramics, catalysis, corrosion, electrochemistry, environmental sciences, ionic liquids, materials science, computational modeling and simulation, nanomaterials, nuclear materials, polymers, separations, solar energy, surface science. *Unit head:* Dr. John M. Gahl, Director of Graduate Studies, 573-884-7414, E-mail: gahlj@missouri.edu. *Application contact:* Dr. Lex Akers, Associate Dean for Academic Programs/Professor of Electrical and Computer Engineering, 573-882-4765, E-mail: akersl@missouri.edu. Web site: http://engineering.missouri.edu/chemical/.

University of Nebraska–Lincoln, Graduate College, College of Engineering, Department of Chemical and Biomolecular Engineering, Lincoln, NE 68588. Offers MS, PhD. *Degree requirements:* For master's, thesis; for doctorate, comprehensive exam, thesis/dissertation. *Entrance requirements:* For master's and doctorate, GRE. Additional exam requirements/recommendations for international students: Required—TOEFL (minimum score 550 paper-based; 213 computer-based). Electronic applications accepted. *Faculty research:* Fermentation, radioactive waste remediation, chemical fuels from renewable feedstocks.

University of Nevada, Reno, Graduate School, College of Engineering, Department of Chemical and Materials Engineering, Program in Chemical Engineering, Reno, NV 89557. Offers MS, PhD. Terminal master's awarded for partial completion of doctoral program. *Degree requirements:* For master's, comprehensive exam, thesis optional; for doctorate, thesis/dissertation. *Entrance requirements:* For master's, GRE General Test, minimum GPA of 2.75; for doctorate, GRE General Test, minimum GPA of 3.0. Additional exam requirements/recommendations for international students: Required—TOEFL (minimum score 500 paper-based; 173 computer-based; 61 iBT), IELTS (minimum score 6). Electronic applications accepted. *Faculty research:* Energy conservation, fuel efficiency, development and fabrication of new materials.

University of New Brunswick Fredericton, School of Graduate Studies, Faculty of Engineering, Department of Chemical Engineering, Fredericton, NB E3B 5A3, Canada. Offers chemical engineering (M Eng, M Sc E, PhD); environmental studies (M Eng). Part-time programs available. *Faculty:* 11 full-time (3 women), 1 part-time/adjunct (0 women). *Students:* 63 full-time (25 women), 4 part-time (1 woman). In 2011, 15 master's, 1 doctorate awarded. *Degree requirements:* For master's, thesis; for doctorate, comprehensive exam, thesis/dissertation, qualifying exam. *Entrance requirements:* For master's and doctorate, minimum GPA of 3.0. Additional exam requirements/recommendations for international students: Required—TOEFL (minimum score 580 paper-based), TWE (minimum score 4). *Application deadline:* For fall admission, 3/1 priority date for domestic students. Application fee: $50 Canadian dollars. Electronic applications accepted. *Financial support:* In 2011–12, 60 fellowships, 5 research assistantships with tuition reimbursements (averaging $18,000 per year), 51 teaching assistantships (averaging $1,500 per year) were awarded. *Faculty research:* Processing and characterizing nanoengineered composite materials based on carbon nanotubes, enhanced oil recovery processes and oil sweep strategies for conventional and heavy oils, pulp and paper, waste-water treatment, chemistry and corrosion of high and lower temperature water systems. *Unit head:* Dr. Kecheng Li, Director of Graduate Studies, 506-451-6861, Fax: 506-453-3591, E-mail: kecheng@unb.ca. *Application contact:* Sylvia Demerson, Graduate Secretary, 506-453-4520, Fax: 506-453-3591, E-mail: sdemerso@unb.ca. Web site: http://www.unbf.ca/eng/che/.

University of New Hampshire, Graduate School, College of Engineering and Physical Sciences, Department of Chemical Engineering, Durham, NH 03824. Offers MS, PhD. *Faculty:* 7 full-time (1 woman). *Students:* 6 full-time (2 women), 9 part-time (5 women); includes 1 minority (Hispanic/Latino), 7 international. Average age 26. 29 applicants, 55% accepted, 4 enrolled. In 2011, 3 master's, 1 doctorate awarded. *Degree requirements:* For master's, thesis; for doctorate, thesis/dissertation. *Entrance requirements:* For master's and doctorate, GRE. Additional exam requirements/recommendations for international students: Required—TOEFL (minimum score 550 paper-based; 213 computer-based). *Application deadline:* For fall admission, 6/1 priority date for domestic students, 4/1 for international students; for spring admission, 12/1 for domestic students. Applications are processed on a rolling basis. Application fee: $65. Electronic applications accepted. *Expenses:* Tuition, state resident: full-time $12,360; part-time $687 per credit hour. Tuition, nonresident: full-time $25,680; part-time $1058 per credit hour. International tuition: $29,550 full-time. *Required fees:* $1666; $833 per course. $416.50 per semester. Tuition and fees vary according to course load and degree level. *Financial support:* In 2011–12, 13 students received support, including 2 research assistantships, 10 teaching assistantships; fellowships, Federal Work-Study, scholarships/grants, and tuition waivers (full and partial) also available. Support available to part-time students. Financial award application deadline: 2/15. *Unit head:* Dr. P. T. Vasudevan, Chairperson, 603-862-3654. *Application contact:* Nancy Littlefield, Administrative Assistant, 603-862-3654, E-mail: chemeng.grad@unh.edu. Web site: http://www.unh.edu/chemical-engineering/.

University of New Mexico, Graduate School, School of Engineering, Department of Chemical and Nuclear Engineering, Program in Chemical Engineering, Albuquerque,

NM 87131-2039. Offers MS, PhD. Part-time programs available. *Students:* 4 full-time (0 women), 3 part-time (1 woman); includes 1 minority (Hispanic/Latino), 1 international. Average age 30. 18 applicants, 22% accepted, 3 enrolled. In 2011, 5 degrees awarded. Terminal master's awarded for partial completion of doctoral program. *Degree requirements:* For master's, thesis (for some programs); for doctorate, comprehensive exam, thesis/dissertation, qualifying exam. *Entrance requirements:* For master's, GRE General Test, minimum GPA of 3.0, 3 letters of reference, letter of intent; for doctorate, GRE General Test, 3 letters of reference, minimum GPA of 3.0, letter of intent. Additional exam requirements/recommendations for international students: Required—TOEFL. *Application deadline:* For fall admission, 1/15 priority date for domestic students, 1/15 for international students; for spring admission, 7/15 priority date for domestic students, 7/15 for international students. Application fee: $50. Electronic applications accepted. *Financial support:* In 2011–12, 34 students received support, including 2 fellowships (averaging $19,909 per year), 30 research assistantships with full tuition reimbursements available (averaging $19,743 per year), 1 teaching assistantship (averaging $5,259 per year); scholarships/grants, traineeships, and health care benefits also available. Financial award application deadline: 1/15; financial award applicants required to submit FAFSA. *Faculty research:* Bioanalytical systems, ceramics, catalysis, colloidal science, bioengineering, biomaterials, fuel cells, protein engineering, semiconductors, tissue engineering. *Total annual research expenditures:* $7.6 million. *Unit head:* Dr. Timothy Ward, Chair, 505-277-5431, Fax: 505-277-5433, E-mail: tward@unm.edu. *Application contact:* Jocelyn White, Coordinator/Program Advisor, 505-277-5606, Fax: 505-277-5433, E-mail: jowhite@unm.edu. Web site: http://www.chne.unm.edu.

University of North Dakota, Graduate School, School of Engineering and Mines, Department of Chemical Engineering, Grand Forks, ND 58202. Offers M Engr, MS. Part-time programs available. *Degree requirements:* For master's, comprehensive exam, thesis or alternative. *Entrance requirements:* For master's, GRE General Test, minimum GPA of 3.0 (MS), 2.5 (M Engr). Additional exam requirements/recommendations for international students: Required—TOEFL (minimum score 550 paper-based; 213 computer-based; 79 iBT), IELTS (minimum score 6.5). Electronic applications accepted. *Faculty research:* Catalysis, fluid flow and heat transfer, application of fractals, modeling and simulation, reaction engineering.

University of Notre Dame, Graduate School, College of Engineering, Department of Chemical and Biomolecular Engineering, Notre Dame, IN 46556. Offers MS Ch E, PhD. *Degree requirements:* For master's, comprehensive exam, thesis; for doctorate, comprehensive exam, thesis/dissertation, candidacy exam. *Entrance requirements:* For master's, GRE General Test; for doctorate, GRE General Test, GRE Subject Test (strongly recommended). Additional exam requirements/recommendations for international students: Required—TOEFL (minimum score 600 paper-based; 250 computer-based; 80 iBT). Electronic applications accepted. *Faculty research:* Biomolecular engineering, green chemistry and engineering for the environment, advanced materials, nanoengineering, catalysis and reaction engineering.

University of Oklahoma, College of Engineering, School of Chemical, Biological and Materials Engineering, Norman, OK 73019. Offers chemical engineering (MS, PhD). *Faculty:* 17 full-time (1 woman), 1 part-time/adjunct (0 women). *Students:* 48 full-time (17 women), 12 part-time (5 women); includes 2 minority (1 Asian, non-Hispanic/Latino; 1 Two or more races, non-Hispanic/Latino), 44 international. Average age 25. 32 applicants, 53% accepted, 14 enrolled. In 2011, 9 master's, 7 doctorates awarded. Terminal master's awarded for partial completion of doctoral program. *Degree requirements:* For master's, thesis, oral exams; for doctorate, thesis/dissertation, oral exam, qualifying exams. *Entrance requirements:* For master's and doctorate, minimum GPA of 3.0. Additional exam requirements/recommendations for international students: Required—TOEFL (minimum score 600 paper-based; 100 iBT). *Application deadline:* For fall admission, 4/1 for domestic students, 3/1 for international students; for spring admission, 11/1 for domestic students, 9/1 for international students. Applications are processed on a rolling basis. Application fee: $40 ($90 for international students). Electronic applications accepted. *Expenses:* Tuition, state resident: full-time $4087; part-time $170.30 per credit hour. Tuition, nonresident: full-time $14,875; part-time $619.80 per credit hour. *Required fees:* $2659; $100.25 per credit hour. Tuition and fees vary according to course load and degree level. *Financial support:* In 2011–12, 4 fellowships with full tuition reimbursements (averaging $2,500 per year), 65 research assistantships with partial tuition reimbursements (averaging $16,550 per year) were awarded; career-related internships or fieldwork, health care benefits, unspecified assistantships, and tuition waivers and waiver of basic health care cost with assistantship also available. Financial award applicants required to submit FAFSA. *Faculty research:* Applied surfactant technologies, biofuels and bio-refining, biomedical and biochemical engineering, catalysis and surface characterization, nanomaterials, polymer processing and characterization. *Total annual research expenditures:* $4.6 million. *Unit head:* Dr. Lance Lobban, Director, 405-325-5811, Fax: 405-325-5813, E-mail: llobban@ou.edu. *Application contact:* Dr. Ulli Nollert, Graduate Program Coordinator and Associate Professor, 405-325-4366, Fax: 405-325-5813, E-mail: nollert@ou.edu. Web site: http://www.ou.edu/coe/cbme.html.

University of Ottawa, Faculty of Graduate and Postdoctoral Studies, Faculty of Engineering, Department of Chemical and Biological Engineering, Ottawa, ON K1N 6N5, Canada. Offers M Eng, MA Sc, PhD. *Degree requirements:* For master's, thesis or alternative; for doctorate, comprehensive exam, thesis/dissertation. *Entrance requirements:* For master's, honors degree or equivalent, minimum B average; for doctorate, master's degree, minimum B+ average. Electronic applications accepted. *Faculty research:* Material development, process engineering, clean technologies.

University of Pennsylvania, School of Engineering and Applied Science, Department of Chemical Engineering, Philadelphia, PA 19104. Offers MSE, PhD, MSE/MBA. Part-time programs available. *Faculty:* 22 full-time (3 women), 2 part-time/adjunct (0 women). *Students:* 108 full-time (34 women), 7 part-time (2 women); includes 17 minority (1 Black or African American, non-Hispanic/Latino; 12 Asian, non-Hispanic/Latino; 4 Hispanic/Latino), 64 international. 376 applicants, 31% accepted, 57 enrolled. In 2011, 17 master's, 9 doctorates awarded. Terminal master's awarded for partial completion of doctoral program. *Degree requirements:* For doctorate, thesis/dissertation. *Entrance requirements:* Additional exam requirements/recommendations for international students: Required—TOEFL. *Application deadline:* For fall admission, 6/1 priority date for domestic students. Applications are processed on a rolling basis. Application fee: $70. Electronic applications accepted. *Expenses:* Tuition: Full-time $26,660; part-time $4944 per course. *Required fees:* $2318; $291 per course. Tuition and fees vary according to course load, degree level and program. *Financial support:* Fellowships, research assistantships, teaching assistantships, institutionally sponsored loans, scholarships/grants, traineeships, health care benefits, and unspecified assistantships available. *Faculty research:* Biochemical engineering, surface and interfacial phenomena, process and design control, zeolites, molecular dynamics. *Unit head:*

Eduardo D. Glandt, Dean, 215-898-7244, Fax: 215-573-2018, E-mail: seasdean@seas.upenn.edu. *Application contact:* 215-898-8351, E-mail: chebiom@seas.upenn.edu. Web site: http://www.seas.upenn.edu/.

University of Pittsburgh, Swanson School of Engineering, Department of Chemical and Petroleum Engineering, Pittsburgh, PA 15260. Offers chemical engineering (MS Ch E, PhD); petroleum engineering (MSPE); MS Ch E/MSPE. Part-time programs available. Postbaccalaureate distance learning degree programs offered. *Faculty:* 18 full-time (3 women), 21 part-time/adjunct (5 women). *Students:* 67 full-time (15 women), 7 part-time (3 women); includes 4 minority (1 Black or African American, non-Hispanic/Latino; 2 Asian, non-Hispanic/Latino; 1 Hispanic/Latino), 35 international. 269 applicants, 28% accepted, 18 enrolled. In 2011, 5 master's, 5 doctorates awarded. *Degree requirements:* For master's, thesis; for doctorate, comprehensive exam, thesis/dissertation, final oral exams. *Entrance requirements:* For master's and doctorate, GRE General Test, minimum QPA of 3.2. Additional exam requirements/recommendations for international students: Required—TOEFL (minimum score 550 paper-based; 213 computer-based; 80 iBT). *Application deadline:* For fall admission, 3/1 priority date for domestic students; for spring admission, 7/1 priority date for domestic students. Applications are processed on a rolling basis. Application fee: $50. Electronic applications accepted. *Expenses:* Tuition, state resident: full-time $18,774; part-time $760 per credit. Tuition, nonresident: full-time $30,736; part-time $1258 per credit. *Required fees:* $740; $200 per term. Tuition and fees vary according to program. *Financial support:* In 2011–12, 36 students received support, including 4 fellowships with full tuition reimbursements available (averaging $29,292 per year), 25 research assistantships with full tuition reimbursements available (averaging $24,048 per year), 7 teaching assistantships with full tuition reimbursements available (averaging $22,296 per year); scholarships/grants, traineeships, and tuition waivers (full and partial) also available. Financial award application deadline: 4/15. *Faculty research:* Biotechnology, polymers, catalysis, energy and environment, computational modeling. *Total annual research expenditures:* $7.7 million. *Unit head:* Dr. J. Karl Johnson, Chairman, 412-624-5644, Fax: 412-624-9639, E-mail: johnson@engr.pitt.edu. *Application contact:* William Federspiel, Associate Professor and Graduate Coordinator, 412-624-9499, Fax: 412-624-9639, E-mail: federspiel@engrng.pitt.edu. Web site: http://www.engineering.pitt.edu/Chemical/.

University of Puerto Rico, Mayagüez Campus, Graduate Studies, College of Engineering, Department of Chemical Engineering, Mayagüez, PR 00681-9000. Offers ME, MS, PhD. Part-time programs available. *Students:* 18 full-time (11 women); includes 14 minority (all Hispanic/Latino), 4 international. 8 applicants, 63% accepted, 4 enrolled. In 2011, 1 master's, 2 doctorates awarded. *Degree requirements:* For master's, comprehensive exam, thesis; for doctorate, comprehensive exam, thesis/dissertation. *Entrance requirements:* For master's, BS in chemical engineering or its equivalent. Additional exam requirements/recommendations for international students: Required—TOEFL. *Application deadline:* For fall admission, 2/15 for domestic and international students; for spring admission, 9/15 for domestic and international students. Applications are processed on a rolling basis. Application fee: $25. Tuition and fees vary according to course level and course load. *Financial support:* In 2011–12, 24 research assistantships (averaging $15,000 per year), 13 teaching assistantships (averaging $8,500 per year) were awarded; Federal Work-Study and institutionally sponsored loans also available. *Faculty research:* Process simulation and optimization, air and water pollution control, mass transport, biochemical engineering. *Total annual research expenditures:* $2.4 million. *Unit head:* Dr. Aldo Acevedo, Chairperson, 787-832-4040 Ext. 2587, Fax: 787-834-3655, E-mail: aldo.acevedo@upr.edu. *Application contact:* Dr. Arturo Hernandez, Graduate Coordinator, 787-832-4040 Ext. 3748, Fax: 787-834-3655, E-mail: arturoj.hernandez@upr.edu. Web site: http://atomo.uprm.edu.

University of Rhode Island, Graduate School, College of Engineering, Department of Chemical Engineering, Kingston, RI 02881. Offers MS, PhD. Part-time programs available. *Faculty:* 11 full-time (2 women). *Students:* 18 full-time (5 women), 3 part-time (0 women); includes 4 minority (2 Black or African American, non-Hispanic/Latino; 2 Asian, non-Hispanic/Latino), 10 international. In 2011, 9 master's, 1 doctorate awarded. *Degree requirements:* For master's, comprehensive exam (for some programs), thesis optional; for doctorate, comprehensive exam, thesis/dissertation. *Entrance requirements:* For master's and doctorate, 3 letters of recommendation. Additional exam requirements/recommendations for international students: Required—TOEFL (minimum score 550 paper-based; 213 computer-based). *Application deadline:* For fall admission, 7/15 for domestic students, 2/1 for international students; for spring admission, 11/15 for domestic students, 7/15 for international students. Application fee: $65. Electronic applications accepted. *Expenses:* Tuition, state resident: full-time $10,432; part-time $580 per credit hour. Tuition, nonresident: full-time $23,130; part-time $1285 per credit hour. *Required fees:* $1362; $36 per credit hour. $35 per semester. One-time fee: $130. *Financial support:* In 2011–12, 6 research assistantships with full and partial tuition reimbursements (averaging $6,474 per year), 2 teaching assistantships with partial tuition reimbursements (averaging $5,630 per year) were awarded. Financial award application deadline: 7/15; financial award applicants required to submit FAFSA. *Faculty research:* Photobioreactors, colloidal and interfacial engineering, biomembrane thermodynamics and transport, degradation of materials, closed loop recycling systems. *Total annual research expenditures:* $1.3 million. *Unit head:* Dr. Michael Greenfield, Chair, 401-874-9289, Fax: 401-874-4689, E-mail: greenfield@uri.edu. *Application contact:* Dr. Richard Brown, Director of Graduate Studies, 401-874-2707, Fax: 401-874-4689, E-mail: rbrown@uri.edu. Web site: http://www.egr.uri.edu/che/index.shtml.

University of Rochester, Hajim School of Engineering and Applied Sciences, Center for Entrepreneurship, Rochester, NY 14627-0360. Offers technical entrepreneurship and management (TEAM) (MS), including biomedical engineering, chemical engineering, computer science, electrical and computer engineering, energy and the environment, materials science, mechanical engineering, optics. *Faculty:* 61 full-time (8 women), 5 part-time/adjunct (1 woman). *Students:* 18 full-time (5 women), 3 part-time (1 woman); includes 4 minority (1 Asian, non-Hispanic/Latino; 3 Hispanic/Latino), 12 international. Average age 23. 134 applicants, 48% accepted, 21 enrolled. *Degree requirements:* For master's, comprehensive exam. *Entrance requirements:* For master's, GRE or GMAT, technical concentration of interest, 3 letters of recommendation, personal statement, official transcript. Additional exam requirements/recommendations for international students: Required—TOEFL or IELTS. *Application deadline:* For fall admission, 2/1 for domestic and international students. Applications are processed on a rolling basis. Application fee: $60. Electronic applications accepted. *Expenses:* Tuition: Full-time $41,040. *Financial support:* Career-related internships or fieldwork and scholarships/grants available. Financial award application deadline: 2/1. *Faculty research:* High efficiency solar cells, macromolecular self-assembly, digital signal processing, memory hierarchy management, molecular and physical mechanisms in cell migration. *Unit head:* Duncan T. Moore, Vice Provost for Entrepreneurship, 585-275-5248, Fax: 585-473-6745, E-mail: moore@optics.rochester.edu. *Application* *contact:* Andrea M. Galati, Executive Director, 585-276-3407, Fax: 585-276-2357, E-mail: andrea.galati@rochester.edu. Web site: http://www.rochester.edu/team.

University of Rochester, Hajim School of Engineering and Applied Sciences, Department of Chemical Engineering, Rochester, NY 14627. Offers alternative energy (MS); chemical engineering (MS, PhD). Part-time programs available. *Faculty:* 10 full-time (1 woman). *Students:* 43 full-time (13 women), 3 part-time (2 women); includes 8 minority (1 Black or African American, non-Hispanic/Latino; 5 Asian, non-Hispanic/Latino; 1 Hispanic/Latino; 1 Two or more races, non-Hispanic/Latino), 22 international. 105 applicants, 37% accepted, 21 enrolled. In 2011, 15 master's, 3 doctorates awarded. Terminal master's awarded for partial completion of doctoral program. *Degree requirements:* For master's, comprehensive exam; for doctorate, thesis/dissertation, preliminary and oral exams. *Entrance requirements:* For master's and doctorate, GRE. Additional exam requirements/recommendations for international students: Required—TOEFL. *Application deadline:* For fall admission, 1/15 for domestic students. Application fee: $60. *Expenses: Tuition:* Full-time $41,040. *Financial support:* Fellowships, research assistantships, teaching assistantships, and tuition waivers (full and partial) available. Financial award application deadline: 2/1. *Faculty research:* Advanced materials, nanotechnology, alternative energy, biotechnology, photovoltaics. *Unit head:* Ching W. Tang, Chairman, 585-275-3552. *Application contact:* Gina Eagan, Graduate Program Coordinator, 585-275-4913. Web site: http://www.che.rochester.edu/graduate/index.html.

See Display below and Close-Up on page 165.

University of Saskatchewan, College of Graduate Studies and Research, College of Engineering, Department of Chemical Engineering, Saskatoon, SK S7N 5A2, Canada. Offers M Eng, M Sc, PhD. *Degree requirements:* For master's, thesis (for some programs); for doctorate, thesis/dissertation. *Entrance requirements:* For master's and doctorate, GRE. Additional exam requirements/recommendations for international students: Required—TOEFL.

University of South Africa, College of Science, Engineering and Technology, Pretoria, South Africa. Offers chemical engineering (M Tech); information technology (M Tech).

University of South Alabama, Graduate School, College of Engineering, Department of Chemical Engineering, Mobile, AL 36688-0002. Offers MS Ch E. *Faculty:* 3 full-time (0 women). *Students:* 8 full-time (4 women), 4 part-time (1 woman); includes 1 minority (Black or African American, non-Hispanic/Latino), 4 international. 113 applicants, 6% accepted, 2 enrolled. In 2011, 3 master's awarded. *Degree requirements:* For master's, project or thesis. *Entrance requirements:* For master's, GRE General Test, BS in engineering, minimum GPA of 3.0. Additional exam requirements/recommendations for international students: Required—TOEFL. *Application deadline:* For fall admission, 7/15 priority date for domestic students, 6/15 for international students; for spring admission, 12/1 priority date for domestic students, 11/1 for international students. Applications are processed on a rolling basis. Application fee: $35. *Expenses:* Tuition, state resident: full-time $7968; part-time $332 per credit hour. Tuition, nonresident: full-time $15,936; part-time $664 per credit hour. *Financial support:* Research assistantships, career-related internships or fieldwork, and institutionally sponsored loans available. Support available to part-time students. Financial award application deadline: 4/1. *Unit head:* Dr. Srinivas Palanki, Chair, 251-460-6160. *Application contact:* Dr. Thomas Thomas, Director of Graduate Studies, 251-460-6160. Web site: http://www.southalabama.edu/engineering/chemical.

University of South Carolina, The Graduate School, College of Engineering and Computing, Department of Chemical Engineering, Columbia, SC 29208. Offers ME, MS, PhD. Part-time and evening/weekend programs available. Postbaccalaureate distance learning degree programs offered (minimal on-campus study). *Degree requirements:* For master's, comprehensive exam, thesis (for some programs); for doctorate, comprehensive exam, thesis/dissertation. *Entrance requirements:* For master's and doctorate, GRE General Test. Additional exam requirements/recommendations for international students: Required—TOEFL. Electronic applications accepted. *Faculty research:* Rheology, liquid and supercritical extractions, electrochemistry, corrosion, heterogeneous and homogeneous catalysis.

University of Southern California, Graduate School, Viterbi School of Engineering, Mork Family Department of Chemical Engineering and Materials Science, Los Angeles, CA 90089. Offers chemical engineering (MS, PhD, Engr); materials engineering (MS); materials science (MS, PhD, Engr); petroleum engineering (MS, PhD, Engr); smart oilfield technologies (MS, Graduate Certificate). Terminal master's awarded for partial completion of doctoral program. *Degree requirements:* For master's, thesis optional; for doctorate, thesis/dissertation. *Entrance requirements:* For master's and doctorate, GRE General Test. Additional exam requirements/recommendations for international students: Recommended—TOEFL. Electronic applications accepted. *Expenses:* Contact institution. *Faculty research:* Heterogeneous materials and porous media, statistical mechanics, molecular simulation, polymer science and engineering, advanced materials, reaction engineering and catalysis, membrane processes and separation, biochemical engineering, cell culture, bioreactor modeling, petroleum engineering.

University of South Florida, Graduate School, College of Engineering, Department of Chemical and Biomedical Engineering, Tampa, FL 33620. Offers biomedical engineering (MSBE, MSES, PhD); chemical engineering (MCH, ME, MSCH, MSES, PhD). Part-time programs available. *Faculty:* 14 full-time (2 women), 6 part-time/adjunct (1 woman). *Students:* 70 full-time (11 women), 18 part-time (0 women); includes 25 minority (10 Black or African American, non-Hispanic/Latino; 4 Asian, non-Hispanic/Latino; 11 Hispanic/Latino), 29 international. Average age 30. 87 applicants, 46% accepted, 20 enrolled. In 2011, 18 master's, 5 doctorates awarded. Terminal master's awarded for partial completion of doctoral program. *Degree requirements:* For master's, comprehensive exam, thesis (for some programs); for doctorate, comprehensive exam, thesis/dissertation. *Entrance requirements:* For master's and doctorate, GRE, minimum GPA of 3.0 in last 60 hours of course work, at least two letters of recommendation, bachelor's degree in engineering or science. Additional exam requirements/recommendations for international students: Required—TOEFL (minimum score 550 paper-based; 213 computer-based; 79 iBT) or IELTS (minimum score 6.5). *Application deadline:* For fall admission, 2/15 for domestic students, 1/2 for international students; for spring admission, 10/15 for domestic students, 6/1 for international students. Application fee: $30. Electronic applications accepted. *Financial support:* In 2011–12, 41 students received support, including 29 research assistantships with tuition reimbursements available (averaging $13,171 per year), 12 teaching assistantships with tuition reimbursements available (averaging $14,017 per year); unspecified assistantships also available. Financial award applicants required to submit FAFSA. *Faculty research:* Biomedical engineering, supercritical fluid technology, advanced materials, surface and interfacial science, alternative and renewable energy. *Total annual research expenditures:* $1.2 million. *Unit head:* Dr. Venkat R. Bhethanabotla, Chair, 813-974-3997, E-mail: bhethana@usf.edu. *Application contact:* Dr. Vinay Gupta, Graduate Admissions Coordinator for Chemical Engineering, 813-974-0851, Fax: 813-974-3651, E-mail: vkgupta@usf.edu. Web site: http://che.eng.usf.edu/.

Chemical Engineering

The University of Tennessee, Graduate School, College of Engineering, Department of Chemical Engineering, Knoxville, TN 37996. Offers chemical engineering (MS, PhD); reliability and maintainability engineering (MS); MS/MBA. Part-time programs available. *Faculty:* 23 full-time (3 women). *Students:* 47 full-time (12 women), 2 part-time (1 woman); includes 6 minority (2 American Indian or Alaska Native, non-Hispanic/Latino; 3 Asian, non-Hispanic/Latino; 1 Hispanic/Latino), 23 international. Average age 26. 129 applicants, 12% accepted, 13 enrolled. In 2011, 5 master's, 2 doctorates awarded. *Degree requirements:* For master's, thesis or alternative; for doctorate, comprehensive exam, thesis/dissertation. *Entrance requirements:* For master's, GRE General Test (for MS students pursuing research thesis), minimum GPA of 2.7 (for U.S. degree holders), 3.0 (for international degree holders); for doctorate, College requires GRE General Test for all PhD candidates, minimum GPA of 3.0 on previous graduate course work. Additional exam requirements/recommendations for international students: Required—TOEFL (minimum score 550 paper-based; 213 computer-based). *Application deadline:* For fall admission, 2/1 priority date for domestic students, 2/1 for international students; for spring admission, 6/15 for domestic and international students. Applications are processed on a rolling basis. Application fee: $35. Electronic applications accepted. *Expenses:* Tuition, state resident: full-time $8332; part-time $464 per credit hour. Tuition, nonresident: full-time $25,174; part-time $1400 per credit hour. *Required fees:* $1162; $56 per credit hour. Tuition and fees vary according to program. *Financial support:* In 2011–12, 43 students received support, including 31 research assistantships with full tuition reimbursements available (averaging $21,863 per year), 12 teaching assistantships with full tuition reimbursements available (averaging $20,357 per year); fellowships, career-related internships or fieldwork, Federal Work-Study, institutionally sponsored loans, health care benefits, and unspecified assistantships also available. Financial award application deadline: 2/1; financial award applicants required to submit FAFSA. *Faculty research:* Bio-fuels; engineering of soft, functional and structural materials; fuel cells and energy storage devices; molecular and cellular bioengineering; molecular modeling and simulations. *Total annual research expenditures:* $4 million. *Unit head:* Dr. Bamin Khomami, Head, 865-974-2421, Fax: 865-974-7076, E-mail: bkhomami@utk.edu. *Application contact:* Dr. Paul Frymier, Graduate Program Coordinator, 865-974-4961, Fax: 865-974-7076, E-mail: pdf@utk.edu. Web site: http://www.engr.utk.edu/cbe/.

The University of Tennessee at Chattanooga, Graduate School, College of Engineering and Computer Science, Program in Engineering, Chattanooga, TN 37403. Offers chemical engineering (MS Engr); civil engineering (MS Engr); computational engineering (MS Engr); electrical engineering (MS Engr); industrial engineering (MS Engr); mechanical engineering (MS Engr). Part-time and evening/weekend programs available. *Faculty:* 27 full-time (3 women), 3 part-time/adjunct (1 woman). *Students:* 40 full-time (7 women), 41 part-time (11 women); includes 23 minority (10 Black or African American, non-Hispanic/Latino; 1 American Indian or Alaska Native, non-Hispanic/Latino; 6 Asian, non-Hispanic/Latino; 4 Hispanic/Latino; 2 Two or more races, non-Hispanic/Latino), 20 international. Average age 28. 89 applicants, 53% accepted, 29 enrolled. In 2011, 8 master's awarded. *Degree requirements:* For master's, comprehensive exam, thesis or alternative, engineering project. *Entrance requirements:* For master's, GRE General Test, minimum undergraduate GPA of 2.5 or 3.0 in last 30 hours of coursework. Additional exam requirements/recommendations for international students: Required—TOEFL (minimum score 550 paper-based; 213 computer-based; 79 iBT), IELTS (minimum score 6). *Application deadline:* For fall admission, 8/1 priority date for domestic students, 6/1 for international students; for spring admission, 12/1 priority date for domestic students, 10/1 for international students. Applications are processed on a rolling basis. Application fee: $35. Electronic applications accepted. *Expenses:* Tuition, state resident: full-time $6472; part-time $359 per credit hour. Tuition, nonresident: full-time $20,006; part-time $1111 per credit hour. *Required fees:* $1320; $160 per credit hour. *Financial support:* Career-related internships or fieldwork, scholarships/grants, and unspecified assistantships available. Support available to part-time students. *Faculty research:* Quality control and reliability engineering, financial management, thermal science, energy conservation, structural analysis. *Total annual research expenditures:* $3.5 million. *Unit head:* Dr. Neslihan Alp, Director, 423-425-4032, Fax: 423-425-5229, E-mail: neslihan-alp@utc.edu. *Application contact:* Dr. Jerald Ainsworth, Dean of Graduate Studies, 423-425-4478, Fax: 423-425-5223, E-mail: jerald-ainsworth@utc.edu. Web site: http://www.utc.edu/Departments/engrcs/ms_engr.php.

The University of Texas at Austin, Graduate School, Cockrell School of Engineering, Department of Chemical Engineering, Austin, TX 78712-1111. Offers MSE, PhD. Terminal master's awarded for partial completion of doctoral program. *Degree requirements:* For master's, thesis (for some programs); for doctorate, comprehensive exam, thesis/dissertation. *Entrance requirements:* For master's and doctorate, GRE General Test. *Application deadline:* For fall admission, 2/1 for domestic and international students; for spring admission, 10/1 for domestic and international students. Application fee: $50 ($75 for international students). Electronic applications accepted. *Financial support:* Fellowships with full tuition reimbursements, research assistantships with full tuition reimbursements, teaching assistantships with full tuition reimbursements, and tuition waivers (full) available. Financial award application deadline: 2/1. *Unit head:* Roger T. Bonnecaze, Chair, 512-471-1497, E-mail: bonnecaze@che.utexas.edu. *Application contact:* T. Stockman, Graduate Coordinator, 512-471-6991, Fax: 512-475-7824, E-mail: t@che.utexas.edu. Web site: http://www.che.utexas.edu/.

The University of Toledo, College of Graduate Studies, College of Engineering, Department of Chemical and Environmental Engineering, Toledo, OH 43606-3390. Offers chemical engineering (MS, PhD). Part-time and evening/weekend programs available. *Degree requirements:* For master's, thesis optional; for doctorate, thesis/dissertation, qualifying exam. *Entrance requirements:* For master's, GRE General Test, minimum GPA of 3.0; for doctorate, GRE General Test, minimum GPA of 3.3. Additional exam requirements/recommendations for international students: Required—TOEFL (minimum score 550 paper-based; 213 computer-based; 80 iBT). Electronic applications accepted. *Faculty research:* Polymers, applied computing, membranes, alternative energy (fuel cells).

University of Toronto, School of Graduate Studies, Faculty of Applied Science and Engineering, Department of Chemical Engineering and Applied Chemistry, Toronto, ON M5S 1A1, Canada. Offers M Eng, MA Sc, PhD. Part-time programs available. *Degree requirements:* For master's, thesis (for some programs); for doctorate, thesis/dissertation. *Entrance requirements:* For master's, minimum B+ average in final 2 years, four-year degree in engineering (M Eng, MA Sc) or physical sciences (MA Sc), 2 letters of reference; for doctorate, research master's degree, minimum B+ average, 2 letters of reference. Additional exam requirements/recommendations for international students: Required—TOEFL (minimum score 580 paper-based; 237 computer-based; 93 iBT), TWE (minimum score 4). Electronic applications accepted.

University of Tulsa, Graduate School, College of Engineering and Natural Sciences, Department of Chemical Engineering, Tulsa, OK 74104-3189. Offers ME, MSE, PhD.

Part-time programs available. *Faculty:* 9 full-time (3 women). *Students:* 24 full-time (10 women), 2 part-time (1 woman); includes 1 minority (Hispanic/Latino), 18 international. Average age 25. 44 applicants, 55% accepted, 6 enrolled. In 2011, 6 master's, 3 doctorates awarded. *Degree requirements:* For master's, thesis (for some programs); for doctorate, comprehensive exam, thesis/dissertation. *Entrance requirements:* For master's and doctorate, GRE General Test. Additional exam requirements/recommendations for international students: Required—TOEFL (minimum score 550 paper-based; 213 computer-based; 80 iBT), IELTS (minimum score 6). *Application deadline:* Applications are processed on a rolling basis. Application fee: $40. Electronic applications accepted. *Expenses: Tuition:* Full-time $17,748; part-time $986 per hour. *Required fees:* $5 per contact hour. $75 per semester. Tuition and fees vary according to program. *Financial support:* In 2011–12, 26 students received support, including 5 fellowships (averaging $3,660 per year), 24 research assistantships with full and partial tuition reimbursements available (averaging $8,903 per year), 9 teaching assistantships with full and partial tuition reimbursements available (averaging $10,750 per year); career-related internships or fieldwork, Federal Work-Study, scholarships/grants, health care benefits, tuition waivers (full and partial), and unspecified assistantships also available. Support available to part-time students. Financial award application deadline: 2/1; financial award applicants required to submit FAFSA. *Faculty research:* Environment, surface science, catalysis, transport phenomena, process systems engineering, bioengineering, alternative energy, petrochemical processes. *Total annual research expenditures:* $3.3 million. *Unit head:* Dr. Geoffrey Price, Chairperson, 918-631-2575, Fax: 918-631-3268, E-mail: chegradadvisor@utulsa.edu. *Application contact:* Dr. Daniel Crunkleton, Advisor, 918-631-2644, Fax: 918-631-3268, E-mail: chegradadvisor@utulsa.edu. Web site: http://www.ce.utulsa.edu/.

University of Utah, Graduate School, College of Engineering, Department of Chemical Engineering, Salt Lake City, UT 84112-1107. Offers ME, MS, PhD. Part-time and evening/weekend programs available. Postbaccalaureate distance learning degree programs offered. *Faculty:* 17 full-time (1 woman), 1 part-time/adjunct (0 women). *Students:* 56 full-time (8 women), 17 part-time (3 women); includes 6 minority (2 Asian, non-Hispanic/Latino; 3 Hispanic/Latino; 1 Two or more races, non-Hispanic/Latino), 27 international. Average age 29. 124 applicants, 17% accepted, 16 enrolled. In 2011, 9 master's, 7 doctorates awarded. Terminal master's awarded for partial completion of doctoral program. *Median time to degree:* Of those who began their doctoral program in fall 2003, 95% received their degree in 8 years or less. *Degree requirements:* For master's, comprehensive exam, thesis (for some programs); for doctorate, comprehensive exam, thesis/dissertation. *Entrance requirements:* For master's, GRE General Test; for doctorate, GRE General Test, minimum GPA of 3.0, degree or course work in chemical engineering. Additional exam requirements/recommendations for international students: Required—TOEFL (minimum score 500 paper-based; 173 computer-based). *Application deadline:* For fall admission, 4/1 priority date for domestic students, 1/15 for international students; for spring admission, 11/1 priority date for domestic students, 10/1 for international students. Applications are processed on a rolling basis. Application fee: $55 ($65 for international students). Electronic applications accepted. *Expenses:* Contact institution. *Financial support:* In 2011–12, 5 fellowships with tuition reimbursements (averaging $25,000 per year), 55 research assistantships with tuition reimbursements (averaging $25,103 per year) were awarded; teaching assistantships with tuition reimbursements, Federal Work-Study, institutionally sponsored loans, scholarships/grants, health care benefits, and unspecified assistantships also available. Financial award application deadline: 4/1; financial award applicants required to submit FAFSA. *Faculty research:* Drug delivery; fossil fuel and biomass combustion and gasification, oil and gas reservoir characteristics and management, multi-scale simulation, micro-scale synthesis. *Total annual research expenditures:* $10 million. *Unit head:* Dr. JoAnn S. Lighty, Chair, 801-581-6715, Fax: 801-585-9291, E-mail: jlighty@utah.edu. *Application contact:* Tracey A. Farnsworth, Academic Advisor, 801-585-7175, Fax: 801-585-9291, E-mail: farnsworth@eng.utah.edu. Web site: http://www.che.utah.edu/.

University of Virginia, School of Engineering and Applied Science, Department of Chemical Engineering, Charlottesville, VA 22903. Offers ME, MS, PhD. Postbaccalaureate distance learning degree programs offered (no on-campus study). *Faculty:* 11 full-time (1 woman). *Students:* 56 full-time (16 women); includes 6 minority (1 Black or African American, non-Hispanic/Latino; 4 Asian, non-Hispanic/Latino; 1 Hispanic/Latino), 27 international. Average age 25. 129 applicants, 24% accepted, 15 enrolled. In 2011, 7 master's, 13 doctorates awarded. *Degree requirements:* For master's, thesis (for some programs); for doctorate, thesis/dissertation. *Entrance requirements:* For master's, GRE General Test, 3 recommendations; for doctorate, GRE General Test, 3 recommendations, essay. Additional exam requirements/recommendations for international students: Required—TOEFL (minimum score 600 paper-based; 250 computer-based; 90 iBT), IELTS (minimum score 7). *Application deadline:* For fall admission, 8/1 for domestic students, 4/1 for international students; for winter admission, 12/1 for domestic students, 8/1 for international students; for spring admission, 5/1 for domestic students, 1/1 for international students. Applications are processed on a rolling basis. Application fee: $60. Electronic applications accepted. *Financial support:* Fellowships, research assistantships, and teaching assistantships available. Financial award application deadline: 1/15; financial award applicants required to submit FAFSA. *Faculty research:* Fluid mechanics, heat and mass transfer, chemical reactor analysis and engineering, biochemical engineering and biotechnology. *Unit head:* Roseanne Ford, Chair, 434-924-7778, Fax: 434-982-2658, E-mail: rmf3f@virginia.edu. *Application contact:* David Green, Graduate Program Coordinator, 434-924-7778, Fax: 434-982-2658, E-mail: dlgreen@virginia.edu. Web site: http://www.che.virginia.edu/.

University of Washington, Graduate School, College of Engineering, Department of Chemical Engineering, Seattle, WA 98195-1750. Offers chemical engineering (MS, MSE, PhD); chemical engineering and nanotechnology (PhD). *Faculty:* 20 full-time (3 women), 5 part-time/adjunct (2 women). *Students:* 75 full-time (20 women), 2 part-time (0 women); includes 17 minority (1 Black or African American, non-Hispanic/Latino; 1 American Indian or Alaska Native, non-Hispanic/Latino; 11 Asian, non-Hispanic/Latino; 4 Hispanic/Latino), 19 international. Average age 25. 250 applicants, 18% accepted, 17 enrolled. In 2011, 17 master's, 7 doctorates awarded. Terminal master's awarded for partial completion of doctoral program. *Degree requirements:* For master's, thesis, final exam, teaching assistantship for 1 quarter, research project; for doctorate, thesis/dissertation, general and final exams, research project, completion of all work for degree within 10 years. *Entrance requirements:* For master's and doctorate, GRE General Test (minimum Quantitative score of 750), minimum GPA of 3.0, official transcripts, personal statement, confidential evaluations by 3 professors or other technical professional, high rank (top 5%) in respected chemical engineering program. Additional exam requirements/recommendations for international students: Required—TOEFL (minimum score 580 paper-based; 237 computer-based; 92 iBT); Recommended—IELTS (minimum score 7). *Application deadline:* For fall admission, 1/15 priority date for domestic students, 12/15 for international students. Applications are processed on a rolling basis. Application fee: $75. Electronic applications accepted. *Expenses:* Contact institution. *Financial support:* In 2011–12, 102 students received support, including 16 fellowships with full tuition reimbursements available (averaging $19,035 per year), 73 research assistantships with full tuition reimbursements available (averaging $19,035 per year), 12 teaching assistantships with full tuition reimbursements available (averaging $19,035 per year); career-related internships or fieldwork, Federal Work-Study, health care benefits, and unspecified assistantships also available. Financial award application deadline: 1/15; financial award applicants required to submit FAFSA. *Faculty research:* Molecular energy processes, living systems and biomolecular processes, molecular aspects of materials and interfaces, molecular/organic electronics. *Total annual research expenditures:* $8.9 million. *Unit head:* Dr. Daniel T. Schwartz, Professor/Chair, 206-543-2250, Fax: 206-543-3778, E-mail: dts@uw.edu. *Application contact:* Dave Drischell, Lead Academic Counselor, 206-543-2252, Fax: 206-543-3778, E-mail: rdd@u.washington.edu. Web site: http://www.cheme.washington.edu/.

University of Waterloo, Graduate Studies, Faculty of Engineering, Department of Chemical Engineering, Waterloo, ON N2L 3G1, Canada. Offers M Eng, MA Sc, PhD. Part-time programs available. *Degree requirements:* For master's, research project or thesis, seminar; for doctorate, comprehensive exam, thesis/dissertation. *Entrance requirements:* For master's, honors degree, minimum B average; for doctorate, master's degree, minimum A- average. Additional exam requirements/recommendations for international students: Required—TOEFL, TWE. Electronic applications accepted. *Faculty research:* Biotechnical and environmental engineering, mathematical analysis, statistics and control, polymer science and engineering.

The University of Western Ontario, Faculty of Graduate Studies, Physical Sciences Division, Faculty of Engineering, London, ON N6A 5B8, Canada. Offers chemical and biochemical engineering (ME Sc, PhD); civil and environmental engineering (M Eng, ME Sc, PhD); electrical and computer engineering (M Eng, ME Sc, PhD); mechanical and materials engineering (M Eng, ME Sc, PhD). Part-time programs available. Terminal master's awarded for partial completion of doctoral program. *Degree requirements:* For master's, thesis; for doctorate, thesis/dissertation. *Entrance requirements:* For master's, minimum B average; for doctorate, minimum B+ average. *Faculty research:* Wind, geotechnical, chemical reactor engineering, applied electrostatics, biochemical engineering.

University of Wisconsin–Madison, Graduate School, College of Engineering, Department of Chemical and Biological Engineering, Madison, WI 53706-0607. Offers chemical engineering (MS, PhD). *Faculty:* 19 full-time (2 women), 1 part-time/adjunct (0 women). *Students:* 131 full-time (38 women); includes 17 minority (1 American Indian or Alaska Native, non-Hispanic/Latino; 9 Asian, non-Hispanic/Latino; 7 Hispanic/Latino), 51 international. Average age 25. 428 applicants, 21% accepted, 28 enrolled. In 2011, 3 master's, 15 doctorates awarded. Terminal master's awarded for partial completion of doctoral program. *Degree requirements:* For master's, thesis or alternative; for doctorate, thesis/dissertation, 2 semesters of teaching assistantship. *Entrance requirements:* For master's and doctorate, GRE General Test. Additional exam requirements/recommendations for international students: Required—TOEFL (minimum score 550 paper-based; 213 computer-based; 80 iBT). *Application deadline:* For fall admission, 1/1 for domestic and international students; for spring admission, 10/15 for domestic and international students. Application fee: $56. Electronic applications accepted. *Expenses:* Tuition, state resident: full-time $10,296; part-time $643.51 per credit. Tuition, nonresident: full-time $24,054; part-time $1503.40 per credit. *Required fees:* $70.06 per credit. Tuition and fees vary according to course load, campus/location, program and reciprocity agreements. *Financial support:* In 2011–12, 122 students received support, including 21 fellowships with full tuition reimbursements available (averaging $28,752 per year), 66 research assistantships with full tuition reimbursements available (averaging $24,000 per year), 45 teaching assistantships with full tuition reimbursements available (averaging $25,167 per year); traineeships and health care benefits also available. Financial award application deadline: 1/15. *Faculty research:* Biotechnology, nanotechnology, complex fluids, molecular and systems modeling, renewable energy and chemicals; materials and processes. *Total annual research expenditures:* $17.7 million. *Unit head:* Prof. Thomas F. Kuech, Chair, 608-263-2922, Fax: 608-262-5434, E-mail: kuech@engr.wisc.edu. *Application contact:* Graduate Coordinator, Graduate Coordinator, 608-263-3138, Fax: 608-262-5434, E-mail: gradoffice@che.wisc.edu. Web site: http://www.engr.wisc.edu/che/.

University of Wyoming, College of Engineering and Applied Sciences, Department of Chemical and Petroleum Engineering, Program in Chemical Engineering, Laramie, WY 82070. Offers MS, PhD. Part-time programs available. Terminal master's awarded for partial completion of doctoral program. *Degree requirements:* For master's, thesis; for doctorate, thesis/dissertation. *Entrance requirements:* For master's and doctorate, GRE General Test, minimum GPA of 3.0. Additional exam requirements/recommendations for international students: Required—TOEFL (minimum score 600 paper-based; 250 computer-based; 76 iBT). Electronic applications accepted. *Faculty research:* Microwave reactor systems, synthetic fuels, fluidization, coal combustion/gasification, flue-gas cleanup.

Vanderbilt University, School of Engineering, Department of Chemical and Biomolecular Engineering, Nashville, TN 37240-1001. Offers M Eng, MS, PhD. MS and PhD offered through the Graduate School. Part-time programs available. *Degree requirements:* For master's, thesis; for doctorate, thesis/dissertation. *Entrance requirements:* For master's and doctorate, GRE General Test. Additional exam requirements/recommendations for international students: Required—TOEFL. Electronic applications accepted. *Faculty research:* Adsorption and surface chemistry; biochemical engineering and biotechnology; chemical reaction engineering, environment, materials, process modeling and control; molecular modeling and thermodynamics.

Villanova University, College of Engineering, Department of Chemical Engineering, Villanova, PA 19085-1699. Offers biochemical engineering (Certificate); chemical engineering (MSChE); environmental protection in the chemical process industries (Certificate). Part-time and evening/weekend programs available. *Degree requirements:* For master's, comprehensive exam, thesis optional. *Entrance requirements:* For master's, GRE General Test (for applicants with degrees from foreign universities), B Ch E, minimum GPA of 3.0. Additional exam requirements/recommendations for international students: Required—TOEFL (minimum score 600 paper-based; 250 computer-based; 100 iBT). *Expenses: Tuition:* Part-time $675 per credit. Part-time tuition and fees vary according to degree level and program. *Faculty research:* Heat transfer, advanced materials, chemical vapor deposition, pyrolysis and combustion chemistry, industrial waste treatment.

Virginia Commonwealth University, Graduate School, School of Engineering, Department of Chemical and Life Science Engineering, Richmond, VA 23284-9005.

Offers MS, PhD. *Entrance requirements:* For master's and doctorate, GRE. Additional exam requirements/recommendations for international students: Required—TOEFL (minimum score 600 paper-based; 250 computer-based; 100 iBT). Electronic applications accepted. *Expenses:* Tuition, state resident: full-time $9133; part-time $507 per credit. Tuition, nonresident: full-time $18,777; part-time $1043 per credit. *Required fees:* $77 per credit. Tuition and fees vary according to degree level, campus/location, program and student level. *Faculty research:* Advanced polymers, including biopolymers and polymers in medicine; chemical and biochemical reactor analysis; the study of supercritical fluids for environmentally favorable processes; systems biological engineering; stem cell engineering; biosensors and biochips; computational bioinformatics and rational drug design.

Virginia Polytechnic Institute and State University, Graduate School, College of Engineering, Department of Chemical Engineering, Blacksburg, VA 24061. Offers M Eng, MS, PhD. *Degree requirements:* For master's, comprehensive exam (for some programs), thesis (for some programs); for doctorate, comprehensive exam (for some programs), thesis/dissertation (for some programs). *Entrance requirements:* For master's and doctorate, GRE. Additional exam requirements/recommendations for international students: Required—TOEFL (minimum score 550 paper-based; 213 computer-based). *Application deadline:* For fall admission, 7/1 for domestic and international students; for spring admission, 12/1 for domestic and international students. Applications are processed on a rolling basis. Application fee: $65. Electronic applications accepted. *Expenses:* Tuition, state resident: full-time $10,048; part-time $558.25 per credit hour. Tuition, nonresident: full-time $19,497; part-time $1083.25 per credit hour. *Required fees:* $405 per semester. Tuition and fees vary according to course load, campus/location and program. *Financial support:* Fellowships with full tuition reimbursements, research assistantships with full tuition reimbursements, teaching assistantships with full tuition reimbursements, career-related internships or fieldwork, Federal Work-Study, scholarships/grants, health care benefits, and unspecified assistantships available. Financial award application deadline: 1/15. *Unit head:* Dr. John Y. Walz, Unit Head, 540-231-4213, Fax: 540-231-5022, E-mail: jywalz@vt.edu. *Application contact:* Luke Achenie, Information Contact, 540-231-4257, Fax: 540-231-5022, E-mail: achenie@vt.edu. Web site: http://www.che.vt.edu/.

Washington State University, Graduate School, College of Engineering and Architecture, School of Chemical Engineering and Bioengineering, Program in Chemical Engineering, Pullman, WA 99164. Offers MS, PhD. *Faculty:* 13. *Students:* 38 full-time (11 women), 2 part-time (1 woman); includes 2 minority (1 Black or African American, non-Hispanic/Latino; 1 Native Hawaiian or other Pacific Islander, non-Hispanic/Latino), 22 international. Average age 27. 75 applicants, 16% accepted, 10 enrolled. In 2011, 2 master's, 2 doctorates awarded. Terminal master's awarded for partial completion of doctoral program. *Degree requirements:* For master's, comprehensive exam (for some programs), thesis, oral exam; for doctorate, one foreign language, comprehensive exam, thesis/dissertation, oral exam. *Entrance requirements:* For master's and doctorate, GRE, minimum GPA of 3.0, 3 letters of recommendation by faculty. Additional exam requirements/recommendations for international students: Required—TOEFL (minimum score 580 paper-based; 190 computer-based). *Application deadline:* For fall admission, 3/1 priority date for domestic students, 3/1 for international students; for spring admission, 7/1 priority date for domestic students, 7/1 for international students. Applications are processed on a rolling basis. Application fee: $75. *Financial support:* In 2011–12, 26 students received support, including 5 fellowships (averaging $4,991 per year), 7 research assistantships with full and partial tuition reimbursements available (averaging $18,204 per year), 4 teaching assistantships with full and partial tuition reimbursements available (averaging $18,204 per year); career-related internships or fieldwork, Federal Work-Study, institutionally sponsored loans, tuition waivers (partial), and teaching associateships also available. Financial award application deadline: 4/1; financial award applicants required to submit FAFSA. *Faculty research:* Bioprocessing, kinetics and catalysis, hazardous waste remediation. *Total annual research expenditures:* $2.3 million. *Unit head:* Dr. James Peterson, Interim Director, 509-335-4332, Fax: 509-335-4806, E-mail: jn_petersen@wsu.edu. *Application contact:* Graduate School Admissions, 800-GRADWSU, Fax: 509-335-1949, E-mail: gradsch@wsu.edu. Web site: http://www.che.wsu.edu/.

Washington University in St. Louis, School of Engineering and Applied Science, Department of Energy, Environmental and Chemical Engineering, St. Louis, MO 63130-4899. Offers chemical engineering (MS, D Sc); environmental engineering (MS, D Sc). Part-time programs available. Terminal master's awarded for partial completion of doctoral program. *Degree requirements:* For master's, thesis optional; for doctorate, thesis/dissertation, preliminary exam, qualifying exam. *Entrance requirements:* For master's and doctorate, GRE, minimum B average during final 2 years of course work. Additional exam requirements/recommendations for international students: Required—TOEFL, TWE. Electronic applications accepted. *Faculty research:* Reaction engineering, materials processing, catalysis, process control, air pollution control.

Wayne State University, College of Engineering, Department of Chemical Engineering and Materials Science, Program in Chemical Engineering, Detroit, MI 48202. Offers MS, PhD. *Students:* 21 full-time (5 women), 8 part-time (3 women); includes 3 minority (all Asian, non-Hispanic/Latino), 18 international. Average age 26. 72 applicants, 49% accepted, 11 enrolled. In 2011, 7 master's, 4 doctorates awarded. *Degree requirements:* For master's, thesis optional; for doctorate, thesis/dissertation. *Entrance requirements:* For master's, GRE (if applying for financial support), letter of recommendation, resume; for doctorate, GRE, recommendations; resume, personal statement. Additional exam requirements/recommendations for international students: Required—TOEFL (minimum score 550 paper-based; 213 computer-based), TWE (minimum score 5.5). *Application deadline:* For fall admission, 6/1 priority date for domestic students, 5/1 for international students; for winter admission, 10/1 priority date for domestic students, 9/1 for international students; for spring admission, 2/1 priority date for domestic students, 1/1 for international students. Applications are processed on a rolling basis. Application fee: $50. Electronic applications accepted. *Expenses:* Tuition, state resident: part-time $512.85 per credit. Tuition, nonresident: part-time $1132.65 per credit. *Required fees:* $26.60 per credit. $199.65 per semester. Tuition and fees vary according to course load and program. *Financial support:* In 2011–12, 16 students received support. Fellowships with tuition reimbursements available, research assistantships with tuition reimbursements available, teaching assistantships with tuition reimbursements available, scholarships/grants, health care benefits, and unspecified assistantships available. Support available to part-time students. *Faculty research:* Environmental management, biochemical engineering, supercritical technology, polymer process catalysis. *Unit head:* Dr. Charles Manke, Chair, 313-577-3800, E-mail: cmanke@eng.wayne.edu. *Application contact:* Dr. Yinlun Huang, Graduate Director, 313-577-3771, E-mail: yhuang@wayne.edu. Web site: http://cheme.eng.wayne.edu/ChE.

Western Michigan University, Graduate College, College of Engineering and Applied Sciences, Department of Paper Engineering, Chemical Engineering, and Imaging,

Chemical Engineering

Kalamazoo, MI 49008. Offers paper and imaging science and engineering (MS, PhD). *Degree requirements:* For master's, thesis optional; for doctorate, one foreign language, comprehensive exam, thesis/dissertation. *Entrance requirements:* For master's, minimum GPA of 3.0. *Faculty research:* Fiber recycling, paper machine wet end operations, paper coating.

West Virginia University, College of Engineering and Mineral Resources, Department of Chemical Engineering, Morgantown, WV 26506. Offers MS Ch E, PhD. Part-time programs available. Terminal master's awarded for partial completion of doctoral program. *Degree requirements:* For master's, thesis; for doctorate, comprehensive exam, thesis/dissertation, original research proposal, dissertation research proposal. *Entrance requirements:* For master's and doctorate, minimum GPA of 3.0. Additional exam requirements/recommendations for international students: Required—TOEFL (minimum score 550 paper-based; 213 computer-based; 80 iBT). Electronic applications accepted. *Faculty research:* Biocatalysis and catalysis, fluid-particle systems, high-value non-fuel uses of coal, opto-electronic materials processing, polymer and polymer-composite nanotechnology.

Widener University, Graduate Programs in Engineering, Program in Chemical Engineering, Chester, PA 19013-5792. Offers M Eng. Part-time and evening/weekend programs available. *Degree requirements:* For master's, thesis optional. *Faculty research:* Biotechnology, environmental engineering, computational fluid mechanics, reaction kinetics, process design.

Worcester Polytechnic Institute, Graduate Studies and Research, Department of Chemical Engineering, Worcester, MA 01609-2280. Offers MS, PhD. Part-time and evening/weekend programs available. *Faculty:* 8 full-time (2 women), 1 part-time/adjunct (0 women). *Students:* 18 full-time (6 women), 7 part-time (6 women); includes 3 minority (2 Asian, non-Hispanic/Latino; 1 Hispanic/Latino), 11 international. 111 applicants, 34% accepted, 7 enrolled. In 2011, 8 master's, 1 doctorate awarded. Terminal master's awarded for partial completion of doctoral program. *Degree requirements:* For master's, thesis; for doctorate, comprehensive exam, thesis/dissertation. *Entrance requirements:* For master's and doctorate, GRE (recommended), 3 letters of recommendation. Additional exam requirements/recommendations for international students: Required—TOEFL (minimum score 563 paper-based; 223 computer-based; 84 iBT), IELTS (minimum score 7), GRE. *Application deadline:* For fall admission, 1/1 priority date for domestic students, 1/1 for international students; for spring admission, 10/1 priority date for domestic students, 10/1 for international students. Applications are processed on a rolling basis. Application fee: $70. Electronic applications accepted. *Financial support:* Fellowships, research assistantships, career-related internships or fieldwork, institutionally sponsored loans, scholarships/grants, and unspecified assistantships available. Financial award application deadline: 1/1; financial award applicants required to submit FAFSA. *Faculty research:* Process analysis in the presence of complexity, performance assessment of energy and environmental systems, process safety and risk analysis, economic assessment of energy technology options, regulation of chemicals. *Unit head:* Dr. David DiBiasio, Head, 508-831-5250, Fax: 508-831-5853, E-mail: dibiasio@wpi.edu. *Application contact:* Dr. Nikolaos Kazantzis, Graduate Coordinator, 508-831-5250, Fax: 508-831-5853, E-mail: nikolas@wp.edu. Web site: http://www.wpi.edu/academics/che.html.

Yale University, Graduate School of Arts and Sciences, School of Engineering and Applied Science, Department of Chemical Engineering, New Haven, CT 06520. Offers MS, PhD. Terminal master's awarded for partial completion of doctoral program. *Degree requirements:* For doctorate, thesis/dissertation, exam. *Entrance requirements:* For master's and doctorate, GRE General Test. Additional exam requirements/recommendations for international students: Required—TOEFL. *Faculty research:* Biochemical engineering, heterogeneous catalysis, high-temperature chemical reaction engineering, separation science and technology, colloids and complex fluids.

UNIVERSITY OF ROCHESTER

Edmund A. Hajim School of Engineering and Applied Sciences
Department of Chemical Engineering

Programs of Study

The interdisciplinary nature of the University of Rochester's chemical engineering program manifests itself in active collaborations with other departments at the school. The faculty enjoys generous research support from government agencies and private industries. The University's graduate programs are among the highest ranked in the nation according to the 2010 National Research Council survey report (www.nap.edu/rdp).

To earn a Ph.D., students must complete 90 credit hours. It typically takes five years to complete the program, which includes successful defense of a dissertation. The first two semesters are devoted to graduate courses in chemical engineering and other sciences. Students are expected to provide undergraduate teaching assistance. At the end of this period, students take a first-year examination as a transition from classroom to full-time research.

Students without prior backgrounds in chemical engineering are encouraged to apply. The Department has a graduate curriculum devised for students with a background in science, such as chemistry, physics, and biology. The curriculum combines courses at the undergraduate and graduate levels and is designed to foster interdisciplinary research in advanced materials, nanotechnology, clean energy, and biotechnology.

The Master of Science degree may be obtained through either a full-time or a part-time program. Graduate students may complete a thesis (Plan A) or choose a nonthesis (Plan B) option. All students who pursue Plan A are expected to earn 30 hours of credit, of which a minimum of 18 and a maximum of 24 hours should be formal course work. The balance of credit hours required for the degree is earned through M.S. research and/or reading courses. Satisfactory completion of the master's thesis is also required. All students who pursue Plan B must earn a minimum of 32 credits of course work. At least 18 credits should be taken from courses within the Department. Overall, no more than 6 credits toward a degree may be earned by research and/or reading courses. Plan B students are required to pass a comprehensive oral exam toward the end of their program.

The Department's 3/2 B.S./M.S. program leads to both the B.S. and M.S. degrees in five years. Students are granted a 75 percent tuition scholarship for their fifth year of study and may earn a stipend in return for their research assistance.

The Department of Chemical Engineering also awards the Master of Science degree in Alternative Energy. Courses and research projects focus on the fundamentals and applications of the generation, storage, and utilization of various forms of alternative energy as well as their impact on sustainability and energy conservation. This program is designed for graduate students with a bachelor's degree in engineering or science who are interested in pursuing a technical career in alternative energy. As with the other M.S. programs, the M.S. degree in Alternative Energy is available as a full- or part-time program, with a thesis (Plan A) or nonthesis (Plan B) option. All students who pursue Plan A are expected to earn 30 hours of credit; at least 18 should be attributed to 400-level courses. The balance of the credit-hour requirement can be satisfied through independent reading (no more than 4 credit hours) and thesis research (at least 6 credit hours), culminating in a master's thesis. All students who pursue Plan B must earn a minimum of 32 credits of course work, with at least 18 credits from 400-level courses and no more than 4 through independent reading. Students may opt for industrial internship (1 credit hour), for which a final essay must be submitted as a part of their degree requirements. In addition to course work and the essay, all Plan B students must pass a comprehensive oral examination as part of the degree requirements.

Research Facilities

The River Campus Libraries hold approximately 2.5 million volumes and provide access to an extensive collection of electronic, multimedia, and interlibrary loan resources. Miner Library includes more than 230,000 volumes of journals, books, theses, and government documents for health-care and medical research. Located at the Medical Center, the library also maintains access to online databases and electronic resources.

The Laboratory for Laser Energetics and the Center for Optoelectronics and Imaging are two state-of-the-art facilities in which specialized material science research is conducted. The Laboratory for Laser Energetics was established in 1970 for the investigation of the interaction of intense radiation with matter, to conduct experiments in support of the National Inertial Confinement Fusion (ICF) program; develop new laser and materials technologies; provide education in electro-optics, high-power lasers, high-energy-density physics, plasma physics, and nuclear fusion technology; operate the National Laser User's Facility; and conduct research in advanced technology related to high-energy-density phenomena.

The renowned Medical Center, which is a few minutes' walk from the River Campus, houses the Peptide Sequencing/Mass Spectrometry Facilities, Cell Sorting Facility, Nucleic Acid Laboratory, Real-Time and Static Confocal Imaging Facility, Functional Genomics Center, and a network of nearly 1,000 investigators providing research, clinical trial, and education services. In addition, a recently founded research institute, the Aab Institute of Biomedical Sciences, is the centerpiece of a ten-year, $400 million strategic plan to expand the Medical Center's research programs in the basic sciences. It is headquartered in a 240,000-square-foot research building on the Medical Center campus.

Financial Aid

The University offers fellowships, scholarships, and assistantships for full-time graduate students, and individual departments provide support through research assistantships. Applicants are encouraged to apply for outside funding such as NSF or New York State fellowships. Full-time Ph.D. students receive an annual stipend of $24,000 plus full graduate tuition.

Cost of Study

In the 2012–13 academic year, tuition is $42,880. Students must also pay additional fees for health services ($480) and health insurance ($1,956). These fee amounts are subject to change.

Living and Housing Costs

Students are eligible to lease a University apartment if enrolled as a full-time graduate student or postgraduate trainee. In the 2012–13 academic year, rent, utilities, food, and supplies are estimated at $11,223 per year; books at $1,290; and personal expenses at $4,500. These amounts are subject to change.

Student Group

The chemical engineering discipline appeals to students who are proficient at both analytical and descriptive sciences, and are intrigued by the prospect of investigating new phenomena, and devising new materials and devices for the technologies of the future. Students in the master's degree program should have acquired technical background in chemistry, mathematics, and physics. For students interested in biotechnology, a technical background in biology is desirable.

University of Rochester

Student Outcomes

In addition to the traditional jobs in the chemical process and petrochemical industries, chemical engineers work in pharmaceuticals, health care, pulp and paper, food processing, polymers, biotechnology, and environmental health and safety industries. Their expertise is also applied in law, education, publishing, finance, and medicine. Chemical engineers also are well equipped to analyze environmental issues and develop solutions to environmental problems, such as pollution control and remediation.

Location

Located at a bend of the Genesee River, the 85-acre River Campus is about 2 miles south of downtown Rochester, New York. Recently ranked as one of the Northeast's ten "Best Places to Live in America" by *Money* magazine, Rochester has also been listed as one of the "Most Livable Cities" in America by the Partners for Livable Communities. Rochester claims more sites on the National Register of Historic Places than any other city its size. With Lake Ontario on its northern border and the scenic Finger Lakes to the south, the Rochester area of about 1 million people offers a wide variety of cultural and recreational opportunities through its museums, parks, orchestras, planetarium, theater companies, and professional sports teams.

The University

Founded in 1850, the University of Rochester ranks among the most highly regarded universities in the country, offering degree programs at the bachelor's, master's, and doctoral levels, as well as in several professional disciplines. In the last eighteen years, 27 faculty members have been named Guggenheim Fellows. Present faculty members include a MacArthur Foundation fellowship recipient and 6 National Endowment for the Humanities Senior Fellows. Past alumni have included 7 Nobel Prize winners and 11 Pulitzer Prize winners. The University's Eastman School of Music is consistently ranked as one of the top music schools in the nation.

Applying

The official graduate application can be found online at https://apply.rochester.edu/graduate-arts-sciences-engineering/Login.aspx. The entire application must be received by January 15 for fall admission. Late applications are considered for exceptional applicants only if scholarship slots are available. Applicants are required to send college transcripts, letters of recommendation, personal/research statement, curriculum vitae, and standardized test results to the Department of Chemical Engineering.

Correspondence and Information

Graduate Program Coordinator
Department of Chemical Engineering
206 Gavett Hall, Box 270166
University of Rochester
Rochester, New York 14627-0166
Phone: 585-275-4913
Fax: 585-273-1348
E-mail: chegradinfo@che.rochester.edu
Web site: http://www.che.rochester.edu

THE FACULTY AND THEIR RESEARCH

Mitchell Anthamatten, Associate Professor and Scientist, LLE; Ph.D., MIT, 2001. Macromolecular self-assembly, associative and functional polymers, nanostructured materials, liquid crystals, interfacial phenomena, optoelectronic materials, vapor deposition polymerization, fuel cell membranes.

Danielle Benoit, Assistant Professor, Biomedical Engineering and Chemical Engineering; Ph.D., Colorado, 2006. The rational design, synthesis, characterization, and employment of materials to treat diseases or control cell behavior for applications in drug therapy, regenerative medicine, and tissue engineering.

Shaw H. Chen, Professor and Senior Scientist, LLE; Ph.D., Minnesota, 1981. Organic semiconductors, glassy liquid crystals, photoalignment of conjugated molecules, bipolar hosts for phosphorescent OLEDs, geometric surfactancy for bulk heterojunction solar cells.

Eldred H. Chimowitz, Professor and Associate Chair; Ph.D., Connecticut, 1982. Critical phenomena, statistical mechanics of fluids, computer-aided design.

David Harding, Professor of Chemical Engineering and Senior Scientist, LLE; Ph.D., Cambridge, 1986. Thin-film deposition, properties of films and composite structures, and developing cryogenic fuel capsules for nuclear fusion experiments.

Stephen Jacobs, Professor of Optics and Chemical Engineering and Senior Scientist, LLE; Ph.D., Rochester, 1975. Optical materials for laser applications, liquid crystal optics, electrooptic devices, optics manufacturing processes, magnetorheological finishing, polishing abrasives and slurries, optical glass.

Jacob Jornè, Professor; Ph.D., Berkeley, 1972. Electrochemical engineering, microelectronics processing, fuel cells, polymer electrolyte membrane fuel cell.

F. Douglas Kelley, Associate Professor; Ph.D., Rochester, 1990. Ways to exploit the divergent transport properties of fluids near the critical point, energy storage technologies that can be useful in balancing energy demand with sustainable energy generation, polymer mixtures and composites.

H. Mukaibo, Assistant Professor, Ph.D., Waseda (Japan), 2006. Template synthesis, microstructured/nanostructured materials, electrochemistry, nanoporous thin film, cell/nanostructure interface, gene delivery, energy.

Lewis Rothberg, Professor of Chemistry and Chemical Engineering; Ph.D., Harvard, 1984. Polymer electronics, optoelectronic devices, light-emitting diodes, thin-film transistors, organic photovoltaics and solar cells, biomolecular sensors, plasmon-enhanced devices.

Yonathon Shapir, Professor of Physics and Chemical Engineering; Ph.D., Tel-Aviv, 1981. Critical phenomena in ordered and disordered systems, classical and quantum transport in dirty metals and the metal-insulator transition, statistical properties of different polymer configurations, fractal properties of percolation and other clusters, kinetic models of growth and aggregation.

Alexander A. Shestopalov, Assistant Professor; Ph.D., Duke, 2009. Development of new unconventional fabrication and patterning techniques and their use in preparation of functional micro- and nanostructured devices.

Ching Tang, Professor of Chemical Engineering, Chemistry, and Physics; Ph.D., Cornell, 1975. Applications of organic electronic devices—organic light-emitting diodes, solar cells, photoconductors, image sensors, photoreceptors; basic studies of organic thin-film devices: charge injection, transport, recombination and luminescence properties; metal-organic and organic-organic junction phenomena; development of flat-panel display technology based on organic light-emitting diodes.

J. H. David Wu, Professor of Chemical Engineering and Biomedical Engineering and Associate Professor of Microbiology and Immunology; Ph.D., MIT, 1987. Biofuels development, molecular enzymology, transcriptional network, genomics and systems biology of biomass degradation for bioenergy conversion, artificial bone marrow and lymphoid tissue engineering, molecular control of hematopoiesis and immune response, stem cell and lymphocyte culture, biochemical engineering, fermentation, molecular biology.

Matthew Yates, Associate Professor and Scientist, LLE; Ph.D., Texas, 1999. Particle synthesis and assembly, crystallization, fuel cell membranes, microemulsions, supercritical fluids, microencapsulation.

Section 7
Civil and Environmental Engineering

This section contains a directory of institutions offering graduate work in civil and environmental engineering. Additional information about programs listed in the directory but not augmented by an in-depth entry may be obtained by writing directly to the dean of a graduate school or chair of a department at the address given in the directory.

For programs offering related work, see also in this book *Agricultural Engineering and Bioengineering, Biomedical Engineering and Biotechnology, Engineering and Applied Sciences, Management of Engineering and Technology,* and *Ocean Engineering.* In the other guides in this series:

Graduate Programs in the Humanities, Arts & Social Sciences

See *Public, Regional, and Industrial Affairs (Urban and Regional Planning and Urban Studies)*

Graduate Programs in the Biological/Biomedical Sciences & Health-Related Medical Professions

See *Ecology, Environmental Biology,* and *Evolutionary Biology*

Graduate Programs in the Physical Sciences, Mathematics, Agricultural Sciences, the Environment & Natural Resources

See *Agricultural and Food Sciences, Environmental Sciences and Management, Geosciences,* and *Marine Sciences and Oceanography*

CONTENTS

Program Directories

Civil Engineering

American University of Beirut, Graduate Programs, Faculty of Engineering and Architecture, Beirut, Lebanon. Offers applied energy (MME); civil engineering (ME, PhD); electrical and computer engineering (ME, PhD); engineering management (MEM); environmental and water resources (ME); environmental and water resources engineering (PhD); environmental technology (MSES); mechanical engineering (ME, PhD); urban design (MUD); urban planning and policy (MUP). Part-time programs available. *Faculty:* 53 full-time (8 women), 10 part-time/adjunct (2 women). *Students:* 290 full-time (101 women), 59 part-time (18 women). Average age 25. 336 applicants, 80% accepted, 83 enrolled. In 2011, 72 master's, 5 doctorates awarded. *Degree requirements:* For master's, one foreign language, comprehensive exam, thesis (for some programs); for doctorate, one foreign language, comprehensive exam, thesis/dissertation, publications. *Entrance requirements:* For master's, GRE (for electrical and computer engineering), letters of recommendation; for doctorate, GRE, letters of recommendation, master's degree, transcripts, curriculum vitae, interview. Additional exam requirements/recommendations for international students: Required—TOEFL (minimum score 600 paper-based; 250 computer-based; 100 iBT), IELTS (minimum score 7.5). *Application deadline:* For fall admission, 2/5 priority date for domestic students, 2/5 for international students; for spring admission, 11/1 priority date for domestic students, 11/1 for international students. Applications are processed on a rolling basis. Application fee: $50. Electronic applications accepted. *Expenses: Tuition:* Full-time $12,780; part-time $710 per credit. *Required fees:* $528; $528 per credit. Tuition and fees vary according to course load and program. *Financial support:* In 2011–12, 9 fellowships with full tuition reimbursements (averaging $24,800 per year), 33 research assistantships with full tuition reimbursements (averaging $24,800 per year), 74 teaching assistantships with full tuition reimbursements (averaging $9,800 per year) were awarded; career-related internships or fieldwork, institutionally sponsored loans, scholarships/grants, health care benefits, and unspecified assistantships also available. *Total annual research expenditures:* $1.1 million. *Unit head:* Prof. Makram T. Suidan, Dean, 961-135-0000 Ext. 3400, Fax: 961-174-4462, E-mail: msuidan@aub.edu.lb. *Application contact:* Dr. Salim Kanaan, Director, Admissions Office, 961-135-0000 Ext. 2594, Fax: 961-175-0775, E-mail: sk00@aub.edu.lb. Web site: http://staff.aub.edu.lb/~webfea.

American University of Sharjah, Graduate Programs, Sharjah, United Arab Emirates. Offers business (EMBA, GEMPA, MBA); chemical engineering (MS Ch E); civil engineering (MSCE); computer engineering (MS); electrical engineering (MSEE); mechanical engineering (MSME); mechatronics engineering (MS); public administration (MPA); teaching English to speakers of other languages (MA); translation and interpreting (MA); urban planning (MUP). Part-time and evening/weekend programs available. *Entrance requirements:* For master's, GMAT (MBA). Additional exam requirements/recommendations for international students: Required—TOEFL (minimum score 550 paper-based; 213 computer-based; 80 iBT), TWE (minimum score 5). Electronic applications accepted. *Faculty research:* Chemical engineering, civil engineering, computer engineering, electrical engineering, linguistics, translation.

Arizona State University, Ira A. Fulton School of Engineering, Del E. Webb School of Construction, Tempe, AZ 85287-5306. Offers civil, environmental and sustainable engineering (MS, MSE, PhD); construction (MS, MSE, PhD); construction engineering (MSE). Part-time and evening/weekend programs available. Postbaccalaureate distance learning degree programs offered (minimal on-campus study). Terminal master's awarded for partial completion of doctoral program. *Degree requirements:* For master's, thesis optional, comprehensive exams (MSE); interactive Program of Study (iPOS) submitted before completing 50 percent of required credit hours; for doctorate, comprehensive exam, thesis/dissertation, interactive Program of Study (iPOS) submitted before completing 50 percent of required credit hours. *Entrance requirements:* For master's, GRE, minimum GPA of 3.0 or equivalent in last 2 years of work leading to bachelor's degree; for doctorate, GRE, minimum GPA of 3.0 in last 2 years of work leading to bachelor's degree, 3.2 in all graduate-level coursework with master's degree; 3 letters of recommendation; resume/curriculum vitae; letter of intent; thesis (if applicable); statement of research interests. Additional exam requirements/recommendations for international students: Required—TOEFL (minimum score 80 iBT), TOEFL, IELTS, or Pearson Test of English. Electronic applications accepted. *Expenses:* Contact institution. *Faculty research:* Water purification, transportation (safety and materials), construction management, environmental biotechnology, environmental nanotechnology, earth systems engineering and management, SMART innovations, project performance metrics, and underground infrastructure.

Auburn University, Graduate School, Ginn College of Engineering, Department of Civil Engineering, Auburn University, AL 36849. Offers construction engineering and management (MCE, MS, PhD); environmental engineering (MCE, MS, PhD); geotechnical/materials engineering (MCE, MS, PhD); hydraulics/hydrology (MCE, MS, PhD); structural engineering (MCE, MS, PhD); transportation engineering (MCE, MS, PhD). Part-time programs available. *Faculty:* 21 full-time (2 women), 1 part-time/adjunct (0 women). *Students:* 48 full-time (16 women), 62 part-time (14 women); includes 6 minority (4 Black or African American, non-Hispanic/Latino; 1 Asian, non-Hispanic/Latino; 1 Hispanic/Latino), 37 international. Average age 26. 111 applicants, 59% accepted, 25 enrolled. In 2011, 26 master's, 2 doctorates awarded. *Degree requirements:* For master's, project (MCE), thesis (MS); for doctorate, comprehensive exam, thesis/dissertation. *Entrance requirements:* For master's and doctorate, GRE General Test. *Application deadline:* For fall admission, 7/7 for domestic students; for spring admission, 11/24 for domestic students. Applications are processed on a rolling basis. Application fee: $50 ($60 for international students). Electronic applications accepted. *Expenses:* Tuition, state resident: full-time $7290; part-time $405 per credit hour. Tuition, nonresident: full-time $21,870; part-time $1215 per credit hour. *International tuition:* $22,000 full-time. *Required fees:* $1402. *Financial support:* Fellowships, research assistantships, teaching assistantships, and Federal Work-Study available. Support available to part-time students. Financial award application deadline: 3/15; financial award applicants required to submit FAFSA. *Unit head:* Dr. J. Michael Stallings, Head, 334-844-4320. *Application contact:* Dr. George Flowers, Dean of the Graduate School, 334-844-2125.

Boise State University, Graduate College, College of Engineering, Department of Civil Engineering, Boise, ID 83725-0399. Offers M Engr, MS. Part-time and evening/weekend programs available. *Degree requirements:* For master's, thesis. *Entrance requirements:* For master's, GRE General Test, minimum GPA of 3.0. Additional exam requirements/recommendations for international students: Required—TOEFL. Electronic applications accepted.

Bradley University, Graduate School, College of Engineering and Technology, Department of Civil Engineering and Construction, Peoria, IL 61625-0002. Offers MSCE. Part-time and evening/weekend programs available. *Degree requirements:* For master's, comprehensive exam. *Entrance requirements:* For master's, minimum GPA of 3.0, 2 letters of recommendation. Additional exam requirements/recommendations for international students: Required—TOEFL (minimum score 550 paper-based; 213 computer-based; 79 iBT).

Brigham Young University, Graduate Studies, Ira A. Fulton College of Engineering and Technology, Department of Civil and Environmental Engineering, Provo, UT 84602. Offers civil engineering (MS, PhD). Part-time programs available. *Faculty:* 16 full-time (0 women), 10 part-time/adjunct (3 women). *Students:* 85 full-time (10 women), 23 part-time (2 women); includes 25 minority (1 Black or African American, non-Hispanic/Latino; 6 Asian, non-Hispanic/Latino; 13 Hispanic/Latino; 5 Native Hawaiian or other Pacific Islander, non-Hispanic/Latino). Average age 28. 58 applicants, 88% accepted, 48 enrolled. In 2011, 42 master's, 2 doctorates awarded. *Degree requirements:* For master's, thesis (for some programs), Fundamentals of Engineering (FE) Exam; for doctorate, comprehensive exam, thesis/dissertation. *Entrance requirements:* For master's, GRE General Test, minimum GPA of 3.0 in last 60 hours of upper-division course work; for doctorate, GRE General Test, minimum graduate GPA of 3.4. Additional exam requirements/recommendations for international students: Required—TOEFL (minimum score 580 paper-based; 237 computer-based; 85 iBT), IELTS (minimum score 7). *Application deadline:* For fall admission, 2/15 for domestic and international students; for winter admission, 9/5 for domestic students, 6/15 for international students; for spring admission, 2/15 for domestic students, 10/15 for international students. Applications are processed on a rolling basis. Application fee: $50. Electronic applications accepted. *Expenses: Tuition:* Full-time $5760; part-time $320 per credit. Tuition and fees vary according to student's religious affiliation. *Financial support:* In 2011–12, 43 students received support, including 74 fellowships with full and partial tuition reimbursements available (averaging $2,452 per year), 47 research assistantships (averaging $3,564 per year), 54 teaching assistantships (averaging $2,115 per year); career-related internships or fieldwork and scholarships/grants also available. Support available to part-time students. Financial award application deadline: 3/1; financial award applicants required to submit FAFSA. *Faculty research:* Structural optimization; finite element modeling and earthquake resistant analysis; groundwater, surface water, watershed and hydrologic modeling and visualization; subsurface environmental issues including transport, remediation, monitoring and characterization; capacity of deep foundations under static and dynamic loading and the behavior and mitigation of liquefiable soils; traffic planning, operations, safety, pavements and materials. *Total annual research expenditures:* $1 million. *Unit head:* Dr. Steven E. Benzley, Department Chair, 801-422-2811, Fax: 801-422-0159, E-mail: seb@byu.edu. *Application contact:* Dr. Grant G. Schultz, Graduate Coordinator, 801-422-2811, Fax: 801-422-0159, E-mail: schultz@byu.edu. Web site: http://ceen.et.byu.edu/.

Bucknell University, Graduate Studies, College of Engineering, Department of Civil and Environmental Engineering, Lewisburg, PA 17837. Offers MSCE, MSEV. *Faculty:* 12 full-time (2 women). *Students:* 6 full-time (1 woman), 1 international. 8 applicants, 63% accepted, 3 enrolled. In 2011, 1 master's awarded. *Degree requirements:* For master's, thesis. *Entrance requirements:* For master's, GRE General Test, minimum GPA of 3.0. Additional exam requirements/recommendations for international students: Required—TOEFL (minimum score 600 paper-based). *Application deadline:* For fall admission, 2/1 priority date for domestic students, 1/1 for international students. Application fee: $25. *Financial support:* In 2011–12, 6 students received support, including 6 research assistantships with full tuition reimbursements available (averaging $28,000 per year); unspecified assistantships also available. Financial award application deadline: 2/1. *Faculty research:* Pile foundations, rehabilitation of bridges, deep-shaft biological-waste treatment, pre-cast concrete structures. *Unit head:* Dr. Matthew Higgins, Head, 570-577-1112. *Application contact:* Gretchen H. Fegley, Coordinator, 570-577-3655, Fax: 570-577-3760, E-mail: gfegley@bucknell.edu. Web site: http://www.bucknell.edu/.

California Institute of Technology, Division of Engineering and Applied Science, Option in Civil Engineering, Pasadena, CA 91125-0001. Offers MS, PhD, Engr. *Degree requirements:* For doctorate, thesis/dissertation. *Faculty research:* Earthquake engineering, soil mechanics, finite-element analysis, hydraulics, coastal engineering.

California Polytechnic State University, San Luis Obispo, College of Engineering, Department of Civil and Environmental Engineering, San Luis Obispo, CA 93407. Offers MS. Part-time programs available. *Faculty:* 6 full-time (0 women), 1 part-time/adjunct (0 women). *Students:* 47 full-time (12 women), 9 part-time (0 women); includes 23 minority (1 Black or African American, non-Hispanic/Latino; 1 American Indian or Alaska Native, non-Hispanic/Latino; 9 Asian, non-Hispanic/Latino; 5 Hispanic/Latino; 7 Two or more races, non-Hispanic/Latino). Average age 24. 87 applicants, 56% accepted, 29 enrolled. In 2011, 24 master's awarded. *Degree requirements:* For master's, comprehensive exam (for some programs), thesis (for some programs). *Entrance requirements:* For master's, GRE General Test, minimum GPA of 3.0 in last 90 quarter units, 3 letters of recommendation. Additional exam requirements/recommendations for international students: Required—TOEFL (minimum score 550 paper-based; 213 computer-based), IELTS (minimum score 6). *Application deadline:* For fall admission, 3/1 for domestic students, 11/30 for international students; for winter admission, 10/1 for domestic students, 6/30 for international students; for spring admission, 1/1 for domestic students. Applications are processed on a rolling basis. Application fee: $55. Electronic applications accepted. *Expenses:* Tuition, state resident: full-time $6738. Tuition, nonresident: full-time $17,898. *Required fees:* $2449. *Financial support:* Fellowships, research assistantships, teaching assistantships, career-related internships or fieldwork, Federal Work-Study, and scholarships/grants available. Support available to part-time students. Financial award application deadline: 3/2; financial award applicants required to submit FAFSA. *Faculty research:* Transportation and traffic, environmental protection, geotechnology, water engineering. *Unit head:* Dr. Robb Moss, Graduate Coordinator, 805-756-6427, Fax: 805-756-6330, E-mail: rmoss@calpoly.edu. *Application contact:* Dr. James Maraviglia, Associate Vice Provost for Marketing and Enrollment Development, 805-756-2311, Fax: 805-756-5400, E-mail: admissions@calpoly.edu. Web site: http://ceenve.calpoly.edu.

California State Polytechnic University, Pomona, Academic Affairs, College of Engineering, Program in Civil Engineering, Pomona, CA 91768-2557. Offers MS. *Students:* 25 full-time (3 women), 78 part-time (6 women); includes 53 minority (1 Black or African American, non-Hispanic/Latino; 31 Asian, non-Hispanic/Latino; 20 Hispanic/Latino; 1 Two or more races, non-Hispanic/Latino), 9 international. Average age 30. 105 applicants, 68% accepted, 39 enrolled. In 2011, 12 master's awarded. *Degree requirements:* For master's, project or thesis. *Application deadline:* Applications are processed on a rolling basis. Application fee: $55. Electronic applications accepted. *Expenses:* Tuition, state resident: full-time $6738. Tuition, nonresident: full-time $12,300. *Required fees:* $657. Tuition and fees vary according to course load and program. *Unit head:* Dr. Francelina A. Neto, Department Chair, 909-869-2488, E-mail: faneto@csupomona.edu. *Application contact:* Dr. Ronald Yeung, Graduate Coordinator,

909-869-2640, E-mail: mryeung@csupomona.edu. Web site: http://www.csupomona.edu/~ce/.

California State University, Fresno, Division of Graduate Studies, College of Engineering and Computer Science, Department of Civil Engineering, Fresno, CA 93740-8027. Offers MS. Part-time and evening/weekend programs available. *Degree requirements:* For master's, thesis or alternative. *Entrance requirements:* For master's, GRE General Test, minimum GPA of 2.75. Additional exam requirements/recommendations for international students: Required—TOEFL. Electronic applications accepted. *Faculty research:* Surveying, water damage, instrumentation equipment, agricultural drainage, aerial triangulation, dairy manure particles.

California State University, Fullerton, Graduate Studies, College of Engineering and Computer Science, Department of Civil Engineering and Engineering Mechanics, Fullerton, CA 92834-9480. Offers MS. Part-time programs available. *Students:* 96 full-time (20 women), 78 part-time (21 women); includes 87 minority (6 Black or African American, non-Hispanic/Latino; 48 Asian, non-Hispanic/Latino; 27 Hispanic/Latino; 6 Two or more races, non-Hispanic/Latino), 27 international. Average age 29. 213 applicants, 64% accepted, 68 enrolled. In 2011, 59 master's awarded. *Degree requirements:* For master's, comprehensive exam, project or thesis. *Entrance requirements:* For master's, minimum undergraduate GPA of 2.5. Application fee: $55. *Financial support:* Career-related internships or fieldwork, Federal Work-Study, institutionally sponsored loans, and scholarships/grants available. Support available to part-time students. Financial award application deadline: 3/1; financial award applicants required to submit FAFSA. *Faculty research:* Soil-structure interaction, finite-element analysis, computer-aided analysis and design. *Unit head:* Dr. Pinaki Chakrabarti, Chair, 657-278-3016. *Application contact:* Admissions/Applications, 657-278-2371.

California State University, Long Beach, Graduate Studies, College of Engineering, Department of Civil Engineering and Construction Engineering Management, Long Beach, CA 90840. Offers civil engineering (MSCE). Part-time programs available. *Faculty:* 6 full-time (3 women), 5 part-time/adjunct (0 women). *Students:* 44 full-time (10 women), 76 part-time (18 women); includes 76 minority (6 Black or African American, non-Hispanic/Latino; 1 American Indian or Alaska Native, non-Hispanic/Latino; 38 Asian, non-Hispanic/Latino; 25 Hispanic/Latino; 2 Native Hawaiian or other Pacific Islander, non-Hispanic/Latino; 4 Two or more races, non-Hispanic/Latino), 16 international. Average age 29. 182 applicants, 55% accepted, 33 enrolled. In 2011, 30 master's awarded. *Degree requirements:* For master's, comprehensive exam or thesis. *Entrance requirements:* Additional exam requirements/recommendations for international students: Required—TOEFL. *Application deadline:* For fall admission, 3/1 for domestic students. Application fee: $55. Electronic applications accepted. *Financial support:* Career-related internships or fieldwork, Federal Work-Study, institutionally sponsored loans, scholarships/grants, and unspecified assistantships available. Financial award application deadline: 3/2. *Faculty research:* Soils, hydraulics, seismic structures, composite metals, computer-aided manufacturing. *Unit head:* Dr. Emelinda Parentela, Chair, 562-985-4932, Fax: 562-985-2380, E-mail: parent@csulb.edu. *Application contact:* Dr. Jeremy Redman, Graduate Advisor, 562-985-5135, Fax: 562-985-2380, E-mail: jredman@csulb.edu.

California State University, Los Angeles, Graduate Studies, College of Engineering, Computer Science, and Technology, Department of Civil Engineering, Los Angeles, CA 90032-8530. Offers MS. Part-time and evening/weekend programs available. *Faculty:* 2 full-time (0 women), 5 part-time/adjunct (0 women). *Students:* 13 full-time (3 women), 47 part-time (12 women); includes 47 minority (5 Black or African American, non-Hispanic/Latino; 25 Asian, non-Hispanic/Latino; 17 Hispanic/Latino), 5 international. Average age 30. 92 applicants, 63% accepted, 22 enrolled. In 2011, 31 master's awarded. *Degree requirements:* For master's, comprehensive exam or thesis. *Entrance requirements:* For master's, GRE or minimum GPA of 2.4. Additional exam requirements/recommendations for international students: Required—TOEFL (minimum score 550 paper-based). *Application deadline:* For fall admission, 5/1 for domestic and international students. Applications are processed on a rolling basis. Application fee: $55. *Expenses:* Tuition, state resident: full-time $8225. *Financial support:* Federal Work-Study available. Support available to part-time students. Financial award application deadline: 3/1. *Faculty research:* Structure, hydraulics, hydrology, soil mechanics. *Unit head:* Dr. Rupa Purasinghe, Chair, 323-343-4450, Fax: 323-343-6316, E-mail: rpurasi@calstatela.edu. *Application contact:* Dr. Karin Brown, Acting Associate Dean of Graduate Studies, 323-343-3820, Fax: 323-343-5653, E-mail: kbrown5@calstatela.edu. Web site: http://www.calstatela.edu/academic/ecst/civil/.

California State University, Northridge, Graduate Studies, College of Engineering and Computer Science, Department of Civil Engineering and Applied Mechanics, Northridge, CA 91330. Offers engineering (MS), including structural engineering. Part-time and evening/weekend programs available. *Degree requirements:* For master's, thesis. *Entrance requirements:* Additional exam requirements/recommendations for international students: Required—TOEFL. *Faculty research:* Composite study.

California State University, Sacramento, Office of Graduate Studies, College of Engineering and Computer Science, Department of Civil Engineering, Sacramento, CA 95819-6029. Offers MS. Part-time and evening/weekend programs available. *Faculty:* 14 full-time (1 woman), 30 part-time/adjunct (4 women). *Students:* 29 full-time, 59 part-time; includes 42 minority (5 Black or African American, non-Hispanic/Latino; 18 Asian, non-Hispanic/Latino; 6 Hispanic/Latino; 5 Native Hawaiian or other Pacific Islander, non-Hispanic/Latino; 8 Two or more races, non-Hispanic/Latino), 7 international. Average age 31. 109 applicants, 63% accepted, 39 enrolled. In 2011, 11 master's awarded. *Degree requirements:* For master's, thesis, project, direct study, or comprehensive exam; writing proficiency exam. *Entrance requirements:* Additional exam requirements/recommendations for international students: Required—TOEFL. *Application deadline:* For fall admission, 3/1 for domestic and international students; for spring admission, 9/15 for domestic students, 9/30 for international students. Applications are processed on a rolling basis. Application fee: $55. Electronic applications accepted. *Financial support:* Research assistantships, teaching assistantships, career-related internships or fieldwork, and Federal Work-Study available. Support available to part-time students. Financial award application deadline: 3/1; financial award applicants required to submit FAFSA. *Unit head:* Ramzi Mahmood, Head, 916-278-6982, Fax: 916-278-7957, E-mail: mahmood@ecs.csus.edu. *Application contact:* Jose Martinez, Outreach and Graduate Diversity Coordinator, 916-278-6470, Fax: 916-278-5669, E-mail: martinj@skymail.csus.edu. Web site: http://www.ecs.csus.edu/ce.

Carleton University, Faculty of Graduate Studies, Faculty of Engineering and Design, Department of Civil and Environmental Engineering, Ottawa, ON K1S 5B6, Canada. Offers M Eng, MA Sc, PhD. *Degree requirements:* For master's, thesis optional; for doctorate, thesis/dissertation. *Entrance requirements:* For master's, honors degree; for doctorate, MA Sc or M Eng. Additional exam requirements/recommendations for international students: Required—TOEFL. *Faculty research:* Pollution and wastewater management, fire safety engineering, earthquake engineering, structural design, bridge engineering.

Carnegie Mellon University, Carnegie Institute of Technology, Department of Civil and Environmental Engineering, Pittsburgh, PA 15213. Offers advanced infrastructure systems (MS, PhD); civil and environmental engineering (MS, PhD); civil and environmental engineering/engineering and public policy (PhD); civil engineering (MS, PhD); computational mechanics (MS, PhD); environmental engineering (MS, PhD); environmental management and science (MS, PhD). Part-time programs available. *Faculty:* 22 full-time (4 women), 24 part-time/adjunct (5 women). *Students:* 147 full-time (64 women), 7 part-time (0 women); includes 13 minority (5 Black or African American, non-Hispanic/Latino; 6 Asian, non-Hispanic/Latino; 2 Hispanic/Latino), 101 international. Average age 26. 487 applicants, 55% accepted, 80 enrolled. In 2011, 84 master's, 12 doctorates awarded. Terminal master's awarded for partial completion of doctoral program. *Degree requirements:* For master's, thesis optional; for doctorate, comprehensive exam, thesis/dissertation, two-part qualifying exam, public defense of dissertation. *Entrance requirements:* For master's and doctorate, GRE General Test. Additional exam requirements/recommendations for international students: Required—TOEFL (minimum score 84 iBT). *Application deadline:* For fall admission, 1/15 priority date for domestic students, 1/15 for international students; for spring admission, 9/30 priority date for domestic students, 9/30 for international students. Application fee: $65. Electronic applications accepted. *Financial support:* In 2011–12, 108 students received support, including 26 fellowships with full and partial tuition reimbursements available (averaging $2,087 per year), 35 research assistantships with full and partial tuition reimbursements available (averaging $2,094 per year); tuition waivers (partial), unspecified assistantships, and service assistantships also available. Financial award application deadline: 1/15. *Faculty research:* Advanced infrastructure systems; environmental engineering science and management; mechanics, materials, and computing; green design; global sustainable construction. *Total annual research expenditures:* $4.9 million. *Unit head:* Dr. James H. Garrett, Jr., Head, 412-268-2941, Fax: 412-268-7813, E-mail: garrett@cmu.edu. *Application contact:* Maxine A. Leffard, Director of the Graduate Program, 412-268-5673, Fax: 412-268-7813, E-mail: ce-admissions@andrew.cmu.edu. Web site: http://www.ce.cmu.edu/.

Case Western Reserve University, School of Graduate Studies, Case School of Engineering, Department of Civil Engineering, Cleveland, OH 44106. Offers civil engineering (MS, PhD). Part-time programs available. Postbaccalaureate distance learning degree programs offered (minimal on-campus study). *Faculty:* 7 full-time (0 women). *Students:* 18 full-time (7 women); includes 1 minority (Black or African American, non-Hispanic/Latino), 15 international. In 2011, 9 master's, 3 doctorates awarded. *Degree requirements:* For master's, thesis (for some programs); for doctorate, thesis/dissertation, qualifying exam, teaching experience. *Entrance requirements:* For master's and doctorate, GRE General Test. Additional exam requirements/recommendations for international students: Required—TOEFL. *Application deadline:* For fall admission, 8/1 priority date for domestic students; for spring admission, 1/1 for domestic students. Application fee: $50. *Financial support:* Fellowships with full and partial tuition reimbursements, research assistantships with full and partial tuition reimbursements, teaching assistantships, and institutionally sponsored loans available. Financial award application deadline: 8/1; financial award applicants required to submit FAFSA. *Faculty research:* Environmental, geotechnical, infrastructure reliability, mechanics, structures. *Total annual research expenditures:* $655,158. *Unit head:* Dr. David Zeng, Chairman/Professor, 216-368-2923, Fax: 216-368-5229, E-mail: xxz16@case.edu. *Application contact:* Carla Wilson, Student Affairs Coordinator, 216-368-4580, Fax: 216-368-3007, E-mail: cxw75@case.edu. Web site: http://civil.case.edu.

The Catholic University of America, School of Engineering, Department of Civil Engineering, Washington, DC 20064. Offers environmental engineering (PhD). Part-time programs available. *Faculty:* 6 full-time (0 women), 4 part-time/adjunct (0 women). *Students:* 6 full-time (2 women), 19 part-time (7 women); includes 8 minority (5 Black or African American, non-Hispanic/Latino; 1 Asian, non-Hispanic/Latino; 2 Hispanic/Latino), 7 international. Average age 35. 28 applicants, 39% accepted, 5 enrolled. In 2011, 4 master's, 1 doctorate awarded. *Degree requirements:* For master's, thesis optional; for doctorate, comprehensive exam, thesis/dissertation. *Entrance requirements:* For master's and doctorate, statement of purpose, official copies of academic transcripts, three letters of recommendation. Additional exam requirements/recommendations for international students: Required—TOEFL (minimum score 580 paper-based; 237 computer-based). *Application deadline:* For fall admission, 8/1 priority date for domestic students, 7/15 for international students; for spring admission, 12/1 priority date for domestic students, 10/15 for international students. Applications are processed on a rolling basis. Application fee: $55. Electronic applications accepted. *Expenses:* Contact institution. *Financial support:* Fellowships, research assistantships, teaching assistantships, Federal Work-Study, scholarships/grants, tuition waivers (full and partial), and unspecified assistantships available. Financial award application deadline: 2/1; financial award applicants required to submit FAFSA. *Faculty research:* Geotechnical engineering, solid mechanics, construction engineering and management, environmental engineering, structural engineering. *Total annual research expenditures:* $325,547. *Unit head:* Dr. Lu Sun, Chair, 202-319-6671, Fax: 202-319-6677, E-mail: sunl@cua.edu. *Application contact:* Andrew Woodall, Director of Graduate Admissions, 202-319-5057, Fax: 202-319-6533, E-mail: cua-admissions@cua.edu. Web site: http://civil.cua.edu/.

The Citadel, The Military College of South Carolina, Citadel Graduate College, Department of Civil Engineering, Charleston, SC 29409. Offers technical project management (MS). Part-time and evening/weekend programs available. *Faculty:* 2 full-time, 3 part-time/adjunct. *Students:* 4 full-time (1 woman), 30 part-time (9 women); includes 4 minority (3 Black or African American, non-Hispanic/Latino; 1 Hispanic/Latino). Average age 37. In 2011, 8 master's awarded. *Entrance requirements:* For master's, GRE or GMAT, evidence of a minimum of one year of professional experience, or permission from department head; two letters of reference; resume detailing previous work. Additional exam requirements/recommendations for international students: Required—TOEFL (minimum score 550 paper-based; 213 computer-based; 79 iBT). *Application deadline:* For fall admission, 8/1 priority date for domestic students. Applications are processed on a rolling basis. Application fee: $30. Electronic applications accepted. *Expenses: Tuition, area resident:* Part-time $501 per credit hour. Tuition, state resident: part-time $501 per credit hour. Tuition, nonresident: part-time $824 per credit hour. *Required fees:* $40 per term. One-time fee: $30. *Financial support:* Health care benefits available. Support available to part-time students. Financial award application deadline: 7/1; financial award applicants required to submit FAFSA. *Unit head:* Dr. Kenneth P. Brannan, Department Head, 843-953-5007, Fax: 843-953-6328, E-mail: ken.brannan@citadel.edu. *Application contact:* Maj. Keith Plemmons, Program Director, 843-953-7677, Fax: 843-953-6328, E-mail: keith.plemmons@citadel.edu. Web site: http://www.citadel.edu/pmgt/.

City College of the City University of New York, Graduate School, Grove School of Engineering, Department of Civil Engineering, New York, NY 10031-9198. Offers ME, MS, PhD. PhD program offered jointly with Graduate School and University Center of the City University of New York. Part-time programs available. *Degree requirements:* For master's, thesis optional; for doctorate, one foreign language, comprehensive exam, thesis/dissertation. *Entrance requirements:* For master's and doctorate, GRE General Test. Additional exam requirements/recommendations for international students: Required—TOEFL (minimum score 500 paper-based; 173 computer-based; 61 iBT). *Faculty research:* Earthquake engineering, transportation systems, groundwater, environmental systems, highway systems.

Clarkson University, Graduate School, Wallace H. Coulter School of Engineering, Department of Civil and Environmental Engineering, Potsdam, NY 13699. Offers civil and environmental engineering (PhD); civil engineering (ME, MS). Part-time programs available. *Faculty:* 28 full-time (3 women), 5 part-time/adjunct (1 woman). *Students:* 42 full-time (14 women); includes 1 minority (Asian, non-Hispanic/Latino), 28 international. Average age 26. 68 applicants, 79% accepted, 15 enrolled. In 2011, 12 master's, 6 doctorates awarded. Terminal master's awarded for partial completion of doctoral program. *Degree requirements:* For master's, thesis; for doctorate, comprehensive exam, thesis/dissertation, departmental qualifying exam. *Entrance requirements:* For master's and doctorate, GRE, transcripts of all college coursework, resume, personal statement, three letters of recommendation. Additional exam requirements/recommendations for international students: Required—TOEFL (minimum score 550 paper-based; 213 computer-based; 80 iBT), IELTS (minimum score 6.5). *Application deadline:* For fall admission, 1/30 priority date for domestic students, 1/30 for international students; for spring admission, 9/1 priority date for domestic students, 9/1 for international students. Applications are processed on a rolling basis. Application fee: $25 ($35 for international students). Electronic applications accepted. *Expenses: Tuition:* Full-time $14,376; part-time $1198 per credit hour. *Required fees:* $295 per semester. *Financial support:* In 2011–12, 39 students received support, including fellowships with full tuition reimbursements available (averaging $21,999 per year), 26 research assistantships with full tuition reimbursements available (averaging $21,999 per year), 14 teaching assistantships with full tuition reimbursements available (averaging $21,999 per year); scholarships/grants, tuition waivers (partial), and unspecified assistantships also available. *Faculty research:* Prognostic algorithm, resuspended particle, load capacity rating, ecosystem, geothermal vents, CO2 bubbles. *Total annual research expenditures:* $4.5 million. *Unit head:* Dr. Stefan Grimberg, Department Chair, 315-268-6529, Fax: 315-268-7985, E-mail: grimberg@clarkson.edu. *Application contact:* Kelly Sharlow, Assistant to the Dean, 315-268-7929, Fax: 315-268-4494, E-mail: ksharlow@clarkson.edu. Web site: http://www.clarkson.edu/cee/.

Clemson University, Graduate School, College of Engineering and Science, Department of Civil Engineering, Clemson, SC 29634. Offers MS, PhD. Part-time programs available. *Faculty:* 22 full-time (2 women), 3 part-time/adjunct (1 woman). *Students:* 115 full-time (27 women), 7 part-time (2 women); includes 6 minority (3 Black or African American, non-Hispanic/Latino; 1 Asian, non-Hispanic/Latino; 1 Hispanic/Latino; 1 Two or more races, non-Hispanic/Latino), 54 international. Average age 27. 211 applicants, 68% accepted, 42 enrolled. In 2011, 47 master's, 9 doctorates awarded. *Degree requirements:* For master's, thesis or alternative, oral exam, seminar; for doctorate, comprehensive exam, thesis/dissertation, oral exam, seminar. *Entrance requirements:* For master's and doctorate, GRE General Test, minimum GPA of 3.0. Additional exam requirements/recommendations for international students: Required—TOEFL. *Application deadline:* For fall admission, 6/1 for domestic students, 4/15 for international students; for spring admission, 9/15 for international students. Applications are processed on a rolling basis. Application fee: $70 ($80 for international students). Electronic applications accepted. *Financial support:* In 2011–12, 98 students received support, including 26 fellowships with full and partial tuition reimbursements available (averaging $10,348 per year), 45 research assistantships with partial tuition reimbursements available (averaging $14,086 per year), 49 teaching assistantships with partial tuition reimbursements available (averaging $9,460 per year); career-related internships or fieldwork, institutionally sponsored loans, scholarships/grants, health care benefits, and unspecified assistantships also available. Support available to part-time students. Financial award application deadline: 2/15; financial award applicants required to submit FAFSA. *Faculty research:* Applied fluid mechanics, construction materials, project management, structural and geotechnical engineering, transportation. *Total annual research expenditures:* $3.2 million. *Unit head:* Dr. Nadim Aziz, Chair, 864-656-3300, Fax: 864-656-2670, E-mail: aziz@clemson.edu. *Application contact:* Dr. Ronald D. Andrus, Graduate Program Coordinator, 864-656-0488, Fax: 864-656-2670, E-mail: randrus@clemson.edu. Web site: http://www.clemson.edu/ce/.

Cleveland State University, College of Graduate Studies, Fenn College of Engineering, Department of Civil and Environmental Engineering, Cleveland, OH 44115. Offers accelerated program civil engineering (MS); accelerated program environmental engineering (MS); civil engineering (MS, D Eng); engineering mechanics (MS); environmental engineering (MS). Part-time and evening/weekend programs available. *Faculty:* 8 full-time (2 women). *Students:* 10 full-time (2 women), 38 part-time (7 women); includes 4 minority (1 Black or African American, non-Hispanic/Latino; 1 American Indian or Alaska Native, non-Hispanic/Latino; 2 Asian, non-Hispanic/Latino), 14 international. Average age 29. 81 applicants, 64% accepted, 11 enrolled. In 2011, 25 master's, 1 doctorate awarded. *Degree requirements:* For master's, project or thesis; for doctorate, comprehensive exam, thesis/dissertation, candidacy and qualifying exams. *Entrance requirements:* For master's, GRE General Test, GRE Subject Test, minimum GPA of 2.75; for doctorate, GRE General Test, GRE Subject Test, minimum GPA of 3.25. Additional exam requirements/recommendations for international students: Required—TOEFL (minimum score 525 paper-based; 197 computer-based). *Application deadline:* For fall admission, 7/15 priority date for domestic students. Applications are processed on a rolling basis. Application fee: $30. *Expenses: Tuition,* state resident: full-time $6416; part-time $494 per credit hour. Tuition, nonresident: full-time $12,074; part-time $929 per credit hour. *Financial support:* In 2011–12, 9 research assistantships with full and partial tuition reimbursements (averaging $3,920 per year) were awarded; teaching assistantships with tuition reimbursements, career-related internships or fieldwork, scholarships/grants, and unspecified assistantships also available. Financial award application deadline: 9/1. *Faculty research:* Solid-waste disposal, constitutive modeling, transportation, safety engineering. *Total annual research expenditures:* $800,000. *Unit head:* Dr. Stephen F. Duffy, Chairperson, 216-687-3874, Fax: 216-687-9280, E-mail: p.bosela@csuohio.edu. *Application contact:* Deborah L. Brown, Interim Assistant Director, Graduate Admissions, 216-523-7572, Fax: 216-687-9214, E-mail: d.l.brown@csuohio.edu. Web site: http://www.csuohio.edu/engineering/civil.

Colorado State University, Graduate School, College of Engineering, Department of Civil and Environmental Engineering, Fort Collins, CO 80523-1372. Offers civil engineering (ME, MS, PhD). Part-time programs available. Postbaccalaureate distance learning degree programs offered (no on-campus study). *Faculty:* 26 full-time (4 women), 5 part-time/adjunct (0 women). *Students:* 97 full-time (25 women), 112 part-time (32 women); includes 14 minority (2 Black or African American, non-Hispanic/Latino; 1 American Indian or Alaska Native, non-Hispanic/Latino; 5 Asian, non-Hispanic/Latino; 4 Hispanic/Latino; 2 Two or more races, non-Hispanic/Latino), 72 international. Average age 30. 253 applicants, 75% accepted, 52 enrolled. In 2011, 37 master's, 13

doctorates awarded. Terminal master's awarded for partial completion of doctoral program. *Degree requirements:* For master's, comprehensive exam (for some programs), thesis with publication (for some programs); for doctorate, comprehensive exam, thesis/dissertation, publication. *Entrance requirements:* For master's, GRE General Test, minimum GPA of 3.0, letters of recommendation, resume; for doctorate, GRE General Test, minimum GPA of 3.0, MS, letters of recommendation, statement of purpose, resume. Additional exam requirements/recommendations for international students: Required—TOEFL (minimum score 550 paper-based; 213 computer-based; 80 iBT); Recommended—IELTS (minimum score 6.5). *Application deadline:* For fall admission, 4/1 priority date for domestic students, 4/1 for international students; for spring admission, 10/1 priority date for domestic students, 10/1 for international students. Applications are processed on a rolling basis. Application fee: $50. Electronic applications accepted. *Expenses:* Tuition, state resident: full-time $7992. Tuition, nonresident: full-time $19,592. *Required fees:* $1735; $58 per credit. *Financial support:* In 2011–12, 68 students received support, including 5 fellowships (averaging $24,122 per year), 47 research assistantships with tuition reimbursements available (averaging $12,616 per year), 16 teaching assistantships with tuition reimbursements available (averaging $9,555 per year); scholarships/grants and unspecified assistantships also available. Financial award application deadline: 2/15; financial award applicants required to submit FAFSA. *Faculty research:* Wind and fluid mechanics, structural engineering and mechanics, hydraulic engineering, geotechnical engineering, environmental and geoenvironmental engineering. *Total annual research expenditures:* $8.1 million. *Unit head:* Dr. Luis Garcia, Head, 970-491-5048, Fax: 970-491-7727, E-mail: luis.garcia@colostate.edu. *Application contact:* Laurie Alburn, Student Advisor, 970-491-5844, Fax: 970-491-7727, E-mail: laurie.alburn@colostate.edu. Web site: http://www.engr.colostate.edu/ce/.

Columbia University, The Fu Foundation School of Engineering and Applied Science, Department of Civil Engineering and Engineering Mechanics, New York, NY 10027. Offers civil engineering (MS, Eng Sc D, PhD, Engr); construction engineering and management (MS); engineering mechanics (MS, Eng Sc D, PhD, Engr). Part-time programs available. Postbaccalaureate distance learning degree programs offered (no on-campus study). *Faculty:* 15 full-time (1 woman), 24 part-time/adjunct (2 women). *Students:* 119 full-time (27 women), 56 part-time (20 women); includes 36 minority (3 Black or African American, non-Hispanic/Latino; 15 Asian, non-Hispanic/Latino; 3 Hispanic/Latino; 15 Two or more races, non-Hispanic/Latino), 93 international. Average age 28. 302 applicants, 36% accepted, 69 enrolled. In 2011, 61 master's, 4 doctorates, 2 other advanced degrees awarded. Terminal master's awarded for partial completion of doctoral program. *Degree requirements:* For doctorate, thesis/dissertation, qualifying exam. *Entrance requirements:* For master's, doctorate, and Engr, GRE General Test. Additional exam requirements/recommendations for international students: Required—TOEFL, IELTS. *Application deadline:* For fall admission, 12/1 priority date for domestic students, 12/1 for international students; for spring admission, 10/1 priority date for domestic students, 10/1 for international students. Application fee: $95. Electronic applications accepted. *Financial support:* In 2011–12, 39 students received support, including 11 fellowships with full tuition reimbursements available (averaging $25,386 per year), 16 research assistantships with full tuition reimbursements available (averaging $31,128 per year), 10 teaching assistantships with full tuition reimbursements available (averaging $31,128 per year); traineeships, health care benefits, and tuition waivers also available. Financial award application deadline: 12/1; financial award applicants required to submit FAFSA. *Faculty research:* Structural dynamics, structural health and monitoring, fatigue and fracture mechanics, geo-enviornmental engineering, multiscale science and engineering. *Unit head:* Dr. Raimondo Betti, Professor and Department Chairman, 212-854-6388, E-mail: betti@civil.columbia.edu. *Application contact:* Dr. Rene B. Testa, Professor, 212-854-6383, Fax: 212-854-6267, E-mail: testa@civil.columbia.edu. Web site: http://www.civil.columbia.edu/.

Concordia University, School of Graduate Studies, Faculty of Engineering and Computer Science, Department of Building, Civil and Environmental Engineering, Montréal, QC H3G 1M8, Canada. Offers building engineering (M Eng, MA Sc, PhD, Certificate); civil engineering (M Eng, MA Sc, PhD); environmental engineering (Certificate). *Degree requirements:* For master's, thesis or alternative; for doctorate, comprehensive exam, thesis/dissertation. *Faculty research:* Structural engineering, geotechnical engineering, water resources and fluid engineering, transportation engineering, systems engineering.

Cooper Union for the Advancement of Science and Art, Albert Nerken School of Engineering, New York, NY 10003-7120. Offers chemical engineering (ME); civil engineering (ME); electrical engineering (ME); mechanical engineering (ME). Part-time programs available. *Faculty:* 27 full-time (1 woman), 15 part-time/adjunct (2 women). *Students:* 39 full-time (10 women), 17 part-time (3 women); includes 18 minority (1 Black or African American, non-Hispanic/Latino; 1 American Indian or Alaska Native, non-Hispanic/Latino; 15 Asian, non-Hispanic/Latino; 1 Hispanic/Latino), 11 international. *Degree requirements:* For master's, thesis. *Entrance requirements:* For master's, GRE, BE, minimum GPA of 3.5. Additional exam requirements/recommendations for international students: Required—TOEFL (minimum score 600 paper-based; 250 computer-based; 100 iBT). *Application deadline:* For fall admission, 2/15 for domestic and international students. Application fee: $65. *Expenses: Tuition:* Full-time $37,500. *Required fees:* $825 per semester. *Financial support:* Fellowships with full tuition reimbursements, career-related internships or fieldwork, Federal Work-Study, tuition waivers (full), and full-tuition scholarships for all admitted students available. Support available to part-time students. Financial award application deadline: 5/1; financial award applicants required to submit CSS PROFILE or FAFSA. *Faculty research:* Civil infrastructure, imaging and sensing technology, biomedical engineering, encryption technology, process engineering. *Unit head:* Dr. Simon Ben-Avi, Acting Dean, 212-353-4286, E-mail: benavi@cooper.edu. *Application contact:* Student Contact, 212-353-4120, E-mail: admissions@cooper.edu. Web site: http://cooper.edu/engineering.

Cornell University, Graduate School, Graduate Fields of Engineering, Field of Civil and Environmental Engineering, Ithaca, NY 14853-0001. Offers engineering management (M Eng, MS, PhD); environmental engineering (M Eng, MS, PhD); environmental fluid mechanics and hydrology (M Eng, MS, PhD); environmental systems engineering (M Eng, MS, PhD); geotechnical engineering (M Eng, MS, PhD); remote sensing (M Eng, MS, PhD); structural engineering (M Eng, MS, PhD); structural mechanics (M Eng, MS); transportation engineering (MS, PhD); transportation systems engineering (M Eng); water resource systems (M Eng, MS, PhD). *Faculty:* 39 full-time (4 women). *Students:* 143 full-time (49 women); includes 20 minority (6 Black or African American, non-Hispanic/Latino; 1 American Indian or Alaska Native, non-Hispanic/Latino; 9 Asian, non-Hispanic/Latino; 4 Hispanic/Latino), 72 international. Average age 25. 574 applicants, 47% accepted, 100 enrolled. In 2011, 88 master's, 13 doctorates awarded. Terminal master's awarded for partial completion of doctoral program. *Degree requirements:* For master's, thesis (MS); for doctorate, comprehensive exam, thesis/dissertation. *Entrance requirements:* For master's and doctorate, GRE General Test (recommended), 2 letters of recommendation. Additional exam requirements/recommendations for international students: Required—TOEFL (minimum score 600 paper-based; 250 computer-based; 77 iBT). *Application deadline:* For fall admission, 1/15 priority date for domestic students; for spring admission, 10/15 for domestic students. Application fee: $95. Electronic applications accepted. *Financial support:* In 2011–12, 50 students received support, including 20 fellowships with full tuition reimbursements available, 27 research assistantships with full tuition reimbursements available, 17 teaching assistantships with full tuition reimbursements available; institutionally sponsored loans, scholarships/grants, health care benefits, tuition waivers (full and partial), and unspecified assistantships also available. Financial award applicants required to submit FAFSA. *Faculty research:* Environmental engineering, geotechnical engineering, remote sensing, environmental fluid mechanics and hydrology, structural engineering. *Unit head:* Director of Graduate Studies, 607-255-7560, Fax: 607-255-9004. *Application contact:* Graduate Field Assistant, 607-255-7560, Fax: 607-255-9004, E-mail: cee_grad@cornell.edu. Web site: http://www.gradschool.cornell.edu/fields.php?id-27&a-2.

Dalhousie University, Faculty of Engineering, Department of Civil and Resource Engineering, Halifax, NS B3J 2X4, Canada. Offers M Eng, MA Sc, PhD. *Degree requirements:* For master's, thesis; for doctorate, thesis/dissertation. *Entrance requirements:* Additional exam requirements/recommendations for international students: Required—TOEFL, IELTS, CANTEST, CAEL, or Michigan English Language Assessment Battery. Electronic applications accepted. *Faculty research:* Environmental/water resources, bridge engineering, geotechnical engineering, pavement design and management/highway materials, composite materials.

Drexel University, College of Engineering, Department of Civil, Architectural, and Environmental Engineering, Program in Civil Engineering, Philadelphia, PA 19104-2875. Offers MS, PhD. Part-time and evening/weekend programs available. *Degree requirements:* For master's, thesis optional; for doctorate, thesis/dissertation. *Entrance requirements:* For master's, minimum GPA of 3.0; for doctorate, minimum GPA of 3.5, MS in civil engineering. Additional exam requirements/recommendations for international students: Required—TOEFL. Electronic applications accepted.

Duke University, Graduate School, Pratt School of Engineering, Department of Civil and Environmental Engineering, Durham, NC 27708. Offers civil and environmental engineering (MS, PhD); environmental engineering (MS, PhD). Part-time programs available. Terminal master's awarded for partial completion of doctoral program. *Degree requirements:* For doctorate, thesis/dissertation. *Entrance requirements:* For master's and doctorate, GRE General Test. Additional exam requirements/recommendations for international students: Required—TOEFL (minimum score 550 paper-based; 213 computer-based; 83 iBT), IELTS (minimum score 7). Electronic applications accepted. *Expenses: Tuition:* Full-time $40,720. *Required fees:* $3107.

Duke University, Graduate School, Pratt School of Engineering, Master of Engineering Program, Durham, NC 27708-0271. Offers biomedical engineering (M Eng); civil engineering (M Eng); electrical and computer engineering (M Eng); environmental engineering (M Eng); materials science and engineering (M Eng); mechanical engineering (M Eng); photonics and optical sciences (M Eng). Part-time programs available. *Entrance requirements:* For master's, GRE General Test, resume, 3 letters of recommendation, statement of purpose. Additional exam requirements/recommendations for international students: Required—TOEFL. *Expenses: Tuition:* Full-time $40,720. *Required fees:* $3107.

École Polytechnique de Montréal, Graduate Programs, Department of Civil, Geological and Mining Engineering, Montréal, QC H3C 3A7, Canada. Offers civil, geological and mining engineering (DESS); environmental engineering (M Eng, M Sc A, PhD); geotechnical engineering (M Eng, M Sc A, PhD); hydraulics engineering (M Eng, M Sc A, PhD); structural engineering (M Eng, M Sc A, PhD); transportation engineering (M Eng, M Sc A, PhD). Part-time programs available. *Degree requirements:* For master's, one foreign language, thesis; for doctorate, one foreign language, thesis/dissertation. *Entrance requirements:* For master's, minimum GPA of 2.75; for doctorate, minimum GPA of 3.0. *Faculty research:* Water resources management, characteristics of building materials, aging of dams, pollution control.

Florida Agricultural and Mechanical University, Division of Graduate Studies, Research, and Continuing Education, FAMU-FSU College of Engineering, Department of Civil and Environmental Engineering, Tallahassee, FL 32307-3200. Offers civil engineering (MS, PhD); environmental engineering (MS, PhD). *Degree requirements:* For master's, comprehensive exam, thesis optional; for doctorate, comprehensive exam, thesis/dissertation. *Entrance requirements:* For master's, GRE General Test, minimum GPA of 3.0; for doctorate, GRE General Test, minimum GPA of 3.0, letters of recommendation (3). Additional exam requirements/recommendations for international students: Required—TOEFL (minimum score 550 paper-based; 213 computer-based). *Faculty research:* Geotechnical, environmental, hydraulic, construction materials, and structures.

Florida Atlantic University, College of Engineering and Computer Science, Department of Civil, Environmental and Geomatics Engineering, Boca Raton, FL 33431-0991. Offers civil engineering (MS). Part-time and evening/weekend programs available. *Faculty:* 15 full-time (3 women). *Students:* 17 full-time (6 women), 11 part-time (0 women); includes 11 minority (3 Black or African American, non-Hispanic/Latino; 1 Asian, non-Hispanic/Latino; 5 Hispanic/Latino; 2 Two or more races, non-Hispanic/Latino), 7 international. Average age 26. 45 applicants, 42% accepted, 8 enrolled. In 2011, 12 master's awarded. *Degree requirements:* For master's, thesis optional. *Entrance requirements:* For master's, GRE General Test, minimum GPA of 3.0 in last 60 hours of undergraduate course work. Additional exam requirements/recommendations for international students: Required—TOEFL (minimum score 550 paper-based; 213 computer-based). *Application deadline:* For fall admission, 7/1 priority date for domestic students, 2/15 for international students; for spring admission, 11/1 for domestic students, 7/15 for international students. Applications are processed on a rolling basis. Application fee: $30. *Expenses: Tuition, area resident:* Part-time $343.02 per credit hour. Tuition, state resident: full-time $8232. Tuition, nonresident: full-time $23,931; part-time $997.14 per credit hour. *Financial support:* Research assistantships with full tuition reimbursements, teaching assistantships with full tuition reimbursements, career-related internships or fieldwork, Federal Work-Study, scholarships/grants, and unspecified assistantships available. Financial award applicants required to submit FAFSA. *Faculty research:* Structures, geotechnical engineering, environmental and water resources engineering, transportation engineering, materials. *Unit head:* Dr. Pete D. Scarlatos, Chair, 561-297-0466, Fax: 561-297-0493, E-mail: scarlatos@fau.edu. *Application contact:* Dr. Frederick Bloetscher, Assistant Professor, 561-297-0744, E-mail: fbloetscher@civil.fau.edu. Web site: http://www.cege.fau.edu/.

Florida Institute of Technology, Graduate Programs, College of Engineering, Civil Engineering Department, Melbourne, FL 32901-6975. Offers MS, PhD. Part-time programs available. *Faculty:* 4 full-time (0 women). *Students:* 22 full-time (3 women), 4 part-time (3 women); includes 2 minority (1 Asian, non-Hispanic/Latino; 1 Hispanic/Latino), 18 international. Average age 32. 61 applicants, 51% accepted, 5 enrolled. In 2011, 3 master's, 1 doctorate awarded. *Degree requirements:* For master's, comprehensive exam (for some programs), thesis optional, teaching or final examinations; for doctorate, comprehensive exam, thesis/dissertation, research project, preliminary examination. *Entrance requirements:* For master's, 2 letters of recommendation, minimum GPA of 3.0, statement of objectives; for doctorate, 3 letters of recommendation, minimum GPA of 3.2, resume, statement of objectives. Additional exam requirements/recommendations for international students: Required—TOEFL (minimum score 550 paper-based; 213 computer-based; 79 iBT). *Application deadline:* For fall admission, 4/1 for international students; for spring admission, 9/30 for international students. Applications are processed on a rolling basis. Electronic applications accepted. *Expenses: Tuition:* Full-time $19,620; part-time $1090 per credit hour. Tuition and fees vary according to campus/location. *Financial support:* In 2011–12, 4 research assistantships with full and partial tuition reimbursements (averaging $6,388 per year), 4 teaching assistantships with full and partial tuition reimbursements (averaging $5,205 per year) were awarded; career-related internships or fieldwork, institutionally sponsored loans, tuition waivers (partial), unspecified assistantships, and tuition remissions also available. Support available to part-time students. Financial award application deadline: 3/1; financial award applicants required to submit FAFSA. *Faculty research:* Groundwater and surface water modeling, pavements, waste materials, in situ soil testing, fiber optic sensors. *Total annual research expenditures:* $430,162. *Unit head:* Dr. Ashok Pandit, Department Head, 321-674-7151, Fax: 321-768-7565, E-mail: apandit@fit.edu. *Application contact:* Cheryl A. Brown, Associate Director of Graduate Admissions, 321-674-7581, Fax: 321-723-9468, E-mail: cbrown@fit.edu. Web site: http://coe.fit.edu/civil/.

Florida International University, College of Engineering and Computing, Department of Civil and Environmental Engineering, Program in Civil Engineering, Miami, FL 33175. Offers MS, PhD. Part-time and evening/weekend programs available. Postbaccalaureate distance learning degree programs offered (no on-campus study). *Degree requirements:* For master's, thesis optional; for doctorate, comprehensive exam, thesis/dissertation. *Entrance requirements:* For master's, bachelor's degree in related field, minimum GPA of 3.0; for doctorate, GRE General Test, minimum graduate GPA of 3.3, master's degree, resume, letters of recommendation, statement of objectives. Additional exam requirements/recommendations for international students: Required—TOEFL (minimum score 550 paper-based; 80 iBT). Electronic applications accepted. *Faculty research:* Structural engineering, wind engineering, sustainable infrastructure engineering, water resources engineering, transportation engineering.

Florida State University, The Graduate School, FAMU-FSU College of Engineering, Department of Civil and Environmental Engineering, Tallahassee, FL 32306. Offers M Eng, MS, PhD. Part-time programs available. *Faculty:* 19 full-time (3 women), 6 part-time/adjunct (0 women). *Students:* 44 full-time (13 women), 13 part-time (2 women); includes 13 minority (6 Black or African American, non-Hispanic/Latino; 2 Asian, non-Hispanic/Latino; 5 Hispanic/Latino), 17 international. Average age 23. 82 applicants, 40% accepted, 17 enrolled. In 2011, 14 master's, 3 doctorates awarded. *Degree requirements:* For master's, thesis optional; for doctorate, thesis/dissertation. *Entrance requirements:* For master's, GRE General Test (minimum score 1000 in old version; 30% Verbal Reasoning/65% Quantitative Reasoning for MS, 35% for Verbal Reasoning and 65% for Quantitative Reasoning for PhD in new format), BS in engineering or related field, minimum GPA of 3.0; for doctorate, GRE General Test (minimum scores of 35% for Verbal Reasoning and 65% for Quantitative Reasoning for PhD), master's degree in engineering or related field, minimum GPA of 3.0. Additional exam requirements/recommendations for international students: Required—TOEFL (minimum score 550 paper-based; 213 computer-based; 80 iBT). *Application deadline:* For fall admission, 7/1 for domestic and international students; for spring admission, 11/1 for domestic and international students. Applications are processed on a rolling basis. Application fee: $30. *Expenses:* Tuition, state resident: full-time $9474; part-time $350.88 per credit hour. Tuition, nonresident: full-time $16,236; part-time $601.34 per credit hour. *Required fees:* $630 per semester. One-time fee: $20. Tuition and fees vary according to course load and campus/location. *Financial support:* In 2011–12, 25 students received support, including 2 fellowships (averaging $12,000 per year), 18 research assistantships with full tuition reimbursements available (averaging $15,000 per year), 26 teaching assistantships with full tuition reimbursements available (averaging $15,000 per year); Federal Work-Study, tuition waivers (full), and unspecified assistantships also available. Financial award application deadline: 6/15; financial award applicants required to submit FAFSA. *Faculty research:* Tidal hydraulics, temperature effects on bridge girders, codes for coastal construction, field performance of pine bridges, river basin management, transportation pavement design, soil dynamics, structural analysis. *Total annual research expenditures:* $1.3 million. *Unit head:* Dr. Kamal S. Tawfiq, Chair and Professor, 850-410-6143, Fax: 850-410-6142, E-mail: tawfiq@eng.fsu.edu. *Application contact:* Johnnye Belinda Morris, Office Manager, 850-410-6139, Fax: 850-410-6142, E-mail: bmorris@eng.fsu.edu. Web site: http://www.eng.fsu.edu/cee/.

George Mason University, Volgenau School of Engineering, Department of Civil, Environmental, and Infrastructure Engineering, Fairfax, VA 22030. Offers civil and infrastructure engineering (MS, PhD); civil infrastructure and security engineering (Certificate); leading technical enterprises (Certificate); sustainability and the environment (Certificate); water resources engineering (Certificate). *Faculty:* 9 full-time (3 women), 22 part-time/adjunct (3 women). *Students:* 26 full-time (9 women), 59 part-time (14 women); includes 18 minority (5 Black or African American, non-Hispanic/Latino; 5 Asian, non-Hispanic/Latino; 7 Hispanic/Latino; 1 Two or more races, non-Hispanic/Latino), 10 international. Average age 31. 73 applicants, 63% accepted, 29 enrolled. In 2011, 16 master's, 7 other advanced degrees awarded. *Degree requirements:* For master's, thesis (for some programs), 30 credits, departmental seminars; for doctorate, thesis/dissertation, qualifying exams. *Entrance requirements:* For master's, GRE, photocopy of passport; 2 official college transcripts; resume; official bank statement; proof of financial support; expanded goals statement; self-evaluation form; BS in engineering or other related science; 3 letters of recommendation; for doctorate, GRE (for those who received degree outside of the U.S.), photocopy of passport; 2 official college transcripts; resume; official bank statement; proof of financial support; expanded goals statement; self-evaluation form; baccalaureate degree in engineering or related science; master's degree (preferred); 3 letters of recommendation; for Certificate, BS in related field; photocopy of passport; 2 official college transcripts; resume; official bank statement; proof of financial support; expanded goals statement; self evaluation form; 3 letters of recommendation. Additional exam requirements/recommendations for international students: Required—TOEFL (minimum score 575 paper-based; 230 computer-based; 88 iBT), IELTS, Pearson Test of English. *Application deadline:* For fall admission, 1/15 priority date for domestic students; for spring admission, 8/1 priority date for domestic students. Application fee: $65 ($80 for international students). Electronic applications accepted. *Expenses:* Tuition, state resident: full-time $8750; part-time $364.58 per credit. Tuition, nonresident: full-time

$24,092; part-time $1003.83 per credit. *Required fees:* $2514; $104.75 per credit. *Financial support:* In 2011–12, 17 students received support, including 3 fellowships (averaging $18,000 per year), 2 research assistantships with full and partial tuition reimbursements available (averaging $17,893 per year), 12 teaching assistantships with full and partial tuition reimbursements available (averaging $8,884 per year); career-related internships or fieldwork, Federal Work-Study, scholarships/grants, unspecified assistantships, and health care benefits (full-time research or teaching assistantship recipients) also available. Support available to part-time students. Financial award application deadline: 3/1; financial award applicants required to submit FAFSA. *Faculty research:* Evolutionary design, infrastructure security, intelligent transportation systems, national transportation networks, water quality modeling. *Total annual research expenditures:* $655,402. *Unit head:* Dr. Deborah J. Goodings, Chair, 703-993-1675, Fax: 703-993-9790, E-mail: goodings@gmu.edu. *Application contact:* Nicole Jerome, Administrative Assistant, 703-993-1675, Fax: 703-993-9790, E-mail: njerome@gmu.edu. Web site: http://civil.gmu.edu/.

The George Washington University, School of Engineering and Applied Science, Department of Civil and Environmental Engineering, Washington, DC 20052. Offers MS, D Sc, App Sc, Engr. Part-time and evening/weekend programs available. *Faculty:* 11 full-time (2 women), 5 part-time/adjunct (0 women). *Students:* 27 full-time (7 women), 26 part-time (6 women); includes 7 minority (3 Black or African American, non-Hispanic/Latino; 4 Hispanic/Latino), 27 international. Average age 29. 111 applicants, 59% accepted, 10 enrolled. In 2011, 7 master's, 4 doctorates awarded. *Degree requirements:* For master's, thesis optional; for doctorate, thesis/dissertation, final and qualifying exams. *Entrance requirements:* For master's, appropriate bachelor's degree, minimum GPA of 3.0; for doctorate, GRE (if highest earned degree is BS), appropriate bachelor's or master's degree, minimum GPA of 3.4; for other advanced degree, appropriate master's degree, minimum GPA of 3.0. Additional exam requirements/recommendations for international students: Required—TOEFL or The George Washington University English as a Foreign Language Test. *Application deadline:* For fall admission, 3/1 priority date for domestic students; for spring admission, 10/1 for domestic students. Applications are processed on a rolling basis. Application fee: $75. *Financial support:* In 2011–12, 42 students received support. Fellowships with tuition reimbursements available, research assistantships, teaching assistantships with tuition reimbursements available, career-related internships or fieldwork, Federal Work-Study, institutionally sponsored loans, and tuition waivers available. Financial award application deadline: 3/1; financial award applicants required to submit FAFSA. *Faculty research:* Computer-integrated manufacturing, materials engineering, electronic materials, fatigue and fracture, reliability. *Unit head:* Dr. Kim Roddis, Chair, 202-994-8515, Fax: 202-994-0127, E-mail: roddis@gwu.edu. *Application contact:* Adina Lav, Marketing, Recruiting and Admissions, 202-994-5827, Fax: 202-994-0909, E-mail: engineering@gwu.edu. Web site: http://www.cee.seas.gwu.edu/.

Georgia Institute of Technology, Graduate Studies and Research, College of Engineering, School of Civil and Environmental Engineering, Program in Civil Engineering, Atlanta, GA 30332-0001. Offers MS, MSCE, PhD. Part-time programs available. Terminal master's awarded for partial completion of doctoral program. *Degree requirements:* For doctorate, thesis/dissertation. *Entrance requirements:* For master's, GRE, minimum GPA of 3.0; for doctorate, GRE, minimum GPA of 3.2. Additional exam requirements/recommendations for international students: Required—TOEFL. *Faculty research:* Structural analysis, fluid mechanics, geotechnical engineering, construction management, transportation engineering.

Graduate School and University Center of the City University of New York, Graduate Studies, Program in Engineering, New York, NY 10016-4039. Offers biomedical engineering (PhD); chemical engineering (PhD); civil engineering (PhD); electrical engineering (PhD); mechanical engineering (PhD). *Degree requirements:* For doctorate, thesis/dissertation. *Entrance requirements:* For doctorate, GRE General Test. Additional exam requirements/recommendations for international students: Required—TOEFL. Electronic applications accepted.

Howard University, College of Engineering, Architecture, and Computer Sciences, School of Engineering and Computer Science, Department of Civil Engineering, Washington, DC 20059-0002. Offers M Eng. Offered through the Graduate School of Arts and Sciences. *Degree requirements:* For master's, comprehensive exam, thesis. *Entrance requirements:* For master's, GRE General Test, minimum GPA of 3.0, bachelor's degree in engineering or related field. Additional exam requirements/recommendations for international students: Required—TOEFL. Electronic applications accepted. *Faculty research:* Modeling of concrete, structures, transportation planning, structural analysis, environmental and water resources.

Idaho State University, Office of Graduate Studies, College of Science and Engineering, Civil and Environmental Engineering Department, Pocatello, ID 83209-8060. Offers civil engineering (MS); environmental engineering (MS); environmental science and management (MS). Part-time programs available. *Degree requirements:* For master's, comprehensive exam (for some programs), thesis optional, thesis project, 2 semesters of seminar. *Entrance requirements:* For master's, GRE. Additional exam requirements/recommendations for international students: Required—TOEFL (minimum score 550 paper-based; 213 computer-based; 80 iBT). Electronic applications accepted. *Faculty research:* Floor vibration investigations, earthquake engineering, base isolation systems and seismic risk assessment, infrastructure revitalization (building foundations and damage, bridge structures, highways, and dams), slope stability and soil erosion, pavement rehabilitation, computational fluid dynamics and flood control structures, microbial fuel cells, water treatment and water quality modeling, environmental risk assessment, biotechnology, nanotechnology.

Illinois Institute of Technology, Graduate College, Armour College of Engineering, Department of Civil, Architectural and Environmental Engineering, Chicago, IL 60616-3793. Offers architectural engineering (M Arch E); civil engineering (MS, PhD), including architectural engineeering (MS), construction engineering and management (MS), geoenvironmental engineering (MS), geotechnical engineering (MS), structural engineering (MS), transportation engineering (MS); construction engineering and management (MCEM); environmental engineering (M Env E, PhD); geoenvironmental engineering (M Geoenv E); geotechnical engineering (MGE); public works (MPW); structural engineering (MSE); transportation engineering (M Trans E). Part-time and evening/weekend programs available. Postbaccalaureate distance learning degree programs offered (minimal on-campus study). Terminal master's awarded for partial completion of doctoral program. *Degree requirements:* For master's, thesis (for some programs); for doctorate, comprehensive exam, thesis/dissertation. *Entrance requirements:* For master's, GRE General Test (minimum score 900 Quantitative and Verbal, 2.5 Analytical Writing), minimum undergraduate GPA of 3.0; for doctorate, GRE General Test (minimum score 1000 Quantitative and Verbal, 3.0 Analytical Writing), minimum undergraduate GPA of 3.0. Additional exam requirements/recommendations for international students: Required—TOEFL (minimum score 523 paper-based; 70 iBT); Recommended—IELTS (minimum score 5.5). Electronic applications accepted. *Faculty research:* Structural, architectural, geotechnical and geoenvironmental engineering; construction engineering and management; transportation engineering; environmental engineering and public works.

Instituto Tecnológico y de Estudios Superiores de Monterrey, Campus Monterrey, Graduate and Research Division, Programs in Engineering, Monterrey, Mexico. Offers applied statistics (M Eng); artificial intelligence (PhD); automation engineering (M Eng); chemical engineering (M Eng); civil engineering (M Eng); electrical engineering (M Eng); electronic engineering (M Eng); environmental engineering (M Eng); industrial engineering (M Eng, PhD); manufacturing engineering (M Eng); mechanical engineering (M Eng); systems and quality engineering (M Eng). M Eng program offered jointly with University of Waterloo; PhD in industrial engineering with Texas A&M University. Part-time and evening/weekend programs available. Terminal master's awarded for partial completion of doctoral program. *Degree requirements:* For master's, one foreign language, thesis; for doctorate, one foreign language, thesis/dissertation. *Entrance requirements:* For master's, EXADEP; for doctorate, GRE, master's degree in related field. Additional exam requirements/recommendations for international students: Required—TOEFL. *Faculty research:* Flexible manufacturing cells, materials, statistical methods, environmental prevention, control and evaluation.

Iowa State University of Science and Technology, Department of Civil and Construction Engineering, Ames, IA 50011-3232. Offers civil engineering (MS, PhD), including civil engineering materials, construction engineering and management, environmental engineering, geometronics, geotechnical engineering, structural engineering, transportation engineering. *Degree requirements:* For master's, thesis or alternative; for doctorate, thesis/dissertation. *Entrance requirements:* For master's and doctorate, GRE General Test. Additional exam requirements/recommendations for international students: Required—TOEFL (minimum score 550 paper-based; 82 iBT), IELTS (minimum score 6.5). *Application deadline:* For fall admission, 2/1 priority date for domestic students, 2/1 for international students; for spring admission, 8/1 priority date for domestic students, 8/1 for international students. Applications are processed on a rolling basis. Application fee: $40 ($90 for international students). Electronic applications accepted. *Unit head:* Dr. Sri Sritharan, Director of Graduate Education, 515-294-4972, Fax: 515-294-8216, E-mail: ccee-grad-inquiry@iastate.edu. *Application contact:* Kathy Petersen, Director of Graduate Education, 515-294-4975, Fax: 515-294-8216, E-mail: ccee-grad-inquiry@iastate.edu. Web site: http://www.ccee.iastate.edu/.

The Johns Hopkins University, Engineering Program for Professionals, Part-time Program in Civil Engineering, Baltimore, MD 21218-2699. Offers MCE. Part-time and evening/weekend programs available. Electronic applications accepted.

The Johns Hopkins University, Whiting School of Engineering, Department of Civil Engineering, Baltimore, MD 21218. Offers MCE, MSE, PhD. Terminal master's awarded for partial completion of doctoral program. *Degree requirements:* For master's, thesis (for some programs); for doctorate, comprehensive exam, thesis/dissertation, qualifying and oral exams. *Entrance requirements:* For master's and doctorate, GRE General Test. Additional exam requirements/recommendations for international students: Required—TOEFL. Electronic applications accepted. *Faculty research:* Geotechnical engineering, structural engineering, structural mechanics, geomechanics, probabilistic modeling.

Kansas State University, Graduate School, College of Engineering, Department of Civil Engineering, Manhattan, KS 66506. Offers MS, PhD. Postbaccalaureate distance learning degree programs offered (no on-campus study). *Faculty:* 14 full-time (2 women), 2 part-time/adjunct (0 women). *Students:* 35 full-time (8 women), 40 part-time (3 women); includes 5 minority (2 Black or African American, non-Hispanic/Latino; 1 Asian, non-Hispanic/Latino; 2 Hispanic/Latino), 23 international. Average age 30. 77 applicants, 47% accepted, 14 enrolled. In 2011, 27 degrees awarded. *Degree requirements:* For master's, thesis or alternative; for doctorate, thesis/dissertation. *Entrance requirements:* For master's, GRE General Test, bachelor's degree or course work in related engineering fields; for doctorate, GRE General Test. Additional exam requirements/recommendations for international students: Required—TOEFL. *Application deadline:* For fall admission, 2/1 priority date for domestic students, 2/1 for international students; for spring admission, 8/1 priority date for domestic students, 8/1 for international students. Applications are processed on a rolling basis. Application fee: $40 ($55 for international students). Electronic applications accepted. *Financial support:* In 2011–12, 31 research assistantships (averaging $11,722 per year), 6 teaching assistantships (averaging $11,700 per year) were awarded; institutionally sponsored loans, scholarships/grants, and tuition waivers also available. Support available to part-time students. Financial award application deadline: 3/1; financial award applicants required to submit FAFSA. *Faculty research:* Transportation and materials engineering, water resources engineering, environmental engineering, geotechnical engineering, structural engineering. *Total annual research expenditures:* $2.4 million. *Unit head:* Alok Bhandari, Interim Head, 785-532-1586, Fax: 785-532-7717, E-mail: bhandari@ksu.edu. *Application contact:* Dunja Peric, Director, 785-532-2468, Fax: 785-532-7717, E-mail: peric@ksu.edu. Web site: http://www.ce.ksu.edu/.

Lamar University, College of Graduate Studies, College of Engineering, Department of Civil Engineering, Beaumont, TX 77710. Offers civil engineering (ME, MES, DE); environmental engineering (MS); environmental studies (MS). Part-time programs available. *Faculty:* 7 full-time (1 woman), 1 part-time/adjunct (0 women). *Students:* 34 full-time (6 women), 13 part-time (4 women); includes 5 minority (1 Black or African American, non-Hispanic/Latino; 3 Asian, non-Hispanic/Latino; 1 Hispanic/Latino), 34 international. Average age 28. 43 applicants, 84% accepted, 9 enrolled. In 2011, 30 master's, 3 doctorates awarded. *Degree requirements:* For master's, thesis optional; for doctorate, thesis/dissertation. *Entrance requirements:* For master's and doctorate, GRE General Test. Additional exam requirements/recommendations for international students: Required—TOEFL. *Application deadline:* For fall admission, 5/15 priority date for domestic students; for spring admission, 10/1 priority date for domestic students. Applications are processed on a rolling basis. Application fee: $25 ($50 for international students). *Expenses:* Tuition, state resident: full-time $5430; part-time $272 per credit hour. Tuition, nonresident: full-time $11,540; part-time $577 per credit hour. *Required fees:* $1916. *Financial support:* In 2011–12, 45 fellowships with partial tuition reimbursements (averaging $1,000 per year), 10 research assistantships with partial tuition reimbursements (averaging $7,200 per year), 3 teaching assistantships with partial tuition reimbursements (averaging $7,200 per year) were awarded; scholarships/grants and tuition waivers (partial) also available. Financial award application deadline: 4/1. *Faculty research:* Environmental remediations, construction productivity, geotechnical soil stabilization, lake/reservoir hydrodynamics, air pollution. *Unit head:* Dr. Enno Koehn, Chair, 409-880-8759, Fax: 409-880-8121, E-mail: koehneu@hal.lamar.edu. *Application contact:* Sandy Drane, Coordinator of Graduate Admissions, 409-880-8356, Fax: 409-880-8414, E-mail: gradmissions@hal.lamar.edu.

Lawrence Technological University, College of Engineering, Southfield, MI 48075-1058. Offers architectural engineering (MS); automotive engineering (MS); civil engineering (MA, MS); construction engineering management (MA); electrical and computer engineering (MS); engineering management (MEM); industrial engineering

(MS); manufacturing systems (ME, DE); mechanical engineering (MS, DE); mechatronic systems engineering (MS). Part-time and evening/weekend programs available. *Faculty:* 25 full-time (4 women), 20 part-time/adjunct (1 woman). *Students:* 8 full-time (0 women), 332 part-time (52 women); includes 58 minority (21 Black or African American, non-Hispanic/Latino; 1 American Indian or Alaska Native, non-Hispanic/Latino; 32 Asian, non-Hispanic/Latino; 2 Hispanic/Latino; 2 Two or more races, non-Hispanic/Latino), 84 international. Average age 32. 652 applicants, 44% accepted, 70 enrolled. In 2011, 127 master's, 2 doctorates awarded. *Degree requirements:* For master's, thesis (for some programs). *Entrance requirements:* Additional exam requirements/recommendations for international students: Required—TOEFL (minimum score 550 paper-based; 213 computer-based; 79 iBT). *Application deadline:* For fall admission, 7/27 priority date for domestic students, 5/23 for international students; for spring admission, 11/15 priority date for domestic students, 11/15 for international students. Applications are processed on a rolling basis. Application fee: $50. Electronic applications accepted. *Financial support:* In 2011–12, 68 students received support, including 6 research assistantships (averaging $8,078 per year); Federal Work-Study and institutionally sponsored loans also available. Support available to part-time students. Financial award application deadline: 4/1; financial award applicants required to submit FAFSA. *Faculty research:* Advanced composite materials in bridges, strengthening existing bridges with carbon and glass fiber sheets, development of drive shafts using composite materials. *Unit head:* Dr. Nabil Grace, Dean, 248-204-2500, Fax: 248-204-2509, E-mail: engrdean@ltu.edu. *Application contact:* Jane Rohrback, Director of Admissions, 248-204-3160, Fax: 248-204-2228, E-mail: admissions@ltu.edu. Web site: http://www.ltu.edu/engineering/index.asp.

Lehigh University, P.C. Rossin College of Engineering and Applied Science, Department of Civil and Environmental Engineering, Bethlehem, PA 18015. Offers civil engineering (M Eng, MS, PhD); environmental engineering (MS, PhD); structural engineering (M Eng, MS, PhD). Part-time programs available. *Faculty:* 15 full-time (3 women), 2 part-time/adjunct (0 women). *Students:* 98 full-time (33 women), 11 part-time (0 women); includes 5 minority (1 Black or African American, non-Hispanic/Latino; 1 Asian, non-Hispanic/Latino; 3 Hispanic/Latino), 67 international. Average age 26. 655 applicants, 31% accepted, 25 enrolled. In 2011, 40 master's, 7 doctorates awarded. Terminal master's awarded for partial completion of doctoral program. *Degree requirements:* For master's, thesis (for some programs); for doctorate, comprehensive exam, thesis/dissertation. *Entrance requirements:* For master's and doctorate, GRE. Additional exam requirements/recommendations for international students: Required—TOEFL (minimum score 550 paper-based; 213 computer-based; 79 iBT). *Application deadline:* For fall admission, 7/15 priority date for domestic students, 7/15 for international students; for spring admission, 12/1 priority date for domestic students, 12/1 for international students. Applications are processed on a rolling basis. Application fee: $75. Electronic applications accepted. *Expenses:* Contact institution. *Financial support:* In 2011–12, 35 students received support, including 8 fellowships with full tuition reimbursements available (averaging $18,560 per year), 7 research assistantships with full tuition reimbursements available (averaging $22,350 per year), 7 teaching assistantships with full tuition reimbursements available (averaging $18,560 per year); institutionally sponsored loans, scholarships/grants, tuition waivers, and unspecified assistantships also available. Financial award application deadline: 1/15. *Faculty research:* Structural engineering, geotechnical engineering, water resources engineering, environmental engineering. *Total annual research expenditures:* $5.4 million. *Unit head:* Dr. Sibel Pamukcu, 610-758-3220, Fax: 610-758-6405, E-mail: sp01@lehigh.edu. *Application contact:* Prisca Vidanage, Graduate Coordinator, 610-758-3530, Fax: 610-758-6405, E-mail: pmv1@lehigh.edu. Web site: http://www.lehigh.edu/~incee/.

Louisiana State University and Agricultural and Mechanical College, Graduate School, College of Engineering, Department of Civil and Environmental Engineering, Baton Rouge, LA 70803. Offers environmental engineering (MSCE, PhD); geotechnical engineering (MSCE, PhD); structural engineering and mechanics (MSCE, PhD); transportation engineering (MSCE, PhD); water resources (MSCE, PhD). Part-time programs available. *Faculty:* 25 full-time (2 women). *Students:* 90 full-time (23 women), 34 part-time (8 women); includes 11 minority (4 Black or African American, non-Hispanic/Latino; 1 American Indian or Alaska Native, non-Hispanic/Latino; 4 Asian, non-Hispanic/Latino; 2 Hispanic/Latino), 73 international. Average age 30. 106 applicants, 67% accepted, 25 enrolled. In 2011, 32 master's, 4 doctorates awarded. *Degree requirements:* For master's, thesis optional; for doctorate, one foreign language, thesis/dissertation. *Entrance requirements:* For master's and doctorate, GRE General Test, minimum GPA of 3.0. Additional exam requirements/recommendations for international students: Required—TOEFL (minimum score 550 paper-based; 213 computer-based; 79 iBT) or IELTS (minimum score 6.5). *Application deadline:* For fall admission, 1/25 priority date for domestic students, 5/15 for international students; for spring admission, 10/15 for international students. Applications are processed on a rolling basis. Application fee: $50 ($70 for international students). Electronic applications accepted. *Financial support:* In 2011–12, 91 students received support, including 3 fellowships with full and partial tuition reimbursements available (averaging $18,050 per year), 72 research assistantships with full and partial tuition reimbursements available (averaging $15,942 per year), 6 teaching assistantships with full and partial tuition reimbursements available (averaging $12,469 per year); career-related internships or fieldwork, institutionally sponsored loans, scholarships/grants, and health care benefits also available. Financial award application deadline: 3/1; financial award applicants required to submit FAFSA. *Faculty research:* Mechanics and structures, environmental, geotechnical transportation, water resources. *Total annual research expenditures:* $3 million. *Unit head:* Dr. George Z. Voyiadjis, Chair/Professor, 225-578-8668, Fax: 225-578-9176, E-mail: voyaidjis@lsu.edu. *Application contact:* Dr. Clinton Willson, Professor, 225-578-8672, E-mail: cwillson@lsu.edu. Web site: http://www.cee.lsu.edu/.

Louisiana Tech University, Graduate School, College of Engineering and Science, Department of Civil Engineering, Ruston, LA 71272. Offers MS, PhD. Part-time programs available. Terminal master's awarded for partial completion of doctoral program. *Degree requirements:* For master's, thesis or alternative; for doctorate, thesis/dissertation. *Entrance requirements:* For master's, GRE General Test, minimum GPA of 3.0 in last 60 hours; for doctorate, minimum graduate GPA of 3.25 (with MS) or GRE General Test. Additional exam requirements/recommendations for international students: Required—TOEFL. *Faculty research:* Environmental engineering, trenchless excavation construction, structural mechanics, transportation materials and planning, water quality modeling.

Loyola Marymount University, College of Science and Engineering, Department of Civil Engineering and Environmental Science, Program in Civil Engineering, Los Angeles, CA 90045. Offers MSE. Part-time programs available. *Faculty:* 7 full-time (1 woman), 2 part-time/adjunct (0 women). *Students:* 9 full-time (4 women), 6 part-time (2 women); includes 8 minority (1 Black or African American, non-Hispanic/Latino; 2 Asian, non-Hispanic/Latino; 3 Hispanic/Latino; 2 Two or more races, non-Hispanic/Latino). Average age 32. 9 applicants, 78% accepted, 3 enrolled. In 2011, 18 master's awarded. *Degree requirements:* For master's, comprehensive exam. *Entrance requirements:* For master's, 2 letters of recommendation, personal statement. Additional exam requirements/recommendations for international students: Required—TOEFL (minimum score 550 paper-based; 213 computer-based; 80 iBT). *Application deadline:* Applications are processed on a rolling basis. Application fee: $50. Electronic applications accepted. *Financial support:* In 2011–12, 6 students received support. Scholarships/grants and laboratory assistantships available. Support available to part-time students. Financial award application deadline: 6/1; financial award applicants required to submit FAFSA. *Total annual research expenditures:* $80,391. *Unit head:* Prof. Joe Reichenberger, Graduate Director, 310-338-2830, E-mail: jreichenberger@lmu.edu. *Application contact:* Chake H. Kouyoumjian, Associate Dean of Graduate Studies, 310-338-2721, E-mail: ckouyoum@lmu.edu. Web site: http://cse.lmu.edu/departments/civilengineering.htm.

Manhattan College, Graduate Division, School of Engineering, Program in Civil Engineering, Riverdale, NY 10471. Offers MS. Part-time and evening/weekend programs available. *Faculty:* 2 full-time (0 women), 15 part-time/adjunct (0 women). *Students:* 4 full-time (0 women), 61 part-time (16 women); includes 18 minority (4 Black or African American, non-Hispanic/Latino; 5 Asian, non-Hispanic/Latino; 4 Hispanic/Latino; 5 Two or more races, non-Hispanic/Latino). Average age 25. 29 applicants, 86% accepted, 20 enrolled. In 2011, 10 master's awarded. *Degree requirements:* For master's, thesis or alternative. *Entrance requirements:* For master's, GRE (recommended), minimum GPA of 3.0. Additional exam requirements/recommendations for international students: Required—TOEFL (minimum score 550 paper-based; 213 computer-based; 80 iBT), IELTS (minimum score 6). *Application deadline:* For fall admission, 8/10 priority date for domestic students, 8/10 for international students; for spring admission, 1/7 for domestic and international students. Applications are processed on a rolling basis. Application fee: $50. Electronic applications accepted. *Expenses: Tuition:* Full-time $14,850; part-time $825 per credit. *Required fees:* $390; $150. *Financial support:* In 2011–12, 2 students received support, including 4 teaching assistantships (averaging $4,000 per year); fellowships, research assistantships, career-related internships or fieldwork, Federal Work-Study, scholarships/grants, and laboratory assistantships also available. Support available to part-time students. Financial award application deadline: 2/1. *Faculty research:* Compressible-inclusion function for geofoams used with rigid walls under static loading, validation of sediment criteria. *Unit head:* Dr. Moujalli Hourani, Chair, 718-862-7172, Fax: 718-862-8035, E-mail: moujalli.hourani@manhattan.edu. *Application contact:* Janet Horgan, Information Contact, 718-862-7171, Fax: 718-862-8035, E-mail: civildept@manhattan.edu. Web site: http://www.engineering.manhattan.edu.

Marquette University, Graduate School, College of Engineering, Department of Civil and Environmental Engineering, Milwaukee, WI 53201-1881. Offers construction and public works management (MS, PhD); construction engineering and management (Certificate); environmental/water resources engineering (MS, PhD); structural design (Certificate); structural/geotechnical engineering (MS, PhD); transportation planning and engineering (MS, PhD); waste and wastewater treatment processes (Certificate). Part-time and evening/weekend programs available. *Faculty:* 13 full-time (0 women), 5 part-time/adjunct (0 women). *Students:* 26 full-time (5 women), 11 part-time (0 women); includes 2 minority (1 Black or African American, non-Hispanic/Latino; 1 Asian, non-Hispanic/Latino), 12 international. Average age 27. 74 applicants, 62% accepted, 9 enrolled. In 2011, 6 master's, 3 doctorates awarded. Terminal master's awarded for partial completion of doctoral program. *Degree requirements:* For master's, comprehensive exam (for some programs), thesis or alternative; for doctorate, thesis/dissertation. *Entrance requirements:* For master's, GRE General Test (recommended), minimum GPA of 3.0, official transcripts from all current and previous colleges/universities except Marquette, three letters of recommendation; for doctorate, GRE General Test, minimum GPA of 3.0, official transcripts from all current and previous colleges/universities except Marquette, three letters of recommendation, brief statement of purpose, submission of any English language publications authored by applicant (strongly recommended). Additional exam requirements/recommendations for international students: Required—TOEFL (minimum score 530 paper-based; 78 computer-based). *Application deadline:* For fall admission, 6/1 priority date for domestic students. Applications are processed on a rolling basis. Application fee: $50. Electronic applications accepted. *Expenses: Tuition:* Full-time $17,010; part-time $945 per credit hour. Tuition and fees vary according to program. *Financial support:* In 2011–12, 21 students received support, including 6 fellowships with partial tuition reimbursements available (averaging $9,177 per year), 1 research assistantship with full tuition reimbursement available (averaging $13,745 per year), 7 teaching assistantships with full tuition reimbursements available (averaging $13,902 per year); scholarships/grants, health care benefits, tuition waivers (partial), and unspecified assistantships also available. Support available to part-time students. Financial award application deadline: 2/15. *Faculty research:* Highway safety, highway performance, and intelligent transportation systems; surface mount technology; watershed management. *Total annual research expenditures:* $826,608. *Unit head:* Dr. Thomas Wenzel, Chair, 414-288-7030, Fax: 414-288-7521, E-mail: thomas.wenzel@marquette.edu. *Application contact:* Dr. Stephen M. Heinrich, Director of Graduate Studies, 414-288-5466, E-mail: stephen.heinrich@marquette.edu. Web site: http://www.marquette.edu/engineering/pages/AllYouNeed/Civil_Environmental/civil.html.

Massachusetts Institute of Technology, School of Engineering, Department of Civil and Environmental Engineering, Cambridge, MA 02139. Offers biological oceanography (PhD, Sc D); chemical oceanography (PhD, Sc D); civil and environmental engineering (PhD, Sc D); civil and environmental systems (PhD, Sc D); civil engineering (PhD, Sc D, CE); coastal engineering (PhD, Sc D); construction engineering and management (PhD, Sc D); environmental and water quality engineering (M Eng); environmental biology (PhD, Sc D); environmental chemistry (PhD, Sc D); environmental engineering (PhD, Sc D); environmental fluid mechanics (PhD, Sc D); environmental science and engineering (SM); geotechnical and geoenvironmental engineering (PhD, Sc D); geotechnology (M Eng); high-performance structures (M Eng); hydrology (PhD, Sc D); information technology (PhD, Sc D); mechanics (SM); oceanographic engineering (PhD, Sc D); structures and materials (PhD, Sc D); transportation (M Eng, PhD, Sc D); SM/MBA. *Faculty:* 35 full-time (6 women), 1 part-time/adjunct (0 women). *Students:* 216 full-time (80 women); includes 30 minority (4 Black or African American, non-Hispanic/Latino; 13 Asian, non-Hispanic/Latino; 8 Hispanic/Latino; 5 Two or more races, non-Hispanic/Latino), 110 international. Average age 27. 589 applicants, 26% accepted, 91 enrolled. In 2011, 62 master's, 14 doctorates awarded. *Degree requirements:* For master's and CE, thesis; for doctorate, comprehensive exam, thesis/dissertation. *Entrance requirements:* For master's and doctorate, GRE General Test. Additional exam requirements/recommendations for international students: Required—TOEFL (minimum score 577 paper-based; 233 computer-based; 90 iBT), IELTS (minimum score 7). *Application deadline:* For fall admission, 12/15 for domestic and international students. Application fee: $75. Electronic applications accepted. *Expenses: Tuition:* Full-time $40,460; part-time $630 per credit hour. *Required fees:* $272. *Financial support:* In

2011–12, 180 students received support, including 51 fellowships (averaging $30,800 per year), 110 research assistantships (averaging $29,500 per year), 19 teaching assistantships (averaging $29,500 per year); career-related internships or fieldwork, Federal Work-Study, institutionally sponsored loans, scholarships/grants, health care benefits, and unspecified assistantships also available. *Faculty research:* Environmental chemistry, environmental fluid mechanics and coastal engineering, environmental microbiology, geotechnical engineering and geomechanics, hydrology and hydroclimatology, infrastructure systems, mechanics of materials and structures, transportation systems. *Total annual research expenditures:* $17.7 million. *Unit head:* Prof. Andrew Whittle, Head, 617-253-7101. *Application contact:* Patricia Glidden, Graduate Admissions Coordinator, 617-253-7119, Fax: 617-258-6775, E-mail: cee-admissions@mit.edu. Web site: http://cee.mit.edu/.

McGill University, Faculty of Graduate and Postdoctoral Studies, Faculty of Engineering, Department of Civil Engineering and Applied Mechanics, Montréal, QC H3A 2T5, Canada. Offers environmental engineering (M Eng, M Sc, PhD); fluid mechanics (M Sc); fluid mechanics and hydraulic engineering (M Eng, PhD); materials engineering (M Eng, PhD); rehabilitation of urban infrastructure (M Eng, PhD); soil behavior (M Eng, PhD); soil mechanics and foundations (M Eng, PhD); structures and structural mechanics (M Eng, PhD); water resources (M Sc); water resources engineering (M Eng, PhD).

McMaster University, School of Graduate Studies, Faculty of Engineering, Department of Civil Engineering, Hamilton, ON L8S 4M2, Canada. Offers M Eng, MA Sc, PhD. *Degree requirements:* For master's, thesis; for doctorate, comprehensive exam, thesis/dissertation. *Entrance requirements:* Additional exam requirements/recommendations for international students: Required—TOEFL (minimum score 550 paper-based; 213 computer-based). *Faculty research:* Building science, environmental hydrology, bolted steel connections, research on highway materials, earthquake engineering.

McNeese State University, Doré School of Graduate Studies, College of Engineering and Engineering Technology, Lake Charles, LA 70609. Offers chemical engineering (M Eng); civil engineering (M Eng); electrical engineering (M Eng); engineering management (M Eng); mechanical engineering (M Eng); pump reliability engineering (Postbaccalaureate Certificate). Part-time and evening/weekend programs available. *Faculty:* 13 full-time (1 woman). *Students:* 21 full-time (4 women), 18 part-time (5 women); includes 5 minority (4 Black or African American, non-Hispanic/Latino; 1 American Indian or Alaska Native, non-Hispanic/Latino), 23 international. In 2011, 28 master's awarded. *Degree requirements:* For master's, thesis or alternative. *Entrance requirements:* For master's, GRE, minimum undergraduate GPA of 3.0. Additional exam requirements/recommendations for international students: Required—TOEFL (minimum score 560 paper-based; 220 computer-based; 83 iBT). *Application deadline:* For fall admission, 5/15 priority date for domestic students, 5/15 for international students; for spring admission, 10/15 priority date for domestic students, 10/15 for international students. Applications are processed on a rolling basis. Application fee: $20 ($30 for international students). *Expenses:* Tuition, state resident: part-time $519 per credit hour. Tuition and fees vary according to course load. *Financial support:* Federal Work-Study available. Support available to part-time students. Financial award application deadline: 5/1. *Unit head:* Dr. Nikos Kiritsis, Dean, 337-475-5875, Fax: 337-475-5237, E-mail: nikosk@mcneese.edu. *Application contact:* Dr. George F. Mead, Jr., Interim Dean of Dore' School of Graduate Studies, 337-475-5396, Fax: 337-475-5397, E-mail: admissions@mcneese.edu.

Memorial University of Newfoundland, School of Graduate Studies, Faculty of Engineering and Applied Science, St. John's, NL A1C 5S7, Canada. Offers civil engineering (M Eng, PhD); electrical and computer engineering (M Eng, PhD); mechanical engineering (M Eng, PhD); ocean and naval architecture engineering (M Eng, PhD). Part-time programs available. *Degree requirements:* For master's, thesis; for doctorate, comprehensive exam, thesis/dissertation, oral thesis defense. *Entrance requirements:* For master's, 2nd class degree; for doctorate, master's degree in engineering. Electronic applications accepted. *Faculty research:* Engineering analysis, environmental and hydrotechnical studies, manufacturing and robotics, mechanics, structures and materials.

Michigan State University, The Graduate School, College of Engineering, Department of Civil and Environmental Engineering, East Lansing, MI 48824. Offers civil engineering (MS, PhD); environmental engineering (MS, PhD); environmental engineering-environmental toxicology (PhD). Part-time programs available. *Entrance requirements:* Additional exam requirements/recommendations for international students: Required—TOEFL. Electronic applications accepted.

Michigan Technological University, Graduate School, College of Engineering, Department of Civil and Environmental Engineering, Houghton, MI 49931. Offers civil engineering (M Eng, MS, PhD); environmental engineering (M Eng, MS); environmental engineering science (MS). Part-time programs available. *Faculty:* 36 full-time (5 women), 8 part-time/adjunct (3 women). *Students:* 72 full-time (24 women), 10 part-time (5 women); includes 6 minority (1 Black or African American, non-Hispanic/Latino; 2 Asian, non-Hispanic/Latino; 3 Hispanic/Latino), 22 international. Average age 27. 258 applicants, 34% accepted, 20 enrolled. In 2011, 28 master's, 3 doctorates awarded. Terminal master's awarded for partial completion of doctoral program. *Degree requirements:* For master's, comprehensive exam (for some programs), thesis (for some programs); for doctorate, comprehensive exam, thesis/dissertation. *Entrance requirements:* For master's, GRE (to be considered for university assistantship), statement of purpose, official transcripts, 3 letters of recommendation; for doctorate, GRE, statement of purpose, official transcripts, 3 letters of recommendation. Additional exam requirements/recommendations for international students: Required—TOEFL (minimum score 100 iBT). *Application deadline:* Applications are processed on a rolling basis. Electronic applications accepted. *Expenses:* Contact institution. *Financial support:* In 2011–12, 75 students received support, including 3 fellowships with full tuition reimbursements available (averaging $6,065 per year), 20 research assistantships with full tuition reimbursements available (averaging $6,065 per year), 16 teaching assistantships with full tuition reimbursements available (averaging $6,065 per year); career-related internships or fieldwork, Federal Work-Study, scholarships/grants, health care benefits, tuition waivers, unspecified assistantships, and cooperative program also available. Financial award applicants required to submit FAFSA. *Faculty research:* Sustainable engineering, water resources, air quality, structural systems, transportation materials, construction, geotechnology. *Total annual research expenditures:* $2.4 million. *Unit head:* Dr. David Hand, Chair, 906-487-2777, Fax: 906-487-2943, E-mail: dwhand@mtu.edu. *Application contact:* Angela Keranen, Administrative Aide, 906-487-2520, Fax: 906-487-2943, E-mail: amkerane@mtu.edu. Web site: http://www.mtu.edu/cee/.

Milwaukee School of Engineering, Civil and Architectural Engineering and Construction Management Department, Program in Civil Engineering, Milwaukee, WI 53202-3109. Offers MS. Five-year freshman-to-master's degree program. Part-time and evening/weekend programs available. *Degree requirements:* For master's, thesis, capstone project. *Entrance requirements:* For master's, GRE General Test or GMAT, 2 letters of recommendation. Additional exam requirements/recommendations for international students: Required—TOEFL (minimum score 79 iBT) or IELTS. *Application deadline:* Applications are processed on a rolling basis. Electronic applications accepted. Application fee is waived when completed online. *Expenses: Tuition:* Full-time $17,550; part-time $650 per credit hour. *Financial support:* Career-related internships or fieldwork available. Support available to part-time students. Financial award applicants required to submit FAFSA. *Unit head:* Dr. Francis Mahuta, Director, 414-277-7599. *Application contact:* Katie Gassenhuber, Graduate Program Associate, 800-321-6763, Fax: 414-277-7208, E-mail: gassenhuber@msoe.edu.

Mississippi State University, Bagley College of Engineering, Department of Civil and Environmental Engineering, Mississippi State, MS 39762. Offers civil engineering (MS); engineering (PhD), including civil engineering. Part-time programs available. Postbaccalaureate distance learning degree programs offered (no on-campus study). *Faculty:* 7 full-time (0 women), 4 part-time/adjunct (0 women). *Students:* 23 full-time (7 women), 56 part-time (10 women); includes 14 minority (5 Black or African American, non-Hispanic/Latino; 1 Asian, non-Hispanic/Latino; 8 Hispanic/Latino), 10 international. Average age 30. 44 applicants, 34% accepted, 8 enrolled. In 2011, 6 master's, 4 doctorates awarded. Terminal master's awarded for partial completion of doctoral program. *Degree requirements:* For master's, thesis (for some programs); for doctorate, thesis/dissertation, research on an approved topic. *Entrance requirements:* For master's and doctorate, GRE, minimum GPA of 3.0. Additional exam requirements/recommendations for international students: Required—TOEFL (minimum score 550 paper-based; 213 computer-based; 79 iBT); Recommended—IELTS (minimum score 6.5). *Application deadline:* For fall admission, 7/1 for domestic students, 5/1 for international students; for spring admission, 11/1 for domestic students, 9/1 for international students. Applications are processed on a rolling basis. Application fee: $40. Electronic applications accepted. *Expenses:* Tuition, state resident: full-time $5805; part-time $322.50 per credit hour. Tuition, nonresident: full-time $14,670; part-time $815 per credit hour. *Financial support:* In 2011–12, 8 research assistantships with full tuition reimbursements (averaging $12,884 per year), 7 teaching assistantships with full tuition reimbursements (averaging $12,340 per year) were awarded; Federal Work-Study, institutionally sponsored loans, and unspecified assistantships also available. Financial award application deadline: 4/1; financial award applicants required to submit FAFSA. *Faculty research:* Transportation, water modeling, construction materials, structures. *Total annual research expenditures:* $5.9 million. *Unit head:* Dr. Dennis D. Truax, Department Head, 662-325-7187, Fax: 662-325-7189, E-mail: truax@cee.msstate.edu. *Application contact:* Dr. James L. Martin, Professor and Graduate Coordinator, 662-325-7194, Fax: 662-325-7189, E-mail: jmartin@cee.msstate.edu. Web site: http://www.cee.msstate.edu/.

Missouri University of Science and Technology, Graduate School, Department of Civil, Architectural, and Environmental Engineering, Rolla, MO 65409. Offers civil engineering (MS, DE, PhD); construction engineering (MS, DE, PhD); environmental engineering (MS); fluid mechanics (MS, DE, PhD); geotechnical engineering (MS, DE, PhD); hydrology and hydraulic engineering (MS, DE, PhD). Part-time and evening/weekend programs available. Terminal master's awarded for partial completion of doctoral program. *Degree requirements:* For master's, thesis optional; for doctorate, comprehensive exam, thesis/dissertation. *Entrance requirements:* For master's, GRE General Test (minimum combined score 1100), minimum GPA of 3.0; for doctorate, GRE General Test (minimum score: verbal and quantitative 400, writing 3.5), minimum GPA of 3.0. Additional exam requirements/recommendations for international students: Required—TOEFL. Electronic applications accepted. *Faculty research:* Earthquake engineering, structural optimization and control systems, structural health monitoring/damage detection, soil-structure interaction, soil mechanics and foundation engineering.

Montana State University, College of Graduate Studies, College of Engineering, Department of Civil Engineering, Bozeman, MT 59717. Offers civil engineering (MS); construction engineering management (MCEM); engineering (PhD), including applied mechanics option, civil engineering option. Part-time programs available. *Degree requirements:* For master's, comprehensive exam, thesis (for some programs); for doctorate, comprehensive exam, thesis/dissertation. *Entrance requirements:* For master's and doctorate, GRE General Test. Additional exam requirements/recommendations for international students: Required—TOEFL (minimum score 550 paper-based; 213 computer-based). Electronic applications accepted. *Faculty research:* Snow and ice mechanics, biofilm engineering, transportation, structural and geo materials, water resources.

Morgan State University, School of Graduate Studies, Clarence M. Mitchell, Jr. School of Engineering, Baltimore, MD 21251. Offers civil engineering (M Eng, D Eng); electrical engineering (M Eng, D Eng); industrial engineering (M Eng, D Eng); transportation (MS). Part-time and evening/weekend programs available. *Degree requirements:* For master's, thesis, comprehensive exam or equivalent; for doctorate, thesis/dissertation, comprehensive exam or equivalent. *Entrance requirements:* For master's, GRE, minimum undergraduate GPA of 2.5; for doctorate, GRE, minimum GPA of 3.0. Additional exam requirements/recommendations for international students: Required—TOEFL (minimum score 550 paper-based; 213 computer-based).

New Jersey Institute of Technology, Office of Graduate Studies, Newark College of Engineering, Department of Civil and Environmental Engineering, Program in Civil Engineering, Newark, NJ 07102. Offers MS, PhD. Part-time and evening/weekend programs available. *Students:* 52 full-time (14 women), 106 part-time (22 women); includes 64 minority (14 Black or African American, non-Hispanic/Latino; 1 American Indian or Alaska Native, non-Hispanic/Latino; 18 Asian, non-Hispanic/Latino; 28 Hispanic/Latino; 3 Two or more races, non-Hispanic/Latino), 26 international. Average age 29. 192 applicants, 61% accepted, 53 enrolled. In 2011, 54 master's, 5 doctorates awarded. Terminal master's awarded for partial completion of doctoral program. *Degree requirements:* For master's, thesis optional; for doctorate, thesis/dissertation. *Entrance requirements:* For master's and doctorate, GRE General Test. Additional exam requirements/recommendations for international students: Required—TOEFL (minimum score 550 paper-based; 213 computer-based; 79 iBT). *Application deadline:* For fall admission, 6/1 priority date for domestic students, 5/1 for international students; for spring admission, 11/15 priority date for domestic students, 11/15 for international students. Applications are processed on a rolling basis. Application fee: $65. Electronic applications accepted. *Expenses:* Tuition, state resident: full-time $7980; part-time $867 per credit. Tuition, nonresident: full-time $11,336; part-time $1196 per credit. *Required fees:* $230 per credit. *Financial support:* Fellowships with full and partial tuition reimbursements, research assistantships with full and partial tuition reimbursements, teaching assistantships with full and partial tuition reimbursements, career-related internships or fieldwork, Federal Work-Study, institutionally sponsored loans, and unspecified assistantships available. Financial award application deadline: 3/15. *Unit head:* Dr. Taha Marhaba, Chair, 973-642-4599, E-mail: taha.f.marhaba@njit.edu. *Application contact:* Kathryn Kelly, Director of Admissions, 973-596-3300, Fax: 973-596-3461, E-mail: admissions@njit.edu.

New Mexico State University, Graduate School, College of Engineering, Department of Civil Engineering, Las Cruces, NM 88003-8001. Offers civil engineering (MSCE, PhD); environmental engineering (MS Env E). Part-time programs available. Postbaccalaureate distance learning degree programs offered. *Faculty:* 13 full-time (2 women). *Students:* 53 full-time (18 women), 13 part-time (3 women); includes 22 minority (3 American Indian or Alaska Native, non-Hispanic/Latino; 18 Hispanic/Latino; 1 Two or more races, non-Hispanic/Latino), 26 international. Average age 29. 33 applicants, 52% accepted, 11 enrolled. In 2011, 15 master's, 2 doctorates awarded. *Degree requirements:* For master's, thesis (for some programs); for doctorate, comprehensive exam (for some programs), thesis/dissertation. *Entrance requirements:* For master's, BS in engineering, minimum GPA of 3.0; for doctorate, qualifying exam, BS in engineering, minimum GPA of 3.0. Additional exam requirements/recommendations for international students: Required—TOEFL (minimum score 550 paper-based; 213 computer-based; 79 iBT), IELTS (minimum score 6). *Application deadline:* For fall admission, 4/1 priority date for domestic students, 4/1 for international students; for spring admission, 9/1 priority date for domestic students, 9/1 for international students. Applications are processed on a rolling basis. Application fee: $40 ($50 for international students). Electronic applications accepted. *Expenses:* Tuition, state resident: full-time $5004; part-time $208.50 per credit. Tuition, nonresident: full-time $17,446; part-time $726.90 per credit. *Financial support:* In 2011–12, 45 students received support, including 9 fellowships (averaging $3,710 per year), 21 research assistantships (averaging $16,842 per year), 25 teaching assistantships (averaging $17,894 per year); career-related internships or fieldwork, Federal Work-Study, and health care benefits also available. Support available to part-time students. Financial award application deadline: 3/1. *Faculty research:* Structural engineering, water resources engineering, environmental engineering, geotechnical engineering, hydraulics/hydrology. *Unit head:* Dr. Adrian Hanson, Interim Head, 575-646-3801, E-mail: athanson@nmsu.edu. *Application contact:* Coordinator, 575-646-2736, Fax: 575-646-7721, E-mail: gradinfo@nmsu.edu. Web site: http://cagesun.nmsu.edu/.

North Carolina Agricultural and Technical State University, School of Graduate Studies, College of Engineering, Department of Civil, Architectural, Agricultural and Environmental Engineering, Greensboro, NC 27411. Offers civil engineering (MSCE). Part-time programs available. *Degree requirements:* For master's, thesis optional. *Entrance requirements:* For master's, GRE General Test, GRE Subject Test (recommended). Additional exam requirements/recommendations for international students: Required—TOEFL. *Faculty research:* Lightning, indoor air quality, material behavior HVAC controls, structural masonry systems.

North Carolina State University, Graduate School, College of Engineering, Department of Civil, Construction, and Environmental Engineering, Raleigh, NC 27695. Offers civil engineering (MCE, MS, PhD). Part-time programs available. Postbaccalaureate distance learning degree programs offered. *Degree requirements:* For master's, thesis optional, oral exams; for doctorate, thesis/dissertation, oral exams. *Entrance requirements:* For master's, GRE General Test, minimum B average in major; for doctorate, GRE General Test. Additional exam requirements/recommendations for international students: Required—TOEFL. Electronic applications accepted. *Faculty research:* Materials; systems, environmental, geotechnical, structural, transportation and water rescue engineering.

North Dakota State University, College of Graduate and Interdisciplinary Studies, College of Engineering and Architecture, Department of Civil Engineering, Fargo, ND 58108. Offers civil engineering (MS, PhD); environmental engineering (MS, PhD); transportation and logistics (PhD). PhD in transportation and logistics offered jointly with Upper Great Plains Transportation Institute. Part-time programs available. Postbaccalaureate distance learning degree programs offered (minimal on-campus study). *Faculty:* 13 full-time (1 woman). *Students:* 25 full-time (2 women), 19 part-time (3 women); includes 3 minority (1 American Indian or Alaska Native, non-Hispanic/Latino; 2 Two or more races, non-Hispanic/Latino), 21 international. 46 applicants, 48% accepted, 8 enrolled. In 2011, 8 master's, 3 doctorates awarded. *Degree requirements:* For master's, thesis; for doctorate, comprehensive exam, thesis/dissertation. *Entrance requirements:* Additional exam requirements/recommendations for international students: Required—TOEFL (minimum score 525 paper-based; 197 computer-based; 71 iBT). *Application deadline:* For fall admission, 2/15 priority date for domestic students, 2/15 for international students; for spring admission, 9/15 priority date for domestic students, 9/15 for international students. Applications are processed on a rolling basis. Application fee: $35. Electronic applications accepted. *Financial support:* Fellowships with full tuition reimbursements, research assistantships with full tuition reimbursements, teaching assistantships with full tuition reimbursements, career-related internships or fieldwork, Federal Work-Study, and institutionally sponsored loans available. Support available to part-time students. Financial award application deadline: 1/15. *Faculty research:* Wastewater, solid waste, composites, nanotechnology. *Unit head:* Dr. Eakalak Khan, Chair, 701-231-7244, Fax: 701-231-6185, E-mail: eakalak.khan@ndsu.edu. *Application contact:* Dr. Kalpana Katti, Professor and Graduate Program Coordinator, 701-231-9504, Fax: 701-231-6185, E-mail: kalpana.katti@ndsu.edu. Web site: http://www.ce.ndsu.nodak.edu/.

Northeastern University, College of Engineering, Department of Civil and Environmental Engineering, Boston, MA 02115-5096. Offers MS, PhD. Part-time programs available. *Faculty:* 15 full-time, 2 part-time/adjunct. *Students:* 97 full-time (41 women), 38 part-time (14 women). 286 applicants, 67% accepted, 56 enrolled. In 2011, 23 master's, 3 doctorates awarded. *Degree requirements:* For master's, thesis optional; for doctorate, thesis/dissertation, departmental qualifying exam. *Entrance requirements:* For master's and doctorate, GRE General Test. Additional exam requirements/recommendations for international students: Required—TOEFL (minimum score 550 paper-based; 213 computer-based; 80 iBT). *Application deadline:* For fall admission, 1/15 priority date for domestic students, 1/15 for international students. Applications are processed on a rolling basis. Application fee: $50. Electronic applications accepted. *Financial support:* In 2011–12, 33 students received support, including 21 research assistantships with full tuition reimbursements available (averaging $18,325 per year), 16 teaching assistantships with full tuition reimbursements available (averaging $18,325 per year); career-related internships or fieldwork, Federal Work-Study, scholarships/grants, tuition waivers (full), and unspecified assistantships also available. Support available to part-time students. Financial award application deadline: 1/15; financial award applicants required to submit FAFSA. *Faculty research:* Earthquake engineering, geotechnical and geoenvironmental engineering, structural engineering, transportation engineering, environmental engineering. *Unit head:* Dr. Jerome Jaffar, Chairman, 617-373-2444, Fax: 617-373-4419. *Application contact:* Jeffery Hengel, Admissions Specialist, 617-373-2711, Fax: 617-373-2501, E-mail: grad-eng@coe.neu.edu. Web site: http://www.coe.neu.edu/.

Northern Arizona University, Graduate College, College of Engineering, Forestry and Natural Sciences, Programs in Engineering, Flagstaff , AZ 86011. Offers civil and environmental engineering (M Eng); civil engineering (MSE); computer science (MSE); electrical engineering (M Eng, MSE); engineering (M Eng, MSE); environmental engineering (M Eng, MSE); mechanical engineering (M Eng, MSE). Part-time programs available. Postbaccalaureate distance learning degree programs offered (no on-campus study). *Faculty:* 42 full-time (10 women). *Students:* 15 full-time (1 woman), 12 part-time (1 woman); includes 2 minority (both Hispanic/Latino), 6 international. Average age 28. 29 applicants, 52% accepted, 8 enrolled. In 2011, 15 degrees awarded. *Degree requirements:* For master's, thesis. *Entrance requirements:* For master's, GRE General Test. Additional exam requirements/recommendations for international students: Required—TOEFL (minimum score 550 paper-based; 213 computer-based; 80 iBT), IELTS (minimum score 7). *Application deadline:* For fall admission, 3/1 priority date for domestic students, 3/1 for international students; for spring admission, 9/15 priority date for domestic students, 9/15 for international students. Applications are processed on a rolling basis. Application fee: $65. Electronic applications accepted. *Expenses:* Tuition, state resident: full-time $7190; part-time $355 per credit hour. Tuition, nonresident: full-time $18,092; part-time $1005 per credit hour. *Required fees:* $818; $328 per semester. *Financial support:* In 2011–12, 3 research assistantships with partial tuition reimbursements (averaging $14,541 per year), 12 teaching assistantships with partial tuition reimbursements (averaging $12,863 per year) were awarded; career-related internships or fieldwork, Federal Work-Study, scholarships/grants, health care benefits, and unspecified assistantships also available. Financial award applicants required to submit FAFSA. *Unit head:* Dr. Ernesto Penado, Chair, 928-523-9453, Fax: 928-523-2300, E-mail: ernesto.penado@nau.edu. *Application contact:* Natasha Kypfer, Program Coordinator, 928-523-1447, Fax: 928-523-2300, E-mail: egrmasters@nau.edu. Web site: http://nau.edu/CEFNS/Engineering/.

Northwestern University, McCormick School of Engineering and Applied Science, Department of Civil and Environmental Engineering, Evanston, IL 60208-3109. Offers environmental engineering and science (MS, PhD); geotechnical engineering (MS, PhD); mechanics of materials and solids (MS, PhD); project management (MS, PhD); structural engineering and materials (MS, PhD); theoretical and applied mechanics (MS, PhD), including fluid mechanics, solid mechanics; transportation systems analysis and planning (MS, PhD). MS and PhD admissions and degrees offered through The Graduate School. Part-time programs available. Terminal master's awarded for partial completion of doctoral program. *Degree requirements:* For master's, thesis (for some programs); for doctorate, thesis/dissertation. *Entrance requirements:* For master's and doctorate, GRE General Test, minimum 2 letters of recommendation, transcripts from all academic institutions attended. Additional exam requirements/recommendations for international students: Required—TOEFL (minimum score 600 paper-based; 250 computer-based; 100 iBT), IELTS (minimum score 7). Electronic applications accepted. *Faculty research:* Environmental engineering and science, geotechnics, mechanics of materials and solids, structural engineering and materials, transportation systems analysis and planning.

Norwich University, College of Graduate and Continuing Studies, Master of Civil Engineering Program, Northfield, VT 05663. Offers construction management (MCE); environmental water resources (MCE); geo-technical (MCE); structural (MCE). Evening/weekend programs available. *Faculty:* 12 part-time/adjunct (1 woman). *Students:* 88 full-time (23 women); includes 15 minority (8 Black or African American, non-Hispanic/Latino; 1 American Indian or Alaska Native, non-Hispanic/Latino; 4 Asian, non-Hispanic/Latino; 2 Hispanic/Latino). Average age 33. In 2011, 44 master's awarded. *Entrance requirements:* For master's, minimum GPA of 2.75. Additional exam requirements/recommendations for international students: Required—TOEFL (minimum score 550 paper-based; 213 computer-based; 83 iBT). *Application deadline:* For fall admission, 8/10 for domestic and international students; for spring admission, 2/6 for domestic and international students. Applications are processed on a rolling basis. Application fee: $50. Electronic applications accepted. *Expenses: Tuition:* Full-time $16,174. *Required fees:* $2130. Full-time tuition and fees vary according to program. *Financial support:* In 2011–12, 5 students received support. Scholarships/grants available. Financial award applicants required to submit FAFSA. *Unit head:* Dr. Thomas Descoteaux, Program Director, 802-485-2730, Fax: 802-485-2533, E-mail: tdescote@norwich.edu. *Application contact:* Rija Ramahatra, Associate Program Director, 802-485-2892, Fax: 802-485-2533, E-mail: ramahatr@norwich.edu. Web site: http://mce.norwich.edu.

The Ohio State University, Graduate School, College of Engineering, Department of Civil and Environmental Engineering and Geodetic Science, Columbus, OH 43210. Offers civil engineering (MS, PhD); geodetic science and surveying (MS, PhD). *Faculty:* 20. *Students:* 66 full-time (23 women), 41 part-time (3 women); includes 8 minority (1 Black or African American, non-Hispanic/Latino; 2 Asian, non-Hispanic/Latino; 3 Hispanic/Latino; 2 Two or more races, non-Hispanic/Latino), 58 international. Average age 27. In 2011, 28 master's, 5 doctorates awarded. *Entrance requirements:* Additional exam requirements/recommendations for international students: Required—TOEFL (minimum score 550 paper-based; 79 iBT), Michigan English Language Assessment Battery (minimum score 82). *Expenses:* Tuition, state resident: full-time $11,400. Tuition, nonresident: full-time $28,125. Tuition and fees vary according to course load, degree level, campus/location and program. *Unit head:* Dr. Carolyn J. Merry, Chair, 614-292-3455, Fax: 614-292-8062, E-mail: merry.1@osu.edu. *Application contact:* Graduate Admissions, 614-292-6301, Fax: 614-292-3656, E-mail: gradadmissions@osu.edu. Web site: http://ceg.osu.edu/.

Ohio University, Graduate College, Russ College of Engineering and Technology, Department of Civil Engineering, Athens, OH 45701-2979. Offers civil engineering (PhD); construction (MS); environmental (MS); geotechnical and geoenvironmental (MS); mechanics (MS); structures (MS); transportation (MS); water resources and structures (MS). Part-time programs available. *Students:* 32 full-time (6 women), 7 part-time (2 women); includes 3 minority (1 Hispanic/Latino; 2 Two or more races, non-Hispanic/Latino), 13 international. 52 applicants, 52% accepted, 4 enrolled. In 2011, 10 degrees awarded. *Degree requirements:* For master's, comprehensive exam (for some programs), thesis or alternative; for doctorate, comprehensive exam, thesis/dissertation. *Entrance requirements:* For master's, GRE General Test, minimum GPA of 3.0, 3 letters of recommendation; for doctorate, GRE General Test. Additional exam requirements/recommendations for international students: Required—TOEFL (minimum score 550 paper-based; 80 iBT) or IELTS (minimum score 6.5). *Application deadline:* For fall admission, 5/1 priority date for domestic students, 2/1 for international students; for winter admission, 8/1 priority date for domestic students, 4/1 for international students; for spring admission, 2/1 priority date for domestic students, 7/1 for international students. Applications are processed on a rolling basis. Application fee: $50 ($55 for international students). Electronic applications accepted. *Financial support:* Research assistantships with full tuition reimbursements, teaching assistantships with full tuition reimbursements, Federal Work-Study, institutionally sponsored loans, scholarships/grants, and unspecified assistantships available. Financial award application deadline: 3/15; financial award applicants required to submit FAFSA. *Faculty research:* Noise abatement, materials and environment, highway infrastructure, subsurface investigation (pavements, pipes, bridges). *Unit head:* Dr. Gayle F. Mitchell, Chair, 740-593-0430, Fax: 740-593-0625, E-mail: mitchelg@ohio.edu. *Application contact:* Dr. Shad M. Sargand,

Graduate Chair, 740-593-1465, Fax: 740-593-0625, E-mail: sargand@ohio.edu. Web site: http://www.ohio.edu/civil/.

Oklahoma State University, College of Engineering, Architecture and Technology, School of Civil and Environmental Engineering, Stillwater, OK 74078. Offers civil engineering (MS); environmental engineering (PhD). *Faculty:* 15 full-time (1 woman), 5 part-time/adjunct (0 women). *Students:* 41 full-time (17 women), 41 part-time (7 women); includes 10 minority (2 Black or African American, non-Hispanic/Latino; 2 American Indian or Alaska Native, non-Hispanic/Latino; 2 Asian, non-Hispanic/Latino; 1 Hispanic/Latino; 3 Two or more races, non-Hispanic/Latino), 44 international. Average age 29. 118 applicants, 37% accepted, 18 enrolled. In 2011, 30 master's, 1 doctorate awarded. *Degree requirements:* For master's, thesis or alternative; for doctorate, comprehensive exam, thesis/dissertation. *Entrance requirements:* For master's and doctorate, GRE or GMAT. Additional exam requirements/recommendations for international students: Required—TOEFL (minimum score 550 paper-based; 79 iBT). *Application deadline:* For fall admission, 3/1 for international students; for spring admission, 8/1 for international students. Applications are processed on a rolling basis. Application fee: $40 ($75 for international students). Electronic applications accepted. *Expenses:* Tuition, state resident: full-time $4044; part-time $168.50 per credit hour. Tuition, nonresident: full-time $16,008; part-time $667 per credit hour. *Required fees:* $2122; $88.45 per credit hour. One-time fee: $50. Tuition and fees vary according to course load and campus/location. *Financial support:* In 2011–12, 28 research assistantships (averaging $13,317 per year), 14 teaching assistantships (averaging $9,013 per year) were awarded; career-related internships or fieldwork, Federal Work-Study, scholarships/grants, health care benefits, tuition waivers (partial), and unspecified assistantships also available. Support available to part-time students. Financial award application deadline: 3/1; financial award applicants required to submit FAFSA. *Unit head:* Dr. John Veenstra, Head, 405-744-5190, Fax: 405-744-7554. *Application contact:* Dr. Sheryl Tucker, Dean, 405-744-7099, Fax: 405-744-0355, E-mail: grad-i@okstate.edu. Web site: http://cive.okstate.edu.

Old Dominion University, Frank Batten College of Engineering and Technology, Program in Civil and Environmental Engineering, Norfolk, VA 23529. Offers D Eng, PhD. Part-time and evening/weekend programs available. Postbaccalaureate distance learning degree programs offered (minimal on-campus study). *Faculty:* 13 full-time (1 woman), 7 part-time/adjunct (0 women). *Students:* 6 full-time (1 woman), 6 part-time (0 women), 5 international. Average age 39. 12 applicants, 100% accepted, 2 enrolled. In 2011, 1 doctorate awarded. *Degree requirements:* For doctorate, thesis/dissertation, candidacy exam. *Entrance requirements:* For doctorate, GRE, minimum GPA of 3.5. Additional exam requirements/recommendations for international students: Required—TOEFL (minimum score 550 paper-based; 213 computer-based; 80 iBT). *Application deadline:* For fall admission, 6/1 priority date for domestic students, 4/15 for international students; for spring admission, 11/1 priority date for domestic students, 10/1 for international students. Applications are processed on a rolling basis. Application fee: $50. Electronic applications accepted. *Expenses:* Tuition, state resident: full-time $9096; part-time $379 per credit. Tuition, nonresident: full-time $23,064; part-time $961 per credit. *Required fees:* $127 per semester. One-time fee: $50. *Financial support:* In 2011–12, 10 research assistantships with full and partial tuition reimbursements (averaging $15,439 per year), 8 teaching assistantships with full and partial tuition reimbursements (averaging $14,244 per year) were awarded; scholarships/grants and unspecified assistantships also available. Support available to part-time students. Financial award application deadline: 4/1. *Faculty research:* Structural engineering, coastal engineering, environmental engineering, geotechnical engineering, water resources, transportation engineering. *Total annual research expenditures:* $557,751. *Unit head:* Dr. Isao Ishibashi, Graduate Program Director, 757-683-4641, Fax: 757-683-5354, E-mail: cegpd@odu.edu. *Application contact:* Dr. Linda Vahala, Associate Dean, 757-683-3789, Fax: 757-683-4898, E-mail: lvahala@odu.edu. Web site: http://eng.odu.edu/cee/.

Old Dominion University, Frank Batten College of Engineering and Technology, Program in Civil Engineering, Norfolk, VA 23529. Offers ME, MS. Part-time and evening/weekend programs available. Postbaccalaureate distance learning degree programs offered (minimal on-campus study). *Faculty:* 13 full-time (1 woman), 7 part-time/adjunct (0 women). *Students:* 25 full-time (4 women), 51 part-time (17 women); includes 14 minority (5 Black or African American, non-Hispanic/Latino; 4 Asian, non-Hispanic/Latino; 4 Hispanic/Latino; 1 Native Hawaiian or other Pacific Islander, non-Hispanic/Latino), 20 international. Average age 31. 23 applicants, 96% accepted, 8 enrolled. In 2011, 11 master's awarded. *Degree requirements:* For master's, comprehensive exam, thesis optional. *Entrance requirements:* For master's, GRE, minimum GPA of 3.0. Additional exam requirements/recommendations for international students: Required—TOEFL (minimum score 550 paper-based; 213 computer-based; 80 iBT). *Application deadline:* For fall admission, 6/1 priority date for domestic students, 4/15 for international students; for spring admission, 11/1 priority date for domestic students, 10/1 for international students. Applications are processed on a rolling basis. Application fee: $50. Electronic applications accepted. *Expenses:* Tuition, state resident: full-time $9096; part-time $379 per credit. Tuition, nonresident: full-time $23,064; part-time $961 per credit. *Required fees:* $127 per semester. One-time fee: $50. *Financial support:* In 2011–12, 4 research assistantships with full and partial tuition reimbursements (averaging $12,177 per year), 1 teaching assistantship (averaging $12,800 per year) were awarded; scholarships/grants and unspecified assistantships also available. Support available to part-time students. Financial award application deadline: 4/1; financial award applicants required to submit FAFSA. *Faculty research:* Structural engineering, coastal engineering, environmental engineering, geotechnical engineering, water resources, transportation engineering. *Total annual research expenditures:* $557,751. *Unit head:* Dr. Isao Ishibashi, Graduate Program Director, 757-683-4641, Fax: 757-683-5354, E-mail: cegpd@odu.edu. *Application contact:* Dr. Linda Vahala, Associate Dean, 757-683-3789, Fax: 757-683-4898, E-mail: lvahala@odu.edu. Web site: http://eng.odu.edu/cee/.

Oregon State University, Graduate School, College of Engineering, School of Civil and Construction Engineering, Corvallis, OR 97331. Offers civil engineering (MS, PhD); coastal and ocean engineering (M Oc E, PhD); coastal engineering (MS); construction engineering management (MBE, PhD); engineering (M Eng, MAIS); geotechnical engineering (MS, PhD); structural engineering (MS, PhD); transportation engineering (MS, PhD); water engineering (MS, PhD). Part-time programs available. Terminal master's awarded for partial completion of doctoral program. *Degree requirements:* For master's, thesis or alternative; for doctorate, one foreign language, thesis/dissertation. *Entrance requirements:* For master's, GRE General Test, minimum GPA of 3.0 in last 90 hours (3.5 for MS); for doctorate, GRE General Test, minimum GPA of 3.0 in last 90 hours of undergraduate course work. Additional exam requirements/recommendations for international students: Required—TOEFL (minimum score 580 paper-based; 237 computer-based). *Faculty research:* Hazardous waste management, carbon cycling, wave forces on structures, pavement design, seismic analysis.

Penn State University Park, Graduate School, College of Engineering, Department of Civil and Environmental Engineering, State College, University Park, PA 16802-1503. Offers civil engineering (M Eng, MS, PhD); environmental engineering (M Eng, MS, PhD). *Unit head:* Dr. David N. Wormley, Dean, 814-865-7537, Fax: 814-865-8767, E-mail: dnw2@engr.psu.edu. *Application contact:* Cynthia E. Nicosia, Director, Graduate Enrollment Services, 814-865-1834, E-mail: cey1@psu.edu. Web site: http://www.engr.psu.edu/CE/.

Polytechnic Institute of New York University, Department of Civil Engineering, Major in Civil Engineering, Brooklyn, NY 11201-2990. Offers MS, PhD. Part-time and evening/weekend programs available. *Students:* 38 full-time (5 women), 62 part-time (9 women); includes 34 minority (5 Black or African American, non-Hispanic/Latino; 18 Asian, non-Hispanic/Latino; 11 Hispanic/Latino), 29 international. Average age 29. 120 applicants, 48% accepted, 82 enrolled. In 2011, 45 master's, 2 doctorates awarded. *Degree requirements:* For master's, comprehensive exam (for some programs), thesis (for some programs); for doctorate, comprehensive exam, thesis/dissertation. *Entrance requirements:* For doctorate, qualifying exam, MS in civil engineering. Additional exam requirements/recommendations for international students: Required—TOEFL (minimum score 550 paper-based; 213 computer-based; 80 iBT); Recommended—IELTS (minimum score 6.5). *Application deadline:* For fall admission, 7/31 priority date for domestic students, 4/30 for international students; for spring admission, 12/31 priority date for domestic students, 10/30 for international students. Applications are processed on a rolling basis. Application fee: $75. Electronic applications accepted. *Expenses:* Tuition: Full-time $22,464; part-time $1248 per credit. *Required fees:* $501 per semester. *Financial support:* Fellowships, research assistantships, teaching assistantships, institutionally sponsored loans, scholarships/grants, and unspecified assistantships available. Support available to part-time students. Financial award applicants required to submit FAFSA. *Unit head:* Dr. Lawrence Chiarelli, Department Head, 718-260-4040, Fax: 718-260-3433, E-mail: lchiarel@poly.edu. *Application contact:* JeanCarlo Bonilla, Director of Graduate Enrollment Management, 718-260-3182, Fax: 718-260-3624, E-mail: gradinfo@poly.edu.

Polytechnic Institute of NYU, Long Island Graduate Center, Graduate Programs, Department of Civil Engineering, Major in Civil Engineering, Melville, NY 11747. Offers MS. *Students:* 1 full-time (0 women). Average age 22. In 2011, 3 master's awarded. *Degree requirements:* For master's, comprehensive exam (for some programs), thesis (for some programs). *Entrance requirements:* Additional exam requirements/recommendations for international students: Required—TOEFL (minimum score 550 paper-based; 213 computer-based; 80 iBT); Recommended—IELTS (minimum score 6.5). *Application deadline:* For fall admission, 7/31 priority date for domestic students, 4/30 for international students; for spring admission, 12/31 priority date for domestic students, 11/30 for international students. Applications are processed on a rolling basis. Application fee: $75. Electronic applications accepted. *Financial support:* Institutionally sponsored loans, scholarships/grants, and unspecified assistantships available. Support available to part-time students. Financial award applicants required to submit FAFSA. *Unit head:* Dr. Roger Peter Roess, Department Head, 718-260-3018, E-mail: rroess@poly.edu. *Application contact:* JeanCarlo Bonilla, Director of Graduate Enrollment Management, 718-260-3182, Fax: 718-260-3624, E-mail: gradinfo@poly.edu.

Polytechnic University of Puerto Rico, Graduate School, Hato Rey, PR 00919. Offers business administration (MBA), including computer information systems, general management, management of information systems, management of international enterprises; civil engineering (ME, MS); computer engineering (ME, MS); computer science (MCS, MS); electrical engineering (ME, MS); engineering management (MEM); environmental management (MEM); landscape architecture (M Land Arch); manufacturing competitiveness (MMC, MS); manufacturing engineering (ME, MS); mechanical engineering (M Mech E). Part-time and evening/weekend programs available. *Entrance requirements:* For master's, 3 letters of recommendation.

Portland State University, Graduate Studies, Maseeh College of Engineering and Computer Science, Department of Civil and Environmental Engineering, Portland, OR 97207-0751. Offers civil and environmental engineering (M Eng, MS, PhD); civil and environmental engineering management (M Eng); environmental sciences and resources (PhD); systems science (PhD). Part-time and evening/weekend programs available. *Degree requirements:* For master's, thesis or alternative, oral exam; for doctorate, one foreign language, thesis/dissertation, oral and written exams. *Entrance requirements:* For master's, minimum GPA of 3.0 in upper-division course work, BS in civil engineering or allied field; for doctorate, GRE General Test, GRE Subject Test, minimum GPA of 3.0 in upper-division course work, master's in civil and environmental engineering, 2 years full-time graduate work beyond master's degree. Additional exam requirements/recommendations for international students: Required—TOEFL (minimum score 550 paper-based; 213 computer-based). *Faculty research:* Structures, water resources, geotechnical engineering, environmental engineering, transportation.

Portland State University, Graduate Studies, Systems Science Program, Portland, OR 97207-0751. Offers computational intelligence (Certificate); computer modeling and simulation (Certificate); systems science (MS); systems science/anthropology (PhD); systems science/business administration (PhD); systems science/civil engineering (PhD); systems science/economics (PhD); systems science/engineering management (PhD); systems science/general (PhD); systems science/mathematical sciences (PhD); systems science/mechanical engineering (PhD); systems science/psychology (PhD); systems science/sociology (PhD). *Degree requirements:* For doctorate, variable foreign language requirement, thesis/dissertation. *Entrance requirements:* For master's, 2 letters of recommendation; for doctorate, GMAT, GRE General Test, minimum undergraduate GPA of 3.0. Additional exam requirements/recommendations for international students: Required—TOEFL. *Faculty research:* Systems theory and methodology, artificial intelligence neural networks, information theory, nonlinear dynamics/chaos, modeling and simulation.

Princeton University, Graduate School, School of Engineering and Applied Science, Department of Civil and Environmental Engineering, Princeton, NJ 08544-1019. Offers civil and environmental engineering (MSE). Terminal master's awarded for partial completion of doctoral program. *Degree requirements:* For master's, thesis (MSE); for doctorate, thesis/dissertation, general exam. *Entrance requirements:* For master's, GRE General Test, 3 letters of recommendation; for doctorate, GRE General Test, official transcript(s), 3 letters of recommendation, personal statement. Additional exam requirements/recommendations for international students: Required—TOEFL. Electronic applications accepted. *Faculty research:* Carbon mitigation; civil engineering materials and structures; climate and atmospheric dynamics; computational mechanics and risk assessment; hydrology, remote sensing, and sustainability.

Purdue University, College of Engineering, School of Civil Engineering, West Lafayette, IN 47907-2051. Offers MS, MSCE, MSE, PhD. Part-time programs available. Terminal master's awarded for partial completion of doctoral program. *Degree requirements:* For master's, thesis (for some programs); for doctorate, thesis/dissertation. *Entrance requirements:* For master's and doctorate, GRE General Test, minimum GPA of 3.0. Additional exam requirements/recommendations for international students: Required—TOEFL (minimum score 575 paper-based; 233 computer-based; 90 iBT); Recommended—TWE. Electronic applications accepted. *Faculty research:* Environmental and hydraulic engineering, geotechnical and materials engineering, structural engineering, construction engineering, infrastructure and transportation systems engineering.

Queen's University at Kingston, School of Graduate Studies and Research, Faculty of Applied Science, Department of Civil Engineering, Kingston, ON K7L 3N6, Canada. Offers M Eng, M Sc Eng, PhD. Part-time programs available. *Degree requirements:* For master's, thesis (for some programs); for doctorate, comprehensive exam, thesis/dissertation. *Entrance requirements:* Additional exam requirements/recommendations for international students: Required—TOEFL. *Faculty research:* Structural, geotechnical, transportation, hydrotechnical, and environmental engineering.

Rensselaer Polytechnic Institute, Graduate School, School of Engineering, Program in Civil Engineering, Troy, NY 12180-3590. Offers geotechnical engineering (M Eng, MS, PhD); mechanics of composite materials and structures (M Eng, MS, PhD); structural engineering (M Eng, MS, PhD); transportation engineering (M Eng, MS, PhD). Part-time programs available. Terminal master's awarded for partial completion of doctoral program. *Degree requirements:* For master's, thesis (for some programs); for doctorate, thesis/dissertation. *Entrance requirements:* For master's and doctorate, GRE. Additional exam requirements/recommendations for international students: Required—TOEFL (minimum score 570 paper-based; 230 computer-based; 89 iBT), IELTS (minimum score 6.5). Electronic applications accepted. *Faculty research:* Computational mechanics, earthquake engineering, geo-environmental engineering.

Rice University, Graduate Programs, George R. Brown School of Engineering, Department of Civil and Environmental Engineering, Houston, TX 77251-1892. Offers civil engineering (MCE, MS, PhD); environmental engineering (MEE, MES, MS, PhD); environmental science (MEE, MES, MS, PhD). Part-time programs available. *Degree requirements:* For master's, thesis (for some programs); for doctorate, thesis/dissertation. *Entrance requirements:* For master's and doctorate, GRE General Test, GRE Subject Test, minimum GPA of 3.25. Additional exam requirements/recommendations for international students: Required—TOEFL (minimum score 600 paper-based; 250 computer-based; 90 iBT). Electronic applications accepted. *Faculty research:* Biology and chemistry of groundwater, pollutant fate in groundwater systems, water quality monitoring, urban storm water runoff, urban air quality.

Rose-Hulman Institute of Technology, Faculty of Engineering and Applied Sciences, Department of Civil Engineering, Terre Haute, IN 47803-3999. Offers civil engineering (MS); environmental engineering (MS). Part-time programs available. *Faculty:* 7 full-time (1 woman). *Students:* 1 full-time (0 women). Average age 23. 3 applicants, 100% accepted, 1 enrolled. In 2011, 1 master's awarded. *Degree requirements:* For master's, thesis. *Entrance requirements:* For master's, GRE, minimum GPA of 3.0. Additional exam requirements/recommendations for international students: Required—TOEFL (minimum score 580 paper-based; 237 computer-based; 92 iBT). *Application deadline:* For fall admission, 2/1 priority date for domestic students. Applications are processed on a rolling basis. Application fee: $0. *Expenses:* Tuition: Full-time $37,197; part-time $1085 per credit hour. *Financial support:* In 2011–12, 1 student received support. Fellowships with full and partial tuition reimbursements available, research assistantships with full and partial tuition reimbursements available, institutionally sponsored loans, scholarships/grants, and tuition waivers (full and partial) available. Financial award application deadline: 2/1. *Faculty research:* Urban stormwater management, groundwater and surface water models, solid and hazardous waste, risk and decision analysis. Total annual research expenditures: $64,522. *Unit head:* Dr. Kevin G. Sutterer, Chairman, 812-877-8959, Fax: 812-877-8440, E-mail: kevin.g.sutterer@rose-hulman.edu. *Application contact:* Dr. Daniel J. Moore, Associate Dean of the Faculty, 812-877-8110, Fax: 812-877-8061, E-mail: daniel.j.moore@rose-hulman.edu. Web site: http://www.rose-hulman.edu/ce/.

Rowan University, Graduate School, College of Engineering, Department of Civil and Environmental Engineering, Program in Civil Engineering, Glassboro, NJ 08028-1701. Offers MS. *Entrance requirements:* For master's, GRE General Test. Additional exam requirements/recommendations for international students: Required—TOEFL. Electronic applications accepted.

Royal Military College of Canada, Division of Graduate Studies and Research, Engineering Division, Department of Civil Engineering, Kingston, ON K7K 7B4, Canada. Offers M Eng, MA Sc, PhD. *Degree requirements:* For master's, thesis; for doctorate, comprehensive exam, thesis/dissertation. *Entrance requirements:* For master's, honours degree with second-class standing; for doctorate, master's degree. Electronic applications accepted.

Rutgers, The State University of New Jersey, New Brunswick, Graduate School-New Brunswick, Department of Civil and Environmental Engineering, Piscataway, NJ 08854-8097. Offers MS, PhD. Part-time and evening/weekend programs available. Terminal master's awarded for partial completion of doctoral program. *Degree requirements:* For master's, comprehensive exam, thesis or alternative; for doctorate, comprehensive exam, thesis/dissertation. *Entrance requirements:* For master's and doctorate, GRE General Test. Additional exam requirements/recommendations for international students: Required—TOEFL (minimum score 580 paper-based; 237 computer-based). Electronic applications accepted. *Faculty research:* Civil engineering materials research, non-destructive evaluation of transportation infrastructure, transportation planning, intelligent transportation systems.

Saint Martin's University, Graduate Programs, Program in Civil Engineering, Lacey, WA 98503. Offers MCE. Part-time and evening/weekend programs available. *Faculty:* 1 full-time (0 women), 2 part-time/adjunct (0 women). *Students:* 8 full-time (1 woman), 1 part-time (0 women); includes 2 minority (1 Black or African American, non-Hispanic/Latino; 1 Asian, non-Hispanic/Latino), 2 international. Average age 31. 6 applicants, 100% accepted, 5 enrolled. In 2011, 3 master's awarded. *Degree requirements:* For master's, thesis optional. *Entrance requirements:* For master's, minimum GPA of 2.8; BS in civil engineering or other engineering/science with completion of calculus, differential equations, physics, chemistry. Additional exam requirements/recommendations for international students: Required—TOEFL (minimum score 525 paper-based; 210 computer-based). *Application deadline:* For fall admission, 6/30 priority date for domestic students, 4/30 for international students; for spring admission, 9/30 priority date for domestic students, 6/30 for international students. Applications are processed on a rolling basis. Application fee: $35. *Expenses:* Tuition: Part-time $910 per credit hour. Tuition and fees vary according to course level, campus/location and program. *Financial support:* Scholarships/grants and tuition waivers (partial) available. Support available to part-time students. Financial award application deadline: 3/1; financial award applicants required to submit FAFSA. *Faculty research:* Transportation engineering, metal fatigue and fracture, environmental engineering. *Unit head:* Dr. Pius O. Igharo, Program Chair, 360-438-4322, Fax: 360-438-4548, E-mail: pigharo@stmartin.edu. *Application contact:* Hopie Lopez, Administrative Assistant, 360-438-4320,

Fax: 360-438-4548, E-mail: hlopez@stmartin.edu. Web site: http://www.stmartin.edu/engineering/mce/.

San Diego State University, Graduate and Research Affairs, College of Engineering, Department of Civil and Environmental Engineering, San Diego, CA 92182. Offers civil engineering (MS). Part-time and evening/weekend programs available. *Degree requirements:* For master's, thesis optional. *Entrance requirements:* For master's, GRE General Test. Additional exam requirements/recommendations for international students: Required—TOEFL. Electronic applications accepted. *Faculty research:* Hydraulics, hydrology, transportation, smart material, concrete material.

San Jose State University, Graduate Studies and Research, Charles W. Davidson College of Engineering, Department of Civil and Environmental Engineering, San Jose, CA 95192-0001. Offers civil engineering (MS). *Degree requirements:* For master's, thesis or alternative. *Entrance requirements:* For master's, minimum GPA of 2.7. Electronic applications accepted.

Santa Clara University, School of Engineering, Department of Civil Engineering, Santa Clara, CA 95053. Offers MS. Part-time and evening/weekend programs available. *Students:* 16 full-time (6 women), 6 part-time (2 women); includes 8 minority (1 Black or African American, non-Hispanic/Latino; 4 Asian, non-Hispanic/Latino; 2 Hispanic/Latino; 1 Native Hawaiian or other Pacific Islander, non-Hispanic/Latino), 3 international. Average age 25. 28 applicants, 54% accepted, 10 enrolled. In 2011, 8 degrees awarded. *Degree requirements:* For master's, thesis (for some programs). *Entrance requirements:* For master's, GRE, transcript. Additional exam requirements/recommendations for international students: Required—TOEFL (minimum score 550 paper-based; 213 computer-based; 79 iBT). *Application deadline:* For fall admission, 8/12 for domestic students, 7/15 for international students; for winter admission, 10/28 for domestic students, 9/23 for international students; for spring admission, 2/25 for domestic students, 1/21 for international students. Applications are processed on a rolling basis. Application fee: $60. Electronic applications accepted. *Expenses:* Contact institution. *Financial support:* Research assistantships and teaching assistantships available. Financial award application deadline: 3/2; financial award applicants required to submit FAFSA. *Unit head:* Dr. Alex Zecevic, Associate Dean for Graduate Studies, 408-554-2394, Fax: 408-554-4323, E-mail: azecevic@scu.edu. *Application contact:* Stacey Tinker, Director of Admissions, Graduate Engineering, 408-554-4748, Fax: 408-554-4323, E-mail: stinker@scu.edu.

South Carolina State University, School of Graduate Studies, Department of Civil and Mechanical Engineering Technology and Nuclear Engineering, Orangeburg, SC 29117-0001. Offers transportation (MS). Part-time and evening/weekend programs available. *Faculty:* 2 full-time (0 women), 3 part-time/adjunct (1 woman). *Students:* 19 full-time (6 women), 3 part-time (1 woman); includes 20 minority (19 Black or African American, non-Hispanic/Latino; 1 Hispanic/Latino), 2 international. Average age 28. 12 applicants, 83% accepted, 5 enrolled. In 2011, 3 master's awarded. *Degree requirements:* For master's, comprehensive exam, thesis, departmental qualifying exam. *Entrance requirements:* For master's, GRE. Additional exam requirements/recommendations for international students: Recommended—TOEFL. *Application deadline:* For fall admission, 6/15 for domestic and international students; for spring admission, 11/1 for domestic and international students. Application fee: $25. Electronic applications accepted. *Expenses:* Tuition, state resident: full-time $8688; part-time $514 per credit hour. Tuition, nonresident: full-time $17,600; part-time $1009 per credit hour. *Required fees:* $570. *Financial support:* In 2011–12, 6 fellowships (averaging $5,150 per year) were awarded; research assistantships, career-related internships or fieldwork, Federal Work-Study, institutionally sponsored loans, and unspecified assistantships also available. Financial award application deadline: 6/1. *Faculty research:* Societal competence, relationship of parent-child interaction to adult, rehabilitation evaluation, vocation, language assessment of rural children. *Unit head:* Dr. Stanley Ihekweazu, Chair, 803-536-7117, Fax: 803-516-4607, E-mail: sihekweazu@scsu.edu. *Application contact:* Annette Hazzard-Jones, Program Coordinator II, 803-536-8809, Fax: 803-536-8812, E-mail: zs_ahazzard@scsu.edu. Web site: http://www.scsu.edu/schoolofgraduatestudies.aspx.

South Dakota School of Mines and Technology, Graduate Division, Program in Civil Engineering, Rapid City, SD 57701-3995. Offers MS. Part-time programs available. *Entrance requirements:* Additional exam requirements/recommendations for international students: Required—TOEFL, TWE. Electronic applications accepted. *Faculty research:* Concrete technology, environmental and sanitation engineering, water resources engineering, composite materials, geotechnical engineering.

South Dakota State University, Graduate School, College of Engineering, Department of Civil and Environmental Engineering, Brookings, SD 57007. Offers engineering (MS). Part-time programs available. Postbaccalaureate distance learning degree programs offered (minimal on-campus study). *Degree requirements:* For master's, thesis (for some programs), oral exam. *Entrance requirements:* Additional exam requirements/recommendations for international students: Required—TOEFL (minimum score 525 paper-based). *Faculty research:* Structural, environmental, geotechnical, transportation engineering and water resources.

Southern Illinois University Carbondale, Graduate School, College of Engineering, Department of Civil and Environmental Engineering, Carbondale, IL 62901-4701. Offers civil engineering (MS). *Faculty:* 10 full-time (1 woman). *Students:* 19 full-time (4 women), 21 part-time (2 women); includes 1 minority (Black or African American, non-Hispanic/Latino), 22 international. Average age 26. 38 applicants, 37% accepted, 9 enrolled. In 2011, 7 master's awarded. *Degree requirements:* For master's, comprehensive exam, thesis. *Entrance requirements:* For master's, minimum GPA of 2.7. Additional exam requirements/recommendations for international students: Required—TOEFL. *Application deadline:* Applications are processed on a rolling basis. Application fee: $20. *Financial support:* In 2011–12, 21 students received support, including 5 research assistantships with full tuition reimbursements available, 9 teaching assistantships with full tuition reimbursements available; fellowships with full tuition reimbursements available, Federal Work-Study, institutionally sponsored loans, and tuition waivers (full) also available. Support available to part-time students. Financial award application deadline: 7/1. *Faculty research:* Composite materials, wastewater treatment, solid waste disposal, slurry transport, geotechnical engineering. Total annual research expenditures: $230,856. *Unit head:* Dr. Lizette Chevalier, Interim Chair, 618-453-7815, E-mail: cheval@engr.siu.edu. *Application contact:* Steve Rogers, Administrative Clerk, 618-536-2368, E-mail: nihil@siu.edu. Web site: http://civil.engr.siu.edu/civil/.

Southern Illinois University Edwardsville, Graduate School, School of Engineering, Department of Civil Engineering, Edwardsville, IL 62026-0001. Offers MS. Part-time and evening/weekend programs available. *Faculty:* 8 full-time (1 woman). *Students:* 7 full-time (3 women), 35 part-time (8 women); includes 2 minority (1 Asian, non-Hispanic/Latino; 1 Two or more races, non-Hispanic/Latino), 9 international. 44 applicants, 52% accepted. In 2011, 17 master's awarded. *Degree requirements:* For master's, thesis (for some programs), research paper. *Entrance requirements:* For master's, minimum undergraduate GPA of 2.75 in science, math, and engineering courses. Additional exam requirements/recommendations for international students: Required—TOEFL (minimum score 550 paper-based; 213 computer-based; 79 iBT), IELTS (minimum score 6.5). *Application deadline:* For fall admission, 7/22 for domestic students, 6/1 for international students; for spring admission, 12/9 for domestic students, 10/1 for international students. Applications are processed on a rolling basis. Application fee: $30. Electronic applications accepted. Tuition and fees vary according to course load and program. *Financial support:* In 2011–12, 1 fellowship with full tuition reimbursement (averaging $8,370 per year), 4 research assistantships with full tuition reimbursements (averaging $9,927 per year), 5 teaching assistantships with full tuition reimbursements (averaging $9,927 per year) were awarded; institutionally sponsored loans, scholarships/grants, and unspecified assistantships also available. Financial award application deadline: 3/1; financial award applicants required to submit FAFSA. *Unit head:* Dr. Susan Morgan, Chair, 618-650-2533, E-mail: smorgan@siue.edu. *Application contact:* Dr. Ryan Fries, Director, 618-650-5026, E-mail: rfries@siue.edu. Web site: http://www.siue.edu/engineering/civilengineering.

Southern Methodist University, Bobby B. Lyle School of Engineering, Department of Environmental and Civil Engineering, Dallas, TX 75275-0340. Offers applied science (MS, PhD); civil and environmental engineering (PhD); civil engineering (MS); environmental engineering (MS); environmental science (MS), including environmental systems management. Part-time and evening/weekend programs available. Postbaccalaureate distance learning degree programs offered (no on-campus study). Terminal master's awarded for partial completion of doctoral program. *Degree requirements:* For master's, thesis optional; for doctorate, thesis/dissertation, oral and written qualifying exams. *Entrance requirements:* For master's, GRE General Test, minimum GPA of 3.0 in last 2 years; bachelor's degree in engineering, mathematics, or sciences; for doctorate, GRE, BS and MS in related field, minimum GPA of 3.3. Additional exam requirements/recommendations for international students: Required—TOEFL. Electronic applications accepted. *Faculty research:* Human and environmental health effects of endocrine disrupters, development of air pollution control systems for diesel engines, structural analysis and design, modeling and design of waste treatment systems.

Stanford University, School of Engineering, Department of Civil and Environmental Engineering, Stanford, CA 94305-9991. Offers MS, PhD, Eng. Terminal master's awarded for partial completion of doctoral program. *Degree requirements:* For doctorate, thesis/dissertation, qualifying exam; for Eng, thesis. *Entrance requirements:* For master's, doctorate, and Eng, GRE General Test. Additional exam requirements/recommendations for international students: Required—TOEFL. Electronic applications accepted. *Expenses:* Tuition: Full-time $40,050; part-time $890 per credit.

Stevens Institute of Technology, Graduate School, Charles V. Schaefer Jr. School of Engineering, Department of Civil, Environmental, and Ocean Engineering, Program in Civil Engineering, Hoboken, NJ 07030. Offers civil engineering (PhD); geotechnical engineering (Certificate); geotechnical/geoenvironmental engineering (M Eng, Engr); hydrologic modeling (M Eng); stormwater management (M Eng); structural engineering (M Eng, Engr); water resources engineering (M Eng). *Degree requirements:* For master's, thesis optional; for doctorate, variable foreign language requirement, thesis/dissertation; for other advanced degree, project or thesis. *Entrance requirements:* For doctorate, GRE. Additional exam requirements/recommendations for international students: Required—TOEFL. Electronic applications accepted.

Syracuse University, L. C. Smith College of Engineering and Computer Science, Program in Civil Engineering, Syracuse, NY 13244. Offers MS, PhD. Part-time programs available. *Students:* 47 full-time (13 women), 5 part-time (2 women); includes 2 minority (1 Hispanic/Latino; 1 Two or more races, non-Hispanic/Latino), 40 international. Average age 27. 75 applicants, 63% accepted, 15 enrolled. In 2011, 9 degrees awarded. *Degree requirements:* For doctorate, thesis/dissertation. *Entrance requirements:* For master's and doctorate, GRE General Test. Additional exam requirements/recommendations for international students: Required—TOEFL (minimum score 100 iBT). *Application deadline:* For fall admission, 6/1 priority date for domestic students, 6/1 for international students. Applications are processed on a rolling basis. Application fee: $75. Electronic applications accepted. *Expenses: Tuition:* Part-time $1206 per credit. *Financial support:* Fellowships with full tuition reimbursements, research assistantships with full and partial tuition reimbursements, teaching assistantships with full and partial tuition reimbursements, and tuition waivers (partial) available. Financial award application deadline: 1/1. *Faculty research:* Fate and transport of pollutants, methods for characterization and remediation of hazardous wastes, response of eco-systems to disturbances, water quality and engineering. *Unit head:* Dr. Chris E. Johnson, Interim Chair, 315-443-2311, E-mail: cejohns@syr.edu. *Application contact:* Elizabeth Buchanan, Information Contact, 315-443-2558, E-mail: ebuchana@syr.edu. Web site: http://lcs.syr.edu/.

Temple University, College of Engineering, Department of Civil and Environmental Engineering, Philadelphia, PA 19122-6096. Offers civil engineering (MSE). Part-time programs available. *Faculty:* 8 full-time (1 woman). *Students:* 8 full-time (4 women), 8 part-time (3 women); includes 5 minority (2 Black or African American, non-Hispanic/Latino; 3 Asian, non-Hispanic/Latino), 4 international. Average age 28. 9 applicants, 78% accepted, 2 enrolled. In 2011, 10 master's awarded. *Degree requirements:* For master's, thesis optional. *Entrance requirements:* For master's, GRE General Test, minimum GPA of 3.0. Additional exam requirements/recommendations for international students: Required—TOEFL (minimum score 550 paper-based; 213 computer-based; 79 iBT). *Application deadline:* For fall admission, 7/1 for domestic students, 12/15 for international students; for spring admission, 11/1 for domestic students, 8/1 for international students. Applications are processed on a rolling basis. Application fee: $50. *Expenses:* Tuition, state resident: full-time $12,366; part-time $687 per credit hour. Tuition, nonresident: full-time $17,298; part-time $961 per credit hour. *Required fees:* $590; $213 per year. *Financial support:* In 2011–12, 1 fellowship was awarded; research assistantships, teaching assistantships, and Federal Work-Study also available. Financial award application deadline: 1/15; financial award applicants required to submit FAFSA. *Faculty research:* Prestressed masonry structure, recycling processes and products, finite element analysis of highways and runways. *Unit head:* Dr. Philip Udo-Inyang, Acting Chair, 215-204-7831, Fax: 215-204-6936, E-mail: udoinyan@temple.edu. *Application contact:* Tara Schumacher, Coordinator of Outreach, 215-204-6575, Fax: 215-204-8781, E-mail: tara.schumacher@temple.edu. Web site: http://www.temple.edu/engineering/civil.

Tennessee Technological University, Graduate School, College of Engineering, Department of Civil and Environmental Engineering, Cookeville, TN 38505. Offers MS. Part-time programs available. *Faculty:* 17 full-time (0 women). *Students:* 18 full-time (4 women), 6 part-time (1 woman); includes 4 minority (3 Black or African American, non-Hispanic/Latino; 1 American Indian or Alaska Native, non-Hispanic/Latino), 2 international. Average age 27. 24 applicants, 75% accepted, 9 enrolled. In 2011, 10 master's awarded. *Degree requirements:* For master's, thesis. *Entrance requirements:* For master's, GRE. Additional exam requirements/recommendations for international

students: Required—TOEFL (minimum score 550 paper-based; 79 iBT), IELTS (minimum score 5.5), PTE Academic. *Application deadline:* For fall admission, 8/1 for domestic students, 5/1 for international students; for spring admission, 12/1 for domestic students, 10/1 for international students. Application fee: $25 ($30 for international students). Electronic applications accepted. *Expenses:* Tuition, state resident: full-time $8094; part-time $422 per credit hour. Tuition, nonresident: full-time $20,574; part-time $1046 per credit hour. *Financial support:* In 2011–12, 6 research assistantships (averaging $8,227 per year), 5 teaching assistantships (averaging $7,200 per year) were awarded; career-related internships or fieldwork also available. Financial award application deadline: 4/1. *Faculty research:* Environmental engineering, transportation, structural engineering, water resources. *Unit head:* Dr. David Huddleston, Interim Chairperson, 931-372-3454, Fax: 931-372-6352, E-mail: dhuddleston@tntech.edu. *Application contact:* Shelia K. Kendrick, Coordinator of Graduate Admissions, 931-372-3808, Fax: 931-372-3497, E-mail: skendrick@tntech.edu.

Texas A&M University, College of Engineering, Zachry Department of Civil Engineering, College Station, TX 77843. Offers coastal and ocean engineering (M Eng, MS, D Eng, PhD); construction engineering and management (M Eng, MS, D Eng, PhD); environmental engineering (M Eng, MS, D Eng, PhD); geotechnical engineering (M Eng, MS, D Eng, PhD); materials engineering (M Eng, MS, D Eng, PhD); structural engineering (M Eng, MS, D Eng, PhD); transportation engineering (M Eng, MS, D Eng, PhD); water resources engineering (M Eng, MS, D Eng, PhD). Part-time programs available. *Faculty:* 57. *Students:* 361 full-time (76 women), 46 part-time (8 women); includes 41 minority (3 Black or African American, non-Hispanic/Latino; 16 Asian, non-Hispanic/Latino; 21 Hispanic/Latino; 1 Two or more races, non-Hispanic/Latino), 247 international. Average age 29. In 2011, 123 master's, 27 doctorates awarded. *Degree requirements:* For master's, thesis (MS); for doctorate, dissertation (PhD), internship (D Eng). *Entrance requirements:* For master's and doctorate, GRE General Test. Additional exam requirements/recommendations for international students: Required—TOEFL. *Application deadline:* Applications are processed on a rolling basis. Application fee: $50 ($75 for international students). Electronic applications accepted. *Expenses:* Tuition, state resident: full-time $5437; part-time $226.55 per credit hour. Tuition, nonresident: full-time $12,949; part-time $539.55 per credit hour. *Required fees:* $2741. *Financial support:* In 2011–12, fellowships (averaging $4,500 per year), research assistantships (averaging $14,000 per year), teaching assistantships (averaging $14,400 per year) were awarded; career-related internships or fieldwork and institutionally sponsored loans also available. Financial award application deadline: 4/15; financial award applicants required to submit FAFSA. *Unit head:* Dr. John Niedzwecki, Head, 979-845-3858, E-mail: j-niedzwecki@tamu.edu. *Application contact:* Graduate Advisor, 979-845-7435, Fax: 979-845-6156, E-mail: info@civil.tamu.edu. Web site: https://www.civil.tamu.edu/.

Texas A&M University–Kingsville, College of Graduate Studies, College of Engineering, Department of Civil Engineering, Kingsville, TX 78363. Offers ME, MS. Part-time and evening/weekend programs available. *Degree requirements:* For master's, comprehensive exam, thesis or alternative. *Entrance requirements:* For master's, GRE General Test. Additional exam requirements/recommendations for international students: Required—TOEFL. *Faculty research:* Geotechnical engineering, structural mechanics, structural design, transportation engineering.

Texas Tech University, Graduate School, Edward E. Whitacre Jr. College of Engineering, Department of Civil and Environmental Engineering, Lubbock, TX 79409. Offers civil engineering (MSCE, PhD); environmental engineering (MENVEGR). *Accreditation:* ABET. Part-time programs available. *Faculty:* 20 full-time (3 women), 1 part-time/adjunct (0 women). *Students:* 68 full-time (18 women), 11 part-time (2 women); includes 10 minority (2 Black or African American, non-Hispanic/Latino; 2 Asian, non-Hispanic/Latino; 6 Hispanic/Latino), 35 international. Average age 26. 91 applicants, 67% accepted, 27 enrolled. In 2011, 34 master's, 2 doctorates awarded. *Degree requirements:* For master's, thesis or alternative; for doctorate, thesis/dissertation. *Entrance requirements:* For master's and doctorate, GRE General Test, minimum GPA of 3.0. Additional exam requirements/recommendations for international students: Required—TOEFL (minimum score 550 paper-based; 213 computer-based; 79 iBT). *Application deadline:* For fall admission, 6/1 priority date for domestic students, 1/15 for international students; for spring admission, 9/1 priority date for domestic students, 6/15 for international students. Applications are processed on a rolling basis. Application fee: $50 ($75 for international students). Electronic applications accepted. *Expenses:* Tuition, state resident: full-time $5899; part-time $245.80 per credit hour. Tuition, nonresident: full-time $13,411; part-time $558.80 per credit hour. *Required fees:* $2680.60; $86.50 per credit hour. $920.30 per semester. *Financial support:* In 2011–12, 40 students received support. Application deadline: 4/15; applicants required to submit FAFSA. *Faculty research:* Wind load/engineering on structures, fluid mechanics, structural dynamics, water resource management, transportation engineering. *Total annual research expenditures:* $2.9 million. *Unit head:* Dr. H. Scott Norville, Chair, 806-742-3523, Fax: 806-742-3488, E-mail: scott.norville@ttu.edu. *Application contact:* Dr. Priyantha Jayawickrama, Graduate Adviser, 806-742-3523, Fax: 806-742-3488, E-mail: priyantha.jayawickrama@ttu.edu. Web site: http://www.ce.ttu.edu/.

Trine University, Allen School of Engineering and Technology, Angola, IN 46703-1764. Offers civil engineering (ME); mechanical engineering (ME). Part-time and evening/weekend programs available. *Degree requirements:* For master's, comprehensive exam, thesis. *Faculty research:* CAD, computer aided MFG, computer numerical control, parametric modeling, megatronics.

Tufts University, School of Engineering, Department of Civil and Environmental Engineering, Medford, MA 02155. Offers bioengineering (ME, MS), including environmental technology; civil engineering (ME, MS, PhD), including geotechnical engineering, structural engineering, water diplomacy (PhD); environmental engineering (ME, MS, PhD), including environmental engineering and environmental sciences, environmental geotechnology, environmental health, environmental science and management, hazardous materials management, water diplomacy (PhD), water resources engineering. Part-time programs available. *Faculty:* 18 full-time, 5 part-time/adjunct. *Students:* 102 full-time (50 women); includes 8 minority (1 Black or African American, non-Hispanic/Latino; 6 Asian, non-Hispanic/Latino; 1 Hispanic/Latino), 37 international. Average age 27. 162 applicants, 59% accepted, 37 enrolled. In 2011, 18 degrees awarded. Terminal master's awarded for partial completion of doctoral program. *Degree requirements:* For master's, thesis or alternative; for doctorate, thesis/dissertation. *Entrance requirements:* For master's and doctorate, GRE General Test. Additional exam requirements/recommendations for international students: Required—TOEFL (minimum score 550 paper-based; 213 computer-based; 80 iBT). *Application deadline:* For fall admission, 1/15 priority date for domestic students, 12/15 for international students; for spring admission, 10/15 for domestic students, 9/15 for international students. Applications are processed on a rolling basis. Application fee: $75. Electronic applications accepted. *Expenses: Tuition:* Full-time $41,208; part-time $1030 per credit hour. Full-time tuition and fees vary according to degree level, program and student level. Part-time tuition and fees vary according to course load. *Financial* *support:* Fellowships with full tuition reimbursements, research assistantships with full and partial tuition reimbursements, teaching assistantships with full and partial tuition reimbursements, Federal Work-Study, scholarships/grants, tuition waivers (partial), and unspecified assistantships available. Financial award application deadline: 1/15; financial award applicants required to submit FAFSA. *Faculty research:* Environmental and water resources engineering, environmental health, geotechnical and geoenvironmental engineering, structural engineering and mechanics, water diplomacy. *Unit head:* Dr. Kurt Penell, Chair, 617-627-3211, Fax: 617-627-3994. *Application contact:* Laura Sacco, Information Contact, 617-627-3211, E-mail: ceeinfo@tufts.edu. Web site: http://www.ase.tufts.edu/cee/.

Université de Moncton, Faculty of Engineering, Program in Civil Engineering, Moncton, NB E1A 3E9, Canada. Offers M Sc A. *Degree requirements:* For master's, thesis, proficiency in French. *Faculty research:* Structures and materials, hydrology and water resources, soil mechanics and statistical analysis, environment, transportation.

Université de Sherbrooke, Faculty of Engineering, Department of Civil Engineering, Sherbrooke, QC J1K 2R1, Canada. Offers M Sc A, PhD. *Degree requirements:* For master's, one foreign language, thesis; for doctorate, comprehensive exam, thesis/dissertation. *Entrance requirements:* For master's, bachelor's degree in engineering or equivalent; for doctorate, master's degree in engineering or equivalent. Electronic applications accepted. *Faculty research:* High-strength concrete, dynamics of structures, solid mechanics, geotechnical engineering, wastewater treatment.

Université Laval, Faculty of Sciences and Engineering, Department of Civil Engineering, Program in Urban Infrastructure Engineering, Québec, QC G1K 7P4, Canada. Offers Diploma. Part-time and evening/weekend programs available. *Entrance requirements:* For degree, knowledge of French. Electronic applications accepted.

Université Laval, Faculty of Sciences and Engineering, Department of Civil Engineering, Programs in Civil Engineering, Québec, QC G1K 7P4, Canada. Offers civil engineering (M Sc, PhD); environmental technology (M Sc). Terminal master's awarded for partial completion of doctoral program. *Degree requirements:* For master's, thesis (for some programs); for doctorate, comprehensive exam, thesis/dissertation. *Entrance requirements:* For master's and doctorate, knowledge of French and English. Electronic applications accepted.

University at Buffalo, the State University of New York, Graduate School, School of Engineering and Applied Sciences, Department of Civil, Structural, and Environmental Engineering, Buffalo, NY 14260. Offers civil engineering (ME, MS, PhD); engineering science (MS). Part-time programs available. Postbaccalaureate distance learning degree programs offered (minimal on-campus study). *Faculty:* 26 full-time (3 women), 4 part-time/adjunct (1 woman). *Students:* 148 full-time (24 women), 10 part-time (2 women); includes 6 minority (1 American Indian or Alaska Native, non-Hispanic/Latino; 2 Asian, non-Hispanic/Latino; 3 Hispanic/Latino), 120 international. Average age 27. 545 applicants, 12% accepted, 58 enrolled. In 2011, 44 master's, 11 doctorates awarded. Terminal master's awarded for partial completion of doctoral program. *Degree requirements:* For master's, thesis optional, project, thesis, or comprehensive exam; for doctorate, thesis/dissertation. *Entrance requirements:* For master's and doctorate, GRE General Test, letters of reference. Additional exam requirements/recommendations for international students: Required—TOEFL (minimum score 550 paper-based; 213 computer-based; 79 iBT). *Application deadline:* For fall admission, 1/15 priority date for domestic students, 1/15 for international students; for spring admission, 9/15 for domestic and international students. Applications are processed on a rolling basis. Application fee: $75. Electronic applications accepted. *Financial support:* In 2011–12, 76 students received support, including 5 fellowships with full tuition reimbursements available (averaging $28,900 per year), 35 research assistantships with full tuition reimbursements available (averaging $27,700 per year), 26 teaching assistantships with full tuition reimbursements available (averaging $20,900 per year); career-related internships or fieldwork, Federal Work-Study, institutionally sponsored loans, scholarships/grants, traineeships, health care benefits, tuition waivers (full and partial), and unspecified assistantships also available. Support available to part-time students. Financial award application deadline: 1/15; financial award applicants required to submit FAFSA. *Faculty research:* Environmental engineering and fluid mechanics, structural dynamics, geomechanics, earthquake engineering computational mechanics. *Total annual research expenditures:* $7 million. *Unit head:* Dr. Andrew S. Whittaker, Chairman, 716-645-2114, Fax: 716-645-3733, E-mail: awhittak@buffalo.edu. *Application contact:* Dr. Adel Sadek, Director of Graduate Studies, 716-645-4367, Fax: 716-645-3733, E-mail: asadek@buffalo.edu. Web site: http://www.csee.buffalo.edu/.

The University of Akron, Graduate School, College of Engineering, Department of Civil Engineering, Akron, OH 44325. Offers MS, PhD. Evening/weekend programs available. *Faculty:* 17 full-time (4 women), 6 part-time/adjunct (0 women). *Students:* 63 full-time (15 women), 20 part-time (4 women); includes 2 minority (1 Asian, non-Hispanic/Latino; 1 Two or more races, non-Hispanic/Latino), 50 international. Average age 28. 72 applicants, 75% accepted, 14 enrolled. In 2011, 10 master's, 4 doctorates awarded. *Degree requirements:* For master's, thesis optional; for doctorate, thesis/dissertation, candidacy exam, qualifying exam. *Entrance requirements:* For master's, GRE, minimum GPA of 2.75, statement of purpose, three letters of recommendation, resume; for doctorate, GRE, minimum GPA of 3.0 with bachelor's degree, 3.5 with master's degree; three letters of recommendation; statement of purpose, resume. Additional exam requirements/recommendations for international students: Required—TOEFL (minimum score 550 paper-based; 213 computer-based; 79 iBT). *Application deadline:* Applications are processed on a rolling basis. Application fee: $30 ($40 for international students). Electronic applications accepted. *Expenses:* Tuition, state resident: full-time $7038; part-time $391 per credit hour. Tuition, nonresident: full-time $12,051; part-time $670 per credit hour. *Required fees:* $1274; $34 per credit hour. *Financial support:* In 2011–12, 15 research assistantships with full tuition reimbursements, 43 teaching assistantships with full tuition reimbursements were awarded; fellowships, career-related internships or fieldwork, and Federal Work-Study also available. *Faculty research:* Development of constitutive laws for numerical analysis of nonlinear problems in structural mechanics, multiscale modeling and simulation of novel materials, water quality and distribution system analysis, safety-related traffic control, dynamic pile testing and analysis. *Total annual research expenditures:* $1.1 million. *Unit head:* Dr. Wieslaw K. Binienda, Chair, 330-972-6693, E-mail: wbinienda@uakron.edu. *Application contact:* Dr. Craig Menzemer, Associate Dean, 330-972-5536, E-mail: ccmenze@uakron.edu. Web site: http://www.uakron.edu/engineering/CE/.

The University of Alabama, Graduate School, College of Engineering, Department of Civil, Construction and Environmental Engineering, Tuscaloosa, AL 35487-0205. Offers civil engineering (MSCE, PhD); environmental engineering (MS). Part-time programs available. *Faculty:* 19 full-time (2 women), 1 part-time/adjunct (0 women). *Students:* 47 full-time (15 women), 11 part-time (5 women); includes 9 minority (8 Black or African American, non-Hispanic/Latino; 1 Asian, non-Hispanic/Latino), 16 international. Average age 28. 93 applicants, 37% accepted, 10 enrolled. In 2011, 27 master's, 3 doctorates awarded. Terminal master's awarded for partial completion of doctoral program. *Median*

time to degree: Of those who began their doctoral program in fall 2003, 100% received their degree in 8 years or less. *Degree requirements:* For master's, thesis or alternative; for doctorate, one foreign language, thesis/dissertation. *Entrance requirements:* For master's and doctorate, GRE General Test, minimum GPA of 3.0 in last 60 hours of course work. Additional exam requirements/recommendations for international students: Required—TOEFL (minimum score 550 paper-based; 213 computer-based), IELTS (minimum score 6.5). *Application deadline:* For fall admission, 7/6 for domestic students, 1/15 for international students; for spring admission, 11/1 for domestic students, 6/1 for international students. Applications are processed on a rolling basis. Application fee: $50 ($60 for international students). Electronic applications accepted. *Expenses:* Tuition, state resident: full-time $8600. Tuition, nonresident: full-time $21,900. *Financial support:* In 2011–12, 40 students received support, including 32 research assistantships with full tuition reimbursements available (averaging $10,489 per year), 12 teaching assistantships with full tuition reimbursements available (averaging $10,489 per year); fellowships, scholarships/grants, tuition waivers (partial), and unspecified assistantships also available. Financial award application deadline: 3/15. *Faculty research:* Experimental structures, modeling of structures, bridge management systems, geotechnological engineering, environmental remediation. *Total annual research expenditures:* $2.2 million. *Unit head:* Dr. Kenneth J. Fridley, Head and Professor, 205-348-6550, Fax: 205-348-0783, E-mail: kfridley@coe.eng.ua.edu. *Application contact:* Dr. David A. Francko, Dean, 205-348-8280, Fax: 205-348-0400, E-mail: dfrancko@ua.edu. Web site: http://www.ce.eng.ua.edu/.

The University of Alabama at Birmingham, School of Engineering, Program in Civil Engineering, Birmingham, AL 35294. Offers MSCE, PhD. Program offered jointly with The University of Alabama in Huntsville. *Expenses:* Tuition, state resident: full-time $5922; part-time $309 per hour. Tuition, nonresident: full-time $13,428; part-time $726 per hour. Tuition and fees vary according to program. *Unit head:* Dr. Fouad H. Fouad, Chair, 205-934-8430, Fax: 205-934-9855, E-mail: ffouad@uab.edu. Web site: http://www.uab.edu/engineering/departments-research/civil/graduate#Master%20of%20Science%20in%20Civil%20Engineering%20%28M.S.C.E.%29%20Program%20Requi.

The University of Alabama in Huntsville, School of Graduate Studies, College of Engineering, Department of Civil and Environmental Engineering, Huntsville, AL 35899. Offers civil and environmental engineering (PhD); civil engineering (MSE), including civil engineering, environmental and water resource engineering, geotechnical engineering, structural engineering and structural mechanics, transportation engineering. PhD offered jointly with The University of Alabama at Birmingham. Part-time and evening/weekend programs available. *Faculty:* 5 full-time (1 woman), 1 part-time/adjunct (0 women). *Students:* 20 full-time (4 women), 12 part-time (6 women); includes 1 minority (Black or African American, non-Hispanic/Latino), 15 international. Average age 29. 26 applicants, 62% accepted, 6 enrolled. In 2011, 3 master's, 1 doctorate awarded. *Degree requirements:* For master's, comprehensive exam, thesis or alternative, oral and written exams; for doctorate, comprehensive exam, thesis/dissertation, oral and written exams. *Entrance requirements:* For master's, GRE General Test, BSE, minimum GPA of 3.0; for doctorate, GRE General Test, minimum GPA of 3.0. Additional exam requirements/recommendations for international students: Required—TOEFL (minimum score 500 paper-based; 173 computer-based; 62 iBT). *Application deadline:* For fall admission, 7/15 for domestic students, 4/1 for international students; for spring admission, 11/30 for domestic students, 9/1 for international students. Applications are processed on a rolling basis. Application fee: $40 ($50 for international students). Electronic applications accepted. *Expenses:* Tuition, state resident: full-time $7830; part-time $473.50 per credit. Tuition, nonresident: full-time $18,748; part-time $1128.33 per credit. Tuition and fees vary according to course load and program. *Financial support:* In 2011–12, 16 students received support, including 10 research assistantships with full and partial tuition reimbursements available (averaging $12,281 per year), 6 teaching assistantships with full and partial tuition reimbursements available (averaging $12,472 per year); career-related internships or fieldwork, Federal Work-Study, institutionally sponsored loans, scholarships/grants, health care benefits, and unspecified assistantships also available. Support available to part-time students. Financial award application deadline: 4/1; financial award applicants required to submit FAFSA. *Faculty research:* Hydrologic modeling, orbital debris impact, hydrogeology, environmental engineering, transportation engineering. *Total annual research expenditures:* $1.1 million. *Unit head:* Dr. Houssam Toutanji, Chair, 256-824-7361, Fax: 256-824-6724, E-mail: toutanji@cee.uah.edu. *Application contact:* Kim Gray, Graduate Studies Admissions Coordinator, 256-824-6002, Fax: 256-824-6405, E-mail: deangrad@uah.edu. Web site: http://www.uah.edu/eng/departments/cee/welcome.

University of Alaska Anchorage, School of Engineering, Program in Civil Engineering, Anchorage, AK 99508. Offers civil engineering (MCE, MS); port and coastal engineering (Certificate). Part-time and evening/weekend programs available. *Degree requirements:* For master's, thesis (for some programs). *Entrance requirements:* For master's, bachelor's degree in engineering. Additional exam requirements/recommendations for international students: Required—TOEFL (minimum score 550 paper-based; 213 computer-based). *Faculty research:* Structural engineering, engineering education, astronomical observations related to engineering.

University of Alaska Fairbanks, College of Engineering and Mines, Department of Civil and Environmental Engineering, Fairbanks, AK 99775-5900. Offers arctic engineering (MS, PhD); civil engineering (MCE, MS, PhD); construction management (Graduate Certificate); engineering (PhD); engineering and science management (MS, PhD), including engineering management, science management (MS); environmental engineering (MS, PhD), including engineering (PhD), environmental engineering (MS); environmental quality science (MS), including environmental contaminants, environmental quality science, environmental science and management, water supply and waste treatment. Part-time programs available. *Faculty:* 11 full-time (2 women). *Students:* 25 full-time (12 women), 16 part-time (6 women); includes 4 minority (1 Black or African American, non-Hispanic/Latino; 1 American Indian or Alaska Native, non-Hispanic/Latino; 1 Asian, non-Hispanic/Latino; 1 Two or more races, non-Hispanic/Latino), 13 international. Average age 32. 21 applicants, 62% accepted, 8 enrolled. In 2011, 10 master's, 1 doctorate awarded. Terminal master's awarded for partial completion of doctoral program. *Degree requirements:* For master's, comprehensive exam, thesis or alternative; for doctorate, comprehensive exam, thesis/dissertation, oral exam, oral defense. *Entrance requirements:* For doctorate, GRE General Test. Additional exam requirements/recommendations for international students: Required—TOEFL (minimum score 550 paper-based; 213 computer-based; 80 iBT). *Application deadline:* For fall admission, 6/1 for domestic students, 3/1 for international students; for spring admission, 10/15 for domestic students, 9/1 for international students. Applications are processed on a rolling basis. Application fee: $60. Electronic applications accepted. *Expenses:* Tuition, state resident: full-time $6696; part-time $372 per credit. Tuition, nonresident: full-time $13,680; part-time $760 per credit. Tuition and fees vary according to course load and reciprocity agreements. *Financial support:* In 2011–12, 12 research assistantships with tuition reimbursements (averaging $12,027 per year), 6 teaching assistantships with tuition reimbursements (averaging $6,390 per year) were awarded; fellowships with tuition reimbursements, career-related internships or fieldwork, Federal Work-Study, scholarships/grants, health care benefits, and unspecified assistantships also available. Support available to part-time students. Financial award application deadline: 7/1; financial award applicants required to submit FAFSA. *Faculty research:* Soils, structures, culvert thawing with solar power, pavement drainage, contaminant hydrogeology. *Unit head:* Dr. David Barnes, Department Chair, 907-474-7241, Fax: 907-474-6087, E-mail: fycee@uaf.edu. *Application contact:* Mike Earnest, Director of Admissions, 907-474-7500, Fax: 907-474-5379, E-mail: admissions@uaf.edu. Web site: http://www.alaska.edu/uaf/cem/cee/.

University of Alberta, Faculty of Graduate Studies and Research, Department of Civil and Environmental Engineering, Edmonton, AB T6G 2E1, Canada. Offers construction engineering and management (M Eng, M Sc, PhD); environmental engineering (M Eng, M Sc, PhD); environmental science (M Sc, PhD); geoenvironmental engineering (M Eng, M Sc, PhD); geotechnical engineering (M Eng, M Sc, PhD); mining engineering (M Eng, M Sc, PhD); petroleum engineering (M Eng, M Sc, PhD); structural engineering (M Eng, M Sc, PhD); water resources (M Eng, M Sc, PhD). Part-time programs available. Postbaccalaureate distance learning degree programs offered (minimal on-campus study). *Degree requirements:* For master's, thesis (for some programs); for doctorate, thesis/dissertation. *Entrance requirements:* For master's, minimum GPA of 3.0 in last 2 years of undergraduate studies; for doctorate, minimum GPA of 3.0. Additional exam requirements/recommendations for international students: Required—TOEFL (minimum score 550 paper-based; 213 computer-based). Electronic applications accepted. *Faculty research:* Mining.

The University of Arizona, College of Engineering, Department of Civil Engineering and Engineering Mechanics, Program in Civil Engineering, Tucson, AZ 85721. Offers MS, PhD. Part-time programs available. *Faculty:* 10 full-time (1 woman). *Students:* 19 full-time (6 women), 8 part-time (0 women); includes 5 minority (1 Asian, non-Hispanic/Latino; 1 Hispanic/Latino; 3 Two or more races, non-Hispanic/Latino), 14 international. Average age 30. 74 applicants, 46% accepted, 7 enrolled. In 2011, 5 master's, 4 doctorates awarded. *Degree requirements:* For master's, thesis; for doctorate, thesis/dissertation, departmental qualifying exam. *Entrance requirements:* For master's, GRE General Test, 3 letters of recommendation, statement of purpose; for doctorate, GRE General Test, minimum GPA of 3.5, 3 letters of recommendation, statement of purpose. Additional exam requirements/recommendations for international students: Required—TOEFL (minimum score 550 paper-based; 213 computer-based; 79 iBT). *Application deadline:* For fall admission, 6/1 for domestic students, 12/1 for international students; for spring admission, 10/1 for domestic students, 6/1 for international students. Applications are processed on a rolling basis. Application fee: $75. Electronic applications accepted. *Expenses:* Tuition, state resident: full-time $10,840. Tuition, nonresident: full-time $25,802. *Financial support:* Institutionally sponsored loans and unspecified assistantships available. Financial award application deadline: 4/6. *Faculty research:* Soil-structure interaction, water resources, waste disposal, concrete and steel structures. *Unit head:* Kevin E. Lansey, Department Head, 520-621-6564, E-mail: lansey@engr.arizona.edu. *Application contact:* Graduate Coordinator, 520-621-2266, Fax: 520-621-2550, E-mail: ceem@engr.arizona.edu. Web site: http://civil.arizona.edu/cms/.

University of Arkansas, Graduate School, College of Engineering, Department of Civil Engineering, Program in Civil Engineering, Fayetteville, AR 72701-1201. Offers MSCE, MSE, PhD. *Students:* 27 full-time (9 women), 23 part-time (1 woman); includes 4 minority (1 Black or African American, non-Hispanic/Latino; 1 Asian, non-Hispanic/Latino; 2 Hispanic/Latino), 15 international. In 2011, 6 master's awarded. *Degree requirements:* For master's, thesis optional; for doctorate, one foreign language, thesis/dissertation. *Application deadline:* For fall admission, 4/1 for international students; for spring admission, 10/1 for international students. Applications are processed on a rolling basis. Application fee: $40 ($50 for international students). Electronic applications accepted. *Financial support:* In 2011–12, 33 research assistantships, 1 teaching assistantship were awarded; fellowships, career-related internships or fieldwork, and Federal Work-Study also available. Support available to part-time students. Financial award application deadline: 4/1; financial award applicants required to submit FAFSA. *Unit head:* Dr. Kevin Hall, Department Chair, 479-575-4954, Fax: 479-575-7168, E-mail: kdhall@uark.edu. *Application contact:* Dr. Paneer Selvam, Graduate Coordinator, 479-575-4954, E-mail: rps@uark.edu. Web site: http://www.cveg.uark.edu/.

The University of British Columbia, Faculty of Applied Science, Department of Civil Engineering, Vancouver, BC V6T 1Z1, Canada. Offers M Eng, MA Sc, PhD. Part-time programs available. *Degree requirements:* For master's, thesis; for doctorate, thesis/dissertation. *Entrance requirements:* Additional exam requirements/recommendations for international students: Required—TOEFL (minimum score 600 paper-based; 250 computer-based), IELTS (minimum score 7), TWE (minimum score 5). Electronic applications accepted. *Faculty research:* Geotechnology; structural, water, and environmental engineering; transportation; materials and construction engineering.

University of Calgary, Faculty of Graduate Studies, Schulich School of Engineering, Department of Civil Engineering, Calgary, AB T2N 1N4, Canada. Offers M Eng, M Sc, MPM, PhD. Part-time and evening/weekend programs available. *Degree requirements:* For master's, thesis (for some programs); for doctorate, thesis/dissertation, candidacy exam. *Entrance requirements:* For master's, minimum GPA of 3.0; for doctorate, minimum GPA of 3.5. Additional exam requirements/recommendations for international students: Required—TOEFL (minimum score 580 paper-based; 230 computer-based). *Faculty research:* Structures, including structural materials; transportation; project management and biomechanics; geotechnical engineering; environmental engineering.

University of California, Berkeley, Graduate Division, College of Engineering, Department of Civil and Environmental Engineering, Berkeley, CA 94720-1500. Offers engineering and project management (M Eng, MS, D Eng, PhD); environmental engineering (M Eng, MS, D Eng, PhD); geoengineering (M Eng, MS, D Eng, PhD); structural engineering, mechanics and materials (M Eng, MS, D Eng, PhD); transportation engineering (M Eng, MS, D Eng, PhD); M Arch/MS; MCP/MS; MPP/MS. *Degree requirements:* For master's, comprehensive exam or thesis (MS); for doctorate, thesis/dissertation, qualifying exam. *Entrance requirements:* For master's, GRE General Test, minimum GPA of 3.0, 3 letters of recommendation; for doctorate, GRE General Test, minimum GPA of 3.5, 3 letters of recommendation. Additional exam requirements/recommendations for international students: Required—TOEFL (minimum score 570 paper-based; 230 computer-based). Electronic applications accepted.

University of California, Davis, College of Engineering, Program in Civil and Environmental Engineering, Davis, CA 95616. Offers M Engr, MS, D Engr, PhD, Certificate, M Engr/MBA. *Degree requirements:* For master's, comprehensive exam (for some programs), thesis (for some programs); for doctorate, thesis/dissertation. *Entrance requirements:* For master's, GRE General Test, minimum GPA of 3.0; for doctorate, GRE, minimum graduate GPA of 3.5. Additional exam requirements/recommendations for international students: Required—TOEFL (minimum score 550 paper-based; 213 computer-based). Electronic applications accepted. *Faculty research:* Environmental water resources, transportation, structural mechanics, structural engineering, geotechnical engineering.

University of California, Irvine, School of Engineering, Department of Civil and Environmental Engineering, Irvine, CA 92697. Offers MS, PhD. Part-time programs available. *Students:* 117 full-time (36 women), 12 part-time (3 women); includes 29 minority (1 American Indian or Alaska Native, non-Hispanic/Latino; 22 Asian, non-Hispanic/Latino; 6 Hispanic/Latino), 63 international. Average age 27. 383 applicants, 27% accepted, 37 enrolled. In 2011, 27 master's, 23 doctorates awarded. Terminal master's awarded for partial completion of doctoral program. *Degree requirements:* For doctorate, thesis/dissertation. *Entrance requirements:* For master's and doctorate, GRE General Test, minimum GPA of 3.0, 3 letters of recommendation. Additional exam requirements/recommendations for international students: Required—TOEFL (minimum score 550 paper-based; 213 computer-based). *Application deadline:* For fall admission, 1/15 priority date for domestic students, 1/15 for international students. Applications are processed on a rolling basis. Application fee: $80 ($100 for international students). Electronic applications accepted. *Financial support:* Fellowships, research assistantships with full tuition reimbursements, teaching assistantships, institutionally sponsored loans, traineeships, health care benefits, and unspecified assistantships available. Financial award application deadline: 3/1; financial award applicants required to submit FAFSA. *Faculty research:* Intelligent transportation systems and transportation economics, risk and reliability, fluid mechanics, environmental hydrodynamics, hydrological and climate systems, water resources. *Unit head:* Prof. Brett F. Sanders, Chair, 949-824-4327, Fax: 949-824-3672, E-mail: bsanders@uci.edu. *Application contact:* April M. Heath, Graduate Coordinator, 949-824-0584, Fax: 949-824-2117, E-mail: a.heath@uci.edu. Web site: http://www.eng.uci.edu/dept/cee.

University of California, Los Angeles, Graduate Division, Henry Samueli School of Engineering and Applied Science, Department of Civil and Environmental Engineering, Los Angeles, CA 90095-1593. Offers MS, PhD. *Faculty:* 17 full-time (4 women), 4 part-time/adjunct (0 women). *Students:* 172 full-time (58 women); includes 57 minority (41 Asian, non-Hispanic/Latino; 14 Hispanic/Latino; 2 Two or more races, non-Hispanic/Latino), 59 international. 389 applicants, 53% accepted, 93 enrolled. In 2011, 66 master's, 6 doctorates awarded. *Degree requirements:* For master's, comprehensive exam or thesis; for doctorate, thesis/dissertation, qualifying exams. *Entrance requirements:* For master's, GRE General Test, minimum GPA of 3.0; for doctorate, GRE General Test, minimum GPA of 3.25. Additional exam requirements/recommendations for international students: Required—TOEFL (minimum score 560 paper-based; 220 computer-based; 87 iBT). *Application deadline:* For fall admission, 12/15 priority date for domestic students, 12/15 for international students. Application fee: $80 ($100 for international students). Electronic applications accepted. *Financial support:* In 2011–12, 105 fellowships, 85 research assistantships, 56 teaching assistantships were awarded; Federal Work-Study, institutionally sponsored loans, and tuition waivers (full and partial) also available. Financial award application deadline: 12/15; financial award applicants required to submit FAFSA. *Faculty research:* Environmental engineering, geotechnical engineering, hydrology and water resources, structures. *Total annual research expenditures:* $3.4 million. *Unit head:* Dr. Jiun-Shyan Chen, Chair, 310-267-4620. *Application contact:* Maida Bassili, Graduate Affairs Officer, 310-825-1851, Fax: 310-206-2222, E-mail: maida@ea.ucla.edu. Web site: http://cee.ucla.edu/.

University of Central Florida, College of Engineering and Computer Science, Department of Civil, Environmental, and Construction Engineering, Program in Civil Engineering, Orlando, FL 32816. Offers civil engineering (MS, MSCE, PhD); construction engineering (Certificate); structural engineering (Certificate); transportation engineering (Certificate). Part-time and evening/weekend programs available. *Students:* 68 full-time (13 women), 87 part-time (16 women); includes 35 minority (7 Black or African American, non-Hispanic/Latino; 6 Asian, non-Hispanic/Latino; 20 Hispanic/Latino; 2 Two or more races, non-Hispanic/Latino), 42 international. Average age 30. 125 applicants, 79% accepted, 45 enrolled. In 2011, 27 master's, 2 doctorates awarded. *Degree requirements:* For master's, thesis or alternative; for doctorate, thesis/dissertation, departmental qualifying exam, candidacy exam. *Entrance requirements:* For master's, GRE General Test, minimum GPA of 3.0 in last 60 hours; for doctorate, GRE General Test, minimum GPA of 3.5 in last 60 hours. Additional exam requirements/recommendations for international students: Required—TOEFL. *Application deadline:* For fall admission, 7/15 priority date for domestic students; for spring admission, 12/15 priority date for domestic students. Application fee: $30. Electronic applications accepted. *Expenses:* Tuition, state resident: part-time $277.08 per credit hour. Tuition, nonresident: part-time $277.08 per credit hour. Part-time tuition and fees vary according to degree level and program. *Financial support:* In 2011–12, 28 students received support, including 6 fellowships with partial tuition reimbursements available (averaging $2,700 per year), 14 research assistantships with partial tuition reimbursements available (averaging $11,800 per year), 15 teaching assistantships with partial tuition reimbursements available (averaging $11,300 per year); career-related internships or fieldwork, Federal Work-Study, institutionally sponsored loans, tuition waivers (partial), and unspecified assistantships also available. Financial award application deadline: 3/1; financial award applicants required to submit FAFSA. *Unit head:* Dr. Essam Radwan, Interim Chair, 407-823-4738, E-mail: ahmed.radwan@ucf.edu. *Application contact:* Barbara Rodriguez, Director, Admissions and Registration, 407-823-2766, Fax: 407-823-6442, E-mail: gradadmissions@ucf.edu. Web site: http://cece.ucf.edu/.

University of Cincinnati, Graduate School, College of Engineering and Applied Science, Department of Civil and Environmental Engineering, Program in Civil Engineering, Cincinnati, OH 45221. Offers MS, PhD. Part-time programs available. Terminal master's awarded for partial completion of doctoral program. *Degree requirements:* For master's, project or thesis; for doctorate, one foreign language, thesis/dissertation. *Entrance requirements:* For master's and doctorate, GRE General Test. Additional exam requirements/recommendations for international students: Required—TOEFL (minimum score 580 paper-based; 237 computer-based; 92 iBT). Electronic applications accepted. *Faculty research:* Soil mechanics and foundations, structures, transportation, water resources systems and hydraulics.

University of Colorado Boulder, Graduate School, College of Engineering and Applied Science, Department of Civil, Environmental, and Architectural Engineering, Boulder, CO 80309. Offers building systems (MS, PhD); construction engineering management (MS, PhD); environmental engineering (MS, PhD); geotechnical engineering and geomechanics (MS, PhD); hydrology, water resources and environmental fluid mechanics (MS, PhD); structural engineering and structural mechanics (MS, PhD). *Faculty:* 37 full-time (8 women). *Students:* 245 full-time (90 women), 53 part-time (15 women); includes 37 minority (1 Black or African American, non-Hispanic/Latino; 2 American Indian or Alaska Native, non-Hispanic/Latino; 15 Asian, non-Hispanic/Latino; 17 Hispanic/Latino; 2 Two or more races, non-Hispanic/Latino), 56 international. Average age 27. 483 applicants, 58% accepted, 83 enrolled. In 2011, 84 master's, 15 doctorates awarded. Terminal master's awarded for partial completion of doctoral program. *Degree requirements:* For master's, comprehensive exam, thesis or alternative; for doctorate, thesis/dissertation. *Entrance requirements:* For master's, GRE General Test, minimum undergraduate GPA of 3.0. *Application deadline:* For fall admission, 3/1 for domestic students, 12/1 for international students; for spring admission, 10/31 for domestic students, 10/1 for international students. Application fee: $50 ($60 for international students). Electronic applications accepted. *Financial support:* In 2011–12, 167 students received support, including 69 fellowships (averaging $12,440 per year), 62 research assistantships with full and partial tuition reimbursements available (averaging $21,979 per year), 20 teaching assistantships with full and partial tuition reimbursements available (averaging $19,877 per year); institutionally sponsored loans, scholarships/grants, health care benefits, and unspecified assistantships also available. Financial award application deadline: 1/15; financial award applicants required to submit FAFSA. *Faculty research:* Building systems engineering, construction engineering and management, environmental engineering, geoenvironmental engineering, geotechnical engineering, materials and mechanics, structural engineering, water resources engineering, life-cycle engineering. *Total annual research expenditures:* $10.9 million. *Application contact:* E-mail: cvengrad@colorado.edu. Web site: http://ceae.colorado.edu/new/.

University of Colorado Denver, College of Engineering and Applied Science, Department of Civil Engineering, Denver, CO 80217. Offers civil engineering (EASPh D); civil engineering systems (PhD); environmental and sustainability engineering (MS, PhD); geographic information systems (MS); geotechnical engineering (MS, PhD); hydrology and hydraulics (MS, PhD); structural engineering (MS, PhD); transportation engineering (MS, PhD). Part-time and evening/weekend programs available. *Faculty:* 14 full-time (1 woman), 6 part-time/adjunct (0 women). *Students:* 66 full-time (11 women), 65 part-time (14 women); includes 30 minority (10 Black or African American, non-Hispanic/Latino; 8 Asian, non-Hispanic/Latino; 10 Hispanic/Latino; 2 Two or more races, non-Hispanic/Latino), 17 international. Average age 34. 67 applicants, 54% accepted, 24 enrolled. In 2011, 30 master's, 2 doctorates awarded. *Degree requirements:* For master's, comprehensive exam, thesis or alternative, 30 credit hours, project or thesis; for doctorate, comprehensive exam, thesis/dissertation, 60 credit hours (30 of which are dissertation research). *Entrance requirements:* For master's, GRE, statement of purpose, transcripts, three references; for doctorate, GRE, statement of purpose, transcripts, references, letter of support from faculty stating willingness to serve as dissertation advisor and outlining plan for financial support. Additional exam requirements/recommendations for international students: Required—TOEFL (minimum score 525 paper-based; 197 computer-based). *Application deadline:* For fall admission, 7/15 for domestic students, 6/15 for international students; for spring admission, 12/1 for domestic students, 11/1 for international students. Applications are processed on a rolling basis. Application fee: $50 ($75 for international students). Electronic applications accepted. *Expenses:* Contact institution. *Financial support:* Research assistantships, teaching assistantships, career-related internships or fieldwork, and Federal Work-Study available. Financial award application deadline: 4/1; financial award applicants required to submit FAFSA. *Faculty research:* Earthquake source physics, environmental biotechnology, hydrologic and hydraulic engineering, sustainability assessments, transportation energy use and greenhouse gas emissions. *Unit head:* Dr. Kevin Rens, Chair, 303-556-8017, Fax: 303-556-2368, E-mail: kevin.rens@ucdenver.edu. *Application contact:* Maria Rase, Program Assistant, 303-556-6712, Fax: 303-556-2368, E-mail: maria.rase@ucdenver.edu. Web site: http://www.ucdenver.edu/academics/colleges/Engineering/Programs/Civil-Engineering/Pages/CivilEngineering.aspx.

University of Colorado Denver, College of Engineering and Applied Science, Master of Engineering Program, Denver, CO 80217-3364. Offers civil engineering (M Eng), including civil engineering, geographic information systems, transportation systems; electrical engineering (M Eng); mechanical engineering (M Eng). Part-time programs available. *Students:* 21 full-time (9 women), 30 part-time (7 women); includes 5 minority (2 Black or African American, non-Hispanic/Latino; 1 Asian, non-Hispanic/Latino; 2 Hispanic/Latino), 1 international. Average age 34. 13 applicants, 69% accepted, 8 enrolled. In 2011, 19 master's awarded. *Degree requirements:* For master's, comprehensive exam, thesis, 27 credit hours of course work, 3 credit hours of report or thesis work. *Entrance requirements:* For master's, GRE (for those with GPA below 2.75), transcripts, references, statement of purpose. Additional exam requirements/recommendations for international students: Required—TOEFL (minimum score 525 paper-based; 197 computer-based; 71 iBT). *Application deadline:* For fall admission, 7/15 for domestic students, 6/15 for international students; for spring admission, 12/1 for domestic students, 11/1 for international students. Applications are processed on a rolling basis. Application fee: $50 ($75 for international students). Electronic applications accepted. *Expenses:* Contact institution. *Financial support:* Federal Work-Study and scholarships/grants available. Financial award application deadline: 4/1; financial award applicants required to submit FAFSA. *Faculty research:* Civil, electrical and mechanical engineering. *Unit head:* 303-556-2870, Fax: 303-556-2511, E-mail: engineering@ucdenver.edu. *Application contact:* Graduate School Admissions, 303-556-2704, E-mail: admissions@ucdenver.edu. Web site: http://ucdenver.edu/academics/colleges/Engineering/admissions/Masters/Pages/MastersAdmissions.aspx.

University of Connecticut, Graduate School, School of Engineering, Department of Civil and Environmental Engineering, Field of Civil Engineering, Storrs, CT 06269. Offers MS, PhD. Terminal master's awarded for partial completion of doctoral program. *Degree requirements:* For master's, comprehensive exam, thesis or alternative; for doctorate, thesis/dissertation. *Entrance requirements:* Additional exam requirements/recommendations for international students: Required—TOEFL (minimum score 550 paper-based; 213 computer-based). Electronic applications accepted.

University of Dayton, Department of Civil and Environmental Engineering and Engineering Mechanics, Dayton, OH 45469-1300. Offers engineering mechanics (MSEM); environmental engineering (MSCE); geotechnical engineering (MSCE); structural engineering (MSCE); transportation engineering (MSCE); water resources engineering (MSCE). Part-time programs available. *Faculty:* 7 full-time (2 women), 2 part-time/adjunct (0 women). *Students:* 16 full-time (4 women), 9 part-time (4 women); includes 1 minority (Asian, non-Hispanic/Latino), 13 international. Average age 27. 53 applicants, 38% accepted, 5 enrolled. In 2011, 7 degrees awarded. *Degree requirements:* For master's, thesis optional. *Entrance requirements:* For master's, minimum GPA of 3.0 in undergraduate work. Additional exam requirements/recommendations for international students: Required—TOEFL (minimum score 550 paper-based; 213 computer-based; 80 iBT). *Application deadline:* For fall admission, 8/1 for domestic students, 3/1 for international students; for winter admission, 7/1 for international students; for spring admission, 1/1 for international students. Applications are processed on a rolling basis. Application fee: $0 ($50 for international students). Electronic applications accepted. *Expenses: Tuition:* Full-time $8400; part-time $700 per credit hour. *Required fees:* $25 per semester. Tuition and fees vary according to degree level. *Financial support:* Research assistantships available. Financial award applicants required to submit FAFSA. *Faculty research:* Physical modeling of hydraulic systems, finite element methods, mechanics of composite materials, transportation systems safety, biological treatment processes. *Total annual research expenditures:* $200,000. *Unit head:* Dr. Donald V. Chase, Chair, 937-229-3847, Fax: 937-229-3491, E-mail: dchase1@udayton.edu. *Application contact:* Dr. Donald Chase, Chair, 937-229-3847, Fax: 937-229-3491, E-mail: dchase1@udayton.edu. Web site: http://www.udayton.edu/engineering/civil.

University of Delaware, College of Engineering, Department of Civil and Environmental Engineering, Newark, DE 19716. Offers environmental engineering (MAS, MCE, PhD); geotechnical engineering (MAS, MCE, PhD); ocean engineering (MAS, MCE, PhD); structural engineering (MAS, MCE, PhD); transportation engineering (MAS, MCE, PhD); water resource engineering (MAS, MCE, PhD). Part-time programs available. Terminal master's awarded for partial completion of doctoral program. *Degree requirements:* For master's, thesis; for doctorate, thesis/dissertation. *Entrance requirements:* For master's and doctorate, GRE General Test. Additional exam requirements/recommendations for international students: Required—TOEFL. Electronic applications accepted. *Faculty research:* Structural engineering and mechanics; transportation engineering; ocean engineering; soil mechanics and foundation; water resources and environmental engineering.

University of Detroit Mercy, College of Engineering and Science, Department of Civil and Environmental Engineering, Detroit, MI 48221. Offers ME, DE. Evening/weekend programs available. *Faculty research:* Geotechnical engineering.

University of Florida, Graduate School, College of Engineering, Department of Civil and Coastal Engineering, Gainesville, FL 32611. Offers civil engineering (MCE, MS, PhD, Engr); coastal and oceanographic engineering (ME, MS, PhD, Engr). Part-time programs available. Postbaccalaureate distance learning degree programs offered (no on-campus study). Terminal master's awarded for partial completion of doctoral program. *Degree requirements:* For master's, thesis (for some programs); for doctorate, comprehensive exam, thesis/dissertation. *Entrance requirements:* For master's and doctorate, GRE General Test, minimum GPA of 3.0. Additional exam requirements/recommendations for international students: Required—TOEFL (minimum score 550 paper-based; 213 computer-based; 80 iBT), IELTS (minimum score 6). Electronic applications accepted. *Faculty research:* Traffic congestion mitigation, wind mitigation, sustainable infrastructure materials, improved sensors for in situ measurements, storm surge modeling.

University of Hawaii at Manoa, Graduate Division, College of Engineering, Department of Civil and Environmental Engineering, Honolulu, HI 96822. Offers MS, PhD. Part-time programs available. *Degree requirements:* For master's, comprehensive exam, thesis; for doctorate, comprehensive exam, thesis/dissertation. *Entrance requirements:* For master's and doctorate, GRE General Test or EIT Exam. Additional exam requirements/recommendations for international students: Required—TOEFL (minimum score 540 paper-based; 207 computer-based; 76 iBT), IELTS (minimum score 5). *Faculty research:* Structures, transportation, environmental engineering, geotechnical engineering, construction.

University of Houston, Cullen College of Engineering, Department of Civil and Environmental Engineering, Houston, TX 77204. Offers civil engineering (MCE, PhD). Part-time programs available. Terminal master's awarded for partial completion of doctoral program. *Entrance requirements:* For master's and doctorate, GRE General Test. Additional exam requirements/recommendations for international students: Required—TOEFL (minimum score 550 paper-based; 213 computer-based; 79 iBT), IELTS (minimum score 6.5). Electronic applications accepted. *Faculty research:* Civil engineering.

University of Idaho, College of Graduate Studies, College of Engineering, Department of Civil Engineering, Moscow, ID 83844-1022. Offers civil engineering (M Engr, MS, PhD); engineering management (M Engr); geological engineering (MS). *Faculty:* 17 full-time, 1 part-time/adjunct. *Students:* 20 full-time, 77 part-time. Average age 35. In 2011, 39 master's, 1 doctorate awarded. *Degree requirements:* For master's, thesis; for doctorate, thesis/dissertation. *Entrance requirements:* For master's, minimum GPA of 2.8; for doctorate, minimum undergraduate GPA of 2.8, 3.0 graduate. *Application deadline:* For fall admission, 8/1 for domestic students; for spring admission, 12/15 for domestic students. Applications are processed on a rolling basis. Application fee: $60. Electronic applications accepted. *Expenses:* Tuition, state resident: full-time $3874; part-time $334 per credit hour. Tuition, nonresident: full-time $16,394; part-time $861 per credit hour. *Required fees:* $2808; $99 per credit hour. Tuition and fees vary according to program. *Financial support:* Fellowships, research assistantships, teaching assistantships, and career-related internships or fieldwork available. Financial award applicants required to submit FAFSA. *Faculty research:* Water resources systems, structural analysis and design, soil mechanics, transportation technology. *Unit head:* Richard J. Nielsen, Chair, 208-885-8961, E-mail: civilengr@uidaho.edu. *Application contact:* Erick Larson, Director of Graduate Admissions, 208-885-4723, E-mail: gadms@uidaho.edu. Web site: http://www.uidaho.edu/engr/ce/.

University of Illinois at Chicago, Graduate College, College of Engineering, Department of Civil and Materials Engineering, Chicago, IL 60607-7128. Offers civil engineering (MS, PhD); materials engineering (MS, PhD). Evening/weekend programs available. *Degree requirements:* For master's, thesis (for some programs); for doctorate, thesis/dissertation, preliminary and qualifying exams. *Entrance requirements:* For master's and doctorate, GRE General Test, minimum GPA of 3.0. Additional exam requirements/recommendations for international students: Required—TOEFL. Electronic applications accepted. *Faculty research:* Transportation and geotechnical engineering, damage and anisotropic behavior, steel processing.

University of Illinois at Urbana–Champaign, Graduate College, College of Engineering, Department of Civil and Environmental Engineering, Champaign, IL 61820. Offers civil engineering (MS); environmental engineering in civil engineering (MS, PhD); environmental science in civil engineering (MS, PhD); M Arch/MS; MBA/MS. *Faculty:* 46 full-time (7 women). *Students:* 421 full-time (123 women), 76 part-time (22 women); includes 54 minority (2 Black or African American, non-Hispanic/Latino; 1 American Indian or Alaska Native, non-Hispanic/Latino; 31 Asian, non-Hispanic/Latino; 14 Hispanic/Latino; 6 Two or more races, non-Hispanic/Latino), 271 international. 1,112 applicants, 41% accepted, 169 enrolled. In 2011, 154 master's, 29 doctorates awarded. *Entrance requirements:* For master's and doctorate, GRE. Additional exam requirements/recommendations for international students: Required—TOEFL (minimum score 550 paper-based; 213 computer-based; 79 iBT) or IELTS (minimum score 6.5). *Application deadline:* Applications are processed on a rolling basis. Application fee: $75 ($90 for international students). Electronic applications accepted. *Financial support:* In 2011–12, 57 fellowships, 258 research assistantships, 90 teaching assistantships were awarded; tuition waivers (full and partial) also available. *Unit head:* Amr S. Elnashai, Jr., Head, 217-265-5497, Fax: 217-265-8040, E-mail: aelnash@illinois.edu. *Application contact:* Maxine M. Peyton, Office Manager, 217-333-6636, Fax: 217-333-9464, E-mail: mpeyton@illinois.edu. Web site: http://cee.illinois.edu/.

Civil Engineering

The University of Iowa, Graduate College, College of Engineering, Department of Civil and Environmental Engineering, Iowa City, IA 52242-1316. Offers MS, PhD. Part-time programs available. *Faculty:* 22 full-time (3 women), 1 part-time/adjunct (0 women). *Students:* 90 full-time (25 women); includes 4 minority (2 Black or African American, non-Hispanic/Latino; 2 Asian, non-Hispanic/Latino), 38 international. Average age 28. 235 applicants, 25% accepted, 20 enrolled. In 2011, 16 master's, 8 doctorates awarded. Terminal master's awarded for partial completion of doctoral program. *Degree requirements:* For master's, thesis optional; exam; for doctorate, comprehensive exam, thesis/dissertation, exam. *Entrance requirements:* For master's, GRE, minimum undergraduate GPA of 3.0; for doctorate, GRE, master's degree or equivalent with minimum GPA of 3.2. Additional exam requirements/recommendations for international students: Required—TOEFL (minimum score 550 paper-based; 213 computer-based; 81 iBT). *Application deadline:* For fall admission, 2/1 priority date for domestic students, 2/1 for international students; for spring admission, 12/1 for domestic students, 10/1 for international students. Applications are processed on a rolling basis. Application fee: $60 ($100 for international students). Electronic applications accepted. *Financial support:* In 2011–12, 8 fellowships with partial tuition reimbursements (averaging $23,480 per year), 73 research assistantships with partial tuition reimbursements (averaging $22,553 per year), 20 teaching assistantships with partial tuition reimbursements (averaging $16,908 per year) were awarded; career-related internships or fieldwork, Federal Work-Study, scholarships/grants, traineeships, and unspecified assistantships also available. Support available to part-time students. Financial award application deadline: 2/1; financial award applicants required to submit FAFSA. *Faculty research:* Water resources; environmental engineering and science; hydraulics and hydrology; structures, mechanics, and materials; transportation engineering. *Total annual research expenditures:* $14.6 million. *Unit head:* Dr. Michelle Scherer, Department Executive Officer, 319-335-5654, Fax: 319-335-5660, E-mail: michelle-scherer@uiowa.edu. *Application contact:* Judy Holland, Secretary, 319-335-5647, Fax: 319-335-5660, E-mail: cee@engineering.uiowa.edu. Web site: http://www.cee.engineering.uiowa.edu/.

The University of Kansas, Graduate Studies, School of Engineering, Program in Civil Engineering, Lawrence, KS 66045. Offers MCE, MS, DE, PhD. Part-time and evening/weekend programs available. *Faculty:* 25 full-time (3 women), 2 part-time/adjunct (0 women). *Students:* 56 full-time (17 women), 48 part-time (11 women); includes 12 minority (1 Black or African American, non-Hispanic/Latino; 1 Asian, non-Hispanic/Latino; 8 Hispanic/Latino; 2 Two or more races, non-Hispanic/Latino), 26 international. Average age 29. 99 applicants, 66% accepted, 28 enrolled. In 2011, 25 master's, 9 doctorates awarded. *Degree requirements:* For master's, thesis or alternative, exam; for doctorate, comprehensive exam, thesis/dissertation. *Entrance requirements:* For master's and doctorate, GRE, BS in engineering. Additional exam requirements/recommendations for international students: Required—TOEFL. *Application deadline:* For fall admission, 7/1 priority date for domestic students, 3/1 for international students; for spring admission, 12/1 priority date for domestic students, 8/15 for international students. Applications are processed on a rolling basis. Application fee: $55 ($65 for international students). Electronic applications accepted. Tuition and fees vary according to course load, campus/location, program and reciprocity agreements. *Financial support:* Fellowships with full tuition reimbursements, research assistantships with full tuition reimbursements, teaching assistantships with full and partial tuition reimbursements, and career-related internships or fieldwork available. Financial award application deadline: 2/7. *Faculty research:* Structural engineering, geotechnical engineering, transportation engineering, water resources engineering, construction engineering. *Unit head:* Craig D. Adams, Chair, 785-864-2700, Fax: 785-864-5631, E-mail: adamscd@ku.edu. *Application contact:* Bruce M. McEnroe, Graduate Advisor, 785-864-2925, Fax: 785-864-2925, E-mail: mcenroe@ku.edu. Web site: http://www.ceae.ku.edu/.

University of Kentucky, Graduate School, College of Engineering, Program in Civil Engineering, Lexington, KY 40506-0032. Offers MCE, MSCE, PhD. *Degree requirements:* For master's, comprehensive exam, thesis optional; for doctorate, comprehensive exam, thesis/dissertation. *Entrance requirements:* For master's, GRE General Test, minimum undergraduate GPA of 2.75; for doctorate, GRE General Test, minimum undergraduate GPA of 3.0. Additional exam requirements/recommendations for international students: Required—TOEFL (minimum score 550 paper-based; 213 computer-based). Electronic applications accepted. *Faculty research:* Geotechnical engineering, structures, construction engineering and management, environmental engineering and water resources, transportation and materials.

University of Louisiana at Lafayette, College of Engineering, Department of Civil Engineering, Lafayette, LA 70504. Offers MSE. Evening/weekend programs available. *Degree requirements:* For master's, comprehensive exam, thesis or alternative. *Entrance requirements:* For master's, GRE General Test, BS in civil engineering, minimum GPA of 2.85. *Faculty research:* Structural mechanics, computer-aided design, environmental engineering.

University of Louisville, J. B. Speed School of Engineering, Department of Civil and Environmental Engineering, Louisville, KY 40292-0001. Offers civil engineering (M Eng, MS, PhD). *Accreditation:* ABET (one or more programs are accredited). Part-time programs available. Postbaccalaureate distance learning degree programs offered (no on-campus study). *Faculty:* 10 full-time (1 woman). *Students:* 38 full-time (5 women), 21 part-time (2 women); includes 2 minority (1 American Indian or Alaska Native, non-Hispanic/Latino; 1 Asian, non-Hispanic/Latino), 12 international. Average age 27. 20 applicants, 45% accepted, 6 enrolled. In 2011, 33 master's, 2 doctorates awarded. Terminal master's awarded for partial completion of doctoral program. *Degree requirements:* For master's, comprehensive exam (for some programs), thesis or alternative; for doctorate, comprehensive exam, thesis/dissertation, minimum GPA of 3.0. *Entrance requirements:* For master's and doctorate, GRE General Test. Additional exam requirements/recommendations for international students: Required—TOEFL (minimum score 550 paper-based; 213 computer-based; 80 iBT), IELTS (minimum score 6.5). *Application deadline:* For fall admission, 5/1 priority date for domestic students, 5/1 for international students; for spring admission, 11/1 priority date for domestic students, 11/1 for international students. Applications are processed on a rolling basis. Application fee: $50. Electronic applications accepted. *Expenses:* Tuition, state resident: full-time $9692; part-time $539 per credit hour. Tuition, nonresident: full-time $20,168; part-time $1121 per credit hour. Tuition and fees vary according to program and reciprocity agreements. *Financial support:* In 2011–12, 7 students received support, including 1 fellowship with full tuition reimbursement available (averaging $20,000 per year), 1 research assistantship with full tuition reimbursement available (averaging $20,000 per year), 5 teaching assistantships with full tuition reimbursements available (averaging $20,000 per year). Financial award application deadline: 1/25; financial award applicants required to submit FAFSA. *Faculty research:* Structures, hydraulics, transportation, environmental engineering, geomechanics. *Total annual research expenditures:* $1.8 million. *Unit head:* Dr. J. P. Mohsen, Chair, 502-852-6276, Fax: 502-852-8851, E-mail: jpmohs01@louisville.edu. *Application contact:* Dr.

Michael Day, Associate Dean, 502-852-6195, Fax: 502-852-7294, E-mail: day@louisville.edu. Web site: http://www.louisville.edu/speed/civil/.

University of Maine, Graduate School, College of Engineering, Department of Civil and Environmental Engineering, Orono, ME 04469. Offers civil engineering (PhD); water resources (MS). *Faculty:* 12 full-time (3 women). *Students:* 33 full-time (11 women), 9 part-time (1 woman); includes 2 minority (1 American Indian or Alaska Native, non-Hispanic/Latino; 1 Two or more races, non-Hispanic/Latino), 4 international. Average age 26. 38 applicants, 66% accepted, 23 enrolled. In 2011, 15 master's, 1 doctorate awarded. *Degree requirements:* For doctorate, thesis/dissertation. *Entrance requirements:* For master's and doctorate, GRE General Test. Additional exam requirements/recommendations for international students: Required—TOEFL. *Application deadline:* For fall admission, 2/1 priority date for domestic students. Applications are processed on a rolling basis. Application fee: $65. Electronic applications accepted. *Expenses:* Tuition, state resident: full-time $5016. Tuition, nonresident: full-time $14,424. *Financial support:* In 2011–12, 15 research assistantships with full tuition reimbursements (averaging $17,387 per year), 3 teaching assistantships with full tuition reimbursements (averaging $13,600 per year) were awarded; Federal Work-Study, institutionally sponsored loans, scholarships/grants, and tuition waivers (full and partial) also available. Financial award application deadline: 3/1. *Total annual research expenditures:* $1.4 million. *Unit head:* Dr. Eric Landis, Chair. *Application contact:* Scott G. Delcourt, Associate Dean of the Graduate School, 207-581-3291, Fax: 207-581-3232, E-mail: graduate@maine.edu. Web site: http://www2.umaine.edu/graduate/.

The University of Manchester, School of Mechanical, Aerospace and Civil Engineering, Manchester, United Kingdom. Offers advanced manufacturing technology (M Ent); aerospace engineering (M Phil, M Sc, PhD); civil engineering (M Phil, M Sc, PhD); environmental engineering (M Phil, PhD); management of projects (M Phil, M Sc, PhD); mechanical engineering (M Phil, M Sc, PhD); mechanical engineering design (M Ent); nuclear engineering (M Phil, D Eng, PhD).

University of Manitoba, Faculty of Graduate Studies, Faculty of Engineering, Department of Civil Engineering, Winnipeg, MB R3T 2N2, Canada. Offers M Eng, M Sc, PhD. *Degree requirements:* For master's, thesis.

University of Maryland, Baltimore County, Graduate School, College of Engineering and Information Technology, Department of Chemical, Biochemical, and Environmental Engineering, Program in Civil Engineering, Baltimore, MD 21250. Offers MS, PhD. Part-time programs available. *Faculty:* 2 full-time (0 women), 1 part-time/adjunct (0 women). *Students:* 13 full-time (8 women), 2 part-time (1 woman); includes 4 minority (1 Black or African American, non-Hispanic/Latino; 1 Asian, non-Hispanic/Latino; 1 Hispanic/Latino; 1 Native Hawaiian or other Pacific Islander, non-Hispanic/Latino), 8 international. Average age 29. 14 applicants, 50% accepted, 3 enrolled. In 2011, 2 degrees awarded. *Degree requirements:* For master's, comprehensive exam (for some programs), thesis (for some programs); for doctorate, comprehensive exam, thesis/dissertation. *Entrance requirements:* For master's and doctorate, GRE General Test, BS in civil and environmental engineering or related field of engineering. Additional exam requirements/recommendations for international students: Required—TOEFL (minimum score 550 paper-based; 213 computer-based; 80 iBT). *Application deadline:* For fall admission, 6/1 for domestic students, 1/1 for international students; for spring admission, 11/1 for domestic students, 6/1 for international students. Applications are processed on a rolling basis. Application fee: $70. Electronic applications accepted. *Financial support:* In 2011–12, 11 research assistantships with full tuition reimbursements (averaging $25,000 per year) were awarded; career-related internships or fieldwork, Federal Work-Study, scholarships/grants, health care benefits, tuition waivers (partial), and unspecified assistantships also available. Support available to part-time students. Financial award application deadline: 6/30; financial award applicants required to submit FAFSA. *Faculty research:* Environmental fate and transport, water resources treatment/remediation. *Unit head:* Dr. Julia M. Ross, Professor and Chair, 410-455-3415, Fax: 410-455-1049, E-mail: jross@umbc.edu. *Application contact:* Dr. Upal Ghosh, Associate Professor and Graduate Program Director, 410-455-8665, Fax: 410-455-6500, E-mail: ughosh@umbc.edu. Web site: http://www.umbc.edu/cbe.

University of Maryland, College Park, Academic Affairs, A. James Clark School of Engineering, Department of Civil and Environmental Engineering, College Park, MD 20742. Offers M Eng, MS, PhD. Part-time and evening/weekend programs available. Postbaccalaureate distance learning degree programs offered. *Faculty:* 67 full-time (14 women), 22 part-time/adjunct (4 women). *Students:* 173 full-time (61 women), 48 part-time (13 women); includes 35 minority (13 Black or African American, non-Hispanic/Latino; 12 Asian, non-Hispanic/Latino; 6 Hispanic/Latino; 4 Two or more races, non-Hispanic/Latino), 112 international. 341 applicants, 32% accepted, 48 enrolled. In 2011, 35 master's, 18 doctorates awarded. *Degree requirements:* For master's, thesis optional; for doctorate, thesis/dissertation, qualifying exam. *Entrance requirements:* For master's and doctorate, GRE General Test, 3 letters of recommendation. *Application deadline:* For fall admission, 5/1 for domestic students, 2/1 for international students; for spring admission, 10/15 for domestic students, 6/1 for international students. Applications are processed on a rolling basis. Application fee: $75. Electronic applications accepted. *Expenses: Tuition, area resident:* Part-time $525 per credit hour. Tuition, state resident: part-time $525 per credit hour. Tuition, nonresident: part-time $1131 per credit hour. *Required fees:* $386.31 per term. Tuition and fees vary according to program. *Financial support:* In 2011–12, 13 fellowships with full and partial tuition reimbursements (averaging $13,372 per year), 83 research assistantships (averaging $19,243 per year), 27 teaching assistantships (averaging $18,634 per year) were awarded; Federal Work-Study and scholarships/grants also available. Support available to part-time students. Financial award applicants required to submit FAFSA. *Faculty research:* Transportation and urban systems, environmental engineering, geotechnical engineering, construction engineering and management, hydraulics. *Total annual research expenditures:* $22.2 million. *Unit head:* Dr. Ali Haghani, Chair, 301-405-1974, E-mail: haghani@umd.edu. *Application contact:* Dr. Charles A. Caramello, Dean of Graduate School, 301-405-0358, Fax: 301-314-9305, E-mail: ccaramel@umd.edu.

University of Maryland, College Park, Academic Affairs, A. James Clark School of Engineering, Department of Continuing and Distance Learning in Engineering, College Park, MD 20742. Offers engineering (M Eng), including aerospace engineering, chemical engineering, civil engineering, electrical engineering, engineering, fire protection engineering, materials science and engineering, mechanical engineering, reliability engineering, systems engineering. *Faculty:* 3 full-time (0 women), 8 part-time/adjunct (0 women). *Students:* 75 full-time (24 women), 418 part-time (81 women); includes 154 minority (62 Black or African American, non-Hispanic/Latino; 64 Asian, non-Hispanic/Latino; 23 Hispanic/Latino; 5 Two or more races, non-Hispanic/Latino), 67 international. 447 applicants, 52% accepted, 154 enrolled. In 2011, 155 master's awarded. *Application deadline:* For fall admission, 8/15 for domestic students, 2/1 for international students; for spring admission, 1/10 for domestic students, 8/1 for international students. Applications are processed on a rolling basis. Application fee:

$75. Electronic applications accepted. *Expenses: Tuition, area resident:* Part-time $525 per credit hour. Tuition, state resident: part-time $525 per credit hour. Tuition, nonresident: part-time $1131 per credit hour. *Required fees:* $386.31 per term. Tuition and fees vary according to program. *Financial support:* In 2011–12, 3 research assistantships (averaging $21,498 per year), 13 teaching assistantships (averaging $16,889 per year) were awarded. *Unit head:* Dr. Darryll Pines, Dean, 301-405-8539, E-mail: pines@umd.edu. *Application contact:* Dr. Charles A. Caramello, Dean of the Graduate School, 301-405-0358, Fax: 301-314-9305.

University of Massachusetts Amherst, Graduate School, College of Engineering, Department of Civil and Environmental Engineering, Amherst, MA 01003. Offers civil engineering (MSCE, PhD); environmental and water resources (MSCE); geotechnical (MSCE); structural engineering and mechanics (MSCE); transportation (MSCE). *Accreditation:* ABET (one or more programs are accredited). Part-time programs available. *Faculty:* 28 full-time (7 women). *Students:* 91 full-time (30 women), 11 part-time (5 women); includes 13 minority (3 Black or African American, non-Hispanic/Latino; 5 Asian, non-Hispanic/Latino; 4 Hispanic/Latino; 1 Two or more races, non-Hispanic/Latino), 29 international. Average age 27. 293 applicants, 53% accepted, 40 enrolled. In 2011, 38 master's, 1 doctorate awarded. Terminal master's awarded for partial completion of doctoral program. *Degree requirements:* For master's, thesis or alternative; for doctorate, comprehensive exam, thesis/dissertation. *Entrance requirements:* For master's and doctorate, GRE General Test. Additional exam requirements/recommendations for international students: Required—TOEFL (minimum score 550 paper-based; 213 computer-based; 80 iBT), IELTS (minimum score 6.5). *Application deadline:* For fall admission, 2/1 for domestic and international students; for spring admission, 10/1 for domestic and international students. Applications are processed on a rolling basis. Application fee: $50 ($65 for international students). Electronic applications accepted. Tuition and fees vary according to course load, campus/location and program. *Financial support:* In 2011–12, 1 fellowship with full tuition reimbursement (averaging $1,000 per year), 74 research assistantships with full tuition reimbursements (averaging $15,151 per year), 6 teaching assistantships with full tuition reimbursements (averaging $15,151 per year) were awarded; career-related internships or fieldwork, Federal Work-Study, scholarships/grants, traineeships, health care benefits, tuition waivers, and unspecified assistantships also available. Support available to part-time students. Financial award application deadline: 2/1; financial award applicants required to submit FAFSA. *Unit head:* Dr. Sanjay Arwade, Graduate Program Director, 413-545-0686, Fax: 413-545-2840. *Application contact:* Lindsay DeSantis, Interim Supervisor of Admissions, 413-545-0722, Fax: 413-577-0100, E-mail: gradadm@grad.umass.edu. Web site: http://cee.umass.edu/.

University of Massachusetts Amherst, Graduate School, Interdisciplinary Programs, Dual Degree Program in Business Administration and Civil Engineering, Amherst, MA 01003. Offers MSCE/MBA. Part-time programs available. *Entrance requirements:* Additional exam requirements/recommendations for international students: Required—TOEFL (minimum score 600 paper-based; 250 computer-based; 100 iBT), IELTS (minimum score 7). *Application deadline:* For fall admission, 2/1 for domestic and international students. Applications are processed on a rolling basis. Application fee: $50 ($65 for international students). Electronic applications accepted. Tuition and fees vary according to course load, campus/location and program. *Financial support:* Career-related internships or fieldwork, Federal Work-Study, scholarships/grants, traineeships, health care benefits, tuition waivers (full), and unspecified assistantships available. Support available to part-time students. Financial award application deadline: 2/1; financial award applicants required to submit FAFSA. *Unit head:* Dr. Sanjay Arwade, Graduate Program Director, 413-545-0686, Fax: 413-545-2840, E-mail: muriel@ecs.umass.edu. *Application contact:* Lindsay DeSantis, Interim Supervisor of Admissions, 413-545-0722, Fax: 413-577-0010, E-mail: gradadm@grad.umass.edu. Web site: http://www-new.ecs.umass.edu/degrees#MBA.

University of Massachusetts Dartmouth, Graduate School, College of Engineering, Program in Civil and Environmental Engineering, North Dartmouth, MA 02747-2300. Offers MS. Part-time programs available. *Faculty:* 8 full-time (2 women), 3 part-time/adjunct (0 women). *Students:* 10 full-time (0 women), 12 part-time (1 woman); includes 3 minority (2 Black or African American, non-Hispanic/Latino; 1 Hispanic/Latino), 8 international. Average age 26. 29 applicants, 97% accepted, 11 enrolled. In 2011, 3 degrees awarded. *Degree requirements:* For master's, thesis or alternative. *Entrance requirements:* For master's, GRE, minimum GPA of 3.0, 3 letters of recommendation, resume, statement of intent. Additional exam requirements/recommendations for international students: Required—TOEFL (minimum score 550 paper-based; 213 computer-based). *Application deadline:* For fall admission, 2/15 priority date for domestic students, 1/15 for international students; for spring admission, 11/15 priority date for domestic students, 10/15 for international students. Application fee: $40 ($60 for international students). *Expenses:* Tuition, state resident: full-time $2071; part-time $86.29 per credit. Tuition, nonresident: full-time $8099; part-time $337.46 per credit. *Required fees:* $438.58 per credit. Part-time tuition and fees vary according to class time, course load, degree level and reciprocity agreements. *Financial support:* In 2011–12, 6 research assistantships with full tuition reimbursements (averaging $12,982 per year), 5 teaching assistantships with full tuition reimbursements (averaging $9,650 per year) were awarded. Financial award application deadline: 3/1; financial award applicants required to submit FAFSA. *Faculty research:* Nutrient removal and recovery, water resources engineering, pavement design and management, waste water treatment systems, hydrology. *Total annual research expenditures:* $556,147. *Unit head:* Dr. Nima Rahbar, Graduate Program Director, 508-999-8467, Fax: 508-999-8964, E-mail: nrahbar@umassd.edu. *Application contact:* Elan Turcotte-Shamski, Graduate Admissions Officer, 508-999-8604, Fax: 508-999-8183, E-mail: graduate@umassd.edu. Web site: http://www.umassd.edu/engineering/cen/graduate/welcome.cfm.

University of Massachusetts Lowell, College of Engineering, Department of Civil and Environmental Engineering, Lowell, MA 01854-2881. Offers civil and environmental engineering (MS Eng, Certificate); environmental engineering (D Eng); environmental studies (MSES, PhD, Certificate), including environmental engineering (MSES), environmental studies (PhD, Certificate); sustainable infrastructure for developing nations (Certificate). Part-time programs available. *Degree requirements:* For master's, thesis optional. *Entrance requirements:* For master's, GRE General Test. *Faculty research:* Bridge design, traffic control, groundwater remediation, pile capacity.

University of Memphis, Graduate School, Herff College of Engineering, Department of Civil Engineering, Memphis, TN 38152. Offers civil engineering (PhD); environmental engineering (MS); foundation engineering (MS); structural engineering (MS); transportation engineering (MS); water resources engineering (MS). Terminal master's awarded for partial completion of doctoral program. *Degree requirements:* For master's, comprehensive exam, thesis optional; for doctorate, comprehensive exam, thesis/dissertation. *Entrance requirements:* For master's, GRE General Test or MAT, minimum undergraduate GPA of 2.5; for doctorate, GRE, 3 letters of recommendation. Additional exam requirements/recommendations for international students: Required—TOEFL (minimum score 550 paper-based; 210 computer-based; 79 iBT). *Faculty research:* Structural response to earthquakes, pavement design, water quality, transportation safety, intermodal transportation,.

University of Miami, Graduate School, College of Engineering, Department of Civil, Architectural, and Environmental Engineering, Coral Gables, FL 33124. Offers architectural engineering (MSAE); civil engineering (MSCE, PhD). Part-time programs available. Terminal master's awarded for partial completion of doctoral program. *Degree requirements:* For master's, thesis (for some programs); for doctorate, comprehensive exam, thesis/dissertation. *Entrance requirements:* For master's, GRE General Test (minimum score 1000 verbal and quantitative), minimum GPA of 3.0; for doctorate, GRE General Test, minimum GPA of 3.5 in preceding degree. Additional exam requirements/recommendations for international students: Required—TOEFL (minimum score 550 paper-based; 213 computer-based). Electronic applications accepted. *Faculty research:* Structural assessment and wind engineering, sustainable construction and materials, moisture transport and management, wastewater and waste engineering, water management and risk analysis.

University of Michigan, College of Engineering, Department of Civil and Environmental Engineering, Ann Arbor, MI 48109. Offers civil engineering (MSE, PhD, CE); construction engineering and management (M Eng, MSE); environmental engineering (MSE, PhD); structural engineering (M Eng); MBA/MSE. Part-time programs available. *Students:* 139 full-time (54 women), 3 part-time (1 woman). 539 applicants, 40% accepted, 66 enrolled. In 2011, 52 master's, 10 doctorates awarded. *Degree requirements:* For master's, thesis optional; for doctorate, comprehensive exam, thesis/dissertation, oral defense of dissertation, preliminary and written exams. *Entrance requirements:* For master's and doctorate, GRE General Test. Additional exam requirements/recommendations for international students: Required—TOEFL (minimum score 560 paper-based; 220 computer-based). *Application deadline:* Applications are processed on a rolling basis. Application fee: $65 ($75 for international students). Electronic applications accepted. *Financial support:* Fellowships, research assistantships, teaching assistantships, institutionally sponsored loans, and tuition waivers (partial) available. Financial award application deadline: 1/19. *Faculty research:* Construction engineering and management, geotechnical engineering, earthquake-resistant design of structures, environmental chemistry and microbiology, cost engineering, environmental and water resources engineering. *Unit head:* Kim Hayes, Chair, 734-764-8495, Fax: 734-764-4292, E-mail: ford@umich.edu. *Application contact:* Kimberly Smith, Student Advisor, 734-764-8405, Fax: 734-647-2127, E-mail: kansmith@umich.edu. Web site: http://www.engin.umich.edu/dept/cee/.

University of Michigan, College of Engineering, Department of Naval Architecture and Marine Engineering, Ann Arbor, MI 48109. Offers concurrent marine design (M Eng); naval architecture and marine engineering (MS, MSE, PhD, Mar Eng, Nav Arch); MBA/MSE. Part-time programs available. *Students:* 90 full-time (14 women), 3 part-time (0 women). 117 applicants, 59% accepted, 43 enrolled. In 2011, 38 master's, 3 doctorates awarded. Terminal master's awarded for partial completion of doctoral program. *Degree requirements:* For master's, thesis (for some programs); for doctorate, comprehensive exam, thesis/dissertation, oral defense of dissertation, preliminary exams (written and oral); for other advanced degree, comprehensive exam, thesis, oral defense of thesis. *Entrance requirements:* For doctorate, GRE General Test, master's degree; for other advanced degree, GRE General Test. Additional exam requirements/recommendations for international students: Required—TOEFL (minimum score 560 paper-based; 220 computer-based). *Application deadline:* Applications are processed on a rolling basis. Application fee: $65 ($75 for international students). Electronic applications accepted. *Financial support:* Fellowships, research assistantships, teaching assistantships, career-related internships or fieldwork, Federal Work-Study, institutionally sponsored loans, scholarships/grants, and unspecified assistantships available. *Faculty research:* System and structural reliability, design and analysis of offshore structures and vehicles, marine systems design, remote sensing of ship wakes and sea surfaces, marine hydrodynamics, nonlinear seakeeping analysis. *Unit head:* Dr. Steven Ceccio, Chair, 734-936-7636, Fax: 734-936-8820, E-mail: kdrake@engin.umich.edu. *Application contact:* Nathalie Fiveland, Unit Administrator, 734-936-0566, Fax: 734-936-8820, E-mail: fiveland@umich.edu. Web site: http://www.engin.umich.edu/dept/name.

University of Minnesota, Twin Cities Campus, College of Science and Engineering, Department of Civil Engineering, Minneapolis, MN 55455-0213. Offers civil engineering (MCE, MS, PhD); geological engineering (M Geo E, MS); stream restoration science and engineering (Certificate). Part-time programs available. *Faculty:* 31 full-time (5 women). *Students:* 153 (33 women); includes 7 minority (2 American Indian or Alaska Native, non-Hispanic/Latino; 3 Asian, non-Hispanic/Latino; 2 Hispanic/Latino), 50 international. *Degree requirements:* For master's, thesis optional; for doctorate, thesis/dissertation. *Entrance requirements:* For master's and doctorate, GRE General Test. Additional exam requirements/recommendations for international students: Required—TOEFL. *Application deadline:* For fall admission, 12/3 for domestic students. Applications are processed on a rolling basis. Application fee: $75 ($95 for international students). *Financial support:* Fellowships with tuition reimbursements, research assistantships with tuition reimbursements, and teaching assistantships with tuition reimbursements available. *Faculty research:* Environmental engineering, geomechanics, structural engineering, transportation, water resources . *Application contact:* Secretary of Graduate Studies, E-mail: civesgs@umn.edu. Web site: http://www.ce.umn.edu/.

University of Missouri, Graduate School, College of Engineering, Department of Civil and Environmental Engineering, Columbia, MO 65211. Offers civil engineering (MS, PhD); environmental engineering (MS, PhD); geotechnical engineering (MS, PhD); structural engineering (MS, PhD); transportation and highway engineering (MS); water resources (MS, PhD). *Faculty:* 18 full-time (2 women), 1 part-time/adjunct (0 women). *Students:* 45 full-time (16 women), 38 part-time (8 women); includes 5 minority (2 Black or African American, non-Hispanic/Latino; 2 Asian, non-Hispanic/Latino; 1 Hispanic/Latino), 49 international. Average age 28. 109 applicants, 28% accepted, 20 enrolled. In 2011, 14 master's, 2 doctorates awarded. *Degree requirements:* For master's, report or thesis; for doctorate, thesis/dissertation. *Entrance requirements:* For master's and doctorate, GRE General Test. Additional exam requirements/recommendations for international students: Required—TOEFL (minimum score 550 paper-based; 213 computer-based; 79 iBT). *Application deadline:* For fall admission, 3/15 priority date for domestic students; for winter admission, 10/15 priority date for domestic students. Application fee: $55 ($75 for international students). *Expenses:* Tuition, state resident: full-time $5881. Tuition, nonresident: full-time $15,183. *Required fees:* $952. Tuition and fees vary according to campus/location and program. *Financial support:* Fellowships, research assistantships, teaching assistantships, and institutionally sponsored loans available. *Unit head:* Dr. Mark Virkler, Department Chair, E-mail: virklerm@missouri.edu. *Application contact:* Jennifer Keyzer-Andre, 573-882-4442, E-mail: keyzerandrej@missouri.edu. Web site: http://engineering.missouri.edu/civil/.

University of Missouri–Kansas City, School of Computing and Engineering, Kansas City, MO 64110-2499. Offers civil engineering (MS); computer and electrical engineering

(PhD); computer science (MS), including bioinformatics, software engineering, telecommunications networking; computer science and informatics (PhD); computing (PhD); electrical engineering (MS); engineering (PhD); mechanical engineering (MS); telecommunications (PhD). PhD (interdisciplinary) offered through the School of Graduate Studies. Part-time programs available. *Faculty:* 36 full-time (6 women), 27 part-time/adjunct (3 women). *Students:* 155 full-time (44 women), 136 part-time (24 women); includes 19 minority (4 Black or African American, non-Hispanic/Latino; 7 Asian, non-Hispanic/Latino; 6 Hispanic/Latino; 2 Two or more races, non-Hispanic/Latino), 201 international. Average age 26. 455 applicants, 46% accepted, 96 enrolled. In 2011, 194 degrees awarded. *Degree requirements:* For doctorate, thesis/dissertation. *Entrance requirements:* For master's, GRE General Test, minimum GPA of 3.0, 3 letters of recommendation from professors; for doctorate, GRE General Test, minimum GPA of 3.5. Additional exam requirements/recommendations for international students: Required—TOEFL (minimum score 550 paper-based; 213 computer-based; 80 iBT). *Application deadline:* For fall admission, 1/15 priority date for domestic students, 1/15 for international students. Applications are processed on a rolling basis. Application fee: $45 ($50 for international students). *Expenses:* Tuition, state resident: full-time $5798; part-time $322.10 per credit hour. Tuition, nonresident: full-time $14,969; part-time $831.60 per credit hour. *Required fees:* $93.51 per credit hour. *Financial support:* In 2011–12, 47 research assistantships with partial tuition reimbursements (averaging $13,190 per year), 10 teaching assistantships with partial tuition reimbursements (averaging $9,815 per year) were awarded; career-related internships or fieldwork, Federal Work-Study, scholarships/grants, tuition waivers (partial), and unspecified assistantships also available. Support available to part-time students. Financial award application deadline: 3/1; financial award applicants required to submit FAFSA. *Faculty research:* Algorithms, bioinformatics and medical informatics, biomechanics/biomaterials, civil engineering materials, networking and telecommunications, thermal science. *Unit head:* Dr. Kevin Z. Truman, Dean, 816-235-2399, Fax: 816-235-5159. *Application contact:* 816-235-2399, Fax: 816-235-5159. Web site: http://sce.umkc.edu/.

University of Nebraska–Lincoln, Graduate College, College of Engineering, Department of Civil Engineering, Lincoln, NE 68588. Offers MS, PhD. *Degree requirements:* For master's, thesis optional; for doctorate, comprehensive exam, thesis/dissertation. *Entrance requirements:* For master's and doctorate, GRE General Test. Additional exam requirements/recommendations for international students: Required—TOEFL (minimum score 550 paper-based; 213 computer-based). Electronic applications accepted. *Faculty research:* Water resources engineering, sediment transport, steel bridge systems, highway safety.

University of Nevada, Las Vegas, Graduate College, Howard R. Hughes College of Engineering, Department of Civil and Environmental Engineering, Las Vegas, NV 89154-4015. Offers civil and environmental engineering (MSE, PhD); transportation (MS). Part-time programs available. *Faculty:* 19 full-time (4 women), 15 part-time/adjunct (1 woman). *Students:* 14 full-time (1 woman), 42 part-time (9 women); includes 12 minority (1 Black or African American, non-Hispanic/Latino; 1 American Indian or Alaska Native, non-Hispanic/Latino; 2 Asian, non-Hispanic/Latino; 4 Hispanic/Latino; 4 Two or more races, non-Hispanic/Latino), 18 international. Average age 32. 36 applicants, 81% accepted, 14 enrolled. In 2011, 16 master's, 2 doctorates awarded. *Degree requirements:* For master's, comprehensive exam (for some programs), thesis (for some programs); for doctorate, comprehensive exam, thesis/dissertation. *Entrance requirements:* For master's and doctorate, GRE General Test. Additional exam requirements/recommendations for international students: Required—TOEFL (minimum score 550 paper-based; 213 computer-based; 80 iBT), IELTS (minimum score 7). *Application deadline:* For fall admission, 6/15 priority date for domestic students, 5/1 for international students; for spring admission, 11/15 priority date for domestic students, 10/1 for international students. Applications are processed on a rolling basis. Application fee: $60 ($95 for international students). Electronic applications accepted. *Financial support:* In 2011–12, 33 students received support, including 15 research assistantships with partial tuition reimbursements available (averaging $8,527 per year), 18 teaching assistantships with partial tuition reimbursements available (averaging $9,210 per year); institutionally sponsored loans, scholarships/grants, health care benefits, and unspecified assistantships also available. Financial award application deadline: 3/1. *Total annual research expenditures:* $340,041. *Unit head:* Dr. David Ashley, Professor, 702-895-4040, Fax: 702-895-3936, E-mail: david.b.ashley@unlv.edu. *Application contact:* Graduate College Admissions Evaluator, 702-895-3320, Fax: 702-895-4180, E-mail: gradcollege@unlv.edu. Web site: http://ce.egr.unlv.edu/.

University of Nevada, Reno, Graduate School, College of Engineering, Department of Civil and Environmental Engineering, Reno, NV 89557. Offers MS, PhD. Terminal master's awarded for partial completion of doctoral program. *Degree requirements:* For master's, thesis optional; for doctorate, thesis/dissertation. *Entrance requirements:* For master's, GRE General Test, minimum GPA of 3.0; for doctorate, GRE General Test, minimum GPA of 3.25. Additional exam requirements/recommendations for international students: Required—TOEFL (minimum score 500 paper-based; 173 computer-based; 61 iBT), IELTS (minimum score 6). Electronic applications accepted. *Faculty research:* Structural and earthquake engineering, geotechnical engineering, environmental engineering, transportation, pavements/materials.

University of New Brunswick Fredericton, School of Graduate Studies, Faculty of Engineering, Department of Civil Engineering, Fredericton, NB E3B 5A3, Canada. Offers construction engineering and management (M Eng, M Sc E, PhD); environmental engineering (M Eng, M Sc E, PhD); environmental studies (M Eng); geotechnical engineering (M Eng, M Sc E, PhD); groundwater/hydrology (M Eng, M Sc E, PhD); materials (M Eng, M Sc E, PhD); pavements (M Eng, M Sc E, PhD); structures (M Eng, M Sc E, PhD); transportation (M Eng, M Sc E, PhD). Part-time programs available. *Faculty:* 13 full-time (1 woman), 7 part-time/adjunct (1 woman). *Students:* 31 full-time (7 women), 17 part-time (2 women). In 2011, 11 master's, 2 doctorates awarded. *Degree requirements:* For master's, thesis, proposal; for doctorate, comprehensive exam, thesis/dissertation, qualifying exam; proposal; 27 credit hours of courses. *Entrance requirements:* For master's, minimum GPA of 3.0; B Sc E in civil engineering or related engineering degree; for doctorate, minimum GPA of 3.0; graduate degree in engineering or applied science. Additional exam requirements/recommendations for international students: Required—TWE (minimum score 4), TOEFL (minimum score 580 paper-based; 237 computer-based) or IELTS (minimum score 7.5). *Application deadline:* For fall admission, 5/1 priority date for domestic students; for winter admission, 11/1 priority date for domestic students. Applications are processed on a rolling basis. Application fee: $50 Canadian dollars. *Financial support:* In 2011–12, 14 fellowships, 30 research assistantships (averaging $7,000 per year), 42 teaching assistantships (averaging $2,000 per year) were awarded; career-related internships or fieldwork and scholarships/grants also available. *Faculty research:* Construction engineering and management; materials and infrastructure renewal; highway and pavement research; structures and solid mechanics; geotechnical, soil; structure interaction; transportation and planning; environment, solid waste management. *Unit head:* Dr. Eric Hildebrand, Director of Graduate Studies, 506-453-5113, Fax: 506-453-3568, E-mail: edh@unb.ca. *Application contact:* Joyce Moore, Graduate Secretary, 506-452-6127, Fax: 506-453-3568, E-mail: civil-grad@unb.ca. Web site: http://www.unbf.ca/eng/civil/.

University of New Hampshire, Graduate School, College of Engineering and Physical Sciences, Department of Civil Engineering, Durham, NH 03824. Offers MS, PhD. Part-time programs available. *Faculty:* 17 full-time (5 women). *Students:* 33 full-time (12 women), 35 part-time (11 women); includes 3 minority (1 American Indian or Alaska Native, non-Hispanic/Latino; 2 Two or more races, non-Hispanic/Latino), 7 international. Average age 26. 63 applicants, 83% accepted, 25 enrolled. In 2011, 18 master's, 1 doctorate awarded. *Degree requirements:* For master's, thesis or alternative; for doctorate, thesis/dissertation. *Entrance requirements:* For master's and doctorate, GRE. Additional exam requirements/recommendations for international students: Required—TOEFL (minimum score 550 paper-based; 213 computer-based; 80 iBT). *Application deadline:* For fall admission, 4/1 priority date for domestic students, 4/1 for international students; for spring admission, 12/1 for domestic students. Applications are processed on a rolling basis. Application fee: $65. *Expenses:* Tuition, state resident: full-time $12,360; part-time $687 per credit hour. Tuition, nonresident: full-time $25,680; part-time $1058 per credit hour. *International tuition:* $29,550 full-time. *Required fees:* $1666; $833 per course. $416.50 per semester. Tuition and fees vary according to course load and degree level. *Financial support:* In 2011–12, 39 students received support, including 1 fellowship, 16 research assistantships, 19 teaching assistantships; Federal Work-Study, scholarships/grants, and tuition waivers (full and partial) also available. Support available to part-time students. Financial award application deadline: 2/15. *Faculty research:* Environmental, structural materials, geotechnical engineering, water resources, systems analysis. *Unit head:* Dr. Robin Collins, Chairperson, 603-862-1419. *Application contact:* Robin Collins, Administrative Assistant, 603-862-1353, E-mail: civil.engineering@unh.edu. Web site: http://www.unh.edu/civil-engineering/.

University of New Mexico, Graduate School, School of Engineering, Department of Civil Engineering, Albuquerque, NM 87131-0001. Offers civil engineering (MSCE); construction management (MCM); engineering (M Eng, PhD). Part-time programs available. *Faculty:* 17 full-time (3 women), 1 part-time/adjunct (0 women). *Students:* 21 full-time (6 women), 45 part-time (12 women); includes 17 minority (1 Black or African American, non-Hispanic/Latino; 4 American Indian or Alaska Native, non-Hispanic/Latino; 1 Asian, non-Hispanic/Latino; 10 Hispanic/Latino; 1 Two or more races, non-Hispanic/Latino), 20 international. Average age 30. 72 applicants, 51% accepted, 23 enrolled. In 2011, 3 master's, 2 doctorates awarded. Terminal master's awarded for partial completion of doctoral program. *Median time to degree:* Of those who began their doctoral program in fall 2003, 100% received their degree in 8 years or less. *Degree requirements:* For master's, comprehensive exam, thesis (for some programs); for doctorate, comprehensive exam, thesis/dissertation. *Entrance requirements:* For master's, GRE General Test (for MSCE and MENG); GRE or GMAT (for MCM), minimum GPA of 3.0; for doctorate, GRE General Test, minimum GPA of 3.0. Additional exam requirements/recommendations for international students: Required—TOEFL (minimum score 550 paper-based; 213 computer-based; 79 iBT). *Application deadline:* For fall admission, 7/15 for domestic students, 3/1 for international students; for spring admission, 11/10 for domestic students, 8/1 for international students. Applications are processed on a rolling basis. Application fee: $50. Electronic applications accepted. *Financial support:* In 2011–12, 63 students received support, including 50 research assistantships with full and partial tuition reimbursements available (averaging $18,648 per year), 4 teaching assistantships with full and partial tuition reimbursements available (averaging $15,000 per year); scholarships/grants, health care benefits, and unspecified assistantships also available. Support available to part-time students. Financial award application deadline: 3/1; financial award applicants required to submit FAFSA. *Faculty research:* Integrating design and construction, project delivery methods, sustainable design and construction, leadership and management in construction, project management and project supervision, production management and improvement. *Total annual research expenditures:* $2.9 million. *Unit head:* Dr. John C. Stormont, Chair, 505-277-2722, Fax: 505-277-1988, E-mail: jcstorm@unm.edu. *Application contact:* Josie Gibson, Professional Academic Advisor, 505-277-2722, Fax: 505-277-1988, E-mail: civil@unm.edu. Web site: http://civil.unm.edu.

The University of North Carolina at Charlotte, Graduate School, The William States Lee College of Engineering, Department of Civil and Environmental Engineering, Charlotte, NC 28223-0001. Offers civil engineering (MSCE); infrastructure and environmental systems (PhD), including infrastructure and environmental systems design. Part-time and evening/weekend programs available. *Faculty:* 20 full-time (2 women). *Students:* 57 full-time (12 women), 41 part-time (10 women); includes 15 minority (3 Black or African American, non-Hispanic/Latino; 2 American Indian or Alaska Native, non-Hispanic/Latino; 3 Asian, non-Hispanic/Latino; 6 Hispanic/Latino; 1 Two or more races, non-Hispanic/Latino), 34 international. Average age 29. 56 applicants, 73% accepted, 24 enrolled. In 2011, 20 master's, 4 doctorates awarded. Terminal master's awarded for partial completion of doctoral program. *Degree requirements:* For master's, thesis or project. *Entrance requirements:* For master's, GRE General Test, minimum GPA of 3.0 in undergraduate major, 2.75 overall. Additional exam requirements/recommendations for international students: Required—TOEFL (minimum score 550 paper-based; 220 computer-based; 83 iBT). *Application deadline:* For fall admission, 7/1 for domestic students, 5/1 for international students; for spring admission, 11/1 for domestic students, 10/1 for international students. Applications are processed on a rolling basis. Application fee: $65 ($75 for international students). Electronic applications accepted. *Expenses:* Tuition, state resident: full-time $3689. Tuition, nonresident: full-time $15,226. *Required fees:* $2198. Tuition and fees vary according to course load and program. *Financial support:* In 2011–12, 44 students received support, including 2 fellowships (averaging $23,547 per year), 25 research assistantships (averaging $5,581 per year), 17 teaching assistantships (averaging $5,679 per year); career-related internships or fieldwork, Federal Work-Study, institutionally sponsored loans, and scholarships/grants also available. Support available to part-time students. Financial award application deadline: 4/1; financial award applicants required to submit FAFSA. *Faculty research:* Structural composite materials, storm water systems, natural and man-made disaster reduction engineering, older drivers and nighttime driving, soil contamination and transport. *Total annual research expenditures:* $1.3 million. *Unit head:* Dr. David T. Young, Chair, 704-687-4175, Fax: 704-687-6953, E-mail: dyoung@.uncc.edu. *Application contact:* Kathy B. Giddings, Director of Graduate Admissions, 704-687-5503, Fax: 704-687-3279, E-mail: gradadm@uncc.edu. Web site: http://cee.uncc.edu/.

University of North Dakota, Graduate School, School of Engineering and Mines, Department of Civil Engineering, Grand Forks, ND 58202. Offers civil engineering (M Engr); sanitary engineering (M Engr), including soils and structures engineering, surface mining engineering. Part-time programs available. *Degree requirements:* For master's, comprehensive exam, thesis or alternative. *Entrance requirements:* For master's, GRE General Test, minimum GPA of 2.5. Additional exam requirements/recommendations for international students: Required—TOEFL (minimum score 550 paper-based; 213 computer-based; 79 iBT), IELTS (minimum score 6.5). Electronic applications accepted. *Faculty research:* Soil-structures, environmental-water resources.

University of North Florida, College of Computing, Engineering, and Construction, School of Engineering, Jacksonville, FL 32224. Offers MSCE, MSEE, MSME. Part-time programs available. *Faculty:* 20 full-time (1 woman). *Students:* 6 full-time (2 women), 35 part-time (6 women); includes 9 minority (1 Black or African American, non-Hispanic/Latino; 3 Asian, non-Hispanic/Latino; 4 Hispanic/Latino; 1 Two or more races, non-Hispanic/Latino), 6 international. Average age 29. 33 applicants, 58% accepted, 6 enrolled. In 2011, 7 master's awarded. *Application deadline:* For fall admission, 7/1 for domestic students, 5/1 for international students; for spring admission, 11/1 for domestic students, 10/1 for international students. Application fee: $30. *Expenses:* Tuition, state resident: full-time $8793; part-time $366.38 per credit hour. Tuition, nonresident: full-time $23,502; part-time $979.24 per credit hour. *Required fees:* $1384; $57.66 per credit hour. Tuition and fees vary according to course load and program. *Financial support:* In 2011–12, 16 students received support, including 14 research assistantships (averaging $3,428 per year), 1 teaching assistantship (averaging $1,600 per year); Federal Work-Study, scholarships/grants, tuition waivers, and unspecified assistantships also available. Financial award application deadline: 4/1; financial award applicants required to submit FAFSA. *Total annual research expenditures:* $5 million. *Unit head:* Gerald Merckel, Associate Dean, 904-620-1390, E-mail: gmerckel@unf.edu. *Application contact:* Lillith Richardson, Assistant Director, The Graduate School, 904-320-1360, Fax: 904-620-1362, E-mail: graduateschool@unf.edu. Web site: http://www.unf.edu/ccec/engineering/.

University of Notre Dame, Graduate School, College of Engineering, Department of Civil Engineering and Geological Sciences, Notre Dame, IN 46556. Offers bioengineering (MS Bio E); civil engineering (MSCE); civil engineering and geological sciences (PhD); environmental engineering (MS Env E); geological sciences (MS). Terminal master's awarded for partial completion of doctoral program. *Degree requirements:* For master's, comprehensive exam; for doctorate, thesis/dissertation, candidacy exam. *Entrance requirements:* For master's and doctorate, GRE General Test. Additional exam requirements/recommendations for international students: Required—TOEFL (minimum score 600 paper-based; 250 computer-based; 80 iBT). Electronic applications accepted. *Faculty research:* Environmental modeling, biological-waste treatment, petrology, environmental geology, geochemistry.

University of Oklahoma, College of Engineering, School of Civil Engineering and Environmental Science, Program in Civil Engineering, Norman, OK 73019. Offers civil engineering (MS, PhD). Part-time programs available. *Students:* 37 full-time (6 women), 15 part-time (2 women); includes 5 minority (2 Black or African American, non-Hispanic/Latino; 1 American Indian or Alaska Native, non-Hispanic/Latino; 1 Asian, non-Hispanic/Latino; 1 Hispanic/Latino), 30 international. Average age 27. 42 applicants, 40% accepted, 9 enrolled. In 2011, 20 master's, 2 doctorates awarded. Terminal master's awarded for partial completion of doctoral program. *Degree requirements:* For master's, comprehensive exam, oral exams; for doctorate, thesis/dissertation, oral and qualifying exams. *Entrance requirements:* For master's, minimum GPA of 3.0; for doctorate, minimum graduate GPA of 3.5. Additional exam requirements/recommendations for international students: Required—TOEFL (minimum score 600 paper-based; 100 iBT). *Application deadline:* For fall admission, 4/1 priority date for domestic students, 3/1 for international students; for spring admission, 11/1 for domestic students, 9/1 for international students. Applications are processed on a rolling basis. Application fee: $40 ($90 for international students). Electronic applications accepted. *Expenses:* Tuition, state resident: full-time $4087; part-time $170.30 per credit hour. Tuition, nonresident: full-time $14,875; part-time $619.80 per credit hour. *Required fees:* $2659; $100.25 per credit hour. Tuition and fees vary according to course load and degree level. *Financial support:* In 2011–12, 52 students received support. Scholarships/grants available. Financial award applicants required to submit FAFSA. *Faculty research:* Intelligent structures, composites, earthquake engineering, intelligent compaction, bridge engineering. *Unit head:* Robert C. Knox, Director, 405-325-5911, Fax: 405-325-4217, E-mail: rknox@ou.edu. *Application contact:* Susan Williams, Graduate Programs Assistant, 405-325-2344, Fax: 405-325-4147, E-mail: srwilliams@ou.edu. Web site: http://cees.ou.edu.

University of Ottawa, Faculty of Graduate and Postdoctoral Studies, Faculty of Engineering, Ottawa-Carleton Institute for Civil Engineering, Ottawa, ON K1N 6N5, Canada. Offers M Eng, MA Sc, PhD. PhD, M Eng, MA Sc offered jointly with Carleton University. *Degree requirements:* For master's, thesis or alternative; for doctorate, comprehensive exam, thesis/dissertation, seminar series. *Entrance requirements:* For master's, honors degree or equivalent, minimum B average; for doctorate, master's degree, minimum B+ average. Electronic applications accepted. *Faculty research:* Environmental engineering, geotechnical engineering, structural engineering, transportation engineering, water resources engineering.

University of Pittsburgh, Swanson School of Engineering, Department of Civil and Environmental Engineering, Pittsburgh, PA 15260. Offers MSCEE, PhD. Part-time programs available. Postbaccalaureate distance learning degree programs offered. *Faculty:* 16 full-time (4 women), 18 part-time/adjunct (1 woman). *Students:* 79 full-time (21 women), 49 part-time (16 women); includes 7 minority (1 Black or African American, non-Hispanic/Latino; 5 Asian, non-Hispanic/Latino; 1 Native Hawaiian or other Pacific Islander, non-Hispanic/Latino), 58 international. 336 applicants, 79% accepted, 42 enrolled. In 2011, 42 master's, 10 doctorates awarded. Terminal master's awarded for partial completion of doctoral program. *Degree requirements:* For master's, thesis optional; for doctorate, comprehensive exam, thesis/dissertation, final oral exams. *Entrance requirements:* For master's and doctorate, minimum QPA of 3.0. Additional exam requirements/recommendations for international students: Required—TOEFL (minimum score 550 paper-based; 213 computer-based; 80 iBT). *Application deadline:* For fall admission, 3/1 priority date for domestic students; for spring admission, 7/1 priority date for domestic students. Applications are processed on a rolling basis. Application fee: $50. Electronic applications accepted. *Expenses:* Tuition, state resident: full-time $18,774; part-time $760 per credit. Tuition, nonresident: full-time $30,736; part-time $1258 per credit. *Required fees:* $740; $200 per term. Tuition and fees vary according to program. *Financial support:* In 2011–12, 39 students received support, including 7 fellowships with tuition reimbursements available (averaging $27,768 per year), 20 research assistantships with full tuition reimbursements available (averaging $22,296 per year), 12 teaching assistantships with full tuition reimbursements available (averaging $22,836 per year); scholarships/grants, traineeships, and tuition waivers (full and partial) also available. Financial award application deadline: 4/15. *Faculty research:* Environmental and water resources, structures and infrastructures, construction management. *Total annual research expenditures:* $4.2 million. *Unit head:* Dr. Radisav Vidic, Chairman, 412-624-9870, Fax: 412-624-0135. *Application contact:* Dr. Leonard Casson, Academic Coordinator, 412-624-9868, Fax: 412-624-0135, E-mail: leonard@pitt.edu. Web site: http://www.engineering.pitt.edu/Civil/.

University of Puerto Rico, Mayagüez Campus, Graduate Studies, College of Engineering, Department of Civil Engineering and Surveying, Mayagüez, PR 00681-9000. Offers civil engineering (ME, MS, PhD). Part-time programs available. *Students:* 113 full-time (49 women), 19 part-time (6 women); includes 108 minority (all Hispanic/Latino), 24 international. 47 applicants, 70% accepted, 23 enrolled. In 2011, 21 master's, 1 doctorate awarded. *Degree requirements:* For master's, comprehensive exam, thesis (MS); for doctorate, one foreign language, thesis/dissertation. *Entrance requirements:* For master's, proficiency in English and Spanish, BS in civil engineering or its equivalent; for doctorate, proficiency in English and Spanish. *Application deadline:* For fall admission, 2/15 for domestic and international students; for spring admission, 9/15 for domestic and international students. Applications are processed on a rolling basis. Application fee: $25. Tuition and fees vary according to course level and course load. *Financial support:* In 2011–12, 55 students received support, including 38 research assistantships (averaging $15,000 per year), 17 teaching assistantships (averaging $8,500 per year); Federal Work-Study and institutionally sponsored loans also available. *Faculty research:* Structural design, concrete structure, finite elements, dynamic analysis, transportation, soils. *Total annual research expenditures:* $2.6 million. *Unit head:* Prof. Ismael Pagan Trinidad, Chairperson, 787-832-4040 Ext. 3434, Fax: 787-833-8260, E-mail: ismael.pagan@upr.edu. *Application contact:* Dr. Ricardo Lopez, Associate Director, 787-832-4040 Ext. 2178, Fax: 787-833-8260, E-mail: rilopez@upr.edu. Web site: http://civil.uprm.edu.

University of Rhode Island, Graduate School, College of Engineering, Department of Civil and Environmental Engineering, Kingston, RI 02881. Offers MS, PhD. Part-time programs available. *Faculty:* 9 full-time (3 women), 2 part-time/adjunct (0 women). *Students:* 33 full-time (7 women), 12 part-time (2 women); includes 4 minority (1 Asian, non-Hispanic/Latino; 2 Hispanic/Latino; 1 Two or more races, non-Hispanic/Latino), 9 international. In 2011, 16 master's, 1 doctorate awarded. *Degree requirements:* For master's, comprehensive exam (for some programs), thesis optional; for doctorate, comprehensive exam, thesis/dissertation. *Entrance requirements:* For master's and doctorate, 2 letters of recommendation. Additional exam requirements/recommendations for international students: Required—TOEFL (minimum score 550 paper-based; 213 computer-based). *Application deadline:* For fall admission, 7/15 for domestic students, 2/1 for international students; for spring admission, 11/15 for domestic students, 7/15 for international students. Application fee: $65. Electronic applications accepted. *Expenses:* Tuition, state resident: full-time $10,432; part-time $580 per credit hour. Tuition, nonresident: full-time $23,130; part-time $1285 per credit hour. *Required fees:* $1362; $36 per credit hour. $35 per semester. One-time fee: $130. *Financial support:* In 2011–12, 3 research assistantships with full and partial tuition reimbursements (averaging $6,482 per year), 4 teaching assistantships with full and partial tuition reimbursements (averaging $8,302 per year) were awarded. Financial award application deadline: 7/15; financial award applicants required to submit FAFSA. *Faculty research:* Industrial waste treatment, structural health monitoring, traffic and transit system operations, computational mechanics, engineering materials design. *Unit head:* Dr. George E. Tsiatas, Chair, 401-874-5117, Fax: 401-874-2786, E-mail: gt@uri.edu. *Application contact:* Dr. Mayrai Gindy, Director of Graduate Studies, 401-874-5587, Fax: 401-874-2786, E-mail: gindy@egr.uri.edu. Web site: http://www.uri.edu/cve/.

University of Saskatchewan, College of Graduate Studies and Research, College of Engineering, Department of Civil and Geological Engineering, Saskatoon, SK S7N 5A2, Canada. Offers M Eng, M Sc, PhD. *Degree requirements:* For master's, thesis (for some programs); for doctorate, thesis/dissertation. *Entrance requirements:* For master's, GRE, minimum GPA of 5.0 on an 8.0 scale; for doctorate, GRE. Additional exam requirements/recommendations for international students: Required—TOEFL. *Faculty research:* Geotechnical engineering, structures, water sciences.

University of South Alabama, Graduate School, College of Engineering, Department of Civil Engineering, Mobile, AL 36688-0002. Offers MSCE. *Faculty:* 5 full-time (0 women). *Students:* 10 full-time (1 woman), 7 part-time (3 women); includes 2 minority (both Hispanic/Latino). 15 applicants, 67% accepted, 7 enrolled. In 2011, 5 master's awarded. *Entrance requirements:* Additional exam requirements/recommendations for international students: Required—TOEFL. *Application deadline:* For fall admission, 7/15 priority date for domestic students, 6/15 for international students; for spring admission, 12/1 priority date for domestic students, 11/1 for international students. Application fee: $35. *Expenses:* Tuition, state resident: full-time $7968; part-time $332 per credit hour. Tuition, nonresident: full-time $15,936; part-time $664 per credit hour. *Unit head:* Dr. Kevin White, Chair, 251-460-6174. *Application contact:* Dr. B. Keith Harrison, Director of Graduate Studies, 251-460-6160. Web site: http://www.eng.usouthal.edu/civil.

University of South Carolina, The Graduate School, College of Engineering and Computing, Department of Civil and Environmental Engineering, Columbia, SC 29208. Offers civil engineering (ME, MS, PhD). Part-time and evening/weekend programs available. Postbaccalaureate distance learning degree programs offered (minimal on-campus study). *Degree requirements:* For master's, comprehensive exam, thesis (for some programs); for doctorate, thesis/dissertation. *Entrance requirements:* For master's and doctorate, GRE General Test, 2 letters of recommendation. Additional exam requirements/recommendations for international students: Required—TOEFL (minimum score 570 paper-based; 230 computer-based). Electronic applications accepted. *Faculty research:* Structures, Water Resources, Environmental, Geotechnical and Transportation.

University of Southern California, Graduate School, Viterbi School of Engineering, Sonny Astani Department of Civil Engineering, Los Angeles, CA 90089. Offers applied mechanics (MS); civil engineering (MS, PhD); computer-aided engineering (ME, Graduate Certificate); construction management (MCM); engineering technology commercialization (Graduate Certificate); environmental engineering (MS, PhD); environmental quality management (ME); structural design (ME); sustainable cities (Graduate Certificate); transportation systems (MS, Graduate Certificate); water and waste management (MS). Part-time and evening/weekend programs available. Terminal master's awarded for partial completion of doctoral program. *Degree requirements:* For master's, thesis optional; for doctorate, thesis/dissertation. *Entrance requirements:* For master's and doctorate, GRE General Test. Additional exam requirements/recommendations for international students: Recommended—TOEFL. Electronic applications accepted. *Faculty research:* Geotechnical engineering, transportation engineering, structural engineering, construction management, environmental engineering, water resources.

University of South Florida, Graduate School, College of Engineering, Department of Civil and Environmental Engineering, Tampa, FL 33620-9951. Offers civil and environmental engineering (MSES); civil engineering (MCE, MSCE, PhD); environmental engineering (MSEV). Part-time programs available. *Faculty:* 20 full-time (5 women), 3 part-time/adjunct (1 woman). *Students:* 116 full-time (40 women), 66 part-time (15 women); includes 38 minority (9 Black or African American, non-Hispanic/Latino; 7 Asian, non-Hispanic/Latino; 20 Hispanic/Latino; 2 Two or more races, non-Hispanic/Latino), 49 international. Average age 30. 184 applicants, 55% accepted, 52 enrolled. In 2011, 51 master's, 7 doctorates awarded. Terminal master's awarded for partial completion of doctoral program. *Degree requirements:* For master's, comprehensive exam, thesis (for some programs); for doctorate, comprehensive exam, thesis/dissertation. *Entrance requirements:* For master's, GRE, minimum GPA of 3.0 in last 60 hours of coursework, two letters of reference, statement of purpose; for doctorate, GRE, minimum GPA of 3.0 in last 60 hours of coursework, three letters of recommendation, statement of purpose, resume. Additional exam requirements/recommendations for international students: Required—TOEFL (minimum score 550 paper-based; 213 computer-based; 79 iBT). *Application deadline:* For fall admission, 2/15 for domestic students, 1/2 for international students; for spring admission, 10/15 for domestic students, 6/1 for international students. Application fee: $30. Electronic applications accepted. *Financial support:* In 2011–12, 65 students received support, including 44 research assistantships (averaging $14,123 per year), 21 teaching assistantships with tuition reimbursements available (averaging $15,329 per year). *Faculty research:* Water resources, structures and materials, transportation, geotechnical engineering, mechanics. *Total annual research expenditures:* $2.6 million. *Unit head:* Dr. Manjriker Gunaratne, Dean, 813-974—5818, Fax: 813-974-5094, E-mail: gunaratn@usf.edu. *Application contact:* Dr. Sarina Ergas, Program Director, 813-974-1119, Fax: 813-974-2957, E-mail: sergas@usf.edu. Web site: http://ce.eng.usf.edu/.

The University of Tennessee, Graduate School, College of Engineering, Department of Civil and Environmental Engineering, Program in Civil Engineering, Knoxville, TN 37996. Offers MS, PhD, MS/MBA. Part-time programs available. Postbaccalaureate distance learning degree programs offered (minimal on-campus study). *Faculty:* 18 full-time (2 women), 12 part-time/adjunct (0 women). *Students:* 66 full-time (11 women), 36 part-time (4 women); includes 7 minority (1 Black or African American, non-Hispanic/Latino; 4 Asian, non-Hispanic/Latino; 2 Hispanic/Latino), 26 international. Average age 23. 103 applicants, 61% accepted, 26 enrolled. In 2011, 24 master's, 8 doctorates awarded. *Degree requirements:* For master's, thesis or alternative; for doctorate, comprehensive exam, thesis/dissertation. *Entrance requirements:* For master's, GRE General Test (for MS students pursuing research thesis), minimum GPA of 2.7 (for U.S. degree holders), 3.0 (for international degree holders); 3 references; statement of purpose; resume; for doctorate, College requires GRE General Test for all PhD candidates, minimum GPA of 3.0 on previous graduate course work; 3 references; statement of purpose; resume. Additional exam requirements/recommendations for international students: Required—TOEFL (minimum score 550 paper-based; 213 computer-based). *Application deadline:* For fall admission, 2/1 priority date for domestic students, 2/1 for international students; for spring admission, 6/15 for domestic and international students. Applications are processed on a rolling basis. Application fee: $35. Electronic applications accepted. *Expenses:* Tuition, state resident: full-time $8332; part-time $464 per credit hour. Tuition, nonresident: full-time $25,174; part-time $1400 per credit hour. *Required fees:* $1162; $56 per credit hour. Tuition and fees vary according to program. *Financial support:* In 2011–12, 57 students received support, including 14 research assistantships with full tuition reimbursements available (averaging $20,464 per year), 37 teaching assistantships with full tuition reimbursements available (averaging $18,874 per year); fellowships, career-related internships or fieldwork, Federal Work-Study, institutionally sponsored loans, health care benefits, and unspecified assistantships also available. Financial award application deadline: 2/1; financial award applicants required to submit FAFSA. *Faculty research:* Multi-functional composites and mechanics of materials, geohydrologic investigations and monitoring, structures and vibrations, geotechnical and earthquake engineering, transportation system planning and design. *Unit head:* Dr. Dayakar Penumadu, Head, 865-974-2355, Fax: 865-974-2355, E-mail: dpenumad@utk.edu. *Application contact:* Dr. Chris Cox, Associate Head, 865-974-7729, Fax: 865-974-2355, E-mail: ccox9@utk.edu. Web site: http://www.engr.utk.edu/civil.

The University of Tennessee at Chattanooga, Graduate School, College of Engineering and Computer Science, Program in Engineering, Chattanooga, TN 37403. Offers chemical engineering (MS Engr); civil engineering (MS Engr); computational engineering (MS Engr); electrical engineering (MS Engr); industrial engineering (MS Engr); mechanical engineering (MS Engr). Part-time and evening/weekend programs available. *Faculty:* 27 full-time (3 women), 3 part-time/adjunct (1 woman). *Students:* 40 full-time (7 women), 41 part-time (11 women); includes 23 minority (10 Black or African American, non-Hispanic/Latino; 1 American Indian or Alaska Native, non-Hispanic/Latino; 6 Asian, non-Hispanic/Latino; 4 Hispanic/Latino; 2 Two or more races, non-Hispanic/Latino), 20 international. Average age 28. 89 applicants, 53% accepted, 29 enrolled. In 2011, 8 master's awarded. *Degree requirements:* For master's, comprehensive exam, thesis or alternative, engineering project. *Entrance requirements:* For master's, GRE General Test, minimum undergraduate GPA of 2.5 or 3.0 in last 30 hours of coursework. Additional exam requirements/recommendations for international students: Required—TOEFL (minimum score 550 paper-based; 213 computer-based; 79 iBT), IELTS (minimum score 6). *Application deadline:* For fall admission, 8/1 priority date for domestic students, 6/1 for international students; for spring admission, 12/1 priority date for domestic students, 10/1 for international students. Applications are processed on a rolling basis. Application fee: $35. Electronic applications accepted. *Expenses:* Tuition, state resident: full-time $6472; part-time $359 per credit hour. Tuition, nonresident: full-time $20,006; part-time $1111 per credit hour. *Required fees:* $1320; $160 per credit hour. *Financial support:* Career-related internships or fieldwork, scholarships/grants, and unspecified assistantships available. Support available to part-time students. *Faculty research:* Quality control and reliability engineering, financial management, thermal science, energy conservation, structural analysis. *Total annual research expenditures:* $3.5 million. *Unit head:* Dr. Neslihan Alp, Director, 423-425-4032, Fax: 423-425-5229, E-mail: neslihan-alp@utc.edu. *Application contact:* Dr. Jerald Ainsworth, Dean of Graduate Studies, 423-425-4478, Fax: 423-425-5223, E-mail: jerald-ainsworth@utc.edu. Web site: http://www.utc.edu/Departments/engrcs/ms_engr.php.

The University of Texas at Arlington, Graduate School, College of Engineering, Department of Civil Engineering, Arlington, TX 76019. Offers M Engr, MS, PhD. Part-time and evening/weekend programs available. Postbaccalaureate distance learning degree programs offered (minimal on-campus study). *Faculty:* 17 full-time (1 woman), 2 part-time/adjunct (0 women). *Students:* 106 full-time (25 women), 105 part-time (24 women); includes 45 minority (12 Black or African American, non-Hispanic/Latino; 20 Asian, non-Hispanic/Latino; 9 Hispanic/Latino; 1 Native Hawaiian or other Pacific Islander, non-Hispanic/Latino; 3 Two or more races, non-Hispanic/Latino), 106 international. 158 applicants, 84% accepted, 50 enrolled. In 2011, 50 master's, 9 doctorates awarded. Terminal master's awarded for partial completion of doctoral program. *Degree requirements:* For master's, comprehensive exam, thesis (for some programs), oral and written exams; for doctorate, comprehensive exam, thesis/dissertation, oral and written defense of dissertation. *Entrance requirements:* For master's, GRE General Test, minimum GPA of 3.0 in last 60 hours of undergraduate course work; for doctorate, GRE General Test, minimum GPA of 3.5. Additional exam requirements/recommendations for international students: Required—TOEFL. *Application deadline:* For fall admission, 6/6 for domestic students, 4/4 for international

students; for spring admission, 10/15 for domestic students, 9/5 for international students. Applications are processed on a rolling basis. Application fee: $35 ($50 for international students). Electronic applications accepted. *Financial support:* In 2011–12, 21 students received support, including 7 fellowships with partial tuition reimbursements available (averaging $1,000 per year), 18 research assistantships with partial tuition reimbursements available (averaging $14,850 per year), 25 teaching assistantships with partial tuition reimbursements available (averaging $16,300 per year); career-related internships or fieldwork, Federal Work-Study, scholarships/grants, tuition waivers (partial), and unspecified assistantships also available. Financial award application deadline: 6/1; financial award applicants required to submit FAFSA. *Faculty research:* Environmental and water resources structures, geotechnical, transportation. *Unit head:* Dr. Ali Abolmaali, Chair, 817-272-5055, Fax: 817-272-2630, E-mail: abolmaali@uta.edu. *Application contact:* Dr. Stephen Mattingly, Graduate Advisor, 817-272-2201, Fax: 817-272-2630, E-mail: mattingly@uta.edu. Web site: http://www.uta.edu/ce/.

The University of Texas at Austin, Graduate School, Cockrell School of Engineering, Department of Civil, Architectural and Environmental Engineering, Austin, TX 78712-1111. Offers architectural engineering (MSE); civil engineering (MS, PhD); environmental and water resources engineering (MS, PhD). *Accreditation:* ABET (one or more programs are accredited). Part-time programs available. *Degree requirements:* For master's, thesis or alternative; for doctorate, comprehensive exam, thesis/dissertation. *Entrance requirements:* For master's and doctorate, GRE General Test. Additional exam requirements/recommendations for international students: Required—TOEFL. *Application deadline:* For fall admission, 1/15 priority date for domestic students, 1/15 for international students; for spring admission, 9/1 priority date for domestic students, 9/1 for international students. Applications are processed on a rolling basis. Application fee: $50 ($75 for international students). Electronic applications accepted. *Financial support:* Fellowships, research assistantships, and teaching assistantships available. Financial award application deadline: 2/1. *Faculty research:* Geotechnical structural engineering, transportation engineering, construction engineering/project management. *Unit head:* Dr. Sharon L. Wood, Chair, 512-471-4558, Fax: 512-471-1944, E-mail: swood@mail.utexas.edu. *Application contact:* Kathy Rose, Graduate Coordinator, 512-232-1702, Fax: 512-471-0592, E-mail: krose@mail.utexas.edu. Web site: http://www.ce.utexas.edu/.

The University of Texas at El Paso, Graduate School, College of Engineering, Department of Civil Engineering, El Paso, TX 79968-0001. Offers civil engineering (MS, PhD); construction management (MS, Certificate); environmental engineering (MEENE, MSENE). Part-time and evening/weekend programs available. *Students:* 106 (25 women); includes 55 minority (2 Asian, non-Hispanic/Latino; 53 Hispanic/Latino), 44 international. Average age 34. 71 applicants, 86% accepted, 47 enrolled. In 2011, 22 master's awarded. *Degree requirements:* For master's, thesis optional. *Entrance requirements:* For master's, GRE General Test, minimum GPA of 3.0. Additional exam requirements/recommendations for international students: Required—TOEFL. *Application deadline:* For fall admission, 7/1 priority date for domestic students, 3/1 for international students; for spring admission, 11/1 priority date for domestic students, 9/1 for international students. Applications are processed on a rolling basis. Application fee: $15 ($65 for international students). Electronic applications accepted. *Financial support:* In 2011–12, research assistantships with partial tuition reimbursements (averaging $21,125 per year), teaching assistantships with partial tuition reimbursements (averaging $16,900 per year) were awarded; fellowships with partial tuition reimbursements, career-related internships or fieldwork, Federal Work-Study, institutionally sponsored loans, scholarships/grants, tuition waivers (partial), and stipends also available. Financial award application deadline: 3/15; financial award applicants required to submit FAFSA. *Faculty research:* On-site wastewater treatment systems, wastewater reuse, disinfection by-product control, water resources, membrane filtration. *Unit head:* Wen-Whai Li, Chair, 915-747-5464, E-mail: wli@utep.edu. *Application contact:* Dr. Benjamin Flores, Interim Dean of the Graduate School, 915-747-5491, Fax: 915-747-5788, E-mail: bflores@utep.edu. Web site: http://ce.utep.edu/.

The University of Texas at San Antonio, College of Engineering, Department of Civil and Environmental Engineering, San Antonio, TX 78249-0617. Offers civil engineering (MCE, MS, MSCE); environmental science and engineering (PhD). Part-time and evening/weekend programs available. *Faculty:* 13 full-time (2 women), 5 part-time/adjunct. *Students:* 48 full-time (13 women), 25 part-time (3 women); includes 27 minority (5 Black or African American, non-Hispanic/Latino; 3 Asian, non-Hispanic/Latino; 19 Hispanic/Latino), 27 international. Average age 30. 58 applicants, 67% accepted, 23 enrolled. In 2011, 21 master's, 2 doctorates awarded. *Degree requirements:* For master's, comprehensive exam (for some programs), thesis (for some programs); for doctorate, comprehensive exam, thesis/dissertation. *Entrance requirements:* For master's, GRE General Test, bachelor's degree with 18 credit hours in field of study or in another appropriate field of study, statement of purpose; for doctorate, GRE, BA or BS and MS from accredited university, minimum GPA of 3.0 in upper-division and graduate courses, resume, three letters of recommendation, statement of purpose. Additional exam requirements/recommendations for international students: Required—TOEFL (minimum score 550 paper-based; 79 iBT), IELTS (minimum score 5). *Application deadline:* For fall admission, 7/1 for domestic students, 4/1 for international students; for spring admission, 11/1 for domestic students, 9/1 for international students. Application fee: $45 ($85 for international students). *Expenses:* Tuition, state resident: full-time $3148; part-time $2176 per semester. Tuition, nonresident: full-time $8782; part-time $5932 per semester. *Required fees:* $719 per semester. *Financial support:* In 2011–12, 29 students received support, including 5 fellowships (averaging $4,100 per year), 18 research assistantships with partial tuition reimbursements available (averaging $19,882 per year), 18 teaching assistantships (averaging $4,680 per year); scholarships/grants and unspecified assistantships also available. Financial award application deadline: 3/31. *Faculty research:* Fate, transport and reactivity of chemicals in natural systems/contaminant adsorption/desorption involving nano-particles; transportation infrastructure management and pavement materials; hydrologic analysis; beneficial use of wastes and industrial by-products; pavement-vehicle interaction. *Unit head:* Dr. Athanassio T. Papagiannakis, Chair, 210-458-7517, Fax: 210-458-6475, E-mail: at.papagiannakis@utsa.edu. *Application contact:* Athanassios Papagiannakis, Graduate Advisor of Record, 210-458-7517, Fax: 210-458-7517, E-mail: at.papagiannakis@utsa.edu.

The University of Texas at Tyler, College of Engineering and Computer Science, Department of Civil Engineering, Tyler, TX 75799-0001. Offers environmental engineering (MS); industrial safety (MS); structural engineering (MS); transportation engineering (MS); water resources engineering (MS). Part-time and evening/weekend programs available. *Degree requirements:* For master's, thesis optional. *Entrance requirements:* For master's, GRE General Test, bachelor's degree in engineering, associated science degree. Additional exam requirements/recommendations for international students: Required—TOEFL (minimum score 79 computer-based). *Faculty research:* Non-destructive strength testing, indoor air quality, transportation routing and signaling, pavement replacement criteria, flood water routing, construction and long-term behavior of innovative geotechnical foundation and embankment construction used in highway construction, engineering education.

The University of Toledo, College of Graduate Studies, College of Engineering, Department of Civil Engineering, Toledo, OH 43606-3390. Offers MS, PhD. Part-time programs available. Terminal master's awarded for partial completion of doctoral program. *Degree requirements:* For master's, thesis or alternative; for doctorate, thesis/dissertation, qualifying exam. *Entrance requirements:* For master's, GRE General Test, minimum GPA of 3.0; for doctorate, GRE General Test, minimum GPA of 3.3. Additional exam requirements/recommendations for international students: Required—TOEFL (minimum score 550 paper-based; 213 computer-based; 80 iBT). Electronic applications accepted. *Faculty research:* Environmental modeling, soil/pavement interaction, structural mechanics, earthquakes, transportation engineering.

University of Toronto, School of Graduate Studies, Faculty of Applied Science and Engineering, Department of Civil Engineering, Toronto, ON M5S 1A1, Canada. Offers M Eng, MA Sc, PhD. Part-time programs available. *Degree requirements:* For master's, thesis and oral presentation (MA Sc); for doctorate, thesis/dissertation, oral presentation. *Entrance requirements:* For master's, bachelor's degree in civil engineering, proficiency in computer usage, minimum B average in final 2 years, 3 letters of reference; for doctorate, proficiency in computer usage, minimum B average in final 2 years, 3 letters of reference. Additional exam requirements/recommendations for international students: Required—TOEFL (minimum score 580 paper-based; 93 iBT). Electronic applications accepted.

University of Utah, Graduate School, College of Engineering, Department of Civil and Environmental Engineering, Salt Lake City, UT 84112. Offers civil and environmental engineering (MS); environmental engineering (ME, MS, PhD); nuclear engineering (MS). Part-time programs available. *Faculty:* 22 full-time (6 women), 2 part-time/adjunct (0 women). *Students:* 75 full-time (23 women), 38 part-time (8 women); includes 3 minority (1 Asian, non-Hispanic/Latino; 2 Hispanic/Latino), 42 international. Average age 29. 157 applicants, 57% accepted, 35 enrolled. In 2011, 39 master's, 8 doctorates awarded. Terminal master's awarded for partial completion of doctoral program. *Median time to degree:* Of those who began their doctoral program in fall 2003, 88% received their degree in 8 years or less. *Degree requirements:* For master's, comprehensive exam, thesis (for some programs); for doctorate, comprehensive exam, thesis/dissertation, departmental qualifying exam. *Entrance requirements:* For master's and doctorate, GRE General Test, minimum GPA of 3.0. Additional exam requirements/recommendations for international students: Required—TOEFL (minimum score 550 paper-based; 213 computer-based; 80 iBT). *Application deadline:* For fall admission, 1/15 for domestic students, 12/15 for international students; for spring admission, 10/1 for domestic and international students. Applications are processed on a rolling basis. Application fee: $55 ($65 for international students). Electronic applications accepted. *Expenses:* Contact institution. *Financial support:* In 2011–12, 63 students received support, including 5 fellowships with full tuition reimbursements available (averaging $22,000 per year), 30 research assistantships with full tuition reimbursements available (averaging $20,016 per year), 17 teaching assistantships with full tuition reimbursements available (averaging $19,200 per year); career-related internships or fieldwork, Federal Work-Study, institutionally sponsored loans, scholarships/grants, health care benefits, tuition waivers (full and partial), and unspecified assistantships also available. Support available to part-time students. Financial award application deadline: 12/15; financial award applicants required to submit FAFSA. *Faculty research:* Structural engineering, geotechnical engineering, transportation engineering, environmental engineering, water resources. *Total annual research expenditures:* $15.1 million. *Unit head:* Dr. Paul J. Tikalsky, Chair, 801-581-6931, Fax: 801-585-5477, E-mail: tikalsky@civil.utah.edu. *Application contact:* Amanda May, Advisor, 801-581-6931, Fax: 801-585-5477, E-mail: amandam@civil.utah.edu. Web site: http://www.civil.utah.edu.

University of Vermont, Graduate College, College of Engineering and Mathematics, Department of Civil and Environmental Engineering, Burlington, VT 05405. Offers MS, PhD. *Students:* 35 (12 women), 9 international. 55 applicants, 49% accepted, 7 enrolled. In 2011, 4 master's, 2 doctorates awarded. *Degree requirements:* For master's, thesis or alternative; for doctorate, thesis/dissertation. *Entrance requirements:* For master's and doctorate, GRE General Test. Additional exam requirements/recommendations for international students: Required—TOEFL (minimum score 550 paper-based; 213 computer-based; 80 iBT). *Application deadline:* For fall admission, 2/1 priority date for domestic students, 2/1 for international students. Applications are processed on a rolling basis. Application fee: $40. Electronic applications accepted. *Financial support:* Research assistantships and teaching assistantships available. Financial award application deadline: 3/1. *Unit head:* Dr. Jason Bates, Interim Director, 802-656-3800. *Application contact:* Dr. Britt Holmen, Coordinator, 802-656-3800.

University of Virginia, School of Engineering and Applied Science, Department of Civil Engineering, Charlottesville, VA 22903. Offers ME, MS, PhD. Part-time programs available. Postbaccalaureate distance learning degree programs offered (no on-campus study). *Faculty:* 14 full-time (3 women). *Students:* 49 full-time (10 women), 1 (woman) part-time; includes 4 minority (all Black or African American, non-Hispanic/Latino), 18 international. Average age 27. 131 applicants, 27% accepted, 16 enrolled. In 2011, 9 master's, 3 doctorates awarded. Terminal master's awarded for partial completion of doctoral program. *Degree requirements:* For master's, thesis (for some programs); for doctorate, comprehensive exam, thesis/dissertation. *Entrance requirements:* For master's and doctorate, GRE General Test, 3 letters of recommendation. Additional exam requirements/recommendations for international students: Required—TOEFL (minimum score 600 paper-based; 250 computer-based; 90 iBT), IELTS (minimum score 7). *Application deadline:* For fall admission, 8/1 for domestic students, 4/1 for international students; for winter admission, 12/1 for domestic students, 8/1 for international students; for spring admission, 5/1 for domestic students, 1/1 for international students. Applications are processed on a rolling basis. Application fee: $60. Electronic applications accepted. *Financial support:* Fellowships with full tuition reimbursements, research assistantships with full tuition reimbursements, and teaching assistantships with full tuition reimbursements available. Financial award application deadline: 1/15. *Faculty research:* Groundwater, surface water, traffic engineering, composite materials. *Unit head:* Bran L. Smith, Chair, 434-924-7464, Fax: 434-982-2951, E-mail: civil@virginia.edu. *Application contact:* Graduate Program Coordinator, 434-924-7464, Fax: 434-982-2951, E-mail: civil@virginia.edu. Web site: http://www.ce.virginia.edu/.

University of Washington, Graduate School, College of Engineering, Department of Civil and Environmental Engineering, Seattle, WA 98195-2700. Offers civil engineering (MS, MSE, PhD); construction engineering (MSCE); environmental engineering (MS, MSCE, MSE, PhD); global trade, transportation and logistics (MS); hydrology, water resources, and environmental fluid mechanics (MS, MSCE, MSE, PhD); structural and geotechnical engineering and mechanics (MS, MSCE, MSE, PhD); transportation and construction engineering (MS, MSE, PhD); transportation engineering (MSCE). Part-time programs available. Postbaccalaureate distance learning degree programs offered (no on-campus study). *Faculty:* 47 full-time (11 women), 9 part-time/adjunct (1 woman). *Students:* 195 full-time (67 women), 72 part-time (19 women); includes 37 minority (4 Black or African American, non-Hispanic/Latino; 27 Asian, non-Hispanic/Latino; 6 Hispanic/Latino), 65 international. 654 applicants, 57% accepted, 100 enrolled. In 2011, 88 master's, 7 doctorates awarded. Terminal master's awarded for partial completion of doctoral program. *Degree requirements:* For master's, thesis (for some programs); for doctorate, comprehensive exam, thesis/dissertation, general, qualifying, and final exams; completion of degree within 10 years. *Entrance requirements:* For master's, GRE General Test, minimum GPA of 3.0, statement of purpose, letters of recommendation, transcripts; for doctorate, GRE General Test, minimum GPA of 3.5, statement of purpose, letters of recommendation, transcripts. Additional exam requirements/recommendations for international students: Required—TOEFL (minimum score 580 paper-based; 237 computer-based; 92 iBT); Recommended—IELTS (minimum score 7). *Application deadline:* For fall admission, 1/10 priority date for domestic students, 1/10 for international students. Applications are processed on a rolling basis. Application fee: $75. Electronic applications accepted. *Expenses:* Contact institution. *Financial support:* In 2011–12, 99 students received support, including 16 fellowships with full and partial tuition reimbursements available (averaging $16,173 per year), 71 research assistantships with full tuition reimbursements available (averaging $16,380 per year), 10 teaching assistantships with full tuition reimbursements available (averaging $16,380 per year); scholarships/grants also available. Financial award application deadline: 1/10; financial award applicants required to submit FAFSA. *Faculty research:* Environmental/water resources, hydrology; construction/transportation; structures/ geotechnical. *Total annual research expenditures:* $13.6 million. *Unit head:* Dr. Gregory R. Miller, Professor/Chair, 206-543-0350, Fax: 206-543-1543, E-mail: gmiller@uw.edu. *Application contact:* Lorna Latal, Graduate Adviser, 206-543-2574, Fax: 206-543-1543, E-mail: llatal@u.washington.edu. Web site: http://www.ce.washington.edu/programs/prospective/grad/applying/gen_admission.html.

University of Waterloo, Graduate Studies, Faculty of Engineering, Department of Civil and Environmental Engineering, Waterloo, ON N2L 3G1, Canada. Offers M Eng, MA Sc, PhD. Part-time programs available. *Degree requirements:* For master's, research paper or thesis; for doctorate, comprehensive exam, thesis/dissertation. *Entrance requirements:* For master's, honors degree, minimum B average; for doctorate, master's degree, minimum A- average. Additional exam requirements/recommendations for international students: Required—TOEFL, TWE. Electronic applications accepted. *Faculty research:* Water resources, structures, construction management, transportation, geotechnical engineering.

The University of Western Ontario, Faculty of Graduate Studies, Physical Sciences Division, Faculty of Engineering, London, ON N6A 5B8, Canada. Offers chemical and biochemical engineering (ME Sc, PhD); civil and environmental engineering (M Eng, ME Sc, PhD); electrical and computer engineering (M Eng, ME Sc, PhD); mechanical and materials engineering (M Eng, ME Sc, PhD). Part-time programs available. Terminal master's awarded for partial completion of doctoral program. *Degree requirements:* For master's, thesis; for doctorate, thesis/dissertation. *Entrance requirements:* For master's, minimum B average; for doctorate, minimum B+ average. *Faculty research:* Wind, geotechnical, chemical reactor engineering, applied electrostatics, biochemical engineering.

University of Windsor, Faculty of Graduate Studies, Faculty of Engineering, Department of Civil and Environmental Engineering, Windsor, ON N9B 3P4, Canada. Offers civil engineering (M Eng, MA Sc, PhD); environmental engineering (M Eng, MA Sc, PhD). Part-time programs available. *Degree requirements:* For master's, thesis; for doctorate, comprehensive exam, thesis/dissertation. *Entrance requirements:* For master's, minimum B average; for doctorate, master's degree, minimum A average. Additional exam requirements/recommendations for international students: Required—TOEFL (minimum score 580 paper-based; 237 computer-based). Electronic applications accepted. *Faculty research:* Odors: sampling, measurement, control; drinking water disinfection, hydrocarbon contaminated soil remediation, structural dynamics, numerical simulation of piezoelectric materials.

University of Wisconsin–Madison, Graduate School, College of Engineering, Department of Civil and Environmental Engineering, Madison, WI 53706-1380. Offers MS, PhD. Part-time programs available. *Faculty:* 31 full-time (3 women), 2 part-time/adjunct (0 women). *Students:* 164 full-time (37 women); includes 9 minority (2 Black or African American, non-Hispanic/Latino; 1 Asian, non-Hispanic/Latino; 5 Hispanic/Latino; 1 Native Hawaiian or other Pacific Islander, non-Hispanic/Latino), 64 international. Average age 29. 508 applicants, 16% accepted, 41 enrolled. In 2011, 46 master's, 12 doctorates awarded. Terminal master's awarded for partial completion of doctoral program. *Degree requirements:* For master's, thesis or alternative; for doctorate, thesis/dissertation, preliminary exam, qualifying exams. *Entrance requirements:* For master's and doctorate, GRE General Test, minimum GPA of 3.0 for last 60 credits of course work. Additional exam requirements/recommendations for international students: Required—TOEFL (minimum score 550 paper-based; 213 computer-based; 80 iBT). *Application deadline:* For fall admission, 12/15 priority date for domestic students, 12/15 for international students; for spring admission, 9/15 for domestic and international students. Application fee: $56. Electronic applications accepted. *Expenses:* Tuition, state resident: full-time $10,296; part-time $643.51 per credit. Tuition, nonresident: full-time $24,054; part-time $1503.40 per credit. *Required fees:* $70.06 per credit. Tuition and fees vary according to course load, campus/location, program and reciprocity agreements. *Financial support:* In 2011–12, 86 students received support, including 5 fellowships with full tuition reimbursements available (averaging $22,440 per year), 59 research assistantships with full tuition reimbursements available (averaging $40,368 per year), 6 teaching assistantships with full tuition reimbursements available (averaging $28,175 per year); Federal Work-Study, scholarships/grants, health care benefits, unspecified assistantships, and project assistantships also available. Support available to part-time students. Financial award application deadline: 12/15. *Faculty research:* Environmental geotechnics and soil mechanics, design and analysis of structures, traffic engineering and intelligent transport systems, industrial pollution control, hydrological monitoring. *Total annual research expenditures:* $11 million. *Unit head:* Craig H. Benson, Chair, 608-262-3491, Fax: 608-262-5199, E-mail: benson@engr.wisc.edu. *Application contact:* Cheryl Loschko, Student Status Examiner, 608-265-5570, Fax: 608-890-1174, E-mail: loschko@wisc.edu. Web site: http://www.engr.wisc.edu/cee/.

University of Wisconsin–Milwaukee, Graduate School, College of Engineering and Applied Science, Program in Engineering, Milwaukee, WI 53201-0413. Offers civil engineering (MS); electrical and computer engineering (MS); energy engineering (Certificate); engineering (PhD); engineering management (MS); engineering mechanics (MS); ergonomics (Certificate); industrial and management engineering (MS); manufacturing engineering (MS); materials engineering (MS); mechanical engineering (MS); MUP/MS. Part-time programs available. *Faculty:* 41 full-time (5 women), 2 part-time/adjunct (0 women). *Students:* 170 full-time (33 women), 101 part-time (18 women); includes 30 minority (6 Black or African American, non-Hispanic/Latino; 15 Asian, non-Hispanic/Latino; 2 Hispanic/Latino; 7 Two or more races, non-Hispanic/Latino), 153 international. Average age 30. 170 applicants, 56% accepted, 48 enrolled. In 2011, 47 master's, 12 doctorates awarded. *Degree requirements:* For master's, comprehensive exam (for some programs), thesis or alternative; for doctorate, comprehensive exam, thesis/dissertation, internship. *Entrance requirements:* For master's, GRE, minimum GPA of 2.75; for doctorate, GRE, minimum GPA of 3.5. Additional exam requirements/recommendations for international students: Required—TOEFL (minimum score 550 paper-based; 79 iBT), IELTS (minimum score 6.5). *Application deadline:* For fall admission, 1/1 priority date for domestic students; for spring admission, 9/1 for domestic students. Applications are processed on a rolling basis. Application fee: $56 ($96 for international students). One-time fee: $506.10 full-time. Tuition and fees vary according to course load and reciprocity agreements. *Financial support:* In 2011–12, 3 fellowships, 55 research assistantships, 77 teaching assistantships were awarded; career-related internships or fieldwork, Federal Work-Study, unspecified assistantships, and project assistantships also available. Support available to part-time students. Financial award application deadline: 4/15. *Total annual research expenditures:* $10.3 million. *Unit head:* David Yu, Representative, 414-229-6169, E-mail: yu@uwm.edu. *Application contact:* Betty Warras, General Information Contact, 414-229-6169, Fax: 414-229-6967, E-mail: bwarras@uwm.edu. Web site: http://www.wum.edu/CEAS/.

University of Wyoming, College of Engineering and Applied Sciences, Department of Civil and Architectural Engineering, Program in Civil Engineering, Laramie, WY 82070. Offers MS, PhD. Part-time programs available. Terminal master's awarded for partial completion of doctoral program. *Degree requirements:* For master's, thesis (for some programs); for doctorate, variable foreign language requirement, comprehensive exam, thesis/dissertation. *Entrance requirements:* For master's, GRE General Test (minimum score 900), minimum GPA of 3.0; for doctorate, GRE General Test (minimum score: 1000), minimum GPA of 3.0. Additional exam requirements/recommendations for international students: Required—TOEFL. Electronic applications accepted. *Faculty research:* Structures, water, resources, geotechnical, transportation.

Utah State University, School of Graduate Studies, College of Engineering, Department of Civil and Environmental Engineering, Logan, UT 84322. Offers ME, MS, PhD, CE. *Degree requirements:* For master's, thesis (for some programs); for doctorate, thesis/dissertation. *Entrance requirements:* For master's and doctorate, GRE General Test, minimum GPA of 3.0. Additional exam requirements/recommendations for international students: Required—TOEFL. Electronic applications accepted. *Faculty research:* Hazardous waste treatment, large space structures, river basin management, earthquake engineering, environmental impact.

Vanderbilt University, School of Engineering, Department of Civil and Environmental Engineering, Program in Civil Engineering, Nashville, TN 37240-1001. Offers M Eng, MS, PhD. MS and PhD offered through the Graduate School. Part-time programs available. *Faculty:* 12 full-time (1 woman), 1 (woman) part-time/adjunct. *Students:* 52 full-time (16 women); includes 5 minority (4 Black or African American, non-Hispanic/Latino; 1 Hispanic/Latino), 16 international. Average age 28. 87 applicants, 11% accepted, 7 enrolled. In 2011, 26 master's, 6 doctorates awarded. Terminal master's awarded for partial completion of doctoral program. *Degree requirements:* For master's, thesis; for doctorate, thesis/dissertation. *Entrance requirements:* For master's and doctorate, GRE General Test. Additional exam requirements/recommendations for international students: Required—TOEFL. *Application deadline:* For fall admission, 1/15 for domestic students; for spring admission, 11/1 for domestic students. Applications are processed on a rolling basis. Application fee: $0. Electronic applications accepted. *Financial support:* In 2011–12, 12 fellowships with full tuition reimbursements (averaging $30,000 per year), 15 research assistantships with full tuition reimbursements (averaging $26,400 per year), 7 teaching assistantships with full tuition reimbursements (averaging $25,020 per year) were awarded; career-related internships or fieldwork, institutionally sponsored loans, scholarships/grants, traineeships, and tuition waivers (full and partial) also available. Financial award application deadline: 1/15. *Faculty research:* Structural mechanics, finite element analysis, urban transportation, hazardous material transport. *Unit head:* Dr. David S. Kosson, Chair, 615-322-2697, Fax: 615-322-3365, E-mail: david.kosson@vanderbilt.edu. *Application contact:* Dr. P. K. Basu, Director of Graduate Studies, 615-322-7477, Fax: 615-322-3365, E-mail: p.k.basu@vanderbilt.edu. Web site: http://www.cee.vanderbilt.edu/.

Villanova University, College of Engineering, Department of Civil and Environmental Engineering, Program in Civil Engineering, Villanova, PA 19085-1699. Offers MSCE. Part-time and evening/weekend programs available. *Degree requirements:* For master's, thesis optional. *Entrance requirements:* For master's, GRE General Test (for applicants with degrees from foreign universities), minimum GPA of 3.0. Additional exam requirements/recommendations for international students: Required—TOEFL (minimum score 600 paper-based; 250 computer-based; 100 iBT). Electronic applications accepted. *Expenses: Tuition:* Part-time $675 per credit. Part-time tuition and fees vary according to degree level and program. *Faculty research:* Bridge inspection, environment maintenance, economy and risk.

Virginia Polytechnic Institute and State University, Graduate School, College of Engineering, Department of Civil and Environmental Engineering, Blacksburg, VA 24061. Offers civil engineering (M Eng, MS, PhD); civil infrastructure systems (Certificate); environmental engineering (MS); environmental sciences and engineering (MS); transportation systems engineering (Certificate); treatment process engineering (Certificate); urban hydrology and stormwater management (Certificate); water quality management (Certificate). *Accreditation:* ABET (one or more programs are accredited). *Degree requirements:* For master's, comprehensive exam (for some programs), thesis (for some programs); for doctorate, comprehensive exam (for some programs), thesis/dissertation (for some programs). *Entrance requirements:* For master's and doctorate, GRE. Additional exam requirements/recommendations for international students: Required—TOEFL (minimum score 550 paper-based; 213 computer-based). *Application deadline:* For fall admission, 7/1 for domestic and international students; for spring admission, 12/1 for domestic and international students. Applications are processed on a rolling basis. Application fee: $65. Electronic applications accepted. *Expenses: Tuition,* state resident: full-time $10,048; part-time $558.25 per credit hour. Tuition, nonresident: full-time $19,497; part-time $1083.25 per credit hour. *Required fees:* $405 per semester. Tuition and fees vary according to course load, campus/location and program. *Financial support:* Fellowships with full tuition reimbursements, research assistantships with full tuition reimbursements, teaching assistantships with full tuition reimbursements, career-related internships or fieldwork, Federal Work-Study, scholarships/grants, health care benefits, and unspecified assistantships available. Financial award application deadline: 1/15. *Faculty research:* Construction, environmental geotechnical hydrosystems, structures and transportation engineering. *Unit head:* Dr. Sam Easterling, Unit Head, 540-231-5143, Fax: 540-231-7532, E-mail: seaster@vt.edu. *Application contact:* Marc Widdowson, Information Contact, 540-231-7153, Fax: 540-231-7532, E-mail: mwiddows@vt.edu. Web site: http://www.cee.vt.edu/.

Virginia Polytechnic Institute and State University, VT Online, Blacksburg, VA 24061. Offers advanced transportation systems (Certificate); aerospace engineering (MS); agricultural and life sciences (MSLFS); business information systems (Graduate Certificate); career and technical education (MS); civil engineering (MS); computer engineering (M Eng, MS); decision support systems (Graduate Certificate); eLearning leadership (MA); electrical engineering (M Eng, MS); engineering administration (MEA); environmental engineering (Certificate); environmental politics and policy (Graduate Certificate); environmental sciences and engineering (MS); foundations of political analysis (Graduate Certificate); health product risk management (Graduate Certificate); industrial and systems engineering (MS); information policy and society (Graduate Certificate); information security (Graduate Certificate); information technology (MIT); instructional technology (MA); integrative STEM education (MA Ed); liberal arts (Graduate Certificate); life sciences: health product risk management (MS); natural resources (MNR, Graduate Certificate); networking (Graduate Certificate); nonprofit and nongovernmental organization management (Graduate Certificate); ocean engineering (MS); political science (MA); security studies (Graduate Certificate); software development (Graduate Certificate). *Expenses:* Tuition, state resident: full-time $10,048; part-time $558.25 per credit hour. Tuition, nonresident: full-time $19,497; part-time $1083.25 per credit hour. *Required fees:* $405 per semester. Tuition and fees vary according to course load, campus/location and program. *Application contact:* Graduate School Applications General Assistance, 540-231-8636, Fax: 540-231-2039, E-mail: gradappl@vt.edu. Web site: http://www.vto.vt.edu/.

Washington State University, Graduate School, College of Engineering and Architecture, Department of Civil and Environmental Engineering, Program in Civil Engineering, Pullman, WA 99164. Offers MS, PhD. *Faculty:* 27. *Students:* 77 full-time (25 women), 7 part-time (3 women); includes 7 minority (2 Black or African American, non-Hispanic/Latino; 2 Asian, non-Hispanic/Latino; 3 Two or more races, non-Hispanic/Latino), 32 international. Average age 28. 138 applicants, 36% accepted, 29 enrolled. In 2011, 31 master's, 4 doctorates awarded. Terminal master's awarded for partial completion of doctoral program. *Degree requirements:* For master's, comprehensive exam (for some programs), thesis (for some programs), oral exam; for doctorate, comprehensive exam, thesis/dissertation, oral exam, written exam. *Entrance requirements:* For master's and doctorate, GRE General Test, official transcripts from all colleges and universities attended; one-page statement of purpose; three letters of recommendation. Additional exam requirements/recommendations for international students: Required—TOEFL, IELTS. *Application deadline:* For fall admission, 1/10 priority date for domestic students, 1/10 for international students; for spring admission, 7/1 for domestic and international students. Applications are processed on a rolling basis. Application fee: $75. Electronic applications accepted. *Financial support:* In 2011–12, research assistantships with full and partial tuition reimbursements (averaging $18,204 per year), teaching assistantships with full and partial tuition reimbursements (averaging $18,204 per year) were awarded; career-related internships or fieldwork, Federal Work-Study, and institutionally sponsored loans also available. Financial award application deadline: 4/1; financial award applicants required to submit FAFSA. *Faculty research:* Environmental geotechnical, hydraulics transportation, structures, wood. *Total annual research expenditures:* $4.1 million. *Unit head:* Dr. David McLean, Chair, 509-335-9578, Fax: 509-335-7632, E-mail: mclean@wsu.edu. *Application contact:* Graduate School Admissions, 800-GRADWSU, Fax: 509-335-1949, E-mail: gradsch@wsu.edu. Web site: http://www.ce.wsu.edu/.

Wayne State University, College of Engineering, Department of Civil and Environmental Engineering, Detroit, MI 48202. Offers MS, PhD. *Students:* 31 full-time (6 women), 42 part-time (12 women); includes 9 minority (3 Black or African American, non-Hispanic/Latino; 4 Asian, non-Hispanic/Latino; 2 Hispanic/Latino), 12 international. Average age 30. 72 applicants, 58% accepted, 18 enrolled. In 2011, 34 master's, 4 doctorates awarded. *Degree requirements:* For master's, thesis optional; for doctorate, thesis/dissertation. *Entrance requirements:* For master's, BS in civil engineering from ABET-accredited institution with minimum GPA of 3.0; for doctorate, GRE if BS in engineering is not from an ABET-accredited institution in the U.S., MS in civil engineering with minimum honor-point average of 3.5; letters of recommendation (for international applicants). Additional exam requirements/recommendations for international students: Required—TOEFL (minimum score 550 paper-based; 213 computer-based); Recommended—TWE (minimum score 5.5). *Application deadline:* For fall admission, 6/1 priority date for domestic students, 5/1 for international students; for winter admission, 10/1 priority date for domestic students, 9/1 for international students; for spring admission, 2/1 priority date for domestic students, 1/1 for international students. Applications are processed on a rolling basis. Application fee: $50. Electronic applications accepted. *Expenses:* Tuition, state resident: part-time $512.85 per credit. Tuition, nonresident: part-time $1132.65 per credit. *Required fees:* $26.60 per credit. $199.65 per semester. Tuition and fees vary according to course load and program. *Financial support:* In 2011–12, 13 students received support, including 3 fellowships with tuition reimbursements available (averaging $17,250 per year), 10 research assistantships with tuition reimbursements available (averaging $14,953 per year), 5 teaching assistantships with tuition reimbursements available (averaging $17,391 per year); career-related internships or fieldwork, scholarships/grants, health care benefits, tuition waivers (partial), and unspecified assistantships also available. Support available to part-time students. *Faculty research:* Environmental geotechnics, civil infrastructure systems and materials, seismic analysis of structures and foundations, traffic and construction safety, transportation planning and economics. *Total annual research expenditures:* $1.5 million. *Unit head:* Dr. Carol Miller, Chair, 313-577-3790, E-mail: cmiller@eng.wayne.edu. Web site: http://engineering.wayne.edu/cee/.

Western Michigan University, Graduate College, College of Engineering and Applied Sciences, Department of Civil and Construction Engineering, Kalamazoo, MI 49008. Offers civil engineering (MS), including construction engineering and management, structural engineering, transportation engineering. *Entrance requirements:* For master's, minimum GPA of 3.0.

West Virginia University, College of Engineering and Mineral Resources, Department of Civil and Environmental Engineering, Morgantown, WV 26506. Offers civil engineering (MSCE, MSE, PhD). Part-time programs available. *Degree requirements:* For master's, thesis; for doctorate, comprehensive exam, thesis/dissertation. *Entrance requirements:* For master's and doctorate, minimum GPA of 3.0. Additional exam requirements/recommendations for international students: Required—TOEFL. *Faculty research:* Habitat restoration, advanced materials for civil infrastructure, pavement modeling, infrastructure condition assessment.

Widener University, Graduate Programs in Engineering, Program in Civil Engineering, Chester, PA 19013-5792. Offers M Eng. Part-time and evening/weekend programs available. *Degree requirements:* For master's, thesis optional. *Faculty research:* Environmental engineering, laws and water supply, structural analysis and design.

Worcester Polytechnic Institute, Graduate Studies and Research, Department of Civil and Environmental Engineering, Worcester, MA 01609-2280. Offers civil and environmental engineering (Advanced Certificate, Graduate Certificate); civil engineering (ME, MS, PhD); construction project management (MS); environmental engineering (MS); master builder environmental engineering (M Eng). Part-time and evening/weekend programs available. Postbaccalaureate distance learning degree programs offered (no on-campus study). *Faculty:* 12 full-time (1 woman), 2 part-time/adjunct (0 women). *Students:* 28 full-time (9 women), 49 part-time (14 women); includes 7 minority (1 Black or African American, non-Hispanic/Latino; 1 American Indian or Alaska Native, non-Hispanic/Latino; 2 Asian, non-Hispanic/Latino; 1 Hispanic/Latino; 2 Two or more races, non-Hispanic/Latino), 17 international. 144 applicants, 44% accepted, 28 enrolled. In 2011, 26 master's, 1 doctorate awarded. *Degree requirements:* For master's, thesis optional; for doctorate, comprehensive exam, thesis/dissertation. *Entrance requirements:* For master's and doctorate, GRE (recommended), 3 letters of recommendation. Additional exam requirements/recommendations for international students: Required—TOEFL (minimum score 563 paper-based; 223 computer-based; 84 iBT), IELTS (minimum score 7). *Application deadline:* For fall admission, 1/1 priority date for domestic students, 1/1 for international students; for spring admission, 10/1 priority date for domestic students, 10/1 for international students. Applications are processed on a rolling basis. Application fee: $70. Electronic applications accepted. *Financial support:* Research assistantships, teaching assistantships, career-related internships or fieldwork, institutionally sponsored loans, scholarships/grants, and unspecified assistantships available. Financial award application deadline: 1/1; financial award applicants required to submit FAFSA. *Faculty research:* Pavement engineering and highway materials, analysis and design of structural systems and smart structures, design-construction integration, water resources and physical and chemical treatment processes, energy and sustainability. *Unit head:* Dr. Tahar El-Korchi, Interim Head, 508-831-5530, Fax: 508-831-5808, E-mail: tek@wpi.edu. *Application contact:* Dr. Paul Mathisen, Graduate Coordinator, 508-831-5530, Fax: 508-831-5808, E-mail: mathisen@wpi.edu. Web site: http://www.wpi.edu/Academics/Depts/CEE/.

Youngstown State University, Graduate School, College of Science, Technology, Engineering and Mathematics, Department of Civil and Environmental Engineering, Youngstown, OH 44555-0001. Offers MSE. Part-time and evening/weekend programs available. *Degree requirements:* For master's, thesis optional. *Entrance requirements:* For master's, minimum GPA of 2.75 in field. Additional exam requirements/recommendations for international students: Required—TOEFL. *Faculty research:* Structural mechanics, water quality modeling, surface and ground water hydrology, physical and chemical processes in aquatic systems.

Construction Engineering

The American University in Cairo, School of Sciences and Engineering, Department of Construction and Architectural Engineering, Cairo, Egypt. Offers construction engineering (M Eng, MS). *Degree requirements:* For master's, thesis. *Entrance requirements:* Additional exam requirements/recommendations for international students: Required—English entrance exam and/or TOEFL. *Application deadline:* For fall admission, 3/31 priority date for domestic students; for spring admission, 1/10 priority date for domestic students. Application fee: $45. *Expenses:* Tuition: Part-time $932 per credit hour. Tuition and fees vary according to course load, degree level and program. *Faculty research:* Composite materials, superelasticity, expert systems, materials selection. *Unit head:* Dr. Mohamed Nagib Abou-Zeid, Chair, 20-2-2615-2516. *Application contact:* Mary Davidson, Coordinator of Student Affairs, 212-730-8800, Fax: 212-730-1600, E-mail: mdavidson@aucnyo.edu. Web site: http://www.aucegypt.edu/sse/ceng/.

Arizona State University, Ira A. Fulton School of Engineering, Del E. Webb School of Construction, Tempe, AZ 85287-5306. Offers civil, environmental and sustainable engineering (MS, MSE, PhD); construction (MS, MSE, PhD); construction engineering (MSE). Part-time and evening/weekend programs available. Postbaccalaureate distance learning degree programs offered (minimal on-campus study). Terminal master's awarded for partial completion of doctoral program. *Degree requirements:* For master's, thesis optional, comprehensive exams (MSE); interactive Program of Study (iPOS) submitted before completing 50 percent of required credit hours; for doctorate, comprehensive exam, thesis/dissertation, interactive Program of Study (iPOS) submitted before completing 50 percent of required credit hours. *Entrance requirements:* For master's, GRE, minimum GPA of 3.0 or equivalent in last 2 years of work leading to bachelor's degree; for doctorate, GRE, minimum GPA of 3.0 in last 2 years of work leading to bachelor's degree, 3.2 in all graduate-level coursework with master's degree; 3 letters of recommendation; resume/curriculum vitae; letter of intent; thesis (if applicable); statement of research interests. Additional exam requirements/recommendations for international students: Required—TOEFL (minimum score 80 iBT), TOEFL, IELTS, or Pearson Test of English. Electronic applications accepted. *Expenses:* Contact institution. *Faculty research:* Water purification, transportation (safety and materials), construction management, environmental biotechnology, environmental nanotechnology, earth systems engineering and management, SMART innovations, project performance metrics, and underground infrastructure.

Auburn University, Graduate School, College of Architecture, Design, and Construction, Department of Building Science, Auburn University, AL 36849. Offers building construction (MBC); construction management (MBC). *Faculty:* 15 full-time (0 women), 1 (woman) part-time/adjunct. *Students:* 10 full-time (0 women), 21 part-time (5 women); includes 3 minority (all Black or African American, non-Hispanic/Latino), 1 international. Average age 30. 36 applicants, 67% accepted, 24 enrolled. In 2011, 31 master's awarded. *Entrance requirements:* For master's, GRE General Test. *Application deadline:* For fall admission, 7/7 for domestic students; for spring admission, 11/24 for domestic students. Applications are processed on a rolling basis. Application fee: $50 ($60 for international students). Electronic applications accepted. *Expenses:* Tuition, state resident: full-time $7290; part-time $405 per credit hour. Tuition, nonresident: full-time $21,870; part-time $1215 per credit hour. *International tuition:* $22,000 full-time. *Required fees:* $1402. *Financial support:* Application deadline: 3/15; applicants required to submit FAFSA. *Unit head:* Dr. Richard Burt, Head, 334-844-5260. *Application contact:* Dr. George Flowers, Dean of the Graduate School, 334-844-2125. Web site: http://www.bsc.auburn.edu/.

Auburn University, Graduate School, Ginn College of Engineering, Department of Civil Engineering, Auburn University, AL 36849. Offers construction engineering and management (MCE, MS, PhD); environmental engineering (MCE, MS, PhD); geotechnical/materials engineering (MCE, MS, PhD); hydraulics/hydrology (MCE, MS, PhD); structural engineering (MCE, MS, PhD); transportation engineering (MCE, MS, PhD). Part-time programs available. *Faculty:* 21 full-time (2 women), 1 part-time/adjunct (0 women). *Students:* 48 full-time (16 women), 62 part-time (14 women); includes 6 minority (4 Black or African American, non-Hispanic/Latino; 1 Asian, non-Hispanic/Latino; 1 Hispanic/Latino), 37 international. Average age 26. 111 applicants, 59% accepted, 25 enrolled. In 2011, 26 master's, 2 doctorates awarded. *Degree requirements:* For master's, project (MCE), thesis (MS); for doctorate, comprehensive exam, thesis/dissertation. *Entrance requirements:* For master's and doctorate, GRE General Test. *Application deadline:* For fall admission, 7/7 for domestic students; for spring admission, 11/24 for domestic students. Applications are processed on a rolling basis. Application fee: $50 ($60 for international students). Electronic applications accepted. *Expenses:* Tuition, state resident: full-time $7290; part-time $405 per credit hour. Tuition, nonresident: full-time $21,870; part-time $1215 per credit hour. *International tuition:* $22,000 full-time. *Required fees:* $1402. *Financial support:* Fellowships, research assistantships, teaching assistantships, and Federal Work-Study available. Support available to part-time students. Financial award application deadline: 3/15; financial award applicants required to submit FAFSA. *Unit head:* Dr. J. Michael Stallings, Head, 334-844-4320. *Application contact:* Dr. George Flowers, Dean of the Graduate School, 334-844-2125.

Bradley University, Graduate School, College of Engineering and Technology, Department of Civil Engineering and Construction, Peoria, IL 61625-0002. Offers MSCE. Part-time and evening/weekend programs available. *Degree requirements:* For master's, comprehensive exam. *Entrance requirements:* For master's, minimum GPA of 3.0, 2 letters of recommendation. Additional exam requirements/recommendations for international students: Required—TOEFL (minimum score 550 paper-based; 213 computer-based; 79 iBT).

Columbia University, The Fu Foundation School of Engineering and Applied Science, Department of Civil Engineering and Engineering Mechanics, New York, NY 10027. Offers civil engineering (MS, Eng Sc D, PhD, Engr); construction engineering and management (MS); engineering mechanics (MS, Eng Sc D, PhD, Engr). Part-time programs available. Postbaccalaureate distance learning degree programs offered (no on-campus study). *Faculty:* 15 full-time (1 woman), 24 part-time/adjunct (2 women). *Students:* 119 full-time (27 women), 56 part-time (20 women); includes 36 minority (3 Black or African American, non-Hispanic/Latino; 15 Asian, non-Hispanic/Latino; 3 Hispanic/Latino; 15 Two or more races, non-Hispanic/Latino), 93 international. Average age 28. 302 applicants, 36% accepted, 69 enrolled. In 2011, 61 master's, 4 doctorates, 2 other advanced degrees awarded. Terminal master's awarded for partial completion of doctoral program. *Degree requirements:* For doctorate, thesis/dissertation, qualifying exam. *Entrance requirements:* For master's, doctorate, and Engr, GRE General Test. Additional exam requirements/recommendations for international students: Required—TOEFL, IELTS. *Application deadline:* For fall admission, 12/1 priority date for domestic students, 12/1 for international students; for spring admission, 10/1 priority date for domestic students, 10/1 for international students. Application fee: $95. Electronic applications accepted. *Financial support:* In 2011–12, 39 students received support, including 11 fellowships with full tuition reimbursements available (averaging $25,386 per year), 16 research assistantships with full tuition reimbursements available (averaging $31,128 per year), 10 teaching assistantships with full tuition reimbursements available (averaging $31,128 per year); traineeships, health care benefits, and tuition waivers also available. Financial award application deadline: 12/1; financial award applicants required to submit FAFSA. *Faculty research:* Structural dynamics, structural health and monitoring, fatigue and fracture mechanics, geo-enviornmental engineering, multiscale science and engineering. *Unit head:* Dr. Raimondo Betti, Professor and Department Chairman, 212-854-6388, E-mail: betti@civil.columbia.edu. *Application contact:* Dr. Rene B. Testa, Professor, 212-854-6383, Fax: 212-854-6267, E-mail: testa@civil.columbia.edu. Web site: http://www.civil.columbia.edu/.

Concordia University, School of Graduate Studies, Faculty of Engineering and Computer Science, Department of Building, Civil and Environmental Engineering, Montréal, QC H3G 1M8, Canada. Offers building engineering (M Eng, MA Sc, PhD, Certificate); civil engineering (M Eng, MA Sc, PhD); environmental engineering (Certificate). *Degree requirements:* For master's, thesis or alternative; for doctorate, comprehensive exam, thesis/dissertation. *Faculty research:* Structural engineering, geotechnical engineering, water resources and fluid engineering, transportation engineering, systems engineering.

Illinois Institute of Technology, Graduate College, Armour College of Engineering, Department of Civil, Architectural and Environmental Engineering, Chicago, IL 60616-3793. Offers architectural engineering (M Arch E); civil engineering (MS, PhD), including architectural engineering (MS), construction engineering and management (MS), geoenvironmental engineering (MS), geotechnical engineering (MS), structural engineering (MS), transportation engineering (MS); construction engineering and management (MCEM); environmental engineering (M Env E, PhD); geoenvironmental engineering (M Geoenv E); geotechnical engineering (MGE); public works (MPW); structural engineering (MSE); transportation engineering (M Trans E). Part-time and evening/weekend programs available. Postbaccalaureate distance learning degree programs offered (minimal on-campus study). Terminal master's awarded for partial completion of doctoral program. *Degree requirements:* For master's, thesis (for some programs); for doctorate, comprehensive exam, thesis/dissertation. *Entrance requirements:* For master's, GRE General Test (minimum score 900 Quantitative and Verbal, 2.5 Analytical Writing), minimum undergraduate GPA of 3.0; for doctorate, GRE General Test (minimum score 1000 Quantitative and Verbal, 3.0 Analytical Writing), minimum undergraduate GPA of 3.0. Additional exam requirements/recommendations for international students: Required—TOEFL (minimum score 523 paper-based; 70 iBT); Recommended—IELTS (minimum score 5.5). Electronic applications accepted. *Faculty research:* Structural, architectural, geotechnical and geoenvironmental engineering; construction engineering and management; transportation engineering; environmental engineering and public works.

Iowa State University of Science and Technology, Department of Civil and Construction Engineering, Ames, IA 50011-3232. Offers civil engineering (MS, PhD), including civil engineering materials, construction engineering and management, environmental engineering, geometronics, geotechnical engineering, structural engineering, transportation engineering. *Degree requirements:* For master's, thesis or alternative; for doctorate, thesis/dissertation. *Entrance requirements:* For master's and doctorate, GRE General Test. Additional exam requirements/recommendations for international students: Required—TOEFL (minimum score 550 paper-based; 82 iBT), IELTS (minimum score 6.5). *Application deadline:* For fall admission, 2/1 priority date for domestic students, 2/1 for international students; for spring admission, 8/1 priority date for domestic students, 8/1 for international students. Applications are processed on a rolling basis. Application fee: $40 ($90 for international students). Electronic applications accepted. *Unit head:* Dr. Sri Sritharan, Director of Graduate Education, 515-294-4972, Fax: 515-294-8216, E-mail: ccee-grad-inquiry@iastate.edu. *Application contact:* Kathy Petersen, Director of Graduate Education, 515-294-4975, Fax: 515-294-8216, E-mail: ccee-grad-inquiry@iastate.edu. Web site: http://www.ccee.iastate.edu/.

Lawrence Technological University, College of Engineering, Southfield, MI 48075-1058. Offers architectural engineering (MS); automotive engineering (MS); civil engineering (MA, MS); construction engineering management (MA); electrical and computer engineering (MS); engineering management (MEM); industrial engineering (MS); manufacturing systems (ME, DE); mechanical engineering (MS, DE); mechatronic systems engineering (MS). Part-time and evening/weekend programs available. *Faculty:* 25 full-time (4 women), 20 part-time/adjunct (1 woman). *Students:* 8 full-time (0 women), 332 part-time (52 women); includes 58 minority (21 Black or African American, non-Hispanic/Latino; 1 American Indian or Alaska Native, non-Hispanic/Latino; 32 Asian, non-Hispanic/Latino; 2 Hispanic/Latino; 2 Two or more races, non-Hispanic/Latino), 84 international. Average age 32. 652 applicants, 44% accepted, 70 enrolled. In 2011, 127 master's, 2 doctorates awarded. *Degree requirements:* For master's, thesis (for some programs). *Entrance requirements:* Additional exam requirements/recommendations for international students: Required—TOEFL (minimum score 550 paper-based; 213 computer-based; 79 iBT). *Application deadline:* For fall admission, 7/27 priority date for domestic students, 5/23 for international students; for spring admission, 11/15 priority date for domestic students, 11/15 for international students. Applications are processed on a rolling basis. Application fee: $50. Electronic applications accepted. *Financial support:* In 2011–12, 68 students received support, including 6 research assistantships (averaging $8,078 per year); Federal Work-Study and institutionally sponsored loans also available. Support available to part-time students. Financial award application deadline: 4/1; financial award applicants required to submit FAFSA. *Faculty research:* Advanced composite materials in bridges, strengthening existing bridges with carbon and glass fiber sheets, development of drive shafts using composite materials. *Unit head:* Dr. Nabil Grace, Dean, 248-204-2500, Fax: 248-204-2509, E-mail: engrdean@ltu.edu. *Application contact:* Jane Rohrback, Director of Admissions, 248-204-3160, Fax: 248-204-2228, E-mail: admissions@ltu.edu. Web site: http://www.ltu.edu/engineering/index.asp.

Marquette University, Graduate School, College of Engineering, Department of Civil and Environmental Engineering, Milwaukee, WI 53201-1881. Offers construction and public works management (MS, PhD); construction engineering and management (Certificate); environmental/water resources engineering (MS, PhD); structural design (Certificate); structural/geotechnical engineering (MS, PhD); transportation planning and engineering (MS, PhD); waste and wastewater treatment processes (Certificate). Part-time and evening/weekend programs available. *Faculty:* 13 full-time (0 women), 5 part-time/adjunct (0 women). *Students:* 26 full-time (5 women), 11 part-time (0 women); includes 2 minority (1 Black or African American, non-Hispanic/Latino; 1 Asian, non-Hispanic/Latino), 12 international. Average age 27. 74 applicants, 62% accepted, 9 enrolled. In 2011, 6 master's, 3 doctorates awarded. Terminal master's awarded for partial completion of doctoral program. *Degree requirements:* For master's, comprehensive exam (for some programs), thesis or alternative; for doctorate, thesis/dissertation. *Entrance requirements:* For master's, GRE General Test (recommended), minimum GPA of 3.0, official transcripts from all current and previous colleges/universities except Marquette, three letters of recommendation; for doctorate, GRE General Test, minimum GPA of 3.0, official transcripts from all current and previous colleges/universities except Marquette, three letters of recommendation, brief statement of purpose, submission of any English language publications authored by applicant (strongly recommended). Additional exam requirements/recommendations for international students: Required—TOEFL (minimum score 530 paper-based; 78 computer-based). *Application deadline:* For fall admission, 6/1 priority date for domestic students. Applications are processed on a rolling basis. Application fee: $50. Electronic applications accepted. *Expenses: Tuition:* Full-time $17,010; part-time $945 per credit hour. Tuition and fees vary according to program. *Financial support:* In 2011–12, 21 students received support, including 6 fellowships with partial tuition reimbursements available (averaging $9,177 per year), 1 research assistantship with full tuition reimbursement available (averaging $13,745 per year), 7 teaching assistantships with full tuition reimbursements available (averaging $13,902 per year); scholarships/grants, health care benefits, tuition waivers (partial), and unspecified assistantships also available. Support available to part-time students. Financial award application deadline: 2/15. *Faculty research:* Highway safety, highway performance, and intelligent transportation systems; surface mount technology; watershed management. *Total annual research expenditures:* $826,608. *Unit head:* Dr. Thomas Wenzel, Chair, 414-288-7030, Fax: 414-288-7521, E-mail: thomas.wenzel@marquette.edu. *Application contact:* Dr. Stephen M. Heinrich, Director of Graduate Studies, 414-288-5466, E-mail: stephen.heinrich@marquette.edu. Web site: http://www.marquette.edu/engineering/pages/AllYouNeed/Civil_Environmental/civil.html.

Massachusetts Institute of Technology, School of Engineering, Department of Civil and Environmental Engineering, Cambridge, MA 02139. Offers biological oceanography (PhD, Sc D); chemical oceanography (PhD, Sc D); civil and environmental engineering (PhD, Sc D); civil and environmental systems (PhD, Sc D); civil engineering (PhD, Sc D, CE); coastal engineering (PhD, Sc D); construction engineering and management (PhD, Sc D); environmental and water quality engineering (M Eng); environmental biology (PhD, Sc D); environmental chemistry (PhD, Sc D); environmental engineering (PhD, Sc D); environmental fluid mechanics (PhD, Sc D); environmental science and engineering (SM); geotechnical and geoenvironmental engineering (PhD, Sc D); geotechnology (M Eng); high-performance structures (M Eng); hydrology (PhD, Sc D); information technology (PhD, Sc D); mechanics (SM); oceanographic engineering (PhD, Sc D); structures and materials (PhD, Sc D); transportation (M Eng, PhD, Sc D); SM/MBA. *Faculty:* 35 full-time (6 women), 1 part-time/adjunct (0 women). *Students:* 216 full-time (80 women); includes 30 minority (4 Black or African American, non-Hispanic/Latino; 13 Asian, non-Hispanic/Latino; 8 Hispanic/Latino; 5 Two or more races, non-Hispanic/Latino), 110 international. Average age 27. 589 applicants, 26% accepted, 91 enrolled. In 2011, 62 master's, 14 doctorates awarded. *Degree requirements:* For master's and CE, thesis; for doctorate, comprehensive exam, thesis/dissertation. *Entrance requirements:* For master's and doctorate, GRE General Test. Additional exam requirements/recommendations for international students: Required—TOEFL (minimum score 577 paper-based; 233 computer-based; 90 iBT), IELTS (minimum score 7). *Application deadline:* For fall admission, 12/15 for domestic and international students. Application fee: $75. Electronic applications accepted. *Expenses: Tuition:* Full-time $40,460; part-time $630 per credit hour. *Required fees:* $272. *Financial support:* In 2011–12, 180 students received support, including 51 fellowships (averaging $30,800 per year), 110 research assistantships (averaging $29,500 per year), 19 teaching assistantships (averaging $29,500 per year); career-related internships or fieldwork, Federal Work-Study, institutionally sponsored loans, scholarships/grants, health care benefits, and unspecified assistantships also available. *Faculty research:* Environmental chemistry, environmental fluid mechanics and coastal engineering, environmental microbiology, geotechnical engineering and geomechanics, hydrology and hydroclimatology, infrastructure systems, mechanics of materials and structures, transportation systems. *Total annual research expenditures:* $17.7 million. *Unit head:* Prof. Andrew Whittle, Head, 617-253-7101. *Application contact:* Patricia Glidden, Graduate Admissions Coordinator, 617-253-7119, Fax: 617-258-6775, E-mail: cee-admissions@mit.edu. Web site: http://cee.mit.edu/.

Missouri University of Science and Technology, Graduate School, Department of Civil, Architectural, and Environmental Engineering, Rolla, MO 65409. Offers civil engineering (MS, DE, PhD); construction engineering (MS, DE, PhD); environmental engineering (MS); fluid mechanics (MS, DE, PhD); geotechnical engineering (MS, DE, PhD); hydrology and hydraulic engineering (MS, DE, PhD). Part-time and evening/weekend programs available. Terminal master's awarded for partial completion of doctoral program. *Degree requirements:* For master's, thesis optional; for doctorate, comprehensive exam, thesis/dissertation. *Entrance requirements:* For master's, GRE General Test (minimum combined score 1100), minimum GPA of 3.0; for doctorate, GRE General Test (minimum score: verbal and quantitative 400, writing 3.5), minimum GPA of 3.0. Additional exam requirements/recommendations for international students: Required—TOEFL. Electronic applications accepted. *Faculty research:* Earthquake engineering, structural optimization and control systems, structural health monitoring/damage detection, soil-structure interaction, soil mechanics and foundation engineering.

Montana State University, College of Graduate Studies, College of Engineering, Department of Civil Engineering, Bozeman, MT 59717. Offers civil engineering (MS); construction engineering management (MCEM); engineering (PhD), including applied mechanics option, civil engineering option. Part-time programs available. *Degree requirements:* For master's, comprehensive exam, thesis (for some programs); for doctorate, comprehensive exam, thesis/dissertation. *Entrance requirements:* For master's and doctorate, GRE General Test. Additional exam requirements/recommendations for international students: Required—TOEFL (minimum score 550 paper-based; 213 computer-based). Electronic applications accepted. *Faculty research:* Snow and ice mechanics, biofilm engineering, transportation, structural and geo materials, water resources.

Ohio University, Graduate College, Russ College of Engineering and Technology, Department of Civil Engineering, Athens, OH 45701-2979. Offers civil engineering (PhD); construction (MS); environmental (MS); geotechnical and geoenvironmental (MS); mechanics (MS); structures (MS); transportation (MS); water resources and structures (MS). Part-time programs available. *Students:* 32 full-time (6 women), 7 part-time (2 women); includes 3 minority (1 Hispanic/Latino; 2 Two or more races, non-Hispanic/Latino), 13 international. 52 applicants, 52% accepted, 4 enrolled. In 2011, 10 degrees awarded. *Degree requirements:* For master's, comprehensive exam (for some programs), thesis or alternative; for doctorate, comprehensive exam, thesis/dissertation. *Entrance requirements:* For master's, GRE General Test, minimum GPA of 3.0, 3 letters of recommendation; for doctorate, GRE General Test. Additional exam requirements/recommendations for international students: Required—TOEFL (minimum score 550 paper-based; 80 iBT) or IELTS (minimum score 6.5). *Application deadline:* For fall admission, 5/1 priority date for domestic students, 2/1 for international students; for winter admission, 8/1 priority date for domestic students, 4/1 for international students; for spring admission, 2/1 priority date for domestic students, 7/1 for international students. Applications are processed on a rolling basis. Application fee: $50 ($55 for international students). Electronic applications accepted. *Financial support:* Research assistantships with full tuition reimbursements, teaching assistantships with full tuition reimbursements, Federal Work-Study, institutionally sponsored loans, scholarships/grants, and unspecified assistantships available. Financial award application deadline: 3/15; financial award applicants required to submit FAFSA. *Faculty research:* Noise abatement, materials and environment, highway infrastructure, subsurface investigation (pavements, pipes, bridges). *Unit head:* Dr. Gayle F. Mitchell, Chair, 740-593-0430, Fax: 740-593-0625, E-mail: mitchelg@ohio.edu. *Application contact:* Dr. Shad M. Sargand, Graduate Chair, 740-593-1465, Fax: 740-593-0625, E-mail: sargand@ohio.edu. Web site: http://www.ohio.edu/civil/.

Oregon State University, Graduate School, College of Engineering, School of Civil and Construction Engineering, Corvallis, OR 97331. Offers civil engineering (MS, PhD); coastal and ocean engineering (M Oc E, PhD); coastal engineering (MS); construction engineering management (MBE, PhD); engineering (M Eng, MAIS); geotechnical engineering (MS, PhD); structural engineering (MS, PhD); transportation engineering (MS, PhD); water engineering (MS, PhD). Part-time programs available. Terminal master's awarded for partial completion of doctoral program. *Degree requirements:* For master's, thesis or alternative; for doctorate, one foreign language, thesis/dissertation. *Entrance requirements:* For master's, GRE General Test, minimum GPA of 3.0 in last 90 hours (3.5 for MS); for doctorate, GRE General Test, minimum GPA of 3.0 in last 90 hours of undergraduate course work. Additional exam requirements/recommendations for international students: Required—TOEFL (minimum score 580 paper-based; 237 computer-based). *Faculty research:* Hazardous waste management, carbon cycling, wave forces on structures, pavement design, seismic analysis.

Pittsburg State University, Graduate School, College of Technology, Department of Construction Management and Construction Engineering Technologies, Pittsburg, KS 66762. Offers construction (MET).

Stevens Institute of Technology, Graduate School, Charles V. Schaefer Jr. School of Engineering, Department of Civil, Environmental, and Ocean Engineering, Program in Construction Management, Hoboken, NJ 07030. Offers construction accounting/estimating (Certificate); construction engineering (Certificate); construction law/disputes (Certificate); construction management (MS); construction/quality management (Certificate). *Degree requirements:* For master's, thesis optional. *Entrance requirements:* For master's, GMAT, GRE General Test. Additional exam requirements/recommendations for international students: Required—TOEFL. Electronic applications accepted.

Texas A&M University, College of Architecture, Department of Construction Science, College Station, TX 77843. Offers construction management (MS). *Faculty:* 16. *Students:* 39 full-time (15 women), 8 part-time (1 woman); includes 6 minority (1 Black or African American, non-Hispanic/Latino; 4 Hispanic/Latino; 1 Two or more races, non-Hispanic/Latino), 24 international. Average age 30. In 2011, 34 master's awarded. *Degree requirements:* For master's, comprehensive exam. *Entrance requirements:* For master's, GRE General Test. Additional exam requirements/recommendations for international students: Required—TOEFL. *Application deadline:* For fall admission, 4/1 priority date for domestic students; for winter admission, 1/1 priority date for domestic students; for spring admission, 9/1 priority date for domestic students. Applications are processed on a rolling basis. Application fee: $50 ($75 for international students). Electronic applications accepted. *Expenses:* Tuition, state resident: full-time $5437; part-time $226.55 per credit hour. Tuition, nonresident: full-time $12,949; part-time $539.55 per credit hour. *Required fees:* $2741. *Financial support:* In 2011–12, fellowships with partial tuition reimbursements (averaging $1,000 per year), research assistantships with partial tuition reimbursements (averaging $9,000 per year), teaching assistantships with partial tuition reimbursements (averaging $9,000 per year) were awarded. Financial award application deadline: 4/1; financial award applicants required to submit FAFSA. *Faculty research:* Fire safety, housing foundations, construction project management, quality management. *Unit head:* Dr. Joe Horlen, Head, 979-458-3477, E-mail: jhorlen@tamu.edu. *Application contact:* Graduate Admissions, 979-458-0427, E-mail: admissions@tamu.edu. Web site: http://cosc.arch.tamu.edu/.

Texas A&M University, College of Engineering, Zachry Department of Civil Engineering, College Station, TX 77843. Offers coastal and ocean engineering (M Eng, MS, D Eng, PhD); construction engineering and management (M Eng, MS, D Eng, PhD); environmental engineering (M Eng, MS, D Eng, PhD); geotechnical engineering (M Eng, MS, D Eng, PhD); materials engineering (M Eng, MS, D Eng, PhD); structural engineering (M Eng, MS, D Eng, PhD); transportation engineering (M Eng, MS, D Eng, PhD); water resources engineering (M Eng, MS, D Eng, PhD). Part-time programs available. *Faculty:* 57. *Students:* 361 full-time (76 women), 46 part-time (8 women); includes 41 minority (3 Black or African American, non-Hispanic/Latino; 16 Asian, non-Hispanic/Latino; 21 Hispanic/Latino; 1 Two or more races, non-Hispanic/Latino), 247 international. Average age 29. In 2011, 123 master's, 27 doctorates awarded. *Degree requirements:* For master's, thesis (MS); for doctorate, dissertation (PhD), internship (D Eng). *Entrance requirements:* For master's and doctorate, GRE General Test. Additional exam requirements/recommendations for international students: Required—TOEFL. *Application deadline:* Applications are processed on a rolling basis. Application fee: $50 ($75 for international students). Electronic applications accepted. *Expenses:* Tuition, state resident: full-time $5437; part-time $226.55 per credit hour. Tuition, nonresident: full-time $12,949; part-time $539.55 per credit hour. *Required fees:* $2741. *Financial support:* In 2011–12, fellowships (averaging $4,500 per year), research assistantships (averaging $14,000 per year), teaching assistantships (averaging $14,400 per year) were awarded; career-related internships or fieldwork and institutionally sponsored loans also available. Financial award application deadline: 4/15; financial award applicants required to submit FAFSA. *Unit head:* Dr. John Niedzwecki, Head, 979-845-3858, E-mail: j-niedzwecki@tamu.edu. *Application contact:* Graduate Advisor, 979-845-7435, Fax: 979-845-6156, E-mail: info@civil.tamu.edu. Web site: https://www.civil.tamu.edu/.

The University of Alabama, Graduate School, College of Engineering, Department of Civil, Construction and Environmental Engineering, Tuscaloosa, AL 35487-0205. Offers civil engineering (MSCE, PhD); environmental engineering (MS). Part-time programs available. *Faculty:* 19 full-time (2 women), 1 part-time/adjunct (0 women). *Students:* 47 full-time (15 women), 11 part-time (5 women); includes 9 minority (8 Black or African American, non-Hispanic/Latino; 1 Asian, non-Hispanic/Latino), 16 international. Average age 28. 93 applicants, 37% accepted, 10 enrolled. In 2011, 27 master's, 3 doctorates awarded. Terminal master's awarded for partial completion of doctoral program. *Median time to degree:* Of those who began their doctoral program in fall 2003, 100% received their degree in 8 years or less. *Degree requirements:* For master's, thesis or alternative; for doctorate, one foreign language, thesis/dissertation. *Entrance requirements:* For master's and doctorate, GRE General Test, minimum GPA of 3.0 in last 60 hours of course work. Additional exam requirements/recommendations for international students: Required—TOEFL (minimum score 550 paper-based; 213 computer-based), IELTS (minimum score 6.5). *Application deadline:* For fall admission, 7/6 for domestic students, 1/15 for international students; for spring admission, 11/1 for domestic students, 6/1 for international students. Applications are processed on a rolling basis. Application fee: $50 ($60 for international students). Electronic applications accepted. *Expenses:* Tuition, state resident: full-time $8600. Tuition, nonresident: full-time $21,900. *Financial support:* In 2011–12, 40 students received support, including 32 research assistantships with full tuition reimbursements available (averaging $10,489 per year), 12 teaching assistantships with full tuition reimbursements available (averaging $10,489 per year); fellowships, scholarships/grants, tuition waivers (partial), and unspecified assistantships also available. Financial award application deadline: 3/15. *Faculty research:* Experimental structures, modeling of structures, bridge management systems, geotechnological engineering, environmental remediation. *Total annual research expenditures:* $2.2 million. *Unit head:* Dr. Kenneth J. Fridley, Head and Professor, 205-348-6550, Fax: 205-348-0783, E-mail: kfridley@coe.eng.ua.edu. *Application contact:* Dr. David A. Francko, Dean, 205-348-8280, Fax: 205-348-0400, E-mail: dfrancko@ua.edu. Web site: http://www.ce.eng.ua.edu/.

The University of Alabama at Birmingham, School of Engineering, Program in Engineering, Birmingham, AL 35294. Offers advanced safety engineering and management (M Eng); construction engineering management (M Eng); information engineering and management (M Eng). *Expenses:* Tuition, state resident: full-time $5922; part-time $309 per hour. Tuition, nonresident: full-time $13,428; part-time $726 per hour. Tuition and fees vary according to program. *Unit head:* Dr. Melinda Lalor, Dean, 205-934-8410, E-mail: mlalor@uab.edu. Web site: http://www.uab.edu/engineering/degrees-cert/master-of-engineering.

University of Alberta, Faculty of Graduate Studies and Research, Department of Civil and Environmental Engineering, Edmonton, AB T6G 2E1, Canada. Offers construction engineering and management (M Eng, M Sc, PhD); environmental engineering (M Eng, M Sc, PhD); environmental science (M Sc, PhD); geoenvironmental engineering (M Eng, M Sc, PhD); geotechnical engineering (M Eng, M Sc, PhD); mining engineering (M Eng, M Sc, PhD); petroleum engineering (M Eng, M Sc, PhD); structural engineering (M Eng, M Sc, PhD); water resources (M Eng, M Sc, PhD). Part-time programs available. Postbaccalaureate distance learning degree programs offered (minimal on-campus study). *Degree requirements:* For master's, thesis (for some programs); for doctorate, thesis/dissertation. *Entrance requirements:* For master's, minimum GPA of 3.0 in last 2 years of undergraduate studies; for doctorate, minimum GPA of 3.0. Additional exam requirements/recommendations for international students: Required—TOEFL (minimum score 550 paper-based; 213 computer-based). Electronic applications accepted. *Faculty research:* Mining.

University of Central Florida, College of Engineering and Computer Science, Department of Civil, Environmental, and Construction Engineering, Program in Civil Engineering, Orlando, FL 32816. Offers civil engineering (MS, MSCE, PhD); construction engineering (Certificate); structural engineering (Certificate); transportation engineering (Certificate). Part-time and evening/weekend programs available. *Students:* 68 full-time (13 women), 87 part-time (16 women); includes 35 minority (7 Black or African American, non-Hispanic/Latino; 6 Asian, non-Hispanic/Latino; 20 Hispanic/Latino; 2 Two or more races, non-Hispanic/Latino), 42 international. Average age 30. 125 applicants, 79% accepted, 45 enrolled. In 2011, 27 master's, 2 doctorates awarded. *Degree requirements:* For master's, thesis or alternative; for doctorate, thesis/dissertation, departmental qualifying exam, candidacy exam. *Entrance requirements:* For master's, GRE General Test, minimum GPA of 3.0 in last 60 hours; for doctorate, GRE General Test, minimum GPA of 3.5 in last 60 hours. Additional exam requirements/recommendations for international students: Required—TOEFL. *Application deadline:* For fall admission, 7/15 priority date for domestic students; for spring admission, 12/15 priority date for domestic students. Application fee: $30. Electronic applications accepted. *Expenses:* Tuition, state resident: part-time $277.08 per credit hour. Tuition, nonresident: part-time $277.08 per credit hour. Part-time tuition and fees vary according to degree level and program. *Financial support:* In 2011–12, 28 students received support, including 6 fellowships with partial tuition reimbursements available (averaging $2,700 per year), 14 research assistantships with partial tuition reimbursements available (averaging $11,800 per year), 15 teaching assistantships with partial tuition reimbursements available (averaging $11,300 per year); career-related internships or fieldwork, Federal Work-Study, institutionally sponsored loans, tuition waivers (partial), and unspecified assistantships also available. Financial award application deadline: 3/1; financial award applicants required to submit FAFSA. *Unit head:* Dr. Essam Radwan, Interim Chair, 407-823-4738, E-mail: ahmed.radwan@ucf.edu. *Application contact:* Barbara Rodriguez, Director, Admissions and Registration, 407-823-2766, Fax: 407-823-6442, E-mail: gradadmissions@ucf.edu. Web site: http://cece.ucf.edu/.

University of Colorado Boulder, Graduate School, College of Engineering and Applied Science, Department of Civil, Environmental, and Architectural Engineering, Boulder, CO 80309. Offers building systems (MS, PhD); construction engineering management (MS, PhD); environmental engineering (MS, PhD); geotechnical engineering and geomechanics (MS, PhD); hydrology, water resources and environmental fluid mechanics (MS, PhD); structural engineering and structural mechanics (MS, PhD). *Faculty:* 37 full-time (8 women). *Students:* 245 full-time (90 women), 53 part-time (15 women); includes 37 minority (1 Black or African American, non-Hispanic/Latino; 2 American Indian or Alaska Native, non-Hispanic/Latino; 15 Asian, non-Hispanic/Latino; 17 Hispanic/Latino; 2 Two or more races, non-Hispanic/Latino), 56 international. Average age 27. 483 applicants, 58% accepted, 83 enrolled. In 2011, 84 master's, 15 doctorates awarded. Terminal master's awarded for partial completion of doctoral program. *Degree requirements:* For master's, comprehensive exam, thesis or alternative; for doctorate, thesis/dissertation. *Entrance requirements:* For master's, GRE General Test, minimum undergraduate GPA of 3.0. *Application deadline:* For fall admission, 3/1 for domestic students, 12/1 for international students; for spring admission, 10/31 for domestic students, 10/1 for international students. Application fee: $50 ($60 for international students). Electronic applications accepted. *Financial support:* In 2011–12, 167 students received support, including 69 fellowships (averaging $12,440 per year), 62 research assistantships with full and partial tuition reimbursements available (averaging $21,979 per year), 20 teaching assistantships with full and partial tuition reimbursements available (averaging $19,877 per year); institutionally sponsored loans, scholarships/grants, health care benefits, and unspecified assistantships also available. Financial award application deadline: 1/15; financial award applicants required to submit FAFSA. *Faculty research:* Building systems engineering, construction engineering and management, environmental engineering, geoenvironmental engineering, geotechnical engineering, materials and mechanics, structural engineering, water resources engineering, life-cycle engineering. *Total annual research expenditures:* $10.9 million. *Application contact:* E-mail: cvengrad@colorado.edu. Web site: http://ceae.colorado.edu/new/.

University of Florida, Graduate School, College of Design, Construction and Planning, M. E. Rinker, Sr. School of Building Construction, Gainesville, FL 32611. Offers building construction (MBC, MSBC); international construction management (MICM). Part-time programs available. *Faculty:* 15 full-time (2 women). *Students:* 34 full-time (13 women), 11 part-time (2 women); includes 7 minority (2 Asian, non-Hispanic/Latino; 5 Hispanic/Latino), 4 international. Average age 29. 66 applicants, 73% accepted, 19 enrolled. In 2011, 58 master's awarded. *Degree requirements:* For master's, thesis. *Entrance requirements:* For master's, GRE General Test, minimum GPA of 3.0. Additional exam requirements/recommendations for international students: Required—TOEFL (minimum score 550 paper-based; 213 computer-based; 80 iBT), IELTS (minimum score 6). *Application deadline:* Applications are processed on a rolling basis. Application fee: $30. Electronic applications accepted. *Financial support:* Research assistantships with full tuition reimbursements, teaching assistantships with full tuition reimbursements, career-related internships or fieldwork, and unspecified assistantships available. Financial award applicants required to submit FAFSA. *Faculty research:* Safety, affordable housing, construction management, environmental issues, sustainable construction. *Unit head:* Dr. Abdol R. Chini, Director, 352-273-1165, Fax: 352-392-9606, E-mail: chini@ufl.edu. *Application contact:* Dr. Ian Flood, Coordinator of PhD Program, 352-273-1159, Fax: 352-392-7266, E-mail: flood@ufl.edu. Web site: http://www.bcn.ufl.edu/.

University of Michigan, College of Engineering, Department of Civil and Environmental Engineering, Ann Arbor, MI 48109. Offers civil engineering (MSE, PhD, CE); construction engineering and management (M Eng, MSE); environmental engineering (MSE, PhD); structural engineering (M Eng); MBA/MSE. Part-time programs available. *Students:* 139 full-time (54 women), 3 part-time (1 woman). 539 applicants, 40% accepted, 66 enrolled. In 2011, 52 master's, 10 doctorates awarded. *Degree requirements:* For master's, thesis optional; for doctorate, comprehensive exam, thesis/dissertation, oral defense of dissertation, preliminary and written exams. *Entrance requirements:* For master's and doctorate, GRE General Test. Additional exam requirements/recommendations for international students: Required—TOEFL (minimum score 560 paper-based; 220 computer-based). *Application deadline:* Applications are processed on a rolling basis. Application fee: $65 ($75 for international students). Electronic applications accepted. *Financial support:* Fellowships, research assistantships, teaching assistantships, institutionally sponsored loans, and tuition waivers (partial) available. Financial award application deadline: 1/19. *Faculty research:* Construction engineering and management, geotechnical engineering, earthquake-resistant design of structures, environmental chemistry and microbiology, cost engineering, environmental and water resources engineering. *Unit head:* Kim Hayes, Chair, 734-764-8495, Fax: 734-764-4292, E-mail: ford@umich.edu. *Application contact:* Kimberly Smith, Student Advisor, 734-764-8405, Fax: 734-647-2127, E-mail: kansmith@umich.edu. Web site: http://www.engin.umich.edu/dept/cee/.

University of New Brunswick Fredericton, School of Graduate Studies, Faculty of Engineering, Department of Civil Engineering, Fredericton, NB E3B 5A3, Canada. Offers construction engineering and management (M Eng, M Sc E, PhD); environmental engineering (M Eng, M Sc E, PhD); environmental studies (M Eng); geotechnical engineering (M Eng, M Sc E, PhD); groundwater/hydrology (M Eng, M Sc E, PhD); materials (M Eng, M Sc E, PhD); pavements (M Eng, M Sc E, PhD); structures (M Eng, M Sc E, PhD); transportation (M Eng, M Sc E, PhD). Part-time programs available. *Faculty:* 13 full-time (1 woman), 7 part-time/adjunct (1 woman). *Students:* 31 full-time (7 women), 17 part-time (2 women). In 2011, 11 master's, 2 doctorates awarded. *Degree requirements:* For master's, thesis, proposal; for doctorate, comprehensive exam, thesis/dissertation, qualifying exam; proposal; 27 credit hours of courses. *Entrance* *requirements:* For master's, minimum GPA of 3.0; B Sc E in civil engineering or related engineering degree; for doctorate, minimum GPA of 3.0; graduate degree in engineering or applied science. Additional exam requirements/recommendations for international students: Required—TWE (minimum score 4), TOEFL (minimum score 580 paper-based; 237 computer-based) or IELTS (minimum score 7.5). *Application deadline:* For fall admission, 5/1 priority date for domestic students; for winter admission, 11/1 priority date for domestic students. Applications are processed on a rolling basis. Application fee: $50 Canadian dollars. *Financial support:* In 2011–12, 14 fellowships, 30 research assistantships (averaging $7,000 per year), 42 teaching assistantships (averaging $2,000 per year) were awarded; career-related internships or fieldwork and scholarships/grants also available. *Faculty research:* Construction engineering and management; materials and infrastructure renewal; highway and pavement research; structures and solid mechanics; geotechnical, soil; structure interaction; transportation and planning; environment, solid waste management. *Unit head:* Dr. Eric Hildebrand, Director of Graduate Studies, 506-453-5113, Fax: 506-453-3568, E-mail: edh@unb.ca. *Application contact:* Joyce Moore, Graduate Secretary, 506-452-6127, Fax: 506-453-3568, E-mail: civil-grad@unb.ca. Web site: http://www.unbf.ca/eng/civil/.

University of Southern Mississippi, Graduate School, College of Science and Technology, School of Construction, Hattiesburg, MS 39406-0001. Offers logistics management and technology (MS). Part-time programs available. *Faculty:* 6 full-time (0 women). *Students:* 7 full-time (2 women), 6 part-time (1 woman); includes 3 minority (all Black or African American, non-Hispanic/Latino), 2 international. Average age 31. 6 applicants, 83% accepted, 4 enrolled. In 2011, 11 degrees awarded. *Degree requirements:* For master's, comprehensive exam, thesis optional. *Entrance requirements:* For master's, GMAT or GRE General Test, minimum GPA of 2.75 in last 60 hours. Additional exam requirements/recommendations for international students: Required—TOEFL, IELTS. *Application deadline:* For fall admission, 3/1 priority date for domestic students, 3/1 for international students. Applications are processed on a rolling basis. Application fee: $50. *Financial support:* In 2011–12, research assistantships with full tuition reimbursements (averaging $7,200 per year), 7 teaching assistantships with full tuition reimbursements (averaging $7,200 per year) were awarded; career-related internships or fieldwork, Federal Work-Study, scholarships/grants, health care benefits, and unspecified assistantships also available. Financial award application deadline: 3/15; financial award applicants required to submit FAFSA. *Faculty research:* Robotics; CAD/CAM; simulation; computer-integrated manufacturing processes; construction scheduling, estimating, and computer systems. *Unit head:* Dr. Desmond Fletcher, Director, 601-266-5185. *Application contact:* Dr. Tulio Sulbaran, Director, Graduate Studies, 601-266-5185. Web site: http://www.usm.edu/graduateschool/table.php.

University of Washington, Graduate School, College of Engineering, Department of Civil and Environmental Engineering, Seattle, WA 98195-2700. Offers civil engineering (MS, MSE, PhD); construction engineering (MSCE); environmental engineering (MS, MSCE, MSE, PhD); global trade, transportation and logistics (MS); hydrology, water resources, and environmental fluid mechanics (MS, MSCE, MSE, PhD); structural and geotechnical engineering and mechanics (MS, MSCE, MSE, PhD); transportation and construction engineering (MS, MSE, PhD); transportation engineering (MSCE). Part-time programs available. Postbaccalaureate distance learning degree programs offered (no on-campus study). *Faculty:* 47 full-time (11 women), 9 part-time/adjunct (1 woman). *Students:* 195 full-time (67 women), 72 part-time (19 women); includes 37 minority (4 Black or African American, non-Hispanic/Latino; 27 Asian, non-Hispanic/Latino; 6 Hispanic/Latino), 65 international. 654 applicants, 57% accepted, 100 enrolled. In 2011, 88 master's, 7 doctorates awarded. Terminal master's awarded for partial completion of doctoral program. *Degree requirements:* For master's, thesis (for some programs); for doctorate, comprehensive exam, thesis/dissertation, general, qualifying, and final exams; completion of degree within 10 years. *Entrance requirements:* For master's, GRE General Test, minimum GPA of 3.0, statement of purpose, letters of recommendation, transcripts; for doctorate, GRE General Test, minimum GPA of 3.5, statement of purpose, letters of recommendation, transcripts. Additional exam requirements/recommendations for international students: Required—TOEFL (minimum score 580 paper-based; 237 computer-based; 92 iBT); Recommended—IELTS (minimum score 7). *Application deadline:* For fall admission, 1/10 priority date for domestic students, 1/10 for international students. Applications are processed on a rolling basis. Application fee: $75. Electronic applications accepted. *Expenses:* Contact institution. *Financial support:* In 2011–12, 99 students received support, including 16 fellowships with full and partial tuition reimbursements available (averaging $16,173 per year), 71 research assistantships with full tuition reimbursements available (averaging $16,380 per year), 10 teaching assistantships with full tuition reimbursements available (averaging $16,380 per year); scholarships/grants also available. Financial award application deadline: 1/10; financial award applicants required to submit FAFSA. *Faculty research:* Environmental/water resources, hydrology; construction/transportation; structures/ geotechnical. *Total annual research expenditures:* $13.6 million. *Unit head:* Dr. Gregory R. Miller, Professor/Chair, 206-543-0350, Fax: 206-543-1543, E-mail: gmiller@uw.edu. *Application contact:* Lorna Latal, Graduate Adviser, 206-543-2574, Fax: 206-543-1543, E-mail: llatal@u.washington.edu. Web site: http://www.ce.washington.edu/programs/prospective/grad/applying/gen_admission.html.

Virginia Polytechnic Institute and State University, Graduate School, College of Architecture and Urban Studies, Department of Building Construction, Blacksburg, VA 24061. Offers building construction science and management (MS); MS/MBA. *Degree requirements:* For master's, comprehensive exam (for some programs), thesis (for some programs); for doctorate, comprehensive exam (for some programs), thesis/dissertation (for some programs). *Entrance requirements:* For master's and doctorate, GRE. Additional exam requirements/recommendations for international students: Required—TOEFL (minimum score 550 paper-based; 213 computer-based). *Application deadline:* For fall admission, 7/1 for domestic and international students; for spring admission, 12/1 for domestic and international students. Applications are processed on a rolling basis. Application fee: $65. Electronic applications accepted. *Expenses:* Tuition, state resident: full-time $10,048; part-time $558.25 per credit hour. Tuition, nonresident: full-time $19,497; part-time $1083.25 per credit hour. *Required fees:* $405 per semester. Tuition and fees vary according to course load, campus/location and program. *Financial support:* Fellowships with full tuition reimbursements, research assistantships with full tuition reimbursements, teaching assistantships with full tuition reimbursements, career-related internships or fieldwork, Federal Work-Study, scholarships/grants, health care benefits, and unspecified assistantships available. Financial award application deadline: 1/15. *Unit head:* Dr. Yvan J. Beliveau, Unit Head, 540-818-4602, Fax: 540-231-7219, E-mail: yvan@vt.edu. *Application contact:* Walid Thabet, Information Contact, 540-818-4604, Fax: 540-231-7219, E-mail: thabet@vt.edu. Web site: http://www.bc.vt.edu/.

Western Michigan University, Graduate College, College of Engineering and Applied Sciences, Department of Civil and Construction Engineering, Kalamazoo, MI 49008. Offers civil engineering (MS), including construction engineering and management, structural engineering, transportation engineering. *Entrance requirements:* For master's, minimum GPA of 3.0.

Environmental Engineering

Air Force Institute of Technology, Graduate School of Engineering and Management, Department of Systems and Engineering Management, Dayton, OH 45433-7765. Offers cost analysis (MS); environmental and engineering management (MS); environmental engineering science (MS); information resource/systems management (MS). *Accreditation:* ABET. Part-time programs available. *Degree requirements:* For master's, thesis. *Entrance requirements:* For master's, GRE, GMAT, minimum GPA of 3.0.

Arizona State University, Ira A. Fulton School of Engineering, Del E. Webb School of Construction, Tempe, AZ 85287-5306. Offers civil, environmental and sustainable engineering (MS, MSE, PhD); construction (MS, MSE, PhD); construction engineering (MSE). Part-time and evening/weekend programs available. Postbaccalaureate distance learning degree programs offered (minimal on-campus study). Terminal master's awarded for partial completion of doctoral program. *Degree requirements:* For master's, thesis optional, comprehensive exams (MSE); interactive Program of Study (iPOS) submitted before completing 50 percent of required credit hours; for doctorate, comprehensive exam, thesis/dissertation, interactive Program of Study (iPOS) submitted before completing 50 percent of required credit hours. *Entrance requirements:* For master's, GRE, minimum GPA of 3.0 or equivalent in last 2 years of work leading to bachelor's degree; for doctorate, GRE, minimum GPA of 3.0 in last 2 years of work leading to bachelor's degree, 3.2 in all graduate-level coursework with master's degree; 3 letters of recommendation; resume/curriculum vitae; letter of intent; thesis (if applicable); statement of research interests. Additional exam requirements/recommendations for international students: Required—TOEFL (minimum score 80 iBT), TOEFL, IELTS, or Pearson Test of English. Electronic applications accepted. *Expenses:* Contact institution. *Faculty research:* Water purification, transportation (safety and materials), construction management, environmental biotechnology, environmental nanotechnology, earth systems engineering and management, SMART innovations, project performance metrics, and underground infrastructure.

Auburn University, Graduate School, Ginn College of Engineering, Department of Civil Engineering, Auburn University, AL 36849. Offers construction engineering and management (MCE, MS, PhD); environmental engineering (MCE, MS, PhD); geotechnical/materials engineering (MCE, MS, PhD); hydraulics/hydrology (MCE, MS, PhD); structural engineering (MCE, MS, PhD); transportation engineering (MCE, MS, PhD). Part-time programs available. *Faculty:* 21 full-time (2 women), 1 part-time/adjunct (0 women). *Students:* 48 full-time (16 women), 62 part-time (14 women); includes 6 minority (4 Black or African American, non-Hispanic/Latino; 1 Asian, non-Hispanic/Latino; 1 Hispanic/Latino), 37 international. Average age 26. 111 applicants, 59% accepted, 25 enrolled. In 2011, 26 master's, 2 doctorates awarded. *Degree requirements:* For master's, project (MCE), thesis (MS); for doctorate, comprehensive exam, thesis/dissertation. *Entrance requirements:* For master's and doctorate, GRE General Test. *Application deadline:* For fall admission, 7/7 for domestic students; for spring admission, 11/24 for domestic students. Applications are processed on a rolling basis. Application fee: $50 ($60 for international students). Electronic applications accepted. *Expenses:* Tuition, state resident: full-time $7290; part-time $405 per credit hour. Tuition, nonresident: full-time $21,870; part-time $1215 per credit hour. *International tuition:* $22,000 full-time. *Required fees:* $1402. *Financial support:* Fellowships, research assistantships, teaching assistantships, and Federal Work-Study available. Support available to part-time students. Financial award application deadline: 3/15; financial award applicants required to submit FAFSA. *Unit head:* Dr. J. Michael Stallings, Head, 334-844-4320. *Application contact:* Dr. George Flowers, Dean of the Graduate School, 334-844-2125.

California Institute of Technology, Division of Engineering and Applied Science, Option in Environmental Science and Engineering, Pasadena, CA 91125-0001. Offers MS, PhD. *Degree requirements:* For doctorate, thesis/dissertation. Electronic applications accepted. *Faculty research:* Chemistry of natural waters, physics and chemistry of particulates, fluid mechanics of the natural environment, pollutant formation and control, environmental modeling systems.

California Institute of Technology, Division of Geological and Planetary Sciences, Pasadena, CA 91125-0001. Offers environmental science and engineering (MS, PhD); geobiology (MS, PhD); geochemistry (MS, PhD); geology (MS, PhD); geophysics (MS, PhD); planetary science (MS, PhD). *Faculty:* 42 full-time (8 women). *Students:* 102 full-time (48 women); includes 10 minority (2 Black or African American, non-Hispanic/Latino; 7 Asian, non-Hispanic/Latino; 1 Hispanic/Latino), 28 international. Average age 26. 188 applicants, 23% accepted, 21 enrolled. In 2011, 11 master's, 12 doctorates awarded. *Degree requirements:* For doctorate, thesis/dissertation. *Entrance requirements:* For doctorate, GRE General Test. Additional exam requirements/recommendations for international students: Required—TOEFL; Recommended—IELTS, TWE. *Application deadline:* For fall admission, 1/1 for domestic and international students. Application fee: $80. Electronic applications accepted. *Financial support:* In 2011–12, 75 students received support, including 16 fellowships with full tuition reimbursements available (averaging $28,000 per year), 86 research assistantships with full tuition reimbursements available (averaging $28,000 per year); teaching assistantships with full tuition reimbursements available, institutionally sponsored loans, scholarships/grants, health care benefits, and unspecified assistantships also available. Financial award applicants required to submit FAFSA. *Faculty research:* Planetary surfaces, evolution of anaerobic respiratory processes, structural geology and tectonics, theoretical and numerical seismology, global biogeochemical cycles. *Unit head:* Dr. Kenneth A. Farley, Chairman, 626-395-6111, Fax: 626-795-6028, E-mail: dianb@gps.caltech.edu. *Application contact:* Dr. Robert W. Clayton, Academic Officer, 626-395-6909, Fax: 626-795-6028, E-mail: dianb@gps.caltech.edu. Web site: http://www.gps.caltech.edu/.

California Polytechnic State University, San Luis Obispo, College of Engineering, Department of Civil and Environmental Engineering, San Luis Obispo, CA 93407. Offers MS. Part-time programs available. *Faculty:* 6 full-time (0 women), 1 part-time/adjunct (0 women). *Students:* 47 full-time (12 women), 9 part-time (0 women); includes 23 minority (1 Black or African American, non-Hispanic/Latino; 1 American Indian or Alaska Native, non-Hispanic/Latino; 9 Asian, non-Hispanic/Latino; 5 Hispanic/Latino; 7 Two or more races, non-Hispanic/Latino). Average age 24. 87 applicants, 56% accepted, 29 enrolled. In 2011, 24 master's awarded. *Degree requirements:* For master's, comprehensive exam (for some programs), thesis (for some programs). *Entrance requirements:* For master's, GRE General Test, minimum GPA of 3.0 in last 90 quarter units, 3 letters of recommendation. Additional exam requirements/recommendations for international students: Required—TOEFL (minimum score 550 paper-based; 213 computer-based), IELTS (minimum score 6). *Application deadline:* For fall admission, 3/1 for domestic students, 11/30 for international students; for winter admission, 10/1 for domestic students, 6/30 for international students; for spring admission, 1/1 for domestic students. Applications are processed on a rolling basis. Application fee: $55. Electronic applications accepted. *Expenses:* Tuition, state resident: full-time $6738. Tuition, nonresident: full-time $17,898. *Required fees:* $2449. *Financial support:* Fellowships, research assistantships, teaching assistantships, career-related internships or fieldwork, Federal Work-Study, and scholarships/grants available. Support available to part-time students. Financial award application deadline: 3/2; financial award applicants required to submit FAFSA. *Faculty research:* Transportation and traffic, environmental protection, geotechnology, water engineering. *Unit head:* Dr. Robb Moss, Graduate Coordinator, 805-756-6427, Fax: 805-756-6330, E-mail: rmoss@calpoly.edu. *Application contact:* Dr. James Maraviglia, Associate Vice Provost for Marketing and Enrollment Development, 805-756-2311, Fax: 805-756-5400, E-mail: admissions@calpoly.edu. Web site: http://ceenve.calpoly.edu.

Carleton University, Faculty of Graduate Studies, Faculty of Engineering and Design, Department of Civil and Environmental Engineering, Ottawa, ON K1S 5B6, Canada. Offers M Eng, MA Sc, PhD. *Degree requirements:* For master's, thesis optional; for doctorate, thesis/dissertation. *Entrance requirements:* For master's, honors degree; for doctorate, MA Sc or M Eng. Additional exam requirements/recommendations for international students: Required—TOEFL. *Faculty research:* Pollution and wastewater management, fire safety engineering, earthquake engineering, structural design, bridge engineering.

Carnegie Mellon University, Carnegie Institute of Technology, Department of Civil and Environmental Engineering, Pittsburgh, PA 15213. Offers advanced infrastructure systems (MS, PhD); civil and environmental engineering (MS, PhD); civil and environmental engineering/engineering and public policy (PhD); civil engineering (MS, PhD); computational mechanics (MS, PhD); environmental engineering (MS, PhD); environmental management and science (MS, PhD). Part-time programs available. *Faculty:* 22 full-time (4 women), 24 part-time/adjunct (5 women). *Students:* 147 full-time (64 women), 7 part-time (0 women); includes 13 minority (5 Black or African American, non-Hispanic/Latino; 6 Asian, non-Hispanic/Latino; 2 Hispanic/Latino), 101 international. Average age 26. 487 applicants, 55% accepted, 80 enrolled. In 2011, 84 master's, 12 doctorates awarded. Terminal master's awarded for partial completion of doctoral program. *Degree requirements:* For master's, thesis optional; for doctorate, comprehensive exam, thesis/dissertation, two-part qualifying exam, public defense of dissertation. *Entrance requirements:* For master's and doctorate, GRE General Test. Additional exam requirements/recommendations for international students: Required—TOEFL (minimum score 84 iBT). *Application deadline:* For fall admission, 1/15 priority date for domestic students, 1/15 for international students; for spring admission, 9/30 priority date for domestic students, 9/30 for international students. Application fee: $65. Electronic applications accepted. *Financial support:* In 2011–12, 108 students received support, including 26 fellowships with full and partial tuition reimbursements available (averaging $2,087 per year), 35 research assistantships with full and partial tuition reimbursements available (averaging $2,094 per year); tuition waivers (partial), unspecified assistantships, and service assistantships also available. Financial award application deadline: 1/15. *Faculty research:* Advanced infrastructure systems; environmental engineering science and management; mechanics, materials, and computing; green design; global sustainable construction. *Total annual research expenditures:* $4.9 million. *Unit head:* Dr. James H. Garrett, Jr., Head, 412-268-2941, Fax: 412-268-7813, E-mail: garrett@cmu.edu. *Application contact:* Maxine A. Leffard, Director of the Graduate Program, 412-268-5673, Fax: 412-268-7813, E-mail: ce-admissions@andrew.cmu.edu. Web site: http://www.ce.cmu.edu/.

Carnegie Mellon University, Tepper School of Business, Pittsburgh, PA 15213-3891. Offers accounting (PhD); algorithms, combinatorics, and optimization (MS, PhD); business management and software engineering (MBMSE); civil engineering and industrial management (MS); computational finance (MSCF); economics (MS, PhD); electronic commerce (MS); environmental engineering and management (MEEM); finance (PhD); financial economics (PhD); industrial administration (MBA), including administration and public management; information systems (PhD); management of manufacturing and automation (PhD); marketing (PhD); mathematical finance (PhD); operations research (PhD); organizational behavior and theory (PhD); political economy (PhD); production and operations management (PhD); public policy and management (MS, MSED); software engineering and business management (MS); JD/MS; JD/MSIA; M Div/MS; MOM/MSIA; MSCF/MSIA. JD/MSIA offered jointly with University of Pittsburgh. Part-time programs available. Terminal master's awarded for partial completion of doctoral program. *Degree requirements:* For doctorate, thesis/dissertation. *Entrance requirements:* For master's, GMAT. Additional exam requirements/recommendations for international students: Required—TOEFL. *Expenses:* Contact institution.

The Catholic University of America, School of Engineering, Department of Civil Engineering, Washington, DC 20064. Offers environmental engineering (PhD). Part-time programs available. *Faculty:* 6 full-time (0 women), 4 part-time/adjunct (0 women). *Students:* 6 full-time (2 women), 19 part-time (7 women); includes 8 minority (5 Black or African American, non-Hispanic/Latino; 1 Asian, non-Hispanic/Latino; 2 Hispanic/Latino), 7 international. Average age 35. 28 applicants, 39% accepted, 5 enrolled. In 2011, 4 master's, 1 doctorate awarded. *Degree requirements:* For master's, thesis optional; for doctorate, comprehensive exam, thesis/dissertation. *Entrance requirements:* For master's and doctorate, statement of purpose, official copies of academic transcripts, three letters of recommendation. Additional exam requirements/recommendations for international students: Required—TOEFL (minimum score 580 paper-based; 237 computer-based). *Application deadline:* For fall admission, 8/1 priority date for domestic students, 7/15 for international students; for spring admission, 12/1 priority date for domestic students, 10/15 for international students. Applications are processed on a rolling basis. Application fee: $55. Electronic applications accepted. *Expenses:* Contact institution. *Financial support:* Fellowships, research assistantships, teaching assistantships, Federal Work-Study, scholarships/grants, tuition waivers (full and partial), and unspecified assistantships available. Financial award application deadline: 2/1; financial award applicants required to submit FAFSA. *Faculty research:* Geotechnical engineering, solid mechanics, construction engineering and management, environmental engineering, structural engineering. *Total annual research expenditures:* $325,547. *Unit head:* Dr. Lu Sun, Chair, 202-319-6671, Fax: 202-319-6677, E-mail: sunl@cua.edu. *Application contact:* Andrew Woodall, Director of Graduate Admissions, 202-319-5057, Fax: 202-319-6533, E-mail: cua-admissions@cua.edu. Web site: http://civil.cua.edu/.

Clarkson University, Graduate School, Institute for a Sustainable Environment, Program in Environmental Science and Engineering, Potsdam, NY 13699. Offers MS, PhD. Part-time programs available. *Faculty:* 8 full-time (4 women). *Students:* 32 full-time (18 women), 1 (woman) part-time; includes 1 minority (Two or more races, non-Hispanic/Latino), 13 international. Average age 26. 55 applicants, 44% accepted, 8 enrolled. In 2011, 7 master's, 4 doctorates awarded. Terminal master's awarded for partial completion of doctoral program. *Degree requirements:* For master's, thesis; for doctorate, comprehensive exam, thesis/dissertation, departmental qualifying exam. *Entrance requirements:* For master's and doctorate, GRE, transcripts of all college coursework, resume, personal statement, three letters of recommendation. Additional exam requirements/recommendations for international students: Required—TOEFL (minimum score 550 paper-based; 213 computer-based; 80 iBT), IELTS (minimum score 6.5). *Application deadline:* For fall admission, 1/30 priority date for domestic students, 1/30 for international students; for spring admission, 9/1 priority date for domestic students, 9/1 for international students. Applications are processed on a rolling basis. Application fee: $25 ($35 for international students). Electronic applications accepted. *Expenses: Tuition:* Full-time $14,376; part-time $1198 per credit hour. *Required fees:* $295 per semester. *Financial support:* In 2011–12, 30 students received support, including fellowships with full tuition reimbursements available (averaging $21,999 per year), 14 research assistantships with full tuition reimbursements available (averaging $21,999 per year), 6 teaching assistantships with full tuition reimbursements available (averaging $21,999 per year); scholarships/grants, tuition waivers (partial), and unspecified assistantships also available. *Faculty research:* Biological, chemical, physical and social systems, renewable energy, environmental health. *Unit head:* Dr. Philip Hopke, Director, 315-268-3856, Fax: 315-268-4291, E-mail: hopkepk@clarkson.edu. *Application contact:* Suzann Cheney, Administrative Secretary, 315-268-3856, Fax: 315-268-4291, E-mail: scheney@clarkson.edu. Web site: http://www.clarkson.edu/ese/.

Clarkson University, Graduate School, Wallace H. Coulter School of Engineering, Department of Civil and Environmental Engineering, Potsdam, NY 13699. Offers civil and environmental engineering (PhD); civil engineering (ME, MS). Part-time programs available. *Faculty:* 28 full-time (3 women), 5 part-time/adjunct (1 woman). *Students:* 42 full-time (14 women); includes 1 minority (Asian, non-Hispanic/Latino), 28 international. Average age 26. 68 applicants, 79% accepted, 15 enrolled. In 2011, 12 master's, 6 doctorates awarded. Terminal master's awarded for partial completion of doctoral program. *Degree requirements:* For master's, thesis; for doctorate, comprehensive exam, thesis/dissertation, departmental qualifying exam. *Entrance requirements:* For master's and doctorate, GRE, transcripts of all college coursework, resume, personal statement, three letters of recommendation. Additional exam requirements/recommendations for international students: Required—TOEFL (minimum score 550 paper-based; 213 computer-based; 80 iBT), IELTS (minimum score 6.5). *Application deadline:* For fall admission, 1/30 priority date for domestic students, 1/30 for international students; for spring admission, 9/1 priority date for domestic students, 9/1 for international students. Applications are processed on a rolling basis. Application fee: $25 ($35 for international students). Electronic applications accepted. *Expenses: Tuition:* Full-time $14,376; part-time $1198 per credit hour. *Required fees:* $295 per semester. *Financial support:* In 2011–12, 39 students received support, including fellowships with full tuition reimbursements available (averaging $21,999 per year), 26 research assistantships with full tuition reimbursements available (averaging $21,999 per year), 14 teaching assistantships with full tuition reimbursements available (averaging $21,999 per year); scholarships/grants, tuition waivers (partial), and unspecified assistantships also available. *Faculty research:* Prognostic algorithm, resuspended particle, load capacity rating, ecosystem, geothermal vents, CO2 bubbles. *Total annual research expenditures:* $4.5 million. *Unit head:* Dr. Stefan Grimberg, Department Chair, 315-268-6529, Fax: 315-268-7985, E-mail: grimberg@clarkson.edu. *Application contact:* Kelly Sharlow, Assistant to the Dean, 315-268-7929, Fax: 315-268-4494, E-mail: ksharlow@clarkson.edu. Web site: http://www.clarkson.edu/cee/.

Clemson University, Graduate School, College of Engineering and Science, Department of Environmental Engineering and Earth Sciences, Programs in Environmental Engineering and Science, Clemson, SC 29634. Offers M Engr, MS, PhD. *Accreditation:* ABET. *Students:* 74 full-time (33 women), 14 part-time (6 women); includes 9 minority (4 Black or African American, non-Hispanic/Latino; 2 Asian, non-Hispanic/Latino; 1 Hispanic/Latino; 2 Two or more races, non-Hispanic/Latino), 41 international. Average age 28. 157 applicants, 42% accepted, 25 enrolled. In 2011, 16 master's, 5 doctorates awarded. *Degree requirements:* For master's, thesis; for doctorate, thesis/dissertation. *Entrance requirements:* For master's and doctorate, GRE General Test, minimum GPA of 3.0. Additional exam requirements/recommendations for international students: Required—TOEFL. *Application deadline:* For fall admission, 3/1 priority date for domestic students, 3/1 for international students; for spring admission, 9/15 for international students. Applications are processed on a rolling basis. Application fee: $70 ($80 for international students). Electronic applications accepted. *Financial support:* In 2011–12, 46 students received support, including 4 fellowships with full and partial tuition reimbursements available (averaging $11,635 per year), 21 research assistantships with partial tuition reimbursements available (averaging $17,399 per year), 15 teaching assistantships with partial tuition reimbursements available (averaging $16,743 per year); career-related internships or fieldwork, institutionally sponsored loans, scholarships/grants, health care benefits, and unspecified assistantships also available. Support available to part-time students. Financial award applicants required to submit FAFSA. *Faculty research:* Water and air pollution control, hazardous waste and environmental management, environmental chemistry and biology, containment transport modeling, risk assessment. *Unit head:* Dr. Tanju Karanfil, Chair, 864-656-1005, E-mail: tkaranf@clemson.edu. *Application contact:* Dr. Cindy Lee, Graduate Program Coordinator, 864-656-1006, Fax: 864-656-5973, E-mail: lc@clemson.edu. Web site: http://www.clemson.edu/ces/departments/eees/.

Cleveland State University, College of Graduate Studies, Fenn College of Engineering, Department of Civil and Environmental Engineering, Cleveland, OH 44115. Offers accelerated program civil engineering (MS); accelerated program environmental engineering (MS); civil engineering (MS, D Eng); engineering mechanics (MS); environmental engineering (MS). Part-time and evening/weekend programs available. *Faculty:* 8 full-time (2 women). *Students:* 10 full-time (2 women), 38 part-time (7 women); includes 4 minority (1 Black or African American, non-Hispanic/Latino; 1 American Indian or Alaska Native, non-Hispanic/Latino; 2 Asian, non-Hispanic/Latino), 14 international. Average age 29. 81 applicants, 64% accepted, 11 enrolled. In 2011, 25 master's, 1 doctorate awarded. *Degree requirements:* For master's, project or thesis; for doctorate, comprehensive exam, thesis/dissertation, candidacy and qualifying exams. *Entrance requirements:* For master's, GRE General Test, GRE Subject Test, minimum

GPA of 2.75; for doctorate, GRE General Test, GRE Subject Test, minimum GPA of 3.25. Additional exam requirements/recommendations for international students: Required—TOEFL (minimum score 525 paper-based; 197 computer-based). *Application deadline:* For fall admission, 7/15 priority date for domestic students. Applications are processed on a rolling basis. Application fee: $30. *Expenses:* Tuition, state resident: full-time $6416; part-time $494 per credit hour. Tuition, nonresident: full-time $12,074; part-time $929 per credit hour. *Financial support:* In 2011–12, 9 research assistantships with full and partial tuition reimbursements (averaging $3,920 per year) were awarded; teaching assistantships with tuition reimbursements, career-related internships or fieldwork, scholarships/grants, and unspecified assistantships also available. Financial award application deadline: 9/1. *Faculty research:* Solid-waste disposal, constitutive modeling, transportation, safety engineering. *Total annual research expenditures:* $800,000. *Unit head:* Dr. Stephen F. Duffy, Chairperson, 216-687-3874, Fax: 216-687-9280, E-mail: p.bosela@csuohio.edu. *Application contact:* Deborah L. Brown, Interim Assistant Director, Graduate Admissions, 216-523-7572, Fax: 216-687-9214, E-mail: d.l.brown@csuohio.edu. Web site: http://www.csuohio.edu/engineering/civil.

Colorado School of Mines, Graduate School, Division of Environmental Science and Engineering, Golden, CO 80401-1887. Offers MS, PhD. Part-time programs available. *Faculty:* 23 full-time (6 women), 8 part-time/adjunct (3 women). *Students:* 98 full-time (46 women), 21 part-time (10 women); includes 15 minority (2 Black or African American, non-Hispanic/Latino; 4 Asian, non-Hispanic/Latino; 8 Hispanic/Latino; 1 Two or more races, non-Hispanic/Latino), 8 international. Average age 28. 175 applicants, 58% accepted, 50 enrolled. In 2011, 20 master's, 2 doctorates awarded. *Degree requirements:* For master's, thesis (for some programs); for doctorate, comprehensive exam, thesis/dissertation. *Entrance requirements:* For master's and doctorate, GRE General Test. Additional exam requirements/recommendations for international students: Required—TOEFL (minimum score 550 paper-based; 213 computer-based; 80 iBT). *Application deadline:* For fall admission, 1/15 priority date for domestic students, 1/15 for international students; for spring admission, 10/15 priority date for domestic students, 10/15 for international students. Application fee: $50 ($70 for international students). Electronic applications accepted. *Expenses:* Tuition, state resident: full-time $12,585; part-time $699 per credit. Tuition, nonresident: full-time $27,270; part-time $1516 per credit. *Required fees:* $1864.20; $670 per semester. *Financial support:* In 2011–12, 49 students received support, including 15 fellowships with full tuition reimbursements available (averaging $20,000 per year), 33 research assistantships with full tuition reimbursements available (averaging $20,000 per year), 1 teaching assistantship with full tuition reimbursement available (averaging $20,000 per year); scholarships/grants, health care benefits, and unspecified assistantships also available. Financial award application deadline: 1/15; financial award applicants required to submit FAFSA. *Faculty research:* Treatment of water and wastes, environmental law: policy and practice, natural environment systems, hazardous waste management, environmental data analysis. *Total annual research expenditures:* $3.3 million. *Unit head:* Dr. John McCray, Director, 303-384-3490, Fax: 303-273-3413, E-mail: jmccray@mines.edu. *Application contact:* Tim VanHaverbeke, Research Faculty, 303-273-3467, Fax: 303-273-3413, E-mail: tvanhave@mines.edu. Web site: http://ese.mines.edu.

Columbia University, The Fu Foundation School of Engineering and Applied Science, Department of Earth and Environmental Engineering, New York, NY 10027. Offers earth and environmental engineering (MS, Eng Sc D, PhD); metallurgical engineering (Engr); mining engineering (Engr); MS/MBA. Part-time programs available. Postbaccalaureate distance learning degree programs offered (minimal on-campus study). *Faculty:* 13 full-time (1 woman), 6 part-time/adjunct (0 women). *Students:* 48 full-time (17 women), 15 part-time (8 women); includes 6 minority (3 Asian, non-Hispanic/Latino; 3 Two or more races, non-Hispanic/Latino), 32 international. Average age 30. 171 applicants, 15% accepted, 14 enrolled. In 2011, 16 master's, 4 doctorates awarded. Terminal master's awarded for partial completion of doctoral program. *Degree requirements:* For master's, thesis; for doctorate, thesis/dissertation, qualifying exam. *Entrance requirements:* For master's, doctorate, and Engr, GRE General Test. Additional exam requirements/recommendations for international students: Required—TOEFL, IELTS. *Application deadline:* For fall admission, 12/1 priority date for domestic students, 12/1 for international students; for spring admission, 10/1 priority date for domestic students, 10/1 for international students. Application fee: $95. Electronic applications accepted. *Financial support:* In 2011–12, 39 students received support, including 6 fellowships with full and partial tuition reimbursements available (averaging $16,478 per year), 26 research assistantships with full tuition reimbursements available (averaging $27,733 per year), 7 teaching assistantships with full tuition reimbursements available (averaging $22,500 per year); health care benefits and unspecified assistantships also available. Financial award application deadline: 12/1; financial award applicants required to submit FAFSA. *Faculty research:* Sustainable energy and materials, waste to energy, water resources and climate risks, environmental health engineering, life cycle analysis. *Unit head:* Dr. Klaus S. Lackner, Professor of Geophysics/Chairman, 212-854-0304, Fax: 212-854-7081, E-mail: kl2010@columbia.edu. *Application contact:* Gary Hill, Administrative Assistant, 212-854-2905, Fax: 212-854-7081, E-mail: gh2206@columbia.edu. Web site: http://www.eee.columbia.edu/.

Concordia University, School of Graduate Studies, Faculty of Engineering and Computer Science, Department of Building, Civil and Environmental Engineering, Montréal, QC H3G 1M8, Canada. Offers building engineering (M Eng, MA Sc, PhD, Certificate); civil engineering (M Eng, MA Sc, PhD); environmental engineering (Certificate). *Degree requirements:* For master's, thesis or alternative; for doctorate, comprehensive exam, thesis/dissertation. *Faculty research:* Structural engineering, geotechnical engineering, water resources and fluid engineering, transportation engineering, systems engineering.

Cornell University, Graduate School, Graduate Fields of Engineering, Field of Civil and Environmental Engineering, Ithaca, NY 14853-0001. Offers engineering management (M Eng, MS, PhD); environmental engineering (M Eng, MS, PhD); environmental fluid mechanics and hydrology (M Eng, MS, PhD); environmental systems engineering (M Eng, MS, PhD); geotechnical engineering (M Eng, MS, PhD); remote sensing (M Eng, MS, PhD); structural engineering (M Eng, MS, PhD); structural mechanics (M Eng, MS); transportation engineering (MS, PhD); transportation systems engineering (M Eng); water resource systems (M Eng, MS, PhD). *Faculty:* 39 full-time (4 women). *Students:* 143 full-time (49 women); includes 20 minority (6 Black or African American, non-Hispanic/Latino; 1 American Indian or Alaska Native, non-Hispanic/Latino; 9 Asian, non-Hispanic/Latino; 4 Hispanic/Latino), 72 international. Average age 25. 574 applicants, 47% accepted, 100 enrolled. In 2011, 88 master's, 13 doctorates awarded. Terminal master's awarded for partial completion of doctoral program. *Degree requirements:* For master's, thesis (MS); for doctorate, comprehensive exam, thesis/dissertation. *Entrance requirements:* For master's and doctorate, GRE General Test (recommended), 2 letters of recommendation. Additional exam requirements/recommendations for international students: Required—TOEFL (minimum score 600 paper-based; 250 computer-based; 77 iBT). *Application deadline:* For fall admission, 1/15 priority date for domestic students; for spring admission, 10/15 for domestic students. Application fee: $95. Electronic applications accepted. *Financial support:* In 2011–12, 50 students received support, including 20 fellowships with full tuition reimbursements available, 27 research assistantships with full tuition reimbursements available, 17 teaching assistantships with full tuition reimbursements available; institutionally sponsored loans, scholarships/grants, health care benefits, tuition waivers (full and partial), and unspecified assistantships also available. Financial award applicants required to submit FAFSA. *Faculty research:* Environmental engineering, geotechnical engineering, remote sensing, environmental fluid mechanics and hydrology, structural engineering. *Unit head:* Director of Graduate Studies, 607-255-7560, Fax: 607-255-9004. *Application contact:* Graduate Field Assistant, 607-255-7560, Fax: 607-255-9004, E-mail: cee_grad@cornell.edu. Web site: http://www.gradschool.cornell.edu/fields.php?id-27&a-2.

Dalhousie University, Faculty of Engineering, Department of Environmental Engineering, Halifax, NS B3J 2X4, Canada. Offers M Eng, MA Sc, PhD. *Entrance requirements:* Additional exam requirements/recommendations for international students: Required—TOEFL, IELTS, CANTEST, CAEL, or Michigan English Language Assessment Battery. Electronic applications accepted.

Dartmouth College, Thayer School of Engineering, Program in Environmental Engineering, Hanover, NH 03755. Offers MS, PhD. Application fee: $45. *Faculty research:* Resource and environmental analysis, decision theory, risk assessment and public policy, environmental fluid mechanics. *Total annual research expenditures:* $261,914. *Unit head:* Dr. Joseph J. Helbie, Dean, 603-646-2238, Fax: 603-646-2580, E-mail: joseph.j.helbie@dartmouth.edu. *Application contact:* Candace S. Potter, Graduate Admissions Administrator, 603-646-3844, Fax: 603-646-1620, E-mail: candace.potter@dartmouth.edu.

Drexel University, College of Engineering, Department of Civil, Architectural, and Environmental Engineering, Program in Environmental Engineering, Philadelphia, PA 19104-2875. Offers MS, PhD. Part-time and evening/weekend programs available. Terminal master's awarded for partial completion of doctoral program. *Degree requirements:* For master's, thesis optional; for doctorate, thesis/dissertation. Electronic applications accepted.

Drexel University, College of Engineering, Department of Civil, Architectural, and Environmental Engineering, Program in Geotechnical, Geoenvironmental and Geosynthetics Engineering, Philadelphia, PA 19104-2875. Offers MS, PhD.

Duke University, Graduate School, Pratt School of Engineering, Department of Civil and Environmental Engineering, Durham, NC 27708. Offers civil and environmental engineering (MS, PhD); environmental engineering (MS, PhD). Part-time programs available. Terminal master's awarded for partial completion of doctoral program. *Degree requirements:* For doctorate, thesis/dissertation. *Entrance requirements:* For master's and doctorate, GRE General Test. Additional exam requirements/recommendations for international students: Required—TOEFL (minimum score 550 paper-based; 213 computer-based; 83 iBT), IELTS (minimum score 7). Electronic applications accepted. *Expenses: Tuition:* Full-time $40,720. *Required fees:* $3107.

Duke University, Graduate School, Pratt School of Engineering, Master of Engineering Program, Durham, NC 27708-0271. Offers biomedical engineering (M Eng); civil engineering (M Eng); electrical and computer engineering (M Eng); environmental engineering (M Eng); materials science and engineering (M Eng); mechanical engineering (M Eng); photonics and optical sciences (M Eng). Part-time programs available. *Entrance requirements:* For master's, GRE General Test, resume, 3 letters of recommendation, statement of purpose. Additional exam requirements/recommendations for international students: Required—TOEFL. *Expenses: Tuition:* Full-time $40,720. *Required fees:* $3107.

École Polytechnique de Montréal, Graduate Programs, Department of Civil, Geological and Mining Engineering, Montréal, QC H3C 3A7, Canada. Offers civil, geological and mining engineering (DESS); environmental engineering (M Eng, M Sc A, PhD); geotechnical engineering (M Eng, M Sc A, PhD); hydraulics engineering (M Eng, M Sc A, PhD); structural engineering (M Eng, M Sc A, PhD); transportation engineering (M Eng, M Sc A, PhD). Part-time programs available. *Degree requirements:* For master's, one foreign language, thesis; for doctorate, one foreign language, thesis/dissertation. *Entrance requirements:* For master's, minimum GPA of 2.75; for doctorate, minimum GPA of 3.0. *Faculty research:* Water resources management, characteristics of building materials, aging of dams, pollution control.

Florida Agricultural and Mechanical University, Division of Graduate Studies, Research, and Continuing Education, FAMU-FSU College of Engineering, Department of Civil and Environmental Engineering, Tallahassee, FL 32307-3200. Offers civil engineering (MS, PhD); environmental engineering (MS, PhD). *Degree requirements:* For master's, comprehensive exam, thesis optional; for doctorate, comprehensive exam, thesis/dissertation. *Entrance requirements:* For master's, GRE General Test, minimum GPA of 3.0; for doctorate, GRE General Test, minimum GPA of 3.0, letters of recommendation (3). Additional exam requirements/recommendations for international students: Required—TOEFL (minimum score 550 paper-based; 213 computer-based). *Faculty research:* Geotechnical, environmental, hydraulic, construction materials, and structures.

Florida International University, College of Engineering and Computing, Department of Civil and Environmental Engineering, Program in Environmental Engineering, Miami, FL 33175. Offers MS. Part-time and evening/weekend programs available. Postbaccalaureate distance learning degree programs offered (no on-campus study). *Degree requirements:* For master's, thesis optional. *Entrance requirements:* For master's, minimum GPA of 3.0; resume, 3 letters of recommendation. Additional exam requirements/recommendations for international students: Required—TOEFL (minimum score 550 paper-based; 80 iBT). Electronic applications accepted. *Faculty research:* Water and wastewater treatment, water quality, solid and hazardous waste, sustainability and green engineering, clean up, remediation and restoration.

Florida State University, The Graduate School, FAMU-FSU College of Engineering, Department of Civil and Environmental Engineering, Tallahassee, FL 32306. Offers M Eng, MS, PhD. Part-time programs available. *Faculty:* 19 full-time (3 women), 6 part-time/adjunct (0 women). *Students:* 44 full-time (13 women), 13 part-time (2 women); includes 13 minority (6 Black or African American, non-Hispanic/Latino; 2 Asian, non-Hispanic/Latino; 5 Hispanic/Latino), 17 international. Average age 23. 82 applicants, 40% accepted, 17 enrolled. In 2011, 14 master's, 3 doctorates awarded. *Degree requirements:* For master's, thesis optional; for doctorate, thesis/dissertation. *Entrance requirements:* For master's, GRE General Test (minimum score 1000 in old version; 30% Verbal Reasoning/65% Quantitative Reasoning for MS, 35% for Verbal Reasoning and 65% for Quantitative Reasoning for PhD in new format), BS in engineering or related field, minimum GPA of 3.0; for doctorate, GRE General Test (minimum scores of 35% for Verbal Reasoning and 65% for Quantitative Reasoning for PhD), master's degree in engineering or related field, minimum GPA of 3.0. Additional exam requirements/recommendations for international students: Required—TOEFL (minimum score 550 paper-based; 213 computer-based; 80 iBT). *Application deadline:* For fall admission, 7/1 for domestic and international students; for spring admission, 11/1 for domestic and international students. Applications are processed on a rolling basis. Application fee: $30. *Expenses:* Tuition, state resident: full-time $9474; part-time $350.88 per credit hour. Tuition, nonresident: full-time $16,236; part-time $601.34 per credit hour. *Required fees:* $630 per semester. One-time fee: $20. Tuition and fees vary according to course load and campus/location. *Financial support:* In 2011–12, 25 students received support, including 2 fellowships (averaging $12,000 per year), 18 research assistantships with full tuition reimbursements available (averaging $15,000 per year), 26 teaching assistantships with full tuition reimbursements available (averaging $15,000 per year); Federal Work-Study, tuition waivers (full), and unspecified assistantships also available. Financial award application deadline: 6/15; financial award applicants required to submit FAFSA. *Faculty research:* Tidal hydraulics, temperature effects on bridge girders, codes for coastal construction, field performance of pine bridges, river basin management, transportation pavement design, soil dynamics, structural analysis. *Total annual research expenditures:* $1.3 million. *Unit head:* Dr. Kamal S. Tawfiq, Chair and Professor, 850-410-6143, Fax: 850-410-6142, E-mail: tawfiq@eng.fsu.edu. *Application contact:* Johnnye Belinda Morris, Office Manager, 850-410-6139, Fax: 850-410-6142, E-mail: bmorris@eng.fsu.edu. Web site: http://www.eng.fsu.edu/cee/.

Gannon University, School of Graduate Studies, College of Engineering and Business, School of Engineering and Computer Science, Program in Environmental Science and Engineering, Erie, PA 16541-0001. Offers MS. Part-time and evening/weekend programs available. *Students:* 7 full-time (3 women), 3 part-time (2 women), 2 international. Average age 26. 31 applicants, 65% accepted, 2 enrolled. In 2011, 4 master's awarded. *Degree requirements:* For master's, thesis, internship, research paper or project. *Entrance requirements:* For master's, GRE. Additional exam requirements/recommendations for international students: Required—TOEFL (minimum score 79 iBT). *Application deadline:* Applications are processed on a rolling basis. Application fee: $25. Electronic applications accepted. *Financial support:* Scholarships/grants and unspecified assistantships available. Financial award application deadline: 7/1; financial award applicants required to submit FAFSA. *Faculty research:* Water quality, renewable energy, human health risk assessment, solid waste management, soil and groundwater contamination. *Unit head:* Dr. Harry Diz, Chair, 814-871-7633, E-mail: diz001@gannon.edu. *Application contact:* Kara Morgan, Director of Graduate Admissions, 814-871-5831, Fax: 814-871-5827, E-mail: graduate@gannon.edu.

The George Washington University, School of Engineering and Applied Science, Department of Civil and Environmental Engineering, Washington, DC 20052. Offers MS, D Sc, App Sc, Engr. Part-time and evening/weekend programs available. *Faculty:* 11 full-time (2 women), 5 part-time/adjunct (0 women). *Students:* 27 full-time (7 women), 26 part-time (6 women); includes 7 minority (3 Black or African American, non-Hispanic/Latino; 4 Hispanic/Latino), 27 international. Average age 29. 111 applicants, 59% accepted, 10 enrolled. In 2011, 7 master's, 4 doctorates awarded. *Degree requirements:* For master's, thesis optional; for doctorate, thesis/dissertation, final and qualifying exams. *Entrance requirements:* For master's, appropriate bachelor's degree, minimum GPA of 3.0; for doctorate, GRE (if highest earned degree is BS), appropriate bachelor's or master's degree, minimum GPA of 3.4; for other advanced degree, appropriate master's degree, minimum GPA of 3.0. Additional exam requirements/recommendations for international students: Required—TOEFL or The George Washington University English as a Foreign Language Test. *Application deadline:* For fall admission, 3/1 priority date for domestic students; for spring admission, 10/1 for domestic students. Applications are processed on a rolling basis. Application fee: $75. *Financial support:* In 2011–12, 42 students received support. Fellowships with tuition reimbursements available, research assistantships, teaching assistantships with tuition reimbursements available, career-related internships or fieldwork, Federal Work-Study, institutionally sponsored loans, and tuition waivers available. Financial award application deadline: 3/1; financial award applicants required to submit FAFSA. *Faculty research:* Computer-integrated manufacturing, materials engineering, electronic materials, fatigue and fracture, reliability. *Unit head:* Dr. Kim Roddis, Chair, 202-994-8515, Fax: 202-994-0127, E-mail: roddis@gwu.edu. *Application contact:* Adina Lav, Marketing, Recruiting and Admissions, 202-994-5827, Fax: 202-994-0909, E-mail: engineering@gwu.edu. Web site: http://www.cee.seas.gwu.edu/.

Georgia Institute of Technology, Graduate Studies and Research, College of Engineering, School of Civil and Environmental Engineering, Program in Environmental Engineering, Atlanta, GA 30332-0001. Offers MS, MS Env E, PhD. *Accreditation:* ABET (one or more programs are accredited). Part-time programs available. Postbaccalaureate distance learning degree programs offered (no on-campus study). *Degree requirements:* For master's, research report or thesis; for doctorate, thesis/dissertation. *Entrance requirements:* For master's and doctorate, GRE, minimum GPA of 3.2. Additional exam requirements/recommendations for international students: Required—TOEFL. *Faculty research:* Advanced microbiology of water and wastes, industrial waste treatment and disposal, air pollution measurements and control.

Idaho State University, Office of Graduate Studies, College of Science and Engineering, Civil and Environmental Engineering Department, Pocatello, ID 83209-8060. Offers civil engineering (MS); environmental engineering (MS); environmental science and management (MS). Part-time programs available. *Degree requirements:* For master's, comprehensive exam (for some programs), thesis optional, thesis project, 2 semesters of seminar. *Entrance requirements:* For master's, GRE. Additional exam requirements/recommendations for international students: Required—TOEFL (minimum score 550 paper-based; 213 computer-based; 80 iBT). Electronic applications accepted. *Faculty research:* Floor vibration investigations, earthquake engineering, base isolation systems and seismic risk assessment, infrastructure revitalization (building foundations and damage, bridge structures, highways, and dams), slope stability and soil erosion, pavement rehabilitation, computational fluid dynamics and flood control structures, microbial fuel cells, water treatment and water quality modeling, environmental risk assessment, biotechnology, nanotechnology.

Illinois Institute of Technology, Graduate College, Armour College of Engineering, Department of Civil, Architectural and Environmental Engineering, Chicago, IL 60616-3793. Offers architectural engineering (M Arch E); civil engineering (MS, PhD), including architectural engineeering (MS), construction engineering and management (MS), geoenvironmental engineering (MS), geotechnical engineering (MS), structural engineering (MS), transportation engineering (MS); construction engineering and management (MCEM); environmental engineering (M Env E, PhD); geoenvironmental engineering (M Geoenv E); geotechnical engineering (MGE); public works (MPW); structural engineering (MSE); transportation engineering (M Trans E). Part-time and evening/weekend programs available. Postbaccalaureate distance learning degree programs offered (minimal on-campus study). Terminal master's awarded for partial completion of doctoral program. *Degree requirements:* For master's, thesis (for some programs); for doctorate, comprehensive exam, thesis/dissertation. *Entrance requirements:* For master's, GRE General Test (minimum score 900 Quantitative and Verbal, 2.5 Analytical Writing), minimum undergraduate GPA of 3.0; for doctorate, GRE General Test (minimum score 1000 Quantitative and Verbal, 3.0 Analytical Writing), minimum undergraduate GPA of 3.0. Additional exam requirements/recommendations for international students: Required—TOEFL (minimum score 523 paper-based; 70 iBT); Recommended—IELTS (minimum score 5.5). Electronic applications accepted. *Faculty research:* Structural, architectural, geotechnical and geoenvironmental engineering; construction engineering and management; transportation engineering; environmental engineering and public works.

Instituto Tecnologico de Santo Domingo, Graduate School, Area of Engineering, Santo Domingo, Dominican Republic. Offers construction administration (MS, Certificate); data telecommunications (M Eng, MS, Certificate); industrial engineering (M Eng, Certificate); industrial management (M Mgmt); information technology (Certificate); maintenance engineering (M Eng); occupational hazard prevention (M Mgmt); production management (Certificate); quantitative methods (Certificate); sanitary and environmental engineering (M Eng); structural engineering (M Eng); systems engineering and electronic data processing (Certificate); transportation (Certificate).

Instituto Tecnológico y de Estudios Superiores de Monterrey, Campus Ciudad de México, Virtual University Division, Ciudad de Mexico, Mexico. Offers administration of information technologies (MA); computer sciences (MA); education (MA, PhD); educational technology (MA); environmental engineering (MA); environmental systems (MA); humanistic studies (MA); industrial engineering (MA); international business for Latin America (MA); quality systems (MA); quality systems and productivity (MA). Part-time and evening/weekend programs available. Postbaccalaureate distance learning degree programs offered (minimal on-campus study). *Entrance requirements:* For master's and doctorate, Instituto entrance exam. Additional exam requirements/recommendations for international students: Required—TOEFL.

Instituto Tecnológico y de Estudios Superiores de Monterrey, Campus Monterrey, Graduate and Research Division, Programs in Engineering, Monterrey, Mexico. Offers applied statistics (M Eng); artificial intelligence (PhD); automation engineering (M Eng); chemical engineering (M Eng); civil engineering (M Eng); electrical engineering (M Eng); electronic engineering (M Eng); environmental engineering (M Eng); industrial engineering (M Eng, PhD); manufacturing engineering (M Eng); mechanical engineering (M Eng); systems and quality engineering (M Eng). M Eng program offered jointly with University of Waterloo; PhD in industrial engineering with Texas A&M University. Part-time and evening/weekend programs available. Terminal master's awarded for partial completion of doctoral program. *Degree requirements:* For master's, one foreign language, thesis; for doctorate, one foreign language, thesis/dissertation. *Entrance requirements:* For master's, EXADEP; for doctorate, GRE, master's degree in related field. Additional exam requirements/recommendations for international students: Required—TOEFL. *Faculty research:* Flexible manufacturing cells, materials, statistical methods, environmental prevention, control and evaluation.

Iowa State University of Science and Technology, Department of Civil and Construction Engineering, Ames, IA 50011-3232. Offers civil engineering (MS, PhD), including civil engineering materials, construction engineering and management, environmental engineering, geometronics, geotechnical engineering, structural engineering, transportation engineering. *Degree requirements:* For master's, thesis or alternative; for doctorate, thesis/dissertation. *Entrance requirements:* For master's and doctorate, GRE General Test. Additional exam requirements/recommendations for international students: Required—TOEFL (minimum score 550 paper-based; 82 iBT), IELTS (minimum score 6.5). *Application deadline:* For fall admission, 2/1 priority date for domestic students, 2/1 for international students; for spring admission, 8/1 priority date for domestic students, 8/1 for international students. Applications are processed on a rolling basis. Application fee: $40 ($90 for international students). Electronic applications accepted. *Unit head:* Dr. Sri Sritharan, Director of Graduate Education, 515-294-4972, Fax: 515-294-8216, E-mail: ccee-grad-inquiry@iastate.edu. *Application contact:* Kathy Petersen, Director of Graduate Education, 515-294-4975, Fax: 515-294-8216, E-mail: ccee-grad-inquiry@iastate.edu. Web site: http://www.ccee.iastate.edu/.

The Johns Hopkins University, Bloomberg School of Public Health, Department of Environmental Health Sciences, Baltimore, MD 21218-2699. Offers environmental health engineering (PhD); environmental health sciences (MHS, Dr PH); occupational and environmental health (PhD); occupational and environmental hygiene (MHS, MHS); physiology (PhD); toxicology (PhD). Postbaccalaureate distance learning degree programs offered (minimal on-campus study). *Degree requirements:* For master's, essay, presentation; for doctorate, comprehensive exam, thesis/dissertation, 1 year full-time residency, oral and written exams. *Entrance requirements:* For master's, GRE General Test or MCAT, 3 letters of recommendation, transcripts; for doctorate, GRE General Test or MCAT, 3 letters of recommendation. Additional exam requirements/recommendations for international students: Required—TOEFL (minimum score 600 paper-based; 250 computer-based). Electronic applications accepted. *Faculty research:* Chemical carcinogenesis/toxicology, lung disease, occupational and environmental health, nuclear imaging, molecular epidemiology.

The Johns Hopkins University, Engineering Program for Professionals, Part-Time Program in Environmental Engineering, Baltimore, MD 21218-2699. Offers MS, Graduate Certificate, Post-Master's Certificate. Part-time and evening/weekend programs available.

The Johns Hopkins University, Engineering Program for Professionals, Part-time Program in Environmental Engineering and Science, Baltimore, MD 21218-2699. Offers MEE, MS, Graduate Certificate, Post-Master's Certificate. Part-time and evening/weekend programs available. Electronic applications accepted.

The Johns Hopkins University, Whiting School of Engineering, Department of Geography and Environmental Engineering, Baltimore, MD 21218-2699. Offers MA, MS, MSE, PhD. Terminal master's awarded for partial completion of doctoral program. *Degree requirements:* For master's, thesis (for some programs), 1 year full-time residency; for doctorate, comprehensive exam, thesis/dissertation, oral exam, 2 year full-time residency. *Entrance requirements:* For master's and doctorate, GRE General Test. Additional exam requirements/recommendations for international students: Required—TOEFL (minimum score 670 paper-based; 300 computer-based; 120 iBT); Recommended—IELTS. Electronic applications accepted. *Faculty research:* Environmental engineering; environmental chemistry; water resources engineering; systems analysis and economics for public decision-making; geomorphology, hydrology and ecology.

Lakehead University, Graduate Studies, Faculty of Engineering, Thunder Bay, ON P7B 5E1, Canada. Offers control engineering (M Sc Engr); electrical/computer engineering (M Sc Engr); environmental engineering (M Sc Engr). Part-time programs available. *Degree requirements:* For master's, thesis. *Entrance requirements:* For master's, bachelor's degree in chemical, electrical or mechanical engineering, minimum B average. Additional exam requirements/recommendations for international students:

Required—TOEFL. *Faculty research:* Pulp and paper, adaptive/process control, robust/interactive learning control, vibration control.

Lamar University, College of Graduate Studies, College of Engineering, Department of Civil Engineering, Beaumont, TX 77710. Offers civil engineering (ME, MES, DE); environmental engineering (MS); environmental studies (MS). Part-time programs available. *Faculty:* 7 full-time (1 woman), 1 part-time/adjunct (0 women). *Students:* 34 full-time (6 women), 13 part-time (4 women); includes 5 minority (1 Black or African American, non-Hispanic/Latino; 3 Asian, non-Hispanic/Latino; 1 Hispanic/Latino), 34 international. Average age 28. 43 applicants, 84% accepted, 9 enrolled. In 2011, 30 master's, 3 doctorates awarded. *Degree requirements:* For master's, thesis optional; for doctorate, thesis/dissertation. *Entrance requirements:* For master's and doctorate, GRE General Test. Additional exam requirements/recommendations for international students: Required—TOEFL. *Application deadline:* For fall admission, 5/15 priority date for domestic students; for spring admission, 10/1 priority date for domestic students. Applications are processed on a rolling basis. Application fee: $25 ($50 for international students). *Expenses:* Tuition, state resident: full-time $5430; part-time $272 per credit hour. Tuition, nonresident: full-time $11,540; part-time $577 per credit hour. *Required fees:* $1916. *Financial support:* In 2011–12, 45 fellowships with partial tuition reimbursements (averaging $1,000 per year), 10 research assistantships with partial tuition reimbursements (averaging $7,200 per year), 3 teaching assistantships with partial tuition reimbursements (averaging $7,200 per year) were awarded; scholarships/grants and tuition waivers (partial) also available. Financial award application deadline: 4/1. *Faculty research:* Environmental remediations, construction productivity, geotechnical soil stabilization, lake/reservoir hydrodynamics, air pollution. *Unit head:* Dr. Enno Koehn, Chair, 409-880-8759, Fax: 409-880-8121, E-mail: koehneu@hal.lamar.edu. *Application contact:* Sandy Drane, Coordinator of Graduate Admissions, 409-880-8356, Fax: 409-880-8414, E-mail: gradmissions@hal.lamar.edu.

Lehigh University, P.C. Rossin College of Engineering and Applied Science, Department of Civil and Environmental Engineering, Bethlehem, PA 18015. Offers civil engineering (M Eng, MS, PhD); environmental engineering (MS, PhD); structural engineering (M Eng, MS, PhD). Part-time programs available. *Faculty:* 15 full-time (3 women), 2 part-time/adjunct (0 women). *Students:* 98 full-time (33 women), 11 part-time (0 women); includes 5 minority (1 Black or African American, non-Hispanic/Latino; 1 Asian, non-Hispanic/Latino; 3 Hispanic/Latino), 67 international. Average age 26. 655 applicants, 31% accepted, 25 enrolled. In 2011, 40 master's, 7 doctorates awarded. Terminal master's awarded for partial completion of doctoral program. *Degree requirements:* For master's, thesis (for some programs); for doctorate, comprehensive exam, thesis/dissertation. *Entrance requirements:* For master's and doctorate, GRE. Additional exam requirements/recommendations for international students: Required—TOEFL (minimum score 550 paper-based; 213 computer-based; 79 iBT). *Application deadline:* For fall admission, 7/15 priority date for domestic students, 7/15 for international students; for spring admission, 12/1 priority date for domestic students, 12/1 for international students. Applications are processed on a rolling basis. Application fee: $75. Electronic applications accepted. *Expenses:* Contact institution. *Financial support:* In 2011–12, 35 students received support, including 8 fellowships with full tuition reimbursements available (averaging $18,560 per year), 7 research assistantships with full tuition reimbursements available (averaging $22,350 per year), 7 teaching assistantships with full tuition reimbursements available (averaging $18,560 per year); institutionally sponsored loans, scholarships/grants, tuition waivers, and unspecified assistantships also available. Financial award application deadline: 1/15. *Faculty research:* Structural engineering, geotechnical engineering, water resources engineering, environmental engineering. *Total annual research expenditures:* $5.4 million. *Unit head:* Dr. Sibel Pamukcu, 610-758-3220, Fax: 610-758-6405, E-mail: sp01@lehigh.edu. *Application contact:* Prisca Vidanage, Graduate Coordinator, 610-758-3530, Fax: 610-758-6405, E-mail: pmv1@lehigh.edu. Web site: http://www.lehigh.edu/~incee/.

Louisiana State University and Agricultural and Mechanical College, Graduate School, College of Engineering, Department of Civil and Environmental Engineering, Baton Rouge, LA 70803. Offers environmental engineering (MSCE, PhD); geotechnical engineering (MSCE, PhD); structural engineering and mechanics (MSCE, PhD); transportation engineering (MSCE, PhD); water resources (MSCE, PhD). Part-time programs available. *Faculty:* 25 full-time (2 women). *Students:* 90 full-time (23 women), 34 part-time (8 women); includes 11 minority (4 Black or African American, non-Hispanic/Latino; 1 American Indian or Alaska Native, non-Hispanic/Latino; 4 Asian, non-Hispanic/Latino; 2 Hispanic/Latino), 73 international. Average age 30. 106 applicants, 67% accepted, 25 enrolled. In 2011, 32 master's, 4 doctorates awarded. *Degree requirements:* For master's, thesis optional; for doctorate, one foreign language, thesis/dissertation. *Entrance requirements:* For master's and doctorate, GRE General Test, minimum GPA of 3.0. Additional exam requirements/recommendations for international students: Required—TOEFL (minimum score 550 paper-based; 213 computer-based; 79 iBT) or IELTS (minimum score 6.5). *Application deadline:* For fall admission, 1/25 priority date for domestic students, 5/15 for international students; for spring admission, 10/15 for international students. Applications are processed on a rolling basis. Application fee: $50 ($70 for international students). Electronic applications accepted. *Financial support:* In 2011–12, 91 students received support, including 3 fellowships with full and partial tuition reimbursements available (averaging $18,050 per year), 72 research assistantships with full and partial tuition reimbursements available (averaging $15,942 per year), 6 teaching assistantships with full and partial tuition reimbursements available (averaging $12,469 per year); career-related internships or fieldwork, institutionally sponsored loans, scholarships/grants, and health care benefits also available. Financial award application deadline: 3/1; financial award applicants required to submit FAFSA. *Faculty research:* Mechanics and structures, environmental, geotechnical transportation, water resources. *Total annual research expenditures:* $3 million. *Unit head:* Dr. George Z. Voyiadjis, Chair/Professor, 225-578-8668, Fax: 225-578-9176, E-mail: voyiadjis@lsu.edu. *Application contact:* Dr. Clinton Willson, Professor, 225-578-8672, E-mail: cwillson@lsu.edu. Web site: http://www.cee.lsu.edu/.

Manhattan College, Graduate Division, School of Engineering, Program in Environmental Engineering, Riverdale, NY 10471. Offers ME, MS. *Accreditation:* ABET. Part-time and evening/weekend programs available. *Faculty:* 4 full-time (0 women), 1 part-time/adjunct (0 women). *Students:* 10 full-time (5 women), 18 part-time (8 women); includes 5 minority (1 Asian, non-Hispanic/Latino; 1 Hispanic/Latino; 3 Two or more races, non-Hispanic/Latino). Average age 25. 13 applicants, 92% accepted, 7 enrolled. In 2011, 10 master's awarded. *Degree requirements:* For master's, thesis optional. *Entrance requirements:* For master's, GRE (recommended), minimum GPA of 3.0. Additional exam requirements/recommendations for international students: Required—TOEFL (minimum score 550 paper-based; 213 computer-based; 80 iBT), IELTS (minimum score 6). *Application deadline:* For fall admission, 8/10 priority date for domestic students, 8/10 for international students; for spring admission, 1/7 for domestic and international students. Applications are processed on a rolling basis. Application fee: $50. *Expenses: Tuition:* Full-time $14,850; part-time $825 per credit. *Required fees:* $390; $150. *Financial support:* In 2011–12, 11 students received support, including 8 teaching assistantships with partial tuition reimbursements available (averaging $4,000 per year); career-related internships or fieldwork, scholarships/grants, tuition waivers (partial), unspecified assistantships, and laboratory assistantships also available. Support available to part-time students. Financial award application deadline: 3/1. *Faculty research:* Water quality modeling, environmental chemistry, air modeling, biological treatment, environmental chemistry. *Total annual research expenditures:* $400,000. *Unit head:* Dr. Robert Sharp, Graduate Program Director, 718-862-7169, Fax: 718-862-8035, E-mail: robert.sharp@manhattan.edu. *Application contact:* Janet Horgan, Information Contact, 718-862-7171, Fax: 718-862-8035, E-mail: janet.horgan@manhattan.edu. Web site: http://www.engineering.manhattan.edu.

Marquette University, Graduate School, College of Engineering, Department of Civil and Environmental Engineering, Milwaukee, WI 53201-1881. Offers construction and public works management (MS, PhD); construction engineering and management (Certificate); environmental/water resources engineering (MS, PhD); structural design (Certificate); structural/geotechnical engineering (MS, PhD); transportation planning and engineering (MS, PhD); waste and wastewater treatment processes (Certificate). Part-time and evening/weekend programs available. *Faculty:* 13 full-time (0 women), 5 part-time/adjunct (0 women). *Students:* 26 full-time (5 women), 11 part-time (0 women); includes 2 minority (1 Black or African American, non-Hispanic/Latino; 1 Asian, non-Hispanic/Latino), 12 international. Average age 27. 74 applicants, 62% accepted, 9 enrolled. In 2011, 6 master's, 3 doctorates awarded. Terminal master's awarded for partial completion of doctoral program. *Degree requirements:* For master's, comprehensive exam (for some programs), thesis or alternative; for doctorate, thesis/dissertation. *Entrance requirements:* For master's, GRE General Test (recommended), minimum GPA of 3.0, official transcripts from all current and previous colleges/universities except Marquette, three letters of recommendation; for doctorate, GRE General Test, minimum GPA of 3.0, official transcripts from all current and previous colleges/universities except Marquette, three letters of recommendation, brief statement of purpose, submission of any English language publications authored by applicant (strongly recommended). Additional exam requirements/recommendations for international students: Required—TOEFL (minimum score 530 paper-based; 78 computer-based). *Application deadline:* For fall admission, 6/1 priority date for domestic students. Applications are processed on a rolling basis. Application fee: $50. Electronic applications accepted. *Expenses: Tuition:* Full-time $17,010; part-time $945 per credit hour. Tuition and fees vary according to program. *Financial support:* In 2011–12, 21 students received support, including 6 fellowships with partial tuition reimbursements available (averaging $9,177 per year), 1 research assistantship with full tuition reimbursement available (averaging $13,745 per year), 7 teaching assistantships with full tuition reimbursements available (averaging $13,902 per year); scholarships/grants, health care benefits, tuition waivers (partial), and unspecified assistantships also available. Support available to part-time students. Financial award application deadline: 2/15. *Faculty research:* Highway safety, highway performance, and intelligent transportation systems; surface mount technology; watershed management. *Total annual research expenditures:* $826,608. *Unit head:* Dr. Thomas Wenzel, Chair, 414-288-7030, Fax: 414-288-7521, E-mail: thomas.wenzel@marquette.edu. *Application contact:* Dr. Stephen M. Heinrich, Director of Graduate Studies, 414-288-5466, E-mail: stephen.heinrich@marquette.edu. Web site: http://www.marquette.edu/engineering/pages/AllYouNeed/Civil_Environmental/civil.html.

Marshall University, Academic Affairs Division, College of Information Technology and Engineering, Weisberg Division of Engineering and Computer Science, Huntington, WV 25755. Offers engineering (MSE); information systems (MS). Part-time and evening/weekend programs available. *Faculty:* 10 full-time (1 woman), 3 part-time/adjunct (1 woman). *Students:* 15 full-time (3 women), 45 part-time (8 women); includes 5 minority (3 Black or African American, non-Hispanic/Latino; 2 Asian, non-Hispanic/Latino), 7 international. Average age 32. In 2011, 23 master's awarded. *Degree requirements:* For master's, final project, oral exam. *Entrance requirements:* For master's, GMAT or GRE General Test, minimum undergraduate GPA of 2.75. Application fee: $40. *Financial support:* Tuition waivers (full) available. Support available to part-time students. Financial award application deadline: 8/1; financial award applicants required to submit FAFSA. *Unit head:* Dr. Bill Pierson, Chair, 304-696-2695, E-mail: pierson@marshall.edu. *Application contact:* Information Contact, 304-746-1900, Fax: 304-746-1902, E-mail: services@marshall.edu. Web site: http://www.marshall.edu/cite/.

Massachusetts Institute of Technology, School of Engineering, Department of Civil and Environmental Engineering, Cambridge, MA 02139. Offers biological oceanography (PhD, Sc D); chemical oceanography (PhD, Sc D); civil and environmental engineering (PhD, Sc D); civil and environmental systems (PhD, Sc D); civil engineering (PhD, Sc D, CE); coastal engineering (PhD, Sc D); construction engineering and management (PhD, Sc D); environmental and water quality engineering (M Eng); environmental biology (PhD, Sc D); environmental chemistry (PhD, Sc D); environmental engineering (PhD, Sc D); environmental fluid mechanics (PhD, Sc D); environmental science and engineering (SM); geotechnical and geoenvironmental engineering (PhD, Sc D); geotechnology (M Eng); high-performance structures (M Eng); hydrology (PhD, Sc D); information technology (PhD, Sc D); mechanics (SM); oceanographic engineering (PhD, Sc D); structures and materials (PhD, Sc D); transportation (M Eng, PhD, Sc D); SM/MBA. *Faculty:* 35 full-time (6 women), 1 part-time/adjunct (0 women). *Students:* 216 full-time (80 women); includes 30 minority (4 Black or African American, non-Hispanic/Latino; 13 Asian, non-Hispanic/Latino; 8 Hispanic/Latino; 5 Two or more races, non-Hispanic/Latino), 110 international. Average age 27. 589 applicants, 26% accepted, 91 enrolled. In 2011, 62 master's, 14 doctorates awarded. *Degree requirements:* For master's and CE, thesis; for doctorate, comprehensive exam, thesis/dissertation. *Entrance requirements:* For master's and doctorate, GRE General Test. Additional exam requirements/recommendations for international students: Required—TOEFL (minimum score 577 paper-based; 233 computer-based; 90 iBT), IELTS (minimum score 7). *Application deadline:* For fall admission, 12/15 for domestic and international students. Application fee: $75. Electronic applications accepted. *Expenses: Tuition:* Full-time $40,460; part-time $630 per credit hour. *Required fees:* $272. *Financial support:* In 2011–12, 180 students received support, including 51 fellowships (averaging $30,800 per year), 110 research assistantships (averaging $29,500 per year), 19 teaching assistantships (averaging $29,500 per year); career-related internships or fieldwork, Federal Work-Study, institutionally sponsored loans, scholarships/grants, health care benefits, and unspecified assistantships also available. *Faculty research:* Environmental chemistry, environmental fluid mechanics and coastal engineering, environmental microbiology, geotechnical engineering and geomechanics, hydrology and hydroclimatology, infrastructure systems, mechanics of materials and structures, transportation systems. *Total annual research expenditures:* $17.7 million. *Unit head:* Prof. Andrew Whittle, Head, 617-253-7101. *Application contact:* Patricia Glidden, Graduate Admissions Coordinator, 617-253-7119, Fax: 617-258-6775, E-mail: cee-admissions@mit.edu. Web site: http://cee.mit.edu/.

McGill University, Faculty of Graduate and Postdoctoral Studies, Faculty of Engineering, Department of Chemical Engineering, Montréal, QC H3A 2T5, Canada. Offers chemical engineering (M Eng, PhD); environmental engineering (M Eng).

McGill University, Faculty of Graduate and Postdoctoral Studies, Faculty of Engineering, Department of Civil Engineering and Applied Mechanics, Montréal, QC H3A 2T5, Canada. Offers environmental engineering (M Eng, M Sc, PhD); fluid mechanics (M Sc); fluid mechanics and hydraulic engineering (M Eng, PhD); materials engineering (M Eng, PhD); rehabilitation of urban infrastructure (M Eng, PhD); soil behavior (M Eng, PhD); soil mechanics and foundations (M Eng, PhD); structures and structural mechanics (M Eng, PhD); water resources (M Sc); water resources engineering (M Eng, PhD).

Memorial University of Newfoundland, School of Graduate Studies, Interdisciplinary Program in Environmental Systems Engineering and Management, St. John's, NL A1C 5S7, Canada. Offers MA Sc. *Degree requirements:* For master's, project course. *Entrance requirements:* For master's, 2nd class engineering degree.

Mercer University, Graduate Studies, Macon Campus, School of Engineering, Macon, GA 31207-0003. Offers biomedical engineering (MSE); computer engineering (MSE); electrical engineering (MSE); engineering management (MSE); environmental engineering (MSE); environmental systems (MS); mechanical engineering (MSE); software engineering (MSE); software systems (MS); technical communications management (MS); technical management (MS). Part-time and evening/weekend programs available. Postbaccalaureate distance learning degree programs offered (no on-campus study). *Faculty:* 17 full-time (3 women), 1 part-time/adjunct (0 women). *Students:* 12 full-time (3 women), 113 part-time (28 women); includes 23 minority (13 Black or African American, non-Hispanic/Latino; 9 Asian, non-Hispanic/Latino; 1 Hispanic/Latino). Average age 31. In 2011, 44 master's awarded. *Degree requirements:* For master's, thesis or alternative. *Entrance requirements:* For master's, minimum undergraduate GPA of 3.0. Additional exam requirements/recommendations for international students: Required—TOEFL. *Application deadline:* For fall admission, 7/1 for domestic students; for spring admission, 11/15 for domestic students. Applications are processed on a rolling basis. Application fee: $35 ($50 for international students). Electronic applications accepted. *Expenses:* Contact institution. *Financial support:* Federal Work-Study available. *Unit head:* Dr. Wade H. Shaw, Dean, 478-301-2459, Fax: 478-301-5593, E-mail: shaw_wh@mercer.edu. *Application contact:* Greg Lofton, Graduate Program Coordinator, 478-301-5480, Fax: 478-301-5434, E-mail: lofton_g@mercer.edu. Web site: http://engineering.mercer.edu/.

Michigan State University, The Graduate School, College of Engineering, Department of Civil and Environmental Engineering, East Lansing, MI 48824. Offers civil engineering (MS, PhD); environmental engineering (MS, PhD); environmental engineering-environmental toxicology (PhD). Part-time programs available. *Entrance requirements:* Additional exam requirements/recommendations for international students: Required—TOEFL. Electronic applications accepted.

Michigan Technological University, Graduate School, College of Engineering, Department of Civil and Environmental Engineering, Houghton, MI 49931. Offers civil engineering (M Eng, MS, PhD); environmental engineering (M Eng, MS); environmental engineering science (MS). Part-time programs available. *Faculty:* 36 full-time (5 women), 8 part-time/adjunct (3 women). *Students:* 72 full-time (24 women), 10 part-time (5 women); includes 6 minority (1 Black or African American, non-Hispanic/Latino; 2 Asian, non-Hispanic/Latino; 3 Hispanic/Latino), 22 international. Average age 27. 258 applicants, 34% accepted, 20 enrolled. In 2011, 28 master's, 3 doctorates awarded. Terminal master's awarded for partial completion of doctoral program. *Degree requirements:* For master's, comprehensive exam (for some programs), thesis (for some programs); for doctorate, comprehensive exam, thesis/dissertation. *Entrance requirements:* For master's, GRE (to be considered for university assistantship), statement of purpose, official transcripts, 3 letters of recommendation; for doctorate, GRE, statement of purpose, official transcripts, 3 letters of recommendation. Additional exam requirements/recommendations for international students: Required—TOEFL (minimum score 100 iBT). *Application deadline:* Applications are processed on a rolling basis. Electronic applications accepted. *Expenses:* Contact institution. *Financial support:* In 2011–12, 75 students received support, including 3 fellowships with full tuition reimbursements available (averaging $6,065 per year), 20 research assistantships with full tuition reimbursements available (averaging $6,065 per year), 16 teaching assistantships with full tuition reimbursements available (averaging $6,065 per year); career-related internships or fieldwork, Federal Work-Study, scholarships/grants, health care benefits, tuition waivers, unspecified assistantships, and cooperative program also available. Financial award applicants required to submit FAFSA. *Faculty research:* Sustainable engineering, water resources, air quality, structural systems, transportation materials, construction, geotechnology. *Total annual research expenditures:* $2.4 million. *Unit head:* Dr. David Hand, Chair, 906-487-2777, Fax: 906-487-2943, E-mail: dwhand@mtu.edu. *Application contact:* Angela Keranen, Administrative Aide, 906-487-2520, Fax: 906-487-2943, E-mail: amkerane@mtu.edu. Web site: http://www.mtu.edu/cee/.

Michigan Technological University, Graduate School, Interdisciplinary Programs, Houghton, MI 49931. Offers atmospheric sciences (PhD); computational sciences and engineering (PhD); engineering - environmental (PhD). *Students:* 28 full-time (14 women), 4 part-time (0 women), 20 international. Average age 29. 73 applicants, 32% accepted, 10 enrolled. In 2011, 3 doctorates awarded. *Degree requirements:* For doctorate, comprehensive exam, thesis/dissertation. *Entrance requirements:* For doctorate, GRE, statement of purpose, official transcripts, 3 letters of recommendation. Additional exam requirements/recommendations for international students: Required—TOEFL or IELTS. *Expenses:* Tuition, state resident: full-time $12,636; part-time $702 per credit. Tuition, nonresident: full-time $12,636; part-time $702 per credit. *Required fees:* $226; $226 per year. *Financial support:* In 2011–12, 28 students received support, including 3 fellowships with full tuition reimbursements available (averaging $6,065 per year), 17 research assistantships with full tuition reimbursements available (averaging $6,065 per year), 3 teaching assistantships with full tuition reimbursements available (averaging $6,065 per year). *Unit head:* Dr. Jacqueline E. Huntoon, Dean, 906-487-2327, Fax: 906-487-2463, E-mail: jeh@mtu.edu. *Application contact:* Carol T. Wingerson, Senior Staff Assistant, 906-487-2327, Fax: 906-487-2463, E-mail: gradadms@mtu.edu.

Milwaukee School of Engineering, Civil and Architectural Engineering and Construction Management Department, Program in Environmental Engineering, Milwaukee, WI 53202-3109. Offers MS. Part-time and evening/weekend programs available. *Faculty:* 2 full-time (1 woman), 5 part-time/adjunct (0 women). *Students:* 1 full-time (0 women), 8 part-time (4 women). Average age 23. 6 applicants, 100% accepted, 3 enrolled. In 2011, 3 master's awarded. *Degree requirements:* For master's, thesis, design project. *Entrance requirements:* For master's, GRE General Test or GMAT, 2 letters of recommendation; BS in architectural, chemical, civil or mechanical engineering or a related field. Additional exam requirements/recommendations for international students: Required—TOEFL (minimum score 79 iBT) or IELTS. *Application deadline:* Applications are processed on a rolling basis. Electronic applications accepted. Application fee is waived when completed online. *Expenses: Tuition:* Full-time $17,550; part-time $650 per credit hour. *Financial support:* In 2011–12, 5 students received support. Career-related internships or fieldwork available. Support available to part-time students. Financial award applicants required to submit FAFSA. *Faculty research:* Environmental systems. *Unit head:* Dr. Francis Manhuta, Director, 414-277-7599. *Application contact:* Katie Gassenhuber, Graduate Program Associate, 800-321-6763, Fax: 414-277-7208, E-mail: gassenhuber@msoe.edu.

Missouri University of Science and Technology, Graduate School, Department of Civil, Architectural, and Environmental Engineering, Rolla, MO 65409. Offers civil engineering (MS, DE, PhD); construction engineering (MS, DE, PhD); environmental engineering (MS); fluid mechanics (MS, DE, PhD); geotechnical engineering (MS, DE, PhD); hydrology and hydraulic engineering (MS, DE, PhD). Part-time and evening/weekend programs available. Terminal master's awarded for partial completion of doctoral program. *Degree requirements:* For master's, thesis optional; for doctorate, comprehensive exam, thesis/dissertation. *Entrance requirements:* For master's, GRE General Test (minimum combined score 1100), minimum GPA of 3.0; for doctorate, GRE General Test (minimum score: verbal and quantitative 400, writing 3.5), minimum GPA of 3.0. Additional exam requirements/recommendations for international students: Required—TOEFL. Electronic applications accepted. *Faculty research:* Earthquake engineering, structural optimization and control systems, structural health monitoring/damage detection, soil-structure interaction, soil mechanics and foundation engineering.

Montana State University, College of Graduate Studies, College of Engineering, Department of Chemical and Biological Engineering, Bozeman, MT 59717. Offers chemical engineering (MS); engineering (PhD), including chemical engineering option, environmental engineering option; environmental engineering (MS). Part-time programs available. *Degree requirements:* For master's, comprehensive exam, thesis (for some programs); for doctorate, comprehensive exam, thesis/dissertation. *Entrance requirements:* For master's and doctorate, GRE General Test. Additional exam requirements/recommendations for international students: Required—TOEFL (minimum score 550 paper-based; 213 computer-based). Electronic applications accepted. *Faculty research:* Biofuels, extremophilic bioprocessing, and situ biocatalyzed heavy metal transformations; metabolic network analysis and engineering; magnetic resonance microscopy; modeling of biological systems; the development of protective coatings on planar solid oxide fuel cell (SOFC) metallic interconnects; characterizing corrosion mechanisms of materials in precisely-controlled exposures; testing materials in poly-crystalline silicon production environments; environmental biotechnology and bioremediation.

Montana Tech of The University of Montana, Graduate School, Department of Environmental Engineering, Butte, MT 59701-8997. Offers MS. Part-time programs available. *Faculty:* 7 full-time (2 women). *Students:* 3 full-time (2 women), 1 part-time (0 women). 2 applicants, 50% accepted, 0 enrolled. In 2011, 4 master's awarded. *Degree requirements:* For master's, thesis. *Entrance requirements:* For master's, GRE General Test, minimum GPA of 3.0. Additional exam requirements/recommendations for international students: Required—TOEFL (minimum score 525 paper-based; 195 computer-based; 71 iBT). *Application deadline:* For fall admission, 4/1 priority date for domestic students, 3/1 for international students; for spring admission, 10/1 priority date for domestic students, 7/1 for international students. Applications are processed on a rolling basis. Application fee: $30. Electronic applications accepted. *Financial support:* In 2011–12, 3 students received support, including 4 teaching assistantships with partial tuition reimbursements available (averaging $4,000 per year); research assistantships with full tuition reimbursements available, career-related internships or fieldwork, tuition waivers (full and partial), and unspecified assistantships also available. Financial award application deadline: 4/1; financial award applicants required to submit FAFSA. *Faculty research:* Mine waste reclamation, modeling, air pollution control, wetlands, water pollution control. *Unit head:* Dr. Kumar Ganesan, Head, 406-496-4239, Fax: 406-496-4650, E-mail: kganesan@mtech.edu. *Application contact:* Fred Sullivan, Administrator, Graduate School, 406-496-4304, Fax: 406-496-4710, E-mail: fsullivan@mtech.edu. Web site: http://www.mtech.edu/academics/gradschool/degreeprograms/degrees-environmental-engineering.htm.

National University, Academic Affairs, School of Engineering, Technology and Media, Department of Applied Engineering, La Jolla, CA 92037-1011. Offers engineering management (MS); environmental engineering (MS); homeland security and safety engineering (MS); project management (Certificate); security and safety engineering (Certificate); sustainability management (MS); wireless communications (MS). Part-time and evening/weekend programs available. Postbaccalaureate distance learning degree programs offered (no on-campus study). *Degree requirements:* For master's, thesis. *Entrance requirements:* For master's, interview, minimum GPA of 2.5. Additional exam requirements/recommendations for international students: Required—TOEFL (minimum score 550 paper-based; 213 computer-based; 79 iBT), IELTS (minimum score 6). *Application deadline:* Applications are processed on a rolling basis. Application fee: $60 ($65 for international students). Electronic applications accepted. *Financial support:* Career-related internships or fieldwork, institutionally sponsored loans, scholarships/grants, and tuition waivers (partial) available. Support available to part-time students. Financial award application deadline: 6/30; financial award applicants required to submit FAFSA. *Unit head:* Dr. Shekar Viswanathan, Chair and Associate Professor, 858-309-3416, Fax: 858-309-3420, E-mail: sviswana@nu.edu. *Application contact:* Dominick Giovanniello, Associate Regional Dean, 800-NAT-UNIV, Fax: 858-541-7792, E-mail: dgiovann@nu.edu. Web site: http://www.nu.edu/OurPrograms/SchoolOfEngineeringAndTechnology/AppliedEngineering.html.

New Jersey Institute of Technology, Office of Graduate Studies, Newark College of Engineering, Department of Civil and Environmental Engineering, Program in Environmental Engineering, Newark, NJ 07102. Offers MS, PhD. Part-time and evening/weekend programs available. *Students:* 22 full-time (9 women), 17 part-time (10 women); includes 11 minority (3 Black or African American, non-Hispanic/Latino; 4 Asian, non-Hispanic/Latino; 4 Hispanic/Latino), 17 international. Average age 29. 77 applicants, 68% accepted, 10 enrolled. In 2011, 6 master's awarded. Terminal master's awarded for partial completion of doctoral program. *Degree requirements:* For master's, thesis or alternative; for doctorate, thesis/dissertation, residency. *Entrance requirements:* For master's, GRE General Test; for doctorate, GRE General Test, minimum graduate GPA of 3.5. Additional exam requirements/recommendations for international students: Required—TOEFL (minimum score 550 paper-based; 213 computer-based; 79 iBT). *Application deadline:* For fall admission, 6/5 priority date for domestic students, 5/1 for international students; for spring admission, 11/15 priority date for domestic students, 11/15 for international students. Applications are processed on a rolling basis. Application fee: $65. Electronic applications accepted. *Expenses:* Tuition, state resident: full-time $7980; part-time $867 per credit. Tuition, nonresident: full-time $11,336; part-time $1196 per credit. *Required fees:* $230 per credit. *Financial support:* Fellowships with full and partial tuition reimbursements, research assistantships with full and partial tuition reimbursements, teaching assistantships with full and partial tuition reimbursements, career-related internships or fieldwork, Federal Work-Study, institutionally sponsored loans, and unspecified assistantships available. Financial award application deadline: 1/15. *Faculty research:* Water resources engineering, solid and hazardous waste management. *Unit head:* Dr. Taha F. Marhaba, Chair, 973-642-4599, E-mail: taha.f.marhaba@njit.edu. *Application contact:* Kathryn Kelly, Director of Admissions, 973-596-3300, Fax: 973-596-3461, E-mail: admissions@njit.edu.

New Mexico Institute of Mining and Technology, Graduate Studies, Department of Civil and Environmental Engineering, Socorro, NM 87801. Offers environmental engineering (MS), including air quality engineering and science, hazardous waste engineering, water quality engineering and science. *Faculty:* 6 full-time (2 women), 2 part-time/adjunct (0 women). *Students:* 6 full-time (3 women); includes 3 minority (1 Black or African American, non-Hispanic/Latino; 1 American Indian or Alaska Native, non-Hispanic/Latino; 1 Hispanic/Latino). Average age 27. 14 applicants, 50% accepted, 3 enrolled. In 2011, 3 master's awarded. *Degree requirements:* For master's, thesis. *Entrance requirements:* For master's, GRE General Test. Additional exam requirements/recommendations for international students: Required—TOEFL (minimum score 540 paper-based; 207 computer-based). *Application deadline:* For fall admission, 3/1 priority date for domestic students; for spring admission, 6/1 for domestic students. Applications are processed on a rolling basis. Application fee: $16 ($30 for international students). *Expenses:* Tuition, state resident: full-time $4849; part-time $269.41 per credit hour. Tuition, nonresident: full-time $16,041; part-time $891.15 per credit hour. *Required fees:* $622; $65 per credit hour. $20 per semester. Part-time tuition and fees vary according to course load. *Financial support:* In 2011–12, 1 fellowship (averaging $7,200 per year), 3 research assistantships (averaging $10,958 per year), 4 teaching assistantships with full and partial tuition reimbursements (averaging $9,350 per year) were awarded; Federal Work-Study, institutionally sponsored loans, and unspecified assistantships also available. Financial award application deadline: 3/1; financial award applicants required to submit CSS PROFILE or FAFSA. *Faculty research:* Air quality, hazardous waste management, wastewater management and treatment, site remediation. *Unit head:* Dr. Mark Cal, Chair, 575-835-5059, Fax: 575-835-5252, E-mail: mcal@nmt.edu. *Application contact:* Dr. Lorie Liebrock, Dean of Graduate Studies, 575-835-5513, Fax: 575-835-5476, E-mail: graduate@nmt.edu. Web site: http://www.nmt.edu/~enve/.

New Mexico State University, Graduate School, College of Engineering, Department of Civil Engineering, Las Cruces, NM 88003-8001. Offers civil engineering (MSCE, PhD); environmental engineering (MS Env E). Part-time programs available. Postbaccalaureate distance learning degree programs offered. *Faculty:* 13 full-time (2 women). *Students:* 53 full-time (18 women), 13 part-time (3 women); includes 22 minority (3 American Indian or Alaska Native, non-Hispanic/Latino; 18 Hispanic/Latino; 1 Two or more races, non-Hispanic/Latino), 26 international. Average age 29. 33 applicants, 52% accepted, 11 enrolled. In 2011, 15 master's, 2 doctorates awarded. *Degree requirements:* For master's, thesis (for some programs); for doctorate, comprehensive exam (for some programs), thesis/dissertation. *Entrance requirements:* For master's, BS in engineering, minimum GPA of 3.0; for doctorate, qualifying exam, BS in engineering, minimum GPA of 3.0. Additional exam requirements/recommendations for international students: Required—TOEFL (minimum score 550 paper-based; 213 computer-based; 79 iBT), IELTS (minimum score 6). *Application deadline:* For fall admission, 4/1 priority date for domestic students, 4/1 for international students; for spring admission, 9/1 priority date for domestic students, 9/1 for international students. Applications are processed on a rolling basis. Application fee: $40 ($50 for international students). Electronic applications accepted. *Expenses:* Tuition, state resident: full-time $5004; part-time $208.50 per credit. Tuition, nonresident: full-time $17,446; part-time $726.90 per credit. *Financial support:* In 2011–12, 45 students received support, including 9 fellowships (averaging $3,710 per year), 21 research assistantships (averaging $16,842 per year), 25 teaching assistantships (averaging $17,894 per year); career-related internships or fieldwork, Federal Work-Study, and health care benefits also available. Support available to part-time students. Financial award application deadline: 3/1. *Faculty research:* Structural engineering, water resources engineering, environmental engineering, geotechnical engineering, hydraulics/hydrology. *Unit head:* Dr. Adrian Hanson, Interim Head, 575-646-3801, E-mail: athanson@nmsu.edu. *Application contact:* Coordinator, 575-646-2736, Fax: 575-646-7721, E-mail: gradinfo@nmsu.edu. Web site: http://cagesun.nmsu.edu/.

New York Institute of Technology, Graduate Division, School of Engineering and Computing Sciences, Program in Environmental Technology, Old Westbury, NY 11568-8000. Offers MS. Part-time and evening/weekend programs available. *Students:* 19 full-time (7 women), 30 part-time (10 women); includes 11 minority (4 Black or African American, non-Hispanic/Latino; 3 Asian, non-Hispanic/Latino; 4 Hispanic/Latino), 23 international. Average age 29. In 2011, 15 master's awarded. *Degree requirements:* For master's, thesis or alternative. *Entrance requirements:* For master's, minimum QPA of 2.85. Additional exam requirements/recommendations for international students: Required—TOEFL (minimum score 550 paper-based; 213 computer-based). *Application deadline:* For fall admission, 7/1 priority date for domestic students; for spring admission, 12/1 priority date for domestic students. Applications are processed on a rolling basis. Application fee: $50. Electronic applications accepted. *Expenses: Tuition:* Part-time $930 per credit hour. *Financial support:* Fellowships, research assistantships with partial tuition reimbursements, career-related internships or fieldwork, institutionally sponsored loans, tuition waivers (full and partial), and unspecified assistantships available. Support available to part-time students. Financial award applicants required to submit FAFSA. *Faculty research:* Development and testing of methodology to assess health risks and environmental impacts from separate sanitary sewage, introduction of technology innovation (including geographical information systems). *Unit head:* Stanley Greenwald, Department Chair, 516-686-7717, Fax: 516-686-7919, E-mail: sgreenwa@nyit.edu. *Application contact:* Dr. Jacquelyn Nealon, Vice President for Enrollment Services, 516-686-7925, Fax: 516-686-7597, E-mail: jnealon@nyit.edu.

North Dakota State University, College of Graduate and Interdisciplinary Studies, College of Engineering and Architecture, Department of Civil Engineering, Fargo, ND 58108. Offers civil engineering (MS, PhD); environmental engineering (MS, PhD); transportation and logistics (PhD). PhD in transportation and logistics offered jointly with Upper Great Plains Transportation Institute. Part-time programs available. Postbaccalaureate distance learning degree programs offered (minimal on-campus study). *Faculty:* 13 full-time (1 woman). *Students:* 25 full-time (2 women), 19 part-time (3 women); includes 3 minority (1 American Indian or Alaska Native, non-Hispanic/Latino; 2 Two or more races, non-Hispanic/Latino), 21 international. 46 applicants, 48% accepted, 8 enrolled. In 2011, 8 master's, 3 doctorates awarded. *Degree requirements:* For master's, thesis; for doctorate, comprehensive exam, thesis/dissertation. *Entrance requirements:* Additional exam requirements/recommendations for international students: Required—TOEFL (minimum score 525 paper-based; 197 computer-based; 71 iBT). *Application deadline:* For fall admission, 2/15 priority date for domestic students, 2/15 for international students; for spring admission, 9/15 priority date for domestic students, 9/15 for international students. Applications are processed on a rolling basis. Application fee: $35. Electronic applications accepted. *Financial support:* Fellowships with full tuition reimbursements, research assistantships with full tuition reimbursements, teaching assistantships with full tuition reimbursements, career-related internships or fieldwork, Federal Work-Study, and institutionally sponsored loans available. Support available to part-time students. Financial award application deadline: 1/15. *Faculty research:* Wastewater, solid waste, composites, nanotechnology. *Unit head:* Dr. Eakalak Khan, Chair, 701-231-7244, Fax: 701-231-6185, E-mail: eakalak.khan@ndsu.edu. *Application contact:* Dr. Kalpana Katti, Professor and Graduate Program Coordinator, 701-231-9504, Fax: 701-231-6185, E-mail: kalpana.katti@ndsu.edu. Web site: http://www.ce.ndsu.nodak.edu/.

Northeastern University, College of Engineering, Department of Civil and Environmental Engineering, Boston, MA 02115-5096. Offers MS, PhD. Part-time programs available. *Faculty:* 15 full-time, 2 part-time/adjunct. *Students:* 97 full-time (41 women), 38 part-time (14 women). 286 applicants, 67% accepted, 56 enrolled. In 2011, 23 master's, 3 doctorates awarded. *Degree requirements:* For master's, thesis optional; for doctorate, thesis/dissertation, departmental qualifying exam. *Entrance requirements:* For master's and doctorate, GRE General Test. Additional exam requirements/recommendations for international students: Required—TOEFL (minimum score 550 paper-based; 213 computer-based; 80 iBT). *Application deadline:* For fall admission, 1/15 priority date for domestic students, 1/15 for international students. Applications are processed on a rolling basis. Application fee: $50. Electronic applications accepted. *Financial support:* In 2011–12, 33 students received support, including 21 research assistantships with full tuition reimbursements available (averaging $18,325 per year), 16 teaching assistantships with full tuition reimbursements available (averaging $18,325 per year); career-related internships or fieldwork, Federal Work-Study, scholarships/grants, tuition waivers (full), and unspecified assistantships also available. Support available to part-time students. Financial award application deadline: 1/15; financial award applicants required to submit FAFSA. *Faculty research:* Earthquake engineering, geotechnical and geoenvironmental engineering, structural engineering, transportation engineering, environmental engineering. *Unit head:* Dr. Jerome Jaffar, Chairman, 617-373-2444, Fax: 617-373-4419. *Application contact:* Jeffery Hengel, Admissions Specialist, 617-373-2711, Fax: 617-373-2501, E-mail: grad-eng@coe.neu.edu. Web site: http://www.coe.neu.edu/.

Northern Arizona University, Graduate College, College of Engineering, Forestry and Natural Sciences, Programs in Engineering, Flagstaff , AZ 86011. Offers civil and environmental engineering (M Eng); civil engineering (MSE); computer science (MSE); electrical engineering (M Eng, MSE); engineering (M Eng, MSE); environmental engineering (M Eng, MSE); mechanical engineering (M Eng, MSE). Part-time programs available. Postbaccalaureate distance learning degree programs offered (no on-campus study). *Faculty:* 42 full-time (10 women). *Students:* 15 full-time (1 woman), 12 part-time (1 woman); includes 2 minority (both Hispanic/Latino), 6 international. Average age 28. 29 applicants, 52% accepted, 8 enrolled. In 2011, 15 degrees awarded. *Degree requirements:* For master's, thesis. *Entrance requirements:* For master's, GRE General Test. Additional exam requirements/recommendations for international students: Required—TOEFL (minimum score 550 paper-based; 213 computer-based; 80 iBT), IELTS (minimum score 7). *Application deadline:* For fall admission, 3/1 priority date for domestic students, 3/1 for international students; for spring admission, 9/15 priority date for domestic students, 9/15 for international students. Applications are processed on a rolling basis. Application fee: $65. Electronic applications accepted. *Expenses:* Tuition, state resident: full-time $7190; part-time $355 per credit hour. Tuition, nonresident: full-time $18,092; part-time $1005 per credit hour. *Required fees:* $818; $328 per semester. *Financial support:* In 2011–12, 3 research assistantships with partial tuition reimbursements (averaging $14,541 per year), 12 teaching assistantships with partial tuition reimbursements (averaging $12,863 per year) were awarded; career-related internships or fieldwork, Federal Work-Study, scholarships/grants, health care benefits, and unspecified assistantships also available. Financial award applicants required to submit FAFSA. *Unit head:* Dr. Ernesto Penado, Chair, 928-523-9453, Fax: 928-523-2300, E-mail: ernesto.penado@nau.edu. *Application contact:* Natasha Kypfer, Program Coordinator, 928-523-1447, Fax: 928-523-2300, E-mail: egrmasters@nau.edu. Web site: http://nau.edu/CEFNS/Engineering/.

Northwestern University, McCormick School of Engineering and Applied Science, Department of Civil and Environmental Engineering, Evanston, IL 60208-3109. Offers environmental engineering and science (MS, PhD); geotechnical engineering (MS, PhD); mechanics of materials and solids (MS, PhD); project management (MS, PhD); structural engineering and materials (MS, PhD); theoretical and applied mechanics (MS, PhD), including fluid mechanics, solid mechanics; transportation systems analysis and planning (MS, PhD). MS and PhD admissions and degrees offered through The Graduate School. Part-time programs available. Terminal master's awarded for partial completion of doctoral program. *Degree requirements:* For master's, thesis (for some programs); for doctorate, thesis/dissertation. *Entrance requirements:* For master's and doctorate, GRE General Test, minimum 2 letters of recommendation, transcripts from all academic institutions attended. Additional exam requirements/recommendations for international students: Required—TOEFL (minimum score 600 paper-based; 250 computer-based; 100 iBT), IELTS (minimum score 7). Electronic applications accepted. *Faculty research:* Environmental engineering and science, geotechnics, mechanics of materials and solids, structural engineering and materials, transportation systems analysis and planning.

Norwich University, College of Graduate and Continuing Studies, Master of Civil Engineering Program, Northfield, VT 05663. Offers construction management (MCE); environmental water resources (MCE); geo-technical (MCE); structural (MCE). Evening/weekend programs available. *Faculty:* 12 part-time/adjunct (1 woman). *Students:* 88 full-time (23 women); includes 15 minority (8 Black or African American, non-Hispanic/Latino; 1 American Indian or Alaska Native, non-Hispanic/Latino; 4 Asian, non-Hispanic/Latino; 2 Hispanic/Latino). Average age 33. In 2011, 44 master's awarded. *Entrance requirements:* For master's, minimum GPA of 2.75. Additional exam requirements/recommendations for international students: Required—TOEFL (minimum score 550 paper-based; 213 computer-based; 83 iBT). *Application deadline:* For fall admission, 8/10 for domestic and international students; for spring admission, 2/6 for domestic and international students. Applications are processed on a rolling basis. Application fee: $50. Electronic applications accepted. *Expenses: Tuition:* Full-time $16,174. *Required fees:* $2130. Full-time tuition and fees vary according to program. *Financial support:* In 2011–12, 5 students received support. Scholarships/grants available. Financial award applicants required to submit FAFSA. *Unit head:* Dr. Thomas Descoteaux, Program Director, 802-485-2730, Fax: 802-485-2533, E-mail: tdescote@norwich.edu. *Application contact:* Rija Ramahatra, Associate Program Director, 802-485-2892, Fax: 802-485-2533, E-mail: ramahatr@norwich.edu. Web site: http://mce.norwich.edu.

Ohio University, Graduate College, Russ College of Engineering and Technology, Department of Civil Engineering, Athens, OH 45701-2979. Offers civil engineering (PhD); construction (MS); environmental (MS); geotechnical and geoenvironmental

(MS); mechanics (MS); structures (MS); transportation (MS); water resources and structures (MS). Part-time programs available. *Students:* 32 full-time (6 women), 7 part-time (2 women); includes 3 minority (1 Hispanic/Latino; 2 Two or more races, non-Hispanic/Latino), 13 international. 52 applicants, 52% accepted, 4 enrolled. In 2011, 10 degrees awarded. *Degree requirements:* For master's, comprehensive exam (for some programs), thesis or alternative; for doctorate, comprehensive exam, thesis/dissertation. *Entrance requirements:* For master's, GRE General Test, minimum GPA of 3.0, 3 letters of recommendation; for doctorate, GRE General Test. Additional exam requirements/recommendations for international students: Required—TOEFL (minimum score 550 paper-based; 80 iBT) or IELTS (minimum score 6.5). *Application deadline:* For fall admission, 5/1 priority date for domestic students, 2/1 for international students; for winter admission, 8/1 priority date for domestic students, 4/1 for international students; for spring admission, 2/1 priority date for domestic students, 7/1 for international students. Applications are processed on a rolling basis. Application fee: $50 ($55 for international students). Electronic applications accepted. *Financial support:* Research assistantships with full tuition reimbursements, teaching assistantships with full tuition reimbursements, Federal Work-Study, institutionally sponsored loans, scholarships/grants, and unspecified assistantships available. Financial award application deadline: 3/15; financial award applicants required to submit FAFSA. *Faculty research:* Noise abatement, materials and environment, highway infrastructure, subsurface investigation (pavements, pipes, bridges). *Unit head:* Dr. Gayle F. Mitchell, Chair, 740-593-0430, Fax: 740-593-0625, E-mail: mitchelg@ohio.edu. *Application contact:* Dr. Shad M. Sargand, Graduate Chair, 740-593-1465, Fax: 740-593-0625, E-mail: sargand@ohio.edu. Web site: http://www.ohio.edu/civil/.

Oklahoma State University, College of Agricultural Science and Natural Resources, Department of Biosystems and Agricultural Engineering, Stillwater, OK 74078. Offers biosystems engineering (MS, PhD); environmental and natural resources (MS, PhD). *Faculty:* 22 full-time (3 women), 3 part-time/adjunct (0 women). *Students:* 18 full-time (6 women), 50 part-time (21 women); includes 7 minority (1 Black or African American, non-Hispanic/Latino; 1 American Indian or Alaska Native, non-Hispanic/Latino; 1 Asian, non-Hispanic/Latino; 2 Hispanic/Latino; 2 Two or more races, non-Hispanic/Latino), 35 international. Average age 31. 57 applicants, 23% accepted, 3 enrolled. In 2011, 6 master's, 4 doctorates awarded. *Degree requirements:* For master's, thesis; for doctorate, comprehensive exam, thesis/dissertation. *Entrance requirements:* For master's and doctorate, GRE or GMAT. Additional exam requirements/recommendations for international students: Required—TOEFL (minimum score 550 paper-based; 79 iBT). *Application deadline:* For fall admission, 3/1 for international students; for spring admission, 8/1 for international students. Applications are processed on a rolling basis. Application fee: $40 ($75 for international students). Electronic applications accepted. *Expenses:* Tuition, state resident: full-time $4044; part-time $168.50 per credit hour. Tuition, nonresident: full-time $16,008; part-time $667 per credit hour. *Required fees:* $2122; $88.45 per credit hour. One-time fee: $50. Tuition and fees vary according to course load and campus/location. *Financial support:* In 2011–12, 43 research assistantships (averaging $17,505 per year) were awarded; teaching assistantships, career-related internships or fieldwork, Federal Work-Study, scholarships/grants, health care benefits, tuition waivers (partial), and unspecified assistantships also available. Support available to part-time students. Financial award application deadline: 3/1; financial award applicants required to submit FAFSA. *Unit head:* Dr. Daniel Thomas, Head, 405-744-5431, Fax: 405-744-6059. *Application contact:* Dr. Sheryl Tucker, Dean, 405-744-7099, Fax: 405-744-0355, E-mail: grad-i@okstate.edu. Web site: http://bioen.okstate.edu/.

Oklahoma State University, College of Engineering, Architecture and Technology, School of Civil and Environmental Engineering, Stillwater, OK 74078. Offers civil engineering (MS); environmental engineering (PhD). *Faculty:* 15 full-time (1 woman), 5 part-time/adjunct (0 women). *Students:* 41 full-time (17 women), 41 part-time (7 women); includes 10 minority (2 Black or African American, non-Hispanic/Latino; 2 American Indian or Alaska Native, non-Hispanic/Latino; 2 Asian, non-Hispanic/Latino; 1 Hispanic/Latino; 3 Two or more races, non-Hispanic/Latino), 44 international. Average age 29. 118 applicants, 37% accepted, 18 enrolled. In 2011, 30 master's, 1 doctorate awarded. *Degree requirements:* For master's, thesis or alternative; for doctorate, comprehensive exam, thesis/dissertation. *Entrance requirements:* For master's and doctorate, GRE or GMAT. Additional exam requirements/recommendations for international students: Required—TOEFL (minimum score 550 paper-based; 79 iBT). *Application deadline:* For fall admission, 3/1 for international students; for spring admission, 8/1 for international students. Applications are processed on a rolling basis. Application fee: $40 ($75 for international students). Electronic applications accepted. *Expenses:* Tuition, state resident: full-time $4044; part-time $168.50 per credit hour. Tuition, nonresident: full-time $16,008; part-time $667 per credit hour. *Required fees:* $2122; $88.45 per credit hour. One-time fee: $50. Tuition and fees vary according to course load and campus/location. *Financial support:* In 2011–12, 28 research assistantships (averaging $13,317 per year), 14 teaching assistantships (averaging $9,013 per year) were awarded; career-related internships or fieldwork, Federal Work-Study, scholarships/grants, health care benefits, tuition waivers (partial), and unspecified assistantships also available. Support available to part-time students. Financial award application deadline: 3/1; financial award applicants required to submit FAFSA. *Unit head:* Dr. John Veenstra, Head, 405-744-5190, Fax: 405-744-7554. *Application contact:* Dr. Sheryl Tucker, Dean, 405-744-7099, Fax: 405-744-0355, E-mail: grad-i@okstate.edu. Web site: http://cive.okstate.edu.

Old Dominion University, Frank Batten College of Engineering and Technology, Program in Civil and Environmental Engineering, Norfolk, VA 23529. Offers D Eng, PhD. Part-time and evening/weekend programs available. Postbaccalaureate distance learning degree programs offered (minimal on-campus study). *Faculty:* 13 full-time (1 woman), 7 part-time/adjunct (0 women). *Students:* 6 full-time (1 woman), 6 part-time (0 women), 5 international. Average age 39. 12 applicants, 100% accepted, 2 enrolled. In 2011, 1 doctorate awarded. *Degree requirements:* For doctorate, thesis/dissertation, candidacy exam. *Entrance requirements:* For doctorate, GRE, minimum GPA of 3.5. Additional exam requirements/recommendations for international students: Required—TOEFL (minimum score 550 paper-based; 213 computer-based; 80 iBT). *Application deadline:* For fall admission, 6/1 priority date for domestic students, 4/15 for international students; for spring admission, 11/1 priority date for domestic students, 10/1 for international students. Applications are processed on a rolling basis. Application fee: $50. Electronic applications accepted. *Expenses:* Tuition, state resident: full-time $9096; part-time $379 per credit. Tuition, nonresident: full-time $23,064; part-time $961 per credit. *Required fees:* $127 per semester. One-time fee: $50. *Financial support:* In 2011–12, 10 research assistantships with full and partial tuition reimbursements (averaging $15,439 per year), 8 teaching assistantships with full and partial tuition reimbursements (averaging $14,244 per year) were awarded; scholarships/grants and unspecified assistantships also available. Support available to part-time students. Financial award application deadline: 4/1. *Faculty research:* Structural engineering, coastal engineering, environmental engineering, geotechnical engineering, water

resources, transportation engineering. *Total annual research expenditures:* $557,751. *Unit head:* Dr. Isao Ishibashi, Graduate Program Director, 757-683-4641, Fax: 757-683-5354, E-mail: cegpd@odu.edu. *Application contact:* Dr. Linda Vahala, Associate Dean, 757-683-3789, Fax: 757-683-4898, E-mail: lvahala@odu.edu. Web site: http://eng.odu.edu/cee/.

Old Dominion University, Frank Batten College of Engineering and Technology, Program in Environmental Engineering, Norfolk, VA 23529. Offers ME, MS. Part-time and evening/weekend programs available. Postbaccalaureate distance learning degree programs offered (minimal on-campus study). *Faculty:* 13 full-time (1 woman), 7 part-time/adjunct (0 women). *Students:* 9 full-time (4 women), 28 part-time (12 women); includes 4 minority (2 Black or African American, non-Hispanic/Latino; 1 American Indian or Alaska Native, non-Hispanic/Latino; 1 Native Hawaiian or other Pacific Islander, non-Hispanic/Latino), 6 international. Average age 30. 18 applicants, 83% accepted, 7 enrolled. In 2011, 7 master's awarded. *Degree requirements:* For master's, comprehensive exam, thesis optional. *Entrance requirements:* For master's, GRE, minimum GPA of 3.0. Additional exam requirements/recommendations for international students: Required—TOEFL (minimum score 550 paper-based; 213 computer-based; 80 iBT). *Application deadline:* For fall admission, 6/1 priority date for domestic students, 4/15 for international students; for spring admission, 11/1 priority date for domestic students, 10/1 for international students. Applications are processed on a rolling basis. Application fee: $50. Electronic applications accepted. *Expenses:* Tuition, state resident: full-time $9096; part-time $379 per credit. Tuition, nonresident: full-time $23,064; part-time $961 per credit. *Required fees:* $127 per semester. One-time fee: $50. *Financial support:* In 2011–12, 3 research assistantships with partial tuition reimbursements (averaging $12,050 per year), 1 teaching assistantship with partial tuition reimbursement (averaging $12,800 per year) were awarded; scholarships/grants and unspecified assistantships also available. Support available to part-time students. Financial award application deadline: 4/1; financial award applicants required to submit FAFSA. *Faculty research:* Aquatic chemistry, physiochemical treatment, waste water treatment, hazardous waste treatment, environmental microbiology. *Total annual research expenditures:* $557,751. *Unit head:* Dr. Isao Ishibashi, Graduate Program Director, 757-683-4641, Fax: 757-683-5354, E-mail: cegpd@odu.edu. *Application contact:* Dr. Linda Vahala, Associate Dean, 757-683-3789, Fax: 757-683-4898, E-mail: lvahala@odu.edu. Web site: http://eng.odu.edu/cee/.

Oregon Health & Science University, School of Medicine, Graduate Programs in Medicine, Department of Environmental and Biomolecular Systems, Portland, OR 97239-3098. Offers biochemistry and molecular biology (MS, PhD); environmental science and engineering (MS, PhD). Part-time programs available. *Faculty:* 14 full-time (4 women), 1 (woman) part-time/adjunct. *Students:* 28 full-time (20 women), 5 part-time (3 women); includes 11 minority (1 Black or African American, non-Hispanic/Latino; 3 American Indian or Alaska Native, non-Hispanic/Latino; 2 Asian, non-Hispanic/Latino; 4 Hispanic/Latino; 1 Two or more races, non-Hispanic/Latino), 5 international. Average age 30. 36 applicants, 25% accepted, 5 enrolled. In 2011, 9 master's, 2 doctorates awarded. Terminal master's awarded for partial completion of doctoral program. *Degree requirements:* For master's, thesis (for some programs); for doctorate, comprehensive exam, thesis/dissertation, qualifying exam. *Entrance requirements:* For master's and doctorate, GRE General Test (minimum scores: 500 Verbal/600 Quantitative/4.5 Analytical) or MCAT (for some programs). Additional exam requirements/recommendations for international students: Required—TOEFL. *Application deadline:* For fall admission, 7/15 for domestic students, 5/15 for international students; for winter admission, 10/15 for domestic students, 9/15 for international students; for spring admission, 1/15 for domestic students, 12/15 for international students. Applications are processed on a rolling basis. Application fee: $70. Electronic applications accepted. *Financial support:* Health care benefits and full tuition and stipends for PhD students available. *Unit head:* Dr. Paul Tratnyek, Program Director, 503-748-1070, E-mail: info@ebs.ogi.edu. *Application contact:* Nancy Christie, Program Coordinator, 503-748-1070, E-mail: info@ebs.ogi.edu.

Oregon State University, Graduate School, College of Engineering, School of Civil and Construction Engineering, Corvallis, OR 97331. Offers civil engineering (MS, PhD); coastal and ocean engineering (M Oc E, PhD); coastal engineering (MS); construction engineering management (MBE, PhD); engineering (M Eng, MAIS); geotechnical engineering (MS, PhD); structural engineering (MS, PhD); transportation engineering (MS, PhD); water engineering (MS, PhD). Part-time programs available. Terminal master's awarded for partial completion of doctoral program. *Degree requirements:* For master's, thesis or alternative; for doctorate, one foreign language, thesis/dissertation. *Entrance requirements:* For master's, GRE General Test, minimum GPA of 3.0 in last 90 hours (3.5 for MS); for doctorate, GRE General Test, minimum GPA of 3.0 in last 90 hours of undergraduate course work. Additional exam requirements/recommendations for international students: Required—TOEFL (minimum score 580 paper-based; 237 computer-based). *Faculty research:* Hazardous waste management, carbon cycling, wave forces on structures, pavement design, seismic analysis.

Penn State Harrisburg, Graduate School, School of Science, Engineering and Technology, Middletown, PA 17057-4898. Offers computer science (MS); electrical engineering (M Eng, MS); engineering management (MPS); engineering science (M Eng); environmental engineering (M Eng); environmental pollution control (MEPC, MS). Part-time and evening/weekend programs available. *Unit head:* Dr. Jerry F. Shoup, Interim Director, 717-948-6352, E-mail: jfs1@psu.edu. *Application contact:* Robert Coffman, Director of Admissions, 717-948-6250, Fax: 717-948-6325, E-mail: ric1@psu.edu. Web site: http://harrisburg.psu.edu/science-engineering-technology.

Penn State University Park, Graduate School, College of Engineering, Department of Civil and Environmental Engineering, State College, University Park, PA 16802-1503. Offers civil engineering (M Eng, MS, PhD); environmental engineering (M Eng, MS, PhD). *Unit head:* Dr. David N. Wormley, Dean, 814-865-7537, Fax: 814-865-8767, E-mail: dnw2@engr.psu.edu. *Application contact:* Cynthia E. Nicosia, Director, Graduate Enrollment Services, 814-865-1834, E-mail: cey1@psu.edu. Web site: http://www.engr.psu.edu/CE/.

Polytechnic Institute of New York University, Department of Civil Engineering, Major in Environmental Engineering, Brooklyn, NY 11201-2990. Offers MS. Part-time and evening/weekend programs available. *Students:* 8 full-time (2 women), 8 part-time (4 women); includes 7 minority (3 Black or African American, non-Hispanic/Latino; 4 Asian, non-Hispanic/Latino), 8 international. Average age 25. 38 applicants, 39% accepted, 5 enrolled. In 2011, 4 degrees awarded. *Degree requirements:* For master's, comprehensive exam (for some programs), thesis (for some programs). *Entrance requirements:* Additional exam requirements/recommendations for international students: Required—TOEFL (minimum score 550 paper-based; 213 computer-based; 80 iBT); Recommended—IELTS (minimum score 6.5). *Application deadline:* For fall admission, 7/31 priority date for domestic students, 4/30 for international students; for spring admission, 12/31 priority date for domestic students, 10/30 for international students. Applications are processed on a rolling basis. Application fee: $75. Electronic applications accepted. *Expenses: Tuition:* Full-time $22,464; part-time $1248 per credit. *Required fees:* $501 per semester. *Financial support:* Fellowships, research assistantships, teaching assistantships, institutionally sponsored loans, scholarships/grants, and unspecified assistantships available. Support available to part-time students. Financial award applicants required to submit FAFSA. *Unit head:* Dr. Lawrence Chiarelli, Head, 718-260-4040, Fax: 718-260-3433, E-mail: lchiarel@poly.edu. *Application contact:* JeanCarlo Bonilla, Director, Graduate Enrollment Management, 718-260-3182, Fax: 718-260-3624, E-mail: gradinfo@poly.edu.

Polytechnic Institute of NYU, Long Island Graduate Center, Graduate Programs, Department of Civil Engineering, Major in Environmental Engineering, Melville, NY 11747. Offers MS. *Degree requirements:* For master's, comprehensive exam, thesis. *Entrance requirements:* Additional exam requirements/recommendations for international students: Required—TOEFL (minimum score 550 paper-based; 213 computer-based; 80 iBT); Recommended—IELTS (minimum score 6.5). *Application deadline:* For fall admission, 7/31 priority date for domestic students, 4/30 for international students; for spring admission, 12/31 priority date for domestic students, 11/30 for international students. Applications are processed on a rolling basis. Application fee: $75. Electronic applications accepted. *Financial support:* Institutionally sponsored loans, scholarships/grants, and unspecified assistantships available. Support available to part-time students. Financial award applicants required to submit FAFSA. *Unit head:* Dr. Roger Peter Roess, Department Head, 718-260-3018, E-mail: rroess@poly.edu. *Application contact:* JeanCarlo Bonilla, Director of Graduate Enrollment Management, 718-260-3182, Fax: 718-260-3624, E-mail: gradinfo@poly.edu.

Polytechnic University of Puerto Rico, Miami Campus, Graduate School, Miami, FL 33166. Offers accounting (MBA); business administration (MBA); construction management (MEM); environmental management (MEM); finance (MBA); human resources management (MBA); logistics and supply chain management (MBA); management of international enterprises (MBA); manufacturing management (MEM); marketing management (MBA); project management (MBA). Part-time and evening/weekend programs available. Postbaccalaureate distance learning degree programs offered (no on-campus study). *Entrance requirements:* For master's, minimum GPA of 3.0. Electronic applications accepted.

Polytechnic University of Puerto Rico, Orlando Campus, Graduate School, Winter Park, FL 32792. Offers accounting (MBA); business administration (MBA); construction management (MEM); engineering management (MEM); environmental management (MEM); finance (MBA); human resources management (MBA); management of international enterprises (MBA); management of technology (MBA); manufacturing management (MEM). Part-time and evening/weekend programs available. Postbaccalaureate distance learning degree programs offered (no on-campus study). *Entrance requirements:* For master's, minimum GPA of 3.0. Additional exam requirements/recommendations for international students: Recommended—TOEFL. Electronic applications accepted.

Portland State University, Graduate Studies, Maseeh College of Engineering and Computer Science, Department of Civil and Environmental Engineering, Portland, OR 97207-0751. Offers civil and environmental engineering (M Eng, MS, PhD); civil and environmental engineering management (M Eng); environmental sciences and resources (PhD); systems science (PhD). Part-time and evening/weekend programs available. *Degree requirements:* For master's, thesis or alternative, oral exam; for doctorate, one foreign language, thesis/dissertation, oral and written exams. *Entrance requirements:* For master's, minimum GPA of 3.0 in upper-division course work, BS in civil engineering or allied field; for doctorate, GRE General Test, GRE Subject Test, minimum GPA of 3.0 in upper-division course work, master's in civil and environmental engineering, 2 years full-time graduate work beyond master's degree. Additional exam requirements/recommendations for international students: Required—TOEFL (minimum score 550 paper-based; 213 computer-based). *Faculty research:* Structures, water resources, geotechnical engineering, environmental engineering, transportation.

Rensselaer Polytechnic Institute, Graduate School, School of Engineering, Program in Environmental Engineering, Troy, NY 12180-3590. Offers M Eng, MS, PhD. Part-time programs available. Terminal master's awarded for partial completion of doctoral program. *Degree requirements:* For master's, thesis (for some programs); for doctorate, thesis/dissertation. *Entrance requirements:* For master's and doctorate, GRE. Additional exam requirements/recommendations for international students: Required—TOEFL (minimum score 570 paper-based; 230 computer-based; 89 iBT), IELTS (minimum score 6.5). Electronic applications accepted. *Faculty research:* Water treatment, bioremediation of hazardous wastes, environmental systems.

Rice University, Graduate Programs, George R. Brown School of Engineering, Department of Civil and Environmental Engineering, Houston, TX 77251-1892. Offers civil engineering (MCE, MS, PhD); environmental engineering (MEE, MES, MS, PhD); environmental science (MEE, MES, MS, PhD). Part-time programs available. *Degree requirements:* For master's, thesis (for some programs); for doctorate, thesis/dissertation. *Entrance requirements:* For master's and doctorate, GRE General Test, GRE Subject Test, minimum GPA of 3.25. Additional exam requirements/recommendations for international students: Required—TOEFL (minimum score 600 paper-based; 250 computer-based; 90 iBT). Electronic applications accepted. *Faculty research:* Biology and chemistry of groundwater, pollutant fate in groundwater systems, water quality monitoring, urban storm water runoff, urban air quality.

Rose-Hulman Institute of Technology, Faculty of Engineering and Applied Sciences, Department of Civil Engineering, Terre Haute, IN 47803-3999. Offers civil engineering (MS); environmental engineering (MS). Part-time programs available. *Faculty:* 7 full-time (1 woman). *Students:* 1 full-time (0 women). Average age 23. 3 applicants, 100% accepted, 1 enrolled. In 2011, 1 master's awarded. *Degree requirements:* For master's, thesis. *Entrance requirements:* For master's, GRE, minimum GPA of 3.0. Additional exam requirements/recommendations for international students: Required—TOEFL (minimum score 580 paper-based; 237 computer-based; 92 iBT). *Application deadline:* For fall admission, 2/1 priority date for domestic students. Applications are processed on a rolling basis. Application fee: $0. *Expenses: Tuition:* Full-time $37,197; part-time $1085 per credit hour. *Financial support:* In 2011–12, 1 student received support. Fellowships with full and partial tuition reimbursements available, research assistantships with full and partial tuition reimbursements available, institutionally sponsored loans, scholarships/grants, and tuition waivers (full and partial) available. Financial award application deadline: 2/1. *Faculty research:* Urban stormwater management, groundwater and surface water models, solid and hazardous waste, risk and decision analysis. *Total annual research expenditures:* $64,522. *Unit head:* Dr. Kevin G. Sutterer, Chairman, 812-877-8959, Fax: 812-877-8440, E-mail: kevin.g.sutterer@rose-hulman.edu. *Application contact:* Dr. Daniel J. Moore, Associate Dean of the Faculty, 812-877-8110, Fax: 812-877-8061, E-mail: daniel.j.moore@rose-hulman.edu. Web site: http://www.rose-hulman.edu/ce/.

Royal Military College of Canada, Division of Graduate Studies and Research, Engineering Division, Department of Chemistry and Chemical Engineering, Program in Environmental Engineering, Kingston, ON K7K 7B4, Canada. Offers chemical and materials (M Eng); chemistry (M Eng); environmental (PhD); nuclear (PhD). *Degree requirements:* For master's, thesis; for doctorate, comprehensive exam, thesis/dissertation. *Entrance requirements:* For master's, honours degree with second-class standing; for doctorate, master's degree. Electronic applications accepted.

Rutgers, The State University of New Jersey, New Brunswick, Graduate School-New Brunswick, Department of Civil and Environmental Engineering, Piscataway, NJ 08854-8097. Offers MS, PhD. Part-time and evening/weekend programs available. Terminal master's awarded for partial completion of doctoral program. *Degree requirements:* For master's, comprehensive exam, thesis or alternative; for doctorate, comprehensive exam, thesis/dissertation. *Entrance requirements:* For master's and doctorate, GRE General Test. Additional exam requirements/recommendations for international students: Required—TOEFL (minimum score 580 paper-based; 237 computer-based). Electronic applications accepted. *Faculty research:* Civil engineering materials research, non-destructive evaluation of transportation infrastructure, transportation planning, intelligent transportation systems.

Southern Methodist University, Bobby B. Lyle School of Engineering, Department of Environmental and Civil Engineering, Dallas, TX 75275-0340. Offers applied science (MS, PhD); civil and environmental engineering (PhD); civil engineering (MS); environmental engineering (MS); environmental science (MS), including environmental systems management. Part-time and evening/weekend programs available. Postbaccalaureate distance learning degree programs offered (no on-campus study). Terminal master's awarded for partial completion of doctoral program. *Degree requirements:* For master's, thesis optional; for doctorate, thesis/dissertation, oral and written qualifying exams. *Entrance requirements:* For master's, GRE General Test, minimum GPA of 3.0 in last 2 years; bachelor's degree in engineering, mathematics, or sciences; for doctorate, GRE, BS and MS in related field, minimum GPA of 3.3. Additional exam requirements/recommendations for international students: Required—TOEFL. Electronic applications accepted. *Faculty research:* Human and environmental health effects of endocrine disrupters, development of air pollution control systems for diesel engines, structural analysis and design, modeling and design of waste treatment systems.

Stanford University, School of Engineering, Department of Civil and Environmental Engineering, Stanford, CA 94305-9991. Offers MS, PhD, Eng. Terminal master's awarded for partial completion of doctoral program. *Degree requirements:* For doctorate, thesis/dissertation, qualifying exam; for Eng, thesis. *Entrance requirements:* For master's, doctorate, and Eng, GRE General Test. Additional exam requirements/recommendations for international students: Required—TOEFL. Electronic applications accepted. *Expenses: Tuition:* Full-time $40,050; part-time $890 per credit.

State University of New York College of Environmental Science and Forestry, Department of Environmental Resources Engineering, Syracuse, NY 13210-2779. Offers ecological engineering (MS, PhD); environmental and resources engineering (MPS, MS, PhD); environmental management (MPS); geospatial information science and engineering (MS, PhD); mapping sciences (MPS); water resources engineering (MS, PhD). *Degree requirements:* For master's, thesis (for some programs); for doctorate, comprehensive exam, thesis/dissertation. *Entrance requirements:* For master's and doctorate, GRE General Test, minimum GPA of 3.0. Additional exam requirements/recommendations for international students: Required—TOEFL (minimum score 550 paper-based; 213 computer-based; 80 iBT), IELTS (minimum score 6). *Application deadline:* For fall admission, 2/1 priority date for domestic students, 2/1 for international students; for spring admission, 11/1 priority date for domestic students, 11/1 for international students. Applications are processed on a rolling basis. Application fee: $60. *Expenses:* Tuition, state resident: full-time $8870; part-time $370 per credit hour. Tuition, nonresident: full-time $15,160; part-time $632 per credit hour. *Required fees:* $60; $370 per credit hour. $350 per semester. One-time fee: $85. *Financial support:* Fellowships with full and partial tuition reimbursements, research assistantships with full and partial tuition reimbursements, teaching assistantships with full and partial tuition reimbursements, Federal Work-Study, institutionally sponsored loans, scholarships/grants, health care benefits, and unspecified assistantships available. Financial award application deadline: 6/30; financial award applicants required to submit FAFSA. *Faculty research:* Forest engineering, paper science and engineering, wood products engineering. *Total annual research expenditures:* $968,412. *Unit head:* Dr. Theodore Endreny, Chair, 315-470-6565, Fax: 315-470-6958, E-mail: te@esf.edu. *Application contact:* Dr. Dudley J. Raynal, Dean, Instruction and Graduate Studies, 315-470-6599, Fax: 315-470-6978, E-mail: esfgrad@esf.edu. Web site: http://www.esf.edu/ere.

Stevens Institute of Technology, Graduate School, Charles V. Schaefer Jr. School of Engineering, Department of Civil, Environmental, and Ocean Engineering, Program in Environmental Engineering, Hoboken, NJ 07030. Offers environmental compatibility in engineering (Certificate); environmental engineering (PhD); environmental processes (M Eng, Certificate); groundwater and soil pollution control (M Eng, Certificate); inland and coastal environmental hydrodynamics (M Eng, Certificate); water quality control (Certificate). *Degree requirements:* For master's, thesis optional; for doctorate, variable foreign language requirement, thesis/dissertation; for Certificate, project or thesis. *Entrance requirements:* For doctorate, GRE. Additional exam requirements/recommendations for international students: Required—TOEFL. Electronic applications accepted.

Syracuse University, L. C. Smith College of Engineering and Computer Science, Program in Environmental Engineering, Syracuse, NY 13244. Offers environmental engineering (MS). Part-time programs available. *Students:* 11 full-time (5 women), 2 part-time (both women), 11 international. Average age 25. 40 applicants, 48% accepted, 7 enrolled. In 2011, 1 degree awarded. *Entrance requirements:* For master's, GRE General Test. Additional exam requirements/recommendations for international students: Required—TOEFL (minimum score 100 iBT). *Application deadline:* For fall admission, 7/1 priority date for domestic students, 6/1 for international students. Applications are processed on a rolling basis. Application fee: $75. Electronic applications accepted. *Expenses: Tuition:* Part-time $1206 per credit. *Financial support:* Fellowships with full tuition reimbursements, research assistantships with full and partial tuition reimbursements, teaching assistantships with full and partial tuition reimbursements, and tuition waivers (partial) available. Financial award application deadline: 1/1. *Unit head:* Dr. Chris E. Johnson, Interim Chair, 315-443-4425, E-mail: cejohns@syr.edu. *Application contact:* Elizabeth Buchanan, Information Contact, 314-443-2558, E-mail: topgrads@syr.edu. Web site: http://lcs.syr.edu.

Syracuse University, L. C. Smith College of Engineering and Computer Science, Program in Environmental Engineering Science, Syracuse, NY 13244. Offers MS. Part-time programs available. *Students:* 3 full-time (1 woman), 1 part-time (0 women), 1 international. Average age 25. 13 applicants, 69% accepted, 4 enrolled. In 2011, 1 master's awarded. *Degree requirements:* For master's, thesis optional. *Entrance requirements:* For master's, GRE General Test. Additional exam requirements/

recommendations for international students: Required—TOEFL (minimum score 100 iBT). *Application deadline:* For fall admission, 7/1 for domestic students, 6/1 for international students. Applications are processed on a rolling basis. Application fee: $75. Electronic applications accepted. *Expenses: Tuition:* Part-time $1206 per credit. *Financial support:* Fellowships with full tuition reimbursements, research assistantships with full and partial tuition reimbursements, teaching assistantships with full and partial tuition reimbursements, and tuition waivers (partial) available. *Unit head:* Dr. Chris Johnson, Department Chair, 315-443-4425, E-mail: cejohns@syr.edu. *Application contact:* Kathleen Joyce, Assistant Dean, 315-443-2219, E-mail: topgrads@syr.edu. Web site: http://lcs.syr.edu/.

Texas A&M University, College of Engineering, Zachry Department of Civil Engineering, College Station, TX 77843. Offers coastal and ocean engineering (M Eng, MS, D Eng, PhD); construction engineering and management (M Eng, MS, D Eng, PhD); environmental engineering (M Eng, MS, D Eng, PhD); geotechnical engineering (M Eng, MS, D Eng, PhD); materials engineering (M Eng, MS, D Eng, PhD); structural engineering (M Eng, MS, D Eng, PhD); transportation engineering (M Eng, MS, D Eng, PhD); water resources engineering (M Eng, MS, D Eng, PhD). Part-time programs available. *Faculty:* 57. *Students:* 361 full-time (76 women), 46 part-time (8 women); includes 41 minority (3 Black or African American, non-Hispanic/Latino; 16 Asian, non-Hispanic/Latino; 21 Hispanic/Latino; 1 Two or more races, non-Hispanic/Latino), 247 international. Average age 29. In 2011, 123 master's, 27 doctorates awarded. *Degree requirements:* For master's, thesis (MS); for doctorate, dissertation (PhD), internship (D Eng). *Entrance requirements:* For master's and doctorate, GRE General Test. Additional exam requirements/recommendations for international students: Required—TOEFL. *Application deadline:* Applications are processed on a rolling basis. Application fee: $50 ($75 for international students). Electronic applications accepted. *Expenses:* Tuition, state resident: full-time $5437; part-time $226.55 per credit hour. Tuition, nonresident: full-time $12,949; part-time $539.55 per credit hour. *Required fees:* $2741. *Financial support:* In 2011–12, fellowships (averaging $4,500 per year), research assistantships (averaging $14,000 per year), teaching assistantships (averaging $14,400 per year) were awarded; career-related internships or fieldwork and institutionally sponsored loans also available. Financial award application deadline: 4/15; financial award applicants required to submit FAFSA. *Unit head:* Dr. John Niedzwecki, Head, 979-845-3858, E-mail: j-niedzwecki@tamu.edu. *Application contact:* Graduate Advisor, 979-845-7435, Fax: 979-845-6156, E-mail: info@civil.tamu.edu. Web site: https://www.civil.tamu.edu/.

Texas A&M University–Kingsville, College of Graduate Studies, College of Engineering, Department of Environmental Engineering, Kingsville, TX 78363. Offers ME, MS, PhD. Part-time and evening/weekend programs available. *Degree requirements:* For master's, comprehensive exam, thesis. *Entrance requirements:* For master's, GRE General Test, bachelor's degree in engineering or physical science, minimum undergraduate GPA of 2.7. Additional exam requirements/recommendations for international students: Required—TOEFL. *Faculty research:* Biodegradation of hazardous waste, air modeling, toxicology and industrial hygiene, water waste treating.

Texas Tech University, Graduate School, Edward E. Whitacre Jr. College of Engineering, Department of Civil and Environmental Engineering, Lubbock, TX 79409. Offers civil engineering (MSCE, PhD); environmental engineering (MENVEGR). *Accreditation:* ABET. Part-time programs available. *Faculty:* 20 full-time (3 women), 1 part-time/adjunct (0 women). *Students:* 68 full-time (18 women), 11 part-time (2 women); includes 10 minority (2 Black or African American, non-Hispanic/Latino; 2 Asian, non-Hispanic/Latino; 6 Hispanic/Latino), 35 international. Average age 26. 91 applicants, 67% accepted, 27 enrolled. In 2011, 34 master's, 2 doctorates awarded. *Degree requirements:* For master's, thesis or alternative; for doctorate, thesis/dissertation. *Entrance requirements:* For master's and doctorate, GRE General Test, minimum GPA of 3.0. Additional exam requirements/recommendations for international students: Required—TOEFL (minimum score 550 paper-based; 213 computer-based; 79 iBT). *Application deadline:* For fall admission, 6/1 priority date for domestic students, 1/15 for international students; for spring admission, 9/1 priority date for domestic students, 6/15 for international students. Applications are processed on a rolling basis. Application fee: $50 ($75 for international students). Electronic applications accepted. *Expenses:* Tuition, state resident: full-time $5899; part-time $245.80 per credit hour. Tuition, nonresident: full-time $13,411; part-time $558.80 per credit hour. *Required fees:* $2680.60; $86.50 per credit hour. $920.30 per semester. *Financial support:* In 2011–12, 40 students received support. Application deadline: 4/15; applicants required to submit FAFSA. *Faculty research:* Wind load/engineering on structures, fluid mechanics, structural dynamics, water resource management, transportation engineering. *Total annual research expenditures:* $2.9 million. *Unit head:* Dr. H. Scott Norville, Chair, 806-742-3523, Fax: 806-742-3488, E-mail: scott.norville@ttu.edu. *Application contact:* Dr. Priyantha Jayawickrama, Graduate Adviser, 806-742-3523, Fax: 806-742-3488, E-mail: priyantha.jayawickrama@ttu.edu. Web site: http://www.ce.ttu.edu/.

Tufts University, School of Engineering, Department of Civil and Environmental Engineering, Medford, MA 02155. Offers bioengineering (ME, MS), including environmental technology; civil engineering (ME, MS, PhD), including geotechnical engineering, structural engineering, water diplomacy (PhD); environmental engineering (ME, MS, PhD), including environmental engineering and environmental sciences, environmental geotechnology, environmental health, environmental science and management, hazardous materials management, water diplomacy (PhD), water resources engineering. Part-time programs available. *Faculty:* 18 full-time, 5 part-time/adjunct. *Students:* 102 full-time (50 women); includes 8 minority (1 Black or African American, non-Hispanic/Latino; 6 Asian, non-Hispanic/Latino; 1 Hispanic/Latino), 37 international. Average age 27. 162 applicants, 59% accepted, 37 enrolled. In 2011, 18 degrees awarded. Terminal master's awarded for partial completion of doctoral program. *Degree requirements:* For master's, thesis or alternative; for doctorate, thesis/dissertation. *Entrance requirements:* For master's and doctorate, GRE General Test. Additional exam requirements/recommendations for international students: Required—TOEFL (minimum score 550 paper-based; 213 computer-based; 80 iBT). *Application deadline:* For fall admission, 1/15 priority date for domestic students, 12/15 for international students; for spring admission, 10/15 for domestic students, 9/15 for international students. Applications are processed on a rolling basis. Application fee: $75. Electronic applications accepted. *Expenses: Tuition:* Full-time $41,208; part-time $1030 per credit hour. Full-time tuition and fees vary according to degree level, program and student level. Part-time tuition and fees vary according to course load. *Financial support:* Fellowships with full tuition reimbursements, research assistantships with full and partial tuition reimbursements, teaching assistantships with full and partial tuition reimbursements, Federal Work-Study, scholarships/grants, tuition waivers (partial), and unspecified assistantships available. Financial award application deadline: 1/15; financial award applicants required to submit FAFSA. *Faculty research:* Environmental and water resources engineering, environmental health, geotechnical and geoenvironmental engineering, structural engineering and mechanics, water diplomacy. *Unit head:* Dr. Kurt Penell, Chair, 617-627-3211, Fax: 617-627-3994. *Application contact:* Laura Sacco, Information Contact, 617-627-3211, E-mail: ceeinfo@tufts.edu. Web site: http://www.ase.tufts.edu/cee/.

Universidad Central del Esté, Graduate School, San Pedro de Macoris, Dominican Republic. Offers environmental engineering (ME); financial management (M Ad); higher education (M Ed), including higher education management, higher education pedagogy; human resources (M Ad). *Entrance requirements:* For master's, letters of recommendation.

Universidad Nacional Pedro Henriquez Urena, Graduate School, Santo Domingo, Dominican Republic. Offers agricultural diversity (MS), including horticultural/fruit production, tropical animal production; conservation of monuments and cultural assets (M Arch); ecology and environment (MS); environmental engineering (MEE); international relations (MA); natural resource management (MS); political science (MA); project optimization (MPM); project feasibility (MPM); project management (MPM); sanitation engineering (ME); science for teachers (MS); tropical Caribbean architecture (M Arch).

Université de Sherbrooke, Faculty of Engineering, Program in the Environment, Sherbrooke, QC J1K 2R1, Canada. Offers M Env. *Degree requirements:* For master's, thesis.

Université Laval, Faculty of Sciences and Engineering, Department of Civil Engineering, Programs in Civil Engineering, Québec, QC G1K 7P4, Canada. Offers civil engineering (M Sc, PhD); environmental technology (M Sc). Terminal master's awarded for partial completion of doctoral program. *Degree requirements:* For master's, thesis (for some programs); for doctorate, comprehensive exam, thesis/dissertation. *Entrance requirements:* For master's and doctorate, knowledge of French and English. Electronic applications accepted.

University at Buffalo, the State University of New York, Graduate School, School of Engineering and Applied Sciences, Department of Civil, Structural, and Environmental Engineering, Buffalo, NY 14260. Offers civil engineering (ME, MS, PhD); engineering science (MS). Part-time programs available. Postbaccalaureate distance learning degree programs offered (minimal on-campus study). *Faculty:* 26 full-time (3 women), 4 part-time/adjunct (1 woman). *Students:* 148 full-time (24 women), 10 part-time (2 women); includes 6 minority (1 American Indian or Alaska Native, non-Hispanic/Latino; 2 Asian, non-Hispanic/Latino; 3 Hispanic/Latino), 120 international. Average age 27. 545 applicants, 12% accepted, 58 enrolled. In 2011, 44 master's, 11 doctorates awarded. Terminal master's awarded for partial completion of doctoral program. *Degree requirements:* For master's, thesis optional, project, thesis, or comprehensive exam; for doctorate, thesis/dissertation. *Entrance requirements:* For master's and doctorate, GRE General Test, letters of reference. Additional exam requirements/recommendations for international students: Required—TOEFL (minimum score 550 paper-based; 213 computer-based; 79 iBT). *Application deadline:* For fall admission, 1/15 priority date for domestic students, 1/15 for international students; for spring admission, 9/15 for domestic and international students. Applications are processed on a rolling basis. Application fee: $75. Electronic applications accepted. *Financial support:* In 2011–12, 76 students received support, including 5 fellowships with full tuition reimbursements available (averaging $28,900 per year), 35 research assistantships with full tuition reimbursements available (averaging $27,700 per year), 26 teaching assistantships with full tuition reimbursements available (averaging $20,900 per year); career-related internships or fieldwork, Federal Work-Study, institutionally sponsored loans, scholarships/grants, traineeships, health care benefits, tuition waivers (full and partial), and unspecified assistantships also available. Support available to part-time students. Financial award application deadline: 1/15; financial award applicants required to submit FAFSA. *Faculty research:* Environmental engineering and fluid mechanics, structural dynamics, geomechanics, earthquake engineering computational mechanics. *Total annual research expenditures:* $7 million. *Unit head:* Dr. Andrew S. Whittaker, Chairman, 716-645-2114, Fax: 716-645-3733, E-mail: awhittak@buffalo.edu. *Application contact:* Dr. Adel Sadek, Director of Graduate Studies, 716-645-4367, Fax: 716-645-3733, E-mail: asadek@buffalo.edu. Web site: http://www.csee.buffalo.edu/.

The University of Alabama, Graduate School, College of Engineering, Department of Civil, Construction and Environmental Engineering, Tuscaloosa, AL 35487-0205. Offers civil engineering (MSCE, PhD); environmental engineering (MS). Part-time programs available. *Faculty:* 19 full-time (2 women), 1 part-time/adjunct (0 women). *Students:* 47 full-time (15 women), 11 part-time (5 women); includes 9 minority (8 Black or African American, non-Hispanic/Latino; 1 Asian, non-Hispanic/Latino), 16 international. Average age 28. 93 applicants, 37% accepted, 10 enrolled. In 2011, 27 master's, 3 doctorates awarded. Terminal master's awarded for partial completion of doctoral program. *Median time to degree:* Of those who began their doctoral program in fall 2003, 100% received their degree in 8 years or less. *Degree requirements:* For master's, thesis or alternative; for doctorate, one foreign language, thesis/dissertation. *Entrance requirements:* For master's and doctorate, GRE General Test, minimum GPA of 3.0 in last 60 hours of course work. Additional exam requirements/recommendations for international students: Required—TOEFL (minimum score 550 paper-based; 213 computer-based), IELTS (minimum score 6.5). *Application deadline:* For fall admission, 7/6 for domestic students, 1/15 for international students; for spring admission, 11/1 for domestic students, 6/1 for international students. Applications are processed on a rolling basis. Application fee: $50 ($60 for international students). Electronic applications accepted. *Expenses:* Tuition, state resident: full-time $8600. Tuition, nonresident: full-time $21,900. *Financial support:* In 2011–12, 40 students received support, including 32 research assistantships with full tuition reimbursements available (averaging $10,489 per year), 12 teaching assistantships with full tuition reimbursements available (averaging $10,489 per year); fellowships, scholarships/grants, tuition waivers (partial), and unspecified assistantships also available. Financial award application deadline: 3/15. *Faculty research:* Experimental structures, modeling of structures, bridge management systems, geotechnological engineering, environmental remediation. *Total annual research expenditures:* $2.2 million. *Unit head:* Dr. Kenneth J. Fridley, Head and Professor, 205-348-6550, Fax: 205-348-0783, E-mail: kfridley@coe.eng.ua.edu. *Application contact:* Dr. David A. Francko, Dean, 205-348-8280, Fax: 205-348-0400, E-mail: dfrancko@ua.edu. Web site: http://www.ce.eng.ua.edu/.

The University of Alabama in Huntsville, School of Graduate Studies, College of Engineering, Department of Civil and Environmental Engineering, Huntsville, AL 35899. Offers civil and environmental engineering (PhD); civil engineering (MSE), including civil engineering, environmental and water resource engineering, geotechnical engineering, structural engineering and structural mechanics, transportation engineering. PhD offered jointly with The University of Alabama at Birmingham. Part-time and evening/weekend programs available. *Faculty:* 5 full-time (1 woman), 1 part-time/adjunct (0 women). *Students:* 20 full-time (4 women), 12 part-time (6 women); includes 1 minority (Black or African American, non-Hispanic/Latino), 15 international. Average age 29. 26 applicants, 62% accepted, 6 enrolled. In 2011, 3 master's, 1 doctorate awarded. *Degree requirements:* For master's, comprehensive exam, thesis or alternative, oral and written exams; for doctorate, comprehensive exam, thesis/dissertation, oral and written exams.

Entrance requirements: For master's, GRE General Test, BSE, minimum GPA of 3.0; for doctorate, GRE General Test, minimum GPA of 3.0. Additional exam requirements/recommendations for international students: Required—TOEFL (minimum score 500 paper-based; 173 computer-based; 62 iBT). *Application deadline:* For fall admission, 7/15 for domestic students, 4/1 for international students; for spring admission, 11/30 for domestic students, 9/1 for international students. Applications are processed on a rolling basis. Application fee: $40 ($50 for international students). Electronic applications accepted. *Expenses:* Tuition, state resident: full-time $7830; part-time $473.50 per credit. Tuition, nonresident: full-time $18,748; part-time $1128.33 per credit. Tuition and fees vary according to course load and program. *Financial support:* In 2011–12, 16 students received support, including 10 research assistantships with full and partial tuition reimbursements available (averaging $12,281 per year), 6 teaching assistantships with full and partial tuition reimbursements available (averaging $12,472 per year); career-related internships or fieldwork, Federal Work-Study, institutionally sponsored loans, scholarships/grants, health care benefits, and unspecified assistantships also available. Support available to part-time students. Financial award application deadline: 4/1; financial award applicants required to submit FAFSA. *Faculty research:* Hydrologic modeling, orbital debris impact, hydrogeology, environmental engineering, transportation engineering. *Total annual research expenditures:* $1.1 million. *Unit head:* Dr. Houssam Toutanji, Chair, 256-824-7361, Fax: 256-824-6724, E-mail: toutanji@cee.uah.edu. *Application contact:* Kim Gray, Graduate Studies Admissions Coordinator, 256-824-6002, Fax: 256-824-6405, E-mail: deangrad@uah.edu. Web site: http://www.uah.edu/eng/departments/cee/welcome.

University of Alaska Anchorage, School of Engineering, Program in Applied Environmental Science and Technology, Anchorage, AK 99508. Offers M AEST, MS. Part-time and evening/weekend programs available. *Degree requirements:* For master's, comprehensive exam, thesis (for some programs). *Entrance requirements:* For master's, GRE General Test. Additional exam requirements/recommendations for international students: Required—TOEFL (minimum score 550 paper-based; 213 computer-based). *Faculty research:* Wastewater treatment, environmental regulations, water resources management, justification of public facilities, rural sanitation, biological treatment process.

University of Alaska Fairbanks, College of Engineering and Mines, Department of Civil and Environmental Engineering, Program in Environmental Engineering, Fairbanks, AK 99775-5900. Offers engineering (PhD), including environmental engineering; environmental engineering (MS), including environmental contaminants, environmental science and management, water supply and waste treatment. Part-time programs available. *Students:* 3 full-time (0 women), 1 (woman) part-time. Average age 26. 5 applicants, 60% accepted, 1 enrolled. In 2011, 2 degrees awarded. *Degree requirements:* For master's, comprehensive exam, thesis or alternative; for doctorate, comprehensive exam, thesis/dissertation, oral exam, oral defense. *Entrance requirements:* For master's, basic computer techniques; for doctorate, GRE General Test. Additional exam requirements/recommendations for international students: Required—TOEFL (minimum score 575 paper-based; 213 computer-based). *Application deadline:* For fall admission, 6/1 for domestic students, 3/1 for international students; for spring admission, 10/15 for domestic students, 9/1 for international students. Applications are processed on a rolling basis. Application fee: $60. Electronic applications accepted. *Expenses:* Tuition, state resident: full-time $6696; part-time $372 per credit. Tuition, nonresident: full-time $13,680; part-time $760 per credit. Tuition and fees vary according to course load and reciprocity agreements. *Financial support:* In 2011–12, 1 research assistantship (averaging $16,834 per year), 2 teaching assistantships (averaging $6,390 per year) were awarded; fellowships, career-related internships or fieldwork, Federal Work-Study, scholarships/grants, health care benefits, and unspecified assistantships also available. Support available to part-time students. Financial award application deadline: 7/1; financial award applicants required to submit FAFSA. *Unit head:* Dr. David Barnes, Department Chair, 907-474-7241, Fax: 907-474-6087, E-mail: fyeqe@uaf.edu. *Application contact:* Mike Earnest, Director of Admissions, 907-474-7500, Fax: 907-474-5379, E-mail: admissions@uaf.edu. Web site: http://www.alaska.edu/uaf/cem/cee/env/.

University of Alberta, Faculty of Graduate Studies and Research, Department of Civil and Environmental Engineering, Edmonton, AB T6G 2E1, Canada. Offers construction engineering and management (M Eng, M Sc, PhD); environmental engineering (M Eng, M Sc, PhD); environmental science (M Sc, PhD); geoenvironmental engineering (M Eng, M Sc, PhD); geotechnical engineering (M Eng, M Sc, PhD); mining engineering (M Eng, M Sc, PhD); petroleum engineering (M Eng, M Sc, PhD); structural engineering (M Eng, M Sc, PhD); water resources (M Eng, M Sc, PhD). Part-time programs available. Postbaccalaureate distance learning degree programs offered (minimal on-campus study). *Degree requirements:* For master's, thesis (for some programs); for doctorate, thesis/dissertation. *Entrance requirements:* For master's, minimum GPA of 3.0 in last 2 years of undergraduate studies; for doctorate, minimum GPA of 3.0. Additional exam requirements/recommendations for international students: Required—TOEFL (minimum score 550 paper-based; 213 computer-based). Electronic applications accepted. *Faculty research:* Mining.

The University of Arizona, College of Engineering, Department of Chemical and Environmental Engineering, Program in Environmental Engineering, Tucson, AZ 85721. Offers MS, PhD. *Faculty:* 13 full-time (1 woman), 1 (woman) part-time/adjunct. *Students:* 30 full-time (12 women), 5 part-time (2 women); includes 5 minority (1 Asian, non-Hispanic/Latino; 3 Hispanic/Latino; 1 Two or more races, non-Hispanic/Latino), 20 international. Average age 30. 54 applicants, 24% accepted, 5 enrolled. In 2011, 7 master's, 3 doctorates awarded. *Entrance requirements:* For master's and doctorate, GRE, 3 letters of recommendation, resume, statement of purpose. Additional exam requirements/recommendations for international students: Required—TOEFL (minimum score 550 paper-based; 213 computer-based; 79 iBT). *Application deadline:* Applications are processed on a rolling basis. Application fee: $75. Electronic applications accepted. *Expenses:* Tuition, state resident: full-time $10,840. Tuition, nonresident: full-time $25,802. *Unit head:* Dr. Jim Field, Department Head, 520-621-2591, Fax: 520-621-6048, E-mail: jimfield@email.arizona.edu. *Application contact:* Jo Leeming, Program Coordinator, 520-621-6044, Fax: 520-621-6048, E-mail: leeming@email.arizona.edu. Web site: http://www.chee.arizona.edu/.

University of Arkansas, Graduate School, College of Engineering, Department of Civil Engineering, Program in Environmental Engineering, Fayetteville, AR 72701-1201. Offers MS En E, MSE. *Accreditation:* ABET. *Students:* 3 full-time (1 woman), 2 part-time (1 woman), 2 international. In 2011, 20 degrees awarded. *Degree requirements:* For master's, thesis optional. *Application deadline:* For fall admission, 4/1 for international students; for spring admission, 10/1 for international students. Applications are processed on a rolling basis. Application fee: $40 ($50 for international students). Electronic applications accepted. *Financial support:* In 2011–12, 4 research assistantships were awarded; fellowships, teaching assistantships, career-related internships or fieldwork, and Federal Work-Study also available. Support available to part-time students. Financial award application deadline: 4/1; financial award applicants required to submit FAFSA. *Unit head:* Dr. Kevin Hall, Department Chair, 479-575-4954, Fax: 479-575-7168, E-mail: kdhall@uark.edu. *Application contact:* Dr. Paneer Selvam, Graduate Coordinator, 479-575-5356, E-mail: rps@uark.edu. Web site: http://www.cveg.uark.edu/.

University of California, Berkeley, Graduate Division, College of Engineering, Department of Civil and Environmental Engineering, Berkeley, CA 94720-1500. Offers engineering and project management (M Eng, MS, D Eng, PhD); environmental engineering (M Eng, MS, D Eng, PhD); geoengineering (M Eng, MS, D Eng, PhD); structural engineering, mechanics and materials (M Eng, MS, D Eng, PhD); transportation engineering (M Eng, MS, D Eng, PhD); M Arch/MS; MCP/MS; MPP/MS. *Degree requirements:* For master's, comprehensive exam or thesis (MS); for doctorate, thesis/dissertation, qualifying exam. *Entrance requirements:* For master's, GRE General Test, minimum GPA of 3.0, 3 letters of recommendation; for doctorate, GRE General Test, minimum GPA of 3.5, 3 letters of recommendation. Additional exam requirements/recommendations for international students: Required—TOEFL (minimum score 570 paper-based; 230 computer-based). Electronic applications accepted.

University of California, Davis, College of Engineering, Program in Civil and Environmental Engineering, Davis, CA 95616. Offers M Engr, MS, D Engr, PhD, Certificate, M Engr/MBA. *Degree requirements:* For master's, comprehensive exam (for some programs), thesis (for some programs); for doctorate, thesis/dissertation. *Entrance requirements:* For master's, GRE General Test, minimum GPA of 3.0; for doctorate, GRE, minimum graduate GPA of 3.5. Additional exam requirements/recommendations for international students: Required—TOEFL (minimum score 550 paper-based; 213 computer-based). Electronic applications accepted. *Faculty research:* Environmental water resources, transportation, structural mechanics, structural engineering, geotechnical engineering.

University of California, Irvine, School of Engineering, Department of Civil and Environmental Engineering, Irvine, CA 92697. Offers MS, PhD. Part-time programs available. *Students:* 117 full-time (36 women), 12 part-time (3 women); includes 29 minority (1 American Indian or Alaska Native, non-Hispanic/Latino; 22 Asian, non-Hispanic/Latino; 6 Hispanic/Latino), 63 international. Average age 27. 383 applicants, 27% accepted, 37 enrolled. In 2011, 27 master's, 23 doctorates awarded. Terminal master's awarded for partial completion of doctoral program. *Degree requirements:* For doctorate, thesis/dissertation. *Entrance requirements:* For master's and doctorate, GRE General Test, minimum GPA of 3.0, 3 letters of recommendation. Additional exam requirements/recommendations for international students: Required—TOEFL (minimum score 550 paper-based; 213 computer-based). *Application deadline:* For fall admission, 1/15 priority date for domestic students, 1/15 for international students. Applications are processed on a rolling basis. Application fee: $80 ($100 for international students). Electronic applications accepted. *Financial support:* Fellowships, research assistantships with full tuition reimbursements, teaching assistantships, institutionally sponsored loans, traineeships, health care benefits, and unspecified assistantships available. Financial award application deadline: 3/1; financial award applicants required to submit FAFSA. *Faculty research:* Intelligent transportation systems and transportation economics, risk and reliability, fluid mechanics, environmental hydrodynamics, hydrological and climate systems, water resources. *Unit head:* Prof. Brett F. Sanders, Chair, 949-824-4327, Fax: 949-824-3672, E-mail: bsanders@uci.edu. *Application contact:* April M. Heath, Graduate Coordinator, 949-824-0584, Fax: 949-824-2117, E-mail: a.heath@uci.edu. Web site: http://www.eng.uci.edu/dept/cee.

University of California, Los Angeles, Graduate Division, Henry Samueli School of Engineering and Applied Science, Department of Civil and Environmental Engineering, Los Angeles, CA 90095-1593. Offers MS, PhD. *Faculty:* 17 full-time (4 women), 4 part-time/adjunct (0 women). *Students:* 172 full-time (58 women); includes 57 minority (41 Asian, non-Hispanic/Latino; 14 Hispanic/Latino; 2 Two or more races, non-Hispanic/Latino), 59 international. 389 applicants, 53% accepted, 93 enrolled. In 2011, 66 master's, 6 doctorates awarded. *Degree requirements:* For master's, comprehensive exam or thesis; for doctorate, thesis/dissertation, qualifying exams. *Entrance requirements:* For master's, GRE General Test, minimum GPA of 3.0; for doctorate, GRE General Test, minimum GPA of 3.25. Additional exam requirements/recommendations for international students: Required—TOEFL (minimum score 560 paper-based; 220 computer-based; 87 iBT). *Application deadline:* For fall admission, 12/15 priority date for domestic students, 12/15 for international students. Application fee: $80 ($100 for international students). Electronic applications accepted. *Financial support:* In 2011–12, 105 fellowships, 85 research assistantships, 56 teaching assistantships were awarded; Federal Work-Study, institutionally sponsored loans, and tuition waivers (full and partial) also available. Financial award application deadline: 12/15; financial award applicants required to submit FAFSA. *Faculty research:* Environmental engineering, geotechnical engineering, hydrology and water resources, structures. *Total annual research expenditures:* $3.4 million. *Unit head:* Dr. Jiun-Shyan Chen, Chair, 310-267-4620. *Application contact:* Maida Bassili, Graduate Affairs Officer, 310-825-1851, Fax: 310-206-2222, E-mail: maida@ea.ucla.edu. Web site: http://cee.ucla.edu/.

University of California, Los Angeles, Graduate Division, School of Public Health, Department of Environmental Health Sciences, Los Angeles, CA 90095. Offers environmental health sciences (MS, PhD); environmental science and engineering (D Env); molecular toxicology (PhD); JD/MPH. *Accreditation:* ABET (one or more programs are accredited). *Degree requirements:* For master's, comprehensive exam or thesis; for doctorate, thesis/dissertation, oral and written qualifying exams. *Entrance requirements:* For master's, GRE General Test, minimum GPA of 3.0; for doctorate, GRE General Test, minimum undergraduate GPA of 3.0. Electronic applications accepted.

University of California, Los Angeles, Graduate Division, School of Public Health, Program in Environmental Science and Engineering, Los Angeles, CA 90095. Offers D Env. *Degree requirements:* For doctorate, thesis/dissertation, oral and written qualifying exams. *Entrance requirements:* For doctorate, GRE General Test, minimum undergraduate GPA of 3.0, master's degree or equivalent in a natural science, engineering, or public health. *Faculty research:* Toxic and hazardous substances, air and water pollution, risk assessment/management, water resources, marine science.

University of California, Riverside, Graduate Division, Department of Chemical and Environmental Engineering, Riverside, CA 92521-0102. Offers MS, PhD. Part-time programs available. Terminal master's awarded for partial completion of doctoral program. *Degree requirements:* For master's, thesis (for some programs); for doctorate, comprehensive exam, thesis/dissertation. *Entrance requirements:* For master's and doctorate, GRE General Test, minimum GPA of 3.0. Additional exam requirements/recommendations for international students: Required—TOEFL (minimum score 550 paper-based; 213 computer-based; 80 iBT). Electronic applications accepted. *Faculty research:* Air quality systems, water quality systems, advanced materials and nanotechnology, energy systems/alternative fuels, theory and molecular modeling.

University of Central Florida, College of Engineering and Computer Science, Department of Civil, Environmental, and Construction Engineering, Program in Environmental Engineering, Orlando, FL 32816. Offers MS, MS Env E, PhD. Part-time and evening/weekend programs available. *Students:* 23 full-time (10 women), 23 part-time (6 women); includes 12 minority (1 Black or African American, non-Hispanic/Latino; 5 Asian, non-Hispanic/Latino; 5 Hispanic/Latino; 1 Two or more races, non-Hispanic/Latino), 4 international. Average age 30. 39 applicants, 56% accepted, 11 enrolled. In 2011, 10 master's, 3 doctorates awarded. *Degree requirements:* For master's, thesis or alternative; for doctorate, thesis/dissertation, departmental qualifying exam, candidacy exam. *Entrance requirements:* For master's, GRE General Test, minimum GPA of 3.0 in last 60 hours of course work; for doctorate, GRE General Test, minimum GPA of 3.5 in last 60 hours of course work, interview. Additional exam requirements/recommendations for international students: Required—TOEFL. *Application deadline:* For fall admission, 7/15 priority date for domestic students; for spring admission, 12/15 priority date for domestic students. Application fee: $30. Electronic applications accepted. *Expenses:* Tuition, state resident: part-time $277.08 per credit hour. Tuition, nonresident: part-time $277.08 per credit hour. Part-time tuition and fees vary according to degree level and program. *Financial support:* In 2011–12, 13 students received support, including 5 fellowships with partial tuition reimbursements available (averaging $2,600 per year), 12 research assistantships with partial tuition reimbursements available (averaging $9,800 per year), 2 teaching assistantships with partial tuition reimbursements available (averaging $11,100 per year); career-related internships or fieldwork, Federal Work-Study, institutionally sponsored loans, tuition waivers (partial), and unspecified assistantships also available. Financial award application deadline: 3/1; financial award applicants required to submit FAFSA. *Unit head:* Dr. Essam Radwan, Interim Chair, 407-823-4738, E-mail: ahmed.radwan@ucf.edu. *Application contact:* Barbara Rodriguez, Director, Admissions and Registration, 407-823-2766, Fax: 407-823-6442, E-mail: gradadmissions@ucf.edu. Web site: http://cece.ucf.edu/.

University of Cincinnati, Graduate School, College of Engineering and Applied Science, Department of Civil and Environmental Engineering, Program in Environmental Engineering, Cincinnati, OH 45221. Offers MS, PhD. *Accreditation:* ABET (one or more programs are accredited). Part-time programs available. *Degree requirements:* For master's, project or thesis; for doctorate, one foreign language, thesis/dissertation. *Entrance requirements:* For master's and doctorate, GRE General Test. Additional exam requirements/recommendations for international students: Required—TOEFL (minimum score 580 paper-based; 237 computer-based; 92 iBT). Electronic applications accepted. *Faculty research:* Environmental microbiology, solid-waste management, air pollution control, water pollution control, aerosols.

University of Colorado Boulder, Graduate School, College of Engineering and Applied Science, Department of Civil, Environmental, and Architectural Engineering, Boulder, CO 80309. Offers building systems (MS, PhD); construction engineering management (MS, PhD); environmental engineering (MS, PhD); geotechnical engineering and geomechanics (MS, PhD); hydrology, water resources and environmental fluid mechanics (MS, PhD); structural engineering and structural mechanics (MS, PhD). *Faculty:* 37 full-time (8 women). *Students:* 245 full-time (90 women), 53 part-time (15 women); includes 37 minority (1 Black or African American, non-Hispanic/Latino; 2 American Indian or Alaska Native, non-Hispanic/Latino; 15 Asian, non-Hispanic/Latino; 17 Hispanic/Latino; 2 Two or more races, non-Hispanic/Latino), 56 international. Average age 27. 483 applicants, 58% accepted, 83 enrolled. In 2011, 84 master's, 15 doctorates awarded. Terminal master's awarded for partial completion of doctoral program. *Degree requirements:* For master's, comprehensive exam, thesis or alternative; for doctorate, thesis/dissertation. *Entrance requirements:* For master's, GRE General Test, minimum undergraduate GPA of 3.0. *Application deadline:* For fall admission, 3/1 for domestic students, 12/1 for international students; for spring admission, 10/31 for domestic students, 10/1 for international students. Application fee: $50 ($60 for international students). Electronic applications accepted. *Financial support:* In 2011–12, 167 students received support, including 69 fellowships (averaging $12,440 per year), 62 research assistantships with full and partial tuition reimbursements available (averaging $21,979 per year), 20 teaching assistantships with full and partial tuition reimbursements available (averaging $19,877 per year); institutionally sponsored loans, scholarships/grants, health care benefits, and unspecified assistantships also available. Financial award application deadline: 1/15; financial award applicants required to submit FAFSA. *Faculty research:* Building systems engineering, construction engineering and management, environmental engineering, geoenvironmental engineering, geotechnical engineering, materials and mechanics, structural engineering, water resources engineering, life-cycle engineering. *Total annual research expenditures:* $10.9 million. *Application contact:* E-mail: cvengrad@colorado.edu. Web site: http://ceae.colorado.edu/new/.

University of Colorado Denver, College of Engineering and Applied Science, Department of Civil Engineering, Denver, CO 80217. Offers civil engineering (EASPh D); civil engineering systems (PhD); environmental and sustainability engineering (MS, PhD); geographic information systems (MS); geotechnical engineering (MS, PhD); hydrology and hydraulics (MS, PhD); structural engineering (MS, PhD); transportation engineering (MS, PhD). Part-time and evening/weekend programs available. *Faculty:* 14 full-time (1 woman), 6 part-time/adjunct (0 women). *Students:* 66 full-time (11 women), 65 part-time (14 women); includes 30 minority (10 Black or African American, non-Hispanic/Latino; 8 Asian, non-Hispanic/Latino; 10 Hispanic/Latino; 2 Two or more races, non-Hispanic/Latino), 17 international. Average age 34. 67 applicants, 54% accepted, 24 enrolled. In 2011, 30 master's, 2 doctorates awarded. *Degree requirements:* For master's, comprehensive exam, thesis or alternative, 30 credit hours, project or thesis; for doctorate, comprehensive exam, thesis/dissertation, 60 credit hours (30 of which are dissertation research). *Entrance requirements:* For master's, GRE, statement of purpose, transcripts, three references; for doctorate, GRE, statement of purpose, transcripts, references, letter of support from faculty stating willingness to serve as dissertation advisor and outlining plan for financial support. Additional exam requirements/recommendations for international students: Required—TOEFL (minimum score 525 paper-based; 197 computer-based). *Application deadline:* For fall admission, 7/15 for domestic students, 6/15 for international students; for spring admission, 12/1 for domestic students, 11/1 for international students. Applications are processed on a rolling basis. Application fee: $50 ($75 for international students). Electronic applications accepted. *Expenses:* Contact institution. *Financial support:* Research assistantships, teaching assistantships, career-related internships or fieldwork, and Federal Work-Study available. Financial award application deadline: 4/1; financial award applicants required to submit FAFSA. *Faculty research:* Earthquake source physics, environmental biotechnology, hydrologic and hydraulic engineering, sustainability assessments, transportation energy use and greenhouse gas emissions. *Unit head:* Dr. Kevin Rens, Chair, 303-556-8017, Fax: 303-556-2368, E-mail: kevin.rens@ucdenver.edu. *Application contact:* Maria Rase, Program Assistant, 303-556-6712, Fax: 303-556-2368, E-mail: maria.rase@ucdenver.edu. Web site: http://www.ucdenver.edu/academics/colleges/Engineering/Programs/Civil-Engineering/Pages/CivilEngineering.aspx.

University of Connecticut, Graduate School, School of Engineering, Department of Civil and Environmental Engineering, Field of Environmental Engineering, Storrs, CT 06269. Offers MS, PhD. *Degree requirements:* For master's, comprehensive exam; for doctorate, thesis/dissertation. *Entrance requirements:* For master's and doctorate, GRE General Test. Additional exam requirements/recommendations for international students: Required—TOEFL (minimum score 550 paper-based; 213 computer-based). Electronic applications accepted.

University of Dayton, Department of Civil and Environmental Engineering and Engineering Mechanics, Dayton, OH 45469-1300. Offers engineering mechanics (MSEM); environmental engineering (MSCE); geotechnical engineering (MSCE); structural engineering (MSCE); transportation engineering (MSCE); water resources engineering (MSCE). Part-time programs available. *Faculty:* 7 full-time (2 women), 2 part-time/adjunct (0 women). *Students:* 16 full-time (4 women), 9 part-time (4 women); includes 1 minority (Asian, non-Hispanic/Latino), 13 international. Average age 27. 53 applicants, 38% accepted, 5 enrolled. In 2011, 7 degrees awarded. *Degree requirements:* For master's, thesis optional. *Entrance requirements:* For master's, minimum GPA of 3.0 in undergraduate work. Additional exam requirements/recommendations for international students: Required—TOEFL (minimum score 550 paper-based; 213 computer-based; 80 iBT). *Application deadline:* For fall admission, 8/1 for domestic students, 3/1 for international students; for winter admission, 7/1 for international students; for spring admission, 1/1 for international students. Applications are processed on a rolling basis. Application fee: $0 ($50 for international students). Electronic applications accepted. *Expenses: Tuition:* Full-time $8400; part-time $700 per credit hour. *Required fees:* $25 per semester. Tuition and fees vary according to degree level. *Financial support:* Research assistantships available. Financial award applicants required to submit FAFSA. *Faculty research:* Physical modeling of hydraulic systems, finite element methods, mechanics of composite materials, transportation systems safety, biological treatment processes. *Total annual research expenditures:* $200,000. *Unit head:* Dr. Donald V. Chase, Chair, 937-229-3847, Fax: 937-229-3491, E-mail: dchase1@udayton.edu. *Application contact:* Dr. Donald Chase, Chair, 937-229-3847, Fax: 937-229-3491, E-mail: dchase1@udayton.edu. Web site: http://www.udayton.edu/engineering/civil.

University of Delaware, College of Engineering, Department of Civil and Environmental Engineering, Newark, DE 19716. Offers environmental engineering (MAS, MCE, PhD); geotechnical engineering (MAS, MCE, PhD); ocean engineering (MAS, MCE, PhD); structural engineering (MAS, MCE, PhD); transportation engineering (MAS, MCE, PhD); water resource engineering (MAS, MCE, PhD). Part-time programs available. Terminal master's awarded for partial completion of doctoral program. *Degree requirements:* For master's, thesis; for doctorate, thesis/dissertation. *Entrance requirements:* For master's and doctorate, GRE General Test. Additional exam requirements/recommendations for international students: Required—TOEFL. Electronic applications accepted. *Faculty research:* Structural engineering and mechanics; transportation engineering; ocean engineering; soil mechanics and foundation; water resources and environmental engineering.

University of Detroit Mercy, College of Engineering and Science, Department of Civil and Environmental Engineering, Detroit, MI 48221. Offers ME, DE. Evening/weekend programs available. *Faculty research:* Geotechnical engineering.

University of Florida, Graduate School, College of Engineering, Department of Environmental Engineering Sciences, Gainesville, FL 32611. Offers ME, MS, PhD, Engr, JD/MS. Part-time and evening/weekend programs available. Postbaccalaureate distance learning degree programs offered (no on-campus study). Terminal master's awarded for partial completion of doctoral program. *Degree requirements:* For master's, comprehensive exam (for some programs), thesis (for some programs), project, thesis or coursework; for doctorate, comprehensive exam, thesis/dissertation; for Engr, project or thesis. *Entrance requirements:* For master's and doctorate, GRE General Test, minimum GPA of 3.0; for Engr, GRE General Test. Additional exam requirements/recommendations for international students: Required—TOEFL (minimum score 550 paper-based; 213 computer-based; 80 iBT), IELTS (minimum score 6). Electronic applications accepted. *Faculty research:* Air resources, ecological systems, solid and hazardous waste, sustainability and environmental nanotechnology, water and wastewater treatment.

University of Georgia, Faculty of Engineering, Athens, GA 30602. Offers MS. *Students:* 13 full-time (4 women), 1 part-time (0 women); includes 3 minority (1 Asian, non-Hispanic/Latino; 1 Hispanic/Latino; 1 Two or more races, non-Hispanic/Latino), 5 international. Average age 27. 15 applicants, 33% accepted, 3 enrolled. In 2011, 5 master's awarded. *Unit head:* Dr. E. Dale Threadgill. *Application contact:* Dr. Melissa Barry, Assistant Dean of The Graduate School, 706-425-2934, Fax: 706-425-3093, E-mail: mjb14@uga.edu. Web site: http://www.engineering.uga.edu/.

University of Guelph, Graduate Studies, College of Physical and Engineering Science, School of Engineering, Guelph, ON N1G 2W1, Canada. Offers biological engineering (M Eng, M Sc, MA Sc, PhD); engineering systems and computing (M Eng, M Sc, MA Sc, PhD); environmental engineering (M Eng, M Sc, MA Sc, PhD); water resources engineering (M Eng, M Sc, MA Sc, PhD). Part-time programs available. *Degree requirements:* For master's, thesis (for some programs); for doctorate, comprehensive exam, thesis/dissertation. *Entrance requirements:* For master's, minimum B- average during previous 2 years of course work; for doctorate, minimum B average. Additional exam requirements/recommendations for international students: Required—TOEFL (minimum score 550 paper-based; 213 computer-based; 89 iBT), IELTS (minimum score 6.5). Electronic applications accepted. *Faculty research:* Water and food safety, environmental contaminant fates and mechanisms, computer systems, robotics and mechatronics, waste treatment.

University of Hawaii at Manoa, Graduate Division, College of Engineering, Department of Civil and Environmental Engineering, Honolulu, HI 96822. Offers MS, PhD. Part-time programs available. *Degree requirements:* For master's, comprehensive exam, thesis; for doctorate, comprehensive exam, thesis/dissertation. *Entrance requirements:* For master's and doctorate, GRE General Test or EIT Exam. Additional exam requirements/recommendations for international students: Required—TOEFL (minimum score 540 paper-based; 207 computer-based; 76 iBT), IELTS (minimum score 5). *Faculty research:* Structures, transportation, environmental engineering, geotechnical engineering, construction.

University of Idaho, College of Graduate Studies, College of Engineering, Department of Engineering, Program in Environmental Engineering, Moscow, ID 83844-2282. Offers M Engr, MS. *Students:* 2 full-time. Average age 27. In 2011, 1 master's awarded. *Application deadline:* For fall admission, 8/1 for domestic students; for spring admission, 12/15 for domestic students. Applications are processed on a rolling basis. Application fee: $60. Electronic applications accepted. *Expenses:* Tuition, state resident: full-time $3874; part-time $334 per credit hour. Tuition, nonresident: full-time $16,394; part-time $861 per credit hour. *Required fees:* $2808; $99 per credit hour. Tuition and fees vary according to program. *Financial support:* Applicants required to submit FAFSA. *Unit* *head:* Dr. Larry Stauffer, Interim Dean, 208-885-7461, E-mail: enve@uidaho.edu. *Application contact:* Erick Larson, Director of Graduate Admissions, 208-885-4723, E-mail: gadms@uidaho.edu. Web site: http://www.webs1.uidaho.edu/enve/.

University of Illinois at Urbana–Champaign, Graduate College, College of Engineering, Department of Civil and Environmental Engineering, Champaign, IL 61820. Offers civil engineering (MS); environmental engineering in civil engineering (MS, PhD); environmental science in civil engineering (MS, PhD); M Arch/MS; MBA/MS. *Faculty:* 46 full-time (7 women). *Students:* 421 full-time (123 women), 76 part-time (22 women); includes 54 minority (2 Black or African American, non-Hispanic/Latino; 1 American Indian or Alaska Native, non-Hispanic/Latino; 31 Asian, non-Hispanic/Latino; 14 Hispanic/Latino; 6 Two or more races, non-Hispanic/Latino), 271 international. 1,112 applicants, 41% accepted, 169 enrolled. In 2011, 154 master's, 29 doctorates awarded. *Entrance requirements:* For master's and doctorate, GRE. Additional exam requirements/recommendations for international students: Required—TOEFL (minimum score 550 paper-based; 213 computer-based; 79 iBT) or IELTS (minimum score 6.5). *Application deadline:* Applications are processed on a rolling basis. Application fee: $75 ($90 for international students). Electronic applications accepted. *Financial support:* In 2011–12, 57 fellowships, 258 research assistantships, 90 teaching assistantships were awarded; tuition waivers (full and partial) also available. *Unit head:* Amr S. Elnashai, Jr., Head, 217-265-5497, Fax: 217-265-8040, E-mail: aelnash@illinois.edu. *Application contact:* Maxine M. Peyton, Office Manager, 217-333-6636, Fax: 217-333-9464, E-mail: mpeyton@illinois.edu. Web site: http://cee.illinois.edu/.

The University of Iowa, Graduate College, College of Engineering, Department of Civil and Environmental Engineering, Iowa City, IA 52242-1316. Offers MS, PhD. Part-time programs available. *Faculty:* 22 full-time (3 women), 1 part-time/adjunct (0 women). *Students:* 90 full-time (25 women); includes 4 minority (2 Black or African American, non-Hispanic/Latino; 2 Asian, non-Hispanic/Latino), 38 international. Average age 28. 235 applicants, 25% accepted, 20 enrolled. In 2011, 16 master's, 8 doctorates awarded. Terminal master's awarded for partial completion of doctoral program. *Degree requirements:* For master's, thesis optional, exam; for doctorate, comprehensive exam, thesis/dissertation, exam. *Entrance requirements:* For master's, GRE, minimum undergraduate GPA of 3.0; for doctorate, GRE, master's degree or equivalent with minimum GPA of 3.2. Additional exam requirements/recommendations for international students: Required—TOEFL (minimum score 550 paper-based; 213 computer-based; 81 iBT). *Application deadline:* For fall admission, 2/1 priority date for domestic students, 2/1 for international students; for spring admission, 12/1 for domestic students, 10/1 for international students. Applications are processed on a rolling basis. Application fee: $60 ($100 for international students). Electronic applications accepted. *Financial support:* In 2011–12, 8 fellowships with partial tuition reimbursements (averaging $23,480 per year), 73 research assistantships with partial tuition reimbursements (averaging $22,553 per year), 20 teaching assistantships with partial tuition reimbursements (averaging $16,908 per year) were awarded; career-related internships or fieldwork, Federal Work-Study, scholarships/grants, traineeships, and unspecified assistantships also available. Support available to part-time students. Financial award application deadline: 2/1; financial award applicants required to submit FAFSA. *Faculty research:* Water resources; environmental engineering and science; hydraulics and hydrology; structures, mechanics, and materials; transportation engineering. *Total annual research expenditures:* $14.6 million. *Unit head:* Dr. Michelle Scherer, Department Executive Officer, 319-335-5654, Fax: 319-335-5660, E-mail: michelle-scherer@uiowa.edu. *Application contact:* Judy Holland, Secretary, 319-335-5647, Fax: 319-335-5660, E-mail: cee@engineering.uiowa.edu. Web site: http://www.cee.engineering.uiowa.edu/.

The University of Kansas, Graduate Studies, School of Engineering, Program in Environmental Engineering, Lawrence, KS 66045. Offers MS, PhD. Part-time programs available. *Faculty:* 9 full-time (1 woman), 1 part-time/adjunct (0 women). *Students:* 13 full-time (6 women), 6 part-time (3 women), 8 international. Average age 28. 27 applicants, 85% accepted, 7 enrolled. In 2011, 4 master's awarded. *Degree requirements:* For master's, thesis or alternative, exam; for doctorate, comprehensive exam, thesis/dissertation. *Entrance requirements:* For master's and doctorate, GRE, BS in engineering. Additional exam requirements/recommendations for international students: Required—TOEFL. *Application deadline:* For fall admission, 3/1 priority date for domestic students, 3/1 for international students; for spring admission, 12/1 priority date for domestic students, 8/15 for international students. Applications are processed on a rolling basis. Application fee: $55 ($65 for international students). Electronic applications accepted. Tuition and fees vary according to course load, campus/location, program and reciprocity agreements. *Financial support:* Fellowships with full tuition reimbursements, research assistantships with full tuition reimbursements, teaching assistantships with full and partial tuition reimbursements, and career-related internships or fieldwork available. Financial award application deadline: 2/7. *Faculty research:* Water quality, water treatment, wastewater treatment, air quality, air pollution control, solid waste, hazardous waste, water resources engineering. *Unit head:* Craig D. Adams, Chair, 785-864-2700, Fax: 785-864-5631, E-mail: adamscd@ku.edu. *Application contact:* Bruce M. McEnroe, Graduate Advisor, 785-864-2925, Fax: 785-864-2925, E-mail: mcenroe@ku.edu. Web site: http://www.ceae.ku.edu/.

University of Louisville, J. B. Speed School of Engineering, Department of Civil and Environmental Engineering, Louisville, KY 40292-0001. Offers civil engineering (M Eng, MS, PhD). *Accreditation:* ABET (one or more programs are accredited). Part-time programs available. Postbaccalaureate distance learning degree programs offered (no on-campus study). *Faculty:* 10 full-time (1 woman). *Students:* 38 full-time (5 women), 21 part-time (2 women); includes 2 minority (1 American Indian or Alaska Native, non-Hispanic/Latino; 1 Asian, non-Hispanic/Latino), 12 international. Average age 27. 20 applicants, 45% accepted, 6 enrolled. In 2011, 33 master's, 2 doctorates awarded. Terminal master's awarded for partial completion of doctoral program. *Degree requirements:* For master's, comprehensive exam (for some programs), thesis or alternative; for doctorate, comprehensive exam, thesis/dissertation, minimum GPA of 3.0. *Entrance requirements:* For master's and doctorate, GRE General Test. Additional exam requirements/recommendations for international students: Required—TOEFL (minimum score 550 paper-based; 213 computer-based; 80 iBT), IELTS (minimum score 6.5). *Application deadline:* For fall admission, 5/1 priority date for domestic students, 5/1 for international students; for spring admission, 11/1 priority date for domestic students, 11/1 for international students. Applications are processed on a rolling basis. Application fee: $50. Electronic applications accepted. *Expenses:* Tuition, state resident: full-time $9692; part-time $539 per credit hour. Tuition, nonresident: full-time $20,168; part-time $1121 per credit hour. Tuition and fees vary according to program and reciprocity agreements. *Financial support:* In 2011–12, 7 students received support, including 1 fellowship with full tuition reimbursement available (averaging $20,000 per year), 1 research assistantship with full tuition reimbursement available (averaging $20,000 per year), 5 teaching assistantships with full tuition reimbursements available (averaging $20,000 per year). Financial award application deadline: 1/25; financial award applicants required to submit FAFSA. *Faculty research:* Structures, hydraulics, transportation, environmental engineering, geomechanics. *Total annual research expenditures:* $1.8 million. *Unit head:* Dr. J. P. Mohsen, Chair, 502-852-6276, Fax: 502-852-8851, E-mail: jpmohs01@louisville.edu. *Application contact:* Dr. Michael Day, Associate Dean, 502-852-6195, Fax: 502-852-7294, E-mail: day@louisville.edu. Web site: http://www.louisville.edu/speed/civil/.

The University of Manchester, School of Mechanical, Aerospace and Civil Engineering, Manchester, United Kingdom. Offers advanced manufacturing technology (M Ent); aerospace engineering (M Phil, M Sc, PhD); civil engineering (M Phil, M Sc, PhD); environmental engineering (M Phil, PhD); management of projects (M Phil, M Sc, PhD); mechanical engineering (M Phil, M Sc, PhD); mechanical engineering design (M Ent); nuclear engineering (M Phil, D Eng, PhD).

University of Maryland, College Park, Academic Affairs, A. James Clark School of Engineering, Department of Civil and Environmental Engineering, College Park, MD 20742. Offers M Eng, MS, PhD. Part-time and evening/weekend programs available. Postbaccalaureate distance learning degree programs offered. *Faculty:* 67 full-time (14 women), 22 part-time/adjunct (4 women). *Students:* 173 full-time (61 women), 48 part-time (13 women); includes 35 minority (13 Black or African American, non-Hispanic/Latino; 12 Asian, non-Hispanic/Latino; 6 Hispanic/Latino; 4 Two or more races, non-Hispanic/Latino), 112 international. 341 applicants, 32% accepted, 48 enrolled. In 2011, 35 master's, 18 doctorates awarded. *Degree requirements:* For master's, thesis optional; for doctorate, thesis/dissertation, qualifying exam. *Entrance requirements:* For master's and doctorate, GRE General Test, 3 letters of recommendation. *Application deadline:* For fall admission, 5/1 for domestic students, 2/1 for international students; for spring admission, 10/15 for domestic students, 6/1 for international students. Applications are processed on a rolling basis. Application fee: $75. Electronic applications accepted. *Expenses: Tuition, area resident:* Part-time $525 per credit hour. Tuition, state resident: part-time $525 per credit hour. Tuition, nonresident: part-time $1131 per credit hour. *Required fees:* $386.31 per term. Tuition and fees vary according to program. *Financial support:* In 2011–12, 13 fellowships with full and partial tuition reimbursements (averaging $13,372 per year), 83 research assistantships (averaging $19,243 per year), 27 teaching assistantships (averaging $18,634 per year) were awarded; Federal Work-Study and scholarships/grants also available. Support available to part-time students. Financial award applicants required to submit FAFSA. *Faculty research:* Transportation and urban systems, environmental engineering, geotechnical engineering, construction engineering and management, hydraulics. *Total annual research expenditures:* $22.2 million. *Unit head:* Dr. Ali Haghani, Chair, 301-405-1974, E-mail: haghani@umd.edu. *Application contact:* Dr. Charles A. Caramello, Dean of Graduate School, 301-405-0358, Fax: 301-314-9305, E-mail: ccaramel@umd.edu.

University of Massachusetts Amherst, Graduate School, College of Engineering, Department of Civil and Environmental Engineering, Amherst, MA 01003. Offers civil engineering (MSCE, PhD); environmental and water resources (MSCE); geotechnical (MSCE); structural engineering and mechanics (MSCE); transportation (MSCE). *Accreditation:* ABET (one or more programs are accredited). Part-time programs available. *Faculty:* 28 full-time (7 women). *Students:* 91 full-time (30 women), 11 part-time (5 women); includes 13 minority (3 Black or African American, non-Hispanic/Latino; 5 Asian, non-Hispanic/Latino; 4 Hispanic/Latino; 1 Two or more races, non-Hispanic/Latino), 29 international. Average age 27. 293 applicants, 53% accepted, 40 enrolled. In 2011, 38 master's, 1 doctorate awarded. Terminal master's awarded for partial completion of doctoral program. *Degree requirements:* For master's, thesis or alternative; for doctorate, comprehensive exam, thesis/dissertation. *Entrance requirements:* For master's and doctorate, GRE General Test. Additional exam requirements/recommendations for international students: Required—TOEFL (minimum score 550 paper-based; 213 computer-based; 80 iBT), IELTS (minimum score 6.5). *Application deadline:* For fall admission, 2/1 for domestic and international students; for spring admission, 10/1 for domestic and international students. Applications are processed on a rolling basis. Application fee: $50 ($65 for international students). Electronic applications accepted. Tuition and fees vary according to course load, campus/location and program. *Financial support:* In 2011–12, 1 fellowship with full tuition reimbursement (averaging $1,000 per year), 74 research assistantships with full tuition reimbursements (averaging $15,151 per year), 6 teaching assistantships with full tuition reimbursements (averaging $15,151 per year) were awarded; career-related internships or fieldwork, Federal Work-Study, scholarships/grants, traineeships, health care benefits, tuition waivers, and unspecified assistantships also available. Support available to part-time students. Financial award application deadline: 2/1; financial award applicants required to submit FAFSA. *Unit head:* Dr. Sanjay Arwade, Graduate Program Director, 413-545-0686, Fax: 413-545-2840. *Application contact:* Lindsay DeSantis, Interim Supervisor of Admissions, 413-545-0722, Fax: 413-577-0100, E-mail: gradadm@grad.umass.edu. Web site: http://cee.umass.edu/.

University of Massachusetts Dartmouth, Graduate School, College of Engineering, Program in Civil and Environmental Engineering, North Dartmouth, MA 02747-2300. Offers MS. Part-time programs available. *Faculty:* 8 full-time (2 women), 3 part-time/adjunct (0 women). *Students:* 10 full-time (0 women), 12 part-time (1 woman); includes 3 minority (2 Black or African American, non-Hispanic/Latino; 1 Hispanic/Latino), 8 international. Average age 26. 29 applicants, 97% accepted, 11 enrolled. In 2011, 3 degrees awarded. *Degree requirements:* For master's, thesis or alternative. *Entrance requirements:* For master's, GRE, minimum GPA of 3.0, 3 letters of recommendation, resume, statement of intent. Additional exam requirements/recommendations for international students: Required—TOEFL (minimum score 550 paper-based; 213 computer-based). *Application deadline:* For fall admission, 2/15 priority date for domestic students, 1/15 for international students; for spring admission, 11/15 priority date for domestic students, 10/15 for international students. Application fee: $40 ($60 for international students). *Expenses:* Tuition, state resident: full-time $2071; part-time $86.29 per credit. Tuition, nonresident: full-time $8099; part-time $337.46 per credit. *Required fees:* $438.58 per credit. Part-time tuition and fees vary according to class time, course load, degree level and reciprocity agreements. *Financial support:* In 2011–12, 6 research assistantships with full tuition reimbursements (averaging $12,982 per year), 5 teaching assistantships with full tuition reimbursements (averaging $9,650 per year) were awarded. Financial award application deadline: 3/1; financial award applicants required to submit FAFSA. *Faculty research:* Nutrient removal and recovery, water resources engineering, pavement design and management, waste water treatment systems, hydrology. *Total annual research expenditures:* $556,147. *Unit head:* Dr. Nima Rahbar, Graduate Program Director, 508-999-8467, Fax: 508-999-8964, E-mail: nrahbar@umassd.edu. *Application contact:* Elan Turcotte-Shamski, Graduate Admissions Officer, 508-999-8604, Fax: 508-999-8183, E-mail: graduate@umassd.edu. Web site: http://www.umassd.edu/engineering/cen/graduate/welcome.cfm.

University of Massachusetts Lowell, College of Engineering, Department of Civil and Environmental Engineering and College of Sciences, Program in Environmental Studies, Lowell, MA 01854-2881. Offers environmental engineering (MSES); environmental studies (PhD, Certificate). Part-time programs available. *Degree requirements:* For master's, thesis optional. *Entrance requirements:* For master's, GRE General Test.

Faculty research: Remote sensing of air pollutants, atmospheric deposition of toxic metals, contaminant transport in groundwater, soil remediation.

University of Memphis, Graduate School, Herff College of Engineering, Department of Civil Engineering, Memphis, TN 38152. Offers civil engineering (PhD); environmental engineering (MS); foundation engineering (MS); structural engineering (MS); transportation engineering (MS); water resources engineering (MS). Terminal master's awarded for partial completion of doctoral program. *Degree requirements:* For master's, comprehensive exam, thesis optional; for doctorate, comprehensive exam, thesis/dissertation. *Entrance requirements:* For master's, GRE General Test or MAT, minimum undergraduate GPA of 2.5; for doctorate, GRE, 3 letters of recommendation. Additional exam requirements/recommendations for international students: Required—TOEFL (minimum score 550 paper-based; 210 computer-based; 79 iBT). *Faculty research:* Structural response to earthquakes, pavement design, water quality, transportation safety, intermodal transportation,.

University of Michigan, College of Engineering, Department of Civil and Environmental Engineering, Ann Arbor, MI 48109. Offers civil engineering (MSE, PhD, CE); construction engineering and management (M Eng, MSE); environmental engineering (MSE, PhD); structural engineering (M Eng); MBA/MSE. Part-time programs available. *Students:* 139 full-time (54 women), 3 part-time (1 woman). 539 applicants, 40% accepted, 66 enrolled. In 2011, 52 master's, 10 doctorates awarded. *Degree requirements:* For master's, thesis optional; for doctorate, comprehensive exam, thesis/dissertation, oral defense of dissertation, preliminary and written exams. *Entrance requirements:* For master's and doctorate, GRE General Test. Additional exam requirements/recommendations for international students: Required—TOEFL (minimum score 560 paper-based; 220 computer-based). *Application deadline:* Applications are processed on a rolling basis. Application fee: $65 ($75 for international students). Electronic applications accepted. *Financial support:* Fellowships, research assistantships, teaching assistantships, institutionally sponsored loans, and tuition waivers (partial) available. Financial award application deadline: 1/19. *Faculty research:* Construction engineering and management, geotechnical engineering, earthquake-resistant design of structures, environmental chemistry and microbiology, cost engineering, environmental and water resources engineering. *Unit head:* Kim Hayes, Chair, 734-764-8495, Fax: 734-764-4292, E-mail: ford@umich.edu. *Application contact:* Kimberly Smith, Student Advisor, 734-764-8405, Fax: 734-647-2127, E-mail: kansmith@umich.edu. Web site: http://www.engin.umich.edu/dept/cee/.

University of Missouri, Graduate School, College of Engineering, Department of Civil and Environmental Engineering, Columbia, MO 65211. Offers civil engineering (MS, PhD); environmental engineering (MS, PhD); geotechnical engineering (MS, PhD); structural engineering (MS, PhD); transportation and highway engineering (MS); water resources (MS, PhD). *Faculty:* 18 full-time (2 women), 1 part-time/adjunct (0 women). *Students:* 45 full-time (16 women), 38 part-time (8 women); includes 5 minority (2 Black or African American, non-Hispanic/Latino; 2 Asian, non-Hispanic/Latino; 1 Hispanic/Latino), 49 international. Average age 28. 109 applicants, 28% accepted, 20 enrolled. In 2011, 14 master's, 2 doctorates awarded. *Degree requirements:* For master's, report or thesis; for doctorate, thesis/dissertation. *Entrance requirements:* For master's and doctorate, GRE General Test. Additional exam requirements/recommendations for international students: Required—TOEFL (minimum score 550 paper-based; 213 computer-based; 79 iBT). *Application deadline:* For fall admission, 3/15 priority date for domestic students; for winter admission, 10/15 priority date for domestic students. Application fee: $55 ($75 for international students). *Expenses:* Tuition, state resident: full-time $5881. Tuition, nonresident: full-time $15,183. *Required fees:* $952. Tuition and fees vary according to campus/location and program. *Financial support:* Fellowships, research assistantships, teaching assistantships, and institutionally sponsored loans available. *Unit head:* Dr. Mark Virkler, Department Chair, E-mail: virklerm@missouri.edu. *Application contact:* Jennifer Keyzer-Andre, 573-882-4442, E-mail: keyzerandrej@missouri.edu. Web site: http://engineering.missouri.edu/civil/.

University of Nebraska–Lincoln, Graduate College, College of Engineering, Interdepartmental Area of Environmental Engineering, Lincoln, NE 68588. Offers MS, PhD. *Degree requirements:* For master's, thesis optional; for doctorate, comprehensive exam, thesis/dissertation. *Entrance requirements:* For master's and doctorate, GRE General Test. Additional exam requirements/recommendations for international students: Required—TOEFL (minimum score 550 paper-based; 213 computer-based). Electronic applications accepted. *Faculty research:* Wastewater engineering, hazardous waste management, solid waste management, groundwater engineering.

University of Nevada, Las Vegas, Graduate College, Howard R. Hughes College of Engineering, Department of Civil and Environmental Engineering, Las Vegas, NV 89154-4015. Offers civil and environmental engineering (MSE, PhD); transportation (MS). Part-time programs available. *Faculty:* 19 full-time (4 women), 15 part-time/adjunct (1 woman). *Students:* 14 full-time (1 woman), 42 part-time (9 women); includes 12 minority (1 Black or African American, non-Hispanic/Latino; 1 American Indian or Alaska Native, non-Hispanic/Latino; 2 Asian, non-Hispanic/Latino; 4 Hispanic/Latino; 4 Two or more races, non-Hispanic/Latino), 18 international. Average age 32. 36 applicants, 81% accepted, 14 enrolled. In 2011, 16 master's, 2 doctorates awarded. *Degree requirements:* For master's, comprehensive exam (for some programs), thesis (for some programs); for doctorate, comprehensive exam, thesis/dissertation. *Entrance requirements:* For master's and doctorate, GRE General Test. Additional exam requirements/recommendations for international students: Required—TOEFL (minimum score 550 paper-based; 213 computer-based; 80 iBT), IELTS (minimum score 7). *Application deadline:* For fall admission, 6/15 priority date for domestic students, 5/1 for international students; for spring admission, 11/15 priority date for domestic students, 10/1 for international students. Applications are processed on a rolling basis. Application fee: $60 ($95 for international students). Electronic applications accepted. *Financial support:* In 2011–12, 33 students received support, including 15 research assistantships with partial tuition reimbursements available (averaging $8,527 per year), 18 teaching assistantships with partial tuition reimbursements available (averaging $9,210 per year); institutionally sponsored loans, scholarships/grants, health care benefits, and unspecified assistantships also available. Financial award application deadline: 3/1. *Total annual research expenditures:* $340,041. *Unit head:* Dr. David Ashley, Professor, 702-895-4040, Fax: 702-895-3936, E-mail: david.b.ashley@unlv.edu. *Application contact:* Graduate College Admissions Evaluator, 702-895-3320, Fax: 702-895-4180, E-mail: gradcollege@unlv.edu. Web site: http://ce.egr.unlv.edu/.

University of New Brunswick Fredericton, School of Graduate Studies, Faculty of Engineering, Department of Civil Engineering, Fredericton, NB E3B 5A3, Canada. Offers construction engineering and management (M Eng, M Sc E, PhD); environmental engineering (M Eng, M Sc E, PhD); environmental studies (M Eng); geotechnical engineering (M Eng, M Sc E, PhD); groundwater/hydrology (M Eng, M Sc E, PhD); materials (M Eng, M Sc E, PhD); pavements (M Eng, M Sc E, PhD); structures (M Eng, M Sc E, PhD); transportation (M Eng, M Sc E, PhD). Part-time programs available. *Faculty:* 13 full-time (1 woman), 7 part-time/adjunct (1 woman). *Students:* 31 full-time (7 women), 17 part-time (2 women). In 2011, 11 master's, 2 doctorates awarded. *Degree requirements:* For master's, thesis, proposal; for doctorate, comprehensive exam, thesis/dissertation, qualifying exam; proposal; 27 credit hours of courses. *Entrance requirements:* For master's, minimum GPA of 3.0; B Sc E in civil engineering or related engineering degree; for doctorate, minimum GPA of 3.0; graduate degree in engineering or applied science. Additional exam requirements/recommendations for international students: Required—TWE (minimum score 4), TOEFL (minimum score 580 paper-based; 237 computer-based) or IELTS (minimum score 7.5). *Application deadline:* For fall admission, 5/1 priority date for domestic students; for winter admission, 11/1 priority date for domestic students. Applications are processed on a rolling basis. Application fee: $50 Canadian dollars. *Financial support:* In 2011–12, 14 fellowships, 30 research assistantships (averaging $7,000 per year), 42 teaching assistantships (averaging $2,000 per year) were awarded; career-related internships or fieldwork and scholarships/grants also available. *Faculty research:* Construction engineering and management; materials and infrastructure renewal; highway and pavement research; structures and solid mechanics; geotechnical, soil; structure interaction; transportation and planning; environment, solid waste management. *Unit head:* Dr. Eric Hildebrand, Director of Graduate Studies, 506-453-5113, Fax: 506-453-3568, E-mail: edh@unb.ca. *Application contact:* Joyce Moore, Graduate Secretary, 506-452-6127, Fax: 506-453-3568, E-mail: civil-grad@unb.ca. Web site: http://www.unbf.ca/eng/civil/.

University of New Haven, Graduate School, Tagliatela College of Engineering, Program in Environmental Engineering, West Haven, CT 06516-1916. Offers environmental engineering (MS); industrial and hazardous wastes (MS); water and wastewater treatment (MS). Part-time and evening/weekend programs available. *Students:* 15 full-time (5 women), 11 part-time (3 women); includes 1 minority (Asian, non-Hispanic/Latino), 18 international. Average age 31. 17 applicants, 100% accepted, 10 enrolled. In 2011, 15 master's awarded. *Degree requirements:* For master's, thesis or alternative. *Entrance requirements:* For master's, bachelor's degree in engineering. Additional exam requirements/recommendations for international students: Required—TOEFL (minimum score 520 paper-based; 190 computer-based; 70 iBT); Recommended—IELTS (minimum score 5.5). *Application deadline:* For fall admission, 5/31 for international students; for winter admission, 10/15 for international students; for spring admission, 1/15 for international students. Applications are processed on a rolling basis. Application fee: $50. Electronic applications accepted. *Expenses: Tuition:* Part-time $750 per credit. *Financial support:* Research assistantships with partial tuition reimbursements, teaching assistantships with partial tuition reimbursements, career-related internships or fieldwork, Federal Work-Study, scholarships/grants, tuition waivers, and unspecified assistantships available. Support available to part-time students. Financial award application deadline: 5/1; financial award applicants required to submit FAFSA. *Unit head:* Dr. Agamemnon D. Koutsospyros, Coordinator, 203-932-7398. *Application contact:* Eloise Gormley, Director of Graduate Admissions, 203-932-7449, Fax: 203-932-7137, E-mail: gradinfo@newhaven.edu. Web site: http://www.newhaven.edu/10140/.

The University of North Carolina at Chapel Hill, Graduate School, School of Public Health, Department of Environmental Sciences and Engineering, Chapel Hill, NC 27599. Offers air, radiation and industrial hygiene (MPH, MS, MSEE, MSPH, PhD); aquatic and atmospheric sciences (MPH, MS, MSPH, PhD); environmental engineering (MPH, MS, MSEE, MSPH, PhD); environmental health sciences (MPH, MS, MSPH, PhD); environmental management and policy (MPH, MS, MSPH, PhD). Terminal master's awarded for partial completion of doctoral program. *Degree requirements:* For master's, comprehensive exam, thesis (for some programs), research paper; for doctorate, comprehensive exam, thesis/dissertation. *Entrance requirements:* For master's and doctorate, GRE General Test, minimum GPA of 3.0. Additional exam requirements/recommendations for international students: Required—TOEFL. Electronic applications accepted. *Faculty research:* Air, radiation and industrial hygiene, aquatic and atmospheric sciences, environmental health sciences, environmental management and policy, water resources engineering.

The University of North Carolina at Charlotte, Graduate School, The William States Lee College of Engineering, Department of Civil and Environmental Engineering, Charlotte, NC 28223-0001. Offers civil engineering (MSCE); infrastructure and environmental systems (PhD), including infrastructure and environmental systems design. Part-time and evening/weekend programs available. *Faculty:* 20 full-time (2 women). *Students:* 57 full-time (12 women), 41 part-time (10 women); includes 15 minority (3 Black or African American, non-Hispanic/Latino; 2 American Indian or Alaska Native, non-Hispanic/Latino; 3 Asian, non-Hispanic/Latino; 6 Hispanic/Latino; 1 Two or more races, non-Hispanic/Latino), 34 international. Average age 29. 56 applicants, 73% accepted, 24 enrolled. In 2011, 20 master's, 4 doctorates awarded. Terminal master's awarded for partial completion of doctoral program. *Degree requirements:* For master's, thesis or project. *Entrance requirements:* For master's, GRE General Test, minimum GPA of 3.0 in undergraduate major, 2.75 overall. Additional exam requirements/recommendations for international students: Required—TOEFL (minimum score 550 paper-based; 220 computer-based; 83 iBT). *Application deadline:* For fall admission, 7/1 for domestic students, 5/1 for international students; for spring admission, 11/1 for domestic students, 10/1 for international students. Applications are processed on a rolling basis. Application fee: $65 ($75 for international students). Electronic applications accepted. *Expenses:* Tuition, state resident: full-time $3689. Tuition, nonresident: full-time $15,226. *Required fees:* $2198. Tuition and fees vary according to course load and program. *Financial support:* In 2011–12, 44 students received support, including 2 fellowships (averaging $23,547 per year), 25 research assistantships (averaging $5,581 per year), 17 teaching assistantships (averaging $5,679 per year); career-related internships or fieldwork, Federal Work-Study, institutionally sponsored loans, and scholarships/grants also available. Support available to part-time students. Financial award application deadline: 4/1; financial award applicants required to submit FAFSA. *Faculty research:* Structural composite materials, storm water systems, natural and man-made disaster reduction engineering, older drivers and nighttime driving, soil contamination and transport. *Total annual research expenditures:* $1.3 million. *Unit head:* Dr. David T. Young, Chair, 704-687-4175, Fax: 704-687-6953, E-mail: dyoung@.uncc.edu. *Application contact:* Kathy B. Giddings, Director of Graduate Admissions, 704-687-5503, Fax: 704-687-3279, E-mail: gradadm@uncc.edu. Web site: http://cee.uncc.edu/.

University of North Dakota, Graduate School, School of Engineering and Mines, Department of Environmental Engineering, Grand Forks, ND 58202. Offers M Engr, MS. *Degree requirements:* For master's, thesis. *Entrance requirements:* For master's, GRE General Test, minimum GPA of 3.0. Additional exam requirements/recommendations for international students: Required—TOEFL (minimum score 550 paper-based; 213 computer-based; 79 iBT), IELTS (minimum score 6.5). Electronic applications accepted.

University of Notre Dame, Graduate School, College of Engineering, Department of Civil Engineering and Geological Sciences, Notre Dame, IN 46556. Offers bioengineering (MS Bio E); civil engineering (MSCE); civil engineering and geological sciences (PhD); environmental engineering (MS Env E); geological sciences (MS).

Terminal master's awarded for partial completion of doctoral program. *Degree requirements:* For master's, comprehensive exam; for doctorate, thesis/dissertation, candidacy exam. *Entrance requirements:* For master's and doctorate, GRE General Test. Additional exam requirements/recommendations for international students: Required—TOEFL (minimum score 600 paper-based; 250 computer-based; 80 iBT). Electronic applications accepted. *Faculty research:* Environmental modeling, biological-waste treatment, petrology, environmental geology, geochemistry.

University of Oklahoma, College of Earth and Energy, School of Petroleum and Geological Engineering, Program in Petroleum Engineering, Norman, OK 73019. Offers natural gas engineering and management (MS); petroleum engineering (MS, PhD). Part-time programs available. *Students:* 64 full-time (12 women), 26 part-time (3 women); includes 5 minority (all Black or African American, non-Hispanic/Latino), 76 international. Average age 28. 237 applicants, 12% accepted, 19 enrolled. In 2011, 31 master's, 5 doctorates awarded. Terminal master's awarded for partial completion of doctoral program. *Degree requirements:* For master's, thesis optional, industrial team project or thesis; for doctorate, thesis/dissertation. *Entrance requirements:* For master's, GRE General Test, bachelor's degree in engineering, 3 letters of recommendation, minimum GPA of 3.0 during final 60 hours of undergraduate course work; for doctorate, GRE General Test, minimum GPA of 3.0, 3 letters of recommendation. Additional exam requirements/recommendations for international students: Required—TOEFL (minimum score 550 paper-based; 79 iBT). *Application deadline:* For fall admission, 6/1 priority date for domestic students, 3/1 for international students; for spring admission, 11/1 for domestic students, 9/1 for international students. Applications are processed on a rolling basis. Application fee: $40 ($90 for international students). Electronic applications accepted. *Expenses:* Tuition, state resident: full-time $4087; part-time $170.30 per credit hour. Tuition, nonresident: full-time $14,875; part-time $619.80 per credit hour. *Required fees:* $2659; $100.25 per credit hour. Tuition and fees vary according to course load and degree level. *Financial support:* In 2011–12, 83 students received support. Traineeships available. Financial award applicants required to submit FAFSA. *Faculty research:* Petrophysics, shale gas, reservoir simulation coiled tubing, poro-mechanics, enhanced oil recovery. *Unit head:* Dr. Chandra Rai, Director, 405-325-2921, Fax: 405-325-7477, E-mail: crai@ou.edu. *Application contact:* Shalli Young, Executive Assistant to the Graduate Liaison, 405-325-2921, Fax: 405-325-7477, E-mail: syoung@ou.edu. Web site: http://mpge.ou.edu/.

University of Oklahoma, College of Engineering, School of Civil Engineering and Environmental Science, Program in Environmental Engineering, Norman, OK 73019. Offers MS, PhD. Part-time programs available. *Students:* 5 full-time (2 women), 5 part-time (1 woman); includes 1 minority (American Indian or Alaska Native, non-Hispanic/Latino), 3 international. Average age 31. 14 applicants, 29% accepted, 3 enrolled. In 2011, 3 degrees awarded. *Entrance requirements:* For master's, undergraduate degree in a related engineering or science discipline. Additional exam requirements/recommendations for international students: Required—TOEFL (minimum score 600 paper-based; 100 iBT). *Application deadline:* For fall admission, 4/1 priority date for domestic students, 3/1 for international students; for spring admission, 11/1 for domestic students, 9/1 for international students. Applications are processed on a rolling basis. Application fee: $40 ($90 for international students). Electronic applications accepted. *Expenses:* Tuition, state resident: full-time $4087; part-time $170.30 per credit hour. Tuition, nonresident: full-time $14,875; part-time $619.80 per credit hour. *Required fees:* $2659; $100.25 per credit hour. Tuition and fees vary according to course load and degree level. *Financial support:* In 2011–12, 10 students received support. Scholarships/grants available. *Faculty research:* Coastal zone flood prediction, inland runoff modeling, flooding and drought due to climate change, water treatment. *Unit head:* Robert C. Knox, Director, 405-325-5911, Fax: 405-325-4217, E-mail: rknox@ou.edu. *Application contact:* Susan Williams, Graduate Programs Specialist, 405-325-2344, Fax: 405-325-4217, E-mail: srwilliams@ou.edu. Web site: http://cees.ou.edu.

University of Pittsburgh, Swanson School of Engineering, Department of Civil and Environmental Engineering, Pittsburgh, PA 15260. Offers MSCEE, PhD. Part-time programs available. Postbaccalaureate distance learning degree programs offered. *Faculty:* 16 full-time (4 women), 18 part-time/adjunct (1 woman). *Students:* 79 full-time (21 women), 49 part-time (16 women); includes 7 minority (1 Black or African American, non-Hispanic/Latino; 5 Asian, non-Hispanic/Latino; 1 Native Hawaiian or other Pacific Islander, non-Hispanic/Latino), 58 international. 336 applicants, 79% accepted, 42 enrolled. In 2011, 42 master's, 10 doctorates awarded. Terminal master's awarded for partial completion of doctoral program. *Degree requirements:* For master's, thesis optional; for doctorate, comprehensive exam, thesis/dissertation, final oral exams. *Entrance requirements:* For master's and doctorate, minimum QPA of 3.0. Additional exam requirements/recommendations for international students: Required—TOEFL (minimum score 550 paper-based; 213 computer-based; 80 iBT). *Application deadline:* For fall admission, 3/1 priority date for domestic students; for spring admission, 7/1 priority date for domestic students. Applications are processed on a rolling basis. Application fee: $50. Electronic applications accepted. *Expenses:* Tuition, state resident: full-time $18,774; part-time $760 per credit. Tuition, nonresident: full-time $30,736; part-time $1258 per credit. *Required fees:* $740; $200 per term. Tuition and fees vary according to program. *Financial support:* In 2011–12, 39 students received support, including 7 fellowships with tuition reimbursements available (averaging $27,768 per year), 20 research assistantships with full tuition reimbursements available (averaging $22,296 per year), 12 teaching assistantships with full tuition reimbursements available (averaging $22,836 per year); scholarships/grants, traineeships, and tuition waivers (full and partial) also available. Financial award application deadline: 4/15. *Faculty research:* Environmental and water resources, structures and infrastructures, construction management. *Total annual research expenditures:* $4.2 million. *Unit head:* Dr. Radisav Vidic, Chairman, 412-624-9870, Fax: 412-624-0135. *Application contact:* Dr. Leonard Casson, Academic Coordinator, 412-624-9868, Fax: 412-624-0135, E-mail: leonard@pitt.edu. Web site: http://www.engineering.pitt.edu/Civil/.

University of Regina, Faculty of Graduate Studies and Research, Faculty of Engineering and Applied Science, Program in Environmental Systems Engineering, Regina, SK S4S 0A2, Canada. Offers M Eng, MA Sc, PhD. Part-time programs available. *Faculty:* 10 full-time (3 women). *Students:* 53 full-time (17 women), 7 part-time (3 women). 62 applicants, 34% accepted. In 2011, 6 master's, 4 doctorates awarded. *Degree requirements:* For master's, thesis (for some programs); for doctorate, thesis/dissertation. *Entrance requirements:* For doctorate, master's degree. Additional exam requirements/recommendations for international students: Required—TOEFL (minimum score 550 paper-based; 80 iBT), IELTS (minimum score 6.5). *Application deadline:* For fall admission, 3/31 for domestic and international students; for winter admission, 7/31 for domestic and international students; for spring admission, 11/30 for domestic and international students. Application fee: $100. Electronic applications accepted. *Financial support:* In 2011–12, 12 fellowships (averaging $6,500 per year), 3 research assistantships (averaging $17,500 per year), 10 teaching assistantships (averaging $2,298 per year) were awarded; career-related internships or fieldwork and scholarships/grants also available. Financial award application deadline: 6/15. *Faculty research:* Design of water and wastewater treatment systems, urban and regional transportation planning, environmental fluid mechanics, air quality management, environmental modeling and decision-making. *Unit head:* Dr. Raphael Idem, Associate Dean, Research and Graduate Studies, 306-585-4770, Fax: 306-585-4855, E-mail: raphael.idem@uregina.ca. *Application contact:* Amy Veawab, Graduate Program Coordinator, 306-585-5665, Fax: 306-585-4855, E-mail: amy.veawab@uregina.ca.

University of Rhode Island, Graduate School, College of Engineering, Department of Civil and Environmental Engineering, Kingston, RI 02881. Offers MS, PhD. Part-time programs available. *Faculty:* 9 full-time (3 women), 2 part-time/adjunct (0 women). *Students:* 33 full-time (7 women), 12 part-time (2 women); includes 4 minority (1 Asian, non-Hispanic/Latino; 2 Hispanic/Latino; 1 Two or more races, non-Hispanic/Latino), 9 international. In 2011, 16 master's, 1 doctorate awarded. *Degree requirements:* For master's, comprehensive exam (for some programs), thesis optional; for doctorate, comprehensive exam, thesis/dissertation. *Entrance requirements:* For master's and doctorate, 2 letters of recommendation. Additional exam requirements/recommendations for international students: Required—TOEFL (minimum score 550 paper-based; 213 computer-based). *Application deadline:* For fall admission, 7/15 for domestic students, 2/1 for international students; for spring admission, 11/15 for domestic students, 7/15 for international students. Application fee: $65. Electronic applications accepted. *Expenses:* Tuition, state resident: full-time $10,432; part-time $580 per credit hour. Tuition, nonresident: full-time $23,130; part-time $1285 per credit hour. *Required fees:* $1362; $36 per credit hour. $35 per semester. One-time fee: $130. *Financial support:* In 2011–12, 3 research assistantships with full and partial tuition reimbursements (averaging $6,482 per year), 4 teaching assistantships with full and partial tuition reimbursements (averaging $8,302 per year) were awarded. Financial award application deadline: 7/15; financial award applicants required to submit FAFSA. *Faculty research:* Industrial waste treatment, structural health monitoring, traffic and transit system operations, computational mechanics, engineering materials design. *Unit head:* Dr. George E. Tsiatas, Chair, 401-874-5117, Fax: 401-874-2786, E-mail: gt@uri.edu. *Application contact:* Dr. Mayrai Gindy, Director of Graduate Studies, 401-874-5587, Fax: 401-874-2786, E-mail: gindy@egr.uri.edu. Web site: http://www.uri.edu/cve/.

University of Saskatchewan, College of Graduate Studies and Research, College of Engineering, Division of Environmental Engineering, Saskatoon, SK S7N 5A2, Canada. Offers M Eng, M Sc, PhD, Diploma. *Degree requirements:* For master's, thesis (for some programs); for doctorate, thesis/dissertation. *Entrance requirements:* For master's and doctorate, GRE. Additional exam requirements/recommendations for international students: Required—TOEFL.

University of Southern California, Graduate School, Viterbi School of Engineering, Sonny Astani Department of Civil Engineering, Los Angeles, CA 90089. Offers applied mechanics (MS); civil engineering (MS, PhD); computer-aided engineering (ME, Graduate Certificate); construction management (MCM); engineering technology commercialization (Graduate Certificate); environmental engineering (MS, PhD); environmental quality management (ME); structural design (ME); sustainable cities (Graduate Certificate); transportation systems (MS, Graduate Certificate); water and waste management (MS). Part-time and evening/weekend programs available. Terminal master's awarded for partial completion of doctoral program. *Degree requirements:* For master's, thesis optional; for doctorate, thesis/dissertation. *Entrance requirements:* For master's and doctorate, GRE General Test. Additional exam requirements/recommendations for international students: Recommended—TOEFL. Electronic applications accepted. *Faculty research:* Geotechnical engineering, transportation engineering, structural engineering, construction management, environmental engineering, water resources.

University of South Florida, Graduate School, College of Engineering, Department of Civil and Environmental Engineering, Tampa, FL 33620-9951. Offers civil and environmental engineering (MSES); civil engineering (MCE, MSCE, PhD); environmental engineering (MSEV). Part-time programs available. *Faculty:* 20 full-time (5 women), 3 part-time/adjunct (1 woman). *Students:* 116 full-time (40 women), 66 part-time (15 women); includes 38 minority (9 Black or African American, non-Hispanic/Latino; 7 Asian, non-Hispanic/Latino; 20 Hispanic/Latino; 2 Two or more races, non-Hispanic/Latino), 49 international. Average age 30. 184 applicants, 55% accepted, 52 enrolled. In 2011, 51 master's, 7 doctorates awarded. Terminal master's awarded for partial completion of doctoral program. *Degree requirements:* For master's, comprehensive exam, thesis (for some programs); for doctorate, comprehensive exam, thesis/dissertation. *Entrance requirements:* For master's, GRE, minimum GPA of 3.0 in last 60 hours of coursework, two letters of reference, statement of purpose; for doctorate, GRE, minimum GPA of 3.0 in last 60 hours of coursework, three letters of recommendation, statement of purpose, resume. Additional exam requirements/recommendations for international students: Required—TOEFL (minimum score 550 paper-based; 213 computer-based; 79 iBT). *Application deadline:* For fall admission, 2/15 for domestic students, 1/2 for international students; for spring admission, 10/15 for domestic students, 6/1 for international students. Application fee: $30. Electronic applications accepted. *Financial support:* In 2011–12, 65 students received support, including 44 research assistantships (averaging $14,123 per year), 21 teaching assistantships with tuition reimbursements available (averaging $15,329 per year). *Faculty research:* Water resources, structures and materials, transportation, geotechnical engineering, mechanics. *Total annual research expenditures:* $2.6 million. *Unit head:* Dr. Manjriker Gunaratne, Dean, 813-974—5818, Fax: 813-974-5094, E-mail: gunaratn@usf.edu. *Application contact:* Dr. Sarina Ergas, Program Director, 813-974-1119, Fax: 813-974-2957, E-mail: sergas@usf.edu. Web site: http://ce.eng.usf.edu/.

The University of Tennessee, Graduate School, College of Engineering, Department of Civil and Environmental Engineering, Program in Environmental Engineering, Knoxville, TN 37996. Offers MS, MS/MBA. Part-time programs available. Postbaccalaureate distance learning degree programs offered (minimal on-campus study). *Faculty:* 13 full-time (0 women), 5 part-time/adjunct (1 woman). *Students:* 13 full-time (3 women), 6 part-time (2 women); includes 1 minority (Black or African American, non-Hispanic/Latino), 2 international. Average age 23. 29 applicants, 76% accepted, 10 enrolled. In 2011, 10 degrees awarded. *Degree requirements:* For master's, thesis or alternative. *Entrance requirements:* For master's, GRE General Test (for MS students pursuing research thesis), minimum GPA of 2.7 (for U.S. degree holders), 3.0 (for international degree holders); 3 references; statement of purpose; resume. Additional exam requirements/recommendations for international students: Required—TOEFL (minimum score 550 paper-based; 213 computer-based). *Application deadline:* For fall admission, 2/1 priority date for domestic students, 2/1 for international students; for spring admission, 6/15 for domestic and international students. Applications are processed on a rolling basis. Application fee: $35. Electronic applications accepted. *Expenses:* Tuition, state resident: full-time $8332; part-time $464 per credit hour. Tuition, nonresident: full-time $25,174; part-time $1400 per credit hour. *Required fees:* $1162; $56 per credit hour. Tuition and fees vary according to program. *Financial support:* In 2011–12, 10 students received support, including 3 research assistantships with full tuition reimbursements available (averaging $16,800 per year), 3 teaching assistantships with full tuition reimbursements available (averaging $16,723 per year); career-related internships or fieldwork, Federal Work-Study, institutionally sponsored loans, health care benefits, and unspecified assistantships also available. Financial award application deadline: 2/1; financial award applicants required to submit FAFSA. *Faculty research:* Air pollution control technologies; climate change and engineering impact on environment; environmental sampling, monitoring, and restoration; soil erosion prediction and control; waste management and utilization. *Unit head:* Dr. Dayakar Penumadu, Head, 865-974-2355, Fax: 865-974-2355, E-mail: dpenumad@utk.edu. *Application contact:* Dr. Chris Cox, Associate Head, 865-974-7729, Fax: 865-974-2355, E-mail: ccox9@utk.edu. Web site: http://www.engr.utk.edu/civil/.

The University of Texas at Austin, Graduate School, Cockrell School of Engineering, Department of Civil, Architectural and Environmental Engineering, Program in Environmental and Water Resources Engineering, Austin, TX 78712-1111. Offers MS, PhD. *Accreditation:* ABET. Part-time programs available. *Degree requirements:* For master's, thesis or alternative. *Entrance requirements:* For master's, GRE General Test. Additional exam requirements/recommendations for international students: Required—TOEFL. *Application deadline:* For fall admission, 1/15 priority date for domestic students, 1/15 for international students; for spring admission, 9/1 priority date for domestic students, 9/1 for international students. Applications are processed on a rolling basis. Application fee: $50 ($75 for international students). Electronic applications accepted. *Financial support:* Fellowships, research assistantships, and teaching assistantships available. Financial award application deadline: 2/1. *Unit head:* Dr. Mary Jo Kirisits, Graduate Advisor, 512-232-7120, E-mail: ewre@mail.ce.utecas.edu. *Application contact:* Kathy Rose, Graduate Coordinator, 512-232-1702, Fax: 512-471-0592, E-mail: krose@mail.utexas.edu. Web site: http://www.caee.utexas.edu/ewre/.

The University of Texas at El Paso, Graduate School, College of Engineering, Department of Civil Engineering, El Paso, TX 79968-0001. Offers civil engineering (MS, PhD); construction management (MS, Certificate); environmental engineering (MEENE, MSENE). Part-time and evening/weekend programs available. *Students:* 106 (25 women); includes 55 minority (2 Asian, non-Hispanic/Latino; 53 Hispanic/Latino), 44 international. Average age 34. 71 applicants, 86% accepted, 47 enrolled. In 2011, 22 master's awarded. *Degree requirements:* For master's, thesis optional. *Entrance requirements:* For master's, GRE General Test, minimum GPA of 3.0. Additional exam requirements/recommendations for international students: Required—TOEFL. *Application deadline:* For fall admission, 7/1 priority date for domestic students, 3/1 for international students; for spring admission, 11/1 priority date for domestic students, 9/1 for international students. Applications are processed on a rolling basis. Application fee: $15 ($65 for international students). Electronic applications accepted. *Financial support:* In 2011–12, research assistantships with partial tuition reimbursements (averaging $21,125 per year), teaching assistantships with partial tuition reimbursements (averaging $16,900 per year) were awarded; fellowships with partial tuition reimbursements, career-related internships or fieldwork, Federal Work-Study, institutionally sponsored loans, scholarships/grants, tuition waivers (partial), and stipends also available. Financial award application deadline: 3/15; financial award applicants required to submit FAFSA. *Faculty research:* On-site wastewater treatment systems, wastewater reuse, disinfection by-product control, water resources, membrane filtration. *Unit head:* Wen-Whai Li, Chair, 915-747-5464, E-mail: wli@utep.edu. *Application contact:* Dr. Benjamin Flores, Interim Dean of the Graduate School, 915-747-5491, Fax: 915-747-5788, E-mail: bflores@utep.edu. Web site: http://ce.utep.edu/.

The University of Texas at El Paso, Graduate School, Interdisciplinary Program in Environmental Science and Engineering, El Paso, TX 79968-0001. Offers PhD. Part-time and evening/weekend programs available. *Students:* 61 (20 women); includes 23 minority (1 American Indian or Alaska Native, non-Hispanic/Latino; 2 Asian, non-Hispanic/Latino; 20 Hispanic/Latino), 30 international. Average age 34. In 2011, 2 doctorates awarded. *Degree requirements:* For doctorate, thesis/dissertation. *Entrance requirements:* For doctorate, GRE, letters of recommendation. Additional exam requirements/recommendations for international students: Required—TOEFL; Recommended—IELTS. *Application deadline:* For fall admission, 8/1 for domestic students, 3/1 for international students; for spring admission, 11/1 for domestic students, 9/3 for international students. Applications are processed on a rolling basis. Application fee: $45 ($80 for international students). Electronic applications accepted. *Financial support:* In 2011–12, research assistantships with partial tuition reimbursements (averaging $22,500 per year), teaching assistantships with partial tuition reimbursements (averaging $18,000 per year) were awarded; fellowships with partial tuition reimbursements, institutionally sponsored loans, scholarships/grants, health care benefits, tuition waivers (partial), and unspecified assistantships also available. Support available to part-time students. Financial award application deadline: 3/15; financial award applicants required to submit FAFSA. *Unit head:* Dr. Barry A. Benedict, Director, 915-747-5604, Fax: 915-747-5145, E-mail: babenedict@utep.edu. *Application contact:* Dr. Benjamin Flores, Interim Dean of the Graduate School, 915-747-5491, Fax: 915-747-5788, E-mail: bflores@utep.edu.

The University of Texas at San Antonio, College of Engineering, Department of Civil and Environmental Engineering, San Antonio, TX 78249-0617. Offers civil engineering (MCE, MS, MSCE); environmental science and engineering (PhD). Part-time and evening/weekend programs available. *Faculty:* 13 full-time (2 women), 5 part-time/adjunct. *Students:* 48 full-time (13 women), 25 part-time (3 women); includes 27 minority (5 Black or African American, non-Hispanic/Latino; 3 Asian, non-Hispanic/Latino; 19 Hispanic/Latino), 27 international. Average age 30. 58 applicants, 67% accepted, 23 enrolled. In 2011, 21 master's, 2 doctorates awarded. *Degree requirements:* For master's, comprehensive exam (for some programs), thesis (for some programs); for doctorate, comprehensive exam, thesis/dissertation. *Entrance requirements:* For master's, GRE General Test, bachelor's degree with 18 credit hours in field of study or in another appropriate field of study, statement of purpose; for doctorate, GRE, BA or BS and MS from accredited university, minimum GPA of 3.0 in upper-division and graduate courses, resume, three letters of recommendation, statement of purpose. Additional exam requirements/recommendations for international students: Required—TOEFL (minimum score 550 paper-based; 79 iBT), IELTS (minimum score 5). *Application deadline:* For fall admission, 7/1 for domestic students, 4/1 for international students; for spring admission, 11/1 for domestic students, 9/1 for international students. Application fee: $45 ($85 for international students). *Expenses:* Tuition, state resident: full-time $3148; part-time $2176 per semester. Tuition, nonresident: full-time $8782; part-time $5932 per semester. *Required fees:* $719 per semester. *Financial support:* In 2011–12, 29 students received support, including 5 fellowships (averaging $4,100 per year), 18 research assistantships with partial tuition reimbursements available (averaging $19,882 per year), 18 teaching assistantships (averaging $4,680 per year); scholarships/grants and unspecified assistantships also available. Financial award application deadline: 3/31. *Faculty research:* Fate, transport and reactivity of chemicals in natural systems/contaminant adsorption/desorption involving nano-particles; transportation infrastructure management and pavement materials; hydrologic analysis; beneficial use of wastes and industrial by-products; pavement-vehicle interaction. *Unit head:* Dr. Athanassio T. Papagiannakis, Chair, 210-458-7517, Fax: 210-458-6475, E-mail: at.papagiannakis@utsa.edu. *Application contact:* Athanassios Papagiannakis, Graduate Advisor of Record, 210-458-7517, Fax: 210-458-7517, E-mail: at.papagiannakis@utsa.edu.

The University of Texas at Tyler, College of Engineering and Computer Science, Department of Civil Engineering, Tyler, TX 75799-0001. Offers environmental engineering (MS); industrial safety (MS); structural engineering (MS); transportation engineering (MS); water resources engineering (MS). Part-time and evening/weekend programs available. *Degree requirements:* For master's, thesis optional. *Entrance requirements:* For master's, GRE General Test, bachelor's degree in engineering, associated science degree. Additional exam requirements/recommendations for international students: Required—TOEFL (minimum score 79 computer-based). *Faculty research:* Non-destructive strength testing, indoor air quality, transportation routing and signaling, pavement replacement criteria, flood water routing, construction and long-term behavior of innovative geotechnical foundation and embankment construction used in highway construction, engineering education.

University of Utah, Graduate School, College of Engineering, Department of Civil and Environmental Engineering, Interdepartmental Program in Environmental Engineering, Salt Lake City, UT 84112-1107. Offers ME, MS, PhD. Part-time programs available. *Students:* 1 full-time (0 women), 1 (woman) part-time. Average age 39. 1 applicant, 0% accepted. Terminal master's awarded for partial completion of doctoral program. *Degree requirements:* For master's, comprehensive exam, thesis (for some programs); for doctorate, comprehensive exam, thesis/dissertation. *Entrance requirements:* For master's and doctorate, GRE, minimum undergraduate GPA of 3.0. Additional exam requirements/recommendations for international students: Required—TOEFL (minimum score 500 paper-based; 173 computer-based). *Application deadline:* For fall admission, 4/1 for domestic and international students; for spring admission, 11/1 for domestic and international students. Applications are processed on a rolling basis. Application fee: $55 ($65 for international students). Electronic applications accepted. *Expenses:* Contact institution. *Financial support:* Application deadline: 2/15; applicants required to submit FAFSA. *Unit head:* Dr. Paul J. Tikalsky, Chair and Professor in Civil and Environmental Engineering, 801-581-6931, Fax: 801-585-5477, E-mail: tikalsky@civil.utah.edu. *Application contact:* Amanda May, Academic Advisor, 801-581-6931, Fax: 850-585-5477, E-mail: amandam@civil.utah.edu. Web site: http://www.eegp.utah.edu.

University of Utah, Graduate School, College of Mines and Earth Sciences, Department of Geology and Geophysics, Salt Lake City, UT 84112. Offers environmental engineering (ME, MS, PhD); geological engineering (ME, MS, PhD); geology (MS, PhD); geophysics (MS, PhD). *Faculty:* 22 full-time (5 women), 4 part-time/adjunct (0 women). *Students:* 55 full-time (16 women), 28 part-time (9 women); includes 2 minority (both Asian, non-Hispanic/Latino), 16 international. Average age 30. 174 applicants, 17% accepted, 21 enrolled. In 2011, 13 master's, 3 doctorates awarded. Terminal master's awarded for partial completion of doctoral program. *Median time to degree:* Of those who began their doctoral program in fall 2003, 76% received their degree in 8 years or less. *Degree requirements:* For master's, comprehensive exam, thesis; for doctorate, thesis/dissertation, qualifying exam (written and oral). *Entrance requirements:* For master's and doctorate, GRE General Test, minimum GPA of 3.25. Additional exam requirements/recommendations for international students: Required—TOEFL (minimum score 500 paper-based; 173 computer-based). *Application deadline:* For fall admission, 1/15 priority date for domestic students, 1/15 for international students. Applications are processed on a rolling basis. Application fee: $55 ($65 for international students). Electronic applications accepted. *Financial support:* In 2011–12, 22 students received support, including 10 fellowships with full tuition reimbursements available (averaging $15,000 per year), 40 research assistantships with full tuition reimbursements available (averaging $22,000 per year), 14 teaching assistantships with full tuition reimbursements available (averaging $15,000 per year); career-related internships or fieldwork, institutionally sponsored loans, scholarships/grants, unspecified assistantships, and stipends also available. Financial award application deadline: 1/15; financial award applicants required to submit FAFSA. *Faculty research:* Igneous, metamorphic, and sedimentary petrology; ore deposits; aqueous geochemistry; isotope geochemistry; heat flow. *Total annual research expenditures:* $3.3 million. *Unit head:* Dr. Kip Solomon, Chair, 801-581-7231, Fax: 801-581-7065, E-mail: kip.solomon@utah.edu. *Application contact:* Dr. Cari L. Johnson, Director of Graduate Studies, 801-585-3782, Fax: 801-581-7065, E-mail: cari.johnson@utah.edu. Web site: http://www.earth.utah.edu/.

University of Vermont, Graduate College, College of Engineering and Mathematics, Department of Civil and Environmental Engineering, Burlington, VT 05405. Offers MS, PhD. *Students:* 35 (12 women), 9 international. 55 applicants, 49% accepted, 7 enrolled. In 2011, 4 master's, 2 doctorates awarded. *Degree requirements:* For master's, thesis or alternative; for doctorate, thesis/dissertation. *Entrance requirements:* For master's and doctorate, GRE General Test. Additional exam requirements/recommendations for international students: Required—TOEFL (minimum score 550 paper-based; 213 computer-based; 80 iBT). *Application deadline:* For fall admission, 2/1 priority date for domestic students, 2/1 for international students. Applications are processed on a rolling basis. Application fee: $40. Electronic applications accepted. *Financial support:* Research assistantships and teaching assistantships available. Financial award application deadline: 3/1. *Unit head:* Dr. Jason Bates, Interim Director, 802-656-3800. *Application contact:* Dr. Britt Holmen, Coordinator, 802-656-3800.

University of Washington, Graduate School, College of Engineering, Department of Civil and Environmental Engineering, Seattle, WA 98195-2700. Offers civil engineering (MS, MSE, PhD); construction engineering (MSCE); environmental engineering (MS, MSCE, MSE, PhD); global trade, transportation and logistics (MS); hydrology, water resources, and environmental fluid mechanics (MS, MSCE, MSE, PhD); structural and geotechnical engineering and mechanics (MS, MSCE, MSE, PhD); transportation and construction engineering (MS, MSE, PhD); transportation engineering (MSCE). Part-time programs available. Postbaccalaureate distance learning degree programs offered (no on-campus study). *Faculty:* 47 full-time (11 women), 9 part-time/adjunct (1 woman). *Students:* 195 full-time (67 women), 72 part-time (19 women); includes 37 minority (4 Black or African American, non-Hispanic/Latino; 27 Asian, non-Hispanic/Latino; 6 Hispanic/Latino), 65 international. 654 applicants, 57% accepted, 100 enrolled. In 2011, 88 master's, 7 doctorates awarded. Terminal master's awarded for partial completion of doctoral program. *Degree requirements:* For master's, thesis (for some programs); for doctorate, comprehensive exam, thesis/dissertation, general, qualifying, and final exams; completion of degree within 10 years. *Entrance requirements:* For master's, GRE General Test, minimum GPA of 3.0, statement of purpose, letters of recommendation, transcripts; for doctorate, GRE General Test, minimum GPA of 3.5, statement of purpose, letters of recommendation, transcripts. Additional exam requirements/recommendations for international students: Required—TOEFL (minimum score 580 paper-based; 237 computer-based; 92 iBT); Recommended—IELTS (minimum score 7). *Application deadline:* For fall admission, 1/10 priority date for domestic students, 1/10 for international students. Applications are processed on a rolling basis. Application fee: $75. Electronic applications accepted. *Expenses:* Contact institution. *Financial support:* In 2011–12, 99 students received support, including 16 fellowships with full and partial tuition reimbursements available (averaging $16,173 per year), 71 research assistantships with full tuition reimbursements available (averaging $16,380 per year), 10 teaching assistantships with full tuition reimbursements available (averaging $16,380 per year); scholarships/grants also available. Financial award application deadline: 1/10; financial award applicants required to submit FAFSA. *Faculty research:* Environmental/water resources, hydrology; construction/transportation; structures/ geotechnical. *Total annual research expenditures:* $13.6 million. *Unit head:* Dr. Gregory R. Miller, Professor/Chair, 206-543-0350, Fax: 206-543-1543, E-mail: gmiller@uw.edu. *Application contact:* Lorna Latal, Graduate Adviser, 206-543-2574, Fax: 206-543-1543, E-mail: llatal@u.washington.edu. Web site: http://www.ce.washington.edu/programs/prospective/grad/applying/gen_admission.html.

University of Waterloo, Graduate Studies, Faculty of Engineering, Department of Civil and Environmental Engineering, Waterloo, ON N2L 3G1, Canada. Offers M Eng, MA Sc, PhD. Part-time programs available. *Degree requirements:* For master's, research paper or thesis; for doctorate, comprehensive exam, thesis/dissertation. *Entrance requirements:* For master's, honors degree, minimum B average; for doctorate, master's degree, minimum A- average. Additional exam requirements/recommendations for international students: Required—TOEFL, TWE. Electronic applications accepted. *Faculty research:* Water resources, structures, construction management, transportation, geotechnical engineering.

The University of Western Ontario, Faculty of Graduate Studies, Physical Sciences Division, Faculty of Engineering, London, ON N6A 5B8, Canada. Offers chemical and biochemical engineering (ME Sc, PhD); civil and environmental engineering (M Eng, ME Sc, PhD); electrical and computer engineering (M Eng, ME Sc, PhD); mechanical and materials engineering (M Eng, ME Sc, PhD). Part-time programs available. Terminal master's awarded for partial completion of doctoral program. *Degree requirements:* For master's, thesis; for doctorate, thesis/dissertation. *Entrance requirements:* For master's, minimum B average; for doctorate, minimum B+ average. *Faculty research:* Wind, geotechnical, chemical reactor engineering, applied electrostatics, biochemical engineering.

University of Windsor, Faculty of Graduate Studies, Faculty of Engineering, Department of Civil and Environmental Engineering, Windsor, ON N9B 3P4, Canada. Offers civil engineering (M Eng, MA Sc, PhD); environmental engineering (M Eng, MA Sc, PhD). Part-time programs available. *Degree requirements:* For master's, thesis; for doctorate, comprehensive exam, thesis/dissertation. *Entrance requirements:* For master's, minimum B average; for doctorate, master's degree, minimum A average. Additional exam requirements/recommendations for international students: Required—TOEFL (minimum score 580 paper-based; 237 computer-based). Electronic applications accepted. *Faculty research:* Odors: sampling, measurement, control; drinking water disinfection, hydrocarbon contaminated soil remediation, structural dynamics, numerical simulation of piezoelectric materials.

University of Wisconsin–Madison, Graduate School, College of Engineering, Department of Civil and Environmental Engineering, Madison, WI 53706-1380. Offers MS, PhD. Part-time programs available. *Faculty:* 31 full-time (3 women), 2 part-time/ adjunct (0 women). *Students:* 164 full-time (37 women); includes 9 minority (2 Black or African American, non-Hispanic/Latino; 1 Asian, non-Hispanic/Latino; 5 Hispanic/Latino; 1 Native Hawaiian or other Pacific Islander, non-Hispanic/Latino), 64 international. Average age 29. 508 applicants, 16% accepted, 41 enrolled. In 2011, 46 master's, 12 doctorates awarded. Terminal master's awarded for partial completion of doctoral program. *Degree requirements:* For master's, thesis or alternative; for doctorate, thesis/ dissertation, preliminary exam, qualifying exams. *Entrance requirements:* For master's and doctorate, GRE General Test, minimum GPA of 3.0 for last 60 credits of course work. Additional exam requirements/recommendations for international students: Required—TOEFL (minimum score 550 paper-based; 213 computer-based; 80 iBT). *Application deadline:* For fall admission, 12/15 priority date for domestic students, 12/15 for international students; for spring admission, 9/15 for domestic and international students. Application fee: $56. Electronic applications accepted. *Expenses:* Tuition, state resident: full-time $10,296; part-time $643.51 per credit. Tuition, nonresident: full-time $24,054; part-time $1503.40 per credit. *Required fees:* $70.06 per credit. Tuition and fees vary according to course load, campus/location, program and reciprocity agreements. *Financial support:* In 2011–12, 86 students received support, including 5 fellowships with full tuition reimbursements available (averaging $22,440 per year), 59 research assistantships with full tuition reimbursements available (averaging $40,368 per year), 6 teaching assistantships with full tuition reimbursements available (averaging $28,175 per year); Federal Work-Study, scholarships/grants, health care benefits, unspecified assistantships, and project assistantships also available. Support available to part-time students. Financial award application deadline: 12/15. *Faculty research:* Environmental geotechnics and soil mechanics, design and analysis of structures, traffic engineering and intelligent transport systems, industrial pollution control, hydrological monitoring. *Total annual research expenditures:* $11 million. *Unit head:* Craig H. Benson, Chair, 608-262-3491, Fax: 608-262-5199, E-mail: benson@engr.wisc.edu. *Application contact:* Cheryl Loschko, Student Status Examiner, 608-265-5570, Fax: 608-890-1174, E-mail: loschko@wisc.edu. Web site: http://www.engr.wisc.edu/cee/.

University of Wyoming, College of Engineering and Applied Sciences, Department of Civil and Architectural Engineering and Department of Chemical and Petroleum Engineering, Program in Environmental Engineering, Laramie, WY 82070. Offers MS. Part-time programs available. *Degree requirements:* For master's, thesis optional. *Entrance requirements:* For master's, GRE General Test, minimum GPA of 3.0. Additional exam requirements/recommendations for international students: Required—TOEFL (minimum score 550 paper-based; 213 computer-based). Electronic applications accepted. *Faculty research:* Water and waste water, solid and hazardous waste management, air pollution control, flue-gas cleanup.

Utah State University, School of Graduate Studies, College of Engineering, Department of Civil and Environmental Engineering, Logan, UT 84322. Offers ME, MS, PhD, CE. *Degree requirements:* For master's, thesis (for some programs); for doctorate, thesis/dissertation. *Entrance requirements:* For master's and doctorate, GRE General Test, minimum GPA of 3.0. Additional exam requirements/recommendations for international students: Required—TOEFL. Electronic applications accepted. *Faculty research:* Hazardous waste treatment, large space structures, river basin management, earthquake engineering, environmental impact.

Vanderbilt University, School of Engineering, Department of Civil and Environmental Engineering, Program in Environmental Engineering, Nashville, TN 37240-1001. Offers environmental engineering (M Eng); environmental management (MS, PhD). MS and PhD offered through the Graduate School. Part-time programs available. *Faculty:* 9 full-time (0 women), 1 (woman) part-time/adjunct. *Students:* 34 full-time (20 women); includes 4 minority (1 Black or African American, non-Hispanic/Latino; 1 Asian, non-

Hispanic/Latino; 1 Hispanic/Latino; 1 Two or more races, non-Hispanic/Latino), 6 international. Average age 30. 111 applicants, 11% accepted, 9 enrolled. In 2011, 5 master's, 2 doctorates awarded. Terminal master's awarded for partial completion of doctoral program. *Degree requirements:* For master's, thesis or alternative; for doctorate, thesis/dissertation. *Entrance requirements:* For master's and doctorate, GRE General Test. Additional exam requirements/recommendations for international students: Required—TOEFL. *Application deadline:* For fall admission, 1/15 for domestic students; for spring admission, 11/1 for domestic students. Applications are processed on a rolling basis. Application fee: $0. Electronic applications accepted. *Financial support:* In 2011–12, 5 fellowships with full tuition reimbursements (averaging $30,000 per year), 12 research assistantships with full tuition reimbursements (averaging $26,400 per year), 7 teaching assistantships with full tuition reimbursements (averaging $25,020 per year) were awarded; career-related internships or fieldwork, institutionally sponsored loans, scholarships/grants, traineeships, and tuition waivers (full and partial) also available. Financial award application deadline: 1/15. *Faculty research:* Waste treatment, hazardous waste management, chemical waste treatment, water quality. *Unit head:* Dr. David S. Kosson, Chair, 615-322-2697, Fax: 615-322-3365, E-mail: david.kosson@vanderbilt.edu. *Application contact:* Dr. James H. Clarke, Administrator, 615-322-3897, Fax: 615-322-3365. Web site: http://www.cee.vanderbilt.edu/.

Villanova University, College of Engineering, Department of Civil and Environmental Engineering, Program in Water Resources and Environmental Engineering, Villanova, PA 19085-1699. Offers urban water resources design (Certificate); water resources and environmental engineering (MSWREE). Part-time and evening/weekend programs available. Postbaccalaureate distance learning degree programs offered (no on-campus study). *Degree requirements:* For master's, thesis optional. *Entrance requirements:* For master's, GRE General Test (for applicants with degrees from foreign universities), BCE or bachelor's degree in science or related engineering field, minimum GPA of 3.0. Additional exam requirements/recommendations for international students: Required—TOEFL (minimum score 600 paper-based; 250 computer-based; 100 iBT). Electronic applications accepted. *Expenses: Tuition:* Part-time $675 per credit. Part-time tuition and fees vary according to degree level and program. *Faculty research:* Photocatalytic decontamination and disinfection of water, urban storm water wetlands, economy and risk, removal and destruction of organic acids in water, sludge treatment.

Virginia Polytechnic Institute and State University, Graduate School, College of Engineering, Department of Civil and Environmental Engineering, Blacksburg, VA 24061. Offers civil engineering (M Eng, MS, PhD); civil infrastructure systems (Certificate); environmental engineering (MS); environmental sciences and engineering (MS); transportation systems engineering (Certificate); treatment process engineering (Certificate); urban hydrology and stormwater management (Certificate); water quality management (Certificate). *Accreditation:* ABET (one or more programs are accredited). *Degree requirements:* For master's, comprehensive exam (for some programs), thesis (for some programs); for doctorate, comprehensive exam (for some programs), thesis/ dissertation (for some programs). *Entrance requirements:* For master's and doctorate, GRE. Additional exam requirements/recommendations for international students: Required—TOEFL (minimum score 550 paper-based; 213 computer-based). *Application deadline:* For fall admission, 7/1 for domestic and international students; for spring admission, 12/1 for domestic and international students. Applications are processed on a rolling basis. Application fee: $65. Electronic applications accepted. *Expenses:* Tuition, state resident: full-time $10,048; part-time $558.25 per credit hour. Tuition, nonresident: full-time $19,497; part-time $1083.25 per credit hour. *Required fees:* $405 per semester. Tuition and fees vary according to course load, campus/location and program. *Financial support:* Fellowships with full tuition reimbursements, research assistantships with full tuition reimbursements, teaching assistantships with full tuition reimbursements, career-related internships or fieldwork, Federal Work-Study, scholarships/grants, health care benefits, and unspecified assistantships available. Financial award application deadline: 1/15. *Faculty research:* Construction, environmental geotechnical hydrosystems, structures and transportation engineering. *Unit head:* Dr. Sam Easterling, Unit Head, 540-231-5143, Fax: 540-231-7532, E-mail: seaster@vt.edu. *Application contact:* Marc Widdowson, Information Contact, 540-231-7153, Fax: 540-231-7532, E-mail: mwiddows@vt.edu. Web site: http://www.cee.vt.edu/.

Virginia Polytechnic Institute and State University, VT Online, Blacksburg, VA 24061. Offers advanced transportation systems (Certificate); aerospace engineering (MS); agricultural and life sciences (MSLFS); business information systems (Graduate Certificate); career and technical education (MS); civil engineering (MS); computer engineering (M Eng, MS); decision support systems (Graduate Certificate); eLearning leadership (MA); electrical engineering (M Eng, MS); engineering administration (MEA); environmental engineering (Certificate); environmental politics and policy (Graduate Certificate); environmental sciences and engineering (MS); foundations of political analysis (Graduate Certificate); health product risk management (Graduate Certificate); industrial and systems engineering (MS); information policy and society (Graduate Certificate); information security (Graduate Certificate); information technology (MIT); instructional technology (MA); integrative STEM education (MA Ed); liberal arts (Graduate Certificate); life sciences: health product risk management (MS); natural resources (MNR, Graduate Certificate); networking (Graduate Certificate); nonprofit and nongovernmental organization management (Graduate Certificate); ocean engineering (MS); political science (MA); security studies (Graduate Certificate); software development (Graduate Certificate). *Expenses:* Tuition, state resident: full-time $10,048; part-time $558.25 per credit hour. Tuition, nonresident: full-time $19,497; part-time $1083.25 per credit hour. *Required fees:* $405 per semester. Tuition and fees vary according to course load, campus/location and program. *Application contact:* Graduate School Applications General Assistance, 540-231-8636, Fax: 540-231-2039, E-mail: gradappl@vt.edu. Web site: http://www.vto.vt.edu/.

Washington State University, Graduate School, College of Engineering and Architecture, Department of Civil and Environmental Engineering, Program in Environmental Engineering, Pullman, WA 99164. Offers MS. *Faculty:* 27. *Students:* 14 full-time (9 women), 1 (woman) part-time; includes 2 minority (1 Asian, non-Hispanic/ Latino; 1 Two or more races, non-Hispanic/Latino), 7 international. Average age 25. 41 applicants, 24% accepted, 8 enrolled. In 2011, 7 master's awarded. *Degree requirements:* For master's, comprehensive exam (for some programs), thesis (for some programs), oral exam. *Entrance requirements:* For master's, GRE General Test, official transcripts from all colleges and universities attended; one-page statement of purpose; three letters of recommendation. Additional exam requirements/recommendations for international students: Required—TOEFL, IELTS. *Application deadline:* For fall admission, 1/10 priority date for domestic students, 1/10 for international students; for spring admission, 7/1 for domestic and international students. Applications are processed on a rolling basis. Application fee: $75. Electronic applications accepted. *Financial support:* In 2011–12, research assistantships with full and partial tuition reimbursements (averaging $18,204 per year), teaching assistantships with full and partial tuition reimbursements (averaging $18,204 per year) were awarded; career-related internships or fieldwork, Federal Work-Study, and institutionally sponsored loans also available. Financial award application deadline: 4/1; financial award applicants required to submit FAFSA. *Faculty research:* Air quality, hazardous waste, soil and ground water contamination, acid precipitation, global climate. *Total annual research expenditures:* $4.1 million. *Unit head:* Dr. David McLean, Chair, 509-335-9578, Fax: 509-335-7632, E-mail: mclean@wsu.edu. *Application contact:* Graduate School Admissions, 800-GRADWSU, Fax: 509-335-1949, E-mail: gradsch@wsu.edu. Web site: http://www.ce.wsu.edu/.

Washington University in St. Louis, School of Engineering and Applied Science, Department of Energy, Environmental and Chemical Engineering, St. Louis, MO 63130-4899. Offers chemical engineering (MS, D Sc); environmental engineering (MS, D Sc). Part-time programs available. Terminal master's awarded for partial completion of doctoral program. *Degree requirements:* For master's, thesis optional; for doctorate, thesis/dissertation, preliminary exam, qualifying exam. *Entrance requirements:* For master's and doctorate, GRE, minimum B average during final 2 years of course work. Additional exam requirements/recommendations for international students: Required—TOEFL, TWE. Electronic applications accepted. *Faculty research:* Reaction engineering, materials processing, catalysis, process control, air pollution control.

West Virginia University, College of Engineering and Mineral Resources, Department of Civil and Environmental Engineering, Morgantown, WV 26506. Offers civil engineering (MSCE, MSE, PhD). Part-time programs available. *Degree requirements:* For master's, thesis; for doctorate, comprehensive exam, thesis/dissertation. *Entrance requirements:* For master's and doctorate, minimum GPA of 3.0. Additional exam requirements/recommendations for international students: Required—TOEFL. *Faculty research:* Habitat restoration, advanced materials for civil infrastructure, pavement modeling, infrastructure condition assessment.

Worcester Polytechnic Institute, Graduate Studies and Research, Department of Civil and Environmental Engineering, Worcester, MA 01609-2280. Offers civil and environmental engineering (Advanced Certificate, Graduate Certificate); civil engineering (ME, MS, PhD); construction project management (MS); environmental engineering (MS); master builder environmental engineering (M Eng). Part-time and evening/weekend programs available. Postbaccalaureate distance learning degree programs offered (no on-campus study). *Faculty:* 12 full-time (1 woman), 2 part-time/adjunct (0 women). *Students:* 28 full-time (9 women), 49 part-time (14 women); includes 7 minority (1 Black or African American, non-Hispanic/Latino; 1 American Indian or Alaska Native, non-Hispanic/Latino; 2 Asian, non-Hispanic/Latino; 1 Hispanic/Latino; 2 Two or more races, non-Hispanic/Latino), 17 international. 144 applicants, 44% accepted, 28 enrolled. In 2011, 26 master's, 1 doctorate awarded. *Degree requirements:* For master's, thesis optional; for doctorate, comprehensive exam, thesis/dissertation. *Entrance requirements:* For master's and doctorate, GRE (recommended), 3 letters of recommendation. Additional exam requirements/recommendations for international students: Required—TOEFL (minimum score 563 paper-based; 223 computer-based; 84 iBT), IELTS (minimum score 7). *Application deadline:* For fall admission, 1/1 priority date for domestic students, 1/1 for international students; for spring admission, 10/1

priority date for domestic students, 10/1 for international students. Applications are processed on a rolling basis. Application fee: $70. Electronic applications accepted. *Financial support:* Research assistantships, teaching assistantships, career-related internships or fieldwork, institutionally sponsored loans, scholarships/grants, and unspecified assistantships available. Financial award application deadline: 1/1; financial award applicants required to submit FAFSA. *Faculty research:* Pavement engineering and highway materials, analysis and design of structural systems and smart structures, design-construction integration, water resources and physical and chemical treatment processes, energy and sustainability. *Unit head:* Dr. Tahar El-Korchi, Interim Head, 508-831-5530, Fax: 508-831-5808, E-mail: tek@wpi.edu. *Application contact:* Dr. Paul Mathisen, Graduate Coordinator, 508-831-5530, Fax: 508-831-5808, E-mail: mathisen@wpi.edu. Web site: http://www.wpi.edu/Academics/Depts/CEE/.

Worcester Polytechnic Institute, Graduate Studies and Research, Programs in Interdisciplinary Studies, Worcester, MA 01609-2280. Offers bioscience administration (MS); impact engineering (MS); manufacturing engineering management (MS); power systems management (MS); social science (PhD); systems modeling (MS). Part-time and evening/weekend programs available. *Faculty:* 1 full-time (0 women). *Students:* 1 full-time (0 women), 201 part-time (30 women); includes 22 minority (2 Black or African American, non-Hispanic/Latino; 11 Asian, non-Hispanic/Latino; 7 Hispanic/Latino; 2 Two or more races, non-Hispanic/Latino), 5 international. 130 applicants, 90% accepted, 107 enrolled. *Degree requirements:* For master's, thesis; for doctorate, comprehensive exam, thesis/dissertation. *Entrance requirements:* For master's and doctorate, 3 letters of recommendation. Additional exam requirements/recommendations for international students: Required—TOEFL (minimum score 563 paper-based; 223 computer-based; 84 iBT), IELTS (minimum score 7). *Application deadline:* For fall admission, 1/1 priority date for domestic students, 1/1 for international students; for spring admission, 10/1 priority date for domestic students, 10/1 for international students. Application fee: $70. *Financial support:* Institutionally sponsored loans, scholarships/grants, and unspecified assistantships available. Financial award application deadline: 1/1; financial award applicants required to submit FAFSA. *Unit head:* Dr. Fred J. Looft, Head, 508-831-5231, Fax: 508-831-5491, E-mail: fjlooft@wpi.edu. *Application contact:* Lynne Dougherty, Administrative Assistant, 508-831-5301, Fax: 508-831-5717, E-mail: grad@wpi.edu.

Yale University, Graduate School of Arts and Sciences, School of Engineering and Applied Science, Program in Environmental Engineering, New Haven, CT 06520. Offers MS, PhD.

Youngstown State University, Graduate School, College of Science, Technology, Engineering and Mathematics, Department of Civil and Environmental Engineering, Youngstown, OH 44555-0001. Offers MSE. Part-time and evening/weekend programs available. *Degree requirements:* For master's, thesis optional. *Entrance requirements:* For master's, minimum GPA of 2.75 in field. Additional exam requirements/recommendations for international students: Required—TOEFL. *Faculty research:* Structural mechanics, water quality modeling, surface and ground water hydrology, physical and chemical processes in aquatic systems.

Fire Protection Engineering

Anna Maria College, Graduate Division, Program in Fire Science, Paxton, MA 01612. Offers MA. Part-time and evening/weekend programs available. *Degree requirements:* For master's, thesis, internship, research project. *Entrance requirements:* For master's, minimum GPA of 2.7, resume, bachelor's degree in fire science or employment in a fire science organization. Additional exam requirements/recommendations for international students: Required—TOEFL (minimum score 500 paper-based). Electronic applications accepted.

Oklahoma State University, College of Arts and Sciences, Department of Political Science, Stillwater, OK 74078. Offers fire and emergency management administration (MS, PhD); political science (MA). *Faculty:* 18 full-time (6 women), 8 part-time/adjunct (2 women). *Students:* 28 full-time (10 women), 93 part-time (19 women); includes 23 minority (7 Black or African American, non-Hispanic/Latino; 4 American Indian or Alaska Native, non-Hispanic/Latino; 7 Hispanic/Latino; 5 Two or more races, non-Hispanic/Latino), 18 international. Average age 36. 71 applicants, 37% accepted, 18 enrolled. In 2011, 22 degrees awarded. *Degree requirements:* For master's, comprehensive exam, thesis or creative component; for doctorate, comprehensive exam, thesis/dissertation. *Entrance requirements:* For master's, GRE; for doctorate, GRE. Additional exam requirements/recommendations for international students: Required—TOEFL (minimum score 550 paper-based; 79 iBT). *Application deadline:* For fall admission, 3/1 for international students; for spring admission, 8/1 for international students. Applications are processed on a rolling basis. Application fee: $40 ($75 for international students). Electronic applications accepted. *Expenses:* Tuition, state resident: full-time $4044; part-time $168.50 per credit hour. Tuition, nonresident: full-time $16,008; part-time $667 per credit hour. *Required fees:* $2122; $88.45 per credit hour. One-time fee: $50. Tuition and fees vary according to course load and campus/location. *Financial support:* In 2011–12, 7 research assistantships (averaging $10,466 per year), 14 teaching assistantships (averaging $7,848 per year) were awarded; career-related internships or fieldwork, Federal Work-Study, scholarships/grants, health care benefits, tuition waivers (partial), and unspecified assistantships also available. Support available to part-time students. Financial award application deadline: 3/1; financial award applicants required to submit FAFSA. *Faculty research:* Fire and emergency management, environmental dispute resolution, voting and elections, women and politics, urban politics. *Unit head:* Dr. Jeanette Mendez, Interim Head, 405-744-5569, Fax: 405-744-6534. *Application contact:* Dr. Sheryl Tucker, Dean, 405-744-7099, Fax: 405-744-0355, E-mail: grad-i@okstate.edu. Web site: http://polsci.okstate.edu.

University of Maryland, College Park, Academic Affairs, A. James Clark School of Engineering, Department of Continuing and Distance Learning in Engineering, College Park, MD 20742. Offers engineering (M Eng), including aerospace engineering, chemical engineering, civil engineering, electrical engineering, engineering, fire protection engineering, materials science and engineering, mechanical engineering, reliability engineering, systems engineering. *Faculty:* 3 full-time (0 women), 8 part-time/adjunct (0 women). *Students:* 75 full-time (24 women), 418 part-time (81 women); includes 154 minority (62 Black or African American, non-Hispanic/Latino; 64 Asian, non-Hispanic/Latino; 23 Hispanic/Latino; 5 Two or more races, non-Hispanic/Latino), 67 international. 447 applicants, 52% accepted, 154 enrolled. In 2011, 155 master's awarded. *Application deadline:* For fall admission, 8/15 for domestic students, 2/1 for international students; for spring admission, 1/10 for domestic students, 8/1 for international students. Applications are processed on a rolling basis. Application fee:

$75. Electronic applications accepted. *Expenses: Tuition, area resident:* Part-time $525 per credit hour. Tuition, state resident: part-time $525 per credit hour. Tuition, nonresident: part-time $1131 per credit hour. *Required fees:* $386.31 per term. Tuition and fees vary according to program. *Financial support:* In 2011–12, 3 research assistantships (averaging $21,498 per year), 13 teaching assistantships (averaging $16,889 per year) were awarded. *Unit head:* Dr. Darryll Pines, Dean, 301-405-8539, E-mail: pines@umd.edu. *Application contact:* Dr. Charles A. Caramello, Dean of the Graduate School, 301-405-0358, Fax: 301-314-9305.

University of Maryland, College Park, Academic Affairs, A. James Clark School of Engineering, Department of Fire Protection Engineering, College Park, MD 20742. Offers M Eng, MS. Part-time and evening/weekend programs available. *Faculty:* 8 full-time (0 women), 4 part-time/adjunct (0 women). *Students:* 20 full-time (3 women), 12 part-time (0 women); includes 3 minority (2 Asian, non-Hispanic/Latino; 1 Two or more races, non-Hispanic/Latino), 5 international. 20 applicants, 50% accepted, 7 enrolled. In 2011, 11 master's awarded. *Degree requirements:* For master's, thesis optional. *Entrance requirements:* For master's, GRE General Test, minimum GPA of 3.0, BS in any engineering or physical science area, 3 letters of recommendation. *Application deadline:* For fall admission, 5/31 for domestic students, 2/1 for international students; for spring admission, 10/31 for domestic students, 6/1 for international students. Applications are processed on a rolling basis. Application fee: $75. Electronic applications accepted. *Expenses: Tuition, area resident:* Part-time $525 per credit hour. Tuition, state resident: part-time $525 per credit hour. Tuition, nonresident: part-time $1131 per credit hour. *Required fees:* $386.31 per term. Tuition and fees vary according to program. *Financial support:* In 2011–12, 12 research assistantships (averaging $22,562 per year), 3 teaching assistantships (averaging $22,570 per year) were awarded; fellowships, career-related internships or fieldwork, Federal Work-Study, institutionally sponsored loans, and scholarships/grants also available. Financial award application deadline: 2/1; financial award applicants required to submit FAFSA. *Faculty research:* Fire and thermal degradation of materials, fire modeling, fire dynamics, smoke detection and management, fire resistance. *Total annual research expenditures:* $1.3 million. *Unit head:* James Milke, Chair, 301-405-3995, E-mail: milke@umd.edu. *Application contact:* Dr. Charles A. Caramello, Dean of Graduate School, 301-405-0358, Fax: 301-405-9305, E-mail: ccaramel@umd.edu. Web site: http://www.enfp.umd.edu/.

University of New Haven, Graduate School, Henry C. Lee College of Criminal Justice and Forensic Sciences, Program in Fire Science, West Haven, CT 06516-1916. Offers emergency management (Certificate); fire administration (MS); fire science technology (Certificate); fire/arson investigation (MS, Certificate); forensic science/fire science (Certificate); public safety management (MS, Certificate). Part-time and evening/weekend programs available. *Students:* 8 full-time (2 women), 12 part-time (1 woman), 1 international. 7 applicants, 100% accepted, 5 enrolled. In 2011, 3 master's, 1 other advanced degree awarded. *Degree requirements:* For master's, thesis or alternative. *Entrance requirements:* Additional exam requirements/recommendations for international students: Required—TOEFL (minimum score 520 paper-based; 190 computer-based; 70 iBT); Recommended—IELTS (minimum score 5.5). *Application deadline:* For fall admission, 5/31 for international students; for winter admission, 10/15 for international students; for spring admission, 1/15 for international students. Applications are processed on a rolling basis. Application fee: $50. Electronic applications accepted. *Expenses: Tuition:* Part-time $750 per credit. *Financial support:*

Research assistantships with partial tuition reimbursements, teaching assistantships with partial tuition reimbursements, career-related internships or fieldwork, Federal Work-Study, scholarships/grants, tuition waivers, and unspecified assistantships available. Support available to part-time students. Financial award applicants required to submit FAFSA. *Unit head:* Sorin Iliescu, Director, 203-932-932-7239, E-mail: silliescu@newhaven.edu. *Application contact:* Eloise Gormley, Director of Graduate Admissions, 203-932-7449, Fax: 203-932-7137, E-mail: gradinfo@newhaven.edu. Web site: http://www.newhaven.edu/5922/.

Worcester Polytechnic Institute, Graduate Studies and Research, Department of Fire Protection Engineering, Worcester, MA 01609-2280. Offers MS, PhD, Advanced Certificate, Graduate Certificate. Part-time and evening/weekend programs available. Postbaccalaureate distance learning degree programs offered (no on-campus study). *Faculty:* 5 full-time (1 woman), 2 part-time/adjunct (0 women). *Students:* 33 full-time (5 women), 66 part-time (16 women); includes 4 minority (2 Asian, non-Hispanic/Latino; 2 Hispanic/Latino), 20 international. 76 applicants, 68% accepted, 43 enrolled. In 2011, 32 master's awarded. *Degree requirements:* For master's, thesis optional; for doctorate, comprehensive exam, thesis/dissertation. *Entrance requirements:* For master's, GRE General Test (recommended), BS in engineering or physical sciences, 3 letters of recommendation, work experience or statement of purpose; for doctorate, GRE General Test, 3 letters of recommendation, statement of purpose. Additional exam requirements/recommendations for international students: Required—TOEFL (minimum score 563 paper-based; 223 computer-based; 84 iBT), IELTS (minimum score 7). *Application deadline:* For fall admission, 1/1 priority date for domestic students, 1/1 for international students; for spring admission, 10/1 priority date for domestic students, 10/1 for international students. Applications are processed on a rolling basis. Electronic applications accepted. *Financial support:* Research assistantships, teaching assistantships, career-related internships or fieldwork, institutionally sponsored loans, scholarships/grants, and unspecified assistantships available. Financial award application deadline: 1/1; financial award applicants required to submit FAFSA. *Faculty research:* Fire and materials, industrial fire protection, wild land fires, tools and technologies for the fire service, building regulatory systems and policy. *Unit head:* Dr. Kathy Notarianni, Head, 508-831-5593, Fax: 508-831-5862, E-mail: kanfpe@wpi.edu. *Application contact:* Dr. Ali Rangwala, Graduate Coordinator, 508-831-5593, Fax: 508-831-5862, E-mail: rangwala@wpi.edu. Web site: http://www.wpi.edu/Academics/Depts/Fire/.

Geotechnical Engineering

Auburn University, Graduate School, Ginn College of Engineering, Department of Civil Engineering, Auburn University, AL 36849. Offers construction engineering and management (MCE, MS, PhD); environmental engineering (MCE, MS, PhD); geotechnical/materials engineering (MCE, MS, PhD); hydraulics/hydrology (MCE, MS, PhD); structural engineering (MCE, MS, PhD); transportation engineering (MCE, MS, PhD). Part-time programs available. *Faculty:* 21 full-time (2 women), 1 part-time/adjunct (0 women). *Students:* 48 full-time (16 women), 62 part-time (14 women); includes 6 minority (4 Black or African American, non-Hispanic/Latino; 1 Asian, non-Hispanic/Latino; 1 Hispanic/Latino), 37 international. Average age 26. 111 applicants, 59% accepted, 25 enrolled. In 2011, 26 master's, 2 doctorates awarded. *Degree requirements:* For master's, project (MCE), thesis (MS); for doctorate, comprehensive exam, thesis/dissertation. *Entrance requirements:* For master's and doctorate, GRE General Test. *Application deadline:* For fall admission, 7/7 for domestic students; for spring admission, 11/24 for domestic students. Applications are processed on a rolling basis. Application fee: $50 ($60 for international students). Electronic applications accepted. *Expenses:* Tuition, state resident: full-time $7290; part-time $405 per credit hour. Tuition, nonresident: full-time $21,870; part-time $1215 per credit hour. *International tuition:* $22,000 full-time. *Required fees:* $1402. *Financial support:* Fellowships, research assistantships, teaching assistantships, and Federal Work-Study available. Support available to part-time students. Financial award application deadline: 3/15; financial award applicants required to submit FAFSA. *Unit head:* Dr. J. Michael Stallings, Head, 334-844-4320. *Application contact:* Dr. George Flowers, Dean of the Graduate School, 334-844-2125.

Cornell University, Graduate School, Graduate Fields of Engineering, Field of Civil and Environmental Engineering, Ithaca, NY 14853-0001. Offers engineering management (M Eng, MS, PhD); environmental engineering (M Eng, MS, PhD); environmental fluid mechanics and hydrology (M Eng, MS, PhD); environmental systems engineering (M Eng, MS, PhD); geotechnical engineering (M Eng, MS, PhD); remote sensing (M Eng, MS, PhD); structural engineering (M Eng, MS, PhD); structural mechanics (M Eng, MS); transportation engineering (MS, PhD); transportation systems engineering (M Eng); water resource systems (M Eng, MS, PhD). *Faculty:* 39 full-time (4 women). *Students:* 143 full-time (49 women); includes 20 minority (6 Black or African American, non-Hispanic/Latino; 1 American Indian or Alaska Native, non-Hispanic/Latino; 9 Asian, non-Hispanic/Latino; 4 Hispanic/Latino), 72 international. Average age 25. 574 applicants, 47% accepted, 100 enrolled. In 2011, 88 master's, 13 doctorates awarded. Terminal master's awarded for partial completion of doctoral program. *Degree requirements:* For master's, thesis (MS); for doctorate, comprehensive exam, thesis/dissertation. *Entrance requirements:* For master's and doctorate, GRE General Test (recommended), 2 letters of recommendation. Additional exam requirements/recommendations for international students: Required—TOEFL (minimum score 600 paper-based; 250 computer-based; 77 iBT). *Application deadline:* For fall admission, 1/15 priority date for domestic students; for spring admission, 10/15 for domestic students. Application fee: $95. Electronic applications accepted. *Financial support:* In 2011–12, 50 students received support, including 20 fellowships with full tuition reimbursements available, 27 research assistantships with full tuition reimbursements available, 17 teaching assistantships with full tuition reimbursements available; institutionally sponsored loans, scholarships/grants, health care benefits, tuition waivers (full and partial), and unspecified assistantships also available. Financial award applicants required to submit FAFSA. *Faculty research:* Environmental engineering, geotechnical engineering, remote sensing, environmental fluid mechanics and hydrology, structural engineering. *Unit head:* Director of Graduate Studies, 607-255-7560, Fax: 607-255-9004. *Application contact:* Graduate Field Assistant, 607-255-7560, Fax: 607-255-9004, E-mail: cee_grad@cornell.edu. Web site: http://www.gradschool.cornell.edu/fields.php?id-27&a-2.

Drexel University, College of Engineering, Department of Civil, Architectural, and Environmental Engineering, Program in Geotechnical, Geoenvironmental and Geosynthetics Engineering, Philadelphia, PA 19104-2875. Offers MS, PhD.

École Polytechnique de Montréal, Graduate Programs, Department of Civil, Geological and Mining Engineering, Montréal, QC H3C 3A7, Canada. Offers civil, geological and mining engineering (DESS); environmental engineering (M Eng, M Sc A, PhD); geotechnical engineering (M Eng, M Sc A, PhD); hydraulics engineering (M Eng, M Sc A, PhD); structural engineering (M Eng, M Sc A, PhD); transportation engineering (M Eng, M Sc A, PhD). Part-time programs available. *Degree requirements:* For master's, one foreign language, thesis; for doctorate, one foreign language, thesis/dissertation. *Entrance requirements:* For master's, minimum GPA of 2.75; for doctorate, minimum GPA of 3.0. *Faculty research:* Water resources management, characteristics of building materials, aging of dams, pollution control.

Illinois Institute of Technology, Graduate College, Armour College of Engineering, Department of Civil, Architectural and Environmental Engineering, Chicago, IL 60616-3793. Offers architectural engineering (M Arch E); civil engineering (MS, PhD), including architectural engineeering (MS), construction engineering and management (MS), geoenvironmental engineering (MS), geotechnical engineering (MS), structural engineering (MS), transportation engineering (MS); construction engineering and management (MCEM); environmental engineering (M Env E, PhD); geoenvironmental engineering (M Geoenv E); geotechnical engineering (MGE); public works (MPW); structural engineering (MSE); transportation engineering (M Trans E). Part-time and evening/weekend programs available. Postbaccalaureate distance learning degree programs offered (minimal on-campus study). Terminal master's awarded for partial completion of doctoral program. *Degree requirements:* For master's, thesis (for some programs); for doctorate, comprehensive exam, thesis/dissertation. *Entrance requirements:* For master's, GRE General Test (minimum score 900 Quantitative and Verbal, 2.5 Analytical Writing), minimum undergraduate GPA of 3.0; for doctorate, GRE General Test (minimum score 1000 Quantitative and Verbal, 3.0 Analytical Writing), minimum undergraduate GPA of 3.0. Additional exam requirements/recommendations for international students: Required—TOEFL (minimum score 523 paper-based; 70 iBT); Recommended—IELTS (minimum score 5.5). Electronic applications accepted. *Faculty research:* Structural, architectural, geotechnical and geoenvironmental engineering; construction engineering and management; transportation engineering; environmental engineering and public works.

Iowa State University of Science and Technology, Department of Civil and Construction Engineering, Ames, IA 50011-3232. Offers civil engineering (MS, PhD), including civil engineering materials, construction engineering and management, environmental engineering, geometronics, geotechnical engineering, structural engineering, transportation engineering. *Degree requirements:* For master's, thesis or alternative; for doctorate, thesis/dissertation. *Entrance requirements:* For master's and doctorate, GRE General Test. Additional exam requirements/recommendations for international students: Required—TOEFL (minimum score 550 paper-based; 82 iBT), IELTS (minimum score 6.5). *Application deadline:* For fall admission, 2/1 priority date for domestic students, 2/1 for international students; for spring admission, 8/1 priority date for domestic students, 8/1 for international students. Applications are processed on a rolling basis. Application fee: $40 ($90 for international students). Electronic applications accepted. *Unit head:* Dr. Sri Sritharan, Director of Graduate Education, 515-294-4972, Fax: 515-294-8216, E-mail: ccee-grad-inquiry@iastate.edu. *Application contact:* Kathy Petersen, Director of Graduate Education, 515-294-4975, Fax: 515-294-8216, E-mail: ccee-grad-inquiry@iastate.edu. Web site: http://www.ccee.iastate.edu/.

Louisiana State University and Agricultural and Mechanical College, Graduate School, College of Engineering, Department of Civil and Environmental Engineering, Baton Rouge, LA 70803. Offers environmental engineering (MSCE, PhD); geotechnical engineering (MSCE, PhD); structural engineering and mechanics (MSCE, PhD); transportation engineering (MSCE, PhD); water resources (MSCE, PhD). Part-time programs available. *Faculty:* 25 full-time (2 women). *Students:* 90 full-time (23 women), 34 part-time (8 women); includes 11 minority (4 Black or African American, non-Hispanic/Latino; 1 American Indian or Alaska Native, non-Hispanic/Latino; 4 Asian, non-Hispanic/Latino; 2 Hispanic/Latino), 73 international. Average age 30. 106 applicants, 67% accepted, 25 enrolled. In 2011, 32 master's, 4 doctorates awarded. *Degree requirements:* For master's, thesis optional; for doctorate, one foreign language, thesis/dissertation. *Entrance requirements:* For master's and doctorate, GRE General Test, minimum GPA of 3.0. Additional exam requirements/recommendations for international students: Required—TOEFL (minimum score 550 paper-based; 213 computer-based; 79 iBT) or IELTS (minimum score 6.5). *Application deadline:* For fall admission, 1/25 priority date for domestic students, 5/15 for international students; for spring admission, 10/15 for international students. Applications are processed on a rolling basis. Application fee: $50 ($70 for international students). Electronic applications accepted. *Financial support:* In 2011–12, 91 students received support, including 3 fellowships with full and partial tuition reimbursements available (averaging $18,050 per year), 72 research assistantships with full and partial tuition reimbursements available (averaging $15,942 per year), 6 teaching assistantships with full and partial tuition reimbursements available (averaging $12,469 per year); career-related internships or fieldwork, institutionally sponsored loans, scholarships/grants, and health care benefits also available. Financial award application deadline: 3/1; financial award applicants required to submit FAFSA. *Faculty research:* Mechanics and structures, environmental, geotechnical transportation, water resources. *Total annual research expenditures:* $3 million. *Unit head:* Dr. George Z. Voyiadjis, Chair/Professor, 225-578-8668, Fax: 225-578-9176, E-mail: voyaidjis@lsu.edu. *Application contact:* Dr. Clinton Willson, Professor, 225-578-8672, E-mail: cwillson@lsu.edu. Web site: http://www.cee.lsu.edu/.

Marquette University, Graduate School, College of Engineering, Department of Civil and Environmental Engineering, Milwaukee, WI 53201-1881. Offers construction and public works management (MS, PhD); construction engineering and management (Certificate); environmental/water resources engineering (MS, PhD); structural design (Certificate); structural/geotechnical engineering (MS, PhD); transportation planning and engineering (MS, PhD); waste and wastewater treatment processes (Certificate). Part-time and evening/weekend programs available. *Faculty:* 13 full-time (0 women), 5 part-time/adjunct (0 women). *Students:* 26 full-time (5 women), 11 part-time (0 women); includes 2 minority (1 Black or African American, non-Hispanic/Latino; 1 Asian, non-Hispanic/Latino), 12 international. Average age 27. 74 applicants, 62% accepted, 9 enrolled. In 2011, 6 master's, 3 doctorates awarded. Terminal master's awarded for partial completion of doctoral program. *Degree requirements:* For master's, comprehensive exam (for some programs), thesis or alternative; for doctorate, thesis/dissertation. *Entrance requirements:* For master's, GRE General Test (recommended), minimum GPA of 3.0, official transcripts from all current and previous colleges/universities except Marquette, three letters of recommendation; for doctorate, GRE General Test, minimum GPA of 3.0, official transcripts from all current and previous colleges/universities except Marquette, three letters of recommendation, brief statement of purpose, submission of any English language publications authored by applicant (strongly recommended). Additional exam requirements/recommendations for international students: Required—TOEFL (minimum score 530 paper-based; 78 computer-based). *Application deadline:* For fall admission, 6/1 priority date for domestic students. Applications are processed on a rolling basis. Application fee: $50. Electronic applications accepted. *Expenses: Tuition:* Full-time $17,010; part-time $945 per credit hour. Tuition and fees vary according to program. *Financial support:* In 2011–12, 21 students received support, including 6 fellowships with partial tuition reimbursements available (averaging $9,177 per year), 1 research assistantship with full tuition reimbursement available (averaging $13,745 per year), 7 teaching assistantships with full tuition reimbursements available (averaging $13,902 per year); scholarships/grants, health care benefits, tuition waivers (partial), and unspecified assistantships also available. Support available to part-time students. Financial award application deadline: 2/15. *Faculty research:* Highway safety, highway performance, and intelligent transportation systems; surface mount technology; watershed management. *Total annual research expenditures:* $826,608. *Unit head:* Dr. Thomas Wenzel, Chair, 414-288-7030, Fax: 414-288-7521, E-mail: thomas.wenzel@marquette.edu. *Application contact:* Dr. Stephen M. Heinrich, Director of Graduate Studies, 414-288-5466, E-mail: stephen.heinrich@marquette.edu. Web site: http://www.marquette.edu/engineering/pages/AllYouNeed/Civil_Environmental/civil.html.

Massachusetts Institute of Technology, School of Engineering, Department of Civil and Environmental Engineering, Cambridge, MA 02139. Offers biological oceanography (PhD, Sc D); chemical oceanography (PhD, Sc D); civil and environmental engineering (PhD, Sc D); civil and environmental systems (PhD, Sc D); civil engineering (PhD, Sc D, CE); coastal engineering (PhD, Sc D); construction engineering and management (PhD, Sc D); environmental and water quality engineering (M Eng); environmental biology (PhD, Sc D); environmental chemistry (PhD, Sc D); environmental engineering (PhD, Sc D); environmental fluid mechanics (PhD, Sc D); environmental science and engineering (SM); geotechnical and geoenvironmental engineering (PhD, Sc D); geotechnology (M Eng); high-performance structures (M Eng); hydrology (PhD, Sc D); information technology (PhD, Sc D); mechanics (SM); oceanographic engineering (PhD, Sc D); structures and materials (PhD, Sc D); transportation (M Eng, PhD, Sc D); SM/MBA. *Faculty:* 35 full-time (6 women), 1 part-time/adjunct (0 women). *Students:* 216 full-time (80 women); includes 30 minority (4 Black or African American, non-Hispanic/Latino; 13 Asian, non-Hispanic/Latino; 8 Hispanic/Latino; 5 Two or more races, non-Hispanic/Latino), 110 international. Average age 27. 589 applicants, 26% accepted, 91 enrolled. In 2011, 62 master's, 14 doctorates awarded. *Degree requirements:* For master's and CE, thesis; for doctorate, comprehensive exam, thesis/dissertation. *Entrance requirements:* For master's and doctorate, GRE General Test. Additional exam requirements/recommendations for international students: Required—TOEFL (minimum score 577 paper-based; 233 computer-based; 90 iBT), IELTS (minimum score 7). *Application deadline:* For fall admission, 12/15 for domestic and international students. Application fee: $75. Electronic applications accepted. *Expenses: Tuition:* Full-time $40,460; part-time $630 per credit hour. *Required fees:* $272. *Financial support:* In 2011–12, 180 students received support, including 51 fellowships (averaging $30,800 per year), 110 research assistantships (averaging $29,500 per year), 19 teaching assistantships (averaging $29,500 per year); career-related internships or fieldwork, Federal Work-Study, institutionally sponsored loans, scholarships/grants, health care benefits, and unspecified assistantships also available. *Faculty research:* Environmental chemistry, environmental fluid mechanics and coastal engineering, environmental microbiology, geotechnical engineering and geomechanics, hydrology and hydroclimatology, infrastructure systems, mechanics of materials and structures, transportation systems. *Total annual research expenditures:* $17.7 million. *Unit head:* Prof. Andrew Whittle, Head, 617-253-7101. *Application contact:* Patricia Glidden, Graduate Admissions Coordinator, 617-253-7119, Fax: 617-258-6775, E-mail: cee-admissions@mit.edu. Web site: http://cee.mit.edu/.

McGill University, Faculty of Graduate and Postdoctoral Studies, Faculty of Engineering, Department of Civil Engineering and Applied Mechanics, Montréal, QC H3A 2T5, Canada. Offers environmental engineering (M Eng, M Sc, PhD); fluid mechanics (M Sc); fluid mechanics and hydraulic engineering (M Eng, PhD); materials engineering (M Eng, PhD); rehabilitation of urban infrastructure (M Eng, PhD); soil behavior (M Eng, PhD); soil mechanics and foundations (M Eng, PhD); structures and structural mechanics (M Eng, PhD); water resources (M Sc); water resources engineering (M Eng, PhD).

Missouri University of Science and Technology, Graduate School, Department of Civil, Architectural, and Environmental Engineering, Rolla, MO 65409. Offers civil engineering (MS, DE, PhD); construction engineering (MS, DE, PhD); environmental engineering (MS); fluid mechanics (MS, DE, PhD); geotechnical engineering (MS, DE, PhD); hydrology and hydraulic engineering (MS, DE, PhD). Part-time and evening/weekend programs available. Terminal master's awarded for partial completion of doctoral program. *Degree requirements:* For master's, thesis optional; for doctorate, comprehensive exam, thesis/dissertation. *Entrance requirements:* For master's, GRE General Test (minimum combined score 1100), minimum GPA of 3.0; for doctorate, GRE General Test (minimum score: verbal and quantitative 400, writing 3.5), minimum GPA of 3.0. Additional exam requirements/recommendations for international students: Required—TOEFL. Electronic applications accepted. *Faculty research:* Earthquake engineering, structural optimization and control systems, structural health monitoring/damage detection, soil-structure interaction, soil mechanics and foundation engineering.

Northwestern University, McCormick School of Engineering and Applied Science, Department of Civil and Environmental Engineering, Evanston, IL 60208-3109. Offers environmental engineering and science (MS, PhD); geotechnical engineering (MS, PhD); mechanics of materials and solids (MS, PhD); project management (MS, PhD); structural engineering and materials (MS, PhD); theoretical and applied mechanics (MS, PhD), including fluid mechanics, solid mechanics; transportation systems analysis and planning (MS, PhD). MS and PhD admissions and degrees offered through The Graduate School. Part-time programs available. Terminal master's awarded for partial completion of doctoral program. *Degree requirements:* For master's, thesis (for some programs); for doctorate, thesis/dissertation. *Entrance requirements:* For master's and doctorate, GRE General Test, minimum 2 letters of recommendation, transcripts from all academic institutions attended. Additional exam requirements/recommendations for international students: Required—TOEFL (minimum score 600 paper-based; 250 computer-based; 100 iBT), IELTS (minimum score 7). Electronic applications accepted. *Faculty research:* Environmental engineering and science, geotechnics, mechanics of materials and solids, structural engineering and materials, transportation systems analysis and planning.

Norwich University, College of Graduate and Continuing Studies, Master of Civil Engineering Program, Northfield, VT 05663. Offers construction management (MCE); environmental water resources (MCE); geo-technical (MCE); structural (MCE). Evening/weekend programs available. *Faculty:* 12 part-time/adjunct (1 woman). *Students:* 88 full-time (23 women); includes 15 minority (8 Black or African American, non-Hispanic/Latino; 1 American Indian or Alaska Native, non-Hispanic/Latino; 4 Asian, non-Hispanic/Latino; 2 Hispanic/Latino). Average age 33. In 2011, 44 master's awarded. *Entrance requirements:* For master's, minimum GPA of 2.75. Additional exam requirements/recommendations for international students: Required—TOEFL (minimum score 550 paper-based; 213 computer-based; 83 iBT). *Application deadline:* For fall admission, 8/10 for domestic and international students; for spring admission, 2/6 for domestic and international students. Applications are processed on a rolling basis. Application fee: $50. Electronic applications accepted. *Expenses: Tuition:* Full-time $16,174. *Required fees:* $2130. Full-time tuition and fees vary according to program. *Financial support:* In 2011–12, 5 students received support. Scholarships/grants available. Financial award applicants required to submit FAFSA. *Unit head:* Dr. Thomas Descoteaux, Program Director, 802-485-2730, Fax: 802-485-2533, E-mail: tdescote@norwich.edu. *Application contact:* Rija Ramahatra, Associate Program Director, 802-485-2892, Fax: 802-485-2533, E-mail: ramahatr@norwich.edu. Web site: http://mce.norwich.edu.

Ohio University, Graduate College, Russ College of Engineering and Technology, Department of Civil Engineering, Athens, OH 45701-2979. Offers civil engineering (PhD); construction (MS); environmental (MS); geotechnical and geoenvironmental (MS); mechanics (MS); structures (MS); transportation (MS); water resources and structures (MS). Part-time programs available. *Students:* 32 full-time (6 women), 7 part-time (2 women); includes 3 minority (1 Hispanic/Latino; 2 Two or more races, non-Hispanic/Latino), 13 international. 52 applicants, 52% accepted, 4 enrolled. In 2011, 10 degrees awarded. *Degree requirements:* For master's, comprehensive exam (for some programs), thesis or alternative; for doctorate, comprehensive exam, thesis/dissertation. *Entrance requirements:* For master's, GRE General Test, minimum GPA of 3.0, 3 letters of recommendation; for doctorate, GRE General Test. Additional exam requirements/recommendations for international students: Required—TOEFL (minimum score 550 paper-based; 80 iBT) or IELTS (minimum score 6.5). *Application deadline:* For fall admission, 5/1 priority date for domestic students, 2/1 for international students; for winter admission, 8/1 priority date for domestic students, 4/1 for international students; for spring admission, 2/1 priority date for domestic students, 7/1 for international students. Applications are processed on a rolling basis. Application fee: $50 ($55 for international students). Electronic applications accepted. *Financial support:* Research assistantships with full tuition reimbursements, teaching assistantships with full tuition reimbursements, Federal Work-Study, institutionally sponsored loans, scholarships/grants, and unspecified assistantships available. Financial award application deadline: 3/15; financial award applicants required to submit FAFSA. *Faculty research:* Noise abatement, materials and environment, highway infrastructure, subsurface investigation (pavements, pipes, bridges). *Unit head:* Dr. Gayle F. Mitchell, Chair, 740-593-0430, Fax: 740-593-0625, E-mail: mitchelg@ohio.edu. *Application contact:* Dr. Shad M. Sargand, Graduate Chair, 740-593-1465, Fax: 740-593-0625, E-mail: sargand@ohio.edu. Web site: http://www.ohio.edu/civil/.

Oregon State University, Graduate School, College of Engineering, School of Civil and Construction Engineering, Corvallis, OR 97331. Offers civil engineering (MS, PhD); coastal and ocean engineering (M Oc E, PhD); coastal engineering (MS); construction engineering management (MBE, PhD); engineering (M Eng, MAIS); geotechnical engineering (MS, PhD); structural engineering (MS, PhD); transportation engineering (MS, PhD); water engineering (MS, PhD). Part-time programs available. Terminal master's awarded for partial completion of doctoral program. *Degree requirements:* For master's, thesis or alternative; for doctorate, one foreign language, thesis/dissertation. *Entrance requirements:* For master's, GRE General Test, minimum GPA of 3.0 in last 90 hours (3.5 for MS); for doctorate, GRE General Test, minimum GPA of 3.0 in last 90 hours of undergraduate course work. Additional exam requirements/recommendations for international students: Required—TOEFL (minimum score 580 paper-based; 237 computer-based). *Faculty research:* Hazardous waste management, carbon cycling, wave forces on structures, pavement design, seismic analysis.

Penn State University Park, Graduate School, College of Earth and Mineral Sciences, Department of Energy and Mineral Engineering, State College, University Park, PA 16802-1503. Offers MS, PhD. *Unit head:* Dr. William E. Easterling, III, Dean, 814-865-6546, Fax: 814-863-7708, E-mail: wee2@psu.edu. *Application contact:* Cynthia E. Nicosia, Director of Graduate Enrollment Services, 814-865-1834, E-mail: cey1@psu.edu. Web site: http://www.eme.psu.edu/.

Rensselaer Polytechnic Institute, Graduate School, School of Engineering, Program in Civil Engineering, Troy, NY 12180-3590. Offers geotechnical engineering (M Eng, MS, PhD); mechanics of composite materials and structures (M Eng, MS, PhD); structural engineering (M Eng, MS, PhD); transportation engineering (M Eng, MS, PhD). Part-time programs available. Terminal master's awarded for partial completion of doctoral program. *Degree requirements:* For master's, thesis (for some programs); for doctorate, thesis/dissertation. *Entrance requirements:* For master's and doctorate, GRE. Additional exam requirements/recommendations for international students: Required—TOEFL (minimum score 570 paper-based; 230 computer-based; 89 iBT), IELTS (minimum score 6.5). Electronic applications accepted. *Faculty research:* Computational mechanics, earthquake engineering, geo-environmental engineering.

Texas A&M University, College of Engineering, Zachry Department of Civil Engineering, College Station, TX 77843. Offers coastal and ocean engineering (M Eng, MS, D Eng, PhD); construction engineering and management (M Eng, MS, D Eng, PhD); environmental engineering (M Eng, MS, D Eng, PhD); geotechnical engineering (M Eng, MS, D Eng, PhD); materials engineering (M Eng, MS, D Eng, PhD); structural engineering (M Eng, MS, D Eng, PhD); transportation engineering (M Eng, MS, D Eng, PhD); water resources engineering (M Eng, MS, D Eng, PhD). Part-time programs available. *Faculty:* 57. *Students:* 361 full-time (76 women), 46 part-time (8 women); includes 41 minority (3 Black or African American, non-Hispanic/Latino; 16 Asian, non-Hispanic/Latino; 21 Hispanic/Latino; 1 Two or more races, non-Hispanic/Latino), 247 international. Average age 29. In 2011, 123 master's, 27 doctorates awarded. *Degree requirements:* For master's, thesis (MS); for doctorate, dissertation (PhD), internship (D Eng). *Entrance requirements:* For master's and doctorate, GRE General Test. Additional exam requirements/recommendations for international students: Required—TOEFL. *Application deadline:* Applications are processed on a rolling basis. Application fee: $50 ($75 for international students). Electronic applications accepted. *Expenses:* Tuition, state resident: full-time $5437; part-time $226.55 per credit hour. Tuition, nonresident: full-time $12,949; part-time $539.55 per credit hour. *Required fees:* $2741. *Financial support:* In 2011–12, fellowships (averaging $4,500 per year), research assistantships (averaging $14,000 per year), teaching assistantships (averaging $14,400 per year) were awarded; career-related internships or fieldwork and institutionally sponsored loans also available. Financial award application deadline: 4/15; financial award applicants required to submit FAFSA. *Unit head:* Dr. John Niedzwecki, Head, 979-845-3858, E-mail: j-niedzwecki@tamu.edu. *Application contact:* Graduate Advisor, 979-845-7435, Fax: 979-845-6156, E-mail: info@civil.tamu.edu. Web site: https://www.civil.tamu.edu/.

Tufts University, School of Engineering, Department of Civil and Environmental Engineering, Medford, MA 02155. Offers bioengineering (ME, MS), including environmental technology; civil engineering (ME, MS, PhD), including geotechnical engineering, structural engineering, water diplomacy (PhD); environmental engineering (ME, MS, PhD), including environmental engineering and environmental sciences, environmental geotechnology, environmental health, environmental science and management, hazardous materials management, water diplomacy (PhD), water resources engineering. Part-time programs available. *Faculty:* 18 full-time, 5 part-time/adjunct. *Students:* 102 full-time (50 women); includes 8 minority (1 Black or African American, non-Hispanic/Latino; 6 Asian, non-Hispanic/Latino; 1 Hispanic/Latino), 37 international. Average age 27. 162 applicants, 59% accepted, 37 enrolled. In 2011, 18 degrees awarded. Terminal master's awarded for partial completion of doctoral program. *Degree requirements:* For master's, thesis or alternative; for doctorate, thesis/dissertation. *Entrance requirements:* For master's and doctorate, GRE General Test. Additional exam requirements/recommendations for international students: Required—TOEFL (minimum score 550 paper-based; 213 computer-based; 80 iBT). *Application deadline:* For fall admission, 1/15 priority date for domestic students, 12/15 for international students; for spring admission, 10/15 for domestic students, 9/15 for international students. Applications are processed on a rolling basis. Application fee: $75. Electronic applications accepted. *Expenses: Tuition:* Full-time $41,208; part-time $1030 per credit hour. Full-time tuition and fees vary according to degree level, program and student level. Part-time tuition and fees vary according to course load. *Financial support:* Fellowships with full tuition reimbursements, research assistantships with full and partial tuition reimbursements, teaching assistantships with full and partial tuition reimbursements, Federal Work-Study, scholarships/grants, tuition waivers (partial), and unspecified assistantships available. Financial award application deadline: 1/15; financial award applicants required to submit FAFSA. *Faculty research:* Environmental and water resources engineering, environmental health, geotechnical and geoenvironmental engineering, structural engineering and mechanics, water diplomacy. *Unit head:* Dr. Kurt Penell, Chair, 617-627-3211, Fax: 617-627-3994. *Application contact:* Laura Sacco, Information Contact, 617-627-3211, E-mail: ceeinfo@tufts.edu. Web site: http://www.ase.tufts.edu/cee/.

The University of Alabama in Huntsville, School of Graduate Studies, College of Engineering, Department of Civil and Environmental Engineering, Huntsville, AL 35899. Offers civil and environmental engineering (PhD); civil engineering (MSE), including civil engineering, environmental and water resource engineering, geotechnical engineering, structural engineering and structural mechanics, transportation engineering. PhD offered jointly with The University of Alabama at Birmingham. Part-time and evening/weekend programs available. *Faculty:* 5 full-time (1 woman), 1 part-time/adjunct (0 women). *Students:* 20 full-time (4 women), 12 part-time (6 women); includes 1 minority (Black or African American, non-Hispanic/Latino), 15 international. Average age 29. 26 applicants, 62% accepted, 6 enrolled. In 2011, 3 master's, 1 doctorate awarded. *Degree requirements:* For master's, comprehensive exam, thesis or alternative, oral and written exams; for doctorate, comprehensive exam, thesis/dissertation, oral and written exams. *Entrance requirements:* For master's, GRE General Test, BSE, minimum GPA of 3.0; for doctorate, GRE General Test, minimum GPA of 3.0. Additional exam requirements/recommendations for international students: Required—TOEFL (minimum score 500 paper-based; 173 computer-based; 62 iBT). *Application deadline:* For fall admission, 7/15 for domestic students, 4/1 for international students; for spring admission, 11/30 for domestic students, 9/1 for international students. Applications are processed on a rolling basis. Application fee: $40 ($50 for international students). Electronic applications accepted. *Expenses:* Tuition, state resident: full-time $7830; part-time $473.50 per credit. Tuition, nonresident: full-time $18,748; part-time $1128.33 per credit. Tuition and fees vary according to course load and program. *Financial support:* In 2011–12, 16 students received support, including 10 research assistantships with full and partial tuition reimbursements available (averaging $12,281 per year), 6 teaching assistantships with full and partial tuition reimbursements available (averaging $12,472 per year); career-related internships or fieldwork, Federal Work-Study, institutionally sponsored loans, scholarships/grants, health care benefits, and unspecified assistantships also available. Support available to part-time students. Financial award application deadline: 4/1; financial award applicants required to submit FAFSA. *Faculty research:* Hydrologic modeling, orbital debris impact, hydrogeology, environmental engineering, transportation engineering. *Total annual research expenditures:* $1.1 million. *Unit head:* Dr. Houssam Toutanji, Chair, 256-824-7361, Fax: 256-824-6724, E-mail: toutanji@cee.uah.edu. *Application contact:* Kim Gray, Graduate Studies Admissions Coordinator, 256-824-6002, Fax: 256-824-6405, E-mail: deangrad@uah.edu. Web site: http://www.uah.edu/eng/departments/cee/welcome.

University of Alberta, Faculty of Graduate Studies and Research, Department of Civil and Environmental Engineering, Edmonton, AB T6G 2E1, Canada. Offers construction engineering and management (M Eng, M Sc, PhD); environmental engineering (M Eng, M Sc, PhD); environmental science (M Sc, PhD); geoenvironmental engineering (M Eng, M Sc, PhD); geotechnical engineering (M Eng, M Sc, PhD); mining engineering (M Eng, M Sc, PhD); petroleum engineering (M Eng, M Sc, PhD); structural engineering (M Eng, M Sc, PhD); water resources (M Eng, M Sc, PhD). Part-time programs available. Postbaccalaureate distance learning degree programs offered (minimal on-campus study). *Degree requirements:* For master's, thesis (for some programs); for doctorate, thesis/dissertation. *Entrance requirements:* For master's, minimum GPA of 3.0 in last 2 years of undergraduate studies; for doctorate, minimum GPA of 3.0. Additional exam requirements/recommendations for international students: Required—TOEFL (minimum score 550 paper-based; 213 computer-based). Electronic applications accepted. *Faculty research:* Mining.

University of Calgary, Faculty of Graduate Studies, Schulich School of Engineering, Department of Geomatics Engineering, Calgary, AB T2N 1N4, Canada. Offers M Eng, M Sc, PhD. Part-time programs available. *Faculty:* 19 full-time (4 women), 4 part-time/adjunct (0 women). *Students:* 118 full-time (35 women), 10 part-time (2 women). 35 applicants, 34% accepted, 11 enrolled. In 2011, 20 master's, 10 doctorates awarded. *Degree requirements:* For master's, thesis (for some programs), minimum of 5 half-courses, completion of seminar course; for doctorate, comprehensive exam, thesis/dissertation, minimum of 3 half-courses beyond M Sc, completion of two seminar courses, candidacy exam. *Entrance requirements:* For master's, B Sc or equivalent with minimum GPA of 3.0; for doctorate, M Sc or transfer from M Sc degree with minimum GPA of 3.5. Additional exam requirements/recommendations for international students: Required—TOEFL (minimum score 550 paper-based; 80 iBT) or IELTS (minimum score 7). *Application deadline:* For fall admission, 8/1 for domestic students, 7/1 for international students; for winter admission, 12/1 for domestic students, 11/1 for international students; for spring admission, 4/1 for domestic students, 3/1 for international students. Applications are processed on a rolling basis. Application fee: $100 ($130 for international students). Electronic applications accepted. *Financial support:* In 2011–12, 63 teaching assistantships (averaging $2,650 per year) were awarded; career-related internships or fieldwork, institutionally sponsored loans, scholarships/grants, health care benefits, tuition waivers (partial), and unspecified assistantships also available. *Faculty research:* Digital imaging systems, earth observation, GIS and land tenurepositioning, navigation and wireless location. *Total annual research expenditures:* $6.3 million. *Unit head:* Dr. Ayman Habib, Professor and Head, 403-220-7105, Fax: 403-284-1980, E-mail: ahabib@ucalgary.ca. *Application contact:* Dr. Danielle Marceau, Professor and Associate Head, Graduate Studies, 403-220-5314, Fax: 403-284-1980, E-mail: dmarceau@ucalgary.ca. Web site: http://www.geomatics.ucalgary.ca/.

University of California, Berkeley, Graduate Division, College of Engineering, Department of Civil and Environmental Engineering, Berkeley, CA 94720-1500. Offers engineering and project management (M Eng, MS, D Eng, PhD); environmental engineering (M Eng, MS, D Eng, PhD); geoengineering (M Eng, MS, D Eng, PhD); structural engineering, mechanics and materials (M Eng, MS, D Eng, PhD); transportation engineering (M Eng, MS, D Eng, PhD); M Arch/MS; MCP/MS; MPP/MS. *Degree requirements:* For master's, comprehensive exam or thesis (MS); for doctorate, thesis/dissertation, qualifying exam. *Entrance requirements:* For master's, GRE General Test, minimum GPA of 3.0, 3 letters of recommendation; for doctorate, GRE General Test, minimum GPA of 3.5, 3 letters of recommendation. Additional exam requirements/recommendations for international students: Required—TOEFL (minimum score 570 paper-based; 230 computer-based). Electronic applications accepted.

University of Colorado Boulder, Graduate School, College of Engineering and Applied Science, Department of Civil, Environmental, and Architectural Engineering, Boulder, CO 80309. Offers building systems (MS, PhD); construction engineering management (MS, PhD); environmental engineering (MS, PhD); geotechnical engineering and geomechanics (MS, PhD); hydrology, water resources and environmental fluid mechanics (MS, PhD); structural engineering and structural mechanics (MS, PhD). *Faculty:* 37 full-time (8 women). *Students:* 245 full-time (90 women), 53 part-time (15 women); includes 37 minority (1 Black or African American, non-Hispanic/Latino; 2 American Indian or Alaska Native, non-Hispanic/Latino; 15 Asian, non-Hispanic/Latino; 17 Hispanic/Latino; 2 Two or more races, non-Hispanic/Latino), 56 international. Average age 27. 483 applicants, 58% accepted, 83 enrolled. In 2011, 84 master's, 15 doctorates awarded. Terminal master's awarded for partial completion of doctoral program. *Degree requirements:* For master's, comprehensive exam, thesis or alternative; for doctorate, thesis/dissertation. *Entrance requirements:* For master's, GRE General Test, minimum undergraduate GPA of 3.0. *Application deadline:* For fall admission, 3/1 for domestic students, 12/1 for international students; for spring admission, 10/31 for domestic students, 10/1 for international students. Application fee: $50 ($60 for international students). Electronic applications accepted. *Financial support:* In 2011–12, 167 students received support, including 69 fellowships (averaging $12,440 per year), 62 research assistantships with full and partial tuition reimbursements available (averaging $21,979 per year), 20 teaching assistantships with full and partial tuition reimbursements available (averaging $19,877 per year); institutionally sponsored loans, scholarships/grants, health care benefits, and unspecified assistantships also available. Financial award application deadline: 1/15; financial award applicants required to submit FAFSA. *Faculty research:* Building systems engineering, construction engineering and management, environmental engineering, geoenvironmental engineering, geotechnical engineering, materials and mechanics, structural engineering, water resources engineering, life-cycle engineering. *Total annual research expenditures:* $10.9 million. *Application contact:* E-mail: cvengrad@colorado.edu. Web site: http://ceae.colorado.edu/new/.

University of Colorado Denver, College of Engineering and Applied Science, Department of Civil Engineering, Denver, CO 80217. Offers civil engineering (EASPh D); civil engineering systems (PhD); environmental and sustainability engineering (MS, PhD); geographic information systems (MS); geotechnical engineering (MS, PhD); hydrology and hydraulics (MS, PhD); structural engineering (MS, PhD); transportation engineering (MS, PhD). Part-time and evening/weekend programs available. *Faculty:* 14 full-time (1 woman), 6 part-time/adjunct (0 women). *Students:* 66 full-time (11 women), 65 part-time (14 women); includes 30 minority (10 Black or African American, non-Hispanic/Latino; 8 Asian, non-Hispanic/Latino; 10 Hispanic/Latino; 2 Two or more races, non-Hispanic/Latino), 17 international. Average age 34. 67 applicants, 54% accepted, 24 enrolled. In 2011, 30 master's, 2 doctorates awarded. *Degree requirements:* For master's, comprehensive exam, thesis or alternative, 30 credit hours, project or thesis; for doctorate, comprehensive exam, thesis/dissertation, 60 credit hours (30 of which are dissertation research). *Entrance requirements:* For master's, GRE, statement of purpose, transcripts, three references; for doctorate, GRE, statement of purpose, transcripts, references, letter of support from faculty stating willingness to serve as dissertation advisor and outlining plan for financial support. Additional exam requirements/recommendations for international students: Required—TOEFL (minimum score 525 paper-based; 197 computer-based). *Application deadline:* For fall admission, 7/15 for domestic students, 6/15 for international students; for spring admission, 12/1 for domestic students, 11/1 for international students. Applications are processed on a rolling basis. Application fee: $50 ($75 for international students). Electronic applications accepted. *Expenses:* Contact institution. *Financial support:* Research assistantships, teaching assistantships, career-related internships or fieldwork, and Federal Work-Study available. Financial award application deadline: 4/1; financial award applicants required to submit FAFSA. *Faculty research:* Earthquake source physics, environmental biotechnology, hydrologic and hydraulic engineering, sustainability assessments, transportation energy use and greenhouse gas emissions. *Unit head:* Dr. Kevin Rens, Chair, 303-556-8017, Fax: 303-556-2368, E-mail: kevin.rens@ucdenver.edu. *Application contact:* Maria Rase, Program Assistant, 303-556-6712, Fax: 303-556-2368, E-mail: maria.rase@ucdenver.edu. Web site: http://www.ucdenver.edu/academics/colleges/Engineering/Programs/Civil-Engineering/Pages/CivilEngineering.aspx.

University of Delaware, College of Engineering, Department of Civil and Environmental Engineering, Newark, DE 19716. Offers environmental engineering (MAS, MCE, PhD); geotechnical engineering (MAS, MCE, PhD); ocean engineering (MAS, MCE, PhD); structural engineering (MAS, MCE, PhD); transportation engineering (MAS, MCE, PhD); water resource engineering (MAS, MCE, PhD). Part-time programs available. Terminal master's awarded for partial completion of doctoral program. *Degree requirements:* For master's, thesis; for doctorate, thesis/dissertation. *Entrance requirements:* For master's and doctorate, GRE General Test. Additional exam requirements/recommendations for international students: Required—TOEFL. Electronic applications accepted. *Faculty research:* Structural engineering and mechanics; transportation engineering; ocean engineering; soil mechanics and foundation; water resources and environmental engineering.

University of Massachusetts Amherst, Graduate School, College of Engineering, Department of Civil and Environmental Engineering, Amherst, MA 01003. Offers civil engineering (MSCE, PhD); environmental and water resources (MSCE); geotechnical (MSCE); structural engineering and mechanics (MSCE); transportation (MSCE). *Accreditation:* ABET (one or more programs are accredited). Part-time programs available. *Faculty:* 28 full-time (7 women). *Students:* 91 full-time (30 women), 11 part-time (5 women); includes 13 minority (3 Black or African American, non-Hispanic/Latino; 5 Asian, non-Hispanic/Latino; 4 Hispanic/Latino; 1 Two or more races, non-Hispanic/Latino), 29 international. Average age 27. 293 applicants, 53% accepted, 40 enrolled. In 2011, 38 master's, 1 doctorate awarded. Terminal master's awarded for partial completion of doctoral program. *Degree requirements:* For master's, thesis or alternative; for doctorate, comprehensive exam, thesis/dissertation. *Entrance requirements:* For master's and doctorate, GRE General Test. Additional exam requirements/recommendations for international students: Required—TOEFL (minimum score 550 paper-based; 213 computer-based; 80 iBT), IELTS (minimum score 6.5). *Application deadline:* For fall admission, 2/1 for domestic and international students; for spring admission, 10/1 for domestic and international students. Applications are processed on a rolling basis. Application fee: $50 ($65 for international students). Electronic applications accepted. Tuition and fees vary according to course load, campus/location and program. *Financial support:* In 2011–12, 1 fellowship with full tuition reimbursement (averaging $1,000 per year), 74 research assistantships with full tuition reimbursements (averaging $15,151 per year), 6 teaching assistantships with full tuition reimbursements (averaging $15,151 per year) were awarded; career-related internships or fieldwork, Federal Work-Study, scholarships/grants, traineeships, health care benefits, tuition waivers, and unspecified assistantships also available. Support available to part-time students. Financial award application deadline: 2/1; financial award applicants required to submit FAFSA. *Unit head:* Dr. Sanjay Arwade, Graduate Program Director, 413-545-0686, Fax: 413-545-2840. *Application contact:* Lindsay DeSantis, Interim Supervisor of Admissions, 413-545-0722, Fax: 413-577-0100, E-mail: gradadm@grad.umass.edu. Web site: http://cee.umass.edu/.

University of Missouri, Graduate School, College of Engineering, Department of Civil and Environmental Engineering, Columbia, MO 65211. Offers civil engineering (MS, PhD); environmental engineering (MS, PhD); geotechnical engineering (MS, PhD); structural engineering (MS, PhD); transportation and highway engineering (MS); water resources (MS, PhD). *Faculty:* 18 full-time (2 women), 1 part-time/adjunct (0 women). *Students:* 45 full-time (16 women), 38 part-time (8 women); includes 5 minority (2 Black or African American, non-Hispanic/Latino; 2 Asian, non-Hispanic/Latino; 1 Hispanic/Latino), 49 international. Average age 28. 109 applicants, 28% accepted, 20 enrolled. In 2011, 14 master's, 2 doctorates awarded. *Degree requirements:* For master's, report or thesis; for doctorate, thesis/dissertation. *Entrance requirements:* For master's and doctorate, GRE General Test. Additional exam requirements/recommendations for international students: Required—TOEFL (minimum score 550 paper-based; 213 computer-based; 79 iBT). *Application deadline:* For fall admission, 3/15 priority date for domestic students; for winter admission, 10/15 priority date for domestic students. Application fee: $55 ($75 for international students). *Expenses:* Tuition, state resident: full-time $5881. Tuition, nonresident: full-time $15,183. *Required fees:* $952. Tuition and fees vary according to campus/location and program. *Financial support:* Fellowships, research assistantships, teaching assistantships, and institutionally sponsored loans available. *Unit head:* Dr. Mark Virkler, Department Chair, E-mail: virklerm@missouri.edu. *Application contact:* Jennifer Keyzer-Andre, 573-882-4442, E-mail: keyzerandrej@missouri.edu. Web site: http://engineering.missouri.edu/civil/.

University of New Brunswick Fredericton, School of Graduate Studies, Faculty of Engineering, Department of Civil Engineering, Fredericton, NB E3B 5A3, Canada. Offers construction engineering and management (M Eng, M Sc E, PhD); environmental engineering (M Eng, M Sc E, PhD); environmental studies (M Eng); geotechnical engineering (M Eng, M Sc E, PhD); groundwater/hydrology (M Eng, M Sc E, PhD); materials (M Eng, M Sc E, PhD); pavements (M Eng, M Sc E, PhD); structures (M Eng, M Sc E, PhD); transportation (M Eng, M Sc E, PhD). Part-time programs available. *Faculty:* 13 full-time (1 woman), 7 part-time/adjunct (1 woman). *Students:* 31 full-time (7 women), 17 part-time (2 women). In 2011, 11 master's, 2 doctorates awarded. *Degree requirements:* For master's, thesis, proposal; for doctorate, comprehensive exam, thesis/dissertation, qualifying exam, proposal; 27 credit hours of courses. *Entrance requirements:* For master's, minimum GPA of 3.0; B Sc E in civil engineering or related engineering degree; for doctorate, minimum GPA of 3.0; graduate degree in engineering or applied science. Additional exam requirements/recommendations for international students: Required—TWE (minimum score 4), TOEFL (minimum score 580 paper-based; 237 computer-based) or IELTS (minimum score 7.5). *Application deadline:* For fall admission, 5/1 priority date for domestic students; for winter admission, 11/1 priority date for domestic students. Applications are processed on a rolling basis. Application fee: $50 Canadian dollars. *Financial support:* In 2011–12, 14 fellowships, 30 research assistantships (averaging $7,000 per year), 42 teaching assistantships (averaging $2,000 per year) were awarded; career-related internships or fieldwork and scholarships/grants also available. *Faculty research:* Construction engineering and management; materials and infrastructure renewal; highway and pavement research; structures and solid mechanics; geotechnical, soil; structure interaction; transportation and planning; environment, solid waste management. *Unit head:* Dr. Eric Hildebrand, Director of Graduate Studies, 506-453-5113, Fax: 506-453-3568, E-mail: edh@unb.ca. *Application contact:* Joyce Moore, Graduate Secretary, 506-452-6127, Fax: 506-453-3568, E-mail: civil-grad@unb.ca. Web site: http://www.unbf.ca/eng/civil/.

The University of Texas at Austin, Graduate School, Cockrell School of Engineering, Department of Petroleum and Geosystems Engineering, Austin, TX 78712-1111. Offers energy and earth resources (MA); petroleum engineering (MS, PhD). Evening/weekend programs available. Postbaccalaureate distance learning degree programs offered (no on-campus study). *Entrance requirements:* For master's and doctorate, GRE General Test. *Application deadline:* For fall admission, 2/1 priority date for domestic students; for spring admission, 10/1 for domestic students. Applications are processed on a rolling basis. Application fee: $50 ($75 for international students). Electronic applications accepted. *Financial support:* Fellowships, research assistantships, and teaching assistantships available. Financial award application deadline: 2/1. *Unit head:* Dr. Tad Patzek, Chairman, 512-471-3161, Fax: 512-471-9605, E-mail: patzek@mail.utexas.edu. *Application contact:* Frankie Hart, Graduate Coordinator, E-mail: pgegradoffice@mail.utexas.edu. Web site: http://www.pge.utexas.edu/current/grad.cfm.

University of Washington, Graduate School, College of Engineering, Department of Civil and Environmental Engineering, Seattle, WA 98195-2700. Offers civil engineering (MS, MSE, PhD); construction engineering (MSCE); environmental engineering (MS, MSCE, MSE, PhD); global trade, transportation and logistics (MS); hydrology, water resources, and environmental fluid mechanics (MS, MSCE, MSE, PhD); structural and geotechnical engineering and mechanics (MS, MSCE, MSE, PhD); transportation and construction engineering (MS, MSE, PhD); transportation engineering (MSCE). Part-time programs available. Postbaccalaureate distance learning degree programs offered (no on-campus study). *Faculty:* 47 full-time (11 women), 9 part-time/adjunct (1 woman). *Students:* 195 full-time (67 women), 72 part-time (19 women); includes 37 minority (4 Black or African American, non-Hispanic/Latino; 27 Asian, non-Hispanic/Latino; 6 Hispanic/Latino), 65 international. 654 applicants, 57% accepted, 100 enrolled. In 2011, 88 master's, 7 doctorates awarded. Terminal master's awarded for partial completion of doctoral program. *Degree requirements:* For master's, thesis (for some programs); for doctorate, comprehensive exam, thesis/dissertation, general, qualifying, and final exams; completion of degree within 10 years. *Entrance requirements:* For master's, GRE General Test, minimum GPA of 3.0, statement of purpose, letters of recommendation, transcripts; for doctorate, GRE General Test, minimum GPA of 3.5, statement of purpose, letters of recommendation, transcripts. Additional exam requirements/recommendations for international students: Required—TOEFL (minimum score 580 paper-based; 237 computer-based; 92 iBT); Recommended—IELTS (minimum score 7). *Application deadline:* For fall admission, 1/10 priority date for domestic students, 1/10 for international students. Applications are processed on a rolling basis. Application fee: $75. Electronic applications accepted. *Expenses:* Contact institution. *Financial support:* In 2011–12, 99 students received support, including 16 fellowships with full and partial tuition reimbursements available (averaging $16,173 per year), 71 research assistantships with full tuition reimbursements available (averaging $16,380 per year), 10 teaching assistantships with full tuition reimbursements available (averaging $16,380 per year); scholarships/grants also available. Financial award application deadline: 1/10; financial award applicants required to submit FAFSA. *Faculty research:* Environmental/water resources, hydrology; construction/transportation; structures/ geotechnical. *Total annual research expenditures:* $13.6 million. *Unit head:* Dr. Gregory R. Miller, Professor/Chair, 206-543-0350, Fax: 206-543-1543, E-mail: gmiller@uw.edu. *Application contact:* Lorna Latal, Graduate Adviser, 206-543-2574, Fax: 206-543-1543, E-mail: llatal@u.washington.edu. Web site: http://www.ce.washington.edu/programs/prospective/grad/applying/gen_admission.html.

Hazardous Materials Management

Humboldt State University, Academic Programs, College of Natural Resources and Sciences, Programs in Natural Resources, Arcata, CA 95521-8299. Offers natural resources (MS), including fisheries, forestry, natural resources planning and interpretation, rangeland resources and wildland soils, wastewater utilization, watershed management, wildlife. *Students:* 45 full-time (26 women), 28 part-time (11 women); includes 4 minority (2 Asian, non-Hispanic/Latino; 1 Hispanic/Latino; 1 Two or more races, non-Hispanic/Latino), 1 international. Average age 30. 100 applicants, 22% accepted, 11 enrolled. In 2011, 25 master's awarded. *Degree requirements:* For master's, thesis or alternative. *Entrance requirements:* For master's, GRE, appropriate bachelor's degree, minimum GPA of 2.5, 3 letters of recommendation, resume. Additional exam requirements/recommendations for international students: Required—TOEFL (minimum score 500 paper-based; 173 computer-based). *Application deadline:* For fall admission, 2/1 for domestic and international students; for spring admission, 9/30 for domestic and international students. Applications are processed on a rolling basis. Application fee: $55. *Expenses:* Tuition, state resident: full-time $6734. Tuition, nonresident: full-time $15,662; part-time $372 per credit. *Required fees:* $903. Tuition and fees vary according to program. *Financial support:* Fellowships, career-related internships or fieldwork, and Federal Work-Study available. Support available to part-time students. Financial award application deadline: 3/1; financial award applicants required to submit FAFSA. *Faculty research:* Spotted owl habitat, pre-settlement vegetation, hardwood utilization, tree physiology, fisheries. *Unit head:* Dr. Robert Van Kirk, Coordinator, 707-826-3744, E-mail: rob.vankirk@humboldt.edu. *Application contact:* Julie Tucker, Administrative Support Coordinator, 707-826-3256, E-mail: jlt7002@humboldt.edu. Web site: http://www.humboldt.edu/cnrs/graduate_programs.

Idaho State University, Office of Graduate Studies, Department of Interdisciplinary Studies, Pocatello, ID 83209. Offers general interdisciplinary (M Ed, MA, MNS); waste management and environmental science (MS). Part-time programs available. *Degree requirements:* For master's, comprehensive exam, thesis optional. *Entrance requirements:* For master's, GRE General Test or MAT, minimum GPA of 3.0. Additional exam requirements/recommendations for international students: Required—TOEFL (minimum score 550 paper-based; 213 computer-based; 80 iBT).

Indiana University Bloomington, School of Public and Environmental Affairs, Public Affairs Programs, Bloomington, IN 47405. Offers comparative and international affairs (MPA); economic development (MPA); energy (MPA); environmental policy (PhD); environmental policy and natural resource management (MPA); hazardous materials management (Certificate); information systems (MPA); international development (MPA); local government management (MPA); nonprofit management (MPA, Certificate); policy analysis (MPA); public budgeting and financial management (Certificate); public finance (PhD); public financial administration (MPA); public management (MPA, PhD, Certificate); public policy analysis (PhD); social entrepreneurship (Certificate); specialized public affairs (MPA); sustainability and sustainable development (MPA); JD/MPA; MPA/MA; MPA/MIS; MPA/MLS; MSES/MPA. *Accreditation:* NASPAA (one or more programs are accredited). Part-time programs available. *Faculty:* 80 full-time (30 women), 102 part-time/adjunct (43 women). *Students:* 338 full-time, 30 part-time; includes 27 minority (7 Black or African American, non-Hispanic/Latino; 2 American Indian or Alaska Native, non-Hispanic/Latino; 10 Asian, non-Hispanic/Latino; 8 Hispanic/Latino), 56 international. Average age 24. 501 applicants, 148 enrolled. In 2011, 172 master's, 7 doctorates awarded. *Degree requirements:* For master's, core classes, capstone, internship; for doctorate, comprehensive exam, thesis/dissertation. *Entrance requirements:* For master's, GRE General Test or GMAT, official transcripts, 3 letters of recommendation, resume, personal statement; for doctorate, GRE General Test or LSAT, official transcripts, 3 letters of recommendation, resume or curriculum vitae, statement of purpose. Additional exam requirements/recommendations for international students: Required—TOEFL (minimum score 600 paper-based; 96 iBT); Recommended—IELTS (minimum score 7). *Application deadline:* For fall admission, 2/1 priority date for domestic students, 12/1 for international students. Applications are processed on a rolling basis. Application fee: $55 ($65 for international students). Electronic applications accepted. *Financial support:* Fellowships with partial tuition reimbursements, research assistantships with partial tuition reimbursements, teaching assistantships with partial tuition reimbursements, career-related internships or fieldwork, Federal Work-Study, scholarships/grants, health care benefits, unspecified assistantships, and Service Corps programs available. Financial award application deadline: 2/1; financial award applicants required to submit FAFSA. *Faculty research:* Comparative and international affairs, environmental policy and resource management, policy analysis, public finance, public management, urban management, nonprofit management, energy policy, social policy, public finance. *Unit head:* Jennifer Forney, Director of Graduate Student Services, 812-855-9485, Fax: 812-856-3665, E-mail: speampo@indiana.edu. *Application contact:* Admissions Assistant, 812-855-2840, E-mail: speaapps@indiana.edu. Web site: http://www.indiana.edu/~spea/prospective_students/masters/.

Marquette University, Graduate School, College of Engineering, Department of Civil and Environmental Engineering, Milwaukee, WI 53201-1881. Offers construction and public works management (MS, PhD); construction engineering and management (Certificate); environmental/water resources engineering (MS, PhD); structural design (Certificate); structural/geotechnical engineering (MS, PhD); transportation planning and engineering (MS, PhD); waste and wastewater treatment processes (Certificate). Part-time and evening/weekend programs available. *Faculty:* 13 full-time (0 women), 5 part-time/adjunct (0 women). *Students:* 26 full-time (5 women), 11 part-time (0 women); includes 2 minority (1 Black or African American, non-Hispanic/Latino; 1 Asian, non-Hispanic/Latino), 12 international. Average age 27. 74 applicants, 62% accepted, 9 enrolled. In 2011, 6 master's, 3 doctorates awarded. Terminal master's awarded for partial completion of doctoral program. *Degree requirements:* For master's, comprehensive exam (for some programs), thesis or alternative; for doctorate, thesis/dissertation. *Entrance requirements:* For master's, GRE General Test (recommended), minimum GPA of 3.0, official transcripts from all current and previous colleges/universities except Marquette, three letters of recommendation; for doctorate, GRE General Test, minimum GPA of 3.0, official transcripts from all current and previous colleges/universities except Marquette, three letters of recommendation, brief statement of purpose, submission of any English language publications authored by applicant (strongly recommended). Additional exam requirements/recommendations for international students: Required—TOEFL (minimum score 530 paper-based; 78 computer-based). *Application deadline:* For fall admission, 6/1 priority date for domestic students. Applications are processed on a rolling basis. Application fee: $50. Electronic applications accepted. *Expenses: Tuition:* Full-time $17,010; part-time $945 per credit hour. Tuition and fees vary according to program. *Financial support:* In 2011–12, 21 students received support, including 6 fellowships with partial tuition reimbursements available (averaging $9,177 per year), 1 research assistantship with full tuition reimbursement available (averaging $13,745 per year), 7 teaching assistantships with full tuition reimbursements available (averaging $13,902 per year); scholarships/grants, health care benefits, tuition waivers (partial), and unspecified assistantships also available. Support available to part-time students. Financial award application deadline: 2/15. *Faculty research:* Highway safety, highway performance, and intelligent transportation systems; surface mount technology; watershed management. *Total annual research expenditures:* $826,608. *Unit head:* Dr. Thomas Wenzel, Chair, 414-288-7030, Fax: 414-288-7521, E-mail: thomas.wenzel@marquette.edu. *Application contact:* Dr. Stephen M. Heinrich, Director of Graduate Studies, 414-288-5466, E-mail: stephen.heinrich@marquette.edu. Web site: http://www.marquette.edu/engineering/pages/AllYouNeed/Civil_Environmental/civil.html.

New Mexico Institute of Mining and Technology, Graduate Studies, Department of Civil and Environmental Engineering, Socorro, NM 87801. Offers environmental engineering (MS), including air quality engineering and science, hazardous waste engineering, water quality engineering and science. *Faculty:* 6 full-time (2 women), 2 part-time/adjunct (0 women). *Students:* 6 full-time (3 women); includes 3 minority (1 Black or African American, non-Hispanic/Latino; 1 American Indian or Alaska Native, non-Hispanic/Latino; 1 Hispanic/Latino). Average age 27. 14 applicants, 50% accepted, 3 enrolled. In 2011, 3 master's awarded. *Degree requirements:* For master's, thesis. *Entrance requirements:* For master's, GRE General Test. Additional exam requirements/recommendations for international students: Required—TOEFL (minimum score 540 paper-based; 207 computer-based). *Application deadline:* For fall admission, 3/1 priority date for domestic students; for spring admission, 6/1 for domestic students. Applications are processed on a rolling basis. Application fee: $16 ($30 for international students). *Expenses:* Tuition, state resident: full-time $4849; part-time $269.41 per credit hour. Tuition, nonresident: full-time $16,041; part-time $891.15 per credit hour. *Required fees:* $622; $65 per credit hour. $20 per semester. Part-time tuition and fees vary according to course load. *Financial support:* In 2011–12, 1 fellowship (averaging $7,200 per year), 3 research assistantships (averaging $10,958 per year), 4 teaching assistantships with full and partial tuition reimbursements (averaging $9,350 per year) were awarded; Federal Work-Study, institutionally sponsored loans, and unspecified assistantships also available. Financial award application deadline: 3/1; financial award applicants required to submit CSS PROFILE or FAFSA. *Faculty research:* Air quality, hazardous waste management, wastewater management and treatment, site remediation. *Unit head:* Dr. Mark Cal, Chair, 575-835-5059, Fax: 575-835-5252, E-mail: mcal@nmt.edu. *Application contact:* Dr. Lorie Liebrock, Dean of Graduate Studies, 575-835-5513, Fax: 575-835-5476, E-mail: graduate@nmt.edu. Web site: http://www.nmt.edu/~enve/.

Rutgers, The State University of New Jersey, New Brunswick, Graduate School-New Brunswick, Department of Environmental Sciences, Piscataway, NJ 08854-8097. Offers air pollution and resources (MS, PhD); aquatic biology (MS, PhD); aquatic chemistry (MS, PhD); atmospheric science (MS, PhD); chemistry and physics of aerosol and hydrosol systems (MS, PhD); environmental chemistry (MS, PhD); environmental microbiology (MS, PhD); environmental toxicology (PhD); exposure assessment (PhD); fate and effects of pollutants (MS, PhD); pollution prevention and control (MS, PhD); water and wastewater treatment (MS, PhD); water resources (MS, PhD). Terminal master's awarded for partial completion of doctoral program. *Degree requirements:* For master's, comprehensive exam, thesis or alternative, oral final exam; for doctorate, comprehensive exam, thesis/dissertation, thesis defense, qualifying exam. *Entrance requirements:* For master's and doctorate, GRE General Test. Additional exam requirements/recommendations for international students: Required—TOEFL. Electronic applications accepted. *Faculty research:* Biological waste treatment; contaminant fate and transport; air, soil and water quality.

Stony Brook University, State University of New York, School of Professional Development, Stony Brook, NY 11794. Offers biology-grade 7-12 (MAT); chemistry-grade 7-12 (MAT); coaching (Graduate Certificate); coaching online (Graduate Certificate); computer integrated engineering (Graduate Certificate); earth science-grade 7-12 (MAT); educational computing (Graduate Certificate); educational leadership (Advanced Certificate); English-grade 7-12 (MAT); environmental management (Graduate Certificate); environmental/occupational health and safety (Graduate

Certificate); French-grade 7-12 (MAT); German-grade 7-12 (MAT); human resource management (Graduate Certificate); human resource management online (Graduate Certificate); information systems management (Graduate Certificate); Italian-grade 7-12 (MAT); liberal studies (MA); liberal studies online (MAT); mathematics-grade 7-12 (MAT); operation research (Graduate Certificate); physics-grade 7-12 (MAT); professional studies online (MPS); school administration and supervision (Graduate Certificate); school building leadership (Graduate Certificate); school district administration (Graduate Certificate); school district business leadership (Advanced Certificate); school district leadership (Graduate Certificate); social science and the professions (MPS), including environmental waste management, human resource management; social studies-grade 7-12 (MAT); Spanish-grade 7-12 (MAT); waste management (Graduate Certificate). Part-time and evening/weekend programs available. Postbaccalaureate distance learning degree programs offered. *Degree requirements:* For master's, one foreign language, thesis or alternative.

Tufts University, School of Engineering, Department of Civil and Environmental Engineering, Medford, MA 02155. Offers bioengineering (ME, MS), including environmental technology; civil engineering (ME, MS, PhD), including geotechnical engineering, structural engineering, water diplomacy (PhD); environmental engineering (ME, MS, PhD), including environmental engineering and environmental sciences, environmental geotechnology, environmental health, environmental science and management, hazardous materials management, water diplomacy (PhD), water resources engineering. Part-time programs available. *Faculty:* 18 full-time, 5 part-time/adjunct. *Students:* 102 full-time (50 women); includes 8 minority (1 Black or African American, non-Hispanic/Latino; 6 Asian, non-Hispanic/Latino; 1 Hispanic/Latino), 37 international. Average age 27. 162 applicants, 59% accepted, 37 enrolled. In 2011, 18 degrees awarded. Terminal master's awarded for partial completion of doctoral program. *Degree requirements:* For master's, thesis or alternative; for doctorate, thesis/dissertation. *Entrance requirements:* For master's and doctorate, GRE General Test. Additional exam requirements/recommendations for international students: Required—TOEFL (minimum score 550 paper-based; 213 computer-based; 80 iBT). *Application deadline:* For fall admission, 1/15 priority date for domestic students, 12/15 for international students; for spring admission, 10/15 for domestic students, 9/15 for international students. Applications are processed on a rolling basis. Application fee: $75. Electronic applications accepted. *Expenses: Tuition:* Full-time $41,208; part-time $1030 per credit hour. Full-time tuition and fees vary according to degree level, program and student level. Part-time tuition and fees vary according to course load. *Financial support:* Fellowships with full tuition reimbursements, research assistantships with full and partial tuition reimbursements, teaching assistantships with full and partial tuition reimbursements, Federal Work-Study, scholarships/grants, tuition waivers (partial), and unspecified assistantships available. Financial award application deadline: 1/15; financial award applicants required to submit FAFSA. *Faculty research:* Environmental and water resources engineering, environmental health, geotechnical and geoenvironmental engineering, structural engineering and mechanics, water diplomacy. *Unit head:* Dr. Kurt Penell, Chair, 617-627-3211, Fax: 617-627-3994. *Application contact:* Laura Sacco, Information Contact, 617-627-3211, E-mail: ceeinfo@tufts.edu. Web site: http://www.ase.tufts.edu/cee/.

University of Colorado Denver, College of Liberal Arts and Sciences, Department of Geography and Environmental Sciences, Denver, CO 80217. Offers environmental sciences (MS), including air quality, ecosystems, environmental health, environmental science education, geo-spatial analysis, hazardous waste, water quality. Part-time and evening/weekend programs available. *Students:* 42 full-time (25 women), 6 part-time (5 women); includes 6 minority (2 Black or African American, non-Hispanic/Latino; 1 Asian, non-Hispanic/Latino; 2 Hispanic/Latino; 1 Two or more races, non-Hispanic/Latino), 10 international. Average age 29. 31 applicants, 68% accepted, 13 enrolled. In 2011, 24 master's awarded. *Degree requirements:* For master's, thesis or alternative, 30 credits including 21 of core requirements and 9 of environmental science electives. *Entrance requirements:* For master's, GRE General Test, BA in one of the natural/physical sciences or engineering (or equivalent background); prerequisite coursework in calculus and physics (one semester each), general chemistry with lab and general biology with lab (two semesters each), three letters of recommendation. Additional exam requirements/recommendations for international students: Required—TOEFL (minimum score 525 paper-based; 197 computer-based). *Application deadline:* For fall admission, 4/1 for domestic and international students; for spring admission, 10/1 for domestic and international students. Application fee: $50 ($75 for international students). Electronic applications accepted. *Financial support:* Research assistantships, teaching assistantships, and Federal Work-Study available. Financial award application deadline: 4/1; financial award applicants required to submit FAFSA. *Faculty research:* Air quality, environmental health, ecosystems, hazardous waste, water quality, geo-spatial analysis and environmental science education. *Unit head:* Dr. Brian K. Page, Department Chair, 303-556-8332, Fax: 303-556-6197, E-mail: john.wyckoff@cudenver.edu. *Application contact:* Sue Eddleman, Program Assistant, 303-556-6197, E-mail: sue.eddleman@ucdenver.edu. Web site: http://www.ucdenver.edu/academics/colleges/CLAS/Departments/ges/Pages/Geography.aspx.

The University of Manchester, School of Materials, Manchester, United Kingdom. Offers advanced aerospace materials engineering (M Sc); advanced metallic systems (PhD); biomedical materials (M Phil, M Sc, PhD); ceramics and glass (M Phil, M Sc, PhD); composite materials (M Sc, PhD); corrosion and protection (M Phil, M Sc, PhD); materials (M Phil, PhD); metallic materials (M Phil, M Sc, PhD); nanostructural materials (M Phil, M Sc, PhD); paper science (M Phil, M Sc, PhD); polymer science and engineering (M Phil, M Sc, PhD); technical textiles (M Sc); textile design, fashion and management (M Phil, M Sc, PhD); textile science and technology (M Phil, M Sc, PhD); textiles (M Phil, PhD); textiles and fashion (M Ent).

University of New Haven, Graduate School, Tagliatela College of Engineering, Program in Environmental Engineering, West Haven, CT 06516-1916. Offers environmental engineering (MS); industrial and hazardous wastes (MS); water and wastewater treatment (MS). Part-time and evening/weekend programs available. *Students:* 15 full-time (5 women), 11 part-time (3 women); includes 1 minority (Asian, non-Hispanic/Latino), 18 international. Average age 31. 17 applicants, 100% accepted, 10 enrolled. In 2011, 15 master's awarded. *Degree requirements:* For master's, thesis or alternative. *Entrance requirements:* For master's, bachelor's degree in engineering. Additional exam requirements/recommendations for international students: Required—TOEFL (minimum score 520 paper-based; 190 computer-based; 70 iBT); Recommended—IELTS (minimum score 5.5). *Application deadline:* For fall admission, 5/31 for international students; for winter admission, 10/15 for international students; for spring admission, 1/15 for international students. Applications are processed on a rolling basis. Application fee: $50. Electronic applications accepted. *Expenses: Tuition:* Part-time $750 per credit. *Financial support:* Research assistantships with partial tuition reimbursements, teaching assistantships with partial tuition reimbursements, career-related internships or fieldwork, Federal Work-Study, scholarships/grants, tuition waivers, and unspecified assistantships available. Support available to part-time students. Financial award application deadline: 5/1; financial award applicants required to submit FAFSA. *Unit head:* Dr. Agamemnon D. Koutsospyros, Coordinator, 203-932-7398. *Application contact:* Eloise Gormley, Director of Graduate Admissions, 203-932-7449, Fax: 203-932-7137, E-mail: gradinfo@newhaven.edu. Web site: http://www.newhaven.edu/10140/.

University of South Carolina, The Graduate School, Arnold School of Public Health, Department of Environmental Health Sciences, Program in Hazardous Materials Management, Columbia, SC 29208. Offers MPH, MSPH, PhD. *Degree requirements:* For master's, comprehensive exam, thesis (for some programs), practicum (MPH); for doctorate, one foreign language, comprehensive exam, thesis/dissertation. *Entrance requirements:* Additional exam requirements/recommendations for international students: Required—TOEFL (minimum score 570 paper-based; 230 computer-based). Electronic applications accepted. *Faculty research:* Environmental/human health protection; use and disposal of hazardous materials; site safety; exposure assessment; migration, fate and transformation of materials.

University of Southern California, Graduate School, Viterbi School of Engineering, Sonny Astani Department of Civil Engineering, Los Angeles, CA 90089. Offers applied mechanics (MS); civil engineering (MS, PhD); computer-aided engineering (ME, Graduate Certificate); construction management (MCM); engineering technology commercialization (Graduate Certificate); environmental engineering (MS, PhD); environmental quality management (ME); structural design (ME); sustainable cities (Graduate Certificate); transportation systems (MS, Graduate Certificate); water and waste management (MS). Part-time and evening/weekend programs available. Terminal master's awarded for partial completion of doctoral program. *Degree requirements:* For master's, thesis optional; for doctorate, thesis/dissertation. *Entrance requirements:* For master's and doctorate, GRE General Test. Additional exam requirements/recommendations for international students: Recommended—TOEFL. Electronic applications accepted. *Faculty research:* Geotechnical engineering, transportation

engineering, structural engineering, construction management, environmental engineering, water resources.

Virginia Polytechnic Institute and State University, Graduate School, College of Engineering, Department of Civil and Environmental Engineering, Blacksburg, VA 24061. Offers civil engineering (M Eng, MS, PhD); civil infrastructure systems (Certificate); environmental engineering (MS); environmental sciences and engineering (MS); transportation systems engineering (Certificate); treatment process engineering (Certificate); urban hydrology and stormwater management (Certificate); water quality management (Certificate). *Accreditation:* ABET (one or more programs are accredited). *Degree requirements:* For master's, comprehensive exam (for some programs), thesis (for some programs); for doctorate, comprehensive exam (for some programs), thesis/dissertation (for some programs). *Entrance requirements:* For master's and doctorate, GRE. Additional exam requirements/recommendations for international students: Required—TOEFL (minimum score 550 paper-based; 213 computer-based). *Application deadline:* For fall admission, 7/1 for domestic and international students; for spring admission, 12/1 for domestic and international students. Applications are processed on a rolling basis. Application fee: $65. Electronic applications accepted. *Expenses:* Tuition, state resident: full-time $10,048; part-time $558.25 per credit hour. Tuition, nonresident: full-time $19,497; part-time $1083.25 per credit hour. *Required fees:* $405 per semester. Tuition and fees vary according to course load, campus/location and program. *Financial support:* Fellowships with full tuition reimbursements, research assistantships with full tuition reimbursements, teaching assistantships with full tuition reimbursements, career-related internships or fieldwork, Federal Work-Study, scholarships/grants, health care benefits, and unspecified assistantships available. Financial award application deadline: 1/15. *Faculty research:* Construction, environmental geotechnical hydrosystems, structures and transportation engineering. *Unit head:* Dr. Sam Easterling, Unit Head, 540-231-5143, Fax: 540-231-7532, E-mail: seaster@vt.edu. *Application contact:* Marc Widdowson, Information Contact, 540-231-7153, Fax: 540-231-7532, E-mail: mwiddows@vt.edu. Web site: http://www.cee.vt.edu/.

Hydraulics

Auburn University, Graduate School, Ginn College of Engineering, Department of Civil Engineering, Auburn University, AL 36849. Offers construction engineering and management (MCE, MS, PhD); environmental engineering (MCE, MS, PhD); geotechnical/materials engineering (MCE, MS, PhD); hydraulics/hydrology (MCE, MS, PhD); structural engineering (MCE, MS, PhD); transportation engineering (MCE, MS, PhD). Part-time programs available. *Faculty:* 21 full-time (2 women), 1 part-time/adjunct (0 women). *Students:* 48 full-time (16 women), 62 part-time (14 women); includes 6 minority (4 Black or African American, non-Hispanic/Latino; 1 Asian, non-Hispanic/Latino; 1 Hispanic/Latino), 37 international. Average age 26. 111 applicants, 59% accepted, 25 enrolled. In 2011, 26 master's, 2 doctorates awarded. *Degree requirements:* For master's, project (MCE), thesis (MS); for doctorate, comprehensive exam, thesis/dissertation. *Entrance requirements:* For master's and doctorate, GRE General Test. *Application deadline:* For fall admission, 7/7 for domestic students; for spring admission, 11/24 for domestic students. Applications are processed on a rolling basis. Application fee: $50 ($60 for international students). Electronic applications accepted. *Expenses:* Tuition, state resident: full-time $7290; part-time $405 per credit hour. Tuition, nonresident: full-time $21,870; part-time $1215 per credit hour. *International tuition:* $22,000 full-time. *Required fees:* $1402. *Financial support:* Fellowships, research assistantships, teaching assistantships, and Federal Work-Study available. Support available to part-time students. Financial award application deadline: 3/15; financial award applicants required to submit FAFSA. *Unit head:* Dr. J. Michael Stallings, Head, 334-844-4320. *Application contact:* Dr. George Flowers, Dean of the Graduate School, 334-844-2125.

Drexel University, College of Engineering, Department of Civil, Architectural, and Environmental Engineering, Philadelphia, PA 19104-2875. Offers architectural / building systems engineering (PhD); architectural/building systems engineering (MS); civil engineering (MS, PhD); environmental engineering (MS, PhD); geotechnical, geoenvironmental and geosynthetics engineering (MS, PhD); hydraulics, hydrology and water resources engineering (MS, PhD); structures (MS). Part-time and evening/weekend programs available. *Degree requirements:* For master's, thesis optional; for doctorate, thesis/dissertation. *Entrance requirements:* For master's, minimum GPA of 3.0; for doctorate, minimum GPA of 3.5, MS in civil engineering. Additional exam requirements/recommendations for international students: Required—TOEFL. Electronic applications accepted. *Faculty research:* Structural dynamics, hazardous wastes, water resources, pavement materials, groundwater.

École Polytechnique de Montréal, Graduate Programs, Department of Civil, Geological and Mining Engineering, Montréal, QC H3C 3A7, Canada. Offers civil, geological and mining engineering (DESS); environmental engineering (M Eng, M Sc A, PhD); geotechnical engineering (M Eng, M Sc A, PhD); hydraulics engineering (M Eng, M Sc A, PhD); structural engineering (M Eng, M Sc A, PhD); transportation engineering (M Eng, M Sc A, PhD). Part-time programs available. *Degree requirements:* For master's, one foreign language, thesis; for doctorate, one foreign language, thesis/dissertation. *Entrance requirements:* For master's, minimum GPA of 2.75; for doctorate, minimum GPA of 3.0. *Faculty research:* Water resources management, characteristics of building materials, aging of dams, pollution control.

McGill University, Faculty of Graduate and Postdoctoral Studies, Faculty of Engineering, Department of Civil Engineering and Applied Mechanics, Montréal, QC H3A 2T5, Canada. Offers environmental engineering (M Eng, M Sc, PhD); fluid mechanics (M Sc); fluid mechanics and hydraulic engineering (M Eng, PhD); materials engineering (M Eng, PhD); rehabilitation of urban infrastructure (M Eng, PhD); soil

behavior (M Eng, PhD); soil mechanics and foundations (M Eng, PhD); structures and structural mechanics (M Eng, PhD); water resources (M Sc); water resources engineering (M Eng, PhD).

Missouri University of Science and Technology, Graduate School, Department of Civil, Architectural, and Environmental Engineering, Rolla, MO 65409. Offers civil engineering (MS, DE, PhD); construction engineering (MS, DE, PhD); environmental engineering (MS); fluid mechanics (MS, DE, PhD); geotechnical engineering (MS, DE, PhD); hydrology and hydraulic engineering (MS, DE, PhD). Part-time and evening/weekend programs available. Terminal master's awarded for partial completion of doctoral program. *Degree requirements:* For master's, thesis optional; for doctorate, comprehensive exam, thesis/dissertation. *Entrance requirements:* For master's, GRE General Test (minimum combined score 1100), minimum GPA of 3.0; for doctorate, GRE General Test (minimum score: verbal and quantitative 400, writing 3.5), minimum GPA of 3.0. Additional exam requirements/recommendations for international students: Required—TOEFL. Electronic applications accepted. *Faculty research:* Earthquake engineering, structural optimization and control systems, structural health monitoring/damage detection, soil-structure interaction, soil mechanics and foundation engineering.

University of Colorado Denver, College of Engineering and Applied Science, Department of Civil Engineering, Denver, CO 80217. Offers civil engineering (EASPh D); civil engineering systems (PhD); environmental and sustainability engineering (MS, PhD); geographic information systems (MS); geotechnical engineering (MS, PhD); hydrology and hydraulics (MS, PhD); structural engineering (MS, PhD); transportation engineering (MS, PhD). Part-time and evening/weekend programs available. *Faculty:* 14 full-time (1 woman), 6 part-time/adjunct (0 women). *Students:* 66 full-time (11 women), 65 part-time (14 women); includes 30 minority (10 Black or African American, non-Hispanic/Latino; 8 Asian, non-Hispanic/Latino; 10 Hispanic/Latino; 2 Two or more races, non-Hispanic/Latino), 17 international. Average age 34. 67 applicants, 54% accepted, 24 enrolled. In 2011, 30 master's, 2 doctorates awarded. *Degree requirements:* For master's, comprehensive exam, thesis or alternative, 30 credit hours, project or thesis; for doctorate, comprehensive exam, thesis/dissertation, 60 credit hours (30 of which are dissertation research). *Entrance requirements:* For master's, GRE, statement of purpose, transcripts, three references; for doctorate, GRE, statement of purpose, transcripts, references, letter of support from faculty stating willingness to serve as dissertation advisor and outlining plan for financial support. Additional exam requirements/recommendations for international students: Required—TOEFL (minimum score 525 paper-based; 197 computer-based). *Application deadline:* For fall admission, 7/15 for domestic students, 6/15 for international students; for spring admission, 12/1 for domestic students, 11/1 for international students. Applications are processed on a rolling basis. Application fee: $50 ($75 for international students). Electronic applications accepted. *Expenses:* Contact institution. *Financial support:* Research assistantships, teaching assistantships, career-related internships or fieldwork, and Federal Work-Study available. Financial award application deadline: 4/1; financial award applicants required to submit FAFSA. *Faculty research:* Earthquake source physics, environmental biotechnology, hydrologic and hydraulic engineering, sustainability assessments, transportation energy use and greenhouse gas emissions. *Unit head:* Dr. Kevin Rens, Chair, 303-556-8017, Fax: 303-556-2368, E-mail: kevin.rens@ucdenver.edu. *Application contact:* Maria Rase, Program Assistant, 303-556-6712, Fax: 303-556-2368, E-mail: maria.rase@ucdenver.edu. Web site: http://www.ucdenver.edu/academics/colleges/Engineering/Programs/Civil-Engineering/Pages/CivilEngineering.aspx.

Structural Engineering

Auburn University, Graduate School, Ginn College of Engineering, Department of Civil Engineering, Auburn University, AL 36849. Offers construction engineering and management (MCE, MS, PhD); environmental engineering (MCE, MS, PhD); geotechnical/materials engineering (MCE, MS, PhD); hydraulics/hydrology (MCE, MS,

PhD); structural engineering (MCE, MS, PhD); transportation engineering (MCE, MS, PhD). Part-time programs available. *Faculty:* 21 full-time (2 women), 1 part-time/adjunct (0 women). *Students:* 48 full-time (16 women), 62 part-time (14 women); includes 6 minority (4 Black or African American, non-Hispanic/Latino; 1 Asian, non-Hispanic/

Latino; 1 Hispanic/Latino), 37 international. Average age 26. 111 applicants, 59% accepted, 25 enrolled. In 2011, 26 master's, 2 doctorates awarded. *Degree requirements:* For master's, project (MCE), thesis (MS); for doctorate, comprehensive exam, thesis/dissertation. *Entrance requirements:* For master's and doctorate, GRE General Test. *Application deadline:* For fall admission, 7/7 for domestic students; for spring admission, 11/24 for domestic students. Applications are processed on a rolling basis. Application fee: $50 ($60 for international students). Electronic applications accepted. *Expenses:* Tuition, state resident: full-time $7290; part-time $405 per credit hour. Tuition, nonresident: full-time $21,870; part-time $1215 per credit hour. *International tuition:* $22,000 full-time. *Required fees:* $1402. *Financial support:* Fellowships, research assistantships, teaching assistantships, and Federal Work-Study available. Support available to part-time students. Financial award application deadline: 3/15; financial award applicants required to submit FAFSA. *Unit head:* Dr. J. Michael Stallings, Head, 334-844-4320. *Application contact:* Dr. George Flowers, Dean of the Graduate School, 334-844-2125.

California State University, Northridge, Graduate Studies, College of Engineering and Computer Science, Department of Civil Engineering and Applied Mechanics, Northridge, CA 91330. Offers engineering (MS), including structural engineering. Part-time and evening/weekend programs available. *Degree requirements:* For master's, thesis. *Entrance requirements:* Additional exam requirements/recommendations for international students: Required—TOEFL. *Faculty research:* Composite study.

Cornell University, Graduate School, Graduate Fields of Engineering, Field of Civil and Environmental Engineering, Ithaca, NY 14853-0001. Offers engineering management (M Eng, MS, PhD); environmental engineering (M Eng, MS, PhD); environmental fluid mechanics and hydrology (M Eng, MS, PhD); environmental systems engineering (M Eng, MS, PhD); geotechnical engineering (M Eng, MS, PhD); remote sensing (M Eng, MS, PhD); structural engineering (M Eng, MS, PhD); structural mechanics (M Eng, MS); transportation engineering (MS, PhD); transportation systems engineering (M Eng); water resource systems (M Eng, MS, PhD). *Faculty:* 39 full-time (4 women). *Students:* 143 full-time (49 women); includes 20 minority (6 Black or African American, non-Hispanic/Latino; 1 American Indian or Alaska Native, non-Hispanic/Latino; 9 Asian, non-Hispanic/Latino; 4 Hispanic/Latino), 72 international. Average age 25. 574 applicants, 47% accepted, 100 enrolled. In 2011, 88 master's, 13 doctorates awarded. Terminal master's awarded for partial completion of doctoral program. *Degree requirements:* For master's, thesis (MS); for doctorate, comprehensive exam, thesis/dissertation. *Entrance requirements:* For master's and doctorate, GRE General Test (recommended), 2 letters of recommendation. Additional exam requirements/recommendations for international students: Required—TOEFL (minimum score 600 paper-based; 250 computer-based; 77 iBT). *Application deadline:* For fall admission, 1/15 priority date for domestic students; for spring admission, 10/15 for domestic students. Application fee: $95. Electronic applications accepted. *Financial support:* In 2011–12, 50 students received support, including 20 fellowships with full tuition reimbursements available, 27 research assistantships with full tuition reimbursements available, 17 teaching assistantships with full tuition reimbursements available; institutionally sponsored loans, scholarships/grants, health care benefits, tuition waivers (full and partial), and unspecified assistantships also available. Financial award applicants required to submit FAFSA. *Faculty research:* Environmental engineering, geotechnical engineering, remote sensing, environmental fluid mechanics and hydrology, structural engineering. *Unit head:* Director of Graduate Studies, 607-255-7560, Fax: 607-255-9004. *Application contact:* Graduate Field Assistant, 607-255-7560, Fax: 607-255-9004, E-mail: cee_grad@cornell.edu. Web site: http://www.gradschool.cornell.edu/fields.php?id-27&a-2.

Drexel University, College of Engineering, Department of Civil, Architectural, and Environmental Engineering, Philadelphia, PA 19104-2875. Offers architectural / building systems engineering (PhD); architectural/building systems engineering (MS); civil engineering (MS, PhD); environmental engineering (MS, PhD); geotechnical, geoenvironmental and geosynthetics engineering (MS, PhD); hydraulics, hydrology and water resources engineering (MS, PhD); structures (MS). Part-time and evening/weekend programs available. *Degree requirements:* For master's, thesis optional; for doctorate, thesis/dissertation. *Entrance requirements:* For master's, minimum GPA of 3.0; for doctorate, minimum GPA of 3.5, MS in civil engineering. Additional exam requirements/recommendations for international students: Required—TOEFL. Electronic applications accepted. *Faculty research:* Structural dynamics, hazardous wastes, water resources, pavement materials, groundwater.

École Polytechnique de Montréal, Graduate Programs, Department of Civil, Geological and Mining Engineering, Montréal, QC H3C 3A7, Canada. Offers civil, geological and mining engineering (DESS); environmental engineering (M Eng, M Sc A, PhD); geotechnical engineering (M Eng, M Sc A, PhD); hydraulics engineering (M Eng, M Sc A, PhD); structural engineering (M Eng, M Sc A, PhD); transportation engineering (M Eng, M Sc A, PhD). Part-time programs available. *Degree requirements:* For master's, one foreign language, thesis; for doctorate, one foreign language, thesis/dissertation. *Entrance requirements:* For master's, minimum GPA of 2.75; for doctorate, minimum GPA of 3.0. *Faculty research:* Water resources management, characteristics of building materials, aging of dams, pollution control.

Illinois Institute of Technology, Graduate College, Armour College of Engineering, Department of Civil, Architectural and Environmental Engineering, Chicago, IL 60616-3793. Offers architectural engineering (M Arch E); civil engineering (MS, PhD), including architectural engineeering (MS), construction engineering and management (MS), geoenvironmental engineering (MS), geotechnical engineering (MS), structural engineering (MS), transportation engineering (MS); construction engineering and management (MCEM); environmental engineering (M Env E, PhD); geoenvironmental engineering (M Geoenv E); geotechnical engineering (MGE); public works (MPW); structural engineering (MSE); transportation engineering (M Trans E). Part-time and evening/weekend programs available. Postbaccalaureate distance learning degree programs offered (minimal on-campus study). Terminal master's awarded for partial completion of doctoral program. *Degree requirements:* For master's, thesis (for some programs); for doctorate, comprehensive exam, thesis/dissertation. *Entrance requirements:* For master's, GRE General Test (minimum score 900 Quantitative and Verbal, 2.5 Analytical Writing), minimum undergraduate GPA of 3.0; for doctorate, GRE General Test (minimum score 1000 Quantitative and Verbal, 3.0 Analytical Writing), minimum undergraduate GPA of 3.0. Additional exam requirements/recommendations for international students: Required—TOEFL (minimum score 523 paper-based; 70 iBT); Recommended—IELTS (minimum score 5.5). Electronic applications accepted. *Faculty research:* Structural, architectural, geotechnical and geoenvironmental engineering; construction engineering and management; transportation engineering; environmental engineering and public works.

Instituto Tecnologico de Santo Domingo, Graduate School, Area of Engineering, Santo Domingo, Dominican Republic. Offers construction administration (MS, Certificate); data telecommunications (M Eng, MS, Certificate); industrial engineering (M Eng, Certificate); industrial management (M Mgmt); information technology (Certificate); maintenance engineering (M Eng); occupational hazard prevention (M Mgmt); production management (Certificate); quantitative methods (Certificate); sanitary and environmental engineering (M Eng); structural engineering (M Eng); systems engineering and electronic data processing (Certificate); transportation (Certificate).

Iowa State University of Science and Technology, Department of Civil and Construction Engineering, Ames, IA 50011-3232. Offers civil engineering (MS, PhD), including civil engineering materials, construction engineering and management, environmental engineering, geometronics, geotechnical engineering, structural engineering, transportation engineering. *Degree requirements:* For master's, thesis or alternative; for doctorate, thesis/dissertation. *Entrance requirements:* For master's and doctorate, GRE General Test. Additional exam requirements/recommendations for international students: Required—TOEFL (minimum score 550 paper-based; 82 iBT), IELTS (minimum score 6.5). *Application deadline:* For fall admission, 2/1 priority date for domestic students, 2/1 for international students; for spring admission, 8/1 priority date for domestic students, 8/1 for international students. Applications are processed on a rolling basis. Application fee: $40 ($90 for international students). Electronic applications accepted. *Unit head:* Dr. Sri Sritharan, Director of Graduate Education, 515-294-4972, Fax: 515-294-8216, E-mail: ccee-grad-inquiry@iastate.edu. *Application contact:* Kathy Petersen, Director of Graduate Education, 515-294-4975, Fax: 515-294-8216, E-mail: ccee-grad-inquiry@iastate.edu. Web site: http://www.ccee.iastate.edu/.

Lehigh University, P.C. Rossin College of Engineering and Applied Science, Department of Civil and Environmental Engineering, Bethlehem, PA 18015. Offers civil engineering (M Eng, MS, PhD); environmental engineering (MS, PhD); structural engineering (M Eng, MS, PhD). Part-time programs available. *Faculty:* 15 full-time (3 women), 2 part-time/adjunct (0 women). *Students:* 98 full-time (33 women), 11 part-time (0 women); includes 5 minority (1 Black or African American, non-Hispanic/Latino; 1 Asian, non-Hispanic/Latino; 3 Hispanic/Latino), 67 international. Average age 26. 655 applicants, 31% accepted, 25 enrolled. In 2011, 40 master's, 7 doctorates awarded. Terminal master's awarded for partial completion of doctoral program. *Degree requirements:* For master's, thesis (for some programs); for doctorate, comprehensive exam, thesis/dissertation. *Entrance requirements:* For master's and doctorate, GRE. Additional exam requirements/recommendations for international students: Required—TOEFL (minimum score 550 paper-based; 213 computer-based; 79 iBT). *Application deadline:* For fall admission, 7/15 priority date for domestic students, 7/15 for international students; for spring admission, 12/1 priority date for domestic students, 12/1 for international students. Applications are processed on a rolling basis. Application fee: $75. Electronic applications accepted. *Expenses:* Contact institution. *Financial support:* In 2011–12, 35 students received support, including 8 fellowships with full tuition reimbursements available (averaging $18,560 per year), 7 research assistantships with full tuition reimbursements available (averaging $22,350 per year), 7 teaching assistantships with full tuition reimbursements available (averaging $18,560 per year); institutionally sponsored loans, scholarships/grants, tuition waivers, and unspecified assistantships also available. Financial award application deadline: 1/15. *Faculty research:* Structural engineering, geotechnical engineering, water resources engineering, environmental engineering. *Total annual research expenditures:* $5.4 million. *Unit head:* Dr. Sibel Pamukcu, 610-758-3220, Fax: 610-758-6405, E-mail: sp01@lehigh.edu. *Application contact:* Prisca Vidanage, Graduate Coordinator, 610-758-3530, Fax: 610-758-6405, E-mail: pmv1@lehigh.edu. Web site: http://www.lehigh.edu/~incee/.

Louisiana State University and Agricultural and Mechanical College, Graduate School, College of Engineering, Department of Civil and Environmental Engineering, Baton Rouge, LA 70803. Offers environmental engineering (MSCE, PhD); geotechnical engineering (MSCE, PhD); structural engineering and mechanics (MSCE, PhD); transportation engineering (MSCE, PhD); water resources (MSCE, PhD). Part-time programs available. *Faculty:* 25 full-time (2 women). *Students:* 90 full-time (23 women), 34 part-time (8 women); includes 11 minority (4 Black or African American, non-Hispanic/Latino; 1 American Indian or Alaska Native, non-Hispanic/Latino; 4 Asian, non-Hispanic/Latino; 2 Hispanic/Latino), 73 international. Average age 30. 106 applicants, 67% accepted, 25 enrolled. In 2011, 32 master's, 4 doctorates awarded. *Degree requirements:* For master's, thesis optional; for doctorate, one foreign language, thesis/dissertation. *Entrance requirements:* For master's and doctorate, GRE General Test, minimum GPA of 3.0. Additional exam requirements/recommendations for international students: Required—TOEFL (minimum score 550 paper-based; 213 computer-based; 79 iBT) or IELTS (minimum score 6.5). *Application deadline:* For fall admission, 1/25 priority date for domestic students, 5/15 for international students; for spring admission, 10/15 for international students. Applications are processed on a rolling basis. Application fee: $50 ($70 for international students). Electronic applications accepted. *Financial support:* In 2011–12, 91 students received support, including 3 fellowships with full and partial tuition reimbursements available (averaging $18,050 per year), 72 research assistantships with full and partial tuition reimbursements available (averaging $15,942 per year), 6 teaching assistantships with full and partial tuition reimbursements available (averaging $12,469 per year); career-related internships or fieldwork, institutionally sponsored loans, scholarships/grants, and health care benefits also available. Financial award application deadline: 3/1; financial award applicants required to submit FAFSA. *Faculty research:* Mechanics and structures, environmental, geotechnical transportation, water resources. *Total annual research expenditures:* $3 million. *Unit head:* Dr. George Z. Voyiadjis, Chair/Professor, 225-578-8668, Fax: 225-578-9176, E-mail: voyaidjis@lsu.edu. *Application contact:* Dr. Clinton Willson, Professor, 225-578-8672, E-mail: cwillson@lsu.edu. Web site: http://www.cee.lsu.edu/.

Marquette University, Graduate School, College of Engineering, Department of Civil and Environmental Engineering, Milwaukee, WI 53201-1881. Offers construction and public works management (MS, PhD); construction engineering and management (Certificate); environmental/water resources engineering (MS, PhD); structural design (Certificate); structural/geotechnical engineering (MS, PhD); transportation planning and engineering (MS, PhD); waste and wastewater treatment processes (Certificate). Part-time and evening/weekend programs available. *Faculty:* 13 full-time (0 women), 5 part-time/adjunct (0 women). *Students:* 26 full-time (5 women), 11 part-time (0 women); includes 2 minority (1 Black or African American, non-Hispanic/Latino; 1 Asian, non-Hispanic/Latino), 12 international. Average age 27. 74 applicants, 62% accepted, 9 enrolled. In 2011, 6 master's, 3 doctorates awarded. Terminal master's awarded for partial completion of doctoral program. *Degree requirements:* For master's, comprehensive exam (for some programs), thesis or alternative; for doctorate, thesis/dissertation. *Entrance requirements:* For master's, GRE General Test (recommended), minimum GPA of 3.0, official transcripts from all current and previous colleges/universities except Marquette, three letters of recommendation; for doctorate, GRE General Test, minimum GPA of 3.0, official transcripts from all current and previous colleges/universities except Marquette, three letters of recommendation, brief statement of purpose, submission of any English language publications authored by applicant (strongly recommended). Additional exam requirements/recommendations for international students: Required—TOEFL (minimum score 530 paper-based; 78 computer-based). *Application deadline:* For fall admission; 6/1 priority date for domestic students. Applications are processed on a rolling basis. Application fee: $50. Electronic applications accepted. *Expenses: Tuition:* Full-time $17,010; part-time $945 per credit hour. Tuition and fees vary according to program. *Financial support:* In 2011–12, 21 students received support, including 6 fellowships with partial tuition reimbursements available (averaging $9,177 per year), 1 research assistantship with full tuition reimbursement available (averaging $13,745 per year), 7 teaching assistantships with full tuition reimbursements available (averaging $13,902 per year); scholarships/grants, health care benefits, tuition waivers (partial), and unspecified assistantships also available. Support available to part-time students. Financial award application deadline: 2/15. *Faculty research:* Highway safety, highway performance, and intelligent transportation systems; surface mount technology; watershed management. *Total annual research expenditures:* $826,608. *Unit head:* Dr. Thomas Wenzel, Chair, 414-288-7030, Fax: 414-288-7521, E-mail: thomas.wenzel@marquette.edu. *Application contact:* Dr. Stephen M. Heinrich, Director of Graduate Studies, 414-288-5466, E-mail: stephen.heinrich@marquette.edu. Web site: http://www.marquette.edu/engineering/pages/AllYouNeed/Civil_Environmental/civil.html.

Massachusetts Institute of Technology, School of Engineering, Department of Civil and Environmental Engineering, Cambridge, MA 02139. Offers biological oceanography (PhD, Sc D); chemical oceanography (PhD, Sc D); civil and environmental engineering (PhD, Sc D); civil and environmental systems (PhD, Sc D); civil engineering (PhD, Sc D, CE); coastal engineering (PhD, Sc D); construction engineering and management (PhD, Sc D); environmental and water quality engineering (M Eng); environmental biology (PhD, Sc D); environmental chemistry (PhD, Sc D); environmental engineering (PhD, Sc D); environmental fluid mechanics (PhD, Sc D); environmental science and engineering (SM); geotechnical and geoenvironmental engineering (PhD, Sc D); geotechnology (M Eng); high-performance structures (M Eng); hydrology (PhD, Sc D); information technology (PhD, Sc D); mechanics (SM); oceanographic engineering (PhD, Sc D); structures and materials (PhD, Sc D); transportation (M Eng, PhD, Sc D); SM/MBA. *Faculty:* 35 full-time (6 women), 1 part-time/adjunct (0 women). *Students:* 216 full-time (80 women); includes 30 minority (4 Black or African American, non-Hispanic/Latino; 13 Asian, non-Hispanic/Latino; 8 Hispanic/Latino; 5 Two or more races, non-Hispanic/Latino), 110 international. Average age 27. 589 applicants, 26% accepted, 91 enrolled. In 2011, 62 master's, 14 doctorates awarded. *Degree requirements:* For master's and CE, thesis; for doctorate, comprehensive exam, thesis/dissertation. *Entrance requirements:* For master's and doctorate, GRE General Test. Additional exam requirements/recommendations for international students: Required—TOEFL (minimum score 577 paper-based; 233 computer-based; 90 iBT), IELTS (minimum score 7). *Application deadline:* For fall admission, 12/15 for domestic and international students. Application fee: $75. Electronic applications accepted. *Expenses: Tuition:* Full-time $40,460; part-time $630 per credit hour. *Required fees:* $272. *Financial support:* In 2011–12, 180 students received support, including 51 fellowships (averaging $30,800 per year), 110 research assistantships (averaging $29,500 per year), 19 teaching assistantships (averaging $29,500 per year); career-related internships or fieldwork, Federal Work-Study, institutionally sponsored loans, scholarships/grants, health care benefits, and unspecified assistantships also available. *Faculty research:* Environmental chemistry, environmental fluid mechanics and coastal engineering, environmental microbiology, geotechnical engineering and geomechanics, hydrology and hydroclimatology, infrastructure systems, mechanics of materials and structures, transportation systems. *Total annual research expenditures:* $17.7 million. *Unit head:* Prof. Andrew Whittle, Head, 617-253-7101. *Application contact:* Patricia Glidden, Graduate Admissions Coordinator, 617-253-7119, Fax: 617-258-6775, E-mail: cee-admissions@mit.edu. Web site: http://cee.mit.edu/.

McGill University, Faculty of Graduate and Postdoctoral Studies, Faculty of Engineering, Department of Civil Engineering and Applied Mechanics, Montréal, QC H3A 2T5, Canada. Offers environmental engineering (M Eng, M Sc, PhD); fluid mechanics (M Sc); fluid mechanics and hydraulic engineering (M Eng, PhD); materials engineering (M Eng, PhD); rehabilitation of urban infrastructure (M Eng, PhD); soil behavior (M Eng, PhD); soil mechanics and foundations (M Eng, PhD); structures and structural mechanics (M Eng, PhD); water resources (M Sc); water resources engineering (M Eng, PhD).

Milwaukee School of Engineering, Civil and Architectural Engineering and Construction Management Department, Program in Structural Engineering, Milwaukee, WI 53202-3109. Offers MS. Part-time and evening/weekend programs available. *Faculty:* 4 full-time (1 woman), 1 (woman) part-time/adjunct. *Students:* 2 full-time (0 women), 11 part-time (2 women). Average age 24. 28 applicants, 75% accepted, 2 enrolled. In 2011, 25 master's awarded. *Degree requirements:* For master's, thesis, design project. *Entrance requirements:* For master's, GRE General Test or GMAT, 2 letters of recommendation, BS in architectural or structural engineering. Additional exam requirements/recommendations for international students: Required—TOEFL (minimum score 79 iBT) or IELTS. *Application deadline:* Applications are processed on a rolling basis. Electronic applications accepted. Application fee is waived when completed online. *Expenses: Tuition:* Full-time $17,550; part-time $650 per credit hour. *Financial support:* In 2011–12, 8 students received support. Research assistantships and career-related internships or fieldwork available. Support available to part-time students. Financial award applicants required to submit FAFSA. *Faculty research:* Steel, materials. *Unit head:* Dr. Richard DeVries, Director, 414-277-7596. *Application contact:* Katie Gassenhuber, Graduate Program Associate, 800-321-6763, Fax: 414-277-7208, E-mail: gassenhuber@msoe.edu.

Northwestern University, McCormick School of Engineering and Applied Science, Department of Civil and Environmental Engineering, Evanston, IL 60208-3109. Offers environmental engineering and science (MS, PhD); geotechnical engineering (MS, PhD); mechanics of materials and solids (MS, PhD); project management (MS, PhD); structural engineering and materials (MS, PhD); theoretical and applied mechanics (MS, PhD), including fluid mechanics, solid mechanics; transportation systems analysis and planning (MS, PhD). MS and PhD admissions and degrees offered through The Graduate School. Part-time programs available. Terminal master's awarded for partial completion of doctoral program. *Degree requirements:* For master's, thesis (for some programs); for doctorate, thesis/dissertation. *Entrance requirements:* For master's and doctorate, GRE General Test, minimum 2 letters of recommendation, transcripts from all academic institutions attended. Additional exam requirements/recommendations for international students: Required—TOEFL (minimum score 600 paper-based; 250 computer-based; 100 iBT), IELTS (minimum score 7). Electronic applications accepted. *Faculty research:* Environmental engineering and science, geotechnics, mechanics of materials and solids, structural engineering and materials, transportation systems analysis and planning.

Norwich University, College of Graduate and Continuing Studies, Master of Civil Engineering Program, Northfield, VT 05663. Offers construction management (MCE); environmental water resources (MCE); geo-technical (MCE); structural (MCE). Evening/weekend programs available. *Faculty:* 12 part-time/adjunct (1 woman). *Students:* 88 full-time (23 women); includes 15 minority (8 Black or African American, non-Hispanic/Latino; 1 American Indian or Alaska Native, non-Hispanic/Latino; 4 Asian, non-Hispanic/Latino; 2 Hispanic/Latino). Average age 33. In 2011, 44 master's awarded. *Entrance requirements:* For master's, minimum GPA of 2.75. Additional exam requirements/recommendations for international students: Required—TOEFL (minimum score 550 paper-based; 213 computer-based; 83 iBT). *Application deadline:* For fall admission, 8/10 for domestic and international students; for spring admission, 2/6 for domestic and international students. Applications are processed on a rolling basis. Application fee: $50. Electronic applications accepted. *Expenses: Tuition:* Full-time $16,174. *Required fees:* $2130. Full-time tuition and fees vary according to program. *Financial support:* In 2011–12, 5 students received support. Scholarships/grants available. Financial award applicants required to submit FAFSA. *Unit head:* Dr. Thomas Descoteaux, Program Director, 802-485-2730, Fax: 802-485-2533, E-mail: tdescote@norwich.edu. *Application contact:* Rija Ramahatra, Associate Program Director, 802-485-2892, Fax: 802-485-2533, E-mail: ramahatr@norwich.edu. Web site: http://mce.norwich.edu.

Ohio University, Graduate College, Russ College of Engineering and Technology, Department of Civil Engineering, Athens, OH 45701-2979. Offers civil engineering (PhD); construction (MS); environmental (MS); geotechnical and geoenvironmental (MS); mechanics (MS); structures (MS); transportation (MS); water resources and structures (MS). Part-time programs available. *Students:* 32 full-time (6 women), 7 part-time (2 women); includes 3 minority (1 Hispanic/Latino; 2 Two or more races, non-Hispanic/Latino), 13 international. 52 applicants, 52% accepted, 4 enrolled. In 2011, 10 degrees awarded. *Degree requirements:* For master's, comprehensive exam (for some programs), thesis or alternative; for doctorate, comprehensive exam, thesis/dissertation. *Entrance requirements:* For master's, GRE General Test, minimum GPA of 3.0, 3 letters of recommendation; for doctorate, GRE General Test. Additional exam requirements/recommendations for international students: Required—TOEFL (minimum score 550 paper-based; 80 iBT) or IELTS (minimum score 6.5). *Application deadline:* For fall admission, 5/1 priority date for domestic students, 2/1 for international students; for winter admission, 8/1 priority date for domestic students, 4/1 for international students; for spring admission, 2/1 priority date for domestic students, 7/1 for international students. Applications are processed on a rolling basis. Application fee: $50 ($55 for international students). Electronic applications accepted. *Financial support:* Research assistantships with full tuition reimbursements, teaching assistantships with full tuition reimbursements, Federal Work-Study, institutionally sponsored loans, scholarships/grants, and unspecified assistantships available. Financial award application deadline: 3/15; financial award applicants required to submit FAFSA. *Faculty research:* Noise abatement, materials and environment, highway infrastructure, subsurface investigation (pavements, pipes, bridges). *Unit head:* Dr. Gayle F. Mitchell, Chair, 740-593-0430, Fax: 740-593-0625, E-mail: mitchelg@ohio.edu. *Application contact:* Dr. Shad M. Sargand, Graduate Chair, 740-593-1465, Fax: 740-593-0625, E-mail: sargand@ohio.edu. Web site: http://www.ohio.edu/civil/.

Oregon State University, Graduate School, College of Engineering, School of Civil and Construction Engineering, Corvallis, OR 97331. Offers civil engineering (MS, PhD); coastal and ocean engineering (M Oc E, PhD); coastal engineering (MS); construction engineering management (MBE, PhD); engineering (M Eng, MAIS); geotechnical engineering (MS, PhD); structural engineering (MS, PhD); transportation engineering (MS, PhD); water engineering (MS, PhD). Part-time programs available. Terminal master's awarded for partial completion of doctoral program. *Degree requirements:* For master's, thesis or alternative; for doctorate, one foreign language, thesis/dissertation. *Entrance requirements:* For master's, GRE General Test, minimum GPA of 3.0 in last 90 hours (3.5 for MS); for doctorate, GRE General Test, minimum GPA of 3.0 in last 90 hours of undergraduate course work. Additional exam requirements/recommendations for international students: Required—TOEFL (minimum score 580 paper-based; 237 computer-based). *Faculty research:* Hazardous waste management, carbon cycling, wave forces on structures, pavement design, seismic analysis.

Pontificia Universidad Catolica Madre y Maestra, Graduate School, Faculty of Engineering Sciences, Santiago, Dominican Republic. Offers earthquake engineering (ME); logistics management (ME).

Rensselaer Polytechnic Institute, Graduate School, School of Engineering, Program in Civil Engineering, Troy, NY 12180-3590. Offers geotechnical engineering (M Eng, MS, PhD); mechanics of composite materials and structures (M Eng, MS, PhD); structural engineering (M Eng, MS, PhD); transportation engineering (M Eng, MS, PhD). Part-time programs available. Terminal master's awarded for partial completion of doctoral program. *Degree requirements:* For master's, thesis (for some programs); for doctorate, thesis/dissertation. *Entrance requirements:* For master's and doctorate, GRE. Additional exam requirements/recommendations for international students: Required—TOEFL (minimum score 570 paper-based; 230 computer-based; 89 iBT), IELTS (minimum score 6.5). Electronic applications accepted. *Faculty research:* Computational mechanics, earthquake engineering, geo-environmental engineering.

Stevens Institute of Technology, Graduate School, Charles V. Schaefer Jr. School of Engineering, Department of Civil, Environmental, and Ocean Engineering, Program in Civil Engineering, Hoboken, NJ 07030. Offers civil engineering (PhD); geotechnical engineering (Certificate); geotechnical/geoenvironmental engineering (M Eng, Engr); hydrologic modeling (M Eng); stormwater management (M Eng); structural engineering (M Eng, Engr); water resources engineering (M Eng). *Degree requirements:* For master's, thesis optional; for doctorate, variable foreign language requirement, thesis/dissertation; for other advanced degree, project or thesis. *Entrance requirements:* For doctorate, GRE. Additional exam requirements/recommendations for international students: Required—TOEFL. Electronic applications accepted.

Texas A&M University, College of Engineering, Zachry Department of Civil Engineering, College Station, TX 77843. Offers coastal and ocean engineering (M Eng, MS, D Eng, PhD); construction engineering and management (M Eng, MS, D Eng, PhD); environmental engineering (M Eng, MS, D Eng, PhD); geotechnical engineering (M Eng, MS, D Eng, PhD); materials engineering (M Eng, MS, D Eng, PhD); structural engineering (M Eng, MS, D Eng, PhD); transportation engineering (M Eng, MS, D Eng, PhD); water resources engineering (M Eng, MS, D Eng, PhD). Part-time programs available. *Faculty:* 57. *Students:* 361 full-time (76 women), 46 part-time (8 women); includes 41 minority (3 Black or African American, non-Hispanic/Latino; 16 Asian, non-Hispanic/Latino; 21 Hispanic/Latino; 1 Two or more races, non-Hispanic/Latino), 247 international. Average age 29. In 2011, 123 master's, 27 doctorates awarded. *Degree requirements:* For master's, thesis (MS); for doctorate, dissertation (PhD), internship (D Eng). *Entrance requirements:* For master's and doctorate, GRE General Test. Additional exam requirements/recommendations for international students: Required—TOEFL. *Application deadline:* Applications are processed on a rolling basis. Application fee: $50 ($75 for international students). Electronic applications accepted. *Expenses: Tuition,* state resident: full-time $5437; part-time $226.55 per credit hour. Tuition, nonresident:

full-time $12,949; part-time $539.55 per credit hour. *Required fees:* $2741. *Financial support:* In 2011–12, fellowships (averaging $4,500 per year), research assistantships (averaging $14,000 per year), teaching assistantships (averaging $14,400 per year) were awarded; career-related internships or fieldwork and institutionally sponsored loans also available. Financial award application deadline: 4/15; financial award applicants required to submit FAFSA. *Unit head:* Dr. John Niedzwecki, Head, 979-845-3858, E-mail: j-niedzwecki@tamu.edu. *Application contact:* Graduate Advisor, 979-845-7435, Fax: 979-845-6156, E-mail: info@civil.tamu.edu. Web site: https://www.civil.tamu.edu/.

Tufts University, School of Engineering, Department of Civil and Environmental Engineering, Medford, MA 02155. Offers bioengineering (ME, MS), including environmental technology; civil engineering (ME, MS, PhD), including geotechnical engineering, structural engineering, water diplomacy (PhD); environmental engineering (ME, MS, PhD), including environmental engineering and environmental sciences, environmental geotechnology, environmental health, environmental science and management, hazardous materials management, water diplomacy (PhD), water resources engineering. Part-time programs available. *Faculty:* 18 full-time, 5 part-time/adjunct. *Students:* 102 full-time (50 women); includes 8 minority (1 Black or African American, non-Hispanic/Latino; 6 Asian, non-Hispanic/Latino; 1 Hispanic/Latino), 37 international. Average age 27. 162 applicants, 59% accepted, 37 enrolled. In 2011, 18 degrees awarded. Terminal master's awarded for partial completion of doctoral program. *Degree requirements:* For master's, thesis or alternative; for doctorate, thesis/dissertation. *Entrance requirements:* For master's and doctorate, GRE General Test. Additional exam requirements/recommendations for international students: Required—TOEFL (minimum score 550 paper-based; 213 computer-based; 80 iBT). *Application deadline:* For fall admission, 1/15 priority date for domestic students, 12/15 for international students; for spring admission, 10/15 for domestic students, 9/15 for international students. Applications are processed on a rolling basis. Application fee: $75. Electronic applications accepted. *Expenses: Tuition:* Full-time $41,208; part-time $1030 per credit hour. Full-time tuition and fees vary according to degree level, program and student level. Part-time tuition and fees vary according to course load. *Financial support:* Fellowships with full tuition reimbursements, research assistantships with full and partial tuition reimbursements, teaching assistantships with full and partial tuition reimbursements, Federal Work-Study, scholarships/grants, tuition waivers (partial), and unspecified assistantships available. Financial award application deadline: 1/15; financial award applicants required to submit FAFSA. *Faculty research:* Environmental and water resources engineering, environmental health, geotechnical and geoenvironmental engineering, structural engineering and mechanics, water diplomacy. *Unit head:* Dr. Kurt Penell, Chair, 617-627-3211, Fax: 617-627-3994. *Application contact:* Laura Sacco, Information Contact, 617-627-3211, E-mail: ceeinfo@tufts.edu. Web site: http://www.ase.tufts.edu/cee/.

University at Buffalo, the State University of New York, Graduate School, School of Engineering and Applied Sciences, Department of Civil, Structural, and Environmental Engineering, Buffalo, NY 14260. Offers civil engineering (ME, MS, PhD); engineering science (MS). Part-time programs available. Postbaccalaureate distance learning degree programs offered (minimal on-campus study). *Faculty:* 26 full-time (3 women), 4 part-time/adjunct (1 woman). *Students:* 148 full-time (24 women), 10 part-time (2 women); includes 6 minority (1 American Indian or Alaska Native, non-Hispanic/Latino; 2 Asian, non-Hispanic/Latino; 3 Hispanic/Latino), 120 international. Average age 27. 545 applicants, 12% accepted, 58 enrolled. In 2011, 44 master's, 11 doctorates awarded. Terminal master's awarded for partial completion of doctoral program. *Degree requirements:* For master's, thesis optional, project, thesis, or comprehensive exam; for doctorate, thesis/dissertation. *Entrance requirements:* For master's and doctorate, GRE General Test, letters of reference. Additional exam requirements/recommendations for international students: Required—TOEFL (minimum score 550 paper-based; 213 computer-based; 79 iBT). *Application deadline:* For fall admission, 1/15 priority date for domestic students, 1/15 for international students; for spring admission, 9/15 for domestic and international students. Applications are processed on a rolling basis. Application fee: $75. Electronic applications accepted. *Financial support:* In 2011–12, 76 students received support, including 5 fellowships with full tuition reimbursements available (averaging $28,900 per year), 35 research assistantships with full tuition reimbursements available (averaging $27,700 per year), 26 teaching assistantships with full tuition reimbursements available (averaging $20,900 per year); career-related internships or fieldwork, Federal Work-Study, institutionally sponsored loans, scholarships/grants, traineeships, health care benefits, tuition waivers (full and partial), and unspecified assistantships also available. Support available to part-time students. Financial award application deadline: 1/15; financial award applicants required to submit FAFSA. *Faculty research:* Environmental engineering and fluid mechanics, structural dynamics, geomechanics, earthquake engineering computational mechanics. *Total annual research expenditures:* $7 million. *Unit head:* Dr. Andrew S. Whittaker, Chairman, 716-645-2114, Fax: 716-645-3733, E-mail: awhittak@buffalo.edu. *Application contact:* Dr. Adel Sadek, Director of Graduate Studies, 716-645-4367, Fax: 716-645-3733, E-mail: asadek@buffalo.edu. Web site: http://www.csee.buffalo.edu/.

The University of Alabama in Huntsville, School of Graduate Studies, College of Engineering, Department of Civil and Environmental Engineering, Huntsville, AL 35899. Offers civil and environmental engineering (PhD); civil engineering (MSE), including civil engineering, environmental and water resource engineering, geotechnical engineering, structural engineering and structural mechanics, transportation engineering. PhD offered jointly with The University of Alabama at Birmingham. Part-time and evening/weekend programs available. *Faculty:* 5 full-time (1 woman), 1 part-time/adjunct (0 women). *Students:* 20 full-time (4 women), 12 part-time (6 women); includes 1 minority (Black or African American, non-Hispanic/Latino), 15 international. Average age 29. 26 applicants, 62% accepted, 6 enrolled. In 2011, 3 master's, 1 doctorate awarded. *Degree requirements:* For master's, comprehensive exam, thesis or alternative, oral and written exams; for doctorate, comprehensive exam, thesis/dissertation, oral and written exams. *Entrance requirements:* For master's, GRE General Test, BSE, minimum GPA of 3.0; for doctorate, GRE General Test, minimum GPA of 3.0. Additional exam requirements/recommendations for international students: Required—TOEFL (minimum score 500 paper-based; 173 computer-based; 62 iBT). *Application deadline:* For fall admission, 7/15 for domestic students, 4/1 for international students; for spring admission, 11/30 for domestic students, 9/1 for international students. Applications are processed on a rolling basis. Application fee: $40 ($50 for international students). Electronic applications accepted. *Expenses:* Tuition, state resident: full-time $7830; part-time $473.50 per credit. Tuition, nonresident: full-time $18,748; part-time $1128.33 per credit. Tuition and fees vary according to course load and program. *Financial support:* In 2011–12, 16 students received support, including 10 research assistantships with full and partial tuition reimbursements available (averaging $12,281 per year), 6 teaching assistantships with full and partial tuition reimbursements available (averaging $12,472 per year); career-related internships or fieldwork, Federal Work-Study, institutionally sponsored loans, scholarships/grants, health care benefits, and unspecified assistantships also available. Support available to part-time students. Financial award application deadline: 4/1; financial award applicants required to submit FAFSA. *Faculty research:* Hydrologic modeling, orbital debris impact, hydrogeology, environmental engineering, transportation engineering. *Total annual research expenditures:* $1.1 million. *Unit head:* Dr. Houssam Toutanji, Chair, 256-824-7361, Fax: 256-824-6724, E-mail: toutanji@cee.uah.edu. *Application contact:* Kim Gray, Graduate Studies Admissions Coordinator, 256-824-6002, Fax: 256-824-6405, E-mail: deangrad@uah.edu. Web site: http://www.uah.edu/eng/departments/cee/welcome.

University of Alberta, Faculty of Graduate Studies and Research, Department of Civil and Environmental Engineering, Edmonton, AB T6G 2E1, Canada. Offers construction engineering and management (M Eng, M Sc, PhD); environmental engineering (M Eng, M Sc, PhD); environmental science (M Sc, PhD); geoenvironmental engineering (M Eng, M Sc, PhD); geotechnical engineering (M Eng, M Sc, PhD); mining engineering (M Eng, M Sc, PhD); petroleum engineering (M Eng, M Sc, PhD); structural engineering (M Eng, M Sc, PhD); water resources (M Eng, M Sc, PhD). Part-time programs available. Postbaccalaureate distance learning degree programs offered (minimal on-campus study). *Degree requirements:* For master's, thesis (for some programs); for doctorate, thesis/dissertation. *Entrance requirements:* For master's, minimum GPA of 3.0 in last 2 years of undergraduate studies; for doctorate, minimum GPA of 3.0. Additional exam requirements/recommendations for international students: Required—TOEFL (minimum score 550 paper-based; 213 computer-based). Electronic applications accepted. *Faculty research:* Mining.

University of California, Berkeley, Graduate Division, College of Engineering, Department of Civil and Environmental Engineering, Berkeley, CA 94720-1500. Offers engineering and project management (M Eng, MS, D Eng, PhD); environmental engineering (M Eng, MS, D Eng, PhD); geoengineering (M Eng, MS, D Eng, PhD); structural engineering, mechanics and materials (M Eng, MS, D Eng, PhD); transportation engineering (M Eng, MS, D Eng, PhD); M Arch/MS; MCP/MS; MPP/MS. *Degree requirements:* For master's, comprehensive exam or thesis (MS); for doctorate, thesis/dissertation, qualifying exam. *Entrance requirements:* For master's, GRE General Test, minimum GPA of 3.0, 3 letters of recommendation; for doctorate, GRE General Test, minimum GPA of 3.5, 3 letters of recommendation. Additional exam requirements/recommendations for international students: Required—TOEFL (minimum score 570 paper-based; 230 computer-based). Electronic applications accepted.

University of California, San Diego, Office of Graduate Studies, Department of Structural Engineering, La Jolla, CA 92093. Offers structural engineering (MS, PhD); structural health monitoring, prognosis, and validated simulations (MS). Applications accepted only for fall quarter. Part-time programs available. *Degree requirements:* For master's, comprehensive exam or thesis; for doctorate, comprehensive exam, thesis/dissertation, candidacy exam. *Entrance requirements:* For master's and doctorate, GRE General Test, minimum GPA of 3.0; BS in engineering, physical sciences, or mathematics; statement of purpose; three letters of recommendation; official transcripts from all institutions attended. Additional exam requirements/recommendations for international students: Required—TOEFL (minimum score 550 paper-based; 213 computer-based; 80 iBT). *Faculty research:* Advanced large-scale civil, mechanical, and aerospace structures.

University of Central Florida, College of Engineering and Computer Science, Department of Civil, Environmental, and Construction Engineering, Program in Civil Engineering, Orlando, FL 32816. Offers civil engineering (MS, MSCE, PhD); construction engineering (Certificate); structural engineering (Certificate); transportation engineering (Certificate). Part-time and evening/weekend programs available. *Students:* 68 full-time (13 women), 87 part-time (16 women); includes 35 minority (7 Black or African American, non-Hispanic/Latino; 6 Asian, non-Hispanic/Latino; 20 Hispanic/Latino; 2 Two or more races, non-Hispanic/Latino), 42 international. Average age 30. 125 applicants, 79% accepted, 45 enrolled. In 2011, 27 master's, 2 doctorates awarded. *Degree requirements:* For master's, thesis or alternative; for doctorate, thesis/dissertation, departmental qualifying exam, candidacy exam. *Entrance requirements:* For master's, GRE General Test, minimum GPA of 3.0 in last 60 hours; for doctorate, GRE General Test, minimum GPA of 3.5 in last 60 hours. Additional exam requirements/recommendations for international students: Required—TOEFL. *Application deadline:* For fall admission, 7/15 priority date for domestic students; for spring admission, 12/15 priority date for domestic students. Application fee: $30. Electronic applications accepted. *Expenses:* Tuition, state resident: part-time $277.08 per credit hour. Tuition, nonresident: part-time $277.08 per credit hour. Part-time tuition and fees vary according to degree level and program. *Financial support:* In 2011–12, 28 students received support, including 6 fellowships with partial tuition reimbursements available (averaging $2,700 per year), 14 research assistantships with partial tuition reimbursements available (averaging $11,800 per year), 15 teaching assistantships with partial tuition reimbursements available (averaging $11,300 per year); career-related internships or fieldwork, Federal Work-Study, institutionally sponsored loans, tuition waivers (partial), and unspecified assistantships also available. Financial award application deadline: 3/1; financial award applicants required to submit FAFSA. *Unit head:* Dr. Essam Radwan, Interim Chair, 407-823-4738, E-mail: ahmed.radwan@ucf.edu. *Application contact:* Barbara Rodriguez, Director, Admissions and Registration, 407-823-2766, Fax: 407-823-6442, E-mail: gradadmissions@ucf.edu. Web site: http://cece.ucf.edu/.

University of Colorado Boulder, Graduate School, College of Engineering and Applied Science, Department of Civil, Environmental, and Architectural Engineering, Boulder, CO 80309. Offers building systems (MS, PhD); construction engineering management (MS, PhD); environmental engineering (MS, PhD); geotechnical engineering and geomechanics (MS, PhD); hydrology, water resources and environmental fluid mechanics (MS, PhD); structural engineering and structural mechanics (MS, PhD). *Faculty:* 37 full-time (8 women). *Students:* 245 full-time (90 women), 53 part-time (15 women); includes 37 minority (1 Black or African American, non-Hispanic/Latino; 2 American Indian or Alaska Native, non-Hispanic/Latino; 15 Asian, non-Hispanic/Latino; 17 Hispanic/Latino; 2 Two or more races, non-Hispanic/Latino), 56 international. Average age 27. 483 applicants, 58% accepted, 83 enrolled. In 2011, 84 master's, 15 doctorates awarded. Terminal master's awarded for partial completion of doctoral program. *Degree requirements:* For master's, comprehensive exam, thesis or alternative; for doctorate, thesis/dissertation. *Entrance requirements:* For master's, GRE General Test, minimum undergraduate GPA of 3.0. *Application deadline:* For fall admission, 3/1 for domestic students, 12/1 for international students; for spring admission, 10/31 for domestic students, 10/1 for international students. Application fee: $50 ($60 for international students). Electronic applications accepted. *Financial support:* In 2011–12, 167 students received support, including 69 fellowships (averaging $12,440 per year), 62 research assistantships with full and partial tuition reimbursements available (averaging $21,979 per year), 20 teaching assistantships with full and partial tuition reimbursements available (averaging $19,877 per year); institutionally sponsored loans, scholarships/grants, health care benefits, and unspecified assistantships also available. Financial award application deadline: 1/15; financial award applicants required to submit FAFSA. *Faculty research:* Building systems engineering, construction engineering and management, environmental engineering, geoenvironmental engineering, geotechnical engineering, materials and mechanics, structural engineering, water resources engineering, life-cycle engineering. *Total annual research expenditures:* $10.9 million. *Application contact:* E-mail: cvengrad@colorado.edu. Web site: http://ceae.colorado.edu/new/.

University of Colorado Denver, College of Engineering and Applied Science, Department of Civil Engineering, Denver, CO 80217. Offers civil engineering (EASPh D); civil engineering systems (PhD); environmental and sustainability engineering (MS, PhD); geographic information systems (MS); geotechnical engineering (MS, PhD); hydrology and hydraulics (MS, PhD); structural engineering (MS, PhD); transportation engineering (MS, PhD). Part-time and evening/weekend programs available. *Faculty:* 14 full-time (1 woman), 6 part-time/adjunct (0 women). *Students:* 66 full-time (11 women), 65 part-time (14 women); includes 30 minority (10 Black or African American, non-Hispanic/Latino; 8 Asian, non-Hispanic/Latino; 10 Hispanic/Latino; 2 Two or more races, non-Hispanic/Latino), 17 international. Average age 34. 67 applicants, 54% accepted, 24 enrolled. In 2011, 30 master's, 2 doctorates awarded. *Degree requirements:* For master's, comprehensive exam, thesis or alternative, 30 credit hours, project or thesis; for doctorate, comprehensive exam, thesis/dissertation, 60 credit hours (30 of which are dissertation research). *Entrance requirements:* For master's, GRE, statement of purpose, transcripts, three references; for doctorate, GRE, statement of purpose, transcripts, references, letter of support from faculty stating willingness to serve as dissertation advisor and outlining plan for financial support. Additional exam requirements/recommendations for international students: Required—TOEFL (minimum score 525 paper-based; 197 computer-based). *Application deadline:* For fall admission, 7/15 for domestic students, 6/15 for international students; for spring admission, 12/1 for domestic students, 11/1 for international students. Applications are processed on a rolling basis. Application fee: $50 ($75 for international students). Electronic applications accepted. *Expenses:* Contact institution. *Financial support:* Research assistantships, teaching assistantships, career-related internships or fieldwork, and Federal Work-Study available. Financial award application deadline: 4/1; financial award applicants required to submit FAFSA. *Faculty research:* Earthquake source physics, environmental biotechnology, hydrologic and hydraulic engineering, sustainability assessments, transportation energy use and greenhouse gas emissions. *Unit head:* Dr. Kevin Rens, Chair, 303-556-8017, Fax: 303-556-2368, E-mail: kevin.rens@ucdenver.edu. *Application contact:* Maria Rase, Program Assistant, 303-556-6712, Fax: 303-556-2368, E-mail: maria.rase@ucdenver.edu. Web site: http://www.ucdenver.edu/academics/colleges/Engineering/Programs/Civil-Engineering/Pages/CivilEngineering.aspx.

University of Dayton, Department of Civil and Environmental Engineering and Engineering Mechanics, Dayton, OH 45469-1300. Offers engineering mechanics (MSEM); environmental engineering (MSCE); geotechnical engineering (MSCE); structural engineering (MSCE); transportation engineering (MSCE); water resources engineering (MSCE). Part-time programs available. *Faculty:* 7 full-time (2 women), 2 part-time/adjunct (0 women). *Students:* 16 full-time (4 women), 9 part-time (4 women); includes 1 minority (Asian, non-Hispanic/Latino), 13 international. Average age 27. 53 applicants, 38% accepted, 5 enrolled. In 2011, 7 degrees awarded. *Degree requirements:* For master's, thesis optional. *Entrance requirements:* For master's, minimum GPA of 3.0 in undergraduate work. Additional exam requirements/recommendations for international students: Required—TOEFL (minimum score 550 paper-based; 213 computer-based; 80 iBT). *Application deadline:* For fall admission, 8/1 for domestic students, 3/1 for international students; for winter admission, 7/1 for international students; for spring admission, 1/1 for international students. Applications are processed on a rolling basis. Application fee: $0 ($50 for international students). Electronic applications accepted. *Expenses: Tuition:* Full-time $8400; part-time $700 per credit hour. *Required fees:* $25 per semester. Tuition and fees vary according to degree level. *Financial support:* Research assistantships available. Financial award applicants required to submit FAFSA. *Faculty research:* Physical modeling of hydraulic systems, finite element methods, mechanics of composite materials, transportation systems safety, biological treatment processes. *Total annual research expenditures:* $200,000. *Unit head:* Dr. Donald V. Chase, Chair, 937-229-3847, Fax: 937-229-3491, E-mail: dchase1@udayton.edu. *Application contact:* Dr. Donald Chase, Chair, 937-229-3847, Fax: 937-229-3491, E-mail: dchase1@udayton.edu. Web site: http://www.udayton.edu/engineering/civil.

University of Delaware, College of Engineering, Department of Civil and Environmental Engineering, Newark, DE 19716. Offers environmental engineering (MAS, MCE, PhD); geotechnical engineering (MAS, MCE, PhD); ocean engineering (MAS, MCE, PhD); structural engineering (MAS, MCE, PhD); transportation engineering (MAS, MCE, PhD); water resource engineering (MAS, MCE, PhD). Part-time programs available. Terminal master's awarded for partial completion of doctoral program. *Degree requirements:* For master's, thesis; for doctorate, thesis/dissertation. *Entrance requirements:* For master's and doctorate, GRE General Test. Additional exam requirements/recommendations for international students: Required—TOEFL. Electronic applications accepted. *Faculty research:* Structural engineering and mechanics; transportation engineering; ocean engineering; soil mechanics and foundation; water resources and environmental engineering.

The University of Manchester, School of Materials, Manchester, United Kingdom. Offers advanced aerospace materials engineering (M Sc); advanced metallic systems (PhD); biomedical materials (M Phil, M Sc, PhD); ceramics and glass (M Phil, M Sc, PhD); composite materials (M Sc, PhD); corrosion and protection (M Phil, M Sc, PhD); materials (M Phil, PhD); metallic materials (M Phil, M Sc, PhD); nanostructural materials (M Phil, M Sc, PhD); paper science (M Phil, M Sc, PhD); polymer science and engineering (M Phil, M Sc, PhD); technical textiles (M Sc); textile design, fashion and management (M Phil, M Sc, PhD); textile science and technology (M Phil, M Sc, PhD); textiles (M Phil, PhD); textiles and fashion (M Ent).

University of Massachusetts Amherst, Graduate School, College of Engineering, Department of Civil and Environmental Engineering, Amherst, MA 01003. Offers civil engineering (MSCE, PhD); environmental and water resources (MSCE); geotechnical (MSCE); structural engineering and mechanics (MSCE); transportation (MSCE). *Accreditation:* ABET (one or more programs are accredited). Part-time programs available. *Faculty:* 28 full-time (7 women). *Students:* 91 full-time (30 women), 11 part-time (5 women); includes 13 minority (3 Black or African American, non-Hispanic/Latino; 5 Asian, non-Hispanic/Latino; 4 Hispanic/Latino; 1 Two or more races, non-Hispanic/Latino), 29 international. Average age 27. 293 applicants, 53% accepted, 40 enrolled. In 2011, 38 master's, 1 doctorate awarded. Terminal master's awarded for partial completion of doctoral program. *Degree requirements:* For master's, thesis or alternative; for doctorate, comprehensive exam, thesis/dissertation. *Entrance requirements:* For master's and doctorate, GRE General Test. Additional exam requirements/recommendations for international students: Required—TOEFL (minimum score 550 paper-based; 213 computer-based; 80 iBT), IELTS (minimum score 6.5). *Application deadline:* For fall admission, 2/1 for domestic and international students; for spring admission, 10/1 for domestic and international students. Applications are processed on a rolling basis. Application fee: $50 ($65 for international students). Electronic applications accepted. Tuition and fees vary according to course load, campus/location and program. *Financial support:* In 2011–12, 1 fellowship with full tuition reimbursement (averaging $1,000 per year), 74 research assistantships with full tuition reimbursements (averaging $15,151 per year), 6 teaching assistantships with full tuition reimbursements (averaging $15,151 per year) were awarded; career-related internships or fieldwork, Federal Work-Study, scholarships/grants, traineeships, health care benefits, tuition waivers, and unspecified assistantships also available. Support available to part-time students. Financial award application deadline: 2/1; financial award applicants required to submit FAFSA. *Unit head:* Dr. Sanjay Arwade, Graduate Program Director, 413-545-0686, Fax: 413-545-2840. *Application contact:* Lindsay DeSantis, Interim Supervisor of Admissions, 413-545-0722, Fax: 413-577-0100, E-mail: gradadm@grad.umass.edu. Web site: http://cee.umass.edu/.

University of Memphis, Graduate School, Herff College of Engineering, Department of Civil Engineering, Memphis, TN 38152. Offers civil engineering (PhD); environmental engineering (MS); foundation engineering (MS); structural engineering (MS); transportation engineering (MS); water resources engineering (MS). Terminal master's awarded for partial completion of doctoral program. *Degree requirements:* For master's, comprehensive exam, thesis optional; for doctorate, comprehensive exam, thesis/dissertation. *Entrance requirements:* For master's, GRE General Test or MAT, minimum undergraduate GPA of 2.5; for doctorate, GRE, 3 letters of recommendation. Additional exam requirements/recommendations for international students: Required—TOEFL (minimum score 550 paper-based; 210 computer-based; 79 iBT). *Faculty research:* Structural response to earthquakes, pavement design, water quality, transportation safety, intermodal transportation,.

University of Michigan, College of Engineering, Department of Civil and Environmental Engineering, Ann Arbor, MI 48109. Offers civil engineering (MSE, PhD, CE); construction engineering and management (M Eng, MSE); environmental engineering (MSE, PhD); structural engineering (M Eng); MBA/MSE. Part-time programs available. *Students:* 139 full-time (54 women), 3 part-time (1 woman). 539 applicants, 40% accepted, 66 enrolled. In 2011, 52 master's, 10 doctorates awarded. *Degree requirements:* For master's, thesis optional; for doctorate, comprehensive exam, thesis/dissertation, oral defense of dissertation, preliminary and written exams. *Entrance requirements:* For master's and doctorate, GRE General Test. Additional exam requirements/recommendations for international students: Required—TOEFL (minimum score 560 paper-based; 220 computer-based). *Application deadline:* Applications are processed on a rolling basis. Application fee: $65 ($75 for international students). Electronic applications accepted. *Financial support:* Fellowships, research assistantships, teaching assistantships, institutionally sponsored loans, and tuition waivers (partial) available. Financial award application deadline: 1/19. *Faculty research:* Construction engineering and management, geotechnical engineering, earthquake-resistant design of structures, environmental chemistry and microbiology, cost engineering, environmental and water resources engineering. *Unit head:* Kim Hayes, Chair, 734-764-8495, Fax: 734-764-4292, E-mail: ford@umich.edu. *Application contact:* Kimberly Smith, Student Advisor, 734-764-8405, Fax: 734-647-2127, E-mail: kansmith@umich.edu. Web site: http://www.engin.umich.edu/dept/cee/.

University of Missouri, Graduate School, College of Engineering, Department of Civil and Environmental Engineering, Columbia, MO 65211. Offers civil engineering (MS, PhD); environmental engineering (MS, PhD); geotechnical engineering (MS, PhD); structural engineering (MS, PhD); transportation and highway engineering (MS); water resources (MS, PhD). *Faculty:* 18 full-time (2 women), 1 part-time/adjunct (0 women). *Students:* 45 full-time (16 women), 38 part-time (8 women); includes 5 minority (2 Black or African American, non-Hispanic/Latino; 2 Asian, non-Hispanic/Latino; 1 Hispanic/Latino), 49 international. Average age 28. 109 applicants, 28% accepted, 20 enrolled. In 2011, 14 master's, 2 doctorates awarded. *Degree requirements:* For master's, report or thesis; for doctorate, thesis/dissertation. *Entrance requirements:* For master's and doctorate, GRE General Test. Additional exam requirements/recommendations for international students: Required—TOEFL (minimum score 550 paper-based; 213 computer-based; 79 iBT). *Application deadline:* For fall admission, 3/15 priority date for domestic students; for winter admission, 10/15 priority date for domestic students. Application fee: $55 ($75 for international students). *Expenses:* Tuition, state resident: full-time $5881. Tuition, nonresident: full-time $15,183. *Required fees:* $952. Tuition and fees vary according to campus/location and program. *Financial support:* Fellowships, research assistantships, teaching assistantships, and institutionally sponsored loans available. *Unit head:* Dr. Mark Virkler, Department Chair, E-mail: virklerm@missouri.edu. *Application contact:* Jennifer Keyzer-Andre, 573-882-4442, E-mail: keyzerandrej@missouri.edu. Web site: http://engineering.missouri.edu/civil/.

University of New Brunswick Fredericton, School of Graduate Studies, Faculty of Engineering, Department of Civil Engineering, Fredericton, NB E3B 5A3, Canada. Offers construction engineering and management (M Eng, M Sc E, PhD); environmental engineering (M Eng, M Sc E, PhD); environmental studies (M Eng); geotechnical engineering (M Eng, M Sc E, PhD); groundwater/hydrology (M Eng, M Sc E, PhD); materials (M Eng, M Sc E, PhD); pavements (M Eng, M Sc E, PhD); structures (M Eng, M Sc E, PhD); transportation (M Eng, M Sc E, PhD). Part-time programs available. *Faculty:* 13 full-time (1 woman), 7 part-time/adjunct (1 woman). *Students:* 31 full-time (7 women), 17 part-time (2 women). In 2011, 11 master's, 2 doctorates awarded. *Degree requirements:* For master's, thesis, proposal; for doctorate, comprehensive exam, thesis/dissertation, qualifying exam; proposal; 27 credit hours of courses. *Entrance requirements:* For master's, minimum GPA of 3.0; B Sc E in civil engineering or related engineering degree; for doctorate, minimum GPA of 3.0; graduate degree in engineering or applied science. Additional exam requirements/recommendations for international students: Required—TWE (minimum score 4), TOEFL (minimum score 580 paper-based; 237 computer-based) or IELTS (minimum score 7.5). *Application deadline:* For fall admission, 5/1 priority date for domestic students; for winter admission, 11/1 priority date for domestic students. Applications are processed on a rolling basis. Application fee: $50 Canadian dollars. *Financial support:* In 2011–12, 14 fellowships, 30 research assistantships (averaging $7,000 per year), 42 teaching assistantships (averaging $2,000 per year) were awarded; career-related internships or fieldwork and scholarships/grants also available. *Faculty research:* Construction engineering and management; materials and infrastructure renewal; highway and pavement research; structures and solid mechanics; geotechnical, soil; structure interaction; transportation and planning; environment, solid waste management. *Unit head:* Dr. Eric Hildebrand, Director of Graduate Studies, 506-453-5113, Fax: 506-453-3568, E-mail: edh@unb.ca. *Application contact:* Joyce Moore, Graduate Secretary, 506-452-6127, Fax: 506-453-3568, E-mail: civil-grad@unb.ca. Web site: http://www.unbf.ca/eng/civil/.

University of North Dakota, Graduate School, School of Engineering and Mines, Department of Civil Engineering, Grand Forks, ND 58202. Offers civil engineering (M Engr); sanitary engineering (M Engr), including soils and structures engineering, surface mining engineering. Part-time programs available. *Degree requirements:* For master's, comprehensive exam, thesis or alternative. *Entrance requirements:* For master's, GRE General Test, minimum GPA of 2.5. Additional exam requirements/ recommendations for international students: Required—TOEFL (minimum score 550 paper-based; 213 computer-based; 79 iBT), IELTS (minimum score 6.5). Electronic applications accepted. *Faculty research:* Soil-structures, environmental-water resources.

The University of Texas at Tyler, College of Engineering and Computer Science, Department of Civil Engineering, Tyler, TX 75799-0001. Offers environmental engineering (MS); industrial safety (MS); structural engineering (MS); transportation engineering (MS); water resources engineering (MS). Part-time and evening/weekend programs available. *Degree requirements:* For master's, thesis optional. *Entrance requirements:* For master's, GRE General Test, bachelor's degree in engineering, associated science degree. Additional exam requirements/recommendations for international students: Required—TOEFL (minimum score 79 computer-based). *Faculty research:* Non-destructive strength testing, indoor air quality, transportation routing and signaling, pavement replacement criteria, flood water routing, construction and long-term behavior of innovative geotechnical foundation and embankment construction used in highway construction, engineering education.

University of Washington, Graduate School, College of Engineering, Department of Civil and Environmental Engineering, Seattle, WA 98195-2700. Offers civil engineering (MS, MSE, PhD); construction engineering (MSCE); environmental engineering (MS, MSCE, MSE, PhD); global trade, transportation and logistics (MS); hydrology, water resources, and environmental fluid mechanics (MS, MSCE, MSE, PhD); structural and geotechnical engineering and mechanics (MS, MSCE, MSE, PhD); transportation and construction engineering (MS, MSE, PhD); transportation engineering (MSCE). Part-time programs available. Postbaccalaureate distance learning degree programs offered (no on-campus study). *Faculty:* 47 full-time (11 women), 9 part-time/adjunct (1 woman). *Students:* 195 full-time (67 women), 72 part-time (19 women); includes 37 minority (4 Black or African American, non-Hispanic/Latino; 27 Asian, non-Hispanic/Latino; 6 Hispanic/Latino), 65 international. 654 applicants, 57% accepted, 100 enrolled. In 2011, 88 master's, 7 doctorates awarded. Terminal master's awarded for partial completion of doctoral program. *Degree requirements:* For master's, thesis (for some programs); for doctorate, comprehensive exam, thesis/dissertation, general, qualifying, and final exams; completion of degree within 10 years. *Entrance requirements:* For master's, GRE General Test, minimum GPA of 3.0, statement of purpose, letters of recommendation, transcripts; for doctorate, GRE General Test, minimum GPA of 3.5, statement of purpose, letters of recommendation, transcripts. Additional exam requirements/recommendations for international students: Required—TOEFL (minimum score 580 paper-based; 237 computer-based; 92 iBT); Recommended—IELTS (minimum score 7). *Application deadline:* For fall admission, 1/10 priority date for domestic students, 1/10 for international students. Applications are processed on a rolling basis. Application fee: $75. Electronic applications accepted. *Expenses:* Contact institution. *Financial support:* In 2011–12, 99 students received support, including 16 fellowships with full and partial tuition reimbursements available (averaging $16,173 per year), 71 research assistantships with full tuition reimbursements available (averaging $16,380 per year), 10 teaching assistantships with full tuition reimbursements available (averaging $16,380 per year); scholarships/grants also available. Financial award application deadline: 1/10; financial award applicants required to submit FAFSA. *Faculty research:* Environmental/water resources, hydrology; construction/transportation; structures/ geotechnical. *Total annual research expenditures:* $13.6 million. *Unit head:* Dr. Gregory R. Miller, Professor/Chair, 206-543-0350, Fax: 206-543-1543, E-mail: gmiller@uw.edu. *Application contact:* Lorna Latal, Graduate Adviser, 206-543-2574, Fax: 206-543-1543, E-mail: llatal@u.washington.edu. Web site: http://www.ce.washington.edu/programs/prospective/grad/applying/gen_admission.html.

Washington University in St. Louis, School of Engineering and Applied Science, Department of Mechanical, Aerospace and Structural Engineering, St. Louis, MO 63130-4899. Offers MS, D Sc, PhD. Part-time programs available. Terminal master's awarded for partial completion of doctoral program. *Degree requirements:* For master's, thesis optional; for doctorate, thesis/dissertation optional. *Entrance requirements:* For master's, GRE; for doctorate, GRE General Test, departmental qualifying exam. *Faculty research:* Aerosols science and technology, applied mechanics, biomechanics and biomedical engineering, design, dynamic systems, combustion science, composite materials, materials science.

Western Michigan University, Graduate College, College of Engineering and Applied Sciences, Department of Civil and Construction Engineering, Kalamazoo, MI 49008. Offers civil engineering (MS), including construction engineering and management, structural engineering, transportation engineering. *Entrance requirements:* For master's, minimum GPA of 3.0.

Surveying Science and Engineering

The Ohio State University, Graduate School, College of Engineering, Department of Civil and Environmental Engineering and Geodetic Science, Columbus, OH 43210. Offers civil engineering (MS, PhD); geodetic science and surveying (MS, PhD). *Faculty:* 20. *Students:* 66 full-time (23 women), 41 part-time (3 women); includes 8 minority (1 Black or African American, non-Hispanic/Latino; 2 Asian, non-Hispanic/Latino; 3 Hispanic/Latino; 2 Two or more races, non-Hispanic/Latino), 58 international. Average age 27. In 2011, 28 master's, 5 doctorates awarded. *Entrance requirements:* Additional exam requirements/recommendations for international students: Required—TOEFL (minimum score 550 paper-based; 79 iBT), Michigan English Language Assessment Battery (minimum score 82). *Expenses:* Tuition, state resident: full-time $11,400. Tuition, nonresident: full-time $28,125. Tuition and fees vary according to course load, degree level, campus/location and program. *Unit head:* Dr. Carolyn J. Merry, Chair, 614-292-3455, Fax: 614-292-8062, E-mail: merry.1@osu.edu. *Application contact:* Graduate Admissions, 614-292-6301, Fax: 614-292-3656, E-mail: gradadmissions@osu.edu. Web site: http://ceg.osu.edu/.

University of New Brunswick Fredericton, School of Graduate Studies, Faculty of Engineering, Department of Geodesy and Geomatics, Fredericton, NB E3B 5A3, Canada. Offers land information management (Diploma); mapping, charting and geodesy (Diploma); surveying engineering (M Eng, M Sc E, PhD). *Faculty:* 9 full-time (1 woman), 13 part-time/adjunct (1 woman). *Students:* 37 full-time (6 women), 6 part-time (0 women). In 2011, 10 master's awarded. *Degree requirements:* For master's, thesis; for doctorate, comprehensive exam, thesis/dissertation, qualifying exam. *Entrance requirements:* For master's and doctorate, minimum GPA of 3.0. Additional exam requirements/recommendations for international students: Required—TOEFL (minimum score 580 paper-based), TWE (minimum score 4). *Application deadline:* For fall admission, 3/1 priority date for domestic students. Applications are processed on a rolling basis. Application fee: $50 Canadian dollars. *Financial support:* In 2011–12, 23 research assistantships, 22 teaching assistantships were awarded; fellowships also available. *Faculty research:* Remote sensing, ocean mapping, land administration. *Unit head:* Dr. Sue Nichols, Director of Graduate Studies, 506-453-5141, Fax: 506-453-4943, E-mail: nichols@unb.ca. *Application contact:* Sylvia Whitaker, Graduate Secretary, 506-458-7085, Fax: 506-453-4943, E-mail: swhitake@unb.ca. Web site: http://www.gge.unb.ca/.

Transportation and Highway Engineering

Arizona State University, College of Liberal Arts and Sciences, School of Geographical Sciences, Tempe, AZ 85287-5302. Offers atmospheric science (Graduate Certificate); geographic education (MAS); geographic information systems (MAS); geographical information science (Graduate Certificate); geography (MA, PhD); transportation systems (Graduate Certificate); urban and environmental planning (MUEP). Terminal master's awarded for partial completion of doctoral program. *Degree requirements:* For master's, thesis, interactive Program of Study (iPOS) submitted before completing 50 percent of required credit hours; for doctorate, comprehensive exam, thesis/dissertation, interactive Program of Study (iPOS) submitted before completing 50 percent of required credit hours. *Entrance requirements:* For master's and doctorate, GRE, minimum GPA of 3.0 or equivalent in last 2 years of work leading to bachelor's degree. Additional exam requirements/recommendations for international students: Required—TOEFL (minimum score 80 iBT), TOEFL, IELTS, or Pearson Test of English. Electronic applications accepted. *Expenses:* Contact institution.

Auburn University, Graduate School, Ginn College of Engineering, Department of Civil Engineering, Auburn University, AL 36849. Offers construction engineering and management (MCE, MS, PhD); environmental engineering (MCE, MS, PhD); geotechnical/materials engineering (MCE, MS, PhD); hydraulics/hydrology (MCE, MS, PhD); structural engineering (MCE, MS, PhD); transportation engineering (MCE, MS, PhD). Part-time programs available. *Faculty:* 21 full-time (2 women), 1 part-time/adjunct (0 women). *Students:* 48 full-time (16 women), 62 part-time (14 women); includes 6 minority (4 Black or African American, non-Hispanic/Latino; 1 Asian, non-Hispanic/Latino; 1 Hispanic/Latino), 37 international. Average age 26. 111 applicants, 59% accepted, 25 enrolled. In 2011, 26 master's, 2 doctorates awarded. *Degree requirements:* For master's, project (MCE), thesis (MS); for doctorate, comprehensive exam, thesis/dissertation. *Entrance requirements:* For master's and doctorate, GRE General Test. *Application deadline:* For fall admission, 7/7 for domestic students; for spring admission, 11/24 for domestic students. Applications are processed on a rolling basis. Application fee: $50 ($60 for international students). Electronic applications accepted. *Expenses:* Tuition, state resident: full-time $7290; part-time $405 per credit hour. Tuition, nonresident: full-time $21,870; part-time $1215 per credit hour. *International tuition:* $22,000 full-time. *Required fees:* $1402. *Financial support:* Fellowships, research assistantships, teaching assistantships, and Federal Work-Study available. Support available to part-time students. Financial award application deadline: 3/15; financial award applicants required to submit FAFSA. *Unit head:* Dr. J. Michael Stallings, Head, 334-844-4320. *Application contact:* Dr. George Flowers, Dean of the Graduate School, 334-844-2125.

Cornell University, Graduate School, Graduate Fields of Engineering, Field of Civil and Environmental Engineering, Ithaca, NY 14853-0001. Offers engineering management (M Eng, MS, PhD); environmental engineering (M Eng, MS, PhD); environmental fluid mechanics and hydrology (M Eng, MS, PhD); environmental systems engineering (M Eng, MS, PhD); geotechnical engineering (M Eng, MS, PhD); remote sensing (M Eng, MS, PhD); structural engineering (M Eng, MS, PhD); structural mechanics (M Eng, MS); transportation engineering (MS, PhD); transportation systems engineering (M Eng); water resource systems (M Eng, MS, PhD). *Faculty:* 39 full-time (4 women). *Students:* 143 full-time (49 women); includes 20 minority (6 Black or African American, non-Hispanic/Latino; 1 American Indian or Alaska Native, non-Hispanic/Latino; 9 Asian, non-Hispanic/Latino; 4 Hispanic/Latino), 72 international. Average age 25. 574 applicants, 47% accepted, 100 enrolled. In 2011, 88 master's, 13 doctorates awarded. Terminal master's awarded for partial completion of doctoral program. *Degree requirements:* For master's, thesis (MS); for doctorate, comprehensive exam, thesis/ dissertation. *Entrance requirements:* For master's and doctorate, GRE General Test (recommended), 2 letters of recommendation. Additional exam requirements/ recommendations for international students: Required—TOEFL (minimum score 600 paper-based; 250 computer-based; 77 iBT). *Application deadline:* For fall admission, 1/15 priority date for domestic students; for spring admission, 10/15 for domestic students. Application fee: $95. Electronic applications accepted. *Financial support:* In 2011–12, 50 students received support, including 20 fellowships with full tuition reimbursements available, 27 research assistantships with full tuition reimbursements available, 17 teaching assistantships with full tuition reimbursements available; institutionally sponsored loans, scholarships/grants, health care benefits, tuition waivers (full and partial), and unspecified assistantships also available. Financial award applicants required to submit FAFSA. *Faculty research:* Environmental engineering, geotechnical engineering, remote sensing, environmental fluid mechanics and hydrology, structural engineering. *Unit head:* Director of Graduate Studies, 607-255-7560, Fax: 607-255-9004. *Application contact:* Graduate Field Assistant, 607-255-7560, Fax: 607-255-9004, E-mail: cee_grad@cornell.edu. Web site: http://www.gradschool.cornell.edu/fields.php?id-27&a-2.

École Polytechnique de Montréal, Graduate Programs, Department of Civil, Geological and Mining Engineering, Montréal, QC H3C 3A7, Canada. Offers civil, geological and mining engineering (DESS); environmental engineering (M Eng, M Sc A, PhD); geotechnical engineering (M Eng, M Sc A, PhD); hydraulics engineering (M Eng, M Sc A, PhD); structural engineering (M Eng, M Sc A, PhD); transportation engineering (M Eng, M Sc A, PhD). Part-time programs available. *Degree requirements:* For master's, one foreign language, thesis; for doctorate, one foreign language, thesis/dissertation. *Entrance requirements:* For master's, minimum GPA of 2.75; for doctorate, minimum GPA of 3.0. *Faculty research:* Water resources management, characteristics of building materials, aging of dams, pollution control.

Illinois Institute of Technology, Graduate College, Armour College of Engineering, Department of Civil, Architectural and Environmental Engineering, Chicago, IL 60616-3793. Offers architectural engineering (M Arch E); civil engineering (MS, PhD), including architectural engineeering (MS), construction engineering and management (MS), geoenvironmental engineering (MS), geotechnical engineering (MS), structural engineering (MS), transportation engineering (MS); construction engineering and management (MCEM); environmental engineering (M Env E, PhD); geoenvironmental engineering (M Geoenv E); geotechnical engineering (MGE); public works (MPW); structural engineering (MSE); transportation engineering (M Trans E). Part-time and evening/weekend programs available. Postbaccalaureate distance learning degree programs offered (minimal on-campus study). Terminal master's awarded for partial completion of doctoral program. *Degree requirements:* For master's, thesis (for some programs); for doctorate, comprehensive exam, thesis/dissertation. *Entrance requirements:* For master's, GRE General Test (minimum score 900 Quantitative and Verbal, 2.5 Analytical Writing), minimum undergraduate GPA of 3.0; for doctorate, GRE General Test (minimum score 1000 Quantitative and Verbal, 3.0 Analytical Writing), minimum undergraduate GPA of 3.0. Additional exam requirements/recommendations for international students: Required—TOEFL (minimum score 523 paper-based; 70 iBT); Recommended—IELTS (minimum score 5.5). Electronic applications accepted. *Faculty research:* Structural, architectural, geotechnical and geoenvironmental engineering; construction engineering and management; transportation engineering; environmental engineering and public works.

Iowa State University of Science and Technology, Department of Civil and Construction Engineering, Ames, IA 50011-3232. Offers civil engineering (MS, PhD), including civil engineering materials, construction engineering and management, environmental engineering, geometronics, geotechnical engineering, structural engineering, transportation engineering. *Degree requirements:* For master's, thesis or alternative; for doctorate, thesis/dissertation. *Entrance requirements:* For master's and doctorate, GRE General Test. Additional exam requirements/recommendations for international students: Required—TOEFL (minimum score 550 paper-based; 82 iBT), IELTS (minimum score 6.5). *Application deadline:* For fall admission, 2/1 priority date for domestic students, 2/1 for international students; for spring admission, 8/1 priority date for domestic students, 8/1 for international students. Applications are processed on a rolling basis. Application fee: $40 ($90 for international students). Electronic applications accepted. *Unit head:* Dr. Sri Sritharan, Director of Graduate Education, 515-294-4972, Fax: 515-294-8216, E-mail: ccee-grad-inquiry@iastate.edu. *Application contact:* Kathy Petersen, Director of Graduate Education, 515-294-4975, Fax: 515-294-8216, E-mail: ccee-grad-inquiry@iastate.edu. Web site: http://www.ccee.iastate.edu/.

Louisiana State University and Agricultural and Mechanical College, Graduate School, College of Engineering, Department of Civil and Environmental Engineering, Baton Rouge, LA 70803. Offers environmental engineering (MSCE, PhD); geotechnical engineering (MSCE, PhD); structural engineering and mechanics (MSCE, PhD); transportation engineering (MSCE, PhD); water resources (MSCE, PhD). Part-time programs available. *Faculty:* 25 full-time (2 women). *Students:* 90 full-time (23 women), 34 part-time (8 women); includes 11 minority (4 Black or African American, non-Hispanic/Latino; 1 American Indian or Alaska Native, non-Hispanic/Latino; 4 Asian, non-Hispanic/Latino; 2 Hispanic/Latino), 73 international. Average age 30. 106 applicants, 67% accepted, 25 enrolled. In 2011, 32 master's, 4 doctorates awarded. *Degree requirements:* For master's, thesis optional; for doctorate, one foreign language, thesis/dissertation. *Entrance requirements:* For master's and doctorate, GRE General Test, minimum GPA of 3.0. Additional exam requirements/recommendations for international students: Required—TOEFL (minimum score 550 paper-based; 213 computer-based; 79 iBT) or IELTS (minimum score 6.5). *Application deadline:* For fall admission, 1/25 priority date for domestic students, 5/15 for international students; for spring admission, 10/15 for international students. Applications are processed on a rolling basis. Application fee: $50 ($70 for international students). Electronic applications accepted. *Financial support:* In 2011–12, 91 students received support, including 3 fellowships with full and partial tuition reimbursements available (averaging $18,050 per year), 72 research assistantships with full and partial tuition reimbursements available (averaging $15,942 per year), 6 teaching assistantships with full and partial tuition reimbursements available (averaging $12,469 per year); career-related internships or fieldwork, institutionally sponsored loans, scholarships/grants, and health care benefits also available. Financial award application deadline: 3/1; financial award applicants required to submit FAFSA. *Faculty research:* Mechanics and structures, environmental, geotechnical transportation, water resources. *Total annual research expenditures:* $3 million. *Unit head:* Dr. George Z. Voyiadjis, Chair/Professor, 225-578-8668, Fax: 225-578-9176, E-mail: voyiadjis@lsu.edu. *Application contact:* Dr. Clinton Willson, Professor, 225-578-8672, E-mail: cwillson@lsu.edu. Web site: http://www.cee.lsu.edu/.

Marquette University, Graduate School, College of Engineering, Department of Civil and Environmental Engineering, Milwaukee, WI 53201-1881. Offers construction and public works management (MS, PhD); construction engineering and management (Certificate); environmental/water resources engineering (MS, PhD); structural design (Certificate); structural/geotechnical engineering (MS, PhD); transportation planning and engineering (MS, PhD); waste and wastewater treatment processes (Certificate). Part-time and evening/weekend programs available. *Faculty:* 13 full-time (0 women), 5 part-time/adjunct (0 women). *Students:* 26 full-time (5 women), 11 part-time (0 women); includes 2 minority (1 Black or African American, non-Hispanic/Latino; 1 Asian, non-Hispanic/Latino), 12 international. Average age 27. 74 applicants, 62% accepted, 9 enrolled. In 2011, 6 master's, 3 doctorates awarded. Terminal master's awarded for partial completion of doctoral program. *Degree requirements:* For master's, comprehensive exam (for some programs), thesis or alternative; for doctorate, thesis/dissertation. *Entrance requirements:* For master's, GRE General Test (recommended), minimum GPA of 3.0, official transcripts from all current and previous colleges/universities except Marquette, three letters of recommendation; for doctorate, GRE

General Test, minimum GPA of 3.0, official transcripts from all current and previous colleges/universities except Marquette, three letters of recommendation, brief statement of purpose, submission of any English language publications authored by applicant (strongly recommended). Additional exam requirements/recommendations for international students: Required—TOEFL (minimum score 530 paper-based; 78 computer-based). *Application deadline:* For fall admission, 6/1 priority date for domestic students. Applications are processed on a rolling basis. Application fee: $50. Electronic applications accepted. *Expenses: Tuition:* Full-time $17,010; part-time $945 per credit hour. Tuition and fees vary according to program. *Financial support:* In 2011–12, 21 students received support, including 6 fellowships with partial tuition reimbursements available (averaging $9,177 per year), 1 research assistantship with full tuition reimbursement available (averaging $13,745 per year), 7 teaching assistantships with full tuition reimbursements available (averaging $13,902 per year); scholarships/grants, health care benefits, tuition waivers (partial), and unspecified assistantships also available. Support available to part-time students. Financial award application deadline: 2/15. *Faculty research:* Highway safety, highway performance, and intelligent transportation systems; surface mount technology; watershed management. *Total annual research expenditures:* $826,608. *Unit head:* Dr. Thomas Wenzel, Chair, 414-288-7030, Fax: 414-288-7521, E-mail: thomas.wenzel@marquette.edu. *Application contact:* Dr. Stephen M. Heinrich, Director of Graduate Studies, 414-288-5466, E-mail: stephen.heinrich@marquette.edu. Web site: http://www.marquette.edu/engineering/pages/AllYouNeed/Civil_Environmental/civil.html.

Massachusetts Institute of Technology, School of Engineering, Department of Civil and Environmental Engineering, Cambridge, MA 02139. Offers biological oceanography (PhD, Sc D); chemical oceanography (PhD, Sc D); civil and environmental engineering (PhD, Sc D); civil and environmental systems (PhD, Sc D); civil engineering (PhD, Sc D, CE); coastal engineering (PhD, Sc D); construction engineering and management (PhD, Sc D); environmental and water quality engineering (M Eng); environmental biology (PhD, Sc D); environmental chemistry (PhD, Sc D); environmental engineering (PhD, Sc D); environmental fluid mechanics (PhD, Sc D); environmental science and engineering (SM); geotechnical and geoenvironmental engineering (PhD, Sc D); geotechnology (M Eng); high-performance structures (M Eng); hydrology (PhD, Sc D); information technology (PhD, Sc D); mechanics (SM); oceanographic engineering (PhD, Sc D); structures and materials (PhD, Sc D); transportation (M Eng, PhD, Sc D); SM/MBA. *Faculty:* 35 full-time (6 women), 1 part-time/adjunct (0 women). *Students:* 216 full-time (80 women); includes 30 minority (4 Black or African American, non-Hispanic/Latino; 13 Asian, non-Hispanic/Latino; 8 Hispanic/Latino; 5 Two or more races, non-Hispanic/Latino), 110 international. Average age 27. 589 applicants, 26% accepted, 91 enrolled. In 2011, 62 master's, 14 doctorates awarded. *Degree requirements:* For master's and CE, thesis; for doctorate, comprehensive exam, thesis/dissertation. *Entrance requirements:* For master's and doctorate, GRE General Test. Additional exam requirements/recommendations for international students: Required—TOEFL (minimum score 577 paper-based; 233 computer-based; 90 iBT), IELTS (minimum score 7). *Application deadline:* For fall admission, 12/15 for domestic and international students. Application fee: $75. Electronic applications accepted. *Expenses: Tuition:* Full-time $40,460; part-time $630 per credit hour. *Required fees:* $272. *Financial support:* In 2011–12, 180 students received support, including 51 fellowships (averaging $30,800 per year), 110 research assistantships (averaging $29,500 per year), 19 teaching assistantships (averaging $29,500 per year); career-related internships or fieldwork, Federal Work-Study, institutionally sponsored loans, scholarships/grants, health care benefits, and unspecified assistantships also available. *Faculty research:* Environmental chemistry, environmental fluid mechanics and coastal engineering, environmental microbiology, geotechnical engineering and geomechanics, hydrology and hydroclimatology, infrastructure systems, mechanics of materials and structures, transportation systems. *Total annual research expenditures:* $17.7 million. *Unit head:* Prof. Andrew Whittle, Head, 617-253-7101. *Application contact:* Patricia Glidden, Graduate Admissions Coordinator, 617-253-7119, Fax: 617-258-6775, E-mail: cee-admissions@mit.edu. Web site: http://cee.mit.edu/.

Morgan State University, School of Graduate Studies, Clarence M. Mitchell, Jr. School of Engineering, Department of Transportation, Baltimore, MD 21251. Offers MS. Part-time and evening/weekend programs available. *Degree requirements:* For master's, thesis optional, comprehensive exam or equivalent. *Entrance requirements:* For master's, minimum undergraduate GPA of 2.5. Additional exam requirements/recommendations for international students: Required—TOEFL (minimum score 550 paper-based; 213 computer-based). *Faculty research:* Distributional impacts of congestion, pricing education and training for intelligent vehicle highway systems.

New Jersey Institute of Technology, Office of Graduate Studies, Newark College of Engineering, Department of Civil and Environmental Engineering, Newark, NJ 07102. Offers civil engineering (MS, PhD); critical infrastructure systems (MS); environmental engineering (MS, PhD); transportation (MS, PhD). Part-time and evening/weekend programs available. *Faculty:* 24 full-time (7 women), 16 part-time/adjunct (0 women). *Students:* 92 full-time (27 women), 145 part-time (37 women); includes 93 minority (21 Black or African American, non-Hispanic/Latino; 1 American Indian or Alaska Native, non-Hispanic/Latino; 32 Asian, non-Hispanic/Latino; 36 Hispanic/Latino; 3 Two or more races, non-Hispanic/Latino), 54 international. Average age 30. 313 applicants, 66% accepted, 70 enrolled. In 2011, 68 master's, 7 doctorates awarded. Terminal master's awarded for partial completion of doctoral program. *Degree requirements:* For master's, thesis optional; for doctorate, thesis/dissertation, residency. *Entrance requirements:* For master's, GRE General Test; for doctorate, GRE General Test, minimum graduate GPA of 3.5. Additional exam requirements/recommendations for international students: Required—TOEFL (minimum score 550 paper-based; 213 computer-based; 79 iBT). *Application deadline:* For fall admission, 6/1 priority date for domestic students, 5/1 for international students; for spring admission, 11/15 priority date for domestic students, 11/15 for international students. Applications are processed on a rolling basis. Application fee: $65. Electronic applications accepted. *Expenses:* Tuition, state resident: full-time $7980; part-time $867 per credit. Tuition, nonresident: full-time $11,336; part-time $1196 per credit. *Required fees:* $230 per credit. *Financial support:* Fellowships with full and partial tuition reimbursements, research assistantships with full and partial tuition reimbursements, teaching assistantships with full and partial tuition reimbursements, career-related internships or fieldwork, Federal Work-Study, institutionally sponsored loans, and unspecified assistantships available. Financial award application deadline: 1/15. *Faculty research:* Geotechnical engineering, water resources engineering, construction engineering, transportation policy, traffic operations. *Total annual research expenditures:* $2.8 million. *Unit head:* Dr. Taha F. Marhaba, Chair, 973-642-4599, E-mail: marhaba@njit.edu. *Application contact:* Kathryn Kelly, Director of Admissions, 973-596-3300, Fax: 973-596-3461, E-mail: admissions@njit.edu. Web site: http://civil.njit.edu/.

New Jersey Institute of Technology, Office of Graduate Studies, Newark College of Engineering, Interdisciplinary Program in Transportation, Newark, NJ 07102. Offers MS, PhD. Part-time and evening/weekend programs available. *Students:* 17 full-time (3

women), 21 part-time (5 women); includes 16 minority (4 Black or African American, non-Hispanic/Latino; 8 Asian, non-Hispanic/Latino; 4 Hispanic/Latino), 11 international. Average age 34. 37 applicants, 81% accepted, 6 enrolled. In 2011, 6 degrees awarded. Terminal master's awarded for partial completion of doctoral program. *Degree requirements:* For master's, thesis or alternative; for doctorate, thesis/dissertation, residency. *Entrance requirements:* For master's, GRE General Test; for doctorate, GRE General Test, minimum graduate GPA of 3.5. Additional exam requirements/recommendations for international students: Required—TOEFL (minimum score 550 paper-based; 213 computer-based; 79 iBT). *Application deadline:* For fall admission, 6/1 priority date for domestic students, 5/1 for international students; for spring admission, 11/15 for domestic and international students. Applications are processed on a rolling basis. Application fee: $65. Electronic applications accepted. *Expenses:* Tuition, state resident: full-time $7980; part-time $867 per credit. Tuition, nonresident: full-time $11,336; part-time $1196 per credit. *Required fees:* $230 per credit. *Financial support:* Fellowships with full and partial tuition reimbursements, research assistantships with full and partial tuition reimbursements, teaching assistantships with full and partial tuition reimbursements, career-related internships or fieldwork, Federal Work-Study, institutionally sponsored loans, and unspecified assistantships available. Financial award application deadline: 1/15. *Faculty research:* Transportation planning, administration, and policy; intelligent vehicle highway systems; bridge maintenance. *Unit head:* Dr. Athanassios Bladikas, Director, 973-596-3653, E-mail: athanassios.bladikas@njit.edu. *Application contact:* Kathryn Kelly, Director of Admissions, 973-596-3300, Fax: 973-596-3461, E-mail: admissions@njit.edu. Web site: http://nce.njit.edu/departments/trans.php.

Northwestern University, McCormick School of Engineering and Applied Science, Department of Civil and Environmental Engineering, Evanston, IL 60208-3109. Offers environmental engineering and science (MS, PhD); geotechnical engineering (MS, PhD); mechanics of materials and solids (MS, PhD); project management (MS, PhD); structural engineering and materials (MS, PhD); theoretical and applied mechanics (MS, PhD), including fluid mechanics, solid mechanics; transportation systems analysis and planning (MS, PhD). MS and PhD admissions and degrees offered through The Graduate School. Part-time programs available. Terminal master's awarded for partial completion of doctoral program. *Degree requirements:* For master's, thesis (for some programs); for doctorate, thesis/dissertation. *Entrance requirements:* For master's and doctorate, GRE General Test, minimum 2 letters of recommendation, transcripts from all academic institutions attended. Additional exam requirements/recommendations for international students: Required—TOEFL (minimum score 600 paper-based; 250 computer-based; 100 iBT), IELTS (minimum score 7). Electronic applications accepted. *Faculty research:* Environmental engineering and science, geotechnics, mechanics of materials and solids, structural engineering and materials, transportation systems analysis and planning.

Ohio University, Graduate College, Russ College of Engineering and Technology, Department of Civil Engineering, Athens, OH 45701-2979. Offers civil engineering (PhD); construction (MS); environmental (MS); geotechnical and geoenvironmental (MS); mechanics (MS); structures (MS); transportation (MS); water resources and structures (MS). Part-time programs available. *Students:* 32 full-time (6 women), 7 part-time (2 women); includes 3 minority (1 Hispanic/Latino; 2 Two or more races, non-Hispanic/Latino), 13 international. 52 applicants, 52% accepted, 4 enrolled. In 2011, 10 degrees awarded. *Degree requirements:* For master's, comprehensive exam (for some programs), thesis or alternative; for doctorate, comprehensive exam, thesis/dissertation. *Entrance requirements:* For master's, GRE General Test, minimum GPA of 3.0, 3 letters of recommendation; for doctorate, GRE General Test. Additional exam requirements/recommendations for international students: Required—TOEFL (minimum score 550 paper-based; 80 iBT) or IELTS (minimum score 6.5). *Application deadline:* For fall admission, 5/1 priority date for domestic students, 2/1 for international students; for winter admission, 8/1 priority date for domestic students, 4/1 for international students; for spring admission, 2/1 priority date for domestic students, 7/1 for international students. Applications are processed on a rolling basis. Application fee: $50 ($55 for international students). Electronic applications accepted. *Financial support:* Research assistantships with full tuition reimbursements, teaching assistantships with full tuition reimbursements, Federal Work-Study, institutionally sponsored loans, scholarships/grants, and unspecified assistantships available. Financial award application deadline: 3/15; financial award applicants required to submit FAFSA. *Faculty research:* Noise abatement, materials and environment, highway infrastructure, subsurface investigation (pavements, pipes, bridges). *Unit head:* Dr. Gayle F. Mitchell, Chair, 740-593-0430, Fax: 740-593-0625, E-mail: mitchelg@ohio.edu. *Application contact:* Dr. Shad M. Sargand, Graduate Chair, 740-593-1465, Fax: 740-593-0625, E-mail: sargand@ohio.edu. Web site: http://www.ohio.edu/civil/.

Oregon State University, Graduate School, College of Engineering, School of Civil and Construction Engineering, Corvallis, OR 97331. Offers civil engineering (MS, PhD); coastal and ocean engineering (M Oc E, PhD); coastal engineering (MS); construction engineering management (MBE, PhD); engineering (M Eng, MAIS); geotechnical engineering (MS, PhD); structural engineering (MS, PhD); transportation engineering (MS, PhD); water engineering (MS, PhD). Part-time programs available. Terminal master's awarded for partial completion of doctoral program. *Degree requirements:* For master's, thesis or alternative; for doctorate, one foreign language, thesis/dissertation. *Entrance requirements:* For master's, GRE General Test, minimum GPA of 3.0 in last 90 hours (3.5 for MS); for doctorate, GRE General Test, minimum GPA of 3.0 in last 90 hours of undergraduate course work. Additional exam requirements/recommendations for international students: Required—TOEFL (minimum score 580 paper-based; 237 computer-based). *Faculty research:* Hazardous waste management, carbon cycling, wave forces on structures, pavement design, seismic analysis.

Polytechnic Institute of New York University, Department of Civil Engineering, Major in Transportation Planning and Engineering, Brooklyn, NY 11201-2990. Offers MS, PhD. Part-time and evening/weekend programs available. *Students:* 25 full-time (5 women), 15 part-time (3 women); includes 8 minority (3 Black or African American, non-Hispanic/Latino; 3 Asian, non-Hispanic/Latino; 2 Hispanic/Latino), 16 international. Average age 30. 41 applicants, 66% accepted, 15 enrolled. In 2011, 9 master's, 1 doctorate awarded. *Degree requirements:* For master's, comprehensive exam (for some programs), thesis (for some programs); for doctorate, comprehensive exam, thesis/dissertation. *Entrance requirements:* Additional exam requirements/recommendations for international students: Required—TOEFL (minimum score 550 paper-based; 213 computer-based; 80 iBT); Recommended—IELTS (minimum score 6.5). *Application deadline:* For fall admission, 7/31 priority date for domestic students, 4/30 for international students; for spring admission, 12/31 priority date for domestic students, 10/30 for international students. Applications are processed on a rolling basis. Application fee: $75. Electronic applications accepted. *Expenses: Tuition:* Full-time $22,464; part-time $1248 per credit. *Required fees:* $501 per semester. *Financial support:* Fellowships, research assistantships, teaching assistantships, institutionally sponsored loans, scholarships/grants, and unspecified assistantships available. Support available to part-time students. Financial award applicants required to submit FAFSA. *Unit head:* Dr. Lawrence Chiarelli, Head, 718-260-4040, Fax: 718-260-3433, E-mail: lchiarel@poly.edu. *Application contact:* JeanCarlo Bonilla, Director of Graduate Enrollment Management, 718-260-3182, Fax: 718-260-3624, E-mail: gradinfo@gmail.com.

Polytechnic Institute of NYU, Long Island Graduate Center, Graduate Programs, Department of Civil Engineering, Major in Transportation Planning and Engineering, Melville, NY 11747. Offers MS. *Students:* 1 part-time (0 women). Average age 25. 1 applicant, 100% accepted, 1 enrolled. *Degree requirements:* For master's, comprehensive exam (for some programs), thesis (for some programs). *Entrance requirements:* Additional exam requirements/recommendations for international students: Required—TOEFL (minimum score 550 paper-based; 213 computer-based; 80 iBT); Recommended—IELTS (minimum score 6.5). *Application deadline:* For fall admission, 7/31 priority date for domestic students, 4/30 for international students; for spring admission, 12/31 priority date for domestic students, 11/30 for international students. Applications are processed on a rolling basis. Application fee: $75. Electronic applications accepted. *Financial support:* Institutionally sponsored loans, scholarships/grants, and unspecified assistantships available. Support available to part-time students. Financial award applicants required to submit FAFSA. *Unit head:* Dr. Roger Peter Roess, Department Head, 718-260-3018, E-mail: rroess@poly.edu. *Application contact:* JeanCarlo Bonilla, Director of Graduate Enrollment Management, 718-260-3182, Fax: 718-260-3624, E-mail: gradinfo@poly.edu.

Rensselaer Polytechnic Institute, Graduate School, School of Engineering, Program in Civil Engineering, Troy, NY 12180-3590. Offers geotechnical engineering (M Eng, MS, PhD); mechanics of composite materials and structures (M Eng, MS, PhD); structural engineering (M Eng, MS, PhD); transportation engineering (M Eng, MS, PhD). Part-time programs available. Terminal master's awarded for partial completion of doctoral program. *Degree requirements:* For master's, thesis (for some programs); for doctorate, thesis/dissertation. *Entrance requirements:* For master's and doctorate, GRE. Additional exam requirements/recommendations for international students: Required—TOEFL (minimum score 570 paper-based; 230 computer-based; 89 iBT), IELTS (minimum score 6.5). Electronic applications accepted. *Faculty research:* Computational mechanics, earthquake engineering, geo-environmental engineering.

Rensselaer Polytechnic Institute, Graduate School, School of Engineering, Program in Transportation Engineering, Troy, NY 12180-3590. Offers M Eng, MS, PhD. Part-time programs available. Terminal master's awarded for partial completion of doctoral program. *Degree requirements:* For master's, thesis (for some programs); for doctorate, thesis/dissertation. *Entrance requirements:* For master's and doctorate, GRE. Additional exam requirements/recommendations for international students: Required—TOEFL (minimum score 570 paper-based; 230 computer-based; 89 iBT), IELTS (minimum score 6.5). Electronic applications accepted. *Faculty research:* Intelligent transportation systems, routing algorithms, dynamic network management, user behavior.

South Carolina State University, School of Graduate Studies, Department of Civil and Mechanical Engineering Technology and Nuclear Engineering, Orangeburg, SC 29117-0001. Offers transportation (MS). Part-time and evening/weekend programs available. *Faculty:* 2 full-time (0 women), 3 part-time/adjunct (1 woman). *Students:* 19 full-time (6 women), 3 part-time (1 woman); includes 20 minority (19 Black or African American, non-Hispanic/Latino; 1 Hispanic/Latino), 2 international. Average age 28. 12 applicants, 83% accepted, 5 enrolled. In 2011, 3 master's awarded. *Degree requirements:* For master's, comprehensive exam, thesis, departmental qualifying exam. *Entrance requirements:* For master's, GRE. Additional exam requirements/recommendations for international students: Recommended—TOEFL. *Application deadline:* For fall admission, 6/15 for domestic and international students; for spring admission, 11/1 for domestic and international students. Application fee: $25. Electronic applications accepted. *Expenses:* Tuition, state resident: full-time $8688; part-time $514 per credit hour. Tuition, nonresident: full-time $17,600; part-time $1009 per credit hour. *Required fees:* $570. *Financial support:* In 2011–12, 6 fellowships (averaging $5,150 per year) were awarded; research assistantships, career-related internships or fieldwork, Federal Work-Study, institutionally sponsored loans, and unspecified assistantships also available. Financial award application deadline: 6/1. *Faculty research:* Societal competence, relationship of parent-child interaction to adult, rehabilitation evaluation, vocation, language assessment of rural children. *Unit head:* Dr. Stanley Ihekweazu, Chair, 803-536-7117, Fax: 803-516-4607, E-mail: sihekweazu@scsu.edu. *Application contact:* Annette Hazzard-Jones, Program Coordinator II, 803-536-8809, Fax: 803-536-8812, E-mail: zs_ahazzard@scsu.edu. Web site: http://www.scsu.edu/schoolofgraduatestudies.aspx.

Texas A&M University, College of Engineering, Zachry Department of Civil Engineering, College Station, TX 77843. Offers coastal and ocean engineering (M Eng, MS, D Eng, PhD); construction engineering and management (M Eng, MS, D Eng, PhD); environmental engineering (M Eng, MS, D Eng, PhD); geotechnical engineering (M Eng, MS, D Eng, PhD); materials engineering (M Eng, MS, D Eng, PhD); structural engineering (M Eng, MS, D Eng, PhD); transportation engineering (M Eng, MS, D Eng, PhD); water resources engineering (M Eng, MS, D Eng, PhD). Part-time programs available. *Faculty:* 57. *Students:* 361 full-time (76 women), 46 part-time (8 women); includes 41 minority (3 Black or African American, non-Hispanic/Latino; 16 Asian, non-Hispanic/Latino; 21 Hispanic/Latino; 1 Two or more races, non-Hispanic/Latino), 247 international. Average age 29. In 2011, 123 master's, 27 doctorates awarded. *Degree requirements:* For master's, thesis (MS); for doctorate, dissertation (PhD), internship (D Eng). *Entrance requirements:* For master's and doctorate, GRE General Test. Additional exam requirements/recommendations for international students: Required—TOEFL. *Application deadline:* Applications are processed on a rolling basis. Application fee: $50 ($75 for international students). Electronic applications accepted. *Expenses:* Tuition, state resident: full-time $5437; part-time $226.55 per credit hour. Tuition, nonresident: full-time $12,949; part-time $539.55 per credit hour. *Required fees:* $2741. *Financial support:* In 2011–12, fellowships (averaging $4,500 per year), research assistantships (averaging $14,000 per year), teaching assistantships (averaging $14,400 per year) were awarded; career-related internships or fieldwork and institutionally sponsored loans also available. Financial award application deadline: 4/15; financial award applicants required to submit FAFSA. *Unit head:* Dr. John Niedzwecki, Head, 979-845-3858, E-mail: j-niedzwecki@tamu.edu. *Application contact:* Graduate Advisor, 979-845-7435, Fax: 979-845-6156, E-mail: info@civil.tamu.edu. Web site: https://www.civil.tamu.edu/.

Texas Southern University, School of Science and Technology, Program in Transportation, Planning and Management, Houston, TX 77004-4584. Offers MS. Part-time and evening/weekend programs available. *Degree requirements:* For master's, comprehensive exam, thesis optional. *Entrance requirements:* For master's, GRE General Test, minimum GPA of 2.5. Additional exam requirements/recommendations for international students: Required—TOEFL. Electronic applications accepted. *Faculty research:* Highway traffic operations, transportation and policy planning, air quality in transportation, transportation modeling.

The University of Alabama in Huntsville, School of Graduate Studies, College of Engineering, Department of Civil and Environmental Engineering, Huntsville, AL 35899. Offers civil and environmental engineering (PhD); civil engineering (MSE), including civil engineering, environmental and water resource engineering, geotechnical engineering, structural engineering and structural mechanics, transportation engineering. PhD offered jointly with The University of Alabama at Birmingham. Part-time and evening/weekend programs available. *Faculty:* 5 full-time (1 woman), 1 part-time/adjunct (0 women). *Students:* 20 full-time (4 women), 12 part-time (6 women); includes 1 minority (Black or African American, non-Hispanic/Latino), 15 international. Average age 29. 26 applicants, 62% accepted, 6 enrolled. In 2011, 3 master's, 1 doctorate awarded. *Degree requirements:* For master's, comprehensive exam, thesis or alternative, oral and written exams; for doctorate, comprehensive exam, thesis/dissertation, oral and written exams. *Entrance requirements:* For master's, GRE General Test, BSE, minimum GPA of 3.0; for doctorate, GRE General Test, minimum GPA of 3.0. Additional exam requirements/recommendations for international students: Required—TOEFL (minimum score 500 paper-based; 173 computer-based; 62 iBT). *Application deadline:* For fall admission, 7/15 for domestic students, 4/1 for international students; for spring admission, 11/30 for domestic students, 9/1 for international students. Applications are processed on a rolling basis. Application fee: $40 ($50 for international students). Electronic applications accepted. *Expenses:* Tuition, state resident: full-time $7830; part-time $473.50 per credit. Tuition, nonresident: full-time $18,748; part-time $1128.33 per credit. Tuition and fees vary according to course load and program. *Financial support:* In 2011–12, 16 students received support, including 10 research assistantships with full and partial tuition reimbursements available (averaging $12,281 per year), 6 teaching assistantships with full and partial tuition reimbursements available (averaging $12,472 per year); career-related internships or fieldwork, Federal Work-Study, institutionally sponsored loans, scholarships/grants, health care benefits, and unspecified assistantships also available. Support available to part-time students. Financial award application deadline: 4/1; financial award applicants required to submit FAFSA. *Faculty research:* Hydrologic modeling, orbital debris impact, hydrogeology, environmental engineering, transportation engineering. *Total annual research expenditures:* $1.1 million. *Unit head:* Dr. Houssam Toutanji, Chair, 256-824-7361, Fax: 256-824-6724, E-mail: toutanji@cee.uah.edu. *Application contact:* Kim Gray, Graduate Studies Admissions Coordinator, 256-824-6002, Fax: 256-824-6405, E-mail: deangrad@uah.edu. Web site: http://www.uah.edu/eng/departments/cee/welcome.

University of Arkansas, Graduate School, College of Engineering, Department of Civil Engineering, Fayetteville, AR 72701-1201. Offers civil engineering (MSCE, MSE, PhD); environmental engineering (MS En E, MSE); transportation engineering (MSE, MSTE). *Students:* 30 full-time (10 women), 25 part-time (2 women); includes 4 minority (1 Black or African American, non-Hispanic/Latino; 1 Asian, non-Hispanic/Latino; 2 Hispanic/Latino), 17 international. In 2011, 9 master's awarded. *Degree requirements:* For master's, thesis optional; for doctorate, one foreign language, thesis/dissertation. *Application deadline:* For fall admission, 4/1 for international students; for spring admission, 10/1 for international students. Applications are processed on a rolling basis. Application fee: $40 ($50 for international students). Electronic applications accepted. *Financial support:* In 2011–12, 37 research assistantships, 1 teaching assistantship were awarded; fellowships with tuition reimbursements, career-related internships or fieldwork, and Federal Work-Study also available. Support available to part-time students. Financial award application deadline: 4/1; financial award applicants required to submit FAFSA. *Unit head:* Dr. Kevin Hall, Departmental Chair, 479-575-4954, Fax: 479-575-7168, E-mail: kdhall@uark.edu. *Application contact:* Dr. Paneer Selvam, Graduate Coordinator, 479-575-4954, E-mail: rps@uark.edu. Web site: http://www.cveg.uark.edu.

University of California, Berkeley, Graduate Division, College of Engineering, Department of Civil and Environmental Engineering, Berkeley, CA 94720-1500. Offers engineering and project management (M Eng, MS, D Eng, PhD); environmental engineering (M Eng, MS, D Eng, PhD); geoengineering (M Eng, MS, D Eng, PhD); structural engineering, mechanics and materials (M Eng, MS, D Eng, PhD); transportation engineering (M Eng, MS, D Eng, PhD); M Arch/MS; MCP/MS; MPP/MS. *Degree requirements:* For master's, comprehensive exam or thesis (MS); for doctorate, thesis/dissertation, qualifying exam. *Entrance requirements:* For master's, GRE General Test, minimum GPA of 3.0, 3 letters of recommendation; for doctorate, GRE General Test, minimum GPA of 3.5, 3 letters of recommendation. Additional exam requirements/recommendations for international students: Required—TOEFL (minimum score 570 paper-based; 230 computer-based). Electronic applications accepted.

University of California, Davis, College of Engineering, Graduate Group in Transportation Technology and Policy, Davis, CA 95616. Offers MS, PhD. Terminal master's awarded for partial completion of doctoral program. *Degree requirements:* For master's, comprehensive exam (for some programs), thesis (for some programs); for doctorate, thesis/dissertation. *Entrance requirements:* For master's, GRE General Test, minimum GPA of 3.0; for doctorate, GRE General Test, minimum GPA of 3.5. Additional exam requirements/recommendations for international students: Required—TOEFL (minimum score 550 paper-based; 213 computer-based). Electronic applications accepted.

University of California, Irvine, School of Social Sciences, Program in Transportation Science, Irvine, CA 92697. Offers MA, PhD. *Students:* 13 full-time (5 women), 1 (woman) part-time; includes 3 minority (all Asian, non-Hispanic/Latino), 8 international. Average age 29. 18 applicants, 61% accepted, 7 enrolled. In 2011, 1 master's, 2 doctorates awarded. *Entrance requirements:* For master's and doctorate, GRE General Test, minimum GPA of 3.0. *Application deadline:* For fall admission, 1/15 for domestic and international students. Application fee: $80 ($100 for international students). *Financial support:* Fellowships, research assistantships with full tuition reimbursements, teaching assistantships, institutionally sponsored loans, traineeships, health care benefits, and unspecified assistantships available. Financial award application deadline: 3/1. *Unit head:* Dr. Jean-Daniel Saphores, Director, 949-824-7334, Fax: 949-824-8385, E-mail: saphores@uci.edu. *Application contact:* Anne Marie Defeo, Administrative Manager, 949-824-6564, Fax: 949-824-8385, E-mail: amdefeo@uci.edu. Web site: http://www.its.uci.edu/.

University of Central Florida, College of Engineering and Computer Science, Department of Civil, Environmental, and Construction Engineering, Program in Civil Engineering, Orlando, FL 32816. Offers civil engineering (MS, MSCE, PhD); construction engineering (Certificate); structural engineering (Certificate); transportation engineering (Certificate). Part-time and evening/weekend programs available. *Students:* 68 full-time (13 women), 87 part-time (16 women); includes 35 minority (7 Black or African American, non-Hispanic/Latino; 6 Asian, non-Hispanic/Latino; 20 Hispanic/Latino; 2 Two or more races, non-Hispanic/Latino), 42 international. Average age 30. 125 applicants, 79% accepted, 45 enrolled. In 2011, 27 master's, 2 doctorates awarded. *Degree requirements:* For master's, thesis or alternative; for doctorate, thesis/dissertation, departmental qualifying exam, candidacy exam. *Entrance requirements:* For master's, GRE General Test, minimum GPA of 3.0 in last 60 hours; for doctorate,

GRE General Test, minimum GPA of 3.5 in last 60 hours. Additional exam requirements/recommendations for international students: Required—TOEFL. *Application deadline:* For fall admission, 7/15 priority date for domestic students; for spring admission, 12/15 priority date for domestic students. Application fee: $30. Electronic applications accepted. *Expenses:* Tuition, state resident: part-time $277.08 per credit hour. Tuition, nonresident: part-time $277.08 per credit hour. Part-time tuition and fees vary according to degree level and program. *Financial support:* In 2011–12, 28 students received support, including 6 fellowships with partial tuition reimbursements available (averaging $2,700 per year), 14 research assistantships with partial tuition reimbursements available (averaging $11,800 per year), 15 teaching assistantships with partial tuition reimbursements available (averaging $11,300 per year); career-related internships or fieldwork, Federal Work-Study, institutionally sponsored loans, tuition waivers (partial), and unspecified assistantships also available. Financial award application deadline: 3/1; financial award applicants required to submit FAFSA. *Unit head:* Dr. Essam Radwan, Interim Chair, 407-823-4738, E-mail: ahmed.radwan@ucf.edu. *Application contact:* Barbara Rodriguez, Director, Admissions and Registration, 407-823-2766, Fax: 407-823-6442, E-mail: gradadmissions@ucf.edu. Web site: http://cece.ucf.edu/.

University of Colorado Denver, College of Engineering and Applied Science, Department of Civil Engineering, Denver, CO 80217. Offers civil engineering (EASPh D); civil engineering systems (PhD); environmental and sustainability engineering (MS, PhD); geographic information systems (MS); geotechnical engineering (MS, PhD); hydrology and hydraulics (MS, PhD); structural engineering (MS, PhD); transportation engineering (MS, PhD). Part-time and evening/weekend programs available. *Faculty:* 14 full-time (1 woman), 6 part-time/adjunct (0 women). *Students:* 66 full-time (11 women), 65 part-time (14 women); includes 30 minority (10 Black or African American, non-Hispanic/Latino; 8 Asian, non-Hispanic/Latino; 10 Hispanic/Latino; 2 Two or more races, non-Hispanic/Latino), 17 international. Average age 34. 67 applicants, 54% accepted, 24 enrolled. In 2011, 30 master's, 2 doctorates awarded. *Degree requirements:* For master's, comprehensive exam, thesis or alternative, 30 credit hours, project or thesis; for doctorate, comprehensive exam, thesis/dissertation, 60 credit hours (30 of which are dissertation research). *Entrance requirements:* For master's, GRE, statement of purpose, transcripts, three references; for doctorate, GRE, statement of purpose, transcripts, references, letter of support from faculty stating willingness to serve as dissertation advisor and outlining plan for financial support. Additional exam requirements/recommendations for international students: Required—TOEFL (minimum score 525 paper-based; 197 computer-based). *Application deadline:* For fall admission, 7/15 for domestic students, 6/15 for international students; for spring admission, 12/1 for domestic students, 11/1 for international students. Applications are processed on a rolling basis. Application fee: $50 ($75 for international students). Electronic applications accepted. *Expenses:* Contact institution. *Financial support:* Research assistantships, teaching assistantships, career-related internships or fieldwork, and Federal Work-Study available. Financial award application deadline: 4/1; financial award applicants required to submit FAFSA. *Faculty research:* Earthquake source physics, environmental biotechnology, hydrologic and hydraulic engineering, sustainability assessments, transportation energy use and greenhouse gas emissions. *Unit head:* Dr. Kevin Rens, Chair, 303-556-8017, Fax: 303-556-2368, E-mail: kevin.rens@ucdenver.edu. *Application contact:* Maria Rase, Program Assistant, 303-556-6712, Fax: 303-556-2368, E-mail: maria.rase@ucdenver.edu. Web site: http://www.ucdenver.edu/academics/colleges/Engineering/Programs/Civil-Engineering/Pages/CivilEngineering.aspx.

University of Colorado Denver, College of Engineering and Applied Science, Master of Engineering Program, Denver, CO 80217-3364. Offers civil engineering (M Eng), including civil engineering, geographic information systems, transportation systems; electrical engineering (M Eng); mechanical engineering (M Eng). Part-time programs available. *Students:* 21 full-time (9 women), 30 part-time (7 women); includes 5 minority (2 Black or African American, non-Hispanic/Latino; 1 Asian, non-Hispanic/Latino; 2 Hispanic/Latino), 1 international. Average age 34. 13 applicants, 69% accepted, 8 enrolled. In 2011, 19 master's awarded. *Degree requirements:* For master's, comprehensive exam, thesis, 27 credit hours of course work, 3 credit hours of report or thesis work. *Entrance requirements:* For master's, GRE (for those with GPA below 2.75), transcripts, references, statement of purpose. Additional exam requirements/recommendations for international students: Required—TOEFL (minimum score 525 paper-based; 197 computer-based; 71 iBT). *Application deadline:* For fall admission, 7/15 for domestic students, 6/15 for international students; for spring admission, 12/1 for domestic students, 11/1 for international students. Applications are processed on a rolling basis. Application fee: $50 ($75 for international students). Electronic applications accepted. *Expenses:* Contact institution. *Financial support:* Federal Work-Study and scholarships/grants available. Financial award application deadline: 4/1; financial award applicants required to submit FAFSA. *Faculty research:* Civil, electrical and mechanical engineering. *Unit head:* 303-556-2870, Fax: 303-556-2511, E-mail: engineering@ucdenver.edu. *Application contact:* Graduate School Admissions, 303-556-2704, E-mail: admissions@ucdenver.edu. Web site: http://ucdenver.edu/academics/colleges/Engineering/admissions/Masters/Pages/MastersAdmissions.aspx.

University of Dayton, Department of Civil and Environmental Engineering and Engineering Mechanics, Dayton, OH 45469-1300. Offers engineering mechanics (MSEM); environmental engineering (MSCE); geotechnical engineering (MSCE); structural engineering (MSCE); transportation engineering (MSCE); water resources engineering (MSCE). Part-time programs available. *Faculty:* 7 full-time (2 women), 2 part-time/adjunct (0 women). *Students:* 16 full-time (4 women), 9 part-time (4 women); includes 1 minority (Asian, non-Hispanic/Latino), 13 international. Average age 27. 53 applicants, 38% accepted, 5 enrolled. In 2011, 7 degrees awarded. *Degree requirements:* For master's, thesis optional. *Entrance requirements:* For master's, minimum GPA of 3.0 in undergraduate work. Additional exam requirements/recommendations for international students: Required—TOEFL (minimum score 550 paper-based; 213 computer-based; 80 iBT). *Application deadline:* For fall admission, 8/1 for domestic students, 3/1 for international students; for winter admission, 7/1 for international students; for spring admission, 1/1 for international students. Applications are processed on a rolling basis. Application fee: $0 ($50 for international students). Electronic applications accepted. *Expenses: Tuition:* Full-time $8400; part-time $700 per credit hour. *Required fees:* $25 per semester. Tuition and fees vary according to degree level. *Financial support:* Research assistantships available. Financial award applicants required to submit FAFSA. *Faculty research:* Physical modeling of hydraulic systems, finite element methods, mechanics of composite materials, transportation systems safety, biological treatment processes. *Total annual research expenditures:* $200,000. *Unit head:* Dr. Donald V. Chase, Chair, 937-229-3847, Fax: 937-229-3491, E-mail: dchase1@udayton.edu. *Application contact:* Dr. Donald Chase, Chair, 937-229-3847, Fax: 937-229-3491, E-mail: dchase1@udayton.edu. Web site: http://www.udayton.edu/engineering/civil.

University of Delaware, College of Engineering, Department of Civil and Environmental Engineering, Newark, DE 19716. Offers environmental engineering (MAS, MCE, PhD); geotechnical engineering (MAS, MCE, PhD); ocean engineering (MAS, MCE, PhD);

structural engineering (MAS, MCE, PhD); transportation engineering (MAS, MCE, PhD); water resource engineering (MAS, MCE, PhD). Part-time programs available. Terminal master's awarded for partial completion of doctoral program. *Degree requirements:* For master's, thesis; for doctorate, thesis/dissertation. *Entrance requirements:* For master's and doctorate, GRE General Test. Additional exam requirements/recommendations for international students: Required—TOEFL. Electronic applications accepted. *Faculty research:* Structural engineering and mechanics; transportation engineering; ocean engineering; soil mechanics and foundation; water resources and environmental engineering.

University of Massachusetts Amherst, Graduate School, College of Engineering, Department of Civil and Environmental Engineering, Amherst, MA 01003. Offers civil engineering (MSCE, PhD); environmental and water resources (MSCE); geotechnical (MSCE); structural engineering and mechanics (MSCE); transportation (MSCE). *Accreditation:* ABET (one or more programs are accredited). Part-time programs available. *Faculty:* 28 full-time (7 women). *Students:* 91 full-time (30 women), 11 part-time (5 women); includes 13 minority (3 Black or African American, non-Hispanic/Latino; 5 Asian, non-Hispanic/Latino; 4 Hispanic/Latino; 1 Two or more races, non-Hispanic/Latino), 29 international. Average age 27. 293 applicants, 53% accepted, 40 enrolled. In 2011, 38 master's, 1 doctorate awarded. Terminal master's awarded for partial completion of doctoral program. *Degree requirements:* For master's, thesis or alternative; for doctorate, comprehensive exam, thesis/dissertation. *Entrance requirements:* For master's and doctorate, GRE General Test. Additional exam requirements/recommendations for international students: Required—TOEFL (minimum score 550 paper-based; 213 computer-based; 80 iBT), IELTS (minimum score 6.5). *Application deadline:* For fall admission, 2/1 for domestic and international students; for spring admission, 10/1 for domestic and international students. Applications are processed on a rolling basis. Application fee: $50 ($65 for international students). Electronic applications accepted. Tuition and fees vary according to course load, campus/location and program. *Financial support:* In 2011–12, 1 fellowship with full tuition reimbursement (averaging $1,000 per year), 74 research assistantships with full tuition reimbursements (averaging $15,151 per year), 6 teaching assistantships with full tuition reimbursements (averaging $15,151 per year) were awarded; career-related internships or fieldwork, Federal Work-Study, scholarships/grants, traineeships, health care benefits, tuition waivers, and unspecified assistantships also available. Support available to part-time students. Financial award application deadline: 2/1; financial award applicants required to submit FAFSA. *Unit head:* Dr. Sanjay Arwade, Graduate Program Director, 413-545-0686, Fax: 413-545-2840. *Application contact:* Lindsay DeSantis, Interim Supervisor of Admissions, 413-545-0722, Fax: 413-577-0100, E-mail: gradadm@grad.umass.edu. Web site: http://cee.umass.edu/.

University of Memphis, Graduate School, Herff College of Engineering, Department of Civil Engineering, Memphis, TN 38152. Offers civil engineering (PhD); environmental engineering (MS); foundation engineering (MS); structural engineering (MS); transportation engineering (MS); water resources engineering (MS). Terminal master's awarded for partial completion of doctoral program. *Degree requirements:* For master's, comprehensive exam, thesis optional; for doctorate, comprehensive exam, thesis/dissertation. *Entrance requirements:* For master's, GRE General Test or MAT, minimum undergraduate GPA of 2.5; for doctorate, GRE, 3 letters of recommendation. Additional exam requirements/recommendations for international students: Required—TOEFL (minimum score 550 paper-based; 210 computer-based; 79 iBT). *Faculty research:* Structural response to earthquakes, pavement design, water quality, transportation safety, intermodal transportation,.

University of Missouri, Graduate School, College of Engineering, Department of Civil and Environmental Engineering, Columbia, MO 65211. Offers civil engineering (MS, PhD); environmental engineering (MS, PhD); geotechnical engineering (MS, PhD); structural engineering (MS, PhD); transportation and highway engineering (MS); water resources (MS, PhD). *Faculty:* 18 full-time (2 women), 1 part-time/adjunct (0 women). *Students:* 45 full-time (16 women), 38 part-time (8 women); includes 5 minority (2 Black or African American, non-Hispanic/Latino; 2 Asian, non-Hispanic/Latino; 1 Hispanic/Latino), 49 international. Average age 28. 109 applicants, 28% accepted, 20 enrolled. In 2011, 14 master's, 2 doctorates awarded. *Degree requirements:* For master's, report or thesis; for doctorate, thesis/dissertation. *Entrance requirements:* For master's and doctorate, GRE General Test. Additional exam requirements/recommendations for international students: Required—TOEFL (minimum score 550 paper-based; 213 computer-based; 79 iBT). *Application deadline:* For fall admission, 3/15 priority date for domestic students; for winter admission, 10/15 priority date for domestic students. Application fee: $55 ($75 for international students). *Expenses:* Tuition, state resident: full-time $5881. Tuition, nonresident: full-time $15,183. *Required fees:* $952. Tuition and fees vary according to campus/location and program. *Financial support:* Fellowships, research assistantships, teaching assistantships, and institutionally sponsored loans available. *Unit head:* Dr. Mark Virkler, Department Chair, E-mail: virklerm@missouri.edu. *Application contact:* Jennifer Keyzer-Andre, 573-882-4442, E-mail: keyzerandrej@missouri.edu. Web site: http://engineering.missouri.edu/civil/.

University of Nevada, Las Vegas, Graduate College, Howard R. Hughes College of Engineering, Department of Civil and Environmental Engineering, Las Vegas, NV 89154-4015. Offers civil and environmental engineering (MSE, PhD); transportation (MS). Part-time programs available. *Faculty:* 19 full-time (4 women), 15 part-time/adjunct (1 woman). *Students:* 14 full-time (1 woman), 42 part-time (9 women); includes 12 minority (1 Black or African American, non-Hispanic/Latino; 1 American Indian or Alaska Native, non-Hispanic/Latino; 2 Asian, non-Hispanic/Latino; 4 Hispanic/Latino; 4 Two or more races, non-Hispanic/Latino), 18 international. Average age 32. 36 applicants, 81% accepted, 14 enrolled. In 2011, 16 master's, 2 doctorates awarded. *Degree requirements:* For master's, comprehensive exam (for some programs), thesis (for some programs); for doctorate, comprehensive exam, thesis/dissertation. *Entrance requirements:* For master's and doctorate, GRE General Test. Additional exam requirements/recommendations for international students: Required—TOEFL (minimum score 550 paper-based; 213 computer-based; 80 iBT), IELTS (minimum score 7). *Application deadline:* For fall admission, 6/15 priority date for domestic students, 5/1 for international students; for spring admission, 11/15 priority date for domestic students, 10/1 for international students. Applications are processed on a rolling basis. Application fee: $60 ($95 for international students). Electronic applications accepted. *Financial support:* In 2011–12, 33 students received support, including 15 research assistantships with partial tuition reimbursements available (averaging $8,527 per year), 18 teaching assistantships with partial tuition reimbursements available (averaging $9,210 per year), institutionally sponsored loans, scholarships/grants, health care benefits, and unspecified assistantships also available. Financial award application deadline: 3/1. *Total annual research expenditures:* $340,041. *Unit head:* Dr. David Ashley, Professor, 702-895-4040, Fax: 702-895-3936, E-mail: david.b.ashley@unlv.edu. *Application contact:* Graduate College Admissions Evaluator, 702-895-3320, Fax: 702-895-4180, E-mail: gradcollege@unlv.edu. Web site: http://ce.egr.unlv.edu/.

University of New Brunswick Fredericton, School of Graduate Studies, Faculty of Engineering, Department of Civil Engineering, Fredericton, NB E3B 5A3, Canada. Offers construction engineering and management (M Eng, M Sc E, PhD); environmental engineering (M Eng, M Sc E, PhD); environmental studies (M Eng); geotechnical engineering (M Eng, M Sc E, PhD); groundwater/hydrology (M Eng, M Sc E, PhD); materials (M Eng, M Sc E, PhD); pavements (M Eng, M Sc E, PhD); structures (M Eng, M Sc E, PhD); transportation (M Eng, M Sc E, PhD). Part-time programs available. *Faculty:* 13 full-time (1 woman), 7 part-time/adjunct (1 woman). *Students:* 31 full-time (7 women), 17 part-time (2 women). In 2011, 11 master's, 2 doctorates awarded. *Degree requirements:* For master's, thesis, proposal; for doctorate, comprehensive exam, thesis/dissertation, qualifying exam; proposal; 27 credit hours of courses. *Entrance requirements:* For master's, minimum GPA of 3.0; B Sc E in civil engineering or related engineering degree; for doctorate, minimum GPA of 3.0; graduate degree in engineering or applied science. Additional exam requirements/recommendations for international students: Required—TWE (minimum score 4), TOEFL (minimum score 580 paper-based; 237 computer-based) or IELTS (minimum score 7.5). *Application deadline:* For fall admission, 5/1 priority date for domestic students; for winter admission, 11/1 priority date for domestic students. Applications are processed on a rolling basis. Application fee: $50 Canadian dollars. *Financial support:* In 2011–12, 14 fellowships, 30 research assistantships (averaging $7,000 per year), 42 teaching assistantships (averaging $2,000 per year) were awarded; career-related internships or fieldwork and scholarships/grants also available. *Faculty research:* Construction engineering and management; materials and infrastructure renewal; highway and pavement research; structures and solid mechanics; geotechnical, soil; structure interaction; transportation and planning; environment, solid waste management. *Unit head:* Dr. Eric Hildebrand, Director of Graduate Studies, 506-453-5113, Fax: 506-453-3568, E-mail: edh@unb.ca. *Application contact:* Joyce Moore, Graduate Secretary, 506-452-6127, Fax: 506-453-3568, E-mail: civil-grad@unb.ca. Web site: http://www.unbf.ca/eng/civil/.

University of Southern California, Graduate School, School of Policy, Planning, and Development, Master of Planning Program, Los Angeles, CA 90089. Offers sustainable cities (Graduate Certificate); transportation systems (Graduate Certificate); urban planning (M Pl); M Arch/M Pl; M Pl/MA; M Pl/MPP; M Pl/MRED; M Pl/MS; M Pl/MSW; MBA/M Pl; ML Arch/M Pl; MPA/M Pl. *Accreditation:* ACSP. Part-time programs available. *Degree requirements:* For master's, comprehensive exam, internship. *Entrance requirements:* For master's, GRE, GMAT. Additional exam requirements/recommendations for international students: Required—TOEFL (minimum score 600 paper-based; 250 computer-based; 100 iBT). Electronic applications accepted. *Faculty research:* Transportation and infrastructure, comparative international development, healthy communities, social economic development, sustainable community planning.

University of Southern California, Graduate School, Viterbi School of Engineering, Daniel J. Epstein Department of Industrial and Systems Engineering, Los Angeles, CA 90089. Offers digital supply chain management (MS); engineering management (MS); engineering technology communication (Graduate Certificate); health systems operations (Graduate Certificate); industrial and systems engineering (MS, PhD, Engr); manufacturing engineering (MS); operations research engineering (MS); optimization and supply chain management (Graduate Certificate); product development engineering (MS); safety systems and security (MS); systems architecting and engineering (MS, Graduate Certificate); systems safety and security (Graduate Certificate); transportation systems (Graduate Certificate); MS/MBA. Part-time and evening/weekend programs available. Postbaccalaureate distance learning degree programs offered (no on-campus study). Terminal master's awarded for partial completion of doctoral program. *Degree requirements:* For master's, thesis optional; for doctorate, thesis/dissertation. *Entrance requirements:* For master's and doctorate, GRE General Test. Additional exam requirements/recommendations for international students: Recommended—TOEFL. Electronic applications accepted. *Faculty research:* Health systems, music cognition and retrieval, transportation and logistics, manufacturing and automation, engineering systems design, risk and economic analysis.

University of Southern California, Graduate School, Viterbi School of Engineering, Sonny Astani Department of Civil Engineering, Los Angeles, CA 90089. Offers applied mechanics (MS); civil engineering (MS, PhD); computer-aided engineering (ME, Graduate Certificate); construction management (MCM); engineering technology commercialization (Graduate Certificate); environmental engineering (MS, PhD); environmental quality management (ME); structural design (ME); sustainable cities (Graduate Certificate); transportation systems (MS, Graduate Certificate); water and waste management (MS). Part-time and evening/weekend programs available. Terminal master's awarded for partial completion of doctoral program. *Degree requirements:* For master's, thesis optional; for doctorate, thesis/dissertation. *Entrance requirements:* For master's and doctorate, GRE General Test. Additional exam requirements/recommendations for international students: Recommended—TOEFL. Electronic applications accepted. *Faculty research:* Geotechnical engineering, transportation engineering, structural engineering, construction management, environmental engineering, water resources.

The University of Texas at Tyler, College of Engineering and Computer Science, Department of Civil Engineering, Tyler, TX 75799-0001. Offers environmental engineering (MS); industrial safety (MS); structural engineering (MS); transportation engineering (MS); water resources engineering (MS). Part-time and evening/weekend programs available. *Degree requirements:* For master's, thesis optional. *Entrance requirements:* For master's, GRE General Test, bachelor's degree in engineering, associated science degree. Additional exam requirements/recommendations for international students: Required—TOEFL (minimum score 79 computer-based). *Faculty research:* Non-destructive strength testing, indoor air quality, transportation routing and signaling, pavement replacement criteria, flood water routing, construction and long-term behavior of innovative geotechnical foundation and embankment construction used in highway construction, engineering education.

University of Washington, Graduate School, College of Engineering, Department of Civil and Environmental Engineering, Seattle, WA 98195-2700. Offers civil engineering (MS, MSE, PhD); construction engineering (MSCE); environmental engineering (MS, MSCE, MSE, PhD); global trade, transportation and logistics (MS); hydrology, water resources, and environmental fluid mechanics (MS, MSCE, MSE, PhD); structural and geotechnical engineering and mechanics (MS, MSCE, MSE, PhD); transportation and construction engineering (MS, MSE, PhD); transportation engineering (MSCE). Part-time programs available. Postbaccalaureate distance learning degree programs offered (no on-campus study). *Faculty:* 47 full-time (11 women), 9 part-time/adjunct (1 woman). *Students:* 195 full-time (67 women), 72 part-time (19 women); includes 37 minority (4 Black or African American, non-Hispanic/Latino; 27 Asian, non-Hispanic/Latino; 6 Hispanic/Latino), 65 international. 654 applicants, 57% accepted, 100 enrolled. In 2011, 88 master's, 7 doctorates awarded. Terminal master's awarded for partial completion of doctoral program. *Degree requirements:* For master's, thesis (for some programs); for doctorate, comprehensive exam, thesis/dissertation, general, qualifying, and final exams; completion of degree within 10 years. *Entrance requirements:* For master's,

GRE General Test, minimum GPA of 3.0, statement of purpose, letters of recommendation, transcripts; for doctorate, GRE General Test, minimum GPA of 3.5, statement of purpose, letters of recommendation, transcripts. Additional exam requirements/recommendations for international students: Required—TOEFL (minimum score 580 paper-based; 237 computer-based; 92 iBT); Recommended—IELTS (minimum score 7). *Application deadline:* For fall admission, 1/10 priority date for domestic students, 1/10 for international students. Applications are processed on a rolling basis. Application fee: $75. Electronic applications accepted. *Expenses:* Contact institution. *Financial support:* In 2011–12, 99 students received support, including 16 fellowships with full and partial tuition reimbursements available (averaging $16,173 per year), 71 research assistantships with full tuition reimbursements available (averaging $16,380 per year), 10 teaching assistantships with full tuition reimbursements available (averaging $16,380 per year); scholarships/grants also available. Financial award application deadline: 1/10; financial award applicants required to submit FAFSA. *Faculty research:* Environmental/water resources, hydrology; construction/transportation; structures/ geotechnical. *Total annual research expenditures:* $13.6 million. *Unit head:* Dr. Gregory R. Miller, Professor/Chair, 206-543-0350, Fax: 206-543-1543, E-mail: gmiller@uw.edu. *Application contact:* Lorna Latal, Graduate Adviser, 206-543-2574, Fax: 206-543-1543, E-mail: llatal@u.washington.edu. Web site: http://www.ce.washington.edu/programs/prospective/grad/applying/gen_admission.html.

Virginia Polytechnic Institute and State University, Graduate School, College of Engineering, Department of Civil and Environmental Engineering, Blacksburg, VA 24061. Offers civil engineering (M Eng, MS, PhD); civil infrastructure systems (Certificate); environmental engineering (MS); environmental sciences and engineering (MS); transportation systems engineering (Certificate); treatment process engineering (Certificate); urban hydrology and stormwater management (Certificate); water quality management (Certificate). *Accreditation:* ABET (one or more programs are accredited). *Degree requirements:* For master's, comprehensive exam (for some programs), thesis (for some programs); for doctorate, comprehensive exam (for some programs), thesis/dissertation (for some programs). *Entrance requirements:* For master's and doctorate, GRE. Additional exam requirements/recommendations for international students: Required—TOEFL (minimum score 550 paper-based; 213 computer-based). *Application deadline:* For fall admission, 7/1 for domestic and international students; for spring admission, 12/1 for domestic and international students. Applications are processed on a rolling basis. Application fee: $65. Electronic applications accepted. *Expenses:* Tuition, state resident: full-time $10,048; part-time $558.25 per credit hour. Tuition, nonresident: full-time $19,497; part-time $1083.25 per credit hour. *Required fees:* $405 per semester. Tuition and fees vary according to course load, campus/location and program. *Financial support:* Fellowships with full tuition reimbursements, research assistantships with full tuition reimbursements, teaching assistantships with full tuition reimbursements, career-related internships or fieldwork, Federal Work-Study, scholarships/grants, health care benefits, and unspecified assistantships available. Financial award application deadline: 1/15. *Faculty research:* Construction, environmental geotechnical hydrosystems, structures and transportation engineering. *Unit head:* Dr. Sam Easterling, Unit Head, 540-231-5143, Fax: 540-231-7532, E-mail: seaster@vt.edu. *Application contact:* Marc Widdowson, Information Contact, 540-231-7153, Fax: 540-231-7532, E-mail: mwiddows@vt.edu. Web site: http://www.cee.vt.edu/.

Virginia Polytechnic Institute and State University, VT Online, Blacksburg, VA 24061. Offers advanced transportation systems (Certificate); aerospace engineering (MS); agricultural and life sciences (MSLFS); business information systems (Graduate Certificate); career and technical education (MS); civil engineering (MS); computer engineering (M Eng, MS); decision support systems (Graduate Certificate); eLearning leadership (MA); electrical engineering (M Eng, MS); engineering administration (MEA); environmental engineering (Certificate); environmental politics and policy (Graduate Certificate); environmental sciences and engineering (MS); foundations of political analysis (Graduate Certificate); health product risk management (Graduate Certificate); industrial and systems engineering (MS); information policy and society (Graduate Certificate); information security (Graduate Certificate); information technology (MIT); instructional technology (MA); integrative STEM education (MA Ed); liberal arts (Graduate Certificate); life sciences: health product risk management (MS); natural resources (MNR, Graduate Certificate); networking (Graduate Certificate); nonprofit and nongovernmental organization management (Graduate Certificate); ocean engineering (MS); political science (MA); security studies (Graduate Certificate); software development (Graduate Certificate). *Expenses:* Tuition, state resident: full-time $10,048; part-time $558.25 per credit hour. Tuition, nonresident: full-time $19,497; part-time $1083.25 per credit hour. *Required fees:* $405 per semester. Tuition and fees vary according to course load, campus/location and program. *Application contact:* Graduate School Applications General Assistance, 540-231-8636, Fax: 540-231-2039, E-mail: gradappl@vt.edu. Web site: http://www.vto.vt.edu/.

Western Michigan University, Graduate College, College of Engineering and Applied Sciences, Department of Civil and Construction Engineering, Kalamazoo, MI 49008. Offers civil engineering (MS), including construction engineering and management, structural engineering, transportation engineering. *Entrance requirements:* For master's, minimum GPA of 3.0.

Water Resources Engineering

American University of Beirut, Graduate Programs, Faculty of Engineering and Architecture, Beirut, Lebanon. Offers applied energy (MME); civil engineering (ME, PhD); electrical and computer engineering (ME, PhD); engineering management (MEM); environmental and water resources (ME); environmental and water resources engineering (PhD); environmental technology (MSES); mechanical engineering (ME, PhD); urban design (MUD); urban planning and policy (MUP). Part-time programs available. *Faculty:* 53 full-time (8 women), 10 part-time/adjunct (2 women). *Students:* 290 full-time (101 women), 59 part-time (18 women). Average age 25. 336 applicants, 80% accepted, 83 enrolled. In 2011, 72 master's, 5 doctorates awarded. *Degree requirements:* For master's, one foreign language, comprehensive exam, thesis (for some programs); for doctorate, one foreign language, comprehensive exam, thesis/dissertation, publications. *Entrance requirements:* For master's, GRE (for electrical and computer engineering), letters of recommendation; for doctorate, GRE, letters of recommendation, master's degree, transcripts, curriculum vitae, interview. Additional exam requirements/recommendations for international students: Required—TOEFL (minimum score 600 paper-based; 250 computer-based; 100 iBT), IELTS (minimum score 7.5). *Application deadline:* For fall admission, 2/5 priority date for domestic students, 2/5 for international students; for spring admission, 11/1 priority date for domestic students, 11/1 for international students. Applications are processed on a rolling basis. Application fee: $50. Electronic applications accepted. *Expenses: Tuition:* Full-time $12,780; part-time $710 per credit. *Required fees:* $528; $528 per credit. Tuition and fees vary according to course load and program. *Financial support:* In 2011–12, 9 fellowships with full tuition reimbursements (averaging $24,800 per year), 33 research assistantships with full tuition reimbursements (averaging $24,800 per year), 74 teaching assistantships with full tuition reimbursements (averaging $9,800 per year) were awarded; career-related internships or fieldwork, institutionally sponsored loans, scholarships/grants, health care benefits, and unspecified assistantships also available. *Total annual research expenditures:* $1.1 million. *Unit head:* Prof. Makram T. Suidan, Dean, 961-135-0000 Ext. 3400, Fax: 961-174-4462, E-mail: msuidan@aub.edu.lb. *Application contact:* Dr. Salim Kanaan, Director, Admissions Office, 961-135-0000 Ext. 2594, Fax: 961-175-0775, E-mail: sk00@aub.edu.lb. Web site: http://staff.aub.edu.lb/~webfea.

Cornell University, Graduate School, Graduate Fields of Engineering, Field of Civil and Environmental Engineering, Ithaca, NY 14853-0001. Offers engineering management (M Eng, MS, PhD); environmental engineering (M Eng, MS, PhD); environmental fluid mechanics and hydrology (M Eng, MS, PhD); environmental systems engineering (M Eng, MS, PhD); geotechnical engineering (M Eng, MS, PhD); remote sensing (M Eng, MS, PhD); structural engineering (M Eng, MS, PhD); structural mechanics (M Eng, MS); transportation engineering (MS, PhD); transportation systems engineering (M Eng); water resource systems (M Eng, MS, PhD). *Faculty:* 39 full-time (4 women). *Students:* 143 full-time (49 women); includes 20 minority (6 Black or African American, non-Hispanic/Latino; 1 American Indian or Alaska Native, non-Hispanic/Latino; 9 Asian, non-Hispanic/Latino; 4 Hispanic/Latino), 72 international. Average age 25. 574 applicants, 47% accepted, 100 enrolled. In 2011, 88 master's, 13 doctorates awarded. Terminal master's awarded for partial completion of doctoral program. *Degree requirements:* For master's, thesis (MS); for doctorate, comprehensive exam, thesis/dissertation. *Entrance requirements:* For master's and doctorate, GRE General Test (recommended), 2 letters of recommendation. Additional exam requirements/recommendations for international students: Required—TOEFL (minimum score 600 paper-based; 250 computer-based; 77 iBT). *Application deadline:* For fall admission, 1/15 priority date for domestic students; for spring admission, 10/15 for domestic students. Application fee: $95. Electronic applications accepted. *Financial support:* In 2011–12, 50 students received support, including 20 fellowships with full tuition reimbursements available, 27 research assistantships with full tuition reimbursements available, 17 teaching assistantships with full tuition reimbursements available; institutionally sponsored loans, scholarships/grants, health care benefits, tuition waivers (full and partial), and unspecified assistantships also available. Financial award applicants required to submit FAFSA. *Faculty research:* Environmental engineering, geotechnical engineering, remote sensing, environmental fluid mechanics and hydrology, structural engineering. *Unit head:* Director of Graduate Studies, 607-255-7560, Fax: 607-255-9004. *Application contact:* Graduate Field Assistant, 607-255-7560, Fax: 607-255-9004, E-mail: cee_grad@cornell.edu. Web site: http://www.gradschool.cornell.edu/fields.php?id-27&a-2.

George Mason University, Volgenau School of Engineering, Department of Civil, Environmental, and Infrastructure Engineering, Fairfax, VA 22030. Offers civil and infrastructure engineering (MS, PhD); civil infrastructure and security engineering (Certificate); leading technical enterprises (Certificate); sustainability and the environment (Certificate); water resources engineering (Certificate). *Faculty:* 9 full-time (3 women), 22 part-time/adjunct (3 women). *Students:* 26 full-time (9 women), 59 part-time (14 women); includes 18 minority (5 Black or African American, non-Hispanic/Latino; 5 Asian, non-Hispanic/Latino; 7 Hispanic/Latino; 1 Two or more races, non-Hispanic/Latino), 10 international. Average age 31. 73 applicants, 63% accepted, 29 enrolled. In 2011, 16 master's, 7 other advanced degrees awarded. *Degree requirements:* For master's, thesis (for some programs), 30 credits, departmental seminars; for doctorate, thesis/dissertation, qualifying exams. *Entrance requirements:* For master's, GRE, photocopy of passport; 2 official college transcripts; resume; official bank statement; proof of financial support; expanded goals statement; self-evaluation form; BS in engineering or other related science; 3 letters of recommendation; for doctorate, GRE (for those who received degree outside of the U.S.), photocopy of passport; 2 official college transcripts; resume; official bank statement; proof of financial support; expanded goals statement; self-evaluation form; baccalaureate degree in engineering or related science; master's degree (preferred); 3 letters of recommendation; for Certificate, BS in related field; photocopy of passport; 2 official college transcripts; resume; official bank statement; proof of financial support; expanded goals statement; self evaluation form; 3 letters of recommendation. Additional exam requirements/recommendations for international students: Required—TOEFL (minimum score 575 paper-based; 230 computer-based; 88 iBT), IELTS, Pearson Test of English. *Application deadline:* For fall admission, 1/15 priority date for domestic students; for spring admission, 8/1 priority date for domestic students. Application fee: $65 ($80 for international students). Electronic applications accepted. *Expenses:* Tuition, state resident: full-time $8750; part-time $364.58 per credit. Tuition, nonresident: full-time $24,092; part-time $1003.83 per credit. *Required fees:* $2514; $104.75 per credit. *Financial support:* In 2011–12, 17 students received support, including 3 fellowships (averaging $18,000 per year), 2 research assistantships with full and partial tuition reimbursements available (averaging $17,893 per year), 12 teaching assistantships with full and partial tuition reimbursements available (averaging $8,884 per year); career-related internships or fieldwork, Federal Work-Study, scholarships/grants, unspecified assistantships, and health care benefits (full-time research or teaching assistantship recipients) also available. Support available to part-time students. Financial award application deadline: 3/1; financial award applicants required to submit FAFSA. *Faculty research:* Evolutionary design, infrastructure security, intelligent transportation systems, national transportation networks, water quality modeling. *Total annual research expenditures:* $655,402. *Unit head:* Dr. Deborah J. Goodings, Chair, 703-993-1675, Fax: 703-993-9790, E-mail: goodings@gmu.edu. *Application contact:* Nicole Jerome, Administrative Assistant, 703-993-1675, Fax: 703-993-9790, E-mail: njerome@gmu.edu. Web site: http://civil.gmu.edu/.

Indiana University Bloomington, School of Public and Environmental Affairs, Environmental Science Programs, Bloomington, IN 47405. Offers applied ecology

(MSES); energy (MSES); environmental chemistry, toxicology, and risk assessment (MSES); environmental science (PhD); specialized environmental science (MSES); water resources (MSES); JD/MSES; MSES/MPA; MSES/MS. Part-time programs available. *Faculty:* 80 full-time (30 women), 102 part-time/adjunct (43 women). *Students:* 142 full-time, 6 part-time; includes 8 minority (2 Black or African American, non-Hispanic/Latino; 5 Asian, non-Hispanic/Latino; 1 Hispanic/Latino), 18 international. Average age 24. 152 applicants, 57 enrolled. In 2011, 58 master's, 2 doctorates awarded. Terminal master's awarded for partial completion of doctoral program. *Degree requirements:* For master's, core classes; capstone or thesis; internship; for doctorate, comprehensive exam, thesis/dissertation. *Entrance requirements:* For master's, GRE General Test or GMAT, official transcripts, 3 letters of recommendation, resume, personal statement; for doctorate, GRE General Test or LSAT, official transcripts, 3 letters of recommendation, resume or curriculum vitae, statement of purpose. Additional exam requirements/recommendations for international students: Required—TOEFL (minimum score 600 paper-based; 96 iBT); Recommended—IELTS (minimum score 7). *Application deadline:* For fall admission, 2/1 priority date for domestic students, 12/1 for international students. Applications are processed on a rolling basis. Application fee: $55 ($65 for international students). Electronic applications accepted. *Financial support:* Fellowships with partial tuition reimbursements, research assistantships with partial tuition reimbursements, teaching assistantships with partial tuition reimbursements, career-related internships or fieldwork, Federal Work-Study, scholarships/grants, health care benefits, unspecified assistantships, and Service Corps programs available. Financial award application deadline: 2/1; financial award applicants required to submit FAFSA. *Faculty research:* Applied ecology, bio-geo chemistry, toxicology, wetlands ecology, environmental microbiology, forest ecology, environmental chemistry. *Unit head:* Jennifer J. Forney, Director, Graduate Student Services, 812-855-9485, Fax: 812-856-3665, E-mail: speampo@indiana.edu. *Application contact:* Admissions Assistant, 812-855-2840, Fax: 812-856-3665, E-mail: speaapps@indiana.edu. Web site: http://www.indiana.edu/~spea/prospective_students/masters/.

Louisiana State University and Agricultural and Mechanical College, Graduate School, College of Engineering, Department of Civil and Environmental Engineering, Baton Rouge, LA 70803. Offers environmental engineering (MSCE, PhD); geotechnical engineering (MSCE, PhD); structural engineering and mechanics (MSCE, PhD); transportation engineering (MSCE, PhD); water resources (MSCE, PhD). Part-time programs available. *Faculty:* 25 full-time (2 women). *Students:* 90 full-time (23 women), 34 part-time (8 women); includes 11 minority (4 Black or African American, non-Hispanic/Latino; 1 American Indian or Alaska Native, non-Hispanic/Latino; 4 Asian, non-Hispanic/Latino; 2 Hispanic/Latino), 73 international. Average age 30. 106 applicants, 67% accepted, 25 enrolled. In 2011, 32 master's, 4 doctorates awarded. *Degree requirements:* For master's, thesis optional; for doctorate, one foreign language, thesis/dissertation. *Entrance requirements:* For master's and doctorate, GRE General Test, minimum GPA of 3.0. Additional exam requirements/recommendations for international students: Required—TOEFL (minimum score 550 paper-based; 213 computer-based; 79 iBT) or IELTS (minimum score 6.5). *Application deadline:* For fall admission, 1/25 priority date for domestic students, 5/15 for international students; for spring admission, 10/15 for international students. Applications are processed on a rolling basis. Application fee: $50 ($70 for international students). Electronic applications accepted. *Financial support:* In 2011–12, 91 students received support, including 3 fellowships with full and partial tuition reimbursements available (averaging $18,050 per year), 72 research assistantships with full and partial tuition reimbursements available (averaging $15,942 per year), 6 teaching assistantships with full and partial tuition reimbursements available (averaging $12,469 per year); career-related internships or fieldwork, institutionally sponsored loans, scholarships/grants, and health care benefits also available. Financial award application deadline: 3/1; financial award applicants required to submit FAFSA. *Faculty research:* Mechanics and structures, environmental, geotechnical transportation, water resources. *Total annual research expenditures:* $3 million. *Unit head:* Dr. George Z. Voyiadjis, Chair/Professor, 225-578-8668, Fax: 225-578-9176, E-mail: voyiadjis@lsu.edu. *Application contact:* Dr. Clinton Willson, Professor, 225-578-8672, E-mail: cwillson@lsu.edu. Web site: http://www.cee.lsu.edu/.

Marquette University, Graduate School, College of Engineering, Department of Civil and Environmental Engineering, Milwaukee, WI 53201-1881. Offers construction and public works management (MS, PhD); construction engineering and management (Certificate); environmental/water resources engineering (MS, PhD); structural design (Certificate); structural/geotechnical engineering (MS, PhD); transportation planning and engineering (MS, PhD); waste and wastewater treatment processes (Certificate). Part-time and evening/weekend programs available. *Faculty:* 13 full-time (0 women), 5 part-time/adjunct (0 women). *Students:* 26 full-time (5 women), 11 part-time (0 women); includes 2 minority (1 Black or African American, non-Hispanic/Latino; 1 Asian, non-Hispanic/Latino), 12 international. Average age 27. 74 applicants, 62% accepted, 9 enrolled. In 2011, 6 master's, 3 doctorates awarded. Terminal master's awarded for partial completion of doctoral program. *Degree requirements:* For master's, comprehensive exam (for some programs), thesis or alternative; for doctorate, thesis/dissertation. *Entrance requirements:* For master's, GRE General Test (recommended), minimum GPA of 3.0, official transcripts from all current and previous colleges/universities except Marquette, three letters of recommendation; for doctorate, GRE General Test, minimum GPA of 3.0, official transcripts from all current and previous colleges/universities except Marquette, three letters of recommendation, brief statement of purpose, submission of any English language publications authored by applicant (strongly recommended). Additional exam requirements/recommendations for international students: Required—TOEFL (minimum score 530 paper-based; 78 computer-based). *Application deadline:* For fall admission, 6/1 priority date for domestic students. Applications are processed on a rolling basis. Application fee: $50. Electronic applications accepted. *Expenses: Tuition:* Full-time $17,010; part-time $945 per credit hour. Tuition and fees vary according to program. *Financial support:* In 2011–12, 21 students received support, including 6 fellowships with partial tuition reimbursements available (averaging $9,177 per year), 1 research assistantship with full tuition reimbursement available (averaging $13,745 per year), 7 teaching assistantships with full tuition reimbursements available (averaging $13,902 per year); scholarships/grants, health care benefits, tuition waivers (partial), and unspecified assistantships also available. Support available to part-time students. Financial award application deadline: 2/15. *Faculty research:* Highway safety, highway performance, and intelligent transportation systems; surface mount technology; watershed management. *Total annual research expenditures:* $826,608. *Unit head:* Dr. Thomas Wenzel, Chair, 414-288-7030, Fax: 414-288-7521, E-mail: thomas.wenzel@marquette.edu. *Application contact:* Dr. Stephen M. Heinrich, Director of Graduate Studies, 414-288-5466, E-mail: stephen.heinrich@marquette.edu. Web site: http://www.marquette.edu/engineering/pages/AllYouNeed/Civil_Environmental/civil.html.

Massachusetts Institute of Technology, School of Engineering, Department of Civil and Environmental Engineering, Cambridge, MA 02139. Offers biological oceanography (PhD, Sc D); chemical oceanography (PhD, Sc D); civil and environmental engineering (PhD, Sc D); civil and environmental systems (PhD, Sc D); civil engineering (PhD, Sc D, CE); coastal engineering (PhD, Sc D); construction engineering and management (PhD, Sc D); environmental and water quality engineering (M Eng); environmental biology (PhD, Sc D); environmental chemistry (PhD, Sc D); environmental engineering (PhD, Sc D); environmental fluid mechanics (PhD, Sc D); environmental science and engineering (SM); geotechnical and geoenvironmental engineering (PhD, Sc D); geotechnology (M Eng); high-performance structures (M Eng); hydrology (PhD, Sc D); information technology (PhD, Sc D); mechanics (SM); oceanographic engineering (PhD, Sc D); structures and materials (PhD, Sc D); transportation (M Eng, PhD, Sc D); SM/MBA. *Faculty:* 35 full-time (6 women), 1 part-time/adjunct (0 women). *Students:* 216 full-time (80 women); includes 30 minority (4 Black or African American, non-Hispanic/Latino; 13 Asian, non-Hispanic/Latino; 8 Hispanic/Latino; 5 Two or more races, non-Hispanic/Latino), 110 international. Average age 27. 589 applicants, 26% accepted, 91 enrolled. In 2011, 62 master's, 14 doctorates awarded. *Degree requirements:* For master's and CE, thesis; for doctorate, comprehensive exam, thesis/dissertation. *Entrance requirements:* For master's and doctorate, GRE General Test. Additional exam requirements/recommendations for international students: Required—TOEFL (minimum score 577 paper-based; 233 computer-based; 90 iBT), IELTS (minimum score 7). *Application deadline:* For fall admission, 12/15 for domestic and international students. Application fee: $75. Electronic applications accepted. *Expenses: Tuition:* Full-time $40,460; part-time $630 per credit hour. *Required fees:* $272. *Financial support:* In 2011–12, 180 students received support, including 51 fellowships (averaging $30,800 per year), 110 research assistantships (averaging $29,500 per year), 19 teaching assistantships (averaging $29,500 per year); career-related internships or fieldwork, Federal Work-Study, institutionally sponsored loans, scholarships/grants, health care benefits, and unspecified assistantships also available. *Faculty research:* Environmental chemistry, environmental fluid mechanics and coastal engineering, environmental microbiology, geotechnical engineering and geomechanics, hydrology and hydroclimatology, infrastructure systems, mechanics of materials and structures, transportation systems. *Total annual research expenditures:* $17.7 million. *Unit head:* Prof. Andrew Whittle, Head, 617-253-7101. *Application contact:* Patricia Glidden, Graduate Admissions Coordinator, 617-253-7119, Fax: 617-258-6775, E-mail: cee-admissions@mit.edu. Web site: http://cee.mit.edu/.

McGill University, Faculty of Graduate and Postdoctoral Studies, Faculty of Engineering, Department of Civil Engineering and Applied Mechanics, Montréal, QC H3A 2T5, Canada. Offers environmental engineering (M Eng, M Sc, PhD); fluid mechanics (M Sc); fluid mechanics and hydraulic engineering (M Eng, PhD); materials engineering (M Eng, PhD); rehabilitation of urban infrastructure (M Eng, PhD); soil behavior (M Eng, PhD); soil mechanics and foundations (M Eng, PhD); structures and structural mechanics (M Eng, PhD); water resources (M Sc); water resources engineering (M Eng, PhD).

New Mexico Institute of Mining and Technology, Graduate Studies, Department of Civil and Environmental Engineering, Socorro, NM 87801. Offers environmental engineering (MS), including air quality engineering and science, hazardous waste engineering, water quality engineering and science. *Faculty:* 6 full-time (2 women), 2 part-time/adjunct (0 women). *Students:* 6 full-time (3 women); includes 3 minority (1 Black or African American, non-Hispanic/Latino; 1 American Indian or Alaska Native, non-Hispanic/Latino; 1 Hispanic/Latino). Average age 27. 14 applicants, 50% accepted, 3 enrolled. In 2011, 3 master's awarded. *Degree requirements:* For master's, thesis. *Entrance requirements:* For master's, GRE General Test. Additional exam requirements/recommendations for international students: Required—TOEFL (minimum score 540 paper-based; 207 computer-based). *Application deadline:* For fall admission, 3/1 priority date for domestic students; for spring admission, 6/1 for domestic students. Applications are processed on a rolling basis. Application fee: $16 ($30 for international students). *Expenses:* Tuition, state resident: full-time $4849; part-time $269.41 per credit hour. Tuition, nonresident: full-time $16,041; part-time $891.15 per credit hour. *Required fees:* $622; $65 per credit hour. $20 per semester. Part-time tuition and fees vary according to course load. *Financial support:* In 2011–12, 1 fellowship (averaging $7,200 per year), 3 research assistantships (averaging $10,958 per year), 4 teaching assistantships with full and partial tuition reimbursements (averaging $9,350 per year) were awarded; Federal Work-Study, institutionally sponsored loans, and unspecified assistantships also available. Financial award application deadline: 3/1; financial award applicants required to submit CSS PROFILE or FAFSA. *Faculty research:* Air quality, hazardous waste management, wastewater management and treatment, site remediation. *Unit head:* Dr. Mark Cal, Chair, 575-835-5059, Fax: 575-835-5252, E-mail: mcal@nmt.edu. *Application contact:* Dr. Lorie Liebrock, Dean of Graduate Studies, 575-835-5513, Fax: 575-835-5476, E-mail: graduate@nmt.edu. Web site: http://www.nmt.edu/~enve/.

Norwich University, College of Graduate and Continuing Studies, Master of Civil Engineering Program, Northfield, VT 05663. Offers construction management (MCE); environmental water resources (MCE); geo-technical (MCE); structural (MCE). Evening/weekend programs available. *Faculty:* 12 part-time/adjunct (1 woman). *Students:* 88 full-time (23 women); includes 15 minority (8 Black or African American, non-Hispanic/Latino; 1 American Indian or Alaska Native, non-Hispanic/Latino; 4 Asian, non-Hispanic/Latino; 2 Hispanic/Latino). Average age 33. In 2011, 44 master's awarded. *Entrance requirements:* For master's, minimum GPA of 2.75. Additional exam requirements/recommendations for international students: Required—TOEFL (minimum score 550 paper-based; 213 computer-based; 83 iBT). *Application deadline:* For fall admission, 8/10 for domestic and international students; for spring admission, 2/6 for domestic and international students. Applications are processed on a rolling basis. Application fee: $50. Electronic applications accepted. *Expenses: Tuition:* Full-time $16,174. *Required fees:* $2130. Full-time tuition and fees vary according to program. *Financial support:* In 2011–12, 5 students received support. Scholarships/grants available. Financial award applicants required to submit FAFSA. *Unit head:* Dr. Thomas Descoteaux, Program Director, 802-485-2730, Fax: 802-485-2533, E-mail: tdescote@norwich.edu. *Application contact:* Rija Ramahatra, Associate Program Director, 802-485-2892, Fax: 802-485-2533, E-mail: ramahatr@norwich.edu. Web site: http://mce.norwich.edu.

Ohio University, Graduate College, Russ College of Engineering and Technology, Department of Civil Engineering, Athens, OH 45701-2979. Offers civil engineering (PhD); construction (MS); environmental (MS); geotechnical and geoenvironmental (MS); mechanics (MS); structures (MS); transportation (MS); water resources and structures (MS). Part-time programs available. *Students:* 32 full-time (6 women), 7 part-time (2 women); includes 3 minority (1 Hispanic/Latino; 2 Two or more races, non-Hispanic/Latino), 13 international. 52 applicants, 52% accepted, 4 enrolled. In 2011, 10 degrees awarded. *Degree requirements:* For master's, comprehensive exam (for some programs), thesis or alternative; for doctorate, comprehensive exam, thesis/dissertation. *Entrance requirements:* For master's, GRE General Test, minimum GPA of 3.0, 3 letters of recommendation; for doctorate, GRE General Test. Additional exam requirements/recommendations for international students: Required—TOEFL (minimum score 550 paper-based; 80 iBT) or IELTS (minimum score 6.5). *Application deadline:* For fall admission, 5/1 priority date for domestic students, 2/1 for international students; for winter admission, 8/1 priority date for domestic students, 4/1 for international students; for spring admission, 2/1 priority date for domestic students, 7/1 for international students. Applications are processed on a rolling basis. Application fee: $50 ($55 for international students). Electronic applications accepted. *Financial support:* Research assistantships with full tuition reimbursements, teaching assistantships with full tuition reimbursements, Federal Work-Study, institutionally sponsored loans, scholarships/grants, and unspecified assistantships available. Financial award application deadline: 3/15; financial award applicants required to submit FAFSA. *Faculty research:* Noise abatement, materials and environment, highway infrastructure, subsurface investigation (pavements, pipes, bridges). *Unit head:* Dr. Gayle F. Mitchell, Chair, 740-593-0430, Fax: 740-593-0625, E-mail: mitchelg@ohio.edu. *Application contact:* Dr. Shad M. Sargand, Graduate Chair, 740-593-1465, Fax: 740-593-0625, E-mail: sargand@ohio.edu. Web site: http://www.ohio.edu/civil/.

Oregon State University, Graduate School, College of Engineering, Department of Biological and Ecological Engineering, Corvallis, OR 97331. Offers M Eng, MS, PhD. Terminal master's awarded for partial completion of doctoral program. *Degree requirements:* For master's, thesis or alternative; for doctorate, thesis/dissertation. *Entrance requirements:* For master's and doctorate, minimum GPA of 3.0 in last 90 hours. Additional exam requirements/recommendations for international students: Required—TOEFL (minimum score 550 paper-based; 213 computer-based). *Expenses:* Contact institution. *Faculty research:* Bioengineering, water resources engineering, food engineering, cell culture and fermentation, vadose zone transport.

Oregon State University, Graduate School, College of Engineering, School of Civil and Construction Engineering, Corvallis, OR 97331. Offers civil engineering (MS, PhD); coastal and ocean engineering (M Oc E, PhD); coastal engineering (MS); construction engineering management (MBE, PhD); engineering .(M Eng, MAIS); geotechnical engineering (MS, PhD); structural engineering (MS, PhD); transportation engineering (MS, PhD); water engineering (MS, PhD). Part-time programs available. Terminal master's awarded for partial completion of doctoral program. *Degree requirements:* For master's, thesis or alternative; for doctorate, one foreign language, thesis/dissertation. *Entrance requirements:* For master's, GRE General Test, minimum GPA of 3.0 in last 90 hours (3.5 for MS); for doctorate, GRE General Test, minimum GPA of 3.0 in last 90 hours of undergraduate course work. Additional exam requirements/recommendations for international students: Required—TOEFL (minimum score 580 paper-based; 237 computer-based). *Faculty research:* Hazardous waste management, carbon cycling, wave forces on structures, pavement design, seismic analysis.

Oregon State University, Graduate School, Program in Water Resources Engineering, Corvallis, OR 97331. Offers MS, PhD.

State University of New York College of Environmental Science and Forestry, Department of Environmental Resources Engineering, Syracuse, NY 13210-2779. Offers ecological engineering (MS, PhD); environmental and resources engineering (MPS, MS, PhD); environmental management (MPS); geospatial information science and engineering (MS, PhD); mapping sciences (MPS); water resources engineering (MS, PhD). *Degree requirements:* For master's, thesis (for some programs); for doctorate, comprehensive exam, thesis/dissertation. *Entrance requirements:* For master's and doctorate, GRE General Test, minimum GPA of 3.0. Additional exam requirements/recommendations for international students: Required—TOEFL (minimum score 550 paper-based; 213 computer-based; 80 iBT), IELTS (minimum score 6). *Application deadline:* For fall admission, 2/1 priority date for domestic students, 2/1 for international students; for spring admission, 11/1 priority date for domestic students, 11/1 for international students. Applications are processed on a rolling basis. Application fee: $60. *Expenses:* Tuition, state resident: full-time $8870; part-time $370 per credit hour. Tuition, nonresident: full-time $15,160; part-time $632 per credit hour. *Required fees:* $60; $370 per credit hour. $350 per semester. One-time fee: $85. *Financial support:* Fellowships with full and partial tuition reimbursements, research assistantships with full and partial tuition reimbursements, teaching assistantships with full and partial tuition reimbursements, Federal Work-Study, institutionally sponsored loans, scholarships/grants, health care benefits, and unspecified assistantships available. Financial award application deadline: 6/30; financial award applicants required to submit FAFSA. *Faculty research:* Forest engineering, paper science and engineering, wood products engineering. *Total annual research expenditures:* $968,412. *Unit head:* Dr. Theodore Endreny, Chair, 315-470-6565, Fax: 315-470-6958, E-mail: te@esf.edu. *Application contact:* Dr. Dudley J. Raynal, Dean, Instruction and Graduate Studies, 315-470-6599, Fax: 315-470-6978, E-mail: esfgrad@esf.edu. Web site: http://www.esf.edu/ere.

Stevens Institute of Technology, Graduate School, Charles V. Schaefer Jr. School of Engineering, Department of Civil, Environmental, and Ocean Engineering, Program in Civil Engineering, Hoboken, NJ 07030. Offers civil engineering (PhD); geotechnical engineering (Certificate); geotechnical/geoenvironmental engineering (M Eng, Engr); hydrologic modeling (M Eng); stormwater management (M Eng); structural engineering (M Eng, Engr); water resources engineering (M Eng). *Degree requirements:* For master's, thesis optional; for doctorate, variable foreign language requirement, thesis/dissertation; for other advanced degree, project or thesis. *Entrance requirements:* For doctorate, GRE. Additional exam requirements/recommendations for international students: Required—TOEFL. Electronic applications accepted.

Texas A&M University, College of Engineering, Zachry Department of Civil Engineering, College Station, TX 77843. Offers coastal and ocean engineering (M Eng, MS, D Eng, PhD); construction engineering and management (M Eng, MS, D Eng, PhD); environmental engineering (M Eng, MS, D Eng, PhD); geotechnical engineering (M Eng, MS, D Eng, PhD); materials engineering (M Eng, MS, D Eng, PhD); structural engineering (M Eng, MS, D Eng, PhD); transportation engineering (M Eng, MS, D Eng, PhD); water resources engineering (M Eng, MS, D Eng, PhD). Part-time programs available. *Faculty:* 57. *Students:* 361 full-time (76 women), 46 part-time (8 women); includes 41 minority (3 Black or African American, non-Hispanic/Latino; 16 Asian, non-Hispanic/Latino; 21 Hispanic/Latino; 1 Two or more races, non-Hispanic/Latino), 247 international. Average age 29. In 2011, 123 master's, 27 doctorates awarded. *Degree requirements:* For master's, thesis (MS); for doctorate, dissertation (PhD), internship (D Eng). *Entrance requirements:* For master's and doctorate, GRE General Test. Additional exam requirements/recommendations for international students: Required—TOEFL. *Application deadline:* Applications are processed on a rolling basis. Application fee: $50 ($75 for international students). Electronic applications accepted. *Expenses:* Tuition, state resident: full-time $5437; part-time $226.55 per credit hour. Tuition, nonresident: full-time $12,949; part-time $539.55 per credit hour. *Required fees:* $2741. *Financial support:* In 2011–12, fellowships (averaging $4,500 per year), research assistantships (averaging $14,000 per year), teaching assistantships (averaging $14,400 per year) were awarded; career-related internships or fieldwork and institutionally sponsored loans also available. Financial award application deadline: 4/15; financial award applicants required to submit FAFSA. *Unit head:* Dr. John Niedzwecki, Head, 979-845-3858, E-mail: j-niedzwecki@tamu.edu. *Application contact:* Graduate Advisor, 979-845-

7435, Fax: 979-845-6156, E-mail: info@civil.tamu.edu. Web site: https://www.civil.tamu.edu/.

Tufts University, School of Engineering, Department of Civil and Environmental Engineering, Medford, MA 02155. Offers bioengineering (ME, MS), including environmental technology; civil engineering (ME, MS, PhD), including geotechnical engineering, structural engineering, water diplomacy (PhD); environmental engineering (ME, MS, PhD), including environmental engineering and environmental sciences, environmental geotechnology, environmental health, environmental science and management, hazardous materials management, water diplomacy (PhD), water resources engineering. Part-time programs available. *Faculty:* 18 full-time, 5 part-time/adjunct. *Students:* 102 full-time (50 women); includes 8 minority (1 Black or African American, non-Hispanic/Latino; 6 Asian, non-Hispanic/Latino; 1 Hispanic/Latino), 37 international. Average age 27. 162 applicants, 59% accepted, 37 enrolled. In 2011, 18 degrees awarded. Terminal master's awarded for partial completion of doctoral program. *Degree requirements:* For master's, thesis or alternative; for doctorate, thesis/dissertation. *Entrance requirements:* For master's and doctorate, GRE General Test. Additional exam requirements/recommendations for international students: Required—TOEFL (minimum score 550 paper-based; 213 computer-based; 80 iBT). *Application deadline:* For fall admission, 1/15 priority date for domestic students, 12/15 for international students; for spring admission, 10/15 for domestic students, 9/15 for international students. Applications are processed on a rolling basis. Application fee: $75. Electronic applications accepted. *Expenses: Tuition:* Full-time $41,208; part-time $1030 per credit hour. Full-time tuition and fees vary according to degree level, program and student level. Part-time tuition and fees vary according to course load. *Financial support:* Fellowships with full tuition reimbursements, research assistantships with full and partial tuition reimbursements, teaching assistantships with full and partial tuition reimbursements, Federal Work-Study, scholarships/grants, tuition waivers (partial), and unspecified assistantships available. Financial award application deadline: 1/15; financial award applicants required to submit FAFSA. *Faculty research:* Environmental and water resources engineering, environmental health, geotechnical and geoenvironmental engineering, structural engineering and mechanics, water diplomacy. *Unit head:* Dr. Kurt Penell, Chair, 617-627-3211, Fax: 617-627-3994. *Application contact:* Laura Sacco, Information Contact, 617-627-3211, E-mail: ceeinfo@tufts.edu. Web site: http://www.ase.tufts.edu/cee/.

The University of Alabama in Huntsville, School of Graduate Studies, College of Engineering, Department of Civil and Environmental Engineering, Huntsville, AL 35899. Offers civil and environmental engineering (PhD); civil engineering (MSE), including civil engineering, environmental and water resource engineering, geotechnical engineering, structural engineering and structural mechanics, transportation engineering. PhD offered jointly with The University of Alabama at Birmingham. Part-time and evening/weekend programs available. *Faculty:* 5 full-time (1 woman), 1 part-time/adjunct (0 women). *Students:* 20 full-time (4 women), 12 part-time (6 women); includes 1 minority (Black or African American, non-Hispanic/Latino), 15 international. Average age 29. 26 applicants, 62% accepted, 6 enrolled. In 2011, 3 master's, 1 doctorate awarded. *Degree requirements:* For master's, comprehensive exam, thesis or alternative, oral and written exams; for doctorate, comprehensive exam, thesis/dissertation, oral and written exams. *Entrance requirements:* For master's, GRE General Test, BSE, minimum GPA of 3.0; for doctorate, GRE General Test, minimum GPA of 3.0. Additional exam requirements/recommendations for international students: Required—TOEFL (minimum score 500 paper-based; 173 computer-based; 62 iBT). *Application deadline:* For fall admission, 7/15 for domestic students, 4/1 for international students; for spring admission, 11/30 for domestic students, 9/1 for international students. Applications are processed on a rolling basis. Application fee: $40 ($50 for international students). Electronic applications accepted. *Expenses:* Tuition, state resident: full-time $7830; part-time $473.50 per credit. Tuition, nonresident: full-time $18,748; part-time $1128.33 per credit. Tuition and fees vary according to course load and program. *Financial support:* In 2011–12, 16 students received support, including 10 research assistantships with full and partial tuition reimbursements available (averaging $12,281 per year), 6 teaching assistantships with full and partial tuition reimbursements available (averaging $12,472 per year); career-related internships or fieldwork, Federal Work-Study, institutionally sponsored loans, scholarships/grants, health care benefits, and unspecified assistantships also available. Support available to part-time students. Financial award application deadline: 4/1; financial award applicants required to submit FAFSA. *Faculty research:* Hydrologic modeling, orbital debris impact, hydrogeology, environmental engineering, transportation engineering. *Total annual research expenditures:* $1.1 million. *Unit head:* Dr. Houssam Toutanji, Chair, 256-824-7361, Fax: 256-824-6724, E-mail: toutanji@cee.uah.edu. *Application contact:* Kim Gray, Graduate Studies Admissions Coordinator, 256-824-6002, Fax: 256-824-6405, E-mail: deangrad@uah.edu. Web site: http://www.uah.edu/eng/departments/cee/welcome.

University of Alberta, Faculty of Graduate Studies and Research, Department of Civil and Environmental Engineering, Edmonton, AB T6G 2E1, Canada. Offers construction engineering and management (M Eng, M Sc, PhD); environmental engineering (M Eng, M Sc, PhD); environmental science (M Sc, PhD); geoenvironmental engineering (M Eng, M Sc, PhD); geotechnical engineering (M Eng, M Sc, PhD); mining engineering (M Eng, M Sc, PhD); petroleum engineering (M Eng, M Sc, PhD); structural engineering (M Eng, M Sc, PhD); water resources (M Eng, M Sc, PhD). Part-time programs available. Postbaccalaureate distance learning degree programs offered (minimal on-campus study). *Degree requirements:* For master's, thesis (for some programs); for doctorate, thesis/dissertation. *Entrance requirements:* For master's, minimum GPA of 3.0 in last 2 years of undergraduate studies; for doctorate, minimum GPA of 3.0. Additional exam requirements/recommendations for international students: Required—TOEFL (minimum score 550 paper-based; 213 computer-based). Electronic applications accepted. *Faculty research:* Mining.

University of California, Berkeley, Graduate Division, College of Engineering, Department of Civil and Environmental Engineering, Berkeley, CA 94720-1500. Offers engineering and project management (M Eng, MS, D Eng, PhD); environmental engineering (M Eng, MS, D Eng, PhD); geoengineering (M Eng, MS, D Eng, PhD); structural engineering, mechanics and materials (M Eng, MS, D Eng, PhD); transportation engineering (M Eng, MS, D Eng, PhD); M Arch/MS; MCP/MS; MPP/MS. *Degree requirements:* For master's, comprehensive exam or thesis (MS); for doctorate, thesis/dissertation, qualifying exam. *Entrance requirements:* For master's, GRE General Test, minimum GPA of 3.0, 3 letters of recommendation; for doctorate, GRE General Test, minimum GPA of 3.5, 3 letters of recommendation. Additional exam requirements/recommendations for international students: Required—TOEFL (minimum score 570 paper-based; 230 computer-based). Electronic applications accepted.

University of Colorado Boulder, Graduate School, College of Engineering and Applied Science, Department of Civil, Environmental, and Architectural Engineering, Boulder, CO 80309. Offers building systems (MS, PhD); construction engineering management (MS, PhD); environmental engineering (MS, PhD); geotechnical engineering and geomechanics (MS, PhD); hydrology, water resources and environmental fluid mechanics (MS, PhD); structural engineering and structural mechanics (MS, PhD). *Faculty:* 37 full-time (8 women). *Students:* 245 full-time (90 women), 53 part-time (15 women); includes 37 minority (1 Black or African American, non-Hispanic/Latino; 2 American Indian or Alaska Native, non-Hispanic/Latino; 15 Asian, non-Hispanic/Latino; 17 Hispanic/Latino; 2 Two or more races, non-Hispanic/Latino), 56 international. Average age 27. 483 applicants, 58% accepted, 83 enrolled. In 2011, 84 master's, 15 doctorates awarded. Terminal master's awarded for partial completion of doctoral program. *Degree requirements:* For master's, comprehensive exam, thesis or alternative; for doctorate, thesis/dissertation. *Entrance requirements:* For master's, GRE General Test, minimum undergraduate GPA of 3.0. *Application deadline:* For fall admission, 3/1 for domestic students, 12/1 for international students; for spring admission, 10/31 for domestic students, 10/1 for international students. Application fee: $50 ($60 for international students). Electronic applications accepted. *Financial support:* In 2011–12, 167 students received support, including 69 fellowships (averaging $12,440 per year), 62 research assistantships with full and partial tuition reimbursements available (averaging $21,979 per year), 20 teaching assistantships with full and partial tuition reimbursements available (averaging $19,877 per year); institutionally sponsored loans, scholarships/grants, health care benefits, and unspecified assistantships also available. Financial award application deadline: 1/15; financial award applicants required to submit FAFSA. *Faculty research:* Building systems engineering, construction engineering and management, environmental engineering, geoenvironmental engineering, geotechnical engineering, materials and mechanics, structural engineering, water resources engineering, life-cycle engineering. *Total annual research expenditures:* $10.9 million. *Application contact:* E-mail: cvengrad@colorado.edu. Web site: http://ceae.colorado.edu/new/.

University of Dayton, Department of Civil and Environmental Engineering and Engineering Mechanics, Dayton, OH 45469-1300. Offers engineering mechanics (MSEM); environmental engineering (MSCE); geotechnical engineering (MSCE); structural engineering (MSCE); transportation engineering (MSCE); water resources engineering (MSCE). Part-time programs available. *Faculty:* 7 full-time (2 women), 2 part-time/adjunct (0 women). *Students:* 16 full-time (4 women), 9 part-time (4 women); includes 1 minority (Asian, non-Hispanic/Latino), 13 international. Average age 27. 53 applicants, 38% accepted, 5 enrolled. In 2011, 7 degrees awarded. *Degree requirements:* For master's, thesis optional. *Entrance requirements:* For master's, minimum GPA of 3.0 in undergraduate work. Additional exam requirements/recommendations for international students: Required—TOEFL (minimum score 550 paper-based; 213 computer-based; 80 iBT). *Application deadline:* For fall admission, 8/1 for domestic students, 3/1 for international students; for winter admission, 7/1 for international students; for spring admission, 1/1 for international students. Applications are processed on a rolling basis. Application fee: $0 ($50 for international students). Electronic applications accepted. *Expenses: Tuition:* Full-time $8400; part-time $700 per credit hour. *Required fees:* $25 per semester. Tuition and fees vary according to degree level. *Financial support:* Research assistantships available. Financial award applicants required to submit FAFSA. *Faculty research:* Physical modeling of hydraulic systems, finite element methods, mechanics of composite materials, transportation systems safety, biological treatment processes. *Total annual research expenditures:* $200,000. *Unit head:* Dr. Donald V. Chase, Chair, 937-229-3847, Fax: 937-229-3491, E-mail: dchase1@udayton.edu. *Application contact:* Dr. Donald Chase, Chair, 937-229-3847, Fax: 937-229-3491, E-mail: dchase1@udayton.edu. Web site: http://www.udayton.edu/engineering/civil.

University of Delaware, College of Engineering, Department of Civil and Environmental Engineering, Newark, DE 19716. Offers environmental engineering (MAS, MCE, PhD); geotechnical engineering (MAS, MCE, PhD); ocean engineering (MAS, MCE, PhD); structural engineering (MAS, MCE, PhD); transportation engineering (MAS, MCE, PhD); water resource engineering (MAS, MCE, PhD). Part-time programs available. Terminal master's awarded for partial completion of doctoral program. *Degree requirements:* For master's, thesis; for doctorate, thesis/dissertation. *Entrance requirements:* For master's and doctorate, GRE General Test. Additional exam requirements/recommendations for international students: Required—TOEFL. Electronic applications accepted. *Faculty research:* Structural engineering and mechanics; transportation engineering; ocean engineering; soil mechanics and foundation; water resources and environmental engineering.

University of Guelph, Graduate Studies, College of Physical and Engineering Science, School of Engineering, Guelph, ON N1G 2W1, Canada. Offers biological engineering (M Eng, M Sc, MA Sc, PhD); engineering systems and computing (M Eng, M Sc, MA Sc, PhD); environmental engineering (M Eng, M Sc, MA Sc, PhD); water resources engineering (M Eng, M Sc, MA Sc, PhD). Part-time programs available. *Degree requirements:* For master's, thesis (for some programs); for doctorate, comprehensive exam, thesis/dissertation. *Entrance requirements:* For master's, minimum B- average during previous 2 years of course work; for doctorate, minimum B average. Additional exam requirements/recommendations for international students: Required—TOEFL (minimum score 550 paper-based; 213 computer-based; 89 iBT), IELTS (minimum score 6.5). Electronic applications accepted. *Faculty research:* Water and food safety, environmental contaminant fates and mechanisms, computer systems, robotics and mechatronics, waste treatment.

University of Maine, Graduate School, College of Engineering, Department of Civil and Environmental Engineering, Orono, ME 04469. Offers civil engineering (PhD); water resources (MS). *Faculty:* 12 full-time (3 women). *Students:* 33 full-time (11 women), 9 part-time (1 woman); includes 2 minority (1 American Indian or Alaska Native, non-Hispanic/Latino; 1 Two or more races, non-Hispanic/Latino), 4 international. Average age 26. 38 applicants, 66% accepted, 23 enrolled. In 2011, 15 master's, 1 doctorate awarded. *Degree requirements:* For doctorate, thesis/dissertation. *Entrance requirements:* For master's and doctorate, GRE General Test. Additional exam requirements/recommendations for international students: Required—TOEFL. *Application deadline:* For fall admission, 2/1 priority date for domestic students. Applications are processed on a rolling basis. Application fee: $65. Electronic applications accepted. *Expenses:* Tuition, state resident: full-time $5016. Tuition, nonresident: full-time $14,424. *Financial support:* In 2011–12, 15 research assistantships with full tuition reimbursements (averaging $17,387 per year), 3 teaching assistantships with full tuition reimbursements (averaging $13,600 per year) were awarded; Federal Work-Study, institutionally sponsored loans, scholarships/grants, and tuition waivers (full and partial) also available. Financial award application deadline: 3/1. *Total annual research expenditures:* $1.4 million. *Unit head:* Dr. Eric Landis, Chair. *Application contact:* Scott G. Delcourt, Associate Dean of the Graduate School, 207-581-3291, Fax: 207-581-3232, E-mail: graduate@maine.edu. Web site: http://www2.umaine.edu/graduate/.

University of Massachusetts Amherst, Graduate School, College of Engineering, Department of Civil and Environmental Engineering, Amherst, MA 01003. Offers civil engineering (MSCE, PhD); environmental and water resources (MSCE); geotechnical (MSCE); structural engineering and mechanics (MSCE); transportation (MSCE). *Accreditation:* ABET (one or more programs are accredited). Part-time programs available. *Faculty:* 28 full-time (7 women). *Students:* 91 full-time (30 women), 11 part-time (5 women); includes 13 minority (3 Black or African American, non-Hispanic/Latino; 5 Asian, non-Hispanic/Latino; 4 Hispanic/Latino; 1 Two or more races, non-Hispanic/Latino), 29 international. Average age 27. 293 applicants, 53% accepted, 40 enrolled. In 2011, 38 master's, 1 doctorate awarded. Terminal master's awarded for partial completion of doctoral program. *Degree requirements:* For master's, thesis or alternative; for doctorate, comprehensive exam, thesis/dissertation. *Entrance requirements:* For master's and doctorate, GRE General Test. Additional exam requirements/recommendations for international students: Required—TOEFL (minimum score 550 paper-based; 213 computer-based; 80 iBT), IELTS (minimum score 6.5). *Application deadline:* For fall admission, 2/1 for domestic and international students; for spring admission, 10/1 for domestic and international students. Applications are processed on a rolling basis. Application fee: $50 ($65 for international students). Electronic applications accepted. Tuition and fees vary according to course load, campus/location and program. *Financial support:* In 2011–12, 1 fellowship with full tuition reimbursement (averaging $1,000 per year), 74 research assistantships with full tuition reimbursements (averaging $15,151 per year), 6 teaching assistantships with full tuition reimbursements (averaging $15,151 per year) were awarded; career-related internships or fieldwork, Federal Work-Study, scholarships/grants, traineeships, health care benefits, tuition waivers, and unspecified assistantships also available. Support available to part-time students. Financial award application deadline: 2/1; financial award applicants required to submit FAFSA. *Unit head:* Dr. Sanjay Arwade, Graduate Program Director, 413-545-0686, Fax: 413-545-2840. *Application contact:* Lindsay DeSantis, Interim Supervisor of Admissions, 413-545-0722, Fax: 413-577-0100, E-mail: gradadm@grad.umass.edu. Web site: http://cee.umass.edu/.

University of Memphis, Graduate School, Herff College of Engineering, Department of Civil Engineering, Memphis, TN 38152. Offers civil engineering (PhD); environmental engineering (MS); foundation engineering (MS); structural engineering (MS); transportation engineering (MS); water resources engineering (MS). Terminal master's awarded for partial completion of doctoral program. *Degree requirements:* For master's, comprehensive exam, thesis optional; for doctorate, comprehensive exam, thesis/dissertation. *Entrance requirements:* For master's, GRE General Test or MAT, minimum undergraduate GPA of 2.5; for doctorate, GRE, 3 letters of recommendation. Additional exam requirements/recommendations for international students: Required—TOEFL (minimum score 550 paper-based; 210 computer-based; 79 iBT). *Faculty research:* Structural response to earthquakes, pavement design, water quality, transportation safety, intermodal transportation,.

University of Missouri, Graduate School, College of Engineering, Department of Civil and Environmental Engineering, Columbia, MO 65211. Offers civil engineering (MS, PhD); environmental engineering (MS, PhD); geotechnical engineering (MS, PhD); structural engineering (MS, PhD); transportation and highway engineering (MS); water resources (MS, PhD). *Faculty:* 18 full-time (2 women), 1 part-time/adjunct (0 women). *Students:* 45 full-time (16 women), 38 part-time (8 women); includes 5 minority (2 Black or African American, non-Hispanic/Latino; 2 Asian, non-Hispanic/Latino; 1 Hispanic/Latino), 49 international. Average age 28. 109 applicants, 28% accepted, 20 enrolled. In 2011, 14 master's, 2 doctorates awarded. *Degree requirements:* For master's, report or thesis; for doctorate, thesis/dissertation. *Entrance requirements:* For master's and doctorate, GRE General Test. Additional exam requirements/recommendations for international students: Required—TOEFL (minimum score 550 paper-based; 213 computer-based; 79 iBT). *Application deadline:* For fall admission, 3/15 priority date for domestic students; for winter admission, 10/15 priority date for domestic students. Application fee: $55 ($75 for international students). *Expenses:* Tuition, state resident: full-time $5881. Tuition, nonresident: full-time $15,183. *Required fees:* $952. Tuition and fees vary according to campus/location and program. *Financial support:* Fellowships, research assistantships, teaching assistantships, and institutionally sponsored loans available. *Unit head:* Dr. Mark Virkler, Department Chair, E-mail: virklerm@missouri.edu. *Application contact:* Jennifer Keyzer-Andre, 573-882-4442, E-mail: keyzerandrej@missouri.edu. Web site: http://engineering.missouri.edu/civil/.

The University of Texas at Austin, Graduate School, Cockrell School of Engineering, Department of Civil, Architectural and Environmental Engineering, Program in Environmental and Water Resources Engineering, Austin, TX 78712-1111. Offers MS, PhD. *Accreditation:* ABET. Part-time programs available. *Degree requirements:* For master's, thesis or alternative. *Entrance requirements:* For master's, GRE General Test. Additional exam requirements/recommendations for international students: Required—TOEFL. *Application deadline:* For fall admission, 1/15 priority date for domestic students, 1/15 for international students; for spring admission, 9/1 priority date for domestic students, 9/1 for international students. Applications are processed on a rolling basis. Application fee: $50 ($75 for international students). Electronic applications accepted. *Financial support:* Fellowships, research assistantships, and teaching assistantships available. Financial award application deadline: 2/1. *Unit head:* Dr. Mary Jo Kirisits, Graduate Advisor, 512-232-7120, E-mail: ewre@mail.ce.utecas.edu. *Application contact:* Kathy Rose, Graduate Coordinator, 512-232-1702, Fax: 512-471-0592, E-mail: krose@mail.utexas.edu. Web site: http://www.caee.utexas.edu/ewre/.

The University of Texas at Tyler, College of Engineering and Computer Science, Department of Civil Engineering, Tyler, TX 75799-0001. Offers environmental engineering (MS); industrial safety (MS); structural engineering (MS); transportation engineering (MS); water resources engineering (MS). Part-time and evening/weekend programs available. *Degree requirements:* For master's, thesis optional. *Entrance requirements:* For master's, GRE General Test, bachelor's degree in engineering, associated science degree. Additional exam requirements/recommendations for international students: Required—TOEFL (minimum score 79 computer-based). *Faculty research:* Non-destructive strength testing, indoor air quality, transportation routing and signaling, pavement replacement criteria, flood water routing, construction and long-term behavior of innovative geotechnical foundation and embankment construction used in highway construction, engineering education.

University of Washington, Graduate School, College of Engineering, Department of Civil and Environmental Engineering, Seattle, WA 98195-2700. Offers civil engineering (MS, MSE, PhD); construction engineering (MSCE); environmental engineering (MS, MSCE, MSE, PhD); global trade, transportation and logistics (MS); hydrology, water resources, and environmental fluid mechanics (MS, MSCE, MSE, PhD); structural and geotechnical engineering and mechanics (MS, MSCE, MSE, PhD); transportation and construction engineering (MS, MSE, PhD); transportation engineering (MSCE). Part-time programs available. Postbaccalaureate distance learning degree programs offered (no on-campus study). *Faculty:* 47 full-time (11 women), 9 part-time/adjunct (1 woman). *Students:* 195 full-time (67 women), 72 part-time (19 women); includes 37 minority (4 Black or African American, non-Hispanic/Latino; 27 Asian, non-Hispanic/Latino; 6 Hispanic/Latino), 65 international. 654 applicants, 57% accepted, 100 enrolled. In 2011, 88 master's, 7 doctorates awarded. Terminal master's awarded for partial completion of doctoral program. *Degree requirements:* For master's, thesis (for some programs); for doctorate, comprehensive exam, thesis/dissertation, general, qualifying, and final exams; completion of degree within 10 years. *Entrance requirements:* For master's, GRE General Test, minimum GPA of 3.0, statement of purpose, letters of recommendation, transcripts; for doctorate, GRE General Test, minimum GPA of 3.5, statement of purpose, letters of recommendation, transcripts. Additional exam requirements/recommendations for international students: Required—TOEFL (minimum score 580 paper-based; 237 computer-based; 92 iBT); Recommended—IELTS (minimum score 7). *Application deadline:* For fall admission, 1/10 priority date for domestic students, 1/10 for international students. Applications are processed on a rolling basis. Application fee: $75. Electronic applications accepted. *Expenses:* Contact institution. *Financial support:* In 2011–12, 99 students received support, including 16 fellowships with full and partial tuition reimbursements available (averaging $16,173 per year), 71 research assistantships with full tuition reimbursements available (averaging $16,380 per year), 10 teaching assistantships with full tuition reimbursements available (averaging $16,380 per year); scholarships/grants also available. Financial award application deadline: 1/10; financial award applicants required to submit FAFSA. *Faculty research:* Environmental/water resources, hydrology; construction/transportation; structures/ geotechnical. *Total annual research expenditures:* $13.6 million. *Unit head:* Dr. Gregory R. Miller, Professor/Chair, 206-543-0350, Fax: 206-543-1543, E-mail: gmiller@uw.edu. *Application contact:* Lorna Latal, Graduate Adviser, 206-543-2574, Fax: 206-543-1543, E-mail: llatal@u.washington.edu. Web site: http://www.ce.washington.edu/programs/prospective/grad/applying/gen_admission.html.

Utah State University, School of Graduate Studies, College of Engineering, Department of Biological and Irrigation Engineering, Logan, UT 84322. Offers biological and agricultural engineering (MS, PhD); irrigation engineering (MS, PhD). Part-time programs available. Terminal master's awarded for partial completion of doctoral program. *Degree requirements:* For master's, thesis (for some programs); for doctorate, thesis/dissertation. *Entrance requirements:* For master's and doctorate, GRE General Test, minimum GPA of 3.0. Additional exam requirements/recommendations for international students: Required—TOEFL. *Faculty research:* On-farm water management, crop-water yield modeling, irrigation, biosensors, biological engineering.

Villanova University, College of Engineering, Department of Civil and Environmental Engineering, Program in Water Resources and Environmental Engineering, Villanova, PA 19085-1699. Offers urban water resources design (Certificate); water resources and environmental engineering (MSWREE). Part-time and evening/weekend programs available. Postbaccalaureate distance learning degree programs offered (no on-campus study). *Degree requirements:* For master's, thesis optional. *Entrance requirements:* For master's, GRE General Test (for applicants with degrees from foreign universities), BCE or bachelor's degree in science or related engineering field, minimum GPA of 3.0. Additional exam requirements/recommendations for international students: Required—TOEFL (minimum score 600 paper-based; 250 computer-based; 100 iBT). Electronic applications accepted. *Expenses: Tuition:* Part-time $675 per credit. Part-time tuition and fees vary according to degree level and program. *Faculty research:* Photocatalytic decontamination and disinfection of water, urban storm water wetlands, economy and risk, removal and destruction of organic acids in water, sludge treatment.

Virginia Polytechnic Institute and State University, Graduate School, College of Engineering, Department of Civil and Environmental Engineering, Blacksburg, VA 24061. Offers civil engineering (M Eng, MS, PhD); civil infrastructure systems (Certificate); environmental engineering (MS); environmental sciences and engineering (MS); transportation systems engineering (Certificate); treatment process engineering (Certificate); urban hydrology and stormwater management (Certificate); water quality management (Certificate). *Accreditation:* ABET (one or more programs are accredited). *Degree requirements:* For master's, comprehensive exam (for some programs), thesis (for some programs); for doctorate, comprehensive exam (for some programs), thesis/dissertation (for some programs). *Entrance requirements:* For master's and doctorate, GRE. Additional exam requirements/recommendations for international students: Required—TOEFL (minimum score 550 paper-based; 213 computer-based). *Application deadline:* For fall admission, 7/1 for domestic and international students; for spring admission, 12/1 for domestic and international students. Applications are processed on a rolling basis. Application fee: $65. Electronic applications accepted. *Expenses:* Tuition, state resident: full-time $10,048; part-time $558.25 per credit hour. Tuition, nonresident: full-time $19,497; part-time $1083.25 per credit hour. *Required fees:* $405 per semester. Tuition and fees vary according to course load, campus/location and program. *Financial support:* Fellowships with full tuition reimbursements, research assistantships with full tuition reimbursements, teaching assistantships with full tuition reimbursements, career-related internships or fieldwork, Federal Work-Study, scholarships/grants, health care benefits, and unspecified assistantships available. Financial award application deadline: 1/15. *Faculty research:* Construction, environmental geotechnical hydrosystems, structures and transportation engineering. *Unit head:* Dr. Sam Easterling, Unit Head, 540-231-5143, Fax: 540-231-7532, E-mail: seaster@vt.edu. *Application contact:* Marc Widdowson, Information Contact, 540-231-7153, Fax: 540-231-7532, E-mail: mwiddows@vt.edu. Web site: http://www.cee.vt.edu/.

Section 8
Computer Science and Information Technology

This section contains a directory of institutions offering graduate work in computer science and information technology, followed by in-depth entries submitted by institutions that chose to prepare detailed program descriptions. Additional information about programs listed in the directory but not augmented by an in-depth entry may be obtained by writing directly to the dean of a graduate school or chair of a department at the address given in the directory.

For programs offering related work, see also in this book *Electrical and Computer Engineering, Engineering and Applied Sciences,* and *Industrial Engineering.* In the other guides in this series:

Graduate Programs in the Humanities, Arts & Social Sciences
See *Communication and Media*

Graduate Programs in the Biological/Biomedical Sciences & Health-Related Medical Professions
See *Allied Health*

Graduate Programs in the Physical Sciences, Mathematics, Agricultural Sciences, the Environment & Natural Resources
See *Mathematical Sciences*

Graduate Programs in Business, Education, Information Studies, Law & Social Work
See *Business Administration and Management* and *Library and Information Studies*

CONTENTS

Program Directories

Displays and Close-Ups

Artificial Intelligence/Robotics

California State University, Northridge, Graduate Studies, College of Engineering and Computer Science, Department of Manufacturing Systems Engineering and Management, Northridge, CA 91330. Offers engineering automation (MS); engineering management (MS); manufacturing systems engineering (MS); materials engineering (MS). Postbaccalaureate distance learning degree programs offered. *Entrance requirements:* For master's, GRE (if cumulative undergraduate GPA less than 3.0).

Carnegie Mellon University, College of Humanities and Social Sciences, Department of Statistics, Pittsburgh, PA 15213-3891. Offers machine learning and statistics (PhD); mathematical finance (PhD); statistics (MS, PhD), including applied statistics (PhD), computational statistics (PhD), theoretical statistics (PhD); statistics and public policy (PhD). Terminal master's awarded for partial completion of doctoral program. *Degree requirements:* For doctorate, comprehensive exam, thesis/dissertation. *Entrance requirements:* For master's and doctorate, GRE General Test. Additional exam requirements/recommendations for international students: Required—TOEFL. *Faculty research:* Stochastic processes, Bayesian statistics, statistical computing, decision theory, psychiatric statistics.

Carnegie Mellon University, School of Computer Science, Department of Machine Learning, Pittsburgh, PA 15213-3891. Offers PhD.

Carnegie Mellon University, School of Computer Science and Carnegie Institute of Technology, Robotics Institute, Pittsburgh, PA 15213-3891. Offers robotic systems development (MS); robotics (MS, PhD); robotics technology (MS). *Degree requirements:* For doctorate, thesis/dissertation. *Entrance requirements:* For doctorate, GRE General Test, GRE Subject Test. Additional exam requirements/recommendations for international students: Required—TOEFL. *Faculty research:* Perception, cognition, manipulation, robot systems, manufacturing.

Cornell University, Graduate School, Graduate Fields of Engineering, Field of Computer Science, Ithaca, NY 14853-0001. Offers algorithms (M Eng, PhD); applied logic and automated reasoning (M Eng, PhD); artificial intelligence (M Eng, PhD); computer graphics (M Eng, PhD); computer science (M Eng, PhD); computer vision (M Eng, PhD); concurrency and distributed computing (M Eng, PhD); information organization and retrieval (M Eng, PhD); operating systems (M Eng, PhD); parallel computing (M Eng, PhD); programming environments (M Eng, PhD); programming languages and methodology (M Eng, PhD); robotics (M Eng, PhD); scientific computing (M Eng, PhD); theory of computation (M Eng, PhD). *Faculty:* 65 full-time (9 women). *Students:* 211 full-time (47 women); includes 24 minority (22 Asian, non-Hispanic/Latino; 2 Hispanic/Latino), 138 international. Average age 25. 1,255 applicants, 20% accepted, 111 enrolled. In 2011, 141 master's, 12 doctorates awarded. *Degree requirements:* For doctorate, comprehensive exam, thesis/dissertation. *Entrance requirements:* For master's, GRE General Test, 2 letters of recommendation; for doctorate, GRE General Test, GRE Subject Test (computer science or mathematics), 3 letters of recommendation. Additional exam requirements/recommendations for international students: Required—TOEFL (minimum score 505 paper-based; 213 computer-based; 77 iBT). *Application deadline:* For fall admission, 1/1 for domestic students. Application fee: $95. Electronic applications accepted. *Financial support:* In 2011–12, 100 students received support, including 13 fellowships with full tuition reimbursements available, 69 research assistantships with full tuition reimbursements available, 28 teaching assistantships with full tuition reimbursements available; institutionally sponsored loans, scholarships/grants, health care benefits, tuition waivers (full and partial), and unspecified assistantships also available. Financial award applicants required to submit FAFSA. *Faculty research:* Artificial intelligence, operating systems and databases, programming languages and security, scientific computing, theory of computing, computational biology and graphics. *Unit head:* Director of Graduate Studies, 607-255-8593, Fax: 607-255-4428. *Application contact:* Graduate Field Assistant, 607-255-8593, Fax: 607-255-4428, E-mail: phd@cs.cornell.edu. Web site: http://www.gradschool.cornell.edu/fields.php?id-28&a-2.

Eastern Michigan University, Graduate School, College of Arts and Sciences, Department of Computer Science, Ypsilanti, MI 48197. Offers artificial intelligence (Graduate Certificate); computer science (MS). Part-time and evening/weekend programs available. Postbaccalaureate distance learning degree programs offered (no on-campus study). *Faculty:* 15 full-time (5 women). *Students:* 12 full-time (6 women), 17 part-time (1 woman); includes 3 minority (1 Black or African American, non-Hispanic/Latino; 2 Asian, non-Hispanic/Latino), 14 international. Average age 29. 93 applicants, 43% accepted, 5 enrolled. In 2011, 10 master's, 1 other advanced degree awarded. *Degree requirements:* For master's, thesis or alternative. *Entrance requirements:* For master's, at least 18 credit hours of 200-level (or above) computer science courses including data structures, programming languages like java, C or C++, computer organization; courses in discrete mathematics, probability and statistics, linear algebra and calculus; minimum GPA of 2.75 in computer science. Additional exam requirements/recommendations for international students: Required—TOEFL. *Application deadline:* For fall admission, 8/1 for domestic students, 5/1 for international students; for winter admission, 12/1 for domestic students, 10/1 for international students; for spring admission, 4/1 for domestic students, 2/1 for international students. Application fee: $35. *Expenses:* Tuition, state resident: full-time $10,367; part-time $432 per credit hour. Tuition, nonresident: full-time $20,435; part-time $851 per credit hour. *Required fees:* $39 per credit hour. $46 per semester. One-time fee: $100. Tuition and fees vary according to course level, degree level and reciprocity agreements. *Financial support:* Fellowships, research assistantships with full tuition reimbursements, teaching assistantships with full tuition reimbursements, career-related internships or fieldwork, Federal Work-Study, institutionally sponsored loans, scholarships/grants, tuition waivers (partial), and unspecified assistantships available. Support available to part-time students. Financial award applicants required to submit FAFSA. *Unit head:* Dr. William McMillan, Department Head, 734-487-1063, Fax: 734-487-6824, E-mail: wmcmillan@emich.edu. *Application contact:* Pamela Moore, Graduate Coordinator, 734-487-1063, Fax: 734-487-6824, E-mail: pmoore@emich.edu. Web site: http://www.emich.edu/compsci.

Eastern Michigan University, Graduate School, College of Arts and Sciences, Department of English Language and Literature, Program in Language Technology, Ypsilanti, MI 48197. Offers Graduate Certificate. Part-time and evening/weekend programs available. In 2011, 1 degree awarded. *Entrance requirements:* Additional exam requirements/recommendations for international students: Required—TOEFL. Application fee: $35. *Expenses:* Tuition, state resident: full-time $10,367; part-time $432 per credit hour. Tuition, nonresident: full-time $20,435; part-time $851 per credit hour. *Required fees:* $39 per credit hour. $46 per semester. One-time fee: $100. Tuition and fees vary according to course level, degree level and reciprocity agreements. *Financial support:* Research assistantships with full tuition reimbursements, teaching assistantships with full tuition reimbursements, career-related internships or fieldwork, Federal Work-Study, institutionally sponsored loans, scholarships/grants, tuition waivers (full and partial), and unspecified assistantships available. Support available to part-time students. *Unit head:* Dr. Joseph Csicsila, Interim Department Head, 734-487-4220, Fax: 734-483-9744, E-mail: jcsicsila@emich.edu. *Application contact:* Dr. Veronica Grondona, Program Advisor, 734-487-0145, Fax: 734-483-9744, E-mail: vgrondona@emich.edu.

Indiana University–Purdue University Indianapolis, School of Engineering and Technology, Department of Electrical Engineering, Indianapolis, IN 46202-2896. Offers biomedical engineering (MS, PhD); electrical and computer engineering (MS, MSECE, PhD), including biomedical engineering (MSECE), control and automation (MSECE), signal processing (MSECE); engineering (interdisciplinary) (MSE). *Students:* 49 full-time (15 women), 48 part-time (5 women); includes 8 minority (2 Black or African American, non-Hispanic/Latino; 2 Asian, non-Hispanic/Latino; 2 Hispanic/Latino; 2 Two or more races, non-Hispanic/Latino), 56 international. Average age 27. 150 applicants, 49% accepted, 45 enrolled. In 2011, 29 degrees awarded. Application fee: $55 ($65 for international students). *Unit head:* Yaobin Chen, Unit Head, 317-274-4032, Fax: 317-274-4493. *Application contact:* Valerie Diemer, Graduate Program, 317-278-4960, Fax: 317-278-1671, E-mail: grad@engr.iupui.edu.

Instituto Tecnológico y de Estudios Superiores de Monterrey, Campus Monterrey, Graduate and Research Division, Program in Computer Science, Monterrey, Mexico. Offers artificial intelligence (PhD); computer science (MS); information systems (MS); information technology (MS). Part-time programs available. *Degree requirements:* For master's, one foreign language, thesis; for doctorate, one foreign language, thesis/dissertation. *Entrance requirements:* For master's, EXADEP; for doctorate, master's degree in related field. Additional exam requirements/recommendations for international students: Required—TOEFL. *Faculty research:* Distributed systems, software engineering, decision support systems.

Instituto Tecnológico y de Estudios Superiores de Monterrey, Campus Monterrey, Graduate and Research Division, Programs in Engineering, Monterrey, Mexico. Offers applied statistics (M Eng); artificial intelligence (PhD); automation engineering (M Eng); chemical engineering (M Eng); civil engineering (M Eng); electrical engineering (M Eng); electronic engineering (M Eng); environmental engineering (M Eng); industrial engineering (M Eng, PhD); manufacturing engineering (M Eng); mechanical engineering (M Eng); systems and quality engineering (M Eng). M Eng program offered jointly with University of Waterloo; PhD in industrial engineering with Texas A&M University. Part-time and evening/weekend programs available. Terminal master's awarded for partial completion of doctoral program. *Degree requirements:* For master's, one foreign language, thesis; for doctorate, one foreign language, thesis/dissertation. *Entrance requirements:* For master's, EXADEP; for doctorate, GRE, master's degree in related field. Additional exam requirements/recommendations for international students: Required—TOEFL. *Faculty research:* Flexible manufacturing cells, materials, statistical methods, environmental prevention, control and evaluation.

Portland State University, Graduate Studies, Systems Science Program, Portland, OR 97207-0751. Offers computational intelligence (Certificate); computer modeling and simulation (Certificate); systems science (MS); systems science/anthropology (PhD); systems science/business administration (PhD); systems science/civil engineering (PhD); systems science/economics (PhD); systems science/engineering management (PhD); systems science/general (PhD); systems science/mathematical sciences (PhD); systems science/mechanical engineering (PhD); systems science/psychology (PhD); systems science/sociology (PhD). *Degree requirements:* For doctorate, variable foreign language requirement, thesis/dissertation. *Entrance requirements:* For master's, 2 letters of recommendation; for doctorate, GMAT, GRE General Test, minimum undergraduate GPA of 3.0. Additional exam requirements/recommendations for international students: Required—TOEFL. *Faculty research:* Systems theory and methodology, artificial intelligence neural networks, information theory, nonlinear dynamics/chaos, modeling and simulation.

South Dakota School of Mines and Technology, Graduate Division, Program in Robotics and Intelligent Autonomous Systems, Rapid City, SD 57701-3995. Offers MS. Part-time programs available. *Entrance requirements:* Additional exam requirements/recommendations for international students: Required—TOEFL, TWE. Electronic applications accepted. *Faculty research:* Database systems, remote sensing, numerical modeling, artificial intelligence, neural networks.

University of California, Riverside, Graduate Division, Department of Electrical Engineering, Riverside, CA 92521-0102. Offers electrical engineering (MS, PhD), including computer engineering, control and robotics, intelligent systems, nanomaterials, devices and circuits, signal processing and communications. Terminal master's awarded for partial completion of doctoral program. *Degree requirements:* For master's, thesis optional; for doctorate, thesis/dissertation, qualifying exams. *Entrance requirements:* For master's and doctorate, GRE General Test, minimum GPA of 3.25. Additional exam requirements/recommendations for international students: Required—TOEFL (minimum score 550 paper-based; 213 computer-based; 80 iBT). Electronic applications accepted. *Faculty research:* Solid state devices, integrated circuits, signal processing.

University of California, San Diego, Office of Graduate Studies, Department of Electrical and Computer Engineering, La Jolla, CA 92093. Offers applied ocean science (MS, PhD); applied physics (MS, PhD); communication theory and systems (MS, PhD); computer engineering (MS, PhD); electrical engineering (M Eng); electronic circuits and systems (MS, PhD); intelligent systems, robotics and control (MS, PhD); photonics (MS, PhD); signal and image processing (MS, PhD). MS only offered to students who have been admitted to the PhD program. *Entrance requirements:* For master's and doctorate, GRE General Test. Electronic applications accepted.

University of Georgia, Franklin College of Arts and Sciences, Artificial Intelligence Center, Athens, GA 30602. Offers MS. *Faculty:* 1 full-time (0 women). *Students:* 21 full-time (4 women), 4 part-time (1 woman); includes 3 minority (2 Black or African American, non-Hispanic/Latino; 1 Two or more races, non-Hispanic/Latino), 11 international. Average age 26. 11 applicants, 82% accepted, 5 enrolled. In 2011, 4 master's awarded. *Degree requirements:* For master's, thesis. *Entrance requirements:* For master's, GRE General Test. *Application deadline:* For fall admission, 7/1 priority date for domestic students; for spring admission, 11/15 for domestic students. Application fee: $50. Electronic applications accepted. *Financial support:* Unspecified assistantships available. *Unit head:* Dr. Walter Don Potter, Director, 706-542-0361, E-mail: potter@uga.edu. *Application contact:* Dr. Khaled M. Rasheed, Graduate Coordinator, 706-542-3444, Fax: 706-542-8864, E-mail: khaled@cs.uga.edu. Web site: http://ai.uga.edu.

University of Michigan, College of Engineering, Interpro Programs in Engineering, Ann Arbor, MI 48109. Offers automotive engineering (M Eng); design science (PhD); energy systems engineering (MS); financial engineering (MS); global automotive and manufacturing engineering (M Eng); manufacturing engineering (M Eng, D Eng); pharmaceutical engineering (M Eng); robotics and autonomous vehicles (M Eng); MBA/

M Eng; MSE/MS. Part-time programs available. Postbaccalaureate distance learning degree programs offered (no on-campus study). *Students:* 225 full-time (55 women), 273 part-time (37 women). In 2011, 145 master's, 1 doctorate awarded. Terminal master's awarded for partial completion of doctoral program. *Degree requirements:* For master's, capstone project; for doctorate, thesis/dissertation. *Entrance requirements:* For master's, GRE; for doctorate, GRE, 2 years of work experience. Additional exam requirements/recommendations for international students: Required—TOEFL (minimum score 560 paper-based; 220 computer-based). *Application deadline:* Applications are processed on a rolling basis. Application fee: $65 ($75 for international students). Electronic applications accepted. *Financial support:* Fellowships, research assistantships with full tuition reimbursements, teaching assistantships with full tuition reimbursements, career-related internships or fieldwork, scholarships/grants, and unspecified assistantships available. Financial award application deadline: 2/15; financial award applicants required to submit FAFSA. *Faculty research:* Automotive engineering, design science, energy systems engineering, engineering sustainable systems dual degree, financial engineering, global automotive and manufacturing engineering, integrated microsystems, manufacturing engineering, pharmaceutical engineering , robotics and autonomous vehicles. *Unit head:* Prof. Panos Papalambros, Director, 734-763-0480, Fax: 734-647-0079, E-mail: pyp@umich.edu. *Application contact:* Patti Mackmiller, Program Manager, 734-764-3071, Fax: 734-647-2243, E-mail: pmackmil@umich.edu. Web site: http://interpro-academics.engin.umich.edu/.

University of Nebraska at Omaha, Graduate Studies, College of Information Science and Technology, Department of Computer Science, Omaha, NE 68182. Offers artificial intelligence (Certificate); communication networks (Certificate); computer science (MA, MS); systems architecture (Certificate). Part-time and evening/weekend programs available. *Faculty:* 15 full-time (2 women). *Students:* 33 full-time (2 women), 53 part-time (5 women); includes 7 minority (2 Black or African American, non-Hispanic/Latino; 5 Asian, non-Hispanic/Latino), 31 international. Average age 30. 65 applicants, 51% accepted, 20 enrolled. In 2011, 22 master's, 2 other advanced degrees awarded. *Degree requirements:* For master's, comprehensive exam, thesis (for some programs). *Entrance requirements:* For master's, GRE General Test, minimum GPA of 3.0, course work in computer science, resume. Additional exam requirements/recommendations for international students: Required—TOEFL (minimum score 500 paper-based; 173 computer-based; 61 iBT). *Application deadline:* For fall admission, 7/1 priority date for domestic students; for spring admission, 11/1 priority date for domestic students. Applications are processed on a rolling basis. Application fee: $45. Electronic applications accepted. *Financial support:* In 2011–12, 9 students received support, including 9 research assistantships with tuition reimbursements available; teaching assistantships with tuition reimbursements available, Federal Work-Study, institutionally sponsored loans, scholarships/grants, tuition waivers (full), and unspecified assistantships also available. Support available to part-time students. Financial award application deadline: 3/1; financial award applicants required to submit FAFSA. *Unit head:* Dr. Qiuming Zhu, Chairperson, 402-554-2423. *Application contact:* Carla Frakes, Information Contact, 402-554-2423.

University of Pittsburgh, Dietrich School of Arts and Sciences, Intelligent Systems Program, Pittsburgh, PA 15260. Offers MS, PhD. *Faculty:* 28 full-time (6 women). *Students:* 23 full-time (6 women); includes 2 minority (both Asian, non-Hispanic/Latino), 15 international. Average age 29. 38 applicants, 21% accepted, 7 enrolled. In 2011, 6 master's, 3 doctorates awarded. Terminal master's awarded for partial completion of doctoral program. *Degree requirements:* For master's, thesis; for doctorate, comprehensive exam, thesis/dissertation. *Entrance requirements:* For master's and doctorate, GRE General Test. Additional exam requirements/recommendations for international students: Required—TOEFL. *Application deadline:* For fall admission, 2/1 priority date for domestic students, 2/1 for international students. Applications are processed on a rolling basis. Application fee: $50. Electronic applications accepted. *Expenses:* Tuition, state resident: full-time $18,774; part-time $760 per credit. Tuition, nonresident: full-time $30,736; part-time $1258 per credit. *Required fees:* $740; $200 per term. Tuition and fees vary according to program. *Financial support:* In 2011–12, 17 students received support, including 9 fellowships with full tuition reimbursements available (averaging $20,932 per year), 8 research assistantships with full tuition reimbursements available (averaging $22,566 per year); Federal Work-Study, institutionally sponsored loans, scholarships/grants, traineeships, health care benefits, and unspecified assistantships also available. Financial award application deadline: 2/1. *Faculty research:* Medical artificial intelligence, expert systems, clinical decision support, plan generation and recognition, special cognition. *Unit head:* Janyce Wiebe, Director, 412-624-9590, Fax: 412-624-8561, E-mail: wiebe@cs.pitt.edu. *Application contact:* Wendy Bergstein, Administrator, 412-624-5755, Fax: 412-624-8561, E-mail: wab23@pitt.edu. Web site: http://www.isp.pitt.edu/.

University of Pittsburgh, Katz Graduate School of Business, Doctoral Program in Business Administration, Pittsburgh, PA 15260. Offers accounting (PhD); finance (PhD); information systems (PhD); marketing (PhD); operations/decision sciences/artificial intelligence (PhD); organizational behavior and human resource management (PhD); strategic planning (PhD). *Accreditation:* AACSB. *Faculty:* 54 full-time (16 women). *Students:* 51 full-time (21 women); includes 9 minority (4 Black or African American, non-Hispanic/Latino; 4 Asian, non-Hispanic/Latino; 1 Hispanic/Latino), 23 international. 373 applicants, 7% accepted, 10 enrolled. In 2011, 6 doctorates awarded. *Degree requirements:* For doctorate, comprehensive exam, thesis/dissertation. *Entrance requirements:* For doctorate, GMAT or GRE. Additional exam requirements/recommendations for international students: Required—TOEFL. *Application deadline:* For fall admission, 2/1 priority date for domestic students, 2/1 for international students. Applications are processed on a rolling basis. Application fee: $50. Electronic applications accepted. *Expenses:* Tuition, state resident: full-time $18,774; part-time $760 per credit. Tuition, nonresident: full-time $30,736; part-time $1258 per credit. *Required fees:* $740; $200 per term. Tuition and fees vary according to program. *Financial support:* In 2011–12, 38 students received support, including 29 research assistantships with full tuition reimbursements available (averaging $19,400 per year), 10 teaching assistantships with full tuition reimbursements available (averaging $24,700 per year); fellowships, Federal Work-Study, scholarships/grants, health care benefits, and unspecified assistantships also available. Financial award application deadline: 2/1. *Faculty research:* Accounting statements and reporting, corporate finance, information systems processes, structures and decision-making, consumer behavior and marketing models. *Total annual research expenditures:* $254,031. *Unit head:* Dr. Dennis Galletta, Director, 412-648-1699, Fax: 412-624-3633, E-mail: galletta@katz.pitt.edu. *Application contact:* Carrie Woods, Assistant Director, 412-648-1525, Fax: 412-624-3633, E-mail: cawoods@katz.pitt.edu. Web site: http://www.business.pitt.edu/katz/phd/.

University of Southern California, Graduate School, Viterbi School of Engineering, Department of Computer Science, Los Angeles, CA 90089. Offers computer networks (MS); computer science (MS, PhD); computer security (MS); game development (MS); high performance computing and simulations (MS); human language technology (MS); intelligent robotics (MS); multimedia and creative technologies (MS); software engineering (MS). Part-time and evening/weekend programs available. Postbaccalaureate distance learning degree programs offered (no on-campus study). *Entrance requirements:* For master's and doctorate, GRE General Test. Additional exam requirements/recommendations for international students: Required—TOEFL. Electronic applications accepted. *Faculty research:* Databases, computer graphics and computer vision, software engineering, networks and security, robotics, multimedia and virtual reality.

Villanova University, College of Engineering, Department of Electrical and Computer Engineering, Program in Computer Engineering, Villanova, PA 19085-1699. Offers computer architectures (Certificate); computer engineering (MSCPE); intelligent control systems (Certificate). Part-time and evening/weekend programs available. *Degree requirements:* For master's, thesis optional. *Entrance requirements:* For master's, GRE General Test (for applicants with degrees from foreign universities), BEE, minimum GPA of 3.0. Additional exam requirements/recommendations for international students: Required—TOEFL (minimum score 600 paper-based; 250 computer-based; 100 iBT). Electronic applications accepted. *Expenses: Tuition:* Part-time $675 per credit. Part-time tuition and fees vary according to degree level and program. *Faculty research:* Expert systems, computer vision, neural networks, image processing, computer architectures.

Villanova University, College of Engineering, Department of Electrical and Computer Engineering, Program in Electrical Engineering, Villanova, PA 19085-1699. Offers electric power systems (Certificate); electrical engineering (MSEE); electro mechanical systems (Certificate); high frequency systems (Certificate); intelligent control systems (Certificate); wireless and digital communications (Certificate). Part-time and evening/weekend programs available. *Degree requirements:* For master's, thesis optional. *Entrance requirements:* For master's, GRE General Test (for applicants with degrees from foreign universities), BEE, minimum GPA of 3.0. Additional exam requirements/recommendations for international students: Required—TOEFL (minimum score 600 paper-based; 250 computer-based; 100 iBT). *Expenses: Tuition:* Part-time $675 per credit. Part-time tuition and fees vary according to degree level and program. *Faculty research:* Signal processing, communications, antennas, devices.

Worcester Polytechnic Institute, Graduate Studies and Research, Department of Computer Science, Worcester, MA 01609-2280. Offers computer and communications networks (MS); computer science (MS, PhD, Advanced Certificate, Graduate Certificate); robotics engineering (MS, PhD). Part-time and evening/weekend programs available. *Faculty:* 21 full-time (4 women), 5 part-time/adjunct (0 women). *Students:* 59 full-time (12 women), 50 part-time (6 women); includes 9 minority (1 Black or African American, non-Hispanic/Latino; 5 Asian, non-Hispanic/Latino; 1 Hispanic/Latino; 2 Two or more races, non-Hispanic/Latino), 51 international. 339 applicants, 56% accepted, 41 enrolled. In 2011, 29 master's, 2 doctorates awarded. Terminal master's awarded for partial completion of doctoral program. *Degree requirements:* For master's, thesis optional; for doctorate, comprehensive exam, thesis/dissertation. *Entrance requirements:* For master's, GRE General Test, 3 letters of recommendation; for doctorate, GRE General Test, 3 letters of recommendation, statement of purpose. Additional exam requirements/recommendations for international students: Required—TOEFL (minimum score 563 paper-based; 223 computer-based; 84 iBT), IELTS (minimum score 7). *Application deadline:* For fall admission, 1/1 priority date for domestic students, 1/1 for international students; for spring admission, 10/1 priority date for domestic students, 10/1 for international students. Applications are processed on a rolling basis. Application fee: $70. Electronic applications accepted. *Financial support:* Research assistantships, teaching assistantships, career-related internships or fieldwork, institutionally sponsored loans, scholarships/grants, and unspecified assistantships available. Financial award application deadline: 1/1; financial award applicants required to submit FAFSA. *Faculty research:* Computer networks and distributed systems, databases and data mining, artificial intelligence and robotics, computer graphics and visualization, applied logic and security. *Unit head:* Dr. Craig Wills, Department Head, 508-831-5357, Fax: 508-831-5776, E-mail: cew@wpi.edu. *Application contact:* Dr. Elke Rundensteiner, Graduate Coordinator, 508-831-5357, Fax: 508-831-5776, E-mail: rundenst@wpi.edu. Web site: http://www.cs.wpi.edu/.

Worcester Polytechnic Institute, Graduate Studies and Research, Program in Robotics Engineering, Worcester, MA 01609-2280. Offers MS, PhD. Part-time and evening/weekend programs available. *Students:* 20 full-time (3 women), 12 part-time (11 women); includes 5 minority (2 Black or African American, non-Hispanic/Latino; 2 Hispanic/Latino; 1 Native Hawaiian or other Pacific Islander, non-Hispanic/Latino), 8 international. 97 applicants, 65% accepted, 23 enrolled. In 2011, 2 master's awarded. *Degree requirements:* For master's, thesis or capstone design project; for doctorate, thesis/dissertation. *Entrance requirements:* For master's and doctorate, GRE, 3 letters of recommendation, statement of purpose. Additional exam requirements/recommendations for international students: Required—TOEFL (minimum score 563 paper-based; 223 computer-based; 84 iBT), IELTS (minimum score 7). *Application deadline:* For fall admission, 1/1 priority date for domestic students, 1/1 for international students; for spring admission, 10/1 priority date for domestic students, 10/1 for international students. Applications are processed on a rolling basis. Electronic applications accepted. *Financial support:* Research assistantships, teaching assistantships, career-related internships or fieldwork, institutionally sponsored loans, scholarships/grants, and unspecified assistantships available. Financial award application deadline: 1/1; financial award applicants required to submit FAFSA. *Faculty research:* Medical robotics, human-robot interaction, robot learning, manipulation, adaptive control, multi-robot systems. *Unit head:* Dr. Michael Gennert, Director, 508-831-5357, Fax: 508-831-5776, E-mail: michaelg@wpi.edu. *Application contact:* Tracey Coetzee, Administrative Assistant, 508-831-5357, Fax: 508-831-5776, E-mail: tcoetzee@wpi.edu.

Bioinformatics

Arizona State University, Graduate College, Department of Biomedical Informatics, Phoenix, AZ 85004. Offers MS, PhD. Terminal master's awarded for partial completion of doctoral program. *Degree requirements:* For master's, interactive Program of Study (iPOS) submitted before completing 50 percent of required credit hours; for doctorate, comprehensive exam, thesis/dissertation, interactive Program of Study (iPOS) submitted before completing 50 percent of required credit hours. *Entrance requirements:* For master's, GRE or MCAT, bachelor's degree with minimum GPA of 3.25 in computer science, biology, physiology, nursing, statistics, engineering, related fields, or unrelated fields with appropriate academic backgrounds; resume/curriculum vitae; statement of purpose; 3 letters of recommendation; all official transcripts; for doctorate, GRE or MCAT, bachelor's degree with minimum GPA of 3.5 in computer science, biology, physiology, nursing, statistics, engineering, related fields, or unrelated fields with appropriate academic backgrounds; resume/curriculum vitae; statement of purpose; 3 letters of recommendation; all official transcripts. Additional exam requirements/recommendations for international students: Required—TOEFL (minimum score 550 paper-based; 213 computer-based; 83 iBT), IELTS (minimum score 6.5). Electronic applications accepted.

Boston University, Graduate School of Arts and Sciences and College of Engineering, Intercollegiate Program in Bioinformatics, Boston, MA 02215. Offers MS, PhD. *Students:* 72 full-time (23 women), 11 part-time (2 women); includes 13 minority (10 Asian, non-Hispanic/Latino; 3 Hispanic/Latino), 34 international. Average age 32. 111 applicants, 30% accepted, 12 enrolled. In 2011, 13 master's, 4 doctorates awarded. *Degree requirements:* For doctorate, thesis/dissertation. *Entrance requirements:* For master's and doctorate, GRE General Test, GRE Subject Test, 3 letters of recommendation, resume. Additional exam requirements/recommendations for international students: Required—TOEFL (minimum score 550 paper-based; 213 computer-based). *Application deadline:* For fall admission, 12/1 for domestic and international students; for spring admission, 10/1 for domestic and international students. Application fee: $70. Electronic applications accepted. *Expenses: Tuition:* Full-time $40,848; part-time $1276 per credit hour. *Required fees:* $572; $286 per semester. *Financial support:* In 2011–12, 35 students received support, including 4 fellowships with full tuition reimbursements available (averaging $19,800 per year), 29 research assistantships with full tuition reimbursements available (averaging $19,300 per year); career-related internships or fieldwork, Federal Work-Study, scholarships/grants, traineeships, and unspecified assistantships also available. Financial award application deadline: 12/1; financial award applicants required to submit FAFSA. *Unit head:* Tom Tullius, Director, 617-353-2482, E-mail: tullius@bu.edu. *Application contact:* David King, Administrator, 617-358-0751, Fax: 617-353-5929, E-mail: dking@bu.edu. Web site: http://www.bu.edu/bioinformatics.

Brandeis University, Rabb School of Continuing Studies, Division of Graduate Professional Studies, Bioinformatics Program, Waltham, MA 02454-9110. Offers MS. Part-time and evening/weekend programs available. *Faculty:* 2 full-time (both women), 34 part-time/adjunct (8 women). *Students:* 23 part-time (13 women); includes 4 minority (all Asian, non-Hispanic/Latino). Average age 35. 2 applicants, 100% accepted, 2 enrolled. In 2011, 2 master's awarded. *Entrance requirements:* For master's, resume, official transcripts, recommendations, goal statements. Additional exam requirements/recommendations for international students: Recommended—TOEFL (minimum score 600 paper-based; 250 computer-based; 100 iBT). *Application deadline:* For fall admission, 6/15 priority date for domestic students; for winter admission, 10/15 priority date for domestic students; for spring admission, 2/15 priority date for domestic students. Applications are processed on a rolling basis. Application fee: $50. Electronic applications accepted. *Unit head:* Dr. Daniel Caffrey, Program Chair, 781-736-8787, Fax: 781-736-3420, E-mail: dcaffrey@brandeis.edu. *Application contact:* Frances Stearns, Associate Director of Admissions and Student Services, 781-736-8785, Fax: 781-736-3420, E-mail: fstearns@brandeis.edu. Web site: http://www.brandeis.edu/rabbgrad.

California State University Channel Islands, Extended Education, Programs in Biotechnology, Camarillo, CA 93012. Offers biotechnology and bioinformatics (MS); MS/MBA. *Entrance requirements:* Additional exam requirements/recommendations for international students: Required—TOEFL (minimum score 550 paper-based).

California State University, Dominguez Hills, College of Natural and Behavioral Sciences, Department of Biology, Carson, CA 90747-0001. Offers MS. Part-time and evening/weekend programs available. *Faculty:* 10 full-time (2 women), 23 part-time/adjunct (10 women). *Students:* 13 full-time (7 women), 34 part-time (17 women); includes 29 minority (6 Black or African American, non-Hispanic/Latino; 8 Asian, non-Hispanic/Latino; 13 Hispanic/Latino; 2 Two or more races, non-Hispanic/Latino), 4 international. Average age 29. 30 applicants, 60% accepted, 15 enrolled. In 2011, 2 master's awarded. *Degree requirements:* For master's, thesis. *Entrance requirements:* For master's, minimum GPA of 2.75. Additional exam requirements/recommendations for international students: Required—TOEFL (minimum score 550 paper-based). *Application deadline:* For fall admission, 6/1 for domestic students, 5/1 for international students; for spring admission, 12/15 for domestic students, 10/1 for international students. Application fee: $55. Electronic applications accepted. *Faculty research:* Cancer biology, infectious diseases, ecology of native plants, remediation, community ecology. *Unit head:* Dr. John Thomlinson, Chair, 310-243-3381, Fax: 310-243-2350, E-mail: jthomlinson@csudh.edu. *Application contact:* Dr. Getachew Kidane, Graduate Program Coordinator, 310-243-3564, Fax: 310-243-2350, E-mail: gkidane@csudh.edu. Web site: http://www.nbs.csudh.edu/biology.

Dalhousie University, Faculty of Computer Science, Halifax , NS B3H 1W5, Canada. Offers computational biology and bioinformatics (M Sc); computer science (PhD); computer science (project-based) (MA Sc); computer science (thesis-based) (MC Sc); electronic commerce (MEC); health informatics (MHI). *Degree requirements:* For master's, thesis (for some programs); for doctorate, thesis/dissertation. *Entrance requirements:* Additional exam requirements/recommendations for international students: Required—1 of 5 approved tests: TOEFL, IELTS, CANTEST, CAEL, Michigan English Language Assessment Battery. Electronic applications accepted.

Duke University, Graduate School, Department of Computational Biology and Bioinformatics, Durham, NC 27705. Offers PhD, Certificate. *Faculty:* 39 full-time. *Students:* 36 full-time (13 women); includes 3 minority (1 Black or African American, non-Hispanic/Latino; 2 Hispanic/Latino), 18 international. 109 applicants, 11% accepted, 4 enrolled. In 2011, 3 doctorates awarded. *Degree requirements:* For doctorate, thesis/dissertation. *Entrance requirements:* For doctorate, GRE General Test. Additional exam requirements/recommendations for international students: Required—TOEFL (minimum score 550 paper-based; 213 computer-based; 83 iBT), IELTS (minimum score 7). *Application deadline:* For fall admission, 12/8 priority date for domestic students, 12/8 for international students. Application fee: $75. Electronic applications accepted. *Expenses: Tuition:* Full-time $40,720. *Required fees:* $3107. *Financial support:* Fellowships, research assistantships, and teaching assistantships available. Financial award application deadline: 12/8. *Unit head:* Jeannette McCarthy, Director of Graduate Studies, 919-684-0881, Fax: 919-668-2465, E-mail: el81@duke.edu. *Application contact:* Elizabeth Hutton, Director, Graduate Admissions, 919-684-3913, Fax: 919-684-2277, E-mail: grad-admissions@duke.edu. Web site: http://cbb.genome.duke.edu/.

Emory University, Rollins School of Public Health, Department of Biostatistics and Bioinformatics, Atlanta, GA 30322-1100. Offers bioinformatics (PhD); biostatistics (MSPH); public health informatics (MSPH). PhD offered through the Graduate School of Arts and Sciences. Part-time programs available. *Students:* 7 full-time. Average age 27. 106 applicants, 18% accepted, 7 enrolled. *Degree requirements:* For master's, thesis, practicum. *Entrance requirements:* For master's, GRE General Test. Additional exam requirements/recommendations for international students: Required—TOEFL (minimum score 550 paper-based; 213 computer-based; 80 iBT). *Application deadline:* For fall admission, 12/15 priority date for domestic students, 12/15 for international students. Application fee: $95. Electronic applications accepted. *Expenses: Tuition:* Full-time $34,800. *Required fees:* $1300. *Financial support:* Fellowships with full and partial tuition reimbursements, career-related internships or fieldwork, Federal Work-Study, institutionally sponsored loans, scholarships/grants, traineeships, health care benefits, and unspecified assistantships available. Support available to part-time students. Financial award application deadline: 1/5; financial award applicants required to submit FAFSA. *Unit head:* Lance A. Waller, Chair, 404-727-1057, Fax: 404-727-1370, E-mail: lwaller@emory.edu.

Florida State University, The Graduate School, College of Arts and Sciences, Department of Scientific Computing, Tallahassee, FL 32306-4120. Offers computational science (MS, PSM, PhD), including atmospheric science (PhD), biochemistry (PhD), biological science (PhD), computational molecular biology/bioinformatics (PSM), computational science (PhD), geological science (PhD), materials science (PhD), physics (PhD). Part-time programs available. *Faculty:* 14 full-time (2 women). *Students:* 32 full-time (6 women), 3 part-time (0 women); includes 13 minority (1 Black or African American, non-Hispanic/Latino; 11 Asian, non-Hispanic/Latino; 1 Hispanic/Latino), 13 international. Average age 28. 29 applicants, 41% accepted, 9 enrolled. In 2011, 14 master's, 3 doctorates awarded. Terminal master's awarded for partial completion of doctoral program. *Degree requirements:* For master's, thesis (for some programs); for doctorate, comprehensive exam, thesis/dissertation. *Entrance requirements:* For master's and doctorate, GRE General Test, knowledge of at least one object-oriented computing language, 3 letters of recommendations. Additional exam requirements/recommendations for international students: Required—TOEFL (minimum score 550 paper-based; 80 iBT). *Application deadline:* For fall admission, 1/15 for domestic and international students. Application fee: $30. Electronic applications accepted. *Expenses:* Tuition, state resident: full-time $9474; part-time $350.88 per credit hour. Tuition, nonresident: full-time $16,236; part-time $601.34 per credit hour. *Required fees:* $630 per semester. One-time fee: $20. Tuition and fees vary according to course load and campus/location. *Financial support:* In 2011–12, 32 students received support, including 12 research assistantships with full tuition reimbursements available (averaging $20,000 per year), 18 teaching assistantships with full tuition reimbursements available (averaging $20,000 per year); unspecified assistantships also available. Financial award application deadline: 4/15. *Faculty research:* Morphometrics, mathematical and systems biology, mining proteomic and metabolic data, computational materials research at Scientific Computing, advanced 4-D Var Data-Assimilation methods in dynamic meteorology and oceanography, computational fluid dynamics, astrophysics. *Unit head:* Dr. Sam Huckaba, Interim Dean, 850-644-1081. *Application contact:* Maribel Amwake, Graduate Academic Coordinator, 850-644-0143, Fax: 850-644-0098, E-mail: mamwake@fsu.edu. Web site: http://www.sc.fsu.edu.

George Mason University, College of Science, School of Systems Biology, Fairfax, VA 22030. Offers bioinformatics and computational biology (MS, PhD, Graduate Certificate); biology (MS); biosciences (PhD). *Faculty:* 15 full-time (5 women), 1 part-time/adjunct. *Students:* 68 full-time (25 women), 66 part-time (36 women); includes 33 minority (3 Black or African American, non-Hispanic/Latino; 28 Asian, non-Hispanic/Latino; 1 Hispanic/Latino; 1 Two or more races, non-Hispanic/Latino), 40 international. Average age 32. 179 applicants, 49% accepted, 34 enrolled. In 2011, 23 master's, 13 doctorates, 1 other advanced degree awarded. *Degree requirements:* For master's, research project or thesis. *Entrance requirements:* For master's, GRE, resume; 3 letters of recommendation; expanded goals statement; 2 copies of official transcripts; bachelor's degree in related field with minimum GPA of 3.0 in last 60 hours; for doctorate, GRE, self-assessment form; resume; 3 letters of recommendation; expanded goals statement; 2 copies of official transcripts; bachelor's degree in related field with minimum GPA of 3.0 in last 60 hours; for Graduate Certificate, resume; 2 copies of official transcripts. Additional exam requirements/recommendations for international students: Required—TOEFL (minimum score 570 paper-based; 230 computer-based; 88 iBT), IELTS, Pearson Test of English. Application fee: $65 ($80 for international students). Electronic applications accepted. *Expenses:* Tuition, state resident: full-time $8750; part-time $364.58 per credit. Tuition, nonresident: full-time $24,092; part-time $1003.83 per credit. *Required fees:* $2514; $104.75 per credit. *Financial support:* In 2011–12, 44 students received support, including 6 fellowships with full tuition reimbursements available (averaging $18,000 per year), 9 research assistantships with full and partial tuition reimbursements available (averaging $13,682 per year), 29 teaching assistantships with full and partial tuition reimbursements available (averaging $12,559 per year); career-related internships or fieldwork, Federal Work-Study, scholarships/grants, unspecified assistantships, and health care benefits (full-time research or teaching assistantship recipients) also available. Support available to part-time students. Financial award application deadline: 3/1; financial award applicants required to submit FAFSA. *Total annual research expenditures:* $1.3 million. *Unit head:* Dr. James D. Willett, Director, 703-993-8311, Fax: 703-993-8976, E-mail: jwillett@gmu.edu. *Application contact:* Diane St. Germain, Graduate Student Services Coordinator, 703-993-4263, Fax: 703-993-8976, E-mail: dstgerma@gmu.edu. Web site: http://ssb.gmu.edu/.

Georgetown University, Graduate School of Arts and Sciences, Programs in Biomedical Sciences, Department of Biostatistics, Bioinformatics and Biomathematics, Washington, DC 20057-1484. Offers biostatistics (MS), including bioinformatics, epidemiology. *Entrance requirements:* For master's, GRE General Test. Additional exam requirements/recommendations for international students: Required—TOEFL. *Faculty research:* Occupation epidemiology, cancer.

The George Washington University, School of Medicine and Health Sciences, Department of Biochemistry and Molecular Biology, Program in Molecular Biochemistry and Bioinformatics, Washington, DC 20052. Offers MS. Part-time programs available. *Students:* 25 full-time (12 women), 4 part-time (2 women); includes 5 minority (4 Asian, non-Hispanic/Latino; 1 Two or more races, non-Hispanic/Latino), 17 international. Average age 25. 58 applicants, 64% accepted. In 2011, 1 master's awarded. *Entrance requirements:* For master's, GRE General Test, minimum GPA of 3.0. Additional exam requirements/recommendations for international students: Required—TOEFL (minimum score 550 paper-based; 213 computer-based). *Application deadline:* For fall admission, 4/1 priority date for domestic students, 4/1 for international students; for spring admission, 10/1 priority date for domestic students, 10/1 for international students. Applications are processed on a rolling basis. Application fee: $75. Electronic applications accepted. *Unit head:* Dr. Jack Vanderhoek, Director, 202-994-2929, E-mail: jyvdh@gwu.edu. *Application contact:* Dr. Fatah Kashanchi, Director, 202-994-1781, Fax: 202-994-6213, E-mail: bcmfxk@gwumc.edu. Web site: http://www.gwumc.edu/bioinformatics/.

Georgia Institute of Technology, Graduate Studies and Research, College of Engineering, The Wallace H. Coulter Department of Biomedical Engineering at Georgia Tech and Emory University, Atlanta, GA 30332-0001. Offers bioengineering (PhD); bioinformatics (PhD); biomedical engineering (PhD); MD/PhD. PhD in biomedical engineering program jointly offered with Emory University (Georgia) and Peking University (China). Terminal master's awarded for partial completion of doctoral program. *Degree requirements:* For doctorate, thesis/dissertation. *Entrance requirements:* Additional exam requirements/recommendations for international students: Required—TOEFL. *Faculty research:* Biomechanics and tissue engineering, bioinstrumentation and medical imaging.

Georgia Institute of Technology, Graduate Studies and Research, College of Sciences, School of Biology, Atlanta, GA 30332-0001. Offers applied biology (MS, PhD); bioinformatics (MS, PhD); biology (MS). Part-time programs available. Terminal master's awarded for partial completion of doctoral program. *Degree requirements:* For master's, thesis; for doctorate, thesis/dissertation, qualifying exam. *Entrance requirements:* For master's, GRE General Test, minimum GPA of 2.9; for doctorate, GRE General Test, minimum GPA of 3.0. Additional exam requirements/recommendations for international students: Required—TOEFL. Electronic applications accepted. *Faculty research:* Microbiology, molecular and cell biology, ecology.

Georgia Institute of Technology, Graduate Studies and Research, College of Sciences, School of Mathematics, Atlanta, GA 30332-0001. Offers algorithms, combinatorics, and optimization (PhD); applied mathematics (MS); bioinformatics (PhD); mathematics (PhD); quantitative and computational finance (MS); statistics (MS Stat). Terminal master's awarded for partial completion of doctoral program. *Degree requirements:* For master's, thesis or alternative; for doctorate, one foreign language, thesis/dissertation. *Entrance requirements:* For master's, GRE General Test, minimum GPA of 3.0; for doctorate, GRE General Test, GRE Subject Test, minimum GPA of 3.0. Additional exam requirements/recommendations for international students: Required—TOEFL. Electronic applications accepted. *Faculty research:* Dynamical systems, discrete mathematics, probability and statistics, mathematical physics.

Grand Valley State University, Padnos College of Engineering and Computing, Medical and Bioinformatics Program, Allendale, MI 49401-9403. Offers MS. Part-time and evening/weekend programs available. *Degree requirements:* For master's, thesis or alternative. *Faculty research:* Biomedical informatics, information visualization, data mining, high-performance computing, computational biology.

Indiana University Bloomington, School of Informatics and Computing, Bloomington, IN 47408. Offers bioinformatics (MS); chemical informatics (MS); computer science (MS, PhD); health informatics (MS); human computer interaction (MS); informatics (PhD); laboratory informatics (MS); media arts and science (MS); music informatics (MS); security informatics (MS); MS/PhD. PhD offered through University Graduate School. Part-time programs available. Postbaccalaureate distance learning degree programs offered (no on-campus study). *Faculty:* 63 full-time (12 women). *Students:* 434 full-time (99 women), 36 part-time (9 women); includes 24 minority (8 Black or African American, non-Hispanic/Latino; 9 Asian, non-Hispanic/Latino; 4 Hispanic/Latino; 3 Two or more races, non-Hispanic/Latino), 309 international. Average age 27. 825 applicants, 58% accepted, 205 enrolled. In 2011, 115 master's, 25 doctorates awarded. Terminal master's awarded for partial completion of doctoral program. *Degree requirements:* For master's, thesis optional; for doctorate, comprehensive exam, thesis/dissertation, oral and written exams. *Entrance requirements:* For master's and doctorate, GRE, letters of reference. Additional exam requirements/recommendations for international students: Required—TOEFL. *Application deadline:* For fall admission, 1/15 for domestic students, 12/1 for international students. Application fee: $55 ($65 for international students). Electronic applications accepted. *Financial support:* In 2011–12, fellowships with full and partial tuition reimbursements (averaging $20,000 per year), research assistantships (averaging $14,000 per year), teaching assistantships (averaging $13,000 per year) were awarded; Federal Work-Study, institutionally sponsored loans, scholarships/grants, health care benefits, tuition waivers (full and partial), and unspecified assistantships also available. Support available to part-time students. *Total annual research expenditures:* $2 million. *Unit head:* Dr. David Leake, Associate Dean for Graduate Studies, 812-855-9756, E-mail: leake@cs.indiana.edu. *Application contact:* Rachel Lawmaster, Manager of Graduate Admissions and Graduate Studies, 812-856-3622, Fax: 812-856-3825, E-mail: raclee@indiana.edu. Web site: http://www.informatics.indiana.edu/.

Iowa State University of Science and Technology, Bioinformatics and Computational Biology Program, Ames, IA 50011-3260. Offers MS, PhD. *Degree requirements:* For doctorate, thesis/dissertation. *Entrance requirements:* For master's and doctorate, GRE General Test. Additional exam requirements/recommendations for international students: Recommended—TOEFL, IELTS. *Application deadline:* For fall admission, 1/15 priority date for domestic students, 1/15 for international students; for spring admission, 10/15 for domestic and international students. Application fee: $40 ($90 for international students). Electronic applications accepted. *Faculty research:* Functional and structural genomics, genome evolution, macromolecular structure and function, mathematical biology and biological statistics, metabolic and developmental networks. *Unit head:* Dr. Julie Dickerson, Chair, Supervising Committee, 515-294-5122, Fax: 515-294-6790, E-mail: bcb@iastate.edu. *Application contact:* Information Contact, 515-294-5836, Fax: 515-294-2592, E-mail: grad_admissions@iastate.edu. Web site: http://www.bcb.iastate.edu/.

The Johns Hopkins University, Bloomberg School of Public Health, Department of Biostatistics, Baltimore, MD 21205-2179. Offers bioinformatics (MHS); biostatistics (MHS, Sc M, PhD). Part-time programs available. *Degree requirements:* For master's, comprehensive exam (for some programs), thesis (for some programs), written exam, final project; for doctorate, comprehensive exam, thesis/dissertation, 1 year full-time residency, oral and written exams. *Entrance requirements:* For master's and doctorate, GRE General Test, course work in calculus and matrix algebra, 3 letters of recommendation, curriculum vitae. Additional exam requirements/recommendations for international students: Required—TOEFL (minimum score 600 paper-based; 250 computer-based). Electronic applications accepted. *Faculty research:* Statistical genetics, bioinformatics, statistical computing, statistical methods, environmental statistics.

The Johns Hopkins University, Engineering Program for Professionals and Advanced Academic Programs, Part-time Program in Bioinformatics, Baltimore, MD 21218-2699. Offers MS, Post-Master's Certificate. Part-time and evening/weekend programs available.

The Johns Hopkins University, Engineering Program for Professionals, Part-Time Program in Computer Science, Baltimore, MD 21218-2699. Offers bioinformatics (MS); computer science (MS, Post-Master's Certificate); telecommunications and networking (MS). Part-time and evening/weekend programs available. Postbaccalaureate distance learning degree programs offered (no on-campus study). Electronic applications accepted.

The Johns Hopkins University, Zanvyl Krieger School of Arts and Sciences, Advanced Academic Programs, Program in Bioinformatics, Baltimore, MD 21218-2699. Offers MS. Part-time and evening/weekend programs available. Postbaccalaureate distance learning degree programs offered (no on-campus study). *Degree requirements:* For master's, thesis (for some programs). *Entrance requirements:* For master's, minimum GPA of 3.0; coursework in programming and data structures, biology, and chemistry. Additional exam requirements/recommendations for international students: Required—TOEFL (minimum score 250 computer-based; 100 iBT). Electronic applications accepted.

Marquette University, Graduate School, College of Arts and Sciences, Department of Mathematics, Statistics, and Computer Science, Milwaukee, WI 53201-1881. Offers bioinformatics (MS); computational sciences (MS, PhD); computing (MS); mathematics education (MS). Part-time and evening/weekend programs available. Postbaccalaureate distance learning degree programs offered (minimal on-campus study). *Faculty:* 28 full-time (9 women), 10 part-time/adjunct (5 women). *Students:* 14 full-time (3 women), 77 part-time (18 women); includes 9 minority (2 Black or African American, non-Hispanic/Latino; 7 Asian, non-Hispanic/Latino), 24 international. Average age 30. 86 applicants, 65% accepted, 24 enrolled. In 2011, 15 master's, 1 doctorate awarded. Terminal master's awarded for partial completion of doctoral program. *Degree requirements:* For master's, thesis (for some programs), essay with oral presentation; for doctorate, comprehensive exam, thesis/dissertation, qualifying examination. *Entrance requirements:* For master's, official transcripts from all current and previous colleges/universities except Marquette, three letters of recommendation; for doctorate, GRE General Test, official transcripts from all current and previous colleges/universities except Marquette, three letters of recommendation. Additional exam requirements/recommendations for international students: Required—TOEFL (minimum score 530 paper-based; 78 computer-based). *Application deadline:* For fall admission, 1/15 for domestic and international students. Applications are processed on a rolling basis. Application fee: $50. Electronic applications accepted. *Expenses: Tuition:* Full-time $17,010; part-time $945 per credit hour. Tuition and fees vary according to program. *Financial support:* In 2011–12, 23 students received support, including 4 fellowships (averaging $1,375 per year), 5 research assistantships with full tuition reimbursements available (averaging $17,000 per year), 15 teaching assistantships with full tuition reimbursements available (averaging $17,000 per year); scholarships/grants, health care benefits, tuition waivers (full and partial), and unspecified assistantships also available. Support available to part-time students. Financial award application deadline: 2/15. *Faculty research:* Models of physiological systems, mathematical immunology, computational group theory, mathematical logic, computational science. *Total annual research expenditures:* $621,359. *Unit head:* Dr. Gary Krenz, Chair, 414-288-7573, Fax: 414-288-1578. *Application contact:* Dr. Francis Pastijn, Director of Graduate Studies, 414-288-5229. Web site: http://www.marquette.edu/mscs/grad.shtml.

Marquette University, Graduate School, College of Arts and Sciences, Program in Bioinformatics, Milwaukee, WI 53201-1881. Offers MS. Program offered jointly with Medical College of Wisconsin. Part-time and evening/weekend programs available. Postbaccalaureate distance learning degree programs offered (minimal on-campus study). *Students:* 3 full-time (1 woman), 7 part-time (4 women), 5 international. Average age 29. 14 applicants, 50% accepted, 3 enrolled. In 2011, 3 master's awarded. *Degree requirements:* For master's, thesis optional, research practicum (for non-thesis option). *Entrance requirements:* For master's, GRE (strongly recommended), official transcripts from all current and previous colleges/universities except Marquette; essay outlining relevant work experience or education, career goals, possible areas of interest, and reasons for seeking admission; three letters of reference. Additional exam requirements/recommendations for international students: Required—TOEFL (minimum score 530 paper-based; 78 computer-based). *Application deadline:* Applications are processed on a rolling basis. Application fee: $50. Electronic applications accepted. *Expenses: Tuition:* Full-time $17,010; part-time $945 per credit hour. Tuition and fees vary according to program. *Financial support:* In 2011–12, 1 fellowship, 3 teaching assistantships were awarded; research assistantships also available. Financial award application deadline: 2/15. *Unit head:* Dr. Craig Struble, Head, 414-288-3783, E-mail: clough@mscs.mu.edu. *Application contact:* Erin Fox, Assistant Director for Recruitment, 414-288-5319, Fax: 414-288-1902, E-mail: erin.fox@marquette.edu. Web site: http://www.brc.mcw.edu/ap.

McGill University, Faculty of Graduate and Postdoctoral Studies, Faculty of Science, Department of Biology, Montréal, QC H3A 2T5, Canada. Offers bioinformatics (M Sc, PhD); environment (M Sc, PhD); neo-tropical environment (M Sc, PhD).

Medical College of Wisconsin, Graduate School of Biomedical Sciences, Program in Bioinformatics, Milwaukee, WI 53226-0509. Offers MS. *Entrance requirements:* For master's, GRE, official transcripts, three letters of recommendation. Additional exam requirements/recommendations for international students: Required—TOEFL.

Mississippi Valley State University, Department of Natural Science and Environmental Health, Itta Bena, MS 38941-1400. Offers bioinformatics (MS); environmental health (MS). Part-time and evening/weekend programs available. *Entrance requirements:* For master's, GRE, minimum GPA of 3.0. *Faculty research:* Toxicology, water equality, microbiology, ecology.

Morgan State University, School of Graduate Studies, School of Computer, Mathematical, and Natural Sciences, Department of Computer Science, Baltimore, MD 21251. Offers bioinformatics (MS). *Entrance requirements:* Additional exam requirements/recommendations for international students: Required—TOEFL (minimum score 550 paper-based; 213 computer-based).

New Jersey Institute of Technology, Office of Graduate Studies, College of Computing Science, Department of Computer Science, Program in Bioinformatics, Newark, NJ 07102. Offers MS. *Students:* 25 full-time (12 women), 9 part-time; includes 8 minority (2 Black or African American, non-Hispanic/Latino; 5 Asian, non-Hispanic/

Latino; 1 Hispanic/Latino), 22 international. Average age 29. 63 applicants, 83% accepted, 19 enrolled. In 2011, 19 master's awarded. *Entrance requirements:* Additional exam requirements/recommendations for international students: Required—TOEFL (minimum score 550 paper-based; 213 computer-based; 79 iBT). *Application deadline:* For fall admission, 6/1 priority date for domestic students, 5/1 for international students; for spring admission, 11/15 priority date for domestic students, 11/15 for international students. Applications are processed on a rolling basis. Application fee: $65. Electronic applications accepted. *Expenses:* Tuition, state resident: full-time $7980; part-time $867 per credit. Tuition, nonresident: full-time $11,336; part-time $1196 per credit. *Required fees:* $230 per credit. *Financial support:* Application deadline: 1/15. *Unit head:* Dr. Michael A. Baltrush, Interim Chair, 973-596-3386, E-mail: michael.a.baltrush@njit.edu. *Application contact:* Kathryn Kelly, Director of Admissions, 973-596-3300, Fax: 973-596-3461, E-mail: admissions@njit.edu. Web site: http://cs.njit.edu/academics/graduate/ms-bioinf/.

New Mexico State University, Graduate School, College of Arts and Sciences, Department of Computer Science, Las Cruces, NM 88003-8001. Offers bioinformatics (MS); computer science (MS, PhD). Part-time programs available. *Faculty:* 9 full-time (3 women). *Students:* 65 full-time (13 women), 20 part-time (4 women); includes 9 minority (1 Asian, non-Hispanic/Latino; 8 Hispanic/Latino), 56 international. Average age 30. 58 applicants, 66% accepted, 14 enrolled. In 2011, 20 master's, 1 doctorate awarded. Terminal master's awarded for partial completion of doctoral program. *Degree requirements:* For master's, comprehensive exam, thesis or alternative; for doctorate, comprehensive exam, thesis/dissertation, qualifying examination, thesis proposal. *Entrance requirements:* For master's and doctorate, BS in computer science. Additional exam requirements/recommendations for international students: Required—TOEFL (minimum score 550 paper-based; 0 computer-based; 79 iBT), IELTS (minimum score 6.5). *Application deadline:* For fall admission, 3/1 priority date for domestic students, 3/1 for international students; for spring admission, 11/1 priority date for domestic students, 11/1 for international students. Applications are processed on a rolling basis. Application fee: $40 ($50 for international students). Electronic applications accepted. *Expenses:* Tuition, state resident: full-time $5004; part-time $208.50 per credit. Tuition, nonresident: full-time $17,446; part-time $726.90 per credit. *Financial support:* In 2011–12, 6 fellowships (averaging $21,370 per year), 13 research assistantships (averaging $26,405 per year), 22 teaching assistantships (averaging $21,764 per year) were awarded; career-related internships or fieldwork, Federal Work-Study, scholarships/grants, health care benefits, and unspecified assistantships also available. Support available to part-time students. Financial award application deadline: 3/1; financial award applicants required to submit FAFSA. *Faculty research:* Programming languages, artificial intelligence, software engineering, bioinformatics, data mining, computer networks, high performance computing. *Total annual research expenditures:* $1.6 million. *Unit head:* Dr. Enrico Pontelli, Head, 575-646-3723, Fax: 575-646-1002, E-mail: epontell@cs.nmsu.edu. *Application contact:* Dr. Son Tran, Chair, Admissions Committee, 575-646-1930, Fax: 575-646-1002, E-mail: tson@cs.nmsu.edu. Web site: http://www.cs.nmsu.edu/.

North Carolina State University, Graduate School, College of Agriculture and Life Sciences and College of Engineering, Program in Bioinformatics, Raleigh, NC 27695. Offers MB, PhD. *Degree requirements:* For master's, thesis optional; for doctorate, thesis/dissertation. *Entrance requirements:* For master's and doctorate, GRE, minimum B average. Additional exam requirements/recommendations for international students: Required—TOEFL. Electronic applications accepted. *Faculty research:* Statistical genetics, molecular evolution, pedigree analysis, quantitative genetics, protein structure.

North Dakota State University, College of Graduate and Interdisciplinary Studies, Interdisciplinary Program in Genomics and Bioinformatics, Fargo, ND 58108. Offers MS, PhD. Part-time programs available. *Faculty:* 21 full-time (3 women). *Students:* 3 full-time (2 women), 3 part-time (1 woman), all international. 13 applicants, 8% accepted, 0 enrolled. In 2011, 1 master's, 1 doctorate awarded. *Degree requirements:* For master's, thesis; for doctorate, comprehensive exam, thesis/dissertation. *Entrance requirements:* For master's and doctorate, minimum GPA of 3.0. Additional exam requirements/recommendations for international students: Required—TOEFL (minimum score 525 paper-based; 197 computer-based; 71 iBT). *Application deadline:* For fall admission, 5/1 for international students; for spring admission, 8/1 for international students. Applications are processed on a rolling basis. Application fee: $35. Electronic applications accepted. *Financial support:* In 2011–12, 12 research assistantships with full tuition reimbursements (averaging $15,000 per year) were awarded; unspecified assistantships also available. *Faculty research:* Genome evolution, genome mapping, genome expression, bioinformatics, data mining. *Unit head:* Dr. Phillip E. McClean, Director, 701-231-8443, Fax: 701-231-8474. *Application contact:* Sonya Goergen, Marketing, Recruitment, and Public Relations Coordinator, 701-231-7033, Fax: 701-231-6524.

Northeastern University, College of Science, Department of Biology, Professional Program in Bioinformatics, Boston, MA 02115-5096. Offers PMS. Part-time programs available. *Faculty:* 6 full-time. *Students:* 25 full-time, 2 part-time. 31 applicants, 90% accepted, 5 enrolled. In 2011, 8 master's awarded. *Degree requirements:* For master's, internship. *Entrance requirements:* For master's, GRE General Test. *Application deadline:* For fall admission, 2/1 priority date for domestic students, 2/1 for international students. Application fee: $50. *Expenses:* Contact institution. *Financial support:* In 2011–12, research assistantships (averaging $18,285 per year) were awarded; Federal Work-Study, scholarships/grants, and tuition waivers (partial) also available. Support available to part-time students. Financial award application deadline: 3/1; financial award applicants required to submit FAFSA. *Unit head:* Dr. Jacqueline Piret, Program Coordinator, 617-373-2260, Fax: 617-373-3724, E-mail: j.piret@neu.edu. *Application contact:* Jo-Anne Dickinson, Admissions Contact, 617-373-5990, Fax: 617-373-7281, E-mail: gsas@neu.edu. Web site: http://www.bioinformatics.neu.edu.

Nova Southeastern University, Health Professions Division, College of Osteopathic Medicine, Fort Lauderdale, FL 33314-7796. Offers biomedical informatics (MS, Graduate Certificate), including biomedical informatics (MS), clinical informatics (Graduate Certificate), public health informatics (Graduate Certificate); disaster and emergency preparedness (MS); osteopathic medicine (DO); public health (MPH). *Accreditation:* AOsA. *Faculty:* 86 full-time (38 women), 1,072 part-time/adjunct (232 women). *Students:* 952 full-time (377 women), 18 part-time (5 women); includes 323 minority (24 Black or African American, non-Hispanic/Latino; 2 American Indian or Alaska Native, non-Hispanic/Latino; 175 Asian, non-Hispanic/Latino; 91 Hispanic/Latino; 31 Native Hawaiian or other Pacific Islander, non-Hispanic/Latino), 22 international. Average age 28. 3,628 applicants, 17% accepted, 241 enrolled. In 2011, 75 master's, 213 doctorates awarded. *Entrance requirements:* For master's, GRE, licensed healthcare professional or GRE; for doctorate, MCAT, biology, chemistry, organic chemistry, physics (all with labs), and English. *Application deadline:* For fall admission, 1/15 for domestic students. Applications are processed on a rolling basis. Application fee: $50. Electronic applications accepted. *Expenses:* Contact institution. *Financial support:* In 2011–12, 80 students received support, including 6 fellowships with full tuition reimbursements available (averaging $40,000 per year); research assistantships, teaching assistantships, career-related internships or fieldwork, Federal Work-Study, institutionally sponsored loans, and scholarships/grants also available. Financial award application deadline: 6/1; financial award applicants required to submit FAFSA. *Faculty research:* Teaching strategies, simulated patient use, HIV-AIDS education, minority health issues, managed care education. *Unit head:* Dr. Anthony J. Silavgni, Dean, 954-262-1407, E-mail: silvagni@hpd.nova.edu. *Application contact:* Anastasia Leveille, College of Medicine Admissions Counselor, 866-817-4068. Web site: http://www.medicine.nova.edu/.

Polytechnic Institute of New York University, Department of Interdisciplinary Studies, Major in Bioinformatics, Brooklyn, NY 11201-2990. Offers MS. *Students:* 12 full-time (6 women), 10 part-time (5 women); includes 6 minority (2 Black or African American, non-Hispanic/Latino; 4 Asian, non-Hispanic/Latino), 7 international. Average age 33. 36 applicants, 42% accepted, 6 enrolled. In 2011, 18 master's awarded. *Degree requirements:* For master's, comprehensive exam (for some programs), thesis (for some programs). *Entrance requirements:* Additional exam requirements/recommendations for international students: Required—TOEFL (minimum score 550 paper-based; 213 computer-based; 80 iBT); Recommended—IELTS (minimum score 6.5). *Application deadline:* For fall admission, 7/31 for domestic students, 4/30 for international students; for spring admission, 12/31 for domestic students, 10/30 for international students. Applications are processed on a rolling basis. Application fee: $75. Electronic applications accepted. *Expenses: Tuition:* Full-time $22,464; part-time $1248 per credit. *Required fees:* $501 per semester. *Financial support:* Institutionally sponsored loans, scholarships/grants, and unspecified assistantships available. Support available to part-time students. *Unit head:* Prof. Michael Greenstein, Department Head, 718-260-3835, E-mail: mgreenst@poly.edu. *Application contact:* JeanCarlo Bonilla, Director, Graduate Enrollment Management, 718-260-3182, Fax: 718-260-3624, E-mail: gradinfo@poly.edu.

Polytechnic Institute of NYU, Long Island Graduate Center, Graduate Programs, Department of Chemical and Biological Sciences, Melville, NY 11747. Offers bioinformatics (MS); chemistry (MS). *Faculty:* 1 part-time/adjunct (0 women). *Students:* 17 applicants, 82% accepted, 13 enrolled. *Entrance requirements:* Additional exam requirements/recommendations for international students: Required—TOEFL (minimum score 550 paper-based; 213 computer-based; 80 iBT); Recommended—IELTS (minimum score 6.5). *Application deadline:* For fall admission, 7/31 priority date for domestic students, 4/30 for international students; for spring admission, 12/31 priority date for domestic students, 11/30 for international students. Applications are processed on a rolling basis. Application fee: $75. Electronic applications accepted. *Financial support:* In 2011–12, 40 fellowships (averaging $2,314 per year), 4 research assistantships (averaging $1,930 per year) were awarded; institutionally sponsored loans, scholarships/grants, and unspecified assistantships also available. Support available to part-time students. *Unit head:* Prof. Bruce A. Garetz, Department Head, 718-260-3287, E-mail: bgaretz@poly.edu. *Application contact:* JeanCarlo Bonilla, Director of Graduate Enrollment Management, 718-260-3182, Fax: 718-260-3624, E-mail: gradinfo@poly.edu.

Polytechnic Institute of NYU, Long Island Graduate Center, Graduate Programs, Major in Bioinformatics, Melville, NY 11747. Offers MS. Part-time and evening/weekend programs available. In 2011, 1 degree awarded. *Entrance requirements:* Additional exam requirements/recommendations for international students: Required—TOEFL (minimum score 550 paper-based; 213 computer-based; 80 iBT); Recommended—IELTS (minimum score 6.5). *Application deadline:* For fall admission, 7/31 priority date for domestic students, 4/30 for international students; for spring admission, 12/31 priority date for domestic students, 11/30 for international students. Applications are processed on a rolling basis. Application fee: $75. Electronic applications accepted. *Financial support:* Institutionally sponsored loans, scholarships/grants, and unspecified assistantships available. Support available to part-time students. *Unit head:* Dr. Frank Cassara, Director, Long Island Graduate Center, 631-755-4360, Fax: 516-755-4404, E-mail: cassara@poly.edu. *Application contact:* JeanCarlo Bonilla, Director of Graduate Enrollment Management, 718-260-3182, Fax: 718-260-3624, E-mail: gradinfo@poly.edu.

Rice University, Graduate Programs, George R. Brown School of Engineering, Department of Statistics, Houston, TX 77251-1892. Offers bioinformatics (PhD); biostatistics (PhD); computational finance (PhD); general statistics (PhD); statistics (M Stat, MA); MBA/M Stat. Part-time programs available. *Degree requirements:* For master's, comprehensive exam; for doctorate, comprehensive exam, thesis/dissertation. *Entrance requirements:* For master's and doctorate, GRE General Test, minimum GPA of 3.0. Additional exam requirements/recommendations for international students: Required—TOEFL (minimum score 630 paper-based; 250 computer-based; 90 iBT). Electronic applications accepted. *Faculty research:* Statistical genetics, non parametric function estimation, computational statistics and visualization, stochastic processes.

Rochester Institute of Technology, Graduate Enrollment Services, College of Science, School of Life Sciences, Program in Bioinformatics, Rochester, NY 14623-5603. Offers MS. Part-time programs available. *Students:* 7 full-time (1 woman), 10 part-time (4 women), 10 international. Average age 26. 44 applicants, 36% accepted, 3 enrolled. In 2011, 10 degrees awarded. *Degree requirements:* For master's, thesis. *Entrance requirements:* For master's, GRE, minimum GPA of 3.2. Additional exam requirements/recommendations for international students: Required—TOEFL (minimum score 570 paper-based; 230 computer-based; 88 iBT) or IELTS (minimum score 6.5). *Application deadline:* For fall admission, 2/15 for domestic and international students. Application fee: $50. Electronic applications accepted. *Expenses: Tuition:* Full-time $34,659; part-time $963 per credit hour. *Required fees:* $228; $76 per quarter. *Financial support:* Fellowships with partial tuition reimbursements, research assistantships with partial tuition reimbursements, teaching assistantships with partial tuition reimbursements, career-related internships or fieldwork, scholarships/grants, and unspecified assistantships available. Support available to part-time students. Financial award applicants required to submit FAFSA. *Faculty research:* Metabolomics analysis, data mining of NHANES III, categorizing mitochondrial genome variation, evolution of viral genomes. *Unit head:* Dr. Michael Osier, Graduate Program Director, 585-475-4392, Fax: 585-475-6970, E-mail: mvosd@rit.edu. *Application contact:* Diane Ellison, Assistant Vice President, Graduate Enrollment Services, 585-475-2229, Fax: 585-475-7164, E-mail: gradinfo@rit.edu.

Stevens Institute of Technology, Graduate School, Charles V. Schaefer Jr. School of Engineering, Department of Chemistry, Chemical Biology and Biomedical Engineering, Hoboken, NJ 07030. Offers analytical chemistry (PhD, Certificate); bioinformatics (PhD, Certificate); biomedical chemistry (Certificate); biomedical engineering (M Eng, Certificate); chemical biology (MS, PhD, Certificate); chemical physiology (Certificate); chemistry (MS, PhD); organic chemistry (PhD); physical chemistry (PhD); polymer chemistry (PhD, Certificate). Part-time and evening/weekend programs available. Postbaccalaureate distance learning degree programs offered (no on-campus study).

Terminal master's awarded for partial completion of doctoral program. *Degree requirements:* For master's, thesis or alternative; for doctorate, one foreign language, thesis/dissertation; for Certificate, project or thesis. *Entrance requirements:* Additional exam requirements/recommendations for international students: Required—TOEFL. Electronic applications accepted. *Faculty research:* Biochemical reaction engineering, polymerization engineering, reactor design, biochemical process control and synthesis.

Tufts University, School of Engineering, Department of Computer Science, Medford, MA 02155. Offers bioengineering (MS), including bioinformatics; computer science (PhD), including cognitive science. Part-time programs available. *Faculty:* 16 full-time, 1 part-time/adjunct. *Students:* 62 (16 women); includes 10 minority (all Asian, non-Hispanic/Latino), 19 international. Average age 27. 169 applicants, 34% accepted, 23 enrolled. In 2011, 13 master's, 9 doctorates awarded. Terminal master's awarded for partial completion of doctoral program. *Degree requirements:* For master's, thesis (for some programs); for doctorate, thesis/dissertation. *Entrance requirements:* For master's and doctorate, GRE. Additional exam requirements/recommendations for international students: Required—TOEFL (minimum score 550 paper-based; 213 computer-based; 80 iBT). *Application deadline:* For fall admission, 1/15 for domestic students, 12/15 for international students; for spring admission, 9/15 for domestic and international students. Applications are processed on a rolling basis. Application fee: $75. Electronic applications accepted. *Expenses: Tuition:* Full-time $41,208; part-time $1030 per credit hour. Full-time tuition and fees vary according to degree level, program and student level. Part-time tuition and fees vary according to course load. *Financial support:* Fellowships with full tuition reimbursements, research assistantships with full and partial tuition reimbursements, teaching assistantships with full and partial tuition reimbursements, Federal Work-Study, scholarships/grants, tuition waivers (partial), and unspecified assistantships available. Financial award application deadline: 1/15; financial award applicants required to submit FAFSA. *Faculty research:* Computational biology, computational geometry, and computational systems biology; cognitive sciences, human-computer interaction, and human robotic interaction; visualization and graphics, educational technologies; machine learning and data mining; programming languages and systems. *Unit head:* Dr. Carla Brodley, Chair, 617-627-2225, Fax: 617-627-2227. *Application contact:* Dr. Lenore Cowen, Information Contact, 617-623-3217, Fax: 617-627-3220, E-mail: csadmin@cs.tufts.edu. Web site: http://www.cs.tufts.edu/.

Tufts University, School of Engineering, Department of Mechanical Engineering, Medford, MA 02155. Offers bioengineering (ME, MS), including bioinformatics (ME), biomechanical systems and devices, signals and systems (ME); human factors (MS); mechanical engineering (ME, MS, PhD). Part-time programs available. *Faculty:* 13 full-time, 5 part-time/adjunct. *Students:* 83 full-time (22 women); includes 13 minority (2 Black or African American, non-Hispanic/Latino; 2 American Indian or Alaska Native, non-Hispanic/Latino; 7 Asian, non-Hispanic/Latino; 2 Hispanic/Latino), 14 international. Average age 27. 126 applicants, 46% accepted, 28 enrolled. In 2011, 21 degrees awarded. Terminal master's awarded for partial completion of doctoral program. *Degree requirements:* For master's, thesis; for doctorate, thesis/dissertation. *Entrance requirements:* For master's and doctorate, GRE General Test. Additional exam requirements/recommendations for international students: Required—TOEFL (minimum score 550 paper-based; 213 computer-based; 80 iBT). *Application deadline:* For fall admission, 1/15 priority date for domestic students, 12/15 for international students; for spring admission, 10/15 for domestic students, 9/15 for international students. Applications are processed on a rolling basis. Application fee: $75. Electronic applications accepted. *Expenses: Tuition:* Full-time $41,208; part-time $1030 per credit hour. Full-time tuition and fees vary according to degree level, program and student level. Part-time tuition and fees vary according to course load. *Financial support:* Fellowships with full tuition reimbursements, research assistantships with full and partial tuition reimbursements, teaching assistantships with full and partial tuition reimbursements, Federal Work-Study, scholarships/grants, tuition waivers (partial), and unspecified assistantships available. Financial award application deadline: 1/15; financial award applicants required to submit FAFSA. *Faculty research:* Applied mechanics, biomaterials, controls/robotics, design/systems, human factors. *Unit head:* Dr. Robert Hannemann, Acting Department Chair, 617-627-3239, Fax: 617-627-3058. *Application contact:* Lorin Polidora, Department Administrator, 617-627-3239, E-mail: meinfo@tufts.edu. Web site: http://engineering.tufts.edu/me.

Université de Montréal, Faculty of Medicine, Biochemistry Department, Montréal, QC H3C 3J7, Canada. Offers M Sc, PhD. Electronic applications accepted.

Université de Montréal, Faculty of Medicine, Program in Bioinformatics, Montréal, QC H3C 3J7, Canada. Offers M Sc, PhD.

University of Arkansas at Little Rock, Graduate School, George W. Donughey College of Engineering and Information Technology, Program in Bioinformatics, Little Rock, AR 72204-1099. Offers MS, PhD.

University of California, Los Angeles, Graduate Division, College of Letters and Science, Interdepartmental Program in Bioinformatics, Los Angeles, CA 90095. Offers MS, PhD. *Students:* 13 full-time (5 women); includes 3 minority (all Asian, non-Hispanic/Latino), 4 international. Average age 29. 54 applicants, 20% accepted, 2 enrolled. In 2011, 1 master's awarded. Application fee: $70 ($90 for international students). Electronic applications accepted. *Financial support:* In 2011–12, 9 fellowships, 5 research assistantships, 5 teaching assistantships were awarded. *Unit head:* Dr. Christopher Lee, Chair, 310-825-7374, E-mail: leec@chem.ucla.edu. *Application contact:* Nancy Purtill, Academic Services Manager, 310-825-7929, E-mail: nancyp@lifesci.ucla.edu. Web site: http://www.bioinformatics.ucla.edu/.

University of California, Riverside, Graduate Division, Graduate Program in Genetics, Genomics, and Bioinformatics, Riverside, CA 92521-0102. Offers genomics and bioinformatics (PhD); molecular genetics (PhD); population and evolutionary genetics (PhD). *Faculty:* 72 full-time (20 women). *Students:* 32 full-time (18 women); includes 2 minority (1 Black or African American, non-Hispanic/Latino; 1 Hispanic/Latino), 15 international. Average age 30. In 2011, 2 doctorates awarded. *Degree requirements:* For doctorate, thesis/dissertation, qualifying exams, teaching experience. *Entrance requirements:* For doctorate, GRE General Test, minimum GPA of 3.2. Additional exam requirements/recommendations for international students: Required—TOEFL (minimum score 550 paper-based; 213 computer-based; 80 iBT). *Application deadline:* For fall admission, 5/1 for domestic students, 2/1 for international students; for winter admission, 9/1 for domestic students, 7/1 for international students; for spring admission, 12/1 for domestic students, 10/1 for international students. Applications are processed on a rolling basis. Application fee: $85 ($100 for international students). Electronic applications accepted. *Financial support:* In 2011–12, fellowships with tuition reimbursements (averaging $12,000 per year), research assistantships with tuition reimbursements (averaging $18,000 per year), teaching assistantships with tuition reimbursements (averaging $16,500 per year) were awarded; career-related internships or fieldwork, Federal Work-Study, institutionally sponsored loans, and tuition waivers (full and partial) also available. *Faculty research:* Molecular genetics, evolution and population genetics, genomics and bioinformatics. *Unit head:* Dr. Shizhong Xu, Director,

951-827-5898. *Application contact:* Deidra Kornfeld, Graduate Program Assistant, 800-735-0717, Fax: 951-827-5517, E-mail: genetics@ucr.edu. Web site: http://ggb.ucr.edu/.

University of California, San Diego, Office of Graduate Studies, PhD Program in Bioinformatics and Systems Biology, La Jolla, CA 92093. Offers PhD. Offered through the Departments of Bioengineering, Biology, Biomedical Sciences, Chemistry and Biochemistry, Computer Sciences and Engineering, Mathematics, and Physics. *Entrance requirements:* For doctorate, GRE General Test. Electronic applications accepted.

University of California, San Diego, School of Medicine and Office of Graduate Studies, Molecular Pathology Program, La Jolla, CA 92093. Offers bioinformatics (PhD); cancer biology/oncology (PhD); cardiovascular sciences and disease (PhD); microbiology (PhD); molecular pathology (PhD); neurological disease (PhD); stem cell and developmental biology (PhD); structural biology/drug design (PhD). *Entrance requirements:* For doctorate, GRE General Test, GRE Subject Test. Additional exam requirements/recommendations for international students: Required—TOEFL. Electronic applications accepted.

University of California, San Francisco, School of Pharmacy and Graduate Division, Graduate Program in Biological and Medical Informatics, San Francisco, CA 94158-2517. Offers PhD. *Faculty:* 35 full-time (6 women). *Students:* 35 full-time (9 women); includes 7 minority (1 Black or African American, non-Hispanic/Latino; 3 Asian, non-Hispanic/Latino; 3 Hispanic/Latino), 3 international. Average age 28. 187 applicants, 20% accepted, 5 enrolled. In 2011, 3 doctorates awarded. Terminal master's awarded for partial completion of doctoral program. *Degree requirements:* For doctorate, thesis/dissertation, cumulative qualifying exams, proposal defense. *Entrance requirements:* For doctorate, GRE General Test, minimum GPA of 3.0. Additional exam requirements/recommendations for international students: Required—TOEFL (minimum score 550 paper-based; 213 computer-based; 80 iBT). *Application deadline:* For fall admission, 12/1 for domestic and international students). Application fee: $70 ($90 for international students). *Financial support:* In 2011–12, 35 students received support, including 6 fellowships with full tuition reimbursements available (averaging $29,500 per year), 29 research assistantships with full tuition reimbursements available (averaging $29,500 per year); career-related internships or fieldwork, scholarships/grants, traineeships, health care benefits, tuition waivers (full), and stipends also available. *Faculty research:* Bioinformatics, biomedical computing, decision science and engineering, imaging informatics, knowledge management/telehealth/health services research. *Unit head:* Thomas E. Ferrin, Director, 415-476-2299, Fax: 415-502-1755, E-mail: tef@cgl.ucsf.edu. *Application contact:* Julia Molla, Program Administrator, 415-476-1914, Fax: 415-502-4690, E-mail: jmolla@cgl.ucsf.edu. Web site: http://www.bioinformatics.ucsf.edu.

University of California, Santa Cruz, Division of Graduate Studies, Jack Baskin School of Engineering, Program in Bioinformatics, Santa Cruz, CA 95064. Offers MS, PhD. *Degree requirements:* For master's, research project with written report; for doctorate, thesis/dissertation. *Entrance requirements:* For master's and doctorate, GRE General Test. Additional exam requirements/recommendations for international students: Required—TOEFL (minimum score 570 paper-based; 230 computer-based; 89 iBT); Recommended—IELTS (minimum score 8). Electronic applications accepted. *Faculty research:* Bioinformatics, genomics, nanopore, stem cell.

University of Cincinnati, Graduate School, College of Engineering and Applied Science, Department of Biomedical Engineering, Cincinnati, OH 45221. Offers bioinformatics (PhD); biomechanics (PhD); medical imaging (PhD); tissue engineering (PhD). Part-time programs available. *Degree requirements:* For doctorate, one foreign language, thesis/dissertation. *Entrance requirements:* For doctorate, GRE General Test. Additional exam requirements/recommendations for international students: Required—TOEFL (minimum score 600 paper-based; 250 computer-based).

University of Colorado Denver, School of Medicine, Program in Pharmacology, Aurora, CO 80045. Offers bioinformatics (PhD); biomolecular structure (PhD); pharmacology (PhD). *Students:* 24 full-time (15 women); includes 4 minority (1 Black or African American, non-Hispanic/Latino; 2 Asian, non-Hispanic/Latino; 1 Hispanic/Latino). Average age 28. 18 applicants, 17% accepted, 3 enrolled. In 2011, 4 doctorates awarded. *Degree requirements:* For doctorate, comprehensive exam, thesis/dissertation, major seminar, 3 research rotations in the first year, 30 hours each of course work and thesis. *Entrance requirements:* For doctorate, GRE General Test. Additional exam requirements/recommendations for international students: Required—TOEFL (minimum score 550 paper-based; 213 computer-based; 80 iBT). *Application deadline:* For fall admission, 12/15 for domestic students, 11/15 for international students. Application fee: $50 ($75 for international students). Electronic applications accepted. *Expenses:* Contact institution. *Financial support:* Fellowships, research assistantships, teaching assistantships, health care benefits, tuition waivers (full), and stipend available. Financial award application deadline: 3/15; financial award applicants required to submit FAFSA. *Faculty research:* Cancer biology, drugs of abuse, neuroscience, signal transduction, structural biology. *Total annual research expenditures:* $16.7 million. *Unit head:* Dr. Andrew Thorburn, Interim Chair, 303-724-3290, Fax: 303-724-3663, E-mail: andrew.thorburn@ucdenver.edu. *Application contact:* Elizabeth Bowen, Graduate Training Coordinator, 303-724-3565, E-mail: elizabeth.bowen@ucdenver.edu. Web site: http://pharmacology.ucdenver.edu/.

University of Georgia, Institute of Bioinformatics, Athens, GA 30602. Offers MS, PhD, Graduate Certificate. *Students:* 46 full-time (23 women), 1 (woman) part-time; includes 4 minority (1 Black or African American, non-Hispanic/Latino; 2 Asian, non-Hispanic/Latino; 1 Hispanic/Latino), 36 international. Average age 29. 51 applicants, 22% accepted, 4 enrolled. In 2011, 1 master's, 2 doctorates awarded. *Unit head:* Dr. Jessica Kissinger, Director, 706-542-6562, E-mail: jkissing@uga.edu. *Application contact:* Dr. Jeffrey Dean, Graduate Coordinator, 706-542-1710, Fax: 706-5428356, E-mail: jeffdean@uga.edu. Web site: http://www.bioinformatics.uga.edu/.

University of Idaho, College of Graduate Studies, Program in Bioinformatics and Computational Biology, Moscow, ID 83844-3051. Offers MS, PhD. *Faculty:* 11 full-time. *Students:* 12 full-time, 4 part-time. Average age 29. *Entrance requirements:* For master's, GRE, minimum GPA of 2.8. *Application deadline:* For fall admission, 8/1 for domestic students; for spring admission, 12/15 for domestic students. Applications are processed on a rolling basis. Application fee: $60. Electronic applications accepted. *Expenses:* Tuition, state resident: full-time $3874; part-time $334 per credit hour. Tuition, nonresident: full-time $16,394; part-time $861 per credit hour. *Required fees:* $2808; $99 per credit hour. Tuition and fees vary according to program. *Financial support:* Applicants required to submit FAFSA. *Unit head:* Dr. Paul Joyce, Director, 208-885-6010, E-mail: bcb@uidaho.edu. *Application contact:* Erick Larson, Director of Graduate Admissions, 208-885-4723, E-mail: gadms@uidaho.edu. Web site: http://www.uidaho.edu/cogs/bcb.

University of Illinois at Urbana–Champaign, Graduate College, College of Agricultural, Consumer and Environmental Sciences, Department of Crop Sciences,

Champaign, IL 61820. Offers bioinformatics: crop sciences (MS); crop sciences (MS, PhD). Postbaccalaureate distance learning degree programs offered (no on-campus study). *Faculty:* 42 full-time (5 women), 1 (woman) part-time/adjunct. *Students:* 101 full-time (30 women), 45 part-time (13 women); includes 8 minority (1 Black or African American, non-Hispanic/Latino; 4 Asian, non-Hispanic/Latino; 3 Hispanic/Latino), 44 international. 121 applicants, 29% accepted, 31 enrolled. In 2011, 26 master's, 5 doctorates awarded. *Entrance requirements:* For master's and doctorate, GRE, minimum GPA of 3.0. Additional exam requirements/recommendations for international students: Required—TOEFL (minimum score 570 paper-based). *Application deadline:* Applications are processed on a rolling basis. Application fee: $75 ($90 for international students). Electronic applications accepted. *Financial support:* In 2011–12, 40 fellowships, 81 research assistantships, 26 teaching assistantships were awarded; tuition waivers (full and partial) also available. *Faculty research:* Plant breeding and genetics, molecular biology, crop production, plant physiology, weed science. *Unit head:* German A. Bollero, Head, 217-333-9475, Fax: 217-333-9817, E-mail: gbollero@illinois.edu. *Application contact:* S. Dianne Carson, Office Support Specialist, 217-244-0396, Fax: 217-333-9817, E-mail: sdcarson@illinois.edu. Web site: http://www.cropsci.illinois.edu.

University of Illinois at Urbana–Champaign, Graduate College, College of Engineering, Department of Computer Science, Champaign, IL 61820. Offers bioinformatics (MS); computer science (MCS, MS, PhD); MCS/JD; MCS/M Arch; MCS/MBA. Part-time programs available. Postbaccalaureate distance learning degree programs offered (no on-campus study). *Faculty:* 51 full-time (5 women), 2 part-time/adjunct (0 women). *Students:* 262 full-time (39 women), 186 part-time (27 women); includes 45 minority (3 Black or African American, non-Hispanic/Latino; 38 Asian, non-Hispanic/Latino; 1 Hispanic/Latino; 3 Two or more races, non-Hispanic/Latino), 269 international. 1,527 applicants, 16% accepted, 105 enrolled. In 2011, 78 master's, 42 doctorates awarded. *Entrance requirements:* For master's and doctorate, minimum GPA of 3.0. Additional exam requirements/recommendations for international students: Required—TOEFL (minimum score 600 paper-based; 250 computer-based; 100 iBT) or IELTS (minimum score 6.5). *Application deadline:* Applications are processed on a rolling basis. Application fee: $75 ($90 for International students). Electronic applications accepted. *Financial support:* In 2011–12, 39 fellowships, 274 research assistantships, 117 teaching assistantships were awarded; tuition waivers (full and partial) also available. *Unit head:* Robin A. Rutenbar, Head, 217-333-3373, Fax: 217-333-3501, E-mail: rutenbar@illinois.edu. *Application contact:* Laura Baylor, Graduate Academic Advisor, 217-333-3425, Fax: 217-244-6073, E-mail: lherriot@illinois.edu. Web site: http://cs.illinois.edu/.

University of Illinois at Urbana–Champaign, Graduate College, Graduate School of Library and Information Science, Champaign, IL 61820. Offers bioinformatics (MS); digital libraries (CAS); library and information science (MS, PhD, CAS). *Accreditation:* ALA (one or more programs are accredited). Postbaccalaureate distance learning degree programs offered. *Faculty:* 25 full-time (12 women), 5 part-time/adjunct (4 women). *Students:* 349 full-time (256 women), 353 part-time (276 women); includes 125 minority (30 Black or African American, non-Hispanic/Latino; 1 American Indian or Alaska Native, non-Hispanic/Latino; 37 Asian, non-Hispanic/Latino; 40 Hispanic/Latino; 1 Native Hawaiian or other Pacific Islander, non-Hispanic/Latino; 16 Two or more races, non-Hispanic/Latino), 27 international. 606 applicants, 68% accepted, 250 enrolled. In 2011, 245 master's, 6 doctorates, 8 other advanced degrees awarded. *Entrance requirements:* For master's, GRE General Test, minimum GPA of 3.0; for doctorate, minimum GPA of 3.0; for CAS, master's degree in library and information science or related field with minimum GPA of 3.0. Additional exam requirements/recommendations for international students: Required—TOEFL (minimum score 620 paper-based; 260 computer-based; 105 iBT) or IELTS (minimum score 7). *Application deadline:* Applications are processed on a rolling basis. Application fee: $75 ($90 for international students). Electronic applications accepted. *Financial support:* In 2011–12, 24 fellowships, 39 research assistantships, 44 teaching assistantships were awarded; tuition waivers (full and partial) also available. *Unit head:* Allen Renear, Dean, 217-265-5216, Fax: 217-244-3302, E-mail: renear@illinois.edu. *Application contact:* Valerie Youngen, Admissions and Records Representative, 217-333-0734, Fax: 217-244-3302, E-mail: vyoungen@illinois.edu. Web site: http://www.lis.illinois.edu.

The University of Manchester, Faculty of Life Sciences, Manchester, United Kingdom. Offers adaptive organismal biology (M Phil, PhD); animal biology (M Phil, PhD); biochemistry (M Phil, PhD); bioinformatics (M Phil, PhD); biomolecular sciences (M Phil, PhD); biotechnology (M Phil, PhD); cell biology (M Phil, PhD); cell matrix research (M Phil, PhD); channels and transporters (M Phil, PhD); developmental biology (M Phil, PhD); Egyptology (M Phil, PhD); environmental biology (M Phil, PhD); evolutionary biology (M Phil, PhD); gene expression (M Phil, PhD); genetics (M Phil, PhD); history of science, technology and medicine (M Phil, PhD); immunology (M Phil, PhD); integrative neurobiology and behavior (M Phil, PhD); membrane trafficking (M Phil, PhD); microbiology (M Phil, PhD); molecular and cellular neuroscience (M Phil, PhD); molecular biology (M Phil, PhD); molecular cancer studies (M Phil, PhD); neuroscience (M Phil, PhD); ophthalmology (M Phil, PhD); optometry (M Phil, PhD); organelle function (M Phil, PhD); pharmacology (M Phil, PhD); physiology (M Phil, PhD); plant sciences (M Phil, PhD); stem cell research (M Phil, PhD); structural biology (M Phil, PhD); systems neuroscience (M Phil, PhD); toxicology (M Phil, PhD).

University of Maryland, College Park, Academic Affairs, College of Computer, Mathematical and Natural Sciences, Department of Biology, PhD Program in Biological Sciences, College Park, MD 20742. Offers behavior, ecology, evolution, and systematics (PhD); computational biology, bioinformatics, and genomics (PhD); molecular and cellular biology (PhD); physiological systems (PhD). *Students:* 68 full-time (41 women), 4 part-time (2 women); includes 13 minority (3 Black or African American, non-Hispanic/Latino; 4 Asian, non-Hispanic/Latino; 5 Hispanic/Latino; 1 Two or more races, non-Hispanic/Latino), 21 international. 380 applicants, 15% accepted, 22 enrolled. *Degree requirements:* For doctorate, comprehensive exam, thesis/dissertation, present thesis work in seminar. *Entrance requirements:* For doctorate, GRE General Test; GRE Subject Test in biology (recommended), academic transcripts, statement of purpose/research interests, 3 letters of recommendation. Additional exam requirements/recommendations for international students: Required—TOEFL. *Application deadline:* For fall admission, 12/15 for domestic and international students. Applications are processed on a rolling basis. Application fee: $75. Electronic applications accepted. *Expenses:* Tuition, area resident: Part-time $525 per credit hour. Tuition, state resident: part-time $525 per credit hour. Tuition, nonresident: part-time $1131 per credit hour. *Required fees:* $386.31 per term. Tuition and fees vary according to program. *Financial support:* In 2011–12, 11 fellowships with full and partial tuition reimbursements (averaging $14,406 per year), 16 research assistantships (averaging $19,495 per year), 41 teaching assistantships (averaging $18,734 per year) were awarded. *Unit head:* Dr. Barbara Thorne, Director, 301-405-6905, E-mail: bthorne@umd.edu. *Application contact:* Dr. Charles A. Caramello, Dean of Graduate School, 301-405-0358, Fax: 301-314-9305. Web site: http://bisi.umd.edu/biologicalsciencesgraduateprogrambisi.

University of Massachusetts Worcester, Graduate School of Biomedical Sciences, Worcester, MA 01655-0115. Offers biochemistry and molecular pharmacology (PhD); bioinformatics and computational biology (PhD); cancer biology (PhD); cell biology (PhD); clinical and population health research (PhD); clinical investigation (MS); immunology and virology (PhD); interdisciplinary graduate program (PhD); molecular genetics and microbiology (PhD); neuroscience (PhD); DVM/PhD; MD/PhD. *Faculty:* 1,427 full-time (526 women), 309 part-time/adjunct (196 women). *Students:* 416 full-time (225 women); includes 47 minority (12 Black or African American, non-Hispanic/Latino; 32 Asian, non-Hispanic/Latino; 3 Hispanic/Latino), 144 international. Average age 29. 623 applicants, 17% accepted, 54 enrolled. In 2011, 5 master's, 63 doctorates awarded. Terminal master's awarded for partial completion of doctoral program. *Degree requirements:* For master's, comprehensive exam, thesis; for doctorate, comprehensive exam, thesis/dissertation. *Entrance requirements:* For master's, bachelor's degree; for doctorate, GRE General Test. Additional exam requirements/recommendations for international students: Required—TOEFL (minimum score 600 paper-based; 250 computer-based; 100 iBT) or IELTS (minimum score 7.5). *Application deadline:* For fall admission, 12/15 for domestic and international students; for spring admission, 5/15 for domestic students. Application fee: $50. Electronic applications accepted. *Expenses:* Contact institution. *Financial support:* In 2011–12, 416 students received support, including 416 research assistantships with full tuition reimbursements available (averaging $29,200 per year); scholarships/grants, health care benefits, tuition waivers (full), and unspecified assistantships also available. Financial award application deadline: 4/16. *Faculty research:* RNA interference, cell biology, bioinformatics, clinical research, infectious disease. *Total annual research expenditures:* $262.7 million. *Unit head:* Dr. Anthony Carruthers, Dean, 508-856-4135, E-mail: anthony.carruthers@umassmed.edu. *Application contact:* Dr. Kendall Knight, Associate Dean and Interim Director of Admissions and Recruitment, 508-856-5628, Fax: 508-856-3659, E-mail: kendall.knight@umassmed.edu. Web site: http://www.umassmed.edu/gsbs/.

University of Medicine and Dentistry of New Jersey, School of Health Related Professions, Department of Health Informatics, Program in Biomedical Informatics, Newark, NJ 07107-1709. Offers MS, PhD, DMD/MS, MD/MS. Part-time and evening/weekend programs available. Postbaccalaureate distance learning degree programs offered (minimal on-campus study). *Faculty:* 4 full-time (0 women), 20 part-time/adjunct (8 women). *Students:* 40 full-time, 63 part-time; includes 61 minority (19 Black or African American, non-Hispanic/Latino; 39 Asian, non-Hispanic/Latino; 3 Hispanic/Latino), 29 international. Average age 37. 95 applicants, 71% accepted, 44 enrolled. In 2011, 16 master's, 6 doctorates awarded. *Degree requirements:* For master's, thesis; for doctorate, comprehensive exam, thesis/dissertation. *Entrance requirements:* For master's, BS, transcript of highest degree, statement of research interests, curriculum vitae, basic understanding of database concepts and calculus, 3 reference letters; for doctorate, master's degree, transcripts of highest degree, statement of research interests, curriculum vitae, basic understanding of database concepts and calculus, 3 reference letters. Additional exam requirements/recommendations for international students: Required—TOEFL. *Application deadline:* For fall admission, 6/1 for domestic students, 3/1 for international students; for winter admission, 4/1 for domestic students; for spring admission, 10/1 for domestic students, 7/1 for international students. Applications are processed on a rolling basis. Application fee: $75. Electronic applications accepted. *Unit head:* Dr. Syed Haque, Chair, 973-972-6871, E-mail: haque@umdnj.edu. *Application contact:* Diane Hanrahan, Assistant Dean, 973-972-5336, Fax: 973-972-7463, E-mail: shrpadm@umdnj.edu.

University of Michigan, Horace H. Rackham School of Graduate Studies, Program in Biomedical Sciences (PIBS) and Horace H. Rackham School of Graduate Studies, Program in Bioinformatics, Ann Arbor, MI 48109-2218. Offers MS, PhD. Part-time programs available. *Faculty:* 122 full-time (27 women). *Students:* 40 full-time (9 women), 1 part-time (0 women); includes 8 minority (1 Black or African American, non-Hispanic/Latino; 1 American Indian or Alaska Native, non-Hispanic/Latino; 4 Asian, non-Hispanic/Latino; 1 Hispanic/Latino; 1 Two or more races, non-Hispanic/Latino), 18 international. 39 applicants, 28% accepted, 6 enrolled. In 2011, 4 master's, 4 doctorates awarded. Terminal master's awarded for partial completion of doctoral program. *Degree requirements:* For master's, thesis optional, summer internship or rotation; for doctorate, thesis/dissertation, oral defense of dissertation, preliminary exam, two rotations. *Entrance requirements:* For master's and doctorate, GRE or MCAT. Additional exam requirements/recommendations for international students: Required—TOEFL (minimum score 100 iBT). *Application deadline:* For fall admission, 12/1 for domestic and international students. Application fee: $60 ($75 for international students). Electronic applications accepted. *Financial support:* In 2011–12, 44 students received support, including 22 fellowships with full tuition reimbursements available (averaging $26,500 per year), 18 research assistantships with full tuition reimbursements available (averaging $26,500 per year), 4 teaching assistantships with full tuition reimbursements available (averaging $26,500 per year); scholarships/grants, traineeships, health care benefits, and unspecified assistantships also available. Financial award application deadline: 12/1. *Faculty research:* Structural and chemical informatics, clinical informatics, databases and computing, genomics, proteomics, statistical applications, systemic modeling. *Unit head:* Dr. Dan Margit, Co-Director, 734-615-5510, Fax: 734-615-6553, E-mail: gradbioinfo@umich.edu. *Application contact:* Michelle S. Melis, Director of Student Life, 734-615-6538, Fax: 734-647-7022, E-mail: msmtegan@umich.edu. Web site: http://www.ccmb.med.umich.edu/graduate-program.

University of Missouri, Graduate School, Informatics Institute, Columbia, MO 65211. Offers PhD. *Students:* 11 full-time (4 women), 19 part-time (8 women); includes 4 minority (1 Black or African American, non-Hispanic/Latino; 1 American Indian or Alaska Native, non-Hispanic/Latino; 2 Hispanic/Latino), 15 international. Average age 35. 15 applicants, 33% accepted, 4 enrolled. In 2011, 1 degree awarded. *Entrance requirements:* Additional exam requirements/recommendations for international students: Required—TOEFL (minimum score 577 paper-based; 233 computer-based; 90 iBT). *Expenses:* Tuition, state resident: full-time $5881. Tuition, nonresident: full-time $15,183. *Required fees:* $952. Tuition and fees vary according to campus/location and program. *Faculty research:* Human-computer interaction, human factors, information technology standards, IT sophistication in nursing homes, data mining and knowledge discovery in genomics and epigenomics, pathology decision support systems, digital image analysis, pathology text mining, computational biophysics, RNA folding and gene regulation, computer graphics and scientific visualization, biomedical imaging and computer vision, 3D shape modeling. *Unit head:* Dr. Chi-Ren Shyu, Director, 573-882-3884, E-mail: shyuc@missouri.edu. *Application contact:* Brenda Montague, 573-882-9007, E-mail: muiiadmissions@missouri.edu. Web site: http://muii.missouri.edu/.

University of Missouri–Kansas City, School of Computing and Engineering, Kansas City, MO 64110-2499. Offers civil engineering (MS); computer and electrical engineering (PhD); computer science (MS), including bioinformatics, software engineering, telecommunications networking; computer science and informatics (PhD); computing (PhD); electrical engineering (MS); engineering (PhD); mechanical engineering (MS);

telecommunications (PhD). PhD (interdisciplinary) offered through the School of Graduate Studies. Part-time programs available. *Faculty:* 36 full-time (6 women), 27 part-time/adjunct (3 women). *Students:* 155 full-time (44 women), 136 part-time (24 women); includes 19 minority (4 Black or African American, non-Hispanic/Latino; 7 Asian, non-Hispanic/Latino; 6 Hispanic/Latino; 2 Two or more races, non-Hispanic/Latino), 201 international. Average age 26. 455 applicants, 46% accepted, 96 enrolled. In 2011, 194 degrees awarded. *Degree requirements:* For doctorate, thesis/dissertation. *Entrance requirements:* For master's, GRE General Test, minimum GPA of 3.0, 3 letters of recommendation from professors; for doctorate, GRE General Test, minimum GPA of 3.5. Additional exam requirements/recommendations for international students: Required—TOEFL (minimum score 550 paper-based; 213 computer-based; 80 iBT). *Application deadline:* For fall admission, 1/15 priority date for domestic students, 1/15 for international students. Applications are processed on a rolling basis. Application fee: $45 ($50 for international students). *Expenses:* Tuition, state resident: full-time $5798; part-time $322.10 per credit hour. Tuition, nonresident: full-time $14,969; part-time $831.60 per credit hour. *Required fees:* $93.51 per credit hour. *Financial support:* In 2011–12, 47 research assistantships with partial tuition reimbursements (averaging $13,190 per year), 10 teaching assistantships with partial tuition reimbursements (averaging $9,815 per year) were awarded; career-related internships or fieldwork, Federal Work-Study, scholarships/grants, tuition waivers (partial), and unspecified assistantships also available. Support available to part-time students. Financial award application deadline: 3/1; financial award applicants required to submit FAFSA. *Faculty research:* Algorithms, bioinformatics and medical informatics, biomechanics/biomaterials, civil engineering materials, networking and telecommunications, thermal science. *Unit head:* Dr. Kevin Z. Truman, Dean, 816-235-2399, Fax: 816-235-5159. *Application contact:* 816-235-2399, Fax: 816-235-5159. Web site: http://sce.umkc.edu/.

University of Missouri–Kansas City, School of Medicine, Kansas City, MO 64110-2499. Offers anesthesia (MS); bioinformatics (MS); medicine (MD); MD/PhD. *Accreditation:* LCME/AMA. *Faculty:* 38 full-time (13 women), 15 part-time/adjunct (4 women). *Students:* 424 full-time (224 women), 11 part-time (7 women); includes 230 minority (25 Black or African American, non-Hispanic/Latino; 1 American Indian or Alaska Native, non-Hispanic/Latino; 190 Asian, non-Hispanic/Latino; 12 Hispanic/Latino; 2 Two or more races, non-Hispanic/Latino), 2 international. Average age 23. 821 applicants, 15% accepted, 107 enrolled. In 2011, 4 master's, 101 doctorates awarded. *Degree requirements:* For doctorate, one foreign language, United States Medical Licensing Exam Step 1 and 2. *Entrance requirements:* For doctorate, interview. *Application deadline:* For fall admission, 11/15 for domestic and international students. Application fee: $50. *Expenses:* Contact institution. *Financial support:* Career-related internships or fieldwork, Federal Work-Study, institutionally sponsored loans, scholarships/grants, and tuition waivers (partial) available. Financial award application deadline: 3/1; financial award applicants required to submit FAFSA. *Faculty research:* Cardiovascular disease, women's and children's health, trauma and infectious diseases, neurological, metabolic disease. *Unit head:* Dr. Betty Drees, Dean, 816-235-1808, E-mail: dreesb@umkc.edu. *Application contact:* Kelly Kasper-Cushman, Interim Admissions Coordinator, 816-235-1870, Fax: 816-235-6579, E-mail: kasperkm@umkc.edu. Web site: http://www.med.umkc.edu/.

University of Nebraska–Lincoln, Graduate College, College of Arts and Sciences and College of Engineering, Department of Computer Science and Engineering, Lincoln, NE 68588. Offers bioinformatics (MS, PhD); computer engineering (MS, PhD); computer science (MS, PhD); information technology (PhD). *Degree requirements:* For master's, thesis optional; for doctorate, comprehensive exam, thesis/dissertation. *Entrance requirements:* For master's and doctorate, GRE General Test. Additional exam requirements/recommendations for international students: Required—TOEFL (minimum score 600 paper-based; 250 computer-based). Electronic applications accepted. *Faculty research:* Software engineering, geo- and bio-informatics, scientific computation, secure communication.

The University of North Carolina at Chapel Hill, School of Medicine and Graduate School, Graduate Programs in Medicine, Curriculum in Bioinformatics and Computational Biology, Chapel Hill, NC 27599. Offers PhD. *Degree requirements:* For doctorate, comprehensive exam, thesis/dissertation. *Entrance requirements:* For doctorate, GRE, minimum GPA of 3.0. Additional exam requirements/recommendations for international students: Required—TOEFL. Electronic applications accepted. *Faculty research:* Protein folding, design and evolution and molecular biophysics of disease; mathematical modeling of signaling pathways and regulatory networks; bioinformatics, medical informatics, user interface design; statistical genetics and genetic epidemiology datamining, classification and clustering analysis of gene-expression data.

The University of North Carolina at Charlotte, Graduate School, College of Computing and Informatics, Department of Bioinformatics and Genomics, Charlotte, NC 28223-0001. Offers bioinformatics (MS, PhD, Certificate). Part-time programs available. *Faculty:* 13 full-time (5 women). *Students:* 31 full-time (14 women), 2 part-time (1 woman); includes 7 minority (3 Black or African American, non-Hispanic/Latino; 2 Asian, non-Hispanic/Latino; 1 Native Hawaiian or other Pacific Islander, non-Hispanic/Latino; 1 Two or more races, non-Hispanic/Latino), 10 international. Average age 28. 25 applicants, 68% accepted, 10 enrolled. In 2011, 8 master's, 2 doctorates, 2 other advanced degrees awarded. Terminal master's awarded for partial completion of doctoral program. *Degree requirements:* For master's, internship, research project, or thesis. *Entrance requirements:* For master's, GRE, minimum undergraduate GPA of 3.0 overall and in undergraduate major. Additional exam requirements/recommendations for international students: Required—TOEFL (minimum score 557 paper-based; 220 computer-based; 83 iBT). *Application deadline:* For fall admission, 7/15 for domestic students, 5/1 for international students; for spring admission, 11/15 for domestic students, 10/1 for international students. Applications are processed on a rolling basis. Application fee: $65 ($75 for international students). Electronic applications accepted. *Expenses:* Tuition, state resident: full-time $3689. Tuition, nonresident: full-time $15,226. *Required fees:* $2198. Tuition and fees vary according to course load and program. *Financial support:* In 2011–12, 26 students received support, including 8 fellowships (averaging $33,557 per year), 10 research assistantships (averaging $13,725 per year), 8 teaching assistantships (averaging $13,938 per year); career-related internships or fieldwork, institutionally sponsored loans, scholarships/grants, and unspecified assistantships also available. Support available to part-time students. *Faculty research:* High-throughput studies, computational biophysics, structural bioinformatics, metagenomics, computational mass spectrometry. *Total annual research expenditures:* $879,165. *Unit head:* Dr. Larry Mays, Chairman, 704-687-8555, E-mail: lemays@uncc.edu. *Application contact:* Kathy B. Giddings, Director of Graduate Admissions, 704-687-5503, Fax: 704-687-3279, E-mail: gradadm@uncc.edu. Web site: http://bioinformatics.uncc.edu/.

University of Oklahoma, College of Arts and Sciences, Department of Chemistry and Biochemistry, Norman, OK 73019. Offers chemistry and biochemistry (MS, PhD), including bioinformatics, cellular and behavioral neurobiology (PhD), chemistry. Part-time programs available. *Faculty:* 27 full-time (6 women). *Students:* 67 full-time (25 women), 22 part-time (9 women); includes 15 minority (5 Black or African American, non-Hispanic/Latino; 1 American Indian or Alaska Native, non-Hispanic/Latino; 3 Asian, non-Hispanic/Latino; 4 Hispanic/Latino; 2 Two or more races, non-Hispanic/Latino), 40 international. Average age 28. 92 applicants, 17% accepted, 15 enrolled. In 2011, 17 master's, 17 doctorates awarded. Terminal master's awarded for partial completion of doctoral program. *Degree requirements:* For master's, thesis optional; for doctorate, thesis/dissertation. *Entrance requirements:* For master's, GRE, BS in chemistry; for doctorate, GRE. Additional exam requirements/recommendations for international students: Required—TOEFL (minimum score 550 paper-based; 79 iBT). *Application deadline:* For fall admission, 4/1 priority date for domestic students, 3/1 for international students; for spring admission, 9/1 priority date for domestic students, 9/1 for international students. Applications are processed on a rolling basis. Application fee: $40 ($90 for international students). Electronic applications accepted. *Expenses:* Tuition, state resident: full-time $4087; part-time $170.30 per credit hour. Tuition, nonresident: full-time $14,875; part-time $619.80 per credit hour. *Required fees:* $2659; $100.25 per credit hour. Tuition and fees vary according to course load and degree level. *Financial support:* In 2011–12, 89 students received support, including 1 fellowship with full tuition reimbursement available (averaging $5,000 per year), 19 research assistantships with partial tuition reimbursements available (averaging $15,794 per year), 58 teaching assistantships with partial tuition reimbursements available (averaging $16,776 per year); scholarships/grants, tuition waivers (full), and unspecified assistantships also available. Financial award applicants required to submit FAFSA. *Faculty research:* Structural biology, synthesis and catalysis, biomaterials, membrane biochemistry, genomics. *Total annual research expenditures:* $7 million. *Unit head:* Dr. George Richter-Addo, Chair, 405-325-4811, Fax: 405-325-6111, E-mail: grichteraddo@ou.edu. *Application contact:* Angelika Tietz, Graduate Program Assistant, 405-325-4811 Ext. 62946, Fax: 405-325-6111, E-mail: atietz@ou.edu. Web site: http://chem.ou.edu.

University of Oklahoma, College of Engineering, School of Computer Science, Norman, OK 73019. Offers computer science (MS, PhD), including bioinformatics, general (MS), standard (PhD). *Faculty:* 19 full-time (4 women), 1 part-time/adjunct (0 women). *Students:* 68 full-time (13 women), 34 part-time (1 woman); includes 4 minority (1 Black or African American, non-Hispanic/Latino; 1 American Indian or Alaska Native, non-Hispanic/Latino; 2 Asian, non-Hispanic/Latino), 65 international. Average age 27. 125 applicants, 50% accepted, 18 enrolled. In 2011, 31 master's, 2 doctorates awarded. Terminal master's awarded for partial completion of doctoral program. *Degree requirements:* For master's, thesis optional, oral exams, qualifying exam; for doctorate, thesis/dissertation, general exam, qualifying exam. *Entrance requirements:* For master's and doctorate, GRE General Test. Additional exam requirements/recommendations for international students: Required—TOEFL (minimum score 550 paper-based; 79 iBT). *Application deadline:* For fall admission, 1/15 priority date for domestic students, 3/1 for international students; for spring admission, 11/1 for domestic students, 9/1 for international students. Applications are processed on a rolling basis. Application fee: $40 ($90 for international students). Electronic applications accepted. *Expenses:* Tuition, state resident: full-time $4087; part-time $170.30 per credit hour. Tuition, nonresident: full-time $14,875; part-time $619.80 per credit hour. *Required fees:* $2659; $100.25 per credit hour. Tuition and fees vary according to course load and degree level. *Financial support:* In 2011–12, 81 students received support, including 3 fellowships with full tuition reimbursements available (averaging $3,000 per year), 18 research assistantships with partial tuition reimbursements available (averaging $15,735 per year), 20 teaching assistantships with partial tuition reimbursements available (averaging $16,144 per year); unspecified assistantships also available. Financial award applicants required to submit FAFSA. *Faculty research:* Artificial intelligence and robotics, scientific computing, computer networks, high performance computing, computer architecture, database management, visual analytics, cryptography. *Total annual research expenditures:* $2.8 million. *Unit head:* Sridhar Radhakrishnan, Professor and Director, 405-325-4042, Fax: 405-325-4044, E-mail: sridhar@ou.edu. *Application contact:* Miranda Sowell, Coordinator of Graduate Admissions, 405-325-3811, Fax: 405-325-5346, E-mail: mgsowell@ou.edu. Web site: http://www.cs.ou.edu/.

University of Pittsburgh, School of Medicine, Biomedical Informatics Training Program, Pittsburgh, PA 15260. Offers MS, PhD, Certificate. Part-time programs available. *Faculty:* 16 full-time (5 women), 11 part-time/adjunct (5 women). *Students:* 23 full-time (9 women), 9 part-time (4 women); includes 9 minority (2 Black or African American, non-Hispanic/Latino; 6 Asian, non-Hispanic/Latino; 1 Hispanic/Latino), 10 international. Average age 28. 51 applicants, 27% accepted, 10 enrolled. In 2011, 4 master's, 2 doctorates awarded. Terminal master's awarded for partial completion of doctoral program. *Median time to degree:* Of those who began their doctoral program in fall 2003, 96% received their degree in 8 years or less. *Degree requirements:* For master's, comprehensive exam, written research report; for doctorate, comprehensive exam, written research report or thesis. *Entrance requirements:* For master's, doctorate, and Certificate, GRE. Additional exam requirements/recommendations for international students: Required—TOEFL. *Application deadline:* For fall admission, 2/1 priority date for domestic students, 2/1 for international students. Application fee: $50. Electronic applications accepted. *Expenses:* Tuition, state resident: full-time $18,774; part-time $760 per credit. Tuition, nonresident: full-time $30,736; part-time $1258 per credit. *Required fees:* $740; $200 per term. Tuition and fees vary according to program. *Financial support:* In 2011–12, 16 students received support, including 10 fellowships with full tuition reimbursements available (averaging $25,500 per year), 6 research assistantships with full tuition reimbursements available (averaging $25,500 per year); health care benefits also available. Financial award application deadline: 2/1. *Faculty research:* Biomedical informatics; bioinformatics; global health informatics; artificial intelligence; probability theory; data mining; machine learning; evaluation methods; dental, radiology, and pathology imaging. *Unit head:* Dr. Rebecca Crowley, Director, 412-647-7113, Fax: 412-647-7190, E-mail: crowleyrs@upmc.edu. *Application contact:* Toni L. Porterfield, Coordinator, 412-647-7176, Fax: 412-647-7190, E-mail: tls18@pitt.edu. Web site: http://www.dbmi.pitt.edu.

University of Southern California, Graduate School, Dana and David Dornsife College of Letters, Arts and Sciences, Department of Biological Sciences, Program in Molecular and Computational Biology, Los Angeles, CA 90089. Offers computational biology and bioinformatics (PhD); molecular biology (PhD). *Degree requirements:* For doctorate, comprehensive exam, thesis/dissertation, qualifying examination, dissertation defense. *Entrance requirements:* For doctorate, GRE, 3 letters of recommendation, personal statement, resume, minimum GPA of 3.0. Additional exam requirements/recommendations for international students: Required—TOEFL (minimum score 600 paper-based; 250 computer-based; 100 iBT). Electronic applications accepted. *Faculty research:* Biochemistry and molecular biology; genomics; computational biology and bioinformatics; cell and developmental biology, and genetics; DNA replication and repair, and cancer biology.

University of South Florida, Graduate School, College of Medicine and Graduate School, Graduate Programs in Medical Sciences, Tampa, FL 33620-9951. Offers bioethics and medical humanities (MABMH); bioinformatics and computational biology

(MSBCB); biotechnology (MSB); medical sciences (MSMS, PhD). *Students:* 439 full-time (235 women), 111 part-time (65 women); includes 258 minority (82 Black or African American, non-Hispanic/Latino; 2 American Indian or Alaska Native, non-Hispanic/Latino; 85 Asian, non-Hispanic/Latino; 77 Hispanic/Latino; 12 Two or more races, non-Hispanic/Latino), 24 international. Average age 27. 1,032 applicants, 53% accepted, 364 enrolled. In 2011, 167 master's, 14 doctorates awarded. Terminal master's awarded for partial completion of doctoral program. *Degree requirements:* For master's, comprehensive exam, thesis; for doctorate, comprehensive exam, thesis/dissertation. *Entrance requirements:* For master's, GRE, MCAT, or GMAT, minimum GPA of 3.0 in last 60 hours of coursework; for doctorate, GRE, minimum GPA of 3.0 in last 60 hours of coursework, three letters of recommendation, personal statement, interview. Additional exam requirements/recommendations for international students: Required—TOEFL (minimum score 550 paper-based; 213 computer-based; 79 iBT) or IELTS (minimum score 6.5). *Application deadline:* For fall admission, 2/15 for domestic students, 1/2 for international students. Application fee: $30. *Expenses:* Contact institution. *Unit head:* Dr. Michael Barber, Program Director, 813-974-9702, Fax: 813-974-4317, E-mail: mbarber@health.usf.edu. *Application contact:* Francisco Vera, Assistant Director for Admissions, 813-974-8800, E-mail: fvera@usf.edu. Web site: http://health.usf.edu/medicine/graduatestudies.

The University of Texas at Dallas, School of Natural Sciences and Mathematics, Department of Mathematical Sciences, Richardson, TX 75080. Offers applied mathematics (MS, PhD); bioinformatics and computational biology (MS); engineering mathematics (MS); mathematics (MS); statistics (MS, PhD). Part-time and evening/weekend programs available. *Faculty:* 15 full-time (2 women). *Students:* 53 full-time (21 women), 17 part-time (3 women); includes 21 minority (5 Black or African American, non-Hispanic/Latino; 12 Asian, non-Hispanic/Latino; 4 Hispanic/Latino), 31 international. Average age 31. 127 applicants, 32% accepted, 28 enrolled. In 2011, 16 master's, 7 doctorates awarded. *Degree requirements:* For master's, thesis optional; for doctorate, thesis/dissertation. *Entrance requirements:* For master's, GRE General Test, minimum GPA of 3.0 in upper-level course work in field; for doctorate, GRE General Test, minimum GPA of 3.5 in upper-level course work in field. Additional exam requirements/recommendations for international students: Required—TOEFL (minimum score 550 paper-based; 215 computer-based). *Application deadline:* For fall admission, 7/15 for domestic students; 5/1 for international students; for spring admission, 11/15 for domestic students, 9/1 for international students. Applications are processed on a rolling basis. Application fee: $50 ($100 for international students). Electronic applications accepted. *Expenses:* Tuition, state resident: full-time $11,170; part-time $620.56 per credit hour. Tuition, nonresident: full-time $20,212; part-time $1122.89 per credit hour. *Financial support:* In 2011–12, 39 students received support, including 2 research assistantships (averaging $20,700 per year), 31 teaching assistantships with partial tuition reimbursements available (averaging $15,503 per year); career-related internships or fieldwork, Federal Work-Study, institutionally sponsored loans, scholarships/grants, and unspecified assistantships also available. Support available to part-time students. Financial award application deadline: 4/30; financial award applicants required to submit FAFSA. *Faculty research:* Sequential analysis, applications in semiconductor manufacturing, medical image analysis, computational anatomy, information theory, probability theory. *Unit head:* Dr. Matthew Goeckner, Department Head, 972-883-4292, Fax: 972-883-6622, E-mail: goeckner@utdallas.edu. *Application contact:* Claire C. Troy, Graduate Support Assistant, 972-883-2163, Fax: 972-883-6622, E-mail: utdmath@utdallas.edu. Web site: http://www.utdallas.edu/math.

The University of Texas at El Paso, Graduate School, College of Science, Department of Biological Sciences, El Paso, TX 79968-0001. Offers bioinformatics (MS); biological sciences (MS, PhD). Part-time and evening/weekend programs available. *Students:* 76 (43 women); includes 49 minority (3 Black or African American, non-Hispanic/Latino; 3 Asian, non-Hispanic/Latino; 42 Hispanic/Latino; 1 Two or more races, non-Hispanic/Latino), 14 international. Average age 34. 38 applicants, 45% accepted, 16 enrolled. In 2011, 4 master's, 1 doctorate awarded. *Degree requirements:* For master's, thesis; for doctorate, thesis/dissertation. *Entrance requirements:* For master's, GRE, minimum GPA of 3.0, letters of recommendation; for doctorate, GRE, statement of purpose, letters of recommendation. Additional exam requirements/recommendations for international students: Required—TOEFL; Recommended—IELTS. *Application deadline:* For fall admission, 8/1 priority date for domestic students, 3/1 for international students; for spring admission, 11/1 priority date for domestic students, 9/1 for international students. Applications are processed on a rolling basis. Application fee: $45 ($80 for international students). Electronic applications accepted. *Financial support:* In 2011–12, research assistantships with partial tuition reimbursements (averaging $22,500 per year), teaching assistantships with partial tuition reimbursements (averaging $18,000 per year) were awarded; fellowships with partial tuition reimbursements, institutionally sponsored loans, scholarships/grants, health care benefits, tuition waivers (partial), and unspecified assistantships also available. Support available to part-time students. Financial award application deadline: 3/15; financial award applicants required to submit FAFSA. *Unit head:* Dr. Robert Kirken, Chair, 915-747-5844, Fax: 915-747-5808, E-mail: rkirken@utep.edu. *Application contact:* Dr. Benjamin Flores, Interim Dean of Graduate School, 915-747-5491, Fax: 915-747-5788, E-mail: bflores@utep.edu.

The University of Texas at El Paso, Graduate School, College of Science, Program in Bioinformatics, El Paso, TX 79968-0001. Offers MS. *Students:* 15 (3 women); includes 3 minority (all Hispanic/Latino), 10 international. In 2011, 1 master's awarded. *Entrance requirements:* For master's, GRE, minimum GPA of 3.0. Additional exam requirements/recommendations for international students: Required—TOEFL. *Application deadline:* For fall admission, 8/1 for domestic students, 3/1 for international students; for spring admission, 11/1 for domestic students, 9/3 for international students. Application fee: $45 ($80 for international students). *Unit head:* Dr. Ming-Ying Leung, Director, 915-747-8484, Fax: 915-747-6502, E-mail: bioinformatics@utep.edu. *Application contact:* Dr. Benjamin Flores, Interim Dean of the Graduate School, 915-747-5844, Fax: 915-747-5788, E-mail: bflores@utep.edu. Web site: http://www.bioinformatics.utep.edu/.

The University of Texas Medical Branch, Graduate School of Biomedical Sciences, Program in Biochemistry and Molecular Biology, Galveston, TX 77555. Offers biochemistry (PhD); bioinformatics (PhD); biophysics (PhD); cell biology (PhD); computational biology (PhD); structural biology (PhD). *Degree requirements:* For doctorate, thesis/dissertation. *Entrance requirements:* Additional exam requirements/recommendations for international students: Required—TOEFL (minimum score 550 paper-based; 213 computer-based). Electronic applications accepted.

University of the Sciences in Philadelphia, College of Graduate Studies, Program in Bioinformatics, Philadelphia, PA 19104-4495. Offers MS. *Entrance requirements:* Additional exam requirements/recommendations for international students: Required—TOEFL, TWE. *Expenses:* Contact institution. *Faculty research:* Genomics, microarray analysis, computer aided drug design, molecular biophysics, cell structure, molecular dynamics, computational chemistry.

The University of Toledo, College of Graduate Studies, College of Medicine and Life Sciences, Interdepartmental Programs, Toledo, OH 43606-3390. Offers bioinformatics/proteomics/genomics (MSBS, Certificate); human donation sciences (MSBS); medical sciences (MSBS). *Faculty:* 37. *Students:* 66 full-time (26 women), 3 part-time (1 woman); includes 17 minority (2 Black or African American, non-Hispanic/Latino; 12 Asian, non-Hispanic/Latino; 2 Hispanic/Latino; 1 Two or more races, non-Hispanic/Latino), 1 international. Average age 25. 12 applicants, 92% accepted, 10 enrolled. In 2011, 54 master's, 1 Certificate awarded. *Degree requirements:* For master's, thesis or alternative. *Entrance requirements:* For master's, GRE, minimum undergraduate GPA of 3.0, three letters of recommendation, statement of purpose, transcripts from all prior institutions attended, resume; for Certificate, minimum undergraduate GPA of 3.0, three letters of recommendation, statement of purpose, transcripts from all prior institutions attended, resume. Additional exam requirements/recommendations for international students: Required—TOEFL (minimum score 550 paper-based; 213 computer-based; 80 iBT), IELTS (minimum score 6.5). *Application deadline:* For fall admission, 1/15 priority date for domestic students, 1/15 for international students. Application fee: $45 ($75 for international students). Electronic applications accepted. *Financial support:* Tuition scholarships available. *Unit head:* Dr. Randall Ruch, Assistant Dean of Admissions for Biomedical Graduate programs. *Application contact:* Admissions Analyst, 419-383-4116, Fax: 419-383-6140. Web site: http://www.utoledo.edu/med/grad/.

University of Utah, School of Medicine and Graduate School, Graduate Programs in Medicine, Department of Biomedical Informatics, Salt Lake City, UT 84112-1107. Offers MS, PhD, Certificate. Part-time programs available. Postbaccalaureate distance learning degree programs offered (minimal on-campus study). *Degree requirements:* For master's, comprehensive exam, thesis; for doctorate, comprehensive exam, thesis/dissertation, qualifying exam. *Entrance requirements:* For master's and doctorate, GRE General Test (minimum 60th percentile), minimum GPA of 3.3. Additional exam requirements/recommendations for international students: Required—TOEFL (minimum score 600 paper-based; 250 computer-based). Electronic applications accepted. *Faculty research:* Health information systems and expert systems, genetic epidemiology, medical imaging, bioinformatics, public health informatics.

University of Washington, Graduate School, School of Medicine, Graduate Programs in Medicine, Department of Medical Education and Biomedical Informatics, Division of Biomedical and Health Informatics, Seattle, WA 98195. Offers MS, PhD. *Entrance requirements:* For master's and doctorate, GRE General Test, minimum GPA of 3.0; previous undergraduate course work in biology, computer programming, and mathematics. Additional exam requirements/recommendations for international students: Required—TOEFL (minimum score 580 paper-based; 237 computer-based; 70 iBT). Electronic applications accepted. *Faculty research:* Bio-clinical informatics, information retrieval, human-computer interaction, knowledge-based systems, telehealth.

University of Washington, Graduate School, School of Public Health, Department of Health Services, Seattle, WA 98195. Offers bioinformatics (PhD); cancer prevention and control (PhD); clinical research (MS); community-oriented public health practice (MPH); economics or finance (PhD); evaluation sciences (PhD); health behavior and health promotion (PhD); health policy research (PhD); health services (MS, PhD); health services administration (EMHA, MHA); health systems policy (MPH); maternal and child health (MPH, PhD); occupational health (PhD); population health and social determinants (PhD); social and behavioral sciences (MPH); sociology and demography (PhD); JD/MHA; MHA/MBA; MHA/MD; MHA/MPA; MPH/JD; MPH/MD; MPH/MN; MPH/MPA; MPH/MS; MPH/MSD; MPH/MSW; MPH/PhD. Part-time and evening/weekend programs available. Postbaccalaureate distance learning degree programs offered (minimal on-campus study). *Faculty:* 40 full-time (23 women), 62 part-time/adjunct (25 women). *Students:* 98 full-time (78 women), 86 part-time (64 women); includes 49 minority (7 Black or African American, non-Hispanic/Latino; 3 American Indian or Alaska Native, non-Hispanic/Latino; 28 Asian, non-Hispanic/Latino; 11 Hispanic/Latino), 3 international. Average age 32. 374 applicants, 49% accepted, 104 enrolled. In 2011, 43 master's, 5 doctorates awarded. Terminal master's awarded for partial completion of doctoral program. *Degree requirements:* For master's, thesis (for some programs), practicum (MPH); for doctorate, comprehensive exam, thesis/dissertation. *Entrance requirements:* For master's and doctorate, GRE General Test, minimum GPA of 3.0. Additional exam requirements/recommendations for international students: Required—TOEFL (minimum score 580 paper-based; 237 computer-based; 92 iBT), IELTS (minimum score 7). *Application deadline:* For fall admission, 1/1 for domestic students, 11/1 for international students. Application fee: 75 Albanian leks. Electronic applications accepted. *Financial support:* In 2011–12, 47 students received support, including 10 fellowships with full and partial tuition reimbursements available (averaging $22,000 per year), 10 research assistantships with full and partial tuition reimbursements available (averaging $18,700 per year), 3 teaching assistantships with full and partial tuition reimbursements available (averaging $4,575 per year); institutionally sponsored loans, traineeships, and health care benefits also available. Financial award application deadline: 2/28; financial award applicants required to submit FAFSA. *Faculty research:* Public health practice, health promotion and disease prevention, maternal and child health, organizational behavior and culture, health policy. *Unit head:* Dr. Larry Kessler, Chair, 206-543-2930. *Application contact:* Kitty A. Andert, MPH/MS/PhD Programs Manager, 206-616-2926, Fax: 206-543-3964, E-mail: kitander@u.washington.edu. Web site: http://depts.washington.edu/hserv/.

Vanderbilt University, Graduate School, Department of Biomedical Informatics, Nashville, TN 37240-1001. Offers MS, PhD, MD/MS, MD/PhD. Part-time programs available. *Faculty:* 24 full-time (4 women). *Students:* 15 full-time (4 women), 2 part-time (1 woman); includes 5 minority (4 Asian, non-Hispanic/Latino; 1 Two or more races, non-Hispanic/Latino), 3 international. Average age 36. 42 applicants, 14% accepted, 3 enrolled. In 2011, 2 master's, 3 doctorates awarded. Terminal master's awarded for partial completion of doctoral program. *Degree requirements:* For master's, thesis; for doctorate, thesis/dissertation, final and qualifying exams. *Entrance requirements:* For master's and doctorate, GRE General Test. Additional exam requirements/recommendations for international students: Required—TOEFL (minimum score 600 paper-based; 230 computer-based; 88 iBT). *Application deadline:* For fall admission, 1/15 for domestic and international students. Application fee: $0. Electronic applications accepted. *Financial support:* Fellowships with full and partial tuition reimbursements, research assistantships with full and partial tuition reimbursements, teaching assistantships with full and partial tuition reimbursements, Federal Work-Study, institutionally sponsored loans, scholarships/grants, traineeships, and health care benefits available. Financial award application deadline: 1/15; financial award applicants required to submit CSS PROFILE or FAFSA. *Faculty research:* Organizational informatics, the application of informatics to the role of information technology in organizational change, clinical research and translational informatics, applications of informatics to facilitating &ITbench to bedside&RO translational research. *Unit head:* Dr. Kevin B. Johnson, Chair, 615-936-3596, Fax: 615-936-1427, E-mail: kevin.b.johnson@

vanderbilt.edu. *Application contact:* Claudia McCarn, Administrative Program Manager, 615-343-9940, Fax: 615-936-1542, E-mail: claudia.mccarn@vanderbilt.edu. Web site: http://dbmi.mc.vanderbilt.edu/.

Virginia Commonwealth University, Graduate School, School of Life Sciences, Center for the Study of Biological Complexity, Richmond, VA 23284-9005. Offers bioinformatics (MS); integrative life sciences (PhD). *Degree requirements:* For master's, thesis optional. *Entrance requirements:* For master's and doctorate, GRE. Additional exam requirements/recommendations for international students: Required—TOEFL (minimum score 600 paper-based; 250 computer-based; 100 iBT). Electronic applications accepted. *Expenses:* Tuition, state resident: full-time $9133; part-time $507 per credit. Tuition, nonresident: full-time $18,777; part-time $1043 per credit. *Required fees:* $77 per credit. Tuition and fees vary according to degree level, campus/location, program and student level.

Virginia Polytechnic Institute and State University, Graduate School, Intercollege, Program in Genetics, Bioinformatics and Computational Biology, Blacksburg, VA 24061. Offers PhD. *Degree requirements:* For doctorate, comprehensive exam (for some programs), thesis/dissertation (for some programs). *Entrance requirements:* For doctorate, GRE. Additional exam requirements/recommendations for international students: Required—TOEFL (minimum score 550 paper-based; 213 computer-based). *Application deadline:* For fall admission, 7/1 for domestic and international students; for spring admission, 12/1 for international students. Applications are processed on a rolling basis. Application fee: $65. Electronic applications accepted. *Expenses:* Tuition, state resident: full-time $10,048; part-time $558.25 per credit hour. Tuition, nonresident: full-time $19,497; part-time $1083.25 per credit hour. *Required fees:* $405 per semester. Tuition and fees vary according to course load, campus/location and program. *Financial support:* Career-related internships or fieldwork, Federal Work-Study, scholarships/grants, health care benefits, and unspecified assistantships available. Financial award application deadline: 1/15. *Unit head:* Dr. David R. Bevan, Unit Head, 540-231-5040, Fax: 540-231-3010, E-mail: drbevan@vt.edu. *Application contact:* Dennie Munson, Information Contact, 540-231-1928, Fax: 540-231-3010, E-mail: dennie@vt.edu. Web site: http://graduateschool.vt.edu/academics/programs/gbcb/.

Wesleyan University, Graduate Programs, Department of Biology, Middletown, CT 06459. Offers animal behavior (PhD); bioformatics/genomics (PhD); cell biology (PhD); developmental biology (PhD); evolution/ecology (PhD); genetics (PhD); neurobiology (PhD); population biology (PhD). *Degree requirements:* For doctorate, variable foreign language requirement, thesis/dissertation. *Entrance requirements:* For doctorate, GRE. Additional exam requirements/recommendations for international students: Required—TOEFL. *Faculty research:* Microbial population genetics, genetic basis of evolutionary adaptation, genetic regulation of differentiation and pattern formation in &ITdrosophila&RO.

Yale University, School of Medicine and Graduate School of Arts and Sciences, Combined Program in Biological and Biomedical Sciences (BBS), Computational Biology and Bioinformatics Track, New Haven, CT 06520. Offers PhD, MD/PhD. *Entrance requirements:* Additional exam requirements/recommendations for international students: Required—TOEFL.

Computer and Information Systems Security

American InterContinental University Online, Program in Information Technology, Hoffman Estates, IL 60192. Offers Internet security (MIT); IT project management (MIT). Evening/weekend programs available. Postbaccalaureate distance learning degree programs offered (no on-campus study). *Entrance requirements:* Additional exam requirements/recommendations for international students: Required—TOEFL (minimum score 550 paper-based; 213 computer-based). Electronic applications accepted.

American InterContinental University South Florida, Program in Information Technology, Weston, FL 33326. Offers Internet security (MIT); wireless computer forensics (MIT). Part-time and evening/weekend programs available. *Entrance requirements:* Additional exam requirements/recommendations for international students: Required—TOEFL (minimum score 670 paper-based). Electronic applications accepted.

American Public University System, AMU/APU Graduate Programs, Charles Town, WV 25414. Offers accounting (MBA, MS); administration and supervision (M Ed); criminal justice (MA); emergency and disaster management (MA); entrepreneurship (MBA); environmental policy and management (MS), including environmental planning, environmental sustainability, fish and wildlife management, general (MA, MS), global environmental management; finance (MBA); general (MBA); global business management (MBA); guidance and counseling (M Ed); history (MA), including American history, ancient and classical history, European history, global history, military and diplomatic history, public history; homeland security (MA); homeland security resource allocation (MBA); humanities (MA); information technology (MS), including digital forensics, enterprise software development, information assurance and security, IT project management; information technology management (MBA); intelligence studies (MA), including criminal intelligence, general (MA, MS), homeland security, intelligence analysis, intelligence collection, intelligence operations, terrorism studies; international relations and conflict resolution (MA), including comparative and security issues, conflict resolution, international and transnational security issues, peacekeeping; legal studies (MA); management (MA), including defense management, general (MA, MS), human resource management, organizational leadership, public administration, reverse logistics, strategic consulting; marketing (MBA); military history (MA), including American military history, American revolution, civil war, war since 1946, World War II; military studies (MA), including air warfare, asymmetrical warfare, joint warfare, land warfare, naval warfare, strategic leadership; national security studies (MA), including general (MA, MS), homeland security, regional security studies, security and intelligence analysis, terrorism studies; nonprofit management (MBA); political science (MA), including American politics and government, comparative government and development, public policy; psychology (MA); public administration (MA, MPA), including disaster management (MPA), environmental policy (MA), health policy (MPA), human resources (MPA), national security (MPA), organizational management (MPA), security management (MPA); public health (MA, MPH), including emergency management (MPH), environmental health (MPH), public administration (MA); reverse logistics management (MA); security management (MA); space studies (MS), including aerospace science, planetary science; sports and health sciences (MS); sports management (MS), including coaching theory and strategy, sports administration; teaching (M Ed), including curriculum and instruction for elementary teachers, elementary, elementary reading, English language learners, instructional leadership, online learning, secondary social sciences, special education; transportation and logistics management (MA), including maritime engineering management. Programs offered via distance learning only. Part-time and evening/weekend programs available. Postbaccalaureate distance learning degree programs offered (no on-campus study). *Faculty:* 445 full-time (241 women), 1,360 part-time/adjunct (617 women). *Students:* 688 full-time (338 women), 10,168 part-time (3,706 women); includes 3,130 minority (1,007 Black or African American, non-Hispanic/Latino; 103 American Indian or Alaska Native, non-Hispanic/Latino; 825 Asian, non-Hispanic/Latino; 810 Hispanic/Latino; 51 Native Hawaiian or other Pacific Islander, non-Hispanic/Latino; 334 Two or more races, non-Hispanic/Latino), 134 international. Average age 35. In 2011, 2,386 master's awarded. *Degree requirements:* For master's, comprehensive exam or practicum. *Entrance requirements:* For master's, official transcript showing earned bachelor's degree from institution accredited by recognized accrediting body. Additional exam requirements/recommendations for international students: Required—TOEFL (minimum score 550 paper-based; 213 computer-based), IELTS (minimum score 6.5). *Application deadline:* Applications are processed on a rolling basis. Application fee: $0. Electronic applications accepted. *Expenses: Tuition:* Part-time $325 per credit hour. *Financial support:* Applicants required to submit FAFSA. *Faculty research:* Military history, criminal justice, management performance, national security. *Unit head:* Dr. Karan Powell, Executive Vice President and Provost, 877-468-6268, Fax: 304-724-3780. *Application contact:* Terry Grant, Vice President of Enrollment Management, 877-468-6268, Fax: 304-724-3780, E-mail: info@apus.edu. Web site: http://www.apus.edu.

Benedictine University, Graduate Programs, Program in Business Administration, Lisle, IL 60532-0900. Offers accounting (MBA); entrepreneurship and managing innovation (MBA); financial management (MBA); health administration (MBA); human resource management (MBA); information systems security (MBA); international business (MBA); management consulting (MBA); management information systems (MBA); marketing management (MBA); operations management and logistics (MBA); organizational leadership (MBA); MBA/MPH; MBA/MS. Part-time and evening/weekend programs available. Postbaccalaureate distance learning degree programs offered (minimal on-campus study). *Faculty:* 4 full-time (2 women), 24 part-time/adjunct (3 women). *Students:* 165 full-time (101 women), 766 part-time (381 women); includes 201 minority (118 Black or African American, non-Hispanic/Latino; 4 American Indian or Alaska Native, non-Hispanic/Latino; 37 Asian, non-Hispanic/Latino; 40 Hispanic/Latino; 2 Native Hawaiian or other Pacific Islander, non-Hispanic/Latino), 14 international. Average age 34. 313 applicants, 73% accepted, 166 enrolled. In 2011, 379 master's awarded. *Entrance requirements:* For master's, GMAT. Additional exam requirements/recommendations for international students: Required—TOEFL (minimum score 550 paper-based; 213 computer-based). *Application deadline:* For fall admission, 9/1 for domestic students; for winter admission, 12/1 for domestic students; for spring admission, 2/15 for domestic students. Applications are processed on a rolling basis. Application fee: $40. Electronic applications accepted. *Financial support:* Career-related internships or fieldwork and health care benefits available. Support available to part-time students. *Faculty research:* Strategic leadership in professional organizations, sociology of professions, organizational change, social identity theory, applications to change management. *Unit head:* Dr. Sharon Borowicz, Director, 630-829-6219, E-mail: sborowicz@ben.edu. *Application contact:* Kari Gibbons, Director, Admissions, 630-829-6200, Fax: 630-829-6584, E-mail: kgibbons@ben.edu.

Boston University, Metropolitan College, Department of Computer Science, Boston, MA 02215. Offers computer information systems (MS), including computer networks, database management and business intelligence, health informatics, IT project management, security, Web application development; computer science (MS), including computer networks, security; telecommunications (MS), including security. Evening/weekend programs available. Postbaccalaureate distance learning degree programs offered. *Faculty:* 12 full-time (2 women), 28 part-time/adjunct (2 women). *Students:* 25 full-time (6 women), 732 part-time (167 women); includes 208 minority (51 Black or African American, non-Hispanic/Latino; 1 American Indian or Alaska Native, non-Hispanic/Latino; 104 Asian, non-Hispanic/Latino; 43 Hispanic/Latino; 1 Native Hawaiian or other Pacific Islander, non-Hispanic/Latino; 8 Two or more races, non-Hispanic/Latino), 86 international. Average age 35. 260 applicants, 67% accepted, 143 enrolled. In 2011, 143 master's awarded. *Degree requirements:* For master's, thesis optional. *Entrance requirements:* For master's, 3 letters of recommendation, professional resume. Additional exam requirements/recommendations for international students: Required—TOEFL (minimum score 550 paper-based; 213 computer-based; 80 iBT). *Application deadline:* For fall admission, 6/1 for international students; for spring admission, 10/1 for international students. Applications are processed on a rolling basis. Application fee: $70. Electronic applications accepted. *Expenses: Tuition:* Full-time $40,848; part-time $1276 per credit hour. *Required fees:* $572; $286 per semester. *Financial support:* In 2011–12, 9 research assistantships (averaging $5,000 per year) were awarded; career-related internships or fieldwork and unspecified assistantships also available. Support available to part-time students. Financial award applicants required to submit FAFSA. *Faculty research:* Medical informatics, Web technologies, telecom and networks, security and forensics, software engineering, programming languages, multimedia and AI, information systems and IT project management. *Unit head:* Dr. Lubomir Chitkushev, Chairman, 617-353-2566, Fax: 617-353-2367, E-mail: csinfo@bu.edu. *Application contact:* Kim Richards, Program Coordinator, 617-353-2566, Fax: 617-353-2367, E-mail: kimrich@bu.edu. Web site: http://www.bu.edu/csmet/.

Brandeis University, Rabb School of Continuing Studies, Division of Graduate Professional Studies, Information Assurance Program, Waltham, MA 02454-9110. Offers MS. Part-time programs available. Postbaccalaureate distance learning degree programs offered (no on-campus study). *Faculty:* 2 full-time (both women), 34 part-time/adjunct (8 women). *Students:* 17 part-time (1 woman); includes 3 minority (1 Black or African American, non-Hispanic/Latino; 2 Asian, non-Hispanic/Latino). Average age 35. 4 applicants, 100% accepted, 4 enrolled. In 2011, 6 degrees awarded. *Entrance requirements:* For master's, resume, official transcripts, recommendations, goal statements. Additional exam requirements/recommendations for international students: Recommended—TOEFL (minimum score 600 paper-based; 250 computer-based; 100 iBT). *Application deadline:* For fall admission, 6/15 priority date for domestic students; for winter admission, 10/15 priority date for domestic students; for spring admission, 2/15 priority date for domestic students. Applications are processed on a rolling basis. Application fee: $50. Electronic applications accepted. *Unit head:* Dr. Cynthia Phillips,

Program Chair, 781-736-8787, Fax: 781-736-3420, E-mail: cynthiap@brandeis.edu. *Application contact:* Frances Stearns, Associate Director of Admissions and Student Services, 781-736-8785, Fax: 781-736-3420, E-mail: fstearns@brandeis.edu. Web site: http://www.brandeis.edu/gps.

California State University, San Bernardino, Graduate Studies, College of Business and Public Administration, Master in Business Administration Program, San Bernardino, CA 92407. Offers accounting (MBA); entrepreneurship (MBA); executives (MBA); finance (MBA); global business (MBA); information assurance and security management (MBA); information management (MBA); management (MBA); marketing (MBA); professionals (MBA); supply chain management (MBA). *Accreditation:* AACSB. Part-time and evening/weekend programs available. Postbaccalaureate distance learning degree programs offered (no on-campus study). *Faculty:* 58 full-time (11 women), 26 part-time/adjunct (9 women). *Students:* 80 full-time (31 women), 137 part-time (56 women); includes 82 minority (19 Black or African American, non-Hispanic/Latino; 3 American Indian or Alaska Native, non-Hispanic/Latino; 20 Asian, non-Hispanic/Latino; 37 Hispanic/Latino; 3 Two or more races, non-Hispanic/Latino), 65 international. Average age 30. 217 applicants, 65% accepted, 79 enrolled. In 2011, 120 master's awarded. *Degree requirements:* For master's, comprehensive exam, thesis optional, portfolio, 48 units, minimum GPA of 3.0. *Entrance requirements:* For master's, GMAT, minimum GPA of 2.5. Additional exam requirements/recommendations for international students: Required—TOEFL (minimum score 550 paper-based; 213 computer-based; 79 iBT). *Application deadline:* For fall admission, 7/12 priority date for domestic students, 7/12 for international students; for winter admission, 10/26 priority date for domestic students, 10/26 for international students; for spring admission, 1/25 priority date for domestic students, 1/25 for international students. Applications are processed on a rolling basis. Application fee: $55. Electronic applications accepted. *Expenses:* Contact institution. *Financial support:* In 2011–12, 56 students received support, including 34 fellowships (averaging $3,732 per year), 18 research assistantships (averaging $2,193 per year), 4 teaching assistantships (averaging $2,606 per year); career-related internships or fieldwork, Federal Work-Study, institutionally sponsored loans, scholarships/grants, and unspecified assistantships also available. Support available to part-time students. Financial award application deadline: 3/1; financial award applicants required to submit FAFSA. *Faculty research:* Fraud, Stock Exchange, small business, logistics, job analysis. *Total annual research expenditures:* $4.8 million. *Unit head:* Dr. Lawrence C. Rose, Dean, 909-537-3703, Fax: 909-537-7026, E-mail: lrose@csusb.edu. *Application contact:* Dr. Sandra Kamusikiri, Associate Vice-President/ Dean of Graduate Studies, 909-537-7058, Fax: 909-537-5078, E-mail: skamusik@csusb.edu. Web site: http://mba.csusb.edu/.

Capella University, School of Business and Technology, Minneapolis, MN 55402. Offers accounting (MBA), including system design and programming; business (Certificate), including human resource management (MS, PhD, Certificate), information technology management (MS, PhD, Certificate), leadership (MBA, MS, PhD, Certificate); finance (MBA); general business (MBA); health care management (MBA); information technology (MS, Certificate), including general information technology (MS), information security, network architecture and design (MS), professional projects management (Certificate), project management and leadership (MS), system design and development (MS),); information technology management (MBA); marketing (MBA); organization and management (MBA, MS, PhD), including general business (PhD), general organization and management (MBA, MS), human resource management (MS, PhD, Certificate), information technology management (MS, PhD, Certificate), leadership (MBA, MS, PhD, Certificate); project management (MBA). Part-time and evening/weekend programs available. Postbaccalaureate distance learning degree programs offered (minimal on-campus study). Terminal master's awarded for partial completion of doctoral program. *Degree requirements:* For master's, thesis optional, integrative project; for doctorate, comprehensive exam, thesis/dissertation. *Entrance requirements:* Additional exam requirements/recommendations for international students: Required—TOEFL (minimum score 550 paper-based; 213 computer-based), TWE (minimum score 4). Electronic applications accepted. *Faculty research:* Business policies: strategic, corporate, and financial management; interplay of technological, organizational and social change.

Capitol College, Graduate Programs, Laurel, MD 20708-9759. Offers business administration (MBA); computer science (MS); electrical engineering (MS); information and telecommunications systems management (MS); information architecture (MS); network security (MS). Part-time and evening/weekend programs available. Postbaccalaureate distance learning degree programs offered (no on-campus study). *Entrance requirements:* For master's, minimum GPA of 3.0. Electronic applications accepted.

Carlow University, School of Management, Program in Fraud and Forensics, Pittsburgh, PA 15213-3165. Offers MS. Postbaccalaureate distance learning degree programs offered (no on-campus study). *Students:* 33 full-time (24 women), 1 (woman) part-time; includes 8 minority (3 Black or African American, non-Hispanic/Latino; 4 Hispanic/Latino; 1 Two or more races, non-Hispanic/Latino). 80 applicants, 46% accepted, 34 enrolled. *Entrance requirements:* For master's, minimum undergraduate GPA of 3.0; essay; resume; transcripts; two recommendations. Additional exam requirements/recommendations for international students: Required—TOEFL (minimum score 550 paper-based; 213 computer-based). *Application deadline:* For fall admission, 7/1 for domestic students. Application fee: $20. Electronic applications accepted. Application fee is waived when completed online. *Expenses: Tuition:* Full-time $10,290; part-time $686 per credit. Tuition and fees vary according to course load, degree level and program. *Unit head:* Dr. Diane Matthews, Director, Fraud and Forensics Program, 412-578-8729, Fax: 412-587-6367, E-mail: damatthews@carlow.edu. *Application contact:* Judy Trosell, Admissions Counselor, 412-578-6671, Fax: 412-578-6321, E-mail: gradstudies@carlow.edu. Web site: http://gradstudies.carlow.edu/fraudforensics/index.html.

Carnegie Mellon University, Carnegie Institute of Technology, Information Networking Institute, Pittsburgh, PA 15213. Offers information networking (MS); information security technology and management (MS); information technology - information security (MS); information technology - mobility (MS); information technology - software management (MS). *Degree requirements:* For master's, thesis optional. *Entrance requirements:* For master's, GRE General Test, bachelor's degree in computer science, computer engineering, or electrical engineering, or related technology degree; programming skills (C/C++ fluency for some programs). Additional exam requirements/recommendations for international students: Required—TOEFL. *Faculty research:* Computer forensics and incident response; dependable systems, embedded systems, mobile systems, and sensor networks; computer and information networks, network and information security, human and socio-economic factors in secure system design; wireless sensor networks, survivable embedded systems, signal processing/compression; strategic management, international strategic management, group dynamics and decision-making structures, simulated competitive environments.

Carnegie Mellon University, Heinz College, School of Information Systems and Management, Master of Science in Information Security Policy and Management Program, Pittsburgh, PA 15213-3891. Offers MSISPM. *Entrance requirements:* For master's, GRE or GMAT, college-level course in advanced algebra/pre-calculus; college-level courses in economics and statistics (recommended). Additional exam requirements/recommendations for international students: Required—TOEFL or IELTS.

City University of Seattle, Graduate Division, School of Management, Bellevue, WA 98005. Offers accounting (Certificate); change leadership (MBA, Certificate); computer systems (MS); finance (Certificate); financial management (MBA); general management (MBA); general management-Europe (MBA); global marketing (MBA); human resources management (Certificate); individualized study (MBA); information security (MS); information systems (MBA); leadership (MA); marketing (MBA, Certificate); project management (MBA, MS, Certificate); sustainable business (Certificate); technology management (MBA, Certificate). Part-time and evening/weekend programs available. Postbaccalaureate distance learning degree programs offered (no on-campus study). *Faculty:* 6 full-time (2 women), 95 part-time/adjunct (33 women). *Students:* 397 full-time (193 women), 283 part-time (137 women); includes 127 minority (67 Black or African American, non-Hispanic/Latino; 5 American Indian or Alaska Native, non-Hispanic/Latino; 33 Asian, non-Hispanic/Latino; 15 Hispanic/Latino; 1 Native Hawaiian or other Pacific Islander, non-Hispanic/Latino; 6 Two or more races, non-Hispanic/Latino), 117 international. Average age 36. 151 applicants, 100% accepted, 151 enrolled. In 2011, 369 master's, 32 other advanced degrees awarded. *Degree requirements:* For master's, comprehensive exam (for some programs), thesis (for some programs). *Entrance requirements:* Additional exam requirements/recommendations for international students: Required—TOEFL (minimum score 567 paper-based; 227 computer-based; 87 iBT); Recommended—IELTS. *Application deadline:* For fall admission, 9/1 for international students; for winter admission, 12/1 for international students; for spring admission, 3/1 for international students. Applications are processed on a rolling basis. Application fee: $50. Electronic applications accepted. *Financial support:* Federal Work-Study and scholarships/grants available. Support available to part-time students. Financial award applicants required to submit FAFSA. *Unit head:* Dr. Kurt Kirstein, Dean, 425-637-1010 Ext. 5456, Fax: 425-709-5363, E-mail: kdkirstein@cityu.edu. *Application contact:* Alysa Borelli, Director, Recruiting, 888-422-4898, Fax: 425-709-5363, E-mail: info@cityu.edu. Web site: http://www.cityu.edu/programs/som/index.aspx.

Colorado Christian University, Program in Business Administration, Lakewood, CO 80226. Offers corporate training (MBA); information security (MA); leadership (MBA); project management (MBA). Part-time and evening/weekend programs available. Postbaccalaureate distance learning degree programs offered (minimal on-campus study). *Degree requirements:* For master's, thesis optional. *Entrance requirements:* For master's, GMAT, 2 letters of recommendation, resume. Additional exam requirements/recommendations for international students: Required—TOEFL. Electronic applications accepted. *Expenses:* Contact institution.

Colorado Technical University Colorado Springs, Graduate Studies, Program in Computer Science, Colorado Springs, CO 80907-3896. Offers computer science (DCS); computer systems security (MSCS); database systems (MSCS); software engineering (MSCS). Part-time and evening/weekend programs available. Postbaccalaureate distance learning degree programs offered. *Degree requirements:* For master's, thesis or alternative; for doctorate, thesis/dissertation. *Entrance requirements:* For doctorate, minimum graduate GPA of 3.0, 5 years of related work experience. *Faculty research:* Software engineering, systems engineering.

Colorado Technical University Colorado Springs, Graduate Studies, Program in Information Science, Colorado Springs, CO 80907-3896. Offers information systems security (MSM). Postbaccalaureate distance learning degree programs offered.

Colorado Technical University Denver South, Program in Computer Science, Aurora, CO 80014. Offers computer systems security (MSCS); database systems (MSCS); software engineering (MSCS). Part-time and evening/weekend programs available. *Degree requirements:* For master's, thesis or alternative. *Entrance requirements:* For master's, minimum undergraduate GPA of 3.0, resume.

Colorado Technical University Denver South, Program in Information Science, Aurora, CO 80014. Offers information systems security (MSM).

Colorado Technical University Sioux Falls, Program in Computing, Sioux Falls, SD 57108. Offers computer systems security (MSCS); software engineering (MSCS).

Concordia University, School of Graduate Studies, Faculty of Engineering and Computer Science, Concordia Institute for Information Systems Engineering (CIISE), Montréal, QC H3G 1M8, Canada. Offers 3D graphics and game development (Certificate); information systems security (M Eng, MA Sc); quality systems engineering (M Eng, MA Sc); service engineering and network management (Certificate).

Concordia University College of Alberta, Program in Information Systems Security Management, Edmonton, AB T5B 4E4, Canada. Offers MA.

Davenport University, Sneden Graduate School, Grand Rapids, MI 49512. Offers accounting (MBA); business administration (EMBA); finance (MBA); health care management (MBA); human resources (MBA); information assurance (MS); public health (MPH); strategic management (MBA). Evening/weekend programs available. *Entrance requirements:* For master's, GMAT, minimum undergraduate GPA of 2.75. Additional exam requirements/recommendations for international students: Required—TOEFL. Electronic applications accepted. *Faculty research:* Leadership, management, marketing, organizational culture.

Davenport University, Sneden Graduate School, Warren, MI 48092-5209. Offers accounting (MBA); business administration (EMBA); finance (MBA); health care management (MBA); human resources management (MBA); information assurance (MS); public health (MPH); strategic management (MBA). *Entrance requirements:* For master's, minimum undergraduate GPA of 2.7.

Davenport University, Sneden Graduate School, Dearborn, MI 48126-3799. Offers accounting (MBA); business administration (EMBA); finance (MBA); health care management (MBA); human resources management (MBA); information assurance (MS); marketing (MBA); public health (MPH); strategic management (MBA). Part-time and evening/weekend programs available. Postbaccalaureate distance learning degree programs offered (no on-campus study). *Entrance requirements:* For master's, minimum GPA of 2.7, previous course work in accounting and statistics. *Faculty research:* Accounting, international accounting, social and environmental accounting, finance.

DePaul University, College of Computing and Digital Media, Chicago, IL 60604. Offers animation (MA, MFA); applied technology (MS); business information technology (MS); cinema (MFA); cinema production (MS); computational finance (MS); computer and information sciences (PhD); computer game development (MS); computer graphics and motion technology (MS); computer information and network security (MS); computer science (MS); e-commerce technology (MS); human-computer interaction (MS);

information systems (MS); information technology (MA); information technology project management (MS); network engineering and management (MS); predictive analytics (MS); screenwriting (MFA); software engineering (MS); JD/MA; JD/MS. Part-time and evening/weekend programs available. Postbaccalaureate distance learning degree programs offered (no on-campus study). *Faculty:* 64 full-time (16 women), 44 part-time/adjunct (5 women). *Students:* 969 full-time (250 women), 936 part-time (231 women); includes 566 minority (204 Black or African American, non-Hispanic/Latino; 3 American Indian or Alaska Native, non-Hispanic/Latino; 166 Asian, non-Hispanic/Latino; 135 Hispanic/Latino; 7 Native Hawaiian or other Pacific Islander, non-Hispanic/Latino; 51 Two or more races, non-Hispanic/Latino; 282 international. Average age 32. 1,040 applicants, 65% accepted, 324 enrolled. In 2011, 478 master's, 4 doctorates awarded. *Degree requirements:* For master's, thesis (for some programs); for doctorate, comprehensive exam, thesis/dissertation. *Entrance requirements:* For master's, GRE or GMAT (MS in computational finance only), bachelor's degree, resume (MS in predictive analytics only), IT experience (MS in information technology project management only), portfolio review (all MFA programs and MA in animation); for doctorate, GRE, master's degree in computer science. Additional exam requirements/recommendations for international students: Required—TOEFL (minimum score 550 paper-based; 213 computer-based; 80 iBT), IELTS (minimum score 6.5), Pearson Test of English (minimum score 53). *Application deadline:* For fall admission, 8/1 priority date for domestic students, 6/1 for international students; for winter admission, 12/1 priority date for domestic students, 10/1 for international students; for spring admission, 3/1 priority date for domestic students, 1/1 for international students. Applications are processed on a rolling basis. Application fee: $25. Electronic applications accepted. *Expenses:* Contact institution. *Financial support:* In 2011–12, 56 students received support, including 3 fellowships with full tuition reimbursements available (averaging $30,000 per year), 3 research assistantships with full and partial tuition reimbursements available (averaging $22,833 per year), 50 teaching assistantships (averaging $6,194 per year); Federal Work-Study, scholarships/grants, tuition waivers (full and partial), and unspecified assistantships also available. Support available to part-time students. Financial award application deadline: 4/30. *Faculty research:* Data mining, theoretical computer science, gaming, security, animation and film. . *Total annual research expenditures:* $3.9 million. *Unit head:* Elly Kafritsas-Wessels, Senior Administrative Assistant, 312-362-5816, Fax: 312-362-5185, E-mail: ekafrits@cdm.depaul.edu. *Application contact:* James Parker, Director of Graduate Admission, 312-362-8714, Fax: 312-362-5179, E-mail: jparke29@cdm.depaul.edu. Web site: http://cdm.depaul.edu.

Eastern Illinois University, Graduate School, Lumpkin College of Business and Applied Sciences, School of Technology, Charleston, IL 61920-3099. Offers computer technology (Certificate); quality systems (Certificate); technology (MS); technology security (Certificate); work performance improvement (Certificate). Part-time and evening/weekend programs available. *Expenses:* Tuition, state resident: part-time $279 per credit hour. Tuition, nonresident: part-time $670 per credit hour. *Required fees:* $179.07 per credit hour. $1253 per semester.

Eastern Michigan University, Graduate School, College of Technology, School of Technology Studies, Program in Information Assurance, Ypsilanti, MI 48197. Offers MLS, Graduate Certificate. Part-time and evening/weekend programs available. Postbaccalaureate distance learning degree programs offered (minimal on-campus study). *Students:* 2 full-time (0 women). Average age 39. 10 applicants, 40% accepted, 2 enrolled. *Entrance requirements:* Additional exam requirements/recommendations for international students: Required—TOEFL. *Application deadline:* Applications are processed on a rolling basis. Application fee: $35. *Expenses:* Tuition, state resident: full-time $10,367; part-time $432 per credit hour. Tuition, nonresident: full-time $20,435; part-time $851 per credit hour. *Required fees:* $39 per credit hour. $46 per semester. One-time fee: $100. Tuition and fees vary according to course level, degree level and reciprocity agreements. *Financial support:* Fellowships, research assistantships with full tuition reimbursements, teaching assistantships with full tuition reimbursements, career-related internships or fieldwork, Federal Work-Study, institutionally sponsored loans, scholarships/grants, tuition waivers (partial), and unspecified assistantships available. Support available to part-time students. Financial award applicants required to submit FAFSA. *Unit head:* Prof. Gerald Lawver, Program Coordinator, 734-487-3170, Fax: 734-487-7690, E-mail: skip.lawver@emich.edu. *Application contact:* Graduate Admissions, 734-487-2400, Fax: 734-487-6559, E-mail: graduate.admissions@emich.edu.

Excelsior College, School of Business and Technology, Albany, NY 12203-5159. Offers business administration (MBA); cybersecurity (MS); cybersecurity management (MBA, Graduate Certificate); human performance technology (MBA); information security (MBA); leadership (MBA); technology management (MBA). Part-time and evening/weekend programs available. Postbaccalaureate distance learning degree programs offered (no on-campus study).

Ferris State University, College of Business, Big Rapids, MI 49307. Offers business intelligence (MBA); design and innovation management (MBA); incident response (MBA); information security and intelligence (MS, MSISM), including business intelligence (MS), incident response (MSISM), project management (MSISM); management tools and concepts (MBA); project management (MBA). *Accreditation:* ACBSP. Part-time and evening/weekend programs available. Postbaccalaureate distance learning degree programs offered (minimal on-campus study). *Faculty:* 9 full-time (3 women), 2 part-time/adjunct (both women). *Students:* 22 full-time (7 women), 98 part-time (50 women); includes 14 minority (3 Black or African American, non-Hispanic/Latino; 4 American Indian or Alaska Native, non-Hispanic/Latino; 2 Asian, non-Hispanic/Latino; 2 Hispanic/Latino; 3 Two or more races, non-Hispanic/Latino), 3 international. Average age 34. 58 applicants, 79% accepted, 10 enrolled. In 2011, 56 master's awarded. *Degree requirements:* For master's, comprehensive exam, thesis (for MSISM). *Entrance requirements:* For master's, GRE or GMAT (waived if GPA is 3.5 or better), minimum GPA of 3.0 in junior/senior level classes, 2.75 overall; writing sample; 3 letters of reference; resume. Additional exam requirements/recommendations for international students: Required—TOEFL (minimum score 500 paper-based; 173 computer-based; 67 iBT). *Application deadline:* For fall admission, 7/1 priority date for domestic students, 6/15 for international students; for winter admission, 11/1 priority date for domestic students, 10/15 for international students; for spring admission, 3/1 priority date for domestic students, 2/15 for international students. Applications are processed on a rolling basis. Application fee: $30. Electronic applications accepted. Application fee is waived when completed online. *Financial support:* Career-related internships or fieldwork, Federal Work-Study, scholarships/grants, and unspecified assistantships available. Support available to part-time students. Financial award application deadline: 3/15; financial award applicants required to submit FAFSA. *Faculty research:* Quality improvement, client/server end-user computing, information management and policy, security, digital forensics. *Unit head:* Dr. David Steenstra, Department Chair, 231-591-2168, Fax: 231-591-3548, E-mail: yosts@ferris.edu. *Application contact:* Shannon Yost, Department Secretary, 231-591-2168, Fax: 231-591-3548, E-mail: yosts@ferris.edu. Web site: http://cbgp.ferris.edu/.

Florida Institute of Technology, Graduate Programs, Nathan M. Bisk College of Business, Online Programs, Melbourne, FL 32901-6975. Offers accounting (MBA); accounting and finance (MBA); business administration (MBA); finance (MBA); healthcare management (MBA); information technology (MS); information technology cybersecurity (MS); information technology management (MBA); international business (MBA); Internet marketing (MBA); management (MBA); marketing (MBA); project management (MBA). Part-time and evening/weekend programs available. Postbaccalaureate distance learning degree programs offered (no on-campus study). *Faculty:* 47 part-time/adjunct (15 women). *Students:* 8 full-time (4 women), 1,122 part-time (547 women); includes 418 minority (271 Black or African American, non-Hispanic/Latino; 5 American Indian or Alaska Native, non-Hispanic/Latino; 55 Asian, non-Hispanic/Latino; 81 Hispanic/Latino; 6 Native Hawaiian or other Pacific Islander, non-Hispanic/Latino), 23 international. Average age 36. In 2011, 329 master's awarded. *Entrance requirements:* For master's, GMAT or resume showing 8 years of supervised experience, 2 letters of recommendation, resume, competency in math past college algebra. Additional exam requirements/recommendations for international students: Required—TOEFL (minimum score 550 paper-based; 213 computer-based; 79 iBT). *Application deadline:* For fall admission, 4/1 for international students; for spring admission, 9/30 for international students. Applications are processed on a rolling basis. Electronic applications accepted. *Expenses:* Contact institution. *Financial support:* Available to part-time students. Application deadline: 3/1; applicants required to submit FAFSA. *Unit head:* Dr. Mary S. Bonhomme, Dean, Florida Tech Online/Associate Provost for Online Learning, 321-674-8202, Fax: 321-674-8216, E-mail: bonhomme@fit.edu. *Application contact:* Carolyn Farrior, Director of Graduate Admissions, Online Learning and Off-Campus Programs, 321-674-7118, Fax: 321-674-8216, E-mail: cfarrior@fit.edu. Web site: http://online.fit.edu.

Florida State University, The Graduate School, College of Arts and Sciences, Department of Computer Science, Tallahassee, FL 32306. Offers computer criminology (MS); computer network and system administration (MS); computer science (MS, PhD); information security (MS). Part-time programs available. *Faculty:* 17 full-time (1 woman), 2 part-time/adjunct (0 women). *Students:* 125 full-time (21 women), 5 part-time (1 woman); includes 11 minority (1 Black or African American, non-Hispanic/Latino; 1 American Indian or Alaska Native, non-Hispanic/Latino; 2 Asian, non-Hispanic/Latino; 7 Hispanic/Latino), 75 international. Average age 26. 294 applicants, 67% accepted, 52 enrolled. In 2011, 29 master's, 6 doctorates awarded. Terminal master's awarded for partial completion of doctoral program. *Degree requirements:* For master's, thesis or alternative; for doctorate, comprehensive exam, thesis/dissertation. *Entrance requirements:* For master's, GRE General Test, minimum undergraduate GPA of 3.0; for doctorate, GRE General Test, minimum GPA of 3.0. Additional exam requirements/recommendations for international students: Required—TOEFL (minimum score 550 paper-based; 213 computer-based; 80 iBT). *Application deadline:* For fall admission, 3/1 priority date for domestic students, 3/1 for international students; for spring admission, 10/1 priority date for domestic students, 10/1 for international students. Application fee: $30. Electronic applications accepted. *Expenses:* Tuition, state resident: full-time $9474; part-time $350.88 per credit hour. Tuition, nonresident: full-time $16,236; part-time $601.34 per credit hour. *Required fees:* $630 per semester. One-time fee: $20. Tuition and fees vary according to course load and campus/location. *Financial support:* In 2011–12, 103 students received support, including 9 fellowships with full tuition reimbursements available (averaging $17,500 per year), 18 research assistantships with full tuition reimbursements available (averaging $17,000 per year), 61 teaching assistantships with full tuition reimbursements available (averaging $16,250 per year); scholarships/grants, health care benefits, tuition waivers (partial), and unspecified assistantships also available. Financial award application deadline: 3/1; financial award applicants required to submit FAFSA. *Faculty research:* Embedded systems, high performance computing, networking, operating systems, security, databases, algorithms. *Total annual research expenditures:* $1.3 million. *Unit head:* Dr. Robert van Engelen, Chairman, 850-645-0309, Fax: 850-644-0058, E-mail: chair@cs.fsu.edu. *Application contact:* Kristan L. McAlpin, Graduate Coordinator, 850-645-4975, Fax: 850-644-0058, E-mail: mcalpin@cs.fsu.edu. Web site: http://www.cs.fsu.edu/.

George Mason University, School of Management, Fairfax, VA 22030. Offers accounting (MS); business administration (EMBA, MBA); management of secure information systems (MS); real estate development (MS); technology management (MS). Part-time and evening/weekend programs available. Postbaccalaureate distance learning degree programs offered. *Faculty:* 79 full-time (25 women), 49 part-time/adjunct (14 women). *Students:* 170 full-time (65 women), 349 part-time (113 women); includes 116 minority (30 Black or African American, non-Hispanic/Latino; 1 American Indian or Alaska Native, non-Hispanic/Latino; 64 Asian, non-Hispanic/Latino; 15 Hispanic/Latino; 1 Native Hawaiian or other Pacific Islander, non-Hispanic/Latino; 5 Two or more races, non-Hispanic/Latino), 49 international. Average age 30. 408 applicants, 58% accepted, 152 enrolled. In 2011, 273 master's awarded. *Entrance requirements:* For master's, GMAT. Additional exam requirements/recommendations for international students: Required—TOEFL (minimum score 570 paper-based; 230 computer-based; 88 iBT), IELTS, Pearson Test of English. *Application deadline:* Applications are processed on a rolling basis. Application fee: $65 ($80 for international students). Electronic applications accepted. *Expenses:* Tuition, state resident: full-time $8750; part-time $364.58 per credit. Tuition, nonresident: full-time $24,092; part-time $1003.83 per credit. *Required fees:* $2514; $104.75 per credit. *Financial support:* In 2011–12, 50 students received support, including 35 research assistantships with full and partial tuition reimbursements available (averaging $9,267 per year), 19 teaching assistantships with full and partial tuition reimbursements available (averaging $8,253 per year); career-related internships or fieldwork, Federal Work-Study, scholarships/grants, unspecified assistantships, and health care benefits (full-time research or teaching assistantship recipients) also available. Financial award application deadline: 3/1; financial award applicants required to submit FAFSA. *Faculty research:* Current leading global issues: offshore outsourcing, international financial risk, comparative systems of innovation. *Total annual research expenditures:* $382,706. *Unit head:* Jorge Haddock, Dean, 703-993-1875, E-mail: jhaddock@gmu.edu. *Application contact:* Melanie Pflugshaupt, Administrative Coordinator to Dean's Office, 703-993-3638, E-mail: mpflugsh@gmu.edu. Web site: http://som.gmu.edu/.

George Mason University, Volgenau School of Engineering, Department of Computer Science, Fairfax, VA 22030. Offers computer games technology (Certificate); computer networking (Certificate); computer science (MS, PhD); database management (Certificate); electronic commerce (Certificate); foundations of information systems (Certificate); information engineering (Certificate); information security and assurance (MS, Certificate); information systems (MS); intelligent agents (Certificate); software architecture (Certificate); software engineering (MS, Certificate); software engineering for C41 (Certificate); Web-based software engineering (Certificate). MS program offered jointly with Old Dominion University, University of Virginia, Virginia Commonwealth University, and Virginia Polytechnic Institute and State University. *Faculty:* 40 full-time (9 women), 17 part-time/adjunct (0 women). *Students:* 208 full-time (52 women), 357 part-time (75 women); includes 98 minority (17 Black or African American, non-Hispanic/Latino; 63 Asian, non-Hispanic/Latino; 14 Hispanic/Latino; 4 Two or more races, non-Hispanic/Latino), 205 international. Average age 30. 882 applicants, 52% accepted, 137 enrolled. In 2011, 164 master's, 5 doctorates, 28 other advanced degrees awarded. *Degree requirements:* For master's, thesis optional; for doctorate, comprehensive exam, thesis/dissertation. *Entrance requirements:* For master's, GRE, proof of financial support; 2 official college transcripts; resume; self-evaluation form; official bank statement; photocopy of passport; 3 letters of recommendation; baccalaureate degree related to computer science; minimum GPA of 3.0 in last 2 years of undergraduate work; 1 year beyond 1st-year calculus; personal goals statement; for doctorate, GRE, personal goals statement; 2 official copies of transcripts; self-evaluation form; 3 letters of recommendation; photocopy of passport; proof of financial support; official bank statement; resume; 4-year baccalaureate degree with strong background in computer science. Additional exam requirements/recommendations for international students: Required—TOEFL (minimum score 575 paper-based; 230 computer-based; 88 iBT), IELTS, Pearson Test of English. *Application deadline:* For fall admission, 1/15 priority date for domestic students; for spring admission, 8/15 priority date for domestic students. Application fee: $65 ($80 for international students). Electronic applications accepted. *Expenses:* Tuition, state resident: full-time $8750; part-time $364.58 per credit. Tuition, nonresident: full-time $24,092; part-time $1003.83 per credit. *Required fees:* $2514; $104.75 per credit. *Financial support:* In 2011–12, 100 students received support, including 3 fellowships (averaging $18,000 per year), 50 research assistantships (averaging $15,232 per year), 47 teaching assistantships (averaging $11,675 per year); career-related internships or fieldwork, Federal Work-Study, scholarships/grants, unspecified assistantships, and health care benefits (full-time research or teaching assistantship recipients) also available. Support available to part-time students. Financial award application deadline: 3/1; financial award applicants required to submit FAFSA. *Faculty research:* Artificial intelligence, image processing/graphics, parallel/distributed systems, software engineering systems. *Total annual research expenditures:* $1.9 million. *Unit head:* Sanjeev Setia, Chair, 703-993-4098, Fax: 703-993-1710, E-mail: setia@gmu.edu. *Application contact:* Michele Pieper, Administrative Assistant, 703-993-9483, Fax: 703-993-1710, E-mail: mpieper@gmu.edu. Web site: http://cs.gmu.edu/.

Georgia Institute of Technology, Graduate Studies and Research, College of Computing, Atlanta, GA 30332-0001. Offers algorithms, combinatorics, and optimization (PhD); computational science and engineering (MS, PhD); computer science (MS, MSCS, PhD); human computer interaction (MSHCI); human-centered computing (PhD); information security (MS). Part-time programs available. Postbaccalaureate distance learning degree programs offered. Terminal master's awarded for partial completion of doctoral program. *Degree requirements:* For master's, thesis optional; for doctorate, comprehensive exam, thesis/dissertation. *Entrance requirements:* For master's, GRE General Test, GRE Subject Test, minimum GPA of 3.0; for doctorate, GRE General Test, GRE Subject Test, minimum GPA of 3.3. Additional exam requirements/recommendations for international students: Required—TOEFL. *Faculty research:* Computer systems, graphics, intelligent systems and artificial intelligence, networks and telecommunications, software engineering.

Henley-Putnam University, Program in Management of Personal Protection, San Jose, CA 95110. Offers MS. Part-time programs available. Postbaccalaureate distance learning degree programs offered.

Hofstra University, College of Liberal Arts and Sciences, Department of Computer Science, Hempstead, NY 11549. Offers networking and security (MS); Web engineering (MS). Part-time and evening/weekend programs available. Postbaccalaureate distance learning degree programs offered (minimal on-campus study). *Faculty:* 4 full-time (1 woman), 3 part-time/adjunct (0 women). *Students:* 4 full-time (1 woman), 16 part-time (3 women); includes 4 minority (2 Black or African American, non-Hispanic/Latino; 1 Asian, non-Hispanic/Latino; 1 Hispanic/Latino), 2 international. Average age 31. 17 applicants, 88% accepted, 6 enrolled. In 2011, 9 master's awarded. *Degree requirements:* For master's, thesis optional, 30 credits; minimum GPA of 3.0. *Entrance requirements:* For master's, GRE, minimum GPA of 3.0. Additional exam requirements/recommendations for international students: Required—TOEFL (minimum score 550 paper-based; 213 computer-based; 80 iBT). *Application deadline:* Applications are processed on a rolling basis. Application fee: $70 ($75 for international students). Electronic applications accepted. *Expenses: Tuition:* Full-time $18,990; part-time $1055 per credit hour. *Required fees:* $970. Tuition and fees vary according to program. *Financial support:* In 2011–12, 12 students received support, including 6 fellowships with full and partial tuition reimbursements available (averaging $2,625 per year); research assistantships with full and partial tuition reimbursements available, Federal Work-Study, institutionally sponsored loans, scholarships/grants, tuition waivers (full and partial), and unspecified assistantships also available. Support available to part-time students. Financial award applicants required to submit FAFSA. *Faculty research:* Computer vision, programming languages, data mining, software engineering, computer security. *Unit head:* Dr. Simona Doboli, Chairperson, 516-463-4786, Fax: 516-463-5790, E-mail: cscxzd@hofstra.edu. *Application contact:* Carol Drummer, Dean of Graduate Admissions, 516-463-4876, Fax: 516-463-4664, E-mail: gradstudent@hofstra.edu. Web site: http://www.hofstra.edu/hclas.

Hood College, Graduate School, Programs in Computer and Information Sciences, Frederick, MD 21701-8575. Offers computer and information sciences (MS); computer science (MS); information security (Certificate). Part-time and evening/weekend programs available. *Degree requirements:* For master's, thesis. *Entrance requirements:* For master's, minimum GPA of 2.75. Additional exam requirements/recommendations for international students: Required—TOEFL (minimum score 575 paper-based; 231 computer-based; 89 iBT). Electronic applications accepted. *Faculty research:* Systems engineering, natural language, processing, database design, artificial intelligence and parallel distributed computing.

Inter American University of Puerto Rico, Guayama Campus, Department of Natural and Applied Sciences, Guayama, PR 00785. Offers computer security and networks (MS); networking and security (MCS).

John Marshall Law School, Graduate and Professional Programs, Chicago, IL 60604-3968. Offers employee benefits (LL M, MS); global legal studies (LL M); information technology (MS); information technology and privacy law (LL M); intellectual property (LL M, MS); international business and trade (LL M); law (JD); real estate (LL M, MS); taxation (LL M, MS); trial advocacy (LL M); JD/LL M; JD/MA; JD/MBA; JD/MPA. JD/MBA offered jointly with Dominican University; JD/MA and JD/MPA with Roosevelt University. *Accreditation:* ABA. Part-time and evening/weekend programs available. *Faculty:* 69 full-time (22 women), 133 part-time/adjunct (40 women). *Students:* 1,305 full-time (598 women), 368 part-time (180 women); includes 385 minority (148 Black or African American, non-Hispanic/Latino; 15 American Indian or Alaska Native, non-Hispanic/Latino; 108 Asian, non-Hispanic/Latino; 110 Hispanic/Latino; 2 Native Hawaiian or other Pacific Islander, non-Hispanic/Latino; 2 Two or more races, non-Hispanic/Latino), 40 international. Average age 27. 3,513 applicants, 48% accepted, 365 enrolled. In 2011, 86 master's, 403 doctorates awarded. *Degree requirements:* For master's, 24 credits; for doctorate, 90 credits. *Entrance requirements:* For master's, JD; for doctorate, LSAT. Additional exam requirements/recommendations for international students: Required—TOEFL. *Application deadline:* For fall admission, 3/1 priority date for domestic students, 3/1 for international students; for spring admission, 10/15 priority date for domestic students, 10/15 for international students. Applications are processed on a rolling basis. Application fee: $0. Electronic applications accepted. *Expenses:* Contact institution. *Financial support:* In 2011–12, 1,350 students received support. Scholarships/grants and tuition waivers (full and partial) available. Support available to part-time students. Financial award application deadline: 6/1; financial award applicants required to submit FAFSA. *Unit head:* John Corkery, Dean, 312-427-2737. *Application contact:* William B. Powers, Associate Dean of Admission and Student Affairs, 800-537-4280, Fax: 312-427-5136, E-mail: admission@jmls.edu.

The Johns Hopkins University, Carey Business School, Information Technology Programs, Baltimore, MD 21218-2699. Offers competitive intelligence (Certificate); information security management (Certificate); information systems (MS); MBA/MSIS. Part-time and evening/weekend programs available. *Degree requirements:* For master's, 36 credits including final project. *Entrance requirements:* For master's and Certificate, minimum GPA of 3.0, resume, work experience, two letters of recommendation. Additional exam requirements/recommendations for international students: Required—TOEFL (minimum score 600 paper-based; 250 computer-based; 100 iBT). Electronic applications accepted. *Faculty research:* Information security, healthcare information systems.

The Johns Hopkins University, Engineering Program for Professionals, Part-Time Program in Information Assurance, Baltimore, MD 21218-2699. Offers MS. Part-time and evening/weekend programs available.

The Johns Hopkins University, Whiting School of Engineering, Information Security Institute, Baltimore, MD 21218-2699. Offers MSSI. Part-time programs available. *Degree requirements:* For master's, project. *Entrance requirements:* For master's, GRE, minimum GPA of 3.0. Additional exam requirements/recommendations for international students: Required—TOEFL (minimum score 600 paper-based; 250 computer-based). Electronic applications accepted. *Faculty research:* Critical infrastructure protection, insider/outsider cryptography and encryption methodologies, international policy protocols, Web-based intellectual property rights.

Jones International University, School of Business, Centennial, CO 80112. Offers accounting (MBA); business communication (MABC); entrepreneurship (MABC, MBA); finance (MBA); global enterprise management (MBA); health care management (MBA); information security management (MBA); information technology management (MBA); leadership and influence (MABC); leading the customer-driven organization (MABC); negotiation and conflict management (MBA); project management (MABC, MBA). Program only offered online. Part-time and evening/weekend programs available. Postbaccalaureate distance learning degree programs offered (no on-campus study). *Degree requirements:* For master's, capstone project. *Entrance requirements:* For master's, minimum cumulative GPA of 2.5. Additional exam requirements/recommendations for international students: Recommended—TOEFL (minimum score 550 paper-based; 213 computer-based). Electronic applications accepted.

Kaplan University, Davenport Campus, School of Information Technology, Davenport, IA 52807-2095. Offers decision support systems (MS); information security and assurance (MS). Part-time and evening/weekend programs available. Postbaccalaureate distance learning degree programs offered (no on-campus study). *Entrance requirements:* Additional exam requirements/recommendations for international students: Required—TOEFL (minimum score 550 paper-based; 218 computer-based; 80 iBT).

Lewis University, College of Business, Graduate School of Management, Program in Business Administration, Romeoville, IL 60446. Offers accounting (MBA); custom elective option (MBA); e-business (MBA); finance (MBA); healthcare management (MBA); human resources management (MBA); information security (MBA); international business (MBA); management information systems (MBA); marketing (MBA); project management (MBA); technology and operations management (MBA). Part-time and evening/weekend programs available. *Students:* 112 full-time (60 women), 232 part-time (118 women); includes 104 minority (62 Black or African American, non-Hispanic/Latino; 1 American Indian or Alaska Native, non-Hispanic/Latino; 7 Asian, non-Hispanic/Latino; 33 Hispanic/Latino; 1 Native Hawaiian or other Pacific Islander, non-Hispanic/Latino), 9 international. Average age 28. In 2011, 99 master's awarded. *Entrance requirements:* For master's, interview, bachelor's degree, resume, 2 recommendations. Additional exam requirements/recommendations for international students: Required—TOEFL (minimum score 550 paper-based; 213 computer-based). *Application deadline:* For fall admission, 8/15 priority date for domestic students, 5/1 for international students; for spring admission, 11/15 for international students. Applications are processed on a rolling basis. Application fee: $40. Electronic applications accepted. *Financial support:* Career-related internships or fieldwork, Federal Work-Study, scholarships/grants, and unspecified assistantships available. Financial award application deadline: 5/1; financial award applicants required to submit FAFSA. *Unit head:* Dr. Maureen Culleeney, Academic Program Director, 815-838-0500 Ext. 5631, E-mail: culleema@lewisu.edu. *Application contact:* Michele Ryan, Director of Admission, 815-838-0500 Ext. 5384, E-mail: gsm@lewisu.edu.

Lewis University, College of Business, Program in Information Security, Romeoville, IL 60446. Offers managerial (MS); technical (MS). Part-time and evening/weekend programs available. Postbaccalaureate distance learning degree programs offered (no on-campus study). *Students:* 35 full-time (6 women), 72 part-time (11 women); includes 34 minority (19 Black or African American, non-Hispanic/Latino; 2 American Indian or Alaska Native, non-Hispanic/Latino; 6 Asian, non-Hispanic/Latino; 5 Hispanic/Latino; 1 Native Hawaiian or other Pacific Islander, non-Hispanic/Latino; 1 Two or more races, non-Hispanic/Latino), 22 international. Average age 35. In 2011, 8 master's awarded. *Entrance requirements:* For master's, bachelor's degree, minimum GPA of 3.0, resume, 2-page statement of purpose, 3 letters of recommendation. Additional exam requirements/recommendations for international students: Required—TOEFL (minimum score 550 paper-based; 213 computer-based; 80 iBT). *Application deadline:* For fall admission, 5/1 for international students; for spring admission, 11/15 for international students. Applications are processed on a rolling basis. Application fee: $40. Electronic applications accepted. *Financial support:* Application deadline: 5/1; applicants required to submit FAFSA. *Unit head:* Dr. Rami Khasawneh, Dean, 815-838-0500 Ext. 5360. *Application contact:* Michele Ryan, Director of Admission, Graduate School of Management, 800-897-9000, E-mail: gsm@lewisu.edu.

Marymount University, School of Business Administration, Program in Information Technology, Arlington, VA 22207-4299. Offers computer security and information assurance (Certificate); health care informatics (Certificate); information technology (MS, Certificate); information technology project management: technology leadership

(Certificate). Part-time and evening/weekend programs available. *Faculty:* 6 full-time (2 women), 9 part-time/adjunct (0 women). *Students:* 37 full-time (14 women), 32 part-time (13 women); includes 19 minority (9 Black or African American, non-Hispanic/Latino; 6 Asian, non-Hispanic/Latino; 3 Hispanic/Latino; 1 Two or more races, non-Hispanic/Latino), 30 international. Average age 30. 47 applicants, 98% accepted, 36 enrolled. In 2011, 28 master's, 10 other advanced degrees awarded. *Degree requirements:* For master's, thesis or alternative. *Entrance requirements:* For master's, GMAT or GRE General Test, interview, resume, bachelor's degree in computer-related field or degree in another subject with a post-baccalaureate certificate in a computer-related field; for Certificate, resume. Additional exam requirements/recommendations for international students: Required—TOEFL (minimum score 600 paper-based; 250 computer-based; 96 iBT), IELTS (minimum score 6.5). *Application deadline:* For fall admission, 7/1 priority date for domestic students, 7/1 for international students; for spring admission, 11/15 for domestic students, 11/16 for international students. Applications are processed on a rolling basis. Application fee: $40. Electronic applications accepted. *Expenses: Tuition:* Part-time $770 per credit hour. *Required fees:* $8 per credit hour. One-time fee: $180 full-time. *Financial support:* In 2011–12, 7 students received support. Research assistantships with full tuition reimbursements available, career-related internships or fieldwork, Federal Work-Study, scholarships/grants, and unspecified assistantships available. Support available to part-time students. Financial award applicants required to submit FAFSA. *Unit head:* Dr. Diane Murphy, Chair, 703-284-5958, Fax: 703-527-3830, E-mail: diane.murphy@marymount.edu. *Application contact:* Francesca Reed, Director, Graduate Admissions, 703-284-5901, Fax: 703-527-3815, E-mail: grad.admissions@marymount.edu. Web site: http://www.marymount.edu/academics/programs/infoTechMS.

Mercy College, School of Liberal Arts, Program in Information Assurance and Security, Dobbs Ferry, NY 10522-1189. Offers cybersecurity (MS). Part-time and evening/weekend programs available. Postbaccalaureate distance learning degree programs offered (no on-campus study). *Degree requirements:* For master's, project or thesis. *Entrance requirements:* For master's, two letters of recommendation, two-page written personal statement; completion of undergraduate prerequisites in local area networks, database management systems, cryptographgy and computer security, operating systems, and statistics. Additional exam requirements/recommendations for international students: Required—TOEFL (minimum score 600 paper-based; 250 computer-based; 100 iBT), IELTS (minimum score 8). Electronic applications accepted. *Expenses:* Contact institution. *Faculty research:* Information security theory, assurance, technical and analytical abilities.

Metropolitan State University, College of Management, St. Paul, MN 55106-5000. Offers business administration (MBA, DBA); database administration (Graduate Certificate); healthcare information technology management (Graduate Certificate); information assurance security (Graduate Certificate); management information systems (MMIS); MIS generalist (Graduate Certificate); MIS systems analysis and design (Graduate Certificate); project management (Graduate Certificate); public and nonprofit administration (MPNA). Part-time and evening/weekend programs available. *Students:* 63 full-time (41 women), 409 part-time (192 women); includes 94 minority (38 Black or African American, non-Hispanic/Latino; 33 Asian, non-Hispanic/Latino; 14 Hispanic/Latino; 9 Two or more races, non-Hispanic/Latino), 61 international. Average age 35. *Degree requirements:* For master's, thesis optional, computer language (MMIS). *Entrance requirements:* For master's, GMAT (MBA), resume. Additional exam requirements/recommendations for international students: Required—TOEFL (minimum score 550 paper-based; 213 computer-based). *Application deadline:* For fall admission, 7/15 for international students; for winter admission, 11/15 for international students; for spring admission, 3/15 for international students. Applications are processed on a rolling basis. Application fee: $20. Electronic applications accepted. *Expenses:* Tuition, state resident: full-time $5799.06; part-time $322.17 per credit. Tuition, nonresident: full-time $11,411; part-time $633.92 per credit. Tuition and fees vary according to degree level, program and reciprocity agreements. *Financial support:* Research assistantships with partial tuition reimbursements, career-related internships or fieldwork, and Federal Work-Study available. Support available to part-time students. Financial award applicants required to submit FAFSA. *Faculty research:* Yugoslav economic system, workers' cooperatives, participative management and job enrichment, global business systems. *Unit head:* Dr. Paul Huo, Dean, 612-659-7271, Fax: 612-659-7268, E-mail: paul.huo@metrostate.edu. Web site: http://choose.metrostate.edu/comgradprograms.

National University, Academic Affairs, School of Engineering, Technology and Media, Department of Computer Science, Information and Media Systems, La Jolla, CA 92037-1011. Offers computer science (MS); cyber security and information assurance (MS); management information systems (MS). Part-time and evening/weekend programs available. Postbaccalaureate distance learning degree programs offered (no on-campus study). *Degree requirements:* For master's, thesis. *Entrance requirements:* For master's, interview, minimum GPA of 2.5. Additional exam requirements/recommendations for international students: Required—TOEFL (minimum score 550 paper-based; 213 computer-based; 79 iBT), IELTS (minimum score 6). *Application deadline:* Applications are processed on a rolling basis. Application fee: $60 ($65 for international students). Electronic applications accepted. *Financial support:* Career-related internships or fieldwork, institutionally sponsored loans, scholarships/grants, and tuition waivers (partial) available. Support available to part-time students. Financial award application deadline: 6/30; financial award applicants required to submit FAFSA. *Unit head:* Dr. Alireza M. Farahani, 858-309-3438, Fax: 858-309-3420, E-mail: afarahan@nu.edu. *Application contact:* Dominick Giovanniello, Associate Regional Dean, 800-NAT-UNIV, Fax: 858-541-7792, E-mail: dgiovann@nu.edu. Web site: http://www.nu.edu/OurPrograms/SchoolOfEngineeringAndTechnology/ComputerScienceAndInformationSystems.html.

Naval Postgraduate School, Departments and Academic Groups, Department of Computer Science, Monterey, CA 93943. Offers computer science (MS, PhD); identity management and cyber security (MA); modeling of virtual environments and simulations (MS, PhD); software engineering (MS, PhD). Program only open to commissioned officers of the United States and friendly nations and selected United States federal civilian employees. Part-time programs available. Postbaccalaureate distance learning degree programs offered (minimal on-campus study). *Faculty:* 89 full-time (13 women), 26 part-time/adjunct (7 women). *Students:* 140 full-time (17 women), 14 part-time (5 women); includes 29 minority (9 Black or African American, non-Hispanic/Latino; 1 American Indian or Alaska Native, non-Hispanic/Latino; 10 Asian, non-Hispanic/Latino; 9 Hispanic/Latino), 26 international. Average age 37. In 2011, 54 master's, 4 doctorates awarded. *Degree requirements:* For master's, thesis; for doctorate, thesis/dissertation. *Total annual research expenditures:* $8.4 million. *Unit head:* Peter Denning, Chairman, 831-656-3603, E-mail: pjd@nps.edu. *Application contact:* Acting Director of Admissions.

New Jersey Institute of Technology, Office of Graduate Studies, College of Computing Science, Department of Computer Science, Program in Cyber Security and Privacy, Newark, NJ 07102. Offers MS. *Students:* 4 part-time (2 women); includes 2 minority (1 Black or African American, non-Hispanic/Latino; 1 Hispanic/Latino), 1

international. Average age 31. 10 applicants, 80% accepted. *Entrance requirements:* Additional exam requirements/recommendations for international students: Required—TOEFL (minimum score 550 paper-based; 213 computer-based; 79 iBT). *Application deadline:* For fall admission, 6/1 priority date for domestic students, 5/1 for international students; for spring admission, 11/15 priority date for domestic students, 11/15 for international students. Applications are processed on a rolling basis. Application fee: $65. Electronic applications accepted. *Expenses:* Tuition, state resident: full-time $7980; part-time $867 per credit. Tuition, nonresident: full-time $11,336; part-time $1196 per credit. *Required fees:* $230 per credit. *Financial support:* Application deadline: 1/15. *Unit head:* Dr. Michael A. Baltrush, Interim Chair, 973-596-3386, E-mail: michael.a.baltrush@njit.edu. *Application contact:* Kathryn Kelly, Director of Admissions, 973-596-3300, Fax: 973-596-3461, E-mail: admissions@njit.edu. Web site: http://cs.njit.edu/academics/graduate/mscsp.php.

New Jersey Institute of Technology, Office of Graduate Studies, College of Computing Science, Department of Information Technology, Program in Information Technology Administration and Security, Newark, NJ 07102. Offers MS. *Students:* 29 full-time (6 women), 56 part-time (6 women); includes 48 minority (11 Black or African American, non-Hispanic/Latino; 17 Asian, non-Hispanic/Latino; 20 Hispanic/Latino), 7 international. Average age 30. 82 applicants, 68% accepted, 35 enrolled. In 2011, 17 master's awarded. *Entrance requirements:* Additional exam requirements/recommendations for international students: Required—TOEFL (minimum score 550 paper-based; 213 computer-based; 79 iBT). *Application deadline:* For fall admission, 6/1 priority date for domestic students, 5/1 for international students; for spring admission, 11/15 priority date for domestic students, 11/15 for international students. Applications are processed on a rolling basis. Application fee: $65. Electronic applications accepted. *Expenses:* Tuition, state resident: full-time $7980; part-time $867 per credit. Tuition, nonresident: full-time $11,336; part-time $1196 per credit. *Required fees:* $230 per credit. *Financial support:* Application deadline: 1/15. *Unit head:* Dr. Narain Gehani, Dean, 973-542-5488, Fax: 973-596-5777, E-mail: narain.gehani@njit.edu. *Application contact:* Kathryn Kelly, Director of Admissions, 973-596-3300, Fax: 973-596-3461, E-mail: admissions@njit.edu.

New York Institute of Technology, Graduate Division, School of Engineering and Computing Sciences, Program in Information, Network, and Computer Security, Old Westbury, NY 11568-8000. Offers MS. Part-time and evening/weekend programs available. Postbaccalaureate distance learning degree programs offered. *Students:* 48 full-time (10 women), 36 part-time (3 women); includes 16 minority (6 Black or African American, non-Hispanic/Latino; 4 Asian, non-Hispanic/Latino; 5 Hispanic/Latino; 1 Two or more races, non-Hispanic/Latino), 25 international. Average age 29. In 2011, 38 master's awarded. *Entrance requirements:* Additional exam requirements/recommendations for international students: Required—TOEFL (minimum score 550 paper-based; 213 computer-based). *Application deadline:* For fall admission, 7/1 priority date for domestic students; for spring admission, 12/1 priority date for domestic students. Applications are processed on a rolling basis. Application fee: $50. Electronic applications accepted. *Expenses: Tuition:* Part-time $930 per credit hour. *Financial support:* Fellowships, research assistantships with partial tuition reimbursements, career-related internships or fieldwork, institutionally sponsored loans, tuition waivers (full and partial), and unspecified assistantships available. Support available to part-time students. Financial award applicants required to submit FAFSA. *Unit head:* Dr. Nada Anid, Dean, 516-686-7931, Fax: 516-625-7933, E-mail: nanid@nyit.edu. *Application contact:* Dr. Jacquelyn Nealon, Vice President for Enrollment Services, 516-686-7925, Fax: 516-686-7597, E-mail: jnealon@nyit.edu.

Northern Kentucky University, Office of Graduate Programs, College of Informatics, Department of Business Informatics, Highland Heights, KY 41099. Offers business informatics (MS, Certificate); corporate information security (Certificate); enterprise resource planning (Certificate). Part-time and evening/weekend programs available. Postbaccalaureate distance learning degree programs offered (no on-campus study). *Faculty:* 9 full-time (3 women), 1 part-time/adjunct (0 women). *Students:* 12 full-time (5 women), 61 part-time (21 women); includes 11 minority (4 Black or African American, non-Hispanic/Latino; 3 Asian, non-Hispanic/Latino; 3 Hispanic/Latino; 1 Native Hawaiian or other Pacific Islander, non-Hispanic/Latino), 5 international. Average age 34. 41 applicants, 80% accepted, 25 enrolled. In 2011, 32 degrees awarded. *Degree requirements:* For master's, capstone and portfolio (some programs), internship. *Entrance requirements:* For master's, GMAT (minimum score 450), GRE General Test (minimum combined score 1000), resume, minimum GPA of 2.5. Additional exam requirements/recommendations for international students: Required—TOEFL (minimum score 550 paper-based; 213 computer-based; 79 iBT); Recommended—IELTS (minimum score 6.5). *Application deadline:* For fall admission, 8/1 for domestic students, 6/1 for international students; for spring admission, 12/1 for domestic students, 10/1 for international students. Applications are processed on a rolling basis. Application fee: $40. Electronic applications accepted. *Expenses:* Tuition, state resident: full-time $7614; part-time $423 per credit hour. Tuition, nonresident: full-time $13,104; part-time $728 per credit hour. Tuition and fees vary according to degree level and reciprocity agreements. *Financial support:* Unspecified assistantships available. Financial award applicants required to submit FAFSA. *Faculty research:* Information systems implementation, information systems security, business analytics, healthcare informatics, project management practices. *Total annual research expenditures:* $50,000. *Unit head:* Dr. Ben Martz, Department Chair, 859-572-6366, E-mail: matrzw1@nku.edu. *Application contact:* Dr. Vijay Raghavan, Director, MBI Program, 859-572-6358, E-mail: raghavan@nku.edu. Web site: http://informatics.nku.edu/bis.

Northwestern University, School of Continuing Studies, Program in Information Systems, Evanston, IL 60208. Offers database and Internet technologies (MS); information systems management (MS); information systems security (MS); software project management and development (MS).

Norwich University, College of Graduate and Continuing Studies, Master of Science in Information Assurance Program, Northfield, VT 05663. Offers business continuity management (MS); continuity of governmental operations (MS); managing cyber crime and digital incidents (MS). Evening/weekend programs available. *Faculty:* 21 part-time/adjunct (4 women). *Students:* 39 full-time (3 women); includes 8 minority (3 Black or African American, non-Hispanic/Latino; 3 Asian, non-Hispanic/Latino; 1 Hispanic/Latino; 1 Native Hawaiian or other Pacific Islander, non-Hispanic/Latino). Average age 39. 13 applicants, 100% accepted, 13 enrolled. In 2011, 67 degrees awarded. *Entrance requirements:* For master's, minimum undergraduate GPA of 2.75. Additional exam requirements/recommendations for international students: Required—TOEFL (minimum score 550 paper-based; 212 computer-based; 83 iBT). *Application deadline:* For fall admission, 8/10 for domestic and international students; for winter admission, 11/7 for domestic and international students; for spring admission, 2/6 for domestic and international students. Applications are processed on a rolling basis. Application fee: $50. Electronic applications accepted. *Expenses: Tuition:* Full-time $16,174. *Required fees:* $2130. Full-time tuition and fees vary according to program. *Financial support:* In 2011–12, 36 students received support. Scholarships/grants available. Financial award applicants required to submit FAFSA. *Unit head:* Dr. Gary Kessler, Director, 802-485-2729, Fax: 802-485-2533, E-mail: kesslerg@norwich.edu. *Application contact:* Elizabeth Templeton, Assistant Director, 802-485-2757, Fax: 802-485-2533, E-mail: etemplet@norwich.edu. Web site: http://infoassurance.norwich.edu/.

Nova Southeastern University, Graduate School of Computer and Information Sciences, Fort Lauderdale, FL 33314-7796. Offers computer information systems (MS, PhD); computer science (MS, PhD); computing technology in education (PhD); information security (MS); information systems (PhD); information technology (MS); information technology in education (MS); management information systems (MS). Part-time and evening/weekend programs available. Postbaccalaureate distance learning degree programs offered (no on-campus study). *Faculty:* 20 full-time (5 women), 21 part-time/adjunct (3 women). *Students:* 130 full-time (37 women), 960 part-time (291 women); includes 496 minority (221 Black or African American, non-Hispanic/Latino; 4 American Indian or Alaska Native, non-Hispanic/Latino; 78 Asian, non-Hispanic/Latino; 178 Hispanic/Latino; 15 Two or more races, non-Hispanic/Latino), 49 international. Average age 41. 486 applicants, 45% accepted. In 2011, 131 master's, 39 doctorates awarded. Terminal master's awarded for partial completion of doctoral program. *Degree requirements:* For master's, thesis optional; for doctorate, thesis/dissertation. *Entrance requirements:* For master's, minimum undergraduate GPA of 2.5; 3.0 in major; for doctorate, master's degree, minimum graduate GPA of 3.25. Additional exam requirements/recommendations for international students: Required—TOEFL (minimum score 213 computer-based; 79 iBT), IELTS (minimum score 6). *Application deadline:* Applications are processed on a rolling basis. Application fee: $50. Electronic applications accepted. *Expenses:* Contact institution. *Financial support:* Federal Work-Study, scholarships/grants, and unspecified assistantships available. Support available to part-time students. Financial award application deadline: 5/1. *Faculty research:* Artificial intelligence, database management, human-computer interaction, distance education, information security. *Unit head:* Dr. Eric S. Ackerman, Interim Dean, 954-262-7300. *Application contact:* 954-262-2000, Fax: 954-262-2752, E-mail: scisinfo@nova.edu. Web site: http://www.scis.nova.edu/.

Our Lady of the Lake University of San Antonio, School of Business and Leadership, Program in Information Systems and Security, San Antonio, TX 78207-4689. Offers MS. Postbaccalaureate distance learning degree programs offered.

Pace University, Seidenberg School of Computer Science and Information Systems, New York, NY 10038. Offers computer communications and networks (Certificate); computer science (MS); computing studies (DPS); information systems (MS); Internet technologies for e-commerce (Certificate); Internet technology (MS); object-oriented programming (Certificate); security and information assurance (Certificate); software development and engineering (MS); telecommunications (MS, Certificate). Part-time and evening/weekend programs available. *Students:* 82 full-time (19 women), 356 part-time (99 women); includes 175 minority (64 Black or African American, non-Hispanic/Latino; 1 American Indian or Alaska Native, non-Hispanic/Latino; 59 Asian, non-Hispanic/Latino; 47 Hispanic/Latino; 4 Two or more races, non-Hispanic/Latino), 72 international. Average age 37. 304 applicants, 67% accepted, 92 enrolled. In 2011, 136 master's, 9 doctorates, 32 other advanced degrees awarded. *Entrance requirements:* For master's, GRE General Test. Additional exam requirements/recommendations for international students: Required—TOEFL. *Application deadline:* For fall admission, 7/31 priority date for domestic students; for spring admission, 11/30 for domestic students. Applications are processed on a rolling basis. Application fee: $70. Electronic applications accepted. *Expenses:* Contact institution. *Financial support:* Research assistantships and career-related internships or fieldwork available. Support available to part-time students. Financial award applicants required to submit FAFSA. *Unit head:* Dr. Constance Knapp, Interim Dean, 914-773-3750, Fax: 914-773-3533, E-mail: cknapp@pace.edu. *Application contact:* Susan Ford-Goldschein, Director of Graduate Admissions, 914-422-4283, Fax: 914-422-4287, E-mail: gradwp@pace.edu. Web site: http://www.pace.edu/.

Polytechnic Institute of New York University, Department of Computer Science and Engineering, Major in Cyber Security, Brooklyn, NY 11201-2990. Offers Graduate Certificate. *Students:* 23 full-time (4 women), 86 part-time (10 women); includes 14 minority (2 Black or African American, non-Hispanic/Latino; 8 Asian, non-Hispanic/Latino; 4 Hispanic/Latino), 15 international. Average age 35. 99 applicants, 70% accepted, 48 enrolled. *Application deadline:* For fall admission, 7/31 priority date for domestic students, 4/30 for international students; for spring admission, 12/31 priority date for domestic students, 11/30 for international students. Applications are processed on a rolling basis. Application fee: $75. Electronic applications accepted. *Expenses: Tuition:* Full-time $22,464; part-time $1248 per credit. *Required fees:* $501 per semester. *Unit head:* Dr. Keith W. Ross, Head, 718-260-3859, Fax: 718-260-3609, E-mail: ross@poly.edu. *Application contact:* JeanCarlo Bonilla, Director, Graduate Enrollment Management, 718-260-3182, Fax: 718-260-3624, E-mail: gradinfo@poly.edu.

Purdue University, Graduate School, Center for Education and Research in Information Assurance and Security (CERIAS), Interdisciplinary Program in Information Security, West Lafayette, IN 47907. Offers MS. *Students:* 9 full-time (4 women), 2 part-time (0 women); includes 3 minority (2 Black or African American, non-Hispanic/Latino; 1 Two or more races, non-Hispanic/Latino), 4 international. Average age 26. 25 applicants, 44% accepted, 4 enrolled. *Entrance requirements:* For master's, GRE test required, minimum undergraduate GPA of 3.0 or equivalent. Additional exam requirements/recommendations for international students: Required—TOEFL (minimum score 550 paper-based; 77 iBT); Recommended—TWE. *Application deadline:* For fall admission, 4/1 priority date for domestic students, 4/1 for international students; for spring admission, 10/1 priority date for domestic students, 10/1 for international students. Applications are processed on a rolling basis. Application fee: $60 ($75 for international students). Electronic applications accepted. *Unit head:* Dr. Eugene Spafford, Head, 765-454-7805. *Application contact:* Marlene Walls, Administrative Assistant, 765-494-7805, E-mail: walls@cerias.purdue.edu.

Regis University, College for Professional Studies, School of Computer and Information Sciences, Denver, CO 80221-1099. Offers database administration with Oracle (Certificate); database development (Certificate); database technologies (M Sc); enterprise Java software development (Certificate); enterprise resource planning (Certificate); executive information technologies (Certificate); information assurance (M Sc, Certificate); information technology management (M Sc); software engineering (M Sc, Certificate); software engineering and database technologies (M Sc); storage area networks (Certificate); systems engineering (M Sc, Certificate). Offered at Boulder Campus, Northwest Denver Campus, Southeast Denver Campus, Fort Collins Campus, Colorado Springs Campus, and Broomfield Campus. Part-time and evening/weekend programs available. Postbaccalaureate distance learning degree programs offered (no on-campus study). *Degree requirements:* For master's, thesis, final research project. *Entrance requirements:* For master's, 2 years of related experience, resume, interview; for Certificate, 2 years of related experience, resumé. Additional exam requirements/

recommendations for international students: Required—TOEFL (minimum score 213 computer-based), TWE (minimum score 5) or university-based test. Electronic applications accepted. *Expenses:* Contact institution. *Faculty research:* Secure Virtual Laboratory Architecture, Joint IA project with W2C06 Institute, Information Policy, OLTP and OLAP Technologies, knowledge management, software architectures.

Robert Morris University, Graduate Studies, School of Communications and Information Systems, Moon Township, PA 15108-1189. Offers communication and information systems (MS); competitive intelligence systems (MS); information security and assurance (MS); information systems and communications (D Sc); information systems management (MS); information technology project management (MS); Internet information systems (MS); organizational leadership (MS). Part-time and evening/weekend programs available. Postbaccalaureate distance learning degree programs offered (no on-campus study). *Faculty:* 28 full-time (9 women), 9 part-time/adjunct (3 women). *Students:* 231 part-time (68 women); includes 41 minority (31 Black or African American, non-Hispanic/Latino; 8 Asian, non-Hispanic/Latino; 2 Hispanic/Latino), 16 international. *Degree requirements:* For doctorate, thesis/dissertation. *Entrance requirements:* For doctorate, employer letter of endorsement, interview. Additional exam requirements/recommendations for international students: Required—TOEFL (minimum score 550 paper-based; 213 computer-based; 79 iBT). *Application deadline:* For fall admission, 7/1 priority date for domestic students, 7/1 for international students; for spring admission, 11/1 priority date for domestic students, 11/1 for international students. Applications are processed on a rolling basis. Application fee: $35. Electronic applications accepted. *Expenses:* Contact institution. *Financial support:* Research assistantships with partial tuition reimbursements, institutionally sponsored loans, and unspecified assistantships available. Support available to part-time students. Financial award application deadline: 5/1. *Unit head:* Dr. Barbara J. Levine, Dean, 412-397-2591, Fax: 412-397-2481, E-mail: levine@rmu.edu. *Application contact:* Deborah Roach, Assistant Dean, Graduate Admissions, 412-397-5200, Fax: 412-397-2425, E-mail: graduateadmissions@rmu.edu. Web site: http://www.rmu.edu/web/cms/schools/scis/.

Rochester Institute of Technology, Graduate Enrollment Services, B. Thomas Golisano College of Computing and Information Sciences, Department of Information Technology, Rochester, NY 14623-5603. Offers database administration (AC); human-computer interaction (MS); information assurance (AC); information technology (MS); interactive multimedia development (AC); medical informatics (MS). Part-time programs available. *Students:* 74 full-time (16 women), 97 part-time (19 women); includes 20 minority (8 Black or African American, non-Hispanic/Latino; 1 American Indian or Alaska Native, non-Hispanic/Latino; 4 Asian, non-Hispanic/Latino; 6 Hispanic/Latino; 1 Two or more races, non-Hispanic/Latino), 78 international. Average age 29. 187 applicants, 60% accepted, 43 enrolled. In 2011, 29 master's, 4 other advanced degrees awarded. *Degree requirements:* For master's, thesis or project. *Entrance requirements:* For master's, GRE, minimum GPA of 3.0. Additional exam requirements/recommendations for international students: Required—TOEFL (minimum score 570 paper-based; 230 computer-based; 99 iBT) or IELTS (minimum score 6.5). *Application deadline:* Applications are processed on a rolling basis. Application fee: $50. Electronic applications accepted. *Expenses: Tuition:* Full-time $34,659; part-time $963 per credit hour. *Required fees:* $228; $76 per quarter. *Financial support:* Research assistantships with partial tuition reimbursements, teaching assistantships with partial tuition reimbursements, career-related internships or fieldwork, scholarships/grants, and unspecified assistantships available. Support available to part-time students. Financial award applicants required to submit FAFSA. *Faculty research:* Human-computer interaction: eye tracking, usability engineering, usability testing, ubiquitous computing, interface design and development; platform-independent Multiuser Online Virtual Environments (MOVEs); simulation; service computing, query optimization, data mining and integration; applications programming, interface designs, needs assessment, data modeling, database administration. *Unit head:* Prof. Jeffrey Lasky, Department Chair, 585-475-2284, Fax: 585-475-6584, E-mail: jeffrey.lasky@rit.edu. *Application contact:* Diane Ellison, Assistant Vice President, Graduate Enrollment Services, 585-475-2229, Fax: 585-475-7164, E-mail: gradinfo@rit.edu. Web site: http://www.it.rit.edu.

Rochester Institute of Technology, Graduate Enrollment Services, B. Thomas Golisano College of Computing and Information Sciences, Department of Networking, Security and Systems Administration, Program in Computing Security and Information Assurance, Rochester, NY 14623-5603. Offers MS. Part-time programs available. *Students:* 14 full-time (1 woman), 12 part-time (2 women), 12 international. Average age 33. 46 applicants, 57% accepted, 12 enrolled. In 2011, 2 master's awarded. *Degree requirements:* For master's, thesis. *Entrance requirements:* For master's, GRE, minimum GPA of 3.0. Additional exam requirements/recommendations for international students: Required—TOEFL (minimum score 600 paper-based; 250 computer-based; 100 iBT) or IELTS (minimum score 7.0). *Application deadline:* Applications are processed on a rolling basis. Application fee: $50. Electronic applications accepted. *Expenses: Tuition:* Full-time $34,659; part-time $963 per credit hour. *Required fees:* $228; $76 per quarter. *Financial support:* Research assistantships with partial tuition reimbursements, teaching assistantships with partial tuition reimbursements, career-related internships or fieldwork, scholarships/grants, and unspecified assistantships available. Support available to part-time students. Financial award applicants required to submit FAFSA. *Unit head:* Prof. Dianne Bills, Graduate Program Director, 585-475-2700, Fax: 585-475-6584, E-mail: informaticsgrad@rit.edu. *Application contact:* Diane Ellison, Assistant Vice President, Graduate Enrollment Services, 585-475-2229, Fax: 585-475-7164, E-mail: gradinfo@rit.edu.

Sacred Heart University, Graduate Programs, College of Arts and Sciences, Department of Computer Science and Information Technology, Fairfield, CT 06825-1000. Offers computer science (MS); database (CPS); information technology (MS, CPS); information technology and network security (CPS); interactive multimedia (CPS); Web development (CPS). Part-time and evening/weekend programs available. *Degree requirements:* For master's, thesis optional. *Entrance requirements:* Additional exam requirements/recommendations for international students: Required—TOEFL (minimum score 550 paper-based; 213 computer-based). Electronic applications accepted. *Faculty research:* Contemporary market software.

St. Cloud State University, School of Graduate Studies, College of Science and Engineering, Program in Information Assurance, St. Cloud, MN 56301-4498. Offers MS.

St. Cloud State University, School of Graduate Studies, G.R. Herberger College of Business, Program in Business Administration, St. Cloud, MN 56301-4498. Offers business administration (MBA); information assurance (MS). Part-time and evening/weekend programs available. *Degree requirements:* For master's, thesis or alternative. *Entrance requirements:* For master's, GMAT, minimum GPA of 2.75. Additional exam requirements/recommendations for international students: Required—Michigan English Language Assessment Battery; Recommended—TOEFL (minimum score 550 paper-based; 213 computer-based), IELTS (minimum score 6.5).

Saint Leo University, Graduate Business Studies, Saint Leo, FL 33574-6665. Offers accounting (MBA); business (MBA); health services management (MBA); human resource management (MBA); information security management (MBA); marketing (MBA); sport business (MBA). Part-time and evening/weekend programs available. Postbaccalaureate distance learning degree programs offered (no on-campus study). *Faculty:* 39 full-time (7 women), 56 part-time/adjunct (17 women). *Students:* 1,506 full-time (901 women); includes 620 minority (480 Black or African American, non-Hispanic/Latino; 5 American Indian or Alaska Native, non-Hispanic/Latino; 21 Asian, non-Hispanic/Latino; 100 Hispanic/Latino; 1 Native Hawaiian or other Pacific Islander, non-Hispanic/Latino; 13 Two or more races, non-Hispanic/Latino), 20 international. Average age 38. In 2011, 574 master's awarded. *Entrance requirements:* For master's, GMAT (minimum score 500 if applicant does not have 5 years of professional work experience), bachelor's degree with minimum GPA of 3.0 in the last 60 hours of coursework from regionally-accredited college or university; 5 years of professional work experience; resume; 2 letters of recommendation. Additional exam requirements/recommendations for international students: Required—TOEFL (minimum score 550 paper-based; 213 computer-based; 80 iBT). *Application deadline:* For fall admission, 7/1 priority date for domestic students, 7/1 for international students; for spring admission, 11/12 priority date for domestic students, 11/1 for international students. Applications are processed on a rolling basis. Application fee: $80. Electronic applications accepted. *Expenses: Tuition:* Full-time $11,340; part-time $630 per semester hour. Tuition and fees vary according to campus/location and program. *Financial support:* In 2011–12, 72 students received support. Career-related internships or fieldwork, Federal Work-Study, scholarships/grants, and health care benefits available. Financial award application deadline: 3/1; financial award applicants required to submit FAFSA. *Unit head:* Dr. Lorrie McGovern, Director, 352-588-7390, Fax: 352-588-8585, E-mail: mbaslu@saintleo.edu. *Application contact:* Jared Welling, Director of Graduate Admission, 800-707-8846, Fax: 352-588-7873, E-mail: grad.admissions@saintleo.edu. Web site: http://www.saintleo.edu/Academics/School-of-Business/Graduate-Degree-Programs.

Salem International University, School of Business, Salem, WV 26426-0500. Offers information security (MBA); international business (MBA). Part-time programs available. Postbaccalaureate distance learning degree programs offered (no on-campus study). *Entrance requirements:* For master's, minimum undergraduate GPA of 2.5, course work in business, resume. Additional exam requirements/recommendations for international students: Recommended—TOEFL (minimum score 550 paper-based; 213 computer-based), IELTS (minimum score 6.5). Electronic applications accepted. *Expenses:* Contact institution. *Faculty research:* Organizational behavior strategy, marketing services.

Salve Regina University, Program in Administration of Justice and Homeland Security, Newport, RI 02840-4192. Offers cybersecurity and intelligence (MS); leadership in justice (MS). Part-time and evening/weekend programs available. *Faculty:* 1 full-time (0 women), 10 part-time/adjunct (2 women). *Students:* 23 full-time (12 women), 34 part-time (5 women); includes 2 minority (1 Black or African American, non-Hispanic/Latino; 1 Hispanic/Latino). *Entrance requirements:* For master's, GMAT, GRE General Test, or MAT. Additional exam requirements/recommendations for international students: Required—TOEFL (minimum score 600 paper-based; 250 computer-based; 100 iBT). *Application deadline:* For fall admission, 3/5 priority date for domestic students, 3/15 for international students; for spring admission, 9/15 priority date for domestic students, 9/5 for international students. Applications are processed on a rolling basis. Application fee: $60. Electronic applications accepted. *Expenses: Tuition:* Full-time $7740; part-time $430 per credit. *Required fees:* $40 per semester. Tuition and fees vary according to program. *Financial support:* Career-related internships or fieldwork and Federal Work-Study available. Support available to part-time students. Financial award application deadline: 3/1; financial award applicants required to submit FAFSA. *Unit head:* David Smith, Director, 401-341-3210, E-mail: david.smith@salve.edu. *Application contact:* Kelly Alverson, Associate Director of Graduate Admissions, 401-341-2153, Fax: 401-341-2973, E-mail: kelly.alverson@salve.edu. Web site: http://www.salve.edu/graduatestudies/programs/gad/.

Sam Houston State University, College of Sciences, Department of Computer Science, Huntsville, TX 77341. Offers computing and information science (MS); digital forensics (MS); information assurance and security (MS). Part-time programs available. *Faculty:* 11 full-time (2 women). *Students:* 38 full-time (8 women), 26 part-time (2 women); includes 14 minority (7 Black or African American, non-Hispanic/Latino; 1 American Indian or Alaska Native, non-Hispanic/Latino; 6 Hispanic/Latino), 34 international. Average age 28. 29 applicants, 83% accepted, 24 enrolled. In 2011, 20 master's awarded. *Entrance requirements:* For master's, GRE General Test. Additional exam requirements/recommendations for international students: Required—TOEFL (minimum score 550 paper-based; 213 computer-based; 79 iBT). *Application deadline:* For fall admission, 8/1 for domestic and international students; for spring admission, 12/1 for domestic and international students. Application fee: $20. *Expenses:* Tuition, state resident: full-time $4420; part-time $221 per credit hour. Tuition, nonresident: full-time $10,680; part-time $534 per credit hour. *Required fees:* $329 per credit hour. *Financial support:* Research assistantships, teaching assistantships, Federal Work-Study, institutionally sponsored loans, and tuition waivers (partial) available. Financial award application deadline: 5/31; financial award applicants required to submit FAFSA. *Unit head:* Dr. Peter Cooper, Chair, 936-294-1569, Fax: 936-294-4312, E-mail: css_pac@shsu.edu. *Application contact:* Dr. Jiuhung Ji, Advisor, 936-294-1579, E-mail: csc_jxj@shsu.edu. Web site: http://cs.shsu.edu/.

Southern Polytechnic State University, School of Computing and Software Engineering, Department of Information Technology, Marietta, GA 30060-2896. Offers health information technology (Graduate Certificate); information security and assurance (Graduate Certificate); information technology (MSIT, Graduate Certificate); information technology fundamentals (Graduate Transition Certificate). Part-time and evening/weekend programs available. Postbaccalaureate distance learning degree programs offered (minimal on-campus study). *Faculty:* 8 full-time (3 women), 2 part-time/adjunct (0 women). *Students:* 49 full-time (15 women), 114 part-time (41 women); includes 81 minority (67 Black or African American, non-Hispanic/Latino; 11 Asian, non-Hispanic/Latino; 1 Hispanic/Latino; 2 Two or more races, non-Hispanic/Latino), 29 international. Average age 33. 82 applicants, 93% accepted, 55 enrolled. In 2011, 43 master's, 5 other advanced degrees awarded. *Degree requirements:* For master's, thesis or alternative. *Entrance requirements:* For master's, minimum GPA of 2.75; for other advanced degree, bachelor's degree. Additional exam requirements/recommendations for international students: Required—TOEFL (minimum score 550 paper-based; 213 computer-based; 79 iBT), IELTS (minimum score 6.5). *Application deadline:* For fall admission, 7/1 priority date for domestic students, 5/1 for international students; for spring admission, 11/1 priority date for domestic students, 9/1 for international students. Applications are processed on a rolling basis. Application fee: $50. Electronic applications accepted. *Expenses:* Tuition, state resident: full-time $2592; part-time $216 per semester hour. Tuition, nonresident: full-time $9408; part-time $784 per semester hour. *Required fees:* $698 per term. *Financial support:* In 2011–12, 12 students received support, including 13 research assistantships with tuition reimbursements available (averaging $3,000 per year); career-related internships or fieldwork, scholarships/grants, and unspecified

assistantships also available. Support available to part-time students. Financial award application deadline: 5/1; financial award applicants required to submit FAFSA. *Faculty research:* IT ethics, user interface design, IT security, IT integration, IT management, health information technology. *Total annual research expenditures:* $50,000. *Unit head:* Dr. Ju Au Wang, Chair, 678-915-3718, Fax: 678-915-5511, E-mail: jwang@spsu.edu. *Application contact:* Nikki Palamiotis, Director of Graduate Studies, 678-915-4276, Fax: 678-915-7292, E-mail: npalamio@spsu.edu. Web site: http://www.spsu.edu/itdegrees/.

Stevens Institute of Technology, Graduate School, Charles V. Schaefer Jr. School of Engineering, Department of Computer Science, Hoboken, NJ 07030. Offers computer graphics (Certificate); computer science (MS, PhD); computer systems (Certificate); database management systems (Certificate); distributed systems (Certificate); elements of computer science (Certificate); enterprise computing (Certificate); enterprise security and information assurance (Certificate); health informatics (Certificate); multimedia experience and management (Certificate); networks and systems administration (Certificate); security and privacy (Certificate); service oriented computing (Certificate); software design (Certificate); theoretical computer science (Certificate). Part-time and evening/weekend programs available. Terminal master's awarded for partial completion of doctoral program. *Degree requirements:* For master's, thesis optional; for doctorate, variable foreign language requirement, comprehensive exam, thesis/dissertation. *Entrance requirements:* For master's and doctorate, GRE, minimum GPA of 3.0. Additional exam requirements/recommendations for international students: Required—TOEFL. Electronic applications accepted. *Faculty research:* Semantics, reliability theory, programming language, cyber security.

Stevens Institute of Technology, Graduate School, Wesley J. Howe School of Technology Management, Program in Information Systems, Hoboken, NJ 07030. Offers computer science (MS); e-commerce (MS); enterprise systems (MS); entrepreneurial information technology (MS); information architecture (MS); information management (MS, Certificate); information security (MS); information technology in financial services industry (MS); information technology in the pharmaceutical industry (MS); information technology outsourcing management (MS); project management (MS, Certificate); software engineering (MS); telecommunications (MS). *Degree requirements:* For master's, thesis optional. *Entrance requirements:* For master's, GMAT, GRE General Test. Additional exam requirements/recommendations for international students: Required—TOEFL. Electronic applications accepted.

Stratford University, School of Graduate Studies, Falls Church, VA 22043. Offers accounting (MS); business administration (IMBA, MBA); enterprise business management (MS); entrepreneurial management (MS); information assurance (MS); information systems (MS); software engineering (MS); telecommunications (MS). Part-time and evening/weekend programs available. Postbaccalaureate distance learning degree programs offered (no on-campus study). *Degree requirements:* For master's, comprehensive exam, capstone project. *Entrance requirements:* For master's, GRE or GMAT, baccalaureate degree. Additional exam requirements/recommendations for international students: Required—TOEFL (minimum score 213 computer-based, 79 iBT) or IELTS (6.5). Electronic applications accepted.

Strayer University, Graduate Studies, Washington, DC 20005-2603. Offers accounting (MS); acquisition (MBA); business administration (MBA); communications technology (MS); educational management (M Ed); finance (MBA); health services administration (MHSA); hospitality and tourism management (MBA); human resource management (MBA); information systems (MS), including computer security management, decision support system management, enterprise resource management, network management, software engineering management, systems development management; management (MBA); management information systems (MS); marketing (MBA); professional accounting (MS), including accounting information systems, controllership, taxation; public administration (MPA); supply chain management (MBA); technology in education (M Ed). Programs also offered at campus locations in Birmingham, AL; Chamblee, GA; Cobb County, GA; Morrow, GA; White Marsh, MD; Charleston, SC; Columbia, SC; Greensboro, NC; Greenville, SC; Lexington, KY; Louisville, KY; Nashville, TN; North Raleigh, NC; Washington, DC. Part-time and evening/weekend programs available. Postbaccalaureate distance learning degree programs offered (minimal on-campus study). *Degree requirements:* For master's, thesis. *Entrance requirements:* For master's, GMAT, GRE General Test, bachelor's degree from an accredited college or university, minimum undergraduate GPA of 2.75. Electronic applications accepted.

Syracuse University, School of Information Studies, Program in Information Security Management, Syracuse, NY 13244. Offers CAS. Part-time and evening/weekend programs available. Postbaccalaureate distance learning degree programs offered. *Students:* 7 part-time (2 women), 3 international. Average age 36. 48 applicants, 73% accepted, 1 enrolled. In 2011, 38 degrees awarded. *Entrance requirements:* Additional exam requirements/recommendations for international students: Required—TOEFL (minimum score 100 iBT). *Application deadline:* For fall admission, 2/1 priority date for domestic students, 2/1 for international students; for spring admission, 10/15 priority date for domestic students, 10/15 for international students. Applications are processed on a rolling basis. Application fee: $75. Electronic applications accepted. *Expenses: Tuition:* Part-time $1206 per credit. *Financial support:* Application deadline: 1/1; applicants required to submit FAFSA. *Unit head:* Joon S. Park, Head, 315-443-2911, E-mail: ischool@syr.edu. *Application contact:* Susan Corieri, Director of Enrollment Management, 315-443-2575, E-mail: ischool@syr.edu. Web site: http://ischool.syr.edu/.

Texas A&M University–San Antonio, School of Business, San Antonio, TX 78224. Offers business administration (MBA); enterprise resource planning systems (MBA); finance (MBA); healthcare management (MBA); human resources management (MBA); information assurance and security (MBA); international business (MBA); professional accounting (MPA); project management (MBA); supply chain management (MBA). Part-time and evening/weekend programs available. *Faculty:* 18 full-time (6 women), 1 part-time/adjunct (0 women). *Students:* 91 full-time (45 women), 278 part-time (150 women). Average age 33. In 2011, 20 master's awarded. *Entrance requirements:* For master's, GMAT. Additional exam requirements/recommendations for international students: Required—TOEFL (minimum score 550 paper-based; 213 computer-based; 80 iBT), IELTS (minimum score 6). *Application deadline:* For fall admission, 7/1 priority date for domestic students, 6/1 for international students; for spring admission, 11/15 priority date for domestic students, 10/1 for international students. Applications are processed on a rolling basis. Application fee: $35 ($50 for international students). Electronic applications accepted. *Expenses:* Tuition, state resident: part-time $691.11 per course. Tuition, nonresident: part-time $1621.11 per course. *Financial support:* Application deadline: 3/31; applicants required to submit FAFSA. *Unit head:* Dr. Tracy Hurley, MBA Coordinator, 210-932-6200, E-mail: tracy.hurley@tamusa.tamus.edu. *Application contact:* Melissa A. Villanueva, Graduate Admissions Specialist, 210-932-6200, Fax: 210-932-6209, E-mail: melissa.villanueva@tamusa.tamus.edu. Web site: http://www.tamusa.tamus.edu.

Towson University, Program in Applied Information Technology, Towson, MD 21252-0001. Offers applied information technology (MS, PhD); database management systems

(Postbaccalaureate Certificate); information security and assurance (Postbaccalaureate Certificate); information systems management (Postbaccalaureate Certificate); Internet applications development (Postbaccalaureate Certificate); networking technologies (Postbaccalaureate Certificate); software engineering (Postbaccalaureate Certificate). *Students:* 145 full-time (32 women), 270 part-time (78 women); includes 151 minority (96 Black or African American, non-Hispanic/Latino; 35 Asian, non-Hispanic/Latino; 17 Hispanic/Latino; 1 Native Hawaiian or other Pacific Islander, non-Hispanic/Latino; 2 Two or more races, non-Hispanic/Latino), 93 international. *Expenses:* Tuition, state resident: part-time $337 per credit. Tuition, nonresident: part-time $709 per credit. *Required fees:* $99 per credit. *Unit head:* Mike O'Leary, Graduate Program Director, 410-704-4757, E-mail: moleary@towson.edu.

Trident University International, College of Business Administration, Program in Business Administration, Cypress, CA 90630. Offers business administration (PhD); conflict and negotiation management (MBA); criminal justice administration (MBA); entrepreneurship (MBA); finance (MBA); general management (MBA); government accounting (MBA); human resource management (MBA); information security and digital assurance management (MBA); information technology management (MBA); international business (MBA); logistics management (MBA); marketing (MBA); project management (MBA); public management (MBA); quality management (MBA); strategic leadership (MBA). Part-time and evening/weekend programs available. Postbaccalaureate distance learning degree programs offered (no on-campus study). *Degree requirements:* For doctorate, comprehensive exam, thesis/dissertation, defense of dissertation. *Entrance requirements:* For master's, minimum GPA of 2.5 (students with GPA 3.0 or greater may transfer up to 30% of graduate level credits); for doctorate, minimum GPA of 3.4, curriculum vitae, course work in research methods or statistics. Additional exam requirements/recommendations for international students: Required—TOEFL. Electronic applications accepted.

Universidad del Este, Graduate School, Carolina, PR 00984. Offers accounting (MBA); adult education (M Ed); agribusiness (MBA); criminal justice and criminology (MA); curriculum and instruction - early education (M Ed); curriculum and instruction - elementary (M Ed); curriculum and instruction - English (M Ed); curriculum and instruction - Spanish (M Ed); human resources (MBA); information security management (MBA); information technology and Web business development (MBA); management (MBA); public policy (MPA); social work (MA), including clinical social work; special education (M Ed); strategic leadership (MBA).

Université de Sherbrooke, Faculty of Administration, Program in Governance, Audit and Security of Information Technology, Longueuil, QC J4K0A8, Canada. Offers M Adm. Part-time and evening/weekend programs available. Postbaccalaureate distance learning degree programs offered. *Faculty:* 1 full-time (0 women), 12 part-time/adjunct (2 women). *Students:* 25 part-time (4 women). Average age 40. 35 applicants, 31% accepted, 8 enrolled. In 2011, 3 master's awarded. *Degree requirements:* For master's, thesis. *Entrance requirements:* For master's, bachelor's degree, related work experience. *Application deadline:* For fall admission, 4/30 priority date for domestic students. Applications are processed on a rolling basis. Application fee: $70. Electronic applications accepted. *Unit head:* Prof. Julien Bilodeau, Director, Graduate Programs in Business, 819-821-8000 Ext. 62355, E-mail: julien.bilodeau@usherbrooke.ca. *Application contact:* Lyne Cantin, Assistant to the Director, 450-463-1835 Ext. 61768, Fax: 450-670-1848, E-mail: lyne.cantin@usherbrooke.ca. Web site: http://gouvauditsecurti.adm@USherbrooke.ca.

University of Advancing Technology, Master of Science Program in Technology, Tempe, AZ 85283-1042. Offers advancing computer science (MS); emerging technologies (MS); game production and management (MS); information assurance (MS); technology leadership (MS). *Degree requirements:* For master's, project or thesis. *Entrance requirements:* Additional exam requirements/recommendations for international students: Required—TOEFL (minimum score 550 paper-based). Electronic applications accepted. *Faculty research:* Artificial intelligence, fractals, organizational management.

The University of Alabama at Birmingham, College of Arts and Sciences, Program in Computer Forensics and Security Management, Birmingham, AL 35294. Offers MS. *Expenses:* Tuition, state resident: full-time $5922; part-time $309 per hour. Tuition, nonresident: full-time $13,428; part-time $726 per hour. Tuition and fees vary according to program. *Unit head:* Dr. John J. Sloan, III, 205-934-2069, Fax: 205-934-2067. Web site: http://www.uab.edu/justice-sciences/justice-science-graduate-programs.

The University of Alabama in Huntsville, School of Graduate Studies, College of Business Administration, Department of Economics and Information Systems, Huntsville, AL 35899. Offers enterprise resource planning (Certificate); information assurance (Certificate); information systems (MSIS). Part-time and evening/weekend programs available. *Faculty:* 11 full-time (2 women), 3 part-time/adjunct (1 woman). *Students:* 11 full-time (4 women), 24 part-time (6 women); includes 6 minority (1 Black or African American, non-Hispanic/Latino; 2 American Indian or Alaska Native, non-Hispanic/Latino; 3 Asian, non-Hispanic/Latino). Average age 34. 31 applicants, 55% accepted, 14 enrolled. In 2011, 12 master's, 10 other advanced degrees awarded. *Degree requirements:* For master's, comprehensive exam, thesis or alternative. *Entrance requirements:* For master's, GMAT (minimum score 500), minimum AACSB index of 1080. Additional exam requirements/recommendations for international students: Required—TOEFL (minimum score 550 paper-based; 213 computer-based; 62 iBT). *Application deadline:* For fall admission, 8/1 for domestic students, 4/1 for international students; for spring admission, 12/1 for domestic students, 9/1 for international students. Applications are processed on a rolling basis. Application fee: $40 ($50 for international students). Electronic applications accepted. *Expenses:* Tuition, state resident: full-time $7830; part-time $473.50 per credit. Tuition, nonresident: full-time $18,748; part-time $1128.33 per credit. Tuition and fees vary according to course load and program. *Financial support:* In 2011–12, 2 students received support, including 1 research assistantship with full tuition reimbursement available (averaging $14,400 per year), 1 teaching assistantship with full tuition reimbursement available (averaging $8,000 per year); career-related internships or fieldwork, Federal Work-Study, institutionally sponsored loans, scholarships/grants, health care benefits, and unspecified assistantships also available. Support available to part-time students. Financial award application deadline: 4/1; financial award applicants required to submit FAFSA. *Faculty research:* Supply chain management, incomplete contract and dynamic bargaining in technology investment, personalization at e-commerce sites, workflow management, real options modeling of technology competition. *Total annual research expenditures:* $306,953. *Unit head:* Dr. Allen W. Wilhite, Chair, 256-824-6591, Fax: 256-824-6328, E-mail: wilhitea@uah.edu. *Application contact:* Jennifer Pettitt, Director of Graduate Programs, 256-824-6681, Fax: 256-824-7571, E-mail: jennifer.pettitt@uah.edu.

The University of Alabama in Huntsville, School of Graduate Studies, College of Engineering, Department of Electrical and Computer Engineering, Huntsville, AL 35899. Offers computer engineering (MSE, PhD), including information assurance (MSE);

electrical engineering (MSE, PhD), including optics and phontonics technology (MSE); opto-electronics (MSE); optics and photonics (MSE); software engineering (MSSE). Part-time and evening/weekend programs available. *Faculty:* 22 full-time (3 women), 4 part-time/adjunct (0 women). *Students:* 52 full-time (12 women), 138 part-time (22 women); includes 20 minority (7 Black or African American, non-Hispanic/Latino; 2 American Indian or Alaska Native, non-Hispanic/Latino; 8 Asian, non-Hispanic/Latino; 2 Hispanic/Latino; 1 Two or more races, non-Hispanic/Latino), 37 international. Average age 31. 157 applicants, 65% accepted, 48 enrolled. In 2011, 26 master's, 6 doctorates awarded. *Degree requirements:* For master's, comprehensive exam, thesis or alternative, oral and written exams; for doctorate, comprehensive exam, thesis/dissertation, oral and written exams. *Entrance requirements:* For master's, GRE General Test, appropriate bachelor's degree, minimum GPA of 3.0; for doctorate, GRE General Test, minimum GPA of 3.0. Additional exam requirements/recommendations for international students: Required—TOEFL (minimum score 500 paper-based; 173 computer-based; 62 iBT). *Application deadline:* For fall admission, 7/15 for domestic students, 4/1 for international students; for spring admission, 11/30 for domestic students, 9/1 for international students. Applications are processed on a rolling basis. Application fee: $40 ($50 for international students). Electronic applications accepted. *Expenses:* Tuition, state resident: full-time $7830; part-time $473.50 per credit. Tuition, nonresident: full-time $18,748; part-time $1128.33 per credit. Tuition and fees vary according to course load and program. *Financial support:* In 2011–12, 29 students received support, including 2 fellowships (averaging $11,154 per year), 9 research assistantships with full and partial tuition reimbursements available (averaging $10,959 per year), 20 teaching assistantships with full and partial tuition reimbursements available (averaging $11,330 per year); career-related internships or fieldwork, Federal Work-Study, institutionally sponsored loans, scholarships/grants, health care benefits, tuition waivers (full), and unspecified assistantships also available. Support available to part-time students. Financial award application deadline: 4/1; financial award applicants required to submit FAFSA. *Faculty research:* Optical signal processing, electromagnetics, photonics, nonlinear waves, computer architecture. *Total annual research expenditures:* $16.5 million. *Unit head:* Dr. Robert Lindquist, Chair, 256-824-6316, Fax: 256-824-6803, E-mail: lindquis@ece.uah.edu. *Application contact:* Kim Gray, Graduate Studies Admissions Coordinator, 256-824-6002, Fax: 256-824-6405, E-mail: deangrad@uah.edu. Web site: http://www.ece.uah.edu/.

University of Dayton, School of Business Administration, Dayton, OH 45469-1300. Offers accounting (MBA); cyber security (MBA); finance (MBA); marketing (MBA); JD/MBA. *Accreditation:* AACSB. Part-time and evening/weekend programs available. *Faculty:* 23 full-time (6 women), 13 part-time/adjunct (2 women). *Students:* 170 full-time (72 women), 117 part-time (43 women); includes 26 minority (16 Black or African American, non-Hispanic/Latino; 6 Asian, non-Hispanic/Latino; 3 Hispanic/Latino; 1 Two or more races, non-Hispanic/Latino), 49 international. Average age 28. 366 applicants, 72% accepted, 126 enrolled. In 2011, 147 master's awarded. *Entrance requirements:* For master's, GMAT or GRE. Additional exam requirements/recommendations for international students: Required—TOEFL (minimum score 550 paper-based; 213 computer-based; 80 iBT); Recommended—IELTS (minimum score 6.5). *Application deadline:* For fall admission, 3/1 for international students; for winter admission, 7/1 for international students; for spring admission, 1/1 for international students. Applications are processed on a rolling basis. Application fee: $0 ($50 for international students). Electronic applications accepted. *Expenses:* Contact institution. *Financial support:* In 2011–12, 12 research assistantships with full and partial tuition reimbursements (averaging $7,020 per year) were awarded; career-related internships or fieldwork, institutionally sponsored loans, scholarships/grants, health care benefits, and unspecified assistantships also available. Support available to part-time students. Financial award application deadline: 3/15; financial award applicants required to submit FAFSA. *Faculty research:* Management information systems, economics, finance, entrepreneurship, marketing, accounting and cyber security. *Unit head:* Janice M. Glynn, Director, MBA Program, 937-229-3733, Fax: 937-229-3882, E-mail: glynn@udayton.edu. *Application contact:* Jeffrey Carter, Assistant Director, MBA Program, 937-229-3733, Fax: 937-229-3882, E-mail: jeff.carter@notes.udayton.edu. Web site: http://business.udayton.edu/mba/.

University of Denver, University College, Denver, CO 80208. Offers arts and culture (MLS, Certificate), including art, literature, and culture, arts development and program management (Certificate); creative writing; environmental policy and management (MAS, Certificate), including energy and sustainability (Certificate), environmental assessment of nuclear power (Certificate), environmental health and safety (Certificate), environmental management, natural resource management (Certificate); geographic information systems (MAS, Certificate); global affairs (MLS, Certificate), including translation studies, world history and culture; healthcare leadership (MPH, Certificate), including healthcare policy, law, and ethics, medical and healthcare information technologies, strategic management of healthcare; information and communications technology (MCIS, Certificate), including database design and administration (Certificate), geographic information systems (MCIS), information security systems security (Certificate), information systems security (MCIS), project management (MCIS, MPS, Certificate), software design and administration (Certificate), software design and programming (MCIS), technology management, telecommunications technology (MCIS), Web design and development; leadership and organizations (MPS, Certificate), including human capital in organizations, philanthropic leadership, project management (MCIS, MPS, Certificate), strategic innovation and change; organizational and professional communication (MPS, Certificate), including alternative dispute resolution, organizational communication, organizational development and training, public relations and marketing; security management (MAS, Certificate), including emergency planning and response, information security (MAS), organizational security; strategic human resource management (MPS, Certificate), including global human resources (MPS), human resource management and development (MPS). Part-time and evening/weekend programs available. Postbaccalaureate distance learning degree programs offered (no on-campus study). *Faculty:* 204 part-time/adjunct (80 women). *Students:* 56 full-time (26 women), 1,096 part-time (647 women); includes 196 minority (81 Black or African American, non-Hispanic/Latino; 7 American Indian or Alaska Native, non-Hispanic/Latino; 30 Asian, non-Hispanic/Latino; 66 Hispanic/Latino; 3 Native Hawaiian or other Pacific Islander, non-Hispanic/Latino; 9 Two or more races, non-Hispanic/Latino), 76 international. Average age 36. 572 applicants, 95% accepted, 410 enrolled. In 2011, 404 master's, 123 other advanced degrees awarded. *Degree requirements:* For master's, capstone project. *Entrance requirements:* For master's, two letters of recommendation, personal statement, resume. Additional exam requirements/recommendations for international students: Required—TOEFL (minimum score 550 paper-based; 80 iBT). *Application deadline:* For fall admission, 7/20 priority date for domestic students, 6/8 for international students; for winter admission, 10/26 priority date for domestic students, 9/14 for international students; for spring admission, 2/1 priority date for domestic students, 12/14 for international students. Applications are processed on a rolling basis. Application fee: $75. Electronic applications accepted. *Expenses:* Contact institution.

Financial support: Applicants required to submit FAFSA. *Unit head:* Dr. James Davis, Dean, 303-871-2291, Fax: 303-871-4047, E-mail: jdavis@du.edu. *Application contact:* Information Contact, 303-871-3155, Fax: 303-871-4047, E-mail: ucolinfo@du.edu. Web site: http://www.universitycollege.du.edu/.

University of Houston, College of Technology, Department of Information and Logistics Technology, Houston, TX 77204. Offers information security (MS); supply chain and logistics technology (MS); technology project management (MS). Part-time programs available. *Degree requirements:* For master's, project or thesis (most programs). *Entrance requirements:* For master's, GMAT. Additional exam requirements/recommendations for international students: Required—TOEFL (minimum score 550 paper-based; 79 iBT). Electronic applications accepted.

University of Louisville, J. B. Speed School of Engineering, Department of Computer Engineering and Computer Science, Louisville, KY 40292-0001. Offers computer engineering and computer science (M Eng); computer science (MS); computer science and engineering (PhD); data mining (Certificate); network and information security (Certificate). *Accreditation:* ABET (one or more programs are accredited). Part-time programs available. Postbaccalaureate distance learning degree programs offered (no on-campus study). *Faculty:* 13 full-time (1 woman). *Students:* 54 full-time (11 women), 40 part-time (8 women); includes 12 minority (6 Black or African American, non-Hispanic/Latino; 6 Asian, non-Hispanic/Latino), 33 international. Average age 27. 49 applicants, 35% accepted, 7 enrolled. In 2011, 38 master's, 7 doctorates awarded. Terminal master's awarded for partial completion of doctoral program. *Degree requirements:* For master's, comprehensive exam (for some programs), thesis or alternative; for doctorate, comprehensive exam, thesis/dissertation, minimum GPA of 3.0. *Entrance requirements:* For master's, doctorate, and Certificate, GRE General Test. Additional exam requirements/recommendations for international students: Required—TOEFL (minimum score 550 paper-based; 213 computer-based; 80 iBT), IELTS (minimum score 6.5). *Application deadline:* For fall admission, 5/1 priority date for domestic students, 5/1 for international students; for spring admission, 11/1 priority date for domestic students, 11/1 for international students. Applications are processed on a rolling basis. Application fee: $50. Electronic applications accepted. *Expenses:* Tuition, state resident: full-time $9692; part-time $539 per credit hour. Tuition, nonresident: full-time $20,168; part-time $1121 per credit hour. Tuition and fees vary according to program and reciprocity agreements. *Financial support:* In 2011–12, 22 students received support, including 1 fellowship with full tuition reimbursement available (averaging $20,000 per year), 15 research assistantships with full tuition reimbursements available (averaging $18,900 per year), 6 teaching assistantships with full tuition reimbursements available (averaging $20,000 per year). Financial award application deadline: 1/25; financial award applicants required to submit FAFSA. *Faculty research:* Software systems engineering, information security and forensics, multimedia and vision, mobile and distributed computing, intelligent systems. *Total annual research expenditures:* $1.3 million. *Unit head:* Dr. Adel S. Elmaghraby, Chair, 502-852-6304, Fax: 502-852-4713, E-mail: adel@louisville.edu. *Application contact:* Dr. Michael Day, Associate Dean, 502-852-6195, Fax: 502-852-6294, E-mail: day@louisville.edu. Web site: http://www.louisville.edu/speed/computer.

University of Maryland, Baltimore County, Graduate School, College of Engineering and Information Technology, Department of Computer Science and Electrical Engineering, Program in Cybersecurity, Baltimore, MD 21250. Offers cybersecurity (MPS); cybersecurity strategy and policy (Postbaccalaureate Certificate). Part-time programs available. *Students:* 10 full-time (1 woman), 77 part-time (21 women); includes 33 minority (15 Black or African American, non-Hispanic/Latino; 11 Asian, non-Hispanic/Latino; 4 Hispanic/Latino; 3 Two or more races, non-Hispanic/Latino), 1 international. Average age 33. 110 applicants, 75% accepted, 59 enrolled. *Degree requirements:* For master's, comprehensive exam (for some programs). *Application deadline:* For fall admission, 8/1 for domestic and international students; for spring admission, 11/1 for international students. Applications are processed on a rolling basis. Application fee: $70. Electronic applications accepted. *Financial support:* Career-related internships or fieldwork, Federal Work-Study, scholarships/grants, health care benefits, and unspecified assistantships available. Support available to part-time students. Financial award application deadline: 6/30; financial award applicants required to submit FAFSA. *Faculty research:* Cyber-security strategy and policy. *Unit head:* Dr. Gary Carter, Professor and Chair, 410-455-3500, E-mail: carter@cs.umbc.edu. *Application contact:* Dr. Rick Forno, Graduate Program Director, 410-455-5536, Fax: 410-455-3969, E-mail: richard.forno@umbc.edu. Web site: http://www.umbc.edu/cyber/.

University of Maryland University College, Graduate School of Management and Technology, Program in Cybersecurity, Adelphi, MD 20783. Offers MS, Certificate. Part-time and evening/weekend programs available. Postbaccalaureate distance learning degree programs offered (no on-campus study). *Students:* 9 full-time (2 women), 1,180 part-time (364 women); includes 571 minority (388 Black or African American, non-Hispanic/Latino; 4 American Indian or Alaska Native, non-Hispanic/Latino; 79 Asian, non-Hispanic/Latino; 55 Hispanic/Latino; 2 Native Hawaiian or other Pacific Islander, non-Hispanic/Latino; 43 Two or more races, non-Hispanic/Latino), 4 international. Average age 37. 679 applicants, 100% accepted, 450 enrolled. In 2011, 44 degrees awarded. *Degree requirements:* For master's, thesis or alternative, capstone course. *Application deadline:* Applications are processed on a rolling basis. Application fee: $50. Electronic applications accepted. *Financial support:* Federal Work-Study and scholarships/grants available. Support available to part-time students. Financial award application deadline: 6/1; financial award applicants required to submit FAFSA. *Unit head:* Alan Carswell, Chair, 240-684-2400, Fax: 240-684-2401, E-mail: alan.carswell@umuc.edu. *Application contact:* Coordinator, Graduate Admissions, 800-888-8682, Fax: 240-684-2151, E-mail: newgrad@umuc.edu. Web site: http://www.umuc.edu/programs/grad/csec/index.shtml.

University of Maryland University College, Graduate School of Management and Technology, Program in Cybersecurity Policy, Adelphi, MD 20783. Offers MS. Part-time and evening/weekend programs available. Postbaccalaureate distance learning degree programs offered (no on-campus study). *Students:* 134 part-time (51 women); includes 63 minority (48 Black or African American, non-Hispanic/Latino; 1 American Indian or Alaska Native, non-Hispanic/Latino; 6 Asian, non-Hispanic/Latino; 7 Hispanic/Latino; 1 Two or more races, non-Hispanic/Latino), 1 international. Average age 40. 150 applicants, 100% accepted, 30 enrolled. *Degree requirements:* For master's, thesis or alternative, capstone course. *Application deadline:* Applications are processed on a rolling basis. Application fee: $50. Electronic applications accepted. *Financial support:* Federal Work-Study and scholarships/grants available. Support available to part-time students. Financial award application deadline: 6/1; financial award applicants required to submit FAFSA. *Unit head:* Dr. Clay Wilson, Director, 240-684-2400, Fax: 240-684-2401, E-mail: clay.wilson@umuc.edu. *Application contact:* Coordinator, Graduate Admissions, 800-888-UMUC, Fax: 240-684-2151, E-mail: newgrad@umuc.edu.

University of Minnesota, Twin Cities Campus, College of Science and Engineering, Technological Leadership Institute, Program in Security Technologies, Minneapolis, MN 55455-0213. Offers MSST. Part-time programs available. *Faculty:* 1 full-time (0 women), 23 part-time/adjunct (2 women). *Students:* 37 (7 women); includes 8 minority (3 Black or African American, non-Hispanic/Latino; 3 Asian, non-Hispanic/Latino; 2 Hispanic/Latino), 1 international. *Degree requirements:* For master's, capstone project. *Entrance requirements:* Additional exam requirements/recommendations for international students: Required—TOEFL (minimum score 580 paper-based; 240 computer-based; 90 iBT). *Application deadline:* For spring admission, 3/15 priority date for domestic students, 3/15 for international students. Applications are processed on a rolling basis. Application fee: $75 ($95 for international students). Electronic applications accepted. *Financial support:* Institutionally sponsored loans available. Financial award applicants required to submit FAFSA. *Unit head:* Dr. Massoud Amin, Director, 612-624-5747, Fax: 612-624-7510. *Application contact:* MSST Program, E-mail: tliss@umn.edu. Web site: http://tli.umn.edu.

University of Nebraska at Omaha, Graduate Studies, College of Information Science and Technology, Department of Information Systems and Quantitative Analysis, Omaha, NE 68182. Offers information assurance (Certificate); information technology (PhD); management information systems (MS); project management (Certificate); systems analysis and design (Certificate). Part-time and evening/weekend programs available. *Faculty:* 14 full-time (7 women). *Students:* 69 full-time (23 women), 87 part-time (26 women); includes 17 minority (4 Black or African American, non-Hispanic/Latino; 7 Asian, non-Hispanic/Latino; 4 Hispanic/Latino; 2 Two or more races, non-Hispanic/Latino), 75 international. Average age 32. 142 applicants, 43% accepted, 49 enrolled. In 2011, 38 master's, 3 doctorates, 29 other advanced degrees awarded. *Degree requirements:* For master's, comprehensive exam, thesis (for some programs); for doctorate, comprehensive exam, thesis/dissertation. *Entrance requirements:* For master's, GMAT or GRE General Test; for doctorate, GMAT or GRE General Test, letters of recommendation, writing sample, resume. Additional exam requirements/recommendations for international students: Required—TOEFL (minimum score 575 paper-based; 230 computer-based; 89 iBT). *Application deadline:* For fall admission, 2/15 for domestic students; for spring admission, 9/15 for domestic students. Applications are processed on a rolling basis. Application fee: $45. Electronic applications accepted. *Financial support:* In 2011–12, 31 students received support, including 25 research assistantships with tuition reimbursements available, 3 teaching assistantships with tuition reimbursements available; fellowships, career-related internships or fieldwork, Federal Work-Study, scholarships/grants, tuition waivers (partial), and unspecified assistantships also available. Financial award application deadline: 3/1; financial award applicants required to submit FAFSA. *Unit head:* Dr. Ilze Zigurs, Chairperson, 402-554-3770. *Application contact:* Carla Frakes, Information Contact, 402-554-2423.

University of New Haven, Graduate School, Henry C. Lee College of Criminal Justice and Forensic Sciences, National Security and Public Safety Program, West Haven, CT 06516-1916. Offers information protection and security (MS); national security (Certificate); national security administration (Certificate). Part-time and evening/weekend programs available. *Students:* 23 full-time (7 women), 23 part-time (9 women); includes 13 minority (5 Black or African American, non-Hispanic/Latino; 2 American Indian or Alaska Native, non-Hispanic/Latino; 1 Asian, non-Hispanic/Latino; 4 Hispanic/Latino; 1 Two or more races, non-Hispanic/Latino), 3 international. 15 applicants, 93% accepted, 7 enrolled. In 2011, 32 master's, 6 other advanced degrees awarded. *Entrance requirements:* Additional exam requirements/recommendations for international students: Required—TOEFL (minimum score 520 paper-based; 190 computer-based; 70 iBT); Recommended—IELTS (minimum score 5.5). *Application deadline:* For fall admission, 5/31 for international students; for winter admission, 10/15 for international students; for spring admission, 1/15 for international students. Applications are processed on a rolling basis. Application fee: $50. Electronic applications accepted. *Expenses:* Tuition: Part-time $750 per credit. *Financial support:* Research assistantships with partial tuition reimbursements, teaching assistantships with partial tuition reimbursements, career-related internships or fieldwork, Federal Work-Study, scholarships/grants, tuition waivers, and unspecified assistantships available. Support available to part-time students. Financial award applicants required to submit FAFSA. *Unit head:* Dr. William L. Tafoya, Dean, 203-932-7260. *Application contact:* Eloise Gormley, Director of Graduate Admissions, 203-932-7449, Fax: 203-932-7137, E-mail: gradinfo@newhaven.edu. Web site: http://www.newhaven.edu/5924/.

University of New Mexico, Robert O. Anderson Graduate School of Management, Department of Marketing, Information and Decision Sciences, Albuquerque, NM 87131. Offers information assurance (MBA); management information systems (MBA); marketing management (MBA); operations management (MBA). Part-time and evening/weekend programs available. *Faculty:* 14 full-time (4 women), 11 part-time/adjunct (5 women). In 2011, 74 master's awarded. *Degree requirements:* For master's, minimum GPA of 3.0. *Entrance requirements:* For master's, GMAT or GRE. Additional exam requirements/recommendations for international students: Required—TOEFL (minimum score 550 paper-based; 213 computer-based; 79 iBT). *Application deadline:* For fall admission, 4/1 priority date for domestic students, 4/1 for international students; for spring admission, 10/1 priority date for domestic students, 10/1 for international students. Applications are processed on a rolling basis. Application fee: $50. Electronic applications accepted. *Financial support:* Fellowships, research assistantships, career-related internships or fieldwork, Federal Work-Study, scholarships/grants, and unspecified assistantships available. Support available to part-time students. Financial award application deadline: 6/1. *Faculty research:* Marketing, operations, information science. *Unit head:* Dr. Steve Yourstone, Chair, 505-277-6471, Fax: 505-277-7108. *Application contact:* Megan Conner, Director, Student Services, 505-277-3290, Fax: 505-277-8436, E-mail: mconner@mgt.unm.edu.

The University of North Carolina at Charlotte, Graduate School, College of Computing and Informatics, Department of Software and Information Systems, Charlotte, NC 28223-0001. Offers game design and development (Certificate); health care information (Certificate); information security/privacy (Certificate); information technology (MS, PhD, Certificate). Part-time programs available. *Faculty:* 14 full-time (3 women), 4 part-time/adjunct (0 women). *Students:* 134 full-time (42 women), 88 part-time (36 women); includes 39 minority (23 Black or African American, non-Hispanic/Latino; 5 Asian, non-Hispanic/Latino; 5 Hispanic/Latino; 6 Two or more races, non-Hispanic/Latino), 102 international. Average age 30. 182 applicants, 75% accepted, 47 enrolled. In 2011, 32 master's, 12 doctorates, 33 other advanced degrees awarded. Terminal master's awarded for partial completion of doctoral program. *Degree requirements:* For master's, thesis optional; for doctorate, comprehensive exam, thesis/dissertation. *Entrance requirements:* For master's, GRE or GMAT, minimum undergraduate GPA of 2.8 overall, 2.0 in last 2 years; for doctorate, GRE or GMAT, working knowledge of 2 high-level programming languages. Additional exam requirements/recommendations for international students: Required—TOEFL (minimum score 557 paper-based; 220 computer-based; 83 iBT). *Application deadline:* For fall admission, 7/1 for domestic students, 5/1 for international students; for spring admission, 11/1 for domestic students, 10/1 for international students. Applications are processed on a rolling basis. Application fee: $65 ($75 for international students). Electronic applications accepted. *Expenses:* Tuition, state resident: full-time $3689. Tuition, nonresident: full-time $15,226. *Required fees:* $2198. Tuition and fees vary according to course load and program. *Financial support:* In 2011–12, 41 students received support, including 1 fellowship (averaging $50,000 per year), 19 research assistantships (averaging $9,874 per year), 21 teaching assistantships (averaging $13,421 per year); career-related internships or fieldwork, institutionally sponsored loans, scholarships/grants, and unspecified assistantships also available. Support available to part-time students. Financial award application deadline: 4/1; financial award applicants required to submit FAFSA. *Faculty research:* Information security, information privacy, information assurance, cryptography, software engineering, enterprise integration, intelligent information systems, human-computer interaction. *Total annual research expenditures:* $1.8 million. *Unit head:* Dr. Ken Chen, Program Director, 704-687-8545, Fax: 704-687-6065, E-mail: chen@uncc.edu. *Application contact:* Kathy B. Giddings, Director of Graduate Admissions, 704-687-5503, Fax: 704-687-3279, E-mail: gradadm@uncc.edu. Web site: http://sis.uncc.edu/.

University of St. Thomas, Graduate Studies, Graduate Programs in Software, Saint Paul, MN 55105. Offers advanced studies in software engineering (Certificate); business analysis (Certificate); computer security (Certificate); information systems (Certificate); software design and development (Certificate); software engineering (MS); software management (MS); software systems (MSS); MS/MBA. Part-time and evening/weekend programs available. *Faculty:* 5 full-time (0 women), 15 part-time/adjunct (1 woman). *Students:* 34 full-time (7 women), 314 part-time (79 women); includes 99 minority (48 Black or African American, non-Hispanic/Latino; 1 American Indian or Alaska Native, non-Hispanic/Latino; 45 Asian, non-Hispanic/Latino; 4 Hispanic/Latino; 1 Two or more races, non-Hispanic/Latino), 70 international. Average age 35. 155 applicants, 85% accepted, 79 enrolled. In 2011, 84 master's, 9 other advanced degrees awarded. *Degree requirements:* For master's, thesis optional. *Entrance requirements:* For master's, bachelor's degree earned in U.S. or equivalent international degree. Additional exam requirements/recommendations for international students: Required—TOEFL (minimum score 80 iBT). *Application deadline:* For fall admission, 8/1 priority date for domestic students, 5/1 for international students; for spring admission, 1/1 priority date for domestic students, 10/1 for international students. Applications are processed on a rolling basis. Application fee: $50. Electronic applications accepted. *Expenses:* Contact institution. *Financial support:* Federal Work-Study, institutionally sponsored loans, and scholarships/grants available. Financial award application deadline: 4/1. *Faculty research:* Data mining, distributed databases, computer security, big data. *Unit head:* Dr. Bhabani Misra, Director, 651-962-5508, Fax: 651-962-5543, E-mail: bsmisra@stthomas.edu. *Application contact:* Douglas J. Stubeda, Assistant Director, 651-962-5503, Fax: 651-962-5543, E-mail: djstubeda@stthomas.edu. Web site: http://www.stthomas.edu/gradsoftware/.

University of Southern California, Graduate School, Viterbi School of Engineering, Department of Computer Science, Los Angeles, CA 90089. Offers computer networks (MS); computer science (MS, PhD); computer security (MS); game development (MS); high performance computing and simulations (MS); human language technology (MS); intelligent robotics (MS); multimedia and creative technologies (MS); software engineering (MS). Part-time and evening/weekend programs available. Postbaccalaureate distance learning degree programs offered (no on-campus study). *Entrance requirements:* For master's and doctorate, GRE General Test. Additional exam requirements/recommendations for international students: Required—TOEFL. Electronic applications accepted. *Faculty research:* Databases, computer graphics and computer vision, software engineering, networks and security, robotics, multimedia and virtual reality.

The University of Texas at Dallas, Naveen Jindal School of Management, Program in Accounting, Richardson, TX 75080. Offers assurance services (MS); corporate accounting (MS); internal audit (MS); taxation (MS). *Accreditation:* AACSB. *Faculty:* 16 full-time (4 women), 11 part-time/adjunct (5 women). *Students:* 398 full-time (258 women), 402 part-time (238 women); includes 136 minority (18 Black or African American, non-Hispanic/Latino; 1 American Indian or Alaska Native, non-Hispanic/Latino; 79 Asian, non-Hispanic/Latino; 28 Hispanic/Latino; 10 Two or more races, non-Hispanic/Latino), 411 international. Average age 28. 825 applicants, 59% accepted, 308 enrolled. In 2011, 314 master's awarded. *Entrance requirements:* For master's, GMAT, minimum GPA of 3.0 in upper-level course work in field. Additional exam requirements/recommendations for international students: Required—TOEFL (minimum score 550 paper-based; 215 computer-based). *Application deadline:* For fall admission, 7/15 for domestic students, 5/1 for international students; for spring admission, 11/15 for domestic students, 9/1 for international students. Applications are processed on a rolling basis. Application fee: $50 ($100 for international students). Electronic applications accepted. *Expenses:* Tuition, state resident: full-time $11,170; part-time $620.56 per credit hour. Tuition, nonresident: full-time $20,212; part-time $1122.89 per credit hour. *Financial support:* In 2011–12, 257 students received support, including 5 teaching assistantships with partial tuition reimbursements available (averaging $10,050 per year); research assistantships with partial tuition reimbursements available, career-related internships or fieldwork, Federal Work-Study, institutionally sponsored loans, scholarships/grants, and unspecified assistantships also available. Support available to part-time students. Financial award application deadline: 4/30; financial award applicants required to submit FAFSA. *Faculty research:* Privatization and accounting/auditing, corporate performance and executive compensation, risk management, information technology in accounting. *Unit head:* Amy Troutman, Associate Area Coordinator, 972-883-6719, Fax: 972-883-6823, E-mail: amybass@utdallas.edu. *Application contact:* Jennifer Johnson, Director, Graduate Accounting Programs, 972-883-5912, E-mail: jennifer.johnson@utdallas.edu. Web site: http://jindal.utdallas.edu/academic-areas/accounting/.

The University of Texas at San Antonio, College of Business, Department of Information Systems and Cyber Security, San Antonio, TX 78249-0617. Offers business (MBA); business administration (PhD); information technology (MSIT); management of technology (MSMOT). Part-time and evening/weekend programs available. *Faculty:* 11 full-time (3 women), 5 part-time/adjunct (1 woman). *Students:* 23 full-time (7 women), 73 part-time (13 women); includes 41 minority (3 Black or African American, non-Hispanic/Latino; 5 Asian, non-Hispanic/Latino; 30 Hispanic/Latino; 1 Native Hawaiian or other Pacific Islander, non-Hispanic/Latino; 2 Two or more races, non-Hispanic/Latino), 4 international. Average age 31. 50 applicants, 40% accepted, 13 enrolled. In 2011, 41 master's awarded. *Degree requirements:* For master's, thesis or alternative; for doctorate, comprehensive exam, thesis/dissertation. *Entrance requirements:* For master's, GMAT, bachelor's degree with 18 credit hours in the field of study or another appropriate field of study, statement of purpose; for doctorate, GMAT or GRE, resume or curriculum vitae, three letters of recommendation from academic or professional sources familiar with the applicant's background. Additional exam requirements/recommendations for international students: Required—TOEFL (minimum score 500 paper-based; 61 iBT), IELTS (minimum score 5). *Application deadline:* For fall admission, 7/1 for domestic students, 4/1 for international students; for spring admission, 11/1 for domestic students, 9/1 for international students. Applications are processed on a rolling basis. Application fee: $45 ($85 for international students). Electronic applications accepted. *Expenses:* Tuition, state resident: full-time $3148; part-time $2176 per semester. Tuition, nonresident: full-time $8782; part-time $5932 per semester. *Required fees:* $719 per semester. *Financial support:* In 2011–12, 23 students received support, including 10 fellowships (averaging $22,000 per year), research assistantships (averaging $10,000 per year), teaching assistantships (averaging $10,000 per year); scholarships/grants, health care benefits, and unspecified assistantships also available. *Faculty research:* economics of information systems, information security, digital forensics, information systems strategy, adoption and diffusion. *Total annual research expenditures:* $300,000. *Unit head:* Dr. Jan Clark, Chair, 210-458-5244, Fax: 210-458-6305, E-mail: jan.clark@utsa.edu. *Application contact:* Katherine Pope, Graduate Advisor of Record, 210-458-7316, Fax: 210-458-4398, E-mail: katherine.pope@utsa.edu.

University of Wisconsin–Madison, Graduate School, Wisconsin School of Business, Wisconsin Full-Time MBA Program, Madison, WI 53706-1380. Offers applied security analysis (MBA); arts administration (MBA); brand and product management (MBA); corporate finance and investment banking (MBA); marketing research (MBA); operations and technology management (MBA); real estate (MBA); risk management and insurance (MBA); strategic human resource management (MBA); supply chain management (MBA). *Faculty:* 32 full-time (6 women), 27 part-time/adjunct (7 women). *Students:* 228 full-time (75 women); includes 53 minority (16 Black or African American, non-Hispanic/Latino; 25 Asian, non-Hispanic/Latino; 10 Hispanic/Latino; 2 Native Hawaiian or other Pacific Islander, non-Hispanic/Latino), 28 international. Average age 28. 509 applicants, 30% accepted, 111 enrolled. In 2011, 120 master's awarded. *Degree requirements:* For master's, thesis (for arts administration). *Entrance requirements:* For master's, GMAT, bachelor's or equivalent degree, 2 years of work experience, letters of recommendation. Additional exam requirements/recommendations for international students: Required—TOEFL (minimum score 600 paper-based; 250 computer-based; 100 iBT), IELTS. *Application deadline:* For fall admission, 11/4 for domestic and international students; for winter admission, 2/3 for domestic and international students; for spring admission, 4/27 for domestic and international students. Applications are processed on a rolling basis. Application fee: $56. Electronic applications accepted. *Expenses:* Tuition, state resident: full-time $10,296; part-time $643.51 per credit. Tuition, nonresident: full-time $24,054; part-time $1503.40 per credit. *Required fees:* $70.06 per credit. Tuition and fees vary according to course load, campus/location, program and reciprocity agreements. *Financial support:* In 2011–12, 176 students received support, including 20 fellowships with full and partial tuition reimbursements available (averaging $18,756 per year), 128 research assistantships with full tuition reimbursements available (averaging $25,185 per year), 28 teaching assistantships with full tuition reimbursements available (averaging $25,097 per year); scholarships/grants, health care benefits, and unspecified assistantships also available. Financial award application deadline: 4/27; financial award applicants required to submit FAFSA. *Faculty research:* Market consequences of International Financial Reporting Standards (IFRS), inter-firm relationships and strategic partnerships, application of Bayesian statistical methods and applied probability models to understanding individuals' behaviors in the context of customer relationship management (CRM) applications, liquidity provision and the structure of financial markets, strategic management of global startups. *Unit head:* Dr. Larry "Chip" W. Hunter, Associate Dean of Master's Programs, 608-265-3494, Fax: 608-265-4192, E-mail: lhunter@bus.wisc.edu. *Application contact:* Maria Reis, Assistant Director of MBA Marketing and Recruiting, 608-262-4000, Fax: 608-265-4192, E-mail: mreis@bus.wisc.edu. Web site: http://www.bus.wisc.edu/mba.

Utica College, Program in Cybersecurity, Utica, NY 13502-4892. Offers MS. Part-time and evening/weekend programs available. Postbaccalaureate distance learning degree programs offered. *Entrance requirements:* Additional exam requirements/recommendations for international students: Recommended—TOEFL. Electronic applications accepted.

Virginia Polytechnic Institute and State University, Graduate School, College of Engineering, Department of Computer Science and Applications, Blacksburg, VA 24061. Offers computer science and applications (MS, PhD); human-computer interactions (Certificate); information assurance engineering (Certificate). *Degree requirements:* For master's, comprehensive exam (for some programs), thesis (for some programs); for doctorate, comprehensive exam (for some programs), thesis/dissertation (for some programs). *Entrance requirements:* For master's and doctorate, GRE. Additional exam requirements/recommendations for international students: Required—TOEFL (minimum score 550 paper-based; 213 computer-based). *Application deadline:* For fall admission, 7/1 for domestic and international students; for spring admission, 12/1 for domestic and international students. Applications are processed on a rolling basis. Application fee: $65. Electronic applications accepted. *Expenses:* Tuition, state resident: full-time $10,048; part-time $558.25 per credit hour. Tuition, nonresident: full-time $19,497; part-time $1083.25 per credit hour. *Required fees:* $405 per semester. Tuition and fees vary according to course load, campus/location and program. *Financial support:* Research assistantships with full tuition reimbursements, teaching assistantships with full tuition reimbursements, career-related internships or fieldwork, Federal Work-Study, scholarships/grants, health care benefits, and unspecified assistantships available. Financial award application deadline: 1/15. *Faculty research:* Bioinformatics, human-computer interaction, problem-solving environments, high performance computing, software engineering. *Unit head:* Dr. Barbara G. Ryder, Unit Head, 540-231-8452, Fax: 540-231-6075, E-mail: ryder@vt.edu. *Application contact:* Naren Ramakrishnan, Information Contact, 540-231-8451, Fax: 540-231-6075, E-mail: naren@vt.edu. Web site: http://www.cs.vt.edu/.

Virginia Polytechnic Institute and State University, VT Online, Blacksburg, VA 24061. Offers advanced transportation systems (Certificate); aerospace engineering (MS); agricultural and life sciences (MSLFS); business information systems (Graduate Certificate); career and technical education (MS); civil engineering (MS); computer engineering (M Eng, MS); decision support systems (Graduate Certificate); eLearning leadership (MA); electrical engineering (M Eng, MS); engineering administration (MEA); environmental engineering (Certificate); environmental politics and policy (Graduate Certificate); environmental sciences and engineering (MS); foundations of political analysis (Graduate Certificate); health product risk management (Graduate Certificate); industrial and systems engineering (MS); information policy and society (Graduate Certificate); information security (Graduate Certificate); information technology (MIT); instructional technology (MA); integrative STEM education (MA Ed); liberal arts (Graduate Certificate); life sciences: health product risk management (MS); natural resources (MNR, Graduate Certificate); networking (Graduate Certificate); nonprofit and nongovernmental organization management (Graduate Certificate); ocean engineering (MS); political science (MA); security studies (Graduate Certificate); software development (Graduate Certificate). *Expenses:* Tuition, state resident: full-time

$10,048; part-time $558.25 per credit hour. Tuition, nonresident: full-time $19,497; part-time $1083.25 per credit hour. *Required fees:* $405 per semester. Tuition and fees vary according to course load, campus/location and program. *Application contact:* Graduate School Applications General Assistance, 540-231-8636, Fax: 540-231-2039, E-mail: gradappl@vt.edu. Web site: http://www.vto.vt.edu/.

West Chester University of Pennsylvania, College of Arts and Sciences, Department of Computer Science, West Chester, PA 19383. Offers computer science (MS); computer security (Certificate); information systems (Certificate); Web technology (Certificate). Part-time and evening/weekend programs available. *Faculty:* 7 part-time/adjunct (1 woman). *Students:* 5 full-time (0 women), 18 part-time (1 woman); includes 1 minority (Black or African American, non-Hispanic/Latino), 6 international. Average age 27. 37 applicants, 49% accepted, 13 enrolled. In 2011, 3 master's, 1 other advanced degree awarded. *Degree requirements:* For master's, thesis optional. *Entrance requirements:* For master's, GRE, two letters of recommendation; for Certificate, BS. Additional exam requirements/recommendations for international students: Required—TOEFL (minimum score 550 paper-based; 213 computer-based; 80 iBT). *Application deadline:* For fall admission, 4/15 priority date for domestic students, 3/15 for international students; for spring admission, 10/15 priority date for domestic students, 9/1 for international students. Applications are processed on a rolling basis. Application fee: $45. Electronic applications accepted. *Expenses:* Tuition, state resident: full-time $7488; part-time $416 per credit. Tuition, nonresident: full-time $11,232; part-time $624 per credit. *Required fees:* $1784.64; $67.59 per credit. Tuition and fees vary according to program. *Financial support:* Unspecified assistantships available. Support available to part-time students. Financial award application deadline: 2/15; financial award applicants required to submit FAFSA. *Faculty research:* Automata theory, compilers, non well-founded sets, security in sensor and mobile ad-hoc networks, intrusion detection, security and trust in pervasive computing, economic modeling of security protocols. *Unit head:* Dr. James Fabrey, Chair, 610-436-2204, E-mail: jfabrey@wcupa.edu. *Application contact:* Dr. Afrand Agah, Graduate Coordinator, 610-430-4419, E-mail: aagah@wcupa.edu. Web site: http://www.cs.wcupa.edu/.

Western Governors University, Program in Information Security and Assurance, Salt Lake City, UT 84107. Offers MS. Postbaccalaureate distance learning degree programs offered. *Degree requirements:* For master's, capstone project. *Expenses: Tuition:* Full-time $6500. Full-time tuition and fees vary according to program. *Financial support:* Institutionally sponsored loans and scholarships/grants available. *Unit head:* Amber Podlucky, Program Coordinator, 801-290-3658, E-mail: apodlucky@wgu.edu. *Application contact:* Enrollment Department, 866-225-5948, Fax: 801-274-3306, E-mail: info@wgu.edu.

Wilmington University, College of Technology, New Castle, DE 19720-6491. Offers corporate training skills (MS); information assurance (MS); information systems technologies (MS); Internet/web design (MS); management and management information systems (MS). Part-time and evening/weekend programs available. *Faculty:* 1 full-time (0 women). *Students:* 21 full-time (8 women), 63 part-time (24 women). Average age 36. *Entrance requirements:* Additional exam requirements/recommendations for international students: Required—TOEFL (minimum score 500 paper-based; 173 computer-based). *Application deadline:* Applications are processed on a rolling basis. Application fee: $35. Electronic applications accepted. *Expenses: Tuition:* Part-time $534 per credit hour. *Required fees:* $25 per term. *Unit head:* Dr. Edward L. Guthrie, Dean, 302-356-6870. *Application contact:* Laura Morris, Director of Admissions, 302-295-1179, Fax: 302-328-5164, E-mail: inquire@wilmcoll.edu. Web site: http://www.wilmu.edu/technology/.

Computer Science

Acadia University, Faculty of Pure and Applied Science, Jodrey School of Computer Science, Wolfville, NS B4P 2R6, Canada. Offers M Sc. *Degree requirements:* For master's, thesis. *Entrance requirements:* For master's, honors degree in computer science. Additional exam requirements/recommendations for international students: Required—TOEFL (minimum score 580 paper-based; 237 computer-based; 93 iBT), IELTS (minimum score 6.5). *Faculty research:* Visual and object-oriented programming, concurrency, artificial intelligence, hypertext and multimedia, algorithm analysis, xml.

Air Force Institute of Technology, Graduate School of Engineering and Management, Department of Electrical and Computer Engineering, Dayton, OH 45433-7765. Offers computer engineering (MS, PhD); computer systems/science (MS); electrical engineering (MS, PhD); electro-optics (MS, PhD). *Accreditation:* ABET (one or more programs are accredited). Part-time programs available. *Degree requirements:* For master's, thesis; for doctorate, thesis/dissertation. *Entrance requirements:* For master's and doctorate, GRE General Test, minimum GPA of 3.0, U.S. citizenship. *Faculty research:* Remote sensing, information survivability, microelectronics, computer networks, artificial intelligence.

Alabama Agricultural and Mechanical University, School of Graduate Studies, School of Engineering and Technology, Department of Computer Science, Huntsville, AL 35811. Offers MS. Evening/weekend programs available. *Degree requirements:* For master's, comprehensive exam, thesis optional. *Entrance requirements:* For master's, GRE General Test. Additional exam requirements/recommendations for international students: Required—TOEFL (minimum score 500 paper-based; 173 computer-based; 61 iBT). Electronic applications accepted. *Faculty research:* Computer-assisted instruction, database management, software engineering, operating systems, neural networks.

Alcorn State University, School of Graduate Studies, School of Arts and Sciences, Department of Mathematical Sciences, Alcorn State, MS 39096-7500. Offers computer and information sciences (MS).

American Sentinel University, Graduate Programs, Aurora, CO 80014. Offers business administration (MBA); business intelligence (MS); computer science (MSCS); health information management (MS); healthcare (MBA); information systems (MSIS); nursing (MSN). Part-time and evening/weekend programs available. Postbaccalaureate distance learning degree programs offered (no on-campus study). *Entrance requirements:* Additional exam requirements/recommendations for international students: Required—TOEFL (minimum score 600 paper-based; 215 computer-based). Electronic applications accepted.

American University, College of Arts and Sciences, Program in Computer Science, Washington, DC 20016-8058. Offers applied science (MS); computer science (MS, Certificate). Part-time and evening/weekend programs available. *Faculty:* 3 full-time (0 women), 1 part-time/adjunct (0 women). *Students:* 1 (woman) part-time; minority (Black or African American, non-Hispanic/Latino). Average age 53. 13 applicants, 54% accepted, 0 enrolled. In 2011, 1 master's awarded. *Degree requirements:* For master's, comprehensive exam, thesis or alternative. *Entrance requirements:* For master's, GRE, minimum GPA of 3.0; for Certificate, bachelor's degree. Additional exam requirements/recommendations for international students: Required—TOEFL. *Application deadline:* For fall admission, 2/1 priority date for domestic students; for spring admission, 10/1 for domestic students. Applications are processed on a rolling basis. Application fee: $80. *Expenses: Tuition:* Full-time $24,264; part-time $1348 per credit hour. *Required fees:* $430. Tuition and fees vary according to course load and program. *Financial support:* Fellowships with full tuition reimbursements, career-related internships or fieldwork, Federal Work-Study, institutionally sponsored loans, tuition waivers (full and partial), and unspecified assistantships available. Financial award application deadline: 2/1. *Faculty research:* Artificial intelligence, database systems, software engineering, expert systems. *Unit head:* Dr. Ulysses J. Sofia, Chair, 202-885-2728, Fax: 202-885-2429, E-mail: sofia@american.edu. *Application contact:* Kathleen Clowery, Director, Graduate Admissions, 202-885-3621, Fax: 202-885-1505, E-mail: clowery@american.edu. Web site: http://www.american.edu/cas/cs.

The American University in Cairo, School of Sciences and Engineering, Department of Computer Science and Engineering, Cairo, Egypt. Offers computer science (Graduate Diploma); computing (M Comp). *Degree requirements:* For master's, thesis. *Entrance requirements:* Additional exam requirements/recommendations for international students: Required—English entrance exam and/or TOEFL. *Application deadline:* For fall admission, 3/31 priority date for domestic students; for spring admission, 1/10 priority date for domestic students. Application fee: $45. *Expenses: Tuition:* Part-time $932 per credit hour. Tuition and fees vary according to course load, degree level and program. *Financial support:* Fellowships and unspecified assistantships available. *Faculty research:* Software engineering, artificial intelligence, robotics, data and knowledge bases. *Unit head:* Dr. Amr El-Kadi, Chair, 20-2-2615-2967, E-mail: elkadi@aucegypt.edu. *Application contact:* Mary Davidson, Coordinator of Student Affairs, 212-730-8800, Fax: 212-730-1600, E-mail: mdavidson@aucnyo.edu. Web site: http://www.aucegypt.edu/sse/csce/.

The American University of Athens, School of Graduate Studies, Athens, Greece. Offers biomedical sciences (MS); business (MBA); business communication (MA); computer sciences (MS); engineering and applied sciences (MS); politics and policy making (MA); systems engineering (MS); telecommunications (MS). *Entrance requirements:* For master's, resume, 2 recommendation letters. Additional exam requirements/recommendations for international students: Required—TOEFL (minimum score 550 paper-based; 213 computer-based). *Faculty research:* Nanotechnology, environmental sciences, rock mechanics, human skin studies, Monte Carlo algorithms and software.

American University of Beirut, Graduate Programs, Faculty of Arts and Sciences, Beirut, Lebanon. Offers anthropology (MA); Arabic language and literature (MA); archaeology (MA); biology (MS); chemistry (MS); computational science (MS); computer science (MS); economics (MA); education (MA); English language (MA); English literature (MA); environmental policy planning (MSES); financial economics (MAFE); geology (MS); history (MA); mathematics (MA, MS); Middle Eastern studies (MA); philosophy (MA); physics (MS); political studies (MA); psychology (MA); public administration (MA); sociology (MA); statistics (MA, MS). Part-time programs available. *Faculty:* 154 full-time (44 women), 12 part-time/adjunct (2 women). *Students:* 180 full-time (122 women), 240 part-time (158 women). Average age 25. 336 applicants, 47% accepted, 86 enrolled. In 2011, 57 master's awarded. *Degree requirements:* For master's, one foreign language, comprehensive exam, thesis (for some programs). *Entrance requirements:* For master's, GRE, letter of recommendation. Additional exam requirements/recommendations for international students: Required—TOEFL (minimum score 600 paper-based; 250 computer-based; 97 iBT), IELTS (minimum score 7). *Application deadline:* For fall admission, 4/30 for domestic and international students; for spring admission, 11/1 for domestic and international students. Application fee: $50. *Expenses: Tuition:* Full-time $12,780; part-time $710 per credit. *Required fees:* $528; $528 per credit. Tuition and fees vary according to course load and program. *Financial support:* In 2011–12, 33 students received support. Career-related internships or fieldwork, institutionally sponsored loans, scholarships/grants, health care benefits, and unspecified assistantships available. Financial award application deadline: 2/4; financial award applicants required to submit FAFSA. *Faculty research:* History of composition studies, syntax of Arabic dialects, Oscar Wilde, decadence, Middle Eastern and international politics, neural mechanisms of creativity and consciousness, personality and psycho-socio-cultural-spiritual correlates of negative and positive mental health, philosophy of mind, metaphysics, micropaleontology and stratigraphy, geochemistry, mineralogy and petrology, tectonophysics, Abbasid, Ottoman and Russian history, landscape, Bronze and Iron Age archaeology. *Unit head:* Dr. Patrick McGreevy, Dean, 961-1374374 Ext. 3800, Fax: 961-1744461, E-mail: pm07@aub.edu.lb. *Application contact:* Dr. Salim Kanaan, Director, Admissions Office, 961-1350000 Ext. 2594, Fax: 961-1750775, E-mail: sk00@aub.edu.lb. Web site: http://staff.aub.edu.lb/~webfas.

Appalachian State University, Cratis D. Williams Graduate School, Department of Computer Science, Boone, NC 28608. Offers MS. Part-time programs available. *Faculty:* 9 full-time (3 women), 1 part-time/adjunct (0 women). *Students:* 11 full-time (0 women), 4 part-time (2 women), 2 international. 13 applicants, 46% accepted, 3 enrolled. In 2011, 12 master's awarded. *Degree requirements:* For master's, comprehensive exam, thesis. *Entrance requirements:* For master's, GRE General Test, 3 letters of recommendation. Additional exam requirements/recommendations for international students: Required—TOEFL (minimum score 570 paper-based; 230 computer-based; 79 iBT), IELTS (minimum score 6.5). *Application deadline:* For fall admission, 3/15 priority date for domestic students, 2/1 for international students; for spring admission, 11/1 for domestic students, 7/1 for international students. Applications are processed on a rolling basis. Application fee: $55. Electronic applications accepted. *Expenses:* Tuition, state resident: full-time $4040; part-time $180 per semester hour. Tuition, nonresident: full-time $15,900; part-time $760 per semester hour. *Required fees:* $2500; $20 per semester hour. Tuition and fees vary according to campus/location. *Financial support:* In 2011–12, 8 teaching assistantships (averaging $9,500 per year) were awarded; fellowships, research assistantships, Federal Work-Study, scholarships/grants, and unspecified assistantships also available. Financial award application deadline: 4/1; financial award applicants required to submit FAFSA. *Faculty* *research:* Graph theory, compilers, parallel architecture, image processing. *Total annual research expenditures:* $609,000. *Unit head:* Dr. James Wilkes, Chairperson, 828-262-2612. *Application contact:* Dr. Jay Fenwick, Advisor, 828-262-3050, Fax: 828-265-8617, E-mail: fenwickjb@appstate.edu. Web site: http://www.cs.appstate.edu.

Arizona State University, College of Technology and Innovation, Department of Engineering, Mesa, AZ 85212. Offers computing studies (MCST); simulation, modeling, and applied cognitive science (PhD). Part-time programs available. *Degree requirements:* For master's, thesis or applied project with oral defense; interactive Program of Study (iPOS) submitted before completing 50 percent of required credit hours; for doctorate, comprehensive exam, thesis/dissertation, interactive Program of Study (iPOS) submitted before completing 50 percent of required credit hours. *Entrance requirements:* For master's, GRE, minimum GPA of 3.0 or equivalent in last 2 years of work leading to bachelor's degree; for doctorate, GRE, master's degree in psychology, engineering, cognitive science, or computer science; 3 letters of recommendation; statement of research interests. Additional exam requirements/recommendations for international students: Required—TOEFL, IELTS, or Pearson Test of English. Electronic applications accepted. *Faculty research:* Software process and automated workflow, software architecture, dotal technologies, relational database systems, embedded systems.

Arizona State University, Ira A. Fulton School of Engineering, School of Computing, Informatics, and Decision Systems Engineering, Tempe, AZ 85287-8809. Offers computer science (MCS, MS, PhD); industrial engineering (MS, PhD). Part-time and evening/weekend programs available. Postbaccalaureate distance learning degree programs offered (minimal on-campus study). Terminal master's awarded for partial completion of doctoral program. *Degree requirements:* For master's, comprehensive exam (for some programs), portfolio (MCS); interactive Program of Study (iPOS) submitted before completing 50 percent of required credit hours; for doctorate, comprehensive exam, thesis/dissertation, interactive Program of Study (iPOS) submitted before completing 50 percent of required credit hours. *Entrance requirements:* For master's, GRE, minimum GPA of 3.0 or equivalent in last 2 years of work leading to bachelor's degree; for doctorate, GRE, minimum GPA of 3.0 in last 2 years of work leading to bachelor's degree. Additional exam requirements/recommendations for international students: Required—TOEFL (minimum score 80 iBT), TOEFL, IELTS, or Pearson Test of English. Electronic applications accepted. *Expenses:* Contact institution. *Faculty research:* Artificial intelligence, cyberphysical and embedded systems, health informatics, information assurance and security, information management/multimedia/visualization, network science, personalized learning/ educational games, production logistics, software and systems engineering, and statistical modeling and data mining.

Arkansas State University, Graduate School, College of Sciences and Mathematics, Department of Computer Science, Jonesboro, State University, AR 72467. Offers MS. Part-time programs available. *Faculty:* 5 full-time (1 woman). *Students:* 41 full-time (10 women), 10 part-time (1 woman); includes 1 minority (Black or African American, non-Hispanic/Latino), 42 international. Average age 26. 131 applicants, 85% accepted, 23 enrolled. In 2011, 15 master's awarded. *Degree requirements:* For master's, comprehensive exam, thesis or alternative. *Entrance requirements:* For master's, GRE General Test or MAT, appropriate bachelor's degree, official transcripts, immunization records. Additional exam requirements/recommendations for international students: Required—TOEFL (minimum score 550 paper-based; 213 computer-based; 79 iBT), IELTS (minimum score 6), PTE: Pearson Test of English Academic (minimum score 56). *Application deadline:* For fall admission, 7/1 for domestic and international students; for spring admission, 11/15 for domestic students, 11/14 for international students. Applications are processed on a rolling basis. Application fee: $30 ($40 for international students). Electronic applications accepted. *Expenses:* Tuition, state resident: full-time $4044; part-time $225 per credit hour. Tuition, nonresident: full-time $8087; part-time $449 per credit hour. *Required fees:* $936; $52 per credit hour. $25 per term. One-time fee: $30. Tuition and fees vary according to course load and program. *Financial support:* In 2011–12, 13 students received support. Career-related internships or fieldwork, scholarships/grants, and unspecified assistantships available. Financial award application deadline: 7/1; financial award applicants required to submit FAFSA. *Unit head:* Dr. Edward Hammerand, Chair, 870-972-3978, Fax: 870-972-3950, E-mail: hammerand@astate.edu. *Application contact:* Dr. Andrew Sustich, Dean of the Graduate School, 870-972-3029, Fax: 870-972-3857, E-mail: sustich@astate.edu. Web site: http://www.cs.astate.edu/.

Armstrong Atlantic State University, School of Graduate Studies, Program in Computer Science, Savannah, GA 31419-1997. Offers MS. Part-time programs available. *Faculty:* 3 full-time (0 women). *Students:* 4 part-time (1 woman); includes 1 minority (Asian, non-Hispanic/Latino), 1 international. Average age 30. 1 applicant, 100% accepted, 0 enrolled. In 2011, 4 master's awarded. *Degree requirements:* For master's, project. *Entrance requirements:* For master's, GRE, minimum GPA of 2.7, letters of recommendation, BS in computer science or related field. Additional exam requirements/recommendations for international students: Required—TOEFL (minimum score 523 paper-based; 193 computer-based). *Application deadline:* For fall admission, 7/1 priority date for domestic students, 5/1 for international students; for spring admission, 11/15 priority date for domestic students, 9/15 for international students. Applications are processed on a rolling basis. Application fee: $30. Electronic applications accepted. *Expenses:* Tuition, state resident: full-time $3402. Tuition, nonresident: full-time $12,636. *Financial support:* In 2011–12, research assistantships with full tuition reimbursements (averaging $5,000 per year) were awarded; career-related internships or fieldwork, Federal Work-Study, scholarships/grants, and unspecified assistantships also available. Support available to part-time students. Financial award applicants required to submit FAFSA. *Unit head:* Dr. Ashraf Saad, Department Head, 912-344-3084, E-mail: ashraf.saad@armstrong.edu. *Application contact:* Jill Bell, Director, Graduate Enrollment Services, 912-344-2798, Fax: 912-344-3488, E-mail: graduate@armstrong.edu. Web site: http://www.armstrong.edu/ Science_and_Technology/ice/ice_ms_in_computer_science.

Auburn University, Graduate School, Ginn College of Engineering, Department of Computer Science and Software Engineering, Auburn University, AL 36849. Offers MS, MSWE, PhD. Part-time programs available. *Faculty:* 15 full-time (1 woman), 1 (woman) part-time/adjunct. *Students:* 58 full-time (11 women), 69 part-time (21 women); includes 18 minority (14 Black or African American, non-Hispanic/Latino; 4 Asian, non-Hispanic/ Latino), 49 international. Average age 29. 203 applicants, 39% accepted, 20 enrolled. In 2011, 27 master's, 13 doctorates awarded. *Degree requirements:* For master's, thesis (for some programs); for doctorate, thesis/dissertation. *Entrance requirements:* For master's and doctorate, GRE General Test, GRE Subject Test. *Application deadline:* For fall admission, 7/7 for domestic students; for spring admission, 11/24 for domestic students. Applications are processed on a rolling basis. Application fee: $50 ($60 for international students). Electronic applications accepted. *Expenses:* Tuition, state resident: full-time $7290; part-time $405 per credit hour. Tuition, nonresident: full-time $21,870; part-time $1215 per credit hour. *International tuition:* $22,000 full-time. *Required fees:* $1402. *Financial support:* Research assistantships, teaching assistantships, and Federal Work-Study available. Support available to part-time students. Financial award application deadline: 3/15; financial award applicants required to submit FAFSA. *Faculty research:* Parallelizable, scalable software translations; graphical representations of algorithms, structures, and processes; graph drawing. *Total annual research expenditures:* $400,000. *Unit head:* Dr. Kai Chang, Chair, 334-844-6310. *Application contact:* Dr. George Flowers, Dean of the Graduate School, 334-844-2125. Web site: http://www.eng.auburn.edu/department/cse/.

Ball State University, Graduate School, College of Sciences and Humanities, Department of Computer Science, Muncie, IN 47306-1099. Offers MA, MS. *Faculty:* 9 full-time (0 women). *Students:* 19 full-time (6 women), 5 part-time (1 woman); includes 1 minority (Black or African American, non-Hispanic/Latino), 13 international. Average age 25. 33 applicants, 30% accepted, 7 enrolled. In 2011, 11 master's awarded. *Entrance requirements:* For master's, GRE General Test. Application fee: $50. Tuition and fees vary according to program and reciprocity agreements. *Financial support:* In 2011–12, 14 students received support, including 12 teaching assistantships with full tuition reimbursements available (averaging $12,472 per year); research assistantships with full tuition reimbursements available also available. Financial award application deadline: 3/1. *Faculty research:* Numerical methods, programmer productivity, graphics. *Unit head:* Dr. Paul Buis, Chairperson, 765-285-8641, Fax: 765-285-2614. *Application contact:* Dr. J. Michael McGrew, Graduate Program Director, 765-285-8641, Fax: 765-285-2614, E-mail: mmcgrew@bsu.edu. Web site: http://www.cs.bsu.edu/.

Baylor University, Graduate School, School of Engineering and Computer Science, Department of Computer Science, Waco, TX 76798. Offers MS. Part-time programs available. *Faculty:* 10 full-time (1 woman). *Students:* 13 full-time (3 women), 2 part-time (0 women); includes 2 minority (1 Asian, non-Hispanic/Latino; 1 Hispanic/Latino), 9 international. 27 applicants, 37% accepted, 10 enrolled. In 2011, 9 master's awarded. *Entrance requirements:* Additional exam requirements/recommendations for international students: Required—TOEFL (minimum score 550 paper-based; 213 computer-based). *Application deadline:* For fall admission, 2/15 priority date for domestic students, 2/15 for international students; for spring admission, 9/1 priority date for domestic students, 9/1 for international students. Applications are processed on a rolling basis. Application fee: $40. Electronic applications accepted. *Faculty research:* Bioinformatics, databases, machine learning, SWE, networking. *Unit head:* Dr. David Sturgill, Chair, 254-710-3876, E-mail: david_sturgill@baylor.edu. *Application contact:* Dr. Sharon Humphrey, Graduate Program Director, 254-710-6821, Fax: 254-710-3870, E-mail: sharon_humphrey@baylor.edu. Web site: http://www.ecs.baylor.edu/ computer_science.

Boise State University, Graduate College, College of Engineering, Program in Computer Science, Boise, ID 83725-0399. Offers MS. Part-time programs available. *Degree requirements:* For master's, comprehensive exam, thesis. *Entrance requirements:* For master's, GRE General Test, minimum GPA of 3.0. Electronic applications accepted.

Boston University, Graduate School of Arts and Sciences, Department of Computer Science, Boston, MA 02215. Offers MA, PhD. *Students:* 55 full-time (10 women), 7 part-time (1 woman); includes 1 minority (Hispanic/Latino), 39 international. Average age 27. 350 applicants, 11% accepted, 20 enrolled. In 2011, 62 master's, 8 doctorates awarded. *Degree requirements:* For master's, one foreign language, thesis optional, project; for doctorate, one foreign language, comprehensive exam, thesis/dissertation. *Entrance requirements:* For master's and doctorate, GRE General Test, 3 letters of recommendation. Additional exam requirements/recommendations for international students: Required—TOEFL (minimum score 550 paper-based; 213 computer-based). *Application deadline:* For fall admission, 12/15 for domestic and international students; for spring admission, 10/1 for domestic and international students. Application fee: $70. *Expenses: Tuition:* Full-time $40,848; part-time $1276 per credit hour. *Required fees:* $572; $286 per semester. *Financial support:* In 2011–12, 1 fellowship with full tuition reimbursement (averaging $19,800 per year), 37 research assistantships with full tuition reimbursements (averaging $19,300 per year), 16 teaching assistantships with full tuition reimbursements (averaging $19,300 per year) were awarded; Federal Work-Study and scholarships/grants also available. Support available to part-time students. Financial award application deadline: 12/15; financial award applicants required to submit FAFSA. *Unit head:* Stan Sclaroff, Chairman, 617-353-8919, Fax: 617-353-6457, E-mail: sclaroff@bu.edu. *Application contact:* Jennifer Streubel, Program Coordinator, 617-353-8919, Fax: 617-353-6457, E-mail: jenn4@bu.edu. Web site: http://cs-www.bu.edu/.

Boston University, Metropolitan College, Department of Computer Science, Boston, MA 02215. Offers computer information systems (MS), including computer networks, database management and business intelligence, health informatics, IT project management, security, Web application development; computer science (MS), including computer networks, security; telecommunications (MS), including security. Evening/ weekend programs available. Postbaccalaureate distance learning degree programs offered. *Faculty:* 12 full-time (2 women), 28 part-time/adjunct (2 women). *Students:* 25 full-time (6 women), 732 part-time (167 women); includes 208 minority (51 Black or African American, non-Hispanic/Latino; 1 American Indian or Alaska Native, non-Hispanic/Latino; 104 Asian, non-Hispanic/Latino; 43 Hispanic/Latino; 1 Native Hawaiian or other Pacific Islander, non-Hispanic/Latino; 8 Two or more races, non-Hispanic/ Latino), 86 international. Average age 35. 260 applicants, 67% accepted, 143 enrolled. In 2011, 143 master's awarded. *Degree requirements:* For master's, thesis optional. *Entrance requirements:* For master's, 3 letters of recommendation, professional resume. Additional exam requirements/recommendations for international students: Required—TOEFL (minimum score 550 paper-based; 213 computer-based; 80 iBT). *Application deadline:* For fall admission, 6/1 for international students; for spring admission, 10/1 for international students. Applications are processed on a rolling basis. Application fee: $70. Electronic applications accepted. *Expenses: Tuition:* Full-time $40,848; part-time $1276 per credit hour. *Required fees:* $572; $286 per semester. *Financial support:* In 2011–12, 9 research assistantships (averaging $5,000 per year) were awarded; career-related internships or fieldwork and unspecified assistantships also available. Support available to part-time students. Financial award applicants required to submit FAFSA. *Faculty research:* Medical informatics, Web technologies, telecom and networks, security and forensics, software engineering, programming languages, multimedia and AI, information systems and IT project management. *Unit head:* Dr. Lubomir Chitkushev, Chairman, 617-353-2566, Fax: 617-353-2367, E-mail: csinfo@bu.edu. *Application contact:* Kim Richards, Program Coordinator, 617-353-2566, Fax: 617-353-2367, E-mail: kimrich@bu.edu. Web site: http://www.bu.edu/csmet/.

Bowie State University, Graduate Programs, Department of Computer Science, Bowie, MD 20715-9465. Offers MS. Part-time and evening/weekend programs available. *Students:* 8 full-time (4 women), 16 part-time (6 women); includes 19 minority (14 Black or African American, non-Hispanic/Latino; 5 Hispanic/Latino), 4 international. Average age 29. 12 applicants, 100% accepted, 6 enrolled. In 2011, 10 master's awarded.

Degree requirements: For master's, comprehensive exam, thesis optional, research paper. *Entrance requirements:* For master's, minimum undergraduate GPA of 2.5. *Application deadline:* For fall admission, 4/1 priority date for domestic students, 4/1 for international students; for spring admission, 11/1 priority date for domestic students, 11/1 for international students. Applications are processed on a rolling basis. Application fee: $40. Electronic applications accepted. *Expenses:* Tuition, state resident: full-time $4140; part-time $3105 per semester. Tuition, nonresident: full-time $7836; part-time $5877 per semester. *Required fees:* $1715; $648 per semester. *Financial support:* Career-related internships or fieldwork and institutionally sponsored loans available. Financial award application deadline: 4/1. *Faculty research:* Holographics, launch vehicle ground truth ephemera. *Unit head:* Dr. Sadanand Srivatava, Chairperson, 301-860-3962, E-mail: ssrivatava@bowiestate.edu. *Application contact:* Angela Issac, Information Contact, 301-860-4000.

Bowie State University, Graduate Programs, Program in Computer Science, Bowie, MD 20715-9465. Offers App Sc D. Part-time and evening/weekend programs available. *Students:* 56 full-time (49 women), 118 part-time (86 women); includes 168 minority (151 Black or African American, non-Hispanic/Latino; 2 American Indian or Alaska Native, non-Hispanic/Latino; 15 Hispanic/Latino), 4 international. *Application deadline:* For fall admission, 4/1 priority date for domestic students, 4/1 for international students; for spring admission, 11/1 priority date for domestic students, 11/1 for international students. Applications are processed on a rolling basis. Application fee: $50. Electronic applications accepted. *Expenses:* Tuition, state resident: full-time $4140; part-time $3105 per semester. Tuition, nonresident: full-time $7836; part-time $5877 per semester. *Required fees:* $1715; $648 per semester. *Unit head:* Dr. Manohar Mareboyana, Director of Doctoral Programs, 301-860-3971, E-mail: manohar@bowiestate.edu. *Application contact:* Angela Issac, Information Contact, 301-860-4000.

Bowling Green State University, Graduate College, College of Arts and Sciences, Department of Computer Science, Bowling Green, OH 43403. Offers computer science (MS), including operations research, parallel and distributed computing, software engineering. Part-time programs available. *Degree requirements:* For master's, thesis or alternative. *Entrance requirements:* For master's, GRE General Test. Additional exam requirements/recommendations for international students: Required—TOEFL. Electronic applications accepted. *Faculty research:* Artificial intelligence, real time and concurrent programming languages, behavioral aspects of computing, network protocols.

Bradley University, Graduate School, College of Liberal Arts and Sciences, Department of Computer Science and Information Systems, Peoria, IL 61625-0002. Offers computer information systems (MS); computer science (MS). Part-time and evening/weekend programs available. *Degree requirements:* For master's, comprehensive exam, thesis or alternative, programming test. *Entrance requirements:* For master's, 2 letters of recommendation. Additional exam requirements/recommendations for international students: Required—TOEFL (minimum score 550 paper-based; 213 computer-based; 79 iBT).

Brandeis University, Graduate School of Arts and Sciences, Department of Computer Science, Waltham, MA 02454-9110. Offers computational linguistics (MA); computer science (MA, PhD, Certificate); computer science and IT entrepreneurship (MA). Part-time programs available. *Degree requirements:* For doctorate, thesis/dissertation, thesis proposal. *Entrance requirements:* For master's, GRE (recommended), official transcript(s), statement of purpose, resume, 2 letters of recommendation; for doctorate, GRE, official transcript(s), statement of purpose, resume, 3 letters of recommendation. Additional exam requirements/recommendations for international students: Required—TOEFL (minimum score 600 paper-based; 250 computer-based; 100 iBT); Recommended—IELTS (minimum score 7). Electronic applications accepted. *Faculty research:* Artificial intelligence, programming languages, parallel computing, computational linguistics, data compression, technology and IT entrepreneurship.

Brandeis University, Graduate School of Arts and Sciences, Program in Computational Linguistics, Waltham, MA 02454-9110. Offers MA. Part-time programs available. *Degree requirements:* For master's, thesis. *Entrance requirements:* For master's, statement of purpose, 2 letters of recommendation, official transcripts, resume or curriculum vitae. Additional exam requirements/recommendations for international students: Required—TOEFL (minimum score 650 paper-based; 250 computer-based; 100 iBT); Recommended—IELTS (minimum score 7). Electronic applications accepted. *Faculty research:* Computer science (artificial intelligence, theory of computation, and programming methods), language and linguistics (phonology, syntax, semantics, and pragmatics).

Brandeis University, Graduate School of Arts and Sciences, Program in Computer Science and IT Entrepreneurship, Waltham, MA 02454-9110. Offers MA. Part-time programs available. *Degree requirements:* For master's, practicum. *Entrance requirements:* For master's, official transcript(s), 2 letters of recommendation, curriculum vitae or resume, statement of purpose. Additional exam requirements/recommendations for international students: Required—TOEFL (minimum score 600 paper-based; 250 computer-based; 100 iBT); Recommended—IELTS (minimum score 7). Electronic applications accepted. *Faculty research:* Software development, IT entrepreneurship, business, computer science, innovation.

Bridgewater State University, School of Graduate Studies, School of Arts and Sciences, Department of Mathematics and Computer Science, Bridgewater, MA 02325-0001. Offers computer science (MS); mathematics (MAT). Part-time and evening/weekend programs available. *Entrance requirements:* For master's, GRE General Test.

Brigham Young University, Graduate Studies, College of Physical and Mathematical Sciences, Department of Computer Science, Provo, UT 84602-1001. Offers MS, PhD. *Faculty:* 27 full-time (0 women), 3 part-time/adjunct (0 women). *Students:* 100 full-time (5 women); includes 14 minority (1 Black or African American, non-Hispanic/Latino; 13 Asian, non-Hispanic/Latino). Average age 28. 41 applicants, 66% accepted, 24 enrolled. In 2011, 29 master's, 5 doctorates awarded. Terminal master's awarded for partial completion of doctoral program. *Degree requirements:* For master's, thesis; for doctorate, comprehensive exam, thesis/dissertation, residency. *Entrance requirements:* For master's, GRE General Test, minimum GPA of 3.25 in last 60 hours; for doctorate, GRE General Test, minimum GPA of 3.5 in last 60 hours, undergraduate degree in computer science. Additional exam requirements/recommendations for international students: Required—TOEFL (minimum score 600 paper-based; 250 computer-based; 85 iBT). *Application deadline:* For fall admission, 1/15 for domestic and international students; for winter admission, 8/15 for domestic and international students. Application fee: $50. Electronic applications accepted. *Expenses: Tuition:* Full-time $5760; part-time $320 per credit. Tuition and fees vary according to student's religious affiliation. *Financial support:* In 2011–12, 43 students received support, including fellowships with full tuition reimbursements available (averaging $22,000 per year), 56 research assistantships with full and partial tuition reimbursements available (averaging $15,000 per year), 23 teaching assistantships with partial tuition reimbursements available (averaging $12,500 per year); scholarships/grants and health care benefits also available. Financial award application deadline: 3/1. *Faculty research:* Graphics, image processing, neural networks and machine learning, formal methods. *Total annual research expenditures:* $851,000. *Unit head:* Dr. Parris K. Egbert, Chair, 801-422-4029, Fax: 801-422-0169, E-mail: egbert@cs.byu.edu. *Application contact:* Dr. Dan A. Ventura, Graduate Coordinator, 801-422-9075, Fax: 801-422-0169, E-mail: ventura@cs.byu.edu. Web site: http://www.cs.byu.edu/.

Brock University, Faculty of Graduate Studies, Faculty of Mathematics and Science, Program in Computer Science, St. Catharines, ON L2S 3A1, Canada. Offers M Sc. Part-time programs available. *Degree requirements:* For master's, thesis. *Entrance requirements:* For master's, honors degree. Additional exam requirements/recommendations for international students: Required—TOEFL (minimum score 550 paper-based; 213 computer-based; 80 iBT), IELTS (minimum score 6.5), TWE (minimum score 4).

Brooklyn College of the City University of New York, Division of Graduate Studies, Department of Computer and Information Science, Brooklyn, NY 11210-2889. Offers computer science (MA, PhD); computer science and health science (MS); information systems (MS); parallel and distributed computing (Advanced Certificate). Part-time and evening/weekend programs available. *Degree requirements:* For master's, comprehensive exam, thesis or alternative. *Entrance requirements:* For master's, previous course work in computer science, 2 letters of recommendation. Additional exam requirements/recommendations for international students: Required—TOEFL (minimum score 525 paper-based; 195 computer-based; 70 iBT). Electronic applications accepted. *Faculty research:* Networks and distributed systems, programming languages, modeling and computer applications, algorithms, artificial intelligence, theoretical computer science.

Brown University, Graduate School, Department of Computer Science, Providence, RI 02912. Offers Sc M, PhD. *Degree requirements:* For master's, thesis or alternative; for doctorate, one foreign language, comprehensive exam, thesis/dissertation. *Entrance requirements:* For master's and doctorate, GRE General Test, GRE Subject Test.

California Institute of Technology, Division of Engineering and Applied Science, Option in Computer Science, Pasadena, CA 91125-0001. Offers MS, PhD. *Degree requirements:* For master's, thesis; for doctorate, thesis/dissertation. Electronic applications accepted. *Faculty research:* VLSI systems, concurrent computation, high-level programming languages, signal and image processing, graphics.

California Polytechnic State University, San Luis Obispo, College of Engineering, Department of Computer Science, San Luis Obispo, CA 93407. Offers MS. Part-time programs available. *Faculty:* 1 (woman) full-time. *Students:* 30 full-time (4 women), 7 part-time (3 women); includes 10 minority (1 Black or African American, non-Hispanic/Latino; 4 Asian, non-Hispanic/Latino; 2 Hispanic/Latino; 3 Two or more races, non-Hispanic/Latino), 1 international. Average age 24. 31 applicants, 39% accepted, 6 enrolled. In 2011, 17 master's awarded. *Degree requirements:* For master's, thesis. *Entrance requirements:* For master's, GRE General Test, minimum GPA of 3.0 in last 90 quarter units. Additional exam requirements/recommendations for international students: Required—TOEFL (minimum score 550 paper-based; 213 computer-based) or IELTS (minimum score 6). *Application deadline:* For fall admission, 4/1 for domestic students, 11/30 for international students; for winter admission, 9/1 for domestic students, 6/30 for international students. Applications are processed on a rolling basis. Application fee: $55. Electronic applications accepted. *Expenses:* Tuition, state resident: full-time $6738. Tuition, nonresident: full-time $17,898. *Required fees:* $2449. *Financial support:* Fellowships, research assistantships, teaching assistantships, career-related internships or fieldwork, Federal Work-Study, institutionally sponsored loans, scholarships/grants, and unspecified assistantships available. Support available to part-time students. Financial award application deadline: 3/2; financial award applicants required to submit FAFSA. *Faculty research:* Human-computer interaction, artificial intelligence, programming languages, computer graphics, database systems. *Unit head:* Dr. Alex Dekhtyar, Graduate Coordinator, 805-756-2387, Fax: 805-756-2956, E-mail: dekhtyar@calpoly.edu. *Application contact:* Dr. James Maraviglia, Associate Vice Provost for Marketing and Enrollment Development, 805-756-2311, Fax: 805-756-5400, E-mail: admissions@calpoly.edu. Web site: http://www.csc.calpoly.edu/programs/ms-csc/.

California State Polytechnic University, Pomona, Academic Affairs, College of Science, Program in Computer Science, Pomona, CA 91768-2557. Offers MS. Part-time programs available. *Students:* 8 full-time (3 women), 48 part-time (9 women); includes 26 minority (1 Black or African American, non-Hispanic/Latino; 18 Asian, non-Hispanic/Latino; 5 Hispanic/Latino; 1 Native Hawaiian or other Pacific Islander, non-Hispanic/Latino; 1 Two or more races, non-Hispanic/Latino), 18 international. Average age 28. 86 applicants, 41% accepted, 16 enrolled. In 2011, 20 master's awarded. *Degree requirements:* For master's, thesis. *Entrance requirements:* For master's, GRE General Test. *Application deadline:* For fall admission, 5/1 priority date for domestic students; for winter admission, 10/15 priority date for domestic students; for spring admission, 1/20 priority date for domestic students. Applications are processed on a rolling basis. Application fee: $55. Electronic applications accepted. *Expenses:* Tuition, state resident: full-time $6738. Tuition, nonresident: full-time $12,300. *Required fees:* $657. Tuition and fees vary according to course load and program. *Financial support:* Career-related internships or fieldwork, Federal Work-Study, and institutionally sponsored loans available. Support available to part-time students. Financial award application deadline: 3/2; financial award applicants required to submit FAFSA. *Unit head:* Dr. Daisy Tang, Graduate Coordinator, 909-869-4733, E-mail: ftang@csupomona.edu. *Application contact:* Deborah L. Brandon, Executive Director, Admissions and Outreach, 909-869-3427, Fax: 909-869-5315, E-mail: dlbrandon@csupomona.edu. Web site: http://www.csupomona.edu/~cs/ms/.

California State University Channel Islands, Extended Education, Program in Computer Science, Camarillo, CA 93012. Offers MS. Part-time and evening/weekend programs available. *Entrance requirements:* Additional exam requirements/recommendations for international students: Required—TOEFL (minimum score 550 paper-based).

California State University, Chico, Office of Graduate Studies, College of Engineering, Computer Science, and Technology, Department of Computer Science, Chico, CA 95929-0722. Offers MS. Postbaccalaureate distance learning degree programs offered. *Faculty:* 3 full-time (0 women). *Students:* 12 full-time (1 woman), 4 part-time (0 women); includes 1 minority (Asian, non-Hispanic/Latino), 8 international. Average age 28. 84 applicants, 65% accepted, 5 enrolled. In 2011, 13 master's awarded. *Degree requirements:* For master's, thesis or project. *Entrance requirements:* For master's, GRE General Test (waived if graduated from ABET-accredited institution), 2 letters of recommendation, statement of purpose. Additional exam requirements/recommendations for international students: Required—TOEFL (minimum score 550 paper-based; 213 computer-based; 80 iBT), IELTS (minimum score 6.5). *Application deadline:* For fall admission, 3/1 priority date for domestic students, 3/1 for international students; for spring admission, 9/15 priority date for domestic students, 9/15 for international students. Application fee: $55. Electronic applications accepted. Tuition and fees vary according to class time, course load and degree level. *Financial support:* Fellowships, research assistantships, teaching assistantships, career-related internships or fieldwork, scholarships/grants, and traineeships available. Financial award application deadline: 3/1; financial award applicants required to submit FAFSA. *Unit head:* Dr. Moaty Fayek, Chair, 530-898-6442, Fax: 530-898-5995, E-mail: csci@csuchico.edu. *Application contact:* Judy L. Rice, Graduate Admissions Coordinator, 530-898-5416, Fax: 530-898-3342, E-mail: jlrice@csuchico.edu. Web site: http://csci.ecst.csuchico.edu.

California State University, Dominguez Hills, College of Natural and Behavioral Sciences, Department of Computer Science, Carson, CA 90747-0001. Offers MSCS. *Faculty:* 5 full-time (1 woman), 1 part-time/adjunct (0 women). *Students:* 8 full-time (1 woman), 13 part-time (3 women); includes 11 minority (1 Black or African American, non-Hispanic/Latino; 3 Asian, non-Hispanic/Latino; 7 Hispanic/Latino), 8 international. Average age 34. 12 applicants, 92% accepted, 4 enrolled. *Degree requirements:* For master's, comprehensive exam (for some programs), thesis (for some programs). *Entrance requirements:* For master's, GRE (minimum score 900), minimum GPA of 2.75. Additional exam requirements/recommendations for international students: Required—TOEFL (minimum score 550 paper-based). Application fee: $55. Electronic applications accepted. *Unit head:* Dr. Mohsen Beheshti, Department Chair, 310-243-3398, E-mail: mbeheshti@csudh.edu. *Application contact:* Brandy McLelland, Interim Director, Student Information Services, 310-243-3654, E-mail: bmclelland@csudh.edu. Web site: http://csc.csudh.edu/.

California State University, East Bay, Office of Academic Programs and Graduate Studies, College of Science, Department of Mathematics and Computer Science, Computer Science Program, Hayward, CA 94542-3000. Offers computer networks (MS); computer science (MS). Part-time programs available. *Faculty:* 12 full-time (5 women). *Students:* 42 full-time (27 women), 131 part-time (63 women); includes 18 minority (16 Asian, non-Hispanic/Latino; 2 Hispanic/Latino), 127 international. Average age 28. 318 applicants, 49% accepted, 34 enrolled. In 2011, 114 master's awarded. *Degree requirements:* For master's, thesis or capstone experience. *Entrance requirements:* For master's, GRE, minimum GPA of 3.0 in field, 2.75 overall; baccalaureate degree in computer science or related field. Additional exam requirements/recommendations for international students: Required—TOEFL (minimum score 550 paper-based; 213 computer-based). *Application deadline:* For fall admission, 6/30 for domestic and international students. Application fee: $55. Electronic applications accepted. *Expenses:* Tuition, state resident: full-time $6738; part-time $1302 per quarter. Tuition, nonresident: full-time $12,690; part-time $2294 per quarter. *Required fees:* $449 per quarter. Tuition and fees vary according to degree level, program and reciprocity agreements. *Financial support:* Fellowships, career-related internships or fieldwork, Federal Work-Study, institutionally sponsored loans, and scholarships/grants available. Support available to part-time students. Financial award application deadline: 3/2; financial award applicants required to submit FAFSA. *Unit head:* Dr. Edna Reiter, Chair, 510-885-3414, Fax: 510-885-4169, E-mail: eddie.reiter@csueastbay.edu. *Application contact:* Prof. Matthew Johnson, Computer Science Graduate Advisor, 510-885-4312, Fax: 510-885-4169, E-mail: matt.johnson@csueastbay.edu. Web site: http://www20.csueastbay.edu/csci/departments/math-cs/.

California State University, Fresno, Division of Graduate Studies, College of Science and Mathematics, Department of Computer Science, Fresno, CA 93740-8027. Offers MS. Part-time and evening/weekend programs available. *Degree requirements:* For master's, thesis or alternative. *Entrance requirements:* For master's, GRE General Test, minimum GPA of 2.75. Additional exam requirements/recommendations for international students: Required—TOEFL. Electronic applications accepted. *Faculty research:* Software design, parallel processing, computer engineering, autoline research.

California State University, Fullerton, Graduate Studies, College of Engineering and Computer Science, Department of Computer Science, Fullerton, CA 92834-9480. Offers computer science (MS); software engineering (MS). Part-time programs available. Postbaccalaureate distance learning degree programs offered. *Students:* 77 full-time (19 women), 242 part-time (53 women); includes 96 minority (7 Black or African American, non-Hispanic/Latino; 64 Asian, non-Hispanic/Latino; 16 Hispanic/Latino; 9 Two or more races, non-Hispanic/Latino), 139 international. Average age 30. 585 applicants, 70% accepted, 113 enrolled. In 2011, 126 master's awarded. *Degree requirements:* For master's, comprehensive exam, project or thesis. *Entrance requirements:* For master's, GRE General Test, minimum undergraduate GPA of 2.5. Application fee: $55. *Financial support:* Career-related internships or fieldwork, Federal Work-Study, institutionally sponsored loans, and scholarships/grants available. Support available to part-time students. Financial award application deadline: 3/1; financial award applicants required to submit FAFSA. *Faculty research:* Software engineering, development of computer networks. *Unit head:* Dr. James Choi, Chair, 657-278-3700. *Application contact:* Admissions/Applications, 657-278-2371.

California State University, Long Beach, Graduate Studies, College of Engineering, Department of Computer Engineering and Computer Science, Long Beach, CA 90840. Offers computer engineering (MSCS); computer science (MSCS). Part-time programs available. *Faculty:* 10 full-time (2 women), 2 part-time/adjunct (0 women). *Students:* 122 full-time (26 women), 99 part-time (13 women); includes 72 minority (5 Black or African American, non-Hispanic/Latino; 1 American Indian or Alaska Native, non-Hispanic/Latino; 49 Asian, non-Hispanic/Latino; 13 Hispanic/Latino; 1 Native Hawaiian or other Pacific Islander, non-Hispanic/Latino; 3 Two or more races, non-Hispanic/Latino), 92 international. Average age 29. 420 applicants, 63% accepted, 62 enrolled. In 2011, 51 master's awarded. *Degree requirements:* For master's, thesis or alternative. *Entrance requirements:* Additional exam requirements/recommendations for international students: Required—TOEFL. *Application deadline:* For fall admission, 3/1 for domestic students. Application fee: $55. Electronic applications accepted. *Financial support:* Teaching assistantships, Federal Work-Study, institutionally sponsored loans, scholarships/grants, and unspecified assistantships available. Financial award application deadline: 3/2. *Faculty research:* Artificial intelligence, software engineering, computer simulation and modeling, user-interface design, networking. *Unit head:* Dr. Kenneth James, Chair, 562-985-5105, Fax: 562-985-7823, E-mail: james@csulb.edu. *Application contact:* Dr. Burkhard Englert, Graduate Advisor, 562-985-7987, Fax: 562-985-7823, E-mail: benglert@.csulb.edu.

California State University, Los Angeles, Graduate Studies, College of Engineering, Computer Science, and Technology, Department of Computer Science, Los Angeles, CA 90032-8530. Offers MS. *Faculty:* 3 full-time (0 women), 2 part-time/adjunct (0 women). *Students:* 41 full-time (15 women), 52 part-time (14 women); includes 31 minority (1 Black or African American, non-Hispanic/Latino; 17 Asian, non-Hispanic/Latino; 12 Hispanic/Latino; 1 Two or more races, non-Hispanic/Latino), 43 international. Average age 29. 102 applicants, 56% accepted, 18 enrolled. In 2011, 39 master's awarded. *Entrance requirements:* Additional exam requirements/recommendations for international students: Required—TOEFL (minimum score 550 paper-based). *Application deadline:* For fall admission, 5/1 for domestic and international students. Applications are processed on a rolling basis. Application fee: $55. Electronic applications accepted. *Expenses:* Tuition, state resident: full-time $8225. *Unit head:* Dr. Raj Pamula, Chair, 323-343-6690, Fax: 323-343-6672, E-mail: rpamula@calstatela.edu. *Application contact:* Dr. Karin Brown, Acting Associate Dean of Graduate Studies, 323-343-3820, Fax: 323-343-5653, E-mail: kbrown5@calstatela.edu. Web site: http://www.calstatela.edu/academic/ecst/cs/.

California State University, Northridge, Graduate Studies, College of Engineering and Computer Science, Department of Computer Science, Northridge, CA 91330. Offers computer science (MS); software engineering (MS). Part-time and evening/weekend programs available. *Degree requirements:* For master's, thesis. *Entrance requirements:* For master's, GRE General Test, minimum GPA of 2.5. Additional exam requirements/recommendations for international students: Required—TOEFL. *Faculty research:* Radar data processing.

California State University, Sacramento, Office of Graduate Studies, College of Engineering and Computer Science, Department of Computer Science, Sacramento, CA 95819-6021. Offers computer systems (MS); software engineering (MS). Part-time and evening/weekend programs available. *Faculty:* 20 full-time (5 women), 4 part-time/adjunct (1 woman). *Students:* 46 full-time, 32 part-time; includes 18 minority (3 Black or African American, non-Hispanic/Latino; 9 Asian, non-Hispanic/Latino; 5 Hispanic/Latino; 1 Two or more races, non-Hispanic/Latino), 51 international. Average age 27. 206 applicants, 51% accepted, 40 enrolled. In 2011, 40 master's awarded. *Degree requirements:* For master's, thesis or comprehensive exam; writing proficiency exam. *Entrance requirements:* For master's, GRE. Additional exam requirements/recommendations for international students: Required—TOEFL. *Application deadline:* For fall admission, 3/1 for domestic and international students; for spring admission, 9/15 for domestic students, 9/30 for international students. Applications are processed on a rolling basis. Application fee: $5. Electronic applications accepted. *Financial support:* Research assistantships, teaching assistantships, career-related internships or fieldwork, and Federal Work-Study available. Support available to part-time students. Financial award application deadline: 3/1; financial award applicants required to submit FAFSA. *Unit head:* Cui Zhang, Chair, 916-278-5843, Fax: 916-278-6774, E-mail: zhangc@ecs.csus.edu. *Application contact:* Jose Martinez, Outreach and Graduate Diversity Coordinator, 916-278-6470, Fax: 916-278-5669, E-mail: martinj@skymail.csus.edu. Web site: http://www.ecs.csus.edu/csc.

California State University, San Bernardino, Graduate Studies, College of Natural Sciences, Department of Computer Science, San Bernardino, CA 92407-2397. Offers MS. *Students:* 33 full-time (6 women), 6 part-time (0 women); includes 10 minority (2 Black or African American, non-Hispanic/Latino; 1 Asian, non-Hispanic/Latino; 7 Hispanic/Latino), 19 international. Average age 29. 41 applicants, 34% accepted, 5 enrolled. In 2011, 12 master's awarded. *Entrance requirements:* For master's, GRE. *Application deadline:* For fall admission, 8/31 priority date for domestic students. Application fee: $55. *Expenses:* Tuition, state resident: full-time $7356. Tuition, nonresident: full-time $7356. *Required fees:* $1077. Tuition and fees vary according to program. *Unit head:* Dr. Kerstin Voigt, Director, 909-537-5326, Fax: 909-537-7004, E-mail: kvoigt@csusb.edu. *Application contact:* Sandra Kamusikiri, Associate Vice-President/Dean of Graduate Studies, 909-537-5058, E-mail: skamusik@csusb.edu.

California State University, San Marcos, College of Arts and Sciences, Program in Computer Science, San Marcos, CA 92096-0001. Offers MS. Part-time programs available. *Entrance requirements:* For master's, GRE General Test, GRE Subject Test (recommended). Additional exam requirements/recommendations for international students: Required—TOEFL. *Faculty research:* Networks, multimedia, parallel algorithms, software engineering, artificial intelligence.

Capitol College, Graduate Programs, Laurel, MD 20708-9759. Offers business administration (MBA); computer science (MS); electrical engineering (MS); information and telecommunications systems management (MS); information architecture (MS); network security (MS). Part-time and evening/weekend programs available. Postbaccalaureate distance learning degree programs offered (no on-campus study). *Entrance requirements:* For master's, minimum GPA of 3.0. Electronic applications accepted.

Carleton University, Faculty of Graduate Studies, Faculty of Science, School of Computer Science, Ottawa, ON K1S 5B6, Canada. Offers computer science (MCS, PhD); information and system science (M Sc). MCS and PhD programs offered jointly with University of Ottawa. Part-time programs available. *Degree requirements:* For master's, thesis optional, project; for doctorate, comprehensive exam, thesis/dissertation. *Entrance requirements:* For master's, honors degree. Additional exam requirements/recommendations for international students: Required—TOEFL. *Faculty research:* Programming systems, theory of computing, computer applications, computer systems.

Carnegie Mellon University, School of Computer Science, Department of Computer Science, Pittsburgh, PA 15213-3891. Offers algorithms, combinatorics, and optimization (PhD); computer science (MS, PhD); pure and applied logic (PhD). *Degree requirements:* For doctorate, thesis/dissertation. *Entrance requirements:* For doctorate, GRE General Test, GRE Subject Test, BS in computer science or equivalent. Additional exam requirements/recommendations for international students: Required—TOEFL. *Faculty research:* Software systems, theory of computations, artificial intelligence, computer systems, programming languages.

Carnegie Mellon University, School of Computer Science, Language Technologies Institute, Pittsburgh, PA 15213-3891. Offers MLT, PhD. Terminal master's awarded for partial completion of doctoral program. *Degree requirements:* For doctorate, thesis/dissertation. *Entrance requirements:* For master's and doctorate, GRE General Test, GRE Subject Test. Additional exam requirements/recommendations for international students: Required—TOEFL. *Faculty research:* Machine translation, natural language processing, speech and information retrieval, literacy.

Case Western Reserve University, School of Graduate Studies, Case School of Engineering, Department of Electrical Engineering and Computer Science, Cleveland, OH 44106. Offers computer engineering (MS, PhD); computing and information sciences (MS, PhD); electrical engineering (MS, PhD); systems and control engineering (MS, PhD). Part-time and evening/weekend programs available. Postbaccalaureate distance learning degree programs offered (minimal on-campus study). *Faculty:* 33 full-time (3 women). *Students:* 188 full-time (34 women), 22 part-time (4 women); includes 6 minority (3 Black or African American, non-Hispanic/Latino; 3 Asian, non-Hispanic/Latino), 132 international. In 2011, 30 master's, 22 doctorates awarded. Terminal master's awarded for partial completion of doctoral program. *Degree requirements:* For master's, thesis; for doctorate, thesis/dissertation, qualifying exam, teaching experience. *Entrance requirements:* For master's and doctorate, GRE General Test. Additional exam requirements/recommendations for international students: Required—TOEFL. *Application deadline:* For fall admission, 2/1 for domestic students; for spring admission,

11/1 for domestic students. Applications are processed on a rolling basis. Application fee: $50. *Financial support:* Fellowships with full and partial tuition reimbursements, research assistantships with full and partial tuition reimbursements, teaching assistantships, career-related internships or fieldwork, Federal Work-Study, and institutionally sponsored loans available. Support available to part-time students. Financial award application deadline: 3/1; financial award applicants required to submit FAFSA. *Faculty research:* Applied artificial intelligence, automation, computer-aided design and testing of digital systems. *Total annual research expenditures:* $6 million. *Unit head:* Dr. Michael Branicky, Department Chair, 216-368-6888, E-mail: branicky@case.edu. *Application contact:* David Easler, Student Affairs Coordinator, 216-368-4080, Fax: 216-368-2801, E-mail: david.easler@case.edu. Web site: http://eecs.cwru.edu/.

The Catholic University of America, School of Engineering, Department of Electrical Engineering and Computer Science, Washington, DC 20064. Offers MEE, MSCS, D Engr, PhD. Part-time programs available. *Faculty:* 10 full-time (3 women), 13 part-time/adjunct (1 woman). *Students:* 14 full-time (3 women), 38 part-time (10 women); includes 9 minority (3 Black or African American, non-Hispanic/Latino; 3 Asian, non-Hispanic/Latino; 3 Hispanic/Latino), 19 international. Average age 33. 38 applicants, 47% accepted, 6 enrolled. In 2011, 13 master's, 4 doctorates awarded. *Degree requirements:* For master's, thesis or alternative; for doctorate, comprehensive exam, thesis/dissertation, oral exams. *Entrance requirements:* For master's and doctorate, statement of purpose, official copies of academic transcripts, three letters of recommendation. Additional exam requirements/recommendations for international students: Required—TOEFL (minimum score 580 paper-based; 237 computer-based). *Application deadline:* For fall admission, 8/1 priority date for domestic students, 7/15 for international students; for spring admission, 12/1 priority date for domestic students, 10/15 for international students. Applications are processed on a rolling basis. Application fee: $55. Electronic applications accepted. *Expenses:* Contact institution. *Financial support:* Fellowships, research assistantships, teaching assistantships, Federal Work-Study, scholarships/grants, tuition waivers (full and partial), and unspecified assistantships available. Financial award application deadline: 2/1; financial award applicants required to submit FAFSA. *Faculty research:* Signal and image processing, computer communications, robotics, intelligent controls, bioelectromagnetics. *Total annual research expenditures:* $443,436. *Unit head:* Dr. Phillip Regalia, Chair, 202-319-5879, Fax: 202-319-5195, E-mail: regalia@cua.edu. *Application contact:* Andrew Woodall, Director of Graduate Admissions, 202-319-5057, Fax: 202-319-6533, E-mail: cua-admissions@cua.edu. Web site: http://eecs.cua.edu/.

Central Connecticut State University, School of Graduate Studies, School of Arts and Sciences, Department of Computer Science, New Britain, CT 06050-4010. Offers computer information technology (MS). Part-time and evening/weekend programs available. *Faculty:* 8 full-time (4 women), 7 part-time/adjunct (0 women). *Students:* 15 full-time (5 women), 41 part-time (10 women); includes 14 minority (5 Black or African American, non-Hispanic/Latino; 3 Asian, non-Hispanic/Latino; 4 Hispanic/Latino; 2 Two or more races, non-Hispanic/Latino), 11 international. Average age 31. 51 applicants, 67% accepted, 20 enrolled. In 2011, 18 master's awarded. *Degree requirements:* For master's, comprehensive exam, thesis or alternative. *Entrance requirements:* For master's, minimum undergraduate GPA of 2.7. Additional exam requirements/recommendations for international students: Required—TOEFL (minimum score 550 paper-based; 213 computer-based). *Application deadline:* For fall admission, 6/1 for domestic students, 5/1 for international students; for spring admission, 11/1 for domestic and international students. Applications are processed on a rolling basis. Application fee: $50. Electronic applications accepted. *Expenses: Tuition, area resident:* Full-time $5137; part-time $482 per credit. Tuition, state resident: full-time $7707; part-time $494 per credit. Tuition, nonresident: full-time $14,311; part-time $494 per credit. *Required fees:* $3865. One-time fee: $62 part-time. *Financial support:* Career-related internships or fieldwork, Federal Work-Study, scholarships/grants, and unspecified assistantships available. Support available to part-time students. Financial award application deadline: 4/15; financial award applicants required to submit FAFSA. *Unit head:* Dr. Bradley Kjell, Chair, 860-832-2710, E-mail: kjell@ccsu.edu. *Application contact:* Patricia Gardner, Associate Director of Graduate Studies, 860-832-2350, Fax: 860-832-2352, E-mail: graduateadmissions@ccsu.edu. Web site: http://www.cs.ccsu.edu/.

Central Connecticut State University, School of Graduate Studies, School of Arts and Sciences, Department of Mathematical Sciences, New Britain, CT 06050-4010. Offers data mining (MS, Certificate); mathematics (MA, MS, Certificate, Sixth Year Certificate), including actuarial science (MA), computer science (MA), statistics (MA). Part-time and evening/weekend programs available. *Faculty:* 33 full-time (10 women), 66 part-time/adjunct (26 women). *Students:* 19 full-time (9 women), 119 part-time (68 women); includes 23 minority (5 Black or African American, non-Hispanic/Latino; 8 Asian, non-Hispanic/Latino; 8 Hispanic/Latino; 2 Two or more races, non-Hispanic/Latino), 4 international. Average age 37. 65 applicants, 57% accepted, 24 enrolled. In 2011, 24 master's awarded. *Degree requirements:* For master's, comprehensive exam, thesis or alternative; for other advanced degree, qualifying exam. *Entrance requirements:* For master's, minimum undergraduate GPA of 2.7. Additional exam requirements/recommendations for international students: Required—TOEFL (minimum score 550 paper-based; 213 computer-based). *Application deadline:* For fall admission, 5/1 for domestic and international students; for spring admission, 11/1 for domestic and international students. Applications are processed on a rolling basis. Application fee: $50. Electronic applications accepted. *Expenses: Tuition, area resident:* Full-time $5137; part-time $482 per credit. Tuition, state resident: full-time $7707; part-time $494 per credit. Tuition, nonresident: full-time $14,311; part-time $494 per credit. *Required fees:* $3865. One-time fee: $62 part-time. *Financial support:* In 2011–12, 5 students received support. Career-related internships or fieldwork, Federal Work-Study, scholarships/grants, and unspecified assistantships available. Support available to part-time students. Financial award application deadline: 4/15; financial award applicants required to submit FAFSA. *Faculty research:* Statistics, actuarial mathematics, computer systems and engineering, computer programming techniques, operations research. *Unit head:* Dr. Jeffrey McGowan, Chair, 860-832-2835, E-mail: mcgowan@ccsu.edu. *Application contact:* Patricia Gardner, Associate Director of Graduate Studies, 860-832-2350, Fax: 860-832-2352, E-mail: graduateadmissions@ccsu.edu. Web site: http://www.math.ccsu.edu/.

Central Michigan University, College of Graduate Studies, College of Science and Technology, Department of Computer Science, Mount Pleasant, MI 48859. Offers MS. Part-time programs available. *Degree requirements:* For master's, thesis or alternative. *Entrance requirements:* For master's, bachelor's degree from accredited institution with minimum GPA of 3.0 in last two years of study. Electronic applications accepted. *Faculty research:* Artificial intelligence, biocomputing, data mining, software engineering, operating systems.

Chicago State University, School of Graduate and Professional Studies, College of Arts and Sciences, Department of Mathematics and Computer Science, Chicago, IL 60628. Offers computer science (MS); mathematics (MS). *Degree requirements:* For master's, thesis optional, oral exam. *Entrance requirements:* For master's, minimum GPA of 2.75.

Christopher Newport University, Graduate Studies, Department of Physics, Computer Science, and Engineering, Newport News, VA 23606-2998. Offers applied physics and computer science (MS). Part-time and evening/weekend programs available. *Degree requirements:* For master's, comprehensive exam (for some programs), thesis optional. *Entrance requirements:* For master's, GRE General Test, minimum GPA of 3.0. Additional exam requirements/recommendations for international students: Required—TOEFL (minimum score 580 paper-based; 237 computer-based; 92 iBT). Electronic applications accepted. *Faculty research:* Advanced programming methodologies, experimental nuclear physics, computer architecture, semiconductor nanophysics, laser and optical fiber sensors.

The Citadel, The Military College of South Carolina, Citadel Graduate College, Department of Mathematics and Computer Science, Charleston, SC 29409. Offers computer and information science (MS); mathematics education (MAE). *Accreditation:* NCATE (one or more programs are accredited). Part-time and evening/weekend programs available. *Faculty:* 3 full-time (0 women), 1 part-time/adjunct (0 women). *Students:* 1 (woman) full-time, 18 part-time (8 women); includes 1 minority (Asian, non-Hispanic/Latino). Average age 35. In 2011, 3 master's awarded. *Degree requirements:* For master's, comprehensive exam (for some programs), thesis (for some programs). *Entrance requirements:* For master's, GRE (minimum score 1000 for MS; 900 verbal and quantitative for MAT, raw score of 396), minimum undergraduate GPA of 3.0 (MS) or 2.5 (MAT); competency, demonstrated through coursework, approved work experience, or a program-administrated competency exam, in the areas of basic computer architecture, object-oriented programming, discrete mathematics, and data structures (MS); successful completion of 7 courses (MAT). Additional exam requirements/recommendations for international students: Required—TOEFL (minimum score 550 paper-based; 213 computer-based; 79 iBT). *Application deadline:* Applications are processed on a rolling basis. Application fee: $30. Electronic applications accepted. *Expenses: Tuition, area resident:* Part-time $501 per credit hour. Tuition, state resident: part-time $501 per credit hour. Tuition, nonresident: part-time $824 per credit hour. *Required fees:* $40 per term. One-time fee: $30. *Financial support:* Health care benefits and unspecified assistantships available. Support available to part-time students. Financial award application deadline: 7/1; financial award applicants required to submit FAFSA. *Faculty research:* Mathematics: numerical linear algebra, inverse problems, operator algebras, geometric group theory, integral equations; computer science: computer networks, database systems, software engineering, computational systems biology, mobile systems. *Unit head:* Dr. John I. Moore, Jr., Department Head, 843-953-5048, Fax: 843-953-7391, E-mail: john.moore@citadel.edu. *Application contact:* Dr. George L. Rudolph, Computer and Information Science Program Director, 843-953-5032, Fax: 843-953-7391, E-mail: george.rudolph@citadel.edu. Web site: http://www.mathcs.citadel.edu/.

City College of the City University of New York, Graduate School, Grove School of Engineering, Department of Computer Sciences, New York, NY 10031-9198. Offers MS, PhD. PhD program offered jointly with Graduate School and University Center of the City University of New York. *Degree requirements:* For master's, thesis optional; for doctorate, one foreign language, comprehensive exam, thesis/dissertation. *Entrance requirements:* For master's and doctorate, GRE General Test. Additional exam requirements/recommendations for international students: Required—TOEFL (minimum score 500 paper-based; 173 computer-based; 61 iBT). *Faculty research:* Complexities of algebraic research, human issues in computer science, scientific computing, supercompilers, parallel algorithms.

City University of Seattle, Graduate Division, School of Management, Bellevue, WA 98005. Offers accounting (Certificate); change leadership (MBA, Certificate); computer systems (MS); finance (Certificate); financial management (MBA); general management (MBA); general management-Europe (MBA); global marketing (MBA); human resources management (Certificate); individualized study (MBA); information security (MS); information systems (MBA); leadership (MA); marketing (MBA, Certificate); project management (MBA, MS, Certificate); sustainable business (Certificate); technology management (MBA, Certificate). Part-time and evening/weekend programs available. Postbaccalaureate distance learning degree programs offered (no on-campus study). *Faculty:* 6 full-time (2 women), 95 part-time/adjunct (33 women). *Students:* 397 full-time (193 women), 283 part-time (137 women); includes 127 minority (67 Black or African American, non-Hispanic/Latino; 5 American Indian or Alaska Native, non-Hispanic/Latino; 33 Asian, non-Hispanic/Latino; 15 Hispanic/Latino; 1 Native Hawaiian or other Pacific Islander, non-Hispanic/Latino; 6 Two or more races, non-Hispanic/Latino), 117 international. Average age 36. 151 applicants, 100% accepted, 151 enrolled. In 2011, 369 master's, 32 other advanced degrees awarded. *Degree requirements:* For master's, comprehensive exam (for some programs), thesis (for some programs). *Entrance requirements:* Additional exam requirements/recommendations for international students: Required—TOEFL (minimum score 567 paper-based; 227 computer-based; 87 iBT); Recommended—IELTS. *Application deadline:* For fall admission, 9/1 for international students; for winter admission, 12/1 for international students; for spring admission, 3/1 for international students. Applications are processed on a rolling basis. Application fee: $50. Electronic applications accepted. *Financial support:* Federal Work-Study and scholarships/grants available. Support available to part-time students. Financial award applicants required to submit FAFSA. *Unit head:* Dr. Kurt Kirstein, Dean, 425-637-1010 Ext. 5456, Fax: 425-709-5363, E-mail: kdkirstein@cityu.edu. *Application contact:* Alysa Borelli, Director, Recruiting, 888-422-4898, Fax: 425-709-5363, E-mail: info@cityu.edu. Web site: http://www.cityu.edu/programs/som/index.aspx.

Clark Atlanta University, School of Arts and Sciences, Department of Computer and Information Science, Atlanta, GA 30314. Offers MS. Part-time programs available. *Faculty:* 3 full-time (0 women). *Students:* 9 full-time (4 women), 7 part-time (2 women); includes 11 minority (10 Black or African American, non-Hispanic/Latino; 1 Asian, non-Hispanic/Latino), 3 international. Average age 33. 13 applicants, 100% accepted, 5 enrolled. In 2011, 2 degrees awarded. *Degree requirements:* For master's, one foreign language, thesis. *Entrance requirements:* For master's, GRE General Test, minimum GPA of 2.5. Additional exam requirements/recommendations for international students: Required—TOEFL (minimum score 500 paper-based; 173 computer-based; 61 iBT). *Application deadline:* For fall admission, 4/1 for domestic and international students; for spring admission, 11/1 for domestic and international students. Applications are processed on a rolling basis. Application fee: $40 ($55 for international students). *Expenses: Tuition:* Full-time $13,572; part-time $754 per credit hour. *Required fees:* $806; $403 per semester. *Financial support:* In 2011–12, 4 fellowships were awarded; career-related internships or fieldwork, Federal Work-Study, scholarships/grants, and unspecified assistantships also available. Support available to part-time students. Financial award application deadline: 4/30; financial award applicants required to submit FAFSA. *Unit head:* Dr. Roy George, Chairperson, 404-880-6945, E-mail: rgeorge@

cau.edu. *Application contact:* Michelle Clark-Davis, Graduate Program Admissions, 404-880-6605, E-mail: cauadmissions@cau.edu.

Clarkson University, Graduate School, School of Arts and Sciences, Program in Computer Science, Potsdam, NY 13699. Offers MS, PhD. Part-time programs available. *Faculty:* 7 full-time (2 women). *Students:* 24 full-time (2 women); includes 1 minority (Hispanic/Latino), 9 international. Average age 26. 13 applicants, 85% accepted, 5 enrolled. In 2011, 2 master's, 1 doctorate awarded. *Degree requirements:* For doctorate, thesis/dissertation, departmental qualifying exam. *Entrance requirements:* For master's and doctorate, GRE, transcripts of all college coursework, three letters of recommendation; resume and personal statement (recommended). Additional exam requirements/recommendations for international students: Required—TOEFL, TSE recommended. *Application deadline:* For fall admission, 1/30 priority date for domestic students, 1/30 for international students; for spring admission, 9/1 priority date for domestic students, 9/1 for international students. Applications are processed on a rolling basis. Application fee: $25 ($35 for international students). Electronic applications accepted. *Expenses: Tuition:* Full-time $14,376; part-time $1198 per credit hour. *Required fees:* $295 per semester. *Financial support:* In 2011–12, 15 students received support, including fellowships with full tuition reimbursements available (averaging $21,999 per year), 4 research assistantships with full tuition reimbursements available (averaging $21,999 per year), 10 teaching assistantships with full tuition reimbursements available (averaging $21,999 per year); scholarships/grants, tuition waivers (partial), and unspecified assistantships also available. *Faculty research:* Security in cyber-physical systems, cryptographic protocol. *Total annual research expenditures:* $266,659. *Unit head:* Dr. Christopher Lynch, Chair, 315-268-2395, Fax: 315-268-2371, E-mail: clynch@clarkson.edu. *Application contact:* Jennifer Reed, Graduate School Coordinator, School of Arts and Sciences, 315-268-3802, Fax: 315-268-3989, E-mail: sciencegrad@clarkson.edu. Web site: http://www.clarkson.edu/cs/.

Clemson University, Graduate School, College of Engineering and Science, School of Computing, Program in Computer Science, Clemson, SC 29634. Offers MS, PhD. *Students:* 132 full-time (23 women), 25 part-time (5 women); includes 5 minority (4 Black or African American, non-Hispanic/Latino; 1 Asian, non-Hispanic/Latino), 109 international. Average age 27. 328 applicants, 60% accepted, 71 enrolled. In 2011, 39 master's, 10 doctorates awarded. Terminal master's awarded for partial completion of doctoral program. *Degree requirements:* For master's, thesis optional; for doctorate, thesis/dissertation. *Entrance requirements:* For master's and doctorate, GRE General Test. Additional exam requirements/recommendations for international students: Required—TOEFL. *Application deadline:* Applications are processed on a rolling basis. Application fee: $70 ($80 for international students). Electronic applications accepted. *Financial support:* In 2011–12, 75 students received support, including 7 fellowships with full and partial tuition reimbursements available (averaging $15,786 per year), 32 research assistantships with partial tuition reimbursements available (averaging $12,730 per year), 25 teaching assistantships with partial tuition reimbursements available (averaging $14,939 per year); career-related internships or fieldwork, institutionally sponsored loans, scholarships/grants, health care benefits, and unspecified assistantships also available. Support available to part-time students. Financial award application deadline: 3/1; financial award applicants required to submit FAFSA. *Unit head:* Dr. Larry F. Hodges, Director, School of Computing, 864-656-7552, Fax: 864-656-0145, E-mail: lfh@clemson.edu. *Application contact:* Dr. Mark Smootherman, Director of Graduate Programs, 864-656-5878, Fax: 864-656-0145, E-mail: mark@clemson.edu. Web site: http://www.clemson.edu/ces/departments/computing/index.html.

Cleveland State University, College of Graduate Studies, Monte Ahuja College of Business, Department of Computer and Information Science, Cleveland, OH 44115. Offers computer and information science (MCIS); information systems (DBA). Part-time and evening/weekend programs available. *Faculty:* 12 full-time (2 women), 3 part-time/adjunct (2 women). *Students:* 18 full-time (8 women), 70 part-time (15 women); includes 6 minority (3 Black or African American, non-Hispanic/Latino; 3 Asian, non-Hispanic/Latino), 51 international. Average age 27. 344 applicants, 71% accepted, 34 enrolled. In 2011, 34 master's awarded. Terminal master's awarded for partial completion of doctoral program. *Degree requirements:* For master's, thesis optional; for doctorate, comprehensive exam, thesis/dissertation. *Entrance requirements:* For master's, GRE or GMAT, minimum GPA of 2.75; for doctorate, GRE or GMAT, MBA, MCIS or equivalent. Additional exam requirements/recommendations for international students: Required—TOEFL (minimum score 525 paper-based; 197 computer-based; 78 iBT). *Application deadline:* For fall admission, 7/15 priority date for domestic students, 5/15 for international students; for spring admission, 12/15 priority date for domestic students. Applications are processed on a rolling basis. Application fee: $30. Electronic applications accepted. *Expenses:* Tuition, state resident: full-time $6416; part-time $494 per credit hour. Tuition, nonresident: full-time $12,074; part-time $929 per credit hour. *Financial support:* In 2011–12, 21 students received support, including 7 research assistantships with full and partial tuition reimbursements available (averaging $7,800 per year), 2 teaching assistantships with full and partial tuition reimbursements available (averaging $16,000 per year); career-related internships or fieldwork, tuition waivers (full), and unspecified assistantships also available. *Faculty research:* Artificial intelligence, object-oriented analysis, database design, software efficiency, distributed system, geographical information systems. *Total annual research expenditures:* $7,500. *Unit head:* Dr. Santosh K. Misra, Chairman, 216-687-4760, Fax: 216-687-5448, E-mail: s.misra@csuohio.edu. *Application contact:* 216-687-4760, Fax: 216-687-9354, E-mail: s.misra@csuohio.edu. Web site: http://cis.csuohio.edu/.

College of Charleston, Graduate School, School of Sciences and Mathematics, Program in Computer and Information Sciences, Charleston, SC 29424-0001. Offers MS. Program offered jointly with The Citadel, The Military College of South Carolina. Part-time and evening/weekend programs available. *Faculty:* 11 full-time (3 women). *Students:* 6 full-time (1 woman), 18 part-time (2 women); includes 2 minority (1 American Indian or Alaska Native, non-Hispanic/Latino; 1 Asian, non-Hispanic/Latino), 2 international. Average age 32. 13 applicants, 62% accepted, 8 enrolled. In 2011, 4 master's awarded. *Degree requirements:* For master's, thesis optional. *Entrance requirements:* For master's, GRE. Additional exam requirements/recommendations for international students: Required—TOEFL (minimum score 81 iBT). *Application deadline:* For fall admission, 6/1 for domestic students; for spring admission, 11/1 for domestic students. Application fee: $45. Electronic applications accepted. *Expenses:* Tuition, state resident: full-time $5455; part-time $455 per credit. Tuition, nonresident: full-time $13,917; part-time $1160 per credit. *Financial support:* In 2011–12, research assistantships (averaging $12,400 per year) were awarded; Federal Work-Study, scholarships/grants, and unspecified assistantships also available. Support available to part-time students. Financial award application deadline: 4/1; financial award applicants required to submit FAFSA. *Unit head:* Dr. Renee McCauley, Director, 843-953-3187, E-mail: mccauleyr@cofc.edu. *Application contact:* Susan Hallatt, Director of Graduate Admissions, 843-953-5614, Fax: 843-953-1434, E-mail: hallatts@cofc.edu.

The College of Saint Rose, Graduate Studies, School of Mathematics and Sciences, Program in Computer Information Systems, Albany, NY 12203-1419. Offers MS. Part-time and evening/weekend programs available. *Degree requirements:* For master's, comprehensive exam, research component. *Entrance requirements:* For master's, minimum GPA of 3.0, 9 undergraduate credits in math. Additional exam requirements/recommendations for international students: Required—TOEFL (minimum score 550 paper-based; 213 computer-based). Electronic applications accepted.

College of Staten Island of the City University of New York, Graduate Programs, Program in Computer Science, Staten Island, NY 10314-6600. Offers MS. Part-time and evening/weekend programs available. *Faculty:* 5 full-time (3 women), 1 (woman) part-time/adjunct. *Students:* 35 (9 women). Average age 28. 36 applicants, 67% accepted, 11 enrolled. In 2011, 9 master's awarded. *Degree requirements:* For master's, thesis optional. *Entrance requirements:* For master's, GRE General Test, previous undergraduate course work in computer science, minimum GPA of 3.0. Additional exam requirements/recommendations for international students: Required—TOEFL (minimum score 550 paper-based; 213 computer-based; 79 iBT), IELTS (minimum score 6.5). *Application deadline:* For fall admission, 4/18 priority date for domestic students, 4/18 for international students; for spring admission, 11/21 priority date for domestic students, 11/21 for international students. Applications are processed on a rolling basis. Application fee: $125. Electronic applications accepted. *Expenses:* Tuition, state resident: full-time $8210; part-time $345 per credit. Tuition, nonresident: part-time $640 per credit. *Required fees:* $128 per semester. *Financial support:* In 2011–12, 2 students received support. Career-related internships or fieldwork and Federal Work-Study available. Support available to part-time students. Financial award applicants required to submit FAFSA. *Total annual research expenditures:* $53,000. *Unit head:* Dr. Shuqun Zhang, Coordinator, 718-982-3178, Fax: 718-982-2856, E-mail: shuqun.zhang@csi.cuny.edu. *Application contact:* Sasha Spence, Assistant Director for Graduate Admissions, 718-982-2699, Fax: 718-982-2500, E-mail: sasha.spence@csi.cuny.edu. Web site: http://www.cs.csi.cuny.edu/content/grad.cs.csi.cuny.new.htm.

The College of William and Mary, Faculty of Arts and Sciences, Department of Computer Science, Williamsburg, VA 23187-8795. Offers computational operations research (MS), including computer science; computer science (MS, PhD), including computational science (PhD). Part-time programs available. *Faculty:* 17 full-time (4 women). *Students:* 83 full-time (18 women), 8 part-time (3 women); includes 8 minority (4 Black or African American, non-Hispanic/Latino; 1 Hispanic/Latino; 3 Two or more races, non-Hispanic/Latino), 45 international. Average age 28. 115 applicants, 59% accepted, 31 enrolled. In 2011, 20 master's, 3 doctorates awarded. *Degree requirements:* For master's, comprehensive exam, thesis optional, research project; for doctorate, comprehensive exam, thesis/dissertation. *Entrance requirements:* For master's, GRE General Test, minimum GPA of 2.5; for doctorate, GRE General Test, minimum GPA of 3.0. Additional exam requirements/recommendations for international students: Required—TOEFL, TWE. *Application deadline:* For fall admission, 3/1 priority date for domestic students, 3/1 for international students; for spring admission, 11/1 for domestic and international students. Applications are processed on a rolling basis. Application fee: $45. Electronic applications accepted. *Expenses:* Tuition, state resident: full-time $6400; part-time $365 per credit hour. Tuition, nonresident: full-time $19,720; part-time $985 per credit hour. *Required fees:* $4562. *Financial support:* In 2011–12, 2 fellowships with full tuition reimbursements (averaging $21,000 per year), 17 research assistantships with full tuition reimbursements (averaging $21,000 per year), 20 teaching assistantships with full tuition reimbursements (averaging $18,000 per year) were awarded; scholarships/grants and unspecified assistantships also available. Financial award application deadline: 3/1; financial award applicants required to submit FAFSA. *Faculty research:* High-performance computing, wireless computing, algorithms, computer systems and network computing, modeling and simulation. *Total annual research expenditures:* $1.1 million. *Unit head:* Dr. Virginia Torczon, Chair, 757-221-3460, Fax: 757-221-1717, E-mail: chair@cs.wm.edu. *Application contact:* Vanessa Godwin, Administrative Director, 757-221-3455, Fax: 757-221-1717, E-mail: gradinfo@cs.wm.edu. Web site: http://www.wm.edu/computerscience.

Colorado School of Mines, Graduate School, Department of Mathematical and Computer Sciences, Golden, CO 80401-1887. Offers MS, PhD. Part-time programs available. *Faculty:* 34 full-time (15 women), 3 part-time/adjunct (0 women). *Students:* 68 full-time (22 women), 9 part-time (2 women); includes 7 minority (1 Black or African American, non-Hispanic/Latino; 1 American Indian or Alaska Native, non-Hispanic/Latino; 3 Asian, non-Hispanic/Latino; 2 Hispanic/Latino), 13 international. Average age 26. 129 applicants, 62% accepted, 36 enrolled. In 2011, 8 master's awarded. *Degree requirements:* For master's, thesis (for some programs); for doctorate, comprehensive exam, thesis/dissertation. *Entrance requirements:* For master's and doctorate, GRE General Test. Additional exam requirements/recommendations for international students: Required—TOEFL (minimum score 550 paper-based; 213 computer-based; 80 iBT). *Application deadline:* For fall admission, 1/15 priority date for domestic students, 1/15 for international students; for spring admission, 10/15 priority date for domestic students, 10/15 for international students. Application fee: $50 ($70 for international students). Electronic applications accepted. *Expenses:* Tuition, state resident: full-time $12,585; part-time $699 per credit. Tuition, nonresident: full-time $27,270; part-time $1516 per credit. *Required fees:* $1864.20; $670 per semester. *Financial support:* In 2011–12, 49 students received support, including 3 fellowships with full tuition reimbursements available (averaging $20,000 per year), 25 research assistantships with full tuition reimbursements available (averaging $20,000 per year), 21 teaching assistantships with full tuition reimbursements available (averaging $20,000 per year); scholarships/grants, health care benefits, and unspecified assistantships also available. Financial award application deadline: 1/15; financial award applicants required to submit FAFSA. *Faculty research:* Applied statistics, numerical computation, artificial intelligence, linear optimization. *Total annual research expenditures:* $949,540. *Unit head:* Dr. Willy Hereman, Interim Head, 303-273-3881, Fax: 303-273-3875, E-mail: whereman@mines.edu. *Application contact:* William Navidi, Professor, 303-273-3489, Fax: 303-273-3875, E-mail: wnavidi@mines.edu. Web site: http://mcs.mines.edu.

Colorado State University, Graduate School, College of Natural Sciences, Department of Computer Science, Fort Collins, CO 80523-1873. Offers MCS, MS, PhD. Postbaccalaureate distance learning degree programs offered (no on-campus study). *Faculty:* 19 full-time (3 women), 1 part-time/adjunct (0 women). *Students:* 54 full-time (11 women), 146 part-time (16 women); includes 24 minority (1 Black or African American, non-Hispanic/Latino; 13 Asian, non-Hispanic/Latino; 8 Hispanic/Latino; 2 Two or more races, non-Hispanic/Latino), 72 international. Average age 33. 207 applicants, 60% accepted, 38 enrolled. In 2011, 42 master's, 7 doctorates awarded. Terminal master's awarded for partial completion of doctoral program. *Degree requirements:* For master's, comprehensive exam (for some programs), thesis (MS); for doctorate, comprehensive exam, thesis/dissertation, qualifying, preliminary, and final exams. *Entrance requirements:* For master's, GRE, computer science background, minimum GPA of 3.0, 3 letters of recommendation, statement of purpose, transcripts; for doctorate, GRE General Test, BSC or master's degree in computer science, minimum GPA of 3.0. Additional exam requirements/recommendations for international students: Required—TOEFL (minimum score 550 paper-based; 213 computer-based; 80 iBT).

Application deadline: For fall admission, 2/1 priority date for domestic students, 2/1 for international students; for spring admission, 10/1 priority date for domestic students, 10/1 for international students. Applications are processed on a rolling basis. Application fee: $50. Electronic applications accepted. *Expenses:* Tuition, state resident: full-time $7992. Tuition, nonresident: full-time $19,592. *Required fees:* $1735; $58 per credit. *Financial support:* In 2011–12, 62 students received support, including 1 fellowship (averaging $45,000 per year), 32 research assistantships with full tuition reimbursements available (averaging $12,082 per year), 29 teaching assistantships with full tuition reimbursements available (averaging $10,572 per year); health care benefits also available. Financial award application deadline: 2/15; financial award applicants required to submit FAFSA. *Faculty research:* Artificial intelligence, parallel and distributed computing, software engineering, computer vision/graphics, security. *Total annual research expenditures:* $2.7 million. *Unit head:* Dr. L. Darrell Whitley, Chairman, 970-491-5373, Fax: 970-491-2466, E-mail: whitley@cs.colostate.edu. *Application contact:* James Peterson, Director of Graduate Admission, 970-491-7137, Fax: 970-491-2466, E-mail: peterson@cs.colostate.edu. Web site: http://www.cs.colostate.edu/cstop/index.

Colorado Technical University Colorado Springs, Graduate Studies, Program in Computer Science, Colorado Springs, CO 80907-3896. Offers computer science (DCS); computer systems security (MSCS); database systems (MSCS); software engineering (MSCS). Part-time and evening/weekend programs available. Postbaccalaureate distance learning degree programs offered. *Degree requirements:* For master's, thesis or alternative; for doctorate, thesis/dissertation. *Entrance requirements:* For doctorate, minimum graduate GPA of 3.0, 5 years of related work experience. *Faculty research:* Software engineering, systems engineering.

Colorado Technical University Denver South, Program in Computer Science, Aurora, CO 80014. Offers computer systems security (MSCS); database systems (MSCS); software engineering (MSCS). Part-time and evening/weekend programs available. *Degree requirements:* For master's, thesis or alternative. *Entrance requirements:* For master's, minimum undergraduate GPA of 3.0, resume.

Colorado Technical University Sioux Falls, Program in Computing, Sioux Falls, SD 57108. Offers computer systems security (MSCS); software engineering (MSCS).

Columbia University, The Fu Foundation School of Engineering and Applied Science, Department of Computer Science, New York, NY 10027. Offers computer science (MS, Eng Sc D, PhD, Engr); computer science and journalism (MS). PhD offered through the Graduate School of Arts and Sciences. Part-time programs available. Postbaccalaureate distance learning degree programs offered (no on-campus study). *Faculty:* 42 full-time (7 women), 9 part-time/adjunct (0 women). *Students:* 242 full-time (52 women), 212 part-time (41 women); includes 24 minority (2 Black or African American, non-Hispanic/Latino; 19 Asian, non-Hispanic/Latino; 3 Two or more races, non-Hispanic/Latino), 330 international. Average age 27. 1,364 applicants, 22% accepted, 163 enrolled. In 2011, 129 master's, 24 doctorates awarded. Terminal master's awarded for partial completion of doctoral program. *Degree requirements:* For master's and Engr, thesis optional; for doctorate, comprehensive exam, thesis/dissertation, candidacy exam. *Entrance requirements:* For master's and Engr, GRE General Test; for doctorate, GRE General Test, GRE Subject Test (computer science). Additional exam requirements/recommendations for international students: Required—TOEFL, IELTS. *Application deadline:* For fall admission, 12/1 priority date for domestic students, 12/1 for international students; for spring admission, 10/1 priority date for domestic students, 10/1 for international students. Application fee: $95. Electronic

applications accepted. *Financial support:* In 2011–12, 121 students received support, including 7 fellowships with full tuition reimbursements available (averaging $26,361 per year), 104 research assistantships with full tuition reimbursements available (averaging $28,861 per year), 10 teaching assistantships with full tuition reimbursements available (averaging $26,361 per year); health care benefits also available. Financial award application deadline: 12/1; financial award applicants required to submit FAFSA. *Faculty research:* Natural language processing, machine learning, software systems, network systems, computer security, computational biology, foundations of computer science, vision and graphics. *Unit head:* Dr. Shree K. Nayar, Professor/Chairman, 212-939-7092, E-mail: nayar@cs.columbia.edu. *Application contact:* Remiko O. Moss, Assistant Director, 212-939-7002, Fax: 212-666-0140, E-mail: remimoss@cs.columbia.edu. Web site: http://www.cs.columbia.edu/.

See Display below and Close-Up on page 339.

Columbus State University, Graduate Studies, D. Abbott Turner College of Business and Computer Science, Columbus, GA 31907-5645. Offers applied computer science (MS); business administration (MBA); modeling and simulation (Certificate); organizational leadership (MS). *Accreditation:* AACSB. *Entrance requirements:* For master's, GMAT, GRE. Additional exam requirements/recommendations for international students: Required—TOEFL (minimum score 550 paper-based; 213 computer-based; 79 iBT). Electronic applications accepted.

Concordia University, School of Graduate Studies, Faculty of Engineering and Computer Science, Department of Computer Science and Software Engineering, Montréal, QC H3G 1M8, Canada. Offers computer science (M App Comp Sc, M Comp Sc, PhD, Diploma); software engineering (MA Sc). *Degree requirements:* For master's, one foreign language, thesis optional; for doctorate, one foreign language, comprehensive exam, thesis/dissertation. *Faculty research:* Computer systems and applications, mathematics of computation, pattern recognition, artificial intelligence and robotics.

Cornell University, Graduate School, Graduate Fields of Engineering, Field of Computer Science, Ithaca, NY 14853-0001. Offers algorithms (M Eng, PhD); applied logic and automated reasoning (M Eng, PhD); artificial intelligence (M Eng, PhD); computer graphics (M Eng, PhD); computer science (M Eng, PhD); computer vision (M Eng, PhD); concurrency and distributed computing (M Eng, PhD); information organization and retrieval (M Eng, PhD); operating systems (M Eng, PhD); parallel computing (M Eng, PhD); programming environments (M Eng, PhD); programming languages and methodology (M Eng, PhD); robotics (M Eng, PhD); scientific computing (M Eng, PhD); theory of computation (M Eng, PhD). *Faculty:* 65 full-time (9 women). *Students:* 211 full-time (47 women); includes 24 minority (22 Asian, non-Hispanic/Latino; 2 Hispanic/Latino), 138 international. Average age 25. 1,255 applicants, 20% accepted, 111 enrolled. In 2011, 141 master's, 12 doctorates awarded. *Degree requirements:* For doctorate, comprehensive exam, thesis/dissertation. *Entrance requirements:* For master's, GRE General Test, 2 letters of recommendation; for doctorate, GRE General Test, GRE Subject Test (computer science or mathematics), 3 letters of recommendation. Additional exam requirements/recommendations for international students: Required—TOEFL (minimum score 505 paper-based; 213 computer-based; 77 iBT). *Application deadline:* For fall admission, 1/1 for domestic students. Application fee: $95. Electronic applications accepted. *Financial support:* In 2011–12, 100 students received support, including 13 fellowships with full tuition reimbursements available, 69 research assistantships with full tuition reimbursements available, 28 teaching

assistantships with full tuition reimbursements available; institutionally sponsored loans, scholarships/grants, health care benefits, tuition waivers (full and partial), and unspecified assistantships also available. Financial award applicants required to submit FAFSA. *Faculty research:* Artificial intelligence, operating systems and databases, programming languages and security, scientific computing, theory of computing, computational biology and graphics. *Unit head:* Director of Graduate Studies, 607-255-8593, Fax: 607-255-4428. *Application contact:* Graduate Field Assistant, 607-255-8593, Fax: 607-255-4428, E-mail: phd@cs.cornell.edu. Web site: http://www.gradschool.cornell.edu/fields.php?id-28&a-2.

Dalhousie University, Faculty of Computer Science, Halifax , NS B3H 1W5, Canada. Offers computational biology and bioinformatics (M Sc); computer science (PhD); computer science (project-based) (MA Sc); computer science (thesis-based) (MC Sc); electronic commerce (MEC); health informatics (MHI). *Degree requirements:* For master's, thesis (for some programs); for doctorate, thesis/dissertation. *Entrance requirements:* Additional exam requirements/recommendations for international students: Required—1 of 5 approved tests: TOEFL, IELTS, CANTEST, CAEL, Michigan English Language Assessment Battery. Electronic applications accepted.

Dartmouth College, Arts and Sciences Graduate Programs, Department of Computer Science, Hanover, NH 03755. Offers MS, PhD. Terminal master's awarded for partial completion of doctoral program. *Degree requirements:* For master's, thesis; for doctorate, thesis/dissertation. *Entrance requirements:* For master's and doctorate, GRE General Test, GRE Subject Test. *Faculty research:* Algorithms, computational geometry and learning, computer vision, information retrieval, robotics.

DePaul University, College of Computing and Digital Media, Chicago, IL 60604. Offers animation (MA, MFA); applied technology (MS); business information technology (MS); cinema (MFA); cinema production (MS); computational finance (MS); computer and information sciences (PhD); computer game development (MS); computer graphics and motion technology (MS); computer information and network security (MS); computer science (MS); e-commerce technology (MS); human-computer interaction (MS); information systems (MS); information technology (MA); information technology project management (MS); network engineering and management (MS); predictive analytics (MS); screenwriting (MFA); software engineering (MS); JD/MA; JD/MS. Part-time and evening/weekend programs available. Postbaccalaureate distance learning degree programs offered (no on-campus study). *Faculty:* 64 full-time (16 women), 44 part-time/adjunct (5 women). *Students:* 969 full-time (250 women), 936 part-time (231 women); includes 566 minority (204 Black or African American, non-Hispanic/Latino; 3 American Indian or Alaska Native, non-Hispanic/Latino; 166 Asian, non-Hispanic/Latino; 135 Hispanic/Latino; 7 Native Hawaiian or other Pacific Islander, non-Hispanic/Latino; 51 Two or more races, non-Hispanic/Latino), 282 international. Average age 32. 1,040 applicants, 65% accepted, 324 enrolled. In 2011, 478 master's, 4 doctorates awarded. *Degree requirements:* For master's, thesis (for some programs); for doctorate, comprehensive exam, thesis/dissertation. *Entrance requirements:* For master's, GRE or GMAT (MS in computational finance only), bachelor's degree, resume (MS in predictive analytics only), IT experience (MS in information technology project management only), portfolio review (all MFA programs and MA in animation); for doctorate, GRE, master's degree in computer science. Additional exam requirements/recommendations for international students: Required—TOEFL (minimum score 550 paper-based; 213 computer-based; 80 iBT), IELTS (minimum score 6.5), Pearson Test of English (minimum score 53). *Application deadline:* For fall admission, 8/1 priority date for domestic students, 6/1 for international students; for winter admission, 12/1 priority date for domestic students, 10/1 for international students; for spring admission, 3/1 priority date for domestic students, 1/1 for international students. Applications are processed on a rolling basis. Application fee: $25. Electronic applications accepted. *Expenses:* Contact institution. *Financial support:* In 2011–12, 56 students received support, including 3 fellowships with full tuition reimbursements available (averaging $30,000 per year), 3 research assistantships with full and partial tuition reimbursements available (averaging $22,833 per year), 50 teaching assistantships (averaging $6,194 per year); Federal Work-Study, scholarships/grants, tuition waivers (full and partial), and unspecified assistantships also available. Support available to part-time students. Financial award application deadline: 4/30. *Faculty research:* Data mining, theoretical computer science, gaming, security, animation and film. . *Total annual research expenditures:* $3.9 million. *Unit head:* Elly Kafritsas-Wessels, Senior Administrative Assistant, 312-362-5816, Fax: 312-362-5185, E-mail: ekafrits@cdm.depaul.edu. *Application contact:* James Parker, Director of Graduate Admission, 312-362-8714, Fax: 312-362-5179, E-mail: jparke29@cdm.depaul.edu. Web site: http://cdm.depaul.edu.

DigiPen Institute of Technology, Graduate Programs, Redmond, WA 98052. Offers computer science (MS). Part-time programs available. *Faculty:* 10 full-time (0 women), 1 part-time/adjunct (0 women). *Students:* 23 full-time (2 women), 30 part-time (4 women); includes 13 minority (1 Black or African American, non-Hispanic/Latino; 4 Asian, non-Hispanic/Latino; 4 Hispanic/Latino; 4 Two or more races, non-Hispanic/Latino), 10 international. Average age 28. 88 applicants, 50% accepted, 27 enrolled. In 2011, 2 master's awarded. *Degree requirements:* For master's, comprehensive exam (for some programs), thesis (for some programs). *Entrance requirements:* For master's, GRE General Test, GRE Subject Test in computer science (for students with non-computer science degrees). Additional exam requirements/recommendations for international students: Required—TOEFL (minimum score 550 paper-based; 213 computer-based; 80 iBT). *Application deadline:* For fall admission, 2/1 priority date for domestic students, 2/1 for international students; for spring admission, 7/1 for domestic and international students. Applications are processed on a rolling basis. Application fee: $35. Electronic applications accepted. Tuition and fees vary according to course load. *Financial support:* In 2011–12, 4 students received support, including 4 fellowships; career-related internships or fieldwork and scholarships/grants also available. Financial award application deadline: 5/1; financial award applicants required to submit FAFSA. *Faculty research:* Procedural modeling, computer graphics and visualization, GPGPU methods, human-computer interaction, fuzzy numbers and fuzzy analysis, modeling under spistemic uncertainty, nonlinear image processing, mathematical representation of surfaces, advanced computer graphic rendering techniques, mathematical physics, computer music and sound synthesis. *Unit head:* Angela Kugler, Vice President of External Affairs, 425-895-4438, Fax: 425-558-0378, E-mail: akugler@digipen.edu. *Application contact:* Danial Powers, Admissions Application Manager, 425-629-5071, Fax: 425-558-0378, E-mail: dpowers@digipen.edu.

Drexel University, College of Engineering, Department of Computer Science, Philadelphia, PA 19104-2875. Offers MS, PhD. *Entrance requirements:* For master's, GRE. Additional exam requirements/recommendations for international students: Required—TOEFL. Electronic applications accepted.

Duke University, Graduate School, Department of Computer Science, Durham, NC 27708. Offers MS, PhD. *Faculty:* 37 full-time. *Students:* 94 full-time (16 women); includes 4 minority (all Asian, non-Hispanic/Latino), 76 international. 553 applicants, 8% accepted, 13 enrolled. In 2011, 10 master's, 6 doctorates awarded. *Degree requirements:* For doctorate, thesis/dissertation. *Entrance requirements:* For master's, GRE General Test; for doctorate, GRE General Test, GRE Subject Test (recommended). Additional exam requirements/recommendations for international students: Required—TOEFL (minimum score 550 paper-based; 213 computer-based; 83 iBT), IELTS (minimum score 7). *Application deadline:* For fall admission, 12/8 priority date for domestic students, 12/8 for international students. Application fee: $75. Electronic applications accepted. *Expenses: Tuition:* Full-time $40,720. *Required fees:* $3107. *Financial support:* Fellowships, research assistantships, teaching assistantships, and Federal Work-Study available. Financial award application deadline: 12/8. *Unit head:* Jun Yang, Director of Graduate Studies, 919-660-6538, Fax: 919-660-6519, E-mail: mkbutler@cs.duke.edu. *Application contact:* Elizabeth Hutton, Director, Graduate Admissions, 919-684-3913, Fax: 919-684-2277, E-mail: grad-admissions@duke.edu. Web site: http://www.cs.duke.edu/.

East Carolina University, Graduate School, College of Technology and Computer Science, Department of Computer Science, Greenville, NC 27858-4353. Offers computer science (MS); software engineering (MS). Part-time and evening/weekend programs available. *Degree requirements:* For master's, comprehensive exam, thesis or alternative. *Entrance requirements:* For master's, GRE General Test. Additional exam requirements/recommendations for international students: Required—TOEFL. *Application deadline:* For fall admission, 11/1 priority date for domestic students, 10/1 for international students; for spring admission, 3/1 priority date for domestic students, 3/1 for international students. Applications are processed on a rolling basis. Application fee: $50. Electronic applications accepted. *Expenses:* Tuition, state resident: full-time $3557; part-time $444.63 per semester hour. Tuition, nonresident: full-time $14,351; part-time $1793.88 per semester hour. *Required fees:* $2016; $252 per semester hour. Part-time tuition and fees vary according to course load, campus/location and program. *Financial support:* Research assistantships, career-related internships or fieldwork, Federal Work-Study, tuition waivers (full), and unspecified assistantships available. Financial award application deadline: 3/1. *Faculty research:* Software development, software engineering, artificial intelligence, bioinformatics, cryptography. *Unit head:* Dr. Karl Abrahamson, Interim Chair, 252-328-9689, E-mail: karl@cs.ecu.edu. Web site: http://www.ecu.edu/cs-tecs/csci/index.cfm.

East Carolina University, Graduate School, College of Technology and Computer Science, Department of Technology Systems, Greenville, NC 27858-4353. Offers computer network professional (Certificate); industrial technology (MS), including computer networking management, digital communications, industrial distribution and logistics, information security, manufacturing, performance improvement, quality systems; information assurance (Certificate); Lean Six Sigma Black Belt (Certificate); occupational safety (MS); technology management (PhD); Website developer (Certificate). *Entrance requirements:* For master's and Certificate, GRE General Test or MAT, minimum GPA of 2.5; for doctorate, GRE General Test, related work experience. *Application deadline:* For fall admission, 6/1 priority date for domestic students. Applications are processed on a rolling basis. Application fee: $50. *Expenses:* Tuition, state resident: full-time $3557; part-time $444.63 per semester hour. Tuition, nonresident: full-time $14,351; part-time $1793.88 per semester hour. *Required fees:* $2016; $252 per semester hour. Part-time tuition and fees vary according to course load, campus/location and program. *Financial support:* Application deadline: 6/1. *Unit head:* Dr. Tijjani Mohammed, Interim Chair, 252-328-9668, E-mail: mohammedt@ecu.edu. Web site: http://www.ecu.edu/cs-tecs/techsystems/.

Eastern Illinois University, Graduate School, College of Sciences, Department of Mathematics and Computer Science, Charleston, IL 61920-3099. Offers mathematics (MA); mathematics education (MA). *Entrance requirements:* For master's, GRE General Test. *Expenses:* Tuition, state resident: part-time $279 per credit hour. Tuition, nonresident: part-time $670 per credit hour. *Required fees:* $179.07 per credit hour. $1253 per semester.

Eastern Illinois University, Graduate School, Lumpkin College of Business and Applied Sciences, School of Technology, Charleston, IL 61920-3099. Offers computer technology (Certificate); quality systems (Certificate); technology (MS); technology security (Certificate); work performance improvement (Certificate). Part-time and evening/weekend programs available. *Expenses:* Tuition, state resident: part-time $279 per credit hour. Tuition, nonresident: part-time $670 per credit hour. *Required fees:* $179.07 per credit hour. $1253 per semester.

Eastern Michigan University, Graduate School, College of Arts and Sciences, Department of Computer Science, Ypsilanti, MI 48197. Offers artificial intelligence (Graduate Certificate); computer science (MS). Part-time and evening/weekend programs available. Postbaccalaureate distance learning degree programs offered (no on-campus study). *Faculty:* 15 full-time (5 women). *Students:* 12 full-time (6 women), 17 part-time (1 woman); includes 3 minority (1 Black or African American, non-Hispanic/Latino; 2 Asian, non-Hispanic/Latino), 14 international. Average age 29. 93 applicants, 43% accepted, 5 enrolled. In 2011, 10 master's, 1 other advanced degree awarded. *Degree requirements:* For master's, thesis or alternative. *Entrance requirements:* For master's, at least 18 credit hours of 200-level (or above) computer science courses including data structures, programming languages like java, C or C++, computer organization; courses in discrete mathematics, probability and statistics, linear algebra and calculus; minimum GPA of 2.75 in computer science. Additional exam requirements/recommendations for international students: Required—TOEFL. *Application deadline:* For fall admission, 8/1 for domestic students, 5/1 for international students; for winter admission, 12/1 for domestic students, 10/1 for international students; for spring admission, 4/1 for domestic students, 2/1 for international students. Application fee: $35. *Expenses:* Tuition, state resident: full-time $10,367; part-time $432 per credit hour. Tuition, nonresident: full-time $20,435; part-time $851 per credit hour. *Required fees:* $39 per credit hour. $46 per semester. One-time fee: $100. Tuition and fees vary according to course level, degree level and reciprocity agreements. *Financial support:* Fellowships, research assistantships with full tuition reimbursements, teaching assistantships with full tuition reimbursements, career-related internships or fieldwork, Federal Work-Study, institutionally sponsored loans, scholarships/grants, tuition waivers (partial), and unspecified assistantships available. Support available to part-time students. Financial award applicants required to submit FAFSA. *Unit head:* Dr. William McMillan, Department Head, 734-487-1063, Fax: 734-487-6824, E-mail: wmcmillan@emich.edu. *Application contact:* Pamela Moore, Graduate Coordinator, 734-487-1063, Fax: 734-487-6824, E-mail: pmoore@emich.edu. Web site: http://www.emich.edu/compsci.

Eastern Michigan University, Graduate School, College of Arts and Sciences, Department of Mathematics, Ypsilanti, MI 48197. Offers applied statistics (MA); computer science (MA); mathematics (MA); mathematics education (MA). Part-time and evening/weekend programs available. Postbaccalaureate distance learning degree programs offered (minimal on-campus study). *Faculty:* 25 full-time (11 women). *Students:* 16 full-time (9 women), 36 part-time (14 women); includes 9 minority (4 Black or African American, non-Hispanic/Latino; 5 Asian, non-Hispanic/Latino), 6 international.

Average age 30. 39 applicants, 82% accepted, 18 enrolled. In 2011, 17 degrees awarded. *Degree requirements:* For master's, thesis optional. *Entrance requirements:* Additional exam requirements/recommendations for international students: Required—TOEFL. *Application deadline:* Applications are processed on a rolling basis. Application fee: $35. *Expenses:* Tuition, state resident: full-time $10,367; part-time $432 per credit hour. Tuition, nonresident: full-time $20,435; part-time $851 per credit hour. *Required fees:* $39 per credit hour. $46 per semester. One-time fee: $100. Tuition and fees vary according to course level, degree level and reciprocity agreements. *Financial support:* Fellowships, research assistantships with full tuition reimbursements, teaching assistantships with full tuition reimbursements, career-related internships or fieldwork, Federal Work-Study, institutionally sponsored loans, scholarships/grants, tuition waivers (partial), and unspecified assistantships available. Support available to part-time students. Financial award applicants required to submit FAFSA. *Unit head:* Dr. Christopher Gardiner, Department Head, 734-487-1444, Fax: 734-487-2489, E-mail: cgardiner@emich.edu. *Application contact:* Dr. Bingwu Wang, Graduate Coordinator, 734-487-5044, Fax: 734-487-2489, E-mail: bwang@emich.edu. Web site: http://www.math.emich.edu.

Eastern Washington University, Graduate Studies, College of Science, Health and Engineering, Department of Computer Science, Cheney, WA 99004-2431. Offers computer and technology-supported education (M Ed); computer science (MS). Part-time programs available. *Faculty:* 13 full-time (1 woman). *Students:* 16 full-time (3 women), 9 part-time; includes 2 minority (1 Asian, non-Hispanic/Latino; 1 Hispanic/Latino), 1 international. Average age 31. 38 applicants, 16% accepted, 6 enrolled. In 2011, 7 master's awarded. *Degree requirements:* For master's, comprehensive exam, thesis or alternative. *Entrance requirements:* For master's, minimum GPA of 3.0. *Application deadline:* For fall admission, 4/1 priority date for domestic students; for spring admission, 1/15 for domestic students. Applications are processed on a rolling basis. Application fee: $50. *Financial support:* In 2011–12, 17 teaching assistantships with partial tuition reimbursements (averaging $12,000 per year) were awarded; career-related internships or fieldwork, Federal Work-Study, institutionally sponsored loans, scholarships/grants, health care benefits, tuition waivers (partial), and unspecified assistantships also available. Support available to part-time students. Financial award application deadline: 2/1. *Unit head:* Dr. Ray Hamel, Chair, 509-359-4758, Fax: 509-358-2061. *Application contact:* Dr. Timothy Rolfe, Adviser, 509-359-4276, Fax: 509-359-2215. Web site: http://www.ewu.edu/cshe/programs/computer-science.xml.

East Stroudsburg University of Pennsylvania, Graduate School, College of Arts and Sciences, Department of Computer Science, East Stroudsburg, PA 18301-2999. Offers MS. Part-time and evening/weekend programs available. *Degree requirements:* For master's, comprehensive exam, thesis or alternative. *Entrance requirements:* For master's, bachelor's degree in computer science or related field. Additional exam requirements/recommendations for international students: Required—TOEFL (minimum score 560 paper-based; 220 computer-based; 83 iBT).

East Tennessee State University, School of Graduate Studies, College of Business and Technology, Department of Computer and Information Sciences, Johnson City, TN 37614. Offers applied computer science (MS); information technology (MS). Part-time and evening/weekend programs available. *Faculty:* 16 full-time (3 women), 1 part-time/adjunct (0 women). *Students:* 33 full-time (2 women), 19 part-time (4 women); includes 2 minority (1 Hispanic/Latino; 1 Two or more races, non-Hispanic/Latino), 10 international. Average age 30. 42 applicants, 55% accepted, 15 enrolled. In 2011, 21 master's awarded. *Degree requirements:* For master's, comprehensive exam, thesis optional, capstone. *Entrance requirements:* For master's, GRE General Test, minimum GPA of 2.5, three letters of recommendation. Additional exam requirements/recommendations for international students: Required—TOEFL (minimum score 550 paper-based; 213 computer-based; 79 iBT). *Application deadline:* For fall admission, 6/1 for domestic students, 4/30 for international students; for spring admission, 11/1 for domestic students, 9/30 for international students. Application fee: $35 ($45 for international students). Electronic applications accepted. *Expenses:* Tuition, state resident: full-time $7312; part-time $350 per credit hour. Tuition, nonresident: full-time $18,490; part-time $621 per credit hour. *Required fees:* $63 per credit hour. Tuition and fees vary according to course load and program. *Financial support:* In 2011–12, 29 students received support, including 9 research assistantships with full tuition reimbursements available (averaging $9,000 per year), 15 teaching assistantships with full tuition reimbursements available (averaging $10,000 per year); career-related internships or fieldwork, institutionally sponsored loans, scholarships/grants, and unspecified assistantships also available. Financial award application deadline: 7/1; financial award applicants required to submit FAFSA. *Faculty research:* Security, enterprise resource planning, high performance computing, optimization, software engineering. *Unit head:* Dr. Terry Countermine, Chair, 423-439-5328, Fax: 423-439-7119, E-mail: counter@etsu.edu. *Application contact:* Bethany Glassbrenner, Graduate Specialist, 423-439-6165, Fax: 423-439-5624, E-mail: glassbrenner@etsu.edu.

École Polytechnique de Montréal, Graduate Programs, Department of Electrical and Computer Engineering, Montréal, QC H3C 3A7, Canada. Offers automation (M Eng, M Sc A, PhD); computer science (M Eng, M Sc A, PhD); electrical engineering (DESS); electrotechnology (M Eng, M Sc A, PhD); microelectronics (M Eng, M Sc A, PhD); microwave technology (M Eng, M Sc A, PhD). Part-time and evening/weekend programs available. *Degree requirements:* For master's, one foreign language, thesis; for doctorate, one foreign language, thesis/dissertation. *Entrance requirements:* For master's, minimum GPA of 2.75; for doctorate, minimum GPA of 3.0. *Faculty research:* Microwaves, telecommunications, software engineering.

Emory University, Laney Graduate School, Department of Mathematics and Computer Science, Atlanta, GA 30322-1100. Offers computer science (MS); computer science and informatics (PhD); mathematics (MS, PhD). *Faculty:* 27 full-time (4 women), 2 part-time/adjunct (0 women). *Students:* 44 full-time (12 women); includes 10 minority (9 Asian, non-Hispanic/Latino; 1 Hispanic/Latino), 15 international. Average age 24. 171 applicants, 23% accepted, 25 enrolled. In 2011, 1 master's, 3 doctorates awarded. Terminal master's awarded for partial completion of doctoral program. *Degree requirements:* For master's, thesis; for doctorate, one foreign language, comprehensive exam, thesis/dissertation. *Entrance requirements:* For master's and doctorate, GRE General Test. *Application deadline:* For fall admission, 1/3 priority date for domestic students, 1/3 for international students. Application fee: $50. Electronic applications accepted. *Expenses:* Tuition: Full-time $34,800. *Required fees:* $1300. *Financial support:* In 2011–12, fellowships (averaging $12,550 per year), teaching assistantships (averaging $16,480 per year) were awarded; scholarships/grants and tuition waivers also available. Financial award application deadline: 1/3. *Total annual research expenditures:* $1.1 million. *Unit head:* Dr. Vaidy Sunderam, Chairman, 404-727-5926, Fax: 404-727-5611, E-mail: vss@emory.edu. *Application contact:* Prof. James Lu, Director of Graduate Studies, 404-712-8638, Fax: 404-727-5611, E-mail: jlu@mathcs.emory.edu. Web site: http://www.mathcs.emory.edu/.

Fairleigh Dickinson University, College at Florham, Maxwell Becton College of Arts and Sciences, Department of Computer Science, Madison, NJ 07940-1099. Offers MS.

Fairleigh Dickinson University, Metropolitan Campus, University College: Arts, Sciences, and Professional Studies, School of Computer Sciences and Engineering, Program in Computer Science, Teaneck, NJ 07666-1914. Offers MS.

Fitchburg State University, Division of Graduate and Continuing Education, Program in Computer Science, Fitchburg, MA 01420-2697. Offers MS. Part-time and evening/weekend programs available. *Students:* 36 full-time (12 women), 21 part-time (6 women); includes 1 minority (Black or African American, non-Hispanic/Latino), 50 international. Average age 27. 51 applicants, 100% accepted, 27 enrolled. In 2011, 28 master's awarded. *Entrance requirements:* Additional exam requirements/recommendations for international students: Required—TOEFL (minimum score 550 paper-based; 213 computer-based; 79 iBT). *Application deadline:* For fall admission, 7/15 for international students; for spring admission, 12/1 for international students. Applications are processed on a rolling basis. Application fee: $25 ($50 for international students). Electronic applications accepted. *Expenses:* Tuition, state resident: full-time $2700; part-time $150 per credit. Tuition, nonresident: full-time $2700; part-time $150 per credit. *Required fees:* $2286; $127 per credit. *Financial support:* In 2011–12, research assistantships with partial tuition reimbursements (averaging $5,500 per year) were awarded; Federal Work-Study, scholarships/grants, and unspecified assistantships also available. Support available to part-time students. Financial award application deadline: 3/1; financial award applicants required to submit FAFSA. *Unit head:* Dr. Stephen Taylor, Chair, 978-665-3704, Fax: 978-665-3658, E-mail: gce@fitchburgstate.edu. *Application contact:* Kay Reynolds, Director of Admissions, 978-665-3144, Fax: 978-665-4540, E-mail: admissions@fitchburgstate.edu. Web site: http://www.fitchburgstate.edu.

Florida Atlantic University, College of Engineering and Computer Science, Department of Computer and Electrical Engineering and Computer Science, Boca Raton, FL 33431-0991. Offers computer engineering (MS, PhD); computer science (MS, PhD); electrical engineering (MS, PhD). Part-time and evening/weekend programs available. *Faculty:* 32 full-time (6 women), 4 part-time/adjunct (0 women). *Students:* 96 full-time (22 women), 106 part-time (21 women); includes 77 minority (16 Black or African American, non-Hispanic/Latino; 23 Asian, non-Hispanic/Latino; 35 Hispanic/Latino; 3 Two or more races, non-Hispanic/Latino), 43 international. Average age 33. 177 applicants, 41% accepted, 35 enrolled. In 2011, 48 master's, 6 doctorates awarded. Terminal master's awarded for partial completion of doctoral program. *Degree requirements:* For master's, thesis optional; for doctorate, thesis/dissertation, qualifying exam. *Entrance requirements:* For master's, GRE General Test, minimum GPA of 3.0; for doctorate, GRE General Test, master's degree, minimum GPA of 3.5. Additional exam requirements/recommendations for international students: Required—TOEFL. *Application deadline:* For fall admission, 7/1 priority date for domestic students, 2/15 for international students; for spring admission, 11/1 for domestic students, 7/15 for international students. Applications are processed on a rolling basis. Application fee: $30. *Expenses: Tuition, area resident:* Part-time $343.02 per credit hour. Tuition, state resident: full-time $8232. Tuition, nonresident: full-time $23,931; part-time $997.14 per credit hour. *Financial support:* Fellowships, research assistantships with partial tuition reimbursements, teaching assistantships with full tuition reimbursements, career-related internships or fieldwork, and Federal Work-Study available. Support available to part-time students. Financial award application deadline: 4/1; financial award applicants required to submit FAFSA. *Faculty research:* VLSI and neural networks, communication networks, software engineering, computer architecture, multimedia and video processing. *Unit head:* Dr. Borko Furht, Chairman, 561-297-3855, Fax: 561-297-2800. *Application contact:* Joanna Arlington, Manager, Graduate Admissions, 561-297-2428, Fax: 561-297-2117, E-mail: arlingto@fau.edu. Web site: http://www.ceecs.fau.edu/.

Florida Gulf Coast University, Lutgert College of Business, Program in Computer and Information Systems, Fort Myers, FL 33965-6565. Offers MS. *Faculty:* 51 full-time (14 women), 11 part-time/adjunct (2 women). *Students:* 5 full-time (1 woman), 4 part-time (0 women), 1 international. Average age 34. 8 applicants, 50% accepted, 3 enrolled. In 2011, 3 master's awarded. *Entrance requirements:* For master's, GMAT, minimum GPA of 3.0. Additional exam requirements/recommendations for international students: Required—TOEFL (minimum score 550 paper-based; 213 computer-based). *Application deadline:* For fall admission, 6/1 priority date for domestic students; for spring admission, 11/1 for domestic students. Applications are processed on a rolling basis. Application fee: $30. Electronic applications accepted. *Expenses:* Tuition, state resident: full-time $8289. Tuition, nonresident: full-time $28,895. *Required fees:* $1831. One-time fee: $30 full-time. *Faculty research:* Advanced distributed learning technologies, object-oriented systems analysis, database management systems, workgroup support systems, software engineering project management. *Unit head:* Dr. Rajesh Srivastava, Chair, 239-590-7372, Fax: 239-590-7330, E-mail: rsrivast@fgcu.edu. *Application contact:* Marisa Ouverson, Director of Enrollment Management, 239-590-7403, Fax: 239-590-7330, E-mail: mouverso@fgcu.edu.

Florida Institute of Technology, Graduate Programs, College of Engineering, Computer Science Department, Melbourne, FL 32901-6975. Offers computer information systems (MS); computer science (MS, PhD); software engineering (MS). Part-time and evening/weekend programs available. *Faculty:* 14 full-time (1 woman), 11 part-time/adjunct (1 woman). *Students:* 73 full-time (14 women), 63 part-time (14 women); includes 9 minority (4 Black or African American, non-Hispanic/Latino; 2 Asian, non-Hispanic/Latino; 2 Hispanic/Latino; 1 Two or more races, non-Hispanic/Latino), 81 international. Average age 29. 342 applicants, 64% accepted, 40 enrolled. In 2011, 37 master's, 4 doctorates awarded. *Degree requirements:* For master's, comprehensive exam (for some programs), thesis optional, final exam, seminar, or internship (for non-thesis option); for doctorate, comprehensive exam, thesis/dissertation, publication in journal, teaching experience (strongly encouraged), specialized research program. *Entrance requirements:* For master's, GRE General Test, minimum GPA of 3.0, 3 letters of recommendation; for doctorate, GRE General Test, GRE Subject Test in computer science (recommended), 3 letters of recommendation, minimum GPA of 3.5, resume, statement of objectives. Additional exam requirements/recommendations for international students: Required—TOEFL (minimum score 550 paper-based; 213 computer-based; 79 iBT). *Application deadline:* For fall admission, 4/1 for international students; for spring admission, 9/30 for international students. Applications are processed on a rolling basis. Application fee: $0. Electronic applications accepted. *Expenses:* Tuition: Full-time $19,620; part-time $1090 per credit hour. Tuition and fees vary according to campus/location. *Financial support:* In 2011–12, 1 research assistantship with full and partial tuition reimbursement (averaging $4,500 per year), 12 teaching assistantships with full and partial tuition reimbursements (averaging $12,103 per year) were awarded; career-related internships or fieldwork, institutionally sponsored loans, tuition waivers (partial), unspecified assistantships, and tuition remissions also available. Support available to part-time students. Financial award application deadline: 3/1; financial award applicants required to submit FAFSA. *Faculty research:* Artificial intelligence, software engineering, management and processes, programming languages, database systems. *Total annual research expenditures:* $741,031. *Unit head:* Dr. William D. Shoaff, Department Head, 321-674-8066, Fax: 321-674-7046, E-mail: wds@cs.fit.edu. *Application contact:* Cheryl A. Brown, Associate Director of Graduate Admissions, 321-674-7581, Fax: 321-723-9468, E-mail: cbrown@fit.edu. Web site: http://coe.fit.edu/cs.

Florida Institute of Technology, Graduate Programs, Extended Studies Division, Melbourne, FL 32901-6975. Offers acquisition and contract management (MS); aerospace engineering (MS); business administration (MBA); computer information systems (MS); computer science (MS); electrical engineering (MS); engineering management (MS); human resources management (MS); logistics management (MS), including humanitarian and disaster relief logistics; management (MS), including acquisition and contract management, e-business, human resources management, information systems, logistics management, management, transportation management; material acquisition management (MS); mechanical engineering (MS); operations research (MS); project management (MS), including information systems, operations research; public administration (MPA); quality management (MS); software engineering (MS); space systems (MS); space systems management (MS); supply chain management (MS); systems management (MS), including information systems, operations research. Part-time and evening/weekend programs available. Postbaccalaureate distance learning degree programs offered (no on-campus study). *Faculty:* 9 full-time (2 women), 105 part-time/adjunct (24 women). *Students:* 113 full-time (52 women), 1,150 part-time (484 women); includes 496 minority (332 Black or African American, non-Hispanic/Latino; 11 American Indian or Alaska Native, non-Hispanic/Latino; 42 Asian, non-Hispanic/Latino; 71 Hispanic/Latino; 2 Native Hawaiian or other Pacific Islander, non-Hispanic/Latino; 38 Two or more races, non-Hispanic/Latino), 11 international. Average age 35. 568 applicants, 56% accepted, 296 enrolled. In 2011, 471 master's awarded. *Degree requirements:* For master's, comprehensive exam (for some programs), capstone course. *Entrance requirements:* For master's, GMAT or resume showing 8 years of supervised experience, minimum GPA of 3.0, 2 letters of recommendation, resume. Additional exam requirements/recommendations for international students: Required—TOEFL (minimum score 550 paper-based; 213 computer-based; 79 iBT). *Application deadline:* For fall admission, 4/1 for international students; for spring admission, 9/30 for international students. Applications are processed on a rolling basis. Application fee: $0. Electronic applications accepted. *Expenses:* Contact institution. *Financial support:* Application deadline: 3/1; applicants required to submit FAFSA. *Unit head:* Dr. Theodore R. Richardson, III, Senior Associate Dean, 321-674-8123, Fax: 321-674-7597, E-mail: trichardson@fit.edu. *Application contact:* Carolyn Farrior, Director of Graduate Admissions, Online Learning and Off-Campus Programs, 321-674-7118, Fax: 321-674-8216, E-mail: cfarrior@fit.edu. Web site: http://es.fit.edu.

Florida International University, College of Engineering and Computing, School of Computing and Information Sciences, Miami, FL 33199. Offers computer science (MS, PhD); computing and information sciences (MS, PhD); telecommunications and networking (MS). Part-time and evening/weekend programs available. *Degree requirements:* For master's, thesis or alternative; for doctorate, comprehensive exam, thesis/dissertation. *Entrance requirements:* For master's and doctorate, GRE General Test, 3 letters of recommendation, minimum GPA of 3.0. Additional exam requirements/recommendations for international students: Required—TOEFL (minimum score 550 paper-based; 80 iBT). Electronic applications accepted. *Faculty research:* Database systems, software engineering, operating systems, networks, bioinformatics and computational biology.

Florida State University, The Graduate School, College of Arts and Sciences, Department of Computer Science, Tallahassee, FL 32306. Offers computer criminology (MS); computer network and system administration (MS); computer science (MS, PhD); information security (MS). Part-time programs available. *Faculty:* 17 full-time (1 woman), 2 part-time/adjunct (0 women). *Students:* 125 full-time (21 women), 5 part-time (1 woman); includes 11 minority (1 Black or African American, non-Hispanic/Latino; 1 American Indian or Alaska Native, non-Hispanic/Latino; 2 Asian, non-Hispanic/Latino; 7 Hispanic/Latino), 75 international. Average age 26. 294 applicants, 67% accepted, 52 enrolled. In 2011, 29 master's, 6 doctorates awarded. Terminal master's awarded for partial completion of doctoral program. *Degree requirements:* For master's, thesis or alternative; for doctorate, comprehensive exam, thesis/dissertation. *Entrance requirements:* For master's, GRE General Test, minimum undergraduate GPA of 3.0; for doctorate, GRE General Test, minimum GPA of 3.0. Additional exam requirements/recommendations for international students: Required—TOEFL (minimum score 550 paper-based; 213 computer-based; 80 iBT). *Application deadline:* For fall admission, 3/1 priority date for domestic students, 3/1 for international students; for spring admission, 10/1 priority date for domestic students, 10/1 for international students. Application fee: $30. Electronic applications accepted. *Expenses:* Tuition, state resident: full-time $9474; part-time $350.88 per credit hour. Tuition, nonresident: full-time $16,236; part-time $601.34 per credit hour. *Required fees:* $630 per semester. One-time fee: $20. Tuition and fees vary according to course load and campus/location. *Financial support:* In 2011–12, 103 students received support, including 9 fellowships with full tuition reimbursements available (averaging $17,500 per year), 18 research assistantships with full tuition reimbursements available (averaging $17,000 per year), 61 teaching assistantships with full tuition reimbursements available (averaging $16,250 per year); scholarships/grants, health care benefits, tuition waivers (partial), and unspecified assistantships also available. Financial award application deadline: 3/1; financial award applicants required to submit FAFSA. *Faculty research:* Embedded systems, high performance computing, networking, operating systems, security, databases, algorithms. *Total annual research expenditures:* $1.3 million. *Unit head:* Dr. Robert van Engelen, Chairman, 850-645-0309, Fax: 850-644-0058, E-mail: chair@cs.fsu.edu. *Application contact:* Kristan L. McAlpin, Graduate Coordinator, 850-645-4975, Fax: 850-644-0058, E-mail: mcalpin@cs.fsu.edu. Web site: http://www.cs.fsu.edu/.

Fordham University, Graduate School of Arts and Sciences, Department of Computer and Information Sciences, New York, NY 10458. Offers biomedical informatics (Advanced Certificate); computer science (MS). Part-time and evening/weekend programs available. *Faculty:* 11 full-time (1 woman). *Students:* 14 full-time (5 women), 11 part-time (2 women); includes 4 minority (1 Asian, non-Hispanic/Latino; 3 Hispanic/Latino), 7 international. Average age 32. 45 applicants, 56% accepted, 12 enrolled. In 2011, 13 master's awarded. *Degree requirements:* For master's, thesis optional. *Entrance requirements:* For master's, GRE General Test. Additional exam requirements/recommendations for international students: Required—TOEFL (minimum score 550 paper-based; 213 computer-based). *Application deadline:* For fall admission, 1/4 priority date for domestic students; for spring admission, 11/1 for domestic students. Application fee: $70. Electronic applications accepted. *Expenses: Tuition:* Full-time $30,480; part-time $1270 per credit. *Required fees:* $586; $293 per semester. *Financial support:* In 2011–12, 5 students received support, including 1 fellowship with tuition reimbursement available (averaging $21,800 per year), 4 research assistantships with tuition reimbursements available (averaging $18,400 per year); career-related internships or

fieldwork, institutionally sponsored loans, tuition waivers (full and partial), and unspecified assistantships also available. Financial award application deadline: 1/4; financial award applicants required to submit CSS PROFILE or FAFSA. *Faculty research:* Robotics and computer vision, data mining and informatics, information and networking, computation and algorithms, biomedical informatics. *Total annual research expenditures:* $7,000. *Unit head:* Dr. Damian Lyons, Chair, 718-817-4480, Fax: 718-817-4488. *Application contact:* Charlene Dundie, Director of Graduate Admissions, 718-817-4420, Fax: 718-817-3566, E-mail: dundie@fordham.edu.

Franklin University, Computer Science Program, Columbus, OH 43215-5399. Offers MS. Part-time and evening/weekend programs available. *Entrance requirements:* For master's, minimum undergraduate GPA of 2.75. Additional exam requirements/recommendations for international students: Required—TOEFL (minimum score 550 paper-based; 213 computer-based). Electronic applications accepted. *Expenses:* Contact institution.

Frostburg State University, Graduate School, College of Liberal Arts and Sciences, Department of Computer Science, Program in Applied Computer Science, Frostburg, MD 21532-1099. Offers MS. *Entrance requirements:* Additional exam requirements/recommendations for international students: Required—TOEFL. Electronic applications accepted.

Gannon University, School of Graduate Studies, College of Engineering and Business, School of Engineering and Computer Science, Program in Computer and Information Science, Erie, PA 16541-0001. Offers MCIS. Part-time and evening/weekend programs available. *Students:* 32 full-time (8 women), 15 part-time (2 women); includes 1 minority (Native Hawaiian or other Pacific Islander, non-Hispanic/Latino), 33 international. Average age 28. 405 applicants, 45% accepted, 13 enrolled. In 2011, 17 master's awarded. *Degree requirements:* For master's, research project or thesis. *Entrance requirements:* For master's, GRE or GMAT, letters of recommendation, resume. Additional exam requirements/recommendations for international students: Required—TOEFL (minimum score 79 iBT). *Application deadline:* Applications are processed on a rolling basis. Application fee: $25. Electronic applications accepted. *Financial support:* Career-related internships or fieldwork, Federal Work-Study, scholarships/grants, traineeships, and unspecified assistantships available. Financial award application deadline: 7/1; financial award applicants required to submit FAFSA. *Faculty research:* Refinement of software engineering processes, graph databases and bioinformatics, aspect-oriented programs and testing, software systems for healthcare applications, game programming. *Unit head:* Dr. Theresa Vitolo, Chair, 814-871-7126, E-mail: vitolo001@gannon.edu. *Application contact:* Kara Morgan, Director of Graduate Admissions, 814-871-5831, Fax: 814-871-5827, E-mail: graduate@gannon.edu.

George Mason University, Volgenau School of Engineering, Department of Computer Science, Fairfax, VA 22030. Offers computer games technology (Certificate); computer networking (Certificate); computer science (MS, PhD); database management (Certificate); electronic commerce (Certificate); foundations of information systems (Certificate); information engineering (Certificate); information security and assurance (MS, Certificate); information systems (MS); intelligent agents (Certificate); software architecture (Certificate); software engineering (MS, Certificate); software engineering for C41 (Certificate); Web-based software engineering (Certificate). MS program offered jointly with Old Dominion University, University of Virginia, Virginia Commonwealth University, and Virginia Polytechnic Institute and State University. *Faculty:* 40 full-time (9 women), 17 part-time/adjunct (0 women). *Students:* 208 full-time (52 women), 357 part-time (75 women); includes 98 minority (17 Black or African American, non-Hispanic/Latino; 63 Asian, non-Hispanic/Latino; 14 Hispanic/Latino; 4 Two or more races, non-Hispanic/Latino), 205 international. Average age 30. 882 applicants, 52% accepted, 137 enrolled. In 2011, 164 master's, 5 doctorates, 28 other advanced degrees awarded. *Degree requirements:* For master's, thesis optional; for doctorate, comprehensive exam, thesis/dissertation. *Entrance requirements:* For master's, GRE, proof of financial support; 2 official college transcripts; resume; self-evaluation form; official bank statement; photocopy of passport; 3 letters of recommendation; baccalaureate degree related to computer science; minimum GPA of 3.0 in last 2 years of undergraduate work; 1 year beyond 1st-year calculus; personal goals statement; for doctorate, GRE, personal goals statement; 2 official copies of transcripts; self-evaluation form; 3 letters of recommendation; photocopy of passport; proof of financial support; official bank statement; resume; 4-year baccalaureate degree with strong background in computer science. Additional exam requirements/recommendations for international students: Required—TOEFL (minimum score 575 paper-based; 230 computer-based; 88 iBT), IELTS, Pearson Test of English. *Application deadline:* For fall admission, 1/15 priority date for domestic students; for spring admission, 8/15 priority date for domestic students. Application fee: $65 ($80 for international students). Electronic applications accepted. *Expenses:* Tuition, state resident: full-time $8750; part-time $364.58 per credit. Tuition, nonresident: full-time $24,092; part-time $1003.83 per credit. *Required fees:* $2514; $104.75 per credit. *Financial support:* In 2011–12, 100 students received support, including 3 fellowships (averaging $18,000 per year), 50 research assistantships (averaging $15,232 per year), 47 teaching assistantships (averaging $11,675 per year); career-related internships or fieldwork, Federal Work-Study, scholarships/grants, unspecified assistantships, and health care benefits (full-time research or teaching assistantship recipients) also available. Support available to part-time students. Financial award application deadline: 3/1; financial award applicants required to submit FAFSA. *Faculty research:* Artificial intelligence, image processing/graphics, parallel/distributed systems, software engineering systems. *Total annual research expenditures:* $1.9 million. *Unit head:* Sanjeev Setia, Chair, 703-993-4098, Fax: 703-993-1710, E-mail: setia@gmu.edu. *Application contact:* Michele Pieper, Administrative Assistant, 703-993-9483, Fax: 703-993-1710, E-mail: mpieper@gmu.edu. Web site: http://cs.gmu.edu/.

Georgetown University, Graduate School of Arts and Sciences, Department of Computer Science, Washington, DC 20057. Offers MS. Part-time and evening/weekend programs available. *Degree requirements:* For master's, thesis optional. *Entrance requirements:* For master's, GRE, basic course work in data structures, advanced math, and programming; 3 letters of recommendation. Additional exam requirements/recommendations for international students: Required—TOEFL. Electronic applications accepted. *Faculty research:* Data mining, artificial intelligence, software engineering, security.

The George Washington University, School of Engineering and Applied Science, Department of Computer Science, Washington, DC 20052. Offers MS, D Sc. Part-time and evening/weekend programs available. *Faculty:* 19 full-time (4 women), 23 part-time/adjunct (4 women). *Students:* 166 full-time (51 women), 173 part-time (47 women); includes 48 minority (24 Black or African American, non-Hispanic/Latino; 3 American Indian or Alaska Native, non-Hispanic/Latino; 16 Asian, non-Hispanic/Latino; 3 Hispanic/Latino; 2 Native Hawaiian or other Pacific Islander, non-Hispanic/Latino), 184 international. Average age 30. 448 applicants, 89% accepted, 111 enrolled. In 2011, 91 master's, 11 doctorates awarded. *Degree requirements:* For master's, thesis optional;

for doctorate, thesis/dissertation, dissertation defense, qualifying exam. *Entrance requirements:* For master's, appropriate bachelor's degree, minimum GPA of 3.0; for doctorate, GRE (if highest earned degree is BS), appropriate bachelor's or master's degree, minimum GPA of 3.3. Additional exam requirements/recommendations for international students: Required—TOEFL or The George Washington University English as a Foreign Language Test. *Application deadline:* For fall admission, 3/1 priority date for domestic students; for spring admission, 10/1 for domestic students. Applications are processed on a rolling basis. Application fee: $75. *Financial support:* In 2011–12, 49 students received support. Fellowships with tuition reimbursements available, research assistantships, teaching assistantships with tuition reimbursements available, career-related internships or fieldwork, institutionally sponsored loans, and tuition waivers available. Financial award application deadline: 3/1; financial award applicants required to submit FAFSA. *Faculty research:* Computer graphics, multimedia, VLSI, parallel processing. *Unit head:* Abdou Youssef, Chair, 202-994-7181, E-mail: ayoussef@gwu.edu. *Application contact:* Adina Lav, Marketing, Recruiting and Admissions, 202-994-5827, Fax: 202-994-0909, E-mail: engineering@gwu.edu. Web site: http://www.cs.gwu.edu/.

Georgia Institute of Technology, Graduate Studies and Research, College of Computing, Atlanta, GA 30332-0001. Offers algorithms, combinatorics, and optimization (PhD); computational science and engineering (MS, PhD); computer science (MS, MSCS, PhD); human computer interaction (MSHCI); human-centered computing (PhD); information security (MS). Part-time programs available. Postbaccalaureate distance learning degree programs offered. Terminal master's awarded for partial completion of doctoral program. *Degree requirements:* For master's, thesis optional; for doctorate, comprehensive exam, thesis/dissertation. *Entrance requirements:* For master's, GRE General Test, GRE Subject Test, minimum GPA of 3.0; for doctorate, GRE General Test, GRE Subject Test, minimum GPA of 3.3. Additional exam requirements/recommendations for international students: Required—TOEFL. *Faculty research:* Computer systems, graphics, intelligent systems and artificial intelligence, networks and telecommunications, software engineering.

Georgia Southern University, Jack N. Averitt College of Graduate Studies, College of Information Technology, Statesboro, GA 30460. Offers computer science (MS). Postbaccalaureate distance learning degree programs offered. *Faculty:* 22 full-time (5 women), 1 part-time/adjunct (0 women). *Students:* 3 full-time (0 women), 34 part-time (11 women); includes 8 minority (4 Black or African American, non-Hispanic/Latino; 1 American Indian or Alaska Native, non-Hispanic/Latino; 2 Asian, non-Hispanic/Latino; 1 Two or more races, non-Hispanic/Latino), 1 international. Average age 32. 35 applicants, 89% accepted, 24 enrolled. *Expenses:* Tuition, state resident: full-time $6300; part-time $263 per semester hour. Tuition, nonresident: full-time $25,174; part-time $1049 per semester hour. *Required fees:* $1872. *Financial support:* In 2011–12, 2 students received support. *Faculty research:* Game programming, software engineering, database, Internet technology, knowledge systems. *Total annual research expenditures:* $50,000. *Unit head:* Dr. Ron Shiffler, Interim Dean, 912-478-7454, E-mail: shiffler@georgiasouthern.edu. *Application contact:* Amanda Gilliland, Coordinator of Graduate Student Recruitment, 912-478-5384, Fax: 912-478-0740, E-mail: gradadmissions@georgiasouthern.edu. Web site: http://cit.georgiasouthern.edu/.

Georgia Southwestern State University, Graduate Studies, School of Computer and Information Sciences, Americus, GA 31709-4693. Offers computer information systems (MS); computer science (MS). Part-time programs available. *Degree requirements:* For master's, thesis (for some programs). *Entrance requirements:* For master's, GRE General Test, minimum GPA of 3.0. Electronic applications accepted. *Faculty research:* Database, Internet technologies, computational complexity, encryption.

Georgia State University, College of Arts and Sciences, Department of Computer Science, Atlanta, GA 30302-3083. Offers MS, PhD. Part-time and evening/weekend programs available. Terminal master's awarded for partial completion of doctoral program. *Degree requirements:* For master's, comprehensive exam, thesis or alternative; for doctorate, thesis/dissertation, qualifying exam. *Entrance requirements:* For master's, GRE General Test, 3 letters of recommendation; for doctorate, 3 letters of recommendation. Additional exam requirements/recommendations for international students: Required—TOEFL. Electronic applications accepted. *Faculty research:* Computer networks, databases, artificial intelligence, bioinformatics, parallel and distributed computing, graphics and visualization.

Governors State University, College of Arts and Sciences, Program in Computer Science, University Park, IL 60484. Offers MS. Part-time and evening/weekend programs available. *Students:* 24 full-time (8 women), 19 part-time (4 women); includes 17 minority (10 Black or African American, non-Hispanic/Latino; 1 Asian, non-Hispanic/Latino; 2 Hispanic/Latino; 1 Native Hawaiian or other Pacific Islander, non-Hispanic/Latino; 3 Two or more races, non-Hispanic/Latino), 9 international. Average age 28. *Degree requirements:* For master's, thesis or alternative. *Entrance requirements:* For master's, minimum GPA of 2.75. *Application deadline:* For fall admission, 7/15 priority date for domestic students; for spring admission, 11/10 for domestic students. Applications are processed on a rolling basis. Application fee: $25. *Financial support:* Research assistantships, career-related internships or fieldwork, Federal Work-Study, institutionally sponsored loans, and scholarships/grants available. Support available to part-time students. Financial award application deadline: 5/1. *Unit head:* Dr. James Howley, Chair, Division of Liberal Arts, 708-534-7893. *Application contact:* Yakeea Daniels, Director of Admission, 708-534-4510, E-mail: ydaniels@govst.edu.

Graduate School and University Center of the City University of New York, Graduate Studies, Program in Computer Science, New York, NY 10016-4039. Offers PhD. Program offered jointly with College of Staten Island of the City University of New York. *Degree requirements:* For doctorate, one foreign language, thesis/dissertation. *Entrance requirements:* For doctorate, GRE General Test. Additional exam requirements/recommendations for international students: Required—TOEFL. Electronic applications accepted.

Grand Valley State University, Padnos College of Engineering and Computing, School of Computing and Information Systems, Allendale, MI 49401-9403. Offers computer information systems (MS), including databases, distributed systems, management of information systems, object-oriented systems, software engineering. Part-time and evening/weekend programs available. *Degree requirements:* For master's, thesis or alternative. *Entrance requirements:* For master's, GMAT or GRE General Test. Additional exam requirements/recommendations for international students: Required—TOEFL. Electronic applications accepted. *Faculty research:* Object technology, distributed computing, information systems management database, software engineering.

Hampton University, Graduate College, Department of Computer Science, Hampton, VA 23668. Offers MS. Part-time and evening/weekend programs available. *Degree requirements:* For master's, thesis or alternative. *Entrance requirements:* For master's, GRE General Test. *Faculty research:* Software testing, neural networks, parallel processing, computer graphics, natural language processing.

Harvard University, Graduate School of Arts and Sciences, School of Engineering and Applied Sciences, Cambridge, MA 02138. Offers applied mathematics (ME, SM, PhD); applied physics (ME, SM, PhD); computer science (ME, SM, PhD); engineering science (ME); engineering sciences (SM, PhD). Part-time programs available. Terminal master's awarded for partial completion of doctoral program. *Degree requirements:* For master's, thesis optional; for doctorate, comprehensive exam, thesis/dissertation. *Entrance requirements:* For master's and doctorate, GRE General Test, GRE Subject Test (recommended), 3 letters of recommendation. Additional exam requirements/recommendations for international students: Required—TOEFL (minimum score 80 iBT). Electronic applications accepted. *Expenses:* Tuition: Full-time $36,304. *Required fees:* $1186. Full-time tuition and fees vary according to program. *Faculty research:* Applied mathematics, applied physics, computer science and electrical engineering, environmental engineering, mechanical and biomedical engineering.

Hofstra University, College of Liberal Arts and Sciences, Department of Computer Science, Hempstead, NY 11549. Offers networking and security (MS); Web engineering (MS). Part-time and evening/weekend programs available. Postbaccalaureate distance learning degree programs offered (minimal on-campus study). *Faculty:* 4 full-time (1 woman), 3 part-time/adjunct (0 women). *Students:* 4 full-time (1 woman), 16 part-time (3 women); includes 4 minority (2 Black or African American, non-Hispanic/Latino; 1 Asian, non-Hispanic/Latino; 1 Hispanic/Latino), 2 international. Average age 31. 17 applicants, 88% accepted, 6 enrolled. In 2011, 9 master's awarded. *Degree requirements:* For master's, thesis optional, 30 credits; minimum GPA of 3.0. *Entrance requirements:* For master's, GRE, minimum GPA of 3.0. Additional exam requirements/recommendations for international students: Required—TOEFL (minimum score 550 paper-based; 213 computer-based; 80 iBT). *Application deadline:* Applications are processed on a rolling basis. Application fee: $70 ($75 for international students). Electronic applications accepted. *Expenses:* Tuition: Full-time $18,990; part-time $1055 per credit hour. *Required fees:* $970. Tuition and fees vary according to program. *Financial support:* In 2011–12, 12 students received support, including 6 fellowships with full and partial tuition reimbursements available (averaging $2,625 per year); research assistantships with full and partial tuition reimbursements available, Federal Work-Study, institutionally sponsored loans, scholarships/grants, tuition waivers (full and partial), and unspecified assistantships also available. Support available to part-time students. Financial award applicants required to submit FAFSA. *Faculty research:* Computer vision, programming languages, data mining, software engineering, computer security. *Unit head:* Dr. Simona Doboli, Chairperson, 516-463-4786, Fax: 516-463-5790, E-mail: cscxzd@hofstra.edu. *Application contact:* Carol Drummer, Dean of Graduate Admissions, 516-463-4876, Fax: 516-463-4664, E-mail: gradstudent@hofstra.edu. Web site: http://www.hofstra.edu/hclas.

Hood College, Graduate School, Programs in Computer and Information Sciences, Frederick, MD 21701-8575. Offers computer and information sciences (MS); computer science (MS); information security (Certificate). Part-time and evening/weekend programs available. *Degree requirements:* For master's, thesis. *Entrance requirements:* For master's, minimum GPA of 2.75. Additional exam requirements/recommendations for international students: Required—TOEFL (minimum score 575 paper-based; 231 computer-based; 89 iBT). Electronic applications accepted. *Faculty research:* Systems engineering, natural language, processing, database design, artificial intelligence and parallel distributed computing.

Howard University, College of Engineering, Architecture, and Computer Sciences, School of Engineering and Computer Science, Department of Systems and Computer Science, Washington, DC 20059-0002. Offers MCS. Offered through the Graduate School of Arts and Sciences. Part-time programs available. *Degree requirements:* For master's, thesis. *Entrance requirements:* For master's, GRE General Test, minimum GPA of 3.0. Additional exam requirements/recommendations for international students: Required—TOEFL (minimum score 213 computer-based). Electronic applications accepted. *Faculty research:* Software engineering, software fault-tolerance, software reliability, artificial intelligence.

Illinois Institute of Technology, Graduate College, College of Science and Letters, Department of Computer Science, Chicago, IL 60616-3793. Offers business (MCS); computer networking and telecommunications (MCS); computer science (MCS, MS, PhD); information systems (MCS); software engineering (MCS); teaching (MST). Part-time and evening/weekend programs available. Postbaccalaureate distance learning degree programs offered (no on-campus study). Terminal master's awarded for partial completion of doctoral program. *Degree requirements:* For master's, thesis optional; for doctorate, comprehensive exam, thesis/dissertation. *Entrance requirements:* For master's, GRE General Test (minimum scores: 1000 Quantitative and Verbal, 3.0 Analytical Writing), minimum undergraduate GPA of 3.0; for doctorate, GRE General Test (minimum scores: 1100 Quantitative and Verbal, 3.5 Analytical Writing), minimum undergraduate GPA of 3.0. Additional exam requirements/recommendations for international students: Required—TOEFL (minimum score 523 paper-based; 70 iBT). Electronic applications accepted. *Faculty research:* Algorithms, data structures, artificial intelligences, computer architecture, computer graphics, computer networking and telecommunications.

Indiana State University, College of Graduate and Professional Studies, College of Arts and Sciences, Department of Mathematics and Computer Science, Terre Haute, IN 47809. Offers math teaching (MA, MS); mathematics and computer science (MA); mathematics and computer sciences (MS). Part-time programs available. *Degree requirements:* For master's, thesis or alternative. *Entrance requirements:* For master's, 24 semester hours of course work in undergraduate mathematics. Electronic applications accepted.

Indiana University Bloomington, School of Informatics and Computing, Program in Computer Science, Bloomington, IN 47405. Offers MS, PhD. *Faculty:* 33 full-time (6 women), 12 part-time/adjunct (1 woman). *Students:* 248 full-time (44 women), 15 part-time (4 women); includes 8 minority (2 Black or African American, non-Hispanic/Latino; 4 Asian, non-Hispanic/Latino; 1 Hispanic/Latino; 1 Two or more races, non-Hispanic/Latino), 208 international. Average age 27. 510 applicants, 60% accepted, 122 enrolled. In 2011, 73 master's, 13 doctorates awarded. Terminal master's awarded for partial completion of doctoral program. *Degree requirements:* For master's, thesis optional; for doctorate, comprehensive exam, thesis/dissertation, oral and written exams. *Entrance requirements:* For master's and doctorate, GRE General Test. Additional exam requirements/recommendations for international students: Required—TOEFL. *Application deadline:* For fall admission, 1/15 priority date for domestic students, 12/1 for international students. Application fee: $55 ($65 for international students). Electronic applications accepted. *Financial support:* In 2011–12, fellowships with full tuition reimbursements (averaging $25,000 per year), research assistantships with full tuition reimbursements (averaging $14,000 per year), teaching assistantships with full tuition reimbursements (averaging $14,000 per year) were awarded; health care benefits and unspecified assistantships also available. *Faculty research:* Artificial intelligence, database and information systems, distributed and parallel systems, foundations, programming languages and compilers. *Unit head:* Dr. Andrew Lumsdaine, Chairman, 812-855-7071, E-mail: lums@cs.indiana.edu. *Application contact:* Debbie Canada, Administrator, 812-855-6487, Fax: 812-855-4829, E-mail: gradvise@cs.indiana.edu. Web site: http://www.cs.indiana.edu/.

Indiana University–Purdue University Fort Wayne, College of Engineering, Technology, and Computer Science, Department of Computer Science, Fort Wayne, IN 46805-1499. Offers applied computer science (MS). Part-time programs available. *Faculty:* 12 full-time (0 women), 1 part-time/adjunct (0 women). *Students:* 7 full-time (2 women), 17 part-time (7 women); includes 2 minority (both Asian, non-Hispanic/Latino), 3 international. Average age 31. 11 applicants, 91% accepted, 6 enrolled. In 2011, 9 master's awarded. *Entrance requirements:* For master's, GRE General Test, minimum GPA of 3.0. Additional exam requirements/recommendations for international students: Required—TOEFL (minimum score 550 paper-based; 213 computer-based; 77 iBT); Recommended—TWE. *Application deadline:* For fall admission, 7/15 for domestic students, 5/15 for international students; for spring admission, 12/1 for domestic students, 10/15 for international students. Applications are processed on a rolling basis. Application fee: $55 ($60 for international students). Electronic applications accepted. *Financial support:* In 2011–12, 3 teaching assistantships with partial tuition reimbursements (averaging $12,930 per year) were awarded; career-related internships or fieldwork, scholarships/grants, and unspecified assistantships also available. Support available to part-time students. Financial award application deadline: 3/1; financial award applicants required to submit FAFSA. *Faculty research:* Elementary education astronomy with 3D visualization, index merging, semantic web queries. *Unit head:* Dr. Peter Ng, Chair, 260-481-6237, Fax: 260-481-5734, E-mail: ngp@ipfw.edu. *Application contact:* Dr. David Liu, Graduate Program Director, 260-481-0182, Fax: 260-481-5734, E-mail: liud@ipfw.edu. Web site: http://www.ipfw.edu/cs.

Indiana University–Purdue University Indianapolis, School of Science, Department of Computer and Information Science, Indianapolis, IN 46202-5132. Offers computer science (MS, PhD). Part-time and evening/weekend programs available. *Faculty:* 3 full-time (0 women). *Students:* 46 full-time (16 women), 60 part-time (9 women); includes 11 minority (2 Black or African American, non-Hispanic/Latino; 7 Asian, non-Hispanic/Latino; 2 Two or more races, non-Hispanic/Latino), 72 international. Average age 28. 131 applicants, 61% accepted, 25 enrolled. In 2011, 45 master's awarded. *Degree requirements:* For master's, thesis optional. *Entrance requirements:* For master's, GRE, BS in computer science or the equivalent. *Application deadline:* For fall admission, 1/15 priority date for domestic students; for spring admission, 9/15 for domestic students. Applications are processed on a rolling basis. Application fee: $55 ($65 for international students). Electronic applications accepted. *Financial support:* In 2011–12, fellowships (averaging $13,125 per year) were awarded; research assistantships with tuition reimbursements, teaching assistantships with tuition reimbursements, career-related internships or fieldwork, institutionally sponsored loans, and tuition waivers (full and partial) also available. Support available to part-time students. Financial award application deadline: 1/15; financial award applicants required to submit FAFSA. *Faculty research:* Artificial intelligence, graphics and visualization, computational geometry, database systems, distributed computing. *Unit head:* Mathew J. Palakal, Chair, 317-274-9727, Fax: 317-274-9742, E-mail: grad_advisor@cs.iupui.edu. *Application contact:* 317-274-9727, Fax: 317-274-9742, E-mail: admissions@cs.iupui.edu. Web site: http://www.cs.iupui.edu/.

Indiana University South Bend, College of Liberal Arts and Sciences, South Bend, IN 46634-7111. Offers applied mathematics and computer science (MS); applied psychology (MA); English (MA); liberal studies (MLS). Part-time and evening/weekend programs available. *Faculty:* 79 full-time (33 women). *Students:* 56 full-time (32 women), 115 part-time (80 women); includes 22 minority (18 Black or African American, non-Hispanic/Latino; 2 American Indian or Alaska Native, non-Hispanic/Latino; 2 Hispanic/Latino), 17 international. Average age 37. 67 applicants, 70% accepted, 35 enrolled. In 2011, 49 master's awarded. *Degree requirements:* For master's, thesis (for some programs). *Entrance requirements:* For master's, minimum GPA of 3.0. Additional exam requirements/recommendations for international students: Required—TOEFL. *Application deadline:* For fall admission, 7/31 priority date for domestic students, 7/1 for international students; for spring admission, 3/31 priority date for domestic students, 11/1 for international students. Applications are processed on a rolling basis. Application fee: $50 ($60 for international students). *Financial support:* In 2011–12, 5 teaching assistantships were awarded; Federal Work-Study also available. Support available to part-time students. *Faculty research:* Artificial intelligence, bioinformatics, English language and literature, creative writing, computer networks. *Total annual research expenditures:* $127,000. *Unit head:* Dr. Lynn R. Williams, Dean, 574-520-4322, Fax: 574-520-4528, E-mail: lwilliam@iusb.edu. *Application contact:* Admissions Counselor, 574-520-4839, Fax: 574-520-4834, E-mail: graduate@iusb.edu. Web site: https://www.iusb.edu/clas/index.php.

Instituto Tecnológico y de Estudios Superiores de Monterrey, Campus Central de Veracruz, Graduate Programs, Córdoba, Mexico. Offers administration (MA); administration of information technologies (MTI); computer sciences (MCC); education (MEE); educational institution administration (MAD); educational technology (MTE); electronic commerce (MCE); finance (MAF); humanistic studies (MEH); international business for Latin America (MNL); marketing (MMT); science (MCP); technology management (MTT). Part-time and evening/weekend programs available. Postbaccalaureate distance learning degree programs offered (minimal on-campus study). *Degree requirements:* For master's, thesis (for some programs). *Entrance requirements:* For master's, PAEP College Board. Electronic applications accepted.

Instituto Tecnológico y de Estudios Superiores de Monterrey, Campus Ciudad de México, Virtual University Division, Ciudad de Mexico, Mexico. Offers administration of information technologies (MA); computer sciences (MA); education (MA, PhD); educational technology (MA); environmental engineering (MA); environmental systems (MA); humanistic studies (MA); industrial engineering (MA); international business for Latin America (MA); quality systems (MA); quality systems and productivity (MA). Part-time and evening/weekend programs available. Postbaccalaureate distance learning degree programs offered (minimal on-campus study). *Entrance requirements:* For master's and doctorate, Instituto entrance exam. Additional exam requirements/recommendations for international students: Required—TOEFL.

Instituto Tecnológico y de Estudios Superiores de Monterrey, Campus Cuernavaca, Programs in Information Science, Temixco, Mexico. Offers administration of information technology (MATI); computer science (MCC, DCC); information technology (MTI).

Instituto Tecnológico y de Estudios Superiores de Monterrey, Campus Estado de México, Professional and Graduate Division, Estado de Mexico, Mexico. Offers administration of information technologies (MITA); architecture (M Arch); business administration (GMBA, MBA); computer sciences (MCS, PhD); education (M Ed); educational institution administration (MAD); educational technology and innovation (PhD); electronic commerce (MEC); environmental systems (MS); finance (MAF); humanistic studies (MHS); information sciences and knowledge management (MISKM); information systems (MS); manufacturing systems (MS); marketing (MEM); quality systems and productivity (MS); science and materials engineering (PhD); telecommunications management (MTM). Part-time programs available. Postbaccalaureate distance learning degree programs offered (minimal on-campus study). *Degree requirements:* For master's, one foreign language, thesis (for some programs); for doctorate, one foreign language, thesis/dissertation. *Entrance requirements:* For master's, E-PAEP 500, interview; for doctorate, E-PAEP 500, research proposal. Additional exam requirements/recommendations for international students: Required—TOEFL (minimum score 550 paper-based). *Faculty research:* Surface treatments by plasmas, mechanical properties, robotics, graphical computing, mechatronics security protocols.

Instituto Tecnológico y de Estudios Superiores de Monterrey, Campus Irapuato, Graduate Programs, Irapuato, Mexico. Offers administration (MBA); administration of information technology (MAIT); administration of telecommunications (MAT); architecture (M Arch); computer science (MCS); education (M Ed); educational administration (MEA); educational innovation and technology (DEIT); educational technology (MET); electronic commerce (MBA); environmental administration and planning (MEAP); environmental systems (MES); finances (MBA); humanistic studies (MHS); international management for Latin American executives (MIMLAE); library and information science (MLIS); manufacturing quality management (MMQM); marketing research (MBA).

Instituto Tecnológico y de Estudios Superiores de Monterrey, Campus Monterrey, Graduate and Research Division, Program in Computer Science, Monterrey, Mexico. Offers artificial intelligence (PhD); computer science (MS); information systems (MS); information technology (MS). Part-time programs available. *Degree requirements:* For master's, one foreign language, thesis; for doctorate, one foreign language, thesis/dissertation. *Entrance requirements:* For master's, EXADEP; for doctorate, master's degree in related field. Additional exam requirements/recommendations for international students: Required—TOEFL. *Faculty research:* Distributed systems, software engineering, decision support systems.

Inter American University of Puerto Rico, Guayama Campus, Department of Natural and Applied Sciences, Guayama, PR 00785. Offers computer security and networks (MS); networking and security (MCS).

Inter American University of Puerto Rico, Metropolitan Campus, Graduate Programs, Program in Open Information Systems, San Juan, PR 00919-1293. Offers MS. *Degree requirements:* For master's, 2 foreign languages.

International Technological University, Program in Computer Science, Santa Clara, CA 95050. Offers MS.

Iona College, School of Arts and Science, Program in Computer Science, New Rochelle, NY 10801-1890. Offers MS. Part-time and evening/weekend programs available. *Faculty:* 8 full-time (4 women), 1 part-time/adjunct (0 women). *Students:* 2 full-time (both women), 13 part-time (3 women); includes 5 minority (3 Black or African American, non-Hispanic/Latino; 2 Hispanic/Latino). Average age 37. 7 applicants, 57% accepted, 3 enrolled. In 2011, 7 master's awarded. *Degree requirements:* For master's, thesis or alternative. *Entrance requirements:* For master's, minimum GPA of 3.0. Additional exam requirements/recommendations for international students: Required—TOEFL (minimum score 550 paper-based; 213 computer-based). *Application deadline:* Applications are processed on a rolling basis. Application fee: $50. Electronic applications accepted. *Expenses:* Contact institution. *Financial support:* Tuition waivers (partial) and unspecified assistantships available. Support available to part-time students. Financial award application deadline: 4/15; financial award applicants required to submit FAFSA. *Unit head:* Dr. Robert Schiaffino, Chair, 914-633-2338, E-mail: rschiaffino@iona.edu. *Application contact:* Dr. Jeanne Zaino, Interim Dean, School of Arts and Science, 914-633-2112, Fax: 914-633-2023, E-mail: jzaino@iona.edu.

Iowa State University of Science and Technology, Department of Computer Science, Ames, IA 50011. Offers MS, PhD. *Degree requirements:* For master's, thesis; for doctorate, thesis/dissertation. *Entrance requirements:* For master's and doctorate, GRE General Test. Additional exam requirements/recommendations for international students: Recommended—TOEFL (minimum score 550 paper-based; 79 iBT), IELTS (minimum score 6.5). *Application deadline:* For fall admission, 1/1 priority date for domestic students, 1/1 for international students; for spring admission, 9/1 priority date for domestic students, 9/1 for international students. Application fee: $40 ($90 for international students). Electronic applications accepted. *Unit head:* Dr. Xiaoqiu Huang, Director of Graduate Education, 515-294-6516, Fax: 515-294-0258, E-mail: grad_adm@cs.iastate.edu. *Application contact:* Ying Cai, Director of Graduate Education, 515-294-6516, Fax: 515-294-0258, E-mail: grad_adm@cs.iastate.edu. Web site: http://www.cs.iastate.edu/.

Jackson State University, Graduate School, College of Science, Engineering and Technology, Department of Computer Science, Jackson, MS 39217. Offers MS. Part-time and evening/weekend programs available. *Degree requirements:* For master's, comprehensive exam, thesis. *Entrance requirements:* For master's, GRE General Test. Additional exam requirements/recommendations for international students: Required—TOEFL (minimum score 520 paper-based; 195 computer-based; 67 iBT).

Jacksonville State University, College of Graduate Studies and Continuing Education, College of Arts and Sciences, Program in Computer Systems and Software Design, Jacksonville, AL 36265-1602. Offers MS. Part-time and evening/weekend programs available. *Degree requirements:* For master's, comprehensive exam, thesis (for some programs). Electronic applications accepted. *Expenses:* Tuition, state resident: part-time $336 per hour. Tuition, nonresident: part-time $672 per hour. Part-time tuition and fees vary according to degree level.

James Madison University, The Graduate School, College of Integrated Science and Technology, Department of Computer Science, Harrisonburg, VA 22807. Offers MS. Postbaccalaureate distance learning degree programs offered. *Faculty:* 8 full-time (0 women), 2 part-time/adjunct (1 woman). *Students:* 16 full-time (3 women), 51 part-time (4 women); includes 8 minority (3 Black or African American, non-Hispanic/Latino; 4 Asian, non-Hispanic/Latino; 1 Hispanic/Latino), 4 international. Average age 27. In 2011, 20 master's awarded. *Degree requirements:* For master's, thesis or alternative. *Entrance requirements:* For master's, GRE General Test. Additional exam requirements/recommendations for international students: Required—TOEFL. *Application deadline:* For fall admission, 5/1 priority date for domestic students; for spring admission, 9/1 priority date for domestic students. Applications are processed on a rolling basis. Application fee: $55. Electronic applications accepted. *Expenses:* Tuition, state resident: full-time $8016; part-time $334 per credit hour. Tuition, nonresident: full-time $22,656; part-time $944 per credit hour. *Financial support:* In 2011–12, 9 students received support. Federal Work-Study and 9 graduate assistantships ($7382) available. Financial award application deadline: 3/1; financial award applicants required to submit

FAFSA. *Unit head:* Dr. Sharon J. Simmons, Academic Unit Head, 540-568-4196. *Application contact:* Katherine R. Laycock, Graduate Coordinator, 540-568-8772.

The Johns Hopkins University, Engineering Program for Professionals, Part-Time Program in Computer Science, Baltimore, MD 21218-2699. Offers bioinformatics (MS); computer science (MS, Post-Master's Certificate); telecommunications and networking (MS). Part-time and evening/weekend programs available. Postbaccalaureate distance learning degree programs offered (no on-campus study). Electronic applications accepted.

The Johns Hopkins University, Whiting School of Engineering, Department of Computer Science, Baltimore, MD 21218-2699. Offers MSE, PhD. Terminal master's awarded for partial completion of doctoral program. *Degree requirements:* For master's, thesis optional; for doctorate, comprehensive exam, thesis/dissertation, oral exam. *Entrance requirements:* For master's and doctorate, GRE General Test. Additional exam requirements/recommendations for international students: Required—TOEFL (minimum score 600 paper-based; 250 computer-based). Electronic applications accepted. *Faculty research:* Computer medical systems, networks/distributed systems, algorithms, security, natural language processing.

The Johns Hopkins University, Whiting School of Engineering, Program in Engineering Management, Baltimore, MD 21218-2699. Offers biomaterials (MSEM); communications science (MSEM); computer science (MSEM); fluid mechanics (MSEM); materials science and engineering (MSEM); mechanical engineering (MSEM); mechanics and materials (MSEM); nano-biotechnology (MSEM); nanomaterials and nanotechnology (MSEM); probability and statistics (MSEM); smart product and device design (MSEM); systems analysis, management and environmental policy (MSEM). *Entrance requirements:* For master's, GRE, 3 letters of recommendation, resume. Additional exam requirements/recommendations for international students: Required—TOEFL (minimum score 600 paper-based; 250 computer-based; 100 iBT) or IELTS (minimum score 7). Electronic applications accepted.

Kansas State University, Graduate School, College of Engineering, Department of Computing and Information Sciences, Manhattan, KS 66506. Offers computer science (MS, PhD); software engineering (MSE). Part-time programs available. Postbaccalaureate distance learning degree programs offered (minimal on-campus study). *Faculty:* 15 full-time (1 woman), 1 part-time/adjunct (0 women). *Students:* 64 full-time (18 women), 19 part-time (2 women); includes 1 minority (Two or more races, non-Hispanic/Latino), 60 international. Average age 27. 258 applicants, 24% accepted, 12 enrolled. In 2011, 31 degrees awarded. Terminal master's awarded for partial completion of doctoral program. *Degree requirements:* For master's, thesis or alternative; for doctorate, thesis/dissertation, preliminary exams. *Entrance requirements:* For master's, GRE, bachelor's degree in computer science, minimum GPA of 3.0; for doctorate, GRE General Test, GRE Subject Test, master's degree in computer science or bachelor's degree and strong advanced computer knowledge. Additional exam requirements/recommendations for international students: Required—TOEFL (minimum score 575 paper-based; 233 computer-based; 90 iBT). *Application deadline:* For fall admission, 2/1 priority date for domestic students, 2/1 for international students; for spring admission, 8/1 priority date for domestic students, 8/1 for international students. Applications are processed on a rolling basis. Application fee: $40 ($55 for international students). Electronic applications accepted. *Financial support:* In 2011–12, 9 fellowships (averaging $30,000 per year), 22 research assistantships (averaging $17,820 per year), 22 teaching assistantships with full tuition reimbursements (averaging $16,000 per year) were awarded; career-related internships or fieldwork, institutionally sponsored loans, scholarships/grants, health care benefits, and unspecified assistantships also available. Support available to part-time students. Financial award application deadline: 3/15; financial award applicants required to submit FAFSA. *Faculty research:* High-assurance software and programming languages, data mining, parallel and distributed computing, computer security, embedded systems. *Total annual research expenditures:* $2.2 million. *Unit head:* Dr. Gurdip E. Singh, Head, 785-532-7945, Fax: 785-532-7353, E-mail: gurdip@ksu.edu. *Application contact:* Susan Cregg, Program Coordinator, 785-532-6350, Fax: 785-532-7353, E-mail: scregg@ksu.edu. Web site: http://www.cis.ksu.edu/.

Kennesaw State University, College of Science and Mathematics, Program in Computer Science, Kennesaw, GA 30144-5591. Offers MS. Part-time programs available. Postbaccalaureate distance learning degree programs offered (minimal on-campus study). *Students:* 18 full-time (4 women), 13 part-time (6 women); includes 8 minority (5 Black or African American, non-Hispanic/Latino; 2 Asian, non-Hispanic/Latino; 1 Hispanic/Latino), 8 international. Average age 33. 17 applicants, 29% accepted, 0 enrolled. In 2011, 24 master's awarded. *Entrance requirements:* For master's, GMAT or GRE, minimum GPA of 2.75. Additional exam requirements/recommendations for international students: Required—TOEFL (minimum score 550 paper-based; 213 computer-based; 80 iBT), IELTS (minimum score 6). *Application deadline:* For fall admission, 7/1 priority date for domestic students, 7/1 for international students; for spring admission, 12/1 priority date for domestic students, 12/1 for international students. Applications are processed on a rolling basis. Application fee: $60. Electronic applications accepted. *Expenses:* Contact institution. *Financial support:* In 2011–12, 2 research assistantships with full tuition reimbursements (averaging $4,000 per year) were awarded; Federal Work-Study and unspecified assistantships also available. Support available to part-time students. Financial award application deadline: 4/1; financial award applicants required to submit FAFSA. *Unit head:* Dr. Victor Clincy, Director, 770-420-4440, E-mail: vclincy@kennesaw.edu. *Application contact:* Tamara Hutto, Admissions Counselor, 770-420-4377, Fax: 770-423-6885, E-mail: ksugrad@kennesaw.edu.

Kent State University, College of Arts and Sciences, Department of Computer Science, Kent, OH 44242-0001. Offers MA, MS, PhD. Part-time and evening/weekend programs available. *Degree requirements:* For master's, thesis (for some programs); for doctorate, comprehensive exam, thesis/dissertation. *Entrance requirements:* Additional exam requirements/recommendations for international students: Required—TOEFL (minimum score 550 paper-based; 213 computer-based). Electronic applications accepted. *Expenses:* Tuition, state resident: full-time $8136; part-time $452 per credit hour. Tuition, nonresident: full-time $14,292; part-time $794 per credit hour. *Faculty research:* Distributed and parallel processing, networking, computational science, graphics and visualization, database and data mining.

Kentucky State University, College of Agriculture, Food Science and Sustainable Systems, Frankfort, KY 40601. Offers aquaculture (MS); environmental studies (MS). Part-time and evening/weekend programs available. *Faculty:* 10 full-time (1 woman), 1 part-time/adjunct (0 women). *Students:* 34 full-time (16 women), 32 part-time (6 women); includes 22 minority (15 Black or African American, non-Hispanic/Latino; 3 Asian, non-Hispanic/Latino; 1 Hispanic/Latino; 1 Native Hawaiian or other Pacific Islander, non-Hispanic/Latino; 2 Two or more races, non-Hispanic/Latino), 12 international. Average age 34. 55 applicants, 51% accepted, 18 enrolled. In 2011, 16 master's awarded. *Degree requirements:* For master's, comprehensive exam, thesis optional. *Entrance requirements:* For master's, GRE, GMAT. Additional exam requirements/recommendations for international students: Required—TOEFL (minimum score 525 paper-based; 173 computer-based). *Application deadline:* Applications are processed on a rolling basis. Application fee: $30 ($100 for international students). Electronic applications accepted. *Expenses:* Tuition, state resident: full-time $6192; part-time $344 per credit hour. Tuition, nonresident: full-time $9522; part-time $529 per credit hour. *Required fees:* $450; $25 per credit hour. Tuition and fees vary according to course load. *Financial support:* In 2011–12, 41 students received support, including 18 research assistantships (averaging $11,378 per year); career-related internships or fieldwork, scholarships/grants, tuition waivers (partial), and unspecified assistantships also available. Financial award application deadline: 4/15; financial award applicants required to submit FAFSA. *Unit head:* Dr. Teferi Tsegaye, Dean, 502-597-6310, E-mail: teferi.tsegaye@kysu.edu. *Application contact:* Dr. Titilayo Ufomata, Acting Director of Graduate Studies, 502-597-6443, E-mail: titilayo.ufomata@kysu.edu. Web site: http://www.kysu.edu/academics/collegesAndSchools/CAFSSS/.

Kentucky State University, College of Business and Computer Science, Frankfort, KY 40601. Offers business administration (MBA); computer science technology (MS). Part-time and evening/weekend programs available. Postbaccalaureate distance learning degree programs offered (minimal on-campus study). *Faculty:* 9 full-time (1 woman). *Students:* 24 full-time (9 women), 29 part-time (14 women); includes 26 minority (22 Black or African American, non-Hispanic/Latino; 2 Asian, non-Hispanic/Latino; 1 Hispanic/Latino; 1 Two or more races, non-Hispanic/Latino), 14 international. Average age 34. 72 applicants, 82% accepted, 15 enrolled. In 2011, 13 degrees awarded. *Degree requirements:* For master's, comprehensive exam, thesis optional. *Entrance requirements:* For master's, GMAT, GRE. Additional exam requirements/recommendations for international students: Required—TOEFL (minimum score 525 paper-based; 173 computer-based). *Application deadline:* Applications are processed on a rolling basis. Application fee: $30 ($100 for international students). Electronic applications accepted. *Expenses:* Tuition, state resident: full-time $6192; part-time $344 per credit hour. Tuition, nonresident: full-time $9522; part-time $529 per credit hour. *Required fees:* $450; $25 per credit hour. Tuition and fees vary according to course load. *Financial support:* In 2011–12, 17 students received support, including 11 research assistantships (averaging $13,449 per year); career-related internships or fieldwork, scholarships/grants, tuition waivers (partial), and unspecified assistantships also available. Financial award application deadline: 4/15; financial award applicants required to submit FAFSA. *Application contact:* Dr. Titilayo Ufomata, Acting Director of Graduate Studies, 502-597-6443, E-mail: titilayo.ufomata@kysu.edu.

Knowledge Systems Institute, Program in Computer and Information Sciences, Skokie, IL 60076. Offers MS. Part-time and evening/weekend programs available. Postbaccalaureate distance learning degree programs offered (minimal on-campus study). *Degree requirements:* For master's, comprehensive exam, thesis. *Entrance requirements:* Additional exam requirements/recommendations for international students: Required—TOEFL (minimum score 550 paper-based; 213 computer-based; 79 iBT). Electronic applications accepted. *Faculty research:* Data mining, web development, database programming and administration.

Kutztown University of Pennsylvania, College of Liberal Arts and Sciences, Program in Computer Science, Kutztown, PA 19530-0730. Offers MS. Part-time and evening/weekend programs available. *Faculty:* 7 full-time (4 women). *Students:* 11 full-time (4 women), 11 part-time (4 women); includes 2 minority (both Asian, non-Hispanic/Latino), 1 international. Average age 31. 14 applicants, 71% accepted, 7 enrolled. In 2011, 6 master's awarded. *Degree requirements:* For master's, comprehensive exam or thesis. *Entrance requirements:* For master's, GRE General Test. Additional exam requirements/recommendations for international students: Required—TOEFL (minimum score 550 paper-based; 79 iBT). *Application deadline:* For fall admission, 8/1 priority date for domestic students, 8/1 for international students; for spring admission, 12/1 priority date for domestic students, 12/1 for international students. Applications are processed on a rolling basis. Application fee: $35. Electronic applications accepted. *Expenses:* Tuition, state resident: full-time $7488; part-time $416 per credit. Tuition, nonresident: full-time $11,232; part-time $624 per credit. *Financial support:* Career-related internships or fieldwork, Federal Work-Study, scholarships/grants, and unspecified assistantships available. Financial award application deadline: 3/1; financial award applicants required to submit FAFSA. *Faculty research:* Artificial intelligence, expert systems, neural networks. *Unit head:* Linda L. Day, Chairperson, 610-683-4340, Fax: 610-683-4129, E-mail: day@kutztown.edu. *Application contact:* Kelly D. Burr, Associate Director, Graduate Admissions, 610-683-4200, Fax: 610-683-1393, E-mail: graduate@kutztown.edu.

Lakehead University, Graduate Studies, School of Mathematical Sciences, Thunder Bay, ON P7B 5E1, Canada. Offers computer science (M Sc); mathematical science (MA). Part-time and evening/weekend programs available. *Degree requirements:* For master's, thesis optional. *Entrance requirements:* For master's, minimum B average, honours degree in mathematics or computer science. Additional exam requirements/recommendations for international students: Required—TOEFL. *Faculty research:* Numerical analysis, classical analysis, theoretical computer science, abstract harmonic analysis, functional analysis.

Lamar University, College of Graduate Studies, College of Arts and Sciences, Department of Computer Science, Beaumont, TX 77710. Offers MS. Part-time programs available. *Faculty:* 6 full-time (2 women). *Students:* 29 full-time (4 women), 9 part-time (2 women); includes 1 minority (Asian, non-Hispanic/Latino), 33 international. Average age 26. 96 applicants, 60% accepted, 13 enrolled. In 2011, 11 master's awarded. *Degree requirements:* For master's, comprehensive exams and project or thesis. *Entrance requirements:* For master's, GRE General Test, minimum GPA of 3.3 in last 60 hours of undergraduate course work or 3.0 overall. Additional exam requirements/recommendations for international students: Required—TOEFL (minimum score 550 paper-based; 213 computer-based). *Application deadline:* For fall admission, 5/15 priority date for domestic students; for spring admission, 10/1 priority date for domestic students. Applications are processed on a rolling basis. Application fee: $25 ($50 for international students). *Expenses:* Tuition, state resident: full-time $5430; part-time $272 per credit hour. Tuition, nonresident: full-time $11,540; part-time $577 per credit hour. *Required fees:* $1916. *Financial support:* In 2011–12, 2 research assistantships with partial tuition reimbursements (averaging $6,000 per year), 4 teaching assistantships with partial tuition reimbursements (averaging $6,000 per year) were awarded; institutionally sponsored loans, scholarships/grants, and tuition waivers (partial) also available. Financial award application deadline: 4/1. *Faculty research:* Computer architecture, network security. *Unit head:* Dr. Lawrence J. Osborne, Chair, 409-880-8775, Fax: 409-880-2364, E-mail: osborne@hal.lamar.edu. *Application contact:* Daisy Estrella, Coordinator of Graduate Admissions, 409-880-8349, Fax: 409-880-8414, E-mail: gradmissions@hal.lamar.edu.

La Salle University, School of Arts and Sciences, Program in Computer Information Science, Philadelphia, PA 19141-1199. Offers MS. Part-time and evening/weekend programs available. *Entrance requirements:* For master's, GRE or MAT, 18 undergraduate credits in computer science, professional experience. *Expenses:* Contact institution. *Faculty research:* Human-computer interaction, networks, technology trends, databases, groupware.

Lawrence Technological University, College of Arts and Sciences, Southfield, MI 48075-1058. Offers computer science (MS); educational technology (MS); educational technology - training and performance (MA); integrated science (MSE); science education (MSE); technical and professional communication (MS). Part-time and evening/weekend programs available. *Faculty:* 9 full-time (5 women), 16 part-time/adjunct (8 women). *Students:* 5 full-time (1 woman), 79 part-time (48 women); includes 30 minority (18 Black or African American, non-Hispanic/Latino; 8 Asian, non-Hispanic/Latino; 1 Hispanic/Latino; 3 Two or more races, non-Hispanic/Latino), 6 international. Average age 37. 382 applicants, 66% accepted, 17 enrolled. In 2011, 32 master's awarded. *Degree requirements:* For master's, thesis (for some programs). *Entrance requirements:* For master's, GRE. Additional exam requirements/recommendations for international students: Required—TOEFL (minimum score 550 paper-based; 213 computer-based; 79 iBT). *Application deadline:* For fall admission, 6/27 priority date for domestic students, 5/23 for international students; for spring admission, 11/15 priority date for domestic students, 11/15 for international students. Applications are processed on a rolling basis. Application fee: $50. Electronic applications accepted. *Financial support:* In 2011–12, 25 students received support, including 3 research assistantships (averaging $18,480 per year); Federal Work-Study also available. Financial award application deadline: 4/1; financial award applicants required to submit FAFSA. *Unit head:* Dr. Hsiao-Ping Moore, Dean, 248-204-3500, Fax: 248-204-3518, E-mail: scidean@ltu.edu. *Application contact:* Jane Rohrback, Director of Admissions, 248-204-3160, Fax: 248-204-2228, E-mail: admissions@ltu.edu. Web site: http://www.ltu.edu/arts_sciences/graduate.asp.

Lebanese American University, School of Arts and Sciences, Beirut, Lebanon. Offers computer science (MS); international affairs (MA).

Lehigh University, P.C. Rossin College of Engineering and Applied Science, Department of Computer Science and Engineering, Bethlehem, PA 18015. Offers computer engineering (M Eng, MS, PhD); computer science (M Eng, MS, PhD, MBA/E); MBA/E. Part-time programs available. *Faculty:* 15 full-time (2 women). *Students:* 52 full-time (9 women), 20 part-time (4 women); includes 2 minority (both Asian, non-Hispanic/Latino), 53 international. Average age 28. 225 applicants, 36% accepted, 20 enrolled. In 2011, 17 master's, 4 doctorates awarded. *Degree requirements:* For master's, oral presentation of thesis; for doctorate, thesis/dissertation, qualifying, general, and oral exams. *Entrance requirements:* For master's, GRE General Test, minimum GPA of 3.0; for doctorate, GRE General Test, minimum GPA of 3.5. Additional exam requirements/recommendations for international students: Required—TOEFL (minimum score 550 paper-based; 213 computer-based; 79 iBT). *Application deadline:* For fall admission, 4/1 for domestic and international students; for spring admission, 11/1 for domestic and international students. Applications are processed on a rolling basis. Application fee: $75. Electronic applications accepted. *Expenses:* Contact institution. *Financial support:* In 2011–12, 2 fellowships with full tuition reimbursements (averaging $18,360 per year), 7 research assistantships with full tuition reimbursements (averaging $18,000 per year), 6 teaching assistantships with full tuition reimbursements (averaging $18,819 per year) were awarded. Financial award application deadline: 1/15. *Faculty research:* Artificial intelligence, networking-pattern recognition, multimedia e-learning/data mining/Web search, mobile robotics, bioinformatics, computer vision. *Total annual research expenditures:* $2.1 million. *Unit head:* Dr. Daniel P. Lopresti, Chairman, 610-758-5782, Fax: 610-758-4096, E-mail: dal9@lehigh.edu. *Application contact:* Judy Frenick, Graduate Coordinator, 610-758-3605, Fax: 610-758-4096, E-mail: jlf2@lehigh.edu. Web site: http://www.cse.lehigh.edu/.

Lehman College of the City University of New York, Division of Natural and Social Sciences, Department of Mathematics and Computer Science, Program in Computer Science, Bronx, NY 10468-1589. Offers MS. *Degree requirements:* For master's, one foreign language, thesis or alternative.

Long Island University–Brooklyn Campus, School of Business, Public Administration and Information Sciences, Department of Computer Science, Brooklyn, NY 11201-8423. Offers MS. *Entrance requirements:* For master's, GMAT or GRE General Test, 2 letters of recommendation. Additional exam requirements/recommendations for international students: Required—TOEFL (minimum score 500 paper-based; 173 computer-based). Electronic applications accepted.

Long Island University–C. W. Post Campus, College of Information and Computer Science, Department of Computer Science/Management Engineering, Brookville, NY 11548-1300. Offers information systems (MS); information technology education (MS); management engineering (MS). Part-time and evening/weekend programs available. *Degree requirements:* For master's, comprehensive exam, thesis or alternative. *Entrance requirements:* For master's, bachelor's degree in science, mathematics, or engineering; minimum GPA of 2.5. Additional exam requirements/recommendations for international students: Required—TOEFL (minimum score 500 paper-based; 173 computer-based). Electronic applications accepted. *Faculty research:* Inductive music learning, re-engineering business process, technology and ethics.

Louisiana State University and Agricultural and Mechanical College, Graduate School, College of Science, Department of Computer Science, Baton Rouge, LA 70803. Offers computer science (MSSS, PhD); systems science (MSSS). Part-time programs available. *Faculty:* 17 full-time (3 women). *Students:* 88 full-time (6 women), 16 part-time (6 women); includes 10 minority (5 Black or African American, non-Hispanic/Latino; 1 American Indian or Alaska Native, non-Hispanic/Latino; 4 Asian, non-Hispanic/Latino), 82 international. Average age 28. 126 applicants, 75% accepted, 20 enrolled. In 2011, 23 master's, 9 doctorates awarded. Terminal master's awarded for partial completion of doctoral program. *Degree requirements:* For master's, thesis; for doctorate, thesis/dissertation. *Entrance requirements:* For master's and doctorate, GRE General Test, minimum GPA of 3.0. Additional exam requirements/recommendations for international students: Required—TOEFL (minimum score 550 paper-based; 213 computer-based; 79 iBT) or IELTS (minimum score 6.5). *Application deadline:* For fall admission, 2/1 for domestic students, 5/15 for international students; for spring admission, 10/1 for domestic students, 10/15 for international students. Applications are processed on a rolling basis. Application fee: $50 ($70 for international students). Electronic applications accepted. *Financial support:* In 2011–12, 80 students received support, including 4 fellowships with full tuition reimbursements available (averaging $18,880 per year), 43 research assistantships with full and partial tuition reimbursements available (averaging $16,225 per year), 30 teaching assistantships with full and partial tuition reimbursements available (averaging $14,146 per year); Federal Work-Study, institutionally sponsored loans, health care benefits, and unspecified assistantships also available. Financial award application deadline: 2/1; financial award applicants required to submit FAFSA. *Faculty research:* Robotics, artificial intelligence, algorithms, database software engineering, high-performance computing. *Total annual research expenditures:* $1.3 million. *Unit head:* Dr. Bijaya S. Karki, Interim Chair, 225-578-1495, Fax: 225-578-1465, E-mail: bbkarki@lsu.edu. *Application contact:* Graduate Coordinator, 225-578-1495, Fax: 225-578-1465. Web site: http://www.csc.lsu.edu/.

Louisiana State University in Shreveport, College of Liberal Arts and Sciences, Program in Computer Systems Technology, Shreveport, LA 71115-2399. Offers MS. *Students:* 7 full-time (3 women), 3 part-time (1 woman). Average age 30. 9 applicants, 89% accepted, 3 enrolled. In 2011, 8 master's awarded. *Degree requirements:* For master's, thesis or alternative. *Entrance requirements:* For master's, GRE, programming course in high-level language, interview. Additional exam requirements/recommendations for international students: Required—TOEFL (minimum score 550 paper-based; 213 computer-based; 80 iBT). *Application deadline:* For fall admission, 6/30 for domestic and international students; for spring admission, 11/30 for domestic and international students. Applications are processed on a rolling basis. Application fee: $10 ($20 for international students). *Financial support:* In 2011–12, 2 research assistantships (averaging $5,000 per year) were awarded. *Unit head:* Dr. Krishna Agarwal, Program Director, 318-795-4283, Fax: 318-795-2419, E-mail: krishna.agarwal@lsus.edu. *Application contact:* Christianne Wojcik, Director of Academic Services, 318-797-5247, Fax: 318-798-4120, E-mail: yyarbrou@lsus.edu.

Louisiana Tech University, Graduate School, College of Engineering and Science, Department of Computer Science, Ruston, LA 71272. Offers MS. Part-time programs available. *Degree requirements:* For master's, thesis or alternative. *Entrance requirements:* For master's, GRE General Test, minimum GPA of 3.0 in last 60 hours. Additional exam requirements/recommendations for international students: Required—TOEFL. *Faculty research:* Computer systems organization, artificial intelligence, expert systems, graphics, program language.

Loyola University Chicago, Graduate School, Department of Computer Science, Chicago, IL 60660. Offers computer science (MS); information technology (MS); software engineering (MS). Part-time and evening/weekend programs available. *Faculty:* 10 full-time (1 woman), 10 part-time/adjunct (2 women). *Students:* 59 full-time (18 women), 29 part-time (8 women); includes 19 minority (9 Black or African American, non-Hispanic/Latino; 9 Asian, non-Hispanic/Latino; 1 Hispanic/Latino), 39 international. Average age 28. 129 applicants, 55% accepted, 29 enrolled. In 2011, 40 master's awarded. *Degree requirements:* For master's, thesis optional, ten courses. *Entrance requirements:* For master's, 3 letters of recommendation, transcripts, statement of purpose. Additional exam requirements/recommendations for international students: Required—TOEFL (minimum score 550 paper-based; 213 computer-based; 79 iBT) or IELTS (minimum score 6.5). *Application deadline:* For fall admission, 8/10 for domestic students, 5/15 for international students; for spring admission, 12/20 for domestic students, 9/15 for international students. Applications are processed on a rolling basis. Electronic applications accepted. *Expenses: Tuition:* Full-time $15,660; part-time $870 per credit hour. *Required fees:* $125 per semester. Tuition and fees vary according to course load and program. *Financial support:* In 2011–12, 20 students received support, including 1 fellowship (averaging $3,000 per year), 16 teaching assistantships with partial tuition reimbursements available (averaging $4,000 per year); career-related internships or fieldwork, Federal Work-Study, scholarships/grants, tuition waivers (partial), and unspecified assistantships also available. Financial award application deadline: 3/15. *Faculty research:* Software engineering, high performance computing, algorithms and complexity, parallel and distributed computing, databases and computer networks. *Total annual research expenditures:* $22,000. *Unit head:* Dr. Chandra Sekharan, Chair, 312-915-7985, Fax: 312-915-7998, E-mail: csekhar@luc.edu. *Application contact:* Cecilia Murphy, Graduate Program Secretary, 312-915-7990, Fax: 312-915-7998, E-mail: gradinfo-cs@luc.edu. Web site: http://cs.luc.edu.

Loyola University Maryland, Graduate Programs, College of Arts and Sciences, Department of Computer Science and Software Engineering, Baltimore, MD 21210-2699. Offers computer science (MS); software engineering (MS). Part-time and evening/weekend programs available. *Faculty:* 3 full-time (1 woman), 6 part-time/adjunct (0 women). *Students:* 5 full-time (1 woman), 59 part-time (16 women); includes 15 minority (7 Black or African American, non-Hispanic/Latino; 4 Asian, non-Hispanic/Latino; 2 Hispanic/Latino; 1 Native Hawaiian or other Pacific Islander, non-Hispanic/Latino; 1 Two or more races, non-Hispanic/Latino), 2 international. Average age 33. In 2011, 11 master's awarded. *Entrance requirements:* For master's, GRE General Test, GRE Subject Test (recommended). Additional exam requirements/recommendations for international students: Required—TOEFL (minimum score 550 paper-based; 213 computer-based). *Application deadline:* For fall admission, 8/1 for domestic students; for spring admission, 12/1 for domestic students. Application fee: $50. Electronic applications accepted. *Financial support:* Research assistantships and unspecified assistantships available. Financial award application deadline: 4/15; financial award applicants required to submit FAFSA. *Unit head:* David W. Binkley, Director of Graduate Programs, 410-617-2281. *Application contact:* Maureen Faux, Executive Director, Graduate Admissions, 410-617-5020, Fax: 410-617-2002, E-mail: graduate@loyola.edu.

Maharishi University of Management, Graduate Studies, Program in Computer Science, Fairfield, IA 52557. Offers MS. *Degree requirements:* For master's, thesis or alternative. *Entrance requirements:* For master's, GRE General Test, minimum GPA of 3.0. Additional exam requirements/recommendations for international students: Required—TOEFL. *Faculty research:* Parallel processing, computer systems in architecture.

Marist College, Graduate Programs, School of Computer Science and Mathematics, Poughkeepsie, NY 12601-1387. Offers computer science/software development (MS); information systems (MS, Adv C); technology management (MS). Part-time and evening/weekend programs available. Postbaccalaureate distance learning degree programs offered (minimal on-campus study). *Entrance requirements:* For master's, resume. Additional exam requirements/recommendations for international students: Required—TOEFL (minimum score 550 paper-based; 213 computer-based; 80 iBT); Recommended—IELTS (minimum score 6.5). Electronic applications accepted. *Faculty research:* Data quality, artificial intelligence, imaging, analysis of algorithms, distributed systems and applications.

Marquette University, Graduate School, College of Arts and Sciences, Department of Mathematics, Statistics, and Computer Science, Milwaukee, WI 53201-1881. Offers bioinformatics (MS); computational sciences (MS, PhD); computing (MS); mathematics education (MS). Part-time and evening/weekend programs available. Postbaccalaureate distance learning degree programs offered (minimal on-campus study). *Faculty:* 28 full-time (9 women), 10 part-time/adjunct (5 women). *Students:* 14 full-time (3 women), 77 part-time (18 women); includes 9 minority (2 Black or African American, non-Hispanic/Latino; 7 Asian, non-Hispanic/Latino), 24 international. Average age 30. 86 applicants, 65% accepted, 24 enrolled. In 2011, 15 master's, 1 doctorate awarded. Terminal master's awarded for partial completion of doctoral program. *Degree requirements:* For master's, thesis (for some programs), essay with oral presentation; for doctorate, comprehensive exam, thesis/dissertation, qualifying examination. *Entrance* *requirements:* For master's, official transcripts from all current and previous colleges/universities except Marquette, three letters of recommendation; for doctorate, GRE General Test, official transcripts from all current and previous colleges/universities except Marquette, three letters of recommendation. Additional exam requirements/recommendations for international students: Required—TOEFL (minimum score 530 paper-based; 78 computer-based). *Application deadline:* For fall admission, 1/15 for domestic and international students. Applications are processed on a rolling basis. Application fee: $50. Electronic applications accepted. *Expenses: Tuition:* Full-time $17,010; part-time $945 per credit hour. Tuition and fees vary according to program. *Financial support:* In 2011–12, 23 students received support, including 4 fellowships (averaging $1,375 per year), 5 research assistantships with full tuition reimbursements available (averaging $17,000 per year), 15 teaching assistantships with full tuition reimbursements available (averaging $17,000 per year); scholarships/grants, health care benefits, tuition waivers (full and partial), and unspecified assistantships also available. Support available to part-time students. Financial award application deadline: 2/15. *Faculty research:* Models of physiological systems, mathematical immunology, computational group theory, mathematical logic, computational science. *Total annual research expenditures:* $621,359. *Unit head:* Dr. Gary Krenz, Chair, 414-288-7573, Fax: 414-288-1578. *Application contact:* Dr. Francis Pastijn, Director of Graduate Studies, 414-288-5229. Web site: http://www.marquette.edu/mscs/grad.shtml.

Marquette University, Graduate School, College of Arts and Sciences, Program in Computing, Milwaukee, WI 53201-1881. Offers MS. Part-time and evening/weekend programs available. Postbaccalaureate distance learning degree programs offered (minimal on-campus study). *Students:* 4 full-time (0 women), 23 part-time (4 women); includes 2 minority (1 Asian, non-Hispanic/Latino; 1 Hispanic/Latino), 9 international. Average age 31. 17 applicants, 88% accepted, 11 enrolled. In 2011, 1 master's awarded. *Degree requirements:* For master's, thesis optional, enrollment in the Professional Seminar in Computing each term. *Entrance requirements:* For master's, official transcripts from all current and previous colleges/universities except Marquette, essay, three letters of reference. Additional exam requirements/recommendations for international students: Required—TOEFL (minimum score 530 paper-based; 78 computer-based). *Application deadline:* Applications are processed on a rolling basis. Application fee: $50. Electronic applications accepted. *Expenses: Tuition:* Full-time $17,010; part-time $945 per credit hour. Tuition and fees vary according to program. *Financial support:* In 2011–12, 1 teaching assistantship was awarded. Financial award application deadline: 2/15. *Unit head:* Dr. Thomas Kaczmarek, Director, 414-288-6734, E-mail: douglas.harris@marquette.edu. *Application contact:* Erin Fox, Assistant Director for Recruitment, 414-288-5319, Fax: 414-288-1902, E-mail: erin.fox@marquette.edu. Web site: http://www.comp.mu.edu/.

Massachusetts Institute of Technology, School of Engineering, Department of Electrical Engineering and Computer Science, Cambridge, MA 02139. Offers computer science (PhD, Sc D, ECS); computer science and engineering (PhD, Sc D); electrical engineering (PhD, Sc D, EE); electrical engineering and computer science (M Eng, SM, PhD, Sc D); SM/MBA. *Faculty:* 125 full-time (17 women). *Students:* 800 full-time (198 women), 3 part-time (1 woman); includes 181 minority (13 Black or African American, non-Hispanic/Latino; 1 American Indian or Alaska Native, non-Hispanic/Latino; 130 Asian, non-Hispanic/Latino; 30 Hispanic/Latino; 7 Two or more races, non-Hispanic/Latino), 365 international. Average age 26. 3,023 applicants, 12% accepted, 259 enrolled. In 2011, 209 master's, 101 doctorates, 5 other advanced degrees awarded. Terminal master's awarded for partial completion of doctoral program. *Degree requirements:* For master's and other advanced degree, thesis; for doctorate, comprehensive exam, thesis/dissertation. *Entrance requirements:* Additional exam requirements/recommendations for international students: Required—TOEFL (minimum score 250 computer-based; 100 iBT), IELTS (minimum score 7). *Application deadline:* For fall admission, 12/15 for domestic and international students. Application fee: $75. Electronic applications accepted. *Expenses: Tuition:* Full-time $40,460; part-time $630 per credit hour. *Required fees:* $272. *Financial support:* In 2011–12, 739 students received support, including 144 fellowships (averaging $31,200 per year), 492 research assistantships (averaging $30,000 per year), 120 teaching assistantships (averaging $31,200 per year); career-related internships or fieldwork, Federal Work-Study, institutionally sponsored loans, scholarships/grants, traineeships, health care benefits, and unspecified assistantships also available. *Faculty research:* Artificial intelligence and applications; robotics; computer architecture, software, systems, and networks; computation theory, cryptography, and algorithms; communications, control, signal processing, and optimization; devices, electronics, electrodynamics, and photonics; bioelectrical engineering; computational biology. *Total annual research expenditures:* $97.5 million. *Unit head:* Prof. Anantha P. Chandrakasan, Head, 617-253-4600, Fax: 617-258-7354, E-mail: hq@eecs.mit.edu. *Application contact:* Graduate Admissions, 617-253-4603, Fax: 617-258-7354, E-mail: grad-ap@eecs.mit.edu. Web site: http://www.eecs.mit.edu/.

McGill University, Faculty of Graduate and Postdoctoral Studies, Faculty of Science, School of Computer Science, Montréal, QC H3A 2T5, Canada. Offers M Sc, PhD.

McMaster University, School of Graduate Studies, Faculty of Engineering, Department of Computing and Software, Hamilton, ON L8S 4M2, Canada. Offers computer science (M Sc, PhD); software engineering (M Eng, MA Sc, PhD). Part-time programs available. *Degree requirements:* For master's, thesis. *Entrance requirements:* Additional exam requirements/recommendations for international students: Required—TOEFL (minimum score 550 paper-based; 213 computer-based). *Faculty research:* Software engineering; theory of non-sequential systems; parallel and distributed computing; artificial intelligence; complexity, design, and analysis of algorithms; combinatorial computing, especially applications to molecular biology.

McNeese State University, Doré School of Graduate Studies, College of Science, Department of Mathematics, Computer Science, and Statistics, Lake Charles, LA 70609. Offers computer science (MS); mathematics (MS); statistics (MS). Evening/weekend programs available. *Faculty:* 13 full-time (4 women). *Students:* 17 full-time (7 women), 6 part-time (2 women); includes 1 minority (Black or African American, non-Hispanic/Latino), 9 international. In 2011, 17 master's awarded. *Degree requirements:* For master's, comprehensive exam, thesis or alternative, written exam. *Entrance requirements:* For master's, GRE. *Application deadline:* For fall admission, 5/15 priority date for domestic students, 5/15 for international students; for spring admission, 10/15 priority date for domestic students, 10/15 for international students. Applications are processed on a rolling basis. Application fee: $20 ($30 for international students). *Expenses:* Tuition, state resident: part-time $519 per credit hour. Tuition and fees vary according to course load. *Financial support:* Teaching assistantships available. Financial award application deadline: 5/1. *Unit head:* Sid Bradley, Head, 337-475-5788, Fax: 337-475-5799, E-mail: sbradley@mcneese.edu. *Application contact:* Dr. George F. Mead, Jr., Interim Dean of Dore' School of Graduate Studies, 337-475-5396, Fax: 337-475-5397, E-mail: admissions@mcneese.edu.

Memorial University of Newfoundland, School of Graduate Studies, Department of Computer Science, St. John's, NL A1C 5S7, Canada. Offers M Sc, PhD. Part-time programs available. *Degree requirements:* For master's, thesis; for doctorate, comprehensive exam, thesis/dissertation, oral thesis defense. *Entrance requirements:* For master's, GRE (strongly recommended), honors degree in computer science or related field; for doctorate, GRE (strongly recommended), master's degree in computer science. Electronic applications accepted. *Faculty research:* Theoretical computer science, parallel and distributed computing, scientific computing, software systems and artificial intelligence.

Metropolitan State University, College of Arts and Sciences, St. Paul, MN 55106-5000. Offers computer science (MS); liberal studies (MA); technical communication (MS). Part-time and evening/weekend programs available. *Students:* 15 full-time (9 women), 129 part-time (81 women); includes 20 minority (6 Black or African American, non-Hispanic/Latino; 10 Asian, non-Hispanic/Latino; 4 Hispanic/Latino), 17 international. Average age 38. *Entrance requirements:* For master's, minimum GPA of 2.75, resume. Additional exam requirements/recommendations for international students: Required—TOEFL (minimum score 550 paper-based; 213 computer-based). *Application deadline:* For fall admission, 8/1 priority date for domestic students, 3/15 for international students; for winter admission, 10/15 for international students; for spring admission, 12/1 priority date for domestic students, 3/15 for international students. Applications are processed on a rolling basis. Application fee: $20. Electronic applications accepted. *Expenses:* Tuition, state resident: full-time $5799.06; part-time $322.17 per credit. Tuition, nonresident: full-time $11,411; part-time $633.92 per credit. Tuition and fees vary according to degree level, program and reciprocity agreements. *Financial support:* Research assistantships available. Financial award applicants required to submit FAFSA. *Unit head:* Dr. Becky Omdahl, Dean, 651-793-1443, Fax: 651-793-1446, E-mail: becky.omdahl@metrostate.edu. *Application contact:* Lucille Maghrak, Graduate Studies Coordinator, 651-793-1932, E-mail: lucille.maghrak@metrostate.edu.

Michigan State University, The Graduate School, College of Engineering, Department of Computer Science and Engineering, East Lansing, MI 48824. Offers computer science (MS, PhD). *Entrance requirements:* Additional exam requirements/recommendations for international students: Required—TOEFL. Electronic applications accepted.

Michigan Technological University, Graduate School, College of Sciences and Arts, Department of Computer Science, Houghton, MI 49931. Offers MS, PhD. Part-time programs available. *Faculty:* 16 full-time (4 women), 2 part-time/adjunct (1 woman). *Students:* 39 full-time (9 women), 8 part-time (3 women), 33 international. Average age 27. 142 applicants, 37% accepted, 12 enrolled. In 2011, 12 master's, 1 doctorate awarded. Terminal master's awarded for partial completion of doctoral program. *Degree requirements:* For master's, comprehensive exam (for some programs), thesis (for some programs); for doctorate, comprehensive exam, thesis/dissertation. *Entrance requirements:* For master's and doctorate, GRE, statement of purpose, official transcripts, 3 letters of recommendation. Additional exam requirements/recommendations for international students: Required—TOEFL (minimum score 90 iBT) or IELTS. *Application deadline:* For fall admission, 7/1 priority date for domestic students, 7/1 for international students; for spring admission, 11/1 for domestic and international students. Applications are processed on a rolling basis. Electronic applications accepted. *Expenses:* Contact institution. *Financial support:* In 2011–12, 32 students received support, including fellowships with full tuition reimbursements available (averaging $6,065 per year), 11 research assistantships with full tuition reimbursements available (averaging $6,065 per year), 11 teaching assistantships with full tuition reimbursements available (averaging $6,065 per year); career-related internships or fieldwork, Federal Work-Study, scholarships/grants, health care benefits, tuition waivers (partial), unspecified assistantships, and cooperative program also available. Financial award applicants required to submit FAFSA. *Faculty research:* Artificial intelligence, graphics/visualization, software engineering, architecture and compiler optimization, human computing interaction. *Total annual research expenditures:* $333,451. *Unit head:* Dr. Steven M. Carr, Department Chair, 906-487-2209, Fax: 906-487-2283, E-mail: carr@mtu.edu. *Application contact:* Sandy J. Kalcich, Graduate Program Coordinator, 906-487-2109, Fax: 906-487-2283, E-mail: sjkalcic@mtu.edu. Web site: http://www.mtu.edu/cs/.

Middle Tennessee State University, College of Graduate Studies, College of Basic and Applied Sciences, Department of Computer Science, Murfreesboro, TN 37132. Offers MS. Part-time and evening/weekend programs available. Postbaccalaureate distance learning degree programs offered. *Faculty:* 11 full-time (4 women). *Students:* 28 part-time (6 women); includes 7 minority (2 Black or African American, non-Hispanic/Latino; 4 Asian, non-Hispanic/Latino; 1 Hispanic/Latino). Average age 27. 56 applicants, 39% accepted. In 2011, 9 master's awarded. *Degree requirements:* For master's, comprehensive exam, thesis. *Entrance requirements:* For master's, GRE. Additional exam requirements/recommendations for international students: Required—TOEFL (minimum score 525 paper-based; 195 computer-based; 71 iBT) or IELTS (minimum score 6). *Application deadline:* For fall admission, 6/1 for domestic and international students. Applications are processed on a rolling basis. Application fee: $25 ($30 for international students). Electronic applications accepted. *Expenses:* Tuition, state resident: full-time $10,008. Tuition, nonresident: full-time $25,056. *Financial support:* In 2011–12, 10 students received support. Tuition waivers available. Support available to part-time students. Financial award application deadline: 5/1; financial award applicants required to submit FAFSA. *Faculty research:* Computational science, parallel processing, AI. *Unit head:* Dr. Chrisila C. Pettey, Chair, 615-898-2397, Fax: 615-898-5567, E-mail: chrisila.pettey@mtsu.edu. *Application contact:* Dr. Michael D. Allen, Dean and Vice Provost for Research, 615-898-2840, Fax: 615-904-8020, E-mail: michael.allen@mtsu.edu.

Midwestern State University, Graduate Studies, College of Science and Mathematics, Computer Science Program, Wichita Falls, TX 76308. Offers MS. Part-time and evening/weekend programs available. *Degree requirements:* For master's, comprehensive exam, thesis. *Entrance requirements:* For master's, GRE General Test. Additional exam requirements/recommendations for international students: Required—TOEFL (minimum score 573 paper-based; 230 computer-based). Electronic applications accepted. *Faculty research:* Software engineering, genetic algorithms and graphics, ASIC design, computational epidemiology, new ways of GPS use.

Mills College, Graduate Studies, Program in Computer Science, Oakland, CA 94613-1000. Offers computer science (Certificate); interdisciplinary computer science (MA). Part-time programs available. *Faculty:* 7 full-time (6 women), 1 part-time/adjunct (0 women). *Students:* 13 full-time (6 women), 2 part-time (both women); includes 4 minority (1 Black or African American, non-Hispanic/Latino; 2 Asian, non-Hispanic/Latino; 1 Hispanic/Latino), 1 international. Average age 29. 12 applicants, 83% accepted, 7 enrolled. In 2011, 2 degrees awarded. *Degree requirements:* For master's, thesis. *Entrance requirements:* For master's, three letters of recommendation. Additional exam requirements/recommendations for international students: Required—TOEFL (minimum score 600 paper-based; 100 iBT) or IELTS (minimum score 7). *Application deadline:* For fall admission, 2/1 priority date for domestic students, 12/15 for international students; for spring admission, 11/1 priority date for domestic students, 10/1 for international students. Applications are processed on a rolling basis. Application fee: $50. Electronic applications accepted. *Expenses: Tuition:* Full-time $28,280; part-time $15,640 per year. *Required fees:* $958. Tuition and fees vary according to program. *Financial support:* In 2011–12, 12 teaching assistantships with full and partial tuition reimbursements (averaging $6,330 per year) were awarded; career-related internships or fieldwork, institutionally sponsored loans, and scholarships/grants also available. Support available to part-time students. Financial award application deadline: 2/1; financial award applicants required to submit FAFSA. *Faculty research:* Dynamical systems, linear programming, theory of computer viruses, interface design, intelligent tutoring systems. *Unit head:* Susan S. Wang, Department Head, 510-430-2138, E-mail: wang@mills.edu. *Application contact:* Tiana Kozoil, Graduate Admission Specialist, 510-430-3305, Fax: 510-430-2159, E-mail: grad-studies@mills.edu. Web site: http://www.mills.edu/ics.

Mississippi College, Graduate School, College of Arts and Sciences, School of Science and Mathematics, Department of Computer Science, Clinton, MS 39058. Offers M Ed, MS. Part-time programs available. *Degree requirements:* For master's, comprehensive exam, thesis or alternative. *Entrance requirements:* For master's, GRE. Additional exam requirements/recommendations for international students: Recommended—TOEFL, IELTS.

Mississippi State University, Bagley College of Engineering, Department of Computer Science and Engineering, Mississippi State, MS 39762. Offers computer science (MS, PhD). Part-time programs available. Postbaccalaureate distance learning degree programs offered (minimal on-campus study). *Faculty:* 15 full-time (2 women), 1 (woman) part-time/adjunct. *Students:* 62 full-time (9 women), 26 part-time (6 women); includes 13 minority (9 Black or African American, non-Hispanic/Latino; 3 Asian, non-Hispanic/Latino; 1 Two or more races, non-Hispanic/Latino), 31 international. Average age 29. 133 applicants, 23% accepted, 16 enrolled. In 2011, 15 master's, 4 doctorates awarded. *Degree requirements:* For master's, thesis, comprehensive oral or written exam; for doctorate, thesis/dissertation, comprehensive oral or written exam. *Entrance requirements:* For master's, GRE, minimum GPA of 2.75; for doctorate, GRE. Additional exam requirements/recommendations for international students: Required—TOEFL (minimum score 550 paper-based; 213 computer-based; 79 iBT); Recommended—IELTS (minimum score 6.5). *Application deadline:* For fall admission, 7/1 for domestic students, 5/1 for international students; for spring admission, 11/1 for domestic students, 9/1 for international students. Applications are processed on a rolling basis. Application fee: $40. Electronic applications accepted. *Expenses:* Tuition, state resident: full-time $5805; part-time $322.50 per credit hour. Tuition, nonresident: full-time $14,670; part-time $815 per credit hour. *Financial support:* In 2011–12, 23 research assistantships with full tuition reimbursements (averaging $13,277 per year), 12 teaching assistantships with full tuition reimbursements (averaging $12,092 per year) were awarded; Federal Work-Study, institutionally sponsored loans, and unspecified assistantships also available. Financial award application deadline: 4/1; financial award applicants required to submit FAFSA. *Faculty research:* Artificial intelligence, software engineering, visualization, high performance computing. *Total annual research expenditures:* $11.3 million. *Unit head:* Dr. Donna Reese, Professor and Department Head, 662-325-2756, Fax: 662-325-8997, E-mail: dreese@cse.msstate.edu. *Application contact:* Dr. Edward B. Allen, Associate Professor and Graduate Coordinator, 662-325-7449, Fax: 662-325-8997, E-mail: edward.allen@computer.org. Web site: http://www.cse.msstate.edu/.

Missouri State University, Graduate College, College of Natural and Applied Sciences, Department of Computer Science, Springfield, MO 65897. Offers MNAS. Part-time programs available. *Faculty:* 5 full-time (1 woman). *Students:* 5 full-time (1 woman), 2 part-time (0 women); includes 1 minority (Hispanic/Latino), 1 international. Average age 28. 2 applicants, 100% accepted, 2 enrolled. In 2011, 2 master's awarded. *Degree requirements:* For master's, comprehensive exam, thesis or alternative. *Entrance requirements:* For master's, GRE, minimum GPA of 3.0. Additional exam requirements/recommendations for international students: Required—TOEFL (minimum score 550 paper-based; 213 computer-based; 79 iBT). *Application deadline:* For fall admission, 7/20 priority date for domestic students, 5/1 for international students; for spring admission, 12/20 priority date for domestic students, 9/1 for international students. Applications are processed on a rolling basis. Application fee: $35 ($50 for international students). Electronic applications accepted. *Expenses:* Tuition, state resident: full-time $4086; part-time $227 per credit hour. Tuition, nonresident: full-time $8172; part-time $454 per credit hour. *Required fees:* $275 per semester. Tuition and fees vary according to course load, campus/location and program. *Financial support:* In 2011–12, 2 teaching assistantships with full tuition reimbursements (averaging $8,000 per year) were awarded; Federal Work-Study, institutionally sponsored loans, scholarships/grants, and unspecified assistantships also available. Financial award application deadline: 3/31; financial award applicants required to submit FAFSA. *Faculty research:* Floating point numbers, data compression, graph theory. *Unit head:* Dr. Kenneth Vollmar, Head, 417-836-4157, Fax: 417-836-6659, E-mail: computerscience@missouristate.edu. *Application contact:* Misty Stewart, Coordinator of Graduate Recruitment, 417-836-6079, Fax: 417-836-6200, E-mail: mistystewart@missouristate.edu. Web site: http://computerscience.missouristate.edu/.

Missouri University of Science and Technology, Graduate School, Department of Computer Science, Rolla, MO 65409. Offers MS, PhD. Part-time programs available. Terminal master's awarded for partial completion of doctoral program. *Degree requirements:* For doctorate, thesis/dissertation, departmental qualifying exam. *Entrance requirements:* For master's, GRE General Test (minimum score 700 quantitative, 4 writing); for doctorate, GRE Subject Test (minimum score: quantitative 600, writing 3.5). Electronic applications accepted. *Faculty research:* Intelligent systems, artificial intelligence software engineering, distributed systems, database systems, computer systems.

Monmouth University, The Graduate School, Program in Computer Science, West Long Branch, NJ 07764-1898. Offers MS. Part-time and evening/weekend programs available. *Faculty:* 4 full-time (2 women), 4 part-time/adjunct (0 women). *Students:* 40 full-time (11 women), 14 part-time (4 women); includes 2 minority (1 Hispanic/Latino; 1 Two or more races, non-Hispanic/Latino), 45 international. Average age 27. 137 applicants, 85% accepted, 22 enrolled. In 2011, 13 degrees awarded. *Degree requirements:* For master's, thesis optional. *Entrance requirements:* For master's, minimum GPA of 3.0 in major, 2.75 overall. Additional exam requirements/recommendations for international students: Required—TOEFL (minimum score 550 paper-based; 213 computer-based; 79 iBT), IELTS (minimum score 5) or Michigan English Language Assessment Battery (minimum score 77), Cambridge A, B, C. *Application deadline:* For fall admission, 7/15 priority date for domestic students, 6/1 for international students; for spring admission, 11/15 priority date for domestic students, 11/1 for international students. Applications are processed on a rolling basis. Application fee: $50. Electronic applications accepted. *Financial support:* In 2011–12, 45 students received support, including 41 fellowships (averaging $1,941 per year), 24 research assistantships (averaging $5,287 per year); career-related internships or fieldwork, scholarships/grants, and unspecified assistantships also available. Support available to part-time students. Financial award application deadline: 3/1; financial award applicants required to submit FAFSA. *Faculty research:* Databases, natural language processing, protocols, performance analysis, communications networks (systems), telecommunications. *Unit head:* Dr. Rich Scherl, Program Director, 732-571-4457, Fax: 732-263-5202, E-mail: rscherl@monmouth.edu. *Application contact:* Kevin Roane, Director, Office of Graduate Admission, 732-571-3452, Fax: 732-263-5123, E-mail: gradadm@monmouth.edu. Web site: http://www.monmouth.edu/academics/CSSE/mscs.asp.

Montana State University, College of Graduate Studies, College of Engineering, Department of Computer Science, Bozeman, MT 59717. Offers computer science (MS, PhD). Part-time programs available. *Degree requirements:* For master's, comprehensive exam; for doctorate, comprehensive exam, thesis/dissertation. *Entrance requirements:* For master's and doctorate, GRE. Additional exam requirements/recommendations for international students: Required—TOEFL (minimum score 550 paper-based; 213 computer-based). Electronic applications accepted. *Faculty research:* Applied algorithms, artificial intelligence, data mining, software engineering, Web-based learning, wireless networking and robotics.

Montclair State University, The Graduate School, College of Science and Mathematics, MS Program in Computer Science, Montclair, NJ 07043-1624. Offers CISCO (Certificate); informatics (MS); object oriented computing (Certificate). Part-time and evening/weekend programs available. *Students:* 11 full-time (6 women), 19 part-time (4 women); includes 7 minority (3 Black or African American, non-Hispanic/Latino; 3 Asian, non-Hispanic/Latino; 1 Hispanic/Latino), 7 international. Average age 31. 40 applicants, 45% accepted, 9 enrolled. In 2011, 9 master's awarded. *Degree requirements:* For master's, comprehensive exam, thesis or alternative. *Entrance requirements:* For master's, GRE General Test, 2 letters of recommendation, essay. Additional exam requirements/recommendations for international students: Required—TOEFL (minimum score 83 iBT) or IELTS (minimum score 6.5). *Application deadline:* For fall admission, 6/1 for international students; for spring admission, 10/1 for international students. Applications are processed on a rolling basis. Application fee: $60. Electronic applications accepted. *Financial support:* In 2011–12, 3 research assistantships with full tuition reimbursements (averaging $7,000 per year) were awarded; Federal Work-Study, scholarships/grants, and unspecified assistantships also available. Support available to part-time students. Financial award application deadline: 3/1; financial award applicants required to submit FAFSA. *Faculty research:* Software engineering, parallel and distributed systems, artificial intelligence, databases, human-computer interaction. *Unit head:* Dr. Michael Oudshoorn, Chairperson, 973-655-4166. *Application contact:* Amy Aiello, Director of Graduate Admissions and Operations, 973-655-5147, Fax: 973-655-7869, E-mail: graduate.school@montclair.edu. Web site: http://cs.montclair.edu/.

National University, Academic Affairs, School of Engineering, Technology and Media, Department of Computer Science, Information and Media Systems, La Jolla, CA 92037-1011. Offers computer science (MS); cyber security and information assurance (MS); management information systems (MS). Part-time and evening/weekend programs available. Postbaccalaureate distance learning degree programs offered (no on-campus study). *Degree requirements:* For master's, thesis. *Entrance requirements:* For master's, interview, minimum GPA of 2.5. Additional exam requirements/recommendations for international students: Required—TOEFL (minimum score 550 paper-based; 213 computer-based; 79 iBT), IELTS (minimum score 6). *Application deadline:* Applications are processed on a rolling basis. Application fee: $60 ($65 for international students). Electronic applications accepted. *Financial support:* Career-related internships or fieldwork, institutionally sponsored loans, scholarships/grants, and tuition waivers (partial) available. Support available to part-time students. Financial award application deadline: 6/30; financial award applicants required to submit FAFSA. *Unit head:* Dr. Alireza M. Farahani, 858-309-3438, Fax: 858-309-3420, E-mail: afarahan@nu.edu. *Application contact:* Dominick Giovanniello, Associate Regional Dean, 800-NAT-UNIV, Fax: 858-541-7792, E-mail: dgiovann@nu.edu. Web site: http://www.nu.edu/OurPrograms/SchoolOfEngineeringAndTechnology/ComputerScienceAndInformationSystems.html.

Naval Postgraduate School, Departments and Academic Groups, Department of Computer Science, Monterey, CA 93943. Offers computer science (MS, PhD); identity management and cyber security (MA); modeling of virtual environments and simulations (MS, PhD); software engineering (MS, PhD). Program only open to commissioned officers of the United States and friendly nations and selected United States federal civilian employees. Part-time programs available. Postbaccalaureate distance learning degree programs offered (minimal on-campus study). *Faculty:* 89 full-time (13 women), 26 part-time/adjunct (7 women). *Students:* 140 full-time (17 women), 14 part-time (5 women); includes 29 minority (9 Black or African American, non-Hispanic/Latino; 1 American Indian or Alaska Native, non-Hispanic/Latino; 10 Asian, non-Hispanic/Latino; 9 Hispanic/Latino), 26 international. Average age 37. In 2011, 54 master's, 4 doctorates awarded. *Degree requirements:* For master's, thesis; for doctorate, thesis/dissertation. *Total annual research expenditures:* $8.4 million. *Unit head:* Peter Denning, Chairman, 831-656-3603, E-mail: pjd@nps.edu. *Application contact:* Acting Director of Admissions.

Naval Postgraduate School, Departments and Academic Groups, Space Systems Academic Group, Monterey, CA 93943. Offers applied physics (MS); astronautical engineering (MS); computer science (MS); electrical engineering (MS); mechanical engineering (MS); space systems (Engr); space systems operations (MS). Program only open to commissioned officers of the United States and friendly nations and selected United States federal civilian employees. Part-time programs available. *Faculty:* 5 full-time, 5 part-time/adjunct (2 women). *Students:* 37 full-time (2 women), 14 part-time; includes 11 minority (5 Black or African American, non-Hispanic/Latino; 2 Asian, non-Hispanic/Latino; 4 Hispanic/Latino), 1 international. Average age 33. In 2011, 20 master's awarded. *Degree requirements:* For master's and Engr, thesis; for doctorate, thesis/dissertation. *Faculty research:* Military applications for space; space reconnaissance and remote sensing; radiation-hardened electronics for space; design, construction and operations of small satellites; satellite communications systems. *Total annual research expenditures:* $2 million. *Unit head:* Dr. Rudy Panholzer, Chairman, 831-656-2154. Web site: http://www.nps.edu/Academics/Schools/GSEAS/Departments/SpaceSystems/.

New Jersey Institute of Technology, Office of Graduate Studies, College of Computing Science, Department of Computer Science, Program in Computer Science, Newark, NJ 07102. Offers MS, PhD. Postbaccalaureate distance learning degree programs offered (no on-campus study). *Students:* 170 full-time (50 women), 90 part-time (18 women); includes 46 minority (8 Black or African American, non-Hispanic/Latino; 30 Asian, non-Hispanic/Latino; 6 Hispanic/Latino; 2 Two or more races, non-Hispanic/Latino), 172 international. Average age 29. 947 applicants, 61% accepted, 90 enrolled. In 2011, 92 master's, 8 doctorates awarded. *Entrance requirements:* For doctorate, GRE General Test, minimum graduate GPA of 3.5. Additional exam requirements/recommendations for international students: Required—TOEFL (minimum score 550 paper-based; 213 computer-based; 79 iBT). *Application deadline:* For fall admission, 6/1 priority date for domestic students, 5/1 for international students; for spring admission, 11/15 priority date for domestic students, 11/15 for international students. Applications are processed on a rolling basis. Application fee: $65. Electronic applications accepted. *Expenses:* Tuition, state resident: full-time $7980; part-time $867 per credit. Tuition, nonresident: full-time $11,336; part-time $1196 per credit. *Required fees:* $230 per credit. *Financial support:* Fellowships with tuition reimbursements, research assistantships with tuition reimbursements, and teaching assistantships with tuition reimbursements available. Financial award application deadline: 1/15. *Faculty research:* Algorithms; bioinformatics/biomedical informatics; database/data mining; image processing; pervasive and mobile computing; systems and software engineering; telecommunications, networking, and security; machine learning; computer vision; pattern recognition; biometrics and security. *Unit head:* Dr. Michael A. Baltrush, Interim Chair, 973-596-3386, E-mail: michael.a.baltrush@njit.edu. *Application contact:* Kathryn Kelly, Director of Admissions, 973-596-3300, Fax: 973-596-3461, E-mail: admissions@njit.edu. Web site: http://cs.njit.edu/academics/graduate/mscs.php.

New Mexico Highlands University, Graduate Studies, College of Arts and Sciences, Department of Computer and Math Sciences, Las Vegas, NM 87701. Offers media arts and computer science (MA, MS). *Faculty:* 5 full-time (0 women). *Students:* 8 full-time (3 women), 8 part-time (3 women); includes 5 minority (1 Black or African American, non-Hispanic/Latino; 4 Hispanic/Latino), 11 international. Average age 26. 13 applicants, 69% accepted, 2 enrolled. In 2011, 3 master's awarded. *Degree requirements:* For master's, comprehensive exam, thesis. *Entrance requirements:* For master's, minimum undergraduate GPA of 3.0. Additional exam requirements/recommendations for international students: Required—TOEFL (minimum score 540 paper-based; 270 computer-based). Application fee: $15. *Expenses:* Tuition, state resident: full-time $2767; part-time $146 per credit hour. Tuition, nonresident: full-time $4879; part-time $234 per credit hour. *International tuition:* $5436 full-time. *Required fees:* $737. *Financial support:* In 2011–12, 7 students received support. Career-related internships or fieldwork, Federal Work-Study, institutionally sponsored loans, scholarships/grants, tuition waivers (full and partial), and unspecified assistantships available. Support available to part-time students. Financial award application deadline: 3/1; financial award applicants required to submit FAFSA. *Faculty research:* Advanced digital compositing, photographic installations and exhibition design, pattern recognition, parallel and distributed computing, computer security education. *Unit head:* Dr. Gil Gallegos, Department Head of Computer and Math Sciences, 505-454-3302, E-mail: grgallegos@nmhu.edu. *Application contact:* Diane Trujillo, Administrative Assistant for Graduate Studies, 505-454-3266, Fax: 505-426-2117, E-mail: dtrujillo@nmhu.edu.

New Mexico Institute of Mining and Technology, Graduate Studies, Department of Computer Science and Engineering, Socorro, NM 87801. Offers computer science (MS, PhD). Part-time programs available. *Faculty:* 7 full-time (1 woman), 3 part-time/adjunct (0 women). *Students:* 22 full-time (4 women), 8 part-time (2 women); includes 14 minority (1 American Indian or Alaska Native, non-Hispanic/Latino; 12 Asian, non-Hispanic/Latino; 1 Hispanic/Latino), 1 international. Average age 30. 15 applicants, 87% accepted, 3 enrolled. In 2011, 6 degrees awarded. *Degree requirements:* For master's, thesis optional; for doctorate, thesis/dissertation. *Entrance requirements:* For master's, GRE General Test; for doctorate, GRE General Test, GRE Subject Test. Additional exam requirements/recommendations for international students: Required—TOEFL. *Application deadline:* For fall admission, 3/1 priority date for domestic students; for spring admission, 6/1 priority date for domestic students. Applications are processed on a rolling basis. Application fee: $16 ($30 for international students). Electronic applications accepted. *Expenses:* Tuition, state resident: full-time $4849; part-time $269.41 per credit hour. Tuition, nonresident: full-time $16,041; part-time $891.15 per credit hour. *Required fees:* $622; $65 per credit hour. $20 per semester. Part-time tuition and fees vary according to course load. *Financial support:* In 2011–12, 8 research assistantships (averaging $21,245 per year), 6 teaching assistantships with full and partial tuition reimbursements (averaging $17,158 per year) were awarded; fellowships, Federal Work-Study, institutionally sponsored loans, and unspecified assistantships also available. Financial award application deadline: 3/1; financial award applicants required to submit CSS PROFILE or FAFSA. *Unit head:* Dr. Lorie Liebrock, Chair, 575-835-6729, E-mail: liebrock@cs.nmt.edu. *Application contact:* Dr. Lorie Liebrock, Dean of Graduate Studies, 575-835-5513, Fax: 575-835-5476, E-mail: graduate@nmt.edu. Web site: http://cs.nmt.edu/.

New Mexico State University, Graduate School, College of Arts and Sciences, Department of Computer Science, Las Cruces, NM 88003-8001. Offers bioinformatics (MS); computer science (MS, PhD). Part-time programs available. *Faculty:* 9 full-time (3 women). *Students:* 65 full-time (13 women), 20 part-time (4 women); includes 9 minority (1 Asian, non-Hispanic/Latino; 8 Hispanic/Latino), 56 international. Average age 30. 58 applicants, 66% accepted, 14 enrolled. In 2011, 20 master's, 1 doctorate awarded. Terminal master's awarded for partial completion of doctoral program. *Degree requirements:* For master's, comprehensive exam, thesis or alternative; for doctorate, comprehensive exam, thesis/dissertation, qualifying examination, thesis proposal. *Entrance requirements:* For master's and doctorate, BS in computer science. Additional exam requirements/recommendations for international students: Required—TOEFL (minimum score 550 paper-based; 0 computer-based; 79 iBT), IELTS (minimum score 6.5). *Application deadline:* For fall admission, 3/1 priority date for domestic students, 3/1 for international students; for spring admission, 11/1 priority date for domestic students, 11/1 for international students. Applications are processed on a rolling basis. Application fee: $40 ($50 for international students). Electronic applications accepted. *Expenses:* Tuition, state resident: full-time $5004; part-time $208.50 per credit. Tuition, nonresident: full-time $17,446; part-time $726.90 per credit. *Financial support:* In 2011–12, 6 fellowships (averaging $21,370 per year), 13 research assistantships (averaging $26,405 per year), 22 teaching assistantships (averaging $21,764 per year) were awarded; career-related internships or fieldwork, Federal Work-Study, scholarships/grants, health care benefits, and unspecified assistantships also available. Support available to part-time students. Financial award application deadline: 3/1; financial award applicants required to submit FAFSA. *Faculty research:* Programming languages, artificial intelligence, software engineering, bioinformatics, data mining, computer networks, high performance computing. *Total annual research expenditures:* $1.6 million. *Unit head:* Dr. Enrico Pontelli, Head, 575-646-3723, Fax: 575-646-1002, E-mail: epontell@cs.nmsu.edu. *Application contact:* Dr. Son Tran, Chair, Admissions Committee, 575-646-1930, Fax: 575-646-1002, E-mail: tson@cs.nmsu.edu. Web site: http://www.cs.nmsu.edu/.

New York Institute of Technology, Graduate Division, School of Engineering and Computing Sciences, Program in Computer Science, Old Westbury, NY 11568-8000. Offers MS. Part-time and evening/weekend programs available. *Students:* 104 full-time (27 women), 51 part-time (11 women); includes 19 minority (2 Black or African American, non-Hispanic/Latino; 9 Asian, non-Hispanic/Latino; 6 Hispanic/Latino; 2 Two or more races, non-Hispanic/Latino), 111 international. Average age 27. In 2011, 66 master's awarded. *Degree requirements:* For master's, project. *Entrance requirements:* For master's, GRE General Test (if QPA less than 2.85), minimum QPA of 2.85, BS in computer science or related field. Additional exam requirements/recommendations for international students: Required—TOEFL (minimum score 550 paper-based; 213 computer-based). *Application deadline:* For fall admission, 7/1 priority date for domestic students; for spring admission, 12/1 priority date for domestic students. Applications are processed on a rolling basis. Application fee: $50. Electronic applications accepted. *Expenses: Tuition:* Part-time $930 per credit hour. *Financial support:* Fellowships, research assistantships with partial tuition reimbursements, institutionally sponsored loans, tuition waivers (partial), and unspecified assistantships available. Support available to part-time students. Financial award applicants required to submit FAFSA. *Faculty research:* Image processing, multimedia CD-ROM, prototype modules of the DTV application environment. *Unit head:* Dr. Ayat Jafari, Chair, 516-686-7569, Fax: 516-686-7439, E-mail: ajafari@nyit.edu. *Application contact:* Dr. Jacquelyn Nealon, Vice President for Enrollment Services, 516-686-7925, Fax: 516-686-7597, E-mail: jnealon@nyit.edu.

New York University, Graduate School of Arts and Science, Courant Institute of Mathematical Sciences, Department of Computer Science, New York, NY 10012-1019. Offers computer science (MS, PhD); information systems (MS); scientific computing (MS). Part-time and evening/weekend programs available. *Faculty:* 30 full-time (1 woman). *Students:* 395 full-time (97 women), 104 part-time (22 women); includes 37 minority (2 Black or African American, non-Hispanic/Latino; 30 Asian, non-Hispanic/Latino; 4 Hispanic/Latino; 1 Two or more races, non-Hispanic/Latino), 392 international. Average age 27. 1,088 applicants, 48% accepted, 236 enrolled. In 2011, 92 master's, 11 doctorates awarded. *Degree requirements:* For doctorate, thesis/dissertation, oral and written exams. *Entrance requirements:* For master's and doctorate, GRE General Test, GRE Subject Test. Additional exam requirements/recommendations for international students: Required—TOEFL. *Application deadline:* For fall admission, 12/12 for domestic students; for spring admission, 11/1 for domestic students. Application fee: $90. *Financial support:* Fellowships with tuition reimbursements, research assistantships with tuition reimbursements, teaching assistantships with tuition reimbursements, Federal Work-Study, institutionally sponsored loans, scholarships/grants, health care benefits, and unspecified assistantships available. Financial award application deadline: 12/15; financial award applicants required to submit FAFSA. *Faculty research:* Distributed parallel and secure computing, computer graphics and vision, algorithmic and theory of computation, natural language processing, computational biology. *Unit head:* Margaret Wright, Director of Graduate Studies, PhD Program, 212-998-3011, Fax: 212-995-4124, E-mail: admissions@cs.nyu.edu. *Application contact:* Benjamin Goldberg, Director of Graduate Studies, Master's Program, 212-998-3011, Fax: 212-995-4124, E-mail: admissions@cs.nyu.edu. Web site: http://cs.nyu.edu/.

Nicholls State University, Graduate Studies, College of Arts and Sciences, Department of Mathematics and Computer Science, Thibodaux, LA 70310. Offers community/technical college mathematics (MS). Part-time and evening/weekend programs available. *Degree requirements:* For master's, comprehensive exam. *Entrance requirements:* For master's, GRE General Test. Electronic applications accepted. *Faculty research:* Operations research, statistics, numerical analysis, algebra, topology.

Norfolk State University, School of Graduate Studies, School of Science and Technology, Department of Computer Science, Norfolk, VA 23504. Offers MS.

North Carolina Agricultural and Technical State University, School of Graduate Studies, College of Engineering, Department of Computer Science, Greensboro, NC 27411. Offers MSCS. Part-time programs available. *Degree requirements:* For master's, thesis optional. *Faculty research:* Object-oriented analysis, artificial intelligence, distributed computing, societal implications of computing, testing.

North Carolina Agricultural and Technical State University, School of Graduate Studies, School of Technology, Department of Electronics, Computer, and Information Technology, Greensboro, NC 27411. Offers electronics and computer technology (MSIT, MSTM); information technology (MSIT, MSTM).

North Carolina State University, Graduate School, College of Engineering, Department of Computer Science, Raleigh, NC 27695. Offers MC Sc, MS, PhD. Part-time programs available. Postbaccalaureate distance learning degree programs offered. *Degree requirements:* For master's, thesis optional; for doctorate, thesis/dissertation. *Entrance requirements:* For master's, GRE General Test, GRE Subject Test, minimum GPA of 3.0; for doctorate, GRE General Test, GRE Subject Test (recommended), minimum GPA of 3.5. Additional exam requirements/recommendations for international students: Required—TOEFL. Electronic applications accepted. *Faculty research:* Networking and performance analysis, theory and algorithms of computation, data mining, graphics and human computer interaction, software engineering and information security.

North Carolina State University, Graduate School, College of Engineering, Department of Electrical and Computer Engineering and Department of Computer Science, Program in Computer Networking, Raleigh, NC 27695. Offers MS. *Degree requirements:* For master's, thesis optional. *Entrance requirements:* For master's, GRE General Test, GRE Subject Test (recommended). Electronic applications accepted. *Faculty research:* High-speed networks, performance modelling, security, wireless and mobile.

North Central College, Graduate and Continuing Education Programs, Department of Computer Science, Naperville, IL 60566-7063. Offers Web and Internet applications (MS). Part-time and evening/weekend programs available. *Faculty:* 4 full-time (1 woman), 2 part-time/adjunct (1 woman). *Students:* 3 full-time (0 women), 8 part-time (3 women), 1 international. Average age 30. 11 applicants, 82% accepted, 5 enrolled. In 2011, 1 master's awarded. *Degree requirements:* For master's, thesis optional, project. *Entrance requirements:* For master's, interview. Additional exam requirements/recommendations for international students: Required—TOEFL (minimum score 577 paper-based; 233 computer-based; 90 iBT). *Application deadline:* For fall admission, 8/15 for domestic students; for winter admission, 12/1 for domestic students; for spring admission, 2/1 for domestic students. Applications are processed on a rolling basis. Application fee: $25. *Expenses:* Contact institution. *Financial support:* In 2011–12, 1 student received support. Scholarships/grants available. Support available to part-time students. *Unit head:* Dr. Caroline St. Clair, Program Coordinator, Web and Internet Applications, 630-637-5171, Fax: 630-637-5172, E-mail: cstclair@noctrl.edu. *Application contact:* Wendy Kulpinski, Director of Graduate and Continuing Education Admission, 630-637-5808, Fax: 630-637-5819, E-mail: wekulpinski@noctrl.edu.

North Dakota State University, College of Graduate and Interdisciplinary Studies, College of Science and Mathematics, Department of Computer Science, Fargo, ND

58108. Offers computer science (MS, PhD); operations research (MS); software engineering (MS, PhD, Certificate). Part-time programs available. *Faculty:* 15 full-time (5 women). *Students:* 99 full-time (16 women), 123 part-time (33 women); includes 9 minority (1 Black or African American, non-Hispanic/Latino; 1 American Indian or Alaska Native, non-Hispanic/Latino; 4 Asian, non-Hispanic/Latino; 1 Hispanic/Latino; 2 Two or more races, non-Hispanic/Latino), 178 international. Average age 24. 146 applicants, 57% accepted, 23 enrolled. In 2011, 28 master's, 6 doctorates, 1 other advanced degree awarded. *Degree requirements:* For master's, comprehensive exam, thesis optional; for doctorate, thesis/dissertation, qualifying exam. *Entrance requirements:* For master's, minimum GPA of 3.0, BS in computer science or related field; for doctorate, minimum GPA of 3.25, MS in computer science or related field. Additional exam requirements/recommendations for international students: Required—TOEFL (minimum score 550 paper-based; 213 computer-based; 79 iBT). *Application deadline:* For fall admission, 3/31 priority date for domestic students. Applications are processed on a rolling basis. Application fee: $35. Electronic applications accepted. *Financial support:* In 2011–12, 37 research assistantships with full tuition reimbursements (averaging $10,000 per year), 17 teaching assistantships with full tuition reimbursements (averaging $4,500 per year) were awarded; career-related internships or fieldwork, Federal Work-Study, institutionally sponsored loans, and tuition waivers (full) also available. Financial award application deadline: 4/15. *Faculty research:* Networking, software engineering, artificial intelligence, database, programming languages. *Unit head:* Dr. Brian Slator, Head, 701-231-8562, Fax: 701-231-8255. *Application contact:* Dr. Ken R. Nygard, Graduate Coordinator, 701-231-9460, Fax: 701-231-8255, E-mail: kendall.nygard@ndsu.edu. Web site: http://www.cs.ndsu.nodak.edu/.

Northeastern Illinois University, Graduate College, College of Arts and Sciences, Department of Computer Science, Program in Computer Science, Chicago, IL 60625-4699. Offers MS. Part-time and evening/weekend programs available. *Degree requirements:* For master's, comprehensive exam, research project or thesis. *Entrance requirements:* For master's, minimum GPA of 2.75, proficiency in 2 higher-level computer languages, 1 course in discrete mathematics. Additional exam requirements/recommendations for international students: Required—TOEFL (minimum score 550 paper-based; 213 computer-based; 79 iBT). Electronic applications accepted. *Faculty research:* Telecommunications, database inference problems, decision-making under uncertainty, belief networks, analysis of algorithms.

Northeastern University, College of Computer and Information Science, Boston, MA 02115-5096. Offers computer and information science (PhD); computer science (MS); health informatics (MS); information assurance (MS). Part-time and evening/weekend programs available. *Faculty:* 28 full-time, 3 part-time/adjunct. *Students:* 337 full-time (91 women), 90 part-time (52 women). 1,045 applicants, 56% accepted, 150 enrolled. In 2011, 88 master's, 7 doctorates awarded. Terminal master's awarded for partial completion of doctoral program. *Degree requirements:* For master's, thesis optional; for doctorate, comprehensive exam, thesis/dissertation. *Entrance requirements:* For master's and doctorate, GRE General Test. Additional exam requirements/recommendations for international students: Required—TOEFL or IELTS. *Application deadline:* For fall admission, 7/15 for domestic students, 5/1 for international students; for spring admission, 10/15 for domestic students, 9/1 for international students. Applications are processed on a rolling basis. Application fee: $50. Electronic applications accepted. *Expenses:* Contact institution. *Financial support:* In 2011–12, 59 students received support, including 1 fellowship, 40 research assistantships with full tuition reimbursements available (averaging $18,260 per year), 33 teaching assistantships with full tuition reimbursements available (averaging $18,260 per year); career-related internships or fieldwork, Federal Work-Study, institutionally sponsored loans, scholarships/grants, and unspecified assistantships also available. Financial award application deadline: 1/15. *Faculty research:* Programming languages, artificial intelligence, human-computer interaction, database management, network security. *Unit head:* Dr. Larry A. Finkelstein, Dean, 617-373-2462, Fax: 617-373-5121. *Application contact:* Dr. Agnes Chan, Associate Dean and Director of Graduate Program, 617-373-2462, Fax: 617-373-5121, E-mail: gradschool@ccs.neu.edu. Web site: http://www.ccs.neu.edu/.

Northern Arizona University, Graduate College, College of Engineering, Forestry and Natural Sciences, Programs in Engineering, Flagstaff , AZ 86011. Offers civil and environmental engineering (M Eng); civil engineering (MSE); computer science (MSE); electrical engineering (M Eng, MSE); engineering (M Eng, MSE); environmental engineering (M Eng, MSE); mechanical engineering (M Eng, MSE). Part-time programs available. Postbaccalaureate distance learning degree programs offered (no on-campus study). *Faculty:* 42 full-time (10 women). *Students:* 15 full-time (1 woman), 12 part-time (1 woman); includes 2 minority (both Hispanic/Latino), 6 international. Average age 28. 29 applicants, 52% accepted, 8 enrolled. In 2011, 15 degrees awarded. *Degree requirements:* For master's, thesis. *Entrance requirements:* For master's, GRE General Test. Additional exam requirements/recommendations for international students: Required—TOEFL (minimum score 550 paper-based; 213 computer-based; 80 iBT), IELTS (minimum score 7). *Application deadline:* For fall admission, 3/1 priority date for domestic students, 3/1 for international students; for spring admission, 9/15 priority date for domestic students, 9/15 for international students. Applications are processed on a rolling basis. Application fee: $65. Electronic applications accepted. *Expenses:* Tuition, state resident: full-time $7190; part-time $355 per credit hour. Tuition, nonresident: full-time $18,092; part-time $1005 per credit hour. *Required fees:* $818; $328 per semester. *Financial support:* In 2011–12, 3 research assistantships with partial tuition reimbursements (averaging $14,541 per year), 12 teaching assistantships with partial tuition reimbursements (averaging $12,863 per year) were awarded; career-related internships or fieldwork, Federal Work-Study, scholarships/grants, health care benefits, and unspecified assistantships also available. Financial award applicants required to submit FAFSA. *Unit head:* Dr. Ernesto Penado, Chair, 928-523-9453, Fax: 928-523-2300, E-mail: ernesto.penado@nau.edu. *Application contact:* Natasha Kypfer, Program Coordinator, 928-523-1447, Fax: 928-523-2300, E-mail: egrmasters@nau.edu. Web site: http://nau.edu/CEFNS/Engineering/.

Northern Illinois University, Graduate School, College of Liberal Arts and Sciences, Department of Computer Science, De Kalb, IL 60115-2854. Offers MS. Part-time and evening/weekend programs available. *Faculty:* 14 full-time (3 women). *Students:* 86 full-time (22 women), 20 part-time (4 women); includes 5 minority (2 Asian, non-Hispanic/Latino; 3 Hispanic/Latino), 82 international. Average age 23. 290 applicants, 62% accepted, 43 enrolled. In 2011, 89 master's awarded. *Degree requirements:* For master's, comprehensive exam. *Entrance requirements:* For master's, GRE General Test, minimum GPA of 2.75. Additional exam requirements/recommendations for international students: Required—TOEFL (minimum score 550 paper-based; 213 computer-based). *Application deadline:* For fall admission, 6/1 for domestic students, 5/1 for international students; for spring admission, 11/1 for domestic students, 10/1 for international students. Applications are processed on a rolling basis. Application fee: $40. Electronic applications accepted. *Financial support:* In 2011–12, 1 research assistantship with full tuition reimbursement, 29 teaching assistantships with full tuition

reimbursements were awarded; fellowships with full tuition reimbursements, career-related internships or fieldwork, Federal Work-Study, scholarships/grants, tuition waivers (full), and unspecified assistantships also available. Support available to part-time students. Financial award applicants required to submit FAFSA. *Faculty research:* Databases, theorem proving, artificial intelligence, neural networks, computer ethics. *Unit head:* Dr. Nicholas Karonis, Chair, 815-753-0349, Fax: 815-753-0342, E-mail: karonis@niu.edu. *Application contact:* Graduate School Office, 815-753-0395, E-mail: gradsch@niu.edu. Web site: http://www.cs.niu.edu/.

Northern Kentucky University, Office of Graduate Programs, College of Informatics, Department of Computer Science, Highland Heights, KY 41099. Offers computer science (MSCS); geographic information systems (Certificate); secure software engineering (Certificate). Part-time and evening/weekend programs available. *Faculty:* 11 full-time (3 women), 1 part-time/adjunct. *Students:* 26 full-time (4 women), 7 part-time (2 women); includes 4 minority (1 Black or African American, non-Hispanic/Latino; 3 Asian, non-Hispanic/Latino), 4 international. Average age 34. 33 applicants, 42% accepted, 7 enrolled. In 2011, 2 master's, 1 Certificate awarded. *Degree requirements:* For master's, thesis optional. *Entrance requirements:* For master's, minimum GPA of 3.0, at least 4 semesters of undergraduate study in computer science including intermediate computer programming and data structures, one year of calculus, one course in discrete mathematics. Additional exam requirements/recommendations for international students: Required—TOEFL (minimum score 550 paper-based; 213 computer-based; 79 iBT); Recommended—IELTS (minimum score 6.5). *Application deadline:* For fall admission, 8/1 for domestic students, 6/1 for international students; for spring admission, 12/1 for domestic students, 10/1 for international students. Applications are processed on a rolling basis. Application fee: $40. Electronic applications accepted. *Expenses:* Tuition, state resident: full-time $7614; part-time $423 per credit hour. Tuition, nonresident: full-time $13,104; part-time $728 per credit hour. Tuition and fees vary according to degree level and reciprocity agreements. *Financial support:* Scholarships/grants and unspecified assistantships available. Financial award applicants required to submit FAFSA. *Faculty research:* Data privacy, data mining, wireless security, secure software engineering, secure networking. *Unit head:* Dr. Wei Hao, Interim MSCS Director, 859-572-5468, Fax: 859-572-6097, E-mail: haow1@nku.edu. *Application contact:* Dr. Peg Griffin, Director of Graduate Programs, 859-572-6934, Fax: 859-572-6670, E-mail: griffinp@nku.edu. Web site: http://informatics.nku.edu/csc/mscs.

Northwestern Polytechnic University, School of Engineering, Fremont, CA 94539-7482. Offers computer science (MS); computer systems engineering (MS); electrical engineering (MS). Part-time and evening/weekend programs available. *Degree requirements:* For master's, thesis optional. *Entrance requirements:* For master's, minimum GPA of 3.0. Additional exam requirements/recommendations for international students: Required—TOEFL (minimum score 550 paper-based; 213 computer-based; 79 iBT). *Faculty research:* Computer networking, database design, Internet technology, software engineering, digital signal processing.

Northwest Missouri State University, Graduate School, Melvin and Valorie Booth College of Business and Professional Studies, Department of Computer Science and Information Systems, Maryville, MO 64468-6001. Offers applied computer science (MS); instructional technology (Certificate); teaching instructional technology (MS Ed). Part-time programs available. *Faculty:* 10 full-time (6 women). *Students:* 98 full-time (19 women), 55 part-time (28 women); includes 2 minority (1 Black or African American, non-Hispanic/Latino; 1 Asian, non-Hispanic/Latino), 120 international. 184 applicants, 83% accepted, 40 enrolled. In 2011, 53 master's awarded. *Degree requirements:* For master's, comprehensive exam. *Entrance requirements:* For master's, GRE General Test, minimum GPA of 3.0. Additional exam requirements/recommendations for international students: Required—TOEFL (minimum score 550 paper-based; 213 computer-based). *Application deadline:* Applications are processed on a rolling basis. Application fee: $0 ($50 for international students). *Financial support:* In 2011–12, research assistantships (averaging $6,000 per year), 21 teaching assistantships with full tuition reimbursements (averaging $6,000 per year) were awarded; unspecified assistantships also available. Financial award application deadline: 4/1; financial award applicants required to submit FAFSA. *Unit head:* Dr. Phillip Heeler, Chairperson, 660-562-1200. *Application contact:* Dr. Gregory Haddock, Dean of Graduate School, 660-562-1145, Fax: 660-562-1096, E-mail: gradsch@nwmissouri.edu.

Notre Dame College, Graduate Programs, South Euclid, OH 44121-4293. Offers mild/moderate needs (M Ed); reading (M Ed); security policy studies (MA, Graduate Certificate); technology (M Ed). Part-time and evening/weekend programs available. *Faculty:* 6 full-time (3 women), 19 part-time/adjunct (16 women). *Students:* 344 part-time (253 women). *Degree requirements:* For master's, thesis. *Entrance requirements:* For master's, GRE General Test, MAT, minimum undergraduate GPA of 2.75, valid teaching certificate, bachelor's degree in an education-related field from accredited college or university, official transcripts of most recent college work. *Application deadline:* For fall admission, 8/1 priority date for domestic students; for spring admission, 1/1 for domestic students. Applications are processed on a rolling basis. Application fee: $40. *Expenses:* Tuition: Part-time $528 per credit. *Financial support:* Tuition waivers (full) available. Support available to part-time students. Financial award application deadline: 4/15; financial award applicants required to submit FAFSA. *Faculty research:* Cognitive psychology, teaching critical thinking in the classroom. *Application contact:* Sarah Palace, Assistant Dean of Adult Enrollment, 216-373-5350, Fax: 216-373-6330, E-mail: spalace@ndc.edu.

Notre Dame de Namur University, Division of Academic Affairs, College of Arts and Sciences, Department of Computer and Information Science, Belmont, CA 94002-1908. Offers MS. Part-time and evening/weekend programs available. Postbaccalaureate distance learning degree programs offered (no on-campus study). *Application deadline:* Applications are processed on a rolling basis. Electronic applications accepted. *Expenses: Tuition:* Full-time $14,220; part-time $790 per credit. *Required fees:* $35 per semester. Tuition and fees vary according to program. *Financial support:* Applicants required to submit FAFSA. *Unit head:* Dr. John Youssefi, Program Director, 650-508-3450, E-mail: jyoussefi@ndnu.edu. *Application contact:* Candace Hallmark, Associate Director of Admissions, 650-508-3600, Fax: 650-508-3426, E-mail: grad.admit@ndnu.edu. Web site: http://onlineprograms.ndnu.edu/mscis/online-computer-science-masters-degree-online.

Nova Southeastern University, Graduate School of Computer and Information Sciences, Fort Lauderdale, FL 33314-7796. Offers computer information systems (MS, PhD); computer science (MS, PhD); computing technology in education (PhD); information security (MS); information systems (PhD); information technology (MS); information technology in education (MS); management information systems (MS). Part-time and evening/weekend programs available. Postbaccalaureate distance learning degree programs offered (no on-campus study). *Faculty:* 20 full-time (5 women), 21 part-time/adjunct (3 women). *Students:* 130 full-time (37 women), 960 part-time (291 women); includes 496 minority (221 Black or African American, non-Hispanic/Latino; 4

American Indian or Alaska Native, non-Hispanic/Latino; 78 Asian, non-Hispanic/Latino; 178 Hispanic/Latino; 15 Two or more races, non-Hispanic/Latino), 49 international. Average age 41. 486 applicants, 45% accepted. In 2011, 131 master's, 39 doctorates awarded. Terminal master's awarded for partial completion of doctoral program. *Degree requirements:* For master's, thesis optional; for doctorate, thesis/dissertation. *Entrance requirements:* For master's, minimum undergraduate GPA of 2.5; 3.0 in major; for doctorate, master's degree, minimum graduate GPA of 3.25. Additional exam requirements/recommendations for international students: Required—TOEFL (minimum score 213 computer-based; 79 iBT), IELTS (minimum score 6). *Application deadline:* Applications are processed on a rolling basis. Application fee: $50. Electronic applications accepted. *Expenses:* Contact institution. *Financial support:* Federal Work-Study, scholarships/grants, and unspecified assistantships available. Support available to part-time students. Financial award application deadline: 5/1. *Faculty research:* Artificial intelligence, database management, human-computer interaction, distance education, information security. *Unit head:* Dr. Eric S. Ackerman, Interim Dean, 954-262-7300. *Application contact:* 954-262-2000, Fax: 954-262-2752, E-mail: scisinfo@nova.edu. Web site: http://www.scis.nova.edu/.

Oakland University, Graduate Study and Lifelong Learning, School of Engineering and Computer Science, Department of Computer Science and Engineering, Rochester, MI 48309-4401. Offers computer science (MS); embedded systems (MS); information systems engineering (MS); software engineering (MS). Part-time and evening/weekend programs available. *Entrance requirements:* For master's, minimum GPA of 3.0 for unconditional admission. Electronic applications accepted. *Expenses:* Contact institution. *Faculty research:* Cyber security, 3D imaging of neurochemicals in rat brains.

The Ohio State University, Graduate School, College of Engineering, Department of Computer Science and Engineering, Columbus, OH 43210. Offers computer and information science (MS, PhD); computer science and engineering (MS). *Faculty:* 33. *Students:* 278 full-time (46 women), 61 part-time (9 women); includes 10 minority (4 Black or African American, non-Hispanic/Latino; 4 Asian, non-Hispanic/Latino; 1 Hispanic/Latino; 1 Two or more races, non-Hispanic/Latino), 274 international. Average age 27. In 2011, 37 master's, 20 doctorates awarded. *Degree requirements:* For master's, thesis optional; for doctorate, thesis/dissertation. *Entrance requirements:* Additional exam requirements/recommendations for international students: Required—Michigan English Language Assessment Battery (minimum score 82); Recommended—TOEFL (minimum score 600 paper-based; 250 computer-based; 79 iBT). *Application deadline:* For fall admission, 8/15 priority date for domestic students, 7/1 for international students; for winter admission, 12/1 priority date for domestic students, 11/1 for international students; for spring admission, 3/1 priority date for domestic students, 2/1 for international students. Applications are processed on a rolling basis. Application fee: $40 ($50 for international students). Electronic applications accepted. *Expenses:* Tuition, state resident: full-time $11,400. Tuition, nonresident: full-time $28,125. Tuition and fees vary according to course load, degree level, campus/location and program. *Financial support:* Fellowships, teaching assistantships, career-related internships or fieldwork, Federal Work-Study, institutionally sponsored loans, and administrative assistantships available. Support available to part-time students. Financial award application deadline: 1/15. *Unit head:* Xiadong Zhang, Chair, 614-292-5973, E-mail: zhang.574@osu.edu. *Application contact:* Graduate Admissions, 614-292-6031, Fax: 614-292-3656, E-mail: gradadmissions@osu.edu. Web site: http://www.cse.ohio-state.edu.

Ohio University, Graduate College, Russ College of Engineering and Technology, School of Electrical Engineering and Computer Science, Athens, OH 45701-2979. Offers computer science (MS); electrical engineering (MS); electrical engineering and computer science (PhD). *Students:* 78 full-time (14 women), 31 part-time (5 women); includes 2 minority (both Hispanic/Latino), 67 international. 172 applicants, 36% accepted, 25 enrolled. In 2011, 26 master's, 3 doctorates awarded. *Degree requirements:* For master's, comprehensive exam (for some programs), thesis; for doctorate, comprehensive exam, thesis/dissertation, qualifying exams. *Entrance requirements:* For master's, GRE, BSEE or BSCS, minimum GPA of 3.0; for doctorate, GRE, MSEE or MSCS, minimum GPA of 3.0. Additional exam requirements/recommendations for international students: Required—TOEFL (minimum score 550 paper-based; 80 iBT) or IELTS (minimum score 6.5). *Application deadline:* For fall admission, 2/1 priority date for domestic students, 1/1 for international students; for winter admission, 6/1 priority date for domestic students, 5/1 for international students; for spring admission, 8/15 priority date for domestic students, 7/15 for international students. Applications are processed on a rolling basis. Application fee: $50 ($55 for international students). Electronic applications accepted. *Financial support:* In 2011–12, 54 research assistantships with full tuition reimbursements, 19 teaching assistantships with full tuition reimbursements were awarded; Federal Work-Study, institutionally sponsored loans, scholarships/grants, and unspecified assistantships also available. Financial award applicants required to submit FAFSA. *Faculty research:* Avionics, networking/communications, intelligent distribution, real-time computing, control systems, optical properties of semiconductors. *Unit head:* Dr. David Juedes, Chair, 740-593-1566, Fax: 740-593-0007, E-mail: juedes@ohio.edu. *Application contact:* Dr. Douglas Lawrence, Graduate Chair, 740-593-1578, Fax: 740-593-0007, E-mail: lawrencd@ohio.edu. Web site: http://www.ohio.edu/eecs.

Oklahoma City University, Meinders School of Business, Division of Computer Science, Oklahoma City, OK 73106-1402. Offers). Part-time and evening/weekend programs available. *Faculty:* 5 full-time (0 women), 1 part-time/adjunct (0 women). *Students:* 45 full-time (9 women), 7 part-time (2 women); includes 1 minority (Asian, non-Hispanic/Latino), 48 international. Average age 25. 451 applicants, 94% accepted, 12 enrolled. In 2011, 21 master's awarded. *Degree requirements:* For master's, comprehensive exam, thesis optional. *Entrance requirements:* Additional exam requirements/recommendations for international students: Required—TOEFL. *Application deadline:* Applications are processed on a rolling basis. Application fee: $50 ($70 for international students). Electronic applications accepted. *Expenses:* Contact institution. *Financial support:* Career-related internships or fieldwork and Federal Work-Study available. Support available to part-time students. Financial award application deadline: 6/1; financial award applicants required to submit FAFSA. *Faculty research:* Parallel processing, pedagogical techniques, databases, numerical analysis, gesture recognition. *Unit head:* Dr. Steve Agee, Dean, 405-208-5130, Fax: 405-208-5098, E-mail: sagee@okcu.edu. *Application contact:* Michelle Cook, Director, Admissions, 800-633-7242, Fax: 405-208-5916, E-mail: gadmissions@okcu.edu. Web site: http://msb.okcu.edu/graduate.

Oklahoma State University, College of Arts and Sciences, Computer Science Department, Stillwater, OK 74078. Offers MS, PhD. *Faculty:* 15 full-time (1 woman), 1 part-time/adjunct (0 women). *Students:* 38 full-time (15 women), 37 part-time (6 women); includes 7 minority (2 Black or African American, non-Hispanic/Latino; 1 American Indian or Alaska Native, non-Hispanic/Latino; 1 Asian, non-Hispanic/Latino; 3 Two or more races, non-Hispanic/Latino), 47 international. Average age 30. 287 applicants, 27% accepted, 27 enrolled. In 2011, 25 master's, 4 doctorates awarded. *Degree*

requirements: For master's, thesis optional; for doctorate, comprehensive exam, thesis/dissertation. *Entrance requirements:* For master's, GRE; for doctorate, GRE General Test, GRE Subject Test in computer science (recommended), 3 letters of recommendation. Additional exam requirements/recommendations for international students: Required—TOEFL (minimum score 550 paper-based; 79 iBT). *Application deadline:* For fall admission, 3/1 for international students; for spring admission, 8/1 for international students. Applications are processed on a rolling basis. Application fee: $40 ($75 for international students). Electronic applications accepted. *Expenses:* Tuition, state resident: full-time $4044; part-time $168.50 per credit hour. Tuition, nonresident: full-time $16,008; part-time $667 per credit hour. *Required fees:* $2122; $88.45 per credit hour. One-time fee: $50. Tuition and fees vary according to course load and campus/location. *Financial support:* In 2011–12, 3 research assistantships (averaging $7,154 per year), 26 teaching assistantships (averaging $10,727 per year) were awarded; career-related internships or fieldwork, Federal Work-Study, scholarships/grants, health care benefits, tuition waivers (partial), and unspecified assistantships also available. Support available to part-time students. Financial award application deadline: 3/1; financial award applicants required to submit FAFSA. *Unit head:* Dr. Subhash Kak, Head, 405-744-5668, Fax: 405-774-9097. *Application contact:* Dr. Sheryl Tucker, Dean, 405-744-7099, Fax: 405-744-0355, E-mail: grad-i@okstate.edu. Web site: http://www.cs.okstate.edu/.

Old Dominion University, College of Sciences, Program in Computer Science, Norfolk, VA 23529. Offers MS, PhD. Part-time programs available. *Faculty:* 16 full-time (5 women). *Students:* 61 full-time (8 women), 55 part-time (10 women); includes 5 minority (2 Black or African American, non-Hispanic/Latino; 1 Asian, non-Hispanic/Latino; 1 Hispanic/Latino; 1 Native Hawaiian or other Pacific Islander, non-Hispanic/Latino), 75 international. Average age 28. 200 applicants, 60% accepted. In 2011, 44 master's, 3 doctorates awarded. Terminal master's awarded for partial completion of doctoral program. *Degree requirements:* For master's, thesis optional, comprehensive diagnostic exam; for doctorate, comprehensive exam, thesis/dissertation. *Entrance requirements:* For master's, GRE General Test, minimum GPA of 3.0; for doctorate, GRE General Test, MS in computer science. Additional exam requirements/recommendations for international students: Required—TOEFL. *Application deadline:* For fall admission, 7/1 for domestic students. Applications are processed on a rolling basis. Application fee: $40. *Expenses:* Tuition, state resident: full-time $9096; part-time $379 per credit. Tuition, nonresident: full-time $23,064; part-time $961 per credit. *Required fees:* $127 per semester. One-time fee: $50. *Financial support:* In 2011–12, 98 students received support, including 1 fellowship (averaging $2,021 per year), 27 research assistantships with tuition reimbursements available (averaging $8,736 per year), 28 teaching assistantships with tuition reimbursements available (averaging $7,926 per year); career-related internships or fieldwork, scholarships/grants, and tuition waivers (partial) also available. Support available to part-time students. Financial award application deadline: 2/15; financial award applicants required to submit FAFSA. *Faculty research:* Software engineering, foundations, high-performance computing, networking, mobile computer. *Total annual research expenditures:* $1.4 million. *Unit head:* Dr. Mohammed Zubair, PhD Director, 757-683-3917, Fax: 757-683-4900, E-mail: csgpd@odu.edu. *Application contact:* Dr. Ravi Mukkamala, MS Director, 757-683-6001, E-mail: rmukkama@odu.edu. Web site: http://www.cs.odu.edu/.

Oregon Health & Science University, School of Medicine, Graduate Programs in Medicine, Department of Biomedical Engineering, Portland, OR 97239-3098. Offers biomedical engineering (MS, PhD); computer science and electrical engineering (PhD). Part-time programs available. *Faculty:* 20 full-time (8 women), 3 part-time/adjunct (1 woman). *Students:* 16 full-time (4 women), 3 part-time (1 woman); includes 1 minority (Hispanic/Latino), 4 international. Average age 29. 28 applicants, 25% accepted, 5 enrolled. In 2011, 1 master's, 4 doctorates awarded. Terminal master's awarded for partial completion of doctoral program. *Degree requirements:* For master's, thesis optional, thesis or capstone project; for doctorate, comprehensive exam, thesis/dissertation, qualifying exam. *Entrance requirements:* For master's and doctorate, GRE General Test (minimum scores: 153 Verbal/148 Quantitative/4.5 Analytical). Additional exam requirements/recommendations for international students: Required—TOEFL. *Application deadline:* For fall admission, 7/15 for domestic students, 5/15 for international students; for winter admission, 10/15 for domestic students, 9/15 for international students; for spring admission, 1/15 for domestic students, 12/15 for international students. Applications are processed on a rolling basis. Application fee: $70. Electronic applications accepted. *Financial support:* Health care benefits, tuition waivers, and full tuition and stipends for PhD students available. *Faculty research:* Blood cells in cancer and cancer biology, smart homes and machine learning, computational mechanics and multiscale modeling, tissue optics and biophotonics, nanomedicine and nanobiotechnology. *Unit head:* Dr. Peter Heeman, Program Director, 503-418-9316, E-mail: info@bme.ogi.edu. *Application contact:* Janet Itami, Administrative Coordinator, 503-418-9304, E-mail: itamij@ohsu.edu.

Oregon Health & Science University, School of Medicine, Graduate Programs in Medicine, Department of Computer Science and Engineering, Portland, OR 97239-3098. Offers computer science and engineering (MS, PhD); electrical engineering (MS, PhD). Part-time programs available. *Faculty:* 7 full-time (2 women), 3 part-time/adjunct (all women). *Students:* 20 full-time (5 women), 4 part-time (all women), 12 international. Average age 33. 8 applicants, 38% accepted, 3 enrolled. In 2011, 1 master's, 3 doctorates awarded. Terminal master's awarded for partial completion of doctoral program. *Degree requirements:* For master's, thesis (for some programs); for doctorate, comprehensive exam, thesis/dissertation, qualifying exam. *Entrance requirements:* For master's and doctorate, GRE General Test (minimum scores: 153 Verbal/148 Quantitative/4.5 Analytical). Additional exam requirements/recommendations for international students: Required—TOEFL. *Application deadline:* For fall admission, 7/15 for domestic students, 5/15 for international students; for winter admission, 10/15 for domestic students, 9/15 for international students; for spring admission, 1/15 for domestic students, 12/15 for international students. Applications are processed on a rolling basis. Application fee: $70. Electronic applications accepted. *Financial support:* Health care benefits, tuition waivers (full), and full tuition and stipends for PhD students available. *Unit head:* Dr. Peter Heeman, Program Director, 503-748-1635, E-mail: cseedept@csee.ogi.edu. *Application contact:* Pat Dickerson, Administrative Coordinator, 503-748-1635, E-mail: cseedept@csee.ogi.edu.

Oregon State University, Graduate School, College of Engineering, School of Electrical Engineering and Computer Science, Corvallis, OR 97331. Offers computer science (M Eng, MAIS, MS, PhD); electrical and computer engineering (M Eng, MS, PhD). *Degree requirements:* For doctorate, thesis/dissertation, qualifying exam, preliminary exam. *Entrance requirements:* For master's and doctorate, minimum GPA of 3.0 in last 90 hours of course work. Additional exam requirements/recommendations for international students: Required—TOEFL (minimum score 600 paper-based; 250 computer-based; 80 iBT). Electronic applications accepted. *Faculty research:* Optical materials and devices, data security and cryptography, analog and mixed-signal integrated circuit design, algorithms, computer graphics and vision.

Computer Science

Pace University, Seidenberg School of Computer Science and Information Systems, New York, NY 10038. Offers computer communications and networks (Certificate); computer science (MS); computing studies (DPS); information systems (MS); Internet technologies for e-commerce (Certificate); Internet technology (MS); object-oriented programming (Certificate); security and information assurance (Certificate); software development and engineering (MS); telecommunications (MS, Certificate). Part-time and evening/weekend programs available. *Students:* 82 full-time (19 women), 356 part-time (99 women); includes 175 minority (64 Black or African American, non-Hispanic/Latino; 1 American Indian or Alaska Native, non-Hispanic/Latino; 59 Asian, non-Hispanic/Latino; 47 Hispanic/Latino; 4 Two or more races, non-Hispanic/Latino), 72 international. Average age 37. 304 applicants, 67% accepted, 92 enrolled. In 2011, 136 master's, 9 doctorates, 32 other advanced degrees awarded. *Entrance requirements:* For master's, GRE General Test. Additional exam requirements/recommendations for international students: Required—TOEFL. *Application deadline:* For fall admission, 7/31 priority date for domestic students; for spring admission, 11/30 for domestic students. Applications are processed on a rolling basis. Application fee: $70. Electronic applications accepted. *Expenses:* Contact institution. *Financial support:* Research assistantships and career-related internships or fieldwork available. Support available to part-time students. Financial award applicants required to submit FAFSA. *Unit head:* Dr. Constance Knapp, Interim Dean, 914-773-3750, Fax: 914-773-3533, E-mail: cknapp@pace.edu. *Application contact:* Susan Ford-Goldschein, Director of Graduate Admissions, 914-422-4283, Fax: 914-422-4287, E-mail: gradwp@pace.edu. Web site: http://www.pace.edu/.

Pacific States University, College of Computer Science and Information Systems, Los Angeles, CA 90006. Offers computer science (MS); information systems (MS). Part-time and evening/weekend programs available. *Faculty:* 4 part-time/adjunct (0 women). *Students:* 19 full-time (3 women); includes 1 minority (Asian, non-Hispanic/Latino), 17 international. Average age 27. 9 applicants, 78% accepted, 6 enrolled. *Entrance requirements:* For master's, bachelor's degree in physics, engineering, computer science, or applied mathematics; minimum undergraduate GPA of 2.5 during last 90 hours of course work. Additional exam requirements/recommendations for international students: Required—TOEFL (minimum score 450 paper-based; 133 computer-based; 45 iBT), IELTS (minimum score 4.5). *Application deadline:* For fall admission, 8/15 priority date for domestic students; for winter admission, 10/15 priority date for domestic students; for spring admission, 1/15 priority date for domestic students. Applications are processed on a rolling basis. Application fee: $100. *Expenses: Tuition:* Full-time $11,040; part-time $345 per credit hour. *Required fees:* $150 per quarter. *Financial support:* Scholarships/grants available. Financial award applicants required to submit FAFSA. *Application contact:* Zolzaya Enkhbayar, Interim Registrar, 323-731-2383, Fax: 323-731-7276, E-mail: registrar@psuca.edu.

Penn State Harrisburg, Graduate School, School of Science, Engineering and Technology, Middletown, PA 17057-4898. Offers computer science (MS); electrical engineering (M Eng, MS); engineering management (MPS); engineering science (M Eng); environmental engineering (M Eng); environmental pollution control (MEPC, MS). Part-time and evening/weekend programs available. *Unit head:* Dr. Jerry F. Shoup, Interim Director, 717-948-6352, E-mail: jfs1@psu.edu. *Application contact:* Robert Coffman, Director of Admissions, 717-948-6250, Fax: 717-948-6325, E-mail: ric1@psu.edu. Web site: http://harrisburg.psu.edu/science-engineering-technology.

Penn State University Park, Graduate School, College of Engineering, Department of Computer Science and Engineering, State College, University Park, PA 16802-1503. Offers M Eng, MS, PhD. *Unit head:* Dr. David N. Wormley, Dean, 814-865-7537, Fax: 814-865-8767, E-mail: dnw2@engr.psu.edu. *Application contact:* Cynthia E. Nicosia, Director, Graduate Enrollment Services, 814-865-1834, E-mail: cey1@psu.edu. Web site: http://www.cse.psu.edu.

Polytechnic Institute of New York University, Department of Computer Science and Engineering, Major in Computer Science, Brooklyn, NY 11201-2990. Offers MS, PhD. Part-time and evening/weekend programs available. *Students:* 263 full-time (50 women), 104 part-time (23 women); includes 46 minority (6 Black or African American, non-Hispanic/Latino; 32 Asian, non-Hispanic/Latino; 8 Hispanic/Latino), 271 international. Average age 26. 932 applicants, 40% accepted, 195 enrolled. In 2011, 114 master's, 1 doctorate awarded. *Degree requirements:* For master's, comprehensive exam (for some programs), thesis (for some programs); for doctorate, comprehensive exam, thesis/dissertation. *Entrance requirements:* For master's, BA or BS in computer science, mathematics, science, or engineering; working knowledge of a high-level program; for doctorate, GRE General Test, GRE Subject Test, qualifying exam, BA or BS in science, engineering, or management; MS or 1 year of graduate course work. Additional exam requirements/recommendations for international students: Required—TOEFL (minimum score 550 paper-based; 213 computer-based; 80 iBT); Recommended—IELTS (minimum score 6.5). *Application deadline:* For fall admission, 7/31 priority date for domestic students, 4/30 for international students; for spring admission, 12/31 priority date for domestic students, 11/30 for international students. Applications are processed on a rolling basis. Application fee: $75. Electronic applications accepted. *Expenses: Tuition:* Full-time $22,464; part-time $1248 per credit. *Required fees:* $501 per semester. *Financial support:* Research assistantships, teaching assistantships, institutionally sponsored loans, scholarships/grants, and unspecified assistantships available. Support available to part-time students. Financial award applicants required to submit FAFSA. *Unit head:* Dr. Keith W. Ross, Head, 718-260-3859, Fax: 718-260-3609, E-mail: ross@poly.edu. *Application contact:* JeanCarlo Bonilla, Director of Graduate Enrollment Management, 718-260-3182, Fax: 718-260-3624, E-mail: gradinfo@poly.edu.

Polytechnic Institute of NYU, Long Island Graduate Center, Graduate Programs, Department of Computer Science and Engineering, Program in Computer Science, Melville, NY 11747. Offers MS. *Students:* 2 full-time (0 women), 2 part-time (0 women); includes 2 minority (1 Black or African American, non-Hispanic/Latino; 1 Asian, non-Hispanic/Latino). Average age 32. 10 applicants, 60% accepted, 4 enrolled. In 2011, 7 master's awarded. *Degree requirements:* For master's, comprehensive exam (for some programs), thesis (for some programs). *Entrance requirements:* Additional exam requirements/recommendations for international students: Required—TOEFL (minimum score 550 paper-based; 213 computer-based; 80 iBT); Recommended—IELTS (minimum score 6.5). *Application deadline:* For fall admission, 7/31 priority date for domestic students, 4/30 for international students; for spring admission, 12/31 priority date for domestic students, 11/30 for international students. Applications are processed on a rolling basis. Application fee: $75. Electronic applications accepted. *Financial support:* Institutionally sponsored loans, scholarships/grants, and unspecified assistantships available. Support available to part-time students. Financial award applicants required to submit FAFSA. *Unit head:* Dr. Keith W. Ross, Department Head, 718-260-3859, E-mail: ross@poly.edu. *Application contact:* JeanCarlo Bonilla, Director of Graduate Enrollment Management, 718-260-3182, Fax: 718-260-3624, E-mail: gradinfo@poly.edu.

Polytechnic Institute of NYU, Westchester Graduate Center, Graduate Programs, Department of Computer Science and Engineering, Major in Computer Science, Hawthorne, NY 10532-1507. Offers MS. *Students:* Average age 35. 4 applicants, 100% accepted, 0 enrolled. In 2011, 4 master's awarded. *Degree requirements:* For master's, comprehensive exam (for some programs), thesis (for some programs). *Entrance requirements:* Additional exam requirements/recommendations for international students: Required—TOEFL (minimum score 550 paper-based; 213 computer-based; 80 iBT); Recommended—IELTS (minimum score 6.5). *Application deadline:* For fall admission, 7/31 priority date for domestic students, 4/30 for international students; for spring admission, 12/31 priority date for domestic students, 11/30 for international students. Applications are processed on a rolling basis. Application fee: $75. Electronic applications accepted. *Financial support:* Institutionally sponsored loans, scholarships/grants, and unspecified assistantships available. Support available to part-time students. *Unit head:* Dr. Keith W. Ross, Department Head, 718-260-3859, E-mail: ross@poly.edu. *Application contact:* JeanCarlo Bonilla, Director of Graduate Enrollment Management, 718-260-3182, Fax: 718-260-3624, E-mail: gradinfo@poly.edu.

Polytechnic University of Puerto Rico, Graduate School, Hato Rey, PR 00919. Offers business administration (MBA), including computer information systems, general management, management of information systems, management of international enterprises; civil engineering (ME, MS); computer engineering (ME, MS); computer science (MCS, MS); electrical engineering (ME, MS); engineering management (MEM); environmental management (MEM); landscape architecture (M Land Arch); manufacturing competitiveness (MMC, MS); manufacturing engineering (ME, MS); mechanical engineering (M Mech E). Part-time and evening/weekend programs available. *Entrance requirements:* For master's, 3 letters of recommendation.

Portland State University, Graduate Studies, Maseeh College of Engineering and Computer Science, Department of Computer Science, Portland, OR 97207-0751. Offers computer science (MS, PhD); software engineering (MSE). Part-time programs available. *Degree requirements:* For master's, thesis or alternative; for doctorate, thesis/dissertation. *Entrance requirements:* For master's, GRE General Test, minimum GPA of 3.0 in upper-division course work, 2 letters of recommendation, BS in computer science or allied field; for doctorate, MS in computer science or allied field. Additional exam requirements/recommendations for international students: Required—TOEFL (minimum score 550 paper-based; 213 computer-based). *Faculty research:* Formal methods, database systems, parallel programming environments, computer security, software tools.

Prairie View A&M University, College of Engineering, Prairie View, TX 77446-0519. Offers computer information systems (MSCIS); computer science (MSCS); electrical engineering (MSEE, PhDEE); engineering (MS Engr). Part-time and evening/weekend programs available. *Degree requirements:* For master's, thesis (for some programs); for doctorate, comprehensive exam, thesis/dissertation. *Entrance requirements:* For master's, GRE General Test, bachelor's degree in engineering from an ABET accredited institution; for doctorate, GRE. Additional exam requirements/recommendations for international students: Required—TOEFL (minimum score 550 paper-based). Electronic applications accepted. *Faculty research:* Applied radiation research, thermal science, computational fluid dynamics, analog mixed signal, aerial space battlefield.

Princeton University, Graduate School, School of Engineering and Applied Science, Department of Computer Science, Princeton, NJ 08544-1019. Offers MSE, PhD. Terminal master's awarded for partial completion of doctoral program. *Degree requirements:* For master's, thesis; for doctorate, thesis/dissertation, general exam. *Entrance requirements:* For master's, GRE General Test, GRE Subject Test (recommended), 3 letters of recommendation; for doctorate, GRE General Test, GRE Subject Test (recommended), official transcript(s), 3 letters of recommendation, personal statement. Additional exam requirements/recommendations for international students: Required—TOEFL. Electronic applications accepted. *Faculty research:* Computational biology and bioinformatics; computer and network systems; graphics, vision, and sound; machine learning, programming languages and security; theory.

Purdue University, Graduate School, College of Science, Department of Computer Sciences, West Lafayette, IN 47907. Offers MS, PhD. Part-time programs available. *Faculty:* 44 full-time (5 women), 3 part-time/adjunct (0 women). *Students:* 175 full-time (29 women), 82 part-time (11 women); includes 9 minority (3 Black or African American, non-Hispanic/Latino; 1 Asian, non-Hispanic/Latino; 5 Hispanic/Latino), 208 international. Average age 27. 1,186 applicants, 22% accepted, 62 enrolled. In 2011, 67 master's, 19 doctorates awarded. Terminal master's awarded for partial completion of doctoral program. *Degree requirements:* For master's, thesis optional; for doctorate, comprehensive exam, thesis/dissertation. *Entrance requirements:* For master's and doctorate, minimum GPA of 3.5. Additional exam requirements/recommendations for international students: Required—TOEFL (minimum score 600 paper-based; 95 iBT), TWE (minimum score 5). *Application deadline:* For fall admission, 12/15 for domestic and international students; for spring admission, 10/1 for domestic and international students. Application fee: $60 ($75 for international students). Electronic applications accepted. *Financial support:* Fellowships with partial tuition reimbursements, research assistantships with partial tuition reimbursements, teaching assistantships with partial tuition reimbursements, health care benefits, and unspecified assistantships available. Financial award application deadline: 12/15. *Faculty research:* Bioinformatics and computational Biology, computational science and engineering, databases, data mining, distributed systems, graphics and visualization, information retrieval, information security and assurance, machine learning, networking and operation systems, programming languages and compilers, software engineering, theory of computing and algorithms. *Unit head:* Prof. Sunil K. Prabhakar, Interim Head, 765-494-6008, E-mail: sunil@cs.purdue.edu. *Application contact:* Renate Mallus, Graduate Contact for Admissions, 765-494-7809, E-mail: mallus@cs.purdue.edu. Web site: http://www.cs.purdue.edu/.

Purdue University Calumet, Graduate Studies Office, School of Engineering, Mathematics, and Science, Department of Mathematics, Computer Science, and Statistics, Hammond, IN 46323-2094. Offers computer science (MS); mathematics (MAT, MS). Part-time programs available. *Entrance requirements:* Additional exam requirements/recommendations for international students: Required—TOEFL. *Faculty research:* Topology, analysis, algebra, mathematics education.

Queens College of the City University of New York, Division of Graduate Studies, Mathematics and Natural Sciences Division, Department of Computer Science, Flushing, NY 11367-1597. Offers MA. Part-time and evening/weekend programs available. *Faculty:* 22 full-time (5 women). *Students:* 13 full-time (3 women), 54 part-time (15 women); includes 28 minority (2 Black or African American, non-Hispanic/Latino; 23 Asian, non-Hispanic/Latino; 3 Hispanic/Latino), 18 international. 67 applicants, 64% accepted, 24 enrolled. In 2011, 22 master's awarded. *Degree requirements:* For master's, comprehensive exam, thesis optional. *Entrance requirements:* For master's, GRE, minimum GPA of 3.0. Additional exam requirements/recommendations for international students: Required—TOEFL. *Application deadline:* For fall admission, 4/1 for domestic students; for spring admission, 11/1 for domestic students. Applications are processed on a rolling basis. Application fee: $125. *Expenses:* Tuition, state resident: part-time $345 per credit. Tuition, nonresident: part-time $640 per credit. *Required fees:* $145.25 per semester. *Financial support:* Career-related internships or fieldwork, Federal Work-Study, institutionally sponsored loans, tuition waivers (partial), and unspecified assistantships available. Support available to part-time students. Financial award application deadline: 4/1; financial award applicants required to submit FAFSA. *Faculty research:* Fifth-generation computing, hardware/software development, analysis of algorithms and theoretical computer science. *Unit head:* Dr. Zhigang Xiang, Chairperson, 718-997-3500. *Application contact:* Dr. Keitaro Yukawa, Graduate Adviser, 718-997-3500, E-mail: keitaro_yukawa@qc.edu.

Queen's University at Kingston, School of Graduate Studies and Research, Faculty of Arts and Sciences, School of Computing, Kingston, ON K7L 3N6, Canada. Offers M Sc, PhD. *Degree requirements:* For master's, thesis; for doctorate, comprehensive exam, thesis/dissertation. *Entrance requirements:* For master's, honours B Sc in computer science; for doctorate, M Sc in computer science. Additional exam requirements/recommendations for international students: Required—TOEFL, TWE. *Faculty research:* Software engineering, human computer interaction, data base, networks, computational geometry.

Regis University, College for Professional Studies, School of Computer and Information Sciences, Denver, CO 80221-1099. Offers database administration with Oracle (Certificate); database development (Certificate); database technologies (M Sc); enterprise Java software development (Certificate); enterprise resource planning (Certificate); executive information technologies (Certificate); information assurance (M Sc, Certificate); information technology management (M Sc); software engineering (M Sc, Certificate); software engineering and database technologies (M Sc); storage area networks (Certificate); systems engineering (M Sc, Certificate). Offered at Boulder Campus, Northwest Denver Campus, Southeast Denver Campus, Fort Collins Campus, Colorado Springs Campus, and Broomfield Campus. Part-time and evening/weekend programs available. Postbaccalaureate distance learning degree programs offered (no on-campus study). *Degree requirements:* For master's, thesis, final research project. *Entrance requirements:* For master's, 2 years of related experience, resume, interview; for Certificate, 2 years of related experience, resumé. Additional exam requirements/recommendations for international students: Required—TOEFL (minimum score 213 computer-based), TWE (minimum score 5) or university-based test. Electronic applications accepted. *Expenses:* Contact institution. *Faculty research:* Secure Virtual Laboratory Architecture, Joint IA project with W2C06 Institute, Information Policy, OLTP and OLAP Technologies, knowledge management, software architectures.

Rensselaer at Hartford, Department of Computer and Information Science, Hartford, CT 06120-2991. Offers computer science (MS); information technology (MS). Part-time and evening/weekend programs available. *Degree requirements:* For master's, thesis optional. *Entrance requirements:* For master's, GRE. Additional exam requirements/recommendations for international students: Required—TOEFL (minimum score 600 paper-based; 250 computer-based; 100 iBT). Electronic applications accepted.

Rensselaer Polytechnic Institute, Graduate School, School of Science, Program in Computer Science, Troy, NY 12180-3590. Offers MS, PhD. Part-time programs available. Terminal master's awarded for partial completion of doctoral program. *Degree requirements:* For master's, thesis; for doctorate, comprehensive exam, thesis/dissertation. *Entrance requirements:* For master's and doctorate, GRE General Test. Additional exam requirements/recommendations for international students: Required—TOEFL (minimum score 570 paper-based; 230 computer-based; 89 iBT). Electronic applications accepted. *Faculty research:* Computer vision and graphics, algorithms and theory, pervasive computing and networking, data mining and machine learning, semantic web.

Rice University, Graduate Programs, George R. Brown School of Engineering, Department of Computer Science, Houston, TX 77251-1892. Offers MCS, MS, PhD. Terminal master's awarded for partial completion of doctoral program. *Degree requirements:* For master's, comprehensive exam; for doctorate, comprehensive exam, thesis/dissertation. *Entrance requirements:* For master's and doctorate, bachelor's degree. Additional exam requirements/recommendations for international students: Required—TOEFL. Electronic applications accepted. *Faculty research:* Programming languages and compiler construction; robotics, bioinformatics, algorithms - motion planning with emphasis on high-dimensional systems; network protocols, distributed systems, and operating systems - adaptive protocols for wireless; computer architecture, aperating systems - virtual machine monitors; computer graphics - application of computers to geometric problems and centered around general problem of representing geometric shapes.

Rivier University, School of Graduate Studies, Department of Computer Science and Mathematics, Nashua, NH 03060. Offers computer science (MS); mathematics (MAT). Part-time and evening/weekend programs available. *Entrance requirements:* For master's, GRE Subject Test. Electronic applications accepted.

Rochester Institute of Technology, Graduate Enrollment Services, B. Thomas Golisano College of Computing and Information Sciences, Department of Computer Science, Rochester, NY 14623-5603. Offers MS. Part-time programs available. *Students:* 198 full-time (31 women), 57 part-time (12 women); includes 14 minority (2 Black or African American, non-Hispanic/Latino; 1 American Indian or Alaska Native, non-Hispanic/Latino; 7 Asian, non-Hispanic/Latino; 3 Hispanic/Latino; 1 Two or more races, non-Hispanic/Latino), 192 international. Average age 25. 539 applicants, 61% accepted, 87 enrolled. In 2011, 46 degrees awarded. *Degree requirements:* For master's, thesis or project. *Entrance requirements:* For master's, GRE, minimum GPA of 3.0. Additional exam requirements/recommendations for international students: Required—TOEFL (minimum score 550 paper-based; 213 computer-based; 80 iBT) or IELTS (minimum score 6.5). *Application deadline:* For fall admission, 2/15 priority date for domestic students, 2/15 for international students; for winter admission, 11/1 priority date for domestic students, 11/1 for international students. Applications are processed on a rolling basis. Application fee: $50. Electronic applications accepted. *Expenses:* Tuition: Full-time $34,659; part-time $963 per credit hour. *Required fees:* $228; $76 per quarter. *Financial support:* Research assistantships with partial tuition reimbursements, teaching assistantships with partial tuition reimbursements, career-related internships or fieldwork, scholarships/grants, and unspecified assistantships available. Support available to part-time students. Financial award applicants required to submit FAFSA. *Faculty research:* Computational vision and acoustics, computer graphics and visualization, data management, distributed systems, intelligent systems, language design, security. *Unit head:* Paul Tymann, Department Chair, 585-475-7908, Fax: 585-475-4935, E-mail: ptt@cs.rit.edu. *Application contact:* Diane Ellison, Assistant Vice President, Graduate Enrollment Services, 585-475-2229, Fax: 585-475-7164, E-mail: gradinfo@rit.edu. Web site: http://www.cs.rit.edu.

Rochester Institute of Technology, Graduate Enrollment Services, B. Thomas Golisano College of Computing and Information Sciences, Department of Networking,

Security and Systems Administration, Program in Networking and Systems Administration, Rochester, NY 14623-5603. Offers network planning and design (AC); networking and systems administration (MS, AC). Part-time programs available. Postbaccalaureate distance learning degree programs offered (no on-campus study). *Students:* 28 full-time (4 women), 53 part-time (6 women); includes 9 minority (4 Black or African American, non-Hispanic/Latino; 5 Hispanic/Latino), 36 international. Average age 31. 108 applicants, 49% accepted, 28 enrolled. In 2011, 12 degrees awarded. *Degree requirements:* For master's, thesis (for some programs). *Entrance requirements:* For master's, GRE, minimum GPA of 3.0. Additional exam requirements/recommendations for international students: Required—TOEFL (minimum score 570 paper-based; 230 computer-based; 88 iBT) or IELTS (minimum score 6.5). *Application deadline:* Applications are processed on a rolling basis. Application fee: $50. Electronic applications accepted. *Expenses:* Tuition: Full-time $34,659; part-time $963 per credit hour. *Required fees:* $228; $76 per quarter. *Financial support:* Research assistantships with partial tuition reimbursements, teaching assistantships with partial tuition reimbursements, career-related internships or fieldwork, scholarships/grants, and unspecified assistantships available. Support available to part-time students. Financial award applicants required to submit FAFSA. *Unit head:* Prof. Dianne Bills, Graduate Program Director, 585-475-2700, Fax: 585-475-6584, E-mail: informaticsgrad@rit.edu. *Application contact:* Diane Ellison, Assistant Vice President, Graduate Enrollment Services, 585-475-2229, Fax: 585-475-7164, E-mail: gradinfo@rit.edu.

Rochester Institute of Technology, Graduate Enrollment Services, B. Thomas Golisano College of Computing and Information Sciences, PhD Program in Computing and Information Sciences, Rochester, NY 14623-5603. Offers PhD. *Students:* 16 full-time (4 women), 16 part-time (1 woman); includes 4 minority (3 Asian, non-Hispanic/Latino; 1 Hispanic/Latino), 23 international. Average age 31. 83 applicants, 17% accepted, 12 enrolled. *Degree requirements:* For doctorate, thesis/dissertation. *Entrance requirements:* For doctorate, GRE, minimum GPA of 3.0. Additional exam requirements/recommendations for international students: Required—TOEFL (minimum score 570 paper-based; 230 computer-based; 88 iBT) or IELTS (minimum score 6.5). *Application deadline:* For fall admission, 1/15 priority date for domestic students, 1/15 for international students. Applications are processed on a rolling basis. Application fee: $50. Electronic applications accepted. *Expenses:* Tuition: Full-time $34,659; part-time $963 per credit hour. *Required fees:* $228; $76 per quarter. *Financial support:* Research assistantships with full and partial tuition reimbursements, teaching assistantships with full and partial tuition reimbursements, career-related internships or fieldwork, scholarships/grants, health care benefits, and unspecified assistantships available. Financial award applicants required to submit FAFSA. *Faculty research:* The Center for Advancing the Study of Cyberinfrastructure (CASCI): the framework supporting science and engineering research, domain-specific informatics. *Unit head:* Dr. Pengcheng Shi, Director, 585-475-6147, E-mail: pengcheng.shi@rit.edu. *Application contact:* Diane Ellison, Assistant Vice President, Graduate Enrollment Services, 585-475-2229, Fax: 585-475-7164, E-mail: gradinfo@rit.edu. Web site: http://www.rit.edu/programs/computing-and-information-sciences.

Roosevelt University, Graduate Division, College of Arts and Sciences, Department of Computer Science and Telecommunications, Program in Computer Science, Chicago, IL 60605. Offers MSC. Part-time and evening/weekend programs available. *Faculty research:* Artificial intelligence, software engineering, distributed databases, parallel processing.

Royal Military College of Canada, Division of Graduate Studies and Research, Science Division, Department of Mathematics and Computer Science, Kingston, ON K7K 7B4, Canada. Offers computer science (M Sc); mathematics (M Sc). *Degree requirements:* For master's, thesis. *Entrance requirements:* For master's, honours degree with second-class standing. Electronic applications accepted.

Rutgers, The State University of New Jersey, Camden, Graduate School of Arts and Sciences, Program in Computer Science, Camden, NJ 08102. Offers MS. Part-time and evening/weekend programs available. *Degree requirements:* For master's, comprehensive exam, thesis (for some programs), 30 credits. *Entrance requirements:* For master's, GRE, 3 letters of recommendation; statement of personal, professional, and academic goals; computer science undergraduate degree (preferred). Additional exam requirements/recommendations for international students: Required—TOEFL, IELTS. Electronic applications accepted. *Faculty research:* Cryptography and computer security, approximation algorithms, optical networks and wireless communications, computational geometry, data compression and encoding.

Rutgers, The State University of New Jersey, New Brunswick, Graduate School-New Brunswick, Program in Computer Science, Piscataway, NJ 08854-8097. Offers MS, PhD. Part-time programs available. Terminal master's awarded for partial completion of doctoral program. *Degree requirements:* For master's, comprehensive exam, thesis; for doctorate, comprehensive exam, thesis/dissertation. *Entrance requirements:* For master's and doctorate, GRE General Test, GRE Subject Test. Additional exam requirements/recommendations for international students: Required—TOEFL. *Faculty research:* Artificial intelligence and machine learning, bioinformatics, algorithms and complexity, networking and operating systems, computational graphics and vision.

Sacred Heart University, Graduate Programs, College of Arts and Sciences, Department of Computer Science and Information Technology, Fairfield, CT 06825-1000. Offers computer science (MS); database (CPS); information technology (MS, CPS); information technology and network security (CPS); interactive multimedia (CPS); Web development (CPS). Part-time and evening/weekend programs available. *Degree requirements:* For master's, thesis optional. *Entrance requirements:* Additional exam requirements/recommendations for international students: Required—TOEFL (minimum score 550 paper-based; 213 computer-based). Electronic applications accepted. *Faculty research:* Contemporary market software.

St. Cloud State University, School of Graduate Studies, College of Science and Engineering, Department of Computer Science, St. Cloud, MN 56301-4498. Offers MS. *Degree requirements:* For master's, thesis or alternative. *Entrance requirements:* For master's, GRE General Test, minimum GPA of 2.75. Additional exam requirements/recommendations for international students: Required—Michigan English Language Assessment Battery; Recommended—TOEFL (minimum score 550 paper-based; 213 computer-based), IELTS (minimum score 6.5). Electronic applications accepted.

St. Francis Xavier University, Graduate Studies, Department of Mathematics, Statistics and Computer Science, Antigonish, NS B2G 2W5, Canada. Offers computer science (M Sc). *Degree requirements:* For master's, thesis. *Entrance requirements:* For master's, bachelor's degree or equivalent in computer science with minimum B average, 2 letters of recommendation. Additional exam requirements/recommendations for international students: Required—TOEFL (minimum score 580 paper-based; 237 computer-based).

Saint Joseph's University, College of Arts and Sciences, Department of Mathematics and Computer Science, Philadelphia, PA 19131-1395. Offers computer science (MS); mathematics and computer science (Post-Master's Certificate). Part-time and evening/weekend programs available. *Faculty:* 5 full-time (2 women). *Students:* 47 full-time (11 women), 20 part-time (10 women); includes 6 minority (2 Black or African American, non-Hispanic/Latino; 3 Asian, non-Hispanic/Latino; 1 Two or more races, non-Hispanic/Latino), 54 international. Average age 27. 49 applicants, 61% accepted, 23 enrolled. In 2011, 31 master's awarded. *Entrance requirements:* For master's, 2 letters of recommendation. *Application deadline:* For fall admission, 7/15 priority date for domestic students, 4/15 for international students; for winter admission, 4/15 for domestic students, 1/15 for international students; for spring admission, 11/15 priority date for domestic students, 10/15 for international students. Applications are processed on a rolling basis. Application fee: $35. Electronic applications accepted. *Expenses: Tuition:* Part-time $735 per credit hour. Tuition and fees vary according to degree level and program. *Financial support:* Teaching assistantships with partial tuition reimbursements and unspecified assistantships available. Financial award applicants required to submit FAFSA. *Faculty research:* Computer vision, pathways to careers. *Unit head:* Dr. George Grevera, Director, Graduate Computer Science, 610-660-1535, Fax: 610-660-3082, E-mail: ggrevera@sju.edu. *Application contact:* Kate McConnell, Director, Graduate College of Arts and Sciences Admissions and Retention, 610-660-3184, Fax: 610-660-3230, E-mail: kate.mcconnell@sju.edu. Web site: http://macs.sju.edu/cscmsprog/index.html.

St. Mary's University, Graduate School, Department of Computer Science, Program in Computer Information Systems, San Antonio, TX 78228-8507. Offers MS. Part-time programs available. *Degree requirements:* For master's, comprehensive exam. *Entrance requirements:* For master's, GMAT or GRE General Test. Additional exam requirements/recommendations for international students: Required—TOEFL (minimum score 530 paper-based; 213 computer-based; 80 iBT). Electronic applications accepted. *Faculty research:* Artificial intelligence, database/knowledge base, software engineering, expert systems.

St. Mary's University, Graduate School, Department of Computer Science, Program in Computer Science, San Antonio, TX 78228-8507. Offers MS, JD/MS. Part-time programs available. *Degree requirements:* For master's, comprehensive exam, internship. *Entrance requirements:* For master's, GRE or GMAT. Additional exam requirements/recommendations for international students: Required—TOEFL (minimum score 550 paper-based; 213 computer-based; 80 iBT). Electronic applications accepted.

Saint Xavier University, Graduate Studies, College of Arts and Sciences, Department of Computer Science, Chicago, IL 60655-3105. Offers MACS. *Degree requirements:* For master's, thesis optional. *Application deadline:* For fall admission, 8/15 for domestic students. Application fee: $35. *Expenses: Tuition:* Part-time $750 per credit hour. *Required fees:* $135 per semester. Tuition and fees vary according to program. *Unit head:* Dr. Florence Appel, Associate Chair, 773-298-3388, Fax: 773-298-3438, E-mail: appel@sxu.edu. *Application contact:* Beth Gierach, Managing Director of Admission, 773-298-3053, Fax: 773-298-3076, E-mail: gierach@sxu.edu.

Sam Houston State University, College of Sciences, Department of Computer Science, Huntsville, TX 77341. Offers computing and information science (MS); digital forensics (MS); information assurance and security (MS). Part-time programs available. *Faculty:* 11 full-time (2 women). *Students:* 38 full-time (8 women), 26 part-time (2 women); includes 14 minority (7 Black or African American, non-Hispanic/Latino; 1 American Indian or Alaska Native, non-Hispanic/Latino; 6 Hispanic/Latino), 34 international. Average age 28. 29 applicants, 83% accepted, 24 enrolled. In 2011, 20 master's awarded. *Entrance requirements:* For master's, GRE General Test. Additional exam requirements/recommendations for international students: Required—TOEFL (minimum score 550 paper-based; 213 computer-based; 79 iBT). *Application deadline:* For fall admission, 8/1 for domestic and international students; for spring admission, 12/1 for domestic and international students. Application fee: $20. *Expenses:* Tuition, state resident: full-time $4420; part-time $221 per credit hour. Tuition, nonresident: full-time $10,680; part-time $534 per credit hour. *Required fees:* $329 per credit hour. *Financial support:* Research assistantships, teaching assistantships, Federal Work-Study, institutionally sponsored loans, and tuition waivers (partial) available. Financial award application deadline: 5/31; financial award applicants required to submit FAFSA. *Unit head:* Dr. Peter Cooper, Chair, 936-294-1569, Fax: 936-294-4312, E-mail: css_pac@shsu.edu. *Application contact:* Dr. Jiuhung Ji, Advisor, 936-294-1579, E-mail: csc_jxj@shsu.edu. Web site: http://cs.shsu.edu/.

San Diego State University, Graduate and Research Affairs, College of Sciences, Program in Computer Science, San Diego, CA 92182. Offers MS. Part-time programs available. *Degree requirements:* For master's, comprehensive exam or thesis. *Entrance requirements:* For master's, GRE General Test. Additional exam requirements/recommendations for international students: Required—TOEFL. Electronic applications accepted.

San Francisco State University, Division of Graduate Studies, College of Science and Engineering, Department of Computer Science, San Francisco, CA 94132-1722. Offers computer science (MS); computer science: computing and business (MS); computer science: computing for life sciences (MS); computer science: software and engineering (MS). Part-time programs available. *Application deadline:* Applications are processed on a rolling basis. *Unit head:* Dr. Dragutin Petkovic, Chair, 415-338-1008, Fax: 415-338-6136, E-mail: csgrad@sfsu.edu. *Application contact:* Barry Levine, Graduate Coordinator, E-mail: levine@sfsu.edu. Web site: http://cs.sfsu.edu/grad/graduate.html.

San Jose State University, Graduate Studies and Research, College of Science, Department of Computer Science, San Jose, CA 95192-0001. Offers MS. Electronic applications accepted.

Santa Clara University, School of Engineering, Program in Computer Science and Engineering, Santa Clara, CA 95053. Offers computer science and engineering (MS, PhD, Engineer); information assurance (Certificate); networking (Certificate); software engineering (MS, Certificate). Part-time and evening/weekend programs available. *Students:* 151 full-time (58 women), 121 part-time (39 women); includes 62 minority (4 Black or African American, non-Hispanic/Latino; 52 Asian, non-Hispanic/Latino; 3 Hispanic/Latino; 1 Native Hawaiian or other Pacific Islander, non-Hispanic/Latino; 2 Two or more races, non-Hispanic/Latino), 156 international. Average age 29. 258 applicants, 48% accepted, 70 enrolled. In 2011, 87 degrees awarded. *Degree requirements:* For master's, thesis (for some programs); for doctorate, thesis/dissertation; for other advanced degree, thesis. *Entrance requirements:* For master's, GRE, transcript; for doctorate, GRE, master's degree or equivalent; for other advanced degree, master's degree, published paper. Additional exam requirements/recommendations for international students: Required—TOEFL (minimum score 550 paper-based; 213 computer-based; 79 iBT). *Application deadline:* For fall admission, 8/12 for domestic students, 7/15 for international students; for winter admission, 10/28 for domestic students, 9/23 for international students; for spring admission, 2/25 for domestic students, 1/21 for international students. Applications are processed on a rolling basis. Application fee: $60. Electronic applications accepted. *Expenses:* Contact institution. *Financial support:* Research assistantships and teaching assistantships available. Financial award application deadline: 3/2; financial award applicants required to submit FAFSA. *Unit head:* Dr. Alex Zecevic, Chair, 408-554-2394, E-mail: azecevic@scu.edu. *Application contact:* Stacey Tinker, Director of Enrollment Management, 408-554-4748, Fax: 408-554-4323, E-mail: stinker@scu.edu.

Shippensburg University of Pennsylvania, School of Graduate Studies, College of Arts and Sciences, Department of Computer Science, Shippensburg, PA 17257-2299. Offers computer science (MS). Part-time and evening/weekend programs available. *Faculty:* 5 full-time (3 women). *Students:* 5 full-time (0 women), 3 part-time (1 woman); includes 3 minority (1 Black or African American, non-Hispanic/Latino; 2 Asian, non-Hispanic/Latino), 1 international. Average age 28. 17 applicants, 53% accepted, 2 enrolled. In 2011, 12 master's awarded. *Entrance requirements:* For master's, GRE (if GPA less than 2.75). Additional exam requirements/recommendations for international students: Required—TOEFL (minimum score 237 computer-based). *Application deadline:* For fall admission, 4/30 for international students; for spring admission, 9/30 for international students. Applications are processed on a rolling basis. Application fee: $30. Electronic applications accepted. *Expenses: Tuition, area resident:* Part-time $416 per credit. Tuition, state resident: part-time $416 per credit. Tuition, nonresident: part-time $624 per credit. *Required fees:* $119 per credit. *Financial support:* In 2011–12, 4 research assistantships with full tuition reimbursements (averaging $5,000 per year) were awarded; career-related internships or fieldwork, scholarships/grants, unspecified assistantships, and resident hall director and student payroll positions also available. Support available to part-time students. Financial award application deadline: 3/1; financial award applicants required to submit FAFSA. *Unit head:* Dr. Jeonghwa Lee, Program Coordinator, 717-477-1178, Fax: 717-477-4002, E-mail: jlee@ship.edu. *Application contact:* Jeremy R. Goshorn, Assistant Dean of Graduate Admissions, 717-477-1231, Fax: 717-477-4016, E-mail: jrgoshorn@ship.edu. Web site: http://www.cs.ship.edu/.

Silicon Valley University, Graduate Programs, San Jose, CA 95131. Offers business administration (MBA); computer engineering (MSCE); computer science (MSCS). *Degree requirements:* For master's, project (MSCS).

Simon Fraser University, Graduate Studies, Faculty of Applied Sciences, School of Computing Science, Burnaby, BC V5A 1S6, Canada. Offers M Sc, PhD. *Degree requirements:* For master's, comprehensive exam, thesis or alternative; for doctorate, comprehensive exam, thesis/dissertation, qualifying exams. *Entrance requirements:* For master's, minimum GPA of 3.0; for doctorate, minimum GPA of 3.5. Additional exam requirements/recommendations for international students: Required—GRE General Test, GRE Subject Test, or IELTS. Electronic applications accepted. *Faculty research:* Artificial intelligence, computer hardware, computer systems, database systems, theory.

Simon Fraser University, Graduate Studies, Faculty of Applied Sciences, School of Interactive Arts and Technology, Surrey, BC V3T 2W1, Canada. Offers information technology (M Sc, PhD); interactive arts (M Sc, PhD). *Degree requirements:* For master's, thesis; for doctorate, comprehensive exam, thesis/dissertation. *Entrance requirements:* For master's, 2 references, curriculum vitae; for doctorate, 3 references, curriculum vitae, minimum GPA of 3.0. Additional exam requirements/recommendations for international students: Required—TOEFL (minimum score 570 paper-based; 230 computer-based), TWE (minimum score 5). Electronic applications accepted.

Southern Arkansas University–Magnolia, Graduate Programs, Magnolia, AR 71754. Offers agriculture (MS); business administration (MBA); computer and information sciences (MS); education (M Ed), including counseling and development, curriculum and instruction, educational administration and supervision, elementary education, middle level, reading, secondary education, TESOL; kinesiology (M Ed); library media and information specialist (M Ed); mental health and clinical counseling (MS); public administration (MPA); school counseling (M Ed); teaching (MAT). *Accreditation:* NCATE. Part-time and evening/weekend programs available. Postbaccalaureate distance learning degree programs offered. *Faculty:* 34 full-time (15 women), 8 part-time/adjunct (5 women). *Students:* 87 full-time (62 women), 320 part-time (224 women); includes 116 minority (111 Black or African American, non-Hispanic/Latino; 2 American Indian or Alaska Native, non-Hispanic/Latino; 2 Asian, non-Hispanic/Latino; 1 Hispanic/Latino), 25 international. Average age 33. 201 applicants, 98% accepted, 156 enrolled. In 2011, 162 master's awarded. *Degree requirements:* For master's, comprehensive exam (for some programs), thesis optional. *Entrance requirements:* For master's, GRE, MAT or GMAT, minimum GPA of 2.5. Additional exam requirements/recommendations for international students: Required—TOEFL (minimum score 173 computer-based). *Application deadline:* For fall admission, 7/15 for domestic and international students; for winter admission, 12/1 for domestic and international students; for spring admission, 12/1 for domestic and international students. Applications are processed on a rolling basis. Application fee: $25 ($35 for international students). Electronic applications accepted. *Expenses:* Tuition, state resident: part-time $232 per credit. Tuition, nonresident: part-time $339 per credit. *Required fees:* $44 per credit. Part-time tuition and fees vary according to course load. *Financial support:* Career-related internships or fieldwork, Federal Work-Study, scholarships/grants, tuition waivers (full), and unspecified assistantships available. Financial award applicants required to submit FAFSA. *Faculty research:* Alternative certification for teachers, supervision of instruction, instructional leadership, counseling. *Unit head:* Dr. Kim Bloss, Dean, School of Graduate Studies, 870-235-4150, Fax: 870-235-5227, E-mail: kkbloss@saumag.edu. *Application contact:* Gaye Calhoun, Admissions Specialist, 870-235-4150, Fax: 870-235-5227, E-mail: glcalhoun@saumag.edu. Web site: http://www.saumag.edu/graduate.

Southern Connecticut State University, School of Graduate Studies, School of Arts and Sciences, Department of Computer Science, New Haven, CT 06515-1355. Offers MS. *Faculty:* 4 full-time (2 women). *Students:* 9 full-time (1 woman), 16 part-time (3 women); includes 4 minority (3 Asian, non-Hispanic/Latino; 1 Hispanic/Latino), 3 international. 41 applicants, 20% accepted, 8 enrolled. In 2011, 4 master's awarded. *Entrance requirements:* For master's, GRE. *Application deadline:* Applications are processed on a rolling basis. Application fee: $50. Electronic applications accepted. *Expenses:* Tuition, state resident: full-time $5137; part-time $413 per credit. *Required fees:* $4008; $55 per term. *Unit head:* Dr. Winnie Yu, Chairperson, 203-392-5812, Fax: 203-392-5898, E-mail: yuw1@southernct.edu. *Application contact:* Dr. Lisa Lancor, Coordinator, 203-392-5890, Fax: 203-392-5898, E-mail: lancorl1@southernct.edu.

Southern Illinois University Carbondale, Graduate School, College of Science, Department of Computer Science, Carbondale, IL 62901-4701. Offers MS, PhD. *Faculty:* 12 full-time (0 women). *Students:* 58 full-time (11 women), 34 part-time (10 women); includes 4 minority (all Asian, non-Hispanic/Latino), 65 international. 180 applicants, 37% accepted, 20 enrolled. In 2011, 28 master's awarded. *Degree requirements:* For master's, thesis. *Entrance requirements:* For master's, previous undergraduate course work in computer science, minimum GPA of 2.7. Additional exam requirements/recommendations for international students: Required—TOEFL. *Application deadline:* Applications are processed on a rolling basis. Application fee: $20.

Financial support: In 2011–12, 32 students received support, including 3 research assistantships with full tuition reimbursements available, 22 teaching assistantships with full tuition reimbursements available; fellowships with full tuition reimbursements available, Federal Work-Study, institutionally sponsored loans, and tuition waivers (full) also available. Support available to part-time students. Financial award application deadline: 3/1. *Faculty research:* Analysis of algorithms, VLSI testing, database systems, artificial intelligence, computer architecture. *Unit head:* Dr. Mehdi Zargham, Chairperson, 618-453-6042, E-mail: mehdi@cs.siu.edu. *Application contact:* Georgia Marine Norman, Graduate Program Secretary, 618-453-6041, Fax: 618-453-6044, E-mail: georgia@cs.siu.edu. Web site: http://www.cs.siu.edu/.

Southern Illinois University Edwardsville, Graduate School, School of Engineering, Department of Computer Science, Edwardsville, IL 62026. Offers MS. Part-time programs available. *Faculty:* 9 full-time (0 women). *Students:* 13 full-time (1 woman), 23 part-time (3 women); includes 2 minority (1 Asian, non-Hispanic/Latino; 1 Two or more races, non-Hispanic/Latino), 18 international. 150 applicants, 27% accepted. In 2011, 8 master's awarded. *Degree requirements:* For master's, thesis (for some programs), final exam. *Entrance requirements:* Additional exam requirements/recommendations for international students: Required—TOEFL (minimum score 550 paper-based; 213 computer-based; 79 iBT), IELTS (minimum score 6.5). *Application deadline:* For fall admission, 7/22 for domestic students, 6/1 for international students; for spring admission, 12/9 for domestic students, 10/1 for international students. Applications are processed on a rolling basis. Application fee: $30. Electronic applications accepted. Tuition and fees vary according to course load and program. *Financial support:* In 2011–12, 4 research assistantships with full tuition reimbursements (averaging $9,927 per year), 8 teaching assistantships with full tuition reimbursements (averaging $9,927 per year) were awarded; fellowships with full tuition reimbursements, institutionally sponsored loans, scholarships/grants, and unspecified assistantships also available. Financial award application deadline: 3/1; financial award applicants required to submit FAFSA. *Unit head:* Dr. Dennis Bouvier, Chair, 618-650-2369, E-mail: dbouvie@siue.edu. *Application contact:* Dr. Xudong Yu, Program Director, 618-650-2321, E-mail: xyu@siue.edu. Web site: http://www.cs.siue.edu/.

Southern Methodist University, Bobby B. Lyle School of Engineering, Department of Computer Science and Engineering, Dallas, TX 75275-0122. Offers computer engineering (MS Cp E, PhD); computer science (MS, PhD); security engineering (MS); software engineering (MS). Part-time and evening/weekend programs available. Postbaccalaureate distance learning degree programs offered (no on-campus study). Terminal master's awarded for partial completion of doctoral program. *Degree requirements:* For master's, thesis optional; for doctorate, thesis/dissertation, oral and written qualifying exams, oral final exam (PhD). *Entrance requirements:* For master's, GRE General Test, minimum GPA of 3.0 in last 2 years; bachelor's degree in engineering, mathematics, or sciences; for doctorate, preliminary counseling exam (PhD), minimum GPA of 3.0, bachelor's degree in related field, MA (DE). Additional exam requirements/recommendations for international students: Required—TOEFL (minimum score 550 paper-based; 213 computer-based). *Faculty research:* Trusted and high performance network computing, software engineering and management, knowledge engineering and management, computer arithmetic, computer architecture and CAD.

Southern Oregon University, Graduate Studies, College of Arts and Sciences, Department of Computer Science, Ashland, OR 97520. Offers applied computer science (PSM). Part-time programs available. *Faculty:* 4 full-time (0 women), 2 part-time/adjunct (1 woman). *Students:* 4 full-time (1 woman), 2 part-time (0 women), 1 international. Average age 33. 5 applicants, 40% accepted, 1 enrolled. In 2011, 2 degrees awarded. *Entrance requirements:* For master's, GRE General Test, minimum GPA of 3.0. *Application deadline:* Applications are processed on a rolling basis. Application fee: $50. *Expenses:* Tuition, state resident: full-time $12,600; part-time $350 per credit. Tuition, nonresident: full-time $16,200; part-time $450 per credit. *Required fees:* $1590. *Financial support:* Research assistantships available. *Unit head:* Dr. Greg Pleva, Chair, 541-552-6973. *Application contact:* Mark Bottorff, Director of Admissions, 541-552-6411, Fax: 541-552-8403, E-mail: admissions@sou.edu. Web site: http://www.sou.edu/cs/.

Southern Polytechnic State University, School of Computing and Software Engineering, Department of Computer Science and Software Engineering, Marietta, GA 30060-2896. Offers computer science (MS, Graduate Transition Certificate); software engineering (MSSWE, Graduate Certificate); software engineering fundamentals (Graduate Transition Certificate). Part-time and evening/weekend programs available. Postbaccalaureate distance learning degree programs offered (no on-campus study). *Faculty:* 12 full-time (1 woman), 3 part-time/adjunct (0 women). *Students:* 63 full-time (14 women), 77 part-time (17 women); includes 43 minority (29 Black or African American, non-Hispanic/Latino; 12 Asian, non-Hispanic/Latino; 2 Hispanic/Latino), 39 international. Average age 31. 94 applicants, 77% accepted, 45 enrolled. In 2011, 29 master's, 2 other advanced degrees awarded. *Degree requirements:* For master's, thesis optional, capstone (software engineering). *Entrance requirements:* For master's, GRE (recommended). Additional exam requirements/recommendations for international students: Required—TOEFL (minimum score 550 paper-based; 213 computer-based; 79 iBT), IELTS (minimum score 6.5). *Application deadline:* For fall admission, 7/1 priority date for domestic students, 5/1 for international students; for spring admission, 11/1 priority date for domestic students, 9/1 for international students. Applications are processed on a rolling basis. Application fee: $50. Electronic applications accepted. *Expenses:* Tuition, state resident: full-time $2592; part-time $216 per semester hour. Tuition, nonresident: full-time $9408; part-time $784 per semester hour. *Required fees:* $698 per term. *Financial support:* In 2011–12, 13 students received support, including 3 research assistantships with tuition reimbursements available, 11 teaching assistantships with tuition reimbursements available; career-related internships or fieldwork, scholarships/grants, unspecified assistantships, and cooperative programs also available. Financial award application deadline: 5/1; financial award applicants required to submit FAFSA. *Faculty research:* Image processing and artificial intelligence information retrieval, distributed computing, telemedicine applications, enterprise architectures, databases, software requirements engineering, software quality and metrics, usability, parallel and distributed computing, information security. *Unit head:* Dr. Venu Dasigi, Chair, 678-915-3571, Fax: 678-915-5511, E-mail: vdasigi@spsu.edu. *Application contact:* Nikki Palamiotis, Director of Graduate Studies, 678-915-4276, Fax: 678-915-7292, E-mail: npalamio@spsu.edu. Web site: http://www.spsu.edu/cswe/.

Southern University and Agricultural and Mechanical College, Graduate School, College of Sciences, Department of Computer Science, Baton Rouge, LA 70813. Offers information systems (MS); micro/minicomputer architecture (MS); operating systems (MS). Part-time programs available. Postbaccalaureate distance learning degree programs offered (minimal on-campus study). *Degree requirements:* For master's, thesis. *Entrance requirements:* For master's, GRE General Test, minimum GPA of 3.0, bachelor's degree in computer science or related field. Additional exam requirements/recommendations for international students: Required—TOEFL (minimum score 525 paper-based; 193 computer-based). *Faculty research:* Network theory, computational complexity, high speed computing, neural networking, data warehousing/mining.

Stanford University, School of Engineering, Department of Computer Science, Stanford, CA 94305-9991. Offers MS, PhD. Terminal master's awarded for partial completion of doctoral program. *Degree requirements:* For doctorate, thesis/dissertation. *Entrance requirements:* For master's, GRE General Test; for doctorate, GRE General Test, GRE Computer Science Subject Test. Additional exam requirements/recommendations for international students: Required—TOEFL. Electronic applications accepted. *Expenses: Tuition:* Full-time $40,050; part-time $890 per credit.

Stanford University, School of Engineering, Program in Scientific Computing and Computational Mathematics, Stanford, CA 94305-9991. Offers MS, PhD. Terminal master's awarded for partial completion of doctoral program. *Degree requirements:* For doctorate, thesis/dissertation, qualifying exam. *Entrance requirements:* For master's, GRE General Test; for doctorate, GRE General Test, GRE Subject Test. Additional exam requirements/recommendations for international students: Required—TOEFL. Electronic applications accepted. *Expenses: Tuition:* Full-time $40,050; part-time $890 per credit.

State University of New York at Binghamton, Graduate School, School of Arts and Sciences, Department of Mathematical Sciences, Binghamton, NY 13902-6000. Offers computer science (MA, PhD); probability and statistics (MA, PhD). Part-time programs available. *Faculty:* 27 full-time (4 women), 18 part-time/adjunct (7 women). *Students:* 45 full-time (11 women), 27 part-time (9 women); includes 5 minority (2 Black or African American, non-Hispanic/Latino; 2 Hispanic/Latino; 1 Native Hawaiian or other Pacific Islander, non-Hispanic/Latino), 31 international. Average age 28. 86 applicants, 45% accepted, 22 enrolled. In 2011, 12 master's, 3 doctorates awarded. Terminal master's awarded for partial completion of doctoral program. *Degree requirements:* For master's, thesis or alternative; for doctorate, 2 foreign languages, thesis/dissertation. *Entrance requirements:* For master's and doctorate, GRE General Test, GRE Subject Test. Additional exam requirements/recommendations for international students: Required—TOEFL (minimum score 550 paper-based; 213 computer-based; 80 iBT). *Application deadline:* For fall admission, 4/15 priority date for domestic students, 4/15 for international students; for spring admission, 11/30 priority date for domestic students, 11/30 for international students. Applications are processed on a rolling basis. Application fee: $60. Electronic applications accepted. *Financial support:* In 2011–12, 58 students received support, including 5 fellowships with full tuition reimbursements available (averaging $16,500 per year), research assistantships with full tuition reimbursements available (averaging $16,500 per year), 51 teaching assistantships with full tuition reimbursements available (averaging $16,500 per year); career-related internships or fieldwork, Federal Work-Study, institutionally sponsored loans, scholarships/grants, health care benefits, tuition waivers (full and partial), and unspecified assistantships also available. Financial award application deadline: 2/15; financial award applicants required to submit FAFSA. *Unit head:* Dr. Fernando Guzman, Chairperson, 607-777-2148, E-mail: fer@math.binghamton.edu. *Application contact:* Catherine Smith, Recruiting and Admissions Coordinator, 607-777-2151, Fax: 607-777-2501, E-mail: cmsmith@binghamton.edu.

State University of New York at Binghamton, Graduate School, Thomas J. Watson School of Engineering and Applied Science, Department of Computer Science, Binghamton, NY 13902-6000. Offers M Eng, MS, PhD. Part-time programs available. *Faculty:* 23 full-time (3 women), 10 part-time/adjunct (4 women). *Students:* 133 full-time (33 women), 114 part-time (18 women); includes 10 minority (1 Black or African American, non-Hispanic/Latino; 1 American Indian or Alaska Native, non-Hispanic/Latino; 3 Hispanic/Latino; 5 Native Hawaiian or other Pacific Islander, non-Hispanic/Latino), 193 international. Average age 27. 372 applicants, 71% accepted, 52 enrolled. In 2011, 81 master's, 7 doctorates awarded. *Degree requirements:* For master's, thesis or alternative; for doctorate, thesis/dissertation. *Entrance requirements:* For master's and doctorate, GRE General Test, GRE Subject Test. Additional exam requirements/recommendations for international students: Required—TOEFL. *Application deadline:* For fall admission, 4/15 priority date for domestic students, 1/15 for international students; for spring admission, 11/1 for domestic students, 10/1 for international students. Applications are processed on a rolling basis. Application fee: $60. Electronic applications accepted. *Financial support:* In 2011–12, 62 students received support, including 1 fellowship with full tuition reimbursement available (averaging $16,500 per year), 23 research assistantships with full tuition reimbursements available (averaging $16,500 per year), 27 teaching assistantships with full tuition reimbursements available (averaging $16,500 per year); career-related internships or fieldwork, Federal Work-Study, institutionally sponsored loans, scholarships/grants, health care benefits, and unspecified assistantships also available. Financial award application deadline: 2/15; financial award applicants required to submit FAFSA. *Unit head:* Dr. Kanad Ghose, Chair, 607-777-4803, E-mail: ghose@cs.binghamton.edu. *Application contact:* Catherine Smith, Recruiting and Admissions Coordinator, 607-777-2151, Fax: 607-777-2501, E-mail: cmsmith@binghamton.edu.

State University of New York at New Paltz, Graduate School, School of Science and Engineering, Department of Computer Science, New Paltz, NY 12561. Offers MS. Part-time and evening/weekend programs available. *Faculty:* 6 full-time (1 woman). *Students:* 29 full-time (7 women), 11 part-time (1 woman); includes 5 minority (1 Black or African American, non-Hispanic/Latino; 3 Hispanic/Latino; 1 Two or more races, non-Hispanic/Latino), 27 international. Average age 26. 79 applicants, 72% accepted, 12 enrolled. In 2011, 21 master's awarded. *Degree requirements:* For master's, comprehensive exam, thesis. *Entrance requirements:* For master's, minimum GPA of 3.0, proficiency in program assembly. Additional exam requirements/recommendations for international students: Required—TOEFL (minimum score 550 paper-based; 213 computer-based; 80 iBT), IELTS (minimum score 6.5). *Application deadline:* For fall admission, 5/15 priority date for domestic students, 5/15 for international students; for spring admission, 11/15 for domestic and international students. Applications are processed on a rolling basis. Application fee: $50. Electronic applications accepted. *Expenses:* Tuition, state resident: full-time $8870; part-time $370 per credit. Tuition, nonresident: full-time $15,160; part-time $632 per credit. *Required fees:* $1188; $34 per credit. $184 per semester. *Financial support:* In 2011–12, 3 students received support, including 3 teaching assistantships with partial tuition reimbursements available (averaging $5,000 per year); unspecified assistantships also available. Financial award application deadline: 8/1; financial award applicants required to submit FAFSA. *Unit head:* Dr. Andrew Pletch, Chair, 845-257-3990, Fax: 845-257-3996, E-mail: pletcha@newpaltz.edu. *Application contact:* Dr. Paul Zuckerman, Graduate Coordinator, 845-257-3516, E-mail: zuckerpr@newpaltz.edu. Web site: http://www.newpaltz.edu/compsci/.

State University of New York Institute of Technology, Program in Computer and Information Science, Utica, NY 13504-3050. Offers MS. Part-time and evening/weekend programs available. *Degree requirements:* For master's, thesis or project. *Entrance* *requirements:* For master's, GRE General Test, minimum GPA of 3.0, letter of recommendation. Additional exam requirements/recommendations for international students: Required—TOEFL (minimum score 550 paper-based; 213 computer-based). *Faculty research:* Cryptography, distributed systems, computer-aided system theory, reasoning with uncertainty, grid computing.

Stephen F. Austin State University, Graduate School, College of Business, Department of Computer Science, Nacogdoches, TX 75962. Offers MS. Part-time programs available. *Degree requirements:* For master's, comprehensive exam, thesis optional. *Entrance requirements:* For master's, GRE General Test. Additional exam requirements/recommendations for international students: Required—TOEFL.

Stevens Institute of Technology, Graduate School, Charles V. Schaefer Jr. School of Engineering, Department of Computer Science, Program in Computer Science, Hoboken, NJ 07030. Offers MS, PhD.

Stevens Institute of Technology, Graduate School, Wesley J. Howe School of Technology Management, Program in Information Systems, Hoboken, NJ 07030. Offers computer science (MS); e-commerce (MS); enterprise systems (MS); entrepreneurial information technology (MS); information architecture (MS); information management (MS, Certificate); information security (MS); information technology in financial services industry (MS); information technology in the pharmaceutical industry (MS); information technology outsourcing management (MS); project management (MS, Certificate); software engineering (MS); telecommunications (MS). *Degree requirements:* For master's, thesis optional. *Entrance requirements:* For master's, GMAT, GRE General Test. Additional exam requirements/recommendations for international students: Required—TOEFL. Electronic applications accepted.

Stony Brook University, State University of New York, Graduate School, College of Engineering and Applied Sciences, Department of Computer Science, Stony Brook, NY 11794. Offers computer science (MS, PhD); information systems (Certificate); information systems engineering (MS); software engineering (Certificate). *Degree requirements:* For master's, thesis or alternative; for doctorate, comprehensive exam, thesis/dissertation. *Entrance requirements:* For master's and doctorate, GRE General Test. Additional exam requirements/recommendations for international students: Required—TOEFL. *Faculty research:* Artificial intelligence, computer architecture, database management systems, VLSI, operating systems.

Suffolk University, College of Arts and Sciences, Department of Mathematics and Computer Science, Boston, MA 02108-2770. Offers software engineering and databases (MSCS). Part-time and evening/weekend programs available. *Faculty:* 6 full-time (0 women), 1 part-time/adjunct (0 women). *Students:* 21 full-time (5 women), 1 part-time (0 women), 19 international. Average age 26. 29 applicants, 79% accepted, 8 enrolled. In 2011, 10 master's awarded. *Degree requirements:* For master's, thesis optional. *Entrance requirements:* For master's, statement of professional goals, official transcripts, 2 letters of recommendation, resume. Additional exam requirements/recommendations for international students: Required—TOEFL (minimum score 550 paper-based; 213 computer-based; 80 iBT). *Application deadline:* For fall admission, 6/15 priority date for domestic students, 6/15 for international students; for spring admission, 11/1 priority date for domestic students, 11/1 for international students. Applications are processed on a rolling basis. Application fee: $50. Electronic applications accepted. *Expenses:* Contact institution. *Financial support:* In 2011–12, 16 students received support, including 16 fellowships with full and partial tuition reimbursements available (averaging $6,764 per year); career-related internships or fieldwork, Federal Work-Study, and institutionally sponsored loans also available. Financial award application deadline: 4/1; financial award applicants required to submit FAFSA. *Faculty research:* Peer-to-peer systems, grid cluster computing, human-computer interaction, large scale, IP networks, distributed load balancing. *Unit head:* Dr. Edith Cook, Chairperson, 617-573-8621, Fax: 617-573-8591, E-mail: ecook@mcs.suffolk.edu. *Application contact:* Ellen Driscoll, Director of Graduate Admissions, 617-573-8302, Fax: 617-305-1733, E-mail: grad.admission@suffolk.edu. Web site: http://www.mcs.suffolk.edu.

Syracuse University, L. C. Smith College of Engineering and Computer Science, Program in Computer Science, Syracuse, NY 13244. Offers MS. Part-time programs available. *Students:* 87 full-time (15 women), 9 part-time (1 woman); includes 4 minority (1 American Indian or Alaska Native, non-Hispanic/Latino; 2 Asian, non-Hispanic/Latino; 1 Hispanic/Latino), 81 international. Average age 24. 695 applicants, 28% accepted, 40 enrolled. In 2011, 44 degrees awarded. *Entrance requirements:* For master's, GRE General Test. Additional exam requirements/recommendations for international students: Required—TOEFL (minimum score 100 iBT). *Application deadline:* For fall admission, 7/1 priority date for domestic students, 6/1 for international students. Applications are processed on a rolling basis. Application fee: $75. Electronic applications accepted. *Expenses: Tuition:* Part-time $1206 per credit. *Financial support:* Fellowships with full tuition reimbursements, research assistantships with full and partial tuition reimbursements, teaching assistantships with full and partial tuition reimbursements, and tuition waivers (partial) available. Financial award application deadline: 1/1; financial award applicants required to submit FAFSA. *Unit head:* Dr. Jae Oh, Program Director, 315-443-4740, Fax: 315-443-2583, E-mail: jcoh@syr.edu. *Application contact:* Barbara Decker, Information Contact, 315-443-2368, E-mail: badecker@syr.edu. Web site: http://lcs.syr.edu/.

Télé-université, Graduate Programs, Québec, QC G1K 9H5, Canada. Offers computer science (PhD); corporate finance (MS); distance learning (MS). Part-time programs available.

Temple University, College of Science and Technology, Department of Computer and Information Sciences, Philadelphia, PA 19122-6096. Offers MS, PhD. Part-time and evening/weekend programs available. *Faculty:* 20 full-time (1 woman). *Students:* 51 full-time (9 women), 9 part-time (2 women); includes 4 minority (3 Black or African American, non-Hispanic/Latino; 1 Asian, non-Hispanic/Latino), 48 international. Average age 29. 40 applicants, 83% accepted, 13 enrolled. In 2011, 5 master's, 3 doctorates awarded. Terminal master's awarded for partial completion of doctoral program. *Degree requirements:* For doctorate, thesis/dissertation. *Entrance requirements:* For master's and doctorate, GRE General Test, minimum GPA of 3.0. Additional exam requirements/recommendations for international students: Required—TOEFL (minimum score 550 paper-based; 213 computer-based; 79 iBT). *Application deadline:* For fall admission, 2/1 for domestic students, 12/15 for international students; for spring admission, 8/1 for domestic and international students. Applications are processed on a rolling basis. Application fee: $50. Electronic applications accepted. *Expenses:* Tuition, state resident: full-time $12,366; part-time $687 per credit hour. Tuition, nonresident: full-time $17,298; part-time $961 per credit hour. *Required fees:* $590; $213 per year. *Financial support:* Fellowships, research assistantships with tuition reimbursements, teaching assistantships with tuition reimbursements, career-related internships or fieldwork, institutionally sponsored loans, and unspecified assistantships available. Financial award application deadline: 1/15; financial award applicants required to submit FAFSA. *Faculty research:* Artificial intelligence, information systems, software engineering, network-distributed systems. *Unit head:* Dr. Jie Wu, Chair, 215-204-8450, Fax: 215-204-5082, E-mail: cis@temple.edu. *Application contact:* Tara Schumacher, Coordinator of Outreach, 215-204-6575, Fax: 215-204-8781, E-mail: tara.schumacher@temple.edu. Web site: http://www.temple.edu/cis.

Tennessee Technological University, Graduate School, College of Engineering, Department of Computer Science, Cookeville, TN 38505. Offers computer software and scientific applications (MS); Internet-based computing (MS). Part-time programs available. *Students:* 4 full-time (2 women), 12 part-time (1 woman), 2 international. 27 applicants, 59% accepted, 5 enrolled. In 2011, 4 master's awarded. *Degree requirements:* For master's, thesis or alternative. *Entrance requirements:* For master's, GRE. Additional exam requirements/recommendations for international students: Required—TOEFL (minimum score 550 paper-based; 79 iBT), IELTS (minimum score 5.5), PTE Academic. *Application deadline:* For fall admission, 8/1 for domestic students, 5/1 for international students; for spring admission, 12/1 for domestic students, 10/1 for international students. Application fee: $25 ($30 for international students). Electronic applications accepted. *Expenses:* Tuition, state resident: full-time $8094; part-time $422 per credit hour. Tuition, nonresident: full-time $20,574; part-time $1046 per credit hour. *Financial support:* In 2011–12, 4 research assistantships (averaging $7,500 per year), 3 teaching assistantships (averaging $7,500 per year) were awarded. Financial award application deadline: 4/1. *Unit head:* Dr. Doug Talbert, Interim Chairperson, 931-372-3691, Fax: 931-372-3686, E-mail: dtalbert@tntech.edu. *Application contact:* Shelia K. Kendrick, Coordinator of Graduate Admissions, 931-372-3808, Fax: 931-372-3497, E-mail: skendrick@tntech.edu.

Texas A&M University, College of Engineering, Department of Computer Science, College Station, TX 77843. Offers computer engineering (M En); computer science (MCS); computer science and engineering (MS, PhD). Part-time programs available. *Faculty:* 37. *Students:* 261 full-time (45 women), 57 part-time (10 women); includes 31 minority (6 Black or African American, non-Hispanic/Latino; 10 Asian, non-Hispanic/Latino; 11 Hispanic/Latino; 1 Native Hawaiian or other Pacific Islander, non-Hispanic/Latino; 3 Two or more races, non-Hispanic/Latino), 217 international. Average age 28. In 2011, 59 master's, 25 doctorates awarded. *Degree requirements:* For master's, thesis (for some programs); for doctorate, thesis/dissertation. *Entrance requirements:* For master's and doctorate, GRE General Test. Additional exam requirements/recommendations for international students: Required—TOEFL (minimum score 213 computer-based). *Application deadline:* For fall admission, 3/1 priority date for domestic students, 3/1 for international students; for spring admission, 8/1 priority date for domestic students, 8/1 for international students. Applications are processed on a rolling basis. Application fee: $50 ($75 for international students). Electronic applications accepted. *Expenses:* Tuition, state resident: full-time $5437; part-time $226.55 per credit hour. Tuition, nonresident: full-time $12,949; part-time $539.55 per credit hour. *Required fees:* $2741. *Financial support:* In 2011–12, research assistantships with tuition reimbursements (averaging $15,478 per year), teaching assistantships (averaging $15,913 per year) were awarded; fellowships with full tuition reimbursements also available. Financial award application deadline: 3/1. *Faculty research:* Software, systems, informatics, human-centered systems, theory. *Unit head:* Dr. Duncan (Hank) M. Walker, Head, 979-845-5820, Fax: 979-847-8578, E-mail: d-walker@tamu.edu. *Application contact:* Dr. Ricardo Gutierrez-Osuna, Graduate Advisor, 979-845-4259, Fax: 979-862-3684, E-mail: grad-admissions@cse.tamu.edu. Web site: http://www.cs.tamu.edu/.

Texas A&M University–Commerce, Graduate School, College of Science, Engineering and Agriculture, Department of Computer Science and Information Systems, Commerce, TX 75429-3011. Offers computer science (MS). Part-time programs available. *Degree requirements:* For master's, comprehensive exam, thesis (for some programs). *Entrance requirements:* For master's, GMAT or GRE General Test. Electronic applications accepted. *Faculty research:* Programming.

Texas A&M University–Corpus Christi, Graduate Studies and Research, College of Science and Technology, Program in Computer Science, Corpus Christi, TX 78412-5503. Offers MS. Part-time and evening/weekend programs available. *Degree requirements:* For master's, comprehensive exam, thesis (for some programs). *Entrance requirements:* For master's, GRE General Test. Additional exam requirements/recommendations for international students: Required—TOEFL. Electronic applications accepted.

Texas A&M University–Kingsville, College of Graduate Studies, College of Engineering, Department of Electrical Engineering and Computer Science, Program in Computer Science, Kingsville, TX 78363. Offers MS. *Degree requirements:* For master's, comprehensive exam, thesis or alternative. *Entrance requirements:* For master's, GRE General Test, minimum GPA of 3.0. Additional exam requirements/recommendations for international students: Required—TOEFL. *Faculty research:* Operating systems, programming languages, database systems, computer architecture, artificial intelligence.

Texas Southern University, School of Science and Technology, Department of Computer Science, Houston, TX 77004-4584. Offers MS. Electronic applications accepted.

Texas State University–San Marcos, Graduate School, College of Science and Engineering, Department of Computer Science, San Marcos, TX 78666. Offers computer science (MA, MS); software engineering (MS). Part-time programs available. *Faculty:* 16 full-time (3 women). *Students:* 104 full-time (29 women), 70 part-time (21 women); includes 37 minority (5 Black or African American, non-Hispanic/Latino; 9 Asian, non-Hispanic/Latino; 21 Hispanic/Latino; 2 Two or more races, non-Hispanic/Latino), 79 international. Average age 29. 233 applicants, 55% accepted, 44 enrolled. In 2011, 35 master's awarded. *Degree requirements:* For master's, comprehensive exam, thesis (for some programs). *Entrance requirements:* For master's, GRE General Test, minimum GPA of 2.75 in last 60 hours of course work. Additional exam requirements/recommendations for international students: Required—TOEFL (minimum score 550 paper-based; 213 computer-based; 78 iBT). *Application deadline:* For fall admission, 6/15 priority date for domestic students, 6/1 for international students; for spring admission, 10/15 priority date for domestic students, 10/1 for international students. Applications are processed on a rolling basis. Application fee: $40 ($90 for international students). Electronic applications accepted. *Expenses:* Tuition, state resident: full-time $6408; part-time $3204 per semester. Tuition, nonresident: full-time $14,832; part-time $7416 per semester. *Required fees:* $1824; $912 per semester. Tuition and fees vary according to course load. *Financial support:* In 2011–12, 38 students received support, including 12 research assistantships (averaging $10,872 per year), 27 teaching assistantships (averaging $10,080 per year); career-related internships or fieldwork, Federal Work-Study, institutionally sponsored loans, scholarships/grants, health care benefits, and unspecified assistantships also available. Support available to part-time students. Financial award application deadline: 4/1; financial award applicants required to submit FAFSA. *Faculty research:* Usability assessment, power consumption, hidden Web databases, REU sites, wireless networks. *Total annual research expenditures:*

$320,196. *Unit head:* Dr. Hongchi Shi, Chair, 512-245-3409, Fax: 512-245-8750, E-mail: hs15@txstate.edu. *Application contact:* Dr. Khosrow Kaikhah, Head, 512-245-3409, Fax: 512-245-8750, E-mail: kk02@txstate.edu. Web site: http://www.cs.txstate.edu/.

Texas Tech University, Graduate School, Edward E. Whitacre Jr. College of Engineering, Department of Computer Science, Lubbock, TX 79409. Offers computer science (MS, PhD); software engineering (MS). Part-time programs available. Postbaccalaureate distance learning degree programs offered (minimal on-campus study). *Faculty:* 18 full-time (3 women), 1 part-time/adjunct (0 women). *Students:* 88 full-time (10 women), 34 part-time (6 women); includes 7 minority (1 Asian, non-Hispanic/Latino; 4 Hispanic/Latino; 2 Two or more races, non-Hispanic/Latino), 93 international. Average age 27. 271 applicants, 48% accepted, 25 enrolled. In 2011, 27 master's, 2 doctorates awarded. *Degree requirements:* For master's, thesis or alternative; for doctorate, thesis/dissertation. *Entrance requirements:* For master's and doctorate, GRE General Test, minimum GPA of 3.0, statement of purpose, 3 letters of recommendation. Additional exam requirements/recommendations for international students: Required—TOEFL (minimum score 600 paper-based; 250 computer-based; 100 iBT). *Application deadline:* For fall admission, 6/1 priority date for domestic students, 1/15 for international students; for spring admission, 9/1 priority date for domestic students, 6/15 for international students. Applications are processed on a rolling basis. Application fee: $50 ($75 for international students). Electronic applications accepted. *Expenses:* Tuition, state resident: full-time $5899; part-time $245.80 per credit hour. Tuition, nonresident: full-time $13,411; part-time $558.80 per credit hour. *Required fees:* $2680.60; $86.50 per credit hour. $920.30 per semester. *Financial support:* In 2011–12, 25 students received support. Application deadline: 4/15; applicants required to submit FAFSA. *Faculty research:* Artificial intelligence, software engineering and languages, high performance computing, logic programming, image processing. *Total annual research expenditures:* $848,686. *Unit head:* Dr. Rattikorn Hewett, Chair, 806-742-3527, Fax: 806-742-3519, E-mail: rattikorn.hewett@ttu.edu. *Application contact:* Jennifer Hearron, Staff Graduate Advisor, 806-742-3527, Fax: 806-742-3519, E-mail: cs.grad_advisor@ttu.edu. Web site: http://www.cs.ttu.edu/.

Towson University, Program in Computer Science, Towson, MD 21252-0001. Offers MS. Part-time and evening/weekend programs available. *Students:* 89 full-time (26 women), 63 part-time (12 women); includes 31 minority (20 Black or African American, non-Hispanic/Latino; 5 Asian, non-Hispanic/Latino; 3 Hispanic/Latino; 3 Two or more races, non-Hispanic/Latino), 50 international. *Degree requirements:* For master's, thesis optional, exam. *Entrance requirements:* For master's, minimum GPA of 3.0, bachelor's degree in computer science or completion of 1-3 preparatory courses. Additional exam requirements/recommendations for international students: Required—TOEFL (minimum score 550 paper-based). *Application deadline:* Applications are processed on a rolling basis. Application fee: $50. Electronic applications accepted. *Expenses:* Tuition, state resident: part-time $337 per credit. Tuition, nonresident: part-time $709 per credit. *Required fees:* $99 per credit. *Financial support:* Application deadline: 4/1; applicants required to submit FAFSA. *Unit head:* Dr. Yanggon Kim, Graduate Program Director, 410-704-3701, E-mail: ykim@towson.edu.

Toyota Technological Institute of Chicago, Program in Computer Science, Chicago, IL 60637. Offers PhD. *Degree requirements:* For doctorate, thesis/dissertation.

Trent University, Graduate Studies, Program in Applications of Modeling in the Natural and Social Sciences, Department of Computer Studies, Peterborough, ON K9J 7B8, Canada. Offers M Sc. *Degree requirements:* For master's, thesis. *Entrance requirements:* For master's, honours degree.

Troy University, Graduate School, College of Arts and Sciences, Program in Computer Science, Troy, AL 36082. Offers MS. Part-time and evening/weekend programs available. *Faculty:* 10 full-time (2 women), 2 part-time/adjunct (0 women). *Students:* 22 full-time (6 women), 27 part-time (8 women); includes 38 minority (11 Black or African American, non-Hispanic/Latino; 1 American Indian or Alaska Native, non-Hispanic/Latino; 6 Asian, non-Hispanic/Latino; 1 Hispanic/Latino; 19 Two or more races, non-Hispanic/Latino). Average age 28. 239 applicants, 40% accepted, 16 enrolled. In 2011, 5 master's awarded. *Degree requirements:* For master's, thesis or research paper and comprehensive exam; minimum GPA of 3.0; admission to candidacy. *Entrance requirements:* For master's, GRE (minimum score of 800), BS in computer science; minimum GPA of 2.5. Additional exam requirements/recommendations for international students: Required—TOEFL (minimum score 523 paper-based; 193 computer-based; 70 iBT), IELTS (minimum score 6). *Application deadline:* For fall admission, 6/1 for international students; for spring admission, 10/15 for international students. Applications are processed on a rolling basis. Application fee: $50. Electronic applications accepted. *Expenses:* Tuition, state resident: full-time $6960; part-time $290 per credit hour. Tuition, nonresident: full-time $13,920; part-time $580 per credit hour. *Required fees:* $386 per term. *Unit head:* Dr. Irem Ozkarahan, Department Chairman/Professor, 334-241-9589, Fax: 334-241-9734, E-mail: iozkarahan@troy.edu. *Application contact:* Brenda K. Campbell, Director of Graduate Admissions, 334-670-3178, Fax: 334-670-3733, E-mail: bcamp@troy.edu.

Tufts University, Graduate School of Arts and Sciences, Graduate Certificate Programs, Computer Science Program, Medford, MA 02155. Offers Certificate. Part-time and evening/weekend programs available. Electronic applications accepted. *Expenses:* Tuition: Full-time $41,208; part-time $1030 per credit hour. Full-time tuition and fees vary according to degree level, program and student level. Part-time tuition and fees vary according to course load.

Tufts University, Graduate School of Arts and Sciences, Graduate Certificate Programs, Post-Baccalaureate Minor Program in Computer Science, Medford, MA 02155. Offers Certificate. Part-time and evening/weekend programs available. Electronic applications accepted. *Expenses: Tuition:* Full-time $41,208; part-time $1030 per credit hour. Full-time tuition and fees vary according to degree level, program and student level. Part-time tuition and fees vary according to course load.

Tufts University, School of Engineering, Department of Computer Science, Medford, MA 02155. Offers bioengineering (MS), including bioinformatics; computer science (PhD), including cognitive science. Part-time programs available. *Faculty:* 16 full-time, 1 part-time/adjunct. *Students:* 62 (16 women); includes 10 minority (all Asian, non-Hispanic/Latino), 19 international. Average age 27. 169 applicants, 34% accepted, 23 enrolled. In 2011, 13 master's, 9 doctorates awarded. Terminal master's awarded for partial completion of doctoral program. *Degree requirements:* For master's, thesis (for some programs); for doctorate, thesis/dissertation. *Entrance requirements:* For master's and doctorate, GRE. Additional exam requirements/recommendations for international students: Required—TOEFL (minimum score 550 paper-based; 213 computer-based; 80 iBT). *Application deadline:* For fall admission, 1/15 for domestic students, 12/15 for international students; for spring admission, 9/15 for domestic and international students. Applications are processed on a rolling basis. Application fee: $75. Electronic applications accepted. *Expenses: Tuition:* Full-time $41,208; part-time $1030 per credit hour. Full-time tuition and fees vary according to degree level, program and student level. Part-time tuition and fees vary according to course load. *Financial support:*

Fellowships with full tuition reimbursements, research assistantships with full and partial tuition reimbursements, teaching assistantships with full and partial tuition reimbursements, Federal Work-Study, scholarships/grants, tuition waivers (partial), and unspecified assistantships available. Financial award application deadline: 1/15; financial award applicants required to submit FAFSA. *Faculty research:* Computational biology, computational geometry, and computational systems biology; cognitive sciences, human-computer interaction, and human robotic interaction; visualization and graphics, educational technologies; machine learning and data mining; programming languages and systems. *Unit head:* Dr. Carla Brodley, Chair, 617-627-2225, Fax: 617-627-2227. *Application contact:* Dr. Lenore Cowen, Information Contact, 617-623-3217, Fax: 617-627-3220, E-mail: csadmin@cs.tufts.edu. Web site: http://www.cs.tufts.edu.

Union Graduate College, School of Engineering and Computer Science, Schenectady, NY 12308-3107. Offers computer science (MS); electrical engineering (MS); engineering and management systems (MS); mechanical engineering (MS). Part-time and evening/weekend programs available. *Faculty:* 3 full-time (0 women), 20 part-time/adjunct (2 women). *Students:* 13 full-time (1 woman), 103 part-time (13 women); includes 15 minority (2 Black or African American, non-Hispanic/Latino; 6 Asian, non-Hispanic/Latino; 6 Hispanic/Latino; 1 Two or more races, non-Hispanic/Latino), 3 international. Average age 28. 62 applicants, 69% accepted, 38 enrolled. In 2011, 29 master's awarded. *Degree requirements:* For master's, capstone course. *Entrance requirements:* For master's, minimum GPA of 3.0, letters of recommendation. Additional exam requirements/recommendations for international students: Required—TOEFL (minimum score 550 paper-based; 213 computer-based). *Application deadline:* Applications are processed on a rolling basis. Application fee: $60. Electronic applications accepted. *Expenses:* Contact institution. *Financial support:* In 2011–12, 2 students received support. Research assistantships, Federal Work-Study, scholarships/grants, health care benefits, and tuition waivers (full and partial) available. Support available to part-time students. Financial award applicants required to submit FAFSA. *Unit head:* Robert Kozik, Dean, 515-631-9881, Fax: 518-631-9902, E-mail: kozikr@union.edu. *Application contact:* Diane Trzaskos, Coordinator, Admissions, 518-631-9837, Fax: 518-631-9901, E-mail: trzaskod@uniongraduatecollege.edu.

Universidad Autonoma de Guadalajara, Graduate Programs, Guadalajara, Mexico. Offers administrative law and justice (LL M); advertising and corporate communications (MA); architecture (M Arch); business (MBA); computational science (MCC); education (Ed M, Ed D); English-Spanish translation (MA); entrepreneurship and management (MBA); integrated management of digital animation (MA); international business (MIB); international corporate law (LL M); internet technologies (MS); manufacturing systems (MMS); occupational health (MS); philosophy (MA, PhD); power electronics (MS); quality systems (MQS); renewable energy (MS); social evaluation of projects (MBA); strategic market research (MBA); tax law (MA); teaching mathematics (MA).

Universidad de las Américas–Puebla, Division of Graduate Studies, School of Engineering, Program in Computer Engineering, Puebla, Mexico. Offers computer science (MS). Part-time and evening/weekend programs available. *Degree requirements:* For master's, one foreign language, thesis. *Faculty research:* Computers in education, robotics, artificial intelligence.

Universidad de las Américas–Puebla, Division of Graduate Studies, School of Engineering, Program in Computer Science, Puebla, Mexico. Offers PhD.

Université de Moncton, Faculty of Sciences, Information Technology Programs, Moncton, NB E1A 3E9, Canada. Offers M Sc, Certificate, Diploma. Part-time programs available. *Degree requirements:* For master's, thesis. Electronic applications accepted. *Faculty research:* Programming, databases, networks.

Université de Montréal, Faculty of Arts and Sciences, Department of Computer Science and Operational Research, Montréal, QC H3C 3J7, Canada. Offers computer systems (M Sc, PhD); electronic commerce (M Sc). Part-time programs available. Terminal master's awarded for partial completion of doctoral program. *Degree requirements:* For master's, one foreign language, thesis; for doctorate, one foreign language, thesis/dissertation, general exam. *Entrance requirements:* For master's, B Sc in related field; for doctorate, MA or M Sc in related field. Electronic applications accepted. *Faculty research:* Optimization statistics, programming languages, telecommunications, theoretical computer science, artificial intelligence.

Université du Québec à Trois-Rivières, Graduate Programs, Program in Mathematics and Computer Science, Trois-Rivières, QC G9A 5H7, Canada. Offers M Sc. *Faculty research:* Probability, statistics.

Université du Québec en Outaouais, Graduate Programs, Program in Computer Network, Gatineau, QC J8X 3X7, Canada. Offers computer science (M Sc, PhD). Part-time and evening/weekend programs available. *Students:* 44 full-time, 17 part-time. *Degree requirements:* For master's, thesis; for doctorate, thesis/dissertation. *Application deadline:* For fall admission, 6/1 priority date for domestic students, 3/1 for international students; for winter admission, 11/1 priority date for domestic students, 10/1 for international students. Application fee: $30 Canadian dollars. *Unit head:* Kamel Adi, Director, 819-595-3900 Ext. 1600, Fax: 819-773-1875, E-mail: kamel.adi@uqo.ca. *Application contact:* Registrar's Office, 819-773-1850, Fax: 819-773-1835, E-mail: registraire@uqo.ca.

Université Laval, Faculty of Sciences and Engineering, Department of Computer Science, Programs in Computer Science, Québec, QC G1K 7P4, Canada. Offers M Sc, PhD. Terminal master's awarded for partial completion of doctoral program. *Degree requirements:* For master's, thesis; for doctorate, thesis/dissertation. *Entrance requirements:* For master's and doctorate, knowledge of French and English. Electronic applications accepted.

University at Albany, State University of New York, College of Computing and Information, Department of Computer Science, Albany, NY 12222-0001. Offers MS, PhD. *Degree requirements:* For master's, comprehensive exam, project or thesis; for doctorate, comprehensive exam, thesis/dissertation, area exams. *Entrance requirements:* For master's and doctorate, GRE General Test. Additional exam requirements/recommendations for international students: Required—TOEFL (minimum score 550 paper-based; 213 computer-based). Electronic applications accepted. *Faculty research:* Algorithm design and analysis, artificial intelligence, computational logic, databases, numerical analysis.

University at Buffalo, the State University of New York, Graduate School, School of Engineering and Applied Sciences, Department of Computer Science and Engineering, Buffalo, NY 14260. Offers computer science and engineering (MS, PhD); information assurance (Certificate). Part-time programs available. *Faculty:* 36 full-time (4 women). *Students:* 367 full-time (73 women), 13 part-time (1 woman); includes 4 minority (2 Black or African American, non-Hispanic/Latino; 1 Asian, non-Hispanic/Latino; 1 Hispanic/Latino), 341 international. Average age 25. 1,632 applicants, 40% accepted, 134 enrolled. In 2011, 120 master's, 12 doctorates awarded. Terminal master's awarded for partial completion of doctoral program. *Degree requirements:* For master's, thesis or alternative; for doctorate, thesis/dissertation, comprehensive qualifying exam. *Entrance* *requirements:* For master's and doctorate, GRE General Test. Additional exam requirements/recommendations for international students: Required—TOEFL (minimum score 550 paper-based; 213 computer-based; 79 iBT). *Application deadline:* For fall admission, 8/15 for domestic and international students. Application fee: $75. Electronic applications accepted. *Financial support:* In 2011–12, 103 students received support, including 5 fellowships with full tuition reimbursements available (averaging $28,900 per year), 53 research assistantships with full tuition reimbursements available (averaging $27,600 per year), 43 teaching assistantships with full tuition reimbursements available (averaging $24,000 per year); career-related internships or fieldwork, Federal Work-Study, institutionally sponsored loans, health care benefits, tuition waivers (partial), and unspecified assistantships also available. Financial award application deadline: 12/15; financial award applicants required to submit FAFSA. *Faculty research:* Bioinformatics, pattern recognition, computer networks and security, theory and algorithms, databases and data mining. *Total annual research expenditures:* $7.1 million. *Unit head:* Dr. Aidong Zhang, Chairman, 716-645-3180, Fax: 716-645-3464, E-mail: azhang@buffalo.edu. *Application contact:* Dr. Jan Chomicki, Director of Graduate Studies, 716-645-4735, Fax: 716-645-3464, E-mail: chomicki@buffalo.edu. Web site: http://www.cse.buffalo.edu/.

University of Advancing Technology, Master of Science Program in Technology, Tempe, AZ 85283-1042. Offers advancing computer science (MS); emerging technologies (MS); game production and management (MS); information assurance (MS); technology leadership (MS). *Degree requirements:* For master's, project or thesis. *Entrance requirements:* Additional exam requirements/recommendations for international students: Required—TOEFL (minimum score 550 paper-based). Electronic applications accepted. *Faculty research:* Artificial intelligence, fractals, organizational management.

The University of Akron, Graduate School, Buchtel College of Arts and Sciences, Department of Computer Science, Akron, OH 44325. Offers MS. *Faculty:* 6 full-time (2 women), 4 part-time/adjunct (1 woman). *Students:* 46 full-time (15 women), 9 part-time (1 woman); includes 3 minority (all Asian, non-Hispanic/Latino), 37 international. Average age 25. 68 applicants, 46% accepted, 9 enrolled. In 2011, 36 master's awarded. *Degree requirements:* For master's, thesis optional, seminar and comprehensive exam or thesis. *Entrance requirements:* For master's, baccalaureate degree in computer science or a related field, minimum GPA of 3.0, three letters of recommendation, statement of purpose, resume. Additional exam requirements/recommendations for international students: Required—TOEFL (minimum score 550 paper-based; 213 computer-based; 79 iBT). *Application deadline:* For fall admission, 3/15 for domestic and international students; for spring admission, 10/15 for domestic and international students. Application fee: $30 ($40 for international students). *Expenses:* Tuition, state resident: full-time $7038; part-time $391 per credit hour. Tuition, nonresident: full-time $12,051; part-time $670 per credit hour. *Required fees:* $1274; $34 per credit hour. *Financial support:* In 2011–12, 8 research assistantships with full tuition reimbursements, 22 teaching assistantships with full tuition reimbursements were awarded. *Faculty research:* Bioinformatics, database/data mining, networking, parallel computing, visualization. *Total annual research expenditures:* $46,748. *Unit head:* Dr. Kathy Liszka, Interim Chair, 330-972-8017, E-mail: liszka@uakron.edu. Web site: http://www.uakron.edu/academics_majors/graduate_programs/programs_detail.dot?programId=7719&pageTitle=Graduate%20Programs&crumbTitle=Computer%20Scienc.

The University of Alabama, Graduate School, College of Engineering, Department of Computer Science, Tuscaloosa, AL 35487-0290. Offers MS, PhD. Part-time programs available. *Faculty:* 16 full-time (2 women). *Students:* 59 full-time (22 women), 22 part-time (14 women); includes 11 minority (7 Black or African American, non-Hispanic/Latino; 1 Asian, non-Hispanic/Latino; 2 Hispanic/Latino; 1 Two or more races, non-Hispanic/Latino), 7 international. Average age 30. 50 applicants, 78% accepted, 20 enrolled. In 2011, 23 master's, 6 doctorates awarded. Terminal master's awarded for partial completion of doctoral program. *Degree requirements:* For master's, comprehensive exam, thesis (for some programs); for doctorate, comprehensive exam, thesis/dissertation. *Entrance requirements:* For master's and doctorate, GRE, minimum undergraduate GPA of 3.0 from ABET-accredited program. Additional exam requirements/recommendations for international students: Required—TOEFL. *Application deadline:* For fall admission, 7/1 priority date for domestic students, 3/15 for international students; for spring admission, 11/1 priority date for domestic students, 7/1 for international students. Applications are processed on a rolling basis. Application fee: $50 ($60 for international students). Electronic applications accepted. *Expenses:* Tuition, state resident: full-time $8600. Tuition, nonresident: full-time $21,900. *Financial support:* In 2011–12, 28 students received support, including 2 fellowships with tuition reimbursements available (averaging $15,000 per year), 10 research assistantships with full tuition reimbursements available (averaging $15,750 per year), 18 teaching assistantships with full tuition reimbursements available (averaging $15,750 per year); health care benefits and unspecified assistantships also available. Financial award application deadline: 4/1. *Faculty research:* Software engineering, networking, database management, robotics, algorithms. *Total annual research expenditures:* $5.6 million. *Unit head:* Dr. David Cordes, Professor and Department Head, 205-348-6363, Fax: 205-348-0219, E-mail: david.cordes@ua.edu. *Application contact:* Dr. Susan Vrbsky, Associate Professor and Graduate Program Director, 205-348-6363, Fax: 205-348-0219, E-mail: vrbsky@cs.ua.edu. Web site: http://cs.ua.edu/.

The University of Alabama at Birmingham, College of Arts and Sciences, Program in Computer and Information Sciences, Birmingham, AL 35294. Offers MS, PhD. Terminal master's awarded for partial completion of doctoral program. *Degree requirements:* For master's, thesis optional; for doctorate, thesis/dissertation. *Entrance requirements:* For master's and doctorate, GRE General Test. Additional exam requirements/recommendations for international students: Required—TOEFL. *Application deadline:* Applications are processed on a rolling basis. Electronic applications accepted. *Expenses:* Tuition, state resident: full-time $5922; part-time $309 per hour. Tuition, nonresident: full-time $13,428; part-time $726 per hour. Tuition and fees vary according to program. *Financial support:* Fellowships with full tuition reimbursements, research assistantships with full tuition reimbursements, teaching assistantships with full tuition reimbursements, career-related internships or fieldwork, Federal Work-Study, institutionally sponsored loans, scholarships/grants, traineeships, health care benefits, and unspecified assistantships available. Support available to part-time students. Financial award application deadline: 3/10. *Faculty research:* Theory and software systems, intelligent systems, systems architecture, high performance computing, computer architecture, computer graphics, data mining, software engineering. *Unit head:* Dr. Anthony Skjellum, Chair, 205-934-2213, Fax: 205-934-5473, E-mail: skjellum@uab.edu. *Application contact:* Dr. John Johnstone, Graduate Program Director/Associate Professor, 205-975-5633, Fax: 205-934-5473, E-mail: jkj@uab.edu. Web site: http://www.cis.uab.edu/.

The University of Alabama in Huntsville, School of Graduate Studies, College of Science, Department of Computer Science, Huntsville, AL 35899. Offers computer science (MS, PhD); software engineering (MSSE, Certificate). Part-time and evening/weekend programs available. Postbaccalaureate distance learning degree programs offered (minimal on-campus study). *Faculty:* 10 full-time (3 women). *Students:* 46 full-time (21 women), 69 part-time (13 women); includes 10 minority (6 Black or African American, non-Hispanic/Latino; 3 Asian, non-Hispanic/Latino; 1 Hispanic/Latino), 37 international. Average age 32. 130 applicants, 53% accepted, 33 enrolled. In 2011, 2 master's, 2 doctorates, 2 other advanced degrees awarded. *Degree requirements:* For master's, comprehensive exam, thesis or alternative, oral and written exams; for doctorate, comprehensive exam, thesis/dissertation, oral and written exams. *Entrance requirements:* For master's, doctorate, and Certificate, GRE General Test, minimum GPA of 3.0. Additional exam requirements/recommendations for international students: Required—TOEFL (minimum score 550 paper-based; 213 computer-based; 62 iBT). *Application deadline:* For fall admission, 7/15 for domestic students, 4/1 for international students; for spring admission, 11/30 for domestic students, 9/1 for international students. Applications are processed on a rolling basis. Application fee: $40 ($50 for international students). Electronic applications accepted. *Expenses:* Tuition, state resident: full-time $7830; part-time $473.50 per credit. Tuition, nonresident: full-time $18,748; part-time $1128.33 per credit. Tuition and fees vary according to course load and program. *Financial support:* In 2011–12, 30 students received support, including 1 fellowship with full tuition reimbursement available (averaging $11,000 per year), 10 research assistantships with full and partial tuition reimbursements available (averaging $9,828 per year), 19 teaching assistantships with full and partial tuition reimbursements available (averaging $8,975 per year); career-related internships or fieldwork, Federal Work-Study, institutionally sponsored loans, scholarships/grants, health care benefits, and unspecified assistantships also available. Support available to part-time students. Financial award application deadline: 4/1; financial award applicants required to submit FAFSA. *Faculty research:* Software engineering and systems, computer graphics and visualization, computer networking, artificial intelligence, modeling and simulation. *Total annual research expenditures:* $5.4 million. *Unit head:* Dr. Heggere Ranganath, Chair, 256-824-6088, Fax: 256-824-6239, E-mail: ranganat@uah.edu. *Application contact:* Kim Gray, Graduate Studies Admissions Manager, 256-824-6002, Fax: 256-824-6405, E-mail: deangrad@uah.edu. Web site: http://www.cs.uah.edu.

University of Alaska Fairbanks, College of Engineering and Mines, Department of Computer Science, Fairbanks, AK 99775-6670. Offers computer science (MS); software engineering (MSE). Part-time programs available. *Faculty:* 8 full-time (1 woman). *Students:* 10 full-time (2 women), 6 part-time (2 women), 2 international. Average age 28. 9 applicants, 33% accepted, 2 enrolled. In 2011, 1 master's awarded. *Degree requirements:* For master's, comprehensive exam, thesis or alternative. *Entrance requirements:* For master's, GRE General Test. Additional exam requirements/recommendations for international students: Required—TOEFL (minimum score 550 paper-based; 213 computer-based; 80 iBT). *Application deadline:* For fall admission, 6/1 for domestic students, 3/1 for international students; for spring admission, 10/15 for domestic students, 9/1 for international students. Application fee: $60. *Expenses:* Tuition, state resident: full-time $6696; part-time $372 per credit. Tuition, nonresident: full-time $13,680; part-time $760 per credit. Tuition and fees vary according to course load and reciprocity agreements. *Financial support:* In 2011–12, 7 research assistantships with tuition reimbursements (averaging $10,886 per year), 3 teaching assistantships with tuition reimbursements (averaging $10,597 per year) were awarded; fellowships with tuition reimbursements, career-related internships or fieldwork, Federal Work-Study, scholarships/grants, health care benefits, and unspecified assistantships also available. Support available to part-time students. Financial award application deadline: 7/1; financial award applicants required to submit FAFSA. *Faculty research:* Interaction with a virtual reality environment, synthetic aperture radar interferometry software. *Total annual research expenditures:* $10,000. *Unit head:* Dr. Jon Genetti, Department Chair, 907-474-2777, Fax: 907-474-5030, E-mail: uaf-cs-dept@alaska.edu. *Application contact:* Mike Earnest, Director of Admissions, 907-474-7500, Fax: 907-474-5379, E-mail: admissions@uaf.edu. Web site: http://www.cs.uaf.edu.

University of Alberta, Faculty of Graduate Studies and Research, Department of Computing Science, Edmonton, AB T6G 2E1, Canada. Offers M Sc, PhD. Part-time programs available. Terminal master's awarded for partial completion of doctoral program. *Degree requirements:* For master's, thesis (for some programs), oral exam, seminar; for doctorate, thesis/dissertation, oral exam, seminar. *Entrance requirements:* For master's and doctorate, GRE General Test. Additional exam requirements/recommendations for international students: Required—TOEFL. *Faculty research:* Artificial intelligence, multimedia, distributed computing, theory, software engineering.

The University of Arizona, College of Science, Department of Computer Science, Tucson, AZ 85721. Offers MS, PhD. Part-time programs available. *Faculty:* 14 full-time (0 women). *Students:* 58 full-time (16 women), 7 part-time (1 woman); includes 4 minority (1 Black or African American, non-Hispanic/Latino; 2 Asian, non-Hispanic/Latino; 1 Hispanic/Latino), 44 international. Average age 29. 256 applicants, 23% accepted, 24 enrolled. In 2011, 21 master's, 6 doctorates awarded. Terminal master's awarded for partial completion of doctoral program. *Degree requirements:* For master's, thesis optional; for doctorate, comprehensive exam, thesis/dissertation. *Entrance requirements:* For master's, GRE General Test, minimum GPA of 3.2; for doctorate, GRE General Test, minimum undergraduate GPA of 3.5. Additional exam requirements/recommendations for international students: Required—TOEFL (minimum score 600 paper-based; 250 computer-based; 100 iBT). *Application deadline:* For fall admission, 1/7 for domestic and international students. Application fee: $75. Electronic applications accepted. *Expenses:* Tuition, state resident: full-time $10,840. Tuition, nonresident: full-time $25,802. *Financial support:* In 2011–12, 53 students received support, including 6 fellowships with full tuition reimbursements available (averaging $25,000 per year), 39 research assistantships with full tuition reimbursements available (averaging $16,597 per year), 7 teaching assistantships with full tuition reimbursements available (averaging $14,858 per year); scholarships/grants, health care benefits, tuition waivers (full and partial), and unspecified assistantships also available. Financial award application deadline: 1/7. *Faculty research:* Operating systems, theory of computation, programming languages, databases, algorithms, networks, cloud computing, green computing, computational biology, machine learning, artificial intelligence. *Total annual research expenditures:* $1.8 million. *Unit head:* Dr. Saumya Debray, Department Head, 520-621-4527, Fax: 520-626-5997. *Application contact:* Holly Brown, Senior Program Coordinator, 520-621-4049, Fax: 520-626-5997, E-mail: gradadmissions@cs.arizona.edu. Web site: http://www.cs.arizona.edu/.

University of Arkansas, Graduate School, College of Engineering, Department of Computer Science and Computer Engineering, Program in Computer Science, Fayetteville, AR 72701-1201. Offers MS, PhD. *Students:* 20 full-time (4 women), 16 part-time (2 women), 24 international. In 2011, 14 master's awarded. *Degree requirements:* For doctorate, thesis/dissertation. *Application deadline:* For fall admission, 4/1 for international students; for spring admission, 10/1 for international students. Applications are processed on a rolling basis. Application fee: $40 ($50 for international students). Electronic applications accepted. *Financial support:* In 2011–12, 16 research assistantships, 6 teaching assistantships were awarded; fellowships with tuition reimbursements, career-related internships or fieldwork, and Federal Work-Study also available. Support available to part-time students. Financial award application deadline: 4/1; financial award applicants required to submit FAFSA. *Unit head:* Dr. Susan Gauch, Departmental Chair, 479-575-6197, Fax: 479-575-5339, E-mail: sgauch@uark.edu. *Application contact:* Dr. Gordon Beavers, Graduate Coordinator, 479-575-6040, Fax: 479-575-5339, E-mail: gordonb@uark.edu. Web site: http://www.csce.uark.edu/.

University of Arkansas at Little Rock, Graduate School, George W. Donughey College of Engineering and Information Technology, Department of Computer Science, Little Rock, AR 72204-1099. Offers computer and information science (MS). Part-time and evening/weekend programs available. *Degree requirements:* For master's, thesis optional. *Entrance requirements:* For master's, GRE General Test, minimum GPA of 3.0; bachelor's degree in computer science, mathematics, or appropriate alternative.

University of Atlanta, Graduate Programs, Atlanta, GA 30360. Offers business (MS); business administration (Exec MBA, MBA); computer science (MS); educational leadership (MS, Ed D); healthcare administration (MS, D Sc, Graduate Certificate); information technology for management (Graduate Certificate); international project management (Graduate Certificate); law (JD); managerial science (DBA); project management (Graduate Certificate); social science (MS). Postbaccalaureate distance learning degree programs offered. *Entrance requirements:* For master's, minimum cumulative GPA of 2.5.

University of Bridgeport, School of Engineering, Departments of Computer Science and Computer Engineering, Bridgeport, CT 06604. Offers computer engineering (MS); computer science (MS); computer science and engineering (PhD). *Faculty:* 10 full-time (1 woman), 5 part-time/adjunct (1 woman). *Students:* 102 full-time (26 women), 95 part-time (16 women); includes 20 minority (6 Black or African American, non-Hispanic/Latino; 8 Asian, non-Hispanic/Latino; 3 Hispanic/Latino; 3 Two or more races, non-Hispanic/Latino), 156 international. Average age 30. 678 applicants, 64% accepted, 34 enrolled. In 2011, 69 master's, 2 doctorates awarded. *Degree requirements:* For master's, thesis optional; for doctorate, comprehensive exam, thesis/dissertation. *Entrance requirements:* Additional exam requirements/recommendations for international students: Recommended—TOEFL (minimum score 550 paper-based; 213 computer-based; 80 iBT), IELTS (minimum score 6.5). *Application deadline:* For fall admission, 8/1 priority date for domestic students, 8/1 for international students; for spring admission, 12/1 priority date for domestic students, 12/1 for international students. Applications are processed on a rolling basis. Application fee: $50. Electronic applications accepted. *Expenses: Tuition:* Full-time $22,880; part-time $700 per credit. *Required fees:* $1870; $95 per semester. Tuition and fees vary according to course load and program. *Financial support:* In 2011–12, 56 students received support. Research assistantships, teaching assistantships, career-related internships or fieldwork, Federal Work-Study, institutionally sponsored loans, and tuition waivers (partial) available. Support available to part-time students. Financial award application deadline: 6/1; financial award applicants required to submit FAFSA. *Unit head:* Dr. Ausif mahmood, Chairman, 203-576-4737, Fax: 203-576-4765, E-mail: mahmood@bridgeport.edu. *Application contact:* Karissa Peckham, Dean of Admissions, 203-576-4552, Fax: 203-576-4941, E-mail: admit@bridgeport.edu.

The University of British Columbia, Faculty of Science, Department of Computer Science, Vancouver, BC V6T 1Z4, Canada. Offers M Sc, PhD. Part-time programs available. *Degree requirements:* For doctorate, comprehensive exam, thesis/dissertation. *Entrance requirements:* For master's and doctorate, GRE. Additional exam requirements/recommendations for international students: Required—TOEFL (minimum score 600 paper-based; 250 computer-based; 100 iBT). Electronic applications accepted. *Faculty research:* Computational intelligence, data management and mining, theory, graphics, network security and systems.

University of Calgary, Faculty of Graduate Studies, Faculty of Science, Department of Computer Science, Calgary, AB T2N 1N4, Canada. Offers computer science (M Sc, PhD); software engineering (M Sc). Part-time programs available. *Degree requirements:* For master's, comprehensive exam (for some programs), thesis (for some programs); for doctorate, thesis/dissertation, oral and written departmental exam. *Entrance requirements:* For master's, bachelor's degree in computer science; for doctorate, M Sc in computer science. Additional exam requirements/recommendations for international students: Required—TOEFL (minimum score 600 paper-based; 250 computer-based); Recommended—TWE. Electronic applications accepted. *Faculty research:* Visual and interactive computing, quantum computing and cryptography, evolutionary software engineering, distributed systems and algorithms.

University of California, Berkeley, Graduate Division, College of Engineering, Department of Electrical Engineering and Computer Sciences, Berkeley, CA 94720-1500. Offers computer science (MS, PhD); electrical engineering (MS, PhD). *Degree requirements:* For master's, comprehensive exam or thesis; for doctorate, thesis/dissertation, qualifying exam. *Entrance requirements:* For master's and doctorate, GRE General Test, minimum GPA of 3.0, 3 letters of recommendation. Additional exam requirements/recommendations for international students: Required—TOEFL. Electronic applications accepted.

University of California, Davis, College of Engineering, Graduate Group in Computer Science, Davis, CA 95616. Offers MS, PhD. Terminal master's awarded for partial completion of doctoral program. *Degree requirements:* For master's, comprehensive exam (for some programs), thesis optional; for doctorate, comprehensive exam, thesis/dissertation. *Entrance requirements:* For master's and doctorate, GRE General Test, GRE Subject Test, minimum GPA of 3.0. Additional exam requirements/recommendations for international students: Required—TOEFL (minimum score 550 paper-based; 213 computer-based). Electronic applications accepted. *Faculty research:* Intrusion detection, malicious code detection, next generation light wave computer networks, biological algorithms, parallel processing.

University of California, Irvine, Donald Bren School of Information and Computer Sciences, Department of Computer Science, Irvine, CA 92697. Offers MS, PhD. *Students:* 188 full-time (22 women), 29 part-time (0 women); includes 32 minority (1 Black or African American, non-Hispanic/Latino; 26 Asian, non-Hispanic/Latino; 2 Hispanic/Latino; 3 Two or more races, non-Hispanic/Latino), 143 international. Average age 28. 1,317 applicants, 19% accepted, 83 enrolled. In 2011, 57 master's, 1 doctorate awarded. Application fee: $80 ($100 for international students). *Unit head:* Sandy Irani, Chair, 949-824-6346, Fax: 949-824-4056, E-mail: irani@ics.uci.edu. *Application contact:* Kris Bolcer, Assistant Director, Graduate Affairs, 949-824-5156, Fax: 949-824-4163, E-mail: kbolcer@uci.edu. Web site: http://www.cs.uci.edu/.

University of California, Irvine, Donald Bren School of Information and Computer Sciences, Program in Networked Systems, Irvine, CA 92697. Offers MS, PhD. *Students:* 27 full-time (3 women), 4 part-time (0 women), 30 international. Average age 28. 125 applicants, 30% accepted, 14 enrolled. In 2011, 8 master's, 2 doctorates awarded. *Application deadline:* For fall admission, 1/15 for domestic students. Application fee: $80 ($100 for international students). *Financial support:* Fellowships, research

assistantships, and teaching assistantships available. *Unit head:* Hamid Jafarkhani, Director, 949-824-1755, Fax: 949-824-2321, E-mail: hamidj@uci.edu. *Application contact:* Kris Bolcer, Assistant Director, Graduate Affairs, 949-824-5156, Fax: 949-824-4163, E-mail: kbolcer@uci.edu. Web site: http://www.networkedsystems.uci.edu/.

University of California, Irvine, School of Engineering, Department of Electrical Engineering and Computer Science, Irvine, CA 92697. Offers electrical engineering and computer science (MS, PhD); networked systems (MS, PhD). Part-time programs available. *Students:* 288 full-time (49 women), 21 part-time (4 women); includes 35 minority (1 Black or African American, non-Hispanic/Latino; 29 Asian, non-Hispanic/Latino; 1 Hispanic/Latino; 4 Two or more races, non-Hispanic/Latino), 237 international. Average age 27. 1,351 applicants, 21% accepted, 135 enrolled. In 2011, 50 master's, 18 doctorates awarded. Terminal master's awarded for partial completion of doctoral program. *Degree requirements:* For doctorate, thesis/dissertation. *Entrance requirements:* For master's and doctorate, GRE General Test, minimum GPA of 3.0, 3 letters of recommendation. Additional exam requirements/recommendations for international students: Required—TOEFL (minimum score 550 paper-based; 213 computer-based). *Application deadline:* For fall admission, 1/15 priority date for domestic students, 1/15 for international students. Applications are processed on a rolling basis. Application fee: $80 ($100 for international students). Electronic applications accepted. *Financial support:* Fellowships, research assistantships with full tuition reimbursements, teaching assistantships, institutionally sponsored loans, traineeships, health care benefits, and unspecified assistantships available. Financial award application deadline: 3/1; financial award applicants required to submit FAFSA. *Faculty research:* Optics and electronic devices and circuits, signal processing, communications, machine vision, power electronics. *Unit head:* Prof. Michael M. Green, Chair, 949-824-1656, Fax: 949-824-3203, E-mail: mgreen@uci.edu. *Application contact:* Ronnie A. Gran, Graduate Admissions Coordinator, 949-824-5489, Fax: 949-824-1853, E-mail: ragran@uci.edu. Web site: http://www.eng.uci.edu/dept/eecs.

University of California, Los Angeles, Graduate Division, Henry Samueli School of Engineering and Applied Science, Department of Computer Science, Los Angeles, CA 90095-1596. Offers MS, PhD, MBA/MS. *Faculty:* 29 full-time (3 women), 2 part-time/adjunct (0 women). *Students:* 320 full-time (49 women); includes 71 minority (4 Black or African American, non-Hispanic/Latino; 55 Asian, non-Hispanic/Latino; 9 Hispanic/Latino; 1 Native Hawaiian or other Pacific Islander, non-Hispanic/Latino; 2 Two or more races, non-Hispanic/Latino), 176 international. 996 applicants, 22% accepted, 78 enrolled. In 2011, 86 master's, 29 doctorates awarded. *Degree requirements:* For master's, comprehensive exam or thesis; for doctorate, thesis/dissertation, qualifying exams. *Entrance requirements:* For master's, GRE General Test, GRE Subject Test, minimum GPA of 3.0; for doctorate, GRE General Test, GRE Subject Test, minimum GPA of 3.25. Additional exam requirements/recommendations for international students: Required—TOEFL (minimum score 560 paper-based; 220 computer-based; 87 iBT). *Application deadline:* For fall admission, 12/1 for domestic and international students. Application fee: $80 ($100 for international students). Electronic applications accepted. *Financial support:* In 2011–12, 43 fellowships, 229 research assistantships, 119 teaching assistantships were awarded; Federal Work-Study, institutionally sponsored loans, and tuition waivers (full and partial) also available. Financial award application deadline: 1/15; financial award applicants required to submit FAFSA. *Faculty research:* Artificial intelligence, computational systems biology, computer network systems, computer systems architecture, information and data management. *Total annual research expenditures:* $10.7 million. *Unit head:* Dr. Jens Palsberg, Chair, 310-825-3886. *Application contact:* Steve Arbuckle, Student Affairs Officer, 310-825-6830, Fax: 310-206-8133, E-mail: arbuckle@cs.ucla.edu. Web site: http://www.cs.ucla.edu/.

University of California, Merced, Division of Graduate Studies, School of Engineering, Merced, CA 95343. Offers electrical engineering and computer science (MS, PhD). *Unit head:* Dr. Samuel J. Traina, Dean, 209-228-4723, Fax: 209-228-6906, E-mail: grad.dean@ucmerced.edu. *Application contact:* Tsu Ya, Graduate Admissions and Academic Services Manager, 209-228-4723, Fax: 209-228-6906, E-mail: tya@ucmerced.edu.

University of California, Riverside, Graduate Division, Department of Computer Science and Engineering, Riverside, CA 92521. Offers computer engineering (MS); computer science (MS, PhD). Part-time programs available. *Faculty:* 22 full-time (1 woman), 1 (woman) part-time/adjunct. *Students:* 167 full-time (38 women), 6 part-time (1 woman); includes 22 minority (5 Black or African American, non-Hispanic/Latino; 14 Asian, non-Hispanic/Latino; 3 Hispanic/Latino), 110 international. Average age 27. 505 applicants, 26% accepted, 45 enrolled. In 2011, 24 master's, 12 doctorates awarded. Terminal master's awarded for partial completion of doctoral program. *Degree requirements:* For master's, thesis or project; for doctorate, thesis/dissertation, qualifying exams. *Entrance requirements:* For master's and doctorate, GRE General Test (minimum score of 1100 or 300 for new format), minimum GPA of 3.2. Additional exam requirements/recommendations for international students: Required—TOEFL (minimum score 550 paper-based; 213 computer-based; 80 iBT). *Application deadline:* For fall admission, 1/5 priority date for domestic students, 1/5 for international students. Application fee: $80 ($100 for international students). Electronic applications accepted. *Financial support:* In 2011–12, 76 students received support, including 26 fellowships with full and partial tuition reimbursements available (averaging $16,000 per year), 53 research assistantships with full and partial tuition reimbursements available (averaging $15,000 per year), 26 teaching assistantships with full and partial tuition reimbursements available (averaging $16,000 per year); institutionally sponsored loans, health care benefits, and unspecified assistantships also available. Financial award applicants required to submit FAFSA. *Faculty research:* Algorithms, bioinformatics, logic; architecture, compilers, embedded systems, verification; databases, data mining, artificial intelligence, graphics; systems, networks. *Unit head:* Dr. Laxmi Bhuyan, Chair, 951-827-5639, Fax: 951-827-4643, E-mail: gradadmission@ucr.edu. *Application contact:* Amy S. Ricks, Graduate Student Affairs Officer, 951-827-5639, Fax: 951-827-4643, E-mail: amy@cs.ucr.edu. Web site: http://www.cs.ucr.edu/.

University of California, San Diego, Office of Graduate Studies, Department of Computer Science and Engineering, La Jolla, CA 92093. Offers computer engineering (MS, PhD); computer science (MS, PhD). *Degree requirements:* For doctorate, thesis/dissertation. *Entrance requirements:* For master's and doctorate, GRE General Test. Electronic applications accepted. *Faculty research:* Analysis of algorithms, combinatorial algorithms, discrete optimization.

University of California, San Diego, Office of Graduate Studies, Interdisciplinary Program in Cognitive Science, La Jolla, CA 92093. Offers cognitive science/anthropology (PhD); cognitive science/communication (PhD); cognitive science/computer science and engineering (PhD); cognitive science/linguistics (PhD); cognitive science/neuroscience (PhD); cognitive science/philosophy (PhD); cognitive science/psychology (PhD); cognitive science/sociology (PhD). Admissions offered through affiliated departments. *Degree requirements:* For doctorate, thesis/dissertation. *Entrance requirements:* For doctorate, GRE General Test, acceptance into one of the eight participating departments. *Faculty research:* Language and cognition, philosophy of mind, visual perception, biological anthropology, sociolinguistics.

University of California, Santa Barbara, Graduate Division, College of Engineering, Department of Computer Science, Santa Barbara, CA 93106-5110. Offers cognitive science (PhD); computational science and engineering (PhD); computer science (MS, PhD); technology and society (PhD). *Faculty:* 32 full-time (5 women), 5 part-time/adjunct (0 women). *Students:* 151 full-time (37 women); includes 9 minority (1 American Indian or Alaska Native, non-Hispanic/Latino; 7 Asian, non-Hispanic/Latino; 1 Two or more races, non-Hispanic/Latino), 101 international. Average age 27. 640 applicants, 20% accepted, 51 enrolled. In 2011, 27 master's, 14 doctorates awarded. Terminal master's awarded for partial completion of doctoral program. *Median time to degree:* Of those who began their doctoral program in fall 2003, 80% received their degree in 8 years or less. *Degree requirements:* For master's, comprehensive exam (for some programs), thesis (for some programs), project (for some programs); for doctorate, thesis/dissertation. *Entrance requirements:* For master's and doctorate, GRE. Additional exam requirements/recommendations for international students: Required—TOEFL (minimum score 600 paper-based; 100 iBT), IELTS (minimum score 7). *Application deadline:* For fall admission, 12/15 for domestic and international students. Application fee: $80 ($100 for international students). Electronic applications accepted. *Expenses:* Tuition, state resident: full-time $12,192. Tuition, nonresident: full-time $27,294. *Required fees:* $764.13. *Financial support:* In 2011–12, 116 students received support, including 36 fellowships with full and partial tuition reimbursements available (averaging $12,330 per year), 63 research assistantships with full and partial tuition reimbursements available (averaging $14,876 per year), 44 teaching assistantships with partial tuition reimbursements available (averaging $17,309 per year); career-related internships or fieldwork, Federal Work-Study, institutionally sponsored loans, scholarships/grants, health care benefits, tuition waivers (full and partial), and unspecified assistantships also available. Financial award application deadline: 12/15; financial award applicants required to submit FAFSA. *Faculty research:* Networking and security, database systems, computational science and engineering, programming languages and software engineering, human-computer interaction. *Unit head:* Subhash Suri, Chair, 805-893-5334, Fax: 805-893-8553, E-mail: suri@cs.ucsb.edu. *Application contact:* Katie Ellis, Graduate Advisor, 805-893-4322, Fax: 805-893-8553, E-mail: kellis@cs.ucsb.edu. Web site: http://www.cs.ucsb.edu/.

University of California, Santa Cruz, Division of Graduate Studies, Jack Baskin School of Engineering, Department of Computer Science, Santa Cruz, CA 95064. Offers MS, PhD. Terminal master's awarded for partial completion of doctoral program. *Degree requirements:* For master's, thesis, project; for doctorate, one foreign language, thesis/dissertation, qualifying exam. *Entrance requirements:* For master's and doctorate, GRE General Test, GRE Subject Test. Additional exam requirements/recommendations for international students: Required—TOEFL (minimum score 570 paper-based; 230 computer-based; 89 iBT); Recommended—IELTS (minimum score 8). Electronic applications accepted. *Faculty research:* Algorithm analysis, artificial intelligence, scientific visualization, computer graphics and gaming, multimodal human-computer interaction.

University of Central Arkansas, Graduate School, College of Natural Sciences and Math, Department of Applied Computing, Conway, AR 72035-0001. Offers MS. *Faculty:* 5 full-time (0 women). *Students:* 7 full-time (2 women), 7 part-time (1 woman); includes 1 minority (Black or African American, non-Hispanic/Latino), 9 international. Average age 25. 5 applicants, 100% accepted, 2 enrolled. In 2011, 2 master's awarded. *Entrance requirements:* For master's, GRE, minimum GPA of 2.7. Additional exam requirements/recommendations for international students: Required—TOEFL (minimum score 550 paper-based; 213 computer-based). *Application deadline:* For fall admission, 3/1 for domestic students. Application fee: $25 ($50 for international students). *Expenses:* Tuition, state resident: full-time $4834; part-time $398.35 per credit hour. Tuition, nonresident: full-time $8686. *Financial support:* Federal Work-Study, scholarships/grants, and unspecified assistantships available. Financial award applicants required to submit FAFSA. *Unit head:* Chenyi Hu, Department Chair, 501-450-3401, Fax: 501-450-5615, E-mail: chu@uca.edu. *Application contact:* Susan Wood, Admissions Assistant, 501-450-3124, Fax: 501-450-5678, E-mail: swood@uca.edu.

University of Central Florida, College of Engineering and Computer Science, Department of Electrical Engineering and Computer Science, Program in Computer Science, Orlando, FL 32816. Offers computer science (MS, PhD); digital forensics (MS). Part-time and evening/weekend programs available. *Students:* 139 full-time (28 women), 168 part-time (30 women); includes 53 minority (15 Black or African American, non-Hispanic/Latino; 15 Asian, non-Hispanic/Latino; 18 Hispanic/Latino; 5 Two or more races, non-Hispanic/Latino), 79 international. Average age 32. 320 applicants, 78% accepted, 106 enrolled. In 2011, 59 master's, 13 doctorates awarded. *Degree requirements:* For master's, thesis or alternative; for doctorate, thesis/dissertation, candidacy exam, departmental qualifying exam. *Entrance requirements:* For master's, GRE General Test, GRE Subject Test, minimum GPA of 3.0 in last 60 hours; for doctorate, GRE Subject Test, minimum GPA of 3.0 in last 60 hours. Additional exam requirements/recommendations for international students: Required—TOEFL. *Application deadline:* For fall admission, 7/15 priority date for domestic students; for spring admission, 12/1 priority date for domestic students. Application fee: $30. Electronic applications accepted. *Expenses:* Tuition, state resident: part-time $277.08 per credit hour. Tuition, nonresident: part-time $277.08 per credit hour. Part-time tuition and fees vary according to degree level and program. *Financial support:* In 2011–12, 75 students received support, including 14 fellowships with partial tuition reimbursements available (averaging $10,100 per year), 49 research assistantships with partial tuition reimbursements available (averaging $10,700 per year), 35 teaching assistantships with partial tuition reimbursements available (averaging $9,100 per year); career-related internships or fieldwork, Federal Work-Study, institutionally sponsored loans, tuition waivers (partial), and unspecified assistantships also available. Financial award application deadline: 3/1; financial award applicants required to submit FAFSA. *Faculty research:* Parallel processing, databases, algorithms, virtual reality. *Unit head:* Dr. Gary L:eavens, Chair, 407-882-0185, E-mail: leavens@ucf.edu. *Application contact:* Barbara Rodriguez, Director, Admissions and Registration, 407-823-2766, Fax: 407-823-6442, E-mail: gradadmissions@ucf.edu. Web site: http://web.eecs.ucf.edu/.

University of Central Missouri, The Graduate School, College of Science and Technology, Warrensburg, MO 64093. Offers applied mathematics (MS); aviation safety (MS); biology (MS); computer science (MS); environmental studies (MA); industrial management (MS); mathematics (MS); technology (MS); technology management (PhD). PhD is offered jointly with Indiana State University. Part-time programs available. Postbaccalaureate distance learning degree programs offered. *Entrance requirements:* Additional exam requirements/recommendations for international students: Required—TOEFL (minimum score 550 paper-based; 79 computer-based). Electronic applications accepted.

University of Central Oklahoma, College of Graduate Studies and Research, College of Mathematics and Science, Department of Mathematics and Statistics, Edmond, OK 73034-5209. Offers applied mathematical sciences (MS), including computer science, mathematics, mathematics/computer science teaching, statistics. Part-time programs available. *Faculty:* 7 full-time (4 women), 3 part-time/adjunct (0 women). *Students:* 20 full-time (7 women), 11 part-time (8 women); includes 5 minority (3 Black or African American, non-Hispanic/Latino; 2 Two or more races, non-Hispanic/Latino), 11 international. Average age 29. In 2011, 5 master's awarded. *Degree requirements:* For master's, thesis. *Entrance requirements:* Additional exam requirements/recommendations for international students: Required—TOEFL (minimum score 550 paper-based; 213 computer-based). *Application deadline:* Applications are processed on a rolling basis. Application fee: $50. Electronic applications accepted. *Expenses:* Tuition, state resident: full-time $3901; part-time $218.30 per credit hour. Tuition, nonresident: full-time $9198; part-time $511.20 per credit hour. Tuition and fees vary according to program. *Financial support:* Federal Work-Study and unspecified assistantships available. Financial award application deadline: 3/31; financial award applicants required to submit FAFSA. *Faculty research:* Curvature, FAA, math education. *Unit head:* Dr. Michael Fulkerson, 405-974-5575, E-mail: mfulkerson@uco.edu. *Application contact:* Dr. Richard Bernard, Adviser, 405-974-3493, Fax: 405-974-3824, E-mail: jyates@aix1.uco.edu. Web site: http://www.ucok.edu/graduate.applied.htm.

University of Chicago, Division of the Physical Sciences, Department of Computer Science, Professional Master's Program in Computer Science, Chicago, IL 60637-1513. Offers SM. Part-time and evening/weekend programs available. *Entrance requirements:* For master's, GRE. Additional exam requirements/recommendations for international students: Required—TOEFL. Electronic applications accepted.

University of Cincinnati, Graduate School, College of Engineering and Applied Science, Department of Electrical and Computer Engineering and Computer Science, Program in Computer Science, Cincinnati, OH 45221. Offers MS. *Degree requirements:* For master's, thesis. *Entrance requirements:* For master's, GRE General Test, GRE Subject Test or BS in computer science. Additional exam requirements/recommendations for international students: Required—TOEFL (minimum score 550 paper-based; 213 computer-based).

University of Cincinnati, Graduate School, College of Engineering and Applied Science, Department of Electrical and Computer Engineering and Computer Science, Program in Computer Science and Engineering, Cincinnati, OH 45221. Offers PhD. *Degree requirements:* For doctorate, thesis/dissertation. *Entrance requirements:* For doctorate, GRE General Test. Additional exam requirements/recommendations for international students: Required—TOEFL.

University of Colorado at Colorado Springs, College of Engineering and Applied Science, Department of Computer Science, Colorado Springs, CO 80933-7150. Offers computer science (MS); engineering (PhD). Part-time programs available. *Faculty:* 10 full-time (2 women), 1 part-time/adjunct (0 women). *Students:* 28 full-time (4 women), 22 part-time (0 women); includes 6 minority (2 Asian, non-Hispanic/Latino; 4 Hispanic/Latino), 12 international. Average age 33. 37 applicants, 68% accepted, 9 enrolled. In 2011, 14 degrees awarded. *Degree requirements:* For master's, thesis optional, oral final exam; for doctorate, comprehensive exam, thesis/dissertation, oral final exam. *Entrance requirements:* For master's, GRE General Test, minimum undergraduate GPA of 3.0, 2 semesters of course work in calculus, 1 other math course, course work in computer science; for doctorate, GRE General Test, GRE Subject Test (computer science), bachelor's or master's degree in computer science; minimum GPA of 3.3 in all previous course work; 2 semesters of calculus and one course in discrete math, statistics, and linear algebra. Additional exam requirements/recommendations for international students: Required—TOEFL (minimum score 550 paper-based; 213 computer-based). *Application deadline:* For fall admission, 6/15 priority date for domestic students, 4/1 for international students; for spring admission, 11/15 for domestic students, 10/1 for international students. Applications are processed on a rolling basis. Application fee: $60 ($75 for international students). *Expenses:* Tuition, state resident: part-time $660 per credit hour. Tuition, nonresident: part-time $1133 per credit hour. Tuition and fees vary according to degree level, program and student level. *Financial support:* In 2011–12, 1 student received support. Teaching assistantships, career-related internships or fieldwork, Federal Work-Study, and scholarships/grants available. Financial award application deadline: 3/1; financial award applicants required to submit FAFSA. *Total annual research expenditures:* $1.1 million. *Unit head:* Dr. Terry Boult, Chair, 719-255-3510, Fax: 719-255-3369, E-mail: tboult@uccs.edu. *Application contact:* Tina Moore, Director, Office of Student Support, 719-255-3347, E-mail: tmoore@uccs.edu. Web site: http://eas.uccs.edu/cs/.

University of Colorado Boulder, Graduate School, College of Engineering and Applied Science, Department of Computer Science, Boulder, CO 80309. Offers ME, MS, PhD. *Faculty:* 28 full-time (7 women). *Students:* 160 full-time (33 women), 51 part-time (6 women); includes 22 minority (4 Black or African American, non-Hispanic/Latino; 2 American Indian or Alaska Native, non-Hispanic/Latino; 13 Asian, non-Hispanic/Latino; 3 Hispanic/Latino), 67 international. Average age 30. 341 applicants, 38% accepted, 50 enrolled. In 2011, 48 master's, 8 doctorates awarded. Terminal master's awarded for partial completion of doctoral program. *Degree requirements:* For master's, comprehensive exam, thesis or alternative; for doctorate, one foreign language, thesis/dissertation. *Entrance requirements:* For master's, minimum undergraduate GPA of 3.0. *Application deadline:* For fall admission, 2/28 priority date for domestic students, 12/1 for international students; for spring admission, 10/15 for domestic students, 9/1 for international students. Applications are processed on a rolling basis. Application fee: $50 ($60 for international students). Electronic applications accepted. *Financial support:* In 2011–12, 127 students received support, including 72 fellowships (averaging $7,900 per year), 52 research assistantships with full and partial tuition reimbursements available (averaging $25,798 per year), 13 teaching assistantships with full and partial tuition reimbursements available (averaging $22,183 per year); institutionally sponsored loans, scholarships/grants, health care benefits, and unspecified assistantships also available. Financial award applicants required to submit FAFSA. *Faculty research:* Artificial intelligence, databases, hardware systems, HCI, hypermedia, machine learning, networks, numerical analysis, parallel computation, program analysis, programming languages. *Total annual research expenditures:* $6 million. *Application contact:* E-mail: csgradinfo@cs.colorado.edu. Web site: http://www.cs.colorado.edu/.

University of Colorado Denver, Business School, Program in Computer Science and Information Systems, Denver, CO 80217. Offers PhD. *Students:* 12 full-time (2 women), 6 part-time (2 women); includes 2 minority (both Asian, non-Hispanic/Latino), 7 international. Average age 37. 16 applicants, 56% accepted, 6 enrolled. In 2011, 1 doctorate awarded. *Degree requirements:* For doctorate, comprehensive exam, thesis/dissertation. *Entrance requirements:* For doctorate, GMAT or GRE General Test, letters of recommendation, portfolio essay describing applicant's motivation and initial plan for doctoral study. Additional exam requirements/recommendations for international students: Required—TOEFL (minimum score 525 paper-based; 197 computer-based; 71 iBT). *Application deadline:* For fall admission, 4/15 priority date for domestic students, 3/15 for international students; for spring admission, 10/15 priority date for domestic students, 10/1 for international students. Applications are processed on a rolling basis. Application fee: $50 ($75 for international students). Electronic applications accepted. *Expenses:* Contact institution. *Financial support:* Research assistantships, teaching assistantships, Federal Work-Study, institutionally sponsored loans, and scholarships/grants available. Support available to part-time students. Financial award application deadline: 4/1; financial award applicants required to submit FAFSA. *Faculty research:* Design science of information systems, information system economics, organizational impacts of information technology, high performance parallel and distributed systems, performance measurement and prediction. *Unit head:* Dr. Michael Mannino, Associate Professor/Co-Director, 303-315-8427, E-mail: michael.mannino@ucdenver.edu. *Application contact:* Shelly Townley, Admissions Coordinator, 303-315-8202, Fax: 303-556-5904, E-mail: shelly.townley@ucdenver.edu. Web site: http://business.cudenver.edu/Disciplines/InfoSystems/PhD/index.htm.

University of Colorado Denver, College of Engineering and Applied Science, Department of Computer Science and Engineering, Denver, CO 80217. Offers computer science (MS); computer science and engineering (EASPh D); computer science and information systems (PhD). Part-time and evening/weekend programs available. *Faculty:* 8 full-time (2 women), 1 part-time/adjunct (0 women). *Students:* 66 full-time (24 women), 31 part-time (10 women); includes 12 minority (3 Black or African American, non-Hispanic/Latino; 7 Asian, non-Hispanic/Latino; 2 Hispanic/Latino), 58 international. Average age 33. 91 applicants, 71% accepted, 27 enrolled. In 2011, 24 master's awarded. *Degree requirements:* For master's, thesis or alternative, at least 30 semester hours of computer science courses while maintaining minimum GPA of 3.0; for doctorate, comprehensive exam, thesis/dissertation, at least 60 hours beyond the master's degree level, 30 of which are dissertation research. *Entrance requirements:* For master's, GRE, minimum GPA of 3.0, 10 semester hours of university-level calculus, at least one math course beyond calculus, statement of purpose, letters of recommendation; for doctorate, GRE or GMAT. Additional exam requirements/recommendations for international students: Required—TOEFL (minimum score 525 paper-based; 197 computer-based; 71 iBT). *Application deadline:* For fall admission, 4/1 for domestic students; for spring admission, 10/1 for domestic students. Applications are processed on a rolling basis. Application fee: $50 ($75 for international students). Electronic applications accepted. *Financial support:* Research assistantships, teaching assistantships, career-related internships or fieldwork, and Federal Work-Study available. Financial award application deadline: 4/1; financial award applicants required to submit FAFSA. *Faculty research:* Algorithms, automata theory, artificial intelligence, communication networks, combinatorial geometry, computational geometry, computer architectures, computer graphics, distributed computing, high performance computing, graph theory, Internet, operating systems, parallel processing, simulation and software engineering. *Unit head:* Dr. Gita Alaghband, Chair, 303-556-2940, Fax: 303-556-8369, E-mail: gita.alaghband@ucdenver.edu. *Application contact:* Frances Moore, Program Assistant, 303-556-4083, Fax: 303-556-8369, E-mail: frances.moore@ucdenver.edu. Web site: http://www.ucdenver.edu/academics/colleges/Engineering/Programs/Computer-Science-and-Engineering/Pages/ComputerScienceEngineering.aspx.

University of Colorado Denver, College of Liberal Arts and Sciences, Program in Integrated Sciences, Denver, CO 80217. Offers applied science (MIS); computer science (MIS); mathematics (MIS). Part-time and evening/weekend programs available. *Students:* 5 full-time (3 women), 2 part-time; includes 3 minority (2 Hispanic/Latino; 1 Two or more races, non-Hispanic/Latino). Average age 38. 4 applicants, 25% accepted, 1 enrolled. In 2011, 1 master's awarded. *Degree requirements:* For master's, thesis or alternative, 30 credit hours; thesis or project. *Entrance requirements:* For master's, GRE if undergraduate GPA is 3.0 or less, minimum of 40 semester hours in mathematics, computer science, physics, biology, chemistry and/or geology; essay; three letters of recommendation. Additional exam requirements/recommendations for international students: Required—TOEFL (minimum score 525 paper-based; 197 computer-based; 71 iBT). *Application deadline:* For fall admission, 4/15 for domestic and international students; for spring admission, 10/15 for domestic and international students. Application fee: $50 ($75 for international students). Electronic applications accepted. *Financial support:* Application deadline: 4/1; applicants required to submit FAFSA. *Faculty research:* Computer science, applied science, mathematics. *Unit head:* Dr. Daniel Howard, Professor and Dean, 303-556-2624, Fax: 303-556-4861, E-mail: dan.howard@ucdenver.edu. *Application contact:* 303-556-2557, Fax: 303-556-4861, E-mail: clas@ucdenver.edu. Web site: http://thunder1.cudenver.edu/clas/mis/index.html.

University of Connecticut, Graduate School, School of Engineering, Department of Computer Science and Engineering, Storrs, CT 06269. Offers computer science (MS, PhD), including artificial intelligence, computer architecture, computer science, operating systems, robotics, software engineering. Terminal master's awarded for partial completion of doctoral program. *Degree requirements:* For master's, comprehensive exam, thesis or alternative; for doctorate, thesis/dissertation. *Entrance requirements:* For master's and doctorate, GRE General Test. Additional exam requirements/recommendations for international students: Required—TOEFL (minimum score 550 paper-based; 213 computer-based). Electronic applications accepted.

University of Dayton, Department of Computer Science, Dayton, OH 45469-1300. Offers MCS. Part-time and evening/weekend programs available. *Faculty:* 8 full-time (3 women), 1 part-time/adjunct (0 women). *Students:* 14 full-time (4 women), 8 part-time (1 woman); includes 1 minority (Black or African American, non-Hispanic/Latino), 12 international. Average age 29. 84 applicants, 45% accepted, 9 enrolled. In 2011, 10 degrees awarded. *Degree requirements:* For master's, software project, additional coursework, or thesis. *Entrance requirements:* For master's, GRE General Test, 3 specified undergraduate courses in computer science, minimum undergraduate GPA of 3.0, or performance on placement exam. Additional exam requirements/recommendations for international students: Required—TOEFL (minimum score 550 paper-based; 213 computer-based; 80 iBT), IELTS (minimum score 6.5). *Application deadline:* For fall admission, 8/1 for domestic students, 3/1 for international students; for winter admission, 7/1 for international students; for spring admission, 1/1 for international students. Applications are processed on a rolling basis. Application fee: $0. Electronic applications accepted. *Expenses: Tuition:* Full-time $8400; part-time $700 per credit hour. *Required fees:* $25 per semester. Tuition and fees vary according to degree level. *Financial support:* In 2011–12, 3 teaching assistantships with tuition reimbursements (averaging $10,290 per year) were awarded; institutionally sponsored loans, health care benefits, and unspecified assistantships also available. Financial award applicants required to submit FAFSA. *Faculty research:* Graph theory, P2P networking, database systems, human-computer interaction, machine learning. *Total annual research expenditures:* $250,000. *Unit head:* Dr. Dale Courte, Chair, 937-229-3831, E-mail: dale.courte@notes.udayton.edu. *Application contact:* Dale Courte,

Assistant Director of Graduate and International Admissions, 937-229-3831, E-mail: dcourte1@udayton.edu. Web site: http://campus.udayton.edu/~cps/.

University of Delaware, College of Engineering, Department of Computer and Information Sciences, Newark, DE 19716. Offers MS, PhD. Part-time programs available. Terminal master's awarded for partial completion of doctoral program. *Degree requirements:* For master's, thesis optional; for doctorate, comprehensive exam, thesis/dissertation. *Entrance requirements:* For master's and doctorate, GRE General Test. Additional exam requirements/recommendations for international students: Required—TOEFL (minimum score 550 paper-based; 213 computer-based). Electronic applications accepted. *Faculty research:* Artificial intelligence, computational theory, graphics and computer vision, networks, systems.

University of Denver, School of Engineering and Computer Science, Department of Computer Science, Denver, CO 80208. Offers computer science (MS, PhD); computer science systems engineering (MS). Part-time programs available. *Faculty:* 10 full-time (2 women), 3 part-time/adjunct (1 woman). *Students:* 2 full-time (1 woman), 58 part-time (10 women); includes 8 minority (1 Black or African American, non-Hispanic/Latino; 4 Asian, non-Hispanic/Latino; 3 Hispanic/Latino), 14 international. Average age 33. 61 applicants, 70% accepted, 16 enrolled. In 2011, 32 master's, 1 doctorate awarded. *Median time to degree:* Of those who began their doctoral program in fall 2003, 100% received their degree in 8 years or less. *Degree requirements:* For doctorate, variable foreign language requirement, comprehensive exam, thesis/dissertation, reading competency in two languages, modern typesetting system, or additional coursework. *Entrance requirements:* For master's and doctorate, GRE General Test, personal statement, three letters of recommendation. Additional exam requirements/recommendations for international students: Required—TOEFL (minimum score 550 paper-based; 80 iBT). *Application deadline:* Applications are processed on a rolling basis. Application fee: $60. Electronic applications accepted. *Financial support:* In 2011–12, 27 students received support, including 1 research assistantship with full and partial tuition reimbursement available (averaging $18,300 per year), 9 teaching assistantships with full and partial tuition reimbursements available (averaging $14,911 per year); career-related internships or fieldwork, Federal Work-Study, institutionally sponsored loans, scholarships/grants, and unspecified assistantships also available. Financial award application deadline: 2/15; financial award applicants required to submit FAFSA. *Faculty research:* Gaming, UML designs, STAMP. *Unit head:* Dr. Ramakrishna Thurimella, Chair, 303-871-3329, E-mail: ramki@cs.du.edu. *Application contact:* Information Contact, 303-871-2458, E-mail: info@cs.du.edu. Web site: http://www.du.edu/cs.

University of Detroit Mercy, College of Engineering and Science, Department of Mathematics and Computer Science, Program in Computer Science, Detroit, MI 48221. Offers computer systems applications (MSCS); software engineering (MSCS). Evening/weekend programs available. *Entrance requirements:* For master's, minimum GPA of 3.0.

University of Evansville, College of Engineering and Computer Science, Department of Electrical Engineering and Computer Science, Evansville, IN 47722. Offers MS. Part-time programs available. *Degree requirements:* For master's, thesis. *Entrance requirements:* For master's, GRE, minimum undergraduate GPA of 2.8, 2 letters of recommendation, BS in electrical engineering or computer science. Additional exam requirements/recommendations for international students: Required—TOEFL (minimum score 550 paper-based; 79 iBT), IELTS (minimum score 6.5). *Expenses:* Contact institution.

University of Florida, Graduate School, College of Engineering and College of Liberal Arts and Sciences, Department of Computer and Information Science and Engineering, Gainesville, FL 32611. Offers computer engineering (ME, MS, PhD); computer science (MS); digital arts and sciences (MS). Part-time programs available. Postbaccalaureate distance learning degree programs offered (minimal on-campus study). Terminal master's awarded for partial completion of doctoral program. *Degree requirements:* For master's, comprehensive exam, thesis optional; for doctorate, comprehensive exam, thesis/dissertation. *Entrance requirements:* For master's and doctorate, GRE General Test, minimum GPA of 3.0. Additional exam requirements/recommendations for international students: Required—TOEFL (minimum score 550 paper-based; 213 computer-based; 80 iBT), IELTS (minimum score 6). Electronic applications accepted. *Faculty research:* Computer systems, database, computer networks, graphics and vision, algorithm and parallel processing.

University of Georgia, Franklin College of Arts and Sciences, Department of Computer Science, Athens, GA 30602. Offers applied mathematical science (MAMS); computer science (MS, PhD). *Faculty:* 18 full-time (3 women). *Students:* 94 full-time (14 women), 19 part-time (5 women); includes 5 minority (2 Black or African American, non-Hispanic/Latino; 2 Asian, non-Hispanic/Latino; 1 Native Hawaiian or other Pacific Islander, non-Hispanic/Latino), 79 international. Average age 29. 195 applicants, 37% accepted, 19 enrolled. In 2011, 13 master's, 6 doctorates awarded. *Degree requirements:* For doctorate, thesis/dissertation. *Entrance requirements:* For master's and doctorate, GRE General Test. *Application deadline:* For fall admission, 7/1 priority date for domestic students, 4/15 for international students; for spring admission, 11/15 for domestic and international students. Applications are processed on a rolling basis. Application fee: $50. Electronic applications accepted. *Financial support:* In 2011–12, 55 students received support, including 20 research assistantships, 31 teaching assistantships; fellowships, tuition waivers (full), and unspecified assistantships also available. *Unit head:* Dr. H. B. Schuttler, Head, 706-542-3455, E-mail: hbs@cs.uga.edu. *Application contact:* Dr. Suchendra Bhandarkar, Graduate Coordinator, 706-542-1082, Fax: 706-542-2966, E-mail: gradadvisor@cs.uga.edu. Web site: http://www.cs.uga.edu/.

University of Guelph, Graduate Studies, College of Physical and Engineering Science, Department of Computing and Information Science, Guelph, ON N1G 2W1, Canada. Offers applied computer science (M Sc); computer science (PhD). *Degree requirements:* For master's, thesis; for doctorate, comprehensive exam, thesis/dissertation. *Entrance requirements:* For master's, major or minor in computer science, honors degree; for doctorate, M Sc in computer science or related discipline. Additional exam requirements/recommendations for international students: Required—TOEFL (minimum score 600 paper-based; 250 computer-based; 89 iBT), IELTS (minimum score 6.5). Electronic applications accepted. *Faculty research:* Modeling and theory, distributed computing, soft computing, software and information systems, data and knowledge management.

University of Hawaii at Manoa, Graduate Division, College of Natural Sciences, Department of Information and Computer Sciences, Honolulu, HI 96822. Offers computer science (MS, PhD); library and information science (MLI Sc, Graduate Certificate), including advanced library and information science (Graduate Certificate), library and information science (MLI Sc). Part-time programs available. *Degree requirements:* For master's, thesis optional; for doctorate, comprehensive exam, thesis/dissertation. *Entrance requirements:* For master's and doctorate, GRE. Additional exam requirements/recommendations for international students: Required—TOEFL (minimum score 580 paper-based; 237 computer-based; 92 iBT), IELTS (minimum score 5). *Faculty research:* Software engineering, telecommunications, artificial intelligence, multimedia.

University of Houston, College of Natural Sciences and Mathematics, Department of Computer Science, Houston, TX 77204. Offers MA, PhD. Part-time programs available. Terminal master's awarded for partial completion of doctoral program. *Degree requirements:* For master's, thesis or alternative; for doctorate, comprehensive exam, thesis/dissertation. *Entrance requirements:* For master's and doctorate, GRE. Additional exam requirements/recommendations for international students: Required—TOEFL (minimum score 550 paper-based; 213 computer-based; 79 iBT), IELTS (minimum score 6.5). Electronic applications accepted. *Faculty research:* Databases, networks, image analysis, security, animation.

University of Houston–Clear Lake, School of Science and Computer Engineering, Program in Computer Science, Houston, TX 77058-1098. Offers MS. Part-time and evening/weekend programs available. *Entrance requirements:* For master's, GRE General Test. Additional exam requirements/recommendations for international students: Required—TOEFL (minimum score 550 paper-based; 213 computer-based).

University of Houston–Victoria, School of Arts and Sciences, Program in Computer Science, Victoria, TX 77901-4450. Offers computer information systems (MS). Part-time and evening/weekend programs available. Postbaccalaureate distance learning degree programs offered (no on-campus study). *Degree requirements:* For master's, comprehensive exam (for some programs), thesis (for some programs). *Entrance requirements:* For master's, GRE. Additional exam requirements/recommendations for international students: Required—TOEFL (minimum score 550 paper-based; 213 computer-based).

University of Idaho, College of Graduate Studies, College of Engineering, Department of Computer Science, Moscow, ID 83844-1010. Offers MS, PhD. *Faculty:* 10 full-time. *Students:* 36 full-time, 24 part-time. Average age 35. In 2011, 5 master's awarded. *Degree requirements:* For master's, thesis; for doctorate, thesis/dissertation. *Entrance requirements:* For master's, GRE General Test, minimum GPA of 3.0; for doctorate, minimum undergraduate GPA of 2.8, 3.0 graduate. Additional exam requirements/recommendations for international students: Required—TOEFL. *Application deadline:* For fall admission, 8/1 for domestic students; for spring admission, 12/15 for domestic students. Applications are processed on a rolling basis. Application fee: $60. Electronic applications accepted. *Expenses:* Tuition, state resident: full-time $3874; part-time $334 per credit hour. Tuition, nonresident: full-time $16,394; part-time $861 per credit hour. *Required fees:* $2808; $99 per credit hour. Tuition and fees vary according to program. *Financial support:* Research assistantships, teaching assistantships, and career-related internships or fieldwork available. Financial award applicants required to submit FAFSA. *Faculty research:* Artificial intelligence, computer and network security, software engineering. *Unit head:* Dr. Greg Donahoe, Chair, 208-885-6589, E-mail: csinfo@uidaho.edu. *Application contact:* Erick Larson, Director of Graduate Admissions, 208-885-4723, E-mail: gadms@uidaho.edu. Web site: http://www.uidaho.edu/engr/cs/.

University of Illinois at Chicago, Graduate College, College of Engineering, Department of Computer Science, Chicago, IL 60607-7128. Offers MS, PhD. Part-time programs available. *Degree requirements:* For master's, thesis or alternative; for doctorate, thesis/dissertation, departmental qualifying exam. *Entrance requirements:* For master's, BS in related field, minimum GPA of 2.75; for doctorate, GRE General Test, minimum GPA of 2.75, MS in related field. Additional exam requirements/recommendations for international students: Required—TOEFL.

University of Illinois at Chicago, Graduate College, College of Liberal Arts and Sciences, Department of Mathematics, Statistics, and Computer Science, Chicago, IL 60607-7128. Offers applied mathematics (MS, PhD); computational finance (MS, PhD); computer science (MS, PhD); mathematics (DA); mathematics and information sciences for industry (MS); probability and statistics (PhD); pure mathematics (MS, PhD); statistics (MS); teaching of mathematics (MST), including elementary, secondary. Part-time programs available. *Degree requirements:* For master's, comprehensive exam; for doctorate, one foreign language, thesis/dissertation. *Entrance requirements:* For master's and doctorate, GRE General Test, minimum GPA of 3.0. Additional exam requirements/recommendations for international students: Required—TOEFL (minimum score 100 iBT). Electronic applications accepted.

University of Illinois at Springfield, Graduate Programs, College of Liberal Arts and Sciences, Program in Computer Science, Springfield, IL 62703-5407. Offers MS. Part-time and evening/weekend programs available. Postbaccalaureate distance learning degree programs offered (no on-campus study). *Faculty:* 6 full-time (0 women), 3 part-time/adjunct (0 women). *Students:* 111 full-time (26 women), 164 part-time (27 women); includes 34 minority (7 Black or African American, non-Hispanic/Latino; 1 American Indian or Alaska Native, non-Hispanic/Latino; 16 Asian, non-Hispanic/Latino; 8 Hispanic/Latino; 2 Two or more races, non-Hispanic/Latino), 121 international. Average age 31. 517 applicants, 74% accepted, 91 enrolled. In 2011, 108 master's awarded. *Degree requirements:* For master's, research seminar. *Entrance requirements:* For master's, GRE General Test, minimum undergraduate GPA of 2.7. Additional exam requirements/recommendations for international students: Required—TOEFL (minimum score 550 paper-based; 213 computer-based; 79 iBT). *Application deadline:* Applications are processed on a rolling basis. Application fee: $50 ($60 for international students). Electronic applications accepted. *Expenses:* Tuition, state resident: full-time $6978; part-time $290.75 per credit hour. Tuition, nonresident: full-time $15,282; part-time $636.75 per credit hour. *Required fees:* $2106; $87.75 per credit hour. *Financial support:* In 2011–12, fellowships with full tuition reimbursements (averaging $8,550 per year), research assistantships with full tuition reimbursements (averaging $8,550 per year), teaching assistantships with full tuition reimbursements (averaging $8,550 per year) were awarded; career-related internships or fieldwork, Federal Work-Study, scholarships/grants, health care benefits, and unspecified assistantships also available. Support available to part-time students. Financial award application deadline: 11/15; financial award applicants required to submit FAFSA. *Unit head:* Dr. Ted Mims, Program Administrator, 217-206-7326, Fax: 217-206-6217, E-mail: mims.ted@uis.edu. *Application contact:* Dr. Lynn Pardie, Office of Graduate Studies, 800-252-8533, Fax: 217-206-7623, E-mail: lpard1@uis.edu.

University of Illinois at Urbana–Champaign, Graduate College, College of Engineering, Department of Computer Science, Champaign, IL 61820. Offers bioinformatics (MS); computer science (MCS, MS, PhD); MCS/JD; MCS/M Arch; MCS/MBA. Part-time programs available. Postbaccalaureate distance learning degree programs offered (no on-campus study). *Faculty:* 51 full-time (5 women), 2 part-time/adjunct (0 women). *Students:* 262 full-time (39 women), 186 part-time (27 women); includes 45 minority (3 Black or African American, non-Hispanic/Latino; 38 Asian, non-Hispanic/Latino; 1 Hispanic/Latino; 3 Two or more races, non-Hispanic/Latino), 269 international. 1,527 applicants, 16% accepted, 105 enrolled. In 2011, 78 master's, 42 doctorates awarded. *Entrance requirements:* For master's and doctorate, minimum GPA of 3.0. Additional exam requirements/recommendations for international students: Required—TOEFL (minimum score 600 paper-based; 250 computer-based; 100 iBT) or IELTS (minimum score 6.5). *Application deadline:* Applications are processed on a rolling basis. Application fee: $75 ($90 for international students). Electronic applications accepted. *Financial support:* In 2011–12, 39 fellowships, 274 research assistantships, 117 teaching assistantships were awarded; tuition waivers (full and partial) also available. *Unit head:* Robin A. Rutenbar, Head, 217-333-3373, Fax: 217-333-3501, E-mail: rutenbar@illinois.edu. *Application contact:* Laura Baylor, Graduate Academic Advisor, 217-333-3425, Fax: 217-244-6073, E-mail: lherriot@illinois.edu. Web site: http://cs.illinois.edu/.

The University of Iowa, Graduate College, College of Liberal Arts and Sciences, Department of Computer Science, Iowa City, IA 52242-1316. Offers MCS, MS, PhD. *Degree requirements:* For master's, thesis optional, exam; for doctorate, comprehensive exam, thesis/dissertation. *Entrance requirements:* For master's, minimum GPA of 3.0; for doctorate, GRE General Test, minimum GPA of 3.0. Additional exam requirements/recommendations for international students: Required—TOEFL (minimum score 550 paper-based; 213 computer-based; 81 iBT). Electronic applications accepted.

The University of Kansas, Graduate Studies, School of Engineering, Program in Computer Science, Lawrence, KS 66045. Offers MS, PhD. Part-time and evening/weekend programs available. *Faculty:* 36. *Students:* 45 full-time (14 women), 17 part-time (4 women); includes 6 minority (1 Black or African American, non-Hispanic/Latino; 4 Asian, non-Hispanic/Latino; 1 Hispanic/Latino), 33 international. Average age 29. 85 applicants, 46% accepted, 12 enrolled. In 2011, 13 master's, 4 doctorates awarded. Terminal master's awarded for partial completion of doctoral program. *Degree requirements:* For master's, thesis optional, exam; for doctorate, one foreign language, comprehensive exam, thesis/dissertation, qualifying exams. *Entrance requirements:* For master's, GRE, minimum GPA of 3.0; for doctorate, GRE, minimum GPA of 3.5. Additional exam requirements/recommendations for international students: Required—TOEFL (minimum score 600 paper-based; 250 computer-based; 100 iBT). *Application deadline:* For fall admission, 3/1 priority date for domestic students, 3/1 for international students; for spring admission, 10/1 priority date for domestic students, 10/1 for international students. Applications are processed on a rolling basis. Application fee: $55 ($65 for international students). Electronic applications accepted. Tuition and fees vary according to course load, campus/location, program and reciprocity agreements. *Financial support:* Fellowships with full and partial tuition reimbursements, research assistantships with full and partial tuition reimbursements, teaching assistantships with full and partial tuition reimbursements, career-related internships or fieldwork, scholarships/grants, and unspecified assistantships available. Financial award application deadline: 1/1. *Faculty research:* Communication systems and networking, computer systems design, interactive intelligent systems, bioinformatics. *Unit head:* Glenn Prescott, Chairperson, 785-864-4620, Fax: 785-864-3226. *Application contact:* Pam Shadoin, Assistant to Graduate Director, 785-864-4487, Fax: 785-864-3226, E-mail: eecs_graduate@.ku.edu. Web site: http://www.eecs.ku.edu/.

University of Kentucky, Graduate School, College of Engineering, Program in Computer Science, Lexington, KY 40506-0032. Offers MS, PhD. *Degree requirements:* For master's, comprehensive exam, thesis optional; for doctorate, one foreign language, comprehensive exam, thesis/dissertation. *Entrance requirements:* For master's, GRE General Test, minimum undergraduate GPA of 2.75; for doctorate, GRE General Test, minimum undergraduate GPA of 3.0. Additional exam requirements/recommendations for international students: Required—TOEFL (minimum score 550 paper-based; 213 computer-based). Electronic applications accepted. *Faculty research:* Artificial intelligence and databases, communication networks and operating systems, graphics and vision, numerical analysis, theory.

University of Lethbridge, School of Graduate Studies, Lethbridge, AB T1K 3M4, Canada. Offers accounting (MScM); addictions counseling (M Sc); agricultural biotechnology (M Sc); agricultural studies (M Sc, MA); anthropology (MA); archaeology (MA); art (MA, MFA); biochemistry (M Sc); biological sciences (M Sc); biomolecular science (PhD); biosystems and biodiversity (PhD); Canadian studies (MA); chemistry (M Sc); computer science (M Sc); computer science and geographical information science (M Sc); counseling psychology (M Ed); dramatic arts (MA); earth, space, and physical science (PhD); economics (MA); educational leadership (M Ed); English (MA); environmental science (M Sc); evolution and behavior (PhD); exercise science (M Sc); finance (MScM); French (MA); French/German (MA); French/Spanish (MA); general education (M Ed); general management (MScM); geography (M Sc, MA); German (MA); health science (M Sc); history (MA); human resource management and labour relations (MScM); individualized multidisciplinary (M Sc, MA); information systems (MScM); international management (MScM); kinesiology (M Sc, MA); management (M Sc, MA); marketing (MScM); mathematics (M Sc); music (M Mus, MA); Native American studies (MA); neuroscience (M Sc, PhD); new media (MA); nursing (M Sc); philosophy (MA); physics (M Sc); policy and strategy (MScM); political science (MA); psychology (M Sc, MA); religious studies (MA); social sciences (MA); sociology (MA); theatre and dramatic arts (MFA); theoretical and computational science (PhD); urban and regional studies (MA); women's studies (MA). Part-time and evening/weekend programs available. *Degree requirements:* For doctorate, comprehensive exam, thesis/dissertation. *Entrance requirements:* For master's, GMAT (M Sc in management), bachelor's degree in related field, minimum GPA of 3.0 during previous 20 graded semester courses, 2 years teaching or related experience (M Ed); for doctorate, master's degree, minimum graduate GPA of 3.5. Additional exam requirements/recommendations for international students: Required—TOEFL. *Faculty research:* Movement and brain plasticity, gibberellin physiology, photosynthesis, carbon cycling, molecular properties of main-group ring components.

University of Louisiana at Lafayette, College of Engineering, Center for Advanced Computer Studies, Lafayette, LA 70504. Offers computer engineering (MS, PhD); computer science (MS, PhD). Part-time programs available. Terminal master's awarded for partial completion of doctoral program. *Degree requirements:* For master's, thesis or alternative; for doctorate, comprehensive exam, thesis/dissertation, final oral exam. *Entrance requirements:* For master's, GRE General Test, minimum GPA of 2.75; for doctorate, GRE General Test, minimum GPA of 3.0. Additional exam requirements/recommendations for international students: Required—TOEFL. Electronic applications accepted.

See Display on next page and Close-Up on page 343.

University of Louisville, J. B. Speed School of Engineering, Department of Computer Engineering and Computer Science, Louisville, KY 40292-0001. Offers computer engineering and computer science (M Eng); computer science (MS); computer science and engineering (PhD); data mining (Certificate); network and information security (Certificate). *Accreditation:* ABET (one or more programs are accredited). Part-time programs available. Postbaccalaureate distance learning degree programs offered (no on-campus study). *Faculty:* 13 full-time (1 woman). *Students:* 54 full-time (11 women), 40 part-time (8 women); includes 12 minority (6 Black or African American, non-Hispanic/Latino; 6 Asian, non-Hispanic/Latino), 33 international. Average age 27. 49

applicants, 35% accepted, 7 enrolled. In 2011, 38 master's, 7 doctorates awarded. Terminal master's awarded for partial completion of doctoral program. *Degree requirements:* For master's, comprehensive exam (for some programs), thesis or alternative; for doctorate, comprehensive exam, thesis/dissertation, minimum GPA of 3.0. *Entrance requirements:* For master's, doctorate, and Certificate, GRE General Test. Additional exam requirements/recommendations for international students: Required—TOEFL (minimum score 550 paper-based; 213 computer-based; 80 iBT), IELTS (minimum score 6.5). *Application deadline:* For fall admission, 5/1 priority date for domestic students, 5/1 for international students; for spring admission, 11/1 priority date for domestic students, 11/1 for international students. Applications are processed on a rolling basis. Application fee: $50. Electronic applications accepted. *Expenses:* Tuition, state resident: full-time $9692; part-time $539 per credit hour. Tuition, nonresident: full-time $20,168; part-time $1121 per credit hour. Tuition and fees vary according to program and reciprocity agreements. *Financial support:* In 2011–12, 22 students received support, including 1 fellowship with full tuition reimbursement available (averaging $20,000 per year), 15 research assistantships with full tuition reimbursements available (averaging $18,900 per year), 6 teaching assistantships with full tuition reimbursements available (averaging $20,000 per year). Financial award application deadline: 1/25; financial award applicants required to submit FAFSA. *Faculty research:* Software systems engineering, information security and forensics, multimedia and vision, mobile and distributed computing, intelligent systems. *Total annual research expenditures:* $1.3 million. *Unit head:* Dr. Adel S. Elmaghraby, Chair, 502-852-6304, Fax: 502-852-4713, E-mail: adel@louisville.edu. *Application contact:* Dr. Michael Day, Associate Dean, 502-852-6195, Fax: 502-852-6294, E-mail: day@louisville.edu. Web site: http://www.louisville.edu/speed/computer.

University of Maine, Graduate School, College of Liberal Arts and Sciences, Department of Computer Science, Orono, ME 04469. Offers MS, PhD. Part-time programs available. *Faculty:* 14 full-time (2 women), 5 part-time/adjunct (1 woman). *Students:* 29 full-time (5 women), 14 part-time (2 women); includes 1 minority (Hispanic/Latino), 12 international. Average age 34. 14 applicants, 64% accepted, 4 enrolled. In 2011, 3 master's, 2 doctorates awarded. *Degree requirements:* For master's, thesis optional; for doctorate, thesis/dissertation. *Entrance requirements:* For master's and doctorate, GRE General Test, GRE Subject Test. Additional exam requirements/recommendations for international students: Required—TOEFL. *Application deadline:* For fall admission, 2/1 priority date for domestic students. Applications are processed on a rolling basis. Application fee: $65. Electronic applications accepted. *Expenses:* Tuition, state resident: full-time $5016. Tuition, nonresident: full-time $14,424. *Financial support:* In 2011–12, 1 fellowship with full tuition reimbursement (averaging $18,000 per year), 2 research assistantships with full tuition reimbursements (averaging $15,300 per year), 9 teaching assistantships with full tuition reimbursements (averaging $16,982 per year) were awarded; career-related internships or fieldwork, Federal Work-Study, institutionally sponsored loans, and tuition waivers (full) also available. Financial award application deadline: 3/1. *Faculty research:* Theory, software engineering, graphics, applications, artificial intelligence. *Total annual research expenditures:* $42,204. *Unit head:* Dr. George Markowsky, Chair, 207-581-3912, Fax: 207-581-4977. *Application contact:* Scott G. Delcourt, Associate Dean of the Graduate School, 207-581-3291, Fax: 207-581-3232, E-mail: graduate@maine.edu. Web site: http://www2.umaine.edu/graduate/.

University of Management and Technology, Program in Computer Science and Information Technology, Arlington, VA 22209. Offers computer science (MS); information technology (AC); information technology project management (MS); management information systems (MS); project management (AC); software engineering (MS). Part-time and evening/weekend programs available. Postbaccalaureate distance learning degree programs offered (no on-campus study). *Entrance requirements:* For master's, 3 recommendations, resume. Additional exam requirements/recommendations for international students: Required—TOEFL (minimum score 550 paper-based; 213 computer-based). Electronic applications accepted.

The University of Manchester, School of Computer Science, Manchester, United Kingdom. Offers M Phil, PhD.

University of Manitoba, Faculty of Graduate Studies, Faculty of Science, Department of Computer Science, Winnipeg, MB R3T 2N2, Canada. Offers M Sc, PhD. *Degree requirements:* For master's, thesis or alternative; for doctorate, thesis/dissertation.

University of Maryland, Baltimore County, Graduate School, College of Engineering and Information Technology, Department of Computer Science and Electrical Engineering, Program in Computer Science, Baltimore, MD 21250. Offers MS, PhD. Part-time programs available. *Students:* 88 full-time (19 women), 44 part-time (9 women); includes 20 minority (5 Black or African American, non-Hispanic/Latino; 2 American Indian or Alaska Native, non-Hispanic/Latino; 7 Asian, non-Hispanic/Latino; 4 Hispanic/Latino; 1 Native Hawaiian or other Pacific Islander, non-Hispanic/Latino; 1 Two or more races, non-Hispanic/Latino), 56 international. Average age 29. 332 applicants, 20% accepted, 24 enrolled. In 2011, 28 master's, 12 doctorates awarded. *Degree requirements:* For master's, comprehensive exam (for some programs), thesis (for some programs); for doctorate, comprehensive exam, thesis/dissertation. *Entrance requirements:* For master's, GRE General Test, strong background in computer science and math courses; for doctorate, GRE General Test, MS in computer science (strongly recommended). Additional exam requirements/recommendations for international students: Required—TOEFL (minimum score 550 paper-based; 213 computer-based; 80 iBT). *Application deadline:* For fall admission, 6/1 for domestic students, 1/1 for international students; for spring admission, 11/1 for domestic students, 6/1 for international students. Applications are processed on a rolling basis. Application fee: $70. Electronic applications accepted. *Financial support:* In 2011–12, 1 fellowship with full tuition reimbursement (averaging $21,500 per year), 21 research assistantships with full tuition reimbursements (averaging $17,000 per year), 25 teaching assistantships with full tuition reimbursements (averaging $17,000 per year) were awarded; career-related internships or fieldwork, Federal Work-Study, scholarships/grants, health care benefits, tuition waivers (partial), and unspecified assistantships also available. Support available to part-time students. Financial award application deadline: 6/30; financial award applicants required to submit FAFSA. *Faculty research:* Artificial intelligence, graphics and visualization, high performance computing, information and knowledge management, networking and systems, security, theory and algorithms. *Unit head:* Dr. Gary Carter, Professor and Chair, 410-455-3500, Fax: 410-455-3969, E-mail: carter@cs.umbc.edu. *Application contact:* Dr. Anupam Joshi, Professor and Graduate Program Director, 410-455-2590, Fax: 410-455-3969, E-mail: joshi@cs.umbc.edu. Web site: http://www.csee.umbc.edu/.

University of Maryland, Baltimore County, Graduate School, College of Engineering and Information Technology, Department of Information Systems, Program in Human-Centered Computing, Baltimore, MD 21250. Offers MS, PhD. Part-time and evening/weekend programs available. *Students:* 26 full-time (14 women), 29 part-time (13 women); includes 11 minority (7 Black or African American, non-Hispanic/Latino; 3 Asian, non-Hispanic/Latino; 1 Two or more races, non-Hispanic/Latino), 11 international.

Average age 31. 59 applicants, 25% accepted, 5 enrolled. In 2011, 6 master's awarded. Terminal master's awarded for partial completion of doctoral program. *Degree requirements:* For master's, comprehensive exam (for some programs), thesis optional; for doctorate, comprehensive exam, thesis/dissertation. *Entrance requirements:* For master's, minimum GPA of 3.0; for doctorate, GRE General Test or GMAT, minimum GPA of 3.0, competence in statistical analysis and experimental design (recommended). Additional exam requirements/recommendations for international students: Required—TOEFL (minimum score 550 paper-based; 213 computer-based; 80 iBT). *Application deadline:* For fall admission, 6/1 for domestic students, 1/1 for international students; for spring admission, 11/1 for domestic students, 6/1 for international students. Applications are processed on a rolling basis. Application fee: $70. Electronic applications accepted. *Financial support:* In 2011–12, 6 research assistantships with full tuition reimbursements (averaging $19,000 per year), 5 teaching assistantships with full tuition reimbursements (averaging $19,000 per year) were awarded; career-related internships or fieldwork, Federal Work-Study, scholarships/grants, health care benefits, tuition waivers (partial), and unspecified assistantships also available. Support available to part-time students. Financial award application deadline: 6/30; financial award applicants required to submit FAFSA. *Faculty research:* Human-centered computing. *Unit head:* Dr. Arrya Gangopadhyay, Professor and Chair, 410-455-2620, Fax: 410-455-1217, E-mail: gangopad@umbc.edu. *Application contact:* Dr. Anita Komlodi, Associate Professor and Graduate Program Director, 410-455-3212, Fax: 410-455-1217, E-mail: komlodi@umbc.edu. Web site: http://www.is.umbc.edu/.

University of Maryland, College Park, Academic Affairs, College of Computer, Mathematical and Natural Sciences, Department of Computer Science, College Park, MD 20742. Offers MS, PhD. Part-time and evening/weekend programs available. *Faculty:* 77 full-time (9 women), 4 part-time/adjunct (0 women). *Students:* 214 full-time (36 women), 21 part-time (4 women); includes 27 minority (2 Black or African American, non-Hispanic/Latino; 21 Asian, non-Hispanic/Latino; 2 Hispanic/Latino; 2 Two or more races, non-Hispanic/Latino), 136 international. 1,184 applicants, 10% accepted, 47 enrolled. In 2011, 23 master's, 27 doctorates awarded. Terminal master's awarded for partial completion of doctoral program. *Degree requirements:* For master's, thesis or scholarly paper and exam; for doctorate, thesis/dissertation. *Entrance requirements:* For master's and doctorate, GRE General Test, GRE Subject Test (recommended), minimum GPA of 3.0, 3 letters of recommendation. Additional exam requirements/recommendations for international students: Required—TOEFL; Recommended—TWE. *Application deadline:* For fall admission, 12/15 for domestic and international students; for spring admission, 10/1 for domestic students, 6/1 for international students. Applications are processed on a rolling basis. Application fee: $75. Electronic applications accepted. *Expenses: Tuition, area resident:* Part-time $525 per credit hour. Tuition, state resident: part-time $525 per credit hour. Tuition, nonresident: part-time $1131 per credit hour. *Required fees:* $386.31 per term. Tuition and fees vary according to program. *Financial support:* In 2011–12, 2 fellowships with partial tuition reimbursements (averaging $10,400 per year), 122 research assistantships with tuition reimbursements (averaging $19,613 per year), 77 teaching assistantships with tuition reimbursements (averaging $18,734 per year) were awarded; career-related internships or fieldwork, Federal Work-Study, and scholarships/grants also available. Support available to part-time students. Financial award applicants required to submit FAFSA. *Faculty research:* Artificial intelligence, computer applications, information processing, bioinformatics and computational biology, human-computer interaction. *Total annual research expenditures:* $4.6 million. *Unit head:* Dr. Larry S. Davis, Chairperson, 301-405-2662, Fax: 301-314-1353, E-mail: lsdavis@umd.edu. *Application contact:* Dr. Charles A. Caramello, Dean of Graduate School, 301-405-0358, Fax: 301-314-9305.

University of Maryland Eastern Shore, Graduate Programs, Department of Mathematics and Computer Sciences, Princess Anne, MD 21853-1299. Offers applied computer science (MS). Part-time and evening/weekend programs available. *Degree requirements:* For master's, thesis or alternative, research project. *Entrance requirements:* For master's, GRE General Test, minimum GPA of 3.0. Additional exam requirements/recommendations for international students: Required—TOEFL (minimum score 213 computer-based; 80 iBT). Electronic applications accepted.

University of Massachusetts Amherst, Graduate School, College of Natural Sciences, Department of Computer Science, Amherst, MA 01003. Offers MS, PhD. Part-time programs available. *Faculty:* 48 full-time (7 women). *Students:* 163 full-time (37 women), 38 part-time (4 women); includes 12 minority (3 Black or African American, non-Hispanic/Latino; 5 Asian, non-Hispanic/Latino; 2 Hispanic/Latino; 2 Two or more races, non-Hispanic/Latino), 109 international. Average age 28. 944 applicants, 14% accepted, 52 enrolled. In 2011, 29 master's, 20 doctorates awarded. Terminal master's awarded for partial completion of doctoral program. *Degree requirements:* For master's, thesis or alternative; for doctorate, comprehensive exam, thesis/dissertation. *Entrance requirements:* For master's and doctorate, GRE General Test. Additional exam requirements/recommendations for international students: Required—TOEFL (minimum score 550 paper-based; 213 computer-based; 80 iBT), IELTS (minimum score 6.5), TWE. *Application deadline:* For fall admission, 12/15 for domestic and international students. Applications are processed on a rolling basis. Application fee: $50 ($65 for international students). Electronic applications accepted. Tuition and fees vary according to course load, campus/location and program. *Financial support:* Fellowships with full and partial tuition reimbursements, research assistantships with full and partial tuition reimbursements, teaching assistantships with full and partial tuition reimbursements, career-related internships or fieldwork, Federal Work-Study, institutionally sponsored loans, scholarships/grants, traineeships, health care benefits, tuition waivers (full and partial), and unspecified assistantships available. Financial award application deadline: 12/15. *Faculty research:* Artificial intelligence, robotics, computer vision, and wearable computing; autonomous and multiagent systems; information retrieval, data mining and machine learning; networking, distributed systems and security. *Unit head:* Dr. Sridhar Mahadevan, Graduate Program Director, 413-545-3640, Fax: 413-545-1249. *Application contact:* Lindsay DeSantis, Interim Supervisor of Admissions, 413-545-0721, Fax: 413-577-0010, E-mail: gradadm@grad.umass.edu. Web site: http://www.cs.umass.edu/.

University of Massachusetts Boston, Office of Graduate Studies, College of Science and Mathematics, Program in Computer Science, Boston, MA 02125-3393. Offers MS, PhD. Part-time and evening/weekend programs available. *Degree requirements:* For master's, comprehensive exam, thesis optional, capstone final project; for doctorate, comprehensive exam, thesis/dissertation, oral exams. *Entrance requirements:* For master's and doctorate, GRE General Test, minimum GPA of 2.75. *Faculty research:* Queuing theory, database design theory, computer networks, theory of database query languages, real-time systems.

University of Massachusetts Lowell, College of Sciences, Department of Computer Science, Lowell, MA 01854-2881. Offers MS, PhD, Sc D. Part-time programs available. *Degree requirements:* For master's, thesis optional; for doctorate, thesis/dissertation. *Entrance requirements:* For master's and doctorate, GRE General Test. *Faculty research:* Networks, multimedia systems, human-computer interaction, graphics and visualization databases.

University of Memphis, Graduate School, College of Arts and Sciences, Department of Computer Science, Memphis, TN 38152. Offers applied computer science (MS); computer science (MS, PhD). *Degree requirements:* For master's, comprehensive exam, thesis; for doctorate, comprehensive exam, thesis/dissertation. *Entrance requirements:* For master's and doctorate, GRE, letters of recommendation. Additional exam requirements/recommendations for international students: Required—TOEFL (minimum score 550 paper-based; 210 computer-based; 80 iBT). *Faculty research:* Network security, biomolecular and distributed computing, wireless sensor networks, artificial intelligence.

University of Memphis, Graduate School, College of Arts and Sciences, Department of Mathematical Sciences, Memphis, TN 38152. Offers applied mathematics (MS); applied statistics (PhD); bioinformatics (MS); computer science (PhD); computer sciences (MS); mathematics (MS, PhD); statistics (MS, PhD). Part-time programs available. Terminal master's awarded for partial completion of doctoral program. *Degree requirements:* For master's, comprehensive exam; for doctorate, one foreign language, thesis/dissertation, oral exams. *Entrance requirements:* For master's and doctorate, GRE General Test, minimum GPA of 2.5. Additional exam requirements/recommendations for international students: Required—TOEFL (minimum score 550 paper-based; 210 computer-based). Electronic applications accepted. *Faculty research:* Combinatorics, ergodic theory, graph theory, Ramsey theory, applied statistics.

University of Miami, Graduate School, College of Arts and Sciences, Department of Computer Science, Coral Gables, FL 33124. Offers MS, PhD. Part-time programs available. Postbaccalaureate distance learning degree programs offered (no on-campus study). *Degree requirements:* For master's, comprehensive exam (for some programs), thesis. *Entrance requirements:* For master's, GRE. Additional exam requirements/recommendations for international students: Required—TOEFL. Electronic applications accepted. *Faculty research:* Algorithm engineering, automated reasoning, computer graphics, cryptography, security network.

University of Michigan, College of Engineering, Department of Computer Science and Engineering, Ann Arbor, MI 48109. Offers MS, MSE, PhD. *Students:* 262 full-time (42 women), 1 part-time (0 women). 1,296 applicants, 19% accepted, 106 enrolled. In 2011, 54 master's, 14 doctorates awarded. *Faculty research:* Solid state electronics and optics; communications, control, signal process; sensors and integrated circuitry; software systems; artificial intelligence; hardware systems. *Unit head:* Prof. Marios Papaefthymiou, Interim Chair, 734-764-8504, Fax: 734-763-1503, E-mail: marios@umich.edu. *Application contact:* Dawn Freysinger, Graduate Programs Coordinator, 734-647-1807, Fax: 734-763-1503, E-mail: dawnf@umich.edu.

University of Michigan, College of Engineering, Department of Electrical Engineering and Computer Science, Ann Arbor, MI 48109. Offers MS, MSE, PhD. *Students:* 607 full-time (90 women), 2 part-time (0 women). 1,879 applicants, 29% accepted, 250 enrolled. In 2011, 116 master's, 33 doctorates awarded. *Faculty research:* Solid state electronics and optics; communications, control, signal process; sensors and integrated circuitry; software systems; artificial intelligence; hardware systems. *Unit head:* Prof. Khalil Najafi, Chair, 734-647-7010, Fax: 734-647-7009, E-mail: najafi@umich.edu. *Application contact:* Beth Stalnaker, Graduate Coordinator, 734-647-1758, Fax: 734-763-1503, E-mail: beths@umich.edu.

University of Michigan–Dearborn, College of Engineering and Computer Science, Department of Computer and Information Science, Dearborn, MI 48128-1491. Offers computer and information science (MS). Part-time and evening/weekend programs available. Postbaccalaureate distance learning degree programs offered (minimal on-campus study). *Faculty:* 15 full-time (1 woman), 3 part-time/adjunct (0 women). *Students:* 18 full-time (6 women), 50 part-time (11 women); includes 12 minority (11 Asian, non-Hispanic/Latino; 1 Hispanic/Latino), 12 international. Average age 33. 33 applicants, 58% accepted, 10 enrolled. In 2011, 14 master's awarded. *Degree requirements:* For master's, thesis optional. *Entrance requirements:* For master's, bachelor's degree in mathematics, computer science, or engineering; minimum GPA of 3.0. Additional exam requirements/recommendations for international students: Required—TOEFL (minimum score 560 paper-based; 220 computer-based; 84 iBT). *Application deadline:* For fall admission, 6/15 priority date for domestic students, 4/1 for international students; for winter admission, 10/15 priority date for domestic students, 8/1 for international students; for spring admission, 2/15 priority date for domestic students, 12/1 for international students. Application fee: $60. *Financial support:* In 2011–12, 3 research assistantships with full and partial tuition reimbursements (averaging $11,961 per year) were awarded; career-related internships or fieldwork also available. Financial award application deadline: 4/1; financial award applicants required to submit FAFSA. *Faculty research:* Information systems, geometric modeling, networks, databases. *Total annual research expenditures:* $54,056. *Unit head:* Dr. William I. Grosky, Chair, 313-583-6424, Fax: 313-593-4256, E-mail: wgrosky@umich.edu. *Application contact:* Katharine R. Markotan, Intermediate Academic Records Assistant, 313-436-9145, Fax: 313-593-4256, E-mail: tabatha@umd.umich.edu. Web site: http://www.engin.umd.umich.edu/CIS/.

University of Michigan–Flint, College of Arts and Sciences, Program in Computer and Information Systems, Flint, MI 48502-1950. Offers computer science and information systems (MS). Part-time programs available. *Degree requirements:* For master's, thesis or alternative. *Entrance requirements:* For master's, minimum undergraduate GPA of 3.0. Additional exam requirements/recommendations for international students: Required—TOEFL (minimum score 560 paper-based; 220 computer-based; 84 iBT), IELTS (minimum score 6.5). *Expenses:* Contact institution.

University of Minnesota, Duluth, Graduate School, Swenson College of Science and Engineering, Department of Computer Science, Duluth, MN 55812-2496. Offers MS. Part-time programs available. *Entrance requirements:* For master's, GRE General Test, minimum GPA of 3.0. Additional exam requirements/recommendations for international students: Required—TOEFL (minimum score 550 paper-based; 213 computer-based). Electronic applications accepted. *Faculty research:* Information retrieval, artificial intelligence, machine learning, parallel/distributed computing, graphics.

University of Minnesota, Twin Cities Campus, College of Science and Engineering, Department of Computer Science and Engineering, Minneapolis, MN 55455-0213. Offers computer science (MCS, MS, PhD); software engineering (MSSE). Part-time programs available. *Faculty:* 36 full-time (3 women). *Students:* 401 (58 women); includes 26 minority (3 Black or African American, non-Hispanic/Latino; 3 American Indian or Alaska Native, non-Hispanic/Latino; 17 Asian, non-Hispanic/Latino; 3 Hispanic/Latino), 225 international. Terminal master's awarded for partial completion of doctoral program. *Degree requirements:* For doctorate, thesis/dissertation. *Entrance requirements:* For master's and doctorate, GRE General Test. Additional exam requirements/recommendations for international students: Required—TOEFL. *Application deadline:* For fall admission, 12/1 priority date for domestic students, 12/1 for international students. Applications are processed on a rolling basis. Application fee: $75 ($95 for international students). Electronic applications accepted. *Financial support:* Fellowships with tuition reimbursements, research assistantships with tuition reimbursements, and teaching assistantships with tuition reimbursements available. *Faculty research:* Computer architecture, bioinformatics and computational biology, data mining; graphics and visualization, high performance computing, human-computer interaction, networks, software systems, theory, artificial intelligence. *Application contact:* Computer Science Graduate Admissions, E-mail: admissions@cs.umn.edu. Web site: http://www.cs.umn.edu/.

University of Minnesota, Twin Cities Campus, Graduate School, Scientific Computation Program, Minneapolis, MN 55455-0213. Offers MS, PhD. Part-time programs available. *Degree requirements:* For master's, thesis; for doctorate, thesis/dissertation. *Entrance requirements:* For doctorate, GRE General Test. Additional exam requirements/recommendations for international students: Required—TOEFL (minimum score 550 paper-based; 213 computer-based; 79 iBT), IELTS (minimum score 6.5). Electronic applications accepted. *Faculty research:* Parallel computations, quantum mechanical dynamics, computational materials science, computational fluid dynamics, computational neuroscience.

University of Missouri, Graduate School, College of Engineering, Department of Computer Science, Columbia, MO 65211. Offers MS, PhD. Part-time programs available. *Faculty:* 19 full-time (4 women). *Students:* 48 full-time (8 women), 43 part-time (9 women); includes 1 minority (Two or more races, non-Hispanic/Latino), 62 international. Average age 29. 95 applicants, 43% accepted, 12 enrolled. In 2011, 12 master's, 8 doctorates awarded. *Degree requirements:* For doctorate, thesis/dissertation. *Entrance requirements:* For master's, GRE General Test, minimum GPA of 3.0; for doctorate, GRE General Test. Additional exam requirements/recommendations for international students: Required—TOEFL (minimum score 577 paper-based; 233 computer-based; 90 iBT). *Application deadline:* For fall admission, 4/15 priority date for domestic students; for winter admission, 9/15 priority date for domestic students. Applications are processed on a rolling basis. Application fee: $55 ($75 for international students). *Expenses:* Tuition, state resident: full-time $5881. Tuition, nonresident: full-time $15,183. *Required fees:* $952. Tuition and fees vary according to campus/location and program. *Financial support:* Fellowships, research assistantships, teaching assistantships, and institutionally sponsored loans available. *Faculty research:* All campus computer science activities involving computational biology and bioinformatics, cyber-security, distributed computing, geospatial information mining and retrieval, intelligent systems, multimedia communications, large dataset scientific visualization, networking, spoken language processing and human-machine interfaces, wireless sensor networks. *Unit head:* Dr. Dong Xu, Department Chair, 573-882-2299, E-mail: xudong@missouri.edu. *Application contact:* Jodie Lenser, Graduate Academic Advisor, 573-882-7037, E-mail: lenserj@missouri.edu. Web site: http://engineering.missouri.edu/cs/.

University of Missouri–Kansas City, School of Computing and Engineering, Kansas City, MO 64110-2499. Offers civil engineering (MS); computer and electrical engineering (PhD); computer science (MS), including bioinformatics, software engineering, telecommunications networking; computer science and informatics (PhD); computing (PhD); electrical engineering (MS); engineering (PhD); mechanical engineering (MS); telecommunications (PhD). PhD (interdisciplinary) offered through the School of Graduate Studies. Part-time programs available. *Faculty:* 36 full-time (6 women), 27 part-time/adjunct (3 women). *Students:* 155 full-time (44 women), 136 part-time (24 women); includes 19 minority (4 Black or African American, non-Hispanic/Latino; 7 Asian, non-Hispanic/Latino; 6 Hispanic/Latino; 2 Two or more races, non-Hispanic/Latino), 201 international. Average age 26. 455 applicants, 46% accepted, 96 enrolled. In 2011, 194 degrees awarded. *Degree requirements:* For doctorate, thesis/dissertation. *Entrance requirements:* For master's, GRE General Test, minimum GPA of 3.0, 3 letters of recommendation from professors; for doctorate, GRE General Test, minimum GPA of 3.5. Additional exam requirements/recommendations for international students: Required—TOEFL (minimum score 550 paper-based; 213 computer-based; 80 iBT). *Application deadline:* For fall admission, 1/15 priority date for domestic students, 1/15 for international students. Applications are processed on a rolling basis. Application fee: $45 ($50 for international students). *Expenses:* Tuition, state resident: full-time $5798; part-time $322.10 per credit hour. Tuition, nonresident: full-time $14,969; part-time $831.60 per credit hour. *Required fees:* $93.51 per credit hour. *Financial support:* In 2011–12, 47 research assistantships with partial tuition reimbursements (averaging $13,190 per year), 10 teaching assistantships with partial tuition reimbursements (averaging $9,815 per year) were awarded; career-related internships or fieldwork, Federal Work-Study, scholarships/grants, tuition waivers (partial), and unspecified assistantships also available. Support available to part-time students. Financial award application deadline: 3/1; financial award applicants required to submit FAFSA. *Faculty research:* Algorithms, bioinformatics and medical informatics, biomechanics/biomaterials, civil engineering materials, networking and telecommunications, thermal science. *Unit head:* Dr. Kevin Z. Truman, Dean, 816-235-2399, Fax: 816-235-5159. *Application contact:* 816-235-2399, Fax: 816-235-5159. Web site: http://sce.umkc.edu/.

University of Missouri–St. Louis, College of Arts and Sciences, Department of Mathematics and Computer Science, St. Louis, MO 63121. Offers applied mathematics (PhD), including computer science, mathematics; computer science (MS); mathematics (MA). Part-time and evening/weekend programs available. *Faculty:* 16 full-time (2 women). *Students:* 28 full-time (16 women), 41 part-time (11 women); includes 6 minority (4 Black or African American, non-Hispanic/Latino; 1 American Indian or Alaska Native, non-Hispanic/Latino; 1 Asian, non-Hispanic/Latino), 18 international. Average age 32. 82 applicants, 57% accepted, 18 enrolled. In 2011, 20 master's, 2 doctorates awarded. *Degree requirements:* For master's, thesis optional; for doctorate, thesis/dissertation. *Entrance requirements:* For master's, GRE (for teaching assistantships), 2 letters of recommendation; C programming, C++ or Java (for computer science); for doctorate, GRE General Test, 3 letters of recommendation. Additional exam requirements/recommendations for international students: Required—TOEFL (minimum score 550 paper-based; 213 computer-based). *Application deadline:* For fall admission, 7/1 priority date for domestic students, 7/1 for international students; for spring admission, 12/1 priority date for domestic students, 12/1 for international students. Applications are processed on a rolling basis. Application fee: $35 ($40 for international students). Electronic applications accepted. *Expenses:* Tuition, state resident: full-time $6273; part-time $3866 per year. Tuition, nonresident: full-time $14,969; part-time $9980 per year. *Required fees:* $315 per year. *Financial support:* In 2011–12, 3 research assistantships with full and partial tuition reimbursements (averaging $14,250 per year), 10 teaching assistantships with full and partial tuition reimbursements (averaging $12,400 per year) were awarded; fellowships with full tuition reimbursements also available. Financial award applicants required to submit FAFSA. *Faculty research:* Statistics, algebra, analysis. *Unit head:* Dr. Shiying Zhao, Director of Graduate Studies, 314-516-5741, Fax: 314-516-5400, E-mail: zhao@arch.cs.umsl.edu. *Application contact:* 314-516-5458, Fax: 314-516-6996, E-mail: gradadm@umsl.edu.

The University of Montana, Graduate School, College of Arts and Sciences, Department of Computer Science, Missoula, MT 59812-0002. Offers MS. Part-time programs available. *Degree requirements:* For master's, project or thesis. *Entrance requirements:* For master's, GRE General Test. Additional exam requirements/recommendations for international students: Required—TOEFL (minimum score 525 paper-based; 197 computer-based). *Faculty research:* Parallel and distributed systems, neural networks, genetic algorithms, machine learning, data visualization, artificial intelligence.

University of Nebraska at Omaha, Graduate Studies, College of Information Science and Technology, Department of Computer Science, Omaha, NE 68182. Offers artificial intelligence (Certificate); communication networks (Certificate); computer science (MA, MS); systems architecture (Certificate). Part-time and evening/weekend programs available. *Faculty:* 15 full-time (2 women). *Students:* 33 full-time (2 women), 53 part-time (5 women); includes 7 minority (2 Black or African American, non-Hispanic/Latino; 5 Asian, non-Hispanic/Latino), 31 international. Average age 30. 65 applicants, 51% accepted, 20 enrolled. In 2011, 22 master's, 2 other advanced degrees awarded. *Degree requirements:* For master's, comprehensive exam, thesis (for some programs). *Entrance requirements:* For master's, GRE General Test, minimum GPA of 3.0, course work in computer science, resume. Additional exam requirements/recommendations for international students: Required—TOEFL (minimum score 500 paper-based; 173 computer-based; 61 iBT). *Application deadline:* For fall admission, 7/1 priority date for domestic students; for spring admission, 11/1 priority date for domestic students. Applications are processed on a rolling basis. Application fee: $45. Electronic applications accepted. *Financial support:* In 2011–12, 9 students received support, including 9 research assistantships with tuition reimbursements available; teaching assistantships with tuition reimbursements available, Federal Work-Study, institutionally sponsored loans, scholarships/grants, tuition waivers (full), and unspecified assistantships also available. Support available to part-time students. Financial award application deadline: 3/1; financial award applicants required to submit FAFSA. *Unit head:* Dr. Qiuming Zhu, Chairperson, 402-554-2423. *Application contact:* Carla Frakes, Information Contact, 402-554-2423.

University of Nebraska–Lincoln, Graduate College, College of Arts and Sciences and College of Engineering, Department of Computer Science and Engineering, Lincoln, NE 68588. Offers bioinformatics (MS, PhD); computer engineering (MS, PhD); computer science (MS, PhD); information technology (PhD). *Degree requirements:* For master's, thesis optional; for doctorate, comprehensive exam, thesis/dissertation. *Entrance requirements:* For master's and doctorate, GRE General Test. Additional exam requirements/recommendations for international students: Required—TOEFL (minimum score 600 paper-based; 250 computer-based). Electronic applications accepted. *Faculty research:* Software engineering, geo- and bio-informatics, scientific computation, secure communication.

University of Nevada, Las Vegas, Graduate College, Howard R. Hughes College of Engineering, School of Computer Science, Las Vegas, NV 89154-4019. Offers MS, PhD. Part-time programs available. *Faculty:* 14 full-time (4 women). *Students:* 11 full-time (5 women), 37 part-time (9 women); includes 8 minority (1 American Indian or Alaska Native, non-Hispanic/Latino; 2 Asian, non-Hispanic/Latino; 4 Hispanic/Latino; 1 Two or more races, non-Hispanic/Latino), 23 international. Average age 28. 28 applicants, 79% accepted, 12 enrolled. In 2011, 15 master's, 1 doctorate awarded. *Degree requirements:* For master's, comprehensive exam, thesis optional, project; for doctorate, comprehensive exam, thesis/dissertation. *Entrance requirements:* For master's, GRE General Test; for doctorate, GRE General Test, GRE Subject Test (computer science). Additional exam requirements/recommendations for international students: Required—TOEFL (minimum score 550 paper-based; 213 computer-based; 80 iBT), IELTS (minimum score 7). *Application deadline:* For fall admission, 6/1 priority date for domestic students, 5/1 for international students; for spring admission, 11/1 priority date for domestic students, 10/1 for international students. Applications are processed on a rolling basis. Application fee: $60 ($95 for international students). Electronic applications accepted. *Financial support:* In 2011–12, 26 students received support, including 5 research assistantships with partial tuition reimbursements available (averaging $7,090 per year), 21 teaching assistantships with partial tuition reimbursements available (averaging $8,572 per year); institutionally sponsored loans, scholarships/grants, health care benefits, and unspecified assistantships also available. Financial award application deadline: 3/1. *Faculty research:* Algorithms, computer graphics, databases and data mining, distributed systems and networks, parallel algorithms. *Total annual research expenditures:* $103,550. *Unit head:* Dr. John Minor, Director/Associate Professor, 702-895-3715, Fax: 702-895-2639, E-mail: minor@cs.unlv.edu. *Application contact:* Graduate College Admissions Evaluator, 702-895-3320, Fax: 702-895-4180, E-mail: gradcollege@unlv.edu. Web site: http://cs.unlv.edu/.

University of Nevada, Reno, Graduate School, College of Engineering, Department of Computer Science and Engineering, Program in Computer Science, Reno, NV 89557. Offers MS. *Degree requirements:* For master's, thesis optional. *Entrance requirements:* For master's, GRE General Test, minimum GPA of 2.75. Additional exam requirements/recommendations for international students: Required—TOEFL (minimum score 500 paper-based; 173 computer-based; 61 iBT), IELTS (minimum score 6). Electronic applications accepted. *Faculty research:* Evolutionary computing systems, computer vision/virtual reality, software engineering.

University of Nevada, Reno, Graduate School, College of Engineering, Department of Computer Science and Engineering, Program in Computer Science and Engineering, Reno, NV 89557. Offers PhD. *Degree requirements:* For doctorate, thesis/dissertation. *Entrance requirements:* For doctorate, GRE General Test, minimum GPA of 3.0. Additional exam requirements/recommendations for international students: Required—TOEFL (minimum score 500 paper-based; 173 computer-based; 61 iBT), IELTS (minimum score 6). Electronic applications accepted. *Faculty research:* Evolutionary computing systems, computer vision/virtual reality, software engineering.

University of New Brunswick Fredericton, School of Graduate Studies, Faculty of Computer Science, Fredericton, NB E3B 5A3, Canada. Offers M Sc CS, PhD. Part-time programs available. *Faculty:* 25 full-time (6 women), 10 part-time/adjunct (0 women). *Students:* 86 full-time (24 women), 12 part-time (2 women). In 2011, 13 master's, 4 doctorates awarded. *Degree requirements:* For master's, thesis; for doctorate, comprehensive exam, thesis/dissertation, qualifying exam. *Entrance requirements:* For master's, minimum GPA of 3.0; undergraduate degree with sufficient computer science background; for doctorate, research-based master's degree in computer science or related area. Additional exam requirements/recommendations for international students: Required—TWE (minimum score 4), TOEFL (minimum score 580 paper-based; 237 computer-based) or IELTS (minimum score 7). *Application deadline:* For fall admission, 3/1 priority date for domestic students. Application fee: $50 Canadian dollars. Electronic applications accepted. *Financial support:* In 2011–12, 2 fellowships, 53 research assistantships, 24 teaching assistantships were awarded. *Faculty research:* Artificial consciousness and intelligence, automated reasoning, biomedical engineering, cloud computing, computer-aided drug design, cryptography, data structures, embedded systems, graph algorithms, health informatics, intelligent adaptive systems, legacy system modernization, machine learning and data mining, multicore computing, Net-centric computing, optimization, parallel and distributed computing, privacy and security, reconfigurable computing, sensor networks, wireless communication. *Unit head:* Dr. Eric Aubanel, Director of Graduate Studies, 506-458-7268, Fax: 506-453-3566, E-mail: aubanel@unb.ca. *Application contact:* Jodi O'Neill, Graduate Secretary, 506-458-7285, Fax: 506-453-3566, E-mail: jodio@unb.ca. Web site: http://www.cs.unb.ca/.

University of New Hampshire, Graduate School, College of Engineering and Physical Sciences, Department of Computer Science, Durham, NH 03824. Offers computer science (MS, PhD); software systems engineering (Postbaccalaureate Certificate). Part-time and evening/weekend programs available. *Faculty:* 10 full-time (2 women). *Students:* 27 full-time (10 women), 51 part-time (3 women); includes 4 minority (1 Black or African American, non-Hispanic/Latino; 2 Asian, non-Hispanic/Latino; 1 Two or more races, non-Hispanic/Latino), 17 international. Average age 31. 69 applicants, 67% accepted, 23 enrolled. In 2011, 17 master's, 18 other advanced degrees awarded. *Degree requirements:* For master's, thesis or alternative; for doctorate, thesis/dissertation. *Entrance requirements:* For master's and doctorate, GRE General Test. Additional exam requirements/recommendations for international students: Required—TOEFL (minimum score 550 paper-based; 213 computer-based; 80 iBT). *Application deadline:* For fall admission, 4/1 priority date for domestic students, 4/1 for international students; for spring admission, 12/1 for domestic students. Applications are processed on a rolling basis. Application fee: $65. Electronic applications accepted. *Expenses:* Tuition, state resident: full-time $12,360; part-time $687 per credit hour. Tuition, nonresident: full-time $25,680; part-time $1058 per credit hour. *International tuition:* $29,550 full-time. *Required fees:* $1666; $833 per course. $416.50 per semester. Tuition and fees vary according to course load and degree level. *Financial support:* In 2011–12, 35 students received support, including 10 research assistantships, 11 teaching assistantships; fellowships, career-related internships or fieldwork, Federal Work-Study, scholarships/grants, and tuition waivers (full and partial) also available. Support available to part-time students. *Faculty research:* Programming languages, compiler design, parallel algorithms, computer graphics, artificial intelligence. *Unit head:* Radim Bartos, Department Chair, 603-862-3792. *Application contact:* Carolyn Kirkpatrick, Administrative Assistant, 603-862-3778, E-mail: office@cs.unh.edu. Web site: http://www.cs.unh.edu/.

University of New Haven, Graduate School, Henry C. Lee College of Criminal Justice and Forensic Sciences, Program in Criminal Justice, West Haven, CT 06516-1916. Offers crime analysis (MS); criminal justice (PhD); criminal justice management (MS); forensic computer investigation (MS, Certificate); forensic psychology (MS); victim advocacy and services management (Certificate); victimology (MS). Part-time and evening/weekend programs available. *Students:* 65 full-time (44 women), 57 part-time (38 women); includes 25 minority (22 Black or African American, non-Hispanic/Latino; 1 Asian, non-Hispanic/Latino; 1 Hispanic/Latino; 1 Two or more races, non-Hispanic/Latino), 10 international. 64 applicants, 97% accepted, 47 enrolled. In 2011, 23 master's, 9 other advanced degrees awarded. *Degree requirements:* For master's, thesis or alternative. *Entrance requirements:* Additional exam requirements/recommendations for international students: Required—TOEFL (minimum score 520 paper-based; 190 computer-based; 70 iBT), IELTS (minimum score 5.5). *Application deadline:* For fall admission, 5/31 for international students; for winter admission, 10/15 for international students; for spring admission, 1/15 for international students. Applications are processed on a rolling basis. Application fee: $50. Electronic applications accepted. *Expenses: Tuition:* Part-time $750 per credit. *Financial support:* Research assistantships with partial tuition reimbursements, teaching assistantships with partial tuition reimbursements, career-related internships or fieldwork, Federal Work-Study, scholarships/grants, tuition waivers, and unspecified assistantships available. Support available to part-time students. Financial award applicants required to submit FAFSA. *Unit head:* Dr. William J. Norton, Director, 203-932-7374, E-mail: wnorton@newhaven.edu. *Application contact:* Eloise Gormley, Director of Graduate Admissions, 203-932-7449, Fax: 203-932-7137, E-mail: gradinfo@newhaven.edu. Web site: http://www.newhaven.edu/5921/.

University of New Haven, Graduate School, Tagliatela College of Engineering, Program in Computer and Information Science, West Haven, CT 06516-1916. Offers computer science (MS, Certificate), including advanced applications (MS), computer programming (Certificate), computer systems (MS), database and information systems (MS), network systems (MS), software engineering and development (MS). Part-time and evening/weekend programs available. *Students:* 53 full-time (16 women), 32 part-time (7 women); includes 4 minority (1 Black or African American, non-Hispanic/Latino; 1 Asian, non-Hispanic/Latino; 2 Hispanic/Latino), 69 international. 133 applicants, 98% accepted, 23 enrolled. In 2011, 19 master's, 1 other advanced degree awarded. *Degree requirements:* For master's, thesis or alternative. *Entrance requirements:* Additional exam requirements/recommendations for international students: Required—TOEFL (minimum score 520 paper-based; 190 computer-based; 70 iBT); Recommended—IELTS (minimum score 5.5). *Application deadline:* For fall admission, 5/31 for international students; for winter admission, 10/15 for international students; for spring admission, 1/15 for international students. Applications are processed on a rolling basis. Application fee: $50. Electronic applications accepted. *Expenses: Tuition:* Part-time $750 per credit. *Financial support:* Research assistantships with partial tuition reimbursements, teaching assistantships with partial tuition reimbursements, career-related internships or fieldwork, Federal Work-Study, scholarships/grants, tuition waivers, and unspecified assistantships available. Support available to part-time students. Financial award applicants required to submit FAFSA. *Unit head:* Dr. David Eggert, Coordinator, 203-932-7097, E-mail: deggert@newhaven.edu. *Application contact:* Eloise Gormley, Director of Graduate Admissions, 203-932-7449, Fax: 203-932-7137, E-mail: gradinfo@newhaven.edu. Web site: http://www.newhaven.edu/9591/.

University of New Mexico, Graduate School, School of Engineering, Department of Computer Science, Albuquerque, NM 87131-2039. Offers MS, PhD. Part-time programs available. *Faculty:* 18 full-time (3 women), 3 part-time/adjunct (0 women). *Students:* 104 full-time (23 women), 44 part-time (11 women); includes 18 minority (1 Black or African American, non-Hispanic/Latino; 2 Asian, non-Hispanic/Latino; 11 Hispanic/Latino; 4 Two or more races, non-Hispanic/Latino), 50 international. Average age 32. 137 applicants, 62% accepted, 52 enrolled. In 2011, 20 master's, 4 doctorates awarded. Terminal master's awarded for partial completion of doctoral program. *Degree requirements:* For master's, thesis or alternative; for doctorate, thesis/dissertation. *Entrance requirements:* For master's and doctorate, GRE General Test, minimum GPA of 3.0. Additional exam requirements/recommendations for international students: Required—TOEFL (minimum score 550 paper-based; 213 computer-based; 79 iBT), IELTS (minimum score 7). *Application deadline:* For fall admission, 1/15 for domestic students, 3/1 for international students; for spring admission, 8/1 for domestic and international students. Applications are processed on a rolling basis. Application fee: $50. Electronic applications accepted. *Financial support:* In 2011–12, 67 students received support, including 5 fellowships with tuition reimbursements available (averaging $16,020 per year), 52 research assistantships with tuition reimbursements available (averaging $16,020 per year), 10 teaching assistantships with tuition reimbursements available (averaging $13,450 per year); career-related internships or fieldwork, scholarships/grants, and health care benefits also available. Financial award application deadline: 1/15; financial award applicants required to submit FAFSA. *Faculty research:* Artificial life, genetic algorithms, computer security, complexity theory, interactive computer graphics, operating systems and networking, biology and computation, machine learning, automated reasoning, quantum computation. *Total annual research expenditures:* $2.4 million. *Unit head:* Dr. Stephanie Forrest, Chairperson, 505-277-3112, Fax: 505-277-6927, E-mail: forrest@cs.unm.edu. *Application contact:* Lynne Jacobsen, Coordinator, Program Advisement, 505-277-3112, Fax: 505-277-6927, E-mail: ljake@cs.unm.edu. Web site: http://cs.unm.edu/.

University of New Orleans, Graduate School, College of Sciences, Department of Computer Science, New Orleans, LA 70148. Offers MS. *Entrance requirements:* For master's, GRE General Test. Additional exam requirements/recommendations for international students: Required—TOEFL (minimum score 550 paper-based; 213 computer-based; 79 iBT). Electronic applications accepted.

The University of North Carolina at Chapel Hill, Graduate School, College of Arts and Sciences, Department of Computer Science, Chapel Hill, NC 27599. Offers MS, PhD. Part-time programs available. Postbaccalaureate distance learning degree programs offered. Terminal master's awarded for partial completion of doctoral program. *Degree requirements:* For master's, comprehensive exam, thesis or alternative, programming product; for doctorate, comprehensive exam, thesis/dissertation, programming product, teaching requirement. *Entrance requirements:* For master's and doctorate, GRE General Test, minimum GPA of 3.0. Additional exam requirements/recommendations for international students: Required—TOEFL (minimum score 575 paper-based; 233 computer-based). Electronic applications accepted. *Faculty research:* Bioinformatics, graphics, hardware, systems, theory.

See Display on next page and Close-Up on page 345.

The University of North Carolina at Charlotte, Graduate School, College of Computing and Informatics, Department of Computer Science, Charlotte, NC 28223-0001. Offers advance databases and knowledge discovery (Certificate); computer science (MS). Part-time programs available. *Faculty:* 21 full-time (5 women), 2 part-time/adjunct (0 women). *Students:* 107 full-time (23 women), 36 part-time (13 women); includes 10 minority (2 Black or African American, non-Hispanic/Latino; 5 Asian, non-Hispanic/Latino; 1 Hispanic/Latino; 2 Two or more races, non-Hispanic/Latino), 106 international. Average age 25. 347 applicants, 50% accepted, 37 enrolled. In 2011, 57 master's, 5 other advanced degrees awarded. *Degree requirements:* For master's, thesis or alternative. *Entrance requirements:* For master's, GRE General Test, minimum GPA of 3.0 during previous 2 years, 2.8 overall. Additional exam requirements/recommendations for international students: Required—TOEFL (minimum score 557 paper-based; 220 computer-based; 83 iBT). *Application deadline:* For fall admission, 7/1 for domestic students, 5/1 for international students; for spring admission, 11/1 for domestic students, 10/1 for international students. Applications are processed on a rolling basis. Application fee: $65 ($75 for international students). Electronic applications accepted. *Expenses:* Tuition, state resident: full-time $3689. Tuition, nonresident: full-time $15,226. *Required fees:* $2198. Tuition and fees vary according to course load and program. *Financial support:* In 2011–12, 38 students received support, including 30 research assistantships (averaging $10,247 per year), 8 teaching assistantships (averaging $9,869 per year); career-related internships or fieldwork, Federal Work-Study, institutionally sponsored loans, scholarships/grants, and unspecified assistantships also available. Support available to part-time students. Financial award application deadline: 4/1; financial award applicants required to submit FAFSA. *Faculty research:* Visualization; visual analytics and computer graphics; intelligent and interactive systems; data mining theory, systems, and application; networked systems; computer game design. *Total annual research expenditures:* $3.1 million. *Unit head:* Dr. Larry F. Hodges, Chair, 704-687-8552, Fax: 704-687-3516, E-mail: lfhodges@uncc.edu. *Application contact:* Kathy B. Giddings, Director of Graduate Admissions, 704-687-3366, Fax: 704-687-3279, E-mail: gradadm@uncc.edu. Web site: http://www.coit.uncc.edu/cs/site/.

The University of North Carolina at Greensboro, Graduate School, College of Arts and Sciences, Department of Computer Science, Greensboro, NC 27412-5001. Offers MS.

The University of North Carolina Wilmington, College of Arts and Sciences, Program in Computer Science and Information Systems, Wilmington, NC 28403-3297. Offers MS. *Entrance requirements:* For master's, GMAT or GRE, 3 letters of recommendation, resume.

University of North Dakota, Graduate School, John D. Odegard School of Aerospace Sciences, Department of Computer Science, Grand Forks, ND 58202. Offers MS, PhD. Part-time programs available. *Degree requirements:* For master's, comprehensive exam, thesis or alternative. *Entrance requirements:* For master's, GRE General Test, minimum GPA of 3.0. Additional exam requirements/recommendations for international students: Required—TOEFL (minimum score 550 paper-based; 213 computer-based; 79 iBT), IELTS (minimum score 6.5). Electronic applications accepted. *Faculty research:* Operating systems, simulation, parallel computation, hypermedia, graph theory.

University of Northern British Columbia, Office of Graduate Studies, Prince George, BC V2N 4Z9, Canada. Offers business administration (Diploma); community health science (M Sc); disability management (MA); education (M Ed); first nations studies (MA); gender studies (MA); history (MA); interdisciplinary studies (MA); international studies (MA); mathematical, computer and physical sciences (M Sc); natural resources and environmental studies (M Sc, MA, MNRES, PhD); political science (MA); psychology (M Sc, PhD); social work (MSW). Part-time and evening/weekend programs available. Postbaccalaureate distance learning degree programs offered (no on-campus study). *Degree requirements:* For master's, thesis; for doctorate, thesis/dissertation. *Entrance requirements:* For master's, GRE, minimum B average in undergraduate course work; for doctorate, candidacy exam, minimum A average in graduate course work.

University of Northern Iowa, Graduate College, College of Humanities, Arts and Sciences, Department of Computer Science, Cedar Falls, IA 50614. Offers MS. *Students:* 10 full-time (2 women), 8 part-time (3 women); includes 1 minority (Asian, non-Hispanic/Latino), 10 international. 34 applicants, 50% accepted, 5 enrolled. In 2011, 1 master's awarded. *Degree requirements:* For master's, comprehensive exam (for some programs), thesis (for some programs). *Entrance requirements:* For master's, GRE, minimum GPA of 3.0. Additional exam requirements/recommendations for international students: Required—TOEFL (minimum score 600 paper-based; 250 computer-based; 100 iBT). *Application deadline:* For fall admission, 8/1 priority date for

domestic students. Applications are processed on a rolling basis. Application fee: $50 ($70 for international students). Electronic applications accepted. *Expenses:* Tuition, state resident: full-time $7476. Tuition, nonresident: full-time $16,410. *Required fees:* $942. *Financial support:* Application deadline: 2/1. *Unit head:* Dr. Eugene Wallingford, Head, 319-273-2618, Fax: 319-273-7123, E-mail: wallingf@cs.uni.edu. *Application contact:* Laurie S. Russell, Record Analyst, 319-273-2623, Fax: 319-273-2885, E-mail: laurie.russell@uni.edu. Web site: http://www.cs.uni.edu/.

University of North Florida, College of Computing, Engineering, and Construction, School of Computing, Jacksonville, FL 32224. Offers computer science (MS); information systems (MS); software engineering (MS). Part-time programs available. *Faculty:* 14 full-time (3 women), 39 part-time (10 women); includes 15 minority (7 Black or African American, non-Hispanic/Latino; 4 Asian, non-Hispanic/Latino; 2 Hispanic/Latino; 2 Two or more races, non-Hispanic/Latino), 14 international. Average age 30. 30 applicants, 63% accepted, 5 enrolled. In 2011, 4 master's awarded. *Degree requirements:* For master's, thesis. *Entrance requirements:* For master's, GRE General Test, minimum GPA of 3.0 in last 60 hours of course work. Additional exam requirements/recommendations for international students: Required—TOEFL (minimum score 500 paper-based; 173 computer-based; 61 iBT). *Application deadline:* For fall admission, 7/1 for domestic students, 5/1 for international students; for spring admission, 11/1 for domestic students, 10/1 for international students. Applications are processed on a rolling basis. Application fee: $30. Electronic applications accepted. *Expenses:* Tuition, state resident: full-time $8793; part-time $366.38 per credit hour. Tuition, nonresident: full-time $23,502; part-time $979.24 per credit hour. *Required fees:* $1384; $57.66 per credit hour. Tuition and fees vary according to course load and program. *Financial support:* In 2011–12, 12 students received support, including 1 research assistantship (averaging $1,000 per year); teaching assistantships, Federal Work-Study, scholarships/grants, and unspecified assistantships also available. Financial award application deadline: 4/1; financial award applicants required to submit FAFSA. *Total annual research expenditures:* $91,012. *Unit head:* Dr. Neal Coulter, Dean, 904-620-1350, E-mail: ncoulter@unf.edu. *Application contact:* Lillith Richardson, Assistant Director, The Graduate School, 904-620-1360, Fax: 904-620-1362, E-mail: graduateschool@unf.edu. Web site: http://www.unf.edu/ccec/computing/.

University of North Texas, Toulouse Graduate School, College of Engineering, Department of Computer Science and Engineering, Denton, TX 76203-5017. Offers computer science (MS); computer science and engineering (PhD). Terminal master's awarded for partial completion of doctoral program. *Degree requirements:* For master's, comprehensive exam (for some programs), thesis (for some programs); for doctorate, comprehensive exam, thesis/dissertation. *Entrance requirements:* For master's, GRE General Test (minimum score 400 verbal, 700 quantitative, 600 analytical or 4.0), minimum GPA of 3.0; for doctorate, GRE General Test (minimum scores: Verbal 50th percentile, Quantitative 700, Analytical 600 or 4.5), minimum GPA of 3.5, 3 letters of recommendation. Additional exam requirements/recommendations for international students: Required—TOEFL (minimum score 550 paper-based; 213 computer-based; 79 iBT); Recommended—IELTS (minimum score 6.5). Electronic applications accepted. *Expenses:* Tuition, state resident: part-time $100 per credit hour. Tuition, nonresident: part-time $413 per credit hour. *Faculty research:* Databases and data mining, computer architecture, cryptography, agent-oriented software engineering, graph theory, low power synthesis.

University of Notre Dame, Graduate School, College of Engineering, Department of Computer Science and Engineering, Notre Dame, IN 46556. Offers MSCSE, PhD. Terminal master's awarded for partial completion of doctoral program. *Degree requirements:* For master's, comprehensive exam; for doctorate, thesis/dissertation, candidacy exam. *Entrance requirements:* For master's and doctorate, GRE General Test. Additional exam requirements/recommendations for international students: Required—TOEFL (minimum score 600 paper-based; 250 computer-based; 80 iBT). Electronic applications accepted. *Faculty research:* Algorithms and theory of computer science, artificial intelligence, behavior-based robotics, biometrics, computer vision.

University of Oklahoma, College of Engineering, School of Computer Science, Norman, OK 73019. Offers computer science (MS, PhD), including bioinformatics, general (MS), standard (PhD). *Faculty:* 19 full-time (4 women), 1 part-time/adjunct (0 women). *Students:* 68 full-time (13 women), 34 part-time (1 woman); includes 4 minority (1 Black or African American, non-Hispanic/Latino; 1 American Indian or Alaska Native, non-Hispanic/Latino; 2 Asian, non-Hispanic/Latino), 65 international. Average age 27. 125 applicants, 50% accepted, 18 enrolled. In 2011, 31 master's, 2 doctorates awarded. Terminal master's awarded for partial completion of doctoral program. *Degree requirements:* For master's, thesis optional, oral exams, qualifying exam; for doctorate, thesis/dissertation, general exam, qualifying exam. *Entrance requirements:* For master's and doctorate, GRE General Test. Additional exam requirements/recommendations for international students: Required—TOEFL (minimum score 550 paper-based; 79 iBT). *Application deadline:* For fall admission, 1/15 priority date for domestic students, 3/1 for international students; for spring admission, 11/1 for domestic students, 9/1 for international students. Applications are processed on a rolling basis. Application fee: $40 ($90 for international students). Electronic applications accepted. *Expenses:* Tuition, state resident: full-time $4087; part-time $170.30 per credit hour. Tuition, nonresident: full-time $14,875; part-time $619.80 per credit hour. *Required fees:* $2659; $100.25 per credit hour. Tuition and fees vary according to course load and degree level. *Financial support:* In 2011–12, 81 students received support, including 3 fellowships with full tuition reimbursements available (averaging $3,000 per year), 18 research assistantships with partial tuition reimbursements available (averaging $15,735 per year), 20 teaching assistantships with partial tuition reimbursements available (averaging $16,144 per year); unspecified assistantships also available. Financial award applicants required to submit FAFSA. *Faculty research:* Artificial intelligence and robotics, scientific computing, computer networks, high performance computing, computer architecture, database management, visual analytics, cryptography. *Total annual research expenditures:* $2.8 million. *Unit head:* Sridhar Radhakrishnan, Professor and Director, 405-325-4042, Fax: 405-325-4044, E-mail: sridhar@ou.edu. *Application contact:* Miranda Sowell, Coordinator of Graduate Admissions, 405-325-3811, Fax: 405-325-5346, E-mail: mgsowell@ou.edu. Web site: http://www.cs.ou.edu/.

University of Oregon, Graduate School, College of Arts and Sciences, Department of Computer and Information Science, Eugene, OR 97403. Offers MA, MS, PhD. Part-time programs available. Terminal master's awarded for partial completion of doctoral program. *Degree requirements:* For doctorate, thesis/dissertation. *Entrance requirements:* For master's and doctorate, GRE General Test, minimum GPA of 3.0. Additional exam requirements/recommendations for international students: Required—TOEFL. *Faculty research:* Artificial intelligence, graphics, natural-language processing, expert systems, operating systems.

University of Ottawa, Faculty of Graduate and Postdoctoral Studies, Faculty of Engineering, Ottawa-Carleton Institute for Computer Science, Ottawa, ON K1N 6N5,

Canada. Offers MCS, PhD. MCS, PhD offered jointly with Carleton University. *Degree requirements:* For master's, thesis or alternative; for doctorate, comprehensive exam, thesis/dissertation, two seminars. *Entrance requirements:* For master's, honors degree or equivalent, minimum B average; for doctorate, minimum B+ average. Electronic applications accepted. *Faculty research:* Knowledge-based and intelligent systems, algorithms, parallel and distributed systems.

University of Pennsylvania, School of Engineering and Applied Science, Department of Computer and Information Science, Philadelphia, PA 19104. Offers MCIT, MSE, PhD. Part-time programs available. *Faculty:* 45 full-time (4 women), 4 part-time/adjunct (1 woman). *Students:* 331 full-time (78 women), 54 part-time (13 women); includes 30 minority (3 Black or African American, non-Hispanic/Latino; 23 Asian, non-Hispanic/Latino; 3 Hispanic/Latino; 1 Two or more races, non-Hispanic/Latino), 253 international. 1,502 applicants, 26% accepted, 118 enrolled. In 2011, 69 master's, 11 doctorates awarded. Terminal master's awarded for partial completion of doctoral program. *Degree requirements:* For master's, thesis optional; for doctorate, thesis/dissertation. *Entrance requirements:* For master's and doctorate, GRE General Test. Additional exam requirements/recommendations for international students: Required—TOEFL. *Application deadline:* For fall admission, 6/1 priority date for domestic students, 5/1 for international students. Applications are processed on a rolling basis. Application fee: $70. Electronic applications accepted. *Expenses: Tuition:* Full-time $26,660; part-time $4944 per course. *Required fees:* $2318; $291 per course. Tuition and fees vary according to course load, degree level and program. *Financial support:* Fellowships with full tuition reimbursements, research assistantships with full tuition reimbursements, teaching assistantships, institutionally sponsored loans, scholarships/grants, traineeships, health care benefits, and unspecified assistantships available. *Faculty research:* AI, computer systems graphics, information management, robotics, software systems theory. *Unit head:* Eduardo D. Glandt, Dean, 215-898-7244, Fax: 215-573-2018, E-mail: seasdean@seas.upenn.edu. *Application contact:* Mike Felker, Graduate Coordinator, 215-898-9672, E-mail: mfelker@cis.upenn.edu. Web site: http://www.seas.upenn.edu.

University of Pittsburgh, Dietrich School of Arts and Sciences, Department of Computer Science, Pittsburgh, PA 15260. Offers MS, PhD. Part-time programs available. *Faculty:* 20 full-time (4 women). *Students:* 86 full-time (13 women), 3 part-time (1 woman); includes 24 minority (1 Black or African American, non-Hispanic/Latino; 21 Asian, non-Hispanic/Latino; 2 Hispanic/Latino), 26 international. Average age 27. 483 applicants, 8% accepted, 20 enrolled. In 2011, 9 master's, 4 doctorates awarded. Terminal master's awarded for partial completion of doctoral program. *Degree requirements:* For master's, thesis or alternative; for doctorate, comprehensive exam, thesis/dissertation, preliminary exams. *Entrance requirements:* For master's and doctorate, GRE General Test. Additional exam requirements/recommendations for international students: Required—TOEFL (minimum score 600 paper-based; 250 computer-based; 90 iBT). *Application deadline:* For fall admission, 1/15 for domestic and international students; for winter admission, 9/15 for domestic and international students. Applications are processed on a rolling basis. Application fee: $50. Electronic applications accepted. *Expenses:* Tuition, state resident: full-time $18,774; part-time $760 per credit. Tuition, nonresident: full-time $30,736; part-time $1258 per credit. *Required fees:* $740; $200 per term. Tuition and fees vary according to program. *Financial support:* In 2011–12, 60 students received support, including 7 fellowships with full tuition reimbursements available (averaging $18,546 per year), 25 research assistantships with full tuition reimbursements available (averaging $17,720 per year), 28 teaching assistantships with full tuition reimbursements available (averaging $15,830 per year); career-related internships or fieldwork, Federal Work-Study, scholarships/grants, health care benefits, and tuition waivers (partial) also available. Financial award application deadline: 1/15. *Faculty research:* Algorithms and theory, artificial intelligence, parallel and distributed systems, software systems and interfaces. *Total annual research expenditures:* $2.7 million. *Unit head:* Dr. Daniel Mosse, Chairman, 412-624-8493, Fax: 412-624-8854, E-mail: mosse@cs.pitt.edu. *Application contact:* Keena Walker, Graduate Secretary, 412-624-8495, Fax: 412-624-8854, E-mail: keena@cs.pitt.edu. Web site: http://www.cs.pitt.edu/.

University of Puerto Rico, Mayagüez Campus, Graduate Studies, College of Engineering, Department of Electrical and Computer Engineering, Mayagüez, PR 00681-9000. Offers computer engineering (ME, MS); computing and information sciences and engineering (PhD); electrical engineering (ME, MS). Part-time programs available. *Students:* 86 full-time (16 women), 8 part-time (1 woman); includes 65 minority (all Hispanic/Latino), 29 international. 42 applicants, 60% accepted, 20 enrolled. In 2011, 19 degrees awarded. *Degree requirements:* For master's, comprehensive exam, thesis; for doctorate, comprehensive exam, thesis/dissertation. *Entrance requirements:* For master's, proficiency in English and Spanish, BS in electrical or computer engineering or equivalent, minimum GPA of 3.0; for doctorate, GRE. Additional exam requirements/recommendations for international students: Required—TOEFL (minimum score 450 paper-based). *Application deadline:* For fall admission, 2/15 for domestic and international students; for spring admission, 9/15 for domestic and international students. Applications are processed on a rolling basis. Application fee: $25. Tuition and fees vary according to course level and course load. *Financial support:* In 2011–12, 46 students received support, including 28 research assistantships (averaging $15,000 per year), 18 teaching assistantships (averaging $8,500 per year); Federal Work-Study and institutionally sponsored loans also available. *Faculty research:* Microcomputer interfacing, control systems, power systems, electronics. *Total annual research expenditures:* $3.8 million. *Unit head:* Dr. Erick Aponte-Diaz, Chairperson, 787-832-4040 Ext. 3821, E-mail: erick.aponte1@upr.edu. *Application contact:* Sandra Montalvo, Administrative Staff, 787-832-4040 Ext. 3094, Fax: 787-831-7564, E-mail: sandra@ece.uprm.edu. Web site: http://www.ece.uprm.edu.

University of Regina, Faculty of Graduate Studies and Research, Faculty of Science, Department of Computer Science, Regina, SK S4S 0A2, Canada. Offers M Sc, PhD. *Faculty:* 16 full-time (3 women). *Students:* 40 full-time (11 women), 10 part-time (2 women). 84 applicants, 38% accepted. In 2011, 10 master's, 1 doctorate awarded. *Degree requirements:* For master's, thesis; for doctorate, thesis/dissertation. *Entrance requirements:* Additional exam requirements/recommendations for international students: Required—TOEFL (minimum score 580 paper-based; 80 iBT), IELTS (minimum score 6.5). *Application deadline:* Applications are processed on a rolling basis. Application fee: $100. Electronic applications accepted. *Financial support:* In 2011–12, 9 fellowships (averaging $6,500 per year), 10 teaching assistantships (averaging $2,298 per year) were awarded; research assistantships, career-related internships or fieldwork, and scholarships/grants also available. Financial award application deadline: 6/15. *Faculty research:* Information retrieval, machine learning, computer visualization, theory and application of rough sets, human-computer interaction. *Unit head:* Dr. Xue Dong Yang, Head, 306-585-4692, Fax: 306-585-4745, E-mail: yang@cs.uregina.ca. *Application contact:* Dr. Boting Yang, Graduate Program Coordinator, 306-585-4774, Fax: 306-585-4745, E-mail: boting@cs.uregina.ca. Web site: http://www.cs.uregina.ca.

University of Rhode Island, Graduate School, College of Arts and Sciences, Department of Computer Science and Statistics, Kingston, RI 02881. Offers applied mathematics (PhD), including computer science, statistics; computer science (MS, PhD); digital forensics (Graduate Certificate); statistics (MS). Part-time programs available. *Faculty:* 10 full-time (4 women), 1 (woman) part-time/adjunct. *Students:* 16 full-time (3 women), 41 part-time (10 women); includes 8 minority (2 Black or African American, non-Hispanic/Latino; 1 Asian, non-Hispanic/Latino; 5 Hispanic/Latino), 7 international. In 2011, 9 master's, 1 doctorate awarded. *Degree requirements:* For master's, comprehensive exam (for some programs), thesis optional; for doctorate, comprehensive exam, thesis/dissertation. *Entrance requirements:* For master's and doctorate, GRE, 2 letters of recommendation. Additional exam requirements/recommendations for international students: Required—TOEFL (minimum score 550 paper-based; 213 computer-based). *Application deadline:* For fall admission, 7/15 for domestic students, 2/1 for international students; for spring admission, 11/15 for domestic students, 7/15 for international students. Application fee: $65. Electronic applications accepted. *Expenses:* Tuition, state resident: full-time $10,432; part-time $580 per credit hour. Tuition, nonresident: full-time $23,130; part-time $1285 per credit hour. *Required fees:* $1362; $36 per credit hour. $35 per semester. One-time fee: $130. *Financial support:* In 2011–12, 2 research assistantships (averaging $7,004 per year), 9 teaching assistantships with full and partial tuition reimbursements (averaging $9,759 per year) were awarded. Financial award application deadline: 2/1; financial award applicants required to submit FAFSA. *Faculty research:* Bioinformatics, computer and digital forensics, behavioral model of pedestrian dynamics, real-time distributed object computing, cryptography. *Unit head:* Dr. James G. Kowalski, Chair, 401-874-2510, Fax: 401-874-4617, E-mail: kowalski@cs.uri.edu. *Application contact:* Dr. Victor Fay-Wolfe, Director of Graduate Studies, 401-874-2701, Fax: 401-874-4617, E-mail: wolfe@cs.uri.edu. Web site: http://www.cs.uri.edu/.

University of Rochester, Hajim School of Engineering and Applied Sciences, Center for Entrepreneurship, Rochester, NY 14627-0360. Offers technical entrepreneurship and management (TEAM) (MS), including biomedical engineering, chemical engineering, computer science, electrical and computer engineering, energy and the environment, materials science, mechanical engineering, optics. *Faculty:* 61 full-time (8 women), 5 part-time/adjunct (1 woman). *Students:* 18 full-time (5 women), 3 part-time (1 woman); includes 4 minority (1 Asian, non-Hispanic/Latino; 3 Hispanic/Latino), 12 international. Average age 23. 134 applicants, 48% accepted, 21 enrolled. *Degree requirements:* For master's, comprehensive exam. *Entrance requirements:* For master's, GRE or GMAT, technical concentration of interest, 3 letters of recommendation, personal statement, official transcript. Additional exam requirements/recommendations for international students: Required—TOEFL or IELTS. *Application deadline:* For fall admission, 2/1 for domestic and international students. Applications are processed on a rolling basis. Application fee: $60. Electronic applications accepted. *Expenses: Tuition:* Full-time $41,040. *Financial support:* Career-related internships or fieldwork and scholarships/grants available. Financial award application deadline: 2/1. *Faculty research:* High efficiency solar cells, macromolecular self-assembly, digital signal processing, memory hierarchy management, molecular and physical mechanisms in cell migration. *Unit head:* Duncan T. Moore, Vice Provost for Entrepreneurship, 585-275-5248, Fax: 585-473-6745, E-mail: moore@optics.rochester.edu. *Application contact:* Andrea M. Galati, Executive Director, 585-276-3407, Fax: 585-276-2357, E-mail: andrea.galati@rochester.edu. Web site: http://www.rochester.edu/team.

University of Rochester, Hajim School of Engineering and Applied Sciences, Department of Computer Science, Rochester, NY 14627. Offers MS, PhD. *Faculty:* 16 full-time (1 woman). *Students:* 53 full-time (12 women), 1 part-time; includes 3 minority (2 Asian, non-Hispanic/Latino; 1 Hispanic/Latino), 35 international. 362 applicants, 11% accepted, 21 enrolled. In 2011, 10 master's, 7 doctorates awarded. *Entrance requirements:* Additional exam requirements/recommendations for international students: Required—TOEFL. *Application deadline:* For fall admission, 1/15 for domestic students. Electronic applications accepted. *Expenses: Tuition:* Full-time $41,040. *Faculty research:* Artificial intelligence, human-computer interaction, systems research, theory research. *Unit head:* Henry Kautz, Chair, 585-275-3772. *Application contact:* JoMarie Carpenter, Graduate Coordinator, 585-275-7737. Web site: http://www.cs.rochester.edu/.

University of San Francisco, College of Arts and Sciences, Computer Science Program, San Francisco, CA 94117-1080. Offers MS. Part-time programs available. *Faculty:* 5 full-time (3 women). *Students:* 48 full-time (9 women), 3 part-time (1 woman); includes 3 minority (1 Asian, non-Hispanic/Latino; 2 Hispanic/Latino), 41 international. Average age 27. 118 applicants, 48% accepted, 8 enrolled. In 2011, 10 master's awarded. *Degree requirements:* For master's, thesis optional. *Entrance requirements:* For master's, GRE General Test, GRE Subject Test, BS in computer science or related field. Additional exam requirements/recommendations for international students: Required—TOEFL. *Application deadline:* For fall admission, 7/1 priority date for domestic students; for spring admission, 12/1 for domestic students. Applications are processed on a rolling basis. Application fee: $55 ($65 for international students). *Expenses: Tuition:* Full-time $20,070; part-time $1115 per unit. Tuition and fees vary according to course load, campus/location and program. *Financial support:* In 2011–12, 22 students received support. Fellowships, teaching assistantships, career-related internships or fieldwork, and Federal Work-Study available. Financial award application deadline: 3/2; financial award applicants required to submit FAFSA. *Faculty research:* Software engineering, computer graphics, computer networks. *Unit head:* Dr. Terence Parr, Chairman, 415-422-6530. *Application contact:* Mark Landerghini, Graduate Adviser, 415-422-5135, E-mail: asgraduate@usfca.edu. Web site: http://www.usfca.edu/artsci/csg/.

University of Saskatchewan, College of Graduate Studies and Research, College of Arts and Science, Department of Computer Science, Saskatoon, SK S7N 5A2, Canada. Offers M Sc, PhD. *Degree requirements:* For master's, thesis; for doctorate, comprehensive exam (for some programs), thesis/dissertation. *Entrance requirements:* For master's and doctorate, GRE. Additional exam requirements/recommendations for international students: Required—TOEFL (minimum score 80 iBT); Recommended—IELTS (minimum score 6.5). Electronic applications accepted.

University of South Alabama, Graduate School, School of Computer and Information Sciences, Mobile, AL 36688-0002. Offers computer science (MS); information systems (MS). Part-time and evening/weekend programs available. *Faculty:* 8 full-time (0 women). *Students:* 70 full-time (18 women), 16 part-time (4 women); includes 6 minority (4 Black or African American, non-Hispanic/Latino; 1 Asian, non-Hispanic/Latino; 1 Native Hawaiian or other Pacific Islander, non-Hispanic/Latino), 51 international. 103 applicants, 74% accepted, 20 enrolled. In 2011, 44 master's awarded. *Degree requirements:* For master's, thesis optional, project. *Entrance requirements:* For master's, GRE General Test. *Application deadline:* For fall admission, 7/15 priority date for domestic students, 6/15 for international students; for spring admission, 12/1 for domestic students, 11/1 for international students. Applications are processed on a rolling basis. Application fee: $35. *Expenses:* Tuition, state resident: full-time $7968;

part-time $332 per credit hour. Tuition, nonresident: full-time $15,936; part-time $664 per credit hour. *Financial support:* Research assistantships, career-related internships or fieldwork, and institutionally sponsored loans available. Support available to part-time students. Financial award application deadline: 4/1. *Faculty research:* Numerical analysis, artificial intelligence, simulation, medical applications, software engineering. *Unit head:* Dr. Roy Daigle, Director of Graduate Studies, 251-460-6390. *Application contact:* Dr. B. Keith Harrison, Dean of the Graduate School, 251-460-6310, Fax: 251-461-1513, E-mail: kharriso@usouthal.edu. Web site: http://www.cis.usouthal.edu.

University of South Carolina, The Graduate School, College of Engineering and Computing, Department of Computer Science and Engineering, Columbia, SC 29208. Offers computer science and engineering (ME, MS, PhD); software engineering (MS). Part-time and evening/weekend programs available. Postbaccalaureate distance learning degree programs offered (minimal on-campus study). *Degree requirements:* For master's, comprehensive exam, thesis (for some programs); for doctorate, comprehensive exam, thesis/dissertation. *Entrance requirements:* For master's and doctorate, GRE General Test. Additional exam requirements/recommendations for international students: Required—TOEFL (minimum score 570 paper-based; 230 computer-based). Electronic applications accepted. *Faculty research:* Computer security, computer vision, artificial intelligence, multiagent systems, bioinformatics.

The University of South Dakota, Graduate School, College of Arts and Sciences, Department of Computer Science, Vermillion, SD 57069-2390. Offers computational sciences and statistics (PhD); computer science (MS). Part-time programs available. *Degree requirements:* For master's, thesis optional. *Entrance requirements:* For master's, GRE General Test, GRE Subject Test (recommended), minimum GPA of 2.7. Additional exam requirements/recommendations for international students: Required—TOEFL (minimum score 550 paper-based; 213 computer-based; 79 iBT). Electronic applications accepted. *Expenses:* Tuition, state resident: full-time $3118.50; part-time $173.25 per credit hour. Tuition, nonresident: full-time $6601; part-time $366.70 per credit hour. *Required fees:* $2268; $126 per credit hour. Tuition and fees vary according to program.

University of Southern California, Graduate School, Viterbi School of Engineering, Department of Computer Science, Los Angeles, CA 90089. Offers computer networks (MS); computer science (MS, PhD); computer security (MS); game development (MS); high performance computing and simulations (MS); human language technology (MS); intelligent robotics (MS); multimedia and creative technologies (MS); software engineering (MS). Part-time and evening/weekend programs available. Postbaccalaureate distance learning degree programs offered (no on-campus study). *Entrance requirements:* For master's and doctorate, GRE General Test. Additional exam requirements/recommendations for international students: Required—TOEFL. Electronic applications accepted. *Faculty research:* Databases, computer graphics and computer vision, software engineering, networks and security, robotics, multimedia and virtual reality.

University of Southern Maine, School of Applied Science, Engineering, and Technology, Department of Computer Science, Portland, ME 04104-9300. Offers MS. Part-time programs available. *Degree requirements:* For master's, thesis. *Entrance requirements:* For master's, GRE General Test, minimum GPA of 3.0. Additional exam requirements/recommendations for international students: Required—TOEFL. Electronic applications accepted. *Faculty research:* Computer networks, database systems, software engineering, theory of computability, human factors.

University of Southern Mississippi, Graduate School, College of Science and Technology, School of Computing, Hattiesburg, MS 39406-0001. Offers computational science (MS, PhD); computer science (MS). *Faculty:* 18 full-time (3 women), 1 (woman) part-time/adjunct. *Students:* 47 full-time (9 women), 20 part-time (4 women); includes 6 minority (2 Black or African American, non-Hispanic/Latino; 2 Asian, non-Hispanic/Latino; 2 Hispanic/Latino), 43 international. Average age 29. 104 applicants, 56% accepted, 21 enrolled. In 2011, 31 master's, 6 doctorates awarded. *Degree requirements:* For master's, comprehensive exam, thesis; for doctorate, comprehensive exam, thesis/dissertation. *Entrance requirements:* For master's, GRE General Test, minimum GPA of 2.75 in last 60 hours; for doctorate, GRE General Test, minimum GPA of 3.5. Additional exam requirements/recommendations for international students: Required—TOEFL, IELTS. *Application deadline:* For fall admission, 3/15 priority date for domestic students, 3/15 for international students; for spring admission, 1/10 priority date for domestic students, 1/10 for international students. Applications are processed on a rolling basis. Application fee: $50. Electronic applications accepted. *Financial support:* In 2011–12, 29 research assistantships with full tuition reimbursements (averaging $8,800 per year), 7 teaching assistantships with full tuition reimbursements (averaging $10,000 per year) were awarded; Federal Work-Study, institutionally sponsored loans, scholarships/grants, health care benefits, and unspecified assistantships also available. Financial award application deadline: 3/15; financial award applicants required to submit FAFSA. *Faculty research:* Satellite telecommunications, advanced life-support systems, artificial intelligence. *Unit head:* Dr. Chaoyang Zhang, Chair, 601-266-4949, Fax: 601-266-6452. *Application contact:* Dr. Chaoyang Zhang, Manager of Graduate Admissions, 601-266-4949, Fax: 601-266-6452. Web site: http://www.usm.edu/graduateschool/table.php.

University of South Florida, Graduate School, College of Engineering, Department of Computer Science and Engineering, Tampa, FL 33620-9951. Offers computer engineering (MSCP); computer science (MSCS); computer science and engineering (PhD). Part-time programs available. *Faculty:* 19 full-time (1 woman), 1 part-time/adjunct (0 women). *Students:* 91 full-time (16 women), 42 part-time (10 women); includes 25 minority (9 Black or African American, non-Hispanic/Latino; 5 Asian, non-Hispanic/Latino; 11 Hispanic/Latino), 59 international. Average age 29. 252 applicants, 38% accepted, 38 enrolled. In 2011, 22 master's, 7 doctorates awarded. Terminal master's awarded for partial completion of doctoral program. *Degree requirements:* For master's, comprehensive exam, thesis or alternative; for doctorate, comprehensive exam, thesis/dissertation, teaching of undergraduate computer science and engineering course. *Entrance requirements:* For master's, GRE, minimum GPA of 3.0 in last 60 hours of coursework, three letters of recommendation, statement of purpose; for doctorate, GRE, minimum GPA of 3.0 in last 60 hours of coursework. Additional exam requirements/recommendations for international students: Required—TOEFL (minimum score 550 paper-based; 213 computer-based; 79 iBT) or IELTS (minimum score 6.5). *Application deadline:* For fall admission, 2/15 for domestic students, 1/2 for international students; for spring admission, 10/15 for domestic students, 6/1 for international students. Application fee: $30. Electronic applications accepted. *Financial support:* In 2011–12, 65 students received support, including 30 research assistantships with tuition reimbursements available (averaging $14,942 per year), 35 teaching assistantships with tuition reimbursements available (averaging $14,003 per year); unspecified assistantships also available. Financial award application deadline: 1/1; financial award applicants required to submit FAFSA. *Faculty research:* Computer vision, networks, artificial intelligence, computer architecture, software security. *Total annual research*

expenditures: $1.4 million. *Unit head:* Dr. Lawrence Hall, Chair, 813-974-4195, Fax: 813-974-5094, E-mail: csechari@cse.usf.edu. *Application contact:* Dr. Miguel Labrador, Program Director, 813-974-3260, Fax: 813-974-5094, E-mail: mlabrador@usf.edu. Web site: http://www.csee.usf.edu/.

The University of Tennessee, Graduate School, College of Arts and Sciences, Department of Computer Science, Knoxville, TN 37996. Offers MS, PhD. Part-time programs available. *Degree requirements:* For master's, thesis or alternative; for doctorate, thesis/dissertation. *Entrance requirements:* For master's and doctorate, GRE General Test, minimum GPA of 2.7. Additional exam requirements/recommendations for international students: Required—TOEFL. Electronic applications accepted. *Expenses:* Tuition, state resident: full-time $8332; part-time $464 per credit hour. Tuition, nonresident: full-time $25,174; part-time $1400 per credit hour. *Required fees:* $1162; $56 per credit hour. Tuition and fees vary according to program.

The University of Tennessee, Graduate School, College of Engineering, Department of Electrical Engineering and Computer Science, Program in Computer Science, Knoxville, TN 37996. Offers MS, PhD. Part-time programs available. *Faculty:* 12 full-time (1 woman), 1 (woman) part-time/adjunct. *Students:* 41 full-time (5 women), 7 part-time; includes 4 minority (1 American Indian or Alaska Native, non-Hispanic/Latino; 3 Asian, non-Hispanic/Latino), 19 international. Average age 31. 178 applicants, 13% accepted, 14 enrolled. In 2011, 13 master's, 3 doctorates awarded. *Degree requirements:* For master's, thesis or alternative; for doctorate, comprehensive exam, thesis/dissertation. *Entrance requirements:* For master's, GRE General Test (for MS students pursuing research thesis), minimum GPA of 2.7 (for U.S. degree holders), 3.0 (for international degree holders); 3 references; personal statement; for doctorate, College requires GRE General Test for all PhD candidates, minimum GPA of 3.0 on previous graduate coursework; 3 references; personal statement. Additional exam requirements/recommendations for international students: Required—TOEFL (minimum score 550 paper-based; 213 computer-based). *Application deadline:* For fall admission, 2/1 priority date for domestic students, 2/1 for international students; for spring admission, 6/15 for domestic and international students. Applications are processed on a rolling basis. Application fee: $35. Electronic applications accepted. *Expenses:* Tuition, state resident: full-time $8332; part-time $464 per credit hour. Tuition, nonresident: full-time $25,174; part-time $1400 per credit hour. *Required fees:* $1162; $56 per credit hour. Tuition and fees vary according to program. *Financial support:* In 2011–12, 47 students received support, including 3 fellowships with full tuition reimbursements available (averaging $9,234 per year), 29 research assistantships with full tuition reimbursements available (averaging $23,903 per year), 15 teaching assistantships with full tuition reimbursements available (averaging $15,700 per year); career-related internships or fieldwork, Federal Work-Study, institutionally sponsored loans, health care benefits, and unspecified assistantships also available. Financial award application deadline: 2/1; financial award applicants required to submit FAFSA. *Unit head:* Dr. Kevin Tomsovic, Head, 865-974-3461, Fax: 865-974-5483, E-mail: tomsovic@eecs.utk.edu. *Application contact:* Dr. Lynne E. Parker, Associate Head, 865-974-4394, Fax: 865-974-5483, E-mail: parker@eecs.utk.edu. Web site: http://www.eecs.utk.edu.

The University of Tennessee at Chattanooga, Graduate School, College of Engineering and Computer Science, Program in Computer Science, Chattanooga, TN 37403-2598. Offers MS, Graduate Certificate. Part-time and evening/weekend programs available. *Faculty:* 7 full-time (4 women). *Students:* 7 full-time (0 women), 15 part-time (2 women); includes 1 minority (Asian, non-Hispanic/Latino), 2 international. Average age 30. 48 applicants, 46% accepted, 8 enrolled. In 2011, 7 master's awarded. *Degree requirements:* For master's, comprehensive exam, thesis. *Entrance requirements:* For master's, GRE General Test. Additional exam requirements/recommendations for international students: Required—TOEFL (minimum score 550 paper-based; 213 computer-based; 79 iBT), IELTS (minimum score 6). *Application deadline:* For fall admission, 8/1 priority date for domestic students, 6/1 for international students; for spring admission, 12/1 priority date for domestic students, 10/1 for international students. Applications are processed on a rolling basis. Application fee: $35. Electronic applications accepted. *Expenses:* Tuition, state resident: full-time $6472; part-time $359 per credit hour. Tuition, nonresident: full-time $20,006; part-time $1111 per credit hour. *Required fees:* $1320; $160 per credit hour. *Financial support:* Career-related internships or fieldwork, scholarships/grants, and unspecified assistantships available. Support available to part-time students. *Faculty research:* Power systems, computer architecture, pattern recognition, artificial intelligence, statistical data analysis. *Total annual research expenditures:* $114,987. *Unit head:* Dr. Joseph Kizza, Department Head, 423-425-4349, Fax: 423-425-5442, E-mail: joseph-kizza@utc.edu. *Application contact:* Dr. Jerald Ainsworth, Dean of Graduate Studies, 423-425-4478, Fax: 423-425-5223, E-mail: jerald-ainsworth@utc.edu. Web site: http://www.utc.edu/Departments/engrcs/ms_cs.php.

The University of Tennessee Space Institute, Graduate Programs, Program in Electrical Engineering and Computer Science, Tullahoma, TN 37388-9700. Offers MS, PhD. *Faculty:* 2 full-time (0 women), 1 part-time/adjunct (0 women). *Students:* 1 part-time (0 women). *Degree requirements:* For master's, thesis (for some programs); for doctorate, one foreign language, thesis/dissertation. *Entrance requirements:* Additional exam requirements/recommendations for international students: Required—TOEFL (minimum score 550 paper-based; 213 computer-based), IELTS (minimum score 6.5). *Application deadline:* For fall admission, 2/1 for international students; for spring admission, 6/15 for international students. Applications are processed on a rolling basis. Application fee: $35. Electronic applications accepted. *Financial support:* Fellowships, research assistantships with full tuition reimbursements, career-related internships or fieldwork, Federal Work-Study, institutionally sponsored loans, health care benefits, tuition waivers (full and partial), and unspecified assistantships available. Financial award applicants required to submit FAFSA. *Unit head:* Dr. Monty Smith, Degree Program Chairman, 931-393-7480, Fax: 931-393-7530, E-mail: msmith@utsi.edu. *Application contact:* Dee Merriman, Coordinator III, 931-393-7213, Fax: 931-393-7211, E-mail: dmerrima@utsi.edu.

The University of Texas at Arlington, Graduate School, College of Engineering, Department of Computer Science and Engineering, Arlington, TX 76019. Offers computer engineering (MS, PhD); computer science (MS, PhD); mathematical sciences, computer science (PhD); software engineering (MS). Part-time programs available. Postbaccalaureate distance learning degree programs offered (minimal on-campus study). *Faculty:* 31 full-time (3 women). *Students:* 206 full-time (46 women), 98 part-time (21 women); includes 7 minority (1 Black or African American, non-Hispanic/Latino; 4 Asian, non-Hispanic/Latino; 1 Hispanic/Latino; 1 Two or more races, non-Hispanic/Latino), 247 international. 752 applicants, 60% accepted, 89 enrolled. In 2011, 60 master's, 12 doctorates awarded. Terminal master's awarded for partial completion of doctoral program. *Degree requirements:* For master's, comprehensive exam (for some programs), thesis; for doctorate, comprehensive exam, thesis/dissertation. *Entrance requirements:* For master's, GRE General Test, minimum GPA of 3.0 (3.2 in computer science-related classes); for doctorate, GRE General Test, minimum GPA of 3.5. Additional exam requirements/recommendations for international students: Required—

TOEFL (minimum score 550 paper-based; 230 computer-based; 92 iBT), IELTS (minimum score 6.5). *Application deadline:* For fall admission, 6/1 for domestic students, 5/1 for international students; for spring admission, 12/1 for domestic students, 10/1 for international students. Applications are processed on a rolling basis. Application fee: $35 ($50 for international students). *Financial support:* In 2011–12, 8 fellowships with full tuition reimbursements (averaging $24,000 per year), 48 research assistantships with partial tuition reimbursements (averaging $19,200 per year), 43 teaching assistantships with partial tuition reimbursements (averaging $18,000 per year) were awarded; career-related internships or fieldwork and scholarships/grants also available. Financial award application deadline: 6/1; financial award applicants required to submit FAFSA. *Faculty research:* Algorithms, homeland security, mobile pervasive computing, high performance computing bioinformation. *Unit head:* Dr. Fillia Makedon, Chairman, 817-272-3605, E-mail: makedon@uta.edu. *Application contact:* Dr. Bahram Khalili, Graduate Advisor, 817-272-5407, Fax: 817-272-3784, E-mail: khalili@uta.edu. Web site: http://www.cse.uta.edu/.

The University of Texas at Austin, Graduate School, College of Natural Sciences, Department of Computer Sciences, Austin, TX 78712-1111. Offers MSCS, PhD. *Degree requirements:* For master's, thesis optional; for doctorate, thesis/dissertation, oral proposal, final defense. *Entrance requirements:* For master's and doctorate, GRE General Test, GRE Subject Test, bachelor's degree in computer sciences (preferred). Additional exam requirements/recommendations for international students: Required—TOEFL. *Application deadline:* For fall admission, 1/2 for domestic and international students; for spring admission, 9/1 for domestic and international students. Applications are processed on a rolling basis. Application fee: $50 ($75 for international students). Electronic applications accepted. *Financial support:* Fellowships with full tuition reimbursements, research assistantships with full tuition reimbursements, teaching assistantships with partial tuition reimbursements, and institutionally sponsored loans available. Financial award application deadline: 1/2. *Faculty research:* Artificial intelligence, distributed computing, networks, algorithms, experimental systems. *Unit head:* Dr. J. Strother Moore, Chairman, 512-471-9590, Fax: 512-471-9500, E-mail: chair@cs.utexas.edu. *Application contact:* Graduate Office, 512-471-9503, Fax: 512-471-7866, E-mail: csadmins@cs.utexas.edu. Web site: http://www.cs.utexas.edu/graduate-program.

The University of Texas at Dallas, Erik Jonsson School of Engineering and Computer Science, Department of Computer Science, Richardson, TX 75080. Offers computer science (MS, PhD); software engineering (PhD). Part-time and evening/weekend programs available. *Faculty:* 41 full-time (6 women), 1 part-time/adjunct (0 women). *Students:* 464 full-time (105 women), 135 part-time (26 women); includes 33 minority (2 Black or African American, non-Hispanic/Latino; 1 American Indian or Alaska Native, non-Hispanic/Latino; 20 Asian, non-Hispanic/Latino; 9 Hispanic/Latino; 1 Two or more races, non-Hispanic/Latino), 485 international. Average age 26. 1,464 applicants, 59% accepted, 264 enrolled. In 2011, 176 master's, 25 doctorates awarded. *Degree requirements:* For master's, thesis optional; for doctorate, comprehensive exam, thesis/dissertation. *Entrance requirements:* For master's, GRE General Test, minimum GPA of 3.0 in undergraduate course work, 3.3 in quantitative course work; for doctorate, GRE General Test, minimum GPA of 3.5. Additional exam requirements/recommendations for international students: Required—TOEFL (minimum score 550 paper-based; 215 computer-based). *Application deadline:* For fall admission, 7/15 for domestic students, 5/1 for international students; for spring admission, 11/15 for domestic students, 9/1 for international students. Applications are processed on a rolling basis. Application fee: $50 ($100 for international students). Electronic applications accepted. *Expenses:* Tuition, state resident: full-time $11,170; part-time $620.56 per credit hour. Tuition, nonresident: full-time $20,212; part-time $1122.89 per credit hour. *Financial support:* In 2011–12, 162 students received support, including 2 fellowships with partial tuition reimbursements available (averaging $12,216 per year), 52 research assistantships with partial tuition reimbursements available (averaging $21,785 per year), 40 teaching assistantships with partial tuition reimbursements available (averaging $16,076 per year); career-related internships or fieldwork, Federal Work-Study, institutionally sponsored loans, and scholarships/grants also available. Support available to part-time students. Financial award application deadline: 4/30; financial award applicants required to submit FAFSA. *Faculty research:* AI-based automated software synthesis and testing, quality of service in computer networks, wireless networks, cloud computing and IT security, speech recognition. *Unit head:* Dr. Gopal Gupta, Department Head, 972-883-4107, Fax: 972-883-2349, E-mail: gupta@utdallas.edu. *Application contact:* Dr. Balaji Raghavachari, Associate Department Head and Director of Graduate Studies, 972-883-2136, Fax: 972-883-2813, E-mail: gradecs@utdallas.edu. Web site: http://cs.utdallas.edu/.

The University of Texas at El Paso, Graduate School, College of Engineering, Department of Computer Science, El Paso, TX 79968-0001. Offers computer science (MS, PhD); information technology (MSIT). Part-time and evening/weekend programs available. *Students:* 48 (10 women); includes 21 minority (1 Asian, non-Hispanic/Latino; 20 Hispanic/Latino), 21 international. Average age 34. 33 applicants, 73% accepted, 12 enrolled. In 2011, 7 master's awarded. *Degree requirements:* For master's, thesis optional; for doctorate, thesis/dissertation. *Entrance requirements:* For master's, GRE, minimum GPA of 3.0; for doctorate, GRE, statement of purpose, letters of reference. Additional exam requirements/recommendations for international students: Required—TOEFL; Recommended—IELTS. *Application deadline:* For fall admission, 8/1 priority date for domestic students, 3/1 for international students; for spring admission, 11/1 priority date for domestic students, 9/1 for international students. Applications are processed on a rolling basis. Application fee: $45 ($80 for international students). Electronic applications accepted. *Financial support:* In 2011–12, research assistantships with partial tuition reimbursements (averaging $21,125 per year), teaching assistantships with partial tuition reimbursements (averaging $16,900 per year) were awarded; fellowships with partial tuition reimbursements, institutionally sponsored loans, scholarships/grants, health care benefits, tuition waivers (partial), and unspecified assistantships also available. Support available to part-time students. Financial award application deadline: 3/15; financial award applicants required to submit FAFSA. *Unit head:* Dr. Eunice E. Santos, Chair, 915-747-5480 Ext. 5480, Fax: 915-747-5030, E-mail: eesantos@utep.edu. *Application contact:* Dr. Benjamin Flores, Interim Dean of the Graduate School, 915-747-5491, Fax: 915-747-5788, E-mail: bflores@utep.edu. Web site: http://www.cs.utep.edu/.

The University of Texas at San Antonio, College of Sciences, Department of Computer Science, San Antonio, TX 78249-0617. Offers MS, PhD. *Faculty:* 20 full-time (4 women), 2 part-time/adjunct (0 women). *Students:* 115 full-time (21 women), 51 part-time (9 women); includes 23 minority (3 Black or African American, non-Hispanic/Latino; 1 American Indian or Alaska Native, non-Hispanic/Latino; 4 Asian, non-Hispanic/Latino; 13 Hispanic/Latino; 2 Two or more races, non-Hispanic/Latino), 104 international. Average age 29. 255 applicants, 40% accepted, 40 enrolled. In 2011, 13 master's, 3 doctorates awarded. *Degree requirements:* For master's, comprehensive exam (for some programs), thesis (for some programs), minimum of 36 semester credit hours of coursework; for doctorate, thesis/dissertation, minimum of 90 semester credit hours of coursework. *Entrance requirements:* For master's, GRE General Test, bachelor's degree in computer science equivalent to that offered at UTSA; for doctorate, GRE General Test, resume, three letters of recommendation, statement of purpose. Additional exam requirements/recommendations for international students: Required—TOEFL (minimum score 550 paper-based; 79 iBT), IELTS (minimum score 6.5). *Application deadline:* For fall admission, 7/1 for domestic students, 4/1 for international students; for spring admission, 11/1 for domestic students, 9/1 for international students. Application fee: $45 ($85 for international students). *Expenses:* Tuition, state resident: full-time $3148; part-time $2176 per semester. Tuition, nonresident: full-time $8782; part-time $5932 per semester. *Required fees:* $719 per semester. *Financial support:* In 2011–12, 17 fellowships (averaging $21,000 per year), 18 research assistantships (averaging $21,000 per year), 36 teaching assistantships (averaging $21,000 per year) were awarded. *Faculty research:* Computer and information security, high performance computing, computational biology, computer networks, artificial intelligence. *Total annual research expenditures:* $2.2 million. *Unit head:* Dr. Daniel Jimenez, Department Chair, 210-458-4436, Fax: 210-458-4437, E-mail: kleanthis.psarris@utsa.edu. *Application contact:* Dr. Weining Zhang, Graduate Advisor of Record, 210-458-5557, Fax: 210-458-557, E-mail: wzhang@cs.utsa.edu. Web site: http://www.cs.utsa.edu/.

The University of Texas at Tyler, College of Engineering and Computer Science, Department of Computer Science, Tyler, TX 75799-0001. Offers computer science (MS); interdisciplinary studies (MSIS). *Degree requirements:* For master's, comprehensive exam, thesis optional. *Entrance requirements:* For master's, GRE General Test, previous course work in data structures and computer organization, 6 hours of course work in calculus and statistics. Additional exam requirements/recommendations for international students: Required—TOEFL (minimum score 79 computer-based). Electronic applications accepted. *Faculty research:* Database design, software engineering, client-server architecture, visual programming, data mining, computer security, digital image processing, simulation and modeling, computer science education.

The University of Texas of the Permian Basin, Office of Graduate Studies, College of Arts and Sciences, Department of Math and Computer Science, Odessa, TX 79762-0001. Offers computer science (MS). Part-time and evening/weekend programs available. *Degree requirements:* For master's, comprehensive exam, thesis or alternative. *Entrance requirements:* For master's, GRE General Test. Additional exam requirements/recommendations for international students: Required—TOEFL (minimum score 550 paper-based; 213 computer-based).

The University of Texas–Pan American, College of Engineering and Computer Science, Department of Computer Science, Edinburg, TX 78539. Offers computer science (MS); information technology (MS). Part-time and evening/weekend programs available. Postbaccalaureate distance learning degree programs offered (minimal on-campus study). *Degree requirements:* For master's, final written exam, project. *Entrance requirements:* For master's, GRE General Test, minimum GPA of 3.0 in last 60 hours. Additional exam requirements/recommendations for international students: Required—TOEFL. *Application deadline:* For fall admission, 7/1 priority date for domestic students; for spring admission, 11/1 priority date for domestic students. Applications are processed on a rolling basis. Application fee: $0. Tuition and fees vary according to course load, program and student level. *Financial support:* Research assistantships, teaching assistantships, career-related internships or fieldwork, Federal Work-Study, and scholarships/grants available. Support available to part-time students. Financial award applicants required to submit FAFSA. *Faculty research:* Artificial intelligence, distributed systems, Internet computing, theoretical computer sciences, information visualization. *Unit head:* Dr. Zhixiang Chen, Chair, 956-665-3520, E-mail: zchen@utpa.edu. *Application contact:* Dr. Richard Fowler, Graduate Coordinator, 956-665-3453, E-mail: fowler@utpa.edu. Web site: http://www.cs.panam.edu/.

University of the District of Columbia, School of Engineering and Applied Science, Department of Computer Science and Information Technology, Program in Computer Science, Washington, DC 20008-1175. Offers MS. *Degree requirements:* For master's, thesis optional. *Expenses: Tuition, area resident:* Full-time $7580; part-time $421 per credit hour. Tuition, state resident: full-time $8580; part-time $477 per credit hour. Tuition, nonresident: full-time $14,580; part-time $810 per credit hour. *Required fees:* $620; $30 per credit hour. $310 per semester.

The University of Toledo, College of Graduate Studies, College of Engineering, Department of Electrical Engineering and Computer Science, Toledo, OH 43606-3390. Offers computer science (MS, PhD); electrical engineering (MS, PhD). Part-time and evening/weekend programs available. *Degree requirements:* For master's, thesis or alternative; for doctorate, thesis/dissertation, qualifying exam. *Entrance requirements:* For master's, GRE General Test, minimum GPA of 3.0; for doctorate, GRE General Test, minimum GPA of 3.3. Additional exam requirements/recommendations for international students: Required—TOEFL (minimum score 550 paper-based; 213 computer-based; 80 iBT). Electronic applications accepted. *Faculty research:* Communication and signal processing, high performance computing systems, intelligent systems, power electronics and energy systems, RF and microwave systems, sensors and medical devices, solid state devices.

University of Toronto, School of Graduate Studies, Faculty of Arts and Science, Department of Computer Science, Toronto, ON M5S 1A1, Canada. Offers applied computing (M Sc AC); computer science (M Sc, PhD). Part-time programs available. *Degree requirements:* For master's, thesis; for doctorate, thesis/dissertation, thesis defense/oral exam. *Entrance requirements:* For master's, GRE (recommended), minimum B+ average overall and in final year; resume; 3 letters of reference; background in computer science and mathematics (preferred); for doctorate, minimum B+ average overall and in final year; resume; 3 letters of reference; background in computer science and mathematics (preferred). Additional exam requirements/recommendations for international students: Required—TOEFL (minimum score 580 paper-based; 237 computer-based), TWE (minimum score 5). *Application deadline:* For fall admission, 12/15 for domestic students. Application fee: $110 Canadian dollars. Electronic applications accepted. *Unit head:* Prof. Sven Dickinson, Chair, 416-978-2980, Fax: 416-946-5464, E-mail: sven@cs.toronto.edu. *Application contact:* Celeste Francis Esteves, Graduate Program Administrator, 416-946-0855, Fax: 416-978-1931, E-mail: celeste@cs.utoronto.edu. Web site: http://web.cs.toronto.edu.

University of Tulsa, Graduate School, College of Engineering and Natural Sciences, Program in Computer Science, Tulsa, OK 74104-3189. Offers MS, PhD, JD/MS, MBA/MS. Part-time programs available. *Faculty:* 10 full-time (1 woman). *Students:* 51 full-time (12 women), 27 part-time (7 women); includes 9 minority (3 Black or African American, non-Hispanic/Latino; 4 American Indian or Alaska Native, non-Hispanic/Latino; 1 Asian, non-Hispanic/Latino; 1 Hispanic/Latino), 14 international. Average age 26. 61 applicants, 72% accepted, 28 enrolled. In 2011, 26 master's, 3 doctorates awarded. Terminal master's awarded for partial completion of doctoral program. *Degree requirements:* For master's, thesis (for some programs); for doctorate, comprehensive exam, thesis/dissertation. *Entrance requirements:* For master's and doctorate, GRE General Test. Additional exam requirements/recommendations for international students: Required—TOEFL (minimum score 550 paper-based; 213 computer-based; 80 iBT), IELTS (minimum score 6). *Application deadline:* Applications are processed on a rolling basis. Application fee: $40. Electronic applications accepted. *Expenses: Tuition:* Full-time $17,748; part-time $986 per hour. *Required fees:* $5 per contact hour. $75 per semester. Tuition and fees vary according to program. *Financial support:* In 2011–12, 45 students received support, including 1 fellowship with full and partial tuition reimbursement available (averaging $30,000 per year), 39 research assistantships with full and partial tuition reimbursements available (averaging $11,886 per year), 9 teaching assistantships with full and partial tuition reimbursements available (averaging $9,605 per year); career-related internships or fieldwork, Federal Work-Study, scholarships/grants, health care benefits, tuition waivers (full and partial), and unspecified assistantships also available. Support available to part-time students. Financial award application deadline: 2/1; financial award applicants required to submit FAFSA. *Faculty research:* Robotics, human-computer interaction, systems security, information assurance, machine learning, intelligent systems, software engineering, distributed systems, evolutionary computation, computational biology, bioinformatics. *Total annual research expenditures:* $7.4 million. *Unit head:* Dr. Roger Wainwright, Chairperson, 918-631-3143, E-mail: rogerw@utulsa.edu. *Application contact:* Dr. Rosanne Gamble, Advisor, 918-631-2988, Fax: 918-631-3077, E-mail: gamble@utulsa.edu. Web site: http://www.utulsa.edu/academics/colleges/college-of-engineering-and-natural-sciences/departments-and-schools/tandy-school-of-computer-science.aspx.

University of Tulsa, Graduate School, Collins College of Business, Business Administration/Computer Science Program, Tulsa, OK 74104-3189. Offers MBA/MS. Part-time programs available. *Students:* 1 full-time (0 women). Average age 24. 1 applicant, 0% accepted, 0 enrolled. *Entrance requirements:* Additional exam requirements/recommendations for international students: Required—TOEFL (minimum score 577 paper-based; 233 computer-based; 91 iBT), IELTS (minimum score 6.5). *Application deadline:* Applications are processed on a rolling basis. Application fee: $40. Electronic applications accepted. *Expenses: Tuition:* Full-time $17,748; part-time $986 per hour. *Required fees:* $5 per contact hour. $75 per semester. Tuition and fees vary according to program. *Financial support:* In 2011–12, 1 student received support, including 1 teaching assistantship with full and partial tuition reimbursement available (averaging $6,061 per year); fellowships with full and partial tuition reimbursements available, research assistantships with full and partial tuition reimbursements available, career-related internships or fieldwork, Federal Work-Study, institutionally sponsored loans, scholarships/grants, health care benefits, tuition waivers, and unspecified assistantships also available. Support available to part-time students. Financial award application deadline: 2/1; financial award applicants required to submit FAFSA. *Unit head:* Dr. Linda Nichols, Associate Dean, 918-631-2242, Fax: 918-631-2142, E-mail: linda-nichols@utulsa.edu. *Application contact:* Information Contact, 918-631-2242, E-mail: graduate-business@utulsa.edu.

University of Utah, Graduate School, College of Engineering, School of Computing, Salt Lake City, UT 84112-9205. Offers computational engineering and science (MS); computer science (M Phil, MS, PhD); computing (MS, PhD). *Faculty:* 37 full-time (4 women), 3 part-time/adjunct (1 woman). *Students:* 186 full-time (26 women), 68 part-time (5 women); includes 18 minority (1 Black or African American, non-Hispanic/Latino; 1 American Indian or Alaska Native, non-Hispanic/Latino; 15 Asian, non-Hispanic/Latino; 1 Two or more races, non-Hispanic/Latino), 150 international. Average age 29. 537 applicants, 18% accepted, 70 enrolled. In 2011, 51 master's, 12 doctorates awarded. Terminal master's awarded for partial completion of doctoral program. *Median time to degree:* Of those who began their doctoral program in fall 2003, 100% received their degree in 8 years or less. *Degree requirements:* For master's, comprehensive exam (for some programs), thesis (for some programs); for doctorate, comprehensive exam, thesis/dissertation. *Entrance requirements:* For master's and doctorate, GRE General Test, minimum GPA of 3.0. Additional exam requirements/recommendations for international students: Required—TOEFL (minimum score 500 paper-based; 173 computer-based; 61 iBT). *Application deadline:* For fall admission, 12/15 for domestic and international students. Application fee: $55 ($65 for international students). Electronic applications accepted. *Expenses:* Contact institution. *Financial support:* In 2011–12, 1 student received support, including 3 fellowships with full tuition reimbursements available (averaging $20,000 per year), 104 research assistantships with full tuition reimbursements available (averaging $25,000 per year), 40 teaching assistantships with full tuition reimbursements available (averaging $12,000 per year); scholarships/grants, traineeships, health care benefits, and unspecified assistantships also available. Financial award application deadline: 12/15; financial award applicants required to submit FAFSA. *Faculty research:* Computer-aided graphic design, VLSI, information retrieval, portable artificial intelligence systems, functional programming, data analysis, image analysis, computer engineering. *Total annual research expenditures:* $20.2 million. *Unit head:* Dr. Alan Davis, Director, 801-581-8224, Fax: 801-581-5843, E-mail: ald@cs.utah.edu. *Application contact:* Ann Carlstrom, Graduate Advisor, 801-581-7631, Fax: 801-581-5843, E-mail: annc@cs.utah.edu. Web site: http://www.cs.utah.edu.

University of Vermont, Graduate College, College of Engineering and Mathematics, Program in Computer Science, Burlington, VT 05405. Offers MS, PhD. *Students:* 25 (7 women); includes 1 minority (Hispanic/Latino), 12 international. 42 applicants, 29% accepted, 2 enrolled. In 2011, 2 master's, 1 doctorate awarded. *Degree requirements:* For master's, thesis or alternative. *Entrance requirements:* For master's and doctorate, GRE General Test. Additional exam requirements/recommendations for international students: Required—TOEFL (minimum score 550 paper-based; 213 computer-based; 80 iBT). *Application deadline:* For fall admission, 2/15 priority date for domestic students, 2/15 for international students. Applications are processed on a rolling basis. Application fee: $40. Electronic applications accepted. *Financial support:* Research assistantships and teaching assistantships available. Financial award application deadline: 3/1. *Unit head:* Jeffrey Dinitz, Chair, 802-656-3330. *Application contact:* Prof. Xindong Wu, Coordinator, 802-656-3330.

University of Victoria, Faculty of Graduate Studies, Faculty of Engineering, Department of Computer Science, Victoria, BC V8W 2Y2, Canada. Offers M Sc, PhD. Part-time programs available. Terminal master's awarded for partial completion of doctoral program. *Degree requirements:* For master's, thesis or alternative; for doctorate, thesis/dissertation, candidacy exam. *Entrance requirements:* For master's, GRE (recommended), B Sc in computer science/software engineering or the equivalent or bachelor's degree in mathematics with emphasis on computer science (recommended); for doctorate, GRE (recommended), MS in computer science or equivalent (recommended). Additional exam requirements/recommendations for international students: Required—TOEFL (minimum score 575 paper-based; 233 computer-based), IELTS (minimum score 7). Electronic applications accepted. *Faculty research:* Functional and logic programming, numerical analysis, parallel and distributed computing, software systems, theoretical computer science, VLSI design and testing.

University of Virginia, School of Engineering and Applied Science, Department of Computer Science, Charlottesville, VA 22903. Offers MCS, MS, PhD. *Faculty:* 23 full-time (1 woman), 1 part-time/adjunct (0 women). *Students:* 81 full-time (17 women); includes 7 minority (1 Black or African American, non-Hispanic/Latino; 5 Asian, non-Hispanic/Latino; 1 Hispanic/Latino), 43 international. Average age 27. 341 applicants, 10% accepted, 21 enrolled. In 2011, 12 master's, 6 doctorates awarded. *Degree requirements:* For master's, thesis (for some programs); for doctorate, comprehensive exam, thesis/dissertation. *Entrance requirements:* For master's, GRE General Test, 3 letters of recommendation; for doctorate, GRE General Test, 3 letters of recommendation; essay. Additional exam requirements/recommendations for international students: Required—TOEFL (minimum score 650 paper-based; 250 computer-based; 90 iBT), IELTS (minimum score 7). *Application deadline:* For fall admission, 8/1 for domestic students, 4/1 for international students; for winter admission, 12/1 for domestic students, 8/1 for international students; for spring admission, 5/1 for domestic students, 1/1 for international students. Applications are processed on a rolling basis. Application fee: $60. Electronic applications accepted. *Financial support:* Fellowships available. Financial award application deadline: 10/15; financial award applicants required to submit FAFSA. *Faculty research:* Systems programming, operating systems, analysis of programs and computation theory, programming languages, software engineering. *Unit head:* Mary Lou Soffa, Chair, 434-982-2200, Fax: 434-982-2214, E-mail: inquiry@cs.virginia.edu. *Application contact:* Kathryn C. Thornton, Assistant Dean for Graduate Programs, 434-924-3897, Fax: 434-982-2214, E-mail: seas-grad-admission@cs.virginia.edu. Web site: http://www.cs.virginia.edu/.

University of Washington, Graduate School, College of Engineering, Department of Computer Science and Engineering, Seattle, WA 98195-2350. Offers MS, PMS, PhD. Postbaccalaureate distance learning degree programs offered. *Faculty:* 55 full-time (8 women), 5 part-time/adjunct (1 woman). *Students:* 164 full-time (36 women), 154 part-time (19 women); includes 47 minority (1 Black or African American, non-Hispanic/Latino; 41 Asian, non-Hispanic/Latino; 5 Hispanic/Latino), 98 international. Average age 28. 1,308 applicants, 11% accepted, 60 enrolled. In 2011, 83 master's, 19 doctorates awarded. *Degree requirements:* For doctorate, thesis/dissertation, independent project. *Entrance requirements:* For doctorate, GRE General Test, minimum GPA of 3.0, statement of purpose, curriculum vitae (academic life), letters of recommendation, transcript. Additional exam requirements/recommendations for international students: Required—TOEFL (minimum score 580 paper-based; 237 computer-based; 92 iBT); Recommended—IELTS (minimum score 7). *Application deadline:* For fall admission, 12/15 priority date for domestic students, 12/15 for international students. Applications are processed on a rolling basis. Application fee: $75. Electronic applications accepted. *Expenses:* Contact institution. *Financial support:* In 2011–12, 171 students received support, including 50 fellowships with full tuition reimbursements available (averaging $20,880 per year), 88 research assistantships with full tuition reimbursements available (averaging $19,692 per year), 27 teaching assistantships with full tuition reimbursements available (averaging $19,359 per year); career-related internships or fieldwork, traineeships, and health care benefits also available. Financial award application deadline: 12/15; financial award applicants required to submit FAFSA. *Faculty research:* Theory, systems, artificial intelligence, graphics, databases. *Total annual research expenditures:* $19.5 million. *Unit head:* Dr. Henry M. Levy, Professor/Chair, 206-543-9204, Fax: 206-543-2969, E-mail: levy@cs.washington.edu. *Application contact:* Lindsay Michimoto, Graduate Admissions Information Contact, 206-543-1695, Fax: 206-543-2969, E-mail: lindsaym@cs.washington.edu. Web site: http://www.cs.washington.edu/.

University of Waterloo, Graduate Studies, Faculty of Mathematics, David R. Cheriton School of Computer Science, Waterloo, ON N2L 3G1, Canada. Offers computer science (M Math, PhD); software engineering (M Math); statistics and computing (M Math). Part-time programs available. *Degree requirements:* For master's, research paper or thesis; for doctorate, comprehensive exam, thesis/dissertation. *Entrance requirements:* For master's, honors degree in field, minimum B+ average; for doctorate, master's degree, minimum B+ average. *Faculty research:* Computer graphics, artificial intelligence, algorithms and complexity, distributed computing and networks, software engineering.

The University of Western Ontario, Faculty of Graduate Studies, Physical Sciences Division, Department of Computer Science, London, ON N6A 5B8, Canada. Offers M Sc, PhD. Part-time programs available. *Degree requirements:* For master's, thesis, project, or course work; for doctorate, thesis/dissertation. *Entrance requirements:* For master's, B Sc in computer science or comparable academic qualifications; for doctorate, M Sc in computer science or comparable academic qualifications. Additional exam requirements/recommendations for international students: Required—TOEFL. *Faculty research:* Artificial intelligence and logic programming, graphics and image processing, software and systems, theory of computing, symbolic mathematical computation.

University of West Florida, College of Arts and Sciences: Sciences, Department of Computer Science, Pensacola, FL 32514-5750. Offers computer science (MS); database systems (MS); software engineering (MS). Part-time and evening/weekend programs available. *Faculty:* 9 full-time (4 women), 5 part-time/adjunct (4 women). *Students:* 22 full-time (8 women), 114 part-time (25 women); includes 38 minority (8 Black or African American, non-Hispanic/Latino; 2 American Indian or Alaska Native, non-Hispanic/Latino; 13 Asian, non-Hispanic/Latino; 13 Hispanic/Latino; 2 Two or more races, non-Hispanic/Latino), 54 international. Average age 37. 53 applicants, 81% accepted, 35 enrolled. In 2011, 64 master's awarded. *Degree requirements:* For master's, thesis optional. *Entrance requirements:* For master's, GRE, MAT, or GMAT, official transcripts; minimum undergraduate GPA of 3.0; letter of intent; three letters of recommendation. Additional exam requirements/recommendations for international students: Required—TOEFL (minimum score 550 paper-based; 213 computer-based). *Application deadline:* For fall admission, 6/1 for domestic and international students; for spring admission, 10/1 for domestic and international students. Applications are processed on a rolling basis. Application fee: $30. *Expenses:* Tuition, state resident: full-time $5729; part-time $302 per credit hour. Tuition, nonresident: full-time $20,059; part-time $961 per credit hour. *Required fees:* $1509; $63 per credit hour. *Financial support:* In 2011–12, 10 fellowships with partial tuition reimbursements (averaging $600 per year), 8 research assistantships with partial tuition reimbursements (averaging $3,280 per year), 2 teaching assistantships with partial tuition reimbursements (averaging $3,760 per year) were awarded; unspecified assistantships also available. Financial award application deadline: 4/15; financial award applicants required to submit FAFSA. *Unit head:* Dr. Leo Ter Haar, Chairperson, 850-474-2542. *Application contact:* Terry McCray, Assistant Director of Graduate Admissions, 850-473-7718, Fax: 850-473-7714, E-mail: gradadmissions@uwf.edu. Web site: http://catalog.uwf.edu/graduate/computerscience/.

University of West Georgia, College of Science and Mathematics, Department of Computer Science, Carrollton, GA 30118. Offers applied computer science (MS). Part-time and evening/weekend programs available. Postbaccalaureate distance learning degree programs offered (no on-campus study). *Faculty:* 7 full-time (2 women). *Students:* 6 full-time (1 woman), 23 part-time (3 women); includes 9 minority (6 Black or African American, non-Hispanic/Latino; 1 Asian, non-Hispanic/Latino; 2 Hispanic/Latino), 2 international. Average age 30. 19 applicants, 74% accepted, 10 enrolled. In 2011, 11 master's awarded. *Entrance requirements:* For master's, bachelor's degree, minimum overall undergraduate GPA of 2.5, 3 letters of reference, resume or curriculum vitae. Additional exam requirements/recommendations for international students: Required—TOEFL (minimum score 523 paper-based; 193 computer-based; 69 iBT); Recommended—IELTS (minimum score 6). *Application deadline:* For fall admission, 8/3 for domestic students. Applications are processed on a rolling basis. Application fee: $30. Electronic applications accepted. *Expenses:* Contact institution. *Financial support:* In 2011–12, 2 students received support, including 2 research assistantships with full tuition reimbursements available (averaging $6,000 per year); unspecified assistantships also available. Financial award application deadline: 7/1; financial award applicants required to submit FAFSA. *Faculty research:* Artificial intelligence, software engineering, Web technologies, database, networks, computer science eduation. *Unit head:* Dr. Adel M. Abunawass, Chair, 678-839-6485, Fax: 678-839-6486, E-mail: adel@westga.edu. *Application contact:* Alice Wesley, Departmental Assistant, 678-839-5192, E-mail: awesley@westga.edu. Web site: http://www.cs.westga.edu/.

University of Windsor, Faculty of Graduate Studies, Faculty of Science, School of Computer Science, Windsor, ON N9B 3P4, Canada. Offers M Sc, PhD. Part-time programs available. *Degree requirements:* For master's, thesis; for doctorate, comprehensive exam, thesis/dissertation. *Entrance requirements:* For master's, GRE, minimum B average; for doctorate, master's degree in computer science, minimum B+ average. Additional exam requirements/recommendations for international students: Required—TOEFL (minimum score 580 paper-based; 237 computer-based). Electronic applications accepted. *Faculty research:* Data mining, distributed query optimization, distributed object based systems, grid computing, querying multimedia database systems.

University of Wisconsin–Madison, Graduate School, College of Letters and Science, Department of Computer Sciences, Madison, WI 53706-1380. Offers MS, PhD. Part-time programs available. Terminal master's awarded for partial completion of doctoral program. *Degree requirements:* For doctorate, thesis/dissertation. *Entrance requirements:* For master's and doctorate, GRE General Test, GRE Subject Test. Electronic applications accepted. *Expenses:* Tuition, state resident: full-time $10,296; part-time $643.51 per credit. Tuition, nonresident: full-time $24,054; part-time $1503.40 per credit. *Required fees:* $70.06 per credit. Tuition and fees vary according to course load, campus/location, program and reciprocity agreements.

University of Wisconsin–Milwaukee, Graduate School, College of Engineering and Applied Science, Program in Computer Science, Milwaukee, WI 53201-0413. Offers computer science (MS, PhD). Part-time programs available. *Faculty:* 24 full-time (4 women). *Students:* 18 full-time (7 women), 31 part-time (6 women); includes 7 minority (6 Asian, non-Hispanic/Latino; 1 Two or more races, non-Hispanic/Latino), 15 international. Average age 31. 79 applicants, 52% accepted, 14 enrolled. In 2011, 16 degrees awarded. *Degree requirements:* For master's, comprehensive exam (for some programs), thesis or alternative; for doctorate, comprehensive exam, thesis/dissertation, internship. *Entrance requirements:* For master's, GRE, minimum GPA of 2.75; for doctorate, GRE, minimum GPA of 3.5. Additional exam requirements/recommendations for international students: Required—TOEFL (minimum score 550 paper-based; 79 iBT), IELTS (minimum score 6.5). *Application deadline:* For fall admission, 1/1 priority date for domestic students; for spring admission, 9/1 for domestic students. Applications are processed on a rolling basis. Application fee: $56 ($96 for international students). Electronic applications accepted. One-time fee: $506.10 full-time. Tuition and fees vary according to course load and reciprocity agreements. *Financial support:* In 2011–12, 4 research assistantships, 10 teaching assistantships were awarded; fellowships, career-related internships or fieldwork, unspecified assistantships, and project assistantships also available. Support available to part-time students. Financial award application deadline: 4/15. *Total annual research expenditures:* $3.2 million. *Unit head:* Seyed Hossein Hosseini, Department Chair, 414-229-5184, E-mail: hosseini@uwm.edu. *Application contact:* General Information Contact, 414-229-4982, Fax: 414-229-6967, E-mail: gradschool@uwm.edu. Web site: http://www.uwm.edu/CEAS/.

University of Wisconsin–Parkside, School of Business and Technology, Program in Computer and Information Systems, Kenosha, WI 53141-2000. Offers MSCIS. *Entrance requirements:* For master's, GRE General Test or GMAT, 3 letters of recommendation, minimum GPA of 3.0. *Faculty research:* Distributed systems, data bases, natural language processing, event-driven systems.

University of Wisconsin–Platteville, School of Graduate Studies, College of Engineering, Mathematics and Science, Program in Computer Science, Platteville, WI 53818-3099. Offers MS. Part-time programs available. *Students:* 2 full-time (1 woman), 2 part-time (0 women), 2 international. 6 applicants, 67% accepted. In 2011, 1 master's awarded. *Degree requirements:* For master's, comprehensive exam, thesis or alternative. *Entrance requirements:* Additional exam requirements/recommendations for international students: Required—TOEFL (minimum score 500 paper-based; 61 iBT), IELTS (minimum score 6). *Application deadline:* For fall admission, 7/1 priority date for domestic students; for spring admission, 11/1 for domestic students. Applications are processed on a rolling basis. Application fee: $56. Electronic applications accepted. *Financial support:* Research assistantships with partial tuition reimbursements available. *Unit head:* Dr. Robert Hasker, Coordinator, 608-342-1561, Fax: 608-342-1965, E-mail: csse@uwplatt.edu. *Application contact:* Lisa Popp, School of Graduate Studies, 608-342-1322, Fax: 608-342-1389, E-mail: poppl@uwplatt.edu.

University of Wyoming, College of Engineering and Applied Sciences, Department of Computer Science, Laramie, WY 82070. Offers MS, PhD. Part-time programs available. Terminal master's awarded for partial completion of doctoral program. *Degree requirements:* For master's, thesis; for doctorate, thesis/dissertation. *Entrance requirements:* For master's and doctorate, GRE General Test, minimum GPA of 3.0. Additional exam requirements/recommendations for international students: Required—TOEFL (minimum score 550 paper-based; 213 computer-based), IELTS (minimum score 6). Electronic applications accepted. *Faculty research:* Fault-tolerant computing, distributed systems, knowledge representation, automated reasoning, parallel database access, formal methods.

Utah State University, School of Graduate Studies, College of Science, Department of Computer Science, Logan, UT 84322. Offers MCS, MS, PhD. Part-time and evening/weekend programs available. Postbaccalaureate distance learning degree programs offered. *Degree requirements:* For master's, thesis (for some programs), research project; for doctorate, thesis/dissertation. *Entrance requirements:* For master's, GRE General Test, GRE Subject Test, minimum GPA of 3.25, prerequisite coursework in math, 3 recommendation letters; for doctorate, GRE General Test, minimum GPA of 3.25, BS or MS. Additional exam requirements/recommendations for international students: Required—TOEFL. Electronic applications accepted. *Faculty research:* Artificial intelligence, software engineering, parallelism.

Vanderbilt University, School of Engineering, Department of Electrical Engineering and Computer Science, Program in Computer Science, Nashville, TN 37240-1001. Offers M Eng, MS, PhD. MS and PhD offered through the Graduate School. Part-time programs available. *Faculty:* 14 full-time (2 women). *Students:* 64 full-time (13 women); includes 3 minority (1 Black or African American, non-Hispanic/Latino; 1 Asian, non-Hispanic/Latino; 1 Hispanic/Latino), 33 international. Average age 26. 226 applicants, 20% accepted, 19 enrolled. In 2011, 18 master's, 12 doctorates awarded. Terminal master's awarded for partial completion of doctoral program. *Degree requirements:* For master's, thesis (for some programs); for doctorate, comprehensive exam, thesis/dissertation. *Entrance requirements:* For master's and doctorate, GRE General Test, 3 letters of recommendation. Additional exam requirements/recommendations for international students: Required—TOEFL. *Application deadline:* For fall admission, 1/15 for domestic and international students; for spring admission, 11/1 for domestic and international students. Application fee: $0. Electronic applications accepted. *Financial support:* In 2011–12, fellowships with full tuition reimbursements (averaging $30,000 per year), research assistantships with full tuition reimbursements (averaging $27,372 per year), teaching assistantships with full tuition reimbursements (averaging $24,552 per year) were awarded; career-related internships or fieldwork, institutionally sponsored loans, scholarships/grants, health care benefits, tuition waivers (full and partial), and unspecified assistantships also available. Support available to part-time students. Financial award application deadline: 1/15. *Faculty research:* Artificial intelligence, performance evaluation, databases, software engineering, computational science. *Unit head:* Dr. Daniel M. Fleetwood, Chair, 615-322-2771, Fax: 615-343-6702, E-mail: dan.fleetwood@vanderbilt.edu. *Application contact:* Dr. Xenofan Koutsoukos, Director of Graduate Studies, 615-322-8283, Fax: 615-322-0677, E-mail: eecsinfo@eecsmail.vuse.vanderbilt.edu. Web site: http://www.eecs.vuse.vanderbilt.edu/.

Villanova University, College of Engineering, Department of Electrical and Computer Engineering, Program in Computer Engineering, Villanova, PA 19085-1699. Offers computer architectures (Certificate); computer engineering (MSCPE); intelligent control systems (Certificate). Part-time and evening/weekend programs available. *Degree requirements:* For master's, thesis optional. *Entrance requirements:* For master's, GRE General Test (for applicants with degrees from foreign universities), BEE, minimum GPA of 3.0. Additional exam requirements/recommendations for international students: Required—TOEFL (minimum score 600 paper-based; 250 computer-based; 100 iBT). Electronic applications accepted. *Expenses: Tuition:* Part-time $675 per credit. Part-time tuition and fees vary according to degree level and program. *Faculty research:* Expert systems, computer vision, neural networks, image processing, computer architectures.

Villanova University, Graduate School, of Liberal Arts and Sciences, Department of Computing Sciences, Villanova, PA 19085-1699. Offers computer science (MS); software engineering (MS). Part-time and evening/weekend programs available. *Faculty:* 8 full-time (1 woman), 4 part-time/adjunct (0 women). *Students:* 75 full-time (25 women), 23 part-time (4 women); includes 9 minority (8 Asian, non-Hispanic/Latino; 1 Native Hawaiian or other Pacific Islander, non-Hispanic/Latino), 54 international. Average age 28. 49 applicants, 88% accepted, 38 enrolled. In 2011, 38 master's awarded. *Degree requirements:* For master's, thesis optional, independent study project. *Entrance requirements:* For master's, GRE, minimum GPA of 3.0. Additional exam requirements/recommendations for international students: Required—TOEFL. *Application deadline:* For fall admission, 5/1 for international students; for spring admission, 11/15 for international students. Applications are processed on a rolling basis. Application fee: $50. Electronic applications accepted. *Expenses:* Contact institution. *Financial support:* Research assistantships, scholarships/grants, and unspecified assistantships available. Financial award applicants required to submit FAFSA. *Unit head:* Dr. Robert Beck, Chair, 610-519-7310. *Application contact:* Dean, Graduate School of Liberal Arts and Sciences. Web site: http://csc.villanova.edu/academics/graduatePrograms.

Virginia Commonwealth University, Graduate School, School of Engineering, Department of Computer Science, Richmond, VA 23284-9005. Offers computer science (MS, PhD); engineering (PhD). *Degree requirements:* For master's, thesis optional. *Entrance requirements:* For master's, GRE General Test; for doctorate, GRE. Additional exam requirements/recommendations for international students: Required—TOEFL (minimum score 600 paper-based; 250 computer-based; 100 iBT). Electronic applications accepted. *Expenses:* Tuition, state resident: full-time $9133; part-time $507 per credit. Tuition, nonresident: full-time $18,777; part-time $1043 per credit. *Required fees:* $77 per credit. Tuition and fees vary according to degree level, campus/location, program and student level.

Virginia International University, School of Computer Information Systems, Fairfax, VA 22030. Offers computer science (MS); information systems (MS). Part-time programs available. *Entrance requirements:* For master's, bachelor's degree. Additional exam requirements/recommendations for international students: Required—TOEFL (minimum score 550 paper-based; 213 computer-based; 80 iBT), IELTS. Electronic applications accepted.

Virginia Polytechnic Institute and State University, VT Online, Blacksburg, VA 24061. Offers advanced transportation systems (Certificate); aerospace engineering (MS); agricultural and life sciences (MSLFS); business information systems (Graduate Certificate); career and technical education (MS); civil engineering (MS); computer engineering (M Eng, MS); decision support systems (Graduate Certificate); eLearning leadership (MA); electrical engineering (M Eng, MS); engineering administration (MEA); environmental engineering (Certificate); environmental politics and policy (Graduate Certificate); environmental sciences and engineering (MS); foundations of political analysis (Graduate Certificate); health product risk management (Graduate Certificate); industrial and systems engineering (MS); information policy and society (Graduate Certificate); information security (Graduate Certificate); information technology (MIT); instructional technology (MA); integrative STEM education (MA Ed); liberal arts (Graduate Certificate); life sciences: health product risk management (MS); natural resources (MNR, Graduate Certificate); networking (Graduate Certificate); nonprofit and nongovernmental organization management (Graduate Certificate); ocean engineering (MS); political science (MA); security studies (Graduate Certificate); software development (Graduate Certificate). *Expenses:* Tuition, state resident: full-time $10,048; part-time $558.25 per credit hour. Tuition, nonresident: full-time $19,497; part-time $1083.25 per credit hour. *Required fees:* $405 per semester. Tuition and fees vary according to course load, campus/location and program. *Application contact:* Graduate School Applications General Assistance, 540-231-8636, Fax: 540-231-2039, E-mail: gradappl@vt.edu. Web site: http://www.vto.vt.edu/.

Virginia State University, School of Graduate Studies, Research, and Outreach, School of Engineering, Science and Technology, Department of Mathematics and

Computer Science, Petersburg, VA 23806-0001. Offers computer science (MS); mathematics (MS); mathematics education (M Ed). *Degree requirements:* For master's, thesis (for some programs).

Wake Forest University, Graduate School of Arts and Sciences, Department of Computer Science, Winston-Salem, NC 27109. Offers MS. Part-time programs available. *Degree requirements:* For master's, one foreign language, thesis optional. *Entrance requirements:* For master's, GRE General Test. Additional exam requirements/recommendations for international students: Required—TOEFL (minimum score 213 computer-based; 79 iBT). Electronic applications accepted.

Washington State University, Graduate School, College of Engineering and Architecture, School of Electrical Engineering and Computer Science, Program in Computer Science, Pullman, WA 99164. Offers MS, PhD. *Faculty:* 24. *Students:* 55 full-time (15 women), 26 part-time (10 women); includes 6 minority (1 Black or African American, non-Hispanic/Latino; 3 Asian, non-Hispanic/Latino; 2 Hispanic/Latino), 46 international. Average age 28. 163 applicants, 20% accepted, 20 enrolled. In 2011, 3 master's, 6 doctorates awarded. *Degree requirements:* For master's, comprehensive exam (for some programs), thesis optional, oral exam; for doctorate, comprehensive exam, thesis/dissertation, oral exam, qualifying exam. *Entrance requirements:* For master's and doctorate, GRE General Test, GRE Subject Test, statement of purpose giving qualifications, research interests, and goals; official college transcripts; three letters of recommendation. Additional exam requirements/recommendations for international students: Required—TOEFL (minimum score 520 paper-based; 190 computer-based), IELTS. *Application deadline:* For fall admission, 1/10 priority date for domestic students, 1/10 for international students; for spring admission, 7/1 for domestic and international students. Applications are processed on a rolling basis. Application fee: $75. *Financial support:* In 2011–12, 2 fellowships (averaging $2,500 per year), 18 research assistantships with full and partial tuition reimbursements (averaging $18,204 per year), 24 teaching assistantships with full and partial tuition reimbursements (averaging $18,204 per year) were awarded; career-related internships or fieldwork, Federal Work-Study, institutionally sponsored loans, tuition waivers (partial), and teaching associateships also available. Financial award application deadline: 2/10; financial award applicants required to submit FAFSA. *Faculty research:* Networks, software engineering, database systems, computer graphics, algorithmics. *Total annual research expenditures:* $3.9 million. *Unit head:* Dr. Anjan Bose, Director, 509-335-1147, Fax: 509-335-3818, E-mail: bose@wsu.edu. *Application contact:* Graduate School Admissions, 800-GRADWSU, Fax: 509-335-1949, E-mail: gradsch@wsu.edu. Web site: http://www.eecs.wsu.edu/.

Washington State University Tri-Cities, Graduate Programs, College of Engineering and Architecture, Richland, WA 99352-1671. Offers computer science (MS, PhD); electrical engineering (MS, PhD); mechanical engineering (MS, PhD). Part-time programs available. *Faculty:* 28. *Students:* 20 full-time (5 women), 37 part-time (10 women); includes 6 minority (1 Black or African American, non-Hispanic/Latino; 2 Asian, non-Hispanic/Latino; 1 Hispanic/Latino; 2 Two or more races, non-Hispanic/Latino), 4 international. Average age 27. 27 applicants, 33% accepted, 6 enrolled. *Degree requirements:* For master's, comprehensive exam, thesis (for some programs); for doctorate, comprehensive exam, thesis/dissertation, oral exam. *Entrance requirements:* For master's and doctorate, GRE, minimum GPA of 3.0, 3 letters of recommendation. Additional exam requirements/recommendations for international students: Required—TOEFL (minimum score 550 paper-based; 213 computer-based). *Application deadline:* For fall admission, 1/10 priority date for domestic students, 1/10 for international students; for spring admission, 7/1 priority date for domestic students, 7/1 for international students. Application fee: $75. *Financial support:* Application deadline: 3/1. *Faculty research:* Positive ion track structure, biological systems computer simulations. *Unit head:* Dr. Ali Saberi, Chair, 509-372-7178, E-mail: sidra@eecs.wsu.edu. *Application contact:* Dr. Scott Hudson, Associate Director, 509-372-7254, Fax: 509-335-1949, E-mail: hudson@tricity.wsu.edu. Web site: http://cea.tricity.wsu.edu/.

Washington State University Vancouver, Graduate Programs, School of Engineering and Computer Science, Vancouver, WA 98686. Offers computer science (MS); mechanical engineering (MS). Part-time programs available. *Faculty:* 9. *Students:* 22 full-time (2 women), 5 part-time (1 woman); includes 2 minority (both Asian, non-Hispanic/Latino), 10 international. Average age 29. 48 applicants, 33% accepted, 13 enrolled. *Degree requirements:* For master's, comprehensive exam (for some programs), thesis, research project. *Entrance requirements:* For master's, minimum GPA of 3.0, 3 letters of recommendation with evaluation forms, resume. Additional exam requirements/recommendations for international students: Required—TOEFL (minimum score 550 paper-based). *Application deadline:* For fall admission, 1/10 priority date for domestic students, 1/10 for international students; for spring admission, 7/1 priority date for domestic students, 7/1 for international students. Applications are processed on a rolling basis. Application fee: $75. *Financial support:* In 2011–12, research assistantships with full tuition reimbursements (averaging $14,634 per year), teaching assistantships with full tuition reimbursements (averaging $13,383 per year) were awarded; health care benefits and unspecified assistantships also available. Financial award application deadline: 2/15. *Faculty research:* Software design, artificial intelligence, sensor networks, robotics, nanotechnology. *Total annual research expenditures:* $3.4 million. *Unit head:* Dr. Hakan Gurocak, Director, 360-546-9637, Fax: 360-546-9438, E-mail: hgurocak@vancouver.wsu.edu. *Application contact:* Peggy Moore, Academic Coordinator, 360-546-9638, Fax: 360-546-9438, E-mail: moorep@vancouver.wsu.edu. Web site: http://ecs.vancouver.wsu.edu/.

Washington University in St. Louis, School of Engineering and Applied Science, Department of Computer Science and Engineering, St. Louis, MO 63130-4899. Offers computer engineering (MS, PhD); computer science (MS, PhD); computer science and engineering (M Eng). Part-time programs available. Terminal master's awarded for partial completion of doctoral program. *Degree requirements:* For master's, thesis optional; for doctorate, thesis/dissertation. *Entrance requirements:* For doctorate, GRE General Test. Additional exam requirements/recommendations for international students: Required—TOEFL. Electronic applications accepted. *Faculty research:* Artificial intelligence, computational genomics, computer and systems architecture, media and machines, networking and communication, software systems.

Wayne State University, College of Engineering, Department of Computer Science, Detroit, MI 48202. Offers computer science (MS, PhD); scientific computing (Certificate). *Students:* 104 full-time (30 women), 38 part-time (9 women); includes 25 minority (7 Black or African American, non-Hispanic/Latino; 1 American Indian or Alaska Native, non-Hispanic/Latino; 17 Asian, non-Hispanic/Latino), 94 international. Average age 30. 222 applicants, 49% accepted, 40 enrolled. In 2011, 17 master's, 7 doctorates awarded. *Degree requirements:* For master's, thesis (for some programs); for doctorate, thesis/dissertation. *Entrance requirements:* For master's, GRE (minimum scores: 450 Verbal, 750 Quantitative, 4.5 Analytical writing), minimum GPA of 3.0, three letters of recommendation, adequate preparation in computer science and mathematics courses, personal statement; for doctorate, GRE (minimum scores: 450 Verbal, 750 Quantitative, 4.5 Analytical writing), minimum GPA of 3.3 in most recent degree; three letters of recommendation; personal statement; adequate preparation in computer science and mathematics courses. Additional exam requirements/recommendations for international students: Required—TOEFL (minimum score 550 paper-based; 213 computer-based); Recommended—TWE (minimum score 5.5). *Application deadline:* For fall admission, 7/1 priority date for domestic students, 5/1 for international students; for winter admission, 11/1 priority date for domestic students, 9/1 for international students; for spring admission, 3/15 priority date for domestic students, 1/2 for international students. Applications are processed on a rolling basis. Application fee: $50. Electronic applications accepted. *Expenses:* Tuition, state resident: part-time $512.85 per credit. Tuition, nonresident: part-time $1132.65 per credit. *Required fees:* $26.60 per credit. $199.65 per semester. Tuition and fees vary according to course load and program. *Financial support:* In 2011–12, 73 students received support, including 7 fellowships with tuition reimbursements available (averaging $26,046 per year), 28 research assistantships with tuition reimbursements available (averaging $19,562 per year), 25 teaching assistantships with tuition reimbursements available (averaging $17,391 per year); career-related internships or fieldwork, Federal Work-Study, scholarships/grants, health care benefits, and unspecified assistantships also available. *Faculty research:* Software engineering, databases, bioinformatics, artificial intelligence, networking, distributed and parallel computing, security, graphics, visualizations. *Total annual research expenditures:* $1.5 million. *Unit head:* Wolfson Seymour, Chair, 313-577-2478, E-mail: wolfson@cs.wayne.edu. *Application contact:* Loren Schwiebert, Associate Professor, 313-577-5474, E-mail: loren@cs.wayne.edu. Web site: http://www.cs.wayne.edu/.

Webster University, George Herbert Walker School of Business and Technology, Department of Mathematics and Computer Science, St. Louis, MO 63119-3194. Offers computer science/distributed systems (MS, Certificate); decision support systems (Certificate); web services (Certificate). Part-time and evening/weekend programs available. Postbaccalaureate distance learning degree programs offered (no on-campus study). *Entrance requirements:* For master's, 36 hours of graduate course work. Additional exam requirements/recommendations for international students: Required—TOEFL. *Expenses: Tuition:* Full-time $10,890; part-time $605 per credit hour. Tuition and fees vary according to campus/location and program. *Faculty research:* Databases, computer information systems networks, operating systems, computer architecture.

Wesleyan University, Graduate Programs, Department of Mathematics and Computer Science, Middletown, CT 06459. Offers MA, PhD. Terminal master's awarded for partial completion of doctoral program. *Degree requirements:* For master's, one foreign language, thesis; for doctorate, 2 foreign languages, thesis/dissertation. *Entrance requirements:* For master's, GRE General Test, GRE Subject Test; for doctorate, GRE Subject Test. Additional exam requirements/recommendations for international students: Required—TOEFL. Electronic applications accepted. *Faculty research:* Topology, analysis.

West Chester University of Pennsylvania, College of Arts and Sciences, Department of Computer Science, West Chester, PA 19383. Offers computer science (MS); computer security (Certificate); information systems (Certificate); Web technology (Certificate). Part-time and evening/weekend programs available. *Faculty:* 7 part-time/adjunct (1 woman). *Students:* 5 full-time (0 women), 18 part-time (1 woman); includes 1 minority (Black or African American, non-Hispanic/Latino), 6 international. Average age 27. 37 applicants, 49% accepted, 13 enrolled. In 2011, 3 master's, 1 other advanced degree awarded. *Degree requirements:* For master's, thesis optional. *Entrance requirements:* For master's, GRE, two letters of recommendation; for Certificate, BS. Additional exam requirements/recommendations for international students: Required—TOEFL (minimum score 550 paper-based; 213 computer-based; 80 iBT). *Application deadline:* For fall admission, 4/15 priority date for domestic students, 3/15 for international students; for spring admission, 10/15 priority date for domestic students, 9/1 for international students. Applications are processed on a rolling basis. Application fee: $45. Electronic applications accepted. *Expenses:* Tuition, state resident: full-time $7488; part-time $416 per credit. Tuition, nonresident: full-time $11,232; part-time $624 per credit. *Required fees:* $1784.64; $67.59 per credit. Tuition and fees vary according to program. *Financial support:* Unspecified assistantships available. Support available to part-time students. Financial award application deadline: 2/15; financial award applicants required to submit FAFSA. *Faculty research:* Automata theory, compilers, non well-founded sets, security in sensor and mobile ad-hoc networks, intrusion detection, security and trust in pervasive computing, economic modeling of security protocols. *Unit head:* Dr. James Fabrey, Chair, 610-436-2204, E-mail: jfabrey@wcupa.edu. *Application contact:* Dr. Afrand Agah, Graduate Coordinator, 610-430-4419, E-mail: aagah@wcupa.edu. Web site: http://www.cs.wcupa.edu/.

Western Carolina University, Graduate School, College of Arts and Sciences, Department of Mathematics and Computer Science, Cullowhee, NC 28723. Offers applied mathematics (MS). Part-time and evening/weekend programs available. *Students:* 11 full-time (6 women), 7 part-time (2 women); includes 1 minority (Two or more races, non-Hispanic/Latino). Average age 27. 16 applicants, 88% accepted, 9 enrolled. In 2011, 7 master's awarded. *Degree requirements:* For master's, thesis or alternative. *Entrance requirements:* For master's, GRE General Test, appropriate undergraduate degree, 3 letters of recommendation. Additional exam requirements/recommendations for international students: Required—TOEFL (minimum score 550 paper-based; 270 computer-based; 79 iBT). *Application deadline:* For fall admission, 5/1 priority date for domestic students; for spring admission, 9/1 priority date for domestic students. Applications are processed on a rolling basis. Application fee: $50. *Expenses:* Tuition, state resident: full-time $3348. Tuition, nonresident: full-time $12,933. *Required fees:* $3155. *Financial support:* Fellowships, research assistantships with full and partial tuition reimbursements, teaching assistantships with full and partial tuition reimbursements, career-related internships or fieldwork, institutionally sponsored loans, scholarships/grants, and unspecified assistantships available. Financial award application deadline: 3/31; financial award applicants required to submit FAFSA. *Unit head:* Dr. Tuval Foguel, Department Head, 828-227-3831, Fax: 828-227-7240, E-mail: tsfoguel@email.wcu.edu. *Application contact:* Admissions Specialist for Applied Mathematics, 828-227-7398, Fax: 828-227-7480, E-mail: gradsch@email.wcu.edu. Web site: http://www.cs.wcu.edu/.

Western Illinois University, School of Graduate Studies, College of Business and Technology, School of Computer Science, Macomb, IL 61455-1390. Offers MS. Part-time programs available. *Students:* 67 full-time (16 women), 16 part-time (0 women); includes 7 minority (6 Black or African American, non-Hispanic/Latino; 1 Asian, non-Hispanic/Latino), 56 international. Average age 26. 168 applicants, 77% accepted. In 2011, 30 master's awarded. *Degree requirements:* For master's, thesis or alternative. *Entrance requirements:* For master's, proficiency in Java. Additional exam requirements/recommendations for international students: Required—TOEFL (minimum score 550 paper-based; 213 computer-based; 80 iBT). *Application deadline:* Applications are processed on a rolling basis. Application fee: $30. Electronic applications accepted. *Expenses:* Tuition, state resident: part-time $281.16 per credit hour. Tuition, nonresident: part-time $562.32 per credit hour. Part-time tuition and fees vary according to campus/location and reciprocity agreements. *Financial support:* In 2011–12, 18 students received support, including 8 research assistantships with full tuition reimbursements available (averaging $7,360 per year), 10 teaching assistantships with full tuition reimbursements available (averaging $8,480 per year). Financial award applicants required to submit FAFSA. *Unit head:* Dr. Dennis DeVolder, Program Director, 309-298-1452. *Application contact:* Dr. Nancy Parsons, Interim Associate Provost and Director of Graduate Studies, 309-298-1806, Fax: 309-298-2345, E-mail: grad-office@wiu.edu. Web site: http://wiu.edu/computerscience.

Western Kentucky University, Graduate Studies, Ogden College of Science and Engineering, Department of Mathematics and Computer Science, Bowling Green, KY 42101. Offers computational mathematics (MS); computer science (MS); mathematics (MA, MS). *Degree requirements:* For master's, comprehensive exam, thesis optional, written exam. *Entrance requirements:* For master's, GRE General Test, minimum GPA of 2.75. Additional exam requirements/recommendations for international students: Required—TOEFL (minimum score 555 paper-based; 213 computer-based; 79 iBT). *Faculty research:* Differential equations numerical analysis, probability statistics, algebra, typology, knot theory.

Western Michigan University, Graduate College, College of Engineering and Applied Sciences, Department of Computer Science, Kalamazoo, MI 49008. Offers MS, PhD. *Degree requirements:* For master's, thesis optional, oral exams; for doctorate, 2 foreign languages, thesis/dissertation. *Entrance requirements:* For master's and doctorate, GRE General Test.

Western Washington University, Graduate School, College of Sciences and Technology, Department of Computer Science, Bellingham, WA 98225-5996. Offers MS. Part-time programs available. *Degree requirements:* For master's, thesis optional, project. *Entrance requirements:* For master's, GRE General Test, minimum GPA of 3.0 in last 60 semester hours or last 90 quarter hours. Additional exam requirements/recommendations for international students: Required—TOEFL (minimum score 567 paper-based; 227 computer-based). Electronic applications accepted. *Faculty research:* Distributed operating systems, data mining, machine learning, robotics, information retrieval, graphics and visualization, parallel and distributed computing.

West Virginia University, College of Engineering and Mineral Resources, Lane Department of Computer Science and Electrical Engineering, Program in Computer Science, Morgantown, WV 26506. Offers MSCS, PhD. Part-time programs available. *Degree requirements:* For master's, thesis; for doctorate, comprehensive exam, thesis/dissertation. *Entrance requirements:* For master's, GRE General Test, letters of recommendation; for doctorate, GRE General Test, GRE Subject Test, MS in computer science, letters of recommendation. Additional exam requirements/recommendations for international students: Required—TOEFL. *Faculty research:* Artificial intelligence, knowledge-based simulation, data communications, mathematical computations, software engineering.

Wichita State University, Graduate School, College of Engineering, Department of Electrical Engineering and Computer Science, Wichita, KS 67260. Offers computer networking (MS); computer science (MS); electrical engineering (MS, PhD). Part-time and evening/weekend programs available. *Expenses:* Tuition, state resident: full-time $4746; part-time $263.65 per credit. Tuition, nonresident: full-time $11,669; part-time $648.30 per credit. *Unit head:* Dr. John Watkins, Chair, 316-978-3156, Fax: 316-978-5408, E-mail: john.watkins@wichita.edu. *Application contact:* Carrie C. Henderson, Admissions Coordinator, 316-978-3095, Fax: 316-978-3253, E-mail: carrie.henderson@wichita.edu. Web site: http://www.wichita.edu/.

Winston-Salem State University, Program in Computer Science and Information Technology, Winston-Salem, NC 27110-0003. Offers MS. Part-time programs available. *Degree requirements:* For master's, thesis optional. *Entrance requirements:* For master's, GRE, resume. Electronic applications accepted. *Faculty research:* Artificial intelligence, network protocols, software engineering.

Worcester Polytechnic Institute, Graduate Studies and Research, Department of Computer Science, Worcester, MA 01609-2280. Offers computer and communications networks (MS); computer science (MS, PhD, Advanced Certificate, Graduate Certificate); robotics engineering (MS, PhD). Part-time and evening/weekend programs available. *Faculty:* 21 full-time (4 women), 5 part-time/adjunct (0 women). *Students:* 59 full-time (12 women), 50 part-time (6 women); includes 9 minority (1 Black or African American, non-Hispanic/Latino; 5 Asian, non-Hispanic/Latino; 1 Hispanic/Latino; 2 Two or more races, non-Hispanic/Latino), 51 international. 339 applicants, 56% accepted, 41 enrolled. In 2011, 29 master's, 2 doctorates awarded. Terminal master's awarded for partial completion of doctoral program. *Degree requirements:* For master's, thesis optional; for doctorate, comprehensive exam, thesis/dissertation. *Entrance requirements:* For master's, GRE General Test, 3 letters of recommendation; for doctorate, GRE General Test, 3 letters of recommendation, statement of purpose. Additional exam requirements/recommendations for international students: Required—TOEFL (minimum score 563 paper-based; 223 computer-based; 84 iBT), IELTS (minimum score 7). *Application deadline:* For fall admission, 1/1 priority date for domestic students, 1/1 for international students; for spring admission, 10/1 priority date for domestic students, 10/1 for international students. Applications are processed on a rolling basis. Application fee: $70. Electronic applications accepted. *Financial support:* Research assistantships, teaching assistantships, career-related internships or fieldwork, institutionally sponsored loans, scholarships/grants, and unspecified assistantships available. Financial award application deadline: 1/1; financial award applicants required to submit FAFSA. *Faculty research:* Computer networks and distributed systems, databases and data mining, artificial intelligence and robotics, computer graphics and visualization, applied logic and security. *Unit head:* Dr. Craig Wills, Department Head, 508-831-5357, Fax: 508-831-5776, E-mail: cew@wpi.edu. *Application contact:* Dr. Elke Rundensteiner, Graduate Coordinator, 508-831-5357, Fax: 508-831-5776, E-mail: rundenst@wpi.edu. Web site: http://www.cs.wpi.edu/.

Wright State University, School of Graduate Studies, College of Engineering and Computer Science, Department of Computer Science and Engineering, Computer Science Program, Dayton, OH 45435. Offers MS. *Degree requirements:* For master's, thesis optional. *Entrance requirements:* For master's, GRE General Test, minimum GPA of 3.0 in major, 2.7 overall. Additional exam requirements/recommendations for international students: Required—TOEFL.

Wright State University, School of Graduate Studies, College of Engineering and Computer Science, Department of Computer Science and Engineering, Program in Computer Science and Engineering, Dayton, OH 45435. Offers PhD. *Degree requirements:* For doctorate, thesis/dissertation, candidacy and general exams. *Entrance requirements:* For doctorate, GRE General Test, minimum GPA of 3.3. Additional exam requirements/recommendations for international students: Required—TOEFL.

Yale University, Graduate School of Arts and Sciences, Department of Computer Science, New Haven, CT 06520. Offers MS, PhD. *Degree requirements:* For doctorate, thesis/dissertation. *Entrance requirements:* For doctorate, GRE General Test, GRE Subject Test.

York University, Faculty of Graduate Studies, Faculty of Science and Engineering, Program in Computer Science, Toronto, ON M3J 1P3, Canada. Offers M Sc, PhD. *Degree requirements:* For master's, thesis or alternative; for doctorate, comprehensive exam, thesis/dissertation, internship or practicum. Electronic applications accepted.

Youngstown State University, Graduate School, College of Science, Technology, Engineering and Mathematics, Department of Computer Science and Information Systems, Youngstown, OH 44555-0001. Offers computing and information systems (MCIS). Part-time programs available. *Degree requirements:* For master's, thesis or capstone project. *Entrance requirements:* For master's, GRE or GMAT. Additional exam requirements/recommendations for international students: Required—TOEFL (minimum score 550 paper-based; 213 computer-based). *Faculty research:* Networking, computational science, graphics and visualization, database and data mining, biometrics, artificial intelligence, online learning environments.

Youngstown State University, Graduate School, College of Science, Technology, Engineering and Mathematics, Department of Mathematics and Statistics, Youngstown, OH 44555-0001. Offers applied mathematics (MS); computer science (MS); secondary mathematics (MS); statistics (MS). Part-time programs available. *Degree requirements:* For master's, comprehensive exam, thesis optional. *Entrance requirements:* For master's, minimum GPA of 2.7 in computer science and mathematics. Additional exam requirements/recommendations for international students: Required—TOEFL. *Faculty research:* Regression analysis, numerical analysis, statistics, Markov chain, topology and fuzzy sets.

Database Systems

Boston University, Metropolitan College, Department of Computer Science, Boston, MA 02215. Offers computer information systems (MS), including computer networks, database management and business intelligence, health informatics, IT project management, security, Web application development; computer science (MS), including computer networks, security; telecommunications (MS), including security. Evening/weekend programs available. Postbaccalaureate distance learning degree programs offered. *Faculty:* 12 full-time (2 women), 28 part-time/adjunct (2 women). *Students:* 25 full-time (6 women), 732 part-time (167 women); includes 208 minority (51 Black or African American, non-Hispanic/Latino; 1 American Indian or Alaska Native, non-Hispanic/Latino; 104 Asian, non-Hispanic/Latino; 43 Hispanic/Latino; 1 Native Hawaiian or other Pacific Islander, non-Hispanic/Latino; 8 Two or more races, non-Hispanic/Latino), 86 international. Average age 35. 260 applicants, 67% accepted, 143 enrolled. In 2011, 143 master's awarded. *Degree requirements:* For master's, thesis optional. *Entrance requirements:* For master's, 3 letters of recommendation, professional resume. Additional exam requirements/recommendations for international students: Required—TOEFL (minimum score 550 paper-based; 213 computer-based; 80 iBT). *Application deadline:* For fall admission, 6/1 for international students; for spring admission, 10/1 for international students. Applications are processed on a rolling basis. Application fee: $70. Electronic applications accepted. *Expenses: Tuition:* Full-time $40,848; part-time $1276 per credit hour. *Required fees:* $572; $286 per semester. *Financial support:* In 2011–12, 9 research assistantships (averaging $5,000 per year) were awarded; career-related internships or fieldwork and unspecified assistantships also available. Support available to part-time students. Financial award applicants required to submit FAFSA. *Faculty research:* Medical informatics, Web technologies, telecom and networks, security and forensics, software engineering, programming languages, multimedia and AI, information systems and IT project management. *Unit head:* Dr. Lubomir Chitkushev, Chairman, 617-353-2566, Fax: 617-353-2367, E-mail: csinfo@bu.edu. *Application contact:* Kim Richards, Program Coordinator, 617-353-2566, Fax: 617-353-2367, E-mail: kimrich@bu.edu. Web site: http://www.bu.edu/csmet/.

Colorado Technical University Colorado Springs, Graduate Studies, Program in Computer Science, Colorado Springs, CO 80907-3896. Offers computer science (DCS); computer systems security (MSCS); database systems (MSCS); software engineering (MSCS). Part-time and evening/weekend programs available. Postbaccalaureate distance learning degree programs offered. *Degree requirements:* For master's, thesis or alternative; for doctorate, thesis/dissertation. *Entrance requirements:* For doctorate, minimum graduate GPA of 3.0, 5 years of related work experience. *Faculty research:* Software engineering, systems engineering.

Colorado Technical University Denver South, Program in Computer Science, Aurora, CO 80014. Offers computer systems security (MSCS); database systems (MSCS); software engineering (MSCS). Part-time and evening/weekend programs available. *Degree requirements:* For master's, thesis or alternative. *Entrance requirements:* For master's, minimum undergraduate GPA of 3.0, resume.

Ferris State University, College of Business, Big Rapids, MI 49307. Offers business intelligence (MBA); design and innovation management (MBA); incident response (MBA); information security and intelligence (MS, MSISM), including business intelligence (MS), incident response (MSISM), project management (MSISM); management tools and concepts (MBA); project management (MBA). *Accreditation:* ACBSP. Part-time and evening/weekend programs available. Postbaccalaureate distance learning degree programs offered (minimal on-campus study). *Faculty:* 9 full-time (3 women), 2 part-time/adjunct (both women). *Students:* 22 full-time (7 women), 98 part-time (50 women); includes 14 minority (3 Black or African American, non-Hispanic/Latino; 4 American Indian or Alaska Native, non-Hispanic/Latino; 2 Asian, non-Hispanic/Latino; 2 Hispanic/Latino; 3 Two or more races, non-Hispanic/Latino), 3 international. Average age 34. 58 applicants, 79% accepted, 10 enrolled. In 2011, 56 master's awarded. *Degree requirements:* For master's, comprehensive exam, thesis (for MSISM). *Entrance requirements:* For master's, GRE or GMAT (waived if GPA is 3.5 or better), minimum GPA of 3.0 in junior/senior level classes, 2.75 overall; writing sample; 3 letters of reference; resume. Additional exam requirements/recommendations for international students: Required—TOEFL (minimum score 500 paper-based; 173 computer-based; 67 iBT). *Application deadline:* For fall admission, 7/1 priority date for domestic students, 6/15 for international students; for winter admission, 11/1 priority date for domestic students, 10/15 for international students; for spring admission, 3/1 priority date for domestic students, 2/15 for international students. Applications are processed on a rolling basis. Application fee: $30. Electronic applications accepted. Application fee is waived when completed online. *Financial support:* Career-related internships or fieldwork, Federal Work-Study, scholarships/grants, and unspecified assistantships available. Support available to part-time students. Financial award application deadline: 3/15; financial award applicants required to submit FAFSA. *Faculty research:* Quality improvement, client/server end-user computing, information management and policy, security, digital forensics. *Unit head:* Dr. David Steenstra, Department Chair, 231-591-2168, Fax: 231-591-3548, E-mail: yosts@ferris.edu. *Application contact:* Shannon Yost, Department Secretary, 231-591-2168, Fax: 231-591-3548, E-mail: yosts@ferris.edu. Web site: http://cbgp.ferris.edu/.

George Mason University, Volgenau School of Engineering, Department of Computer Science, Fairfax, VA 22030. Offers computer games technology (Certificate); computer networking (Certificate); computer science (MS, PhD); database management (Certificate); electronic commerce (Certificate); foundations of information systems (Certificate); information engineering (Certificate); information security and assurance (MS, Certificate); information systems (MS); intelligent agents (Certificate); software architecture (Certificate); software engineering (MS, Certificate); software engineering for C41 (Certificate); Web-based software engineering (Certificate). MS program offered jointly with Old Dominion University, University of Virginia, Virginia Commonwealth University, and Virginia Polytechnic Institute and State University. *Faculty:* 40 full-time (9 women), 17 part-time/adjunct (0 women). *Students:* 208 full-time (52 women), 357 part-time (75 women); includes 98 minority (17 Black or African American, non-Hispanic/Latino; 63 Asian, non-Hispanic/Latino; 14 Hispanic/Latino; 4 Two or more races, non-Hispanic/Latino), 205 international. Average age 30. 882 applicants, 52% accepted, 137 enrolled. In 2011, 164 master's, 5 doctorates, 28 other advanced degrees awarded. *Degree requirements:* For master's, thesis optional; for doctorate, comprehensive exam, thesis/dissertation. *Entrance requirements:* For master's, GRE, proof of financial support; 2 official college transcripts; resume; self-evaluation form; official bank statement; photocopy of passport; 3 letters of recommendation; baccalaureate degree related to computer science; minimum GPA of 3.0 in last 2 years of undergraduate work; 1 year beyond 1st-year calculus; personal goals statement; for doctorate, GRE, personal goals statement; 2 official copies of transcripts; self-evaluation form; 3 letters of recommendation; photocopy of passport; proof of financial support; official bank statement; resume; 4-year baccalaureate degree with strong background in computer science. Additional exam requirements/recommendations for international students: Required—TOEFL (minimum score 575 paper-based; 230 computer-based; 88 iBT), IELTS, Pearson Test of English. *Application deadline:* For fall admission, 1/15 priority date for domestic students; for spring admission, 8/15 priority date for domestic students. Application fee: $65 ($80 for international students). Electronic applications accepted. *Expenses:* Tuition, state resident: full-time $8750; part-time $364.58 per credit. Tuition, nonresident: full-time $24,092; part-time $1003.83 per credit. *Required fees:* $2514; $104.75 per credit. *Financial support:* In 2011–12, 100 students received support, including 3 fellowships (averaging $18,000 per year), 50 research assistantships (averaging $15,232 per year), 47 teaching assistantships (averaging $11,675 per year); career-related internships or fieldwork, Federal Work-Study, scholarships/grants, unspecified assistantships, and health care benefits (full-time research or teaching assistantship recipients) also available. Support available to part-time students. Financial award application deadline: 3/1; financial award applicants required to submit FAFSA. *Faculty research:* Artificial intelligence, image processing/graphics, parallel/distributed systems, software engineering systems. *Total annual research expenditures:* $1.9 million. *Unit head:* Sanjeev Setia, Chair, 703-993-4098, Fax: 703-993-1710, E-mail: setia@gmu.edu. *Application contact:* Michele Pieper, Administrative Assistant, 703-993-9483, Fax: 703-993-1710, E-mail: mpieper@gmu.edu. Web site: http://cs.gmu.edu/.

Metropolitan State University, College of Management, St. Paul, MN 55106-5000. Offers business administration (MBA, DBA); database administration (Graduate Certificate); healthcare information technology management (Graduate Certificate); information assurance security (Graduate Certificate); management information systems (MMIS); MIS generalist (Graduate Certificate); MIS systems analysis and design (Graduate Certificate); project management (Graduate Certificate); public and nonprofit administration (MPNA). Part-time and evening/weekend programs available. *Students:* 63 full-time (41 women), 409 part-time (192 women); includes 94 minority (38 Black or African American, non-Hispanic/Latino; 33 Asian, non-Hispanic/Latino; 14 Hispanic/Latino; 9 Two or more races, non-Hispanic/Latino), 61 international. Average age 35. *Degree requirements:* For master's, thesis optional, computer language (MMIS). *Entrance requirements:* For master's, GMAT (MBA), resume. Additional exam requirements/recommendations for international students: Required—TOEFL (minimum score 550 paper-based; 213 computer-based). *Application deadline:* For fall admission, 7/15 for international students; for winter admission, 11/15 for international students; for spring admission, 3/15 for international students. Applications are processed on a rolling basis. Application fee: $20. Electronic applications accepted. *Expenses:* Tuition, state resident: full-time $5799.06; part-time $322.17 per credit. Tuition, nonresident: full-time $11,411; part-time $633.92 per credit. Tuition and fees vary according to degree level, program and reciprocity agreements. *Financial support:* Research assistantships with partial tuition reimbursements, career-related internships or fieldwork, and Federal Work-Study available. Support available to part-time students. Financial award applicants required to submit FAFSA. *Faculty research:* Yugoslav economic system, workers' cooperatives, participative management and job enrichment, global business systems. *Unit head:* Dr. Paul Huo, Dean, 612-659-7271, Fax: 612-659-7268, E-mail: paul.huo@metrostate.edu. Web site: http://choose.metrostate.edu/comgradprograms.

Minnesota State University Mankato, College of Graduate Studies, College of Science, Engineering and Technology, Department of Information Systems and Technology, Mankato, MN 56001. Offers database technologies (Certificate); information technology (MS). *Students:* 9 full-time (1 woman), 22 part-time (4 women). *Degree requirements:* For master's, comprehensive exam, thesis or alternative. *Entrance requirements:* For master's, GRE General Test, minimum GPA of 3.0 during previous 2 years. Additional exam requirements/recommendations for international students: Required—TOEFL (minimum score 550 paper-based; 213 computer-based; 80 iBT). *Application deadline:* For fall admission, 7/1 priority date for domestic students; for spring admission, 11/1 for domestic students. Applications are processed on a rolling basis. Electronic applications accepted. *Financial support:* Research assistantships with full tuition reimbursements, teaching assistantships with full tuition reimbursements, and unspecified assistantships available. Financial award application deadline: 3/15; financial award applicants required to submit FAFSA. *Unit head:* Dr. Mahbubur Syed,

Graduate Coordinator, 507-389-3226. *Application contact:* 507-389-2321, E-mail: grad@mnsu.edu. Web site: http://cset.mnsu.edu/ist/.

New York University, School of Continuing and Professional Studies, Division of Programs in Business, Graduate Programs in Management and Systems, New York, NY 10012-1019. Offers core business competencies (Advanced Certificate); database technologies (MS); enterprise and risk management (Advanced Certificate); enterprise risk management (MS); information technologies (Advanced Certificate); strategy and leadership (MS, Advanced Certificate); systems management (MS). Part-time and evening/weekend programs available. Postbaccalaureate distance learning degree programs offered (no on-campus study). *Faculty:* 2 full-time (0 women), 43 part-time/adjunct (7 women). *Students:* 30 full-time (15 women), 222 part-time (89 women); includes 49 minority (14 Black or African American, non-Hispanic/Latino; 20 Asian, non-Hispanic/Latino; 14 Hispanic/Latino; 1 Two or more races, non-Hispanic/Latino), 39 international. Average age 35. 178 applicants, 54% accepted, 50 enrolled. In 2011, 69 master's, 15 other advanced degrees awarded. *Degree requirements:* For master's, thesis, capstone project. *Entrance requirements:* For master's, GRE/GMAT only upon request, relevant professional work, internship or volunteer experience. Additional exam requirements/recommendations for international students: Required—TOEFL (minimum score 600 paper-based; 250 computer-based; 100 iBT), IELTS (minimum score 7). *Application deadline:* For fall admission, 2/1 priority date for domestic students, 2/1 for international students; for spring admission, 10/15 priority date for domestic students, 8/15 for international students. Applications are processed on a rolling basis. Application fee: $150. Electronic applications accepted. *Financial support:* In 2011–12, 94 students received support, including 94 fellowships (averaging $1,704 per year). *Unit head:* Anthony Pennings, Visiting Clinical Assistant Professor. *Application contact:* Admissions Office, 212-998-7100, E-mail: scps.gradadmissions@nyu.edu. Web site: http://www.scps.nyu.edu/areas-of-study/information-technology/.

Northwestern University, School of Continuing Studies, Program in Information Systems, Evanston, IL 60208. Offers database and Internet technologies (MS); information systems management (MS); information systems security (MS); software project management and development (MS).

Regis University, College for Professional Studies, School of Computer and Information Sciences, Denver, CO 80221-1099. Offers database administration with Oracle (Certificate); database development (Certificate); database technologies (M Sc); enterprise Java software development (Certificate); enterprise resource planning (Certificate); executive information technologies (Certificate); information assurance (M Sc, Certificate); information technology management (M Sc); software engineering (M Sc, Certificate); software engineering and database technologies (M Sc); storage area networks (Certificate); systems engineering (M Sc, Certificate). Offered at Boulder Campus, Northwest Denver Campus, Southeast Denver Campus, Fort Collins Campus, Colorado Springs Campus, and Broomfield Campus. Part-time and evening/weekend programs available. Postbaccalaureate distance learning degree programs offered (no on-campus study). *Degree requirements:* For master's, thesis, final research project. *Entrance requirements:* For master's, 2 years of related experience, resume, interview; for Certificate, 2 years of related experience, resumé. Additional exam requirements/recommendations for international students: Required—TOEFL (minimum score 213 computer-based), TWE (minimum score 5) or university-based test. Electronic applications accepted. *Expenses:* Contact institution. *Faculty research:* Secure Virtual Laboratory Architecture, Joint IA project with W2C06 Institute, Information Policy, OLTP and OLAP Technologies, knowledge management, software architectures.

Rochester Institute of Technology, Graduate Enrollment Services, B. Thomas Golisano College of Computing and Information Sciences, Department of Information Technology, Rochester, NY 14623-5603. Offers database administration (AC); human-computer interaction (MS); information assurance (AC); information technology (MS); interactive multimedia development (AC); medical informatics (MS). Part-time programs available. *Students:* 74 full-time (16 women), 97 part-time (19 women); includes 20 minority (8 Black or African American, non-Hispanic/Latino; 1 American Indian or Alaska Native, non-Hispanic/Latino; 4 Asian, non-Hispanic/Latino; 6 Hispanic/Latino; 1 Two or more races, non-Hispanic/Latino), 78 international. Average age 29. 187 applicants, 60% accepted, 43 enrolled. In 2011, 29 master's, 4 other advanced degrees awarded. *Degree requirements:* For master's, thesis or project. *Entrance requirements:* For master's, GRE, minimum GPA of 3.0. Additional exam requirements/recommendations for international students: Required—TOEFL (minimum score 570 paper-based; 230 computer-based; 99 iBT) or IELTS (minimum score 6.5). *Application deadline:* Applications are processed on a rolling basis. Application fee: $50. Electronic applications accepted. *Expenses:* Tuition: Full-time $34,659; part-time $963 per credit hour. *Required fees:* $228; $76 per quarter. *Financial support:* Research assistantships with partial tuition reimbursements, teaching assistantships with partial tuition reimbursements, career-related internships or fieldwork, scholarships/grants, and unspecified assistantships available. Support available to part-time students. Financial award applicants required to submit FAFSA. *Faculty research:* Human-computer interaction: eye tracking, usability engineering, usability testing, ubiquitous computing, interface design and development; platform-independent Multiuser Online Virtual Environments (MOVEs); simulation; service computing, query optimization, data mining and integration; applications programming, interface designs, needs assessment, data modeling, database administration. *Unit head:* Prof. Jeffrey Lasky, Department Chair, 585-475-2284, Fax: 585-475-6584, E-mail: jeffrey.lasky@rit.edu. *Application contact:* Diane Ellison, Assistant Vice President, Graduate Enrollment Services, 585-475-2229, Fax: 585-475-7164, E-mail: gradinfo@rit.edu. Web site: http://www.it.rit.edu.

Sacred Heart University, Graduate Programs, College of Arts and Sciences, Department of Computer Science and Information Technology, Fairfield, CT 06825-1000. Offers computer science (MS); database (CPS); information technology (MS, CPS); information technology and network security (CPS); interactive multimedia (CPS); Web development (CPS). Part-time and evening/weekend programs available. *Degree requirements:* For master's, thesis optional. *Entrance requirements:* Additional exam requirements/recommendations for international students: Required—TOEFL (minimum score 550 paper-based; 213 computer-based). Electronic applications accepted. *Faculty research:* Contemporary market software.

Stevens Institute of Technology, Graduate School, Charles V. Schaefer Jr. School of Engineering, Department of Computer Science, Hoboken, NJ 07030. Offers computer graphics (Certificate); computer science (MS, PhD); computer systems (Certificate); database management systems (Certificate); distributed systems (Certificate); elements of computer science (Certificate); enterprise computing (Certificate); enterprise security and information assurance (Certificate); health informatics (Certificate); multimedia experience and management (Certificate); networks and systems administration (Certificate); security and privacy (Certificate); service oriented computing (Certificate); software design (Certificate); theoretical computer science (Certificate). Part-time and evening/weekend programs available. Terminal master's awarded for partial completion of doctoral program. *Degree requirements:* For master's, thesis optional; for doctorate, variable foreign language requirement, comprehensive exam, thesis/dissertation. *Entrance requirements:* For master's and doctorate, GRE, minimum GPA of 3.0. Additional exam requirements/recommendations for international students: Required—TOEFL. Electronic applications accepted. *Faculty research:* Semantics, reliability theory, programming language, cyber security.

Towson University, Program in Applied Information Technology, Towson, MD 21252-0001. Offers applied information technology (MS, PhD); database management systems (Postbaccalaureate Certificate); information security and assurance (Postbaccalaureate Certificate); information systems management (Postbaccalaureate Certificate); Internet applications development (Postbaccalaureate Certificate); networking technologies (Postbaccalaureate Certificate); software engineering (Postbaccalaureate Certificate). *Students:* 145 full-time (32 women), 270 part-time (78 women); includes 151 minority (96 Black or African American, non-Hispanic/Latino; 35 Asian, non-Hispanic/Latino; 17 Hispanic/Latino; 1 Native Hawaiian or other Pacific Islander, non-Hispanic/Latino; 2 Two or more races, non-Hispanic/Latino), 93 international. *Expenses:* Tuition, state resident: part-time $337 per credit. Tuition, nonresident: part-time $709 per credit. *Required fees:* $99 per credit. *Unit head:* Mike O'Leary, Graduate Program Director, 410-704-4757, E-mail: moleary@towson.edu.

University of Denver, University College, Denver, CO 80208. Offers arts and culture (MLS, Certificate), including art, literature, and culture, arts development and program management (Certificate), creative writing; environmental policy and management (MAS, Certificate), including energy and sustainability (Certificate), environmental assessment of nuclear power (Certificate), environmental health and safety (Certificate), environmental management, natural resource management (Certificate); geographic information systems (MAS, Certificate); global affairs (MLS, Certificate), including translation studies, world history and culture; healthcare leadership (MPH, Certificate), including healthcare policy, law, and ethics, medical and healthcare information technologies, strategic management of healthcare; information and communications technology (MCIS, Certificate), including database design and administration (Certificate), geographic information systems (MCIS), information security systems security (Certificate), information systems security (MCIS), project management (MCIS, MPS, Certificate), software design and administration (Certificate), software design and programming (MCIS), technology management, telecommunications technology (MCIS), Web design and development; leadership and organizations (MPS, Certificate), including human capital in organizations, philanthropic leadership, project management (MCIS, MPS, Certificate), strategic innovation and change; organizational and professional communication (MPS, Certificate), including alternative dispute resolution, organizational communication, organizational development and training, public relations and marketing; security management (MAS, Certificate), including emergency planning and response, information security (MAS), organizational security; strategic human resource management (MPS, Certificate), including global human resources (MPS), human resource management and development (MPS). Part-time and evening/weekend programs available. Postbaccalaureate distance learning degree programs offered (no on-campus study). *Faculty:* 204 part-time/adjunct (80 women). *Students:* 56 full-time (26 women), 1,096 part-time (647 women); includes 196 minority (81 Black or African American, non-Hispanic/Latino; 7 American Indian or Alaska Native, non-Hispanic/Latino; 30 Asian, non-Hispanic/Latino; 66 Hispanic/Latino; 3 Native Hawaiian or other Pacific Islander, non-Hispanic/Latino; 9 Two or more races, non-Hispanic/Latino), 76 international. Average age 36. 572 applicants, 95% accepted, 410 enrolled. In 2011, 404 master's, 123 other advanced degrees awarded. *Degree requirements:* For master's, capstone project. *Entrance requirements:* For master's, two letters of recommendation, personal statement, resume. Additional exam requirements/recommendations for international students: Required—TOEFL (minimum score 550 paper-based; 80 iBT). *Application deadline:* For fall admission, 7/20 priority date for domestic students, 6/8 for international students; for winter admission, 10/26 priority date for domestic students, 9/14 for international students; for spring admission, 2/1 priority date for domestic students, 12/14 for international students. Applications are processed on a rolling basis. Application fee: $75. Electronic applications accepted. *Expenses:* Contact institution. *Financial support:* Applicants required to submit FAFSA. *Unit head:* Dr. James Davis, Dean, 303-871-2291, Fax: 303-871-4047, E-mail: jdavis@du.edu. *Application contact:* Information Contact, 303-871-3155, Fax: 303-871-4047, E-mail: ucolinfo@du.edu. Web site: http://www.universitycollege.du.edu/.

University of New Haven, Graduate School, Tagliatela College of Engineering, Program in Computer and Information Science, West Haven, CT 06516-1916. Offers computer science (MS, Certificate), including advanced applications (MS), computer programming (Certificate), computer systems (MS), database and information systems (MS), network systems (MS), software engineering and development (MS). Part-time and evening/weekend programs available. *Students:* 53 full-time (16 women), 32 part-time (7 women); includes 4 minority (1 Black or African American, non-Hispanic/Latino; 1 Asian, non-Hispanic/Latino; 2 Hispanic/Latino), 69 international. 133 applicants, 98% accepted, 23 enrolled. In 2011, 19 master's, 1 other advanced degree awarded. *Degree requirements:* For master's, thesis or alternative. *Entrance requirements:* Additional exam requirements/recommendations for international students: Required—TOEFL (minimum score 520 paper-based; 190 computer-based; 70 iBT); Recommended—IELTS (minimum score 5.5). *Application deadline:* For fall admission, 5/31 for international students; for winter admission, 10/15 for international students; for spring admission, 1/15 for international students. Applications are processed on a rolling basis. Application fee: $50. Electronic applications accepted. *Expenses: Tuition:* Part-time $750 per credit. *Financial support:* Research assistantships with partial tuition reimbursements, teaching assistantships with partial tuition reimbursements, career-related internships or fieldwork, Federal Work-Study, scholarships/grants, tuition waivers, and unspecified assistantships available. Support available to part-time students. Financial award applicants required to submit FAFSA. *Unit head:* Dr. David Eggert, Coordinator, 203-932-7097, E-mail: deggert@newhaven.edu. *Application contact:* Eloise Gormley, Director of Graduate Admissions, 203-932-7449, Fax: 203-932-7137, E-mail: gradinfo@newhaven.edu. Web site: http://www.newhaven.edu/9591/.

The University of North Carolina at Charlotte, Graduate School, College of Computing and Informatics, Department of Computer Science, Charlotte, NC 28223-0001. Offers advance databases and knowledge discovery (Certificate); computer science (MS). Part-time programs available. *Faculty:* 21 full-time (5 women), 2 part-time/adjunct (0 women). *Students:* 107 full-time (23 women), 36 part-time (13 women); includes 10 minority (2 Black or African American, non-Hispanic/Latino; 5 Asian, non-Hispanic/Latino; 1 Hispanic/Latino; 2 Two or more races, non-Hispanic/Latino), 106 international. Average age 25. 347 applicants, 50% accepted, 37 enrolled. In 2011, 57 master's, 5 other advanced degrees awarded. *Degree requirements:* For master's, thesis or alternative. *Entrance requirements:* For master's, GRE General Test, minimum GPA of 3.0 during previous 2 years, 2.8 overall. Additional exam requirements/recommendations for international students: Required—TOEFL (minimum score 557 paper-based; 220 computer-based; 83 iBT). *Application deadline:* For fall admission, 7/1 for domestic students, 5/1 for international students; for spring admission, 11/1 for domestic students, 10/1 for international students. Applications are processed on a rolling basis. Application fee: $65 ($75 for international students). Electronic applications accepted. *Expenses:* Tuition, state resident: full-time $3689. Tuition, nonresident: full-time $15,226. *Required fees:* $2198. Tuition and fees vary according to course load and program. *Financial support:* In 2011–12, 38 students received support, including 30 research assistantships (averaging $10,247 per year), 8 teaching assistantships (averaging $9,869 per year); career-related internships or fieldwork, Federal Work-Study, institutionally sponsored loans, scholarships/grants, and unspecified assistantships also available. Support available to part-time students. Financial award application deadline: 4/1; financial award applicants required to submit FAFSA. *Faculty research:* Visualization; visual analytics and computer graphics; intelligent and interactive systems; data mining theory, systems, and application; networked systems; computer game design. *Total annual research expenditures:* $3.1 million. *Unit head:* Dr. Larry F. Hodges, Chair, 704-687-8552, Fax: 704-687-3516, E-mail: lfhodges@uncc.edu. *Application contact:* Kathy B. Giddings, Director of Graduate Admissions, 704-687-3366, Fax: 704-687-3279, E-mail: gradadm@uncc.edu. Web site: http://www.coit.uncc.edu/cs/site/.

University of San Francisco, College of Arts and Sciences, Analytics Program, San Francisco, CA 94117-1080. Offers MS. Program offered jointly with School of Management. *Expenses: Tuition:* Full-time $20,070; part-time $1115 per unit. Tuition and fees vary according to course load, campus/location and program.

University of West Florida, College of Arts and Sciences: Sciences, Department of Computer Science, Pensacola, FL 32514-5750. Offers computer science (MS); database systems (MS); software engineering (MS). Part-time and evening/weekend programs available. *Faculty:* 9 full-time (4 women), 5 part-time/adjunct (4 women). *Students:* 22 full-time (8 women), 114 part-time (25 women); includes 38 minority (8 Black or African American, non-Hispanic/Latino; 2 American Indian or Alaska Native, non-Hispanic/Latino; 13 Asian, non-Hispanic/Latino; 13 Hispanic/Latino; 2 Two or more races, non-Hispanic/Latino), 54 international. Average age 37. 53 applicants, 81% accepted, 35 enrolled. In 2011, 64 master's awarded. *Degree requirements:* For master's, thesis optional. *Entrance requirements:* For master's, GRE, MAT, or GMAT, official transcripts; minimum undergraduate GPA of 3.0; letter of intent; three letters of recommendation. Additional exam requirements/recommendations for international students: Required—TOEFL (minimum score 550 paper-based; 213 computer-based). *Application deadline:* For fall admission, 6/1 for domestic and international students; for spring admission, 10/1 for domestic and international students. Applications are processed on a rolling basis. Application fee: $30. *Expenses:* Tuition, state resident: full-time $5729; part-time $302 per credit hour. Tuition, nonresident: full-time $20,059; part-time $961 per credit hour. *Required fees:* $1509; $63 per credit hour. *Financial support:* In 2011–12, 10 fellowships with partial tuition reimbursements (averaging $600 per year), 8 research assistantships with partial tuition reimbursements (averaging $3,280 per year), 2 teaching assistantships with partial tuition reimbursements (averaging $3,760 per year) were awarded; unspecified assistantships also available. Financial award application deadline: 4/15; financial award applicants required to submit FAFSA. *Unit head:* Dr. Leo Ter Haar, Chairperson, 850-474-2542. *Application contact:* Terry McCray, Assistant Director of Graduate Admissions, 850-473-7718, Fax: 850-473-7714, E-mail: gradadmissions@uwf.edu. Web site: http://catalog.uwf.edu/graduate/computerscience/.

University of West Florida, College of Professional Studies, Department of Applied Science, Technology and Administration, Program in Administration, Pensacola, FL 32514-5750. Offers acquisition and contract administration (MSA); biomedical/pharmaceutical (MSA); criminal justice administration (MSA); database administration (MSA); education leadership (MSA); healthcare administration (MSA); human performance technology (MSA); leadership (MSA); nursing administration (MSA); public administration (MSA); software engineering administration (MSA). Part-time and evening/weekend programs available. Postbaccalaureate distance learning degree programs offered (no on-campus study). *Students:* 36 full-time (28 women), 158 part-time (95 women); includes 61 minority (31 Black or African American, non-Hispanic/Latino; 4 American Indian or Alaska Native, non-Hispanic/Latino; 4 Asian, non-Hispanic/Latino; 17 Hispanic/Latino; 2 Native Hawaiian or other Pacific Islander, non-Hispanic/Latino; 3 Two or more races, non-Hispanic/Latino), 1 international. Average age 34. 102 applicants, 59% accepted, 40 enrolled. In 2011, 62 master's awarded. *Entrance requirements:* For master's, GRE General Test, letter of intent, names of references. Additional exam requirements/recommendations for international students: Required—TOEFL (minimum score 550 paper-based; 213 computer-based). *Application deadline:* For fall admission, 6/1 for domestic and international students; for spring admission, 10/1 for domestic and international students. Applications are processed on a rolling basis. Application fee: $30. *Expenses:* Tuition, state resident: full-time $5729; part-time $302 per credit hour. Tuition, nonresident: full-time $20,059; part-time $961 per credit hour. *Required fees:* $1509; $63 per credit hour. *Financial support:* Unspecified assistantships available. Financial award application deadline: 4/15; financial award applicants required to submit FAFSA. *Unit head:* Dr. Karen Rasmussen, Chairperson, 850-474-2301, Fax: 850-474-2804, E-mail: krasmuss@uwf.edu. *Application contact:* Terry McCray, Assistant Director of Graduate Admissions, 850-473-7718, Fax: 850-473-7714, E-mail: gradadmissions@uwf.edu. Web site: http://uwf.edu/msaprogram/.

University of West Florida, College of Professional Studies, Department of Research and Applied Studies, Pensacola, FL 32514-5750. Offers administration (MSA), including acquisition and contract administration, biomedical/pharmaceutical, criminal justice administration, database administration, education leadership, healthcare administration, human performance technology, leadership, nursing administration, public administration, software engineering and administration; college student personnel administration (M Ed), including college personnel administration, guidance and counseling; curriculum and instruction (M Ed, Ed S); educational leadership (M Ed); middle and secondary level education and ESOL (M Ed). Part-time and evening/weekend programs available. *Faculty:* 2 full-time (both women), 3 part-time/adjunct (2 women). *Students:* 26 full-time (15 women), 13 part-time (9 women); includes 8 minority (4 Black or African American, non-Hispanic/Latino; 2 American Indian or Alaska Native, non-Hispanic/Latino; 1 Hispanic/Latino; 1 Two or more races, non-Hispanic/Latino), 1 international. Average age 26. 51 applicants, 51% accepted, 16 enrolled. In 2011, 17 master's, 49 Ed Ss awarded. *Entrance requirements:* For master's, GRE or MAT, official transcripts; minimum undergraduate GPA of 3.0; letter of intent; three letters of recommendation; resume. Additional exam requirements/recommendations for international students: Required—TOEFL (minimum score 550 paper-based; 213 computer-based). *Application deadline:* For fall admission, 6/1 for domestic and international students; for spring admission, 10/1 for domestic and international students. Applications are processed on a rolling basis. Application fee: $30. *Expenses:* Tuition, state resident: full-time $5729; part-time $302 per credit hour. Tuition, nonresident: full-time $20,059; part-time $961 per credit hour. *Required fees:* $1509; $63 per credit hour. *Financial support:* In 2011–12, 33 fellowships (averaging $860 per year), 10 research assistantships (averaging $3,280 per year), 2 teaching assistantships (averaging $3,760 per year) were awarded; unspecified assistantships also available. Financial award application deadline: 4/15; financial award applicants required to submit FAFSA. *Unit head:* Dr. Joyce Nichols, Chairperson, 850-857-6042, E-mail: jcoleman0@ uwf.edu. *Application contact:* Terry McCray, Assistant Director of Graduate Admissions, 850-473-7718, Fax: 850-473-7714, E-mail: gradadmissions@uwf.edu. Web site: http://uwf.edu/pcl/.

Financial Engineering

Claremont Graduate University, Graduate Programs, Financial Engineering Program, Claremont, CA 91711-6160. Offers MSFE, MS/EMBA, MS/MBA, MS/PhD. *Students:* 62 full-time (19 women), 2 part-time (both women); includes 9 minority (1 Black or African American, non-Hispanic/Latino; 5 Asian, non-Hispanic/Latino; 3 Hispanic/Latino), 43 international. Average age 27. In 2011, 26 master's awarded. *Entrance requirements:* For master's, GRE General Test or GMAT. Additional exam requirements/recommendations for international students: Required—TOEFL (minimum score 550 paper-based; 213 computer-based; 80 iBT). *Application deadline:* For fall admission, 2/1 priority date for domestic students. Applications are processed on a rolling basis. Application fee: $60. Electronic applications accepted. *Expenses: Tuition:* Full-time $36,374; part-time $1581 per unit. *Required fees:* $165 per semester. *Financial support:* Fellowships, Federal Work-Study, institutionally sponsored loans, and scholarships/grants available. Support available to part-time students. Financial award application deadline: 2/15; financial award applicants required to submit FAFSA. *Unit head:* Jim Mills, Co-Director, 909-607-3310, E-mail: jim.mills@cgu.edu. *Application contact:* Martha Lua, 909-607-7811, E-mail: drucker@cgu.edu. Web site: http://www.cgu.edu/fineng.

Columbia University, The Fu Foundation School of Engineering and Applied Science, Department of Industrial Engineering and Operations Research, New York, NY 10027. Offers financial engineering (MS); industrial engineering (Engr); industrial engineering and operations research (MS, Eng Sc D, PhD); MS/MBA. Part-time and evening/weekend programs available. Postbaccalaureate distance learning degree programs offered (no on-campus study). *Faculty:* 22 full-time (3 women), 27 part-time/adjunct (2 women). *Students:* 344 full-time (99 women), 205 part-time (54 women); includes 34 minority (28 Asian, non-Hispanic/Latino; 2 Hispanic/Latino; 1 Native Hawaiian or other Pacific Islander, non-Hispanic/Latino; 3 Two or more races, non-Hispanic/Latino), 460 international. Average age 26. 2,041 applicants, 19% accepted, 311 enrolled. In 2011, 229 master's, 6 doctorates, 1 other advanced degree awarded. *Degree requirements:* For doctorate, thesis/dissertation, oral and written qualifying exams. *Entrance requirements:* For master's, doctorate, and Engr, GRE General Test. Additional exam requirements/recommendations for international students: Required—TOEFL, IELTS. *Application deadline:* For fall admission, 12/1 priority date for domestic students, 12/1 for international students; for spring admission, 10/1 priority date for domestic students, 10/1 for international students. Application fee: $95. Electronic applications accepted. *Financial support:* In 2011–12, 44 students received support, including 2 fellowships with full tuition reimbursements available (averaging $35,968 per year), 22 research assistantships with full tuition reimbursements available (averaging $31,380 per year), 20 teaching assistantships with full tuition reimbursements available (averaging $31,380 per year); career-related internships or fieldwork and health care benefits also available. Financial award application deadline: 12/1; financial award applicants required to submit FAFSA. *Faculty research:* Applied probability and optimization; financial engineering, modeling risk including credit risk and systemic risk, asset allocation, portfolio execution, behavioral finance, agent-based model in finance; revenue management; management and optimization of service systems, call centers, capacity allocation in healthcare systems, inventory control for vaccines; energy, smart grids, demand shaping, managing renewable energy sources, energy-aware scheduling. *Unit head:* Dr. Cliff S. Stein, Professor and Department Chairman, 212-854-5238, Fax: 212-854-8103, E-mail: cliff@ieor.columbia.edu. *Application contact:* Adina Berrios Brooks, Student Affairs Manager, 212-854-1934, Fax: 212-854-8103, E-mail: admit@ieor.columbia.edu. Web site: http://www.ieor.columbia.edu/.

HEC Montreal, School of Business Administration, Master of Science Programs in Administration, Program in Financial Engineering, Montréal, QC H3T 2A7, Canada. Offers M Sc. Part-time programs available. *Students:* 56 full-time (7 women), 20 part-time (2 women). 60 applicants, 58% accepted, 23 enrolled. In 2011, 18 master's awarded. *Degree requirements:* For master's, one foreign language, thesis. *Entrance requirements:* For master's, Test de francais international (TFI) with minimum score of 850 (for those who have never studied in French), BBA, undergraduate degree in another field, degree deemed equivalent by program director and minimum GPA of 3.0 on 4.3 scale. *Application deadline:* For fall admission, 3/15 for domestic and international students; for winter admission, 9/15 for domestic and international students. Application fee: $80 Canadian dollars. Electronic applications accepted. Application fee is waived when completed online. *Expenses:* Contact institution. *Financial support:* Fellowships, research assistantships, teaching assistantships, and scholarships/grants available. Financial award application deadline: 9/2. *Unit head:* Dr. Claude Laurin, Director, 514-340-6485, Fax: 514-340-6880, E-mail: claude.laurin@hec.ca. *Application contact:* Virginie Lefebvre, Administrative Director, 514-340-6112, Fax: 514-340-6411, E-mail: virginie.lefebvre@hec.ca. Web site: http://www.hec.ca/en/programs_training/msc/options/finance/financial_engineering/index.html.

The International University of Monaco, Graduate Programs, Monte Carlo, Monaco. Offers entrepreneurship (EMBA, MBA); financial engineering (M Sc); hedge fund and private equity (M Sc); international marketing (EMBA, MBA); international wealth management (M Sc); luxury goods and services (EMBA, M Sc, MBA); wealth and asset management (EMBA, MBA). Part-time programs available. *Degree requirements:* For master's, comprehensive exam (for some programs), applied research project. *Entrance requirements:* Additional exam requirements/recommendations for international students: Required—TOEFL (minimum score 550 paper-based; 213 computer-based), IELTS. Electronic applications accepted. *Faculty research:* Gaming, leadership, disintermediation.

North Carolina State University, Graduate School, College of Agriculture and Life Sciences and College of Engineering and College of Physical and Mathematical Sciences, Program in Financial Mathematics, Raleigh, NC 27695. Offers MFM. Part-time programs available. *Degree requirements:* For master's, thesis optional, project/internship. *Entrance requirements:* For master's, GRE General Test. Additional exam requirements/recommendations for international students: Required—TOEFL (minimum score 550 paper-based; 213 computer-based). Electronic applications accepted. *Faculty research:* Financial mathematics modeling and computation, futures, options and commodities markets, real options, credit risk, portfolio optimization.

Polytechnic Institute of New York University, Department of Finance and Risk Engineering, Brooklyn, NY 11201-2990. Offers financial engineering (MS, Advanced Certificate), including capital markets (MS), computational finance (MS), financial technology (MS); financial technology management (Advanced Certificate); organizational behavior (Advanced Certificate); risk management (Advanced Certificate); technology management (Advanced Certificate). Part-time and evening/weekend programs available. *Faculty:* 6 full-time (2 women), 23 part-time/adjunct (5 women). *Students:* 149 full-time (49 women), 44 part-time (8 women); includes 30 minority (6 Black or African American, non-Hispanic/Latino; 22 Asian, non-Hispanic/Latino; 2 Hispanic/Latino), 135 international. Average age 27. 515 applicants, 36% accepted, 102 enrolled. In 2011, 95 degrees awarded. *Degree requirements:* For master's, comprehensive exam (for some programs), thesis (for some programs). *Entrance requirements:* For master's, GMAT, minimum B average in undergraduate course work. Additional exam requirements/recommendations for international students: Required—TOEFL (minimum score 550 paper-based; 213 computer-based; 80 iBT); Recommended—IELTS (minimum score 6.5). *Application deadline:* For fall admission, 7/31 priority date for domestic students, 4/30 for international students; for spring admission, 12/31 priority date for domestic students, 11/30 for international students. Applications are processed on a rolling basis. Application fee: $75. Electronic applications accepted. *Expenses: Tuition:* Full-time $22,464; part-time $1248 per credit. *Required fees:* $501 per semester. *Financial support:* Institutionally sponsored loans, scholarships/grants, and unspecified assistantships available. Support available to part-time students. Financial award applicants required to submit FAFSA. *Unit head:* Prof. Charles S. Tapiero, Academic Director, 718-260-3653, Fax: 718-260-3874, E-mail: ctapiero@poly.edu. *Application contact:* JeanCarlo Bonilla, Director, Graduate Enrollment Management, 718-260-3182, Fax: 718-260-3624.

Polytechnic Institute of NYU, Long Island Graduate Center, Graduate Programs, Department of Finance and Risk Engineering, Major in Financial Engineering, Melville, NY 11747. Offers MS, AC. Part-time and evening/weekend programs available. *Students:* 1 part-time (0 women), all international. Average age 24. 1 applicant, 100% accepted, 1 enrolled. *Entrance requirements:* Additional exam requirements/recommendations for international students: Required—TOEFL (minimum score 550 paper-based; 213 computer-based; 80 iBT); Recommended—IELTS (minimum score 6.5). *Application deadline:* For fall admission, 7/31 priority date for domestic students, 4/30 for international students; for spring admission, 12/31 priority date for domestic students, 11/30 for international students. Applications are processed on a rolling basis. Application fee: $75. Electronic applications accepted. *Financial support:* Institutionally sponsored loans, scholarships/grants, and unspecified assistantships available. Support available to part-time students. *Unit head:* Dr. Charles S. Tapiero, Department Head, 718-260-3653, E-mail: ctapiero@poly.edu. *Application contact:* JeanCarlo Bonilla, Director of Graduate Enrollment Management, 718-260-3182, Fax: 718-260-3624, E-mail: gradinfo@poly.edu.

Princeton University, Graduate School, School of Engineering and Applied Science, Department of Operations Research and Financial Engineering, Princeton, NJ 08544-1019. Offers M Eng, MSE, PhD. Terminal master's awarded for partial completion of doctoral program. *Degree requirements:* For master's, thesis (MSE); for doctorate, thesis/dissertation, general exam. *Entrance requirements:* For master's and doctorate, GRE General Test, official transcript(s), 3 letters of recommendation, personal statement. Additional exam requirements/recommendations for international students: Required—TOEFL. Electronic applications accepted. *Faculty research:* Applied and computational mathematics; financial mathematics; optimization, queuing theory, and machine learning; statistics and stochastic analysis; transportation and logistics.

Rensselaer Polytechnic Institute, Graduate School, Lally School of Management and Technology, Troy, NY 12180-3590. Offers business (MBA); financial engineering and risk analysis (MS); management (MS, PhD); technology, commercialization, and entrepreneurship (MS). *Accreditation:* AACSB. Part-time and evening/weekend programs available. *Degree requirements:* For doctorate, thesis/dissertation. *Entrance requirements:* For master's, GMAT, 2 letters of recommendation, resume; for doctorate, GMAT or GRE General Test, 2 letters of recommendation. Additional exam requirements/recommendations for international students: Required—TOEFL (minimum score 600 paper-based; 250 computer-based; 100 iBT); Recommended—IELTS (minimum score 7). Electronic applications accepted. *Faculty research:* Technological entrepreneurship, operations management, new product development and marketing, finance and financial engineering and risk analytics, information systems.

Stevens Institute of Technology, Graduate School, School of Systems and Enterprises, Program in Financial Engineering, Hoboken, NJ 07030. Offers MS.

Temple University, Fox School of Business, Specialized Master's Programs, Philadelphia, PA 19122-6096. Offers accountancy (MS); actuarial science (MS); finance (MS); financial engineering (MS); human resource management (MS); marketing (MS); statistics (MS). *Accreditation:* AACSB. Part-time programs available. *Entrance requirements:* For master's, GRE General Test or GMAT, minimum undergraduate GPA of 3.0. Additional exam requirements/recommendations for international students: Required—TOEFL (minimum score 600 paper-based; 250 computer-based; 100 iBT), IELTS (minimum score 7.5). *Expenses:* Tuition, state resident: full-time $12,366; part-time $687 per credit hour. Tuition, nonresident: full-time $17,298; part-time $961 per credit hour. *Required fees:* $590; $213 per year.

University at Buffalo, the State University of New York, Graduate School, School of Management, Buffalo, NY 14260. Offers accounting (MS); business administration (EMBA, MBA, PMBA); finance (MS), including financial engineering, financial management; management (PhD); management information systems (MS); supply chains and operations management (MS); Au D/MBA; JD/MBA; M Arch/MBA; MA/MBA; MD/MBA; MPH/MBA; MSW/MBA; Pharm D/MBA. *Accreditation:* AACSB. Part-time and evening/weekend programs available. *Degree requirements:* For master's, thesis (for some programs); for doctorate, comprehensive exam, thesis/dissertation. *Entrance requirements:* For master's, GMAT (MBA, MS in accounting), GRE or GMAT (for all other MS concentrations); for doctorate, GMAT or GRE. Additional exam requirements/recommendations for international students: Required—TOEFL (minimum score 230 computer-based; 95 iBT). Electronic applications accepted. *Expenses:* Contact institution. *Faculty research:* Earnings management and electronic information assurance, supply chains and operations management, corporate financing and asset pricing, consumer behavior and quantitative modeling of marketing behavior, leadership and politics in organizations.

University of California, Berkeley, Graduate Division, Haas School of Business, Master of Financial Engineering Program, Berkeley, CA 94720-1500. Offers MFE. *Students:* 68 full-time (8 women); includes 15 minority (13 Asian, non-Hispanic/Latino; 2 Hispanic/Latino), 44 international. Average age 28. 404 applicants, 22% accepted, 68 enrolled. In 2011, 66 master's awarded. *Degree requirements:* For master's, comprehensive exam, internship/applied finance project. *Entrance requirements:* For master's, GMAT or GRE (waived if candidate holds PhD), bachelor's degree with minimum GPA of 3.0 or equivalent; two recommendation letters. Additional exam requirements/recommendations for international students: Required—TOEFL (minimum score 570 paper-based; 230 computer-based; 68 iBT). *Application deadline:* For spring admission, 9/1 for domestic and international students. Applications are processed on a rolling basis. Application fee: $225. Electronic applications accepted. *Expenses:* Contact institution. *Financial support:* Teaching assistantships available. Financial award applicants required to submit FAFSA. *Faculty research:* Financial economics, modern portfolio theory, valuation of exotic options, mortgage markets. *Unit head:* Linda Kreitzman, Executive Director, 510-643-4329, Fax: 510-643-4345, E-mail: lindak@haas.berkeley.edu. *Application contact:* Christina Henri, Associate Director, 510-642-4417, Fax: 510-643-4345, E-mail: mfe@haas.berkeley.edu. Web site: http://mfe.haas.berkeley.edu.

University of California, Los Angeles, Graduate Division, UCLA Anderson School of Management, Los Angeles, CA 90095-1481. Offers accounting (PhD); Asia Pacific (EMBA); business administration (EMBA, MBA); decisions, operations and technology management (PhD); finance (PhD); financial engineering (MFE); global economics and management (PhD); Latin America (EMBA); management and organizations (PhD); marketing (PhD); strategy (PhD); DDS/MBA; MBA/JD; MBA/MD; MBA/MLAS; MBA/MLIS; MBA/MPH; MBA/MPP; MBA/MSCS; MBA/MSN; MBA/MUP. *Accreditation:* AACSB. Part-time programs available. *Faculty:* 90 full-time (14 women), 62 part-time/adjunct (14 women). *Students:* 1,103 full-time (312 women), 842 part-time (223 women); includes 663 minority (18 Black or African American, non-Hispanic/Latino; 510 Asian, non-Hispanic/Latino; 46 Hispanic/Latino; 2 Native Hawaiian or other Pacific Islander, non-Hispanic/Latino; 87 Two or more races, non-Hispanic/Latino), 469 international. 4,737 applicants, 32% accepted, 875 enrolled. In 2011, 759 master's, 6 doctorates awarded. *Degree requirements:* For master's, comprehensive exam, field study consulting project (for MBA); thesis/dissertation (for MFE); for doctorate, comprehensive exam, thesis/dissertation, oral and written qualifying exams. *Entrance requirements:* For master's, GMAT (for MBA); GMAT or GRE General Test (for MFE), 4-year bachelor's degree or equivalent; for doctorate, GMAT or GRE General Test, 4-year bachelor's degree from regionally-accredited institution; minimum GPA of 3.0. Additional exam requirements/recommendations for international students: Required—TOEFL (minimum score 560 paper-based; 220 computer-based; 87 iBT), IELTS (minimum score 7). *Application deadline:* For fall admission, 10/26 for domestic and international students; for winter admission, 1/11 for domestic and international students; for spring admission, 4/18 for domestic and international students. Application fee: $200. Electronic applications accepted. *Expenses:* Contact institution. *Financial support:* In 2011–12, 600 students received support. Fellowships, research assistantships, teaching assistantships, career-related internships or fieldwork, institutionally sponsored loans, scholarships/grants, health care benefits, and tuition waivers (partial) available. Financial award application deadline: 4/15; financial award applicants required to submit FAFSA. *Unit head:* Judy D. Olian, Dean, 310-825-7982, Fax: 310-206-2073, E-mail: judy.olian@anderson.ucla.edu. *Application contact:* Robert Weiler, Assistant Dean, Director of MBA Admissions and Financial Aid, 310-825-6944, Fax: 310-825-8582, E-mail: mba.admissions@anderson.ucla.edu. Web site: http://www.anderson.ucla.edu/.

University of Hawaii at Manoa, Graduate Division, Shidler College of Business, Program in Financial Engineering, Honolulu, HI 96822. Offers MS. Part-time programs available. *Degree requirements:* For master's, thesis optional. *Entrance requirements:* For master's, GRE General Test. Additional exam requirements/recommendations for international students: Required—TOEFL (minimum score 600 paper-based; 250 computer-based; 100 iBT), IELTS (minimum score 7).

University of Illinois at Urbana–Champaign, Graduate College, College of Engineering, Joint Program in Financial Engineering, Champaign, IL 61820. Offers MS. Program offered jointly with College of Business. Part-time programs available. *Students:* 69 full-time (17 women); includes 6 minority (all Asian, non-Hispanic/Latino), 54 international. 513 applicants, 30% accepted, 43 enrolled. *Degree requirements:* For master's, thesis or alternative. *Entrance requirements:* For master's, one year of calculus, one semester each of linear algebra, differential equations, and programming (preferably in C/C++). Additional exam requirements/recommendations for international students: Required—TOEFL (minimum score 103 iBT), TOEFL (minimum score 613 paper-based; 257 computer-based; 79 iBT) or IELTS (minimum score 7). *Application deadline:* Applications are processed on a rolling basis. Application fee: $75 ($90 for international students). Electronic applications accepted. *Financial support:* Scholarships/grants available. *Unit head:* Morton Lane, Director, 217-333-3284, Fax: 217-333-1486, E-mail: msfe@illinois.edu. *Application contact:* Sabria Kushad, Assistant Director, 217-333-3284, E-mail: skushad2@illinois.edu. Web site: http://msfe.illinois.edu/.

University of Michigan, College of Engineering, Interpro Programs in Engineering, Ann Arbor, MI 48109. Offers automotive engineering (M Eng); design science (PhD); energy systems engineering (MS); financial engineering (MS); global automotive and manufacturing engineering (M Eng); manufacturing engineering (M Eng, D Eng); pharmaceutical engineering (M Eng); robotics and autonomous vehicles (M Eng); MBA/M Eng; MSE/MS. Part-time programs available. Postbaccalaureate distance learning degree programs offered (no on-campus study). *Students:* 225 full-time (55 women), 273 part-time (37 women). In 2011, 145 master's, 1 doctorate awarded. Terminal master's awarded for partial completion of doctoral program. *Degree requirements:* For master's, capstone project; for doctorate, thesis/dissertation. *Entrance requirements:* For master's, GRE; for doctorate, GRE, 2 years of work experience. Additional exam requirements/recommendations for international students: Required—TOEFL (minimum score 560 paper-based; 220 computer-based). *Application deadline:* Applications are processed on a rolling basis. Application fee: $65 ($75 for international students). Electronic applications accepted. *Financial support:* Fellowships, research assistantships with full tuition reimbursements, teaching assistantships with full tuition reimbursements, career-related internships or fieldwork, scholarships/grants, and unspecified assistantships available. Financial award application deadline: 2/15; financial award applicants required to submit FAFSA. *Faculty research:* Automotive engineering, design science, energy systems engineering, engineering sustainable systems dual degree, financial engineering, global automotive and manufacturing engineering, integrated microsystems, manufacturing engineering, pharmaceutical engineering , robotics and autonomous vehicles. *Unit head:* Prof. Panos Papalambros, Director, 734-763-0480, Fax: 734-647-0079, E-mail: pyp@umich.edu. *Application contact:* Patti Mackmiller, Program Manager, 734-764-3071, Fax: 734-647-2243, E-mail: pmackmil@umich.edu. Web site: http://interpro-academics.engin.umich.edu/.

The University of Texas at Dallas, Naveen Jindal School of Management, Program in Finance, Richardson, TX 75080. Offers finance (MS); financial analysis (MS); financial engineering and risk management (MS); investment management (MS). Part-time and evening/weekend programs available. *Faculty:* 18 full-time (3 women), 8 part-time/adjunct (1 woman). *Students:* 358 full-time (187 women), 81 part-time (19 women); includes 34 minority (1 Black or African American, non-Hispanic/Latino; 24 Asian, non-Hispanic/Latino; 6 Hispanic/Latino; 3 Two or more races, non-Hispanic/Latino), 352 international. Average age 25. 864 applicants, 56% accepted, 235 enrolled. In 2011, 93 master's awarded. *Entrance requirements:* For master's, GMAT. Additional exam requirements/recommendations for international students: Required—TOEFL (minimum score 550 paper-based; 215 computer-based). *Application deadline:* For fall admission, 7/15 for domestic students, 5/1 for international students; for spring admission, 11/15 for domestic students, 9/1 for international students. Applications are processed on a rolling basis. Application fee: $50 ($100 for international students). Electronic applications accepted. *Expenses:* Tuition, state resident: full-time $11,170; part-time $620.56 per credit hour. Tuition, nonresident: full-time $20,212; part-time $1122.89 per credit hour. *Financial support:* In 2011–12, 161 students received support. Research assistantships with partial tuition reimbursements available, teaching assistantships with partial tuition reimbursements available, career-related internships or fieldwork, Federal Work-Study, institutionally sponsored loans, scholarships/grants, and unspecified assistantships available. Support available to part-time students. Financial award application deadline: 4/30; financial award applicants required to submit FAFSA. *Faculty research:* Econometrics, industrial organization, auction theory, file-sharing copyrights and bundling, international financial management, entrepreneurial finance. *Unit head:* Dr. Robert Kieschnick, Area Coordinator, 972-883-6273, E-mail: rkiesch@utdallas.edu. *Application contact:* James Parker, Assistant Director, 972-883-5842, E-mail: jparker@utdallas.edu. Web site: http://jindal.utdallas.edu/academic-areas/finance-and-managerial-economics/.

University of Tulsa, Graduate School, Collins College of Business, Program in Finance, Tulsa, OK 74104-3189. Offers corporate finance (MS); investments and portfolio management (MS); risk management (MS); JD/MSF; MBA/MSF; MSF/MSAM. Part-time and evening/weekend programs available. *Faculty:* 10 full-time (1 woman). *Students:* 33 full-time (14 women), 2 part-time (0 women), 25 international. Average age 24. 121 applicants, 59% accepted, 21 enrolled. In 2011, 12 master's awarded. *Degree requirements:* For master's, thesis optional. *Entrance requirements:* For master's, GMAT. Additional exam requirements/recommendations for international students: Required—TOEFL (minimum score 577 paper-based; 233 computer-based; 91 iBT), IELTS (minimum score 6.5). *Application deadline:* Applications are processed on a rolling basis. Application fee: $40. Electronic applications accepted. *Expenses: Tuition:* Full-time $17,748; part-time $986 per hour. *Required fees:* $5 per contact hour. $75 per semester. Tuition and fees vary according to program. *Financial support:* In 2011–12, 4 students received support, including 4 teaching assistantships with full and partial tuition reimbursements available (averaging $12,355 per year); fellowships with full and partial tuition reimbursements available, research assistantships with full and partial tuition reimbursements available, career-related internships or fieldwork, Federal Work-Study, institutionally sponsored loans, scholarships/grants, health care benefits, tuition waivers (full and partial), and unspecified assistantships also available. Support available to part-time students. Financial award application deadline: 2/1; financial award applicants required to submit FAFSA. *Unit head:* Dr. Linda Nichols, Associate Dean, 918-631-2242, Fax: 918-631-2142, E-mail: linda-nichols@utulsa.edu. *Application contact:* Information Contact, 918-631-2242, E-mail: graduate-business@utulsa.edu. Web site: http://www.utulsa.edu/academics/colleges/collins-college-of-business/bus-dept-schools/School-of-Finance-Operations-Management-and-International-Busine.

Game Design and Development

Academy of Art University, Graduate Program, School of Game Design, San Francisco, CA 94105-3410. Offers MFA. Part-time programs available. Postbaccalaureate distance learning degree programs offered (no on-campus study). *Faculty:* 5 full-time (0 women), 10 part-time/adjunct (2 women). *Students:* 95 full-time (26 women), 51 part-time (12 women); includes 24 minority (5 Black or African American, non-Hispanic/Latino; 11 Asian, non-Hispanic/Latino; 6 Hispanic/Latino; 1 Native Hawaiian or other Pacific Islander, non-Hispanic/Latino; 1 Two or more races, non-Hispanic/Latino), 49 international. Average age 28. 58 applicants. *Degree requirements:* For master's, final review. *Entrance requirements:* For master's, statement of intent; resume; portfolio/reel; official college transcripts. *Application deadline:* Applications are processed on a rolling basis. Application fee: $100. Electronic applications accepted. *Expenses: Tuition:* Full-time $20,160; part-time $840 per unit. *Required fees:* $90. *Financial support:* Career-related internships or fieldwork and Federal Work-Study available. Support available to part-time students. Financial award application deadline: 8/10; financial award applicants required to submit FAFSA. *Unit head:* 800-544-ARTS, E-mail: info@academyart.edu. *Application contact:* 800-544-ARTS, Fax: 415-263-4130, E-mail: info@academyart.edu. Web site: http://www.academyart.edu/game-design-school/index.html.

Concordia University, School of Graduate Studies, Faculty of Engineering and Computer Science, Concordia Institute for Information Systems Engineering (CIISE), Montréal, QC H3G 1M8, Canada. Offers 3D graphics and game development (Certificate); information systems security (M Eng, MA Sc); quality systems engineering (M Eng, MA Sc); service engineering and network management (Certificate).

DePaul University, College of Computing and Digital Media, Chicago, IL 60604. Offers animation (MA, MFA); applied technology (MS); business information technology (MS);

cinema (MFA); cinema production (MS); computational finance (MS); computer and information sciences (PhD); computer game development (MS); computer graphics and motion technology (MS); computer information and network security (MS); computer science (MS); e-commerce technology (MS); human-computer interaction (MS); information systems (MS); information technology (MA); information technology project management (MS); network engineering and management (MS); predictive analytics (MS); screenwriting (MFA); software engineering (MS); JD/MA; JD/MS. Part-time and evening/weekend programs available. Postbaccalaureate distance learning degree programs offered (no on-campus study). *Faculty:* 64 full-time (16 women), 44 part-time/adjunct (5 women). *Students:* 969 full-time (250 women), 936 part-time (231 women); includes 566 minority (204 Black or African American, non-Hispanic/Latino; 3 American Indian or Alaska Native, non-Hispanic/Latino; 166 Asian, non-Hispanic/Latino; 135 Hispanic/Latino; 7 Native Hawaiian or other Pacific Islander, non-Hispanic/Latino; 51 Two or more races, non-Hispanic/Latino), 282 international. Average age 32. 1,040 applicants, 65% accepted, 324 enrolled. In 2011, 478 master's, 4 doctorates awarded. *Degree requirements:* For master's, thesis (for some programs); for doctorate, comprehensive exam, thesis/dissertation. *Entrance requirements:* For master's, GRE or GMAT (MS in computational finance only), bachelor's degree, resume (MS in predictive analytics only), IT experience (MS in information technology project management only), portfolio review (all MFA programs and MA in animation); for doctorate, GRE, master's degree in computer science. Additional exam requirements/recommendations for international students: Required—TOEFL (minimum score 550 paper-based; 213 computer-based; 80 iBT), IELTS (minimum score 6.5), Pearson Test of English (minimum score 53). *Application deadline:* For fall admission, 8/1 priority date for domestic students, 6/1 for international students; for winter admission, 12/1 priority date for domestic students, 10/1 for international students; for spring admission, 3/1 priority date for domestic students, 1/1 for international students. Applications are processed on a rolling basis. Application fee: $25. Electronic applications accepted. *Expenses:* Contact institution. *Financial support:* In 2011–12, 56 students received support, including 3 fellowships with full tuition reimbursements available (averaging $30,000 per year), 3 research assistantships with full and partial tuition reimbursements available (averaging $22,833 per year), 50 teaching assistantships (averaging $6,194 per year); Federal Work-Study, scholarships/grants, tuition waivers (full and partial), and unspecified assistantships also available. Support available to part-time students. Financial award application deadline: 4/30. *Faculty research:* Data mining, theoretical computer science, gaming, security, animation and film. *Total annual research expenditures:* $3.9 million. *Unit head:* Elly Kafritsas-Wessels, Senior Administrative Assistant, 312-362-5816, Fax: 312-362-5185, E-mail: ekafrits@cdm.depaul.edu. *Application contact:* James Parker, Director of Graduate Admission, 312-362-8714, Fax: 312-362-5179, E-mail: jparke29@cdm.depaul.edu. Web site: http://cdm.depaul.edu.

Full Sail University, Game Design Master of Science Program - Campus, Winter Park, FL 32792-7437. Offers MS.

George Mason University, Volgenau School of Engineering, Department of Computer Science, Fairfax, VA 22030. Offers computer games technology (Certificate); computer networking (Certificate); computer science (MS, PhD); database management (Certificate); electronic commerce (Certificate); foundations of information systems (Certificate); information engineering (Certificate); information security and assurance (MS, Certificate); information systems (MS); intelligent agents (Certificate); software architecture (Certificate); software engineering (MS, Certificate); software engineering for C41 (Certificate); Web-based software engineering (Certificate). MS program offered jointly with Old Dominion University, University of Virginia, Virginia Commonwealth University, and Virginia Polytechnic Institute and State University. *Faculty:* 40 full-time (9 women), 17 part-time/adjunct (0 women). *Students:* 208 full-time (52 women), 357 part-time (75 women); includes 98 minority (17 Black or African American, non-Hispanic/Latino; 63 Asian, non-Hispanic/Latino; 14 Hispanic/Latino; 4 Two or more races, non-Hispanic/Latino), 205 international. Average age 30. 882 applicants, 52% accepted, 137 enrolled. In 2011, 164 master's, 5 doctorates, 28 other advanced degrees awarded. *Degree requirements:* For master's, thesis optional; for doctorate, comprehensive exam, thesis/dissertation. *Entrance requirements:* For master's, GRE, proof of financial support; 2 official college transcripts; resume; self-evaluation form; official bank statement; photocopy of passport; 3 letters of recommendation; baccalaureate degree related to computer science; minimum GPA of 3.0 in last 2 years of undergraduate work; 1 year beyond 1st-year calculus; personal goals statement; for doctorate, GRE, personal goals statement; 2 official copies of transcripts; self-evaluation form; 3 letters of recommendation; photocopy of passport; proof of financial support; official bank statement; resume; 4-year baccalaureate degree with strong background in computer science. Additional exam requirements/recommendations for international students: Required—TOEFL (minimum score 575 paper-based; 230 computer-based; 88 iBT), IELTS, Pearson Test of English. *Application deadline:* For fall admission, 1/15 priority date for domestic students; for spring admission, 8/15 priority date for domestic students. Application fee: $65 ($80 for international students). Electronic applications accepted. *Expenses:* Tuition, state resident: full-time $8750; part-time $364.58 per credit. Tuition, nonresident: full-time $24,092; part-time $1003.83 per credit. *Required fees:* $2514; $104.75 per credit. *Financial support:* In 2011–12, 100 students received support, including 3 fellowships (averaging $18,000 per year), 50 research assistantships (averaging $15,232 per year), 47 teaching assistantships (averaging $11,675 per year); career-related internships or fieldwork, Federal Work-Study, scholarships/grants, unspecified assistantships, and health care benefits (full-time research or teaching assistantship recipients) also available. Support available to part-time students. Financial award application deadline: 3/1; financial award applicants required to submit FAFSA. *Faculty research:* Artificial intelligence, image processing/graphics, parallel/distributed systems, software engineering systems. *Total annual research expenditures:* $1.9 million. *Unit head:* Sanjeev Setia, Chair, 703-993-4098, Fax: 703-993-1710, E-mail: setia@gmu.edu. *Application contact:* Michele Pieper, Administrative Assistant, 703-993-9483, Fax: 703-993-1710, E-mail: mpieper@gmu.edu. Web site: http://cs.gmu.edu/.

Michigan State University, The Graduate School, College of Communication Arts and Sciences, Department of Telecommunication, Information Studies, and Media, East Lansing, MI 48824. Offers digital media arts and technology (MA); information and telecommunication management (MA); information, policy and society (MA); serious game design (MA). *Entrance requirements:* Additional exam requirements/recommendations for international students: Required—TOEFL. Electronic applications accepted.

Rochester Institute of Technology, Graduate Enrollment Services, B. Thomas Golisano College of Computing and Information Sciences, School of Interactive Games and Media, Rochester, NY 14623-5603. Offers game design and development (MS). Part-time programs available. *Students:* 17 full-time (3 women); includes 2 minority (1 Black or African American, non-Hispanic/Latino; 1 Hispanic/Latino), 5 international. Average age 24. 51 applicants, 37% accepted, 9 enrolled. In 2011, 11 degrees awarded. *Degree requirements:* For master's, thesis. *Entrance requirements:* For master's, GRE, minimum GPA of 3.25. Additional exam requirements/recommendations for international students: Required—TOEFL (minimum score 570 paper-based; 230 computer-based; 88 iBT) or IELTS (minimum score 6.5). *Application deadline:* For fall admission, 1/15 priority date for domestic students, 1/1 for international students. Applications are processed on a rolling basis. Application fee: $50. Electronic applications accepted. *Expenses: Tuition:* Full-time $34,659; part-time $963 per credit hour. *Required fees:* $228; $76 per quarter. *Financial support:* Research assistantships with partial tuition reimbursements, teaching assistantships with partial tuition reimbursements, career-related internships or fieldwork, scholarships/grants, and unspecified assistantships available. Support available to part-time students. Financial award applicants required to submit FAFSA. *Faculty research:* Experimental game design and development; exploratory research in visualization environments and integrated media frameworks; outreach efforts that surround games and underlying technologies; support of STEM learning through games and interactive entertainment; the application of games and game technology to non-entertainment domains (Serious Games); small, discrete play experiences (Casual Games). *Unit head:* Andrew Phelps, Director, 585-475-6758, E-mail: andy@mail.rit.edu. *Application contact:* Diane Ellison, Assistant Vice President, Graduate Enrollment Services, 585-475-2229, Fax: 585-475-7164, E-mail: gradinfo@rit.edu. Web site: http://igm.rit.edu.

Savannah College of Art and Design, Graduate School, Program in Interactive Design and Game Development, Savannah, GA 31402-3146. Offers MA, MFA, Graduate Certificate. Part-time programs available. Postbaccalaureate distance learning degree programs offered (no on-campus study). *Faculty:* 15 full-time (4 women), 7 part-time/adjunct (1 woman). *Students:* 62 full-time (22 women), 42 part-time (16 women); includes 16 minority (6 Black or African American, non-Hispanic/Latino; 3 Asian, non-Hispanic/Latino; 7 Hispanic/Latino), 26 international. Average age 29. 98 applicants, 44% accepted, 25 enrolled. In 2011, 24 master's, 2 other advanced degrees awarded. *Degree requirements:* For master's, thesis, internships. *Entrance requirements:* For master's, portfolio (in digital or multimedia format). Additional exam requirements/recommendations for international students: Required—TOEFL (minimum score 400 paper-based; 50 computer-based). *Application deadline:* For fall admission, 4/1 priority date for domestic students, 4/1 for international students. Applications are processed on a rolling basis. Application fee: $35. Electronic applications accepted. *Expenses: Tuition:* Full-time $30,960; part-time $6880 per quarter. One-time fee: $500. *Financial support:* Fellowships, career-related internships or fieldwork, Federal Work-Study, and scholarships/grants available. Financial award application deadline: 4/1; financial award applicants required to submit FAFSA. *Unit head:* Luis Cataldi, Chair, 912-525-8577, E-mail: lcataldi@scad.edu. *Application contact:* Elizabeth Mathis, Director of Graduate Recruitment, 912-525-5965, Fax: 912-525-5985, E-mail: emathis@scad.edu.

University of Advancing Technology, Master of Science Program in Technology, Tempe, AZ 85283-1042. Offers advancing computer science (MS); emerging technologies (MS); game production and management (MS); information assurance (MS); technology leadership (MS). *Degree requirements:* For master's, project or thesis. *Entrance requirements:* Additional exam requirements/recommendations for international students: Required—TOEFL (minimum score 550 paper-based). Electronic applications accepted. *Faculty research:* Artificial intelligence, fractals, organizational management.

University of Central Florida, College of Arts and Humanities, Florida Interactive Entertainment Academy, Orlando, FL 32816. Offers MS. *Students:* 66 full-time (14 women), 55 part-time (10 women); includes 34 minority (6 Black or African American, non-Hispanic/Latino; 10 Asian, non-Hispanic/Latino; 17 Hispanic/Latino; 1 Two or more races, non-Hispanic/Latino), 7 international. Average age 26. 130 applicants, 55% accepted, 65 enrolled. In 2011, 48 master's awarded. *Expenses:* Tuition, state resident: part-time $277.08 per credit hour. Tuition, nonresident: part-time $277.08 per credit hour. Part-time tuition and fees vary according to degree level and program. *Unit head:* Ben Noel, Executive Director, 407-235-3612, Fax: 407-317-7094, E-mail: bnoel@fiea.ucf.edu. *Application contact:* Barbara Rodriguez, Director, Admissions and Registration, 407-823-2766, Fax: 407-823-6442, E-mail: gradadmissions@ucf.edu. Web site: http://www.fiea.ucf.edu/.

The University of North Carolina at Charlotte, Graduate School, College of Computing and Informatics, Department of Software and Information Systems, Charlotte, NC 28223-0001. Offers game design and development (Certificate); health care information (Certificate); information security/privacy (Certificate); information technology (MS, PhD, Certificate). Part-time programs available. *Faculty:* 14 full-time (3 women), 4 part-time/adjunct (0 women). *Students:* 134 full-time (42 women), 88 part-time (36 women); includes 39 minority (23 Black or African American, non-Hispanic/Latino; 5 Asian, non-Hispanic/Latino; 5 Hispanic/Latino; 6 Two or more races, non-Hispanic/Latino), 102 international. Average age 30. 182 applicants, 75% accepted, 47 enrolled. In 2011, 32 master's, 12 doctorates, 33 other advanced degrees awarded. Terminal master's awarded for partial completion of doctoral program. *Degree requirements:* For master's, thesis optional; for doctorate, comprehensive exam, thesis/dissertation. *Entrance requirements:* For master's, GRE or GMAT, minimum undergraduate GPA of 2.8 overall, 2.0 in last 2 years; for doctorate, GRE or GMAT, working knowledge of 2 high-level programming languages. Additional exam requirements/recommendations for international students: Required—TOEFL (minimum score 557 paper-based; 220 computer-based; 83 iBT). *Application deadline:* For fall admission, 7/1 for domestic students, 5/1 for international students; for spring admission, 11/1 for domestic students, 10/1 for international students. Applications are processed on a rolling basis. Application fee: $65 ($75 for international students). Electronic applications accepted. *Expenses:* Tuition, state resident: full-time $3689. Tuition, nonresident: full-time $15,226. *Required fees:* $2198. Tuition and fees vary according to course load and program. *Financial support:* In 2011–12, 41 students received support, including 1 fellowship (averaging $50,000 per year), 19 research assistantships (averaging $9,874 per year), 21 teaching assistantships (averaging $13,421 per year); career-related internships or fieldwork, institutionally sponsored loans, scholarships/grants, and unspecified assistantships also available. Support available to part-time students. Financial award application deadline: 4/1; financial award applicants required to submit FAFSA. *Faculty research:* Information security, information privacy, information assurance, cryptography, software engineering, enterprise integration, intelligent information systems, human-computer interaction. *Total annual research expenditures:* $1.8 million. *Unit head:* Dr. Ken Chen, Program Director, 704-687-8545, Fax: 704-687-6065, E-mail: chen@uncc.edu. *Application contact:* Kathy B. Giddings, Director of Graduate Admissions, 704-687-5503, Fax: 704-687-3279, E-mail: gradadm@uncc.edu. Web site: http://sis.uncc.edu/.

University of Southern California, Graduate School, Viterbi School of Engineering, Department of Computer Science, Los Angeles, CA 90089. Offers computer networks (MS); computer science (MS, PhD); computer security (MS); game development (MS); high performance computing and simulations (MS); human language technology (MS); intelligent robotics (MS); multimedia and creative technologies (MS); software engineering (MS). Part-time and evening/weekend programs available.

Postbaccalaureate distance learning degree programs offered (no on-campus study). *Entrance requirements:* For master's and doctorate, GRE General Test. Additional exam requirements/recommendations for international students: Required—TOEFL. Electronic applications accepted. *Faculty research:* Databases, computer graphics and computer vision, software engineering, networks and security, robotics, multimedia and virtual reality.

West Virginia University, College of Engineering and Mineral Resources, Lane Department of Computer Science and Electrical Engineering, Program in Interactive Technologies and Serious Gaming, Morgantown, WV 26506. Offers Graduate Certificate. *Entrance requirements:* Additional exam requirements/recommendations for international students: Required—TOEFL or IELTS. Electronic applications accepted.

Worcester Polytechnic Institute, Graduate Studies and Research, Program in Interactive Media and Game Development, Worcester, MA 01609-2280. Offers MS. Part-time and evening/weekend programs available. *Students:* 3 full-time (0 women), 2 part-time (0 women), 1 international. 10 applicants, 90% accepted, 5 enrolled. *Entrance requirements:* For master's, GRE (recommended), 3 letters of recommendation. Additional exam requirements/recommendations for international students: Required—TOEFL (minimum score 563 paper-based; 223 computer-based; 84 iBT), IELTS (minimum score 7). *Application deadline:* For fall admission, 1/1 for domestic and international students; for spring admission, 10/1 for domestic and international students. Applications are processed on a rolling basis. Electronic applications accepted. *Financial support:* Research assistantships and teaching assistantships available. *Faculty research:* Artificial intelligence, human-robot interaction, intelligent user interfaces, serious games. *Unit head:* Charles Rich, Graduate Coordinator, 508-831-4977, Fax: 508-831-5776, E-mail: rich@wpi.edu. *Application contact:* Tracy Coetzee, Administrative Assistant, 508-831-4977, Fax: 508-831-5776, E-mail: tcoetzee@wpi.edu. Web site: http://imgd.wpi.edu/.

Health Informatics

American Sentinel University, Graduate Programs, Aurora, CO 80014. Offers business administration (MBA); business intelligence (MS); computer science (MSCS); health information management (MS); healthcare (MBA); information systems (MSIS); nursing (MSN). Part-time and evening/weekend programs available. Postbaccalaureate distance learning degree programs offered (no on-campus study). *Entrance requirements:* Additional exam requirements/recommendations for international students: Required—TOEFL (minimum score 600 paper-based; 215 computer-based). Electronic applications accepted.

Arkansas Tech University, Center for Leadership and Learning, College of Natural and Health Sciences, Russellville, AR 72801. Offers fisheries and wildlife biology (MS); health informatics (MS); nursing (MSN). Part-time programs available. *Students:* 6 full-time (4 women), 45 part-time (34 women); includes 2 minority (1 Black or African American, non-Hispanic/Latino; 1 American Indian or Alaska Native, non-Hispanic/Latino), 1 international. Average age 40. In 2011, 9 master's awarded. *Degree requirements:* For master's, thesis (for some programs), project. *Entrance requirements:* For master's, GRE General Test. Additional exam requirements/recommendations for international students: Required—TOEFL (minimum score 550 paper-based; 213 computer-based; 79 iBT), IELTS (minimum score 6). *Application deadline:* For fall admission, 3/1 priority date for domestic students, 5/1 for international students; for spring admission, 10/1 priority date for domestic students, 10/1 for international students. Applications are processed on a rolling basis. Application fee: $25 ($75 for international students). Electronic applications accepted. *Expenses:* Tuition, state resident: full-time $4968; part-time $207 per credit hour. Tuition, nonresident: full-time $9936; part-time $414 per credit hour. *Required fees:* $375 per semester. Tuition and fees vary according to course load. *Financial support:* In 2011–12, teaching assistantships with full tuition reimbursements (averaging $4,800 per year) were awarded; research assistantships with full tuition reimbursements, career-related internships or fieldwork, Federal Work-Study, scholarships/grants, health care benefits, and unspecified assistantships also available. Support available to part-time students. Financial award application deadline: 4/15; financial award applicants required to submit FAFSA. *Unit head:* Dr. Jeff Robertson, Dean, 479-968-0498, E-mail: jrobertson@atu.edu. *Application contact:* Dr. Mary B. Gunter, Dean of Graduate College, 479-968-0398, Fax: 479-964-0542, E-mail: gradcollege@atu.edu. Web site: http://www.atu.edu/nhs/.

Barry University, College of Health Sciences, Graduate Certificate Programs, Miami Shores, FL 33161-6695. Offers health care leadership (Certificate); health care planning and informatics (Certificate); histotechnology (Certificate); long term care management (Certificate); medical group practice management (Certificate); quality improvement and outcomes management (Certificate).

Benedictine University, Graduate Programs, Program in Public Health, Lisle, IL 60532-0900. Offers administration of health care institutions (MPH); dietetics (MPH); disaster management (MPH); health education (MPH); health information systems (MPH); MBA/MPH; MPH/MS. Part-time and evening/weekend programs available. Postbaccalaureate distance learning degree programs offered. *Faculty:* 2 full-time (0 women), 8 part-time/adjunct (3 women). *Students:* 85 full-time (61 women), 437 part-time (333 women); includes 217 minority (133 Black or African American, non-Hispanic/Latino; 1 American Indian or Alaska Native, non-Hispanic/Latino; 65 Asian, non-Hispanic/Latino; 18 Hispanic/Latino), 28 international. Average age 33. 172 applicants, 80% accepted, 113 enrolled. In 2011, 116 master's awarded. *Entrance requirements:* For master's, MAT, GRE, or GMAT. Additional exam requirements/recommendations for international students: Required—TOEFL (minimum score 550 paper-based; 213 computer-based). *Application deadline:* For fall admission, 9/1 for domestic students; for winter admission, 12/1 for domestic students; for spring admission, 2/15 for domestic students. Application fee: $40. *Financial support:* Career-related internships or fieldwork and health care benefits available. Support available to part-time students. *Unit head:* Dr. Georgeen Polyak, Director, 630-829-6217, E-mail: gpolyak@ben.edu. *Application contact:* Kari Gibbons, Associate Vice President, Enrollment Center, 630-829-6200, Fax: 630-829-6584, E-mail: kgibbons@ben.edu.

Boston University, Metropolitan College, Department of Computer Science, Boston, MA 02215. Offers computer information systems (MS), including computer networks, database management and business intelligence, health informatics, IT project management, security, Web application development; computer science (MS), including computer networks, security; telecommunications (MS), including security. Evening/weekend programs available. Postbaccalaureate distance learning degree programs offered. *Faculty:* 12 full-time (2 women), 28 part-time/adjunct (2 women). *Students:* 25 full-time (6 women), 732 part-time (167 women); includes 208 minority (51 Black or African American, non-Hispanic/Latino; 1 American Indian or Alaska Native, non-Hispanic/Latino; 104 Asian, non-Hispanic/Latino; 43 Hispanic/Latino; 1 Native Hawaiian or other Pacific Islander, non-Hispanic/Latino; 8 Two or more races, non-Hispanic/Latino), 86 international. Average age 35. 260 applicants, 67% accepted, 143 enrolled. In 2011, 143 master's awarded. *Degree requirements:* For master's, thesis optional. *Entrance requirements:* For master's, 3 letters of recommendation, professional resume. Additional exam requirements/recommendations for international students: Required—TOEFL (minimum score 550 paper-based; 213 computer-based; 80 iBT). *Application deadline:* For fall admission, 6/1 for international students; for spring admission, 10/1 for international students. Applications are processed on a rolling basis. Application fee: $70. Electronic applications accepted. *Expenses: Tuition:* Full-time $40,848; part-time $1276 per credit hour. *Required fees:* $572; $286 per semester. *Financial support:* In 2011–12, 9 research assistantships (averaging $5,000 per year) were awarded; career-related internships or fieldwork and unspecified assistantships also available. Support available to part-time students. Financial award applicants required to submit FAFSA. *Faculty research:* Medical informatics, Web technologies, telecom and networks, security and forensics, software engineering, programming languages, multimedia and AI, information systems and IT project management. *Unit head:* Dr. Lubomir Chitkushev, Chairman, 617-353-2566, Fax: 617-353-2367, E-mail: csinfo@bu.edu. *Application contact:* Kim Richards, Program Coordinator, 617-353-2566, Fax: 617-353-2367, E-mail: kimrich@bu.edu. Web site: http://www.bu.edu/csmet/.

Brandeis University, Rabb School of Continuing Studies, Division of Graduate Professional Studies, Health and Medical Informatics Program, Waltham, MA 02454-9110. Offers MS. Part-time programs available. Postbaccalaureate distance learning degree programs offered (no on-campus study). *Faculty:* 2 full-time (both women), 34 part-time/adjunct (8 women). *Students:* 1 (woman) full-time, 16 part-time (12 women); includes 3 minority (2 Black or African American, non-Hispanic/Latino; 1 Asian, non-Hispanic/Latino). Average age 35. 9 applicants, 100% accepted, 8 enrolled. *Entrance requirements:* For master's, resume, official transcripts, recommendations, goal statements. Additional exam requirements/recommendations for international students: Recommended—TOEFL (minimum score 600 paper-based; 250 computer-based; 100 iBT). *Application deadline:* For fall admission, 6/15 priority date for domestic students; for winter admission, 10/15 for domestic students; for spring admission, 2/15 for domestic students. Application fee: $50. *Unit head:* Dr. Cynthia Phillips, Program Chair, 781-736-8787, Fax: 781-736-3420, E-mail: cynthiap@brandeis.edu. *Application contact:* Frances Stearns, Associate Director of Admissions and Student Services, 781-736-8785, Fax: 781-736-3420, E-mail: fstearns@brandeis.edu. Web site: http://www.brandeis.edu/gps/.

Claremont Graduate University, Graduate Programs, School of Information Systems and Technology, Claremont, CA 91711-6160. Offers electronic commerce (MS, PhD); health information management (MS); information systems (Certificate); knowledge management (MS, PhD); systems development (MS, PhD); telecommunications and networking (MS, PhD); MBA/MS. Part-time programs available. *Faculty:* 7 full-time (1 woman), 1 part-time/adjunct (0 women). *Students:* 68 full-time (20 women), 26 part-time (10 women); includes 31 minority (5 Black or African American, non-Hispanic/Latino; 14 Asian, non-Hispanic/Latino; 9 Hispanic/Latino; 1 Native Hawaiian or other Pacific Islander, non-Hispanic/Latino; 2 Two or more races, non-Hispanic/Latino), 31 international. Average age 37. In 2011, 16 master's, 5 doctorates awarded. *Degree requirements:* For doctorate, comprehensive exam, thesis/dissertation, portfolio. *Entrance requirements:* For master's and doctorate, GMAT, GRE General Test. Additional exam requirements/recommendations for international students: Required—TOEFL (minimum score 550 paper-based; 213 computer-based; 80 iBT). *Application deadline:* For fall admission, 2/1 priority date for domestic students. Applications are processed on a rolling basis. Application fee: $60. Electronic applications accepted. *Expenses: Tuition:* Full-time $36,374; part-time $1581 per unit. *Required fees:* $165 per semester. *Financial support:* Fellowships, research assistantships, teaching assistantships, Federal Work-Study, institutionally sponsored loans, and scholarships/grants available. Support available to part-time students. Financial award application deadline: 2/15; financial award applicants required to submit FAFSA. *Faculty research:* GPSS, man-machine interaction, organizational aspects of computing, implementation of information systems, information systems practice. *Unit head:* Tom Horan, Dean, 909-607-9302, Fax: 909-621-8564, E-mail: tom.horan@cgu.edu. *Application contact:* Anondah Saide, Program Coordinator, 909-607-6006, E-mail: anonda.saide@cgu.edu. Web site: http://www.cgu.edu/pages/153.asp.

The College of St. Scholastica, Graduate Studies, Department of Health Information Management, Duluth, MN 55811-4199. Offers MA, Certificate. Part-time programs available. Postbaccalaureate distance learning degree programs offered (minimal on-campus study). *Faculty:* 4 full-time (all women), 12 part-time/adjunct (10 women). *Students:* 174 full-time (132 women), 46 part-time (40 women); includes 75 minority (42 Black or African American, non-Hispanic/Latino; 2 American Indian or Alaska Native, non-Hispanic/Latino; 22 Asian, non-Hispanic/Latino; 3 Hispanic/Latino; 2 Native Hawaiian or other Pacific Islander, non-Hispanic/Latino; 4 Two or more races, non-Hispanic/Latino). Average age 40. 71 applicants, 59% accepted. In 2011, 27 master's awarded. *Degree requirements:* For master's, thesis. *Entrance requirements:* For master's, minimum GPA of 3.0. Additional exam requirements/recommendations for international students: Required—TOEFL (minimum score 550 paper-based; 213 computer-based; 79 iBT). *Application deadline:* For fall admission, 8/1 priority date for domestic students, 8/1 for international students; for spring admission, 11/1 priority date for domestic students, 11/1 for international students. Applications are processed on a rolling basis. Electronic applications accepted. *Expenses:* Contact institution. *Financial support:* In 2011–12, 55 students received support. Scholarships/grants available. Support available to part-time students. Financial award applicants required to submit FAFSA. *Faculty research:* Electronic health record implementation, personal health records, Athens project. *Unit head:* Amy Watters, Director, 218-723-7094, Fax: 218-733-2239, E-mail: awatters@css.edu. *Application contact:* Lindsay Lahti, Director of Graduate and Extended Studies Recruitment, 218-733-2240, Fax: 218-733-2275, E-mail: gradstudies@css.edu. Web site: http://www.css.edu/Academics/School-of-Health-Sciences/Health-Information-Management.html.

Drexel University, The iSchool at Drexel, College of Information Science and Technology, Master of Science in Health Informatics Program, Philadelphia, PA 19104-2875. Offers MS. Postbaccalaureate distance learning degree programs offered (no on-campus study). *Unit head:* Dr. David E. Fenske, Dean/Professor of Information Science, 215-895-2475, Fax: 215-895-6378, E-mail: fenske@drexel.edu. *Application contact:* Matthew Lechtenberg, Graduate Admissions Manager, 215-895-1951, Fax: 215-895-2303, E-mail: ml333@drexel.edu. Web site: http://www.ischool.drexel.edu/PS/GraduatePrograms/Degrees/MSHI.

Emory University, Rollins School of Public Health, Department of Biostatistics and Bioinformatics, Atlanta, GA 30322-1100. Offers bioinformatics (PhD); biostatistics (MSPH); public health informatics (MSPH). PhD offered through the Graduate School of Arts and Sciences. Part-time programs available. *Students:* 7 full-time. Average age 27. 106 applicants, 18% accepted, 7 enrolled. *Degree requirements:* For master's, thesis, practicum. *Entrance requirements:* For master's, GRE General Test. Additional exam requirements/recommendations for international students: Required—TOEFL (minimum score 550 paper-based; 213 computer-based; 80 iBT). *Application deadline:* For fall admission, 12/15 priority date for domestic students, 12/15 for international students. Application fee: $95. Electronic applications accepted. *Expenses: Tuition:* Full-time $34,800. *Required fees:* $1300. *Financial support:* Fellowships with full and partial tuition reimbursements, career-related internships or fieldwork, Federal Work-Study, institutionally sponsored loans, scholarships/grants, traineeships, health care benefits, and unspecified assistantships available. Support available to part-time students. Financial award application deadline: 1/5; financial award applicants required to submit FAFSA. *Unit head:* Lance A. Waller, Chair, 404-727-1057, Fax: 404-727-1370, E-mail: lwaller@emory.edu.

Emory University, Rollins School of Public Health, Online Program in Public Health, Atlanta, GA 30322-1100. Offers applied epidemiology (MPH); applied public health informatics (MPH); prevention science (MPH). Part-time and evening/weekend programs available. Postbaccalaureate distance learning degree programs offered (minimal on-campus study). *Students:* 35 full-time. Average age 40. *Degree requirements:* For master's, thesis, practicum. *Entrance requirements:* For master's, GRE. Additional exam requirements/recommendations for international students: Required—TOEFL (minimum score 550 paper-based; 213 computer-based; 80 iBT). *Application deadline:* For fall admission, 1/5 priority date for domestic students, 1/5 for international students. Applications are processed on a rolling basis. Application fee: $95. Electronic applications accepted. *Expenses: Tuition:* Full-time $34,800. *Required fees:* $1300. *Financial support:* Fellowships with full and partial tuition reimbursements, career-related internships or fieldwork, Federal Work-Study, institutionally sponsored loans, scholarships/grants, traineeships, health care benefits, and unspecified assistantships available. Support available to part-time students. Financial award application deadline: 1/5; financial award applicants required to submit FAFSA. *Unit head:* Melissa Alperin, Director, 404-727-2928, Fax: 404-727-3996, E-mail: malperi@emory.edu. Web site: http://www.sph.emory.edu/CMPH/.

George Mason University, College of Health and Human Services, Department of Health Administration and Policy, Fairfax, VA 22030. Offers health and medical policy (MS); health information systems (Certificate); health systems management (MS); quality improvement and outcomes management in health care systems (Certificate); senior housing administration (MS, Certificate). *Accreditation:* CAHME. *Faculty:* 18 full-time (5 women), 11 part-time/adjunct (7 women). *Students:* 45 full-time (31 women), 110 part-time (77 women); includes 75 minority (27 Black or African American, non-Hispanic/Latino; 32 Asian, non-Hispanic/Latino; 12 Hispanic/Latino; 4 Two or more races, non-Hispanic/Latino), 8 international. Average age 32. 113 applicants, 60% accepted, 49 enrolled. In 2011, 31 master's, 6 other advanced degrees awarded. *Degree requirements:* For master's, comprehensive exam, internship. *Entrance requirements:* For master's, GRE recommended if undergraduate GPA is below 3.0 (for senior housing administration MS only), 2 official transcripts; expanded goals statement; 3 letters of recommendation; resume; 1 year of work experience (for MHA in health systems management); for Certificate, 2 official transcripts; expanded goals statement; 3 letters of recommendation; resume. Additional exam requirements/recommendations for international students: Required—TOEFL (minimum score 575 paper-based; 230 computer-based; 88 iBT), IELTS, Pearson Test of English. *Application deadline:* For fall admission, 4/1 priority date for domestic students; for spring admission, 11/1 priority date for domestic students. Applications are processed on a rolling basis. Application fee: $65 ($80 for international students). Electronic applications accepted. *Expenses:* Tuition, state resident: full-time $8750; part-time $364.58 per credit. Tuition, nonresident: full-time $24,092; part-time $1003.83 per credit. *Required fees:* $2514; $104.75 per credit. *Financial support:* In 2011–12, 3 students received support, including 2 research assistantships with full and partial tuition reimbursements available (averaging $15,000 per year), 1 teaching assistantship (averaging $12,760 per year); career-related internships or fieldwork, Federal Work-Study, scholarships/grants, unspecified assistantships, and health care benefits (full-time research or teaching assistantship recipients) also available. Support available to part-time students. Financial award application deadline: 3/1; financial award applicants required to submit FAFSA. *Faculty research:* Universal health care, publications, relationships between malpractice pressure and rates of Cesarean section and VBAC, seniors and Wii gaming, relationships between changes in physician's incomes and practice settings and their care to Medicaid and charity patients. *Total annual research expenditures:* $517,468. *Unit head:* Dr. P. J. Maddox, Chair, 703-993-1982, Fax: 703-993-1982, E-mail: pmaddox@gmu.edu. *Application contact:* Valerie Bartush, Office Manager, 703-993-1929, Fax: 703-993-1953, E-mail: vbartush@gmu.edu. Web site: http://chhs.gmu.edu/hap/index.

Georgia Health Sciences University, College of Graduate Studies, Program in Public Health–Informatics, Augusta, GA 30912. Offers MPH. Part-time programs available. *Faculty:* 7 full-time (5 women). *Students:* 11 full-time (9 women), 10 part-time (6 women); includes 10 minority (4 Black or African American, non-Hispanic/Latino; 4 Asian, non-Hispanic/Latino; 2 Hispanic/Latino), 1 international. Average age 32. 28 applicants, 39% accepted, 7 enrolled. In 2011, 5 master's awarded. *Degree requirements:* For master's, thesis (for some programs). *Entrance requirements:* For master's, GRE General Test. Additional exam requirements/recommendations for international students: Required—TOEFL. *Application deadline:* For fall admission, 6/1 for domestic and international students. Application fee: $50. Electronic applications accepted. *Financial support:* Federal Work-Study available. Financial award application deadline: 5/31; financial award applicants required to submit FAFSA. *Unit head:* Dr. Douglas Keskula, Interim Dean, 706-721-2621, Fax: 706-721-7312, E-mail: dkeskula@georgiahealth.edu. *Application contact:* Lori Prince, Interim Chair, 706-721-3436, E-mail: lprince@georgiahealth.edu. Web site: http://www.georgiahealth.edu/alliedhealth/mph/index.html.

Golden Gate University, Ageno School of Business, San Francisco, CA 94105-2968. Offers accounting (MBA); business administration (EMBA, MBA, PMBA, DBA); finance (MBA, MS, Certificate); financial planning (MS, Certificate); healthcare information systems (Certificate); human resource management (MBA, MS); human resources management (Certificate); information systems (MS); information technology (MBA); information technology management (Certificate); integrated marketing and communications (MS, Certificate); international business (MBA); management (MBA); marketing (MBA, MS, Certificate); operations supply chain management (Certificate); psychology (MA, Certificate); public administration (EMPA); public relations (MS, Certificate); technical market analysis (Certificate); JD/MBA. Part-time and evening/weekend programs available. *Faculty:* 19 full-time (6 women), 241 part-time/adjunct (72 women). *Students:* 397 full-time (230 women), 779 part-time (432 women); includes 376 minority (105 Black or African American, non-Hispanic/Latino; 5 American Indian or Alaska Native, non-Hispanic/Latino; 161 Asian, non-Hispanic/Latino; 77 Hispanic/Latino; 12 Native Hawaiian or other Pacific Islander, non-Hispanic/Latino; 16 Two or more races, non-Hispanic/Latino), 265 international. Average age 34. 871 applicants, 64% accepted, 271 enrolled. In 2011, 550 master's, 13 doctorates awarded. *Degree requirements:* For doctorate, thesis/dissertation, qualifying examination. *Entrance requirements:* For master's, GMAT (MBA), minimum GPA of 2.5 (MS). Additional exam requirements/recommendations for international students: Required—TOEFL (minimum score 550 paper-based; 213 computer-based; 79 iBT). *Application deadline:* For fall admission, 5/15 for domestic and international students; for winter admission, 1/15 for domestic and international students; for spring admission, 9/15 for domestic and international students. Applications are processed on a rolling basis. Application fee: $70 ($110 for international students). Electronic applications accepted. *Expenses:* Contact institution. *Financial support:* Career-related internships or fieldwork, Federal Work-Study, institutionally sponsored loans, and scholarships/grants available. Support available to part-time students. Financial award applicants required to submit FAFSA. *Unit head:* Dr. Paul Fouts, Dean, 415-442-7026, Fax: 415-442-6579. *Application contact:* Angela Melero, Enrollment Services, 415-442-7800, Fax: 415-442-7807, E-mail: info@ggu.edu. Web site: http://www.ggu.edu/programs/business-and-management.

Grand Canyon University, College of Nursing and Health Sciences, Phoenix, AZ 85017-1097. Offers addiction counseling (MS); health care administration (MS); health care informatics (MS); marriage and family therapy (MS); professional counseling (MS); public health (MS). Part-time and evening/weekend programs available. Postbaccalaureate distance learning degree programs offered (no on-campus study). *Entrance requirements:* For master's, undergraduate degree with minimum GPA of 2.8. Additional exam requirements/recommendations for international students: Required—TOEFL (minimum score 575 paper-based; 233 computer-based; 90 iBT), IELTS (minimum score 7).

Indiana University Bloomington, School of Informatics and Computing, Bloomington, IN 47408. Offers bioinformatics (MS); chemical informatics (MS); computer science (MS, PhD); health informatics (MS); human computer interaction (MS); informatics (PhD); laboratory informatics (MS); media arts and science (MS); music informatics (MS); security informatics (MS); MS/PhD. PhD offered through University Graduate School. Part-time programs available. Postbaccalaureate distance learning degree programs offered (no on-campus study). *Faculty:* 63 full-time (12 women). *Students:* 434 full-time (99 women), 36 part-time (9 women); includes 24 minority (8 Black or African American, non-Hispanic/Latino; 9 Asian, non-Hispanic/Latino; 4 Hispanic/Latino; 3 Two or more races, non-Hispanic/Latino), 309 international. Average age 27. 825 applicants, 58% accepted, 205 enrolled. In 2011, 115 master's, 25 doctorates awarded. Terminal master's awarded for partial completion of doctoral program. *Degree requirements:* For master's, thesis optional; for doctorate, comprehensive exam, thesis/dissertation, oral and written exams. *Entrance requirements:* For master's and doctorate, GRE, letters of reference. Additional exam requirements/recommendations for international students: Required—TOEFL. *Application deadline:* For fall admission, 1/15 for domestic students, 12/1 for international students. Application fee: $55 ($65 for international students). Electronic applications accepted. *Financial support:* In 2011–12, fellowships with full and partial tuition reimbursements (averaging $20,000 per year), research assistantships (averaging $14,000 per year), teaching assistantships (averaging $13,000 per year) were awarded; Federal Work-Study, institutionally sponsored loans, scholarships/grants, health care benefits, tuition waivers (full and partial), and unspecified assistantships also available. Support available to part-time students. *Total annual research expenditures:* $2 million. *Unit head:* Dr. David Leake, Associate Dean for Graduate Studies, 812-855-9756, E-mail: leake@cs.indiana.edu. *Application contact:* Rachel Lawmaster, Manager of Graduate Admissions and Graduate Studies, 812-856-3622, Fax: 812-856-3825, E-mail: raclee@indiana.edu. Web site: http://www.informatics.indiana.edu/.

The Johns Hopkins University, School of Medicine, Division of Health Sciences Informatics, Baltimore, MD 21218-2699. Offers applied health sciences informatics (MS); health sciences informatics research (MS). *Degree requirements:* For master's, thesis, publications, practica. *Entrance requirements:* Additional exam requirements/recommendations for international students: Recommended—TOEFL. Electronic applications accepted. *Faculty research:* Decision modeling, consumer health informatics, digital libraries, data standards, patient safety.

Lipscomb University, Program in Health Care Informatics, Nashville, TN 37204-3951. Offers MHCI. Part-time and evening/weekend programs available. *Faculty:* 1 (woman) full-time, 1 (woman) part-time/adjunct. *Students:* 22 full-time (11 women), 3 part-time (2 women); includes 7 minority (6 Black or African American, non-Hispanic/Latino; 1 Asian, non-Hispanic/Latino). Average age 38. 37 applicants, 84% accepted, 25 enrolled. *Entrance requirements:* For master's, bachelor's degree in relevant area of study and 5 years experience or advanced degree in relevant area of study, 2 references, resume, and personal statement. Additional exam requirements/recommendations for international students: Required—TOEFL (minimum score 570 paper-based; 230 computer-based). *Application deadline:* Applications are processed on a rolling basis. Application fee: $50 ($75 for international students). Electronic applications accepted. *Expenses: Tuition:* Full-time $16,830; part-time $935 per credit hour. Tuition and fees vary according to degree level and program. *Financial support:* Scholarships/grants available. Financial award applicants required to submit FAFSA. *Unit head:* Dr. Beth Breeden, Director, 615-966-7112, E-mail: beth.breeden@lipscomb.edu. *Application contact:* Kaci Allen, Director of Enrollment Management, 615-966-1195, E-mail: kaci.allen@lipscomb.edu. Web site: http://www.lipscomb.edu/technology/Health-Care-Informatics.

Marshall University, Academic Affairs Division, College of Health Professions, Department of Health Informatics, Huntington, WV 25755. Offers MS. Offered jointly with Lewis College of Business and College of Information Technology and Engineering. *Students:* 10 full-time (7 women), 4 part-time (1 woman); includes 5 minority (2 Black or African American, non-Hispanic/Latino; 2 Asian, non-Hispanic/Latino; 1 Hispanic/Latino), 3 international. Average age 32. *Unit head:* Dr. Girmay Berhie, Program Director, 304-696-2718, E-mail: berhie@marshall.edu. *Application contact:* Information Contact, 304-746-1900, Fax: 304-746-1902, E-mail: services@marshall.edu.

Metropolitan State University, College of Management, St. Paul, MN 55106-5000. Offers business administration (MBA, DBA); database administration (Graduate Certificate); healthcare information technology management (Graduate Certificate); information assurance security (Graduate Certificate); management information systems (MMIS); MIS generalist (Graduate Certificate); MIS systems analysis and design (Graduate Certificate); project management (Graduate Certificate); public and nonprofit administration (MPNA). Part-time and evening/weekend programs available. *Students:* 63 full-time (41 women), 409 part-time (192 women); includes 94 minority (38 Black or African American, non-Hispanic/Latino; 33 Asian, non-Hispanic/Latino; 14 Hispanic/Latino; 9 Two or more races, non-Hispanic/Latino), 61 international. Average age 35. *Degree requirements:* For master's, thesis optional, computer language (MMIS). *Entrance requirements:* For master's, GMAT (MBA), resume. Additional exam requirements/recommendations for international students: Required—TOEFL (minimum score 550 paper-based; 213 computer-based). *Application deadline:* For fall admission, 7/15 for international students; for winter admission, 11/15 for international students; for spring admission, 3/15 for international students. Applications are processed on a rolling basis. Application fee: $20. Electronic applications accepted. *Expenses:* Tuition, state resident: full-time $5799.06; part-time $322.17 per credit. Tuition, nonresident: full-time $11,411; part-time $633.92 per credit. Tuition and fees vary according to degree level, program and reciprocity agreements. *Financial support:* Research assistantships with partial tuition reimbursements, career-related internships or fieldwork, and Federal Work-Study available. Support available to part-time students. Financial award applicants required to submit FAFSA. *Faculty research:* Yugoslav economic system, workers' cooperatives, participative management and job enrichment, global business systems. *Unit head:* Dr. Paul Huo, Dean, 612-659-7271, Fax: 612-659-7268, E-mail: paul.huo@metrostate.edu. Web site: http://choose.metrostate.edu/comgradprograms.

Montana Tech of The University of Montana, Graduate School, Health Care Informatics Program, Butte, MT 59701-8997. Offers Certificate. Part-time and evening/weekend programs available. Postbaccalaureate distance learning degree programs offered (no on-campus study). *Faculty:* 4 full-time (2 women). *Students:* 6 full-time (all women), 1 (woman) part-time. 8 applicants, 88% accepted, 7 enrolled. *Entrance requirements:* Additional exam requirements/recommendations for international students: Required—TOEFL (minimum score 525 paper-based; 195 computer-based; 71 iBT). *Application deadline:* For fall admission, 4/1 priority date for domestic students, 3/1 for international students; for spring admission, 10/1 priority date for domestic students, 7/1 for international students. Applications are processed on a rolling basis. Application fee: $30. Electronic applications accepted. *Financial support:* In 2011–12, 7 students received support. Scholarships/grants available. Financial award application deadline: 4/1; financial award applicants required to submit FAFSA. *Faculty research:* Informatics, Healthcare, Computer Science. *Unit head:* Dr. Gary Mannix, Department Head, 406-496-4345, Fax: 406-496-4435, E-mail: gmannix@mtech.edu. *Application contact:* Fred Sullivan, Administrator, Graduate School, 406-496-4304, Fax: 406-496-4710, E-mail: fsullivan@mtech.edu. Web site: http://www.mtech.edu/academics/gradschool/distancelearning/distancelearning-hci.htm.

National University, Academic Affairs, School of Health and Human Services, Department of Community Health, La Jolla, CA 92037-1011. Offers health informatics (MS); healthcare administration (MHA); public health (MPH). Part-time and evening/weekend programs available. Postbaccalaureate distance learning degree programs offered. *Degree requirements:* For master's, thesis. *Entrance requirements:* Additional exam requirements/recommendations for international students: Required—TOEFL (minimum score 550 paper-based; 213 computer-based; 79 iBT). Application fee: $60 ($65 for international students). *Financial support:* Career-related internships or fieldwork, institutionally sponsored loans, and scholarships/grants available. Support available to part-time students. Financial award application deadline: 6/30; financial award applicants required to submit FAFSA. *Unit head:* Dr. Gina Piane, 858-309-3474, E-mail: gpiane@nu.edu. *Application contact:* Dominick Giovanniello, Associate Regional Dean, 800-NAT-UNIV, Fax: 858-541-7792, E-mail: dgiovann@nu.edu. Web site: http://www.nu.edu/OurPrograms/SchoolOfHealthAndHumanServices/CommunityHealth.html.

Northeastern University, College of Computer and Information Science, Boston, MA 02115-5096. Offers computer and information science (PhD); computer science (MS); health informatics (MS); information assurance (MS). Part-time and evening/weekend programs available. *Faculty:* 28 full-time, 3 part-time/adjunct. *Students:* 337 full-time (91 women), 90 part-time (52 women). 1,045 applicants, 56% accepted, 150 enrolled. In 2011, 88 master's, 7 doctorates awarded. Terminal master's awarded for partial completion of doctoral program. *Degree requirements:* For master's, thesis optional; for doctorate, comprehensive exam, thesis/dissertation. *Entrance requirements:* For master's and doctorate, GRE General Test. Additional exam requirements/recommendations for international students: Required—TOEFL or IELTS. *Application deadline:* For fall admission, 7/15 for domestic students, 5/1 for international students; for spring admission, 10/15 for domestic students, 9/1 for international students. Applications are processed on a rolling basis. Application fee: $50. Electronic applications accepted. *Expenses:* Contact institution. *Financial support:* In 2011–12, 59 students received support, including 1 fellowship, 40 research assistantships with full tuition reimbursements available (averaging $18,260 per year), 33 teaching assistantships with full tuition reimbursements available (averaging $18,260 per year); career-related internships or fieldwork, Federal Work-Study, institutionally sponsored loans, scholarships/grants, and unspecified assistantships also available. Financial award application deadline: 1/15. *Faculty research:* Programming languages, artificial intelligence, human-computer interaction, database management, network security. *Unit head:* Dr. Larry A. Finkelstein, Dean, 617-373-2462, Fax: 617-373-5121. *Application contact:* Dr. Agnes Chan, Associate Dean and Director of Graduate Program, 617-373-2462, Fax: 617-373-5121, E-mail: gradschool@ccs.neu.edu. Web site: http://www.ccs.neu.edu/.

Northern Kentucky University, Office of Graduate Programs, College of Informatics, Program in Health Informatics, Highland Heights, KY 41099. Offers MS, Certificate. Part-time and evening/weekend programs available. Postbaccalaureate distance learning degree programs offered (no on-campus study). *Students:* 10 full-time (5 women), 70 part-time (49 women); includes 11 minority (5 Black or African American, non-Hispanic/Latino; 4 Asian, non-Hispanic/Latino; 2 Hispanic/Latino), 4 international. Average age 40. 59 applicants, 68% accepted, 28 enrolled. In 2011, 11 master's, 20 other advanced degrees awarded. *Degree requirements:* For master's, capstone. *Entrance requirements:* For master's, MAT, GRE, or GMAT, minimum GPA of 3.0. Additional exam requirements/recommendations for international students: Required—TOEFL (minimum score 550 paper-based; 213 computer-based; 79 iBT); Recommended—IELTS (minimum score 6.5). *Application deadline:* For fall admission, 8/1 for domestic students, 6/1 for international students; for spring admission, 12/1 for domestic students, 10/1 for international students. Applications are processed on a rolling basis. Application fee: $40. Electronic applications accepted. *Expenses:* Tuition, state resident: full-time $7614; part-time $423 per credit hour. Tuition, nonresident: full-time $13,104; part-time $728 per credit hour. Tuition and fees vary according to degree level and reciprocity agreements. *Financial support:* Unspecified assistantships available. Financial award applicants required to submit FAFSA. *Faculty research:* Health informatics course development, healthcare analytics, technology acceptance in healthcare. *Unit head:* Dr. Ben Martz, Chair, Department of Business Informatics, 859-572-6366, Fax: 859-572-6187, E-mail: martzzw1@nku.edu. *Application contact:* Pam Atkinson, MHI Program Coordinator, 859-572-5992, Fax: 859-572-6187, E-mail: atkinsonpa@nku.edu. Web site: http://informatics.nku.edu/bis/mhi/.

Nova Southeastern University, Health Professions Division, College of Osteopathic Medicine, Fort Lauderdale, FL 33314-7796. Offers biomedical informatics (MS, Graduate Certificate), including biomedical informatics (MS), clinical informatics (Graduate Certificate), public health informatics (Graduate Certificate); disaster and emergency preparedness (MS); osteopathic medicine (DO); public health (MPH). *Accreditation:* AOsA. *Faculty:* 86 full-time (38 women), 1,072 part-time/adjunct (232 women). *Students:* 952 full-time (377 women), 18 part-time (5 women); includes 323 minority (24 Black or African American, non-Hispanic/Latino; 2 American Indian or Alaska Native, non-Hispanic/Latino; 175 Asian, non-Hispanic/Latino; 91 Hispanic/Latino; 31 Native Hawaiian or other Pacific Islander, non-Hispanic/Latino), 22 international. Average age 28. 3,628 applicants, 17% accepted, 241 enrolled. In 2011, 75 master's, 213 doctorates awarded. *Entrance requirements:* For master's, GRE, licensed healthcare professional or GRE; for doctorate, MCAT, biology, chemistry, organic chemistry, physics (all with labs), and English. *Application deadline:* For fall admission, 1/15 for domestic students. Applications are processed on a rolling basis. Application fee: $50. Electronic applications accepted. *Expenses:* Contact institution. *Financial support:* In 2011–12, 80 students received support, including 6 fellowships with full tuition reimbursements available (averaging $40,000 per year); research assistantships, teaching assistantships, career-related internships or fieldwork, Federal Work-Study, institutionally sponsored loans, and scholarships/grants also available. Financial award application deadline: 6/1; financial award applicants required to submit FAFSA. *Faculty research:* Teaching strategies, simulated patient use, HIV-AIDS education, minority health issues, managed care education. *Unit head:* Dr. Anthony J. Silavgni, Dean, 954-262-1407, E-mail: silvagni@hpd.nova.edu. *Application contact:* Anastasia Leveille, College of Medicine Admissions Counselor, 866-817-4068. Web site: http://www.medicine.nova.edu/.

Oregon Health & Science University, School of Medicine, Graduate Programs in Medicine, Department of Medical Informatics and Clinical Epidemiology, Portland, OR 97239-3098. Offers clinical informatics (MS, PhD, Certificate); computational biology (MS, PhD); health information management (Certificate). Part-time programs available. Postbaccalaureate distance learning degree programs offered (minimal on-campus study). *Faculty:* 10 full-time (3 women), 13 part-time/adjunct (8 women). *Students:* 40 full-time (18 women), 151 part-time (61 women); includes 46 minority (7 Black or African American, non-Hispanic/Latino; 4 American Indian or Alaska Native, non-Hispanic/Latino; 23 Asian, non-Hispanic/Latino; 2 Hispanic/Latino; 1 Native Hawaiian or other Pacific Islander, non-Hispanic/Latino; 9 Two or more races, non-Hispanic/Latino), 9 international. Average age 41. 78 applicants, 44% accepted, 34 enrolled. In 2011, 12 master's, 6 doctorates, 32 other advanced degrees awarded. Terminal master's awarded for partial completion of doctoral program. *Degree requirements:* For master's, thesis optional, thesis or capstone project; for doctorate, comprehensive exam, thesis/dissertation, qualifying exam. *Entrance requirements:* For master's and doctorate, GRE General Test (minimum scores: 153 Verbal/148 Quantitative/4.5 Analytical), coursework in computer programming, human anatomy and physiology. Additional exam requirements/recommendations for international students: Required—TOEFL. *Application deadline:* For fall admission, 12/1 for domestic students; for winter admission, 11/1 for domestic students; for spring admission, 2/1 for domestic students. Applications are processed on a rolling basis. Application fee: $70. Electronic applications accepted. *Expenses:* Contact institution. *Financial support:* Fellowships with full tuition reimbursements, research assistantships, Federal Work-Study, institutionally sponsored loans, scholarships/grants, health care benefits, and full tuition and stipends for PhD students available. Financial award application deadline: 3/1; financial award applicants required to submit FAFSA. *Faculty research:* Use of knowledge-based information by healthcare practitioners and researchers, application of text mining and machine learning techniques to the scientific literature curated databases, examining factors that affect quality of data collected in healthcare databases and the subsequent uses of that data, statistical analysis of microarray data with emphasis on time series analysis, computational biology and automatic speech recognition. *Unit head:* Andrea Ilg, 503-494-2547, E-mail: informat@ohsu.edu. *Application contact:* Lauren Ludwig, 503-494-2547, E-mail: informat@ohsu.edu. Web site: http://www.ohsu.edu/dmice/.

Regis University, Rueckert-Hartman College for Health Professions, Denver, CO 80221-1099. Offers family nurse practitioner (MSN); health informatics (Postbaccalaureate Certificate); health services administration (MS); leadership in healthcare systems (MSN); neonatal nurse practitioner (MSN); nursing (MSN); pharmacy (Pharm D); physical therapy (DPT, TDPT). *Entrance requirements:* Additional exam requirements/recommendations for international students: Required—TOEFL (minimum score 550 paper-based; 213 computer-based; 82 iBT). Electronic applications accepted. *Expenses:* Contact institution. *Faculty research:* Normal and pathological balance and gait research, normal/pathological upper limb motor control/biomechanics, exercise energy/metabolism research, optical treatment protocols for therapeutic modalities.

Sacred Heart University, Graduate Programs, College of Health Professions, Program in Healthcare Information Systems, Fairfield, CT 06825-1000. Offers MS.

Saint Joseph's University, College of Arts and Sciences, Department of Health Services, Philadelphia, PA 19131-1395. Offers health administration (MS, Post-Master's Certificate); health care ethics (Post-Master's Certificate); health education (MS, Post-Master's Certificate); health informatics (Post-Master's Certificate); healthcare ethics (MS); long-term care administration (MS); nurse anesthesia (MS); school nurse certification (MS). Part-time and evening/weekend programs available. *Faculty:* 9 full-time (1 woman), 21 part-time/adjunct (11 women). *Students:* 76 full-time (53 women), 261 part-time (204 women); includes 106 minority (79 Black or African American, non-Hispanic/Latino; 2 American Indian or Alaska Native, non-Hispanic/Latino; 12 Asian, non-Hispanic/Latino; 10 Hispanic/Latino; 1 Native Hawaiian or other Pacific Islander, non-Hispanic/Latino; 2 Two or more races, non-Hispanic/Latino), 17 international. Average age 35. 143 applicants, 69% accepted, 91 enrolled. In 2011, 67 master's awarded. *Entrance requirements:* For master's, GRE (if GPA less than 2.75), 2 letters of recommendation, minimum GPA of 2.75, resume. Additional exam requirements/recommendations for international students: Required—TOEFL (minimum score 550 paper-based; 213 computer-based; 79 iBT). *Application deadline:* For fall admission, 7/15 priority date for domestic students, 4/15 for international students; for winter admission, 1/15 for international students; for spring admission, 11/15 priority date for domestic students, 10/15 for international students. Applications are processed on a rolling basis. Application fee: $35. Electronic applications accepted. *Expenses:* Tuition:

Part-time $735 per credit hour. Tuition and fees vary according to degree level and program. *Financial support:* Career-related internships or fieldwork and unspecified assistantships available. Financial award applicants required to submit FAFSA. *Unit head:* Nakia Henderson, Director, 610-660-2952, E-mail: nakia.henderson@sju.edu. *Application contact:* Kate McConnell, Director, Graduate College of Arts and Sciences Admissions and Retention, 610-660-3184, Fax: 610-660-3230, E-mail: kate.mcconnell@sju.edu.

Southern Polytechnic State University, School of Computing and Software Engineering, Department of Information Technology, Marietta, GA 30060-2896. Offers health information technology (Graduate Certificate); information security and assurance (Graduate Certificate); information technology (MSIT, Graduate Certificate); information technology fundamentals (Graduate Transition Certificate). Part-time and evening/weekend programs available. Postbaccalaureate distance learning degree programs offered (minimal on-campus study). *Faculty:* 8 full-time (3 women), 2 part-time/adjunct (0 women). *Students:* 49 full-time (15 women), 114 part-time (41 women); includes 81 minority (67 Black or African American, non-Hispanic/Latino; 11 Asian, non-Hispanic/Latino; 1 Hispanic/Latino; 2 Two or more races, non-Hispanic/Latino), 29 international. Average age 33. 82 applicants, 93% accepted, 55 enrolled. In 2011, 43 master's, 5 other advanced degrees awarded. *Degree requirements:* For master's, thesis or alternative. *Entrance requirements:* For master's, minimum GPA of 2.75; for other advanced degree, bachelor's degree. Additional exam requirements/recommendations for international students: Required—TOEFL (minimum score 550 paper-based; 213 computer-based; 79 iBT), IELTS (minimum score 6.5). *Application deadline:* For fall admission, 7/1 priority date for domestic students, 5/1 for international students; for spring admission, 11/1 priority date for domestic students, 9/1 for international students. Applications are processed on a rolling basis. Application fee: $50. Electronic applications accepted. *Expenses:* Tuition, state resident: full-time $2592; part-time $216 per semester hour. Tuition, nonresident: full-time $9408; part-time $784 per semester hour. *Required fees:* $698 per term. *Financial support:* In 2011–12, 12 students received support, including 13 research assistantships with tuition reimbursements available (averaging $3,000 per year); career-related internships or fieldwork, scholarships/grants, and unspecified assistantships also available. Support available to part-time students. Financial award application deadline: 5/1; financial award applicants required to submit FAFSA. *Faculty research:* IT ethics, user interface design, IT security, IT integration, IT management, health information technology. *Total annual research expenditures:* $50,000. *Unit head:* Dr. Ju Au Wang, Chair, 678-915-3718, Fax: 678-915-5511, E-mail: jwang@spsu.edu. *Application contact:* Nikki Palamiotis, Director of Graduate Studies, 678-915-4276, Fax: 678-915-7292, E-mail: npalamio@spsu.edu. Web site: http://www.spsu.edu/itdegrees/.

Stephens College, Division of Graduate and Continuing Studies, Columbia, MO 65215-0002. Offers business (MBA, MSL); counseling (M Ed), including counseling; curriculum and instruction (M Ed); health information administration (Postbaccalaureate Certificate). Part-time and evening/weekend programs available. Postbaccalaureate distance learning degree programs offered (minimal on-campus study). *Faculty:* 4 full-time (all women), 25 part-time/adjunct (17 women). *Students:* 198 full-time (182 women), 48 part-time (43 women); includes 33 minority (18 Black or African American, non-Hispanic/Latino; 1 American Indian or Alaska Native, non-Hispanic/Latino; 5 Asian, non-Hispanic/Latino; 4 Hispanic/Latino; 5 Two or more races, non-Hispanic/Latino). Average age 35. 60 applicants, 65% accepted, 34 enrolled. In 2011, 84 master's awarded. *Entrance requirements:* For master's, minimum GPA of 3.0 in last 60 hours. Additional exam requirements/recommendations for international students: Required—TOEFL (minimum score 213 computer-based). *Application deadline:* For fall admission, 7/25 priority date for domestic students, 7/25 for international students; for winter admission, 12/1 priority date for domestic students, 12/1 for international students; for spring admission, 4/25 priority date for domestic students, 4/25 for international students. Applications are processed on a rolling basis. Application fee: $50. Electronic applications accepted. *Expenses: Tuition:* Full-time $2220; part-time $370 per credit hour. *Required fees:* $228; $38 per credit hour. *Financial support:* In 2011–12, 12 fellowships with full tuition reimbursements (averaging $7,971 per year) were awarded; scholarships/grants and unspecified assistantships also available. Financial award applicants required to submit FAFSA. *Faculty research:* Educational psychology, outcomes assessment. *Unit head:* Dr. Nicole House, Director of Graduate and Continuing Studies, 573-876-7290, Fax: 573-876-7237, E-mail: online@stephens.edu. *Application contact:* Jennifer Deaver, Director of Marketing and Recruitment, 800-388-7579, E-mail: online@stephens.edu. Web site: http://www.stephens.edu/gcs/.

Stevens Institute of Technology, Graduate School, Charles V. Schaefer Jr. School of Engineering, Department of Computer Science, Hoboken, NJ 07030. Offers computer graphics (Certificate); computer science (MS, PhD); computer systems (Certificate); database management systems (Certificate); distributed systems (Certificate); elements of computer science (Certificate); enterprise computing (Certificate); enterprise security and information assurance (Certificate); health informatics (Certificate); multimedia experience and management (Certificate); networks and systems administration (Certificate); security and privacy (Certificate); service oriented computing (Certificate); software design (Certificate); theoretical computer science (Certificate). Part-time and evening/weekend programs available. Terminal master's awarded for partial completion of doctoral program. *Degree requirements:* For master's, thesis optional; for doctorate, variable foreign language requirement, comprehensive exam, thesis/dissertation. *Entrance requirements:* For master's and doctorate, GRE, minimum GPA of 3.0. Additional exam requirements/recommendations for international students: Required—TOEFL. Electronic applications accepted. *Faculty research:* Semantics, reliability theory, programming language, cyber security.

Temple University, Health Sciences Center, College of Health Professions and Social Work, Department of Health Information Management, Philadelphia, PA 19122-6096. Offers health informatics (MS). Part-time and evening/weekend programs available. *Students:* 19 full-time (10 women); includes 5 minority (4 Black or African American, non-Hispanic/Latino; 1 Asian, non-Hispanic/Latino). Average age 39. 8 applicants, 100% accepted, 8 enrolled. *Entrance requirements:* Additional exam requirements/recommendations for international students: Required—TOEFL (minimum score 550 paper-based; 213 computer-based; 79 iBT). Application fee: $50. Electronic applications accepted. *Expenses:* Tuition, state resident: full-time $12,366; part-time $687 per credit hour. Tuition, nonresident: full-time $17,298; part-time $961 per credit hour. *Required fees:* $590; $213 per year. *Financial support:* Application deadline: 1/15; applicants required to submit FAFSA. *Unit head:* Cindy Marselis, Interim Chair, 215-707-4811, Fax: 215-707-5852, E-mail: hlthinfo@temple.edu. *Application contact:* Tara Schumacher, Coordinator of Outreach, 215-204-6575, Fax: 215-204-8781, E-mail: tara.schumacher@temple.edu. Web site: http://www.temple.edu/chpsw/departments/him/index.html.

Trident University International, College of Health Sciences, Program in Health Sciences, Cypress, CA 90630. Offers clinical research administration (MS, Certificate); emergency and disaster management (MS, Certificate); environmental health science (Certificate); health care administration (PhD); health care management (MS), including health informatics; health education (MS, Certificate); health informatics (Certificate); health sciences (PhD); international health (MS); international health: educator or researcher option (PhD); international health: practitioner option (PhD); law and expert witness studies (MS, Certificate); public health (MS); quality assurance (Certificate). Part-time and evening/weekend programs available. Postbaccalaureate distance learning degree programs offered (no on-campus study). *Degree requirements:* For doctorate, comprehensive exam, thesis/dissertation, defense of dissertation. *Entrance requirements:* For master's, minimum GPA of 2.5 (students with GPA 3.0 or greater may transfer up to 30% of graduate level credits); for doctorate, minimum GPA of 3.4, curriculum vitae, course work in research methods or statistics. Additional exam requirements/recommendations for international students: Required—TOEFL. Electronic applications accepted.

University at Buffalo, the State University of New York, Graduate School, School of Medicine and Biomedical Sciences, Program in Medical/Health Informatics, Buffalo, NY 14260. Offers Certificate. Part-time programs available. *Faculty:* 4 part-time/adjunct. *Students:* 2 part-time (both women). Average age 35. In 2011, 1 Certificate awarded. *Degree requirements:* For Certificate, 24 credit hours of coursework (18 required courses, 6 electives). *Entrance requirements:* For degree, all previous college/university transcripts; 2 letters of recommendation; personal letter with career objectives. Additional exam requirements/recommendations for international students: Required—TOEFL (minimum score 600 paper-based; 100 computer-based). *Application deadline:* For fall admission, 8/15 priority date for domestic students, 7/15 for international students. Application fee: $50. *Faculty research:* Integrated information systems planning and evaluation, management of knowledge-based information resources, scholarly communication in the health sciences , the economic value of health information, electronic health records, natural language understanding, ontologies, telemedicine/telehealth systems of healthcare, quality management information systems, implementation and evaluation of electronic health record systems, ethical and social issues in informatics. *Unit head:* Dr. Michael E. Cain, Dean, 716-829-3955, Fax: 716-829-3395, E-mail: mcain@buffalo.edu. *Application contact:* Amy J. Kuzdale, Staff Associate, 716-829-3399, Fax: 716-829-2437, E-mail: akuzdale@buffalo.edu. Web site: http://www.smbs.buffalo.edu/medinformatics/.

The University of Alabama at Birmingham, School of Health Professions, Program in Health Informatics, Birmingham, AL 35294. Offers MSHI. *Degree requirements:* For master's, thesis or alternative. *Entrance requirements:* For master's, GRE General Test, MAT, minimum GPA of 3.0, course work in computing fundamentals and programming. Electronic applications accepted. *Expenses:* Tuition, state resident: full-time $5922; part-time $309 per hour. Tuition, nonresident: full-time $13,428; part-time $726 per hour. Tuition and fees vary according to program. *Financial support:* Career-related internships or fieldwork and Federal Work-Study available. *Faculty research:* Healthcare/medical informatics, natural language processing, application of expert systems, graphical user interface design. *Unit head:* Dr. Gerald Glandon, Director, 205-934-5665, Fax: 205-975-6608. *Application contact:* Julie Bryant, Director of Graduate Admissions, 205-934-8227, Fax: 205-934-8413, E-mail: jbryant@uab.edu. Web site: http://www.uab.edu/hsa/academic-programs/hi.

University of Central Florida, College of Health and Public Affairs, Department of Health Management and Informatics, Orlando, FL 32816. Offers health care informatics (MS, Certificate); health sciences (MS). *Accreditation:* CAHME. Part-time and evening/weekend programs available. *Faculty:* 17 full-time (8 women), 25 part-time/adjunct (18 women). *Students:* 146 full-time (100 women), 248 part-time (178 women); includes 175 minority (90 Black or African American, non-Hispanic/Latino; 1 American Indian or Alaska Native, non-Hispanic/Latino; 32 Asian, non-Hispanic/Latino; 47 Hispanic/Latino; 5 Two or more races, non-Hispanic/Latino), 9 international. Average age 29. 288 applicants, 81% accepted, 138 enrolled. In 2011, 44 master's, 2 other advanced degrees awarded. *Degree requirements:* For master's, comprehensive exam, thesis or alternative, research report. *Entrance requirements:* For master's, GRE General Test. Additional exam requirements/recommendations for international students: Required—TOEFL. *Application deadline:* For fall admission, 7/15 for domestic students; for spring admission, 10/1 for domestic students. Application fee: $30. Electronic applications accepted. *Expenses:* Tuition, state resident: part-time $277.08 per credit hour. Tuition, nonresident: part-time $277.08 per credit hour. Part-time tuition and fees vary according to degree level and program. *Financial support:* In 2011–12, 4 students received support, including 1 fellowship with partial tuition reimbursement available (averaging $10,000 per year), 3 research assistantships (averaging $4,600 per year), 1 teaching assistantship (averaging $6,700 per year); career-related internships or fieldwork, Federal Work-Study, institutionally sponsored loans, and unspecified assistantships also available. Financial award application deadline: 3/1; financial award applicants required to submit FAFSA. *Unit head:* Dr. Dawn Oetjen, Interim Chair, 407-823-3729, E-mail: dawn.oetjen@ucf.edu. *Application contact:* Barbara Rodriguez, Director, Admissions and Registration, 407-823-2766, Fax: 407-823-6442, E-mail: gradadmissions@ucf.edu. Web site: http://www.cohpa.ucf.edu/hmi/.

University of Illinois at Chicago, Graduate College, College of Applied Health Sciences, Program in Health Informatics, Chicago, IL 60607-7128. Offers MS. Postbaccalaureate distance learning degree programs offered (no on-campus study).

University of Illinois at Urbana–Champaign, Graduate College, Graduate School of Library and Information Science, Champaign, IL 61820. Offers bioinformatics (MS); digital libraries (CAS); library and information science (MS, PhD, CAS). *Accreditation:* ALA (one or more programs are accredited). Postbaccalaureate distance learning degree programs offered. *Faculty:* 25 full-time (12 women), 5 part-time/adjunct (4 women). *Students:* 349 full-time (256 women), 353 part-time (276 women); includes 125 minority (30 Black or African American, non-Hispanic/Latino; 1 American Indian or Alaska Native, non-Hispanic/Latino; 37 Asian, non-Hispanic/Latino; 40 Hispanic/Latino; 1 Native Hawaiian or other Pacific Islander, non-Hispanic/Latino; 16 Two or more races, non-Hispanic/Latino), 27 international. 606 applicants, 68% accepted, 250 enrolled. In 2011, 245 master's, 6 doctorates, 8 other advanced degrees awarded. *Entrance requirements:* For master's, GRE General Test, minimum GPA of 3.0; for doctorate, minimum GPA of 3.0; for CAS, master's degree in library and information science or related field with minimum GPA of 3.0. Additional exam requirements/recommendations for international students: Required—TOEFL (minimum score 620 paper-based; 260 computer-based; 105 iBT) or IELTS (minimum score 7). *Application deadline:* Applications are processed on a rolling basis. Application fee: $75 ($90 for international students). Electronic applications accepted. *Financial support:* In 2011–12, 24 fellowships, 39 research assistantships, 44 teaching assistantships were awarded; tuition waivers (full and partial) also available. *Unit head:* Allen Renear, Dean, 217-265-5216, Fax: 217-244-3302, E-mail: renear@illinois.edu. *Application contact:* Valerie Youngen, Admissions and Records Representative, 217-333-0734, Fax: 217-244-3302, E-mail: vyoungen@llinois.edu. Web site: http://www.lis.illinois.edu.

The University of Iowa, Graduate College, Program in Informatics, Iowa City, IA 52242-1316. Offers bioinformatics and computational biology (Certificate); health informatics (MS, PhD, Certificate); information science (MS, PhD, Certificate). *Degree* *requirements:* For master's, thesis optional; for doctorate, comprehensive exam, thesis/dissertation. *Entrance requirements:* For master's and doctorate, GRE General Test, minimum GPA of 3.0. Additional exam requirements/recommendations for international students: Required—TOEFL (minimum score 550 paper-based; 213 computer-based; 81 iBT). Electronic applications accepted.

The University of Kansas, University of Kansas Medical Center, Program in Health Informatics, Lawrence, KS 66045. Offers MS. Part-time programs available. Postbaccalaureate distance learning degree programs offered (minimal on-campus study). *Faculty:* 6. *Students:* 4 full-time (2 women), 4 part-time (1 woman); includes 2 minority (both Black or African American, non-Hispanic/Latino), 2 international. Average age 33. 4 applicants, 100% accepted, 4 enrolled. *Degree requirements:* For master's, comprehensive exam, thesis or alternative. *Entrance requirements:* For master's, GRE, minimum GPA of 3.0, 3 references, personal statement of career goals. Additional exam requirements/recommendations for international students: Required—TOEFL. *Application deadline:* For fall admission, 3/1 for domestic and international students; for spring admission, 9/1 for domestic and international students. Application fee: $60. Electronic applications accepted. Tuition and fees vary according to course load, campus/location, program and reciprocity agreements. *Financial support:* Application deadline: 2/14; applicants required to submit FAFSA. *Faculty research:* GIS in public health, symbolic representation of health data, smoking cessation. *Unit head:* Dr. Allen Rawitch, Vice Chancellor for Academic Affairs/Dean of Graduate Studies, 913-588-1258, E-mail: arawitch@kumc.edu. *Application contact:* Dr. Eva LaVerne Manos, Director, 913-588-1671, Fax: 913-588-1660, E-mail: lmanos@kumc.edu. Web site: http://www2.kumc.edu/healthinformatics/mshi.htm.

University of La Verne, College of Business and Public Management, Program in Health Administration, La Verne, CA 91750-4443. Offers financial management (MHA); health administration (MHA); human resources (MHA); information management (MHA); leadership and management (MHA); managed care (MHA); marketing and business development (MHA). Part-time programs available. *Faculty:* 34 full-time (15 women), 28 part-time/adjunct (13 women). *Students:* 55 full-time (37 women), 35 part-time (27 women); includes 52 minority (15 Black or African American, non-Hispanic/Latino; 9 Asian, non-Hispanic/Latino; 27 Hispanic/Latino; 1 Native Hawaiian or other Pacific Islander, non-Hispanic/Latino), 13 international. Average age 32. In 2011, 16 master's awarded. *Entrance requirements:* For master's, minimum undergraduate GPA of 2.5, 3 letters of reference, curriculum vitae or resume, writing sample. Additional exam requirements/recommendations for international students: Required—TOEFL (minimum score 550 paper-based; 213 computer-based). *Application deadline:* Applications are processed on a rolling basis. Application fee: $50. *Expenses:* Contact institution. *Financial support:* Application deadline: 3/2; applicants required to submit FAFSA. *Unit head:* Terrell Ford, Program Director, 909-593-3511 Ext. 4796, E-mail: tford@laverne.edu. *Application contact:* Barbara Cox, Program and Admissions Specialist, 909-593-3511 Ext. 4004, Fax: 909-392-2761, E-mail: bcox@laverne.edu. Web site: http://laverne.edu/catalog/program/mha-master-of-health-administration/.

University of Maryland University College, Graduate School of Management and Technology, Program in Health Administration Informatics, Adelphi, MD 20783. Offers MS, Certificate. Part-time and evening/weekend programs available. Postbaccalaureate distance learning degree programs offered (no on-campus study). *Students:* 9 full-time (7 women), 186 part-time (124 women); includes 119 minority (96 Black or African American, non-Hispanic/Latino; 2 American Indian or Alaska Native, non-Hispanic/Latino; 13 Asian, non-Hispanic/Latino; 6 Hispanic/Latino; 1 Native Hawaiian or other Pacific Islander, non-Hispanic/Latino; 1 Two or more races, non-Hispanic/Latino), 1 international. Average age 40. 60 applicants, 100% accepted, 30 enrolled. In 2011, 23 master's, 8 other advanced degrees awarded. *Degree requirements:* For master's, thesis or alternative, capstone course. *Application deadline:* Applications are processed on a rolling basis. Application fee: $40. Electronic applications accepted. *Financial support:* Federal Work-Study and scholarships/grants available. Support available to part-time students. Financial award application deadline: 6/1; financial award applicants required to submit FAFSA. *Unit head:* Dr. Kathrine Marconi, Director, 240-684-2400, Fax: 240-684-2401, E-mail: katherine.marconi@umuc.edu. *Application contact:* Coordinator, Graduate Admissions, 800-888-8682, Fax: 240-684-2151, E-mail: newgrad@umuc.edu. Web site: http://www.umuc.edu/grad/gradprograms/mshai.cfm.

University of Massachusetts Lowell, School of Health and Environment, Department of Community Health and Sustainability, Lowell, MA 01854-2881. Offers health management and policy (MS, Graduate Certificate). Part-time programs available. *Degree requirements:* For master's, thesis optional. *Entrance requirements:* For master's, GRE General Test. *Faculty research:* Alzheimer's disease, total quality management systems, information systems, market analysis.

University of Michigan, Horace H. Rackham School of Graduate Studies, School of Information, Ann Arbor, MI 48109-1285. Offers archives and records management (MSI); community informatics (MSI); health informatics (MS); human computer interaction (MSI); information (PhD); information analysis and retrieval (MSI); information economics for management (MSI); information policy (MSI); library and information science (MSI); preservation of information (MSI); school library media (MSI); social computing (MSI). *Accreditation:* ALA (one or more programs are accredited). *Entrance requirements:* For master's and doctorate, GRE General Test. Additional exam requirements/recommendations for international students: Required—TOEFL (minimum score 600 paper-based; 100 iBT). Electronic applications accepted.

University of Minnesota, Twin Cities Campus, Graduate School, Program in Health Informatics, Minneapolis, MN 55455-0213. Offers MHI, MS, PhD, MD/MHI. Part-time programs available. *Degree requirements:* For master's, thesis or alternative; for doctorate, thesis/dissertation. *Entrance requirements:* For master's and doctorate, GRE General Test, previous course work in life sciences, programming, calculus. Additional exam requirements/recommendations for international students: Required—TOEFL (minimum score 550 paper-based; 237 computer-based). Electronic applications accepted. *Faculty research:* Medical decision making, physiological control systems, population studies, clinical information systems, telemedicine.

University of Missouri, Graduate School, Department of Health Management and Informatics, Columbia, MO 65211. Offers health administration (MHA); health ethics (Graduate Certificate); health informatics (MS, Graduate Certificate). *Accreditation:* CAHME. Part-time programs available. *Faculty:* 18 full-time (5 women), 2 part-time/adjunct (0 women). *Students:* 89 full-time (38 women), 42 part-time (23 women); includes 25 minority (14 Black or African American, non-Hispanic/Latino; 6 Asian, non-Hispanic/Latino; 3 Hispanic/Latino; 2 Two or more races, non-Hispanic/Latino), 19 international. Average age 31. 72 applicants, 60% accepted, 37 enrolled. In 2011, 54 master's, 3 other advanced degrees awarded. *Entrance requirements:* For master's, GRE General Test or GMAT, minimum GPA of 3.0. Additional exam requirements/recommendations for international students: Required—TOEFL (minimum score 500 paper-based; 173 computer-based; 61 iBT). Application fee: $55 ($75 for international students). *Expenses:* Tuition, state resident: full-time $5881. Tuition, nonresident: full-time $15,183. *Required fees:* $952. Tuition and fees vary according to campus/location and program. *Financial support:* Fellowships, research assistantships, teaching assistantships, and institutionally sponsored loans available. *Faculty research:* GUI aesthetics for physician use, application of informatics tools to day-to-day clinical operations, consumer health informatics, decision support, health literacy and numeracy, information interventions for persons with chronic illnesses, use of simulation in the education of health care professionals, statistical bioinformatics, classification, dimension reduction, ethics and end of life care, telehealth and teleethics, research ethics, health literacy, clinical informatics, human factors. *Unit head:* Dr. Robert DeGraaff, Director of Graduate Studies, 573-882-1783, E-mail: degraaffr@missouri.edu. *Application contact:* Adrienne Vogt, 573-884-0698, E-mail: vogtb@health.missouri.edu. Web site: http://www.hmi.missouri.edu/.

The University of North Carolina at Charlotte, Graduate School, College of Computing and Informatics, Department of Software and Information Systems, Charlotte, NC 28223-0001. Offers game design and development (Certificate); health care information (Certificate); information security/privacy (Certificate); information technology (MS, PhD, Certificate). Part-time programs available. *Faculty:* 14 full-time (3 women), 4 part-time/adjunct (0 women). *Students:* 134 full-time (42 women), 88 part-time (36 women); includes 39 minority (23 Black or African American, non-Hispanic/Latino; 5 Asian, non-Hispanic/Latino; 5 Hispanic/Latino; 6 Two or more races, non-Hispanic/Latino), 102 international. Average age 30. 182 applicants, 75% accepted, 47 enrolled. In 2011, 32 master's, 12 doctorates, 33 other advanced degrees awarded. Terminal master's awarded for partial completion of doctoral program. *Degree requirements:* For master's, thesis optional; for doctorate, comprehensive exam, thesis/dissertation. *Entrance requirements:* For master's, GRE or GMAT, minimum undergraduate GPA of 2.8 overall, 2.0 in last 2 years; for doctorate, GRE or GMAT, working knowledge of 2 high-level programming languages. Additional exam requirements/recommendations for international students: Required—TOEFL (minimum score 557 paper-based; 220 computer-based; 83 iBT). *Application deadline:* For fall admission, 7/1 for domestic students, 5/1 for international students; for spring admission, 11/1 for domestic students, 10/1 for international students. Applications are processed on a rolling basis. Application fee: $65 ($75 for international students). Electronic applications accepted. *Expenses:* Tuition, state resident: full-time $3689. Tuition, nonresident: full-time $15,226. *Required fees:* $2198. Tuition and fees vary according to course load and program. *Financial support:* In 2011–12, 41 students received support, including 1 fellowship (averaging $50,000 per year), 19 research assistantships (averaging $9,874 per year), 21 teaching assistantships (averaging $13,421 per year); career-related internships or fieldwork, institutionally sponsored loans, scholarships/grants, and unspecified assistantships also available. Support available to part-time students. Financial award application deadline: 4/1; financial award applicants required to submit FAFSA. *Faculty research:* Information security, information privacy, information assurance, cryptography, software engineering, enterprise integration, intelligent information systems, human-computer interaction. *Total annual research expenditures:* $1.8 million. *Unit head:* Dr. Ken Chen, Program Director, 704-687-8545, Fax: 704-687-6065, E-mail: chen@uncc.edu. *Application contact:* Kathy B. Giddings, Director of Graduate Admissions, 704-687-5503, Fax: 704-687-3279, E-mail: gradadm@uncc.edu. Web site: http://sis.uncc.edu/.

University of Phoenix–Birmingham Campus, College of Health and Human Services, Birmingham, AL 35244. Offers education (MHA); gerontology (MHA); health administration (MHA); health care management (MBA); informatics (MHA); nursing (MSN); nursing/health care education (MSN); MSN/MBA; MSN/MHA.

University of Phoenix–Charlotte Campus, College of Nursing, Charlotte, NC 28273-3409. Offers education (MHA); gerontology (MHA); health administration (MHA); informatics (MHA, MSN); nursing (MSN); nursing/health care education (MSN). Evening/weekend programs available. *Degree requirements:* For master's, thesis (for some programs). *Entrance requirements:* For master's, minimum undergraduate GPA of 2.5, 3 years work experience. Additional exam requirements/recommendations for international students: Required—TOEFL (minimum score 550 paper-based; 213 computer-based; 79 iBT). Electronic applications accepted.

University of Phoenix–Des Moines Campus, College of Nursing, Des Moines, IA 50266. Offers education (MHA); gerontology (MHA); health administration (MHA, DHA); informatics (MHA, MSN); nursing (MSN, PhD); nursing/health care education (MSN).

University of Phoenix–Milwaukee Campus, College of Nursing, Milwaukee, WI 53045. Offers education (MHA); gerontology (MHA); health administration (MHA, DHA); informatics (MHA, MSN); nursing (MSN, PhD); nursing/health care education (MSN); MSN/MBA; MSN/MHA.

University of Phoenix–Online Campus, College of Natural Sciences, Phoenix, AZ 85034-7209. Offers education (MHA); gerontology (MHA, Graduate Certificate); health administration (MHA); health care informatics (Graduate Certificate); health care management (Graduate Certificate), including lifelong learning; informatics (MHA). Evening/weekend programs available. Postbaccalaureate distance learning degree programs offered. *Students:* 2,854 full-time (2,408 women); includes 1,137 minority (855 Black or African American, non-Hispanic/Latino; 24 American Indian or Alaska Native, non-Hispanic/Latino; 73 Asian, non-Hispanic/Latino; 140 Hispanic/Latino; 18 Native Hawaiian or other Pacific Islander, non-Hispanic/Latino; 27 Two or more races, non-Hispanic/Latino), 91 international. Average age 39. *Entrance requirements:* Additional exam requirements/recommendations for international students: Required—TOEFL, TOEIC (Test of English as an International Communication), Berlitz Online English Proficiency Exam, PTE (Pearson Test of English), or IELTS. *Application deadline:* Applications are processed on a rolling basis. Application fee: $45. Electronic applications accepted. *Expenses: Tuition:* Full-time $17,160. *Required fees:* $920. One-time fee: $45 full-time. Full-time tuition and fees vary according to course load, degree level, campus/location and program. *Financial support:* Scholarships/grants available. Financial award applicants required to submit FAFSA. *Unit head:* Dr. Hinrich Eylers, Dean/Associate Provost. *Application contact:* 866-766-0766. Web site: http://www.phoenix.edu/colleges_divisions/natural-sciences.html.

University of Phoenix–Phoenix Main Campus, College of Natural Science, Tempe, AZ 85282-2371. Offers education (MHA); gerontology (MHA); gerontology health care (Certificate); health administration (MHA); informatics (MHA). Evening/weekend programs available. Postbaccalaureate distance learning degree programs offered. *Students:* 27 full-time (17 women); includes 10 minority (4 Black or African American, non-Hispanic/Latino; 1 American Indian or Alaska Native, non-Hispanic/Latino; 1 Asian, non-Hispanic/Latino; 4 Hispanic/Latino). Average age 42. *Entrance requirements:* Additional exam requirements/recommendations for international students: Required—TOEFL, TOEIC (Test of English as an International Communication), Berlitz Online English Proficiency Exam, PTE (Pearson Test of English), or IELTS. *Application deadline:* Applications are processed on a rolling basis. Application fee: $45. Electronic applications accepted. *Expenses:* Contact institution. *Financial support:* Scholarships/grants available. Financial award applicants required to submit FAFSA. *Unit head:* Dr.

Hinrich Eylers, Dean/Associate Provost. *Application contact:* 866-766-0766. Web site: http://www.phoenix.edu/colleges_divisions/natural-sciences.html.

University of Phoenix–Raleigh Campus, College of Nursing, Raleigh, NC 27606. Offers education (MHA); gerontology (MHA); health administration (MHA, DHA); informatics (MHA, MSN); nursing (MSN, PhD); nursing/health care education (MSN).

University of Phoenix–Washington D.C. Campus, College of Nursing, Washington, DC 20001. Offers education (MHA); gerontology (MHA); health administration (MHA, DHA); informatics (MHA, MSN); nursing (MSN, PhD); nursing/health care education (MSN); MSN/MBA; MSN/MHA.

University of Pittsburgh, School of Health and Rehabilitation Sciences, Master's Programs in Health and Rehabilitation Sciences, Pittsburgh, PA 15260. Offers health and rehabilitation sciences (MS), including clinical dietetics and nutrition, health care supervision and management, health information systems, occupational therapy, physical therapy, rehabilitation counseling, rehabilitation science and technology, sports medicine, wellness and human performance. *Accreditation:* APTA. Part-time and evening/weekend programs available. *Faculty:* 22 full-time (16 women), 4 part-time/ adjunct (2 women). *Students:* 144 full-time (91 women), 35 part-time (23 women); includes 23 minority (8 Black or African American, non-Hispanic/Latino; 8 Asian, non-Hispanic/Latino; 3 Hispanic/Latino; 4 Two or more races, non-Hispanic/Latino), 74 international. Average age 28. 399 applicants, 61% accepted, 121 enrolled. In 2011, 86 master's awarded. *Degree requirements:* For master's, comprehensive exam (for some programs), thesis optional. *Entrance requirements:* For master's, minimum GPA of 3.0. Additional exam requirements/recommendations for international students: Required—TOEFL (minimum score 550 paper-based; 213 computer-based; 80 iBT), IELTS (minimum score 6.5). *Application deadline:* For fall admission, 3/1 for international students; for spring admission, 7/31 for international students. Applications are processed on a rolling basis. Application fee: $50. Electronic applications accepted. *Expenses:* Contact institution. *Financial support:* Research assistantships, teaching assistantships, Federal Work-Study, institutionally sponsored loans, traineeships, and unspecified assistantships available. Financial award applicants required to submit FAFSA. *Faculty research:* Assistive technology, seating and wheeled mobility, cellular neurophysiology, low back syndrome, augmentative communication. *Total annual research expenditures:* $7.8 million. *Unit head:* Dr. Clifford E. Brubaker, Dean, 412-383-6560, Fax: 412-383-6535, E-mail: cliffb@pitt.edu. *Application contact:* Shameem Gangjee, Director of Admissions, 412-383-6558, Fax: 412-383-6535, E-mail: admissions@shrs.pitt.edu. Web site: http://www.shrs.pitt.edu/.

University of Puerto Rico, Medical Sciences Campus, School of Health Professions, Program in Health Information Administration, San Juan, PR 00936-5067. Offers MS. Part-time programs available. *Degree requirements:* For master's, one foreign language, thesis or alternative, internship. *Entrance requirements:* For master's, EXADEP or GRE General Test, minimum GPA of 2.5, interview, fluency in Spanish. *Faculty research:* Quality of medical records, health information data.

University of San Diego, Hahn School of Nursing and Health Science, San Diego, CA 92110-2492. Offers adult-gerontology clinical nurse specialist (MSN); adult-gerontology nurse practitioner/family nurse practitioner (MSN); clinical nursing (MSN); entry-level nursing (for non-RNs) (MSN); executive nurse leader (MSN); family nurse practitioner (MSN); family/lifespan psychiatric-mental health nurse practitioner (MSN); healthcare informatics (MS, MSN); nursing (PhD); nursing practice (DNP); pediatric nurse practitioner/family nurse practitioner (MSN). *Accreditation:* AACN. Part-time and evening/weekend programs available. *Faculty:* 23 full-time (21 women), 37 part-time/ adjunct (34 women). *Students:* 157 full-time (131 women), 182 part-time (162 women); includes 121 minority (21 Black or African American, non-Hispanic/Latino; 6 American Indian or Alaska Native, non-Hispanic/Latino; 51 Asian, non-Hispanic/Latino; 36 Hispanic/Latino; 2 Native Hawaiian or other Pacific Islander, non-Hispanic/Latino; 5 Two or more races, non-Hispanic/Latino), 7 international. Average age 36. 506 applicants, 47% accepted, 150 enrolled. In 2011, 87 master's, 26 doctorates awarded. *Degree requirements:* For doctorate, thesis/dissertation (for some programs), residency (DNP). *Entrance requirements:* For master's, GRE General Test (entry-level nursing), BSN, current California RN licensure (except for entry-level nursing); minimum GPA of 3.0; for doctorate, minimum GPA of 3.5, MSN, current California RN licensure. Additional exam requirements/recommendations for international students: Required—TOEFL (minimum score 580 paper-based; 237 computer-based; 83 iBT), TWE. *Application deadline:* For fall admission, 3/1 priority date for domestic students, 3/1 for international students; for spring admission, 11/1 priority date for domestic students, 11/1 for international students. Applications are processed on a rolling basis. Application fee: $45. Electronic applications accepted. *Expenses: Tuition:* Full-time $22,482; part-time $1249 per unit. *Required fees:* $224. Full-time tuition and fees vary according to course load and degree level. *Financial support:* In 2011–12, 232 students received support. Scholarships/ grants and traineeships available. Support available to part-time students. Financial award application deadline: 4/1; financial award applicants required to submit FAFSA. *Faculty research:* Palliative and end of life care, maternal/child health, childhood obesity, health care disparities, cognitive functioning. *Unit head:* Dr. Sally Hardin, Dean, 619-260-4550, Fax: 619-260-6814. *Application contact:* Monica Mahon, Associate Director of Graduate Admissions, 619-260-4524, Fax: 619-260-4158, E-mail: grads@sandiego.edu. Web site: http://www.sandiego.edu/academics/nursing/.

The University of Texas Health Science Center at Houston, School of Health Information Sciences, Houston, TX 77225-0036. Offers health informatics (MS, PhD, Certificate); MPH/MS; MPH/PhD. Part-time programs available. Postbaccalaureate distance learning degree programs offered (no on-campus study). *Degree requirements:* For master's, thesis; for doctorate, thesis/dissertation. *Entrance requirements:* For master's and doctorate, GRE or MAT. Additional exam requirements/recommendations for international students: Required—TOEFL (minimum score 550 paper-based; 213 computer-based; 87 iBT). Electronic applications accepted. *Faculty research:* Patient safety, human computer interface, artificial intelligence, decision support tools, 3-D visualization, biomedical engineering.

University of Toronto, Faculty of Medicine, Program in Health Informatics, Toronto, ON M5S 1A1, Canada. Offers MHI. *Entrance requirements:* For master's, minimum B average in last academic year. Additional exam requirements/recommendations for international students: Required—TOEFL (minimum score 580 paper-based; 93 iBT), TWE (minimum score 5). Electronic applications accepted.

University of Victoria, Faculty of Graduate Studies, Faculty of Human and Social Development, School of Health Information Science, Victoria, BC V8W 2Y2, Canada. Offers M Sc. *Degree requirements:* For master's, thesis or research project. *Entrance requirements:* Additional exam requirements/recommendations for international students: Required—TOEFL (minimum score 575 paper-based).

University of Virginia, School of Medicine, Department of Public Health Sciences, Program in Clinical Research, Charlottesville, VA 22903. Offers clinical investigation and patient-oriented research (MS); informatics in medicine (MS). Part-time programs available. *Students:* 5 full-time (2 women), 13 part-time (7 women); includes 5 minority (3 Asian, non-Hispanic/Latino; 2 Hispanic/Latino), 1 international. Average age 37. 11 applicants, 73% accepted, 8 enrolled. In 2011, 16 master's awarded. *Degree requirements:* For master's, thesis (for some programs). *Entrance requirements:* For master's, 2 letters of recommendation. Additional exam requirements/recommendations for international students: Required—TOEFL (minimum score 600 paper-based; 250 computer-based; 90 iBT). *Application deadline:* For fall admission, 3/1 priority date for domestic students, 3/1 for international students. Application fee: $60. Electronic applications accepted. *Financial support:* Career-related internships or fieldwork available. Financial award applicants required to submit FAFSA. *Unit head:* Dr. Ruth Gaare Bernheim, Chair, 434-924-8430, Fax: 434-924-8437. *Application contact:* Tracey L. Brookman, Academic Programs Administrator, 434-924-8430, Fax: 434-924-8437, E-mail: ms-hes@virginia.edu. Web site: http://www.healthsystem.virginia.edu/internet/phs/ms/mshome.cfm.

University of Washington, Graduate School, School of Medicine, Graduate Programs in Medicine, Department of Medical Education and Biomedical Informatics, Division of Biomedical and Health Informatics, Seattle, WA 98195. Offers MS, PhD. *Entrance requirements:* For master's and doctorate, GRE General Test, minimum GPA of 3.0; previous undergraduate course work in biology, computer programming, and mathematics. Additional exam requirements/recommendations for international students: Required—TOEFL (minimum score 580 paper-based; 237 computer-based; 70 iBT). Electronic applications accepted. *Faculty research:* Bio-clinical informatics, information retrieval, human-computer interaction, knowledge-based systems, telehealth.

University of Wisconsin–Milwaukee, Graduate School, College of Health Sciences, Interdepartmental Program in Healthcare Informatics, Milwaukee, WI 53201-0413. Offers MS, Certificate. *Students:* 12 full-time (7 women), 6 part-time (2 women); includes 1 minority (Hispanic/Latino), 2 international. Average age 32. 11 applicants, 45% accepted, 2 enrolled. In 2011, 2 master's awarded. *Degree requirements:* For master's, comprehensive exam, thesis optional. *Entrance requirements:* For master's, GRE General Test. Additional exam requirements/recommendations for international students: Required—TOEFL (minimum score 550 paper-based; 79 iBT), IELTS (minimum score 6.5). Application fee: $56 ($96 for international students). One-time fee: $506.10 full-time. Tuition and fees vary according to course load and reciprocity agreements. *Financial support:* Fellowships, research assistantships, and teaching assistantships available. *Unit head:* Timothy Patrick, Representative, 414-229-6849, Fax: 414-229-2619, E-mail: tp5@uwm.edu. *Application contact:* General Information Contact, 414-229-4982, Fax: 414-229-6967, E-mail: gradschool@uwm.edu. Web site: http://www4.uwm.edu/chs/academics/graduate/healthgraduate/index.html.

Walden University, Graduate Programs, School of Health Sciences, Minneapolis, MN 55401. Offers clinical research administration (MS, Postbaccalaureate Certificate); health informatics (MS); health services (PhD), including community health education and advocacy, general program, healthcare administration, leadership, public health policy, self-designed; healthcare administration (MHA); public health (MPH, PhD), including community health and education (PhD), epidemiology (PhD). Part-time and evening/weekend programs available. Postbaccalaureate distance learning degree programs offered (minimal on-campus study). *Faculty:* 20 full-time (13 women), 175 part-time/adjunct (81 women). *Students:* 2,777 full-time (2,158 women), 1,350 part-time (1,038 women); includes 2,379 minority (1,935 Black or African American, non-Hispanic/Latino; 33 American Indian or Alaska Native, non-Hispanic/Latino; 173 Asian, non-Hispanic/Latino; 180 Hispanic/Latino; 9 Native Hawaiian or other Pacific Islander, non-Hispanic/Latino; 49 Two or more races, non-Hispanic/Latino), 247 international. Average age 40. In 2011, 528 master's, 79 doctorates, 1 other advanced degree awarded. *Degree requirements:* For doctorate, thesis/dissertation, residency. *Entrance requirements:* For master's, bachelor's degree or equivalent in related field, minimum GPA of 2.5; for doctorate, master's degree or equivalent in related field; minimum GPA of 3.0; official transcripts; three years of related professional/academic experience (preferred); access to computer and Internet. Additional exam requirements/recommendations for international students: Required—TOEFL (minimum score 550 paper-based; 213 computer-based), IELTS (minimum score 6.5), or Michigan English Language Assessment Battery (minimum score 82). *Application deadline:* Applications are processed on a rolling basis. Application fee: $50. Electronic applications accepted. *Financial support:* Federal Work-Study, scholarships/grants, unspecified assistantships, and family tuition reduction, active duty/veteran tuition reduction, group tuition reduction, interest-free payment plans, employee tuition reduction available. Support available to part-time students. Financial award applicants required to submit FAFSA. *Unit head:* Dr. Jorg Westermann, Associate Dean, 800-925-3368. *Application contact:* Jennifer Hall, Vice President of Enrollment Management, 866-4-WALDEN, E-mail: info@waldenu.edu. Web site: http://www.waldenu.edu/Colleges-and-Schools/College-of-Health-Sciences/School-of-Health-Sciences.htm.

Human-Computer Interaction

Carnegie Mellon University, School of Computer Science, Department of Human-Computer Interaction, Pittsburgh, PA 15213-3891. Offers MHCI, PhD. *Entrance requirements:* For master's, GRE General Test, GRE Subject Test.

Clemson University, Graduate School, College of Engineering and Science, School of Computing, Program in Human-Centered Computing, Clemson, SC 29634. Offers PhD. *Students:* 11 full-time (5 women), 1 (woman) part-time; includes 7 minority (all Black or African American, non-Hispanic/Latino), 3 international. Average age 31. 1 applicant, 100% accepted, 1 enrolled. *Degree requirements:* For doctorate, comprehensive exam, thesis/dissertation. *Entrance requirements:* For doctorate, GRE General Test. Additional exam requirements/recommendations for international students: Required—TOEFL. *Application deadline:* For fall admission, 1/1 priority date for domestic students, 1/1 for international students; for spring admission, 9/15 priority date for domestic students, 9/

15 for international students. Applications are processed on a rolling basis. Electronic applications accepted. *Financial support:* In 2011–12, 10 students received support, including 3 fellowships with full and partial tuition reimbursements available (averaging $3,013 per year), 7 research assistantships with partial tuition reimbursements available (averaging $14,143 per year), 2 teaching assistantships with partial tuition reimbursements available (averaging $15,000 per year). Financial award applicants required to submit FAFSA. *Faculty research:* Virtual worlds and virtual humans, user interfaces and user experience, identity science and biometrics, affective computing, advanced learning technologies. *Unit head:* Dr. Larry F. Hodges, Director, 864-656-7552, Fax: 864-656-0145, E-mail: lfh@clemson.edu. *Application contact:* Dr. Juan Gilbert, Professor and Chair, 864-656-4846, E-mail: mark@clemson.edu. Web site: http://www.clemson.edu/ces/computing/current/curr_grad/phd_hcc/.

Cornell University, Graduate School, Graduate Fields of Arts and Sciences, Field of Information Science, Ithaca, NY 14853-0001. Offers cognition (PhD); human computer interaction (PhD); information systems (PhD); social aspects of information (PhD). *Faculty:* 38 full-time (11 women). *Students:* 31 full-time (12 women); includes 3 minority (1 Black or African American, non-Hispanic/Latino; 2 Asian, non-Hispanic/Latino), 18 international. Average age 27. 152 applicants, 14% accepted, 17 enrolled. In 2011, 3 doctorates awarded. *Degree requirements:* For doctorate, comprehensive exam, thesis/dissertation. *Entrance requirements:* For doctorate, GRE General Test, 3 letters of recommendation. Additional exam requirements/recommendations for international students: Required—TOEFL (minimum score 550 paper-based; 213 computer-based; 77 iBT). *Application deadline:* For fall admission, 1/1 for domestic students. Application fee: $95. Electronic applications accepted. *Financial support:* In 2011–12, 2 fellowships with full tuition reimbursements, 8 research assistantships with full tuition reimbursements, 6 teaching assistantships with full tuition reimbursements were awarded; institutionally sponsored loans, scholarships/grants, tuition waivers (full and partial), and unspecified assistantships also available. Financial award applicants required to submit FAFSA. *Faculty research:* Digital libraries, game theory, data mining, human-computer interaction, computational linguistics. *Unit head:* Director of Graduate Studies, 607-255-5925. *Application contact:* Graduate Field Assistant, 607-255-5925, E-mail: info@infosci.cornell.edu. Web site: http://www.gradschool.cornell.edu/fields.php?id-9A&a-2.

Dalhousie University, Faculty of Engineering, Department of Internetworking, Halifax, NS B3J 1Z1, Canada. Offers M Eng. *Entrance requirements:* Additional exam requirements/recommendations for international students: Required—TOEFL, IELTS, CANTEST, CAEL, or Michigan English Language Assessment Battery. Electronic applications accepted.

DePaul University, College of Computing and Digital Media, Chicago, IL 60604. Offers animation (MA, MFA); applied technology (MS); business information technology (MS); cinema (MFA); cinema production (MS); computational finance (MS); computer and information sciences (PhD); computer game development (MS); computer graphics and motion technology (MS); computer information and network security (MS); computer science (MS); e-commerce technology (MS); human-computer interaction (MS); information systems (MS); information technology (MA); information technology project management (MS); network engineering and management (MS); predictive analytics (MS); screenwriting (MFA); software engineering (MS); JD/MA; JD/MS. Part-time and evening/weekend programs available. Postbaccalaureate distance learning degree programs offered (no on-campus study). *Faculty:* 64 full-time (16 women), 44 part-time/adjunct (5 women). *Students:* 969 full-time (250 women), 936 part-time (231 women); includes 566 minority (204 Black or African American, non-Hispanic/Latino; 3 American Indian or Alaska Native, non-Hispanic/Latino; 166 Asian, non-Hispanic/Latino; 135 Hispanic/Latino; 7 Native Hawaiian or other Pacific Islander, non-Hispanic/Latino; 51 Two or more races, non-Hispanic/Latino), 282 international. Average age 32. 1,040 applicants, 65% accepted, 324 enrolled. In 2011, 478 master's, 4 doctorates awarded. *Degree requirements:* For master's, thesis (for some programs); for doctorate, comprehensive exam, thesis/dissertation. *Entrance requirements:* For master's, GRE or GMAT (MS in computational finance only), bachelor's degree, resume (MS in predictive analytics only), IT experience (MS in information technology project management only), portfolio review (all MFA programs and MA in animation); for doctorate, GRE, master's degree in computer science. Additional exam requirements/recommendations for international students: Required—TOEFL (minimum score 550 paper-based; 213 computer-based; 80 iBT), IELTS (minimum score 6.5), Pearson Test of English (minimum score 53). *Application deadline:* For fall admission, 8/1 priority date for domestic students, 6/1 for international students; for winter admission, 12/1 priority date for domestic students, 10/1 for international students; for spring admission, 3/1 priority date for domestic students, 1/1 for international students. Applications are processed on a rolling basis. Application fee: $25. Electronic applications accepted. *Expenses:* Contact institution. *Financial support:* In 2011–12, 56 students received support, including 3 fellowships with full tuition reimbursements available (averaging $30,000 per year), 3 research assistantships with full and partial tuition reimbursements available (averaging $22,833 per year), 50 teaching assistantships (averaging $6,194 per year); Federal Work-Study, scholarships/grants, tuition waivers (full and partial), and unspecified assistantships also available. Support available to part-time students. Financial award application deadline: 4/30. *Faculty research:* Data mining, theoretical computer science, gaming, security, animation and film. *Total annual research expenditures:* $3.9 million. *Unit head:* Elly Kafritsas-Wessels, Senior Administrative Assistant, 312-362-5816, Fax: 312-362-5185, E-mail: ekafrits@cdm.depaul.edu. *Application contact:* James Parker, Director of Graduate Admission, 312-362-8714, Fax: 312-362-5179, E-mail: jparke29@cdm.depaul.edu. Web site: http://cdm.depaul.edu.

Georgia Institute of Technology, Graduate Studies and Research, College of Computing, Multidisciplinary Program in Human Computer Interaction, Atlanta, GA 30332-0001. Offers MSHCI. Part-time programs available. *Degree requirements:* For master's, project. *Entrance requirements:* For master's, GRE General Test. Additional exam requirements/recommendations for international students: Required—TOEFL (minimum score 600 paper-based; 250 computer-based). Electronic applications accepted.

Indiana University Bloomington, School of Informatics and Computing, Bloomington, IN 47408. Offers bioinformatics (MS); chemical informatics (MS); computer science (MS, PhD); health informatics (MS); human computer interaction (MS); informatics (PhD); laboratory informatics (MS); media arts and science (MS); music informatics (MS); security informatics (MS); MS/PhD. PhD offered through University Graduate School. Part-time programs available. Postbaccalaureate distance learning degree programs offered (no on-campus study). *Faculty:* 63 full-time (12 women). *Students:* 434 full-time (99 women), 36 part-time (9 women); includes 24 minority (8 Black or African American, non-Hispanic/Latino; 9 Asian, non-Hispanic/Latino; 4 Hispanic/Latino; 3 Two or more races, non-Hispanic/Latino), 309 international. Average age 27. 825 applicants, 58% accepted, 205 enrolled. In 2011, 115 master's, 25 doctorates awarded. Terminal master's awarded for partial completion of doctoral program. *Degree requirements:* For master's, thesis optional; for doctorate, comprehensive exam, thesis/dissertation, oral and written exams. *Entrance requirements:* For master's and doctorate, GRE, letters of reference. Additional exam requirements/recommendations for international students: Required—TOEFL. *Application deadline:* For fall admission, 1/15 for domestic students, 12/1 for international students. Application fee: $55 ($65 for international students). Electronic applications accepted. *Financial support:* In 2011–12, fellowships with full and partial tuition reimbursements (averaging $20,000 per year), research assistantships (averaging $14,000 per year), teaching assistantships (averaging $13,000 per year) were awarded; Federal Work-Study, institutionally sponsored loans, scholarships/grants, health care benefits, tuition waivers (full and partial), and unspecified assistantships also available. Support available to part-time students. *Total annual research expenditures:* $2 million. *Unit head:* Dr. David Leake, Associate Dean for Graduate Studies, 812-855-9756, E-mail: leake@cs.indiana.edu. *Application contact:* Rachel Lawmaster, Manager of Graduate Admissions and Graduate Studies, 812-856-3622, Fax: 812-856-3825, E-mail: raclee@indiana.edu. Web site: http://www.informatics.indiana.edu/.

Iowa State University of Science and Technology, Program in Human-Computer Interaction, Ames, IA 50011-2274. Offers MS, PhD. *Degree requirements:* For master's, thesis; for doctorate, thesis/dissertation. *Entrance requirements:* For master's, GRE General Test; for doctorate, GRE General Test, e-portfolio of research. Additional exam requirements/recommendations for international students: Required—TOEFL (minimum score 580 paper-based; 95 iBT), IELTS (minimum score 7). *Application deadline:* For fall admission, 1/15 priority date for domestic students, 1/15 for international students. Application fee: $40 ($90 for international students). Electronic applications accepted. *Unit head:* Dr. James Oliver, Director of Graduate Education, 515-294-2089, Fax: 515-294-5530, E-mail: info@hci.iastate.edu. *Application contact:* Pam Shill, Application Contact, 515-294-2089, Fax: 515-294-5530, E-mail: info@hci.iastaate.edu. Web site: http://www.hci.iastate.edu/.

Rensselaer Polytechnic Institute, Graduate School, School of Humanities, Arts, and Social Sciences, Program in Human-Computer Interaction, Troy, NY 12180-3590. Offers MS. Part-time programs available. *Degree requirements:* For master's, thesis optional. *Entrance requirements:* For master's, GRE General Test, resume. Additional exam requirements/recommendations for international students: Required—TOEFL (minimum score 570 paper-based; 230 computer-based; 89 iBT). Electronic applications accepted. *Faculty research:* Usability testing and evaluation; games research and design; Web, interface, and interaction analysis and design; information architecture; human-media interaction.

Rochester Institute of Technology, Graduate Enrollment Services, B. Thomas Golisano College of Computing and Information Sciences, Department of Information Technology, Program in Human-Computer Interaction, Rochester, NY 14623-5603. Offers MS. Part-time programs available. Postbaccalaureate distance learning degree programs offered (minimal on-campus study). *Students:* 18 full-time (8 women), 14 part-time (4 women); includes 4 minority (1 Black or African American, non-Hispanic/Latino; 1 Asian, non-Hispanic/Latino; 1 Hispanic/Latino; 1 Two or more races, non-Hispanic/Latino), 11 international. Average age 30. 38 applicants, 58% accepted, 4 enrolled. In 2011, 1 master's awarded. *Degree requirements:* For master's, thesis or project. *Entrance requirements:* For master's, GRE, minimum GPA of 3.0. Additional exam requirements/recommendations for international students: Required—TOEFL (minimum score 570 paper-based; 230 computer-based; 88 iBT) or IELTS (minimum score 6.5). *Application deadline:* Applications are processed on a rolling basis. Application fee: $50. Electronic applications accepted. *Expenses: Tuition:* Full-time $34,659; part-time $963 per credit hour. *Required fees:* $228; $76 per quarter. *Financial support:* Research assistantships with partial tuition reimbursements, teaching assistantships with partial tuition reimbursements, career-related internships or fieldwork, scholarships/grants, and unspecified assistantships available. Support available to part-time students. Financial award applicants required to submit FAFSA. *Unit head:* Prof. Dianne Bills, Graduate Program Director, 585-475-2700, Fax: 585-475-6584, E-mail: informaticsgrad@rit.edu. *Application contact:* Diane Ellison, Assistant Vice President, Graduate Enrollment Services, 585-475-2229, Fax: 585-475-7164, E-mail: gradinfo@rit.edu.

State University of New York at Oswego, Graduate Studies, College of Liberal Arts and Sciences, Interdisciplinary Program in Human Computer Interaction, Oswego, NY 13126. Offers MA. Part-time programs available. *Entrance requirements:* For master's, GRE, minimum GPA of 3.0. Additional exam requirements/recommendations for international students: Required—TOEFL (minimum score 560 paper-based; 220 computer-based).

Tufts University, Graduate School of Arts and Sciences, Graduate Certificate Programs, Human-Computer Interaction Program, Medford, MA 02155. Offers Certificate. Part-time and evening/weekend programs available. Electronic applications accepted. *Expenses: Tuition:* Full-time $41,208; part-time $1030 per credit hour. Full-time tuition and fees vary according to degree level, program and student level. Part-time tuition and fees vary according to course load.

University of Baltimore, Graduate School, The Yale Gordon College of Liberal Arts, School of Information Arts and Technologies, Baltimore, MD 21201-5779. Offers communications design (DCD); human-computer interaction (MS); interaction design and information technology (MS). Part-time and evening/weekend programs available. *Entrance requirements:* For master's, GRE or MAT, minimum undergraduate GPA of 3.0. Additional exam requirements/recommendations for international students: Required—TOEFL (minimum score 550 paper-based; 213 computer-based).

University of Illinois at Urbana–Champaign, Graduate College, Graduate School of Library and Information Science, Champaign, IL 61820. Offers bioinformatics (MS); digital libraries (CAS); library and information science (MS, PhD, CAS). *Accreditation:* ALA (one or more programs are accredited). Postbaccalaureate distance learning degree programs offered. *Faculty:* 25 full-time (12 women), 5 part-time/adjunct (4 women). *Students:* 349 full-time (256 women), 353 part-time (276 women); includes 125 minority (30 Black or African American, non-Hispanic/Latino; 1 American Indian or Alaska Native, non-Hispanic/Latino; 37 Asian, non-Hispanic/Latino; 40 Hispanic/Latino; 1 Native Hawaiian or other Pacific Islander, non-Hispanic/Latino; 16 Two or more races, non-Hispanic/Latino), 27 international. 606 applicants, 68% accepted, 250 enrolled. In 2011, 245 master's, 6 doctorates, 8 other advanced degrees awarded. *Entrance requirements:* For master's, GRE General Test, minimum GPA of 3.0; for doctorate, minimum GPA of 3.0; for CAS, master's degree in library and information science or related field with minimum GPA of 3.0. Additional exam requirements/recommendations for international students: Required—TOEFL (minimum score 620 paper-based; 260 computer-based; 105 iBT) or IELTS (minimum score 7). *Application deadline:* Applications are processed on a rolling basis. Application fee: $75 ($90 for international students). Electronic applications accepted. *Financial support:* In 2011–12, 24 fellowships, 39 research assistantships, 44 teaching assistantships were awarded; tuition waivers (full and partial) also available. *Unit head:* Allen Renear, Dean, 217-265-5216, Fax: 217-244-3302, E-mail: renear@illinois.edu. *Application contact:* Valerie

Youngen, Admissions and Records Representative, 217-333-0734, Fax: 217-244-3302, E-mail: vyoungen@llinois.edu. Web site: http://www.lis.illinois.edu.

University of Michigan, Horace H. Rackham School of Graduate Studies, School of Information, Ann Arbor, MI 48109-1285. Offers archives and records management (MSI); community informatics (MSI); health informatics (MS); human computer interaction (MSI); information (PhD); information analysis and retrieval (MSI); information economics for management (MSI); information policy (MSI); library and information science (MSI); preservation of information (MSI); school library media (MSI); social computing (MSI). *Accreditation:* ALA (one or more programs are accredited). *Entrance requirements:* For master's and doctorate, GRE General Test. Additional exam requirements/recommendations for international students: Required—TOEFL (minimum score 600 paper-based; 100 iBT). Electronic applications accepted.

Virginia Polytechnic Institute and State University, Graduate School, College of Engineering, Department of Computer Science and Applications, Blacksburg, VA 24061. Offers computer science and applications (MS, PhD); human-computer interactions (Certificate); information assurance engineering (Certificate). *Degree requirements:* For master's, comprehensive exam (for some programs), thesis (for some programs); for doctorate, comprehensive exam (for some programs), thesis/dissertation (for some programs). *Entrance requirements:* For master's and doctorate, GRE. Additional exam requirements/recommendations for international students: Required—TOEFL (minimum score 550 paper-based; 213 computer-based). *Application deadline:* For fall admission, 7/1 for domestic and international students; for spring admission, 12/1 for domestic and international students. Applications are processed on a rolling basis. Application fee: $65. Electronic applications accepted. *Expenses:* Tuition, state resident: full-time $10,048; part-time $558.25 per credit hour. Tuition, nonresident: full-time $19,497; part-time $1083.25 per credit hour. *Required fees:* $405 per semester. Tuition and fees vary according to course load, campus/location and program. *Financial support:* Research assistantships with full tuition reimbursements, teaching assistantships with full tuition reimbursements, career-related internships or fieldwork, Federal Work-Study, scholarships/grants, health care benefits, and unspecified assistantships available. Financial award application deadline: 1/15. *Faculty research:* Bioinformatics, human-computer interaction, problem-solving environments, high performance computing, software engineering. *Unit head:* Dr. Barbara G. Ryder, Unit Head, 540-231-8452, Fax: 540-231-6075, E-mail: ryder@vt.edu. *Application contact:* Naren Ramakrishnan, Information Contact, 540-231-8451, Fax: 540-231-6075, E-mail: naren@vt.edu. Web site: http://www.cs.vt.edu/.

Virginia Polytechnic Institute and State University, Graduate School, College of Engineering, Department of Industrial and Systems Engineering, Blacksburg, VA 24061. Offers human-system integration (Certificate); industrial and systems engineering (MEA, MS, PhD). *Degree requirements:* For master's, comprehensive exam (for some programs), thesis (for some programs); for doctorate, comprehensive exam (for some programs), thesis/dissertation (for some programs). *Entrance requirements:* For master's and doctorate, GRE. Additional exam requirements/recommendations for international students: Required—TOEFL (minimum score 550 paper-based; 213 computer-based). *Application deadline:* For fall admission, 7/1 for domestic and international students; for spring admission, 12/1 for domestic and international students. Applications are processed on a rolling basis. Application fee: $65. Electronic applications accepted. *Expenses:* Tuition, state resident: full-time $10,048; part-time $558.25 per credit hour. Tuition, nonresident: full-time $19,497; part-time $1083.25 per credit hour. *Required fees:* $405 per semester. Tuition and fees vary according to course load, campus/location and program. *Financial support:* Fellowships with full tuition reimbursements, research assistantships with full tuition reimbursements, teaching assistantships with full tuition reimbursements, career-related internships or fieldwork, Federal Work-Study, scholarships/grants, health care benefits, and unspecified assistantships available. Financial award application deadline: 1/15. *Unit head:* Dr. Gaylon D. Taylor, Unit Head, 540-231-4771, Fax: 540-231-3322, E-mail: taylorgd@vt.edu. *Application contact:* Jaime Camelio, Information Contact, 540-231-8976, Fax: 540-231-3322, E-mail: jcamelio@vt.edu. Web site: http://ise.vt.edu/.

Information Science

Alcorn State University, School of Graduate Studies, School of Arts and Sciences, Department of Mathematical Sciences, Alcorn State, MS 39096-7500. Offers computer and information sciences (MS).

American InterContinental University Atlanta, Program in Information Technology, Atlanta, GA 30328. Offers MIT. Part-time and evening/weekend programs available. *Degree requirements:* For master's, technical proficiency demonstration. *Entrance requirements:* For master's, Computer Programmer Aptitude Battery Exam, interview. Electronic applications accepted. *Faculty research:* Operating systems, security issues, networks and routing, computer hardware.

American InterContinental University Online, Program in Information Technology, Hoffman Estates, IL 60192. Offers Internet security (MIT); IT project management (MIT). Evening/weekend programs available. Postbaccalaureate distance learning degree programs offered (no on-campus study). *Entrance requirements:* Additional exam requirements/recommendations for international students: Required—TOEFL (minimum score 550 paper-based; 213 computer-based). Electronic applications accepted.

American InterContinental University South Florida, Program in Information Technology, Weston, FL 33326. Offers Internet security (MIT); wireless computer forensics (MIT). Part-time and evening/weekend programs available. *Entrance requirements:* Additional exam requirements/recommendations for international students: Required—TOEFL (minimum score 670 paper-based). Electronic applications accepted.

Arizona State University, College of Technology and Innovation, Department of Technology Management, Mesa, AZ 85212. Offers technology (aviation management and human factors) (MS); technology (environmental technology management) (MS); technology (global technology and development) (MS); technology (graphic information technology) (MS); technology (management of technology) (MS). Part-time and evening/weekend programs available. Postbaccalaureate distance learning degree programs offered (minimal on-campus study). *Degree requirements:* For master's, thesis or applied project and oral defense; interactive Program of Study (iPOS) submitted before completing 50 percent of required credit hours. *Entrance requirements:* For master's, GRE, minimum GPA of 3.0 or equivalent in last 2 years of work leading to bachelor's degree. Additional exam requirements/recommendations for international students: Required—TOEFL (minimum score 83 iBT), TOEFL, IELTS, or Pearson Test of English. Electronic applications accepted. *Faculty research:* Digital imaging, digital publishing, Internet development/e-commerce, information aviation human factors, pilot selection, databases, multimedia, commercial digital photography, digital workflow, computer graphics modeling and animation, information design, sociotechnology, visual and technical literacy, environmental management, quality management, project management, industrial ethics, hazardous materials, environmental chemistry.

Arkansas Tech University, Center for Leadership and Learning, College of Applied Sciences, Russellville, AR 72801. Offers emergency management (MS); engineering (M Engr); information technology (MS). Part-time programs available. Postbaccalaureate distance learning degree programs offered (no on-campus study). *Students:* 81 full-time (29 women), 53 part-time (15 women); includes 15 minority (7 Black or African American, non-Hispanic/Latino; 1 American Indian or Alaska Native, non-Hispanic/Latino; 1 Asian, non-Hispanic/Latino; 2 Hispanic/Latino; 1 Native Hawaiian or other Pacific Islander, non-Hispanic/Latino; 3 Two or more races, non-Hispanic/Latino), 55 international. Average age 30. In 2011, 52 master's awarded. *Degree requirements:* For master's, comprehensive exam (for some programs), thesis (for some programs), internship. *Entrance requirements:* For master's, GRE General Test. Additional exam requirements/recommendations for international students: Required—TOEFL (minimum score 550 paper-based; 213 computer-based; 79 iBT), IELTS (minimum score 6). *Application deadline:* For fall admission, 3/1 priority date for domestic students, 5/1 for international students; for spring admission, 10/1 priority date for domestic students, 10/1 for international students. Applications are processed on a rolling basis. Application fee: $25 ($75 for international students). Electronic applications accepted. *Expenses:* Tuition, state resident: full-time $4968; part-time $207 per credit hour. Tuition, nonresident: full-time $9936; part-time $414 per credit hour. *Required fees:* $375 per semester. Tuition and fees vary according to course load. *Financial support:* In 2011–12, teaching assistantships with full tuition reimbursements (averaging $4,800 per year) were awarded; research assistantships with full tuition reimbursements, career-related internships or fieldwork, Federal Work-Study, scholarships/grants, health care benefits, and unspecified assistantships also available. Support available to part-time students. Financial award application deadline: 4/15; financial award applicants required to submit FAFSA. *Unit head:* Dr. William Hoefler, Dean, 479-968-0353 Ext. 501, E-mail: whoeflerjr@atu.edu. *Application contact:* Dr. Mary B. Gunter, Dean of Graduate College, 479-968-0398, Fax: 479-964-0542, E-mail: gradcollege@atu.edu. Web site: http://www.atu.edu/appliedsci/.

Aspen University, Program in Information Technology, Denver, CO 80246. Offers MS, Certificate. Part-time and evening/weekend programs available. Postbaccalaureate distance learning degree programs offered (no on-campus study). Electronic applications accepted.

Athabasca University, School of Computing and Information Systems, Athabasca, AB T9S 3A3, Canada. Offers information systems (M Sc). Part-time programs available. Postbaccalaureate distance learning degree programs offered (no on-campus study). *Degree requirements:* For master's, thesis optional. *Entrance requirements:* For master's, B Sc in computing or other bachelor's degree and IT experience. Electronic applications accepted. *Expenses:* Contact institution. *Faculty research:* Distributed systems multimedia, computer science education, e-services.

Ball State University, Graduate School, College of Communication, Information, and Media, Center for Information and Communication Sciences, Muncie, IN 47306-1099. Offers MS. *Faculty:* 7 full-time (0 women). *Students:* 43 full-time (9 women), 23 part-time (11 women); includes 3 minority (2 Black or African American, non-Hispanic/Latino; 1 Asian, non-Hispanic/Latino), 6 international. Average age 25. 75 applicants, 73% accepted, 44 enrolled. In 2011, 57 master's awarded. Application fee: $50. Tuition and fees vary according to program and reciprocity agreements. *Financial support:* In 2011–12, 51 students received support, including 44 teaching assistantships with full tuition reimbursements available (averaging $11,125 per year). Financial award application deadline: 3/1. *Unit head:* Dr. Stephan Jones, Director, 765-285-1889, Fax: 765-285-1516. *Application contact:* Dr. Robert Morris, Associate Provost for Research and Dean of the Graduate School, 765-285-4723, Fax: 765-285-1328, E-mail: rmorris@bsu.edu. Web site: http://www.cics.bsu.edu/.

Barry University, School of Adult and Continuing Education, Program in Information Technology, Miami Shores, FL 33161-6695. Offers MS. Part-time and evening/weekend programs available. *Entrance requirements:* For master's, GMAT, GRE or MAT, bachelor's degree in information technology, related area or professional experience. Electronic applications accepted.

Bellevue University, Graduate School, College of Information Technology, Bellevue, NE 68005-3098. Offers computer information systems (MS); cybersecurity (MS); management of information systems (MS); project management (MPM).

Bentley University, McCallum Graduate School of Business, Program in Information Technology, Waltham, MA 02452-4705. Offers MSIT. Part-time and evening/weekend programs available. *Entrance requirements:* For master's, GMAT or GRE General Test. Additional exam requirements/recommendations for international students: Required—TOEFL (minimum score 600 paper-based; 250 computer-based; 100 iBT) or IELTS (minimum score 7). Electronic applications accepted. *Faculty research:* Business intelligence, enterprise networks and services, telemedicine, ERP usability, information visualization.

Bradley University, Graduate School, College of Liberal Arts and Sciences, Department of Computer Science and Information Systems, Peoria, IL 61625-0002. Offers computer information systems (MS); computer science (MS). Part-time and evening/weekend programs available. *Degree requirements:* For master's, comprehensive exam, thesis or alternative, programming test. *Entrance requirements:* For master's, 2 letters of recommendation. Additional exam requirements/recommendations for international students: Required—TOEFL (minimum score 550 paper-based; 213 computer-based; 79 iBT).

Brigham Young University, Graduate Studies, Ira A. Fulton College of Engineering and Technology, School of Technology, Provo, UT 84602-1001. Offers construction management (MS); information technology (MS); manufacturing systems (MS); technology and engineering education (MS). *Faculty:* 26 full-time (0 women). *Students:* 25 full-time (2 women), 9 part-time (3 women); includes 3 minority (1 Asian, non-Hispanic/Latino; 2 Hispanic/Latino), 5 international. Average age 25. 27 applicants, 59% accepted, 14 enrolled. In 2011, 12 master's awarded. *Degree requirements:* For master's, thesis. *Entrance requirements:* For master's, GRE General Test; GMAT or GRE (for construction management emphasis), minimum GPA of 3.0 in last 60 hours of course work. Additional exam requirements/recommendations for international students: Required—TOEFL (minimum score 580 paper-based; 237 computer-based; 85 iBT). *Application deadline:* For fall admission, 2/15 for domestic and international students; for winter admission, 9/15 for domestic and international students; for spring admission, 2/15 for domestic and international students. Application fee: $50. Electronic applications accepted. *Expenses: Tuition:* Full-time $5760; part-time $320 per credit. Tuition and fees vary according to student's religious affiliation. *Financial support:* In 2011–12, 34 students received support, including 11 research assistantships (averaging $3,506 per year), 7 teaching assistantships (averaging $3,254 per year); scholarships/grants also available. *Faculty research:* Information assurance and security, computerized systems in CM, pedagogy in technology and engineering, manufacturing planning. *Total annual research expenditures:* $220,300. *Unit head:* Val D. Hawks, Director, 801-422-6300, Fax: 801-422-0490, E-mail: hawksv@byu.edu. *Application contact:* Barry M. Lunt, Graduate Coordinator, 801-422-2264, Fax: 801-422-0490, E-mail: ralowe@byu.edu. Web site: http://www.et.byu.edu/sot/.

Brooklyn College of the City University of New York, Division of Graduate Studies, Department of Computer and Information Science, Brooklyn, NY 11210-2889. Offers computer science (MA, PhD); computer science and health science (MS); information systems (MS); parallel and distributed computing (Advanced Certificate). Part-time and evening/weekend programs available. *Degree requirements:* For master's, comprehensive exam, thesis or alternative. *Entrance requirements:* For master's, previous course work in computer science, 2 letters of recommendation. Additional exam requirements/recommendations for international students: Required—TOEFL (minimum score 525 paper-based; 195 computer-based; 70 iBT). Electronic applications accepted. *Faculty research:* Networks and distributed systems, programming languages, modeling and computer applications, algorithms, artificial intelligence, theoretical computer science.

California State University, Fullerton, Graduate Studies, College of Business and Economics, Department of Information Systems and Decision Sciences, Fullerton, CA 92834-9480. Offers information systems (MS); information systems (decision sciences) (MS); information systems (e-commerce) (MS); information technology (MS); management science (MBA). Part-time programs available. *Students:* 15 full-time (2 women), 66 part-time (10 women); includes 35 minority (1 Black or African American, non-Hispanic/Latino; 23 Asian, non-Hispanic/Latino; 9 Hispanic/Latino; 2 Two or more races, non-Hispanic/Latino), 9 international. Average age 33. 82 applicants, 44% accepted, 30 enrolled. In 2011, 36 master's awarded. *Degree requirements:* For master's, project or thesis. *Entrance requirements:* For master's, GMAT, minimum AACSB index of 950. Application fee: $55. *Financial support:* Career-related internships or fieldwork, Federal Work-Study, institutionally sponsored loans, and scholarships/grants available. Support available to part-time students. Financial award application deadline: 3/1; financial award applicants required to submit FAFSA. *Unit head:* Dr. Bhushan Kapoor, Chair, 657-278-2221. *Application contact:* Admissions/Applications, 657-278-2371.

Capitol College, Graduate Programs, Laurel, MD 20708-9759. Offers business administration (MBA); computer science (MS); electrical engineering (MS); information and telecommunications systems management (MS); information architecture (MS); network security (MS). Part-time and evening/weekend programs available. Postbaccalaureate distance learning degree programs offered (no on-campus study). *Entrance requirements:* For master's, minimum GPA of 3.0. Electronic applications accepted.

Carleton University, Faculty of Graduate Studies, Faculty of Engineering and Design, Ottawa-Carleton Institute for Electrical Engineering, Department of Systems and Computer Engineering, Program in Information and Systems Science, Ottawa, ON K1S 5B6, Canada. Offers M Sc.

Carleton University, Faculty of Graduate Studies, Faculty of Science, Information and Systems Science Program, Ottawa, ON K1S 5B6, Canada. Offers M Sc. *Degree requirements:* For master's, thesis optional. *Entrance requirements:* For master's, honors degree. Additional exam requirements/recommendations for international students: Required—TOEFL. *Faculty research:* Software engineering, real-time and microprocessor programming, computer communications.

Carleton University, Faculty of Graduate Studies, Faculty of Science, School of Computer Science, Ottawa, ON K1S 5B6, Canada. Offers computer science (MCS, PhD); information and system science (M Sc). MCS and PhD programs offered jointly with University of Ottawa. Part-time programs available. *Degree requirements:* For master's, thesis optional, project; for doctorate, comprehensive exam, thesis/dissertation. *Entrance requirements:* For master's, honors degree. Additional exam requirements/recommendations for international students: Required—TOEFL. *Faculty research:* Programming systems, theory of computing, computer applications, computer systems.

Carnegie Mellon University, Heinz College Australia, Master of Science in Information Technology Program (Adelaide, South Australia), Adelaide, PA 5000, Australia. Offers MSIT. *Entrance requirements:* For master's, GRE or GMAT, college-level course in advanced algebra/pre-calculus; college-level courses in economics and statistics (recommended). Additional exam requirements/recommendations for international students: Required—TOEFL or IELTS.

Carnegie Mellon University, Heinz College, School of Information Systems and Management, Master of Information Systems Management Program, Pittsburgh, PA 15213-3891. Offers MISM. *Entrance requirements:* For master's, GRE or GMAT, college-level course in advanced algebra/pre-calculus; college-level courses in economics and statistics (recommended). Additional exam requirements/recommendations for international students: Required—TOEFL or IELTS.

Carnegie Mellon University, School of Computer Science, Language Technologies Institute, Pittsburgh, PA 15213-3891. Offers MLT, PhD. Terminal master's awarded for partial completion of doctoral program. *Degree requirements:* For doctorate, thesis/dissertation. *Entrance requirements:* For master's and doctorate, GRE General Test, GRE Subject Test. Additional exam requirements/recommendations for international students: Required—TOEFL. *Faculty research:* Machine translation, natural language processing, speech and information retrieval, literacy.

Case Western Reserve University, School of Graduate Studies, Case School of Engineering, Department of Electrical Engineering and Computer Science, Cleveland, OH 44106. Offers computer engineering (MS, PhD); computing and information sciences (MS, PhD); electrical engineering (MS, PhD); systems and control engineering (MS, PhD). Part-time and evening/weekend programs available. Postbaccalaureate distance learning degree programs offered (minimal on-campus study). *Faculty:* 33 full-time (3 women). *Students:* 188 full-time (34 women), 22 part-time (4 women); includes 6 minority (3 Black or African American, non-Hispanic/Latino; 3 Asian, non-Hispanic/Latino), 132 international. In 2011, 30 master's, 22 doctorates awarded. Terminal master's awarded for partial completion of doctoral program. *Degree requirements:* For master's, thesis; for doctorate, thesis/dissertation, qualifying exam, teaching experience. *Entrance requirements:* For master's and doctorate, GRE General Test. Additional exam requirements/recommendations for international students: Required—TOEFL. *Application deadline:* For fall admission, 2/1 for domestic students; for spring admission, 11/1 for domestic students. Applications are processed on a rolling basis. Application fee: $50. *Financial support:* Fellowships with full and partial tuition reimbursements, research assistantships with full and partial tuition reimbursements, teaching assistantships, career-related internships or fieldwork, Federal Work-Study, and institutionally sponsored loans available. Support available to part-time students. Financial award application deadline: 3/1; financial award applicants required to submit FAFSA. *Faculty research:* Applied artificial intelligence, automation, computer-aided design and testing of digital systems. *Total annual research expenditures:* $6 million. *Unit head:* Dr. Michael Branicky, Department Chair, 216-368-6888, E-mail: branicky@case.edu. *Application contact:* David Easler, Student Affairs Coordinator, 216-368-4080, Fax: 216-368-2801, E-mail: david.easler@case.edu. Web site: http://eecs.cwru.edu/.

The Citadel, The Military College of South Carolina, Citadel Graduate College, Department of Mathematics and Computer Science, Charleston, SC 29409. Offers computer and information science (MS); mathematics education (MAE). *Accreditation:* NCATE (one or more programs are accredited). Part-time and evening/weekend programs available. *Faculty:* 3 full-time (0 women), 1 part-time/adjunct (0 women). *Students:* 1 (woman) full-time, 18 part-time (8 women); includes 1 minority (Asian, non-Hispanic/Latino). Average age 35. In 2011, 3 master's awarded. *Degree requirements:* For master's, comprehensive exam (for some programs), thesis (for some programs). *Entrance requirements:* For master's, GRE (minimum score 1000 for MS; 900 verbal and quantitative for MAT, raw score of 396), minimum undergraduate GPA of 3.0 (MS) or 2.5 (MAT); competency, demonstrated through coursework, approved work experience, or a program-administrated competency exam, in the areas of basic computer architecture, object-oriented programming, discrete mathematics, and data structures (MS); successful completion of 7 courses (MAT). Additional exam requirements/recommendations for international students: Required—TOEFL (minimum score 550 paper-based; 213 computer-based; 79 iBT). *Application deadline:* Applications are processed on a rolling basis. Application fee: $30. Electronic applications accepted. *Expenses: Tuition, area resident:* Part-time $501 per credit hour. Tuition, state resident: part-time $501 per credit hour. Tuition, nonresident: part-time $824 per credit hour. *Required fees:* $40 per term. One-time fee: $30. *Financial support:* Health care benefits and unspecified assistantships available. Support available to part-time students. Financial award application deadline: 7/1; financial award applicants required to submit FAFSA. *Faculty research:* Mathematics: numerical linear algebra, inverse problems, operator algebras, geometric group theory, integral equations; computer science: computer networks, database systems, software engineering, computational systems biology, mobile systems. *Unit head:* Dr. John I. Moore, Jr., Department Head, 843-953-5048, Fax: 843-953-7391, E-mail: john.moore@citadel.edu. *Application contact:* Dr. George L. Rudolph, Computer and Information Science Program Director, 843-953-5032, Fax: 843-953-7391, E-mail: george.rudolph@citadel.edu. Web site: http://www.mathcs.citadel.edu/.

Claremont Graduate University, Graduate Programs, School of Information Systems and Technology, Claremont, CA 91711-6160. Offers electronic commerce (MS, PhD); health information management (MS); information systems (Certificate); knowledge management (MS, PhD); systems development (MS, PhD); telecommunications and networking (MS, PhD); MBA/MS. Part-time programs available. *Faculty:* 7 full-time (1 woman), 1 part-time/adjunct (0 women). *Students:* 68 full-time (20 women), 26 part-time (10 women); includes 31 minority (5 Black or African American, non-Hispanic/Latino; 14 Asian, non-Hispanic/Latino; 9 Hispanic/Latino; 1 Native Hawaiian or other Pacific Islander, non-Hispanic/Latino; 2 Two or more races, non-Hispanic/Latino), 31 international. Average age 37. In 2011, 16 master's, 5 doctorates awarded. *Degree requirements:* For doctorate, comprehensive exam, thesis/dissertation, portfolio. *Entrance requirements:* For master's and doctorate, GMAT, GRE General Test. Additional exam requirements/recommendations for international students: Required—TOEFL (minimum score 550 paper-based; 213 computer-based; 80 iBT). *Application deadline:* For fall admission, 2/1 priority date for domestic students. Applications are processed on a rolling basis. Application fee: $60. Electronic applications accepted. *Expenses: Tuition:* Full-time $36,374; part-time $1581 per unit. *Required fees:* $165 per semester. *Financial support:* Fellowships, research assistantships, teaching assistantships, Federal Work-Study, institutionally sponsored loans, and scholarships/grants available. Support available to part-time students. Financial award application deadline: 2/15; financial award applicants required to submit FAFSA. *Faculty research:* GPSS, man-machine interaction, organizational aspects of computing, implementation of information systems, information systems practice. *Unit head:* Tom Horan, Dean, 909-607-9302, Fax: 909-621-8564, E-mail: tom.horan@cgu.edu. *Application contact:* Anondah Saide, Program Coordinator, 909-607-6006, E-mail: anonda.saide@cgu.edu. Web site: http://www.cgu.edu/pages/153.asp.

Clark Atlanta University, School of Arts and Sciences, Department of Computer and Information Science, Atlanta, GA 30314. Offers MS. Part-time programs available. *Faculty:* 3 full-time (0 women). *Students:* 9 full-time (4 women), 7 part-time (2 women); includes 11 minority (10 Black or African American, non-Hispanic/Latino; 1 Asian, non-Hispanic/Latino), 3 international. Average age 33. 13 applicants, 100% accepted, 5 enrolled. In 2011, 2 degrees awarded. *Degree requirements:* For master's, one foreign language, thesis. *Entrance requirements:* For master's, GRE General Test, minimum GPA of 2.5. Additional exam requirements/recommendations for international students: Required—TOEFL (minimum score 500 paper-based; 173 computer-based; 61 iBT). *Application deadline:* For fall admission, 4/1 for domestic and international students; for spring admission, 11/1 for domestic and international students. Applications are processed on a rolling basis. Application fee: $40 ($55 for international students). *Expenses: Tuition:* Full-time $13,572; part-time $754 per credit hour. *Required fees:* $806; $403 per semester. *Financial support:* In 2011–12, 4 fellowships were awarded; career-related internships or fieldwork, Federal Work-Study, scholarships/grants, and unspecified assistantships also available. Support available to part-time students. Financial award application deadline: 4/30; financial award applicants required to submit FAFSA. *Unit head:* Dr. Roy George, Chairperson, 404-880-6945, E-mail: rgeorge@cau.edu. *Application contact:* Michelle Clark-Davis, Graduate Program Admissions, 404-880-6605, E-mail: cauadmissions@cau.edu.

Clarkson University, Graduate School, School of Arts and Sciences, Program in Information Technology, Potsdam, NY 13699. Offers MS. Part-time programs available. *Students:* 5 full-time (1 woman), 3 part-time (1 woman), 5 international. Average age 32. 15 applicants, 80% accepted, 2 enrolled. In 2011, 5 master's awarded. *Entrance requirements:* For master's, GRE, transcripts of all college coursework, three letters of recommendation; resume and personal statement (recommended). Additional exam requirements/recommendations for international students: Required—TOEFL, TSE recommended. *Application deadline:* For fall admission, 1/30 priority date for domestic students, 1/30 for international students; for spring admission, 9/1 priority date for domestic students, 9/1 for international students. Applications are processed on a rolling basis. Application fee: $25 ($35 for international students). Electronic applications accepted. *Expenses: Tuition:* Full-time $14,376; part-time $1198 per credit hour. *Required fees:* $295 per semester. *Financial support:* In 2011–12, 5 students received support, including 1 research assistantship with full tuition reimbursement available (averaging $21,999 per year); scholarships/grants, tuition waivers (partial), and unspecified assistantships also available. *Faculty research:* Information networks, technical communications, networking management information systems. *Total annual research expenditures:* $1,452. *Unit head:* Dr. William Dennis Horn, Director, 315-268-6420, Fax: 315-268-2335, E-mail: horn@clarkson.edu. *Application contact:* Jennifer Reed, Graduate School Coordinator, School of Arts and Sciences, 315-268-3802, Fax: 315-268-3989, E-mail: sciencegrad@clarkson.edu. Web site: http://www.clarkson.edu/it/.

Clark University, Graduate School, College of Professional and Continuing Education, Program in Information Technology, Worcester, MA 01610-1477. Offers MSIT. *Students:* 13 full-time (7 women), 18 part-time (3 women); includes 6 minority (1 Black or African American, non-Hispanic/Latino; 3 Asian, non-Hispanic/Latino; 1 Hispanic/Latino; 1 Two or more races, non-Hispanic/Latino), 16 international. Average age 32. 22 applicants, 100% accepted, 12 enrolled. In 2011, 15 master's awarded. *Degree requirements:* For master's, thesis or alternative. *Application deadline:* Applications are processed on a rolling basis. Application fee: $50. Electronic applications accepted. *Expenses: Tuition:* Full-time $37,000; part-time $1156 per credit hour. *Financial support:* Tuition waivers (partial) available. *Unit head:* Max E. Hess, Director of Graduate Studies, 508-793-7217, Fax: 508-793-7232. *Application contact:* Julia Parent, Director of Marketing, Communications, and Admissions, 508-793-7217, Fax: 508-793-7232, E-mail: jparent@clarku.edu. Web site: http://copace.clarku.edu/c/academics/ma/msit.cfm.

Cleveland State University, College of Graduate Studies, Monte Ahuja College of Business, Department of Computer and Information Science, Cleveland, OH 44115. Offers computer and information science (MCIS); information systems (DBA). Part-time and evening/weekend programs available. *Faculty:* 12 full-time (2 women), 3 part-time/adjunct (2 women). *Students:* 18 full-time (8 women), 70 part-time (15 women); includes 6 minority (3 Black or African American, non-Hispanic/Latino; 3 Asian, non-Hispanic/Latino), 51 international. Average age 27. 344 applicants, 71% accepted, 34 enrolled. In 2011, 34 master's awarded. Terminal master's awarded for partial completion of doctoral program. *Degree requirements:* For master's, thesis optional; for doctorate, comprehensive exam, thesis/dissertation. *Entrance requirements:* For master's, GRE or GMAT, minimum GPA of 2.75; for doctorate, GRE or GMAT, MBA, MCIS or equivalent. Additional exam requirements/recommendations for international students: Required—TOEFL (minimum score 525 paper-based; 197 computer-based; 78 iBT). *Application deadline:* For fall admission, 7/15 priority date for domestic students, 5/15 for international students; for spring admission, 12/15 priority date for domestic students. Applications are processed on a rolling basis. Application fee: $30. Electronic applications accepted. *Expenses: Tuition,* state resident: full-time $6416; part-time $494 per credit hour. Tuition, nonresident: full-time $12,074; part-time $929 per credit hour. *Financial support:* In 2011–12, 21 students received support, including 7 research assistantships with full and partial tuition reimbursements available (averaging $7,800 per year), 2 teaching assistantships with full and partial tuition reimbursements available (averaging $16,000 per year); career-related internships or fieldwork, tuition waivers (full), and unspecified assistantships also available. *Faculty research:* Artificial intelligence, object-oriented analysis, database design, software efficiency, distributed system, geographical information systems. *Total annual research expenditures:* $7,500. *Unit head:* Dr. Santosh K. Misra, Chairman, 216-687-4760, Fax: 216-687-5448, E-mail: s.misra@csuohio.edu. *Application contact:* 216-687-4760, Fax: 216-687-9354, E-mail: s.misra@csuohio.edu. Web site: http://cis.csuohio.edu/.

Coleman University, Program in Information Technology, San Diego, CA 92123. Offers MSIT. Evening/weekend programs available. *Entrance requirements:* For master's, bachelor's degree in computer field, minimum GPA of 3.0. Additional exam requirements/recommendations for international students: Required—TOEFL (minimum score 500 paper-based).

The College of Saint Rose, Graduate Studies, School of Mathematics and Sciences, Program in Computer Information Systems, Albany, NY 12203-1419. Offers MS. Part-time and evening/weekend programs available. *Degree requirements:* For master's, comprehensive exam, research component. *Entrance requirements:* For master's, minimum GPA of 3.0, 9 undergraduate credits in math. Additional exam requirements/recommendations for international students: Required—TOEFL (minimum score 550 paper-based; 213 computer-based). Electronic applications accepted.

Cornell University, Graduate School, Graduate Fields of Arts and Sciences, Field of Information Science, Ithaca, NY 14853-0001. Offers cognition (PhD); human computer interaction (PhD); information systems (PhD); social aspects of information (PhD). *Faculty:* 38 full-time (11 women). *Students:* 31 full-time (12 women); includes 3 minority (1 Black or African American, non-Hispanic/Latino; 2 Asian, non-Hispanic/Latino), 18 international. Average age 27. 152 applicants, 14% accepted, 17 enrolled. In 2011, 3 doctorates awarded. *Degree requirements:* For doctorate, comprehensive exam, thesis/dissertation. *Entrance requirements:* For doctorate, GRE General Test, 3 letters of recommendation. Additional exam requirements/recommendations for international students: Required—TOEFL (minimum score 550 paper-based; 213 computer-based; 77 iBT). *Application deadline:* For fall admission, 1/1 for domestic students. Application fee: $95. Electronic applications accepted. *Financial support:* In 2011–12, 2 fellowships with full tuition reimbursements, 8 research assistantships with full tuition reimbursements, 6 teaching assistantships with full tuition reimbursements were awarded; institutionally sponsored loans, scholarships/grants, tuition waivers (full and partial), and unspecified assistantships also available. Financial award applicants required to submit FAFSA. *Faculty research:* Digital libraries, game theory, data mining, human-computer interaction, computational linguistics. *Unit head:* Director of Graduate Studies, 607-255-5925. *Application contact:* Graduate Field Assistant, 607-255-5925, E-mail: info@infosci.cornell.edu. Web site: http://www.gradschool.cornell.edu/fields.php?id-9A&a-2.

Dakota State University, College of Business and Information Systems, Madison, SD 57042-1799. Offers MBA, MSHI, MSIA, MSIS, D Sc IS. *Accreditation:* ACBSP. Part-time and evening/weekend programs available. Postbaccalaureate distance learning degree programs offered (minimal on-campus study). *Faculty:* 28 full-time (7 women), 2 part-time/adjunct (1 woman). *Students:* 53 full-time (10 women), 157 part-time (43 women); includes 32 minority (8 Black or African American, non-Hispanic/Latino; 2 American Indian or Alaska Native, non-Hispanic/Latino; 12 Asian, non-Hispanic/Latino; 7 Hispanic/Latino; 1 Native Hawaiian or other Pacific Islander, non-Hispanic/Latino; 2 Two or more races, non-Hispanic/Latino), 37 international. Average age 36. 173 applicants, 53%

accepted, 55 enrolled. In 2011, 58 master's, 1 doctorate awarded. *Degree requirements:* For master's, comprehensive exam, thesis optional, examination, integrative project; for doctorate, comprehensive exam, thesis/dissertation, portfolio. *Entrance requirements:* For master's, GRE General Test, demonstration of information systems skills, minimum GPA of 2.75 (MSIS); for doctorate, GRE General Test, demonstration of information systems skills. Additional exam requirements/recommendations for international students: Required—TOEFL (minimum score 550 paper-based; 213 computer-based; 78 iBT). *Application deadline:* For fall admission, 6/15 for domestic and international students; for spring admission, 11/15 for domestic and international students. Applications are processed on a rolling basis. Application fee: $35 ($85 for international students). *Financial support:* In 2011–12, 71 students received support, including 13 fellowships with partial tuition reimbursements available (averaging $31,837 per year), 13 research assistantships with partial tuition reimbursements available (averaging $11,116 per year); teaching assistantships, Federal Work-Study, scholarships/grants, unspecified assistantships, and administrative assistantships also available. Support available to part-time students. Financial award applicants required to submit FAFSA. *Faculty research:* E-commerce, data mining and data warehousing, effectiveness of hybrid learning environments, biometrics and information assurance, decision support systems. *Unit head:* Dr. Tom Halverson, Dean, 605-256-5165, Fax: 605-256-5060, E-mail: tom.halverson@dsu.edu. *Application contact:* Erin Blankespoor, Secretary, Office of Graduate Studies and Research, 605-256-5799, Fax: 605-256-5093, E-mail: erin.blankespoor@dsu.edu. Web site: http://www.dsu.edu/bis/index.aspx.

See Display on next page and Close-Up on page 341.

DePaul University, College of Computing and Digital Media, Chicago, IL 60604. Offers animation (MA, MFA); applied technology (MS); business information technology (MS); cinema (MFA); cinema production (MS); computational finance (MS); computer and information sciences (PhD); computer game development (MS); computer graphics and motion technology (MS); computer information and network security (MS); computer science (MS); e-commerce technology (MS); human-computer interaction (MS); information systems (MS); information technology (MA); information technology project management (MS); network engineering and management (MS); predictive analytics (MS); screenwriting (MFA); software engineering (MS); JD/MA; JD/MS. Part-time and evening/weekend programs available. Postbaccalaureate distance learning degree programs offered (no on-campus study). *Faculty:* 64 full-time (16 women), 44 part-time/adjunct (5 women). *Students:* 969 full-time (250 women), 936 part-time (231 women); includes 566 minority (204 Black or African American, non-Hispanic/Latino; 3 American Indian or Alaska Native, non-Hispanic/Latino; 166 Asian, non-Hispanic/Latino; 135 Hispanic/Latino; 7 Native Hawaiian or other Pacific Islander, non-Hispanic/Latino; 51 Two or more races, non-Hispanic/Latino), 282 international. Average age 32. 1,040 applicants, 65% accepted, 324 enrolled. In 2011, 478 master's, 4 doctorates awarded. *Degree requirements:* For master's, thesis (for some programs); for doctorate, comprehensive exam, thesis/dissertation. *Entrance requirements:* For master's, GRE or GMAT (MS in computational finance only), bachelor's degree, resume (MS in predictive analytics only), IT experience (MS in information technology project management only), portfolio review (all MFA programs and MA in animation); for doctorate, GRE, master's degree in computer science. Additional exam requirements/recommendations for international students: Required—TOEFL (minimum score 550 paper-based; 213 computer-based; 80 iBT), IELTS (minimum score 6.5), Pearson Test of English (minimum score 53). *Application deadline:* For fall admission, 8/1 priority date for domestic students, 6/1 for international students; for winter admission, 12/1 priority date for domestic students, 10/1 for international students; for spring admission, 3/1 priority date for domestic students, 1/1 for international students. Applications are processed on a rolling basis. Application fee: $25. Electronic applications accepted. *Expenses:* Contact institution. *Financial support:* In 2011–12, 56 students received support, including 3 fellowships with full tuition reimbursements available (averaging $30,000 per year), 3 research assistantships with full and partial tuition reimbursements available (averaging $22,833 per year), 50 teaching assistantships (averaging $6,194 per year); Federal Work-Study, scholarships/grants, tuition waivers (full and partial), and unspecified assistantships also available. Support available to part-time students. Financial award application deadline: 4/30. *Faculty research:* Data mining, theoretical computer science, gaming, security, animation and film. *Total annual research expenditures:* $3.9 million. *Unit head:* Elly Kafritsas-Wessels, Senior Administrative Assistant, 312-362-5816, Fax: 312-362-5185, E-mail: ekafrits@cdm.depaul.edu. *Application contact:* James Parker, Director of Graduate Admission, 312-362-8714, Fax: 312-362-5179, E-mail: jparke29@cdm.depaul.edu. Web site: http://cdm.depaul.edu.

DeSales University, Graduate Division, Program in Information Systems, Center Valley, PA 18034-9568. Offers MSIS. Part-time programs available. *Degree requirements:* For master's, comprehensive exam, thesis optional. *Entrance requirements:* Additional exam requirements/recommendations for international students: Required—TOEFL. *Application deadline:* Applications are processed on a rolling basis. Application fee: $35. Electronic applications accepted. Tuition and fees vary according to degree level. *Financial support:* Applicants required to submit FAFSA. *Faculty research:* Digital communication, numerical analysis, database design. *Unit head:* Fr. Peter J. Leonard, Acting Director, 610-282-1100 Ext. 1289, Fax: 610-282-2254, E-mail: peter.leonard@desales.edu. *Application contact:* Caryn Stopper, Director of Graduate Admissions, 610-282-1100 Ext. 1768, Fax: 610-282-2254, E-mail: caryn.stopper@desales.edu.

Drexel University, The iSchool at Drexel, College of Information Science and Technology, Master of Science in Library and Information Science Program, Philadelphia, PA 19104-2875. Offers archival studies (MS); competitive intelligence and knowledge management (MS); digital libraries (MS); library and information services (MS); school library media (MS); youth services (MS). Part-time and evening/weekend programs available. Postbaccalaureate distance learning degree programs offered (no on-campus study). *Faculty:* 30 full-time (20 women), 29 part-time/adjunct (15 women). *Students:* 198 full-time (155 women), 437 part-time (353 women); includes 79 minority (30 Black or African American, non-Hispanic/Latino; 6 American Indian or Alaska Native, non-Hispanic/Latino; 20 Asian, non-Hispanic/Latino; 23 Hispanic/Latino), 15 international. Average age 33. 464 applicants, 72% accepted, 202 enrolled. In 2011, 261 master's awarded. *Entrance requirements:* For master's, GRE General Test. Additional exam requirements/recommendations for international students: Required—TOEFL (minimum score 600 paper-based; 250 computer-based; 100 iBT). *Application deadline:* For fall admission, 8/1 for domestic and international students; for spring admission, 2/1 for domestic and international students. Applications are processed on a rolling basis. Electronic applications accepted. *Expenses:* Contact institution. *Financial support:* In 2011–12, 217 students received support, including 252 fellowships with partial tuition reimbursements available (averaging $22,500 per year); institutionally sponsored loans and scholarships/grants also available. Support available to part-time students. Financial award application deadline: 3/1; financial award applicants required to submit FAFSA. *Faculty research:* Library and information resources and services, knowledge organization and representation, information retrieval/information visualization/

bibliometrics, information needs and behaviors, digital libraries. *Total annual research expenditures:* $2 million. *Unit head:* Dr. David E. Fenske, Dean/Professor of Information Science, 215-895-2475, Fax: 215-895-6378, E-mail: fenske@drexel.edu. *Application contact:* Matthew Lechtenberg, Graduate Admissions Manager, 215-895-1951, Fax: 215-895-2303, E-mail: ml333@drexel.edu.

Drexel University, The iSchool at Drexel, College of Information Science and Technology, PhD in Information Studies Program, Philadelphia, PA 19104-2875. Offers PhD. Part-time and evening/weekend programs available. *Students:* 37 full-time (16 women), 19 part-time (9 women); includes 9 minority (5 Black or African American, non-Hispanic/Latino; 2 Asian, non-Hispanic/Latino; 1 Hispanic/Latino; 1 Native Hawaiian or other Pacific Islander, non-Hispanic/Latino), 26 international. Average age 33. 83 applicants, 14% accepted, 9 enrolled. In 2011, 9 doctorates awarded. *Degree requirements:* For doctorate, thesis/dissertation. *Entrance requirements:* For doctorate, GRE General Test. Additional exam requirements/recommendations for international students: Required—TOEFL (minimum score 600 paper-based; 250 computer-based; 100 iBT). *Application deadline:* For fall admission, 2/1 for domestic and international students. Applications are processed on a rolling basis. Electronic applications accepted. Application fee is waived when completed online. *Financial support:* In 2011–12, 25 research assistantships with full tuition reimbursements (averaging $22,500 per year), 10 teaching assistantships with full tuition reimbursements (averaging $22,500 per year) were awarded; career-related internships or fieldwork, institutionally sponsored loans, scholarships/grants, traineeships, health care benefits, tuition waivers (partial), and unspecified assistantships also available. Financial award application deadline: 2/1. *Faculty research:* Information retrieval/information visualization/bibliometrics, human-computer interaction, digital libraries, databases, text/data mining, healthcare informatics, school library media, social media, information behavior, information ethics, information policy and archives. *Total annual research expenditures:* $2 million. *Unit head:* Dr. David E. Fenske, Dean/Professor of Information Science, 215-895-2475, Fax: 215-895-6378, E-mail: fenske@drexel.edu. *Application contact:* Matthew Lechtenberg, Graduate Admissions Manager, 215-895-1951, Fax: 215-895-2303, E-mail: ml333@drexel.edu.

East Tennessee State University, School of Graduate Studies, College of Business and Technology, Department of Computer and Information Sciences, Johnson City, TN 37614. Offers applied computer science (MS); information technology (MS). Part-time and evening/weekend programs available. *Faculty:* 16 full-time (3 women), 1 part-time/adjunct (0 women). *Students:* 33 full-time (2 women), 19 part-time (4 women); includes 2 minority (1 Hispanic/Latino; 1 Two or more races, non-Hispanic/Latino), 10 international. Average age 30. 42 applicants, 55% accepted, 15 enrolled. In 2011, 21 master's awarded. *Degree requirements:* For master's, comprehensive exam, thesis optional, capstone. *Entrance requirements:* For master's, GRE General Test, minimum GPA of 2.5, three letters of recommendation. Additional exam requirements/recommendations for international students: Required—TOEFL (minimum score 550 paper-based; 213 computer-based; 79 iBT). *Application deadline:* For fall admission, 6/1 for domestic students, 4/30 for international students; for spring admission, 11/1 for domestic students, 9/30 for international students. Application fee: $35 ($45 for international students). Electronic applications accepted. *Expenses:* Tuition, state resident: full-time $7312; part-time $350 per credit hour. Tuition, nonresident: full-time $18,490; part-time $621 per credit hour. *Required fees:* $63 per credit hour. Tuition and fees vary according to course load and program. *Financial support:* In 2011–12, 29 students received support, including 9 research assistantships with full tuition reimbursements available

(averaging $9,000 per year), 15 teaching assistantships with full tuition reimbursements available (averaging $10,000 per year); career-related internships or fieldwork, institutionally sponsored loans, scholarships/grants, and unspecified assistantships also available. Financial award application deadline: 7/1; financial award applicants required to submit FAFSA. *Faculty research:* Security, enterprise resource planning, high performance computing, optimization, software engineering. *Unit head:* Dr. Terry Countermine, Chair, 423-439-5328, Fax: 423-439-7119, E-mail: counter@etsu.edu. *Application contact:* Bethany Glassbrenner, Graduate Specialist, 423-439-6165, Fax: 423-439-5624, E-mail: glassbrenner@etsu.edu.

Everglades University, Graduate Programs, Program in Information Technology, Boca Raton, FL 33431. Offers MIT. *Entrance requirements:* Additional exam requirements/recommendations for international students: Recommended—TOEFL (minimum score 500 paper-based; 173 computer-based). Electronic applications accepted.

Florida Gulf Coast University, Lutgert College of Business, Program in Computer and Information Systems, Fort Myers, FL 33965-6565. Offers MS. *Faculty:* 51 full-time (14 women), 11 part-time/adjunct (2 women). *Students:* 5 full-time (1 woman), 4 part-time (0 women), 1 international. Average age 34. 8 applicants, 50% accepted, 3 enrolled. In 2011, 3 master's awarded. *Entrance requirements:* For master's, GMAT, minimum GPA of 3.0. Additional exam requirements/recommendations for international students: Required—TOEFL (minimum score 550 paper-based; 213 computer-based). *Application deadline:* For fall admission, 6/1 priority date for domestic students; for spring admission, 11/1 for domestic students. Applications are processed on a rolling basis. Application fee: $30. Electronic applications accepted. *Expenses:* Tuition, state resident: full-time $8289. Tuition, nonresident: full-time $28,895. *Required fees:* $1831. One-time fee: $30 full-time. *Faculty research:* Advanced distributed learning technologies, object-oriented systems analysis, database management systems, workgroup support systems, software engineering project management. *Unit head:* Dr. Rajesh Srivastava, Chair, 239-590-7372, Fax: 239-590-7330, E-mail: rsrivast@fgcu.edu. *Application contact:* Marisa Ouverson, Director of Enrollment Management, 239-590-7403, Fax: 239-590-7330, E-mail: mouverso@fgcu.edu.

Florida International University, College of Engineering and Computing, School of Computing and Information Sciences, Miami, FL 33199. Offers computer science (MS, PhD); computing and information sciences (MS, PhD); telecommunications and networking (MS). Part-time and evening/weekend programs available. *Degree requirements:* For master's, thesis or alternative; for doctorate, comprehensive exam, thesis/dissertation. *Entrance requirements:* For master's and doctorate, GRE General Test, 3 letters of recommendation, minimum GPA of 3.0. Additional exam requirements/recommendations for international students: Required—TOEFL (minimum score 550 paper-based; 80 iBT). Electronic applications accepted. *Faculty research:* Database systems, software engineering, operating systems, networks, bioinformatics and computational biology.

Gannon University, School of Graduate Studies, College of Engineering and Business, School of Engineering and Computer Science, Program in Computer and Information Science, Erie, PA 16541-0001. Offers MCIS. Part-time and evening/weekend programs available. *Students:* 32 full-time (8 women), 15 part-time (2 women); includes 1 minority (Native Hawaiian or other Pacific Islander, non-Hispanic/Latino), 33 international. Average age 28. 405 applicants, 45% accepted, 13 enrolled. In 2011, 17 master's awarded. *Degree requirements:* For master's, research project or thesis. *Entrance requirements:* For master's, GRE or GMAT, letters of recommendation, resume. Additional exam requirements/recommendations for international students: Required—

TOEFL (minimum score 79 iBT). *Application deadline:* Applications are processed on a rolling basis. Application fee: $25. Electronic applications accepted. *Financial support:* Career-related internships or fieldwork, Federal Work-Study, scholarships/grants, traineeships, and unspecified assistantships available. Financial award application deadline: 7/1; financial award applicants required to submit FAFSA. *Faculty research:* Refinement of software engineering processes, graph databases and bioinformatics, aspect-oriented programs and testing, software systems for healthcare applications, game programming. *Unit head:* Dr. Theresa Vitolo, Chair, 814-871-7126, E-mail: vitolo001@gannon.edu. *Application contact:* Kara Morgan, Director of Graduate Admissions, 814-871-5831, Fax: 814-871-5827, E-mail: graduate@gannon.edu.

George Mason University, Volgenau School of Engineering, Department of Applied Information Technology, Fairfax, VA 22030. Offers MS. *Faculty:* 20 full-time (5 women), 54 part-time/adjunct (12 women). *Students:* 25 full-time (6 women), 80 part-time (22 women); includes 46 minority (11 Black or African American, non-Hispanic/Latino; 29 Asian, non-Hispanic/Latino; 3 Hispanic/Latino; 1 Native Hawaiian or other Pacific Islander, non-Hispanic/Latino; 2 Two or more races, non-Hispanic/Latino), 6 international. Average age 30. 67 applicants, 82% accepted, 45 enrolled. In 2011, 34 master's awarded. *Degree requirements:* For master's, capstone course. *Entrance requirements:* For master's, GRE/GMAT, personal goals statement; 2 copies of official transcripts; 3 letters of recommendation; resume; official bank statement; proof of financial support; photocopy of passport; baccalaureate degree from an accredited program with minimum B average in last 60 credit hours. Additional exam requirements/recommendations for international students: Required—TOEFL (minimum score 575 paper-based; 230 computer-based; 88 iBT), IELTS, Pearson Test of English. *Application deadline:* For fall admission, 1/15 priority date for domestic students; for spring admission, 8/15 priority date for domestic students. Application fee: $65 ($80 for international students). Electronic applications accepted. *Expenses:* Tuition, state resident: full-time $8750; part-time $364.58 per credit. Tuition, nonresident: full-time $24,092; part-time $1003.83 per credit. *Required fees:* $2514; $104.75 per credit. *Financial support:* In 2011–12, 4 students received support, including 1 research assistantship with full and partial tuition reimbursement available (averaging $8,304 per year), 3 teaching assistantships with full and partial tuition reimbursements available (averaging $10,435 per year); career-related internships or fieldwork, Federal Work-Study, scholarships/grants, unspecified assistantships, and health care benefits (full-time research or teaching assistantship recipients) also available. Support available to part-time students. Financial award application deadline: 3/1; financial award applicants required to submit FAFSA. *Total annual research expenditures:* $454,023. *Unit head:* Donald Gantz, Chair, 703-993-3565, Fax: 703-993-1734, E-mail: dgantz@gmu.edu. *Application contact:* Patty Holly, Information Contact, 703-993-2799, E-mail: pholly@gmu.edu. Web site: http://ait.gmu.edu.

George Mason University, Volgenau School of Engineering, Program in Information Technology, Fairfax, VA 22030. Offers PhD, Engr. *Faculty:* 40 full-time (9 women), 17 part-time/adjunct. *Students:* 55 full-time (14 women), 102 part-time (14 women); includes 26 minority (7 Black or African American, non-Hispanic/Latino; 1 American Indian or Alaska Native, non-Hispanic/Latino; 13 Asian, non-Hispanic/Latino; 2 Hispanic/Latino; 3 Two or more races, non-Hispanic/Latino), 55 international. Average age 38. 91 applicants, 55% accepted, 22 enrolled. In 2011, 14 degrees awarded. *Median time to degree:* Of those who began their doctoral program in fall 2003, 10% received their degree in 8 years or less. *Degree requirements:* For doctorate, comprehensive exam, thesis/dissertation, internship. *Entrance requirements:* For doctorate, GRE, MS and BS earned in a related field; 2 official copies of transcripts; 3 letters of recommendation; resume; expanded goals statement; self assessment; photocopy of passport; official bank statement; proof of financial support;. Additional exam requirements/recommendations for international students: Required—TOEFL (minimum score 575 paper-based; 230 computer-based), Pearson Test of English. *Application deadline:* For fall admission, 1/1 priority date for domestic students; for spring admission, 8/1 priority date for domestic students. Application fee: $65 ($80 for international students). Electronic applications accepted. *Expenses:* Tuition, state resident: full-time $8750; part-time $364.58 per credit. Tuition, nonresident: full-time $24,092; part-time $1003.83 per credit. *Required fees:* $2514; $104.75 per credit. *Financial support:* In 2011–12, 34 students received support, including 11 research assistantships with full and partial tuition reimbursements available (averaging $15,602 per year), 23 teaching assistantships with full and partial tuition reimbursements available (averaging $13,486 per year); career-related internships or fieldwork, Federal Work-Study, scholarships/grants, unspecified assistantships, and health care benefits (full-time research or teaching assistantship recipients) also available. Support available to part-time students. Financial award application deadline: 3/1; financial award applicants required to submit FAFSA. *Faculty research:* Rapid pace of technological innovation, need for efficient and effective technology development, unwavering interoperability challenges, the scope and complexity of major system design requirements. *Unit head:* Stephen Nash, Senior Associate Dean, 703-993-1505, Fax: 703-993-1633, E-mail: snash@gmu.edu. *Application contact:* Lisa Nolder, Director of Graduate Student Services, 703-993-1499, Fax: 703-993-1633, E-mail: snolder@gmu.edu. Web site: http://volgenau.gmu.edu/PhDprogr.

Georgia Southwestern State University, Graduate Studies, School of Computer and Information Sciences, Americus, GA 31709-4693. Offers computer information systems (MS); computer science (MS). Part-time programs available. *Degree requirements:* For master's, thesis (for some programs). *Entrance requirements:* For master's, GRE General Test, minimum GPA of 3.0. Electronic applications accepted. *Faculty research:* Database, Internet technologies, computational complexity, encryption.

Georgia State University, J. Mack Robinson College of Business, Program in General Business Administration, Atlanta, GA 30302-3083. Offers accounting/information systems (MBA); economics (MBA, MS); enterprise risk management (MBA); general business (MBA); general business administration (EMBA, PMBA); information systems consulting (MBA); information systems risk management (MBA); international business and information technology (MBA); international entrepreneurship (MBA); MBA/JD. *Accreditation:* AACSB. Part-time and evening/weekend programs available. *Entrance requirements:* For master's, GMAT. Additional exam requirements/recommendations for international students: Required—TOEFL (minimum score 610 paper-based; 255 computer-based; 101 iBT). Electronic applications accepted.

Grand Valley State University, Padnos College of Engineering and Computing, School of Computing and Information Systems, Allendale, MI 49401-9403. Offers computer information systems (MS), including databases, distributed systems, management of information systems, object-oriented systems, software engineering. Part-time and evening/weekend programs available. *Degree requirements:* For master's, thesis or alternative. *Entrance requirements:* For master's, GMAT or GRE General Test. Additional exam requirements/recommendations for international students: Required—TOEFL. Electronic applications accepted. *Faculty research:* Object technology, distributed computing, information systems management database, software engineering.

Harvard University, Extension School, Cambridge, MA 02138-3722. Offers applied sciences (CAS); biotechnology (ALM); educational technologies (ALM); educational technology (CET); English for graduate and professional studies (DGP); environmental management (ALM, CEM); information technology (ALM); journalism (ALM); liberal arts (ALM); management (ALM, CM); mathematics for teaching (ALM); museum studies (ALM); premedical studies (Diploma); publication and communication (CPC). Part-time and evening/weekend programs available. *Degree requirements:* For master's, thesis. *Entrance requirements:* For master's, 3 completed graduate courses with grade of B or higher. Additional exam requirements/recommendations for international students: Required—TOEFL (minimum score 600 paper-based; 250 computer-based), TWE (minimum score 5). *Expenses:* Contact institution.

Harvard University, Graduate School of Arts and Sciences, Program in Information, Technology and Management, Cambridge, MA 02138. Offers PhD. *Expenses: Tuition:* Full-time $36,304. *Required fees:* $1186. Full-time tuition and fees vary according to program.

Hood College, Graduate School, Program in Management of Information Technology, Frederick, MD 21701-8575. Offers MS. Part-time and evening/weekend programs available. *Degree requirements:* For master's, thesis. *Entrance requirements:* For master's, minimum GPA of 2.75. Additional exam requirements/recommendations for international students: Required—TOEFL (minimum score 575 paper-based; 231 computer-based; 89 iBT). Electronic applications accepted. *Faculty research:* Systems engineering, parallel distributed computing, strategy, business ethics, entrepreneurship.

Hood College, Graduate School, Programs in Computer and Information Sciences, Frederick, MD 21701-8575. Offers computer and information sciences (MS); computer science (MS); information security (Certificate). Part-time and evening/weekend programs available. *Degree requirements:* For master's, thesis. *Entrance requirements:* For master's, minimum GPA of 2.75. Additional exam requirements/recommendations for international students: Required—TOEFL (minimum score 575 paper-based; 231 computer-based; 89 iBT). Electronic applications accepted. *Faculty research:* Systems engineering, natural language, processing, database design, artificial intelligence and parallel distributed computing.

Indiana University Bloomington, School of Informatics and Computing, Bloomington, IN 47408. Offers bioinformatics (MS); chemical informatics (MS); computer science (MS, PhD); health informatics (MS); human computer interaction (MS); informatics (PhD); laboratory informatics (MS); media arts and science (MS); music informatics (MS); security informatics (MS); MS/PhD. PhD offered through University Graduate School. Part-time programs available. Postbaccalaureate distance learning degree programs offered (no on-campus study). *Faculty:* 63 full-time (12 women). *Students:* 434 full-time (99 women), 36 part-time (9 women); includes 24 minority (8 Black or African American, non-Hispanic/Latino; 9 Asian, non-Hispanic/Latino; 4 Hispanic/Latino; 3 Two or more races, non-Hispanic/Latino), 309 international. Average age 27. 825 applicants, 58% accepted, 205 enrolled. In 2011, 115 master's, 25 doctorates awarded. Terminal master's awarded for partial completion of doctoral program. *Degree requirements:* For master's, thesis optional; for doctorate, comprehensive exam, thesis/dissertation, oral and written exams. *Entrance requirements:* For master's and doctorate, GRE, letters of reference. Additional exam requirements/recommendations for international students: Required—TOEFL. *Application deadline:* For fall admission, 1/15 for domestic students, 12/1 for international students. Application fee: $55 ($65 for international students). Electronic applications accepted. *Financial support:* In 2011–12, fellowships with full and partial tuition reimbursements (averaging $20,000 per year), research assistantships (averaging $14,000 per year), teaching assistantships (averaging $13,000 per year) were awarded; Federal Work-Study, institutionally sponsored loans, scholarships/grants, health care benefits, tuition waivers (full and partial), and unspecified assistantships also available. Support available to part-time students. *Total annual research expenditures:* $2 million. *Unit head:* Dr. David Leake, Associate Dean for Graduate Studies, 812-855-9756, E-mail: leake@cs.indiana.edu. *Application contact:* Rachel Lawmaster, Manager of Graduate Admissions and Graduate Studies, 812-856-3622, Fax: 812-856-3825, E-mail: raclee@indiana.edu. Web site: http://www.informatics.indiana.edu/.

Indiana University Bloomington, School of Library and Information Science, Bloomington, IN 47405-3907. Offers MIS, MLS, PhD, Sp LIS, JD/MLS, MIS/MA, MLS/MA, MPA/MIS, MPA/MLS. *Accreditation:* ALA (one or more programs are accredited). Part-time programs available. *Faculty:* 16 full-time (7 women). *Students:* 256 full-time (176 women), 67 part-time (49 women); includes 46 minority (13 Black or African American, non-Hispanic/Latino; 2 American Indian or Alaska Native, non-Hispanic/Latino; 23 Asian, non-Hispanic/Latino; 4 Hispanic/Latino; 4 Two or more races, non-Hispanic/Latino), 28 international. Average age 29. 286 applicants, 79% accepted, 101 enrolled. In 2011, 143 master's, 7 doctorates, 2 other advanced degrees awarded. *Degree requirements:* For doctorate, thesis/dissertation. *Entrance requirements:* For master's and doctorate, GRE General Test, 3 letters of reference. Additional exam requirements/recommendations for international students: Required—TOEFL (minimum score 600 paper-based; 250 computer-based; 100 iBT). *Application deadline:* For fall admission, 5/15 priority date for domestic students, 12/1 for international students; for spring admission, 10/15 priority date for domestic students, 9/1 for international students. Applications are processed on a rolling basis. Application fee: $55 ($65 for international students). Electronic applications accepted. *Expenses:* Contact institution. *Financial support:* Fellowships with full and partial tuition reimbursements, research assistantships with full and partial tuition reimbursements, career-related internships or fieldwork, Federal Work-Study, institutionally sponsored loans, scholarships/grants, tuition waivers (partial), and unspecified assistantships available. Support available to part-time students. Financial award application deadline: 1/15. *Faculty research:* Scholarly communication, interface design, library and management policy, computer-mediated communication, information retrieval. *Application contact:* Rhonda Spencer, Director of Admissions, 812-855-2018, Fax: 812-855-6166, E-mail: slis@indiana.edu. Web site: http://www.slis.indiana.edu/.

Indiana University–Purdue University Fort Wayne, College of Engineering, Technology, and Computer Science, Program in Technology, Fort Wayne, IN 46805-1499. Offers facilities and construction management (MS); industrial technology/manufacturing (MS); information technology/advanced computer applications (MS). Part-time programs available. *Faculty:* 14 full-time (5 women). *Students:* 1 full-time (0 women), 18 part-time (1 woman); includes 3 minority (1 Black or African American, non-Hispanic/Latino; 1 Asian, non-Hispanic/Latino; 1 Hispanic/Latino), 3 international. Average age 32. 9 applicants, 100% accepted, 7 enrolled. In 2011, 5 master's awarded. *Entrance requirements:* For master's, minimum GPA of 3.0. Additional exam requirements/recommendations for international students: Required—TOEFL (minimum score 550 paper-based; 213 computer-based; 77 iBT), TWE. *Application deadline:* For fall admission, 7/15 for domestic students, 5/15 for international students; for spring admission, 12/1 for domestic students, 10/15 for international students. Applications are processed on a rolling basis. Application fee: $55 ($60 for international students).

Electronic applications accepted. *Financial support:* Career-related internships or fieldwork, scholarships/grants, and unspecified assistantships available. Support available to part-time students. Financial award application deadline: 3/1; financial award applicants required to submit FAFSA. *Unit head:* Dr. Max Yen, Dean, 260-481-6839, Fax: 260-481-5734, E-mail: yens@ipfw.edu. *Application contact:* Dr. Gary Steffen, Chair, 260-481-6344, Fax: 260-481-5734, E-mail: steffen@ipfw.edu. Web site: http://www.ipfw.edu/etcs.

Indiana University–Purdue University Indianapolis, School of Informatics, Indianapolis, IN 46202-2896. Offers informatics (PhD); media arts and science (MS). Part-time and evening/weekend programs available. *Faculty:* 3 full-time (0 women). *Students:* 48 full-time (24 women), 80 part-time (24 women); includes 26 minority (13 Black or African American, non-Hispanic/Latino; 9 Asian, non-Hispanic/Latino; 2 Hispanic/Latino; 2 Two or more races, non-Hispanic/Latino), 30 international. Average age 34. 135 applicants, 61% accepted, 45 enrolled. In 2011, 36 master's awarded. *Degree requirements:* For master's, multimedia project. *Entrance requirements:* For master's, minimum undergraduate GPA of 3.0, graduate 3.2; interview; portfolio; BA with demonstrated media arts skills. Additional exam requirements/recommendations for international students: Required—TOEFL. *Application deadline:* For fall admission, 3/15 for domestic students; for spring admission, 11/15 for domestic students. Application fee: $55 ($65 for international students). *Financial support:* In 2011–12, fellowships (averaging $17,447 per year), teaching assistantships (averaging $9,392 per year) were awarded; career-related internships or fieldwork, Federal Work-Study, institutionally sponsored loans, and scholarships/grants also available. Support available to part-time students. *Unit head:* Darrell L. Bailey, Executive Associate Dean, 317-278-4636, Fax: 317-278-7769. *Application contact:* Dr. Sherry Queener, Director, Graduate Studies and Associate Dean, 317-274-1577, Fax: 317-278-2380. Web site: http://www.newmedia.iupui.edu/.

Indiana University–Purdue University Indianapolis, School of Library and Information Science, Indianapolis, IN 46202-2896. Offers MLS. Part-time and evening/weekend programs available. *Faculty:* 3 full-time (2 women). *Students:* 66 full-time (46 women), 169 part-time (133 women); includes 21 minority (11 Black or African American, non-Hispanic/Latino; 2 Asian, non-Hispanic/Latino; 5 Hispanic/Latino; 3 Two or more races, non-Hispanic/Latino). Average age 34. 53 applicants, 96% accepted, 33 enrolled. In 2011, 110 master's awarded. *Entrance requirements:* For master's, GRE General Test. Additional exam requirements/recommendations for international students: Required—TOEFL (minimum score 600 paper-based). *Application deadline:* For fall admission, 7/15 priority date for domestic students; for spring admission, 11/15 priority date for domestic students. Applications are processed on a rolling basis. Application fee: $55 ($65 for international students). *Financial support:* In 2011–12, teaching assistantships (averaging $9,500 per year) were awarded; career-related internships or fieldwork, Federal Work-Study, institutionally sponsored loans, and scholarships/grants also available. Support available to part-time students. *Unit head:* Dr. Daniel Collison, Executive Associate Dean, 317-278-2375, Fax: 317-278-1807, E-mail: slisindy@iupui.edu. *Application contact:* Dr. Sherry Queener, Director, Graduate Studies and Associate Dean, 317-274-1577, Fax: 317-278-2380. Web site: http://www.slis.indiana.edu/.

Instituto Tecnologico de Santo Domingo, Graduate School, Area of Engineering, Santo Domingo, Dominican Republic. Offers construction administration (MS, Certificate); data telecommunications (M Eng, MS, Certificate); industrial engineering (M Eng, Certificate); industrial management (M Mgmt); information technology (Certificate); maintenance engineering (M Eng); occupational hazard prevention (M Mgmt); production management (Certificate); quantitative methods (Certificate); sanitary and environmental engineering (M Eng); structural engineering (M Eng); systems engineering and electronic data processing (Certificate); transportation (Certificate).

Instituto Tecnológico y de Estudios Superiores de Monterrey, Campus Cuernavaca, Programs in Information Science, Temixco, Mexico. Offers administration of information technology (MATI); computer science (MCC, DCC); information technology (MTI).

Instituto Tecnológico y de Estudios Superiores de Monterrey, Campus Estado de México, Professional and Graduate Division, Estado de Mexico, Mexico. Offers administration of information technologies (MITA); architecture (M Arch); business administration (GMBA, MBA); computer sciences (MCS, PhD); education (M Ed); educational institution administration (MAD); educational technology and innovation (PhD); electronic commerce (MEC); environmental systems (MS); finance (MAF); humanistic studies (MHS); information sciences and knowledge management (MISKM); information systems (MS); manufacturing systems (MS); marketing (MEM); quality systems and productivity (MS); science and materials engineering (PhD); telecommunications management (MTM). Part-time programs available. Postbaccalaureate distance learning degree programs offered (minimal on-campus study). *Degree requirements:* For master's, one foreign language, thesis (for some programs); for doctorate, one foreign language, thesis/dissertation. *Entrance requirements:* For master's, E-PAEP 500, interview; for doctorate, E-PAEP 500, research proposal. Additional exam requirements/recommendations for international students: Required—TOEFL (minimum score 550 paper-based). *Faculty research:* Surface treatments by plasmas, mechanical properties, robotics, graphical computing, mechatronics security protocols.

Instituto Tecnológico y de Estudios Superiores de Monterrey, Campus Irapuato, Graduate Programs, Irapuato, Mexico. Offers administration (MBA); administration of information technology (MAIT); administration of telecommunications (MAT); architecture (M Arch); computer science (MCS); education (M Ed); educational administration (MEA); educational innovation and technology (DEIT); educational technology (MET); electronic commerce (MBA); environmental administration and planning (MEAP); environmental systems (MES); finances (MBA); humanistic studies (MHS); international management for Latin American executives (MIMLAE); library and information science (MLIS); manufacturing quality management (MMQM); marketing research (MBA).

Instituto Tecnológico y de Estudios Superiores de Monterrey, Campus Monterrey, Graduate and Research Division, Program in Computer Science, Monterrey, Mexico. Offers artificial intelligence (PhD); computer science (MS); information systems (MS); information technology (MS). Part-time programs available. *Degree requirements:* For master's, one foreign language, thesis; for doctorate, one foreign language, thesis/dissertation. *Entrance requirements:* For master's, EXADEP; for doctorate, master's degree in related field. Additional exam requirements/recommendations for international students: Required—TOEFL. *Faculty research:* Distributed systems, software engineering, decision support systems.

Instituto Tecnológico y de Estudios Superiores de Monterrey, Campus Monterrey, Graduate and Research Division, Program in Informatics, Monterrey, Mexico. Offers PhD. Part-time programs available. *Degree requirements:* For doctorate, one foreign language, thesis/dissertation, technological project, arbitrated publication of articles. *Entrance requirements:* For doctorate, GRE General Test, GRE Subject Test, master's degree in related field. Additional exam requirements/recommendations for international students: Required—TOEFL. *Faculty research:* Artificial intelligence, distributed systems, software engineering, decision support systems.

Instituto Tecnológico y de Estudios Superiores de Monterrey, Campus Sonora Norte, Program in Technological Information Management, Hermosillo, Mexico. Offers MA.

Inter American University of Puerto Rico, San Germán Campus, Graduate Studies Center, Program in Business Administration, San Germán, PR 00683-5008. Offers accounting (MBA); finance (MBA); human resources (MBA, PhD); industrial relations (MBA); information sciences (MBA); management (MBA); marketing (MBA). Part-time and evening/weekend programs available. *Degree requirements:* For master's, comprehensive exam. *Entrance requirements:* For master's, GRE General Test or EXADEP, minimum GPA of 3.0. *Application deadline:* For fall admission, 4/30 priority date for domestic students; for spring admission, 11/15 for domestic students. Applications are processed on a rolling basis. Application fee: $31. *Expenses: Required fees:* $213 per semester. *Financial support:* Teaching assistantships, Federal Work-Study, and unspecified assistantships available. *Unit head:* Dr. Elba T. Irizarry, Director of Graduate Studies Center, 787-264-1912 Ext. 7357, Fax: 787-892-6350, E-mail: elbat@sg.inter.edu.

Iowa State University of Science and Technology, Program in Information Assurance, Ames, IA 50011-3060. Offers MS. *Degree requirements:* For master's, thesis or alternative. *Entrance requirements:* For master's, GRE General Test. Additional exam requirements/recommendations for international students: Required—TOEFL (minimum score 570 paper-based; 79 iBT), IELTS (minimum score 6.5). *Application deadline:* For fall admission, 5/1 priority date for domestic students, 5/1 for international students; for spring admission, 11/1 priority date for domestic students, 11/1 for international students. Application fee: $40 ($90 for international students). Electronic applications accepted. *Unit head:* Dr. Doug Jacobson, Director of Graduate Education, 515-294-8307, Fax: 515-294-7582, E-mail: dougj@iastate.edu. *Application contact:* Virginia Anderson, Application Contact, 515-294-0659, Fax: 515-294-7582, E-mail: ginny@iastate.edu. Web site: http://www.iac.iastate.edu.

The Johns Hopkins University, Whiting School of Engineering, Information Security Institute, Baltimore, MD 21218-2699. Offers MSSI. Part-time programs available. *Degree requirements:* For master's, project. *Entrance requirements:* For master's, GRE, minimum GPA of 3.0. Additional exam requirements/recommendations for international students: Required—TOEFL (minimum score 600 paper-based; 250 computer-based). Electronic applications accepted. *Faculty research:* Critical infrastructure protection, insider/outsider cryptography and encryption methodologies, international policy protocols, Web-based intellectual property rights.

Kansas State University, Graduate School, College of Engineering, Department of Computing and Information Sciences, Manhattan, KS 66506. Offers computer science (MS, PhD); software engineering (MSE). Part-time programs available. Postbaccalaureate distance learning degree programs offered (minimal on-campus study). *Faculty:* 15 full-time (1 woman), 1 part-time/adjunct (0 women). *Students:* 64 full-time (18 women), 19 part-time (2 women); includes 1 minority (Two or more races, non-Hispanic/Latino), 60 international. Average age 27. 258 applicants, 24% accepted, 12 enrolled. In 2011, 31 degrees awarded. Terminal master's awarded for partial completion of doctoral program. *Degree requirements:* For master's, thesis or alternative; for doctorate, thesis/dissertation, preliminary exams. *Entrance requirements:* For master's, GRE, bachelor's degree in computer science, minimum GPA of 3.0; for doctorate, GRE General Test, GRE Subject Test, master's degree in computer science or bachelor's degree and strong advanced computer knowledge. Additional exam requirements/recommendations for international students: Required—TOEFL (minimum score 575 paper-based; 233 computer-based; 90 iBT). *Application deadline:* For fall admission, 2/1 priority date for domestic students, 2/1 for international students; for spring admission, 8/1 priority date for domestic students, 8/1 for international students. Applications are processed on a rolling basis. Application fee: $40 ($55 for international students). Electronic applications accepted. *Financial support:* In 2011–12, 9 fellowships (averaging $30,000 per year), 22 research assistantships (averaging $17,820 per year), 22 teaching assistantships with full tuition reimbursements (averaging $16,000 per year) were awarded; career-related internships or fieldwork, institutionally sponsored loans, scholarships/grants, health care benefits, and unspecified assistantships also available. Support available to part-time students. Financial award application deadline: 3/15; financial award applicants required to submit FAFSA. *Faculty research:* High-assurance software and programming languages, data mining, parallel and distributed computing, computer security, embedded systems. *Total annual research expenditures:* $2.2 million. *Unit head:* Dr. Gurdip E. Singh, Head, 785-532-7945, Fax: 785-532-7353, E-mail: gurdip@ksu.edu. *Application contact:* Susan Cregg, Program Coordinator, 785-532-6350, Fax: 785-532-7353, E-mail: scregg@ksu.edu. Web site: http://www.cis.ksu.edu/.

Kennesaw State University, Michael J. Coles College of Business, Program in Information Systems, Kennesaw, GA 30144-5591. Offers MSIS. Part-time programs available. *Students:* 19 full-time (4 women), 37 part-time (13 women); includes 21 minority (13 Black or African American, non-Hispanic/Latino; 4 Asian, non-Hispanic/Latino; 4 Hispanic/Latino), 3 international. Average age 35. 28 applicants, 54% accepted, 10 enrolled. In 2011, 20 master's awarded. *Entrance requirements:* For master's, GMAT or GRE General Test, minimum GPA of 2.75. Additional exam requirements/recommendations for international students: Required—TOEFL (minimum score 550 paper-based; 213 computer-based; 80 iBT), IELTS (minimum score 6). *Application deadline:* For fall admission, 7/1 for domestic and international students; for spring admission, 11/1 for domestic and international students. Applications are processed on a rolling basis. Application fee: $60. Electronic applications accepted. *Expenses:* Tuition, state resident: full-time $3000; part-time $250 per semester hour. Tuition, nonresident: full-time $10,836; part-time $903 per semester hour. *Required fees:* $774 per semester. *Financial support:* In 2011–12, 2 research assistantships with full tuition reimbursements (averaging $4,000 per year) were awarded; Federal Work-Study and unspecified assistantships also available. Support available to part-time students. Financial award application deadline: 4/1; financial award applicants required to submit FAFSA. *Unit head:* Dr. Amy Woszczynski, Director, 770-423-6005, Fax: 770-423-6731, E-mail: awoszczy@kennesaw.edu. *Application contact:* Tamara Hutto, Admissions Counselor, 770-420-4377, Fax: 770-423-6885, E-mail: ksugrad@kennesaw.edu. Web site: http://www.kennesaw.edu/.

Kent State University, College of Communication and Information, Interdisciplinary Program in Information Architecture and Knowledge Management, Kent, OH 44242-0001. Offers MS. Part-time and evening/weekend programs available. *Degree requirements:* For master's, capstone or thesis. *Entrance requirements:* For master's, GRE (recommended). *Expenses:* Tuition, state resident: full-time $8136; part-time $452 per credit hour. Tuition, nonresident: full-time $14,292; part-time $794 per credit hour. *Faculty research:* Information architecture, knowledge management, usability, organizational memory management, information design, user interface design.

Knowledge Systems Institute, Program in Computer and Information Sciences, Skokie, IL 60076. Offers MS. Part-time and evening/weekend programs available. Postbaccalaureate distance learning degree programs offered (minimal on-campus study). *Degree requirements:* For master's, comprehensive exam, thesis. *Entrance requirements:* Additional exam requirements/recommendations for international students: Required—TOEFL (minimum score 550 paper-based; 213 computer-based; 79 iBT). Electronic applications accepted. *Faculty research:* Data mining, web development, database programming and administration.

Lamar University, College of Graduate Studies, College of Business, Beaumont, TX 77710. Offers accounting (MBA); experiential business and entrepreneurship (MBA); financial management (MBA); healthcare administration (MBA); information systems (MBA); management (MBA). *Accreditation:* AACSB. Part-time and evening/weekend programs available. *Faculty:* 18 full-time (5 women), 5 part-time/adjunct (0 women). *Students:* 74 full-time (33 women), 72 part-time (27 women); includes 24 minority (7 Black or African American, non-Hispanic/Latino; 9 Asian, non-Hispanic/Latino; 8 Hispanic/Latino), 34 international. Average age 29. 69 applicants, 84% accepted, 16 enrolled. In 2011, 62 master's awarded. *Degree requirements:* For master's, comprehensive exam (for some programs), thesis optional. *Entrance requirements:* For master's, GMAT. Additional exam requirements/recommendations for international students: Required—TOEFL (minimum score 525 paper-based; 197 computer-based). *Application deadline:* For fall admission, 3/15 priority date for domestic students; for spring admission, 10/1 priority date for domestic students. Applications are processed on a rolling basis. Application fee: $25 ($50 for international students). *Expenses:* Tuition, state resident: full-time $5430; part-time $272 per credit hour. Tuition, nonresident: full-time $11,540; part-time $577 per credit hour. *Required fees:* $1916. *Financial support:* In 2011–12, 12 students received support, including 4 research assistantships with partial tuition reimbursements available; fellowships with tuition reimbursements available, career-related internships or fieldwork, Federal Work-Study, institutionally sponsored loans, scholarships/grants, and tuition waivers (partial) also available. Support available to part-time students. Financial award application deadline: 4/1; financial award applicants required to submit FAFSA. *Faculty research:* Marketing, finance, quantitative methods, management information systems, legal, environmental. *Unit head:* Dr. Enrique R. Venta, Dean, 409-880-8604, Fax: 409-880-8088, E-mail: henry.venta@lamar.edu. *Application contact:* Dr. Brad Mayer, Professor and Associate Dean, 409-880-2383, Fax: 409-880-8605, E-mail: bradley.mayer@lamar.edu. Web site: http://mba.lamar.edu.

Lehigh University, College of Business and Economics, Department of Accounting, Bethlehem, PA 18015. Offers accounting and information analysis (MS). *Accreditation:* AACSB. *Faculty:* 6 full-time (0 women). *Students:* 43 full-time (29 women), 17 part-time (14 women); includes 1 minority (Hispanic/Latino), 46 international. Average age 23. 149 applicants, 68% accepted, 19 enrolled. In 2011, 23 master's awarded. *Entrance requirements:* For master's, GMAT. Additional exam requirements/recommendations for international students: Required—TOEFL (minimum score 105 iBT). *Application deadline:* For fall admission, 5/1 for domestic and international students. Applications are processed on a rolling basis. Application fee: $100. Electronic applications accepted. *Expenses:* Contact institution. *Financial support:* In 2011–12, 6 research assistantships with partial tuition reimbursements (averaging $2,500 per year) were awarded; scholarships/grants and tuition waivers (partial) also available. Financial award application deadline: 1/15. *Faculty research:* Behavioral accounting, internal control, information systems, supply chain management, financial accounting. *Unit head:* Dr. Heibatollah Sami, Director, 610-758-3407, Fax: 610-758-6429, E-mail: hes205@lehigh.edu. *Application contact:* Corinn McBride, Director of Recruitment and Admissions, 610-758-3418, Fax: 610-758-5283, E-mail: com207@lehigh.edu. Web site: http://www4.lehigh.edu/business/academics/depts/accounting.

Long Island University–C. W. Post Campus, College of Information and Computer Science, Department of Computer Science/Management Engineering, Brookville, NY 11548-1300. Offers information systems (MS); information technology education (MS); management engineering (MS). Part-time and evening/weekend programs available. *Degree requirements:* For master's, comprehensive exam, thesis or alternative. *Entrance requirements:* For master's, bachelor's degree in science, mathematics, or engineering; minimum GPA of 2.5. Additional exam requirements/recommendations for international students: Required—TOEFL (minimum score 500 paper-based; 173 computer-based). Electronic applications accepted. *Faculty research:* Inductive music learning, re-engineering business process, technology and ethics.

Loyola University Chicago, Graduate School, Department of Computer Science, Chicago, IL 60660. Offers computer science (MS); information technology (MS); software engineering (MS). Part-time and evening/weekend programs available. *Faculty:* 10 full-time (1 woman), 10 part-time/adjunct (2 women). *Students:* 59 full-time (18 women), 29 part-time (8 women); includes 19 minority (9 Black or African American, non-Hispanic/Latino; 9 Asian, non-Hispanic/Latino; 1 Hispanic/Latino), 39 international. Average age 28. 129 applicants, 55% accepted, 29 enrolled. In 2011, 40 master's awarded. *Degree requirements:* For master's, thesis optional, ten courses. *Entrance requirements:* For master's, 3 letters of recommendation, transcripts, statement of purpose. Additional exam requirements/recommendations for international students: Required—TOEFL (minimum score 550 paper-based; 213 computer-based; 79 iBT) or IELTS (minimum score 6.5). *Application deadline:* For fall admission, 8/10 for domestic students, 5/15 for international students; for spring admission, 12/20 for domestic students, 9/15 for international students. Applications are processed on a rolling basis. Electronic applications accepted. *Expenses: Tuition:* Full-time $15,660; part-time $870 per credit hour. *Required fees:* $125 per semester. Tuition and fees vary according to course load and program. *Financial support:* In 2011–12, 20 students received support, including 1 fellowship (averaging $3,000 per year), 16 teaching assistantships with partial tuition reimbursements available (averaging $4,000 per year); career-related internships or fieldwork, Federal Work-Study, scholarships/grants, tuition waivers (partial), and unspecified assistantships also available. Financial award application deadline: 3/15. *Faculty research:* Software engineering, high performance computing, algorithms and complexity, parallel and distributed computing, databases and computer networks. *Total annual research expenditures:* $22,000. *Unit head:* Dr. Chandra Sekharan, Chair, 312-915-7985, Fax: 312-915-7998, E-mail: csekhar@luc.edu. *Application contact:* Cecilia Murphy, Graduate Program Secretary, 312-915-7990, Fax: 312-915-7998, E-mail: gradinfo-cs@luc.edu. Web site: http://cs.luc.edu.

Marlboro College, Graduate School, Program in Information Technologies, Marlboro, VT 05344. Offers information technologies (MS); open source Web development (Certificate); project management (Certificate). Part-time and evening/weekend programs available. Postbaccalaureate distance learning degree programs offered (minimal on-campus study). *Degree requirements:* For master's, 30 credits including

capstone project. *Entrance requirements:* For master's, letter of intent, 2 letters of recommendation, transcripts. Electronic applications accepted.

Marshall University, Academic Affairs Division, College of Information Technology and Engineering, Weisberg Division of Engineering and Computer Science, Program in Information Systems, Huntington, WV 25755. Offers MS. Part-time and evening/weekend programs available. *Students:* 10 full-time (2 women), 13 part-time (3 women); includes 1 minority (Black or African American, non-Hispanic/Latino), 6 international. Average age 30. In 2011, 11 master's awarded. *Degree requirements:* For master's, final project, oral exam. *Entrance requirements:* For master's, GRE General Test or MAT, minimum undergraduate GPA of 2.5. Application fee: $40. *Financial support:* Tuition waivers (full) available. Support available to part-time students. Financial award application deadline: 8/1; financial award applicants required to submit FAFSA. *Unit head:* Dr. William Pierson, Professor, 304-696-2695, E-mail: pierson@marshall.edu. *Application contact:* Information Contact, 304-746-1900, Fax: 304-746-1902, E-mail: services@marshall.edu. Web site: http://www.marshall.edu/cite/.

Massachusetts Institute of Technology, School of Engineering, Department of Civil and Environmental Engineering, Cambridge, MA 02139. Offers biological oceanography (PhD, Sc D); chemical oceanography (PhD, Sc D); civil and environmental engineering (PhD, Sc D); civil and environmental systems (PhD, Sc D); civil engineering (PhD, Sc D, CE); coastal engineering (PhD, Sc D); construction engineering and management (PhD, Sc D); environmental and water quality engineering (M Eng); environmental biology (PhD, Sc D); environmental chemistry (PhD, Sc D); environmental engineering (PhD, Sc D); environmental fluid mechanics (PhD, Sc D); environmental science and engineering (SM); geotechnical and geoenvironmental engineering (PhD, Sc D); geotechnology (M Eng); high-performance structures (M Eng); hydrology (PhD, Sc D); information technology (PhD, Sc D); mechanics (SM); oceanographic engineering (PhD, Sc D); structures and materials (PhD, Sc D); transportation (M Eng, PhD, Sc D); SM/MBA. *Faculty:* 35 full-time (6 women), 1 part-time/adjunct (0 women). *Students:* 216 full-time (80 women); includes 30 minority (4 Black or African American, non-Hispanic/Latino; 13 Asian, non-Hispanic/Latino; 8 Hispanic/Latino; 5 Two or more races, non-Hispanic/Latino), 110 international. Average age 27. 589 applicants, 26% accepted, 91 enrolled. In 2011, 62 master's, 14 doctorates awarded. *Degree requirements:* For master's and CE, thesis; for doctorate, comprehensive exam, thesis/dissertation. *Entrance requirements:* For master's and doctorate, GRE General Test. Additional exam requirements/recommendations for international students: Required—TOEFL (minimum score 577 paper-based; 233 computer-based; 90 iBT), IELTS (minimum score 7). *Application deadline:* For fall admission, 12/15 for domestic and international students. Application fee: $75. Electronic applications accepted. *Expenses: Tuition:* Full-time $40,460; part-time $630 per credit hour. *Required fees:* $272. *Financial support:* In 2011–12, 180 students received support, including 51 fellowships (averaging $30,800 per year), 110 research assistantships (averaging $29,500 per year), 19 teaching assistantships (averaging $29,500 per year); career-related internships or fieldwork, Federal Work-Study, institutionally sponsored loans, scholarships/grants, health care benefits, and unspecified assistantships also available. *Faculty research:* Environmental chemistry, environmental fluid mechanics and coastal engineering, environmental microbiology, geotechnical engineering and geomechanics, hydrology and hydroclimatology, infrastructure systems, mechanics of materials and structures, transportation systems. *Total annual research expenditures:* $17.7 million. *Unit head:* Prof. Andrew Whittle, Head, 617-253-7101. *Application contact:* Patricia Glidden, Graduate Admissions Coordinator, 617-253-7119, Fax: 617-258-6775, E-mail: cee-admissions@mit.edu. Web site: http://cee.mit.edu/.

Missouri University of Science and Technology, Graduate School, Department of Business and Information Technology, Rolla, MO 65409. Offers business and information technology (MBA); information science and technology (MS). *Degree requirements:* For master's, thesis or alternative. *Entrance requirements:* Additional exam requirements/recommendations for international students: Required—TOEFL (minimum score 600 paper-based; 250 computer-based).

Montclair State University, The Graduate School, College of Science and Mathematics, MS Program in Computer Science, Montclair, NJ 07043-1624. Offers CISCO (Certificate); informatics (MS); object oriented computing (Certificate). Part-time and evening/weekend programs available. *Students:* 11 full-time (6 women), 19 part-time (4 women); includes 7 minority (3 Black or African American, non-Hispanic/Latino; 3 Asian, non-Hispanic/Latino; 1 Hispanic/Latino), 7 international. Average age 31. 40 applicants, 45% accepted, 9 enrolled. In 2011, 9 master's awarded. *Degree requirements:* For master's, comprehensive exam, thesis or alternative. *Entrance requirements:* For master's, GRE General Test, 2 letters of recommendation, essay. Additional exam requirements/recommendations for international students: Required—TOEFL (minimum score 83 iBT) or IELTS (minimum score 6.5). *Application deadline:* For fall admission, 6/1 for international students; for spring admission, 10/1 for international students. Applications are processed on a rolling basis. Application fee: $60. Electronic applications accepted. *Financial support:* In 2011–12, 3 research assistantships with full tuition reimbursements (averaging $7,000 per year) were awarded; Federal Work-Study, scholarships/grants, and unspecified assistantships also available. Support available to part-time students. Financial award application deadline: 3/1; financial award applicants required to submit FAFSA. *Faculty research:* Software engineering, parallel and distributed systems, artificial intelligence, databases, human-computer interaction. *Unit head:* Dr. Michael Oudshoorn, Chairperson, 973-655-4166. *Application contact:* Amy Aiello, Director of Graduate Admissions and Operations, 973-655-5147, Fax: 973-655-7869, E-mail: graduate.school@montclair.edu. Web site: http://cs.montclair.edu/.

National University, Academic Affairs, School of Engineering, Technology and Media, Department of Computer Science, Information and Media Systems, La Jolla, CA 92037-1011. Offers computer science (MS); cyber security and information assurance (MS); management information systems (MS). Part-time and evening/weekend programs available. Postbaccalaureate distance learning degree programs offered (no on-campus study). *Degree requirements:* For master's, thesis. *Entrance requirements:* For master's, interview, minimum GPA of 2.5. Additional exam requirements/recommendations for international students: Required—TOEFL (minimum score 550 paper-based; 213 computer-based; 79 iBT), IELTS (minimum score 6). *Application deadline:* Applications are processed on a rolling basis. Application fee: $60 ($65 for international students). Electronic applications accepted. *Financial support:* Career-related internships or fieldwork, institutionally sponsored loans, scholarships/grants, and tuition waivers (partial) available. Support available to part-time students. Financial award application deadline: 6/30; financial award applicants required to submit FAFSA. *Unit head:* Dr. Alireza M. Farahani, 858-309-3438, Fax: 858-309-3420, E-mail: afarahan@nu.edu. *Application contact:* Dominick Giovanniello, Associate Regional Dean, 800-NAT-UNIV, Fax: 858-541-7792, E-mail: dgiovann@nu.edu.

Web site: http://www.nu.edu/OurPrograms/SchoolOfEngineeringAndTechnology/ComputerScienceAndInformationSystems.html.

Information Science

Naval Postgraduate School, Departments and Academic Groups, Department of Information Sciences, Monterey, CA 93943. Offers electronic warfare systems engineering (MS); information sciences (PhD); information systems and operations (MS); information technology management (MS); information warfare systems engineering (MS); knowledge superiority (Certificate); remote sensing intelligence (MS); system technology (command, control and communications) (MS). Program open only to commissioned officers of the United States and friendly nations and selected United States federal civilian employees. Part-time programs available. *Faculty:* 54 full-time (5 women), 5 part-time/adjunct (1 woman). *Students:* 169 full-time (2 women), 38 part-time (4 women); includes 51 minority (19 Black or African American, non-Hispanic/Latino; 1 American Indian or Alaska Native, non-Hispanic/Latino; 16 Asian, non-Hispanic/Latino; 15 Hispanic/Latino), 36 international. Average age 41. In 2011, 65 master's, 1 doctorate awarded. *Degree requirements:* For master's, thesis (for some programs); for doctorate, thesis/dissertation. *Faculty research:* Designing inter-organisational collectivities for dynamic fit: stability, manoeuvrability and application in disaster relief endeavours; system self-awareness and related methods for Improving the use and understanding of data within DoD3; evaluating a macrocognition model of team collaboration using real-world data from the Haiti relief effort; cyber distortion in command and control; performance and QoS in service-based systems. *Total annual research expenditures:* $12.4 million. *Unit head:* Prof. Dan Boger, Department Chair, 831-656-3671, E-mail: dboger@nps.edu. Web site: http://nps.edu/Academics/Schools/GSOIS/Departments/IS/index.html.

New Jersey Institute of Technology, Office of Graduate Studies, College of Computing Science, Program in Information Systems, Newark, NJ 07102. Offers business and information systems (MS); emergency management and business continuity (MS); information systems (MS, PhD). Part-time and evening/weekend programs available. *Faculty:* 9 full-time (2 women), 3 part-time/adjunct (0 women). *Students:* 85 full-time (28 women), 145 part-time (40 women); includes 96 minority (26 Black or African American, non-Hispanic/Latino; 42 Asian, non-Hispanic/Latino; 27 Hispanic/Latino; 1 Native Hawaiian or other Pacific Islander, non-Hispanic/Latino), 58 international. Average age 32. 373 applicants, 64% accepted, 72 enrolled. In 2011, 99 master's, 1 doctorate awarded. Terminal master's awarded for partial completion of doctoral program. *Degree requirements:* For master's, thesis optional; for doctorate, thesis/dissertation. *Entrance requirements:* For master's, GRE General Test; for doctorate, GRE General Test, minimum graduate GPA of 3.5. Additional exam requirements/recommendations for international students: Required—TOEFL (minimum score 550 paper-based; 213 computer-based; 79 iBT). *Application deadline:* For fall admission, 6/1 priority date for domestic students, 5/1 for international students; for spring admission, 11/15 for domestic and international students. Applications are processed on a rolling basis. Application fee: $65. Electronic applications accepted. *Expenses:* Tuition, state resident: full-time $7980; part-time $867 per credit. Tuition, nonresident: full-time $11,336; part-time $1196 per credit. *Required fees:* $230 per credit. *Financial support:* Fellowships with full and partial tuition reimbursements, research assistantships with full and partial tuition reimbursements, teaching assistantships with full and partial tuition reimbursements, career-related internships or fieldwork, Federal Work-Study, institutionally sponsored loans, and unspecified assistantships available. Financial award application deadline: 1/15. *Total annual research expenditures:* $366,728. *Unit head:* Dr. Michael P. Bieber, Associate Chair, 973-596-2681, Fax: 973-596-2986, E-mail: michael.p.bieber@njit.edu. *Application contact:* Kathryn Kelly, Director of Admissions, 973-596-3300, Fax: 973-596-3461, E-mail: admissions@njit.edu. Web site: http://is.njit.edu/.

Northeastern University, College of Computer and Information Science, Boston, MA 02115-5096. Offers computer and information science (PhD); computer science (MS); health informatics (MS); information assurance (MS). Part-time and evening/weekend programs available. *Faculty:* 28 full-time, 3 part-time/adjunct. *Students:* 337 full-time (91 women), 90 part-time (52 women). 1,045 applicants, 56% accepted, 150 enrolled. In 2011, 88 master's, 7 doctorates awarded. Terminal master's awarded for partial completion of doctoral program. *Degree requirements:* For master's, thesis optional; for doctorate, comprehensive exam, thesis/dissertation. *Entrance requirements:* For master's and doctorate, GRE General Test. Additional exam requirements/recommendations for international students: Required—TOEFL or IELTS. *Application deadline:* For fall admission, 7/15 for domestic students, 5/1 for international students; for spring admission, 10/15 for domestic students, 9/1 for international students. Applications are processed on a rolling basis. Application fee: $50. Electronic applications accepted. *Expenses:* Contact institution. *Financial support:* In 2011–12, 59 students received support, including 1 fellowship, 40 research assistantships with full tuition reimbursements available (averaging $18,260 per year), 33 teaching assistantships with full tuition reimbursements available (averaging $18,260 per year); career-related internships or fieldwork, Federal Work-Study, institutionally sponsored loans, scholarships/grants, and unspecified assistantships also available. Financial award application deadline: 1/15. *Faculty research:* Programming languages, artificial intelligence, human-computer interaction, database management, network security. *Unit head:* Dr. Larry A. Finkelstein, Dean, 617-373-2462, Fax: 617-373-5121. *Application contact:* Dr. Agnes Chan, Associate Dean and Director of Graduate Program, 617-373-2462, Fax: 617-373-5121, E-mail: gradschool@ccs.neu.edu. Web site: http://www.ccs.neu.edu/.

Northeastern University, College of Engineering, Program in Information Systems, Boston, MA 02115-5096. Offers MS, Certificate. Part-time programs available. Postbaccalaureate distance learning degree programs offered (no on-campus study). *Students:* 152 full-time, 11 part-time. Average age 26. 188 applicants, 91% accepted, 68 enrolled. In 2011, 58 master's awarded. *Degree requirements:* For master's, thesis optional. *Entrance requirements:* For master's, GRE General Test. Additional exam requirements/recommendations for international students: Required—TOEFL (minimum score 600 paper-based; 250 computer-based; 80 iBT). *Application deadline:* For fall admission, 1/15 priority date for domestic students, 1/15 for international students. Applications are processed on a rolling basis. Application fee: $50. Electronic applications accepted. *Financial support:* In 2011–12, 18 students received support, including 1 fellowship with full tuition reimbursement available (averaging $18,325 per year), 1 research assistantship with full tuition reimbursement available, 12 teaching assistantships with full tuition reimbursements available; career-related internships or fieldwork, Federal Work-Study, scholarships/grants, tuition waivers (full), and unspecified assistantships also available. Support available to part-time students. Financial award application deadline: 1/15; financial award applicants required to submit FAFSA. *Faculty research:* Simulation analysis, software architecture. *Unit head:* Dr. Khaled Bugrara, Director, 617-373-3699. *Application contact:* Jeffrey Hengel, Admissions Specialist, 617-373-2711, Fax: 617-373-2501, E-mail: grad-eng@coe.neu.edu. Web site: http://www.coe.neu.edu/.

Northern Kentucky University, Office of Graduate Programs, College of Informatics, Department of Business Informatics, Highland Heights, KY 41099. Offers business informatics (MS, Certificate); corporate information security (Certificate); enterprise resource planning (Certificate). Part-time and evening/weekend programs available. Postbaccalaureate distance learning degree programs offered (no on-campus study). *Faculty:* 9 full-time (3 women), 1 part-time/adjunct (0 women). *Students:* 12 full-time (5 women), 61 part-time (21 women); includes 11 minority (4 Black or African American, non-Hispanic/Latino; 3 Asian, non-Hispanic/Latino; 3 Hispanic/Latino; 1 Native Hawaiian or other Pacific Islander, non-Hispanic/Latino), 5 international. Average age 34. 41 applicants, 80% accepted, 25 enrolled. In 2011, 32 degrees awarded. *Degree requirements:* For master's, capstone and portfolio (some programs), internship. *Entrance requirements:* For master's, GMAT (minimum score 450), GRE General Test (minimum combined score 1000), resume, minimum GPA of 2.5. Additional exam requirements/recommendations for international students: Required—TOEFL (minimum score 550 paper-based; 213 computer-based; 79 iBT); Recommended—IELTS (minimum score 6.5). *Application deadline:* For fall admission, 8/1 for domestic students, 6/1 for international students; for spring admission, 12/1 for domestic students, 10/1 for international students. Applications are processed on a rolling basis. Application fee: $40. Electronic applications accepted. *Expenses:* Tuition, state resident: full-time $7614; part-time $423 per credit hour. Tuition, nonresident: full-time $13,104; part-time $728 per credit hour. Tuition and fees vary according to degree level and reciprocity agreements. *Financial support:* Unspecified assistantships available. Financial award applicants required to submit FAFSA. *Faculty research:* Information systems implementation, information systems security, business analytics, healthcare informatics, project management practices. *Total annual research expenditures:* $50,000. *Unit head:* Dr. Ben Martz, Department Chair, 859-572-6366, E-mail: matrzw1@nku.edu. *Application contact:* Dr. Vijay Raghavan, Director, MBI Program, 859-572-6358, E-mail: raghavan@nku.edu. Web site: http://informatics.nku.edu/bis.

Northwestern University, McCormick School of Engineering and Applied Science, Department of Electrical Engineering and Computer Science, MS in Information Technology Program, Evanston, IL 60208. Offers MS. Part-time and evening/weekend programs available. *Faculty:* 15 part-time/adjunct (0 women). *Students:* 4 full-time (2 women), 40 part-time (6 women); includes 21 minority (10 Black or African American, non-Hispanic/Latino; 9 Asian, non-Hispanic/Latino; 1 Hispanic/Latino; 1 Native Hawaiian or other Pacific Islander, non-Hispanic/Latino), 9 international. Average age 32. 82 applicants, 39% accepted, 26 enrolled. In 2011, 21 master's awarded. *Entrance requirements:* For master's, work experience in an IT-related position. *Application deadline:* For fall admission, 8/1 for domestic students, 6/1 for international students. Applications are processed on a rolling basis. Application fee: $50. Electronic applications accepted. *Financial support:* Institutionally sponsored loans available. Financial award application deadline: 1/15; financial award applicants required to submit FAFSA. *Unit head:* Dr. Abraham Haddad, Director, 847-491-8175, Fax: 847-467-3550, E-mail: ahaddad@northwestern.edu. *Application contact:* Trista Wdziekonski, Associate Director, 847-467-6557, Fax: 847-467-3550, E-mail: trista@northwestern.edu. Web site: http://www.infotech.northwestern.edu/index.shtml.

Notre Dame de Namur University, Division of Academic Affairs, College of Arts and Sciences, Department of Computer and Information Science, Belmont, CA 94002-1908. Offers MS. Part-time and evening/weekend programs available. Postbaccalaureate distance learning degree programs offered (no on-campus study). *Application deadline:* Applications are processed on a rolling basis. Electronic applications accepted. *Expenses: Tuition:* Full-time $14,220; part-time $790 per credit. *Required fees:* $35 per semester. Tuition and fees vary according to program. *Financial support:* Applicants required to submit FAFSA. *Unit head:* Dr. John Youssefi, Program Director, 650-508-3450, E-mail: jyoussefi@ndnu.edu. *Application contact:* Candace Hallmark, Associate Director of Admissions, 650-508-3600, Fax: 650-508-3426, E-mail: grad.admit@ndnu.edu. Web site: http://onlineprograms.ndnu.edu/mscis/online-computer-science-masters-degree-online.

Nova Southeastern University, Graduate School of Computer and Information Sciences, Fort Lauderdale, FL 33314-7796. Offers computer information systems (MS, PhD); computer science (MS, PhD); computing technology in education (PhD); information security (MS); information systems (PhD); information technology (MS); information technology in education (MS); management information systems (MS). Part-time and evening/weekend programs available. Postbaccalaureate distance learning degree programs offered (no on-campus study). *Faculty:* 20 full-time (5 women), 21 part-time/adjunct (3 women). *Students:* 130 full-time (37 women), 960 part-time (291 women); includes 496 minority (221 Black or African American, non-Hispanic/Latino; 4 American Indian or Alaska Native, non-Hispanic/Latino; 78 Asian, non-Hispanic/Latino; 178 Hispanic/Latino; 15 Two or more races, non-Hispanic/Latino), 49 international. Average age 41. 486 applicants, 45% accepted. In 2011, 131 master's, 39 doctorates awarded. Terminal master's awarded for partial completion of doctoral program. *Degree requirements:* For master's, thesis optional; for doctorate, thesis/dissertation. *Entrance requirements:* For master's, minimum undergraduate GPA of 2.5; 3.0 in major; for doctorate, master's degree, minimum graduate GPA of 3.25. Additional exam requirements/recommendations for international students: Required—TOEFL (minimum score 213 computer-based; 79 iBT), IELTS (minimum score 6). *Application deadline:* Applications are processed on a rolling basis. Application fee: $50. Electronic applications accepted. *Expenses:* Contact institution. *Financial support:* Federal Work-Study, scholarships/grants, and unspecified assistantships available. Support available to part-time students. Financial award application deadline: 5/1. *Faculty research:* Artificial intelligence, database management, human-computer interaction, distance education, information security. *Unit head:* Dr. Eric S. Ackerman, Interim Dean, 954-262-7300. *Application contact:* 954-262-2000, Fax: 954-262-2752, E-mail: scisinfo@nova.edu. Web site: http://www.scis.nova.edu/.

The Ohio State University, Graduate School, College of Engineering, Department of Computer Science and Engineering, Columbus, OH 43210. Offers computer and information science (MS, PhD); computer science and engineering (MS). *Faculty:* 33. *Students:* 278 full-time (46 women), 61 part-time (9 women); includes 10 minority (4 Black or African American, non-Hispanic/Latino; 4 Asian, non-Hispanic/Latino; 1 Hispanic/Latino; 1 Two or more races, non-Hispanic/Latino), 274 international. Average age 27. In 2011, 37 master's, 20 doctorates awarded. *Degree requirements:* For master's, thesis optional; for doctorate, thesis/dissertation. *Entrance requirements:* Additional exam requirements/recommendations for international students: Required—Michigan English Language Assessment Battery (minimum score 82); Recommended—TOEFL (minimum score 600 paper-based; 250 computer-based; 79 iBT). *Application deadline:* For fall admission, 8/15 priority date for domestic students, 7/1 for international students; for winter admission, 12/1 priority date for domestic students, 11/1 for international students; for spring admission, 3/1 priority date for domestic students, 2/1 for international students. Applications are processed on a rolling basis. Application fee: $40 ($50 for international students). Electronic applications accepted. *Expenses:* Tuition, state resident: full-time $11,400. Tuition, nonresident: full-time $28,125. Tuition and fees vary according to course load, degree level, campus/location and program. *Financial support:* Fellowships, teaching assistantships, career-related internships or fieldwork, Federal Work-Study, institutionally sponsored loans, and administrative assistantships available. Support available to part-time students. Financial award application deadline: 1/15. *Unit head:* Xiadong Zhang, Chair, 614-292-5973, E-mail: zhang.574@osu.edu. *Application contact:* Graduate Admissions, 614-292-6031`, Fax: 614-292-3656, E-mail: gradadmissions@osu.edu. Web site: http://www.cse.ohio-state.edu.

Oklahoma State University, Spears School of Business, Department of Management Science and Information Systems, Stillwater, OK 74078. Offers management information systems (MS); management science and information systems (PhD); telecommunications management (MS). Part-time programs available. Postbaccalaureate distance learning degree programs offered. *Faculty:* 17 full-time (3 women), 2 part-time/adjunct (0 women). *Students:* 57 full-time (12 women), 75 part-time (9 women); includes 10 minority (3 Black or African American, non-Hispanic/Latino; 3 American Indian or Alaska Native, non-Hispanic/Latino; 1 Asian, non-Hispanic/Latino; 2 Hispanic/Latino; 1 Two or more races, non-Hispanic/Latino), 54 international. Average age 30. 280 applicants, 37% accepted, 50 enrolled. In 2011, 60 degrees awarded. *Degree requirements:* For master's, thesis or alternative; for doctorate, comprehensive exam, thesis/dissertation. *Entrance requirements:* For master's and doctorate, GRE or GMAT. Additional exam requirements/recommendations for international students: Required—TOEFL (minimum score 550 paper-based; 79 iBT). *Application deadline:* For fall admission, 3/1 for international students; for spring admission, 8/1 for international students. Applications are processed on a rolling basis. Application fee: $40 ($75 for international students). Electronic applications accepted. *Expenses:* Tuition, state resident: full-time $4044; part-time $168.50 per credit hour. Tuition, nonresident: full-time $16,008; part-time $667 per credit hour. *Required fees:* $2122; $88.45 per credit hour. One-time fee: $50. Tuition and fees vary according to course load and campus/location. *Financial support:* In 2011–12, 1 research assistantship (averaging $4,200 per year), 12 teaching assistantships (averaging $13,083 per year) were awarded; career-related internships or fieldwork, Federal Work-Study, scholarships/grants, health care benefits, tuition waivers (partial), and unspecified assistantships also available. Support available to part-time students. Financial award application deadline: 3/1; financial award applicants required to submit FAFSA. *Unit head:* Dr. Rick Wilson, Head, 405-744-3551, Fax: 405-744-5180. *Application contact:* Dr. Sheryl Tucker, Dean, 405-744-7099, Fax: 405-744-0355, E-mail: grad-i@okstate.edu. Web site: http://spears.okstate.edu/msis.

Old Dominion University, College of Business and Public Administration, Doctoral Program in Business Administration, Norfolk, VA 23529. Offers finance (PhD); information technology (PhD); marketing (PhD); strategic management (PhD). *Accreditation:* AACSB. *Faculty:* 21 full-time (2 women). *Students:* 51 full-time (17 women); includes 5 minority (3 Black or African American, non-Hispanic/Latino; 1 Asian, non-Hispanic/Latino; 1 Native Hawaiian or other Pacific Islander, non-Hispanic/Latino), 29 international. Average age 35. 47 applicants, 60% accepted, 12 enrolled. In 2011, 7 doctorates awarded. *Degree requirements:* For doctorate, comprehensive exam, thesis/dissertation. *Entrance requirements:* For doctorate, GMAT. Additional exam requirements/recommendations for international students: Required—TOEFL (minimum score 550 paper-based; 213 computer-based; 79 iBT). *Application deadline:* For fall admission, 4/1 priority date for domestic students, 4/1 for international students. Application fee: $50. Electronic applications accepted. *Expenses:* Tuition, state resident: full-time $9096; part-time $379 per credit. Tuition, nonresident: full-time $23,064; part-time $961 per credit. *Required fees:* $127 per semester. One-time fee: $50. *Financial support:* In 2011–12, 27 students received support, including 2 fellowships with full tuition reimbursements available (averaging $7,500 per year), 32 research assistantships with full tuition reimbursements available (averaging $7,500 per year), 12 teaching assistantships with full tuition reimbursements available (averaging $7,500 per year); scholarships/grants and unspecified assistantships also available. Financial award application deadline: 4/1; financial award applicants required to submit FAFSA. *Faculty research:* International business, buyer behavior, financial markets, strategy, operations research. *Unit head:* Dr. John B. Ford, Graduate Program Director, 757-683-3587, Fax: 757-683-4076, E-mail: jford@odu.edu. *Application contact:* Katrina Davenport, Program Coordinator, 757-683-5138, Fax: 757-683-4076, E-mail: kdavenpo@odu.edu. Web site: http://bpa.odu.edu/bpa/academics/baphd.shtml.

Pace University, Seidenberg School of Computer Science and Information Systems, New York, NY 10038. Offers computer communications and networks (Certificate); computer science (MS); computing studies (DPS); information systems (MS); Internet technologies for e-commerce (Certificate); Internet technology (MS); object-oriented programming (Certificate); security and information assurance (Certificate); software development and engineering (MS); telecommunications (MS, Certificate). Part-time and evening/weekend programs available. *Students:* 82 full-time (19 women), 356 part-time (99 women); includes 175 minority (64 Black or African American, non-Hispanic/Latino; 1 American Indian or Alaska Native, non-Hispanic/Latino; 59 Asian, non-Hispanic/Latino; 47 Hispanic/Latino; 4 Two or more races, non-Hispanic/Latino), 72 international. Average age 37. 304 applicants, 67% accepted, 92 enrolled. In 2011, 136 master's, 9 doctorates, 32 other advanced degrees awarded. *Entrance requirements:* For master's, GRE General Test. Additional exam requirements/recommendations for international students: Required—TOEFL. *Application deadline:* For fall admission, 7/31 priority date for domestic students; for spring admission, 11/30 for domestic students. Applications are processed on a rolling basis. Application fee: $70. Electronic applications accepted. *Expenses:* Contact institution. *Financial support:* Research assistantships and career-related internships or fieldwork available. Support available to part-time students. Financial award applicants required to submit FAFSA. *Unit head:* Dr. Constance Knapp, Interim Dean, 914-773-3750, Fax: 914-773-3533, E-mail: cknapp@pace.edu. *Application contact:* Susan Ford-Goldschein, Director of Graduate Admissions, 914-422-4283, Fax: 914-422-4287, E-mail: gradwp@pace.edu. Web site: http://www.pace.edu/.

Penn State Great Valley, Graduate Studies, Engineering Division, Malvern, PA 19355-1488. Offers engineering management (MEM); information science (MS); software engineering (MSE); systems engineering (M Eng). Postbaccalaureate distance learning degree programs offered (no on-campus study). *Unit head:* Dr. James A. Nemes, Interim Director, Academic Affairs, 610-648-3335 Ext. 610, Fax: 648-648-3377, E-mail: jan16@psu.edu. *Application contact:* 610-648-3242, Fax: 610-889-1334. Web site: http://www.sgps.psu.edu/Level3.aspx?id=662.

Penn State University Park, Graduate School, College of Information Sciences and Technology, State College, University Park, PA 16802-1503. Offers MPS, MS, PhD. *Students:* 84 full-time (31 women), 13 part-time (2 women). Average age 30. 151 applicants, 20% accepted, 17 enrolled. In 2011, 10 master's, 12 doctorates awarded. *Entrance requirements:* Additional exam requirements/recommendations for international students: Required—TOEFL (minimum score 550 paper-based; 213 computer-based; 80 iBT). *Application deadline:* Applications are processed on a rolling basis. Application fee: $65. Electronic applications accepted. *Financial support:* Fellowships, research assistantships, and teaching assistantships available. Financial award applicants required to submit FAFSA. *Unit head:* Dr. David L. Hall, Interim Dean,

814-863-3528, Fax: 814-865-5604, E-mail: dlh28@psu.edu. *Application contact:* Cynthia E. Nicosia, Director, Graduate Enrollment Services, 814-865-1795, Fax: 814-865-4627, E-mail: cey1@psu.edu. Web site: http://ist.psu.edu.

Polytechnic Institute of NYU, Westchester Graduate Center, Graduate Programs, Department of Computer Science and Engineering, Major in Information Systems Engineering, Hawthorne, NY 10532-1507. Offers MS. Evening/weekend programs available. *Students:* 2 full-time (1 woman), 1 international. 21 applicants, 57% accepted, 2 enrolled. In 2011, 1 master's awarded. *Degree requirements:* For master's, comprehensive exam (for some programs), thesis (for some programs). *Entrance requirements:* Additional exam requirements/recommendations for international students: Required—TOEFL (minimum score 550 paper-based; 213 computer-based; 80 iBT); Recommended—IELTS (minimum score 6.5). *Application deadline:* For fall admission, 7/31 priority date for domestic students, 4/30 for international students; for spring admission, 12/31 priority date for domestic students, 11/30 for international students. Applications are processed on a rolling basis. Application fee: $75. Electronic applications accepted. *Financial support:* Institutionally sponsored loans, scholarships/grants, and unspecified assistantships available. Support available to part-time students. *Unit head:* Dr. Keith W. Ross, Department Head, 718-260-3859, E-mail: ross@poly.edu. *Application contact:* JeanCarlo Bonilla, Director of Graduate Enrollment Management, 718-260-3182, Fax: 718-260-3624, E-mail: gradinfo@poly.edu.

Regis University, College for Professional Studies, School of Computer and Information Sciences, Denver, CO 80221-1099. Offers database administration with Oracle (Certificate); database development (Certificate); database technologies (M Sc); enterprise Java software development (Certificate); enterprise resource planning (Certificate); executive information technologies (Certificate); information assurance (M Sc, Certificate); information technology management (M Sc); software engineering (M Sc, Certificate); software engineering and database technologies (M Sc); storage area networks (Certificate); systems engineering (M Sc, Certificate). Offered at Boulder Campus, Northwest Denver Campus, Southeast Denver Campus, Fort Collins Campus, Colorado Springs Campus, and Broomfield Campus. Part-time and evening/weekend programs available. Postbaccalaureate distance learning degree programs offered (no on-campus study). *Degree requirements:* For master's, thesis, final research project. *Entrance requirements:* For master's, 2 years of related experience, resume, interview; for Certificate, 2 years of related experience, resumé. Additional exam requirements/recommendations for international students: Required—TOEFL (minimum score 213 computer-based), TWE (minimum score 5) or university-based test. Electronic applications accepted. *Expenses:* Contact institution. *Faculty research:* Secure Virtual Laboratory Architecture, Joint IA project with W2C06 Institute, Information Policy, OLTP and OLAP Technologies, knowledge management, software architectures.

Rensselaer at Hartford, Department of Computer and Information Science, Program in Information Technology, Hartford, CT 06120-2991. Offers MS. Part-time and evening/weekend programs available. *Entrance requirements:* For master's, GRE. Additional exam requirements/recommendations for international students: Required—TOEFL (minimum score 600 paper-based; 250 computer-based; 100 iBT). Electronic applications accepted.

Rensselaer Polytechnic Institute, Graduate School, School of Science, Program in Information Technology and Web Science, Troy, NY 12180-3590. Offers MS. Part-time programs available. *Degree requirements:* For master's, capstone course. *Entrance requirements:* For master's, GRE. Additional exam requirements/recommendations for international students: Required—TOEFL. Electronic applications accepted. *Faculty research:* Web science, database systems, software design, human-computer interaction, networking, information technology, financial engineering, electronic arts, management, information security.

Robert Morris University, Graduate Studies, School of Communications and Information Systems, Moon Township, PA 15108-1189. Offers communication and information systems (MS); competitive intelligence systems (MS); information security and assurance (MS); information systems and communications (D Sc); information systems management (MS); information technology project management (MS); Internet information systems (MS); organizational leadership (MS). Part-time and evening/weekend programs available. Postbaccalaureate distance learning degree programs offered (no on-campus study). *Faculty:* 28 full-time (9 women), 9 part-time/adjunct (3 women). *Students:* 231 part-time (68 women); includes 41 minority (31 Black or African American, non-Hispanic/Latino; 8 Asian, non-Hispanic/Latino; 2 Hispanic/Latino), 16 international. *Degree requirements:* For doctorate, thesis/dissertation. *Entrance requirements:* For doctorate, employer letter of endorsement, interview. Additional exam requirements/recommendations for international students: Required—TOEFL (minimum score 550 paper-based; 213 computer-based; 79 iBT). *Application deadline:* For fall admission, 7/1 priority date for domestic students, 7/1 for international students; for spring admission, 11/1 priority date for domestic students, 11/1 for international students. Applications are processed on a rolling basis. Application fee: $35. Electronic applications accepted. *Expenses:* Contact institution. *Financial support:* Research assistantships with partial tuition reimbursements, institutionally sponsored loans, and unspecified assistantships available. Support available to part-time students. Financial award application deadline: 5/1. *Unit head:* Dr. Barbara J. Levine, Dean, 412-397-2591, Fax: 412-397-2481, E-mail: levine@rmu.edu. *Application contact:* Deborah Roach, Assistant Dean, Graduate Admissions, 412-397-5200, Fax: 412-397-2425, E-mail: graduateadmissions@rmu.edu. Web site: http://www.rmu.edu/web/cms/schools/scis/.

Rochester Institute of Technology, Graduate Enrollment Services, B. Thomas Golisano College of Computing and Information Sciences, Department of Information Technology, Program in Information Technology, Rochester, NY 14623-5603. Offers MS. Part-time programs available. *Students:* 53 full-time (7 women), 59 part-time (11 women); includes 11 minority (3 Black or African American, non-Hispanic/Latino; 1 American Indian or Alaska Native, non-Hispanic/Latino; 2 Asian, non-Hispanic/Latino; 5 Hispanic/Latino), 65 international. Average age 27. 127 applicants, 63% accepted, 33 enrolled. In 2011, 20 degrees awarded. *Degree requirements:* For master's, thesis or project. *Entrance requirements:* For master's, GRE, minimum GPA of 3.0. Additional exam requirements/recommendations for international students: Required—TOEFL (minimum score 570 paper-based; 230 computer-based; 88 iBT) or IELTS (minimum score 6.5). *Application deadline:* Applications are processed on a rolling basis. Application fee: $50. Electronic applications accepted. *Expenses:* Tuition: Full-time $34,659; part-time $963 per credit hour. *Required fees:* $228; $76 per quarter. *Financial support:* Research assistantships with partial tuition reimbursements, teaching assistantships with partial tuition reimbursements, career-related internships or fieldwork, scholarships/grants, and unspecified assistantships available. Support available to part-time students. Financial award applicants required to submit FAFSA. *Unit head:* Prof. Dianne Bills, Graduate Program Director, 585-475-2700, Fax: 585-475-6584, E-mail: informaticsgrad@rit.edu. *Application contact:* Diane Ellison, Assistant Vice President, Graduate Enrollment Services, 585-475-2229, Fax: 585-475-7164, E-mail: gradinfo@rit.edu. Web site: http://www.ist.rit.edu/?q-node/18.

Rochester Institute of Technology, Graduate Enrollment Services, B. Thomas Golisano College of Computing and Information Sciences, PhD Program in Computing and Information Sciences, Rochester, NY 14623-5603. Offers PhD. *Students:* 16 full-time (4 women), 16 part-time (1 woman); includes 4 minority (3 Asian, non-Hispanic/Latino; 1 Hispanic/Latino), 23 international. Average age 31. 83 applicants, 17% accepted, 12 enrolled. *Degree requirements:* For doctorate, thesis/dissertation. *Entrance requirements:* For doctorate, GRE, minimum GPA of 3.0. Additional exam requirements/recommendations for international students: Required—TOEFL (minimum score 570 paper-based; 230 computer-based; 88 iBT) or IELTS (minimum score 6.5). *Application deadline:* For fall admission, 1/15 priority date for domestic students, 1/15 for international students. Applications are processed on a rolling basis. Application fee: $50. Electronic applications accepted. *Expenses: Tuition:* Full-time $34,659; part-time $963 per credit hour. *Required fees:* $228; $76 per quarter. *Financial support:* Research assistantships with full and partial tuition reimbursements, teaching assistantships with full and partial tuition reimbursements, career-related internships or fieldwork, scholarships/grants, health care benefits, and unspecified assistantships available. Financial award applicants required to submit FAFSA. *Faculty research:* The Center for Advancing the Study of Cyberinfrastructure (CASCI): the framework supporting science and engineering research, domain-specific informatics. *Unit head:* Dr. Pengcheng Shi, Director, 585-475-6147, E-mail: pengcheng.shi@rit.edu. *Application contact:* Diane Ellison, Assistant Vice President, Graduate Enrollment Services, 585-475-2229, Fax: 585-475-7164, E-mail: gradinfo@rit.edu. Web site: http://www.rit.edu/programs/computing-and-information-sciences.

Sacred Heart University, Graduate Programs, College of Arts and Sciences, Department of Computer Science and Information Technology, Fairfield, CT 06825-1000. Offers computer science (MS); database (CPS); information technology (MS, CPS); information technology and network security (CPS); interactive multimedia (CPS); Web development (CPS). Part-time and evening/weekend programs available. *Degree requirements:* For master's, thesis optional. *Entrance requirements:* Additional exam requirements/recommendations for international students: Required—TOEFL (minimum score 550 paper-based; 213 computer-based). Electronic applications accepted. *Faculty research:* Contemporary market software.

St. Mary's University, Graduate School, Department of Computer Science, Program in Computer Information Systems, San Antonio, TX 78228-8507. Offers MS. Part-time programs available. *Degree requirements:* For master's, comprehensive exam. *Entrance requirements:* For master's, GMAT or GRE General Test. Additional exam requirements/recommendations for international students: Required—TOEFL (minimum score 530 paper-based; 213 computer-based; 80 iBT). Electronic applications accepted. *Faculty research:* Artificial intelligence, database/knowledge base, software engineering, expert systems.

Sam Houston State University, College of Sciences, Department of Computer Science, Huntsville, TX 77341. Offers computing and information science (MS); digital forensics (MS); information assurance and security (MS). Part-time programs available. *Faculty:* 11 full-time (2 women). *Students:* 38 full-time (8 women), 26 part-time (2 women); includes 14 minority (7 Black or African American, non-Hispanic/Latino; 1 American Indian or Alaska Native, non-Hispanic/Latino; 6 Hispanic/Latino), 34 international. Average age 28. 29 applicants, 83% accepted, 24 enrolled. In 2011, 20 master's awarded. *Entrance requirements:* For master's, GRE General Test. Additional exam requirements/recommendations for international students: Required—TOEFL (minimum score 550 paper-based; 213 computer-based; 79 iBT). *Application deadline:* For fall admission, 8/1 for domestic and international students; for spring admission, 12/1 for domestic and international students. Application fee: $20. *Expenses:* Tuition, state resident: full-time $4420; part-time $221 per credit hour. Tuition, nonresident: full-time $10,680; part-time $534 per credit hour. *Required fees:* $329 per credit hour. *Financial support:* Research assistantships, teaching assistantships, Federal Work-Study, institutionally sponsored loans, and tuition waivers (partial) available. Financial award application deadline: 5/31; financial award applicants required to submit FAFSA. *Unit head:* Dr. Peter Cooper, Chair, 936-294-1569, Fax: 936-294-4312, E-mail: css_pac@shsu.edu. *Application contact:* Dr. Jiuhung Ji, Advisor, 936-294-1579, E-mail: csc_jxj@shsu.edu. Web site: http://cs.shsu.edu/.

Simmons College, Graduate School of Library and Information Science, Boston, MA 02115. Offers archives management (MS, Certificate); instructional technology licensure (Certificate); library and information science (MS, PhD); managerial leadership in the informational professions (PhD); school library teacher (MS, Certificate); MS/MA. *Accreditation:* ALA (one or more programs are accredited). *Unit head:* Dr. Michele V. Cloonan, Dean, 617-521-2806, Fax: 617-521-3192, E-mail: michele.cloonan@simmons.edu. *Application contact:* Sarah Petrakos, Assistant Dean, Admission and Recruitment, 617-521-2868, Fax: 617-521-3192, E-mail: gslisadm@simmons.edu. Web site: http://www.simmons.edu/gslis/.

Simon Fraser University, Graduate Studies, Faculty of Applied Sciences, School of Interactive Arts and Technology, Surrey, BC V3T 2W1, Canada. Offers information technology (M Sc, PhD); interactive arts (M Sc, PhD). *Degree requirements:* For master's, thesis; for doctorate, comprehensive exam, thesis/dissertation. *Entrance requirements:* For master's, 2 references, curriculum vitae; for doctorate, 3 references, curriculm vitae, minimum GPA of 3.0. Additional exam requirements/recommendations for international students: Required—TOEFL (minimum score 570 paper-based; 230 computer-based), TWE (minimum score 5). Electronic applications accepted.

Southern Methodist University, Bobby B. Lyle School of Engineering, Department of Engineering Management, Information, and Systems, Dallas, TX 75275. Offers applied science (MS); engineering management (MSEM, DE); information engineering and management (MSIEM); operations research (MS, PhD); systems engineering (MS, PhD). Part-time and evening/weekend programs available. Postbaccalaureate distance learning degree programs offered. Terminal master's awarded for partial completion of doctoral program. *Degree requirements:* For master's, thesis optional; for doctorate, thesis/dissertation, oral and written qualifying exams. *Entrance requirements:* For master's, minimum GPA of 3.0 in last 2 years; bachelor's degree in engineering, mathematics, sciences, or technical area; for doctorate, GRE General Test (operations research, engineering management), bachelor's degree in related field. Additional exam requirements/recommendations for international students: Required—TOEFL. *Faculty research:* Telecommunications, decision systems, information engineering, operations research, software.

Southern Polytechnic State University, School of Arts and Sciences, Department of English, Technical Communication, and Media Arts, Marietta, GA 30060-2896. Offers communications management (AGC); content development (AGC); information and instructional design (MSIID); information design and communication (MS); instructional design (AGC); technical communication (Graduate Certificate); visual communication and graphics (AGC). Part-time and evening/weekend programs available. Postbaccalaureate distance learning degree programs offered (no on-campus study). *Faculty:* 5 full-time (3 women), 2 part-time/adjunct (both women). *Students:* 1 full-time (0 women), 44 part-time (34 women); includes 13 minority (all Black or African American, non-Hispanic/Latino), 1 international. Average age 36. 24 applicants, 88% accepted, 16 enrolled. In 2011, 7 master's, 5 other advanced degrees awarded. *Degree requirements:* For master's, thesis optional; for other advanced degree, thesis optional, 18 hours completed through thesis option (6 hours), internship option (6 hours) or advanced coursework option (6 hours). *Entrance requirements:* For master's, GRE, statement of purpose, writing sample, timed essay; for other advanced degree, writing sample, professional recommendations. Additional exam requirements/recommendations for international students: Required—TOEFL (minimum score 550 paper-based; 213 computer-based; 79 iBT), IELTS (minimum score 6.5). *Application deadline:* For fall admission, 7/1 priority date for domestic students, 5/1 for international students; for spring admission, 11/1 priority date for domestic students, 9/1 for international students. Applications are processed on a rolling basis. Application fee: $50. Electronic applications accepted. *Expenses:* Tuition, state resident: full-time $2592; part-time $216 per semester hour. Tuition, nonresident: full-time $9408; part-time $784 per semester hour. *Required fees:* $698 per term. *Financial support:* Research assistantships with tuition reimbursements, teaching assistantships with tuition reimbursements, career-related internships or fieldwork, Federal Work-Study, scholarships/grants, and unspecified assistantships available. Support available to part-time students. Financial award application deadline: 5/1; financial award applicants required to submit FAFSA. *Faculty research:* Usability, user-centered design, instructional design, information architecture, information design, content strategy. *Unit head:* Dr. Mark Nunes, Chair, 678-915-7202, Fax: 678-915-7425, E-mail: mnunes@spsu.edu. *Application contact:* Donna McPherson, Program Assistant, 678-915-7202, Fax: 678-915-7425, E-mail: donna@@spsu.edu. Web site: http://www.spsu.edu/arts/departments.htm.

Southern Polytechnic State University, School of Computing and Software Engineering, Department of Information Technology, Marietta, GA 30060-2896. Offers health information technology (Graduate Certificate); information security and assurance (Graduate Certificate); information technology (MSIT, Graduate Certificate); information technology fundamentals (Graduate Transition Certificate). Part-time and evening/weekend programs available. Postbaccalaureate distance learning degree programs offered (minimal on-campus study). *Faculty:* 8 full-time (3 women), 2 part-time/adjunct (0 women). *Students:* 49 full-time (15 women), 114 part-time (41 women); includes 81 minority (67 Black or African American, non-Hispanic/Latino; 11 Asian, non-Hispanic/Latino; 1 Hispanic/Latino; 2 Two or more races, non-Hispanic/Latino), 29 international. Average age 33. 82 applicants, 93% accepted, 55 enrolled. In 2011, 43 master's, 5 other advanced degrees awarded. *Degree requirements:* For master's, thesis or alternative. *Entrance requirements:* For master's, minimum GPA of 2.75; for other advanced degree, bachelor's degree. Additional exam requirements/recommendations for international students: Required—TOEFL (minimum score 550 paper-based; 213 computer-based; 79 iBT), IELTS (minimum score 6.5). *Application deadline:* For fall admission, 7/1 priority date for domestic students, 5/1 for international students; for spring admission, 11/1 priority date for domestic students, 9/1 for international students. Applications are processed on a rolling basis. Application fee: $50. Electronic applications accepted. *Expenses:* Tuition, state resident: full-time $2592; part-time $216 per semester hour. Tuition, nonresident: full-time $9408; part-time $784 per semester hour. *Required fees:* $698 per term. *Financial support:* In 2011–12, 12 students received support, including 13 research assistantships with tuition reimbursements available (averaging $3,000 per year); career-related internships or fieldwork, scholarships/grants, and unspecified assistantships also available. Support available to part-time students. Financial award application deadline: 5/1; financial award applicants required to submit FAFSA. *Faculty research:* IT ethics, user interface design, IT security, IT integration, IT management, health information technology. *Total annual research expenditures:* $50,000. *Unit head:* Dr. Ju Au Wang, Chair, 678-915-3718, Fax: 678-915-5511, E-mail: jwang@spsu.edu. *Application contact:* Nikki Palamiotis, Director of Graduate Studies, 678-915-4276, Fax: 678-915-7292, E-mail: npalamio@spsu.edu. Web site: http://www.spsu.edu/itdegrees/.

State University of New York Institute of Technology, Program in Computer and Information Science, Utica, NY 13504-3050. Offers MS. Part-time and evening/weekend programs available. *Degree requirements:* For master's, thesis or project. *Entrance requirements:* For master's, GRE General Test, minimum GPA of 3.0, letter of recommendation. Additional exam requirements/recommendations for international students: Required—TOEFL (minimum score 550 paper-based; 213 computer-based). *Faculty research:* Cryptography, distributed systems, computer-aided system theory, reasoning with uncertainty, grid computing.

State University of New York Institute of Technology, Program in Information Design and Technology, Utica, NY 13504-3050. Offers MS. Part-time and evening/weekend programs available. *Degree requirements:* For master's, thesis or project. *Entrance requirements:* For master's, minimum GPA of 3.0; 2 letters of recommendation; portfolio; bachelor's degree in communication, rhetoric, journalism, English, or computer science, or 15 hours of communication. Additional exam requirements/recommendations for international students: Required—TOEFL (minimum score 550 paper-based; 213 computer-based). *Faculty research:* Textual-visualization, ethics and technology, behavioral information security.

Stevens Institute of Technology, Graduate School, Wesley J. Howe School of Technology Management, Program in Information Systems, Hoboken, NJ 07030. Offers computer science (MS); e-commerce (MS); enterprise systems (MS); entrepreneurial information technology (MS); information architecture (MS); information management (MS, Certificate); information security (MS); information technology in financial services industry (MS); information technology in the pharmaceutical industry (MS); information technology outsourcing management (MS); project management (MS, Certificate); software engineering (MS); telecommunications (MS). *Degree requirements:* For master's, thesis optional. *Entrance requirements:* For master's, GMAT, GRE General Test. Additional exam requirements/recommendations for international students: Required—TOEFL. Electronic applications accepted.

Strayer University, Graduate Studies, Washington, DC 20005-2603. Offers accounting (MS); acquisition (MBA); business administration (MBA); communications technology (MS); educational management (M Ed); finance (MBA); health services administration (MHSA); hospitality and tourism management (MBA); human resource management (MBA); information systems (MS), including computer security management, decision support system management, enterprise resource management, network management, software engineering management, systems development management; management (MBA); management information systems (MS); marketing (MBA); professional accounting (MS), including accounting information systems, controllership, taxation; public administration (MPA); supply chain management (MBA); technology in education (M Ed). Programs also offered at campus locations in Birmingham, AL; Chamblee, GA; Cobb County, GA; Morrow, GA; White Marsh, MD; Charleston, SC; Columbia, SC; Greensboro, NC; Greenville, SC; Lexington, KY; Louisville, KY; Nashville, TN; North Raleigh, NC; Washington, DC. Part-time and evening/weekend programs available. Postbaccalaureate distance learning degree programs offered (minimal on-campus study). *Degree requirements:* For master's, thesis. *Entrance requirements:* For master's,

GMAT, GRE General Test, bachelor's degree from an accredited college or university, minimum undergraduate GPA of 2.75. Electronic applications accepted.

Syracuse University, L. C. Smith College of Engineering and Computer Science, Program in Computer and Information Science and Engineering, Syracuse, NY 13244. Offers PhD. *Students:* 30 full-time (8 women), 6 part-time (1 woman); includes 2 minority (both Asian, non-Hispanic/Latino), 24 international. Average age 29. 105 applicants, 18% accepted, 12 enrolled. In 2011, 2 degrees awarded. *Degree requirements:* For doctorate, thesis/dissertation. *Entrance requirements:* For doctorate, GRE General Test, GRE Subject Test (computer science). Additional exam requirements/recommendations for international students: Required—TOEFL (minimum score 100 iBT). *Application deadline:* For fall admission, 7/1 priority date for domestic students, 6/1 for international students. Applications are processed on a rolling basis. Application fee: $75. Electronic applications accepted. *Expenses: Tuition:* Part-time $1206 per credit. *Financial support:* Fellowships with full tuition reimbursements, research assistantships with full and partial tuition reimbursements, teaching assistantships with full and partial tuition reimbursements, and tuition waivers (partial) available. *Unit head:* Dr. Chilukuri Mohan, Department Chair, 315-443-2322, Fax: 315-443-2583, E-mail: ckmohan@syr.edu. *Application contact:* Barbara Decker, Information Contact, 315-443-2368, Fax: 315-443-2583, E-mail: badecker@syr.edu. Web site: http://lcs.syr.edu/.

Syracuse University, School of Information Studies, Program in Information Innovation, Syracuse, NY 13244. Offers CAS. Part-time and evening/weekend programs available. Postbaccalaureate distance learning degree programs offered. *Students:* 3 applicants, 100% accepted, 0 enrolled. *Entrance requirements:* Additional exam requirements/recommendations for international students: Required—TOEFL (minimum score 100 iBT). *Application deadline:* For fall admission, 2/1 priority date for domestic students, 1/1 for international students. Applications are processed on a rolling basis. Application fee: $75. Electronic applications accepted. *Expenses: Tuition:* Part-time $1206 per credit. *Unit head:* Elizabeth Liddy, Dean, 315-443-2736. *Application contact:* Susan Corieri, Director of Enrollment Management, 315-443-2575, E-mail: ischool@syr.edu. Web site: http://ischool.syr.edu/academics/graduate/infoinnovation/index.aspx.

Syracuse University, School of Information Studies, Program in Information Science and Technology, Syracuse, NY 13244. Offers PhD. *Students:* 39 full-time (22 women), 11 part-time (6 women); includes 8 minority (5 Black or African American, non-Hispanic/Latino; 2 Asian, non-Hispanic/Latino; 1 Hispanic/Latino), 21 international. Average age 36. 57 applicants, 7% accepted, 3 enrolled. In 2011, 7 degrees awarded. *Degree requirements:* For doctorate, thesis/dissertation. *Entrance requirements:* For doctorate, GRE General Test (recommended), interview. Additional exam requirements/recommendations for international students: Required—TOEFL (minimum score 100 iBT). *Application deadline:* For fall admission, 1/8 priority date for domestic students, 1/8 for international students. Application fee: $75. Electronic applications accepted. *Expenses: Tuition:* Part-time $1206 per credit. *Financial support:* Fellowships with full tuition reimbursements, research assistantships with partial tuition reimbursements, and teaching assistantships with partial tuition reimbursements available. Financial award application deadline: 1/1; financial award applicants required to submit FAFSA. *Unit head:* Prof. Ping Zang, Director, 315-443-5617, Fax: 315-443-6886, E-mail: pzhang@syr.edu. *Application contact:* Susan Corieri, Director of Enrollment Management, 315-443-2575, E-mail: ischool@syr.edu. Web site: http://ischool.syr.edu/.

Temple University, College of Science and Technology, Department of Computer and Information Sciences, Philadelphia, PA 19122-6096. Offers MS, PhD. Part-time and evening/weekend programs available. *Faculty:* 20 full-time (1 woman). *Students:* 51 full-time (9 women), 9 part-time (2 women); includes 4 minority (3 Black or African American, non-Hispanic/Latino; 1 Asian, non-Hispanic/Latino), 48 international. Average age 29. 40 applicants, 83% accepted, 13 enrolled. In 2011, 5 master's, 3 doctorates awarded. Terminal master's awarded for partial completion of doctoral program. *Degree requirements:* For doctorate, thesis/dissertation. *Entrance requirements:* For master's and doctorate, GRE General Test, minimum GPA of 3.0. Additional exam requirements/recommendations for international students: Required—TOEFL (minimum score 550 paper-based; 213 computer-based; 79 iBT). *Application deadline:* For fall admission, 2/1 for domestic students, 12/15 for international students; for spring admission, 8/1 for domestic and international students. Applications are processed on a rolling basis. Application fee: $50. Electronic applications accepted. *Expenses:* Tuition, state resident: full-time $12,366; part-time $687 per credit hour. Tuition, nonresident: full-time $17,298; part-time $961 per credit hour. *Required fees:* $590; $213 per year. *Financial support:* Fellowships, research assistantships with tuition reimbursements, teaching assistantships with tuition reimbursements, career-related internships or fieldwork, institutionally sponsored loans, and unspecified assistantships available. Financial award application deadline: 1/15; financial award applicants required to submit FAFSA. *Faculty research:* Artificial intelligence, information systems, software engineering, network-distributed systems. *Unit head:* Dr. Jie Wu, Chair, 215-204-8450, Fax: 215-204-5082, E-mail: cis@temple.edu. *Application contact:* Tara Schumacher, Coordinator of Outreach, 215-204-6575, Fax: 215-204-8781, E-mail: tara.schumacher@temple.edu. Web site: http://www.temple.edu/cis.

Towson University, Program in Applied Information Technology, Towson, MD 21252-0001. Offers applied information technology (MS, PhD); database management systems (Postbaccalaureate Certificate); information security and assurance (Postbaccalaureate Certificate); information systems management (Postbaccalaureate Certificate); Internet applications development (Postbaccalaureate Certificate); networking technologies (Postbaccalaureate Certificate); software engineering (Postbaccalaureate Certificate). *Students:* 145 full-time (32 women), 270 part-time (78 women); includes 151 minority (96 Black or African American, non-Hispanic/Latino; 35 Asian, non-Hispanic/Latino; 17 Hispanic/Latino; 1 Native Hawaiian or other Pacific Islander, non-Hispanic/Latino; 2 Two or more races, non-Hispanic/Latino), 93 international. *Expenses:* Tuition, state resident: part-time $337 per credit. Tuition, nonresident: part-time $709 per credit. *Required fees:* $99 per credit. *Unit head:* Mike O'Leary, Graduate Program Director, 410-704-4757, E-mail: moleary@towson.edu.

Trevecca Nazarene University, College of Lifelong Learning, School of Education, Major in Library and Information Science, Nashville, TN 37210-2877. Offers MLI Sc. Part-time and evening/weekend programs available. *Students:* 19 full-time (16 women), 6 part-time (all women); includes 2 minority (1 Asian, non-Hispanic/Latino; 1 Two or more races, non-Hispanic/Latino). Average age 36. In 2011, 28 master's awarded. *Degree requirements:* For master's, exit assessment. *Entrance requirements:* For master's, GRE General Test, MAT, technology pre-assessment, minimum GPA of 2.7, 2 reference forms. Additional exam requirements/recommendations for international students: Required—TOEFL (minimum score 550 paper-based; 213 computer-based). *Application deadline:* Applications are processed on a rolling basis. Application fee: $25. *Expenses:* Contact institution. *Financial support:* Applicants required to submit FAFSA. *Unit head:* Dr. Esther Swink, Dean, School of Education/Director of Graduate Education Program, 615-248-1201, Fax: 615-248-1597, E-mail: admissions_ged@trevecca.edu. *Application contact:* Melanie Eaton, Admissions, 615-248-1498, E-mail: admissions_ged@trevecca.edu. Web site: http://www.trevecca.edu/.

Université de Sherbrooke, Faculty of Sciences, Department of Informatics, Sherbrooke, QC J1K 2R1, Canada. Offers M Sc, PhD. *Degree requirements:* For master's, thesis. Electronic applications accepted.

University at Albany, State University of New York, College of Computing and Information, Albany, NY 12222-0001. Offers computer science (MS, PhD); information science (PhD); information studies (MS, CAS), including information science. *Accreditation:* ALA (one or more programs are accredited). Part-time programs available. *Degree requirements:* For doctorate, thesis/dissertation. *Entrance requirements:* For doctorate, GRE General Test. Additional exam requirements/recommendations for international students: Required—TOEFL (minimum score 550 paper-based; 213 computer-based). Electronic applications accepted. *Faculty research:* Human-computer interaction, government information management, library information science, web development, social implications of technology.

The University of Alabama at Birmingham, College of Arts and Sciences, Program in Computer and Information Sciences, Birmingham, AL 35294. Offers MS, PhD. Terminal master's awarded for partial completion of doctoral program. *Degree requirements:* For master's, thesis optional; for doctorate, thesis/dissertation. *Entrance requirements:* For master's and doctorate, GRE General Test. Additional exam requirements/recommendations for international students: Required—TOEFL. *Application deadline:* Applications are processed on a rolling basis. Electronic applications accepted. *Expenses:* Tuition, state resident: full-time $5922; part-time $309 per hour. Tuition, nonresident: full-time $13,428; part-time $726 per hour. Tuition and fees vary according to program. *Financial support:* Fellowships with full tuition reimbursements, research assistantships with full tuition reimbursements, teaching assistantships with full tuition reimbursements, career-related internships or fieldwork, Federal Work-Study, institutionally sponsored loans, scholarships/grants, traineeships, health care benefits, and unspecified assistantships available. Support available to part-time students. Financial award application deadline: 3/10. *Faculty research:* Theory and software systems, intelligent systems, systems architecture, high performance computing, computer architecture, computer graphics, data mining, software engineering. *Unit head:* Dr. Anthony Skjellum, Chair, 205-934-2213, Fax: 205-934-5473, E-mail: skjellum@uab.edu. *Application contact:* Dr. John Johnstone, Graduate Program Director/Associate Professor, 205-975-5633, Fax: 205-934-5473, E-mail: jkj@uab.edu. Web site: http://www.cis.uab.edu/.

University of Arkansas at Little Rock, Graduate School, George W. Donughey College of Engineering and Information Technology, Program in Information Quality, Little Rock, AR 72204-1099. Offers MS.

University of Baltimore, Graduate School, The Yale Gordon College of Liberal Arts, School of Information Arts and Technologies, Baltimore, MD 21201-5779. Offers communications design (DCD); human-computer interaction (MS); interaction design and information technology (MS). Part-time and evening/weekend programs available. *Entrance requirements:* For master's, GRE or MAT, minimum undergraduate GPA of 3.0. Additional exam requirements/recommendations for international students: Required—TOEFL (minimum score 550 paper-based; 213 computer-based).

University of California, Irvine, Donald Bren School of Information and Computer Sciences, Department of Informatics, Irvine, CA 92697. Offers information and computer science (MS, PhD). *Students:* 115 full-time (34 women), 6 part-time (1 woman); includes 19 minority (1 Black or African American, non-Hispanic/Latino; 12 Asian, non-Hispanic/Latino; 5 Hispanic/Latino; 1 Two or more races, non-Hispanic/Latino), 61 international. Average age 28. 286 applicants, 30% accepted, 30 enrolled. In 2011, 23 master's, 25 doctorates awarded. Application fee: $80 ($100 for international students). *Unit head:* Adriaan Van der Hoek, Chair, 949-824-6326, Fax: 949-824-4056, E-mail: andre@uci.edu. *Application contact:* Kris Bolcer, Assistant Director, Graduate Affairs, 949-824-5156, Fax: 949-824-4163, E-mail: kbolcer@uci.edu. Web site: http://www.informatics.uci.edu/.

University of Central Missouri, The Graduate School, College of Education, Warrensburg, MO 64093. Offers career and technical education administration (MS); career and technical education industry training (MS); career and technical education leadership/teaching (MS); college student personnel administration (MS); counseling (MS); curriculum and instruction (Ed S); educational leadership (Ed D); educational technology (MS); elementary education/educational foundations and literacy (MSE); elementary school administration (MSE); elementary school principalship (Ed S); human services/learning resources (Ed S); human services/professional counseling (Ed S); human services/special education (Ed S); human services/technology and occupational education (Ed S); K-12 education/educational foundations and literacy (MSE); K-12 special education (MSE); library science and information services (MS); literacy education (MSE); secondary education/educational foundations & literacy (MSE); secondary school administration (MSE); secondary school principalship (Ed S); superintendency (Ed S); teaching (MAT). Ed D offered jointly with University of Missouri. Part-time programs available. Postbaccalaureate distance learning degree programs offered. *Entrance requirements:* Additional exam requirements/recommendations for international students: Required—TOEFL (minimum score 550 paper-based; 79 computer-based). Electronic applications accepted.

University of Colorado at Colorado Springs, College of Engineering and Applied Science, Department of Mechanical and Aerospace Engineering, Colorado Springs, CO 80933-7150. Offers engineering management (ME); information operations (ME); manufacturing (ME); mechanical engineering (MS); software engineering (ME); space operations (ME); space systems (MS). Part-time and evening/weekend programs available. *Faculty:* 11 full-time (2 women). *Students:* 48 full-time (14 women), 44 part-time (11 women); includes 15 minority (3 Black or African American, non-Hispanic/Latino; 6 Asian, non-Hispanic/Latino; 5 Hispanic/Latino; 1 Two or more races, non-Hispanic/Latino), 3 international. Average age 33. 40 applicants, 60% accepted, 13 enrolled. In 2011, 31 degrees awarded. *Degree requirements:* For master's, thesis optional. *Entrance requirements:* For master's, GRE General Test, bachelor's degree in engineering or related degree, minimum GPA of 3.0. Additional exam requirements/recommendations for international students: Required—TOEFL (minimum score 550 paper-based; 213 computer-based; 79 iBT). *Application deadline:* For fall admission, 3/1 for domestic and international students; for spring admission, 10/1 for domestic and international students. Applications are processed on a rolling basis. Application fee: $60 ($75 for international students). *Expenses:* Tuition, state resident: part-time $660 per credit hour. Tuition, nonresident: part-time $1133 per credit hour. Tuition and fees vary according to degree level, program and student level. *Financial support:* In 2011–12, 5 students received support. Federal Work-Study and scholarships/grants available. Support available to part-time students. Financial award application deadline: 3/1; financial award applicants required to submit FAFSA. *Faculty research:* Neural networks, artificial intelligence, robust control, space operations, space propulsion. *Total annual research expenditures:* $163,405. *Unit head:* Rebecca Webb, Director, 719-255-

3581, Fax: 719-255-3674, E-mail: rwebb@uccs.edu. *Application contact:* Siew Nylund, Academic Adviser, 719-255-3243, Fax: 719-255-3589, E-mail: snylund@eas.uccs.edu. Web site: http://eas.uccs.edu/mae/.

University of Colorado Denver, College of Engineering and Applied Science, Department of Computer Science and Engineering, Denver, CO 80217. Offers computer science (MS); computer science and engineering (EASPh D); computer science and information systems (PhD). Part-time and evening/weekend programs available. *Faculty:* 8 full-time (2 women), 1 part-time/adjunct (0 women). *Students:* 66 full-time (24 women), 31 part-time (10 women); includes 12 minority (3 Black or African American, non-Hispanic/Latino; 7 Asian, non-Hispanic/Latino; 2 Hispanic/Latino), 58 international. Average age 33. 91 applicants, 71% accepted, 27 enrolled. In 2011, 24 master's awarded. *Degree requirements:* For master's, thesis or alternative, at least 30 semester hours of computer science courses while maintaining minimum GPA of 3.0; for doctorate, comprehensive exam, thesis/dissertation, at least 60 hours beyond the master's degree level, 30 of which are dissertation research. *Entrance requirements:* For master's, GRE, minimum GPA of 3.0, 10 semester hours of university-level calculus, at least one math course beyond calculus, statement of purpose, letters of recommendation; for doctorate, GRE or GMAT. Additional exam requirements/recommendations for international students: Required—TOEFL (minimum score 525 paper-based; 197 computer-based; 71 iBT). *Application deadline:* For fall admission, 4/1 for domestic students; for spring admission, 10/1 for domestic students. Applications are processed on a rolling basis. Application fee: $50 ($75 for international students). Electronic applications accepted. *Financial support:* Research assistantships, teaching assistantships, career-related internships or fieldwork, and Federal Work-Study available. Financial award application deadline: 4/1; financial award applicants required to submit FAFSA. *Faculty research:* Algorithms, automata theory, artificial intelligence, communication networks, combinatorial geometry, computational geometry, computer architectures, computer graphics, distributed computing, high performance computing, graph theory, Internet, operating systems, parallel processing, simulation and software engineering. *Unit head:* Dr. Gita Alaghband, Chair, 303-556-2940, Fax: 303-556-8369, E-mail: gita.alaghband@ucdenver.edu. *Application contact:* Frances Moore, Program Assistant, 303-556-4083, Fax: 303-556-8369, E-mail: frances.moore@ucdenver.edu. Web site: http://www.ucdenver.edu/academics/colleges/Engineering/Programs/Computer-Science-and-Engineering/Pages/ComputerScienceEngineering.aspx.

University of Delaware, College of Engineering, Department of Computer and Information Sciences, Newark, DE 19716. Offers MS, PhD. Part-time programs available. Terminal master's awarded for partial completion of doctoral program. *Degree requirements:* For master's, thesis optional; for doctorate, comprehensive exam, thesis/dissertation. *Entrance requirements:* For master's and doctorate, GRE General Test. Additional exam requirements/recommendations for international students: Required—TOEFL (minimum score 550 paper-based; 213 computer-based). Electronic applications accepted. *Faculty research:* Artificial intelligence, computational theory, graphics and computer vision, networks, systems.

University of Detroit Mercy, College of Business Administration, Program in Information Assurance, Detroit, MI 48221. Offers MS.

University of Florida, Graduate School, College of Engineering and College of Liberal Arts and Sciences, Department of Computer and Information Science and Engineering, Gainesville, FL 32611. Offers computer engineering (ME, MS, PhD); computer science (MS); digital arts and sciences (MS). Part-time programs available. Postbaccalaureate distance learning degree programs offered (minimal on-campus study). Terminal master's awarded for partial completion of doctoral program. *Degree requirements:* For master's, comprehensive exam, thesis optional; for doctorate, comprehensive exam, thesis/dissertation. *Entrance requirements:* For master's and doctorate, GRE General Test, minimum GPA of 3.0. Additional exam requirements/recommendations for international students: Required—TOEFL (minimum score 550 paper-based; 213 computer-based; 80 iBT), IELTS (minimum score 6). Electronic applications accepted. *Faculty research:* Computer systems, database, computer networks, graphics and vision, algorithm and parallel processing.

University of Hawaii at Manoa, Graduate Division, Interdisciplinary Program in Communication and Information Sciences, Honolulu, HI 96822. Offers PhD. Part-time programs available. *Degree requirements:* For doctorate, comprehensive exam, thesis/dissertation. *Entrance requirements:* For doctorate, GRE or GMAT. Additional exam requirements/recommendations for international students: Required—TOEFL (minimum score 600 paper-based; 250 computer-based; 100 iBT), IELTS (minimum score 7).

University of Hawaii at Manoa, Graduate Division, Shidler College of Business, Program in Business Administration, Honolulu, HI 96822. Offers Asian business studies (MBA); Chinese business studies (MBA); decision sciences (MBA); entrepreneurship (MBA); finance (MBA); finance and banking (MBA); human resources management (MBA); information management (MBA); information technology (MBA); international business (MBA); Japanese business studies (MBA); marketing (MBA); organizational behavior (MBA); organizational management (MBA); real estate (MBA); student-designed track (MBA). *Accreditation:* AACSB. Part-time and evening/weekend programs available. *Degree requirements:* For master's, thesis optional. *Entrance requirements:* For master's, GMAT, minimum GPA of 3.0. Additional exam requirements/recommendations for international students: Required—TOEFL (minimum score 600 paper-based; 250 computer-based; 100 iBT), IELTS (minimum score 7). *Expenses:* Contact institution.

University of Houston, Bauer College of Business, Decision and Information Sciences Program, Houston, TX 77204. Offers PhD. Evening/weekend programs available.

University of Houston, College of Technology, Department of Information and Logistics Technology, Houston, TX 77204. Offers information security (MS); supply chain and logistics technology (MS); technology project management (MS). Part-time programs available. *Degree requirements:* For master's, project or thesis (most programs). *Entrance requirements:* For master's, GMAT. Additional exam requirements/recommendations for international students: Required—TOEFL (minimum score 550 paper-based; 79 iBT). Electronic applications accepted.

University of Houston–Clear Lake, School of Science and Computer Engineering, Program in Computer Information Systems, Houston, TX 77058-1098. Offers MS. Part-time and evening/weekend programs available. *Entrance requirements:* For master's, GRE General Test. Additional exam requirements/recommendations for international students: Required—TOEFL (minimum score 550 paper-based; 213 computer-based).

University of Illinois at Urbana–Champaign, Graduate College, Graduate School of Library and Information Science, Champaign, IL 61820. Offers bioinformatics (MS); digital libraries (CAS); library and information science (MS, PhD, CAS). *Accreditation:* ALA (one or more programs are accredited). Postbaccalaureate distance learning degree programs offered. *Faculty:* 25 full-time (12 women), 5 part-time/adjunct (4 women). *Students:* 349 full-time (256 women), 353 part-time (276 women); includes 125 minority (30 Black or African American, non-Hispanic/Latino; 1 American Indian or

Alaska Native, non-Hispanic/Latino; 37 Asian, non-Hispanic/Latino; 40 Hispanic/Latino; 1 Native Hawaiian or other Pacific Islander, non-Hispanic/Latino; 16 Two or more races, non-Hispanic/Latino), 27 international. 606 applicants, 68% accepted, 250 enrolled. In 2011, 245 master's, 6 doctorates, 8 other advanced degrees awarded. *Entrance requirements:* For master's, GRE General Test, minimum GPA of 3.0; for doctorate, minimum GPA of 3.0; for CAS, master's degree in library and information science or related field with minimum GPA of 3.0. Additional exam requirements/recommendations for international students: Required—TOEFL (minimum score 620 paper-based; 260 computer-based; 105 iBT) or IELTS (minimum score 7). *Application deadline:* Applications are processed on a rolling basis. Application fee: $75 ($90 for international students). Electronic applications accepted. *Financial support:* In 2011–12, 24 fellowships, 39 research assistantships, 44 teaching assistantships were awarded; tuition waivers (full and partial) also available. *Unit head:* Allen Renear, Dean, 217-265-5216, Fax: 217-244-3302, E-mail: renear@illinois.edu. *Application contact:* Valerie Youngen, Admissions and Records Representative, 217-333-0734, Fax: 217-244-3302, E-mail: vyoungen@llinois.edu. Web site: http://www.lis.illinois.edu.

University of Illinois at Urbana–Champaign, Informatics Institute, Champaign, IL 61820. Offers PhD. Part-time programs available. *Students:* 1 full-time, 1 part-time; includes 1 minority (Two or more races, non-Hispanic/Latino). *Degree requirements:* For doctorate, thesis/dissertation. *Entrance requirements:* Additional exam requirements/recommendations for international students: Required—TOEFL (minimum score 600 paper-based; 250 computer-based; 100 iBT); Recommended—IELTS (minimum score 6.5). Application fee: $75 ($90 for international students). *Financial support:* In 2011–12, 1 fellowship, 1 research assistantship were awarded; teaching assistantships and tuition waivers (full and partial) also available. *Unit head:* Guy Garnett, Director, 217-333-3281, E-mail: garnett@illinois.edu. *Application contact:* Judy Tolliver, Coordinator for Informatics Education Programs, 217-333-2322, E-mail: tolliver@illinois.edu. Web site: https://www.informatics.illinois.edu/icubed/.

The University of Iowa, Graduate College, Program in Informatics, Iowa City, IA 52242-1316. Offers bioinformatics and computational biology (Certificate); health informatics (MS, PhD, Certificate); information science (MS, PhD, Certificate). *Degree requirements:* For master's, thesis optional; for doctorate, comprehensive exam, thesis/dissertation. *Entrance requirements:* For master's and doctorate, GRE General Test, minimum GPA of 3.0. Additional exam requirements/recommendations for international students: Required—TOEFL (minimum score 550 paper-based; 213 computer-based; 81 iBT). Electronic applications accepted.

University of Kentucky, Graduate School, College of Communications and Information Studies, Program in Library and Information Science, Lexington, KY 40506-0032. Offers MA, MSLS. *Accreditation:* ALA (one or more programs are accredited). Part-time programs available. *Degree requirements:* For master's, variable foreign language requirement, comprehensive exam. *Entrance requirements:* For master's, GRE General Test, minimum undergraduate GPA of 2.75. Additional exam requirements/recommendations for international students: Required—TOEFL (minimum score 550 paper-based; 213 computer-based). *Faculty research:* Information retrieval systems, information-seeking behavior, organizational behavior, computer cataloging, library resource sharing.

University of Management and Technology, Program in Computer Science and Information Technology, Arlington, VA 22209. Offers computer science (MS); information technology (AC); information technology project management (MS); management information systems (MS); project management (AC); software engineering (MS). Part-time and evening/weekend programs available. Postbaccalaureate distance learning degree programs offered (no on-campus study). *Entrance requirements:* For master's, 3 recommendations, resume. Additional exam requirements/recommendations for international students: Required—TOEFL (minimum score 550 paper-based; 213 computer-based). Electronic applications accepted.

University of Maryland, Baltimore County, Graduate School, College of Engineering and Information Technology, Department of Information Systems, Program in Information Systems, Baltimore, MD 21250. Offers MS, PhD. Part-time programs available. Postbaccalaureate distance learning degree programs offered (no on-campus study). *Students:* 89 full-time (35 women), 229 part-time (58 women); includes 85 minority (43 Black or African American, non-Hispanic/Latino; 36 Asian, non-Hispanic/Latino; 4 Hispanic/Latino; 2 Two or more races, non-Hispanic/Latino), 83 international. Average age 33. 268 applicants, 67% accepted, 77 enrolled. In 2011, 118 master's, 7 doctorates awarded. *Median time to degree:* Of those who began their doctoral program in fall 2003, 11% received their degree in 8 years or less. *Degree requirements:* For master's, comprehensive exam (for some programs), thesis optional; for doctorate, comprehensive exam, thesis/dissertation. *Entrance requirements:* For master's, minimum GPA of 3.0; for doctorate, GRE General Test or GMAT, minimum GPA of 3.0, competence in statistical analysis and experimental design (recommended). Additional exam requirements/recommendations for international students: Required—TOEFL (minimum score 550 paper-based; 213 computer-based; 80 iBT). *Application deadline:* For fall admission, 6/1 for domestic students, 1/1 for international students; for spring admission, 11/1 for domestic students, 6/1 for international students. Applications are processed on a rolling basis. Application fee: $70. Electronic applications accepted. *Financial support:* In 2011–12, 1 fellowship with full tuition reimbursement (averaging $30,000 per year), 9 research assistantships with full tuition reimbursements (averaging $19,000 per year), 12 teaching assistantships with full tuition reimbursements (averaging $17,000 per year) were awarded; career-related internships or fieldwork, Federal Work-Study, scholarships/grants, health care benefits, tuition waivers (partial), and unspecified assistantships also available. Support available to part-time students. Financial award application deadline: 6/30; financial award applicants required to submit FAFSA. *Faculty research:* Artificial intelligence/knowledge management, database/data mining, decision-making support systems, software engineering/systems analysis and design. *Unit head:* Dr. Arrya Gangopadhyay, Professor and Chair, 410-455-2620, Fax: 410-455-1217, E-mail: gangopad@umbc.edu. *Application contact:* Dr. George Karabatis, Associate Professor and Graduate Program Director, 410-455-3940, Fax: 410-455-1217, E-mail: georgek@umbc.edu. Web site: http://www.is.umbc.edu/.

University of Maryland University College, Graduate School of Management and Technology, Program in Accounting and Information Technology, Adelphi, MD 20783. Offers MS, Certificate. *Accreditation:* AACSB. Part-time and evening/weekend programs available. Postbaccalaureate distance learning degree programs offered (no on-campus study). *Students:* 2 full-time (both women), 216 part-time (137 women); includes 137 minority (111 Black or African American, non-Hispanic/Latino; 14 Asian, non-Hispanic/Latino; 11 Hispanic/Latino; 1 Two or more races, non-Hispanic/Latino), 3 international. Average age 36. 62 applicants, 100% accepted, 39 enrolled. In 2011, 34 master's, 6 other advanced degrees awarded. *Degree requirements:* For master's, thesis or alternative, capstone course. *Application deadline:* Applications are processed on a rolling basis. Application fee: $50. Electronic applications accepted. *Financial support:* Federal Work-Study and scholarships/grants available. Support available to part-time students. Financial award application deadline: 6/1; financial award applicants required to submit FAFSA. *Unit head:* Dr. Kathryn Klose, Director, 240-684-2400, Fax: 240-684-2401, E-mail: kklose@umuc.edu. *Application contact:* Coordinator, Graduate Admissions, 800-888-8682, Fax: 240-684-2151, E-mail: newgrad@umuc.edu.

University of Maryland University College, Graduate School of Management and Technology, Program in Information Technology, Adelphi, MD 20783. Offers MS, Certificate. Part-time and evening/weekend programs available. Postbaccalaureate distance learning degree programs offered (no on-campus study). *Students:* 33 full-time (13 women), 2,032 part-time (701 women); includes 1,027 minority (733 Black or African American, non-Hispanic/Latino; 8 American Indian or Alaska Native, non-Hispanic/Latino; 153 Asian, non-Hispanic/Latino; 107 Hispanic/Latino; 2 Native Hawaiian or other Pacific Islander, non-Hispanic/Latino; 24 Two or more races, non-Hispanic/Latino; 58 international. Average age 37. 462 applicants, 100% accepted, 318 enrolled. In 2011, 493 master's, 141 other advanced degrees awarded. *Degree requirements:* For master's, thesis or alternative, capstone course. *Application deadline:* Applications are processed on a rolling basis. Application fee: $50. Electronic applications accepted. *Financial support:* Federal Work-Study and scholarships/grants available. Support available to part-time students. Financial award application deadline: 6/1; financial award applicants required to submit FAFSA. *Unit head:* Dr. Garth MacKenzie, Associate Chair and Program Director, ITEC Core, 240-684-2400, Fax: 240-684-2401, E-mail: gmackenzie@umuc.edu. *Application contact:* Coordinator, Graduate Admissions, 800-888-8682, Fax: 240-684-2151, E-mail: newgrad@umuc.edu. Web site: http://www.umuc.edu/grad/msit/msit_home.shtml.

University of Michigan, Horace H. Rackham School of Graduate Studies, School of Information, Ann Arbor, MI 48109-1285. Offers archives and records management (MSI); community informatics (MSI); health informatics (MS); human computer interaction (MSI); information (PhD); information analysis and retrieval (MSI); information economics for management (MSI); information policy (MSI); library and information science (MSI); preservation of information (MSI); school library media (MSI); social computing (MSI). *Accreditation:* ALA (one or more programs are accredited). *Entrance requirements:* For master's and doctorate, GRE General Test. Additional exam requirements/recommendations for international students: Required—TOEFL (minimum score 600 paper-based; 100 iBT). Electronic applications accepted.

University of Michigan–Dearborn, College of Engineering and Computer Science, Department of Computer and Information Science, Program in Computer and Information Science, Dearborn, MI 48128-1491. Offers MS. Part-time and evening/weekend programs available. Postbaccalaureate distance learning degree programs offered (minimal on-campus study). *Faculty:* 15 full-time (1 woman), 3 part-time/adjunct (0 women). *Students:* 18 full-time (6 women), 50 part-time (11 women); includes 12 minority (11 Asian, non-Hispanic/Latino; 1 Hispanic/Latino), 12 international. Average age 33. 33 applicants, 58% accepted, 10 enrolled. In 2011, 14 master's awarded. *Degree requirements:* For master's, thesis optional. *Entrance requirements:* For master's, bachelor's degree in mathematics, computer science or engineering; minimum GPA of 3.0. Additional exam requirements/recommendations for international students: Required—TOEFL (minimum score 560 paper-based; 220 computer-based; 84 iBT). *Application deadline:* For fall admission, 6/15 priority date for domestic students, 4/1 for international students; for winter admission, 10/15 priority date for domestic students, 8/1 for international students; for spring admission, 2/15 priority date for domestic students, 12/1 for international students. Application fee: $60. *Financial support.* In 2011–12, 3 research assistantships with full and partial tuition reimbursements (averaging $11,961 per year) were awarded; career-related internships or fieldwork also available. Financial award application deadline: 4/1; financial award applicants required to submit FAFSA. *Faculty research:* Information systems, geometric modeling, networks, databases. *Total annual research expenditures:* $54,056. *Unit head:* Dr. William I. Grosky, Chair, 313-583-6424, Fax: 313-593-4256, E-mail: wgrosky@umich.edu. *Application contact:* Katharine R. Markotan, Intermediate Academic Records Assistant, 313-436-9145, Fax: 313-593-4256, E-mail: tabatha@umd.umich.edu. Web site: http://cis.umd.umich.edu.

University of Michigan–Flint, College of Arts and Sciences, Program in Computer and Information Systems, Flint, MI 48502-1950. Offers computer science and information systems (MS). Part-time programs available. *Degree requirements:* For master's, thesis or alternative. *Entrance requirements:* For master's, minimum undergraduate GPA of 3.0. Additional exam requirements/recommendations for international students: Required—TOEFL (minimum score 560 paper-based; 220 computer-based; 84 iBT), IELTS (minimum score 6.5). *Expenses:* Contact institution.

University of Nebraska at Omaha, Graduate Studies, College of Information Science and Technology, Department of Information Systems and Quantitative Analysis, Omaha, NE 68182. Offers information assurance (Certificate); information technology (PhD); management information systems (MS); project management (Certificate); systems analysis and design (Certificate). Part-time and evening/weekend programs available. *Faculty:* 14 full-time (7 women). *Students:* 69 full-time (23 women), 87 part-time (26 women); includes 17 minority (4 Black or African American, non-Hispanic/Latino; 7 Asian, non-Hispanic/Latino; 4 Hispanic/Latino; 2 Two or more races, non-Hispanic/Latino), 75 international. Average age 32. 142 applicants, 43% accepted, 49 enrolled. In 2011, 38 master's, 3 doctorates, 29 other advanced degrees awarded. *Degree requirements:* For master's, comprehensive exam, thesis (for some programs); for doctorate, comprehensive exam, thesis/dissertation. *Entrance requirements:* For master's, GMAT or GRE General Test; for doctorate, GMAT or GRE General Test, letters of recommendation, writing sample, resume. Additional exam requirements/recommendations for international students: Required—TOEFL (minimum score 575 paper-based; 230 computer-based; 89 iBT). *Application deadline:* For fall admission, 2/15 for domestic students; for spring admission, 9/15 for domestic students. Applications are processed on a rolling basis. Application fee: $45. Electronic applications accepted. *Financial support:* In 2011–12, 31 students received support, including 25 research assistantships with tuition reimbursements available, 3 teaching assistantships with tuition reimbursements available; fellowships, career-related internships or fieldwork, Federal Work-Study, scholarships/grants, tuition waivers (partial), and unspecified assistantships also available. Financial award application deadline: 3/1; financial award applicants required to submit FAFSA. *Unit head:* Dr. Ilze Zigurs, Chairperson, 402-554-3770. *Application contact:* Carla Frakes, Information Contact, 402-554-2423.

University of Nebraska–Lincoln, Graduate College, College of Arts and Sciences and College of Engineering, Department of Computer Science and Engineering, Lincoln, NE 68588. Offers bioinformatics (MS, PhD); computer engineering (MS, PhD); computer science (MS, PhD); information technology (PhD). *Degree requirements:* For master's, thesis optional; for doctorate, comprehensive exam, thesis/dissertation. *Entrance requirements:* For master's and doctorate, GRE General Test. Additional exam requirements/recommendations for international students: Required—TOEFL (minimum score 600 paper-based; 250 computer-based). Electronic applications accepted. *Faculty*

research: Software engineering, geo- and bio-informatics, scientific computation, secure communication.

University of Nevada, Las Vegas, Graduate College, Howard R. Hughes College of Engineering, School of Informatics, Las Vegas, NV 89154-4054. Offers MS, PhD. *Faculty:* 5 full-time (3 women), 1 part-time/adjunct (0 women). *Students:* 1 part-time (0 women); minority (Black or African American, non-Hispanic/Latino). Average age 26. 11 applicants, 1 enrolled. In 2011, 4 master's awarded. *Degree requirements:* For master's, project; for doctorate, comprehensive exam, thesis/dissertation. *Entrance requirements:* For master's and doctorate, GRE General Test (verbal and quantitative), GMAT. Additional exam requirements/recommendations for international students: Required—TOEFL (minimum score 550 paper-based; 213 computer-based; 80 iBT), IELTS (minimum score 7). *Application deadline:* For fall admission, 5/1 for international students; for spring admission, 10/1 for international students. Application fee: $60 ($95 for international students). Electronic applications accepted. *Financial support:* In 2011–12, 1 research assistantship with partial tuition reimbursement (averaging $10,000 per year), 2 teaching assistantships with partial tuition reimbursements (averaging $12,000 per year) were awarded; institutionally sponsored loans, scholarships/grants, health care benefits, and unspecified assistantships also available. Financial award application deadline: 3/1. *Faculty research:* Digital security, healthcare informatics, human-computer interaction, ecology informatics, hospitality, gaming informatics. *Unit head:* Dr. Hal Berghel, Director/Associate Dean, 702-895-2441, Fax: 702-895-0577, E-mail: hlb@berghel.net. *Application contact:* Graduate College Admissions Evaluator, 702-895-3320, Fax: 702-895-4180, E-mail: gradcollege@univ.edu. Web site: http://informatics.unlv.edu/index.html.

University of New Haven, Graduate School, Tagliatela College of Engineering, Program in Computer and Information Science, West Haven, CT 06516-1916. Offers computer science (MS, Certificate), including advanced applications (MS), computer programming (Certificate), computer systems (MS), database and information systems (MS), network systems (MS), software engineering and development (MS). Part-time and evening/weekend programs available. *Students:* 53 full-time (16 women), 32 part-time (7 women); includes 4 minority (1 Black or African American, non-Hispanic/Latino; 1 Asian, non-Hispanic/Latino; 2 Hispanic/Latino), 69 international. 133 applicants, 98% accepted, 23 enrolled. In 2011, 19 master's, 1 other advanced degree awarded. *Degree requirements:* For master's, thesis or alternative. *Entrance requirements:* Additional exam requirements/recommendations for international students: Required—TOEFL (minimum score 520 paper-based; 190 computer-based; 70 iBT), Recommended—IELTS (minimum score 5.5). *Application deadline:* For fall admission, 5/31 for international students; for winter admission, 10/15 for international students; for spring admission, 1/15 for international students. Applications are processed on a rolling basis. Application fee: $50. Electronic applications accepted. *Expenses: Tuition:* Part-time $750 per credit. *Financial support:* Research assistantships with partial tuition reimbursements, teaching assistantships with partial tuition reimbursements, career-related internships or fieldwork, Federal Work-Study, scholarships/grants, tuition waivers, and unspecified assistantships available. Support available to part-time students. Financial award applicants required to submit FAFSA. *Unit head:* Dr. David Eggert, Coordinator, 203-932-7097, E-mail: deggert@newhaven.edu. *Application contact:* Eloise Gormley, Director of Graduate Admissions, 203-932-7449, Fax: 203-932-7137, E-mail: gradinfo@newhaven.edu. Web site: http://www.newhaven.edu/9591/

The University of North Carolina at Charlotte, Graduate School, College of Computing and Informatics, Department of Software and Information Systems, Charlotte, NC 28223-0001. Offers game design and development (Certificate); health care information (Certificate); information security/privacy (Certificate); information technology (MS, PhD, Certificate). Part-time programs available. *Faculty:* 14 full-time (3 women), 4 part-time/adjunct (0 women). *Students:* 134 full-time (42 women), 88 part-time (36 women); includes 39 minority (23 Black or African American, non-Hispanic/Latino; 5 Asian, non-Hispanic/Latino; 5 Hispanic/Latino; 6 Two or more races, non-Hispanic/Latino), 102 international. Average age 30. 182 applicants, 75% accepted, 47 enrolled. In 2011, 32 master's, 12 doctorates, 33 other advanced degrees awarded. Terminal master's awarded for partial completion of doctoral program. *Degree requirements:* For master's, thesis optional; for doctorate, comprehensive exam, thesis/dissertation. *Entrance requirements:* For master's, GRE or GMAT, minimum undergraduate GPA of 2.8 overall, 2.0 in last 2 years; for doctorate, GRE or GMAT, working knowledge of 2 high-level programming languages. Additional exam requirements/recommendations for international students: Required—TOEFL (minimum score 557 paper-based; 220 computer-based; 83 iBT). *Application deadline:* For fall admission, 7/1 for domestic students, 5/1 for international students; for spring admission, 11/1 for domestic students, 10/1 for international students. Applications are processed on a rolling basis. Application fee: $65 ($75 for international students). Electronic applications accepted. *Expenses:* Tuition, state resident: full-time $3689. Tuition, nonresident: full-time $15,226. *Required fees:* $2198. Tuition and fees vary according to course load and program. *Financial support:* In 2011–12, 41 students received support, including 1 fellowship (averaging $50,000 per year), 19 research assistantships (averaging $9,874 per year), 21 teaching assistantships (averaging $13,421 per year); career-related internships or fieldwork, institutionally sponsored loans, scholarships/grants, and unspecified assistantships also available. Support available to part-time students. Financial award application deadline: 4/1; financial award applicants required to submit FAFSA. *Faculty research:* Information security, information privacy, information assurance, cryptography, software engineering, enterprise integration, intelligent information systems, human-computer interaction. *Total annual research expenditures:* $1.8 million. *Unit head:* Dr. Ken Chen, Program Director, 704-687-8545, Fax: 704-687-6065, E-mail: chen@uncc.edu. *Application contact:* Kathy B. Giddings, Director of Graduate Admissions, 704-687-5503, Fax: 704-687-3279, E-mail: gradadm@uncc.edu. Web site: http://sis.uncc.edu/.

University of Oregon, Graduate School, College of Arts and Sciences, Department of Computer and Information Science, Eugene, OR 97403. Offers MA, MS, PhD. Part-time programs available. Terminal master's awarded for partial completion of doctoral program. *Degree requirements:* For doctorate, thesis/dissertation. *Entrance requirements:* For master's and doctorate, GRE General Test, minimum GPA of 3.0. Additional exam requirements/recommendations for international students: Required—TOEFL. *Faculty research:* Artificial intelligence, graphics, natural-language processing, expert systems, operating systems.

University of Ottawa, Faculty of Graduate and Postdoctoral Studies, Faculty of Engineering, Engineering Management Program, Ottawa, ON K1N 6N5, Canada. Offers engineering management (M Eng); information technology (Certificate); project management (Certificate). *Degree requirements:* For master's, thesis or alternative. *Entrance requirements:* For master's and Certificate, honors degree or equivalent, minimum B average. Electronic applications accepted.

University of Pennsylvania, School of Engineering and Applied Science, Department of Computer and Information Science, Philadelphia, PA 19104. Offers MCIT, MSE, PhD. Part-time programs available. *Faculty:* 45 full-time (4 women), 4 part-time/adjunct (1 woman). *Students:* 331 full-time (78 women), 54 part-time (13 women); includes 30 minority (3 Black or African American, non-Hispanic/Latino; 23 Asian, non-Hispanic/Latino; 3 Hispanic/Latino; 1 Two or more races, non-Hispanic/Latino), 253 international. 1,502 applicants, 26% accepted, 118 enrolled. In 2011, 69 master's, 11 doctorates awarded. Terminal master's awarded for partial completion of doctoral program. *Degree requirements:* For master's, thesis optional; for doctorate, thesis/dissertation. *Entrance requirements:* For master's and doctorate, GRE General Test. Additional exam requirements/recommendations for international students: Required—TOEFL. *Application deadline:* For fall admission, 6/1 priority date for domestic students, 5/1 for international students. Applications are processed on a rolling basis. Application fee: $70. Electronic applications accepted. *Expenses: Tuition:* Full-time $26,660; part-time $4944 per course. *Required fees:* $2318; $291 per course. Tuition and fees vary according to course load, degree level and program. *Financial support:* Fellowships with full tuition reimbursements, research assistantships with full tuition reimbursements, teaching assistantships, institutionally sponsored loans, scholarships/grants, traineeships, health care benefits, and unspecified assistantships available. *Faculty research:* AI, computer systems graphics, information management, robotics, software systems theory. *Unit head:* Eduardo D. Glandt, Dean, 215-898-7244, Fax: 215-573-2018, E-mail: seasdean@seas.upenn.edu. *Application contact:* Mike Felker, Graduate Coordinator, 215-898-9672, E-mail: mfelker@cis.upenn.edu. Web site: http://www.seas.upenn.edu.

University of Phoenix–Cincinnati Campus, College of Information Systems and Technology, West Chester, OH 45069-4875. Offers electronic business (MBA); information systems (MIS); technology management (MBA). Evening/weekend programs available. Postbaccalaureate distance learning degree programs offered. *Degree requirements:* For master's, thesis (for some programs). *Entrance requirements:* For master's, minimum undergraduate GPA of 2.5, 3 years of work experience. Additional exam requirements/recommendations for international students: Required—TOEFL (minimum score 550 paper-based; 213 computer-based; 79 iBT). Electronic applications accepted.

University of Pittsburgh, School of Information Sciences, Information Science and Technology Program, Pittsburgh, PA 15260. Offers MSIS, PhD, Certificate. Part-time and evening/weekend programs available. *Faculty:* 11 full-time (0 women), 1 part-time/adjunct (0 women). *Students:* 128 full-time (41 women), 48 part-time (12 women); includes 12 minority (2 Black or African American, non-Hispanic/Latino; 7 Asian, non-Hispanic/Latino; 3 Hispanic/Latino), 112 international. 326 applicants, 79% accepted, 58 enrolled. In 2011, 62 master's, 5 doctorates awarded. *Median time to degree:* Of those who began their doctoral program in fall 2003, 44% received their degree in 8 years or less. *Degree requirements:* For master's, thesis optional; for doctorate, comprehensive exam, thesis/dissertation. *Entrance requirements:* For master's, GRE General Test, bachelor's degree with minimum GPA of 3.0; course work in structured programming language, statistics, mathematics; for doctorate, GRE General Test, master's degree; minimum QPA of 3.3; course work in statistics or mathematics, programming, cognitive psychology, systems analysis and design, data structures database management; for Certificate, master's degree in information science, telecommunications, or related field. Additional exam requirements/recommendations for international students: Required—TOEFL (minimum score 550 paper-based; 80 iBT). *Application deadline:* For fall admission, 7/15 priority date for domestic students, 1/15 for international students; for winter admission, 11/1 priority date for domestic students, 6/15 for international students; for spring admission, 3/15 priority date for domestic students, 12/15 for international students. Applications are processed on a rolling basis. Application fee: $50. Electronic applications accepted. *Expenses:* Contact institution. *Financial support:* Fellowships with full and partial tuition reimbursements, research assistantships with full and partial tuition reimbursements, teaching assistantships with full and partial tuition reimbursements, career-related internships or fieldwork, scholarships/grants, health care benefits, tuition waivers (full and partial), and unspecified assistantships available. Financial award application deadline: 1/15; financial award applicants required to submit FAFSA. *Faculty research:* Adaptive Web systems, systems analysis and design, geoinformatics, database and Web systems, information assurance and security. *Unit head:* Dr. Paul Munro, Program Chair, 412-624-4427, Fax: 421-624-2788, E-mail: pmunro@sis.pitt.edu. *Application contact:* Shabana Reza, Student Recruiting Coordinator, 412-624-3988, Fax: 412-624-5231, E-mail: isinq@sis.pitt.edu. Web site: http://www.ischool.pitt.edu/ist/.

University of Puerto Rico, Mayagüez Campus, Graduate Studies, College of Engineering, Department of Electrical and Computer Engineering, Mayagüez, PR 00681-9000. Offers computer engineering (ME, MS); computing and information sciences and engineering (PhD); electrical engineering (ME, MS). Part-time programs available. *Students:* 86 full-time (16 women), 8 part-time (1 woman); includes 65 minority (all Hispanic/Latino), 29 international. 42 applicants, 60% accepted, 20 enrolled. In 2011, 19 degrees awarded. *Degree requirements:* For master's, comprehensive exam, thesis; for doctorate, comprehensive exam, thesis/dissertation. *Entrance requirements:* For master's, proficiency in English and Spanish, BS in electrical or computer engineering or equivalent, minimum GPA of 3.0; for doctorate, GRE. Additional exam requirements/recommendations for international students: Required—TOEFL (minimum score 450 paper-based). *Application deadline:* For fall admission, 2/15 for domestic and international students; for spring admission, 9/15 for domestic and international students. Applications are processed on a rolling basis. Application fee: $25. Tuition and fees vary according to course level and course load. *Financial support:* In 2011–12, 46 students received support, including 28 research assistantships (averaging $15,000 per year), 18 teaching assistantships (averaging $8,500 per year); Federal Work-Study and institutionally sponsored loans also available. *Faculty research:* Microcomputer interfacing, control systems, power systems, electronics. *Total annual research expenditures:* $3.8 million. *Unit head:* Dr. Erick Aponte-Diaz, Chairperson, 787-832-4040 Ext. 3821, E-mail: erick.aponte1@upr.edu. *Application contact:* Sandra Montalvo, Administrative Staff, 787-832-4040 Ext. 3094, Fax: 787-831-7564, E-mail: sandra@ece.uprm.edu. Web site: http://www.ece.uprm.edu.

University of Puerto Rico, Mayagüez Campus, Graduate Studies, College of Engineering, Program in Computer and Information Sciences and Engineering, Mayagüez, PR 00681-9000. Offers PhD. Part-time programs available. *Students:* 17 full-time (5 women), 2 part-time (0 women); includes 6 minority (all Hispanic/Latino), 13 international. 9 applicants, 67% accepted, 6 enrolled. *Degree requirements:* For doctorate, comprehensive exam, thesis/dissertation. *Entrance requirements:* For doctorate, GRE, BS in engineering or science; the equivalent of undergraduate courses in data structures, programming language, calculus III and linear algebra. *Application deadline:* For fall admission, 2/15 for domestic and international students; for spring admission, 9/15 for domestic and international students. Application fee: $25. Tuition and fees vary according to course level and course load. *Financial support:* In 2011–12,

1 student received support, including 1 research assistantship (averaging $15,000 per year). *Faculty research:* Algorithms, computer architectures. *Unit head:* Dr. Nestor Rodriguez, 787-832-4040 Ext. 5217, E-mail: nestor@ece.uprm.edu. Web site: http://www.cisephd.ece.uprm.edu.

University of Puerto Rico, Río Piedras, Graduate School of Information Sciences and Technologies, San Juan, PR 00931-3300. Offers administration of academic libraries (PMC); administration of public libraries (PMC); administration of special libraries (PMC); consultant in information services (PMC); documents and files administration (Post-Graduate Certificate); electronic information resources analyst (Post-Graduate Certificate); information science (MIS); librarianship and information services (MLS); school librarian (Post-Graduate Certificate); school librarian distance education mode (Post-Graduate Certificate); specialist in legal information (PMC). *Accreditation:* ALA. Part-time programs available. *Degree requirements:* For master's, comprehensive exam, thesis, portfolio. *Entrance requirements:* For master's, PAEG, GRE, interview, minimum GPA of 3.0, 3 letters of recommendation; for other advanced degree, PAEG, GRE, minimum GPA of 3.0, IST master's degree. *Faculty research:* Investigating the users needs and preferences for a specialized environmental library.

University of South Africa, College of Human Sciences, Pretoria, South Africa. Offers adult education (M Ed); African languages (MA, PhD); African politics (MA, PhD); Afrikaans (MA, PhD); ancient history (MA, PhD); ancient Near Eastern studies (MA, PhD); anthropology (MA, PhD); applied linguistics (MA); Arabic (MA, PhD); archaeology (MA); art history (MA); Biblical archaeology (MA); Biblical studies (M Th, D Th, PhD); Christian spirituality (M Th, D Th); church history (M Th, D Th); classical studies (MA, PhD); clinical psychology (MA); communication (MA, PhD); comparative education (M Ed, Ed D); consulting psychology (D Admin, D Com, PhD); curriculum studies (M Ed, Ed D); development studies (M Admin, MA, D Admin, PhD); didactics (M Ed, Ed D); education (M Tech); education management (M Ed, Ed D); educational psychology (M Ed); English (MA); environmental education (M Ed); French (MA, PhD); German (MA, PhD); Greek (MA); guidance and counseling (M Ed); health studies (MA, PhD), including health sciences education (MA), health services management (MA), medical and surgical nursing science (critical care general) (MA), midwifery and neonatal nursing science (MA), trauma and emergency care (MA); history (MA, PhD); history of education (Ed D); inclusive education (M Ed, Ed D); information and communications technology policy and regulation (MA); information science (MA, MIS, PhD); international politics (MA, PhD); Islamic studies (MA, PhD); Italian (MA, PhD); Judaica (MA, PhD); linguistics (MA, PhD); mathematical education (M Ed); mathematics education (MA); missiology (M Th, D Th); modern Hebrew (MA, PhD); musicology (MA, MMus, D Mus, PhD); natural science education (M Ed); New Testament (M Th, D Th); Old Testament (D Th); pastoral therapy (M Th, D Th); philosophy (MA); philosophy of education (M Ed, Ed D); politics (MA, PhD); Portuguese (MA, PhD); practical theology (M Th, D Th); psychology (MA, MS, PhD); psychology of education (M Ed, Ed D); public health (MA); religious studies (MA, D Th, PhD); Romance languages (MA); Russian (MA, PhD); Semitic languages (MA, PhD); social behavior studies in HIV/AIDS (MA); social science (mental health) (MA); social science in development studies (MA); social science in psychology (MA); social science in social work (MA); social science in sociology (MA); social work (MSW, DSW, PhD); socio-education (M Ed, Ed D); sociolinguistics (MA); sociology (MA, PhD); Spanish (MA, PhD); systematic theology (M Th, D Th); TESOL (teaching English to speakers of other languages) (MA); theological ethics (M Th, D Th); theory of literature (MA, PhD); urban ministries (D Th); urban ministry (M Th).

University of South Alabama, Graduate School, School of Computer and Information Sciences, Mobile, AL 36688-0002. Offers computer science (MS); information systems (MS). Part-time and evening/weekend programs available. *Faculty:* 8 full-time (0 women). *Students:* 70 full-time (18 women), 16 part-time (4 women); includes 6 minority (4 Black or African American, non-Hispanic/Latino; 1 Asian, non-Hispanic/Latino; 1 Native Hawaiian or other Pacific Islander, non-Hispanic/Latino), 51 international. 103 applicants, 74% accepted, 20 enrolled. In 2011, 44 master's awarded. *Degree requirements:* For master's, thesis optional, project. *Entrance requirements:* For master's, GRE General Test. *Application deadline:* For fall admission, 7/15 priority date for domestic students, 6/15 for international students; for spring admission, 12/1 for domestic students, 11/1 for international students. Applications are processed on a rolling basis. Application fee: $35. *Expenses:* Tuition, state resident: full-time $7968; part-time $332 per credit hour. Tuition, nonresident: full-time $15,936; part-time $664 per credit hour. *Financial support:* Research assistantships, career-related internships or fieldwork, and institutionally sponsored loans available. Support available to part-time students. Financial award application deadline: 4/1. *Faculty research:* Numerical analysis, artificial intelligence, simulation, medical applications, software engineering. *Unit head:* Dr. Roy Daigle, Director of Graduate Studies, 251-460-6390. *Application contact:* Dr. B. Keith Harrison, Dean of the Graduate School, 251-460-6310, Fax: 251-461-1513, E-mail: kharriso@usouthal.edu. Web site: http://www.cis.usouthal.edu.

The University of Tennessee, Graduate School, College of Communication and Information, School of Information Sciences, Knoxville, TN 37996. Offers MS, PhD. *Accreditation:* ALA (one or more programs are accredited). Part-time programs available. Postbaccalaureate distance learning degree programs offered (no on-campus study). *Degree requirements:* For master's, thesis or alternative. *Entrance requirements:* For master's, GRE General Test, minimum GPA of 2.7. Additional exam requirements/recommendations for international students: Required—TOEFL. Electronic applications accepted. *Expenses:* Tuition, state resident: full-time $8332; part-time $464 per credit hour. Tuition, nonresident: full-time $25,174; part-time $1400 per credit hour. *Required fees:* $1162; $56 per credit hour. Tuition and fees vary according to program.

The University of Texas at El Paso, Graduate School, College of Engineering, Department of Computer Science, El Paso, TX 79968-0001. Offers computer science (MS, PhD); information technology (MSIT). Part-time and evening/weekend programs available. *Students:* 48 (10 women); includes 21 minority (1 Asian, non-Hispanic/Latino; 20 Hispanic/Latino), 21 international. Average age 34. 33 applicants, 73% accepted, 12 enrolled. In 2011, 7 master's awarded. *Degree requirements:* For master's, thesis optional; for doctorate, thesis/dissertation. *Entrance requirements:* For master's, GRE, minimum GPA of 3.0; for doctorate, GRE, statement of purpose, letters of reference. Additional exam requirements/recommendations for international students: Required—TOEFL; Recommended—IELTS. *Application deadline:* For fall admission, 8/1 priority date for domestic students, 3/1 for international students; for spring admission, 11/1 priority date for domestic students, 9/1 for international students. Applications are processed on a rolling basis. Application fee: $45 ($80 for international students). Electronic applications accepted. *Financial support:* In 2011–12, research assistantships with partial tuition reimbursements (averaging $21,125 per year), teaching assistantships with partial tuition reimbursements (averaging $16,900 per year) were awarded; fellowships with partial tuition reimbursements, institutionally sponsored loans, scholarships/grants, health care benefits, tuition waivers (partial), and unspecified assistantships also available. Support available to part-time students. Financial award application deadline: 3/15; financial award applicants required to submit FAFSA. *Unit head:* Dr. Eunice E. Santos, Chair, 915-747-5480 Ext. 5480, Fax: 915-747-5030, E-mail:

eesantos@utep.edu. *Application contact:* Dr. Benjamin Flores, Interim Dean of the Graduate School, 915-747-5491, Fax: 915-747-5788, E-mail: bflores@utep.edu. Web site: http://www.cs.utep.edu/.

The University of Texas at San Antonio, College of Business, Department of Information Systems and Cyber Security, San Antonio, TX 78249-0617. Offers business (MBA); business administration (PhD); information technology (MSIT); management of technology (MSMOT). Part-time and evening/weekend programs available. *Faculty:* 11 full-time (3 women), 5 part-time/adjunct (1 woman). *Students:* 23 full-time (7 women), 73 part-time (13 women); includes 41 minority (3 Black or African American, non-Hispanic/Latino; 5 Asian, non-Hispanic/Latino; 30 Hispanic/Latino; 1 Native Hawaiian or other Pacific Islander, non-Hispanic/Latino; 2 Two or more races, non-Hispanic/Latino), 4 international. Average age 31. 50 applicants, 40% accepted, 13 enrolled. In 2011, 41 master's awarded. *Degree requirements:* For master's, thesis or alternative; for doctorate, comprehensive exam, thesis/dissertation. *Entrance requirements:* For master's, GMAT, bachelor's degree with 18 credit hours in the field of study or another appropriate field of study, statement of purpose; for doctorate, GMAT or GRE, resume or curriculum vitae, three letters of recommendation from academic or professional sources familiar with the applicant's background. Additional exam requirements/recommendations for international students: Required—TOEFL (minimum score 500 paper-based; 61 iBT), IELTS (minimum score 5). *Application deadline:* For fall admission, 7/1 for domestic students, 4/1 for international students; for spring admission, 11/1 for domestic students, 9/1 for international students. Applications are processed on a rolling basis. Application fee: $45 ($85 for international students). Electronic applications accepted. *Expenses:* Tuition, state resident: full-time $3148; part-time $2176 per semester. Tuition, nonresident: full-time $8782; part-time $5932 per semester. *Required fees:* $719 per semester. *Financial support:* In 2011–12, 23 students received support, including 10 fellowships (averaging $22,000 per year), research assistantships (averaging $10,000 per year), teaching assistantships (averaging $10,000 per year); scholarships/grants, health care benefits, and unspecified assistantships also available. *Faculty research:* economics of information systems, information security, digital forensics, information systems strategy, adoption and diffusion. *Total annual research expenditures:* $300,000. *Unit head:* Dr. Jan Clark, Chair, 210-458-5244, Fax: 210-458-6305, E-mail: jan.clark@utsa.edu. *Application contact:* Katherine Pope, Graduate Advisor of Record, 210-458-7316, Fax: 210-458-4398, E-mail: katherine.pope@utsa.edu.

University of the Sacred Heart, Graduate Programs, Department of Business Administration, Program in Information Technology, San Juan, PR 00914-0383. Offers Certificate.

University of Washington, Graduate School, The Information School, Seattle, WA 98195. Offers information management (MSIM); information science (PhD); library and information science (MLIS). *Accreditation:* ALA (one or more programs are accredited). Part-time and evening/weekend programs available. Postbaccalaureate distance learning degree programs offered (minimal on-campus study). *Faculty:* 37 full-time (17 women), 17 part-time/adjunct (10 women). *Students:* 282 full-time (185 women), 257 part-time (184 women); includes 93 minority (9 Black or African American, non-Hispanic/Latino; 7 American Indian or Alaska Native, non-Hispanic/Latino; 54 Asian, non-Hispanic/Latino; 20 Hispanic/Latino; 3 Native Hawaiian or other Pacific Islander, non-Hispanic/Latino), 72 international. Average age 31. 775 applicants, 61% accepted, 239 enrolled. In 2011, 219 master's, 5 doctorates awarded. Terminal master's awarded for partial completion of doctoral program. *Degree requirements:* For master's, comprehensive exam (for some programs), thesis optional, culminating experience project (thesis, capstone or portfolio), internship; for doctorate, comprehensive exam, thesis/dissertation. *Entrance requirements:* For master's, GRE General Test, GMAT, minimum GPA of 3.0; for doctorate, GRE General Test, minimum GPA of 3.0. Additional

exam requirements/recommendations for international students: Required—TOEFL (minimum score 580 paper-based; 237 computer-based; 92 iBT), IELTS (minimum score 7), MLT (minimum score 90). *Application deadline:* For fall admission, 12/1 priority date for domestic students, 12/1 for international students. Application fee: $75. Electronic applications accepted. *Expenses:* Contact institution. *Financial support:* In 2011–12, 57 students received support, including 8 fellowships with full tuition reimbursements available (averaging $12,942 per year), 19 research assistantships with full and partial tuition reimbursements available (averaging $11,270 per year), 18 teaching assistantships with full and partial tuition reimbursements available (averaging $18,205 per year); career-related internships or fieldwork, Federal Work-Study, institutionally sponsored loans, scholarships/grants, health care benefits, tuition waivers (full and partial), unspecified assistantships, and graduate assistantships (17 awards averaging $14,090) also available. Support available to part-time students. Financial award application deadline: 2/28; financial award applicants required to submit FAFSA. *Faculty research:* Human/computer interaction, information policy and ethics, knowledge organization, information literacy and access, information assurance and cyber security. *Total annual research expenditures:* $4.5 million. *Unit head:* Dr. Harry Bruce, Dean, 206-616-0985, E-mail: harryb@uw.edu. *Application contact:* Kari Brothers, Admissions Counselor, 206-616-5541, Fax: 206-616-3152, E-mail: kari683@uw.edu. Web site: http://ischool.uw.edu/.

University of Waterloo, Graduate Studies, Faculty of Engineering, Department of Management Sciences, Waterloo, ON N2L 3G1, Canada. Offers applied operations research (MA Sc, MMS, PhD); information systems (MA Sc, MMS, PhD); management of technology (MA Sc, MMS, PhD). Part-time programs available. Postbaccalaureate distance learning degree programs offered (no on-campus study). *Degree requirements:* For master's, research paper or thesis; for doctorate, comprehensive exam, thesis/dissertation. *Entrance requirements:* For master's, GMAT or GRE, honors degree, minimum B average, resume; for doctorate, GMAT or GRE, master's degree, minimum A- average, resumé. Additional exam requirements/recommendations for international students: Required—TOEFL, TWE. *Faculty research:* Operations research, manufacturing systems, scheduling, information systems.

University of Wisconsin–Parkside, School of Business and Technology, Program in Computer and Information Systems, Kenosha, WI 53141-2000. Offers MSCIS. *Entrance requirements:* For master's, GRE General Test or GMAT, 3 letters of recommendation, minimum GPA of 3.0. *Faculty research:* Distributed systems, data bases, natural language processing, event-driven systems.

University of Wisconsin–Stout, Graduate School, College of Technology, Engineering, and Management, Program in Information and Communication Technologies, Menomonie, WI 54751. Offers MS. Part-time programs available. Postbaccalaureate distance learning degree programs offered (minimal on-campus study). *Degree requirements:* For master's, thesis. *Entrance requirements:* For master's, minimum GPA of 2.75. Additional exam requirements/recommendations for international students: Required—TOEFL (minimum score 500 paper-based; 173 computer-based; 61 iBT). Electronic applications accepted.

Youngstown State University, Graduate School, College of Science, Technology, Engineering and Mathematics, Department of Computer Science and Information Systems, Youngstown, OH 44555-0001. Offers computing and information systems (MCIS). Part-time programs available. *Degree requirements:* For master's, thesis or capstone project. *Entrance requirements:* For master's, GRE or GMAT. Additional exam requirements/recommendations for international students: Required—TOEFL (minimum score 550 paper-based; 213 computer-based). *Faculty research:* Networking, computational science, graphics and visualization, database and data mining, biometrics, artificial intelligence, online learning environments.

Internet Engineering

Hofstra University, College of Liberal Arts and Sciences, Department of Computer Science, Hempstead, NY 11549. Offers networking and security (MS); Web engineering (MS). Part-time and evening/weekend programs available. Postbaccalaureate distance learning degree programs offered (minimal on-campus study). *Faculty:* 4 full-time (1 woman), 3 part-time/adjunct (0 women). *Students:* 4 full-time (1 woman), 16 part-time (3 women); includes 4 minority (2 Black or African American, non-Hispanic/Latino; 1 Asian, non-Hispanic/Latino; 1 Hispanic/Latino), 2 international. Average age 31. 17 applicants, 88% accepted, 6 enrolled. In 2011, 9 master's awarded. *Degree requirements:* For master's, thesis optional, 30 credits; minimum GPA of 3.0. *Entrance requirements:* For master's, GRE, minimum GPA of 3.0. Additional exam requirements/recommendations for international students: Required—TOEFL (minimum score 550 paper-based; 213 computer-based; 80 iBT). *Application deadline:* Applications are processed on a rolling basis. Application fee: $70 ($75 for international students). Electronic applications accepted. *Expenses: Tuition:* Full-time $18,990; part-time $1055 per credit hour. *Required fees:* $970. Tuition and fees vary according to program. *Financial support:* In 2011–12, 12 students received support, including 6 fellowships with full and partial tuition reimbursements available (averaging $2,625 per year); research assistantships with full and partial tuition reimbursements available, Federal Work-Study, institutionally sponsored loans, scholarships/grants, tuition waivers (full and partial), and unspecified assistantships also available. Support available to part-time students. Financial award applicants required to submit FAFSA. *Faculty research:* Computer vision, programming languages, data mining, software engineering, computer security. *Unit head:* Dr. Simona Doboli, Chairperson, 516-463-4786, Fax: 516-463-5790, E-mail: cscxzd@hofstra.edu. *Application contact:* Carol Drummer, Dean of Graduate Admissions, 516-463-4876, Fax: 516-463-4664, E-mail: gradstudent@hofstra.edu. Web site: http://www.hofstra.edu/hclas.

New Jersey Institute of Technology, Office of Graduate Studies, Newark College of Engineering, Department of Electrical and Computer Engineering, Program in Internet Engineering, Newark, NJ 07102. Offers MS. Part-time and evening/weekend programs available. *Students:* 2 full-time (0 women), 3 part-time (0 women); includes 1 minority (Asian, non-Hispanic/Latino), 3 international. Average age 33. 16 applicants, 81% accepted, 5 enrolled. In 2011, 3 master's awarded. *Degree requirements:* For master's, thesis optional. *Entrance requirements:* For master's, GRE General Test. Additional exam requirements/recommendations for international students: Required—TOEFL (minimum score 550 paper-based; 213 computer-based; 79 iBT). *Application deadline:* For fall admission, 6/1 priority date for domestic students, 5/1 for international students; for spring admission, 11/15 for domestic and international students. Applications are processed on a rolling basis. Application fee: $65. Electronic applications accepted.

Expenses: Tuition, state resident: full-time $7980; part-time $867 per credit. Tuition, nonresident: full-time $11,336; part-time $1196 per credit. *Required fees:* $230 per credit. *Financial support:* Fellowships with full and partial tuition reimbursements, research assistantships with full and partial tuition reimbursements, teaching assistantships with full and partial tuition reimbursements, career-related internships or fieldwork, Federal Work-Study, institutionally sponsored loans, and unspecified assistantships available. Financial award application deadline: 3/15. *Unit head:* Dr. Leonid Tsybeskov, 973-596-6594, E-mail: leonid.tsybeskov@njit.edu. *Application contact:* Kathryn Kelly, Director of Admissions, 973-596-3300, Fax: 973-596-3461, E-mail: admissions@njit.edu.

University of Denver, University College, Denver, CO 80208. Offers arts and culture (MLS, Certificate), including art, literature, and culture, arts development and program management (Certificate), creative writing; environmental policy and management (MAS, Certificate), including energy and sustainability (Certificate), environmental assessment of nuclear power (Certificate), environmental health and safety (Certificate), environmental management, natural resource management (Certificate); geographic information systems (MAS, Certificate); global affairs (MLS, Certificate), including translation studies, world history and culture; healthcare leadership (MPH, Certificate), including healthcare policy, law, and ethics, medical and healthcare information technologies, strategic management of healthcare; information and communications technology (MCIS, Certificate), including database design and administration (Certificate), geographic information systems (MCIS), information security systems security (Certificate), information systems security (MCIS), project management (MCIS, MPS, Certificate), software design and administration (Certificate), software design and programming (MCIS), technology management, telecommunications technology (MCIS), Web design and development; leadership and organizations (MPS, Certificate), including human capital in organizations, philanthropic leadership, project management (MCIS, MPS, Certificate), strategic innovation and change; organizational and professional communication (MPS, Certificate), including alternative dispute resolution, organizational communication, organizational development and training, public relations and marketing; security management (MAS, Certificate), including emergency planning and response, information security (MAS), organizational security; strategic human resource management (MPS, Certificate), including global human resources (MPS), human resource management and development (MPS). Part-time and evening/weekend programs available. Postbaccalaureate distance learning degree programs offered (no on-campus study). *Faculty:* 204 part-time/adjunct (80 women). *Students:* 56 full-time (26 women), 1,096 part-time (647 women); includes 196 minority (81 Black or African American, non-Hispanic/Latino; 7 American Indian or Alaska Native, non-Hispanic/

Latino; 30 Asian, non-Hispanic/Latino; 66 Hispanic/Latino; 3 Native Hawaiian or other Pacific Islander, non-Hispanic/Latino; 9 Two or more races, non-Hispanic/Latino), 76 international. Average age 36. 572 applicants, 95% accepted, 410 enrolled. In 2011, 404 master's, 123 other advanced degrees awarded. *Degree requirements:* For master's, capstone project. *Entrance requirements:* For master's, two letters of recommendation, personal statement, resume. Additional exam requirements/recommendations for international students: Required—TOEFL (minimum score 550 paper-based; 80 iBT). *Application deadline:* For fall admission, 7/20 priority date for domestic students, 6/8 for international students; for winter admission, 10/26 priority date for domestic students, 9/14 for international students; for spring admission, 2/1 priority date for domestic students, 12/14 for international students. Applications are processed on a rolling basis. Application fee: $75. Electronic applications accepted. *Expenses:* Contact institution. *Financial support:* Applicants required to submit FAFSA. *Unit head:* Dr. James Davis, Dean, 303-871-2291, Fax: 303-871-4047, E-mail: jdavis@du.edu. *Application contact:* Information Contact, 303-871-3155, Fax: 303-871-4047, E-mail: ucolinfo@du.edu. Web site: http://www.universitycollege.du.edu/.

University of San Francisco, College of Arts and Sciences, Web Science Program, San Francisco, CA 94117-1080. Offers MS. *Faculty:* 5 full-time (3 women). *Students:* 16 full-time (1 woman), 5 part-time (0 women); includes 4 minority (2 Black or African American, non-Hispanic/Latino; 1 Asian, non-Hispanic/Latino; 1 Hispanic/Latino), 7 international. Average age 29. 30 applicants, 67% accepted, 8 enrolled. In 2011, 12 master's awarded. *Expenses: Tuition:* Full-time $20,070; part-time $1115 per unit. Tuition and fees vary according to course load, campus/location and program. *Financial support:* In 2011–12, 6 students received support. *Unit head:* Terence Parr, Graduate Director, 415-422-6530, Fax: 415-422-5800. *Application contact:* Mark Landerghini, Graduate Adviser, 415-422-5135, E-mail: asgraduate@usfca.edu. Web site: http://www1.cs.usfca.edu/grad/msws.

Wilmington University, College of Technology, New Castle, DE 19720-6491. Offers corporate training skills (MS); information assurance (MS); information systems technologies (MS); Internet/web design (MS); management and management information systems (MS). Part-time and evening/weekend programs available. *Faculty:* 1 full-time (0 women). *Students:* 21 full-time (8 women), 63 part-time (24 women). Average age 36. *Entrance requirements:* Additional exam requirements/recommendations for international students: Required—TOEFL (minimum score 500 paper-based; 173 computer-based). *Application deadline:* Applications are processed on a rolling basis. Application fee: $35. Electronic applications accepted. *Expenses: Tuition:* Part-time $534 per credit hour. *Required fees:* $25 per term. *Unit head:* Dr. Edward L. Guthrie, Dean, 302-356-6870. *Application contact:* Laura Morris, Director of Admissions, 302-295-1179, Fax: 302-328-5164, E-mail: inquire@wilmcoll.edu. Web site: http://www.wilmu.edu/technology/.

Medical Informatics

Arizona State University, Graduate College, Department of Biomedical Informatics, Phoenix, AZ 85004. Offers MS, PhD. Terminal master's awarded for partial completion of doctoral program. *Degree requirements:* For master's, interactive Program of Study (iPOS) submitted before completing 50 percent of required credit hours; for doctorate, comprehensive exam, thesis/dissertation, interactive Program of Study (iPOS) submitted before completing 50 percent of required credit hours. *Entrance requirements:* For master's, GRE or MCAT, bachelor's degree with minimum GPA of 3.25 in computer science, biology, physiology, nursing, statistics, engineering, related fields, or unrelated fields with appropriate academic backgrounds; resume/curriculum vitae; statement of purpose; 3 letters of recommendation; all official transcripts; for doctorate, GRE or MCAT, bachelor's degree with minimum GPA of 3.5 in computer science, biology, physiology, nursing, statistics, engineering, related fields, or unrelated fields with appropriate academic backgrounds; resume/curriculum vitae; statement of purpose; 3 letters of recommendation; all official transcripts. Additional exam requirements/recommendations for international students: Required—TOEFL (minimum score 550 paper-based; 213 computer-based; 83 iBT), IELTS (minimum score 6.5). Electronic applications accepted.

Cambridge College, School of Management, Cambridge, MA 02138-5304. Offers business negotiation and conflict resolution (M Mgt); general business (M Mgt); health care informatics (M Mgt); health care management (M Mgt); leadership in human and organizational dynamics (M Mgt); non-profit and public organization management (M Mgt); small business development (M Mgt); technology management (M Mgt). Part-time and evening/weekend programs available. *Degree requirements:* For master's, thesis, seminars. *Entrance requirements:* For master's, resume, 2 professional references. Additional exam requirements/recommendations for international students: Required—TOEFL (minimum score 550 paper-based; 213 computer-based; 79 iBT); Recommended—IELTS (minimum score 6). Electronic applications accepted. *Expenses:* Contact institution. *Faculty research:* Negotiation, mediation and conflict resolution; leadership; management of diverse organizations; case studies and simulation methodologies for management education, digital as a second language; social networking for digital immigrants, non-profit and public management.

Columbia University, College of Dental Medicine and Graduate School of Arts and Sciences, Programs in Dental Specialties, New York, NY 10027. Offers advanced education in general dentistry (Certificate); biomedical informatics (MA, PhD); endodontics (Certificate); orthodontics (MS, Certificate); periodontics (MS, Certificate); prosthodontics (MS, Certificate); science education (MA). *Degree requirements:* For master's, thesis, presentation of seminar. *Entrance requirements:* For master's, GRE General Test, DDS or equivalent. *Expenses:* Contact institution. *Faculty research:* Analysis of growth/form, pulpal microcirculation, implants, microbiology of oral environment, calcified tissues.

Columbia University, College of Physicians and Surgeons, Department of Biomedical Informatics, New York, NY 10032. Offers M Phil, MA, PhD, MD/PhD. *Degree requirements:* For doctorate, thesis/dissertation. *Entrance requirements:* For master's and doctorate, GRE General Test, knowledge of computational techniques. Additional exam requirements/recommendations for international students: Required—TOEFL. Electronic applications accepted. *Faculty research:* Bioinformatics, bioimaging, clinical informatics, public health informatics.

Dalhousie University, Faculty of Computer Science, Halifax , NS B3H 1W5, Canada. Offers computational biology and bioinformatics (M Sc); computer science (PhD); computer science (project-based) (MA Sc); computer science (thesis-based) (MC Sc); electronic commerce (MEC); health informatics (MHI). *Degree requirements:* For master's, thesis (for some programs); for doctorate, thesis/dissertation. *Entrance requirements:* Additional exam requirements/recommendations for international students: Required—1 of 5 approved tests: TOEFL, IELTS, CANTEST, CAEL, Michigan English Language Assessment Battery. Electronic applications accepted.

Excelsior College, School of Health Sciences, Albany, NY 12203-5159. Offers health care informatics (Certificate). Part-time and evening/weekend programs available. Postbaccalaureate distance learning degree programs offered (no on-campus study). *Entrance requirements:* For degree, bachelor's degree in applicable field. Electronic applications accepted. *Faculty research:* Use of technology in online learning.

Grand Valley State University, Padnos College of Engineering and Computing, Medical and Bioinformatics Program, Allendale, MI 49401-9403. Offers MS. Part-time and evening/weekend programs available. *Degree requirements:* For master's, thesis or alternative. *Faculty research:* Biomedical informatics, information visualization, data mining, high-performance computing, computational biology.

Marymount University, School of Business Administration, Program in Information Technology, Arlington, VA 22207-4299. Offers computer security and information assurance (Certificate); health care informatics (Certificate); information technology (MS, Certificate); information technology project management: technology leadership (Certificate). Part-time and evening/weekend programs available. *Faculty:* 6 full-time (2 women), 9 part-time/adjunct (0 women). *Students:* 37 full-time (14 women), 32 part-time (13 women); includes 19 minority (9 Black or African American, non-Hispanic/Latino; 6 Asian, non-Hispanic/Latino; 3 Hispanic/Latino; 1 Two or more races, non-Hispanic/Latino), 30 international. Average age 30. 47 applicants, 98% accepted, 36 enrolled. In 2011, 28 master's, 10 other advanced degrees awarded. *Degree requirements:* For master's, thesis or alternative. *Entrance requirements:* For master's, GMAT or GRE General Test, interview, resume, bachelor's degree in computer-related field or degree in another subject with a post-baccalaureate certificate in a computer-related field; for Certificate, resume. Additional exam requirements/recommendations for international students: Required—TOEFL (minimum score 600 paper-based; 250 computer-based; 96 iBT), IELTS (minimum score 6.5). *Application deadline:* For fall admission, 7/1 priority date for domestic students, 7/1 for international students; for spring admission, 11/15 for domestic students, 11/16 for international students. Applications are processed on a rolling basis. Application fee: $40. Electronic applications accepted. *Expenses: Tuition:* Part-time $770 per credit hour. *Required fees:* $8 per credit hour. One-time fee: $180 full-time. *Financial support:* In 2011–12, 7 students received support. Research assistantships with full tuition reimbursements available, career-related internships or fieldwork, Federal Work-Study, scholarships/grants, and unspecified assistantships available. Support available to part-time students. Financial award applicants required to submit FAFSA. *Unit head:* Dr. Diane Murphy, Chair, 703-284-5958, Fax: 703-527-3830, E-mail: diane.murphy@marymount.edu. *Application contact:* Francesca Reed, Director, Graduate Admissions, 703-284-5901, Fax: 703-527-3815, E-mail: grad.admissions@marymount.edu. Web site: http://www.marymount.edu/academics/programs/infoTechMS.

Medical College of Wisconsin, Graduate School of Biomedical Sciences, Program in Medical Informatics, Milwaukee, WI 53226-0509. Offers MS. Program offered jointly with Milwaukee School of Engineering. Part-time and evening/weekend programs available. *Degree requirements:* For master's, thesis or alternative. *Entrance requirements:* For master's, GRE, official transcripts, three letters of recommendation. Additional exam requirements/recommendations for international students: Required—TOEFL. *Faculty research:* Computer science.

Middle Tennessee State University, College of Graduate Studies, College of Basic and Applied Sciences, Program in Professional Science, Murfreesboro, TN 37132. Offers biostatistics (MS); health care informatics (MS). Part-time and evening/weekend programs available. Postbaccalaureate distance learning degree programs offered. *Students:* 4 full-time (1 woman), 72 part-time (43 women); includes 34 minority (15 Black or African American, non-Hispanic/Latino; 17 Asian, non-Hispanic/Latino; 2 Two or more races, non-Hispanic/Latino). Average age 28. In 2011, 22 master's awarded. *Degree requirements:* For master's, comprehensive exam. *Entrance requirements:* For master's, GRE. Additional exam requirements/recommendations for international students: Required—TOEFL (minimum score 525 paper-based; 195 computer-based; 71 iBT) or IELTS (minimum score 6). *Application deadline:* For fall admission, 6/1 for domestic and international students. Applications are processed on a rolling basis. Application fee: $25 ($30 for international students). *Expenses:* Tuition, state resident: full-time $10,008. Tuition, nonresident: full-time $25,056. *Financial support:* In 2011–12, 7 students received support. Tuition waivers available. Support available to part-time students. Financial award application deadline: 5/1. *Faculty research:* Biotechnology, biostatistics, informatics. *Unit head:* Dr. Robert W. Fischer, Jr., Dean, 615-898-2613, Fax: 615-898-2615. *Application contact:* Dr. Michael D. Allen, Dean and Vice Provost for Research, 615-898-2840, Fax: 615-904-8020, E-mail: michael.allen@mtsu.edu.

Milwaukee School of Engineering, Rader School of Business, Program in Medical Informatics, Milwaukee, WI 53202-3109. Offers MS. Part-time and evening/weekend programs available. *Faculty:* 1 full-time (0 women), 4 part-time/adjunct (1 woman). *Students:* 12 part-time (7 women); includes 2 minority (1 Asian, non-Hispanic/Latino; 1 Two or more races, non-Hispanic/Latino). Average age 25. 4 applicants, 75% accepted, 4 enrolled. In 2011, 2 master's awarded. *Degree requirements:* For master's, thesis, capstone course, research project. *Entrance requirements:* For master's, GRE General Test or GMAT, 2 letters of recommendation. Additional exam requirements/recommendations for international students: Required—TOEFL (minimum score 79 iBT) or IELTS. *Application deadline:* Applications are processed on a rolling basis. Electronic applications accepted. Application fee is waived when completed online. *Expenses: Tuition:* Full-time $17,550; part-time $650 per credit hour. *Financial support:* In 2011–12, 7 students received support. Career-related internships or fieldwork available. Support available to part-time students. Financial award applicants required to submit FAFSA. *Faculty research:* Information technology, databases. *Unit head:* Dr. John Traxler, Director, 414-277-2218, Fax: 414-277-7279, E-mail: traxler@msoe.edu. *Application contact:* Katie Gassenhuber, Graduate Program Associate, 800-321-6763, Fax: 414-277-7208, E-mail: gassenhuber@msoe.edu.

Northwestern University, School of Continuing Studies, Program in Medical Informatics, Evanston, IL 60208. Offers MS. Postbaccalaureate distance learning degree programs offered.

Nova Southeastern University, Health Professions Division, College of Osteopathic Medicine, Fort Lauderdale, FL 33314-7796. Offers biomedical informatics (MS, Graduate Certificate), including biomedical informatics (MS), clinical informatics (Graduate Certificate), public health informatics (Graduate Certificate); disaster and emergency preparedness (MS); osteopathic medicine (DO); public health (MPH). *Accreditation:* AOsA. *Faculty:* 86 full-time (38 women), 1,072 part-time/adjunct (232 women). *Students:* 952 full-time (377 women), 18 part-time (5 women); includes 323 minority (24 Black or African American, non-Hispanic/Latino; 2 American Indian or Alaska Native, non-Hispanic/Latino; 175 Asian, non-Hispanic/Latino; 91 Hispanic/Latino; 31 Native Hawaiian or other Pacific Islander, non-Hispanic/Latino), 22 international. Average age 28. 3,628 applicants, 17% accepted, 241 enrolled. In 2011, 75 master's, 213 doctorates awarded. *Entrance requirements:* For master's, GRE, licensed healthcare professional or GRE; for doctorate, MCAT, biology, chemistry, organic chemistry, physics (all with labs), and English. *Application deadline:* For fall admission, 1/15 for domestic students. Applications are processed on a rolling basis. Application fee: $50. Electronic applications accepted. *Expenses:* Contact institution. *Financial support:* In 2011–12, 80 students received support, including 6 fellowships with full tuition reimbursements available (averaging $40,000 per year); research assistantships, teaching assistantships, career-related internships or fieldwork, Federal Work-Study, institutionally sponsored loans, and scholarships/grants also available. Financial award application deadline: 6/1; financial award applicants required to submit FAFSA. *Faculty research:* Teaching strategies, simulated patient use, HIV-AIDS education, minority health issues, managed care education. *Unit head:* Dr. Anthony J. Silavgni, Dean, 954-262-1407, E-mail: silvagni@hpd.nova.edu. *Application contact:* Anastasia Leveille, College of Medicine Admissions Counselor, 866-817-4068. Web site: http://www.medicine.nova.edu/.

Oregon Health & Science University, School of Medicine, Graduate Programs in Medicine, Department of Medical Informatics and Clinical Epidemiology, Portland, OR 97239-3098. Offers clinical informatics (MS, PhD, Certificate); computational biology (MS, PhD); health information management (Certificate). Part-time programs available. Postbaccalaureate distance learning degree programs offered (minimal on-campus study). *Faculty:* 10 full-time (3 women), 13 part-time/adjunct (8 women). *Students:* 40 full-time (18 women), 151 part-time (61 women); includes 46 minority (7 Black or African American, non-Hispanic/Latino; 4 American Indian or Alaska Native, non-Hispanic/Latino; 23 Asian, non-Hispanic/Latino; 2 Hispanic/Latino; 1 Native Hawaiian or other Pacific Islander, non-Hispanic/Latino; 9 Two or more races, non-Hispanic/Latino), 9 international. Average age 41. 78 applicants, 44% accepted, 34 enrolled. In 2011, 12 master's, 6 doctorates, 32 other advanced degrees awarded. Terminal master's awarded for partial completion of doctoral program. *Degree requirements:* For master's, thesis optional, thesis or capstone project; for doctorate, comprehensive exam, thesis/dissertation, qualifying exam. *Entrance requirements:* For master's and doctorate, GRE General Test (minimum scores: 153 Verbal/148 Quantitative/4.5 Analytical), coursework in computer programming, human anatomy and physiology. Additional exam requirements/recommendations for international students: Required—TOEFL. *Application deadline:* For fall admission, 12/1 for domestic students; for winter admission, 11/1 for domestic students; for spring admission, 2/1 for domestic students. Applications are processed on a rolling basis. Application fee: $70. Electronic applications accepted. *Expenses:* Contact institution. *Financial support:* Fellowships with full tuition reimbursements, research assistantships, Federal Work-Study, institutionally sponsored loans, scholarships/grants, health care benefits, and full tuition and stipends for PhD students available. Financial award application deadline: 3/1; financial award applicants required to submit FAFSA. *Faculty research:* Use of knowledge-based information by healthcare practitioners and researchers, application of text mining and machine learning techniques to the scientific literature curated databases, examining factors that affect quality of data collected in healthcare databases and the subsequent uses of that data, statistical analysis of microarray data with emphasis on time series analysis, computational biology and automatic speech recognition. *Unit head:* Andrea Ilg, 503-494-2547, E-mail: informat@ohsu.edu. *Application contact:* Lauren Ludwig, 503-494-2547, E-mail: informat@ohsu.edu. Web site: http://www.ohsu.edu/dmice/.

Rochester Institute of Technology, Graduate Enrollment Services, B. Thomas Golisano College of Computing and Information Sciences, Department of Information Technology, Program in Medical Informatics, Rochester, NY 14623-5603. Offers MS. Part-time programs available. *Students:* 3 full-time (1 woman), 1 part-time (0 women). 19 applicants, 47% accepted, 4 enrolled. *Degree requirements:* For master's, thesis or alternative, capstone. *Entrance requirements:* Additional exam requirements/recommendations for international students: Required—TOEFL (minimum score 570 paper-based; 230 computer-based; 88 iBT). *Application deadline:* Applications are processed on a rolling basis. Application fee: $50. Electronic applications accepted. *Expenses: Tuition:* Full-time $34,659; part-time $963 per credit hour. *Required fees:* $228; $76 per quarter. *Financial support:* Applicants required to submit FAFSA. *Faculty research:* Electronic health record development, database systems, clinical systems integration, Web applications for medicine, management, public health. *Unit head:* Prof. Dianne Bills, Graduate Program Director, 585-475-2700, E-mail: informaticsgrad@rit.edu. *Application contact:* Diane Ellison, Assistant Vice President, Graduate Enrollment Services, 585-475-2229, Fax: 585-475-7164, E-mail: gradinfo@rit.edu. Web site: http://medinfo.rit.edu/main/index.maml.

Stanford University, School of Medicine, Graduate Programs in Medicine, Biomedical Informatics Program, Stanford, CA 94305-9991. Offers MS, PhD. Terminal master's awarded for partial completion of doctoral program. *Degree requirements:* For master's, thesis; for doctorate, thesis/dissertation. *Entrance requirements:* For doctorate, GRE or MCAT. Additional exam requirements/recommendations for international students: Required—TOEFL. Electronic applications accepted. *Expenses: Tuition:* Full-time $40,050; part-time $890 per credit.

University at Buffalo, the State University of New York, Graduate School, School of Medicine and Biomedical Sciences, Program in Medical/Health Informatics, Buffalo, NY 14260. Offers Certificate. Part-time programs available. *Faculty:* 4 part-time/adjunct. *Students:* 2 part-time (both women). Average age 35. In 2011, 1 Certificate awarded. *Degree requirements:* For Certificate, 24 credit hours of coursework (18 required courses, 6 electives). *Entrance requirements:* For degree, all previous college/university transcripts; 2 letters of recommendation; personal letter with career objectives. Additional exam requirements/recommendations for international students: Required—TOEFL (minimum score 600 paper-based; 100 computer-based). *Application deadline:* For fall admission, 8/15 priority date for domestic students, 7/15 for international students. Application fee: $50. *Faculty research:* Integrated information systems planning and evaluation, management of knowledge-based information resources, scholarly communication in the health sciences , the economic value of health information, electronic health records, natural language understanding, ontologies, telemedicine/telehealth systems of healthcare, quality management information systems, implementation and evaluation of electronic health record systems, ethical and social issues in informatics. *Unit head:* Dr. Michael E. Cain, Dean, 716-829-3955, Fax: 716-829-3395, E-mail: mcain@buffalo.edu. *Application contact:* Amy J. Kuzdale, Staff Associate, 716-829-3399, Fax: 716-829-2437, E-mail: akuzdale@buffalo.edu. Web site: http://www.smbs.buffalo.edu/medinformatics/.

The University of Arizona, College of Nursing, Tucson, AZ 85721. Offers health care informatics (Certificate); nurse practitioner (MS, Certificate); nursing (DNP, PhD); rural health (Certificate). *Accreditation:* AACN. Part-time programs available. Postbaccalaureate distance learning degree programs offered (minimal on-campus study). *Faculty:* 19 full-time (18 women). *Students:* 279 full-time (241 women), 36 part-time (32 women); includes 84 minority (13 Black or African American, non-Hispanic/Latino; 4 American Indian or Alaska Native, non-Hispanic/Latino; 19 Asian, non-Hispanic/Latino; 31 Hispanic/Latino; 1 Native Hawaiian or other Pacific Islander, non-Hispanic/Latino; 16 Two or more races, non-Hispanic/Latino), 3 international. Average age 38. In 2011, 1 master's, 19 doctorates awarded. Terminal master's awarded for partial completion of doctoral program. *Degree requirements:* For master's, thesis optional; for doctorate, comprehensive exam, thesis/dissertation. *Entrance requirements:* For master's, BSN, eligibility for RN license; for doctorate, BSN; for Certificate, GRE General Test, Arizona RN license, BSN, minimum GPA of 3.0. Additional exam requirements/recommendations for international students: Required—TOEFL (minimum score 550 paper-based; 213 computer-based; 79 iBT). *Application deadline:* For fall admission, 1/15 for domestic and international students. Applications are processed on a rolling basis. Application fee: $75. Electronic applications accepted. *Expenses:* Contact institution. *Financial support:* In 2011–12, 4 research assistantships with full tuition reimbursements (averaging $18,220 per year), 3 teaching assistantships (averaging $18,327 per year) were awarded; career-related internships or fieldwork, institutionally sponsored loans, scholarships/grants, traineeships, health care benefits, tuition waivers (full), and unspecified assistantships also available. Financial award application deadline: 6/1. *Faculty research:* Vulnerable populations, injury mechanisms and biobehavioral responses, health care systems, informatics, rural health. *Total annual research expenditures:* $5.5 million. *Unit head:* Dr. Joan Shaver, Dean, 520-626-7124, Fax: 520-626-6424, E-mail: cmurdaugh@nursing.arizona.edu. *Application contact:* Sally J. Reel, Assistant Dean, Student Affairs, 520-626-6154, Fax: 520-626-2211, E-mail: info@nursing.arizona.edu. Web site: http://www.nursing.arizona.edu/.

University of California, Davis, Graduate Studies, Graduate Group in Health Informatics, Davis, CA 95616. Offers MS. *Entrance requirements:* Additional exam requirements/recommendations for international students: Required—TOEFL (minimum score 550 paper-based; 213 computer-based).

University of California, San Francisco, School of Pharmacy and Graduate Division, Graduate Program in Biological and Medical Informatics, San Francisco, CA 94158-2517. Offers PhD. *Faculty:* 35 full-time (6 women). *Students:* 35 full-time (9 women); includes 7 minority (1 Black or African American, non-Hispanic/Latino; 3 Asian, non-Hispanic/Latino; 3 Hispanic/Latino), 3 international. Average age 28. 187 applicants, 20% accepted, 5 enrolled. In 2011, 3 doctorates awarded. Terminal master's awarded for partial completion of doctoral program. *Degree requirements:* For doctorate, thesis/dissertation, cumulative qualifying exams, proposal defense. *Entrance requirements:* For doctorate, GRE General Test, minimum GPA of 3.0. Additional exam requirements/recommendations for international students: Required—TOEFL (minimum score 550 paper-based; 213 computer-based; 80 iBT). *Application deadline:* For fall admission, 12/1 for domestic and international students. Application fee: $70 ($90 for international students). *Financial support:* In 2011–12, 35 students received support, including 6 fellowships with full tuition reimbursements available (averaging $29,500 per year), 29 research assistantships with full tuition reimbursements available (averaging $29,500 per year); career-related internships or fieldwork, scholarships/grants, traineeships, health care benefits, tuition waivers (full), and stipends also available. *Faculty research:* Bioinformatics, biomedical computing, decision science and engineering, imaging informatics, knowledge management/telehealth/health services research. *Unit head:* Thomas E. Ferrin, Director, 415-476-2299, Fax: 415-502-1755, E-mail: tef@cgl.ucsf.edu. *Application contact:* Julia Molla, Program Administrator, 415-476-1914, Fax: 415-502-4690, E-mail: jmolla@cgl.ucsf.edu. Web site: http://www.bioinformatics.ucsf.edu.

University of Colorado Denver, College of Nursing, Aurora, CO 80045. Offers adult clinical nurse specialist (MS); adult nurse practitioner (MS); family nurse practitioner (MS); family psychiatric mental health nurse practitioner (MS); health care informatics (MS); nurse-midwifery (MS); nursing (DNP, PhD); nursing leadership and health care systems (MS); pediatric nurse practitioner (MS); pediatric nursing leadership (MS); special studies (MS); women's health care (MS); MS/PhD. *Accreditation:* ACNM/ACME (one or more programs are accredited); NLN (one or more programs are accredited). Part-time and evening/weekend programs available. Postbaccalaureate distance learning degree programs offered (minimal on-campus study). *Faculty:* 69 full-time (65 women), 68 part-time/adjunct (64 women). *Students:* 308 full-time (288 women), 134 part-time (118 women); includes 59 minority (11 Black or African American, non-Hispanic/Latino; 8 American Indian or Alaska Native, non-Hispanic/Latino; 10 Asian, non-Hispanic/Latino; 27 Hispanic/Latino; 3 Two or more races, non-Hispanic/Latino), 8 international. Average age 39. 298 applicants, 46% accepted, 110 enrolled. In 2011, 72 master's, 19 doctorates awarded. Terminal master's awarded for partial completion of doctoral program. *Degree requirements:* For master's, thesis optional; for doctorate, comprehensive exam, thesis/dissertation, 42 credits of coursework, 30 credits of dissertation. *Entrance requirements:* For master's, GRE if cumulative undergraduate GPA is less than 3.0, undergraduate nursing degree from NLNAC- or CCNE-accredited school or university; completion of research and statistics courses with minimum grade of C; copy of current and unencumbered nursing license; for doctorate, GRE, bachelor's and/or master's degrees in nursing from NLN- or CCNE-accredited institution; portfolio; minimum undergraduate GPA of 3.0, graduate 3.5; graduate-level intermediate statistics and master's-level nursing theory courses with minimum B grade; interview. Additional exam requirements/recommendations for international students: Required—TOEFL (minimum score 560 paper-based; 220 computer-based; 83 iBT). *Application deadline:* For fall admission, 4/1 for domestic students; for spring admission, 9/1 for domestic students. Application fee: $65. Electronic applications accepted. *Expenses:* Contact institution. *Financial support:* In 2011–12, 40 students received support. Fellowships, research assistantships, teaching assistantships, Federal Work-Study, scholarships/grants, and unspecified assistantships available. Support available to part-time students. Financial award application deadline: 4/1; financial award applicants required to submit FAFSA. *Faculty research:* Biological and behavioral phenomena in pregnancy and postpartum; patterns of glycemia during the insulin resistance of pregnancy; obesity, gestational diabetes, and relationship to neonatal adiposity; men's awareness and knowledge of male breast cancer; cognitive-behavioral therapy for chronic insomnia after breast cancer treatment; massage therapy for the treatment of tension-type headaches. *Total annual research expenditures:* $5.2 million. *Unit head:* Dr. Patricia Moritz, Dean, 303-724-1679, E-mail: pat.moritz@ucdenver.edu. *Application contact:* Judy Campbell, Graduate Programs Coordinator, 303-724-8503, E-mail:

judy.campbell@ucdenver.edu. Web site: http://www.ucdenver.edu/academics/colleges/nursing/Pages/default.aspx.

University of Illinois at Urbana–Champaign, Graduate College, Graduate School of Library and Information Science, Champaign, IL 61820. Offers bioinformatics (MS); digital libraries (CAS); library and information science (MS, PhD, CAS). *Accreditation:* ALA (one or more programs are accredited). Postbaccalaureate distance learning degree programs offered. *Faculty:* 25 full-time (12 women), 5 part-time/adjunct (4 women). *Students:* 349 full-time (256 women), 353 part-time (276 women); includes 125 minority (30 Black or African American, non-Hispanic/Latino; 1 American Indian or Alaska Native, non-Hispanic/Latino; 37 Asian, non-Hispanic/Latino; 40 Hispanic/Latino; 1 Native Hawaiian or other Pacific Islander, non-Hispanic/Latino; 16 Two or more races, non-Hispanic/Latino), 27 international. 606 applicants, 68% accepted, 250 enrolled. In 2011, 245 master's, 6 doctorates, 8 other advanced degrees awarded. *Entrance requirements:* For master's, GRE General Test, minimum GPA of 3.0; for doctorate, minimum GPA of 3.0; for CAS, master's degree in library and information science or related field with minimum GPA of 3.0. Additional exam requirements/recommendations for international students: Required—TOEFL (minimum score 620 paper-based; 260 computer-based; 105 iBT) or IELTS (minimum score 7). *Application deadline:* Applications are processed on a rolling basis. Application fee: $75 ($90 for international students). Electronic applications accepted. *Financial support:* In 2011–12, 24 fellowships, 39 research assistantships, 44 teaching assistantships were awarded; tuition waivers (full and partial) also available. *Unit head:* Allen Renear, Dean, 217-265-5216, Fax: 217-244-3302, E-mail: renear@illinois.edu. *Application contact:* Valerie Youngen, Admissions and Records Representative, 217-333-0734, Fax: 217-244-3302, E-mail: vyoungen@llinois.edu. Web site: http://www.lis.illinois.edu.

The University of Kansas, University of Kansas Medical Center, School of Nursing, Kansas City, KS 66160. Offers adult/gerontological clinical nurse specialist (PMC); adult/gerontological nurse practitioner (PMC); clinical research management (PMC); family nurse practitioner (PMC); health care informatics (PMC); health professions educator (PMC); nurse midwife (PMC); nursing (MS, DNP, PhD); organizational leadership (PMC); psychiatric/mental health nurse practitioner (PMC); public health nursing (PMC). *Accreditation:* AACN; ACNM/ACME. Part-time programs available. Postbaccalaureate distance learning degree programs offered (minimal on-campus study). *Faculty:* 80. *Students:* 79 full-time (71 women), 336 part-time (317 women); includes 63 minority (24 Black or African American, non-Hispanic/Latino; 2 American Indian or Alaska Native, non-Hispanic/Latino; 18 Asian, non-Hispanic/Latino; 15 Hispanic/Latino; 4 Two or more races, non-Hispanic/Latino), 6 international. Average age 37. 155 applicants, 82% accepted, 127 enrolled. In 2011, 79 master's, 15 doctorates, 12 other advanced degrees awarded. Terminal master's awarded for partial completion of doctoral program. *Degree requirements:* For master's, comprehensive exam, thesis optional, general oral exam; for doctorate, variable foreign language requirement, thesis/dissertation, comprehensive oral exam (for DNP); comprehensive written and oral exam (for PhD). *Entrance requirements:* For master's, bachelor's degree in nursing, minimum GPA of 3.0, RN license, 1 year of clinical experience, RN license in KS and MO; for doctorate, GRE General Test, master's degree in nursing, minimum GPA of 3.5, RN license in KS and MO; national certification (for some specialties). Additional exam requirements/recommendations for international students: Required—TOEFL. *Application deadline:* For fall admission, 4/1 for domestic and international students; for spring admission, 9/1 for domestic and international students. Application fee: $60. Electronic applications accepted. Tuition and fees vary according to course load, campus/location, program and reciprocity agreements. *Financial support:* Research assistantships with full and partial tuition reimbursements, teaching assistantships with full and partial tuition reimbursements, and traineeships available. Financial award application deadline: 2/14; financial award applicants required to submit FAFSA. *Faculty research:* Breastfeeding practices of teen mothers, national database of nursing quality indicators, caregiving of families of patients using technology in the home, simulation in nursing education, diaphragm fatigue. *Total annual research expenditures:* $6.1 million. *Unit head:* Dr. Karen L. Miller, Dean, 913-588-1601, Fax: 913-588-1660, E-mail: kmiller@kumc.edu. *Application contact:* Dr. Debra J. Ford, Associate Dean, Student Affairs, 913-588-1619, Fax: 913-588-1615, E-mail: dford@kumc.edu. Web site: http://nursing.kumc.edu.

University of Medicine and Dentistry of New Jersey, School of Health Related Professions, Department of Health Informatics, Program in Biomedical Informatics, Newark, NJ 07107-1709. Offers MS, PhD, DMD/MS, MD/MS. Part-time and evening/weekend programs available. Postbaccalaureate distance learning degree programs offered (minimal on-campus study). *Faculty:* 4 full-time (0 women), 20 part-time/adjunct (8 women). *Students:* 40 full-time, 63 part-time; includes 61 minority (19 Black or African American, non-Hispanic/Latino; 39 Asian, non-Hispanic/Latino; 3 Hispanic/Latino), 29 international. Average age 37. 95 applicants, 71% accepted, 44 enrolled. In 2011, 16 master's, 6 doctorates awarded. *Degree requirements:* For master's, thesis; for doctorate, comprehensive exam, thesis/dissertation. *Entrance requirements:* For master's, BS, transcript of highest degree, statement of research interests, curriculum vitae, basic understanding of database concepts and calculus, 3 reference letters; for doctorate, master's degree, transcripts of highest degree, statement of research interests, curriculum vitae, basic understanding of database concepts and calculus, 3 reference letters. Additional exam requirements/recommendations for international students: Required—TOEFL. *Application deadline:* For fall admission, 6/1 for domestic students, 3/1 for international students; for winter admission, 4/1 for domestic students; for spring admission, 10/1 for domestic students, 7/1 for international students. Applications are processed on a rolling basis. Application fee: $75. Electronic applications accepted. *Unit head:* Dr. Syed Haque, Chair, 973-972-6871, E-mail: haque@umdnj.edu. *Application contact:* Diane Hanrahan, Assistant Dean, 973-972-5336, Fax: 973-972-7463, E-mail: shrpadm@umdnj.edu.

University of Medicine and Dentistry of New Jersey, School of Health Related Professions, Department of Health Informatics, Program in Health Care Informatics, Newark, NJ 07107-1709. Offers Certificate. Part-time and evening/weekend programs available. Postbaccalaureate distance learning degree programs offered (minimal on-campus study). *Students:* 5 applicants, 60% accepted. In 2011, 2 Certificates awarded. *Entrance requirements:* For degree, all transcripts, basic proficiency in programming language, BS, 3 reference letters. Additional exam requirements/recommendations for international students: Required—TOEFL (minimum score 500 paper-based; 79 iBT). *Application deadline:* For fall admission, 6/1 for domestic students, 3/1 for international students; for spring admission, 10/1 for domestic students, 7/1 for international students. Applications are processed on a rolling basis. Application fee: $75. Electronic applications accepted. *Unit head:* Dr. Syed Haque, Director, 973-972-6871, E-mail: haque@umdnj.edu. *Application contact:* Diane Hanrahan, Assistant Dean, 973-972-5336, Fax: 973-972-7463, E-mail: shrpadm@umdnj.edu.

The University of Tennessee at Chattanooga, Graduate School, College of Health, Education and Professional Studies, School of Nursing, Chattanooga, TN 37403. Offers administration (MSN); certified nurse anesthetist (Post-Master's Certificate); education (MSN); family nurse practitioner (MSN, Post-Master's Certificate); health care informatics (Post-Master's Certificate); nurse anesthesia (MSN); nurse education (Post-Master's Certificate); nursing (DNP). *Accreditation:* AACN; AANA/CANAEP (one or more programs are accredited). *Faculty:* 15 full-time (13 women), 4 part-time/adjunct (all women). *Students:* 68 full-time (45 women), 37 part-time (33 women); includes 8 minority (6 Black or African American, non-Hispanic/Latino; 2 Hispanic/Latino). Average age 33. 5 applicants, 100% accepted, 3 enrolled. In 2011, 52 degrees awarded. *Degree requirements:* For master's, thesis optional, qualifying exams, professional project; for Post-Master's Certificate, thesis or alternative, practicum, seminar. *Entrance requirements:* For master's, GRE General Test, MAT, BSN, minimum GPA of 3.0, eligibility for Tennessee RN license, 1 year direct patient care experience; for Post-Master's Certificate, GRE General Test, MAT, MSN, minimum GPA of 3.0, eligibility for Tennessee RN license, one year of direct patient care experience. Additional exam requirements/recommendations for international students: Required—TOEFL (minimum score 550 paper-based; 213 computer-based; 79 iBT), IELTS (minimum score 6). *Application deadline:* For fall admission, 8/1 priority date for domestic students, 6/1 for international students; for spring admission, 12/1 priority date for domestic students, 10/1 for international students. Applications are processed on a rolling basis. Application fee: $35. Electronic applications accepted. *Expenses:* Tuition, state resident: full-time $6472; part-time $359 per credit hour. Tuition, nonresident: full-time $20,006; part-time $1111 per credit hour. *Required fees:* $1320; $160 per credit hour. *Financial support:* Career-related internships or fieldwork and scholarships/grants available. Support available to part-time students. *Faculty research:* Diabetes in women, health care for elderly, alternative medicine, hypertension, nurse anesthesia. *Total annual research expenditures:* $1.9 million. *Unit head:* Dr. Kay R. Lindgren, Head, 423-425-4646, Fax: 423-425-4668, E-mail: kay-lindgren@utc.edu. *Application contact:* Dr. Jerald Ainsworth, Dean of Graduate Studies, 423-425-4478, Fax: 423-425-5223, E-mail: jerald-ainsworth@utc.edu. Web site: http://www.utc.edu/Academic/Nursing/.

University of Washington, Graduate School, School of Medicine, Graduate Programs in Medicine, Department of Medical Education and Biomedical Informatics, Division of Biomedical and Health Informatics, Seattle, WA 98195. Offers MS, PhD. *Entrance requirements:* For master's and doctorate, GRE General Test, minimum GPA of 3.0; previous undergraduate course work in biology, computer programming, and mathematics. Additional exam requirements/recommendations for international students: Required—TOEFL (minimum score 580 paper-based; 237 computer-based; 70 iBT). Electronic applications accepted. *Faculty research:* Bio-clinical informatics, information retrieval, human-computer interaction, knowledge-based systems, telehealth.

University of Wisconsin–Milwaukee, Graduate School, College of Engineering and Applied Science, Program in Medical Informatics, Milwaukee, WI 53201-0413. Offers PhD. *Students:* 16 full-time (4 women), 9 part-time (4 women); includes 1 minority (Two or more races, non-Hispanic/Latino), 6 international. Average age 32. 20 applicants, 35% accepted, 4 enrolled. *Degree requirements:* For doctorate, comprehensive exam, thesis/dissertation. *Entrance requirements:* For doctorate, GRE, GMAT or MCAT. Additional exam requirements/recommendations for international students: Required—TOEFL (minimum score 600 paper-based; 250 computer-based; 79 iBT), IELTS (minimum score 6.5). Application fee: $56 ($96 for international students). One-time fee: $506.10 full-time. Tuition and fees vary according to course load and reciprocity agreements. *Financial support:* In 2011–12, 6 research assistantships, 4 teaching assistantships were awarded; fellowships and project assistantships also available. *Total annual research expenditures:* $1,744. *Unit head:* Susan McRoy, Representative, 414-229-4677, Fax: 414-229-4677, E-mail: mcroy@uwm.edu. *Application contact:* General Information Contact, 414-229-4982, Fax: 414-229-6967, E-mail: gradschool@uwm.edu. Web site: http://www.uwm.edu/dept/medinf/.

Modeling and Simulation

Academy of Art University, Graduate Program, School of Animation and Visual Effects, San Francisco, CA 94105-3410. Offers 2D animation (MFA); 3D animation (MFA); 3D modeling (MFA); visual effects (MFA). Part-time programs available. Postbaccalaureate distance learning degree programs offered (no on-campus study). *Faculty:* 17 full-time (3 women), 72 part-time/adjunct (19 women). *Students:* 593 full-time (227 women), 337 part-time (124 women); includes 144 minority (32 Black or African American, non-Hispanic/Latino; 3 American Indian or Alaska Native, non-Hispanic/Latino; 70 Asian, non-Hispanic/Latino; 37 Hispanic/Latino; 1 Native Hawaiian or other Pacific Islander, non-Hispanic/Latino; 1 Two or more races, non-Hispanic/Latino), 454 international. Average age 29. 263 applicants. In 2011, 166 master's awarded. *Degree requirements:* For master's, final review. *Entrance requirements:* For master's, statement of intent; resume; portfolio/reel; official college transcripts. *Application deadline:* Applications are processed on a rolling basis. Application fee: $100. Electronic applications accepted. *Expenses:* *Tuition:* Full-time $20,160; part-time $840 per unit. *Required fees:* $90. *Financial support:* Career-related internships or fieldwork and Federal Work-Study available. Support available to part-time students. Financial award application deadline: 8/10; financial award applicants required to submit FAFSA. *Unit head:* 800-544-ARTS, Fax: 415-263-4130, E-mail: info@academyart.edu. *Application contact:* 800-544-ARTS, Fax: 415-263-4130, E-mail: info@academyart.edu. Web site: http://www.academyart.edu/animation-school/index.html.

Arizona State University, College of Technology and Innovation, Department of Engineering, Mesa, AZ 85212. Offers computing studies (MCST); simulation, modeling, and applied cognitive science (PhD). Part-time programs available. *Degree requirements:* For master's, thesis or applied project with oral defense; interactive Program of Study (iPOS) submitted before completing 50 percent of required credit hours; for doctorate, comprehensive exam, thesis/dissertation, interactive Program of Study (iPOS) submitted before completing 50 percent of required credit hours. *Entrance requirements:* For master's, GRE, minimum GPA of 3.0 or equivalent in last 2 years of work leading to bachelor's degree; for doctorate, GRE, master's degree in psychology, engineering, cognitive science, or computer science; 3 letters of recommendation; statement of research interests. Additional exam requirements/recommendations for international students: Required—TOEFL, IELTS, or Pearson Test of English. Electronic applications accepted. *Faculty research:* Software process and automated workflow, software architecture, dotal technologies, relational database systems, embedded systems.

Arizona State University, Ira A. Fulton School of Engineering, ASU Engineering Online Programs, Tempe, AZ 85287. Offers construction (MS); embedded systems (M Eng); enterprise systems innovation and management (MSE); modeling and simulation (M Eng); quality and reliability engineering (M Eng); software engineering (MSE); systems engineering (M Eng).

Columbus State University, Graduate Studies, D. Abbott Turner College of Business and Computer Science, Columbus, GA 31907-5645. Offers applied computer science (MS); business administration (MBA); modeling and simulation (Certificate); organizational leadership (MS). *Accreditation:* AACSB. *Entrance requirements:* For master's, GMAT, GRE. Additional exam requirements/recommendations for international students: Required—TOEFL (minimum score 550 paper-based; 213 computer-based; 79 iBT). Electronic applications accepted.

Embry-Riddle Aeronautical University–Worldwide, Worldwide Headquarters - Graduate Degrees and Programs, Program in Business Administration for Aviation, Daytona Beach, FL 32114-3900. Offers business administration (MBAA); modeling and simulation management (Graduate Certificate). *Faculty:* 14 full-time (3 women), 102 part-time/adjunct (26 women). *Students:* 964 full-time (216 women), 882 part-time (180 women); includes 320 minority (123 Black or African American, non-Hispanic/Latino; 9 American Indian or Alaska Native, non-Hispanic/Latino; 40 Asian, non-Hispanic/Latino; 143 Hispanic/Latino; 2 Native Hawaiian or other Pacific Islander, non-Hispanic/Latino; 3 Two or more races, non-Hispanic/Latino), 20 international. Average age 37. 735 applicants, 76% accepted, 280 enrolled. In 2011, 278 master's awarded. *Degree requirements:* For master's, comprehensive exam (for some programs), thesis (for some programs). *Entrance requirements:* Additional exam requirements/recommendations for international students: Recommended—TOEFL (minimum score 550 paper-based; 213 computer-based; 79 iBT). Application fee: $50. *Expenses: Tuition:* Part-time $395 per credit hour. Tuition and fees vary according to degree level and program. *Financial support:* In 2011–12, 221 students received support. *Faculty research:* Healthcare operations management, humanitarian logistics, supply chain risk management, collaborative supply chain management, intersection of collaborative supply chain management and the learning organization, development of assessment tool measuring supply chain collaborative capacity, teaching effectiveness, teaching quality, management style effectiveness, aeronautics, small/medium-sized business leadership study, leadership factors, critical thinking, efficacy of ePortfolio. *Total annual research expenditures:* $16,331. *Unit head:* Dr. Kees Rietsema, Department Chair, 602-904-1295, E-mail: kees.rietsema@erau.edu. *Application contact:* Linda Dammer, Director of Admissions, 386-226-6396 Ext. 1, Fax: 386-226-6984, E-mail: worldwide@erau.edu.

George Mason University, Volgenau School of Engineering, Department of Systems Engineering and Operations Research, Fairfax, VA 22030. Offers architecture-based systems integration (Certificate); command, control, communication, computing and intelligence (Certificate); computational modeling (Certificate); discovery, design and innovation (Certificate); military operations research (Certificate); operations research (MS); systems engineering (MS); systems engineering analysis and architecture (Certificate); systems engineering and operations research (PhD); systems engineering of software intensive systems (Certificate). MS programs offered jointly with Old Dominion University, University of Virginia, Virginia Commonwealth University, and Virginia Polytechnic Institute and State University. *Faculty:* 16 full-time (4 women), 15 part-time/adjunct (4 women). *Students:* 42 full-time (5 women), 153 part-time (31 women); includes 46 minority (5 Black or African American, non-Hispanic/Latino; 2 American Indian or Alaska Native, non-Hispanic/Latino; 27 Asian, non-Hispanic/Latino; 11 Hispanic/Latino; 1 Two or more races, non-Hispanic/Latino), 13 international. Average age 32. 124 applicants, 74% accepted, 51 enrolled. In 2011, 50 master's, 1 doctorate, 11 other advanced degrees awarded. *Degree requirements:* For master's, thesis optional; for doctorate, comprehensive exam, thesis/dissertation, qualifying exams. *Entrance requirements:* For master's, GRE General Test, BS in related field; minimum GPA of 3.0; 3 letters of recommendation; 2 official transcripts; expanded goals statement; proof of financial support; photocopy of passport; official bank statement; multivariable calculus, applied probability, statistics and a computer language course; self evaluation form; for doctorate, GRE, MS with minimum GPA of 3.5; BS with minimum GPA of 3.0 in systems or operational research; 2 official transcripts; 3 letters of recommendation; resume; expanded goals statement; self evaluation form; photocopy of passport; official bank statement; proof of financial support; for Certificate, personal goals statement; 2 official transcripts; self-evaluation form; 1 letter of recommendation; resume; official bank statement; photocopy of passport; proof of financial support; baccalaureate degree in related field. Additional exam requirements/recommendations for international students: Required—TOEFL (minimum score 575 paper-based; 230 computer-based; 88 iBT), IELTS, Pearson Test of English. *Application deadline:* For fall admission, 1/15 priority date for domestic students; for spring admission, 8/15 priority date for domestic students. Application fee: $65 ($80 for international students). Electronic applications accepted. *Expenses:* Tuition, state resident: full-time $8750; part-time $364.58 per credit. Tuition, nonresident: full-time $24,092; part-time $1003.83 per credit. *Required fees:* $2514; $104.75 per credit. *Financial support:* In 2011–12, 12 students received support, including 7 research assistantships with full and partial tuition reimbursements available (averaging $15,028 per year), 5 teaching assistantships with full and partial tuition reimbursements available (averaging $12,474 per year); career-related internships or fieldwork, Federal Work-Study, scholarships/grants, unspecified assistantships, and health care benefits (full-time research or teaching assistantship recipients) also available. Support available to part-time students. Financial award application deadline: 3/1; financial award applicants required to submit FAFSA. *Faculty research:* Requirements engineering, signal processing, systems architecture, data fusion. *Total annual research expenditures:* $1.5 million. *Unit head:* Dr. Ariela Sofer, Chair, 703-993-1692, Fax: 703-993-1521, E-mail: asofer@gmu.edu. *Application contact:* Josefine Wiecks, Administrative Assistant, 703-993-1785, Fax: 703-993-1521, E-mail: jwiecks@gmu.edu. Web site: http://seor.gmu.edu.

Louisiana Tech University, Graduate School, College of Engineering and Science, Department of Physics, Ruston, LA 71272. Offers applied computational analysis and modeling (PhD); physics (MS). Part-time programs available. *Degree requirements:* For master's, thesis or alternative; for doctorate, thesis/dissertation. *Entrance requirements:* For master's, GRE General Test, minimum GPA of 3.0 in last 60 hours. Additional exam requirements/recommendations for international students: Required—TOEFL. *Faculty research:* Experimental high energy physics, laser/optics, computational physics, quantum gravity.

Naval Postgraduate School, Departments and Academic Groups, Department of Computer Science, Monterey, CA 93943. Offers computer science (MS, PhD); identity management and cyber security (MA); modeling of virtual environments and simulations (MS, PhD); software engineering (MS, PhD). Program only open to commissioned officers of the United States and friendly nations and selected United States federal civilian employees. Part-time programs available. Postbaccalaureate distance learning degree programs offered (minimal on-campus study). *Faculty:* 89 full-time (13 women), 26 part-time/adjunct (7 women). *Students:* 140 full-time (17 women), 14 part-time (5 women); includes 29 minority (9 Black or African American, non-Hispanic/Latino; 1 American Indian or Alaska Native, non-Hispanic/Latino; 10 Asian, non-Hispanic/Latino; 9 Hispanic/Latino), 26 international. Average age 37. In 2011, 54 master's, 4 doctorates awarded. *Degree requirements:* For master's, thesis; for doctorate, thesis/dissertation. *Total annual research expenditures:* $8.4 million. *Unit head:* Peter Denning, Chairman, 831-656-3603, E-mail: pjd@nps.edu. *Application contact:* Acting Director of Admissions.

Old Dominion University, College of Arts and Letters, Graduate Program in International Studies, Norfolk, VA 23529. Offers comparative and regional studies (MA, PhD); conflict and cooperation (MA, PhD); interdependence and transnationalism (MA, PhD); international cultural studies (MA, PhD); international political economy and development (MA, PhD); modeling and simulation (MA, PhD); U. S. foreign policy and international relations (MA); U. S. foreign policy and international relations (PhD). Part-time programs available. *Faculty:* 14 full-time (3 women). *Students:* 47 full-time (21 women), 46 part-time (14 women); includes 7 minority (2 Black or African American, non-Hispanic/Latino; 5 Hispanic/Latino), 35 international. Average age 32. 99 applicants, 54% accepted, 30 enrolled. In 2011, 24 master's, 3 doctorates awarded. Terminal master's awarded for partial completion of doctoral program. *Degree requirements:* For master's, one foreign language, comprehensive exam, thesis optional; for doctorate, one foreign language, comprehensive exam, thesis/dissertation. *Entrance requirements:* For master's, GRE General Test, sample of written work, 2 letters of recommendation; for doctorate, GRE General Test, sample of written work, 3 letters of recommendation. Additional exam requirements/recommendations for international students: Required—TOEFL (minimum score 570 paper-based; 230 computer-based). *Application deadline:* For fall admission, 1/15 for domestic and international students; for spring admission, 10/15 for domestic and international students. Application fee: $40. Electronic applications accepted. *Expenses:* Tuition, state resident: full-time $9096; part-time $379 per credit. Tuition, nonresident: full-time $23,064; part-time $961 per credit. *Required fees:* $127 per semester. One-time fee: $50. *Financial support:* In 2011–12, 20 students received support, including 2 fellowships (averaging $13,000 per year), 5 research assistantships with tuition reimbursements available (averaging $15,000 per year), 7 teaching assistantships with tuition reimbursements available (averaging $15,000 per year); career-related internships or fieldwork, institutionally sponsored loans, scholarships/grants, and unspecified assistantships also available. Support available to part-time students. Financial award application deadline: 2/15; financial award applicants required to submit FAFSA. *Faculty research:* U. S. foreign policy, international security, transatlantic and transpacific relations, transnational issues, IPE and development. *Total annual research expenditures:* $330,391. *Unit head:* Dr. Regina Karp, Graduate Program Director, 757-683-5700, Fax: 757-683-5701, E-mail: rkarp@odu.edu. *Application contact:* Dr. Regina Karp, Graduate Program Director, 757-683-5700, Fax: 757-683-5701, E-mail: rkarp@odu.edu. Web site: http://www.al.odu.edu/gpis/.

Old Dominion University, Frank Batten College of Engineering and Technology, Program in Modeling and Simulation, Norfolk, VA 23529. Offers ME, MS, D Eng, PhD. Part-time and evening/weekend programs available. Postbaccalaureate distance learning degree programs offered (no on-campus study). *Faculty:* 8 full-time (0 women), 8 part-time/adjunct (1 woman). *Students:* 21 full-time (6 women), 45 part-time (6 women); includes 9 minority (5 Black or African American, non-Hispanic/Latino; 1 Asian, non-Hispanic/Latino; 1 Hispanic/Latino; 2 Two or more races, non-Hispanic/Latino), 19 international. Average age 35. 38 applicants, 100% accepted, 21 enrolled. In 2011, 10 master's, 3 doctorates awarded. Terminal master's awarded for partial completion of doctoral program. *Degree requirements:* For master's, comprehensive exam (for some programs), thesis (for some programs); for doctorate, comprehensive exam, thesis/dissertation, candidacy exam. *Entrance requirements:* For master's, GRE, proficiency in calculus, calculus-based statistics, and computer science; for doctorate, GRE, graduate-level proficiency in calculus, calculus-based statistics, and computer science. Additional exam requirements/recommendations for international students: Required—TOEFL (minimum score 550 paper-based; 213 computer-based; 79 iBT). *Application deadline:* For fall admission, 6/1 for domestic students, 4/15 for international students; for spring admission, 11/1 for domestic students, 10/1 for international students. Applications are processed on a rolling basis. Application fee: $50. Electronic applications accepted. *Expenses:* Tuition, state resident: full-time $9096; part-time $379 per credit. Tuition, nonresident: full-time $23,064; part-time $961 per credit. *Required fees:* $127 per semester. One-time fee: $50. *Financial support:* In 2011–12, 18 students received support, including 2 fellowships with full tuition reimbursements available (averaging $16,000 per year), 16 research assistantships with full tuition reimbursements available (averaging $18,000 per year); career-related internships or fieldwork, scholarships/grants, and unspecified assistantships also available. Financial award application deadline: 4/15; financial award applicants required to submit FAFSA. *Faculty research:* Distributed simulation and interoperability, medical modeling and simulation, transportation modeling and simulation, human factors, discrete event systems. *Total annual research expenditures:* $1.5 million. *Unit head:* Dr. Rick McKenzie, Graduate Program Director, 757-683-5590, Fax: 757-683-3200, E-mail: rdmckenz@odu.edu. *Application contact:* Dr. Linda Vahala, Associate Dean, 757-683-3789, Fax: 757-683-4898, E-mail: lvahala@odu.edu. Web site: http://eng.odu.edu/msve.

Portland State University, Graduate Studies, Systems Science Program, Portland, OR 97207-0751. Offers computational intelligence (Certificate); computer modeling and simulation (Certificate); systems science (MS); systems science/anthropology (PhD); systems science/business administration (PhD); systems science/civil engineering (PhD); systems science/economics (PhD); systems science/engineering management (PhD); systems science/general (PhD); systems science/mathematical sciences (PhD); systems science/mechanical engineering (PhD); systems science/psychology (PhD); systems science/sociology (PhD). *Degree requirements:* For doctorate, variable foreign language requirement, thesis/dissertation. *Entrance requirements:* For master's, 2 letters of recommendation; for doctorate, GMAT, GRE General Test, minimum undergraduate GPA of 3.0. Additional exam requirements/recommendations for international students: Required—TOEFL. *Faculty research:* Systems theory and methodology, artificial intelligence neural networks, information theory, nonlinear dynamics/chaos, modeling and simulation.

Stevens Institute of Technology, Graduate School, Charles V. Schaefer Jr. School of Engineering, Department of Civil, Environmental, and Ocean Engineering, Program in Civil Engineering, Hoboken, NJ 07030. Offers civil engineering (PhD); geotechnical engineering (Certificate); geotechnical/geoenvironmental engineering (M Eng, Engr);

hydrologic modeling (M Eng); stormwater management (M Eng); structural engineering (M Eng, Engr); water resources engineering (M Eng). *Degree requirements:* For master's, thesis optional; for doctorate, variable foreign language requirement, thesis/dissertation; for other advanced degree, project or thesis. *Entrance requirements:* For doctorate, GRE. Additional exam requirements/recommendations for international students: Required—TOEFL. Electronic applications accepted.

Trent University, Graduate Studies, Program in Applications of Modeling in the Natural and Social Sciences, Peterborough, ON K9J 7B8, Canada. Offers applications of modeling in the natural and social sciences (MA); biology (M Sc, PhD); chemistry (M Sc); computer studies (M Sc); geography (M Sc, PhD); physics (M Sc). Part-time programs available. *Degree requirements:* For master's, thesis. *Entrance requirements:* For master's, honours degree. *Faculty research:* Computation of heat transfer, atmospheric physics, statistical mechanics, stress and coping, evolutionary ecology.

Université Laval, Faculty of Administrative Sciences, Programs in Business Administration, Québec, QC G1K 7P4, Canada. Offers accounting (MBA); agri-food management (MBA); electronic business (MBA, Diploma); factory management and logistics (MBA); finance (MBA); firm management (MBA); geomatic management (MBA); information technology management (MBA); international management (MBA); management (MBA); management accounting (MBA, Diploma); marketing (MBA); modeling and organizational decision (MBA); occupational health and safety management (MBA); pharmacy management (MBA); social and environmental responsibility (MBA); technological entrepreneurship (Diploma). *Accreditation:* AACSB. Part-time and evening/weekend programs available. Postbaccalaureate distance learning degree programs offered (no on-campus study). *Entrance requirements:* For master's and Diploma, knowledge of French and English. Electronic applications accepted.

University at Buffalo, the State University of New York, Graduate School, College of Arts and Sciences, Department of Geography, Buffalo, NY 14260. Offers earth systems science (MA); economic geography and international business and world trade (MA); environmental modeling and analysis (MA); geographic information science (MA, Certificate); geography (MA, PhD); transportation and business geographics (MA, Certificate); urban and regional geography (MA); MA/MBA. *Faculty:* 15 full-time (7 women), 1 part-time/adjunct (0 women). *Students:* 102 full-time (38 women), 20 part-time (10 women); includes 61 minority (1 Black or African American, non-Hispanic/Latino; 55 Asian, non-Hispanic/Latino; 5 Hispanic/Latino), 1 international. 167 applicants, 33% accepted, 29 enrolled. In 2011, 21 master's, 5 doctorates awarded. Terminal master's awarded for partial completion of doctoral program. *Degree requirements:* For master's, thesis (for some programs), project or portfolio; for doctorate, thesis/dissertation. *Entrance requirements:* For master's, GRE General Test, minimum GPA of 2.9; for doctorate, GRE General Test, minimum GPA of 3.0. Additional exam requirements/recommendations for international students: Required—TOEFL (minimum score 550 paper-based; 213 computer-based; 79 iBT). *Application deadline:* For fall admission, 7/1 priority date for domestic students, 1/10 for international students; for spring admission, 12/1 priority date for domestic students, 10/1 for international students. Applications are processed on a rolling basis. Application fee: $75. Electronic applications accepted. *Financial support:* In 2011–12, 13 students received support, including 8 fellowships with full tuition reimbursements available (averaging $4,750 per year), 13 teaching assistantships with full tuition reimbursements available (averaging $13,520 per year); research assistantships with full tuition reimbursements available, career-related internships or fieldwork, Federal Work-Study, institutionally sponsored loans, traineeships, health care benefits, and unspecified assistantships also available. Financial award application deadline: 1/10. *Faculty research:* International business and world trade, geographic information systems and cartography, transportation, urban and regional analysis, physical and environmental geography. *Total annual research expenditures:* $630,314. *Unit head:* Dr. Sharmistha Bagchi-Sen, Chairman, 716-645-0473, Fax: 716-645-2329, E-mail: geosbs@buffalo.edu. *Application contact:* Betsy Abraham, Graduate Secretary, 716-645-0471, Fax: 716-645-2329, E-mail: babraham@buffalo.edu. Web site: http://www.geog.buffalo.edu/.

The University of Alabama in Huntsville, School of Graduate Studies, Interdisciplinary Studies, Interdisciplinary Program of Modeling and Simulation, Huntsville, AL 35899. Offers MS, PhD, Certificate. Part-time and evening/weekend programs available. Postbaccalaureate distance learning degree programs offered (minimal on-campus study). *Faculty:* 12 full-time (2 women), 2 part-time/adjunct (0 women). *Students:* 2 full-time (1 woman), 7 part-time (0 women); includes 1 minority (Black or African American, non-Hispanic/Latino). Average age 38. 9 applicants, 67% accepted, 4 enrolled. In 2011, 1 other advanced degree awarded. *Degree requirements:* For master's, comprehensive exam, thesis or alternative, 24 hours course work plus 6 hours thesis; for doctorate, comprehensive exam, thesis/dissertation, 54 hours course work plus 18 hours dissertation. *Entrance requirements:* For master's, doctorate, and Certificate, GRE General Test, minimum GPA of 3.0. Additional exam requirements/recommendations for international students: Required—TOEFL (minimum score 500 paper-based; 173 computer-based; 62 iBT). *Application deadline:* For fall admission, 7/15 for domestic students, 4/1 for international students; for spring admission, 11/30 for domestic students, 9/1 for international students. Applications are processed on a rolling basis. Application fee: $40 ($50 for international students). Electronic applications accepted. *Expenses:* Tuition, state resident: full-time $7830; part-time $473.50 per credit. Tuition, nonresident: full-time $18,748; part-time $1128.33 per credit. Tuition and fees vary according to course load and program. *Financial support:* In 2011–12, 1 student received support, including 1 research assistantship with full tuition reimbursement available (averaging $13,568 per year); career-related internships or fieldwork, Federal Work-Study, institutionally sponsored loans, scholarships/grants, health care benefits, and unspecified assistantships also available. Support available to part-time students. Financial award application deadline: 4/1; financial award applicants required to submit FAFSA. *Faculty research:* Simulation interoperability and composability, discrete event simulation, mathematical modeling and analysis, system-level modeling, technical team performance. *Unit head:* Dr. Mikel D. Petty, Director, Center for Modeling, Simulation, and Analysis, 256-824-4368, Fax: 256-824-6405, E-mail: pettym@uah.edu. *Application contact:* Kim Gray, Graduate Studies Admissions Coordinator, 256-824-6002, Fax: 256-824-6405, E-mail: deangrad@uah.edu. Web site: http://cmsa.uah.edu/?info&page=about.

University of California, San Diego, Office of Graduate Studies, Department of Structural Engineering, La Jolla, CA 92093. Offers structural engineering (MS, PhD); structural health monitoring, prognosis, and validated simulations (MS). Applications accepted only for fall quarter. Part-time programs available. *Degree requirements:* For master's, comprehensive exam or thesis; for doctorate, comprehensive exam, thesis/dissertation, candidacy exam. *Entrance requirements:* For master's and doctorate, GRE General Test, minimum GPA of 3.0; BS in engineering, physical sciences, or mathematics; statement of purpose; three letters of recommendation; official transcripts from all institutions attended. Additional exam requirements/recommendations for international students: Required—TOEFL (minimum score 550 paper-based; 213

computer-based; 80 iBT). *Faculty research:* Advanced large-scale civil, mechanical, and aerospace structures.

University of Central Florida, College of Education, Department of Educational and Human Sciences, Program in Instructional Systems, Orlando, FL 32816. Offers instructional design for simulations (Certificate); instructional systems (MA). *Students:* 17 full-time (9 women), 43 part-time (29 women); includes 15 minority (5 Black or African American, non-Hispanic/Latino; 3 Asian, non-Hispanic/Latino; 6 Hispanic/Latino; 1 Two or more races, non-Hispanic/Latino), 3 international. Average age 35. 25 applicants, 88% accepted, 17 enrolled. In 2011, 6 master's, 6 other advanced degrees awarded. Application fee: $30. Electronic applications accepted. *Expenses:* Tuition, state resident: part-time $277.08 per credit hour. Tuition, nonresident: part-time $277.08 per credit hour. Part-time tuition and fees vary according to degree level and program. *Financial support:* Fellowships with partial tuition reimbursements, research assistantships with partial tuition reimbursements, and teaching assistantships with partial tuition reimbursements available. *Unit head:* Dr. Atsusi Hirumi, Program Coordinator, 407-823-1760, E-mail: atsusi.hirumi@ucf.edu. *Application contact:* Barbara Rodriguez, Director, Admissions and Registration, 407-823-2766, Fax: 407-823-6442, E-mail: gradadmissions@ucf.edu.

University of Central Florida, College of Engineering and Computer Science, Department of Industrial Engineering and Management Systems, Orlando, FL 32816. Offers applied operations research (Certificate); design for usability (Certificate); engineering management (PSM); industrial engineering (MSIE, PhD); industrial engineering and management systems (MS); industrial ergonomics and safety (Certificate); project engineering (Certificate); quality assurance (Certificate); systems engineering (Certificate); systems simulation for engineers (Certificate); training simulation (Certificate). Part-time and evening/weekend programs available. *Faculty:* 18 full-time (4 women), 5 part-time/adjunct (1 woman). *Students:* 105 full-time (27 women), 151 part-time (47 women); includes 84 minority (20 Black or African American, non-Hispanic/Latino; 1 American Indian or Alaska Native, non-Hispanic/Latino; 20 Asian, non-Hispanic/Latino; 37 Hispanic/Latino; 1 Native Hawaiian or other Pacific Islander, non-Hispanic/Latino; 5 Two or more races, non-Hispanic/Latino), 52 international. Average age 32. 199 applicants, 79% accepted, 75 enrolled. In 2011, 83 master's, 11 doctorates, 40 other advanced degrees awarded. *Degree requirements:* For master's, thesis; for doctorate, thesis/dissertation, departmental qualifying exam, candidacy exam. *Entrance requirements:* For master's, GRE General Test, minimum GPA of 3.0 in last 60 hours of course work; for doctorate, minimum GPA of 3.5 in last 60 hours of course work. Additional exam requirements/recommendations for international students: Required—TOEFL. *Application deadline:* For fall admission, 7/15 priority date for domestic students; for spring admission, 12/1 priority date for domestic students. Application fee: $30. Electronic applications accepted. *Expenses:* Tuition, state resident: part-time $277.08 per credit hour. Tuition, nonresident: part-time $277.08 per credit hour. Part-time tuition and fees vary according to degree level and program. *Financial support:* In 2011–12, 19 students received support, including 8 fellowships with partial tuition reimbursements available (averaging $3,500 per year), 10 research assistantships with partial tuition reimbursements available (averaging $11,100 per year), 6 teaching assistantships with partial tuition reimbursements available (averaging $12,300 per year); career-related internships or fieldwork, Federal Work-Study, institutionally sponsored loans, tuition waivers (partial), and unspecified assistantships also available. Financial award application deadline: 3/1; financial award applicants required to submit FAFSA. *Unit head:* Dr. Waldemar Karwowski, Chair, 407-823-2204, E-mail: wkar@ucf.edu. *Application contact:* Barbara Rodriguez, Director, Admissions and Registration, 407-823-2766, Fax: 407-823-6442, E-mail: gradadmissions@ucf.edu. Web site: http://iems.ucf.edu/.

University of Central Florida, College of Graduate Studies, Program in Modeling and Simulation, Orlando, FL 32816. Offers MS, PhD. *Students:* 60 full-time (17 women), 65 part-time (18 women); includes 37 minority (8 Black or African American, non-Hispanic/Latino; 9 Asian, non-Hispanic/Latino; 19 Hispanic/Latino; 1 Native Hawaiian or other Pacific Islander, non-Hispanic/Latino), 9 international. Average age 35. 44 applicants, 91% accepted, 31 enrolled. In 2011, 24 master's, 7 doctorates awarded. *Expenses:* Tuition, state resident: part-time $277.08 per credit hour. Tuition, nonresident: part-time $277.08 per credit hour. Part-time tuition and fees vary according to degree level and program. *Financial support:* In 2011–12, 23 students received support, including 3 fellowships (averaging $6,000 per year), 27 research assistantships (averaging $10,500 per year). *Unit head:* Dr. Peter Kincaid, Program Director, 407-882-1330, E-mail: pkincaid@ist.ucf.edu. *Application contact:* Barbara Rodriguez, Director, Admissions and Registration, 407-823-2766, Fax: 407-823-6442, E-mail: gradadmissions@ucf.edu. Web site: http://www.ist.ucf.edu/.

The University of Manchester, School of Chemical Engineering and Analytical Science, Manchester, United Kingdom. Offers biocatalysis (M Phil, PhD); chemical engineering (M Phil, PhD); chemical engineering and analytical science (M Phil, D Eng, PhD); colloids, crystals, interfaces and materials (M Phil, PhD); environment and sustainable technology (M Phil, PhD); instrumentation (M Phil, PhD); multi-scale modeling (M Phil, PhD); process integration (M Phil, PhD); systems biology (M Phil, PhD).

University of Northern Iowa, Graduate College, College of Humanities, Arts and Sciences, Department of Mathematics, Cedar Falls, IA 50614. Offers industrial mathematics (PSM), including actuarial science, continuous quality improvement, mathematical computing and modeling; mathematics (MA), including mathematics, secondary; mathematics for middle grades 4-8 (MA). Part-time programs available. *Students:* 13 full-time (6 women), 23 part-time (17 women); includes 2 minority (1 Black or African American, non-Hispanic/Latino; 1 Asian, non-Hispanic/Latino), 6 international. 35 applicants, 74% accepted, 11 enrolled. In 2011, 19 master's awarded. *Degree requirements:* For master's, comprehensive exam (for some programs), thesis or alternative. *Entrance requirements:* For master's, minimum GPA of 3.0. Additional exam requirements/recommendations for international students: Required—TOEFL (minimum score 600 paper-based; 250 computer-based; 100 iBT). *Application deadline:* For fall admission, 8/1 priority date for domestic students. Applications are processed on a rolling basis. Application fee: $50 ($70 for international students). Electronic applications accepted. *Expenses:* Tuition, state resident: full-time $7476. Tuition, nonresident: full-time $16,410. *Required fees:* $942. *Financial support:* Career-related internships or fieldwork, Federal Work-Study, scholarships/grants, and tuition waivers (full and partial) available. Support available to part-time students. Financial award application deadline: 2/1. *Unit head:* Dr. Douglas Mupasiri, Interim Head, 319-273-2012, Fax: 319-273-2546, E-mail: douglas.mupasiri@uni.edu. *Application contact:* Laurie S. Russell, Record Analyst, 319-273-2623, Fax: 319-273-2885, E-mail: laurie.russell@uni.edu. Web site: http://www.math.uni.edu/.

University of Southern California, Graduate School, Viterbi School of Engineering, Department of Computer Science, Los Angeles, CA 90089. Offers computer networks (MS); computer science (MS, PhD); computer security (MS); game development (MS);

high performance computing and simulations (MS); human language technology (MS); intelligent robotics (MS); multimedia and creative technologies (MS); software engineering (MS). Part-time and evening/weekend programs available. Postbaccalaureate distance learning degree programs offered (no on-campus study). *Entrance requirements:* For master's and doctorate, GRE General Test. Additional exam requirements/recommendations for international students: Required—TOEFL. Electronic applications accepted. *Faculty research:* Databases, computer graphics and computer vision, software engineering, networks and security, robotics, multimedia and virtual reality.

Virginia Commonwealth University, Graduate School, College of Humanities and Sciences, Department of Statistical Sciences and Operations Research, Richmond, VA 23284-9005. Offers operations research (MS); statistics (MS); systems modeling and analysis (PhD). *Students:* 20 applicants, 70% accepted, 11 enrolled. *Entrance requirements:* For master's, GRE General Test, 30 undergraduate credits in mathematics, statistics, or operations research, including calculus I and II, multivariate calculus, linear algebra, probability and statistics. Additional exam requirements/recommendations for international students: Required—TOEFL (minimum score 600 paper-based; 250 computer-based; 100 iBT); Recommended—IELTS (minimum score 6.5). *Application deadline:* For fall admission, 3/1 for domestic students; for spring admission, 10/15 for domestic students. Applications are processed on a rolling basis. Application fee: $50. Electronic applications accepted. *Expenses:* Tuition, state resident: full-time $9133; part-time $507 per credit. Tuition, nonresident: full-time $18,777; part-time $1043 per credit. *Required fees:* $77 per credit. Tuition and fees vary according to degree level, campus/location, program and student level. *Unit head:* Dr.

D'Arcy P. Mays, Chair, 804-828-1301 Ext. 151, E-mail: jemays@vcu.edu. *Application contact:* Dr. Edward L. Boone, Director, 804-828-4637, E-mail: elboone@VCU.edu. Web site: http://www.stat.vcu.edu/.

Worcester Polytechnic Institute, Graduate Studies and Research, Programs in Interdisciplinary Studies, Worcester, MA 01609-2280. Offers bioscience administration (MS); impact engineering (MS); manufacturing engineering management (MS); power systems management (MS); social science (PhD); systems modeling (MS). Part-time and evening/weekend programs available. *Faculty:* 1 full-time (0 women). *Students:* 1 full-time (0 women), 201 part-time (30 women); includes 22 minority (2 Black or African American, non-Hispanic/Latino; 11 Asian, non-Hispanic/Latino; 7 Hispanic/Latino; 2 Two or more races, non-Hispanic/Latino), 5 international. 130 applicants, 90% accepted, 107 enrolled. *Degree requirements:* For master's, thesis; for doctorate, comprehensive exam, thesis/dissertation. *Entrance requirements:* For master's and doctorate, 3 letters of recommendation. Additional exam requirements/recommendations for international students: Required—TOEFL (minimum score 563 paper-based; 223 computer-based; 84 iBT), IELTS (minimum score 7). *Application deadline:* For fall admission, 1/1 priority date for domestic students, 1/1 for international students; for spring admission, 10/1 priority date for domestic students, 10/1 for international students. Application fee: $70. *Financial support:* Institutionally sponsored loans, scholarships/grants, and unspecified assistantships available. Financial award application deadline: 1/1; financial award applicants required to submit FAFSA. *Unit head:* Dr. Fred J. Looft, Head, 508-831-5231, Fax: 508-831-5491, E-mail: fjlooft@wpi.edu. *Application contact:* Lynne Dougherty, Administrative Assistant, 508-831-5301, Fax: 508-831-5717, E-mail: grad@wpi.edu.

Software Engineering

American Public University System, AMU/APU Graduate Programs, Charles Town, WV 25414. Offers accounting (MBA, MS); administration and supervision (M Ed); criminal justice (MA); emergency and disaster management (MA); entrepreneurship (MBA); environmental policy and management (MS), including environmental planning, environmental sustainability, fish and wildlife management, general (MA, MS), global environmental management; finance (MBA); general (MBA); global business management (MBA); guidance and counseling (M Ed); history (MA), including American history, ancient and classical history, European history, global history, military and diplomatic history, public history; homeland security (MA); homeland security resource allocation (MBA); humanities (MA); information technology (MS), including digital forensics, enterprise software development, information assurance and security, IT project management; information technology management (MBA); intelligence studies (MA), including criminal intelligence, general (MA, MS), homeland security, intelligence analysis, intelligence collection, intelligence operations, terrorism studies; international relations and conflict resolution (MA), including comparative and security issues, conflict resolution, international and transnational security issues, peacekeeping; legal studies (MA); management (MA), including defense management, general (MA, MS), human resource management, organizational leadership, public administration, reverse logistics, strategic consulting; marketing (MBA); military history (MA), including American military history, American revolution, civil war, war since 1946, World War II; military studies (MA), including air warfare, asymmetrical warfare, joint warfare, land warfare, naval warfare, strategic leadership; national security studies (MA), including general (MA, MS), homeland security, regional security studies, security and intelligence analysis, terrorism studies; nonprofit management (MBA); political science (MA), including American politics and government, comparative government and development, public policy; psychology (MA); public administration (MA, MPA), including disaster management (MPA), environmental policy (MA), health policy (MPA), human resources (MPA), national security (MPA), organizational management (MPA), security management (MPA); public health (MA, MPH), including emergency management (MPH), environmental health (MPH), public administration (MA); reverse logistics management (MA); security management (MA); space studies (MS), including aerospace science, planetary science; sports and health sciences (MS); sports management (MS), including coaching theory and strategy, sports administration; teaching (M Ed), including curriculum and instruction for elementary teachers, elementary, elementary reading, English language learners, instructional leadership, online learning, secondary social sciences, special education; transportation and logistics management (MA), including maritime engineering management. Programs offered via distance learning only. Part-time and evening/weekend programs available. Postbaccalaureate distance learning degree programs offered (no on-campus study). *Faculty:* 445 full-time (241 women), 1,360 part-time/adjunct (617 women). *Students:* 688 full-time (338 women), 10,168 part-time (3,706 women); includes 3,130 minority (1,007 Black or African American, non-Hispanic/Latino; 103 American Indian or Alaska Native, non-Hispanic/Latino; 825 Asian, non-Hispanic/Latino; 810 Hispanic/Latino; 51 Native Hawaiian or other Pacific Islander, non-Hispanic/Latino; 334 Two or more races, non-Hispanic/Latino), 134 international. Average age 35. In 2011, 2,386 master's awarded. *Degree requirements:* For master's, comprehensive exam or practicum. *Entrance requirements:* For master's, official transcript showing earned bachelor's degree from institution accredited by recognized accrediting body. Additional exam requirements/recommendations for international students: Required—TOEFL (minimum score 550 paper-based; 213 computer-based), IELTS (minimum score 6.5). *Application deadline:* Applications are processed on a rolling basis. Application fee: $0. Electronic applications accepted. *Expenses:* Tuition: Part-time $325 per credit hour. *Financial support:* Applicants required to submit FAFSA. *Faculty research:* Military history, criminal justice, management performance, national security. *Unit head:* Dr. Karan Powell, Executive Vice President and Provost, 877-468-6268, Fax: 304-724-3780. *Application contact:* Terry Grant, Vice President of Enrollment Management, 877-468-6268, Fax: 304-724-3780, E-mail: info@apus.edu. Web site: http://www.apus.edu.

Andrews University, School of Graduate Studies, College of Technology, Department of Engineering, Computer Science, and Engineering Technology, Berrien Springs, MI 49104. Offers software engineering (MS). *Faculty:* 6 full-time (1 woman). *Students:* 1 full-time (0 women), all international. Average age 28. 8 applicants, 38% accepted, 1 enrolled. In 2011, 1 master's awarded. *Entrance requirements:* For master's, GRE, minimum GPA of 2.6. Additional exam requirements/recommendations for international students: Required—TOEFL. *Application deadline:* Applications are processed on a rolling basis. Application fee: $40. *Unit head:* Dr. George Agoki, Chairman, 269-471-3420. *Application contact:* Carolyn Hurst, Supervisor of Graduate Admission, 800-253-2874, Fax: 269-471-6321, E-mail: graduate@andrews.edu.

Arizona State University, Ira A. Fulton School of Engineering, ASU Engineering Online Programs, Tempe, AZ 85287. Offers construction (MS); embedded systems (M Eng); enterprise systems innovation and management (MSE); modeling and simulation (M Eng); quality and reliability engineering (M Eng); software engineering (MSE); systems engineering (M Eng).

Auburn University, Graduate School, Ginn College of Engineering, Department of Computer Science and Software Engineering, Auburn University, AL 36849. Offers MS, MSWE, PhD. Part-time programs available. *Faculty:* 15 full-time (1 woman), 1 (woman) part-time/adjunct. *Students:* 58 full-time (11 women), 69 part-time (21 women); includes 18 minority (14 Black or African American, non-Hispanic/Latino; 4 Asian, non-Hispanic/Latino), 49 international. Average age 29. 203 applicants, 39% accepted, 20 enrolled. In 2011, 27 master's, 13 doctorates awarded. *Degree requirements:* For master's, thesis (for some programs); for doctorate, thesis/dissertation. *Entrance requirements:* For master's and doctorate, GRE General Test, GRE Subject Test. *Application deadline:* For fall admission, 7/7 for domestic students; for spring admission, 11/24 for domestic students. Applications are processed on a rolling basis. Application fee: $50 ($60 for international students). Electronic applications accepted. *Expenses:* Tuition, state resident: full-time $7290; part-time $405 per credit hour. Tuition, nonresident: full-time $21,870; part-time $1215 per credit hour. *International tuition:* $22,000 full-time. *Required fees:* $1402. *Financial support:* Research assistantships, teaching assistantships, and Federal Work-Study available. Support available to part-time students. Financial award application deadline: 3/15; financial award applicants required to submit FAFSA. *Faculty research:* Parallelizable, scalable software translations; graphical representations of algorithms, structures, and processes; graph drawing. *Total annual research expenditures:* $400,000. *Unit head:* Dr. Kai Chang, Chair, 334-844-6310. *Application contact:* Dr. George Flowers, Dean of the Graduate School, 334-844-2125. Web site: http://www.eng.auburn.edu/department/cse/.

Bowling Green State University, Graduate College, College of Arts and Sciences, Department of Computer Science, Bowling Green, OH 43403. Offers computer science (MS), including operations research, parallel and distributed computing, software engineering. Part-time programs available. *Degree requirements:* For master's, thesis or alternative. *Entrance requirements:* For master's, GRE General Test. Additional exam requirements/recommendations for international students: Required—TOEFL. Electronic applications accepted. *Faculty research:* Artificial intelligence, real time and concurrent programming languages, behavioral aspects of computing, network protocols.

Brandeis University, Rabb School of Continuing Studies, Division of Graduate Professional Studies, Software Engineering Program, Waltham, MA 02454-9110. Offers MSE. Part-time programs available. Postbaccalaureate distance learning degree programs offered (no on-campus study). *Faculty:* 2 full-time (both women), 34 part-time/adjunct (8 women). *Students:* 1 (woman) full-time, 76 part-time (15 women); includes 19 minority (1 Black or African American, non-Hispanic/Latino; 13 Asian, non-Hispanic/Latino; 5 Hispanic/Latino), 1 international. Average age 35. 16 applicants, 94% accepted, 13 enrolled. In 2011, 62 master's awarded. *Entrance requirements:* For master's, resume, official transcripts, recommendations, goal statements. Additional exam requirements/recommendations for international students: Recommended—TOEFL (minimum score 600 paper-based; 250 computer-based; 100 iBT). *Application deadline:* For fall admission, 6/15 priority date for domestic students; for winter admission, 10/15 priority date for domestic students; for spring admission, 2/15 priority date for domestic students. Application fee: $50. *Unit head:* Erik Hemdal, Program Chair, 781-736-8787, Fax: 781-736-3420, E-mail: ehemdal@brandeis.edu. *Application contact:* Frances Stearns, Associate Director of Admissions and Student Services, 781-736-8785, Fax: 781-736-3420, E-mail: fstearns@brandeis.edu. Web site: http://www.brandeis.edu/gps.

California State University, Fullerton, Graduate Studies, College of Engineering and Computer Science, Department of Computer Science, Fullerton, CA 92834-9480. Offers computer science (MS); software engineering (MS). Part-time programs available. Postbaccalaureate distance learning degree programs offered. *Students:* 77 full-time (19 women), 242 part-time (53 women); includes 96 minority (7 Black or African American, non-Hispanic/Latino; 64 Asian, non-Hispanic/Latino; 16 Hispanic/Latino; 9 Two or more races, non-Hispanic/Latino), 139 international. Average age 30. 585 applicants, 70% accepted, 113 enrolled. In 2011, 126 master's awarded. *Degree requirements:* For master's, comprehensive exam, project or thesis. *Entrance requirements:* For master's, GRE General Test, minimum undergraduate GPA of 2.5. Application fee: $55. *Financial support:* Career-related internships or fieldwork, Federal Work-Study, institutionally sponsored loans, and scholarships/grants available. Support available to part-time students. Financial award application deadline: 3/1; financial award applicants required to submit FAFSA. *Faculty research:* Software engineering, development of computer networks. *Unit head:* Dr. James Choi, Chair, 657-278-3700. *Application contact:* Admissions/Applications, 657-278-2371.

California State University, Northridge, Graduate Studies, College of Engineering and Computer Science, Department of Computer Science, Northridge, CA 91330. Offers computer science (MS); software engineering (MS). Part-time and evening/weekend programs available. *Degree requirements:* For master's, thesis. *Entrance requirements:* For master's, GRE General Test, minimum GPA of 2.5. Additional exam requirements/recommendations for international students: Required—TOEFL. *Faculty research:* Radar data processing.

California State University, Sacramento, Office of Graduate Studies, College of Engineering and Computer Science, Department of Computer Science, Sacramento, CA 95819-6021. Offers computer systems (MS); software engineering (MS). Part-time and evening/weekend programs available. *Faculty:* 20 full-time (5 women), 4 part-time/adjunct (1 woman). *Students:* 46 full-time, 32 part-time; includes 18 minority (3 Black or African American, non-Hispanic/Latino; 9 Asian, non-Hispanic/Latino; 5 Hispanic/Latino; 1 Two or more races, non-Hispanic/Latino), 51 international. Average age 27. 206 applicants, 51% accepted, 40 enrolled. In 2011, 40 master's awarded. *Degree requirements:* For master's, thesis or comprehensive exam; writing proficiency exam. *Entrance requirements:* For master's, GRE. Additional exam requirements/recommendations for international students: Required—TOEFL. *Application deadline:* For fall admission, 3/1 for domestic and international students; for spring admission, 9/15 for domestic students, 9/30 for international students. Applications are processed on a rolling basis. Application fee: $5. Electronic applications accepted. *Financial support:* Research assistantships, teaching assistantships, career-related internships or fieldwork, and Federal Work-Study available. Support available to part-time students. Financial award application deadline: 3/1; financial award applicants required to submit FAFSA. *Unit head:* Cui Zhang, Chair, 916-278-5843, Fax: 916-278-6774, E-mail: zhangc@ecs.csus.edu. *Application contact:* Jose Martinez, Outreach and Graduate Diversity Coordinator, 916-278-6470, Fax: 916-278-5669, E-mail: martinj@skymail.csus.edu. Web site: http://www.ecs.csus.edu/csc.

Carnegie Mellon University, Carnegie Institute of Technology, Information Networking Institute, Pittsburgh, PA 15213. Offers information networking (MS); information security technology and management (MS); information technology - information security (MS); information technology - mobility (MS); information technology - software management (MS). *Degree requirements:* For master's, thesis optional. *Entrance requirements:* For master's, GRE General Test, bachelor's degree in computer science, computer engineering, or electrical engineering, or related technology degree; programming skills (C/C++ fluency for some programs). Additional exam requirements/recommendations for international students: Required—TOEFL. *Faculty research:* Computer forensics and incident response; dependable systems, embedded systems, mobile systems, and sensor networks; computer and information networks, network and information security, human and socio-economic factors in secure system design; wireless sensor networks, survivable embedded systems, signal processing/compression; strategic management, international strategic management, group dynamics and decision-making structures, simulated competitive environments.

Carnegie Mellon University, School of Computer Science, Software Engineering Program, Pittsburgh, PA 15213-3891. Offers MSE, PhD. *Entrance requirements:* For master's, GRE General Test, GRE Subject Test (computer science), 2 years of experience in large-scale software development project.

Carnegie Mellon University, Tepper School of Business, Pittsburgh, PA 15213-3891. Offers accounting (PhD); algorithms, combinatorics, and optimization (MS, PhD); business management and software engineering (MBMSE); civil engineering and industrial management (MS); computational finance (MSCF); economics (MS, PhD); electronic commerce (MS); environmental engineering and management (MEEM); finance (PhD); financial economics (PhD); industrial administration (MBA), including administration and public management; information systems (PhD); management of manufacturing and automation (PhD); marketing (PhD); mathematical finance (PhD); operations research (PhD); organizational behavior and theory (PhD); political economy (PhD); production and operations management (PhD); public policy and management (MS, MSED); software engineering and business management (MS); JD/MS; JD/MSIA; M Div/MS; MOM/MSIA; MSCF/MSIA. JD/MSIA offered jointly with University of Pittsburgh. Part-time programs available. Terminal master's awarded for partial completion of doctoral program. *Degree requirements:* For doctorate, thesis/dissertation. *Entrance requirements:* For master's, GMAT. Additional exam requirements/recommendations for international students: Required—TOEFL. *Expenses:* Contact institution.

Carroll University, Program in Software Engineering, Waukesha, WI 53186-5593. Offers MSE. Part-time and evening/weekend programs available. *Degree requirements:* For master's, professional experience, capstone project. *Entrance requirements:* For master's, BA or BS, 2 years professional experience. Additional exam requirements/recommendations for international students: Required—TOEFL. Electronic applications accepted. *Faculty research:* Networking, artificial intelligence, virtual reality, effective teaching of software design, computer science pedagogy.

Cleveland State University, College of Graduate Studies, Fenn College of Engineering, Department of Electrical and Computer Engineering, Cleveland, OH 44115. Offers electrical engineering (MS, D Eng); software engineering (MS). Part-time and evening/weekend programs available. *Faculty:* 15 full-time (2 women), 1 part-time/adjunct (0 women). *Students:* 14 full-time (4 women), 187 part-time (35 women); includes 13 minority (4 Black or African American, non-Hispanic/Latino; 8 Asian, non-Hispanic/Latino; 1 Hispanic/Latino), 146 international. Average age 27. 372 applicants, 63% accepted, 41 enrolled. In 2011, 63 master's, 1 doctorate awarded. *Degree requirements:* For master's, thesis optional; for doctorate, thesis/dissertation, qualifying and candidacy exams. *Entrance requirements:* For master's, GRE General Test (minimum score 650 quantitative), minimum GPA of 2.75; for doctorate, GRE General Test (minimum quantitative score in 80th percentile), minimum GPA of 3.25. Additional exam requirements/recommendations for international students: Required—TOEFL (minimum score 535 paper-based; 197 computer-based; 65 iBT) or IELTS (minimum score 6.0). *Application deadline:* For fall admission, 7/15 priority date for domestic students. Applications are processed on a rolling basis. Application fee: $30. *Expenses:* Contact institution. *Financial support:* In 2011–12, 31 students received support, including 23 research assistantships with full and partial tuition reimbursements available (averaging $4,242 per year), 8 teaching assistantships with full and partial tuition reimbursements available (averaging $4,242 per year); career-related internships or fieldwork, scholarships/grants, and unspecified assistantships also available. *Faculty research:* Computer networks, computer security and privacy, mobile computing, distributed computing, software engineering, knowledge-based control systems, artificial intelligence, digital communications, MEMS, sensors, power systems, power electronics. *Total annual research expenditures:* $484,362. *Unit head:* Dr. Fuqin Xiong, Chairperson, 216-687-2127, E-mail: f.xiong@csuohio.edu. *Application contact:* Deborah L. Brown, Interim Assistant Director, Graduate Admissions, 216-523-7572, Fax: 216-687-9214, E-mail: d.l.brown@csuohio.edu. Web site: http://www.csuohio.edu/ece.

Colorado Technical University Colorado Springs, Graduate Studies, Program in Computer Science, Colorado Springs, CO 80907-3896. Offers computer science (DCS); computer systems security (MSCS); database systems (MSCS); software engineering (MSCS). Part-time and evening/weekend programs available. Postbaccalaureate distance learning degree programs offered. *Degree requirements:* For master's, thesis or alternative; for doctorate, thesis/dissertation. *Entrance requirements:* For doctorate, minimum graduate GPA of 3.0, 5 years of related work experience. *Faculty research:* Software engineering, systems engineering.

Colorado Technical University Denver South, Program in Computer Science, Aurora, CO 80014. Offers computer systems security (MSCS); database systems (MSCS); software engineering (MSCS). Part-time and evening/weekend programs available. *Degree requirements:* For master's, thesis or alternative. *Entrance requirements:* For master's, minimum undergraduate GPA of 3.0, resume.

Colorado Technical University Sioux Falls, Program in Computing, Sioux Falls, SD 57108. Offers computer systems security (MSCS); software engineering (MSCS).

Concordia University, School of Graduate Studies, Faculty of Engineering and Computer Science, Department of Computer Science and Software Engineering, Montréal, QC H3G 1M8, Canada. Offers computer science (M App Comp Sc, M Comp Sc, PhD, Diploma); software engineering (MA Sc). *Degree requirements:* For master's, one foreign language, thesis optional; for doctorate, one foreign language, comprehensive exam, thesis/dissertation. *Faculty research:* Computer systems and applications, mathematics of computation, pattern recognition, artificial intelligence and robotics.

Concordia University, School of Graduate Studies, Faculty of Engineering and Computer Science, Department of Mechanical and Industrial Engineering, Montréal, QC H3G 1M8, Canada. Offers composites (M Eng); industrial engineering (M Eng, MA Sc); mechanical engineering (M Eng, MA Sc, PhD, Certificate); software systems for industrial engineering (Certificate). M Eng in composites program offered jointly with École Polytechnique de Montréal. *Degree requirements:* For master's, variable foreign language requirement, thesis or alternative; for doctorate, comprehensive exam, thesis/dissertation. *Faculty research:* Mechanical systems, fluid control systems, thermofluids engineering and robotics, industrial control systems.

DePaul University, College of Computing and Digital Media, Chicago, IL 60604. Offers animation (MA, MFA); applied technology (MS); business information technology (MS); cinema (MFA); cinema production (MS); computational finance (MS); computer and information sciences (PhD); computer game development (MS); computer graphics and motion technology (MS); computer information and network security (MS); computer science (MS); e-commerce technology (MS); human-computer interaction (MS); information systems (MS); information technology (MA); information technology project management (MS); network engineering and management (MS); predictive analytics (MS); screenwriting (MFA); software engineering (MS); JD/MA; JD/MS. Part-time and evening/weekend programs available. Postbaccalaureate distance learning degree programs offered (no on-campus study). *Faculty:* 64 full-time (16 women), 44 part-time/adjunct (5 women). *Students:* 969 full-time (250 women), 936 part-time (231 women); includes 566 minority (204 Black or African American, non-Hispanic/Latino; 3 American Indian or Alaska Native, non-Hispanic/Latino; 166 Asian, non-Hispanic/Latino; 135 Hispanic/Latino; 7 Native Hawaiian or other Pacific Islander, non-Hispanic/Latino; 51 Two or more races, non-Hispanic/Latino), 282 international. Average age 32. 1,040 applicants, 65% accepted, 324 enrolled. In 2011, 478 master's, 4 doctorates awarded. *Degree requirements:* For master's, thesis (for some programs); for doctorate, comprehensive exam, thesis/dissertation. *Entrance requirements:* For master's, GRE or GMAT (MS in computational finance only), bachelor's degree, resume (MS in predictive analytics only), IT experience (MS in information technology project management only), portfolio review (all MFA programs and MA in animation); for doctorate, GRE, master's degree in computer science. Additional exam requirements/recommendations for international students: Required—TOEFL (minimum score 550 paper-based; 213 computer-based; 80 iBT), IELTS (minimum score 6.5), Pearson Test of English (minimum score 53). *Application deadline:* For fall admission, 8/1 priority date for domestic students, 6/1 for international students; for winter admission, 12/1 priority date for domestic students, 10/1 for international students; for spring admission, 3/1 priority date for domestic students, 1/1 for international students. Applications are processed on a rolling basis. Application fee: $25. Electronic applications accepted. *Expenses:* Contact institution. *Financial support:* In 2011–12, 56 students received support, including 3 fellowships with full tuition reimbursements available (averaging $30,000 per year), 3 research assistantships with full and partial tuition reimbursements available (averaging $22,833 per year), 50 teaching assistantships (averaging $6,194 per year); Federal Work-Study, scholarships/grants, tuition waivers (full and partial), and unspecified assistantships also available. Support available to part-time students. Financial award application deadline: 4/30. *Faculty research:* Data mining, theoretical computer science, gaming, security, animation and film. *Total annual research expenditures:* $3.9 million. *Unit head:* Elly Kafritsas-Wessels, Senior Administrative Assistant, 312-362-5816, Fax: 312-362-5185, E-mail: ekafrits@cdm.depaul.edu. *Application contact:* James Parker, Director of Graduate Admission, 312-362-8714, Fax: 312-362-5179, E-mail: jparke29@cdm.depaul.edu. Web site: http://cdm.depaul.edu.

Drexel University, College of Engineering, Department of Electrical and Computer Engineering, Program in Software Engineering, Philadelphia, PA 19104-2875. Offers MSSE. *Entrance requirements:* For master's, GRE. Additional exam requirements/recommendations for international students: Required—TOEFL. Electronic applications accepted.

East Carolina University, Graduate School, College of Technology and Computer Science, Department of Computer Science, Greenville, NC 27858-4353. Offers computer science (MS); software engineering (MS). Part-time and evening/weekend programs available. *Degree requirements:* For master's, comprehensive exam, thesis or alternative. *Entrance requirements:* For master's, GRE General Test. Additional exam requirements/recommendations for international students: Required—TOEFL. *Application deadline:* For fall admission, 11/1 priority date for domestic students, 10/1 for international students; for spring admission, 3/1 priority date for domestic students, 3/1 for international students. Applications are processed on a rolling basis. Application fee: $50. Electronic applications accepted. *Expenses:* Tuition, state resident: full-time $3557; part-time $444.63 per semester hour. Tuition, nonresident: full-time $14,351; part-time $1793.88 per semester hour. *Required fees:* $2016; $252 per semester hour. Part-time tuition and fees vary according to course load, campus/location and program. *Financial support:* Research assistantships, career-related internships or fieldwork, Federal Work-Study, tuition waivers (full), and unspecified assistantships available. Financial award application deadline: 3/1. *Faculty research:* Software development, software engineering, artificial intelligence, bioinformatics, cryptography. *Unit head:* Dr.

Karl Abrahamson, Interim Chair, 252-328-9689, E-mail: karl@cs.ecu.edu. Web site: http://www.ecu.edu/cs-tecs/csci/index.cfm.

Embry-Riddle Aeronautical University–Daytona, Daytona Beach Campus Graduate Program, Department of Electrical, Computer and Software Engineering, Daytona Beach, FL 32114-3900. Offers electrical/computer engineering (MSECE); engineering (MMSE); software engineering (MSE). Part-time and evening/weekend programs available. *Faculty:* 11 full-time (0 women), 3 part-time/adjunct (1 woman). *Students:* 36 full-time (9 women), 20 part-time (1 woman); includes 4 minority (1 Black or African American, non-Hispanic/Latino; 3 Hispanic/Latino), 16 international. Average age 27. 40 applicants, 70% accepted, 18 enrolled. In 2011, 12 master's awarded. *Degree requirements:* For master's, thesis or alternative. *Entrance requirements:* For master's, minimum GPA of 3.0 in senior year, 2.5 overall; course work in computer science. Additional exam requirements/recommendations for international students: Required—TOEFL (minimum score 550 paper-based; 213 computer-based; 79 iBT). *Application deadline:* For fall admission, 6/1 priority date for domestic students, 6/1 for international students; for spring admission, 11/1 priority date for domestic students, 10/1 for international students. Applications are processed on a rolling basis. Application fee: $50. Electronic applications accepted. *Expenses: Tuition:* Full-time $14,340; part-time $1195 per credit hour. *Financial support:* In 2011–12, 24 students received support, including 8 research assistantships with full and partial tuition reimbursements available (averaging $3,772 per year), 4 teaching assistantships with full and partial tuition reimbursements available (averaging $3,514 per year); career-related internships or fieldwork, Federal Work-Study, and unspecified assistantships also available. Financial award application deadline: 4/15; financial award applicants required to submit FAFSA. *Faculty research:* Safety-critical software, qualification and certification of digital hardware and softwae, next-generation air transportation system, unmanned aircraft systems, regulatory issues in unmanned aircraft systems. *Total annual research expenditures:* $800,000. *Unit head:* Dr. Timothy Wilson, Department Chair, 386-226-6454, E-mail: timothy.wilson@erau.edu. *Application contact:* Flavia Carreiro, Assistant Director, International and Graduate Admissions, 800-388-3728, Fax: 386-226-7070, E-mail: graduate.admissions@erau.edu.

Fairfield University, School of Engineering, Fairfield, CT 06824-5195. Offers electrical and computer engineering (MS); management of technology (MS); mechanical engineering (MS); software engineering (MS). Part-time and evening/weekend programs available. *Faculty:* 10 full-time (2 women), 11 part-time/adjunct. *Students:* 44 full-time (15 women), 86 part-time (22 women); includes 19 minority (4 Black or African American, non-Hispanic/Latino; 8 Asian, non-Hispanic/Latino; 4 Hispanic/Latino; 1 Native Hawaiian or other Pacific Islander, non-Hispanic/Latino; 2 Two or more races, non-Hispanic/Latino), 21 international. Average age 34. 100 applicants, 76% accepted, 27 enrolled. In 2011, 38 master's awarded. *Degree requirements:* For master's, thesis, capstone course. *Entrance requirements:* For master's, interview, minimum GPA of 2.8, resume, 2 recommendations. Additional exam requirements/recommendations for international students: Required—TOEFL (minimum score 550 paper-based; 213 computer-based; 80 iBT)or IELTS (minimum score 6.5). *Application deadline:* For fall admission, 5/15 for international students; for spring admission, 10/15 for international students. Applications are processed on a rolling basis. Application fee: $60. Electronic applications accepted. *Expenses:* Contact institution. *Financial support:* In 2011–12, 50 students received support. Scholarships/grants and unspecified assistantships available. Financial award applicants required to submit FAFSA. *Faculty research:* Vehicle dynamics, image processing, multimedia in instruction, thermal packaging, character recognition, photovoltaics and nanotechnology, Web technology. *Unit head:* Dr. Jack Beal, Dean, 203-254-4000 Ext. 4147, Fax: 203-254-4013, E-mail: jwbeal@fairfield.edu. *Application contact:* Marianne Gumpper, Director of Graduate and Continuing Studies Admission, 203-254-4184, Fax: 203-254-4073, E-mail: gradadmis@fairfield.edu. Web site: http://www.fairfield.edu/soe/soe_grad_1.html.

Florida Agricultural and Mechanical University, Division of Graduate Studies, Research, and Continuing Education, College of Arts and Sciences, Department of Computer Information Sciences, Tallahassee, FL 32307-3200. Offers software engineering (MS). *Entrance requirements:* Additional exam requirements/recommendations for international students: Required—TOEFL.

Florida Institute of Technology, Graduate Programs, College of Engineering, Computer Science Department, Melbourne, FL 32901-6975. Offers computer information systems (MS); computer science (MS, PhD); software engineering (MS). Part-time and evening/weekend programs available. *Faculty:* 14 full-time (1 woman), 11 part-time/adjunct (1 woman). *Students:* 73 full-time (14 women), 63 part-time (14 women); includes 9 minority (4 Black or African American, non-Hispanic/Latino; 2 Asian, non-Hispanic/Latino; 2 Hispanic/Latino; 1 Two or more races, non-Hispanic/Latino), 81 international. Average age 29. 342 applicants, 64% accepted, 40 enrolled. In 2011, 37 master's, 4 doctorates awarded. *Degree requirements:* For master's, comprehensive exam (for some programs), thesis optional, final exam, seminar, or internship (for non-thesis option); for doctorate, comprehensive exam, thesis/dissertation, publication in journal, teaching experience (strongly encouraged), specialized research program. *Entrance requirements:* For master's, GRE General Test, minimum GPA of 3.0, 3 letters of recommendation; for doctorate, GRE General Test, GRE Subject Test in computer science (recommended), 3 letters of recommendation, minimum GPA of 3.5, resume, statement of objectives. Additional exam requirements/recommendations for international students: Required—TOEFL (minimum score 550 paper-based; 213 computer-based; 79 iBT). *Application deadline:* For fall admission, 4/1 for international students; for spring admission, 9/30 for international students. Applications are processed on a rolling basis. Application fee: $0. Electronic applications accepted. *Expenses: Tuition:* Full-time $19,620; part-time $1090 per credit hour. Tuition and fees vary according to campus/location. *Financial support:* In 2011–12, 1 research assistantship with full and partial tuition reimbursement (averaging $4,500 per year), 12 teaching assistantships with full and partial tuition reimbursements (averaging $12,103 per year) were awarded; career-related internships or fieldwork, institutionally sponsored loans, tuition waivers (partial), unspecified assistantships, and tuition remissions also available. Support available to part-time students. Financial award application deadline: 3/1; financial award applicants required to submit FAFSA. *Faculty research:* Artificial intelligence, software engineering, management and processes, programming languages, database systems. *Total annual research expenditures:* $741,031. *Unit head:* Dr. William D. Shoaff, Department Head, 321-674-8066, Fax: 321-674-7046, E-mail: wds@cs.fit.edu. *Application contact:* Cheryl A. Brown, Associate Director of Graduate Admissions, 321-674-7581, Fax: 321-723-9468, E-mail: cbrown@fit.edu. Web site: http://coe.fit.edu/cs.

Florida Institute of Technology, Graduate Programs, Extended Studies Division, Melbourne, FL 32901-6975. Offers acquisition and contract management (MS); aerospace engineering (MS); business administration (MBA); computer information systems (MS); computer science (MS); electrical engineering (MS); engineering management (MS); human resources management (MS); logistics management (MS), including humanitarian and disaster relief logistics; management (MS), including acquisition and contract management, e-business, human resources management, information systems, logistics management, management, transportation management; material acquisition management (MS); mechanical engineering (MS); operations research (MS); project management (MS), including information systems, operations research; public administration (MPA); quality management (MS); software engineering (MS); space systems (MS); space systems management (MS); supply chain management (MS); systems management (MS), including information systems, operations research. Part-time and evening/weekend programs available. Postbaccalaureate distance learning degree programs offered (no on-campus study). *Faculty:* 9 full-time (2 women), 105 part-time/adjunct (24 women). *Students:* 113 full-time (52 women), 1,150 part-time (484 women); includes 496 minority (332 Black or African American, non-Hispanic/Latino; 11 American Indian or Alaska Native, non-Hispanic/Latino; 42 Asian, non-Hispanic/Latino; 71 Hispanic/Latino; 2 Native Hawaiian or other Pacific Islander, non-Hispanic/Latino; 38 Two or more races, non-Hispanic/Latino), 11 international. Average age 35. 568 applicants, 56% accepted, 296 enrolled. In 2011, 471 master's awarded. *Degree requirements:* For master's, comprehensive exam (for some programs), capstone course. *Entrance requirements:* For master's, GMAT or resume showing 8 years of supervised experience, minimum GPA of 3.0, 2 letters of recommendation, resume. Additional exam requirements/recommendations for international students: Required—TOEFL (minimum score 550 paper-based; 213 computer-based; 79 iBT). *Application deadline:* For fall admission, 4/1 for international students; for spring admission, 9/30 for international students. Applications are processed on a rolling basis. Application fee: $0. Electronic applications accepted. *Expenses:* Contact institution. *Financial support:* Application deadline: 3/1; applicants required to submit FAFSA. *Unit head:* Dr. Theodore R. Richardson, III, Senior Associate Dean, 321-674-8123, Fax: 321-674-7597, E-mail: trichardson@fit.edu. *Application contact:* Carolyn Farrior, Director of Graduate Admissions, Online Learning and Off-Campus Programs, 321-674-7118, Fax: 321-674-8216, E-mail: cfarrior@fit.edu. Web site: http://es.fit.edu.

Gannon University, School of Graduate Studies, College of Engineering and Business, School of Engineering and Computer Science, Program in Embedded Software Engineering, Erie, PA 16541-0001. Offers MSES. Part-time and evening/weekend programs available. *Students:* 12 full-time (1 woman), 6 part-time (0 women); includes 1 minority (Black or African American, non-Hispanic/Latino), 10 international. Average age 25. 27 applicants, 78% accepted, 2 enrolled. In 2011, 5 master's awarded. *Degree requirements:* For master's, thesis or project. *Entrance requirements:* For master's, GRE or GMAT, bachelor's degree in engineering, minimum GPA of 2.5. Additional exam requirements/recommendations for international students: Required—TOEFL (minimum score 79 iBT). *Application deadline:* Applications are processed on a rolling basis. Application fee: $25. Electronic applications accepted. *Financial support:* Career-related internships or fieldwork, Federal Work-Study, scholarships/grants, traineeships, and unspecified assistantships available. Financial award application deadline: 7/1; financial award applicants required to submit FAFSA. *Unit head:* Dr. Fong Mak, Chair, 814-871-7625, E-mail: mak001@gannon.edu. *Application contact:* Kara Morgan, Director of Graduate Admissions, 814-871-5831, Fax: 814-871-5827, E-mail: graduate@gannon.edu.

George Mason University, Volgenau School of Engineering, Department of Computer Science, Fairfax, VA 22030. Offers computer games technology (Certificate); computer networking (Certificate); computer science (MS, PhD); database management (Certificate); electronic commerce (Certificate); foundations of information systems (Certificate); information engineering (Certificate); information security and assurance (MS, Certificate); information systems (MS); intelligent agents (Certificate); software architecture (Certificate); software engineering (MS, Certificate); software engineering for C4I (Certificate); Web-based software engineering (Certificate). MS program offered jointly with Old Dominion University, University of Virginia, Virginia Commonwealth University, and Virginia Polytechnic Institute and State University. *Faculty:* 40 full-time (9 women), 17 part-time/adjunct (0 women). *Students:* 208 full-time (52 women), 357 part-time (75 women); includes 98 minority (17 Black or African American, non-Hispanic/Latino; 63 Asian, non-Hispanic/Latino; 14 Hispanic/Latino; 4 Two or more races, non-Hispanic/Latino), 205 international. Average age 30. 882 applicants, 52% accepted, 137 enrolled. In 2011, 164 master's, 5 doctorates, 28 other advanced degrees awarded. *Degree requirements:* For master's, thesis optional; for doctorate, comprehensive exam, thesis/dissertation. *Entrance requirements:* For master's, GRE, proof of financial support; 2 official college transcripts; resume; self-evaluation form; official bank statement; photocopy of passport; 3 letters of recommendation; baccalaureate degree related to computer science; minimum GPA of 3.0 in last 2 years of undergraduate work; 1 year beyond 1st-year calculus; personal goals statement; for doctorate, GRE, personal goals statement; 2 official copies of transcripts; self-evaluation form; 3 letters of recommendation; photocopy of passport; proof of financial support; official bank statement; resume; 4-year baccalaureate degree with strong background in computer science. Additional exam requirements/recommendations for international students: Required—TOEFL (minimum score 575 paper-based; 230 computer-based; 88 iBT), IELTS, Pearson Test of English. *Application deadline:* For fall admission, 1/15 priority date for domestic students; for spring admission, 8/15 priority date for domestic students. Application fee: $65 ($80 for international students). Electronic applications accepted. *Expenses:* Tuition, state resident: full-time $8750; part-time $364.58 per credit. Tuition, nonresident: full-time $24,092; part-time $1003.83 per credit. *Required fees:* $2514; $104.75 per credit. *Financial support:* In 2011–12, 100 students received support, including 3 fellowships (averaging $18,000 per year), 50 research assistantships (averaging $15,232 per year), 47 teaching assistantships (averaging $11,675 per year); career-related internships or fieldwork, Federal Work-Study, scholarships/grants, unspecified assistantships, and health care benefits (full-time research or teaching assistantship recipients) also available. Support available to part-time students. Financial award application deadline: 3/1; financial award applicants required to submit FAFSA. *Faculty research:* Artificial intelligence, image processing/graphics, parallel/distributed systems, software engineering systems. *Total annual research expenditures:* $1.9 million. *Unit head:* Sanjeev Setia, Chair, 703-993-4098, Fax: 703-993-1710, E-mail: setia@gmu.edu. *Application contact:* Michele Pieper, Administrative Assistant, 703-993-9483, Fax: 703-993-1710, E-mail: mpieper@gmu.edu. Web site: http://cs.gmu.edu/.

Grand Valley State University, Padnos College of Engineering and Computing, School of Computing and Information Systems, Allendale, MI 49401-9403. Offers computer information systems (MS), including databases, distributed systems, management of information systems, object-oriented systems, software engineering. Part-time and evening/weekend programs available. *Degree requirements:* For master's, thesis or alternative. *Entrance requirements:* For master's, GMAT or GRE General Test. Additional exam requirements/recommendations for international students: Required—TOEFL. Electronic applications accepted. *Faculty research:* Object technology, distributed computing, information systems management database, software engineering.

Hawai`i Pacific University, College of Business Administration, Program in Information Systems, Honolulu, HI 96813. Offers knowledge management (MSIS); software engineering (MSIS); telecommunications security (MSIS). Part-time and evening/weekend programs available. *Faculty:* 9 full-time (2 women), 3 part-time/adjunct (1 woman). *Students:* 46 full-time (7 women), 51 part-time (9 women); includes 64 minority (6 Black or African American, non-Hispanic/Latino; 29 Asian, non-Hispanic/Latino; 10 Hispanic/Latino; 2 Native Hawaiian or other Pacific Islander, non-Hispanic/Latino; 17 Two or more races, non-Hispanic/Latino). Average age 32. 52 applicants, 83% accepted, 23 enrolled. In 2011, 52 master's awarded. *Expenses: Tuition:* Full-time $13,230; part-time $735 per credit. Tuition and fees vary according to course load and program. *Financial support:* In 2011–12, 12 students received support. Career-related internships or fieldwork, Federal Work-Study, scholarships/grants, tuition waivers, and unspecified assistantships available. *Unit head:* Dr. Gordon Jones, Dean, 808-544-1181, Fax: 808-544-0247, E-mail: gjones@hpu.edu. *Application contact:* Chad Schempp, Director of Graduate Admissions, 808-543-8035, Fax: 808-544-0280, E-mail: graduate@hpu.edu.

Illinois Institute of Technology, Graduate College, Armour College of Engineering, Department of Electrical and Computer Engineering, Chicago, IL 60616-3793. Offers biomedical imaging and signals (MBMI); computer engineering (MS, PhD); electrical and computer engineering (MECE); electrical engineering (MS, PhD); electricity markets (MEM); network engineering (MNE); power engineering (MPE); telecommunications and software engineering (MTSE); VLSI and microelectronics (MVM). Part-time and evening/weekend programs available. Postbaccalaureate distance learning degree programs offered (minimal on-campus study). Terminal master's awarded for partial completion of doctoral program. *Degree requirements:* For master's, comprehensive exam (for some programs), thesis (for some programs); for doctorate, comprehensive exam, thesis/dissertation. *Entrance requirements:* For master's and doctorate, GRE General Test (minimum score 1100 Quantitative and Verbal, 3.5 Analytical Writing), minimum undergraduate GPA of 3.0. Additional exam requirements/recommendations for international students: Required—TOEFL (minimum score 523 paper-based; 70 iBT); Recommended—IELTS (minimum score 5.5). Electronic applications accepted. *Faculty research:* Communication systems, computer systems and micro-electronics, electromagnetics and electronics, power and control systems, signal and image processing.

Illinois Institute of Technology, Graduate College, College of Science and Letters, Department of Computer Science, Chicago, IL 60616-3793. Offers business (MCS); computer networking and telecommunications (MCS); computer science (MCS, MS, PhD); information systems (MCS); software engineering (MCS); teaching (MST). Part-time and evening/weekend programs available. Postbaccalaureate distance learning degree programs offered (no on-campus study). Terminal master's awarded for partial completion of doctoral program. *Degree requirements:* For master's, thesis optional; for doctorate, comprehensive exam, thesis/dissertation. *Entrance requirements:* For master's, GRE General Test (minimum scores: 1000 Quantitative and Verbal, 3.0 Analytical Writing), minimum undergraduate GPA of 3.0; for doctorate, GRE General Test (minimum scores: 1100 Quantitative and Verbal, 3.5 Analytical Writing), minimum undergraduate GPA of 3.0. Additional exam requirements/recommendations for international students: Required—TOEFL (minimum score 523 paper-based; 70 iBT). Electronic applications accepted. *Faculty research:* Algorithms, data structures, artificial intelligences, computer architecture, computer graphics, computer networking and telecommunications.

Instituto Tecnologico de Santo Domingo, Graduate School, Area of Engineering, Santo Domingo, Dominican Republic. Offers construction administration (MS, Certificate); data telecommunications (M Eng, MS, Certificate); industrial engineering (M Eng, Certificate); industrial management (M Mgmt); information technology (Certificate); maintenance engineering (M Eng); occupational hazard prevention (M Mgmt); production management (Certificate); quantitative methods (Certificate); sanitary and environmental engineering (M Eng); structural engineering (M Eng); systems engineering and electronic data processing (Certificate); transportation (Certificate).

International Technological University, Program in Software Engineering, Santa Clara, CA 95050. Offers MSSE, PhD. *Degree requirements:* For master's, thesis or alternative. *Entrance requirements:* For master's, 3 semesters of calculus, minimum GPA of 2.5. Additional exam requirements/recommendations for international students: Required—TOEFL. *Faculty research:* Software testing, web management, client service and the Internet.

Jacksonville State University, College of Graduate Studies and Continuing Education, College of Arts and Sciences, Program in Computer Systems and Software Design, Jacksonville, AL 36265-1602. Offers MS. Part-time and evening/weekend programs available. *Degree requirements:* For master's, comprehensive exam, thesis (for some programs). Electronic applications accepted. *Expenses:* Tuition, state resident: part-time $336 per hour. Tuition, nonresident: part-time $672 per hour. Part-time tuition and fees vary according to degree level.

Kansas State University, Graduate School, College of Engineering, Department of Computing and Information Sciences, Manhattan, KS 66506. Offers computer science (MS, PhD); software engineering (MSE). Part-time programs available. Postbaccalaureate distance learning degree programs offered (minimal on-campus study). *Faculty:* 15 full-time (1 woman), 1 part-time/adjunct (0 women). *Students:* 64 full-time (18 women), 19 part-time (2 women); includes 1 minority (Two or more races, non-Hispanic/Latino), 60 international. Average age 27. 258 applicants, 24% accepted, 12 enrolled. In 2011, 31 degrees awarded. Terminal master's awarded for partial completion of doctoral program. *Degree requirements:* For master's, thesis or alternative; for doctorate, thesis/dissertation, preliminary exams. *Entrance requirements:* For master's, GRE, bachelor's degree in computer science, minimum GPA of 3.0; for doctorate, GRE General Test, GRE Subject Test, master's degree in computer science or bachelor's degree and strong advanced computer knowledge. Additional exam requirements/recommendations for international students: Required—TOEFL (minimum score 575 paper-based; 233 computer-based; 90 iBT). *Application deadline:* For fall admission, 2/1 priority date for domestic students, 2/1 for international students; for spring admission, 8/1 priority date for domestic students, 8/1 for international students. Applications are processed on a rolling basis. Application fee: $40 ($55 for international students). Electronic applications accepted. *Financial support:* In 2011–12, 9 fellowships (averaging $30,000 per year), 22 research assistantships (averaging $17,820 per year), 22 teaching assistantships with full tuition reimbursements (averaging $16,000 per year) were awarded; career-related internships or fieldwork, institutionally sponsored loans, scholarships/grants, health care benefits, and unspecified assistantships also available. Support available to part-time students. Financial award application deadline: 3/15; financial award applicants required to submit FAFSA. *Faculty research:* High-assurance software and programming languages, data mining, parallel and distributed computing, computer security, embedded systems. *Total annual research expenditures:* $2.2 million. *Unit head:* Dr. Gurdip E. Singh, Head, 785-532-7945, Fax: 785-532-7353, E-mail: gurdip@ksu.edu. *Application contact:* Susan Cregg, Program Coordinator, 785-532-6350, Fax: 785-532-7353, E-mail: scregg@ksu.edu. Web site: http://www.cis.ksu.edu/.

Loyola University Chicago, Graduate School, Department of Computer Science, Chicago, IL 60660. Offers computer science (MS); information technology (MS); software engineering (MS). Part-time and evening/weekend programs available. *Faculty:* 10 full-time (1 woman), 10 part-time/adjunct (2 women). *Students:* 59 full-time (18 women), 29 part-time (8 women); includes 19 minority (9 Black or African American, non-Hispanic/Latino; 9 Asian, non-Hispanic/Latino; 1 Hispanic/Latino), 39 international. Average age 28. 129 applicants, 55% accepted, 29 enrolled. In 2011, 40 master's awarded. *Degree requirements:* For master's, thesis optional, ten courses. *Entrance requirements:* For master's, 3 letters of recommendation, transcripts, statement of purpose. Additional exam requirements/recommendations for international students: Required—TOEFL (minimum score 550 paper-based; 213 computer-based; 79 iBT) or IELTS (minimum score 6.5). *Application deadline:* For fall admission, 8/10 for domestic students, 5/15 for international students; for spring admission, 12/20 for domestic students, 9/15 for international students. Applications are processed on a rolling basis. Electronic applications accepted. *Expenses: Tuition:* Full-time $15,660; part-time $870 per credit hour. *Required fees:* $125 per semester. Tuition and fees vary according to course load and program. *Financial support:* In 2011–12, 20 students received support, including 1 fellowship (averaging $3,000 per year), 16 teaching assistantships with partial tuition reimbursements available (averaging $4,000 per year); career-related internships or fieldwork, Federal Work-Study, scholarships/grants, tuition waivers (partial), and unspecified assistantships also available. Financial award application deadline: 3/15. *Faculty research:* Software engineering, high performance computing, algorithms and complexity, parallel and distributed computing, databases and computer networks. *Total annual research expenditures:* $22,000. *Unit head:* Dr. Chandra Sekharan, Chair, 312-915-7985, Fax: 312-915-7998, E-mail: csekhar@luc.edu. *Application contact:* Cecilia Murphy, Graduate Program Secretary, 312-915-7990, Fax: 312-915-7998, E-mail: gradinfo-cs@luc.edu. Web site: http://cs.luc.edu.

Loyola University Maryland, Graduate Programs, College of Arts and Sciences, Department of Computer Science and Software Engineering, Baltimore, MD 21210-2699. Offers computer science (MS); software engineering (MS). Part-time and evening/weekend programs available. *Faculty:* 3 full-time (1 woman), 6 part-time/adjunct (0 women). *Students:* 5 full-time (1 woman), 59 part-time (16 women); includes 15 minority (7 Black or African American, non-Hispanic/Latino; 4 Asian, non-Hispanic/Latino; 2 Hispanic/Latino; 1 Native Hawaiian or other Pacific Islander, non-Hispanic/Latino; 1 Two or more races, non-Hispanic/Latino), 2 international. Average age 33. In 2011, 11 master's awarded. *Entrance requirements:* For master's, GRE General Test, GRE Subject Test (recommended). Additional exam requirements/recommendations for international students: Required—TOEFL (minimum score 550 paper-based; 213 computer-based). *Application deadline:* For fall admission, 8/1 for domestic students; for spring admission, 12/1 for domestic students. Application fee: $50. Electronic applications accepted. *Financial support:* Research assistantships and unspecified assistantships available. Financial award application deadline: 4/15; financial award applicants required to submit FAFSA. *Unit head:* David W. Binkley, Director of Graduate Programs, 410-617-2281. *Application contact:* Maureen Faux, Executive Director, Graduate Admissions, 410-617-5020, Fax: 410-617-2002, E-mail: graduate@loyola.edu.

Marist College, Graduate Programs, School of Computer Science and Mathematics, Poughkeepsie, NY 12601-1387. Offers computer science/software development (MS); information systems (MS, Adv C); technology management (MS). Part-time and evening/weekend programs available. Postbaccalaureate distance learning degree programs offered (minimal on-campus study). *Entrance requirements:* For master's, resume. Additional exam requirements/recommendations for international students: Required—TOEFL (minimum score 550 paper-based; 213 computer-based; 80 iBT); Recommended—IELTS (minimum score 6.5). Electronic applications accepted. *Faculty research:* Data quality, artificial intelligence, imaging, analysis of algorithms, distributed systems and applications.

McMaster University, School of Graduate Studies, Faculty of Engineering, Department of Computing and Software, Hamilton, ON L8S 4M2, Canada. Offers computer science (M Sc, PhD); software engineering (M Eng, MA Sc, PhD). Part-time programs available. *Degree requirements:* For master's, thesis. *Entrance requirements:* Additional exam requirements/recommendations for international students: Required—TOEFL (minimum score 550 paper-based; 213 computer-based). *Faculty research:* Software engineering; theory of non-sequential systems; parallel and distributed computing; artificial intelligence; complexity, design, and analysis of algorithms; combinatorial computing, especially applications to molecular biology.

Mercer University, Graduate Studies, Macon Campus, School of Engineering, Macon, GA 31207-0003. Offers biomedical engineering (MSE); computer engineering (MSE); electrical engineering (MSE); engineering management (MSE); environmental engineering (MSE); environmental systems (MS); mechanical engineering (MSE); software engineering (MSE); software systems (MS); technical communications management (MS); technical management (MS). Part-time and evening/weekend programs available. Postbaccalaureate distance learning degree programs offered (no on-campus study). *Faculty:* 17 full-time (3 women), 1 part-time/adjunct (0 women). *Students:* 12 full-time (3 women), 113 part-time (28 women); includes 23 minority (13 Black or African American, non-Hispanic/Latino; 9 Asian, non-Hispanic/Latino; 1 Hispanic/Latino). Average age 31. In 2011, 44 master's awarded. *Degree requirements:* For master's, thesis or alternative. *Entrance requirements:* For master's, minimum undergraduate GPA of 3.0. Additional exam requirements/recommendations for international students: Required—TOEFL. *Application deadline:* For fall admission, 7/1 for domestic students; for spring admission, 11/15 for domestic students. Applications are processed on a rolling basis. Application fee: $35 ($50 for international students). Electronic applications accepted. *Expenses:* Contact institution. *Financial support:* Federal Work-Study available. *Unit head:* Dr. Wade H. Shaw, Dean, 478-301-2459, Fax: 478-301-5593, E-mail: shaw_wh@mercer.edu. *Application contact:* Greg Lofton, Graduate Program Coordinator, 478-301-5480, Fax: 478-301-5434, E-mail: lofton_g@mercer.edu. Web site: http://engineering.mercer.edu/.

Miami University, School of Engineering and Applied Science, Oxford, OH 45056. Offers chemical and paper engineering (MS); computational science and engineering (MS); computer science and software engineering (MCS), including computer science; software development (Certificate). *Entrance requirements:* For master's, GRE, minimum undergraduate GPA of 3.0 during previous 2 years or 2.75 overall. Additional exam requirements/recommendations for international students: Required—TOEFL. *Expenses:* Tuition, state resident: full-time $12,023; part-time $501 per credit hour. Tuition, nonresident: full-time $26,554; part-time $1107 per credit hour. *Required fees:* $528. *Unit head:* Dr. Marek Dollar, Dean, 513-529-0700, E-mail: seasfyi@muohio.edu.

Application contact: Graduate Admission Coordinator, 513-529-3734, Fax: 513-529-3734, E-mail: gradschool@muohio.edu. Web site: http://www.eas.muohio.edu/.

Monmouth University, The Graduate School, Program in Software Engineering, West Long Branch, NJ 07764-1898. Offers software development (Certificate); software engineering (MS, Certificate). Part-time and evening/weekend programs available. *Faculty:* 6 full-time (1 woman), 3 part-time/adjunct (0 women). *Students:* 14 full-time (3 women), 12 part-time (4 women); includes 5 minority (2 Black or African American, non-Hispanic/Latino; 1 Asian, non-Hispanic/Latino; 2 Hispanic/Latino), 11 international. Average age 29. 45 applicants, 91% accepted, 11 enrolled. In 2011, 9 master's awarded. *Degree requirements:* For master's, thesis or alternative, practicum. *Entrance requirements:* For master's, bachelor's degree in computer science, engineering, mathematics, or physics; minimum GPA of 3.0; 1 year of software development experience. Additional exam requirements/recommendations for international students: Required—TOEFL (minimum score 550 paper-based; 213 computer-based; 79 iBT), IELTS (minimum score 5) or Michigan English Language Assessment Battery (minimum score 77), Cambridge A, B, C. *Application deadline:* For fall admission, 7/15 priority date for domestic students, 6/1 for international students; for spring admission, 11/15 priority date for domestic students, 11/1 for international students. Applications are processed on a rolling basis. Application fee: $50. Electronic applications accepted. *Expenses:* Contact institution. *Financial support:* In 2011–12, 15 students received support, including 14 fellowships (averaging $2,111 per year), 8 research assistantships (averaging $4,438 per year); career-related internships or fieldwork, scholarships/grants, and unspecified assistantships also available. Support available to part-time students. Financial award applicants required to submit FAFSA. *Faculty research:* Conceptual structures, real time software, business rules, project management, software related to homeland security. *Unit head:* Dr. Daniela Rosca, Program Director, 732-571-4459, Fax: 732-263-5253, E-mail: drosca@monmouth.edu. *Application contact:* Kevin Roane, Director, Office of Graduate Admission, 732-571-3452, Fax: 732-263-5123, E-mail: gradadm@monmouth.edu. Web site: http://www.monmouth.edu/graduate_se.

Naval Postgraduate School, Departments and Academic Groups, Department of Computer Science, Monterey, CA 93943. Offers computer science (MS, PhD); identity management and cyber security (MA); modeling of virtual environments and simulations (MS, PhD); software engineering (MS, PhD). Program only open to commissioned officers of the United States and friendly nations and selected United States federal civilian employees. Part-time programs available. Postbaccalaureate distance learning degree programs offered (minimal on-campus study). *Faculty:* 89 full-time (13 women), 26 part-time/adjunct (7 women). *Students:* 140 full-time (17 women), 14 part-time (5 women); includes 29 minority (9 Black or African American, non-Hispanic/Latino; 1 American Indian or Alaska Native, non-Hispanic/Latino; 10 Asian, non-Hispanic/Latino; 9 Hispanic/Latino), 26 international. Average age 37. In 2011, 54 master's, 4 doctorates awarded. *Degree requirements:* For master's, thesis; for doctorate, thesis/dissertation. *Total annual research expenditures:* $8.4 million. *Unit head:* Peter Denning, Chairman, 831-656-3603, E-mail: pjd@nps.edu. *Application contact:* Acting Director of Admissions.

New Jersey Institute of Technology, Office of Graduate Studies, College of Computing Science, Department of Computer Science, Program in Software Engineering, Newark, NJ 07102. Offers MS. *Students:* 6 full-time (0 women), 5 part-time (1 woman); includes 8 minority (1 Black or African American, non-Hispanic/Latino; 1 American Indian or Alaska Native, non-Hispanic/Latino; 3 Asian, non-Hispanic/Latino; 2 Hispanic/Latino; 1 Two or more races, non-Hispanic/Latino), 1 international. Average age 33. 53 applicants, 62% accepted, 3 enrolled. In 2011, 1 master's awarded. *Entrance requirements:* Additional exam requirements/recommendations for international students: Required—TOEFL (minimum score 550 paper-based; 213 computer-based; 79 iBT). *Application deadline:* For fall admission, 6/1 priority date for domestic students, 5/1 for international students; for spring admission, 11/15 priority date for domestic students, 11/15 for international students. Applications are processed on a rolling basis. Application fee: $65. Electronic applications accepted. *Expenses:* Tuition, state resident: full-time $7980; part-time $867 per credit. Tuition, nonresident: full-time $11,336; part-time $1196 per credit. *Required fees:* $230 per credit. *Financial support:* Application deadline: 1/15. *Unit head:* Dr. Michael A. Baltrush, Interim Chair, 973-596-3386, E-mail: michael.a.baltrush@njit.edu. *Application contact:* Kathryn Kelly, Director of Admissions, 973-596-3300, Fax: 973-596-3461, E-mail: admissions@njit.edu. Web site: http://cs.njit.edu/academics/graduate/ms-se/index.php.

North Dakota State University, College of Graduate and Interdisciplinary Studies, College of Science and Mathematics, Department of Computer Science, Program in Software Engineering, Fargo, ND 58108. Offers MS, PhD, Certificate. Part-time programs available. Postbaccalaureate distance learning degree programs offered (minimal on-campus study). *Students:* 45 full-time (8 women), 44 part-time (11 women); includes 7 minority (1 Black or African American, non-Hispanic/Latino; 1 American Indian or Alaska Native, non-Hispanic/Latino; 3 Asian, non-Hispanic/Latino; 1 Hispanic/Latino; 1 Two or more races, non-Hispanic/Latino), 64 international. 40 applicants, 78% accepted, 14 enrolled. In 2011, 2 master's, 2 doctorates, 1 other advanced degree awarded. Terminal master's awarded for partial completion of doctoral program. *Degree requirements:* For master's, comprehensive exam, thesis optional; for doctorate, thesis/dissertation, qualifying exam. *Entrance requirements:* For master's and doctorate, minimum GPA of 3.0 in software engineering or related field. Additional exam requirements/recommendations for international students: Required—TOEFL (minimum score 550 paper-based; 213 computer-based; 79 iBT). *Application deadline:* For fall admission, 3/31 priority date for domestic students. Applications are processed on a rolling basis. Application fee: $35. Electronic applications accepted. *Financial support:* Research assistantships with full tuition reimbursements, teaching assistantships with full tuition reimbursements, career-related internships or fieldwork, Federal Work-Study, institutionally sponsored loans, and tuition waivers (full) available. Financial award application deadline: 4/15. *Faculty research:* Data knowledge and engineering requirements, formal methods for software, software measurement and mobile agents, software development process. *Unit head:* Dr. Brian Slator, Head, 701-231-8562, Fax: 701-231-8255. *Application contact:* Dr. Ken R. Nygard, Graduate Coordinator, 701-231-9460, Fax: 701-231-8255, E-mail: kendall.nygard@ndsu.edu.

Northern Kentucky University, Office of Graduate Programs, College of Informatics, Department of Computer Science, Highland Heights, KY 41099. Offers computer science (MSCS); geographic information systems (Certificate); secure software engineering (Certificate). Part-time and evening/weekend programs available. *Faculty:* 11 full-time (3 women), 1 part-time/adjunct. *Students:* 26 full-time (4 women), 7 part-time (2 women); includes 4 minority (1 Black or African American, non-Hispanic/Latino; 3 Asian, non-Hispanic/Latino), 4 international. Average age 34. 33 applicants, 42% accepted, 7 enrolled. In 2011, 2 master's, 1 Certificate awarded. *Degree requirements:* For master's, thesis optional. *Entrance requirements:* For master's, minimum GPA of 3.0, at least 4 semesters of undergraduate study in computer science including intermediate computer programming and data structures, one year of calculus, one course in discrete mathematics. Additional exam requirements/recommendations for

international students: Required—TOEFL (minimum score 550 paper-based; 213 computer-based; 79 iBT); Recommended—IELTS (minimum score 6.5). *Application deadline:* For fall admission, 8/1 for domestic students, 6/1 for international students; for spring admission, 12/1 for domestic students, 10/1 for international students. Applications are processed on a rolling basis. Application fee: $40. Electronic applications accepted. *Expenses:* Tuition, state resident: full-time $7614; part-time $423 per credit hour. Tuition, nonresident: full-time $13,104; part-time $728 per credit hour. Tuition and fees vary according to degree level and reciprocity agreements. *Financial support:* Scholarships/grants and unspecified assistantships available. Financial award applicants required to submit FAFSA. *Faculty research:* Data privacy, data mining, wireless security, secure software engineering, secure networking. *Unit head:* Dr. Wei Hao, Interim MSCS Director, 859-572-5468, Fax: 859-572-6097, E-mail: haow1@nku.edu. *Application contact:* Dr. Peg Griffin, Director of Graduate Programs, 859-572-6934, Fax: 859-572-6670, E-mail: griffinp@nku.edu. Web site: http://informatics.nku.edu/csc/mscs.

Northwestern University, School of Continuing Studies, Program in Information Systems, Evanston, IL 60208. Offers database and Internet technologies (MS); information systems management (MS); information systems security (MS); software project management and development (MS).

Oakland University, Graduate Study and Lifelong Learning, School of Engineering and Computer Science, Department of Computer Science and Engineering, Rochester, MI 48309-4401. Offers computer science (MS); embedded systems (MS); information systems engineering (MS); software engineering (MS). Part-time and evening/weekend programs available. *Entrance requirements:* For master's, minimum GPA of 3.0 for unconditional admission. Electronic applications accepted. *Expenses:* Contact institution. *Faculty research:* Cyber security, 3D imaging of neurochemicals in rat brains.

Pace University, Seidenberg School of Computer Science and Information Systems, New York, NY 10038. Offers computer communications and networks (Certificate); computer science (MS); computing studies (DPS); information systems (MS); Internet technologies for e-commerce (Certificate); Internet technology (MS); object-oriented programming (Certificate); security and information assurance (Certificate); software development and engineering (MS); telecommunications (MS, Certificate). Part-time and evening/weekend programs available. *Students:* 82 full-time (19 women), 356 part-time (99 women); includes 175 minority (64 Black or African American, non-Hispanic/Latino; 1 American Indian or Alaska Native, non-Hispanic/Latino; 59 Asian, non-Hispanic/Latino; 47 Hispanic/Latino; 4 Two or more races, non-Hispanic/Latino), 72 international. Average age 37. 304 applicants, 67% accepted, 92 enrolled. In 2011, 136 master's, 9 doctorates, 32 other advanced degrees awarded. *Entrance requirements:* For master's, GRE General Test. Additional exam requirements/recommendations for international students: Required—TOEFL. *Application deadline:* For fall admission, 7/31 priority date for domestic students; for spring admission, 11/30 for domestic students. Applications are processed on a rolling basis. Application fee: $70. Electronic applications accepted. *Expenses:* Contact institution. *Financial support:* Research assistantships and career-related internships or fieldwork available. Support available to part-time students. Financial award applicants required to submit FAFSA. *Unit head:* Dr. Constance Knapp, Interim Dean, 914-773-3750, Fax: 914-773-3533, E-mail: cknapp@pace.edu. *Application contact:* Susan Ford-Goldschein, Director of Graduate Admissions, 914-422-4283, Fax: 914-422-4287, E-mail: gradwp@pace.edu. Web site: http://www.pace.edu/.

Penn State Great Valley, Graduate Studies, Engineering Division, Malvern, PA 19355-1488. Offers engineering management (MEM); information science (MS); software engineering (MSE); systems engineering (M Eng). Postbaccalaureate distance learning degree programs offered (no on-campus study). *Unit head:* Dr. James A. Nemes, Interim Director, Academic Affairs, 610-648-3335 Ext. 610, Fax: 648-648-3377, E-mail: jan16@psu.edu. *Application contact:* 610-648-3242, Fax: 610-889-1334. Web site: http://www.sgps.psu.edu/Level3.aspx?id=662.

Polytechnic Institute of New York University, Department of Computer Science and Engineering, Major in Software Engineering, Brooklyn, NY 11201-2990. Offers Graduate Certificate. *Application deadline:* For fall admission, 7/31 priority date for domestic students, 4/30 for international students; for spring admission, 12/31 priority date for domestic students, 11/30 for international students. Applications are processed on a rolling basis. Application fee: $75. Electronic applications accepted. *Expenses:* Tuition: Full-time $22,464; part-time $1248 per credit. *Required fees:* $501 per semester. *Unit head:* Dr. Keith W. Ross, Head, 718-260-3859, Fax: 718-260-3609, E-mail: ross@poly.edu. *Application contact:* JeanCarlo Bonilla, Director, Graduate Enrollment Management, 718-260-3182, Fax: 718-260-3624, E-mail: gradinfo@poly.edu. Web site: http://www.poly.edu/cis/graduate/certificates/.

Portland State University, Graduate Studies, Maseeh College of Engineering and Computer Science, Department of Computer Science, Portland, OR 97207-0751. Offers computer science (MS, PhD); software engineering (MSE). Part-time programs available. *Degree requirements:* For master's, thesis or alternative; for doctorate, thesis/dissertation. *Entrance requirements:* For master's, GRE General Test, minimum GPA of 3.0 in upper-division course work, 2 letters of recommendation, BS in computer science or allied field; for doctorate, MS in computer science or allied field. Additional exam requirements/recommendations for international students: Required—TOEFL (minimum score 550 paper-based; 213 computer-based). *Faculty research:* Formal methods, database systems, parallel programming environments, computer security, software tools.

Regis University, College for Professional Studies, School of Computer and Information Sciences, Denver, CO 80221-1099. Offers database administration with Oracle (Certificate); database development (Certificate); database technologies (M Sc); enterprise Java software development (Certificate); enterprise resource planning (Certificate); executive information technologies (Certificate); information assurance (M Sc, Certificate); information technology management (M Sc); software engineering (M Sc, Certificate); software engineering and database technologies (M Sc); storage area networks (Certificate); systems engineering (M Sc, Certificate). Offered at Boulder Campus, Northwest Denver Campus, Southeast Denver Campus, Fort Collins Campus, Colorado Springs Campus, and Broomfield Campus. Part-time and evening/weekend programs available. Postbaccalaureate distance learning degree programs offered (no on-campus study). *Degree requirements:* For master's, thesis, final research project. *Entrance requirements:* For master's, 2 years of related experience, resume, interview; for Certificate, 2 years of related experience, resumé. Additional exam requirements/recommendations for international students: Required—TOEFL (minimum score 213 computer-based), TWE (minimum score 5) or university-based test. Electronic applications accepted. *Expenses:* Contact institution. *Faculty research:* Secure Virtual Laboratory Architecture, Joint IA project with W2C06 Institute, Information Policy, OLTP and OLAP Technologies, knowledge management, software architectures.

Rochester Institute of Technology, Graduate Enrollment Services, B. Thomas Golisano College of Computing and Information Sciences, Department of Software

Engineering, Rochester, NY 14623-5603. Offers MS. Part-time programs available. *Students:* 19 full-time (2 women), 5 part-time (0 women); includes 1 minority (Black or African American, non-Hispanic/Latino), 16 international. Average age 27. 38 applicants, 79% accepted, 16 enrolled. In 2011, 5 master's awarded. *Degree requirements:* For master's, thesis or project. *Entrance requirements:* For master's, GRE, minimum GPA of 3.0. Additional exam requirements/recommendations for international students: Required—TOEFL (minimum score 570 paper-based; 230 computer-based; 88 iBT) or IELTS (minimum score 6.5). *Application deadline:* For fall admission, 2/15 priority date for domestic students, 2/15 for international students; for winter admission, 11/1 priority date for domestic students, 11/1 for international students; for spring admission, 2/1 priority date for domestic students, 2/1 for international students. Applications are processed on a rolling basis. Application fee: $50. Electronic applications accepted. *Expenses: Tuition:* Full-time $34,659; part-time $963 per credit hour. *Required fees:* $228; $76 per quarter. *Financial support:* Research assistantships with partial tuition reimbursements, teaching assistantships with partial tuition reimbursements, career-related internships or fieldwork, scholarships/grants, and unspecified assistantships available. Support available to part-time students. Financial award applicants required to submit FAFSA. *Faculty research:* Software engineering education, software architecture and design, architectural styles and design patterns, mathematical foundations of software engineering, object-oriented software development, augmented and virtual reality systems, engineering of real-time and embedded software systems, concurrent systems, distributed systems, data communications and networking, programming environments and tools, computer graphics, computer vision. *Unit head:* Dr. Stephanie Ludi, Graduate Program Director, 585-475-7407, E-mail: sal@se.rit.edu. *Application contact:* Diane Ellison, Assistant Vice President, Graduate Enrollment Services, 585-475-2229, Fax: 585-475-7164, E-mail: gradinfo@rit.edu. Web site: http://www.se.rit.edu.

Rose-Hulman Institute of Technology, Faculty of Engineering and Applied Sciences, Department of Computer Science and Software Engineering, Terre Haute, IN 47803-3999. Offers software engineering (MS). Part-time programs available. *Faculty:* 14 full-time (1 woman). *Students:* 5 part-time (0 women). Average age 29. 2 applicants, 100% accepted, 2 enrolled. *Degree requirements:* For master's, thesis. *Entrance requirements:* For master's, GRE, minimum GPA of 3.0. Additional exam requirements/recommendations for international students: Required—TOEFL (minimum score 580 paper-based; 237 computer-based; 92 iBT). *Application deadline:* For fall admission, 2/1 priority date for domestic students. Applications are processed on a rolling basis. Application fee: $0. *Expenses: Tuition:* Full-time $37,197; part-time $1085 per credit hour. *Financial support:* Fellowships with full and partial tuition reimbursements, research assistantships with full and partial tuition reimbursements, and tuition waivers (full and partial) available. *Total annual research expenditures:* $64,236. *Unit head:* Dr. Cary Laxer, Chairman, 812-877-8429, Fax: 812-872-6060, E-mail: laxer@rose-hulman.edu. *Application contact:* Dr. Daniel J. Moore, Associate Dean of the Faculty, 812-877-8110, Fax: 812-877-8061, E-mail: daniel.j.moore@rose-hulman.edu. Web site: http://www.cs.rose-hulman.edu/.

Royal Military College of Canada, Division of Graduate Studies and Research, Engineering Division, Department of Electrical and Computer Engineering, Kingston, ON K7K 7B4, Canada. Offers computer engineering (M Eng, PhD); electrical engineering (M Eng, PhD); software engineering (M Eng, PhD). *Degree requirements:* For master's, thesis; for doctorate, comprehensive exam, thesis/dissertation. *Entrance requirements:* For master's, honours degree with second-class standing in the appropriate field; for doctorate, master's degree. Electronic applications accepted.

St. Mary's University, Graduate School, Department of Engineering, Program in Software Engineering, San Antonio, TX 78228-8507. Offers MS. Part-time programs available. *Degree requirements:* For master's, comprehensive exam. *Entrance requirements:* For master's, GRE. Additional exam requirements/recommendations for international students: Required—TOEFL (minimum score 550 paper-based; 213 computer-based; 80 iBT). Electronic applications accepted.

San Francisco State University, Division of Graduate Studies, College of Science and Engineering, Department of Computer Science, San Francisco, CA 94132-1722. Offers computer science (MS); computer science: computing and business (MS); computer science: computing for life sciences (MS); computer science: software and engineering (MS). Part-time programs available. *Application deadline:* Applications are processed on a rolling basis. *Unit head:* Dr. Dragutin Petkovic, Chair, 415-338-1008, Fax: 415-338-6136, E-mail: csgrad@sfsu.edu. *Application contact:* Barry Levine, Graduate Coordinator, E-mail: levine@sfsu.edu. Web site: http://cs.sfsu.edu/grad/graduate.html.

San Jose State University, Graduate Studies and Research, Charles W. Davidson College of Engineering, Department of Computer Engineering, San Jose, CA 95192-0001. Offers computer engineering (MS); software engineering (MS). *Degree requirements:* For master's, comprehensive exam, thesis. *Entrance requirements:* For master's, GRE General Test. Electronic applications accepted. *Faculty research:* Robotics, database management systems, computer networks.

Santa Clara University, School of Engineering, Program in Computer Science and Engineering, Santa Clara, CA 95053. Offers computer science and engineering (MS, PhD, Engineer); information assurance (Certificate); networking (Certificate); software engineering (MS, Certificate). Part-time and evening/weekend programs available. *Students:* 151 full-time (58 women), 121 part-time (39 women); includes 62 minority (4 Black or African American, non-Hispanic/Latino; 52 Asian, non-Hispanic/Latino; 3 Hispanic/Latino; 1 Native Hawaiian or other Pacific Islander, non-Hispanic/Latino; 2 Two or more races, non-Hispanic/Latino), 156 international. Average age 29. 258 applicants, 48% accepted, 70 enrolled. In 2011, 87 degrees awarded. *Degree requirements:* For master's, thesis (for some programs); for doctorate, thesis/dissertation; for other advanced degree, thesis. *Entrance requirements:* For master's, GRE, transcript; for doctorate, GRE, master's degree or equivalent; for other advanced degree, master's degree, published paper. Additional exam requirements/recommendations for international students: Required—TOEFL (minimum score 550 paper-based; 213 computer-based; 79 iBT). *Application deadline:* For fall admission, 8/12 for domestic students, 7/15 for international students; for winter admission, 10/28 for domestic students, 9/23 for international students; for spring admission, 2/25 for domestic students, 1/21 for international students. Applications are processed on a rolling basis. Application fee: $60. Electronic applications accepted. *Expenses:* Contact institution. *Financial support:* Research assistantships and teaching assistantships available. Financial award application deadline: 3/2; financial award applicants required to submit FAFSA. *Unit head:* Dr. Alex Zecevic, Chair, 408-554-2394, E-mail: azecevic@scu.edu. *Application contact:* Stacey Tinker, Director of Enrollment Management, 408-554-4748, Fax: 408-554-4323, E-mail: stinker@scu.edu.

Seattle University, College of Science and Engineering, Program in Software Engineering, Seattle, WA 98122-1090. Offers MSE. Part-time and evening/weekend programs available. *Faculty:* 10 full-time (4 women), 1 (woman) part-time/adjunct. *Students:* 16 full-time (7 women), 30 part-time (8 women); includes 13 minority (1 Black or African American, non-Hispanic/Latino; 10 Asian, non-Hispanic/Latino; 2 Hispanic/Latino), 15 international. Average age 30. 45 applicants, 49% accepted, 10 enrolled. In 2011, 17 master's awarded. *Degree requirements:* For master's, thesis. *Entrance requirements:* For master's, GRE General Test, 2 years of related work experience. *Application deadline:* For fall admission, 7/1 for domestic students. Application fee: $55. *Financial support:* Career-related internships or fieldwork and Federal Work-Study available. Support available to part-time students. Financial award applicants required to submit FAFSA. *Unit head:* Dr. Everald Mills, Director, 206-296-5511, Fax: 206-296-2071. *Application contact:* Janet Shandley, Associate Dean of Graduate Admissions, 206-296-5900, Fax: 206-298-5656, E-mail: grad_admissions@seattleu.edu. Web site: http://www.seattleu.edu/.

Southern Methodist University, Bobby B. Lyle School of Engineering, Department of Computer Science and Engineering, Dallas, TX 75275-0122. Offers computer engineering (MS Cp E, PhD); computer science (MS, PhD); security engineering (MS); software engineering (MS). Part-time and evening/weekend programs available. Postbaccalaureate distance learning degree programs offered (no on-campus study). Terminal master's awarded for partial completion of doctoral program. *Degree requirements:* For master's, thesis optional; for doctorate, thesis/dissertation, oral and written qualifying exams, oral final exam (PhD). *Entrance requirements:* For master's, GRE General Test, minimum GPA of 3.0 in last 2 years; bachelor's degree in engineering, mathematics, or sciences; for doctorate, preliminary counseling exam (PhD), minimum GPA of 3.0, bachelor's degree in related field, MA (DE). Additional exam requirements/recommendations for international students: Required—TOEFL (minimum score 550 paper-based; 213 computer-based). *Faculty research:* Trusted and high performance network computing, software engineering and management, knowledge engineering and management, computer arithmetic, computer architecture and CAD.

Southern Polytechnic State University, School of Computing and Software Engineering, Department of Computer Science and Software Engineering, Marietta, GA 30060-2896. Offers computer science (MS, Graduate Transition Certificate); software engineering (MSSWE, Graduate Certificate); software engineering fundamentals (Graduate Transition Certificate). Part-time and evening/weekend programs available. Postbaccalaureate distance learning degree programs offered (no on-campus study). *Faculty:* 12 full-time (1 woman), 3 part-time/adjunct (0 women). *Students:* 63 full-time (14 women), 77 part-time (17 women); includes 43 minority (29 Black or African American, non-Hispanic/Latino; 12 Asian, non-Hispanic/Latino; 2 Hispanic/Latino), 39 international. Average age 31. 94 applicants, 77% accepted, 45 enrolled. In 2011, 29 master's, 2 other advanced degrees awarded. *Degree requirements:* For master's, thesis optional, capstone (software engineering). *Entrance requirements:* For master's, GRE (recommended). Additional exam requirements/recommendations for international students: Required—TOEFL (minimum score 550 paper-based; 213 computer-based; 79 iBT), IELTS (minimum score 6.5). *Application deadline:* For fall admission, 7/1 priority date for domestic students, 5/1 for international students; for spring admission, 11/1 priority date for domestic students, 9/1 for international students. Applications are processed on a rolling basis. Application fee: $50. Electronic applications accepted. *Expenses:* Tuition, state resident: full-time $2592; part-time $216 per semester hour. Tuition, nonresident: full-time $9408; part-time $784 per semester hour. *Required fees:* $698 per term. *Financial support:* In 2011–12, 13 students received support, including 3 research assistantships with tuition reimbursements available, 11 teaching assistantships with tuition reimbursements available; career-related internships or fieldwork, scholarships/grants, unspecified assistantships, and cooperative programs also available. Financial award application deadline: 5/1; financial award applicants required to submit FAFSA. *Faculty research:* Image processing and artificial intelligence information retrieval, distributed computing, telemedicine applications, enterprise architectures, databases, software requirements engineering, software quality and metrics, usability, parallel and distributed computing, information security. *Unit head:* Dr. Venu Dasigi, Chair, 678-915-3571, Fax: 678-915-5511, E-mail: vdasigi@spsu.edu. *Application contact:* Nikki Palamiotis, Director of Graduate Studies, 678-915-4276, Fax: 678-915-7292, E-mail: npalamio@spsu.edu. Web site: http://www.spsu.edu/cswe/.

Stevens Institute of Technology, Graduate School, Charles V. Schaefer Jr. School of Engineering, Department of Computer Science, Hoboken, NJ 07030. Offers computer graphics (Certificate); computer science (MS, PhD); computer systems (Certificate); database management systems (Certificate); distributed systems (Certificate); elements of computer science (Certificate); enterprise computing (Certificate); enterprise security and information assurance (Certificate); health informatics (Certificate); multimedia experience and management (Certificate); networks and systems administration (Certificate); security and privacy (Certificate); service oriented computing (Certificate); software design (Certificate); theoretical computer science (Certificate). Part-time and evening/weekend programs available. Terminal master's awarded for partial completion of doctoral program. *Degree requirements:* For master's, thesis optional; for doctorate, variable foreign language requirement, comprehensive exam, thesis/dissertation. *Entrance requirements:* For master's and doctorate, GRE, minimum GPA of 3.0. Additional exam requirements/recommendations for international students: Required—TOEFL. Electronic applications accepted. *Faculty research:* Semantics, reliability theory, programming language, cyber security.

Stevens Institute of Technology, Graduate School, School of Systems and Enterprises, Program in Software Engineering, Hoboken, NJ 07030. Offers MS. *Entrance requirements:* Additional exam requirements/recommendations for international students: Required—TOEFL.

Stony Brook University, State University of New York, Graduate School, College of Engineering and Applied Sciences, Department of Computer Science, Stony Brook, NY 11794. Offers computer science (MS, PhD); information systems (Certificate); information systems engineering (MS); software engineering (Certificate). *Degree requirements:* For master's, thesis or alternative; for doctorate, comprehensive exam, thesis/dissertation. *Entrance requirements:* For master's and doctorate, GRE General Test. Additional exam requirements/recommendations for international students: Required—TOEFL. *Faculty research:* Artificial intelligence, computer architecture, database management systems, VLSI, operating systems.

Stratford University, School of Graduate Studies, Falls Church, VA 22043. Offers accounting (MS); business administration (IMBA, MBA); enterprise business management (MS); entrepreneurial management (MS); information assurance (MS); information systems (MS); software engineering (MS); telecommunications (MS). Part-time and evening/weekend programs available. Postbaccalaureate distance learning degree programs offered (no on-campus study). *Degree requirements:* For master's, comprehensive exam, capstone project. *Entrance requirements:* For master's, GRE or GMAT, baccalaureate degree. Additional exam requirements/recommendations for international students: Required—TOEFL (minimum score 213 computer-based, 79 iBT) or IELTS (6.5). Electronic applications accepted.

Strayer University, Graduate Studies, Washington, DC 20005-2603. Offers accounting (MS); acquisition (MBA); business administration (MBA); communications technology (MS); educational management (M Ed); finance (MBA); health services administration (MHSA); hospitality and tourism management (MBA); human resource management (MBA); information systems (MS), including computer security management, decision support system management, enterprise resource management, network management, software engineering management, systems development management; management (MBA); management information systems (MS); marketing (MBA); professional accounting (MS), including accounting information systems, controllership, taxation; public administration (MPA); supply chain management (MBA); technology in education (M Ed). Programs also offered at campus locations in Birmingham, AL; Chamblee, GA; Cobb County, GA; Morrow, GA; White Marsh, MD; Charleston, SC; Columbia, SC; Greensboro, NC; Greenville, SC; Lexington, KY; Louisville, KY; Nashville, TN; North Raleigh, NC; Washington, DC. Part-time and evening/weekend programs available. Postbaccalaureate distance, learning degree programs offered (minimal on-campus study). *Degree requirements:* For master's, thesis. *Entrance requirements:* For master's, GMAT, GRE General Test, bachelor's degree from an accredited college or university, minimum undergraduate GPA of 2.75. Electronic applications accepted.

Tennessee Technological University, Graduate School, College of Engineering, Department of Computer Science, Cookeville, TN 38505. Offers computer software and scientific applications (MS); Internet-based computing (MS). Part-time programs available. *Students:* 4 full-time (2 women), 12 part-time (1 woman), 2 international. 27 applicants, 59% accepted, 5 enrolled. In 2011, 4 master's awarded. *Degree requirements:* For master's, thesis or alternative. *Entrance requirements:* For master's, GRE. Additional exam requirements/recommendations for international students: Required—TOEFL (minimum score 550 paper-based; 79 iBT), IELTS (minimum score 5.5), PTE Academic. *Application deadline:* For fall admission, 8/1 for domestic students, 5/1 for international students; for spring admission, 12/1 for domestic students, 10/1 for international students. Application fee: $25 ($30 for international students). Electronic applications accepted. *Expenses:* Tuition, state resident: full-time $8094; part-time $422 per credit hour. Tuition, nonresident: full-time $20,574; part-time $1046 per credit hour. *Financial support:* In 2011–12, 4 research assistantships (averaging $7,500 per year), 3 teaching assistantships (averaging $7,500 per year) were awarded. Financial award application deadline: 4/1. *Unit head:* Dr. Doug Talbert, Interim Chairperson, 931-372-3691, Fax: 931-372-3686, E-mail: dtalbert@tntech.edu. *Application contact:* Shelia K. Kendrick, Coordinator of Graduate Admissions, 931-372-3808, Fax: 931-372-3497, E-mail: skendrick@tntech.edu.

Texas State University–San Marcos, Graduate School, College of Science and Engineering, Department of Computer Science, Program in Software Engineering, San Marcos, TX 78666. Offers MS. *Faculty:* 4 full-time (1 woman). *Students:* 8 full-time (0 women), 9 part-time (2 women); includes 7 minority (1 Black or African American, non-Hispanic/Latino; 2 Asian, non-Hispanic/Latino; 4 Hispanic/Latino), 2 international. Average age 35. 19 applicants, 53% accepted, 4 enrolled. In 2011, 4 master's awarded. *Degree requirements:* For master's, comprehensive exam, thesis (for some programs). *Entrance requirements:* For master's, GRE General Test, minimum GPA of 2.75 in last 60 hours of course work. Additional exam requirements/recommendations for international students: Required—TOEFL (minimum score 550 paper-based; 213 computer-based; 78 iBT). *Application deadline:* For fall admission, 6/15 priority date for domestic students, 6/1 for international students; for spring admission, 10/15 priority date for domestic students, 10/1 for international students. Applications are processed on a rolling basis. Application fee: $40 ($90 for international students). Electronic applications accepted. *Expenses:* Tuition, state resident: full-time $6408; part-time $3204 per semester. Tuition, nonresident: full-time $14,832; part-time $7416 per semester. *Required fees:* $1824; $912 per semester. Tuition and fees vary according to course load. *Financial support:* In 2011–12, 4 students received support, including 3 teaching assistantships (averaging $10,152 per year); research assistantships, Federal Work-Study, institutionally sponsored loans, scholarships/grants, health care benefits, and unspecified assistantships also available. Support available to part-time students. Financial award application deadline: 4/1; financial award applicants required to submit FAFSA. *Unit head:* Dr. Wuxu Peng, Head, 512-245-3874, Fax: 512-245-8750, E-mail: wp01@txstate.edu. *Application contact:* Dr. Wuxu Peng, Head, 512-245-3874, Fax: 512-245-8750, E-mail: wp01@txstate.edu. Web site: http://www.cstxstate.edu/.

Texas Tech University, Graduate School, Edward E. Whitacre Jr. College of Engineering, Department of Computer Science, Lubbock, TX 79409. Offers computer science (MS, PhD); software engineering (MS). Part-time programs available. Postbaccalaureate distance learning degree programs offered (minimal on-campus study). *Faculty:* 18 full-time (3 women), 1 part-time/adjunct (0 women). *Students:* 88 full-time (10 women), 34 part-time (6 women); includes 7 minority (1 Asian, non-Hispanic/Latino; 4 Hispanic/Latino; 2 Two or more races, non-Hispanic/Latino), 93 international. Average age 27. 271 applicants, 48% accepted, 25 enrolled. In 2011, 27 master's, 2 doctorates awarded. *Degree requirements:* For master's, thesis or alternative; for doctorate, thesis/dissertation. *Entrance requirements:* For master's and doctorate, GRE General Test, minimum GPA of 3.0, statement of purpose, 3 letters of recommendation. Additional exam requirements/recommendations for international students: Required—TOEFL (minimum score 600 paper-based; 250 computer-based; 100 iBT). *Application deadline:* For fall admission, 6/1 priority date for domestic students, 1/15 for international students; for spring admission, 9/1 priority date for domestic students, 6/15 for international students. Applications are processed on a rolling basis. Application fee: $50 ($75 for international students). Electronic applications accepted. *Expenses:* Tuition, state resident: full-time $5899; part-time $245.80 per credit hour. Tuition, nonresident: full-time $13,411; part-time $558.80 per credit hour. *Required fees:* $2680.60; $86.50 per credit hour. $920.30 per semester. *Financial support:* In 2011–12, 25 students received support. Application deadline: 4/15; applicants required to submit FAFSA. *Faculty research:* Artificial intelligence, software engineering and languages, high performance computing, logic programming, image processing. *Total annual research expenditures:* $848,686. *Unit head:* Dr. Rattikorn Hewett, Chair, 806-742-3527, Fax: 806-742-3519, E-mail: rattikorn.hewett@ttu.edu. *Application contact:* Jennifer Hearron, Staff Graduate Advisor, 806-742-3527, Fax: 806-742-3519, E-mail: cs.grad_advisor@ttu.edu. Web site: http://www.cs.ttu.edu/.

Towson University, Program in Applied Information Technology, Towson, MD 21252-0001. Offers applied information technology (MS, PhD); database management systems (Postbaccalaureate Certificate); information security and assurance (Postbaccalaureate Certificate); information systems management (Postbaccalaureate Certificate); Internet applications development (Postbaccalaureate Certificate); networking technologies (Postbaccalaureate Certificate); software engineering (Postbaccalaureate Certificate). *Students:* 145 full-time (32 women), 270 part-time (78 women); includes 151 minority (96 Black or African American, non-Hispanic/Latino; 35 Asian, non-Hispanic/Latino; 17 Hispanic/Latino; 1 Native Hawaiian or other Pacific Islander, non-Hispanic/Latino; 2 Two or more races, non-Hispanic/Latino), 93 international. *Expenses:* Tuition, state resident: part-time $337 per credit. Tuition, nonresident: part-time $709 per credit. *Required fees:*

$99 per credit. *Unit head:* Mike O'Leary, Graduate Program Director, 410-704-4757, E-mail: moleary@towson.edu.

Université du Québec en Outaouais, Graduate Programs, Department of Language Studies, Gatineau, QC J8X 3X7, Canada. Offers localization (DESS); second and foreign language teaching (Diploma). *Students:* 20 part-time. *Application deadline:* For fall admission, 6/1 priority date for domestic students, 3/1 for international students; for winter admission, 11/1 priority date for domestic students, 10/1 for international students. Application fee: $30. *Financial support:* Research assistantships available. *Unit head:* Georges Farid, Director, 819-595-3900 Ext. 4444, Fax: 819-595-4450, E-mail: georges.farid@uqo.ca. *Application contact:* Registrar's Office, 819-773-1850, Fax: 819-773-1835, E-mail: registraire@uqo.ca.

Université Laval, Faculty of Sciences and Engineering, Program in Software Engineering, Québec, QC G1K 7P4, Canada. Offers Diploma. Part-time programs available. *Entrance requirements:* For degree, knowledge of French. Electronic applications accepted.

The University of Alabama in Huntsville, School of Graduate Studies, College of Engineering, Department of Electrical and Computer Engineering, Huntsville, AL 35899. Offers computer engineering (MSE, PhD), including information assurance (MSE); electrical engineering (MSE, PhD), including optics and phontonics technology (MSE), opto-electronics (MSE); optics and photonics (MSE); software engineering (MSSE). Part-time and evening/weekend programs available. *Faculty:* 22 full-time (3 women), 4 part-time/adjunct (0 women). *Students:* 52 full-time (12 women), 138 part-time (22 women); includes 20 minority (7 Black or African American, non-Hispanic/Latino; 2 American Indian or Alaska Native, non-Hispanic/Latino; 8 Asian, non-Hispanic/Latino; 2 Hispanic/Latino; 1 Two or more races, non-Hispanic/Latino), 37 international. Average age 31. 157 applicants, 65% accepted, 48 enrolled. In 2011, 26 master's, 6 doctorates awarded. *Degree requirements:* For master's, comprehensive exam, thesis or alternative, oral and written exams; for doctorate, comprehensive exam, thesis/dissertation, oral and written exams. *Entrance requirements:* For master's, GRE General Test, appropriate bachelor's degree, minimum GPA of 3.0; for doctorate, GRE General Test, minimum GPA of 3.0. Additional exam requirements/recommendations for international students: Required—TOEFL (minimum score 500 paper-based; 173 computer-based; 62 iBT). *Application deadline:* For fall admission, 7/15 for domestic students, 4/1 for international students; for spring admission, 11/30 for domestic students, 9/1 for international students. Applications are processed on a rolling basis. Application fee: $40 ($50 for international students). Electronic applications accepted. *Expenses:* Tuition, state resident: full-time $7830; part-time $473.50 per credit. Tuition, nonresident: full-time $18,748; part-time $1128.33 per credit. Tuition and fees vary according to course load and program. *Financial support:* In 2011–12, 29 students received support, including 2 fellowships (averaging $11,154 per year), 9 research assistantships with full and partial tuition reimbursements available (averaging $10,959 per year), 20 teaching assistantships with full and partial tuition reimbursements available (averaging $11,330 per year); career-related internships or fieldwork, Federal Work-Study, institutionally sponsored loans, scholarships/grants, health care benefits, tuition waivers (full), and unspecified assistantships also available. Support available to part-time students. Financial award application deadline: 4/1; financial award applicants required to submit FAFSA. *Faculty research:* Optical signal processing, electromagnetics, photonics, nonlinear waves, computer architecture. *Total annual research expenditures:* $16.5 million. *Unit head:* Dr. Robert Lindquist, Chair, 256-824-6316, Fax: 256-824-6803, E-mail: lindquis@ece.uah.edu. *Application contact:* Kim Gray, Graduate Studies Admissions Coordinator, 256-824-6002, Fax: 256-824-6405, E-mail: deangrad@uah.edu. Web site: http://www.ece.uah.edu/.

The University of Alabama in Huntsville, School of Graduate Studies, College of Science, Department of Computer Science, Huntsville, AL 35899. Offers computer science (MS, PhD); software engineering (MSSE, Certificate). Part-time and evening/weekend programs available. Postbaccalaureate distance learning degree programs offered (minimal on-campus study). *Faculty:* 10 full-time (3 women). *Students:* 46 full-time (21 women), 69 part-time (13 women); includes 10 minority (6 Black or African American, non-Hispanic/Latino; 3 Asian, non-Hispanic/Latino; 1 Hispanic/Latino), 37 international. Average age 32. 130 applicants, 53% accepted, 33 enrolled. In 2011, 2 master's, 2 doctorates, 2 other advanced degrees awarded. *Degree requirements:* For master's, comprehensive exam, thesis or alternative, oral and written exams; for doctorate, comprehensive exam, thesis/dissertation, oral and written exams. *Entrance requirements:* For master's, doctorate, and Certificate, GRE General Test, minimum GPA of 3.0. Additional exam requirements/recommendations for international students: Required—TOEFL (minimum score 550 paper-based; 213 computer-based; 62 iBT). *Application deadline:* For fall admission, 7/15 for domestic students, 4/1 for international students; for spring admission, 11/30 for domestic students, 9/1 for international students. Applications are processed on a rolling basis. Application fee: $40 ($50 for international students). Electronic applications accepted. *Expenses:* Tuition, state resident: full-time $7830; part-time $473.50 per credit. Tuition, nonresident: full-time $18,748; part-time $1128.33 per credit. Tuition and fees vary according to course load and program. *Financial support:* In 2011–12, 30 students received support, including 1 fellowship with full tuition reimbursement available (averaging $11,000 per year), 10 research assistantships with full and partial tuition reimbursements available (averaging $9,828 per year), 19 teaching assistantships with full and partial tuition reimbursements available (averaging $8,975 per year); career-related internships or fieldwork, Federal Work-Study, institutionally sponsored loans, scholarships/grants, health care benefits, and unspecified assistantships also available. Support available to part-time students. Financial award application deadline: 4/1; financial award applicants required to submit FAFSA. *Faculty research:* Software engineering and systems, computer graphics and visualization, computer networking, artificial intelligence, modeling and simulation. *Total annual research expenditures:* $5.4 million. *Unit head:* Dr. Heggere Ranganath, Chair, 256-824-6088, Fax: 256-824-6239, E-mail: ranganat@uah.edu. *Application contact:* Kim Gray, Graduate Studies Admissions Manager, 256-824-6002, Fax: 256-824-6405, E-mail: deangrad@uah.edu. Web site: http://www.cs.uah.edu.

University of Alaska Fairbanks, College of Engineering and Mines, Department of Computer Science, Fairbanks, AK 99775-6670. Offers computer science (MS); software engineering (MSE). Part-time programs available. *Faculty:* 8 full-time (1 woman). *Students:* 10 full-time (2 women), 6 part-time (2 women), 2 international. Average age 28. 9 applicants, 33% accepted, 2 enrolled. In 2011, 1 master's awarded. *Degree requirements:* For master's, comprehensive exam, thesis or alternative. *Entrance requirements:* For master's, GRE General Test. Additional exam requirements/recommendations for international students: Required—TOEFL (minimum score 550 paper-based; 213 computer-based; 80 iBT). *Application deadline:* For fall admission, 6/1 for domestic students, 3/1 for international students; for spring admission, 10/15 for domestic students, 9/1 for international students. Application fee: $60. *Expenses:* Tuition, state resident: full-time $6696; part-time $372 per credit. Tuition, nonresident: full-time $13,680; part-time $760 per credit. Tuition and fees vary according to course load and reciprocity agreements. *Financial support:* In 2011–12, 7 research assistantships with tuition reimbursements (averaging $10,886 per year), 3 teaching assistantships with tuition reimbursements (averaging $10,597 per year) were awarded; fellowships with tuition reimbursements, career-related internships or fieldwork, Federal Work-Study, scholarships/grants, health care benefits, and unspecified assistantships also available. Support available to part-time students. Financial award application deadline: 7/1; financial award applicants required to submit FAFSA. *Faculty research:* Interaction with a virtual reality environment, synthetic aperture radar interferometry software. *Total annual research expenditures:* $10,000. *Unit head:* Dr. Jon Genetti, Department Chair, 907-474-2777, Fax: 907-474-5030, E-mail: uaf-cs-dept@alaska.edu. *Application contact:* Mike Earnest, Director of Admissions, 907-474-7500, Fax: 907-474-5379, E-mail: admissions@uaf.edu. Web site: http://www.cs.uaf.edu.

The University of British Columbia, Faculty of Applied Science, Program in Software Systems, Vancouver, BC V6T 1Z1, Canada. Offers MSS. *Degree requirements:* For master's, internship. *Entrance requirements:* For master's, bachelor's degree in science, engineering, business or technology (non-computer science). Additional exam requirements/recommendations for international students: Required—TOEFL (minimum score 600 paper-based; 250 computer-based; 100 iBT), IELTS (minimum score 6.5). Electronic applications accepted. *Expenses:* Contact institution.

University of Calgary, Faculty of Graduate Studies, Faculty of Science, Department of Computer Science, Calgary, AB T2N 1N4, Canada. Offers computer science (M Sc, PhD); software engineering (M Sc). Part-time programs available. *Degree requirements:* For master's, comprehensive exam (for some programs), thesis (for some programs); for doctorate, thesis/dissertation, oral and written departmental exam. *Entrance requirements:* For master's, bachelor's degree in computer science; for doctorate, M Sc in computer science. Additional exam requirements/recommendations for international students: Required—TOEFL (minimum score 600 paper-based; 250 computer-based); Recommended—TWE. Electronic applications accepted. *Faculty research:* Visual and interactive computing, quantum computing and cryptography, evolutionary software engineering, distributed systems and algorithms.

University of Colorado at Colorado Springs, College of Engineering and Applied Science, Department of Mechanical and Aerospace Engineering, Colorado Springs, CO 80933-7150. Offers engineering management (ME); information operations (ME); manufacturing (ME); mechanical engineering (MS); software engineering (ME); space operations (ME); space systems (MS). Part-time and evening/weekend programs available. *Faculty:* 11 full-time (2 women). *Students:* 48 full-time (14 women), 44 part-time (11 women); includes 15 minority (3 Black or African American, non-Hispanic/Latino; 6 Asian, non-Hispanic/Latino; 5 Hispanic/Latino; 1 Two or more races, non-Hispanic/Latino), 3 international. Average age 33. 40 applicants, 60% accepted, 13 enrolled. In 2011, 31 degrees awarded. *Degree requirements:* For master's, thesis optional. *Entrance requirements:* For master's, GRE General Test, bachelor's degree in engineering or related degree, minimum GPA of 3.0. Additional exam requirements/recommendations for international students: Required—TOEFL (minimum score 550 paper-based; 213 computer-based; 79 iBT). *Application deadline:* For fall admission, 3/1 for domestic and international students; for spring admission, 10/1 for domestic and international students. Applications are processed on a rolling basis. Application fee: $60 ($75 for international students). *Expenses:* Tuition, state resident: part-time $660 per credit hour. Tuition, nonresident: part-time $1133 per credit hour. Tuition and fees vary according to degree level, program and student level. *Financial support:* In 2011–12, 5 students received support. Federal Work-Study and scholarships/grants available. Support available to part-time students. Financial award application deadline: 3/1; financial award applicants required to submit FAFSA. *Faculty research:* Neural networks, artificial intelligence, robust control, space operations, space propulsion. *Total annual research expenditures:* $163,405. *Unit head:* Rebecca Webb, Director, 719-255-3581, Fax: 719-255-3674, E-mail: rwebb@uccs.edu. *Application contact:* Siew Nylund, Academic Adviser, 719-255-3243, Fax: 719-255-3589, E-mail: snylund@eas.uccs.edu. Web site: http://eas.uccs.edu/mae/.

University of Connecticut, Graduate School, School of Engineering, Department of Computer Science and Engineering, Storrs, CT 06269. Offers computer science (MS, PhD), including artificial intelligence, computer architecture, computer science, operating systems, robotics, software engineering. Terminal master's awarded for partial completion of doctoral program. *Degree requirements:* For master's, comprehensive exam, thesis or alternative; for doctorate, thesis/dissertation. *Entrance requirements:* For master's and doctorate, GRE General Test. Additional exam requirements/recommendations for international students: Required—TOEFL (minimum score 550 paper-based; 213 computer-based). Electronic applications accepted.

University of Denver, University College, Denver, CO 80208. Offers arts and culture (MLS, Certificate), including art, literature, and culture, arts development and program management (Certificate), creative writing; environmental policy and management (MAS, Certificate), including energy and sustainability (Certificate), environmental assessment of nuclear power (Certificate), environmental health and safety (Certificate), environmental management, natural resource management (Certificate); geographic information systems (MAS, Certificate); global affairs (MLS, Certificate), including translation studies, world history and culture; healthcare leadership (MPH, Certificate), including healthcare policy, law, and ethics, medical and healthcare information technologies, strategic management of healthcare; information and communications technology (MCIS, Certificate), including database design and administration (Certificate), geographic information systems (MCIS), information security systems security (Certificate), information systems security (MCIS), project management (MCIS, MPS, Certificate), software design and administration (Certificate), software design and programming (MCIS), technology management, telecommunications technology (MCIS), Web design and development; leadership and organizations (MPS, Certificate), including human capital in organizations, philanthropic leadership, project management (MCIS, MPS, Certificate), strategic innovation and change; organizational and professional communication (MPS, Certificate), including alternative dispute resolution, organizational communication, organizational development and training, public relations and marketing; security management (MAS, Certificate), including emergency planning and response, information security (MAS), organizational security; strategic human resource management (MPS, Certificate), including global human resources (MPS), human resource management and development (MPS). Part-time and evening/weekend programs available. Postbaccalaureate distance learning degree programs offered (no on-campus study). *Faculty:* 204 part-time/adjunct (80 women). *Students:* 56 full-time (26 women), 1,096 part-time (647 women); includes 196 minority (81 Black or African American, non-Hispanic/Latino; 7 American Indian or Alaska Native, non-Hispanic/Latino; 30 Asian, non-Hispanic/Latino; 66 Hispanic/Latino; 3 Native Hawaiian or other Pacific Islander, non-Hispanic/Latino; 9 Two or more races, non-Hispanic/Latino), 76 international. Average age 36. 572 applicants, 95% accepted, 410 enrolled. In 2011, 404 master's, 123 other advanced degrees awarded. *Degree requirements:* For master's, capstone project. *Entrance requirements:* For master's, two letters of recommendation, personal statement, resume. Additional exam requirements/recommendations for international students: Required—TOEFL (minimum score 550 paper-based; 80 iBT). *Application deadline:* For fall admission, 7/20 priority date for domestic students, 6/8 for international students; for winter admission, 10/26 priority date for domestic students, 9/14 for international students; for spring admission, 2/1 priority date for domestic students, 12/14 for international students. Applications are processed on a rolling basis. Application fee: $75. Electronic applications accepted. *Expenses:* Contact institution. *Financial support:* Applicants required to submit FAFSA. *Unit head:* Dr. James Davis, Dean, 303-871-2291, Fax: 303-871-4047, E-mail: jdavis@du.edu. *Application contact:* Information Contact, 303-871-3155, Fax: 303-871-4047, E-mail: ucolinfo@du.edu. Web site: http://www.universitycollege.du.edu/.

University of Detroit Mercy, College of Engineering and Science, Department of Mathematics and Computer Science, Program in Computer Science, Detroit, MI 48221. Offers computer systems applications (MSCS); software engineering (MSCS). Evening/weekend programs available. *Entrance requirements:* For master's, minimum GPA of 3.0.

University of Houston–Clear Lake, School of Science and Computer Engineering, Program in Software Engineering, Houston, TX 77058-1098. Offers MS. Part-time and evening/weekend programs available. *Entrance requirements:* For master's, GRE General Test. Additional exam requirements/recommendations for international students: Required—TOEFL (minimum score 550 paper-based; 213 computer-based).

University of Management and Technology, Program in Computer Science and Information Technology, Arlington, VA 22209. Offers computer science (MS); information technology (AC); information technology project management (MS); management information systems (MS); project management (AC); software engineering (MS). Part-time and evening/weekend programs available. Postbaccalaureate distance learning degree programs offered (no on-campus study). *Entrance requirements:* For master's, 3 recommendations, resume. Additional exam requirements/recommendations for international students: Required—TOEFL (minimum score 550 paper-based; 213 computer-based). Electronic applications accepted.

University of Massachusetts Dartmouth, Graduate School, College of Engineering, Program in Computer Science, North Dartmouth, MA 02747-2300. Offers computer networks and distributed systems (Postbaccalaureate Certificate); computer science (MS); computer systems (Postbaccalaureate Certificate); software development and design (Postbaccalaureate Certificate). Part-time programs available. Postbaccalaureate distance learning degree programs offered. *Faculty:* 8 full-time (2 women), 2 part-time/adjunct (0 women). *Students:* 37 full-time (7 women), 17 part-time (5 women); includes 2 minority (1 Hispanic/Latino; 1 Two or more races, non-Hispanic/Latino), 37 international. Average age 26. 94 applicants, 90% accepted, 22 enrolled. In 2011, 25 degrees awarded. *Degree requirements:* For master's, thesis or alternative. *Entrance requirements:* For master's, GRE General Test, 3 letters of recommendation, resume, statement of intent; for Postbaccalaureate Certificate, 3 letters of recommendation, resume, statement of intent. Additional exam requirements/recommendations for international students: Required—TOEFL (minimum score 533 paper-based; 200 computer-based; 72 iBT). *Application deadline:* For fall admission, 2/15 priority date for domestic students, 1/15 for international students; for spring admission, 11/15 priority date for domestic students, 10/15 for international students. Applications are processed on a rolling basis. Application fee: $40 ($60 for international students). Electronic applications accepted. *Expenses:* Tuition, state resident: full-time $2071; part-time $86.29 per credit. Tuition, nonresident: full-time $8099; part-time $337.46 per credit. *Required fees:* $438.58 per credit. Part-time tuition and fees vary according to class time, course load, degree level and reciprocity agreements. *Financial support:* In 2011–12, 3 research assistantships with full tuition reimbursements (averaging $12,122 per year), 8 teaching assistantships with partial tuition reimbursements (averaging $4,453 per year) were awarded; Federal Work-Study and unspecified assistantships also available. Support available to part-time students. Financial award application deadline: 3/1; financial award applicants required to submit FAFSA. *Faculty research:* Self-organizing feature maps, location-based services, brain modeling, software engineering, multi-agent systems. *Total annual research expenditures:* $149,926. *Unit head:* Dr. Shelley Zhang, Graduate Program Director, 508-999-8294, Fax: 508-999-9144, E-mail: x2zhang@umassd.edu. *Application contact:* Elan Turcotte-Shamski, Graduate Admissions Officer, 508-999-8604, Fax: 508-999-8183, E-mail: graduate@umassd.edu. Web site: http://www.umassd.edu/engineering/cis/graduate/welcome.cfm.

University of Michigan–Dearborn, College of Engineering and Computer Science, Department of Electrical and Computer Engineering, Program in Software Engineering, Dearborn, MI 48128-1491. Offers MS. Part-time and evening/weekend programs available. Postbaccalaureate distance learning degree programs offered (no on-campus study). *Faculty:* 9 full-time (1 woman), 4 part-time/adjunct (1 woman). *Students:* 2 full-time (0 women), 22 part-time (2 women); includes 6 minority (3 Black or African American, non-Hispanic/Latino; 2 Asian, non-Hispanic/Latino; 1 Hispanic/Latino). Average age 34. 9 applicants, 22% accepted, 1 enrolled. In 2011, 3 master's awarded. *Degree requirements:* For master's, thesis optional. *Entrance requirements:* For master's, bachelor's degree in mathematics, computer science or engineering, minimum GPA of 3.0. Additional exam requirements/recommendations for international students: Required—TOEFL (minimum score 560 paper-based; 220 computer-based; 84 iBT). *Application deadline:* For fall admission, 6/15 for domestic students, 4/1 for international students; for winter admission, 10/15 for domestic students, 8/1 for international students; for spring admission, 2/15 for domestic students, 12/1 for international students. Applications are processed on a rolling basis. Application fee: $60. Electronic applications accepted. *Faculty research:* Information systems, geometric modeling, networks, databases. *Unit head:* Dr. YiLu Murphey, Chair, 313-593-5028, Fax: 313-583-6336, E-mail: yilu@umich.edu. *Application contact:* Michael Patrick Hicks, Academic Records Intermediate Assistant, 313-593-5420, Fax: 313-583-6336, E-mail: ece-grad@umd.umich.edu. Web site: http://www.engin.umd.umich.edu/ECE.

University of Minnesota, Twin Cities Campus, College of Science and Engineering, Department of Computer Science and Engineering, Minneapolis, MN 55455-0213. Offers computer science (MCS, MS, PhD); software engineering (MSSE). Part-time programs available. *Faculty:* 36 full-time (3 women). *Students:* 401 (58 women); includes 26 minority (3 Black or African American, non-Hispanic/Latino; 3 American Indian or Alaska Native, non-Hispanic/Latino; 17 Asian, non-Hispanic/Latino; 3 Hispanic/Latino), 225 international. Terminal master's awarded for partial completion of doctoral program. *Degree requirements:* For doctorate, thesis/dissertation. *Entrance requirements:* For master's and doctorate, GRE General Test. Additional exam requirements/recommendations for international students: Required—TOEFL. *Application deadline:* For fall admission, 12/1 priority date for domestic students, 12/1 for international students. Applications are processed on a rolling basis. Application fee: $75 ($95 for international students). Electronic applications accepted. *Financial support:* Fellowships with tuition reimbursements, research assistantships with tuition reimbursements, and teaching assistantships with tuition reimbursements available. *Faculty research:* Computer architecture, bioinformatics and computational biology, data mining; graphics and visualization, high performance computing, human-computer interaction, networks, software systems, theory, artificial intelligence. *Application contact:* Computer Science Graduate Admissions, E-mail: admissions@cs.umn.edu. Web site: http://www.cs.umn.edu/.

University of Missouri–Kansas City, School of Computing and Engineering, Kansas City, MO 64110-2499. Offers civil engineering (MS); computer and electrical engineering (PhD); computer science (MS), including bioinformatics, software engineering, telecommunications networking; computer science and informatics (PhD); computing (PhD); electrical engineering (MS); engineering (PhD); mechanical engineering (MS); telecommunications (PhD). PhD (interdisciplinary) offered through the School of Graduate Studies. Part-time programs available. *Faculty:* 36 full-time (6 women), 27 part-time/adjunct (3 women). *Students:* 155 full-time (44 women), 136 part-time (24 women); includes 19 minority (4 Black or African American, non-Hispanic/Latino; 7 Asian, non-Hispanic/Latino; 6 Hispanic/Latino; 2 Two or more races, non-Hispanic/Latino), 201 international. Average age 26. 455 applicants, 46% accepted, 96 enrolled. In 2011, 194 degrees awarded. *Degree requirements:* For doctorate, thesis/dissertation. *Entrance requirements:* For master's, GRE General Test, minimum GPA of 3.0, 3 letters of recommendation from professors; for doctorate, GRE General Test, minimum GPA of 3.5. Additional exam requirements/recommendations for international students: Required—TOEFL (minimum score 550 paper-based; 213 computer-based; 80 iBT). *Application deadline:* For fall admission, 1/15 priority date for domestic students, 1/15 for international students. Applications are processed on a rolling basis. Application fee: $45 ($50 for international students). *Expenses:* Tuition, state resident: full-time $5798; part-time $322.10 per credit hour. Tuition, nonresident: full-time $14,969; part-time $831.60 per credit hour. *Required fees:* $93.51 per credit hour. *Financial support:* In 2011–12, 47 research assistantships with partial tuition reimbursements (averaging $13,190 per year), 10 teaching assistantships with partial tuition reimbursements (averaging $9,815 per year) were awarded; career-related internships or fieldwork, Federal Work-Study, scholarships/grants, tuition waivers (partial), and unspecified assistantships also available. Support available to part-time students. Financial award application deadline: 3/1; financial award applicants required to submit FAFSA. *Faculty research:* Algorithms, bioinformatics and medical informatics, biomechanics/biomaterials, civil engineering materials, networking and telecommunications, thermal science. *Unit head:* Dr. Kevin Z. Truman, Dean, 816-235-2399, Fax: 816-235-5159. *Application contact:* 816-235-2399, Fax: 816-235-5159. Web site: http://sce.umkc.edu/.

University of New Hampshire, Graduate School, College of Engineering and Physical Sciences, Department of Computer Science, Durham, NH 03824. Offers computer science (MS, PhD); software systems engineering (Postbaccalaureate Certificate). Part-time and evening/weekend programs available. *Faculty:* 10 full-time (2 women). *Students:* 27 full-time (10 women), 51 part-time (3 women); includes 4 minority (1 Black or African American, non-Hispanic/Latino; 2 Asian, non-Hispanic/Latino; 1 Two or more races, non-Hispanic/Latino), 17 international. Average age 31. 69 applicants, 67% accepted, 23 enrolled. In 2011, 17 master's, 18 other advanced degrees awarded. *Degree requirements:* For master's, thesis or alternative; for doctorate, thesis/dissertation. *Entrance requirements:* For master's and doctorate, GRE General Test. Additional exam requirements/recommendations for international students: Required—TOEFL (minimum score 550 paper-based; 213 computer-based; 80 iBT). *Application deadline:* For fall admission, 4/1 priority date for domestic students, 4/1 for international students; for spring admission, 12/1 for domestic students. Applications are processed on a rolling basis. Application fee: $65. Electronic applications accepted. *Expenses:* Tuition, state resident: full-time $12,360; part-time $687 per credit hour. Tuition, nonresident: full-time $25,680; part-time $1058 per credit hour. *International tuition:* $29,550 full-time. *Required fees:* $1666; $833 per course. $416.50 per semester. Tuition and fees vary according to course load and degree level. *Financial support:* In 2011–12, 35 students received support, including 10 research assistantships, 11 teaching assistantships; fellowships, career-related internships or fieldwork, Federal Work-Study, scholarships/grants, and tuition waivers (full and partial) also available. Support available to part-time students. *Faculty research:* Programming languages, compiler design, parallel algorithms, computer graphics, artificial intelligence. *Unit head:* Radim Bartos, Department Chair, 603-862-3792. *Application contact:* Carolyn Kirkpatrick, Administrative Assistant, 603-862-3778, E-mail: office@cs.unh.edu. Web site: http://www.cs.unh.edu/.

University of New Hampshire, Graduate School Manchester Campus, Manchester, NH 03101. Offers business administration (MBA); counseling (M Ed); education (M Ed, MAT); educational administration and supervision (M Ed, Ed S); information technology (MS); management of technology (MS); public administration (MPA); public health (MPH, Certificate); social work (MSW); software systems engineering (Certificate). Part-time and evening/weekend programs available. *Students:* 78 full-time (50 women), 130 part-time (65 women); includes 62 minority (2 Black or African American, non-Hispanic/Latino; 56 Asian, non-Hispanic/Latino; 4 Hispanic/Latino), 4 international. Average age 34. 132 applicants, 55% accepted, 57 enrolled. In 2011, 66 master's, 9 other advanced degrees awarded. *Degree requirements:* For master's, thesis or alternative. *Entrance requirements:* Additional exam requirements/recommendations for international students: Required—TOEFL (minimum score 550 paper-based; 213 computer-based; 80 iBT). *Application deadline:* For fall admission, 6/1 for domestic students, 4/1 for international students; for spring admission, 12/1 for domestic students. Applications are processed on a rolling basis. Application fee: $65. Electronic applications accepted. *Expenses:* Tuition, state resident: full-time $12,360; part-time $687 per credit hour. Tuition, nonresident: full-time $25,680; part-time $1058 per credit hour. *International tuition:* $29,550 full-time. *Required fees:* $1666; $833 per course. $416.50 per semester. Tuition and fees vary according to course load and degree level. *Financial support:* In 2011–12, 11 students received support, including 2 teaching assistantships; fellowships, research assistantships, Federal Work-Study, scholarships/grants, health care benefits, and unspecified assistantships also available. Support available to part-time students. Financial award application deadline: 3/1; financial award applicants required to submit FAFSA. *Unit head:* Candice Brown, Director, 603-641-4313, E-mail: unhm.gradcenter@unh.edu. *Application contact:* Graduate Admissions Office, 603-862-3000, Fax: 603-862-0275, E-mail: grad.school@unh.edu. Web site: http://www.gradschool.unh.edu/manchester/.

University of New Haven, Graduate School, Tagliatela College of Engineering, Program in Computer and Information Science, West Haven, CT 06516-1916. Offers computer science (MS, Certificate), including advanced applications (MS), computer programming (Certificate), computer systems (MS), database and information systems (MS), network systems (MS), software engineering and development (MS). Part-time and evening/weekend programs available. *Students:* 53 full-time (16 women), 32 part-time (7 women); includes 4 minority (1 Black or African American, non-Hispanic/Latino; 1 Asian, non-Hispanic/Latino; 2 Hispanic/Latino), 69 international. 133 applicants, 98% accepted, 23 enrolled. In 2011, 19 master's, 1 other advanced degree awarded. *Degree requirements:* For master's, thesis or alternative. *Entrance requirements:* Additional exam requirements/recommendations for international students: Required—TOEFL

(minimum score 520 paper-based; 190 computer-based; 70 iBT); Recommended—IELTS (minimum score 5.5). *Application deadline:* For fall admission, 5/31 for international students; for winter admission, 10/15 for international students; for spring admission, 1/15 for international students. Applications are processed on a rolling basis. Application fee: $50. Electronic applications accepted. *Expenses:* Tuition: Part-time $750 per credit. *Financial support:* Research assistantships with partial tuition reimbursements, teaching assistantships with partial tuition reimbursements, career-related internships or fieldwork, Federal Work-Study, scholarships/grants, tuition waivers, and unspecified assistantships available. Support available to part-time students. Financial award applicants required to submit FAFSA. *Unit head:* Dr. David Eggert, Coordinator, 203-932-7097, E-mail: deggert@newhaven.edu. *Application contact:* Eloise Gormley, Director of Graduate Admissions, 203-932-7449, Fax: 203-932-7137, E-mail: gradinfo@newhaven.edu. Web site: http://www.newhaven.edu/9591/

University of North Florida, College of Computing, Engineering, and Construction, School of Computing, Jacksonville, FL 32224. Offers computer science (MS); information systems (MS); software engineering (MS). Part-time programs available. *Faculty:* 14 full-time (3 women). *Students:* 7 full-time (3 women), 39 part-time (10 women); includes 15 minority (7 Black or African American, non-Hispanic/Latino; 4 Asian, non-Hispanic/Latino; 2 Hispanic/Latino; 2 Two or more races, non-Hispanic/Latino), 14 international. Average age 30. 30 applicants, 63% accepted, 5 enrolled. In 2011, 4 master's awarded. *Degree requirements:* For master's, thesis. *Entrance requirements:* For master's, GRE General Test, minimum GPA of 3.0 in last 60 hours of course work. Additional exam requirements/recommendations for international students: Required—TOEFL (minimum score 500 paper-based; 173 computer-based; 61 iBT). *Application deadline:* For fall admission, 7/1 for domestic students, 5/1 for international students; for spring admission, 11/1 for domestic students, 10/1 for international students. Applications are processed on a rolling basis. Application fee: $30. Electronic applications accepted. *Expenses:* Tuition, state resident: full-time $8793; part-time $366.38 per credit hour. Tuition, nonresident: full-time $23,502; part-time $979.24 per credit hour. *Required fees:* $1384; $57.66 per credit hour. Tuition and fees vary according to course load and program. *Financial support:* In 2011–12, 12 students received support, including 1 research assistantship (averaging $1,000 per year); teaching assistantships, Federal Work-Study, scholarships/grants, and unspecified assistantships also available. Financial award application deadline: 4/1; financial award applicants required to submit FAFSA. *Total annual research expenditures:* $91,012. *Unit head:* Dr. Neal Coulter, Dean, 904-620-1350, E-mail: ncoulter@unf.edu. *Application contact:* Lillith Richardson, Assistant Director, The Graduate School, 904-620-1360, Fax: 904-620-1362, E-mail: graduateschool@unf.edu. Web site: http://www.unf.edu/ccec/computing/.

University of Regina, Faculty of Graduate Studies and Research, Faculty of Engineering and Applied Science, Program in Software Systems Engineering, Regina, SK S4S 0A2, Canada. Offers M Eng, MA Sc, PhD. Part-time programs available. *Faculty:* 7 full-time (1 woman). *Students:* 16 full-time (1 woman), 3 part-time (1 woman). 20 applicants, 50% accepted. In 2011, 2 degrees awarded. *Degree requirements:* For master's, comprehensive exam, thesis. *Entrance requirements:* Additional exam requirements/recommendations for international students: Required—TOEFL (minimum score 550 paper-based; 80 iBT), IELTS (minimum score 6.5). *Application deadline:* For fall admission, 3/31 for domestic and international students; for winter admission, 7/31 for domestic and international students; for spring admission, 11/30 for domestic and international students. Application fee: $100. Electronic applications accepted. *Financial support:* In 2011–12, 3 fellowships (averaging $6,000 per year), 2 teaching assistantships (averaging $2,298 per year) were awarded; research assistantships, career-related internships or fieldwork, and scholarships/grants also available. Financial award application deadline: 6/15. *Faculty research:* Software design and development, network computing, multimedia communication, computational theories to real-life programming techniques, embedded systems construction. *Unit head:* Dr. Christine Chan, Chair/Graduate Program Coordinator, 306-585-5225, Fax: 306-585-4855, E-mail: christine.chan@uregina.ca. *Application contact:* Melissa Dyck, Administrative Contact, 306-337-2603, Fax: 306-585-4855, E-mail: melissa.dyck@uregina.ca. Web site: http://www.urengineering.ca/programs/software-systems-engineering.

University of St. Thomas, Graduate Studies, Graduate Programs in Software, Saint Paul, MN 55105. Offers advanced studies in software engineering (Certificate); business analysis (Certificate); computer security (Certificate); information systems (Certificate); software design and development (Certificate); software engineering (MS); software management (MS); software systems (MSS); MS/MBA. Part-time and evening/weekend programs available. *Faculty:* 5 full-time (0 women), 15 part-time/adjunct (1 woman). *Students:* 34 full-time (7 women), 314 part-time (79 women); includes 99 minority (48 Black or African American, non-Hispanic/Latino; 1 American Indian or Alaska Native, non-Hispanic/Latino; 45 Asian, non-Hispanic/Latino; 4 Hispanic/Latino; 1 Two or more races, non-Hispanic/Latino), 70 international. Average age 35. 155 applicants, 85% accepted, 79 enrolled. In 2011, 84 master's, 9 other advanced degrees awarded. *Degree requirements:* For master's, thesis optional. *Entrance requirements:* For master's, bachelor's degree earned in U.S. or equivalent international degree. Additional exam requirements/recommendations for international students: Required—TOEFL (minimum score 80 iBT). *Application deadline:* For fall admission, 8/1 priority date for domestic students, 5/1 for international students; for spring admission, 1/1 priority date for domestic students, 10/1 for international students. Applications are processed on a rolling basis. Application fee: $50. Electronic applications accepted. *Expenses:* Contact institution. *Financial support:* Federal Work-Study, institutionally sponsored loans, and scholarships/grants available. Financial award application deadline: 4/1. *Faculty research:* Data mining, distributed databases, computer security, big data. *Unit head:* Dr. Bhabani Misra, Director, 651-962-5508, Fax: 651-962-5543, E-mail: bsmisra@stthomas.edu. *Application contact:* Douglas J. Stubeda, Assistant Director, 651-962-5503, Fax: 651-962-5543, E-mail: djstubeda@stthomas.edu. Web site: http://www.stthomas.edu/gradsoftware/.

University of St. Thomas, Graduate Studies, School of Engineering, St. Paul, MN 55105-1096. Offers manufacturing engineering and operations (MS); mechanical engineering (MS); medical device development (Certificate); regulatory science (MS); software engineering (MS); software management (MS); software systems (MSS); systems engineering (MS); technology management (MS). *Accreditation:* ABET (one or more programs are accredited). *Students:* 8 full-time, 210 part-time (38 women); includes 47 minority (22 Black or African American, non-Hispanic/Latino; 4 Asian, non-Hispanic/Latino; 6 Hispanic/Latino; 1 Native Hawaiian or other Pacific Islander, non-Hispanic/Latino; 14 Two or more races, non-Hispanic/Latino), 14 international. Average age 33. *Entrance requirements:* For master's, resume, official transcripts. Additional exam requirements/recommendations for international students: Required—TOEFL (minimum score 550 paper-based). *Application deadline:* For fall admission, 8/1 priority date for domestic students; for spring admission, 1/1 priority date for domestic students. Applications are processed on a rolling basis. Application fee: $30. Electronic applications accepted. *Expenses:* Contact institution. *Financial support:* Fellowships, research assistantships, institutionally sponsored loans, and scholarships/grants available. Support available to part-time students. Financial award application deadline: 4/1; financial award applicants required to submit FAFSA. *Unit head:* Don Weinkauf, Dean, 651-962-5760, Fax: 651-962-6419, E-mail: dhweinkauf@stthomas.edu. *Application contact:* Joyce A. Taylor, Graduate Programs Coordinator, 651-962-5756, Fax: 651-962-6419, E-mail: jataylor1@stthomas.edu.

The University of Scranton, College of Graduate and Continuing Education, Program in Software Engineering, Scranton, PA 18510. Offers MS. Part-time and evening/weekend programs available. *Faculty:* 8 full-time (0 women). *Students:* 17 full-time (2 women), 4 part-time (2 women); includes 1 minority (Asian, non-Hispanic/Latino), 1 international. Average age 29. 22 applicants, 86% accepted. In 2011, 4 master's awarded. *Degree requirements:* For master's, thesis, capstone experience. *Entrance requirements:* For master's, GMAT or GRE, minimum GPA of 3.0. Additional exam requirements/recommendations for international students: Required—TOEFL (minimum score 500 paper-based; 173 computer-based), IELTS (minimum score 5.5). *Application deadline:* For fall admission, 3/1 priority date for domestic students. Applications are processed on a rolling basis. Application fee: $0. *Financial support:* In 2011–12, 7 students received support, including 7 teaching assistantships with full tuition reimbursements available (averaging $8,800 per year); fellowships, career-related internships or fieldwork, Federal Work-Study, and unspecified assistantships also available. Support available to part-time students. Financial award application deadline: 3/1. *Faculty research:* Database, parallel and distributed systems, computer network, real time systems. *Unit head:* Dr. Yaodong Bi, Director, 570-941-6108, Fax: 570-941-4250, E-mail: biy1@scranton.edu. *Application contact:* Joseph M. Roback, Director of Admissions, 570-941-4385, Fax: 570-941-5928, E-mail: robackj2@scranton.edu. Web site: http://www.cs.uofs.edu/.

University of South Carolina, The Graduate School, College of Engineering and Computing, Department of Computer Science and Engineering, Columbia, SC 29208. Offers computer science and engineering (ME, MS, PhD); software engineering (MS). Part-time and evening/weekend programs available. Postbaccalaureate distance learning degree programs offered (minimal on-campus study). *Degree requirements:* For master's, comprehensive exam, thesis (for some programs); for doctorate, comprehensive exam, thesis/dissertation. *Entrance requirements:* For master's and doctorate, GRE General Test. Additional exam requirements/recommendations for international students: Required—TOEFL (minimum score 570 paper-based; 230 computer-based). Electronic applications accepted. *Faculty research:* Computer security, computer vision, artificial intelligence, multiagent systems, bioinformatics.

University of Southern California, Graduate School, Viterbi School of Engineering, Department of Computer Science, Los Angeles, CA 90089. Offers computer networks (MS); computer science (MS, PhD); computer security (MS); game development (MS); high performance computing and simulations (MS); human language technology (MS); intelligent robotics (MS); multimedia and creative technologies (MS); software engineering (MS). Part-time and evening/weekend programs available. Postbaccalaureate distance learning degree programs offered (no on-campus study). *Entrance requirements:* For master's and doctorate, GRE General Test. Additional exam requirements/recommendations for international students: Required—TOEFL. Electronic applications accepted. *Faculty research:* Databases, computer graphics and computer vision, software engineering, networks and security, robotics, multimedia and virtual reality.

The University of Texas at Arlington, Graduate School, College of Engineering, Department of Computer Science and Engineering, Arlington, TX 76019. Offers computer engineering (MS, PhD); computer science (MS, PhD); mathematical sciences, computer science (PhD); software engineering (MS). Part-time programs available. Postbaccalaureate distance learning degree programs offered (minimal on-campus study). *Faculty:* 31 full-time (3 women). *Students:* 206 full-time (46 women), 98 part-time (21 women); includes 7 minority (1 Black or African American, non-Hispanic/Latino; 4 Asian, non-Hispanic/Latino; 1 Hispanic/Latino; 1 Two or more races, non-Hispanic/Latino), 247 international. 752 applicants, 60% accepted, 89 enrolled. In 2011, 60 master's, 12 doctorates awarded. Terminal master's awarded for partial completion of doctoral program. *Degree requirements:* For master's, comprehensive exam (for some programs), thesis; for doctorate, comprehensive exam, thesis/dissertation. *Entrance requirements:* For master's, GRE General Test, minimum GPA of 3.0 (3.2 in computer science-related classes); for doctorate, GRE General Test, minimum GPA of 3.5. Additional exam requirements/recommendations for international students: Required—TOEFL (minimum score 550 paper-based; 230 computer-based; 92 iBT), IELTS (minimum score 6.5). *Application deadline:* For fall admission, 6/1 for domestic students, 5/1 for international students; for spring admission, 12/1 for domestic students, 10/1 for international students. Applications are processed on a rolling basis. Application fee: $35 ($50 for international students). *Financial support:* In 2011–12, 8 fellowships with full tuition reimbursements (averaging $24,000 per year), 48 research assistantships with partial tuition reimbursements (averaging $19,200 per year), 43 teaching assistantships with partial tuition reimbursements (averaging $18,000 per year) were awarded; career-related internships or fieldwork and scholarships/grants also available. Financial award application deadline: 6/1; financial award applicants required to submit FAFSA. *Faculty research:* Algorithms, homeland security, mobile pervasive computing, high performance computing bioinformation. *Unit head:* Dr. Fillia Makedon, Chairman, 817-272-3605, E-mail: makedon@uta.edu. *Application contact:* Dr. Bahram Khalili, Graduate Advisor, 817-272-5407, Fax: 817-272-3784, E-mail: khalili@uta.edu. Web site: http://www.cse.uta.edu/.

The University of Texas at Dallas, Erik Jonsson School of Engineering and Computer Science, Department of Computer Science, Richardson, TX 75080. Offers computer science (MS, PhD); software engineering (PhD). Part-time and evening/weekend programs available. *Faculty:* 41 full-time (6 women), 1 part-time/adjunct (0 women). *Students:* 464 full-time (105 women), 135 part-time (26 women); includes 33 minority (2 Black or African American, non-Hispanic/Latino; 1 American Indian or Alaska Native, non-Hispanic/Latino; 20 Asian, non-Hispanic/Latino; 9 Hispanic/Latino; 1 Two or more races, non-Hispanic/Latino), 485 international. Average age 26. 1,464 applicants, 59% accepted, 264 enrolled. In 2011, 176 master's, 25 doctorates awarded. *Degree requirements:* For master's, thesis optional; for doctorate, comprehensive exam, thesis/dissertation. *Entrance requirements:* For master's, GRE General Test, minimum GPA of 3.0 in undergraduate course work, 3.3 in quantitative course work; for doctorate, GRE General Test, minimum GPA of 3.5. Additional exam requirements/recommendations for international students: Required—TOEFL (minimum score 550 paper-based; 215 computer-based). *Application deadline:* For fall admission, 7/15 for domestic students, 5/1 for international students; for spring admission, 11/15 for domestic students, 9/1 for international students. Applications are processed on a rolling basis. Application fee: $50 ($100 for international students). Electronic applications accepted. *Expenses:* Tuition, state resident: full-time $11,170; part-time $620.56 per credit hour. Tuition, nonresident: full-time $20,212; part-time $1122.89 per credit hour. *Financial support:* In 2011–12, 162 students received support, including 2 fellowships with partial tuition reimbursements available (averaging $12,216 per year), 52 research assistantships with partial tuition reimbursements available (averaging $21,785 per year), 40 teaching assistantships with partial tuition reimbursements available (averaging $16,076 per year); career-related internships or fieldwork, Federal Work-Study, institutionally sponsored loans, and scholarships/grants also available. Support available to part-time students. Financial award application deadline: 4/30; financial award applicants required to submit FAFSA. *Faculty research:* AI-based automated software synthesis and testing, quality of service in computer networks, wireless networks, cloud computing and IT security, speech recognition. *Unit head:* Dr. Gopal Gupta, Department Head, 972-883-4107, Fax: 972-883-2349, E-mail: gupta@utdallas.edu. *Application contact:* Dr. Balaji Raghavachari, Associate Department Head and Director of Graduate Studies, 972-883-2136, Fax: 972-883-2813, E-mail: gradecs@utdallas.edu. Web site: http://cs.utdallas.edu/.

University of Washington, Bothell, Program in Computing and Software Systems, Bothell, WA 98011-8246. Offers MS. Part-time and evening/weekend programs available. *Faculty:* 5 full-time (3 women), 66 part-time/adjunct (16 women). *Students:* 7 full-time (6 women), 51 part-time (6 women); includes 15 minority (1 Black or African American, non-Hispanic/Latino; 10 Asian, non-Hispanic/Latino; 1 Hispanic/Latino; 1 Native Hawaiian or other Pacific Islander, non-Hispanic/Latino; 2 Two or more races, non-Hispanic/Latino), 12 international. Average age 33. 35 applicants, 63% accepted, 16 enrolled. In 2011, 3 master's awarded. *Degree requirements:* For master's, comprehensive exam (for some programs), thesis optional. *Entrance requirements:* For master's, GRE. Additional exam requirements/recommendations for international students: Required—TOEFL (minimum score 580 paper-based; 237 computer-based; 92 iBT) or IELTS (minimum score 7). *Application deadline:* For fall admission, 7/1 for domestic students, 4/1 for international students; for winter admission, 11/1 for domestic students; for spring admission, 2/1 for domestic students. Application fee: $75. Electronic applications accepted. *Expenses:* Contact institution. *Financial support:* Applicants required to submit FAFSA. *Faculty research:* Computer science, software engineering, computer graphics, parallel and distributed systems, computer vision. *Unit head:* Dr. Michael Stiber, Professor and Director, 425-352-5279, E-mail: cssinfo@uwb.edu. *Application contact:* Megan Jewell, Graduate Advisor, 425-352-5279, E-mail: mjewell@uwb.edu. Web site: http://www.uwb.edu/mscss.

University of Washington, Tacoma, Graduate Programs, Program in Computing and Software Systems, Tacoma, WA 98402-3100. Offers MS. Part-time programs available. *Degree requirements:* For master's, capstone project/thesis or 15 credits elective coursework. *Entrance requirements:* For master's, GRE, personal statement, resume, transcripts, 3 recommendations. Additional exam requirements/recommendations for international students: Required—TOEFL (minimum score 580 paper-based; 237 computer-based; 92 iBT), IELTS (minimum score 7). Electronic applications accepted. *Faculty research:* Data stream analysis, formal methods, data mining, robotic systems, software development processes.

University of Waterloo, Graduate Studies, Faculty of Engineering, Department of Electrical and Computer Engineering, Waterloo, ON N2L 3G1, Canada. Offers electrical and computer engineering (M Eng, MA Sc, PhD); electrical and computer engineering (software engineering) (MA Sc). Part-time programs available. *Degree requirements:* For master's, research paper or thesis; for doctorate, comprehensive exam, thesis/dissertation. *Entrance requirements:* For master's, honors degree, minimum B+ average; for doctorate, master's degree, minimum A- average. Additional exam requirements/recommendations for international students: Required—TOEFL (minimum score 550 paper-based; 213 computer-based), TWE (minimum score 4). Electronic applications accepted. *Faculty research:* Communications, computers, systems and control, silicon devices, power engineering.

University of Waterloo, Graduate Studies, Faculty of Mathematics, David R. Cheriton School of Computer Science, Waterloo, ON N2L 3G1, Canada. Offers computer science (M Math, PhD); software engineering (M Math); statistics and computing (M Math). Part-time programs available. *Degree requirements:* For master's, research paper or thesis; for doctorate, comprehensive exam, thesis/dissertation. *Entrance requirements:* For master's, honors degree in field, minimum B+ average; for doctorate, master's degree, minimum B+ average. *Faculty research:* Computer graphics, artificial intelligence, algorithms and complexity, distributed computing and networks, software engineering.

University of West Florida, College of Arts and Sciences: Sciences, Department of Computer Science, Pensacola, FL 32514-5750. Offers computer science (MS); database systems (MS); software engineering (MS). Part-time and evening/weekend programs available. *Faculty:* 9 full-time (4 women), 5 part-time/adjunct (4 women). *Students:* 22 full-time (8 women), 114 part-time (25 women); includes 38 minority (8 Black or African American, non-Hispanic/Latino; 2 American Indian or Alaska Native, non-Hispanic/Latino; 13 Asian, non-Hispanic/Latino; 13 Hispanic/Latino; 2 Two or more races, non-Hispanic/Latino), 54 international. Average age 37. 53 applicants, 81% accepted, 35 enrolled. In 2011, 64 master's awarded. *Degree requirements:* For master's, thesis optional. *Entrance requirements:* For master's, GRE, MAT, or GMAT, official transcripts; minimum undergraduate GPA of 3.0; letter of intent; three letters of recommendation. Additional exam requirements/recommendations for international students: Required—TOEFL (minimum score 550 paper-based; 213 computer-based). *Application deadline:* For fall admission, 6/1 for domestic and international students; for spring admission, 10/1 for domestic and international students. Applications are processed on a rolling basis. Application fee: $30. *Expenses:* Tuition, state resident: full-time $5729; part-time $302 per credit hour. Tuition, nonresident: full-time $20,059; part-time $961 per credit hour. *Required fees:* $1509; $63 per credit hour. *Financial support:* In 2011–12, 10 fellowships with partial tuition reimbursements (averaging $600 per year), 8 research assistantships with partial tuition reimbursements (averaging $3,280 per year), 2 teaching assistantships with partial tuition reimbursements (averaging $3,760 per year) were awarded; unspecified assistantships also available. Financial award application deadline: 4/15; financial award applicants required to submit FAFSA. *Unit head:* Dr. Leo Ter Haar, Chairperson, 850-474-2542. *Application contact:* Terry McCray, Assistant Director of Graduate Admissions, 850-473-7718, Fax: 850-473-7714, E-mail: gradadmissions@uwf.edu. Web site: http://catalog.uwf.edu/graduate/computerscience/.

University of West Florida, College of Professional Studies, Department of Applied Science, Technology and Administration, Program in Administration, Pensacola, FL 32514-5750. Offers acquisition and contract administration (MSA); biomedical/pharmaceutical (MSA); criminal justice administration (MSA); database administration (MSA); education leadership (MSA); healthcare administration (MSA); human performance technology (MSA); leadership (MSA); nursing administration (MSA); public administration (MSA); software engineering administration (MSA). Part-time and evening/weekend programs available. Postbaccalaureate distance learning degree programs offered (no on-campus study). *Students:* 36 full-time (28 women), 158 part-time (95 women); includes 61 minority (31 Black or African American, non-Hispanic/

Latino; 4 American Indian or Alaska Native, non-Hispanic/Latino; 4 Asian, non-Hispanic/Latino; 17 Hispanic/Latino; 2 Native Hawaiian or other Pacific Islander, non-Hispanic/Latino; 3 Two or more races, non-Hispanic/Latino), 1 international. Average age 34. 102 applicants, 59% accepted, 40 enrolled. In 2011, 62 master's awarded. *Entrance requirements:* For master's, GRE General Test, letter of intent, names of references. Additional exam requirements/recommendations for international students: Required—TOEFL (minimum score 550 paper-based; 213 computer-based). *Application deadline:* For fall admission, 6/1 for domestic and international students; for spring admission, 10/1 for domestic and international students. Applications are processed on a rolling basis. Application fee: $30. *Expenses:* Tuition, state resident: full-time $5729; part-time $302 per credit hour. Tuition, nonresident: full-time $20,059; part-time $961 per credit hour. *Required fees:* $1509; $63 per credit hour. *Financial support:* Unspecified assistantships available. Financial award application deadline: 4/15; financial award applicants required to submit FAFSA. *Unit head:* Dr. Karen Rasmussen, Chairperson, 850-474-2301, Fax: 850-474-2804, E-mail: krasmuss@uwf.edu. *Application contact:* Terry McCray, Assistant Director of Graduate Admissions, 850-473-7718, Fax: 850-473-7714, E-mail: gradadmissions@uwf.edu. Web site: http://uwf.edu/msaprogram/.

University of West Florida, College of Professional Studies, Department of Research and Applied Studies, Pensacola, FL 32514-5750. Offers administration (MSA), including acquisition and contract administration, biomedical/pharmaceutical, criminal justice administration, database administration, education leadership, healthcare administration, human performance technology, leadership, nursing administration, public administration, software engineering and administration; college student personnel administration (M Ed), including college personnel administration, guidance and counseling; curriculum and instruction (M Ed, Ed S); educational leadership (M Ed); middle and secondary level education and ESOL (M Ed). Part-time and evening/weekend programs available. *Faculty:* 2 full-time (both women), 3 part-time/adjunct (2 women). *Students:* 26 full-time (15 women), 13 part-time (9 women); includes 8 minority (4 Black or African American, non-Hispanic/Latino; 2 American Indian or Alaska Native, non-Hispanic/Latino; 1 Hispanic/Latino; 1 Two or more races, non-Hispanic/Latino), 1 international. Average age 26. 51 applicants, 51% accepted, 16 enrolled. In 2011, 17 master's, 49 Ed Ss awarded. *Entrance requirements:* For master's, GRE or MAT, official transcripts; minimum undergraduate GPA of 3.0; letter of intent; three letters of recommendation; resume. Additional exam requirements/recommendations for international students: Required—TOEFL (minimum score 550 paper-based; 213 computer-based). *Application deadline:* For fall admission, 6/1 for domestic and international students; for spring admission, 10/1 for domestic and international students. Applications are processed on a rolling basis. Application fee: $30. *Expenses:* Tuition, state resident: full-time $5729; part-time $302 per credit hour. Tuition, nonresident: full-time $20,059; part-time $961 per credit hour. *Required fees:* $1509; $63 per credit hour. *Financial support:* In 2011–12, 33 fellowships (averaging $860 per year), 10 research assistantships (averaging $3,280 per year), 2 teaching assistantships (averaging $3,760 per year) were awarded; unspecified assistantships also available. Financial award application deadline: 4/15; financial award applicants required to submit FAFSA. *Unit head:* Dr. Joyce Nichols, Chairperson, 850-857-6042, E-mail: jcoleman0@uwf.edu. *Application contact:* Terry McCray, Assistant Director of Graduate Admissions, 850-473-7718, Fax: 850-473-7714, E-mail: gradadmissions@uwf.edu. Web site: http://uwf.edu/pcl/.

University of Wisconsin–La Crosse, Office of University Graduate Studies, College of Science and Health, Department of Computer Science, La Crosse, WI 54601-3742. Offers software engineering (MSE). Part-time programs available. *Faculty:* 7 full-time (1 woman). *Students:* 25 full-time (6 women), 17 part-time (2 women); includes 1 minority (Two or more races, non-Hispanic/Latino), 20 international. Average age 28. 35 applicants, 40% accepted, 9 enrolled. In 2011, 24 master's awarded. *Degree requirements:* For master's, thesis. *Entrance requirements:* Additional exam requirements/recommendations for international students: Required—TOEFL (minimum score 550 paper-based; 213 computer-based; 79 iBT). *Application deadline:* For fall admission, 5/1 priority date for domestic students, 5/1 for international students; for spring admission, 11/1 priority date for domestic students, 11/1 for international students. Applications are processed on a rolling basis. Application fee: $56. Electronic applications accepted. *Expenses:* Tuition, state resident: full-time $8391; part-time $481.17 per credit. Tuition, nonresident: full-time $17,850; part-time $1006.68 per credit. *Required fees:* $2 per credit. $18.25 per semester. Tuition and fees vary according to course load, program, reciprocity agreements and student level. *Financial support:* In 2011–12, 3 research assistantships with partial tuition reimbursements (averaging $8,437 per year) were awarded; Federal Work-Study, scholarships/grants, health care benefits, and tuition waivers (partial) also available. Support available to part-time students. *Unit head:* Dr. Kasi Periyasamy, Software Engineering Program Director, 608-785-6823, E-mail: periyasa.kas2@uwlax.edu. *Application contact:* Kathryn Kiefer, Director of Admissions, 608-785-8939, E-mail: admissions@uwlax.edu. Web site: http://www.cs.uwlax.edu/mse.htm.

Villanova University, Graduate School of Liberal Arts and Sciences, Department of Computing Sciences, Villanova, PA 19085-1699. Offers computer science (MS); software engineering (MS). Part-time and evening/weekend programs available. *Faculty:* 8 full-time (1 woman), 4 part-time/adjunct (0 women). *Students:* 75 full-time (25 women), 23 part-time (4 women); includes 9 minority (8 Asian, non-Hispanic/Latino; 1 Native Hawaiian or other Pacific Islander, non-Hispanic/Latino), 54 international. Average age 28. 49 applicants, 88% accepted, 38 enrolled. In 2011, 38 master's awarded. *Degree requirements:* For master's, thesis optional, independent study project. *Entrance requirements:* For master's, GRE, minimum GPA of 3.0. Additional exam requirements/recommendations for international students: Required—TOEFL. *Application deadline:* For fall admission, 5/1 for international students; for spring admission, 11/15 for international students. Applications are processed on a rolling basis. Application fee: $50. Electronic applications accepted. *Expenses:* Contact institution. *Financial support:* Research assistantships, scholarships/grants, and unspecified assistantships available. Financial award applicants required to submit FAFSA. *Unit head:* Dr. Robert Beck, Chair, 610-519-7310. *Application contact:* Dean, Graduate School of Liberal Arts and Sciences. Web site: http://csc.villanova.edu/academics/graduatePrograms.

Virginia Polytechnic Institute and State University, VT Online, Blacksburg, VA 24061. Offers advanced transportation systems (Certificate); aerospace engineering (MS); agricultural and life sciences (MSLFS); business information systems (Graduate Certificate); career and technical education (MS); civil engineering (MS); computer engineering (M Eng, MS); decision support systems (Graduate Certificate); eLearning leadership (MA); electrical engineering (M Eng, MS); engineering administration (MEA); environmental engineering (Certificate); environmental politics and policy (Graduate Certificate); environmental sciences and engineering (MS); foundations of political analysis (Graduate Certificate); health product risk management (Graduate Certificate); industrial and systems engineering (MS); information policy and society (Graduate Certificate); information security (Graduate Certificate); information technology (MIT); instructional technology (MA); integrative STEM education (MA Ed); liberal arts (Graduate Certificate); life sciences: health product risk management (MS); natural resources (MNR, Graduate Certificate); networking (Graduate Certificate); nonprofit and nongovernmental organization management (Graduate Certificate); ocean engineering (MS); political science (MA); security studies (Graduate Certificate); software development (Graduate Certificate). *Expenses:* Tuition, state resident: full-time $10,048; part-time $558.25 per credit hour. Tuition, nonresident: full-time $19,497; part-time $1083.25 per credit hour. *Required fees:* $405 per semester. Tuition and fees vary according to course load, campus/location and program. *Application contact:* Graduate School Applications General Assistance, 540-231-8636, Fax: 540-231-2039, E-mail: gradappl@vt.edu. Web site: http://www.vto.vt.edu/.

West Virginia University, College of Engineering and Mineral Resources, Lane Department of Computer Science and Electrical Engineering, Program in Software Engineering, Morgantown, WV 26506. Offers MSSE. *Entrance requirements:* For master's, GRE or work experience.

Widener University, Graduate Programs in Engineering, Program in Computer and Software Engineering, Chester, PA 19013-5792. Offers M Eng. Part-time and evening/weekend programs available. *Degree requirements:* For master's, thesis optional. *Faculty research:* Computer and software engineering, computer network fault-tolerant computing, optical computing.

Winthrop University, College of Business Administration, Program in Software Project Management, Rock Hill, SC 29733. Offers software development (MS); software project management (Certificate). *Entrance requirements:* For master's, GMAT.

Systems Science

Arizona State University, Ira A. Fulton School of Engineering, ASU Engineering Online Programs, Tempe, AZ 85287. Offers construction (MS); embedded systems (M Eng); enterprise systems innovation and management (MSE); modeling and simulation (M Eng); quality and reliability engineering (M Eng); software engineering (MSE); systems engineering (M Eng).

Carleton University, Faculty of Graduate Studies, Faculty of Engineering and Design, Ottawa-Carleton Institute for Electrical Engineering, Department of Systems and Computer Engineering, Program in Information and Systems Science, Ottawa, ON K1S 5B6, Canada. Offers M Sc.

Carleton University, Faculty of Graduate Studies, Faculty of Science, Information and Systems Science Program, Ottawa, ON K1S 5B6, Canada. Offers M Sc. *Degree requirements:* For master's, thesis optional. *Entrance requirements:* For master's, honors degree. Additional exam requirements/recommendations for international students: Required—TOEFL. *Faculty research:* Software engineering, real-time and microprocessor programming, computer communications.

Carleton University, Faculty of Graduate Studies, Faculty of Science, School of Computer Science, Ottawa, ON K1S 5B6, Canada. Offers computer science (MCS, PhD); information and system science (M Sc). MCS and PhD programs offered jointly with University of Ottawa. Part-time programs available. *Degree requirements:* For master's, thesis optional, project; for doctorate, comprehensive exam, thesis/dissertation. *Entrance requirements:* For master's, honors degree. Additional exam requirements/recommendations for international students: Required—TOEFL. *Faculty research:* Programming systems, theory of computing, computer applications, computer systems.

Claremont Graduate University, Graduate Programs, School of Information Systems and Technology, Claremont, CA 91711-6160. Offers electronic commerce (MS, PhD); health information management (MS); information systems (Certificate); knowledge management (MS, PhD); systems development (MS, PhD); telecommunications and networking (MS, PhD); MBA/MS. Part-time programs available. *Faculty:* 7 full-time (1 woman), 1 part-time/adjunct (0 women). *Students:* 68 full-time (20 women), 26 part-time (10 women); includes 31 minority (5 Black or African American, non-Hispanic/Latino; 14 Asian, non-Hispanic/Latino; 9 Hispanic/Latino; 1 Native Hawaiian or other Pacific Islander, non-Hispanic/Latino; 2 Two or more races, non-Hispanic/Latino), 31 international. Average age 37. In 2011, 16 master's, 5 doctorates awarded. *Degree requirements:* For doctorate, comprehensive exam, thesis/dissertation, portfolio. *Entrance requirements:* For master's and doctorate, GMAT, GRE General Test. Additional exam requirements/recommendations for international students: Required—TOEFL (minimum score 550 paper-based; 213 computer-based; 80 iBT). *Application deadline:* For fall admission, 2/1 priority date for domestic students. Applications are processed on a rolling basis. Application fee: $60. Electronic applications accepted. *Expenses:* Tuition: Full-time $36,374; part-time $1581 per unit. *Required fees:* $165 per semester. *Financial support:* Fellowships, research assistantships, teaching assistantships, Federal Work-Study, institutionally sponsored loans, and scholarships/grants available. Support available to part-time students. Financial award application deadline: 2/15; financial award applicants required to submit FAFSA. *Faculty research:* GPSS, man-machine interaction, organizational aspects of computing, implementation of information systems, information systems practice. *Unit head:* Tom Horan, Dean, 909-607-9302, Fax: 909-621-8564, E-mail: tom.horan@cgu.edu. *Application contact:* Anondah Saide, Program Coordinator, 909-607-6006, E-mail: anonda.saide@cgu.edu. Web site: http://www.cgu.edu/pages/153.asp.

Eastern Illinois University, Graduate School, Lumpkin College of Business and Applied Sciences, School of Technology, Charleston, IL 61920-3099. Offers computer technology (Certificate); quality systems (Certificate); technology (MS); technology security (Certificate); work performance improvement (Certificate). Part-time and evening/weekend programs available. *Expenses:* Tuition, state resident: part-time $279 per credit hour. Tuition, nonresident: part-time $670 per credit hour. *Required fees:* $179.07 per credit hour. $1253 per semester.

Systems Science

Fairleigh Dickinson University, Metropolitan Campus, University College: Arts, Sciences, and Professional Studies, Program in Systems Science, Teaneck, NJ 07666-1914. Offers MS. *Entrance requirements:* For master's, GRE General Test.

Hood College, Graduate School, Program in Management of Information Technology, Frederick, MD 21701-8575. Offers MS. Part-time and evening/weekend programs available. *Degree requirements:* For master's, thesis. *Entrance requirements:* For master's, minimum GPA of 2.75. Additional exam requirements/recommendations for international students: Required—TOEFL (minimum score 575 paper-based; 231 computer-based; 89 iBT). Electronic applications accepted. *Faculty research:* Systems engineering, parallel distributed computing, strategy, business ethics, entrepreneurship.

Louisiana State University and Agricultural and Mechanical College, Graduate School, College of Science, Department of Computer Science, Baton Rouge, LA 70803. Offers computer science (MSSS, PhD); systems science (MSSS). Part-time programs available. *Faculty:* 17 full-time (3 women). *Students:* 88 full-time (6 women), 16 part-time (6 women); includes 10 minority (5 Black or African American, non-Hispanic/Latino; 1 American Indian or Alaska Native, non-Hispanic/Latino; 4 Asian, non-Hispanic/Latino), 82 international. Average age 28. 126 applicants, 75% accepted, 20 enrolled. In 2011, 23 master's, 9 doctorates awarded. Terminal master's awarded for partial completion of doctoral program. *Degree requirements:* For master's, thesis; for doctorate, thesis/dissertation. *Entrance requirements:* For master's and doctorate, GRE General Test, minimum GPA of 3.0. Additional exam requirements/recommendations for international students: Required—TOEFL (minimum score 550 paper-based; 213 computer-based; 79 iBT) or IELTS (minimum score 6.5). *Application deadline:* For fall admission, 2/1 for domestic students, 5/15 for international students; for spring admission, 10/1 for domestic students, 10/15 for international students. Applications are processed on a rolling basis. Application fee: $50 ($70 for international students). Electronic applications accepted. *Financial support:* In 2011–12, 80 students received support, including 4 fellowships with full tuition reimbursements available (averaging $18,880 per year), 43 research assistantships with full and partial tuition reimbursements available (averaging $16,225 per year), 30 teaching assistantships with full and partial tuition reimbursements available (averaging $14,146 per year); Federal Work-Study, institutionally sponsored loans, health care benefits, and unspecified assistantships also available. Financial award application deadline: 2/1; financial award applicants required to submit FAFSA. *Faculty research:* Robotics, artificial intelligence, algorithms, database software engineering, high-performance computing. *Total annual research expenditures:* $1.3 million. *Unit head:* Dr. Bijaya S. Karki, Interim Chair, 225-578-1495, Fax: 225-578-1465, E-mail: bbkarki@lsu.edu. *Application contact:* Graduate Coordinator, 225-578-1495, Fax: 225-578-1465. Web site: http://www.csc.lsu.edu/.

Louisiana State University in Shreveport, College of Liberal Arts and Sciences, Program in Computer Systems Technology, Shreveport, LA 71115-2399. Offers MS. *Students:* 7 full-time (3 women), 3 part-time (1 woman). Average age 30. 9 applicants, 89% accepted, 3 enrolled. In 2011, 8 master's awarded. *Degree requirements:* For master's, thesis or alternative. *Entrance requirements:* For master's, GRE, programming course in high-level language, interview. Additional exam requirements/recommendations for international students: Required—TOEFL (minimum score 550 paper-based; 213 computer-based; 80 iBT). *Application deadline:* For fall admission, 6/30 for domestic and international students; for spring admission, 11/30 for domestic and international students. Applications are processed on a rolling basis. Application fee: $10 ($20 for international students). *Financial support:* In 2011–12, 2 research assistantships (averaging $5,000 per year) were awarded. *Unit head:* Dr. Krishna Agarwal, Program Director, 318-795-4283, Fax: 318-795-2419, E-mail: krishna.agarwal@lsus.edu. *Application contact:* Christianne Wojcik, Director of Academic Services, 318-797-5247, Fax: 318-798-4120, E-mail: yyarbrou@lsus.edu.

Miami University, School of Engineering and Applied Science, Department of Computer Science and Software Engineering, Oxford, OH 45056. Offers computer science (MCS). *Students:* 15 full-time (3 women), 1 (woman) part-time; includes 4 minority (3 Asian, non-Hispanic/Latino; 1 Hispanic/Latino), 5 international. Average age 24. In 2011, 7 master's awarded. *Entrance requirements:* For master's, GRE, minimum cumulative undergraduate GPA of 3.0. Additional exam requirements/recommendations for international students: Required—TOEFL (minimum score 500 paper-based; 250 computer-based). *Application deadline:* For fall admission, 2/1 for domestic and international students. Application fee: $50. Electronic applications accepted. *Expenses:* Tuition, state resident: full-time $12,023; part-time $501 per credit hour. Tuition, nonresident: full-time $26,554; part-time $1107 per credit hour. *Required fees:* $528. *Financial support:* Fellowships, research assistantships, teaching assistantships, Federal Work-Study, health care benefits, tuition waivers (full), and unspecified assistantships available. Financial award application deadline: 2/1; financial award applicants required to submit FAFSA. *Unit head:* Dr. James Kiper, Chair, 513-529-0345, E-mail: kiperjd@muohio.edu. *Application contact:* 513-529-0340, E-mail: seasgrad@muohio.edu. Web site: http://www.eas.muohio.edu/csa/.

New Jersey Institute of Technology, Office of Graduate Studies, College of Computing Science, Department of Computer Science, Program in Computing and Business, Newark, NJ 07102. Offers MS. *Students:* 5 full-time (3 women), 8 part-time; includes 6 minority (5 Black or African American, non-Hispanic/Latino; 1 Asian, non-Hispanic/Latino), 2 international. Average age 29. 25 applicants, 60% accepted, 4 enrolled. In 2011, 3 master's awarded. *Entrance requirements:* Additional exam requirements/recommendations for international students: Required—TOEFL (minimum score 550 paper-based; 213 computer-based; 79 iBT). *Application deadline:* For fall admission, 6/1 priority date for domestic students, 5/1 for international students; for spring admission, 11/15 priority date for domestic students, 11/15 for international students. Applications are processed on a rolling basis. Application fee: $65. Electronic applications accepted. *Expenses:* Tuition, state resident: full-time $7980; part-time $867 per credit. Tuition, nonresident: full-time $11,336; part-time $1196 per credit. *Required fees:* $230 per credit. *Financial support:* Application deadline: 1/15. *Unit head:* Dr. Michael A. Baltrush, Interim Chair, 973-596-3386, E-mail: michael.a.baltrush@njit.edu. *Application contact:* Kathryn Kelly, Director of Admissions, 973-596-3300, Fax: 973-596-3461, E-mail: admissions@njit.edu. Web site: http://cs.njit.edu/academics/graduate/mscb.php.

Oakland University, Graduate Study and Lifelong Learning, School of Engineering and Computer Science, Department of Computer Science and Engineering, Rochester, MI 48309-4401. Offers computer science (MS); embedded systems (MS); information systems engineering (MS); software engineering (MS). Part-time and evening/weekend programs available. *Entrance requirements:* For master's, minimum GPA of 3.0 for unconditional admission. Electronic applications accepted. *Expenses:* Contact institution. *Faculty research:* Cyber security, 3D imaging of neurochemicals in rat brains.

Portland State University, Graduate Studies, Maseeh College of Engineering and Computer Science, Department of Engineering and Technology Management, Portland, OR 97207-0751. Offers engineering and technology management (M Eng); engineering management (MS); manufacturing engineering (ME); manufacturing management (M Eng); systems science/engineering management (PhD); MS/MBA; MS/MS. Part-time and evening/weekend programs available. *Degree requirements:* For master's, thesis optional; for doctorate, one foreign language, thesis/dissertation, oral and written exams. *Entrance requirements:* For master's, minimum GPA of 3.0 in upper-division course work, BS in civil engineering; for doctorate, GRE General Test, GRE Subject Test, minimum GPA of 3.0 in upper-division course work. Additional exam requirements/recommendations for international students: Required—TOEFL (minimum score 550 paper-based; 213 computer-based). *Faculty research:* Scheduling, hierarchical decision modeling, operations research, knowledge-based information systems.

Portland State University, Graduate Studies, Systems Science Program, Portland, OR 97207-0751. Offers computational intelligence (Certificate); computer modeling and simulation (Certificate); systems science (MS); systems science/anthropology (PhD); systems science/business administration (PhD); systems science/civil engineering (PhD); systems science/economics (PhD); systems science/engineering management (PhD); systems science/general (PhD); systems science/mathematical sciences (PhD); systems science/mechanical engineering (PhD); systems science/psychology (PhD); systems science/sociology (PhD). *Degree requirements:* For doctorate, variable foreign language requirement, thesis/dissertation. *Entrance requirements:* For master's, 2 letters of recommendation; for doctorate, GMAT, GRE General Test, minimum undergraduate GPA of 3.0. Additional exam requirements/recommendations for international students: Required—TOEFL. *Faculty research:* Systems theory and methodology, artificial intelligence neural networks, information theory, nonlinear dynamics/chaos, modeling and simulation.

Rensselaer at Hartford, Department of Engineering, Program in Computer and Systems Engineering, Hartford, CT 06120-2991. Offers ME. *Entrance requirements:* For master's, GRE.

Southern Methodist University, Bobby B. Lyle School of Engineering, Department of Engineering Management, Information, and Systems, Dallas, TX 75275. Offers applied science (MS); engineering management (MSEM, DE); information engineering and management (MSIEM); operations research (MS, PhD); systems engineering (MS, PhD). Part-time and evening/weekend programs available. Postbaccalaureate distance learning degree programs offered. Terminal master's awarded for partial completion of doctoral program. *Degree requirements:* For master's, thesis optional; for doctorate, thesis/dissertation, oral and written qualifying exams. *Entrance requirements:* For master's, minimum GPA of 3.0 in last 2 years; bachelor's degree in engineering, mathematics, sciences, or technical area; for doctorate, GRE General Test (operations research, engineering management), bachelor's degree in related field. Additional exam requirements/recommendations for international students: Required—TOEFL. *Faculty research:* Telecommunications, decision systems, information engineering, operations research, software.

State University of New York at Binghamton, Graduate School, Thomas J. Watson School of Engineering and Applied Science, Department of Systems Science and Industrial Engineering, Binghamton, NY 13902-6000. Offers M Eng, MS, MSAT, PhD. Part-time and evening/weekend programs available. *Faculty:* 10 full-time (2 women), 4 part-time/adjunct (1 woman). *Students:* 80 full-time (21 women), 75 part-time (13 women); includes 20 minority (5 Black or African American, non-Hispanic/Latino; 2 American Indian or Alaska Native, non-Hispanic/Latino; 5 Asian, non-Hispanic/Latino; 4 Hispanic/Latino; 4 Native Hawaiian or other Pacific Islander, non-Hispanic/Latino), 82 international. Average age 30. 164 applicants, 68% accepted, 40 enrolled. In 2011, 49 master's, 8 doctorates awarded. Terminal master's awarded for partial completion of doctoral program. *Degree requirements:* For master's, thesis or alternative; for doctorate, thesis/dissertation. *Entrance requirements:* For master's and doctorate, GRE General Test, GRE Subject Test. Additional exam requirements/recommendations for international students: Required—TOEFL. *Application deadline:* For fall admission, 4/15 priority date for domestic students, 1/15 for international students; for spring admission, 11/1 for domestic students, 10/1 for international students. Applications are processed on a rolling basis. Application fee: $60. Electronic applications accepted. *Financial support:* In 2011–12, 72 students received support, including 1 fellowship with full tuition reimbursement available (averaging $16,500 per year), 50 research assistantships with full tuition reimbursements available (averaging $16,500 per year), 15 teaching assistantships with full tuition reimbursements available (averaging $16,500 per year); career-related internships or fieldwork, Federal Work-Study, institutionally sponsored loans, scholarships/grants, health care benefits, tuition waivers (full and partial), and unspecified assistantships also available. Financial award application deadline: 2/15; financial award applicants required to submit FAFSA. *Faculty research:* Problem restructuring, protein modeling. *Unit head:* Dr. Nagen Nagarur, Chair, 607-777-3027, E-mail: nnagarur@binghamton.edu. *Application contact:* Catherine Smith, Recruiting and Admissions Coordinator, 607-777-2151, Fax: 607-777-2501, E-mail: cmsmith@binghamton.edu. Web site: http://www.ssie.binghamton.edu.

Stevens Institute of Technology, Graduate School, Charles V. Schaefer Jr. School of Engineering, Department of Mechanical Engineering, Program in Integrated Product Development, Hoboken, NJ 07030. Offers armament engineering (M Eng); computer and electrical engineering (M Eng); manufacturing technologies (M Eng); systems reliability and design (M Eng).

Stevens Institute of Technology, Graduate School, School of Systems and Enterprises, Program in Enterprise Systems, Hoboken, NJ 07030. Offers MS, PhD.

Strayer University, Graduate Studies, Washington, DC 20005-2603. Offers accounting (MS); acquisition (MBA); business administration (MBA); communications technology (MS); educational management (M Ed); finance (MBA); health services administration (MHSA); hospitality and tourism management (MBA); human resource management (MBA); information systems (MS), including computer security management, decision support system management, enterprise resource management, network management, software engineering management, systems development management; management (MBA); management information systems (MS); marketing (MBA); professional accounting (MS), including accounting information systems, controllership, taxation; public administration (MPA); supply chain management (MBA); technology in education (M Ed). Programs also offered at campus locations in Birmingham, AL; Chamblee, GA; Cobb County, GA; Morrow, GA; White Marsh, MD; Charleston, SC; Columbia, SC; Greensboro, NC; Greenville, SC; Lexington, KY; Louisville, KY; Nashville, TN; North Raleigh, NC; Washington, DC. Part-time and evening/weekend programs available. Postbaccalaureate distance learning degree programs offered (minimal on-campus study). *Degree requirements:* For master's, thesis. *Entrance requirements:* For master's, GMAT, GRE General Test, bachelor's degree from an accredited college or university, minimum undergraduate GPA of 2.75. Electronic applications accepted.

Universidad Autonoma de Guadalajara, Graduate Programs, Guadalajara, Mexico. Offers administrative law and justice (LL M); advertising and corporate communications (MA); architecture (M Arch); business (MBA); computational science (MCC); education (Ed M, Ed D); English-Spanish translation (MA); entrepreneurship and management (MBA); integrated management of digital animation (MA); international business (MIB);

international corporate law (LL M); internet technologies (MS); manufacturing systems (MMS); occupational health (MS); philosophy (MA, PhD); power electronics (MS); quality systems (MQS); renewable energy (MS); social evaluation of projects (MBA); strategic market research (MBA); tax law (MA); teaching mathematics (MA).

The University of North Carolina Wilmington, College of Arts and Sciences, Program in Computer Science and Information Systems, Wilmington, NC 28403-3297. Offers MS. *Entrance requirements:* For master's, GMAT or GRE, 3 letters of recommendation, resume.

University of Ottawa, Faculty of Graduate and Postdoctoral Studies, Interdisciplinary Programs, Ottawa, ON K1N 6N5, Canada. Offers e-business (Certificate); e-commerce (Certificate); finance (Certificate); health services and policies research (Diploma); population health (PhD); population health risk assessment and management (Certificate); public management and governance (Certificate); systems science (Certificate).

University of Ottawa, Faculty of Graduate and Postdoctoral Studies, Systems Science Program, Ottawa, ON K1N 6N5, Canada. Offers M Sc, M Sys Sc, Certificate. Part-time and evening/weekend programs available. *Degree requirements:* For master's and Certificate, thesis optional. *Entrance requirements:* For master's, bachelor's degree or equivalent, minimum B average; for Certificate, honors degree or equivalent, minimum B average. Additional exam requirements/recommendations for international students: Recommended—TOEFL (minimum score 237 computer-based). Electronic applications accepted. *Faculty research:* Software engineering, communication systems, information systems, production management, corporate managerial modeling.

Washington University in St. Louis, School of Engineering and Applied Science, Department of Electrical and Systems Engineering, St. Louis, MO 63130-4899. Offers electrical engineering (MS, D Sc, PhD); systems science and mathematics (MS, D Sc, PhD). Part-time programs available. Terminal master's awarded for partial completion of doctoral program. *Degree requirements:* For master's, thesis or alternative; for doctorate, comprehensive exam, thesis/dissertation. *Entrance requirements:* For master's, minimum GPA of 3.0 in the last 2 years of undergraduate course work; for doctorate, GRE. Additional exam requirements/recommendations for international students: Required—TOEFL (minimum score 550 paper-based; 213 computer-based; 80 iBT). Electronic applications accepted. *Faculty research:* Applied physics and electronics, signal and image processing, systems analysis, biomedicine, and energy.

Worcester Polytechnic Institute, Graduate Studies and Research, Department of Social Science and Policy Studies, Worcester, MA 01609-2280. Offers interdisciplinary social science (PhD); system dynamics (MS, Graduate Certificate). Part-time and evening/weekend programs available. Postbaccalaureate distance learning degree programs offered (no on-campus study). *Faculty:* 5 full-time (1 woman), 1 part-time/adjunct (0 women). *Students:* 7 part-time (3 women), 1 international. 3 applicants, 100% accepted, 3 enrolled. In 2011, 6 master's awarded. *Entrance requirements:* For master's, GRE General Test, 3 letters of recommendation. Additional exam requirements/recommendations for international students: Required—TOEFL (minimum score 563 paper-based; 223 computer-based; 84 iBT), IELTS (minimum score 7). *Application deadline:* For fall admission, 1/1 priority date for domestic students, 1/1 for international students; for spring admission, 10/1 priority date for domestic students, 10/1 for international students. Applications are processed on a rolling basis. Application fee: $70. Electronic applications accepted. *Financial support:* Research assistantships, teaching assistantships, career-related internships or fieldwork, institutionally sponsored loans, scholarships/grants, and unspecified assistantships available. Financial award application deadline: 1/1; financial award applicants required to submit FAFSA. *Faculty research:* Feedback economics, political economy, system dynamics, systems thinking, social simulation. *Unit head:* Dr. James K. Doyle, Head, 508-831-5296, Fax: 508-831-5896, E-mail: doyle@wpi.edu. *Application contact:* Dr. Oleg Pavlov, Graduate Coordinator, 508-831-5296, Fax: 508-831-5896, E-mail: opavlov@wpi.edu. Web site: http://www.wpi.edu/academics/Depts/SSPS/.

COLUMBIA UNIVERSITY
Department of Computer Science

Programs of Study

The doctoral program of the Department of Computer Science is geared toward the exceptional student. The faculty believes that the best way to learn how to do research is by doing it; therefore, starting in their first semester, students conduct joint research with faculty members. In addition to conducting research they also prepare themselves for the Ph.D. comprehensive examinations, which test breadth in computer science. The primary educational goal is to prepare students for research and teaching careers either in universities or in industry. The Department enjoys a low doctoral student–faculty ratio (about 4:1).

Current research areas include artificial intelligence, collaborative work, computational biology, computational complexity, computational learning theory, computer architecture, computer-aided design of digital systems, databases, digital libraries, distributed computing, graphics, HCI, digital system design, mobile and wearable computing, multimedia, natural-language processing, networking, network management, operating systems, parallel processing, robotics, security, software engineering, user interfaces, virtual and augmented reality, vision, and Web technologies.

The Department also offers the Master of Science degree in computer science. This program can be completed within three semesters of full-time classwork. Completing the optional thesis generally stretches the program to two years. The M.S. degree can also be earned through part-time study. An interdepartmental M.S. degree in computer engineering is also offered between the computer science and electrical engineering departments.

Research Facilities

The Department has well-equipped lab areas for research in computer graphics, computer-aided digital design, computer vision, databases and digital libraries, data mining and knowledge discovery, distributed systems, mobile and wearable computing, natural-language processing, networking, operating systems, programming systems, robotics, user interfaces, and real-time multimedia.

The computer facilities include a gigabit network with 3-GB uplink, NetApp file servers, a student interactive teaching and research lab of high-end multimedia workstations, a large VMware system for teaching, a programming laboratory with eighteen Windows workstations and sixty-three Linux workstations, a cluster of Linux servers for computational work, a cluster of Sun servers, and a compute cluster consisting of a Linux cloud that can support approximately 5,000 VMware instances. The research infrastructure includes hundreds of workstations and PCs running Solaris, Windows, Linux, and Mac OSX; terabytes of disk space are backed up to disks and also to tapes.

Research labs contain several large Linux and Solaris clusters; Puma 500 and IBM robotic arms; a UTAH-MIT dexterous hand; an Adept-1 robot; mobile research robots; a real-time defocus range sensor; interactive 3-D graphics workstations with 3-D position and orientation trackers; prototype wearable computers; wall-sized stereo projection systems; see-through head-mounted displays; a networking testbed with three Cisco 7500 backbone routers; traffic generators; Ethernet switches; and a network security testbed with secure LAN, Cisco routers, EMC storage and a Linux server. The Department uses a 3COM SIP IP phone system. The protocol was developed in the Department. The Department is on a gigabit network which has direct connectivity to the campus OC-3 Internet and Internet 2 gateways.

The campus has 802.11 a/b wireless LAN coverage.

The research facility is supported by a full-time staff of professional system administrators and programmers aided by a number of part-time student system administrators.

Financial Aid

Most doctoral students and a few master's students receive graduate research assistantships. The stipend for 2011–12 was $2829 per month for the academic year. In addition, graduate research assistants receive full tuition exemption. A limited number of teaching assistantships are available to doctoral students.

Cost of Study

Tuition and fees totaled approximately $44,160 for the M.S. program and $36,500 for the Ph.D. program for the 2011–12 academic year.

Living and Housing Costs

In 2011–12, apartments in University-owned buildings cost $775–$1325 and up per month. Rooms are also available at International House; these cost $815–$1355 and up per month.

Student Group

There are 120 Ph.D. students in the Department. A large proportion of Columbia University's student body is at the graduate level; of the 25,459 students, 15,819 are in the graduate or professional schools.

Location

New York City is the intellectual, artistic, cultural, gastronomic, corporate, financial, and media center of the United States, and perhaps of the world. The city is renowned for its theaters, museums, libraries, restaurants, opera, and music. Inexpensive student tickets for cultural and sporting events are frequently available, and the museums are open to students at very modest cost or are free. The ethnic variety of the city adds to its appeal. The city is bordered by uncongested areas of great beauty that provide varied types of recreation, such as hiking, camping, skiing, and ocean and lake swimming. There are superb beaches on Long Island and in New Jersey, while to the north lie the Catskill, Green, Berkshire, and Adirondack mountains. Close at hand is the beautiful Hudson River valley.

The University

Columbia University was established as King's College in 1754. Today it consists of sixteen schools and faculties and is one of the leading universities in the world. The University draws students from many countries. The high caliber of the students and faculty makes it an intellectually stimulating place to be. Columbia University is located on Morningside Heights, close to Lincoln Center for the Performing Arts, Greenwich Village, Central Park, and midtown Manhattan. Columbia athletic teams compete in the Ivy League.

Applying

For maximum consideration for admission to the doctoral program, students should submit the required application materials before December 1 for the fall term and before October 1 for the spring term. Applicants must submit official applications, transcripts, at least three recommendation letters, and an application fee. The General and Subject Tests of the Graduate Record Examinations are required for all computer science graduate applicants. The deadlines for applications to the master's program are February 15 for fall admission and October 1 for spring admission.

Program information can be found at http://www.cs.columbia.edu. Further details on admission and online application for the M.S. program are on the Web at http://www.cs.columbia.edu/education/

admissions#msadmissions and for the Ph.D. program at http://www.
cs.columbia.edu/education/admissions#phd.

Correspondence and Information
Fu Foundation School of Engineering and Applied Science
Department of Computer Science
450 Computer Science Building
Mail Code 0401
Columbia University
1214 Amsterdam Avenue
New York, New York 10027-7003
Phone: 212-939-7000
Web site: http://www.cs.columbia.edu/education/admissions

THE FACULTY AND THEIR RESEARCH

Alfred V. Aho, Lawrence Gussman Professor. Programming languages, compilers, software, quantum computing.

Peter K. Allen, Professor. Robotics, computer vision, 3-D modeling.

Peter Belhumeur, Professor. Computer vision, biometrics, face recognition, computational photography, computer graphics, biological species identification.

Steven M. Bellovin, Professor. Internet security, computer security, privacy, information technology policy.

Adam H. Cannon, Lecturer in Discipline. Machine learning, statistical pattern recognition, computer science education.

Luca Carloni, Associate Professor. Computer-aided design, embedded systems, multi-core platform architectures, cyber-physical systems.

Augustin Chaintreau, Assistant Professor. Networked algorithms, social networks, mobile computing, stochastic networks.

Shih-Fu Chang, Richard Dicker Professor. Multimedia, computer vision, machine learning, signal processing, information retrieval, visual search.

Xi Chen, Assistant Professor. Algorithmic game theory and economics, computational complexity theory.

Michael Collins, Vikram S. Pandit Professor. Natural language processing and machine learning.

Stephen A. Edwards, Associate Professor. Embedded systems, domain-specific languages, compilers, hardware-software codesign, computer-aided design.

Steven K. Feiner, Professor. Human-computer interaction, augmented reality and virtual environments, 3-D user interfaces, knowledge-based design of graphics and multimedia, mobile and wearable computing, computer games, health-management user interfaces, information visualization.

Luis Gravano, Associate Professor. Databases, digital libraries, distributed search over text databases, Web search, "top-k" query processing, information extraction, text mining.

Eitan Grinspun, Associate Professor. Computer graphics, geometry processing, computational mechanics, scientific computing, discrete differential geometry.

Jonathan L. Gross, Professor of Computer Science, Mathematics, and Mathematical Statistics. Computational aspects of topological graph theory and knot theory, enumerative analysis, and combinatorial models; applications to network layouts on higher-order surfaces and to interactive computer graphics of weaves and links.

Julia Hirschberg, Professor. Natural-language processing, spoken language processing, spoken dialogue systems, deceptive speech.

Tony Jebara, Associate Professor. Machine learning, social networks, graphs, vision, spatio-temporal modeling.

Gail E. Kaiser, Professor. Social software engineering, collaborative work, privacy and security, software reliability, self-managing systems, parallel and distributed systems, Web technologies, information management, software development environments and tools.

John R. Kender, Professor. Computer vision, video understanding, visual user interfaces, medical imaging processing, artificial intelligence.

Angelos D. Keromytis, Associate Professor. Computer and network security.

Martha A. Kim, Assistant Professor. Computer architecture, hardware systems, hardware/software interaction, parallel hardware and software systems.

Tal G. Malkin, Associate Professor. Cryptography, information and network security, foundations of computer science, computational complexity, distributed computation, randomness in computation.

Kathleen R. McKeown, Henry and Gertrude Rothschild Professor. Artificial intelligence, natural-language processing, language generation, multimedia explanation, text summarization, user interfaces, user modeling, digital libraries.

Vishal Misra, Associate Professor. Networking, modeling and performance evaluation, Internet economics.

Shree K. Nayar, T. C. Chang Professor. Computer vision, computational imaging, computer graphics, robotics, human-computer interfaces.

Jason Nieh, Associate Professor. Operating systems, distributed systems, mobile computing, thin-client computing, performance evaluation.

Steven M. Nowick, Professor. Asynchronous and mixed-timing digital circuits and systems, computer-aided design, networks-on-chip, interconnection networks for parallel processors, low-power digital design.

Dana Pe'er, Associate Professor. Computational biology, machine learning, biological networks, genomics and systems biology.

Itsik Pe'er, Associate Professor. Computational biology, genomics, medical and population genetics, isolated and admixed populations, analysis of heritable variation in cancer.

Kenneth A. Ross, Professor. Databases, query optimization, declarative languages for database systems, logic programming, architecture-sensitive software design.

Dan Rubenstein, Associate Professor. Computer networks, network robustness and security, multimedia networking, performance evaluation, algorithms, low-power networking.

Henning G. Schulzrinne, Julian Clarence Levi Professor. Computer networks, multimedia systems, mobile and wireless systems, ubiquitous and pervasive computing.

Rocco A. Servedio, Associate Professor. Computational learning theory, computational complexity theory, randomness in computation, combinatorics, cryptography.

Simha Sethumadhavan, Assistant Professor. Computer architecture, hardware security.

Clifford Stein, Professor. Algorithms, combinatorial optimization, scheduling, network algorithms.

Salvatore J. Stolfo, Professor. Computer security, intrusion detection systems, parallel computing, artificial intelligence, machine learning.

Joseph F. Traub, Edwin Howard Armstrong Professor. Quantum computing, computational complexity, information-based complexity, financial computations.

Henryk Woniakowski, Professor. Computational complexity, information-based complexity, quantum computing, algorithmic analysis, numerical mathematics.

Junfeng Yang, Assistant Professor. Operating systems, software reliability, programming languages, security, distributed systems, software engineering.

Mihalis Yannakakis, Percy K. and Vida L. W. Hudson Professor. Algorithms, complexity theory, combinatorial optimization, databases, testing and verification.

Changxi Zheng, Assistant Professor. Computer graphics, physically-based multi-sensory animation, physically-based sound rendering, scientific computing, robotics.

Associated Faculty/Research Scientists
Edward G. Coffman, Jr., Professor Emeritus. Computer and network performance evaluation, analysis of algorithms, mathematical models of molecular computing.

Stephen H. Unger, Professor Emeritus of Computer Science and Electrical Engineering. Logic circuits theory, digital systems, self-timed systems, parallel processing, technology-society interface, engineering ethics.

Vladimir Vapnik, Professor, Computer Science and Center for Computational Learning Systems. Empirical inference, support vector machines, kernel methods, transductive inference.

Yechiam Yemini, Professor Emeritus. Computer networks.

DAKOTA STATE UNIVERSITY
Department of Information Systems and Technology

Programs of Study

Dakota State University (DSU) offers graduate degree programs in educational technology (M.S.E.T.), information assurance (M.S.I.A.), health informatics (M.S.H.I.), and information systems (M.S.I.S. and D.Sc.). The programs are available online or on campus. Educational technology requires a one-week residency on campus. There are no other required graduate program residencies.

The Master of Science in Educational Technology program (M.S.E.T) empowers educators and trainers to meet the increasing demands of integrating technology in curriculum and instruction. Specializations include distance education, technology systems, and a K–12 educational technology endorsement. Students take 36 credits in common core courses, which are shared between DSU and the University of South Dakota. GetEducated.com rates the program a best buy. Students should visit http://www.dsu.edu/mset/index.aspx for more information.

The Master of Science in Information Assurance program (M.S.I.A.) prepares graduates to protect an organization's information assets. Both the National Security Agency and the Department of Homeland Security have designated DSU as a National Center of Academic Excellence in Information Assurance Education (CAEIAE). The program requires 30 hours beyond the baccalaureate, including six core courses (18 credit hours) and a four-course sequence (12 credit hours) in a specialization. Specializations include banking and financial security, and cybersecurity. GetEducated.com rates the program a best buy. For more information, students should visit http://www.dsu.edu/msia/index.aspx.

The Master of Science in Health Informatics (M.S.H.I.) is intended to produce graduates who are expected to play a key role in the design, development, and management of health information systems in health-care related facilities, agencies, and organizations, in integrated delivery systems, and in interconnected, community-wide health data exchanges and regional networks. The program is intended to attract students with a variety of educational backgrounds and disciplines. The program requires 33 hours beyond the baccalaureate, including seven core courses (21 credit hours), three elective courses (9 credit hours), and a three-credit capstone experience. For more information, students should visit http://www.dsu.edu/mshi/index.aspx.

The Master of Science in Information Systems program (M.S.I.S.) focuses on the integration of information technology with business problems and opportunities. Specializations include data management, application development, network administration and security, and health-care information systems. GetEducated.com rates it a best buy. For more information, students should visit http://www.dsu.edu/msis/index.aspx.

The Doctor of Science (D.Sc.) in information systems program prepares students for careers in teaching, research, consulting, and corporate employment. Specializations include decision support, knowledge and data management, information assurance and computer security, and health-care information systems. The D.Sc. requires 88 semester credit hours. Students take 63 credit hours of graduate course work: 27 credit hours of master's-level information systems, which may be waived for students who have completed the M.S.I.S. program or equivalent; 9 credit hours of research methods; and 27 credit hours of research specialization, including research seminars and core and elective courses. D.Sc. students must also complete a screening examination, a qualifying portfolio, and 25 credit hours of dissertation. For more information, students should visit http://www.dsu.edu/doctor-of-science/index.aspx.

Research Facilities

The Karl E. Mundt Library provides access to an extensive collection of materials through its online library catalog, which includes more than 4.5 million holdings of more than seventy libraries in the South Dakota Library Network (SDLN). In addition to being an online catalog of library holdings, the SDLN has been enriched by the addition of a number of external databases, most notably, EBSCO's Academic Search Premier, Lexis-Nexis Academic, ProQuest Research Library, and ABI-Inform. Many of these databases provide the full text and images of articles and books. Web-based access to the information services provides students with access to databases critical to their disciplines. Materials held by other libraries are readily available through the electronic interlibrary loan system or full text. The library also provides online access to tutorials and other research aides.

DSU also offers an Advanced Informatics Research Lab (AIRL) which is a state-of-the-art computing lab supporting applied information systems research in the areas of decision support data and knowledge management, information assurance, and health care. It supports the information systems faculty, graduate assistants, and students (online and on-campus) involved in the D.Sc. in information systems program. The lab includes infrastructure to support development and deployment of prototypes and other research results and computing capacity for conducting statistical analysis and running and solving models. It allows distance students access to computing resources and specialized workstations and software. The AIRL also has a variety of decision support tools and technologies for building and deploying DSS. Its servers run Windows and Linux operating systems and the lab provides support for .NET, JAVA and other development environment/technologies, e.g., MS SQL, Visual Studio 2005, etc.

An excellent computer environment is found at DSU. Computer laboratories are available in every academic building on campus. To provide ample facilities for both instruction and outside course work, labs are used directly in teaching and for general access. For the convenience of students, microcomputers are located in the dorms, in the Trojan Center (student union), and the library. In addition to cabled connections, a wireless network also supports mobile computing devices in each academic building, the Trojan Center, and the library.

Financial Aid

Graduate students apply for federal financial aid with the Free Application for Federal Student Aid (FAFSA), either online or with a paper form. Graduate students may be eligible to receive Federal Stafford Loans and Federal Perkins Loans but not Federal Pell Grants or Federal Supplemental Education Opportunity Grants. In addition, graduate assistantships are available to qualified graduate students, based on need and/or merit and available funds. Recipients of an assistantship receive a reduced tuition rate (student pays one third the state-support tuition rate) and a stipend as established by the Board of Regents. More information is available online at http://www.dsu.edu/gradoffice/grad-assistantships.aspx or by phone at 605-256-5799.

Dakota State University

Cost of Study

For the academic year 2012–13, tuition per credit hour ranges from $189 to $399 depending on residency and delivery of the courses. Online courses are $383 per credit for both in-state and out-of-state students. Fees total around $116 per credit hour for all students in classes on the DSU campus. More information is available at http://www.dsu.edu/gradoffice/grad-tuition-fees.aspx.

Living and Housing Costs

On-campus housing is available. Local telephone service, cable TV, and Internet access are included in the semester room fee. Students are expected to provide their own phone. Each hall has one or more kitchens, TV lounges, and card/coin-operated washers and dryers. Residence hall rates range between $1385 and $1818 per semester, whereas apartments are $1675 per person per semester. Meal plans range from $1088 to $1541 per semester. The Madison community has several apartment complexes and other off-campus housing.

Location

DSU is in Madison, South Dakota, less than an hour northwest of Sioux Falls. Madison is in the state's southern lakes region, which offers great outdoor recreation. The University is minutes from Lake Herman State Park and Walker's Point Recreation Area. Madison offers a variety of options for dining, shopping, and entertainment. For fitness and other recreation, students can easily walk to Madison's excellent Community Center. Madison is a safe town, with little traffic and a high quality of life as well as job opportunities for students and spouses.

The University

Dakota State University (DSU) strives to be one of the best technological universities in the Midwest. *U.S. News & World Report* ranked DSU the number 1 public baccalaureate college in the Midwest five years in a row in 2007, 2008, 2009, 2010, and again in 2011. DSU is accredited by the North Central Association of Colleges and Schools, and GetEducated.com rates its online master's degree programs as best buys.

Applying

In general, students should have earned a baccalaureate degree from a regionally accredited college or university. Each applicant must provide a completed application form, the $35 application fee, one official transcript for all college work, three forms of recommendation, and official scores on the standardized graduate admission test (see specific programs for what test is required). All international applicants must take the Test of English as a Foreign Language (TOEFL) and score at least 550 on the PBT (213 on the CBT or 79 on the iBT). Students should check online for program-specific requirements and deadlines.

Correspondence and Information

Office of Graduate Studies & Research
Dakota State University
Madison, South Dakota 57042-1799
Phone: 605-256-5799
Fax: 605-256-5093
E-mail: gradoffice@dsu.edu
Web site: http://www.dsu.edu/gradoffice/index.aspx

THE FACULTY

Richard Avery, Associate Professor of Mathematics; Ph.D., Nebraska–Lincoln.

Richard Christoph, Professor of Computer Information Systems; Ph.D., Clemson.

Amit Deokar, Assistant Professor of Information Systems; Ph.D., Arizona.

Omar El-Gayar, Associate Professor and Dean of Graduate Studies and Research; Ph.D., Hawaii at Manoa.

William Figg, Associate Professor of Computer Information Systems; Ph.D., Capella.

Mark Geary, Assistant Professor of Education, Ph.D.

Steve Graham, Assistant Professor of Computer Science; Ph.D., Kansas.

Tom Halverson, Associate Professor of Computer Science and Dean of the College of Business and Information Systems; Ph.D., Iowa.

Mark Hawkes, Associate Professor of Instructional Technology and Program Coordinator of the Master of Science in Educational Technology; Ph.D., Syracuse.

Stephen Krebsbach, Associate Professor of Computer Science; Ph.D., North Dakota State.

Jeff Palmer, Professor of Mathematics; Ph.D., Washington State.

Josh Pauli, Assistant Professor of Information Systems; Ph.D., North Dakota State.

Wayne Pauli, Assistant Professor of Information Systems and Director of Center of Excellence in Computer Information Systems; Ph.D., Capella.

Ronghua Shan, Associate Professor of Computer Science/Information Systems; Ph.D., Nebraska–Lincoln.

Kevin Streff, Assistant Professor of Information Assurance, Director of Center of Excellence in Information Assurance, and MSIA Program Coordinator; Ph.D., Capella.

Daniel Talley, Associate Professor of Economics; Ph.D., Oregon.

Haomin Wang, Associate Professor of Instructional Technology and Webmaster; Ed.D., Northern Arizona.

Don Wiken, Associate Professor of Education; Ed.D., South Dakota.

Dakota State University is among the best technological universities in the Midwest.

UNIVERSITY OF LOUISIANA AT LAFAYETTE
The Center for Advanced Computer Studies

Programs of Study

The primary missions of The Center for Advanced Computer Studies (CACS) at the University of Louisiana at Lafayette (UL Lafayette) are to conduct research and provide graduate-level education in computer engineering and computer science. CACS offers four graduate degrees: the Ph.D. in computer engineering and the Ph.D. in computer science, the Master of Science in Computer Engineering (M.S.C.E.), and the Master of Science in Computer Science (M.S.C.S.). Areas of specialization are bioinformatics and biocomputing; computer and sensor networks; computer architecture and prototyping; computer visualization and graphics; cryptography and data security; entertainment computing and video game design; grid computing; image, video, and multimedia systems; information processing and data mining; intelligent systems and knowledge engineering; parallel and distributed systems; secure systems and networks; software engineering; software-hardware codesign and reconfigurable computing; virtual reality; VLSI and embedded systems; Web technologies and Internet computing; and wireless communications and mobile computing.

Research Facilities

CACS research computing facilities include over 325 mixed-base workstations, numerous laptops, several miniclusters, and about seventy servers. The computers run on multiple versions of Linux, Solaris, Microsoft Windows, and Apple operating systems supporting CACS's research diversity. To communicate with the world and within, CACS's extensive Ethernet network consists of more than twenty routers (five SuperStacks) capable of connecting up to 1,000 devices throughout the building. A wide variety of software is available and ranges from artificial intelligence to VLSI design and other well-known tools such as Cadence, Synopsys, QualNet, Mentor Graphics, Oracle, Maya, and MATLAB. CACS provides five miniclusters, including one in the making, for student research involving high performance, grid, and cloud computing. CACS has a high-performance grid that is connected to LONI (Louisiana Optical Network Initiative), which is part of the National High Speed Network. CACS houses state-of-the-art research laboratories that specialize in a number of fields, including bioinformatics, CajunBot, computer architecture and networking (CAN), entertainment computing/video game design, FPGA and reconfigurable computing, integrated wireless information network (iWIN), Internet computing (LINC), neurocomputing and brain simulation, micro/nano-electronic embedded computing, software systems research, virtual reality, VLSI and SoC, and wireless systems and performance engineering research (WiSPER).

Financial Aid

Fellowships are available for entering students with superior academic records and strong GRE scores, valued at up to $15,775 for Ph.D. students and $9,500 for M.S. students. In addition, all tuition is waived. All fellowship application materials must be received by February 15 for consideration. CACS has a large number of teaching and research assistantships that include a waiver of tuition and most fees. Stipends range from about $7500 to more than $16,000 for the academic year.

Cost of Study

In spring 2012, Louisiana resident tuition totaled $2632.75 per semester. Nonresident students paid $6943.75 per semester. Tuition amounts are subject to change without notice.

Living and Housing Costs

Rooms and/or apartments are available on a first-come, first-served basis to single and married students. The typical cost is $3595 (including board) for married students. Room and board charges vary according to the board plan.

Student Group

Total University enrollment is more than 16,000 students. In fall 2012, there were approximately 200 students enrolled in CACS's graduate programs. UL Lafayette is known to attract international graduate students in the fields of computer science and engineering at both the master's and Ph.D. levels.

Student Outcomes

Among the universities employing/employed some of CACS's recent graduates are Penn State; Notre Dame; California, Davis; Arizona State; Alaska at Fairbanks; West Virginia Tech; Emory; George Mason; Columbia State; Alexandria (Egypt); Calgary (Canada); Arkansas; South Carolina; Houston; Stevens; South Alabama; Tulane; Louisiana Tech; Mississippi State; Haceteppe (Turkey); National Institute of Saudi Arabia; and Chungbuk National University (Korea). Some Ph.D. graduates have accepted employment in industry with Microsoft, IBM (Durham, Boca Raton), Schlumberger (Austin), Intel (San Jose, Portland), LSI Logic (Milpitas, California), Centigram Communication (San Jose), and the Stock Exchange of Thailand.

Location

The University of Louisiana is located in Lafayette, the central city of the geographic area known as Acadiana. The more than 500,000 inhabitants of this locale are mainly descendants of the exiled Acadians of Nova Scotia. Culturally, the region is characterized by a joie de vivre that has given it an international reputation. Lafayette is located approximately 52 miles from the state capital of Baton Rouge and 129 miles from New Orleans.

The University and The Center

The University has an impressive physical plant that is steadily being enlarged on all parts of the campus. It includes the administrative complex; Dupre Library; French House; academic buildings; athletic facilities; housing for men, women, and married students; an art museum; and a Student Union Complex situated on Cypress Lake. Located on the agricultural extension of the campus are Blackham Coliseum, Cajun Field, and the Cajun Dome, which seats approximately 12,000. Since its inception in 1984, The Center for Advanced Computer Studies has demonstrated a strong contribution to high-quality education and research in the fields of computer science and engineering. The University and CACS have created an environment unique in the nation. CACS is one of the first to merge the overlapping,

University of Louisiana at Lafayette

yet disjointed, disciplines of computer science and computer engineering into a successful graduate program. CACS has 15 tenure-track faculty members, 2 research scientists, and 4 support staff members.

Applying

Applications for admission for the fall semester must be submitted to the Graduate School thirty days before classes begin. Applications for graduate assistantships for the fall semester must be submitted to the Graduate School by March 1 and for the spring semester by November 1. Students are notified by April 1 and December 1, respectively, of their acceptance. Requirements for admission include a baccalaureate degree from an accredited institution, an excellent GPA, GRE and TOEFL scores (if the degree is earned outside the United States), three letters of recommendation, and a fluent command of English. Application fees (nonrefundable) are $25 for U.S. citizens, permanent residents, and refugees and $30 for international students. Applications, inquiries, letters of recommendation, transcripts, and GRE and TOEFL scores should be sent to the Graduate School.

Correspondence and Information

Dr. Magdy Bayoumi, Director
Dr. Anthony Maida, Graduate Coordinator
The Center for Advanced Computer Studies
University of Louisiana at Lafayette
P.O. Box 44330
Lafayette, Louisiana 70504-4330
United States
Phone: 337-482-6308
E-mail: info@louisiana.edu
Web site: http://www.cacs.louisiana.edu

THE FACULTY AND THEIR RESEARCH

Professors

Magdy A. Bayoumi, Director of CACS; Ph.D., Windsor, 1984. VLSI design, image and video signal processing, parallel processing, neural networks, wideband, multimedia network architectures, Smart Systems, WSN.

Chee-Hung Henry Chu, Ph.D., Purdue, 1988. Computer vision, signal and image processing, pattern recognition.

Arun Lakhotia, Ph.D., Case Western Reserve, 1989. Computer security, malware analysis, robotics, autonomous ground vehicles.

Vijay V. Raghavan, Ph.D., Alberta, 1978. Information retrieval and extraction; conceptual categorization of text/images; knowledge discovery in databases; integration of unstructured, semi-structured, and structured data; bioinformatics.

Nian-Feng Tzeng, Ph.D., Illinois, 1986. Networked and distributed computer systems, wireless and sensor networks.

Hongyi Wu, Ph.D., SUNY at Buffalo, 2002. Computer networks, mobile computing, wireless sensors networks.

Associate Professors

Christoph Borst, Ph.D., Texas A&M, 2002. Virtual reality, computer graphics, visualization.

Kemal Efe, Ph.D., Leeds (England), 1985. Parallel and distributed systems, Internet computing, search engines, information retrieval.

Gui-Liang Feng, Ph.D., Lehigh, 1990. Error-correcting codes, data compression, fault-tolerant computing, cryptography, network coding, wireless network coding.

Rasiah Loganantharaj, Ph.D., Colorado State, 1985. Bioinformatics including gene regulation, functional annotations, microarray analysis, mining for interesting patterns from genomic sequences and databases.

Anthony S. Maida, Ph.D., SUNY at Buffalo, 1980. Neurocomputing, artificial intelligence, cognitive science.

Dmitri Perkins, Ph.D., Michigan State, 2002. Wireless networks, mobile computing, communication systems.

Dirk Reiners, Ph.D., TU Darmstadt (Germany), 2002. Software systems for interactive 3-D graphics, complex problem visualization, virtual reality, high-reality displays.

Danella Zhao, Ph.D., SUNY at Buffalo, 2004. VLSI testing, embedded systems, wireless.

Assistant Professors

Miao Jin, Ph.D., Stony Brook, SUNY, 2008. Computer graphics, geometric modeling, medical imaging, computer vision, visualization, computational conformal geometry.

Research Scientists

Ryan Benton, Ph.D., Louisiana at Lafayette, 2001. Internet and grid computing.

Suresh Golconda, Ph.D., Louisiana at Lafayette, 2010. Robotics.

UNIVERSITY OF NORTH CAROLINA AT CHAPEL HILL
Department of Computer Science

Programs of Study

The Department offers the Ph.D. and a professional M.S. degree. Study for the M.S. degree includes algorithms, programming languages, and hardware as well as important areas of application. The Ph.D. program includes courses in specialized areas and preparation for teaching and advanced research. Students pursue particular areas of their choice and are actively involved in research. The curricula emphasize the design and application of real computer systems and the portion of theory that guides and supports practice. The Department's orientation is experimental, with clusters of research in bioinformatics and computational biology, computer architecture, computer graphics, computer-supported collaborative work, computer vision, databases and data mining, geometric computing, high-performance computing, human-computer interaction, medical image analysis, networking, real-time systems, robotics, security, software engineering, and theory. Students holding an assistantship can typically expect to earn the M.S. degree in two academic years and the Ph.D. in four or five years.

Research Facilities

All of the Department's computing facilities are housed in two adjoining four-story computer science buildings that feature specialized research laboratories for graphics and image processing, telepresence and computer vision, computer building and design, robotics, computer security, and collaborative, distributed, and parallel systems. The labs, offices, conference areas, and classrooms are bound together by the Department's fully integrated distributed computing environment, which includes more than 1,000 computers, ranging from older systems used for generating network traffic for simulated Internet experiments to state-of-the-art workstations and clusters for graphics- and compute-intensive research. These systems are integrated by high-speed networks and by software that is consistent at the user level over the many architectural platforms. Each student is assigned a computer, with computer assignments based on the students' research or teaching responsibilities and their seniority within the Department. In addition to the Departmental servers and office systems, the research laboratories contain a wide variety of specialized equipment and facilities. The nearby Kenan Science Library has extensive holdings in mathematics, physics, statistics, operations research, and computer science.

Financial Aid

During the academic year, many students are supported by assistantships and fellowships. The stipend for research and teaching assistantships for the nine-month academic year in 2011–12 was $17,000 (20 hours per week). Full-time summer employment on a research project is normally available to students who would like to receive support. The rate for summer 2012 was $850 (40 hours per week) for ten to twelve weeks. This produces a combined annual financial package for graduate assistants of approximately $27,200. Students with assistantships qualify for a Graduate Student Tuition Grant and pay no tuition; they are responsible for paying student fees of $935 per semester. Graduate Student Tuition Grants typically cover M.S. students for four semesters of study and Ph.D. students for ten semesters of study. At no additional cost to them, students are also covered by a comprehensive major medical insurance program, underwritten by Blue Cross/Blue Shield of North Carolina. Each semester, the Department provides a $500 educational fund to any student who receives a competitive fellowship that is not granted by the University of North Carolina at Chapel Hill (UNC–Chapel Hill). The fund may be used for education-related expenses, including books, journals, travel, computer supplies and accessories, and professional memberships. The Department also awards a $1500 supplement each semester to nonservice fellowship holders who join a research team. To apply for an assistantship, the applicant should check the appropriate item on the admission application form. Applicants for assistantships are automatically considered for all available fellowships. Students can expect continued support, contingent upon satisfactory work performance and academic progress. Students are not assigned to specific research projects or teaching assistant positions immediately upon being admitted to the department. Assignments are made just prior to the start of each semester, after faculty members and students have had an opportunity to meet and to discuss their interests. Students are encouraged to gain professional experience through summer internships with companies in the Research Triangle area or in other parts of the country.

Cost of Study

For the 2012–13 academic year, tuition and fees for graduate students at the University of North Carolina at Chapel Hill are $9689 for state residents and $25,779 for nonresidents. A large number of graduate students in computer science pay no tuition, as mentioned in the Financial Aid section.

Living and Housing Costs

Annual living costs for single graduate students in the Chapel Hill area are estimated by University staff members to be $18,000 or higher. On-campus housing is available for both married and single students attending the University.

Student Group

The Department of Computer Science enrolls approximately 160 graduate students; the majority of them attend full-time.

Student Outcomes

A majority of the Department's master's graduates work in industry, in companies ranging from small start-up operations to government research labs and large research and development corporations. Ph.D. graduates work in both academia and industry. Academic employment ranges from positions in four-year colleges, where teaching is the primary focus, to positions at major research universities. Some graduates take postdoctoral positions at research laboratories prior to continuing in industry or joining academia.

Location

Chapel Hill (population 58,000) is a scenic college town located in the heart of North Carolina, where small-town charm mixes with a cosmopolitan atmosphere to provide students with a rich and varied living experience. The town and the surrounding area offer many cultural advantages, including excellent theater and music, museums, and a planetarium. There are also many opportunities to watch and to participate in sports. The Carolina beaches, the Outer Banks, Great Smoky Mountains National Park, and the Blue Ridge Mountains are only a few hours' drive away. The Research Triangle of North Carolina is formed by the University of North Carolina at Chapel Hill, Duke University in Durham, and North Carolina State University in Raleigh. The universities have a combined enrollment of more than 77,000 students, have libraries with more than 14 million volumes with interconnected catalogs and have national prominence in a variety of disciplines. Collectively, they conduct more than $1.5 billion in research each year.

The University and The Department

The 729-acre central campus of UNC–Chapel Hill is among the most beautiful in the country. Of the approximately 29,300 students enrolled, nearly 10,500 are graduate and professional students. The Department's primary missions are research and graduate and undergraduate teaching. It offers the B.A., B.S., M.S., and Ph.D. degrees. The Computer Science Students' Association sponsors both professional and social events and represents the students in Departmental matters. Its president is a voting member at faculty meetings. There is much interaction between students and faculty members, and students contribute to nearly every aspect of the Department's operation.

Applying

Applications for fall admission, complete with a personal statement, all transcripts, three letters of recommendation, and official GRE and/or TOEFL scores should be received by the Graduate School no later than April 10. Application deadlines may be earlier for applicants who wish to be considered for financial aid and fellowships. International applicants should consider completing their applications no later than December 1 to allow time for processing financial and visa documents. Applicants should check the Department Web site for the latest information regarding application deadlines. Early submission is encouraged.

Correspondence and Information

For written information about graduate study:

Admissions and Graduate Studies
Department of Computer Science
Campus Box 3175, Brooks Computer Science Building
University of North Carolina
Chapel Hill, North Carolina 27599-3175
Phone: 919-962-1900
Fax: 919-962-1799
E-mail: admit@cs.unc.edu
Web site: http://www.cs.unc.edu

For applications and admissions information:

The Graduate School
Campus Box 4010, 200 Bynum Hall
University of North Carolina
Chapel Hill, North Carolina 27599-4010
Phone: 919-966-2611
E-mail: gradinfo@unc.edu
Web site: http://gradschool.unc.edu/

THE FACULTY AND THEIR RESEARCH

Stan Ahalt, Professor and Director of the Renaissance Computing Institute (RENCI); Ph.D., Clemson, 1986. Signal, image, and video processing; high-performance scientific and industrial computing; pattern recognition applied to national security problems; high-productivity, domain-specific languages.

Jay Aikat, Research Assistant Professor; Ph.D., North Carolina at Chapel Hill, 2010. Experimental methods and models in networking research and education; measurement and modeling of Internet traffic, protocol benchmarking; Internet traffic generation, wireless networks, congestion control and active queue management.

Ron Alterovitz, Assistant Professor; Ph.D., Berkeley, 2006. Medical robotics, motion planning, physically-based simulation, assistive robotics, medical image analysis.

James Anderson, Professor and Director of Graduate Admissions; Ph.D., Texas at Austin, 1990. Real-time systems, distributed and concurrent algorithms, multicore computing, operating systems.

University of North Carolina at Chapel Hill

Sanjoy K. Baruah, Professor; Ph.D., Texas at Austin, 1993. Scheduling theory, real-time and safety-critical system design, computer networks, resource allocation and sharing in distributed computing environments.
Gary Bishop, Professor; Ph.D., North Carolina at Chapel Hill, 1984. Hardware and software for man-machine interaction, assistive technology, 3-D interactive computer graphics, virtual environments, tracking technologies, image-based rendering.
Frederick P. Brooks Jr., Kenan Professor; Ph.D., Harvard, 1956. 3-D interactive computer graphics, human-computer interaction, virtual worlds, computer architecture, the design process.
Peter Calingaert, Professor Emeritus; Ph.D., Harvard, 1955.
Prasun Dewan, Professor; Ph.D., Wisconsin–Madison, 1986. User interfaces, distributed collaboration, software engineering environments, mobile computing, access control.
Enrique Dunn, Research Assistant Professor; Ph.D. CICESE (Mexico), 2006. Computer vision, evolutionary computation.
Jan-Michael Frahm, Assistant Professor; Ph.D., Kiel (Germany), 2005. Structure from motion, camera self-calibration, camera sensor systems, multicamera systems, multiview stereo, robust estimation, fast-tracking of salient features in images and video, computer vision, active vision for model improvement, markerless augmented reality.
Henry Fuchs, Federico Gil Professor; Ph.D., Utah, 1975. Virtual environments, telepresence, future office environments, 3-D medical imaging, computer vision, robotics.
John H. Halton, Professor Emeritus; D.Phil., Oxford, 1960.
Kye S. Hedlund, Associate Professor; Ph.D., Purdue, 1982. Computer-aided design tools, software engineering.
Kevin Jeffay, Gillian Cell Distinguished Professor and Associate Chairman for Academic Affairs; Ph.D., Washington (Seattle), 1989. Computer networking, operating systems, real-time systems, multimedia networking, performance evaluation.
Vladimir Jojic, Assistant Professor; Ph.D. Toronto (Canada), 2007. Bioinformatics, computational biology, machine learning.
Jasleen Kaur, Associate Professor; Ph.D., Texas at Austin, 2002. Design and analysis of networks and operating systems, specifically resource management for providing service guarantees, Internet measurements, transport protocols and congestion control.
Anselmo A. Lastra, Professor and Chairman; Ph.D., Duke, 1988. Interactive 3-D computer graphics, hardware architectures for computer graphics.
Ming C. Lin, John R. and Louise S. Parker Distinguished Professor; Ph.D., Berkeley, 1993. Physically based and geometric modeling, applied computational geometry, robotics, distributed interactive simulation, virtual environments, algorithm analysis, many-core computing.
Gyula A. Magó, Professor Emeritus; Ph.D., Cambridge, 1970.
Dinesh Manocha, Phi Delta Theta/Matthew Mason Distinguished Professor; Ph.D., Berkeley, 1992. Interactive computer graphics, geometric and solid modeling, robotics, motion planning, many-core algorithms.
Ketan Mayer-Patel, Associate Professor; Ph.D., Berkeley, 1999. Multimedia systems, networking, multicast applications.
Leonard McMillan, Associate Professor, Ph.D., North Carolina at Chapel Hill, 1997. Computational biology, genetics, bioinformatics, information visualization, data-driven modeling, image processing, imaging technologies, computer graphics.
Fabian Monrose, Associate Professor; Ph.D., NYU, 1999. Computer and network security, biometrics and techniques for strong user authentication.
Tessa Joseph Nicholas, Lecturer; Ph.D., North Carolina at Chapel Hill, 2008. New media arts and poetics, digital communities, digital-age ethics.
Marc Niethammer, Assistant Professor; Ph.D., Georgia Tech, 2004. Medical image analysis, shape analysis, image segmentation, deformable registration, image-based estimation methods.
Stephen M. Pizer, Kenan Professor; Ph.D., Harvard, 1967. Image analysis and display, human and computer vision, graphics, medical imaging.
David A. Plaisted, Professor; Ph.D., Stanford, 1976. Mechanical theorem proving, term rewriting systems, logic programming, algorithms.
Marc Pollefeys, Research Professor; Ph.D., Leuven (Belgium), 1999. Computer vision, image-based modeling and rendering, image and video analysis, multiview geometry.
Diane Pozefsky, Research Professor; Ph.D., North Carolina at Chapel Hill, 1979. Software engineering and environments; computer education; serious games design and development; social, legal, and ethical issues concerning information technology.
Jan F. Prins, Professor and Director of Graduate Studies; Ph.D., Cornell, 1987. High-performance computing: parallel algorithms, programming languages, compilers, and architectures; scientific computing with focus on computational biology and bioinformatics.
Timothy L. Quigg, Lecturer and Associate Chairman for Administration, Finance and Entrepreneurship; M.P.A., North Carolina State, 1979. Management and organization dynamics in research-intensive organizations, intellectual property rights, creative methods for capturing and commercializing university technology.
Michael K. Reiter, Lawrence M. Slifkin Distinguished Professor; Ph.D., Cornell, 1993. Computer and network security, distributed systems, applied cryptography.
Montek Singh, Associate Professor; Ph.D., Columbia, 2002. High-performance and low-power digital systems, asynchronous and mixed-timing circuits and systems, VLSI CAD tools, energy-efficient graphics hardware, applications to computer security, emerging computing technologies.
F. Donelson Smith, Research Professor; Ph.D., North Carolina at Chapel Hill, 1978. Computer networks, operating systems, distributed systems, multimedia.
John B. Smith, Professor Emeritus; Ph.D., North Carolina at Chapel Hill, 1970.
Jack Snoeyink, Professor; Ph.D., Stanford, 1990. Computational geometry, algorithms for geographical information systems and structural biology, geometric modeling and computation, algorithms and data structures, theory of computation.
Donald F. Stanat, Professor Emeritus; Ph.D., Michigan, 1966.
David Stotts, Professor; Ph.D., Virginia, 1985. Computer-supported cooperative work, especially collaborative user interfaces; software engineering, design patterns and formal methods; hypermedia and Web technology.
Martin Styner, Research Assistant Professor; Ph.D., North Carolina at Chapel Hill, 2001. Medical image processing and analysis including anatomical structure and tissue segmentation, morphometry using shape analysis, modeling and atlas building, intramodality and intermodality registration.
Russell M. Taylor II, Research Professor; Ph.D., North Carolina at Chapel Hill, 1994. 3-D interactive computer graphics, virtual worlds, distributed computing, scientific visualization, human-computer interaction.
Leandra Vicci, Lecturer and Director, Applied Engineering Laboratory; B.S., Antioch (Ohio), 1964. Information processing hardware: theory, practice, systems, and applications; computer-integrated magnetic force systems; wave optics; tracking and imaging; electricity and magnetism; low Reynolds number fluid dynamics; biophysical models of mitotic spindles; quantum theory.
Stephen F. Weiss, Professor Emeritus; Ph.D., Cornell, 1970.
Mary C. Whitton, Research Associate Professor; M.S., North Carolina State, 1984. Developing and evaluating technology for virtual and augmented reality systems, virtual locomotion, tools for serious games.
William V. Wright, Research Professor Emeritus; Ph.D., North Carolina at Chapel Hill, 1972.

Adjunct Faculty

Stephen Aylward, Adjunct Associate Professor; Ph.D., North Carolina at Chapel Hill, 1997. Computer-aided diagnosis, computer-aided surgical planning, statistical pattern recognition, image processing, neural networks.
Derek Chiang, Adjunct Assistant Professor; Ph.D., Berkeley, 2005. Bioinformatics, liver cancer, sequencing technologies.
Larry Conrad, Professor of the Practice, Vice Chancellor for Information Technology, and Chief Information Officer; M.S., Arizona State.
Brad Davis, Adjunct Assistant Professor; Ph.D., North Carolina at Chapel Hill, 2008. Image analysis, shape analysis, image processing, statistical methods in nonlinear spaces, medical applications, visualization, software engineering.
Nick England, Adjunct Research Professor; E.E., North Carolina State, 1974. Systems architectures for graphics and imaging, scientific visualization, volume rendering, interactive surface modeling.
Mark Foskey, Adjunct Research Assistant Professor; Ph.D., California, San Diego, 1994. Medical image analysis, especially in cancer therapy; geometric computation.
Rob Fowler, Adjunct Professor; Ph.D., Washington (Seattle), 1985. High-performance computing.
Guido Gerig, Adjunct Professor; Ph.D., Swiss Federal Institute of Technology, 1987. Image analysis, shape-based object recognition, 3-D object representation and quantitative analysis, medical image processing.
Shawn Gomez, Adjunct Assistant Professor; Eng.Sc.D., Columbia, 2000. Bioinformatics, computational biology, systems biology, bioimage informatics.
Chris Healey, Adjunct Associate Professor; Ph.D., British Columbia, 1996. Computer graphics, scientific visualization, perception and cognitive vision, color, texture, databases, computational geometry.
M. Gail Jones, Adjunct Professor; Ph.D., North Carolina State, 1987. Science education, gender and science, high-stakes assessment nanotechnology education, haptics and learning.
Hye-Chung Kum, Adjunct Assistant Professor; Ph.D., North Carolina at Chapel Hill, 2004. Social welfare intelligence and informatics, health informatics, government informatics, data mining, KDD (Knowledge Discovery in Databases), government administrative data.
Svetlana Lazebnik, Adjunct Assistant Professor; Ph.D. Illinois at Urbana-Champaign, 2006. Object recognition and scene interpretation, modeling and organizing large-scale photo collections, machine learning.
Yun Li, Adjunct Assistant Professor; Ph.D. Michigan, 2009. Statistical genetics.
J. Stephen Marron, Adjunct Professor; Ph.D., UCLA, 1982. Smoothing methods for curve estimation.
John McHugh, Adjunct Professor; Ph.D. Texas at Austin. Computer and network security.
Steven E. Molnar, Adjunct Associate Professor; Ph.D., North Carolina at Chapel Hill, 1991. Architectures for real-time computer graphics, VLSI-based system design, parallel rendering algorithms.
Frank Mueller, Adjunct Associate Professor; Ph.D., Florida State, 1994.
Lars S. Nyland, Adjunct Research Associate Professor; Ph.D., Duke, 1991. High-performance computing, hardware systems, computer graphics and image analysis, geometric modeling and computation.
Ipek Oguz, Adjunct Assistant Professor; Ph.D., North Carolina at Chapel Hill, 2009. Medical image analysis.
John Poulton, Adjunct Professor; Ph.D., North Carolina at Chapel Hill, 1980. Graphics architectures, VLSI-based system design, design tools, rapid system prototyping.
Julian Rosenman, Adjunct Professor; Ph.D., Texas at Austin, 1971; M.D., Texas Health Science Center at Dallas, 1977. Computer graphics for treatment of cancer patients, contrast enhancement for x-rays.
Dinggang Shen, Adjunct Associate Professor; Ph.D., Shanghai Jiao Tong (China), 1995. Medical image analysis, computer vision, pattern recognition.
Diane H. Sonnenwald, Adjunct Professor; Ph.D., Rutgers, 1993. Collaboration among multidisciplinary, cross-organizational teams, human information behavior, digital libraries.
Richard Superfine, Adjunct Professor; Ph.D., Berkeley, 1991. Condensed-matter physics, biophysics, microscopy.
Alexander Tropsha, Adjunct Professor; Ph.D., Moscow State (Russia), 1986. Computer-assisted drug design, computational toxicology, cheminformatics, structural bioinformatics.
William Valdar, Adjunct Assistant Professor; Ph.D., University College London, 2001.
Wei Wang, Adjunct Professor; Ph.D., UCLA, 1999. Bioinformatics and computational biology, data mining, database systems.
Sean Washburn, Adjunct Professor; Ph.D., Duke, 1982. Condensed-matter physics, materials science.
Turner Whitted, Adjunct Research Professor; Ph.D., North Carolina State, 1978.

The Frederick P. Brooks, Jr. Building is the home of the Department of Computer Science at UNC-Chapel Hill.

Section 9
Electrical and Computer Engineering

This section contains a directory of institutions offering graduate work in electrical and computer engineering, followed by in-depth entries submitted by institutions that chose to prepare detailed program descriptions. Additional information about programs listed in the directory but not augmented by an in-depth entry may be obtained by writing directly to the dean of a graduate school or chair of a department at the address given in the directory.

For programs offering related work, see also in this book *Computer Science and Information Technology, Energy and Power Engineering, Engineering and Applied Sciences, Industrial Engineering,* and *Mechanical Engineering and Mechanics.* In another guide in this series:

Graduate Programs in the Physical Sciences, Mathematics, Agricultural Sciences, the Environment & Natural Resources

See *Mathematical Sciences* and *Physics*

CONTENTS

Computer Engineering

Air Force Institute of Technology, Graduate School of Engineering and Management, Department of Electrical and Computer Engineering, Dayton, OH 45433-7765. Offers computer engineering (MS, PhD); computer systems/science (MS); electrical engineering (MS, PhD); electro-optics (MS, PhD). *Accreditation:* ABET (one or more programs are accredited). Part-time programs available. *Degree requirements:* For master's, thesis; for doctorate, thesis/dissertation. *Entrance requirements:* For master's and doctorate, GRE General Test, minimum GPA of 3.0, U.S. citizenship. *Faculty research:* Remote sensing, information survivability, microelectronics, computer networks, artificial intelligence.

American University of Beirut, Graduate Programs, Faculty of Engineering and Architecture, Beirut, Lebanon. Offers applied energy (MME); civil engineering (ME, PhD); electrical and computer engineering (ME, PhD); engineering management (MEM); environmental and water resources (ME); environmental and water resources engineering (PhD); environmental technology (MSES); mechanical engineering (ME, PhD); urban design (MUD); urban planning and policy (MUP). Part-time programs available. *Faculty:* 53 full-time (8 women), 10 part-time/adjunct (2 women). *Students:* 290 full-time (101 women), 59 part-time (18 women). Average age 25. 336 applicants, 80% accepted, 83 enrolled. In 2011, 72 master's, 5 doctorates awarded. *Degree requirements:* For master's, one foreign language, comprehensive exam, thesis (for some programs); for doctorate, one foreign language, comprehensive exam, thesis/dissertation, publications. *Entrance requirements:* For master's, GRE (for electrical and computer engineering), letters of recommendation; for doctorate, GRE, letters of recommendation, master's degree, transcripts, curriculum vitae, interview. Additional exam requirements/recommendations for international students: Required—TOEFL (minimum score 600 paper-based; 250 computer-based; 100 iBT), IELTS (minimum score 7.5). *Application deadline:* For fall admission, 2/5 priority date for domestic students, 2/5 for international students; for spring admission, 11/1 priority date for domestic students, 11/1 for international students. Applications are processed on a rolling basis. Application fee: $50. Electronic applications accepted. *Expenses: Tuition:* Full-time $12,780; part-time $710 per credit. *Required fees:* $528; $528 per credit. Tuition and fees vary according to course load and program. *Financial support:* In 2011–12, 9 fellowships with full tuition reimbursements (averaging $24,800 per year), 33 research assistantships with full tuition reimbursements (averaging $24,800 per year), 74 teaching assistantships with full tuition reimbursements (averaging $9,800 per year) were awarded; career-related internships or fieldwork, institutionally sponsored loans, scholarships/grants, health care benefits, and unspecified assistantships also available. *Total annual research expenditures:* $1.1 million. *Unit head:* Prof. Makram T. Suidan, Dean, 961-135-0000 Ext. 3400, Fax: 961-174-4462, E-mail: msuidan@aub.edu.lb. *Application contact:* Dr. Salim Kanaan, Director, Admissions Office, 961-135-0000 Ext. 2594, Fax: 961-175-0775, E-mail: sk00@aub.edu.lb. Web site: http://staff.aub.edu.lb/~webfea.

American University of Sharjah, Graduate Programs, Sharjah, United Arab Emirates. Offers business (EMBA, GEMPA, MBA); chemical engineering (MS Ch E); civil engineering (MSCE); computer engineering (MS); electrical engineering (MSEE); mechanical engineering (MSME); mechatronics engineering (MS); public administration (MPA); teaching English to speakers of other languages (MA); translation and interpreting (MA); urban planning (MUP). Part-time and evening/weekend programs available. *Entrance requirements:* For master's, GMAT (MBA). Additional exam requirements/recommendations for international students: Required—TOEFL (minimum score 550 paper-based; 213 computer-based; 80 iBT), TWE (minimum score 5). Electronic applications accepted. *Faculty research:* Chemical engineering, civil engineering, computer engineering, electrical engineering, linguistics, translation.

Auburn University, Graduate School, Ginn College of Engineering, Department of Electrical and Computer Engineering, Auburn University, AL 36849. Offers MEE, MS, PhD. Part-time programs available. *Faculty:* 28 full-time (2 women), 1 part-time/adjunct (0 women). *Students:* 105 full-time (21 women), 59 part-time (13 women); includes 9 minority (3 Black or African American, non-Hispanic/Latino; 4 Asian, non-Hispanic/Latino; 2 Hispanic/Latino), 118 international. Average age 26. 388 applicants, 57% accepted, 43 enrolled. In 2011, 29 master's, 11 doctorates awarded. *Degree requirements:* For master's, comprehensive exam, thesis (for some programs); for doctorate, thesis/dissertation. *Entrance requirements:* For master's and doctorate, GRE General Test, GRE Subject Test. *Application deadline:* For fall admission, 7/7 for domestic students; for spring admission, 11/24 for domestic students. Applications are processed on a rolling basis. Application fee: $50 ($60 for international students). Electronic applications accepted. *Expenses:* Tuition, state resident: full-time $7290; part-time $405 per credit hour. Tuition, nonresident: full-time $21,870; part-time $1215 per credit hour. *International tuition:* $22,000 full-time. *Required fees:* $1402. *Financial support:* Fellowships, research assistantships, teaching assistantships, and Federal Work-Study available. Support available to part-time students. Financial award application deadline: 3/15; financial award applicants required to submit FAFSA. *Faculty research:* Power systems, energy conversion, electronics, electromagnetics, digital systems. *Unit head:* Dr. Mark Nelms, Head, 334-844-1830. *Application contact:* Dr. George Flowers, Dean of the Graduate School, 334-844-2125. Web site: http://www.eng.auburn.edu/department/ee/.

Baylor University, Graduate School, School of Engineering and Computer Science, Department of Engineering, Waco, TX 76798. Offers biomedical engineering (MSBE); electrical and computer engineering (MSECE, PhD); engineering (ME); mechanical engineering (MSME). *Faculty:* 14 full-time (1 woman). *Students:* 25 full-time (2 women), 7 part-time (1 woman); includes 6 minority (2 Black or African American, non-Hispanic/Latino; 1 Asian, non-Hispanic/Latino; 1 Hispanic/Latino; 2 Two or more races, non-Hispanic/Latino), 6 international. In 2011, 19 master's awarded. *Unit head:* Dr. Mike Thompson, Graduate Director, 254-710-4188. *Application contact:* Linda Keer, Administrative Assistant, 254-710-4188, Fax: 254-710-3870, E-mail: linda_kerr@baylor.edu. Web site: http://www.ecs.baylor.edu/engineering.

Boise State University, Graduate College, College of Engineering, Department of Electrical and Computer Engineering, Boise, ID 83725-0399. Offers computer engineering (M Engr, MS); electrical and computer engineering (PhD); electrical engineering (M Engr, MS). Part-time and evening/weekend programs available. *Degree requirements:* For master's, thesis. *Entrance requirements:* For master's, GRE General Test, minimum GPA of 3.0. Additional exam requirements/recommendations for international students: Required—TOEFL. Electronic applications accepted.

Boston University, College of Engineering, Department of Electrical and Computer Engineering, Boston, MA 02215. Offers computer engineering (M Eng, MS, PhD); electrical engineering (M Eng, MS, PhD); photonics (M Eng, MS). Part-time programs available. *Faculty:* 40 full-time (3 women), 5 part-time/adjunct (0 women). *Students:* 221 full-time (43 women), 23 part-time (0 women); includes 21 minority (1 Black or African American, non-Hispanic/Latino; 1 American Indian or Alaska Native, non-Hispanic/Latino; 15 Asian, non-Hispanic/Latino; 2 Hispanic/Latino; 2 Two or more races, non-Hispanic/Latino), 165 international. Average age 25. 810 applicants, 25% accepted, 112 enrolled. In 2011, 56 master's, 21 doctorates awarded. Terminal master's awarded for partial completion of doctoral program. *Degree requirements:* For master's, thesis (for some programs); for doctorate, comprehensive exam, thesis/dissertation. *Entrance requirements:* For master's and doctorate, GRE General Test. Additional exam requirements/recommendations for international students: Required—TOEFL (minimum score 550 paper-based; 213 computer-based; 84 iBT), IELTS (minimum score 6.5). *Application deadline:* For fall admission, 3/15 for domestic and international students; for spring admission, 10/1 for domestic and international students. Applications are processed on a rolling basis. Application fee: $70. Electronic applications accepted. *Expenses: Tuition:* Full-time $40,848; part-time $1276 per credit hour. *Required fees:* $572; $286 per semester. *Financial support:* In 2011–12, 126 students received support, including 8 fellowships with full tuition reimbursements available (averaging $28,950 per year), 82 research assistantships with full tuition reimbursements available (averaging $19,300 per year), 18 teaching assistantships with full tuition reimbursements available (averaging $19,300 per year); career-related internships or fieldwork, Federal Work-Study, institutionally sponsored loans, scholarships/grants, traineeships, and health care benefits also available. Financial award application deadline: 1/15; financial award applicants required to submit FAFSA. *Faculty research:* Communications and computer networks; signal, image, video, and multimedia processing; solid-state materials, devices, and photonics; systems, control, and reliable computing; VLSI, computer engineering and high-performance computing. *Unit head:* Dr. David Castanon, Interim Chairman, 617-353-9880, Fax: 617-353-6440, E-mail: dac@bu.edu. *Application contact:* Stephen Doherty, Director of Graduate Programs, 617-353-9760, Fax: 617-353-0259, E-mail: enggrad@bu.edu. Web site: http://www.bu.edu/ece/.

Boston University, Metropolitan College, Department of Computer Science, Boston, MA 02215. Offers computer information systems (MS), including computer networks, database management and business intelligence, health informatics, IT project management, security, Web application development; computer science (MS), including computer networks, security; telecommunications (MS), including security. Evening/weekend programs available. Postbaccalaureate distance learning degree programs offered. *Faculty:* 12 full-time (2 women), 28 part-time/adjunct (2 women). *Students:* 25 full-time (6 women), 732 part-time (167 women); includes 208 minority (51 Black or African American, non-Hispanic/Latino; 1 American Indian or Alaska Native, non-Hispanic/Latino; 104 Asian, non-Hispanic/Latino; 43 Hispanic/Latino; 1 Native Hawaiian or other Pacific Islander, non-Hispanic/Latino; 8 Two or more races, non-Hispanic/Latino), 86 international. Average age 35. 260 applicants, 67% accepted, 143 enrolled. In 2011, 143 master's awarded. *Degree requirements:* For master's, thesis optional. *Entrance requirements:* For master's, 3 letters of recommendation, professional resume. Additional exam requirements/recommendations for international students: Required—TOEFL (minimum score 550 paper-based; 213 computer-based; 80 iBT). *Application deadline:* For fall admission, 6/1 for international students; for spring admission, 10/1 for international students. Applications are processed on a rolling basis. Application fee: $70. Electronic applications accepted. *Expenses: Tuition:* Full-time $40,848; part-time $1276 per credit hour. *Required fees:* $572; $286 per semester. *Financial support:* In 2011–12, 9 research assistantships (averaging $5,000 per year) were awarded; career-related internships or fieldwork and unspecified assistantships also available. Support available to part-time students. Financial award applicants required to submit FAFSA. *Faculty research:* Medical informatics, Web technologies, telecom and networks, security and forensics, software engineering, programming languages, multimedia and AI, information systems and IT project management. *Unit head:* Dr. Lubomir Chitkushev, Chairman, 617-353-2566, Fax: 617-353-2367, E-mail: csinfo@bu.edu. *Application contact:* Kim Richards, Program Coordinator, 617-353-2566, Fax: 617-353-2367, E-mail: kimrich@bu.edu. Web site: http://www.bu.edu/csmet/.

Brigham Young University, Graduate Studies, Ira A. Fulton College of Engineering and Technology, Department of Electrical and Computer Engineering, Provo, UT 84602. Offers MS, PhD. *Faculty:* 23 full-time (0 women). *Students:* 92 full-time (4 women); includes 6 minority (3 Asian, non-Hispanic/Latino; 3 Hispanic/Latino), 25 international. Average age 28. 41 applicants, 78% accepted, 19 enrolled. In 2011, 17 master's, 11 doctorates awarded. *Degree requirements:* For master's, thesis optional; for doctorate, comprehensive exam, thesis/dissertation. *Entrance requirements:* For master's and doctorate, GRE General Test, minimum GPA of 3.2 in last 60 hours of course work. Additional exam requirements/recommendations for international students: Required—TOEFL (minimum score 580 paper-based; 237 computer-based; 85 iBT). *Application deadline:* For fall admission, 1/15 for domestic and international students; for winter admission, 8/15 for domestic and international students. Application fee: $50. Electronic applications accepted. *Expenses: Tuition:* Full-time $5760; part-time $320 per credit. Tuition and fees vary according to student's religious affiliation. *Financial support:* In 2011–12, 74 students received support, including 6 fellowships with full tuition reimbursements available (averaging $19,500 per year), 54 research assistantships with full tuition reimbursements available (averaging $19,500 per year), 14 teaching assistantships with full tuition reimbursements available (averaging $19,500 per year); scholarships/grants also available. Financial award application deadline: 5/15; financial award applicants required to submit FAFSA. *Faculty research:* Microwave remote sensing, reconfigurable computing, microelectronics, wireless communications, computer architecture, biomedical imaging, bio-chemical sensing. *Total annual research expenditures:* $3.2 million. *Unit head:* Dr. Michael A. Jensen, Chair, 801-422-4012, Fax: 801-422-0201, E-mail: jensen@ee.byu.edu. *Application contact:* Janalyn L. Mergist, Graduate Secretary, 801-422-4013, Fax: 801-422-0201, E-mail: janalyn@ee.byu.edu. Web site: http://www.ee.byu.edu/.

Brown University, Graduate School, Division of Engineering, Program in Electrical Sciences and Computer Engineering, Providence, RI 02912. Offers Sc M, PhD. *Degree requirements:* For doctorate, thesis/dissertation, preliminary exam.

California State University, Chico, Office of Graduate Studies, College of Engineering, Computer Science, and Technology, Department of Electrical and Computer Engineering, Option in Computer Engineering, Chico, CA 95929-0722. Offers MS. *Students:* 1 full-time (0 women), 1 part-time (0 women), 1 international. Average age 26. 11 applicants, 73% accepted, 2 enrolled. In 2011, 2 master's awarded. *Degree requirements:* For master's, comprehensive oral examination. *Entrance requirements:* For master's, GRE General Test, 2 letters of recommendation, statement of purpose, resume. Additional exam requirements/recommendations for international students: Required—TOEFL (minimum score 550 paper-based; 213 computer-based; 80 iBT), IELTS (minimum score 6.8), Pearson Test of English (minimum score 59). *Application deadline:* For fall admission, 3/1 priority date for domestic students, 3/1 for international students; for spring admission, 9/15 priority date for domestic students, 9/15 for international students. Applications are processed on a rolling basis. Application fee: $55. Electronic applications accepted. Tuition and fees vary according to class time, course load and degree level. *Financial support:* Career-related internships or fieldwork, scholarships/grants, and traineeships available. *Unit head:* Dr. Ben Juliano, Interim Dean, 530-898-5343, Fax: 530-898-4956, E-mail: elce@csuchico.edu. *Application contact:* Judy L. Rice, Graduate Admissions Coordinator, 530-898-5416, Fax: 530-898-3342, E-mail: jlrice@csuchico.edu. Web site: http://catalog.csuchico.edu/viewer/12/ENGR/ELCENONEMS.html.

California State University, Long Beach, Graduate Studies, College of Engineering, Department of Computer Engineering and Computer Science, Long Beach, CA 90840. Offers computer engineering (MSCS); computer science (MSCS). Part-time programs available. *Faculty:* 10 full-time (2 women), 2 part-time/adjunct (0 women). *Students:* 122 full-time (26 women), 99 part-time (13 women); includes 72 minority (5 Black or African American, non-Hispanic/Latino; 1 American Indian or Alaska Native, non-Hispanic/Latino; 49 Asian, non-Hispanic/Latino; 13 Hispanic/Latino; 1 Native Hawaiian or other Pacific Islander, non-Hispanic/Latino; 3 Two or more races, non-Hispanic/Latino), 92 international. Average age 29. 420 applicants, 63% accepted, 62 enrolled. In 2011, 51 master's awarded. *Degree requirements:* For master's, thesis or alternative. *Entrance requirements:* Additional exam requirements/recommendations for international students: Required—TOEFL. *Application deadline:* For fall admission, 3/1 for domestic students. Application fee: $55. Electronic applications accepted. *Financial support:* Teaching assistantships, Federal Work-Study, institutionally sponsored loans, scholarships/grants, and unspecified assistantships available. Financial award application deadline: 3/2. *Faculty research:* Artificial intelligence, software engineering, computer simulation and modeling, user-interface design, networking. *Unit head:* Dr. Kenneth James, Chair, 562-985-5105, Fax: 562-985-7823, E-mail: james@csulb.edu. *Application contact:* Dr. Burkhard Englert, Graduate Advisor, 562-985-7987, Fax: 562-985-7823, E-mail: benglert@.csulb.edu.

Carnegie Mellon University, Carnegie Institute of Technology, Department of Electrical and Computer Engineering, Pittsburgh, PA 15213-3891. Offers MS, PhD. Part-time programs available. *Degree requirements:* For master's, thesis; for doctorate, thesis/dissertation, qualifying exam, teaching experience. *Entrance requirements:* For master's and doctorate, GRE General Test. Additional exam requirements/recommendations for international students: Required—TOEFL. *Faculty research:* Computer-aided design, solid-state devices, VLSI, processing, robotics and controls, signal processing, data systems storage.

Case Western Reserve University, School of Graduate Studies, Case School of Engineering, Department of Electrical Engineering and Computer Science, Cleveland, OH 44106. Offers computer engineering (MS, PhD); computing and information sciences (MS, PhD); electrical engineering (MS, PhD); systems and control engineering (MS, PhD). Part-time and evening/weekend programs available. Postbaccalaureate distance learning degree programs offered (minimal on-campus study). *Faculty:* 33 full-time (3 women). *Students:* 188 full-time (34 women), 22 part-time (4 women); includes 6 minority (3 Black or African American, non-Hispanic/Latino; 3 Asian, non-Hispanic/Latino), 132 international. In 2011, 30 master's, 22 doctorates awarded. Terminal master's awarded for partial completion of doctoral program. *Degree requirements:* For master's, thesis; for doctorate, thesis/dissertation, qualifying exam, teaching experience. *Entrance requirements:* For master's and doctorate, GRE General Test. Additional exam requirements/recommendations for international students: Required—TOEFL. *Application deadline:* For fall admission, 2/1 for domestic students; for spring admission, 11/1 for domestic students. Applications are processed on a rolling basis. Application fee: $50. *Financial support:* Fellowships with full and partial tuition reimbursements, research assistantships with full and partial tuition reimbursements, teaching assistantships, career-related internships or fieldwork, Federal Work-Study, and institutionally sponsored loans available. Support available to part-time students. Financial award application deadline: 3/1; financial award applicants required to submit FAFSA. *Faculty research:* Applied artificial intelligence, automation, computer-aided design and testing of digital systems. *Total annual research expenditures:* $6 million. *Unit head:* Dr. Michael Branicky, Department Chair, 216-368-6888, E-mail: branicky@case.edu. *Application contact:* David Easler, Student Affairs Coordinator, 216-368-4080, Fax: 216-368-2801, E-mail: david.easler@case.edu. Web site: http://eecs.cwru.edu/.

Clarkson University, Graduate School, Wallace H. Coulter School of Engineering, Department of Electrical and Computer Engineering, Potsdam, NY 13699. Offers electrical and computer engineering (PhD); electrical engineering (ME, MS). Part-time programs available. *Faculty:* 22 full-time (5 women), 1 (woman) part-time/adjunct. *Students:* 41 full-time (5 women), 2 part-time (1 woman); includes 3 minority (1 Asian, non-Hispanic/Latino; 2 Hispanic/Latino), 16 international. Average age 28. 72 applicants, 88% accepted, 13 enrolled. In 2011, 12 master's, 6 doctorates awarded. Terminal master's awarded for partial completion of doctoral program. *Degree requirements:* For master's, thesis; for doctorate, comprehensive exam, thesis/dissertation, departmental qualifying exam. *Entrance requirements:* For master's and doctorate, GRE, transcripts of all college coursework, resume, personal statement, three letters of recommendation. Additional exam requirements/recommendations for international students: Required—TOEFL (minimum score 550 paper-based; 213 computer-based; 80 iBT), IELTS (minimum score 6.5). *Application deadline:* For fall admission, 1/30 priority date for domestic students, 1/30 for international students; for spring admission, 9/1 priority date for domestic students, 9/1 for international students. Applications are processed on a rolling basis. Application fee: $25 ($35 for international students). Electronic applications accepted. *Expenses:* Tuition: Full-time $14,376; part-time $1198 per credit hour. *Required fees:* $295 per semester. *Financial support:* In 2011–12, 33 students received support, including 3 fellowships with full tuition reimbursements available (averaging $21,999 per year), 14 research assistantships with full tuition reimbursements available (averaging $21,999 per year), 13 teaching assistantships with full tuition reimbursements available (averaging $21,999 per year); scholarships/grants, tuition waivers (partial), and unspecified assistantships also available. *Faculty research:* Thoracic biometrics, hybrid lidar, microwave frequency, biometrics, DNA sample analysis. *Total annual research expenditures:* $1.3 million. *Unit head:* Dr. William Jemison, Chair, 315-268-7648, Fax: 315-268-7600, E-mail: wjemison@clarkson.edu. *Application contact:* Kelly Sharlow, Assistant to the Dean, 315-268-7929, Fax: 315-268-4494, E-mail: ksharlow@clarkson.edu. Web site: http://www.clarkson.edu/ece/.

Clemson University, Graduate School, College of Engineering and Science, Department of Electrical and Computer Engineering, Program in Computer Engineering, Clemson, SC 29634. Offers MS, PhD. *Students:* 42 full-time (6 women), 6 part-time (0 women); includes 8 minority (4 Black or African American, non-Hispanic/Latino; 4 Asian, non-Hispanic/Latino), 29 international. Average age 27. 106 applicants, 40% accepted, 20 enrolled. In 2011, 9 master's, 2 doctorates awarded. *Degree requirements:* For master's, thesis or alternative; for doctorate, thesis/dissertation, departmental qualifying exam. *Entrance requirements:* For master's and doctorate, GRE General Test. Additional exam requirements/recommendations for international students: Required—TOEFL. *Application deadline:* Applications are processed on a rolling basis. Application fee: $70 ($80 for international students). Electronic applications accepted. *Financial*

support: In 2011–12, 36 students received support, including 3 fellowships with full and partial tuition reimbursements available (averaging $10,500 per year), 22 research assistantships with partial tuition reimbursements available (averaging $14,511 per year), 21 teaching assistantships with partial tuition reimbursements available (averaging $6,799 per year); career-related internships or fieldwork, institutionally sponsored loans, scholarships/grants, health care benefits, and unspecified assistantships also available. Support available to part-time students. Financial award applicants required to submit FAFSA. *Faculty research:* Interface applications, software development, multisystem communications, artificial intelligence, robotics. *Unit head:* Dr. Darren Dawson, Chair, 864-656-5249, Fax: 864-656-5917, E-mail: ddarren@clemson.edu. *Application contact:* Dr. Daniel Noneaker, 864-656-0100, Fax: 864-656-5917, E-mail: ece-grad-program@ces.clemson.edu. Web site: http://www.clemson.edu/ces/departments/ece/index.html.

Colorado Technical University Colorado Springs, Graduate Studies, Program in Computer Engineering, Colorado Springs, CO 80907-3896. Offers MSCE. Part-time and evening/weekend programs available. Postbaccalaureate distance learning degree programs offered. *Degree requirements:* For master's, thesis or alternative.

Colorado Technical University Denver South, Program in Computer Engineering, Aurora, CO 80014. Offers MS.

Columbia University, The Fu Foundation School of Engineering and Applied Science, Department of Electrical Engineering, New York, NY 10027. Offers computer engineering (MS); electrical engineering (MS, Eng Sc D, PhD, Engr); solid state science and engineering (MS, Eng Sc D, PhD). PhD offered through the Graduate School of Arts and Sciences. Part-time programs available. Postbaccalaureate distance learning degree programs offered (no on-campus study). *Faculty:* 27 full-time (1 woman), 15 part-time/adjunct (1 woman). *Students:* 336 full-time (74 women), 155 part-time (38 women); includes 36 minority (2 Black or African American, non-Hispanic/Latino; 1 American Indian or Alaska Native, non-Hispanic/Latino; 26 Asian, non-Hispanic/Latino; 2 Hispanic/Latino; 5 Two or more races, non-Hispanic/Latino), 375 international. Average age 26. 1,385 applicants, 37% accepted, 250 enrolled. In 2011, 117 master's, 17 doctorates, 2 other advanced degrees awarded. *Degree requirements:* For doctorate, thesis/dissertation, qualifying exam. *Entrance requirements:* For master's, doctorate, and Engr, GRE General Test. Additional exam requirements/recommendations for international students: Required—TOEFL, IELTS. *Application deadline:* For fall admission, 12/1 priority date for domestic students, 12/1 for international students; for spring admission, 10/1 priority date for domestic students, 10/1 for international students. Application fee: $95. Electronic applications accepted. *Financial support:* In 2011–12, 99 students received support, including 8 fellowships with full tuition reimbursements available (averaging $35,000 per year), 66 research assistantships with full tuition reimbursements available (averaging $31,133 per year), 25 teaching assistantships with full tuition reimbursements available (averaging $31,133 per year); health care benefits also available. Financial award application deadline: 12/1; financial award applicants required to submit FAFSA. *Faculty research:* Media informatics and signal processing, integrated circuits and cyberphysical systems, communications systems and networking, nanoscale electronics and photonics, systems biology and neuroengineering. *Unit head:* Dr. Keren Bergman, Professor and Department Chair, 212-854-2280, Fax: 212-854-0300, E-mail: bergman@ee.columbia.edu. *Application contact:* Michal Zussman, Staff Associate, 212-854-3105, Fax: 212-932-9421, E-mail: mz2344@columbia.edu. Web site: http://www.ee.columbia.edu/.

See Display on page 371 and Close-Up on page 397.

Concordia University, School of Graduate Studies, Faculty of Engineering and Computer Science, Department of Electrical and Computer Engineering, Montréal, QC H3G 1M8, Canada. Offers M Eng, MA Sc, PhD. *Degree requirements:* For master's, thesis optional; for doctorate, comprehensive exam, thesis/dissertation. *Faculty research:* Computer communications and protocols, circuits and systems, graph theory, VLSI systems, microelectronics.

Cornell University, Graduate School, Graduate Fields of Engineering, Field of Electrical and Computer Engineering, Ithaca, NY 14853. Offers computer engineering (M Eng, PhD); electrical engineering (M Eng, PhD); electrical systems (M Eng, PhD); electrophysics (M Eng, PhD). *Faculty:* 61 full-time (5 women). *Students:* 235 full-time (52 women); includes 26 minority (3 Black or African American, non-Hispanic/Latino; 18 Asian, non-Hispanic/Latino; 5 Hispanic/Latino), 165 international. Average age 26. 1,234 applicants, 25% accepted, 111 enrolled. In 2011, 94 master's, 19 doctorates awarded. *Degree requirements:* For doctorate, comprehensive exam, thesis/dissertation. *Entrance requirements:* For master's, GRE General Test, 2 letters of recommendation; for doctorate, GRE General Test, 3 letters of recommendation. Additional exam requirements/recommendations for international students: Required—TOEFL (minimum score 600 paper-based; 250 computer-based; 77 iBT). *Application deadline:* For fall admission, 1/15 priority date for domestic students. Application fee: $70. Electronic applications accepted. *Financial support:* In 2011–12, 150 students received support, including 38 fellowships with full tuition reimbursements available, 94 research assistantships with full tuition reimbursements available, 19 teaching assistantships with full tuition reimbursements available; institutionally sponsored loans, scholarships/grants, health care benefits, tuition waivers (full and partial), and unspecified assistantships also available. Financial award applicants required to submit FAFSA. *Faculty research:* Communications, information theory, signal processing and power control, computer engineering, microelectromechanical systems and nanotechnology. *Unit head:* Director of Graduate Studies, 607-255-4304. *Application contact:* Graduate Field Assistant, 607-255-4304, E-mail: meng@ece.cornell.edu. Web site: http://www.gradschool.cornell.edu/fields.php?id-29&a-2.

Dalhousie University, Faculty of Engineering, Department of Electrical and Computer Engineering, Halifax, NS B3J 1Z1, Canada. Offers M Eng, MA Sc, PhD. *Degree requirements:* For master's, thesis; for doctorate, thesis/dissertation. *Entrance requirements:* Additional exam requirements/recommendations for international students: Required—TOEFL, IELTS, CANTEST, CAEL, or Michigan English Language Assessment Battery. Electronic applications accepted. *Faculty research:* Communications, computer engineering, power engineering, electronics, systems engineering.

Dartmouth College, Thayer School of Engineering, Program in Computer Engineering, Hanover, NH 03755. Offers MS, PhD. *Degree requirements:* For master's, thesis; for doctorate, thesis/dissertation, candidacy oral exam. *Entrance requirements:* For master's and doctorate, GRE General Test. *Application deadline:* For fall admission, 1/1 priority date for domestic students. Application fee: $45. *Financial support:* Fellowships, research assistantships, teaching assistantships, career-related internships or fieldwork, Federal Work-Study, institutionally sponsored loans, and tuition waivers (full and partial) available. Financial award application deadline: 1/15. *Faculty research:* Analog VLSI, electromagnetic fields and waves, electronic instrumentation, microelectromechanical systems, optics, lasers and non-linear optics, power electronics and integrated power converters, networking, parallel and distributed computing, simulation, VLSI design and testing, wireless networking. *Total annual research expenditures:* $4.5 million. *Unit head:* Dr. Joseph J. Helbie, Dean, 603-646-2238, Fax: 603-646-2580, E-mail: joseph.j.helbie@dartmouth.edu. *Application contact:* Candace S. Potter, Graduate Admissions Administrator, 603-646-3844, Fax: 603-646-1620, E-mail: candace.potter@dartmouth.edu. Web site: http://engineering.dartmouth.edu/.

Drexel University, College of Engineering, Department of Electrical and Computer Engineering, Program in Computer Engineering, Philadelphia, PA 19104-2875. Offers MS. Part-time and evening/weekend programs available. *Degree requirements:* For master's, thesis (for some programs). Electronic applications accepted.

Duke University, Graduate School, Pratt School of Engineering, Department of Electrical and Computer Engineering, Durham, NC 27708. Offers MS, PhD, JD/MS. Part-time programs available. Terminal master's awarded for partial completion of doctoral program. *Degree requirements:* For doctorate, thesis/dissertation. *Entrance requirements:* For master's and doctorate, GRE General Test. Additional exam requirements/recommendations for international students: Required—TOEFL (minimum score 550 paper-based; 213 computer-based; 83 iBT), IELTS (minimum score 7). Electronic applications accepted. *Expenses: Tuition:* Full-time $40,720. *Required fees:* $3107.

See Display on page 372 and Close-Up on page 399.

Duke University, Graduate School, Pratt School of Engineering, Master of Engineering Program, Durham, NC 27708-0271. Offers biomedical engineering (M Eng); civil engineering (M Eng); electrical and computer engineering (M Eng); environmental engineering (M Eng); materials science and engineering (M Eng); mechanical engineering (M Eng); photonics and optical sciences (M Eng). Part-time programs available. *Entrance requirements:* For master's, GRE General Test, resume, 3 letters of recommendation, statement of purpose. Additional exam requirements/recommendations for international students: Required—TOEFL. *Expenses: Tuition:* Full-time $40,720. *Required fees:* $3107.

École Polytechnique de Montréal, Graduate Programs, Department of Electrical and Computer Engineering, Montréal, QC H3C 3A7, Canada. Offers automation (M Eng, M Sc A, PhD); computer science (M Eng, M Sc A, PhD); electrical engineering (DESS); electrotechnology (M Eng, M Sc A, PhD); microelectronics (M Eng, M Sc A, PhD); microwave technology (M Eng, M Sc A, PhD). Part-time and evening/weekend programs available. *Degree requirements:* For master's, one foreign language, thesis; for doctorate, one foreign language, thesis/dissertation. *Entrance requirements:* For master's, minimum GPA of 2.75; for doctorate, minimum GPA of 3.0. *Faculty research:* Microwaves, telecommunications, software engineering.

Embry-Riddle Aeronautical University–Daytona, Daytona Beach Campus Graduate Program, Department of Electrical, Computer and Software Engineering, Daytona Beach, FL 32114-3900. Offers electrical/computer engineering (MSECE); engineering (MMSE); software engineering (MSE). Part-time and evening/weekend programs available. *Faculty:* 11 full-time (0 women), 3 part-time/adjunct (1 woman). *Students:* 36 full-time (9 women), 20 part-time (1 woman); includes 4 minority (1 Black or African American, non-Hispanic/Latino; 3 Hispanic/Latino), 16 international. Average age 27. 40 applicants, 70% accepted, 18 enrolled. In 2011, 12 master's awarded. *Degree requirements:* For master's, thesis or alternative. *Entrance requirements:* For master's, minimum GPA of 3.0 in senior year, 2.5 overall; course work in computer science. Additional exam requirements/recommendations for international students: Required—TOEFL (minimum score 550 paper-based; 213 computer-based; 79 iBT). *Application deadline:* For fall admission, 6/1 priority date for domestic students, 6/1 for international students; for spring admission, 11/1 priority date for domestic students, 10/1 for international students. Applications are processed on a rolling basis. Application fee: $50. Electronic applications accepted. *Expenses: Tuition:* Full-time $14,340; part-time $1195 per credit hour. *Financial support:* In 2011–12, 24 students received support, including 8 research assistantships with full and partial tuition reimbursements available (averaging $3,772 per year), 4 teaching assistantships with full and partial tuition reimbursements available (averaging $3,514 per year); career-related internships or fieldwork, Federal Work-Study, and unspecified assistantships also available. Financial award application deadline: 4/15; financial award applicants required to submit FAFSA. *Faculty research:* Safety-critical software, qualification and certification of digital hardware and softwae, next-generation air transportation system, unmanned aircraft systems, regulatory issues in unmanned aircraft systems. *Total annual research expenditures:* $800,000. *Unit head:* Dr. Timothy Wilson, Department Chair, 386-226-6454, E-mail: timothy.wilson@erau.edu. *Application contact:* Flavia Carreiro, Assistant Director, International and Graduate Admissions, 800-388-3728, Fax: 386-226-7070, E-mail: graduate.admissions@erau.edu.

Fairfield University, School of Engineering, Fairfield, CT 06824-5195. Offers electrical and computer engineering (MS); management of technology (MS); mechanical engineering (MS); software engineering (MS). Part-time and evening/weekend programs available. *Faculty:* 10 full-time (2 women), 11 part-time/adjunct. *Students:* 44 full-time (15 women), 86 part-time (22 women); includes 19 minority (4 Black or African American, non-Hispanic/Latino; 8 Asian, non-Hispanic/Latino; 4 Hispanic/Latino; 1 Native Hawaiian or other Pacific Islander, non-Hispanic/Latino; 2 Two or more races, non-Hispanic/Latino), 21 international. Average age 34. 100 applicants, 76% accepted, 27 enrolled. In 2011, 38 master's awarded. *Degree requirements:* For master's, thesis, capstone course. *Entrance requirements:* For master's, interview, minimum GPA of 2.8, resume, 2 recommendations. Additional exam requirements/recommendations for international students: Required—TOEFL (minimum score 550 paper-based; 213 computer-based; 80 iBT)or IELTS (minimum score 6.5). *Application deadline:* For fall admission, 5/15 for international students; for spring admission, 10/15 for international students. Applications are processed on a rolling basis. Application fee: $60. Electronic applications accepted. *Expenses:* Contact institution. *Financial support:* In 2011–12, 50 students received support. Scholarships/grants and unspecified assistantships available. Financial award applicants required to submit FAFSA. *Faculty research:* Vehicle dynamics, image processing, multimedia in instruction, thermal packaging, character recognition, photovoltaics and nanotechnology, Web technology. *Unit head:* Dr. Jack Beal, Dean, 203-254-4000 Ext. 4147, Fax: 203-254-4013, E-mail: jwbeal@fairfield.edu. *Application contact:* Marianne Gumpper, Director of Graduate and Continuing Studies Admission, 203-254-4184, Fax: 203-254-4073, E-mail: gradadmis@fairfield.edu. Web site: http://www.fairfield.edu/soe/soe_grad_1.html.

Fairleigh Dickinson University, Metropolitan Campus, University College: Arts, Sciences, and Professional Studies, School of Computer Sciences and Engineering, Program in Computer Engineering, Teaneck, NJ 07666-1914. Offers MS.

Florida Atlantic University, College of Engineering and Computer Science, Department of Computer and Electrical Engineering and Computer Science, Boca Raton, FL 33431-0991. Offers computer engineering (MS, PhD); computer science (MS, PhD); electrical engineering (MS, PhD). Part-time and evening/weekend programs available. *Faculty:* 32 full-time (6 women), 4 part-time/adjunct (0 women). *Students:* 96 full-time (22 women), 106 part-time (21 women); includes 77 minority (16 Black or African American, non-Hispanic/Latino; 23 Asian, non-Hispanic/Latino; 35 Hispanic/Latino; 3 Two or more races, non-Hispanic/Latino), 43 international. Average age 33. 177 applicants, 41% accepted, 35 enrolled. In 2011, 48 master's, 6 doctorates awarded. Terminal master's awarded for partial completion of doctoral program. *Degree requirements:* For master's, thesis optional; for doctorate, thesis/dissertation, qualifying exam. *Entrance requirements:* For master's, GRE General Test, minimum GPA of 3.0; for doctorate, GRE General Test, master's degree, minimum GPA of 3.5. Additional exam requirements/recommendations for international students: Required—TOEFL. *Application deadline:* For fall admission, 7/1 priority date for domestic students, 2/15 for international students; for spring admission, 11/1 for domestic students, 7/15 for international students. Applications are processed on a rolling basis. Application fee: $30. *Expenses: Tuition, area resident:* Part-time $343.02 per credit hour. Tuition, state resident: full-time $8232. Tuition, nonresident: full-time $23,931; part-time $997.14 per credit hour. *Financial support:* Fellowships, research assistantships with partial tuition reimbursements, teaching assistantships with full tuition reimbursements, career-related internships or fieldwork, and Federal Work-Study available. Support available to part-time students. Financial award application deadline: 4/1; financial award applicants required to submit FAFSA. *Faculty research:* VLSI and neural networks, communication networks, software engineering, computer architecture, multimedia and video processing. *Unit head:* Dr. Borko Furht, Chairman, 561-297-3855, Fax: 561-297-2800. *Application contact:* Joanna Arlington, Manager, Graduate Admissions, 561-297-2428, Fax: 561-297-2117, E-mail: arlingto@fau.edu. Web site: http://www.ceecs.fau.edu/.

Florida Institute of Technology, Graduate Programs, College of Engineering, Electrical and Computer Engineering Department, Melbourne, FL 32901-6975. Offers computer engineering (MS, PhD); electrical engineering (MS, PhD). Part-time and evening/weekend programs available. *Faculty:* 9 full-time (1 woman), 2 part-time/adjunct (0 women). *Students:* 87 full-time (20 women), 27 part-time (5 women); includes 9 minority (3 Black or African American, non-Hispanic/Latino; 2 Asian, non-Hispanic/Latino; 3 Hispanic/Latino; 1 Two or more races, non-Hispanic/Latino), 83 international. Average age 29. 323 applicants, 65% accepted, 31 enrolled. In 2011, 29 master's, 4 doctorates awarded. *Degree requirements:* For master's, comprehensive exam (for some programs), thesis optional, final exam, faculty-supervised specialized research; for doctorate, comprehensive exam (for some programs), thesis/dissertation, complete program of significant original research. *Entrance requirements:* For master's, GRE, minimum GPA of 3.0, bachelor's degree from an ABET-accredited program; for doctorate, 3 letters of recommendation, resume, minimum GPA of 3.2, statement of objectives, on-campus interview (highly recommended). Additional exam requirements/recommendations for international students: Required—TOEFL (minimum score 550 paper-based; 213 computer-based; 79 iBT). *Application deadline:* For fall admission, 4/1 for international students; for spring admission, 9/30 for international students. Applications are processed on a rolling basis. Application fee: $0. Electronic applications accepted. *Expenses: Tuition:* Full-time $19,620; part-time $1090 per credit hour. Tuition and fees vary according to campus/location. *Financial support:* In 2011–12, 3 research assistantships with full and partial tuition reimbursements (averaging $8,287 per year), 8 teaching assistantships with full and partial tuition reimbursements (averaging $3,265 per year) were awarded; career-related internships or fieldwork, institutionally sponsored loans, tuition waivers (partial), unspecified assistantships, and tuition remissions also available. Support available to part-time students. Financial award application deadline: 3/1; financial award applicants required to submit FAFSA. *Faculty research:* Electro-optics, electromagnetics, microelectronics, communications, computer architecture, neural networks. *Total annual research expenditures:* $458,364. *Unit head:* Dr. Samuel P. Kozaitis, Department Head, 321-674-8060, Fax: 321-674-8192, E-mail: kozaitis@fit.edu. *Application contact:* Cheryl A. Brown, Associate Director of Graduate Admissions, 321-674-7581, Fax: 321-723-9468, E-mail: cbrown@fit.edu. Web site: http://coe.fit.edu/ee/.

Florida International University, College of Engineering and Computing, Department of Electrical and Computer Engineering, Program in Computer Engineering, Miami, FL 33175. Offers MS. Part-time and evening/weekend programs available. *Degree requirements:* For master's, thesis optional. *Entrance requirements:* For master's, minimum GPA of 3.0, resume, 3 letters of recommendation, letter of intent. Additional exam requirements/recommendations for international students: Required—TOEFL (minimum score 550 paper-based; 80 iBT). Electronic applications accepted.

George Mason University, Volgenau School of Engineering, Department of Electrical and Computer Engineering, Fairfax, VA 22030. Offers advanced networking protocols for telecommunications (Certificate); communications and networking (Certificate); computer engineering (MS); computer forensics (MS); electrical and computer engineering (PhD); electrical engineering (MS); network technology and applications (Certificate); networks, system integration and testing (Certificate); signal processing (Certificate); telecommunications (MS); telecommunications forensics and security (Certificate); wireless communication (Certificate). MS program offered jointly with Old Dominion University, University of Virginia, Virginia Commonwealth University, and Virginia Polytechnic Institute and State University. *Faculty:* 29 full-time (4 women), 36 part-time/adjunct (2 women). *Students:* 162 full-time (49 women), 284 part-time (52 women); includes 101 minority (30 Black or African American, non-Hispanic/Latino; 1 American Indian or Alaska Native, non-Hispanic/Latino; 47 Asian, non-Hispanic/Latino; 19 Hispanic/Latino; 1 Native Hawaiian or other Pacific Islander, non-Hispanic/Latino; 3 Two or more races, non-Hispanic/Latino), 169 international. Average age 30. 478 applicants, 68% accepted, 106 enrolled. In 2011, 129 master's, 5 doctorates, 45 other advanced degrees awarded. *Degree requirements:* For master's, thesis optional; for doctorate, comprehensive exam, thesis or scholarly paper. *Entrance requirements:* For master's, GRE, personal goals statement; 2 official copies of transcripts; self-evaluation form; 3 letters of recommendation; resume; official bank statement; photocopy of passport; proof of financial support; for doctorate, GRE (waived for GMU electrical and computer engineering master's graduates with minimum GPA of 3.0), personal goals statement; 2 official copies of transcripts; self-evaluation form; 3 letters of recommendation; resume; official bank statement; photocopy of passport; proof of financial support. Additional exam requirements/recommendations for international students: Required—TOEFL (minimum score 575 paper-based; 230 computer-based; 88 iBT), IELTS, Pearson Test of English. *Application deadline:* For fall admission, 1/15 priority date for domestic students; for spring admission, 8/15 priority date for domestic students. Applications are processed on a rolling basis. Application fee: $65 ($80 for international students). Electronic applications accepted. *Expenses:* Tuition, state resident: full-time $8750; part-time $364.58 per credit. Tuition, nonresident: full-time $24,092; part-time $1003.83 per credit. *Required fees:* $2514; $104.75 per credit. *Financial support:* In 2011–12, 77 students received support, including 3 fellowships with full tuition reimbursements available (averaging $18,000 per year), 24 research assistantships with full and partial tuition reimbursements available (averaging $15,736 per year), 50 teaching assistantships with full and partial tuition reimbursements available (averaging $10,961 per year); career-related internships or fieldwork, Federal Work-Study, scholarships/grants, unspecified assistantships, and health care benefits (full-time research or teaching assistantship recipients) also available. Support available to part-time students. Financial award application deadline: 3/1; financial award applicants required to submit FAFSA. *Faculty research:* Communication networks, signal processing, system failure diagnosis, multiprocessors, material processing using microwave energy. *Total annual research expenditures:* $4.4 million. *Unit head:* Dr. Andre Manitius, Chairperson, 703-993-1569, Fax: 703-993-1601, E-mail: amanitiu@gmu.edu. *Application contact:* Jammie Chang, Academic Program Coordinator, 703-993-1523, Fax: 703-993-1601, E-mail: jchangn@gmu.edu. Web site: http://ece.gmu.edu/#.

The George Washington University, School of Engineering and Applied Science, Department of Electrical and Computer Engineering, Washington, DC 20052. Offers electrical and computer engineering (MS, D Sc); telecommunication and computers (MS). Part-time and evening/weekend programs available. *Faculty:* 24 full-time (2 women), 9 part-time/adjunct (0 women). *Students:* 131 full-time (25 women), 101 part-time (14 women); includes 40 minority (16 Black or African American, non-Hispanic/Latino; 18 Asian, non-Hispanic/Latino; 5 Hispanic/Latino; 1 Native Hawaiian or other Pacific Islander, non-Hispanic/Latino), 136 international. Average age 29. 362 applicants, 86% accepted, 68 enrolled. In 2011, 78 master's, 12 doctorates awarded. *Degree requirements:* For master's, thesis optional; for doctorate, comprehensive exam, thesis/dissertation, dissertation defense, qualifying exam. *Entrance requirements:* For master's, appropriate bachelor's degree, minimum GPA of 3.0; for doctorate, GRE (if highest earned degree is BS), appropriate bachelor's or master's degree, minimum GPA of 3.3. Additional exam requirements/recommendations for international students: Required—TOEFL or The George Washington University English as a Foreign Language Test. *Application deadline:* For fall admission, 3/1 priority date for domestic students; for spring admission, 10/1 for domestic students. Applications are processed on a rolling basis. Application fee: $75. *Financial support:* In 2011–12, 39 students received support. Fellowships with tuition reimbursements available, research assistantships, teaching assistantships with tuition reimbursements available, career-related internships or fieldwork, and institutionally sponsored loans available. Financial award application deadline: 3/1; financial award applicants required to submit FAFSA. *Faculty research:* Computer graphics, multimedia systems. *Unit head:* Can E. Korman, Chair, 202-994-4952, E-mail: korman@gwu.edu. *Application contact:* Adina Lav, Marketing, Recruiting and Admissions, 202-994-5827, Fax: 202-994-0909, E-mail: engineering@gwu.edu. Web site: http://www.ece.gwu.edu/.

Georgia Institute of Technology, Graduate Studies and Research, College of Computing, Atlanta, GA 30332-0001. Offers algorithms, combinatorics, and optimization (PhD); computational science and engineering (MS, PhD); computer science (MS, MSCS, PhD); human computer interaction (MSHCI); human-centered computing (PhD); information security (MS). Part-time programs available. Postbaccalaureate distance learning degree programs offered. Terminal master's awarded for partial completion of doctoral program. *Degree requirements:* For master's, thesis optional; for doctorate, comprehensive exam, thesis/dissertation. *Entrance requirements:* For master's, GRE General Test, GRE Subject Test, minimum GPA of 3.0; for doctorate, GRE General Test, GRE Subject Test, minimum GPA of 3.3. Additional exam requirements/recommendations for international students: Required—TOEFL. *Faculty research:* Computer systems, graphics, intelligent systems and artificial intelligence, networks and telecommunications, software engineering.

Georgia Institute of Technology, Graduate Studies and Research, College of Engineering, School of Electrical and Computer Engineering, Atlanta, GA 30332-0001. Offers MS, MSEE, PhD. Part-time programs available. Postbaccalaureate distance learning degree programs offered (minimal on-campus study). Terminal master's awarded for partial completion of doctoral program. *Degree requirements:* For master's, thesis optional; for doctorate, thesis/dissertation. *Entrance requirements:* For master's, GRE General Test, minimum GPA of 3.0; for doctorate, GRE General Test, minimum GPA of 3.5. Additional exam requirements/recommendations for international students: Required—TOEFL. *Faculty research:* Telecommunications, computer systems, microelectronics, optical engineering, digital signal processing.

Grand Valley State University, Padnos College of Engineering and Computing, School of Engineering, Allendale, MI 49401-9403. Offers electrical and computer engineering (MSE); manufacturing operations (MSE); mechanical engineering (MSE); product design and manufacturing engineering (MSE). Part-time and evening/weekend programs available. *Degree requirements:* For master's, project or thesis. *Entrance requirements:* For master's, engineering degree, minimum GPA of 3.0. Additional exam requirements/recommendations for international students: Required—TOEFL. Electronic applications accepted. *Faculty research:* Digital signal processing, computer aided design, computer aided manufacturing, manufacturing simulation, biomechanics, product design.

Illinois Institute of Technology, Graduate College, Armour College of Engineering, Department of Electrical and Computer Engineering, Chicago, IL 60616-3793. Offers biomedical imaging and signals (MBMI); computer engineering (MS, PhD); electrical and computer engineering (MECE); electrical engineering (MS, PhD); electricity markets (MEM); network engineering (MNE); power engineering (MPE); telecommunications and software engineering (MTSE); VLSI and microelectronics (MVM). Part-time and evening/weekend programs available. Postbaccalaureate distance learning degree programs offered (minimal on-campus study). Terminal master's awarded for partial completion of doctoral program. *Degree requirements:* For master's, comprehensive exam (for some programs), thesis (for some programs); for doctorate, comprehensive exam, thesis/dissertation. *Entrance requirements:* For master's and doctorate, GRE General Test (minimum score 1100 Quantitative and Verbal, 3.5 Analytical Writing), minimum undergraduate GPA of 3.0. Additional exam requirements/recommendations for international students: Required—TOEFL (minimum score 523 paper-based; 70 iBT); Recommended—IELTS (minimum score 5.5). Electronic applications accepted. *Faculty research:* Communication systems, computer systems and micro-electronics, electromagnetics and electronics, power and control systems, signal and image processing.

Indiana State University, College of Graduate and Professional Studies, College of Technology, Department of Electronics and Computer Technology, Terre Haute, IN 47809. Offers MS. *Degree requirements:* For master's, thesis or alternative. *Entrance requirements:* For master's, bachelor's degree in industrial technology or related field. Additional exam requirements/recommendations for international students: Required—TOEFL. Electronic applications accepted.

Indiana University–Purdue University Fort Wayne, College of Engineering, Technology, and Computer Science, Department of Engineering, Fort Wayne, IN 46805-1499. Offers computer engineering (MSE); electrical engineering (MSE); mechanical engineering (MSE); systems engineering (MSE). Part-time programs available. *Faculty:* 21 full-time (0 women), 2 part-time/adjunct (0 women). *Students:* 6 full-time (0 women),

29 part-time (5 women); includes 3 minority (2 Asian, non-Hispanic/Latino; 1 Hispanic/Latino), 3 international. Average age 28. 26 applicants, 96% accepted, 17 enrolled. In 2011, 16 master's awarded. *Entrance requirements:* For master's, minimum GPA of 3.0, bachelor's degree in engineering discipline. Additional exam requirements/recommendations for international students: Required—TOEFL (minimum score 550 paper-based; 213 computer-based; 77 iBT); Recommended—TWE. *Application deadline:* For fall admission, 7/15 priority date for domestic students, 5/15 for international students; for spring admission, 12/1 priority date for domestic students, 10/15 for international students. Applications are processed on a rolling basis. Application fee: $55 ($60 for international students). Electronic applications accepted. *Financial support:* In 2011–12, 7 research assistantships with partial tuition reimbursements (averaging $12,930 per year), 3 teaching assistantships with partial tuition reimbursements (averaging $12,930 per year) were awarded. Financial award application deadline: 3/1; financial award applicants required to submit FAFSA. *Faculty research:* Thermal science, robot prototypes, worm-scanning strategies. *Total annual research expenditures:* $185,757. *Unit head:* Dr. Donald Mueller, Chair, 260-481-5707, Fax: 260-481-6281, E-mail: mueller@engr.ipfw.edu. *Application contact:* Dr. Carlos Pomalaza-Raez, Program Director/Professor, 260-481-6353, Fax: 260-481-5734, E-mail: carlos-pomalaza-raez@purdue.edu. Web site: http://www.ipfw.edu/engr.

Indiana University–Purdue University Indianapolis, School of Engineering and Technology, Department of Electrical Engineering, Indianapolis, IN 46202-2896. Offers biomedical engineering (MS, PhD); electrical and computer engineering (MS, MSECE, PhD), including biomedical engineering (MSECE), control and automation (MSECE), signal processing (MSECE); engineering (interdisciplinary) (MSE). *Students:* 49 full-time (15 women), 48 part-time (5 women); includes 8 minority (2 Black or African American, non-Hispanic/Latino; 2 Asian, non-Hispanic/Latino; 2 Hispanic/Latino; 2 Two or more races, non-Hispanic/Latino), 56 international. Average age 27. 150 applicants, 49% accepted, 45 enrolled. In 2011, 29 degrees awarded. Application fee: $55 ($65 for international students). *Unit head:* Yaobin Chen, Unit Head, 317-274-4032, Fax: 317-274-4493. *Application contact:* Valerie Diemer, Graduate Program, 317-278-4960, Fax: 317-278-1671, E-mail: grad@engr.iupui.edu.

Instituto Tecnológico y de Estudios Superiores de Monterrey, Campus Chihuahua, Graduate Programs, Chihuahua, Mexico. Offers computer systems engineering (Ingeniero); electrical engineering (Ingeniero); electromechanical engineering (Ingeniero); electronic engineering (Ingeniero); engineering administration (MEA); industrial engineering (MIE, Ingeniero); international trade (MIT); mechanical engineering (Ingeniero).

International Technological University, Program in Computer Engineering, Santa Clara, CA 95050. Offers MSCE. *Degree requirements:* For master's, thesis or alternative. *Entrance requirements:* For master's, 3 semesters of calculus, minimum GPA of 2.5. Additional exam requirements/recommendations for international students: Required—TOEFL. *Faculty research:* Computer networking management, digital systems, embedded system design.

Iowa State University of Science and Technology, Department of Electrical and Computer Engineering, Ames, IA 50011. Offers computer engineering (M Eng, MS, PhD); electrical engineering (M Eng, MS, PhD). *Degree requirements:* For master's, thesis or alternative; for doctorate, thesis/dissertation. *Entrance requirements:* For master's and doctorate, GRE General Test. Additional exam requirements/recommendations for international students: Required—TOEFL (minimum score 570 paper-based; 79 iBT), IELTS (minimum score 6.5). *Application deadline:* For fall admission, 1/15 priority date for domestic students, 1/15 for international students; for spring admission, 9/15 for domestic and international students. Application fee: $40 ($90 for international students). Electronic applications accepted. *Unit head:* Dr. Zhengdao Wang, Director of Graduate Education, 515-294-8403, E-mail: ecegrad@ee.iastate.edu. *Application contact:* Director of Graduate Education, 515-294-8403, E-mail: ecegrad@iastate.edu. Web site: http://www.ece.iastate.edu/.

Iowa State University of Science and Technology, Program in Computer Engineering, Ames, IA 50011. Offers M Eng, MS, PhD. *Entrance requirements:* For master's and doctorate, GRE. Additional exam requirements/recommendations for international students: Required—TOEFL (minimum score 570 paper-based; 79 iBT), IELTS (minimum score 6.5). *Application deadline:* For fall admission, 1/15 for domestic students; for spring admission, 9/15 for domestic students. *Unit head:* Zhengdao Wang, Director of Graduate Education, 515-294-8403, E-mail: ecpegrad@iastate.edu. *Application contact:* Vicky Thorland-Oster, Application Contact, 515-294-8403, E-mail: ecpegrad@iastate.edu. Web site: http://www.ece.iastate.edu/.

The Johns Hopkins University, Engineering Program for Professionals, Part-time Program in Electrical and Computer Engineering, Baltimore, MD 21218-2699. Offers MS, Post-Master's Certificate. Part-time and evening/weekend programs available. Electronic applications accepted.

The Johns Hopkins University, Whiting School of Engineering, Department of Electrical and Computer Engineering, Baltimore, MD 21218-2699. Offers MSE, PhD. Terminal master's awarded for partial completion of doctoral program. *Degree requirements:* For master's, thesis optional; for doctorate, thesis/dissertation, qualifying and oral exams, seminar. *Entrance requirements:* For master's and doctorate, GRE General Test, transcripts, 3 letters of recommendation, statement of purpose. Additional exam requirements/recommendations for international students: Required—TOEFL (minimum score 600 paper-based; 250 computer-based; 100 iBT). Electronic applications accepted. *Faculty research:* Computer engineering, systems and control, language and speech processing, photonics and optoelectronics, signal and image processing.

Lakehead University, Graduate Studies, Faculty of Engineering, Thunder Bay, ON P7B 5E1, Canada. Offers control engineering (M Sc Engr); electrical/computer engineering (M Sc Engr); environmental engineering (M Sc Engr). Part-time programs available. *Degree requirements:* For master's, thesis. *Entrance requirements:* For master's, bachelor's degree in chemical, electrical or mechanical engineering, minimum B average. Additional exam requirements/recommendations for international students: Required—TOEFL. *Faculty research:* Pulp and paper, adaptive/process control, robust/interactive learning control, vibration control.

Lawrence Technological University, College of Engineering, Southfield, MI 48075-1058. Offers architectural engineering (MS); automotive engineering (MS); civil engineering (MA, MS); construction engineering management (MA); electrical and computer engineering (MS); engineering management (MEM); industrial engineering (MS); manufacturing systems (ME, DE); mechanical engineering (MS, DE); mechatronic systems engineering (MS). Part-time and evening/weekend programs available. *Faculty:* 25 full-time (4 women), 20 part-time/adjunct (1 woman). *Students:* 8 full-time (0 women), 332 part-time (52 women); includes 58 minority (21 Black or African American, non-Hispanic/Latino; 1 American Indian or Alaska Native, non-Hispanic/Latino; 32 Asian, non-Hispanic/Latino; 2 Hispanic/Latino; 2 Two or more races, non-Hispanic/Latino), 84 international. Average age 32. 652 applicants, 44% accepted, 70 enrolled. In 2011, 127 master's, 2 doctorates awarded. *Degree requirements:* For master's, thesis (for some programs). *Entrance requirements:* Additional exam requirements/recommendations for international students: Required—TOEFL (minimum score 550 paper-based; 213 computer-based; 79 iBT). *Application deadline:* For fall admission, 7/27 priority date for domestic students, 5/23 for international students; for spring admission, 11/15 priority date for domestic students, 11/15 for international students. Applications are processed on a rolling basis. Application fee: $50. Electronic applications accepted. *Financial support:* In 2011–12, 68 students received support, including 6 research assistantships (averaging $8,078 per year); Federal Work-Study and institutionally sponsored loans also available. Support available to part-time students. Financial award application deadline: 4/1; financial award applicants required to submit FAFSA. *Faculty research:* Advanced composite materials in bridges, strengthening existing bridges with carbon and glass fiber sheets, development of drive shafts using composite materials. *Unit head:* Dr. Nabil Grace, Dean, 248-204-2500, Fax: 248-204-2509, E-mail: engrdean@ltu.edu. *Application contact:* Jane Rohrback, Director of Admissions, 248-204-3160, Fax: 248-204-2228, E-mail: admissions@ltu.edu. Web site: http://www.ltu.edu/engineering/index.asp.

Lehigh University, P.C. Rossin College of Engineering and Applied Science, Department of Computer Science and Engineering, Bethlehem, PA 18015. Offers computer engineering (M Eng, MS, PhD); computer science (M Eng, MS, PhD, MBA/E); MBA/E. Part-time programs available. *Faculty:* 15 full-time (2 women). *Students:* 52 full-time (9 women), 20 part-time (4 women); includes 2 minority (both Asian, non-Hispanic/Latino), 53 international. Average age 28. 225 applicants, 36% accepted, 20 enrolled. In 2011, 17 master's, 4 doctorates awarded. *Degree requirements:* For master's, oral presentation of thesis; for doctorate, thesis/dissertation, qualifying, general, and oral exams. *Entrance requirements:* For master's, GRE General Test, minimum GPA of 3.0; for doctorate, GRE General Test, minimum GPA of 3.5. Additional exam requirements/recommendations for international students: Required—TOEFL (minimum score 550 paper-based; 213 computer-based; 79 iBT). *Application deadline:* For fall admission, 4/1 for domestic and international students; for spring admission, 11/1 for domestic and international students. Applications are processed on a rolling basis. Application fee: $75. Electronic applications accepted. *Expenses:* Contact institution. *Financial support:* In 2011–12, 2 fellowships with full tuition reimbursements (averaging $18,360 per year), 7 research assistantships with full tuition reimbursements (averaging $18,000 per year), 6 teaching assistantships with full tuition reimbursements (averaging $18,819 per year) were awarded. Financial award application deadline: 1/15. *Faculty research:* Artificial intelligence, networking-pattern recognition, multimedia e-learning/data mining/Web search, mobile robotics, bioinformatics, computer vision. *Total annual research expenditures:* $2.1 million. *Unit head:* Dr. Daniel P. Lopresti, Chairman, 610-758-5782, Fax: 610-758-4096, E-mail: dal9@lehigh.edu. *Application contact:* Judy Frenick, Graduate Coordinator, 610-758-3605, Fax: 610-758-4096, E-mail: jlf2@lehigh.edu. Web site: http://www.cse.lehigh.edu/.

Louisiana State University and Agricultural and Mechanical College, Graduate School, College of Engineering, Department of Electrical and Computer Engineering, Baton Rouge, LA 70803. Offers MSEE, PhD. *Faculty:* 26 full-time (1 woman), 1 part-time/adjunct (0 women). *Students:* 92 full-time (11 women), 11 part-time (2 women); includes 5 minority (1 Black or African American, non-Hispanic/Latino; 2 Asian, non-Hispanic/Latino; 2 Hispanic/Latino), 89 international. Average age 27. 207 applicants, 65% accepted, 14 enrolled. In 2011, 37 master's, 11 doctorates awarded. Terminal master's awarded for partial completion of doctoral program. *Degree requirements:* For master's, thesis optional; for doctorate, thesis/dissertation. *Entrance requirements:* For master's, GRE General Test, minimum GPA of 3.0; for doctorate, GRE General Test, minimum GPA of 3.5. Additional exam requirements/recommendations for international students: Required—TOEFL (minimum score 550 paper-based; 213 computer-based; 79 iBT) or IELTS (minimum score 6.5). *Application deadline:* For fall admission, 1/25 priority date for domestic students, 5/15 for international students; for spring admission, 10/15 for international students. Applications are processed on a rolling basis. Application fee: $50 ($70 for international students). Electronic applications accepted. *Financial support:* In 2011–12, 79 students received support, including 5 fellowships with full and partial tuition reimbursements available (averaging $18,269 per year), 40 research assistantships with full and partial tuition reimbursements available (averaging $14,678 per year), 29 teaching assistantships with full and partial tuition reimbursements available (averaging $13,194 per year); Federal Work-Study, institutionally sponsored loans, health care benefits, tuition waivers (full and partial), and unspecified assistantships also available. Financial award application deadline: 2/28; financial award applicants required to submit FAFSA. *Faculty research:* Computer engineering, electronics, control systems and signal processing, communications. *Total annual research expenditures:* $1.3 million. *Unit head:* Dr. Pratul Ajmera, Interim Chair, 225-578-5534, Fax: 225-578-5200, E-mail: ajmera@lsu.edu. *Application contact:* Dr. Guoxiang GuU, Graduate Adviser, 225-578-5534, Fax: 225-578-5200, E-mail: ggu@lsu.edu. Web site: http://www.ece.lsu.edu/.

Manhattan College, Graduate Division, School of Engineering, Program in Computer Engineering, Riverdale, NY 10471. Offers MS. Part-time and evening/weekend programs available. *Faculty:* 7 full-time (1 woman), 2 part-time/adjunct (0 women). *Students:* 1 full-time (0 women), 1 part-time (0 women), 1 international. Average age 24. In 2011, 1 master's awarded. *Degree requirements:* For master's, thesis or alternative. *Entrance requirements:* For master's, GRE (recommended), minimum GPA of 3.0. Additional exam requirements/recommendations for international students: Required—TOEFL (minimum score 550 paper-based; 213 computer-based; 80 iBT), IELTS (minimum score 6). *Application deadline:* For fall admission, 8/10 priority date for domestic students, 8/10 for international students; for spring admission, 1/7 for domestic and international students. Applications are processed on a rolling basis. Application fee: $50. *Expenses: Tuition:* Full-time $14,850; part-time $825 per credit. *Required fees:* $390; $150. *Financial support:* Fellowships, research assistantships, teaching assistantships, career-related internships or fieldwork, Federal Work-Study, scholarships/grants, and tuition waivers (partial) available. Support available to part-time students. Financial award application deadline: 5/15. *Unit head:* Dr. Gordon Silverman, Chairperson, 718-862-7153, Fax: 718-862-7162, E-mail: gordon.silverman@manhattan.edu. *Application contact:* Coralie Gale, 718-862-7153, Fax: 718-862-7162, E-mail: coralie.gale@manhattan.edu. Web site: http://www.engineering.manhattan.edu.

Marquette University, Graduate School, College of Engineering, Department of Electrical and Computer Engineering, Milwaukee, WI 53201-1881. Offers digital signal processing (Certificate); electric machines, drives, and controls (Certificate); electrical and computer engineering (MS, PhD); microwaves and antennas (Certificate); sensors and smart systems (Certificate). Part-time and evening/weekend programs available. *Faculty:* 15 full-time (2 women), 5 part-time/adjunct (0 women). *Students:* 33 full-time (8 women), 27 part-time (6 women); includes 8 minority (2 Black or African American, non-Hispanic/Latino; 3 Asian, non-Hispanic/Latino; 2 Hispanic/Latino; 1 Two or more races, non-Hispanic/Latino), 29 international. Average age 25. 85 applicants, 60% accepted, 14 enrolled. In 2011, 13 master's, 3 doctorates awarded. Terminal master's awarded for partial completion of doctoral program. *Degree requirements:* For master's, comprehensive exam (for some programs), thesis optional; for doctorate, thesis/dissertation, dissertation defense, qualifying exam. *Entrance requirements:* For master's, GRE General Test (recommended), official transcripts from all current and previous colleges/universities except Marquette, three letters of recommendation; for doctorate, GRE General Test, minimum GPA of 3.0, official transcripts from all current and previous colleges/universities except Marquette, three letters of recommendation, statement of purpose, submission of any English language publications authored by applicant (strongly recommended). Additional exam requirements/recommendations for international students: Required—TOEFL (minimum score 530 paper-based; 78 computer-based). *Application deadline:* For fall admission, 7/15 priority date for domestic students; for spring admission, 11/15 for domestic students. Applications are processed on a rolling basis. Application fee: $50. Electronic applications accepted. *Expenses: Tuition:* Full-time $17,010; part-time $945 per credit hour. Tuition and fees vary according to program. *Financial support:* In 2011–12, 22 students received support, including 3 fellowships with partial tuition reimbursements available (averaging $9,826 per year), 1 research assistantship with full tuition reimbursement available (averaging $13,745 per year), 9 teaching assistantships with full tuition reimbursements available (averaging $14,020 per year); scholarships/grants, health care benefits, tuition waivers (partial), and unspecified assistantships also available. Support available to part-time students. Financial award application deadline: 2/15. *Faculty research:* Electric machines, drives, and controls; applied solid-state electronics; computers and signal processing; microwaves and antennas; solid state devices and acoustic wave sensors. *Total annual research expenditures:* $885,354. *Unit head:* Dr. Edwin E. Yaz, Chair, 414-288-6820, Fax: 414-288-5579, E-mail: edwin.yaz@marquette.edu. *Application contact:* Dr. Michael Johnson, Director of Graduate Studies, 414-288-0631, Fax: 414-288-5579, E-mail: michael.johnson@marquette.edu. Web site: http://www.marquette.edu/engineering/electrical_computer/grad.shtml.

Massachusetts Institute of Technology, School of Engineering, Department of Electrical Engineering and Computer Science, Cambridge, MA 02139. Offers computer science (PhD, Sc D, ECS); computer science and engineering (PhD, Sc D); electrical engineering (PhD, Sc D, EE); electrical engineering and computer science (M Eng, SM, PhD, Sc D); SM/MBA. *Faculty:* 125 full-time (17 women). *Students:* 800 full-time (198 women), 3 part-time (1 woman); includes 181 minority (13 Black or African American, non-Hispanic/Latino; 1 American Indian or Alaska Native, non-Hispanic/Latino; 130 Asian, non-Hispanic/Latino; 30 Hispanic/Latino; 7 Two or more races, non-Hispanic/Latino), 365 international. Average age 26. 3,023 applicants, 12% accepted, 259 enrolled. In 2011, 209 master's, 101 doctorates, 5 other advanced degrees awarded. Terminal master's awarded for partial completion of doctoral program. *Degree requirements:* For master's and other advanced degree, thesis; for doctorate, comprehensive exam, thesis/dissertation. *Entrance requirements:* Additional exam requirements/recommendations for international students: Required—TOEFL (minimum score 250 computer-based; 100 iBT), IELTS (minimum score 7). *Application deadline:* For fall admission, 12/15 for domestic and international students. Application fee: $75. Electronic applications accepted. *Expenses: Tuition:* Full-time $40,460; part-time $630 per credit hour. *Required fees:* $272. *Financial support:* In 2011–12, 739 students received support, including 144 fellowships (averaging $31,200 per year), 492 research assistantships (averaging $30,000 per year), 120 teaching assistantships (averaging $31,200 per year); career-related internships or fieldwork, Federal Work-Study, institutionally sponsored loans, scholarships/grants, traineeships, health care benefits, and unspecified assistantships also available. *Faculty research:* Artificial intelligence and applications; robotics; computer architecture, software, systems, and networks; computation theory, cryptography, and algorithms; communications, control, signal processing, and optimization; devices, electronics, electrodynamics, and photonics; bioelectrical engineering; computational biology. *Total annual research expenditures:* $97.5 million. *Unit head:* Prof. Anantha P. Chandrakasan, Head, 617-253-4600, Fax: 617-258-7354, E-mail: hq@eecs.mit.edu. *Application contact:* Graduate Admissions, 617-253-4603, Fax: 617-258-7354, E-mail: grad-ap@eecs.mit.edu. Web site: http://www.eecs.mit.edu/.

McGill University, Faculty of Graduate and Postdoctoral Studies, Faculty of Engineering, Department of Electrical and Computer Engineering, Montréal, QC H3A 2T5, Canada. Offers M Eng, PhD.

Memorial University of Newfoundland, School of Graduate Studies, Faculty of Engineering and Applied Science, St. John's, NL A1C 5S7, Canada. Offers civil engineering (M Eng, PhD); electrical and computer engineering (M Eng, PhD); mechanical engineering (M Eng, PhD); ocean and naval architecture engineering (M Eng, PhD). Part-time programs available. *Degree requirements:* For master's, thesis; for doctorate, comprehensive exam, thesis/dissertation, oral thesis defense. *Entrance requirements:* For master's, 2nd class degree; for doctorate, master's degree in engineering. Electronic applications accepted. *Faculty research:* Engineering analysis, environmental and hydrotechnical studies, manufacturing and robotics, mechanics, structures and materials.

Memorial University of Newfoundland, School of Graduate Studies, Interdisciplinary Program in Computer Engineering, St. John's, NL A1C 5S7, Canada. Offers MA Sc. *Degree requirements:* For master's, project course. *Entrance requirements:* For master's, 2nd class engineering degree.

Mercer University, Graduate Studies, Macon Campus, School of Engineering, Macon, GA 31207-0003. Offers biomedical engineering (MSE); computer engineering (MSE); electrical engineering (MSE); engineering management (MSE); environmental engineering (MSE); environmental systems (MS); mechanical engineering (MSE); software engineering (MSE); software systems (MS); technical communications management (MS); technical management (MS). Part-time and evening/weekend programs available. Postbaccalaureate distance learning degree programs offered (no on-campus study). *Faculty:* 17 full-time (3 women), 1 part-time/adjunct (0 women). *Students:* 12 full-time (3 women), 113 part-time (28 women); includes 23 minority (13 Black or African American, non-Hispanic/Latino; 9 Asian, non-Hispanic/Latino; 1 Hispanic/Latino). Average age 31. In 2011, 44 master's awarded. *Degree requirements:* For master's, thesis or alternative. *Entrance requirements:* For master's, minimum undergraduate GPA of 3.0. Additional exam requirements/recommendations for international students: Required—TOEFL. *Application deadline:* For fall admission, 7/1 for domestic students; for spring admission, 11/15 for domestic students. Applications are processed on a rolling basis. Application fee: $35 ($50 for international students). Electronic applications accepted. *Expenses:* Contact institution. *Financial support:* Federal Work-Study available. *Unit head:* Dr. Wade H. Shaw, Dean, 478-301-2459, Fax: 478-301-5593, E-mail: shaw_wh@mercer.edu. *Application contact:* Greg Lofton, Graduate Program Coordinator, 478-301-5480, Fax: 478-301-5434, E-mail: lofton_g@mercer.edu. Web site: http://engineering.mercer.edu/.

Michigan Technological University, Graduate School, College of Engineering, Department of Electrical and Computer Engineering, Houghton, MI 49931. Offers advanced electric power engineering (Graduate Certificate); computer engineering (MS, PhD); electrical engineering (MS, PhD). Part-time programs available. Postbaccalaureate distance learning degree programs offered (minimal on-campus study). *Faculty:* 31 full-time (3 women), 8 part-time/adjunct (3 women). *Students:* 123 full-time (20 women), 57 part-time (5 women); includes 10 minority (4 Black or African American, non-Hispanic/Latino; 1 Asian, non-Hispanic/Latino; 4 Hispanic/Latino; 1 Two or more races, non-Hispanic/Latino), 111 international. Average age 29. 513 applicants, 50% accepted, 55 enrolled. In 2011, 43 master's, 5 doctorates, 2 other advanced degrees awarded. Terminal master's awarded for partial completion of doctoral program. *Degree requirements:* For master's, comprehensive exam (for some programs), thesis (for some programs); for doctorate, comprehensive exam, thesis/dissertation. *Entrance requirements:* For master's and doctorate, GRE, statement of purpose, official transcripts, 3 letters of recommendation. Additional exam requirements/recommendations for international students: Required—TOEFL (minimum score 100 iBT) or IELTS. *Application deadline:* For fall admission, 2/15 for domestic and international students; for spring admission, 8/15 for domestic and international students. Applications are processed on a rolling basis. Electronic applications accepted. *Expenses:* Contact institution. *Financial support:* In 2011–12, 100 students received support, including 7 fellowships with full tuition reimbursements available (averaging $6,065 per year), 31 research assistantships with full tuition reimbursements available (averaging $6,065 per year), 19 teaching assistantships with full tuition reimbursements available (averaging $6,065 per year); career-related internships or fieldwork, Federal Work-Study, scholarships/grants, health care benefits, tuition waivers (partial), unspecified assistantships, and cooperative program also available. Financial award applicants required to submit FAFSA. *Faculty research:* Information systems (signal processing and communications), solid-state electronics, power and energy systems, computer engineering. *Total annual research expenditures:* $2.4 million. *Unit head:* Dr. Daniel R. Fuhrmann, Department Chair, 906-487-2550, Fax: 906-487-2949, E-mail: ljbohman@mtu.edu. *Application contact:* Michele L. Kamppinen, Secretary 6, 906-487-2550, Fax: 906-487-2949, E-mail: mlkamppi@mtu.edu. Web site: http://www.mtu.edu/ece/.

Michigan Technological University, Graduate School, Interdisciplinary Programs, Houghton, MI 49931. Offers atmospheric sciences (PhD); computational sciences and engineering (PhD); engineering - environmental (PhD). *Students:* 28 full-time (14 women), 4 part-time (0 women), 20 international. Average age 29. 73 applicants, 32% accepted, 10 enrolled. In 2011, 3 doctorates awarded. *Degree requirements:* For doctorate, comprehensive exam, thesis/dissertation. *Entrance requirements:* For doctorate, GRE, statement of purpose, official transcripts, 3 letters of recommendation. Additional exam requirements/recommendations for international students: Required—TOEFL or IELTS. *Expenses:* Tuition, state resident: full-time $12,636; part-time $702 per credit. Tuition, nonresident: full-time $12,636; part-time $702 per credit. *Required fees:* $226; $226 per year. *Financial support:* In 2011–12, 28 students received support, including 3 fellowships with full tuition reimbursements available (averaging $6,065 per year), 17 research assistantships with full tuition reimbursements available (averaging $6,065 per year), 3 teaching assistantships with full tuition reimbursements available (averaging $6,065 per year). *Unit head:* Dr. Jacqueline E. Huntoon, Dean, 906-487-2327, Fax: 906-487-2463, E-mail: jeh@mtu.edu. *Application contact:* Carol T. Wingerson, Senior Staff Assistant, 906-487-2327, Fax: 906-487-2463, E-mail: gradadms@mtu.edu.

Mississippi State University, Bagley College of Engineering, Department of Electrical and Computer Engineering, Mississippi State, MS 39762. Offers computer engineering (MS, PhD); electrical engineering (MS, PhD). Part-time programs available. Postbaccalaureate distance learning degree programs offered (minimal on-campus study). *Faculty:* 22 full-time (1 woman). *Students:* 70 full-time (9 women), 36 part-time (3 women); includes 6 minority (3 Black or African American, non-Hispanic/Latino; 3 Asian, non-Hispanic/Latino), 58 international. Average age 29. 204 applicants, 24% accepted, 16 enrolled. In 2011, 18 master's, 9 doctorates awarded. Terminal master's awarded for partial completion of doctoral program. *Degree requirements:* For master's, comprehensive exam, thesis optional; for doctorate, comprehensive exam, thesis/dissertation, written exam. *Entrance requirements:* For master's, GRE General Test, minimum undergraduate GPA of 3.0; for doctorate, GRE, minimum graduate GPA of 3.5. Additional exam requirements/recommendations for international students: Required—TOEFL (minimum score 550 paper-based; 213 computer-based; 79 iBT); Recommended—IELTS (minimum score 6.5). *Application deadline:* For fall admission, 7/1 for domestic students, 5/1 for international students; for spring admission, 11/1 for domestic students, 9/1 for international students. Applications are processed on a rolling basis. Application fee: $40. Electronic applications accepted. *Expenses:* Tuition, state resident: full-time $5805; part-time $322.50 per credit hour. Tuition, nonresident: full-time $14,670; part-time $815 per credit hour. *Financial support:* In 2011–12, 22 research assistantships with full tuition reimbursements (averaging $16,419 per year), 18 teaching assistantships with full tuition reimbursements (averaging $14,450 per year) were awarded; Federal Work-Study, institutionally sponsored loans, scholarships/grants, and unspecified assistantships also available. Financial award application deadline: 4/1; financial award applicants required to submit FAFSA. *Faculty research:* Digital computing, power, controls, communication systems, microelectronics. *Total annual research expenditures:* $21.9 million. *Unit head:* Dr. Nicholas H. Younan, Jr., Professor and Department Head, 662-325-3912, Fax: 662-325-2298, E-mail: ece-head@ece.msstate.edu. *Application contact:* Dr. James E. Fowler, Professor and Interim Graduate Program Director, 662-325-3640, Fax: 662-325-2298, E-mail: fowler@ece.msstate.edu. Web site: http://www.ece.msstate.edu/.

Missouri University of Science and Technology, Graduate School, School of Engineering, Department of Electrical and Computer Engineering, Rolla, MO 65409. Offers computer engineering (MS, DE, PhD); electrical engineering (MS, DE, PhD). Part-time and evening/weekend programs available. Terminal master's awarded for partial completion of doctoral program. *Degree requirements:* For master's, thesis optional; for doctorate, comprehensive exam, thesis/dissertation, departmental qualifying exam. *Entrance requirements:* For master's, GRE General Test (minimum score 1100 verbal and quantitative, writing 4.5); for doctorate, GRE General Test (minimum score: verbal and quantitative 1100, writing 3.5). Additional exam requirements/recommendations for international students: Required—TOEFL. Electronic applications accepted. *Faculty research:* Power systems, computer/communication networks, intelligent control/robotics, robust control, nanotechnologies.

Montana State University, College of Graduate Studies, College of Engineering, Department of Electrical and Computer Engineering, Bozeman, MT 59717. Offers electrical engineering (MS); engineering (PhD), including electrical and computer engineering option. Part-time programs available. *Degree requirements:* For master's, comprehensive exam, thesis (for some programs); for doctorate, comprehensive exam, thesis/dissertation. *Entrance requirements:* For master's, GRE, BS in electrical or computer engineering or related field; for doctorate, GRE, MS in electrical or computer engineering or related field. Additional exam requirements/recommendations for international students: Required—TOEFL (minimum score 550 paper-based; 213 computer-based). Electronic applications accepted. *Faculty research:* Optics and optoelectonics, communications and signal processing, microfabrication, complex systems and control, energy systems.

Naval Postgraduate School, Departments and Academic Groups, Department of Electrical and Computer Engineering, Monterey, CA 93943-5216. Offers computer engineering (MS); electrical engineer (EE); electrical engineering (PhD); engineering acoustics (MS); engineering science (MS). Program only open to commissioned officers of the United States and friendly nations and selected United States federal civilian employees. *Accreditation:* ABET (one or more programs are accredited). Part-time programs available. Postbaccalaureate distance learning degree programs offered (minimal on-campus study). *Faculty:* 32 full-time (5 women), 4 part-time/adjunct (1 woman). *Students:* 59 full-time (4 women), 66 part-time (8 women); includes 27 minority (7 Black or African American, non-Hispanic/Latino; 12 Asian, non-Hispanic/Latino; 8 Hispanic/Latino), 11 international. In 2011, 38 master's, 8 other advanced degrees awarded. *Degree requirements:* For master's and EE, thesis (for some programs), capstone project or research/dissertation paper (for some programs); for doctorate, thesis/dissertation. *Faculty research:* Theory and design of digital communication systems; behavior modeling for detection, identification, prediction and reaction in AI systems solutions; waveform design for target class discrimination with closed-loop radar; iterative technique for system identification with adaptive signal design. *Total annual research expenditures:* $3.5 million. *Unit head:* Prof. Clark Robertson, Department Chair, 831-656-2082, E-mail: crobertson@nps.edu. Web site: http://www.nps.edu/Academics/Schools/GSEAS/Departments/ECE/.

New Jersey Institute of Technology, Office of Graduate Studies, Newark College of Engineering, Department of Electrical and Computer Engineering, Program in Computer Engineering, Newark, NJ 07102. Offers MS, PhD. Part-time and evening/weekend programs available. *Students:* 11 full-time (1 woman), 10 part-time (0 women); includes 6 minority (2 Black or African American, non-Hispanic/Latino; 3 Asian, non-Hispanic/Latino; 1 Hispanic/Latino), 11 international. Average age 27. 131 applicants, 57% accepted, 7 enrolled. In 2011, 17 master's, 2 doctorates awarded. Terminal master's awarded for partial completion of doctoral program. *Degree requirements:* For master's, thesis optional; for doctorate, thesis/dissertation, residency. *Entrance requirements:* For master's, GRE General Test; for doctorate, GRE General Test, minimum graduate GPA of 3.5. Additional exam requirements/recommendations for international students: Required—TOEFL (minimum score 550 paper-based; 213 computer-based; 79 iBT). *Application deadline:* For fall admission, 6/5 priority date for domestic students, 5/1 for international students; for spring admission, 11/15 priority date for domestic students, 11/15 for international students. Applications are processed on a rolling basis. Application fee: $65. Electronic applications accepted. *Expenses:* Tuition, state resident: full-time $7980; part-time $867 per credit. Tuition, nonresident: full-time $11,336; part-time $1196 per credit. *Required fees:* $230 per credit. *Financial support:* Fellowships with full and partial tuition reimbursements, research assistantships with full and partial tuition reimbursements, teaching assistantships with full and partial tuition reimbursements, career-related internships or fieldwork, Federal Work-Study, institutionally sponsored loans, and unspecified assistantships available. Financial award application deadline: 1/15. *Unit head:* Dr. Leonid Tsybeskov, Interim Chair, 973-596-6594, E-mail: leonid.tsybeskov@njit.edu. *Application contact:* Kathryn Kelly, Director of Admissions, 973-596-3300, Fax: 973-596-3461, E-mail: admissions@njit.edu.

New Mexico State University, Graduate School, College of Engineering, Klipsch School of Electrical and Computer Engineering, Las Cruces, NM 88003-8001. Offers MSEE, PhD. Part-time and evening/weekend programs available. Postbaccalaureate distance learning degree programs offered (no on-campus study). *Faculty:* 20 full-time (2 women), 1 part-time/adjunct (0 women). *Students:* 92 full-time (17 women), 46 part-time (5 women); includes 27 minority (2 American Indian or Alaska Native, non-Hispanic/Latino; 1 Asian, non-Hispanic/Latino; 23 Hispanic/Latino; 1 Two or more races, non-Hispanic/Latino), 73 international. Average age 30. 44 applicants, 68% accepted, 11 enrolled. In 2011, 34 master's, 1 doctorate awarded. Terminal master's awarded for partial completion of doctoral program. *Degree requirements:* For master's, thesis (for some programs), final oral or written exam; for doctorate, comprehensive exam, thesis/dissertation. *Entrance requirements:* For master's, GRE, minimum GPA of 3.0; for doctorate, departmental qualifying exam, minimum GPA of 3.0. Additional exam requirements/recommendations for international students: Required—TOEFL (minimum score 550 paper-based; 79 iBT), IELTS (minimum score 6.5). *Application deadline:* For fall admission, 3/1 priority date for domestic students, 3/1 for international students; for spring admission, 8/1 priority date for domestic students, 8/1 for international students. Applications are processed on a rolling basis. Application fee: $40 ($50 for international students). Electronic applications accepted. *Expenses:* Tuition, state resident: full-time $5004; part-time $208.50 per credit. Tuition, nonresident: full-time $17,446; part-time $726.90 per credit. *Financial support:* In 2011–12, 4 fellowships (averaging $10,061 per year), 35 research assistantships (averaging $20,720 per year), 29 teaching assistantships (averaging $20,642 per year) were awarded; career-related internships or fieldwork, Federal Work-Study, health care benefits, and unspecified assistantships also available. Support available to part-time students. Financial award application deadline: 3/1. *Faculty research:* Image and digital signal processing, energy systems, wireless communication, analog VLSI design, electro-optics. *Unit head:* Dr. Vojin Oklobdzija, Head, 575-646-3115, Fax: 575-646-1435, E-mail: vojin@nmsu.edu. *Application contact:* Sue Kord, Records Technician I, 575-646-6440, Fax: 575-646-1435, E-mail: kkord@nmsu.edu. Web site: http://ece.nmsu.edu/index.php.

New York Institute of Technology, Graduate Division, School of Engineering and Computing Sciences, Program in Electrical Engineering and Computer Engineering, Old Westbury, NY 11568-8000. Offers MS. Part-time and evening/weekend programs available. *Students:* 69 full-time (5 women), 59 part-time (5 women); includes 30 minority (9 Black or African American, non-Hispanic/Latino; 1 American Indian or Alaska Native, non-Hispanic/Latino; 17 Asian, non-Hispanic/Latino; 2 Hispanic/Latino; 1 Two or more races, non-Hispanic/Latino), 71 international. Average age 27. In 2011, 62 master's awarded. *Degree requirements:* For master's, project. *Entrance requirements:* For master's, GRE General Test (if QPA less than 2.85), BS in electrical engineering or related field, minimum QPA of 2.85. Additional exam requirements/recommendations for international students: Required—TOEFL (minimum score 550 paper-based; 213 computer-based). *Application deadline:* For fall admission, 7/1 priority date for domestic students; for spring admission, 12/1 priority date for domestic students. Applications are processed on a rolling basis. Application fee: $50. Electronic applications accepted. *Expenses: Tuition:* Part-time $930 per credit hour. *Financial support:* Fellowships, research assistantships with partial tuition reimbursements, institutionally sponsored loans, tuition waivers (full and partial), and unspecified assistantships available. Support available to part-time students. Financial award applicants required to submit FAFSA.

Faculty research: Computer networks, control theory, light waves and optics, robotics, signal processing. *Unit head:* Dr. Ayat Jafari, Chair, 516-686-7569, Fax: 516-686-7439, E-mail: ajafari@nyit.edu. *Application contact:* Dr. Jacquelyn Nealon, Vice President for Enrollment Services, 516-686-7925, Fax: 516-686-7597, E-mail: jnealon@nyit.edu.

Norfolk State University, School of Graduate Studies, School of Science and Technology, Program in Electronics Engineering, Norfolk, VA 23504. Offers MS.

North Carolina Agricultural and Technical State University, School of Graduate Studies, College of Engineering, Department of Electrical and Computer Engineering, Greensboro, NC 27411. Offers electrical engineering (MSEE, PhD), including communications and signal processing, computer engineering, electronic and optical materials and devices, power systems and control. Part-time programs available. *Degree requirements:* For master's, project, thesis defense; for doctorate, thesis/dissertation. *Entrance requirements:* For master's, GRE General Test, GRE Subject Test, minimum GPA of 2.8; for doctorate, GRE General Test, minimum GPA of 3.0. *Faculty research:* Semiconductor compounds, VLSI design, image processing, optical systems and devices, fault-tolerant computing.

North Carolina State University, Graduate School, College of Engineering, Department of Electrical and Computer Engineering, Program in Computer Engineering, Raleigh, NC 27695. Offers MS, PhD. *Degree requirements:* For master's, thesis (for some programs); for doctorate, thesis/dissertation. *Entrance requirements:* For master's and doctorate, GRE. Additional exam requirements/recommendations for international students: Required—TOEFL (minimum score 575 paper-based). Electronic applications accepted. *Faculty research:* Computer architecture, parallel processing, embedded computer systems, VLSI design, computer networking performance and control.

North Dakota State University, College of Graduate and Interdisciplinary Studies, College of Engineering and Architecture, Department of Electrical and Computer Engineering, Fargo, ND 58108. Offers MS, PhD. Part-time programs available. *Faculty:* 15 full-time (0 women). *Students:* 34 full-time (7 women), 18 part-time (7 women); includes 1 minority (Asian, non-Hispanic/Latino), 41 international. Average age 28. 88 applicants, 42% accepted, 18 enrolled. In 2011, 5 master's, 1 doctorate awarded. Terminal master's awarded for partial completion of doctoral program. *Degree requirements:* For master's, comprehensive exam, thesis; for doctorate, comprehensive exam, thesis/dissertation. *Entrance requirements:* Additional exam requirements/recommendations for international students: Required—TOEFL (minimum score 525 paper-based; 197 computer-based; 71 iBT). *Application deadline:* For fall admission, 2/28 priority date for domestic students, 2/28 for international students; for spring admission, 10/15 for domestic and international students. Application fee: $35. Electronic applications accepted. *Financial support:* In 2011–12, 30 students received support, including 2 fellowships with full tuition reimbursements available (averaging $25,000 per year), 6 research assistantships with full tuition reimbursements available (averaging $8,100 per year), 10 teaching assistantships with full tuition reimbursements available (averaging $8,100 per year); career-related internships or fieldwork, Federal Work-Study, institutionally sponsored loans, and tuition waivers (full) also available. Financial award application deadline: 3/1. *Faculty research:* Computers, power and control systems, microwaves, communications and signal processing, bioengineering. *Unit head:* Dr. Jacob Glower, Chair, 701-231-7608, Fax: 701-231-8677, E-mail: jacob.glower@ndsu.edu. *Application contact:* Dr. Rajesh Kavasseri, Associate Professor, 701-231-7019, E-mail: rajesh.kavasseri@ndsu.edu. Web site: http://www.ece.ndsu.nodak.edu/.

Northeastern University, College of Engineering, Department of Electrical and Computer Engineering, Boston, MA 02115-5096. Offers computer engineering (PhD); electrical engineering (MS, PhD); engineering leadership (MS). *Faculty:* 45 full-time, 2 part-time/adjunct. *Students:* 257 full-time (49 women), 98 part-time (6 women). 1,054 applicants, 47% accepted, 122 enrolled. In 2011, 83 master's, 13 doctorates awarded. *Degree requirements:* For master's, thesis optional; for doctorate, thesis/dissertation, departmental qualifying exam. *Entrance requirements:* For master's and doctorate, GRE General Test. Additional exam requirements/recommendations for international students: Required—TOEFL (minimum score 550 paper-based; 213 computer-based). *Application deadline:* For fall admission, 1/15 priority date for domestic students, 1/15 for international students. Applications are processed on a rolling basis. Application fee: $50. Electronic applications accepted. *Financial support:* In 2011–12, 136 students received support, including 1 fellowship with full tuition reimbursement available, 102 research assistantships with full tuition reimbursements available (averaging $18,325 per year), 32 teaching assistantships with full tuition reimbursements available (averaging $18,325 per year); career-related internships or fieldwork, Federal Work-Study, scholarships/grants, tuition waivers (full), and unspecified assistantships also available. Support available to part-time students. Financial award application deadline: 1/15; financial award applicants required to submit FAFSA. *Faculty research:* Signal processing and sensor data fusion, plasma science, sensing and imaging, power electronics, computer engineering. *Unit head:* Dr. Ali Abur, Chairman, 617-373-4159, Fax: 617-373-8970. *Application contact:* Jeffery Hengel, Admissions Specialist, 617-373-2711, Fax: 617-373-2501, E-mail: grad-eng@coe.neu.edu. Web site: http://www.coe.neu.edu/.

Northwestern Polytechnic University, School of Engineering, Fremont, CA 94539-7482. Offers computer science (MS); computer systems engineering (MS); electrical engineering (MS). Part-time and evening/weekend programs available. *Degree requirements:* For master's, thesis optional. *Entrance requirements:* For master's, minimum GPA of 3.0. Additional exam requirements/recommendations for international students: Required—TOEFL (minimum score 550 paper-based; 213 computer-based; 79 iBT). *Faculty research:* Computer networking, database design, Internet technology, software engineering, digital signal processing.

Northwestern University, McCormick School of Engineering and Applied Science, Department of Electrical Engineering and Computer Science, Evanston, IL 60208. Offers MS, PhD. MS and PhD admissions and degrees offered through The Graduate School. Part-time programs available. *Faculty:* 52 full-time (10 women). *Students:* 246 full-time (43 women), 15 part-time (6 women); includes 28 minority (1 Black or African American, non-Hispanic/Latino; 20 Asian, non-Hispanic/Latino; 5 Hispanic/Latino; 2 Two or more races, non-Hispanic/Latino), 179 international. Average age 26. 1,203 applicants, 16% accepted, 76 enrolled. In 2011, 43 master's, 24 doctorates awarded. Terminal master's awarded for partial completion of doctoral program. *Degree requirements:* For master's, comprehensive exam (for some programs), thesis optional; for doctorate, comprehensive exam, thesis/dissertation. *Entrance requirements:* For master's and doctorate, GRE General Test. Additional exam requirements/recommendations for international students: Required—TOEFL (minimum score 577 paper-based, 233 computer-based, 90 iBT) or IELTS. *Application deadline:* For fall admission, 12/31 for domestic and international students; for winter admission, 11/15 for domestic students, 11/1 for international students; for spring admission, 2/15 for domestic students, 2/1 for international students. Application fee: $75. Electronic applications accepted. *Financial support:* Fellowships with full tuition reimbursements,

research assistantships with full tuition reimbursements, teaching assistantships with full tuition reimbursements, career-related internships or fieldwork, institutionally sponsored loans, health care benefits, and unspecified assistantships available. Financial award application deadline: 1/15; financial award applicants required to submit FAFSA. *Faculty research:* Solid state and photonics; computing, algorithms, and applications; computer engineering and systems; cognitive systems; graphics and interactive media; signals and systems. *Total annual research expenditures:* $19.2 million. *Unit head:* Dr. Alan Sahakian, Chair, 847-491-7007, Fax: 847-491-4455, E-mail: sahakian@ece.northwestern.edu. *Application contact:* Dr. Chris Riesbeck, Director of Graduate Admissions, 847-491-7279, Fax: 847-491-4455, E-mail: c-riesbeck@northwestern.edu. Web site: http://www.eecs.northwestern.edu/.

Oakland University, Graduate Study and Lifelong Learning, School of Engineering and Computer Science, Department of Computer Science and Engineering, Rochester, MI 48309-4401. Offers computer science (MS); embedded systems (MS); information systems engineering (MS); software engineering (MS). Part-time and evening/weekend programs available. *Entrance requirements:* For master's, minimum GPA of 3.0 for unconditional admission. Electronic applications accepted. *Expenses:* Contact institution. *Faculty research:* Cyber security, 3D imaging of neurochemicals in rat brains.

Oakland University, Graduate Study and Lifelong Learning, School of Engineering and Computer Science, Department of Electrical and Systems Engineering, Program in Electrical and Computer Engineering, Rochester, MI 48309-4401. Offers MS. Part-time and evening/weekend programs available. *Entrance requirements:* For master's, minimum GPA of 3.0 for unconditional admission. Additional exam requirements/recommendations for international students: Required—TOEFL (minimum score 550 paper-based; 213 computer-based). Electronic applications accepted. *Expenses:* Contact institution.

The Ohio State University, Graduate School, College of Engineering, Department of Computer Science and Engineering, Columbus, OH 43210. Offers computer and information science (MS, PhD); computer science and engineering (MS). *Faculty:* 33. *Students:* 278 full-time (46 women), 61 part-time (9 women); includes 10 minority (4 Black or African American, non-Hispanic/Latino; 4 Asian, non-Hispanic/Latino; 1 Hispanic/Latino; 1 Two or more races, non-Hispanic/Latino), 274 international. Average age 27. In 2011, 37 master's, 20 doctorates awarded. *Degree requirements:* For master's, thesis optional; for doctorate, thesis/dissertation. *Entrance requirements:* Additional exam requirements/recommendations for international students: Required—Michigan English Language Assessment Battery (minimum score 82); Recommended—TOEFL (minimum score 600 paper-based; 250 computer-based; 79 iBT). *Application deadline:* For fall admission, 8/15 priority date for domestic students, 7/1 for international students; for winter admission, 12/1 priority date for domestic students, 11/1 for international students; for spring admission, 3/1 priority date for domestic students, 2/1 for international students. Applications are processed on a rolling basis. Application fee: $40 ($50 for international students). Electronic applications accepted. *Expenses:* Tuition, state resident: full-time $11,400. Tuition, nonresident: full-time $28,125. Tuition and fees vary according to course load, degree level, campus/location and program. *Financial support:* Fellowships, teaching assistantships, career-related internships or fieldwork, Federal Work-Study, institutionally sponsored loans, and administrative assistantships available. Support available to part-time students. Financial award application deadline: 1/15. *Unit head:* Xiadong Zhang, Chair, 614-292-5973, E-mail: zhang.574@osu.edu. *Application contact:* Graduate Admissions, 614-292-6031, Fax: 614-292-3656, E-mail: gradadmissions@osu.edu. Web site: http://www.cse.ohio-state.edu.

Oklahoma State University, College of Engineering, Architecture and Technology, School of Electrical and Computer Engineering, Stillwater, OK 74078. Offers MS, PhD. Postbaccalaureate distance learning degree programs offered. *Faculty:* 26 full-time (2 women), 1 part-time/adjunct (0 women). *Students:* 91 full-time (20 women), 95 part-time (14 women); includes 14 minority (3 Black or African American, non-Hispanic/Latino; 1 American Indian or Alaska Native, non-Hispanic/Latino; 3 Asian, non-Hispanic/Latino; 5 Hispanic/Latino; 2 Two or more races, non-Hispanic/Latino), 143 international. Average age 28. 399 applicants, 31% accepted, 37 enrolled. In 2011, 47 master's, 6 doctorates awarded. *Degree requirements:* For master's, thesis or alternative; for doctorate, comprehensive exam, thesis/dissertation. *Entrance requirements:* For master's and doctorate, GRE or GMAT. Additional exam requirements/recommendations for international students: Required—TOEFL (minimum score 550 paper-based; 79 iBT). *Application deadline:* For fall admission, 3/1 for international students; for spring admission, 8/1 for international students. Applications are processed on a rolling basis. Application fee: $40 ($75 for international students). Electronic applications accepted. *Expenses:* Tuition, state resident: full-time $4044; part-time $168.50 per credit hour. Tuition, nonresident: full-time $16,008; part-time $667 per credit hour. *Required fees:* $2122; $88.45 per credit hour. One-time fee: $50. Tuition and fees vary according to course load and campus/location. *Financial support:* In 2011–12, 70 research assistantships (averaging $12,128 per year), 25 teaching assistantships (averaging $8,748 per year) were awarded; career-related internships or fieldwork, Federal Work-Study, scholarships/grants, health care benefits, tuition waivers (partial), and unspecified assistantships also available. Support available to part-time students. Financial award application deadline: 3/1; financial award applicants required to submit FAFSA. *Unit head:* Dr. Keith Teague, Head, 405-744-5151, Fax: 405-744-9198. *Application contact:* Dr. Sheryl Tucker, Dean, 405-744-7099, Fax: 405-744-0355, E-mail: grad-i@okstate.edu. Web site: http://www.ece.okstate.edu.

Old Dominion University, Frank Batten College of Engineering and Technology, Program in Electrical and Computer Engineering, Norfolk, VA 23529. Offers ME, MS, PhD. Part-time programs available. Postbaccalaureate distance learning degree programs offered (minimal on-campus study). *Faculty:* 21 full-time (1 woman), 2 part-time/adjunct (both women). *Students:* 74 full-time (15 women), 15 part-time (3 women); includes 9 minority (4 Black or African American, non-Hispanic/Latino; 4 Asian, non-Hispanic/Latino; 1 Hispanic/Latino), 51 international. Average age 30. 144 applicants, 62% accepted, 16 enrolled. In 2011, 18 master's, 14 doctorates awarded. *Degree requirements:* For master's, comprehensive exam (for some programs), thesis (for some programs); for doctorate, thesis/dissertation, candidacy exam, diagnostic exam. *Entrance requirements:* For master's, GRE, two letters of recommendation; for doctorate, GRE, three letters of recommendation, resume, personal statement of objective. Additional exam requirements/recommendations for international students: Required—TOEFL (minimum score 550 paper-based; 79 iBT). *Application deadline:* For fall admission, 6/1 for domestic students, 4/15 for international students; for spring admission, 11/1 for domestic students, 10/1 for international students. Applications are processed on a rolling basis. Application fee: $50. Electronic applications accepted. *Expenses:* Tuition, state resident: full-time $9096; part-time $379 per credit. Tuition, nonresident: full-time $23,064; part-time $961 per credit. *Required fees:* $127 per semester. One-time fee: $50. *Financial support:* In 2011–12, 2 fellowships with full tuition reimbursements (averaging $17,500 per year), 24 research assistantships with full and partial tuition reimbursements (averaging $15,000 per year), 25 teaching assistantships with full and partial tuition reimbursements (averaging $15,000 per year) were awarded; career-related internships or fieldwork, Federal Work-Study, scholarships/grants, tuition waivers (full), and unspecified assistantships also available. Support available to part-time students. Financial award application deadline: 2/15; financial award applicants required to submit FAFSA. *Faculty research:* Signal and image processing biomedical and target detection applications, renewal energy applications including the development of high efficiency solar cells, nanotechnology and nanoscale thin film techniques, ultrafast (femtosecond) laser applications, linear and nonlinear systems theory. *Total annual research expenditures:* $3 million. *Unit head:* Dr. Oscar Gonzalez, Graduate Program Director, 757-683-4966, Fax: 757-683-3220, E-mail: ecegpd@odu.edu. *Application contact:* Linda Marshall, Senior Secretary, 757-683-3741, Fax: 757-683-3220, E-mail: lmarshal@odu.edu. Web site: http://eng.odu.edu/ece/.

Oregon Health & Science University, School of Medicine, Graduate Programs in Medicine, Department of Computer Science and Engineering, Portland, OR 97239-3098. Offers computer science and engineering (MS, PhD); electrical engineering (MS, PhD). Part-time programs available. *Faculty:* 7 full-time (2 women), 3 part-time/adjunct (all women). *Students:* 20 full-time (5 women), 4 part-time (all women), 12 international. Average age 33. 8 applicants, 38% accepted, 3 enrolled. In 2011, 1 master's, 3 doctorates awarded. Terminal master's awarded for partial completion of doctoral program. *Degree requirements:* For master's, thesis (for some programs); for doctorate, comprehensive exam, thesis/dissertation, qualifying exam. *Entrance requirements:* For master's and doctorate, GRE General Test (minimum scores: 153 Verbal/148 Quantitative/4.5 Analytical). Additional exam requirements/recommendations for international students: Required—TOEFL. *Application deadline:* For fall admission, 7/15 for domestic students, 5/15 for international students; for winter admission, 10/15 for domestic students, 9/15 for international students; for spring admission, 1/15 for domestic students, 12/15 for international students. Applications are processed on a rolling basis. Application fee: $70. Electronic applications accepted. *Financial support:* Health care benefits, tuition waivers (full), and full tuition and stipends for PhD students available. *Unit head:* Dr. Peter Heeman, Program Director, 503-748-1635, E-mail: cseedept@csee.ogi.edu. *Application contact:* Pat Dickerson, Administrative Coordinator, 503-748-1635, E-mail: cseedept@csee.ogi.edu.

Oregon State University, Graduate School, College of Engineering, School of Electrical Engineering and Computer Science, Corvallis, OR 97331. Offers computer science (M Eng, MAIS, MS, PhD); electrical and computer engineering (M Eng, MS, PhD). *Degree requirements:* For doctorate, thesis/dissertation, qualifying exam, preliminary exam. *Entrance requirements:* For master's and doctorate, minimum GPA of 3.0 in last 90 hours of course work. Additional exam requirements/recommendations for international students: Required—TOEFL (minimum score 600 paper-based; 250 computer-based; 80 iBT). Electronic applications accepted. *Faculty research:* Optical materials and devices, data security and cryptography, analog and mixed-signal integrated circuit design, algorithms, computer graphics and vision.

Penn State University Park, Graduate School, College of Engineering, Department of Computer Science and Engineering, State College, University Park, PA 16802-1503. Offers M Eng, MS, PhD. *Unit head:* Dr. David N. Wormley, Dean, 814-865-7537, Fax: 814-865-8767, E-mail: dnw2@engr.psu.edu. *Application contact:* Cynthia E. Nicosia, Director, Graduate Enrollment Services, 814-865-1834, E-mail: cey1@psu.edu. Web site: http://www.cse.psu.edu.

Polytechnic Institute of New York University, Department of Electrical and Computer Engineering, Major in Computer Engineering, Brooklyn, NY 11201-2990. Offers MS, Certificate. *Students:* 23 full-time (1 woman), 16 part-time (2 women); includes 9 minority (1 Black or African American, non-Hispanic/Latino; 6 Asian, non-Hispanic/Latino; 2 Hispanic/Latino), 20 international. 60 applicants, 37% accepted, 22 enrolled. In 2011, 16 master's awarded. *Degree requirements:* For master's, comprehensive exam (for some programs), thesis (for some programs). *Entrance requirements:* For master's, BS in electrical engineering. Additional exam requirements/recommendations for international students: Required—TOEFL (minimum score 550 paper-based; 213 computer-based; 80 iBT); Recommended—IELTS (minimum score 6.5). *Application deadline:* For fall admission, 7/31 priority date for domestic students, 4/30 for international students; for spring admission, 12/31 priority date for domestic students, 11/30 for international students. Applications are processed on a rolling basis. Application fee: $75. Electronic applications accepted. *Expenses: Tuition:* Full-time $22,464; part-time $1248 per credit. *Required fees:* $501 per semester. *Financial support:* Applicants required to submit FAFSA. *Unit head:* Dr. Jonathan Chao, Head, 718-860-3478, Fax: 718-260-3302, E-mail: chao@poly.edu. *Application contact:* JeanCarlo Bonilla, Director, Graduate Enrollment Management, 718-260-3182, Fax: 718-260-3624.

Polytechnic Institute of NYU, Long Island Graduate Center, Graduate Programs, Department of Electrical and Computer Engineering, Major in Computer Engineering, Melville, NY 11747. Offers MS. *Students:* Average age 27. 1 applicant, 0% accepted, 0 enrolled. In 2011, 3 master's awarded. *Degree requirements:* For master's, comprehensive exam (for some programs), thesis (for some programs). *Entrance requirements:* Additional exam requirements/recommendations for international students: Required—TOEFL (minimum score 550 paper-based; 213 computer-based; 80 iBT); Recommended—IELTS (minimum score 6.5). *Application deadline:* For fall admission, 7/31 priority date for domestic students, 4/30 for international students; for spring admission, 12/31 priority date for domestic students, 11/30 for international students. Applications are processed on a rolling basis. Application fee: $75. Electronic applications accepted. *Financial support:* Institutionally sponsored loans, scholarships/grants, and unspecified assistantships available. Support available to part-time students. *Unit head:* Dr. Jonathan Chao, Department Head, 718-260-3302, E-mail: chao@poly.edu. *Application contact:* JeanCarlo Bonilla, Director of Graduate Enrollment Management, 718-260-3182, Fax: 718-260-3624, E-mail: gradinfo@poly.edu.

Polytechnic Institute of NYU, Westchester Graduate Center, Graduate Programs, Department of Electrical and Computer Engineering, Major in Computer Engineering, Hawthorne, NY 10532-1507. Offers MS. *Students:* 1 applicant, 100% accepted, 1 enrolled. *Degree requirements:* For master's, comprehensive exam (for some programs), thesis (for some programs). *Entrance requirements:* Additional exam requirements/recommendations for international students: Required—TOEFL (minimum score 550 paper-based; 213 computer-based; 80 iBT); Recommended—IELTS (minimum score 6.5). *Application deadline:* For fall admission, 7/31 priority date for domestic students, 4/30 for international students; for spring admission, 12/31 priority date for domestic students, 11/30 for international students. Applications are processed on a rolling basis. Application fee: $75. Electronic applications accepted. *Financial support:* Institutionally sponsored loans, scholarships/grants, and unspecified assistantships available. Support available to part-time students. Financial award applicants required to submit FAFSA. *Unit head:* Dr. Jonathan Chao, Department Head, 718-260-3302, E-mail: chao@poly.edu. *Application contact:* JeanCarlo Bonilla, Director of Graduate Enrollment Management, 718-260-3182, Fax: 718-260-3624, E-mail: gradinfo@poly.edu.

Polytechnic University of Puerto Rico, Graduate School, Hato Rey, PR 00919. Offers business administration (MBA), including computer information systems, general management, management of information systems, management of international enterprises; civil engineering (ME, MS); computer engineering (ME, MS); computer science (MCS, MS); electrical engineering (ME, MS); engineering management (MEM); environmental management (MEM); landscape architecture (M Land Arch); manufacturing competitiveness (MMC, MS); manufacturing engineering (ME, MS); mechanical engineering (M Mech E). Part-time and evening/weekend programs available. *Entrance requirements:* For master's, 3 letters of recommendation.

Portland State University, Graduate Studies, Maseeh College of Engineering and Computer Science, Department of Electrical and Computer Engineering, Portland, OR 97207-0751. Offers M Eng, MS, PhD. Part-time and evening/weekend programs available. *Degree requirements:* For master's, variable foreign language requirement, oral exam; for doctorate, one foreign language, comprehensive exam, thesis/dissertation, oral and written exams. *Entrance requirements:* For master's, minimum GPA of 3.0 in upper-division course work or 2.75 overall, BS in electrical or computer engineering or allied field; for doctorate, GRE General Test, GRE Subject Test, minimum GPA of 3.0 in upper-division course work, MS in electrical engineering or allied field. Additional exam requirements/recommendations for international students: Required—TOEFL (minimum score 550 paper-based; 213 computer-based). *Faculty research:* Optics and laser systems, design automation, VLSI design, computer systems, power electronics.

Purdue University, College of Engineering, School of Electrical and Computer Engineering, West Lafayette, IN 47907-2035. Offers MS, MSE, MSECE, PhD. MS and PhD degree programs in biomedical engineering offered jointly with School of Mechanical Engineering and School of Chemical Engineering. Part-time programs available. Postbaccalaureate distance learning degree programs offered (no on-campus study). Terminal master's awarded for partial completion of doctoral program. *Entrance requirements:* For master's and doctorate, GRE General Test, minimum GPA of 3.25. Additional exam requirements/recommendations for international students: Required—TOEFL (minimum score 550 paper-based; 213 computer-based; 77 iBT). Electronic applications accepted. *Faculty research:* Automatic controls; biomedical imaging; computer engineering; communications, networking signal and image processing; fields and optics.

Purdue University Calumet, Graduate Studies Office, School of Engineering, Mathematics, and Science, Department of Engineering, Hammond, IN 46323-2094. Offers computer engineering (MSE); electrical engineering (MSE); engineering (MS); mechanical engineering (MSE). Evening/weekend programs available. *Entrance requirements:* Additional exam requirements/recommendations for international students: Required—TOEFL.

Queen's University at Kingston, School of Graduate Studies and Research, Faculty of Applied Science, Department of Electrical and Computer Engineering, Kingston, ON K7L 3N6, Canada. Offers M Eng, M Sc, M Sc Eng, PhD. Part-time programs available. *Degree requirements:* For master's, thesis optional; for doctorate, comprehensive exam, thesis/dissertation. *Entrance requirements:* Additional exam requirements/recommendations for international students: Required—TOEFL (minimum score 580 paper-based; 237 computer-based). *Faculty research:* Communications and signal processing systems, computer engineering systems.

Rensselaer at Hartford, Department of Engineering, Program in Computer and Systems Engineering, Hartford, CT 06120-2991. Offers ME. *Entrance requirements:* For master's, GRE.

Rensselaer Polytechnic Institute, Graduate School, School of Engineering, Program in Computer and Systems Engineering, Troy, NY 12180-3590. Offers M Eng, MS, PhD. Part-time programs available. Terminal master's awarded for partial completion of doctoral program. *Degree requirements:* For master's, thesis (for some programs); for doctorate, thesis/dissertation. *Entrance requirements:* For master's, GRE; for doctorate, GRE, qualifying exam, candidacy exam. Additional exam requirements/recommendations for international students: Required—TOEFL (minimum score 570 paper-based; 89 iBT). Electronic applications accepted. *Faculty research:* Multimedia via ATM, mobile robotics, thermophotovoltaic devices, microelectronic interconnections, agile manufacturing.

Rice University, Graduate Programs, George R. Brown School of Engineering, Department of Electrical and Computer Engineering, Houston, TX 77251-1892. Offers bioengineering (MS, PhD); circuits, controls, and communication systems (MS, PhD); computer science and engineering (MS, PhD); electrical engineering (MEE); lasers, microwaves, and solid-state electronics (MS, PhD); MBA/MEE. Part-time programs available. *Degree requirements:* For master's, thesis (for some programs); for doctorate, thesis/dissertation. *Entrance requirements:* For master's and doctorate, GRE General Test, GRE Subject Test, minimum GPA of 3.0. Additional exam requirements/recommendations for international students: Required—TOEFL (minimum score 600 paper-based; 250 computer-based; 90 iBT). Electronic applications accepted. *Faculty research:* Physical electronics, systems, computer engineering, bioengineering.

Rice University, Graduate Programs, George R. Brown School of Engineering, Program in Computational Science and Engineering, Houston, TX 77251-1892. Offers MCSE.

Rochester Institute of Technology, Graduate Enrollment Services, Kate Gleason College of Engineering, Department of Computer Engineering, Rochester, NY 14623-5603. Offers MS. Part-time programs available. *Students:* 29 full-time (4 women), 12 part-time (1 woman); includes 4 minority (3 Asian, non-Hispanic/Latino; 1 Hispanic/Latino), 16 international. Average age 24. 73 applicants, 38% accepted, 8 enrolled. In 2011, 18 degrees awarded. *Degree requirements:* For master's, thesis. *Entrance requirements:* For master's, GRE, minimum GPA of 3.0. Additional exam requirements/recommendations for international students: Required—TOEFL (minimum score 550 paper-based; 213 computer-based; 79 iBT) or IELTS (minimum score 6). *Application deadline:* For fall admission, 2/15 priority date for domestic students, 2/15 for international students; for winter admission, 10/15 priority date for domestic students, 10/15 for international students. Applications are processed on a rolling basis. Application fee: $50. Electronic applications accepted. *Expenses: Tuition:* Full-time $34,659; part-time $963 per credit hour. *Required fees:* $228; $76 per quarter. *Financial support:* Fellowships with partial tuition reimbursements, research assistantships with partial tuition reimbursements, teaching assistantships with partial tuition reimbursements, career-related internships or fieldwork, institutionally sponsored loans, scholarships/grants, and unspecified assistantships available. Support available to part-time students. Financial award applicants required to submit FAFSA. *Faculty research:* Object detection and tracking using multiple cameras; face detection and recognition; pose and gaze estimation; activity recognition; power-constrained processing; lossless image compression; color forms processing; adaptive thresholding; automatic albuming; MPEG-7 color, shape and motion descriptors; Web printing. *Unit head:* Dr. S. Jay Yang, Graduate Program Director, 585-475-2987, E-mail: sjyeec@rit.edu. *Application contact:* Diane Ellison, Assistant Vice President, Graduate Enrollment Services, 585-475-2229, Fax: 585-475-7164, E-mail: gradinfo@rit.edu. Web site: http://www.ce.rit.edu/.

Rose-Hulman Institute of Technology, Faculty of Engineering and Applied Sciences, Department of Electrical and Computer Engineering, Terre Haute, IN 47803-3999. Offers electrical and computer engineering (M Eng); electrical engineering (MS). Part-time programs available. Postbaccalaureate distance learning degree programs offered (minimal on-campus study). *Faculty:* 19 full-time (5 women), 1 part-time/adjunct (0 women). *Students:* 8 full-time (2 women), 2 part-time (0 women); includes 1 minority (Asian, non-Hispanic/Latino), 6 international. Average age 23. 15 applicants, 80% accepted, 5 enrolled. In 2011, 15 master's awarded. *Degree requirements:* For master's, thesis (for some programs). *Entrance requirements:* For master's, GRE, minimum GPA of 3.0. Additional exam requirements/recommendations for international students: Required—TOEFL (minimum score 580 paper-based; 237 computer-based; 92 iBT). *Application deadline:* For fall admission, 2/1 priority date for domestic students. Applications are processed on a rolling basis. Application fee: $0. *Expenses: Tuition:* Full-time $37,197; part-time $1085 per credit hour. *Financial support:* In 2011–12, 9 students received support. Fellowships with full and partial tuition reimbursements available, research assistantships with full and partial tuition reimbursements available, institutionally sponsored loans, scholarships/grants, and tuition waivers (full and partial) available. *Faculty research:* Wireless systems, VLSI design, aerial robotics, power system dynamics and control, image and speech processing. *Total annual research expenditures:* $140,727. *Unit head:* Dr. Robert Throne, Interim Chairman, 812-877-8414, Fax: 812-877-8895, E-mail: robert.d.throne@rose-hulman.edu. *Application contact:* Dr. Daniel J. Moore, Associate Dean of the Faculty, 812-877-8110, Fax: 812-877-8061, E-mail: daniel.j.moore@rose-hulman.edu. Web site: http://www.rose-hulman.edu/ece/.

Royal Military College of Canada, Division of Graduate Studies and Research, Engineering Division, Department of Electrical and Computer Engineering, Kingston, ON K7K 7B4, Canada. Offers computer engineering (M Eng, PhD); electrical engineering (M Eng, PhD); software engineering (M Eng, PhD). *Degree requirements:* For master's, thesis; for doctorate, comprehensive exam, thesis/dissertation. *Entrance requirements:* For master's, honours degree with second-class standing in the appropriate field; for doctorate, master's degree. Electronic applications accepted.

Rutgers, The State University of New Jersey, New Brunswick, Graduate School-New Brunswick, Department of Electrical and Computer Engineering, Piscataway, NJ 08854-8097. Offers communications and solid-state electronics (MS, PhD); computer engineering (MS, PhD); control systems (MS, PhD); digital signal processing (MS, PhD). Part-time programs available. Terminal master's awarded for partial completion of doctoral program. *Degree requirements:* For master's, thesis or alternative; for doctorate, thesis/dissertation. *Entrance requirements:* For master's and doctorate, GRE General Test. Additional exam requirements/recommendations for international students: Required—TOEFL. Electronic applications accepted. *Faculty research:* Communication and information processing, wireless information networks, micro-vacuum devices, machine vision, VLSI design.

St. Mary's University, Graduate School, Department of Engineering, Program in Electrical Engineering, San Antonio, TX 78228-8507. Offers electrical engineering (MS); electrical/computer engineering (MS). Part-time programs available. *Degree requirements:* For master's, comprehensive exam. *Entrance requirements:* For master's, GRE General Test. Additional exam requirements/recommendations for international students: Required—TOEFL (minimum score 550 paper-based; 213 computer-based; 80 iBT). Electronic applications accepted. *Faculty research:* Image processing, control, communication, artificial intelligence, robotics.

San Jose State University, Graduate Studies and Research, Charles W. Davidson College of Engineering, Department of Computer Engineering, San Jose, CA 95192-0001. Offers computer engineering (MS); software engineering (MS). *Degree requirements:* For master's, comprehensive exam, thesis. *Entrance requirements:* For master's, GRE General Test. Electronic applications accepted. *Faculty research:* Robotics, database management systems, computer networks.

Santa Clara University, School of Engineering, Program in Computer Science and Engineering, Santa Clara, CA 95053. Offers computer science and engineering (MS, PhD, Engineer); information assurance (Certificate); networking (Certificate); software engineering (MS, Certificate). Part-time and evening/weekend programs available. *Students:* 151 full-time (58 women), 121 part-time (39 women); includes 62 minority (4 Black or African American, non-Hispanic/Latino; 52 Asian, non-Hispanic/Latino; 3 Hispanic/Latino; 1 Native Hawaiian or other Pacific Islander, non-Hispanic/Latino; 2 Two or more races, non-Hispanic/Latino), 156 international. Average age 29. 258 applicants, 48% accepted, 70 enrolled. In 2011, 87 degrees awarded. *Degree requirements:* For master's, thesis (for some programs); for doctorate, thesis/dissertation; for other advanced degree, thesis. *Entrance requirements:* For master's, GRE, transcript; for doctorate, GRE, master's degree or equivalent; for other advanced degree, master's degree, published paper. Additional exam requirements/recommendations for international students: Required—TOEFL (minimum score 550 paper-based; 213 computer-based; 79 iBT). *Application deadline:* For fall admission, 8/12 for domestic students, 7/15 for international students; for winter admission, 10/28 for domestic students, 9/23 for international students; for spring admission, 2/25 for domestic students, 1/21 for international students. Applications are processed on a rolling basis. Application fee: $60. Electronic applications accepted. *Expenses:* Contact institution. *Financial support:* Research assistantships and teaching assistantships available. Financial award application deadline: 3/2; financial award applicants required to submit FAFSA. *Unit head:* Dr. Alex Zecevic, Chair, 408-554-2394, E-mail: azecevic@scu.edu. *Application contact:* Stacey Tinker, Director of Enrollment Management, 408-554-4748, Fax: 408-554-4323, E-mail: stinker@scu.edu.

Silicon Valley University, Graduate Programs, San Jose, CA 95131. Offers business administration (MBA); computer engineering (MSCE); computer science (MSCS). *Degree requirements:* For master's, project (MSCS).

Southern Illinois University Carbondale, Graduate School, College of Engineering, Department of Electrical and Computer Engineering, Carbondale, IL 62901-4701. Offers MS, PhD. *Faculty:* 15 full-time (1 woman), 1 part-time/adjunct (0 women). *Students:* 168 full-time (31 women), 88 part-time (12 women); includes 7 minority (4 Black or African American, non-Hispanic/Latino; 2 Asian, non-Hispanic/Latino; 1 Hispanic/Latino), 240 international. 358 applicants, 62% accepted, 61 enrolled. In 2011, 90 master's, 10 doctorates awarded. *Degree requirements:* For master's, comprehensive exam, thesis. *Entrance requirements:* For master's, minimum GPA of 2.7. Additional exam requirements/recommendations for international students: Required—TOEFL. *Application deadline:* Applications are processed on a rolling basis. Application fee: $20. *Financial support:* In 2011–12, 21 students received support, including 6 research

assistantships with full tuition reimbursements available; fellowships with full tuition reimbursements available, teaching assistantships with full tuition reimbursements available, Federal Work-Study, institutionally sponsored loans, and tuition waivers (full) also available. Support available to part-time students. Financial award application deadline: 1/15. *Faculty research:* Circuits and power systems, communications and signal processing, controls and systems, electromagnetics and optics, electronics instrumentation and bioengineering. *Total annual research expenditures:* $254,257. *Unit head:* Dr. Glafkos D. Galanos, Chair, 618-536-2364, E-mail: ggalanos@siu.edu. *Application contact:* Jill Allison, Administrative Clerk, 618-453-2110, E-mail: ecedept@siu.edu.

Southern Methodist University, Bobby B. Lyle School of Engineering, Department of Computer Science and Engineering, Dallas, TX 75275-0122. Offers computer engineering (MS Cp E, PhD); computer science (MS, PhD); security engineering (MS); software engineering (MS). Part-time and evening/weekend programs available. Postbaccalaureate distance learning degree programs offered (no on-campus study). Terminal master's awarded for partial completion of doctoral program. *Degree requirements:* For master's, thesis optional; for doctorate, thesis/dissertation, oral and written qualifying exams, oral final exam (PhD). *Entrance requirements:* For master's, GRE General Test, minimum GPA of 3.0 in last 2 years; bachelor's degree in engineering, mathematics, or sciences; for doctorate, preliminary counseling exam (PhD), minimum GPA of 3.0, bachelor's degree in related field, MA (DE). Additional exam requirements/recommendations for international students: Required—TOEFL (minimum score 550 paper-based; 213 computer-based). *Faculty research:* Trusted and high performance network computing, software engineering and management, knowledge engineering and management, computer arithmetic, computer architecture and CAD.

Southern Polytechnic State University, School of Engineering Technology and Management, Department of Electrical and Computer Engineering Technology, Marietta, GA 30060-2896. Offers engineering technology/electrical (MS). Part-time and evening/weekend programs available. *Faculty:* 8 full-time (1 woman), 3 part-time/adjunct (0 women). *Students:* 20 full-time (5 women), 6 part-time (0 women); includes 8 minority (5 Black or African American, non-Hispanic/Latino; 3 Asian, non-Hispanic/Latino), 11 international. Average age 29. 14 applicants, 79% accepted, 5 enrolled. In 2011, 9 master's awarded. *Degree requirements:* For master's, thesis. *Entrance requirements:* For master's, GRE (minimum scores: 147 Verbal, 147 Quantitative, 3.5 Analytical), minimum GPA of 2.7. Additional exam requirements/recommendations for international students: Required—TOEFL (minimum score 550 paper-based; 213 computer-based; 79 iBT), IELTS (minimum score 6.5). *Application deadline:* For fall admission, 7/1 priority date for domestic students, 5/1 for international students; for spring admission, 11/1 priority date for domestic students, 9/1 for international students. Applications are processed on a rolling basis. Application fee: $50. Electronic applications accepted. *Expenses:* Tuition, state resident: full-time $2592; part-time $216 per semester hour. Tuition, nonresident: full-time $9408; part-time $784 per semester hour. *Required fees:* $698 per term. *Financial support:* In 2011–12, 5 students received support, including 5 teaching assistantships with partial tuition reimbursements available (averaging $3,000 per year); career-related internships or fieldwork, scholarships/grants, and unspecified assistantships also available. Support available to part-time students. Financial award application deadline: 5/1; financial award applicants required to submit FAFSA. *Faculty research:* Analog and digital communications, computer networking, analog and low power electronics design, control systems and digital signal processing, instrumentation (medical and industrial), biomedical signal analysis, biomedical imaging, renewable energy systems, electronics, power distribution. *Unit head:* Dr. Austin Asgill, Chair, 678-915-7796, Fax: 678-915-7285, E-mail: aasgill@spsu.edu. *Application contact:* Nikki Palamiotis, Director of Graduate Studies, 678-915-4276, Fax: 678-915-7292, E-mail: npalamio@spsu.edu. Web site: http://www.spsu.edu/ecet/index.htm.

Stevens Institute of Technology, Graduate School, Charles V. Schaefer Jr. School of Engineering, Department of Electrical and Computer Engineering, Program in Computer Engineering, Hoboken, NJ 07030. Offers computer engineering (PhD); computer systems (M Eng); data communications and networks (M Eng); digital signal processing (Certificate); digital systems design (M Eng); engineered software systems (M Eng); image processing and multimedia (M Eng); information system security (M Eng); information systems (M Eng); real-time and embedded systems (Certificate). Part-time and evening/weekend programs available. Terminal master's awarded for partial completion of doctoral program. *Degree requirements:* For doctorate, thesis/dissertation. *Entrance requirements:* For master's, doctorate, and Certificate, GRE. Additional exam requirements/recommendations for international students: Required—TOEFL. Electronic applications accepted.

Stevens Institute of Technology, Graduate School, Charles V. Schaefer Jr. School of Engineering, Department of Mechanical Engineering, Program in Integrated Product Development, Hoboken, NJ 07030. Offers armament engineering (M Eng); computer and electrical engineering (M Eng); manufacturing technologies (M Eng); systems reliability and design (M Eng).

Stony Brook University, State University of New York, Graduate School, College of Engineering and Applied Sciences, Department of Electrical and Computer Engineering, Program in Computer Engineering, Stony Brook, NY 11794. Offers MS, PhD.

Stony Brook University, State University of New York, School of Professional Development, Stony Brook, NY 11794. Offers biology-grade 7-12 (MAT); chemistry-grade 7-12 (MAT); coaching (Graduate Certificate); coaching online (Graduate Certificate); computer integrated engineering (Graduate Certificate); earth science-grade 7-12 (MAT); educational computing (Graduate Certificate); educational leadership (Advanced Certificate); English-grade 7-12 (MAT); environmental management (Graduate Certificate); environmental/occupational health and safety (Graduate Certificate); French-grade 7-12 (MAT); German-grade 7-12 (MAT); human resource management (Graduate Certificate); human resource management online (Graduate Certificate); information systems management (Graduate Certificate); Italian-grade 7-12 (MAT); liberal studies (MA); liberal studies online (MAT); mathematics-grade 7-12 (MAT); operation research (Graduate Certificate); physics-grade 7-12 (MAT); professional studies online (MPS); school administration and supervision (Graduate Certificate); school building leadership (Graduate Certificate); school district administration (Graduate Certificate); school district business leadership (Advanced Certificate); school district leadership (Graduate Certificate); social science and the professions (MPS), including environmental waste management, human resource management; social studies-grade 7-12 (MAT); Spanish-grade 7-12 (MAT); waste management (Graduate Certificate). Part-time and evening/weekend programs available. Postbaccalaureate distance learning degree programs offered. *Degree requirements:* For master's, one foreign language, thesis or alternative.

Syracuse University, L. C. Smith College of Engineering and Computer Science, Program in Computer Engineering, Syracuse, NY 13244. Offers MS, CE. Part-time and evening/weekend programs available. *Students:* 112 full-time (25 women), 16 part-time

(1 woman); includes 8 minority (3 Black or African American, non-Hispanic/Latino; 5 Asian, non-Hispanic/Latino), 104 international. Average age 25. 140 applicants, 60% accepted, 28 enrolled. In 2011, 77 degrees awarded. *Degree requirements:* For CE, thesis. *Entrance requirements:* For master's and CE, GRE General Test. Additional exam requirements/recommendations for international students: Required—TOEFL (minimum score 100 iBT). *Application deadline:* For fall admission, 6/1 priority date for domestic students, 6/1 for international students. Applications are processed on a rolling basis. Application fee: $75. Electronic applications accepted. *Expenses: Tuition:* Part-time $1206 per credit. *Financial support:* Fellowships with full tuition reimbursements, research assistantships with full and partial tuition reimbursements, teaching assistantships with full and partial tuition reimbursements, and tuition waivers (partial) available. Financial award application deadline: 1/1. *Faculty research:* Hardware, software, computer applications. *Unit head:* Dr. Roger Chen, Program Director, 315-443-4179, E-mail: crchen@syr.edu. *Application contact:* Barbara Decker, 315-443-2369, Fax: 315-443-2369, E-mail: badecker@syr.edu. Web site: http://lcs.syr.edu/.

Syracuse University, L. C. Smith College of Engineering and Computer Science, Program in Electrical and Computer Engineering, Syracuse, NY 13244. Offers PhD. *Students:* 57 full-time (16 women), 10 part-time (2 women); includes 1 minority (Asian, non-Hispanic/Latino), 57 international. Average age 27. 175 applicants, 21% accepted, 21 enrolled. In 2011, 5 doctorates awarded. *Degree requirements:* For doctorate, comprehensive exam, thesis/dissertation. *Entrance requirements:* For doctorate, GRE General Test. Additional exam requirements/recommendations for international students: Required—TOEFL (minimum score 100 iBT). *Application deadline:* For fall admission, 7/1 priority date for domestic students, 6/1 for international students. Application fee: $75. Electronic applications accepted. *Expenses: Tuition:* Part-time $1206 per credit. *Financial support:* Fellowships with full tuition reimbursements, research assistantships with full and partial tuition reimbursements, teaching assistantships with full and partial tuition reimbursements, and tuition waivers (partial) available. Financial award application deadline: 1/1. *Unit head:* Prof. Chilukuri Mohan, Chair, 315-443-2583, E-mail: mohan@syr.edu. *Application contact:* Barbara Decker, Information Contact, 315-443-2368, Fax: 315-443-2583, E-mail: badecker@syr.edu. Web site: http://lcs.syr.edu/.

Temple University, College of Engineering, Department of Electrical and Computer Engineering, Philadelphia, PA 19122-6096. Offers electrical engineering (MSE). Part-time and evening/weekend programs available. *Faculty:* 10 full-time (1 woman). *Students:* 14 full-time (1 woman), 9 part-time (2 women); includes 4 minority (1 Black or African American, non-Hispanic/Latino; 3 Asian, non-Hispanic/Latino), 9 international. Average age 27. 26 applicants, 88% accepted, 7 enrolled. In 2011, 26 master's awarded. *Degree requirements:* For master's, thesis optional. *Entrance requirements:* For master's, GRE General Test, minimum GPA of 3.0. Additional exam requirements/recommendations for international students: Required—TOEFL (minimum score 550 paper-based; 213 computer-based; 79 iBT). *Application deadline:* For fall admission, 7/1 for domestic students, 12/15 for international students; for spring admission, 11/1 for domestic students, 8/1 for international students. Applications are processed on a rolling basis. Application fee: $50. Electronic applications accepted. *Expenses:* Tuition, state resident: full-time $12,366; part-time $687 per credit hour. Tuition, nonresident: full-time $17,298; part-time $961 per credit hour. *Required fees:* $590; $213 per year. *Financial support:* In 2011–12, 1 fellowship with full tuition reimbursement, 1 research assistantship with full tuition reimbursement, 9 teaching assistantships with full tuition reimbursements were awarded; Federal Work-Study and institutionally sponsored loans also available. Financial award application deadline: 1/15; financial award applicants required to submit FAFSA. *Faculty research:* Computer engineering, intelligent control, microprocessors, digital processing, neutral networks. *Unit head:* Dr. Joseph Picone, Chair, 215-204-7597, Fax: 215-204-5960, E-mail: picone@temple.edu. *Application contact:* Tara Schumacher, Coordinator of Outreach, 215-204-6575, Fax: 215-204-8781, E-mail: tara.schumacher@temple.edu. Web site: http://www.temple.edu/engineering/ece.

Texas A&M University, College of Engineering, Department of Computer Science, College Station, TX 77843. Offers computer engineering (M En); computer science (MCS); computer science and engineering (MS, PhD). Part-time programs available. *Faculty:* 37. *Students:* 261 full-time (45 women), 57 part-time (10 women); includes 31 minority (6 Black or African American, non-Hispanic/Latino; 10 Asian, non-Hispanic/Latino; 11 Hispanic/Latino; 1 Native Hawaiian or other Pacific Islander, non-Hispanic/Latino; 3 Two or more races, non-Hispanic/Latino), 217 international. Average age 28. In 2011, 59 master's, 25 doctorates awarded. *Degree requirements:* For master's, thesis (for some programs); for doctorate, thesis/dissertation. *Entrance requirements:* For master's and doctorate, GRE General Test. Additional exam requirements/recommendations for international students: Required—TOEFL (minimum score 213 computer-based). *Application deadline:* For fall admission, 3/1 priority date for domestic students, 3/1 for international students; for spring admission, 8/1 priority date for domestic students, 8/1 for international students. Applications are processed on a rolling basis. Application fee: $50 ($75 for international students). Electronic applications accepted. *Expenses:* Tuition, state resident: full-time $5437; part-time $226.55 per credit hour. Tuition, nonresident: full-time $12,949; part-time $539.55 per credit hour. *Required fees:* $2741. *Financial support:* In 2011–12, research assistantships with tuition reimbursements (averaging $15,478 per year), teaching assistantships (averaging $15,913 per year) were awarded; fellowships with full tuition reimbursements also available. Financial award application deadline: 3/1. *Faculty research:* Software, systems, informatics, human-centered systems, theory. *Unit head:* Dr. Duncan (Hank) M. Walker, Head, 979-845-5820, Fax: 979-847-8578, E-mail: d-walker@tamu.edu. *Application contact:* Dr. Ricardo Gutierrez-Osuna, Graduate Advisor, 979-845-4259, Fax: 979-862-3684, E-mail: grad-admissions@cse.tamu.edu. Web site: http://www.cs.tamu.edu/.

Texas A&M University, College of Engineering, Department of Electrical and Computer Engineering, College Station, TX 77843. Offers computer engineering (M Eng, MS, PhD); electrical engineering (MS, PhD). *Faculty:* 63. *Students:* 480 full-time (73 women), 53 part-time (5 women); includes 52 minority (9 Black or African American, non-Hispanic/Latino; 21 Asian, non-Hispanic/Latino; 18 Hispanic/Latino; 4 Two or more races, non-Hispanic/Latino), 422 international. Average age 28. In 2011, 119 master's, 36 doctorates awarded. *Degree requirements:* For master's, thesis (MS); for doctorate, thesis/dissertation. *Entrance requirements:* For master's and doctorate, GRE General Test. Additional exam requirements/recommendations for international students: Required—TOEFL. Application fee: $50 ($75 for international students). *Expenses:* Tuition, state resident: full-time $5437; part-time $226.55 per credit hour. Tuition, nonresident: full-time $12,949; part-time $539.55 per credit hour. *Required fees:* $2741. *Financial support:* Fellowships, research assistantships, teaching assistantships, and career-related internships or fieldwork available. Financial award application deadline: 4/1; financial award applicants required to submit FAFSA. *Faculty research:* Solid-state, electric power systems, and communications engineering. *Unit head:* Dr. Costas N. Georghiades, Head, 979-845-7441, E-mail: c-georghiades@tamu.edu. *Application contact:* Graduate Advisor, 979-845-7441, E-mail: gradinfo@ece.tamu.edu. Web site: http://www.ece.tamu.edu/.

The University of Akron, Graduate School, College of Engineering, Department of Electrical and Computer Engineering, Akron, OH 44325. Offers MS, PhD. Evening/weekend programs available. *Faculty:* 17 full-time (1 woman), 2 part-time/adjunct (0 women). *Students:* 55 full-time (8 women), 19 part-time (3 women); includes 2 minority (1 Asian, non-Hispanic/Latino; 1 Native Hawaiian or other Pacific Islander, non-Hispanic/Latino), 60 international. Average age 27. 116 applicants, 24% accepted, 6 enrolled. In 2011, 3 master's, 1 doctorate awarded. *Degree requirements:* For master's, thesis optional, oral comprehensive exam or thesis; for doctorate, one foreign language, thesis/dissertation, candidacy exam, qualifying exam. *Entrance requirements:* For master's, GRE, minimum GPA of 2.75, three letters of recommendation, statement of purpose; for doctorate, GRE, minimum GPA of 3.0 with bachelor's degree, 3.5 with master's degree; three letters of recommendation; statement of purpose. Additional exam requirements/recommendations for international students: Required—TOEFL (minimum score 550 paper-based; 213 computer-based; 79 iBT). *Application deadline:* Applications are processed on a rolling basis. Application fee: $30 ($40 for international students). Electronic applications accepted. *Expenses:* Tuition, state resident: full-time $7038; part-time $391 per credit hour. Tuition, nonresident: full-time $12,051; part-time $670 per credit hour. *Required fees:* $1274; $34 per credit hour. *Financial support:* In 2011–12, 27 research assistantships with full tuition reimbursements, 26 teaching assistantships with full tuition reimbursements were awarded; career-related internships or fieldwork also available. *Faculty research:* Computational electromagnetics and nondestructive testing, control systems, sensors and actuators applications and networks, alternative energy systems and hybrid vehicles, analog IC design embedded systems. *Total annual research expenditures:* $435,958. *Unit head:* Dr. Jose De Abreu-Garcia, Chair, 330-972-6709, E-mail: jdeabreu-garcia@uakron.edu. *Application contact:* Dr. Craig Menzemer, Associate Dean, 330-972-5536, E-mail: ccmenze@uakron.edu. Web site: http://www.uakron.edu/engineering/ECE/.

The University of Alabama, Graduate School, College of Engineering, Department of Electrical and Computer Engineering, Tuscaloosa, AL 35487-0286. Offers electrical engineering (MS, PhD). Part-time programs available. Postbaccalaureate distance learning degree programs offered (minimal on-campus study). *Faculty:* 16 full-time (4 women). *Students:* 53 full-time (7 women), 8 part-time (1 woman); includes 5 minority (1 Black or African American, non-Hispanic/Latino; 2 Asian, non-Hispanic/Latino; 2 Hispanic/Latino), 31 international. Average age 28. 88 applicants, 48% accepted, 15 enrolled. In 2011, 7 master's, 1 doctorate awarded. *Median time to degree:* Of those who began their doctoral program in fall 2003, 80% received their degree in 8 years or less. *Degree requirements:* For master's, thesis or alternative; for doctorate, one foreign language, comprehensive exam, thesis/dissertation. *Entrance requirements:* For master's, GRE (for students from non ABET-accredited schools), minimum GPA of 3.0 in last 60 hours of course work or overall; for doctorate, GRE (for students from non ABET-accredited schools), minimum GPA of 3.0 overall. Additional exam requirements/recommendations for international students: Required—TOEFL (minimum score 550 paper-based; 213 computer-based). *Application deadline:* For fall admission, 7/1 priority date for domestic students, 1/15 for international students; for spring admission, 11/1 priority date for domestic students, 6/1 for international students. Applications are processed on a rolling basis. Application fee: $50 ($60 for international students). Electronic applications accepted. *Expenses:* Tuition, state resident: full-time $8600. Tuition, nonresident: full-time $21,900. *Financial support:* In 2011–12, 1 fellowship with full tuition reimbursement (averaging $15,000 per year), 14 research assistantships with full tuition reimbursements (averaging $14,000 per year), 6 teaching assistantships with full tuition reimbursements (averaging $11,025 per year) were awarded; health care benefits and unspecified assistantships also available. *Faculty research:* Devices and materials, electromechanical systems, embedded systems. *Total annual research expenditures:* $2.5 million. *Unit head:* Dr. D. Jeff Jackson, Department Head, 205-348-2919, Fax: 205-348-6959, E-mail: jjackson@eng.ua.edu. *Application contact:* Dr. Tim Haskew, Graduate Program Director, 205-348-1766, Fax: 205-348-6959, E-mail: thaskew@eng.ua.edu. Web site: http://ece.eng.ua.edu.

The University of Alabama at Birmingham, School of Engineering, Program in Computer Engineering, Birmingham, AL 35294. Offers PhD. Program offered jointly with The University of Alabama in Huntsville. *Expenses:* Tuition, state resident: full-time $5922; part-time $309 per hour. Tuition, nonresident: full-time $13,428; part-time $726 per hour. Tuition and fees vary according to program. *Unit head:* Dr. Yehia Massoud, Chair, 205-934-8440. Web site: http://www.uab.edu/engineering/departments-research/ece/grad#phd.

The University of Alabama in Huntsville, School of Graduate Studies, College of Engineering, Department of Electrical and Computer Engineering, Huntsville, AL 35899. Offers computer engineering (MSE, PhD), including information assurance (MSE); electrical engineering (MSE, PhD), including optics and phontonics technology (MSE), opto-electronics (MSE); optics and photonics (MSE); software engineering (MSSE). Part-time and evening/weekend programs available. *Faculty:* 22 full-time (3 women), 4 part-time/adjunct (0 women). *Students:* 52 full-time (12 women), 138 part-time (22 women); includes 20 minority (7 Black or African American, non-Hispanic/Latino; 2 American Indian or Alaska Native, non-Hispanic/Latino; 8 Asian, non-Hispanic/Latino; 2 Hispanic/Latino; 1 Two or more races, non-Hispanic/Latino), 37 international. Average age 31. 157 applicants, 65% accepted, 48 enrolled. In 2011, 26 master's, 6 doctorates awarded. *Degree requirements:* For master's, comprehensive exam, thesis or alternative, oral and written exams; for doctorate, comprehensive exam, thesis/dissertation, oral and written exams. *Entrance requirements:* For master's, GRE General Test, appropriate bachelor's degree, minimum GPA of 3.0; for doctorate, GRE General Test, minimum GPA of 3.0. Additional exam requirements/recommendations for international students: Required—TOEFL (minimum score 500 paper-based; 173 computer-based; 62 iBT). *Application deadline:* For fall admission, 7/15 for domestic students, 4/1 for international students; for spring admission, 11/30 for domestic students, 9/1 for international students. Applications are processed on a rolling basis. Application fee: $40 ($50 for international students). Electronic applications accepted. *Expenses:* Tuition, state resident: full-time $7830; part-time $473.50 per credit. Tuition, nonresident: full-time $18,748; part-time $1128.33 per credit. Tuition and fees vary according to course load and program. *Financial support:* In 2011–12, 29 students received support, including 2 fellowships (averaging $11,154 per year), 9 research assistantships with full and partial tuition reimbursements available (averaging $10,959 per year), 20 teaching assistantships with full and partial tuition reimbursements available (averaging $11,330 per year); career-related internships or fieldwork, Federal Work-Study, institutionally sponsored loans, scholarships/grants, health care benefits, tuition waivers (full), and unspecified assistantships also available. Support available to part-time students. Financial award application deadline: 4/1; financial award applicants required to submit FAFSA. *Faculty research:* Optical signal processing, electromagnetics, photonics, nonlinear waves, computer architecture. *Total annual research expenditures:* $16.5 million. *Unit head:* Dr. Robert Lindquist, Chair, 256-824-

6316, Fax: 256-824-6803, E-mail: lindquis@ece.uah.edu. *Application contact:* Kim Gray, Graduate Studies Admissions Coordinator, 256-824-6002, Fax: 256-824-6405, E-mail: deangrad@uah.edu. Web site: http://www.ece.uah.edu/.

The University of Alabama in Huntsville, School of Graduate Studies, Interdisciplinary Studies, Interdisciplinary Program in Information Assurance and Cybersecurity, Huntsville, AL 35899. Offers computer engineering (MS), including computer science; information systems (Certificate). Part-time and evening/weekend programs available. *Faculty:* 6 full-time (0 women), 3 part-time/adjunct (0 women). *Students:* 5 full-time (4 women), 17 part-time (5 women); includes 7 minority (4 Black or African American, non-Hispanic/Latino; 2 Asian, non-Hispanic/Latino; 1 Hispanic/Latino). Average age 37. 15 applicants, 67% accepted, 8 enrolled. In 2011, 2 master's awarded. *Degree requirements:* For master's, comprehensive exam, thesis or alternative, thesis: 24 hours course work plus 6-hour thesis. *Entrance requirements:* For master's, GRE General Test, minimum GPA of 3.0; for Certificate, GMAT, minimum GPA of 3.0. Additional exam requirements/recommendations for international students: Required—TOEFL (minimum score 550 paper-based; 213 computer-based; 62 iBT). *Application deadline:* For fall admission, 7/15 for domestic students, 4/1 for international students; for spring admission, 11/30 for domestic students, 9/1 for international students. Applications are processed on a rolling basis. Application fee: $40 ($50 for international students). Electronic applications accepted. *Expenses:* Tuition, state resident: full-time $7830; part-time $473.50 per credit. Tuition, nonresident: full-time $18,748; part-time $1128.33 per credit. Tuition and fees vary according to course load and program. *Financial support:* Career-related internships or fieldwork, Federal Work-Study, institutionally sponsored loans, scholarships/grants, health care benefits, and unspecified assistantships available. Support available to part-time students. Financial award application deadline: 4/1; financial award applicants required to submit FAFSA. *Faculty research:* Service discovery, enterprise security, security metrics, cryptography, network security. *Unit head:* Dr. Rhonda Kay Gaede, Dean of Graduate Studies, 256-824-6002, Fax: 256-824-6405, E-mail: deangrad@uah.edu. *Application contact:* Jennifer Pettitt, College of Business Administration Director of Graduate Programs, 256-824-6681, Fax: 256-824-7572, E-mail: jennifer.pettitt@uah.edu. Web site: http://www.cs.uah.edu/admissions/msias.html.

University of Alaska Fairbanks, College of Engineering and Mines, Department of Electrical and Computer Engineering, Fairbanks, AK 99775-5915. Offers electrical engineering (MEE, MS, PhD); engineering (PhD). Part-time programs available. *Faculty:* 9 full-time (2 women). *Students:* 17 full-time (4 women), 8 international. Average age 24. 21 applicants, 29% accepted, 5 enrolled. In 2011, 4 master's awarded. Terminal master's awarded for partial completion of doctoral program. *Degree requirements:* For master's, comprehensive exam, thesis or alternative; for doctorate, comprehensive exam, thesis/dissertation, oral exam, oral defense. *Entrance requirements:* For master's and doctorate, GRE General Test. Additional exam requirements/recommendations for international students: Required—TOEFL (minimum score 550 paper-based; 213 computer-based; 80 iBT). *Application deadline:* For fall admission, 6/1 for domestic students, 3/1 for international students; for spring admission, 10/15 for domestic students, 9/1 for international students. Applications are processed on a rolling basis. Application fee: $60. Electronic applications accepted. *Expenses:* Tuition, state resident: full-time $6696; part-time $372 per credit. Tuition, nonresident: full-time $13,680; part-time $760 per credit. Tuition and fees vary according to course load and reciprocity agreements. *Financial support:* In 2011–12, 11 research assistantships with tuition reimbursements (averaging $12,733 per year), 7 teaching assistantships with tuition reimbursements (averaging $5,216 per year) were awarded; fellowships with tuition reimbursements, career-related internships or fieldwork, Federal Work-Study, scholarships/grants, health care benefits, and unspecified assistantships also available. Support available to part-time students. Financial award application deadline: 7/1; financial award applicants required to submit FAFSA. *Faculty research:* Geomagnetically-induced currents in power lines, electromagnetic wave propagation, laser radar systems, bioinformatics, distributed sensor networks. *Unit head:* Dr. Charles Mayer, Chair, 907-474-7137, Fax: 907-474-5135, E-mail: fyee@uaf.edu. *Application contact:* Mike Earnest, Director of Admissions, 907-474-7500, Fax: 907-474-5379, E-mail: admissions@uaf.edu. Web site: http://cem.uaf.edu/ece/.

University of Alberta, Faculty of Graduate Studies and Research, Department of Electrical and Computer Engineering, Edmonton, AB T6G 2E1, Canada. Offers communications (M Eng, M Sc, PhD); computer engineering (M Eng, M Sc, PhD); electromagnetics (M Eng, M Sc, PhD); nanotechnology and microdevices (M Eng, M Sc, PhD); power/power electronics (M Eng, M Sc, PhD); systems (M Eng, M Sc, PhD). Terminal master's awarded for partial completion of doctoral program. *Degree requirements:* For master's, thesis; for doctorate, thesis/dissertation. *Entrance requirements:* Additional exam requirements/recommendations for international students: Required—TOEFL. Electronic applications accepted. *Faculty research:* Controls, communications, microelectronics, electromagnetics.

The University of Arizona, College of Engineering, Department of Electrical and Computer Engineering, Tucson, AZ 85721. Offers M Eng, MS, PhD. Part-time programs available. *Faculty:* 20 full-time (2 women), 8 part-time/adjunct (3 women). *Students:* 123 full-time (17 women), 33 part-time (5 women); includes 27 minority (1 Black or African American, non-Hispanic/Latino; 7 Asian, non-Hispanic/Latino; 11 Hispanic/Latino; 8 Two or more races, non-Hispanic/Latino), 93 international. Average age 30. 514 applicants, 23% accepted, 38 enrolled. In 2011, 34 master's, 12 doctorates awarded. *Degree requirements:* For master's, thesis (for some programs); for doctorate, thesis/dissertation. *Entrance requirements:* For master's, GRE General Test, 3 letters of recommendation, statement of purpose; for doctorate, GRE General Test, master's degree in related field, 3 letters of recommendation, statement of purpose. Additional exam requirements/recommendations for international students: Required—TOEFL (minimum score 550 paper-based; 213 computer-based; 79 iBT). *Application deadline:* For fall admission, 12/15 for domestic and international students; for spring admission, 7/15 for domestic and international students. Applications are processed on a rolling basis. Application fee: $75. Electronic applications accepted. *Expenses:* Tuition, state resident: full-time $10,840. Tuition, nonresident: full-time $25,802. *Financial support:* In 2011–12, 68 research assistantships with full tuition reimbursements (averaging $23,715 per year), 16 teaching assistantships with full tuition reimbursements (averaging $23,585 per year) were awarded; institutionally sponsored loans, scholarships/grants, health care benefits, and unspecified assistantships also available. Financial award application deadline: 3/15. *Faculty research:* Communication systems, control systems, signal processing, computer-aided logic. *Total annual research expenditures:* $7.1 million. *Unit head:* Dr. Tamal Bose, Head, 520-621-6193, E-mail: head@ece.arizona.edu. *Application contact:* Tami J. Whelan, Senior Graduate Academic Adviser, 520-621-6195, Fax: 520-621-8076, E-mail: whelan@ece.arizona.edu. Web site: http://www.ece.arizona.edu/.

University of Arkansas, Graduate School, College of Engineering, Department of Computer Science and Computer Engineering, Program in Computer Engineering, Fayetteville, AR 72701-1201. Offers MS Cmp E, MSE, PhD. *Students:* 2 full-time (0 women), 15 part-time (2 women); includes 2 minority (1 American Indian or Alaska Native, non-Hispanic/Latino; 1 Two or more races, non-Hispanic/Latino), 4 international. In 2011, 5 degrees awarded. *Degree requirements:* For master's, thesis optional; for doctorate, one foreign language, thesis/dissertation. *Application deadline:* For fall admission, 4/1 for international students; for spring admission, 10/1 for international students. Applications are processed on a rolling basis. Application fee: $40 ($50 for international students). Electronic applications accepted. *Financial support:* In 2011–12, 8 research assistantships, 2 teaching assistantships were awarded; fellowships with tuition reimbursements, career-related internships or fieldwork, and Federal Work-Study also available. Support available to part-time students. Financial award application deadline: 4/1; financial award applicants required to submit FAFSA. *Unit head:* Dr. Susan Gauch, Department Chair, 479-575-6197, Fax: 479-575-5339, E-mail: sgauch@uark.edu. *Application contact:* Dr. Gordon Beavers, Graduate Coordinator, 479-575-6040, Fax: 479-575-5339, E-mail: gordonb@uark.edu. Web site: http://www.csce.uark.edu/.

University of Bridgeport, School of Engineering, Departments of Computer Science and Computer Engineering, Bridgeport, CT 06604. Offers computer engineering (MS); computer science (MS); computer science and engineering (PhD). *Faculty:* 10 full-time (1 woman), 5 part-time/adjunct (1 woman). *Students:* 102 full-time (26 women), 95 part-time (16 women); includes 20 minority (6 Black or African American, non-Hispanic/Latino; 8 Asian, non-Hispanic/Latino; 3 Hispanic/Latino; 3 Two or more races, non-Hispanic/Latino), 156 international. Average age 30. 678 applicants, 64% accepted, 34 enrolled. In 2011, 69 master's, 2 doctorates awarded. *Degree requirements:* For master's, thesis optional; for doctorate, comprehensive exam, thesis/dissertation. *Entrance requirements:* Additional exam requirements/recommendations for international students: Recommended—TOEFL (minimum score 550 paper-based; 213 computer-based; 80 iBT), IELTS (minimum score 6.5). *Application deadline:* For fall admission, 8/1 priority date for domestic students, 8/1 for international students; for spring admission, 12/1 priority date for domestic students, 12/1 for international students. Applications are processed on a rolling basis. Application fee: $50. Electronic applications accepted. *Expenses: Tuition:* Full-time $22,880; part-time $700 per credit. *Required fees:* $1870; $95 per semester. Tuition and fees vary according to course load and program. *Financial support:* In 2011–12, 56 students received support. Research assistantships, teaching assistantships, career-related internships or fieldwork, Federal Work-Study, institutionally sponsored loans, and tuition waivers (partial) available. Support available to part-time students. Financial award application deadline: 6/1; financial award applicants required to submit FAFSA. *Unit head:* Dr. Ausif mahmood, Chairman, 203-576-4737, Fax: 203-576-4765, E-mail: mahmood@bridgeport.edu. *Application contact:* Karissa Peckham, Dean of Admissions, 203-576-4552, Fax: 203-576-4941, E-mail: admit@bridgeport.edu.

The University of British Columbia, Faculty of Applied Science, Program in Electrical and Computer Engineering, Vancouver, BC V6T 1Z1, Canada. Offers M Eng, MA Sc, PhD. Part-time programs available. *Degree requirements:* For master's, thesis (for some programs); for doctorate, thesis/dissertation. *Entrance requirements:* Additional exam requirements/recommendations for international students: Required—TOEFL (minimum score 600 paper-based; 250 computer-based; 100 iBT), TWE. Electronic applications accepted. *Faculty research:* Applied electromagnetics, biomedical engineering, communications and signal processing, computer and software engineering, power engineering, robotics, solid-state, systems and control.

University of Calgary, Faculty of Graduate Studies, Schulich School of Engineering, Department of Electrical and Computer Engineering, Calgary, AB T2N 1N4, Canada. Offers M Eng, M Sc, PhD. Part-time programs available. *Degree requirements:* For master's, thesis (M Sc); for doctorate, thesis/dissertation, candidacy exam. *Entrance requirements:* For master's and doctorate, minimum GPA of 3.0. Additional exam requirements/recommendations for international students: Required—TOEFL (minimum score 550 paper-based; 213 computer-based) or IELTS (minimum score 7). Electronic applications accepted. *Faculty research:* Biomedical and bioelectrics, telecommunications and signal processing, software and computer engineering, power and control, microelectronics and instrumentation.

University of California, Davis, College of Engineering, Program in Electrical and Computer Engineering, Davis, CA 95616. Offers MS, PhD. Terminal master's awarded for partial completion of doctoral program. *Degree requirements:* For master's, comprehensive exam (for some programs), thesis (for some programs); for doctorate, thesis/dissertation, preliminary and qualifying exams, thesis defense. *Entrance requirements:* For master's, GRE General Test, minimum GPA of 3.2; for doctorate, GRE, minimum graduate GPA of 3.5. Additional exam requirements/recommendations for international students: Required—TOEFL (minimum score 550 paper-based; 213 computer-based). Electronic applications accepted.

University of California, Riverside, Graduate Division, Department of Computer Science and Engineering, Riverside, CA 92521. Offers computer engineering (MS); computer science (MS, PhD). Part-time programs available. *Faculty:* 22 full-time (1 woman), 1 (woman) part-time/adjunct. *Students:* 167 full-time (38 women), 6 part-time (1 woman); includes 22 minority (5 Black or African American, non-Hispanic/Latino; 14 Asian, non-Hispanic/Latino; 3 Hispanic/Latino), 110 international. Average age 27. 505 applicants, 26% accepted, 45 enrolled. In 2011, 24 master's, 12 doctorates awarded. Terminal master's awarded for partial completion of doctoral program. *Degree requirements:* For master's, thesis or project; for doctorate, thesis/dissertation, qualifying exams. *Entrance requirements:* For master's and doctorate, GRE General Test (minimum score of 1100 or 300 for new format), minimum GPA of 3.2. Additional exam requirements/recommendations for international students: Required—TOEFL (minimum score 550 paper-based; 213 computer-based; 80 iBT). *Application deadline:* For fall admission, 1/5 priority date for domestic students, 1/5 for international students. Application fee: $80 ($100 for international students). Electronic applications accepted. *Financial support:* In 2011–12, 76 students received support, including 26 fellowships with full and partial tuition reimbursements available (averaging $16,000 per year), 53 research assistantships with full and partial tuition reimbursements available (averaging $15,000 per year), 26 teaching assistantships with full and partial tuition reimbursements available (averaging $16,000 per year); institutionally sponsored loans, health care benefits, and unspecified assistantships also available. Financial award applicants required to submit FAFSA. *Faculty research:* Algorithms, bioinformatics, logic; architecture, compilers, embedded systems, verification; databases, data mining, artificial intelligence, graphics; systems, networks. *Unit head:* Dr. Laxmi Bhuyan, Chair, 951-827-5639, Fax: 951-827-4643, E-mail: gradadmission@ucr.edu. *Application contact:* Amy S. Ricks, Graduate Student Affairs Officer, 951-827-5639, Fax: 951-827-4643, E-mail: amy@cs.ucr.edu. Web site: http://www.cs.ucr.edu/.

University of California, Riverside, Graduate Division, Department of Electrical Engineering, Riverside, CA 92521-0102. Offers electrical engineering (MS, PhD), including computer engineering, control and robotics, intelligent systems, nanomaterials, devices and circuits, signal processing and communications. Terminal master's awarded for partial completion of doctoral program. *Degree requirements:* For master's, thesis optional; for doctorate, thesis/dissertation, qualifying exams. *Entrance requirements:* For master's and doctorate, GRE General Test, minimum GPA of 3.25. Additional exam requirements/recommendations for international students: Required—TOEFL (minimum score 550 paper-based; 213 computer-based; 80 iBT). Electronic applications accepted. *Faculty research:* Solid state devices, integrated circuits, signal processing.

University of California, San Diego, Office of Graduate Studies, Department of Computer Science and Engineering, La Jolla, CA 92093. Offers computer engineering (MS, PhD); computer science (MS, PhD). *Degree requirements:* For doctorate, thesis/dissertation. *Entrance requirements:* For master's and doctorate, GRE General Test. Electronic applications accepted. *Faculty research:* Analysis of algorithms, combinatorial algorithms, discrete optimization.

University of California, San Diego, Office of Graduate Studies, Department of Electrical and Computer Engineering, La Jolla, CA 92093. Offers applied ocean science (MS, PhD); applied physics (MS, PhD); communication theory and systems (MS, PhD); computer engineering (MS, PhD); electrical engineering (M Eng); electronic circuits and systems (MS, PhD); intelligent systems, robotics and control (MS, PhD); photonics (MS, PhD); signal and image processing (MS, PhD). MS only offered to students who have been admitted to the PhD program. *Entrance requirements:* For master's and doctorate, GRE General Test. Electronic applications accepted.

University of California, San Diego, Office of Graduate Studies, Interdisciplinary Program in Cognitive Science, La Jolla, CA 92093. Offers cognitive science/ anthropology (PhD); cognitive science/communication (PhD); cognitive science/ computer science and engineering (PhD); cognitive science/linguistics (PhD); cognitive science/neuroscience (PhD); cognitive science/philosophy (PhD); cognitive science/ psychology (PhD); cognitive science/sociology (PhD). Admissions offered through affiliated departments. *Degree requirements:* For doctorate, thesis/dissertation. *Entrance requirements:* For doctorate, GRE General Test, acceptance into one of the eight participating departments. *Faculty research:* Language and cognition, philosophy of mind, visual perception, biological anthropology, sociolinguistics.

University of California, Santa Barbara, Graduate Division, College of Engineering, Department of Computer Science, Santa Barbara, CA 93106-5110. Offers cognitive science (PhD); computational science and engineering (PhD); computer science (MS, PhD); technology and society (PhD). *Faculty:* 32 full-time (5 women), 5 part-time/adjunct (0 women). *Students:* 151 full-time (37 women); includes 9 minority (1 American Indian or Alaska Native, non-Hispanic/Latino; 7 Asian, non-Hispanic/Latino; 1 Two or more races, non-Hispanic/Latino), 101 international. Average age 27. 640 applicants, 20% accepted, 51 enrolled. In 2011, 27 master's, 14 doctorates awarded. Terminal master's awarded for partial completion of doctoral program. *Median time to degree:* Of those who began their doctoral program in fall 2003, 80% received their degree in 8 years or less. *Degree requirements:* For master's, comprehensive exam (for some programs), thesis (for some programs), project (for some programs); for doctorate, thesis/ dissertation. *Entrance requirements:* For master's and doctorate, GRE. Additional exam requirements/recommendations for international students: Required—TOEFL (minimum score 600 paper-based; 100 iBT), IELTS (minimum score 7). *Application deadline:* For fall admission, 12/15 for domestic and international students. Application fee: $80 ($100 for international students). Electronic applications accepted. *Expenses:* Tuition, state resident: full-time $12,192. Tuition, nonresident: full-time $27,294. *Required fees:* $764.13. *Financial support:* In 2011–12, 116 students received support, including 36 fellowships with full and partial tuition reimbursements available (averaging $12,330 per year), 63 research assistantships with full and partial tuition reimbursements available (averaging $14,876 per year), 44 teaching assistantships with partial tuition reimbursements available (averaging $17,309 per year); career-related internships or fieldwork, Federal Work-Study, institutionally sponsored loans, scholarships/grants, health care benefits, tuition waivers (full and partial), and unspecified assistantships also available. Financial award application deadline: 12/15; financial award applicants required to submit FAFSA. *Faculty research:* Networking and security, database systems, computational science and engineering, programming languages and software engineering, human-computer interaction. *Unit head:* Subhash Suri, Chair, 805-893-5334, Fax: 805-893-8553, E-mail: suri@cs.ucsb.edu. *Application contact:* Katie Ellis, Graduate Advisor, 805-893-4322, Fax: 805-893-8553, E-mail: kellis@cs.ucsb.edu. Web site: http://www.cs.ucsb.edu/.

University of California, Santa Barbara, Graduate Division, College of Engineering, Department of Electrical and Computer Engineering, Santa Barbara, CA 93106-2014. Offers communications, control and signal processing (MS, PhD); computer engineering (MS, PhD); electronics and photonics (MS, PhD); MS/PhD. *Faculty:* 37 full-time (3 women), 1 part-time/adjunct (0 women). *Students:* 272 full-time (52 women); includes 40 minority (2 American Indian or Alaska Native, non-Hispanic/Latino; 30 Asian, non-Hispanic/Latino; 6 Hispanic/Latino; 1 Native Hawaiian or other Pacific Islander, non-Hispanic/Latino; 1 Two or more races, non-Hispanic/Latino), 159 international. Average age 26. 1,252 applicants, 27% accepted, 95 enrolled. In 2011, 49 master's, 33 doctorates awarded. Terminal master's awarded for partial completion of doctoral program. *Median time to degree:* Of those who began their doctoral program in fall 2003, 44% received their degree in 8 years or less. *Degree requirements:* For master's, comprehensive exam, thesis; for doctorate, thesis/dissertation. *Entrance requirements:* For master's and doctorate, GRE General Test. Additional exam requirements/ recommendations for international students: Required—TOEFL (minimum score 550 paper-based; 80 iBT), IELTS (minimum score 7). *Application deadline:* For fall admission, 12/15 for domestic and international students; for winter admission, 11/1 for domestic and international students; for spring admission, 1/1 for domestic and international students. Application fee: $80 ($100 for international students). Electronic applications accepted. *Expenses:* Tuition, state resident: full-time $12,192. Tuition, nonresident: full-time $27,294. *Required fees:* $764.13. *Financial support:* In 2011–12, 196 students received support, including 70 fellowships with full and partial tuition reimbursements available (averaging $7,181 per year), 155 research assistantships with full and partial tuition reimbursements available (averaging $15,235 per year), 54 teaching assistantships with full and partial tuition reimbursements available (averaging $9,910 per year); tuition waivers (full and partial) also available. Financial award application deadline: 12/15; financial award applicants required to submit FAFSA. *Faculty research:* Communications, signal processing, computer engineering, control, electronics and photonics. *Total annual research expenditures:* $25.5 million. *Unit head:* Prof. Jerry Gibson, Chair, 805-893-3821, Fax: 805-893-6262, E-mail: gibson@ece.ucsb.edu. *Application contact:* Erika Raquel Klukovich, Graduate Admissions Coordinator, 805-893-3114, Fax: 805-893-5402, E-mail: erika@ece.ucsb.edu. Web site: http://www.ece.ucsb.edu/.

University of California, Santa Barbara, Graduate Division, College of Engineering, Department of Mechanical Engineering, Santa Barbara, CA 93106-5070. Offers computational science and engineering (MS, PhD); mechanical engineering (MS, PhD);

MS/PhD. *Faculty:* 28 full-time (4 women), 8 part-time/adjunct (3 women). *Students:* 80 full-time (9 women); includes 10 minority (1 Black or African American, non-Hispanic/ Latino; 7 Asian, non-Hispanic/Latino; 2 Hispanic/Latino), 28 international. Average age 27. 279 applicants, 19% accepted, 19 enrolled. In 2011, 7 master's, 8 doctorates awarded. *Median time to degree:* Of those who began their doctoral program in fall 2003, 100% received their degree in 8 years or less. *Degree requirements:* For master's, thesis; for doctorate, comprehensive exam, thesis/dissertation. *Entrance requirements:* For master's and doctorate, GRE. Additional exam requirements/recommendations for international students: Required—TOEFL (minimum score 550 paper-based; 213 computer-based; 80 iBT), IELTS (minimum score 7). *Application deadline:* For fall admission, 12/15 for domestic and international students. Application fee: $80 ($100 for international students). Electronic applications accepted. *Expenses:* Tuition, state resident: full-time $12,192. Tuition, nonresident: full-time $27,294. *Required fees:* $764.13. *Financial support:* In 2011–12, 72 students received support, including 7 fellowships with full and partial tuition reimbursements available (averaging $22,000 per year), 27 research assistantships with full and partial tuition reimbursements available (averaging $19,099 per year), 24 teaching assistantships with full and partial tuition reimbursements available (averaging $17,308 per year); scholarships/grants, health care benefits, tuition waivers (full and partial), and unspecified assistantships also available. Financial award application deadline: 12/15; financial award applicants required to submit FAFSA. *Faculty research:* Micro/nanoscale technology; computational science and engineering; dynamics systems, controls and robotics; thermofluid sciences; solid mechanics, materials, and structures. *Total annual research expenditures:* $5.7 million. *Unit head:* Dr. Kimberly Turner, Chair, 805-893-8080, Fax: 805-893-8651, E-mail: turner@engineering.ucsb.edu. *Application contact:* Laura L. Reynolds, Staff Graduate Program Advisor, 805-893-2239, Fax: 805-893-8651, E-mail: megrad@engineering.ucsb.edu. Web site: http://www.me.ucsb.edu/.

University of California, Santa Barbara, Graduate Division, College of Letters and Sciences, Division of Mathematics, Life, and Physical Sciences, Department of Ecology, Evolution, and Marine Biology, Santa Barbara, CA 93106-9620. Offers computational science and engineering (MA); computational sciences and engineering (PhD); ecology, evolution, and marine biology (MA, PhD); MA/PhD. *Faculty:* 27 full-time (7 women). *Students:* 58 full-time (39 women); includes 9 minority (1 Black or African American, non-Hispanic/Latino; 5 Asian, non-Hispanic/Latino; 2 Hispanic/Latino; 1 Two or more races, non-Hispanic/Latino), 4 international. Average age 30. 131 applicants, 15% accepted, 8 enrolled. In 2011, 4 master's, 4 doctorates awarded. *Median time to degree:* Of those who began their doctoral program in fall 2003, 100% received their degree in 8 years or less. *Degree requirements:* For master's, comprehensive exam (for some programs), thesis (for some programs); for doctorate, comprehensive exam, thesis/ dissertation. *Entrance requirements:* For master's and doctorate, GRE General Test. Additional exam requirements/recommendations for international students: Required— TOEFL (minimum score 550 paper-based; 80 iBT), IELTS. *Application deadline:* For fall admission, 12/15 for domestic and international students. Application fee: $80 ($100 for international students). Electronic applications accepted. *Expenses:* Tuition, state resident: full-time $12,192. Tuition, nonresident: full-time $27,294. *Required fees:* $764.13. *Financial support:* In 2011–12, 54 students received support, including 44 fellowships with full and partial tuition reimbursements available (averaging $10,812 per year), 13 research assistantships with full and partial tuition reimbursements available (averaging $8,441 per year), 22 teaching assistantships with partial tuition reimbursements available (averaging $9,346 per year); Federal Work-Study, scholarships/grants, traineeships, health care benefits, and tuition waivers (full and partial) also available. Financial award application deadline: 12/15; financial award applicants required to submit FAFSA. *Faculty research:* Community ecology, evolution, marine biology, population genetics, stream ecology. *Unit head:* Dr. Cheryl Briggs, Chair, 805-893-2415, Fax: 805-893-5885. *Application contact:* Melanie Fujii, Staff Graduate Advisor, 805-893-2979, Fax: 805-893-5885, E-mail: eemb-info@ lifesci.ucsb.edu. Web site: http://www.lifesci.ucsb.edu/EEMB/index.html.

University of California, Santa Cruz, Division of Graduate Studies, Jack Baskin School of Engineering, Program in Computer Engineering, Santa Cruz, CA 95064. Offers computer engineering (MS, PhD); network engineering (MS). Part-time programs available. Terminal master's awarded for partial completion of doctoral program. *Degree requirements:* For master's, thesis; for doctorate, comprehensive exam, thesis/ dissertation, oral qualifying exams. *Entrance requirements:* For master's and doctorate, GRE General Test, GRE Subject Test. Additional exam requirements/recommendations for international students: Required—TOEFL (minimum score 570 paper-based; 230 computer-based; 89 iBT); Recommended—IELTS (minimum score 8). Electronic applications accepted. *Faculty research:* Computer-aided design of digital systems, networks, robotics and control, sensing and interaction.

University of Central Florida, College of Engineering and Computer Science, Department of Electrical Engineering and Computer Science, Program in Computer Engineering, Orlando, FL 32816. Offers computer engineering (MS Cp E, PhD). Part-time and evening/weekend programs available. *Students:* 48 full-time (6 women), 37 part-time (9 women); includes 18 minority (3 Black or African American, non-Hispanic/ Latino; 5 Asian, non-Hispanic/Latino; 10 Hispanic/Latino), 30 international. Average age 30. 68 applicants, 65% accepted, 11 enrolled. In 2011, 25 master's, 6 doctorates awarded. *Degree requirements:* For master's, thesis or alternative; for doctorate, thesis/ dissertation, departmental qualifying exam, candidacy exam. *Entrance requirements:* For master's, GRE General Test, minimum GPA of 3.0 in last 60 hours; for doctorate, GRE General Test, minimum GPA of 3.5 in last 60 hours. Additional exam requirements/ recommendations for international students: Required—TOEFL. *Application deadline:* For fall admission, 7/15 priority date for domestic students; for spring admission, 12/1 priority date for domestic students. Electronic applications accepted. *Expenses:* Tuition, state resident: part-time $277.08 per credit hour. Tuition, nonresident: part-time $277.08 per credit hour. Part-time tuition and fees vary according to degree level and program. *Financial support:* In 2011–12, 25 students received support, including 9 fellowships (averaging $3,800 per year), 15 research assistantships (averaging $9,900 per year), 9 teaching assistantships (averaging $9,300 per year); tuition waivers (partial) also available. *Unit head:* Dr. Zhihua Qu, Interim Chair, 407-823-5976, Fax: 407-823-5835, E-mail: qu@ucf.edu. *Application contact:* Barbara Rodriguez, Director, Admissions and Registration, 407-823-2766, Fax: 407-823-6442, E-mail: gradadmissions@ucf.edu.

University of Cincinnati, Graduate School, College of Engineering and Applied Science, Department of Electrical and Computer Engineering and Computer Science, Program in Computer Engineering, Cincinnati, OH 45221. Offers MS. *Degree requirements:* For master's, thesis. *Entrance requirements:* For master's, GRE General Test. Additional exam requirements/recommendations for international students: Required—TOEFL (minimum score 550 paper-based; 213 computer-based). Electronic applications accepted. *Faculty research:* Digital signal processing, large-scale systems, picture processing.

University of Cincinnati, Graduate School, College of Engineering and Applied Science, Department of Electrical and Computer Engineering and Computer Science,

Program in Computer Science and Engineering, Cincinnati, OH 45221. Offers PhD. *Degree requirements:* For doctorate, thesis/dissertation. *Entrance requirements:* For doctorate, GRE General Test. Additional exam requirements/recommendations for international students: Required—TOEFL.

University of Colorado Boulder, Graduate School, College of Engineering and Applied Science, Department of Electrical, Computer and Energy Engineering, Boulder, CO 80309. Offers ME, MS, PhD. *Faculty:* 32 full-time (5 women). *Students:* 243 full-time (46 women), 75 part-time (10 women); includes 20 minority (2 Black or African American, non-Hispanic/Latino; 12 Asian, non-Hispanic/Latino; 5 Hispanic/Latino; 1 Two or more races, non-Hispanic/Latino), 149 international. Average age 28. 759 applicants, 41% accepted, 75 enrolled. In 2011, 88 master's, 22 doctorates awarded. Terminal master's awarded for partial completion of doctoral program. *Degree requirements:* For master's, thesis or alternative; for doctorate, one foreign language, thesis/dissertation, departmental qualifying exam. *Entrance requirements:* For master's, GRE General Test, minimum undergraduate GPA of 3.0; for doctorate, GRE General Test, minimum undergraduate GPA of 3.5. *Application deadline:* For fall admission, 1/15 priority date for domestic students, 12/1 for international students; for spring admission, 10/1 for domestic and international students. Applications are processed on a rolling basis. Application fee: $50 ($60 for international students). Electronic applications accepted. *Financial support:* In 2011–12, 167 students received support, including 61 fellowships (averaging $9,329 per year), 72 research assistantships with full and partial tuition reimbursements available (averaging $20,840 per year), 29 teaching assistantships with full and partial tuition reimbursements available (averaging $14,759 per year); institutionally sponsored loans, scholarships/grants, health care benefits, and unspecified assistantships also available. Financial award application deadline: 1/15; financial award applicants required to submit FAFSA. *Faculty research:* Biomedical engineering and cognitive disabilities, computer engineering VLSI CAD, dynamics and control systems, digital signal processing communications, electromagnetics, RF and microwaves, nanostructures and devices, optics and optoelectronics, power electronics and renewable energy systems. *Total annual research expenditures:* $9.1 million. *Application contact:* E-mail: ecegrad@colorado.edu. Web site: http://ece-www.colorado.edu/.

University of Dayton, Department of Electrical and Computer Engineering, Dayton, OH 45469-1300. Offers MSEE, DE, PhD. Part-time and evening/weekend programs available. *Faculty:* 15 full-time (0 women), 4 part-time/adjunct (1 woman). *Students:* 114 full-time (14 women), 35 part-time (7 women); includes 7 minority (1 Black or African American, non-Hispanic/Latino; 4 Asian, non-Hispanic/Latino; 2 Hispanic/Latino), 103 international. Average age 27. 285 applicants, 51% accepted, 57 enrolled. In 2011, 55 master's, 3 doctorates awarded. *Degree requirements:* For master's, thesis optional; for doctorate, variable foreign language requirement, thesis/dissertation, departmental qualifying exam. *Entrance requirements:* Additional exam requirements/recommendations for international students: Required—TOEFL (minimum score 550 paper-based; 213 computer-based; 80 iBT). *Application deadline:* For fall admission, 8/1 for domestic students, 3/1 for international students; for winter admission, 7/1 for international students; for spring admission, 1/1 for international students. Applications are processed on a rolling basis. Application fee: $0 ($50 for international students). Electronic applications accepted. *Expenses: Tuition:* Full-time $8400; part-time $700 per credit hour. *Required fees:* $25 per semester. Tuition and fees vary according to degree level. *Financial support:* In 2011–12, 1 fellowship (averaging $27,500 per year), 24 research assistantships with full tuition reimbursements (averaging $12,500 per year), 6 teaching assistantships with full tuition reimbursements (averaging $10,065 per year) were awarded. Financial award application deadline: 5/1; financial award applicants required to submit FAFSA. *Faculty research:* Electrical engineering, video processing, leaky wave antenna. *Total annual research expenditures:* $1.1 million. *Unit head:* Dr. Guru Subramanyam, Chair, 937-229-3188, Fax: 937-229-4529, E-mail: gsubramanyam1@udayton.edu. *Application contact:* Dr. Gurur Subramanyam, Chair, 937-229-3188, Fax: 937-229-4529, E-mail: gsubramanyam1@udayton.edu.

University of Delaware, College of Engineering, Department of Electrical and Computer Engineering, Newark, DE 19716. Offers MSECE, PhD. Part-time programs available. Postbaccalaureate distance learning degree programs offered (no on-campus study). Terminal master's awarded for partial completion of doctoral program. *Degree requirements:* For master's, thesis optional; for doctorate, thesis/dissertation. *Entrance requirements:* For master's, GRE General Test; for doctorate, GRE General Test, qualifying exam. Additional exam requirements/recommendations for international students: Required—TOEFL. Electronic applications accepted. *Faculty research:* HIV Evolution During Dynamic Therapy, compressive sensing in imaging, sensor, networks, and UWB radios, computer network time synchronization, silicon spintronics, devices and imaging in the high-terahertz band.

University of Denver, School of Engineering and Computer Science, Department of Electrical and Computer Engineering, Denver, CO 80210. Offers computer engineering (MS); electrical and computer engineering (PhD); electrical engineering (MS); engineering (MS); mechatronic systems engineering (MS). Part-time and evening/weekend programs available. *Faculty:* 11 full-time (0 women), 3 part-time/adjunct (1 woman). *Students:* 3 full-time (1 woman), 115 part-time (18 women); includes 14 minority (6 Asian, non-Hispanic/Latino; 7 Hispanic/Latino; 1 Two or more races, non-Hispanic/Latino), 29 international. Average age 29. 121 applicants, 77% accepted, 27 enrolled. In 2011, 29 master's, 2 doctorates awarded. Terminal master's awarded for partial completion of doctoral program. *Degree requirements:* For master's, thesis optional, proficiency in high- or low-level computer language; for doctorate, comprehensive exam, thesis/dissertation, proficiency in high- or low-level computer language. *Entrance requirements:* For master's and doctorate, GRE General Test, personal statement, three letters of recommendation. Additional exam requirements/recommendations for international students: Required—TOEFL (minimum score 550 paper-based; 80 iBT). *Application deadline:* Applications are processed on a rolling basis. Application fee: $60. Electronic applications accepted. *Financial support:* In 2011–12, 67 students received support, including 12 research assistantships with full and partial tuition reimbursements available (averaging $16,291 per year), 9 teaching assistantships with full and partial tuition reimbursements available (averaging $16,264 per year); Federal Work-Study, scholarships/grants, and unspecified assistantships also available. Financial award application deadline: 2/15; financial award applicants required to submit FAFSA. *Faculty research:* Energy and power, MEMS, unmanned systems, image processing/pattern recognition. *Total annual research expenditures:* $1.6 million. *Unit head:* Dr. Kimon Valavanis, Chair, 303-871-2586, Fax: 303-871-2194, E-mail: kvalavan@du.edu. *Application contact:* Crystal Harris, Assistant to the Chair, 303-871-6618, Fax: 303-871-2194, E-mail: crystal.harris@du.edu. Web site: http://www.ece.du.edu.

University of Detroit Mercy, College of Engineering and Science, Department of Electrical and Computer Engineering, Detroit, MI 48221. Offers computer engineering (ME, DE); mechatronics systems (ME, DE); signals and systems (ME, DE). Evening/weekend programs available. *Degree requirements:* For doctorate, thesis/dissertation. *Faculty research:* Electromagnetics, computer architecture, systems.

University of Florida, Graduate School, College of Engineering and College of Liberal Arts and Sciences, Department of Computer and Information Science and Engineering, Gainesville, FL 32611. Offers computer engineering (ME, MS, PhD); computer science (MS); digital arts and sciences (MS). Part-time programs available. Postbaccalaureate distance learning degree programs offered (minimal on-campus study). Terminal master's awarded for partial completion of doctoral program. *Degree requirements:* For master's, comprehensive exam, thesis optional; for doctorate, comprehensive exam, thesis/dissertation. *Entrance requirements:* For master's and doctorate, GRE General Test, minimum GPA of 3.0. Additional exam requirements/recommendations for international students: Required—TOEFL (minimum score 550 paper-based; 213 computer-based; 80 iBT), IELTS (minimum score 6). Electronic applications accepted. *Faculty research:* Computer systems, database, computer networks, graphics and vision, algorithm and parallel processing.

University of Florida, Graduate School, College of Engineering, Department of Electrical and Computer Engineering, Gainesville, FL 32611. Offers ME, MS, PhD, Engr. Part-time programs available. Postbaccalaureate distance learning degree programs offered. Terminal master's awarded for partial completion of doctoral program. *Degree requirements:* For master's, comprehensive exam (for some programs), thesis (for some programs); for doctorate, comprehensive exam, thesis/dissertation; for Engr, thesis. *Entrance requirements:* For master's, GRE General Test, minimum GPA of 3.0; for doctorate, GRE General Test, minimum GPA of 3.5; for Engr, GRE General Test. Additional exam requirements/recommendations for international students: Required—TOEFL (minimum score 550 paper-based; 213 computer-based; 80 iBT), IELTS (minimum score 6). Electronic applications accepted. *Faculty research:* Computer engineering, devices, electromagnetics and energy systems, electronics and signals and systems.

University of Houston–Clear Lake, School of Science and Computer Engineering, Program in Computer Engineering, Houston, TX 77058-1098. Offers MS. Part-time and evening/weekend programs available. *Entrance requirements:* For master's, GRE General Test. Additional exam requirements/recommendations for international students: Required—TOEFL (minimum score 550 paper-based; 213 computer-based).

University of Idaho, College of Graduate Studies, College of Engineering, Department of Electrical and Computer Engineering, Program in Computer Engineering, Moscow, ID 83844-2282. Offers M Engr, MS. *Students:* 2 full-time, 4 part-time. Average age 30. In 2011, 3 master's awarded. *Degree requirements:* For master's, thesis. *Entrance requirements:* For master's, minimum GPA of 2.8. *Application deadline:* For fall admission, 8/1 for domestic students; for spring admission, 12/15 for domestic students. Applications are processed on a rolling basis. Application fee: $60. Electronic applications accepted. *Expenses:* Tuition, state resident: full-time $3874; part-time $334 per credit hour. Tuition, nonresident: full-time $16,394; part-time $861 per credit hour. *Required fees:* $2808; $99 per credit hour. Tuition and fees vary according to program. *Financial support:* Federal Work-Study available. Financial award applicants required to submit FAFSA. *Unit head:* Dr. Brian Johnson, Chair, 208-885-6902. *Application contact:* Erick Larson, Director of Graduate Admissions, 208-885-4723, E-mail: gadms@uidaho.edu. Web site: http://www.uidaho.edu/engr/ece/mscompengr.

University of Illinois at Chicago, Graduate College, College of Engineering, Department of Electrical and Computer Engineering, Program in Electrical and Computer Engineering, Chicago, IL 60607-7128. Offers MS, PhD. Part-time programs available. *Degree requirements:* For master's, thesis or alternative; for doctorate, thesis/dissertation, departmental qualifying exam. *Entrance requirements:* For master's, minimum GPA of 2.75, BS in related field; for doctorate, GRE General Test, minimum GPA of 2.75, MS in related field. Additional exam requirements/recommendations for international students: Required—TOEFL.

University of Illinois at Urbana–Champaign, Graduate College, College of Engineering, Department of Electrical and Computer Engineering, Champaign, IL 61820. Offers electrical and computer engineering (MS, PhD); MS/MBA. *Faculty:* 75 full-time (6 women), 3 part-time/adjunct (0 women). *Students:* 446 full-time (55 women), 28 part-time (4 women); includes 71 minority (8 Black or African American, non-Hispanic/Latino; 41 Asian, non-Hispanic/Latino; 14 Hispanic/Latino; 8 Two or more races, non-Hispanic/Latino), 267 international. 1,831 applicants, 11% accepted, 77 enrolled. In 2011, 86 master's, 72 doctorates awarded. *Entrance requirements:* For master's, GRE, minimum GPA of 3.0; for doctorate, GRE. Additional exam requirements/recommendations for international students: Required—TOEFL (minimum score 590 paper-based; 243 computer-based; 96 iBT) or IELTS (minimum score 6.5). *Application deadline:* Applications are processed on a rolling basis. Application fee: $75 ($90 for international students). Electronic applications accepted. *Financial support:* In 2011–12, 52 fellowships, 353 research assistantships, 162 teaching assistantships were awarded; tuition waivers (full and partial) also available. *Unit head:* Andreas C. Cangellaris, Head, 217-333-6037, Fax: 217-244-7075, E-mail: cangella@illinois.edu. *Application contact:* Laurie A. Fisher, Administrative Aide, 217-333-9709, Fax: 217-333-8582, E-mail: fisher2@illinois.edu. Web site: http://www.ece.illinois.edu/.

The University of Iowa, Graduate College, College of Engineering, Department of Electrical and Computer Engineering, Iowa City, IA 52242-1316. Offers MS, PhD. Part-time programs available. *Faculty:* 18 full-time (2 women), 2 part-time/adjunct (0 women). *Students:* 74 full-time (15 women); includes 5 minority (1 Black or African American, non-Hispanic/Latino; 1 Asian, non-Hispanic/Latino; 3 Hispanic/Latino), 47 international. Average age 27. 125 applicants, 19% accepted, 16 enrolled. In 2011, 17 master's, 11 doctorates awarded. *Degree requirements:* For master's, comprehensive exam, thesis optional; for doctorate, comprehensive exam, thesis/dissertation, qualifying exam. *Entrance requirements:* For master's and doctorate, GRE. Additional exam requirements/recommendations for international students: Required—TOEFL (minimum score 550 paper-based; 213 computer-based; 81 iBT). *Application deadline:* For fall admission, 2/1 priority date for domestic students, 2/1 for international students. Applications are processed on a rolling basis. Application fee: $60 ($100 for international students). Electronic applications accepted. *Financial support:* In 2011–12, 5 fellowships with full tuition reimbursements (averaging $19,146 per year), 44 research assistantships with full and partial tuition reimbursements (averaging $21,511 per year), 16 teaching assistantships with full tuition reimbursements (averaging $17,600 per year) were awarded; scholarships/grants and unspecified assistantships also available. Financial award application deadline: 2/1; financial award applicants required to submit FAFSA. *Faculty research:* Applied optics and nanotechnology, compressive sensing, computational genomics, database management systems, large-scale intelligent and control systems, medical image processing, VLSI design and test. *Total annual research expenditures:* $6.7 million. *Unit head:* Dr. Milan Sonka, Department Executive Officer, 319-335-6052, Fax: 319-335-6028, E-mail: milan-sonka@uiowa.edu. *Application contact:* Cathy Kern, Secretary, 319-335-5197, Fax: 319-335-6028, E-mail: ece@engineering.uiowa.edu. Web site: http://www.ece.engineering.uiowa.edu/.

The University of Kansas, Graduate Studies, School of Engineering, Program in Computer Engineering, Lawrence, KS 66045. Offers MS. Part-time programs available. *Faculty:* 36. *Students:* 5 full-time (2 women), 5 part-time (2 women); includes 1 minority (Black or African American, non-Hispanic/Latino), 8 international. Average age 26. 18 applicants, 39% accepted, 2 enrolled. In 2011, 10 degrees awarded. *Degree requirements:* For master's, thesis optional, exam. *Entrance requirements:* For master's, GRE, minimum GPA of 3.0. Additional exam requirements/recommendations for international students: Required—TOEFL (minimum score 600 paper-based; 250 computer-based; 100 iBT). *Application deadline:* For fall admission, 3/1 priority date for domestic students, 3/1 for international students; for spring admission, 10/1 priority date for domestic students, 10/1 for international students. Applications are processed on a rolling basis. Application fee: $55 ($65 for international students). Electronic applications accepted. Tuition and fees vary according to course load, campus/location, program and reciprocity agreements. *Financial support:* Fellowships with full and partial tuition reimbursements, research assistantships with full and partial tuition reimbursements, teaching assistantships with full and partial tuition reimbursements, career-related internships or fieldwork, scholarships/grants, and unspecified assistantships available. Financial award application deadline: 1/1. *Faculty research:* Communication systems and networking, computer systems design, interactive intelligent systems, radar systems and remote sensing, bioinformatics. *Unit head:* Glenn Prescott, Chairperson, 785-864-4620, Fax: 785-864-3226. *Application contact:* Pam Shadoin, Assistant to Graduate Director, 785-864-4487, Fax: 785-864-3226, E-mail: eecs_graduate@ku.edu. Web site: http://www.eecs.ku.edu/.

University of Louisiana at Lafayette, College of Engineering, Center for Advanced Computer Studies, Lafayette, LA 70504. Offers computer engineering (MS, PhD); computer science (MS, PhD). Part-time programs available. Terminal master's awarded for partial completion of doctoral program. *Degree requirements:* For master's, thesis or alternative; for doctorate, comprehensive exam, thesis/dissertation, final oral exam. *Entrance requirements:* For master's, GRE General Test, minimum GPA of 2.75; for doctorate, GRE General Test, minimum GPA of 3.0. Additional exam requirements/recommendations for international students: Required—TOEFL. Electronic applications accepted.

See Display on page 281 and Close-Up on page 343.

University of Louisiana at Lafayette, College of Engineering, Department of Electrical and Computer Engineering, Lafayette, LA 70504. Offers computer engineering (MS, PhD); telecommunications (MSTC). *Degree requirements:* For master's, thesis or alternative; for doctorate, comprehensive exam, thesis/dissertation, final oral exam. *Entrance requirements:* For master's, GRE General Test, minimum GPA of 2.75. Additional exam requirements/recommendations for international students: Required—TOEFL (minimum score 550 paper-based; 213 computer-based). Electronic applications accepted.

University of Louisville, J. B. Speed School of Engineering, Department of Computer Engineering and Computer Science, Louisville, KY 40292-0001. Offers computer engineering and computer science (M Eng); computer science (MS); computer science and engineering (PhD); data mining (Certificate); network and information security (Certificate). *Accreditation:* ABET (one or more programs are accredited). Part-time programs available. Postbaccalaureate distance learning degree programs offered (no on-campus study). *Faculty:* 13 full-time (1 woman). *Students:* 54 full-time (11 women), 40 part-time (8 women); includes 12 minority (6 Black or African American, non-Hispanic/Latino; 6 Asian, non-Hispanic/Latino), 33 international. Average age 27. 49 applicants, 35% accepted, 7 enrolled. In 2011, 38 master's, 7 doctorates awarded. Terminal master's awarded for partial completion of doctoral program. *Degree requirements:* For master's, comprehensive exam (for some programs), thesis or alternative; for doctorate, comprehensive exam, thesis/dissertation, minimum GPA of 3.0. *Entrance requirements:* For master's, doctorate, and Certificate, GRE General Test. Additional exam requirements/recommendations for international students: Required—TOEFL (minimum score 550 paper-based; 213 computer-based; 80 iBT), IELTS (minimum score 6.5). *Application deadline:* For fall admission, 5/1 priority date for domestic students, 5/1 for international students; for spring admission, 11/1 priority date for domestic students, 11/1 for international students. Applications are processed on a rolling basis. Application fee: $50. Electronic applications accepted. *Expenses:* Tuition, state resident: full-time $9692; part-time $539 per credit hour. Tuition, nonresident: full-time $20,168; part-time $1121 per credit hour. Tuition and fees vary according to program and reciprocity agreements. *Financial support:* In 2011–12, 22 students received support, including 1 fellowship with full tuition reimbursement available (averaging $20,000 per year), 15 research assistantships with full tuition reimbursements available (averaging $18,900 per year), 6 teaching assistantships with full tuition reimbursements available (averaging $20,000 per year). Financial award application deadline: 1/25; financial award applicants required to submit FAFSA. *Faculty research:* Software systems engineering, information security and forensics, multimedia and vision, mobile and distributed computing, intelligent systems. *Total annual research expenditures:* $1.3 million. *Unit head:* Dr. Adel S. Elmaghraby, Chair, 502-852-6304, Fax: 502-852-4713, E-mail: adel@louisville.edu. *Application contact:* Dr. Michael Day, Associate Dean, 502-852-6195, Fax: 502-852-6294, E-mail: day@louisville.edu. Web site: http://www.louisville.edu/speed/computer.

University of Louisville, J. B. Speed School of Engineering, Department of Electrical and Computer Engineering, Louisville, KY 40292-0001. Offers M Eng, MS, PhD. *Accreditation:* ABET (one or more programs are accredited). Part-time programs available. *Faculty:* 15 full-time (2 women). *Students:* 74 full-time (7 women), 20 part-time (4 women); includes 6 minority (2 Black or African American, non-Hispanic/Latino; 2 Asian, non-Hispanic/Latino; 1 Hispanic/Latino; 1 Two or more races, non-Hispanic/Latino), 42 international. Average age 28. 38 applicants, 45% accepted, 6 enrolled. In 2011, 36 master's, 4 doctorates awarded. Terminal master's awarded for partial completion of doctoral program. *Degree requirements:* For master's, comprehensive exam (for some programs), thesis or alternative; for doctorate, comprehensive exam, thesis/dissertation, minimum GPA of 3.0. *Entrance requirements:* For master's and doctorate, GRE General Test. Additional exam requirements/recommendations for international students: Required—TOEFL (minimum score 550 paper-based; 213 computer-based; 80 iBT), IELTS (minimum score 6.5). *Application deadline:* For fall admission, 5/1 priority date for domestic students, 5/1 for international students; for spring admission, 11/1 priority date for domestic students, 11/1 for international students. Applications are processed on a rolling basis. Application fee: $50. Electronic applications accepted. *Expenses:* Tuition, state resident: full-time $9692; part-time $539 per credit hour. Tuition, nonresident: full-time $20,168; part-time $1121 per credit hour. Tuition and fees vary according to program and reciprocity agreements. *Financial support:* In 2011–12, 16 students received support, including 4 fellowships with full tuition reimbursements available (averaging $20,000 per year), 4 research assistantships with full tuition reimbursements available (averaging $21,000 per year), 8 teaching assistantships with full tuition reimbursements available (averaging $20,000

per year). Financial award application deadline: 1/25; financial award applicants required to submit FAFSA. *Faculty research:* Nanotechnology; microfabrication; computer engineering; control, communication and signal processing; electronic devices and systems. *Total annual research expenditures:* $5.8 million. *Unit head:* James H. Graham, Acting Chair, 502-852-6289, Fax: 502-852-6807, E-mail: jhgrah01@louisville.edu. *Application contact:* Dr. Michael Day, Associate Dean, 502-852-6195, Fax: 502-852-7294, E-mail: day@louisville.edu. Web site: http://www.louisville.edu/speed/electrical/.

University of Maine, Graduate School, College of Engineering, Department of Electrical and Computer Engineering, Orono, ME 04469. Offers computer engineering (MS); electrical engineering (MS, PhD). Part-time programs available. *Faculty:* 12 full-time (1 woman). *Students:* 21 full-time (4 women), 16 part-time (3 women); includes 4 minority (3 Asian, non-Hispanic/Latino; 1 Hispanic/Latino), 16 international. Average age 28. 35 applicants, 49% accepted, 12 enrolled. In 2011, 8 master's, 3 doctorates awarded. *Degree requirements:* For master's, thesis (for some programs); for doctorate, thesis/dissertation. *Entrance requirements:* For master's and doctorate, GRE General Test. Additional exam requirements/recommendations for international students: Required—TOEFL. *Application deadline:* For fall admission, 2/1 priority date for domestic students. Applications are processed on a rolling basis. Application fee: $65. Electronic applications accepted. *Expenses:* Tuition, state resident: full-time $5016. Tuition, nonresident: full-time $14,424. *Financial support:* In 2011–12, 15 research assistantships with full tuition reimbursements (averaging $18,720 per year), 2 teaching assistantships with full tuition reimbursements (averaging $13,600 per year) were awarded; Federal Work-Study, institutionally sponsored loans, and tuition waivers (full and partial) also available. Financial award application deadline: 3/1. *Total annual research expenditures:* $289,054. *Unit head:* Dr. Donald Hummels, Chair, 207-581-2244. *Application contact:* Scott G. Delcourt, Associate Dean of the Graduate School, 207-581-3291, Fax: 207-581-3232, E-mail: graduate@maine.edu. Web site: http://www2.umaine.edu/graduate/.

University of Manitoba, Faculty of Graduate Studies, Faculty of Engineering, Department of Electrical and Computer Engineering, Winnipeg, MB R3T 2N2, Canada. Offers M Eng, M Sc, PhD. *Degree requirements:* For master's, thesis; for doctorate, thesis/dissertation.

University of Maryland, Baltimore County, Graduate School, College of Engineering and Information Technology, Department of Computer Science and Electrical Engineering, Program in Computer Engineering, Baltimore, MD 21250. Offers MS, PhD. Part-time programs available. *Students:* 14 full-time (3 women), 8 part-time (1 woman); includes 2 minority (1 Black or African American, non-Hispanic/Latino; 1 Asian, non-Hispanic/Latino), 11 international. Average age 27. 25 applicants, 44% accepted, 6 enrolled. In 2011, 3 degrees awarded. *Degree requirements:* For master's, comprehensive exam (for some programs), thesis or alternative; for doctorate, comprehensive exam, thesis/dissertation. *Entrance requirements:* For master's, GRE General Test, strong background in computer engineering, computer science, and math courses; for doctorate, GRE General Test, MS in computer science (strongly recommended). Additional exam requirements/recommendations for international students: Required—TOEFL (minimum score 550 paper-based; 213 computer-based; 80 iBT). *Application deadline:* For fall admission, 6/1 for domestic students, 1/1 for international students; for spring admission, 11/1 for domestic students, 6/1 for international students. Applications are processed on a rolling basis. Application fee: $70. Electronic applications accepted. *Financial support:* In 2011–12, 2 research assistantships with full tuition reimbursements (averaging $18,000 per year), 10 teaching assistantships with full tuition reimbursements (averaging $18,000 per year) were awarded; career-related internships or fieldwork, Federal Work-Study, scholarships/grants, health care benefits, tuition waivers (partial), and unspecified assistantships also available. Support available to part-time students. Financial award application deadline: 6/30; financial award applicants required to submit FAFSA. *Faculty research:* Communication and signal processing, photonics and micro electronics, sensor systems, signal processing architectures, VLSI design and test. *Unit head:* Dr. Gary Carter, Professor and Chair, 410-455-3500, Fax: 410-455-3969, E-mail: carter@cs.umbc.edu. *Application contact:* 410-455-3000, Fax: 410-455-3969. Web site: http://www.cs.umbc.edu/.

University of Maryland, College Park, Academic Affairs, A. James Clark School of Engineering, Department of Electrical and Computer Engineering, College Park, MD 20742. Offers electrical and computer engineering (M Eng, MS, PhD); electrical engineering (MS, PhD); telecommunications (MS). Part-time and evening/weekend programs available. Postbaccalaureate distance learning degree programs offered. *Faculty:* 99 full-time (9 women), 27 part-time/adjunct (3 women). *Students:* 493 full-time (101 women), 65 part-time (7 women); includes 57 minority (7 Black or African American, non-Hispanic/Latino; 37 Asian, non-Hispanic/Latino; 10 Hispanic/Latino; 3 Two or more races, non-Hispanic/Latino), 419 international. 1,578 applicants, 34% accepted, 231 enrolled. In 2011, 104 master's, 45 doctorates awarded. *Degree requirements:* For master's, thesis optional; for doctorate, thesis/dissertation, oral exam, qualifying exam. *Entrance requirements:* For master's and doctorate, GRE General Test, 3 letters of recommendation. *Application deadline:* For fall admission, 5/1 for domestic students, 2/1 for international students; for spring admission, 6/1 for international students. Applications are processed on a rolling basis. Application fee: $75. Electronic applications accepted. *Expenses: Tuition, area resident:* Part-time $525 per credit hour. Tuition, state resident: part-time $525 per credit hour. Tuition, nonresident: part-time $1131 per credit hour. *Required fees:* $386.31 per term. Tuition and fees vary according to program. *Financial support:* In 2011–12, 13 fellowships with full and partial tuition reimbursements (averaging $20,640 per year), 172 research assistantships with tuition reimbursements (averaging $17,823 per year), 82 teaching assistantships with tuition reimbursements (averaging $16,768 per year) were awarded; career-related internships or fieldwork also available. Financial award applicants required to submit FAFSA. *Faculty research:* Communications and control, electrophysics, micro-electronics, robotics, computer engineering. *Total annual research expenditures:* $11.6 million. *Unit head:* Rama Chellappa, Interim Chair, 301-405-3683, E-mail: chella@umd.edu. *Application contact:* Dr. Charles A. Caramello, Dean of Graduate School, 301-405-0358, Fax: 301-314-9305, E-mail: ccaramel@umd.edu.

University of Massachusetts Amherst, Graduate School, College of Engineering, Department of Electrical and Computer Engineering, Amherst, MA 01003. Offers MSECE, PhD. Part-time programs available. *Faculty:* 41 full-time (2 women). *Students:* 196 full-time (38 women), 23 part-time (6 women); includes 13 minority (3 Black or African American, non-Hispanic/Latino; 6 Asian, non-Hispanic/Latino; 4 Hispanic/Latino), 175 international. Average age 26. 776 applicants, 29% accepted, 71 enrolled. In 2011, 53 master's, 12 doctorates awarded. Terminal master's awarded for partial completion of doctoral program. *Degree requirements:* For master's, thesis or alternative; for doctorate, comprehensive exam, thesis/dissertation. *Entrance requirements:* For master's and doctorate, GRE General Test. Additional exam requirements/recommendations for international students: Required—TOEFL (minimum score 550 paper-based; 213 computer-based; 80 iBT), IELTS (minimum score 6.5). *Application deadline:* For fall admission, 1/15 for domestic and international students; for spring admission, 10/1 for domestic and international students. Applications are processed on a rolling basis. Application fee: $50 ($65 for international students). Electronic applications accepted. Tuition and fees vary according to course load, campus/location and program. *Financial support:* Fellowships with full and partial tuition reimbursements, research assistantships with full tuition reimbursements, teaching assistantships with full tuition reimbursements, career-related internships or fieldwork, Federal Work-Study, scholarships/grants, traineeships, health care benefits, tuition waivers (full and partial), and unspecified assistantships available. Support available to part-time students. Financial award application deadline: 1/15. *Unit head:* Dr. C. Mani Krishna, Graduate Program Director, 413-545-4583, Fax: 413-545-4611, E-mail: ecegrad@ecs.umass.edu. *Application contact:* Lindsay DeSantis, Supervisor of Admissions, 413-545-0722, Fax: 413-577-0010, E-mail: gradadm@grad.umass.edu. Web site: http://ece.umass.edu/.

University of Massachusetts Dartmouth, Graduate School, College of Engineering, Department of Electrical and Computer Engineering, North Dartmouth, MA 02747-2300. Offers acoustics (Postbaccalaureate Certificate); communications (Postbaccalaureate Certificate); computer engineering (MS, PhD); computer systems engineering (Postbaccalaureate Certificate); digital signal processing (Postbaccalaureate Certificate); electrical engineering (MS, PhD); electrical engineering systems (Postbaccalaureate Certificate). Part-time programs available. *Faculty:* 15 full-time (3 women), 4 part-time/adjunct (1 woman). *Students:* 37 full-time (5 women), 52 part-time (8 women); includes 9 minority (2 Black or African American, non-Hispanic/Latino; 2 Asian, non-Hispanic/Latino; 1 Hispanic/Latino; 4 Two or more races, non-Hispanic/Latino), 45 international. Average age 29. 83 applicants, 93% accepted, 26 enrolled. In 2011, 17 master's, 1 doctorate awarded. *Degree requirements:* For master's, culminating project or thesis; for doctorate, comprehensive exam, thesis/dissertation. *Entrance requirements:* For master's, GRE, minimum undergraduate GPA of 3.0, 3 letters of recommendation, statement of intent, resume; for doctorate, GRE, 3 letters of recommendation, resume, statement of intent; for Postbaccalaureate Certificate, 3 letters of recommendation, resume, statement of intent. Additional exam requirements/recommendations for international students: Required—TOEFL (minimum score 533 paper-based; 200 computer-based; 72 iBT). *Application deadline:* For fall admission, 2/15 priority date for domestic students, 1/15 for international students; for spring admission, 11/1 priority date for domestic students, 10/1 for international students. Applications are processed on a rolling basis. Application fee: $40 ($60 for international students). Electronic applications accepted. *Expenses:* Tuition, state resident: full-time $2071; part-time $86.29 per credit. Tuition, nonresident: full-time $8099; part-time $337.46 per credit. *Required fees:* $438.58 per credit. Part-time tuition and fees vary according to class time, course load, degree level and reciprocity agreements. *Financial support:* In 2011–12, 10 research assistantships with full tuition reimbursements (averaging $12,720 per year), 14 teaching assistantships with full tuition reimbursements (averaging $10,385 per year) were awarded; fellowships, Federal Work-Study, and unspecified assistantships also available. Support available to part-time students. Financial award application deadline: 3/1; financial award applicants required to submit FAFSA. *Faculty research:* Speech acoustics, marine applications, signals and systems, applied electromagnetics, intelligent agency. *Total annual research expenditures:* $921,048. *Unit head:* Dr. Karen Payton, Graduate Program Director, 508-999-8434, Fax: 508-999-8489, E-mail: kpayton@umassd.edu. *Application contact:* Elan Turcotte-Shamski, Graduate Admissions Officer, 508-999-8604, Fax: 508-999-8183, E-mail: graduate@umassd.edu. Web site: http://www.umassd.edu/engineering/ece/graduate/welcome.cfm.

University of Massachusetts Lowell, College of Engineering, Department of Electrical and Computer Engineering, Program in Computer Engineering, Lowell, MA 01854-2881. Offers MS Eng. *Degree requirements:* For master's, thesis optional.

University of Memphis, Graduate School, Herff College of Engineering, Department of Electrical and Computer Engineering, Memphis, TN 38152. Offers automatic control systems (MS); biomedical systems (MS); communications and propagation systems (MS); computer engineering (PhD); electrical engineering (PhD); engineering computer systems (MS). *Degree requirements:* For master's, comprehensive exam, thesis or alternative. *Entrance requirements:* For master's, GRE General Test or MAT, minimum undergraduate GPA of 2.5. *Faculty research:* Image processing, imaging sensors, biomedical systems, intelligent systems.

University of Memphis, Graduate School, Herff College of Engineering, Department of Engineering Technology, Memphis, TN 38152. Offers computer engineering technology (MS); electronics engineering technology (MS); manufacturing engineering technology (MS). Part-time and evening/weekend programs available. *Degree requirements:* For master's, comprehensive exam, thesis optional. *Entrance requirements:* For master's, GRE General Test, minimum undergraduate GPA of 2.5. Electronic applications accepted. *Faculty research:* Teacher education services-technology education; flexible manufacturing control systems; embedded, dedicated, and real-time computer systems; network, Internet, and Web-based programming; analog and digital electronic communication systems.

University of Miami, Graduate School, College of Engineering, Department of Electrical and Computer Engineering, Coral Gables, FL 33124. Offers MSECE, PhD. Part-time programs available. *Degree requirements:* For master's, thesis (for some programs); for doctorate, comprehensive exam, thesis/dissertation, dissertation proposal defense. *Entrance requirements:* For master's, GRE General Test, minimum GPA of 3.0; for doctorate, GRE General Test, minimum undergraduate GPA of 3.3, graduate 3.5. Additional exam requirements/recommendations for international students: Required—TOEFL (minimum score 550 paper-based; 213 computer-based; 59 iBT), IELTS (minimum score 7). Electronic applications accepted. *Faculty research:* Computer network, image processing, database systems, digital signal processing, machine intelligence.

University of Michigan, College of Engineering, Department of Computer Science and Engineering, Ann Arbor, MI 48109. Offers MS, MSE, PhD. *Students:* 262 full-time (42 women), 1 part-time (0 women). 1,296 applicants, 19% accepted, 106 enrolled. In 2011, 54 master's, 14 doctorates awarded. *Faculty research:* Solid state electronics and optics; communications, control, signal process; sensors and integrated circuitry; software systems; artificial intelligence; hardware systems. *Unit head:* Prof. Marios Papaefthymiou, Interim Chair, 734-764-8504, Fax: 734-763-1503, E-mail: marios@umich.edu. *Application contact:* Dawn Freysinger, Graduate Programs Coordinator, 734-647-1807, Fax: 734-763-1503, E-mail: dawnf@umich.edu.

University of Michigan–Dearborn, College of Engineering and Computer Science, Department of Electrical and Computer Engineering, Dearborn, MI 48128-1491. Offers computer engineering (MSE); electrical engineering (MSE); software engineering (MS). Part-time and evening/weekend programs available. Postbaccalaureate distance learning degree programs offered (no on-campus study). *Faculty:* 9 full-time (1 woman), 9 part-time/adjunct (1 woman). *Students:* 15 full-time (4 women), 90 part-time (9 women); includes 36 minority (6 Black or African American, non-Hispanic/Latino; 28 Asian, non-Hispanic/Latino; 1 Hispanic/Latino; 1 Two or more races, non-Hispanic/Latino). Average age 32. 74 applicants, 50% accepted, 24 enrolled. In 2011, 33 master's awarded. *Degree requirements:* For master's, thesis optional. *Entrance requirements:* For master's, bachelor's degree in electrical and computer engineering or equivalent, minimum GPA of 3.0. Additional exam requirements/recommendations for international students: Required—TOEFL (minimum score 560 paper-based; 220 computer-based; 84 iBT). *Application deadline:* For fall admission, 8/1 priority date for domestic students, 4/1 for international students; for winter admission, 12/1 priority date for domestic students, 8/1 for international students; for spring admission, 4/1 priority date for domestic students, 2/1 for international students. Applications are processed on a rolling basis. Application fee: $60. Electronic applications accepted. *Financial support:* In 2011–12, 6 research assistantships with partial tuition reimbursements (averaging $8,815 per year), 2 teaching assistantships with partial tuition reimbursements (averaging $8,851 per year) were awarded; scholarships/grants and health care benefits also available. *Faculty research:* Fuzzy systems and applications, machine vision, pattern recognition and machine intelligence, vehicle electronics, wireless communications. *Unit head:* Dr. YiLu Murphey, Chair, 313-593-5028, Fax: 313-583-6336, E-mail: yilu@umich.edu. *Application contact:* Michael Patrick Hicks, Academic Records Intermediate Assistant, 313-593-5420, Fax: 313-583-6336, E-mail: ece-grad@umd.umich.edu. Web site: http://www.engin.umd.umich.edu/ECE/.

University of Minnesota, Duluth, Graduate School, Swenson College of Science and Engineering, Department of Electrical and Computer Engineering, Duluth, MN 55812-2496. Offers MSECE. Part-time programs available. *Degree requirements:* For master's, thesis. *Entrance requirements:* Additional exam requirements/recommendations for international students: Recommended—TOEFL, IELTS, TWE. *Faculty research:* Biomedical instrumentation, transportation systems, computer hardware and software, signal processing, optical communications.

University of Minnesota, Twin Cities Campus, College of Science and Engineering, Department of Computer Science and Engineering, Minneapolis, MN 55455-0213. Offers computer science (MCS, MS, PhD); software engineering (MSSE). Part-time programs available. *Faculty:* 36 full-time (3 women). *Students:* 401 (58 women); includes 26 minority (3 Black or African American, non-Hispanic/Latino; 3 American Indian or Alaska Native, non-Hispanic/Latino; 17 Asian, non-Hispanic/Latino; 3 Hispanic/Latino), 225 international. Terminal master's awarded for partial completion of doctoral program. *Degree requirements:* For doctorate, thesis/dissertation. *Entrance requirements:* For master's and doctorate, GRE General Test. Additional exam requirements/recommendations for international students: Required—TOEFL. *Application deadline:* For fall admission, 12/1 priority date for domestic students, 12/1 for international students. Applications are processed on a rolling basis. Application fee: $75 ($95 for international students). Electronic applications accepted. *Financial support:* Fellowships with tuition reimbursements, research assistantships with tuition reimbursements, and teaching assistantships with tuition reimbursements available. *Faculty research:* Computer architecture, bioinformatics and computational biology, data mining; graphics and visualization, high performance computing, human-computer interaction, networks, software systems, theory, artificial intelligence. *Application contact:* Computer Science Graduate Admissions, E-mail: admissions@cs.umn.edu. Web site: http://www.cs.umn.edu/.

University of Minnesota, Twin Cities Campus, College of Science and Engineering, Department of Electrical and Computer Engineering, Minneapolis, MN 55455-0213. Offers MSEE, PhD. Part-time programs available. *Faculty:* 42 full-time (2 women). *Students:* 486 (82 women); includes 32 minority (8 Black or African American, non-Hispanic/Latino; 21 Asian, non-Hispanic/Latino; 3 Hispanic/Latino), 326 international. *Degree requirements:* For master's, thesis or alternative; for doctorate, thesis/dissertation. *Entrance requirements:* Additional exam requirements/recommendations for international students: Required—TOEFL (minimum score 550 paper-based; 213 computer-based). *Application deadline:* For fall admission, 12/1 priority date for domestic students, 12/1 for international students. Applications are processed on a rolling basis. Application fee: $75 ($95 for international students). Electronic applications accepted. *Financial support:* Fellowships, research assistantships, and teaching assistantships available. *Faculty research:* Signal processing, micro and nano structures, computers, controls, power electronics. *Application contact:* Electrical Engineering Graduate Program, E-mail: newgrad@umn.edu. Web site: http://www.ece.umn.edu/.

University of Missouri–Kansas City, School of Computing and Engineering, Kansas City, MO 64110-2499. Offers civil engineering (MS); computer and electrical engineering (PhD); computer science (MS), including bioinformatics, software engineering, telecommunications networking; computer science and informatics (PhD); computing (PhD); electrical engineering (MS); engineering (PhD); mechanical engineering (MS); telecommunications (PhD). PhD (interdisciplinary) offered through the School of Graduate Studies. Part-time programs available. *Faculty:* 36 full-time (6 women), 27 part-time/adjunct (3 women). *Students:* 155 full-time (44 women), 136 part-time (24 women); includes 19 minority (4 Black or African American, non-Hispanic/Latino; 7 Asian, non-Hispanic/Latino; 6 Hispanic/Latino; 2 Two or more races, non-Hispanic/Latino), 201 international. Average age 26. 455 applicants, 46% accepted, 96 enrolled. In 2011, 194 degrees awarded. *Degree requirements:* For doctorate, thesis/dissertation. *Entrance requirements:* For master's, GRE General Test, minimum GPA of 3.0, 3 letters of recommendation from professors; for doctorate, GRE General Test, minimum GPA of 3.5. Additional exam requirements/recommendations for international students: Required—TOEFL (minimum score 550 paper-based; 213 computer-based; 80 iBT). *Application deadline:* For fall admission, 1/15 priority date for domestic students, 1/15 for international students. Applications are processed on a rolling basis. Application fee: $45 ($50 for international students). *Expenses:* Tuition, state resident: full-time $5798; part-time $322.10 per credit hour. Tuition, nonresident: full-time $14,969; part-time $831.60 per credit hour. *Required fees:* $93.51 per credit hour. *Financial support:* In 2011–12, 47 research assistantships with partial tuition reimbursements (averaging $13,190 per year), 10 teaching assistantships with partial tuition reimbursements (averaging $9,815 per year) were awarded; career-related internships or fieldwork, Federal Work-Study, scholarships/grants, tuition waivers (partial), and unspecified assistantships also available. Support available to part-time students. Financial award application deadline: 3/1; financial award applicants required to submit FAFSA. *Faculty research:* Algorithms, bioinformatics and medical informatics, biomechanics/biomaterials, civil engineering materials, networking and telecommunications, thermal science. *Unit head:* Dr. Kevin Z. Truman, Dean, 816-235-2399, Fax: 816-235-5159. *Application contact:* 816-235-2399, Fax: 816-235-5159. Web site: http://sce.umkc.edu/.

University of Nebraska–Lincoln, Graduate College, College of Arts and Sciences and College of Engineering, Department of Computer Science and Engineering, Lincoln, NE 68588. Offers bioinformatics (MS, PhD); computer engineering (MS, PhD); computer science (MS, PhD); information technology (PhD). *Degree requirements:* For master's, thesis optional; for doctorate, comprehensive exam, thesis/dissertation. *Entrance requirements:* For master's and doctorate, GRE General Test. Additional exam requirements/recommendations for international students: Required—TOEFL (minimum score 600 paper-based; 250 computer-based). Electronic applications accepted. *Faculty research:* Software engineering, geo- and bio-informatics, scientific computation, secure communication.

University of Nevada, Las Vegas, Graduate College, Howard R. Hughes College of Engineering, Department of Electrical and Computer Engineering, Las Vegas, NV 89154-4026. Offers MSE, PhD. Part-time programs available. *Faculty:* 20 full-time (3 women), 6 part-time/adjunct (1 woman). *Students:* 13 full-time (0 women), 28 part-time (4 women); includes 4 minority (1 Black or African American, non-Hispanic/Latino; 2 Hispanic/Latino; 1 Two or more races, non-Hispanic/Latino), 27 international. Average age 29. 33 applicants, 61% accepted, 10 enrolled. In 2011, 9 master's, 3 doctorates awarded. *Degree requirements:* For master's, comprehensive exam, thesis, project; for doctorate, comprehensive exam, thesis/dissertation. *Entrance requirements:* Additional exam requirements/recommendations for international students: Required—TOEFL (minimum score 550 paper-based; 213 computer-based; 80 iBT), IELTS (minimum score 7). *Application deadline:* For fall admission, 6/1 priority date for domestic students, 5/1 for international students; for spring admission, 10/1 priority date for domestic students, 10/1 for international students. Applications are processed on a rolling basis. Application fee: $60 ($95 for international students). Electronic applications accepted. *Financial support:* In 2011–12, 41 students received support, including 21 research assistantships with partial tuition reimbursements available (averaging $9,997 per year), 20 teaching assistantships with partial tuition reimbursements available (averaging $8,504 per year); institutionally sponsored loans, scholarships/grants, health care benefits, tuition waivers (full), and unspecified assistantships also available. Financial award application deadline: 3/1. *Faculty research:* Computer engineering, power engineering, semiconductor and nanotechnology, electronics and VLSI, telecommunications and control. *Total annual research expenditures:* $1.4 million. *Unit head:* Dr. Henry Selvaraj, Chair/Professor, 702-895-4183, Fax: 702-895-4075, E-mail: ece.chair@unlv.edu. *Application contact:* Graduate College Admissions Evaluator, 702-895-3320, Fax: 702-895-4180, E-mail: gradcollege@unlv.edu. Web site: http://ece.unlv.edu/.

University of Nevada, Reno, Graduate School, College of Engineering, Department of Computer Science and Engineering, Program in Computer Engineering, Reno, NV 89557. Offers MS. *Degree requirements:* For master's, thesis optional. *Entrance requirements:* For master's, GRE General Test, minimum GPA of 2.75. Additional exam requirements/recommendations for international students: Required—TOEFL (minimum score 500 paper-based; 173 computer-based; 61 iBT), IELTS (minimum score 6). Electronic applications accepted. *Faculty research:* Evolutionary computing systems, computer vision/virtual reality, software engineering.

University of Nevada, Reno, Graduate School, College of Engineering, Department of Computer Science and Engineering, Program in Computer Science and Engineering, Reno, NV 89557. Offers PhD. *Degree requirements:* For doctorate, thesis/dissertation. *Entrance requirements:* For doctorate, GRE General Test, minimum GPA of 3.0. Additional exam requirements/recommendations for international students: Required—TOEFL (minimum score 500 paper-based; 173 computer-based; 61 iBT), IELTS (minimum score 6). Electronic applications accepted. *Faculty research:* Evolutionary computing systems, computer vision/virtual reality, software engineering.

University of New Brunswick Fredericton, School of Graduate Studies, Faculty of Engineering, Department of Electrical and Computer Engineering, Fredericton, NB E3B 5A3, Canada. Offers M Eng, M Sc E, PhD. Part-time programs available. *Faculty:* 14 full-time (1 woman), 1 (woman) part-time/adjunct. *Students:* 69 full-time (6 women), 8 part-time (2 women). 45 applicants, 44% accepted. In 2011, 8 master's awarded. *Degree requirements:* For master's, thesis, research proposal; 10 courses (for M Eng); for doctorate, comprehensive exam, thesis/dissertation, research proposal. *Entrance requirements:* For master's, minimum GPA of 3.0; references; for doctorate, M Sc; minimum GPA of 3.0 or B average; previous transcripts; references. Additional exam requirements/recommendations for international students: Required—TWE, TOEFL (minimum score 580 paper-based; 237 computer-based) or IELTS (minimum score 7). *Application deadline:* Applications are processed on a rolling basis. Application fee: $50 Canadian dollars. *Financial support:* In 2011–12, 16 fellowships, 51 research assistantships (averaging $14,400 per year), 35 teaching assistantships were awarded. *Faculty research:* Biomedical engineering, communications, robotics and control systems, electromagnetic systems, embedded systems, optical fiber systems, sustainable energy and power systems, signal processing, software systems. *Unit head:* Dr. Julian Meng, Director of Graduate Studies, 504-458-7453, Fax: 504-453-3589, E-mail: jmeng@unb.ca. *Application contact:* Shelley Cormier, Graduate Secretary, 506-452-6142, Fax: 506-453-3589, E-mail: scormier@unb.ca. Web site: http://www.ee.unb.ca/.

University of New Haven, Graduate School, Tagliatela College of Engineering, Program in Electrical Engineering, West Haven, CT 06516-1916. Offers communications/digital signal processing (MS); control system (MS); electrical and computer engineering (MS); electrical engineering (MS). Part-time and evening/weekend programs available. *Students:* 62 full-time (14 women), 22 part-time (1 woman); includes 4 minority (1 Black or African American, non-Hispanic/Latino; 3 Asian, non-Hispanic/Latino), 76 international. 140 applicants, 99% accepted, 28 enrolled. In 2011, 26 master's awarded. *Degree requirements:* For master's, thesis or alternative. *Entrance requirements:* For master's, bachelor's degree in electrical engineering. Additional exam requirements/recommendations for international students: Required—TOEFL (minimum score 520 paper-based; 190 computer-based; 70 iBT); Recommended—IELTS (minimum score 5.5). *Application deadline:* For fall admission, 5/31 for international students; for winter admission, 10/15 for international students; for spring admission, 1/15 for international students. Applications are processed on a rolling basis. Application fee: $50. Electronic applications accepted. *Expenses: Tuition:* Part-time $750 per credit. *Financial support:* Research assistantships with partial tuition reimbursements, teaching assistantships with partial tuition reimbursements, career-related internships or fieldwork, Federal Work-Study, scholarships/grants, tuition waivers, and unspecified assistantships available. Support available to part-time students. Financial award applicants required to submit FAFSA. *Unit head:* Dr. Bouzid Aliane, Coordinator, 203-932-7160, E-mail: baliane@newhaven.edu. *Application contact:* Eloise Gormley, Director of Graduate Admissions, 203-932-7449, Fax: 203-932-7137, E-mail: gradinfo@newhaven.edu. Web site: http://www.newhaven.edu/9592/

University of New Haven, Graduate School, Tagliatela College of Engineering, Program in Network Systems, West Haven, CT 06516-1916. Offers MS. *Students:* 6 full-time (2 women), 4 part-time (1 woman), 4 international. 11 applicants, 100% accepted, 3 enrolled. *Degree requirements:* For master's, project. *Expenses: Tuition:* Part-time $750 per credit. *Unit head:* Dr. David Eggert, Graduate Advisor, 203-932-7097. *Application*

contact: Eloise Gormley, Director of Graduate Admissions, 203-932-7449, Fax: 203-932-7137, E-mail: gradinfo@newhaven.edu. Web site: http://www.newhaven.edu/32755/.

University of New Mexico, Graduate School, School of Engineering, Department of Electrical and Computer Engineering, Albuquerque, NM 87131-2039. Offers computational science and engineering (Post-Doctoral Certificate); computer engineering (MS, PhD); electrical engineering (MS, PhD). Part-time and evening/weekend programs available. Postbaccalaureate distance learning degree programs offered (no on-campus study). *Faculty:* 36 full-time (5 women), 8 part-time/adjunct (0 women). *Students:* 71 full-time (12 women), 64 part-time (13 women); includes 35 minority (1 Black or African American, non-Hispanic/Latino; 2 American Indian or Alaska Native, non-Hispanic/Latino; 8 Asian, non-Hispanic/Latino; 21 Hispanic/Latino; 3 Two or more races, non-Hispanic/Latino), 49 international. Average age 31. 184 applicants, 35% accepted, 47 enrolled. In 2011, 33 master's, 11 doctorates awarded. Terminal master's awarded for partial completion of doctoral program. *Degree requirements:* For master's, thesis; for doctorate, comprehensive exam, thesis/dissertation. *Entrance requirements:* For master's, GRE General Test, minimum GPA of 3.0; for doctorate, GRE General Test, minimum GPA of 3.5. Additional exam requirements/recommendations for international students: Required—TOEFL (minimum score 550 paper-based; 213 computer-based; 79 iBT). *Application deadline:* For fall admission, 7/15 for domestic students, 2/15 for international students; for spring admission, 11/1 for domestic students, 6/15 for international students. Application fee: $50. Electronic applications accepted. *Financial support:* In 2011–12, 124 students received support, including 2 fellowships with tuition reimbursements available (averaging $11,500 per year), 95 research assistantships with tuition reimbursements available (averaging $16,097 per year), 4 teaching assistantships with tuition reimbursements available (averaging $11,093 per year); scholarships/grants, health care benefits, and unspecified assistantships also available. Financial award application deadline: 2/15; financial award applicants required to submit FAFSA. *Faculty research:* Advanced graphics and visualization, biomedical engineering, communications and networking, networked control systems, photonics and microelectronics, pulsed power and high-power electromagnetics, reconfigurable systems. *Total annual research expenditures:* $3.2 million. *Unit head:* Dr. Chaouki T. Abdallah, Chair, 505-277-0298, Fax: 505-277-1439, E-mail: chaouki@ece.unm.edu. *Application contact:* Elmyra Grelle, Coordinator, Graduate Programs, 505-277-2600, Fax: 505-277-1439, E-mail: egrelle@ece.unm.edu. Web site: http://ece.unm.edu/.

See Display on page 389 and Close-Up on page 401.

The University of North Carolina at Charlotte, Graduate School, The William States Lee College of Engineering, Department of Electrical and Computer Engineering, Charlotte, NC 28223-0001. Offers electrical engineering (MSEE, PhD). Part-time and evening/weekend programs available. *Faculty:* 31 full-time (2 women). *Students:* 97 full-time (23 women), 63 part-time (9 women); includes 13 minority (4 Black or African American, non-Hispanic/Latino; 1 American Indian or Alaska Native, non-Hispanic/Latino; 6 Asian, non-Hispanic/Latino; 2 Hispanic/Latino), 98 international. Average age 27. 286 applicants, 64% accepted, 45 enrolled. In 2011, 52 master's, 2 doctorates awarded. Terminal master's awarded for partial completion of doctoral program. *Degree requirements:* For master's, thesis optional, thesis or project; for doctorate, thesis/dissertation. *Entrance requirements:* For master's, GRE General Test, minimum GPA of 3.0 in undergraduate major, 2.75 overall; for doctorate, GRE General Test, 3 letters of reference. Additional exam requirements/recommendations for international students: Required—TOEFL (minimum score 557 paper-based; 220 computer-based; 83 iBT). *Application deadline:* For fall admission, 7/1 for domestic students, 5/1 for international students; for spring admission, 11/1 for domestic students, 10/1 for international students. Applications are processed on a rolling basis. Application fee: $65 ($75 for international students). Electronic applications accepted. *Expenses:* Tuition, state resident: full-time $3689. Tuition, nonresident: full-time $15,226. *Required fees:* $2198. Tuition and fees vary according to course load and program. *Financial support:* In 2011–12, 47 students received support, including 2 fellowships (averaging $43,625 per year), 24 research assistantships (averaging $9,327 per year), 21 teaching assistantships (averaging $9,950 per year); career-related internships or fieldwork, institutionally sponsored loans, scholarships/grants, and unspecified assistantships also available. Support available to part-time students. Financial award application deadline: 4/1; financial award applicants required to submit FAFSA. *Faculty research:* Integrated circuits self test, control systems, optoelectronics/microelectronics devices and systems, communications, computer engineering. *Total annual research expenditures:* $1.2 million. *Unit head:* Dr. Ian Ferguson, Chair, 704-687-8404, Fax: 704-687-4762, E-mail: ianf@uncc.edu. *Application contact:* Kathy B. Giddings, Director of Graduate Admissions, 704-687-5503, Fax: 704-687-3279, E-mail: gradadm@uncc.edu. Web site: http://coe.uncc.edu/students/prospective/graduate.htm.

University of North Texas, Toulouse Graduate School, College of Engineering, Department of Computer Science and Engineering, Denton, TX 76203-5017. Offers computer science (MS); computer science and engineering (PhD). Terminal master's awarded for partial completion of doctoral program. *Degree requirements:* For master's, comprehensive exam (for some programs), thesis (for some programs); for doctorate, comprehensive exam, thesis/dissertation. *Entrance requirements:* For master's, GRE General Test (minimum score 400 verbal, 700 quantitative, 600 analytical or 4.0), minimum GPA of 3.0; for doctorate, GRE General Test (minimum scores: Verbal 50th percentile, Quantitative 700, Analytical 600 or 4.5), minimum GPA of 3.5, 3 letters of recommendation. Additional exam requirements/recommendations for international students: Required—TOEFL (minimum score 550 paper-based; 213 computer-based; 79 iBT); Recommended—IELTS (minimum score 6.5). Electronic applications accepted. *Expenses:* Tuition, state resident: part-time $100 per credit hour. Tuition, nonresident: part-time $413 per credit hour. *Faculty research:* Databases and data mining, computer architecture, cryptography, agent-oriented software engineering, graph theory, low power synthesis.

University of Notre Dame, Graduate School, College of Engineering, Department of Computer Science and Engineering, Notre Dame, IN 46556. Offers MSCSE, PhD. Terminal master's awarded for partial completion of doctoral program. *Degree requirements:* For master's, comprehensive exam; for doctorate, thesis/dissertation, candidacy exam. *Entrance requirements:* For master's and doctorate, GRE General Test. Additional exam requirements/recommendations for international students: Required—TOEFL (minimum score 600 paper-based; 250 computer-based; 80 iBT). Electronic applications accepted. *Faculty research:* Algorithms and theory of computer science, artificial intelligence, behavior-based robotics, biometrics, computer vision.

University of Oklahoma, College of Engineering, Department of Electrical and Computer Engineering, Program in Electrical and Computer Engineering, Norman, OK 73019. Offers MS, PhD. Part-time programs available. *Students:* 81 full-time (14 women), 52 part-time (10 women); includes 11 minority (2 Black or African American, non-Hispanic/Latino; 4 American Indian or Alaska Native, non-Hispanic/Latino; 4 Asian, non-Hispanic/Latino; 1 Two or more races, non-Hispanic/Latino), 80 international. Average age 28. 102 applicants, 32% accepted, 18 enrolled. In 2011, 24 master's, 4 doctorates awarded. Terminal master's awarded for partial completion of doctoral program. *Degree requirements:* For master's, thesis, oral exam; for doctorate, thesis/dissertation, general exam, oral exam, qualifying exam. *Entrance requirements:* For master's and doctorate, GRE General Test. Additional exam requirements/recommendations for international students: Required—TOEFL (minimum score 550 paper-based; 79 iBT). *Application deadline:* For fall admission, 5/15 for domestic students, 3/1 for international students; for spring admission, 9/1 for domestic and international students. Applications are processed on a rolling basis. Application fee: $40 ($90 for international students). Electronic applications accepted. *Expenses:* Tuition, state resident: full-time $4087; part-time $170.30 per credit hour. Tuition, nonresident: full-time $14,875; part-time $619.80 per credit hour. *Required fees:* $2659; $100.25 per credit hour. Tuition and fees vary according to course load and degree level. *Financial support:* In 2011–12, 133 students received support. Career-related internships or fieldwork, scholarships/grants, health care benefits, and unspecified assistantships available. Financial award applicants required to submit FAFSA. *Faculty research:* Signal/image processing, biomedical imaging, computer hardware design, weather radar, solid state electronics, intelligent transportation systems, navigation systems, power/electrical energy, control systems, communications. *Unit head:* Dr. James Sluss, Director, 405-325-4721, Fax: 405-325-7066, E-mail: sluss@ou.edu. *Application contact:* Lynn Hall, Graduate Program Assistant/Student Services Coordinator, 405-325-4285, Fax: 405-325-7066, E-mail: srg@ou.edu. Web site: http://ece.ou.edu.

University of Ottawa, Faculty of Graduate and Postdoctoral Studies, Faculty of Engineering, Ottawa-Carleton Institute for Electrical and Computer Engineering, Ottawa, ON K1N 6N5, Canada. Offers M Eng, MA Sc, PhD. *Degree requirements:* For master's, thesis or alternative, project; for doctorate, comprehensive exam, thesis/dissertation. *Entrance requirements:* For master's, honors degree or equivalent, minimum B average; for doctorate, minimum A- average. Electronic applications accepted. *Faculty research:* CAD, CSE, distributed systems and BISDN, CCN, DOC.

University of Pittsburgh, Swanson School of Engineering, Computer Engineering Program, Pittsburgh, PA 15260. Offers MS, PhD. Terminal master's awarded for partial completion of doctoral program. *Degree requirements:* For master's, thesis; for doctorate, comprehensive exam, thesis/dissertation, preliminary exams. *Entrance requirements:* For master's and doctorate, GRE General Test. Additional exam requirements/recommendations for international students: Required—TOEFL. *Application deadline:* For fall admission, 1/15 priority date for domestic students, 1/15 for international students. Applications are processed on a rolling basis. Application fee: $50. Electronic applications accepted. *Expenses:* Tuition, state resident: full-time $18,774; part-time $760 per credit. Tuition, nonresident: full-time $30,736; part-time $1258 per credit. *Required fees:* $740; $200 per term. Tuition and fees vary according to program. *Financial support:* Research assistantships with full tuition reimbursements, teaching assistantships with full tuition reimbursements, and health care benefits available. Support available to part-time students. Financial award application deadline: 1/15. *Faculty research:* Computer architecture, high performance parallel and distributed systems, electronic design automation, reconfigurable computing systems and wireless networks. *Unit head:* Dr. Donald M. Chiarulli, Co-Director, 412-624-8839, Fax: 412-624-5249, E-mail: don@cs.pitt.edu. *Application contact:* Keena M. Walker, Graduate Secretary, 412-624-8495, Fax: 412-624-8854, E-mail: keena@cs.pitt.edu. Web site: http://www.cs.pitt.edu/coe/.

University of Puerto Rico, Mayagüez Campus, Graduate Studies, College of Engineering, Department of Electrical and Computer Engineering, Mayagüez, PR 00681-9000. Offers computer engineering (ME, MS); computing and information sciences and engineering (PhD); electrical engineering (ME, MS). Part-time programs available. *Students:* 86 full-time (16 women), 8 part-time (1 woman); includes 65 minority (all Hispanic/Latino), 29 international. 42 applicants, 60% accepted, 20 enrolled. In 2011, 19 degrees awarded. *Degree requirements:* For master's, comprehensive exam, thesis; for doctorate, comprehensive exam, thesis/dissertation. *Entrance requirements:* For master's, proficiency in English and Spanish, BS in electrical or computer engineering or equivalent, minimum GPA of 3.0; for doctorate, GRE. Additional exam requirements/recommendations for international students: Required—TOEFL (minimum score 450 paper-based). *Application deadline:* For fall admission, 2/15 for domestic and international students; for spring admission, 9/15 for domestic and international students. Applications are processed on a rolling basis. Application fee: $25. Tuition and fees vary according to course level and course load. *Financial support:* In 2011–12, 46 students received support, including 28 research assistantships (averaging $15,000 per year), 18 teaching assistantships (averaging $8,500 per year); Federal Work-Study and institutionally sponsored loans also available. *Faculty research:* Microcomputer interfacing, control systems, power systems, electronics. *Total annual research expenditures:* $3.8 million. *Unit head:* Dr. Erick Aponte-Diaz, Chairperson, 787-832-4040 Ext. 3821, E-mail: erick.aponte1@upr.edu. *Application contact:* Sandra Montalvo, Administrative Staff, 787-832-4040 Ext. 3094, Fax: 787-831-7564, E-mail: sandra@ece.uprm.edu. Web site: http://www.ece.uprm.edu.

University of Regina, Faculty of Graduate Studies and Research, Faculty of Engineering and Applied Science, Program in Electronic Systems Engineering, Regina, SK S4S 0A2, Canada. Offers M Eng, MA Sc, PhD. Part-time programs available. *Faculty:* 8 full-time (0 women), 2 part-time/adjunct (0 women). *Students:* 26 full-time (6 women), 7 part-time (0 women). 140 applicants, 24% accepted. In 2011, 7 master's, 1 doctorate awarded. *Degree requirements:* For master's, thesis (for some programs); for doctorate, thesis/dissertation. *Entrance requirements:* For doctorate, master's degree. Additional exam requirements/recommendations for international students: Required—TOEFL (minimum score 550 paper-based; 80 iBT), IELTS (minimum score 6.5). *Application deadline:* For fall admission, 3/31 for domestic and international students; for winter admission, 7/31 for domestic and international students; for spring admission, 11/30 for domestic and international students. Application fee: $100. Electronic applications accepted. *Financial support:* In 2011–12, 6 fellowships (averaging $6,500 per year), 6 teaching assistantships (averaging $2,298 per year) were awarded; research assistantships, career-related internships or fieldwork, and scholarships/grants also available. Financial award application deadline: 6/15. *Faculty research:* Local area networks, digital and data communications systems design, telecommunications and computer networks, image processing, RF and microwave engineering. *Unit head:* Dr. Thomas Conroy, Department Coordinator, 306-585-4397, Fax: 306-585-4855, E-mail: thomas.conroy@uregina.ca.

University of Rhode Island, Graduate School, College of Engineering, Department of Electrical, Computer and Biomedical Engineering, Kingston, RI 02881. Offers MS, PhD, Graduate Certificate. Part-time programs available. *Faculty:* 18 full-time (3 women), 2 part-time/adjunct (1 woman). *Students:* 32 full-time (6 women), 25 part-time (1 woman); includes 8 minority (5 Asian, non-Hispanic/Latino; 3 Hispanic/Latino), 14 international. In 2011, 4 master's, 2 doctorates awarded. *Degree requirements:* For master's, comprehensive exam (for some programs), thesis optional; for doctorate, comprehensive exam, thesis/dissertation. *Entrance requirements:* For master's and doctorate, 2 letters of recommendation. Additional exam requirements/recommendations for international students: Required—TOEFL (minimum score 550 paper-based; 213 computer-based). *Application deadline:* For fall admission, 7/15 for domestic students, 2/1 for international students; for spring admission, 11/15 for domestic students, 7/15 for international students. Application fee: $65. Electronic applications accepted. *Expenses:* Tuition, state resident: full-time $10,432; part-time $580 per credit hour. Tuition, nonresident: full-time $23,130; part-time $1285 per credit hour. *Required fees:* $1362; $36 per credit hour. $35 per semester. One-time fee: $130. *Financial support:* In 2011–12, 9 research assistantships with full and partial tuition reimbursements (averaging $9,465 per year), 5 teaching assistantships with full and partial tuition reimbursements (averaging $8,520 per year) were awarded. Financial award application deadline: 7/15; financial award applicants required to submit FAFSA. *Faculty research:* Biomedical Instrumentation, cardiac physiology and computational modeling, analog/digital CMOS circuits, neural-machine interface, digital circuit design and VLSI testing. *Total annual research expenditures:* $985,856. *Unit head:* Dr. Godi Fischer, Chair, 401-874-5879, Fax: 401-782-6422, E-mail: fischer@ele.uri.edu. *Application contact:* Dr. Godi Fischer, Director of Graduate Studies, 401-874-5879, Fax: 401-782-6422, E-mail: fischer@ele.uri.edu. Web site: http://www.ele.uri.edu/.

University of Rochester, Hajim School of Engineering and Applied Sciences, Center for Entrepreneurship, Rochester, NY 14627-0360. Offers technical entrepreneurship and management (TEAM) (MS), including biomedical engineering, chemical engineering, computer science, electrical and computer engineering, energy and the environment, materials science, mechanical engineering, optics. *Faculty:* 61 full-time (8 women), 5 part-time/adjunct (1 woman). *Students:* 18 full-time (5 women), 3 part-time (1 woman); includes 4 minority (1 Asian, non-Hispanic/Latino; 3 Hispanic/Latino), 12 international. Average age 23. 134 applicants, 48% accepted, 21 enrolled. *Degree requirements:* For master's, comprehensive exam. *Entrance requirements:* For master's, GRE or GMAT, technical concentration of interest, 3 letters of recommendation, personal statement, official transcript. Additional exam requirements/recommendations for international students: Required—TOEFL or IELTS. *Application deadline:* For fall admission, 2/1 for domestic and international students. Applications are processed on a rolling basis. Application fee: $60. Electronic applications accepted. *Expenses: Tuition:* Full-time $41,040. *Financial support:* Career-related internships or fieldwork and scholarships/grants available. Financial award application deadline: 2/1. *Faculty research:* High efficiency solar cells, macromolecular self-assembly, digital signal processing, memory hierarchy management, molecular and physical mechanisms in cell migration. *Unit head:* Duncan T. Moore, Vice Provost for Entrepreneurship, 585-275-5248, Fax: 585-473-6745, E-mail: moore@optics.rochester.edu. *Application contact:* Andrea M. Galati, Executive Director, 585-276-3407, Fax: 585-276-2357, E-mail: andrea.galati@rochester.edu. Web site: http://www.rochester.edu/team.

University of Rochester, Hajim School of Engineering and Applied Sciences, Department of Electrical and Computer Engineering, Rochester, NY 14627. Offers MS, PhD. *Faculty:* 20 full-time (2 women). *Students:* 107 full-time (21 women), 5 part-time (3 women); includes 5 minority (2 Black or African American, non-Hispanic/Latino; 3 Asian, non-Hispanic/Latino), 89 international. 441 applicants, 37% accepted, 60 enrolled. In 2011, 27 master's, 15 doctorates awarded. Terminal master's awarded for partial completion of doctoral program. *Degree requirements:* For master's, comprehensive exam; for doctorate, thesis/dissertation, preliminary and oral exams. *Entrance requirements:* For master's and doctorate, GRE. Additional exam requirements/recommendations for international students: Required—TOEFL. *Application deadline:* For fall admission, 1/15 for domestic students. Application fee: $0. *Expenses: Tuition:* Full-time $41,040. *Financial support:* Fellowships, research assistantships, teaching assistantships, and tuition waivers (full and partial) available. Financial award application deadline: 2/1. *Faculty research:* Bio-informatics, communications, digital audio, image processing, medical imaging. *Unit head:* Philippe M. Fauchet, Chair, 585-275-1487. *Application contact:* Barbara Dick, Administrative Assistant/Academic Coordinator, 585-275-5719. Web site: http://www.ece.rochester.edu/graduate/index.html.

University of South Carolina, The Graduate School, College of Engineering and Computing, Department of Computer Science and Engineering, Columbia, SC 29208. Offers computer science and engineering (ME, MS, PhD); software engineering (MS). Part-time and evening/weekend programs available. Postbaccalaureate distance learning degree programs offered (minimal on-campus study). *Degree requirements:* For master's, comprehensive exam, thesis (for some programs); for doctorate, comprehensive exam, thesis/dissertation. *Entrance requirements:* For master's and doctorate, GRE General Test. Additional exam requirements/recommendations for international students: Required—TOEFL (minimum score 570 paper-based; 230 computer-based). Electronic applications accepted. *Faculty research:* Computer security, computer vision, artificial intelligence, multiagent systems, bioinformatics.

University of Southern California, Graduate School, Viterbi School of Engineering, Department of Computer Science, Los Angeles, CA 90089. Offers computer networks (MS); computer science (MS, PhD); computer security (MS); game development (MS); high performance computing and simulations (MS); human language technology (MS); intelligent robotics (MS); multimedia and creative technologies (MS); software engineering (MS). Part-time and evening/weekend programs available. Postbaccalaureate distance learning degree programs offered (no on-campus study). *Entrance requirements:* For master's and doctorate, GRE General Test. Additional exam requirements/recommendations for international students: Required—TOEFL. Electronic applications accepted. *Faculty research:* Databases, computer graphics and computer vision, software engineering, networks and security, robotics, multimedia and virtual reality.

University of Southern California, Graduate School, Viterbi School of Engineering, Ming Hsieh Department of Electrical Engineering, Los Angeles, CA 90089. Offers computer engineering (MS, PhD); electric power (MS); electrical engineering (MS, PhD, Engr); engineering technology commercialization (Graduate Certificate); multimedia and creative technologies (MS); telecommunications (MS); VLSI design (MS); wireless health technology (MS). Part-time programs available. Postbaccalaureate distance learning degree programs offered (no on-campus study). Terminal master's awarded for partial completion of doctoral program. *Degree requirements:* For master's, thesis optional; for doctorate, thesis/dissertation. *Entrance requirements:* For master's and doctorate, GRE General Test. Additional exam requirements/recommendations for international students: Recommended—TOEFL. Electronic applications accepted. *Faculty research:* Communications, computer engineering and networks, control systems, integrated circuits and systems, electromagnetics and energy conversion, micro electro-mechanical systems and nanotechnology, photonics and quantum electronics, plasma research, signal and image processing.

University of South Florida, Graduate School, College of Engineering, Department of Computer Science and Engineering, Tampa, FL 33620-9951. Offers computer engineering (MSCP); computer science (MSCS); computer science and engineering (PhD). Part-time programs available. *Faculty:* 19 full-time (1 woman), 1 part-time/adjunct (0 women). *Students:* 91 full-time (16 women), 42 part-time (10 women); includes 25 minority (9 Black or African American, non-Hispanic/Latino; 5 Asian, non-Hispanic/Latino; 11 Hispanic/Latino), 59 international. Average age 29. 252 applicants, 38% accepted, 38 enrolled. In 2011, 22 master's, 7 doctorates awarded. Terminal master's awarded for partial completion of doctoral program. *Degree requirements:* For master's, comprehensive exam, thesis or alternative; for doctorate, comprehensive exam, thesis/dissertation, teaching of undergraduate computer science and engineering course. *Entrance requirements:* For master's, GRE, minimum GPA of 3.0 in last 60 hours of coursework, three letters of recommendation, statement of purpose; for doctorate, GRE, minimum GPA of 3.0 in last 60 hours of coursework. Additional exam requirements/recommendations for international students: Required—TOEFL (minimum score 550 paper-based; 213 computer-based; 79 iBT) or IELTS (minimum score 6.5). *Application deadline:* For fall admission, 2/15 for domestic students, 1/2 for international students; for spring admission, 10/15 for domestic students, 6/1 for international students. Application fee: $30. Electronic applications accepted. *Financial support:* In 2011–12, 65 students received support, including 30 research assistantships with tuition reimbursements available (averaging $14,942 per year), 35 teaching assistantships with tuition reimbursements available (averaging $14,003 per year); unspecified assistantships also available. Financial award application deadline: 1/1; financial award applicants required to submit FAFSA. *Faculty research:* Computer vision, networks, artificial intelligence, computer architecture, software security. *Total annual research expenditures:* $1.4 million. *Unit head:* Dr. Lawrence Hall, Chair, 813-974-4195, Fax: 813-974-5094, E-mail: csechari@cse.usf.edu. *Application contact:* Dr. Miguel Labrador, Program Director, 813-974-3260, Fax: 813-974-5094, E-mail: mlabrador@usf.edu. Web site: http://www.csee.usf.edu/.

The University of Tennessee, Graduate School, College of Engineering, Department of Electrical Engineering and Computer Science, Program in Computer Engineering, Knoxville, TN 37996. Offers MS, PhD. Part-time programs available. *Faculty:* 7 full-time (2 women). *Students:* 35 full-time (3 women), 7 part-time (1 woman); includes 3 minority (2 Asian, non-Hispanic/Latino; 1 Hispanic/Latino), 17 international. Average age 27. 117 applicants, 7% accepted, 7 enrolled. In 2011, 6 master's, 3 doctorates awarded. *Degree requirements:* For master's, thesis or alternative; for doctorate, comprehensive exam, thesis/dissertation. *Entrance requirements:* For master's, GRE General Test (for MS students pursuing research thesis), minimum GPA of 2.7 (for U.S. degree holders), 3.0 (for international degree holders); 3 references; personal statement; for doctorate, College requires GRE General Test for all PhD candidates, minimum GPA of 3.0 on previous graduate course work; 3 references; personal statement. Additional exam requirements/recommendations for international students: Required—TOEFL (minimum score 550 paper-based; 213 computer-based). *Application deadline:* For fall admission, 2/1 priority date for domestic students, 2/1 for international students; for spring admission, 6/15 for domestic and international students. Applications are processed on a rolling basis. Application fee: $35. Electronic applications accepted. *Expenses:* Tuition, state resident: full-time $8332; part-time $464 per credit hour. Tuition, nonresident: full-time $25,174; part-time $1400 per credit hour. *Required fees:* $1162; $56 per credit hour. Tuition and fees vary according to program. *Financial support:* In 2011–12, 33 students received support, including 3 fellowships with full tuition reimbursements available (averaging $9,234 per year), 16 research assistantships with full tuition reimbursements available (averaging $22,639 per year), 13 teaching assistantships with full tuition reimbursements available (averaging $15,607 per year); career-related internships or fieldwork, Federal Work-Study, institutionally sponsored loans, health care benefits, and unspecified assistantships also available. Financial award application deadline: 2/1; financial award applicants required to submit FAFSA. *Unit head:* Dr. Kevin Tomsovic, Head, 865-974-3461, Fax: 865-974-5483, E-mail: tomsovic@eecs.utk.edu. *Application contact:* Dr. Lynne E. Parker, Associate Head, 865-974-4394, Fax: 865-974-5483, E-mail: parker@eecs.utk.edu. Web site: http://www.eecs.utk.edu.

The University of Texas at Arlington, Graduate School, College of Engineering, Department of Computer Science and Engineering, Arlington, TX 76019. Offers computer engineering (MS, PhD); computer science (MS, PhD); mathematical sciences, computer science (PhD); software engineering (MS). Part-time programs available. Postbaccalaureate distance learning degree programs offered (minimal on-campus study). *Faculty:* 31 full-time (3 women). *Students:* 206 full-time (46 women), 98 part-time (21 women); includes 7 minority (1 Black or African American, non-Hispanic/Latino; 4 Asian, non-Hispanic/Latino; 1 Hispanic/Latino; 1 Two or more races, non-Hispanic/Latino), 247 international. 752 applicants, 60% accepted, 89 enrolled. In 2011, 60 master's, 12 doctorates awarded. Terminal master's awarded for partial completion of doctoral program. *Degree requirements:* For master's, comprehensive exam (for some programs), thesis; for doctorate, comprehensive exam, thesis/dissertation. *Entrance requirements:* For master's, GRE General Test, minimum GPA of 3.0 (3.2 in computer science-related classes); for doctorate, GRE General Test, minimum GPA of 3.5. Additional exam requirements/recommendations for international students: Required—TOEFL (minimum score 550 paper-based; 230 computer-based; 92 iBT), IELTS (minimum score 6.5). *Application deadline:* For fall admission, 6/1 for domestic students, 5/1 for international students; for spring admission, 12/1 for domestic students, 10/1 for international students. Applications are processed on a rolling basis. Application fee: $35 ($50 for international students). *Financial support:* In 2011–12, 8 fellowships with full tuition reimbursements (averaging $24,000 per year), 48 research assistantships with partial tuition reimbursements (averaging $19,200 per year), 43 teaching assistantships with partial tuition reimbursements (averaging $18,000 per year) were awarded; career-related internships or fieldwork and scholarships/grants also available. Financial award application deadline: 6/1; financial award applicants required to submit FAFSA. *Faculty research:* Algorithms, homeland security, mobile pervasive computing, high performance computing bioinformation. *Unit head:* Dr. Fillia Makedon, Chairman, 817-272-3605, E-mail: makedon@uta.edu. *Application contact:* Dr. Bahram Khalili, Graduate Advisor, 817-272-5407, Fax: 817-272-3784, E-mail: khalili@uta.edu. Web site: http://www.cse.uta.edu/.

The University of Texas at Austin, Graduate School, Cockrell School of Engineering, Department of Electrical and Computer Engineering, Austin, TX 78712-1111. Offers MS, PhD. Part-time programs available. *Entrance requirements:* For master's, GRE General Test, minimum GPA of 3.3 in upper-division course work; for doctorate, GRE General Test. *Application deadline:* For fall admission, 1/2 for domestic students. Applications are processed on a rolling basis. Application fee: $50 ($75 for international students). Electronic applications accepted. *Financial support:* Fellowships, research assistantships, and teaching assistantships available. Financial award application deadline: 1/2. *Unit head:* Dr. L. Frank Register, Graduate Advisor, 512-232-1868, E-mail: register@mer.utexas.edu. *Application contact:* Susanne Graves, Graduate Coordinator, 521-471-8044, E-mail: susanne.graves@mail.utexas.edu. Web site: http://www.ece.utexas.edu/.

The University of Texas at Dallas, Erik Jonsson School of Engineering and Computer Science, Department of Electrical Engineering, Richardson, TX 75080. Offers computer engineering (MS, PhD); electrical engineering (MSEE, PhD); systems engineering and management (MS); telecommunications (MSTE, PhD). Part-time and evening/weekend programs available. *Faculty:* 44 full-time (2 women), 4 part-time/adjunct (0 women). *Students:* 510 full-time (108 women), 279 part-time (53 women); includes 110 minority (17 Black or African American, non-Hispanic/Latino; 65 Asian, non-Hispanic/Latino; 25 Hispanic/Latino; 3 Two or more races, non-Hispanic/Latino), 555 international. Average age 27. 1,933 applicants, 42% accepted, 265 enrolled. In 2011, 168 master's, 30 doctorates awarded. *Degree requirements:* For master's, thesis or major design project; for doctorate, thesis/dissertation. *Entrance requirements:* For master's, GRE General Test, minimum GPA of 3.0 in related bachelor's degree; for doctorate, GRE General Test, minimum GPA of 3.5. Additional exam requirements/recommendations for international students: Required—TOEFL (minimum score 550 paper-based; 215 computer-based). *Application deadline:* For fall admission, 7/15 for domestic students, 5/1 for international students; for spring admission, 11/15 for domestic students, 9/1 for international students. Applications are processed on a rolling basis. Application fee: $50 ($100 for international students). Electronic applications accepted. *Expenses:* Tuition, state resident: full-time $11,170; part-time $620.56 per credit hour. Tuition, nonresident: full-time $20,212; part-time $1122.89 per credit hour. *Financial support:* In 2011–12, 224 students received support, including 132 research assistantships with partial tuition reimbursements available (averaging $21,532 per year), 47 teaching assistantships with partial tuition reimbursements available (averaging $14,850 per year); fellowships with partial tuition reimbursements available, Federal Work-Study, institutionally sponsored loans, scholarships/grants, unspecified assistantships, and cooperative positions also available. Support available to part-time students. Financial award application deadline: 4/30; financial award applicants required to submit FAFSA. *Faculty research:* Semiconductor device manufacturing, photonics devices and systems, signal processing and language technology, nano-fabrication, energy efficient digital systems. *Unit head:* Dr. John H. L. Hansen, Department Head, 972-883-6755, Fax: 972-883-2710, E-mail: john.hansen@utdallas.edu. *Application contact:* Kathy Gribble, Graduate Program Coordinator, 972-883-2649, Fax: 972-883-2710, E-mail: gradecs@utdallas.edu. Web site: http://www.ee.utdallas.edu.

The University of Texas at El Paso, Graduate School, College of Engineering, Department of Electrical and Computer Engineering, El Paso, TX 79968-0001. Offers computer engineering (MS); electrical and computer engineering (PhD); electrical engineering (MS). Part-time and evening/weekend programs available. *Students:* 123 (17 women); includes 55 minority (1 Black or African American, non-Hispanic/Latino; 2 Asian, non-Hispanic/Latino; 52 Hispanic/Latino), 61 international. Average age 34. 52 applicants, 81% accepted, 16 enrolled. In 2011, 14 master's, 2 doctorates awarded. *Degree requirements:* For master's, thesis optional; for doctorate, thesis/dissertation. *Entrance requirements:* For master's, GRE General Test, minimum GPA of 3.0; for doctorate, GRE General Test, qualifying exam, minimum graduate GPA of 3.0. Additional exam requirements/recommendations for international students: Required—TOEFL. *Application deadline:* For fall admission, 7/1 priority date for domestic students, 3/1 for international students; for spring admission, 11/1 priority date for domestic students, 9/1 for international students. Applications are processed on a rolling basis. Application fee: $15 ($65 for international students). Electronic applications accepted. *Financial support:* In 2011–12, 60 students received support, including research assistantships with partial tuition reimbursements available (averaging $22,375 per year), teaching assistantships with partial tuition reimbursements available (averaging $17,900 per year); fellowships with partial tuition reimbursements available, Federal Work-Study, institutionally sponsored loans, scholarships/grants, and tuition waivers (partial) also available. Financial award application deadline: 3/15; financial award applicants required to submit FAFSA. *Faculty research:* Signal and image processing, computer architecture, fiber optics, computational electromagnetics, electronic displays and thin films. *Unit head:* Patricia Nava, Chair, 915-747-5994, E-mail: pnava@utep.edu. *Application contact:* Dr. Benjamin Flores, Interim Dean of the Graduate School, 915-747-5491, Fax: 915-747-5788, E-mail: bflores@utep.edu.

The University of Texas at San Antonio, College of Engineering, Department of Electrical and Computer Engineering, San Antonio, TX 78249-0617. Offers computer engineering (MS); electrical engineering (MSEE, PhD); materials engineering (MS). Part-time programs available. *Faculty:* 21 full-time (3 women), 2 part-time/adjunct (0 women). *Students:* 111 full-time (34 women), 56 part-time (11 women); includes 32 minority (6 Black or African American, non-Hispanic/Latino; 4 Asian, non-Hispanic/Latino; 19 Hispanic/Latino; 3 Two or more races, non-Hispanic/Latino), 106 international. Average age 28. 228 applicants, 67% accepted, 47 enrolled. In 2011, 33 master's, 4 doctorates awarded. Terminal master's awarded for partial completion of doctoral program. *Degree requirements:* For master's, comprehensive exam, thesis (for some programs); for doctorate, comprehensive exam, thesis/dissertation. *Entrance requirements:* For master's, GRE General Test, bachelor's degree in electrical or computer engineering from ABET-accredited institution of higher education or related field; minimum GPA of 3.0 on the last 60 semester credit hours of undergraduate studies; for doctorate, GRE General Test, master's degree or minimum GPA of 3.3 in last 60 semester credit hours of undergraduate level coursework in electrical engineering; statement of purpose. Additional exam requirements/recommendations for international students: Required—TOEFL (minimum score 550 paper-based; 79 iBT), IELTS (minimum score 6.5). *Application deadline:* For fall admission, 7/1 for domestic students, 4/1 for international students; for spring admission, 11/1 for domestic students, 9/1 for international students. Applications are processed on a rolling basis. Application fee: $45 ($85 for international students). Electronic applications accepted. *Expenses:* Tuition, state resident: full-time $3148; part-time $2176 per semester. Tuition, nonresident: full-time $8782; part-time $5932 per semester. *Required fees:* $719 per semester. *Financial support:* In 2011–12, 60 students received support, including 11 fellowships (averaging $24,500 per year), 26 research assistantships (averaging $21,653 per year), 11 teaching assistantships (averaging $15,200 per year); unspecified assistantships and Valero Residency Fellowships, travel grants also available. Financial award application deadline: 3/31. *Faculty research:* Computer engineering, digital signal processing, systems and controls, communications, electronics materials and devices, electric power engineering. *Unit head:* Dr. Ruyan Guo, Interim Department Chair, 210-458-7057/7076, Fax: 210-458-5947, E-mail: electrical.engineering@utsa.edu. *Application contact:* Dr. Chunjiang Qian, Graduate Advisor of Record, 210-458-5587, Fax: 210-458-5947, E-mail: graduate.ece@utsa.edu. Web site: http://ece.utsa.edu/.

University of Toronto, School of Graduate Studies, Faculty of Applied Science and Engineering, Department of Electrical and Computer Engineering, Toronto, ON M5S 1A1, Canada. Offers M Eng, MA Sc, PhD. Part-time programs available. *Degree requirements:* For master's, thesis (for some programs), oral thesis defense (MA Sc); for doctorate, thesis/dissertation, qualifying exam, thesis defense. *Entrance requirements:*

For master's, four-year degree in electrical or computer engineering, minimum B average, 2 letters of reference; for doctorate, minimum B+ average, MA Sc in electrical or computer engineering, 2 letters of reference. Additional exam requirements/recommendations for international students: Required—TOEFL (minimum score 580 paper-based; 93 iBT). Electronic applications accepted.

University of Victoria, Faculty of Graduate Studies, Faculty of Engineering, Department of Electrical and Computer Engineering, Victoria, BC V8W 2Y2, Canada. Offers M Eng, MA Sc, PhD. *Degree requirements:* For master's, thesis; for doctorate, thesis/dissertation, candidacy exam. *Entrance requirements:* For master's, GRE (recommended), bachelor's degree in engineering; for doctorate, GRE (recommended), master's degree. Additional exam requirements/recommendations for international students: Required—TOEFL (minimum score 575 paper-based; 233 computer-based), IELTS (minimum score 7). Electronic applications accepted. *Faculty research:* Communications and computers; electromagnetics, microwaves, and optics; electronics; power systems, signal processing, and control.

University of Virginia, School of Engineering and Applied Science, Department of Electrical and Computer Engineering, Program in Computer Engineering, Charlottesville, VA 22903. Offers ME, MS, PhD. Postbaccalaureate distance learning degree programs offered (no on-campus study). *Students:* 21 full-time (2 women), 1 part-time (0 women); includes 1 minority (Asian, non-Hispanic/Latino), 17 international. Average age 26. 66 applicants, 18% accepted, 7 enrolled. In 2011, 3 master's, 2 doctorates awarded. Terminal master's awarded for partial completion of doctoral program. *Degree requirements:* For master's, thesis (for some programs); for doctorate, comprehensive exam, thesis/dissertation. *Entrance requirements:* For master's, GRE General Test, 3 letters of recommendation; for doctorate, GRE General Test, 3 letters of recommendation; essay. Additional exam requirements/recommendations for international students: Required—TOEFL (minimum score 650 paper-based; 250 computer-based; 90 iBT), IELTS (minimum score 7). *Application deadline:* For fall admission, 8/1 for domestic students, 4/1 for international students; for winter admission, 12/1 for domestic students, 8/1 for international students; for spring admission, 5/1 for domestic students, 1/1 for international students. Applications are processed on a rolling basis. Application fee: $60. Electronic applications accepted. *Financial support:* Fellowships, research assistantships, and teaching assistantships available. Financial award application deadline: 1/15; financial award applicants required to submit FAFSA. *Faculty research:* Computer architecture, VLSI, switching theory, operating systems, real-time and embedded systems, compiler, software systems and software engineering, fault-tolerant computing and reliability engineering. *Unit head:* Joanne B. Dugan, Director, 434-924-3198, Fax: 434-924-8818, E-mail: compe@virginia.edu. *Application contact:* Kathryn C. Thornton, Assistant Dean for Graduate Programs, 434-924-3897, Fax: 434-982-2214, E-mail: seas-grad-admission@cs.virginia.edu.

University of Washington, Bothell, Program in Computing and Software Systems, Bothell, WA 98011-8246. Offers MS. Part-time and evening/weekend programs available. *Faculty:* 5 full-time (3 women), 66 part-time/adjunct (16 women). *Students:* 7 full-time (6 women), 51 part-time (6 women); includes 15 minority (1 Black or African American, non-Hispanic/Latino; 10 Asian, non-Hispanic/Latino; 1 Hispanic/Latino; 1 Native Hawaiian or other Pacific Islander, non-Hispanic/Latino; 2 Two or more races, non-Hispanic/Latino), 12 international. Average age 33. 35 applicants, 63% accepted, 16 enrolled. In 2011, 3 master's awarded. *Degree requirements:* For master's, comprehensive exam (for some programs), thesis optional. *Entrance requirements:* For master's, GRE. Additional exam requirements/recommendations for international students: Required—TOEFL (minimum score 580 paper-based; 237 computer-based; 92 iBT) or IELTS (minimum score 7). *Application deadline:* For fall admission, 7/1 for domestic students, 4/1 for international students; for winter admission, 11/1 for domestic students; for spring admission, 2/1 for domestic students. Application fee: $75. Electronic applications accepted. *Expenses:* Contact institution. *Financial support:* Applicants required to submit FAFSA. *Faculty research:* Computer science, software engineering, computer graphics, parallel and distributed systems, computer vision. *Unit head:* Dr. Michael Stiber, Professor and Director, 425-352-5279, E-mail: cssinfo@uwb.edu. *Application contact:* Megan Jewell, Graduate Advisor, 425-352-5279, E-mail: mjewell@uwb.edu. Web site: http://www.uwb.edu/mscss.

University of Washington, Tacoma, Graduate Programs, Program in Computing and Software Systems, Tacoma, WA 98402-3100. Offers MS. Part-time programs available. *Degree requirements:* For master's, capstone project/thesis or 15 credits elective coursework. *Entrance requirements:* For master's, GRE, personal statement, resume, transcripts, 3 recommendations. Additional exam requirements/recommendations for international students: Required—TOEFL (minimum score 580 paper-based; 237 computer-based; 92 iBT), IELTS (minimum score 7). Electronic applications accepted. *Faculty research:* Data stream analysis, formal methods, data mining, robotic systems, software development processes.

University of Waterloo, Graduate Studies, Faculty of Engineering, Department of Electrical and Computer Engineering, Waterloo, ON N2L 3G1, Canada. Offers electrical and computer engineering (M Eng, MA Sc, PhD); electrical and computer engineering (software engineering) (MA Sc). Part-time programs available. *Degree requirements:* For master's, research paper or thesis; for doctorate, comprehensive exam, thesis/dissertation. *Entrance requirements:* For master's, honors degree, minimum B+ average; for doctorate, master's degree, minimum A- average. Additional exam requirements/recommendations for international students: Required—TOEFL (minimum score 550 paper-based; 213 computer-based), TWE (minimum score 4). Electronic applications accepted. *Faculty research:* Communications, computers, systems and control, silicon devices, power engineering.

The University of Western Ontario, Faculty of Graduate Studies, Physical Sciences Division, Faculty of Engineering, London, ON N6A 5B8, Canada. Offers chemical and biochemical engineering (ME Sc, PhD); civil and environmental engineering (M Eng, ME Sc, PhD); electrical and computer engineering (M Eng, ME Sc, PhD); mechanical and materials engineering (M Eng, ME Sc, PhD). Part-time programs available. Terminal master's awarded for partial completion of doctoral program. *Degree requirements:* For master's, thesis; for doctorate, thesis/dissertation. *Entrance requirements:* For master's, minimum B average; for doctorate, minimum B+ average. *Faculty research:* Wind, geotechnical, chemical reactor engineering, applied electrostatics, biochemical engineering.

University of Wisconsin–Milwaukee, Graduate School, College of Engineering and Applied Science, Program in Engineering, Milwaukee, WI 53201-0413. Offers civil engineering (MS); electrical and computer engineering (MS); energy engineering (Certificate); engineering (PhD); engineering management (MS); engineering mechanics (MS); ergonomics (Certificate); industrial and management engineering (MS); manufacturing engineering (MS); materials engineering (MS); mechanical engineering (MS); MUP/MS. Part-time programs available. *Faculty:* 41 full-time (5 women), 2 part-time/adjunct (0 women). *Students:* 170 full-time (33 women), 101 part-time (18 women); includes 30 minority (6 Black or African American, non-Hispanic/Latino; 15 Asian, non-

Hispanic/Latino; 2 Hispanic/Latino; 7 Two or more races, non-Hispanic/Latino), 153 international. Average age 30. 170 applicants, 56% accepted, 48 enrolled. In 2011, 47 master's, 12 doctorates awarded. *Degree requirements:* For master's, comprehensive exam (for some programs), thesis or alternative; for doctorate, comprehensive exam, thesis/dissertation, internship. *Entrance requirements:* For master's, GRE, minimum GPA of 2.75; for doctorate, GRE, minimum GPA of 3.5. Additional exam requirements/recommendations for international students: Required—TOEFL (minimum score 550 paper-based; 79 iBT), IELTS (minimum score 6.5). *Application deadline:* For fall admission, 1/1 priority date for domestic students; for spring admission, 9/1 for domestic students. Applications are processed on a rolling basis. Application fee: $56 ($96 for international students). One-time fee: $506.10 full-time. Tuition and fees vary according to course load and reciprocity agreements. *Financial support:* In 2011–12, 3 fellowships, 55 research assistantships, 77 teaching assistantships were awarded; career-related internships or fieldwork, Federal Work-Study, unspecified assistantships, and project assistantships also available. Support available to part-time students. Financial award application deadline: 4/15. *Total annual research expenditures:* $10.3 million. *Unit head:* David Yu, Representative, 414-229-6169, E-mail: yu@uwm.edu. *Application contact:* Betty Warras, General Information Contact, 414-229-6169, Fax: 414-229-6967, E-mail: bwarras@uwm.edu. Web site: http://www.wum.edu/CEAS/.

Villanova University, College of Engineering, Department of Electrical and Computer Engineering, Program in Computer Engineering, Villanova, PA 19085-1699. Offers computer architectures (Certificate); computer engineering (MSCPE); intelligent control systems (Certificate). Part-time and evening/weekend programs available. *Degree requirements:* For master's, thesis optional. *Entrance requirements:* For master's, GRE General Test (for applicants with degrees from foreign universities), BEE, minimum GPA of 3.0. Additional exam requirements/recommendations for international students: Required—TOEFL (minimum score 600 paper-based; 250 computer-based; 100 iBT). Electronic applications accepted. *Expenses: Tuition:* Part-time $675 per credit. Part-time tuition and fees vary according to degree level and program. *Faculty research:* Expert systems, computer vision, neural networks, image processing, computer architectures.

Virginia Polytechnic Institute and State University, Graduate School, College of Engineering, Department of Electrical and Computer Engineering, Blacksburg, VA 24061. Offers air transportation systems (Certificate); computer engineering (M Eng, MS, PhD); electrical engineering (M Eng, MS, PhD); emerging devices technologies (Certificate); traffic control and operations (Certificate). *Degree requirements:* For master's, comprehensive exam (for some programs), thesis (for some programs); for doctorate, comprehensive exam (for some programs), thesis/dissertation (for some programs). *Entrance requirements:* For master's and doctorate, GRE. Additional exam requirements/recommendations for international students: Required—TOEFL (minimum score 590 paper-based; 213 computer-based). *Application deadline:* For fall admission, 7/1 for domestic and international students; for spring admission, 12/1 for domestic and international students. Applications are processed on a rolling basis. Application fee: $65. Electronic applications accepted. *Expenses:* Tuition, state resident: full-time $10,048; part-time $558.25 per credit hour. Tuition, nonresident: full-time $19,497; part-time $1083.25 per credit hour. *Required fees:* $405 per semester. Tuition and fees vary according to course load, campus/location and program. *Financial support:* Fellowships with full tuition reimbursements, research assistantships with full tuition reimbursements, teaching assistantships with full tuition reimbursements, career-related internships or fieldwork, Federal Work-Study, scholarships/grants, health care benefits, and unspecified assistantships available. Financial award application deadline: 1/15. *Faculty research:* Electromagnetics, controls, electronics, power, communications. *Unit head:* Dr. James S. Thorp, Unit Head, 540-231-2946, Fax: 540-231-3362, E-mail: jsthorp@vt.edu. *Application contact:* Paul Plassmann, Information Contact, 540-231-5379, Fax: 540-231-3362, E-mail: plassmann@vt.edu. Web site: http://www.ece.vt.edu/.

Virginia Polytechnic Institute and State University, VT Online, Blacksburg, VA 24061. Offers advanced transportation systems (Certificate); aerospace engineering (MS); agricultural and life sciences (MSLFS); business information systems (Graduate Certificate); career and technical education (MS); civil engineering (MS); computer engineering (M Eng, MS); decision support systems (Graduate Certificate); eLearning leadership (MA); electrical engineering (M Eng, MS); engineering administration (MEA); environmental engineering (Certificate); environmental politics and policy (Graduate Certificate); environmental sciences and engineering (MS); foundations of political analysis (Graduate Certificate); health product risk management (Graduate Certificate); industrial and systems engineering (MS); information policy and society (Graduate Certificate); information security (Graduate Certificate); information technology (MIT); instructional technology (MA); integrative STEM education (MA Ed); liberal arts (Graduate Certificate); life sciences: health product risk management (MS); natural resources (MNR, Graduate Certificate); networking (Graduate Certificate); nonprofit and nongovernmental organization management (Graduate Certificate); ocean engineering (MS); political science (MA); security studies (Graduate Certificate); software development (Graduate Certificate). *Expenses:* Tuition, state resident: full-time $10,048; part-time $558.25 per credit hour. Tuition, nonresident: full-time $19,497; part-time $1083.25 per credit hour. *Required fees:* $405 per semester. Tuition and fees vary according to course load, campus/location and program. *Application contact:* Graduate School Applications General Assistance, 540-231-8636, Fax: 540-231-2039, E-mail: gradappl@vt.edu. Web site: http://www.vto.vt.edu/.

Washington State University, Graduate School, College of Engineering and Architecture, School of Electrical Engineering and Computer Science, Program in Computer Engineering, Pullman, WA 99164. Offers MS, PhD. *Faculty:* 24. *Students:* 4 full-time (0 women), 5 part-time (1 woman); includes 2 minority (1 Asian, non-Hispanic/Latino; 1 Native Hawaiian or other Pacific Islander, non-Hispanic/Latino), 3 international. Average age 30. 29 applicants, 7% accepted, 1 enrolled. In 2011, 2 master's awarded. *Degree requirements:* For master's, comprehensive exam (for some programs), thesis optional, research project; for doctorate, comprehensive exam, thesis/dissertation. *Entrance requirements:* For master's, GRE, 3 letters of recommendation; for doctorate, 3 letters of recommendation. Additional exam requirements/recommendations for international students: Required—TOEFL. *Application deadline:* For fall admission, 3/1 for domestic and international students; for spring admission, 9/1 for domestic students, 7/1 for international students. Application fee: $75. *Financial support:* In 2011–12, research assistantships with tuition reimbursements (averaging $18,204 per year), teaching assistantships with tuition reimbursements (averaging $18,204 per year) were awarded. *Total annual research expenditures:* $3.9 million. *Unit head:* Behrooz Shirazi, Director, 509-335-8148, E-mail: shirazi@wsu.edu. *Application contact:* Graduate School Admissions, 800-GRADWSU, Fax: 509-335-1949, E-mail: gradsch@wsu.edu. Web site: http://school.eecs.wsu.edu/graduate/programs/index.htm.

Washington University in St. Louis, School of Engineering and Applied Science, Department of Computer Science and Engineering, St. Louis, MO 63130-4899. Offers computer engineering (MS, PhD); computer science (MS, PhD); computer science and engineering (M Eng). Part-time programs available. Terminal master's awarded for partial completion of doctoral program. *Degree requirements:* For master's, thesis

optional; for doctorate, thesis/dissertation. *Entrance requirements:* For doctorate, GRE General Test. Additional exam requirements/recommendations for international students: Required—TOEFL. Electronic applications accepted. *Faculty research:* Artificial intelligence, computational genomics, computer and systems architecture, media and machines, networking and communication, software systems.

Wayne State University, College of Engineering, Department of Electrical and Computer Engineering, Program in Computer Engineering, Detroit, MI 48202. Offers MS, PhD. *Students:* 27 full-time (4 women), 10 part-time (0 women); includes 3 minority (all Asian, non-Hispanic/Latino), 25 international. Average age 29. 56 applicants, 45% accepted, 8 enrolled. In 2011, 10 master's, 5 doctorates awarded. *Degree requirements:* For master's, thesis optional; for doctorate, thesis/dissertation. *Entrance requirements:* Additional exam requirements/recommendations for international students: Required—TOEFL (minimum score 550 paper-based; 213 computer-based), Michigan English Language Assessment Battery (minimum score 85); Recommended—TWE (minimum score 5.5). *Application deadline:* For fall admission, 6/1 priority date for domestic students, 5/1 for international students; for winter admission, 10/1 priority date for domestic students, 9/1 for international students; for spring admission, 2/1 priority date for domestic students, 1/1 for international students. Applications are processed on a rolling basis. Application fee: $50. Electronic applications accepted. *Expenses:* Tuition, state resident: part-time $512.85 per credit. Tuition, nonresident: part-time $1132.65 per credit. *Required fees:* $26.60 per credit. $199.65 per semester. Tuition and fees vary according to course load and program. *Financial support:* In 2011–12, 16 students received support. Fellowships with tuition reimbursements available, research assistantships with tuition reimbursements available, teaching assistantships with tuition reimbursements available, scholarships/grants, health care benefits, and unspecified assistantships available. Financial award application deadline: 3/16. *Faculty research:* Neural networks, parallel processing, pattern recognition, VLSI, computer architecture. *Unit head:* Yang Zhao, Chair, 313-577-3920, Fax: 313-577-1101, E-mail: aa3606@wayne.edu. *Application contact:* Pepe Siy, Graduate Director, 313-577-3841, Fax: 313-577-1101, E-mail: psiy@ece.eng.wayne.edu. Web site: http://www.eng.wayne.edu/page.php?id=62.

Western Michigan University, Graduate College, College of Engineering and Applied Sciences, Department of Electrical and Computer Engineering, Kalamazoo, MI 49008. Offers computer engineering (MSE); electrical and computer engineering (PhD); electrical engineering (MSE). Part-time programs available. *Degree requirements:* For master's, thesis optional. *Entrance requirements:* For master's, minimum GPA of 3.0. *Faculty research:* Fiber optics, computer architecture, bioelectromagnetics, acoustics.

West Virginia University, College of Engineering and Mineral Resources, Lane Department of Computer Science and Electrical Engineering, Program in Computer Engineering, Morgantown, WV 26506. Offers PhD. *Degree requirements:* For doctorate, comprehensive exam, thesis/dissertation. *Entrance requirements:* For doctorate, GRE General Test, minimum GPA of 3.0, letters of recommendation. Additional exam requirements/recommendations for international students: Required—TOEFL. *Faculty research:* Software engineering, microprocessor applications, microelectronic systems, fault tolerance, advanced computer architectures and networks.

Wichita State University, Graduate School, College of Engineering, Department of Electrical Engineering and Computer Science, Wichita, KS 67260. Offers computer networking (MS); computer science (MS); electrical engineering (MS, PhD). Part-time and evening/weekend programs available. *Expenses:* Tuition, state resident: full-time $4746; part-time $263.65 per credit. Tuition, nonresident: full-time $11,669; part-time $648.30 per credit. *Unit head:* Dr. John Watkins, Chair, 316-978-3156, Fax: 316-978-5408, E-mail: john.watkins@wichita.edu. *Application contact:* Carrie C. Henderson, Admissions Coordinator, 316-978-3095, Fax: 316-978-3253, E-mail: carrie.henderson@wichita.edu. Web site: http://www.wichita.edu/.

Widener University, Graduate Programs in Engineering, Program in Computer and Software Engineering, Chester, PA 19013-5792. Offers M Eng. Part-time and evening/weekend programs available. *Degree requirements:* For master's, thesis optional. *Faculty research:* Computer and software engineering, computer network fault-tolerant computing, optical computing.

Worcester Polytechnic Institute, Graduate Studies and Research, Department of Electrical and Computer Engineering, Worcester, MA 01609-2280. Offers electrical and computer engineering (Advanced Certificate, Graduate Certificate); electrical engineering (M Eng, MS, PhD). Part-time and evening/weekend programs available. *Faculty:* 16 full-time (0 women), 6 part-time/adjunct (2 women). *Students:* 101 full-time (28 women), 114 part-time (16 women); includes 28 minority (3 Black or African American, non-Hispanic/Latino; 16 Asian, non-Hispanic/Latino; 7 Hispanic/Latino; 2 Two or more races, non-Hispanic/Latino), 109 international. 636 applicants, 46% accepted, 101 enrolled. In 2011, 89 master's, 6 doctorates awarded. Terminal master's awarded for partial completion of doctoral program. *Degree requirements:* For master's, thesis optional; for doctorate, comprehensive exam, thesis/dissertation. *Entrance requirements:* For master's, 3 letters of recommendation; for doctorate, 3 letters of recommendation, statement of purpose. Additional exam requirements/recommendations for international students: Required—TOEFL (minimum score 563 paper-based; 223 computer-based; 84 iBT), IELTS (minimum score 7). *Application deadline:* For fall admission, 1/1 priority date for domestic students, 1/1 for international students; for spring admission, 10/1 priority date for domestic students, 10/1 for international students. Applications are processed on a rolling basis. Application fee: $70. Electronic applications accepted. *Financial support:* Research assistantships, teaching assistantships, career-related internships or fieldwork, institutionally sponsored loans, scholarships/grants, and unspecified assistantships available. Financial award application deadline: 1/1; financial award applicants required to submit FAFSA. *Faculty research:* Analog and mixed signal IC design, RF electronics and antenna design, computational modeling, cryptography, data and system security, networking and communication systems (including sw defined radios), biomedical signal processing and medical systems, indoor/outdoor localization and navigation systems. *Unit head:* Dr. Fred Looft, Department Head, 508-831-5231, Fax: 508-831-5491, E-mail: fjlooft@wpi.edu. *Application contact:* Dr. Reinhold Ludwig, Graduate Coordinator, 508-831-5231, Fax: 508-831-5491, E-mail: ludwig@wpi.edu. Web site: http://www.ece.wpi.edu/.

Wright State University, School of Graduate Studies, College of Engineering and Computer Science, Department of Computer Science and Engineering, Computer Engineering Program, Dayton, OH 45435. Offers MSCE. *Degree requirements:* For master's, thesis optional. *Entrance requirements:* For master's, GRE General Test, minimum GPA of 3.0 in major, 2.7 overall. Additional exam requirements/recommendations for international students: Required—TOEFL. *Faculty research:* Networking and digital communications, parallel and concurrent computing, robotics and control, computer vision, optical computing.

Wright State University, School of Graduate Studies, College of Engineering and Computer Science, Department of Computer Science and Engineering, Program in Computer Science and Engineering, Dayton, OH 45435. Offers PhD. *Degree requirements:* For doctorate, thesis/dissertation, candidacy and general exams. *Entrance requirements:* For doctorate, GRE General Test, minimum GPA of 3.3. Additional exam requirements/recommendations for international students: Required—TOEFL.

Youngstown State University, Graduate School, College of Science, Technology, Engineering and Mathematics, Department of Electrical and Computer Engineering, Youngstown, OH 44555-0001. Offers computer engineering (MSE); electrical engineering (MSE). Part-time and evening/weekend programs available. *Degree requirements:* For master's, thesis optional. *Entrance requirements:* For master's, minimum GPA of 2.75 in field. Additional exam requirements/recommendations for international students: Required—TOEFL. *Faculty research:* Computer-aided design, power systems, electromagnetic energy conversion, sensors, control systems.

Electrical Engineering

Air Force Institute of Technology, Graduate School of Engineering and Management, Department of Electrical and Computer Engineering, Dayton, OH 45433-7765. Offers computer engineering (MS, PhD); computer systems/science (MS); electrical engineering (MS, PhD); electro-optics (MS, PhD). *Accreditation:* ABET (one or more programs are accredited). Part-time programs available. *Degree requirements:* For master's, thesis; for doctorate, thesis/dissertation. *Entrance requirements:* For master's and doctorate, GRE General Test, minimum GPA of 3.0, U.S. citizenship. *Faculty research:* Remote sensing, information survivability, microelectronics, computer networks, artificial intelligence.

Alfred University, Graduate School, New York State College of Ceramics, School of Engineering, Alfred, NY 14802-1205. Offers biomedical materials engineering science (MS); ceramic engineering (MS); ceramics (PhD); electrical engineering (MS); glass science (MS, PhD); materials science and engineering (MS, PhD); mechanical engineering (MS). *Degree requirements:* For master's, thesis; for doctorate, thesis/dissertation. *Entrance requirements:* Additional exam requirements/recommendations for international students: Required—TOEFL (minimum score 590 paper-based; 243 computer-based). Electronic applications accepted. *Expenses:* Contact institution. *Faculty research:* Fine-particle technology, X-ray diffraction, superconductivity, electronic materials.

American University of Beirut, Graduate Programs, Faculty of Engineering and Architecture, Beirut, Lebanon. Offers applied energy (MME); civil engineering (ME, PhD); electrical and computer engineering (ME, PhD); engineering management (MEM); environmental and water resources (ME); environmental and water resources engineering (PhD); environmental technology (MSES); mechanical engineering (ME, PhD); urban design (MUD); urban planning and policy (MUP). Part-time programs available. *Faculty:* 53 full-time (8 women), 10 part-time/adjunct (2 women). *Students:* 290 full-time (101 women), 59 part-time (18 women). Average age 25. 336 applicants, 80% accepted, 83 enrolled. In 2011, 72 master's, 5 doctorates awarded. *Degree requirements:* For master's, one foreign language, comprehensive exam, thesis (for some programs); for doctorate, one foreign language, comprehensive exam, thesis/dissertation, publications. *Entrance requirements:* For master's, GRE (for electrical and computer engineering), letters of recommendation; for doctorate, GRE, letters of recommendation, master's degree, transcripts, curriculum vitae, interview. Additional exam requirements/recommendations for international students: Required—TOEFL (minimum score 600 paper-based; 250 computer-based; 100 iBT), IELTS (minimum score 7.5). *Application deadline:* For fall admission, 2/5 priority date for domestic students, 2/5 for international students; for spring admission, 11/1 priority date for domestic students, 11/1 for international students. Applications are processed on a rolling basis. Application fee: $50. Electronic applications accepted. *Expenses: Tuition:* Full-time $12,780; part-time $710 per credit. *Required fees:* $528; $528 per credit. Tuition and fees vary according to course load and program. *Financial support:* In 2011–12, 9 fellowships with full tuition reimbursements (averaging $24,800 per year), 83 research assistantships with full tuition reimbursements (averaging $24,800 per year), 74 teaching assistantships with full tuition reimbursements (averaging $9,800 per year) were awarded; career-related internships or fieldwork, institutionally sponsored loans, scholarships/grants, health care benefits, and unspecified assistantships also available. *Total annual research expenditures:* $1.1 million. *Unit head:* Prof. Makram T. Suidan, Dean, 961-135-0000 Ext. 3400, Fax: 961-174-4462, E-mail: msuidan@aub.edu.lb. *Application contact:* Dr. Salim Kanaan, Director, Admissions Office, 961-135-0000 Ext. 2594, Fax: 961-175-0775, E-mail: sk00@aub.edu.lb. Web site: http://staff.aub.edu.lb/~webfea.

American University of Sharjah, Graduate Programs, Sharjah, United Arab Emirates. Offers business (EMBA, GEMPA, MBA); chemical engineering (MS Ch E); civil engineering (MSCE); computer engineering (MS); electrical engineering (MSEE); mechanical engineering (MSME); mechatronics engineering (MS); public administration (MPA); teaching English to speakers of other languages (MA); translation and interpreting (MA); urban planning (MUP). Part-time and evening/weekend programs available. *Entrance requirements:* For master's, GMAT (MBA). Additional exam requirements/recommendations for international students: Required—TOEFL (minimum score 550 paper-based; 213 computer-based; 80 iBT), TWE (minimum score 5). Electronic applications accepted. *Faculty research:* Chemical engineering, civil engineering, computer engineering, electrical engineering, linguistics, translation.

Arizona State University, Ira A. Fulton School of Engineering, Department of Electrical Engineering, Tempe, AZ 85287-5706. Offers electrical engineering (MS, MSE, PhD); nuclear power generation (Graduate Certificate). Part-time and evening/weekend programs available. Postbaccalaureate distance learning degree programs offered (minimal on-campus study). Terminal master's awarded for partial completion of doctoral program. *Degree requirements:* For master's, thesis and defense (MS); comprehensive exams (MSE); interactive Program of Study (iPOS) submitted before completing 50 percent of required credit hours; for doctorate, comprehensive exam, thesis/dissertation, interactive Program of Study (iPOS) submitted before completing 50 percent of required credit hours. *Entrance requirements:* For master's, GRE, minimum GPA of 3.0 in last 2 years of work leading to bachelor's degree, 3.5 if from non-ABET accredited school; for doctorate, GRE, master's degree with minimum GPA of 3.5 or 3.6 in last 2 years of ABET-accredited undergraduate program. Additional exam requirements/recommendations for international students: Required—TOEFL (minimum score 80 iBT), TOEFL, IELTS, or Pearson Test of English. Electronic applications accepted. *Expenses:* Contact institution. *Faculty research:* Power and energy systems, signal processing and communications, solid state devices and modeling, wireless communications and circuits, photovoltaics, biosignatures discovery automation, flexible electronics, and nanostructures.

Auburn University, Graduate School, Ginn College of Engineering, Department of Electrical and Computer Engineering, Auburn University, AL 36849. Offers MEE, MS, PhD. Part-time programs available. *Faculty:* 28 full-time (2 women), 1 part-time/adjunct (0 women). *Students:* 105 full-time (21 women), 59 part-time (13 women); includes 9 minority (3 Black or African American, non-Hispanic/Latino; 4 Asian, non-Hispanic/Latino; 2 Hispanic/Latino), 118 international. Average age 26. 388 applicants, 57% accepted, 43 enrolled. In 2011, 29 master's, 11 doctorates awarded. *Degree requirements:* For master's, comprehensive exam, thesis (for some programs); for doctorate, thesis/dissertation. *Entrance requirements:* For master's and doctorate, GRE General Test, GRE Subject Test. *Application deadline:* For fall admission, 7/7 for domestic students; for spring admission, 11/24 for domestic students. Applications are processed on a rolling basis. Application fee: $50 ($60 for international students). Electronic applications accepted. *Expenses:* Tuition, state resident: full-time $7290; part-time $405 per credit hour. Tuition, nonresident: full-time $21,870; part-time $1215 per credit hour. *International tuition:* $22,000 full-time. *Required fees:* $1402. *Financial support:* Fellowships, research assistantships, teaching assistantships, and Federal Work-Study available. Support available to part-time students. Financial award application deadline: 3/15; financial award applicants required to submit FAFSA. *Faculty research:* Power systems, energy conversion, electronics, electromagnetics, digital systems. *Unit head:* Dr. Mark Nelms, Head, 334-844-1830. *Application contact:* Dr. George Flowers, Dean of the Graduate School, 334-844-2125. Web site: http://www.eng.auburn.edu/department/ee/.

Baylor University, Graduate School, School of Engineering and Computer Science, Department of Engineering, Waco, TX 76798. Offers biomedical engineering (MSBE); electrical and computer engineering (MSECE, PhD); engineering (ME); mechanical engineering (MSME). *Faculty:* 14 full-time (1 woman). *Students:* 25 full-time (2 women), 7 part-time (1 woman); includes 6 minority (2 Black or African American, non-Hispanic/Latino; 1 Asian, non-Hispanic/Latino; 1 Hispanic/Latino; 2 Two or more races, non-Hispanic/Latino), 6 international. In 2011, 19 master's awarded. *Unit head:* Dr. Mike Thompson, Graduate Director, 254-710-4188. *Application contact:* Linda Keer, Administrative Assistant, 254-710-4188, Fax: 254-710-3870, E-mail: linda_kerr@baylor.edu. Web site: http://www.ecs.baylor.edu/engineering.

Boise State University, Graduate College, College of Engineering, Department of Electrical and Computer Engineering, Boise, ID 83725-0399. Offers computer engineering (M Engr, MS); electrical and computer engineering (PhD); electrical engineering (M Engr, MS). Part-time and evening/weekend programs available. *Degree requirements:* For master's, thesis. *Entrance requirements:* For master's, GRE General Test, minimum GPA of 3.0. Additional exam requirements/recommendations for international students: Required—TOEFL. Electronic applications accepted.

Boston University, College of Engineering, Department of Electrical and Computer Engineering, Boston, MA 02215. Offers computer engineering (M Eng, MS, PhD); electrical engineering (M Eng, MS, PhD); photonics (M Eng, MS). Part-time programs available. *Faculty:* 40 full-time (3 women), 5 part-time/adjunct (0 women). *Students:* 221 full-time (43 women), 23 part-time (0 women); includes 21 minority (1 Black or African American, non-Hispanic/Latino; 1 American Indian or Alaska Native, non-Hispanic/Latino; 15 Asian, non-Hispanic/Latino; 2 Hispanic/Latino; 2 Two or more races, non-Hispanic/Latino), 165 international. Average age 25. 810 applicants, 25% accepted, 112 enrolled. In 2011, 56 master's, 21 doctorates awarded. Terminal master's awarded for partial completion of doctoral program. *Degree requirements:* For master's, thesis (for some programs); for doctorate, comprehensive exam, thesis/dissertation. *Entrance requirements:* For master's and doctorate, GRE General Test. Additional exam requirements/recommendations for international students: Required—TOEFL (minimum score 550 paper-based; 213 computer-based; 84 iBT), IELTS (minimum score 6.5). *Application deadline:* For fall admission, 3/15 for domestic and international students; for spring admission, 10/1 for domestic and international students. Applications are processed on a rolling basis. Application fee: $70. Electronic applications accepted. *Expenses: Tuition:* Full-time $40,848; part-time $1276 per credit hour. *Required fees:* $572; $286 per semester. *Financial support:* In 2011–12, 126 students received support, including 8 fellowships with full tuition reimbursements available (averaging $28,950 per year), 82 research assistantships with full tuition reimbursements available (averaging $19,300 per year), 18 teaching assistantships with full tuition reimbursements available (averaging $19,300 per year); career-related internships or fieldwork, Federal Work-Study, institutionally sponsored loans, scholarships/grants, traineeships, and health care benefits also available. Financial award application deadline: 1/15; financial award applicants required to submit FAFSA. *Faculty research:* Communications and computer networks; signal, image, video, and multimedia processing; solid-state materials, devices, and photonics; systems, control, and reliable computing; VLSI, computer engineering and high-performance computing. *Unit head:* Dr. David Castanon, Interim Chairman, 617-353-9880, Fax: 617-353-6440, E-mail: dac@bu.edu. *Application contact:* Stephen Doherty, Director of Graduate Programs, 617-353-9760, Fax: 617-353-0259, E-mail: enggrad@bu.edu. Web site: http://www.bu.edu/ece/.

Bradley University, Graduate School, College of Engineering and Technology, Department of Electrical Engineering, Peoria, IL 61625-0002. Offers MSEE. Part-time and evening/weekend programs available. *Degree requirements:* For master's, comprehensive exam. *Entrance requirements:* For master's, GRE, minimum GPA of 3.0. Additional exam requirements/recommendations for international students: Required—TOEFL (minimum score 550 paper-based; 213 computer-based; 79 iBT).

Brigham Young University, Graduate Studies, Ira A. Fulton College of Engineering and Technology, Department of Electrical and Computer Engineering, Provo, UT 84602. Offers MS, PhD. *Faculty:* 23 full-time (0 women). *Students:* 92 full-time (4 women); includes 6 minority (3 Asian, non-Hispanic/Latino; 3 Hispanic/Latino), 25 international. Average age 28. 41 applicants, 78% accepted, 19 enrolled. In 2011, 17 master's, 11 doctorates awarded. *Degree requirements:* For master's, thesis optional; for doctorate, comprehensive exam, thesis/dissertation. *Entrance requirements:* For master's and doctorate, GRE General Test, minimum GPA of 3.2 in last 60 hours of course work. Additional exam requirements/recommendations for international students: Required—TOEFL (minimum score 580 paper-based; 237 computer-based; 85 iBT). *Application deadline:* For fall admission, 1/15 for domestic and international students; for winter admission, 8/15 for domestic and international students. Application fee: $50. Electronic applications accepted. *Expenses: Tuition:* Full-time $5760; part-time $320 per credit. Tuition and fees vary according to student's religious affiliation. *Financial support:* In 2011–12, 74 students received support, including 6 fellowships with full tuition reimbursements available (averaging $19,500 per year), 54 research assistantships with full tuition reimbursements available (averaging $19,500 per year), 14 teaching assistantships with full tuition reimbursements available (averaging $19,500 per year); scholarships/grants also available. Financial award application deadline: 5/15; financial award applicants required to submit FAFSA. *Faculty research:* Microwave remote sensing, reconfigurable computing, microelectronics, wireless communications, computer architecture, biomedical imaging, bio-chemical sensing. *Total annual research expenditures:* $3.2 million. *Unit head:* Dr. Michael A. Jensen, Chair, 801-422-4012, Fax: 801-422-0201, E-mail: jensen@ee.byu.edu. *Application contact:* Janalyn L. Mergist, Graduate Secretary, 801-422-4013, Fax: 801-422-0201, E-mail: janalyn@ee.byu.edu. Web site: http://www.ee.byu.edu/.

Brown University, Graduate School, Division of Engineering, Program in Electrical Sciences and Computer Engineering, Providence, RI 02912. Offers Sc M, PhD. *Degree requirements:* For doctorate, thesis/dissertation, preliminary exam.

Bucknell University, Graduate Studies, College of Engineering, Department of Electrical Engineering, Lewisburg, PA 17837. Offers MSEE. Part-time programs available. *Faculty:* 9 full-time (1 woman). *Students:* 1 applicant, 0% accepted. *Degree requirements:* For master's, thesis. *Entrance requirements:* For master's, GRE General Test, minimum GPA of 3.0. Additional exam requirements/recommendations for international students: Required—TOEFL (minimum score 600 paper-based). *Application deadline:* For fall admission, 2/1 priority date for domestic students, 1/1 for international students. Application fee: $25. *Financial support:* Unspecified assistantships available. Financial award application deadline: 3/1. *Unit head:* Dr. Robert Nickel, Head, 570-577-1234. *Application contact:* Gretchen H. Fegley, Coordinator, 570-577-3655, Fax: 570-577-3760, E-mail: gfegley@bucknell.edu. Web site: http://www.bucknell.edu/.

California Institute of Technology, Division of Engineering and Applied Science, Option in Electrical Engineering, Pasadena, CA 91125-0001. Offers MS, PhD, Engr. *Degree requirements:* For doctorate, thesis/dissertation. Electronic applications accepted. *Faculty research:* Solid-state electronics, power electronics, communications, controls, submillimeter-wave integrated circuits.

California Polytechnic State University, San Luis Obispo, College of Engineering, Department of Electrical Engineering, San Luis Obispo, CA 93407. Offers MS. Part-time programs available. *Faculty:* 1 full-time (0 women), 1 part-time/adjunct (0 women). *Students:* 51 full-time (2 women), 14 part-time (1 woman); includes 32 minority (21 Asian, non-Hispanic/Latino; 9 Hispanic/Latino; 2 Two or more races, non-Hispanic/Latino), 5 international. Average age 25. 52 applicants, 65% accepted, 21 enrolled. In 2011, 31 master's awarded. *Degree requirements:* For master's, comprehensive exam (for some programs), thesis (for some programs). *Entrance requirements:* For master's, GRE General Test, minimum GPA of 3.0 in last 90 quarter units. Additional exam requirements/recommendations for international students: Required—TOEFL (minimum score 550 paper-based; 213 computer-based) or IELTS (minimum score 6). *Application deadline:* For fall admission, 7/1 for domestic students, 11/30 for international students; for winter admission, 11/1 for domestic students, 6/30 for international students; for spring admission, 2/1 for domestic students. Applications are processed on a rolling basis. Application fee: $55. Electronic applications accepted. *Expenses:* Tuition, state resident: full-time $6738. Tuition, nonresident: full-time $17,898. *Required fees:* $2449. *Financial support:* Fellowships, research assistantships, teaching assistantships, career-related internships or fieldwork, Federal Work-Study, scholarships/grants, and unspecified assistantships available. Support available to part-time students. Financial award application deadline: 3/2; financial award applicants required to submit FAFSA. *Faculty research:* Communications, systems design and analysis, control systems, electronic devices, microprocessors. *Unit head:* Dr. Dennis Derickson, Graduate Coordinator, 805-756-7584, Fax: 805-756-1456, E-mail: ddericks@calpoly.edu. *Application contact:* Dr. James Maraviglia, Associate Vice Provost for Marketing and Enrollment Development, 805-756-2311, Fax: 805-756-5400, E-mail: admissions@calpoly.edu. Web site: http://www.ee.calpoly.edu/.

California State Polytechnic University, Pomona, Academic Affairs, College of Engineering, Program in Electrical Engineering, Pomona, CA 91768-2557. Offers MSEE. *Students:* 14 full-time (1 woman), 56 part-time (6 women); includes 42 minority (1 American Indian or Alaska Native, non-Hispanic/Latino; 28 Asian, non-Hispanic/Latino; 12 Hispanic/Latino; 1 Two or more races, non-Hispanic/Latino), 9 international. Average age 32. 106 applicants, 43% accepted, 24 enrolled. In 2011, 38 master's awarded. *Application deadline:* Applications are processed on a rolling basis. Application fee: $55. Electronic applications accepted. *Expenses:* Tuition, state resident: full-time $6738. Tuition, nonresident: full-time $12,300. *Required fees:* $657. Tuition and fees vary according to course load and program. *Unit head:* Dr. Zekeriya Aliyazicioglu, Graduate Coordinator, 909-869-4609, E-mail: zaliyazici@csupomona.edu. *Application contact:* Deborah L. Brandon, Executive Director, Admissions and Outreach, 909-869-3427, Fax: 909-869-5315, E-mail: dlbrandon@csupomona.edu. Web site: http://www.csupomona.edu/~ece/msee.

California State University, Chico, Office of Graduate Studies, College of Engineering, Computer Science, and Technology, Department of Electrical and Computer Engineering, Option in Electronics Engineering, Chico, CA 95929-0722. Offers MS. *Faculty:* 2 full-time (0 women). *Students:* 6 full-time (2 women), 12 part-time (1 woman), 15 international. Average age 24. 29 applicants, 66% accepted, 7 enrolled. In 2011, 2 master's awarded. *Degree requirements:* For master's, thesis or project plan. *Entrance requirements:* For master's, GRE General Test, 2 letters of recommendation, statement of purpose, resume. Additional exam requirements/recommendations for international students: Required—TOEFL (minimum score 550 paper-based; 213 computer-based; 80 iBT), IELTS (minimum score 6.5), Pearson Test of English (minimum score 59). *Application deadline:* For fall admission, 3/1 priority date for domestic students, 3/1 for international students; for spring admission, 9/15 priority date for domestic students, 9/15 for international students. Application fee: $55. Electronic applications accepted. Tuition and fees vary according to class time, course load and degree level. *Unit head:* Dr. Ben Juliano, Interim Chair, 530-898-5343, Fax: 530-898-4956, E-mail: elce@csuchico.edu. *Application contact:* Judy L. Rice, Graduate Admissions Coordinator, 530-898-5416, Fax: 530-898-3342, E-mail: jlrice@csuchico.edu.

California State University, Fresno, Division of Graduate Studies, College of Engineering and Computer Science, Program in Electrical Engineering, Fresno, CA 93740-8027. Offers MS. Offered at Edwards Air Force Base. Part-time and evening/weekend programs available. *Degree requirements:* For master's, thesis or alternative. *Entrance requirements:* For master's, GRE General Test, minimum GPA of 2.7. Additional exam requirements/recommendations for international students: Required—

TOEFL. Electronic applications accepted. *Faculty research:* Research in electromagnetic devices.

California State University, Fullerton, Graduate Studies, College of Engineering and Computer Science, Department of Electrical Engineering, Fullerton, CA 92834-9480. Offers electrical engineering (MS); systems engineering (MS). Part-time programs available. *Students:* 52 full-time (12 women), 89 part-time (18 women); includes 46 minority (3 Black or African American, non-Hispanic/Latino; 37 Asian, non-Hispanic/Latino; 5 Hispanic/Latino; 1 Two or more races, non-Hispanic/Latino), 62 international. Average age 27. 264 applicants, 75% accepted, 35 enrolled. In 2011, 67 master's awarded. *Degree requirements:* For master's, comprehensive exam, project or thesis. *Entrance requirements:* For master's, GRE General Test, GRE Subject Test, minimum undergraduate GPA of 2.5, 3.0 graduate. Application fee: $55. *Financial support:* Career-related internships or fieldwork, Federal Work-Study, institutionally sponsored loans, and scholarships/grants available. Support available to part-time students. Financial award application deadline: 3/1; financial award applicants required to submit FAFSA. *Unit head:* Dr. Mostafa Shiva, Chair, 657-278-3013. *Application contact:* Admissions/Applications, 657-278-2371.

California State University, Long Beach, Graduate Studies, College of Engineering, Department of Electrical Engineering, Long Beach, CA 90840. Offers MSEE. Part-time programs available. *Faculty:* 13 full-time (1 woman), 3 part-time/adjunct (0 women). *Students:* 78 full-time (12 women), 82 part-time (13 women); includes 69 minority (6 Black or African American, non-Hispanic/Latino; 41 Asian, non-Hispanic/Latino; 17 Hispanic/Latino; 4 Native Hawaiian or other Pacific Islander, non-Hispanic/Latino; 1 Two or more races, non-Hispanic/Latino), 60 international. Average age 28. 293 applicants, 74% accepted, 63 enrolled. In 2011, 98 master's awarded. *Degree requirements:* For master's, comprehensive exam or thesis. *Entrance requirements:* Additional exam requirements/recommendations for international students: Required—TOEFL. *Application deadline:* For fall admission, 3/1 for domestic students. Application fee: $55. Electronic applications accepted. *Financial support:* Teaching assistantships, career-related internships or fieldwork, Federal Work-Study, institutionally sponsored loans, scholarships/grants, and unspecified assistantships available. Financial award application deadline: 3/2. *Faculty research:* Health care systems, VLSI, communications, CAD/CAM. *Unit head:* Dr. Bahram Shahian, Chair, 562-985-8041, Fax: 562-985-5327, E-mail: shahian@csulb.edu. *Application contact:* Dr. Fumio Hamano, Graduate Adviser, 562-985-7580, Fax: 562-985-5327, E-mail: fhamano@csulb.edu.

California State University, Los Angeles, Graduate Studies, College of Engineering, Computer Science, and Technology, Department of Electrical and Computer Engineering, Los Angeles, CA 90032-8530. Offers electrical engineering (MS). Part-time and evening/weekend programs available. *Faculty:* 1 full-time (0 women), 7 part-time/adjunct (3 women). *Students:* 44 full-time (10 women), 82 part-time (8 women); includes 75 minority (10 Black or African American, non-Hispanic/Latino; 1 American Indian or Alaska Native, non-Hispanic/Latino; 31 Asian, non-Hispanic/Latino; 32 Hispanic/Latino; 1 Native Hawaiian or other Pacific Islander, non-Hispanic/Latino), 31 international. Average age 30. 99 applicants, 60% accepted, 38 enrolled. In 2011, 112 master's awarded. *Degree requirements:* For master's, comprehensive exam or thesis. *Entrance requirements:* For master's, GRE General Test, GRE Subject Test. Additional exam requirements/recommendations for international students: Required—TOEFL (minimum score 550 paper-based). *Application deadline:* For fall admission, 5/1 for domestic and international students. Applications are processed on a rolling basis. Application fee: $55. Electronic applications accepted. *Expenses:* Tuition, state resident: full-time $8225. *Financial support:* Federal Work-Study available. Support available to part-time students. Financial award application deadline: 3/1. *Unit head:* Dr. Fred Daneshgaran, Chair, 323-343-4470, Fax: 323-343-4547, E-mail: fdanesh@calstatela.edu. *Application contact:* Dr. Karin Brown, Acting Associate Dean of Graduate Studies, 323-343-3820, Fax: 323-343-5653, E-mail: kbrown5@calstatela.edu. Web site: http://www.calstatela.edu/academic/ecst/ee/.

California State University, Northridge, Graduate Studies, College of Engineering and Computer Science, Department of Electrical and Computer Engineering, Northridge, CA 91330. Offers electrical engineering (MS). Part-time and evening/weekend programs available. *Degree requirements:* For master's, thesis or alternative. *Entrance requirements:* For master's, GRE General Test, minimum GPA of 2.75. Additional exam requirements/recommendations for international students: Required—TOEFL. *Faculty research:* Reflector antenna study.

California State University, Sacramento, Office of Graduate Studies, College of Engineering and Computer Science, Department of Electrical and Electronic Engineering, Sacramento, CA 95819-6019. Offers electrical engineering (MS). Part-time and evening/weekend programs available. *Faculty:* 14 full-time (3 women), 6 part-time/adjunct (3 women). *Students:* 52 full-time, 46 part-time; includes 22 minority (4 Black or African American, non-Hispanic/Latino; 12 Asian, non-Hispanic/Latino; 3 Hispanic/Latino; 1 Native Hawaiian or other Pacific Islander, non-Hispanic/Latino; 2 Two or more races, non-Hispanic/Latino), 59 international. Average age 24. 127 applicants, 69% accepted, 35 enrolled. In 2011, 117 master's awarded. *Degree requirements:* For master's, thesis or comprehensive exam, writing proficiency exam. *Entrance requirements:* Additional exam requirements/recommendations for international students: Required—TOEFL. *Application deadline:* For fall admission, 3/1 for domestic and international students; for spring admission, 9/15 for domestic students, 9/30 for international students. Applications are processed on a rolling basis. Application fee: $55. Electronic applications accepted. *Financial support:* Research assistantships, teaching assistantships, career-related internships or fieldwork, and Federal Work-Study available. Support available to part-time students. Financial award application deadline: 3/1; financial award applicants required to submit FAFSA. *Unit head:* Dr. Suresh Vadhva, Chair, 916-278-7944, Fax: 916-278-7215, E-mail: vadhva@csus.edu. *Application contact:* Jose Martinez, Outreach and Graduate Diversity Coordinator, 916-278-6470, Fax: 916-278-5669, E-mail: martinj@skymail.csus.edu. Web site: http://www.ecs.csus.edu/eee.

Capitol College, Graduate Programs, Laurel, MD 20708-9759. Offers business administration (MBA); computer science (MS); electrical engineering (MS); information and telecommunications systems management (MS); information architecture (MS); network security (MS). Part-time and evening/weekend programs available. Postbaccalaureate distance learning degree programs offered (no on-campus study). *Entrance requirements:* For master's, minimum GPA of 3.0. Electronic applications accepted.

Carleton University, Faculty of Graduate Studies, Faculty of Engineering and Design, Ottawa-Carleton Institute for Electrical Engineering, Department of Electronics, Ottawa, ON K1S 5B6, Canada. Offers electrical engineering (M Eng, MA Sc, PhD). *Degree requirements:* For master's, thesis optional; for doctorate, comprehensive exam, thesis/dissertation. *Entrance requirements:* For master's, honors degree; for doctorate, MA Sc or M Eng. Additional exam requirements/recommendations for international students: Required—TOEFL.

Carleton University, Faculty of Graduate Studies, Faculty of Engineering and Design, Ottawa-Carleton Institute for Electrical Engineering, Department of Systems and Computer Engineering, Ottawa, ON K1S 5B6, Canada. Offers electrical engineering (MA Sc, PhD); information and systems science (M Sc); technology innovation management (M Eng, MA Sc). PhD program offered jointly with University of Ottawa. *Degree requirements:* For master's, thesis optional. *Entrance requirements:* For master's, honors degree. Additional exam requirements/recommendations for international students: Required—TOEFL. *Faculty research:* Design manufacturing management; network design, protocols, and performance; software engineering; wireless and satellite communications.

Carnegie Mellon University, Carnegie Institute of Technology, Department of Electrical and Computer Engineering, Pittsburgh, PA 15213-3891. Offers MS, PhD. Part-time programs available. *Degree requirements:* For master's, thesis; for doctorate, thesis/dissertation, qualifying exam, teaching experience. *Entrance requirements:* For master's and doctorate, GRE General Test. Additional exam requirements/recommendations for international students: Required—TOEFL. *Faculty research:* Computer-aided design, solid-state devices, VLSI, processing, robotics and controls, signal processing, data systems storage.

Case Western Reserve University, School of Graduate Studies, Case School of Engineering, Department of Electrical Engineering and Computer Science, Cleveland, OH 44106. Offers computer engineering (MS, PhD); computing and information sciences (MS, PhD); electrical engineering (MS, PhD); systems and control engineering (MS, PhD). Part-time and evening/weekend programs available. Postbaccalaureate distance learning degree programs offered (minimal on-campus study). *Faculty:* 33 full-time (3 women). *Students:* 188 full-time (34 women), 22 part-time (4 women); includes 6 minority (3 Black or African American, non-Hispanic/Latino; 3 Asian, non-Hispanic/Latino), 132 international. In 2011, 30 master's, 22 doctorates awarded. Terminal master's awarded for partial completion of doctoral program. *Degree requirements:* For master's, thesis; for doctorate, thesis/dissertation, qualifying exam, teaching experience. *Entrance requirements:* For master's and doctorate, GRE General Test. Additional exam requirements/recommendations for international students: Required—TOEFL. *Application deadline:* For fall admission, 2/1 for domestic students; for spring admission, 11/1 for domestic students. Applications are processed on a rolling basis. Application fee: $50. *Financial support:* Fellowships with full and partial tuition reimbursements, research assistantships with full and partial tuition reimbursements, teaching assistantships, career-related internships or fieldwork, Federal Work-Study, and institutionally sponsored loans available. Support available to part-time students. Financial award application deadline: 3/1; financial award applicants required to submit FAFSA. *Faculty research:* Applied artificial intelligence, automation, computer-aided design and testing of digital systems. *Total annual research expenditures:* $6 million. *Unit head:* Dr. Michael Branicky, Department Chair, 216-368-6888, E-mail: branicky@case.edu. *Application contact:* David Easler, Student Affairs Coordinator, 216-368-4080, Fax: 216-368-2801, E-mail: david.easler@case.edu. Web site: http://eecs.cwru.edu/.

The Catholic University of America, School of Engineering, Department of Electrical Engineering and Computer Science, Washington, DC 20064. Offers MEE, MSCS, D Engr, PhD. Part-time programs available. *Faculty:* 10 full-time (3 women), 13 part-time/adjunct (1 woman). *Students:* 14 full-time (3 women), 38 part-time (10 women); includes 9 minority (3 Black or African American, non-Hispanic/Latino; 3 Asian, non-Hispanic/Latino; 3 Hispanic/Latino), 19 international. Average age 33. 38 applicants, 47% accepted, 6 enrolled. In 2011, 13 master's, 4 doctorates awarded. *Degree requirements:* For master's, thesis or alternative; for doctorate, comprehensive exam, thesis/dissertation, oral exams. *Entrance requirements:* For master's and doctorate, statement of purpose, official copies of academic transcripts, three letters of recommendation. Additional exam requirements/recommendations for international students: Required—TOEFL (minimum score 580 paper-based; 237 computer-based). *Application deadline:* For fall admission, 8/1 priority date for domestic students, 7/15 for international students; for spring admission, 12/1 priority date for domestic students, 10/15 for international students. Applications are processed on a rolling basis. Application fee: $55. Electronic applications accepted. *Expenses:* Contact institution. *Financial support:* Fellowships, research assistantships, teaching assistantships, Federal Work-Study, scholarships/grants, tuition waivers (full and partial), and unspecified assistantships available. Financial award application deadline: 2/1; financial award applicants required to submit FAFSA. *Faculty research:* Signal and image processing, computer communications, robotics, intelligent controls, bioelectromagnetics. *Total annual research expenditures:* $443,436. *Unit head:* Dr. Phillip Regalia, Chair, 202-319-5879, Fax: 202-319-5195, E-mail: regalia@cua.edu. *Application contact:* Andrew Woodall, Director of Graduate Admissions, 202-319-5057, Fax: 202-319-6533, E-mail: cua-admissions@cua.edu. Web site: http://eecs.cua.edu/.

City College of the City University of New York, Graduate School, Grove School of Engineering, Department of Electrical Engineering, New York, NY 10031-9198. Offers ME, MS, PhD. PhD program offered jointly with Graduate School and University Center of the City University of New York. Part-time programs available. *Degree requirements:* For master's, thesis optional; for doctorate, one foreign language, comprehensive exam, thesis/dissertation. *Entrance requirements:* For master's and doctorate, GRE General Test. Additional exam requirements/recommendations for international students: Required—TOEFL (minimum score 500 paper-based; 173 computer-based; 61 iBT). *Faculty research:* Optical electronics, microwaves, communication, signal processing, control systems.

Clarkson University, Graduate School, Wallace H. Coulter School of Engineering, Department of Electrical and Computer Engineering, Potsdam, NY 13699. Offers electrical and computer engineering (PhD); electrical engineering (ME, MS). Part-time programs available. *Faculty:* 22 full-time (5 women), 1 (woman) part-time/adjunct. *Students:* 41 full-time (5 women), 2 part-time (1 woman); includes 3 minority (1 Asian, non-Hispanic/Latino; 2 Hispanic/Latino), 16 international. Average age 28. 72 applicants, 88% accepted, 13 enrolled. In 2011, 12 master's, 6 doctorates awarded. Terminal master's awarded for partial completion of doctoral program. *Degree requirements:* For master's, thesis; for doctorate, comprehensive exam, thesis/dissertation, departmental qualifying exam. *Entrance requirements:* For master's and doctorate, GRE, transcripts of all college coursework, resume, personal statement, three letters of recommendation. Additional exam requirements/recommendations for international students: Required—TOEFL (minimum score 550 paper-based; 213 computer-based; 80 iBT), IELTS (minimum score 6.5). *Application deadline:* For fall admission, 1/30 priority date for domestic students, 1/30 for international students; for spring admission, 9/1 priority date for domestic students, 9/1 for international students. Applications are processed on a rolling basis. Application fee: $25 ($35 for international students). Electronic applications accepted. *Expenses: Tuition:* Full-time $14,376; part-time $1198 per credit hour. *Required fees:* $295 per semester. *Financial support:* In 2011–12, 33 students received support, including 3 fellowships with full tuition reimbursements available (averaging $21,999 per year), 14 research assistantships with full tuition reimbursements available (averaging $21,999 per year), 13 teaching assistantships with full tuition reimbursements available (averaging $21,999 per year); scholarships/grants, tuition waivers (partial), and unspecified assistantships also available. *Faculty research:* Thoracic biometrics, hybrid lidar, microwave frequency, biometrics, DNA sample analysis. *Total annual research expenditures:* $1.3 million. *Unit head:* Dr. William Jemison, Chair, 315-268-7648, Fax: 315-268-7600, E-mail: wjemison@clarkson.edu. *Application contact:* Kelly Sharlow, Assistant to the Dean, 315-268-7929, Fax: 315-268-4494, E-mail: ksharlow@clarkson.edu. Web site: http://www.clarkson.edu/ece/.

Clemson University, Graduate School, College of Engineering and Science, Department of Electrical and Computer Engineering, Program in Electrical Engineering, Clemson, SC 29634. Offers M Engr, MS, PhD. *Students:* 111 full-time (26 women), 7 part-time (1 woman); includes 8 minority (4 Black or African American, non-Hispanic/Latino; 4 Asian, non-Hispanic/Latino), 82 international. Average age 27. 604 applicants, 22% accepted, 37 enrolled. In 2011, 19 master's, 8 doctorates awarded. *Degree requirements:* For master's, thesis or alternative; for doctorate, thesis/dissertation, departmental qualifying exam. *Entrance requirements:* For master's, GRE General Test (MS); for doctorate, GRE General Test. Additional exam requirements/recommendations for international students: Required—TOEFL. *Application deadline:* For fall admission, 6/1 for domestic students, 4/15 for international students; for spring admission, 9/15 for international students. Applications are processed on a rolling basis. Application fee: $70 ($80 for international students). Electronic applications accepted. *Financial support:* In 2011–12, 82 students received support, including 6 fellowships with full and partial tuition reimbursements available (averaging $3,590 per year), 44 research assistantships with partial tuition reimbursements available (averaging $13,336 per year), 64 teaching assistantships with partial tuition reimbursements available (averaging $7,029 per year); career-related internships or fieldwork, institutionally sponsored loans, scholarships/grants, health care benefits, and unspecified assistantships also available. Support available to part-time students. Financial award applicants required to submit FAFSA. *Faculty research:* Microelectronics, robotics, signal processing/communications, power systems, control. *Unit head:* Dr. Darren Dawson, Chair, 864-656-5249, Fax: 864-656-5917, E-mail: ddarren@clemson.edu. *Application contact:* Dr. Daniel Noneaker, 864-656-0100, Fax: 864-656-5917, E-mail: ece-grad-program@ces.clemson.edu. Web site: http://www.clemson.edu/ces/departments/ece/index.html.

Cleveland State University, College of Graduate Studies, Fenn College of Engineering, Department of Electrical and Computer Engineering, Cleveland, OH 44115. Offers electrical engineering (MS, D Eng); software engineering (MS). Part-time and evening/weekend programs available. *Faculty:* 15 full-time (2 women), 1 part-time/adjunct (0 women). *Students:* 14 full-time (4 women), 187 part-time (35 women); includes 13 minority (4 Black or African American, non-Hispanic/Latino; 8 Asian, non-Hispanic/Latino; 1 Hispanic/Latino), 146 international. Average age 27. 372 applicants, 63% accepted, 41 enrolled. In 2011, 63 master's, 1 doctorate awarded. *Degree requirements:* For master's, thesis optional; for doctorate, thesis/dissertation, qualifying and candidacy exams. *Entrance requirements:* For master's, GRE General Test (minimum score 650 quantitative), minimum GPA of 2.75; for doctorate, GRE General Test (minimum quantitative score in 80th percentile), minimum GPA of 3.25. Additional exam requirements/recommendations for international students: Required—TOEFL (minimum score 535 paper-based; 197 computer-based; 65 iBT) or IELTS (minimum score 6.0). *Application deadline:* For fall admission, 7/15 priority date for domestic students. Applications are processed on a rolling basis. Application fee: $30. *Expenses:* Contact institution. *Financial support:* In 2011–12, 31 students received support, including 23 research assistantships with full and partial tuition reimbursements available (averaging $4,242 per year), 8 teaching assistantships with full and partial tuition reimbursements available (averaging $4,242 per year); career-related internships or fieldwork, scholarships/grants, and unspecified assistantships also available. *Faculty research:* Computer networks, computer security and privacy, mobile computing, distributed computing, software engineering, knowledge-based control systems, artificial intelligence, digital communications, MEMS, sensors, power systems, power electronics. *Total annual research expenditures:* $484,362. *Unit head:* Dr. Fuqin Xiong, Chairperson, 216-687-2127, E-mail: f.xiong@csuohio.edu. *Application contact:* Deborah L. Brown, Interim Assistant Director, Graduate Admissions, 216-523-7572, Fax: 216-687-9214, E-mail: d.l.brown@csuohio.edu. Web site: http://www.csuohio.edu/ece.

Colorado State University, Graduate School, College of Engineering, Department of Electrical and Computer Engineering, Fort Collins, CO 80523-1373. Offers electrical engineering (MEE, MS, PhD). Part-time and evening/weekend programs available. Postbaccalaureate distance learning degree programs offered (no on-campus study). *Faculty:* 24 full-time (3 women), 1 part-time/adjunct (0 women). *Students:* 63 full-time (7 women), 90 part-time (20 women); includes 11 minority (2 Asian, non-Hispanic/Latino; 6 Hispanic/Latino; 3 Two or more races, non-Hispanic/Latino), 96 international. Average age 27. 157 applicants, 49% accepted, 34 enrolled. In 2011, 14 master's, 1 doctorate awarded. Terminal master's awarded for partial completion of doctoral program. *Degree requirements:* For master's, comprehensive exam (for some programs), thesis (for some programs), final exam; for doctorate, comprehensive exam, thesis/dissertation, qualifying, preliminary, and final exams. *Entrance requirements:* For master's, GRE General Test, minimum GPA of 3.5, BA/BS from ABET-accredited institution, 3 letters of recommendation; for doctorate, GRE General Test, minimum GPA of 3.5, transcripts, 3 letters of recommendation, statement of purpose. Additional exam requirements/recommendations for international students: Required—TOEFL (minimum score 550 paper-based; 213 computer-based; 80 iBT); Recommended—IELTS (minimum score 6). *Application deadline:* For fall admission, 2/1 priority date for domestic students, 2/1 for international students; for spring admission, 9/1 priority date for domestic students, 9/1 for international students. Applications are processed on a rolling basis. Application fee: $50. Electronic applications accepted. *Expenses:* Tuition, state resident: full-time $7992. Tuition, nonresident: full-time $19,592. *Required fees:* $1735; $58 per credit. *Financial support:* In 2011–12, 80 students received support, including 9 fellowships (averaging $29,389 per year), 59 research assistantships with tuition reimbursements available (averaging $18,089 per year), 12 teaching assistantships with tuition reimbursements available (averaging $8,159 per year); unspecified assistantships also available. Financial award application deadline: 2/1; financial award applicants required to submit FAFSA. *Faculty research:* Communications, optoelectronics, controls and robotics, computer engineering, biomedical engineering. *Total annual research expenditures:* $12.6 million. *Unit head:* Dr. Anthony A. Maciejewski, Head, 970-491-6600, Fax: 970-491-2249, E-mail: aam@engr.colostate.edu. *Application contact:* Karen Ungerer, Academic Advisor, 970-491-0500, Fax: 970-491-2249, E-mail: karen.ungerer@colostate.edu. Web site: http://www.engr.colostate.edu/ece/.

Colorado Technical University Colorado Springs, Graduate Studies, Program in Electrical Engineering, Colorado Springs, CO 80907-3896. Offers MSEE. Part-time and evening/weekend programs available. Postbaccalaureate distance learning degree programs offered. *Degree requirements:* For master's, thesis or alternative. *Faculty research:* Electronic systems design, communication systems design.

Colorado Technical University Denver South, Program in Electrical Engineering, Aurora, CO 80014. Offers MS.

Columbia University, The Fu Foundation School of Engineering and Applied Science, Department of Electrical Engineering, New York, NY 10027. Offers computer engineering (MS); electrical engineering (MS, Eng Sc D, PhD, Engr); solid state science and engineering (MS, Eng Sc D, PhD). PhD offered through the Graduate School of Arts and Sciences. Part-time programs available. Postbaccalaureate distance learning degree programs offered (no on-campus study). *Faculty:* 27 full-time (1 woman), 15 part-time/adjunct (1 woman). *Students:* 336 full-time (74 women), 155 part-time (38 women); includes 36 minority (2 Black or African American, non-Hispanic/Latino; 1 American Indian or Alaska Native, non-Hispanic/Latino; 26 Asian, non-Hispanic/Latino; 2 Hispanic/Latino; 5 Two or more races, non-Hispanic/Latino), 375 international. Average age 26. 1,385 applicants, 37% accepted, 250 enrolled. In 2011, 117 master's, 17 doctorates, 2 other advanced degrees awarded. *Degree requirements:* For doctorate, thesis/dissertation, qualifying exam. *Entrance requirements:* For master's, doctorate, and Engr, GRE General Test. Additional exam requirements/recommendations for international students: Required—TOEFL, IELTS. *Application deadline:* For fall admission, 12/1 priority date for domestic students, 12/1 for international students; for spring admission, 10/1 priority date for domestic students, 10/1 for international students. Application fee: $95. Electronic applications accepted. *Financial support:* In 2011–12, 99 students received support, including 8 fellowships with full tuition reimbursements available (averaging $35,000 per year), 66 research assistantships with full tuition reimbursements available (averaging $31,133 per year), 25 teaching assistantships with full tuition reimbursements available (averaging $31,133 per year); health care benefits also available. Financial award application deadline: 12/1; financial award applicants required to submit FAFSA. *Faculty research:* Media informatics and signal processing, integrated circuits and cyberphysical systems, communications systems and networking, nanoscale electronics and photonics, systems biology and neuroengineering. *Unit head:* Dr. Keren Bergman, Professor and Department Chair, 212-854-2280, Fax: 212-854-0300, E-mail: bergman@ee.columbia.edu. *Application contact:* Michal Zussman, Staff Associate, 212-854-3105, Fax: 212-932-9421, E-mail: mz2344@columbia.edu. Web site: http://www.ee.columbia.edu/.

See Display on next page and Close-Up on page 397.

Concordia University, School of Graduate Studies, Faculty of Engineering and Computer Science, Department of Electrical and Computer Engineering, Montréal, QC H3G 1M8, Canada. Offers M Eng, MA Sc, PhD. *Degree requirements:* For master's, thesis optional; for doctorate, comprehensive exam, thesis/dissertation. *Faculty research:* Computer communications and protocols, circuits and systems, graph theory, VLSI systems, microelectronics.

Cooper Union for the Advancement of Science and Art, Albert Nerken School of Engineering, New York, NY 10003-7120. Offers chemical engineering (ME); civil engineering (ME); electrical engineering (ME); mechanical engineering (ME). Part-time programs available. *Faculty:* 27 full-time (1 woman), 15 part-time/adjunct (2 women). *Students:* 39 full-time (10 women), 17 part-time (3 women); includes 18 minority (1 Black or African American, non-Hispanic/Latino; 1 American Indian or Alaska Native, non-Hispanic/Latino; 15 Asian, non-Hispanic/Latino; 1 Hispanic/Latino), 11 international. *Degree requirements:* For master's, thesis. *Entrance requirements:* For master's, GRE, BE, minimum GPA of 3.5. Additional exam requirements/recommendations for international students: Required—TOEFL (minimum score 600 paper-based; 250 computer-based; 100 iBT). *Application deadline:* For fall admission, 2/15 for domestic and international students. Application fee: $65. *Expenses: Tuition:* Full-time $37,500. *Required fees:* $825 per semester. *Financial support:* Fellowships with full tuition reimbursements, career-related internships or fieldwork, Federal Work-Study, tuition waivers (full), and full-tuition scholarships for all admitted students available. Support available to part-time students. Financial award application deadline: 5/1; financial award applicants required to submit CSS PROFILE or FAFSA. *Faculty research:* Civil infrastructure, imaging and sensing technology, biomedical engineering, encryption technology, process engineering. *Unit head:* Dr. Simon Ben-Avi, Acting Dean, 212-353-4286, E-mail: benavi@cooper.edu. *Application contact:* Student Contact, 212-353-4120, E-mail: admissions@cooper.edu. Web site: http://cooper.edu/engineering.

Cornell University, Graduate School, Graduate Fields of Engineering, Field of Electrical and Computer Engineering, Ithaca, NY 14853. Offers computer engineering (M Eng, PhD); electrical engineering (M Eng, PhD); electrical systems (M Eng, PhD); electrophysics (M Eng, PhD). *Faculty:* 61 full-time (5 women). *Students:* 235 full-time (52 women); includes 26 minority (3 Black or African American, non-Hispanic/Latino; 18 Asian, non-Hispanic/Latino; 5 Hispanic/Latino), 165 international. Average age 26. 1,234 applicants, 25% accepted, 111 enrolled. In 2011, 94 master's, 19 doctorates awarded. *Degree requirements:* For doctorate, comprehensive exam, thesis/dissertation. *Entrance requirements:* For master's, GRE General Test, 2 letters of recommendation; for doctorate, GRE General Test, 3 letters of recommendation. Additional exam requirements/recommendations for international students: Required—TOEFL (minimum score 600 paper-based; 250 computer-based; 77 iBT). *Application deadline:* For fall admission, 1/15 priority date for domestic students. Application fee: $70. Electronic applications accepted. *Financial support:* In 2011–12, 150 students received support, including 38 fellowships with full tuition reimbursements available, 94 research assistantships with full tuition reimbursements available, 19 teaching assistantships with full tuition reimbursements available; institutionally sponsored loans, scholarships/grants, health care benefits, tuition waivers (full and partial), and unspecified assistantships also available. Financial award applicants required to submit FAFSA. *Faculty research:* Communications, information theory, signal processing and power control, computer engineering, microelectromechanical systems and nanotechnology. *Unit head:* Director of Graduate Studies, 607-255-4304. *Application contact:* Graduate Field Assistant, 607-255-4304, E-mail: meng@ece.cornell.edu. Web site: http://www.gradschool.cornell.edu/fields.php?id-29&a-2.

Dalhousie University, Faculty of Engineering, Department of Electrical and Computer Engineering, Halifax, NS B3J 1Z1, Canada. Offers M Eng, MA Sc, PhD. *Degree requirements:* For master's, thesis; for doctorate, thesis/dissertation. *Entrance requirements:* Additional exam requirements/recommendations for international students: Required—TOEFL, IELTS, CANTEST, CAEL, or Michigan English Language Assessment Battery. Electronic applications accepted. *Faculty research:* Communications, computer engineering, power engineering, electronics, systems engineering.

Dartmouth College, Thayer School of Engineering, Program in Electrical Engineering, Hanover, NH 03755. Offers MS, PhD. *Degree requirements:* For master's, thesis; for doctorate, thesis/dissertation, candidacy oral exam. *Entrance requirements:* For master's and doctorate, GRE General Test. *Application deadline:* For fall admission, 1/1 priority date for domestic students. Application fee: $40 ($50 for international students). *Financial support:* Career-related internships or fieldwork, Federal Work-Study, institutionally sponsored loans, and tuition waivers (full and partial) available. Financial award application deadline: 1/15. *Faculty research:* Power electronics and microengineering, signal/image processing and communications, optics, lasers and optoelectronics, electromagnetic fields and waves. *Unit head:* Dr. Joseph J. Helbie, Dean, 603-646-2238, Fax: 603-646-2580, E-mail: joseph.j.helbie@dartmouth.edu. *Application contact:* Candace S. Potter, Graduate Admissions Administrator, 603-646-3844, Fax: 603-646-1620, E-mail: candace.potter@dartmouth.edu. Web site: http://engineering.dartmouth.edu/.

Drexel University, College of Engineering, Department of Electrical and Computer Engineering, Program in Electrical Engineering, Philadelphia, PA 19104-2875. Offers MSEE. Part-time and evening/weekend programs available. Terminal master's awarded for partial completion of doctoral program. *Degree requirements:* For master's, thesis (for some programs). Electronic applications accepted.

Duke University, Graduate School, Pratt School of Engineering, Department of Electrical and Computer Engineering, Durham, NC 27708. Offers MS, PhD, JD/MS. Part-time programs available. Terminal master's awarded for partial completion of doctoral program. *Degree requirements:* For doctorate, thesis/dissertation. *Entrance requirements:* For master's and doctorate, GRE General Test. Additional exam requirements/recommendations for international students: Required—TOEFL (minimum score 550 paper-based; 213 computer-based; 83 iBT), IELTS (minimum score 7). Electronic applications accepted. *Expenses: Tuition:* Full-time $40,720. *Required fees:* $3107.

See Display on next page and Close-Up on page 399.

Duke University, Graduate School, Pratt School of Engineering, Master of Engineering Program, Durham, NC 27708-0271. Offers biomedical engineering (M Eng); civil engineering (M Eng); electrical and computer engineering (M Eng); environmental engineering (M Eng); materials science and engineering (M Eng); mechanical engineering (M Eng); photonics and optical sciences (M Eng). Part-time programs available. *Entrance requirements:* For master's, GRE General Test, resume, 3 letters of recommendation, statement of purpose. Additional exam requirements/recommendations for international students: Required—TOEFL. *Expenses: Tuition:* Full-time $40,720. *Required fees:* $3107.

École Polytechnique de Montréal, Graduate Programs, Department of Electrical and Computer Engineering, Montréal, QC H3C 3A7, Canada. Offers automation (M Eng, M Sc A, PhD); computer science (M Eng, M Sc A, PhD); electrical engineering (DESS); electrotechnology (M Eng, M Sc A, PhD); microelectronics (M Eng, M Sc A, PhD); microwave technology (M Eng, M Sc A, PhD). Part-time and evening/weekend programs available. *Degree requirements:* For master's, one foreign language, thesis; for doctorate, one foreign language, thesis/dissertation. *Entrance requirements:* For master's, minimum GPA of 2.75; for doctorate, minimum GPA of 3.0. *Faculty research:* Microwaves, telecommunications, software engineering.

Embry-Riddle Aeronautical University–Daytona, Daytona Beach Campus Graduate Program, Department of Electrical, Computer and Software Engineering, Daytona Beach, FL 32114-3900. Offers electrical/computer engineering (MSECE); engineering (MMSE); software engineering (MSE). Part-time and evening/weekend programs available. *Faculty:* 11 full-time (0 women), 3 part-time/adjunct (1 woman). *Students:* 36 full-time (9 women), 20 part-time (1 woman); includes 4 minority (1 Black or African American, non-Hispanic/Latino; 3 Hispanic/Latino), 16 international. Average age 27. 40 applicants, 70% accepted, 18 enrolled. In 2011, 12 master's awarded. *Degree requirements:* For master's, thesis or alternative. *Entrance requirements:* For master's,

minimum GPA of 3.0 in senior year, 2.5 overall; course work in computer science. Additional exam requirements/recommendations for international students: Required—TOEFL (minimum score 550 paper-based; 213 computer-based; 79 iBT). *Application deadline:* For fall admission, 6/1 priority date for domestic students, 6/1 for international students; for spring admission, 11/1 priority date for domestic students, 10/1 for international students. Applications are processed on a rolling basis. Application fee: $50. Electronic applications accepted. *Expenses: Tuition:* Full-time $14,340; part-time $1195 per credit hour. *Financial support:* In 2011–12, 24 students received support, including 8 research assistantships with full and partial tuition reimbursements available (averaging $3,772 per year), 4 teaching assistantships with full and partial tuition reimbursements available (averaging $3,514 per year); career-related internships or fieldwork, Federal Work-Study, and unspecified assistantships also available. Financial award application deadline: 4/15; financial award applicants required to submit FAFSA. *Faculty research:* Safety-critical software, qualification and certification of digital hardware and softwae, next-generation air transportation system, unmanned aircraft systems, regulatory issues in unmanned aircraft systems. *Total annual research expenditures:* $800,000. *Unit head:* Dr. Timothy Wilson, Department Chair, 386-226-6454, E-mail: timothy.wilson@erau.edu. *Application contact:* Flavia Carreiro, Assistant Director, International and Graduate Admissions, 800-388-3728, Fax: 386-226-7070, E-mail: graduate.admissions@erau.edu.

Fairfield University, School of Engineering, Fairfield, CT 06824-5195. Offers electrical and computer engineering (MS); management of technology (MS); mechanical engineering (MS); software engineering (MS). Part-time and evening/weekend programs available. *Faculty:* 10 full-time (2 women), 11 part-time/adjunct. *Students:* 44 full-time (15 women), 86 part-time (22 women); includes 19 minority (4 Black or African American, non-Hispanic/Latino; 8 Asian, non-Hispanic/Latino; 4 Hispanic/Latino; 1 Native Hawaiian or other Pacific Islander, non-Hispanic/Latino; 2 Two or more races, non-Hispanic/Latino), 21 international. Average age 34. 100 applicants, 76% accepted, 27 enrolled. In 2011, 38 master's awarded. *Degree requirements:* For master's, thesis, capstone course. *Entrance requirements:* For master's, interview, minimum GPA of 2.8, resume, 2 recommendations. Additional exam requirements/recommendations for international students: Required—TOEFL (minimum score 550 paper-based; 213 computer-based; 80 iBT)or IELTS (minimum score 6.5). *Application deadline:* For fall admission, 5/15 for international students; for spring admission, 10/15 for international students. Applications are processed on a rolling basis. Application fee: $60. Electronic applications accepted. *Expenses:* Contact institution. *Financial support:* In 2011–12, 50 students received support. Scholarships/grants and unspecified assistantships available. Financial award applicants required to submit FAFSA. *Faculty research:* Vehicle dynamics, image processing, multimedia in instruction, thermal packaging, character recognition, photovoltaics and nanotechnology, Web technology. *Unit head:* Dr. Jack Beal, Dean, 203-254-4000 Ext. 4147, Fax: 203-254-4013, E-mail: jwbeal@fairfield.edu. *Application contact:* Marianne Gumpper, Director of Graduate and Continuing Studies Admission, 203-254-4184, Fax: 203-254-4073, E-mail: gradadmis@fairfield.edu. Web site: http://www.fairfield.edu/soe/soe_grad_1.html.

Fairleigh Dickinson University, Metropolitan Campus, University College: Arts, Sciences, and Professional Studies, School of Computer Sciences and Engineering, Program in Electrical Engineering, Teaneck, NJ 07666-1914. Offers MSEE. *Entrance requirements:* For master's, GRE General Test.

Florida Agricultural and Mechanical University, Division of Graduate Studies, Research, and Continuing Education, FAMU-FSU College of Engineering, Department

---

DUKE UNIVERSITY

Electrical & Computer Engineering M.S. and Ph.D.

Why Duke?

Duke's Pratt School of Engineering students work in a supportive, close-knit community which gives them ample opportunities to:

- publish with their faculty adviser,
- present research at professional conferences,
- work in a highly collaborative, cross-disciplinary environment, &
- make significant contributions to their field.

Our Electrical and Computer Engineering Department is ranked seventh in faculty scholarly productivity.

Research Areas

Graduate students and faculty collaborate in cutting edge research in these areas:

- architecture & networking
- biological applications circuits & systems
- nanosystems, devices & materials
- quantum computing & photonics
- sensing & signals visualization
- waves & metamaterials

Why Durham, NC?

Duke is located in the Research Triangle region of North Carolina which is known for having the highest concentration of Ph.D.'s and M.D.'s in the world.

Durham is a vibrant, culturally rich city with affordable housing and a warm climate.

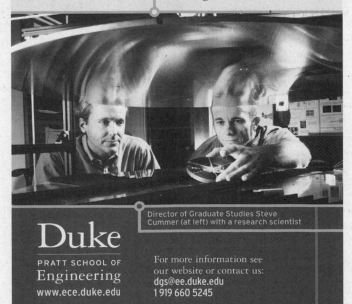

Director of Graduate Studies Steve Cummer (at left) with a research scientist

Duke
PRATT SCHOOL OF Engineering
www.ece.duke.edu

For more information see our website or contact us:
dgs@ee.duke.edu
1 919 660 5245

---

of Electrical Engineering, Tallahassee, FL 32307-3200. Offers MS, PhD. *Degree requirements:* For master's, comprehensive exam, thesis, conference paper; for doctorate, comprehensive exam, thesis/dissertation, publishable paper. *Entrance requirements:* For master's, GRE General Test, minimum GPA of 3.0; for doctorate, minimum GPA of 3.3. Additional exam requirements/recommendations for international students: Required—TOEFL (minimum score 550 paper-based; 213 computer-based). *Faculty research:* Electromagnetics, computer security, advanced power systems, sensor systems.

Florida Atlantic University, College of Engineering and Computer Science, Department of Computer and Electrical Engineering and Computer Science, Boca Raton, FL 33431-0991. Offers computer engineering (MS, PhD); computer science (MS, PhD); electrical engineering (MS, PhD). Part-time and evening/weekend programs available. *Faculty:* 32 full-time (6 women), 4 part-time/adjunct (0 women). *Students:* 96 full-time (22 women), 106 part-time (21 women); includes 77 minority (16 Black or African American, non-Hispanic/Latino; 23 Asian, non-Hispanic/Latino; 35 Hispanic/Latino; 3 Two or more races, non-Hispanic/Latino), 43 international. Average age 33. 177 applicants, 41% accepted, 35 enrolled. In 2011, 48 master's, 6 doctorates awarded. Terminal master's awarded for partial completion of doctoral program. *Degree requirements:* For master's, thesis optional; for doctorate, thesis/dissertation, qualifying exam. *Entrance requirements:* For master's, GRE General Test, minimum GPA of 3.0; for doctorate, GRE General Test, master's degree, minimum GPA of 3.5. Additional exam requirements/recommendations for international students: Required—TOEFL. *Application deadline:* For fall admission, 7/1 priority date for domestic students, 2/15 for international students; for spring admission, 11/1 for domestic students, 7/15 for international students. Applications are processed on a rolling basis. Application fee: $30. *Expenses: Tuition, area resident:* Part-time $343.02 per credit hour. Tuition, state resident: full-time $8232. Tuition, nonresident: full-time $23,931; part-time $997.14 per credit hour. *Financial support:* Fellowships, research assistantships with partial tuition reimbursements, teaching assistantships with full tuition reimbursements, career-related internships or fieldwork, and Federal Work-Study available. Support available to part-time students. Financial award application deadline: 4/1; financial award applicants required to submit FAFSA. *Faculty research:* VLSI and neural networks, communication networks, software engineering, computer architecture, multimedia and video processing. *Unit head:* Dr. Borko Furht, Chairman, 561-297-3855, Fax: 561-297-2800. *Application contact:* Joanna Arlington, Manager, Graduate Admissions, 561-297-2428, Fax: 561-297-2117, E-mail: arlingto@fau.edu. Web site: http://www.ceecs.fau.edu/.

Florida Institute of Technology, Graduate Programs, College of Engineering, Electrical and Computer Engineering Department, Melbourne, FL 32901-6975. Offers computer engineering (MS, PhD); electrical engineering (MS, PhD). Part-time and evening/weekend programs available. *Faculty:* 9 full-time (1 woman), 2 part-time/adjunct (0 women). *Students:* 87 full-time (20 women), 27 part-time (5 women); includes 9 minority (3 Black or African American, non-Hispanic/Latino; 2 Asian, non-Hispanic/Latino; 3 Hispanic/Latino; 1 Two or more races, non-Hispanic/Latino), 83 international. Average age 29. 323 applicants, 65% accepted, 31 enrolled. In 2011, 29 master's, 4 doctorates awarded. *Degree requirements:* For master's, comprehensive exam (for some programs), thesis optional, final exam, faculty-supervised specialized research; for doctorate, comprehensive exam (for some programs), thesis/dissertation, complete program of significant original research. *Entrance requirements:* For master's, GRE, minimum GPA of 3.0, bachelor's degree from an ABET-accredited program; for doctorate, 3 letters of recommendation, resume, minimum GPA of 3.2, statement of objectives, on-campus interview (highly recommended). Additional exam requirements/recommendations for international students: Required—TOEFL (minimum score 550 paper-based; 213 computer-based; 79 iBT). *Application deadline:* For fall admission, 4/1 for international students; for spring admission, 9/30 for international students. Applications are processed on a rolling basis. Application fee: $0. Electronic applications accepted. *Expenses: Tuition:* Full-time $19,620; part-time $1090 per credit hour. Tuition and fees vary according to campus/location. *Financial support:* In 2011–12, 3 research assistantships with full and partial tuition reimbursements (averaging $8,287 per year), 8 teaching assistantships with full and partial tuition reimbursements (averaging $3,265 per year) were awarded; career-related internships or fieldwork, institutionally sponsored loans, tuition waivers (partial), unspecified assistantships, and tuition remissions also available. Support available to part-time students. Financial award application deadline: 3/1; financial award applicants required to submit FAFSA. *Faculty research:* Electro-optics, electromagnetics, microelectronics, communications, computer architecture, neural networks. *Total annual research expenditures:* $458,364. *Unit head:* Dr. Samuel P. Kozaitis, Department Head, 321-674-8060, Fax: 321-674-8192, E-mail: kozaitis@fit.edu. *Application contact:* Cheryl A. Brown, Associate Director of Graduate Admissions, 321-674-7581, Fax: 321-723-9468, E-mail: cbrown@fit.edu. Web site: http://coe.fit.edu/ee/.

Florida Institute of Technology, Graduate Programs, Extended Studies Division, Melbourne, FL 32901-6975. Offers acquisition and contract management (MS); aerospace engineering (MS); business administration (MBA); computer information systems (MS); computer science (MS); electrical engineering (MS); engineering management (MS); human resources management (MS); logistics management (MS), including humanitarian and disaster relief logistics; management (MS), including acquisition and contract management, e-business, human resources management, information systems, logistics management, management, transportation management; material acquisition management (MS); mechanical engineering (MS); operations research (MS); project management (MS), including information systems, operations research; public administration (MPA); quality management (MS); software engineering (MS); space systems (MS); space systems management (MS); supply chain management (MS); systems management (MS), including information systems, operations research. Part-time and evening/weekend programs available. Postbaccalaureate distance learning degree programs offered (no on-campus study). *Faculty:* 9 full-time (2 women), 105 part-time/adjunct (24 women). *Students:* 113 full-time (52 women), 1,150 part-time (484 women); includes 496 minority (332 Black or African American, non-Hispanic/Latino; 11 American Indian or Alaska Native, non-Hispanic/Latino; 42 Asian, non-Hispanic/Latino; 71 Hispanic/Latino; 2 Native Hawaiian or other Pacific Islander, non-Hispanic/Latino; 38 Two or more races, non-Hispanic/Latino), 11 international. Average age 35. 568 applicants, 56% accepted, 296 enrolled. In 2011, 471 master's awarded. *Degree requirements:* For master's, comprehensive exam (for some programs), capstone course. *Entrance requirements:* For master's, GMAT or resume showing 8 years of supervised experience, minimum GPA of 3.0, 2 letters of recommendation, resume. Additional exam requirements/recommendations for international students: Required—TOEFL (minimum score 550 paper-based; 213 computer-based; 79 iBT). *Application deadline:* For fall admission, 4/1 for international students; for spring admission, 9/30 for international students. Applications are processed on a rolling basis. Application fee: $0. Electronic applications accepted. *Expenses:* Contact institution. *Financial support:* Application deadline: 3/1; applicants required to submit FAFSA. *Unit head:* Dr. Theodore R. Richardson, III, Senior Associate

Dean, 321-674-8123, Fax: 321-674-7597, E-mail: trichardson@fit.edu. *Application contact:* Carolyn Farrior, Director of Graduate Admissions, Online Learning and Off-Campus Programs, 321-674-7118, Fax: 321-674-8216, E-mail: cfarrior@fit.edu. Web site: http://es.fit.edu.

Florida International University, College of Engineering and Computing, Department of Electrical and Computer Engineering, Program in Electrical Engineering, Miami, FL 33175. Offers MS, PhD. Part-time and evening/weekend programs available. Terminal master's awarded for partial completion of doctoral program. *Degree requirements:* For master's, thesis optional; for doctorate, comprehensive exam, thesis/dissertation. *Entrance requirements:* For master's, minimum undergraduate GPA of 3.0 in upper-level coursework, resume, letters of recommendation, letter of intent; for doctorate, GRE General Test, minimum graduate GPA of 3.3, resume, master's degree, letters of recommendation, letter of intent. Additional exam requirements/recommendations for international students: Required—TOEFL (minimum score 550 paper-based; 80 iBT). Electronic applications accepted.

Florida State University, The Graduate School, FAMU-FSU College of Engineering, Department of Electrical and Computer Engineering, Tallahassee, FL 32306. Offers electrical engineering (MS, PhD). Part-time programs available. *Faculty:* 19 full-time (2 women), 1 part-time/adjunct (0 women). *Students:* 66 full-time (9 women), 12 part-time (1 woman); includes 10 minority (8 Black or African American, non-Hispanic/Latino; 2 Hispanic/Latino), 46 international. Average age 26. 200 applicants, 47% accepted, 26 enrolled. In 2011, 23 master's, 3 doctorates awarded. *Degree requirements:* For master's, thesis; for doctorate, comprehensive exam, thesis/dissertation, preliminary exam, qualifying exam. *Entrance requirements:* For master's, GRE General Test, minimum GPA of 3.0, BS in electrical engineering; for doctorate, GRE General Test, minimum graduate GPA of 3.3, MS in electrical engineering. Additional exam requirements/recommendations for international students: Required—TOEFL (minimum score 550 paper-based; 213 computer-based). *Application deadline:* For fall admission, 3/1 for domestic and international students; for spring admission, 10/1 for domestic and international students. Applications are processed on a rolling basis. Application fee: $30. Electronic applications accepted. *Expenses:* Tuition, state resident: full-time $9474; part-time $350.88 per credit hour. Tuition, nonresident: full-time $16,236; part-time $601.34 per credit hour. *Required fees:* $630 per semester. One-time fee: $20. Tuition and fees vary according to course load and campus/location. *Financial support:* In 2011–12, 1 fellowship with full tuition reimbursement (averaging $12,000 per year), 11 research assistantships with full tuition reimbursements (averaging $15,800 per year), 26 teaching assistantships with full tuition reimbursements (averaging $15,800 per year) were awarded; career-related internships or fieldwork, institutionally sponsored loans, scholarships/grants, and tuition waivers (full) also available. Financial award application deadline: 6/15. *Faculty research:* Electromagnetics, digital signal processing, computer systems, image processing, laser optics. *Total annual research expenditures:* $816,000. *Unit head:* Dr. Simon Foo, Chair and Professor, 850-410-6474, Fax: 850-410-6479, E-mail: foo@eng.fsu.edu. *Application contact:* Melissa Jackson, Graduate Program Assistant, 850-410-6454, Fax: 850-410-6479, E-mail: ecegrad@eng.fsu.edu. Web site: http://www.eng.fsu.edu/ece/.

Gannon University, School of Graduate Studies, College of Engineering and Business, School of Engineering and Computer Science, Program in Electrical Engineering, Erie, PA 16541-0001. Offers MSEE. Part-time and evening/weekend programs available. *Students:* 55 full-time (9 women), 23 part-time (3 women); includes 4 minority (3 Black or African American, non-Hispanic/Latino; 1 Asian, non-Hispanic/Latino), 68 international. Average age 24. 420 applicants, 88% accepted, 16 enrolled. In 2011, 47 master's awarded. *Degree requirements:* For master's, thesis or project. *Entrance requirements:* For master's, GRE or GMAT, bachelor's degree in engineering, minimum QPA of 2.5. Additional exam requirements/recommendations for international students: Required—TOEFL (minimum score 79 iBT). *Application deadline:* Applications are processed on a rolling basis. Application fee: $25. Electronic applications accepted. *Financial support:* Career-related internships or fieldwork, scholarships/grants, traineeships, and unspecified assistantships available. Financial award application deadline: 7/1; financial award applicants required to submit FAFSA. *Faculty research:* Electronics system integration, real-time implementation andapplications, renewable energy control and application, smart-grid communication, electric drives control and modeling. *Unit head:* Dr. Fong Mak, Chair, 814-871-7625, E-mail: mak001@gannon.edu. *Application contact:* Kara Morgan, Director of Graduate Admissions, 814-871-5831, Fax: 814-871-5827, E-mail: graduate@gannon.edu.

George Mason University, Volgenau School of Engineering, Department of Electrical and Computer Engineering, Fairfax, VA 22030. Offers advanced networking protocols for telecommunications (Certificate); communications and networking (Certificate); computer engineering (MS); computer forensics (MS); electrical and computer engineering (PhD); electrical engineering (MS); network technology and applications (Certificate); networks, system integration and testing (Certificate); signal processing (Certificate); telecommunications (MS); telecommunications forensics and security (Certificate); wireless communication (Certificate). MS program offered jointly with Old Dominion University, University of Virginia, Virginia Commonwealth University, and Virginia Polytechnic Institute and State University. *Faculty:* 29 full-time (4 women), 36 part-time/adjunct (2 women). *Students:* 162 full-time (49 women), 284 part-time (52 women); includes 101 minority (30 Black or African American, non-Hispanic/Latino; 1 American Indian or Alaska Native, non-Hispanic/Latino; 47 Asian, non-Hispanic/Latino; 19 Hispanic/Latino; 1 Native Hawaiian or other Pacific Islander, non-Hispanic/Latino; 3 Two or more races, non-Hispanic/Latino), 169 international. Average age 30. 478 applicants, 68% accepted, 106 enrolled. In 2011, 129 master's, 5 doctorates, 45 other advanced degrees awarded. *Degree requirements:* For master's, thesis optional; for doctorate, comprehensive exam, thesis or scholarly paper. *Entrance requirements:* For master's, GRE, personal goals statement; 2 official copies of transcripts; self-evaluation form; 3 letters of recommendation; resume; official bank statement; photocopy of passport; proof of financial support; for doctorate, GRE (waived for GMU electrical and computer engineering master's graduates with minimum GPA of 3.0), personal goals statement; 2 official copies of transcripts; self-evaluation form; 3 letters of recommendation; resume; official bank statement; photocopy of passport; proof of financial support. Additional exam requirements/recommendations for international students: Required—TOEFL (minimum score 575 paper-based; 230 computer-based; 88 iBT), IELTS, Pearson Test of English. *Application deadline:* For fall admission, 1/15 priority date for domestic students; for spring admission, 8/15 priority date for domestic students. Applications are processed on a rolling basis. Application fee: $65 ($80 for international students). Electronic applications accepted. *Expenses:* Tuition, state resident: full-time $8750; part-time $364.58 per credit. Tuition, nonresident: full-time $24,092; part-time $1003.83 per credit. *Required fees:* $2514; $104.75 per credit. *Financial support:* In 2011–12, 77 students received support, including 3 fellowships with full tuition reimbursements available (averaging $18,000 per year), 24 research assistantships with full and partial tuition reimbursements available (averaging $15,736 per year), 50 teaching assistantships with full and partial tuition reimbursements available (averaging $10,961 per year); career-related internships or fieldwork, Federal Work-Study, scholarships/grants, unspecified assistantships, and health care benefits (full-time research or teaching assistantship recipients) also available. Support available to part-time students. Financial award application deadline: 3/1; financial award applicants required to submit FAFSA. *Faculty research:* Communication networks, signal processing, system failure diagnosis, multiprocessors, material processing using microwave energy. *Total annual research expenditures:* $4.4 million. *Unit head:* Dr. Andre Manitius, Chairperson, 703-993-1569, Fax: 703-993-1601, E-mail: amanitiu@gmu.edu. *Application contact:* Jammie Chang, Academic Program Coordinator, 703-993-1523, Fax: 703-993-1601, E-mail: jchangn@gmu.edu. Web site: http://ece.gmu.edu/#.

The George Washington University, School of Engineering and Applied Science, Department of Electrical and Computer Engineering, Washington, DC 20052. Offers electrical and computer engineering (MS, D Sc); telecommunication and computers (MS). Part-time and evening/weekend programs available. *Faculty:* 24 full-time (2 women), 9 part-time/adjunct (0 women). *Students:* 131 full-time (25 women), 101 part-time (14 women); includes 40 minority (16 Black or African American, non-Hispanic/Latino; 18 Asian, non-Hispanic/Latino; 5 Hispanic/Latino; 1 Native Hawaiian or other Pacific Islander, non-Hispanic/Latino), 136 international. Average age 29. 362 applicants, 86% accepted, 68 enrolled. In 2011, 78 master's, 12 doctorates awarded. *Degree requirements:* For master's, thesis optional; for doctorate, comprehensive exam, thesis/dissertation, dissertation defense, qualifying exam. *Entrance requirements:* For master's, appropriate bachelor's degree, minimum GPA of 3.0; for doctorate, GRE (if highest earned degree is BS), appropriate bachelor's or master's degree, minimum GPA of 3.3. Additional exam requirements/recommendations for international students: Required—TOEFL or The George Washington University English as a Foreign Language Test. *Application deadline:* For fall admission, 3/1 priority date for domestic students; for spring admission, 10/1 for domestic students. Applications are processed on a rolling basis. Application fee: $75. *Financial support:* In 2011–12, 39 students received support. Fellowships with tuition reimbursements available, research assistantships, teaching assistantships with tuition reimbursements available, career-related internships or fieldwork, and institutionally sponsored loans available. Financial award application deadline: 3/1; financial award applicants required to submit FAFSA. *Faculty research:* Computer graphics, multimedia systems. *Unit head:* Can E. Korman, Chair, 202-994-4952, E-mail: korman@gwu.edu. *Application contact:* Adina Lav, Marketing, Recruiting and Admissions, 202-994-5827, Fax: 202-994-0909, E-mail: engineering@gwu.edu. Web site: http://www.ece.gwu.edu/.

Georgia Institute of Technology, Graduate Studies and Research, College of Engineering, School of Electrical and Computer Engineering, Atlanta, GA 30332-0001. Offers MS, MSEE, PhD. Part-time programs available. Postbaccalaureate distance learning degree programs offered (minimal on-campus study). Terminal master's awarded for partial completion of doctoral program. *Degree requirements:* For master's, thesis optional; for doctorate, thesis/dissertation. *Entrance requirements:* For master's, GRE General Test, minimum GPA of 3.0; for doctorate, GRE General Test, minimum GPA of 3.5. Additional exam requirements/recommendations for international students: Required—TOEFL. *Faculty research:* Telecommunications, computer systems, microelectronics, optical engineering, digital signal processing.

Georgia Southern University, Jack N. Averitt College of Graduate Studies, Allen E. Paulson College of Science and Technology, Department of Mechanical and Electrical Engineering Technology, Statesboro, GA 30460. Offers M Tech, MSAE, Certificate. Part-time and evening/weekend programs available. *Students:* 38 full-time (4 women), 19 part-time (3 women); includes 19 minority (11 Black or African American, non-Hispanic/Latino; 1 Asian, non-Hispanic/Latino; 4 Hispanic/Latino; 3 Two or more races, non-Hispanic/Latino), 5 international. Average age 27. 30 applicants, 90% accepted, 21 enrolled. In 2011, 14 master's awarded. *Degree requirements:* For master's, comprehensive exam, thesis optional. *Entrance requirements:* For master's, GRE. Additional exam requirements/recommendations for international students: Required—TOEFL (minimum score 550 paper-based; 213 computer-based; 80 iBT). *Application deadline:* For fall admission, 3/1 priority date for domestic students, 3/1 for international students; for spring admission, 10/1 priority date for domestic students, 10/1 for international students. Applications are processed on a rolling basis. Application fee: $50. Electronic applications accepted. *Expenses:* Tuition, state resident: full-time $6300; part-time $263 per semester hour. Tuition, nonresident: full-time $25,174; part-time $1049 per semester hour. *Required fees:* $1872. *Financial support:* In 2011–12, 23 students received support, including 4 research assistantships with partial tuition reimbursements available (averaging $7,200 per year); tuition waivers (partial) and unspecified assistantships also available. Financial award application deadline: 4/15; financial award applicants required to submit FAFSA. *Faculty research:* Interdisciplinary research in computational mechanics, experimental and computational biofuel combustion and tribology, mechatronics and control, thermomechanical and thermofluid finite element modeling, information technology. *Total annual research expenditures:* $458,293. *Unit head:* Dr. Mohammad S. Davoud, Chair, 912-478-0540, Fax: 912-478-1455, E-mail: mdavoud@georgiasouthern.edu. *Application contact:* Amanda Gilliland, Coordinator for Graduate Student Recruitment, 912-478-5384, Fax: 912-478-0740, E-mail: gradadmissions@georgiasouthern.edu.

Graduate School and University Center of the City University of New York, Graduate Studies, Program in Engineering, New York, NY 10016-4039. Offers biomedical engineering (PhD); chemical engineering (PhD); civil engineering (PhD); electrical engineering (PhD); mechanical engineering (PhD). *Degree requirements:* For doctorate, thesis/dissertation. *Entrance requirements:* For doctorate, GRE General Test. Additional exam requirements/recommendations for international students: Required—TOEFL. Electronic applications accepted.

Grand Valley State University, Padnos College of Engineering and Computing, School of Engineering, Allendale, MI 49401-9403. Offers electrical and computer engineering (MSE); manufacturing operations (MSE); mechanical engineering (MSE); product design and manufacturing engineering (MSE). Part-time and evening/weekend programs available. *Degree requirements:* For master's, project or thesis. *Entrance requirements:* For master's, engineering degree, minimum GPA of 3.0. Additional exam requirements/recommendations for international students: Required—TOEFL. Electronic applications accepted. *Faculty research:* Digital signal processing, computer aided design, computer aided manufacturing, manufacturing simulation, biomechanics, product design.

Howard University, College of Engineering, Architecture, and Computer Sciences, School of Engineering and Computer Science, Department of Electrical Engineering, Washington, DC 20059-0002. Offers M Eng, PhD. Offered through the Graduate School of Arts and Sciences. Part-time programs available. *Degree requirements:* For master's, thesis (for some programs), qualifying exam; for doctorate, thesis/dissertation, preliminary exam. *Entrance requirements:* For master's, GRE General Test, bachelor's degree in electrical engineering, minimum GPA of 3.0; for doctorate, GRE General Test, minimum GPA of 3.0. Additional exam requirements/recommendations for international students: Required—TOEFL. Electronic applications accepted. *Faculty research:* Solid-state electronics, antennas and microwaves, communications and signal processing, controls and power systems, nanotechnology.

Illinois Institute of Technology, Graduate College, Armour College of Engineering, Department of Electrical and Computer Engineering, Chicago, IL 60616-3793. Offers biomedical imaging and signals (MBMI); computer engineering (MS, PhD); electrical and computer engineering (MECE); electrical engineering (MS, PhD); electricity markets (MEM); network engineering (MNE); power engineering (MPE); telecommunications and software engineering (MTSE); VLSI and microelectronics (MVM). Part-time and evening/weekend programs available. Postbaccalaureate distance learning degree programs offered (minimal on-campus study). Terminal master's awarded for partial completion of doctoral program. *Degree requirements:* For master's, comprehensive exam (for some programs), thesis (for some programs); for doctorate, comprehensive exam, thesis/dissertation. *Entrance requirements:* For master's and doctorate, GRE General Test (minimum score 1100 Quantitative and Verbal, 3.5 Analytical Writing), minimum undergraduate GPA of 3.0. Additional exam requirements/recommendations for international students: Required—TOEFL (minimum score 523 paper-based; 70 iBT); Recommended—IELTS (minimum score 5.5). Electronic applications accepted. *Faculty research:* Communication systems, computer systems and micro-electronics, electromagnetics and electronics, power and control systems, signal and image processing.

Indiana University–Purdue University Fort Wayne, College of Engineering, Technology, and Computer Science, Department of Engineering, Fort Wayne, IN 46805-1499. Offers computer engineering (MSE); electrical engineering (MSE); mechanical engineering (MSE); systems engineering (MSE). Part-time programs available. *Faculty:* 21 full-time (0 women), 2 part-time/adjunct (0 women). *Students:* 6 full-time (0 women), 29 part-time (5 women); includes 3 minority (2 Asian, non-Hispanic/Latino; 1 Hispanic/Latino), 3 international. Average age 28. 26 applicants, 96% accepted, 17 enrolled. In 2011, 16 master's awarded. *Entrance requirements:* For master's, minimum GPA of 3.0, bachelor's degree in engineering discipline. Additional exam requirements/recommendations for international students: Required—TOEFL (minimum score 550 paper-based; 213 computer-based; 77 iBT); Recommended—TWE. *Application deadline:* For fall admission, 7/15 priority date for domestic students, 5/15 for international students; for spring admission, 12/1 priority date for domestic students, 10/15 for international students. Applications are processed on a rolling basis. Application fee: $55 ($60 for international students). Electronic applications accepted. *Financial support:* In 2011–12, 7 research assistantships with partial tuition reimbursements (averaging $12,930 per year), 3 teaching assistantships with partial tuition reimbursements (averaging $12,930 per year) were awarded. Financial award application deadline: 3/1; financial award applicants required to submit FAFSA. *Faculty research:* Thermal science, robot prototypes, worm-scanning strategies. *Total annual research expenditures:* $185,757. *Unit head:* Dr. Donald Mueller, Chair, 260-481-5707, Fax: 260-481-6281, E-mail: mueller@engr.ipfw.edu. *Application contact:* Dr. Carlos Pomalaza-Raez, Program Director/Professor, 260-481-6353, Fax: 260-481-5734, E-mail: carlos-pomalaza-raez@purdue.edu. Web site: http://www.ipfw.edu/engr.

Indiana University–Purdue University Indianapolis, School of Engineering and Technology, Department of Electrical Engineering, Indianapolis, IN 46202-2896. Offers biomedical engineering (MS, PhD); electrical and computer engineering (MS, MSECE, PhD), including biomedical engineering (MSECE), control and automation (MSECE), signal processing (MSECE); engineering (interdisciplinary) (MSE). *Students:* 49 full-time (15 women), 48 part-time (5 women); includes 8 minority (2 Black or African American, non-Hispanic/Latino; 2 Asian, non-Hispanic/Latino; 2 Hispanic/Latino; 2 Two or more races, non-Hispanic/Latino), 56 international. Average age 27. 150 applicants, 49% accepted, 45 enrolled. In 2011, 29 degrees awarded. Application fee: $55 ($65 for international students). *Unit head:* Yaobin Chen, Unit Head, 317-274-4032, Fax: 317-274-4493. *Application contact:* Valerie Diemer, Graduate Program, 317-278-4960, Fax: 317-278-1671, E-mail: grad@engr.iupui.edu.

Instituto Tecnológico y de Estudios Superiores de Monterrey, Campus Chihuahua, Graduate Programs, Chihuahua, Mexico. Offers computer systems engineering (Ingeniero); electrical engineering (Ingeniero); electromechanical engineering (Ingeniero); electronic engineering (Ingeniero); engineering administration (MEA); industrial engineering (MIE, Ingeniero); international trade (MIT); mechanical engineering (Ingeniero).

Instituto Tecnológico y de Estudios Superiores de Monterrey, Campus Monterrey, Graduate and Research Division, Programs in Engineering, Monterrey, Mexico. Offers applied statistics (M Eng); artificial intelligence (PhD); automation engineering (M Eng); chemical engineering (M Eng); civil engineering (M Eng); electrical engineering (M Eng); electronic engineering (M Eng); environmental engineering (M Eng); industrial engineering (M Eng, PhD); manufacturing engineering (M Eng); mechanical engineering (M Eng); systems and quality engineering (M Eng). M Eng program offered jointly with University of Waterloo; PhD in industrial engineering with Texas A&M University. Part-time and evening/weekend programs available. Terminal master's awarded for partial completion of doctoral program. *Degree requirements:* For master's, one foreign language, thesis; for doctorate, one foreign language, thesis/dissertation. *Entrance requirements:* For master's, EXADEP; for doctorate, GRE, master's degree in related field. Additional exam requirements/recommendations for international students: Required—TOEFL. *Faculty research:* Flexible manufacturing cells, materials, statistical methods, environmental prevention, control and evaluation.

International Technological University, Program in Electrical Engineering, Santa Clara, CA 95050. Offers MSEE, PhD. Part-time and evening/weekend programs available. *Degree requirements:* For master's, thesis or alternative. *Entrance requirements:* For master's, 3 semesters of calculus, minimum GPA of 2.5. Additional exam requirements/recommendations for international students: Required—TOEFL. *Faculty research:* VLSI design, digital systems, routing and optimization theory.

Iowa State University of Science and Technology, Department of Electrical and Computer Engineering, Ames, IA 50011. Offers computer engineering (M Eng, MS, PhD); electrical engineering (M Eng, MS, PhD). *Degree requirements:* For master's, thesis or alternative; for doctorate, thesis/dissertation. *Entrance requirements:* For master's and doctorate, GRE General Test. Additional exam requirements/recommendations for international students: Required—TOEFL (minimum score 570 paper-based; 79 iBT), IELTS (minimum score 6.5). *Application deadline:* For fall admission, 1/15 priority date for domestic students, 1/15 for international students; for spring admission, 9/15 for domestic and international students. Application fee: $40 ($90 for international students). Electronic applications accepted. *Unit head:* Dr. Zhengdao Wang, Director of Graduate Education, 515-294-8403, E-mail: ecegrad@ee.iastate.edu. *Application contact:* Director of Graduate Education, 515-294-8403, E-mail: ecegrad@iastate.edu. Web site: http://www.ece.iastate.edu/.

The Johns Hopkins University, Engineering Program for Professionals, Part-time Program in Electrical and Computer Engineering, Baltimore, MD 21218-2699. Offers MS, Post-Master's Certificate. Part-time and evening/weekend programs available. Electronic applications accepted.

The Johns Hopkins University, Whiting School of Engineering, Department of Electrical and Computer Engineering, Baltimore, MD 21218-2699. Offers MSE, PhD. Terminal master's awarded for partial completion of doctoral program. *Degree requirements:* For master's, thesis optional; for doctorate, thesis/dissertation, qualifying and oral exams, seminar. *Entrance requirements:* For master's and doctorate, GRE General Test, transcripts, 3 letters of recommendation, statement of purpose. Additional exam requirements/recommendations for international students: Required—TOEFL (minimum score 600 paper-based; 250 computer-based; 100 iBT). Electronic applications accepted. *Faculty research:* Computer engineering, systems and control, language and speech processing, photonics and optoelectronics, signal and image processing.

Kansas State University, Graduate School, College of Engineering, Department of Electrical and Computer Engineering, Manhattan, KS 66506. Offers electrical engineering (MS, PhD). Postbaccalaureate distance learning degree programs offered (no on-campus study). *Faculty:* 16 full-time (3 women), 3 part-time/adjunct (1 woman). *Students:* 50 full-time (13 women), 44 part-time (5 women); includes 19 minority (8 Black or African American, non-Hispanic/Latino; 6 Asian, non-Hispanic/Latino; 5 Hispanic/Latino), 31 international. Average age 29. 176 applicants, 28% accepted, 14 enrolled. In 2011, 30 master's, 5 doctorates awarded. *Degree requirements:* For master's, thesis or alternative, final exam; for doctorate, thesis/dissertation, preliminary exams. *Entrance requirements:* For master's, GRE General Test, bachelor's degree in electrical engineering or computer science, minimum GPA of 3.0; for doctorate, GRE General Test. Additional exam requirements/recommendations for international students: Required—TOEFL (minimum score 600 paper-based). *Application deadline:* For fall admission, 2/1 priority date for domestic students, 2/1 for international students; for spring admission, 8/1 priority date for domestic students, 8/1 for international students. Applications are processed on a rolling basis. Application fee: $40 ($55 for international students). Electronic applications accepted. *Financial support:* In 2011–12, 40 research assistantships (averaging $16,874 per year), 11 teaching assistantships with full tuition reimbursements (averaging $16,213 per year) were awarded; career-related internships or fieldwork, institutionally sponsored loans, and scholarships/grants also available. Support available to part-time students. Financial award application deadline: 3/1; financial award applicants required to submit FAFSA. *Faculty research:* Energy systems and renewable energy, computer systems and real time embedded systems, communication systems and signal processing, integrated circuits and devices, bioengineering. *Total annual research expenditures:* $1.3 million. *Unit head:* Don Gruenbacher, Head, 785-532-4692, Fax: 785-532-1188, E-mail: grue@ksu.edu. *Application contact:* Andrew Rys, Director, 785-532-4665, Fax: 785-532-1188, E-mail: andrys@ksu.edu. Web site: http://www.ece.ksu.edu/.

Kettering University, Graduate School, Electrical and Computer Engineering Department, Flint, MI 48504. Offers engineering (MS). Part-time and evening/weekend programs available. Postbaccalaureate distance learning degree programs offered (no on-campus study). *Faculty:* 6 full-time (0 women). *Students:* 1 full-time (0 women), 10 part-time (1 woman); includes 1 minority (Black or African American, non-Hispanic/Latino), 3 international. Average age 28. 17 applicants, 35% accepted, 2 enrolled. In 2011, 3 master's awarded. *Degree requirements:* For master's, thesis optional. *Entrance requirements:* Additional exam requirements/recommendations for international students: Required—TOEFL (minimum score 550 paper-based; 213 computer-based; 79 iBT). *Application deadline:* For fall admission, 9/15 for domestic students, 6/15 for international students; for winter admission, 12/15 for domestic students, 9/15 for international students; for spring admission, 3/15 for domestic students, 12/15 for international students. Applications are processed on a rolling basis. Application fee: $0. Electronic applications accepted. *Expenses: Tuition:* Full-time $11,456; part-time $716 per credit hour. *Financial support:* In 2011–12, 1 student received support, including fellowships with full tuition reimbursements available (averaging $13,000 per year), research assistantships with full tuition reimbursements available (averaging $13,000 per year), teaching assistantships with full tuition reimbursements available (averaging $13,000 per year); Federal Work-Study, scholarships/grants, and tuition waivers (partial) also available. Support available to part-time students. Financial award application deadline: 7/15; financial award applicants required to submit CSS PROFILE or FAFSA. *Faculty research:* Batteries, battery testing, robotics, hepatics. *Total annual research expenditures:* $761,000. *Unit head:* Dr. James McDonald, Department Head, 810-762-9500 Ext. 5690, Fax: 810-762-9830, E-mail: jmcdonal@kettering.edu. *Application contact:* Bonnie Switzer, Admissions Representative, 810-762-7953, Fax: 810-762-9935, E-mail: bswitzer@kettering.edu.

Lakehead University, Graduate Studies, Faculty of Engineering, Thunder Bay, ON P7B 5E1, Canada. Offers control engineering (M Sc Engr); electrical/computer engineering (M Sc Engr); environmental engineering (M Sc Engr). Part-time programs available. *Degree requirements:* For master's, thesis. *Entrance requirements:* For master's, bachelor's degree in chemical, electrical or mechanical engineering, minimum B average. Additional exam requirements/recommendations for international students: Required—TOEFL. *Faculty research:* Pulp and paper, adaptive/process control, robust/interactive learning control, vibration control.

Lamar University, College of Graduate Studies, College of Engineering, Department of Electrical Engineering, Beaumont, TX 77710. Offers ME, MES, DE. Part-time programs available. *Faculty:* 6 full-time (0 women). *Students:* 26 full-time (3 women), 32 part-time (4 women); includes 2 minority (1 Black or African American, non-Hispanic/Latino; 1 Asian, non-Hispanic/Latino), 50 international. Average age 26. 103 applicants, 62% accepted, 20 enrolled. In 2011, 112 master's awarded. *Degree requirements:* For master's, thesis (for some programs); for doctorate, thesis/dissertation. *Entrance requirements:* For master's and doctorate, GRE General Test. Additional exam requirements/recommendations for international students: Required—TOEFL. *Application deadline:* For fall admission, 5/15 priority date for domestic students; for spring admission, 10/1 priority date for domestic students. Applications are processed on a rolling basis. Application fee: $25 ($50 for international students). *Expenses:* Tuition, state resident: full-time $5430; part-time $272 per credit hour. Tuition, nonresident: full-time $11,540; part-time $577 per credit hour. *Required fees:* $1916. *Financial support:* In 2011–12, 2 fellowships with partial tuition reimbursements (averaging $6,000 per year), 20 research assistantships with partial tuition reimbursements (averaging $6,000 per year), 2 teaching assistantships with partial tuition reimbursements (averaging $4,500 per year) were awarded; tuition waivers (partial) also available. Financial award application deadline: 4/1. *Faculty research:* Video processing, photonics, VLSI design, computer networking. *Unit head:* Dr. Harley Ross Myler, Chair, 409-880-8746, Fax: 409-880-8121, E-mail: mylerhr@hal.lamar.edu. *Application contact:* Jane Stanley McCabe, Information Contact, 409-880-8746, Fax: 409-880-8121, E-mail: eece@hal.lamar.edu. Web site: http://ee.lamar.edu.

Lawrence Technological University, College of Engineering, Southfield, MI 48075-1058. Offers architectural engineering (MS); automotive engineering (MS); civil engineering (MA, MS); construction engineering management (MA); electrical and computer engineering (MS); engineering management (MEM); industrial engineering (MS); manufacturing systems (ME, DE); mechanical engineering (MS, DE); mechatronic systems engineering (MS). Part-time and evening/weekend programs available. *Faculty:* 25 full-time (4 women), 20 part-time/adjunct (1 woman). *Students:* 8 full-time (0 women), 332 part-time (52 women); includes 58 minority (21 Black or African American, non-Hispanic/Latino; 1 American Indian or Alaska Native, non-Hispanic/Latino; 32 Asian, non-Hispanic/Latino; 2 Hispanic/Latino; 2 Two or more races, non-Hispanic/Latino), 84 international. Average age 32. 652 applicants, 44% accepted, 70 enrolled. In 2011, 127 master's, 2 doctorates awarded. *Degree requirements:* For master's, thesis (for some programs). *Entrance requirements:* Additional exam requirements/recommendations for international students: Required—TOEFL (minimum score 550 paper-based; 213 computer-based; 79 iBT). *Application deadline:* For fall admission, 7/27 priority date for domestic students, 5/23 for international students; for spring admission, 11/15 priority date for domestic students, 11/15 for international students. Applications are processed on a rolling basis. Application fee: $50. Electronic applications accepted. *Financial support:* In 2011–12, 68 students received support, including 6 research assistantships (averaging $8,078 per year); Federal Work-Study and institutionally sponsored loans also available. Support available to part-time students. Financial award application deadline: 4/1; financial award applicants required to submit FAFSA. *Faculty research:* Advanced composite materials in bridges, strengthening existing bridges with carbon and glass fiber sheets, development of drive shafts using composite materials. *Unit head:* Dr. Nabil Grace, Dean, 248-204-2500, Fax: 248-204-2509, E-mail: engrdean@ltu.edu. *Application contact:* Jane Rohrback, Director of Admissions, 248-204-3160, Fax: 248-204-2228, E-mail: admissions@ltu.edu. Web site: http://www.ltu.edu/engineering/index.asp.

Lehigh University, P.C. Rossin College of Engineering and Applied Science, Department of Electrical and Computer Engineering, Bethlehem, PA 18015. Offers electrical engineering (M Eng, MS, PhD); photonics (MS); wireless network engineering (MS). Part-time programs available. *Faculty:* 19 full-time (4 women). *Students:* 43 full-time (7 women), 14 part-time (4 women); includes 2 minority (1 Asian, non-Hispanic/Latino; 1 Hispanic/Latino), 49 international. Average age 26. 383 applicants, 5% accepted, 12 enrolled. In 2011, 15 master's, 14 doctorates awarded. Terminal master's awarded for partial completion of doctoral program. *Degree requirements:* For master's, thesis optional; for doctorate, thesis/dissertation, qualifying or comprehensive exam for all 1st year PhD's; general exam 7 months or more prior to completion/dissertation defense. *Entrance requirements:* For master's and doctorate, GRE General Test, BS in field or related field. Additional exam requirements/recommendations for international students: Required—TOEFL (minimum score 79 iBT). *Application deadline:* For fall admission, 1/15 priority date for domestic students, 1/15 for international students; for spring admission, 11/1 for domestic and international students. Application fee: $75. Electronic applications accepted. *Financial support:* In 2011–12, 48 students received support, including 4 fellowships with full tuition reimbursements available (averaging $18,360 per year), 42 research assistantships with full tuition reimbursements available (averaging $21,600 per year), 5 teaching assistantships with full tuition reimbursements available (averaging $18,819 per year); career-related internships or fieldwork, Federal Work-Study, institutionally sponsored loans, scholarships/grants, tuition waivers (full and partial), and unspecified assistantships also available. Support available to part-time students. Financial award application deadline: 1/15. *Faculty research:* Nanostructures/nanodevices, terahertz generation, analog devices, mixed mode design and signal circuits, optoelectronic sensors, micro-fabrication technology and design, packaging/reliability of microsensors, coding and networking information theory, radio frequency, wireless and optical wireless communication, wireless networks. *Total annual research expenditures:* $3.2 million. *Unit head:* Dr. Filbert J. Bartoli, Chair, 610-758-4069, Fax: 610-758-6279, E-mail: fjb205@lehigh.edu. *Application contact:* Coley B. Burke, Graduate Coordinator, 610-758-4072, Fax: 610-758-6279, E-mail: cbb310@lehigh.edu. Web site: http://www.ece.lehigh.edu/.

Louisiana State University and Agricultural and Mechanical College, Graduate School, College of Engineering, Department of Electrical and Computer Engineering, Baton Rouge, LA 70803. Offers MSEE, PhD. *Faculty:* 26 full-time (1 woman), 1 part-time/adjunct (0 women). *Students:* 92 full-time (11 women), 11 part-time (2 women); includes 5 minority (1 Black or African American, non-Hispanic/Latino; 2 Asian, non-Hispanic/Latino; 2 Hispanic/Latino), 89 international. Average age 27. 207 applicants, 65% accepted, 14 enrolled. In 2011, 37 master's, 11 doctorates awarded. Terminal master's awarded for partial completion of doctoral program. *Degree requirements:* For master's, thesis optional; for doctorate, thesis/dissertation. *Entrance requirements:* For master's, GRE General Test, minimum GPA of 3.0; for doctorate, GRE General Test, minimum GPA of 3.5. Additional exam requirements/recommendations for international students: Required—TOEFL (minimum score 550 paper-based; 213 computer-based; 79 iBT) or IELTS (minimum score 6.5). *Application deadline:* For fall admission, 1/25 priority date for domestic students, 5/15 for international students; for spring admission, 10/15 for international students. Applications are processed on a rolling basis. Application fee: $50 ($70 for international students). Electronic applications accepted. *Financial support:* In 2011–12, 79 students received support, including 5 fellowships with full and partial tuition reimbursements available (averaging $18,269 per year), 40 research assistantships with full and partial tuition reimbursements available (averaging $14,678 per year), 29 teaching assistantships with full and partial tuition reimbursements available (averaging $13,194 per year); Federal Work-Study, institutionally sponsored loans, health care benefits, tuition waivers (full and partial), and unspecified assistantships also available. Financial award application deadline: 2/28; financial award applicants required to submit FAFSA. *Faculty research:* Computer engineering, electronics, control systems and signal processing, communications. *Total annual research expenditures:* $1.3 million. *Unit head:* Dr. Pratul Ajmera, Interim Chair, 225-578-5534, Fax: 225-578-5200, E-mail: ajmera@lsu.edu. *Application contact:* Dr. Guoxiang GuU, Graduate Adviser, 225-578-5534, Fax: 225-578-5200, E-mail: ggu@lsu.edu. Web site: http://www.ece.lsu.edu/.

Louisiana Tech University, Graduate School, College of Engineering and Science, Department of Electrical Engineering, Ruston, LA 71272. Offers MS, PhD. Part-time programs available. Terminal master's awarded for partial completion of doctoral program. *Degree requirements:* For master's, thesis; for doctorate, thesis/dissertation. *Entrance requirements:* For master's, GRE General Test, minimum GPA of 3.0 in last 60 hours; for doctorate, minimum graduate GPA of 3.25 (with MS) or GRE General Test. Additional exam requirements/recommendations for international students: Required—TOEFL. *Faculty research:* Communications, computers and microprocessors, electrical and power systems, pattern recognition, robotics.

Manhattan College, Graduate Division, School of Engineering, Program in Electrical Engineering, Riverdale, NY 10471. Offers MS. Part-time and evening/weekend programs available. *Faculty:* 7 full-time (1 woman), 2 part-time/adjunct (0 women).

Students: 8 full-time (1 woman), 12 part-time (all women); includes 11 minority (6 Black or African American, non-Hispanic/Latino; 2 Asian, non-Hispanic/Latino; 3 Hispanic/Latino), 2 international. Average age 24. 9 applicants, 56% accepted, 2 enrolled. In 2011, 10 master's awarded. *Degree requirements:* For master's, thesis or alternative. *Entrance requirements:* For master's, GRE (recommended), minimum GPA of 3.0. Additional exam requirements/recommendations for international students: Required—TOEFL (minimum score 550 paper-based; 213 computer-based; 80 iBT), IELTS (minimum score 6). *Application deadline:* For fall admission, 8/10 priority date for domestic students, 8/10 for international students; for spring admission, 1/7 for domestic and international students. Applications are processed on a rolling basis. Application fee: $50. *Expenses: Tuition:* Full-time $14,850; part-time $825 per credit. *Required fees:* $390; $150. *Financial support:* In 2011–12, 3 students received support, including 5 teaching assistantships with partial tuition reimbursements available (averaging $8,000 per year); career-related internships or fieldwork, Federal Work-Study, scholarships/grants, and laboratory assistantships also available. Support available to part-time students. Financial award application deadline: 5/15. *Faculty research:* Multimedia tools, neural networks, robotic control systems, magnetic resonance imaging, telemedicine, computer-based instruction. *Unit head:* Dr. Gordon Silverman, Chairperson, 718-862-7153, Fax: 718-862-7162, E-mail: gordon.silverman@manhattan.edu. *Application contact:* Coralie Gale, Chairperson, 718-862-7153, Fax: 718-862-7162, E-mail: coralie.gale@manhattan.edu. Web site: http://www.engineering.manhattan.edu.

Marquette University, Graduate School, College of Engineering, Department of Electrical and Computer Engineering, Milwaukee, WI 53201-1881. Offers digital signal processing (Certificate); electric machines, drives, and controls (Certificate); electrical and computer engineering (MS, PhD); microwaves and antennas (Certificate); sensors and smart systems (Certificate). Part-time and evening/weekend programs available. *Faculty:* 15 full-time (2 women), 5 part-time/adjunct (0 women). *Students:* 33 full-time (8 women), 27 part-time (6 women); includes 8 minority (2 Black or African American, non-Hispanic/Latino; 3 Asian, non-Hispanic/Latino; 2 Hispanic/Latino; 1 Two or more races, non-Hispanic/Latino), 29 international. Average age 25. 85 applicants, 60% accepted, 14 enrolled. In 2011, 13 master's, 3 doctorates awarded. Terminal master's awarded for partial completion of doctoral program. *Degree requirements:* For master's, comprehensive exam (for some programs), thesis optional; for doctorate, thesis/dissertation, dissertation defense, qualifying exam. *Entrance requirements:* For master's, GRE General Test (recommended), official transcripts from all current and previous colleges/universities except Marquette, three letters of recommendation; for doctorate, GRE General Test, minimum GPA of 3.0, official transcripts from all current and previous colleges/universities except Marquette, three letters of recommendation, statement of purpose, submission of any English language publications authored by applicant (strongly recommended). Additional exam requirements/recommendations for international students: Required—TOEFL (minimum score 530 paper-based; 78 computer-based). *Application deadline:* For fall admission, 7/15 priority date for domestic students; for spring admission, 11/15 for domestic students. Applications are processed on a rolling basis. Application fee: $50. Electronic applications accepted. *Expenses: Tuition:* Full-time $17,010; part-time $945 per credit hour. Tuition and fees vary according to program. *Financial support:* In 2011–12, 22 students received support, including 3 fellowships with partial tuition reimbursements available (averaging $9,826 per year), 1 research assistantship with full tuition reimbursement available (averaging $13,745 per year), 9 teaching assistantships with full tuition reimbursements available (averaging $14,020 per year); scholarships/grants, health care benefits, tuition waivers (partial), and unspecified assistantships also available. Support available to part-time students. Financial award application deadline: 2/15. *Faculty research:* Electric machines, drives, and controls; applied solid-state electronics; computers and signal processing; microwaves and antennas; solid state devices and acoustic wave sensors. *Total annual research expenditures:* $885,354. *Unit head:* Dr. Edwin E. Yaz, Chair, 414-288-6820, Fax: 414-288-5579, E-mail: edwin.yaz@marquette.edu. *Application contact:* Dr. Michael Johnson, Director of Graduate Studies, 414-288-0631, Fax: 414-288-5579, E-mail: michael.johnson@marquette.edu. Web site: http://www.marquette.edu/engineering/electrical_computer/grad.shtml.

Massachusetts Institute of Technology, School of Engineering, Department of Electrical Engineering and Computer Science, Cambridge, MA 02139. Offers computer science (PhD, Sc D, ECS); computer science and engineering (PhD, Sc D); electrical engineering (PhD, Sc D, EE); electrical engineering and computer science (M Eng, SM, PhD, Sc D); SM/MBA. *Faculty:* 125 full-time (17 women). *Students:* 800 full-time (198 women), 3 part-time (1 woman); includes 181 minority (13 Black or African American, non-Hispanic/Latino; 1 American Indian or Alaska Native, non-Hispanic/Latino; 130 Asian, non-Hispanic/Latino; 30 Hispanic/Latino; 7 Two or more races, non-Hispanic/Latino), 365 international. Average age 26. 3,023 applicants, 12% accepted, 259 enrolled. In 2011, 209 master's, 101 doctorates, 5 other advanced degrees awarded. Terminal master's awarded for partial completion of doctoral program. *Degree requirements:* For master's and other advanced degree, thesis; for doctorate, comprehensive exam, thesis/dissertation. *Entrance requirements:* Additional exam requirements/recommendations for international students: Required—TOEFL (minimum score 250 computer-based; 100 iBT), IELTS (minimum score 7). *Application deadline:* For fall admission, 12/15 for domestic and international students. Application fee: $75. Electronic applications accepted. *Expenses: Tuition:* Full-time $40,460; part-time $630 per credit hour. *Required fees:* $272. *Financial support:* In 2011–12, 739 students received support, including 144 fellowships (averaging $31,200 per year), 492 research assistantships (averaging $30,000 per year), 120 teaching assistantships (averaging $31,200 per year); career-related internships or fieldwork, Federal Work-Study, institutionally sponsored loans, scholarships/grants, traineeships, health care benefits, and unspecified assistantships also available. *Faculty research:* Artificial intelligence and applications; robotics; computer architecture, software, systems, and networks; computation theory, cryptography, and algorithms; communications, control, signal processing, and optimization; devices, electronics, electrodynamics, and photonics; bioelectrical engineering; computational biology. *Total annual research expenditures:* $97.5 million. *Unit head:* Prof. Anantha P. Chandrakasan, Head, 617-253-4600, Fax: 617-258-7354, E-mail: hq@eecs.mit.edu. *Application contact:* Graduate Admissions, 617-253-4603, Fax: 617-258-7354, E-mail: grad-ap@eecs.mit.edu. Web site: http://www.eecs.mit.edu/.

McGill University, Faculty of Graduate and Postdoctoral Studies, Faculty of Engineering, Department of Electrical and Computer Engineering, Montréal, QC H3A 2T5, Canada. Offers M Eng, PhD.

McMaster University, School of Graduate Studies, Faculty of Engineering, Department of Electrical and Computer Engineering, Hamilton, ON L8S 4M2, Canada. Offers electrical engineering (M Eng, MA Sc, PhD). *Degree requirements:* For master's, thesis; for doctorate, comprehensive exam, thesis/dissertation. *Entrance requirements:* Additional exam requirements/recommendations for international students: Required—TOEFL (minimum score 550 paper-based; 213 computer-based). *Faculty research:*

Robust and blind adaptive filtering, topics in statistical signal processing, local and metropolitan area networks, smart antennas, embedded wireless communications.

McNeese State University, Doré School of Graduate Studies, College of Engineering and Engineering Technology, Lake Charles, LA 70609. Offers chemical engineering (M Eng); civil engineering (M Eng); electrical engineering (M Eng); engineering management (M Eng); mechanical engineering (M Eng); pump reliability engineering (Postbaccalaureate Certificate). Part-time and evening/weekend programs available. *Faculty:* 13 full-time (1 woman). *Students:* 21 full-time (4 women), 18 part-time (5 women); includes 5 minority (4 Black or African American, non-Hispanic/Latino; 1 American Indian or Alaska Native, non-Hispanic/Latino), 23 international. In 2011, 28 master's awarded. *Degree requirements:* For master's, thesis or alternative. *Entrance requirements:* For master's, GRE, minimum undergraduate GPA of 3.0. Additional exam requirements/recommendations for international students: Required—TOEFL (minimum score 560 paper-based; 220 computer-based; 83 iBT). *Application deadline:* For fall admission, 5/15 priority date for domestic students, 5/15 for international students; for spring admission, 10/15 priority date for domestic students, 10/15 for international students. Applications are processed on a rolling basis. Application fee: $20 ($30 for international students). *Expenses:* Tuition, state resident: part-time $519 per credit hour. Tuition and fees vary according to course load. *Financial support:* Federal Work-Study available. Support available to part-time students. Financial award application deadline: 5/1. *Unit head:* Dr. Nikos Kiritsis, Dean, 337-475-5875, Fax: 337-475-5237, E-mail: nikosk@mcneese.edu. *Application contact:* Dr. George F. Mead, Jr., Interim Dean of Dore' School of Graduate Studies, 337-475-5396, Fax: 337-475-5397, E-mail: admissions@mcneese.edu.

Memorial University of Newfoundland, School of Graduate Studies, Faculty of Engineering and Applied Science, St. John's, NL A1C 5S7, Canada. Offers civil engineering (M Eng, PhD); electrical and computer engineering (M Eng, PhD); mechanical engineering (M Eng, PhD); ocean and naval architecture engineering (M Eng, PhD). Part-time programs available. *Degree requirements:* For master's, thesis; for doctorate, comprehensive exam, thesis/dissertation, oral thesis defense. *Entrance requirements:* For master's, 2nd class degree; for doctorate, master's degree in engineering. Electronic applications accepted. *Faculty research:* Engineering analysis, environmental and hydrotechnical studies, manufacturing and robotics, mechanics, structures and materials.

Mercer University, Graduate Studies, Macon Campus, School of Engineering, Macon, GA 31207-0003. Offers biomedical engineering (MSE); computer engineering (MSE); electrical engineering (MSE); engineering management (MSE); environmental engineering (MSE); environmental systems (MS); mechanical engineering (MSE); software engineering (MSE); software systems (MS); technical communications management (MS); technical management (MS). Part-time and evening/weekend programs available. Postbaccalaureate distance learning degree programs offered (no on-campus study). *Faculty:* 17 full-time (3 women), 1 part-time/adjunct (0 women). *Students:* 12 full-time (3 women), 113 part-time (28 women); includes 23 minority (13 Black or African American, non-Hispanic/Latino; 9 Asian, non-Hispanic/Latino; 1 Hispanic/Latino). Average age 31. In 2011, 44 master's awarded. *Degree requirements:* For master's, thesis or alternative. *Entrance requirements:* For master's, minimum undergraduate GPA of 3.0. Additional exam requirements/recommendations for international students: Required—TOEFL. *Application deadline:* For fall admission, 7/1 for domestic students; for spring admission, 11/15 for domestic students. Applications are processed on a rolling basis. Application fee: $35 ($50 for international students). Electronic applications accepted. *Expenses:* Contact institution. *Financial support:* Federal Work-Study available. *Unit head:* Dr. Wade H. Shaw, Dean, 478-301-2459, Fax: 478-301-5593, E-mail: shaw_wh@mercer.edu. *Application contact:* Greg Lofton, Graduate Program Coordinator, 478-301-5480, Fax: 478-301-5434, E-mail: lofton_g@mercer.edu. Web site: http://engineering.mercer.edu/.

Michigan State University, The Graduate School, College of Engineering, Department of Electrical and Computer Engineering, East Lansing, MI 48824. Offers electrical engineering (MS, PhD). *Entrance requirements:* Additional exam requirements/recommendations for international students: Required—TOEFL. Electronic applications accepted.

Michigan Technological University, Graduate School, College of Engineering, Department of Electrical and Computer Engineering, Houghton, MI 49931. Offers advanced electric power engineering (Graduate Certificate); computer engineering (MS, PhD); electrical engineering (MS, PhD). Part-time programs available. Postbaccalaureate distance learning degree programs offered (minimal on-campus study). *Faculty:* 31 full-time (3 women), 8 part-time/adjunct (3 women). *Students:* 123 full-time (20 women), 57 part-time (5 women); includes 10 minority (4 Black or African American, non-Hispanic/Latino; 1 Asian, non-Hispanic/Latino; 4 Hispanic/Latino; 1 Two or more races, non-Hispanic/Latino), 111 international. Average age 29. 513 applicants, 50% accepted, 55 enrolled. In 2011, 43 master's, 5 doctorates, 2 other advanced degrees awarded. Terminal master's awarded for partial completion of doctoral program. *Degree requirements:* For master's, comprehensive exam (for some programs), thesis (for some programs); for doctorate, comprehensive exam, thesis/dissertation. *Entrance requirements:* For master's and doctorate, GRE, statement of purpose, official transcripts, 3 letters of recommendation. Additional exam requirements/recommendations for international students: Required—TOEFL (minimum score 100 iBT) or IELTS. *Application deadline:* For fall admission, 2/15 for domestic and international students; for spring admission, 8/15 for domestic and international students. Applications are processed on a rolling basis. Electronic applications accepted. *Expenses:* Contact institution. *Financial support:* In 2011–12, 100 students received support, including 7 fellowships with full tuition reimbursements available (averaging $6,065 per year), 31 research assistantships with full tuition reimbursements available (averaging $6,065 per year), 19 teaching assistantships with full tuition reimbursements available (averaging $6,065 per year); career-related internships or fieldwork, Federal Work-Study, scholarships/grants, health care benefits, tuition waivers (partial), unspecified assistantships, and cooperative program also available. Financial award applicants required to submit FAFSA. *Faculty research:* Information systems (signal processing and communications), solid-state electronics, power and energy systems, computer engineering. *Total annual research expenditures:* $2.4 million. *Unit head:* Dr. Daniel R. Fuhrmann, Department Chair, 906-487-2550, Fax: 906-487-2949, E-mail: ljbohman@mtu.edu. *Application contact:* Michele L. Kamppinen, Secretary 6, 906-487-2550, Fax: 906-487-2949, E-mail: mlkamppi@mtu.edu. Web site: http://www.mtu.edu/ece/.

Minnesota State University Mankato, College of Graduate Studies, College of Science, Engineering and Technology, Department of Electrical and Computer Engineering and Technology, Mankato, MN 56001. Offers MSE. *Students:* 9 full-time (2 women), 12 part-time (0 women). *Degree requirements:* For master's, comprehensive exam, thesis. *Entrance requirements:* For master's, GRE General Test, minimum GPA of 3.0 during previous 2 years. Additional exam requirements/recommendations for international students: Required—TOEFL (minimum score 550 paper-based; 213 computer-based; 80 iBT). *Application deadline:* For fall admission, 7/1 priority date for domestic students; for spring admission, 11/1 for domestic students. Applications are processed on a rolling basis. Application fee: $40. Electronic applications accepted. *Financial support:* Research assistantships with full tuition reimbursements, teaching assistantships with full tuition reimbursements, and unspecified assistantships available. Financial award application deadline: 3/15. *Unit head:* Dr. Vince Winstead, Graduate Coordinator, 507-389-5747. *Application contact:* 507-389-2321, E-mail: grad@mnsu.edu. Web site: http://cset.mnsu.edu/ecet/.

Mississippi State University, Bagley College of Engineering, Department of Electrical and Computer Engineering, Mississippi State, MS 39762. Offers computer engineering (MS, PhD); electrical engineering (MS, PhD). Part-time programs available. Postbaccalaureate distance learning degree programs offered (minimal on-campus study). *Faculty:* 22 full-time (1 woman). *Students:* 70 full-time (9 women), 36 part-time (3 women); includes 6 minority (3 Black or African American, non-Hispanic/Latino; 3 Asian, non-Hispanic/Latino), 58 international. Average age 29. 204 applicants, 24% accepted, 16 enrolled. In 2011, 18 master's, 9 doctorates awarded. Terminal master's awarded for partial completion of doctoral program. *Degree requirements:* For master's, comprehensive exam, thesis optional; for doctorate, comprehensive exam, thesis/dissertation, written exam. *Entrance requirements:* For master's, GRE General Test, minimum undergraduate GPA of 3.0; for doctorate, GRE, minimum graduate GPA of 3.5. Additional exam requirements/recommendations for international students: Required—TOEFL (minimum score 550 paper-based; 213 computer-based; 79 iBT); Recommended—IELTS (minimum score 6.5). *Application deadline:* For fall admission, 7/1 for domestic students, 5/1 for international students; for spring admission, 11/1 for domestic students, 9/1 for international students. Applications are processed on a rolling basis. Application fee: $40. Electronic applications accepted. *Expenses:* Tuition, state resident: full-time $5805; part-time $322.50 per credit hour. Tuition, nonresident: full-time $14,670; part-time $815 per credit hour. *Financial support:* In 2011–12, 22 research assistantships with full tuition reimbursements (averaging $16,419 per year), 18 teaching assistantships with full tuition reimbursements (averaging $14,450 per year) were awarded; Federal Work-Study, institutionally sponsored loans, scholarships/grants, and unspecified assistantships also available. Financial award application deadline: 4/1; financial award applicants required to submit FAFSA. *Faculty research:* Digital computing, power, controls, communication systems, microelectronics. *Total annual research expenditures:* $21.9 million. *Unit head:* Dr. Nicholas H. Younan, Jr., Professor and Department Head, 662-325-3912, Fax: 662-325-2298, E-mail: ece-head@ece.msstate.edu. *Application contact:* Dr. James E. Fowler, Professor and Interim Graduate Program Director, 662-325-3640, Fax: 662-325-2298, E-mail: fowler@ece.msstate.edu. Web site: http://www.ece.msstate.edu/.

Missouri University of Science and Technology, Graduate School, School of Engineering, Department of Electrical and Computer Engineering, Rolla, MO 65409. Offers computer engineering (MS, DE, PhD); electrical engineering (MS, DE, PhD). Part-time and evening/weekend programs available. Terminal master's awarded for partial completion of doctoral program. *Degree requirements:* For master's, thesis optional; for doctorate, comprehensive exam, thesis/dissertation, departmental qualifying exam. *Entrance requirements:* For master's, GRE General Test (minimum score 1100 verbal and quantitative, writing 4.5); for doctorate, GRE General Test (minimum score: verbal and quantitative 1100, writing 3.5). Additional exam requirements/recommendations for international students: Required—TOEFL. Electronic applications accepted. *Faculty research:* Power systems, computer/communication networks, intelligent control/robotics, robust control, nanotechnologies.

Montana State University, College of Graduate Studies, College of Engineering, Department of Electrical and Computer Engineering, Bozeman, MT 59717. Offers electrical engineering (MS); engineering (PhD), including electrical and computer engineering option. Part-time programs available. *Degree requirements:* For master's, comprehensive exam, thesis (for some programs); for doctorate, comprehensive exam, thesis/dissertation. *Entrance requirements:* For master's, GRE, BS in electrical or computer engineering or related field; for doctorate, GRE, MS in electrical or computer engineering or related field. Additional exam requirements/recommendations for international students: Required—TOEFL (minimum score 550 paper-based; 213 computer-based). Electronic applications accepted. *Faculty research:* Optics and optoelectonics, communications and signal processing, microfabrication, complex systems and control, energy systems.

Montana Tech of The University of Montana, Graduate School, Electrical Engineering Program, Butte, MT 59701-8997. Offers MS. Part-time programs available. *Faculty:* 5 full-time (0 women). *Students:* 5 full-time (0 women), 1 part-time (0 women), 1 international. 6 applicants, 67% accepted, 4 enrolled. In 2011, 3 master's awarded. *Degree requirements:* For master's, comprehensive exam (for some programs), thesis optional. *Entrance requirements:* For master's, minimum GPA of 3.0. Additional exam requirements/recommendations for international students: Required—TOEFL (minimum score 525 paper-based; 195 computer-based; 71 iBT). *Application deadline:* For fall admission, 4/1 priority date for domestic students, 3/1 for international students; for spring admission, 10/1 priority date for domestic students, 7/1 for international students. Applications are processed on a rolling basis. Application fee: $30. Electronic applications accepted. *Financial support:* In 2011–12, 3 students received support, including 5 teaching assistantships with partial tuition reimbursements available (averaging $4,000 per year); research assistantships with full tuition reimbursements available, career-related internships or fieldwork, tuition waivers (full and partial), and unspecified assistantships also available. Financial award application deadline: 4/1. *Faculty research:* Energy grid modernization, battery diagnostics instrumentation, wind turbine research, improving energy efficiency. *Unit head:* Dr. Daniel Trudnowski, Professor, 406-496-4681, Fax: 406-496-4849, E-mail: dtrudnowski@mtech.edu. *Application contact:* Fred Sullivan, Administrator, Graduate School, 406-496-4304, Fax: 406-496-4710, E-mail: fsullivan@mtech.edu. Web site: http://www.mtech.edu/academics/gradschool/degreeprograms/degrees-electrical-engineering.htm.

Morgan State University, School of Graduate Studies, Clarence M. Mitchell, Jr. School of Engineering, Baltimore, MD 21251. Offers civil engineering (M Eng, D Eng); electrical engineering (M Eng, D Eng); industrial engineering (M Eng, D Eng); transportation (MS). Part-time and evening/weekend programs available. *Degree requirements:* For master's, thesis, comprehensive exam or equivalent; for doctorate, thesis/dissertation, comprehensive exam or equivalent. *Entrance requirements:* For master's, GRE, minimum undergraduate GPA of 2.5; for doctorate, GRE, minimum GPA of 3.0. Additional exam requirements/recommendations for international students: Required—TOEFL (minimum score 550 paper-based; 213 computer-based).

Naval Postgraduate School, Departments and Academic Groups, Department of Electrical and Computer Engineering, Monterey, CA 93943-5216. Offers computer engineering (MS); electrical engineer (EE); electrical engineering (PhD); engineering acoustics (MS); engineering science (MS). Program only open to commissioned officers of the United States and friendly nations and selected United States federal civilian employees. *Accreditation:* ABET (one or more programs are accredited). Part-time programs available. Postbaccalaureate distance learning degree programs offered (minimal on-campus study). *Faculty:* 32 full-time (5 women), 4 part-time/adjunct (1 woman). *Students:* 59 full-time (4 women), 66 part-time (8 women); includes 27 minority (7 Black or African American, non-Hispanic/Latino; 12 Asian, non-Hispanic/Latino; 8 Hispanic/Latino), 11 international. In 2011, 38 master's, 8 other advanced degrees awarded. *Degree requirements:* For master's and EE, thesis (for some programs), capstone project or research/dissertation paper (for some programs); for doctorate, thesis/dissertation. *Faculty research:* Theory and design of digital communication systems; behavior modeling for detection, identification, prediction and reaction in AI systems solutions; waveform design for target class discrimination with closed-loop radar; iterative technique for system identification with adaptive signal design. *Total annual research expenditures:* $3.5 million. *Unit head:* Prof. Clark Robertson, Department Chair, 831-656-2082, E-mail: crobertson@nps.edu. Web site: http://www.nps.edu/Academics/Schools/GSEAS/Departments/ECE/.

Naval Postgraduate School, Departments and Academic Groups, Space Systems Academic Group, Monterey, CA 93943. Offers applied physics (MS); astronautical engineering (MS); computer science (MS); electrical engineering (MS); mechanical engineering (MS); space systems (Engr); space systems operations (MS). Program only open to commissioned officers of the United States and friendly nations and selected United States federal civilian employees. Part-time programs available. *Faculty:* 5 full-time, 5 part-time/adjunct (2 women). *Students:* 37 full-time (2 women), 14 part-time; includes 11 minority (5 Black or African American, non-Hispanic/Latino; 2 Asian, non-Hispanic/Latino; 4 Hispanic/Latino), 1 international. Average age 33. In 2011, 20 master's awarded. *Degree requirements:* For master's and Engr, thesis; for doctorate, thesis/dissertation. *Faculty research:* Militaryapplications for space; space reconnaissance and remote sensing; radiation-hardened electronics for space; design, construction and operations of small satellites; satellite communications systems. *Total annual research expenditures:* $2 million. *Unit head:* Dr. Rudy Panholzer, Chairman, 831-656-2154. Web site: http://www.nps.edu/Academics/Schools/GSEAS/Departments/SpaceSystems/.

Naval Postgraduate School, Departments and Academic Groups, Undersea Warfare Academic Group, Monterey, CA 93943. Offers applied mathematics (MS); applied physics (MS); applied science (MS), including acoustics, operations research, physical oceanography, signal processing; electrical engineering (MS); engineering acoustics (MS, PhD); engineering science (MS), including electrical engineering, mechanical engineering; mechanical engineer (ME); mechanical engineering (MS, MSME); meteorology (MS); operations research (MS); physical oceanography (MS). Program only open to commissioned officers of the United States and friendly nations and selected United States federal civilian employees. Part-time programs available. *Students:* 2 full-time, both international. Average age 36. *Degree requirements:* For master's, thesis. *Faculty research:* Unmanned/autonomous vehicles, sea mines and countermeasures, submarine warfare in the twentieth and twenty-first centuries. *Unit head:* Dr. Clyde Scandrett, Academic Group Chairman, 831-656-2027. Web site: http://www.nps.edu/Academics/Schools/GSEAS/Departments/USW/USW-Index.html.

New Jersey Institute of Technology, Office of Graduate Studies, Newark College of Engineering, Department of Electrical and Computer Engineering, Program in Bioelectronics, Newark, NJ 07102. Offers MS. *Students:* 7 full-time (1 woman), 1 part-time; includes 1 minority (Asian, non-Hispanic/Latino), 4 international. Average age 26. 11 applicants, 82% accepted, 4 enrolled. *Entrance requirements:* For master's, GRE General Test. Additional exam requirements/recommendations for international students: Required—TOEFL (minimum score 550 paper-based; 213 computer-based; 79 iBT). *Application deadline:* For fall admission, 6/1 priority date for domestic students, 5/1 for international students; for spring admission, 11/15 priority date for domestic students, 11/15 for international students. Applications are processed on a rolling basis. Application fee: $65. Electronic applications accepted. *Expenses:* Tuition, state resident: full-time $7980; part-time $867 per credit. Tuition, nonresident: full-time $11,336; part-time $1196 per credit. *Required fees:* $230 per credit. *Financial support:* Application deadline: 1/15. *Unit head:* Dr. Leonid Tsybeskov, Chair, 973-596-6594, E-mail: leonid.tsybeskov@njit.edu. *Application contact:* Kathryn Kelly, Director of Admissions, 973-596-3300, Fax: 973-596-3461, E-mail: admissions@njit.edu. Web site: http://ece.njit.edu/academics/graduate/ms-bioelectronics/index.php.

New Jersey Institute of Technology, Office of Graduate Studies, Newark College of Engineering, Department of Electrical and Computer Engineering, Program in Electrical Engineering, Newark, NJ 07102. Offers MS, PhD. Part-time and evening/weekend programs available. *Students:* 195 full-time (47 women), 62 part-time (7 women); includes 35 minority (8 Black or African American, non-Hispanic/Latino; 19 Asian, non-Hispanic/Latino; 8 Hispanic/Latino), 195 international. Average age 26. 809 applicants, 73% accepted, 105 enrolled. In 2011, 68 master's, 8 doctorates awarded. Terminal master's awarded for partial completion of doctoral program. *Degree requirements:* For master's, thesis optional; for doctorate, thesis/dissertation, residency. *Entrance requirements:* For master's, GRE General Test; for doctorate, GRE General Test, minimum graduate GPA of 3.5. Additional exam requirements/recommendations for international students: Required—TOEFL (minimum score 550 paper-based; 213 computer-based; 79 iBT). *Application deadline:* For fall admission, 6/1 priority date for domestic students, 5/1 for international students; for spring admission, 11/15 priority date for domestic students, 11/15 for international students. Applications are processed on a rolling basis. Application fee: $65. Electronic applications accepted. *Expenses:* Tuition, state resident: full-time $7980; part-time $867 per credit. Tuition, nonresident: full-time $11,336; part-time $1196 per credit. *Required fees:* $230 per credit. *Financial support:* Fellowships with full and partial tuition reimbursements, research assistantships with full and partial tuition reimbursements, teaching assistantships with full and partial tuition reimbursements, career-related internships or fieldwork, Federal Work-Study, institutionally sponsored loans, and unspecified assistantships available. Financial award application deadline: 3/15. *Unit head:* Dr. Leonid Tsybeskov, Interim Chair, 973-596-6594, E-mail: leonid.tsybeskov@njit.edu. *Application contact:* Kathryn Kelly, Director of Admissions, 973-596-3300, Fax: 973-596-3461, E-mail: admissions@njit.edu.

New Mexico Institute of Mining and Technology, Graduate Studies, Department of Electrical Engineering, Socorro, NM 87801. Offers MS. *Faculty:* 9 full-time (0 women), 2 part-time/adjunct (0 women). *Students:* 12 full-time (0 women), 1 part-time (0 women); includes 4 minority (1 Black or African American, non-Hispanic/Latino; 1 American Indian or Alaska Native, non-Hispanic/Latino; 2 Two or more races, non-Hispanic/Latino). Average age 25. 12 applicants, 67% accepted, 6 enrolled. In 2011, 3 master's awarded. *Entrance requirements:* Additional exam requirements/recommendations for international students: Required—TOEFL (minimum score 540 paper-based; 207 computer-based). *Application deadline:* For fall admission, 3/1 priority date for domestic students; for spring admission, 6/1 priority date for domestic students. Applications are processed on a rolling basis. Electronic applications accepted. *Expenses:* Tuition, state

resident: full-time $4849; part-time $269.41 per credit hour. Tuition, nonresident: full-time $16,041; part-time $891.15 per credit hour. *Required fees:* $622; $65 per credit hour. $20 per semester. Part-time tuition and fees vary according to course load. *Financial support:* In 2011–12, 1 fellowship (averaging $7,200 per year), 2 research assistantships (averaging $25,587 per year), 7 teaching assistantships (averaging $9,691 per year) were awarded. *Unit head:* Dr. Kevin Wedeward, Chair, 575-835-5708, Fax: 575-835-5332, E-mail: wedeward@ee.nmt.edu. *Application contact:* Dr. Lorie Liebrock, Dean of Graduate Studies, 575-835-5513, Fax: 575-835-5476, E-mail: graduate@nmt.edu. Web site: http://www.ee.nmt.edu/.

New Mexico State University, Graduate School, College of Engineering, Klipsch School of Electrical and Computer Engineering, Las Cruces, NM 88003-8001. Offers MSEE, PhD. Part-time and evening/weekend programs available. Postbaccalaureate distance learning degree programs offered (no on-campus study). *Faculty:* 20 full-time, (2 women), 1 part-time/adjunct (0 women). *Students:* 92 full-time (17 women), 46 part-time (5 women); includes 27 minority (2 American Indian or Alaska Native, non-Hispanic/Latino; 1 Asian, non-Hispanic/Latino; 23 Hispanic/Latino; 1 Two or more races, non-Hispanic/Latino), 73 international. Average age 30. 44 applicants, 68% accepted, 11 enrolled. In 2011, 34 master's, 1 doctorate awarded. Terminal master's awarded for partial completion of doctoral program. *Degree requirements:* For master's, thesis (for some programs), final oral or written exam; for doctorate, comprehensive exam, thesis/dissertation. *Entrance requirements:* For master's, GRE, minimum GPA of 3.0; for doctorate, departmental qualifying exam, minimum GPA of 3.0. Additional exam requirements/recommendations for international students: Required—TOEFL (minimum score 550 paper-based; 79 iBT), IELTS (minimum score 6.5). *Application deadline:* For fall admission, 3/1 priority date for domestic students, 3/1 for international students; for spring admission, 8/1 priority date for domestic students, 8/1 for international students. Applications are processed on a rolling basis. Application fee: $40 ($50 for international students). Electronic applications accepted. *Expenses:* Tuition, state resident: full-time $5004; part-time $208.50 per credit. Tuition, nonresident: full-time $17,446; part-time $726.90 per credit. *Financial support:* In 2011–12, 4 fellowships (averaging $10,061 per year), 35 research assistantships (averaging $20,720 per year), 29 teaching assistantships (averaging $20,642 per year) were awarded; career-related internships or fieldwork, Federal Work-Study, health care benefits, and unspecified assistantships also available. Support available to part-time students. Financial award application deadline: 3/1. *Faculty research:* Image and digital signal processing, energy systems, wireless communication, analog VLSI design, electro-optics. *Unit head:* Dr. Vojin Oklobdzija, Head, 575-646-3115, Fax: 575-646-1435, E-mail: vojin@nmsu.edu. *Application contact:* Sue Kord, Records Technician I, 575-646-6440, Fax: 575-646-1435, E-mail: kkord@nmsu.edu. Web site: http://ece.nmsu.edu/index.php.

New York Institute of Technology, Graduate Division, School of Engineering and Computing Sciences, Program in Electrical Engineering and Computer Engineering, Old Westbury, NY 11568-8000. Offers MS. Part-time and evening/weekend programs available. *Students:* 69 full-time (5 women), 59 part-time (5 women); includes 30 minority (9 Black or African American, non-Hispanic/Latino; 1 American Indian or Alaska Native, non-Hispanic/Latino; 17 Asian, non-Hispanic/Latino; 2 Hispanic/Latino; 1 Two or more races, non-Hispanic/Latino), 71 international. Average age 27. In 2011, 62 master's awarded. *Degree requirements:* For master's, project. *Entrance requirements:* For master's, GRE General Test (if QPA less than 2.85), BS in electrical engineering or related field, minimum QPA of 2.85. Additional exam requirements/recommendations for international students: Required—TOEFL (minimum score 550 paper-based; 213 computer-based). *Application deadline:* For fall admission, 7/1 priority date for domestic students; for spring admission, 12/1 priority date for domestic students. Applications are processed on a rolling basis. Application fee: $50. Electronic applications accepted. *Expenses:* Tuition: Part-time $930 per credit hour. *Financial support:* Fellowships, research assistantships with partial tuition reimbursements, institutionally sponsored loans, tuition waivers (full and partial), and unspecified assistantships available. Support available to part-time students. Financial award applicants required to submit FAFSA. *Faculty research:* Computer networks, control theory, light waves and optics, robotics, signal processing. *Unit head:* Dr. Ayat Jafari, Chair, 516-686-7569, Fax: 516-686-7439, E-mail: ajafari@nyit.edu. *Application contact:* Dr. Jacquelyn Nealon, Vice President for Enrollment Services, 516-686-7925, Fax: 516-686-7597, E-mail: jnealon@nyit.edu.

Norfolk State University, School of Graduate Studies, School of Science and Technology, Program in Electronics Engineering, Norfolk, VA 23504. Offers MS.

North Carolina Agricultural and Technical State University, School of Graduate Studies, College of Engineering, Department of Electrical and Computer Engineering, Greensboro, NC 27411. Offers electrical engineering (MSEE, PhD), including communications and signal processing, computer engineering, electronic and optical materials and devices, power systems and control. Part-time programs available. *Degree requirements:* For master's, project, thesis defense; for doctorate, thesis/dissertation. *Entrance requirements:* For master's, GRE General Test, GRE Subject Test, minimum GPA of 2.8; for doctorate, GRE General Test, minimum GPA of 3.0. *Faculty research:* Semiconductor compounds, VLSI design, image processing, optical systems and devices, fault-tolerant computing.

North Carolina Agricultural and Technical State University, School of Graduate Studies, School of Technology, Department of Electronics, Computer, and Information Technology, Greensboro, NC 27411. Offers electronics and computer technology (MSIT, MSTM); information technology (MSIT, MSTM).

North Carolina State University, Graduate School, College of Engineering, Department of Electrical and Computer Engineering, Program in Electrical Engineering, Raleigh, NC 27695. Offers MS, PhD. *Degree requirements:* For master's, thesis (for some programs); for doctorate, thesis/dissertation. *Entrance requirements:* For master's and doctorate, GRE. Additional exam requirements/recommendations for international students: Required—TOEFL (minimum score 575 paper-based). Electronic applications accepted. *Faculty research:* Microwave devices, wireless communications, nanoelectronics and photonics, robotic and mechatronics, power electronics.

North Dakota State University, College of Graduate and Interdisciplinary Studies, College of Engineering and Architecture, Department of Electrical and Computer Engineering, Fargo, ND 58108. Offers MS, PhD. Part-time programs available. *Faculty:* 15 full-time (0 women). *Students:* 34 full-time (7 women), 18 part-time (7 women); includes 1 minority (Asian, non-Hispanic/Latino), 41 international. Average age 28. 88 applicants, 42% accepted, 18 enrolled. In 2011, 5 master's, 1 doctorate awarded. Terminal master's awarded for partial completion of doctoral program. *Degree requirements:* For master's, comprehensive exam, thesis; for doctorate, comprehensive exam, thesis/dissertation. *Entrance requirements:* Additional exam requirements/recommendations for international students: Required—TOEFL (minimum score 525 paper-based; 197 computer-based; 71 iBT). *Application deadline:* For fall admission, 2/28 priority date for domestic students, 2/28 for international students; for spring admission, 10/15 for domestic and international students. Application fee: $35. Electronic applications accepted. *Financial support:* In 2011–12, 30 students received support, including 2 fellowships with full tuition reimbursements available (averaging $25,000 per year), 6 research assistantships with full tuition reimbursements available (averaging $8,100 per year), 10 teaching assistantships with full tuition reimbursements available (averaging $8,100 per year); career-related internships or fieldwork, Federal Work-Study, institutionally sponsored loans, and tuition waivers (full) also available. Financial award application deadline: 3/1. *Faculty research:* Computers, power and control systems, microwaves, communications and signal processing, bioengineering. *Unit head:* Dr. Jacob Glower, Chair, 701-231-7608, Fax: 701-231-8677, E-mail: jacob.glower@ndsu.edu. *Application contact:* Dr. Rajesh Kavasseri, Associate Professor, 701-231-7019, E-mail: rajesh.kavasseri@ndsu.edu. Web site: http://www.ece.ndsu.nodak.edu/.

Northeastern University, College of Engineering, Department of Electrical and Computer Engineering, Boston, MA 02115-5096. Offers computer engineering (PhD); electrical engineering (MS, PhD); engineering leadership (MS). *Faculty:* 45 full-time, 2 part-time/adjunct. *Students:* 257 full-time (49 women), 98 part-time (6 women). 1,054 applicants, 47% accepted, 122 enrolled. In 2011, 83 master's, 13 doctorates awarded. *Degree requirements:* For master's, thesis optional; for doctorate, thesis/dissertation, departmental qualifying exam. *Entrance requirements:* For master's and doctorate, GRE General Test. Additional exam requirements/recommendations for international students: Required—TOEFL (minimum score 550 paper-based; 213 computer-based). *Application deadline:* For fall admission, 1/15 priority date for domestic students, 1/15 for international students. Applications are processed on a rolling basis. Application fee: $50. Electronic applications accepted. *Financial support:* In 2011–12, 136 students received support, including 1 fellowship with full tuition reimbursement available, 102 research assistantships with full tuition reimbursements available (averaging $18,325 per year), 32 teaching assistantships with full tuition reimbursements available (averaging $18,325 per year); career-related internships or fieldwork, Federal Work-Study, scholarships/grants, tuition waivers (full), and unspecified assistantships also available. Support available to part-time students. Financial award application deadline: 1/15; financial award applicants required to submit FAFSA. *Faculty research:* Signal processing and sensor data fusion, plasma science, sensing and imaging, power electronics, computer engineering. *Unit head:* Dr. Ali Abur, Chairman, 617-373-4159, Fax: 617-373-8970. *Application contact:* Jeffery Hengel, Admissions Specialist, 617-373-2711, Fax: 617-373-2501, E-mail: grad-eng@coe.neu.edu. Web site: http://www.coe.neu.edu/.

Northern Arizona University, Graduate College, College of Engineering, Forestry and Natural Sciences, Programs in Engineering, Flagstaff , AZ 86011. Offers civil and environmental engineering (M Eng); civil engineering (MSE); computer science (MSE); electrical engineering (M Eng, MSE); engineering (M Eng, MSE); environmental engineering (M Eng, MSE); mechanical engineering (M Eng, MSE). Part-time programs available. Postbaccalaureate distance learning degree programs offered (no on-campus study). *Faculty:* 42 full-time (10 women). *Students:* 15 full-time (1 woman), 12 part-time (1 woman); includes 2 minority (both Hispanic/Latino), 6 international. Average age 28. 29 applicants, 52% accepted, 8 enrolled. In 2011, 15 degrees awarded. *Degree requirements:* For master's, thesis. *Entrance requirements:* For master's, GRE General Test. Additional exam requirements/recommendations for international students: Required—TOEFL (minimum score 550 paper-based; 213 computer-based; 80 iBT), IELTS (minimum score 7). *Application deadline:* For fall admission, 3/1 priority date for domestic students, 3/1 for international students; for spring admission, 9/15 priority date for domestic students, 9/15 for international students. Applications are processed on a rolling basis. Application fee: $65. Electronic applications accepted. *Expenses:* Tuition, state resident: full-time $7190; part-time $355 per credit hour. Tuition, nonresident: full-time $18,092; part-time $1005 per credit hour. *Required fees:* $818; $328 per semester. *Financial support:* In 2011–12, 3 research assistantships with partial tuition reimbursements (averaging $14,541 per year), 12 teaching assistantships with partial tuition reimbursements (averaging $12,863 per year) were awarded; career-related internships or fieldwork, Federal Work-Study, scholarships/grants, health care benefits, and unspecified assistantships also available. Financial award applicants required to submit FAFSA. *Unit head:* Dr. Ernesto Penado, Chair, 928-523-9453, Fax: 928-523-2300, E-mail: ernesto.penado@nau.edu. *Application contact:* Natasha Kypfer, Program Coordinator, 928-523-1447, Fax: 928-523-2300, E-mail: egrmasters@nau.edu. Web site: http://nau.edu/CEFNS/Engineering/.

Northern Illinois University, Graduate School, College of Engineering and Engineering Technology, Department of Electrical Engineering, De Kalb, IL 60115-2854. Offers MS. Part-time and evening/weekend programs available. *Faculty:* 9 full-time (0 women). *Students:* 19 full-time (5 women), 34 part-time (8 women); includes 4 minority (all Asian, non-Hispanic/Latino), 44 international. Average age 24. 161 applicants, 25% accepted, 10 enrolled. In 2011, 27 master's awarded. *Degree requirements:* For master's, comprehensive exam, thesis optional. *Entrance requirements:* For master's, GRE General Test, minimum GPA of 2.75. Additional exam requirements/recommendations for international students: Required—TOEFL (minimum score 550 paper-based; 213 computer-based). *Application deadline:* For fall admission, 6/1 for domestic students, 5/1 for international students; for spring admission, 11/1 for domestic students, 10/1 for international students. Applications are processed on a rolling basis. Application fee: $40. Electronic applications accepted. *Financial support:* In 2011–12, 4 research assistantships with full tuition reimbursements, 14 teaching assistantships with full tuition reimbursements were awarded; fellowships with full tuition reimbursements, career-related internships or fieldwork, Federal Work-Study, scholarships/grants, tuition waivers (full), and staff assistantships also available. Support available to part-time students. Financial award applicants required to submit FAFSA. *Faculty research:* Digital signal processing, optics, nano-electronic devices, physion electronics, VLSI. *Unit head:* Dr. Ibrahim Abdel-motaleb, Chair, 815-753-1290, Fax: 815-753-1289, E-mail: ibrahim@niu.edu. *Application contact:* Graduate School Office, 815-753-0395, E-mail: gradsch@niu.edu. Web site: http://www.niu.edu/ee/.

Northwestern Polytechnic University, School of Engineering, Fremont, CA 94539-7482. Offers computer science (MS); computer systems engineering (MS); electrical engineering (MS). Part-time and evening/weekend programs available. *Degree requirements:* For master's, thesis optional. *Entrance requirements:* For master's, minimum GPA of 3.0. Additional exam requirements/recommendations for international students: Required—TOEFL (minimum score 550 paper-based; 213 computer-based; 79 iBT). *Faculty research:* Computer networking, database design, Internet technology, software engineering, digital signal processing.

Northwestern University, McCormick School of Engineering and Applied Science, Department of Electrical Engineering and Computer Science, Evanston, IL 60208. Offers MS, PhD. MS and PhD admissions and degrees offered through The Graduate School. Part-time programs available. *Faculty:* 52 full-time (10 women). *Students:* 246 full-time (43 women), 15 part-time (6 women); includes 28 minority (1 Black or African American, non-Hispanic/Latino; 20 Asian, non-Hispanic/Latino; 5 Hispanic/Latino; 2 Two or more races, non-Hispanic/Latino), 179 international. Average age 26. 1,203 applicants, 16% accepted, 76 enrolled. In 2011, 43 master's, 24 doctorates awarded.

Terminal master's awarded for partial completion of doctoral program. *Degree requirements:* For master's, comprehensive exam (for some programs), thesis optional; for doctorate, comprehensive exam, thesis/dissertation. *Entrance requirements:* For master's and doctorate, GRE General Test. Additional exam requirements/recommendations for international students: Required—TOEFL (minimum score 577 paper-based, 233 computer-based, 90 iBT) or IELTS. *Application deadline:* For fall admission, 12/31 for domestic and international students; for winter admission, 11/15 for domestic students, 11/1 for international students; for spring admission, 2/15 for domestic students, 2/1 for international students. Application fee: $75. Electronic applications accepted. *Financial support:* Fellowships with full tuition reimbursements, research assistantships with full tuition reimbursements, teaching assistantships with full tuition reimbursements, career-related internships or fieldwork, institutionally sponsored loans, health care benefits, and unspecified assistantships available. Financial award application deadline: 1/15; financial award applicants required to submit FAFSA. *Faculty research:* Solid state and photonics; computing, algorithms, and applications; computer engineering and systems; cognitive systems; graphics and interactive media; signals and systems. *Total annual research expenditures:* $19.2 million. *Unit head:* Dr. Alan Sahakian, Chair, 847-491-7007, Fax: 847-491-4455, E-mail: sahakian@ece.northwestern.edu. *Application contact:* Dr. Chris Riesbeck, Director of Graduate Admissions, 847-491-7279, Fax: 847-491-4455, E-mail: c-riesbeck@northwestern.edu. Web site: http://www.eecs.northwestern.edu/.

Oakland University, Graduate Study and Lifelong Learning, School of Engineering and Computer Science, Department of Electrical and Systems Engineering, Program in Electrical and Computer Engineering, Rochester, MI 48309-4401. Offers MS. Part-time and evening/weekend programs available. *Entrance requirements:* For master's, minimum GPA of 3.0 for unconditional admission. Additional exam requirements/recommendations for international students: Required—TOEFL (minimum score 550 paper-based; 213 computer-based). Electronic applications accepted. *Expenses:* Contact institution.

The Ohio State University, Graduate School, College of Engineering, Department of Electrical and Computer Engineering, Columbus, OH 43210. Offers electrical engineering (MS, PhD). Part-time programs available. *Faculty:* 50. *Students:* 321 full-time (57 women), 89 part-time (10 women); includes 22 minority (3 Black or African American, non-Hispanic/Latino; 13 Asian, non-Hispanic/Latino; 5 Hispanic/Latino; 1 Two or more races, non-Hispanic/Latino), 291 international. Average age 27. In 2011, 52 master's, 30 doctorates awarded. Terminal master's awarded for partial completion of doctoral program. *Degree requirements:* For master's, thesis optional; for doctorate, thesis/dissertation. *Entrance requirements:* Additional exam requirements/recommendations for international students: Required—TOEFL (minimum score 580 paper-based; 237 computer-based; 79 iBT), Michigan English Language Assessment Battery (minimum score 82). *Application deadline:* For fall admission, 8/15 priority date for domestic students, 7/1 for international students; for winter admission, 12/1 priority date for domestic students, 11/1 for international students; for spring admission, 3/1 priority date for domestic students, 2/1 for international students. Applications are processed on a rolling basis. Application fee: $40 ($50 for international students). Electronic applications accepted. *Expenses:* Tuition, state resident: full-time $11,400. Tuition, nonresident: full-time $28,125. Tuition and fees vary according to course load, degree level, campus/location and program. *Financial support:* In 2011–12, 25 fellowships with full tuition reimbursements (averaging $18,000 per year), 100 research assistantships with full tuition reimbursements (averaging $18,000 per year), 30 teaching assistantships with full tuition reimbursements (averaging $15,000 per year) were awarded; career-related internships or fieldwork, Federal Work-Study, institutionally sponsored loans, scholarships/grants, traineeships, health care benefits, and unspecified assistantships also available. Support available to part-time students. *Total annual research expenditures:* $13 million. *Unit head:* Robert Lee, Chair, 614-292-2571, Fax: 614-292-7596, E-mail: lee.146@osu.edu. *Application contact:* Electrical and Computer Engineering Graduate Program, 614-292-2572, Fax: 614-292-7596, E-mail: ecegrad@ece.osu.edu. Web site: http://www.ece.ohio-state.edu/.

Ohio University, Graduate College, Russ College of Engineering and Technology, School of Electrical Engineering and Computer Science, Athens, OH 45701-2979. Offers computer science (MS); electrical engineering (MS); electrical engineering and computer science (PhD). *Students:* 78 full-time (14 women), 31 part-time (5 women); includes 2 minority (both Hispanic/Latino), 67 international. 172 applicants, 36% accepted, 25 enrolled. In 2011, 26 master's, 3 doctorates awarded. *Degree requirements:* For master's, comprehensive exam (for some programs), thesis; for doctorate, comprehensive exam, thesis/dissertation, qualifying exams. *Entrance requirements:* For master's, GRE, BSEE or BSCS, minimum GPA of 3.0; for doctorate, GRE, MSEE or MSCS, minimum GPA of 3.0. Additional exam requirements/recommendations for international students: Required—TOEFL (minimum score 550 paper-based; 80 iBT) or IELTS (minimum score 6.5). *Application deadline:* For fall admission, 2/1 priority date for domestic students, 1/1 for international students; for winter admission, 6/1 priority date for domestic students, 5/1 for international students; for spring admission, 8/15 priority date for domestic students, 7/15 for international students. Applications are processed on a rolling basis. Application fee: $50 ($55 for international students). Electronic applications accepted. *Financial support:* In 2011–12, 54 research assistantships with full tuition reimbursements, 19 teaching assistantships with full tuition reimbursements were awarded; Federal Work-Study, institutionally sponsored loans, scholarships/grants, and unspecified assistantships also available. Financial award applicants required to submit FAFSA. *Faculty research:* Avionics, networking/communications, intelligent distribution, real-time computing, control systems, optical properties of semiconductors. *Unit head:* Dr. David Juedes, Chair, 740-593-1566, Fax: 740-593-0007, E-mail: juedes@ohio.edu. *Application contact:* Dr. Douglas Lawrence, Graduate Chair, 740-593-1578, Fax: 740-593-0007, E-mail: lawrencd@ohio.edu. Web site: http://www.ohio.edu/eecs.

Oklahoma State University, College of Engineering, Architecture and Technology, School of Electrical and Computer Engineering, Stillwater, OK 74078. Offers MS, PhD. Postbaccalaureate distance learning degree programs offered. *Faculty:* 26 full-time (2 women), 1 part-time/adjunct (0 women). *Students:* 91 full-time (20 women), 95 part-time (14 women); includes 14 minority (3 Black or African American, non-Hispanic/Latino; 1 American Indian or Alaska Native, non-Hispanic/Latino; 3 Asian, non-Hispanic/Latino; 5 Hispanic/Latino; 2 Two or more races, non-Hispanic/Latino), 143 international. Average age 28. 399 applicants, 31% accepted, 37 enrolled. In 2011, 47 master's, 6 doctorates awarded. *Degree requirements:* For master's, thesis or alternative; for doctorate, comprehensive exam, thesis/dissertation. *Entrance requirements:* For master's and doctorate, GRE or GMAT. Additional exam requirements/recommendations for international students: Required—TOEFL (minimum score 550 paper-based; 79 iBT). *Application deadline:* For fall admission, 3/1 for international students; for spring admission, 8/1 for international students. Applications are processed on a rolling basis. Application fee: $40 ($75 for international students). Electronic applications accepted. *Expenses:* Tuition, state resident: full-time $4044; part-time $168.50 per credit hour.

Tuition, nonresident: full-time $16,008; part-time $667 per credit hour. *Required fees:* $2122; $88.45 per credit hour. One-time fee: $50. Tuition and fees vary according to course load and campus/location. *Financial support:* In 2011–12, 70 research assistantships (averaging $12,128 per year), 25 teaching assistantships (averaging $8,748 per year) were awarded; career-related internships or fieldwork, Federal Work-Study, scholarships/grants, health care benefits, tuition waivers (partial), and unspecified assistantships also available. Support available to part-time students. Financial award application deadline: 3/1; financial award applicants required to submit FAFSA. *Unit head:* Dr. Keith Teague, Head, 405-744-5151, Fax: 405-744-9198. *Application contact:* Dr. Sheryl Tucker, Dean, 405-744-7099, Fax: 405-744-0355, E-mail: grad-i@okstate.edu. Web site: http://www.ece.okstate.edu.

Old Dominion University, Frank Batten College of Engineering and Technology, Program in Electrical and Computer Engineering, Norfolk, VA 23529. Offers ME, MS, PhD. Part-time programs available. Postbaccalaureate distance learning degree programs offered (minimal on-campus study). *Faculty:* 21 full-time (1 woman), 2 part-time/adjunct (both women). *Students:* 74 full-time (15 women), 15 part-time (3 women); includes 9 minority (4 Black or African American, non-Hispanic/Latino; 4 Asian, non-Hispanic/Latino; 1 Hispanic/Latino), 51 international. Average age 30. 144 applicants, 62% accepted, 16 enrolled. In 2011, 18 master's, 14 doctorates awarded. *Degree requirements:* For master's, comprehensive exam (for some programs), thesis (for some programs); for doctorate, thesis/dissertation, candidacy exam, diagnostic exam. *Entrance requirements:* For master's, GRE, two letters of recommendation; for doctorate, GRE, three letters of recommendation, resume, personal statement of objective. Additional exam requirements/recommendations for international students: Required—TOEFL (minimum score 550 paper-based; 79 iBT). *Application deadline:* For fall admission, 6/1 for domestic students, 4/15 for international students; for spring admission, 11/1 for domestic students, 10/1 for international students. Applications are processed on a rolling basis. Application fee: $50. Electronic applications accepted. *Expenses:* Tuition, state resident: full-time $9096; part-time $379 per credit. Tuition, nonresident: full-time $23,064; part-time $961 per credit. *Required fees:* $127 per semester. One-time fee: $50. *Financial support:* In 2011–12, 2 fellowships with full tuition reimbursements (averaging $17,500 per year), 24 research assistantships with full and partial tuition reimbursements (averaging $15,000 per year), 25 teaching assistantships with full and partial tuition reimbursements (averaging $15,000 per year) were awarded; career-related internships or fieldwork, Federal Work-Study, scholarships/grants, tuition waivers (full), and unspecified assistantships also available. Support available to part-time students. Financial award application deadline: 2/15; financial award applicants required to submit FAFSA. *Faculty research:* Signal and image processing biomedical and target detection applications, renewal energy applications including the development of high efficiency solar cells, nanotechnology and nanoscale thin film techniques, ultrafast (femtosecond) laser applications, linear and nonlinear systems theory. *Total annual research expenditures:* $3 million. *Unit head:* Dr. Oscar Gonzalez, Graduate Program Director, 757-683-4966, Fax: 757-683-3220, E-mail: ecegpd@odu.edu. *Application contact:* Linda Marshall, Senior Secretary, 757-683-3741, Fax: 757-683-3220, E-mail: lmarshal@odu.edu. Web site: http://eng.odu.edu/ece/.

Oregon Health & Science University, School of Medicine, Graduate Programs in Medicine, Department of Biomedical Engineering, Portland, OR 97239-3098. Offers biomedical engineering (MS, PhD); computer science and electrical engineering (PhD). Part-time programs available. *Faculty:* 20 full-time (8 women), 3 part-time/adjunct (1 woman). *Students:* 16 full-time (4 women), 3 part-time (1 woman); includes 1 minority (Hispanic/Latino), 4 international. Average age 29. 28 applicants, 25% accepted, 5 enrolled. In 2011, 1 master's, 4 doctorates awarded. Terminal master's awarded for partial completion of doctoral program. *Degree requirements:* For master's, thesis optional, thesis or capstone project; for doctorate, comprehensive exam, thesis/dissertation, qualifying exam. *Entrance requirements:* For master's and doctorate, GRE General Test (minimum scores: 153 Verbal/148 Quantitative/4.5 Analytical). Additional exam requirements/recommendations for international students: Required—TOEFL. *Application deadline:* For fall admission, 7/15 for domestic students, 5/15 for international students; for winter admission, 10/15 for domestic students, 9/15 for international students; for spring admission, 1/15 for domestic students, 12/15 for international students. Applications are processed on a rolling basis. Application fee: $70. Electronic applications accepted. *Financial support:* Health care benefits, tuition waivers, and full tuition and stipends for PhD students available. *Faculty research:* Blood cells in cancer and cancer biology, smart homes and machine learning, computational mechanics and multiscale modeling, tissue optics and biophotonics, nanomedicine and nanobiotechnology. *Unit head:* Dr. Peter Heeman, Program Director, 503-418-9316, E-mail: info@bme.ogi.edu. *Application contact:* Janet Itami, Administrative Coordinator, 503-418-9304, E-mail: itamij@ohsu.edu.

Oregon Health & Science University, School of Medicine, Graduate Programs in Medicine, Department of Computer Science and Engineering, Portland, OR 97239-3098. Offers computer science and engineering (MS, PhD); electrical engineering (MS, PhD). Part-time programs available. *Faculty:* 7 full-time (2 women), 3 part-time/adjunct (all women). *Students:* 20 full-time (5 women), 4 part-time (all women), 12 international. Average age 33. 8 applicants, 38% accepted, 3 enrolled. In 2011, 1 master's, 3 doctorates awarded. Terminal master's awarded for partial completion of doctoral program. *Degree requirements:* For master's, thesis (for some programs); for doctorate, comprehensive exam, thesis/dissertation, qualifying exam. *Entrance requirements:* For master's and doctorate, GRE General Test (minimum scores: 153 Verbal/148 Quantitative/4.5 Analytical). Additional exam requirements/recommendations for international students: Required—TOEFL. *Application deadline:* For fall admission, 7/15 for domestic students, 5/15 for international students; for winter admission, 10/15 for domestic students, 9/15 for international students; for spring admission, 1/15 for domestic students, 12/15 for international students. Applications are processed on a rolling basis. Application fee: $70. Electronic applications accepted. *Financial support:* Health care benefits, tuition waivers (full), and full tuition and stipends for PhD students available. *Unit head:* Dr. Peter Heeman, Program Director, 503-748-1635, E-mail: cseedept@csee.ogi.edu. *Application contact:* Pat Dickerson, Administrative Coordinator, 503-748-1635, E-mail: cseedept@csee.ogi.edu.

Oregon State University, Graduate School, College of Engineering, School of Electrical Engineering and Computer Science, Corvallis, OR 97331. Offers computer science (M Eng, MAIS, MS, PhD); electrical and computer engineering (M Eng, MS, PhD). *Degree requirements:* For doctorate, thesis/dissertation, qualifying exam, preliminary exam. *Entrance requirements:* For master's and doctorate, minimum GPA of 3.0 in last 90 hours of course work. Additional exam requirements/recommendations for international students: Required—TOEFL (minimum score 600 paper-based; 250 computer-based; 80 iBT). Electronic applications accepted. *Faculty research:* Optical materials and devices, data security and cryptography, analog and mixed-signal integrated circuit design, algorithms, computer graphics and vision.

Penn State Harrisburg, Graduate School, School of Science, Engineering and Technology, Middletown, PA 17057-4898. Offers computer science (MS); electrical engineering (M Eng, MS); engineering management (MPS); engineering science (M Eng); environmental engineering (M Eng); environmental pollution control (MEPC, MS). Part-time and evening/weekend programs available. *Unit head:* Dr. Jerry F. Shoup, Interim Director, 717-948-6352, E-mail: jfs1@psu.edu. *Application contact:* Robert Coffman, Director of Admissions, 717-948-6250, Fax: 717-948-6325, E-mail: ric1@psu.edu. Web site: http://harrisburg.psu.edu/science-engineering-technology.

Penn State University Park, Graduate School, College of Engineering, Department of Electrical Engineering, State College, University Park, PA 16802-1503. Offers M Eng, MS, PhD. *Unit head:* Dr. David N. Wormley, Dean, 814-865-7537, Fax: 814-865-8767, E-mail: dnw2@engr.psu.edu. *Application contact:* Cynthia E. Nicosia, Director, Graduate Enrollment Services, 814-865-1834, E-mail: cey1@psu.edu. Web site: http://www.ee.psu.edu.

Polytechnic Institute of New York University, Department of Electrical and Computer Engineering, Major in Electrical Engineering, Brooklyn, NY 11201-2990. Offers MS, PhD. Part-time and evening/weekend programs available. *Students:* 332 full-time (58 women), 183 part-time (23 women); includes 70 minority (19 Black or African American, non-Hispanic/Latino; 41 Asian, non-Hispanic/Latino; 10 Hispanic/Latino), 370 international. Average age 26. 1,034 applicants, 53% accepted, 171 enrolled. In 2011, 123 master's, 1 doctorate awarded. *Degree requirements:* For master's, comprehensive exam (for some programs), thesis (for some programs); for doctorate, comprehensive exam, thesis/dissertation. *Entrance requirements:* For master's, BS in electrical engineering; for doctorate, qualifying exam, MS in electrical engineering. Additional exam requirements/recommendations for international students: Required—TOEFL (minimum score 550 paper-based; 213 computer-based; 80 iBT); Recommended—IELTS (minimum score 6.5). *Application deadline:* For fall admission, 7/31 priority date for domestic students, 4/30 for international students; for spring admission, 12/31 priority date for domestic students, 11/30 for international students. Applications are processed on a rolling basis. Application fee: $75. Electronic applications accepted. *Expenses:* Tuition: Full-time $22,464; part-time $1248 per credit. *Required fees:* $501 per semester. *Financial support:* Fellowships, research assistantships, teaching assistantships, institutionally sponsored loans, scholarships/grants, and unspecified assistantships available. Support available to part-time students. Financial award applicants required to submit FAFSA. *Unit head:* Dr. Jonathan Chao, Head, 718-860-3478, Fax: 718-260-3302, E-mail: chao@poly.edu. *Application contact:* JeanCarlo Bonilla, Director of Graduate Enrollment Management, 718-260-3182, Fax: 718-260-3624, E-mail: gradinfo@poly.edu.

Polytechnic Institute of NYU, Long Island Graduate Center, Graduate Programs, Department of Electrical and Computer Engineering, Major in Electrical Engineering, Melville, NY 11747. Offers MS. Part-time and evening/weekend programs available. *Students:* 9 full-time (2 women), 15 part-time (3 women); includes 7 minority (1 Black or African American, non-Hispanic/Latino; 4 Asian, non-Hispanic/Latino; 2 Hispanic/Latino), 5 international. Average age 32. 24 applicants, 100% accepted, 24 enrolled. In 2011, 21 master's awarded. *Degree requirements:* For master's, comprehensive exam, thesis. *Entrance requirements:* Additional exam requirements/recommendations for international students: Required—TOEFL (minimum score 550 paper-based; 213 computer-based; 80 iBT); Recommended—IELTS (minimum score 6.5). *Application deadline:* For fall admission, 7/31 priority date for domestic students, 4/30 for international students; for spring admission, 12/31 priority date for domestic students, 11/30 for international students. Applications are processed on a rolling basis. Application fee: $75. Electronic applications accepted. *Financial support:* Institutionally sponsored loans, scholarships/grants, and unspecified assistantships available. Support available to part-time students. Financial award applicants required to submit FAFSA. *Unit head:* Dr. Jonathan Chao, Department Head, 718-260-3302, E-mail: chao@poly.edu. *Application contact:* JeanCarlo Bonilla, Director of Graduate Enrollment Management, 718-260-3182, Fax: 718-260-3624, E-mail: gradinfo@poly.edu.

Polytechnic Institute of NYU, Westchester Graduate Center, Graduate Programs, Department of Electrical and Computer Engineering, Major in Electrical Engineering, Hawthorne, NY 10532-1507. Offers MS. *Students:* 2 part-time (0 women). Average age 32. 8 applicants, 75% accepted, 2 enrolled. In 2011, 11 master's awarded. *Degree requirements:* For master's, comprehensive exam (for some programs), thesis (for some programs). *Entrance requirements:* Additional exam requirements/recommendations for international students: Required—TOEFL (minimum score 550 paper-based; 213 computer-based; 80 iBT); Recommended—IELTS (minimum score 6.5). *Application deadline:* For fall admission, 7/31 priority date for domestic students, 4/30 for international students; for spring admission, 12/31 priority date for domestic students, 11/30 for international students. Applications are processed on a rolling basis. Application fee: $75. Electronic applications accepted. *Financial support:* Institutionally sponsored loans, scholarships/grants, and unspecified assistantships available. Support available to part-time students. *Unit head:* Dr. Jonathan Chao, Department Head, 718-260-3302, E-mail: chao@poly.edu. *Application contact:* JeanCarlo Bonilla, Director of Graduate Enrollment Management, 718-260-3182, Fax: 718-260-3624, E-mail: gradinfo@poly.edu.

Polytechnic University of Puerto Rico, Graduate School, Hato Rey, PR 00919. Offers business administration (MBA), including computer information systems, general management, management of information systems, management of international enterprises; civil engineering (ME, MS); computer engineering (ME, MS); computer science (MCS, MS); electrical engineering (ME, MS); engineering management (MEM); environmental management (MEM); landscape architecture (M Land Arch); manufacturing competitiveness (MMC, MS); manufacturing engineering (ME, MS); mechanical engineering (M Mech E). Part-time and evening/weekend programs available. *Entrance requirements:* For master's, 3 letters of recommendation.

Portland State University, Graduate Studies, Maseeh College of Engineering and Computer Science, Department of Electrical and Computer Engineering, Portland, OR 97207-0751. Offers M Eng, MS, PhD. Part-time and evening/weekend programs available. *Degree requirements:* For master's, variable foreign language requirement, oral exam; for doctorate, one foreign language, comprehensive exam, thesis/dissertation, oral and written exams. *Entrance requirements:* For master's, minimum GPA of 3.0 in upper-division course work or 2.75 overall, BS in electrical or computer engineering or allied field; for doctorate, GRE General Test, GRE Subject Test, minimum GPA of 3.0 in upper-division course work, MS in electrical engineering or allied field. Additional exam requirements/recommendations for international students: Required—TOEFL (minimum score 550 paper-based; 213 computer-based). *Faculty research:* Optics and laser systems, design automation, VLSI design, computer systems, power electronics.

Prairie View A&M University, College of Engineering, Prairie View, TX 77446-0519. Offers computer information systems (MSCIS); computer science (MSCS); electrical engineering (MSEE, PhDEE); engineering (MS Engr). Part-time and evening/weekend programs available. *Degree requirements:* For master's, thesis (for some programs); for doctorate, comprehensive exam, thesis/dissertation. *Entrance requirements:* For master's, GRE General Test, bachelor's degree in engineering from an ABET accredited institution; for doctorate, GRE. Additional exam requirements/recommendations for international students: Required—TOEFL (minimum score 550 paper-based). Electronic applications accepted. *Faculty research:* Applied radiation research, thermal science, computational fluid dynamics, analog mixed signal, aerial space battlefield.

Princeton University, Graduate School, School of Engineering and Applied Science, Department of Electrical Engineering, Princeton, NJ 08544-1019. Offers M Eng, PhD. Terminal master's awarded for partial completion of doctoral program. *Degree requirements:* For doctorate, thesis/dissertation, general exam. *Entrance requirements:* For master's, GRE General Test, 3 letters of recommendation; for doctorate, GRE General Test, official transcript(s), 3 letters of recommendation, personal statement. Additional exam requirements/recommendations for international students: Required—TOEFL. Electronic applications accepted. *Faculty research:* Computer engineering, electronic materials and devices, information sciences and systems, optics and optical electronics.

Purdue University, College of Engineering, School of Electrical and Computer Engineering, West Lafayette, IN 47907-2035. Offers MS, MSE, MSECE, PhD. MS and PhD degree programs in biomedical engineering offered jointly with School of Mechanical Engineering and School of Chemical Engineering. Part-time programs available. Postbaccalaureate distance learning degree programs offered (no on-campus study). Terminal master's awarded for partial completion of doctoral program. *Entrance requirements:* For master's and doctorate, GRE General Test, minimum GPA of 3.25. Additional exam requirements/recommendations for international students: Required—TOEFL (minimum score 550 paper-based; 213 computer-based; 77 iBT). Electronic applications accepted. *Faculty research:* Automatic controls; biomedical imaging; computer engineering; communications, networking signal and image processing; fields and optics.

Purdue University Calumet, Graduate Studies Office, School of Engineering, Mathematics, and Science, Department of Engineering, Hammond, IN 46323-2094. Offers computer engineering (MSE); electrical engineering (MSE); engineering (MS); mechanical engineering (MSE). Evening/weekend programs available. *Entrance requirements:* Additional exam requirements/recommendations for international students: Required—TOEFL.

Queen's University at Kingston, School of Graduate Studies and Research, Faculty of Applied Science, Department of Electrical and Computer Engineering, Kingston, ON K7L 3N6, Canada. Offers M Eng, M Sc, M Sc Eng, PhD. Part-time programs available. *Degree requirements:* For master's, thesis optional; for doctorate, comprehensive exam, thesis/dissertation. *Entrance requirements:* Additional exam requirements/recommendations for international students: Required—TOEFL (minimum score 580 paper-based; 237 computer-based). *Faculty research:* Communications and signal processing systems, computer engineering systems.

Rensselaer at Hartford, Department of Engineering, Program in Electrical Engineering, Hartford, CT 06120-2991. Offers ME, MS. Part-time and evening/weekend programs available. *Degree requirements:* For master's, thesis optional. *Entrance requirements:* For master's, GRE. Additional exam requirements/recommendations for international students: Required—TOEFL (minimum score 600 paper-based; 250 computer-based; 100 iBT).

Rensselaer Polytechnic Institute, Graduate School, School of Engineering, Program in Electrical Engineering, Troy, NY 12180-3590. Offers M Eng, MS, PhD. Part-time programs available. Terminal master's awarded for partial completion of doctoral program. *Degree requirements:* For master's, thesis (for some programs); for doctorate, thesis/dissertation. *Entrance requirements:* For master's, GRE; for doctorate, GRE, qualifying exam, candidacy exam. Additional exam requirements/recommendations for international students: Required—TOEFL (minimum score 570 paper-based; 89 iBT). Electronic applications accepted. *Faculty research:* Networking and multimedia via ATM, thermophotovoltaic devices, microelectronic interconnections, agile manufacturing, mobile robotics.

Rice University, Graduate Programs, George R. Brown School of Engineering, Department of Electrical and Computer Engineering, Houston, TX 77251-1892. Offers bioengineering (MS, PhD); circuits, controls, and communication systems (MS, PhD); computer science and engineering (MS, PhD); electrical engineering (MEE); lasers, microwaves, and solid-state electronics (MS, PhD); MBA/MEE. Part-time programs available. *Degree requirements:* For master's, thesis (for some programs); for doctorate, thesis/dissertation. *Entrance requirements:* For master's and doctorate, GRE General Test, GRE Subject Test, minimum GPA of 3.0. Additional exam requirements/recommendations for international students: Required—TOEFL (minimum score 600 paper-based; 250 computer-based; 90 iBT). Electronic applications accepted. *Faculty research:* Physical electronics, systems, computer engineering, bioengineering.

Rochester Institute of Technology, Graduate Enrollment Services, Kate Gleason College of Engineering, Department of Electrical Engineering, Rochester, NY 14623-5603. Offers MSEE. Part-time programs available. *Students:* 97 full-time (8 women), 73 part-time (9 women); includes 7 minority (1 Black or African American, non-Hispanic/Latino; 1 American Indian or Alaska Native, non-Hispanic/Latino; 4 Asian, non-Hispanic/Latino; 1 Hispanic/Latino), 95 international. Average age 26. 387 applicants, 63% accepted, 50 enrolled. In 2011, 27 degrees awarded. *Degree requirements:* For master's, thesis optional. *Entrance requirements:* For master's, GRE, minimum GPA of 3.0. Additional exam requirements/recommendations for international students: Required—TOEFL (minimum score 570 paper-based; 230 computer-based; 88 iBT) or IELTS (minimum score 6.5). *Application deadline:* For fall admission, 2/15 priority date for domestic students, 2/15 for international students; for winter admission, 10/15 for domestic and international students. Applications are processed on a rolling basis. Application fee: $50. Electronic applications accepted. *Expenses: Tuition:* Full-time $34,659; part-time $963 per credit hour. *Required fees:* $228; $76 per quarter. *Financial support:* Research assistantships with partial tuition reimbursements, teaching assistantships with partial tuition reimbursements, career-related internships or fieldwork, institutionally sponsored loans, scholarships/grants, and unspecified assistantships available. Support available to part-time students. Financial award applicants required to submit FAFSA. *Faculty research:* Integrated optics, control systems, digital signal processing, robotic vision. *Unit head:* Dr. Eli Saber, Graduate Program Director, 585-475-6927, Fax: 585-475-5845, E-mail: ee@rit.edu. *Application contact:* Diane Ellison, Assistant Vice President, Graduate Enrollment Services, 585-475-2229, Fax: 585-475-7164, E-mail: gradinfo@rit.edu. Web site: http://www.rit.edu/kgcoe/electrical/.

Rochester Institute of Technology, Graduate Enrollment Services, Kate Gleason College of Engineering, Department of Microelectronic Engineering, Program in Microelectronic Engineering, Rochester, NY 14623-5603. Offers MS. Part-time

programs available. *Students:* 12 full-time (0 women), 6 part-time (2 women); includes 2 minority (both Hispanic/Latino), 11 international. Average age 27. 15 applicants, 47% accepted, 5 enrolled. In 2011, 2 degrees awarded. *Degree requirements:* For master's, thesis. *Entrance requirements:* Additional exam requirements/recommendations for international students: Required—TOEFL (minimum score 570 paper-based; 230 computer-based; 88 iBT) or IELTS (minimum score 6.5). *Application deadline:* For fall admission, 2/15 priority date for domestic students, 2/15 for international students; for winter admission, 10/15 for domestic and international students. Applications are processed on a rolling basis. Application fee: $50. Electronic applications accepted. *Expenses: Tuition:* Full-time $34,659; part-time $963 per credit hour. *Required fees:* $228; $76 per quarter. *Financial support:* Research assistantships with partial tuition reimbursements, teaching assistantships with partial tuition reimbursements, career-related internships or fieldwork, institutionally sponsored loans, scholarships/grants, and unspecified assistantships available. Support available to part-time students. Financial award applicants required to submit FAFSA. *Faculty research:* Electromagnetics, MEMs and microfludics. *Unit head:* Dr. Robert Pearson, Graduate Program Director, 585-475-2923, Fax: 585-475-5845, E-mail: eme@rit.edu. *Application contact:* Diane Ellison, Assistant Vice President, Graduate Enrollment Services, 585-475-2229, Fax: 585-475-7164, E-mail: gradinfo@rit.edu.

Rose-Hulman Institute of Technology, Faculty of Engineering and Applied Sciences, Department of Electrical and Computer Engineering, Terre Haute, IN 47803-3999. Offers electrical and computer engineering (M Eng); electrical engineering (MS). Part-time programs available. Postbaccalaureate distance learning degree programs offered (minimal on-campus study). *Faculty:* 19 full-time (5 women), 1 part-time/adjunct (0 women). *Students:* 8 full-time (2 women), 2 part-time (0 women); includes 1 minority (Asian, non-Hispanic/Latino), 6 international. Average age 23. 15 applicants, 80% accepted, 5 enrolled. In 2011, 15 master's awarded. *Degree requirements:* For master's, thesis (for some programs). *Entrance requirements:* For master's, GRE, minimum GPA of 3.0. Additional exam requirements/recommendations for international students: Required—TOEFL (minimum score 580 paper-based; 237 computer-based; 92 iBT). *Application deadline:* For fall admission, 2/1 priority date for domestic students. Applications are processed on a rolling basis. Application fee: $0. *Expenses: Tuition:* Full-time $37,197; part-time $1085 per credit hour. *Financial support:* In 2011–12, 9 students received support. Fellowships with full and partial tuition reimbursements available, research assistantships with full and partial tuition reimbursements available, institutionally sponsored loans, scholarships/grants, and tuition waivers (full and partial) available. *Faculty research:* Wireless systems, VLSI design, aerial robotics, power system dynamics and control, image and speech processing. *Total annual research expenditures:* $140,727. *Unit head:* Dr. Robert Throne, Interim Chairman, 812-877-8414, Fax: 812-877-8895, E-mail: robert.d.throne@rose-hulman.edu. *Application contact:* Dr. Daniel J. Moore, Associate Dean of the Faculty, 812-877-8110, Fax: 812-877-8061, E-mail: daniel.j.moore@rose-hulman.edu. Web site: http://www.rose-hulman.edu/ece/.

Rowan University, Graduate School, College of Engineering, Department of Electrical Engineering, Glassboro, NJ 08028-1701. Offers MS. Part-time and evening/weekend programs available. *Degree requirements:* For master's, thesis. *Entrance requirements:* For master's, GRE General Test. Additional exam requirements/recommendations for international students: Required—TOEFL. Electronic applications accepted.

Royal Military College of Canada, Division of Graduate Studies and Research, Engineering Division, Department of Electrical and Computer Engineering, Kingston, ON K7K 7B4, Canada. Offers computer engineering (M Eng, PhD); electrical engineering (M Eng, PhD); software engineering (M Eng, PhD). *Degree requirements:* For master's, thesis; for doctorate, comprehensive exam, thesis/dissertation. *Entrance requirements:* For master's, honours degree with second-class standing in the appropriate field; for doctorate, master's degree. Electronic applications accepted.

Rutgers, The State University of New Jersey, New Brunswick, Graduate School-New Brunswick, Department of Electrical and Computer Engineering, Piscataway, NJ 08854-8097. Offers communications and solid-state electronics (MS, PhD); computer engineering (MS, PhD); control systems (MS, PhD); digital signal processing (MS, PhD). Part-time programs available. Terminal master's awarded for partial completion of doctoral program. *Degree requirements:* For master's, thesis or alternative; for doctorate, thesis/dissertation. *Entrance requirements:* For master's and doctorate, GRE General Test. Additional exam requirements/recommendations for international students: Required—TOEFL. Electronic applications accepted. *Faculty research:* Communication and information processing, wireless information networks, micro-vacuum devices, machine vision, VLSI design.

St. Cloud State University, School of Graduate Studies, College of Science and Engineering, Department of Electrical and Computer Engineering, St. Cloud, MN 56301-4498. Offers electrical engineering (MS). *Degree requirements:* For master's, thesis or alternative. *Entrance requirements:* For master's, GRE General Test, minimum GPA of 2.75. Additional exam requirements/recommendations for international students: Required—Michigan English Language Assessment Battery; Recommended—TOEFL (minimum score 550 paper-based; 213 computer-based), IELTS (minimum score 6.5). Electronic applications accepted.

St. Mary's University, Graduate School, Department of Engineering, Program in Electrical Engineering, San Antonio, TX 78228-8507. Offers electrical engineering (MS); electrical/computer engineering (MS). Part-time programs available. *Degree requirements:* For master's, comprehensive exam. *Entrance requirements:* For master's, GRE General Test. Additional exam requirements/recommendations for international students: Required—TOEFL (minimum score 550 paper-based; 213 computer-based; 80 iBT). Electronic applications accepted. *Faculty research:* Image processing, control, communication, artificial intelligence, robotics.

San Diego State University, Graduate and Research Affairs, College of Engineering, Department of Electrical and Computer Engineering, San Diego, CA 92182. Offers electrical engineering (MS). Evening/weekend programs available. *Entrance requirements:* For master's, GRE General Test. Additional exam requirements/recommendations for international students: Required—TOEFL. Electronic applications accepted. *Faculty research:* Ultra-high speed integral circuits and systems, naval command control and ocean surveillance, signal processing and analysis.

San Jose State University, Graduate Studies and Research, Charles W. Davidson College of Engineering, Department of Electrical Engineering, San Jose, CA 95192-0001. Offers MS. *Degree requirements:* For master's, thesis. *Entrance requirements:* For master's, GRE General Test. Electronic applications accepted.

Santa Clara University, School of Engineering, Program in Electrical Engineering, Santa Clara, CA 95053. Offers analog circuit design (Certificate); ASIC design and test (Certificate); digital signal processing (Certificate); electrical engineering (MS, PhD, Engineer); fundamentals of electrical engineering (Certificate); microwave and antennas (Certificate); renewable energy (Certificate). Part-time and evening/weekend programs available. *Students:* 46 full-time (11 women), 93 part-time (14 women); includes 48 minority (2 Black or African American, non-Hispanic/Latino; 43 Asian, non-Hispanic/Latino; 2 Hispanic/Latino; 1 Native Hawaiian or other Pacific Islander, non-Hispanic/Latino), 47 international. Average age 32. 128 applicants, 46% accepted, 30 enrolled. In 2011, 59 master's, 5 doctorates, 7 other advanced degrees awarded. *Degree requirements:* For master's, thesis (for some programs); for doctorate, thesis/dissertation; for other advanced degree, thesis. *Entrance requirements:* For master's, GRE, transcript; for doctorate, GRE, master's degree or equivalent; for other advanced degree, master's degree, published paper. Additional exam requirements/recommendations for international students: Required—TOEFL (minimum score 550 paper-based; 213 computer-based; 79 iBT). *Application deadline:* For fall admission, 8/12 for domestic students, 7/15 for international students; for winter admission, 10/28 for domestic students, 9/23 for international students; for spring admission, 2/25 for domestic students, 1/21 for international students. Applications are processed on a rolling basis. Application fee: $60. Electronic applications accepted. *Expenses:* Contact institution. *Financial support:* Research assistantships and teaching assistantships available. Financial award application deadline: 3/2; financial award applicants required to submit FAFSA. *Faculty research:* Thermal and electrical nanoscale transport (TENT). *Unit head:* Dr. Alex Zecevic, Associate Dean for Graduate Studies, 408-554-2394, E-mail: azecevic@scu.edu. *Application contact:* Stacey Tinker, Director of Enrollment Management, 408-554-4748, Fax: 408-554-4323, E-mail: stinker@scu.edu.

South Dakota School of Mines and Technology, Graduate Division, Program in Electrical Engineering, Rapid City, SD 57701-3995. Offers MS. Part-time programs available. *Degree requirements:* For master's, thesis. *Entrance requirements:* Additional exam requirements/recommendations for international students: Required—TOEFL, TWE. Electronic applications accepted. *Faculty research:* Semiconductors, systems, digital systems, computers, superconductivity.

South Dakota State University, Graduate School, College of Engineering, Department of Electrical Engineering and Computer Science, Brookings, SD 57007. Offers electrical engineering (PhD); engineering (MS). Part-time programs available. *Degree requirements:* For master's, thesis (for some programs), oral exam; for doctorate, comprehensive exam, thesis/dissertation, oral exam. *Entrance requirements:* For master's and doctorate, GRE. Additional exam requirements/recommendations for international students: Required—TOEFL (minimum score 575 paper-based). *Faculty research:* Image processing, communications, power systems, electronic materials and devices, nanotechnology, photovoltaics.

Southern Illinois University Carbondale, Graduate School, College of Engineering, Department of Electrical and Computer Engineering, Carbondale, IL 62901-4701. Offers MS, PhD. *Faculty:* 15 full-time (1 woman), 1 part-time/adjunct (0 women). *Students:* 168 full-time (31 women), 88 part-time (12 women); includes 7 minority (4 Black or African American, non-Hispanic/Latino; 2 Asian, non-Hispanic/Latino; 1 Hispanic/Latino), 240 international. 358 applicants, 62% accepted, 61 enrolled. In 2011, 90 master's, 10 doctorates awarded. *Degree requirements:* For master's, comprehensive exam, thesis. *Entrance requirements:* For master's, minimum GPA of 2.7. Additional exam requirements/recommendations for international students: Required—TOEFL. *Application deadline:* Applications are processed on a rolling basis. Application fee: $20. *Financial support:* In 2011–12, 21 students received support, including 6 research assistantships with full tuition reimbursements available; fellowships with full tuition reimbursements available, teaching assistantships with full tuition reimbursements available, Federal Work-Study, institutionally sponsored loans, and tuition waivers (full) also available. Support available to part-time students. Financial award application deadline: 1/15. *Faculty research:* Circuits and power systems, communications and signal processing, controls and systems, electromagnetics and optics, electronics instrumentation and bioengineering. *Total annual research expenditures:* $254,257. *Unit head:* Dr. Glafkos D. Galanos, Chair, 618-536-2364, E-mail: ggalanos@siu.edu. *Application contact:* Jill Allison, Administrative Clerk, 618-453-2110, E-mail: ecedept@siu.edu.

Southern Illinois University Carbondale, Graduate School, College of Engineering, Program in Engineering Science, Carbondale, IL 62901-4701. Offers electrical systems (PhD); fossil energy (PhD); mechanics (PhD). *Faculty:* 55 full-time (3 women), 3 part-time/adjunct (0 women). *Students:* 12 full-time (1 woman), 34 part-time (7 women); includes 5 minority (2 Black or African American, non-Hispanic/Latino; 3 Asian, non-Hispanic/Latino), 28 international. 22 applicants, 55% accepted, 7 enrolled. In 2011, 3 doctorates awarded. *Degree requirements:* For doctorate, thesis/dissertation. *Entrance requirements:* For doctorate, GRE General Test, minimum GPA of 3.5. Additional exam requirements/recommendations for international students: Required—TOEFL. Application fee: $20. *Financial support:* In 2011–12, 13 students received support. Fellowships with full tuition reimbursements available, research assistantships with full tuition reimbursements available, teaching assistantships with full tuition reimbursements available, Federal Work-Study, institutionally sponsored loans, and tuition waivers (full) available. Support available to part-time students. *Unit head:* Dr. Josh Nicklow, Associate Dean, 618-453-7746, Fax: 618-453-4235. *Application contact:* Anna Maria Alms, Student Contact, 618-453-4321, Fax: 618-453-4235, E-mail: amalms@siu.edu.

Southern Illinois University Edwardsville, Graduate School, School of Engineering, Department of Electrical and Computer Engineering, Edwardsville, IL 62026-0001. Offers electrical engineering (MS). Part-time and evening/weekend programs available. *Faculty:* 10 full-time (0 women). *Students:* 42 full-time (8 women), 34 part-time (9 women); includes 5 minority (3 Black or African American, non-Hispanic/Latino; 1 Asian, non-Hispanic/Latino; 1 Hispanic/Latino), 52 international. 139 applicants, 51% accepted. In 2011, 45 master's awarded. *Degree requirements:* For master's, thesis (for some programs), research paper, final exam. *Entrance requirements:* For master's, minimum undergraduate GPA of 2.75 in engineering, mathematics, and science courses. Additional exam requirements/recommendations for international students: Required—TOEFL (minimum score 550 paper-based; 213 computer-based; 79 iBT), IELTS (minimum score 6.5). *Application deadline:* For fall admission, 7/22 for domestic students, 6/1 for international students; for spring admission, 12/9 for domestic students, 10/1 for international students. Applications are processed on a rolling basis. Application fee: $30. Electronic applications accepted. Tuition and fees vary according to course load and program. *Financial support:* In 2011–12, 10 research assistantships with full tuition reimbursements (averaging $9,927 per year), 23 teaching assistantships with full tuition reimbursements (averaging $9,927 per year) were awarded; fellowships with full tuition reimbursements, institutionally sponsored loans, scholarships/grants, and unspecified assistantships also available. Financial award application deadline: 3/1; financial award applicants required to submit FAFSA. *Unit head:* Dr. Luis Youn, Chair, 618-650-2524, E-mail: lyoun@siue.edu. *Application contact:* Dr. Scott Umbaugh, Program Director, 618-650-2948, E-mail: sumbaug@siue.edu. Web ,site: http://www.siue.edu/engineering/ece/.

Southern Methodist University, Bobby B. Lyle School of Engineering, Department of Electrical Engineering, Dallas, TX 75275-0338. Offers electrical engineering (MSEE, PhD); telecommunications (MS). Part-time and evening/weekend programs available. Postbaccalaureate distance learning degree programs offered (no on-campus study). Terminal master's awarded for partial completion of doctoral program. *Degree requirements:* For master's, thesis optional; for doctorate, thesis/dissertation, oral and written qualifying exams, oral final exam. *Entrance requirements:* For master's, GRE General Test, minimum GPA of 3.0 in last 2 years; bachelor's degree in engineering, mathematics, or sciences; for doctorate, preliminary counseling exam, minimum GPA of 3.0, bachelor's degree in related field. Additional exam requirements/recommendations for international students: Required—TOEFL. Electronic applications accepted. *Faculty research:* Mobile communications, optical communications, digital signal processing, photonics.

Southern Polytechnic State University, School of Engineering Technology and Management, Department of Electrical and Computer Engineering Technology, Marietta, GA 30060-2896. Offers engineering technology/electrical (MS). Part-time and evening/weekend programs available. *Faculty:* 8 full-time (1 woman), 3 part-time/adjunct (0 women). *Students:* 20 full-time (5 women), 6 part-time (0 women); includes 8 minority (5 Black or African American, non-Hispanic/Latino; 3 Asian, non-Hispanic/Latino; 11 international. Average age 29. 14 applicants, 79% accepted, 5 enrolled. In 2011, 9 master's awarded. *Degree requirements:* For master's, thesis. *Entrance requirements:* For master's, GRE (minimum scores: 147 Verbal, 147 Quantitative, 3.5 Analytical), minimum GPA of 2.7. Additional exam requirements/recommendations for international students: Required—TOEFL (minimum score 550 paper-based; 213 computer-based; 79 iBT), IELTS (minimum score 6.5). *Application deadline:* For fall admission, 7/1 priority date for domestic students, 5/1 for international students; for spring admission, 11/1 priority date for domestic students, 9/1 for international students. Applications are processed on a rolling basis. Application fee: $50. Electronic applications accepted. *Expenses:* Tuition, state resident: full-time $2592; part-time $216 per semester hour. Tuition, nonresident: full-time $9408; part-time $784 per semester hour. *Required fees:* $698 per term. *Financial support:* In 2011–12, 5 students received support, including 5 teaching assistantships with partial tuition reimbursements available (averaging $3,000 per year); career-related internships or fieldwork, scholarships/grants, and unspecified assistantships also available. Support available to part-time students. Financial award application deadline: 5/1; financial award applicants required to submit FAFSA. *Faculty research:* Analog and digital communications, computer networking, analog and low power electronics design, control systems and digital signal processing, instrumentation (medical and industrial), biomedical signal analysis, biomedical imaging, renewable energy systems, electronics, power distribution. *Unit head:* Dr. Austin Asgill, Chair, 678-915-7796, Fax: 678-915-7285, E-mail: aasgill@spsu.edu. *Application contact:* Nikki Palamiotis, Director of Graduate Studies, 678-915-4276, Fax: 678-915-7292, E-mail: npalamio@spsu.edu. Web site: http://www.spsu.edu/ecet/index.htm.

Stanford University, School of Engineering, Department of Electrical Engineering, Stanford, CA 94305-9991. Offers MS, PhD, Eng. Terminal master's awarded for partial completion of doctoral program. *Degree requirements:* For doctorate, thesis/dissertation; for Eng, thesis. *Entrance requirements:* For master's, doctorate, and Eng, GRE General Test. Additional exam requirements/recommendations for international students: Required—TOEFL. Electronic applications accepted. *Expenses: Tuition:* Full-time $40,050; part-time $890 per credit.

State University of New York at Binghamton, Graduate School, Thomas J. Watson School of Engineering and Applied Science, Department of Electrical and Computer Engineering, Binghamton, NY 13902-6000. Offers M Eng, MS, PhD. Part-time and evening/weekend programs available. *Faculty:* 15 full-time (2 women), 3 part-time/adjunct (0 women). *Students:* 62 full-time (6 women), 79 part-time (10 women); includes 23 minority (2 Black or African American, non-Hispanic/Latino; 5 Asian, non-Hispanic/Latino; 3 Hispanic/Latino; 13 Native Hawaiian or other Pacific Islander, non-Hispanic/Latino), 58 international. Average age 29. 220 applicants, 50% accepted, 39 enrolled. In 2011, 53 master's, 3 doctorates awarded. *Degree requirements:* For master's, thesis or alternative; for doctorate, thesis/dissertation. *Entrance requirements:* For master's and doctorate, GRE General Test, GRE Subject Test. Additional exam requirements/recommendations for international students: Required—TOEFL. *Application deadline:* For fall admission, 4/15 priority date for domestic students, 1/15 for international students; for spring admission, 11/1 for domestic students, 10/1 for international students. Applications are processed on a rolling basis. Application fee: $60. Electronic applications accepted. *Financial support:* In 2011–12, 36 students received support, including fellowships with full tuition reimbursements available (averaging $16,500 per year), 20 research assistantships with full tuition reimbursements available (averaging $16,500 per year), 13 teaching assistantships with full tuition reimbursements available (averaging $16,500 per year); career-related internships or fieldwork, Federal Work-Study, institutionally sponsored loans, scholarships/grants, health care benefits, tuition waivers (full and partial), and unspecified assistantships also available. Financial award application deadline: 2/15; financial award applicants required to submit FAFSA. *Unit head:* Dr. Stephen Zahorian, Chairperson, 607-777-4846, E-mail: zahorian@binghamton.edu. *Application contact:* Catherine Smith, Recruiting and Admissions Coordinator, 607-777-2151, Fax: 607-777-2501, E-mail: cmsmith@binghamton.edu.

State University of New York at New Paltz, Graduate School, School of Science and Engineering, Department of Electrical and Computer Engineering, New Paltz, NY 12561. Offers electrical engineering (MS). Part-time and evening/weekend programs available. *Faculty:* 7 full-time, 3 part-time/adjunct. *Students:* 65 full-time (14 women), 17 part-time (4 women), 78 international. Average age 24. 95 applicants, 73% accepted, 19 enrolled. In 2011, 57 master's awarded. *Degree requirements:* For master's, comprehensive exam, thesis optional. *Entrance requirements:* For master's, GRE General Test, minimum GPA of 3.0. Additional exam requirements/recommendations for international students: Required—TOEFL (minimum score 550 paper-based; 213 computer-based; 80 iBT), IELTS (minimum score 6.5). *Application deadline:* For fall admission, 5/15 priority date for domestic students, 5/15 for international students; for spring admission, 11/15 for domestic and international students. Applications are processed on a rolling basis. Application fee: $50. Electronic applications accepted. *Expenses:* Tuition, state resident: full-time $8870; part-time $370 per credit. Tuition, nonresident: full-time $15,160; part-time $632 per credit. *Required fees:* $1188; $34 per credit. $184 per semester. *Financial support:* In 2011–12, 11 students received support, including 11 fellowships with partial tuition reimbursements available (averaging $1,100 per year); tuition waivers (partial) also available. *Unit head:* Dr. Baback Izadi, Chair, 845-257-3823, E-mail: bai@eng.newpaltz.edu. *Application contact:* Prof. Damodaran Radhakrishnan, Graduate Coordinator, 845-257-3772, E-mail: damu@newpaltz.edu. Web site: http://www.engr.newpaltz.edu/.

Stevens Institute of Technology, Graduate School, Charles V. Schaefer Jr. School of Engineering, Department of Electrical and Computer Engineering, Program in Electrical Engineering, Hoboken, NJ 07030. Offers computer architecture and digital systems (M Eng); electrical engineering (PhD); microelectronics and photonics science and technology (M Eng); signal processing for communications (M Eng); telecommunications systems engineering (M Eng); wireless communications (M Eng, Certificate). *Degree requirements:* For master's, thesis optional; for doctorate, variable foreign language requirement, thesis/dissertation. *Entrance requirements:* For master's, doctorate, and Certificate, GRE. Additional exam requirements/recommendations for international students: Required—TOEFL. Electronic applications accepted.

Stevens Institute of Technology, Graduate School, Charles V. Schaefer Jr. School of Engineering, Department of Mechanical Engineering, Program in Integrated Product Development, Hoboken, NJ 07030. Offers armament engineering (M Eng); computer and electrical engineering (M Eng); manufacturing technologies (M Eng); systems reliability and design (M Eng).

Stevens Institute of Technology, Graduate School, Charles V. Schaefer Jr. School of Engineering, Interdisciplinary Program in Microelectronics and Photonics, Hoboken, NJ 07030. Offers Certificate.

Stony Brook University, State University of New York, Graduate School, College of Engineering and Applied Sciences, Department of Electrical and Computer Engineering, Program in Electrical Engineering, Stony Brook, NY 11794. Offers MS, PhD.

Syracuse University, L. C. Smith College of Engineering and Computer Science, Program in Electrical and Computer Engineering, Syracuse, NY 13244. Offers PhD. *Students:* 57 full-time (16 women), 10 part-time (2 women); includes 1 minority (Asian, non-Hispanic/Latino), 57 international. Average age 27. 175 applicants, 21% accepted, 21 enrolled. In 2011, 5 doctorates awarded. *Degree requirements:* For doctorate, comprehensive exam, thesis/dissertation. *Entrance requirements:* For doctorate, GRE General Test. Additional exam requirements/recommendations for international students: Required—TOEFL (minimum score 100 iBT). *Application deadline:* For fall admission, 7/1 priority date for domestic students, 6/1 for international students. Application fee: $75. Electronic applications accepted. *Expenses: Tuition:* Part-time $1206 per credit. *Financial support:* Fellowships with full tuition reimbursements, research assistantships with full and partial tuition reimbursements, teaching assistantships with full and partial tuition reimbursements, and tuition waivers (partial) available. Financial award application deadline: 1/1. *Unit head:* Prof. Chilukuri Mohan, Chair, 315-443-2583, E-mail: mohan@syr.edu. *Application contact:* Barbara Decker, Information Contact, 315-443-2368, Fax: 315-443-2583, E-mail: badecker@syr.edu. Web site: http://lcs.syr.edu/.

Syracuse University, L. C. Smith College of Engineering and Computer Science, Program in Electrical Engineering, Syracuse, NY 13244. Offers MS, EE. Part-time programs available. *Students:* 114 full-time (25 women), 24 part-time (1 woman); includes 7 minority (1 Black or African American, non-Hispanic/Latino; 4 Asian, non-Hispanic/Latino; 2 Hispanic/Latino), 109 international. Average age 24. 670 applicants, 37% accepted, 67 enrolled. In 2011, 38 degrees awarded. *Entrance requirements:* For master's, GRE General Test. Additional exam requirements/recommendations for international students: Required—TOEFL (minimum score 100 iBT). *Application deadline:* For fall admission, 7/1 priority date for domestic students, 6/1 for international students. Applications are processed on a rolling basis. Application fee: $75. Electronic applications accepted. *Expenses: Tuition:* Part-time $1206 per credit. *Financial support:* Fellowships with full tuition reimbursements, research assistantships with full and partial tuition reimbursements, teaching assistantships with full and partial tuition reimbursements, scholarships/grants, and tuition waivers (partial) available. Financial award application deadline: 1/1; financial award applicants required to submit FAFSA. *Faculty research:* Electromagnetics, electronic devices, systems. *Unit head:* Dr. Chilukuri K. Mohan, Department Chair, 315-443-2322, Fax: 315-443-2583, E-mail: ckmohan@syr.edu. *Application contact:* Heather Paris, 315-443-2368, Fax: 315-443-2583, E-mail: hdparis@syr.edu. Web site: http://lcs.syr.edu.

Syracuse University, L. C. Smith College of Engineering and Computer Science, Program in Microwave Engineering, Syracuse, NY 13244. Offers CAS. Part-time programs available. *Students:* 1 full-time (0 women), 1 part-time (0 women); includes 1 minority (Asian, non-Hispanic/Latino), 1 international. Average age 27. 1 applicant, 100% accepted, 1 enrolled. *Degree requirements:* For CAS, thesis. *Entrance requirements:* For degree, GRE General Test. Additional exam requirements/recommendations for international students: Required—TOEFL (minimum score 100 iBT). *Application deadline:* For fall admission, 7/1 priority date for domestic students, 6/1 for international students. Applications are processed on a rolling basis. Application fee: $75. Electronic applications accepted. *Expenses: Tuition:* Part-time $1206 per credit. *Faculty research:* Software engineering, parallel and high-performance computing, computer aided design and architectures, coding theory, neural networks. *Unit head:* 315-443-5807. *Application contact:* Barbara Decker, Information Contact, 315-443-2655, Fax: 315-443-2583, E-mail: badecker@syr.edu. Web site: http://lcs.syr.edu/.

Temple University, College of Engineering, Department of Electrical and Computer Engineering, Philadelphia, PA 19122-6096. Offers electrical engineering (MSE). Part-time and evening/weekend programs available. *Faculty:* 10 full-time (1 woman). *Students:* 14 full-time (1 woman), 9 part-time (2 women); includes 4 minority (1 Black or African American, non-Hispanic/Latino; 3 Asian, non-Hispanic/Latino), 9 international. Average age 27. 26 applicants, 88% accepted, 7 enrolled. In 2011, 26 master's awarded. *Degree requirements:* For master's, thesis optional. *Entrance requirements:* For master's, GRE General Test, minimum GPA of 3.0. Additional exam requirements/recommendations for international students: Required—TOEFL (minimum score 550 paper-based; 213 computer-based; 79 iBT). *Application deadline:* For fall admission, 7/1 for domestic students, 12/15 for international students; for spring admission, 11/1 for domestic students, 8/1 for international students. Applications are processed on a rolling basis. Application fee: $50. Electronic applications accepted. *Expenses:* Tuition, state resident: full-time $12,366; part-time $687 per credit hour. Tuition, nonresident: full-time $17,298; part-time $961 per credit hour. *Required fees:* $590; $213 per year. *Financial support:* In 2011–12, 1 fellowship with full tuition reimbursement, 1 research assistantship with full tuition reimbursement, 9 teaching assistantships with full tuition reimbursements were awarded; Federal Work-Study and institutionally sponsored loans also available. Financial award application deadline: 1/15; financial award applicants required to submit FAFSA. *Faculty research:* Computer engineering, intelligent control, microprocessors, digital processing, neutral networks. *Unit head:* Dr. Joseph Picone, Chair, 215-204-7597, Fax: 215-204-5960, E-mail: picone@temple.edu. *Application contact:* Tara Schumacher, Coordinator of Outreach, 215-204-6575, Fax: 215-204-8781, E-mail: tara.schumacher@temple.edu. Web site: http://www.temple.edu/engineering/ece.

Tennessee Technological University, Graduate School, College of Engineering, Department of Electrical and Computer Engineering, Cookeville, TN 38505. Offers MS. Part-time programs available. *Faculty:* 19 full-time (0 women). *Students:* 22 full-time (1 woman), 12 part-time (2 women), 22 international. Average age 27. 76 applicants, 70% accepted, 11 enrolled. In 2011, 12 master's awarded. *Degree requirements:* For master's, thesis. *Entrance requirements:* For master's, GRE. Additional exam requirements/recommendations for international students: Required—TOEFL (minimum score 550 paper-based; 79 iBT), IELTS (minimum score 5.5), PTE Academic. *Application deadline:* For fall admission, 8/1 for domestic students, 5/1 for international students; for spring admission, 12/1 for domestic students, 10/1 for international students. Application fee: $25 ($30 for international students). Electronic applications accepted. *Expenses:* Tuition, state resident: full-time $8094; part-time $422 per credit hour. Tuition, nonresident: full-time $20,574; part-time $1046 per credit hour. *Financial support:* In 2011–12, 1 fellowship (averaging $8,000 per year), 9 research assistantships (averaging $7,650 per year), 15 teaching assistantships (averaging $7,500 per year) were awarded; career-related internships or fieldwork also available. Financial award application deadline: 4/1. *Faculty research:* Control, digital, and power systems. *Unit head:* Dr. P. K. Rajan, Chairperson, 931-372-3397, Fax: 931-372-3436, E-mail: pkrajan@tntech.edu. *Application contact:* Shelia K. Kendrick, Coordinator of Graduate Admissions, 931-372-3808, Fax: 931-372-3497, E-mail: skendrick@tntech.edu.

Texas A&M University, College of Engineering, Department of Electrical and Computer Engineering, College Station, TX 77843. Offers computer engineering (M Eng, MS, PhD); electrical engineering (MS, PhD). *Faculty:* 63. *Students:* 480 full-time (73 women), 53 part-time (5 women); includes 52 minority (9 Black or African American, non-Hispanic/Latino; 21 Asian, non-Hispanic/Latino; 18 Hispanic/Latino; 4 Two or more races, non-Hispanic/Latino), 422 international. Average age 28. In 2011, 119 master's, 36 doctorates awarded. *Degree requirements:* For master's, thesis (MS); for doctorate, thesis/dissertation. *Entrance requirements:* For master's and doctorate, GRE General Test. Additional exam requirements/recommendations for international students: Required—TOEFL. Application fee: $50 ($75 for international students). *Expenses:* Tuition, state resident: full-time $5437; part-time $226.55 per credit hour. Tuition, nonresident: full-time $12,949; part-time $539.55 per credit hour. *Required fees:* $2741. *Financial support:* Fellowships, research assistantships, teaching assistantships, and career-related internships or fieldwork available. Financial award application deadline: 4/1; financial award applicants required to submit FAFSA. *Faculty research:* Solid-state, electric power systems, and communications engineering. *Unit head:* Dr. Costas N. Georghiades, Head, 979-845-7441, E-mail: c-georghiades@tamu.edu. *Application contact:* Graduate Advisor, 979-845-7441, E-mail: gradinfo@ece.tamu.edu. Web site: http://www.ece.tamu.edu/.

Texas A&M University–Kingsville, College of Graduate Studies, College of Engineering, Department of Electrical Engineering and Computer Science, Program in Electrical Engineering, Kingsville, TX 78363. Offers ME, MS. *Degree requirements:* For master's, comprehensive exam, thesis or alternative. *Entrance requirements:* For master's, GRE General Test, minimum GPA of 3.0. Additional exam requirements/recommendations for international students: Required—TOEFL.

Texas Tech University, Graduate School, Edward E. Whitacre Jr. College of Engineering, Department of Electrical and Computer Engineering, Lubbock, TX 79409. Offers electrical engineering (MSEE, PhD). Part-time programs available. *Faculty:* 23 full-time (3 women), 2 part-time/adjunct (1 woman). *Students:* 153 full-time (24 women), 40 part-time (6 women); includes 16 minority (1 Black or African American, non-Hispanic/Latino; 5 Asian, non-Hispanic/Latino; 9 Hispanic/Latino; 1 Two or more races, non-Hispanic/Latino), 126 international. Average age 26. 506 applicants, 30% accepted, 44 enrolled. In 2011, 64 master's, 4 doctorates awarded. *Degree requirements:* For master's, thesis or alternative; for doctorate, thesis/dissertation. *Entrance requirements:* For master's and doctorate, GRE General Test, minimum GPA of 3.0, statement of purpose, 3 letters of recommendation, resume. Additional exam requirements/recommendations for international students: Required—TOEFL (minimum score 550 paper-based; 213 computer-based; 79 iBT). *Application deadline:* For fall admission, 6/1 priority date for domestic students, 1/15 for international students; for spring admission, 9/1 priority date for domestic students, 6/15 for international students. Applications are processed on a rolling basis. Application fee: $50 ($75 for international students). Electronic applications accepted. *Expenses:* Tuition, state resident: full-time $5899; part-time $245.80 per credit hour. Tuition, nonresident: full-time $13,411; part-time $558.80 per credit hour. *Required fees:* $2680.60; $86.50 per credit hour. $920.30 per semester. *Financial support:* In 2011–12, 123 students received support. Application deadline: 4/15; applicants required to submit FAFSA. *Faculty research:* Computer vision in image processing, pulsed power, power electronics, nanotechnology, advanced vehicle engineering. *Total annual research expenditures:* $8.8 million. *Unit head:* Dr. Vittal Rao, Chair, 806-742-3533, Fax: 806-742-1245, E-mail: vittal.rao@ttu.edu. *Application contact:* Dr. John E. Kobza, Senior Associate Dean, 806-742-3451, Fax: 806-742-3493, E-mail: john.kobza@ttu.edu. Web site: http://www.depts.ttu.edu/ece/.

Tufts University, Graduate School of Arts and Sciences, Graduate Certificate Programs, Microwave and Wireless Engineering Program, Medford, MA 02155. Offers Certificate. Part-time and evening/weekend programs available. Electronic applications accepted. *Expenses: Tuition:* Full-time $41,208; part-time $1030 per credit hour. Full-time tuition and fees vary according to degree level, program and student level. Part-time tuition and fees vary according to course load.

Tufts University, School of Engineering, Department of Electrical and Computer Engineering, Medford, MA 02155. Offers bioengineering (MS), including signals and systems; electrical engineering (MS, PhD). Part-time programs available. *Faculty:* 12 full-time, 3 part-time/adjunct. *Students:* 70 full-time (13 women); includes 10 minority (2 Black or African American, non-Hispanic/Latino; 6 Asian, non-Hispanic/Latino; 2 Hispanic/Latino), 31 international. Average age 27. 157 applicants, 28% accepted, 16 enrolled. In 2011, 10 master's, 3 doctorates awarded. Terminal master's awarded for partial completion of doctoral program. *Degree requirements:* For master's, thesis or alternative; for doctorate, thesis/dissertation. *Entrance requirements:* For master's and doctorate, GRE General Test. Additional exam requirements/recommendations for international students: Required—TOEFL (minimum score 550 paper-based; 213 computer-based; 80 iBT). *Application deadline:* For fall admission, 1/15 priority date for domestic students, 12/15 for international students; for spring admission, 10/15 for domestic students, 9/15 for international students. Applications are processed on a rolling basis. Application fee: $75. Electronic applications accepted. *Expenses: Tuition:* Full-time $41,208; part-time $1030 per credit hour. Full-time tuition and fees vary according to degree level, program and student level. Part-time tuition and fees vary according to course load. *Financial support:* Fellowships with full tuition reimbursements, research assistantships with full and partial tuition reimbursements, teaching assistantships with full and partial tuition reimbursements, Federal Work-Study, scholarships/grants, tuition waivers (partial), and unspecified assistantships available. Financial award application deadline: 2/1; financial award applicants required to submit FAFSA. *Faculty research:* Communication theory, networks, protocol, and transmission technology; simulation and modeling; digital processing technology; image and signal processing for security and medical applications; integrated circuits and VLSI. *Unit head:* Dr. Jeffrey Hopwood, Chair, 617-627-3217, Fax: 617-627-3220. *Application contact:* Dr. Eric Miller, Graduate Advisor, 617-627-3217, E-mail: eceadmin@ece.tufts.edu. Web site: http://www.ece.tufts.edu/.

Tuskegee University, Graduate Programs, College of Engineering, Architecture and Physical Sciences, Department of Electrical Engineering, Tuskegee, AL 36088. Offers MSEE. *Faculty:* 8 full-time (0 women). *Students:* 20 full-time (9 women), 3 part-time (1 woman); includes 12 minority (all Black or African American, non-Hispanic/Latino), 9 international. Average age 26. In 2011, 44 master's awarded. *Degree requirements:* For master's, thesis or alternative. *Entrance requirements:* For master's, GRE General Test, GRE Subject Test. Additional exam requirements/recommendations for international students: Required—TOEFL (minimum score 500 paper-based; 69 computer-based). *Application deadline:* For fall admission, 7/15 for domestic students. Applications are processed on a rolling basis. Application fee: $25 ($35 for international students). *Expenses: Tuition:* Full-time $17,070; part-time $705 per credit hour. *Financial support:* Fellowships, research assistantships, teaching assistantships, career-related internships or fieldwork, Federal Work-Study, and institutionally sponsored loans available. Support available to part-time students. Financial award application deadline: 4/15. *Faculty research:* Photovoltaic insulation, automatic guidance and control, wind energy. *Unit head:* Dr. Sammie Giles, Director, 334-727-8298. *Application contact:* Dr. Robert L. Laney, Jr., Vice President/Director of Admissions and Enrollment Management, 334-727-8580, Fax: 334-727-5750, E-mail: planey@tuskegee.edu.

Union Graduate College, School of Engineering and Computer Science, Schenectady, NY 12308-3107. Offers computer science (MS); electrical engineering (MS); engineering and management systems (MS); mechanical engineering (MS). Part-time and evening/weekend programs available. *Faculty:* 3 full-time (0 women), 20 part-time/adjunct (2 women). *Students:* 13 full-time (1 woman), 103 part-time (13 women); includes 15 minority (2 Black or African American, non-Hispanic/Latino; 6 Asian, non-Hispanic/Latino; 6 Hispanic/Latino; 1 Two or more races, non-Hispanic/Latino), 3 international. Average age 28. 62 applicants, 69% accepted, 38 enrolled. In 2011, 29 master's awarded. *Degree requirements:* For master's, capstone course. *Entrance requirements:* For master's, minimum GPA of 3.0, letters of recommendation. Additional exam requirements/recommendations for international students: Required—TOEFL (minimum score 550 paper-based; 213 computer-based). *Application deadline:* Applications are processed on a rolling basis. Application fee: $60. Electronic applications accepted. *Expenses:* Contact institution. *Financial support:* In 2011–12, 2 students received support. Research assistantships, Federal Work-Study, scholarships/grants, health care benefits, and tuition waivers (full and partial) available. Support available to part-time students. Financial award applicants required to submit FAFSA. *Unit head:* Robert Kozik, Dean, 515-631-9881, Fax: 518-631-9902, E-mail: kozikr@union.edu. *Application contact:* Diane Trzaskos, Coordinator, Admissions, 518-631-9837, Fax: 518-631-9901, E-mail: trzaskod@uniongraduatecollege.edu.

Universidad de las Américas–Puebla, Division of Graduate Studies, School of Engineering, Program in Electronic Engineering, Puebla, Mexico. Offers MS. Part-time and evening/weekend programs available. *Faculty research:* Telecommunications, data processing, digital systems.

Université de Moncton, Faculty of Engineering, Program in Electrical Engineering, Moncton, NB E1A 3E9, Canada. Offers M Sc A. *Degree requirements:* For master's, thesis, proficiency in French. *Faculty research:* Telecommunications, electronics and instrumentation, analog and digital electronics, electronic control of machines, energy systems, electronic design.

Université de Sherbrooke, Faculty of Engineering, Department of Electrical Engineering and Computer Engineering, Sherbrooke, QC J1K 2R1, Canada. Offers electrical engineering (M Sc A, PhD). *Degree requirements:* For master's, one foreign language, thesis; for doctorate, comprehensive exam, thesis/dissertation. *Entrance requirements:* For master's, bachelor's degree in engineering or equivalent. Electronic applications accepted. *Faculty research:* Minielectronics, biomedical engineering, digital signal prolonging and telecommunications, software engineering and artificial intelligence.

Université du Québec à Trois-Rivières, Graduate Programs, Program in Electrical Engineering, Trois-Rivières, QC G9A 5H7, Canada. Offers M Sc A, PhD. Part-time programs available. *Degree requirements:* For master's, thesis; for doctorate, thesis/dissertation. *Entrance requirements:* For master's, appropriate bachelor's degree, proficiency in French; for doctorate, appropriate master's degree, proficiency in French. *Faculty research:* Industrial electronics.

Université Laval, Faculty of Sciences and Engineering, Department of Electrical and Computer Engineering, Programs in Electrical Engineering, Québec, QC G1K 7P4, Canada. Offers M Sc, PhD. Terminal master's awarded for partial completion of doctoral program. *Degree requirements:* For master's, thesis (for some programs); for doctorate, thesis/dissertation. *Entrance requirements:* For master's and doctorate, knowledge of French and English. Electronic applications accepted.

University at Buffalo, the State University of New York, Graduate School, School of Engineering and Applied Sciences, Department of Electrical Engineering, Buffalo, NY 14260. Offers ME, MS, PhD. Part-time programs available. *Faculty:* 30 full-time (5 women), 3 part-time/adjunct (0 women). *Students:* 197 full-time (46 women), 15 part-time (1 woman); includes 10 minority (5 Black or African American, non-Hispanic/Latino; 3 Asian, non-Hispanic/Latino; 2 Hispanic/Latino), 173 international. Average age 26. 1,011 applicants, 27% accepted, 88 enrolled. In 2011, 118 master's, 14 doctorates awarded. Terminal master's awarded for partial completion of doctoral program. *Degree requirements:* For master's, comprehensive exam (for some programs), thesis or exam; for doctorate, comprehensive exam, thesis/dissertation. *Entrance requirements:* For master's and doctorate, GRE General Test. Additional exam requirements/recommendations for international students: Required—TOEFL (minimum score 550 paper-based; 213 computer-based; 79 iBT). *Application deadline:* For fall admission, 12/31 for domestic and international students; for spring admission, 8/31 for domestic and international students. Applications are processed on a rolling basis. Application fee: $75. Electronic applications accepted. *Financial support:* In 2011–12, 76 students received support, including 8 fellowships with full tuition reimbursements available (averaging $28,900 per year), 36 research assistantships with full tuition reimbursements available (averaging $20,700 per year), 27 teaching assistantships with full tuition reimbursements available (averaging $20,900 per year); career-related internships or fieldwork, Federal Work-Study, institutionally sponsored loans, tuition waivers (full and partial), and unspecified assistantships also available. Financial award application deadline: 2/1; financial award applicants required to submit FAFSA. *Faculty research:* High power electronics and plasmas, electronic materials signal and image processing, photonics and communications, optics, nanoelectronics. *Total annual research expenditures:* $5.3 million. *Unit head:* Dr. Stella N. Batalama, Chairman, 716-645-3115, Fax: 716-645-3656, E-mail: batalama@buffalo.edu. *Application contact:* Dr. Chu Wie, Director of Graduate Admissions, 716-645-1023, Fax: 716-645-3656, E-mail: eegradapply@buffalo.edu. Web site: http://www.ee.buffalo.edu/.

The University of Akron, Graduate School, College of Engineering, Department of Electrical and Computer Engineering, Akron, OH 44325. Offers MS, PhD. Evening/weekend programs available. *Faculty:* 17 full-time (1 woman), 2 part-time/adjunct (0 women). *Students:* 55 full-time (8 women), 19 part-time (3 women); includes 2 minority (1 Asian, non-Hispanic/Latino; 1 Native Hawaiian or other Pacific Islander, non-Hispanic/Latino), 60 international. Average age 27. 116 applicants, 24% accepted, 6 enrolled. In 2011, 3 master's, 1 doctorate awarded. *Degree requirements:* For master's, thesis optional, oral comprehensive exam or thesis; for doctorate, one foreign language, thesis/dissertation, candidacy exam, qualifying exam. *Entrance requirements:* For master's, GRE, minimum GPA of 2.75, three letters of recommendation, statement of purpose; for doctorate, GRE, minimum GPA of 3.0 with bachelor's degree, 3.5 with master's degree; three letters of recommendation; statement of purpose. Additional exam requirements/recommendations for international students: Required—TOEFL (minimum score 550 paper-based; 213 computer-based; 79 iBT). *Application deadline:* Applications are processed on a rolling basis. Application fee: $30 ($40 for international students). Electronic applications accepted. *Expenses:* Tuition, state resident: full-time $7038; part-time $391 per credit hour. Tuition, nonresident: full-time $12,051; part-time $670 per credit hour. *Required fees:* $1274; $34 per credit hour. *Financial support:* In 2011–12, 27 research assistantships with full tuition reimbursements, 26 teaching assistantships with full tuition reimbursements were awarded; career-related internships or fieldwork also available. *Faculty research:* Computational electromagnetics and nondestructive testing, control systems, sensors and actuators applications and networks, alternative energy systems and hybrid vehicles, analog IC design embedded systems. *Total annual research expenditures:* $435,958. *Unit head:* Dr. Jose De Abreu-Garcia, Chair, 330-972-6709, E-mail: jdeabreu-garcia@uakron.edu. *Application contact:* Dr. Craig Menzemer, Associate Dean, 330-972-5536, E-mail: ccmenze@uakron.edu. Web site: http://www.uakron.edu/engineering/ECE/.

The University of Alabama, Graduate School, College of Engineering, Department of Electrical and Computer Engineering, Tuscaloosa, AL 35487-0286. Offers electrical engineering (MS, PhD). Part-time programs available. Postbaccalaureate distance learning degree programs offered (minimal on-campus study). *Faculty:* 16 full-time (4 women). *Students:* 53 full-time (7 women), 8 part-time (1 woman); includes 5 minority (1 Black or African American, non-Hispanic/Latino; 2 Asian, non-Hispanic/Latino; 2 Hispanic/Latino), 31 international. Average age 28. 88 applicants, 48% accepted, 15 enrolled. In 2011, 7 master's, 1 doctorate awarded. *Median time to degree:* Of those who began their doctoral program in fall 2003, 80% received their degree in 8 years or less. *Degree requirements:* For master's, thesis or alternative; for doctorate, one foreign language, comprehensive exam, thesis/dissertation. *Entrance requirements:* For master's, GRE (for students from non ABET-accredited schools), minimum GPA of 3.0 in last 60 hours of course work or overall; for doctorate, GRE (for students from non ABET-accredited schools), minimum GPA of 3.0 overall. Additional exam requirements/recommendations for international students: Required—TOEFL (minimum score 550 paper-based; 213 computer-based). *Application deadline:* For fall admission, 7/1 priority date for domestic students, 1/15 for international students; for spring admission, 11/1 priority date for domestic students, 6/1 for international students. Applications are processed on a rolling basis. Application fee: $50 ($60 for international students). Electronic applications accepted. *Expenses:* Tuition, state resident: full-time $8600. Tuition, nonresident: full-time $21,900. *Financial support:* In 2011–12, 1 fellowship with full tuition reimbursement (averaging $15,000 per year), 14 research assistantships with full tuition reimbursements (averaging $14,000 per year), 6 teaching assistantships with full tuition reimbursements (averaging $11,025 per year) were awarded; health care benefits and unspecified assistantships also available. *Faculty research:* Devices and materials, electromechanical systems, embedded systems. *Total annual research expenditures:* $2.5 million. *Unit head:* Dr. D. Jeff Jackson, Department Head, 205-348-2919, Fax: 205-348-6959, E-mail: jjackson@eng.ua.edu. *Application contact:* Dr. Tim Haskew, Graduate Program Director, 205-348-1766, Fax: 205-348-6959, E-mail: thaskew@eng.ua.edu. Web site: http://ece.eng.ua.edu.

The University of Alabama at Birmingham, School of Engineering, Program in Electrical Engineering, Birmingham, AL 35294. Offers MSEE. *Expenses:* Tuition, state resident: full-time $5922; part-time $309 per hour. Tuition, nonresident: full-time $13,428; part-time $726 per hour. Tuition and fees vary according to program. *Unit head:* Dr. Yehia Massoud, Chair, 205-934-8440, Fax: 205-975-3337. Web site: http://www.uab.edu/engineering/departments-research/ece/grad.

The University of Alabama in Huntsville, School of Graduate Studies, College of Engineering, Department of Electrical and Computer Engineering, Huntsville, AL 35899. Offers computer engineering (MSE, PhD), including information assurance (MSE); electrical engineering (MSE, PhD), including optics and phontonics technology (MSE), opto-electronics (MSE); optics and photonics (MSE); software engineering (MSSE). Part-time and evening/weekend programs available. *Faculty:* 22 full-time (3 women), 4 part-time/adjunct (0 women). *Students:* 52 full-time (12 women), 138 part-time (22 women); includes 20 minority (7 Black or African American, non-Hispanic/Latino; 2 American Indian or Alaska Native, non-Hispanic/Latino; 8 Asian, non-Hispanic/Latino; 2 Hispanic/Latino; 1 Two or more races, non-Hispanic/Latino), 37 international. Average age 31. 157 applicants, 65% accepted, 48 enrolled. In 2011, 26 master's, 6 doctorates awarded. *Degree requirements:* For master's, comprehensive exam, thesis or alternative, oral and written exams; for doctorate, comprehensive exam, thesis/dissertation, oral and written exams. *Entrance requirements:* For master's, GRE General Test, appropriate bachelor's degree, minimum GPA of 3.0; for doctorate, GRE General Test, minimum GPA of 3.0. Additional exam requirements/recommendations for international students: Required—TOEFL (minimum score 500 paper-based; 173 computer-based; 62 iBT). *Application deadline:* For fall admission, 7/15 for domestic students, 4/1 for international students; for spring admission, 11/30 for domestic students, 9/1 for international students. Applications are processed on a rolling basis. Application fee: $40 ($50 for international students). Electronic applications accepted. *Expenses:* Tuition, state resident: full-time $7830; part-time $473.50 per credit. Tuition, nonresident: full-time $18,748; part-time $1128.33 per credit. Tuition and fees vary according to course load and program. *Financial support:* In 2011–12, 29 students received support, including 2 fellowships (averaging $11,154 per year), 9 research assistantships with full and partial tuition reimbursements available (averaging $10,959 per year), 20 teaching assistantships with full and partial tuition reimbursements available (averaging $11,330 per year); career-related internships or fieldwork, Federal Work-Study, institutionally sponsored loans, scholarships/grants, health care benefits, tuition waivers (full), and unspecified assistantships also available. Support available to part-time students. Financial award application deadline: 4/1; financial award applicants required to submit FAFSA. *Faculty research:* Optical signal processing, electromagnetics, photonics, nonlinear waves, computer architecture. *Total annual research expenditures:* $16.5 million. *Unit head:* Dr. Robert Lindquist, Chair, 256-824-6316, Fax: 256-824-6803, E-mail: lindquis@ece.uah.edu. *Application contact:* Kim Gray, Graduate Studies Admissions Coordinator, 256-824-6002, Fax: 256-824-6405, E-mail: deangrad@uah.edu. Web site: http://www.ece.uah.edu/.

University of Alaska Fairbanks, College of Engineering and Mines, Department of Electrical and Computer Engineering, Fairbanks, AK 99775-5915. Offers electrical engineering (MEE, MS, PhD); engineering (PhD). Part-time programs available. *Faculty:*

9 full-time (2 women). *Students:* 17 full-time (4 women), 8 international. Average age 24. 21 applicants, 29% accepted, 5 enrolled. In 2011, 4 master's awarded. Terminal master's awarded for partial completion of doctoral program. *Degree requirements:* For master's, comprehensive exam, thesis or alternative; for doctorate, comprehensive exam, thesis/dissertation, oral exam, oral defense. *Entrance requirements:* For master's and doctorate, GRE General Test. Additional exam requirements/recommendations for international students: Required—TOEFL (minimum score 550 paper-based; 213 computer-based; 80 iBT). *Application deadline:* For fall admission, 6/1 for domestic students, 3/1 for international students; for spring admission, 10/15 for domestic students, 9/1 for international students. Applications are processed on a rolling basis. Application fee: $60. Electronic applications accepted. *Expenses:* Tuition, state resident: full-time $6696; part-time $372 per credit. Tuition, nonresident: full-time $13,680; part-time $760 per credit. Tuition and fees vary according to course load and reciprocity agreements. *Financial support:* In 2011–12, 11 research assistantships with tuition reimbursements (averaging $12,733 per year), 7 teaching assistantships with tuition reimbursements (averaging $5,216 per year) were awarded; fellowships with tuition reimbursements, career-related internships or fieldwork, Federal Work-Study, scholarships/grants, health care benefits, and unspecified assistantships also available. Support available to part-time students. Financial award application deadline: 7/1; financial award applicants required to submit FAFSA. *Faculty research:* Geomagnetically-induced currents in power lines, electromagnetic wave propagation, laser radar systems, bioinformatics, distributed sensor networks. *Unit head:* Dr. Charles Mayer, Chair, 907-474-7137, Fax: 907-474-5135, E-mail: fyee@uaf.edu. *Application contact:* Mike Earnest, Director of Admissions, 907-474-7500, Fax: 907-474-5379, E-mail: admissions@uaf.edu. Web site: http://cem.uaf.edu/ece/.

University of Alberta, Faculty of Graduate Studies and Research, Department of Electrical and Computer Engineering, Edmonton, AB T6G 2E1, Canada. Offers communications (M Eng, M Sc, PhD); computer engineering (M Eng, M Sc, PhD); electromagnetics (M Eng, M Sc, PhD); nanotechnology and microdevices (M Eng, M Sc, PhD); power/power electronics (M Eng, M Sc, PhD); systems (M Eng, M Sc, PhD). Terminal master's awarded for partial completion of doctoral program. *Degree requirements:* For master's, thesis; for doctorate, thesis/dissertation. *Entrance requirements:* Additional exam requirements/recommendations for international students: Required—TOEFL. Electronic applications accepted. *Faculty research:* Controls, communications, microelectronics, electromagnetics.

The University of Arizona, College of Engineering, Department of Electrical and Computer Engineering, Tucson, AZ 85721. Offers M Eng, MS, PhD. Part-time programs available. *Faculty:* 20 full-time (2 women), 8 part-time/adjunct (3 women). *Students:* 123 full-time (17 women), 33 part-time (5 women); includes 27 minority (1 Black or African American, non-Hispanic/Latino; 7 Asian, non-Hispanic/Latino; 11 Hispanic/Latino; 8 Two or more races, non-Hispanic/Latino), 93 international. Average age 30. 514 applicants, 23% accepted, 38 enrolled. In 2011, 34 master's, 12 doctorates awarded. *Degree requirements:* For master's, thesis (for some programs); for doctorate, thesis/dissertation. *Entrance requirements:* For master's, GRE General Test, 3 letters of recommendation, statement of purpose; for doctorate, GRE General Test, master's degree in related field, 3 letters of recommendation, statement of purpose. Additional exam requirements/recommendations for international students: Required—TOEFL (minimum score 550 paper-based; 213 computer-based; 79 iBT). *Application deadline:* For fall admission, 12/15 for domestic and international students; for spring admission, 7/15 for domestic and international students. Applications are processed on a rolling basis. Application fee: $75. Electronic applications accepted. *Expenses:* Tuition, state resident: full-time $10,840. Tuition, nonresident: full-time $25,802. *Financial support:* In 2011–12, 68 research assistantships with full tuition reimbursements (averaging $23,715 per year), 16 teaching assistantships with full tuition reimbursements (averaging $23,585 per year) were awarded; institutionally sponsored loans, scholarships/grants, health care benefits, and unspecified assistantships also available. Financial award application deadline: 3/15. *Faculty research:* Communication systems, control systems, signal processing, computer-aided logic. *Total annual research expenditures:* $7.1 million. *Unit head:* Dr. Tamal Bose, Head, 520-621-6193, E-mail: head@ece.arizona.edu. *Application contact:* Tami J. Whelan, Senior Graduate Academic Adviser, 520-621-6195, Fax: 520-621-8076, E-mail: whelan@ece.arizona.edu. Web site: http://www.ece.arizona.edu/.

University of Arkansas, Graduate School, College of Engineering, Department of Electrical Engineering, Fayetteville, AR 72701-1201. Offers electrical engineering (MSEE, PhD); telecommunications engineering (MS Tc E). *Students:* 14 full-time (3 women), 65 part-time (7 women); includes 5 minority (4 Black or African American, non-Hispanic/Latino; 1 Asian, non-Hispanic/Latino), 47 international. In 2011, 12 master's awarded. *Degree requirements:* For master's, thesis optional; for doctorate, one foreign language, thesis/dissertation. *Entrance requirements:* For master's and doctorate, GRE General Test. *Application deadline:* For fall admission, 4/1 for international students; for spring admission, 10/1 for international students. Applications are processed on a rolling basis. Application fee: $40 ($50 for international students). Electronic applications accepted. *Financial support:* In 2011–12, 48 research assistantships, 8 teaching assistantships were awarded; fellowships with tuition reimbursements, career-related internships or fieldwork, and Federal Work-Study also available. Support available to part-time students. Financial award application deadline: 4/1; financial award applicants required to submit FAFSA. *Unit head:* Dr. Juan Balda, Department Chair, 479-575-3005, Fax: 479-575-7967, E-mail: jbalda@uark.edu. *Application contact:* Dr. Randy Brown, Graduate Coordinator, 479-575-6581, E-mail: rlb02@uark.edu. Web site: http://www.eleg.uark.edu/.

University of Bridgeport, School of Engineering, Department of Electrical Engineering, Bridgeport, CT 06604. Offers MS. Part-time and evening/weekend programs available. *Faculty:* 4 full-time (1 woman), 15 part-time/adjunct (1 woman). *Students:* 129 full-time (26 women), 56 part-time (7 women); includes 2 minority (both Asian, non-Hispanic/Latino), 181 international. Average age 26. 373 applicants, 74% accepted, 23 enrolled. In 2011, 157 master's awarded. *Degree requirements:* For master's, thesis optional. *Entrance requirements:* Additional exam requirements/recommendations for international students: Recommended—TOEFL (minimum score 550 paper-based; 213 computer-based; 80 iBT), IELTS (minimum score 6.5). *Application deadline:* For fall admission, 8/1 priority date for domestic students, 8/1 for international students; for spring admission, 12/1 priority date for domestic students, 12/1 for international students. Applications are processed on a rolling basis. Application fee: $50. Electronic applications accepted. *Expenses: Tuition:* Full-time $22,880; part-time $700 per credit. *Required fees:* $1870; $95 per semester. Tuition and fees vary according to course load and program. *Financial support:* In 2011–12, 20 students received support. Research assistantships, teaching assistantships, career-related internships or fieldwork, Federal Work-Study, institutionally sponsored loans, and tuition waivers (partial) available. Support available to part-time students. Financial award application deadline: 6/1; financial award applicants required to submit FAFSA. *Unit head:* Dr. Lawrence Hmurcik, Chairman, 203-576-4296, Fax: 203-576-4105, E-mail: hmurcik@bridgeport.edu.

Application contact: Karissa Peckham, Vice President of Enrollment Management, 203-576-4552, Fax: 203-576-4941, E-mail: admit@bridgeport.edu.

The University of British Columbia, Faculty of Applied Science, Program in Electrical and Computer Engineering, Vancouver, BC V6T 1Z1, Canada. Offers M Eng, MA Sc, PhD. Part-time programs available. *Degree requirements:* For master's, thesis (for some programs); for doctorate, thesis/dissertation. *Entrance requirements:* Additional exam requirements/recommendations for international students: Required—TOEFL (minimum score 600 paper-based; 250 computer-based; 100 iBT), TWE. Electronic applications accepted. *Faculty research:* Applied electromagnetics, biomedical engineering, communications and signal processing, computer and software engineering, power engineering, robotics, solid-state, systems and control.

University of Calgary, Faculty of Graduate Studies, Schulich School of Engineering, Department of Electrical and Computer Engineering, Calgary, AB T2N 1N4, Canada. Offers M Eng, M Sc, PhD. Part-time programs available. *Degree requirements:* For master's, thesis (M Sc); for doctorate, thesis/dissertation, candidacy exam. *Entrance requirements:* For master's and doctorate, minimum GPA of 3.0. Additional exam requirements/recommendations for international students: Required—TOEFL (minimum score 550 paper-based; 213 computer-based) or IELTS (minimum score 7). Electronic applications accepted. *Faculty research:* Biomedical and bioelectrics, telecommunications and signal processing, software and computer engineering, power and control, microelectronics and instrumentation.

University of California, Berkeley, Graduate Division, College of Engineering, Department of Electrical Engineering and Computer Sciences, Berkeley, CA 94720-1500. Offers computer science (MS, PhD); electrical engineering (MS, PhD). *Degree requirements:* For master's, comprehensive exam or thesis; for doctorate, thesis/dissertation, qualifying exam. *Entrance requirements:* For master's and doctorate, GRE General Test, minimum GPA of 3.0, 3 letters of recommendation. Additional exam requirements/recommendations for international students: Required—TOEFL. Electronic applications accepted.

University of California, Davis, College of Engineering, Program in Electrical and Computer Engineering, Davis, CA 95616. Offers MS, PhD. Terminal master's awarded for partial completion of doctoral program. *Degree requirements:* For master's, comprehensive exam (for some programs), thesis (for some programs); for doctorate, thesis/dissertation, preliminary and qualifying exams, thesis defense. *Entrance requirements:* For master's, GRE General Test, minimum GPA of 3.2; for doctorate, GRE, minimum graduate GPA of 3.5. Additional exam requirements/recommendations for international students: Required—TOEFL (minimum score 550 paper-based; 213 computer-based). Electronic applications accepted.

University of California, Irvine, School of Engineering, Department of Electrical Engineering and Computer Science, Irvine, CA 92697. Offers electrical engineering and computer science (MS, PhD); networked systems (MS, PhD). Part-time programs available. *Students:* 288 full-time (49 women), 21 part-time (4 women); includes 35 minority (1 Black or African American, non-Hispanic/Latino; 29 Asian, non-Hispanic/Latino; 1 Hispanic/Latino; 4 Two or more races, non-Hispanic/Latino), 237 international. Average age 27. 1,351 applicants, 21% accepted, 135 enrolled. In 2011, 50 master's, 18 doctorates awarded. Terminal master's awarded for partial completion of doctoral program. *Degree requirements:* For doctorate, thesis/dissertation. *Entrance requirements:* For master's and doctorate, GRE General Test, minimum GPA of 3.0, 3 letters of recommendation. Additional exam requirements/recommendations for international students: Required—TOEFL (minimum score 550 paper-based; 213 computer-based). *Application deadline:* For fall admission, 1/15 priority date for domestic students, 1/15 for international students. Applications are processed on a rolling basis. Application fee: $80 ($100 for international students). Electronic applications accepted. *Financial support:* Fellowships, research assistantships with full tuition reimbursements, teaching assistantships, institutionally sponsored loans, traineeships, health care benefits, and unspecified assistantships available. Financial award application deadline: 3/1; financial award applicants required to submit FAFSA. *Faculty research:* Optics and electronic devices and circuits, signal processing, communications, machine vision, power electronics. *Unit head:* Prof. Michael M. Green, Chair, 949-824-1656, Fax: 949-824-3203, E-mail: mgreen@uci.edu. *Application contact:* Ronnie A. Gran, Graduate Admissions Coordinator, 949-824-5489, Fax: 949-824-1853, E-mail: ragran@uci.edu. Web site: http://www.eng.uci.edu/dept/eecs.

University of California, Los Angeles, Graduate Division, Henry Samueli School of Engineering and Applied Science, Department of Electrical Engineering, Los Angeles, CA 90095-1594. Offers electrical engineering (MS, PhD). *Faculty:* 46 full-time (6 women), 7 part-time/adjunct (0 women). *Students:* 470 full-time (71 women); includes 94 minority (2 Black or African American, non-Hispanic/Latino; 1 American Indian or Alaska Native, non-Hispanic/Latino; 80 Asian, non-Hispanic/Latino; 8 Hispanic/Latino; 3 Two or more races, non-Hispanic/Latino), 315 international. 1,702 applicants, 24% accepted, 179 enrolled. In 2011, 72 master's, 43 doctorates awarded. *Degree requirements:* For master's, comprehensive exam or thesis; for doctorate, thesis/dissertation, qualifying exams. *Entrance requirements:* For master's, GRE General Test, minimum GPA of 3.0; for doctorate, GRE General Test, minimum GPA of 3.25. Additional exam requirements/recommendations for international students: Required—TOEFL (minimum score 560 paper-based; 220 computer-based; 87 iBT). *Application deadline:* For fall admission, 12/15 for domestic and international students. Application fee: $80 ($100 for international students). Electronic applications accepted. *Financial support:* In 2011–12, 143 fellowships, 501 research assistantships, 106 teaching assistantships were awarded; career-related internships or fieldwork, Federal Work-Study, institutionally sponsored loans, and tuition waivers (full and partial) also available. Financial award application deadline: 12/15; financial award applicants required to submit FAFSA. *Faculty research:* Circuits and embedded systems, physical and wave electronics, signals and systems. *Total annual research expenditures:* $15.7 million. *Unit head:* Dr. M.-C. Frank Chang, Chair, 310-825-2647. *Application contact:* Deeona Columbia, Student Affairs Officer, 310-825-7574, E-mail: deeona@ea.ucla.edu. Web site: http://www.ee.ucla.edu/.

University of California, Merced, Division of Graduate Studies, School of Engineering, Merced, CA 95343. Offers electrical engineering and computer science (MS, PhD). *Unit head:* Dr. Samuel J. Traina, Dean, 209-228-4723, Fax: 209-228-6906, E-mail: grad.dean@ucmerced.edu. *Application contact:* Tsu Ya, Graduate Admissions and Academic Services Manager, 209-228-4723, Fax: 209-228-6906, E-mail: tya@ucmerced.edu.

University of California, Riverside, Graduate Division, Department of Electrical Engineering, Riverside, CA 92521-0102. Offers electrical engineering (MS, PhD), including computer engineering, control and robotics, intelligent systems, nano-materials, devices and circuits, signal processing and communications. Terminal master's awarded for partial completion of doctoral program. *Degree requirements:* For master's, thesis optional; for doctorate, thesis/dissertation, qualifying exams. *Entrance requirements:* For master's and doctorate, GRE General Test, minimum GPA of 3.25. Additional exam requirements/recommendations for international students: Required—

TOEFL (minimum score 550 paper-based; 213 computer-based; 80 iBT). Electronic applications accepted. *Faculty research:* Solid state devices, integrated circuits, signal processing.

University of California, San Diego, Office of Graduate Studies, Department of Electrical and Computer Engineering, La Jolla, CA 92093. Offers applied ocean science (MS, PhD); applied physics (MS, PhD); communication theory and systems (MS, PhD); computer engineering (MS, PhD); electrical engineering (M Eng); electronic circuits and systems (MS, PhD); intelligent systems, robotics and control (MS, PhD); photonics (MS, PhD); signal and image processing (MS, PhD). MS only offered to students who have been admitted to the PhD program. *Entrance requirements:* For master's and doctorate, GRE General Test. Electronic applications accepted.

University of California, Santa Barbara, Graduate Division, College of Engineering, Department of Electrical and Computer Engineering, Santa Barbara, CA 93106-2014. Offers communications, control and signal processing (MS, PhD); computer engineering (MS, PhD); electronics and photonics (MS, PhD); MS/PhD. *Faculty:* 37 full-time (3 women), 1 part-time/adjunct (0 women). *Students:* 272 full-time (52 women); includes 40 minority (2 American Indian or Alaska Native, non-Hispanic/Latino; 30 Asian, non-Hispanic/Latino; 6 Hispanic/Latino; 1 Native Hawaiian or other Pacific Islander, non-Hispanic/Latino; 1 Two or more races, non-Hispanic/Latino), 159 international. Average age 26. 1,252 applicants, 27% accepted, 95 enrolled. In 2011, 49 master's, 33 doctorates awarded. Terminal master's awarded for partial completion of doctoral program. *Median time to degree:* Of those who began their doctoral program in fall 2003, 44% received their degree in 8 years or less. *Degree requirements:* For master's, comprehensive exam, thesis; for doctorate, thesis/dissertation. *Entrance requirements:* For master's and doctorate, GRE General Test. Additional exam requirements/recommendations for international students: Required—TOEFL (minimum score 550 paper-based; 80 iBT), IELTS (minimum score 7). *Application deadline:* For fall admission, 12/15 for domestic and international students; for winter admission, 11/1 for domestic and international students; for spring admission, 1/1 for domestic and international students. Application fee: $80 ($100 for international students). Electronic applications accepted. *Expenses:* Tuition, state resident: full-time $12,192. Tuition, nonresident: full-time $27,294. *Required fees:* $764.13. *Financial support:* In 2011–12, 196 students received support, including 70 fellowships with full and partial tuition reimbursements available (averaging $7,181 per year), 155 research assistantships with full and partial tuition reimbursements available (averaging $15,235 per year), 54 teaching assistantships with full and partial tuition reimbursements available (averaging $9,910 per year); tuition waivers (full and partial) also available. Financial award application deadline: 12/15; financial award applicants required to submit FAFSA. *Faculty research:* Communications, signal processing, computer engineering, control, electronics and photonics. *Total annual research expenditures:* $25.5 million. *Unit head:* Prof. Jerry Gibson, Chair, 805-893-3821, Fax: 805-893-6262, E-mail: gibson@ece.ucsb.edu. *Application contact:* Erika Raquel Klukovich, Graduate Admissions Coordinator, 805-893-3114, Fax: 805-893-5402, E-mail: erika@ece.ucsb.edu. Web site: http://www.ece.ucsb.edu/.

University of California, Santa Cruz, Division of Graduate Studies, Jack Baskin School of Engineering, Department of Electrical Engineering, Santa Cruz, CA 95064. Offers MS, PhD. *Degree requirements:* For master's, thesis; for doctorate, thesis/dissertation, qualifying exam. *Entrance requirements:* For master's and doctorate, GRE General Test. Additional exam requirements/recommendations for international students: Required—TOEFL (minimum score 570 paper-based; 230 computer-based; 89 iBT); Recommended—IELTS (minimum score 8). Electronic applications accepted. *Faculty research:* Photonics and electronics, signal processing and communications, remote sensing, nanotechnology.

University of Central Florida, College of Engineering and Computer Science, Department of Electrical Engineering and Computer Science, Program in Electrical Engineering, Orlando, FL 32816. Offers electrical engineering (MSEE, PhD); electronic circuits (Certificate). Part-time and evening/weekend programs available. *Students:* 143 full-time (33 women), 73 part-time (12 women); includes 43 minority (10 Black or African American, non-Hispanic/Latino; 11 Asian, non-Hispanic/Latino; 21 Hispanic/Latino; 1 Two or more races, non-Hispanic/Latino), 104 international. Average age 29. 303 applicants, 73% accepted, 55 enrolled. In 2011, 62 master's, 13 doctorates awarded. *Degree requirements:* For master's, thesis or alternative; for doctorate, thesis/dissertation, departmental qualifying exam, candidacy exam. *Entrance requirements:* For master's, GRE General Test, minimum GPA of 3.0 in last 60 hours; for doctorate, GRE General Test, minimum GPA of 3.5 in last 60 hours. Additional exam requirements/recommendations for international students: Required—TOEFL. *Application deadline:* For fall admission, 7/15 priority date for domestic students; for spring admission, 12/1 priority date for domestic students. Application fee: $30. Electronic applications accepted. *Expenses:* Tuition, state resident: part-time $277.08 per credit hour. Tuition, nonresident: part-time $277.08 per credit hour. Part-time tuition and fees vary according to degree level and program. *Financial support:* In 2011–12, 65 students received support, including 28 fellowships (averaging $7,100 per year), 43 research assistantships (averaging $10,800 per year), 18 teaching assistantships (averaging $7,000 per year); tuition waivers (partial) also available. *Unit head:* Dr. Zhihua Qu, Interim Chair, 407-823-5976, Fax: 407-823-5835, E-mail: qu@ucf.edu. *Application contact:* Barbara Rodriguez, Director, Admissions and Registration, 407-823-2766, Fax: 407-823-6442, E-mail: gradadmissions@ucf.edu. Web site: http://web.eecs.ucf.edu/.

University of Cincinnati, Graduate School, College of Engineering and Applied Science, Department of Electrical and Computer Engineering and Computer Science, Program in Electrical Engineering, Cincinnati, OH 45221. Offers MS, PhD. *Degree requirements:* For master's, thesis; for doctorate, thesis/dissertation. *Entrance requirements:* For master's and doctorate, GRE General Test. Additional exam requirements/recommendations for international students: Required—TOEFL (minimum score 550 paper-based; 213 computer-based). *Faculty research:* Integrated circuits and optical devices, charge-coupled devices, photosensitive devices.

University of Colorado at Colorado Springs, College of Engineering and Applied Science, Department of Electrical and Computer Engineering, Colorado Springs, CO 80933-7150. Offers electrical engineering (ME, MS, PhD). Part-time and evening/weekend programs available. *Faculty:* 7 full-time (1 woman), 1 part-time/adjunct (0 women). *Students:* 22 full-time (4 women), 23 part-time (0 women); includes 6 minority (2 Asian, non-Hispanic/Latino; 4 Hispanic/Latino), 9 international. Average age 32. 22 applicants, 82% accepted, 13 enrolled. In 2011, 6 master's, 1 doctorate awarded. *Degree requirements:* For master's, thesis (for some programs), final oral exam (for non-thesis option); for doctorate, comprehensive exam, thesis/dissertation, preliminary exam. *Entrance requirements:* For master's, GRE General Test, minimum GPA of 3.0, BS or course work in electrical engineering; for doctorate, GRE General Test, minimum GPA of 3.3. Additional exam requirements/recommendations for international students: Required—TOEFL (minimum score 550 paper-based; 213 computer-based; 78 iBT). *Application deadline:* For fall admission, 4/1 for domestic and international students; for spring admission, 10/1 for domestic and international students. Applications are processed on a rolling basis. Application fee: $60 ($75 for international students). *Expenses:* Tuition, state resident: part-time $660 per credit hour. Tuition, nonresident: part-time $1133 per credit hour. Tuition and fees vary according to degree level, program and student level. *Financial support:* In 2011–12, 3 students received support. Fellowships, research assistantships, teaching assistantships, career-related internships or fieldwork, Federal Work-Study, and scholarships/grants available. Support available to part-time students. Financial award application deadline: 3/1; financial award applicants required to submit FAFSA. *Faculty research:* Integrated ferroelectric devices; applied electromagnetics; digital/mixed-signal circuit design, test and design for testability; signal processing for communications and controls. *Total annual research expenditures:* $335,241. *Unit head:* Dr. T. S. Kalkur, Chair, 719-255-3147, Fax: 719-255-3589. *Application contact:* Brianne Powell, Director, 719-255-3548, Fax: 719-255-3589, E-mail: bpowell@uccs.ede. Web site: http://ece.uccs.edu/.

University of Colorado Boulder, Graduate School, College of Engineering and Applied Science, Department of Electrical, Computer and Energy Engineering, Boulder, CO 80309. Offers ME, MS, PhD. *Faculty:* 32 full-time (5 women). *Students:* 243 full-time (46 women), 75 part-time (10 women); includes 20 minority (2 Black or African American, non-Hispanic/Latino; 12 Asian, non-Hispanic/Latino; 5 Hispanic/Latino; 1 Two or more races, non-Hispanic/Latino), 149 international. Average age 28. 759 applicants, 41% accepted, 75 enrolled. In 2011, 88 master's, 22 doctorates awarded. Terminal master's awarded for partial completion of doctoral program. *Degree requirements:* For master's, thesis or alternative; for doctorate, one foreign language, thesis/dissertation, departmental qualifying exam. *Entrance requirements:* For master's, GRE General Test, minimum undergraduate GPA of 3.0; for doctorate, GRE General Test, minimum undergraduate GPA of 3.5. *Application deadline:* For fall admission, 1/15 priority date for domestic students, 12/1 for international students; for spring admission, 10/1 for domestic and international students. Applications are processed on a rolling basis. Application fee: $50 ($60 for international students). Electronic applications accepted. *Financial support:* In 2011–12, 167 students received support, including 61 fellowships (averaging $9,329 per year), 72 research assistantships with full and partial tuition reimbursements available (averaging $20,840 per year), 29 teaching assistantships with full and partial tuition reimbursements available (averaging $14,759 per year); institutionally sponsored loans, scholarships/grants, health care benefits, and unspecified assistantships also available. Financial award application deadline: 1/15; financial award applicants required to submit FAFSA. *Faculty research:* Biomedical engineering and cognitive disabilities, computer engineering VLSI CAD, dynamics and control systems, digital signal processing communications, electromagnetics, RF and microwaves, nanostructures and devices, optics and optoelectronics, power electronics and renewable energy systems. *Total annual research expenditures:* $9.1 million. *Application contact:* E-mail: ecegrad@colorado.edu. Web site: http://ece-www.colorado.edu/.

University of Colorado Denver, College of Engineering and Applied Science, Department of Electrical Engineering, Denver, CO 80217. Offers MS, EASPh D. Part-time and evening/weekend programs available. *Faculty:* 11 full-time (1 woman), 3 part-time/adjunct (1 woman). *Students:* 56 full-time (10 women), 21 part-time (4 women); includes 8 minority (3 Black or African American, non-Hispanic/Latino; 3 Asian, non-Hispanic/Latino; 2 Hispanic/Latino), 48 international. Average age 30. 95 applicants, 68% accepted, 20 enrolled. In 2011, 25 master's awarded. *Degree requirements:* For master's, thesis or project, 30 credit hours; for doctorate, 60 credit hours beyond master's work (30 of which are for dissertation research). *Entrance requirements:* For master's, GRE; for doctorate, GRE, three letters of recommendation, personal statement. Additional exam requirements/recommendations for international students: Required—TOEFL (minimum score 550 paper-based; 213 computer-based; 80 iBT), TOEFL (minimum score 600 paper-based, 250 computer-based) for EASPh D. *Application deadline:* For fall admission, 4/1 for domestic students; for spring admission, 10/1 for domestic students. Applications are processed on a rolling basis. Application fee: $50 ($75 for international students). Electronic applications accepted. *Expenses:* Contact institution. *Financial support:* Research assistantships, teaching assistantships, career-related internships or fieldwork, and Federal Work-Study available. Financial award application deadline: 4/1; financial award applicants required to submit FAFSA. *Faculty research:* Communication and signal processing, embedded systems, electromagnetic fields and matter, energy and power systems, photonics and biomedical imaging. *Unit head:* Dr. Miloje (Mike) Radenkovic, Professor/Chair, 303-556-3616, E-mail: miloje.radenkovic@ucdenver.edu. *Application contact:* Janiece Hockaday, Administrative Assistant, 303-556-4718, E-mail: janiece.hockaday@ucdenver.edu. Web site: http://www.ucdenver.edu/academics/colleges/Engineering/Programs/Electrical-Engineering/Pages/ElectricalEngineering.aspx.

University of Colorado Denver, College of Engineering and Applied Science, Master of Engineering Program, Denver, CO 80217-3364. Offers civil engineering (M Eng), including civil engineering, geographic information systems, transportation systems; electrical engineering (M Eng); mechanical engineering (M Eng). Part-time programs available. *Students:* 21 full-time (9 women), 30 part-time (7 women); includes 5 minority (2 Black or African American, non-Hispanic/Latino; 1 Asian, non-Hispanic/Latino; 2 Hispanic/Latino), 1 international. Average age 34. 13 applicants, 69% accepted, 8 enrolled. In 2011, 19 master's awarded. *Degree requirements:* For master's, comprehensive exam, thesis, 27 credit hours of course work, 3 credit hours of report or thesis work. *Entrance requirements:* For master's, GRE (for those with GPA below 2.75), transcripts, references, statement of purpose. Additional exam requirements/recommendations for international students: Required—TOEFL (minimum score 525 paper-based; 197 computer-based; 71 iBT). *Application deadline:* For fall admission, 7/15 for domestic students, 6/15 for international students; for spring admission, 12/1 for domestic students, 11/1 for international students. Applications are processed on a rolling basis. Application fee: $50 ($75 for international students). Electronic applications accepted. *Expenses:* Contact institution. *Financial support:* Federal Work-Study and scholarships/grants available. Financial award application deadline: 4/1; financial award applicants required to submit FAFSA. *Faculty research:* Civil, electrical and mechanical engineering. *Unit head:* 303-556-2870, Fax: 303-556-2511, E-mail: engineering@ucdenver.edu. *Application contact:* Graduate School Admissions, 303-556-2704, E-mail: admissions@ucdenver.edu. Web site: http://ucdenver.edu/academics/colleges/Engineering/admissions/Masters/Pages/MastersAdmissions.aspx.

University of Connecticut, Graduate School, School of Engineering, Department of Electrical and Computer Engineering, Field of Electrical Engineering, Storrs, CT 06269. Offers MS, PhD. Terminal master's awarded for partial completion of doctoral program. *Degree requirements:* For master's, comprehensive exam; for doctorate, thesis/dissertation. *Entrance requirements:* For master's and doctorate, GRE General Test. Additional exam requirements/recommendations for international students: Required—TOEFL (minimum score 550 paper-based; 213 computer-based). Electronic applications accepted.

Electrical Engineering

University of Dayton, Department of Electrical and Computer Engineering, Dayton, OH 45469-1300. Offers MSEE, DE, PhD. Part-time and evening/weekend programs available. *Faculty:* 15 full-time (0 women), 4 part-time/adjunct (1 woman). *Students:* 114 full-time (14 women), 35 part-time (7 women); includes 7 minority (1 Black or African American, non-Hispanic/Latino; 4 Asian, non-Hispanic/Latino; 2 Hispanic/Latino), 103 international. Average age 27. 285 applicants, 51% accepted, 57 enrolled. In 2011, 55 master's, 3 doctorates awarded. *Degree requirements:* For master's, thesis optional; for doctorate, variable foreign language requirement, thesis/dissertation, departmental qualifying exam. *Entrance requirements:* Additional exam requirements/recommendations for international students: Required—TOEFL (minimum score 550 paper-based; 213 computer-based; 80 iBT). *Application deadline:* For fall admission, 8/1 for domestic students, 3/1 for international students; for winter admission, 7/1 for international students; for spring admission, 1/1 for international students. Applications are processed on a rolling basis. Application fee: $0 ($50 for international students). Electronic applications accepted. *Expenses: Tuition:* Full-time $8400; part-time $700 per credit hour. *Required fees:* $25 per semester. Tuition and fees vary according to degree level. *Financial support:* In 2011–12, 1 fellowship (averaging $27,500 per year), 24 research assistantships with full tuition reimbursements (averaging $12,500 per year), 6 teaching assistantships with full tuition reimbursements (averaging $10,065 per year) were awarded. Financial award application deadline: 5/1; financial award applicants required to submit FAFSA. *Faculty research:* Electrical engineering, video processing, leaky wave antenna. *Total annual research expenditures:* $1.1 million. *Unit head:* Dr. Guru Subramanyam, Chair, 937-229-3188, Fax: 937-229-4529, E-mail: gsubramanyam1@udayton.edu. *Application contact:* Dr. Gurur Subramanyam, Chair, 937-229-3188, Fax: 937-229-4529, E-mail: gsubramanyam1@udayton.edu.

University of Delaware, College of Engineering, Department of Electrical and Computer Engineering, Newark, DE 19716. Offers MSECE, PhD. Part-time programs available. Postbaccalaureate distance learning degree programs offered (no on-campus study). Terminal master's awarded for partial completion of doctoral program. *Degree requirements:* For master's, thesis optional; for doctorate, thesis/dissertation. *Entrance requirements:* For master's, GRE General Test; for doctorate, GRE General Test, qualifying exam. Additional exam requirements/recommendations for international students: Required—TOEFL. Electronic applications accepted. *Faculty research:* HIV Evolution During Dynamic Therapy, compressive sensing in imaging, sensor, networks, and UWB radios, computer network time synchronization, silicon spintronics, devices and imaging in the high-terahertz band.

University of Denver, School of Engineering and Computer Science, Department of Electrical and Computer Engineering, Denver, CO 80210. Offers computer engineering (MS); electrical and computer engineering (PhD); electrical engineering (MS); engineering (MS); mechatronic systems engineering (MS). Part-time and evening/weekend programs available. *Faculty:* 11 full-time (0 women), 3 part-time/adjunct (1 woman). *Students:* 3 full-time (1 woman), 115 part-time (18 women); includes 14 minority (6 Asian, non-Hispanic/Latino; 7 Hispanic/Latino; 1 Two or more races, non-Hispanic/Latino), 29 international. Average age 29. 121 applicants, 77% accepted, 27 enrolled. In 2011, 29 master's, 2 doctorates awarded. Terminal master's awarded for partial completion of doctoral program. *Degree requirements:* For master's, thesis optional, proficiency in high- or low-level computer language; for doctorate, comprehensive exam, thesis/dissertation, proficiency in high- or low-level computer language. *Entrance requirements:* For master's and doctorate, GRE General Test, personal statement, three letters of recommendation. Additional exam requirements/recommendations for international students: Required—TOEFL (minimum score 550 paper-based; 80 iBT). *Application deadline:* Applications are processed on a rolling basis. Application fee: $60. Electronic applications accepted. *Financial support:* In 2011–12, 67 students received support, including 12 research assistantships with full and partial tuition reimbursements available (averaging $16,291 per year), 9 teaching assistantships with full and partial tuition reimbursements available (averaging $16,264 per year); Federal Work-Study, scholarships/grants, and unspecified assistantships also available. Financial award application deadline: 2/15; financial award applicants required to submit FAFSA. *Faculty research:* Energy and power, MEMS, unmanned systems, image processing/pattern recognition. *Total annual research expenditures:* $1.6 million. *Unit head:* Dr. Kimon Valavanis, Chair, 303-871-2586, Fax: 303-871-2194, E-mail: kvalavan@du.edu. *Application contact:* Crystal Harris, Assistant to the Chair, 303-871-6618, Fax: 303-871-2194, E-mail: crystal.harris@du.edu. Web site: http://www.ece.du.edu.

University of Detroit Mercy, College of Engineering and Science, Department of Electrical and Computer Engineering, Detroit, MI 48221. Offers computer engineering (ME, DE); mechatronics systems (ME, DE); signals and systems (ME, DE). Evening/weekend programs available. *Degree requirements:* For doctorate, thesis/dissertation. *Faculty research:* Electromagnetics, computer architecture, systems.

University of Evansville, College of Engineering and Computer Science, Department of Electrical Engineering and Computer Science, Evansville, IN 47722. Offers MS. Part-time programs available. *Degree requirements:* For master's, thesis. *Entrance requirements:* For master's, GRE, minimum undergraduate GPA of 2.8, 2 letters of recommendation, BS in electrical engineering or computer science. Additional exam requirements/recommendations for international students: Required—TOEFL (minimum score 550 paper-based; 79 iBT), IELTS (minimum score 6.5). *Expenses:* Contact institution.

University of Florida, Graduate School, College of Engineering, Department of Electrical and Computer Engineering, Gainesville, FL 32611. Offers ME, MS, PhD, Engr. Part-time programs available. Postbaccalaureate distance learning degree programs offered. Terminal master's awarded for partial completion of doctoral program. *Degree requirements:* For master's, comprehensive exam (for some programs), thesis (for some programs); for doctorate, comprehensive exam, thesis/dissertation; for Engr, thesis. *Entrance requirements:* For master's, GRE General Test, minimum GPA of 3.0; for doctorate, GRE General Test, minimum GPA of 3.5; for Engr, GRE General Test. Additional exam requirements/recommendations for international students: Required—TOEFL (minimum score 550 paper-based; 213 computer-based; 80 iBT), IELTS (minimum score 6). Electronic applications accepted. *Faculty research:* Computer engineering, devices, electromagnetics and energy systems, electronics and signals and systems.

University of Hawaii at Manoa, Graduate Division, College of Engineering, Department of Electrical Engineering, Honolulu, HI 96822. Offers MS, PhD. Part-time programs available. *Degree requirements:* For master's, comprehensive exam, thesis; for doctorate, comprehensive exam, thesis/dissertation. *Entrance requirements:* For master's and doctorate, GRE General Test. Additional exam requirements/recommendations for international students: Required—TOEFL (minimum score 540 paper-based; 207 computer-based; 76 iBT), IELTS (minimum score 5). *Faculty research:* Computers and artificial intelligence, communication and networking, control theory, physical electronics, VLSI design, micromillimeter waves.

University of Houston, Cullen College of Engineering, Department of Electrical and Computer Engineering, Houston, TX 77204. Offers electrical engineering (MEE, MSEE, PhD). Part-time programs available. Terminal master's awarded for partial completion of doctoral program. *Degree requirements:* For master's, thesis (for some programs); for doctorate, comprehensive exam, thesis/dissertation. *Entrance requirements:* For master's and doctorate, GRE General Test. Additional exam requirements/recommendations for international students: Required—TOEFL (minimum score 580 paper-based; 237 computer-based; 92 iBT). Electronic applications accepted. *Faculty research:* Applied electromagnetics and microelectronics, signal and image processing, biomedical engineering, geophysical applications, control engineering.

University of Idaho, College of Graduate Studies, College of Engineering, Department of Electrical and Computer Engineering, Program in Electrical Engineering, Moscow, ID 83844-2282. Offers M Engr, MS, PhD. *Students:* 34 full-time, 103 part-time. Average age 34. In 2011, 28 master's, 1 doctorate awarded. *Application deadline:* Applications are processed on a rolling basis. Application fee: $60. Electronic applications accepted. *Expenses:* Tuition, state resident: full-time $3874; part-time $334 per credit hour. Tuition, nonresident: full-time $16,394; part-time $861 per credit hour. *Required fees:* $2808; $99 per credit hour. Tuition and fees vary according to program. *Financial support:* Applicants required to submit FAFSA. *Unit head:* Dr. Brian Johnson, Chair, 208-885-6902. *Application contact:* Erick Larson, Director of Graduate Admissions, 208-885-4723, E-mail: gadms@uidaho.edu. Web site: http://www.uidaho.edu/engr/ece/mselectricalengr.

University of Illinois at Chicago, Graduate College, College of Engineering, Department of Electrical and Computer Engineering, Program in Electrical and Computer Engineering, Chicago, IL 60607-7128. Offers MS, PhD. Part-time programs available. *Degree requirements:* For master's, thesis or alternative; for doctorate, thesis/dissertation, departmental qualifying exam. *Entrance requirements:* For master's, minimum GPA of 2.75, BS in related field; for doctorate, GRE General Test, minimum GPA of 2.75, MS in related field. Additional exam requirements/recommendations for international students: Required—TOEFL.

University of Illinois at Urbana–Champaign, Graduate College, College of Engineering, Department of Electrical and Computer Engineering, Champaign, IL 61820. Offers electrical and computer engineering (MS, PhD); MS/MBA. *Faculty:* 75 full-time (6 women), 3 part-time/adjunct (0 women). *Students:* 446 full-time (55 women), 28 part-time (4 women); includes 71 minority (8 Black or African American, non-Hispanic/Latino; 41 Asian, non-Hispanic/Latino; 14 Hispanic/Latino; 8 Two or more races, non-Hispanic/Latino), 267 international. 1,831 applicants, 11% accepted, 77 enrolled. In 2011, 86 master's, 72 doctorates awarded. *Entrance requirements:* For master's, GRE, minimum GPA of 3.0; for doctorate, GRE. Additional exam requirements/recommendations for international students: Required—TOEFL (minimum score 590 paper-based; 243 computer-based; 96 iBT) or IELTS (minimum score 6.5). *Application deadline:* Applications are processed on a rolling basis. Application fee: $75 ($90 for international students). Electronic applications accepted. *Financial support:* In 2011–12, 52 fellowships, 353 research assistantships, 162 teaching assistantships were awarded; tuition waivers (full and partial) also available. *Unit head:* Andreas C. Cangellaris, Head, 217-333-6037, Fax: 217-244-7075, E-mail: cangella@illinois.edu. *Application contact:* Laurie A. Fisher, Administrative Aide, 217-333-9709, Fax: 217-333-8582, E-mail: fisher2@illinois.edu. Web site: http://www.ece.illinois.edu/.

The University of Iowa, Graduate College, College of Engineering, Department of Electrical and Computer Engineering, Iowa City, IA 52242-1316. Offers MS, PhD. Part-time programs available. *Faculty:* 18 full-time (2 women), 2 part-time/adjunct (0 women). *Students:* 74 full-time (15 women); includes 5 minority (1 Black or African American, non-Hispanic/Latino; 1 Asian, non-Hispanic/Latino; 3 Hispanic/Latino), 47 international. Average age 27. 125 applicants, 19% accepted, 16 enrolled. In 2011, 17 master's, 11 doctorates awarded. *Degree requirements:* For master's, comprehensive exam, thesis optional; for doctorate, comprehensive exam, thesis/dissertation, qualifying exam. *Entrance requirements:* For master's and doctorate, GRE. Additional exam requirements/recommendations for international students: Required—TOEFL (minimum score 550 paper-based; 213 computer-based; 81 iBT). *Application deadline:* For fall admission, 2/1 priority date for domestic students, 2/1 for international students. Applications are processed on a rolling basis. Application fee: $60 ($100 for international students). Electronic applications accepted. *Financial support:* In 2011–12, 5 fellowships with full tuition reimbursements (averaging $19,146 per year), 44 research assistantships with full and partial tuition reimbursements (averaging $21,511 per year), 16 teaching assistantships with full tuition reimbursements (averaging $17,600 per year) were awarded; scholarships/grants and unspecified assistantships also available. Financial award application deadline: 2/1; financial award applicants required to submit FAFSA. *Faculty research:* Applied optics and nanotechnology, compressive sensing, computational genomics, database management systems, large-scale intelligent and control systems, medical image processing, VLSI design and test. *Total annual research expenditures:* $6.7 million. *Unit head:* Dr. Milan Sonka, Department Executive Officer, 319-335-6052, Fax: 319-335-6028, E-mail: milan-sonka@uiowa.edu. *Application contact:* Cathy Kern, Secretary, 319-335-5197, Fax: 319-335-6028, E-mail: ece@engineering.uiowa.edu. Web site: http://www.ece.engineering.uiowa.edu/.

The University of Kansas, Graduate Studies, School of Engineering, Program in Electrical Engineering, Lawrence, KS 66045. Offers MS, DE, PhD. Part-time programs available. *Faculty:* 36. *Students:* 59 full-time (10 women), 9 part-time (0 women); includes 3 minority (1 Asian, non-Hispanic/Latino; 1 Hispanic/Latino; 1 Native Hawaiian or other Pacific Islander, non-Hispanic/Latino), 39 international. Average age 27. 95 applicants, 59% accepted, 17 enrolled. In 2011, 14 master's, 2 doctorates awarded. Terminal master's awarded for partial completion of doctoral program. *Degree requirements:* For master's, thesis optional, exam; for doctorate, one foreign language, comprehensive exam, thesis/dissertation, qualifying exams. *Entrance requirements:* For master's, GRE, minimum GPA of 3.0; for doctorate, GRE, minimum GPA of 3.5. Additional exam requirements/recommendations for international students: Required—TOEFL (minimum score 600 paper-based; 250 computer-based; 100 iBT). *Application deadline:* For fall admission, 3/1 priority date for domestic students, 3/1 for international students; for spring admission, 10/1 priority date for domestic students, 10/1 for international students. Applications are processed on a rolling basis. Application fee: $55 ($65 for international students). Electronic applications accepted. Tuition and fees vary according to course load, campus/location, program and reciprocity agreements. *Financial support:* Fellowships with full and partial tuition reimbursements, research assistantships with full and partial tuition reimbursements, teaching assistantships with full and partial tuition reimbursements, career-related internships or fieldwork, scholarships/grants, and unspecified assistantships available. Financial award application deadline: 1/1. *Faculty research:* Communication systems and networking, computer systems design, radar systems and remote sensing. *Unit head:* Glenn Prescott, Chairperson, 785-864-4620, Fax: 785-864-3226. *Application contact:* Pam Shadoin, Assistant to Graduate Director, 785-864-4487, Fax: 785-864-3226, E-mail: eecs_graduate@.ku.edu. Web site: http://www.eecs.ku.edu

University of Kentucky, Graduate School, College of Engineering, Program in Electrical Engineering, Lexington, KY 40506-0032. Offers MSEE, PhD. *Degree requirements:* For master's, comprehensive exam, thesis optional; for doctorate, one foreign language, comprehensive exam, thesis/dissertation. *Entrance requirements:* For master's, GRE General Test, minimum undergraduate GPA of 2.75; for doctorate, GRE General Test, minimum undergraduate GPA of 3.0. Additional exam requirements/recommendations for international students: Required—TOEFL (minimum score 550 paper-based; 213 computer-based). Electronic applications accepted. *Faculty research:* Signal processing, systems, and control; electromagnetic field theory; power electronics and machines; computer engineering and VLSI; materials and devices.

University of Louisville, J. B. Speed School of Engineering, Department of Electrical and Computer Engineering, Louisville, KY 40292-0001. Offers M Eng, MS, PhD. *Accreditation:* ABET (one or more programs are accredited). Part-time programs available. *Faculty:* 15 full-time (2 women). *Students:* 74 full-time (7 women), 20 part-time (4 women); includes 6 minority (2 Black or African American, non-Hispanic/Latino; 2 Asian, non-Hispanic/Latino; 1 Hispanic/Latino; 1 Two or more races, non-Hispanic/Latino), 42 international. Average age 28. 38 applicants, 45% accepted, 6 enrolled. In 2011, 36 master's, 4 doctorates awarded. Terminal master's awarded for partial completion of doctoral program. *Degree requirements:* For master's, comprehensive exam (for some programs), thesis or alternative; for doctorate, comprehensive exam, thesis/dissertation, minimum GPA of 3.0. *Entrance requirements:* For master's and doctorate, GRE General Test. Additional exam requirements/recommendations for international students: Required—TOEFL (minimum score 550 paper-based; 213 computer-based; 80 iBT), IELTS (minimum score 6.5). *Application deadline:* For fall admission, 5/1 priority date for domestic students, 5/1 for international students; for spring admission, 11/1 priority date for domestic students, 11/1 for international students. Applications are processed on a rolling basis. Application fee: $50. Electronic applications accepted. *Expenses:* Tuition, state resident: full-time $9692; part-time $539 per credit hour. Tuition, nonresident: full-time $20,168; part-time $1121 per credit hour. Tuition and fees vary according to program and reciprocity agreements. *Financial support:* In 2011–12, 16 students received support, including 4 fellowships with full tuition reimbursements available (averaging $20,000 per year), 4 research assistantships with full tuition reimbursements available (averaging $21,000 per year), 8 teaching assistantships with full tuition reimbursements available (averaging $20,000 per year). Financial award application deadline: 1/25; financial award applicants required to submit FAFSA. *Faculty research:* Nanotechnology; microfabrication; computer engineering; control, communication and signal processing; electronic devices and systems. *Total annual research expenditures:* $5.8 million. *Unit head:* James H. Graham, Acting Chair, 502-852-6289, Fax: 502-852-6807, E-mail: jhgrah01@louisville.edu. *Application contact:* Dr. Michael Day, Associate Dean, 502-852-6195, Fax: 502-852-7294, E-mail: day@louisville.edu. Web site: http://www.louisville.edu/speed/electrical/.

University of Maine, Graduate School, College of Engineering, Department of Electrical and Computer Engineering, Orono, ME 04469. Offers computer engineering (MS); electrical engineering (MS, PhD). Part-time programs available. *Faculty:* 12 full-time (1 woman). *Students:* 21 full-time (4 women), 16 part-time (3 women); includes 4 minority (3 Asian, non-Hispanic/Latino; 1 Hispanic/Latino), 16 international. Average age 28. 35 applicants, 49% accepted, 12 enrolled. In 2011, 8 master's, 3 doctorates awarded. *Degree requirements:* For master's, thesis (for some programs); for doctorate, thesis/dissertation. *Entrance requirements:* For master's and doctorate, GRE General Test. Additional exam requirements/recommendations for international students: Required—TOEFL. *Application deadline:* For fall admission, 2/1 priority date for domestic students. Applications are processed on a rolling basis. Application fee: $65. Electronic applications accepted. *Expenses:* Tuition, state resident: full-time $5016. Tuition, nonresident: full-time $14,424. *Financial support:* In 2011–12, 15 research assistantships with full tuition reimbursements (averaging $18,720 per year), 2 teaching assistantships with full tuition reimbursements (averaging $13,600 per year) were awarded; Federal Work-Study, institutionally sponsored loans, and tuition waivers (full and partial) also available. Financial award application deadline: 3/1. *Total annual research expenditures:* $289,054. *Unit head:* Dr. Donald Hummels, Chair, 207-581-2244. *Application contact:* Scott G. Delcourt, Associate Dean of the Graduate School, 207-581-3291, Fax: 207-581-3232, E-mail: graduate@maine.edu. Web site: http://www2.umaine.edu/graduate/.

The University of Manchester, School of Electrical and Electronic Engineering, Manchester, United Kingdom. Offers M Phil, PhD.

University of Manitoba, Faculty of Graduate Studies, Faculty of Engineering, Department of Electrical and Computer Engineering, Winnipeg, MB R3T 2N2, Canada. Offers M Eng, M Sc, PhD. *Degree requirements:* For master's, thesis; for doctorate, thesis/dissertation.

University of Maryland, Baltimore County, Graduate School, College of Engineering and Information Technology, Department of Computer Science and Electrical Engineering, Program in Electrical Engineering, Baltimore, MD 21250. Offers MS, PhD. Part-time programs available. *Students:* 31 full-time (5 women), 15 part-time (4 women); includes 12 minority (4 Black or African American, non-Hispanic/Latino; 4 Asian, non-Hispanic/Latino; 2 Hispanic/Latino; 1 Native Hawaiian or other Pacific Islander, non-Hispanic/Latino; 1 Two or more races, non-Hispanic/Latino), 19 international. Average age 32. 57 applicants, 58% accepted, 9 enrolled. In 2011, 1 master's, 5 doctorates awarded. *Degree requirements:* For master's, thesis optional; for doctorate, comprehensive exam, thesis/dissertation. *Entrance requirements:* For master's, GRE General Test, BS from ABET-accredited undergraduate program in electrical engineering or strong background in computer science, math, physics, or other engineering science; for doctorate, GRE General Test, BS from ABET-accredited undergraduate program in electrical engineering or strong background in computer science. Additional exam requirements/recommendations for international students: Required—TOEFL (minimum score 550 paper-based; 213 computer-based; 80 iBT). *Application deadline:* For fall admission, 6/1 for domestic students, 1/1 for international students; for spring admission, 11/1 for domestic students, 6/1 for international students. Applications are processed on a rolling basis. Application fee: $70. Electronic applications accepted. *Financial support:* In 2011–12, 2 fellowships, 9 research assistantships with full tuition reimbursements (averaging $22,000 per year), 5 teaching assistantships with partial tuition reimbursements (averaging $17,000 per year) were awarded; career-related internships or fieldwork, Federal Work-Study, scholarships/grants, health care benefits, tuition waivers (partial), and unspecified assistantships also available. Support available to part-time students. Financial award application deadline: 6/30; financial award applicants required to submit FAFSA. *Faculty research:* Communication and signal processing, photonics and micro electronics, sensor systems, signal processing architectures, VLSI design and test. *Unit head:* Dr. Gary Carter, Professor and Chair, 410-455-3500, Fax: 410-455-3969, E-mail: carter@cs.umbc.edu. *Application contact:* 410-455-3500, Fax: 410-455-3969. Web site: http://www.cs.umbc.edu/.

University of Maryland, College Park, Academic Affairs, A. James Clark School of Engineering, Department of Continuing and Distance Learning in Engineering, College Park, MD 20742. Offers engineering (M Eng), including aerospace engineering, chemical engineering, civil engineering, electrical engineering, engineering, fire protection engineering, materials science and engineering, mechanical engineering, reliability engineering, systems engineering. *Faculty:* 3 full-time (0 women), 8 part-time/adjunct (0 women). *Students:* 75 full-time (24 women), 418 part-time (81 women); includes 154 minority (62 Black or African American, non-Hispanic/Latino; 64 Asian, non-Hispanic/Latino; 23 Hispanic/Latino; 5 Two or more races, non-Hispanic/Latino), 67 international. 447 applicants, 52% accepted, 154 enrolled. In 2011, 155 master's awarded. *Application deadline:* For fall admission, 8/15 for domestic students, 2/1 for international students; for spring admission, 1/10 for domestic students, 8/1 for international students. Applications are processed on a rolling basis. Application fee: $75. Electronic applications accepted. *Expenses: Tuition, area resident:* Part-time $525 per credit hour. Tuition, state resident: part-time $525 per credit hour. Tuition, nonresident: part-time $1131 per credit hour. *Required fees:* $386.31 per term. Tuition and fees vary according to program. *Financial support:* In 2011–12, 3 research assistantships (averaging $21,498 per year), 13 teaching assistantships (averaging $16,889 per year) were awarded. *Unit head:* Dr. Darryll Pines, Dean, 301-405-8539, E-mail: pines@umd.edu. *Application contact:* Dr. Charles A. Caramello, Dean of the Graduate School, 301-405-0358, Fax: 301-314-9305.

University of Maryland, College Park, Academic Affairs, A. James Clark School of Engineering, Department of Electrical and Computer Engineering, College Park, MD 20742. Offers electrical and computer engineering (M Eng, MS, PhD); electrical engineering (MS, PhD); telecommunications (MS). Part-time and evening/weekend programs available. Postbaccalaureate distance learning degree programs offered. *Faculty:* 99 full-time (9 women), 27 part-time/adjunct (3 women). *Students:* 493 full-time (101 women), 65 part-time (7 women); includes 57 minority (7 Black or African American, non-Hispanic/Latino; 37 Asian, non-Hispanic/Latino; 10 Hispanic/Latino; 3 Two or more races, non-Hispanic/Latino), 419 international. 1,578 applicants, 34% accepted, 231 enrolled. In 2011, 104 master's, 45 doctorates awarded. *Degree requirements:* For master's, thesis optional; for doctorate, thesis/dissertation, oral exam, qualifying exam. *Entrance requirements:* For master's and doctorate, GRE General Test, 3 letters of recommendation. *Application deadline:* For fall admission, 5/1 for domestic students, 2/1 for international students; for spring admission, 6/1 for international students. Applications are processed on a rolling basis. Application fee: $75. Electronic applications accepted. *Expenses: Tuition, area resident:* Part-time $525 per credit hour. Tuition, state resident: part-time $525 per credit hour. Tuition, nonresident: part-time $1131 per credit hour. *Required fees:* $386.31 per term. Tuition and fees vary according to program. *Financial support:* In 2011–12, 13 fellowships with full and partial tuition reimbursements (averaging $20,640 per year), 172 research assistantships with tuition reimbursements (averaging $17,823 per year), 82 teaching assistantships with tuition reimbursements (averaging $16,768 per year) were awarded; career-related internships or fieldwork also available. Financial award applicants required to submit FAFSA. *Faculty research:* Communications and control, electrophysics, micro-electronics, robotics, computer engineering. *Total annual research expenditures:* $11.6 million. *Unit head:* Rama Chellappa, Interim Chair, 301-405-3683, E-mail: chella@umd.edu. *Application contact:* Dr. Charles A. Caramello, Dean of Graduate School, 301-405-0358, Fax: 301-314-9305, E-mail: ccaramel@umd.edu.

University of Massachusetts Amherst, Graduate School, College of Engineering, Department of Electrical and Computer Engineering, Amherst, MA 01003. Offers MSECE, PhD. Part-time programs available. *Faculty:* 41 full-time (2 women). *Students:* 196 full-time (38 women), 23 part-time (6 women); includes 13 minority (3 Black or African American, non-Hispanic/Latino; 6 Asian, non-Hispanic/Latino; 4 Hispanic/Latino), 175 international. Average age 26. 776 applicants, 29% accepted, 71 enrolled. In 2011, 53 master's, 12 doctorates awarded. Terminal master's awarded for partial completion of doctoral program. *Degree requirements:* For master's, thesis or alternative; for doctorate, comprehensive exam, thesis/dissertation. *Entrance requirements:* For master's and doctorate, GRE General Test. Additional exam requirements/recommendations for international students: Required—TOEFL (minimum score 550 paper-based; 213 computer-based; 80 iBT), IELTS (minimum score 6.5). *Application deadline:* For fall admission, 1/15 for domestic and international students; for spring admission, 10/1 for domestic and international students. Applications are processed on a rolling basis. Application fee: $50 ($65 for international students). Electronic applications accepted. Tuition and fees vary according to course load, campus/location and program. *Financial support:* Fellowships with full and partial tuition reimbursements, research assistantships with full tuition reimbursements, teaching assistantships with full tuition reimbursements, career-related internships or fieldwork, Federal Work-Study, scholarships/grants, traineeships, health care benefits, tuition waivers (full and partial), and unspecified assistantships available. Support available to part-time students. Financial award application deadline: 1/15. *Unit head:* Dr. C. Mani Krishna, Graduate Program Director, 413-545-4583, Fax: 413-545-4611, E-mail: ecegrad@ecs.umass.edu. *Application contact:* Lindsay DeSantis, Supervisor of Admissions, 413-545-0722, Fax: 413-577-0010, E-mail: gradadm@grad.umass.edu. Web site: http://ece.umass.edu/.

University of Massachusetts Dartmouth, Graduate School, College of Engineering, Department of Electrical and Computer Engineering, North Dartmouth, MA 02747-2300. Offers acoustics (Postbaccalaureate Certificate); communications (Postbaccalaureate Certificate); computer engineering (MS, PhD); computer systems engineering (Postbaccalaureate Certificate); digital signal processing (Postbaccalaureate Certificate); electrical engineering (MS, PhD); electrical engineering systems (Postbaccalaureate Certificate). Part-time programs available. *Faculty:* 15 full-time (3 women), 4 part-time/adjunct (1 woman). *Students:* 37 full-time (5 women), 52 part-time (8 women); includes 9 minority (2 Black or African American, non-Hispanic/Latino; 2 Asian, non-Hispanic/Latino; 1 Hispanic/Latino; 4 Two or more races, non-Hispanic/Latino), 45 international. Average age 29. 83 applicants, 93% accepted, 26 enrolled. In 2011, 17 master's, 1 doctorate awarded. *Degree requirements:* For master's, culminating project or thesis; for doctorate, comprehensive exam, thesis/dissertation. *Entrance requirements:* For master's, GRE, minimum undergraduate GPA of 3.0, 3 letters of recommendation, statement of intent, resume; for doctorate, GRE, 3 letters of recommendation, resume, statement of intent; for Postbaccalaureate Certificate, 3 letters of recommendation, resume, statement of intent. Additional exam requirements/recommendations for international students: Required—TOEFL (minimum score 533 paper-based; 200 computer-based; 72 iBT). *Application deadline:* For fall admission, 2/15 priority date for domestic students, 1/15 for international students; for spring admission, 11/1 priority date for domestic students, 10/1 for international students. Applications are processed on a rolling basis. Application fee: $40 ($60 for international students). Electronic applications accepted. *Expenses:* Tuition, state resident: full-time $2071; part-time $86.29 per credit. Tuition, nonresident: full-time $8099; part-time $337.46 per credit. *Required fees:* $438.58 per credit. Part-time tuition and fees vary according to class time, course load, degree level and reciprocity agreements. *Financial support:* In 2011–12, 10 research assistantships with full tuition reimbursements (averaging $12,720 per year), 14 teaching assistantships with full tuition reimbursements (averaging $10,385 per year) were awarded; fellowships, Federal Work-Study, and unspecified assistantships also available. Support available to part-time students. Financial award application deadline: 3/1; financial award applicants required to submit FAFSA. *Faculty research:* Speech acoustics, marine applications, signals and systems, applied electromagnetics, intelligent agency. *Total annual research expenditures:* $921,048. *Unit head:* Dr. Karen Payton, Graduate Program Director, 508-999-8434, Fax: 508-999-8489, E-mail: kpayton@umassd.edu. *Application contact:* Elan Turcotte-Shamski, Graduate Admissions Officer, 508-999-8604, Fax: 508-999-8183, E-mail: graduate@umassd.edu. Web site: http://www.umassd.edu/engineering/ece/graduate/welcome.cfm.

University of Massachusetts Lowell, College of Engineering, Department of Electrical and Computer Engineering, Program in Electrical Engineering, Lowell, MA 01854-2881. Offers MS Eng, D Eng. Part-time and evening/weekend programs available. Terminal master's awarded for partial completion of doctoral program. *Degree requirements:* For master's, thesis; for doctorate, 2 foreign languages, thesis/dissertation. *Entrance requirements:* For master's and doctorate, GRE General Test.

University of Memphis, Graduate School, Herff College of Engineering, Department of Electrical and Computer Engineering, Memphis, TN 38152. Offers automatic control systems (MS); biomedical systems (MS); communications and propagation systems (MS); computer engineering (PhD); electrical engineering (PhD); engineering computer systems (MS). *Degree requirements:* For master's, comprehensive exam, thesis or alternative. *Entrance requirements:* For master's, GRE General Test or MAT, minimum undergraduate GPA of 2.5. *Faculty research:* Image processing, imaging sensors, biomedical systems, intelligent systems.

University of Miami, Graduate School, College of Engineering, Department of Electrical and Computer Engineering, Coral Gables, FL 33124. Offers MSECE, PhD. Part-time programs available. *Degree requirements:* For master's, thesis (for some programs); for doctorate, comprehensive exam, thesis/dissertation, dissertation proposal defense. *Entrance requirements:* For master's, GRE General Test, minimum GPA of 3.0; for doctorate, GRE General Test, minimum undergraduate GPA of 3.3, graduate 3.5. Additional exam requirements/recommendations for international students: Required—TOEFL (minimum score 550 paper-based; 213 computer-based; 59 iBT), IELTS (minimum score 7). Electronic applications accepted. *Faculty research:* Computer network, image processing, database systems, digital signal processing, machine intelligence.

University of Michigan, College of Engineering, Department of Electrical Engineering and Computer Science, Ann Arbor, MI 48109. Offers MS, MSE, PhD. *Students:* 607 full-time (90 women), 2 part-time (0 women). 1,879 applicants, 29% accepted, 250 enrolled. In 2011, 116 master's, 33 doctorates awarded. *Faculty research:* Solid state electronics and optics; communications, control, signal process; sensors and integrated circuitry; software systems; artificial intelligence; hardware systems. *Unit head:* Prof. Khalil Najafi, Chair, 734-647-7010, Fax: 734-647-7009, E-mail: najafi@umich.edu. *Application contact:* Beth Stalnaker, Graduate Coordinator, 734-647-1758, Fax: 734-763-1503, E-mail: beths@umich.edu.

University of Michigan–Dearborn, College of Engineering and Computer Science, Department of Electrical and Computer Engineering, Dearborn, MI 48128-1491. Offers computer engineering (MSE); electrical engineering (MSE); software engineering (MS). Part-time and evening/weekend programs available. Postbaccalaureate distance learning degree programs offered (no on-campus study). *Faculty:* 9 full-time (1 woman), 9 part-time/adjunct (1 woman). *Students:* 15 full-time (4 women), 90 part-time (9 women); includes 36 minority (6 Black or African American, non-Hispanic/Latino; 28 Asian, non-Hispanic/Latino; 1 Hispanic/Latino; 1 Two or more races, non-Hispanic/Latino). Average age 32. 74 applicants, 50% accepted, 24 enrolled. In 2011, 33 master's awarded. *Degree requirements:* For master's, thesis optional. *Entrance requirements:* For master's, bachelor's degree in electrical and computer engineering or equivalent, minimum GPA of 3.0. Additional exam requirements/recommendations for international students: Required—TOEFL (minimum score 560 paper-based; 220 computer-based; 84 iBT). *Application deadline:* For fall admission, 8/1 priority date for domestic students, 4/1 for international students; for winter admission, 12/1 priority date for domestic students, 8/1 for international students; for spring admission, 4/1 priority date for domestic students, 2/1 for international students. Applications are processed on a rolling basis. Application fee: $60. Electronic applications accepted. *Financial support:* In 2011–12, 6 research assistantships with partial tuition reimbursements (averaging $8,815 per year), 2 teaching assistantships with partial tuition reimbursements (averaging $8,851 per year) were awarded; scholarships/grants and health care benefits also available. *Faculty research:* Fuzzy systems and applications, machine vision, pattern recognition and machine intelligence, vehicle electronics, wireless communications. *Unit head:* Dr. YiLu Murphey, Chair, 313-593-5028, Fax: 313-583-6336, E-mail: yilu@umich.edu. *Application contact:* Michael Patrick Hicks, Academic Records Intermediate Assistant, 313-593-5420, Fax: 313-583-6336, E-mail: ece-grad@umd.umich.edu. Web site: http://www.engin.umd.umich.edu/ECE/.

University of Minnesota, Duluth, Graduate School, Swenson College of Science and Engineering, Department of Electrical and Computer Engineering, Duluth, MN 55812-2496. Offers MSECE. Part-time programs available. *Degree requirements:* For master's, thesis. *Entrance requirements:* Additional exam requirements/recommendations for international students: Recommended—TOEFL, IELTS, TWE. *Faculty research:* Biomedical instrumentation, transportation systems, computer hardware and software, signal processing, optical communications.

University of Minnesota, Twin Cities Campus, College of Science and Engineering, Department of Electrical and Computer Engineering, Minneapolis, MN 55455-0213. Offers MSEE, PhD. Part-time programs available. *Faculty:* 42 full-time (2 women). *Students:* 486 (82 women); includes 32 minority (8 Black or African American, non-Hispanic/Latino; 21 Asian, non-Hispanic/Latino; 3 Hispanic/Latino), 326 international. *Degree requirements:* For master's, thesis or alternative; for doctorate, thesis/dissertation. *Entrance requirements:* Additional exam requirements/recommendations for international students: Required—TOEFL (minimum score 550 paper-based; 213 computer-based). *Application deadline:* For fall admission, 12/1 priority date for domestic students, 12/1 for international students. Applications are processed on a rolling basis. Application fee: $75 ($95 for international students). Electronic applications accepted. *Financial support:* Fellowships, research assistantships, and teaching assistantships available. *Faculty research:* Signal processing, micro and nano structures, computers, controls, power electronics. *Application contact:* Electrical Engineering Graduate Program, E-mail: newgrad@umn.edu. Web site: http://www.ece.umn.edu/.

University of Missouri, Graduate School, College of Engineering, Department of Electrical and Computer Engineering, Columbia, MO 65211. Offers MS, PhD. *Faculty:* 26 full-time (4 women), 3 part-time/adjunct (0 women). *Students:* 66 full-time (12 women), 76 part-time (10 women); includes 7 minority (3 Black or African American, non-Hispanic/Latino; 3 Asian, non-Hispanic/Latino; 1 Two or more races, non-Hispanic/Latino), 102 international. Average age 26. 166 applicants, 37% accepted, 27 enrolled. In 2011, 31 master's, 14 doctorates awarded. *Degree requirements:* For master's, thesis or alternative; for doctorate, thesis/dissertation. *Entrance requirements:* For master's, GRE General Test, minimum GPA of 3.0; for doctorate, GRE General Test, GRE Subject Test, minimum GPA of 3.0. Additional exam requirements/recommendations for international students: Required—TOEFL (minimum score 550 paper-based; 213 computer-based; 80 iBT). *Application deadline:* For fall admission, 2/15 priority date for domestic students. Applications are processed on a rolling basis. Application fee: $55 ($75 for international students). *Expenses:* Tuition, state resident: full-time $5881. Tuition, nonresident: full-time $15,183. *Required fees:* $952. Tuition and fees vary according to campus/location and program. *Financial support:* Fellowships, research assistantships, teaching assistantships, and institutionally sponsored loans available. *Faculty research:* Communication and signal processing, physical electronics, intelligent systems, systems modeling and control, nano and micro electronics, digital/computer systems. *Unit head:* Dr. William C. Nunnally, Department Chair, E-mail: nunnallyw@missouri.edu. *Application contact:* Shirley Holdmeier, 573-882-4436, E-mail: holdmeiers@missouri.edu. Web site: http://engineering.missouri.edu/ece/.

University of Missouri–Kansas City, School of Computing and Engineering, Kansas City, MO 64110-2499. Offers civil engineering (MS); computer and electrical engineering (PhD); computer science (MS), including bioinformatics, software engineering, telecommunications networking; computer science and informatics (PhD); computing (PhD); electrical engineering (MS); engineering (PhD); mechanical engineering (MS); telecommunications (PhD). PhD (interdisciplinary) offered through the School of Graduate Studies. Part-time programs available. *Faculty:* 36 full-time (6 women), 27 part-time/adjunct (3 women). *Students:* 155 full-time (44 women), 136 part-time (24 women); includes 19 minority (4 Black or African American, non-Hispanic/Latino; 7 Asian, non-Hispanic/Latino; 6 Hispanic/Latino; 2 Two or more races, non-Hispanic/Latino), 201 international. Average age 26. 455 applicants, 46% accepted, 96 enrolled. In 2011, 194 degrees awarded. *Degree requirements:* For doctorate, thesis/dissertation. *Entrance requirements:* For master's, GRE General Test, minimum GPA of 3.0, 3 letters of recommendation from professors; for doctorate, GRE General Test, minimum GPA of 3.5. Additional exam requirements/recommendations for international students: Required—TOEFL (minimum score 550 paper-based; 213 computer-based; 80 iBT). *Application deadline:* For fall admission, 1/15 priority date for domestic students, 1/15 for international students. Applications are processed on a rolling basis. Application fee: $45 ($50 for international students). *Expenses:* Tuition, state resident: full-time $5798; part-time $322.10 per credit hour. Tuition, nonresident: full-time $14,969; part-time $831.60 per credit hour. *Required fees:* $93.51 per credit hour. *Financial support:* In 2011–12, 47 research assistantships with partial tuition reimbursements (averaging $13,190 per year), 10 teaching assistantships with partial tuition reimbursements (averaging $9,815 per year) were awarded; career-related internships or fieldwork, Federal Work-Study, scholarships/grants, tuition waivers (partial), and unspecified assistantships also available. Support available to part-time students. Financial award application deadline: 3/1; financial award applicants required to submit FAFSA. *Faculty research:* Algorithms, bioinformatics and medical informatics, biomechanics/biomaterials, civil engineering materials, networking and telecommunications, thermal science. *Unit head:* Dr. Kevin Z. Truman, Dean, 816-235-2399, Fax: 816-235-5159. *Application contact:* 816-235-2399, Fax: 816-235-5159. Web site: http://sce.umkc.edu/.

University of Nebraska–Lincoln, Graduate College, College of Engineering, Department of Electrical Engineering, Lincoln, NE 68588. Offers MS, PhD. *Degree requirements:* For master's, thesis optional; for doctorate, comprehensive exam, thesis/dissertation. *Entrance requirements:* For master's and doctorate, GRE General Test. Additional exam requirements/recommendations for international students: Required—TOEFL (minimum score 550 paper-based; 213 computer-based). Electronic applications accepted. *Faculty research:* Electromagnetics, communications, biomedical digital signal processing, electrical breakdown of gases, optical properties of microelectronic materials.

University of Nevada, Las Vegas, Graduate College, Howard R. Hughes College of Engineering, Department of Electrical and Computer Engineering, Las Vegas, NV 89154-4026. Offers MSE, PhD. Part-time programs available. *Faculty:* 20 full-time (3 women), 6 part-time/adjunct (1 woman). *Students:* 13 full-time (0 women), 28 part-time (4 women); includes 4 minority (1 Black or African American, non-Hispanic/Latino; 2 Hispanic/Latino; 1 Two or more races, non-Hispanic/Latino), 27 international. Average age 29. 33 applicants, 61% accepted, 10 enrolled. In 2011, 9 master's, 3 doctorates awarded. *Degree requirements:* For master's, comprehensive exam, thesis, project; for doctorate, comprehensive exam, thesis/dissertation. *Entrance requirements:* Additional exam requirements/recommendations for international students: Required—TOEFL (minimum score 550 paper-based; 213 computer-based; 80 iBT), IELTS (minimum score 7). *Application deadline:* For fall admission, 6/1 priority date for domestic students, 5/1 for international students; for spring admission, 10/1 priority date for domestic students, 10/1 for international students. Applications are processed on a rolling basis. Application fee: $60 ($95 for international students). Electronic applications accepted. *Financial support:* In 2011–12, 41 students received support, including 21 research assistantships with partial tuition reimbursements available (averaging $9,997 per year), 20 teaching assistantships with partial tuition reimbursements available (averaging $8,504 per year); institutionally sponsored loans, scholarships/grants, health care benefits, tuition waivers (full), and unspecified assistantships also available. Financial award application deadline: 3/1. *Faculty research:* Computer engineering, power engineering, semiconductor and nanotechnology, electronics and VLSI, telecommunications and control. *Total annual research expenditures:* $1.4 million. *Unit head:* Dr. Henry Selvaraj, Chair/Professor, 702-895-4183, Fax: 702-895-4075, E-mail: ece.chair@unlv.edu. *Application contact:* Graduate College Admissions Evaluator, 702-895-3320, Fax: 702-895-4180, E-mail: gradcollege@unlv.edu. Web site: http://ece.unlv.edu/.

University of Nevada, Reno, Graduate School, College of Engineering, Department of Electrical Engineering, Reno, NV 89557. Offers MS, PhD. Terminal master's awarded for partial completion of doctoral program. *Degree requirements:* For master's, thesis optional; for doctorate, thesis/dissertation. *Entrance requirements:* For master's, GRE General Test, minimum GPA of 2.75; for doctorate, GRE General Test, minimum GPA of 3.0. Additional exam requirements/recommendations for international students: Required—TOEFL (minimum score 500 paper-based; 173 computer-based; 61 iBT), IELTS (minimum score 6). Electronic applications accepted. *Faculty research:* Acoustics, neural networking, synthetic aperture radar simulation, optical fiber communications and sensors.

University of New Brunswick Fredericton, School of Graduate Studies, Faculty of Engineering, Department of Electrical and Computer Engineering, Fredericton, NB E3B 5A3, Canada. Offers M Eng, M Sc E, PhD. Part-time programs available. *Faculty:* 14

full-time (1 woman), 1 (woman) part-time/adjunct. *Students:* 69 full-time (6 women), 8 part-time (2 women). 45 applicants, 44% accepted. In 2011, 8 master's awarded. *Degree requirements:* For master's, thesis, research proposal; 10 courses (for M Eng); for doctorate, comprehensive exam, thesis/dissertation, research proposal. *Entrance requirements:* For master's, minimum GPA of 3.0; references; for doctorate, M Sc; minimum GPA of 3.0 or B average; previous transcripts; references. Additional exam requirements/recommendations for international students: Required—TWE, TOEFL (minimum score 580 paper-based; 237 computer-based) or IELTS (minimum score 7). *Application deadline:* Applications are processed on a rolling basis. Application fee: $50 Canadian dollars. *Financial support:* In 2011–12, 16 fellowships, 51 research assistantships (averaging $14,400 per year), 35 teaching assistantships were awarded. *Faculty. research:* Biomedical engineering, communications, robotics and control systems, electromagnetic systems, embedded systems, optical fiber systems, sustainable energy and power systems, signal processing, software systems. *Unit head:* Dr. Julian Meng, Director of Graduate Studies, 504-458-7453, Fax: 504-453-3589, E-mail: jmeng@unb.ca. *Application contact:* Shelley Cormier, Graduate Secretary, 506-452-6142, Fax: 506-453-3589, E-mail: scormier@unb.ca. Web site: http://www.ee.unb.ca/.

University of New Hampshire, Graduate School, College of Engineering and Physical Sciences, Department of Electrical and Computer Engineering, Durham, NH 03824. Offers electrical engineering (MS, PhD). Part-time and evening/weekend programs available. *Faculty:* 11 full-time (0 women). *Students:* 8 full-time (1 woman), 20 part-time (2 women); includes 5 minority (3 Asian, non-Hispanic/Latino; 2 Hispanic/Latino), 4 international. Average age 25. 58 applicants, 45% accepted, 10 enrolled. In 2011, 9 master's, 1 doctorate awarded. *Degree requirements:* For master's, thesis or alternative; for doctorate, thesis/dissertation. *Entrance requirements:* For master's and doctorate, GRE (for non-U.S. university bachelor's degree holders). Additional exam requirements/recommendations for international students: Required—TOEFL (minimum score 550 paper-based; 213 computer-based; 80 iBT). *Application deadline:* For fall admission, 4/1 priority date for domestic students, 4/1 for international students; for spring admission, 12/1 for domestic students. Applications are processed on a rolling basis. Application fee: $65. Electronic applications accepted. *Expenses:* Tuition, state resident: full-time $12,360; part-time $687 per credit hour. Tuition, nonresident: full-time $25,680; part-time $1058 per credit hour. *International tuition:* $29,550 full-time. *Required fees:* $1666; $833 per course. $416.50 per semester. Tuition and fees vary according to course load and degree level. *Financial support:* In 2011–12, 17 students received support, including 8 research assistantships, 7 teaching assistantships; fellowships, Federal Work-Study, scholarships/grants, and tuition waivers (full and partial) also available. Support available to part-time students. Financial award application deadline: 2/15. *Faculty research:* Biomedical engineering, communications systems and information theory, digital systems, illumination engineering. *Unit head:* John LaCourse, III, Chairperson, 603-862-1357. *Application contact:* Kathryn Reynolds, Administrative Assistant, 603-862-1358, E-mail: ece.dept@unh.edu. Web site: http://www.ece.unh.edu/.

University of New Haven, Graduate School, Tagliatela College of Engineering, Program in Electrical Engineering, West Haven, CT 06516-1916. Offers communications/digital signal processing (MS); control system (MS); electrical and computer engineering (MS); electrical engineering (MS). Part-time and evening/weekend programs available. *Students:* 62 full-time (14 women), 22 part-time (1 woman); includes 4 minority (1 Black or African American, non-Hispanic/Latino; 3 Asian, non-Hispanic/Latino), 76 international. 140 applicants, 99% accepted, 28 enrolled. In 2011, 26 master's awarded. *Degree requirements:* For master's, thesis or alternative. *Entrance requirements:* For master's, bachelor's degree in electrical engineering. Additional exam requirements/recommendations for international students: Required—TOEFL (minimum score 520 paper-based; 190 computer-based; 70 iBT); Recommended—IELTS (minimum score 5.5). *Application deadline:* For fall admission, 5/31 for international students; for winter admission, 10/15 for international students; for spring admission, 1/15 for international students. Applications are processed on a rolling basis. Application fee: $50. Electronic applications accepted. *Expenses: Tuition:* Part-time $750 per credit. *Financial support:* Research assistantships with partial tuition reimbursements, teaching assistantships with partial tuition reimbursements, career-related internships or fieldwork, Federal Work-Study, scholarships/grants, tuition waivers, and unspecified assistantships available. Support available to part-time students. Financial award applicants required to submit FAFSA. *Unit head:* Dr. Bouzid Aliane, Coordinator, 203-932-7160, E-mail: baliane@newhaven.edu. *Application contact:* Eloise Gormley, Director of Graduate Admissions, 203-932-7449, Fax: 203-932-7137, E-mail: gradinfo@newhaven.edu. Web site: http://www.newhaven.edu/9592/.

University of New Mexico, Graduate School, School of Engineering, Department of Electrical and Computer Engineering, Albuquerque, NM 87131-2039. Offers computational science and engineering (Post-Doctoral Certificate); computer engineering (MS, PhD); electrical engineering (MS, PhD). Part-time and evening/weekend programs available. Postbaccalaureate distance learning degree programs offered (no on-campus study). *Faculty:* 36 full-time (5 women), 8 part-time/adjunct (0 women). *Students:* 71 full-time (12 women), 64 part-time (13 women); includes 35 minority (1 Black or African American, non-Hispanic/Latino; 2 American Indian or Alaska Native, non-Hispanic/Latino; 8 Asian, non-Hispanic/Latino; 21 Hispanic/Latino; 3 Two or more races, non-Hispanic/Latino), 49 international. Average age 31. 184 applicants, 35% accepted, 47 enrolled. In 2011, 33 master's, 11 doctorates awarded. Terminal master's awarded for partial completion of doctoral program. *Degree requirements:* For master's, thesis; for doctorate, comprehensive exam, thesis/dissertation. *Entrance requirements:* For master's, GRE General Test, minimum GPA of 3.0; for doctorate, GRE General Test, minimum GPA of 3.5. Additional exam requirements/recommendations for international students: Required—TOEFL (minimum score 550 paper-based; 213 computer-based; 79 iBT). *Application deadline:* For fall admission, 7/15 for domestic students, 2/15 for international students; for spring admission, 11/1 for domestic students, 6/15 for international students. Application fee: $50. Electronic applications accepted. *Financial support:* In 2011–12, 124 students received support, including 2 fellowships with tuition reimbursements available (averaging $11,500 per year), 95 research assistantships with tuition reimbursements available (averaging $16,097 per year), 4 teaching assistantships with tuition reimbursements available (averaging $11,093 per year); scholarships/grants, health care benefits, and unspecified assistantships also available. Financial award application deadline: 2/15; financial award applicants required to submit FAFSA. *Faculty research:* Advanced graphics and visualization, biomedical engineering, communications and networking, networked control systems, photonics and microelectronics, pulsed power and high-power electromagnetics, reconfigurable systems. *Total annual research expenditures:* $3.2 million. *Unit head:* Dr. Chaouki T. Abdallah, Chair, 505-277-0298, Fax: 505-277-1439, E-mail: chaouki@ece.unm.edu. *Application contact:* Elmyra Grelle, Coordinator, Graduate Programs, 505-277-2600, Fax: 505-277-1439, E-mail: egrelle@ece.unm.edu. Web site: http://ece.unm.edu/.

See Display below and Close-Up on page 401.

Electrical Engineering

The University of North Carolina at Charlotte, Graduate School, The William States Lee College of Engineering, Department of Electrical and Computer Engineering, Charlotte, NC 28223-0001. Offers electrical engineering (MSEE, PhD). Part-time and evening/weekend programs available. *Faculty:* 31 full-time (2 women). *Students:* 97 full-time (23 women), 63 part-time (9 women); includes 13 minority (4 Black or African American, non-Hispanic/Latino; 1 American Indian or Alaska Native, non-Hispanic/Latino; 6 Asian, non-Hispanic/Latino; 2 Hispanic/Latino), 98 international. Average age 27. 286 applicants, 64% accepted, 45 enrolled. In 2011, 52 master's, 2 doctorates awarded. Terminal master's awarded for partial completion of doctoral program. *Degree requirements:* For master's, thesis optional, thesis or project; for doctorate, thesis/dissertation. *Entrance requirements:* For master's, GRE General Test, minimum GPA of 3.0 in undergraduate major, 2.75 overall; for doctorate, GRE General Test, 3 letters of reference. Additional exam requirements/recommendations for international students: Required—TOEFL (minimum score 557 paper-based; 220 computer-based; 83 iBT). *Application deadline:* For fall admission, 7/1 for domestic students, 5/1 for international students; for spring admission, 11/1 for domestic students, 10/1 for international students. Applications are processed on a rolling basis. Application fee: $65 ($75 for international students). Electronic applications accepted. *Expenses:* Tuition, state resident: full-time $3689. Tuition, nonresident: full-time $15,226. *Required fees:* $2198. Tuition and fees vary according to course load and program. *Financial support:* In 2011–12, 47 students received support, including 2 fellowships (averaging $43,625 per year), 24 research assistantships (averaging $9,327 per year), 21 teaching assistantships (averaging $9,950 per year); career-related internships or fieldwork, institutionally sponsored loans, scholarships/grants, and unspecified assistantships also available. Support available to part-time students. Financial award application deadline: 4/1; financial award applicants required to submit FAFSA. *Faculty research:* Integrated circuits self test, control systems, optoelectronics/microelectronics devices and systems, communications, computer engineering. *Total annual research expenditures:* $1.2 million. *Unit head:* Dr. Ian Ferguson, Chair, 704-687-8404, Fax: 704-687-4762, E-mail: ianf@uncc.edu. *Application contact:* Kathy B. Giddings, Director of Graduate Admissions, 704-687-5503, Fax: 704-687-3279, E-mail: gradadm@uncc.edu. Web site: http://coe.uncc.edu/students/prospective/graduate.htm.

University of North Dakota, Graduate School, School of Engineering and Mines, Department of Electrical Engineering, Grand Forks, ND 58202. Offers M Engr, MS. Part-time programs available. *Degree requirements:* For master's, comprehensive exam, thesis or alternative. *Entrance requirements:* For master's, GRE General Test, minimum GPA of 3.0 (MS), 2.5 (M Engr). Additional exam requirements/recommendations for international students: Required—TOEFL (minimum score 550 paper-based; 213 computer-based; 79 iBT), IELTS (minimum score 6.5). Electronic applications accepted. *Faculty research:* Controls and robotics, signal processing, energy conversion, microwaves, computer engineering.

University of North Florida, College of Computing, Engineering, and Construction, School of Engineering, Jacksonville, FL 32224. Offers MSCE, MSEE, MSME. Part-time programs available. *Faculty:* 20 full-time (1 woman). *Students:* 6 full-time (2 women), 35 part-time (6 women); includes 9 minority (1 Black or African American, non-Hispanic/Latino; 3 Asian, non-Hispanic/Latino; 4 Hispanic/Latino; 1 Two or more races, non-Hispanic/Latino), 6 international. Average age 29. 33 applicants, 58% accepted, 6 enrolled. In 2011, 7 master's awarded. *Application deadline:* For fall admission, 7/1 for domestic students, 5/1 for international students; for spring admission, 11/1 for domestic students, 10/1 for international students. Application fee: $30. *Expenses:* Tuition, state resident: full-time $8793; part-time $366.38 per credit hour. Tuition, nonresident: full-time $23,502; part-time $979.24 per credit hour. *Required fees:* $1384; $57.66 per credit hour. Tuition and fees vary according to course load and program. *Financial support:* In 2011–12, 16 students received support, including 14 research assistantships (averaging $3,428 per year), 1 teaching assistantship (averaging $1,600 per year); Federal Work-Study, scholarships/grants, tuition waivers, and unspecified assistantships also available. Financial award application deadline: 4/1; financial award applicants required to submit FAFSA. *Total annual research expenditures:* $5 million. *Unit head:* Gerald Merckel, Associate Dean, 904-620-1390, E-mail: gmerckel@unf.edu. *Application contact:* Lillith Richardson, Assistant Director, The Graduate School, 904-320-1360, Fax: 904-620-1362, E-mail: graduateschool@unf.edu. Web site: http://www.unf.edu/ccec/engineering/.

University of North Texas, Toulouse Graduate School, College of Engineering, Department of Electrical Engineering, Denton, TX 76203. Offers MS. Part-time programs available. *Degree requirements:* For master's, thesis optional. *Entrance requirements:* For master's, GRE, minimum GPA of 3.0. Additional exam requirements/recommendations for international students: Required—TOEFL (minimum score 550 paper-based; 213 computer-based; 79 iBT). *Expenses:* Tuition, state resident: part-time $100 per credit hour. Tuition, nonresident: part-time $413 per credit hour. *Faculty research:* Ecological and environmental modeling, radar systems, wireless communication, human-computer interaction, computer vision, signal processing, information assurance, VISI design.

University of Notre Dame, Graduate School, College of Engineering, Department of Electrical Engineering, Notre Dame, IN 46556. Offers MSEE, PhD. Terminal master's awarded for partial completion of doctoral program. *Degree requirements:* For master's, comprehensive exam; for doctorate, thesis/dissertation, candidacy exam. *Entrance requirements:* For master's and doctorate, GRE General Test. Additional exam requirements/recommendations for international students: Required—TOEFL (minimum score 600 paper-based; 250 computer-based; 80 iBT). Electronic applications accepted. *Faculty research:* Electronic properties of materials and devices, signal and imaging processing, communication theory, control theory and applications, optoelectronics.

University of Oklahoma, College of Engineering, Department of Electrical and Computer Engineering, Program in Electrical and Computer Engineering, Norman, OK 73019. Offers MS, PhD. Part-time programs available. *Students:* 81 full-time (14 women), 52 part-time (10 women); includes 11 minority (2 Black or African American, non-Hispanic/Latino; 4 American Indian or Alaska Native, non-Hispanic/Latino; 4 Asian, non-Hispanic/Latino; 1 Two or more races, non-Hispanic/Latino), 80 international. Average age 28. 102 applicants, 32% accepted, 18 enrolled. In 2011, 24 master's, 4 doctorates awarded. Terminal master's awarded for partial completion of doctoral program. *Degree requirements:* For master's, thesis, oral exam; for doctorate, thesis/dissertation, general exam, oral exam, qualifying exam. *Entrance requirements:* For master's and doctorate, GRE General Test. Additional exam requirements/recommendations for international students: Required—TOEFL (minimum score 550 paper-based; 79 iBT). *Application deadline:* For fall admission, 5/15 for domestic students, 3/1 for international students; for spring admission, 9/1 for domestic and international students. Applications are processed on a rolling basis. Application fee: $40 ($90 for international students). Electronic applications accepted. *Expenses:* Tuition, state resident: full-time $4087; part-time $170.30 per credit hour. Tuition, nonresident: full-time $14,875; part-time $619.80 per credit hour. *Required fees:* $2659; $100.25 per credit hour. Tuition and fees vary according to course load and degree

level. *Financial support:* In 2011–12, 133 students received support. Career-related internships or fieldwork, scholarships/grants, health care benefits, and unspecified assistantships available. Financial award applicants required to submit FAFSA. *Faculty research:* Signal/image processing, biomedical imaging, computer hardware design, weather radar, solid state electronics, intelligent transportation systems, navigation systems, power/electrical energy, control systems, communications. *Unit head:* Dr. James Sluss, Director, 405-325-4721, Fax: 405-325-7066, E-mail: sluss@ou.edu. *Application contact:* Lynn Hall, Graduate Program Assistant/Student Services Coordinator, 405-325-4285, Fax: 405-325-7066, E-mail: srg@ou.edu. Web site: http://ece.ou.edu.

University of Ottawa, Faculty of Graduate and Postdoctoral Studies, Faculty of Engineering, Ottawa-Carleton Institute for Electrical and Computer Engineering, Ottawa, ON K1N 6N5, Canada. Offers M Eng, MA Sc, PhD. *Degree requirements:* For master's, thesis or alternative, project; for doctorate, comprehensive exam, thesis/dissertation. *Entrance requirements:* For master's, honors degree or equivalent, minimum B average; for doctorate, minimum A- average. Electronic applications accepted. *Faculty research:* CAD, CSE, distributed systems and BISDN, CCN, DOC.

University of Pennsylvania, School of Engineering and Applied Science, Department of Electrical and Systems Engineering, Philadelphia, PA 19104. Offers MSE, PhD. Part-time programs available. *Faculty:* 27 full-time (2 women), 5 part-time/adjunct (0 women). *Students:* 199 full-time (49 women), 38 part-time (5 women); includes 16 minority (1 Black or African American, non-Hispanic/Latino; 14 Asian, non-Hispanic/Latino; 1 Two or more races, non-Hispanic/Latino), 182 international. 1,027 applicants, 30% accepted, 134 enrolled. In 2011, 69 master's, 9 doctorates awarded. Terminal master's awarded for partial completion of doctoral program. *Degree requirements:* For master's, thesis optional; for doctorate, comprehensive exam, thesis/dissertation. *Entrance requirements:* For master's and doctorate, GRE General Test. Additional exam requirements/recommendations for international students: Required—TOEFL. *Application deadline:* For fall admission, 6/1 priority date for domestic students, 5/1 for international students; for spring admission, 11/1 priority date for domestic students, 10/1 for international students. Applications are processed on a rolling basis. Application fee: $70. Electronic applications accepted. *Expenses: Tuition:* Full-time $26,660; part-time $4944 per course. *Required fees:* $2318; $291 per course. Tuition and fees vary according to course load, degree level and program. *Financial support:* Fellowships, research assistantships, teaching assistantships, institutionally sponsored loans, scholarships/grants, traineeships, health care benefits, and unspecified assistantships available. *Faculty research:* Electro-optics, microwave and millimeter-wave optics, solid-state and chemical electronics, electromagnetic propagation, telecommunications. *Unit head:* Eduardo D. Glandt, Dean, 215-898-7244, Fax: 215-573-2018, E-mail: seasdean@seas.upenn.edu. *Application contact:* Nichole Wood, Graduate Coordinator, 215-898-9390, E-mail: woodn@seas.upenn.edu. Web site: http://www.seas.upenn.edu/.

University of Pittsburgh, Swanson School of Engineering, Program in Electrical Engineering, Pittsburgh, PA 15260. Offers MSEE, PhD. Part-time programs available. Postbaccalaureate distance learning degree programs offered. *Faculty:* 17 full-time (1 woman), 16 part-time/adjunct (1 woman). *Students:* 91 full-time (13 women), 58 part-time (8 women); includes 11 minority (8 Black or African American, non-Hispanic/Latino; 3 Asian, non-Hispanic/Latino), 79 international. 768 applicants, 15% accepted, 40 enrolled. In 2011, 28 master's, 8 doctorates awarded. Terminal master's awarded for partial completion of doctoral program. *Degree requirements:* For master's, thesis optional; for doctorate, comprehensive exam, thesis/dissertation, final oral exams. *Entrance requirements:* For master's and doctorate, GRE General Test, minimum QPA of 3.0. Additional exam requirements/recommendations for international students: Required—TOEFL (minimum score 550 paper-based; 213 computer-based; 80 iBT). *Application deadline:* For fall admission, 3/1 priority date for domestic students; for spring admission, 7/1 priority date for domestic students. Applications are processed on a rolling basis. Application fee: $50. Electronic applications accepted. *Expenses:* Tuition, state resident: full-time $18,774; part-time $760 per credit. Tuition, nonresident: full-time $30,736; part-time $1258 per credit. *Required fees:* $740; $200 per term. Tuition and fees vary according to program. *Financial support:* In 2011–12, 52 students received support, including 3 fellowships with full tuition reimbursements available (averaging $29,280 per year), 30 research assistantships with full tuition reimbursements available (averaging $22,584 per year), 19 teaching assistantships with full tuition reimbursements available (averaging $23,532 per year); scholarships/grants and tuition waivers (full and partial) also available. Financial award application deadline: 4/15. *Faculty research:* Computer engineering, image processing, signal processing, electro-optic devices, controls/power. *Total annual research expenditures:* $6.4 million. *Unit head:* Dr. William Stanchina, Chairman, 412-624-8000, Fax: 412-624-8003, E-mail: wstasnchina@engr.bitt.edu. *Application contact:* Dr. Steven Levitan, Graduate Coordinator, 412-624-8001, Fax: 412-624-8003, E-mail: levitan@engr.pitt.edu.

University of Puerto Rico, Mayagüez Campus, Graduate Studies, College of Engineering, Department of Electrical and Computer Engineering, Mayagüez, PR 00681-9000. Offers computer engineering (ME, MS); computing and information sciences and engineering (PhD); electrical engineering (ME, MS). Part-time programs available. *Students:* 86 full-time (16 women), 8 part-time (1 woman); includes 65 minority (all Hispanic/Latino), 29 international. 42 applicants, 60% accepted, 20 enrolled. In 2011, 19 degrees awarded. *Degree requirements:* For master's, comprehensive exam, thesis; for doctorate, comprehensive exam, thesis/dissertation. *Entrance requirements:* For master's, proficiency in English and Spanish, BS in electrical or computer engineering or equivalent, minimum GPA of 3.0; for doctorate, GRE. Additional exam requirements/recommendations for international students: Required—TOEFL (minimum score 450 paper-based). *Application deadline:* For fall admission, 2/15 for domestic and international students; for spring admission, 9/15 for domestic and international students. Applications are processed on a rolling basis. Application fee: $25. Tuition and fees vary according to course level and course load. *Financial support:* In 2011–12, 46 students received support, including 28 research assistantships (averaging $15,000 per year), 18 teaching assistantships (averaging $8,500 per year); Federal Work-Study and institutionally sponsored loans also available. *Faculty research:* Microcomputer interfacing, control systems, power systems, electronics. *Total annual research expenditures:* $3.8 million. *Unit head:* Dr. Erick Aponte-Diaz, Chairperson, 787-832-4040 Ext. 3821, E-mail: erick.aponte1@upr.edu. *Application contact:* Sandra Montalvo, Administrative Staff, 787-832-4040 Ext. 3094, Fax: 787-831-7564, E-mail: sandra@ece.uprm.edu. Web site: http://www.ece.uprm.edu.

University of Rhode Island, Graduate School, College of Engineering, Department of Electrical, Computer and Biomedical Engineering, Kingston, RI 02881. Offers MS, PhD, Graduate Certificate. Part-time programs available. *Faculty:* 18 full-time (3 women), 2 part-time/adjunct (1 woman). *Students:* 32 full-time (6 women), 25 part-time (1 woman); includes 8 minority (5 Asian, non-Hispanic/Latino; 3 Hispanic/Latino), 14 international. In 2011, 4 master's, 2 doctorates awarded. *Degree requirements:* For master's, comprehensive exam (for some programs), thesis optional; for doctorate, comprehensive exam, thesis/dissertation. *Entrance requirements:* For master's and doctorate, 2 letters of recommendation. Additional exam requirements/recommendations for international students: Required—TOEFL (minimum score 550 paper-based; 213 computer-based). *Application deadline:* For fall admission, 7/15 for domestic students, 2/1 for international students; for spring admission, 11/15 for domestic students, 7/15 for international students. Application fee: $65. Electronic applications accepted. *Expenses:* Tuition, state resident: full-time $10,432; part-time $580 per credit hour. Tuition, nonresident: full-time $23,130; part-time $1285 per credit hour. *Required fees:* $1362; $36 per credit hour. $35 per semester. One-time fee: $130. *Financial support:* In 2011–12, 9 research assistantships with full and partial tuition reimbursements (averaging $9,465 per year), 5 teaching assistantships with full and partial tuition reimbursements (averaging $8,520 per year) were awarded. Financial award application deadline: 7/15; financial award applicants required to submit FAFSA. *Faculty research:* Biomedical Instrumentation, cardiac physiology and computational modeling, analog/digital CMOS circuits, neural-machine interface, digital circuit design and VLSI testing. *Total annual research expenditures:* $985,856. *Unit head:* Dr. Godi Fischer, Chair, 401-874-5879, Fax: 401-782-6422, E-mail: fischer@ele.uri.edu. *Application contact:* Dr. Godi Fischer, Director of Graduate Studies, 401-874-5879, Fax: 401-782-6422, E-mail: fischer@ele.uri.edu. Web site: http://www.ele.uri.edu/.

University of Rochester, Hajim School of Engineering and Applied Sciences, Center for Entrepreneurship, Rochester, NY 14627-0360. Offers technical entrepreneurship and management (TEAM) (MS), including biomedical engineering, chemical engineering, computer science, electrical and computer engineering, energy and the environment, materials science, mechanical engineering, optics. *Faculty:* 61 full-time (8 women), 5 part-time/adjunct (1 woman). *Students:* 18 full-time (5 women), 3 part-time (1 woman); includes 4 minority (1 Asian, non-Hispanic/Latino; 3 Hispanic/Latino), 12 international. Average age 23. 134 applicants, 48% accepted, 21 enrolled. *Degree requirements:* For master's, comprehensive exam. *Entrance requirements:* For master's, GRE or GMAT, technical concentration of interest, 3 letters of recommendation, personal statement, official transcript. Additional exam requirements/recommendations for international students: Required—TOEFL or IELTS. *Application deadline:* For fall admission, 2/1 for domestic and international students. Applications are processed on a rolling basis. Application fee: $60. Electronic applications accepted. *Expenses: Tuition:* Full-time $41,040. *Financial support:* Career-related internships or fieldwork and scholarships/grants available. Financial award application deadline: 2/1. *Faculty research:* High efficiency solar cells, macromolecular self-assembly, digital signal processing, memory hierarchy management, molecular and physical mechanisms in cell migration. *Unit head:* Duncan T. Moore, Vice Provost for Entrepreneurship, 585-275-5248, Fax: 585-473-6745, E-mail: moore@optics.rochester.edu. *Application contact:* Andrea M. Galati, Executive Director, 585-276-3407, Fax: 585-276-2357, E-mail: andrea.galati@rochester.edu. Web site: http://www.rochester.edu/team.

University of Rochester, Hajim School of Engineering and Applied Sciences, Department of Electrical and Computer Engineering, Rochester, NY 14627. Offers MS, PhD. *Faculty:* 20 full-time (2 women). *Students:* 107 full-time (21 women), 5 part-time (3 women); includes 5 minority (2 Black or African American, non-Hispanic/Latino; 3 Asian, non-Hispanic/Latino), 89 international. 441 applicants, 37% accepted, 60 enrolled. In 2011, 27 master's, 15 doctorates awarded. Terminal master's awarded for partial completion of doctoral program. *Degree requirements:* For master's, comprehensive exam; for doctorate, thesis/dissertation, preliminary and oral exams. *Entrance requirements:* For master's and doctorate, GRE. Additional exam requirements/recommendations for international students: Required—TOEFL. *Application deadline:* For fall admission, 1/15 for domestic students. Application fee: $0. *Expenses: Tuition:* Full-time $41,040. *Financial support:* Fellowships, research assistantships, teaching assistantships, and tuition waivers (full and partial) available. Financial award application deadline: 2/1. *Faculty research:* Bio-informatics, communications, digital audio, image processing, medical imaging. *Unit head:* Philippe M. Fauchet, Chair, 585-275-1487. *Application contact:* Barbara Dick, Administrative Assistant/Academic Coordinator, 585-275-5719. Web site: http://www.ece.rochester.edu/graduate/index.html.

University of Saskatchewan, College of Graduate Studies and Research, College of Engineering, Department of Electrical Engineering, Saskatoon, SK S7N 5A2, Canada. Offers M Eng, M Sc, PhD. *Degree requirements:* For master's, thesis (for some programs); for doctorate, thesis/dissertation. *Entrance requirements:* For master's and doctorate, GRE. Additional exam requirements/recommendations for international students: Required—TOEFL.

University of South Alabama, Graduate School, College of Engineering, Department of Electrical and Computer Engineering, Mobile, AL 36688-0002. Offers electrical engineering (MSEE). Part-time programs available. *Faculty:* 12 full-time (0 women). *Students:* 46 full-time (7 women), 6 part-time (1 woman); includes 2 minority (both Asian, non-Hispanic/Latino), 46 international. 82 applicants, 65% accepted, 17 enrolled. In 2011, 74 master's awarded. *Degree requirements:* For master's, project or thesis. *Entrance requirements:* For master's, GRE General Test, BS in engineering, minimum GPA of 3.0. *Application deadline:* For fall admission, 7/15 priority date for domestic students, 6/15 for international students; for spring admission, 12/1 priority date for domestic students, 11/1 for international students. Applications are processed on a rolling basis. Application fee: $35. *Expenses:* Tuition, state resident: full-time $7968; part-time $332 per credit hour. Tuition, nonresident: full-time $15,936; part-time $664 per credit hour. *Financial support:* Research assistantships, career-related internships or fieldwork, and institutionally sponsored loans available. Support available to part-time students. Financial award application deadline: 4/1. *Unit head:* Dr. Mohammed Alam, Chair, 251-460-6117. *Application contact:* Dr. B. Keith Harrison, Director of Graduate Studies, 251-460-6160. Web site: http://www.southalabama.edu/engineering/ece/.

University of South Carolina, The Graduate School, College of Engineering and Computing, Department of Electrical Engineering, Columbia, SC 29208. Offers ME, MS, PhD. Part-time and evening/weekend programs available. Postbaccalaureate distance learning degree programs offered (minimal on-campus study). *Degree requirements:* For master's, comprehensive exam, thesis (for some programs); for doctorate, comprehensive exam, thesis/dissertation, qualifying exam. *Entrance requirements:* For master's and doctorate, GRE General Test. Additional exam requirements/recommendations for international students: Required—TOEFL (minimum score 570 paper-based; 230 computer-based; 88 iBT). Electronic applications accepted. *Faculty research:* Microelectronics, photonics, wireless communications, signal integrity, energy and control systems.

University of Southern California, Graduate School, Viterbi School of Engineering, Ming Hsieh Department of Electrical Engineering, Los Angeles, CA 90089. Offers computer engineering (MS, PhD); electric power (MS); electrical engineering (MS, PhD, Engr); engineering technology commercialization (Graduate Certificate); multimedia and creative technologies (MS); telecommunications (MS); VLSI design (MS); wireless health technology (MS). Part-time programs available. Postbaccalaureate distance learning degree programs offered (no on-campus study). Terminal master's awarded for partial completion of doctoral program. *Degree requirements:* For master's, thesis optional; for doctorate, thesis/dissertation. *Entrance requirements:* For master's and doctorate, GRE General Test. Additional exam requirements/recommendations for international students: Recommended—TOEFL. Electronic applications accepted. *Faculty research:* Communications, computer engineering and networks, control systems, integrated circuits and systems, electromagnetics and energy conversion, micro electro-mechanical systems and nanotechnology, photonics and quantum electronics, plasma research, signal and image processing.

University of South Florida, Graduate School, College of Engineering, Department of Electrical Engineering, Tampa, FL 33620-9951. Offers ME, MSEE, MSES, PhD. Part-time programs available. Postbaccalaureate distance learning degree programs offered (no on-campus study). *Faculty:* 25 full-time (3 women), 5 part-time/adjunct (0 women). *Students:* 122 full-time (26 women), 58 part-time (6 women); includes 42 minority (12 Black or African American, non-Hispanic/Latino; 17 Asian, non-Hispanic/Latino; 9 Hispanic/Latino; 1 Native Hawaiian or other Pacific Islander, non-Hispanic/Latino; 3 Two or more races, non-Hispanic/Latino), 96 international. Average age 31. 187 applicants, 49% accepted, 31 enrolled. In 2011, 69 master's, 10 doctorates awarded. Terminal master's awarded for partial completion of doctoral program. *Degree requirements:* For master's, comprehensive exam, thesis or alternative; for doctorate, comprehensive exam, thesis/dissertation. *Entrance requirements:* For master's, GRE, minimum GPA of 3.0 in last 60 hours of coursework, three letters of recommendation; educational experience (for MSEE); for doctorate, GRE, minimum GPA of 3.0 in last 60 hours of coursework, three letters of recommendation, statement of purpose. Additional exam requirements/recommendations for international students: Required—TOEFL (minimum score 550 paper-based; 213 computer-based; 79 iBT) or IELTS (minimum score 6.5). *Application deadline:* For fall admission, 2/15 for domestic students, 1/2 for international students; for spring admission, 10/15 for domestic students, 6/1 for international students. Application fee: $30. Electronic applications accepted. *Financial support:* In 2011–12, 98 students received support, including 57 research assistantships (averaging $12,357 per year), 41 teaching assistantships with tuition reimbursements available (averaging $13,528 per year). Financial award applicants required to submit FAFSA. *Faculty research:* Silicon processing, micro/millimeter waves, communication and signal processing, clean energy and sustainability, bioengineering. *Total annual research expenditures:* $3.4 million. *Unit head:* Dr. Salvatore Morgera, Chair, 813-974-1004, E-mail: morgera@usf.edu. *Application contact:* Dr. Kenneth A. Buckle, Program Director, 813-974-4772, Fax: 813-974-5250, E-mail: buckle@usf.edu. Web site: http://ee.eng.usf.edu/.

The University of Tennessee, Graduate School, College of Engineering, Department of Electrical Engineering and Computer Science, Program in Electrical Engineering, Knoxville, TN 37996. Offers MS, PhD. Part-time programs available. *Faculty:* 17 full-time (3 women), 2 part-time/adjunct (1 woman). *Students:* 105 full-time (25 women), 15 part-time (2 women); includes 1 minority (Black or African American, non-Hispanic/Latino), 88 international. Average age 28. 382 applicants, 12% accepted, 31 enrolled. In 2011, 17 master's, 4 doctorates awarded. *Degree requirements:* For master's, thesis or alternative; for doctorate, comprehensive exam, thesis/dissertation. *Entrance requirements:* For master's, GRE General Test (for MS students pursuing research thesis), minimum GPA of 2.7 (U.S. degree holders), 3.0 (international degree holders); 3 references; personal statement; for doctorate, College requires GRE General Test for all PhD candidates, minimum GPA of 3.0 on previous graduate coursework; 3 references; personal statement. Additional exam requirements/recommendations for international students: Required—TOEFL (minimum score 550 paper-based; 213 computer-based). *Application deadline:* For fall admission, 2/1 priority date for domestic students, 2/1 for international students; for spring admission, 6/15 for domestic and international students. Applications are processed on a rolling basis. Application fee: $35. Electronic applications accepted. *Expenses:* Tuition, state resident: full-time $8332; part-time $464 per credit hour. Tuition, nonresident: full-time $25,174; part-time $1400 per credit hour. *Required fees:* $1162; $56 per credit hour. Tuition and fees vary according to program. *Financial support:* In 2011–12, 103 students received support, including 7 fellowships with full tuition reimbursements available (averaging $9,234 per year), 43 research assistantships with full tuition reimbursements available (averaging $19,843 per year), 43 teaching assistantships with full tuition reimbursements available (averaging $16,705 per year); career-related internships or fieldwork, Federal Work-Study, institutionally sponsored loans, health care benefits, and unspecified assistantships also available. Financial award application deadline: 2/1; financial award applicants required to submit FAFSA. *Unit head:* Dr. Kevin Tomsovic, Head, 865-974-3461, Fax: 865-974-5483, E-mail: tomsovic@eecs.utk.edu. *Application contact:* Dr. Lynne E. Parker, Associate Head, 865-974-4394, Fax: 865-974-5483, E-mail: parker@eecs.utk.edu. Web site: http://www.eecs.utk.edu.

The University of Tennessee at Chattanooga, Graduate School, College of Engineering and Computer Science, Program in Engineering, Chattanooga, TN 37403. Offers chemical engineering (MS Engr); civil engineering (MS Engr); computational engineering (MS Engr); electrical engineering (MS Engr); industrial engineering (MS Engr); mechanical engineering (MS Engr). Part-time and evening/weekend programs available. *Faculty:* 27 full-time (3 women), 3 part-time/adjunct (1 woman). *Students:* 40 full-time (7 women), 41 part-time (11 women); includes 23 minority (10 Black or African American, non-Hispanic/Latino; 1 American Indian or Alaska Native, non-Hispanic/Latino; 6 Asian, non-Hispanic/Latino; 4 Hispanic/Latino; 2 Two or more races, non-Hispanic/Latino), 20 international. Average age 28. 89 applicants, 53% accepted, 29 enrolled. In 2011, 8 master's awarded. *Degree requirements:* For master's, comprehensive exam, thesis or alternative, engineering project. *Entrance requirements:* For master's, GRE General Test, minimum undergraduate GPA of 2.5 or 3.0 in last 30 hours of coursework. Additional exam requirements/recommendations for international students: Required—TOEFL (minimum score 550 paper-based; 213 computer-based; 79 iBT), IELTS (minimum score 6). *Application deadline:* For fall admission, 8/1 priority date for domestic students, 6/1 for international students; for spring admission, 12/1 priority date for domestic students, 10/1 for international students. Applications are processed on a rolling basis. Application fee: $35. Electronic applications accepted. *Expenses:* Tuition, state resident: full-time $6472; part-time $359 per credit hour. Tuition, nonresident: full-time $20,006; part-time $1111 per credit hour. *Required fees:* $1320; $160 per credit hour. *Financial support:* Career-related internships or fieldwork, scholarships/grants, and unspecified assistantships available. Support available to part-time students. *Faculty research:* Quality control and reliability engineering, financial management, thermal science, energy conservation, structural analysis. *Total annual research expenditures:* $3.5 million. *Unit head:* Dr. Neslihan Alp, Director, 423-425-4032, Fax: 423-425-5229, E-mail: neslihan-alp@utc.edu. *Application contact:* Dr. Jerald Ainsworth, Dean of Graduate Studies, 423-425-4478, Fax: 423-425-5223, E-mail: jerald-ainsworth@utc.edu. Web site: http://www.utc.edu/Departments/engrcs/ms_engr.php.

The University of Tennessee Space Institute, Graduate Programs, Program in Electrical Engineering and Computer Science, Tullahoma, TN 37388-9700. Offers MS, PhD. *Faculty:* 2 full-time (0 women), 1 part-time/adjunct (0 women). *Students:* 1 part-time (0 women). *Degree requirements:* For master's, thesis (for some programs); for doctorate, one foreign language, thesis/dissertation. *Entrance requirements:* Additional exam requirements/recommendations for international students: Required—TOEFL (minimum score 550 paper-based; 213 computer-based), IELTS (minimum score 6.5). *Application deadline:* For fall admission, 2/1 for international students; for spring admission, 6/15 for international students. Applications are processed on a rolling basis. Application fee: $35. Electronic applications accepted. *Financial support:* Fellowships, research assistantships with full tuition reimbursements, career-related internships or fieldwork, Federal Work-Study, institutionally sponsored loans, health care benefits, tuition waivers (full and partial), and unspecified assistantships available. Financial award applicants required to submit FAFSA. *Unit head:* Dr. Monty Smith, Degree Program Chairman, 931-393-7480, Fax: 931-393-7530, E-mail: msmith@utsi.edu. *Application contact:* Dee Merriman, Coordinator III, 931-393-7213, Fax: 931-393-7211, E-mail: dmerrima@utsi.edu.

The University of Texas at Arlington, Graduate School, College of Engineering, Department of Electrical Engineering, Arlington, TX 76019. Offers M Engr, MS, PhD. Part-time and evening/weekend programs available. Postbaccalaureate distance learning degree programs offered (no on-campus study). *Faculty:* 27 full-time (1 woman), 1 part-time/adjunct (0 women). *Students:* 198 full-time (34 women), 119 part-time (23 women); includes 18 minority (4 Black or African American, non-Hispanic/Latino; 11 Asian, non-Hispanic/Latino; 3 Hispanic/Latino), 266 international. 643 applicants, 43% accepted, 65 enrolled. In 2011, 144 master's, 9 doctorates awarded. Terminal master's awarded for partial completion of doctoral program. *Degree requirements:* For master's, thesis optional; for doctorate, comprehensive exam, thesis/dissertation, written diagnostic exam. *Entrance requirements:* For master's, GRE General Test, minimum GPA of 3.25; for doctorate, GRE General Test, minimum GPA of 3.5. Additional exam requirements/recommendations for international students: Required—TOEFL (minimum score 560 paper-based; 220 computer-based); Recommended—TWE (minimum score 4). *Application deadline:* For fall admission, 6/1 for domestic students, 4/1 for international students; for spring admission, 10/15 for domestic students, 9/15 for international students. Applications are processed on a rolling basis. Application fee: $35 ($50 for international students). *Financial support:* In 2011–12, 202 students received support, including 23 fellowships (averaging $1,000 per year), 60 research assistantships (averaging $14,400 per year), 40 teaching assistantships (averaging $10,800 per year); Federal Work-Study, institutionally sponsored loans, scholarships/grants, and unspecified assistantships also available. Financial award application deadline: 6/1; financial award applicants required to submit FAFSA. *Faculty research:* Nanotech and MEMS, digital image processing, telecommunications and optics, energy systems and power electronics, VLSI and semiconductors. *Total annual research expenditures:* $1 million. *Unit head:* Dr. Jonathan Bredow, Chair, 817-272-3266, Fax: 817-272-2253, E-mail: jbredow@uta.edu. *Application contact:* Dr. William E. Dillon, Graduate Adviser, 817-272-2671, Fax: 817-272-1509, E-mail: eedept@uta.edu. Web site: http://www.ee.uta.edu/ee.

The University of Texas at Austin, Graduate School, Cockrell School of Engineering, Department of Electrical and Computer Engineering, Austin, TX 78712-1111. Offers MS, PhD. Part-time programs available. *Entrance requirements:* For master's, GRE General Test, minimum GPA of 3.3 in upper-division course work; for doctorate, GRE General Test. *Application deadline:* For fall admission, 1/2 for domestic students. Applications are processed on a rolling basis. Application fee: $50 ($75 for international students). Electronic applications accepted. *Financial support:* Fellowships, research assistantships, and teaching assistantships available. Financial award application deadline: 1/2. *Unit head:* Dr. L. Frank Register, Graduate Advisor, 512-232-1868, E-mail: register@mer.utexas.edu. *Application contact:* Susanne Graves, Graduate Coordinator, 521-471-8044, E-mail: susanne.graves@mail.utexas.edu. Web site: http://www.ece.utexas.edu/.

The University of Texas at Dallas, Erik Jonsson School of Engineering and Computer Science, Department of Electrical Engineering, Richardson, TX 75080. Offers computer engineering (MS, PhD); electrical engineering (MSEE, PhD); systems engineering and management (MS); telecommunications (MSTE, PhD). Part-time and evening/weekend programs available. *Faculty:* 44 full-time (2 women), 4 part-time/adjunct (0 women). *Students:* 510 full-time (108 women), 279 part-time (53 women); includes 110 minority (17 Black or African American, non-Hispanic/Latino; 65 Asian, non-Hispanic/Latino; 25 Hispanic/Latino; 3 Two or more races, non-Hispanic/Latino), 555 international. Average age 27. 1,933 applicants, 42% accepted, 265 enrolled. In 2011, 168 master's, 30 doctorates awarded. *Degree requirements:* For master's, thesis or major design project; for doctorate, thesis/dissertation. *Entrance requirements:* For master's, GRE General Test, minimum GPA of 3.0 in related bachelor's degree; for doctorate, GRE General Test, minimum GPA of 3.5. Additional exam requirements/recommendations for international students: Required—TOEFL (minimum score 550 paper-based; 215 computer-based). *Application deadline:* For fall admission, 7/15 for domestic students, 5/1 for international students; for spring admission, 11/15 for domestic students, 9/1 for international students. Applications are processed on a rolling basis. Application fee: $50 ($100 for international students). Electronic applications accepted. *Expenses:* Tuition, state resident: full-time $11,170; part-time $620.56 per credit hour. Tuition, nonresident: full-time $20,212; part-time $1122.89 per credit hour. *Financial support:* In 2011–12, 224 students received support, including 132 research assistantships with partial tuition reimbursements available (averaging $21,532 per year), 47 teaching assistantships with partial tuition reimbursements available (averaging $14,850 per year); fellowships with partial tuition reimbursements available, Federal Work-Study, institutionally sponsored loans, scholarships/grants, unspecified assistantships, and cooperative positions also available. Support available to part-time students. Financial award application deadline: 4/30; financial award applicants required to submit FAFSA. *Faculty research:* Semiconductor device manufacturing, photonics devices and systems, signal processing and language technology, nano-fabrication, energy efficient digital systems. *Unit head:* Dr. John H. L. Hansen, Department Head, 972-883-6755, Fax: 972-883-2710, E-mail: john.hansen@utdallas.edu. *Application contact:* Kathy Gribble, Graduate Program Coordinator, 972-883-2649, Fax: 972-883-2710, E-mail: gradecs@utdallas.edu. Web site: http://www.ee.utdallas.edu.

The University of Texas at El Paso, Graduate School, College of Engineering, Department of Electrical and Computer Engineering, El Paso, TX 79968-0001. Offers computer engineering (MS); electrical and computer engineering (PhD); electrical engineering (MS). Part-time and evening/weekend programs available. *Students:* 123 (17 women); includes 55 minority (1 Black or African American, non-Hispanic/Latino; 2 Asian, non-Hispanic/Latino; 52 Hispanic/Latino), 61 international. Average age 34. 52 applicants, 81% accepted, 16 enrolled. In 2011, 14 master's, 2 doctorates awarded. *Degree requirements:* For master's, thesis optional; for doctorate, thesis/dissertation. *Entrance requirements:* For master's, GRE General Test, minimum GPA of 3.0; for doctorate, GRE General Test, qualifying exam, minimum graduate GPA of 3.0. Additional exam requirements/recommendations for international students: Required—TOEFL. *Application deadline:* For fall admission, 7/1 priority date for domestic students, 3/1 for international students; for spring admission, 11/1 priority date for domestic students, 9/1 for international students. Applications are processed on a rolling basis. Application fee: $15 ($65 for international students). Electronic applications accepted. *Financial support:* In 2011–12, 60 students received support, including research assistantships with partial tuition reimbursements available (averaging $22,375 per year), teaching assistantships with partial tuition reimbursements available (averaging $17,900 per year); fellowships with partial tuition reimbursements available, Federal Work-Study, institutionally sponsored loans, scholarships/grants, and tuition waivers (partial) also available. Financial award application deadline: 3/15; financial award applicants required to submit FAFSA. *Faculty research:* Signal and image processing, computer architecture, fiber optics, computational electromagnetics, electronic displays and thin films. *Unit head:* Patricia Nava, Chair, 915-747-5994, E-mail: pnava@utep.edu. *Application contact:* Dr. Benjamin Flores, Interim Dean of the Graduate School, 915-747-5491, Fax: 915-747-5788, E-mail: bflores@utep.edu.

The University of Texas at San Antonio, College of Engineering, Department of Electrical and Computer Engineering, San Antonio, TX 78249-0617. Offers computer engineering (MS); electrical engineering (MSEE, PhD); materials engineering (MS). Part-time programs available. *Faculty:* 21 full-time (3 women), 2 part-time/adjunct (0 women). *Students:* 111 full-time (34 women), 56 part-time (11 women); includes 32 minority (6 Black or African American, non-Hispanic/Latino; 4 Asian, non-Hispanic/Latino; 19 Hispanic/Latino; 3 Two or more races, non-Hispanic/Latino), 106 international. Average age 28. 228 applicants, 67% accepted, 47 enrolled. In 2011, 33 master's, 4 doctorates awarded. Terminal master's awarded for partial completion of doctoral program. *Degree requirements:* For master's, comprehensive exam, thesis (for some programs); for doctorate, comprehensive exam, thesis/dissertation. *Entrance requirements:* For master's, GRE General Test, bachelor's degree in electrical or computer engineering from ABET-accredited institution of higher education or related field; minimum GPA of 3.0 on the last 60 semester credit hours of undergraduate studies; for doctorate, GRE General Test, master's degree or minimum GPA of 3.3 in last 60 semester credit hours of undergraduate level coursework in electrical engineering; statement of purpose. Additional exam requirements/recommendations for international students: Required—TOEFL (minimum score 550 paper-based; 79 iBT), IELTS (minimum score 6.5). *Application deadline:* For fall admission, 7/1 for domestic students, 4/1 for international students; for spring admission, 11/1 for domestic students, 9/1 for international students. Applications are processed on a rolling basis. Application fee: $45 ($85 for international students). Electronic applications accepted. *Expenses:* Tuition, state resident: full-time $3148; part-time $2176 per semester. Tuition, nonresident: full-time $8782; part-time $5932 per semester. *Required fees:* $719 per semester. *Financial support:* In 2011–12, 60 students received support, including 11 fellowships (averaging $24,500 per year), 26 research assistantships (averaging $21,653 per year), 11 teaching assistantships (averaging $15,200 per year); unspecified assistantships and Valero Residency Fellowships, travel grants also available. Financial award application deadline: 3/31. *Faculty research:* Computer engineering, digital signal processing, systems and controls, communications, electronics materials and devices, electric power engineering. *Unit head:* Dr. Ruyan Guo, Interim Department Chair, 210-458-7057/7076, Fax: 210-458-5947, E-mail: electrical.engineering@utsa.edu. *Application contact:* Dr. Chunjiang Qian, Graduate Advisor of Record, 210-458-5587, Fax: 210-458-5947, E-mail: graduate.ece@utsa.edu. Web site: http://ece.utsa.edu/.

The University of Texas at Tyler, College of Engineering and Computer Science, Department of Electrical Engineering, Tyler, TX 75799-0001. Offers MS. Part-time and evening/weekend programs available. *Degree requirements:* For master's, comprehensive exam (for some programs). *Entrance requirements:* For master's, GRE General Test, bachelor's degree in electrical engineering. Additional exam requirements/recommendations for international students: Required—TOEFL (minimum score 79 computer-based). *Faculty research:* Electronics, digital sign processing, real time systems electromagnetic fields, semiconductor modeling.

The University of Texas–Pan American, College of Engineering and Computer Science, Department of Electrical Engineering, Edinburg, TX 78539. Offers MS. Tuition and fees vary according to course load, program and student level. *Unit head:* Dr. Heinrich Foltz, Chair, 956-381-2609, Fax: 956-381-3527, E-mail: hfoltz@utpa.edu. *Application contact:* Dr. Junfei Li, Graduate Program Director, 956-316-7148, Fax: 956-381-3527, E-mail: fei@utpa.edu. Web site: http://portal.utpa.edu/utpa_main/daa_home/coecs_home/ee_home.

University of the District of Columbia, School of Engineering and Applied Science, Department of Electrical and Computer Engineering, Washington, DC 20008-1175. Offers electrical engineering (MS). *Expenses: Tuition, area resident:* Full-time $7580; part-time $421 per credit hour. Tuition, state resident: full-time $8580; part-time $477 per credit hour. Tuition, nonresident: full-time $14,580; part-time $810 per credit hour. *Required fees:* $620; $30 per credit hour. $310 per semester.

The University of Toledo, College of Graduate Studies, College of Engineering, Department of Electrical Engineering and Computer Science, Toledo, OH 43606-3390. Offers computer science (MS, PhD); electrical engineering (MS, PhD). Part-time and evening/weekend programs available. *Degree requirements:* For master's, thesis or alternative; for doctorate, thesis/dissertation, qualifying exam. *Entrance requirements:* For master's, GRE General Test, minimum GPA of 3.0; for doctorate, GRE General Test, minimum GPA of 3.3. Additional exam requirements/recommendations for international students: Required—TOEFL (minimum score 550 paper-based; 213 computer-based; 80 iBT). Electronic applications accepted. *Faculty research:* Communication and signal processing, high performance computing systems, intelligent systems, power electronics and energy systems, RF and microwave systems, sensors and medical devices, solid state devices.

University of Toronto, School of Graduate Studies, Faculty of Applied Science and Engineering, Department of Electrical and Computer Engineering, Toronto, ON M5S 1A1, Canada. Offers M Eng, MA Sc, PhD. Part-time programs available. *Degree requirements:* For master's, thesis (for some programs), oral thesis defense (MA Sc); for doctorate, thesis/dissertation, qualifying exam, thesis defense. *Entrance requirements:* For master's, four-year degree in electrical or computer engineering, minimum B average, 2 letters of reference; for doctorate, minimum B+ average, MA Sc in electrical or computer engineering, 2 letters of reference. Additional exam requirements/recommendations for international students: Required—TOEFL (minimum score 580 paper-based; 93 iBT). Electronic applications accepted.

University of Tulsa, Graduate School, College of Engineering and Natural Sciences, Department of Electrical Engineering, Tulsa, OK 74104-3189. Offers ME, MSE. Part-time programs available. *Faculty:* 7 full-time (0 women). *Students:* 7 full-time (0 women), 6 part-time (1 woman); includes 1 minority (American Indian or Alaska Native, non-Hispanic/Latino), 5 international. Average age 24. 25 applicants, 60% accepted, 4 enrolled. In 2011, 7 master's awarded. *Degree requirements:* For master's, comprehensive exam (for some programs), design report (ME), thesis (MS). *Entrance requirements:* For master's, GRE General Test. Additional exam requirements/

recommendations for international students: Required—TOEFL (minimum score 550 paper-based; 213 computer-based; 80 iBT), IELTS (minimum score 6). *Application deadline:* Applications are processed on a rolling basis. Application fee: $40. Electronic applications accepted. *Expenses: Tuition:* Full-time $17,748; part-time $986 per hour. *Required fees:* $5 per contact hour. $75 per semester. Tuition and fees vary according to program. *Financial support:* In 2011–12, 8 students received support, including 3 research assistantships with full and partial tuition reimbursements available (averaging $8,434 per year), 6 teaching assistantships with full and partial tuition reimbursements available (averaging $11,111 per year); fellowships with full and partial tuition reimbursements available, career-related internships or fieldwork, Federal Work-Study, scholarships/grants, health care benefits, tuition waivers (full and partial), and unspecified assistantships also available. Support available to part-time students. Financial award application deadline: 2/1; financial award applicants required to submit FAFSA. *Faculty research:* VLSI microprocessors, intelligent systems, electromagnetics, intrusion detection systems, digital electronics. *Total annual research expenditures:* $6.1 million. *Unit head:* Dr. Gerald R. Kane, Chairperson, 918-631-3280. *Application contact:* Dr. Heng-Ming Tai, Adviser, 918-631-3271, Fax: 918-631-3344, E-mail: tai@utulsa.edu. Web site: http://www.utulsa.edu/academics/colleges/college-of-engineering-and-natural-sciences/departments-and-schools/Department-of-Electrical-Engineering.aspx.

University of Utah, Graduate School, College of Engineering, Department of Electrical and Computer Engineering, Salt Lake City, UT 84112. Offers electrical engineering (ME, MS, PhD). Part-time programs available. *Faculty:* 29 full-time (2 women), 2 part-time/adjunct (0 women). *Students:* 97 full-time (11 women), 35 part-time (3 women); includes 9 minority (5 Asian, non-Hispanic/Latino; 3 Hispanic/Latino; 1 Two or more races, non-Hispanic/Latino), 65 international. Average age 29. 284 applicants, 45% accepted, 50 enrolled. In 2011, 44 master's, 12 doctorates awarded. Terminal master's awarded for partial completion of doctoral program. *Degree requirements:* For master's, comprehensive exam (for some programs), thesis (for some programs); for doctorate, comprehensive exam, thesis/dissertation. *Entrance requirements:* For master's, GRE General Test, minimum GPA of 3.2; for doctorate, GRE General Test, minimum GPA of 3.5. Additional exam requirements/recommendations for international students: Required—TOEFL (minimum score 600 paper-based; 250 computer-based; 100 iBT); Recommended—IELTS (minimum score 7.5). *Application deadline:* For fall admission, 1/15 priority date for domestic students, 1/15 for international students; for spring admission, 10/1 for domestic students. Application fee: $55 ($65 for international students). *Expenses:* Contact institution. *Financial support:* In 2011–12, 2 students received support, including 4 fellowships with full tuition reimbursements available (averaging $20,000 per year), 68 research assistantships with full tuition reimbursements available (averaging $15,100 per year), 15 teaching assistantships with full tuition reimbursements available (averaging $14,000 per year); Federal Work-Study, institutionally sponsored loans, health care benefits, and unspecified assistantships also available. Financial award application deadline: 2/15; financial award applicants required to submit FAFSA. *Faculty research:* Semiconductors, VLSI design, control systems, electromagnetics and applied optics, communication theory and digital signal processing, power systems. *Total annual research expenditures:* $11.1 million. *Unit head:* Dr. Gianluca Lazzi, Chair, 801-581-6941, Fax: 801-581-5281, E-mail: lazzi@utah.edu. *Application contact:* Lori Sather, Graduate Coordinator, 801-581-6943, Fax: 801-581-5281, E-mail: sather@ece.utah.edu. Web site: http://www.ece.utah.edu/.

University of Vermont, Graduate College, College of Engineering and Mathematics, Department of Electrical Engineering, Burlington, VT 05405. Offers MS, PhD. *Students:* 39 (5 women); includes 4 minority (1 Black or African American, non-Hispanic/Latino; 3 Asian, non-Hispanic/Latino), 11 international. 36 applicants, 56% accepted, 7 enrolled. In 2011, 1 degree awarded. *Degree requirements:* For master's, thesis or alternative; for doctorate, one foreign language, thesis/dissertation. *Entrance requirements:* For master's, GRE General Test. Additional exam requirements/recommendations for international students: Required—TOEFL (minimum score 550 paper-based; 213 computer-based; 80 iBT). *Application deadline:* For fall admission, 4/1 priority date for domestic students, 4/1 for international students. Applications are processed on a rolling basis. Application fee: $40. Electronic applications accepted. *Financial support:* Fellowships, research assistantships, and teaching assistantships available. Financial award application deadline: 3/1. *Unit head:* Jason Bates, Interim Director, 802-656-3331. *Application contact:* Prof. Kurt Oughstun, Coordinator, 802-656-3331.

University of Victoria, Faculty of Graduate Studies, Faculty of Engineering, Department of Electrical and Computer Engineering, Victoria, BC V8W 2Y2, Canada. Offers M Eng, MA Sc, PhD. *Degree requirements:* For master's, thesis; for doctorate, thesis/dissertation, candidacy exam. *Entrance requirements:* For master's, GRE (recommended), bachelor's degree in engineering; for doctorate, GRE (recommended), master's degree. Additional exam requirements/recommendations for international students: Required—TOEFL (minimum score 575 paper-based; 233 computer-based), IELTS (minimum score 7). Electronic applications accepted. *Faculty research:* Communications and computers; electromagnetics, microwaves, and optics; electronics; power systems, signal processing, and control.

University of Virginia, School of Engineering and Applied Science, Department of Electrical and Computer Engineering, Program in Electrical Engineering, Charlottesville, VA 22903. Offers ME, MS, PhD. *Students:* 100 full-time (24 women), 12 part-time (1 woman); includes 18 minority (6 Black or African American, non-Hispanic/Latino; 10 Asian, non-Hispanic/Latino; 1 Hispanic/Latino; 1 Two or more races, non-Hispanic/Latino), 63 international. Average age 27. 238 applicants, 12% accepted, 16 enrolled. In 2011, 16 master's, 17 doctorates awarded. *Degree requirements:* For doctorate, thesis/dissertation. *Entrance requirements:* For master's, GRE General Test, 3 letters of recommendation; for doctorate, GRE General Test, 3 letters of recommendation; essay. Additional exam requirements/recommendations for international students: Required—TOEFL (minimum score 650 paper-based; 250 computer-based; 100 iBT), IELTS (minimum score 7). *Application deadline:* For fall admission, 8/1 for domestic students, 1/15 for international students; for winter admission, 12/1 for domestic students, 8/1 for international students; for spring admission, 5/1 for domestic students. Applications are processed on a rolling basis. Application fee: $60. Electronic applications accepted. *Financial support:* Fellowships, research assistantships, and teaching assistantships available. Financial award application deadline: 1/15; financial award applicants required to submit FAFSA. *Unit head:* Lloyd R. Harriott, Chair, 434-924-3960, Fax: 434-924-8818, E-mail: lrharriott@virginia.edu. *Application contact:* Nathan Swami, Graduate Program Director, 434-924-3960, Fax: 434-924-8818, E-mail: nathanswami@virginia.edu. Web site: http://www.ee.virginia.edu/.

University of Washington, Graduate School, College of Engineering, Department of Electrical Engineering, Seattle, WA 98195-2500. Offers electrical engineering (MS, PhD); electrical engineering and nanotechnology (PhD). Postbaccalaureate distance learning degree programs offered (no on-campus study). *Faculty:* 58 full-time (9 women), 14 part-time/adjunct (3 women). *Students:* 199 full-time (39 women), 135 part-time (19 women); includes 72 minority (10 Black or African American, non-Hispanic/Latino; 1 American Indian or Alaska Native, non-Hispanic/Latino; 51 Asian, non-Hispanic/Latino; 10 Hispanic/Latino), 130 international. 1,061 applicants, 21% accepted, 94 enrolled. In 2011, 60 master's, 32 doctorates awarded. *Degree requirements:* For master's, thesis optional; for doctorate, thesis/dissertation, qualifying, general, and final exams. *Entrance requirements:* For master's and doctorate, GRE General Test (recommended minimum scores: Verbal 500, Quantitative 720, Analytical 600), minimum GPA of 3.2, resume or curriculum vitae, statement of purpose, 3 letters of recommendation, undergraduate and graduate transcripts. Additional exam requirements/recommendations for international students: Required—TOEFL (minimum score 600 paper-based; 250 computer-based; 92 iBT); Recommended—IELTS (minimum score 7). *Application deadline:* For fall admission, 1/1 priority date for domestic students, 12/15 for international students. Applications are processed on a rolling basis. Application fee: $75. Electronic applications accepted. *Expenses:* Contact institution. *Financial support:* In 2011–12, 143 students received support, including 5 fellowships with full tuition reimbursements available (averaging $19,485 per year), 98 research assistantships with partial tuition reimbursements available (averaging $19,485 per year), 34 teaching assistantships with partial tuition reimbursements available (averaging $14,751 per year); career-related internships or fieldwork, Federal Work-Study, and institutionally sponsored loans also available. Financial award application deadline: 1/1; financial award applicants required to submit FAFSA. *Faculty research:* Controls and robotics, communications and signal processing, electromagnetics, optics and acoustics, electronic devices and photonics. *Total annual research expenditures:* $15.7 million. *Unit head:* Dr. Vikram Jandhyala, Professor/Chair, 206-616-0959, Fax: 206-543-3842, E-mail: vj@uw.edu. *Application contact:* Scott Latiolais, Lead Graduate Program Academic Counselor, 206-221-7913, Fax: 206-543-3842, E-mail: latiolais@ee.washington.edu. Web site: http://www.ee.washington.edu/.

University of Waterloo, Graduate Studies, Faculty of Engineering, Department of Electrical and Computer Engineering, Waterloo, ON N2L 3G1, Canada. Offers electrical and computer engineering (M Eng, MA Sc, PhD); electrical and computer engineering (software engineering) (MA Sc). Part-time programs available. *Degree requirements:* For master's, research paper or thesis; for doctorate, comprehensive exam, thesis/dissertation. *Entrance requirements:* For master's, honors degree, minimum B+ average; for doctorate, master's degree, minimum A- average. Additional exam requirements/recommendations for international students: Required—TOEFL (minimum score 550 paper-based; 213 computer-based), TWE (minimum score 4). Electronic applications accepted. *Faculty research:* Communications, computers, systems and control, silicon devices, power engineering.

The University of Western Ontario, Faculty of Graduate Studies, Physical Sciences Division, Faculty of Engineering, London, ON N6A 5B8, Canada. Offers chemical and biochemical engineering (ME Sc, PhD); civil and environmental engineering (M Eng, ME Sc, PhD); electrical and computer engineering (M Eng, ME Sc, PhD); mechanical and materials engineering (M Eng, ME Sc, PhD). Part-time programs available. Terminal master's awarded for partial completion of doctoral program. *Degree requirements:* For master's, thesis; for doctorate, thesis/dissertation. *Entrance requirements:* For master's, minimum B average; for doctorate, minimum B+ average. *Faculty research:* Wind, geotechnical, chemical reactor engineering, applied electrostatics, biochemical engineering.

University of Windsor, Faculty of Graduate Studies, Faculty of Engineering, Department of Electrical and Computer Engineering, Windsor, ON N9B 3P4, Canada. Offers electrical engineering (M Eng, MA Sc, PhD). Part-time programs available. *Degree requirements:* For master's, thesis; for doctorate, comprehensive exam, thesis/dissertation. *Entrance requirements:* For master's, minimum B average; for doctorate, master's degree, minimum B+ average. Additional exam requirements/recommendations for international students: Required—TOEFL (minimum score 600 paper-based; 250 computer-based). Electronic applications accepted. *Faculty research:* Systems, signals, power.

University of Wisconsin–Madison, Graduate School, College of Engineering, Department of Electrical and Computer Engineering, Madison, WI 53706. Offers electrical engineering (MS, PhD). Part-time programs available. Postbaccalaureate distance learning degree programs offered (minimal on-campus study). *Faculty:* 39 full-time (5 women), 2 part-time/adjunct (0 women). *Students:* 356 full-time (46 women); includes 23 minority (3 Black or African American, non-Hispanic/Latino; 15 Asian, non-Hispanic/Latino; 5 Hispanic/Latino), 221 international. Average age 27. 1,514 applicants, 18% accepted, 93 enrolled. In 2011, 99 master's, 51 doctorates awarded. Terminal master's awarded for partial completion of doctoral program. *Degree requirements:* For master's, thesis or alternative; for doctorate, thesis/dissertation, exam. *Entrance requirements:* For master's and doctorate, GRE General Test. Additional exam requirements/recommendations for international students: Required—TOEFL (minimum score 550 paper-based; 213 computer-based; 80 iBT). *Application deadline:* For fall admission, 12/15 for domestic and international students; for spring admission, 9/15 for domestic and international students. Application fee: $56. Electronic applications accepted. *Expenses:* Tuition, state resident: full-time $10,296; part-time $643.51 per credit. Tuition, nonresident: full-time $24,054; part-time $1503.40 per credit. *Required fees:* $70.06 per credit. Tuition and fees vary according to course load, campus/location, program and reciprocity agreements. *Financial support:* In 2011–12, 230 students received support, including 20 fellowships with full tuition reimbursements available (averaging $13,000 per year), 126 research assistantships with full tuition reimbursements available (averaging $20,400 per year), 84 teaching assistantships with full tuition reimbursements available (averaging $9,392 per year); career-related internships or fieldwork, Federal Work-Study, institutionally sponsored loans, health care benefits, unspecified assistantships, and Project Assistantships also available. Support available to part-time students. Financial award application deadline: 12/15. *Faculty research:* Microelectronics, computer architecture, power electronics and systems, communications, signal processing. *Total annual research expenditures:* $19.5 million. *Unit head:* John Booske, Chair, 608-262-3840, Fax: 608-262-1267, E-mail: ecechair@engr.wisc.edu. *Application contact:* Cheryl Loschko, Graduate Admissions Coordinator, 608-265-5570, Fax: 608-890-1174, E-mail: ece.gradadmissions@uwalumni.com. Web site: http://www.engr.wisc.edu/ece/.

University of Wisconsin–Milwaukee, Graduate School, College of Engineering and Applied Science, Program in Engineering, Milwaukee, WI 53201-0413. Offers civil engineering (MS); electrical and computer engineering (MS); energy engineering (Certificate); engineering (PhD); engineering management (MS); engineering mechanics (MS); ergonomics (Certificate); industrial and management engineering (MS); manufacturing engineering (MS); materials engineering (MS); mechanical engineering (MS); MUP/MS. Part-time programs available. *Faculty:* 41 full-time (5 women), 2 part-time/adjunct (0 women). *Students:* 170 full-time (33 women), 101 part-time (18 women); includes 30 minority (6 Black or African American, non-Hispanic/Latino; 15 Asian, non-Hispanic/Latino; 2 Hispanic/Latino; 7 Two or more races, non-Hispanic/Latino), 153 international. Average age 30. 170 applicants, 56% accepted, 48 enrolled. In 2011, 47 master's, 12 doctorates awarded. *Degree requirements:* For master's, comprehensive exam (for some programs), thesis or alternative; for doctorate, comprehensive exam, thesis/dissertation, internship. *Entrance requirements:* For master's, GRE, minimum GPA of 2.75; for doctorate, GRE, minimum GPA of 3.5. Additional exam requirements/recommendations for international students: Required—TOEFL (minimum score 550 paper-based; 79 iBT), IELTS (minimum score 6.5). *Application deadline:* For fall admission, 1/1 priority date for domestic students; for spring admission, 9/1 for domestic students. Applications are processed on a rolling basis. Application fee: $56 ($96 for international students). One-time fee: $506.10 full-time. Tuition and fees vary according to course load and reciprocity agreements. *Financial support:* In 2011–12, 3 fellowships, 55 research assistantships, 77 teaching assistantships were awarded; career-related internships or fieldwork, Federal Work-Study, unspecified assistantships, and project assistantships also available. Support available to part-time students. Financial award application deadline: 4/15. *Total annual research expenditures:* $10.3 million. *Unit head:* David Yu, Representative, 414-229-6169, E-mail: yu@uwm.edu. *Application contact:* Betty Warras, General Information Contact, 414-229-6169, Fax: 414-229-6967, E-mail: bwarras@uwm.edu. Web site: http://www.wum.edu/CEAS/.

University of Wyoming, College of Engineering and Applied Sciences, Department of Electrical and Computer Engineering, Laramie, WY 82070. Offers electrical engineering (MS, PhD). Part-time programs available. *Degree requirements:* For master's, thesis (for some programs); for doctorate, comprehensive exam, thesis/dissertation, dissertation proposal/presentation. *Entrance requirements:* For master's, GRE General Test, minimum undergraduate GPA of 3.0; for doctorate, GRE General Test, minimum GPA of 3.0. Additional exam requirements/recommendations for international students: Required—TOEFL (minimum score 550 paper-based; 213 computer-based; 79 iBT). Electronic applications accepted. *Faculty research:* Robotics and controls, signal and image processing, power electronics, power systems, computer networks, wind energy.

Utah State University, School of Graduate Studies, College of Engineering, Department of Electrical and Computer Engineering, Logan, UT 84322. Offers electrical engineering (ME, MS, PhD). Part-time programs available. *Degree requirements:* For master's, thesis (for some programs); for doctorate, comprehensive exam, thesis/dissertation. *Entrance requirements:* For master's, GRE General Test, minimum GPA of 3.0, BS in electrical engineering, 3 recommendation letters; for doctorate, GRE General Test, minimum GPA of 3.0, MS in electrical engineering, 3 recommendation letters. Additional exam requirements/recommendations for international students: Required—TOEFL. Electronic applications accepted. *Faculty research:* Parallel processing, networking, control systems, digital signal processing, communications.

Vanderbilt University, School of Engineering, Department of Electrical Engineering and Computer Science, Program in Electrical Engineering, Nashville, TN 37240-1001. Offers M Eng, MS, PhD. MS and PhD offered through the Graduate School. Part-time programs available. *Faculty:* 22 full-time (1 woman). *Students:* 98 full-time (22 women); includes 9 minority (2 Black or African American, non-Hispanic/Latino; 1 Asian, non-Hispanic/Latino; 3 Hispanic/Latino; 3 Two or more races, non-Hispanic/Latino), 60 international. Average age 27. 355 applicants, 10% accepted, 16 enrolled. In 2011, 15 master's, 11 doctorates awarded. Terminal master's awarded for partial completion of doctoral program. *Degree requirements:* For master's, thesis; for doctorate, comprehensive exam, thesis/dissertation. *Entrance requirements:* For master's and doctorate, GRE General Test, 3 letters of recommendation. Additional exam requirements/recommendations for international students: Required—TOEFL. *Application deadline:* For fall admission, 1/15 for domestic and international students; for spring admission, 11/1 for domestic and international students. Application fee: $0. Electronic applications accepted. *Financial support:* In 2011–12, 85 students received support, including fellowships with full and partial tuition reimbursements available (averaging $30,000 per year), research assistantships with full tuition reimbursements available (averaging $27,372 per year), teaching assistantships with full tuition reimbursements available (averaging $24,552 per year); career-related internships or fieldwork, institutionally sponsored loans, scholarships/grants, health care benefits, tuition waivers (full and partial), and unspecified assistantships also available. Support available to part-time students. Financial award application deadline: 1/15. *Faculty research:* Robotics, microelectronics, signal and image processing, VLSI, solid-state sensors, radiation effects and reliability. *Unit head:* Dr. Daniel M. Fleetwood, Chair, 615-322-2771, Fax: 615-343-6702, E-mail: dan.fleetwood@vanderbilt.edu. *Application contact:* Dr. Sharon M. Weiss, Director of Graduate Studies, 615-343-8311, Fax: 615-343-6702, E-mail: sharon.weiss@Vanderbilt.Edu. Web site: http://www.eecs.vuse.vanderbilt.edu/.

Villanova University, College of Engineering, Department of Electrical and Computer Engineering, Program in Electrical Engineering, Villanova, PA 19085-1699. Offers electric power systems (Certificate); electrical engineering (MSEE); electro mechanical systems (Certificate); high frequency systems (Certificate); intelligent control systems (Certificate); wireless and digital communications (Certificate). Part-time and evening/weekend programs available. *Degree requirements:* For master's, thesis optional. *Entrance requirements:* For master's, GRE General Test (for applicants with degrees from foreign universities), BEE, minimum GPA of 3.0. Additional exam requirements/recommendations for international students: Required—TOEFL (minimum score 600 paper-based; 250 computer-based; 100 iBT). *Expenses: Tuition:* Part-time $675 per credit. Part-time tuition and fees vary according to degree level and program. *Faculty research:* Signal processing, communications, antennas, devices.

Virginia Commonwealth University, Graduate School, School of Engineering, Department of Electrical and Computer Engineering, Richmond, VA 23284-9005. Offers electrical engineering (MS, PhD). *Entrance requirements:* For master's and doctorate, GRE. Additional exam requirements/recommendations for international students: Required—TOEFL (minimum score 600 paper-based; 250 computer-based; 100 iBT). Electronic applications accepted. *Expenses:* Tuition, state resident: full-time $9133; part-time $507 per credit. Tuition, nonresident: full-time $18,777; part-time $1043 per credit. *Required fees:* $77 per credit. Tuition and fees vary according to degree level, campus/location, program and student level.

Virginia Polytechnic Institute and State University, Graduate School, College of Engineering, Department of Electrical and Computer Engineering, Blacksburg, VA 24061. Offers air transportation systems (Certificate); computer engineering (M Eng, MS, PhD); electrical engineering (M Eng, MS, PhD); emerging devices technologies (Certificate); traffic control and operations (Certificate). *Degree requirements:* For master's, comprehensive exam (for some programs), thesis (for some programs); for doctorate, comprehensive exam (for some programs), thesis/dissertation (for some programs). *Entrance requirements:* For master's and doctorate, GRE. Additional exam requirements/recommendations for international students: Required—TOEFL (minimum score 590 paper-based; 213 computer-based). *Application deadline:* For fall admission, 7/1 for domestic and international students; for spring admission, 12/1 for domestic and international students. Applications are processed on a rolling basis. Application fee: $65. Electronic applications accepted. *Expenses:* Tuition, state resident: full-time $10,048; part-time $558.25 per credit hour. Tuition, nonresident: full-time $19,497; part-time $1083.25 per credit hour. *Required fees:* $405 per semester. Tuition and fees vary according to course load, campus/location and program. *Financial support:* Fellowships with full tuition reimbursements, research assistantships with full tuition reimbursements, teaching assistantships with full tuition reimbursements, career-related internships or fieldwork, Federal Work-Study, scholarships/grants, health care benefits, and unspecified assistantships available. Financial award application deadline: 1/15. *Faculty research:* Electromagnetics, controls, electronics, power, communications. *Unit head:* Dr. James S. Thorp, Unit Head, 540-231-2946, Fax: 540-231-3362, E-mail: jsthorp@vt.edu. *Application contact:* Paul Plassmann, Information Contact, 540-231-5379, Fax: 540-231-3362, E-mail: plassmann@vt.edu. Web site: http://www.ece.vt.edu/.

Virginia Polytechnic Institute and State University, VT Online, Blacksburg, VA 24061. Offers advanced transportation systems (Certificate); aerospace engineering (MS); agricultural and life sciences (MSLFS); business information systems (Graduate Certificate); career and technical education (MS); civil engineering (MS); computer engineering (M Eng, MS); decision support systems (Graduate Certificate); eLearning leadership (MA); electrical engineering (M Eng, MS); engineering administration (MEA); environmental engineering (Certificate); environmental politics and policy (Graduate Certificate); environmental sciences and engineering (MS); foundations of political analysis (Graduate Certificate); health product risk management (Graduate Certificate); industrial and systems engineering (MS); information policy and society (Graduate Certificate); information security (Graduate Certificate); information technology (MIT); instructional technology (MA); integrative STEM education (MA Ed); liberal arts (Graduate Certificate); life sciences: health product risk management (MS); natural resources (MNR, Graduate Certificate); networking (Graduate Certificate); nonprofit and nongovernmental organization management (Graduate Certificate); ocean engineering (MS); political science (MA); security studies (Graduate Certificate); software development (Graduate Certificate). *Expenses:* Tuition, state resident: full-time $10,048; part-time $558.25 per credit hour. Tuition, nonresident: full-time $19,497; part-time $1083.25 per credit hour. *Required fees:* $405 per semester. Tuition and fees vary according to course load, campus/location and program. *Application contact:* Graduate School Applications General Assistance, 540-231-8636, Fax: 540-231-2039, E-mail: gradappl@vt.edu. Web site: http://www.vto.vt.edu/.

Washington State University, Graduate School, College of Engineering and Architecture, School of Electrical Engineering and Computer Science, Program in Electrical Engineering, Pullman, WA 99164. Offers MS, PhD. *Faculty:* 30. *Students:* 75 full-time (14 women), 22 part-time (0 women); includes 3 minority (1 Black or African American, non-Hispanic/Latino; 2 Asian, non-Hispanic/Latino), 60 international. Average age 26. 237 applicants, 18% accepted, 24 enrolled. In 2011, 5 master's, 6 doctorates awarded. *Degree requirements:* For master's, comprehensive exam (for some programs), thesis, oral exam; for doctorate, comprehensive exam, thesis/dissertation, oral exam, qualifying exam, preliminary exam, oral defense of dissertation. *Entrance requirements:* For master's and doctorate, GRE General Test, major in computer engineering, electrical engineering, or computer science; statement of purpose giving qualifications, research interests, and goals; official college transcripts; three letters of recommendation. Additional exam requirements/recommendations for international students: Required—TOEFL (minimum score 520 paper-based; 190 computer-based), IELTS. *Application deadline:* For fall admission, 1/10 priority date for domestic students, 1/10 for international students; for spring admission, 7/1 for domestic and international students. Applications are processed on a rolling basis. Application fee: $75. *Financial support:* In 2011–12, 3 fellowships with full tuition reimbursements (averaging $2,500 per year), 18 research assistantships with full tuition reimbursements (averaging $13,917 per year), 24 teaching assistantships with full tuition reimbursements (averaging $13,056 per year) were awarded; career-related internships or fieldwork, Federal Work-Study, and institutionally sponsored loans also available. Financial award application deadline: 2/10; financial award applicants required to submit FAFSA. *Faculty research:* Energy and power systems, microelectronics, electrophysics controls, systems telecommunications. *Unit head:* Dr. Anjan Bose, Chair, 509-335-1147, Fax: 509-335-3818, E-mail: bose@wsu.edu. *Application contact:* Graduate School Admissions, 800-GRADWSU, Fax: 509-335-1949, E-mail: gradsch@wsu.edu. Web site: http://www.eecs.wsu.edu/.

Washington State University Tri-Cities, Graduate Programs, College of Engineering and Architecture, Richland, WA 99352-1671. Offers computer science (MS, PhD); electrical engineering (MS, PhD); mechanical engineering (MS, PhD). Part-time programs available. *Faculty:* 28. *Students:* 20 full-time (5 women), 37 part-time (10 women); includes 6 minority (1 Black or African American, non-Hispanic/Latino; 2 Asian, non-Hispanic/Latino; 1 Hispanic/Latino; 2 Two or more races, non-Hispanic/Latino), 4 international. Average age 27. 27 applicants, 33% accepted, 6 enrolled. *Degree requirements:* For master's, comprehensive exam, thesis (for some programs); for doctorate, comprehensive exam, thesis/dissertation, oral exam. *Entrance requirements:* For master's and doctorate, GRE, minimum GPA of 3.0, 3 letters of recommendation. Additional exam requirements/recommendations for international students: Required—TOEFL (minimum score 550 paper-based; 213 computer-based). *Application deadline:* For fall admission, 1/10 priority date for domestic students, 1/10 for international students; for spring admission, 7/1 priority date for domestic students, 7/1 for international students. Application fee: $75. *Financial support:* Application deadline: 3/1. *Faculty research:* Positive ion track structure, biological systems computer simulations. *Unit head:* Dr. Ali Saberi, Chair, 509-372-7178, E-mail: sidra@eecs.wsu.edu. *Application contact:* Dr. Scott Hudson, Associate Director, 509-372-7254, Fax: 509-335-1949, E-mail: hudson@tricity.wsu.edu. Web site: http://cea.tricity.wsu.edu/.

Washington University in St. Louis, School of Engineering and Applied Science, Department of Electrical and Systems Engineering, St. Louis, MO 63130-4899. Offers electrical engineering (MS, D Sc, PhD); systems science and mathematics (MS, D Sc, PhD). Part-time programs available. Terminal master's awarded for partial completion of doctoral program. *Degree requirements:* For master's, thesis or alternative; for doctorate, comprehensive exam, thesis/dissertation. *Entrance requirements:* For master's, minimum GPA of 3.0 in the last 2 years of undergraduate course work; for doctorate, GRE. Additional exam requirements/recommendations for international students: Required—TOEFL (minimum score 550 paper-based; 213 computer-based; 80 iBT). Electronic applications accepted. *Faculty research:* Applied physics and electronics, signal and image processing, systems analysis, biomedicine, and energy.

Wayne State University, College of Engineering, Department of Electrical and Computer Engineering, Program in Electrical Engineering, Detroit, MI 48202. Offers MS, PhD. *Students:* 57 full-time (6 women), 21 part-time (2 women); includes 17 minority (2 Black or African American, non-Hispanic/Latino; 13 Asian, non-Hispanic/Latino; 1 Hispanic/Latino; 1 Native Hawaiian or other Pacific Islander, non-Hispanic/Latino), 47 international. Average age 28. 180 applicants, 52% accepted, 16 enrolled. In 2011, 27 master's, 3 doctorates awarded. *Degree requirements:* For master's, thesis optional; for doctorate, thesis/dissertation. *Entrance requirements:* Additional exam requirements/recommendations for international students: Required—TOEFL (minimum score 550 paper-based; 213 computer-based), Michigan English Language Assessment Battery (minimum score 85); Recommended—TWE (minimum score 5.5). *Application deadline:*

For fall admission, 6/1 priority date for domestic students, 5/1 for international students; for winter admission, 10/1 priority date for domestic students, 9/1 for international students; for spring admission, 2/1 priority date for domestic students, 1/1 for international students. Applications are processed on a rolling basis. Application fee: $50. Electronic applications accepted. *Expenses:* Tuition, state resident: part-time $512.85 per credit. Tuition, nonresident: part-time $1132.65 per credit. *Required fees:* $26.60 per credit. $199.65 per semester. Tuition and fees vary according to course load and program. *Financial support:* In 2011–12, 16 students received support. Fellowships with tuition reimbursements available, research assistantships with tuition reimbursements available, teaching assistantships with tuition reimbursements available, scholarships/grants, health care benefits, and unspecified assistantships available. Support available to part-time students. Financial award application deadline: 3/15. *Faculty research:* Biomedical systems, control systems, solid state materials, optical materials, hybrid vehicle. *Unit head:* Yang Zhao, Chair, 313-577-3920, Fax: 313-577-1101, E-mail: aa3606@wayne.edu. *Application contact:* Pepe Siy, Graduate Director, 313-577-3841, Fax: 313-577-1101, E-mail: psiy@ece.eng.wayne.edu. Web site: http://www.eng.wayne.edu/page.php?id=62.

Western Michigan University, Graduate College, College of Engineering and Applied Sciences, Department of Electrical and Computer Engineering, Kalamazoo, MI 49008. Offers computer engineering (MSE); electrical and computer engineering (PhD); electrical engineering (MSE). Part-time programs available. *Degree requirements:* For master's, thesis optional. *Entrance requirements:* For master's, minimum GPA of 3.0. *Faculty research:* Fiber optics, computer architecture, bioelectromagnetics, acoustics.

Western New England University, College of Engineering, Department of Electrical Engineering, Springfield, MA 01119. Offers MSEE. Part-time and evening/weekend programs available. *Students:* 5 part-time (0 women), 1 international. *Degree requirements:* For master's, comprehensive exam, thesis optional. *Entrance requirements:* For master's, GRE, bachelor's degree in engineering or related field, two recommendations, resume. *Application deadline:* Applications are processed on a rolling basis. Application fee: $30. *Financial support:* Available to part-time students. Applicants required to submit FAFSA. *Faculty research:* Superconductors, microwave cooking, computer voice output, digital filters, computer engineering. *Unit head:* Dr. James J. Moriarty, Chair, 413-782-1272, E-mail: jmoriart@wne.edu. *Application contact:* Matt Fox, Director of Recruiting and Marketing for Adult Learners, 413-782-1249, Fax: 413-782-1779, E-mail: learn@wne.edu. Web site: http://www1.wnec.edu/engineering/index.cfm?selection-doc.8531.

West Virginia University, College of Engineering and Mineral Resources, Lane Department of Computer Science and Electrical Engineering, Program in Electrical Engineering, Morgantown, WV 26506. Offers MSEE, PhD. Terminal master's awarded for partial completion of doctoral program. *Degree requirements:* For master's, thesis or alternative; for doctorate, comprehensive exam, thesis/dissertation. *Entrance requirements:* For master's and doctorate, GRE General Test, minimum GPA of 3.0, letters of recommendation. Additional exam requirements/recommendations for international students: Required—TOEFL. *Faculty research:* Power and control systems, communications and signal processing, electromechanical systems, microelectronics and photonics.

Wichita State University, Graduate School, College of Engineering, Department of Electrical Engineering and Computer Science, Wichita, KS 67260. Offers computer networking (MS); computer science (MS); electrical engineering (MS, PhD). Part-time and evening/weekend programs available. *Expenses:* Tuition, state resident: full-time $4746; part-time $263.65 per credit. Tuition, nonresident: full-time $11,669; part-time $648.30 per credit. *Unit head:* Dr. John Watkins, Chair, 316-978-3156, Fax: 316-978-5408, E-mail: john.watkins@wichita.edu. *Application contact:* Carrie C. Henderson, Admissions Coordinator, 316-978-3095, Fax: 316-978-3253, E-mail: carrie.henderson@wichita.edu. Web site: http://www.wichita.edu/.

Wilkes University, College of Graduate and Professional Studies, College of Science and Engineering, Division of Engineering and Physics, Wilkes-Barre, PA 18766-0002. Offers electrical engineering (MSEE); engineering management (MS); mechanical engineering (MS). Part-time programs available. *Students:* 27 full-time (2 women), 26 part-time (4 women); includes 2 minority (both Asian, non-Hispanic/Latino), 19 international. Average age 30. In 2011, 11 master's awarded. *Entrance requirements:* For master's, GRE General Test. Additional exam requirements/recommendations for international students: Required—TOEFL (minimum score 550 paper-based; 213 computer-based; 79 iBT). *Application deadline:* Applications are processed on a rolling basis. Application fee: $45 ($65 for international students). Electronic applications accepted. *Financial support:* Federal Work-Study and unspecified assistantships available. Financial award application deadline: 3/1; financial award applicants required to submit FAFSA. *Unit head:* Dr. Rodney Ridley, Director, 570-408-4824, Fax: 570-408-7846, E-mail: rodney.ridley@wilkes.edu. *Application contact:* Erin Sutzko, Director of Extended Learning, 570-408-4253, Fax: 570-408-7846, E-mail: erin.sutzko@wilkes.edu. Web site: http://www.wilkes.edu/pages/387.asp.

Worcester Polytechnic Institute, Graduate Studies and Research, Department of Electrical and Computer Engineering, Worcester, MA 01609-2280. Offers electrical and computer engineering (Advanced Certificate, Graduate Certificate); electrical engineering (M Eng, MS, PhD). Part-time and evening/weekend programs available. *Faculty:* 16 full-time (0 women), 6 part-time/adjunct (2 women). *Students:* 101 full-time (28 women), 114 part-time (16 women); includes 28 minority (3 Black or African American, non-Hispanic/Latino; 16 Asian, non-Hispanic/Latino; 7 Hispanic/Latino; 2 Two or more races, non-Hispanic/Latino), 109 international. 636 applicants, 46% accepted, 101 enrolled. In 2011, 89 master's, 6 doctorates awarded. Terminal master's awarded for partial completion of doctoral program. *Degree requirements:* For master's, thesis optional; for doctorate, comprehensive exam, thesis/dissertation. *Entrance requirements:* For master's, 3 letters of recommendation; for doctorate, 3 letters of recommendation, statement of purpose. Additional exam requirements/recommendations for international students: Required—TOEFL (minimum score 563 paper-based; 223 computer-based; 84 iBT), IELTS (minimum score 7). *Application deadline:* For fall admission, 1/1 priority date for domestic students, 1/1 for international students; for spring admission, 10/1 priority date for domestic students, 10/1 for international students. Applications are processed on a rolling basis. Application fee: $70. Electronic applications accepted. *Financial support:* Research assistantships, teaching assistantships, career-related internships or fieldwork, institutionally sponsored loans, scholarships/grants, and unspecified assistantships available. Financial award application deadline: 1/1; financial award applicants required to submit FAFSA. *Faculty research:* Analog and mixed signal IC design, RF electronics and antenna design, computational modeling, cryptography, data and system security, networking and communication systems (including sw defined radios), biomedical signal processing and medical systems, indoor/outdoor localization and navigation systems. *Unit head:* Dr. Fred Looft, Department Head, 508-831-5231, Fax: 508-831-5491, E-mail: fjlooft@wpi.edu. *Application contact:* Dr. Reinhold Ludwig, Graduate Coordinator, 508-831-5231, Fax: 508-831-5491, E-mail: ludwig@wpi.edu. Web site: http://www.ece.wpi.edu/.

Wright State University, School of Graduate Studies, College of Engineering and Computer Science, Programs in Engineering, Program in Electrical Engineering, Dayton, OH 45435. Offers MSE. Part-time and evening/weekend programs available. *Degree requirements:* For master's, thesis or course option alternative. *Entrance requirements:* Additional exam requirements/recommendations for international students: Required—TOEFL. *Faculty research:* Robotics, circuit design, power electronics, image processing, communication systems.

Yale University, Graduate School of Arts and Sciences, School of Engineering and Applied Science, Department of Electrical Engineering, New Haven, CT 06520. Offers MS, PhD. Terminal master's awarded for partial completion of doctoral program. *Degree requirements:* For doctorate, thesis/dissertation, exam. *Entrance requirements:* For master's and doctorate, GRE General Test. Additional exam requirements/recommendations for international students: Required—TOEFL. *Faculty research:* Signal processing, control, and communications; digital systems and computer engineering; microelectronics and photonics; nanotechnology; computers, sensors, and networking.

Youngstown State University, Graduate School, College of Science, Technology, Engineering and Mathematics, Department of Electrical and Computer Engineering, Youngstown, OH 44555-0001. Offers computer engineering (MSE); electrical engineering (MSE). Part-time and evening/weekend programs available. *Degree requirements:* For master's, thesis optional. *Entrance requirements:* For master's, minimum GPA of 2.75 in field. Additional exam requirements/recommendations for international students: Required—TOEFL. *Faculty research:* Computer-aided design, power systems, electromagnetic energy conversion, sensors, control systems.

COLUMBIA UNIVERSITY
Department of Electrical Engineering

Programs of Study

The Department of Electrical Engineering offers programs of study leading to the degrees of Master of Science (M.S.), Electrical Engineer (E.E.), Doctor of Engineering Science (Eng.Sc.D.), and Doctor of Philosophy (Ph.D.). Registration as a nondegree candidate (special student) is also permitted.

There are no prescribed course requirements for these degrees. Students, in consultation with their faculty advisers, design their own programs, focusing on particular fields. Among them are semiconductor physics materials and devices; telecommunication systems and computer networks; high-speed analog, RF analog, and mixed analog/digital integrated circuits and systems; image, video, audio, and speech processing; electromagnetic theory and applications; plasma physics; quantum electronics; photonics; and sensory perception.

Graduate studies are closely associated with research. Faculty members are engaged in theoretical and experimental research in various areas of their disciplines.

Access also exists to a number of interdisciplinary programs, such as Computer Engineering, Solid-State Science and Engineering, and Bioengineering. In addition, substantial research interactions occur with the Departments of Applied Physics, Computer Science, and Industrial Engineering and Operations Research and with the College of Physicians and Surgeons.

The requirements for the Ph.D. and Eng.Sc.D. degrees are essentially identical. Both require a dissertation based on the candidate's original research, conducted under the supervision of a faculty member. The work may be theoretical or experimental or both. The E.E. professional degree program does not require a thesis. It provides specialization beyond the M.S. degree in a field chosen by the student and is particularly suited to those who wish to advance their professional development after a period of industrial employment.

Research Facilities

Every phase of current research activities is fully supported and carried out in one of more than a dozen well-equipped research laboratories run by the Department. Specifically, laboratory research is conducted in the following laboratories: Multimedia Networking Laboratory, Ultrafast Opto-Electronics Laboratory, Photonics Laboratory, Microelectronics Device Fabrication Laboratory, Digital Video and Multimedia Laboratory, Molecular Beam Epitaxy Laboratory, Laser Processing and Quantum Physics Laboratory, Integrated Systems Laboratory, Laboratory for Recognition and Organization of Speech and Audio, Lightwave Communications Laboratory, Bioelectronic Systems Laboratory, Columbia Laboratory for Unconventional Electronics, and Plasma Physics Laboratory (in conjunction with the Department of Applied Physics).

Financial Aid

Teaching assistantships and graduate research assistantships are available. For the 2012–13 academic year, stipends are $2639 per month plus tuition exemption.

Cost of Study

The annual tuition for 2011–12 was about $43,088, plus fees.

Living and Housing Costs

The University provides limited housing for graduate men and women who are registered either for an approved program of full-time academic study or for doctoral dissertation research. University residence halls include traditional dormitory facilities as well as suites and apartments for single and married students; furnishings and utilities may be included. An estimated minimum of $20,000 should be allowed for board, room, and personal expenses for the academic year.

University Real Estate properties include apartments owned and managed by the University in the immediate vicinity of the Morningside Heights campus. These are leased yearly, as they become available, to single and married students at rates that reflect the size and location of each apartment as well as whether furnishings or utilities are included.

Requests for additional information and application forms should be directed to the Assignments Office, 111 Wallach Hall, Columbia University, New York, New York 10027.

Student Group

In 2012–13, enrollment in the Department of Electrical Engineering is projected to be 709 students and included 95 undergraduates (52 electrical engineering juniors and seniors and 34 computer engineering juniors and seniors), 408 electrical engineering master's degree candidates, 56 computer engineering master's candidates, 153 doctoral candidates with master's degrees, and 6 professional candidates. The student population has a diverse and international character.

Location

The proximity of many local industries provides strong student-industry contact and excellent job opportunities. Cooperative research projects are available in neighboring industrial laboratories, which are engaged in research and development in computers, telecommunications, electronics, defense, and health care. Adjunct faculty members from industry provide courses in areas of current professional interest. Frequent colloquia are given on current research by distinguished speakers from industry and neighboring universities.

The University

Since its founding in 1754, Columbia University has attracted students interested in the issues of their times. Opened as King's College under charter of King George II to "prevent the growth of republican principles which prevail already too much in the colonies," it instead educated founders of a new and powerful nation: Alexander Hamilton, John Jay, Robert Livingston, and Gouverneur Morris. Since then such notable figures as Michael Pupin, Edwin Armstrong, and Jacob Millman have served as professors of electrical engineering at Columbia.

Applying

The Department of Electrical Engineering uses an online application that can be found at http://www.engineering.columbia.edu/admissions. October 1 is the priority deadline for all spring applicants. December 1 is the priority deadline for fall doctoral applicants. February 15 is the priority deadline for fall M.S. and professional degree applicants. Notification of admission decisions are mailed beginning March 1.

Correspondence and Information

Office of Engineering Admissions
Department of Electrical Engineering
524 S.W. Mudd, Mail Code 4708
Columbia University
500 West 120th Street
New York, New York 10027
Phone: 212-854-6438
E-mail: seasgradmit@columbia.edu
Web site: http://www.engineering.columbia.edu/admissions (admissions home page)
     http://www.ee.columbia.edu (Department home page)

Columbia University

THE FACULTY AND THEIR RESEARCH

Dimitris Anastassiou, Professor; Ph.D., Berkeley, 1979. Computational biology, with emphasis on systems-based gene expression analysis and comparative genomics. (phone: 212-854-3113; e-mail: anastas@ee.columbia.edu)

Keren Bergman, Professor; Ph.D., MIT, 1994. Optical interconnection networks for high-performance data centers, photonic networks-on-chip, silicon photonics, optically interconnected memory, WDM optical networking, cross-layer networking, multiwavelength optical packet switching. (phone: 212-854-2280; e-mail: bergman@ee.columbia.edu)

Shih-Fu Chang, Professor; Ph.D., Berkeley, 1993. Multimedia, computer vision, signal processing, machine learning, digital video, multimedia communication. (phone: 212-854-6894; e-mail: sfchang@ee.columbia.edu)

Paul Diament, Professor; Ph.D., Columbia, 1963. Electromagnetics, microwaves, antennas, biological and medical applications of electromagnetics, mutual coupling in arrays, fiber optics, wave interactions. (phone: 212-854-3111; e-mail: diament@ee.columbia.edu)

Dan Ellis, Associate Professor; Ph.D., MIT, 1996. Audio information extraction, speech recognition, source separation, music information retrieval, computational hearing, sound visualization. (phone: 212-854-8928; e-mail: dpwe@ee.columbia.edu)

Dirk Englund, Assistant Professor; Ph.D., Stanford, 2008. Quantum information and metrology, nanophotonics, advanced optoelectronic devices, nuclear spin dynamics in semiconductors. (phone: 212-851-5958; email: englund@columbia.edu)

Christine P. Fleming, Assistant Professor; Ph.D., Case Western Reserve, 2010. Optical coherence tomography, near-infrared spectroscopy, cardiovascular imaging, cardiac electrophysiology, medical image analysis. (e-mail: cfleming@ee.columbia.edu)

Tony F. Heinz, David M. Rickey Professor; Ph.D., Berkeley, 1982. Ultrafast optics and spectroscopy, nonlinear optics, properties of nanostructures and interfaces. (phone: 212-854-6564; e-mail: tony.heinz@columbia.edu)

Predrag Jelenkovic, Associate Professor; Ph.D., Columbia, 1996. Mathematical modeling and analysis of resource control and management in multimedia communication networks. (phone: 212-854-8174; e-mail: predrag@ee.columbia.edu)

Peter Kinget, Professor; Ph.D., Leuven (Belgium), 1996. Design of analog, radio-frequency (RF) and power integrated circuits for applications in communications, sensing, and power management. (phone: 212-854-0309; e-mail: kinget@ee.columbia.edu)

Harish Krishnaswamy, Assistant Professor, Ph.D., USC, 2009. Radio-frequency (RF), millimeter-wave (mm-Wave) and sub-mmWave integrated circuits, with an emphasis on multiple-antenna systems, efficient, high-power transmitters, sub-mmWave signal sources, and low-phase-noise oscillators. (phone: 212-854-8496; email: harish@ee.columbia.edu)

Ioannis Kymissis, Associate Professor; Ph.D., MIT, 2003. Organic semiconductors, OFETs, photodetectors, OLEDs, large-area thin-film electronics, hybrid device integration. (phone: 212-854-4023; e-mail: johnkym@ee.columbia.edu)

Javad Lavaei, Assistant Professor; Ph.D., Caltech, 2011. Control and optimization for large-scale networks such as power systems, smart grids, and communication networks. (e-mail: jl4006@columbia.edu)

Aurel A. Lazar, Professor; Ph.D., Princeton, 1980. Time encoding and information representation in sensory systems, spike processing and neural computation in the cortex. (phone: 212-854-1747; e-mail: aurel@ee.columbia.edu)

Nicholas Maxemchuk, Professor; Ph.D., Pennsylvania, 1975. Communications networks: protocols, topological design, applications. (phone: 212-854-0580; e-mail: nick@ee.columbia.edu)

Vishal Misra, Associate Professor; Ph.D., Massachusetts Amherst, 2000. Networking, modeling and performance evaluation, information theory. (phone: 212-939-7061; e-mail: misra@cs.columbia.edu)

Steven M. Nowick, Professor; Ph.D., Stanford, 1993. Chair, Computer Engineering Program. Asynchronous And mixed-timing digital circuits And systems, computer-aided design, networks-on-chip, interconnection networks for parallel processors, low-power digital design. (phone: 212-939-7056; e-mail: nowick@cs.columbia.edu)

Richard M. Osgood Jr., Higgins Professor; Ph.D., MIT, 1973. Integrated and guided-wave SI and other optoelectronic devices and their design, semiconductor and nanoscale surface physics and chemistry, ultrafast laser sources, quantum size studies. (phone: 212-854-4462; e-mail: osgood@columbia.edu)

Henning Schulzrinne, Professor; Ph.D., Massachusetts Amherst. Internet real-time and multimedia services and protocols, wireless networks, modeling and analysis of computer communication networks, network security. (phone: 212-939-7004; e-mail: hgs@cs.columbia.edu)

Amiya K. Sen, Professor; Ph.D., Columbia, 1963. Plasma instabilities and their feedback control, plasma turbulence and anomalous transport. (phone: 212-854-3124; e-mail: amiya@ee.columbia.edu)

Mingoo Seok, Assistant Professor; Ph.D., Michigan, 2011. Low-power integrated circuit and digital VLSI design, robust and high-performance circuit and system design, computer-aided design for VLSI, computing systems for cyber physical systems. (phone: 212-854-3105 email: mgseok@ee.columbia.edu)

Kenneth Shepard, Associate Professor; Ph.D., Stanford, 1992. Design and analysis of mixed-signal CMOS integrated circuits, bioelectronics, application of CMOS circuit design to biological applications, carbon-based electronics integrated with CMOS. (phone: 212-854-2529; e-mail: shepard@ee.columbia.edu)

Yannis Tsividis, Charles Batchelor Professor; Ph.D., Berkeley, 1976. Analog and mixed-signal integrated circuits, RF integrated circuits, circuit theory, analog and mixed signal processing. (phone: 212-854-4229; e-mail: tsividis@ee.columbia.edu)

Wen I. Wang, Thayer Lindsley Professor; Ph.D., Cornell, 1981. Quantum and heterostructure optoelectronics, materials and devices, photovoltaics, molecular beam epitaxy. (phone: 212-854-1748; e-mail: wen@ee.columbia.edu)

Xiaodong Wang, Associate Professor; Ph.D., Princeton, 1998. Statistical signal processing, multiuser communication theory, wireless communications. (phone: 212-854-6592; e-mail: wangx@ee.columbia.edu)

John Wright, Assistant Professor; Ph.D., Illinois at Urbana-Champaign, 2009. Signal processing, sparse signal representation, robust estimation, computer vision. (phone: 212-854-3105; e-mail: johnwright@ee.columbia.edu)

Charles A. Zukowski, Professor; Ph.D., MIT, 1985. Design and analysis of digital VLSI circuits, simulation of circuits and biological networks, communication circuits. (phone: 212-854-2073; e-mail: caz@columbia.edu)

Gil Zussman, Assistant Professor; Ph.D., Technion–Israel Institute of Technology, 2004. Wireless and mobile networks, including ad hoc, mesh, sensor, vehicular, and cognitive radio networks. (phone: 212-854-8670; e-mail: gil@ee.columbia.edu)

DUKE UNIVERSITY
Department of Electrical and Computer Engineering

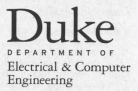

Duke
DEPARTMENT OF
Electrical & Computer
Engineering

Programs of Study

Graduate study in the Department of Electrical and Computer Engineering (ECE) is intended to prepare students for leadership roles in academia, industry, and government that require creative technical problem-solving skills. The Department offers both Ph.D. and M.S. degree programs, with opportunities for study in a broad spectrum of areas within the disciplines of electrical and computer engineering. Research and course offerings in the Department are organized into four areas of specialization: computer engineering; information physics; microelectronics, photonics, and nanotechnology; and signal and information processing. Interdisciplinary programs are also available that connect the above programs with those in other engineering departments and computer science, the natural sciences, and the Medical School. Students in the Department may also be involved in research conducted in one of the Duke centers, e.g., the Fitzpatrick Institute for Photonics. Under a reciprocal agreement with neighboring universities, a student may elect to enroll in some courses offered at the University of North Carolina at Chapel Hill and North Carolina State University in Raleigh. Since an important criterion for admitting new students is the match between student and faculty research interests, prospective students are encouraged to indicate in which Departmental specialization areas they are interested when applying.

Research Facilities

The ECE department currently occupies approximately 47,000 square feet in two buildings: the Fitzpatrick Center for Interdisciplinary Engineering, Medicine and Applied Sciences (FCIEMAS) and Hudson Hall. CIEMAS houses cross-disciplinary activities involving the Pratt School and its partners in the fields of bioengineering, photonics, microsystems integration, sensing and simulation, and materials science and materials engineering. This comprehensive facility provides extensive fabrication and test laboratories, Departmental offices, teaching labs, and other lab support spaces as well as direct access to a café. In addition, the Shared Materials Instrumentation Facility (SMiF), a state-of-the-art clean room for nanotechnology research, is housed on its main floor. Hudson Hall is the oldest of the buildings in the engineering complex. It was built in 1948 when the Engineering School moved to Duke's West Campus and was known as Old Red. An annex was built onto the back of the building in 1972, and in 1992, the building was expanded again and renamed Hudson Hall to honor Fitzgerald S. (Jerry) Hudson E'46. Hudson Hall is home to all four departments in the Pratt School of Engineering, as well as the school's laboratories, computing facilities, offices, and classrooms.

Financial Aid

Financial support is available for the majority of Ph.D. students. Graduate fellowships for the first two semesters of study provide a stipend, registration fees, and full tuition. Beyond this initial period, most students receive research assistantships funded by faculty research grants, which, together with financial aid, cover their full registration fees, tuition, and stipend until completion of the Ph.D. degree.

Cost of Study

For the 2012–13 academic year, tuition for doctoral students is $42,350. Tuition for terminal master's students is $18,410 per semester.

Living and Housing Costs

Duke has a limited number of residential apartment facilities available to graduate students through an application process. These furnished apartments are available for continuous occupancy throughout the calendar year. Academic-year rates in central campus apartments begin at $7582 per person. There are also a wide variety of options for off-campus housing near campus and in the greater Durham area.

Student Group

In the 2012–13 academic year a total of 200 students are enrolled, of whom 135 are doctoral students and 65 are master's students.

Location

Located in the rolling central Piedmont area of North Carolina, the Duke University campus is widely regarded as one of the most beautiful in the nation. The four-season climate is mild, but winter skiing is available in the North Carolina mountains a few hours' drive to the west, and ocean recreation is a similar distance away to the east. Duke is readily accessible by Interstates 85 and 40 and from Raleigh-Durham International Airport, which is about a 20-minute drive from the campus via Interstate 40 and the Durham expressway.

The University and The Department

Trinity College, founded in 1859, was selected by James B. Duke as the major recipient of a 1924 endowment that enabled a university to be organized around the college and to be named for Washington B. Duke, the family patriarch. A department of engineering was established at Trinity College in 1910, and the Department of Electrical Engineering was formed in 1920. Its name changed to the Department of Electrical and Computer Engineering in 1996. Duke University remains a privately supported university, with more than 11,000 students in degree programs.

Applying

Admission to the Department is based on a review of previous education and experience, the applicant's statement of intent, letters of evaluation, standardized test scores (GRE and TOEFL), and grade point average. The application deadline for spring admission is October 15. December 8 is the priority deadline for submission of Ph.D. applications for admission and financial award for the fall semester. January 30 is the priority deadline for submission of M.S. applications for admission.

Correspondence and Information

Steven A. Cummer
Professor and Director of Graduate Studies
Department of Electrical and Computer Engineering
Pratt School of Engineering, Box 90291
Duke University
Durham, North Carolina 27708-0291
Phone: 919-660-5245
E-mail: dgs@ee.duke.edu
Web site: http://www.ee.duke.edu

THE FACULTY AND THEIR RESEARCH

John A. Board, Associate Professor of ECE and Computer Science; D.Phil., Oxford. High performance scientific computing and simulation, novel computer architectures, cluster computing and parallel processing, ubiquitous computing.

David J. Brady, Michael J. Fitzpatrick Professor; Ph.D., Caltech. Computational optical sensor systems, hyperspectral microscopy, Raman spectroscopy for tissue chemometrics, optical coherence sensors and infrared spectral filters.

Duke University

Martin A. Brooke, Associate Professor; Ph.D., USC. Integrated analog CMOS circuit design, integrated nanoscale systems, mixed signal VLSI design, sensing and sensor systems, optical imaging and communications, analog and power electronics, electronic circuit assembly and testing.

April S. Brown, John Cocke Professor; D.Sc., Cornell. Nanomaterial manufacturing and characterization, sensing and sensor systems, nanoscale/microscale computing systems, integrated nanoscale systems.

Robert Calderbank, Dean of Natural Sciences and Professor of ECE, Math, and Computer Science; Ph.D., Caltech. Computer engineering, computer architecture, information theory.

Lawrence Carin, William H. Younger Professor and Chair; Ph.D., Maryland, College Park, Homeland security, sensing and sensor systems, signal processing, land mine detection.

Krishnendu Chakrabarty, Professor; Ph.D., Michigan. Computer engineering, nanoscale/microscale computing systems, self-assembled computer architecture, micro-electronic mechanical machines, failure analysis, integrated nanoscale systems, microsystems.

Leslie M. Collins, Professor; Ph.D., Michigan. Sensing and sensor systems, homeland security, land mine detection, neural prosthesis, geophysics, signal processing.

Steven A. Cummer, Professor and Director of Graduate Studies; Ph.D., Stanford. Geophysics, photonics, atmospheric science, metamaterials, electromagnetics.

Chris Dwyer, Associate Professor; Ph.D., North Carolina at Chapel Hill. Self-assembled computer architecture, nanoscale/microscale computing systems, nanomaterial manufacturing and characterization, computer engineering, biological computing, computer architecture, nanoscience, materials.

Richard B. Fair, Lord-Chandran Professor; Ph.D., Duke. Computer engineering, sensing and sensor systems, electronic devices, integrated nanoscale systems, medical diagnostics, microsystems, semiconductors.

Jeffrey T. Glass, Professor and Hogg Family Director, Engineering Management and Entrepreneurship; Ph.D., Virginia. Micro-electronic mechanical machines, engineering management, entrepreneurship, social entrepreneurship, sensing and sensor systems, materials.

Michael R. Gustafson, Associate Professor of the Practice; Ph.D., Duke. Engineering education, electronic circuit assembly and testing, electronic devices.

Lisa G. Huettel, Associate Professor of the Practice, Associate Chair, and Director of Undergraduate Studies; Ph.D., Duke. Sensing and sensor systems, engineering education, signal processing, distributed systems.

William T. Joines, Professor; Ph.D., Duke. Photonics and electromagnetics.

Nan M. Jokerst, J. A. Jones Professor; Ph.D., USC. Photonics, sensing and sensor systems, nanomaterial manufacturing and characterization, semiconductors, integrated nanoscale systems, microsystems.

Tom Katsouleas, Professor and Dean; Ph.D., Physics, UCLA. Use of plasmas as novel particle accelerators and light sources.

Jungsang Kim, Associate Professor; Ph.D., Stanford. Photonics, micro-electronic mechanical machines, sensing and sensor systems, semiconductors, quantum information, integrated nanoscale systems.

Jeffrey L. Krolik, Professor; Ph.D., Toronto (Canada). Sensing and sensor systems, signal processing, acoustics, medical imaging, homeland security, electromagnetics, antennas.

Benjamin C. Lee, Assistant Professor; Ph.D., Harvard. Scalable technologies, power-efficient computer architectures, high-performance applications.

Xuejun Liao, Assistant Research Professor; Ph.D., Xidian University, Xi'an (China). Pattern recognition and machine learning, bioinformatics, signal processing.

Qing H. Liu, Professor; Ph.D., Illinois at Urbana-Champaign. Electromagnetics, antennas, medical imaging, photonics, acoustics, computational electromagnetics.

Daniel L. Marks, Assistant Research Professor; Ph.D., Illinois at Urbana-Champaign. Imaging and spectroscopy.

Hisham Z. Massoud, Professor; Ph.D., Stanford. Nanomaterial manufacturing and characterization, nanoscale/microscale computing systems, computer engineering, engineering education, electronic devices, manufacturing, semiconductors, microsystems.

James Morizio, Assistant Research Professor; Ph.D., Duke. Computer engineering, nanoscale/microscale computing systems, biological computing, mixed signal VLSI design, integrated analog CMOS circuit design.

Kenneth D. Morton Jr., Assistant Research Professor; Ph.D., Duke. Statistical signal processing, sensing and sensor systems, machine learning, land mine detection, acoustics.

Loren W. Nolte, Professor; Ph.D., Michigan. Sensing and sensor systems, medical imaging, signal processing.

Douglas P. Nowacek, Repass-Rodgers University Associate Professor of Conservation Technology and Associate Professor of ECE; Ph.D., MIT/Woods Hole Oceanographic Institution. Acoustics, micro-electronic mechanical machines.

Ekaterina Poutrina, Assistant Research Professor; Ph.D., Rochester. Theory of active and nonlinear metamaterials.

Matthew S. Reynolds, Nortel Networks Assistant Professor; Ph.D., MIT. RFID and its applications to robotics and human-computer interaction, ultra-low power sensing and computation, parasitic power and smart materials, surfaces, spaces.

Romit Roy Choudhury, Nortel Networks Associate Professor; Ph.D., Illinois at Urbana-Champaign. Computer engineering, antennas, electronic devices, wireless networking, mobile computing, distributed systems.

Guillermo Sapiro, Professor; D.Sc., Technion, Haifa (Israel). Image and video processing, computer graphics, computational vision, biomedical imaging, cryotomography of viruses.

David R. Smith, William Bevan Professor; Ph.D., California, San Diego. Photonics, metamaterials, electromagnetic, plasmonics.

Daniel J. Sorin, Associate Professor; Ph.D., Wisconsin–Madison. Computer engineering, computer architecture, fault tolerance, reliability.

Adrienne D. Stiff-Roberts, Associate Professor; Ph.D., Michigan. Nanomaterial manufacturing and characterization, semiconductor photonic devices, photonics, nanoscience.

Peter A. Torrione; Assistant Research Professor; Ph.D., Duke. Statistical signal processing, machine learning, pattern recognition, buried threat detection.

Kishor S. Trivedi; Hudson Professor (joint with Computer Science); Ph.D., Illinois at Urbana-Champaign. Computer engineering, failure analysis, fault tolerance, reliability, computer architecture.

Yaroslav A. Urzhumov, Assistant Research Professor; Ph.D., Texas at Austin. Numerical simulation of metamaterials and plasmonic nanosystems.

Rebecca Willett, Assistant Professor; Ph.D., Rice. Sensing and sensor systems, homeland security, medical imaging, K–12 education in science and mathematics, signal processing, photonics, distributed systems.

Gary A. Ybarra, Professor of the Practice; Ph.D., North Carolina State. Engineering education, K–12 education in science and mathematics, medical imaging.

Tomoyuki Yoshie, Assistant Professor; Ph.D., Caltech. Photonics, semiconductor photonic devices, nanoscale/microscale computing systems, quantum information, integrated nanoscale systems.

ECE Student, Duke Pratt School of Engineering.

Hudson Hall, Duke Pratt School of Engineering.

UNIVERSITY OF NEW MEXICO
Department of Electrical and Computer Engineering

The University of New Mexico

Programs of Study

Graduate work leading to the M.S. and Ph.D. degrees is offered by the Department in the areas of bioengineering, communications, computational intelligence, computer architecture, computer networks and systems, control systems, electromagnetics, image processing, microelectronics and optoelectronics, plasma science, and signal processing. The M.S. degree is also offered in optical science and engineering. The master's degree program requires 30 semester credit hours for a thesis option and 33 semester credit hours for a nonthesis option. The Ph.D. program requires that a minimum of 24 graduate credit hours beyond the master's degree be completed at the University of New Mexico (UNM). Additional course work and research leading to the dissertation are geared to the individual student's needs and interests. As a potential candidate for the Ph.D. program, each student must pass the Ph.D. qualifying examination to establish levels and areas of scholastic competence.

Research Facilities

The Department maintains state-of-the-art laboratories for computer vision and image processing, wireless communications, high-performance computing and networking, laser and electrooptics, microprocessors (including advanced DSP platforms and emerging architectures), microwaves and antennas, pulsed power and plasma science, real-time computing and embedded systems (including a number of mobile robots and advanced real-time development systems), solid-state fabrication, and virtual reality/advanced human-computer interfaces. In addition, the Department has a close affiliation with world-class research laboratories and terascale supercomputing platforms at the Sandia National Laboratories, the Air Force Research Laboratory, the Los Alamos National Laboratory, and the Mind Research Network. Sponsored research expenditures for the past three years were approximately $13 million each year.

Financial Aid

Support is available in the form of teaching, graduate, and research assistantships. Graduate internship programs are conducted with local industries, such as Sandia National Laboratories and the Air Force Research Laboratories. Annual stipends for full-time assistantships require no more than 20 hours of service per week for the academic year and include a tuition waiver of up to 12 credit hours per semester. Assistants are paid on a scale of $1250 to $2400 per month.

Cost of Study

In 2012–13, the tuition for students carrying 12 or more credit hours is $3296 for state residents and $10,604 for nonresidents per semester. All residents carrying 11 or fewer credit hours paid $277 per semester credit hour. Domestic students can meet the requirements for resident status by living continuously in New Mexico for at least one year prior to registration for the following semester and by providing satisfactory evidence of their intent to retain residency in New Mexico. International students must provide proof of financial support prior to admission to UNM.

Living and Housing Costs

Living costs in Albuquerque are somewhat lower than those in other cities of comparable size. In addition to tuition and fees, a single domestic student's expenses are estimated at $16,000 per year; expenses for a single international student are approximately $24,000 per year, including tuition and fees.

Student Group

Students come from all parts of the United States as well as from many other countries around the world. The graduate enrollment in the Department, including part-time students, is about 275, of whom 150 are post-M.S. or Ph.D. candidates. During the past two years, the Department has awarded seventy master's degrees and thirty-nine Ph.D. degrees.

Student Outcomes

The current demand for graduate engineers is excellent, and the employment rate for electrical engineering and computer engineering graduates has been almost 100 percent. Graduates of the Department have been employed in various positions, such as senior engineer, vice president, manufacturing, electronics engineer, and systems engineer. Examples of companies that hire the Department's graduates include Intel, Motorola, IBM, Ford, Agilent, Northrop Grumman, Boeing, ATK Mission Research, Microsoft, and Honeywell in addition to small entrepreneurial companies and the National Labs (Sandia, Los Alamos, etc.).

Location

Albuquerque's greater metropolitan population is more than 670,000 and is the largest city in New Mexico. The city offers a delightful and interesting blend of several cultures; a wide variety of cultural, artistic, and aesthetic events are available year-round. Many of these take place on the campus, while others are located in the city and neighboring pueblos. The Indian Pueblo Cultural Center, the National Atomic Museum, and the UNM Maxwell Museum of Anthropology are facilities of particular interest. Albuquerque lies between the low land of the Rio Grande and the towering 11,000-foot Sandia Mountains. In this "Land of Enchantment" environment, the climate is dry and warm, and sunny days are followed by cool nights. Hiking, fishing, ballooning, mountain climbing, and skiing are only a few of the recreational activities that are readily available.

The University and The Department

The University of New Mexico was established in 1889 and is situated on 600 acres in the center of metropolitan Albuquerque. It is the largest university in the state, with more than 30,000 students. UNM is a Carnegie-designated Doctoral/Research-Extensive University, one of only three in the U.S. In the most recent *U.S. News & World Report*, the electrical engineering program was ranked fifty-third in the nation and twenty-eighth among all public universities, while the computer engineering program was ranked seventy-second in the nation and forty-eighth among all public universities.

The resources of the University and its proximity to Sandia National Laboratories, Kirtland Air Force Base, and the Los Alamos National Laboratory provide an excellent environment for advanced studies and research.

Applying

Prospective domestic applicants should contact the Office of Graduate Studies as well as the Department of Electrical and Computer Engineering for the latest information and dates. The GRE General Test is required for admission to both the M.S. and Ph.D. programs. Applications, fees, and transcripts should be on file with the Office of Graduate Studies by July 1 for domestic students and February 15 for international students for the fall semester, by November 1 for domestic students and June 15 for international students for the spring semester, and by April 30 for the summer session.

Correspondence and Information

Graduate Office
Department of Electrical and Computer Engineering
MSC01 1100
1 University of New Mexico
Albuquerque, New Mexico 87131-0001
Phone: 505-277-2600
Fax: 505-277-1439
E-mail: gradinfo@ece.unm.edu
Web site: http://www.ece.unm.edu

THE FACULTY AND THEIR RESEARCH

Chaouki T. Abdallah, Professor, Provost and Executive Vice President for Academic Affairs; Ph.D., Georgia Tech. Control systems, control of computing systems, reconfigurable systems and networks.

Ganesh Balakrishnan, Assistant Professor; Ph.D., New Mexico. Semiconductor device development including epitaxy and characterization, high-power vertical-external-cavity surface-emitting lasers, novel semiconductor material development for mid-infrared lasers.

Steven R. J. Brueck, Distinguished Professor and Director, Center for High Technology Materials (CHTM); Ph.D., MIT. Nanoscale lithography and nanofabrication with applications to nanophotonics, nanofluidics, and nanoscale epitaxial growth and sources/detectors; tunable infrared lasers; ultrahigh resolution optical microscopy.

Vince D. Calhoun, Professor and Chief Technology Officer, The Research Network; Ph.D., Maryland, Baltimore County. Biomedical engineering, psychiatric neuroimaging, functional and structural magnetic resonance imaging (MRI), multimodal data fusion, neuroimaging genetics, medical image analysis.

Thomas P. Caudell, Professor; Ph.D., Arizona. Computational cognitive neurosciences, neural networks theory and simulation, virtual reality and visualization, art/science collaborations, evolutionary computation, high-performance computing, autonomous robotics.

Christos G. Christodoulou, Professor and Director, COSMIAC; Ph.D., North Carolina State. Modeling of electromagnetic systems, smart antennas, reconfigurable antennas, machine learning applications in electromagnetics, cognitive radio, RF/photonics.

Daniel F. Feezell, Assistant Professor; Ph.D., California, Santa Barbara. Group III-nitride semiconductors, solid-state lighting, visible lasers, vertical-cavity surface-emitting lasers, epitaxial growth and device fabrication, energy efficiency, renewable energy.

Rafael Fierro, Associate Professor; Ph.D., Texas at Arlington. Cooperative control of multi-agent systems, cyber-physical systems, mobile sensor and robotic networks, motion planning under sensing/communication constraints, optimization-based multivehicle coordination.

Charles B. Fleddermann, Professor; Associate Dean (Academic Affairs), School of Engineering; Ph.D., Illinois at Urbana-Champaign. Plasma processing, physical electronics, photovoltaics.

Nasir Ghani, Associate Professor, Associate Chair and Director of Graduate Programs; Ph.D., Waterloo. High-speed networking, cyber-infrastructures, protocols and architectures, cloud computing systems, network virtualization, traffic engineering, routing, routing, optical networks, integrated smart grids and power, performance evaluation, survivability, network simulation, stochastic modeling.

Mark A. Gilmore, Associate Professor; Ph.D., UCLA. Plasma physics, plasma diagnostics, magnetic confinement fusion, microwave engineering.

Majeed M. Hayat, Professor, Associate Director of CHTM, General Chair of Optical Science in Engineering; Ph.D., Wisconsin–Madison. Statistical communication theory, signal and image processing, algorithms for spectral sensing, avalanche photodiodes, optical communication, distributed computing, network modeling, applied probability and stochastic processes.

Gregory L. Heileman, Professor, Associate Provost for Curriculum; Ph.D., Central Florida. Data structures and algorithmic analysis; theory of information, security and computing; machine learning and pattern recognition.

Mani Hossein-Zadeh, Assistant Professor; Ph.D., USC. Electrooptics, microwave-photonic devices and systems, ultra-high-Q optical microresonators, optomechanical interaction in UH-Q optical resonators, optical communication, photonic sensors, optofluidics and plasmonics.

Ravinder K. Jain, Professor; Ph.D., Berkeley. Quantum electronics, optoelectronics, electrooptics, experimental solid-state physics.

Sudharman K. Jayaweera, Associate Professor; Ph.D., Princeton. Wireless communications, statistical signal processing, network information theory, cognitive radios, cooperative communications, information theoretic aspects of networked control systems, smart-grid communications and control, wireless mobile sensor networks.

Ramiro Jordan, Associate Professor, Associate Chair and Director of Undergraduate Programs, Founder and Executive VP, Ibero American Science and Technology Consortium (ISTEC); Ph.D., Kansas State. Communications, wireless sensor networks, multidimensional signal processing and embedded systems.

Sanjay Krishna, Professor; Ph.D., Michigan. Investigation of nanostructured semiconductor materials for mid infrared lasers, detectors, nanoscale materials consisting of self-assembled quantum dots, strain-layer superlattices for next generation bio-inspired sensors using metamaterials and plasmonics.

Olga Lavrova, Assistant Professor; Ph.D., California, Santa Barbara. Photovoltaics and nanoscale semiconductor structures for photovoltaic applications; smart-grid and emerging energy generation, distribution, and storage technologies.

Luke F. Lester, Professor and Interim Chair; Ph.D., Cornell. RF photonics, solar cells, semiconductor lasers, and quantum dot devices.

Meeko Oishi, Assistant Professor, Ph.D., Stanford. Cyber-physical systems, hybrid control theory, nonlinear dynamical systems, verification of human-automation interaction, assistive technologies, control-based modeling of Parkinson's disease.

Marek Osinski, Professor; Ph.D., Institute of Physics, Polish Academy of Sciences. Magnetic nanoparticles, nanotechnology, colloidal nanocrystals, nuclear radiation detectors, semiconductor lasers, optoelectronic devices and materials, integrated optoelectronic circuits, group-III nitrides, degradation mechanisms and reliability, computer simulation, biomedical applications of nanocrystals.

Marios S. Pattichis, Professor; Ph.D., Texas at Austin. Biomedical image and video processing and communications, medical imaging, dynamically reconfigurable systems, general methods for image and video analysis.

Fernando Perez-Gonzalez, Professor, Prince of Asturias Endowed Chair; Ph.D., Vigo (Spain). Information forensics and security, digital watermarking, cognitive radio, digital communications, adaptive algorithms.

James F. Plusquellic, Associate Professor; Ph.D., Pittsburgh. IC Trust, design for manufacturability, defect-based and data-driven VLSI test, small delay faulty test, model-to-hardware correlation and IC fabrication process monitors.

L. Howard Pollard, Assistant Professor; Ph.D., Illinois at Urbana-Champaign. Computer architecture, digital design, fault tolerance, microprocessors, FPGA systems, space electronics.

Balu Santhanam, Associate Professor; Ph.D., Georgia Tech. Digital signal processing, statistical communication theory, adaptive filtering, time-frequency analysis and representations, multicomponent AM-FM signal modeling, SAR-based vibrometry and related nonstationary signal analysis, ICA-related signal separation and classification.

Edl Schamiloglu, Professor; Ph.D., Cornell. Physics and technology of charged particle beam generation and propagation, high-power microwave sources and effects, pulsed-power science and technologies, plasma physics and diagnostics, electromagnetics and wave propagation, neurosystems engineering.

Wei Wennie Shu, Associate Professor, Associate Dean for Graduate Recruitment; Ph.D., Illinois at Urbana-Champaign. Distributed systems, high performance computing, wireless networking, mobile ad-hoc and sensor networks, biomed modeling and simulation.

Payman Zarkesh-Ha, Associate Professor; Ph.D., Georgia Tech. Statistical modeling of VLSI systems, design for manufacturability, low-power and high-performance VLSI design.

Joint Appointees

Edward S. Angel, Professor Emeritus; Ph.D., USC. Computer graphics, scientific visualization.

Jean-Claude M. Diels, Professor; Ph.D., Brussels (Belgium). Laser physics and nonlinear optics, ultrafast phenomena.

Frank L. Gilfeather, Professor; Ph.D., California, Irvine. High-performance computing applications, intelligence analysis, functional analysis.

Sang M. Han, Professor; Ph.D., California, Santa Barbara. Heteroepitaxial integration of Ge and III-V material systems on Si for photovolatic and high-speed transistor applications; integration of semiconductor nanocrystals (NCs) in usable matrices for photovoltaic, nonlinear optical, and biological applications;

synthetic modification of semiconductor surfaces for sensing applications; hybrid micro/nanofluidic systems for advanced bioseparation and analysis.

Terran D. R. Lane, Associate Professor; Ph.D., Purdue. Machine learning, including applications to bioinformatics, information security, user and cognitive modeling, and neuroimaging; reinforcement learning, behavior, and control; artificial intelligence in general.

Zayd Chad Leseman, Associate Professor; Ph.D., Illinois at Urbana-Champaign. MEMS, NEMS, photonic and phononic crystals, thin film growth and characterization, carbon nanostructures.

Ronald Lumia, Professor; Ph.D., Virginia. Robotics, automation, image processing.

Stefan Posse, Professor; Ph.D., Berne (Switzerland). Biomedical MR imaging and spectroscopy, basic research and clinical applications in human brain and breast, real-time functional MRI and high-speed metabolic imaging.

Timothy J. Ross, Professor; Ph.D., Stanford. Structural system reliability, structural dynamics, autonomous control, fuzzy logic, fuzzy set theory, risk assessment.

Wolfgang G. Rudolph, Professor; Ph.D., Jena (Germany). Laser physics, ultrashort light pulses, time-resolved spectroscopy and imaging.

Mansoor Sheik-Bahae, Professor; Ph.D., SUNY at Buffalo. Lasers and photonics, coherent and ultrafast processes in semiconductors, laser cooling of solids, nonlinear optics.

Mahmoud Reda Taha, Professor; Ph.D., Calgary (Canada). Structural health monitoring, application of artificial intelligence in structural engineering and biomechanics.

Research Professors

Alexander Albrecht, Research Assistant Professor; Ph.D., New Mexico.

Ladan Arissian, Research Assistant Professor; Ph.D., New Mexico.

Jerald C. Buchenauer, Research Professor; Ph.D., Cornell.

Hyun Ju Connor, Postdoctoral Fellow; Ph.D., New Hampshire.

Larry Ralph Dawson, Research Professor; Ph.D., USC.

David Dietz, Research Professor; Ph.D., Indiana.

Abdel-Rahman A. El-Emawy, Research Associate Professor; Ph.D., Colorado State.

Mikhail Isaakovich Fuks, Research Professor; Ph.D., Gorky State (Russia).

John A. Gaudet, Research Professor; Ph.D., Air Force Tech.

Edward D. Graham, Lecturer and Research Professor; Ph.D., North Carolina State.

Michael John Healy, Research Scholar; M.S., Idaho.

Craig Kief, Research Scholar; M.S., New Mexico.

Daryl O. Lee, Lecturer and Research Professor; Ph.D., SMU.

Seung-Chang Lee, Research Associate Professor; Ph.D., Hanyang (Seoul).

Alan G. Lynn, Research Assistant Professor; Ph.D., Texas at Austin.

Sayan D. Mukherjee, Research Professor; Ph.D.

Asal Naseri-Kouzehgarani, Research Assistant Professor; Ph.D., Illinois at Urbana-Champaign.

Matthew P. Pepin, Postdoctoral Fellow; Ph.D., Air Force Tech.

Andrew C. Pineda, Senior Research Scientist; Ph.D., Harvard.

Sarita D. Prasad, Postdoctoral Fellow; Ph.D., New Mexico.

Elena A. Plis, Research Assistant Professor; Ph.D., New Mexico.

Thomas J. Rotter, Research Assistant Professor; Ph.D., New Mexico.

Yagyadeva D. Sharma, Research Assistant Professor; Ph.D., New Delhi (India).

Gennady Smolyakov, Research Assistant Professor; Ph.D., Saratov State (Russia).

Mehmet F. Su, Research Assistant Professor; Ph.D., New Mexico.

Steven C. Suddarth, Research Professor; Ph.D., Washington (Seattle).

Youssef A. Tawk, Postdoctoral Fellow; Ph.D., New Mexico.

G. Alonzo Vera, Research Assistant Professor; Ph.D., New Mexico.

Gregory von Winckel, Research Associate Professor; Ph.D., New Mexic

Research Centers Associated with The Department

Center for High Technology Materials (CHTM). Creating a leading optoelectronics and nanotechnology research center is the primary goal of the CHTM, an interdisciplinary organization that sponsors and encourages research efforts in the Departments of Electrical and Computer Engineering, Physics and Astronomy, Chemistry, and Chemical and Nuclear Engineering. CHTM's multilateral mission involves both research and education. It is dedicated to encouraging and strengthening interactions and the flow of technology among the University, government laboratories, and private industry, while promoting economic development in the state.

The Mind Research Network (MRN). MRN is a nonprofit partnership dedicated to the discovery and advancement of clinical solutions for the prevention, diagnosis, and treatment of mental illness and other brain disorders. Headquartered in Albuquerque, New Mexico, MRN consists of in-house scientists, as well as an interdisciplinary association of research partners located at universities, national laboratories, and research centers around the country that are focused on imaging technology and its emergence as an integral element of neurodiagnostic discovery. MRN has a strong relationship with and hosts faculty and graduate students from multiple UNM departments including Electrical and Computer Engineering, Math and Statistics, Computer Science, Biology, Neurosciences, and Psychiatry.

MRN specializes in the following areas of research: schizophrenia, addiction, forensic and social cognitive neuroscience, neuroinformatics, image/signal processing, machine learning, autism, traumatic brain injury (TBI), and neurodevelopment. In addition to advanced information technology and neuroinformatics capabilities, MRN also has MRI (3.0 Tesla Siemens TIM Trio, 1.5 Tesla mobile Siemens Avanto), magnetoencephalography (MEG), electroencephalography (EEG), and neurogenetics resources available.

Section 10
Energy and Power Engineering

This section contains a directory of institutions offering graduate work in energy and power engineering. Additional information about programs listed in the directory but not augmented by an in-depth entry may be obtained by writing directly to the dean of a graduate school or chair of a department at the address given in the directory.

For programs offering related work, see also in this book *Computer Science and Information Technology, Engineering and Applied Sciences, Industrial Engineering,* and *Mechanical Engineering and Mechanics.* In another guide in this series:

Graduate Programs in the Physical Sciences, Mathematics, Agricultural Sciences, the Environment & Natural Resources

See *Physics* and *Mathematical Sciences*

CONTENTS

Program Directories

Energy and Power Engineering

Appalachian State University, Cratis D. Williams Graduate School, Department of Technology, Boone, NC 28608. Offers appropriate technology (MS); renewable energy engineering (MS). Part-time programs available. *Faculty:* 18 full-time (5 women), 4 part-time/adjunct (1 woman). *Students:* 38 full-time (7 women), 5 part-time (1 woman); includes 3 minority (1 Black or African American, non-Hispanic/Latino; 1 American Indian or Alaska Native, non-Hispanic/Latino; 1 Asian, non-Hispanic/Latino), 1 international. 28 applicants, 82% accepted, 12 enrolled. In 2011, 19 master's awarded. *Degree requirements:* For master's, comprehensive exam, thesis optional. *Entrance requirements:* For master's, GRE General Test, 3 letters of recommendation. Additional exam requirements/recommendations for international students: Required—TOEFL (minimum score 550 paper-based; 230 computer-based; 79 iBT), IELTS (minimum score 6.5). *Application deadline:* For fall admission, 3/15 priority date for domestic students, 2/1 for international students; for spring admission, 11/1 for domestic students, 7/1 for international students. Applications are processed on a rolling basis. Application fee: $55. Electronic applications accepted. *Expenses:* Tuition, state resident: full-time $4040; part-time $180 per semester hour. Tuition, nonresident: full-time $15,900; part-time $760 per semester hour. *Required fees:* $2500; $20 per semester hour. Tuition and fees vary according to campus/location. *Financial support:* In 2011–12, 14 research assistantships (averaging $9,000 per year) were awarded; fellowships, teaching assistantships, career-related internships or fieldwork, Federal Work-Study, institutionally sponsored loans, scholarships/grants, and unspecified assistantships also available. Financial award application deadline: 4/1; financial award applicants required to submit FAFSA. *Faculty research:* Wind power, biofuels, green construction, solar energy production. *Total annual research expenditures:* $322,000. *Unit head:* Dr. Jeff Tiller, Chair, 828-262-6351, E-mail: tillerjs@appstate.edu. *Application contact:* Dr. Marie Hoepfl, Graduate Program Director, 828-262-6351, E-mail: hoepflmc@appstate.edu. Web site: http://www.tec.appstate.edu.

Florida State University, The Graduate School, FAMU-FSU College of Engineering, Department of Mechanical Engineering, Tallahassee, FL 32310-6046. Offers mechanical engineering (MS, PhD); sustainable energy (MS). Part-time programs available. *Faculty:* 17 full-time (1 woman), 4 part-time/adjunct (0 women). *Students:* 72 full-time (12 women); includes 8 minority (5 Black or African American, non-Hispanic/Latino; 3 Hispanic/Latino), 25 international. 113 applicants, 72% accepted, 15 enrolled. In 2011, 18 master's, 9 doctorates awarded. Terminal master's awarded for partial completion of doctoral program. *Degree requirements:* For master's, thesis optional; for doctorate, thesis/dissertation, 45 credit hours (21 coursework, 24 research). *Entrance requirements:* For master's and doctorate, GRE General Test (minimum scores: Verbal 150, Quantitative 155), minimum GPA of 3.0, official transcripts, resume, personal statement, 3 letters of recommendation. Additional exam requirements/recommendations for international students: Required—TOEFL (minimum score 550 paper-based; 213 computer-based; 80 iBT), IELTS (minimum score 6.5), Michigan English Language Assessment Battery (minimum score 77). *Application deadline:* For fall admission, 5/1 for domestic and international students; for spring admission, 10/1 for domestic and international students. Applications are processed on a rolling basis. Application fee: $30. Electronic applications accepted. *Expenses:* Tuition, state resident: full-time $9474; part-time $350.88 per credit hour. Tuition, nonresident: full-time $16,236; part-time $601.34 per credit hour. *Required fees:* $630 per semester. One-time fee: $20. Tuition and fees vary according to course load and campus/location. *Financial support:* In 2011–12, fellowships with full tuition reimbursements (averaging $30,000 per year), 55 research assistantships with full tuition reimbursements (averaging $20,000 per year), 11 teaching assistantships with full tuition reimbursements (averaging $20,000 per year) were awarded; career-related internships or fieldwork, institutionally sponsored loans, scholarships/grants, health care benefits, tuition waivers (partial), and unspecified assistantships also available. Support available to part-time students. Financial award applicants required to submit FAFSA. *Faculty research:* Aero-propulsion, superconductivity, smart materials, nano-materials, intelligent robotic systems, robotic locomotion, sustainable energy. *Total annual research expenditures:* $5 million. *Unit head:* Dr. Emmanuel Collins, Chair, 850-410-6373, Fax: 850-410-6337, E-mail: ecollins@eng.fsu.edu. *Application contact:* George Green, Coordinator of Graduate Studies, 850-410-6196, Fax: 850-410-6337, E-mail: ggreen@admin.fsu.edu. Web site: http://www.eng.fsu.edu/me/.

Instituto Tecnologico de Santo Domingo, Graduate School, Area of Basic And Environmental Sciences, Santo Domingo, Dominican Republic. Offers environmental science (M En S), including environmental education, environmental management, marine resources, natural resources management; mathematics (MS, PhD); renewable energy technology (MS, Certificate).

Lehigh University, P.C. Rossin College of Engineering and Applied Science, Program in Energy Systems Engineering, Bethlehem, PA 18015. Offers M Eng. *Faculty:* 1 part-time/adjunct (0 women). *Students:* 20 full-time (0 women), 3 part-time (0 women), 4 international. Average age 24. 162 applicants, 24% accepted, 0 enrolled. In 2011, 22 master's awarded. *Entrance requirements:* For master's, GRE. Additional exam requirements/recommendations for international students: Required—TOEFL (minimum score 79 iBT). *Application deadline:* For fall admission, 5/15 for domestic and international students. Applications are processed on a rolling basis. Application fee: $75. Electronic applications accepted. *Financial support:* In 2011–12, 14 students received support. Scholarships/grants available. Financial award application deadline: 1/15. *Unit head:* Martha Dodge, Director, 610-758-3529, E-mail: mds482@lehigh.edu. *Application contact:* Emily Kissel, Graduate Coordinator, 610-758-3650, E-mail: inesei@lehigh.edu. Web site: http://www.lehigh.edu/esei.

Marylhurst University, Department of Business Administration, Marylhurst, OR 97036-0261. Offers finance (MBA); general management (MBA); government policy and administration (MBA); green development (MBA); health care management (MBA); marketing (MBA); natural and organic resources (MBA); nonprofit management (MBA); organizational behavior (MBA); real estate (MBA); renewable energy (MBA); sustainable business (MBA). Part-time and evening/weekend programs available. Postbaccalaureate distance learning degree programs offered (no on-campus study). *Faculty:* 3 full-time (0 women), 36 part-time/adjunct (6 women). *Students:* 29 full-time (15 women), 675 part-time (373 women); includes 178 minority (59 Black or African American, non-Hispanic/Latino; 6 American Indian or Alaska Native, non-Hispanic/Latino; 34 Asian, non-Hispanic/Latino; 46 Hispanic/Latino; 4 Native Hawaiian or other Pacific Islander, non-Hispanic/Latino; 29 Two or more races, non-Hispanic/Latino), 14 international. Average age 37. 262 applicants, 91% accepted, 194 enrolled. In 2011, 352 master's awarded. *Degree requirements:* For master's, comprehensive exam, capstone course. *Entrance requirements:* For master's, GMAT (if GPA less than 3.0 and fewer than 5 years of work experience), interview, resume, 2 letters of recommendation. Additional exam requirements/recommendations for international students: Recommended—TOEFL (minimum score 550 paper-based; 213 computer-based; 80 iBT). *Application deadline:* For fall admission, 9/11 priority date for domestic students, 9/11 for international students; for winter admission, 12/15 priority date for domestic students, 12/15 for international students; for spring admission, 3/15 priority date for domestic students, 3/17 for international students. Applications are processed on a rolling basis. Application fee: $50. Electronic applications accepted. *Expenses:* Tuition: Full-time $14,796; part-time $548 per quarter hour. Tuition and fees vary according to program. *Financial support:* Scholarships/grants available. Support available to part-time students. Financial award applicants required to submit FAFSA. *Unit head:* David McNamee, Interim Chair, 503-636-8141, Fax: 503-697-5597, E-mail: mba@marylhurst.edu. *Application contact:* Maruska Lynch, Graduate Admissions Specialist, 800-634-9982 Ext. 6322, Fax: 503-699-6320, E-mail: admissions@marylhurst.edu. Web site: http://www.marylhurst.edu/.

New Jersey Institute of Technology, Office of Graduate Studies, Newark College of Engineering, Department of Electrical and Computer Engineering, Program in Power and Energy Systems, Newark, NJ 07102. Offers MS. Part-time and evening/weekend programs available. Postbaccalaureate distance learning degree programs offered. *Students:* 15 full-time (3 women), 21 part-time (1 woman); includes 20 minority (3 Black or African American, non-Hispanic/Latino; 9 Asian, non-Hispanic/Latino; 8 Hispanic/Latino), 9 international. Average age 29. 73 applicants, 53% accepted, 10 enrolled. In 2011, 4 master's awarded. *Degree requirements:* For master's, thesis optional. *Entrance requirements:* For master's, GRE General Test. Additional exam requirements/recommendations for international students: Required—TOEFL (minimum score 550 paper-based; 213 computer-based; 79 iBT). *Application deadline:* For fall admission, 6/1 priority date for domestic students, 5/1 for international students; for spring admission, 11/15 priority date for domestic students, 11/15 for international students. Applications are processed on a rolling basis. Application fee: $65. Electronic applications accepted. *Expenses:* Tuition, state resident: full-time $7980; part-time $867 per credit. Tuition, nonresident: full-time $11,336; part-time $1196 per credit. *Required fees:* $230 per credit. *Financial support:* Application deadline: 3/15. *Unit head:* Dr. Nirwan Ansari, Director, 973-596-3670, E-mail: nirwan.ansari@njit.edu. *Application contact:* Kathryn Kelly, Director of Admissions, 973-596-3300, Fax: 973-596-3461, E-mail: admissions@njit.edu. Web site: http://ece.njit.edu/academics/graduate/ms-powerandenergy/.

New York Institute of Technology, Graduate Division, School of Engineering and Computing Sciences, Program in Energy Management, Old Westbury, NY 11568-8000. Offers energy management (MS); energy technology (Advanced Certificate); environmental management (Advanced Certificate); facilities management (Advanced Certificate). Part-time and evening/weekend programs available. Postbaccalaureate distance learning degree programs offered. *Students:* 48 full-time (8 women), 97 part-time (17 women); includes 32 minority (11 Black or African American, non-Hispanic/Latino; 1 American Indian or Alaska Native, non-Hispanic/Latino; 4 Asian, non-Hispanic/Latino; 15 Hispanic/Latino; 1 Two or more races, non-Hispanic/Latino), 31 international. Average age 32. In 2011, 53 master's, 28 other advanced degrees awarded. *Degree requirements:* For master's, comprehensive exam, thesis or alternative. *Entrance requirements:* For master's, minimum QPA of 2.85. Additional exam requirements/recommendations for international students: Required—TOEFL (minimum score 550 paper-based; 213 computer-based). *Application deadline:* For fall admission, 7/1 priority date for domestic students; for spring admission, 12/1 priority date for domestic students. Applications are processed on a rolling basis. Application fee: $50. Electronic applications accepted. *Expenses:* Tuition: Part-time $930 per credit hour. *Financial support:* Fellowships, research assistantships with partial tuition reimbursements, institutionally sponsored loans, tuition waivers (full and partial), and unspecified assistantships available. Support available to part-time students. Financial award applicants required to submit FAFSA. *Unit head:* Dr. Robert Amundsen, Department Chair, 516-686-7578, E-mail: ramundse@nyit.edu. *Application contact:* Dr. Jacquelyn Nealon, Vice President for Enrollment Services, 516-686-7925, Fax: 516-686-7597, E-mail: jnealon@nyit.edu.

North Carolina Agricultural and Technical State University, School of Graduate Studies, College of Engineering, Department of Electrical and Computer Engineering, Greensboro, NC 27411. Offers electrical engineering (MSEE, PhD), including communications and signal processing, computer engineering, electronic and optical materials and devices, power systems and control. Part-time programs available. *Degree requirements:* For master's, project, thesis defense; for doctorate, thesis/dissertation. *Entrance requirements:* For master's, GRE General Test, GRE Subject Test, minimum GPA of 2.8; for doctorate, GRE General Test, minimum GPA of 3.0. *Faculty research:* Semiconductor compounds, VLSI design, image processing, optical systems and devices, fault-tolerant computing.

Northeastern University, College of Engineering, Program in Energy Systems, Boston, MA 02115-5096. Offers MS. Part-time programs available. *Students:* 31 full-time, 7 part-time. Average age 25. 58 applicants, 76% accepted, 26 enrolled. *Entrance requirements:* For master's, GRE General Test. Additional exam requirements/recommendations for international students: Required—TOEFL (minimum score 550 paper-based; 213 computer-based). *Application deadline:* For fall admission, 1/15 for domestic and international students. Applications are processed on a rolling basis. Application fee: $50. Electronic applications accepted. *Financial support:* Career-related internships or fieldwork, Federal Work-Study, scholarships/grants, tuition waivers (full), and unspecified assistantships available. Support available to part-time students. Financial award application deadline: 1/15; financial award applicants required to submit FAFSA. *Unit head:* Dr. Yaman Yener, Associate Dean of Engineering for Research and Graduate Studies, 617-373-2711, Fax: 617-373-2501. *Application contact:* Jeffrey Hengel, Admissions Specialist, 617-373-2711, Fax: 617-373-2501, E-mail: grad-eng@coe.neu.edu. Web site: http://www.coe.neu.edu/gse/programs/ES/.

Santa Clara University, School of Engineering, Program in Electrical Engineering, Santa Clara, CA 95053. Offers analog circuit design (Certificate); ASIC design and test (Certificate); digital signal processing (Certificate); electrical engineering (MS, PhD, Engineer); fundamentals of electrical engineering (Certificate); microwave and antennas (Certificate); renewable energy (Certificate). Part-time and evening/weekend programs available. *Students:* 46 full-time (11 women), 93 part-time (14 women); includes 48 minority (2 Black or African American, non-Hispanic/Latino; 43 Asian, non-Hispanic/Latino; 2 Hispanic/Latino; 1 Native Hawaiian or other Pacific Islander, non-Hispanic/Latino), 47 international. Average age 32. 128 applicants, 46% accepted, 30 enrolled. In 2011, 59 master's, 5 doctorates, 7 other advanced degrees awarded. *Degree requirements:* For master's, thesis (for some programs); for doctorate, thesis/dissertation; for other advanced degree, thesis. *Entrance requirements:* For master's, GRE, transcript; for doctorate, GRE, master's degree or equivalent; for other advanced degree, master's degree, published paper. Additional exam requirements/recommendations for international students: Required—TOEFL (minimum score 550 paper-based; 213 computer-based; 79 iBT). *Application deadline:* For fall admission, 8/12 for domestic students, 7/15 for international students; for winter admission, 10/28 for domestic students, 9/23 for international students; for spring admission, 2/25 for domestic students, 1/21 for international students. Applications are processed on a rolling basis. Application fee: $60. Electronic applications accepted. *Expenses:* Contact institution. *Financial support:* Research assistantships and teaching assistantships available. Financial award application deadline: 3/2; financial award applicants required to submit FAFSA. *Faculty research:* Thermal and electrical nanoscale transport (TENT). *Unit head:* Dr. Alex Zecevic, Associate Dean for Graduate Studies, 408-554-2394, E-mail: azecevic@scu.edu. *Application contact:* Stacey Tinker, Director of Enrollment Management, 408-554-4748, Fax: 408-554-4323, E-mail: stinker@scu.edu.

Santa Clara University, School of Engineering, Program in Sustainable Energy, Santa Clara, CA 95053. Offers MS. Part-time and evening/weekend programs available. *Students:* 4 full-time (2 women), 2 part-time (0 women); includes 2 minority (both Asian, non-Hispanic/Latino), 3 international. Average age 28. 6 applicants, 100% accepted, 5 enrolled. *Entrance requirements:* For master's, GRE, undergraduate degree in a field of engineering or physics. Additional exam requirements/recommendations for international students: Required—TOEFL (minimum score 550 paper-based; 213 computer-based; 79 iBT) or IELTS. *Application deadline:* For fall admission, 8/12 for domestic students, 7/15 for international students; for winter admission, 10/28 for domestic students, 9/23 for international students; for spring admission, 2/25 for domestic students, 1/21 for international students. Applications are processed on a rolling basis. Application fee: $60. Electronic applications accepted. *Financial support:* Application deadline: 3/2; applicants required to submit FAFSA. *Unit head:* Dr. Samiha Mourad, Advisor, 408-554-4313, E-mail: smourad@scu.edu. *Application contact:* Stacey Tinker, Director of Enrollment Management, 408-554-4748, Fax: 408-554-4323, E-mail: stinker@scu.edu. Web site: http://www.scu.edu/engineering/graduate/academics/msenergy.cfm.

Southern Illinois University Carbondale, Graduate School, College of Engineering, Program in Engineering Science, Carbondale, IL 62901-4701. Offers electrical systems (PhD); fossil energy (PhD); mechanics (PhD). *Faculty:* 55 full-time (3 women), 3 part-time/adjunct (0 women). *Students:* 12 full-time (1 woman), 34 part-time (7 women); includes 5 minority (2 Black or African American, non-Hispanic/Latino; 3 Asian, non-Hispanic/Latino), 28 international. 22 applicants, 55% accepted, 7 enrolled. In 2011, 3 doctorates awarded. *Degree requirements:* For doctorate, thesis/dissertation. *Entrance requirements:* For doctorate, GRE General Test, minimum GPA of 3.5. Additional exam requirements/recommendations for international students: Required—TOEFL. Application fee: $20. *Financial support:* In 2011–12, 13 students received support. Fellowships with full tuition reimbursements available, research assistantships with full tuition reimbursements available, teaching assistantships with full tuition reimbursements available, Federal Work-Study, institutionally sponsored loans, and tuition waivers (full) available. Support available to part-time students. *Unit head:* Dr. Josh Nicklow, Associate Dean, 618-453-7746, Fax: 618-453-4235. *Application contact:* Anna Maria Alms, Student Contact, 618-453-4321, Fax: 618-453-4235, E-mail: amalms@siu.edu.

Universidad Autonoma de Guadalajara, Graduate Programs, Guadalajara, Mexico. Offers administrative law and justice (LL M); advertising and corporate communications (MA); architecture (M Arch); business (MBA); computational science (MCC); education (Ed M, Ed D); English-Spanish translation (MA); entrepreneurship and management (MBA); integrated management of digital animation (MA); international business (MIB); international corporate law (LL M); internet technologies (MS); manufacturing systems (MMS); occupational health (MS); philosophy (MA, PhD); power electronics (MS); quality systems (MQS); renewable energy (MS); social evaluation of projects (MBA); strategic market research (MBA); tax law (MA); teaching mathematics (MA).

University of Alberta, Faculty of Graduate Studies and Research, Department of Electrical and Computer Engineering, Edmonton, AB T6G 2E1, Canada. Offers communications (M Eng, M Sc, PhD); computer engineering (M Eng, M Sc, PhD); electromagnetics (M Eng, M Sc, PhD); nanotechnology and microdevices (M Eng, M Sc, PhD); power/power electronics (M Eng, M Sc, PhD); systems (M Eng, M Sc, PhD). Terminal master's awarded for partial completion of doctoral program. *Degree requirements:* For master's, thesis; for doctorate, thesis/dissertation. *Entrance requirements:* Additional exam requirements/recommendations for international students: Required—TOEFL. Electronic applications accepted. *Faculty research:* Controls, communications, microelectronics, electromagnetics.

University of Massachusetts Lowell, College of Engineering, Program in Energy Engineering, Lowell, MA 01854-2881. Offers MS Eng, D Eng, PhD. *Degree requirements:* For master's, thesis optional. *Entrance requirements:* For master's, GRE General Test. Additional exam requirements/recommendations for international students: Required—TOEFL.

University of Memphis, Graduate School, Herff College of Engineering, Department of Mechanical Engineering, Memphis, TN 38152. Offers design and mechanical engineering (MS); energy systems (MS); industrial engineering (MS); mechanical engineering (PhD); mechanical systems (MS); power systems (MS). Part-time programs available. Terminal master's awarded for partial completion of doctoral program. *Degree requirements:* For master's, comprehensive exam, thesis; for doctorate, comprehensive exam, thesis/dissertation. *Entrance requirements:* For master's, GRE General Test, BS in mechanical engineering, minimum undergraduate GPA of 3.0. *Faculty research:* Computational fluid dynamics, computational mechanics, integrated design, nondestructive testing, operations research.

University of Michigan, College of Engineering, Interpro Programs in Engineering, Ann Arbor, MI 48109. Offers automotive engineering (M Eng); design science (PhD); energy systems engineering (MS); financial engineering (MS); global automotive and manufacturing engineering (M Eng); manufacturing engineering (M Eng, D Eng); pharmaceutical engineering (M Eng); robotics and autonomous vehicles (M Eng); MBA/M Eng; MSE/MS. Part-time programs available. Postbaccalaureate distance learning degree programs offered (no on-campus study). *Students:* 225 full-time (55 women), 273 part-time (37 women). In 2011, 145 master's, 1 doctorate awarded. Terminal master's awarded for partial completion of doctoral program. *Degree requirements:* For master's, capstone project; for doctorate, thesis/dissertation. *Entrance requirements:* For master's, GRE; for doctorate, GRE, 2 years of work experience. Additional exam requirements/recommendations for international students: Required—TOEFL (minimum score 560 paper-based; 220 computer-based). *Application deadline:* Applications are processed on a rolling basis. Application fee: $65 ($75 for international students). Electronic applications accepted. *Financial support:* Fellowships, research assistantships with full tuition reimbursements, teaching assistantships with full tuition reimbursements, career-related internships or fieldwork, scholarships/grants, and unspecified assistantships available. Financial award application deadline: 2/15; financial award applicants required to submit FAFSA. *Faculty research:* Automotive engineering, design science, energy systems engineering, engineering sustainable systems dual degree, financial engineering, global automotive and manufacturing engineering, integrated microsystems, manufacturing engineering, pharmaceutical engineering, robotics and autonomous vehicles. *Unit head:* Prof. Panos Papalambros,

Director, 734-763-0480, Fax: 734-647-0079, E-mail: pyp@umich.edu. *Application contact:* Patti Mackmiller, Program Manager, 734-764-3071, Fax: 734-647-2243, E-mail: pmackmil@umich.edu. Web site: http://interpro-academics.engin.umich.edu/.

University of Nevada, Las Vegas, Graduate College, Greenspun College of Urban Affairs, School of Environmental and Public Affairs, Las Vegas, NV 89154-4030. Offers crisis and emergency management (MS); environmental science (MS, PhD); non-profit management (Certificate); public administration (MPA); public affairs (PhD); public management (Certificate); solar and renewabale energy (Certificate); urban leadership (MA); workforce development and organizational leadership (PhD). Part-time programs available. *Faculty:* 28 full-time (10 women), 53 part-time/adjunct (11 women). *Students:* 49 full-time (19 women), 117 part-time (57 women); includes 62 minority (31 Black or African American, non-Hispanic/Latino; 1 American Indian or Alaska Native, non-Hispanic/Latino; 4 Asian, non-Hispanic/Latino; 21 Hispanic/Latino; 5 Two or more races, non-Hispanic/Latino), 5 international. Average age 36. 94 applicants, 66% accepted, 47 enrolled. In 2011, 46 master's, 4 doctorates, 4 other advanced degrees awarded. *Degree requirements:* For master's, comprehensive exam (for some programs), thesis; for doctorate, comprehensive exam (for some programs), thesis/dissertation. *Entrance requirements:* Additional exam requirements/recommendations for international students: Required—TOEFL (minimum score 550 paper-based; 213 computer-based; 80 iBT), IELTS (minimum score 7). *Application deadline:* For fall admission, 2/15 priority date for domestic students, 5/1 for international students; for spring admission, 11/15 priority date for domestic students, 10/1 for international students. Applications are processed on a rolling basis. Application fee: $60 ($95 for international students). Electronic applications accepted. *Financial support:* In 2011–12, 33 students received support, including 20 research assistantships with partial tuition reimbursements available (averaging $11,193 per year), 13 teaching assistantships with partial tuition reimbursements available (averaging $10,928 per year); institutionally sponsored loans, scholarships/grants, health care benefits, and unspecified assistantships also available. Financial award application deadline: 3/1. *Faculty research:* Community and organizational resilience; environmental decision-making and management; budgeting and human resource/workforce management; urban design, sustainability and governance; public and non-profit management. *Total annual research expenditures:* $1.3 million. *Unit head:* Dr. Christopher Stream, Chair/Associate Professor, 702-895-5120, Fax: 702-895-4436, E-mail: chris.stream@unlv.edu. *Application contact:* Graduate College Admissions Evaluator, 702-895-3320, Fax: 702-895-4180, E-mail: gradcollege@unlv.edu. Web site: http://sepa.unlv.edu/.

University of Rochester, Hajim School of Engineering and Applied Sciences, Department of Chemical Engineering, Program in Alternative Energy, Rochester, NY 14627. Offers MS. *Students:* 6 full-time (2 women); includes 1 minority (Asian, non-Hispanic/Latino), 5 international. 15 applicants, 60% accepted, 4 enrolled. In 2011, 1 master's awarded. *Entrance requirements:* For master's, GRE. Additional exam requirements/recommendations for international students: Required—TOEFL. *Application deadline:* For fall admission, 1/15 for domestic students. Electronic applications accepted. *Expenses:* Tuition: Full-time $41,040. *Faculty research:* Solar cells, fuel cells, biofuels, nuclear fusion, nanotechnology. *Application contact:* Gina Eagan, Coordinator, 585-275-4913. Web site: http://www.che.rochester.edu/graduate/index.html.

The University of Tennessee, Graduate School, College of Engineering, Center for Interdisciplinary Research and Graduate Education, Knoxville, TN 37996. Offers energy science and engineering (PhD). *Students:* 8 full-time (2 women); includes 2 minority (1 Black or African American, non-Hispanic/Latino; 1 Asian, non-Hispanic/Latino), 1 international. Average age 29. 100 applicants, 28% accepted, 8 enrolled. *Degree requirements:* For doctorate, comprehensive exam, thesis/dissertation, qualifying examination. *Entrance requirements:* For doctorate, GRE General Test, research interest letter, resume/curriculum vitae; 3 letters of recommendation. Additional exam requirements/recommendations for international students: Required—TOEFL (minimum score 550 paper-based; 213 computer-based). *Application deadline:* For fall admission, 1/31 for domestic and international students. Applications are processed on a rolling basis. Application fee: $35. Electronic applications accepted. *Expenses:* Tuition, state resident: full-time $8332; part-time $464 per credit hour. Tuition, nonresident: full-time $25,174; part-time $1400 per credit hour. *Required fees:* $1162; $56 per credit hour. Tuition and fees vary according to program. *Financial support:* In 2011–12, 8 students received support, including 8 fellowships with full tuition reimbursements available (averaging $28,000 per year); health care benefits also available. Financial award application deadline: 1/31. *Faculty research:* Biomass processing for biofuels, cellulosic ethanol, and lignin repurposing; applied photosynthesis; nuclear fusion, reactor design and modeling; design and distribution of wind power; development of photovoltaic materials; fuel cell and battery design for energy conversion and storage; development of next generation SMART grid systems and novel grid management tools; climate change modeling, environmental, and planetary sciences as they relate to energy usage. *Unit head:* Dr. Lee Riedinger, Director, 865-974-7999, Fax: 865-974-9482, E-mail: lrieding@utk.edu. *Application contact:* 865-974-7999, Fax: 865-974-9482, E-mail: cire@utk.edu. Web site: http://cire.utk.edu/.

The University of Tennessee at Chattanooga, Graduate School, College of Engineering and Computer Science, Program in Engineering Management, Chattanooga, TN 37403. Offers engineering management (MS); fundamentals of engineering management (Graduate Certificate); power systems management (Graduate Certificate); project and value management (Graduate Certificate); quality management (Graduate Certificate). Postbaccalaureate distance learning degree programs offered (no on-campus study). *Faculty:* 5 full-time (1 woman), 2 part-time/adjunct (1 woman). *Students:* 14 full-time (2 women), 72 part-time (14 women); includes 17 minority (13 Black or African American, non-Hispanic/Latino; 2 Asian, non-Hispanic/Latino; 2 Hispanic/Latino). Average age 32. 52 applicants, 52% accepted, 14 enrolled. In 2011, 37 master's, 4 other advanced degrees awarded. *Degree requirements:* For master's, thesis. *Entrance requirements:* For master's, GRE General Test, letters of recommendation; minimum undergraduate GPA of 2.5 overall or 3.0 in senior year. Additional exam requirements/recommendations for international students: Required—TOEFL (minimum score 550 paper-based; 213 computer-based; 79 iBT), IELTS (minimum score 6). *Application deadline:* For fall admission, 8/1 priority date for domestic students, 6/1 for international students; for spring admission, 12/1 priority date for domestic students, 10/1 for international students. Applications are processed on a rolling basis. Application fee: $35. Electronic applications accepted. *Expenses:* Tuition, state resident: full-time $6472; part-time $359 per credit hour. Tuition, nonresident: full-time $20,006; part-time $1111 per credit hour. *Required fees:* $1320; $160 per credit hour. *Financial support:* Career-related internships or fieldwork, scholarships/grants, and unspecified assistantships available. Support available to part-time students. Financial award applicants required to submit FAFSA. *Faculty research:* Plant layout design, lean manufacturing, six sigma, value management, product development. *Unit head:* Dr. Neslihan Alp, Director, 423-425-4032, Fax: 423-425-5229, E-mail: neslihan-alp@utc.edu. *Application contact:* Dr. Jerald Ainsworth, Dean of Graduate Studies, 423-

425-4478, Fax: 423-425-5223, E-mail: jerald-ainsworth@utc.edu. Web site: http://www.utc.edu/Departments/engrcs/engm/index.php.

University of Wisconsin–Madison, Graduate School, College of Engineering, Department of Mechanical Engineering, Madison, WI 53706-1380. Offers energy systems (ME); engine systems (ME); mechanical engineering (MS, PhD); polymers (ME). Part-time programs available. Postbaccalaureate distance learning degree programs offered (no on-campus study). *Faculty:* 33 full-time (3 women), 1 part-time/adjunct (0 women). *Students:* 191 full-time (17 women), 18 part-time (1 woman); includes 23 minority (1 Black or African American, non-Hispanic/Latino; 1 American Indian or Alaska Native, non-Hispanic/Latino; 10 Asian, non-Hispanic/Latino; 10 Hispanic/Latino; 1 Native Hawaiian or other Pacific Islander, non-Hispanic/Latino). Average age 25. 615 applicants, 19% accepted, 46 enrolled. In 2011, 56 master's, 16 doctorates awarded. Terminal master's awarded for partial completion of doctoral program. *Degree requirements:* For master's, thesis optional; for doctorate, thesis/dissertation, qualifying exam, preliminary exam. *Entrance requirements:* For master's, GRE, BS in mechanical engineering or related field, minimum GPA of 3.0 in last 60 hours of course work; for doctorate, GRE, BS in mechanical engineering or related field, minimum undergraduate GPA of 3.0 in last 60 hours of course work. Additional exam requirements/recommendations for international students: Required—TOEFL (minimum score 550 paper-based; 213 computer-based; 80 iBT). *Application deadline:* For fall admission, 5/1 for domestic students, 6/1 for international students; for spring admission, 11/30 for domestic students, 10/1 for international students. Applications are processed on a rolling basis. Application fee: $56. Electronic applications accepted. *Expenses:* Tuition, state resident: full-time $10,296; part-time $643.51 per credit. Tuition, nonresident: full-time $24,054; part-time $1503.40 per credit. *Required fees:* $70.06 per credit. Tuition and fees vary according to course load, campus/location, program and reciprocity agreements. *Financial support:* In 2011–12, 168 students received support, including 11 fellowships with full tuition reimbursements available (averaging $22,224 per year), 121 research assistantships with full tuition reimbursements available (averaging $19,596 per year), 37 teaching assistantships with full tuition reimbursements available (averaging $8,595 per year); career-related internships or fieldwork, institutionally sponsored loans, scholarships/grants, traineeships, health care benefits, and unspecified assistantships also available. *Faculty research:* Design and manufacturing, materials processing, combustion, energy systems nanotechnology. *Total annual research expenditures:* $10 million. *Unit head:* Roxann L. Engelstad, Chair, 608-262-5745, Fax: 608-265-2316, E-mail: engelsta@engr.wisc.edu. *Application contact:* 608-262-2433, Fax: 608-262-5134, E-mail: gradadmiss@mail.bascom.wisc.edu. Web site: http://www.engr.wisc.edu/me/.

Wayne State University, College of Engineering, Department of Chemical Engineering and Materials Science, Detroit, MI 48202. Offers alternative energy technologies (Certificate); chemical engineering (MS, PhD); materials science and engineering (MS, PhD, Certificate), including materials science and engineering (MS, PhD), polymer engineering (Certificate); sustainable engineering (Certificate). Part-time programs available. *Students:* 33 full-time (9 women), 11 part-time (5 women); includes 5 minority (1 Black or African American, non-Hispanic/Latino; 4 Asian, non-Hispanic/Latino), 28 international. Average age 27. 114 applicants, 46% accepted, 15 enrolled. In 2011, 11 master's, 4 doctorates, 1 other advanced degree awarded. Terminal master's awarded for partial completion of doctoral program. *Degree requirements:* For master's, thesis optional; for doctorate, thesis/dissertation. *Entrance requirements:* For master's, GRE (if applying for financial support), minimum GPA of 3.0; for doctorate, GRE (if applying for financial support). Additional exam requirements/recommendations for international students: Required—TOEFL (minimum score 550 paper-based; 213 computer-based), TWE (minimum score 5.5). *Application deadline:* For fall admission, 6/1 priority date for domestic students, 5/1 for international students; for winter admission, 10/1 priority date for domestic students, 9/1 for international students; for spring admission, 2/1 priority date for domestic students, 1/1 for international students. Applications are processed on a rolling basis. Application fee: $50. Electronic applications accepted. *Expenses:* Tuition, state resident: part-time $512.85 per credit. Tuition, nonresident: part-time $1132.65 per credit. *Required fees:* $26.60 per credit. $199.65 per semester. Tuition and fees vary according to course load and program. *Financial support:* In 2011–12, 2 fellowships with tuition reimbursements (averaging $20,475 per year), 14 research assistantships with tuition reimbursements (averaging $17,560 per year), 10 teaching assistantships with tuition reimbursements (averaging $17,445 per year) were awarded; scholarships/grants, health care benefits, and unspecified assistantships also available. *Faculty research:* Polymer solutions and processing, catalysis, environmental transport, waste minimization, transport in biological systems. *Total annual research expenditures:* $985,618. *Unit head:* Dr. Charles Manke, Chair, 313-577-3849, E-mail: cmanke@eng.wayne.edu. *Application contact:* Dr. Yinlun Huang, Graduate Director, 313-577-3771, E-mail: yhuang@wayne.edu. Web site: http://cheme.eng.wayne.edu/ChE.

Worcester Polytechnic Institute, Graduate Studies and Research, Programs in Interdisciplinary Studies, Worcester, MA 01609-2280. Offers bioscience administration (MS); impact engineering (MS); manufacturing engineering management (MS); power systems management (MS); social science (PhD); systems modeling (MS). Part-time and evening/weekend programs available. *Faculty:* 1 full-time (0 women). *Students:* 1 full-time (0 women), 201 part-time (30 women); includes 22 minority (2 Black or African American, non-Hispanic/Latino; 11 Asian, non-Hispanic/Latino; 7 Hispanic/Latino; 2 Two or more races, non-Hispanic/Latino), 5 international. 130 applicants, 90% accepted, 107 enrolled. *Degree requirements:* For master's, thesis; for doctorate, comprehensive exam, thesis/dissertation. *Entrance requirements:* For master's and doctorate, 3 letters of recommendation. Additional exam requirements/recommendations for international students: Required—TOEFL (minimum score 563 paper-based; 223 computer-based; 84 iBT), IELTS (minimum score 7). *Application deadline:* For fall admission, 1/1 priority date for domestic students, 1/1 for international students; for spring admission, 10/1 priority date for domestic students, 10/1 for international students. Application fee: $70. *Financial support:* Institutionally sponsored loans, scholarships/grants, and unspecified assistantships available. Financial award application deadline: 1/1; financial award applicants required to submit FAFSA. *Unit head:* Dr. Fred J. Looft, Head, 508-831-5231, Fax: 508-831-5491, E-mail: fjlooft@wpi.edu. *Application contact:* Lynne Dougherty, Administrative Assistant, 508-831-5301, Fax: 508-831-5717, E-mail: grad@wpi.edu.

Nuclear Engineering

Air Force Institute of Technology, Graduate School of Engineering and Management, Department of Engineering Physics, Dayton, OH 45433-7765. Offers applied physics (MS, PhD); electro-optics (MS, PhD); materials science (PhD); nuclear engineering (MS, PhD); space physics (MS). Part-time programs available. *Degree requirements:* For master's, thesis; for doctorate, thesis/dissertation. *Entrance requirements:* For master's and doctorate, GRE General Test, minimum GPA of 3.0, U.S. citizenship. *Faculty research:* High-energy lasers, space physics, nuclear weapon effects, semiconductor physics.

Arizona State University, Ira A. Fulton School of Engineering, Department of Electrical Engineering, Tempe, AZ 85287-5706. Offers electrical engineering (MS, MSE, PhD); nuclear power generation (Graduate Certificate). Part-time and evening/weekend programs available. Postbaccalaureate distance learning degree programs offered (minimal on-campus study). Terminal master's awarded for partial completion of doctoral program. *Degree requirements:* For master's, thesis and defense (MS); comprehensive exams (MSE); interactive Program of Study (iPOS) submitted before completing 50 percent of required credit hours; for doctorate, comprehensive exam, thesis/dissertation, interactive Program of Study (iPOS) submitted before completing 50 percent of required credit hours. *Entrance requirements:* For master's, GRE, minimum GPA of 3.0 in last 2 years of work leading to bachelor's degree, 3.5 if from non-ABET accredited school; for doctorate, GRE, master's degree with minimum GPA of 3.5 or 3.6 in last 2 years of ABET-accredited undergraduate program. Additional exam requirements/recommendations for international students: Required—TOEFL (minimum score 80 iBT), TOEFL, IELTS, or Pearson Test of English. Electronic applications accepted. *Expenses:* Contact institution. *Faculty research:* Power and energy systems, signal processing and communications, solid state devices and modeling, wireless communications and circuits, photovoltaics, biosignatures discovery automation, flexible electronics, and nanostructures.

Colorado School of Mines, Graduate School, Program in Nuclear Engineering, Golden, CO 80401-1887. Offers MS, PhD. Part-time programs available. *Students:* 28 full-time (5 women), 2 part-time (0 women); includes 3 minority (all Hispanic/Latino), 5 international. Average age 27. 28 applicants, 71% accepted, 13 enrolled. In 2011, 5 master's awarded. *Degree requirements:* For master's, thesis (for some programs); for doctorate, comprehensive exam, thesis/dissertation. *Entrance requirements:* For master's and doctorate, GRE General Test. Additional exam requirements/recommendations for international students: Required—TOEFL (minimum score 550 paper-based; 213 computer-based; 80 iBT). *Application deadline:* For fall admission, 1/15 priority date for domestic students, 1/15 for international students; for spring admission, 10/15 priority date for domestic students, 10/15 for international students. Electronic applications accepted. *Expenses:* Tuition, state resident: full-time $12,585; part-time $699 per credit. Tuition, nonresident: full-time $27,270; part-time $1516 per credit. *Required fees:* $1864.20; $670 per semester. *Financial support:* In 2011–12, 22 students received support, including 3 fellowships with full tuition reimbursements available (averaging $20,000 per year), 13 research assistantships with full tuition reimbursements available (averaging $20,000 per year), 6 teaching assistantships with full tuition reimbursements available (averaging $20,000 per year); career-related internships or fieldwork, Federal Work-Study, institutionally sponsored loans, scholarships/grants, health care benefits, and unspecified assistantships also available. Financial award application deadline: 1/15; financial award applicants required to submit FAFSA. *Faculty research:* Nuclear materials and nuclear fuel cycle. *Unit head:* Dr. Jeff King, Director, 303-273-3618, Fax: 303-279-3919, E-mail: kingjc@mines.edu. Web site: http://subatomic.mines.edu/.

École Polytechnique de Montréal, Graduate Programs, Institute of Nuclear Engineering, Montréal, QC H3C 3A7, Canada. Offers nuclear engineering (M Eng, PhD, DESS); nuclear engineering, socio-economics of energy (M Sc A). *Degree requirements:* For master's, one foreign language, thesis; for doctorate, one foreign language, thesis/dissertation. *Entrance requirements:* For master's, minimum GPA of 2.75; for doctorate, minimum GPA of 3.0. *Faculty research:* Nuclear technology, thermohydraulics.

Georgia Institute of Technology, Graduate Studies and Research, College of Engineering, George W. Woodruff School of Mechanical Engineering, Nuclear and Radiological Engineering and Medical Physics Programs, Atlanta, GA 30332-0001. Offers medical physics (MS); nuclear and radiological engineering (MSNE, PhD). Part-time programs available. Postbaccalaureate distance learning degree programs offered (no on-campus study). Terminal master's awarded for partial completion of doctoral program. *Degree requirements:* For master's, thesis optional; for doctorate, comprehensive exam, thesis/dissertation. *Entrance requirements:* For master's and doctorate, GRE General Test, minimum GPA of 3.0. Additional exam requirements/recommendations for international students: Required—TOEFL (minimum score 580 paper-based; 240 computer-based). *Faculty research:* Reactor physics, nuclear materials, plasma physics, radiation detection, radiological assessment.

Idaho State University, Office of Graduate Studies, College of Science and Engineering, Nuclear Engineering and Health Physics Department, Pocatello, ID 83209. Offers nuclear science and engineering (MS, PhD). Part-time programs available. *Degree requirements:* For master's, comprehensive exam (for some programs), thesis, seminar; for doctorate, comprehensive exam, thesis/dissertation, oral and written exams at the end of 1st year. *Entrance requirements:* For master's, GRE; for doctorate, master's degree in engineering, physics, geosciences, math, etc.; 3 letters of recommendation. Additional exam requirements/recommendations for international students: Required—TOEFL (minimum score 550 paper-based; 213 computer-based; 80 iBT). Electronic applications accepted.

Kansas State University, Graduate School, College of Engineering, Department of Mechanical and Nuclear Engineering, Manhattan, KS 66506. Offers mechanical engineering (MS, PhD); nuclear engineering (MS, PhD). *Faculty:* 18 full-time (2 women), 2 part-time/adjunct (0 women). *Students:* 42 full-time (8 women), 22 part-time (3 women); includes 2 minority (1 Black or African American, non-Hispanic/Latino; 1 Two or more races, non-Hispanic/Latino), 24 international. Average age 29. 97 applicants, 29% accepted, 9 enrolled. In 2011, 22 master's, 6 doctorates awarded. *Degree requirements:* For master's, thesis or alternative; for doctorate, comprehensive exam, thesis/dissertation. *Entrance requirements:* For master's, GRE General Test, minimum GPA of 3.0 in physics, mathematics, and chemistry; for doctorate, GRE General Test, master's degree in mechanical engineering. Additional exam requirements/recommendations for international students: Required—TOEFL. *Application deadline:* For fall admission, 2/1 priority date for domestic students, 2/1 for international students;

for spring admission, 7/1 priority date for domestic students, 8/1 for international students. Applications are processed on a rolling basis. Application fee: $40 ($55 for international students). Electronic applications accepted. *Financial support:* In 2011–12, 33 research assistantships (averaging $19,839 per year), 5 teaching assistantships with full and partial tuition reimbursements (averaging $14,400 per year) were awarded; career-related internships or fieldwork, institutionally sponsored loans, and scholarships/grants also available. Support available to part-time students. Financial award application deadline: 3/1; financial award applicants required to submit FAFSA. *Faculty research:* Radiation detection and protection, heat and mass transfer, machine design, control systems, nuclear reactor physics and engineering. *Total annual research expenditures:* $3.6 million. *Unit head:* Donald Fenton, Head, 785-532-2321, Fax: 785-532-7057, E-mail: fenton@ksu.edu. *Application contact:* Steve Eckels, Director, 785-532-2283, Fax: 785-532-7057, E-mail: grad@mne.ksu.edu. Web site: http://www.mne.ksu.edu/.

Massachusetts Institute of Technology, School of Engineering, Department of Nuclear Science and Engineering, Cambridge, MA 02139. Offers SM, PhD, Sc D, NE. *Faculty:* 14 full-time (3 women). *Students:* 121 full-time (18 women); includes 12 minority (4 Black or African American, non-Hispanic/Latino; 1 American Indian or Alaska Native, non-Hispanic/Latino; 3 Asian, non-Hispanic/Latino; 4 Two or more races, non-Hispanic/Latino), 38 international. Average age 26. 172 applicants, 28% accepted, 31 enrolled. In 2011, 18 master's, 15 doctorates, 1 other advanced degree awarded. Terminal master's awarded for partial completion of doctoral program. *Degree requirements:* For master's and NE, thesis; for doctorate, comprehensive exam, thesis/dissertation. *Entrance requirements:* For master's, doctorate, and NE, GRE General Test. Additional exam requirements/recommendations for international students: Required—TOEFL (minimum score 577 paper-based; 233 computer-based; 90 iBT), IELTS (minimum score 7). *Application deadline:* For fall admission, 1/7 for domestic and international students. Application fee: $75. Electronic applications accepted. *Expenses: Tuition:* Full-time $40,460; part-time $630 per credit hour. *Required fees:* $272. *Financial support:* In 2011–12, 105 students received support, including 32 fellowships (averaging $32,400 per year), 76 research assistantships (averaging $28,500 per year), 6 teaching assistantships (averaging $30,800 per year); career-related internships or fieldwork, Federal Work-Study, institutionally sponsored loans, scholarships/grants, health care benefits, and unspecified assistantships also available. *Faculty research:* Advanced reactor design and innovation; nuclear fuel cycle technology and economics; plasma physics and fusion engineering; materials in extreme environments; radiation science, nuclear imaging and quantum information; nuclear systems engineering, management and policy. *Total annual research expenditures:* $12.7 million. *Unit head:* Prof. Richard Lester, Head, 617-253-7522, E-mail: nse-info@mit.edu. *Application contact:* Academic Programs Administrator, 617-253-3814, Fax: 617-258-7437. Web site: http://web.mit.edu/nse.

McMaster University, School of Graduate Studies, Faculty of Engineering, Department of Engineering Physics, Hamilton, ON L8S 4M2, Canada. Offers engineering physics (M Eng, MA Sc, PhD); nuclear engineering (PhD). *Degree requirements:* For master's, thesis or alternative; for doctorate, comprehensive exam, thesis/dissertation. *Entrance requirements:* For master's, minimum B average in engineering, mathematics, or physical sciences. Additional exam requirements/recommendations for international students: Required—TOEFL (minimum score 550 paper-based; 213 computer-based). *Faculty research:* Non-thermal plasmas for pollution control and electrostatic precipitation, bulk and thin film luminescent materials, devices and systems for optical fiber communications, physics and applications of III-V materials and devices, defect spectroscopy in semiconductors.

Missouri University of Science and Technology, Graduate School, Department of Mining and Nuclear Engineering, Rolla, MO 65409. Offers mining engineering (MS, DE, PhD); nuclear engineering (MS, DE, PhD). *Degree requirements:* For master's, thesis optional; for doctorate, comprehensive exam. *Entrance requirements:* For master's, GRE (minimum score 600 quantitative, 3 writing); for doctorate, GRE (minimum score: quantitative 600, writing 3.5). Additional exam requirements/recommendations for international students: Required—TOEFL (minimum score 550 paper-based; 213 computer-based). *Faculty research:* Mine health and safety, nuclear radiation transport, modeling of mining operations, radiation effects, blasting.

North Carolina State University, Graduate School, College of Engineering, Department of Nuclear Engineering, Raleigh, NC 27695. Offers MNE, MS, PhD. *Degree requirements:* For master's, thesis (for some programs); for doctorate, thesis/dissertation. *Entrance requirements:* For master's, bachelor's degree in engineering or GRE; for doctorate, engineering degree or GRE. Electronic applications accepted. *Faculty research:* Computational reactor engineering, plasma applications, waste management, materials, radiation applications and measurement.

The Ohio State University, Graduate School, College of Engineering, Department of Mechanical and Aerospace Engineering, Program in Nuclear Engineering, Columbus, OH 43210. Offers MS, PhD. *Faculty:* 6. *Students:* 27 full-time (2 women), 4 part-time; includes 2 minority (1 Asian, non-Hispanic/Latino; 1 Hispanic/Latino), 7 international. Average age 28. In 2011, 3 master's, 4 doctorates awarded. *Degree requirements:* For master's, thesis optional; for doctorate, thesis/dissertation. *Entrance requirements:* Additional exam requirements/recommendations for international students: Required—Michigan English Language Assessment Battery (minimum score 82); Recommended—TOEFL (minimum score 600 paper-based; 250 computer-based; 79 iBT). *Application deadline:* For fall admission, 8/15 priority date for domestic students, 7/1 for international students; for winter admission, 12/1 priority date for domestic students, 11/1 for international students; for spring admission, 3/1 priority date for domestic students, 2/1 for international students. Applications are processed on a rolling basis. Application fee: $40 ($50 for international students). Electronic applications accepted. *Expenses:* Tuition, state resident: full-time $11,400. Tuition, nonresident: full-time $28,125. Tuition and fees vary according to course load, degree level, campus/location and program. *Financial support:* Fellowships, research assistantships, teaching assistantships, career-related internships or fieldwork, Federal Work-Study, and institutionally sponsored loans available. Support available to part-time students. *Unit head:* Tunc Aldemir, Graduate Studies Committee Chair, 614-292-4627, E-mail: aldemir.1@osu.edu. *Application contact:* Janeen Sands, Graduate Programs Coordinator, 614-247-6605, Fax: 614-292-3656, E-mail: sands.3@osu.edu. Web site: http://mae.osu.edu/graduate/nuclear-engineering.

Oregon State University, Graduate School, College of Engineering, Department of Nuclear Engineering and Radiation Health Physics, Corvallis, OR 97331. Offers nuclear engineering (M Eng, MS, PhD); radiation health physics (MA, MHP, MS, PhD). Part-time programs available. Terminal master's awarded for partial completion of doctoral program. *Degree requirements:* For master's, thesis; for doctorate, thesis/dissertation. *Entrance requirements:* For master's and doctorate, GRE General Test, minimum GPA of 3.0 in last 90 hours. Additional exam requirements/recommendations for international students: Required—TOEFL (minimum score 550 paper-based; 213 computer-based). *Faculty research:* Reactor thermal hydraulics and safety, applications of radiation and nuclear techniques, computational methods development, environmental transport of radioactive materials.

Penn State University Park, Graduate School, College of Engineering, Department of Mechanical and Nuclear Engineering, State College, University Park, PA 16802-1503. Offers mechanical engineering (MS, PhD); nuclear engineering (M Eng, MS, PhD). *Faculty research:* Reactor safety, radiation damage, advanced controls, radiation instrumentation, computational methods. *Unit head:* Dr. David N. Wormley, Dean, 814-865-7537, Fax: 814-865-8767, E-mail: dnw2@engr.psu.edu. *Application contact:* Cynthia E. Nicosia, Director, Graduate Enrollment Services, 814-865-1834, E-mail: cey1@psu.edu. Web site: http://www.mne.psu.edu.

Purdue University, College of Engineering, School of Nuclear Engineering, West Lafayette, IN 47907-2017. Offers MS, MSNE, PhD. Part-time programs available. Terminal master's awarded for partial completion of doctoral program. *Entrance requirements:* For master's and doctorate, GRE General Test, minimum GPA of 3.0. Additional exam requirements/recommendations for international students: Required—TOEFL (minimum score 550 paper-based; 213 computer-based; 77 iBT); Recommended—TWE. Electronic applications accepted. *Faculty research:* Nuclear reactor safety, thermal hydraulics, fusion technology, reactor materials, reactor physics.

Rensselaer Polytechnic Institute, Graduate School, School of Engineering, Program in Nuclear Engineering, Troy, NY 12180-3590. Offers nuclear engineering (M Eng, MS); nuclear engineering and science (PhD). Part-time programs available. *Degree requirements:* For master's, thesis (for some programs); for doctorate, thesis/dissertation. *Entrance requirements:* For master's and doctorate, GRE. Additional exam requirements/recommendations for international students: Required—TOEFL (minimum score 600 paper-based; 250 computer-based; 100 iBT). Electronic applications accepted. *Faculty research:* Nuclear data measurement, multiphase flow and heat transfer, environmental and operational health physics, fusion reactor engineering and safety.

Royal Military College of Canada, Division of Graduate Studies and Research, Engineering Division, Program in Nuclear Engineering, Kingston, ON K7K 7B4, Canada. Offers M Eng, MA Sc, PhD. *Degree requirements:* For master's, thesis; for doctorate, comprehensive exam, thesis/dissertation. *Entrance requirements:* For master's, honours degree with second-class standing; for doctorate, master's degree. Electronic applications accepted.

Royal Military College of Canada, Division of Graduate Studies and Research, Engineering Division, Program in Nuclear Science, Kingston, ON K7K 7B4, Canada. Offers M Sc, PhD. *Degree requirements:* For master's, thesis; for doctorate, comprehensive exam, thesis/dissertation. *Entrance requirements:* For master's, honour's degree with second-class standing; for doctorate, master's degree. Electronic applications accepted.

Texas A&M University, College of Engineering, Department of Nuclear Engineering, College Station, TX 77843. Offers health physics (MS, PhD); nuclear engineering (M Eng, MS, PhD). *Faculty:* 17. *Students:* 110 full-time (20 women), 24 part-time (3 women); includes 18 minority (2 Black or African American, non-Hispanic/Latino; 5 Asian, non-Hispanic/Latino; 9 Hispanic/Latino; 2 Two or more races, non-Hispanic/Latino), 38 international. Average age 28. In 2011, 20 master's, 5 doctorates awarded. *Degree requirements:* For master's, thesis or alternative; for doctorate, thesis/dissertation, departmental qualifying exams. *Entrance requirements:* For master's and doctorate, GRE General Test, 3 letters of recommendation. Additional exam requirements/recommendations for international students: Required—TOEFL. *Application deadline:* For fall admission, 3/1 for domestic and international students; for spring admission, 8/1 for domestic and international students. Applications are processed on a rolling basis. Application fee: $50 ($75 for international students). Electronic applications accepted. *Expenses:* Tuition, state resident: full-time $5437; part-time $226.55 per credit hour. Tuition, nonresident: full-time $12,949; part-time $539.55 per credit hour. *Required fees:* $2741. *Financial support:* Fellowships, research assistantships, career-related internships or fieldwork, scholarships/grants, and unspecified assistantships available. Financial award application deadline: 4/1; financial award applicants required to submit FAFSA. *Faculty research:* Accelerators, aerosols, computational transport, fission, fusion. *Total annual research expenditures:* $4.2 million. *Unit head:* Dr. Yassin A. Hassan, Head, 979-845-7090, E-mail: y-hassan@tamu.edu. *Application contact:* Graduate Coordinator, 979-845-7090, E-mail: nuclear@tamu.edu. Web site: http://nuclear.tamu.edu/.

University of California, Berkeley, Graduate Division, College of Engineering, Department of Nuclear Engineering, Berkeley, CA 94720-1730. Offers M Eng, MS, D Eng, PhD. *Degree requirements:* For master's, project or thesis; for doctorate, thesis/dissertation, oral exam. *Entrance requirements:* For master's and doctorate, GRE General Test, minimum GPA of 3.0, 3 letters of recommendation. Additional exam requirements/recommendations for international students: Required—TOEFL. *Faculty research:* Applied nuclear reactions and instrumentation, fission reactor engineering, fusion reactor technology, nuclear waste and materials management, radiation protection and environmental effects.

University of Cincinnati, Graduate School, College of Engineering and Applied Science, Department of Mechanical, Industrial and Nuclear Engineering, Program in Nuclear Engineering, Cincinnati, OH 45221. Offers MS, PhD. Part-time programs available. Terminal master's awarded for partial completion of doctoral program. *Degree requirements:* For master's, project or thesis; for doctorate, thesis/dissertation. *Entrance requirements:* For master's and doctorate, GRE General Test. Additional exam requirements/recommendations for international students: Required—TOEFL (minimum score 575 paper-based; 233 computer-based). Electronic applications accepted. *Faculty research:* Nuclear fission reactor engineering, reduction and fusion effects, health and medical physics, radiological assessment.

University of Florida, Graduate School, College of Engineering, Department of Nuclear and Radiological Engineering, Gainesville, FL 32611. Offers nuclear engineering sciences (ME, MS, PhD, Engr). Part-time programs available. Terminal master's awarded for partial completion of doctoral program. *Degree requirements:* For master's, comprehensive exam, thesis; for doctorate, comprehensive exam, thesis/dissertation; for Engr, thesis. *Entrance requirements:* For master's and doctorate, GRE General Test, minimum GPA of 3.0; for Engr, GRE General Test. Additional exam requirements/recommendations for international students: Required—TOEFL (minimum score 550 paper-based; 213 computer-based; 80 iBT), IELTS (minimum score 6). Electronic applications accepted. *Faculty research:* Nuclear materials, radiation detection, thermal hydraulics, reactor physics and transport, generation 4 reactor technology.

University of Idaho, College of Graduate Studies, College of Engineering, Department of Engineering, Program in Nuclear Engineering, Moscow, ID 83844-2282. Offers M Engr, MS, PhD. *Faculty:* 6 full-time, 1 part-time/adjunct. *Students:* 14 full-time, 28 part-time. Average age 34. In 2011, 9 master's awarded. *Degree requirements:* For master's, thesis or alternative; for doctorate, thesis/dissertation. *Entrance requirements:* For master's, minimum GPA of 2.8; for doctorate, minimum undergraduate GPA of 2.8, 3.0 graduate. Additional exam requirements/recommendations for international students: Required—TOEFL. *Application deadline:* For fall admission, 8/1 for domestic students; for spring admission, 12/15 for domestic students. Applications are processed on a rolling basis. Application fee: $60. Electronic applications accepted. *Expenses:* Tuition, state resident: full-time $3874; part-time $334 per credit hour. Tuition, nonresident: full-time $16,394; part-time $861 per credit hour. *Required fees:* $2808; $99 per credit hour. Tuition and fees vary according to program. *Financial support:* Applicants required to submit FAFSA. *Unit head:* Dr. Larry Stauffer, Interim Dean, 208-282-6479, E-mail: wadmassu@uidaho.edu. *Application contact:* Erick Larson, Director of Graduate Admissions, 208-885-4723, E-mail: gadms@uidaho.edu. Web site: http://www.if.uidaho.edu/ne/.

University of Illinois at Urbana–Champaign, Graduate College, College of Engineering, Department of Nuclear, Plasma, and Radiological Engineering, Champaign, IL 61820. Offers nuclear engineering (MS, PhD). *Faculty:* 8 full-time (0 women), 2 part-time/adjunct (0 women). *Students:* 58 full-time (10 women), 4 part-time (0 women); includes 6 minority (5 Asian, non-Hispanic/Latino; 1 Hispanic/Latino), 37 international. 76 applicants, 53% accepted, 18 enrolled. In 2011, 19 master's, 6 doctorates awarded. *Entrance requirements:* For master's and doctorate, minimum GPA of 3.0. Additional exam requirements/recommendations for international students: Required—TOEFL (minimum score 550 paper-based; 213 computer-based; 79 iBT) or IELTS. *Application deadline:* Applications are processed on a rolling basis. Application fee: $75 ($90 for international students). Electronic applications accepted. *Financial support:* In 2011–12, 11 fellowships, 33 research assistantships, 32 teaching assistantships were awarded; tuition waivers (full and partial) also available. *Unit head:* James F. Stubbins, Head, 217-333-6474, Fax: 217-333-3906, E-mail: jstubbin@illinois.edu. *Application contact:* Becky J. Meline, Admissions and Records Officer, 217-333-3598, Fax: 217-333-3906, E-mail: bmeline@illinois.edu. Web site: http://npre.illinois.edu/.

The University of Manchester, School of Mechanical, Aerospace and Civil Engineering, Manchester, United Kingdom. Offers advanced manufacturing technology (M Ent); aerospace engineering (M Phil, M Sc, PhD); civil engineering (M Phil, M Sc, PhD); environmental engineering (M Phil, PhD); management of projects (M Phil, M Sc, PhD); mechanical engineering (M Phil, M Sc, PhD); mechanical engineering design (M Ent); nuclear engineering (M Phil, D Eng, PhD).

University of Maryland, College Park, Academic Affairs, A. James Clark School of Engineering, Department of Materials Science and Engineering, Nuclear Engineering Program, College Park, MD 20742. Offers ME, MS, PhD. Part-time and evening/weekend programs available. Postbaccalaureate distance learning degree programs offered. *Students:* 11 full-time (6 women), 1 part-time (0 women); includes 3 minority (1 Asian, non-Hispanic/Latino; 1 Hispanic/Latino; 1 Two or more races, non-Hispanic/Latino), 1 international. 8 applicants, 25% accepted, 2 enrolled. In 2011, 2 master's awarded. *Degree requirements:* For master's, thesis optional; for doctorate, variable foreign language requirement, thesis/dissertation, oral exam. *Entrance requirements:* For master's and doctorate, GRE General Test, minimum GPA of 3.0. Additional exam requirements/recommendations for international students: Required—TOEFL. *Application deadline:* For fall admission, 1/15 for domestic and international students; for spring admission, 6/1 for domestic and international students. Applications are processed on a rolling basis. Application fee: $75. Electronic applications accepted. *Expenses: Tuition, area resident:* Part-time $525 per credit hour. Tuition, state resident: part-time $525 per credit hour. Tuition, nonresident: part-time $1131 per credit hour. *Required fees:* $386.31 per term. Tuition and fees vary according to program. *Financial support:* In 2011–12, 5 research assistantships (averaging $24,515 per year) were awarded; fellowships, teaching assistantships, and tuition waivers (full) also available. Financial award applicants required to submit FAFSA. *Faculty research:* Reliability and risk assessment, heat transfer and two-phase flow, reactor safety analysis, nuclear reactor, radiation/polymers. *Unit head:* Robert M. Briber, Head, 301-405-7313, Fax: 301-314-2029, E-mail: rbriber@umd.edu. *Application contact:* Dr. Charles A. Caramello, Dean of Graduate School, 301-405-0358, Fax: 301-314-9305, E-mail: ccaramel@umd.edu.

University of Massachusetts Lowell, College of Engineering, Program in Energy Engineering, Lowell, MA 01854-2881. Offers MS Eng, D Eng, PhD. *Degree requirements:* For master's, thesis optional. *Entrance requirements:* For master's, GRE General Test. Additional exam requirements/recommendations for international students: Required—TOEFL.

University of Michigan, College of Engineering, Department of Nuclear Engineering and Radiological Sciences, Ann Arbor, MI 48109. Offers nuclear engineering (Nuc E); nuclear engineering and radiological sciences (MSE, PhD); nuclear science (MS, PhD). *Students:* 135 full-time (21 women). 145 applicants, 50% accepted, 39 enrolled. In 2011, 28 master's, 11 doctorates awarded. Terminal master's awarded for partial completion of doctoral program. *Degree requirements:* For master's, thesis optional; for doctorate, thesis/dissertation, oral defense of dissertation, preliminary exams. *Entrance requirements:* For master's and doctorate, GRE General Test. Additional exam requirements/recommendations for international students: Required—TOEFL (minimum score 560 paper-based; 220 computer-based). *Application deadline:* Applications are processed on a rolling basis. Application fee: $65 ($75 for international students). Electronic applications accepted. *Financial support:* Fellowships, research assistantships, teaching assistantships, career-related internships or fieldwork, institutionally sponsored loans, scholarships/grants, traineeships, health care benefits, and unspecified assistantships available. *Faculty research:* Radiation safety, environmental sciences, medical physics, fission systems and radiation transport, materials, plasmas and fusion, radiation measurements and imaging. *Unit head:* Dr. Ronald Gilgenbach, Chair, 734-936-0122, Fax: 734-763-4540, E-mail: rongilg@umich.edu. *Application contact:* Peggy Jo Gramer, Graduate Program Coordinator, 734-615-8810, Fax: 734-763-4540, E-mail: pjgramer@umich.edu. Web site: http://www.ners.engin.umich.edu/.

University of Missouri, Graduate School, Nuclear Science and Engineering Institute, Columbia, MO 65211. Offers nuclear power engineering (MS, PhD), including health physics (MS), medical physics (MS), nuclear power engineering (MS). *Faculty:* 5 full-time (0 women). *Students:* 58 full-time (11 women), 7 part-time (2 women); includes 8 minority (5 Asian, non-Hispanic/Latino; 3 Hispanic/Latino), 15 international. Average age 29. 44 applicants, 48% accepted, 8 enrolled. In 2011, 6 master's, 8 doctorates awarded. *Degree requirements:* For master's, research project; for doctorate, thesis/dissertation. *Entrance requirements:* For master's and doctorate, GRE General Test. Additional exam requirements/recommendations for international students: Required—TOEFL (minimum score 500 paper-based; 173 computer-based; 61 iBT). *Application deadline:* For fall admission, 3/15 priority date for domestic students. Application fee: $55 ($75 for international students). *Expenses:* Tuition, state resident: full-time $5881. Tuition,

nonresident: full-time $15,183. *Required fees:* $952. Tuition and fees vary according to campus/location and program. *Financial support:* Fellowships, research assistantships, teaching assistantships, and institutionally sponsored loans available. *Unit head:* Dr. Wynn Volkert, Department Chair, E-mail: volkertw@missouri.edu. *Application contact:* Latricia Vaughn, 573-882-8201, E-mail: vaughnlj@missouri.edu. Web site: http://nsei.missouri.edu/.

University of Nevada, Las Vegas, Graduate College, Howard R. Hughes College of Engineering, Department of Mechanical Engineering, Las Vegas, NV 89154-4027. Offers aerospace engineering (MS); biomedical engineering (MS); materials and nuclear engineering (MS); mechanical engineering (MSE, PhD). Part-time programs available. *Faculty:* 14 full-time (0 women), 19 part-time/adjunct (1 woman). *Students:* 14 full-time (2 women), 40 part-time (8 women); includes 12 minority (1 Black or African American, non-Hispanic/Latino; 4 Asian, non-Hispanic/Latino; 3 Hispanic/Latino; 1 Native Hawaiian or other Pacific Islander, non-Hispanic/Latino; 3 Two or more races, non-Hispanic/Latino), 13 international. Average age 31. 31 applicants, 74% accepted, 8 enrolled. In 2011, 18 master's, 3 doctorates awarded. *Degree requirements:* For master's, comprehensive exam, thesis (for some programs), project; for doctorate, comprehensive exam, thesis/dissertation. *Entrance requirements:* For master's and doctorate, GRE General Test. Additional exam requirements/recommendations for international students: Required—TOEFL (minimum score 550 paper-based; 213 computer-based; 80 iBT), IELTS (minimum score 7). *Application deadline:* For fall admission, 8/1 priority date for domestic students, 5/1 for international students; for spring admission, 12/1 priority date for domestic students, 10/1 for international students. Applications are processed on a rolling basis. Application fee: $60 ($95 for international students). Electronic applications accepted. *Financial support:* In 2011–12, 29 students received support, including 14 research assistantships with partial tuition reimbursements available (averaging $9,415 per year), 15 teaching assistantships with partial tuition reimbursements available (averaging $10,934 per year); institutionally sponsored loans, scholarships/grants, health care benefits, and unspecified assistantships also available. Financial award application deadline: 3/1. *Faculty research:* Dynamics and control systems; energy systems including renewable and nuclear; computational fluid and solid mechanics; structures, materials and manufacturing; vibrations and acoustics. *Total annual research expenditures:* $2.9 million. *Unit head:* Dr. Woosoon Yim, Chair/Professor, 702-895-0956, Fax: 702-895-3936, E-mail: wy@me.unlv.edu. *Application contact:* Graduate College Admissions Evaluator, 702-895-3320, Fax: 702-895-4180, E-mail: gradcollege@unlv.edu. Web site: http://www.me.unlv.edu/.

University of New Mexico, Graduate School, School of Engineering, Department of Chemical and Nuclear Engineering, Program in Nuclear Engineering, Albuquerque, NM 87131-2039. Offers MS, PhD. Part-time programs available. Postbaccalaureate distance learning degree programs offered (no on-campus study). *Students:* 15 full-time (5 women), 19 part-time (3 women); includes 11 minority (9 Hispanic/Latino; 1 Native Hawaiian or other Pacific Islander, non-Hispanic/Latino; 1 Two or more races, non-Hispanic/Latino), 1 international. Average age 33. 70 applicants, 27% accepted, 7 enrolled. In 2011, 5 master's, 2 doctorates awarded. Terminal master's awarded for partial completion of doctoral program. *Degree requirements:* For master's, thesis (for some programs); for doctorate, comprehensive exam, thesis/dissertation. *Entrance requirements:* For master's, GRE General Test, minimum GPA of 3.0, 3 letters of recommendation, letter of intent; for doctorate, GRE General Test, 3 letters of recommendation, letter of intent. Additional exam requirements/recommendations for international students: Required—TOEFL. *Application deadline:* For fall admission, 1/15 priority date for domestic students, 3/1 for international students; for spring admission, 7/15 priority date for domestic students, 8/1 for international students. Application fee: $50. Electronic applications accepted. *Financial support:* In 2011–12, 21 students received support, including 4 fellowships (averaging $4,875 per year), 15 research assistantships with full tuition reimbursements available (averaging $17,613 per year); teaching assistantships, scholarships/grants, health care benefits, and tuition waivers (full) also available. Financial award application deadline: 3/1; financial award applicants required to submit FAFSA. *Faculty research:* Plasma science, space power, thermal hydraulics, radiation measurement and protection, fusion plasma measurements, medical physics, nuclear criticality safety, radiation measurements and protection, radiation transport modeling and simulation, Monte Carlo methods. *Total annual research expenditures:* $1 million. *Unit head:* Dr. Timothy Ward, Chair, 505-277-5431, Fax: 505-277-5433, E-mail: tward@unm.edu. *Application contact:* Jocelyn White, Coordinator/Program Advisor, 505-277-5606, Fax: 505-277-5433, E-mail: jowhite@unm.edu. Web site: http://www-chne.unm.edu.

University of South Carolina, The Graduate School, College of Engineering and Computing, Department of Nuclear Engineering, Columbia, SC 29208. Offers ME, MS, PhD. Part-time and evening/weekend programs available. Postbaccalaureate distance learning degree programs offered. *Degree requirements:* For master's, thesis (for some programs); for doctorate, thesis/dissertation. *Entrance requirements:* For master's and doctorate, GRE General Test. Additional exam requirements/recommendations for international students: Required—TOEFL (minimum score 600 paper-based; 250 computer-based; 100 iBT). Electronic applications accepted.

The University of Tennessee, Graduate School, College of Engineering, Department of Nuclear and Radiological Engineering, Program in Nuclear Engineering, Knoxville, TN 37996. Offers MS, PhD. Part-time programs available. *Faculty:* 13 full-time, 25 part-time/adjunct (2 women). *Students:* 77 full-time (12 women), 36 part-time (5 women); includes 7 minority (3 Black or African American, non-Hispanic/Latino; 3 Asian, non-Hispanic/Latino; 1 Hispanic/Latino), 8 international. Average age 31. 111 applicants, 54% accepted, 29 enrolled. In 2011, 17 master's, 6 doctorates awarded. *Degree requirements:* For master's, thesis or alternative; for doctorate, comprehensive exam, thesis/dissertation. *Entrance requirements:* For master's, GRE General Test (for MS students pursuing research thesis), minimum GPA of 2.7 (for U.S. degree holders), 3.0 (for international degree holders); for doctorate, College requires GRE General Test for all PhD candidates, minimum GPA of 3.0 on previous graduate course work. Additional exam requirements/recommendations for international students: Required—TOEFL (minimum score 550 paper-based; 213 computer-based). *Application deadline:* For fall admission, 2/1 priority date for domestic students, 2/1 for international students; for spring admission, 6/15 for domestic students, 5/15 for international students. Applications are processed on a rolling basis. Application fee: $35. Electronic applications accepted. *Expenses:* Tuition, state resident: full-time $8332; part-time $464 per credit hour. Tuition, nonresident: full-time $25,174; part-time $1400 per credit hour. *Required fees:* $1162; $56 per credit hour. Tuition and fees vary according to program. *Financial support:* In 2011–12, 74 students received support, including 16 fellowships with full tuition reimbursements available (averaging $18,900 per year), 55 research assistantships with full tuition reimbursements available (averaging $24,345 per year), 7 teaching assistantships with full tuition reimbursements available (averaging $23,770 per year); career-related internships or fieldwork, Federal Work-Study, institutionally sponsored loans, health care benefits, and unspecified assistantships also available. Financial award application deadline: 2/1; financial award applicants required to submit

FAFSA. *Faculty research:* Heat transfer and fluid dynamics; instrumentation, sensors and controls; nuclear materials and nuclear security; radiological engineering; reactor system design and safety. *Unit head:* Dr. J. Wesley Hines, Head, 865-974-2525, Fax: 865-974-0668, E-mail: jhines2@utk.edu. *Application contact:* Dr. Masood Parang, Associate Dean of Student Affairs, 865-974-2454, Fax: 865-974-9871, E-mail: mparang@utk.edu.

University of Utah, Graduate School, College of Engineering, Department of Civil and Environmental Engineering, Program in Nuclear Engineering, Salt Lake City, UT 84112. Offers ME, MS, PhD. Part-time programs available. *Students:* 7 full-time (0 women), 4 part-time (0 women); includes 1 minority (Hispanic/Latino), 3 international. Average age 30. 12 applicants, 50% accepted, 4 enrolled. In 2011, 1 degree awarded. Terminal master's awarded for partial completion of doctoral program. *Degree requirements:* For master's, comprehensive exam, thesis (for some programs); for doctorate, comprehensive exam, thesis/dissertation, qualifying exam. *Entrance requirements:* For master's and doctorate, GRE General Test, minimum GPA of 3.0. Additional exam requirements/recommendations for international students: Required—TOEFL (minimum score 550 paper-based; 213 computer-based; 80 iBT). *Application deadline:* For fall admission, 1/15 for domestic students, 12/15 for international students; for spring admission, 10/1 for domestic and international students. Applications are processed on a rolling basis. Application fee: $55 ($65 for international students). Electronic applications accepted. *Expenses:* Contact institution. *Financial support:* In 2011–12, 6 students received support, including 5 research assistantships with full tuition reimbursements available (averaging $20,016 per year), 1 teaching assistantship with full tuition reimbursement available (averaging $19,200 per year); fellowships, career-related internships or fieldwork, institutionally sponsored loans, scholarships/grants, traineeships, health care benefits, and unspecified assistantships also available. Support available to part-time students. Financial award application deadline: 12/15; financial award applicants required to submit FAFSA. *Faculty research:* Dosimetry, material damage, energy, foresnsics. *Unit head:* Dr. Paul J. Tikalsky, Department Chair, Civil and Environmental Engineering, 801-581-6931, Fax: 801-585-5477, E-mail: tikalsky@civil.utah.edu. *Application contact:* Amanda May, Academic Advisor, 801-581-6931, Fax: 801-585-5477, E-mail: amandam@civil.utah.edu. Web site: http://www.nuclear.utah.edu/.

University of Wisconsin–Madison, Graduate School, College of Engineering, Department of Engineering Physics, Madison, WI 53706. Offers engineering mechanics (MS, PhD); nuclear engineering and engineering physics (MS, PhD). Part-time programs available. Postbaccalaureate distance learning degree programs offered (minimal on-campus study). *Faculty:* 20 full-time (0 women), 9 part-time/adjunct (4 women). *Students:* 102 full-time (11 women), 16 part-time (1 woman); includes 12 minority (3 Black or African American, non-Hispanic/Latino; 1 American Indian or Alaska Native, non-Hispanic/Latino; 1 Asian, non-Hispanic/Latino; 7 Hispanic/Latino), 18 international. Average age 25. 198 applicants, 37% accepted, 38 enrolled. In 2011, 43 master's, 8 doctorates awarded. Terminal master's awarded for partial completion of doctoral program. *Degree requirements:* For master's, thesis optional; for doctorate, thesis/dissertation. *Entrance requirements:* For master's and doctorate, GRE General Test, minimum GPA of 3.0 in last 60 hours, appropriate bachelor's degree. Additional exam requirements/recommendations for international students: Required—TOEFL (minimum score 600 paper-based; 245 computer-based). *Application deadline:* For fall admission, 1/15 priority date for domestic students, 1/15 for international students. Applications are processed on a rolling basis. Application fee: $56. Electronic applications accepted. *Expenses:* Tuition, state resident: full-time $10,296; part-time $643.51 per credit. Tuition, nonresident: full-time $24,054; part-time $1503.40 per credit. *Required fees:* $70.06 per credit. Tuition and fees vary according to course load, campus/location, program and reciprocity agreements. *Financial support:* In 2011–12, 106 students received support, including 20 fellowships with full tuition reimbursements available (averaging $25,000 per year), 76 research assistantships with full tuition reimbursements available (averaging $20,400 per year), 10 teaching assistantships with full tuition reimbursements available (averaging $12,633 per year); career-related internships or fieldwork, Federal Work-Study, institutionally sponsored loans, and unspecified assistantships also available. Support available to part-time students. Financial award application deadline: 1/15. *Faculty research:* Fission reactor engineering and safety, plasma physics and fusion technology, plasma processing and ion implantation, nanotechnology, engineering mechanics and astronautics. *Total annual research expenditures:* $18.8 million. *Unit head:* Dr. James P. Blanchard, Chair, 608-263-0391, Fax: 608-263-7451, E-mail: blanchard@engr.wisc.edu. *Application contact:* Betsy A. Wood, Graduate Coordinator, 608-263-7038, Fax: 608-263-7451, E-mail: bwood@engr.wisc.edu. Web site: http://www.engr.wisc.edu/ep/.

Section 11
Engineering Design

This section contains a directory of institutions offering graduate work in engineering design. Additional information about programs listed in the directory but not augmented by an in-depth entry may be obtained by writing directly to the dean of a graduate school or chair of a department at the address given in the directory.

For programs offering related work, see also in this book *Aerospace/ Aeronautical Engineering; Agricultural Engineering and Bioengineering; Biomedical Engineering and Biotechnology; Computer Science and Information Technology; Electrical and Computer Engineering; Energy and Power Engineering; Engineering and Applied Sciences; Industrial Engineering; Man-* *agement of Engineering and Technology;* and *Mechanical Engineering and Mechanics.* In another guide in this series:
Graduate Programs in the Biological/Biomedical Sciences & Health-Related Medical Professions
See *Biological and Biomedical Sciences*

CONTENTS

Program Directory

Engineering Design

Northwestern University, McCormick School of Engineering and Applied Science, Segal Design Institute, MS in Engineering Design and Innovation Program, Evanston, IL 60208. Offers MS. *Faculty:* 9 full-time (4 women). *Students:* 16 full-time (4 women); includes 5 minority (1 Black or African American, non-Hispanic/Latino; 3 Asian, non-Hispanic/Latino; 1 Hispanic/Latino). Average age 23. 56 applicants, 66% accepted, 16 enrolled. In 2011, 16 master's awarded. *Entrance requirements:* For master's, GRE General Test, 2 letters of recommendation. Additional exam requirements/recommendations for international students: Required—TOEFL (minimum score 550 paper-based, 233 computer-based, 90 iBT) or IELTS (minimum score 7). *Application deadline:* For fall admission, 7/15 for domestic students, 7/1 for international students. Applications are processed on a rolling basis. Application fee: $75. Electronic applications accepted. *Financial support:* Career-related internships or fieldwork, health care benefits, and unspecified assistantships available. Financial award application deadline: 1/15; financial award applicants required to submit FAFSA. *Unit head:* Kim Hoffmann, Associate Director, 847-467-3534, Fax: 847-491-2603, E-mail: kimhoffmann@northwestern.edu. *Application contact:* Kim Hoffmann, Admission Officer, 847-491-5434, Fax: 847-491-2603, E-mail: kimhoffmann@northwestern.edu. Web site: http://www.segal.northwestern.edu/.

Polytechnic Institute of NYU, Long Island Graduate Center, Graduate Programs, Department of Electrical and Computer Engineering, Interdisciplinary Major in Wireless Innovations, Melville, NY 11747. Offers M Engr. Part-time and evening/weekend programs available. *Students:* 11 full-time (2 women), 3 part-time; includes 3 minority (all Asian, non-Hispanic/Latino), 10 international. Average age 29. 14 applicants, 100% accepted, 14 enrolled. In 2011, 1 master's awarded. *Degree requirements:* For master's, comprehensive exam (for some programs), thesis (for some programs). *Entrance requirements:* Additional exam requirements/recommendations for international students: Required—TOEFL (minimum score 550 paper-based; 213 computer-based; 80 iBT); Recommended—IELTS (minimum score 6.5). *Application deadline:* For fall admission, 7/31 priority date for domestic students, 4/30 for international students; for spring admission, 12/31 priority date for domestic students, 11/30 for international students. Applications are processed on a rolling basis. Application fee: $75. Electronic applications accepted. *Financial support:* Institutionally sponsored loans, scholarships/grants, and unspecified assistantships available. Support available to part-time students. *Unit head:* Dr. Jonathan Chao, Department Head, 718-260-3302, Fax: 718-260-3906, E-mail: chao@poly.edu. *Application contact:* JeanCarlo Bonilla, Director of Graduate Enrollment Management, 718-260-3182, Fax: 718-260-3624, E-mail: gradinfo@poly.edu.

San Diego State University, Graduate and Research Affairs, College of Engineering, Department of Mechanical Engineering, San Diego, CA 92182. Offers engineering sciences and applied mechanics (PhD); manufacture and design (MS); mechanical engineering (MS). PhD offered jointly with University of California, San Diego and Department of Aerospace Engineering and Engineering Mechanics. Evening/weekend programs available. *Degree requirements:* For master's, comprehensive exam (for some programs), thesis (for some programs); for doctorate, thesis/dissertation. *Entrance requirements:* For master's, GRE General Test; for doctorate, GRE, 3 letters of recommendation. Additional exam requirements/recommendations for international students: Required—TOEFL. Electronic applications accepted. *Faculty research:* Energy analysis and diagnosis, seawater pump design, space-related research.

Santa Clara University, School of Engineering, Program in Mechanical Engineering, Santa Clara, CA 95053. Offers controls (Certificate); dynamics (Certificate); materials engineering (Certificate); mechanical design analysis (Certificate); mechanical engineering (MS, PhD, Engineer); mechatronics systems engineering (Certificate); technology jump-start (Certificate); thermofluids (Certificate). Part-time and evening/weekend programs available. *Students:* 36 full-time (5 women), 68 part-time (11 women); includes 42 minority (33 Asian, non-Hispanic/Latino; 9 Hispanic/Latino), 16 international. Average age 27. 109 applicants, 56% accepted, 36 enrolled. In 2011, 33 master's, 1 doctorate, 1 other advanced degree awarded. *Degree requirements:* For master's, thesis (for some programs); for doctorate, thesis/dissertation; for other advanced degree, thesis. *Entrance requirements:* For master's, GRE, transcript; for doctorate, GRE, master's degree or equivalent; for other advanced degree, master's degree, published paper. Additional exam requirements/recommendations for international students: Required—TOEFL (minimum score 550 paper-based; 213 computer-based; 79 iBT). *Application deadline:* For fall admission, 8/12 for domestic students, 7/15 for international students; for winter admission, 10/28 for domestic students, 9/23 for international students; for spring admission, 2/25 for domestic students, 1/21 for international students. Applications are processed on a rolling basis. Application fee: $60. Electronic applications accepted. *Expenses:* Contact institution. *Financial support:* Research assistantships and teaching assistantships available. Financial award application deadline: 3/2; financial award applicants required to submit FAFSA. *Faculty research:* Development of small satellite design, tests and operations technology. *Unit head:* Dr. Alex Zecevic, Associate Dean for Graduate Studies, 408-554-2394, E-mail: azecevic@scu.edu. *Application contact:* Stacey Tinker, Director of Admissions, Graduate Engineering, 408-554-4748, Fax: 408-554-4323, E-mail: stinker@scu.edu.

Stanford University, School of Engineering, Department of Mechanical Engineering, Program in Product Design, Stanford, CA 94305-9991. Offers MS. *Entrance requirements:* For master's, GRE General Test, undergraduate degree in engineering, math or sciences. Additional exam requirements/recommendations for international students: Required—TOEFL. *Expenses: Tuition:* Full-time $40,050; part-time $890 per credit.

Stevens Institute of Technology, Graduate School, Charles V. Schaefer Jr. School of Engineering, Department of Mechanical Engineering, Program in Product Architecture and Engineering, Hoboken, NJ 07030. Offers M Eng.

University of Central Florida, College of Engineering and Computer Science, Department of Industrial Engineering and Management Systems, Orlando, FL 32816. Offers applied operations research (Certificate); design for usability (Certificate); engineering management (PSM); industrial engineering (MSIE, PhD); industrial engineering and management systems (MS); industrial ergonomics and safety (Certificate); project engineering (Certificate); quality assurance (Certificate); systems engineering (Certificate); systems simulation for engineers (Certificate); training simulation (Certificate). Part-time and evening/weekend programs available. *Faculty:* 18 full-time (4 women), 5 part-time/adjunct (1 woman). *Students:* 105 full-time (27 women), 151 part-time (47 women); includes 84 minority (20 Black or African American, non-Hispanic/Latino; 1 American Indian or Alaska Native, non-Hispanic/Latino; 20 Asian, non-Hispanic/Latino; 37 Hispanic/Latino; 1 Native Hawaiian or other Pacific Islander, non-Hispanic/Latino; 5 Two or more races, non-Hispanic/Latino), 52 international. Average age 32. 199 applicants, 79% accepted, 75 enrolled. In 2011, 83 master's, 11 doctorates, 40 other advanced degrees awarded. *Degree requirements:* For master's, thesis; for doctorate, thesis/dissertation, departmental qualifying exam, candidacy exam. *Entrance requirements:* For master's, GRE General Test, minimum GPA of 3.0 in last 60 hours of course work; for doctorate, minimum GPA of 3.5 in last 60 hours of course work. Additional exam requirements/recommendations for international students: Required—TOEFL. *Application deadline:* For fall admission, 7/15 priority date for domestic students; for spring admission, 12/1 priority date for domestic students. Application fee: $30. Electronic applications accepted. *Expenses:* Tuition, state resident: part-time $277.08 per credit hour. Tuition, nonresident: part-time $277.08 per credit hour. Part-time tuition and fees vary according to degree level and program. *Financial support:* In 2011–12, 19 students received support, including 8 fellowships with partial tuition reimbursements available (averaging $3,500 per year), 10 research assistantships with partial tuition reimbursements available (averaging $11,100 per year), 6 teaching assistantships with partial tuition reimbursements available (averaging $12,300 per year); career-related internships or fieldwork, Federal Work-Study, institutionally sponsored loans, tuition waivers (partial), and unspecified assistantships also available. Financial award application deadline: 3/1; financial award applicants required to submit FAFSA. *Unit head:* Dr. Waldemar Karwowski, Chair, 407-823-2204, E-mail: wkar@ucf.edu. *Application contact:* Barbara Rodriguez, Director, Admissions and Registration, 407-823-2766, Fax: 407-823-6442, E-mail: gradadmissions@ucf.edu. Web site: http://iems.ucf.edu/.

Worcester Polytechnic Institute, Graduate Studies and Research, School of Business, Worcester, MA 01609-2280. Offers information technology (MS), including information security management; management (Graduate Certificate); marketing and technological innovation (MS); operations design and leadership (MS); technology (MBA, MS). *Accreditation:* AACSB. Part-time and evening/weekend programs available. Postbaccalaureate distance learning degree programs offered (minimal on-campus study). *Faculty:* 12 full-time (7 women), 12 part-time/adjunct (2 women). *Students:* 108 full-time (64 women), 206 part-time (55 women); includes 27 minority (4 Black or African American, non-Hispanic/Latino; 12 Asian, non-Hispanic/Latino; 4 Hispanic/Latino; 7 Two or more races, non-Hispanic/Latino), 131 international. 596 applicants, 48% accepted, 131 enrolled. In 2011, 75 master's awarded. *Degree requirements:* For master's, thesis optional. *Entrance requirements:* For master's, GMAT (MBA), GMAT or GRE General Test (MS), resume; for Graduate Certificate, GMAT or GRE General Test, statement of purpose, 3 letters of recommendation. Additional exam requirements/recommendations for international students: Required—TOEFL (minimum score 563 paper-based; 223 computer-based; 84 iBT), IELTS (minimum score 7). *Application deadline:* For fall admission, 6/1 priority date for domestic students, 6/1 for international students; for spring admission, 11/1 priority date for domestic students, 10/1 for international students. Applications are processed on a rolling basis. Application fee: $70. Electronic applications accepted. *Financial support:* Career-related internships or fieldwork, institutionally sponsored loans, scholarships/grants, and unspecified assistantships available. Financial award application deadline: 6/1; financial award applicants required to submit FAFSA. *Faculty research:* Organizational aesthetics, resistance in organizations, dynamics of product innovation, economic approaches to productivity, corporate earnings forecasts and value relevance, ERP implementation, improving Web accessibility, information quality assessment, measuring strategic and transactional IT, website quality, service operations modeling, healthcare operations and performance analysis, entrepreneurship, leadership and change. *Unit head:* Dr. Mark Rice, Dean, 508-831-4665, Fax: 508-831-5218, E-mail: rice@wpi.edu. *Application contact:* Peggy Caisse, Recruiting Operations Coordinator, 508-831-4665, Fax: 508-831-5720, E-mail: mcaisse@wpi.edu. Web site: http://www.biz.wpi.edu/Graduate/.

Section 12
Engineering Physics

This section contains a directory of institutions offering graduate work in engineering physics. Additional information about programs listed in the directory but not augmented by an in-depth entry may be obtained by writing directly to the dean of a graduate school or chair of a department at the address given in the directory.

For programs offering related work, see also in this book *Electrical and Computer Engineering, Energy and Power Engineering (Nuclear Engineering), Engineering and Applied Sciences,* and *Materials Sciences and Engineering.* In the other guides in this series:

Graduate Programs in the Biological/Biomedical Sciences & Health-Related Medical Professions
See *Biophysics* and *Health Sciences (Medical Physics)*

Graduate Programs in the Physical Sciences, Mathematics, Agricultural Sciences, the Environment & Natural Resources
See *Physics*

CONTENTS

Program Directory

Engineering Physics

Air Force Institute of Technology, Graduate School of Engineering and Management, Department of Engineering Physics, Dayton, OH 45433-7765. Offers applied physics (MS, PhD); electro-optics (MS, PhD); materials science (PhD); nuclear engineering (MS, PhD); space physics (MS). Part-time programs available. *Degree requirements:* For master's, thesis; for doctorate, thesis/dissertation. *Entrance requirements:* For master's and doctorate, GRE General Test, minimum GPA of 3.0, U.S. citizenship. *Faculty research:* High-energy lasers, space physics, nuclear weapon effects, semiconductor physics.

Appalachian State University, Cratis D. Williams Graduate School, Department of Physics and Astronomy, Boone, NC 28608. Offers engineering physics (MS), including systems and lab automation. Part-time programs available. *Faculty:* 18 full-time (9 women), 2 part-time/adjunct (1 woman). *Students:* 14 full-time (2 women), 4 part-time (1 woman); includes 2 minority (1 Black or African American, non-Hispanic/Latino; 1 Hispanic/Latino). 17 applicants, *76% accepted, 6 enrolled. In 2011, 10 master's awarded. *Degree requirements:* For master's, comprehensive exam, thesis optional. *Entrance requirements:* For master's, GRE General Test, 3 letters of recommendation. Additional exam requirements/recommendations for international students: Required—TOEFL (minimum score 570 paper-based; 230 computer-based; 79 iBT), IELTS (minimum score 6.5). *Application deadline:* For fall admission, 3/15 priority date for domestic students, 2/1 for international students; for spring admission, 11/1 for domestic students, 7/1 for international students. Applications are processed on a rolling basis. Application fee: $55. Electronic applications accepted. *Expenses:* Tuition, state resident: full-time $4040; part-time $180 per semester hour. Tuition, nonresident: full-time $15,900; part-time $760 per semester hour. *Required fees:* $2500; $20 per semester hour. Tuition and fees vary according to campus/location. *Financial support:* In 2011–12, 1 research assistantship with tuition reimbursement (averaging $10,000 per year), 7 teaching assistantships with tuition reimbursements (averaging $9,500 per year) were awarded; fellowships, career-related internships or fieldwork, Federal Work-Study, scholarships/grants, and unspecified assistantships also available. Financial award application deadline: 4/1. *Faculty research:* Raman spectroscopy, applied electrostatics, scanning tunneling microscope/atomic force microscope (STM/AFM), stellar spectroscopy and photometry, surface physics, remote sensing. *Total annual research expenditures:* $35,000. *Unit head:* Dr. Michael Briley, Chairperson, 828-262-3090, E-mail: brileymm@appstate.edu. *Application contact:* Dr. Sid Clements, Director, 828-262-2447, E-mail: clementsjs@appstate.edu. Web site: http://www.phys.appstate.edu/.

Cornell University, Graduate School, Graduate Fields of Engineering, Field of Applied Physics, Ithaca, NY 14853-0001. Offers applied physics (PhD); engineering physics (M Eng). *Faculty:* 44 full-time (4 women). *Students:* 93 full-time (16 women); includes 11 minority (6 Asian, non-Hispanic/Latino; 5 Hispanic/Latino), 40 international. Average age 25. 201 applicants, 41% accepted, 30 enrolled. In 2011, 22 master's, 6 doctorates awarded. *Degree requirements:* For doctorate, comprehensive exam, thesis/dissertation, written exams. *Entrance requirements:* For master's, GRE General Test, 3 letters of recommendation; for doctorate, GRE General Test, GRE Subject Test (physics), GRE Writing Assessment, 3 letters of recommendation. Additional exam requirements/recommendations for international students: Required—TOEFL (minimum score 600 paper-based; 250 computer-based; 77 iBT). *Application deadline:* For fall admission, 1/15 for domestic students. Application fee: $95. Electronic applications accepted. *Financial support:* In 2011–12, 70 students received support, including 7 fellowships with full tuition reimbursements available, 49 research assistantships with full tuition reimbursements available, 11 teaching assistantships with full tuition reimbursements available; institutionally sponsored loans, scholarships/grants, health care benefits, tuition waivers (full and partial), and unspecified assistantships also available. *Faculty research:* Quantum and nonlinear optics, plasma physics, solid state physics, condensed matter physics and nanotechnology, electron and x-ray spectroscopy. *Unit head:* Graduate Faculty Representative, 607-255-0638. *Application contact:* Graduate Field Assistant, 607-255-0638, E-mail: aep_info@cornell.edu. Web site: http://www.gradschool.cornell.edu/fields.php?id-23&a-2.

Dartmouth College, Thayer School of Engineering, Program in Engineering Physics, Hanover, NH 03755. Offers MS, PhD. Application fee: $45. *Faculty research:* Computational physics, medical physics, radiation physics, plasma science and magneto hydro-dynamics, magnetospheric and ionospheric physics. *Unit head:* Dr. Joseph J. Helbie, Dean, 603-646-2238, Fax: 603-646-2580, E-mail: joseph.j.helbie@dartmouth.edu. *Application contact:* Candace S. Potter, Graduate Admissions Administrator, 603-646-3844, Fax: 603-646-1620, E-mail: candace.potter@dartmouth.edu.

École Polytechnique de Montréal, Graduate Programs, Department of Engineering Physics, Montréal, QC H3C 3A7, Canada. Offers optical engineering (M Eng, M Sc A, PhD); solid-state physics and engineering (M Eng, M Sc A, PhD). Part-time programs available. *Degree requirements:* For master's, one foreign language, thesis; for doctorate, one foreign language, thesis/dissertation. *Entrance requirements:* For master's, minimum GPA of 2.75; for doctorate, minimum GPA of 3.0. *Faculty research:* Optics, thin-film physics, laser spectroscopy, plasmas, photonic devices.

Embry-Riddle Aeronautical University–Daytona, Daytona Beach Campus Graduate Program, Department of Physical Sciences, Daytona Beach, FL 32114-3900. Offers engineering physics (MS, PhD). Part-time and evening/weekend programs available. *Faculty:* 7 full-time (0 women). *Students:* 25 full-time (4 women), 1 part-time (0 women); includes 7 minority (1 Black or African American, non-Hispanic/Latino; 3 Asian, non-Hispanic/Latino; 3 Hispanic/Latino), 5 international. Average age 25. 16 applicants, 88% accepted, 11 enrolled. In 2011, 6 degrees awarded. *Degree requirements:* For master's, thesis; for doctorate, comprehensive exam, thesis/dissertation. *Entrance requirements:* For doctorate, GRE (minimum score verbal plus quantitative of 1200 obtained within previous two years of application), master's degree in physics or engineering, minimum GPA of 3.2, statement of goals, 3 letters of recommendation. Additional exam requirements/recommendations for international students: Required—TOEFL (minimum score 550 paper-based; 213 computer-based; 79 iBT). *Application deadline:* For fall admission, 5/1 priority date for domestic students, 6/1 for international students; for spring admission, 11/1 priority date for domestic students, 10/1 for international students. Applications are processed on a rolling basis. Application fee: $50. Electronic applications accepted. *Expenses:* Tuition: Full-time $14,340; part-time $1195 per credit hour. *Financial support:* In 2011–12, 22 students received support, including 11 research assistantships with full and partial tuition reimbursements available (averaging $8,364 per year), 1 teaching assistantship with full and partial tuition reimbursement available (averaging $4,001 per year); career-related internships or fieldwork and unspecified assistantships also available. Financial award application deadline: 4/15; financial award applicants required to submit FAFSA. *Faculty research:* Aeronomy/upper atmospheric physics, space physics, spacecraft instrumentation, spacecraft systems engineering, spacecraft power and thermal control. *Unit head:* Dr. Robert Fleck, Interim Department Chair, 386-226-7059, E-mail: robert.fleck@erau.edu. *Application contact:* Flavia Carreiro, Assistant Director, International and Graduate Admissions, 800-388-3728, Fax: 386-226-7070, E-mail: graduate.admissions@erau.edu. Web site: http://daytonabeach.erau.edu/coas/physical-sciences/graduate-degrees/index.html.

George Mason University, College of Science, School of Physics, Astronomy and Computational Sciences, Fairfax, VA 22030. Offers applied and engineering physics (MS); computational science (PhD); computational sciences and informatics (MS); physics (PhD). *Faculty:* 55 full-time (11 women), 10 part-time/adjunct (1 woman). *Students:* 49 full-time (12 women), 98 part-time (26 women); includes 23 minority (5 Black or African American, non-Hispanic/Latino; 12 Asian, non-Hispanic/Latino; 6 Hispanic/Latino), 25 international. Average age 35. 79 applicants, 49% accepted, 19 enrolled. In 2011, 12 master's, 17 doctorates, 2 other advanced degrees awarded. *Degree requirements:* For master's, thesis optional. *Entrance requirements:* For master's and doctorate, GRE, baccalaureate degree in related field with minimum GPA of 3.0 in last 60 credit hours; 3 letters of recommendation; expanded goals statement; resume; 2 copies of official transcripts. Additional exam requirements/recommendations for international students: Required—TOEFL (minimum score 570 paper-based; 230 computer-based; 88 iBT), IELTS, Pearson Test of English. *Application deadline:* For fall admission, 4/15 priority date for domestic students; for spring admission, 11/15 priority date for domestic students. Application fee: $65 ($80 for international students). Electronic applications accepted. *Expenses:* Tuition, state resident: full-time $8750; part-time $364.58 per credit. Tuition, nonresident: full-time $24,092; part-time $1003.83 per credit. *Required fees:* $2514; $104.75 per credit. *Financial support:* In 2011–12, 48 students received support, including 5 fellowships with full tuition reimbursements available (averaging $18,000 per year), 33 research assistantships with full and partial tuition reimbursements available (averaging $15,744 per year), 15 teaching assistantships with full and partial tuition reimbursements available (averaging $13,827 per year); career-related internships or fieldwork, Federal Work-Study, scholarships/grants, unspecified assistantships, and health care benefits (full-time research or teaching assistantship recipients) also available. Support available to part-time students. Financial award application deadline: 3/1; financial award applicants required to submit FAFSA. *Faculty research:* Astronomy, astrophysics, and space and planetary science; astronomy and physics education; atomic physics; biophysics and neuroscience. *Total annual research expenditures:* $6.7 million. *Unit head:* Dr. Michael Summers, Chairman, 703-993-3971, Fax: 703-993-1269, E-mail: msummers@gmu.edu. *Application contact:* Dr. Paul So, Information Contact, 703-993-4377, Fax: 703-993-1269, E-mail: paso@gmu.edu. Web site: http://spacs.gmu.edu/.

McMaster University, School of Graduate Studies, Faculty of Engineering, Department of Engineering Physics, Hamilton, ON L8S 4M2, Canada. Offers engineering physics (M Eng, MA Sc, PhD); nuclear engineering (PhD). *Degree requirements:* For master's, thesis or alternative; for doctorate, comprehensive exam, thesis/dissertation. *Entrance requirements:* For master's, minimum B average in engineering, mathematics, or physical sciences. Additional exam requirements/recommendations for international students: Required—TOEFL (minimum score 550 paper-based; 213 computer-based). *Faculty research:* Non-thermal plasmas for pollution control and electrostatic precipitation, bulk and thin film luminescent materials, devices and systems for optical fiber communications, physics and applications of III-V materials and devices, defect spectroscopy in semiconductors.

Michigan Technological University, Graduate School, College of Sciences and Arts, Department of Physics, Houghton, MI 49931. Offers engineering physics (PhD); physics (MS, PhD). Part-time programs available. *Faculty:* 24 full-time (2 women), 3 part-time/adjunct (0 women). *Students:* 28 full-time (5 women), 3 part-time (1 woman), 23 international. Average age 29. 94 applicants, 13% accepted, 3 enrolled. In 2011, 4 master's, 7 doctorates awarded. Terminal master's awarded for partial completion of doctoral program. *Degree requirements:* For master's, comprehensive exam (for some programs), thesis (for some programs); for doctorate, comprehensive exam, thesis/dissertation, preliminary exam, research proposal. *Entrance requirements:* For master's and doctorate, GRE (recommended minimum quantitative score of 156 [720 old version] and analytical score of 3.0), statement of purpose, official transcripts, 3 letters of recommendation. Additional exam requirements/recommendations for international students: Required—TOEFL (minimum score 88 iBT) or IELTS. *Application deadline:* For fall admission, 3/1 for domestic students, 1/15 for international students. Applications are processed on a rolling basis. Electronic applications accepted. *Expenses:* Tuition, state resident: full-time $12,636; part-time $702 per credit. Tuition, nonresident: full-time $12,636; part-time $702 per credit. *Required fees:* $226; $226 per year. *Financial support:* In 2011–12, 31 students received support, including 1 fellowship with full tuition reimbursement available (averaging $6,065 per year), 12 research assistantships with full tuition reimbursements available (averaging $6,065 per year), 15 teaching assistantships with full tuition reimbursements available (averaging $6,065 per year); career-related internships or fieldwork, Federal Work-Study, scholarships/grants, health care benefits, tuition waivers (partial), unspecified assistantships, and cooperative program also available. Financial award applicants required to submit FAFSA. *Faculty research:* Atmospheric physics, astrophysics, biophysics, materials physics, atomic/molecular physics. *Total annual research expenditures:* $2 million. *Unit head:* Dr. Ravindra Pandey, Chair, 906-487-2831, Fax: 906-487-2933, E-mail: pandey@mtu.edu. *Application contact:* Kathleen S. Wollan, Secretary, 906-487-2086, Fax: 906-487-2933, E-mail: kswollan@mtu.edu. Web site: http://www.phy.mtu.edu/.

Polytechnic Institute of New York University, Department of Electrical and Computer Engineering, Major in Electrophysics, Brooklyn, NY 11201-2990. Offers MS. Part-time and evening/weekend programs available. *Students:* 2 full-time (0 women), 2 part-time (0 women); includes 1 minority (Black or African American, non-Hispanic/Latino). Average age 27. 9 applicants, 56% accepted, 4 enrolled. In 2011, 1 master's awarded. *Degree requirements:* For master's, comprehensive exam (for some programs), thesis (for some programs). *Entrance requirements:* For master's, BS in electrical engineering. Additional exam requirements/recommendations for international students: Required—TOEFL (minimum score 550 paper-based; 213 computer-based; 80 iBT); Recommended—IELTS (minimum score 6.5). *Application deadline:* For fall admission, 7/31 priority date for domestic students, 4/30 for international students; for spring admission, 12/31 priority date for domestic students, 11/30 for international students. Applications are processed on a rolling basis. Application fee: $75. Electronic applications accepted. *Expenses:* Tuition: Full-time $22,464; part-time $1248 per credit. *Required fees:* $501 per semester. *Financial support:* Fellowships, research assistantships, teaching assistantships, institutionally sponsored loans, scholarships/grants, and unspecified assistantships available. Support available to part-time students. Financial award applicants required to submit FAFSA. *Unit head:* Dr. Jonathan Chao, Head, 718-860-3478, Fax: 718-260-3302, E-mail: chao@poly.edu. *Application contact:* JeanCarlo Bonilla, Director of Graduate Enrollment Management, 718-260-3182, Fax: 718-260-3624.

Polytechnic Institute of NYU, Long Island Graduate Center, Graduate Programs, Department of Electrical and Computer Engineering, Major in Electrophysics, Melville, NY 11747. Offers MS. Part-time and evening/weekend programs available. In 2011, 1 master's awarded. *Degree requirements:* For master's, comprehensive exam (for some programs), thesis (for some programs). *Entrance requirements:* Additional exam requirements/recommendations for international students: Required—TOEFL (minimum score 550 paper-based; 213 computer-based; 80 iBT); Recommended—IELTS (minimum score 6.5). *Application deadline:* For fall admission, 7/31 priority date for domestic students, 4/30 for international students; for spring admission, 12/31 priority date for domestic students, 11/30 for international students. Applications are processed on a rolling basis. Application fee: $75. Electronic applications accepted. *Financial support:* Institutionally sponsored loans, scholarships/grants, and unspecified assistantships available. Support available to part-time students. Financial award applicants required to submit FAFSA. *Unit head:* Dr. Jonathan Chao, Department Head, 718-260-3302, E-mail: chao@poly.edu. *Application contact:* JeanCarlo Bonilla, Director of Graduate Enrollment Management, 718-260-3182, Fax: 718-260-3624, E-mail: gradinfo@poly.edu.

Rensselaer Polytechnic Institute, Graduate School, School of Engineering, Program in Engineering Physics, Troy, NY 12180-3590. Offers MS, PhD. Part-time programs available. Terminal master's awarded for partial completion of doctoral program. *Degree requirements:* For master's, thesis (for some programs); for doctorate, thesis/dissertation. *Entrance requirements:* For master's and doctorate, GRE. Additional exam requirements/recommendations for international students: Required—TOEFL (minimum score 600 paper-based; 250 computer-based; 100 iBT). Electronic applications accepted. *Faculty research:* Nuclear data management, multiphase flow and heat transfer, environmental and operational health physics, fusion reactor engineering and safety, radiation destruction of hazardous chemicals.

Stevens Institute of Technology, Graduate School, Charles V. Schaefer Jr. School of Engineering, Department of Physics and Engineering Physics, Hoboken, NJ 07030. Offers applied optics (Certificate); engineering physics (M Eng); microdevices and microsystems (Certificate); physics (MS, PhD); plasma and surface physics (Certificate). Part-time and evening/weekend programs available. Terminal master's awarded for partial completion of doctoral program. *Degree requirements:* For master's, thesis optional; for doctorate, thesis/dissertation. *Entrance requirements:* For master's and doctorate, GRE. Additional exam requirements/recommendations for international students: Required—TOEFL. Electronic applications accepted. *Faculty research:* Laser spectroscopy, physical kinetics, semiconductor-device physics, condensed-matter theory.

University of California, San Diego, Office of Graduate Studies, Department of Mechanical and Aerospace Engineering, Program in Engineering Physics, La Jolla, CA 92093. Offers MS, PhD. Part-time programs available. *Degree requirements:* For master's, comprehensive exam or thesis; for doctorate, thesis/dissertation, qualifying exam. *Entrance requirements:* For master's and doctorate, GRE General Test, minimum GPA of 3.0. Additional exam requirements/recommendations for international students: Required—TOEFL. Electronic applications accepted. *Faculty research:* Combustion engineering, environmental mechanics, magnetic recording, materials processing, computational fluid dynamics.

University of Maine, Graduate School, College of Liberal Arts and Sciences, Department of Physics and Astronomy, Program in Engineering Physics, Orono, ME 04469. Offers M Eng. *Students:* 2 full-time (0 women). Average age 26. 4 applicants, 25% accepted, 1 enrolled. In 2011, 3 degrees awarded. *Degree requirements:* For master's, thesis or alternative. *Entrance requirements:* For master's, GRE General Test, GRE Subject Test. Additional exam requirements/recommendations for international students: Required—TOEFL. *Application deadline:* For fall admission, 2/1 priority date for domestic students; for spring admission, 10/15 for domestic students. Applications are processed on a rolling basis. Application fee: $65. *Expenses:* Tuition, state resident: full-time $5016. Tuition, nonresident: full-time $14,424. *Financial support:* In 2011–12, 1 teaching assistantship with full tuition reimbursement (averaging $13,600 per year) was awarded. Financial award application deadline: 3/1. *Unit head:* Dr. Susan McKay, Chair, 207-581-1015, Fax: 207-581-3410. *Application contact:* Scott G. Delcourt, Associate Dean of the Graduate School, 207-581-3291, Fax: 207-581-3232, E-mail: graduate@maine.edu. Web site: http://www2.umaine.edu/graduate/.

University of Oklahoma, College of Engineering, Program in Engineering Physics, Norman, OK 73019. Offers MS, PhD. Terminal master's awarded for partial completion of doctoral program. *Degree requirements:* For master's, thesis or alternative, departmental qualifying exam; for doctorate, thesis/dissertation, comprehensive, departmental qualifying, oral, and written exams. *Entrance requirements:* For master's and doctorate, GRE General Test, GRE Subject Test (physics), previous course work in physics. Additional exam requirements/recommendations for international students: Required—TOEFL (minimum score 550 paper-based; 79 iBT). *Application deadline:* For fall admission, 3/1 priority date for domestic students, 3/1 for international students; for spring admission, 10/1 for domestic students, 9/1 for international students. Applications are processed on a rolling basis. Application fee: $40 ($90 for international students). Electronic applications accepted. *Expenses:* Tuition, state resident: full-time $4087; part-time $170.30 per credit hour. Tuition, nonresident: full-time $14,875; part-time $619.80 per credit hour. *Required fees:* $2659; $100.25 per credit hour. Tuition and fees vary according to course load and degree level. *Financial support:* Scholarships/grants, health care benefits, tuition waivers (full), and unspecified assistantships available. Financial award applicants required to submit FAFSA. *Faculty research:* Nanoscience, ultra cold atoms, high energy physics. *Unit head:* Mike Santos, Director, 405-325-3961, Fax: 405-325-7557, E-mail: msantos@ou.edu. *Application contact:* Miranda Sowell, Coordinator of Graduate Admissions, 405-325-3811, Fax: 405-325-5346, E-mail: mgsowell@ou.edu. Web site: http://www.nhn.ou.edu/ephys/.

University of Saskatchewan, College of Graduate Studies and Research, College of Arts and Science, Department of Physics and Engineering Physics, Saskatoon, SK S7N 5A2, Canada. Offers M Sc, PhD. *Degree requirements:* For master's, thesis; for doctorate, comprehensive exam (for some programs), thesis/dissertation. *Entrance requirements:* Additional exam requirements/recommendations for international students: Required—TOEFL (minimum score 80 iBT); Recommended—IELTS (minimum score 6.5). Electronic applications accepted.

University of Tulsa, Graduate School, College of Engineering and Natural Sciences, Department of Physics and Engineering Physics, Program in Engineering Physics, Tulsa, OK 74104-3189. Offers MS. Part-time programs available. *Students:* 1 full-time (0 women). Average age 24. 1 applicant, 0% accepted, 0 enrolled. In 2011, 2 master's awarded. *Degree requirements:* For master's, thesis. *Entrance requirements:* For master's, GRE General Test. Additional exam requirements/recommendations for international students: Required—TOEFL (minimum score 550 paper-based; 213 computer-based; 80 iBT), IELTS (minimum score 6). *Application deadline:* Applications are processed on a rolling basis. Application fee: $40. Electronic applications accepted. *Expenses:* Tuition: Full-time $17,748; part-time $986 per hour. *Required fees:* $5 per contact hour. $75 per semester. Tuition and fees vary according to program. *Financial support:* In 2011–12, 1 student received support, including 2 teaching assistantships (averaging $9,091 per year); fellowships, research assistantships, career-related internships or fieldwork, Federal Work-Study, scholarships/grants, health care benefits, tuition waivers (full and partial), and unspecified assistantships also available. Support available to part-time students. *Faculty research:* Nanotechnology, theoretical plasma physics/fusion, condensed matter, laser spectroscopy, optics and optical applications for environmental applications. *Unit head:* Dr. George Miller, Program Chair, 918-631-3021, Fax: 918-631-2995, E-mail: george-miller@utulsa.edu. *Application contact:* Dr. Scott Holmstrom, Advisor, 918-631-3031, Fax: 918-631-2995, E-mail: scott-holmstrom@utulsa.edu.

University of Virginia, School of Engineering and Applied Science, Program in Engineering Physics, Charlottesville, VA 22903. Offers MEP, MS, PhD. Postbaccalaureate distance learning degree programs offered (no on-campus study). *Students:* 20 full-time (4 women), 1 part-time (0 women); includes 4 minority (2 Black or African American, non-Hispanic/Latino; 2 Asian, non-Hispanic/Latino), 3 international. Average age 29. 19 applicants, 42% accepted, 1 enrolled. In 2011, 3 master's, 6 doctorates awarded. *Degree requirements:* For master's, comprehensive exam; for doctorate, comprehensive exam, thesis/dissertation. *Entrance requirements:* For master's and doctorate, GRE General Test, 3 recommendations. Additional exam requirements/recommendations for international students: Required—TOEFL. *Application deadline:* For fall admission, 1/15 for domestic and international students. Applications are processed on a rolling basis. Application fee: $60. Electronic applications accepted. *Financial support:* Fellowships, research assistantships, and teaching assistantships available. Financial award application deadline: 2/1; financial award applicants required to submit FAFSA. *Faculty research:* Continuum and rarefied gas dynamics, ultracentrifuge isotope enrichment, solid-state physics, atmospheric physics, atomic collisions. *Unit head:* Petra Reinke, Co-Chair, 434-924-7237, Fax: 434-982-5660, E-mail: pr6e@virginia.edu. *Application contact:* Kathryn C. Thornton, Assistant Dean for Graduate Programs, 434-924-3897, Fax: 434-982-2214, E-mail: seas-grad-admission@cs.virginia.edu. Web site: http://www.virginia.edu/ep/.

University of Wisconsin–Madison, Graduate School, College of Engineering, Department of Engineering Physics, Madison, WI 53706. Offers engineering mechanics (MS, PhD); nuclear engineering and engineering physics (MS, PhD). Part-time programs available. Postbaccalaureate distance learning degree programs offered (minimal on-campus study). *Faculty:* 20 full-time (0 women), 9 part-time/adjunct (4 women). *Students:* 102 full-time (11 women), 16 part-time (1 woman); includes 12 minority (3 Black or African American, non-Hispanic/Latino; 1 American Indian or Alaska Native, non-Hispanic/Latino; 1 Asian, non-Hispanic/Latino; 7 Hispanic/Latino), 18 international. Average age 25. 198 applicants, 37% accepted, 38 enrolled. In 2011, 43 master's, 8 doctorates awarded. Terminal master's awarded for partial completion of doctoral program. *Degree requirements:* For master's, thesis optional; for doctorate, thesis/dissertation. *Entrance requirements:* For master's and doctorate, GRE General Test, minimum GPA of 3.0 in last 60 hours, appropriate bachelor's degree. Additional exam requirements/recommendations for international students: Required—TOEFL (minimum score 600 paper-based; 245 computer-based). *Application deadline:* For fall admission, 1/15 priority date for domestic students, 1/15 for international students. Applications are processed on a rolling basis. Application fee: $56. Electronic applications accepted. *Expenses:* Tuition, state resident: full-time $10,296; part-time $643.51 per credit. Tuition, nonresident: full-time $24,054; part-time $1503.40 per credit. *Required fees:* $70.06 per credit. Tuition and fees vary according to course load, campus/location, program and reciprocity agreements. *Financial support:* In 2011–12, 106 students received support, including 20 fellowships with full tuition reimbursements available (averaging $25,000 per year), 76 research assistantships with full tuition reimbursements available (averaging $20,400 per year), 10 teaching assistantships with full tuition reimbursements available (averaging $12,633 per year); career-related internships or fieldwork, Federal Work-Study, institutionally sponsored loans, and unspecified assistantships also available. Support available to part-time students. Financial award application deadline: 1/15. *Faculty research:* Fission reactor engineering and safety, plasma physics and fusion technology, plasma processing and ion implantation, nanotechnology, engineering mechanics and astronautics. *Total annual research expenditures:* $18.8 million. *Unit head:* Dr. James P. Blanchard, Chair, 608-263-0391, Fax: 608-263-7451, E-mail: blanchard@engr.wisc.edu. *Application contact:* Betsy A. Wood, Graduate Coordinator, 608-263-7038, Fax: 608-263-7451, E-mail: bwood@engr.wisc.edu. Web site: http://www.engr.wisc.edu/ep/.

Yale University, Graduate School of Arts and Sciences, School of Engineering and Applied Science, Department of Applied Physics, New Haven, CT 06520. Offers MS, PhD. Terminal master's awarded for partial completion of doctoral program. *Degree requirements:* For doctorate, thesis/dissertation, area exam. *Entrance requirements:* For master's and doctorate, GRE General Test. Additional exam requirements/recommendations for international students: Required—TOEFL. *Faculty research:* Condensed-matter physics, optical physics, materials science.

Section 13
Geological, Mineral/Mining, and Petroleum Engineering

This section contains a directory of institutions offering graduate work in geological, mineral/mining, and petroleum engineering. Additional information about programs listed in the directory but not augmented by an in-depth entry may be obtained by writing directly to the dean of a graduate school or chair of a department at the address given in the directory.

For programs offering related work, see also in this book *Chemical Engineering, Civil and Environmental Engineering, Electrical and Computer Engineering, Energy and Power Engineering, Engineering and Applied Sciences, Management of Engineering and Technology,* and *Materials Sciences and Engineering.* In another guide in this series:

Graduate Programs in the Physical Sciences, Mathematics, Agricultural Sciences, the Environment & Natural Resources
See *Geosciences* and *Marine Sciences and Oceanography*

CONTENTS

Program Directories

Geological Engineering

Arizona State University, College of Liberal Arts and Sciences, School of Earth and Space Exploration, Tempe, AZ 85287-1404. Offers astrophysics (MS, PhD); exploration systems design (PhD); geological sciences (MS, PhD). PhD in exploration systems design is offered in collaboration with the Fulton Schools of Engineering. Terminal master's awarded for partial completion of doctoral program. *Degree requirements:* For master's, thesis, interactive Program of Study (iPOS) submitted before completing 50 percent of required credit hours; for doctorate, thesis/dissertation, interactive Program of Study (iPOS) submitted before completing 50 percent of required credit hours. *Entrance requirements:* For master's and doctorate, GRE, minimum GPA of 3.0 or equivalent in last 2 years of work leading to bachelor's degree. Additional exam requirements/recommendations for international students: Required—TOEFL (minimum score 80 iBT), TOEFL, IELTS, or Pearson Test of English. Electronic applications accepted.

Colorado School of Mines, Graduate School, Department of Geology and Geological Engineering, Golden, CO 80401-1887. Offers geochemistry (MS, PMS, PhD); geological engineering (ME, MS, PhD); geology (MS, PhD). Part-time programs available. *Faculty:* 22 full-time (7 women), 4 part-time/adjunct (2 women). *Students:* 147 full-time (51 women), 31 part-time (11 women); includes 15 minority (2 Black or African American, non-Hispanic/Latino; 2 American Indian or Alaska Native, non-Hispanic/Latino; 2 Asian, non-Hispanic/Latino; 8 Hispanic/Latino; 1 Two or more races, non-Hispanic/Latino), 29 international. Average age 30. 241 applicants, 55% accepted, 55 enrolled. In 2011, 26 master's, 1 doctorate awarded. *Degree requirements:* For master's, thesis (for some programs); for doctorate, comprehensive exam, thesis/dissertation. *Entrance requirements:* For master's and doctorate, GRE General Test. Additional exam requirements/recommendations for international students: Required—TOEFL (minimum score 550 paper-based; 213 computer-based; 80 iBT). *Application deadline:* For fall admission, 1/15 for domestic and international students; for spring admission, 10/15 for domestic and international students. Application fee: $50 ($70 for international students). Electronic applications accepted. *Expenses:* Tuition, state resident: full-time $12,585; part-time $699 per credit. Tuition, nonresident: full-time $27,270; part-time $1516 per credit. *Required fees:* $1864.20; $670 per semester. *Financial support:* In 2011–12, 79 students received support, including 14 fellowships with full tuition reimbursements available (averaging $20,000 per year), 47 research assistantships with full tuition reimbursements available (averaging $20,000 per year), 18 teaching assistantships with full tuition reimbursements available (averaging $20,000 per year); scholarships/grants, health care benefits, and unspecified assistantships also available. Financial award application deadline: 1/15; financial award applicants required to submit FAFSA. *Faculty research:* Predictive sediment modeling, petrophysics, aquifer-contaminant flow modeling, water-rock interactions, geotechnical engineering. *Total annual research expenditures:* $3.3 million. *Unit head:* Dr. John Humphrey, Head, 303-273-3819, Fax: 303-273-3859, E-mail: jhumphre@mines.edu. *Application contact:* Dr. Christian Shorey, Lecturer, 303-273-3556, Fax: 303-273-3859, E-mail: cshorey@mines.edu. Web site: http://geology.mines.edu.

Colorado School of Mines, Graduate School, Department of Geophysics, Golden, CO 80401-1887. Offers geophysical engineering (ME, MS, PhD); geophysics (MS, PhD); mineral exploration and mining geosciences (PMS). Part-time programs available. *Faculty:* 18 full-time (1 woman), 2 part-time/adjunct (0 women). *Students:* 85 full-time (28 women), 7 part-time (2 women); includes 9 minority (1 American Indian or Alaska Native, non-Hispanic/Latino; 3 Asian, non-Hispanic/Latino; 5 Hispanic/Latino), 47 international. Average age 28. 163 applicants, 24% accepted, 28 enrolled. In 2011, 14 master's, 3 doctorates awarded. *Degree requirements:* For master's, thesis (for some programs); for doctorate, one foreign language, comprehensive exam, thesis/dissertation, oral exams. *Entrance requirements:* For master's and doctorate, GRE General Test. Additional exam requirements/recommendations for international students: Required—TOEFL (minimum score 550 paper-based; 213 computer-based; 80 iBT). *Application deadline:* For fall admission, 1/15 for domestic and international students; for spring admission, 10/15 for domestic and international students. Application fee: $50 ($70 for international students). Electronic applications accepted. *Expenses:* Tuition, state resident: full-time $12,585; part-time $699 per credit. Tuition, nonresident: full-time $27,270; part-time $1516 per credit. *Required fees:* $1864.20; $670 per semester. *Financial support:* In 2011–12, 74 students received support, including 7 fellowships with full tuition reimbursements available (averaging $20,000 per year), 60 research assistantships with full tuition reimbursements available (averaging $20,000 per year), 7 teaching assistantships with full tuition reimbursements available (averaging $20,000 per year); scholarships/grants, health care benefits, and unspecified assistantships also available. Financial award application deadline: 1/15; financial award applicants required to submit FAFSA. *Faculty research:* Seismic exploration, gravity and geomagnetic fields, electrical mapping and sounding, bore hole measurements, environmental physics. *Total annual research expenditures:* $4.3 million. *Unit head:* Dr. Terence K. Young, Head, 303-273-3454, Fax: 303-273-3478, E-mail: tkyoung@mines.edu. *Application contact:* Michelle Szobody, Office Manager, 303-273-3935, Fax: 303-273-3478, E-mail: mszobody@mines.edu. Web site: http://geophysics.mines.edu.

Michigan Technological University, Graduate School, College of Engineering, Department of Geological and Mining Engineering and Sciences, Houghton, MI 49931. Offers geological engineering (MS, PhD); geology (MS, PhD); geophysics (MS, PhD); mining engineering (MS, PhD). Part-time programs available. *Faculty:* 20 full-time (2 women), 21 part-time/adjunct (1 woman). *Students:* 52 full-time (28 women), 8 part-time (3 women); includes 3 minority (all Hispanic/Latino), 20 international. Average age 29. 114 applicants, 33% accepted, 15 enrolled. In 2011, 10 master's, 1 doctorate awarded. Terminal master's awarded for partial completion of doctoral program. *Degree requirements:* For master's, comprehensive exam (for some programs), thesis (for some programs); for doctorate, comprehensive exam, thesis/dissertation. *Entrance requirements:* For master's and doctorate, GRE, statement of purpose, official transcripts, 3 letters of recommendation. Additional exam requirements/recommendations for international students: Required—TOEFL (minimum score 79 iBT) or IELTS. *Application deadline:* Applications are processed on a rolling basis. Electronic applications accepted. *Expenses:* Tuition, state resident: full-time $12,636; part-time $702 per credit. Tuition, nonresident: full-time $12,636; part-time $702 per credit. *Required fees:* $226; $226 per year. *Financial support:* In 2011–12, 45 students received support, including 4 fellowships with full tuition reimbursements available (averaging $6,065 per year), 22 research assistantships with full tuition reimbursements available (averaging $6,065 per year), teaching assistantships with full tuition reimbursements available (averaging $6,065 per year); career-related internships or fieldwork, Federal Work-Study, scholarships/grants, health care benefits, tuition waivers (partial), unspecified assistantships, and cooperative program also available. Financial award applicants required to submit FAFSA. *Faculty research:* Volcanic hazards and volcanic clouds, oil and gas exploration and development, groundwater measurement and modeling, geophysics, environmental paleomagnetism. *Total annual research expenditures:* $1.3 million. *Unit head:* Dr. Wayne D. Pennington, Chair, 906-487-3573,

Fax: 906-487-3371, E-mail: wayne@mtu.edu. *Application contact:* Amie S. Ledgerwood, Secretary 5, 906-487-2531, Fax: 906-487-3371, E-mail: asledger@mtu.edu. Web site: http://www.mtu.edu/geo/.

Missouri University of Science and Technology, Graduate School, Department of Geological Sciences and Engineering, Rolla, MO 65409. Offers geological engineering (MS, DE, PhD); geology and geophysics (MS, PhD), including geochemistry, geology, geophysics, groundwater and environmental geology; petroleum engineering (MS, DE, PhD). Part-time programs available. *Degree requirements:* For master's, thesis optional; for doctorate, comprehensive exam, thesis/dissertation. *Entrance requirements:* For master's, GRE General Test (minimum score 600 quantitative, writing 3.5), minimum GPA of 3.0 in last 4 semesters; for doctorate, GRE General Test (minimum: Q 600, GRE WR 3.5). Additional exam requirements/recommendations for international students: Required—TOEFL. Electronic applications accepted. *Faculty research:* Digital image processing and geographic information systems, mineralogy, igneous and sedimentary petrology-geochemistry, sedimentology groundwater hydrology and contaminant transport.

Montana Tech of The University of Montana, Graduate School, Geosciences Programs, Butte, MT 59701-8997. Offers geochemistry (MS); geological engineering (MS); geology (MS); geophysical engineering (MS); hydrogeological engineering (MS); hydrogeology (MS). Part-time programs available. *Faculty:* 16 full-time (4 women), 4 part-time/adjunct (0 women). *Students:* 16 full-time (7 women), 12 part-time (6 women); includes 2 minority (1 Black or African American, non-Hispanic/Latino; 1 American Indian or Alaska Native, non-Hispanic/Latino), 1 international. 23 applicants, 65% accepted, 13 enrolled. In 2011, 9 master's awarded. *Degree requirements:* For master's, comprehensive exam (for some programs), thesis (for some programs). *Entrance requirements:* For master's, GRE General Test, minimum GPA of 3.0. Additional exam requirements/recommendations for international students: Required—TOEFL (minimum score 525 paper-based; 195 computer-based; 71 iBT). *Application deadline:* For fall admission, 4/1 priority date for domestic students, 3/1 for international students; for spring admission, 10/1 priority date for domestic students, 7/1 for international students. Applications are processed on a rolling basis. Application fee: $30. Electronic applications accepted. *Financial support:* In 2011–12, 15 students received support, including 10 teaching assistantships with partial tuition reimbursements available (averaging $5,000 per year); research assistantships with partial tuition reimbursements available, career-related internships or fieldwork, tuition waivers (full and partial), and unspecified assistantships also available. Financial award application deadline: 4/1; financial award applicants required to submit FAFSA. *Faculty research:* Water resource development, seismic processing, petroleum reservoir characterization, environmental geochemistry, geologic mapping. *Unit head:* Dr. Mary MacLaughlin, Department Head, 406-496-4655, Fax: 406-496-4260, E-mail: mmaclaughlin@mtech.edu. *Application contact:* Fred Sullivan, Administrator, Graduate School, 406-496-4304, Fax: 406-496-4710, E-mail: fsullivan@mtech.edu. Web site: http://www.mtech.edu/academics/gradschool/degreeprograms/degrees.htm.

South Dakota School of Mines and Technology, Graduate Division, Department of Geology and Geological Engineering, Rapid City, SD 57701-3995. Offers geology and geological engineering (MS, PhD); paleontology (MS). Part-time programs available. *Degree requirements:* For master's, thesis; for doctorate, thesis/dissertation. *Entrance requirements:* For master's and doctorate, GRE General Test, GRE Subject Test. Additional exam requirements/recommendations for international students: Required—TOEFL, TWE. Electronic applications accepted. *Faculty research:* Contaminants in soil, nitrate leaching, environmental changes, fracture formations, greenhouse effect.

University of Alaska Anchorage, School of Engineering, Program in Arctic Engineering, Anchorage, AK 99508. Offers MS. Part-time and evening/weekend programs available. *Degree requirements:* For master's, thesis or alternative, engineering project report. *Entrance requirements:* For master's, bachelor's degree in engineering. Additional exam requirements/recommendations for international students: Required—TOEFL (minimum score 550 paper-based; 213 computer-based). *Faculty research:* Load-bearing ice, control of drifting snow, permafrost and foundations, frozen ground engineering.

University of Alaska Fairbanks, College of Engineering and Mines, Department of Mining and Geological Engineering, Fairbanks, AK 99775-5800. Offers geological engineering (MS, PhD); mineral preparation engineering (MS); mining engineering (MS, PhD). Part-time programs available. *Faculty:* 7 full-time (1 woman). *Students:* 13 full-time (4 women), 3 part-time (1 woman); includes 4 minority (3 Asian, non-Hispanic/Latino; 1 Two or more races, non-Hispanic/Latino), 4 international. Average age 30. 20 applicants, 20% accepted, 2 enrolled. In 2011, 2 degrees awarded. Terminal master's awarded for partial completion of doctoral program. *Degree requirements:* For master's, comprehensive exam, thesis or alternative; for doctorate, comprehensive exam, thesis/dissertation, oral exam, oral defense. *Entrance requirements:* For doctorate, GRE General Test. Additional exam requirements/recommendations for international students: Required—TOEFL (minimum score 550 paper-based; 213 computer-based; 80 iBT). *Application deadline:* For fall admission, 6/1 for domestic students, 3/1 for international students; for spring admission, 10/15 for domestic students, 9/1 for international students. Applications are processed on a rolling basis. Application fee: $60. Electronic applications accepted. *Expenses:* Tuition, state resident: full-time $6696; part-time $372 per credit. Tuition, nonresident: full-time $13,680; part-time $760 per credit. Tuition and fees vary according to course load and reciprocity agreements. *Financial support:* In 2011–12, 9 research assistantships with tuition reimbursements (averaging $10,283 per year), 2 teaching assistantships with tuition reimbursements (averaging $7,302 per year) were awarded; fellowships with tuition reimbursements, career-related internships or fieldwork, Federal Work-Study, scholarships/grants, health care benefits, and unspecified assistantships also available. Support available to part-time students. Financial award application deadline: 7/1; financial award applicants required to submit FAFSA. *Faculty research:* Underground mining in permafrost, testing of ultra clean diesel, slope stability, fractal and mathematical morphology, soil and rock mechanics. *Unit head:* Dr. Rajive Ganguli, Chair, 907-474-7388, Fax: 907-474-6635, E-mail: fyminge@uaf.edu. *Application contact:* Mike Earnest, Director of Admissions, 907-474-7500, Fax: 907-474-5379, E-mail: admissions@uaf.edu. Web site: http://www.alaska.edu/uaf/cem/min.

The University of Arizona, College of Engineering, Department of Mining, Geological and Geophysical Engineering, Tucson, AZ 85721. Offers geological engineering (MS, PhD); mining engineering (M Eng, Certificate), including mine health and safety (Certificate), mine information and production technology (Certificate), mining engineering (M Eng), rock mechanics (Certificate). Part-time programs available. Postbaccalaureate distance learning degree programs offered (minimal on-campus study). *Faculty:* 7 full-time (0 women), 1 part-time/adjunct (0 women). *Students:* 16 full-time (2 women), 9 part-time (1 woman); includes 1 minority (Asian, non-Hispanic/Latino), 12 international. Average age 34. 28 applicants, 32% accepted, 4 enrolled. In 2011, 3 master's, 1 doctorate awarded. *Degree requirements:* For master's, thesis; for doctorate, thesis/dissertation. *Entrance requirements:* For master's, GRE General Test, 3 letters of recommendation; for doctorate, GRE General Test, 3 letters of recommendation, statements of purpose. Additional exam requirements/recommendations for international students: Required—TOEFL (minimum score 550 paper-based; 213 computer-based; 79 iBT). *Application deadline:* For fall admission, 6/1 for domestic students, 12/1 for international students; for spring admission, 10/1 for domestic students, 6/1 for international students. Applications are processed on a rolling basis. Application fee: $75. *Expenses:* Tuition, state resident: full-time $10,840. Tuition, nonresident: full-time $25,802. *Financial support:* In 2011–12, 19 research assistantships with full tuition reimbursements (averaging $25,063 per year), 1 teaching assistantship with full tuition reimbursement (averaging $23,586 per year) were awarded; institutionally sponsored loans, scholarships/grants, health care benefits, tuition waivers (partial), and unspecified assistantships also available. Financial award application deadline: 4/1. *Faculty research:* Geomechanics, mineral processing, information technology, automation, geosensing. *Total annual research expenditures:* $420,172. *Unit head:* Dr. Mary M. Poulton, Head, 520-621-6063, Fax: 520-621-8330, E-mail: mpoulton@u.arizona.edu. *Application contact:* Olivia Hanson, Graduate Advisor, 520-621-6063, Fax: 520-621-8330, E-mail: ohanson@engr.arizona.edu. Web site: http://www.mge.arizona.edu.

The University of British Columbia, Faculty of Science, Department of Earth and Ocean Sciences, Vancouver, BC V6T 1Z4, Canada. Offers atmospheric science (M Sc, PhD); geological engineering (M Eng, MA Sc, PhD); geological sciences (M Sc, PhD); geophysics (M Sc, MA Sc, PhD); oceanography (M Sc, PhD). *Degree requirements:* For master's, thesis (for some programs); for doctorate, comprehensive exam, thesis/dissertation. *Entrance requirements:* Additional exam requirements/recommendations for international students: Required—TOEFL (minimum score 600 paper-based; 250 computer-based; 100 iBT). Electronic applications accepted. *Faculty research:* Oceans and atmosphere, environmental earth science, hydro geology, mineral deposits, geophysics.

University of Hawaii at Manoa, Graduate Division, School of Ocean and Earth Science and Technology, Department of Geology and Geophysics, Honolulu, HI 96822. Offers high-pressure geophysics and geochemistry (MS, PhD); hydrogeology and engineering geology (MS, PhD); marine geology and geophysics (MS, PhD); planetary geosciences and remote sensing (MS, PhD); seismology and solid-earth geophysics (MS, PhD); volcanology, petrology, and geochemistry (MS, PhD). Part-time programs available. Terminal master's awarded for partial completion of doctoral program. *Degree requirements:* For master's, thesis optional; for doctorate, comprehensive exam, thesis/dissertation. *Entrance requirements:* For master's and doctorate, GRE General Test, minimum GPA of 3.0. Additional exam requirements/recommendations for international students: Required—TOEFL (minimum score 580 paper-based; 237 computer-based; 92 iBT), IELTS (minimum score 5).

University of Idaho, College of Graduate Studies, College of Engineering, Department of Civil Engineering, Program in Geological Engineering, Moscow, ID 83844-2282. Offers MS. *Students:* 9 part-time. Average age 36. *Degree requirements:* For master's, one foreign language, thesis. *Entrance requirements:* For master's, minimum GPA of 2.8. *Application deadline:* For fall admission, 8/1 for domestic students; for spring admission, 12/15 for domestic students. Applications are processed on a rolling basis. Application fee: $60. Electronic applications accepted. *Expenses:* Tuition, state resident: full-time $3874; part-time $334 per credit hour. Tuition, nonresident: full-time $16,394; part-time $861 per credit hour. *Required fees:* $2808; $99 per credit hour. Tuition and fees vary according to program. *Financial support:* Applicants required to submit FAFSA. *Faculty research:* Slope stability and landslide mitigation, erosion and sediment control for construction sites, rock engineering and rock reinforcement, underground natural gas storage. *Unit head:* Dr. Richard Nielsen, Chair, 208-885-6782. *Application contact:* Erick Larson, Director of Graduate Admissions, 208-885-4723, E-mail: gadms@uidaho.edu. Web site: http://www.uidaho.edu/engr/ce/academics/graduateprogram/msgeoe.

University of Minnesota, Twin Cities Campus, College of Science and Engineering, Department of Civil Engineering, Minneapolis, MN 55455-0213. Offers civil engineering (MCE, MS, PhD); geological engineering (M Geo E, MS); stream restoration science and engineering (Certificate). Part-time programs available. *Faculty:* 31 full-time (5 women). *Students:* 153 (33 women); includes 7 minority (2 American Indian or Alaska Native, non-Hispanic/Latino; 3 Asian, non-Hispanic/Latino; 2 Hispanic/Latino), 50 international. *Degree requirements:* For master's, thesis optional; for doctorate, thesis/dissertation. *Entrance requirements:* For master's and doctorate, GRE General Test. Additional exam requirements/recommendations for international students: Required—TOEFL. *Application deadline:* For fall admission, 12/3 for domestic students. Applications are processed on a rolling basis. Application fee: $75 ($95 for international students). *Financial support:* Fellowships with tuition reimbursements, research assistantships with tuition reimbursements, and teaching assistantships with tuition reimbursements available. *Faculty research:* Environmental engineering, geomechanics, structural engineering, transportation, water resources . *Application contact:* Secretary of Graduate Studies, E-mail: civesgs@umn.edu. Web site: http://www.ce.umn.edu/.

University of Nevada, Reno, Graduate School, College of Science, Mackay School of Earth Sciences and Engineering, Department of Geological Sciences, Program in Geological Engineering, Reno, NV 89557. Offers MS, PhD. Terminal master's awarded for partial completion of doctoral program. *Degree requirements:* For master's, thesis optional; for doctorate, thesis/dissertation. *Entrance requirements:* For master's and doctorate, GRE General Test, minimum GPA of 2.75. Additional exam requirements/recommendations for international students: Required—TOEFL (minimum score 500 paper-based; 173 computer-based; 61 iBT), IELTS (minimum score 6). Electronic applications accepted. *Faculty research:* Reclamation, remediation, restoration .

University of North Dakota, Graduate School, School of Engineering and Mines, Department of Geological Engineering, Grand Forks, ND 58202. Offers M Engr, MS. *Degree requirements:* For master's, thesis. *Entrance requirements:* For master's, GRE General Test. Additional exam requirements/recommendations for international students: Required—TOEFL (minimum score 550 paper-based; 213 computer-based; 79 iBT), IELTS (minimum score 6.5). Electronic applications accepted.

University of Oklahoma, College of Earth and Energy, School of Petroleum and Geological Engineering, Program in Geological Engineering, Norman, OK 73019. Offers MS, PhD. Part-time programs available. *Students:* 1 (woman) part-time, all international. Average age 26. 3 applicants, 0% accepted, 0 enrolled. In 2011, 1 degree awarded. *Entrance requirements:* Additional exam requirements/recommendations for international students: Required—TOEFL (minimum score 550 paper-based; 79 iBT). *Application deadline:* For fall admission, 6/1 for domestic students, 3/1 for international students; for spring admission, 11/1 for domestic students, 9/1 for international students. Applications are processed on a rolling basis. Application fee: $40 ($90 for international students). Electronic applications accepted. *Expenses:* Tuition, state resident: full-time $4087; part-time $170.30 per credit hour. Tuition, nonresident: full-time $14,875; part-time $619.80 per credit hour. *Required fees:* $2659; $100.25 per credit hour. Tuition and fees vary according to course load and degree level. *Financial support:* Traineeships available. *Faculty research:* Hydraulic fracturing, geothermal energy. *Unit head:* Dr. Chandra Rai, Director, 405-325-2921, Fax: 405-325-7477, E-mail: crai@ou.edu. *Application contact:* Shalli Young, Executive Assistant to Graduate Liaison, 405-325-2921, Fax: 405-325-7477, E-mail: syoung@ou.edu. Web site: http://mpge.ou.edu.

University of Utah, Graduate School, College of Mines and Earth Sciences, Department of Geology and Geophysics, Salt Lake City, UT 84112. Offers environmental engineering (ME, MS, PhD); geological engineering (ME, MS, PhD); geology (MS, PhD); geophysics (MS, PhD). *Faculty:* 22 full-time (5 women), 4 part-time/adjunct (0 women). *Students:* 55 full-time (16 women), 28 part-time (9 women); includes 2 minority (both Asian, non-Hispanic/Latino), 16 international. Average age 30. 174 applicants, 17% accepted, 21 enrolled. In 2011, 13 master's, 3 doctorates awarded. Terminal master's awarded for partial completion of doctoral program. *Median time to degree:* Of those who began their doctoral program in fall 2003, 76% received their degree in 8 years or less. *Degree requirements:* For master's, comprehensive exam, thesis; for doctorate, thesis/dissertation, qualifying exam (written and oral). *Entrance requirements:* For master's and doctorate, GRE General Test, minimum GPA of 3.25. Additional exam requirements/recommendations for international students: Required—TOEFL (minimum score 500 paper-based; 173 computer-based). *Application deadline:* For fall admission, 1/15 priority date for domestic students, 1/15 for international students. Applications are processed on a rolling basis. Application fee: $55 ($65 for international students). Electronic applications accepted. *Financial support:* In 2011–12, 22 students received support, including 10 fellowships with full tuition reimbursements available (averaging $15,000 per year), 40 research assistantships with full tuition reimbursements available (averaging $22,000 per year), 14 teaching assistantships with full tuition reimbursements available (averaging $15,000 per year); career-related internships or fieldwork, institutionally sponsored loans, scholarships/grants, unspecified assistantships, and stipends also available. Financial award application deadline: 1/15; financial award applicants required to submit FAFSA. *Faculty research:* Igneous, metamorphic, and sedimentary petrology; ore deposits; aqueous geochemistry; isotope geochemistry; heat flow. *Total annual research expenditures:* $3.3 million. *Unit head:* Dr. Kip Solomon, Chair, 801-581-7231, Fax: 801-581-7065, E-mail: kip.solomon@utah.edu. *Application contact:* Dr. Cari L. Johnson, Director of Graduate Studies, 801-585-3782, Fax: 801-581-7065, E-mail: cari.johnson@utah.edu. Web site: http://www.earth.utah.edu/.

University of Wisconsin–Madison, Graduate School, College of Engineering, Geological Engineering Program, Madison, WI 53706-1380. Offers MS, PhD. Part-time programs available. *Faculty:* 16 full-time (3 women). *Students:* 10 full-time (4 women), 3 international. Average age 25. 26 applicants, 27% accepted, 3 enrolled. In 2011, 3 master's, 2 doctorates awarded. *Degree requirements:* For doctorate, thesis/dissertation. *Entrance requirements:* For master's and doctorate, GRE. Additional exam requirements/recommendations for international students: Required—TOEFL (minimum score 550 paper-based; 213 computer-based; 80 iBT). *Application deadline:* For fall admission, 3/15 priority date for domestic students, 3/15 for international students; for spring admission, 10/15 priority date for domestic students, 10/15 for international students. Application fee: $56. Electronic applications accepted. *Expenses:* Tuition, state resident: full-time $10,296; part-time $643.51 per credit. Tuition, nonresident: full-time $24,054; part-time $1503.40 per credit. *Required fees:* $70.06 per credit. Tuition and fees vary according to course load, campus/location, program and reciprocity agreements. *Financial support:* In 2011–12, 5 students received support, including fellowships with full tuition reimbursements available (averaging $22,224 per year), 3 research assistantships with full tuition reimbursements available (averaging $40,368 per year), 2 teaching assistantships with full tuition reimbursements available (averaging $28,175 per year); Federal Work-Study, scholarships/grants, and unspecified assistantships also available. Support available to part-time students. Financial award application deadline: 12/15. *Faculty research:* Constitute models for geomaterials, rock fracture, in situ stress determination, environmental geotechnics, site remediation. *Total annual research expenditures:* $1.2 million. *Unit head:* Craig H. Benson, Chair, 608-262-3491, Fax: 608-263-2453, E-mail: benson@engr.wisc.edu. *Application contact:* Cheryl Loschko, Program Coordinator, 608-265-5570, Fax: 608-890-1174, E-mail: loschko@wisc.edu. Web site: http://www.eng.wisc.edu/interd/gep/.

Mineral/Mining Engineering

Colorado School of Mines, Graduate School, Department of Geophysics, Golden, CO 80401-1887. Offers geophysical engineering (ME, MS, PhD); geophysics (MS, PhD); mineral exploration and mining geosciences (PMS). Part-time programs available. *Faculty:* 18 full-time (1 woman), 2 part-time/adjunct (0 women). *Students:* 85 full-time (28 women), 7 part-time (2 women); includes 9 minority (1 American Indian or Alaska Native, non-Hispanic/Latino; 3 Asian, non-Hispanic/Latino; 5 Hispanic/Latino), 47 international. Average age 28. 163 applicants, 24% accepted, 28 enrolled. In 2011, 14 master's, 3 doctorates awarded. *Degree requirements:* For master's, thesis (for some programs); for doctorate, one foreign language, comprehensive exam, thesis/dissertation, oral exams. *Entrance requirements:* For master's and doctorate, GRE General Test. Additional exam requirements/recommendations for international students: Required—TOEFL (minimum score 550 paper-based; 213 computer-based; 80 iBT). *Application deadline:* For fall admission, 1/15 for domestic and international students; for spring admission, 10/15 for domestic and international students. Application fee: $50 ($70 for international students). Electronic applications accepted. *Expenses:* Tuition, state resident: full-time $12,585; part-time $699 per credit. Tuition, nonresident: full-time $27,270; part-time $1516 per credit. *Required fees:* $1864.20; $670 per semester. *Financial support:* In 2011–12, 74 students received support, including 7 fellowships with full tuition reimbursements available (averaging $20,000 per year), 60 research assistantships with full tuition reimbursements available (averaging $20,000 per year), 7 teaching assistantships with full tuition reimbursements available (averaging $20,000 per year); scholarships/grants, health care benefits, and unspecified assistantships also available. Financial award application deadline: 1/15; financial award applicants required to submit FAFSA. *Faculty research:* Seismic exploration, gravity and geomagnetic fields, electrical mapping and sounding, bore hole measurements, environmental physics. *Total annual research expenditures:* $4.3 million. *Unit head:* Dr. Terence K. Young, Head, 303-273-3454, Fax: 303-273-3478, E-mail: tkyoung@mines.edu. *Application contact:* Michelle Szobody, Office Manager, 303-273-3935, Fax: 303-273-3478, E-mail: mszobody@mines.edu. Web site: http://geophysics.mines.edu.

Colorado School of Mines, Graduate School, Department of Mining Engineering, Golden, CO 80401-1887. Offers engineer of mines (ME); mining and earth systems engineering (MS); mining engineering (PhD). Part-time programs available. *Faculty:* 11 full-time (0 women), 4 part-time/adjunct (0 women). *Students:* 27 full-time (4 women), 8 part-time (0 women); includes 3 minority (1 Asian, non-Hispanic/Latino; 2 Hispanic/Latino), 18 international. Average age 35. 48 applicants, 71% accepted, 10 enrolled. In 2011, 3 master's, 1 doctorate awarded. *Degree requirements:* For master's, thesis (for some programs); for doctorate, one foreign language, comprehensive exam, thesis/dissertation. *Entrance requirements:* For master's and doctorate, GRE General Test. Additional exam requirements/recommendations for international students: Required—TOEFL (minimum score 550 paper-based; 213 computer-based; 80 iBT). *Application deadline:* For fall admission, 1/15 priority date for domestic students, 1/15 for international students; for spring admission, 10/15 priority date for domestic students, 10/15 for international students. Application fee: $50 ($70 for international students). Electronic applications accepted. *Expenses:* Tuition, state resident: full-time $12,585; part-time $699 per credit. Tuition, nonresident: full-time $27,270; part-time $1516 per credit. *Required fees:* $1864.20; $670 per semester. *Financial support:* In 2011–12, 16 students received support, including 3 fellowships with full tuition reimbursements available (averaging $20,000 per year), 9 research assistantships with full tuition reimbursements available (averaging $20,000 per year), 4 teaching assistantships with full tuition reimbursements available (averaging $20,000 per year); scholarships/grants, health care benefits, and unspecified assistantships also available. Financial award application deadline: 1/15; financial award applicants required to submit FAFSA. *Faculty research:* Mine evaluation and planning, geostatistics, mining robotics, water jet cutting, rock mechanics. *Total annual research expenditures:* $1.2 million. *Unit head:* Dr. Kadri Dagdelen, Head, 303-273-3711, Fax: 303-273-3719, E-mail: kdagdele@mines.edu. *Application contact:* Christine Monroe, Administrative Assistant, 303-273-3992, Fax: 303-273-3719, E-mail: cmonroe@mines.edu. Web site: http://mining.mines.edu.

Columbia University, The Fu Foundation School of Engineering and Applied Science, Department of Earth and Environmental Engineering, New York, NY 10027. Offers earth and environmental engineering (MS, Eng Sc D, PhD); metallurgical engineering (Engr); mining engineering (Engr); MS/MBA. Part-time programs available. Postbaccalaureate distance learning degree programs offered (minimal on-campus study). *Faculty:* 13 full-time (1 woman), 6 part-time/adjunct (0 women). *Students:* 48 full-time (17 women), 15 part-time (8 women); includes 6 minority (3 Asian, non-Hispanic/Latino; 3 Two or more races, non-Hispanic/Latino), 32 international. Average age 30. 171 applicants, 15% accepted, 14 enrolled. In 2011, 16 master's, 4 doctorates awarded. Terminal master's awarded for partial completion of doctoral program. *Degree requirements:* For master's, thesis; for doctorate, thesis/dissertation, qualifying exam. *Entrance requirements:* For master's, doctorate, and Engr, GRE General Test. Additional exam requirements/recommendations for international students: Required—TOEFL, IELTS. *Application deadline:* For fall admission, 12/1 priority date for domestic students, 12/1 for international students; for spring admission, 10/1 priority date for domestic students, 10/1 for international students. Application fee: $95. Electronic applications accepted. *Financial support:* In 2011–12, 39 students received support, including 6 fellowships with full and partial tuition reimbursements available (averaging $16,478 per year), 26 research assistantships with full tuition reimbursements available (averaging $27,733 per year), 7 teaching assistantships with full tuition reimbursements available (averaging $22,500 per year); health care benefits and unspecified assistantships also available. Financial award application deadline: 12/1; financial award applicants required to submit FAFSA. *Faculty research:* Sustainable energy and materials, waste to energy, water resources and climate risks, environmental health engineering, life cycle analysis. *Unit head:* Dr. Klaus S. Lackner, Professor of Geophysics/Chairman, 212-854-0304, Fax: 212-854-7081, E-mail: kl2010@columbia.edu. *Application contact:* Gary Hill, Administrative Assistant, 212-854-2905, Fax: 212-854-7081, E-mail: gh2206@columbia.edu. Web site: http://www.eee.columbia.edu/.

Dalhousie University, Faculty of Engineering, Department of Mineral Resource Engineering, Halifax, NS B3J 1Z1, Canada. Offers mineral resource engineering (M Eng, MA Sc, PhD). *Degree requirements:* For master's, thesis; for doctorate, thesis/dissertation. *Entrance requirements:* Additional exam requirements/recommendations for international students: Required—TOEFL, IELTS, CANTEST, CAEL, or Michigan English Language Assessment Battery. Electronic applications accepted. *Faculty research:* Mining technology, environmental impact, petroleum engineering, mine waste management, rock mechanics.

Laurentian University, School of Graduate Studies and Research, Programme in Geology (Earth Sciences), Sudbury, ON P3E 2C6, Canada. Offers geology (M Sc); mineral deposits and precambrian geology (PhD); mineral exploration (M Sc). Part-time programs available. *Degree requirements:* For master's, thesis. *Entrance requirements:* For master's, honors degree with second class or better. *Faculty research:* Localization and metallogenesis of Ni-Cu-(PGE) sulfide mineralization in the Thompson Nickel Belt, mapping lithology and ore-grade and monitoring dissolved organic carbon in lakes using remote sensing, global reefs, volcanic effects on VMS deposits.

Laurentian University, School of Graduate Studies and Research, School of Engineering, Sudbury, ON P3E 2C6, Canada. Offers mineral resources engineering (M Eng, MA Sc); natural resources engineering (PhD). Part-time programs available. *Faculty research:* Mining engineering, rock mechanics (tunneling, rockbursts, rock support), metallurgy (mineral processing, hydro and pyrometallurgy), simulations and remote mining, simulations and scheduling.

McGill University, Faculty of Graduate and Postdoctoral Studies, Faculty of Engineering, Department of Mining and Materials Engineering, Montréal, QC H3A 2T5, Canada. Offers materials engineering (M Eng, PhD); mining engineering (M Eng, M Sc, PhD, Diploma).

Michigan Technological University, Graduate School, College of Engineering, Department of Geological and Mining Engineering and Sciences, Houghton, MI 49931.

Offers geological engineering (MS, PhD); geology (MS, PhD); geophysics (MS, PhD); mining engineering (MS, PhD). Part-time programs available. *Faculty:* 20 full-time (2 women), 21 part-time/adjunct (1 woman). *Students:* 52 full-time (28 women), 8 part-time (3 women); includes 3 minority (all Hispanic/Latino), 20 international. Average age 29. 114 applicants, 33% accepted, 15 enrolled. In 2011, 10 master's, 1 doctorate awarded. Terminal master's awarded for partial completion of doctoral program. *Degree requirements:* For master's, comprehensive exam (for some programs), thesis (for some programs); for doctorate, comprehensive exam, thesis/dissertation. *Entrance requirements:* For master's and doctorate, GRE, statement of purpose, official transcripts, 3 letters of recommendation. Additional exam requirements/recommendations for international students: Required—TOEFL (minimum score 79 iBT) or IELTS. *Application deadline:* Applications are processed on a rolling basis. Electronic applications accepted. *Expenses:* Tuition, state resident: full-time $12,636; part-time $702 per credit. Tuition, nonresident: full-time $12,636; part-time $702 per credit. *Required fees:* $226; $226 per year. *Financial support:* In 2011–12, 45 students received support, including 4 fellowships with full tuition reimbursements available (averaging $6,065 per year), 22 research assistantships with full tuition reimbursements available (averaging $6,065 per year), teaching assistantships with full tuition reimbursements available (averaging $6,065 per year); career-related internships or fieldwork, Federal Work-Study, scholarships/grants, health care benefits, tuition waivers (partial), unspecified assistantships, and cooperative program also available. Financial award applicants required to submit FAFSA. *Faculty research:* Volcanic hazards and volcanic clouds, oil and gas exploration and development, groundwater measurement and modeling, geophysics, environmental paleomagnetism. *Total annual research expenditures:* $1.3 million. *Unit head:* Dr. Wayne D. Pennington, Chair, 906-487-3573, Fax: 906-487-3371, E-mail: wayne@mtu.edu. *Application contact:* Amie S. Ledgerwood, Secretary 5, 906-487-2531, Fax: 906-487-3371, E-mail: asledger@mtu.edu. Web site: http://www.mtu.edu/geo/.

Missouri University of Science and Technology, Graduate School, Department of Mining and Nuclear Engineering, Rolla, MO 65409. Offers mining engineering (MS, DE, PhD); nuclear engineering (MS, DE, PhD). *Degree requirements:* For master's, thesis optional; for doctorate, comprehensive exam. *Entrance requirements:* For master's, GRE (minimum score 600 quantitative, 3 writing); for doctorate, GRE (minimum score: quantitative 600, writing 3.5). Additional exam requirements/recommendations for international students: Required—TOEFL (minimum score 550 paper-based; 213 computer-based). *Faculty research:* Mine health and safety, nuclear radiation transport, modeling of mining operations, radiation effects, blasting.

Montana Tech of The University of Montana, Graduate School, Metallurgical/Mineral Processing Engineering Programs, Butte, MT 59701-8997. Offers MS. Part-time programs available. *Faculty:* 6 full-time (0 women). *Students:* 3 full-time (1 woman), 1 (woman) part-time. 5 applicants, 40% accepted, 1 enrolled. In 2011, 3 master's awarded. *Degree requirements:* For master's, comprehensive exam (for some programs), thesis optional. *Entrance requirements:* For master's, GRE General Test, minimum GPA of 3.0. Additional exam requirements/recommendations for international students: Required—TOEFL (minimum score 525 paper-based; 195 computer-based; 71 iBT). *Application deadline:* For fall admission, 4/1 priority date for domestic students, 3/1 for international students; for spring admission, 10/1 priority date for domestic students, 7/1 for international students. Applications are processed on a rolling basis. Application fee: $30. Electronic applications accepted. *Financial support:* In 2011–12, 4 students received support, including 2 teaching assistantships with partial tuition reimbursements available (averaging $5,000 per year); research assistantships with partial tuition reimbursements available, career-related internships or fieldwork, tuition waivers (full and partial), and unspecified assistantships also available. Financial award application deadline: 4/1; financial award applicants required to submit FAFSA. *Faculty research:* Stabilizing hazardous waste, decontamination of metals by melt refining, ultraviolet enhancement of stabilization reactions, extractive metallurgy, fuel cells. *Unit head:* Dr. Courtney Young, Department Head, 406-496-4158, Fax: 406-496-4664, E-mail: cyoung@mtech.edu. *Application contact:* Fred Sullivan, Administrator, Graduate School, 406-496-4304, Fax: 406-496-4710, E-mail: fsullivan@mtech.edu. Web site: http://www.mtech.edu/academics/gradschool/degreeprograms/degrees-metallurgical.htm.

Montana Tech of The University of Montana, Graduate School, Mining Engineering Program, Butte, MT 59701-8997. Offers MS. Part-time programs available. *Faculty:* 4 full-time (0 women). *Students:* 1 full-time (0 women), 1 part-time (0 women). 8 applicants, 38% accepted, 2 enrolled. In 2011, 3 master's awarded. *Degree requirements:* For master's, thesis optional. *Entrance requirements:* For master's, minimum GPA of 3.0. Additional exam requirements/recommendations for international students: Required—TOEFL (minimum score 525 paper-based; 195 computer-based; 71 iBT). *Application deadline:* For fall admission, 4/1 priority date for domestic students, 3/1 for international students; for spring admission, 10/1 priority date for domestic students, 7/1 for international students. Applications are processed on a rolling basis. Application fee: $30. Electronic applications accepted. *Financial support:* In 2011–12, 2 students received support, including 2 teaching assistantships with partial tuition reimbursements available (averaging $4,000 per year); research assistantships, career-related internships or fieldwork, tuition waivers (full and partial), and unspecified assistantships also available. Financial award application deadline: 4/1; financial award applicants required to submit FAFSA. *Faculty research:* Geostatistics, geomechanics, mine planning, economic models, equipment selection. *Unit head:* Dr. David Armstrong, Department Head, 406-496-4867, Fax: 406-496-4260, E-mail: darmstrong@mtech.edu. *Application contact:* Fred Sullivan, Administrator, Graduate School, 406-496-4304, Fax: 406-496-4710, E-mail: fsullivan@mtech.edu. Web site: http://www.mtech.edu/academics/gradschool/degreeprograms/degrees-mining-engineering.htm.

New Mexico Institute of Mining and Technology, Graduate Studies, Department of Mineral Engineering, Socorro, NM 87801. Offers MS. *Faculty:* 4 full-time (1 woman), 6 part-time/adjunct (3 women). *Students:* 11 full-time (4 women), 1 part-time (0 women); includes 7 minority (4 Black or African American, non-Hispanic/Latino; 1 American Indian or Alaska Native, non-Hispanic/Latino; 2 Asian, non-Hispanic/Latino), 2 international. Average age 30. 20 applicants, 75% accepted, 11 enrolled. In 2011, 5 master's awarded. *Degree requirements:* For master's, thesis. *Entrance requirements:* Additional exam requirements/recommendations for international students: Required—TOEFL (minimum score 540 paper-based; 207 computer-based). *Expenses:* Tuition, state resident: full-time $4849; part-time $269.41 per credit hour. Tuition, nonresident: full-time $16,041; part-time $891.15 per credit hour. *Required fees:* $622; $65 per credit hour. $20 per semester. Part-time tuition and fees vary according to course load. *Financial support:* In 2011–12, 7 research assistantships (averaging $10,507 per year), 4 teaching assistantships with full and partial tuition reimbursements (averaging $9,730 per year) were awarded; fellowships, scholarships/grants, and unspecified assistantships also available. *Faculty research:* Drilling and blasting, geological engineering, mine design, applied mineral exploration, rock mechanics. *Unit head:* Dr.

Navid Mojtabai, Chair, 575-835-5345, Fax: 575-835-5252, E-mail: mojtabai@nmt.edu. *Application contact:* Dr. Lorie Liebrock, Dean of Graduate Studies, 575-835-5513, Fax: 575-835-5476, E-mail: graduate@nmt.edu. Web site: http://infohost.nmt.edu/~mining/.

Penn State University Park, Graduate School, College of Earth and Mineral Sciences, Department of Energy and Mineral Engineering, State College, University Park, PA 16802-1503. Offers MS, PhD. *Unit head:* Dr. William E. Easterling, III, Dean, 814-865-6546, Fax: 814-863-7708, E-mail: wee2@psu.edu. *Application contact:* Cynthia E. Nicosia, Director of Graduate Enrollment Services, 814-865-1834, E-mail: cey1@psu.edu. Web site: http://www.eme.psu.edu/.

Queen's University at Kingston, School of Graduate Studies and Research, Faculty of Applied Science, Department of Mining Engineering, Kingston, ON K7L 3N6, Canada. Offers M Eng, M Sc, M Sc Eng, PhD. Part-time programs available. *Degree requirements:* For master's, thesis optional; for doctorate, comprehensive exam, thesis/dissertation. *Entrance requirements:* Additional exam requirements/recommendations for international students: Required—TOEFL (minimum score 550 paper-based; 213 computer-based). Electronic applications accepted. *Faculty research:* Rock mechanics, drilling, ventilation/environmental control, gold extraction.

Southern Illinois University Carbondale, Graduate School, College of Engineering, Department of Mining and Mineral Resources Engineering, Carbondale, IL 62901-4701. Offers mining engineering (MS). *Faculty:* 3 full-time (0 women), 1 part-time/adjunct (0 women). *Students:* 4 full-time (0 women), 1 part-time (0 women); includes 1 minority (Black or African American, non-Hispanic/Latino), 2 international. Average age 25. 9 applicants, 22% accepted, 1 enrolled. In 2011, 2 master's awarded. *Degree requirements:* For master's, comprehensive exam, thesis. *Entrance requirements:* For master's, minimum GPA of 2.7. Additional exam requirements/recommendations for international students: Required—TOEFL. *Application deadline:* Applications are processed on a rolling basis. Application fee: $20. *Financial support:* Fellowships with full tuition reimbursements, research assistantships with full tuition reimbursements, teaching assistantships with full tuition reimbursements, Federal Work-Study, institutionally sponsored loans, and tuition waivers (full) available. Support available to part-time students. Financial award application deadline: 3/1. *Faculty research:* Rock mechanics and ground control, mine subsidence, mine systems analysis, fine coal cleaning, surface mine reclamation. *Total annual research expenditures:* $1.7 million. *Unit head:* Dr. Satya Harpalani, Chairperson, 618-536-6637, Fax: 618-453-4235, E-mail: satya@engr.siu.edu. *Application contact:* Diane Lyall, Administrative Clerk, 618-536-6637, E-mail: lyall@siu.edu.

Université du Québec en Abitibi-Témiscamingue, Graduate Programs, Program in Engineering, Rouyn-Noranda, QC J9X 5E4, Canada. Offers engineering (ME); mineral engineering (ME); mining engineering (DESS).

Université Laval, Faculty of Sciences and Engineering, Department of Mining, Metallurgical and Materials Engineering, Programs in Mining Engineering, Québec, QC G1K 7P4, Canada. Offers M Sc, PhD. Terminal master's awarded for partial completion of doctoral program. *Degree requirements:* For master's, thesis; for doctorate, comprehensive exam, thesis/dissertation. *Entrance requirements:* For master's and doctorate, knowledge of French and English. Electronic applications accepted.

University of Alaska Fairbanks, College of Engineering and Mines, Department of Mining and Geological Engineering, Program in Mineral Preparation Engineering, Fairbanks, AK 99775. Offers MS. Part-time programs available. *Students:* 1 (woman) full-time, all international. Average age 23. *Degree requirements:* For master's, comprehensive exam, thesis or alternative. *Entrance requirements:* For master's, GRE General Test. Additional exam requirements/recommendations for international students: Required—TOEFL (minimum score 550 paper-based; 213 computer-based; 80 iBT). *Application deadline:* For fall admission, 6/1 for domestic students, 3/1 for international students; for spring admission, 10/15 for domestic students, 9/1 for international students. Applications are processed on a rolling basis. Application fee: $60. Electronic applications accepted. *Expenses:* Tuition, state resident: full-time $6696; part-time $372 per credit. Tuition, nonresident: full-time $13,680; part-time $760 per credit. Tuition and fees vary according to course load and reciprocity agreements. *Financial support:* Fellowships, research assistantships, teaching assistantships, career-related internships or fieldwork, Federal Work-Study, scholarships/grants, health care benefits, and unspecified assistantships available. Support available to part-time students. Financial award application deadline: 7/1; financial award applicants required to submit FAFSA. *Faculty research:* Washability of coal, microbial mining, mineral leaching, pollution control technology, concentration of target minerals. *Unit head:* Dr. Rajive Ganguli, Department Chair, 907-474-7388, Fax: 907-474-6635, E-mail: fyminge@uaf.edu. *Application contact:* Mike Earnest, Director of Admissions, 907-474-7500, Fax: 907-474-5379, E-mail: admissions@uaf.edu. Web site: http://www.alaska.edu/uaf/cem/min/grad/index.xml.

University of Alberta, Faculty of Graduate Studies and Research, Department of Civil and Environmental Engineering, Edmonton, AB T6G 2E1, Canada. Offers construction engineering and management (M Eng, M Sc, PhD); environmental engineering (M Eng, M Sc, PhD); environmental science (M Sc, PhD); geoenvironmental engineering (M Eng, M Sc, PhD); geotechnical engineering (M Eng, M Sc, PhD); mining engineering (M Eng, M Sc, PhD); petroleum engineering (M Eng, M Sc, PhD); structural engineering (M Eng, M Sc, PhD); water resources (M Eng, M Sc, PhD). Part-time programs available. Postbaccalaureate distance learning degree programs offered (minimal on-campus study). *Degree requirements:* For master's, thesis (for some programs); for doctorate, thesis/dissertation. *Entrance requirements:* For master's, minimum GPA of 3.0 in last 2 years of undergraduate studies; for doctorate, minimum GPA of 3.0. Additional exam requirements/recommendations for international students: Required—TOEFL (minimum score 550 paper-based; 213 computer-based). Electronic applications accepted. *Faculty research:* Mining.

The University of Arizona, College of Engineering, Department of Mining, Geological and Geophysical Engineering, Program in Mining Engineering, Tucson, AZ 85721. Offers mine health and safety (Certificate); mine information and production technology (Certificate); mining engineering (M Eng); rock mechanics (Certificate). Part-time programs available. Postbaccalaureate distance learning degree programs offered (minimal on-campus study). *Faculty:* 7 full-time (0 women), 1 part-time/adjunct (0 women). *Students:* 16 full-time (2 women), 9 part-time (1 woman); includes 1 minority (Asian, non-Hispanic/Latino), 12 international. Average age 34. In 2011, 3 master's awarded. *Degree requirements:* For master's, thesis. *Entrance requirements:* For master's, GRE General Test, 3 letters of recommendation, statement of purpose. Additional exam requirements/recommendations for international students: Required—TOEFL (minimum score 550 paper-based; 213 computer-based; 79 iBT). *Application deadline:* For fall admission, 6/1 for domestic students, 12/1 for international students; for spring admission, 10/1 for domestic students, 6/1 for international students.

Applications are processed on a rolling basis. Application fee: $75. Electronic applications accepted. *Expenses:* Tuition, state resident: full-time $10,840. Tuition, nonresident: full-time $25,802. *Financial support:* In 2011–12, 19 research assistantships with full tuition reimbursements (averaging $23,488 per year) were awarded; institutionally sponsored loans, scholarships/grants, health care benefits, tuition waivers (partial), and unspecified assistantships also available. Financial award application deadline: 4/1. *Faculty research:* Mine system design, in-site leaching, fluid flow in rocks, geostatistics, rock mechanics. *Unit head:* Dr. Mary M. Poulton, Head, 520-621-6063, Fax: 520-621-8330, E-mail: mpoulton@u.arizona.edu. *Application contact:* Olivia Hanson, Graduate Advisor, 520-621-6063, Fax: 520-621-8330, E-mail: ohanson@engr.arizona.edu. Web site: http://www.mge.arizona.edu.

The University of British Columbia, Faculty of Applied Science, Program in Mining Engineering, Vancouver, BC V6T 1Z4, Canada. Offers M Eng, MA Sc, PhD. *Degree requirements:* For master's, thesis; for doctorate, thesis/dissertation. *Entrance requirements:* Additional exam requirements/recommendations for international students: Required—TOEFL (minimum score 213 computer-based; 80 iBT), IELTS. *Faculty research:* Advanced mining methods and automation, rock mechanics, mine economics, operations research, mine waste management, environmental aspects of mining, process control, fine particle processing, surface chemistry.

University of Kentucky, Graduate School, College of Engineering, Program in Mining Engineering, Lexington, KY 40506-0032. Offers MME, MS Min, PhD. *Degree requirements:* For master's, comprehensive exam, thesis optional; for doctorate, one foreign language, comprehensive exam, thesis/dissertation. *Entrance requirements:* For master's, GRE General Test, minimum undergraduate GPA of 2.75; for doctorate, GRE General Test, minimum undergraduate GPA of 3.0. Additional exam requirements/recommendations for international students: Required—TOEFL (minimum score 550 paper-based; 213 computer-based). Electronic applications accepted. *Faculty research:* Benefication of fine and ultrafine particles, operation research in mining and mineral processing, land reclamation.

University of Nevada, Reno, Graduate School, College of Science, Mackay School of Earth Sciences and Engineering, Department of Mining Engineering, Reno, NV 89557. Offers MS. *Degree requirements:* For master's, thesis optional. *Entrance requirements:* For master's, GRE, minimum GPA of 2.75. Additional exam requirements/recommendations for international students: Required—TOEFL (minimum score 500 paper-based; 173 computer-based; 61 iBT), IELTS (minimum score 6). Electronic applications accepted. *Faculty research:* Mine ventilation, rock mechanics, mine design.

University of North Dakota, Graduate School, School of Engineering and Mines, Department of Civil Engineering, Grand Forks, ND 58202. Offers civil engineering (M Engr); sanitary engineering (M Engr), including soils and structures engineering, surface mining engineering. Part-time programs available. *Degree requirements:* For master's, comprehensive exam, thesis or alternative. *Entrance requirements:* For master's, GRE General Test, minimum GPA of 2.5. Additional exam requirements/recommendations for international students: Required—TOEFL (minimum score 550 paper-based; 213 computer-based; 79 iBT), IELTS (minimum score 6.5). Electronic applications accepted. *Faculty research:* Soil-structures, environmental-water resources.

The University of Texas at Austin, Graduate School, Cockrell School of Engineering, Department of Petroleum and Geosystems Engineering, Program in Energy and Earth Resources, Austin, TX 78712-1111. Offers MA. *Degree requirements:* For master's, thesis, seminar. *Entrance requirements:* For master's, GRE General Test. Additional exam requirements/recommendations for international students: Required—TOEFL. *Application deadline:* For fall admission, 4/30 priority date for domestic students. Applications are processed on a rolling basis. Application fee: $50 ($75 for international students). Electronic applications accepted. *Unit head:* Stephen P. Grand, Chair, 512-471-3005, E-mail: steveg@geo.utexas.edu. *Application contact:* Philip Guerrero, Graduate Coordinator, 512-471-6098, E-mail: philipg@mail.utexas.edu. Web site: http://www.jsg.utexas.edu/eer/.

University of Utah, Graduate School, College of Mines and Earth Sciences, Department of Mining Engineering, Salt Lake City, UT 84112. Offers ME, MS, PhD. Part-time programs available. *Faculty:* 4 full-time (1 woman), 1 part-time/adjunct (0 women). *Students:* 10 full-time (1 woman), 2 part-time (0 women); includes 1 minority (Hispanic/Latino), 6 international. Average age 36. 19 applicants, 32% accepted, 5 enrolled. In 2011, 2 master's, 1 doctorate awarded. *Degree requirements:* For master's, comprehensive exam (ME), thesis (MS); for doctorate, one foreign language, thesis/dissertation. *Entrance requirements:* For master's, minimum undergraduate GPA of 3.0; for doctorate, GRE General Test. Additional exam requirements/recommendations for international students: Required—TOEFL (minimum score 550 paper-based; 173 computer-based; 61 iBT). *Application deadline:* For fall admission, 4/1 for domestic and international students; for spring admission, 11/1 priority date for domestic students, 11/1 for international students. Application fee: $55 ($65 for international students). Electronic applications accepted. *Financial support:* In 2011–12, 3 fellowships with tuition reimbursements (averaging $17,000 per year), 4 research assistantships with tuition reimbursements (averaging $17,000 per year) were awarded; career-related internships or fieldwork and institutionally sponsored loans also available. Support available to part-time students. Financial award application deadline: 2/15. *Faculty research:* Blasting, underground coal mine design and operations, rock mechanics, mine ventilation, 2-D and 3-D visualization, mine automation, mine safety. *Total annual research expenditures:* $324,354. *Unit head:* Dr. Michael Gordon Nelson, Chair, 801-585-3064, Fax: 801-585-5410, E-mail: mike.nelson@utah.edu. *Application contact:* Pam Hofmann, Administrative Assistant, 801-581-7198, Fax: 801-585-5410, E-mail: pamhofmann@utah.edu. Web site: http://www.mining.utah.edu/.

Virginia Polytechnic Institute and State University, Graduate School, College of Engineering, Department of Mining and Minerals Engineering, Blacksburg, VA 24061. Offers M Eng, MS, PhD. *Degree requirements:* For master's, comprehensive exam (for some programs), thesis (for some programs); for doctorate, comprehensive exam (for some programs), thesis/dissertation (for some programs). *Entrance requirements:* For master's and doctorate, GRE. Additional exam requirements/recommendations for international students: Required—TOEFL (minimum score 550 paper-based; 213 computer-based). *Application deadline:* For fall admission, 7/1 for domestic and international students; for spring admission, 12/1 for domestic and international students. Applications are processed on a rolling basis. Application fee: $65. Electronic applications accepted. *Expenses:* Tuition, state resident: full-time $10,048; part-time $558.25 per credit hour. Tuition, nonresident: full-time $19,497; part-time $1083.25 per credit hour. *Required fees:* $405 per semester. Tuition and fees vary according to course load, campus/location and program. *Financial support:* Research assistantships with full tuition reimbursements, teaching assistantships with full tuition reimbursements, career-related internships or fieldwork, Federal Work-Study, scholarships/grants, health care benefits, and unspecified assistantships available. Financial award application deadline: 1/15. *Faculty research:* Sensor development, slope stability, rock fracture, mechanics, ground control, environmental remediation. *Unit head:* Dr. Gregory Adel, Unit Head, 540-231-6671, E-mail: adel@vt.edu. *Application contact:* Gerald Luttrell, Information Contact, 540-231-6314, Fax: 540-231-4070, E-mail: luttrell@vt.edu. Web site: http://www.mining.vt.edu/.

West Virginia University, College of Engineering and Mineral Resources, Department of Mining Engineering, Morgantown, WV 26506. Offers MS Min E, PhD. Part-time programs available. *Degree requirements:* For master's, thesis; for doctorate, comprehensive exam, thesis/dissertation. *Entrance requirements:* For master's, minimum GPA of 3.0; for doctorate, GRE General Test, MS in mineral engineering, minimum GPA of 3.5. Additional exam requirements/recommendations for international students: Required—TOEFL. *Faculty research:* Mine safety.

Petroleum Engineering

Colorado School of Mines, Graduate School, Department of Petroleum Engineering, Golden, CO 80401-1887. Offers petroleum engineering (ME, MS, PhD); petroleum reservoir systems (PMS). Part-time programs available. *Faculty:* 15 full-time (5 women), 5 part-time/adjunct (2 women). *Students:* 93 full-time (13 women), 7 part-time (1 woman); includes 3 minority (1 Black or African American, non-Hispanic/Latino; 1 Asian, non-Hispanic/Latino; 1 Hispanic/Latino), 80 international. Average age 29. 282 applicants, 29% accepted, 31 enrolled. In 2011, 17 master's, 7 doctorates awarded. *Degree requirements:* For master's, thesis (for some programs); for doctorate, comprehensive exam, thesis/dissertation. *Entrance requirements:* For master's and doctorate, GRE General Test. Additional exam requirements/recommendations for international students: Required—TOEFL (minimum score 550 paper-based; 213 computer-based; 80 iBT). *Application deadline:* For fall admission, 1/15 priority date for domestic students, 1/15 for international students; for spring admission, 10/15 priority date for domestic students, 10/15 for international students. Application fee: $50 ($70 for international students). Electronic applications accepted. *Expenses:* Tuition, state resident: full-time $12,585; part-time $699 per credit. Tuition, nonresident: full-time $27,270; part-time $1516 per credit. *Required fees:* $1864.20; $670 per semester. *Financial support:* In 2011–12, 58 students received support, including 1 fellowship with full tuition reimbursement available (averaging $20,000 per year), 32 research assistantships with full tuition reimbursements available (averaging $20,000 per year), 25 teaching assistantships with full tuition reimbursements available (averaging $20,000 per year); career-related internships or fieldwork, scholarships/grants, health care benefits, and unspecified assistantships also available. Financial award application deadline: 1/15; financial award applicants required to submit FAFSA. *Faculty research:* Dynamic rock mechanics, deflagration theory, geostatistics, geochemistry, petrophysics. *Total annual research expenditures:* $2.2 million. *Unit head:* Dr. Ramona Graves, Head, 303-273-3746, Fax: 303-273-3189, E-mail: rgraves@mines.edu. *Application contact:* Denise Winn-Bower, Administrative Assistant, 303-273-3740, Fax: 303-273-3189, E-mail: dwinnbow@mines.edu. Web site: http://petroleum.mines.edu.

Louisiana State University and Agricultural and Mechanical College, Graduate School, College of Engineering, Department of Petroleum Engineering, Baton Rouge, LA 70803. Offers MS Pet E, PhD. *Faculty:* 10 full-time (1 woman). *Students:* 44 full-time (10 women), 4 part-time (0 women); includes 2 minority (both Black or African American, non-Hispanic/Latino), 35 international. Average age 30. 247 applicants, 6% accepted, 9 enrolled. In 2011, 7 master's, 3 doctorates awarded. *Degree requirements:* For master's, thesis or alternative; for doctorate, thesis/dissertation, exam. *Entrance requirements:* For master's and doctorate, GRE General Test, minimum GPA of 3.0. Additional exam requirements/recommendations for international students: Required—TOEFL (minimum score 550 paper-based; 213 computer-based; 79 iBT) or IELTS (minimum score 6.5). *Application deadline:* For fall admission, 1/25 priority date for domestic students, 5/15 for international students; for spring admission, 10/15 for international students. Applications are processed on a rolling basis. Application fee: $50 ($70 for international students). Electronic applications accepted. *Financial support:* In 2011–12, 34 students received support, including 28 research assistantships with full and partial tuition reimbursements available (averaging $13,696 per year), 6 teaching assistantships with full and partial tuition reimbursements available (averaging $12,539 per year); fellowships, Federal Work-Study, institutionally sponsored loans, health care benefits, and unspecified assistantships also available. Financial award applicants required to submit FAFSA. *Faculty research:* Rock properties, well logging, production engineering, drilling, reservoir engineering. *Total annual research expenditures:* $524,034. *Unit head:* Dr. Stephen O. Sears, Chair, 225-578-6055, Fax: 225-578-6039, E-mail: sosears@lsu.edu. *Application contact:* Dr. Andrew Wojtanowicz, Graduate Adviser, 225-578-6049, Fax: 225-578-6039, E-mail: awojtan@lsu.edu. Web site: http://www.pete.lsu.edu/.

Missouri University of Science and Technology, Graduate School, Department of Geological Sciences and Engineering, Rolla, MO 65409. Offers geological engineering (MS, DE, PhD); geology and geophysics (MS, PhD), including geochemistry, geology, geophysics, groundwater and environmental geology; petroleum engineering (MS, DE, PhD). Part-time programs available. *Degree requirements:* For master's, thesis optional; for doctorate, comprehensive exam, thesis/dissertation. *Entrance requirements:* For master's, GRE General Test (minimum score 600 quantitative, writing 3.5), minimum GPA of 3.0 in last 4 semesters; for doctorate, GRE General Test (minimum: Q 600, GRE WR 3.5). Additional exam requirements/recommendations for international students: Required—TOEFL. Electronic applications accepted. *Faculty research:* Digital image processing and geographic information systems, mineralogy, igneous and sedimentary petrology-geochemistry, sedimentology groundwater hydrology and contaminant transport.

Montana Tech of The University of Montana, Graduate School, Department of Petroleum Engineering, Butte, MT 59701-8997. Offers MS. Part-time and evening/weekend programs available. *Faculty:* 7 full-time (2 women), 1 part-time/adjunct (0 women). *Students:* 7 full-time (1 woman), 2 part-time (0 women); includes 1 minority (Black or African American, non-Hispanic/Latino), 5 international. 40 applicants, 8% accepted, 2 enrolled. In 2011, 2 master's awarded. *Degree requirements:* For master's, comprehensive exam, thesis optional. *Entrance requirements:* For master's, minimum GPA of 3.0. Additional exam requirements/recommendations for international students: Required—TOEFL (minimum score 525 paper-based; 195 computer-based; 71 iBT). *Application deadline:* For fall admission, 4/1 priority date for domestic students, 3/1 for international students; for spring admission, 10/1 priority date for domestic students, 7/1 for international students. Applications are processed on a rolling basis. Application fee: $30. Electronic applications accepted. *Financial support:* In 2011–12, 6 students received support, including 5 teaching assistantships with partial tuition reimbursements available (averaging $4,800 per year); research assistantships, career-related internships or fieldwork, institutionally sponsored loans, tuition waivers (full and partial), and unspecified assistantships also available. Financial award application deadline: 4/1;

financial award applicants required to submit FAFSA. *Faculty research:* Reservoir characterization, simulations, near well bore problems, PVT, environmental waste. *Unit head:* Leo Heath, Head, 406-496-4507, Fax: 406-496-4417, E-mail: lheath@mtech.edu. *Application contact:* Fred Sullivan, Administrator, Graduate School, 406-496-4304, Fax: 406-496-4710, E-mail: fsullivan@mtech.edu. Web site: http://www.mtech.edu/academics/gradschool/degreeprograms/degrees-petroleum-engineering.htm.

New Mexico Institute of Mining and Technology, Graduate Studies, Program in Petroleum Engineering, Socorro, NM 87801. Offers MS, PhD. *Faculty:* 9 full-time (0 women), 14 part-time/adjunct (1 woman). *Students:* 36 full-time (5 women), 4 part-time (1 woman); includes 30 minority (8 Black or African American, non-Hispanic/Latino; 20 Asian, non-Hispanic/Latino; 1 Hispanic/Latino; 1 Two or more races, non-Hispanic/Latino), 7 international. Average age 26. 124 applicants, 31% accepted, 20 enrolled. In 2011, 16 degrees awarded. *Degree requirements:* For master's, thesis optional; for doctorate, thesis/dissertation. *Entrance requirements:* For master's, GRE General Test; for doctorate, GRE General Test, GRE Subject Test. Additional exam requirements/recommendations for international students: Required—TOEFL (minimum score 540 paper-based; 207 computer-based). *Application deadline:* For fall admission, 3/1 priority date for domestic students; for spring admission, 6/1 for domestic students. Applications are processed on a rolling basis. Application fee: $16 ($30 for international students). *Expenses:* Tuition, state resident: full-time $4849; part-time $269.41 per credit hour. Tuition, nonresident: full-time $16,041; part-time $891.15 per credit hour. *Required fees:* $622; $65 per credit hour. $20 per semester. Part-time tuition and fees vary according to course load. *Financial support:* In 2011–12, 13 research assistantships (averaging $27,398 per year), 4 teaching assistantships with full and partial tuition reimbursements (averaging $18,842 per year) were awarded; fellowships, Federal Work-Study, and institutionally sponsored loans also available. Financial award application deadline: 3/1; financial award applicants required to submit CSS PROFILE or FAFSA. *Faculty research:* Enhanced recovery processes, drilling and production, reservoir evaluation, produced water management, wettability and phase behavior. *Unit head:* Dr. Thomas Engler, Chairman, 575-835-5412, Fax: 575-835-5210, E-mail: engler@nmt.edu. *Application contact:* Dr. Lorie Liebrock, Dean of Graduate Studies, 575-835-5513, Fax: 575-835-5476, E-mail: graduate@nmt.edu. Web site: http://www.nmt.edu/~petro/.

Stanford University, School of Earth Sciences, Department of Petroleum Engineering, Stanford, CA 94305-9991. Offers MS, PhD, Eng. Terminal master's awarded for partial completion of doctoral program. *Degree requirements:* For doctorate, thesis/dissertation; for Eng, thesis. *Entrance requirements:* For master's, doctorate, and Eng, GRE General Test. Additional exam requirements/recommendations for international students: Required—TOEFL. Electronic applications accepted. *Expenses: Tuition:* Full-time $40,050; part-time $890 per credit.

Texas A&M University, College of Engineering, Department of Petroleum Engineering, College Station, TX 77843. Offers M Eng, MS, PhD. Part-time programs available. Postbaccalaureate distance learning degree programs offered (no on-campus study). *Faculty:* 29. *Students:* 234 full-time (53 women), 100 part-time (10 women); includes 43 minority (10 Black or African American, non-Hispanic/Latino; 11 Asian, non-Hispanic/Latino; 20 Hispanic/Latino; 2 Two or more races, non-Hispanic/Latino), 219 international. Average age 25. In 2011, 72 master's, 16 doctorates awarded. *Degree requirements:* For master's, comprehensive exam, thesis (MS); for doctorate, comprehensive exam, thesis/dissertation. *Entrance requirements:* For master's and doctorate, GRE General Test. Additional exam requirements/recommendations for international students: Required—TOEFL (minimum score 550 paper-based; 213 computer-based). *Application deadline:* Applications are processed on a rolling basis. Application fee: $50 ($75 for international students). Electronic applications accepted. *Expenses:* Tuition, state resident: full-time $5437; part-time $226.55 per credit hour. Tuition, nonresident: full-time $12,949; part-time $539.55 per credit hour. *Required fees:* $2741. *Financial support:* In 2011–12, fellowships (averaging $1,000 per year), research assistantships (averaging $15,000 per year), teaching assistantships (averaging $15,000 per year) were awarded; career-related internships or fieldwork and tuition waivers (partial) also available. Financial award application deadline: 3/1; financial award applicants required to submit FAFSA. *Faculty research:* Drilling and well stimulation, well completions and well performance, reservoir modeling and reservoir description, reservoir simulation, improved/enhanced recovery. *Unit head:* Dr. Dan Hill, Head, 979-845-2255, E-mail: dan.hill@pe.tamu.edu. *Application contact:* Graduate Advisor, 979-847-9095, E-mail: graduate_program@pe.tamu.edu. Web site: http://www.pe.tamu.edu.

Texas A&M University–Kingsville, College of Graduate Studies, College of Engineering, Department of Chemical Engineering and Natural Gas Engineering, Program in Natural Gas Engineering, Kingsville, TX 78363. Offers ME, MS. *Degree requirements:* For master's, comprehensive exam, thesis or alternative. *Entrance requirements:* For master's, GRE General Test, minimum GPA of 3.0. Additional exam requirements/recommendations for international students: Required—TOEFL. *Faculty research:* Gas processing, coal gasification and liquefaction, enhanced oil recovery, gas measurement, unconventional gas recovery.

Texas Tech University, Graduate School, Edward E. Whitacre Jr. College of Engineering, Bob L. Herd Department of Petroleum Engineering, Lubbock, TX 79409. Offers MSPE, PhD. Part-time programs available. *Faculty:* 8 full-time (1 woman). *Students:* 47 full-time (7 women), 5 part-time (1 woman); includes 2 minority (1 Black or African American, non-Hispanic/Latino; 1 Asian, non-Hispanic/Latino), 46 international. Average age 27. 226 applicants, 25% accepted, 22 enrolled. In 2011, 15 master's, 3 doctorates awarded. Terminal master's awarded for partial completion of doctoral program. *Degree requirements:* For master's, thesis or alternative; for doctorate, thesis/dissertation. *Entrance requirements:* For master's and doctorate, GRE General Test, minimum GPA of 3.0. Additional exam requirements/recommendations for international students: Required—TOEFL (minimum score 550 paper-based; 213 computer-based; 79 iBT). *Application deadline:* For fall admission, 6/1 priority date for domestic students, 1/15 for international students; for spring admission, 9/1 priority date for domestic students, 6/15 for international students. Applications are processed on a rolling basis. Application fee: $50 ($75 for international students). Electronic applications accepted. *Expenses:* Tuition, state resident: full-time $5899; part-time $245.80 per credit hour. Tuition, nonresident: full-time $13,411; part-time $558.80 per credit hour. *Required fees:* $2680.60; $86.50 per credit hour. $920.30 per semester. *Financial support:* In 2011–12, 43 students received support. *Application deadline:* 4/15; applicants required to submit FAFSA. *Faculty research:* Stimulation (fracturing) wells including unconventional resources, EOR techniques, reservoir characterization and effect of carbon dioxide on hydrocarbon recovery. *Total annual research expenditures:* $516,632. *Unit head:* Dr. M. Y. Soliman, Chair, 806-742-3573, Fax: 806-742-3502, E-mail: mohame.soliman@ttu.edu. *Application contact:* Jamie L. Perez, Advisor, 806-742-3573 Ext. 223, Fax: 806-742-3502, E-mail: jamie.l.perez@ttu.edu. Web site: http://www.pe.ttu.edu/.

University of Alaska Fairbanks, College of Engineering and Mines, Department of Petroleum Engineering, Fairbanks, AK 99775. Offers MS, PhD. Part-time programs available. *Faculty:* 7 full-time (2 women). *Students:* 17 full-time (1 woman), 10 part-time (2 women); includes 2 minority (1 Black or African American, non-Hispanic/Latino; 1 Asian, non-Hispanic/Latino), 16 international. Average age 27. 59 applicants, 12% accepted, 4 enrolled. In 2011, 8 master's awarded. Terminal master's awarded for partial completion of doctoral program. *Degree requirements:* For master's, comprehensive exam, thesis or alternative; for doctorate, comprehensive exam, thesis/dissertation, oral exam, oral defense. *Entrance requirements:* For doctorate, GRE General Test. Additional exam requirements/recommendations for international students: Required—TOEFL (minimum score 550 paper-based; 213 computer-based; 80 iBT). *Application deadline:* For fall admission, 6/1 for domestic students, 3/1 for international students; for spring admission, 10/15 for domestic students, 9/1 for international students. Applications are processed on a rolling basis. Application fee: $60. Electronic applications accepted. *Expenses:* Tuition, state resident: full-time $6696; part-time $372 per credit. Tuition, nonresident: full-time $13,680; part-time $760 per credit. Tuition and fees vary according to course load and reciprocity agreements. *Financial support:* In 2011–12, 7 research assistantships with tuition reimbursements (averaging $8,721 per year), 7 teaching assistantships with tuition reimbursements (averaging $4,924 per year) were awarded; fellowships with tuition reimbursements, career-related internships or fieldwork, Federal Work-Study, scholarships/grants, health care benefits, and unspecified assistantships also available. Support available to part-time students. Financial award application deadline: 7/1; financial award applicants required to submit FAFSA. *Faculty research:* Gas-to-liquid transportation hydraulics and issues, carbon sequestration, enhanced oil recovery, reservoir engineering, coalbed methane. *Unit head:* Dr. Catherine Hanks, Chair, 907-474-7734, Fax: 907-474-5912, E-mail: fyipete@uaf.edu. *Application contact:* Mike Earnest, Director of Admissions, 907-474-7500, Fax: 907-474-5379, E-mail: admissions@uaf.edu. Web site: http://cem.uaf.edu/pete/.

University of Alberta, Faculty of Graduate Studies and Research, Department of Civil and Environmental Engineering, Edmonton, AB T6G 2E1, Canada. Offers construction engineering and management (M Eng, M Sc, PhD); environmental engineering (M Eng, M Sc, PhD); environmental science (M Sc, PhD); geoenvironmental engineering (M Eng, M Sc, PhD); geotechnical engineering (M Eng, M Sc, PhD); mining engineering (M Eng, M Sc, PhD); petroleum engineering (M Eng, M Sc, PhD); structural engineering (M Eng, M Sc, PhD); water resources (M Eng, M Sc, PhD). Part-time programs available. Postbaccalaureate distance learning degree programs offered (minimal on-campus study). *Degree requirements:* For master's, thesis (for some programs); for doctorate, thesis/dissertation. *Entrance requirements:* For master's, minimum GPA of 3.0 in last 2 years of undergraduate studies; for doctorate, minimum GPA of 3.0. Additional exam requirements/recommendations for international students: Required—TOEFL (minimum score 550 paper-based; 213 computer-based). Electronic applications accepted. *Faculty research:* Mining.

University of Calgary, Faculty of Graduate Studies, Schulich School of Engineering, Department of Chemical and Petroleum Engineering, Calgary, AB T2N 1N4, Canada. Offers M Eng, M Sc, PhD. Part-time programs available. *Degree requirements:* For master's, thesis (for some programs); for doctorate, comprehensive exam, thesis/dissertation, candidacy exam. *Entrance requirements:* For master's, minimum GPA of 3.0; for doctorate, minimum GPA of 3.5. Additional exam requirements/recommendations for international students: Required—TOEFL (minimum score 550 paper-based; 213 computer-based; 80 iBT), IELTS (minimum score 7). Electronic applications accepted. *Faculty research:* Environmental engineering, biomedical engineering modeling, simulation and control, petroleum recovery and reservoir engineering, phase equilibria and transport properties.

University of Houston, Cullen College of Engineering, Department of Chemical and Biomolecular Engineering, Houston, TX 77204. Offers chemical engineering (MCHE, PhD); petroleum engineering (M Pet E). Part-time programs available. Terminal master's awarded for partial completion of doctoral program. *Entrance requirements:* For master's and doctorate, GRE General Test. Additional exam requirements/recommendations for international students: Required—TOEFL (minimum score 550 paper-based; 79 iBT), IELTS (minimum score 6.5). *Faculty research:* Chemical engineering.

The University of Kansas, Graduate Studies, School of Engineering, Program in Chemical and Petroleum Engineering, Lawrence, KS 66045. Offers MS, PhD. *Faculty:* 14 full-time (4 women). *Students:* 32 full-time (14 women), 5 part-time (3 women); includes 3 minority (1 American Indian or Alaska Native, non-Hispanic/Latino; 2 Asian, non-Hispanic/Latino), 25 international. Average age 27. 101 applicants, 13% accepted, 1 enrolled. In 2011, 6 master's, 7 doctorates awarded. *Degree requirements:* For master's, thesis (for some programs), exam; for doctorate, comprehensive exam, thesis/dissertation, qualifying exams. *Entrance requirements:* For master's, GRE General Test, minimum GPA of 3.0; for doctorate, GRE General Test, minimum GPA of 3.5. Additional exam requirements/recommendations for international students: Required—TOEFL. *Application deadline:* For fall admission, 1/10 priority date for domestic students, 1/10 for international students; for spring admission, 6/10 priority date for domestic students, 6/10 for international students. Applications are processed on a rolling basis. Application fee: $55 ($65 for international students). Electronic applications accepted. Tuition and fees vary according to course load, campus/location, program and reciprocity agreements. *Financial support:* Fellowships, research assistantships with full and partial tuition reimbursements, teaching assistantships with full and partial tuition reimbursements, career-related internships or fieldwork, Federal Work-Study, scholarships/grants, traineeships, and unspecified assistantships available. Financial award application deadline: 4/1; financial award applicants required to submit FAFSA.

Faculty research: Enhanced oil recovery, catalysis and kinetics, electrochemical engineering, biomedical engineering, semiconductor materials processing. *Unit head:* Prof. Laurence Weatherley, Chairperson, 785-864-4965, Fax: 785-864-4967, E-mail: lweather@ku.edu. *Application contact:* Prof. Marylee Southard, Graduate Recruiting Officer, 785-864-4965, Fax: 785-864-4967, E-mail: marylee@ku.edu. Web site: http://www.cpe.engr.ku.edu.

The University of Kansas, Graduate Studies, School of Engineering, Program in Petroleum Engineering, Lawrence, KS 66045. Offers MS. Tuition and fees vary according to course load, campus/location, program and reciprocity agreements. *Unit head:* Dr. Stuart R. Bell, Dean, 785-864-3881, E-mail: kuengr@ku.edu. *Application contact:* Dr. Glen Marotz, Associate Dean, 785-864-2980, Fax: 785-864-5445, E-mail: gama@ku.edu.

University of Louisiana at Lafayette, College of Engineering, Department of Petroleum Engineering, Lafayette, LA 70504. Offers MSE. Evening/weekend programs available. *Degree requirements:* For master's, comprehensive exam, thesis or alternative. *Entrance requirements:* For master's, GRE General Test, minimum GPA of 2.85. Electronic applications accepted.

University of Oklahoma, College of Earth and Energy, School of Petroleum and Geological Engineering, Program in Natural Gas Engineering and Management, Norman, OK 73019. Offers MS. Part-time programs available. *Students:* 11 full-time (2 women), 4 part-time (1 woman); includes 3 minority (1 Black or African American, non-Hispanic/Latino; 2 Hispanic/Latino), 9 international. Average age 26. 28 applicants, 29% accepted, 5 enrolled. In 2011, 5 degrees awarded. *Entrance requirements:* Additional exam requirements/recommendations for international students: Required—TOEFL (minimum score 550 paper-based; 79 iBT). *Application deadline:* For fall admission, 6/1 for domestic students, 3/1 for international students; for spring admission, 11/1 for domestic students, 9/1 for international students. Applications are processed on a rolling basis. Application fee: $40 ($90 for international students). Electronic applications accepted. *Expenses:* Tuition, state resident: full-time $4087; part-time $170.30 per credit hour. Tuition, nonresident: full-time $14,875; part-time $619.80 per credit hour. *Required fees:* $2659; $100.25 per credit hour. Tuition and fees vary according to course load and degree level. *Financial support:* In 2011–12, 8 students received support. Traineeships available. Financial award applicants required to submit FAFSA. *Unit head:* Dr. Chandra Rai, Chair, 405-325-6866, Fax: 405-325-7477, E-mail: crai@ou.edu. *Application contact:* Shalli Young, Executive Assistant to the Graduate Liaison, 405-325-2921, Fax: 405-325-7477, E-mail: syoung@ou.edu. Web site: http://mpge.ou.edu.

University of Oklahoma, College of Earth and Energy, School of Petroleum and Geological Engineering, Program in Petroleum Engineering, Norman, OK 73019. Offers natural gas engineering and management (MS); petroleum engineering (MS, PhD). Part-time programs available. *Students:* 64 full-time (12 women), 26 part-time (3 women); includes 5 minority (all Black or African American, non-Hispanic/Latino), 76 international. Average age 28. 237 applicants, 12% accepted, 19 enrolled. In 2011, 31 master's, 5 doctorates awarded. Terminal master's awarded for partial completion of doctoral program. *Degree requirements:* For master's, thesis optional, industrial team project or thesis; for doctorate, thesis/dissertation. *Entrance requirements:* For master's, GRE General Test, bachelor's degree in engineering, 3 letters of recommendation, minimum GPA of 3.0 during final 60 hours of undergraduate course work; for doctorate, GRE General Test, minimum GPA of 3.0, 3 letters of recommendation. Additional exam requirements/recommendations for international students: Required—TOEFL (minimum score 550 paper-based; 79 iBT). *Application deadline:* For fall admission, 6/1 priority date for domestic students, 3/1 for international students; for spring admission, 11/1 for domestic students, 9/1 for international students. Applications are processed on a rolling basis. Application fee: $40 ($90 for international students). Electronic applications accepted. *Expenses:* Tuition, state resident: full-time $4087; part-time $170.30 per credit hour. Tuition, nonresident: full-time $14,875; part-time $619.80 per credit hour. *Required fees:* $2659; $100.25 per credit hour. Tuition and fees vary according to course load and degree level. *Financial support:* In 2011–12, 83 students received support. Traineeships available. Financial award applicants required to submit FAFSA. *Faculty research:* Petrophysics, shale gas, reservoir simulation coiled tubing, poro-mechanics, enhanced oil recovery. *Unit head:* Dr. Chandra Rai, Director, 405-325-2921, Fax: 405-325-7477, E-mail: crai@ou.edu. *Application contact:* Shalli Young, Executive Assistant to the Graduate Liaison, 405-325-2921, Fax: 405-325-7477, E-mail: syoung@ou.edu. Web site: http://mpge.ou.edu/.

University of Pittsburgh, Swanson School of Engineering, Department of Chemical and Petroleum Engineering, Pittsburgh, PA 15260. Offers chemical engineering (MS Ch E, PhD); petroleum engineering (MSPE); MS Ch E/MSPE. Part-time programs available. Postbaccalaureate distance learning degree programs offered. *Faculty:* 18 full-time (3 women), 21 part-time/adjunct (5 women). *Students:* 67 full-time (15 women), 7 part-time (3 women); includes 4 minority (1 Black or African American, non-Hispanic/Latino; 2 Asian, non-Hispanic/Latino; 1 Hispanic/Latino), 35 international. 269 applicants, 28% accepted, 18 enrolled. In 2011, 5 master's, 5 doctorates awarded. *Degree requirements:* For master's, thesis; for doctorate, comprehensive exam, thesis/dissertation, final oral exams. *Entrance requirements:* For master's and doctorate, GRE General Test, minimum QPA of 3.2. Additional exam requirements/recommendations for international students: Required—TOEFL (minimum score 550 paper-based; 213 computer-based; 80 iBT). *Application deadline:* For fall admission, 3/1 priority date for domestic students; for spring admission, 7/1 priority date for domestic students. Applications are processed on a rolling basis. Application fee: $50. Electronic applications accepted. *Expenses:* Tuition, state resident: full-time $18,774; part-time $760 per credit. Tuition, nonresident: full-time $30,736; part-time $1258 per credit. *Required fees:* $740; $200 per term. Tuition and fees vary according to program. *Financial support:* In 2011–12, 36 students received support, including 4 fellowships with full tuition reimbursements available (averaging $29,292 per year), 25 research assistantships with full tuition reimbursements available (averaging $24,048 per year), 7 teaching assistantships with full tuition reimbursements available (averaging $22,296 per year); scholarships/grants, traineeships, and tuition waivers (full and partial) also available. Financial award application deadline: 4/15. *Faculty research:* Biotechnology, polymers, catalysis, energy and environment, computational modeling. *Total annual research expenditures:* $7.7 million. *Unit head:* Dr. J. Karl Johnson, Chairman, 412-624-5644, Fax: 412-624-9639, E-mail: johnson@engr.pitt.edu. *Application contact:* William Federspiel, Associate Professor and Graduate Coordinator, 412-624-9499, Fax: 412-624-9639, E-mail: federspiel@engrng.pitt.edu. Web site: http://www.engineering.pitt.edu/Chemical/.

University of Regina, Faculty of Graduate Studies and Research, Faculty of Engineering and Applied Science, Program in Petroleum Systems Engineering, Regina, SK S4S 0A2, Canada. Offers M Eng, MA Sc, PhD. Part-time programs available.

Petroleum Engineering

Faculty: 7 full-time (1 woman). *Students:* 44 full-time (11 women), 3 part-time (0 women). 110 applicants, 13% accepted. In 2011, 5 master's, 1 doctorate awarded. *Degree requirements:* For master's, thesis; for doctorate, thesis/dissertation. *Entrance requirements:* Additional exam requirements/recommendations for international students: Required—TOEFL (minimum score 550 paper-based; 80 iBT), IELTS (minimum score 6.5). *Application deadline:* For fall admission, 3/31 for domestic and international students; for winter admission, 7/31 for domestic and international students; for spring admission, 11/30 for domestic and international students. Application fee: $100. Electronic applications accepted. *Financial support:* In 2011–12, 6 fellowships (averaging $6,500 per year), 2 research assistantships (averaging $17,250 per year), 12 teaching assistantships (averaging $2,298 per year) were awarded; career-related internships or fieldwork and scholarships/grants also available. Financial award application deadline: 6/15. *Faculty research:* Enhanced oil recovery, production engineering, reservoir engineering, surface thermodynamics, geostatistics. *Unit head:* Dr. Raphael Idem, Associate Dean, Research and Graduate Studies, 306-337-3287, Fax: 306-585-4855, E-mail: raphael.idem@uregina.ca. *Application contact:* Dr. Farshid Torabi, Graduate Program Coordinator, 306-337-3287, Fax: 306-585-4855, E-mail: farshid.torabi@uregina.ca.

University of Southern California, Graduate School, Viterbi School of Engineering, Mork Family Department of Chemical Engineering and Materials Science, Los Angeles, CA 90089. Offers chemical engineering (MS, PhD, Engr); materials engineering (MS); materials science (MS, PhD, Engr); petroleum engineering (MS, PhD, Engr); smart oilfield technologies (MS, Graduate Certificate). Terminal master's awarded for partial completion of doctoral program. *Degree requirements:* For master's, thesis optional; for doctorate, thesis/dissertation. *Entrance requirements:* For master's and doctorate, GRE General Test. Additional exam requirements/recommendations for international students: Recommended—TOEFL. Electronic applications accepted. *Expenses:* Contact institution. *Faculty research:* Heterogeneous materials and porous media, statistical mechanics, molecular simulation, polymer science and engineering, advanced materials, reaction engineering and catalysis, membrane processes and separation, biochemical engineering, cell culture, bioreactor modeling, petroleum engineering.

The University of Texas at Austin, Graduate School, Cockrell School of Engineering, Department of Petroleum and Geosystems Engineering, Austin, TX 78712-1111. Offers energy and earth resources (MA); petroleum engineering (MS, PhD). Evening/weekend programs available. Postbaccalaureate distance learning degree programs offered (no on-campus study). *Entrance requirements:* For master's and doctorate, GRE General Test. *Application deadline:* For fall admission, 2/1 priority date for domestic students; for spring admission, 10/1 for domestic students. Applications are processed on a rolling basis. Application fee: $50 ($75 for international students). Electronic applications accepted. *Financial support:* Fellowships, research assistantships, and teaching assistantships available. Financial award application deadline: 2/1. *Unit head:* Dr. Tad Patzek, Chairman, 512-471-3161, Fax: 512-471-9605, E-mail: patzek@mail.utexas.edu. *Application contact:* Frankie Hart, Graduate Coordinator, E-mail: pgegradoffice@mail.utexas.edu. Web site: http://www.pge.utexas.edu/current/grad.cfm.

University of Tulsa, Graduate School, College of Engineering and Natural Sciences, McDougall School of Petroleum Engineering, Tulsa, OK 74104-3189. Offers ME, MSE, PhD. Part-time programs available. *Faculty:* 11 full-time (0 women). *Students:* 60 full-time (10 women), 17 part-time (4 women); includes 1 minority (Asian, non-Hispanic/Latino), 74 international. Average age 27. 314 applicants, 9% accepted, 17 enrolled. In 2011, 30 master's, 5 doctorates awarded. *Degree requirements:* For master's, thesis (MSE); for doctorate, one foreign language, comprehensive exam, thesis/dissertation. *Entrance requirements:* For master's and doctorate, GRE General Test. Additional exam requirements/recommendations for international students: Required—TOEFL (minimum score 550 paper-based; 213 computer-based; 80 iBT), IELTS (minimum score 6). *Application deadline:* Applications are processed on a rolling basis. Application fee: $40. Electronic applications accepted. *Expenses: Tuition:* Full-time $17,748; part-time $986 per hour. *Required fees:* $5 per contact hour. $75 per semester. Tuition and fees vary according to program. *Financial support:* In 2011–12, 62 students received support, including 6 fellowships with partial tuition reimbursements available (averaging $5,209 per year), 56 research assistantships with full and partial tuition reimbursements available (averaging $11,168 per year), 18 teaching assistantships with full and partial tuition reimbursements available (averaging $7,886 per year); career-related internships or fieldwork, Federal Work-Study, scholarships/grants, health care benefits, tuition waivers (full and partial), and unspecified assistantships also available. Support available to part-time students. Financial award application deadline: 2/1; financial award applicants required to submit FAFSA. *Faculty research:* Artificial lift, drilling, multiphase flow in pipes, separation technology, horizontal well technology, reservoir characterization, well testing, reservoir simulation, unconventional natural gas. *Total annual research expenditures:* $8.5 million. *Unit head:* Dr. Mohan Kelkar, Chairperson, 918-631-3036, Fax: 915-631-2059, E-mail: mohan@utulsa.edu. *Application contact:* Dr. Jagan Mahadevan, Adviser, 918-631-3906, Fax: 918-631-5142, E-mail: jmahadevan@utulsa.edu. Web site: http://www.utulsa.edu/academics/colleges/college-of-engineering-and-natural-sciences/departments-and-schools/mcdougall-school-of-petroleum-engineering.

University of Wyoming, College of Engineering and Applied Sciences, Department of Chemical and Petroleum Engineering, Program in Petroleum Engineering, Laramie, WY 82070. Offers MS, PhD. Part-time programs available. Terminal master's awarded for partial completion of doctoral program. *Degree requirements:* For master's, thesis; for doctorate, thesis/dissertation. *Entrance requirements:* For master's and doctorate, GRE General Test, minimum GPA of 3.0. Additional exam requirements/recommendations for international students: Required—TOEFL (minimum score 600 paper-based; 250 computer-based). Electronic applications accepted. *Faculty research:* Oil recovery methods, oil production, coal bed methane.

West Virginia University, College of Engineering and Mineral Resources, Department of Petroleum and Natural Gas Engineering, Morgantown, WV 26506. Offers MSPNGE, PhD. Part-time programs available. *Degree requirements:* For master's, thesis; for doctorate, thesis/dissertation. *Entrance requirements:* For master's, minimum GPA of 3.0, BS or equivalent in petroleum or natural gas engineering; for doctorate, minimum GPA of 3.0, BS or MS in petroleum engineering from an ABET accredited or an internationally recognized petroleum engineering program or equivalent. Additional exam requirements/recommendations for international students: Required—TOEFL. *Faculty research:* Gas reservoir engineering, well logging, environment artificial intelligence.

Section 14
Industrial Engineering

This section contains a directory of institutions offering graduate work in industrial engineering. Additional information about programs listed in the directory but not augmented by an in-depth entry may be obtained by writing directly to the dean of a graduate school or chair of a department at the address given in the directory.

For programs offering related work, see also in this book *Computer Science and Information Technology, Electrical and Computer Engineering, Energy and Power Engineering, Engineering and Applied Sciences,* and *Management of Engineering and Technology.* In the other guides in this series:

Graduate Programs in the Physical Sciences, Mathematics, Agricultural Sciences, the Environment & Natural Resources
See *Mathematical Sciences*

Graduate Programs in Business, Education, Information Studies, Law & Social Work
See *Business Administration and Management*

CONTENTS

Program Directories

Automotive Engineering

Clemson University, Graduate School, College of Engineering and Science, Department of Automotive Engineering, Clemson, SC 29634. Offers MS, PhD. *Faculty:* 8 full-time (0 women). *Students:* 125 full-time (7 women), 4 part-time; includes 6 minority (2 Black or African American, non-Hispanic/Latino; 1 Asian, non-Hispanic/Latino; 1 Hispanic/Latino; 2 Two or more races, non-Hispanic/Latino), 92 international. Average age 26. 233 applicants, 73% accepted, 58 enrolled. In 2011, 30 master's, 4 doctorates awarded. *Degree requirements:* For master's, one foreign language, industrial internship; for doctorate, one foreign language, thesis/dissertation. *Entrance requirements:* For master's, GRE; for doctorate, GRE, MS or 2 years post-bachelor's experience. Additional exam requirements/recommendations for international students: Required—TOEFL. *Application deadline:* Applications are processed on a rolling basis. Application fee: $70 ($80 for international students). Electronic applications accepted. *Expenses:* Contact institution. *Financial support:* In 2011–12, 43 students received support, including 32 research assistantships with partial tuition reimbursements available (averaging $16,875 per year), 6 teaching assistantships with partial tuition reimbursements available (averaging $14,777 per year); fellowships with partial tuition reimbursements available, career-related internships or fieldwork, institutionally sponsored loans, scholarships/grants, traineeships, health care benefits, and unspecified assistantships also available. Support available to part-time students. Financial award application deadline: 2/1. *Faculty research:* Systems integration, manufacturing product design/development/vehicle electronics. *Total annual research expenditures:* $1.4 million. *Unit head:* Imtiaz Haque, Chair, 864-283-7212, E-mail: sih@clemson.edu. *Application contact:* Dr. Mohammed Omar, Coordinator, 864-656-5537, Fax: 864-656-4435, E-mail: momar@clemson.edu. Web site: http://www.clemson.edu/centers-institutes/cu-icar/education/automotive/.

Lawrence Technological University, College of Engineering, Southfield, MI 48075-1058. Offers architectural engineering (MS); automotive engineering (MS); civil engineering (MA, MS); construction engineering management (MA); electrical and computer engineering (MS); engineering management (MEM); industrial engineering (MS); manufacturing systems (ME, DE); mechanical engineering (MS, DE); mechatronic systems engineering (MS). Part-time and evening/weekend programs available. *Faculty:* 25 full-time (4 women), 20 part-time/adjunct (1 woman). *Students:* 8 full-time (0 women), 332 part-time (52 women); includes 58 minority (21 Black or African American, non-Hispanic/Latino; 1 American Indian or Alaska Native, non-Hispanic/Latino; 32 Asian, non-Hispanic/Latino; 2 Hispanic/Latino; 2 Two or more races, non-Hispanic/Latino), 84 international. Average age 32. 652 applicants, 44% accepted, 70 enrolled. In 2011, 127 master's, 2 doctorates awarded. *Degree requirements:* For master's, thesis (for some programs). *Entrance requirements:* Additional exam requirements/recommendations for international students: Required—TOEFL (minimum score 550 paper-based; 213 computer-based; 79 iBT). *Application deadline:* For fall admission, 7/27 priority date for domestic students, 5/23 for international students; for spring admission, 11/15 priority date for domestic students, 11/15 for international students. Applications are processed on a rolling basis. Application fee: $50. Electronic applications accepted. *Financial support:* In 2011–12, 68 students received support, including 6 research assistantships (averaging $8,078 per year); Federal Work-Study and institutionally sponsored loans also available. Support available to part-time students. Financial award application deadline: 4/1; financial award applicants required to submit FAFSA. *Faculty research:* Advanced composite materials in bridges, strengthening existing bridges with carbon and glass fiber sheets, development of drive shafts using composite materials. *Unit head:* Dr. Nabil Grace, Dean, 248-204-2500, Fax: 248-204-2509, E-mail: engrdean@ltu.edu. *Application contact:* Jane Rohrback, Director of Admissions, 248-204-3160, Fax: 248-204-2228, E-mail: admissions@ltu.edu. Web site: http://www.ltu.edu/engineering/index.asp.

Minnesota State University Mankato, College of Graduate Studies, College of Science, Engineering and Technology, Department of Automotive and Manufacturing Engineering Technology, Mankato, MN 56001. Offers manufacturing engineering technology (MS). *Students:* 9 full-time (2 women), 10 part-time (1 woman). *Degree requirements:* For master's, comprehensive exam, thesis. *Entrance requirements:* For master's, GRE General Test (if GPA less than 3.0), minimum GPA of 3.0 during previous 2 years. Additional exam requirements/recommendations for international students: Required—TOEFL. *Application deadline:* For fall admission, 7/1 priority date for domestic students; for spring admission, 11/1 for domestic students. Applications are processed on a rolling basis. Application fee: $40. Electronic applications accepted. *Financial support:* Research assistantships with full tuition reimbursements, teaching assistantships with full tuition reimbursements, and unspecified assistantships available. Financial award application deadline: 3/15; financial award applicants required to submit FAFSA. *Unit head:* Dr. Bruce Jones, Graduate Coordinator, 507-389-6700. *Application contact:* 507-389-2321, E-mail: grad@mnsu.edu.

University of Michigan, College of Engineering, Interpro Programs in Engineering, Ann Arbor, MI 48109. Offers automotive engineering (M Eng); design science (PhD); energy systems engineering (MS); financial engineering (MS); global automotive and manufacturing engineering (M Eng); manufacturing engineering (M Eng, D Eng); pharmaceutical engineering (M Eng); robotics and autonomous vehicles (M Eng); MBA/M Eng; MSE/MS. Part-time programs available. Postbaccalaureate distance learning degree programs offered (no on-campus study). *Students:* 225 full-time (55 women), 273 part-time (37 women). In 2011, 145 master's, 1 doctorate awarded. Terminal master's awarded for partial completion of doctoral program. *Degree requirements:* For master's, capstone project; for doctorate, thesis/dissertation. *Entrance requirements:* For master's, GRE; for doctorate, GRE, 2 years of work experience. Additional exam requirements/recommendations for international students: Required—TOEFL (minimum score 560 paper-based; 220 computer-based). *Application deadline:* Applications are processed on a rolling basis. Application fee: $65 ($75 for international students). Electronic applications accepted. *Financial support:* Fellowships, research assistantships with full tuition reimbursements, teaching assistantships with full tuition reimbursements, career-related internships or fieldwork, scholarships/grants, and unspecified assistantships available. Financial award application deadline: 2/15; financial award applicants required to submit FAFSA. *Faculty research:* Automotive engineering, design science, energy systems engineering, engineering sustainable systems dual degree, financial engineering, global automotive and manufacturing engineering, integrated microsystems, manufacturing engineering, pharmaceutical engineering , robotics and autonomous vehicles. *Unit head:* Prof. Panos Papalambros, Director, 734-763-0480, Fax: 734-647-0079, E-mail: pyp@umich.edu. *Application contact:* Patti Mackmiller, Program Manager, 734-764-3071, Fax: 734-647-2243, E-mail: pmackmil@umich.edu. Web site: http://interpro-academics.engin.umich.edu/.

University of Michigan–Dearborn, College of Engineering and Computer Science, Interdisciplinary Programs, MSE Program in Automotive Systems Engineering, Dearborn, MI 48128-1491. Offers MSE. Part-time and evening/weekend programs available. Postbaccalaureate distance learning degree programs offered. *Faculty:* 1 full-time (0 women). *Students:* 12 full-time (1 woman), 22 part-time (3 women); includes 5 minority (1 Black or African American, non-Hispanic/Latino; 4 Hispanic/Latino), 21 international. Average age 30. 52 applicants, 50% accepted, 12 enrolled. In 2011, 21 master's awarded. *Degree requirements:* For master's, thesis optional. *Entrance requirements:* For master's, bachelor's degree in applied mathematics, computer science, engineering, or physical science; minimum GPA of 3.0. Additional exam requirements/recommendations for international students: Required—TOEFL (minimum score 560 paper-based; 220 computer-based; 84 iBT). *Application deadline:* For fall admission, 8/1 priority date for domestic students, 4/1 for international students; for winter admission, 12/1 priority date for domestic students, 8/1 for international students; for spring admission, 4/1 priority date for domestic students, 12/1 for international students. Applications are processed on a rolling basis. Application fee: $60. Electronic applications accepted. *Financial support:* In 2011–12, 1 research assistantship with full tuition reimbursement (averaging $21,156 per year) was awarded; scholarships/grants and unspecified assistantships also available. Financial award application deadline: 4/1; financial award applicants required to submit FAFSA. *Faculty research:* Performance of lightweight automotive materials, stamping, hydroforming, tailor-welded blanking, automotive composites processing and design, thermoplastic matrix composites, injection molding. *Unit head:* Dr. Pankaj K. Mallick, Director/Professor, 313-593-5119, Fax: 313-593-5386, E-mail: pkm@umich.edu. *Application contact:* Sherry Boyd, Intermediate Administrative Assistant, 313-593-5582, Fax: 313-593-5386, E-mail: idpgrad@umd.umich.edu. Web site: http://www.engin.umd.umich.edu/IDP/mse_ase/.

University of Michigan–Dearborn, College of Engineering and Computer Science, Interdisciplinary Programs, PhD Program in Automotive Systems Engineering, Dearborn, MI 48128-1491. Offers PhD. Part-time and evening/weekend programs available. *Faculty:* 1 full-time (0 women). *Students:* 9 full-time (0 women), 6 part-time (0 women), 9 international. Average age 29. 6 applicants, 83% accepted, 4 enrolled. *Degree requirements:* For doctorate, thesis/dissertation. *Entrance requirements:* For doctorate, GRE. Additional exam requirements/recommendations for international students: Required—TOEFL (minimum score 560 paper-based; 220 computer-based; 84 iBT). *Application deadline:* For fall admission, 1/15 priority date for domestic students, 1/15 for international students; for winter admission, 4/15 priority date for domestic students, 4/15 for international students. Applications are processed on a rolling basis. Application fee: $60. Electronic applications accepted. *Financial support:* In 2011–12, 5 research assistantships with full tuition reimbursements (averaging $26,500 per year) were awarded; scholarships/grants and unspecified assistantships also available. Financial award applicants required to submit FAFSA. *Unit head:* Dr. Pankaj K. Mallick, Director/Professor, 313-593-5119, Fax: 313-593-5386, E-mail: pkm@umich.edu. *Application contact:* Sherry Boyd, Intermediate Administrative Assistant, 313-593-5582, Fax: 313-593-5386, E-mail: idpgrad@umd.umich.edu. Web site: http://www.engin.umd.umich.edu/IDP/phd_ase/.

Wayne State University, College of Engineering, Program in Electric-drive Vehicle Engineering, Detroit, MI 48202. Offers MS, Graduate Certificate. *Students:* 6 full-time (0 women), 28 part-time (1 woman); includes 13 minority (7 Asian, non-Hispanic/Latino; 5 Hispanic/Latino; 1 Two or more races, non-Hispanic/Latino), 3 international. Average age 39. 45 applicants, 51% accepted, 14 enrolled. In 2011, 1 master's awarded. *Degree requirements:* For master's, thesis optional. *Entrance requirements:* For master's, bachelor's degree in engineering from accredited institution with minimum GPA of 3.0; for Graduate Certificate, bachelor's degree in engineering from accredited institution with minimum GPA of 2.7. Additional exam requirements/recommendations for international students: Required—TOEFL (minimum score 550 paper-based; 213 computer-based), TWE (minimum score 5.5). *Application deadline:* For fall admission, 6/1 priority date for domestic students, 5/1 for international students; for winter admission, 10/1 priority date for domestic students, 9/1 for international students; for spring admission, 2/1 priority date for domestic students, 1/1 for international students. Applications are processed on a rolling basis. Application fee: $50. Electronic applications accepted. *Expenses:* Tuition, state resident: part-time $512.85 per credit. Tuition, nonresident: part-time $1132.65 per credit. *Required fees:* $26.60 per credit. $199.65 per semester. Tuition and fees vary according to course load and program. *Unit head:* Dr. Simon Ng, Program Director, 313-577-3805, E-mail: sng@wayne.edu. Web site: http://www.eng.wayne.edu/page.php?id=5909.

Industrial/Management Engineering

Arizona State University, Ira A. Fulton School of Engineering, School of Computing, Informatics, and Decision Systems Engineering, Tempe, AZ 85287-8809. Offers computer science (MCS, MS, PhD); industrial engineering (MS, PhD). Part-time and evening/weekend programs available. Postbaccalaureate distance learning degree programs offered (minimal on-campus study). Terminal master's awarded for partial completion of doctoral program. *Degree requirements:* For master's, comprehensive exam (for some programs), portfolio (MCS); interactive Program of Study (iPOS) submitted before completing 50 percent of required credit hours; for doctorate, comprehensive exam, thesis/dissertation, interactive Program of Study (iPOS) submitted before completing 50 percent of required credit hours. *Entrance requirements:* For master's, GRE, minimum GPA of 3.0 or equivalent in last 2 years of work leading to bachelor's degree; for doctorate, GRE, minimum GPA of 3.0 in last 2 years of work leading to bachelor's degree. Additional exam requirements/recommendations for international students: Required—TOEFL (minimum score 80 iBT), TOEFL, IELTS, or Pearson Test of English. Electronic applications accepted. *Expenses:* Contact institution. *Faculty research:* Artificial intelligence, cyberphysical and embedded systems, health informatics, information assurance and security, information management/multimedia/visualization, network science, personalized learning/educational games, production logistics, software and systems engineering, and statistical modeling and data mining.

Auburn University, Graduate School, Ginn College of Engineering, Department of Industrial and Systems Engineering, Auburn University, AL 36849. Offers MISE, MS, PhD, Graduate Certificate. Part-time programs available. *Faculty:* 8 full-time (1 woman), 3 part-time/adjunct (0 women). *Students:* 79 full-time (21 women), 45 part-time (12 women); includes 15 minority (10 Black or African American, non-Hispanic/Latino; 1 American Indian or Alaska Native, non-Hispanic/Latino; 2 Asian, non-Hispanic/Latino; 2 Hispanic/Latino), 68 international. Average age 29. 154 applicants, 80% accepted, 30 enrolled. In 2011, 46 master's, 5 doctorates awarded. *Degree requirements:* For master's, thesis (MS); for doctorate, thesis/dissertation. *Entrance requirements:* For master's and doctorate, GRE General Test. *Application deadline:* For fall admission, 7/7 for domestic students; for spring admission, 11/24 for domestic students. Applications are processed on a rolling basis. Application fee: $50 ($60 for international students). *Expenses:* Tuition, state resident: full-time $7290; part-time $405 per credit hour. Tuition, nonresident: full-time $21,870; part-time $1215 per credit hour. *International tuition:* $22,000 full-time. *Required fees:* $1402. *Financial support:* Fellowships, research assistantships, teaching assistantships, and Federal Work-Study available. Support available to part-time students. Financial award application deadline: 3/15; financial award applicants required to submit FAFSA. *Unit head:* Dr. Jorge Valenzuela, Chair, 334-844-1400. *Application contact:* Dr. George Flowers, Dean of the Graduate School, 334-844-2125. Web site: http://www.eng.auburn.edu/department/ie.

Bradley University, Graduate School, College of Engineering and Technology, Department of Industrial and Manufacturing Engineering and Technology, Peoria, IL 61625-0002. Offers industrial engineering (MSIE); manufacturing engineering (MSIE). Part-time and evening/weekend programs available. *Degree requirements:* For master's, comprehensive exam, project. *Entrance requirements:* For master's, minimum GPA of 3.0. Additional exam requirements/recommendations for international students: Required—TOEFL (minimum score 550 paper-based; 213 computer-based; 79 iBT).

Buffalo State College, State University of New York, The Graduate School, Faculty of Applied Science and Education, Department of Technology, Program in Industrial Technology, Buffalo, NY 14222-1095. Offers MS. *Degree requirements:* For master's, thesis or project. *Entrance requirements:* For master's, minimum GPA of 2.5. Additional exam requirements/recommendations for international students: Required—TOEFL (minimum score 550 paper-based; 213 computer-based).

California Polytechnic State University, San Luis Obispo, College of Engineering, Department of Industrial Engineering, San Luis Obispo, CA 93407. Offers MS. Part-time programs available. *Faculty:* 1 (woman) full-time. *Students:* 17 full-time (5 women); includes 7 minority (4 Asian, non-Hispanic/Latino; 2 Hispanic/Latino; 1 Two or more races, non-Hispanic/Latino). Average age 23. 9 applicants, 78% accepted, 5 enrolled. In 2011, 8 master's awarded. *Degree requirements:* For master's, comprehensive exam (for some programs), thesis (for some programs). *Entrance requirements:* For master's, GRE General Test, minimum GPA of 3.0 in last 90 quarter units of course work. Additional exam requirements/recommendations for international students: Required—TOEFL (minimum score 550 paper-based; 213 computer-based) or IELTS (minimum score 6). *Application deadline:* For fall admission, 7/1 for domestic students, 11/30 for international students; for winter admission, 11/1 for domestic students, 6/30 for international students; for spring admission, 2/1 for domestic students. Applications are processed on a rolling basis. Application fee: $55. Electronic applications accepted. *Expenses:* Tuition, state resident: full-time $6738. Tuition, nonresident: full-time $17,898. *Required fees:* $2449. *Financial support:* Fellowships, research assistantships, teaching assistantships, career-related internships or fieldwork, Federal Work-Study, institutionally sponsored loans, and scholarships/grants available. Support available to part-time students. Financial award application deadline: 3/2; financial award applicants required to submit FAFSA. *Faculty research:* Operations research, simulation, project management, supply chain and logistics, quality engineering. *Unit head:* Dr. Liz Schlemer, Graduate Coordinator, 805-756-2183, Fax: 805-756-5439, E-mail: lschleme@calpoly.edu. *Application contact:* Dr. James Maraviglia, Associate Vice Provost for Marketing and Enrollment Development, 805-756-2311, Fax: 805-756-5400, E-mail: admissions@calpoly.edu. Web site: http://www.ime.calpoly.edu/programs/graduate/.

California State University, Fresno, Division of Graduate Studies, College of Agricultural Sciences and Technology, Department of Industrial Technology, Fresno, CA 93740-8027. Offers MS. Part-time and evening/weekend programs available. *Degree requirements:* For master's, comprehensive exam (for some programs), thesis (for some programs). *Entrance requirements:* For master's, GRE General Test, minimum GPA of 2.5. Additional exam requirements/recommendations for international students: Required—TOEFL. Electronic applications accepted. *Faculty research:* Fuels/pollution, energy, outdoor storage methods.

California State University, Northridge, Graduate Studies, College of Engineering and Computer Science, Department of Manufacturing Systems Engineering and Management, Northridge, CA 91330. Offers engineering automation (MS); engineering management (MS); manufacturing systems engineering (MS); materials engineering (MS). Postbaccalaureate distance learning degree programs offered. *Entrance requirements:* For master's, GRE (if cumulative undergraduate GPA less than 3.0).

Central Washington University, Graduate Studies and Research, College of Education and Professional Studies, Department of Industrial and Engineering Technology, Ellensburg, WA 98926. Offers engineering technology (MS). Part-time programs available. *Faculty:* 18 full-time (0 women). *Students:* 23 full-time (5 women), 16 part-time (0 women); includes 14 minority (1 Black or African American, non-Hispanic/Latino; 12 Asian, non-Hispanic/Latino; 1 Native Hawaiian or other Pacific Islander, non-Hispanic/Latino). 20 applicants, 90% accepted, 18 enrolled. In 2011, 24 master's awarded. *Degree requirements:* For master's, thesis or alternative. *Entrance requirements:* For master's, minimum GPA of 3.0. Additional exam requirements/recommendations for international students: Required—TOEFL (minimum score 550 paper-based; 213 computer-based; 79 iBT), IELTS (minimum score 6.5). *Application deadline:* For fall admission, 2/1 priority date for domestic students; for winter admission, 10/1 for domestic students; for spring admission, 1/1 for domestic students. Applications are processed on a rolling basis. Application fee: $50. Electronic applications accepted. *Expenses:* Tuition, state resident: full-time $8112; part-time $270 per credit. Tuition, nonresident: full-time $18,069; part-time $602 per credit. *Required fees:* $924. *Financial support:* In 2011–12, 4 teaching assistantships with full and partial tuition reimbursements (averaging $9,234 per year) were awarded; career-related internships or fieldwork, Federal Work-Study, and health care benefits also available. *Unit head:* Dr. Darren Olson, Graduate Coordinator, 509-963-1756. *Application contact:* Justine Eason, Admissions Program Coordinator, 509-963-3103, Fax: 509-963-1799, E-mail: masters@cwu.edu. Web site: http://www.cwu.edu/~iet/.

Clemson University, Graduate School, College of Engineering and Science, Department of Industrial Engineering, Clemson, SC 29634. Offers M Eng, MS, PhD. Part-time programs available. Postbaccalaureate distance learning degree programs offered (no on-campus study). *Faculty:* 10 full-time (2 women), 1 (woman) part-time/ adjunct. *Students:* 62 full-time (18 women), 111 part-time (32 women); includes 22 minority (7 Black or African American, non-Hispanic/Latino; 2 American Indian or Alaska Native, non-Hispanic/Latino; 5 Asian, non-Hispanic/Latino; 5 Hispanic/Latino; 3 Two or more races, non-Hispanic/Latino), 63 international. Average age 28. 251 applicants, 66% accepted, 56 enrolled. In 2011, 19 master's, 11 doctorates awarded. Terminal master's awarded for partial completion of doctoral program. *Degree requirements:* For master's, thesis or alternative; for doctorate, comprehensive exam, thesis/dissertation. *Entrance requirements:* Additional exam requirements/recommendations for international students: Required—TOEFL. *Application deadline:* For fall admission, 6/1 for domestic students, 11/30 for international students. Applications are processed on a rolling basis. Application fee: $70 ($80 for international students). Electronic applications accepted. *Financial support:* In 2011–12, 37 students received support, including 1 fellowship with full and partial tuition reimbursement available (averaging $2,040 per year), 22 research assistantships with partial tuition reimbursements available (averaging $7,966 per year), 26 teaching assistantships with partial tuition reimbursements available (averaging $7,371 per year); career-related internships or fieldwork, institutionally sponsored loans, scholarships/grants, health care benefits, and unspecified assistantships also available. Support available to part-time students. Financial award applicants required to submit FAFSA. *Faculty research:* System optimization, health care engineering, human factors and safety, human-computer interaction, quality. *Total annual research expenditures:* $1.4 million. *Unit head:* Dr. Anand Gramopadhye, Head, 864-656-4716, E-mail: agramop@ces.clemson.edu. *Application contact:* Kevin M. Taaffe, Graduate Coordinator, 864-656-0291, E-mail: taaffe@clemson.edu. Web site: http://www.clemson.edu/ces/departments/ie/index.html.

Cleveland State University, College of Graduate Studies, Fenn College of Engineering, Department of Industrial and Manufacturing Engineering, Cleveland, OH 44115. Offers industrial engineering (MS, D Eng). Part-time programs available. *Faculty:* 5 full-time (0 women), 2 part-time/adjunct (0 women). *Students:* 12 full-time (1 woman), 14 part-time (4 women); includes 4 minority (3 Black or African American, non-Hispanic/Latino; 1 Asian, non-Hispanic/Latino), 13 international. Average age 29. 58 applicants, 60% accepted, 8 enrolled. In 2011, 21 master's, 2 doctorates awarded. Terminal master's awarded for partial completion of doctoral program. *Degree requirements:* For master's, thesis or alternative; for doctorate, thesis/dissertation, candidacy and qualifying exams. *Entrance requirements:* For master's, GRE General Test, minimum GPA of 2.75; for doctorate, GRE General Test, minimum GPA of 3.25. Additional exam requirements/recommendations for international students: Required—TOEFL (minimum score 525 paper-based; 197 computer-based). *Application deadline:* For fall admission, 7/15 priority date for domestic students, 6/1 for international students; for spring admission, 11/1 for international students. Applications are processed on a rolling basis. Application fee: $30. *Expenses:* Tuition, state resident: full-time $6416; part-time $494 per credit hour. Tuition, nonresident: full-time $12,074; part-time $929 per credit hour. *Financial support:* In 2011–12, 4 research assistantships with full and partial tuition reimbursements (averaging $3,550 per year), 2 teaching assistantships with tuition reimbursements (averaging $3,725 per year) were awarded; fellowships, career-related internships or fieldwork, institutionally sponsored loans, tuition waivers (partial), and unspecified assistantships also available. Support available to part-time students. *Faculty research:* Modeling of manufacturing systems, statistical process control, computerized production planning and facilities design, cellular manufacturing, artificial intelligence and sensors. *Unit head:* Dr. Joseph A. Svestka, Chairperson, 216-687-4662, Fax: 216-687-9330, E-mail: j.svestka@csuohio.edu. *Application contact:* Shirley A. Love, Administrative Services Coordinator, 216-687-2044, Fax: 216-687-9330, E-mail: s.love@csuohio.edu. Web site: http://www.csuohio.edu/ime.

Colorado State University–Pueblo, College of Education, Engineering and Professional Studies, Department of Engineering, Pueblo, CO 81001-4901. Offers industrial and systems engineering (MS). *Degree requirements:* For master's, thesis optional. *Entrance requirements:* For master's, GRE General Test. Additional exam requirements/recommendations for international students: Required—TOEFL (minimum score 500 paper-based). *Faculty research:* Nanotechnology, applied operations, research transportation, decision analysis.

Columbia University, The Fu Foundation School of Engineering and Applied Science, Department of Industrial Engineering and Operations Research, New York, NY 10027. Offers financial engineering (MS); industrial engineering (Engr); industrial engineering and operations research (MS, Eng Sc D, PhD); MS/MBA. Part-time and evening/weekend programs available. Postbaccalaureate distance learning degree programs offered (no on-campus study). *Faculty:* 22 full-time (3 women), 27 part-time/adjunct (2 women). *Students:* 344 full-time (99 women), 205 part-time (54 women); includes 34 minority (28 Asian, non-Hispanic/Latino; 2 Hispanic/Latino; 1 Native Hawaiian or other Pacific Islander, non-Hispanic/Latino; 3 Two or more races, non-Hispanic/Latino), 460 international. Average age 26. 2,041 applicants, 19% accepted, 311 enrolled. In 2011, 229 master's, 6 doctorates, 1 other advanced degree awarded. *Degree requirements:* For doctorate, thesis/dissertation, oral and written qualifying exams. *Entrance requirements:* For master's, doctorate, and Engr, GRE General Test. Additional exam requirements/recommendations for international students: Required—TOEFL, IELTS. *Application deadline:* For fall admission, 12/1 priority date for domestic students, 12/1 for international students; for spring admission, 10/1 priority date for domestic students, 10/1 for international students. Application fee: $95. Electronic applications accepted. *Financial support:* In 2011–12, 44 students received support, including 2 fellowships with full tuition reimbursements available (averaging $35,968 per year), 22 research assistantships with full tuition reimbursements available (averaging $31,380 per year), 20 teaching assistantships with full tuition reimbursements available (averaging $31,380 per year); career-related internships or fieldwork and health care benefits also available. Financial award application deadline: 12/1; financial award applicants required to submit FAFSA. *Faculty research:* Applied probability and optimization; financial engineering, modeling risk including credit risk and systemic risk, asset allocation, portfolio execution, behavioral finance, agent-based model in finance; revenue management; management and optimization of service systems, call centers, capacity allocation in healthcare systems, inventory control for vaccines; energy, smart grids, demand shaping, managing renewable energy sources, energy-aware scheduling. *Unit head:* Dr. Cliff S. Stein, Professor and Department Chairman, 212-854-5238, Fax: 212-854-8103, E-mail: cliff@ieor.columbia.edu. *Application contact:* Adina Berrios Brooks, Student Affairs Manager, 212-854-1934, Fax: 212-854-8103, E-mail: admit@ieor.columbia.edu. Web site: http://www.ieor.columbia.edu/.

Concordia University, School of Graduate Studies, Faculty of Engineering and Computer Science, Department of Mechanical and Industrial Engineering, Montréal, QC H3G 1M8, Canada. Offers composites (M Eng); industrial engineering (M Eng, MA Sc); mechanical engineering (M Eng, MA Sc, PhD, Certificate); software systems for industrial engineering (Certificate). M Eng in composites program offered jointly with École Polytechnique de Montréal. *Degree requirements:* For master's, variable foreign language requirement, thesis or alternative; for doctorate, comprehensive exam, thesis/

dissertation. *Faculty research:* Mechanical systems, fluid control systems, thermofluids engineering and robotics, industrial control systems.

Cornell University, Graduate School, Graduate Fields of Engineering, Field of Operations Research and Information Engineering, Ithaca, NY 14853. Offers applied probability and statistics (PhD); manufacturing systems engineering (PhD); mathematical programming (PhD); operations research and industrial engineering (M Eng). *Faculty:* 38 full-time (6 women). *Students:* 172 full-time (47 women); includes 25 minority (2 Black or African American, non-Hispanic/Latino; 19 Asian, non-Hispanic/Latino; 4 Hispanic/Latino), 120 international. Average age 24. 1,070 applicants, 24% accepted, 106 enrolled. In 2011, 93 master's, 6 doctorates awarded. *Degree requirements:* For doctorate, comprehensive exam, thesis/dissertation. *Entrance requirements:* For master's and doctorate, GRE General Test, 3 letters of recommendation. Additional exam requirements/recommendations for international students: Required—TOEFL (minimum score 600 paper-based; 250 computer-based; 100 iBT). *Application deadline:* For fall admission, 12/15 for domestic students. Application fee: $95. Electronic applications accepted. *Financial support:* In 2011–12, 44 students received support, including 11 fellowships with full tuition reimbursements available, 13 research assistantships with full tuition reimbursements available, 19 teaching assistantships with full tuition reimbursements available; institutionally sponsored loans, scholarships/grants, health care benefits, tuition waivers (full and partial), and unspecified assistantships also available. Financial award applicants required to submit FAFSA. *Faculty research:* Mathematical programming and combinatorial optimization, statistics, stochastic processes, mathematical finance, simulation, manufacturing, e-commerce. *Unit head:* Director of Graduate Studies, 607-255-9128, Fax: 607-255-9129. *Application contact:* Graduate Field Assistant, 607-255-9128, Fax: 607-255-9129, E-mail: orie@cornell.edu. Web site: http://www.gradschool.cornell.edu/fields.php?id-35&a-2.

Dalhousie University, Faculty of Engineering, Department of Industrial Engineering, Halifax, NS B3J 2X4, Canada. Offers M Eng, MA Sc, PhD. *Degree requirements:* For master's, thesis; for doctorate, thesis/dissertation. *Entrance requirements:* Additional exam requirements/recommendations for international students: Required—TOEFL, IELTS, CANTEST, CAEL, or Michigan English Language Assessment Battery. Electronic applications accepted. *Faculty research:* Industrial ergonomics, operations research, production manufacturing systems, scheduling stochastic models.

East Carolina University, Graduate School, College of Technology and Computer Science, Department of Technology Systems, Greenville, NC 27858-4353. Offers computer network professional (Certificate); industrial technology (MS), including computer networking management, digital communications, industrial distribution and logistics, information security, manufacturing, performance improvement, quality systems; information assurance (Certificate); Lean Six Sigma Black Belt (Certificate); occupational safety (MS); technology management (PhD); Website developer (Certificate). *Entrance requirements:* For master's and Certificate, GRE General Test or MAT, minimum GPA of 2.5; for doctorate, GRE General Test, related work experience. *Application deadline:* For fall admission, 6/1 priority date for domestic students. Applications are processed on a rolling basis. Application fee: $50. *Expenses:* Tuition, state resident: full-time $3557; part-time $444.63 per semester hour. Tuition, nonresident: full-time $14,351; part-time $1793.88 per semester hour. *Required fees:* $2016; $252 per semester hour. Part-time tuition and fees vary according to course load, campus/location and program. *Financial support:* Application deadline: 6/1. *Unit head:* Dr. Tijjani Mohammed, Interim Chair, 252-328-9668, E-mail: mohammedt@ecu.edu. Web site: http://www.ecu.edu/cs-tecs/techsystems/.

Eastern Kentucky University, The Graduate School, College of Business and Technology, Department of Technology, Program in Industrial Technology, Richmond, KY 40475-3102. Offers MS. Part-time programs available. *Entrance requirements:* For master's, GRE General Test, minimum GPA of 2.5. *Faculty research:* Quality control, dental implants, manufacturing technology.

École Polytechnique de Montréal, Graduate Programs, Department of Mathematics and Industrial Engineering, Montréal, QC H3C 3A7, Canada. Offers ergonomy (M Eng, M Sc A, DESS); mathematical method in CA engineering (M Eng, M Sc A, PhD); operational research (M Eng, M Sc A, PhD); production (M Eng, M Sc A); technology management (M Eng, M Sc A). DESS program offered jointly with HEC Montreal and Université de Montréal. Part-time programs available. *Degree requirements:* For master's, one foreign language, thesis. *Entrance requirements:* For master's, minimum GPA of 2.75. *Faculty research:* Use of computers in organizations.

Florida Agricultural and Mechanical University, Division of Graduate Studies, Research, and Continuing Education, FAMU-FSU College of Engineering, Department of Industrial Engineering, Tallahassee, FL 32307-3200. Offers MS, PhD. *Degree requirements:* For master's, thesis optional. *Entrance requirements:* For master's, GRE General Test, minimum GPA of 3.0. Additional exam requirements/recommendations for international students: Required—TOEFL (minimum score 550 paper-based; 213 computer-based). *Faculty research:* Design for environmentally conscious manufacturing, affordable composite manufacturing, integrated product and process design, precision machining research.

Florida State University, The Graduate School, FAMU-FSU College of Engineering, Department of Industrial and Manufacturing Engineering, Tallahassee, FL 32306. Offers industrial engineering (MS, PhD). *Faculty:* 10 full-time (1 woman), 1 (woman) part-time/adjunct. *Students:* 34 full-time (6 women), 2 part-time (1 woman); includes 9 minority (8 Black or African American, non-Hispanic/Latino; 1 Hispanic/Latino), 18 international. Average age 24. 66 applicants, 26% accepted, 8 enrolled. In 2011, 7 degrees awarded. *Degree requirements:* For master's, thesis; for doctorate, thesis/dissertation, preliminary exam, qualifying exam. *Entrance requirements:* For master's, GRE General Test (minimum score of 400 Verbal and 650 Quantitative), minimum GPA of 3.0; for doctorate, GRE General Test (minimum score of 450 Verbal and 700 Quantitative), minimum GPA of 3.0 (without MS in industrial engineering), 3.4 (with MS in industrial engineering). Additional exam requirements/recommendations for international students: Required—TOEFL (minimum score 550 paper-based; 213 computer-based; 80 iBT). *Application deadline:* For fall admission, 7/1 for domestic students, 3/1 for international students; for spring admission, 11/1 for domestic students, 7/1 for international students. Applications are processed on a rolling basis. Application fee: $30. *Expenses:* Tuition, state resident: full-time $9474; part-time $350.88 per credit hour. Tuition, nonresident: full-time $16,236; part-time $601.34 per credit hour. *Required fees:* $630 per semester. One-time fee: $20. Tuition and fees vary according to course load and campus/location. *Financial support:* In 2011–12, 33 students received support, including 1 fellowship with full and partial tuition reimbursement available (averaging $42,000 per year), 28 research assistantships with full tuition reimbursements available (averaging $18,361 per year), 5 teaching assistantships with full tuition reimbursements available (averaging $15,628 per year); tuition waivers (full) also available. Financial award application deadline: 6/15. *Faculty research:* Precision manufacturing, composite manufacturing, green manufacturing, applied optimization,

simulation. *Unit head:* Dr. Chun Zhang, Chair and Professor, 850-410-6355, Fax: 850-410-6342, E-mail: chzhang@eng.fsu.edu. *Application contact:* Stephanie Salters, Office Manager, 850-410-6345, Fax: 850-410-6342, E-mail: salters@eng.fsu.edu. Web site: http://www.eng.fsu.edu/departments/industrial/.

Georgia Institute of Technology, Graduate Studies and Research, College of Engineering, School of Industrial and Systems Engineering, Program in Industrial and Systems Engineering, Atlanta, GA 30332-0001. Offers algorithms, combinatorics, and optimization (PhD); industrial and systems engineering (PhD); industrial engineering (MS, MSIE); statistics (MS Stat). Part-time programs available. Terminal master's awarded for partial completion of doctoral program. *Degree requirements:* For master's, thesis optional; for doctorate, thesis/dissertation. *Entrance requirements:* For master's and doctorate, GRE General Test, minimum GPA of 3.0. Additional exam requirements/recommendations for international students: Required—TOEFL. Electronic applications accepted. *Faculty research:* Computer-integrated manufacturing systems, materials handling systems, production and distribution.

Illinois State University, Graduate School, College of Applied Science and Technology, Department of Technology, Normal, IL 61790-2200. Offers MS. *Degree requirements:* For master's, thesis or alternative. *Entrance requirements:* For master's, GRE General Test, minimum GPA of 2.8. *Faculty research:* National Center for Engineering and Technology Education, Illinois Manufacturing Extension Center Field Office hosting, model for the professional development of K-12 technology education teachers, Illinois State University Illinois Mathermatics and Science Partnership, Illinois University council for career and technical education.

Indiana State University, College of Graduate and Professional Studies, College of Technology, Program in Industrial Technology, Terre Haute, IN 47809. Offers MS. *Entrance requirements:* For master's, bachelor's degree in industrial technology or related field. Additional exam requirements/recommendations for international students: Required—TOEFL. Electronic applications accepted.

Indiana University–Purdue University Fort Wayne, College of Engineering, Technology, and Computer Science, Program in Technology, Fort Wayne, IN 46805-1499. Offers facilities and construction management (MS); industrial technology/manufacturing (MS); information technology/advanced computer applications (MS). Part-time programs available. *Faculty:* 14 full-time (5 women). *Students:* 1 full-time (0 women), 18 part-time (1 woman); includes 3 minority (1 Black or African American, non-Hispanic/Latino; 1 Asian, non-Hispanic/Latino; 1 Hispanic/Latino), 3 international. Average age 32. 9 applicants, 100% accepted, 7 enrolled. In 2011, 5 master's awarded. *Entrance requirements:* For master's, minimum GPA of 3.0. Additional exam requirements/recommendations for international students: Required—TOEFL (minimum score 550 paper-based; 213 computer-based; 77 iBT), TWE. *Application deadline:* For fall admission, 7/15 for domestic students, 5/15 for international students; for spring admission, 12/1 for domestic students, 10/15 for international students. Applications are processed on a rolling basis. Application fee: $55 ($60 for international students). Electronic applications accepted. *Financial support:* Career-related internships or fieldwork, scholarships/grants, and unspecified assistantships available. Support available to part-time students. Financial award application deadline: 3/1; financial award applicants required to submit FAFSA. *Unit head:* Dr. Max Yen, Dean, 260-481-6839, Fax: 260-481-5734, E-mail: yens@ipfw.edu. *Application contact:* Dr. Gary Steffen, Chair, 260-481-6344, Fax: 260-481-5734, E-mail: steffen@ipfw.edu. Web site: http://www.ipfw.edu/etcs.

Instituto Tecnologico de Santo Domingo, Graduate School, Area of Engineering, Santo Domingo, Dominican Republic. Offers construction administration (MS, Certificate); data telecommunications (M Eng, MS, Certificate); industrial engineering (M Eng, Certificate); industrial management (M Mgmt); information technology (Certificate); maintenance engineering (M Eng); occupational hazard prevention (M Mgmt); production management (Certificate); quantitative methods (Certificate); sanitary and environmental engineering (M Eng); structural engineering (M Eng); systems engineering and electronic data processing (Certificate); transportation (Certificate).

Instituto Tecnológico y de Estudios Superiores de Monterrey, Campus Chihuahua, Graduate Programs, Chihuahua, Mexico. Offers computer systems engineering (Ingeniero); electrical engineering (Ingeniero); electromechanical engineering (Ingeniero); electronic engineering (Ingeniero); engineering administration (MEA); industrial engineering (MIE, Ingeniero); international trade (MIT); mechanical engineering (Ingeniero).

Instituto Tecnológico y de Estudios Superiores de Monterrey, Campus Ciudad de México, Virtual University Division, Ciudad de Mexico, Mexico. Offers administration of information technologies (MA); computer sciences (MA); education (MA, PhD); educational technology (MA); environmental engineering (MA); environmental systems (MA); humanistic studies (MA); industrial engineering (MA); international business for Latin America (MA); quality systems (MA); quality systems and productivity (MA). Part-time and evening/weekend programs available. Postbaccalaureate distance learning degree programs offered (minimal on-campus study). *Entrance requirements:* For master's and doctorate, Instituto entrance exam. Additional exam requirements/recommendations for international students: Required—TOEFL.

Instituto Tecnológico y de Estudios Superiores de Monterrey, Campus Laguna, Graduate School, Torreón, Mexico. Offers business administration (MBA); industrial engineering (MIE); management information systems (MS). Part-time programs available. *Entrance requirements:* For master's, GMAT. *Faculty research:* Computer communications from home to the university.

Instituto Tecnológico y de Estudios Superiores de Monterrey, Campus Monterrey, Graduate and Research Division, Programs in Engineering, Monterrey, Mexico. Offers applied statistics (M Eng); artificial intelligence (PhD); automation engineering (M Eng); chemical engineering (M Eng); civil engineering (M Eng); electrical engineering (M Eng); electronic engineering (M Eng); environmental engineering (M Eng); industrial engineering (M Eng, PhD); manufacturing engineering (M Eng); mechanical engineering (M Eng); systems and quality engineering (M Eng). M Eng program offered jointly with University of Waterloo; PhD in industrial engineering with Texas A&M University. Part-time and evening/weekend programs available. Terminal master's awarded for partial completion of doctoral program. *Degree requirements:* For master's, one foreign language, thesis; for doctorate, one foreign language, thesis/dissertation. *Entrance requirements:* For master's, EXADEP; for doctorate, GRE, master's degree in related field. Additional exam requirements/recommendations for international students: Required—TOEFL. *Faculty research:* Flexible manufacturing cells, materials, statistical methods, environmental prevention, control and evaluation.

Iowa State University of Science and Technology, Department of Industrial and Manufacturing Systems Engineering, Ames, IA 50011. Offers industrial engineering (M Eng, MS, PhD); operations research (MS); systems engineering (M Eng). *Degree requirements:* For master's, thesis or alternative; for doctorate, thesis/dissertation.

Entrance requirements: For master's and doctorate, GRE General Test. Additional exam requirements/recommendations for international students: Required—TOEFL (minimum score 550 paper-based; 79 iBT), IELTS (minimum score 6.5). *Application deadline:* For fall admission, 1/15 for international students; for spring admission, 7/15 for international students. Application fee: $40 ($90 for international students). Electronic applications accepted. *Faculty research:* Economic modeling, valuation techniques, robotics, digital controls, systems reliability. *Unit head:* Dr. Sarah Ryan, Director of Graduate Education, 515-294-0129, Fax: 515-294-3524, E-mail: bushore@iastate.edu. *Application contact:* Lori Bushore, Director of Graduate Studies, 515-294-0129, Fax: 515-294-3524, E-mail: bushore@iastate.edu. Web site: http://www.imse.iastate.edu.

Kansas State University, Graduate School, College of Engineering, Department of Industrial and Manufacturing Systems Engineering, Manhattan, KS 66506. Offers engineering management (MEM); industrial engineering (MS, PhD); operations research (MS). Part-time programs available. Postbaccalaureate distance learning degree programs offered. *Faculty:* 12 full-time (3 women), 4 part-time/adjunct (1 woman). *Students:* 43 full-time (11 women), 57 part-time (14 women); includes 8 minority (1 Black or African American, non-Hispanic/Latino; 1 Asian, non-Hispanic/Latino; 2 Hispanic/Latino; 4 Two or more races, non-Hispanic/Latino), 34 international. Average age 29. 94 applicants, 46% accepted, 14 enrolled. In 2011, 21 master's, 3 doctorates awarded. *Degree requirements:* For master's, thesis or alternative; for doctorate, thesis/dissertation. *Entrance requirements:* For master's, GRE General Test (minimum 750 [old version], 159 [new format] on Quantitative portion of exam), bachelor's degree in engineering, mathematics, or physical science; for doctorate, GRE General Test (minimum 770 [old version], 164 [new format] on Quantitative portion of exam), master's degree in engineering or industrial manufacturing. Additional exam requirements/recommendations for international students: Required—TOEFL (minimum score 550 paper-based; 79 iBT) or IELTS (minimum score 6.5). *Application deadline:* For fall admission, 6/1 priority date for domestic students, 2/1 for international students; for spring admission, 11/1 priority date for domestic students, 8/1 for international students. Applications are processed on a rolling basis. Application fee: $40 ($55 for international students). Electronic applications accepted. *Financial support:* In 2011–12, 15 research assistantships (averaging $12,412 per year), 1 teaching assistantship with full tuition reimbursement (averaging $12,000 per year) were awarded; Federal Work-Study, institutionally sponsored loans, and scholarships/grants also available. Support available to part-time students. Financial award application deadline: 3/1; financial award applicants required to submit FAFSA. *Faculty research:* Industrial engineering, ergonomics, healthcare systems engineering, manufacturing processes, operations research, engineering management. *Total annual research expenditures:* $645,655. *Unit head:* Bradley Kramer, Head, 785-532-5606, Fax: 785-532-3738, E-mail: bradleyk@ksu.edu. *Application contact:* David Ben-Arieh, Chair of Graduate Committee, 785-532-5606, Fax: 785-532-3738, E-mail: imse@ksu.edu. Web site: http://imse.ksu.edu/.

Lamar University, College of Graduate Studies, College of Engineering, Department of Industrial Engineering, Beaumont, TX 77710. Offers engineering management (MEM); industrial engineering (ME, MES, DE). *Faculty:* 8 full-time (0 women). *Students:* 27 full-time (4 women), 10 part-time (3 women); includes 5 minority (1 Black or African American, non-Hispanic/Latino; 2 Asian, non-Hispanic/Latino; 2 Hispanic/Latino), 30 international. Average age 28. 39 applicants, 79% accepted, 8 enrolled. In 2011, 24 master's, 2 doctorates awarded. *Degree requirements:* For doctorate, thesis/dissertation. *Entrance requirements:* For master's and doctorate, GRE General Test. Additional exam requirements/recommendations for international students: Required—TOEFL. *Application deadline:* For fall admission, 5/15 priority date for domestic students; for spring admission, 10/1 priority date for domestic students. Applications are processed on a rolling basis. Application fee: $25 ($50 for international students). *Expenses:* Tuition, state resident: full-time $5430; part-time $272 per credit hour. Tuition, nonresident: full-time $11,540; part-time $577 per credit hour. *Required fees:* $1916. *Financial support:* In 2011–12, 2 fellowships (averaging $6,000 per year), 4 research assistantships (averaging $1,000 per year), 2 teaching assistantships (averaging $4,500 per year) were awarded. Financial award application deadline: 4/1. *Faculty research:* Process simulation, total quality management, ergonomics and safety, scheduling. *Unit head:* Dr. Victor Zaloom, Chair, 409-880-8804, Fax: 409-880-8121. *Application contact:* Dr. Hsing-Wei Chu, Professor, 409-880-8804, Fax: 409-880-8121. Web site: http://dept.lamar.edu/industrial/.

Lawrence Technological University, College of Engineering, Southfield, MI 48075-1058. Offers architectural engineering (MS); automotive engineering (MS); civil engineering (MA, MS); construction engineering management (MA); electrical and computer engineering (MS); engineering management (MEM); industrial engineering (MS); manufacturing systems (ME, DE); mechanical engineering (MS, DE); mechatronic systems engineering (MS). Part-time and evening/weekend programs available. *Faculty:* 25 full-time (4 women), 20 part-time/adjunct (1 woman). *Students:* 8 full-time (0 women), 332 part-time (52 women); includes 58 minority (21 Black or African American, non-Hispanic/Latino; 1 American Indian or Alaska Native, non-Hispanic/Latino; 32 Asian, non-Hispanic/Latino; 2 Hispanic/Latino; 2 Two or more races, non-Hispanic/Latino), 84 international. Average age 32. 652 applicants, 44% accepted, 70 enrolled. In 2011, 127 master's, 2 doctorates awarded. *Degree requirements:* For master's, thesis (for some programs). *Entrance requirements:* Additional exam requirements/recommendations for international students: Required—TOEFL (minimum score 550 paper-based; 213 computer-based; 79 iBT). *Application deadline:* For fall admission, 7/27 priority date for domestic students, 5/23 for international students; for spring admission, 11/15 priority date for domestic students, 11/15 for international students. Applications are processed on a rolling basis. Application fee: $50. Electronic applications accepted. *Financial support:* In 2011–12, 68 students received support, including 6 research assistantships (averaging $8,078 per year); Federal Work-Study and institutionally sponsored loans also available. Support available to part-time students. Financial award application deadline: 4/1; financial award applicants required to submit FAFSA. *Faculty research:* Advanced composite materials in bridges, strengthening existing bridges with carbon and glass fiber sheets, development of drive shafts using composite materials. *Unit head:* Dr. Nabil Grace, Dean, 248-204-2500, Fax: 248-204-2509, E-mail: engrdean@ltu.edu. *Application contact:* Jane Rohrback, Director of Admissions, 248-204-3160, Fax: 248-204-2228, E-mail: admissions@ltu.edu. Web site: http://www.ltu.edu/engineering/index.asp.

Lehigh University, P.C. Rossin College of Engineering and Applied Science, Department of Industrial and Systems Engineering, Bethlehem, PA 18015. Offers analytical finance (MS); healthcare systems engineering (M Eng); industrial and systems engineering (M Eng, MS); industrial engineering (PhD); management science and engineering (M Eng, MS); MBA/E. Part-time programs available. Postbaccalaureate distance learning degree programs offered (no on-campus study). *Faculty:* 14 full-time (2 women). *Students:* 73 full-time (28 women), 12 part-time (3 women); includes 2 minority (both Black or African American, non-Hispanic/Latino), 70 international. Average age 27. 275 applicants, 25% accepted, 20 enrolled. In 2011, 28 master's, 2

doctorates awarded. *Degree requirements:* For master's, thesis (MS); project (M Eng); for doctorate, comprehensive exam, thesis/dissertation. *Entrance requirements:* For master's and doctorate, GRE General Test. Additional exam requirements/recommendations for international students: Required—TOEFL (minimum score 550 paper-based; 213 computer-based; 79 iBT). *Application deadline:* For fall admission, 7/15 for domestic and international students; for spring admission, 12/1 for domestic and international students. Applications are processed on a rolling basis. Application fee: $75. Electronic applications accepted. *Financial support:* In 2011–12, 36 students received support, including 3 fellowships with full tuition reimbursements available (averaging $17,460 per year), 16 research assistantships with full tuition reimbursements available (averaging $15,300 per year), 11 teaching assistantships with full tuition reimbursements available (averaging $18,360 per year); career-related internships or fieldwork, scholarships/grants, tuition waivers, and unspecified assistantships also available. Financial award application deadline: 1/15. *Faculty research:* Optimization, mathematical programming; logistics and supply chain, stochastic processes and simulation; computational optimization and high performance computing; financial engineering and robust optimization. *Total annual research expenditures:* $1.5 million. *Unit head:* Dr. Tamas Terlaky, Chair, 610-758-4050, Fax: 610-758-4886, E-mail: terlaky@lehigh.edu. *Application contact:* Rita Frey, Graduate Coordinator, 610-758-4051, Fax: 610-758-4886, E-mail: ise@lehigh.edu. Web site: http://www.lehigh.edu/ise.

Louisiana State University and Agricultural and Mechanical College, Graduate School, College of Engineering, Department of Construction Management and Industrial Engineering, Baton Rouge, LA 70803. Offers engineering science (PhD); industrial engineering (MSIE). *Faculty:* 11 full-time (5 women), 1 part-time/adjunct (0 women). *Students:* 11 full-time (3 women), 3 part-time (0 women); includes 1 minority (Black or African American, non-Hispanic/Latino), 8 international. Average age 27. 20 applicants, 55% accepted, 1 enrolled. In 2011, 3 master's awarded. Terminal master's awarded for partial completion of doctoral program. *Degree requirements:* For master's, thesis; for doctorate, thesis/dissertation. *Entrance requirements:* For master's and doctorate, GRE General Test, minimum GPA of 3.0. Additional exam requirements/recommendations for international students: Required—TOEFL (minimum score 550 paper-based; 213 computer-based; 79 iBT) or IELTS (minimum score 6.5). *Application deadline:* For fall admission, 1/25 priority date for domestic students, 5/15 for international students; for spring admission, 10/15 for international students. Applications are processed on a rolling basis. Application fee: $50 ($70 for international students). Electronic applications accepted. *Financial support:* In 2011–12, 9 students received support, including 5 research assistantships with partial tuition reimbursements available (averaging $10,240 per year), 2 teaching assistantships with partial tuition reimbursements available (averaging $12,400 per year); fellowships, Federal Work-Study, institutionally sponsored loans, health care benefits, and unspecified assistantships also available. Financial award application deadline: 5/1; financial award applicants required to submit FAFSA. *Faculty research:* Ergonomics and occupational health, information technology, production systems, supply management, construction safety and methods. *Total annual research expenditures:* $434,200. *Unit head:* Dr. Craig Harvey, Chair, 225-578-5112, Fax: 225-578-5109, E-mail: harvey@lsu.edu. *Application contact:* Dr. Pius Egbelu, Graduate Adviser, 225-578-5112, Fax: 225-578-5109, E-mail: pegbelu@eng.lsu.edu. Web site: http://www.cm.lsu.edu/.

Louisiana Tech University, Graduate School, College of Engineering and Science, Department of Industrial Engineering, Ruston, LA 71272. Offers MS.

Mississippi State University, Bagley College of Engineering, Department of Industrial and Systems Engineering, Mississippi State, MS 39762. Offers industrial and systems engineering (PhD); industrial engineering (MS). Part-time programs available. Postbaccalaureate distance learning degree programs offered (no on-campus study). *Faculty:* 8 full-time (3 women), 1 part-time/adjunct (0 women). *Students:* 30 full-time (9 women), 55 part-time (9 women); includes 19 minority (10 Black or African American, non-Hispanic/Latino; 5 Asian, non-Hispanic/Latino; 4 Hispanic/Latino), 20 international. Average age 34. 80 applicants, 35% accepted, 16 enrolled. In 2011, 8 master's, 4 doctorates awarded. *Degree requirements:* For master's, thesis (for some programs), comprehensive oral or written exam; for doctorate, thesis/dissertation, candidacy exam. *Entrance requirements:* For master's, GRE General Test, minimum GPA of 3.0; for doctorate, GRE General Test, minimum GPA of 3.3. Additional exam requirements/recommendations for international students: Required—TOEFL (minimum score 550 paper-based; 213 computer-based; 79 iBT); Recommended—IELTS (minimum score 6.5). *Application deadline:* For fall admission, 7/1 for domestic students, 5/1 for international students; for spring admission, 11/1 for domestic students, 9/1 for international students. Applications are processed on a rolling basis. Application fee: $40. *Expenses:* Tuition, state resident: full-time $5805; part-time $322.50 per credit hour. Tuition, nonresident: full-time $14,670; part-time $815 per credit hour. *Financial support:* In 2011–12, 15 research assistantships with full tuition reimbursements (averaging $15,051 per year), 6 teaching assistantships with full tuition reimbursements (averaging $12,230 per year) were awarded; Federal Work-Study, institutionally sponsored loans, and unspecified assistantships also available. Financial award application deadline: 4/1; financial award applicants required to submit FAFSA. *Faculty research:* Operations research, ergonomics, production systems, management systems, transportation. *Unit head:* Dr. John Usher, Professor/Interim Head/Graduate Coordinator, 662-325-7624, Fax: 662-325-7618, E-mail: usher@ise.msstate.edu. Web site: http://www.ie.msstate.edu/.

Montana State University, College of Graduate Studies, College of Engineering, Department of Mechanical and Industrial Engineering, Bozeman, MT 59717. Offers engineering (PhD), including industrial engineering, mechanical engineering; industrial and management engineering (MS); mechanical engineering (MS). Part-time programs available. *Degree requirements:* For master's, comprehensive exam, thesis, oral exams; for doctorate, comprehensive exam, thesis/dissertation, qualifying exam. *Entrance requirements:* For master's, GRE, official transcript, minimum GPA of 3.0, demonstrated potential for success, statement of goals, three letters of recommendation, proof of funds affidavit; for doctorate, minimum undergraduate GPA of 3.0, 3.2 graduate; three letters of recommendation; statement of objectives. Additional exam requirements/recommendations for international students: Required—TOEFL or IELTS. Electronic applications accepted. *Faculty research:* Human factors engineering, energy, design and manufacture, systems modeling, materials and structures, measurement systems.

Montana Tech of The University of Montana, Graduate School, Project Engineering and Management Program, Butte, MT 59701-8997. Offers MPEM. Part-time and evening/weekend programs available. Postbaccalaureate distance learning degree programs offered (no on-campus study). *Faculty:* 1 full-time (0 women), 7 part-time/adjunct (1 woman). *Students:* 2 full-time (0 women), 10 part-time (6 women), 1 international. 4 applicants, 100% accepted, 4 enrolled. In 2011, 4 master's awarded. *Degree requirements:* For master's, comprehensive exam, final project presentation. *Entrance requirements:* For master's, minimum GPA of 3.0. Additional exam requirements/recommendations for international students: Required—TOEFL (minimum score 550 paper-based; 213 computer-based; 71 iBT). *Application deadline:* For fall admission, 4/1 priority date for domestic students, 3/1 for international students; for spring admission, 10/1 priority date for domestic students, 7/1 for international students. Applications are processed on a rolling basis. Application fee: $30. Electronic applications accepted. *Financial support:* Application deadline: 4/1; applicants required to submit FAFSA. *Unit head:* Dr. Kumar Ganesan, Director, 406-496-4239, Fax: 406-496-4650, E-mail: kganesan@mtech.edu. *Application contact:* Fred Sullivan, Administrator, Graduate School, 406-496-4304, Fax: 406-496-4710, E-mail: fsullivan@mtech.edu. Web site: http://www.mtech.edu/academics/gradschool/distancelearning/distancelearning-pem.htm.

Morehead State University, Graduate Programs, College of Science and Technology, Department of Industrial and Engineering Technology, Morehead, KY 40351. Offers career and technical education (MS); engineering technology (MS). Part-time and evening/weekend programs available. *Degree requirements:* For master's, completion and defense of thesis or written and oral comprehensive exit exams. *Entrance requirements:* For master's, GRE, minimum undergraduate GPA of 3.0 in major. Additional exam requirements/recommendations for international students: Required—TOEFL (minimum score 500 paper-based; 173 computer-based). Electronic applications accepted.

Morgan State University, School of Graduate Studies, Clarence M. Mitchell, Jr. School of Engineering, Baltimore, MD 21251. Offers civil engineering (M Eng, D Eng); electrical engineering (M Eng, D Eng); industrial engineering (M Eng, D Eng); transportation (MS). Part-time and evening/weekend programs available. *Degree requirements:* For master's, thesis, comprehensive exam or equivalent; for doctorate, thesis/dissertation, comprehensive exam or equivalent. *Entrance requirements:* For master's, GRE, minimum undergraduate GPA of 2.5; for doctorate, GRE, minimum GPA of 3.0. Additional exam requirements/recommendations for international students: Required—TOEFL (minimum score 550 paper-based; 213 computer-based).

New Jersey Institute of Technology, Office of Graduate Studies, Newark College of Engineering, Department of Mechanical Engineering, Program in Industrial Engineering, Newark, NJ 07102. Offers MS, PhD. Part-time and evening/weekend programs available. *Students:* 29 full-time (6 women), 21 part-time (5 women); includes 14 minority (5 Black or African American, non-Hispanic/Latino; 6 Asian, non-Hispanic/Latino; 3 Hispanic/Latino), 26 international. Average age 28. 152 applicants, 71% accepted, 17 enrolled. In 2011, 24 master's, 3 doctorates awarded. Terminal master's awarded for partial completion of doctoral program. *Degree requirements:* For master's, thesis or alternative; for doctorate, thesis/dissertation. *Entrance requirements:* For master's, GRE General Test; for doctorate, GRE General Test, minimum graduate GPA of 3.5. Additional exam requirements/recommendations for international students: Required—TOEFL (minimum score 550 paper-based; 213 computer-based; 79 iBT). *Application deadline:* For fall admission, 6/1 priority date for domestic students, 5/1 for international students; for spring admission, 11/15 for domestic and international students. Applications are processed on a rolling basis. Application fee: $65. Electronic applications accepted. *Expenses:* Tuition, state resident: full-time $7980; part-time $867 per credit. Tuition, nonresident: full-time $11,336; part-time $1196 per credit. *Required fees:* $230 per credit. *Financial support:* Fellowships with full and partial tuition reimbursements, research assistantships with full and partial tuition reimbursements, teaching assistantships with full and partial tuition reimbursements, career-related internships or fieldwork, Federal Work-Study, institutionally sponsored loans, and unspecified assistantships available. Financial award application deadline: 3/15. *Faculty research:* Knowledge-based systems, CAS/CAM simulation and interface, expert system. *Unit head:* Dr. Sanchoy K. Das, Director, 973-596-3654, Fax: 973-596-3652, E-mail: sanchoy.k.das@njit.edu. *Application contact:* Kathryn Kelly, Director of Admissions, 973-596-3300, Fax: 973-596-3461, E-mail: admissions@njit.edu.

New Mexico State University, Graduate School, College of Engineering, Department of Industrial Engineering, Las Cruces, NM 88003-8001. Offers industrial engineering (MSIE, PhD); systems engineering (Graduate Certificate). Part-time and evening/weekend programs available. Postbaccalaureate distance learning degree programs offered (no on-campus study). *Faculty:* 6 full-time (2 women). *Students:* 45 full-time (11 women), 90 part-time (25 women); includes 41 minority (7 Black or African American, non-Hispanic/Latino; 1 American Indian or Alaska Native, non-Hispanic/Latino; 2 Asian, non-Hispanic/Latino; 29 Hispanic/Latino; 2 Two or more races, non-Hispanic/Latino), 25 international. Average age 31. 58 applicants, 76% accepted, 39 enrolled. In 2011, 41 master's, 2 doctorates, 6 other advanced degrees awarded. *Degree requirements:* For master's, thesis optional; for doctorate, comprehensive exam, thesis/dissertation. *Entrance requirements:* For doctorate, qualifying exam. Additional exam requirements/recommendations for international students: Required—TOEFL (minimum score 550 paper-based; 79 iBT), IELTS (minimum score 6.5). *Application deadline:* For fall admission, 7/1 priority date for domestic students, 3/1 for international students; for spring admission, 11/1 for domestic students, 10/1 for international students. Applications are processed on a rolling basis. Application fee: $40 ($50 for international students). Electronic applications accepted. *Expenses:* Tuition, state resident: full-time $5004; part-time $208.50 per credit. Tuition, nonresident: full-time $17,446; part-time $726.90 per credit. *Financial support:* In 2011–12, 2 fellowships (averaging $37,852 per year), 6 research assistantships (averaging $12,804 per year), 8 teaching assistantships (averaging $20,231 per year) were awarded; career-related internships or fieldwork, Federal Work-Study, health care benefits, and unspecified assistantships also available. Financial award application deadline: 3/1. *Faculty research:* Optimization, healthcare systems, manufacturing engineering, systems engineering. *Unit head:* Dr. Edward Pines, Head, 575-646-4923, Fax: 575-646-2976, E-mail: epines@nmsu.edu. *Application contact:* Sarah Deyoe, Department Secretary, 575-646-4923, Fax: 575-646-2976, E-mail: sdeyoe@nmsu.edu. Web site: http://ie.nmsu.edu.

North Carolina Agricultural and Technical State University, School of Graduate Studies, College of Engineering, Department of Industrial and Systems Engineering, Greensboro, NC 27411. Offers industrial engineering (MSIE, PhD). Part-time programs available. *Degree requirements:* For master's, thesis, project; for doctorate, thesis/dissertation. *Entrance requirements:* For master's, GRE General Test (recommended); for doctorate, GRE General Test, degree in engineering, BS in industrial engineering from ABET-accredited program with minimum cumulative credit point average of 3.7 or MS in discipline related to industrial engineering from college or university recognized by a regional or general accrediting agency with minimum cumulative GPA of 3.3. Additional exam requirements/recommendations for international students: Required—TOEFL (minimum score 550 paper-based; 213 computer-based; 79 iBT). *Faculty research:* Human-machine systems engineering, management systems engineering, operations research and systems analysis, production systems engineering.

North Carolina State University, Graduate School, College of Engineering, Edward P. Fitts Department of Industrial and Systems Engineering, Raleigh, NC 27695. Offers industrial engineering (MIE, MS, PhD). PhD offered jointly with North Carolina Agricultural and Technical State University, The University of North Carolina at Charlotte. Part-time programs available. Terminal master's awarded for partial completion of doctoral program. *Degree requirements:* For master's, thesis optional; for doctorate, thesis/dissertation. *Entrance requirements:* For master's, GRE General Test, minimum GPA of 3.0; for doctorate, GRE General Test. Additional exam requirements/recommendations for international students: Required—TOEFL. Electronic applications accepted.

North Dakota State University, College of Graduate and Interdisciplinary Studies, College of Engineering and Architecture, Department of Industrial and Manufacturing Engineering, Fargo, ND 58108. Offers industrial and manufacturing engineering (PhD); industrial engineering and management (MS); manufacturing engineering (MS). Part-time programs available. *Faculty:* 9 full-time (2 women). *Students:* 12 full-time (1 woman), 15 part-time (4 women); includes 1 minority (Asian, non-Hispanic/Latino), 25 international. Average age 26. 25 applicants, 36% accepted, 3 enrolled. In 2011, 4 master's awarded. *Degree requirements:* For doctorate, comprehensive exam, thesis/dissertation. *Entrance requirements:* For master's, GRE General Test, bachelor's degree in engineering; for doctorate, GRE General Test, master's degree in engineering. Additional exam requirements/recommendations for international students: Required—TOEFL (minimum score 550 paper-based; 213 computer-based; 79 iBT), TWE (minimum score 4). *Application deadline:* For fall admission, 5/1 for international students; for spring admission, 8/1 for international students. Applications are processed on a rolling basis. Application fee: $35. Electronic applications accepted. *Financial support:* In 2011–12, 2 fellowships with full tuition reimbursements (averaging $15,000 per year), 9 research assistantships with full tuition reimbursements (averaging $12,000 per year), 16 teaching assistantships with full tuition reimbursements (averaging $12,000 per year) were awarded; Federal Work-Study, institutionally sponsored loans, scholarships/grants, and unspecified assistantships also available. Financial award application deadline: 4/1. *Faculty research:* Electronics manufacturing, quality engineering, manufacturing process science, healthcare, lean manufacturing. *Unit head:* Dr. John Cook, Chair, 701-231-7285, Fax: 701-231-7195, E-mail: john.cook@ndsu.edu. *Application contact:* Dr. Om Prakash Yadav, Graduate Program Coordinator, 701-231-7285, Fax: 701-231-7195, E-mail: om.yadav@ndsu.edu.

Northeastern University, College of Engineering, Department of Mechanical, Industrial, and Manufacturing Engineering, Boston, MA 02115-5096. Offers engineering management (MS); industrial engineering (MS, PhD); mechanical engineering (MS, PhD); operations research (MS). Part-time programs available. *Faculty:* 34 full-time, 7 part-time/adjunct. *Students:* 297 full-time (70 women), 103 part-time (20 women). 616 applicants, 77% accepted, 140 enrolled. In 2011, 107 master's, 5 doctorates awarded. *Degree requirements:* For master's, thesis (for some programs); for doctorate, thesis/dissertation, departmental qualifying exam. *Entrance requirements:* For master's and doctorate, GRE General Test. Additional exam requirements/recommendations for international students: Required—TOEFL (minimum score 550 paper-based; 213 computer-based; 80 iBT). *Application deadline:* For fall admission, 1/15 priority date for domestic students, 1/15 for international students; for spring admission, 11/1 priority date for domestic students. Applications are processed on a rolling basis. Application fee: $50. Electronic applications accepted. *Financial support:* In 2011–12, 79 students received support, including 50 research assistantships with full tuition reimbursements available (averaging $18,325 per year), 33 teaching assistantships with full tuition reimbursements available (averaging $18,325 per year); fellowships with full tuition reimbursements available, career-related internships or fieldwork, Federal Work-Study, scholarships/grants, health care benefits, and unspecified assistantships also available. Support available to part-time students. Financial award application deadline: 1/15; financial award applicants required to submit FAFSA. *Faculty research:* Dry sliding instabilities, droplet deposition, combustion, manufacturing systems, nano-manufacturing, advanced materials processing, bio-nano robotics, burning speed measurement, virtual environments. *Unit head:* Dr. Hameed Metghalchi, Chairman, 617-373-2973, Fax: 617-373-2921. *Application contact:* Jeffery Hengel, Admissions Specialist, 617-373-2711, Fax: 617-373-2501, E-mail: grad-eng@coe.neu.edu.

Northern Illinois University, Graduate School, College of Engineering and Engineering Technology, Department of Industrial Engineering, De Kalb, IL 60115-2854. Offers MS. Part-time programs available. *Faculty:* 4 full-time (1 woman), 1 part-time/adjunct (0 women). *Students:* 18 full-time (3 women), 13 part-time (3 women); includes 4 minority (1 Black or African American, non-Hispanic/Latino; 3 Asian, non-Hispanic/Latino), 14 international. Average age 26. 44 applicants, 55% accepted, 7 enrolled. In 2011, 33 master's awarded. *Degree requirements:* For master's, comprehensive exam, thesis optional. *Entrance requirements:* For master's, GRE General Test, minimum GPA of 2.75. Additional exam requirements/recommendations for international students: Required—TOEFL (minimum score 550 paper-based; 213 computer-based). *Application deadline:* For fall admission, 6/1 for domestic students, 5/1 for international students; for spring admission, 11/1 for domestic students, 10/1 for international students. Applications are processed on a rolling basis. Application fee: $40. Electronic applications accepted. *Financial support:* In 2011–12, 13 research assistantships, 7 teaching assistantships were awarded; fellowships, Federal Work-Study, scholarships/grants, tuition waivers (full), and staff assistantships also available. Support available to part-time students. Financial award applicants required to submit FAFSA. *Faculty research:* Assembly robots, engineering ethics, quality cost models, data mining. *Unit head:* Dr. Omar Ghrayeb, Chair, 815-753-1349, Fax: 815-753-0823. *Application contact:* Graduate School Office, 815-753-0395, E-mail: gradsch@niu.edu. Web site: http://www.ceet.niu.edu/depts/ie/.

Northwestern University, McCormick School of Engineering and Applied Science, Department of Industrial Engineering and Management Sciences, Evanston, IL 60208. Offers engineering management (MEM); industrial engineering and management science (MS, PhD). MS and PhD admissions and degrees offered through The Graduate School. *Faculty:* 20 full-time (2 women). *Students:* 63 full-time (19 women); includes 3 minority (2 Hispanic/Latino; 1 Two or more races, non-Hispanic/Latino), 49 international. Average age 23. 260 applicants, 8% accepted, 10 enrolled. In 2011, 12 master's, 4 doctorates awarded. Terminal master's awarded for partial completion of doctoral program. *Degree requirements:* For master's, comprehensive exam; for doctorate, comprehensive exam, thesis/dissertation. *Entrance requirements:* For master's and doctorate, GRE General Test. Additional exam requirements/recommendations for international students: Required—TOEFL (minimum score 577 paper-based; 233 computer-based; 90 iBT), IELTS (minimum score 7). *Application deadline:* For fall admission, 12/31 for domestic and international students. Application fee: $75. Electronic applications accepted. *Financial support:* Fellowships with full tuition reimbursements, research assistantships with full tuition reimbursements, teaching assistantships with full tuition reimbursements, career-related internships or fieldwork, institutionally sponsored loans, health care benefits, and unspecified assistantships available. Financial award application deadline: 1/15; financial award applicants required to submit FAFSA. *Faculty research:* Decision and risk analysis, financial engineering, healthcare engineering, humanitarian logistics, optimization, organization behavior and technology management, production and logistics, social and organizational networks, statistics for enterprise engineering, stochastic modeling and simulation. *Total annual research expenditures:* $2.9 million. *Unit head:* Dr. Barry Nelson, Chair, 847-491-3747, Fax: 847-491-8005, E-mail: nelsonb@northwestern.edu. *Application contact:* Dr. Jeremy Staum, Admission Officer, 847-491-3383, Fax: 847-491-8005, E-mail: j-staum@northwestern.edu. Web site: http://www.iems.northwestern.edu/

The Ohio State University, Graduate School, College of Engineering, Program in Industrial and Systems Engineering, Columbus, OH 43210. Offers industrial and systems engineering (MS, PhD); welding engineering (MS, MWE, PhD). *Faculty:* 20. *Students:* 66 full-time (22 women), 34 part-time (8 women); includes 6 minority (1 Black or African American, non-Hispanic/Latino; 3 Asian, non-Hispanic/Latino; 1 Hispanic/Latino; 1 Two or more races, non-Hispanic/Latino), 57 international. Average age 28. In 2011, 12 master's, 6 doctorates awarded. *Degree requirements:* For master's, thesis optional; for doctorate, thesis/dissertation. *Entrance requirements:* For master's and doctorate, GRE General Test. Additional exam requirements/recommendations for international students: Required—Michigan English Language Assessment Battery (minimum score 82); Recommended—TOEFL (minimum score 600 paper-based; 250 computer-based; 79 iBT). *Application deadline:* For fall admission, 8/15 priority date for domestic students, 11/1 for international students; for winter admission, 12/1 priority date for domestic students, 7/1 for international students; for spring admission, 3/1 priority date for domestic students, 2/1 for international students. Applications are processed on a rolling basis. Application fee: $40 ($50 for international students). Electronic applications accepted. *Expenses:* Tuition, state resident: full-time $11,400. Tuition, nonresident: full-time $28,125. Tuition and fees vary according to course load, degree level, campus/location and program. *Financial support:* Fellowships, research assistantships, teaching assistantships, career-related internships or fieldwork, Federal Work-Study, institutionally sponsored loans, and unspecified assistantships available. Support available to part-time students. *Unit head:* Dr. Philip J. Smith, Interim Department Chair, 614-292-4120, E-mail: smith.131@osu.edu. *Application contact:* Dr. Jerald Brevik, Graduate Studies Chair, 614-292-0177, Fax: 614-292-7852, E-mail: brevik.1@osu.edu. Web site: http://ise.osu.edu/.

Ohio University, Graduate College, Russ College of Engineering and Technology, Department of Industrial and Systems Engineering, Athens, OH 45701-2979. Offers M Eng Mgt, MS. Part-time and evening/weekend programs available. *Students:* 50 full-time (16 women), 23 part-time (5 women); includes 8 minority (3 Black or African American, non-Hispanic/Latino; 1 Asian, non-Hispanic/Latino; 3 Hispanic/Latino; 1 Two or more races, non-Hispanic/Latino), 14 international. 67 applicants, 57% accepted, 29 enrolled. In 2011, 26 master's awarded. *Degree requirements:* For master's, comprehensive exam (for some programs), thesis optional, research project. *Entrance requirements:* For master's, GRE General Test. Additional exam requirements/recommendations for international students: Required—TOEFL (minimum score 550 paper-based; 80 iBT) or IELTS (minimum score 6.5). *Application deadline:* For fall admission, 3/1 priority date for domestic students, 3/1 for international students; for winter admission, 9/1 priority date for domestic students, 9/1 for international students; for spring admission, 1/1 priority date for domestic students, 1/1 for international students. Applications are processed on a rolling basis. Application fee: $50 ($55 for international students). Electronic applications accepted. *Financial support:* In 2011–12, research assistantships with full tuition reimbursements (averaging $9,000 per year) were awarded; Federal Work-Study, institutionally sponsored loans, tuition waivers (full), and unspecified assistantships also available. Financial award application deadline: 2/15; financial award applicants required to submit FAFSA. *Faculty research:* Software systems integration, human factors and ergonomics. *Total annual research expenditures:* $350,000. *Unit head:* Dr. Robert P. Judd, Chairman, 740-593-0106, Fax: 740-593-0778, E-mail: judd@ohio.edu. *Application contact:* Dr. Gursel Suer, Graduate Chairman, 740-593-1542, Fax: 740-593-0778, E-mail: suer@ohio.edu. Web site: http://www.ohio.edu/industrial/.

Ohio University, Graduate College, Russ College of Engineering and Technology, Program in Mechanical and Systems Engineering, Athens, OH 45701-2979. Offers industrial engineering (PhD); mechanical engineering (PhD). *Students:* 14 full-time (2 women), 2 part-time (1 woman), 13 international. 18 applicants, 6% accepted, 1 enrolled. In 2011, 2 doctorates awarded. *Degree requirements:* For doctorate, comprehensive exam, thesis/dissertation. *Entrance requirements:* For doctorate, GRE General Test, MS in engineering or related field. Additional exam requirements/recommendations for international students: Required—TOEFL (minimum score 550 paper-based; 80 iBT) or IELTS (minimum score 6.5). *Application deadline:* For fall admission, 3/15 priority date for domestic students, 3/15 for international students. Applications are processed on a rolling basis. Application fee: $50 ($55 for international students). Electronic applications accepted. *Financial support:* In 2011–12, 4 research assistantships with full tuition reimbursements (averaging $14,000 per year) were awarded; Federal Work-Study, institutionally sponsored loans, and unspecified assistantships also available. Financial award application deadline: 3/15; financial award applicants required to submit FAFSA. *Faculty research:* Material processing, expert systems, environmental geotechnical manufacturing, thermal systems, robotics. *Total annual research expenditures:* $1.8 million. *Unit head:* Dr. Shawn Ostermann, Associate Dean, 740-593-1482, Fax: 740-593-0659, E-mail: ostermann@ohio.edu. *Application contact:* Dr. Shawn Ostermann, Associate Dean, 740-593-1482, Fax: 740-593-0659, E-mail: ostermann@ohio.edu. Web site: http://www.ohio.edu/engineering/msephd/.

Oklahoma State University, College of Engineering, Architecture and Technology, School of Industrial Engineering and Management, Stillwater, OK 74078. Offers MS, PhD. Postbaccalaureate distance learning degree programs offered. *Faculty:* 11 full-time (1 woman), 3 part-time/adjunct (2 women). *Students:* 88 full-time (14 women), 194 part-time (36 women); includes 52 minority (18 Black or African American, non-Hispanic/Latino; 8 American Indian or Alaska Native, non-Hispanic/Latino; 11 Asian, non-Hispanic/Latino; 9 Hispanic/Latino; 6 Two or more races, non-Hispanic/Latino), 97 international. Average age 32. 272 applicants, 46% accepted, 59 enrolled. In 2011, 101 master's, 1 doctorate awarded. *Degree requirements:* For master's, creative component or thesis; for doctorate, comprehensive exam, thesis/dissertation. *Entrance requirements:* For master's and doctorate, GRE or GMAT. Additional exam requirements/recommendations for international students: Required—TOEFL (minimum score 550 paper-based; 79 iBT). *Application deadline:* For fall admission, 3/1 for international students; for spring admission, 8/1 for international students. Applications are processed on a rolling basis. Application fee: $40 ($75 for international students). Electronic applications accepted. *Expenses:* Tuition, state resident: full-time $4044; part-time $168.50 per credit hour. Tuition, nonresident: full-time $16,008; part-time $667 per credit hour. *Required fees:* $2122; $88.45 per credit hour. One-time fee: $50. Tuition and fees vary according to course load and campus/location. *Financial support:* In 2011–12, 31 research assistantships (averaging $10,813 per year), 22 teaching assistantships (averaging $7,284 per year) were awarded; career-related internships or fieldwork, Federal Work-Study, scholarships/grants, health care benefits, tuition waivers (partial), and unspecified assistantships also available. Support available to part-time

students. Financial award application deadline: 3/1; financial award applicants required to submit FAFSA. *Unit head:* Dr. William J. Kolarik, Head, 405-744-6055, Fax: 405-744-4654. *Application contact:* Dr. Sheryl Tucker, Dean, 405-744-7099, Fax: 405-744-0355, E-mail: grad-i@okstate.edu. Web site: http://iem2.okstate.edu/.

Oregon State University, Graduate School, College of Engineering, School of Mechanical, Industrial, and Manufacturing Engineering, Corvallis, OR 97331. Offers human systems engineering (MS, PhD); industrial engineering (MS, PhD); information systems engineering (MS, PhD); manufacturing engineering (M Engr); manufacturing systems engineering (MS, PhD); materials science (MAIS, MS, PhD); mechanical engineering (MS, PhD); nano/micro fabrication (MS, PhD). Part-time programs available. Postbaccalaureate distance learning degree programs offered (minimal on-campus study). *Degree requirements:* For master's, thesis or alternative; for doctorate, thesis/dissertation. *Entrance requirements:* For master's, placement exam, minimum GPA of 3.0 in last 90 hours of course work; for doctorate, GRE, placement exam, minimum GPA of 3.0 in last 90 hours of course work. Additional exam requirements/recommendations for international students: Required—TOEFL (minimum score 550 paper-based; 213 computer-based). *Faculty research:* Computer-integrated manufacturing, human factors, robotics, decision support systems, simulation modeling and analysis.

Penn State University Park, Graduate School, College of Engineering, Department of Industrial and Manufacturing Engineering, State College, University Park, PA 16802-1503. Offers industrial engineering (M Eng, MS, PhD). *Unit head:* Dr. David N. Wormley, Dean, 814-865-7537, Fax: 814-865-8767, E-mail: dnw2@engr.psu.edu. *Application contact:* Cynthia E. Nicosia, Director, Graduate Enrollment Services, 814-865-1834, E-mail: cey1@psu.edu. Web site: http://www.ie.psu.edu.

Polytechnic Institute of New York University, Department of Interdisciplinary Studies, Major in Industrial Engineering, Brooklyn, NY 11201-2990. Offers MS. Part-time and evening/weekend programs available. *Students:* 46 full-time (18 women), 16 part-time (4 women); includes 8 minority (2 Black or African American, non-Hispanic/Latino; 3 Asian, non-Hispanic/Latino; 3 Hispanic/Latino), 43 international. Average age 26. 97 applicants, 43% accepted, 22 enrolled. In 2011, 15 master's awarded. *Degree requirements:* For master's, comprehensive exam (for some programs), thesis (for some programs). *Entrance requirements:* For master's, BE or BS in engineering, physics, chemistry, mathematical sciences, or biological sciences or MBA. Additional exam requirements/recommendations for international students: Required—TOEFL (minimum score 550 paper-based; 213 computer-based; 80 iBT); Recommended—IELTS (minimum score 6.5). *Application deadline:* For fall admission, 7/31 priority date for domestic students, 4/30 for international students; for spring admission, 12/31 priority date for domestic students, 11/30 for international students. Applications are processed on a rolling basis. Application fee: $75. Electronic applications accepted. *Expenses:* Tuition: Full-time $22,464; part-time $1248 per credit. *Required fees:* $501 per semester. *Financial support:* Institutionally sponsored loans, scholarships/grants, and unspecified assistantships available. Support available to part-time students. Financial award applicants required to submit FAFSA. *Unit head:* Prof. Michael Greenstein, Department Head, 718-260-3835, E-mail: mgreenst@poly.edu. *Application contact:* JeanCarlo Bonilla, Director of Graduate Enrollment Management, 718-260-3182, Fax: 718-260-3624, E-mail: gradinfo@poly.edu.

Polytechnic Institute of NYU, Long Island Graduate Center, Graduate Programs, Department of Mechanical and Aerospace Engineering, Melville, NY 11747. Offers aeronautics and astronautics (MS); industrial engineering (MS); manufacturing engineering (MS); mechanical engineering (MS). Part-time and evening/weekend programs available. *Students:* 1 full-time (0 women). Average age 28. In 2011, 2 master's awarded. *Degree requirements:* For master's, comprehensive exam (for some programs), thesis (for some programs). *Entrance requirements:* Additional exam requirements/recommendations for international students: Required—TOEFL (minimum score 550 paper-based; 213 computer-based; 80 iBT); Recommended—IELTS (minimum score 6.5). *Application deadline:* For fall admission, 7/31 priority date for domestic students, 4/30 for international students; for spring admission, 12/31 priority date for domestic students, 11/30 for international students. Applications are processed on a rolling basis. Application fee: $75. Electronic applications accepted. *Financial support:* In 2011–12, 16 fellowships with tuition reimbursements (averaging $1,394 per year) were awarded; research assistantships with tuition reimbursements, institutionally sponsored loans, scholarships/grants, and unspecified assistantships also available. Support available to part-time students. Financial award applicants required to submit FAFSA. *Faculty research:* UV filter, fuel efficient hydrodynamic containment for gas core fission, turbulent boundary layer research. *Unit head:* Dr. George Vradis, Department Head, 718-260-3875, E-mail: gvradis@duke.poly.edu. *Application contact:* JeanCarlo Bonilla, Director of Graduate Enrollment Management, 718-260-3182, Fax: 718-260-3624, E-mail: gradinfo@poly.edu.

Polytechnic Institute of NYU, Long Island Graduate Center, Graduate Programs, Major in Industrial Engineering, Melville, NY 11747. Offers MS. Part-time and evening/weekend programs available. *Students:* 1 part-time (0 women). Average age 34. 1 applicant, 100% accepted, 1 enrolled. In 2011, 1 master's awarded. *Entrance requirements:* Additional exam requirements/recommendations for international students: Required—TOEFL (minimum score 550 paper-based; 213 computer-based; 80 iBT); Recommended—IELTS (minimum score 6.5). *Application deadline:* For fall admission, 7/31 priority date for domestic students, 4/30 for international students; for spring admission, 12/31 priority date for domestic students, 11/30 for international students. Applications are processed on a rolling basis. Application fee: $75. Electronic applications accepted. *Financial support:* Institutionally sponsored loans, scholarships/grants, and unspecified assistantships available. Support available to part-time students. *Unit head:* Dr. Frank Cassara, Director, Long Island Graduate Center, 631-755-4360, Fax: 516-755-4404, E-mail: cassara@poly.edu. *Application contact:* JeanCarlo Bonilla, Director of Graduate Enrollment Management, 718-260-3182, Fax: 718-260-3624, E-mail: gradinfo@poly.edu.

Purdue University, College of Engineering, School of Industrial Engineering, West Lafayette, IN 47907-2023. Offers MS, MSIE, PhD. Part-time programs available. Postbaccalaureate distance learning degree programs offered (no on-campus study). Terminal master's awarded for partial completion of doctoral program. *Entrance requirements:* For master's and doctorate, GRE General Test, minimum GPA of 3.0. Additional exam requirements/recommendations for international students: Required—TOEFL (minimum score 570 paper-based; 220 computer-based); Recommended—TWE. Electronic applications accepted. *Faculty research:* Precision manufacturing process, computer-aided manufacturing, computer-aided process planning, knowledge-based systems, combinatorics.

Rensselaer Polytechnic Institute, Graduate School, School of Engineering, Program in Decision Sciences and Engineering Systems, Troy, NY 12180-3590. Offers industrial and systems engineering (PhD). Part-time programs available. Terminal master's awarded for partial completion of doctoral program. *Degree requirements:* For doctorate, thesis/dissertation. *Entrance requirements:* For doctorate, GRE General Test (minimum score 550 verbal). Additional exam requirements/recommendations for international students: Required—TOEFL (minimum score 570 paper-based). Electronic applications accepted. *Faculty research:* Decision support systems, simulation and modeling, statistical methods/computing, operations research, supply chain logistics.

Rensselaer Polytechnic Institute, Graduate School, School of Engineering, Program in Industrial and Management Engineering, Troy, NY 12180-3590. Offers M Eng, MS. Part-time programs available. *Degree requirements:* For master's, thesis (for some programs). *Entrance requirements:* For master's, GRE General Test (minimum score 550 verbal). Additional exam requirements/recommendations for international students: Required—TOEFL (minimum score 570 paper-based). Electronic applications accepted. *Faculty research:* Decision support systems, simulation and modeling, statistical methods/computing, operations research, supply chain logistics.

Rochester Institute of Technology, Graduate Enrollment Services, Kate Gleason College of Engineering, Department of Industrial and Systems Engineering, Rochester, NY 14623-5603. Offers engineering management (ME); industrial engineering (ME, MS); manufacturing engineering (ME, MS); systems engineering (ME). Part-time programs available. *Students:* 58 full-time (13 women), 31 part-time (13 women); includes 3 minority (1 Black or African American, non-Hispanic/Latino; 1 Asian, non-Hispanic/Latino; 1 Hispanic/Latino), 59 international. Average age 25. 231 applicants, 44% accepted, 34 enrolled. In 2011, 49 degrees awarded. *Degree requirements:* For master's, internship. *Entrance requirements:* For master's, GRE, minimum GPA of 3.0. Additional exam requirements/recommendations for international students: Required—TOEFL (minimum score 570 paper-based; 230 computer-based; 88 iBT) or IELTS (minimum score 6.5). *Application deadline:* For fall admission, 2/15 priority date for domestic students, 2/15 for international students. Applications are processed on a rolling basis. Application fee: $50. *Expenses: Tuition:* Full-time $34,659; part-time $963 per credit hour. *Required fees:* $228; $76 per quarter. *Financial support:* Research assistantships with partial tuition reimbursements, teaching assistantships with partial tuition reimbursements, career-related internships or fieldwork, institutionally sponsored loans, scholarships/grants, tuition waivers (partial), and unspecified assistantships available. Support available to part-time students. Financial award applicants required to submit FAFSA. *Faculty research:* Operations; manufacturing systems and sustainable product design; product development and design robustness; lean manufacturing; ergonomics/human factors; simulation, systems engineering; rapid prototyping, rapid manufacturing. *Unit head:* Dr. Scott E. Grasman, Interim Department Head, 585-475-2598, E-mail: scott.grasman@rit.edu. *Application contact:* Diane Ellison, Assistant Vice President, Graduate Enrollment Services, 585-475-2229, Fax: 585-475-7164, E-mail: gradinfo@rit.edu.

Rutgers, The State University of New Jersey, New Brunswick, Graduate School-New Brunswick, Department of Industrial and Systems Engineering, Piscataway, NJ 08854-8097. Offers industrial and systems engineering (MS, PhD); information technology (MS); manufacturing systems engineering (MS); quality and reliability engineering (MS). Part-time and evening/weekend programs available. Terminal master's awarded for partial completion of doctoral program. *Degree requirements:* For master's, thesis or alternative, seminar; for doctorate, comprehensive exam, thesis/dissertation. *Entrance requirements:* For master's and doctorate, GRE General Test. Additional exam requirements/recommendations for international students: Required—TOEFL. *Faculty research:* Production and manufacturing systems, quality and reliability engineering, systems engineering and aviation safety.

St. Mary's University, Graduate School, Department of Engineering, Program in Industrial Engineering, San Antonio, TX 78228-8507. Offers engineering computer applications (MS); engineering management (MS); industrial engineering (MS); operations research (MS); JD/MS. Part-time programs available. *Degree requirements:* For master's, comprehensive exam. *Entrance requirements:* For master's, GRE General Test, BS in science or engineering, minimum GPA of 3.0. Additional exam requirements/recommendations for international students: Required—TOEFL (minimum score 550 paper-based; 213 computer-based; 80 iBT). Electronic applications accepted. *Faculty research:* Robotics, artificial intelligence, manufacturing engineering.

San Jose State University, Graduate Studies and Research, Charles W. Davidson College of Engineering, Department of Industrial and Systems Engineering, San Jose, CA 95192-0001. Offers industrial and systems engineering (MS). Part-time programs available. *Degree requirements:* For master's, comprehensive exam. Electronic applications accepted.

South Dakota State University, Graduate School, College of Engineering, Department of Engineering Technology and Management, Brookings, SD 57007. Offers industrial management (MS). *Degree requirements:* For master's, comprehensive exam, thesis (for some programs), oral exam. *Entrance requirements:* Additional exam requirements/recommendations for international students: Required—TOEFL (minimum score 575 paper-based). *Faculty research:* Query, economic development, statistical process control, foreign business plans, operations management.

Southern Illinois University Edwardsville, Graduate School, School of Engineering, Department of Mechanical and Industrial Engineering, Program in Industrial Engineering, Edwardsville, IL 62026-0001. Offers MS. Part-time programs available. *Students:* 13 full-time (2 women), 11 part-time (2 women); includes 7 minority (all Black or African American, non-Hispanic/Latino), 9 international. 31 applicants, 61% accepted. In 2011, 2 master's awarded. *Degree requirements:* For master's, thesis (for some programs), final exam. *Entrance requirements:* For master's, GRE (for applicants whose degree is from non-ABET accredited institution). Additional exam requirements/recommendations for international students: Required—TOEFL (minimum score 550 paper-based; 213 computer-based; 79 iBT), IELTS (minimum score 6.5). *Application deadline:* For fall admission, 7/22 for domestic students, 6/1 for international students; for spring admission, 12/9 for domestic students, 10/1 for international students. Applications are processed on a rolling basis. Electronic applications accepted. Tuition and fees vary according to course load and program. *Financial support:* In 2011–12, 1 fellowship (averaging $8,370 per year), 5 research assistantships with full tuition reimbursements (averaging $9,927 per year), 13 teaching assistantships with full tuition reimbursements (averaging $9,927 per year) were awarded; institutionally sponsored loans, scholarships/grants, and unspecified assistantships also available. Financial award application deadline: 3/1; financial award applicants required to submit FAFSA. *Unit head:* Dr. Felix Lee, Director, 618-650-2805, E-mail: hflee@siue.edu. *Application contact:* Dr. Xin Chen, Program Director, 618-650-3185, E-mail: xchen@siue.edu. Web site: http://www.siue.edu/ENGINEER/IE/.

Southern Polytechnic State University, School of Engineering Technology and Management, Department of Industrial Engineering Technology, Marietta, GA 30060-2896. Offers quality assurance (MS, Graduate Certificate). Part-time and evening/weekend programs available. Postbaccalaureate distance learning degree programs offered (no on-campus study). *Faculty:* 3 full-time (2 women), 6 part-time/adjunct (4 women). *Students:* 13 full-time (6 women), 61 part-time (22 women); includes 30 minority (22 Black or African American, non-Hispanic/Latino; 2 Asian, non-Hispanic/Latino; 5 Hispanic/Latino; 1 Two or more races, non-Hispanic/Latino), 4 international. Average age 39. 24 applicants, 92% accepted, 15 enrolled. In 2011, 19 master's awarded. *Degree requirements:* For master's and Graduate Certificate, comprehensive exam (for some programs). *Entrance requirements:* For master's, 3 reference forms, minimum GPA of 2.7, statement of purpose; for Graduate Certificate, minimum GPA of 2.7, statement of purpose. Additional exam requirements/recommendations for international students: Required—TOEFL (minimum score 550 paper-based; 213 computer-based; 79 iBT), IELTS (minimum score 6.5). *Application deadline:* For fall admission, 7/1 priority date for domestic students, 5/1 for international students; for spring admission, 11/1 priority date for domestic students, 9/1 for international students. Applications are processed on a rolling basis. Application fee: $50. Electronic applications accepted. *Expenses:* Tuition, state resident: full-time $2592; part-time $216 per semester hour. Tuition, nonresident: full-time $9408; part-time $784 per semester hour. *Required fees:* $698 per term. *Financial support:* In 2011–12, 1 research assistantship with partial tuition reimbursement (averaging $1,500 per year) was awarded; career-related internships or fieldwork and unspecified assistantships also available. Support available to part-time students. Financial award application deadline: 5/1; financial award applicants required to submit FAFSA. *Faculty research:* Application on industrial engineering to public sector, investigation of the response model method in robust design, effectiveness of online education, learning community, physical and mechanical properties of shape-wear garments to their functional performance, the advantage of tablet computer technology in a distance learning format, health care, BRIGE: Optimization Models for Public Health Policy. *Unit head:* Thomas Ball, Chair, 678-915-7162, Fax: 678-915-4991, E-mail: tball@spsu.edu. *Application contact:* Nikki Palamiotis, Director of Graduate Studies, 678-915-4276, Fax: 678-915-7292, E-mail: npalamio@spsu.edu. Web site: http://www.spsu.edu/iet/index.htm.

Stanford University, School of Engineering, Department of Management Science and Engineering, Stanford, CA 94305-9991. Offers management science and engineering (MS, PhD). Terminal master's awarded for partial completion of doctoral program. *Degree requirements:* For doctorate, thesis/dissertation, qualification procedure. *Entrance requirements:* For master's and doctorate, GRE General Test. Additional exam requirements/recommendations for international students: Required—TOEFL. Electronic applications accepted. *Expenses: Tuition:* Full-time $40,050; part-time $890 per credit.

State University of New York at Binghamton, Graduate School, Thomas J. Watson School of Engineering and Applied Science, Department of Systems Science and Industrial Engineering, Binghamton, NY 13902-6000. Offers M Eng, MS, MSAT, PhD. Part-time and evening/weekend programs available. *Faculty:* 10 full-time (2 women), 4 part-time/adjunct (1 woman). *Students:* 80 full-time (21 women), 75 part-time (13 women); includes 20 minority (5 Black or African American, non-Hispanic/Latino; 2 American Indian or Alaska Native, non-Hispanic/Latino; 5 Asian, non-Hispanic/Latino; 4 Hispanic/Latino; 4 Native Hawaiian or other Pacific Islander, non-Hispanic/Latino), 82 international. Average age 30. 164 applicants, 68% accepted, 40 enrolled. In 2011, 49 master's, 8 doctorates awarded. Terminal master's awarded for partial completion of doctoral program. *Degree requirements:* For master's, thesis or alternative; for doctorate, thesis/dissertation. *Entrance requirements:* For master's and doctorate, GRE General Test, GRE Subject Test. Additional exam requirements/recommendations for international students: Required—TOEFL. *Application deadline:* For fall admission, 4/15 priority date for domestic students, 1/15 for international students; for spring admission, 11/1 for domestic students, 10/1 for international students. Applications are processed on a rolling basis. Application fee: $60. Electronic applications accepted. *Financial support:* In 2011–12, 72 students received support, including 1 fellowship with full tuition reimbursement available (averaging $16,500 per year), 50 research assistantships with full tuition reimbursements available (averaging $16,500 per year), 15 teaching assistantships with full tuition reimbursements available (averaging $16,500 per year); career-related internships or fieldwork, Federal Work-Study, institutionally sponsored loans, scholarships/grants, health care benefits, tuition waivers (full and partial), and unspecified assistantships also available. Financial award application deadline: 2/15; financial award applicants required to submit FAFSA. *Faculty research:* Problem restructuring, protein modeling. *Unit head:* Dr. Nagen Nagarur, Chair, 607-777-3027, E-mail: nnagarur@binghamton.edu. *Application contact:* Catherine Smith, Recruiting and Admissions Coordinator, 607-777-2151, Fax: 607-777-2501, E-mail: cmsmith@binghamton.edu. Web site: http://www.ssie.binghamton.edu.

Texas A&M University, College of Engineering, Department of Industrial and Systems Engineering, College Station, TX 77843. Offers industrial and systems engineering (M Eng, MS); industrial engineering (D Eng, PhD). Part-time programs available. Postbaccalaureate distance learning degree programs offered (no on-campus study). *Faculty:* 19. *Students:* 201 full-time (61 women), 39 part-time (8 women); includes 30 minority (7 Black or African American, non-Hispanic/Latino; 9 Asian, non-Hispanic/Latino; 13 Hispanic/Latino; 1 Two or more races, non-Hispanic/Latino), 178 international. Average age 28. In 2011, 108 master's, 8 doctorates awarded. *Degree requirements:* For master's, comprehensive exam (for some programs), thesis optional; for doctorate, comprehensive exam, dissertation (PhD). *Entrance requirements:* For master's and doctorate, GRE General Test. Additional exam requirements/recommendations for international students: Required—TOEFL. *Application deadline:* For fall admission, 3/1 priority date for domestic students, 3/1 for international students; for spring admission, 8/1 priority date for domestic students, 8/1 for international students. Applications are processed on a rolling basis. Application fee: $50 ($75 for international students). Electronic applications accepted. *Expenses:* Tuition, state resident: full-time $5437; part-time $226.55 per credit hour. Tuition, nonresident: full-time $12,949; part-time $539.55 per credit hour. *Required fees:* $2741. *Financial support:* In 2011–12, fellowships with partial tuition reimbursements (averaging $25,000 per year), research assistantships with partial tuition reimbursements (averaging $12,000 per year), teaching assistantships with partial tuition reimbursements (averaging $12,000 per year) were awarded; career-related internships or fieldwork, scholarships/grants, and unspecified assistantships also available. Financial award application deadline: 2/1. *Faculty research:* Manufacturing systems, computer integration, operations research, logistics, simulation. *Unit head:* Dr. Cesar O. Malave, Head, 979-845-5576, Fax: 979-458-4299, E-mail: malave@tamu.edu. *Application contact:* Judy Meeks, Administrative Assistant, Graduate Programs, 979-845-5536, Fax: 979-458-4299, E-mail: judym@tamu.edu. Web site: http://ise.tamu.edu.

Texas A&M University–Kingsville, College of Graduate Studies, College of Engineering, Department of Mechanical and Industrial Engineering, Program in Industrial Engineering, Kingsville, TX 78363. Offers ME, MS. *Degree requirements:* For master's, comprehensive exam, thesis or alternative. *Entrance requirements:* For master's, GRE General Test, minimum GPA of 3.0. Additional exam requirements/recommendations for international students: Required—TOEFL. *Faculty research:* Robotics and automation, neural networks and fuzzy logic, systems engineering/simulation modeling, integrated manufacturing and production systems.

Texas Southern University, School of Science and Technology, Department of Industrial Technology, Houston, TX 77004-4584. Offers MS. *Degree requirements:* For master's, comprehensive exam. *Entrance requirements:* For master's, GRE General Test, minimum GPA of 2.5. Additional exam requirements/recommendations for international students: Required—TOEFL. Electronic applications accepted.

Texas State University–San Marcos, Graduate School, College of Science and Engineering, Department of Engineering Technology, Program in Industrial Technology, San Marcos, TX 78666. Offers MST. Part-time and evening/weekend programs available. *Faculty:* 11 full-time (0 women). *Students:* 21 full-time (3 women), 17 part-time (1 woman); includes 9 minority (2 Black or African American, non-Hispanic/Latino; 1 Asian, non-Hispanic/Latino; 5 Hispanic/Latino; 1 Two or more races, non-Hispanic/Latino), 7 international. Average age 31. 23 applicants, 43% accepted, 4 enrolled. In 2011, 15 master's awarded. *Degree requirements:* For master's, comprehensive exam, thesis optional. *Entrance requirements:* For master's, minimum GPA of 2.75 in last 60 hours of undergraduate work. Additional exam requirements/recommendations for international students: Required—TOEFL (minimum score 550 paper-based; 213 computer-based; 78 iBT). *Application deadline:* For fall admission, 6/15 priority date for domestic students, 6/1 for international students; for spring admission, 10/15 priority date for domestic students, 10/1 for international students. Applications are processed on a rolling basis. Application fee: $40 ($90 for international students). *Expenses:* Tuition, state resident: full-time $6408; part-time $3204 per semester. Tuition, nonresident: full-time $14,832; part-time $7416 per semester. *Required fees:* $1824; $912 per semester. Tuition and fees vary according to course load. *Financial support:* In 2011–12, 9 students received support, including 3 research assistantships (averaging $16,002 per year), 8 teaching assistantships (averaging $10,341 per year); career-related internships or fieldwork, Federal Work-Study, and institutionally sponsored loans also available. Support available to part-time students. Financial award application deadline: 4/1; financial award applicants required to submit FAFSA. *Unit head:* Dr. Andy Batey, Interim Chair, 512-245-2137, Fax: 512-245-3052, E-mail: ab08@txstate.edu. *Application contact:* Dr. Andy Batey, Graduate Adviser, 512-245-2137, Fax: 512-245-3052, E-mail: ab08@txstate.edu. Web site: http://www.txstate.edu/technology/.

Texas Tech University, Graduate School, Edward E. Whitacre Jr. College of Engineering, Department of Industrial Engineering, Lubbock, TX 79409. Offers industrial engineering (MSIE, PhD); systems and engineering management (MSSEM, PhD). Part-time programs available. Postbaccalaureate distance learning degree programs offered (minimal on-campus study). *Faculty:* 13 full-time (2 women), 2 part-time/adjunct (1 woman). *Students:* 66 full-time (13 women), 47 part-time (7 women); includes 12 minority (3 Black or African American, non-Hispanic/Latino; 1 Asian, non-Hispanic/Latino; 7 Hispanic/Latino; 1 Two or more races, non-Hispanic/Latino), 57 international. Average age 31. 201 applicants, 50% accepted, 22 enrolled. In 2011, 28 master's, 9 doctorates awarded. *Degree requirements:* For master's, thesis or alternative; for doctorate, thesis/dissertation. *Entrance requirements:* For master's, GRE General Test; for doctorate, GRE General Test, MS. Additional exam requirements/recommendations for international students: Required—TOEFL (minimum score 550 paper-based; 213 computer-based; 79 iBT). *Application deadline:* For fall admission, 6/1 priority date for domestic students, 1/15 for international students; for spring admission, 9/1 priority date for domestic students, 6/15 for international students. Applications are processed on a rolling basis. Application fee: $50 ($75 for international students). Electronic applications accepted. *Expenses:* Tuition, state resident: full-time $5899; part-time $245.80 per credit hour. Tuition, nonresident: full-time $13,411; part-time $558.80 per credit hour. *Required fees:* $2680.60; $86.50 per credit hour. $920.30 per semester. *Financial support:* In 2011–12, 32 students received support. Application deadline: 4/15; applicants required to submit FAFSA. *Faculty research:* Knowledge and engineering management, environmentally conscious manufacturing, biomechanical simulation, aviation security, supply chain management. *Total annual research expenditures:* $924,834. *Unit head:* Dr. Pat Patterson, Chair, 806-742-3543, Fax: 806-742-3411, E-mail: pat.patterson@ttu.edu. *Application contact:* Dr. Mario Beruvides, Professor, 806-742-3543, Fax: 806-742-3411, E-mail: mario.beruvides@ttu.edu. Web site: http://www.ie.ttu.edu/.

Universidad de las Américas–Puebla, Division of Graduate Studies, School of Engineering, Program in Industrial Engineering, Puebla, Mexico. Offers industrial engineering (MS); production management (M Adm). Part-time and evening/weekend programs available. *Degree requirements:* For master's, one foreign language, thesis. *Faculty research:* Textile industry, quality control.

Université de Moncton, Faculty of Engineering, Program in Industrial Engineering, Moncton, NB E1A 3E9, Canada. Offers M Sc A. *Degree requirements:* For master's, thesis, proficiency in French. *Faculty research:* Production systems, optimization, simulation and expert systems, modeling and warehousing systems, quality control.

Université du Québec à Trois-Rivières, Graduate Programs, Program in Industrial Engineering, Trois-Rivières, QC G9A 5H7, Canada. Offers M Sc, DESS. *Entrance requirements:* For degree, appropriate bachelor's degree, proficiency in French. *Faculty research:* Production.

Université Laval, Faculty of Sciences and Engineering, Programs in Industrial Engineering, Québec, QC G1K 7P4, Canada. Offers Diploma. Part-time programs available. *Entrance requirements:* For degree, knowledge of French. Electronic applications accepted.

University at Buffalo, the State University of New York, Graduate School, School of Engineering and Applied Sciences, Department of Industrial and Systems Engineering, Buffalo, NY 14260. Offers ME, MS, PhD. Part-time programs available. Postbaccalaureate distance learning degree programs offered (minimal on-campus study). *Faculty:* 12 full-time (1 woman), 3 part-time/adjunct (0 women). *Students:* 145 full-time (35 women), 8 part-time (2 women); includes 7 minority (1 American Indian or Alaska Native, non-Hispanic/Latino; 4 Asian, non-Hispanic/Latino; 2 Hispanic/Latino), 113 international. Average age 27. 564 applicants, 28% accepted, 46 enrolled. In 2011, 62 master's, 12 doctorates awarded. Terminal master's awarded for partial completion of doctoral program. *Degree requirements:* For master's, comprehensive exam (for some programs), thesis or alternative; for doctorate, thesis/dissertation. *Entrance requirements:* For master's and doctorate, GRE General Test. Additional exam requirements/recommendations for international students: Required—TOEFL (minimum score 550 paper-based; 213 computer-based; 79 iBT). *Application deadline:* For fall admission, 2/1 priority date for domestic students; for spring admission, 8/1 for domestic students. Applications are processed on a rolling basis. Application fee: $75. Electronic applications accepted. *Financial support:* In 2011–12, 67 students received support, including 9 fellowships with full tuition reimbursements available (averaging $28,900 per year), 39 research assistantships with full and partial tuition reimbursements available (averaging $24,000 per year), 15 teaching assistantships with partial tuition reimbursements available (averaging $20,900 per year); Federal Work-Study, institutionally sponsored loans, tuition waivers (full and partial), and unspecified assistantships also available. Financial award application deadline: 2/1; financial award applicants required to submit FAFSA. *Faculty research:* Ergonomics, operations research, production systems, human factors. *Total annual research expenditures:* $13.6 million. *Unit head:* Dr. Rakesh Nagl, Chairman, 716-645-2357, Fax: 716-645-3302, E-mail: iegrad@buffalo.edu. *Application contact:* Dr. Victor Paquet, Director of Graduate Studies, 716-645-4712, Fax: 716-645-3302, E-mail: iegrad@buffalo.edu. Web site: http://www.ise.buffalo.edu/index.php.

The University of Alabama in Huntsville, School of Graduate Studies, College of Engineering, Department of Industrial and Systems Engineering and Engineering Management, Huntsville, AL 35899. Offers industrial and systems engineering (MSE, PhD); industrial engineering (MSE, PhD); operations research (MSOR); systems engineering (MSE). Part-time and evening/weekend programs available. Postbaccalaureate distance learning degree programs offered (minimal on-campus study). *Faculty:* 9 full-time (2 women), 3 part-time/adjunct (1 woman). *Students:* 13 full-time (7 women), 147 part-time (39 women); includes 25 minority (14 Black or African American, non-Hispanic/Latino; 3 American Indian or Alaska Native, non-Hispanic/Latino; 4 Asian, non-Hispanic/Latino; 3 Hispanic/Latino; 1 Two or more races, non-Hispanic/Latino), 4 international. Average age 35. 98 applicants, 56% accepted, 32 enrolled. In 2011, 23 master's, 5 doctorates awarded. *Degree requirements:* For master's, comprehensive exam, thesis or alternative, oral and written exams; for doctorate, comprehensive exam, thesis/dissertation, oral and written exams. *Entrance requirements:* For master's and doctorate, GRE General Test, minimum GPA of 3.0. Additional exam requirements/recommendations for international students: Required—TOEFL (minimum score 500 paper-based; 173 computer-based; 62 iBT). *Application deadline:* For fall admission, 7/15 for domestic students, 4/1 for international students; for spring admission, 11/30 for domestic students, 9/1 for international students. Applications are processed on a rolling basis. Application fee: $40 ($50 for international students). Electronic applications accepted. *Expenses:* Tuition, state resident: full-time $7830; part-time $473.50 per credit. Tuition, nonresident: full-time $18,748; part-time $1128.33 per credit. Tuition and fees vary according to course load and program. *Financial support:* In 2011–12, 8 students received support, including 2 research assistantships with full tuition reimbursements available (averaging $6,784 per year), 5 teaching assistantships with full tuition reimbursements available (averaging $12,080 per year); career-related internships or fieldwork, Federal Work-Study, institutionally sponsored loans, scholarships/grants, health care benefits, and unspecified assistantships also available. Support available to part-time students. Financial award application deadline: 4/1; financial award applicants required to submit FAFSA. *Faculty research:* Engineering management, systems engineering, manufacturing, logistics, simulation. *Total annual research expenditures:* $8.4 million. *Unit head:* Dr. James Swain, Chair, 256-824-6749, Fax: 256-824-6733, E-mail: jswain@ise.uah.edu. *Application contact:* Kim Gray, Graduate Studies Admissions Coordinator, 256-824-6002, Fax: 256-824-6405, E-mail: deangrad@uah.edu. Web site: http://www.uah.edu/eng/departments/iseem/welcome.

The University of Arizona, College of Engineering, Department of Systems and Industrial Engineering, Program in Industrial Engineering, Tucson, AZ 85721. Offers MS. Part-time programs available. Postbaccalaureate distance learning degree programs offered. *Students:* 2 full-time (1 woman), 1 part-time (0 women), 12 international. Average age 25. 25 applicants, 40% accepted. In 2011, 5 master's awarded. *Entrance requirements:* Additional exam requirements/recommendations for international students: Required—TOEFL (minimum score 575 paper-based; 233 computer-based; 80 iBT). *Application deadline:* For fall admission, 6/1 for domestic students, 12/1 for international students; for spring admission, 9/1 for domestic students, 6/1 for international students. Applications are processed on a rolling basis. Application fee: $75. Electronic applications accepted. *Expenses:* Tuition, state resident: full-time $10,840. Tuition, nonresident: full-time $25,802. *Financial support:* Institutionally sponsored loans, scholarships/grants, and unspecified assistantships available. *Faculty research:* Operations research, manufacturing systems, quality and reliability, statistical/engineering design. *Unit head:* Dr. K. Larry Head, Head, 520-621-6551, E-mail: larry@sie.arizona.edu. *Application contact:* Linda Cramer, Graduate Secretary, 520-626-4644, Fax: 520-621-6555, E-mail: gradapp@sie.arizona.edu. Web site: http://www.sie.arizona.edu.

The University of Arizona, College of Engineering, Department of Systems and Industrial Engineering, Program in Systems and Industrial Engineering, Tucson, AZ 85721. Offers MS, PhD. Postbaccalaureate distance learning degree programs offered. *Faculty:* 7 full-time (1 woman). *Students:* 29 full-time (5 women), 1 part-time (0 women), all international. Average age 27. 24 applicants, 75% accepted, 6 enrolled. In 2011, 3 doctorates awarded. *Degree requirements:* For doctorate, thesis/dissertation. *Entrance requirements:* For master's, GRE General Test (minimum score: 500 Verbal, 700 Quantitative), 3 letters of recommendation, letter of intent; for doctorate, GRE General Test (minimum score: 500 Verbal, 750 Quantitative), 3 letters of recommendation, letter of intent. Additional exam requirements/recommendations for international students: Required—TOEFL (minimum score 575 paper-based; 233 computer-based; 80 iBT). *Application deadline:* For fall admission, 6/1 for domestic students, 12/1 for international students; for spring admission, 9/1 for domestic students, 6/1 for international students. Applications are processed on a rolling basis. Application fee: $75. Electronic applications accepted. *Expenses:* Tuition, state resident: full-time $10,840. Tuition, nonresident: full-time $25,802. *Financial support:* Tuition waivers (full) and unspecified assistantships available. *Faculty research:* Optimization, systems theory, logistics, transportation, embedded systems. *Unit head:* Dr. K. Larry Head, Head, 520-621-6551, E-mail: larry@sie.arizona.edu. *Application contact:* Linda Cramer, Graduate Secretary, 520-626-4644, Fax: 520-621-6555, E-mail: gradapp@sie.arizona.edu. Web site: http://www.sie.arizona.edu.

University of Arkansas, Graduate School, College of Engineering, Department of Industrial Engineering, Program in Industrial Engineering, Fayetteville, AR 72701-1201. Offers MSE, MSIE, PhD. *Students:* 23 full-time (6 women), 24 part-time (8 women); includes 1 minority (Asian, non-Hispanic/Latino), 27 international. 61 applicants, 59% accepted. In 2011, 8 master's awarded. *Degree requirements:* For master's, thesis optional; for doctorate, one foreign language, thesis/dissertation. *Application deadline:* For fall admission, 4/1 for international students; for spring admission, 10/1 for international students. Applications are processed on a rolling basis. Application fee: $40 ($50 for international students). Electronic applications accepted. *Financial support:* In 2011–12, 32 research assistantships were awarded; fellowships, teaching assistantships, career-related internships or fieldwork, and Federal Work-Study also available. Support available to part-time students. Financial award application deadline: 4/1; financial award applicants required to submit FAFSA. *Unit head:* Dr. Kim Needy, Department Chairperson, 479-575-3157, Fax: 479-575-8431, E-mail: kneedy@uark.edu. *Application contact:* Dr. Justin Chimka, Graduate Coordinator, 479-575-7392, E-mail: jchimka@uark.edu. Web site: http://www.ineg.uark.edu/.

University of California, Berkeley, Graduate Division, College of Engineering, Department of Industrial Engineering and Operations Research, Berkeley, CA 94720-1500. Offers M Eng, MS, D Eng, PhD. *Degree requirements:* For master's, comprehensive exam or thesis (MS); for doctorate, thesis/dissertation, qualifying exam. *Entrance requirements:* For master's and doctorate, GRE General Test, minimum GPA of 3.0, 3 letters of recommendation. *Faculty research:* Mathematical programming, robotics and manufacturing, linear and nonlinear optimization, production planning and scheduling, queuing theory.

University of Central Florida, College of Engineering and Computer Science, Department of Industrial Engineering and Management Systems, Orlando, FL 32816. Offers applied operations research (Certificate); design for usability (Certificate); engineering management (PSM); industrial engineering (MSIE, PhD); industrial engineering and management systems (MS); industrial ergonomics and safety (Certificate); project engineering (Certificate); quality assurance (Certificate); systems engineering (Certificate); systems simulation for engineers (Certificate); training simulation (Certificate). Part-time and evening/weekend programs available. *Faculty:* 18 full-time (4 women), 5 part-time/adjunct (1 woman). *Students:* 105 full-time (27 women), 151 part-time (47 women); includes 84 minority (20 Black or African American, non-Hispanic/Latino; 1 American Indian or Alaska Native, non-Hispanic/Latino; 20 Asian, non-Hispanic/Latino; 37 Hispanic/Latino; 1 Native Hawaiian or other Pacific Islander, non-Hispanic/Latino; 5 Two or more races, non-Hispanic/Latino), 52 international. Average age 32. 199 applicants, 79% accepted, 75 enrolled. In 2011, 83 master's, 11 doctorates, 40 other advanced degrees awarded. *Degree requirements:* For master's, thesis; for doctorate, thesis/dissertation, departmental qualifying exam, candidacy exam. *Entrance requirements:* For master's, GRE General Test, minimum GPA of 3.0 in last 60 hours of course work; for doctorate, minimum GPA of 3.5 in last 60 hours of course work. Additional exam requirements/recommendations for international students: Required—TOEFL. *Application deadline:* For fall admission, 7/15 priority date for domestic students; for spring admission, 12/1 priority date for domestic students. Application fee: $30. Electronic applications accepted. *Expenses:* Tuition, state resident: part-time $277.08 per credit hour. Tuition, nonresident: part-time $277.08 per credit hour. Part-time tuition and fees vary according to degree level and program. *Financial support:* In 2011–12, 19 students received support, including 8 fellowships with partial tuition reimbursements available (averaging $3,500 per year), 10 research assistantships with partial tuition reimbursements available (averaging $11,100 per year), 6 teaching assistantships with partial tuition reimbursements available (averaging $12,300 per year); career-related internships or fieldwork, Federal Work-Study, institutionally sponsored loans, tuition waivers (partial), and unspecified assistantships also available. Financial award application deadline: 3/1; financial award applicants required to submit FAFSA. *Unit head:* Dr. Waldemar Karwowski, Chair, 407-823-2204, E-mail: wkar@ucf.edu. *Application contact:* Barbara Rodriguez, Director, Admissions and Registration, 407-823-2766, Fax: 407-823-6442, E-mail: gradadmissions@ucf.edu. Web site: http://iems.ucf.edu/.

University of Cincinnati, Graduate School, College of Engineering and Applied Science, Department of Mechanical, Industrial and Nuclear Engineering, Program in Industrial Engineering, Cincinnati, OH 45221. Offers MS, PhD, MBA/MS. Part-time and evening/weekend programs available. *Degree requirements:* For master's, oral exam, thesis defense; for doctorate, variable foreign language requirement, thesis/dissertation, oral exam. *Entrance requirements:* For master's and doctorate, GRE General Test. Additional exam requirements/recommendations for international students: Required—TOEFL (minimum score 575 paper-based; 233 computer-based). Electronic applications accepted. *Faculty research:* Operations research, engineering administration, safety.

University of Florida, Graduate School, College of Engineering, Department of Industrial and Systems Engineering, Gainesville, FL 32611. Offers ME, MS, PhD, Engr. Part-time and evening/weekend programs available. Postbaccalaureate distance learning degree programs offered (minimal on-campus study). Terminal master's awarded for partial completion of doctoral program. *Degree requirements:* For master's, thesis (for some programs); for doctorate, comprehensive exam (for some programs), thesis/dissertation (for some programs). *Entrance requirements:* For master's and doctorate, GRE General Test, minimum GPA of 3.0; for Engr, GRE General Test. Additional exam requirements/recommendations for international students: Required—TOEFL (minimum score 550 paper-based; 213 computer-based; 80 iBT), IELTS (minimum score 6). Electronic applications accepted. *Faculty research:* Operations research; financial engineering; logistics and supply chain management; energy, healthcare, and transportation applications of operations research.

University of Houston, Cullen College of Engineering, Department of Industrial Engineering, Houston, TX 77204. Offers MIE, PhD. Part-time programs available. Terminal master's awarded for partial completion of doctoral program. *Degree requirements:* For master's, thesis (for some programs); for doctorate, thesis/dissertation, departmental qualifying exam. *Entrance requirements:* For master's and doctorate, GRE General Test. Additional exam requirements/recommendations for international students: Required—TOEFL; Recommended—IELTS. Electronic applications accepted.

University of Illinois at Chicago, Graduate College, College of Engineering, Department of Mechanical and Industrial Engineering, Program in Industrial Engineering, Chicago, IL 60607-7128. Offers MS. Part-time programs available. *Degree requirements:* For master's, thesis. *Entrance requirements:* For master's, GRE General Test, minimum GPA of 2.75. Additional exam requirements/recommendations for international students: Required—TOEFL. Electronic applications accepted. *Faculty research:* Systems modeling.

University of Illinois at Chicago, Graduate College, College of Engineering, Department of Mechanical and Industrial Engineering, Program in Industrial Engineering and Operations Research, Chicago, IL 60607-7128. Offers PhD. Part-time programs available. *Degree requirements:* For doctorate, thesis/dissertation. *Entrance requirements:* For doctorate, GRE General Test, minimum GPA of 2.75. Additional exam requirements/recommendations for international students: Required—TOEFL. Electronic applications accepted.

University of Illinois at Urbana–Champaign, Graduate College, College of Engineering, Department of Industrial and Enterprise Systems Engineering, Champaign, IL 61820. Offers industrial engineering (MS, PhD); systems and entrepreneurial engineering (MS, PhD); MBA/MS. *Faculty:* 18 full-time (5 women). *Students:* 42 full-time (12 women), 20 part-time (8 women); includes 3 minority (1 Black or African American, non-Hispanic/Latino; 1 Asian, non-Hispanic/Latino; 1 Hispanic/Latino), 48 international. 233 applicants, 14% accepted, 14 enrolled. In 2011, 14 master's, 7 doctorates awarded. *Entrance requirements:* For master's and doctorate, GRE, minimum GPA of 3.25. Additional exam requirements/recommendations for international students: Required—TOEFL (minimum score 613 paper-based; 257 computer-based; 103 iBT) or IELTS (minimum score 7). *Application deadline:* Applications are processed on a rolling basis. Application fee: $75 ($90 for international students). Electronic applications accepted. *Financial support:* In 2011–12, 7 fellowships, 43 research assistantships, 49 teaching assistantships were awarded; tuition waivers (full and partial) also available. *Unit head:* Jong-Shi Pang, Head, 217-244-5703, Fax: 217-244-5705, E-mail: jspang@illinois.edu. *Application contact:* Michelle Holly Tipsword, Graduate Programs Specialist, 217-333-2730, Fax: 217-244-5705, E-mail: tippy6@illinois.edu. Web site: http://www.iese.illinois.edu.

University of Illinois at Urbana–Champaign, Graduate College, College of Engineering, Department of Mechanical Science and Engineering, Champaign, IL 61820. Offers mechanical engineering (MS, PhD); theoretical and applied mechanics (MS, PhD); MS/MBA. *Faculty:* 52 full-time (5 women), 2 part-time/adjunct (0 women). *Students:* 323 full-time (42 women), 35 part-time (5 women); includes 30 minority (16 Asian, non-Hispanic/Latino; 12 Hispanic/Latino; 2 Two or more races, non-Hispanic/Latino), 211 international. 807 applicants, 26% accepted, 75 enrolled. In 2011, 90 master's, 31 doctorates awarded. Terminal master's awarded for partial completion of doctoral program. *Entrance requirements:* For master's, GRE General Test, minimum GPA of 3.25; for doctorate, GRE General Test, minimum GPA of 3.5. Additional exam requirements/recommendations for international students: Required—TOEFL (minimum score 613 paper-based; 257 computer-based; 103 iBT). *Application deadline:* Applications are processed on a rolling basis. Application fee: $75 ($90 for international students). Electronic applications accepted. *Financial support:* In 2011–12, 44 fellowships, 244 research assistantships, 109 teaching assistantships were awarded; tuition waivers (full and partial) also available. *Faculty research:* Combustion and propulsion, design methodology, dynamic systems and controls, energy transfer, materials behavior and processing, manufacturing systems operations, management. *Unit head:* Placid Mathew Ferreira, Head, 217-333-0639, Fax: 217-244-6534, E-mail: pferreir@illinois.edu. *Application contact:* Katrina Hagler, Graduate Admissions Coordinator, 217-244-3416, Fax: 217-244-6534, E-mail: kkappes2@illinois.edu. Web site: http://mechse.illinois.edu.

The University of Iowa, Graduate College, College of Engineering, Department of Industrial Engineering, Iowa City, IA 52242-1316. Offers engineering design and manufacturing (MS, PhD); ergonomics (MS, PhD); information and engineering management (MS, PhD); operations research (MS, PhD); quality engineering (MS, PhD). *Faculty:* 7 full-time (0 women). *Students:* 21 full-time (6 women); includes 2 minority (1 Black or African American, non-Hispanic/Latino; 1 Asian, non-Hispanic/Latino), 14 international. Average age 27. 69 applicants, 13% accepted, 5 enrolled. In 2011, 8 master's, 6 doctorates awarded. *Degree requirements:* For master's, thesis optional, exam; for doctorate, comprehensive exam, thesis/dissertation, final defense exam. *Entrance requirements:* For master's and doctorate, GRE General Test. Additional exam requirements/recommendations for international students: Required—TOEFL (minimum score 550 paper-based; 213 computer-based; 81 iBT). *Application deadline:* For fall admission, 7/15 for domestic students, 4/15 for international students; for spring admission, 12/1 for domestic students, 10/1 for international students. Applications are processed on a rolling basis. Application fee: $60 ($100 for international students). Electronic applications accepted. *Financial support:* In 2011–12, 5 fellowships with partial tuition reimbursements (averaging $30,450 per year), 17 research assistantships with partial tuition reimbursements (averaging $20,000 per year), 5 teaching assistantships with partial tuition reimbursements (averaging $16,630 per year) were awarded; career-related internships or fieldwork, scholarships/grants, and unspecified assistantships also available. Support available to part-time students. Financial award applicants required to submit FAFSA. *Faculty research:* Operations research, informatics, human factors engineering, manufacturing systems, human-machine interaction. *Total annual research expenditures:* $4.6 million. *Unit head:* Dr. Andrew Kusiak, Department Executive Officer, 319-335-5934, Fax: 319-335-5669, E-mail: andrew-kusiak@uiowa.edu. *Application contact:* Andrea Flaherty, Academic Program Specialist, 319-335-5939, Fax: 319-335-5669, E-mail: indeng@engineering.uiowa.edu. Web site: http://www.mie.engineering.uiowa.edu/.

University of Louisville, J. B. Speed School of Engineering, Department of Industrial Engineering, Louisville, KY 40292-0001. Offers engineering management (M Eng); industrial engineering (M Eng, MS, PhD); logistics and distribution (Certificate). *Accreditation:* ABET (one or more programs are accredited). Part-time programs available. *Faculty:* 10 full-time (1 woman). *Students:* 42 full-time (13 women), 11 part-time (6 women); includes 5 minority (4 Black or African American, non-Hispanic/Latino; 1 Hispanic/Latino), 21 international. Average age 28. 52 applicants, 33% accepted, 11 enrolled. In 2011, 43 master's, 3 doctorates awarded. Terminal master's awarded for partial completion of doctoral program. *Degree requirements:* For master's, comprehensive exam (for some programs), thesis or alternative; for doctorate, comprehensive exam, thesis/dissertation, minimum GPA of 3.0. *Entrance requirements:* For master's and doctorate, GRE General Test. Additional exam requirements/recommendations for international students: Required—TOEFL (minimum score 550 paper-based; 213 computer-based; 80 iBT), IELTS (minimum score 6.5). *Application deadline:* For fall admission, 5/1 priority date for domestic students, 5/1 for international students; for spring admission, 11/1 priority date for domestic students, 11/1 for international students. Applications are processed on a rolling basis. Application fee: $50. Electronic applications accepted. *Expenses:* Tuition, state resident: full-time $9692; part-time $539 per credit hour. Tuition, nonresident: full-time $20,168; part-time $1121 per credit hour. Tuition and fees vary according to program and reciprocity agreements. *Financial support:* In 2011–12, 15 students received support, including 7 fellowships with full tuition reimbursements available (averaging $20,000 per year), 2 research assistantships with full tuition reimbursements available (averaging $20,000 per year), 6 teaching assistantships with full tuition reimbursements available (averaging $20,000 per year). Financial award application deadline: 1/25; financial award applicants required to submit FAFSA. *Faculty research:* Optimization, computer simulation, logistics and distribution, ergonomics and human factors, advanced manufacturing process. *Total annual research expenditures:* $748,000. *Unit head:* Dr. John S. Usher, Chair, 502-852-6342, Fax: 502-852-5633, E-mail: usher@louisville.edu. *Application contact:* Dr. Michael Day, Associate Dean, 502-852-6195, Fax: 502-852-7294, E-mail: day@louisville.edu. Web site: http://www.louisville.edu/speed/industrial/.

University of Manitoba, Faculty of Graduate Studies, Faculty of Engineering, Department of Mechanical and Manufacturing Engineering, Winnipeg, MB R3T 2N2, Canada. Offers M Eng, M Sc, PhD. *Degree requirements:* For master's, thesis; for doctorate, thesis/dissertation.

University of Massachusetts Amherst, Graduate School, College of Engineering, Department of Mechanical and Industrial Engineering, Amherst, MA 01003. Offers industrial engineering and operations research (MS, PhD); mechanical engineering (MSME, PhD). Part-time programs available. *Faculty:* 36 full-time (3 women). *Students:* 103 full-time (26 women), 14 part-time (3 women); includes 10 minority (2 Black or African American, non-Hispanic/Latino; 4 Asian, non-Hispanic/Latino; 3 Hispanic/Latino; 1 Native Hawaiian or other Pacific Islander, non-Hispanic/Latino), 60 international. Average age 28. 350 applicants, 32% accepted, 29 enrolled. In 2011, 16 master's, 4 doctorates awarded. Terminal master's awarded for partial completion of doctoral program. *Degree requirements:* For master's, thesis or alternative; for doctorate, comprehensive exam, thesis/dissertation. *Entrance requirements:* For master's and doctorate, GRE General Test. Additional exam requirements/recommendations for international students: Required—TOEFL (minimum score 550 paper-based; 213 computer-based; 80 iBT), IELTS (minimum score 6.5). *Application deadline:* For fall admission, 1/15 for domestic and international students; for spring admission, 10/1 for domestic and international students. Applications are processed on a rolling basis. Application fee: $50 ($65 for international students). Electronic applications accepted. Tuition and fees vary according to course load, campus/location and program. *Financial support:* Fellowships with full and partial tuition reimbursements, research assistantships with full tuition reimbursements, teaching assistantships with full tuition reimbursements, career-related internships or fieldwork, Federal Work-Study, scholarships/grants, traineeships, health care benefits, tuition waivers (full and partial), and unspecified assistantships available. Support available to part-time students. Financial award application deadline: 1/15. *Unit head:* Dr. David P. Schmidt, Graduate Program Director, 413-545-3827, Fax: 413-545-1027. *Application contact:* Lindsay DeSantis, Interim Supervisor of Admissions, 413-545-0722, Fax: 413-577-0100, E-mail: gradadm@grad.umass.edu. Web site: http://mie.umass.edu/.

University of Massachusetts Amherst, Graduate School, Interdisciplinary Programs, Dual Degree Program in Business Administration and Industrial Engineering, Amherst, MA 01003. Offers MBA/MSIE. Part-time programs available. *Entrance requirements:* Additional exam requirements/recommendations for international students: Required— TOEFL (minimum score 600 paper-based; 250 computer-based; 100 iBT), IELTS (minimum score 7). *Application deadline:* For fall admission, 1/15 for domestic and international students. Applications are processed on a rolling basis. Application fee: $50 ($65 for international students). Electronic applications accepted. Tuition and fees vary according to course load, campus/location and program. *Financial support:* Career-related internships or fieldwork, Federal Work-Study, scholarships/grants, traineeships, health care benefits, tuition waivers (full), and unspecified assistantships available. Support available to part-time students. *Unit head:* Dr. David P. Schmidt, Graduate Program Director, 413-545-3827, Fax: 413-545-1027. *Application contact:* Lindsay DeSantis, Interim Supervisor of Admissions, 413-545-0722, Fax: 413-577-0010, E-mail: gradadm@grad.umass.edu. Web site: http://www-new.ecs.umass.edu/ degrees#MBA.

University of Massachusetts Lowell, School of Health and Environment, Department of Work Environment, Lowell, MA 01854-2881. Offers cleaner production and pollution prevention (MS, Sc D); environmental risk assessment (Certificate); epidemiology (MS, Sc D); ergonomics and safety (MS, Sc D); identification and control of ergonomic hazards (Certificate); job stress and healthy job redesign (Certificate); occupational and environmental hygiene (MS, Sc D); radiological health physics and general work environment protection (Certificate); work environment policy (MS, Sc D). *Accreditation:* ABET (one or more programs are accredited). Part-time programs available. Terminal master's awarded for partial completion of doctoral program. *Degree requirements:* For master's, thesis optional; for doctorate, thesis/dissertation. *Entrance requirements:* For master's and doctorate, GRE General Test. Additional exam requirements/ recommendations for international students: Required—TOEFL.

University of Memphis, Graduate School, Herff College of Engineering, Department of Mechanical Engineering, Memphis, TN 38152. Offers design and mechanical engineering (MS); energy systems (MS); industrial engineering (MS); mechanical engineering (PhD); mechanical systems (MS); power systems (MS). Part-time programs available. Terminal master's awarded for partial completion of doctoral program. *Degree requirements:* For master's, comprehensive exam, thesis; for doctorate, comprehensive exam, thesis/dissertation. *Entrance requirements:* For master's, GRE General Test, BS in mechanical engineering, minimum undergraduate GPA of 3.0. *Faculty research:* Computational fluid dynamics, computational mechanics, integrated design, nondestructive testing, operations research.

University of Miami, Graduate School, College of Engineering, Department of Industrial Engineering, Coral Gables, FL 33124. Offers ergonomics (PhD); industrial engineering (MSIE, PhD); management of technology (MS); occupational ergonomics and safety (MS, MSOES), including environmental health and safety (MS), occupational ergonomics and safety (MSOES); MBA/MSIE. Part-time programs available. *Degree requirements:* For master's, thesis (for some programs); for doctorate, comprehensive exam, thesis/dissertation. *Entrance requirements:* For master's and doctorate, GRE General Test, minimum GPA of 3.0. Additional exam requirements/recommendations for international students: Required—TOEFL (minimum score 550 paper-based; 213 computer-based). *Faculty research:* Logistics, supply chain management, industrial applications of biomechanics and ergonomics, technology management, back pain, aging, operations research, manufacturing, safety, human reliability, energy assessment.

University of Michigan, College of Engineering, Department of Industrial and Operations Engineering, Ann Arbor, MI 48109. Offers MS, MSE, PhD, MBA/MS, MBA/ MSE. *Accreditation:* ABET. Part-time programs available. *Students:* 210 full-time (71 women), 2 part-time (0 women). 534 applicants, 42% accepted, 92 enrolled. In 2011, 79 master's, 8 doctorates awarded. Terminal master's awarded for partial completion of doctoral program. *Degree requirements:* For doctorate, oral defense of dissertation, preliminary exams, qualifying exam. *Entrance requirements:* For master's, GRE General Test, minimum GPA of 3.2; for doctorate, GRE General Test, minimum GPA of 3.5. Additional exam requirements/recommendations for international students: Required— TOEFL. *Application deadline:* Applications are processed on a rolling basis. Application fee: $65 ($75 for international students). Electronic applications accepted. *Financial support:* In 2011–12, 71 students received support. Fellowships, research assistantships, teaching assistantships, Federal Work-Study, institutionally sponsored loans, scholarships/grants, traineeships, health care benefits, and unspecified assistantships available. Financial award applicants required to submit FAFSA. *Faculty research:* Production/distribution/logistics, financial engineering and enterprise systems, ergonomics (physical and cognitive), stochastic processes, linear and nonlinear optimization, operations research. *Unit head:* Mark Daskin, Chair, 734-764-9422, Fax: 734-764-3451, E-mail: msdaskin@umich.edu. *Application contact:* Matt Irelan, Graduate Student Advisor/Program Coordinator, 734-764-6480, Fax: 734-764-3451, E-mail: mirelan@umich.edu. Web site: http://ioe.engin.umich.edu/.

University of Michigan–Dearborn, College of Engineering and Computer Science, Department of Industrial and Manufacturing Systems Engineering, Dearborn, MI 48128-1491. Offers program and project management (MS); MBA/MSE. Part-time and evening/ weekend programs available. *Faculty:* 13 full-time (0 women), 3 part-time/adjunct (0 women). *Students:* 18 full-time (6 women), 147 part-time (32 women); includes 49 minority (7 Black or African American, non-Hispanic/Latino; 1 American Indian or Alaska Native, non-Hispanic/Latino; 34 Asian, non-Hispanic/Latino; 7 Hispanic/Latino), 20 international. Average age 31. 98 applicants, 51% accepted, 45 enrolled. In 2011, 38 master's awarded. *Degree requirements:* For master's, thesis optional. *Entrance requirements:* For master's, bachelor's degree in applied mathematics, computer science, engineering, or physical science; minimum GPA of 3.0. Additional exam requirements/recommendations for international students: Required—TOEFL (minimum

score 560 paper-based; 220 computer-based; 84 iBT). *Application deadline:* For fall admission, 8/1 priority date for domestic students, 4/1 for international students; for winter admission, 12/1 priority date for domestic students, 8/1 for international students; for spring admission, 4/1 for domestic students, 12/1 for international students. Applications are processed on a rolling basis. Application fee: $60. *Financial support:* Fellowships, research assistantships, teaching assistantships, and Federal Work-Study available. Financial award application deadline: 4/1; financial award applicants required to submit FAFSA. *Faculty research:* Health care systems, data and knowledge management, human factors engineering, machine diagnostics, precision machining. *Unit head:* Dr. Armen Zakarian, Chair, 313-593-5361, Fax: 313-593-3692, E-mail: zakarian@umd.umich.edu. *Application contact:* Joey W. Woods, Graduate Program Assistant, 313-593-5361, Fax: 313-593-3692, E-mail: jwwoods@umd.umich.edu. Web site: http://www.engin.umd.umich.edu/IMSE/.

University of Minnesota, Twin Cities Campus, College of Science and Engineering, Program in Industrial and Systems Engineering, Minneapolis, MN 55455-0213. Offers MS, PhD. Part-time programs available. *Faculty:* 7 full-time (0 women). *Students:* 45 (14 women); includes 3 minority (1 American Indian or Alaska Native, non-Hispanic/Latino; 1 Asian, non-Hispanic/Latino; 1 Hispanic/Latino), 32 international. *Degree requirements:* For doctorate, thesis/dissertation. *Entrance requirements:* For master's, GRE General Test, minimum GPA of 3.0; for doctorate, GRE General Test. Additional exam requirements/recommendations for international students: Required—TOEFL. *Application deadline:* For fall admission, 12/15 for domestic and international students. Applications are processed on a rolling basis. Application fee: $75 ($95 for international students). Electronic applications accepted. *Financial support:* Fellowships, research assistantships, and teaching assistantships available. *Faculty research:* Operations research, supply chains and logistics, health care, revenue management, transportation, service and manufacturing operations. *Application contact:* John Gardner, Assistant Academic Adviser, E-mail: jgardner@me.umn.edu. Web site: http://www.isye.umn.edu/ program/.

University of Missouri, Graduate School, College of Engineering, Department of Industrial and Manufacturing Systems Engineering, Columbia, MO 65211. Offers MS, PhD. *Faculty:* 11 full-time (2 women). *Students:* 18 full-time (1 woman), 19 part-time (7 women), 33 international. Average age 28. 63 applicants, 40% accepted, 12 enrolled. In 2011, 11 master's, 1 doctorate awarded. *Degree requirements:* For master's, thesis or alternative; for doctorate, thesis/dissertation. *Entrance requirements:* For master's and doctorate, GRE General Test, minimum GPA of 3.0. Additional exam requirements/ recommendations for international students: Required—TOEFL (minimum score 550 paper-based; 213 computer-based; 80 iBT). *Application deadline:* For fall admission, 5/1 priority date for domestic students. Applications are processed on a rolling basis. Application fee: $55 ($75 for international students). *Expenses:* Tuition, state resident: full-time $5881. Tuition, nonresident: full-time $15,183. *Required fees:* $952. Tuition and fees vary according to campus/location and program. *Financial support:* Research assistantships, teaching assistantships, and institutionally sponsored loans available. *Faculty research:* Logistics systems analysis and design, supply chain modeling, material flow design and improvement, intelligent systems. *Unit head:* Dr. Luis Occena, Department Chair, E-mail: occenal@missouri.edu. *Application contact:* Sally Schwartz, 573-882-2692, E-mail: schwartzs@missouri.edu. Web site: http:// engineering.missouri.edu/imse/.

University of Nebraska–Lincoln, Graduate College, College of Engineering, Department of Industrial and Management Systems Engineering, Lincoln, NE 68588. Offers engineering management (M Eng); industrial and management systems engineering (MS, PhD); manufacturing systems engineering (MS). Postbaccalaureate distance learning degree programs offered. *Degree requirements:* For master's, thesis optional; for doctorate, comprehensive exam, thesis/dissertation. *Entrance requirements:* For master's and doctorate, GRE. Additional exam requirements/ recommendations for international students: Required—TOEFL (minimum score 525 paper-based; 195 computer-based). Electronic applications accepted. *Faculty research:* Ergonomics, occupational safety, quality control, industrial packaging, facility design.

University of New Haven, Graduate School, Tagliatela College of Engineering, Program in Industrial Engineering, West Haven, CT 06516-1916. Offers industrial engineering (MSIE); lean-Six Sigma (Certificate); quality engineering (Certificate). Part-time and evening/weekend programs available. *Students:* 18 full-time (5 women), 8 part-time (1 woman); includes 3 minority (1 Black or African American, non-Hispanic/Latino; 2 Asian, non-Hispanic/Latino), 18 international. 26 applicants, 100% accepted, 6 enrolled. In 2011, 9 master's, 6 Certificates awarded. *Degree requirements:* For master's, project or thesis. *Entrance requirements:* For master's, bachelor's degree in engineering. Additional exam requirements/recommendations for international students: Required—TOEFL (minimum score 520 paper-based; 190 computer-based; 70 iBT); Recommended—IELTS (minimum score 5.5). *Application deadline:* For fall admission, 5/31 for international students; for winter admission, 10/15 for international students; for spring admission, 1/15 for international students. Applications are processed on a rolling basis. Application fee: $50. Electronic applications accepted. *Expenses: Tuition:* Part-time $750 per credit. *Financial support:* Research assistantships with partial tuition reimbursements, teaching assistantships with partial tuition reimbursements, career-related internships or fieldwork, Federal Work-Study, scholarships/grants, tuition waivers, and unspecified assistantships available. Support available to part-time students. Financial award applicants required to submit FAFSA. *Unit head:* Dr. John Sarris, Department Head, 203-932-7146, E-mail: jsarris@newhaven.edu. *Application contact:* Eloise Gormley, Director of Graduate Admissions, 203-932-7449, Fax: 203-932-7137, E-mail: gradinfo@newhaven.edu. Web site: http://www.newhaven.edu/9595/

University of Oklahoma, College of Engineering, School of Industrial Engineering, Norman, OK 73019. Offers industrial engineering (MS, PhD), including engineering management (MS), general (MS). Part-time programs available. *Faculty:* 14 full-time (4 women). *Students:* 40 full-time (15 women), 31 part-time (10 women); includes 13 minority (4 Black or African American, non-Hispanic/Latino; 1 American Indian or Alaska Native, non-Hispanic/Latino; 3 Asian, non-Hispanic/Latino; 2 Hispanic/Latino; 3 Two or more races, non-Hispanic/Latino), 32 international. Average age 30. 88 applicants, 76% accepted, 31 enrolled. In 2011, 20 master's, 3 doctorates awarded. *Degree requirements:* For master's, comprehensive exam, thesis (for some programs); for doctorate, thesis/dissertation, qualifying exam. *Entrance requirements:* For master's and doctorate, GRE, minimum GPA of 3.0, 3 letters of reference, resume or curriculum vitae. Additional exam requirements/recommendations for international students: Required— TOEFL (minimum score 550 paper-based; 79 iBT). *Application deadline:* For fall admission, 6/1 priority date for domestic students, 3/1 for international students; for spring admission, 11/1 for domestic students, 9/1 for international students. Applications are processed on a rolling basis. Application fee: $40 ($90 for international students). Electronic applications accepted. *Expenses:* Tuition, state resident: full-time $4087; part-time $170.30 per credit hour. Tuition, nonresident: full-time $14,875; part-time $619.80 per credit hour. *Required fees:* $2659; $100.25 per credit hour. Tuition and fees vary according to course load and degree level. *Financial support:* In 2011–12, 44 students received support, including 18 research assistantships with partial tuition reimbursements available (averaging $13,795 per year), 4 teaching assistantships with partial tuition reimbursements available (averaging $11,335 per year); scholarships/grants and unspecified assistantships also available. Financial award applicants required to submit FAFSA. *Faculty research:* Computational optimization, logistics and supply chain management, human factors, design and manufacturing, systems modeling, engineering education. *Total annual research expenditures:* $2.1 million. *Unit head:* Dr. Randa Shehab, Director, 405-325-3721, Fax: 405-325-7555, E-mail: rlshehab@ou.edu. *Application contact:* Amy J. Piper, Student Services Coordinator, 405-325-3721, Fax: 405-325-7555, E-mail: ajpiper@ou.edu. Web site: http://www.ou.edu/coe/ie.

University of Pittsburgh, Swanson School of Engineering, Department of Industrial Engineering, Pittsburgh, PA 15260. Offers MSIE, PhD. Part-time programs available. Postbaccalaureate distance learning degree programs offered. *Faculty:* 13 full-time (2 women), 13 part-time/adjunct (3 women). *Students:* 60 full-time (17 women), 23 part-time (6 women); includes 8 minority (1 Black or African American, non-Hispanic/Latino; 5 Asian, non-Hispanic/Latino; 2 Hispanic/Latino), 53 international. 342 applicants, 45% accepted, 32 enrolled. In 2011, 33 master's, 5 doctorates awarded. Terminal master's awarded for partial completion of doctoral program. *Degree requirements:* For master's, thesis optional; for doctorate, comprehensive exam, thesis/dissertation, final oral exams. *Entrance requirements:* For master's and doctorate, GRE General Test, minimum QPA of 3.0. Additional exam requirements/recommendations for international students: Required—TOEFL (minimum score 550 paper-based; 213 computer-based; 80 iBT). *Application deadline:* For fall admission, 3/1 priority date for domestic students; for spring admission, 7/1 priority date for domestic students. Applications are processed on a rolling basis. Application fee: $50. Electronic applications accepted. *Expenses:* Tuition, state resident: full-time $18,774; part-time $760 per credit. Tuition, nonresident: full-time $30,736; part-time $1258 per credit. *Required fees:* $740; $200 per term. Tuition and fees vary according to program. *Financial support:* In 2011–12, 33 students received support, including 3 fellowships with full tuition reimbursements available (averaging $27,624 per year), 25 research assistantships with full tuition reimbursements available (averaging $23,832 per year), 5 teaching assistantships with full tuition reimbursements available (averaging $20,028 per year); scholarships/grants and tuition waivers (full and partial) also available. Financial award application deadline: 4/15. *Faculty research:* Operations research, engineering management, computational intelligence, manufacturing, information systems. *Total annual research expenditures:* $4.4 million. *Unit head:* Dr. Bopaya Bidanda, Chairman, 412-624-9830, Fax: 412-624-9831. *Application contact:* Dr. Jayant Rajgopal, Graduate Coordinator, 412-624-9840, Fax: 412-624-9831, E-mail: rajgopal@engrng.pitt.edu.

University of Puerto Rico, Mayagüez Campus, Graduate Studies, College of Engineering, Department of Industrial Engineering, Mayagüez, PR 00681-9000. Offers industrial engineering (ME, MS); management systems engineering (ME). Part-time programs available. *Students:* 23 full-time (15 women), 2 part-time (both women); includes 17 minority (all Hispanic/Latino), 8 international. 11 applicants, 73% accepted, 5 enrolled. In 2011, 4 master's awarded. *Degree requirements:* For master's, comprehensive exam, thesis, project. *Entrance requirements:* For master's, minimum GPA of 2.5; proficiency in English and Spanish; BS in engineering. Additional exam requirements/recommendations for international students: Required—TOEFL. *Application deadline:* For fall admission, 2/15 for domestic and international students; for spring admission, 9/15 for domestic and international students. Applications are processed on a rolling basis. Application fee: $25. Tuition and fees vary according to course level and course load. *Financial support:* In 2011–12, 14 students received support, including 2 research assistantships (averaging $15,000 per year), 12 teaching assistantships (averaging $8,500 per year); Federal Work-Study and institutionally sponsored loans also available. *Total annual research expenditures:* $141,455. *Unit head:* Dr. Viviana Cesani, Chairperson, 787-265-3819, Fax: 787-265-3820, E-mail: viviana.cesani@upr.edu. Web site: http://ininweb.uprm.edu.

University of Regina, Faculty of Graduate Studies and Research, Faculty of Engineering and Applied Science, Program in Industrial Systems Engineering, Regina, SK S4S 0A2, Canada. Offers M Eng, MA Sc, PhD. Part-time programs available. *Faculty:* 13 full-time (2 women). *Students:* 47 full-time (8 women), 5 part-time (0 women). 72 applicants, 38% accepted. In 2011, 8 master's, 1 doctorate awarded. *Degree requirements:* For master's, thesis (for some programs); for doctorate, thesis/dissertation. *Entrance requirements:* For doctorate, master's degree. Additional exam requirements/recommendations for international students: Required—TOEFL (minimum score 550 paper-based; 80 iBT), IELTS (minimum score 6.5). *Application deadline:* For fall admission, 3/31 for domestic and international students; for winter admission, 7/31 for domestic and international students; for spring admission, 11/30 for domestic and international students. Applications are processed on a rolling basis. Application fee: $100. *Financial support:* In 2011–12, 4 fellowships (averaging $6,500 per year), 1 research assistantship (averaging $5,500 per year), 6 teaching assistantships (averaging $2,298 per year) were awarded; career-related internships or fieldwork and scholarships/grants also available. Financial award application deadline: 6/15. *Faculty research:* Stochastic systems simulation, metallurgy of welding, computer-aided engineering, finite element method of engineering systems, manufacturing systems. *Unit head:* Dr. Raphael Idem, Associate Dean, Research and Graduate Studies, 306-337-2696, E-mail: raphael.idem@uregina.ca. *Application contact:* Dr. Andy Aroonwilas, Graduate Program Coordinator, 306-337-2469, Fax: 306-585-4855, E-mail: adisorn.aroonwilas@uregina.ca.

University of Southern California, Graduate School, Viterbi School of Engineering, Daniel J. Epstein Department of Industrial and Systems Engineering, Los Angeles, CA 90089. Offers digital supply chain management (MS); engineering management (MS); engineering technology communication (Graduate Certificate); health systems operations (Graduate Certificate); industrial and systems engineering (MS, PhD, Engr); manufacturing engineering (MS); operations research engineering (MS); optimization and supply chain management (Graduate Certificate); product development engineering (MS); safety systems and security (MS); systems architecting and engineering (MS, Graduate Certificate); systems safety and security (Graduate Certificate); transportation systems (Graduate Certificate); MS/MBA. Part-time and evening/weekend programs available. Postbaccalaureate distance learning degree programs offered (no on-campus study). Terminal master's awarded for partial completion of doctoral program. *Degree requirements:* For master's, thesis optional; for doctorate, thesis/dissertation. *Entrance requirements:* For master's and doctorate, GRE General Test. Additional exam requirements/recommendations for international students: Recommended—TOEFL. Electronic applications accepted. *Faculty research:* Health systems, music cognition and retrieval, transportation and logistics, manufacturing and automation, engineering systems design, risk and economic analysis.

University of South Florida, Graduate School, College of Engineering, Department of Industrial and Management Systems Engineering, Tampa, FL 33620-9951. Offers engineering management (MSEM, MSIE); engineering science (PhD); industrial engineering (MIE, MSIE, PhD). Part-time programs available. Postbaccalaureate distance learning degree programs offered (minimal on-campus study). *Faculty:* 11 full-time (3 women), 10 part-time/adjunct (2 women). *Students:* 61 full-time (14 women), 64 part-time (18 women); includes 32 minority (5 Black or African American, non-Hispanic/Latino; 2 Asian, non-Hispanic/Latino; 24 Hispanic/Latino; 1 Two or more races, non-Hispanic/Latino), 40 international. Average age 31. 124 applicants, 44% accepted, 20 enrolled. In 2011, 46 master's, 4 doctorates awarded. Terminal master's awarded for partial completion of doctoral program. *Degree requirements:* For master's, comprehensive exam, thesis (for some programs); for doctorate, comprehensive exam, thesis/dissertation, 2 tools of research as specified by dissertation committee. *Entrance requirements:* For master's, GRE, minimum GPA of 3.0 in last 60 hours of coursework, three letters of recommendation; one letter of recommendation, BS in engineering, and resume (for MSEM in engineering management); for doctorate, GRE, minimum GPA of 3.0 in last 60 hours of coursework, three letters of recommendation, statement of purpose. Additional exam requirements/recommendations for international students: Required—TOEFL (minimum score 550 paper-based; 213 computer-based; 79 iBT) or IELTS (minimum score 6.5). *Application deadline:* For fall admission, 2/15 for domestic students, 1/2 for international students; for spring admission, 10/15 for domestic students, 6/1 for international students. Application fee: $30. Electronic applications accepted. *Financial support:* In 2011–12, 31 students received support, including 20 research assistantships with partial tuition reimbursements available (averaging $16,748 per year), 11 teaching assistantships with partial tuition reimbursements available (averaging $15,000 per year); tuition waivers (partial) also available. Financial award applicants required to submit FAFSA. *Faculty research:* Bio-health engineering, engineering health care systems, energy markets, nanotechnology and nanomanufacturing, transportation and logistics, innovation in education. *Total annual research expenditures:* $501,470. *Unit head:* Dr. Jose Zayas-Castro, Chair, 813-974-2269, Fax: 813-974-5953, E-mail: josezaya@usf.edu. *Application contact:* Dr. Ali Yalcin, Program Coordinator, 813-974-5590, Fax: 813-974-5953, E-mail: ayalcin@usf.edu. Web site: http://imse.eng.usf.edu.

The University of Tennessee, Graduate School, College of Engineering, Department of Industrial and Information Engineering, Knoxville, TN 37966. Offers engineering management (MS); industrial engineering (MS, PhD); reliability and maintainability engineering (MS); MS/MBA. Part-time programs available. Postbaccalaureate distance learning degree programs offered (minimal on-campus study). *Faculty:* 7 full-time (1 woman), 14 part-time/adjunct (1 woman). *Students:* 51 full-time (11 women), 64 part-time (21 women); includes 21 minority (11 Black or African American, non-Hispanic/Latino; 1 American Indian or Alaska Native, non-Hispanic/Latino; 7 Asian, non-Hispanic/Latino; 1 Hispanic/Latino; 1 Native Hawaiian or other Pacific Islander, non-Hispanic/Latino), 27 international. Average age 28. 119 applicants, 50% accepted, 47 enrolled. In 2011, 13 master's, 4 doctorates awarded. *Degree requirements:* For master's, thesis or alternative; for doctorate, comprehensive exam, thesis/dissertation. *Entrance requirements:* For master's, GRE General Test (for MS students pursuing research thesis), minimum GPA of 2.7 (for U.S. degree holders), 3.0 (for international degree holders); for doctorate, College requires GRE General Test for all PhD candidates, minimum GPA of 3.0 on previous graduate course work. Additional exam requirements/recommendations for international students: Required—TOEFL (minimum score 550 paper-based; 213 computer-based). *Application deadline:* For fall admission, 2/1 priority date for domestic students, 2/1 for international students; for spring admission, 6/15 for domestic and international students. Applications are processed on a rolling basis. Application fee: $35. Electronic applications accepted. *Expenses:* Tuition, state resident: full-time $8332; part-time $464 per credit hour. Tuition, nonresident: full-time $25,174; part-time $1400 per credit hour. *Required fees:* $1162; $56 per credit hour. Tuition and fees vary according to program. *Financial support:* In 2011–12, 27 students received support, including 13 research assistantships with full tuition reimbursements available (averaging $17,355 per year), 10 teaching assistantships with full tuition reimbursements available (averaging $16,985 per year); career-related internships or fieldwork, Federal Work-Study, institutionally sponsored loans, health care benefits, and unspecified assistantships also available. Financial award application deadline: 2/1; financial award applicants required to submit FAFSA. *Faculty research:* Defense-oriented supply chain modeling; dependability and reliability of large computer networks; design of lean, reliable systems; new product development; operations research in the automotive industry. *Total annual research expenditures:* $800,000. *Unit head:* Dr. Rapinder Sawhney, Department Head, 865-974-3333, Fax: 865-974-0588, E-mail: sawhney@utk.edu. *Application contact:* Dr. Denise Jackson, Graduate Representative, 865-946-3248, E-mail: djackson@utk.edu. Web site: http://www.engr.utk.edu/ie/.

The University of Tennessee at Chattanooga, Graduate School, College of Engineering and Computer Science, Program in Engineering, Chattanooga, TN 37403. Offers chemical engineering (MS Engr); civil engineering (MS Engr); computational engineering (MS Engr); electrical engineering (MS Engr); industrial engineering (MS Engr); mechanical engineering (MS Engr). Part-time and evening/weekend programs available. *Faculty:* 27 full-time (3 women), 3 part-time/adjunct (1 woman). *Students:* 40 full-time (7 women), 41 part-time (11 women); includes 23 minority (10 Black or African American, non-Hispanic/Latino; 1 American Indian or Alaska Native, non-Hispanic/Latino; 6 Asian, non-Hispanic/Latino; 4 Hispanic/Latino; 2 Two or more races, non-Hispanic/Latino), 20 international. Average age 28. 89 applicants, 53% accepted, 29 enrolled. In 2011, 8 master's awarded. *Degree requirements:* For master's, comprehensive exam, thesis or alternative, engineering project. *Entrance requirements:* For master's, GRE General Test, minimum undergraduate GPA of 2.5 or 3.0 in last 30 hours of coursework. Additional exam requirements/recommendations for international students: Required—TOEFL (minimum score 550 paper-based; 213 computer-based; 79 iBT), IELTS (minimum score 6). *Application deadline:* For fall admission, 8/1 priority date for domestic students, 6/1 for international students; for spring admission, 12/1 priority date for domestic students, 10/1 for international students. Applications are processed on a rolling basis. Application fee: $35. Electronic applications accepted. *Expenses:* Tuition, state resident: full-time $6472; part-time $359 per credit hour. Tuition, nonresident: full-time $20,006; part-time $1111 per credit hour. *Required fees:* $1320; $160 per credit hour. *Financial support:* Career-related internships or fieldwork, scholarships/grants, and unspecified assistantships available. Support available to part-time students. *Faculty research:* Quality control and reliability engineering, financial management, thermal science, energy conservation, structural analysis. *Total annual research expenditures:* $3.5 million. *Unit head:* Dr. Neslihan Alp, Director, 423-425-4032, Fax: 423-425-5229, E-mail: neslihan-alp@utc.edu. *Application contact:* Dr. Jerald Ainsworth, Dean of Graduate Studies, 423-425-4478, Fax: 423-425-5223, E-mail: jerald-ainsworth@utc.edu. Web site: http://www.utc.edu/Departments/engrcs/ms_engr.php.

The University of Texas at Arlington, Graduate School, College of Engineering, Department of Industrial and Manufacturing Systems Engineering, Arlington, TX 76019. Offers engineering management (MS); industrial engineering (MS, PhD); logistics (MS); systems engineering (MS). Part-time and evening/weekend programs available.

Postbaccalaureate distance learning degree programs offered (no on-campus study). *Faculty:* 11 full-time (4 women). *Students:* 124 full-time (33 women), 80 part-time (16 women); includes 37 minority (12 Black or African American, non-Hispanic/Latino; 10 Asian, non-Hispanic/Latino; 14 Hispanic/Latino; 1 Two or more races, non-Hispanic/Latino), 125 international. 263 applicants, 80% accepted, 49 enrolled. In 2011, 66 master's, 8 doctorates awarded. Terminal master's awarded for partial completion of doctoral program. *Degree requirements:* For master's, comprehensive exam, thesis optional; for doctorate, comprehensive exam, thesis/dissertation. *Entrance requirements:* For master's and doctorate, GRE General Test, minimum GPA of 3.0. Additional exam requirements/recommendations for international students: Required—TOEFL (minimum score 550 paper-based; 213 computer-based). *Application deadline:* For fall admission, 6/6 for domestic students, 4/4 for international students; for spring admission, 10/15 for domestic students, 9/5 for international students. Applications are processed on a rolling basis. Application fee: $35 ($50 for international students). *Financial support:* In 2011–12, 50 students received support, including 9 fellowships (averaging $1,000 per year), 17 research assistantships (averaging $8,400 per year), 15 teaching assistantships (averaging $9,000 per year); career-related internships or fieldwork, Federal Work-Study, institutionally sponsored loans, scholarships/grants, and unspecified assistantships also available. Financial award application deadline: 6/1; financial award applicants required to submit FAFSA. *Faculty research:* Manufacturing, healthcare logistics, environmental systems, operations research, statistics. *Unit head:* Dr. Donald H. Liles, Chair, 817-272-3092, Fax: 817-272-3406, E-mail: dliles@uta.edu. *Application contact:* Dr. Sheik Imrhan, Graduate Advisor, 817-272-3167, Fax: 817-272-3406, E-mail: imrhan@uta.edu. Web site: http://ie.uta.edu/.

The University of Texas at Austin, Graduate School, Cockrell School of Engineering, Department of Mechanical Engineering, Program in Operations Research and Industrial Engineering, Austin, TX 78712-1111. Offers MS, PhD. *Entrance requirements:* For master's and doctorate, GRE General Test. Additional exam requirements/recommendations for international students: Required—TOEFL. Application fee: $50 ($75 for international students). *Financial support:* Fellowships, research assistantships, and teaching assistantships available. Financial award application deadline: 2/1. *Unit head:* David Morton, Program Coordinator, 512-471-4104, Fax: 512-471-8727, E-mail: morton@mail.utexas.edu. *Application contact:* John J. Hasenbein, Graduate Advisor, 512-471-3079, Fax: 512-471-1494, E-mail: jhas@mail.utexas.edu. Web site: http://www.me.utexas.edu/areas/orie/.

The University of Texas at El Paso, Graduate School, College of Engineering, Department of Industrial Engineering, El Paso, TX 79968-0001. Offers industrial engineering (MS); manufacturing engineering (MS); systems engineering (MS, Certificate). Part-time and evening/weekend programs available. *Students:* 107 (28 women); includes 60 minority (2 Black or African American, non-Hispanic/Latino; 1 Asian, non-Hispanic/Latino; 57 Hispanic/Latino), 44 international. Average age 34. 56 applicants, 91% accepted, 43 enrolled. In 2011, 27 master's awarded. *Degree requirements:* For master's, thesis optional. *Entrance requirements:* For master's, GRE General Test, minimum GPA of 3.0 in major. Additional exam requirements/recommendations for international students: Required—TOEFL. *Application deadline:* For fall admission, 7/1 priority date for domestic students, 3/1 for international students; for spring admission, 11/1 priority date for domestic students, 9/1 for international students. Applications are processed on a rolling basis. Application fee: $15 ($65 for international students). Electronic applications accepted. *Financial support:* In 2011–12, research assistantships with partial tuition reimbursements (averaging $21,125 per year), teaching assistantships with partial tuition reimbursements (averaging $16,900 per year) were awarded; fellowships with partial tuition reimbursements, Federal Work-Study, institutionally sponsored loans, scholarships/grants, and tuition waivers (partial) also available. Financial award application deadline: 3/15; financial award applicants required to submit FAFSA. *Faculty research:* Computer vision, automated inspection, simulation and modeling. *Unit head:* Dr. Rafael S. Gutierrez, Chair, 915-747-5450, Fax: 915-747-5019, E-mail: rsgutier@utep.edu. *Application contact:* Dr. Benjamin Flores, Interim Dean of the Graduate School, 915-747-5491, Fax: 915-747-5788, E-mail: bflores@utep.edu.

The University of Toledo, College of Graduate Studies, College of Engineering, Department of Mechanical, Industrial, and Manufacturing Engineering, Toledo, OH 43606-3390. Offers industrial engineering (MS, PhD); mechanical engineering (MS, PhD). Part-time programs available. Postbaccalaureate distance learning degree programs offered (minimal on-campus study). *Degree requirements:* For master's, thesis optional; for doctorate, thesis/dissertation, qualifying exam. *Entrance requirements:* For master's, GRE General Test, minimum GPA of 3.0; for doctorate, GRE General Test, minimum GPA of 3.3. Additional exam requirements/recommendations for international students: Required—TOEFL (minimum score 550 paper-based; 213 computer-based; 80 iBT). Electronic applications accepted. *Faculty research:* Computational and experimental thermal sciences, manufacturing process and systems, mechanics, materials, design, quality and management engineering systems.

University of Toronto, School of Graduate Studies, Faculty of Applied Science and Engineering, Department of Mechanical and Industrial Engineering, Toronto, ON M5S 1A1, Canada. Offers M Eng, MA Sc, PhD. Part-time programs available. *Degree requirements:* For master's, thesis (for some programs), oral exam/thesis defense (MA Sc); for doctorate, thesis/dissertation, thesis defense, qualifying examination. *Entrance requirements:* For master's, GRE (recommended), minimum B+ average in last 2 years of undergraduate study, 2 letters of reference, resume, Canadian citizenship or permanent residency (M Eng); for doctorate, GRE (recommended), minimum B+ average, 2 letters of reference, resume. Additional exam requirements/recommendations for international students: Required—TOEFL (580 paper-based, 237 computer-based), Michigan English Language Assessment Battery (85), IELTS (7) or COPE (4). Electronic applications accepted.

University of Washington, Graduate School, College of Engineering, Department of Industrial and Systems Engineering, Seattle, WA 98195-2650. Offers MS, PhD. Part-time programs available. Postbaccalaureate distance learning degree programs offered (no on-campus study). *Faculty:* 13 full-time (5 women), 4 part-time/adjunct (1 woman). *Students:* 22 full-time (8 women), 15 part-time (2 women); includes 6 minority (1 Black or African American, non-Hispanic/Latino; 3 Asian, non-Hispanic/Latino; 2 Hispanic/Latino), 19 international. Average age 29. 168 applicants, 27% accepted, 10 enrolled. In 2011, 13 master's, 6 doctorates awarded. Terminal master's awarded for partial completion of doctoral program. *Degree requirements:* For master's, thesis optional; for doctorate, comprehensive exam, thesis/dissertation, qualifying, general, and final exams. *Entrance requirements:* For master's, GRE General Test, minimum GPA of 3.0; bachelor's degree in engineering, math, or science; transcripts; letters of recommendation; resume; statement of objectives; for doctorate, GRE General Test, minimum GPA of 3.0; transcripts; letters of recommendation; resume; statement of objectives. Additional exam requirements/recommendations for international students: Required—TOEFL (minimum score 580 paper-based; 237 computer-based; 92 iBT);

Recommended—IELTS (minimum score 7). *Application deadline:* For fall admission, 2/1 priority date for domestic students, 1/1 for international students. Applications are processed on a rolling basis. Application fee: $75. Electronic applications accepted. *Expenses:* Contact institution. *Financial support:* In 2011–12, 58 students received support, including 3 fellowships (averaging $10,440 per year), 36 research assistantships with full tuition reimbursements available (averaging $14,751 per year), 18 teaching assistantships with full tuition reimbursements available (averaging $14,751 per year); career-related internships or fieldwork, scholarships/grants, traineeships, and tuition waivers (full) also available. Financial award application deadline: 2/1; financial award applicants required to submit FAFSA. *Faculty research:* Manufacturing, operations research, supply chain systems, human interface technology, quality control, logistics systems, bio-industrial systems. *Total annual research expenditures:* $645,000. *Unit head:* Dr. Richard Lee Storch, Professor/Chair, 206-543-1427, Fax: 206-685-3072, E-mail: rlstorch@u.washington.edu. *Application contact:* Jennifer W. Tsai, Academic Counselor, 206-543-5041, Fax: 206-685-3072, E-mail: ieadvise@u.washington.edu. Web site: http://depts.washington.edu/ie/.

University of Windsor, Faculty of Graduate Studies, Faculty of Engineering, Department of Industrial and Manufacturing Systems Engineering, Windsor, ON N9B 3P4, Canada. Offers industrial engineering (M Eng, MA Sc); manufacturing systems engineering (PhD). Part-time programs available. *Degree requirements:* For master's, thesis; for doctorate, comprehensive exam, thesis/dissertation. *Entrance requirements:* For master's, minimum B average; for doctorate, master's degree, minimum B average. Additional exam requirements/recommendations for international students: Required—TOEFL (minimum score 560 paper-based; 220 computer-based). Electronic applications accepted. *Faculty research:* Human factors, operations research.

University of Wisconsin–Madison, Graduate School, College of Engineering, Department of Industrial and Systems Engineering, Madison, WI 53706. Offers MS, PhD. Part-time programs available. *Faculty:* 21 full-time (6 women), 12 part-time/adjunct (4 women). *Students:* 99 full-time (32 women), 20 part-time (7 women); includes 12 minority (8 Black or African American, non-Hispanic/Latino; 1 American Indian or Alaska Native, non-Hispanic/Latino; 2 Asian, non-Hispanic/Latino; 1 Hispanic/Latino), 83 international. Average age 27. 500 applicants, 11% accepted, 39 enrolled. In 2011, 71 master's, 11 doctorates awarded. Terminal master's awarded for partial completion of doctoral program. *Degree requirements:* For master's, thesis optional; for doctorate, comprehensive exam, thesis/dissertation. *Entrance requirements:* For master's, GRE General Test, minimum GPA of 3.0, BS in engineering or equivalent, course work in computer programming and statistics; for doctorate, GRE General Test, minimum GPA of 3.0. Additional exam requirements/recommendations for international students: Required—IELTS (minimum score 6); Recommended—TOEFL (minimum score 550 paper-based; 213 computer-based; 80 iBT). *Application deadline:* For fall admission, 2/1 priority date for domestic students, 2/1 for international students; for spring admission, 10/1 priority date for domestic students, 10/1 for international students. Application fee: $56. Electronic applications accepted. *Expenses:* Tuition, state resident: full-time $10,296; part-time $643.51 per credit. Tuition, nonresident: full-time $24,054; part-time $1503.40 per credit. Required fees: $70.06 per credit. Tuition and fees vary according to course load, campus/location, program and reciprocity agreements. *Financial support:* In 2011–12, 87 students received support, including fellowships with full tuition reimbursements available (averaging $21,760 per year), 46 research assistantships with full tuition reimbursements available (averaging $40,800 per year), 8 teaching assistantships with full tuition reimbursements available (averaging $28,175 per year); career-related internships or fieldwork, Federal Work-Study, institutionally sponsored loans, scholarships/grants, traineeships, health care benefits, and unspecified assistantships also available. *Faculty research:* Human factors and ergonomics, manufacturing and production systems, health systems engineering, decision science/operations research, quality engineering. *Total annual research expenditures:* $10.2 million. *Unit head:* Dr. Vicki M. Bier, Chair, 608-262-2064, Fax: 608-262-8454, E-mail: bier@engr.wisc.edu. *Application contact:* Staci Rubenzer, Graduate Admissions Coordinator, 608-890-2248, Fax: 608-890-2204, E-mail: srubenzer@engr.wisc.edu. Web site: http://www.engr.wisc.edu/ie/.

University of Wisconsin–Milwaukee, Graduate School, College of Engineering and Applied Science, Program in Engineering, Milwaukee, WI 53201-0413. Offers civil engineering (MS); electrical and computer engineering (MS); energy engineering (Certificate); engineering (PhD); engineering management (MS); engineering mechanics (MS); ergonomics (Certificate); industrial and management engineering (MS); manufacturing engineering (MS); materials engineering (MS); mechanical engineering (MS); MUP/MS. Part-time programs available. *Faculty:* 41 full-time (5 women), 2 part-time/adjunct (0 women). *Students:* 170 full-time (33 women), 101 part-time (18 women); includes 30 minority (6 Black or African American, non-Hispanic/Latino; 15 Asian, non-Hispanic/Latino; 2 Hispanic/Latino; 7 Two or more races, non-Hispanic/Latino), 153 international. Average age 30. 170 applicants, 56% accepted, 48 enrolled. In 2011, 47 master's, 12 doctorates awarded. *Degree requirements:* For master's, comprehensive exam (for some programs), thesis or alternative; for doctorate, comprehensive exam, thesis/dissertation, internship. *Entrance requirements:* For master's, GRE, minimum GPA of 2.75; for doctorate, GRE, minimum GPA of 3.5. Additional exam requirements/recommendations for international students: Required—TOEFL (minimum score 550 paper-based; 79 iBT), IELTS (minimum score 6.5). *Application deadline:* For fall admission, 1/1 priority date for domestic students; for spring admission, 9/1 for domestic students. Applications are processed on a rolling basis. Application fee: $56 ($96 for international students). One-time fee: $506.10 full-time. Tuition and fees vary according to course load and reciprocity agreements. *Financial support:* In 2011–12, 3 fellowships, 55 research assistantships, 77 teaching assistantships were awarded; career-related internships or fieldwork, Federal Work-Study, unspecified assistantships, and project assistantships also available. Support available to part-time students. Financial award application deadline: 4/15. *Total annual research expenditures:* $10.3 million. *Unit head:* David Yu, Representative, 414-229-6169, E-mail: yu@uwm.edu. *Application contact:* Betty Warras, General Information Contact, 414-229-6169, Fax: 414-229-6967, E-mail: bwarras@uwm.edu. Web site: http://www.wum.edu/CEAS/.

University of Wisconsin–Stout, Graduate School, College of Technology, Engineering, and Management, MS Program in Risk Control, Menomonie, WI 54751. Offers MS. Part-time programs available. *Degree requirements:* For master's, thesis. *Entrance requirements:* For master's, minimum GPA of 3.0. Additional exam requirements/recommendations for international students: Required—TOEFL (minimum score 500 paper-based; 173 computer-based; 61 iBT). Electronic applications accepted. *Faculty research:* Environmental microbiology, water supply safety, facilities planning, industrial ventilation, bioterrorist.

Virginia Polytechnic Institute and State University, Graduate School, College of Engineering, Department of Industrial and Systems Engineering, Blacksburg, VA 24061. Offers human-system integration (Certificate); industrial and systems engineering (MEA, MS, PhD). *Degree requirements:* For master's, comprehensive exam (for some programs), thesis (for some programs); for doctorate, comprehensive exam (for some programs), thesis/dissertation (for some programs). *Entrance requirements:* For master's and doctorate, GRE. Additional exam requirements/recommendations for international students: Required—TOEFL (minimum score 550 paper-based; 213 computer-based). *Application deadline:* For fall admission, 7/1 for domestic and international students; for spring admission, 12/1 for domestic and international students. Applications are processed on a rolling basis. Application fee: $65. Electronic applications accepted. *Expenses:* Tuition, state resident: full-time $10,048; part-time $558.25 per credit hour. Tuition, nonresident: full-time $19,497; part-time $1083.25 per credit hour. *Required fees:* $405 per semester. Tuition and fees vary according to course load, campus/location and program. *Financial support:* Fellowships with full tuition reimbursements, research assistantships with full tuition reimbursements, teaching assistantships with full tuition reimbursements, career-related internships or fieldwork, Federal Work-Study, scholarships/grants, health care benefits, and unspecified assistantships available. Financial award application deadline: 1/15. *Unit head:* Dr. Gaylon D. Taylor, Unit Head, 540-231-4771, Fax: 540-231-3322, E-mail: taylorgd@vt.edu. *Application contact:* Jaime Camelio, Information Contact, 540-231-8976, Fax: 540-231-3322, E-mail: jcamelio@vt.edu. Web site: http://ise.vt.edu/.

Virginia Polytechnic Institute and State University, VT Online, Blacksburg, VA 24061. Offers advanced transportation systems (Certificate); aerospace engineering (MS); agricultural and life sciences (MSLFS); business information systems (Graduate Certificate); career and technical education (MS); civil engineering (MS); computer engineering (M Eng, MS); decision support systems (Graduate Certificate); eLearning leadership (MA); electrical engineering (M Eng, MS); engineering administration (MEA); environmental engineering (Certificate); environmental politics and policy (Graduate Certificate); environmental sciences and engineering (MS); foundations of political analysis (Graduate Certificate); health product risk management (Graduate Certificate); industrial and systems engineering (MS); information policy and society (Graduate Certificate); information security (Graduate Certificate); information technology (MIT); instructional technology (MA); integrative STEM education (MA Ed); liberal arts (Graduate Certificate); life sciences: health product risk management (MS); natural resources (MNR, Graduate Certificate); networking (Graduate Certificate); nonprofit and nongovernmental organization management (Graduate Certificate); ocean engineering (MS); political science (MA); security studies (Graduate Certificate); software development (Graduate Certificate). *Expenses:* Tuition, state resident: full-time $10,048; part-time $558.25 per credit hour. Tuition, nonresident: full-time $19,497; part-time $1083.25 per credit hour. *Required fees:* $405 per semester. Tuition and fees vary according to course load, campus/location and program. *Application contact:* Graduate School Applications General Assistance, 540-231-8636, Fax: 540-231-2039, E-mail: gradappl@vt.edu. Web site: http://www.vto.vt.edu/.

Wayne State University, College of Engineering, Department of Industrial and Manufacturing Engineering, Program in Industrial Engineering, Detroit, MI 48202. Offers MS, PhD. *Students:* 32 full-time (10 women), 38 part-time (11 women); includes 16 minority (7 Black or African American, non-Hispanic/Latino; 8 Asian, non-Hispanic/Latino; 1 Hispanic/Latino), 31 international. Average age 34. 129 applicants, 40% accepted, 11 enrolled. In 2011, 26 master's, 2 doctorates awarded. *Degree requirements:* For master's, thesis optional; for doctorate, thesis/dissertation. *Entrance requirements:* For master's, baccalaureate degree in engineering from an ABET-accredited institution, minimum undergraduate upper division GPA of 2.8; for doctorate, minimum graduate GPA of 3.5 in MS in industrial engineering or operations research. Additional exam requirements/recommendations for international students: Required—TOEFL (minimum score 550 paper-based; 213 computer-based); Recommended—TWE (minimum score 5.5). *Application deadline:* For fall admission, 6/1 priority date for domestic students, 5/1 for international students; for winter admission, 10/1 priority date for domestic students, 9/1 for international students; for spring admission, 2/1 priority date for domestic students, 1/1 for international students. Applications are processed on a rolling basis. Application fee: $50. Electronic applications accepted. *Expenses:* Tuition, state resident: part-time $512.85 per credit. Tuition, nonresident: part-time $1132.65 per credit. *Required fees:* $26.60 per credit. $199.65 per semester. Tuition and fees vary according to course load and program. *Financial support:* In 2011–12, 20 students received support. Fellowships with tuition reimbursements available, research assistantships with tuition reimbursements available, teaching assistantships with tuition reimbursements available, career-related internships or fieldwork, scholarships/grants, health care benefits, and unspecified assistantships available. *Faculty research:* Reliability and quality, technology management, manufacturing systems, operations research, concurrent engineering. *Unit head:* Dr. Leslie Monplaisir, Chair, 313-577-1645, E-mail: ad5365@wayne.edu. *Application contact:* Ratna Chinnam, Graduate Director, 313-577-4846, E-mail: ratna.chinnam@wayne.edu. Web site: http://ise.wayne.edu/.

Western Carolina University, Graduate School, Kimmel School of Construction Management and Technology, Department of Engineering and Technology, Cullowhee, NC 28723. Offers MS. Part-time programs available. *Students:* 12 full-time (1 woman), 7 part-time (2 women); includes 3 minority (1 Asian, non-Hispanic/Latino; 1 Hispanic/Latino; 1 Two or more races, non-Hispanic/Latino), 2 international. Average age 30. 15 applicants, 100% accepted, 11 enrolled. In 2011, 8 master's awarded. *Degree requirements:* For master's, comprehensive exam. *Entrance requirements:* For master's, GRE, appropriate undergraduate degree with minimum GPA of 3.0, 3 letters of recommendation. Additional exam requirements/recommendations for international students: Required—TOEFL (minimum score 550 paper-based; 270 computer-based; 79 iBT). *Application deadline:* For fall admission, 5/1 priority date for domestic students; for spring admission, 9/1 priority date for domestic students. Applications are processed on a rolling basis. Application fee: $50. *Expenses:* Tuition, state resident: full-time $3348. Tuition, nonresident: full-time $12,933. *Required fees:* $3155. *Financial support:* Fellowships, research assistantships with full and partial tuition reimbursements, teaching assistantships with full and partial tuition reimbursements, institutionally sponsored loans, scholarships/grants, and unspecified assistantships available. Financial award application deadline: 3/31; financial award applicants required to submit FAFSA. *Faculty research:* Electrophysiology, 3D graphics, digital signal processing, CAM and advanced machining, fluid power, polymer science, wireless communication. *Unit head:* Dr. Chip Ferguson, Department Head, 828-227-7368, Fax: 828-227-7838, E-mail: cferguson@wcu.edu. *Application contact:* Admissions Specialist for Engineering and Technology, 828-227-7398, Fax: 828-227-7480, E-mail: gradsch@email.wcu.edu. Web site: http://www.wcu.edu/3626.asp.

Western Michigan University, Graduate College, College of Engineering and Applied Sciences, Department of Industrial and Manufacturing Engineering, Program in Industrial Engineering, Kalamazoo, MI 49008. Offers MSE, PhD. *Entrance requirements:* For master's, minimum GPA of 3.0.

Western New England University, College of Engineering, Department of Industrial and Manufacturing Engineering, Springfield, MA 01119. Offers production management (MSEM). Part-time and evening/weekend programs available. *Students:* 36 part-time (7 women); includes 6 minority (1 Asian, non-Hispanic/Latino; 5 Hispanic/Latino), 1 international. *Degree requirements:* For master's, comprehensive exam, thesis optional. *Entrance requirements:* For master's, GRE, bachelor's degree in engineering or related field, two letters of recommendation, resume. *Application deadline:* Applications are processed on a rolling basis. Application fee: $30. *Financial support:* Available to part-time students. Applicants required to submit FAFSA. *Faculty research:* Project scheduling, flexible manufacturing systems, facility layout, energy management. *Unit head:* Dr. Eric W. Haffner, Chair, 413-782-1272, E-mail: ehaffner@wne.edu. *Application contact:* Matt Fox, Director of Recruiting and Marketing for Adult Learners, 413-782-1249, Fax: 413-782-1779, E-mail: study@wne.edu. Web site: http://www1.wne.edu/engineering/ie/index.cfm?selection-doc.2328.

West Virginia University, College of Engineering and Mineral Resources, Department of Industrial and Management Systems Engineering, Program in Industrial Engineering, Morgantown, WV 26506. Offers engineering (MSE); industrial engineering (MSIE, PhD). Part-time programs available. *Degree requirements:* For master's, thesis or alternative; for doctorate, comprehensive exam, thesis/dissertation. *Entrance requirements:* For master's, GRE General Test, minimum GPA of 3.0 Regular; 2.75 Provisional; for doctorate, GRE General Test, minimum GPA of 3.5. Additional exam requirements/recommendations for international students: Required—TOEFL (minimum score 550 paper-based; 213 computer-based; 80 iBT). Electronic applications accepted. *Faculty research:* Production planning and control, quality control, robotics and CIMS, ergonomics, castings.

Wichita State University, Graduate School, College of Engineering, Department of Industrial and Manufacturing Engineering, Wichita, KS 67260. Offers engineering management (MEM); industrial engineering (MS, PhD). Part-time programs available. In 2011, 37 master's, 3 doctorates awarded. *Entrance requirements:* Additional exam requirements/recommendations for international students: Required—TOEFL. *Expenses:* Tuition, state resident: full-time $4746; part-time $263.65 per credit. Tuition, nonresident: full-time $11,669; part-time $648.30 per credit. *Financial support:* Teaching assistantships available. *Unit head:* Dr. Krishna Krishnan, Chair, 316-978-3425, Fax: 316-978-3742, E-mail: krishna.krishnan@wichita.edu. *Application contact:* Carrie C. Henderson, Admissions Coordinator, 316-978-3095, Fax: 316-978-3253, E-mail: carrie.henderson@wichita.edu. Web site: http://www.wichita.edu/.

Youngstown State University, Graduate School, College of Science, Technology, Engineering and Mathematics, Department of Industrial and Systems Engineering, Youngstown, OH 44555-0001. Offers MSE.

Manufacturing Engineering

Arizona State University, College of Technology and Innovation, Department of Engineering Technology, Mesa, AZ 85212. Offers technology (alternative energy technologies) (MS); technology (electronic systems engineering technology) (MS); technology (integrated electronic systems) (MS); technology (manufacturing engineering technology) (MS). Part-time and evening/weekend programs available. *Degree requirements:* For master's, thesis or applied project and oral defense, final examination, interactive Program of Study (iPOS) submitted before completing 50 percent of required credit hours. *Entrance requirements:* For master's, bachelor's degree with minimum of 30 credit hours or equivalent in a technology area including course work applicable to the concentration being sought and minimum of 16 credit hours of math and science; industrial experience beyond bachelor's degree (recommended). Additional exam requirements/recommendations for international students: Required—TOEFL (minimum score 83 iBT), TOEFL, IELTS, or Pearson Test of English. Electronic applications accepted. *Faculty research:* Manufacturing modeling and simulation &ITsmart&RO and composite materials, optimization of turbine engines, machinability and manufacturing processes design, fuel cells and other alternative energy sources.

Boston University, College of Engineering, Department of Mechanical Engineering, Boston, MA 02215. Offers global manufacturing (MS); manufacturing engineering (M Eng, MS); mechanical engineering (M Eng, MS, PhD); MS/MBA. Part-time programs available. Postbaccalaureate distance learning degree programs offered (no on-campus study). *Faculty:* 38 full-time (5 women), 1 part-time/adjunct (0 women). *Students:* 109 full-time (13 women), 19 part-time (8 women); includes 15 minority (2 Black or African American, non-Hispanic/Latino; 6 Asian, non-Hispanic/Latino; 3 Hispanic/Latino; 4 Two or more races, non-Hispanic/Latino), 58 international. Average age 26. 298 applicants, 21% accepted, 30 enrolled. In 2011, 45 master's, 13 doctorates awarded. Terminal master's awarded for partial completion of doctoral program. *Degree requirements:* For master's, thesis (for some programs); for doctorate, comprehensive exam, thesis/dissertation. *Entrance requirements:* For master's and doctorate, GRE General Test. Additional exam requirements/recommendations for international students: Required—TOEFL (minimum score 550 paper-based; 213 computer-based; 84 iBT), IELTS (minimum score 6.5). *Application deadline:* For fall admission, 3/15 for domestic and international students; for spring admission, 10/1 for domestic and international students. Application fee: $70. Electronic applications accepted. *Expenses: Tuition:* Full-time $40,848; part-time $1276 per credit hour. *Required fees:* $572; $286 per semester. *Financial support:* In 2011–12, 81 students received support, including 13 fellowships with full tuition reimbursements available (averaging $28,950 per year), 41 research assistantships with full tuition reimbursements available (averaging $19,300 per year), 19 teaching assistantships with full tuition reimbursements available (averaging $19,300 per year); career-related internships or fieldwork, Federal Work-Study, institutionally sponsored loans, scholarships/grants, health care benefits, and tuition waivers (full and partial) also available. Financial award application deadline: 1/15; financial award applicants required to submit FAFSA. *Faculty research:* Acoustics, ultrasound, and vibrations; biomechanics; dynamics, control, and robotics; energy and thermofluid sciences; MEMS and nanotechnology. *Total annual research expenditures:* $11 million. *Unit head:* Dr. Ronald A. Roy, Chairman, 617-353-2814, Fax: 617-353-5866, E-mail: ronroy@bu.edu. *Application contact:* Stephen Doherty, Director of Graduate Programs, 617-353-9760, Fax: 617-353-0259, E-mail: enggrad@bu.edu. Web site: http://www.bu.edu/me/.

Bowling Green State University, Graduate College, College of Technology, Department of Technology Systems, Bowling Green, OH 43403. Offers construction management (MIT); manufacturing technology (MIT). Part-time programs available. *Degree requirements:* For master's, thesis or alternative. *Entrance requirements:* For master's, GRE General Test. Additional exam requirements/recommendations for international students: Required—TOEFL. Electronic applications accepted.

Bradley University, Graduate School, College of Engineering and Technology, Department of Industrial and Manufacturing Engineering and Technology, Peoria, IL 61625-0002. Offers industrial engineering (MSIE); manufacturing engineering (MSIE). Part-time and evening/weekend programs available. *Degree requirements:* For master's, comprehensive exam, project. *Entrance requirements:* For master's, minimum GPA of 3.0. Additional exam requirements/recommendations for international students: Required—TOEFL (minimum score 550 paper-based; 213 computer-based; 79 iBT).

California State University, Northridge, Graduate Studies, College of Engineering and Computer Science, Department of Manufacturing Systems Engineering and Management, Northridge, CA 91330. Offers engineering automation (MS); engineering management (MS); manufacturing systems engineering (MS); materials engineering (MS). Postbaccalaureate distance learning degree programs offered. *Entrance requirements:* For master's, GRE (if cumulative undergraduate GPA less than 3.0).

Clemson University, Graduate School, College of Agriculture, Forestry and Life Sciences, Department of Food, Nutrition and Packaging Sciences, Program of Packaging Science, Clemson, SC 29634. Offers MS. *Faculty:* 7 full-time (2 women), 1 part-time/adjunct (0 women). *Students:* 11 full-time (7 women), 2 part-time (1 woman); includes 2 minority (1 Asian, non-Hispanic/Latino; 1 Hispanic/Latino). Average age 27. 29 applicants, 21% accepted, 3 enrolled. In 2011, 2 master's awarded. *Entrance requirements:* For master's, GRE General Test. *Application deadline:* For fall admission, 4/15 for international students; for spring admission, 9/15 for international students. Applications are processed on a rolling basis. Application fee: $70 ($80 for international students). Electronic applications accepted. *Expenses:* Contact institution. *Financial support:* In 2011–12, 10 students received support, including 5 research assistantships with partial tuition reimbursements available (averaging $7,708 per year), 3 teaching assistantships with partial tuition reimbursements available (averaging $9,333 per year); fellowships with full and partial tuition reimbursements available, career-related internships or fieldwork, institutionally sponsored loans, scholarships/grants, health care benefits, and unspecified assistantships also available. Support available to part-time students. *Total annual research expenditures:* $143,855. *Unit head:* Dr. Anthony Pometto, III, Department Chair, 864-656-4382, Fax: 864-656-0331, E-mail: pometto@clemson.edu. *Application contact:* Dr. Ron Thomas, Coordinator, 864-656-5697, Fax: 864-656-4395, E-mail: rthms@clemson.edu. Web site: http://workgroups.clemson.edu/CAFLS0320_PACKAGING_SCIENCE/index.php.

Cornell University, Graduate School, Graduate Fields of Engineering, Field of Operations Research and Information Engineering, Ithaca, NY 14853. Offers applied probability and statistics (PhD); manufacturing systems engineering (PhD); mathematical programming (PhD); operations research and industrial engineering (M Eng). *Faculty:* 38 full-time (6 women). *Students:* 172 full-time (47 women); includes 25 minority (2 Black or African American, non-Hispanic/Latino; 19 Asian, non-Hispanic/Latino; 4 Hispanic/Latino), 120 international. Average age 24. 1,070 applicants, 24% accepted, 106 enrolled. In 2011, 93 master's, 6 doctorates awarded. *Degree requirements:* For doctorate, comprehensive exam, thesis/dissertation. *Entrance requirements:* For master's and doctorate, GRE General Test, 3 letters of recommendation. Additional exam requirements/recommendations for international students: Required—TOEFL (minimum score 600 paper-based; 250 computer-based; 100 iBT). *Application deadline:* For fall admission, 12/15 for domestic students. Application fee: $95. Electronic applications accepted. *Financial support:* In 2011–12, 44 students received support, including 11 fellowships with full tuition reimbursements available, 13 research assistantships with full tuition reimbursements available, 19 teaching assistantships with full tuition reimbursements available; institutionally sponsored loans, scholarships/grants, health care benefits, tuition waivers (full and partial), and unspecified assistantships also available. Financial award applicants required to submit FAFSA. *Faculty research:* Mathematical programming and combinatorial optimization, statistics, stochastic processes, mathematical finance, simulation, manufacturing, e-commerce. *Unit head:* Director of Graduate Studies, 607-255-9128, Fax: 607-255-9129. *Application contact:* Graduate Field Assistant, 607-255-9128, Fax: 607-255-9129, E-mail: orie@cornell.edu. Web site: http://www.gradschool.cornell.edu/fields.php?id-35&a-2.

East Carolina University, Graduate School, College of Technology and Computer Science, Department of Technology Systems, Greenville, NC 27858-4353. Offers computer network professional (Certificate); industrial technology (MS), including computer networking management, digital communications, industrial distribution and logistics, information security, manufacturing, performance improvement, quality systems; information assurance (Certificate); Lean Six Sigma Black Belt (Certificate); occupational safety (MS); technology management (PhD); Website developer (Certificate). *Entrance requirements:* For master's and Certificate, GRE General Test or MAT, minimum GPA of 2.5; for doctorate, GRE General Test, related work experience. *Application deadline:* For fall admission, 6/1 priority date for domestic students. Applications are processed on a rolling basis. Application fee: $50. *Expenses:* Tuition, state resident: full-time $3557; part-time $444.63 per semester hour. Tuition, nonresident: full-time $14,351; part-time $1793.88 per semester hour. *Required fees:* $2016; $252 per semester hour. Part-time tuition and fees vary according to course load, campus/location and program. *Financial support:* Application deadline: 6/1. *Unit head:* Dr. Tijjani Mohammed, Interim Chair, 252-328-9668, E-mail: mohammedt@ecu.edu. Web site: http://www.ecu.edu/cs-tecs/techsystems/.

Eastern Kentucky University, The Graduate School, College of Business and Technology, Department of Technology, Richmond, KY 40475-3102. Offers industrial education (MS), including occupational training and development, technical administration, technology education; industrial technology (MS). Part-time and evening/weekend programs available. *Entrance requirements:* For master's, GRE General Test, minimum GPA of 2.5. *Faculty research:* Lunar excavation, computer networking, integrating academic and vocational education.

East Tennessee State University, School of Graduate Studies, College of Business and Technology, Department of Engineering Technology, Surveying and Digital Media, Johnson City, TN 37614. Offers entrepreneurial leadership (Postbaccalaureate Certificate); technology (MS), including digital media, engineering technology, entrepreneurial leadership. Part-time programs available. *Faculty:* 16 full-time (1 woman), 2 part-time/adjunct (0 women). *Students:* 24 full-time (7 women), 17 part-time (2 women); includes 9 minority (4 Black or African American, non-Hispanic/Latino; 2 Asian, non-Hispanic/Latino; 2 Hispanic/Latino; 1 Two or more races, non-Hispanic/Latino), 2 international. Average age 32. 37 applicants, 68% accepted, 9 enrolled. In 2011, 24 master's awarded. *Degree requirements:* For master's, comprehensive exam,

thesis optional, strategic experience, capstone; for Postbaccalaureate Certificate, strategic experience. *Entrance requirements:* For master's, bachelor's degree in technical or related area, minimum GPA of 3.0; for Postbaccalaureate Certificate, minimum GPA of 2.5, three letters of recommendation. Additional exam requirements/recommendations for international students: Required—TOEFL (minimum score 550 paper-based; 213 computer-based; 79 iBT). *Application deadline:* For fall admission, 6/1 for domestic students, 4/30 for international students; for spring admission, 11/1 for domestic students, 9/30 for international students. Application fee: $35 ($45 for international students). Electronic applications accepted. *Expenses:* Tuition, state resident: full-time $7312; part-time $350 per credit hour. Tuition, nonresident: full-time $18,490; part-time $621 per credit hour. *Required fees:* $63 per credit hour. Tuition and fees vary according to course load and program. *Financial support:* In 2011–12, 20 students received support, including 12 research assistantships with full tuition reimbursements available (averaging $6,000 per year); career-related internships or fieldwork, institutionally sponsored loans, scholarships/grants, and unspecified assistantships also available. Financial award application deadline: 7/1; financial award applicants required to submit FAFSA. *Faculty research:* Computer-integrated manufacturing, alternative energy, sustainability, CAD/CAM, organizational change. *Unit head:* Dr. Keith V. Johnson, Chair, 423-439-7822, Fax: 423-439-7750, E-mail: johnsonk@etsu.edu. *Application contact:* Bethany Glassbrenner, Graduate Specialist, 423-439-6165, Fax: 423-439-5624, E-mail: glassbrenner@etsu.edu.

Florida State University, The Graduate School, FAMU-FSU College of Engineering, Department of Industrial and Manufacturing Engineering, Tallahassee, FL 32306. Offers industrial engineering (MS, PhD). *Faculty:* 10 full-time (1 woman), 1 (woman) part-time/adjunct. *Students:* 34 full-time (6 women), 2 part-time (1 woman); includes 9 minority (8 Black or African American, non-Hispanic/Latino; 1 Hispanic/Latino), 18 international. Average age 24. 66 applicants, 26% accepted, 8 enrolled. In 2011, 7 degrees awarded. *Degree requirements:* For master's, thesis; for doctorate, thesis/dissertation, preliminary exam, qualifying exam. *Entrance requirements:* For master's, GRE General Test (minimum score of 400 Verbal and 650 Quantitative), minimum GPA of 3.0; for doctorate, GRE General Test (minimum score of 450 Verbal and 700 Quantitative), minimum GPA of 3.0 (without MS in industrial engineering), 3.4 (with MS in industrial engineering). Additional exam requirements/recommendations for international students: Required—TOEFL (minimum score 550 paper-based; 213 computer-based; 80 iBT). *Application deadline:* For fall admission, 7/1 for domestic students, 3/1 for international students; for spring admission, 11/1 for domestic students, 7/1 for international students. Applications are processed on a rolling basis. Application fee: $30. *Expenses:* Tuition, state resident: full-time $9474; part-time $350.88 per credit hour. Tuition, nonresident: full-time $16,236; part-time $601.34 per credit hour. *Required fees:* $630 per semester. One-time fee: $20. Tuition and fees vary according to course load and campus/location. *Financial support:* In 2011–12, 33 students received support, including 1 fellowship with full and partial tuition reimbursement available (averaging $42,000 per year), 28 research assistantships with full tuition reimbursements available (averaging $18,361 per year), 5 teaching assistantships with full tuition reimbursements available (averaging $15,628 per year); tuition waivers (full) also available. Financial award application deadline: 6/15. *Faculty research:* Precision manufacturing, composite manufacturing, green manufacturing, applied optimization, simulation. *Unit head:* Dr. Chun Zhang, Chair and Professor, 850-410-6355, Fax: 850-410-6342, E-mail: chzhang@eng.fsu.edu. *Application contact:* Stephanie Salters, Office Manager, 850-410-6345, Fax: 850-410-6342, E-mail: salters@eng.fsu.edu. Web site: http://www.eng.fsu.edu/departments/industrial/.

Grand Valley State University, Padnos College of Engineering and Computing, School of Engineering, Allendale, MI 49401-9403. Offers electrical and computer engineering (MSE); manufacturing operations (MSE); mechanical engineering (MSE); product design and manufacturing engineering (MSE). Part-time and evening/weekend programs available. *Degree requirements:* For master's, project or thesis. *Entrance requirements:* For master's, engineering degree, minimum GPA of 3.0. Additional exam requirements/recommendations for international students: Required—TOEFL. Electronic applications accepted. *Faculty research:* Digital signal processing, computer aided design, computer aided manufacturing, manufacturing simulation, biomechanics, product design.

Illinois Institute of Technology, Graduate College, Armour College of Engineering, Department of Mechanical, Materials and Aerospace Engineering, Chicago, IL 60616-3793. Offers manufacturing engineering (MME, MS); materials science and engineering (MMME, MS, PhD); mechanical and aerospace engineering (MMAE, MS, PhD), including economics (MS), energy (MS), environment (MS). Part-time and evening/weekend programs available. Postbaccalaureate distance learning degree programs offered (minimal on-campus study). Terminal master's awarded for partial completion of doctoral program. *Degree requirements:* For master's, comprehensive exam (for some programs), thesis (for some programs); for doctorate, comprehensive exam, thesis/dissertation. *Entrance requirements:* For master's and doctorate, GRE General Test (minimum score 1000 Quantitative and Verbal, 3.0 Analytical Writing), minimum undergraduate GPA of 3.0. Additional exam requirements/recommendations for international students: Required—TOEFL (minimum score 523 paper-based; 70 iBT); Recommended—IELTS (minimum score 5.5). Electronic applications accepted. *Faculty research:* Fluid dynamics, metallurgical and materials engineering, solids and structures, computational mechanics, theoretical mechanics.

Instituto Tecnológico y de Estudios Superiores de Monterrey, Campus Monterrey, Graduate and Research Division, Programs in Engineering, Monterrey, Mexico. Offers applied statistics (M Eng); artificial intelligence (PhD); automation engineering (M Eng); chemical engineering (M Eng); civil engineering (M Eng); electrical engineering (M Eng); electronic engineering (M Eng); environmental engineering (M Eng); industrial engineering (M Eng, PhD); manufacturing engineering (M Eng); mechanical engineering (M Eng); systems and quality engineering (M Eng). M Eng program offered jointly with University of Waterloo; PhD in industrial engineering with Texas A&M University. Part-time and evening/weekend programs available. Terminal master's awarded for partial completion of doctoral program. *Degree requirements:* For master's, one foreign language, thesis; for doctorate, one foreign language, thesis/dissertation. *Entrance requirements:* For master's, EXADEP; for doctorate, GRE, master's degree in related field. Additional exam requirements/recommendations for international students: Required—TOEFL. *Faculty research:* Flexible manufacturing cells, materials, statistical methods, environmental prevention, control and evaluation.

Kansas State University, Graduate School, College of Engineering, Department of Industrial and Manufacturing Systems Engineering, Manhattan, KS 66506. Offers engineering management (MEM); industrial engineering (MS, PhD); operations research (MS). Part-time programs available. Postbaccalaureate distance learning degree programs offered. *Faculty:* 12 full-time (3 women), 4 part-time/adjunct (1 woman). *Students:* 43 full-time (11 women), 57 part-time (14 women); includes 8 minority (1 Black or African American, non-Hispanic/Latino; 1 Asian, non-Hispanic/Latino; 2 Hispanic/Latino; 4 Two or more races, non-Hispanic/Latino), 34 international. Average age 29. 94

applicants, 46% accepted, 14 enrolled. In 2011, 21 master's, 3 doctorates awarded. *Degree requirements:* For master's, thesis or alternative; for doctorate, thesis/dissertation. *Entrance requirements:* For master's, GRE General Test (minimum 750 [old version], 159 [new format] on Quantitative portion of exam), bachelor's degree in engineering, mathematics, or physical science; for doctorate, GRE General Test (minimum 770 [old version], 164 [new format] on Quantitative portion of exam), master's degree in engineering or industrial manufacturing. Additional exam requirements/recommendations for international students: Required—TOEFL (minimum score 550 paper-based; 79 iBT) or IELTS (minimum score 6.5). *Application deadline:* For fall admission, 6/1 priority date for domestic students, 2/1 for international students; for spring admission, 11/1 priority date for domestic students, 8/1 for international students. Applications are processed on a rolling basis. Application fee: $40 ($55 for international students). Electronic applications accepted. *Financial support:* In 2011–12, 15 research assistantships (averaging $12,412 per year), 1 teaching assistantship with full tuition reimbursement (averaging $12,000 per year) were awarded; Federal Work-Study, institutionally sponsored loans, and scholarships/grants also available. Support available to part-time students. Financial award application deadline: 3/1; financial award applicants required to submit FAFSA. *Faculty research:* Industrial engineering, ergonomics, healthcare systems engineering, manufacturing processes, operations research, engineering management. *Total annual research expenditures:* $645,655. *Unit head:* Bradley Kramer, Head, 785-532-5606, Fax: 785-532-3738, E-mail: bradleyk@ksu.edu. *Application contact:* David Ben-Arieh, Chair of Graduate Committee, 785-532-5606, Fax: 785-532-3738, E-mail: imse@ksu.edu. Web site: http://imse.ksu.edu/.

Kettering University, Graduate School, Department of Industrial and Manufacturing Engineering, Flint, MI 48504. Offers engineering (MS). Part-time and evening/weekend programs available. Postbaccalaureate distance learning degree programs offered (no on-campus study). *Faculty:* 3 full-time (2 women), 1 part-time/adjunct (0 women). *Students:* 8 part-time (0 women); includes 1 minority (Asian, non-Hispanic/Latino). Average age 36. 2 applicants, 100% accepted, 0 enrolled. In 2011, 3 master's awarded. *Degree requirements:* For master's, thesis optional. *Entrance requirements:* Additional exam requirements/recommendations for international students: Required—TOEFL (minimum score 550 paper-based; 213 computer-based; 79 iBT). *Application deadline:* For fall admission, 9/15 for domestic students, 6/15 for international students; for winter admission, 12/15 for domestic students, 9/5 for international students; for spring admission, 3/15 for domestic students, 12/5 for international students. Applications are processed on a rolling basis. Application fee: $0. Electronic applications accepted. *Expenses: Tuition:* Full-time $11,456; part-time $716 per credit hour. *Financial support:* In 2011–12, 1 student received support, including fellowships with full tuition reimbursements available (averaging $13,000 per year), research assistantships with full tuition reimbursements available (averaging $13,000 per year), teaching assistantships with full tuition reimbursements available (averaging $13,000 per year); Federal Work-Study, scholarships/grants, and tuition waivers (partial) also available. Support available to part-time students. Financial award application deadline: 7/15; financial award applicants required to submit CSS PROFILE or FAFSA. *Faculty research:* Machine part testing, office procedure study. *Total annual research expenditures:* $25,000. *Unit head:* Dr. W. L. Scheller, Department Head, 810-762-7974, Fax: 810-762-9924, E-mail: wschelle@kettering.edu. *Application contact:* Bonnie Switzer, Admissions Representative, 810-762-7953, Fax: 810-762-9935, E-mail: bswitzer@kettering.edu. Web site: http://www.kettering.edu/.

Lawrence Technological University, College of Engineering, Southfield, MI 48075-1058. Offers architectural engineering (MS); automotive engineering (MS); civil engineering (MA, MS); construction engineering management (MA); electrical and computer engineering (MS); engineering management (MEM); industrial engineering (MS); manufacturing systems (ME, DE); mechanical engineering (MS, DE); mechatronic systems engineering (MS). Part-time and evening/weekend programs available. *Faculty:* 25 full-time (4 women), 20 part-time/adjunct (1 woman). *Students:* 8 full-time (0 women), 332 part-time (52 women); includes 58 minority (21 Black or African American, non-Hispanic/Latino; 1 American Indian or Alaska Native, non-Hispanic/Latino; 32 Asian, non-Hispanic/Latino; 2 Hispanic/Latino; 2 Two or more races, non-Hispanic/Latino), 84 international. Average age 32. 652 applicants, 44% accepted, 70 enrolled. In 2011, 127 master's, 2 doctorates awarded. *Degree requirements:* For master's, thesis (for some programs). *Entrance requirements:* Additional exam requirements/recommendations for international students: Required—TOEFL (minimum score 550 paper-based; 213 computer-based; 79 iBT). *Application deadline:* For fall admission, 7/27 priority date for domestic students, 5/23 for international students; for spring admission, 11/15 priority date for domestic students, 11/15 for international students. Applications are processed on a rolling basis. Application fee: $50. Electronic applications accepted. *Financial support:* In 2011–12, 68 students received support, including 6 research assistantships (averaging $8,078 per year); Federal Work-Study and institutionally sponsored loans also available. Support available to part-time students. Financial award application deadline: 4/1; financial award applicants required to submit FAFSA. *Faculty research:* Advanced composite materials in bridges, strengthening existing bridges with carbon and glass fiber sheets, development of drive shafts using composite materials. *Unit head:* Dr. Nabil Grace, Dean, 248-204-2500, Fax: 248-204-2509, E-mail: engrdean@ltu.edu. *Application contact:* Jane Rohrback, Director of Admissions, 248-204-3160, Fax: 248-204-2228, E-mail: admissions@ltu.edu. Web site: http://www.ltu.edu/engineering/index.asp.

Lehigh University, P.C. Rossin College of Engineering and Applied Science, Program in Manufacturing Systems Engineering, Bethlehem, PA 18015. Offers MS, MBA/E. Part-time and evening/weekend programs available. Postbaccalaureate distance learning degree programs offered (no on-campus study). *Faculty:* 1 full-time (0 women). *Students:* 27 part-time (10 women); includes 3 minority (1 Asian, non-Hispanic/Latino; 2 Hispanic/Latino). Average age 35. 38 applicants, 26% accepted, 9 enrolled. In 2011, 5 degrees awarded. *Degree requirements:* For master's, comprehensive exam, project or thesis. *Entrance requirements:* For master's, GRE General Test, minimum GPA of 2.75. Additional exam requirements/recommendations for international students: Required—TOEFL (minimum score 620 paper-based; 260 computer-based; 85 iBT). *Application deadline:* For fall admission, 7/15 for domestic and international students; for spring admission, 12/1 for domestic and international students. Applications are processed on a rolling basis. Application fee: $75. Electronic applications accepted. *Faculty research:* Manufacturing systems design, development, and implementation; accounting and management; agile/lean systems; supply chain issues; sustainable systems design; product design. *Unit head:* Dr. Keith M. Gardiner, Director, 610-758-5070, Fax: 610-758-6527, E-mail: kg03@lehigh.edu. *Application contact:* Carolyn C. Jones, Graduate Coordinator, 610-758-5157, Fax: 610-758-6527, E-mail: ccj1@lehigh.edu. Web site: http://www.lehigh.edu/~inmse/gradprogram/.

Massachusetts Institute of Technology, School of Engineering, Department of Mechanical Engineering, Cambridge, MA 02139. Offers manufacturing (M Eng); mechanical engineering (SM, PhD, Sc D, Mech E); naval architecture and marine engineering (SM, PhD, Sc D); naval engineering (Naval E); ocean engineering (SM, PhD, Sc D), including); oceanographic engineering (SM, PhD, Sc D); SM/MBA. *Faculty:* 68 full-time (8 women). *Students:* 540 full-time (111 women), 1 part-time (0 women); includes 98 minority (9 Black or African American, non-Hispanic/Latino; 1 American Indian or Alaska Native, non-Hispanic/Latino; 52 Asian, non-Hispanic/Latino; 29 Hispanic/Latino; 7 Two or more races, non-Hispanic/Latino), 220 international. Average age 26. 881 applicants, 27% accepted, 142 enrolled. In 2011, 123 master's, 56 doctorates, 11 other advanced degrees awarded. Terminal master's awarded for partial completion of doctoral program. *Degree requirements:* For master's and other advanced degree, thesis; for doctorate, comprehensive exam, thesis/dissertation. *Entrance requirements:* For master's, doctorate, and other advanced degree, GRE General Test. Additional exam requirements/recommendations for international students: Required—IELTS (minimum score 7). *Application deadline:* For fall admission, 12/15 for domestic and international students. Application fee: $75. Electronic applications accepted. *Expenses: Tuition:* Full-time $40,460; part-time $630 per credit hour. *Required fees:* $272. *Financial support:* In 2011–12, 447 students received support, including 95 fellowships (averaging $30,800 per year), 318 research assistantships (averaging $29,200 per year), 45 teaching assistantships (averaging $33,000 per year); career-related internships or fieldwork, Federal Work-Study, institutionally sponsored loans, scholarships/grants, health care benefits, and unspecified assistantships also available. *Faculty research:* Mechanics: modeling, experimentation and computation; design, manufacturing, and product development; controls, instrumentation, and robotics; energy science and engineering; ocean science and engineering; bioengineering; micro and nano engineering. *Total annual research expenditures:* $50.9 million. *Unit head:* Prof. Mary C. Boyce, Head, 617-253-2201, Fax: 617-258-6156, E-mail: mehq@mit.edu. *Application contact:* Graduate Office, 617-253-2291, Fax: 617-258-5802, E-mail: me-gradoffice@mit.edu. Web site: http://meche.mit.edu.

Michigan State University, The Graduate School, College of Agriculture and Natural Resources, School of Packaging, East Lansing, MI 48824. Offers MS, PhD. *Entrance requirements:* Additional exam requirements/recommendations for international students: Required—TOEFL. Electronic applications accepted.

Minnesota State University Mankato, College of Graduate Studies, College of Science, Engineering and Technology, Department of Automotive and Manufacturing Engineering Technology, Mankato, MN 56001. Offers manufacturing engineering technology (MS). *Students:* 9 full-time (2 women), 10 part-time (1 woman). *Degree requirements:* For master's, comprehensive exam, thesis. *Entrance requirements:* For master's, GRE General Test (if GPA less than 3.0), minimum GPA of 3.0 during previous 2 years. Additional exam requirements/recommendations for international students: Required—TOEFL. *Application deadline:* For fall admission, 7/1 priority date for domestic students; for spring admission, 11/1 for domestic students. Applications are processed on a rolling basis. Application fee: $40. Electronic applications accepted. *Financial support:* Research assistantships with full tuition reimbursements, teaching assistantships with full tuition reimbursements, and unspecified assistantships available. Financial award application deadline: 3/15; financial award applicants required to submit FAFSA. *Unit head:* Dr. Bruce Jones, Graduate Coordinator, 507-389-6700. *Application contact:* 507-389-2321, E-mail: grad@mnsu.edu.

Missouri University of Science and Technology, Graduate School, Department of Engineering Management and Systems Engineering, Rolla, MO 65409. Offers engineering management (MS, DE, PhD); manufacturing engineering (M Eng, MS); systems engineering (MS, PhD). *Degree requirements:* For master's, thesis optional; for doctorate, comprehensive exam. *Entrance requirements:* For master's, GRE (minimum score 1150 verbal and quantitative, 4.5 writing); for doctorate, GRE (minimum score: 1100 verbal and quantitative, 3.5 writing). Additional exam requirements/recommendations for international students: Required—TOEFL (minimum score 580 paper-based; 213 computer-based). *Faculty research:* Management of technology, industrial engineering, manufacturing engineering, packaging engineering, quality engineering.

New Jersey Institute of Technology, Office of Graduate Studies, Newark College of Engineering, Department of Mechanical Engineering, Program in Manufacturing Engineering, Newark, NJ 07102. Offers MS. Part-time and evening/weekend programs available. *Students:* 1 full-time (0 women), 4 part-time (1 woman); includes 4 minority (1 Asian, non-Hispanic/Latino; 3 Hispanic/Latino). Average age 30. 13 applicants, 85% accepted, 3 enrolled. In 2011, 5 master's awarded. *Degree requirements:* For master's, thesis or alternative. *Entrance requirements:* For master's, GRE General Test. Additional exam requirements/recommendations for international students: Required—TOEFL (minimum score 550 paper-based; 213 computer-based; 79 iBT). *Application deadline:* For fall admission, 6/1 priority date for domestic students, 5/1 for international students; for spring admission, 11/15 priority date for domestic students, 11/15 for international students. Applications are processed on a rolling basis. Application fee: $65. Electronic applications accepted. *Expenses:* Tuition, state resident: full-time $7980; part-time $867 per credit. Tuition, nonresident: full-time $11,336; part-time $1196 per credit. *Required fees:* $230 per credit. *Financial support:* Fellowships with full and partial tuition reimbursements, research assistantships with full and partial tuition reimbursements, teaching assistantships with full and partial tuition reimbursements, career-related internships or fieldwork, Federal Work-Study, institutionally sponsored loans, and unspecified assistantships available. Financial award application deadline: 3/15. *Faculty research:* Knowledge-based systems, CAS/CAM simulation and interface, expert system. *Unit head:* Dr. Sanchoy Das, Director, 973-596-3654, Fax: 973-596-3652, E-mail: sanchoy.k.das@njit.edu. *Application contact:* Kathryn Kelly, Director of Admissions, 973-596-3300, Fax: 973-596-3461, E-mail: admissions@njit.edu. Web site: http://mechanical.njit.edu/academics/graduate/ms-manufacturing.php.

North Carolina State University, Graduate School, College of Engineering, Integrated Manufacturing Systems Engineering Institute, Raleigh, NC 27695. Offers MIMS. Part-time programs available. *Degree requirements:* For master's, thesis optional. *Entrance requirements:* For master's, GRE. Additional exam requirements/recommendations for international students: Required—TOEFL. Electronic applications accepted. *Faculty research:* Mechatronics, manufacturing systems modeling, systems integration product and process engineering, logistics.

North Dakota State University, College of Graduate and Interdisciplinary Studies, College of Engineering and Architecture, Department of Industrial and Manufacturing Engineering, Fargo, ND 58108. Offers industrial and manufacturing engineering (PhD); industrial engineering and management (MS); manufacturing engineering (MS). Part-time programs available. *Faculty:* 9 full-time (2 women). *Students:* 12 full-time (1 woman), 15 part-time (4 women); includes 1 minority (Asian, non-Hispanic/Latino), 25 international. Average age 26. 25 applicants, 36% accepted, 3 enrolled. In 2011, 4 master's awarded. *Degree requirements:* For doctorate, comprehensive exam, thesis/dissertation. *Entrance requirements:* For master's, GRE General Test, bachelor's degree in engineering; for doctorate, GRE General Test, master's degree in engineering. Additional exam requirements/recommendations for international students:

Required—TOEFL (minimum score 550 paper-based; 213 computer-based; 79 iBT), TWE (minimum score 4). *Application deadline:* For fall admission, 5/1 for international students; for spring admission, 8/1 for international students. Applications are processed on a rolling basis. Application fee: $35. Electronic applications accepted. *Financial support:* In 2011–12, 2 fellowships with full tuition reimbursements (averaging $15,000 per year), 9 research assistantships with full tuition reimbursements (averaging $12,000 per year), 16 teaching assistantships with full tuition reimbursements (averaging $12,000 per year) were awarded; Federal Work-Study, institutionally sponsored loans, scholarships/grants, and unspecified assistantships also available. Financial award application deadline: 4/1. *Faculty research:* Electronics manufacturing, quality engineering, manufacturing process science, healthcare, lean manufacturing. *Unit head:* Dr. John Cook, Chair, 701-231-7285, Fax: 701-231-7195, E-mail: john.cook@ndsu.edu. *Application contact:* Dr. Om Prakash Yadav, Graduate Program Coordinator, 701-231-7285, Fax: 701-231-7195, E-mail: om.yadav@ndsu.edu.

Northeastern University, College of Engineering, Department of Mechanical, Industrial, and Manufacturing Engineering, Boston, MA 02115-5096. Offers engineering management (MS); industrial engineering (MS, PhD); mechanical engineering (MS, PhD); operations research (MS). Part-time programs available. *Faculty:* 34 full-time, 7 part-time/adjunct. *Students:* 297 full-time (70 women), 103 part-time (20 women). 616 applicants, 77% accepted, 140 enrolled. In 2011, 107 master's, 5 doctorates awarded. *Degree requirements:* For master's, thesis (for some programs); for doctorate, thesis/dissertation, departmental qualifying exam. *Entrance requirements:* For master's and doctorate, GRE General Test. Additional exam requirements/recommendations for international students: Required—TOEFL (minimum score 550 paper-based; 213 computer-based; 80 iBT). *Application deadline:* For fall admission, 1/15 priority date for domestic students, 1/15 for international students; for spring admission, 11/1 priority date for domestic students. Applications are processed on a rolling basis. Application fee: $50. Electronic applications accepted. *Financial support:* In 2011–12, 79 students received support, including 50 research assistantships with full tuition reimbursements available (averaging $18,325 per year), 33 teaching assistantships with full tuition reimbursements available (averaging $18,325 per year); fellowships with full tuition reimbursements available, career-related internships or fieldwork, Federal Work-Study, scholarships/grants, health care benefits, and unspecified assistantships also available. Support available to part-time students. Financial award application deadline: 1/15; financial award applicants required to submit FAFSA. *Faculty research:* Dry sliding instabilities, droplet deposition, combustion, manufacturing systems, nano-manufacturing, advanced materials processing, bio-nano robotics, burning speed measurement, virtual environments. *Unit head:* Dr. Hameed Metghalchi, Chairman, 617-373-2973, Fax: 617-373-2921. *Application contact:* Jeffery Hengel, Admissions Specialist, 617-373-2711, Fax: 617-373-2501, E-mail: grad-eng@coe.neu.edu.

Oregon State University, Graduate School, College of Engineering, School of Mechanical, Industrial, and Manufacturing Engineering, Corvallis, OR 97331. Offers human systems engineering (MS, PhD); industrial engineering (MS, PhD); information systems engineering (MS, PhD); manufacturing engineering (M Engr); manufacturing systems engineering (MS, PhD); materials science (MAIS, MS, PhD); mechanical engineering (MS, PhD); nano/micro fabrication (MS, PhD). Part-time programs available. Postbaccalaureate distance learning degree programs offered (minimal on-campus study). *Degree requirements:* For master's, thesis or alternative; for doctorate, thesis/dissertation. *Entrance requirements:* For master's, placement exam, minimum GPA of 3.0 in last 90 hours of course work; for doctorate, GRE, placement exam, minimum GPA of 3.0 in last 90 hours of course work. Additional exam requirements/recommendations for international students: Required—TOEFL (minimum score 550 paper-based; 213 computer-based). *Faculty research:* Computer-integrated manufacturing, human factors, robotics, decision support systems, simulation modeling and analysis.

Polytechnic Institute of New York University, Department of Interdisciplinary Studies, Major in Manufacturing Engineering, Brooklyn, NY 11201-2990. Offers MS. Part-time and evening/weekend programs available. *Students:* 4 full-time (0 women), 8 part-time (1 woman); includes 5 minority (3 Black or African American, non-Hispanic/Latino; 2 Asian, non-Hispanic/Latino), 3 international. Average age 29. 14 applicants, 71% accepted, 1 enrolled. In 2011, 18 master's awarded. *Degree requirements:* For master's, comprehensive exam (for some programs), thesis (for some programs). *Entrance requirements:* For master's, BE or BS in engineering, physics, chemistry, mathematical sciences, or biological sciences or MBA. Additional exam requirements/recommendations for international students: Required—TOEFL (minimum score 550 paper-based; 213 computer-based; 80 iBT); Recommended—IELTS (minimum score 6.5). *Application deadline:* For fall admission, 7/31 priority date for domestic students, 4/30 for international students; for spring admission, 12/31 priority date for domestic students, 11/30 for international students. Applications are processed on a rolling basis. Application fee: $75. Electronic applications accepted. *Expenses: Tuition:* Full-time $22,464; part-time $1248 per credit. *Required fees:* $501 per semester. *Financial support:* Institutionally sponsored loans, scholarships/grants, and unspecified assistantships available. Support available to part-time students. Financial award applicants required to submit FAFSA. *Unit head:* Prof. Michael Greenstein, Department Head, 718-260-3835, E-mail: mgreenst@poly.edu. *Application contact:* JeanCarlo Bonilla, Director, Graduate Enrollment Management, 718-260-3182, Fax: 718-260-3624, E-mail: gradinfo@poly.edu.

Polytechnic Institute of NYU, Long Island Graduate Center, Graduate Programs, Department of Mechanical and Aerospace Engineering, Melville, NY 11747. Offers aeronautics and astronautics (MS); industrial engineering (MS); manufacturing engineering (MS); mechanical engineering (MS). Part-time and evening/weekend programs available. *Students:* 1 full-time (0 women). Average age 28. In 2011, 2 master's awarded. *Degree requirements:* For master's, comprehensive exam (for some programs), thesis (for some programs). *Entrance requirements:* Additional exam requirements/recommendations for international students: Required—TOEFL (minimum score 550 paper-based; 213 computer-based; 80 iBT); Recommended—IELTS (minimum score 6.5). *Application deadline:* For fall admission, 7/31 priority date for domestic students, 4/30 for international students; for spring admission, 12/31 priority date for domestic students, 11/30 for international students. Applications are processed on a rolling basis. Application fee: $75. Electronic applications accepted. *Financial support:* In 2011–12, 16 fellowships with tuition reimbursements (averaging $1,394 per year) were awarded; research assistantships with tuition reimbursements, institutionally sponsored loans, scholarships/grants, and unspecified assistantships also available. Support available to part-time students. Financial award applicants required to submit FAFSA. *Faculty research:* UV filter, fuel efficient hydrodynamic containment for gas core fission, turbulent boundary layer research. *Unit head:* Dr. George Vradis, Department Head, 718-260-3875, E-mail: gvradis@duke.poly.edu. *Application contact:* JeanCarlo Bonilla, Director of Graduate Enrollment Management, 718-260-3182, Fax: 718-260-3624, E-mail: gradinfo@poly.edu.

Polytechnic Institute of NYU, Long Island Graduate Center, Graduate Programs, Major in Manufacturing Engineering, Melville, NY 11747. Offers MS. Part-time and evening/weekend programs available. *Entrance requirements:* Additional exam requirements/recommendations for international students: Required—TOEFL (minimum score 550 paper-based; 213 computer-based; 80 iBT); Recommended—IELTS (minimum score 6.5). *Application deadline:* For fall admission, 7/31 priority date for domestic students, 4/30 for international students; for spring admission, 12/31 priority date for domestic students, 11/30 for international students. Applications are processed on a rolling basis. Application fee: $75. Electronic applications accepted. *Financial support:* Institutionally sponsored loans, scholarships/grants, and unspecified assistantships available. Support available to part-time students. *Unit head:* Dr. Frank Cassara, Director, Long Island Graduate Center, 631-755-4360, Fax: 516-755-4404, E-mail: cassara@poly.edu. *Application contact:* JeanCarlo Bonilla, Director of Graduate Enrollment Management, 718-260-3182, Fax: 718-260-3624, E-mail: gradinfo@poly.edu.

Polytechnic University of Puerto Rico, Graduate School, Hato Rey, PR 00919. Offers business administration (MBA), including computer information systems, general management, management of information systems, management of international enterprises; civil engineering (ME, MS); computer engineering (ME, MS); computer science (MCS, MS); electrical engineering (ME, MS); engineering management (MEM); environmental management (MEM); landscape architecture (M Land Arch); manufacturing competitiveness (MMC, MS); manufacturing engineering (ME, MS); mechanical engineering (M Mech E). Part-time and evening/weekend programs available. *Entrance requirements:* For master's, 3 letters of recommendation.

Portland State University, Graduate Studies, Maseeh College of Engineering and Computer Science, Department of Engineering and Technology Management, Portland, OR 97207-0751. Offers engineering and technology management (M Eng); engineering management (MS); manufacturing engineering (ME); manufacturing management (M Eng); systems science/engineering management (PhD); MS/MBA; MS/MS. Part-time and evening/weekend programs available. *Degree requirements:* For master's, thesis optional; for doctorate, one foreign language, thesis/dissertation, oral and written exams. *Entrance requirements:* For master's, minimum GPA of 3.0 in upper-division course work, BS in civil engineering; for doctorate, GRE General Test, GRE Subject Test, minimum GPA of 3.0 in upper-division course work. Additional exam requirements/recommendations for international students: Required—TOEFL (minimum score 550 paper-based; 213 computer-based). *Faculty research:* Scheduling, hierarchical decision modeling, operations research, knowledge-based information systems.

Rochester Institute of Technology, Graduate Enrollment Services, College of Applied Science and Technology, School of Engineering Technology, Department of Electrical, Computer and Telecommunications Engineering Technology, Rochester, NY 14623-5603. Offers facility management (MS); manufacturing and mechanical systems integration (MS); telecommunications engineering technology (MS). Part-time and evening/weekend programs available. Postbaccalaureate distance learning degree programs offered (no on-campus study). *Students:* 54 full-time (13 women), 34 part-time (6 women); includes 7 minority (4 Black or African American, non-Hispanic/Latino; 1 Asian, non-Hispanic/Latino; 1 Hispanic/Latino; 1 Two or more races, non-Hispanic/Latino), 70 international. Average age 26. 154 applicants, 55% accepted, 32 enrolled. In 2011, 24 master's awarded. *Degree requirements:* For master's, thesis. *Entrance requirements:* For master's, GRE, minimum GPA of 3.0. Additional exam requirements/recommendations for international students: Required—TOEFL (minimum score 550 paper-based; 213 computer-based; 79 iBT) or IELTS (minimum score 6.5). *Application deadline:* For fall admission, 2/15 priority date for domestic students, 2/15 for international students; for winter admission, 11/1 for domestic and international students; for spring admission, 2/1 for domestic and international students. Applications are processed on a rolling basis. Application fee: $50. Electronic applications accepted. *Expenses: Tuition:* Full-time $34,659; part-time $963 per credit hour. *Required fees:* $228; $76 per quarter. *Financial support:* Research assistantships with partial tuition reimbursements, teaching assistantships with partial tuition reimbursements, career-related internships or fieldwork, and unspecified assistantships available. Support available to part-time students. Financial award application deadline: 2/15; financial award applicants required to submit FAFSA. *Faculty research:* Fiber optic networks, next generation networks, project management. *Unit head:* Michael Eastman, Department Chair, 585-475-7787, Fax: 585-475-2178, E-mail: mgeiee@rit.edu. *Application contact:* Diane Ellison, Assistant Vice President, Graduate Enrollment Services, 585-475-2229, Fax: 585-475-7164, E-mail: gradinfo@rit.edu. Web site: http://www.rit.edu/cast/ectet/.

Rochester Institute of Technology, Graduate Enrollment Services, College of Applied Science and Technology, School of Engineering Technology, Department of Manufacturing and Mechanical Engineering Technology/Packaging Science, Program in Manufacturing and Mechanical Systems Integration, Rochester, NY 14623-5603. Offers MS. Part-time and evening/weekend programs available. *Students:* 13 full-time (3 women), 13 part-time (0 women), 8 international. Average age 25. 18 applicants, 67% accepted, 8 enrolled. In 2011, 10 master's awarded. *Degree requirements:* For master's, thesis. *Entrance requirements:* For master's, GRE, minimum GPA of 3.0. Additional exam requirements/recommendations for international students: Required—TOEFL (minimum score 550 paper-based; 213 computer-based; 79 iBT) or IELTS (minimum score 6.5). *Application deadline:* For fall admission, 2/15 priority date for domestic students, 2/15 for international students; for winter admission, 11/1 for domestic and international students; for spring admission, 2/1 for domestic and international students. Applications are processed on a rolling basis. Application fee: $50. Electronic applications accepted. *Expenses: Tuition:* Full-time $34,659; part-time $963 per credit hour. *Required fees:* $228; $76 per quarter. *Financial support:* Research assistantships with partial tuition reimbursements, teaching assistantships with partial tuition reimbursements, career-related internships or fieldwork, scholarships/grants, and unspecified assistantships available. Support available to part-time students. Financial award application deadline: 2/15; financial award applicants required to submit FAFSA. *Faculty research:* Biodegradable plastics, health physics, nuclear engineering technology, solidworks, automative engineering, compression strength, protective package development. *Unit head:* Dr. S. Manian Ramkumar, Graduate Program Director, 585-475-6081, Fax: 585-475-5227, E-mail: smrmet@rit.edu. *Application contact:* Diane Ellison, Assistant Vice President, Graduate Enrollment Services, 585-475-2229, Fax: 585-475-7164, E-mail: gradinfo@rit.edu. Web site: http://www.rit.edu/cast/mmetps/ms-in-manufacturing-and-mechanical-systems-integration.php.

Rochester Institute of Technology, Graduate Enrollment Services, College of Applied Science and Technology, School of Engineering Technology, Department of Manufacturing and Mechanical Engineering Technology/Packaging Science, Program in Packaging Science, Rochester, NY 14623-5603. Offers MS. Part-time programs available. *Students:* 22 full-time (9 women), 5 part-time (3 women); includes 1 minority (Asian, non-Hispanic/Latino), 17 international. Average age 28. 28 applicants, 86% accepted, 12 enrolled. In 2011, 9 degrees awarded. *Degree requirements:* For master's, thesis or project. *Entrance requirements:* Additional exam requirements/recommendations for international students: Required—TOEFL (minimum score 550 paper-based; 213 computer-based; 79 iBT) or IELTS (minimum score 6). *Application deadline:* Applications are processed on a rolling basis. Application fee: $50. Electronic applications accepted. *Expenses: Tuition:* Full-time $34,659; part-time $963 per credit hour. *Required fees:* $228; $76 per quarter. *Unit head:* Deanna Jacobs, Chair, 585-475-6801, E-mail: dmjipk@rit.edu. *Application contact:* Diane Ellison, Assistant Vice President, Graduate Enrollment Services, 585-475-2229, Fax: 585-475-7164, E-mail: gradinfo@rit.edu. Web site: http://www.rit.edu/cast/mmetps/ms-in-packaging-science.php.

Rochester Institute of Technology, Graduate Enrollment Services, Kate Gleason College of Engineering, Department of Industrial and Systems Engineering, Rochester, NY 14623-5603. Offers engineering management (ME); industrial engineering (ME, MS); manufacturing engineering (ME, MS); systems engineering (ME). Part-time programs available. *Students:* 58 full-time (13 women), 31 part-time (13 women); includes 3 minority (1 Black or African American, non-Hispanic/Latino; 1 Asian, non-Hispanic/Latino; 1 Hispanic/Latino), 59 international. Average age 25. 231 applicants, 44% accepted, 34 enrolled. In 2011, 49 degrees awarded. *Degree requirements:* For master's, internship. *Entrance requirements:* For master's, GRE, minimum GPA of 3.0. Additional exam requirements/recommendations for international students: Required—TOEFL (minimum score 570 paper-based; 230 computer-based; 88 iBT) or IELTS (minimum score 6.5). *Application deadline:* For fall admission, 2/15 priority date for domestic students, 2/15 for international students. Applications are processed on a rolling basis. Application fee: $50. *Expenses: Tuition:* Full-time $34,659; part-time $963 per credit hour. *Required fees:* $228; $76 per quarter. *Financial support:* Research assistantships with partial tuition reimbursements, teaching assistantships with partial tuition reimbursements, career-related internships or fieldwork, institutionally sponsored loans, scholarships/grants, tuition waivers (partial), and unspecified assistantships available. Support available to part-time students. Financial award applicants required to submit FAFSA. *Faculty research:* Operations; manufacturing systems and sustainable product design; product development and design robustness; lean manufacturing; ergonomics/human factors; simulation, systems engineering; rapid prototyping, rapid manufacturing. *Unit head:* Dr. Scott E. Grasman, Interim Department Head, 585-475-2598, E-mail: scott.grasman@rit.edu. *Application contact:* Diane Ellison, Assistant Vice President, Graduate Enrollment Services, 585-475-2229, Fax: 585-475-7164, E-mail: gradinfo@rit.edu.

Rochester Institute of Technology, Graduate Enrollment Services, Kate Gleason College of Engineering, Department of Microelectronic Engineering, Program in Microelectronic Manufacturing Engineering, Rochester, NY 14623-5603. Offers ME, MS. Part-time programs available. *Students:* 4 full-time (0 women), 7 part-time (3 women); includes 1 minority (Asian, non-Hispanic/Latino), 6 international. Average age 29. 14 applicants, 57% accepted, 4 enrolled. In 2011, 2 degrees awarded. *Degree requirements:* For master's, thesis (for some programs). *Entrance requirements:* Additional exam requirements/recommendations for international students: Required—TOEFL (minimum score 570 paper-based; 230 computer-based; 88 iBT) or IELTS (minimum score 6.5). *Application deadline:* For fall admission, 2/15 for domestic and international students. *Expenses: Tuition:* Full-time $34,659; part-time $963 per credit hour. *Required fees:* $228; $76 per quarter. *Financial support:* Available to part-time students. Applicants required to submit FAFSA. *Faculty research:* Semiconductor modeling; analog integrated circuits; thin-film transistors; signal/image processing, digital communications, and control; semiconductor devices, processes and electrical characterization; phase adaptive optics, nano/microlithography and design of experiments. *Unit head:* Dr. Robert Pearson, Graduate Program Director, 585-475-2923, Fax: 585-475-5845, E-mail: eme@rit.edu. *Application contact:* Diane Ellison, Assistant Vice President, Graduate Enrollment Services, 585-475-2229, Fax: 585-475-7164, E-mail: gradinfo@rit.edu.

Southern Illinois University Carbondale, Graduate School, College of Engineering, Program in Manufacturing Systems, Carbondale, IL 62901-4701. Offers MS. *Faculty:* 11 full-time (1 woman). *Students:* 18 full-time (3 women), 9 part-time (0 women); includes 6 minority (4 Black or African American, non-Hispanic/Latino; 1 Asian, non-Hispanic/Latino; 1 Hispanic/Latino), 3 international. Average age 25. 21 applicants, 95% accepted, 9 enrolled. In 2011, 11 master's awarded. *Degree requirements:* For master's, comprehensive exam, thesis. *Entrance requirements:* For master's, minimum GPA of 2.7. Additional exam requirements/recommendations for international students: Required—TOEFL. *Application deadline:* Applications are processed on a rolling basis. Application fee: $20. *Financial support:* In 2011–12, 1 fellowship with full tuition reimbursement, 3 research assistantships with full tuition reimbursements, 9 teaching assistantships with full tuition reimbursements were awarded; tuition waivers (full) also available. Financial award application deadline: 7/1. *Faculty research:* Computer-aided manufacturing, robotics, quality assurance. *Total annual research expenditures:* $205,198. *Unit head:* Mandara Savage, Interim Chair, 618-536-3396. *Application contact:* Jeanne Baker, Administrative Clerk, 618-536-3396, E-mail: jeanne@engr.siu.edu.

Southern Methodist University, Bobby B. Lyle School of Engineering, Department of Mechanical Engineering, Dallas, TX 75205. Offers electronic and optical packaging (MS); manufacturing systems management (MS); mechanical engineering (MSME, PhD). Part-time and evening/weekend programs available. Postbaccalaureate distance learning degree programs offered (no on-campus study). Terminal master's awarded for partial completion of doctoral program. *Degree requirements:* For master's, thesis optional; for doctorate, thesis/dissertation, oral and written qualifying exams, oral final exam. *Entrance requirements:* For master's, GRE General Test, minimum GPA of 3.0 in last 2 years; bachelor's degree in engineering, mathematics, or sciences; for doctorate, preliminary counseling exam, minimum graduate GPA of 3.0, bachelor's degree in related field. Additional exam requirements/recommendations for international students: Required—TOEFL. *Faculty research:* Design, systems, and controls; thermal and fluid sciences.

Stevens Institute of Technology, Graduate School, Charles V. Schaefer Jr. School of Engineering, Department of Mechanical Engineering, Program in Integrated Product Development, Hoboken, NJ 07030. Offers armament engineering (M Eng); computer and electrical engineering (M Eng); manufacturing technologies (M Eng); systems reliability and design (M Eng).

Texas A&M University, College of Engineering, Department of Engineering Technology and Industrial Distribution, College Station, TX 77843. Offers industrial distribution (MID). *Faculty:* 11. *Students:* 27 full-time (2 women); includes 5 minority (all Hispanic/Latino), 1 international. In 2011, 11 master's awarded. *Entrance requirements:* Additional exam requirements/recommendations for international students: Required—TOEFL. *Application deadline:* For fall admission, 3/1 priority date for domestic students, 3/1 for international students; for spring admission, 8/1 priority date for domestic students, 8/1 for international students. Applications are processed on a rolling basis. Application fee: $50 ($75 for international students). Electronic applications accepted. *Expenses:* Tuition, state resident: full-time $5437; part-time $226.55 per credit hour. Tuition, nonresident: full-time $12,949; part-time $539.55 per credit hour. *Required fees:* $2741. *Financial support:* Application deadline: 2/1. *Unit head:* Dr. Walter W. Buchanan, Head, 979-862-4945, E-mail: buchanan@entc.tamu.edu. *Application contact:* Graduate Admissions, 979-458-0427, E-mail: admissions@tamu.edu. Web site: http://etidweb.tamu.edu.

Tufts University, Graduate School of Arts and Sciences, Graduate Certificate Programs, Manufacturing Engineering Program, Medford, MA 02155. Offers Certificate. Part-time and evening/weekend programs available. Electronic applications accepted. *Expenses: Tuition:* Full-time $41,208; part-time $1030 per credit hour. Full-time tuition and fees vary according to degree level, program and student level. Part-time tuition and fees vary according to course load.

Universidad Autonoma de Guadalajara, Graduate Programs, Guadalajara, Mexico. Offers administrative law and justice (LL M); advertising and corporate communications (MA); architecture (M Arch); business (MBA); computational science (MCC); education (Ed M, Ed D); English-Spanish translation (MA); entrepreneurship and management (MBA); integrated management of digital animation (MA); international business (MIB); international corporate law (LL M); internet technologies (MS); manufacturing systems (MMS); occupational health (MS); philosophy (MA, PhD); power electronics (MS); quality systems (MQS); renewable energy (MS); social evaluation of projects (MBA); strategic market research (MBA); tax law (MA); teaching mathematics (MA).

Universidad de las Américas–Puebla, Division of Graduate Studies, School of Engineering, Program in Manufacturing Administration, Puebla, Mexico. Offers MS. *Faculty research:* Operations research, construction.

University of Calgary, Faculty of Graduate Studies, Schulich School of Engineering, Department of Mechanical and Manufacturing Engineering, Calgary, AB T2N 1N4, Canada. Offers M Eng, M Sc, PhD. *Degree requirements:* For master's, thesis (for some programs); for doctorate, thesis/dissertation, candidacy exam. *Entrance requirements:* For master's, minimum GPA of 3.0; for doctorate, minimum GPA of 3.3. Additional exam requirements/recommendations for international students: Required—TOEFL (minimum score 550 paper-based; 213 computer-based), IELTS (minimum score 7). *Faculty research:* Thermofluids, solid mechanics, materials, biomechanics, manufacturing.

University of California, Los Angeles, Graduate Division, Henry Samueli School of Engineering and Applied Science, Department of Mechanical and Aerospace Engineering, Program in Manufacturing Engineering, Los Angeles, CA 90095-1597. Offers MS. *Faculty:* 29 full-time (2 women), 6 part-time/adjunct. *Students:* 8 applicants, 25% accepted, 0 enrolled. *Degree requirements:* For master's, comprehensive exam or thesis. *Entrance requirements:* For master's, GRE General Test, minimum GPA of 3.0. Additional exam requirements/recommendations for international students: Required—TOEFL (minimum score 560 paper-based; 87 iBT). *Application deadline:* For fall admission, 12/15 for domestic and international students; for winter admission, 10/1 for domestic students; for spring admission, 12/31 for domestic students. Application fee: $80 ($100 for international students). Electronic applications accepted. *Financial support:* Fellowships, research assistantships, teaching assistantships, Federal Work-Study, institutionally sponsored loans, and tuition waivers (full and partial) available. Financial award application deadline: 12/15; financial award applicants required to submit FAFSA. *Unit head:* Dr. Tsu-Chin Tsao, Chair, 310-206-2819, E-mail: ttsao@seas.ucla.edu. *Application contact:* Angie Castillo, Student Affairs Officer, 310-825-7793, Fax: 310-206-4830, E-mail: angie@ea.ucla.edu. Web site: http://www.mae.ucla.edu/.

University of Colorado at Colorado Springs, College of Engineering and Applied Science, Department of Mechanical and Aerospace Engineering, Colorado Springs, CO 80933-7150. Offers engineering management (ME); information operations (ME); manufacturing (ME); mechanical engineering (MS); software engineering (ME); space operations (ME); space systems (MS). Part-time and evening/weekend programs available. *Faculty:* 11 full-time (2 women). *Students:* 48 full-time (14 women), 44 part-time (11 women); includes 15 minority (3 Black or African American, non-Hispanic/Latino; 6 Asian, non-Hispanic/Latino; 5 Hispanic/Latino; 1 Two or more races, non-Hispanic/Latino), 3 international. Average age 33. 40 applicants, 60% accepted, 13 enrolled. In 2011, 31 degrees awarded. *Degree requirements:* For master's, thesis optional. *Entrance requirements:* For master's, GRE General Test, bachelor's degree in engineering or related degree, minimum GPA of 3.0. Additional exam requirements/recommendations for international students: Required—TOEFL (minimum score 550 paper-based; 213 computer-based; 79 iBT). *Application deadline:* For fall admission, 3/1 for domestic and international students; for spring admission, 10/1 for domestic and international students. Applications are processed on a rolling basis. Application fee: $60 ($75 for international students). *Expenses:* Tuition, state resident: part-time $660 per credit hour. Tuition, nonresident: part-time $1133 per credit hour. Tuition and fees vary according to degree level, program and student level. *Financial support:* In 2011–12, 5 students received support. Federal Work-Study and scholarships/grants available. Support available to part-time students. Financial award application deadline: 3/1; financial award applicants required to submit FAFSA. *Faculty research:* Neural networks, artificial intelligence, robust control, space operations, space propulsion. *Total annual research expenditures:* $163,405. *Unit head:* Rebecca Webb, Director, 719-255-3581, Fax: 719-255-3674, E-mail: rwebb@uccs.edu. *Application contact:* Siew Nylund, Academic Adviser, 719-255-3243, Fax: 719-255-3589, E-mail: snylund@eas.uccs.edu. Web site: http://eas.uccs.edu/mae/.

The University of Iowa, Graduate College, College of Engineering, Department of Industrial Engineering, Iowa City, IA 52242-1316. Offers engineering design and manufacturing (MS, PhD); ergonomics (MS, PhD); information and engineering management (MS, PhD); operations research (MS, PhD); quality engineering (MS, PhD). *Faculty:* 7 full-time (0 women). *Students:* 21 full-time (6 women); includes 2 minority (1 Black or African American, non-Hispanic/Latino; 1 Asian, non-Hispanic/Latino), 14 international. Average age 27. 69 applicants, 13% accepted, 5 enrolled. In 2011, 8 master's, 6 doctorates awarded. *Degree requirements:* For master's, thesis optional, exam; for doctorate, comprehensive exam, thesis/dissertation, final defense exam. *Entrance requirements:* For master's and doctorate, GRE General Test. Additional exam requirements/recommendations for international students: Required—TOEFL (minimum score 550 paper-based; 213 computer-based; 81 iBT). *Application deadline:* For fall admission, 7/15 for domestic students, 4/15 for international students; for spring admission, 12/1 for domestic students, 10/1 for international students. Applications are processed on a rolling basis. Application fee: $60 ($100 for international students). Electronic applications accepted. *Financial support:* In 2011–12, 5 fellowships with partial tuition reimbursements (averaging $30,450 per year), 17 research assistantships with partial tuition reimbursements (averaging $20,000 per year), 5 teaching assistantships with partial tuition reimbursements (averaging $16,630 per year) were awarded; career-related internships or fieldwork, scholarships/grants, and unspecified assistantships also available. Support available to part-time students.

Financial award applicants required to submit FAFSA. *Faculty research:* Operations research, informatics, human factors engineering, manufacturing systems, human-machine interaction. *Total annual research expenditures:* $4.6 million. *Unit head:* Dr. Andrew Kusiak, Department Executive Officer, 319-335-5934, Fax: 319-335-5669, E-mail: andrew-kusiak@uiowa.edu. *Application contact:* Andrea Flaherty, Academic Program Specialist, 319-335-5939, Fax: 319-335-5669, E-mail: indeng@engineering.uiowa.edu. Web site: http://www.mie.engineering.uiowa.edu/.

University of Kentucky, Graduate School, College of Engineering, Program in Manufacturing Systems Engineering, Lexington, KY 40506-0032. Offers MSMSE. *Degree requirements:* For master's, comprehensive exam. *Entrance requirements:* For master's, GRE General Test, minimum undergraduate GPA of 2.75. Additional exam requirements/recommendations for international students: Required—TOEFL (minimum score 550 paper-based; 213 computer-based). Electronic applications accepted. *Faculty research:* Manufacturing processes and equipment, manufacturing systems and control, computer-aided design and manufacturing, automation in manufacturing, electric manufacturing and packaging.

University of Manitoba, Faculty of Graduate Studies, Faculty of Engineering, Department of Mechanical and Manufacturing Engineering, Winnipeg, MB R3T 2N2, Canada. Offers M Eng, M Sc, PhD. *Degree requirements:* For master's, thesis; for doctorate, thesis/dissertation.

University of Maryland, College Park, Academic Affairs, A. James Clark School of Engineering, Department of Mechanical Engineering, College Park, MD 20742. Offers electronic packaging and reliability (MS, PhD); manufacturing and design (MS, PhD); mechanics and materials (MS, PhD); reliability engineering (M Eng, MS, PhD); thermal and fluid sciences (MS, PhD). Part-time and evening/weekend programs available. Postbaccalaureate distance learning degree programs offered. *Faculty:* 88 full-time (8 women), 20 part-time/adjunct. *Students:* 240 full-time (36 women), 72 part-time (6 women); includes 54 minority (14 Black or African American, non-Hispanic/Latino; 2 American Indian or Alaska Native, non-Hispanic/Latino; 23 Asian, non-Hispanic/Latino; 11 Hispanic/Latino; 4 Two or more races, non-Hispanic/Latino; 145 international. 457 applicants, 19% accepted, 61 enrolled. In 2011, 35 master's, 29 doctorates awarded. *Degree requirements:* For master's, thesis optional; for doctorate, thesis/dissertation, qualifying exam. *Entrance requirements:* For master's, GRE General Test, 3 letters of recommendation; for doctorate, GRE General Test, minimum GPA of 3.0. Additional exam requirements/recommendations for international students: Required—TOEFL. *Application deadline:* For fall admission, 5/15 for domestic students, 2/1 for international students; for spring admission, 10/15 for domestic students, 6/1 for international students. Applications are processed on a rolling basis. Application fee: $75. Electronic applications accepted. *Expenses: Tuition, area resident:* Part-time $525 per credit hour. Tuition, state resident: part-time $525 per credit hour. Tuition, nonresident: part-time $1131 per credit hour. *Required fees:* $386.31 per term. Tuition and fees vary according to program. *Financial support:* In 2011–12, 7 fellowships with full and partial tuition reimbursements (averaging $24,003 per year), 166 research assistantships (averaging $23,766 per year), 17 teaching assistantships (averaging $17,967 per year) were awarded; Federal Work-Study and scholarships/grants also available. Support available to part-time students. Financial award applicants required to submit FAFSA. *Faculty research:* Injection molding, electronic packaging, fluid mechanics, product engineering. *Total annual research expenditures:* $19 million. *Unit head:* Dr. B. Balachandran, Chair, 301-405-5309, E-mail: balab@umd.edu. *Application contact:* Dr. Charles A. Caramello, Graduate Director, 301-405-0358, Fax: 301-314-9305, E-mail: ccaramel@umd.edu.

University of Memphis, Graduate School, Herff College of Engineering, Department of Engineering Technology, Memphis, TN 38152. Offers computer engineering technology (MS); electronics engineering technology (MS); manufacturing engineering technology (MS). Part-time and evening/weekend programs available. *Degree requirements:* For master's, comprehensive exam, thesis optional. *Entrance requirements:* For master's, GRE General Test, minimum undergraduate GPA of 2.5. Electronic applications accepted. *Faculty research:* Teacher education services-technology education; flexible manufacturing control systems; embedded, dedicated, and real-time computer systems; network, Internet, and Web based programming; analog and digital electronic communication systems.

University of Michigan, College of Engineering, Interpro Programs in Engineering, Ann Arbor, MI 48109. Offers automotive engineering (M Eng); design science (PhD); energy systems engineering (MS); financial engineering (MS); global automotive and manufacturing engineering (M Eng); manufacturing engineering (M Eng, D Eng); pharmaceutical engineering (M Eng); robotics and autonomous vehicles (M Eng); MBA/M Eng; MSE/MS. Part-time programs available. Postbaccalaureate distance learning degree programs offered (no on-campus study). *Students:* 225 full-time (55 women), 273 part-time (37 women). In 2011, 145 master's, 1 doctorate awarded. Terminal master's awarded for partial completion of doctoral program. *Degree requirements:* For master's, capstone project; for doctorate, thesis/dissertation. *Entrance requirements:* For master's, GRE; for doctorate, GRE, 2 years of work experience. Additional exam requirements/recommendations for international students: Required—TOEFL (minimum score 560 paper-based; 220 computer-based). *Application deadline:* Applications are processed on a rolling basis. Application fee: $65 ($75 for international students). Electronic applications accepted. *Financial support:* Fellowships, research assistantships with full tuition reimbursements, teaching assistantships with full tuition reimbursements, career-related internships or fieldwork, scholarships/grants, and unspecified assistantships available. Financial award application deadline: 2/15; financial award applicants required to submit FAFSA. *Faculty research:* Automotive engineering, design science, energy systems engineering, engineering sustainable systems dual degree, financial engineering, global automotive and manufacturing engineering, integrated microsystems, manufacturing engineering, pharmaceutical engineering, robotics and autonomous vehicles. *Unit head:* Prof. Panos Papalambros, Director, 734-763-0480, Fax: 734-647-0079, E-mail: pyp@umich.edu. *Application contact:* Patti Mackmiller, Program Manager, 734-764-3071, Fax: 734-647-2243, E-mail: pmackmil@umich.edu. Web site: http://interpro-academics.engin.umich.edu/.

University of Michigan–Dearborn, College of Engineering and Computer Science, Interdisciplinary Programs, Program in Manufacturing Systems Engineering, Dearborn, MI 48128-1491. Offers MSE. Part-time and evening/weekend programs available. *Faculty:* 1 full-time (0 women). *Students:* 1 full-time (0 women), 10 part-time (2 women); includes 4 minority (3 Black or African American, non-Hispanic/Latino; 1 Hispanic/Latino), 1 international. Average age 30. 3 applicants, 33% accepted, 1 enrolled. In 2011, 3 master's awarded. *Degree requirements:* For master's, thesis optional. *Entrance requirements:* For master's, bachelor's degree in applied mathematics, computer science, engineering, or physical science; minimum GPA of 3.0. Additional exam requirements/recommendations for international students: Required—TOEFL (minimum score 560 paper-based; 220 computer-based; 84 iBT). *Application deadline:* For fall admission, 8/1 priority date for domestic students, 4/1 for international students; for winter admission, 12/1 priority date for domestic students, 8/1 for international students;

for spring admission, 4/1 priority date for domestic students, 12/1 for international students. Applications are processed on a rolling basis. Application fee: $60. Electronic applications accepted. *Financial support:* Scholarships/grants and unspecified assistantships available. Financial award application deadline: 4/1; financial award applicants required to submit FAFSA. *Faculty research:* Toolwear metrology, paper handling, grinding wheel imbalance, machine mission. *Unit head:* Dr. Pankaj K. Mallick, Director/Professor, 313-593-5119, Fax: 313-593-5386, E-mail: pkm@umich.edu. *Application contact:* Sherry Boyd, Intermediate Administrative Assistant, 313-593-5582, Fax: 313-593-5386, E-mail: idpgrad@umd.umich.edu. Web site: http://www.engin.umd.umich.edu/.

University of Missouri, Graduate School, College of Engineering, Department of Industrial and Manufacturing Systems Engineering, Columbia, MO 65211. Offers MS, PhD. *Faculty:* 11 full-time (2 women). *Students:* 18 full-time (1 woman), 19 part-time (7 women), 33 international. Average age 28. 63 applicants, 40% accepted, 12 enrolled. In 2011, 11 master's, 1 doctorate awarded. *Degree requirements:* For master's, thesis or alternative; for doctorate, thesis/dissertation. *Entrance requirements:* For master's and doctorate, GRE General Test, minimum GPA of 3.0. Additional exam requirements/recommendations for international students: Required—TOEFL (minimum score 550 paper-based; 213 computer-based; 80 iBT). *Application deadline:* For fall admission, 5/1 priority date for domestic students. Applications are processed on a rolling basis. Application fee: $55 ($75 for international students). *Expenses:* Tuition, state resident: full-time $5881. Tuition, nonresident: full-time $15,183. *Required fees:* $952. Tuition and fees vary according to campus/location and program. *Financial support:* Research assistantships, teaching assistantships, and institutionally sponsored loans available. *Faculty research:* Logistics systems analysis and design, supply chain modeling, material flow design and improvement, intelligent systems. *Unit head:* Dr. Luis Occena, Department Chair, E-mail: occenal@missouri.edu. *Application contact:* Sally Schwartz, 573-882-2692, E-mail: schwartzs@missouri.edu. Web site: http://engineering.missouri.edu/imse/.

University of Nebraska–Lincoln, Graduate College, College of Engineering, Department of Industrial and Management Systems Engineering, Lincoln, NE 68588. Offers engineering management (M Eng); industrial and management systems engineering (MS, PhD); manufacturing systems engineering (MS). Postbaccalaureate distance learning degree programs offered. *Degree requirements:* For master's, thesis optional; for doctorate, comprehensive exam, thesis/dissertation. *Entrance requirements:* For master's and doctorate, GRE. Additional exam requirements/recommendations for international students: Required—TOEFL (minimum score 525 paper-based; 195 computer-based). Electronic applications accepted. *Faculty research:* Ergonomics, occupational safety, quality control, industrial packaging, facility design.

University of New Mexico, Graduate School, School of Engineering, Manufacturing Engineering Program, Albuquerque, NM 87131-2039. Offers MEME, MBA/MEME. Part-time programs available. *Students:* 2 full-time (0 women), 4 part-time (0 women); includes 3 minority (1 American Indian or Alaska Native, non-Hispanic/Latino; 2 Hispanic/Latino), 1 international. Average age 31. 7 applicants, 57% accepted, 1 enrolled. In 2011, 2 degrees awarded. *Degree requirements:* For master's, 500 hours relevant industry experience, paid or unpaid. *Entrance requirements:* For master's, GRE General Test (minimum score: 400 verbal, 600 quantitative, 3.5 analytical writing), minimum GPA of 3.0. Additional exam requirements/recommendations for international students: Required—TOEFL (minimum score 550 paper-based; 213 computer-based; 79 iBT). *Application deadline:* For fall admission, 7/30 priority date for domestic students, 3/1 for international students; for spring admission, 11/30 priority date for domestic students, 8/1 for international students. Application fee: $50. Electronic applications accepted. *Financial support:* In 2011–12, 2 students received support, including 1 teaching assistantship (averaging $5,045 per year); career-related internships or fieldwork and health care benefits also available. Support available to part-time students. Financial award application deadline: 3/1; financial award applicants required to submit FAFSA. *Faculty research:* Robotics, automation control and machine vision, microsystems and microgrippers, semiconductor manufacturing and metrology, cross-training and operations of technicians and engineers. *Total annual research expenditures:* $1.1 million. *Unit head:* Dr. John E. Wood, Director, 505-272-7000, Fax: 505-272-7152, E-mail: jw@unm.edu. *Application contact:* Arden L. Ballantine, Information Contact, 505-272-7000, Fax: 505-272-7152, E-mail: aballant@unm.edu. Web site: http://www.mfg.unm.edu.

University of St. Thomas, Graduate Studies, School of Engineering, St. Paul, MN 55105-1096. Offers manufacturing engineering and operations (MS); mechanical engineering (MS); medical device development (Certificate); regulatory science (MS); software engineering (MS); software management (MS); software systems (MSS); systems engineering (MS); technology management (MS). *Accreditation:* ABET (one or more programs are accredited). *Students:* 8 full-time, 210 part-time (38 women); includes 47 minority (22 Black or African American, non-Hispanic/Latino; 4 Asian, non-Hispanic/Latino; 6 Hispanic/Latino; 1 Native Hawaiian or other Pacific Islander, non-Hispanic/Latino; 14 Two or more races, non-Hispanic/Latino), 14 international. Average age 33. *Entrance requirements:* For master's, resume, official transcripts. Additional exam requirements/recommendations for international students: Required—TOEFL (minimum score 550 paper-based). *Application deadline:* For fall admission, 8/1 priority date for domestic students; for spring admission, 1/1 priority date for domestic students. Applications are processed on a rolling basis. Application fee: $30. Electronic applications accepted. *Expenses:* Contact institution. *Financial support:* Fellowships, research assistantships, institutionally sponsored loans, and scholarships/grants available. Support available to part-time students. Financial award application deadline: 4/1; financial award applicants required to submit FAFSA. *Unit head:* Don Weinkauf, Dean, 651-962-5760, Fax: 651-962-6419, E-mail: dhweinkauf@stthomas.edu. *Application contact:* Joyce A. Taylor, Graduate Programs Coordinator, 651-962-5756, Fax: 651-962-6419, E-mail: jataylor1@stthomas.edu.

University of Southern California, Graduate School, Viterbi School of Engineering, Daniel J. Epstein Department of Industrial and Systems Engineering, Los Angeles, CA 90089. Offers digital supply chain management (MS); engineering management (MS); engineering technology communication (Graduate Certificate); health systems operations (Graduate Certificate); industrial and systems engineering (MS, PhD, Engr); manufacturing engineering (MS); operations research engineering (MS); optimization and supply chain management (Graduate Certificate); product development engineering (MS); safety systems and security (MS); systems architecting and engineering (MS, Graduate Certificate); systems safety and security (Graduate Certificate); transportation systems (Graduate Certificate); MS/MBA. Part-time and evening/weekend programs available. Postbaccalaureate distance learning degree programs offered (no on-campus study). Terminal master's awarded for partial completion of doctoral program. *Degree requirements:* For master's, thesis optional; for doctorate, thesis/dissertation. *Entrance requirements:* For master's and doctorate, GRE General Test. Additional exam requirements/recommendations for international students: Recommended—TOEFL. Electronic applications accepted. *Faculty research:* Health systems, music cognition and retrieval, transportation and logistics, manufacturing and automation, engineering systems design, risk and economic analysis.

University of Southern Maine, School of Applied Science, Engineering, and Technology, Department of Technology, Portland, ME 04104-9300. Offers manufacturing systems (MS). *Entrance requirements:* Additional exam requirements/recommendations for international students: Required—TOEFL. Electronic applications accepted.

The University of Texas at El Paso, Graduate School, College of Engineering, Department of Industrial Engineering, El Paso, TX 79968-0001. Offers industrial engineering (MS); manufacturing engineering (MS); systems engineering (MS, Certificate). Part-time and evening/weekend programs available. *Students:* 107 (28 women); includes 60 minority (2 Black or African American, non-Hispanic/Latino; 1 Asian, non-Hispanic/Latino; 57 Hispanic/Latino), 44 international. Average age 34. 56 applicants, 91% accepted, 43 enrolled. In 2011, 27 master's awarded. *Degree requirements:* For master's, thesis optional. *Entrance requirements:* For master's, GRE General Test, minimum GPA of 3.0 in major. Additional exam requirements/recommendations for international students: Required—TOEFL. *Application deadline:* For fall admission, 7/1 priority date for domestic students, 3/1 for international students; for spring admission, 11/1 priority date for domestic students, 9/1 for international students. Applications are processed on a rolling basis. Application fee: $15 ($65 for international students). Electronic applications accepted. *Financial support:* In 2011–12, research assistantships with partial tuition reimbursements (averaging $21,125 per year), teaching assistantships with partial tuition reimbursements (averaging $16,900 per year) were awarded; fellowships with partial tuition reimbursements, Federal Work-Study, institutionally sponsored loans, scholarships/grants, and tuition waivers (partial) also available. Financial award application deadline: 3/15; financial award applicants required to submit FAFSA. *Faculty research:* Computer vision, automated inspection, simulation and modeling. *Unit head:* Dr. Rafael S. Gutierrez, Chair, 915-747-5450, Fax: 915-747-5019, E-mail: rsgutier@utep.edu. *Application contact:* Dr. Benjamin Flores, Interim Dean of the Graduate School, 915-747-5491, Fax: 915-747-5788, E-mail: bflores@utep.edu.

The University of Texas at San Antonio, College of Engineering, Department of Mechanical Engineering, San Antonio, TX 78249-0617. Offers advanced manufacturing and enterprise engineering (MS); mechanical engineering (MSME, PhD). Part-time and evening/weekend programs available. *Faculty:* 14 full-time (1 woman), 4 part-time/adjunct (0 women). *Students:* 37 full-time (4 women), 38 part-time (3 women); includes 21 minority (4 Asian, non-Hispanic/Latino; 14 Hispanic/Latino; 3 Two or more races, non-Hispanic/Latino), 32 international. Average age 27. 98 applicants, 69% accepted, 29 enrolled. In 2011, 24 master's awarded. Terminal master's awarded for partial completion of doctoral program. *Degree requirements:* For master's, comprehensive exam (for some programs), thesis; for doctorate, comprehensive exam (for some programs), thesis/dissertation, oral and written qualifying exams, dissertation proposal. *Entrance requirements:* For master's, GRE General Test, bachelor's degree in mechanical engineering or related field from accredited institution of higher education; for doctorate, GRE, master's degree in mechanical engineering or exceptionally outstanding undergraduate record in mechanical engineering or related field. Additional exam requirements/recommendations for international students: Required—TOEFL (minimum score 500 paper-based; 61 iBT), IELTS (minimum score 5). *Application deadline:* For fall admission, 7/1 for domestic students, 4/1 for international students; for spring admission, 11/1 for domestic students, 9/1 for international students. Application fee: $45 ($85 for international students). *Expenses:* Tuition, state resident: full-time $3148; part-time $2176 per semester. Tuition, nonresident: full-time $8782; part-time $5932 per semester. *Required fees:* $719 per semester. *Financial support:* In 2011–12, 33 students received support, including 4 fellowships, 16 research assistantships, 34 teaching assistantships; scholarships/grants and unspecified assistantships also available. Financial award application deadline: 3/31. *Faculty research:* Mechanics of materials, biomechanics and bioengineering, manufacturing and engineering enterprise, mechanical systems and design, thermal and fluid systems. *Unit head:* Dr. Harry R. Millwater, Department Chair, 210-458-4481, Fax: 210-458-6504, E-mail: harry.millwater@utsa.edu. *Application contact:* Dr. Xiaodu Wang, Assistant Dean of the Graduate School, 210-458-5565, Fax: 210-458-5565, E-mail: xiaodu.wang@utsa.edu.

The University of Texas–Pan American, College of Engineering and Computer Science, Department of Manufacturing Engineering, Edinburg, TX 78539. Offers engineering management (MS); manufacturing engineering (MS); systems engineering (MS). Tuition and fees vary according to course load, program and student level. *Unit head:* Dr. Rajiv Nambiar, Dean, 956-665-7056, E-mail: nambiar@utpa.edu. Web site: http://portal.utpa.edu/portal/page/portal/utpa_main/daa_home/cose_home/manu_home.

University of Toronto, School of Graduate Studies, Advanced Design and Manufacturing Institute, Toronto, ON M5S 1A1, Canada. Offers M Eng. Program offered jointly with McMaster University, Queen's University, University of Waterloo, and The University of Western Ontario; available only to Canadian citizens and permanent residents of Canada. Part-time programs available. *Entrance requirements:* For master's, honours bachelor's degree in engineering with grades equivalent to a mid-B or better. Additional exam requirements/recommendations for international students: Required—TOEFL (minimum score 580 paper-based; 93 iBT), TWE (minimum score 4). Electronic applications accepted.

University of Windsor, Faculty of Graduate Studies, Faculty of Engineering, Department of Industrial and Manufacturing Systems Engineering, Windsor, ON N9B 3P4, Canada. Offers industrial engineering (M Eng, MA Sc); manufacturing systems engineering (PhD). Part-time programs available. *Degree requirements:* For master's, thesis; for doctorate, comprehensive exam, thesis/dissertation. *Entrance requirements:* For master's, minimum B average; for doctorate, master's degree, minimum B average. Additional exam requirements/recommendations for international students: Required—TOEFL (minimum score 560 paper-based; 220 computer-based). Electronic applications accepted. *Faculty research:* Human factors, operations research.

University of Wisconsin–Madison, Graduate School, College of Engineering, Manufacturing Systems Engineering Program, Madison, WI 53706. Offers MS. Part-time programs available. Postbaccalaureate distance learning degree programs offered (minimal on-campus study). *Degree requirements:* For master's, thesis (for some programs), independent research projects. *Entrance requirements:* For master's, GRE General Test. Additional exam requirements/recommendations for international students: Required—TOEFL. Electronic applications accepted. *Expenses:* Tuition, state resident: full-time $10,296; part-time $643.51 per credit. Tuition, nonresident: full-time $24,054; part-time $1503.40 per credit. *Required fees:* $70.06 per credit. Tuition and fees vary according to course load, campus/location, program and reciprocity agreements. *Faculty research:* CAD/CAM, rapid prototyping, lead time reduction, quick response manufacturing.

University of Wisconsin–Milwaukee, Graduate School, College of Engineering and Applied Science, Program in Engineering, Milwaukee, WI 53201-0413. Offers civil engineering (MS); electrical and computer engineering (MS); energy engineering (Certificate); engineering (PhD); engineering management (MS); engineering mechanics (MS); ergonomics (Certificate); industrial and management engineering (MS); manufacturing engineering (MS); materials engineering (MS); mechanical engineering (MS); MUP/MS. Part-time programs available. *Faculty:* 41 full-time (5 women), 2 part-time/adjunct (0 women). *Students:* 170 full-time (33 women), 101 part-time (18 women); includes 30 minority (6 Black or African American, non-Hispanic/Latino; 15 Asian, non-Hispanic/Latino; 2 Hispanic/Latino; 7 Two or more races, non-Hispanic/Latino), 153 international. Average age 30. 170 applicants, 56% accepted, 48 enrolled. In 2011, 47 master's, 12 doctorates awarded. *Degree requirements:* For master's, comprehensive exam (for some programs), thesis or alternative; for doctorate, comprehensive exam, thesis/dissertation, internship. *Entrance requirements:* For master's, GRE, minimum GPA of 2.75; for doctorate, GRE, minimum GPA of 3.5. Additional exam requirements/recommendations for international students: Required—TOEFL (minimum score 550 paper-based; 79 iBT), IELTS (minimum score 6.5). *Application deadline:* For fall admission, 1/1 priority date for domestic students; for spring admission, 9/1 for domestic students. Applications are processed on a rolling basis. Application fee: $56 ($96 for international students). One-time fee: $506.10 full-time. Tuition and fees vary according to course load and reciprocity agreements. *Financial support:* In 2011–12, 3 fellowships, 55 research assistantships, 77 teaching assistantships were awarded; career-related internships or fieldwork, Federal Work-Study, unspecified assistantships, and project assistantships also available. Support available to part-time students. Financial award application deadline: 4/15. *Total annual research expenditures:* $10.3 million. *Unit head:* David Yu, Representative, 414-229-6169, E-mail: yu@uwm.edu. *Application contact:* Betty Warras, General Information Contact, 414-229-6169, Fax: 414-229-6967, E-mail: bwarras@uwm.edu. Web site: http://www.wum.edu/CEAS/.

University of Wisconsin–Stout, Graduate School, College of Technology, Engineering, and Management, Program in Manufacturing Engineering, Menomonie, WI 54751. Offers MS. Postbaccalaureate distance learning degree programs offered (minimal on-campus study). *Degree requirements:* For master's, thesis. *Entrance requirements:* For master's, minimum GPA of 3.0. Additional exam requirements/recommendations for international students: Required—TOEFL (minimum score 500 paper-based; 173 computer-based; 61 iBT). Electronic applications accepted. *Faculty research:* General ceramics patents, metal matrix composites, solidification processing, high temperature processing.

Villanova University, College of Engineering, Department of Mechanical Engineering, Villanova, PA 19085-1699. Offers electro-mechanical systems (Certificate); machinery dynamics (Certificate); mechanical engineering (MSME); nonlinear dynamics and control (Certificate); thermofluid systems (Certificate). Part-time and evening/weekend programs available. Postbaccalaureate distance learning degree programs offered (no on-campus study). *Degree requirements:* For master's, thesis optional. *Entrance requirements:* For master's, GRE General Test (for applicants with degrees from foreign universities), BME, minimum GPA of 3.0. Additional exam requirements/recommendations for international students: Required—TOEFL (minimum score 600 paper-based; 250 computer-based; 100 iBT). Electronic applications accepted. *Expenses: Tuition:* Part-time $675 per credit. Part-time tuition and fees vary according to degree level and program. *Faculty research:* Composite materials, power plant systems, fluid mechanics, automated manufacturing, dynamic analysis.

Wayne State University, College of Engineering, Department of Industrial and Manufacturing Engineering, Program in Manufacturing Engineering, Detroit, MI 48202. Offers MS. *Students:* 3 full-time (0 women), 2 part-time (0 women); includes 1 minority (Black or African American, non-Hispanic/Latino), 3 international. Average age 28. 12 applicants, 75% accepted, 1 enrolled. In 2011, 3 master's awarded. *Degree requirements:* For master's, thesis optional. *Entrance requirements:* For master's, minimum undergraduate upper-division GPA of 2.8, baccalaureate degree in engineering from ABET-accredited institution. Additional exam requirements/recommendations for international students: Required—TOEFL (minimum score 550 paper-based; 213 computer-based), GRE; Recommended—TWE (minimum score 5.5). *Application deadline:* For fall admission, 6/1 priority date for domestic students, 5/1 for international students; for winter admission, 10/1 priority date for domestic students, 9/1 for international students; for spring admission, 2/1 priority date for domestic students, 1/1 for international students. Applications are processed on a rolling basis. Application fee: $50. Electronic applications accepted. *Expenses:* Tuition, state resident: part-time $512.85 per credit. Tuition, nonresident: part-time $1132.65 per credit. *Required fees:* $26.60 per credit. $199.65 per semester. Tuition and fees vary according to course load and program. *Financial support:* Fellowships with tuition reimbursements, research assistantships with tuition reimbursements, teaching assistantships with tuition reimbursements, career-related internships or fieldwork, scholarships/grants, health care benefits, and unspecified assistantships available. *Faculty research:* Design for manufacturing, machine tools, manufacturing processes, material selection for manufacturing, manufacturing systems. *Unit head:* Dr. Leslie Monplaisir, Chair, 313-577-1645, E-mail: ad5365@wayne.edu. *Application contact:* Dr. Ratna Chinnam, Graduate Director, 313-577-7846, E-mail: ratna.chinnam@wayne.edu. Web site: http://ise.wayne.edu/.

Western Illinois University, School of Graduate Studies, College of Business and Technology, Department of Engineering Technology, Macomb, IL 61455-1390. Offers manufacturing engineering systems (MS). Part-time programs available. *Students:* 14 full-time (3 women), 10 part-time (1 woman); includes 4 minority (all Black or African American, non-Hispanic/Latino), 9 international. Average age 29. 16 applicants, 81% accepted. In 2011, 12 master's awarded. *Degree requirements:* For master's, thesis or alternative. *Entrance requirements:* Additional exam requirements/recommendations for international students: Required—TOEFL (minimum score 550 paper-based; 213 computer-based; 80 iBT). *Application deadline:* Applications are processed on a rolling basis. Application fee: $30. Electronic applications accepted. *Expenses:* Tuition, state resident: part-time $281.16 per credit hour. Tuition, nonresident: part-time $562.32 per credit hour. Part-time tuition and fees vary according to campus/location and reciprocity agreements. *Financial support:* In 2011–12, 8 students received support, including 8 research assistantships with full tuition reimbursements available (averaging $7,360 per year). Financial award applicants required to submit FAFSA. *Unit head:* Dr. Ray Diez, Chairperson, 309-298-1091. *Application contact:* Dr. Nancy Parsons, Interim Associate Provost and Director of Graduate Studies, 309-298-1806, Fax: 309-298-2345, E-mail: grad-office@wiu.edu. Web site: http://wiu.edu/engrtech.

Western Michigan University, Graduate College, College of Engineering and Applied Sciences, Department of Industrial and Manufacturing Engineering, Program in Manufacturing Engineering, Kalamazoo, MI 49008. Offers MS. *Entrance requirements:* For master's, GRE General Test, minimum GPA of 3.0.

Western New England University, College of Engineering, Department of Industrial and Manufacturing Engineering, Springfield, MA 01119. Offers production management (MSEM). Part-time and evening/weekend programs available. *Students:* 36 part-time (7 women); includes 6 minority (1 Asian, non-Hispanic/Latino; 5 Hispanic/Latino), 1 international. *Degree requirements:* For master's, comprehensive exam, thesis optional. *Entrance requirements:* For master's, GRE, bachelor's degree in engineering or related field, two letters of recommendation, resume. *Application deadline:* Applications are processed on a rolling basis. Application fee: $30. *Financial support:* Available to part-time students. Applicants required to submit FAFSA. *Faculty research:* Project scheduling, flexible manufacturing systems, facility layout, energy management. *Unit head:* Dr. Eric W. Haffner, Chair, 413-782-1272, E-mail: ehaffner@wne.edu. *Application contact:* Matt Fox, Director of Recruiting and Marketing for Adult Learners, 413-782-1249, Fax: 413-782-1779, E-mail: study@wne.edu. Web site: http://www1.wne.edu/engineering/ie/index.cfm?selection-doc.2328.

Western New England University, College of Engineering, Master's Program in Engineering Management, Springfield, MA 01119. Offers business and engineering information systems (MSEM); general engineering management (MSEM); production and manufacturing systems (MSEM); quality engineering (MSEM). Evening/weekend programs available. Postbaccalaureate distance learning degree programs offered (no on-campus study). *Students:* 36 part-time (7 women); includes 6 minority (1 Asian, non-Hispanic/Latino; 5 Hispanic/Latino), 1 international. *Degree requirements:* For master's, thesis optional. *Unit head:* Dr. S. Hossein Cheraghi, Dean, 413-782-1272, E-mail: cheraghi@wnec.edu. *Application contact:* Matt Fox, Director of Recruiting and Marketing for Adult Learners, 413-782-1517, Fax: 413-782-1777, E-mail: study@wnec.edu.

Wichita State University, Graduate School, College of Engineering, Department of Industrial and Manufacturing Engineering, Wichita, KS 67260. Offers engineering management (MEM); industrial engineering (MS, PhD). Part-time programs available. In 2011, 37 master's, 3 doctorates awarded. *Entrance requirements:* Additional exam requirements/recommendations for international students: Required—TOEFL. *Expenses:* Tuition, state resident: full-time $4746; part-time $263.65 per credit. Tuition, nonresident: full-time $11,669; part-time $648.30 per credit. *Financial support:* Teaching assistantships available. *Unit head:* Dr. Krishna Krishnan, Chair, 316-978-3425, Fax: 316-978-3742, E-mail: krishna.krishnan@wichita.edu. *Application contact:* Carrie C. Henderson, Admissions Coordinator, 316-978-3095, Fax: 316-978-3253, E-mail: carrie.henderson@wichita.edu. Web site: http://www.wichita.edu/.

Worcester Polytechnic Institute, Graduate Studies and Research, Department of Mechanical Engineering, Program in Manufacturing Engineering, Worcester, MA 01609-2280. Offers MS, PhD. Part-time and evening/weekend programs available. *Students:* 12 full-time (1 woman), 24 part-time (8 women); includes 3 minority (1 Black or African American, non-Hispanic/Latino; 2 Hispanic/Latino), 14 international. 52 applicants, 85% accepted, 20 enrolled. In 2011, 14 master's, 2 doctorates awarded. *Degree requirements:* For master's, thesis optional; for doctorate, comprehensive exam, thesis/dissertation, research proposal. *Entrance requirements:* For master's and doctorate, GRE (recommended), 3 letters of recommendation. Additional exam requirements/recommendations for international students: Required—TOEFL (minimum score 563 paper-based; 223 computer-based; 84 iBT), IELTS (minimum score 7), GRE. *Application deadline:* For fall admission, 1/1 priority date for domestic students, 1/1 for international students; for spring admission, 10/1 priority date for domestic students, 10/1 for international students. Applications are processed on a rolling basis. Application fee: $70. Electronic applications accepted. *Financial support:* Research assistantships, teaching assistantships, career-related internships or fieldwork, institutionally sponsored loans, scholarships/grants, and unspecified assistantships available. Financial award application deadline: 1/1; financial award applicants required to submit FAFSA. *Faculty research:* Manufacturing processes and systems, design for manufacturability, CAD/CAM applications, surface metrology, materials processing. *Unit head:* Dr. Kevin Rong, Director, 508-831-6088, Fax: 508-831-5673, E-mail: rong@wpi.edu. *Application contact:* Susan Milkman, Graduate Secretary, 508-831-6088, Fax: 508-831-5673, E-mail: smilkman@wpi.edu. Web site: http://www.me.wpi.edu/MFE/.

Worcester Polytechnic Institute, Graduate Studies and Research, Programs in Interdisciplinary Studies, Worcester, MA 01609-2280. Offers bioscience administration (MS); impact engineering (MS); manufacturing engineering management (MS); power systems management (MS); social science (PhD); systems modeling (MS). Part-time and evening/weekend programs available. *Faculty:* 1 full-time (0 women). *Students:* 1 full-time (0 women), 201 part-time (30 women); includes 22 minority (2 Black or African American, non-Hispanic/Latino; 11 Asian, non-Hispanic/Latino; 7 Hispanic/Latino; 2 Two or more races, non-Hispanic/Latino), 5 international. 130 applicants, 90% accepted, 107 enrolled. *Degree requirements:* For master's, thesis; for doctorate, comprehensive exam, thesis/dissertation. *Entrance requirements:* For master's and doctorate, 3 letters of recommendation. Additional exam requirements/recommendations for international students: Required—TOEFL (minimum score 563 paper-based; 223 computer-based; 84 iBT), IELTS (minimum score 7). *Application deadline:* For fall admission, 1/1 priority date for domestic students, 1/1 for international students; for spring admission, 10/1 priority date for domestic students, 10/1 for international students. Application fee: $70. *Financial support:* Institutionally sponsored loans, scholarships/grants, and unspecified assistantships available. Financial award application deadline: 1/1; financial award applicants required to submit FAFSA. *Unit head:* Dr. Fred J. Looft, Head, 508-831-5231, Fax: 508-831-5491, E-mail: fjlooft@wpi.edu. *Application contact:* Lynne Dougherty, Administrative Assistant, 508-831-5301, Fax: 508-831-5717, E-mail: grad@wpi.edu.

Pharmaceutical Engineering

New Jersey Institute of Technology, Office of Graduate Studies, Newark College of Engineering, Department of Chemical Engineering, Interdisciplinary Program in Pharmaceutical Engineering, Newark, NJ 07102. Offers MS. Part-time and evening/weekend programs available. *Students:* 60 full-time (34 women), 20 part-time (10 women); includes 19 minority (4 Black or African American, non-Hispanic/Latino; 13 Asian, non-Hispanic/Latino; 1 Hispanic/Latino; 1 Native Hawaiian or other Pacific Islander, non-Hispanic/Latino), 52 international. Average age 27. 161 applicants, 76% accepted, 38 enrolled. In 2011, 37 master's awarded. *Degree requirements:* For master's, thesis optional. *Entrance requirements:* For master's, GRE General Test. Additional exam requirements/recommendations for international students: Required—TOEFL (minimum score 550 paper-based; 213 computer-based; 79 iBT). *Application deadline:* For fall admission, 6/1 priority date for domestic students, 5/1 for international students; for spring admission, 11/15 for domestic and international students. Applications are processed on a rolling basis. Application fee: $65. Electronic applications accepted. *Expenses:* Tuition, state resident: full-time $7980; part-time $867 per credit. Tuition, nonresident: full-time $11,336; part-time $1196 per credit. *Required fees:* $230 per credit. *Financial support:* Fellowships with full and partial tuition reimbursements, research assistantships with full and partial tuition reimbursements, teaching assistantships with full and partial tuition reimbursements, career-related internships or fieldwork, Federal Work-Study, institutionally sponsored loans, and unspecified assistantships available. Financial award application deadline: 1/15. *Unit head:* Dr. Piero Armenante, Director, 973-596-3548, Fax: 973-596-8436, E-mail: piero.armenante@njit.edu. *Application contact:* Kathryn Kelly, Director of Admissions, 973-596-3300, Fax: 973-596-3461, E-mail: admissions@njit.edu. Web site: http://chemicaleng.njit.edu/academics/graduate/masters/pharm.php.

University of Michigan, College of Engineering, Interpro Programs in Engineering, Ann Arbor, MI 48109. Offers automotive engineering (M Eng); design science (PhD); energy systems engineering (MS); financial engineering (MS); global automotive and manufacturing engineering (M Eng); manufacturing engineering (M Eng, D Eng); pharmaceutical engineering (M Eng); robotics and autonomous vehicles (M Eng); MBA/M Eng; MSE/MS. Part-time programs available. Postbaccalaureate distance learning degree programs offered (no on-campus study). *Students:* 225 full-time (55 women), 273 part-time (37 women). In 2011, 145 master's, 1 doctorate awarded. Terminal master's awarded for partial completion of doctoral program. *Degree requirements:* For master's, capstone project; for doctorate, thesis/dissertation. *Entrance requirements:* For master's, GRE; for doctorate, GRE, 2 years of work experience. Additional exam requirements/recommendations for international students: Required—TOEFL (minimum score 560 paper-based; 220 computer-based). *Application deadline:* Applications are processed on a rolling basis. Application fee: $65 ($75 for international students). Electronic applications accepted. *Financial support:* Fellowships, research assistantships with full tuition reimbursements, teaching assistantships with full tuition reimbursements, career-related internships or fieldwork, scholarships/grants, and unspecified assistantships available. Financial award application deadline: 2/15; financial award applicants required to submit FAFSA. *Faculty research:* Automotive engineering, design science, energy systems engineering, engineering sustainable systems dual degree, financial engineering, global automotive and manufacturing engineering, integrated microsystems, manufacturing engineering, pharmaceutical engineering, robotics and autonomous vehicles. *Unit head:* Prof. Panos Papalambros, Director, 734-763-0480, Fax: 734-647-0079, E-mail: pyp@umich.edu. *Application contact:* Patti Mackmiller, Program Manager, 734-764-3071, Fax: 734-647-2243, E-mail: pmackmil@umich.edu. Web site: http://interpro-academics.engin.umich.edu/.

Reliability Engineering

Arizona State University, Ira A. Fulton School of Engineering, ASU Engineering Online Programs, Tempe, AZ 85287. Offers construction (MS); embedded systems (M Eng); enterprise systems innovation and management (MSE); modeling and simulation (M Eng); quality and reliability engineering (M Eng); software engineering (MSE); systems engineering (M Eng).

The University of Arizona, College of Engineering, Department of Systems and Industrial Engineering, Program in Reliability and Quality Engineering, Tucson, AZ 85721. Offers MS. Part-time programs available. Postbaccalaureate distance learning degree programs offered. *Students:* 1 (woman) full-time, all international. Average age 27. 1 applicant, 0% accepted. *Entrance requirements:* Additional exam requirements/recommendations for international students: Required—TOEFL (minimum score 550 paper-based; 213 computer-based; 79 iBT). *Application deadline:* Applications are processed on a rolling basis. Application fee: $75. Electronic applications accepted. *Expenses:* Tuition, state resident: full-time $10,840. Tuition, nonresident: full-time $25,802. *Financial support:* Unspecified assistantships available. *Unit head:* Dr. K. Larry Head, Head, 520-621-6551, E-mail: larry@sie.arizona.edu. *Application contact:* Graduate Secretary, 520-626-4644, Fax: 520-621-6555, E-mail: gradapp@sie.arizona.edu. Web site: http://www.sie.arizona.edu.

University of Maryland, College Park, Academic Affairs, A. James Clark School of Engineering, Department of Continuing and Distance Learning in Engineering, College Park, MD 20742. Offers engineering (M Eng), including aerospace engineering, chemical engineering, civil engineering, electrical engineering, engineering, fire protection engineering, materials science and engineering, mechanical engineering, reliability engineering, systems engineering. *Faculty:* 3 full-time (0 women), 8 part-time/adjunct (0 women). *Students:* 75 full-time (24 women), 418 part-time (81 women); includes 154 minority (62 Black or African American, non-Hispanic/Latino; 64 Asian, non-Hispanic/Latino; 23 Hispanic/Latino; 5 Two or more races, non-Hispanic/Latino), 67 international. 447 applicants, 52% accepted, 154 enrolled. In 2011, 155 master's awarded. *Application deadline:* For fall admission, 8/15 for domestic students, 2/1 for international students; for spring admission, 1/10 for domestic students, 8/1 for international students. Applications are processed on a rolling basis. Application fee: $75. Electronic applications accepted. *Expenses: Tuition, area resident:* Part-time $525 per credit hour. Tuition, state resident: part-time $525 per credit hour. Tuition, nonresident: part-time $1131 per credit hour. *Required fees:* $386.31 per term. Tuition and fees vary according to program. *Financial support:* In 2011–12, 3 research assistantships (averaging $21,498 per year), 13 teaching assistantships (averaging $16,889 per year) were awarded. *Unit head:* Dr. Darryll Pines, Dean, 301-405-8539,

E-mail: pines@umd.edu. *Application contact:* Dr. Charles A. Caramello, Dean of the Graduate School, 301-405-0358, Fax: 301-314-9305.

University of Maryland, College Park, Academic Affairs, A. James Clark School of Engineering, Department of Mechanical Engineering, Reliability Engineering Program, College Park, MD 20742. Offers M Eng, MS, PhD. Part-time and evening/weekend programs available. Postbaccalaureate distance learning degree programs offered. *Students:* 32 full-time (10 women), 25 part-time (4 women); includes 6 minority (4 Black or African American, non-Hispanic/Latino; 2 Hispanic/Latino), 26 international. 31 applicants, 45% accepted, 13 enrolled. In 2011, 9 master's, 8 doctorates awarded. *Degree requirements:* For master's, thesis optional; for doctorate, thesis/dissertation. *Entrance requirements:* For master's, GRE General Test, 3 letters of recommendation; for doctorate, GRE General Test, minimum GPA of 3.0. Additional exam requirements/recommendations for international students: Required—TOEFL. *Application deadline:* For fall admission, 5/1 for domestic students, 2/1 for international students; for spring admission, 10/15 for domestic students, 6/1 for international students. Applications are processed on a rolling basis. Application fee: $75. Electronic applications accepted. *Expenses: Tuition, area resident:* Part-time $525 per credit hour. Tuition, state resident: part-time $525 per credit hour. Tuition, nonresident: part-time $1131 per credit hour. *Required fees:* $386.31 per term. Tuition and fees vary according to program. *Financial support:* In 2011–12, 9 research assistantships (averaging $24,093 per year), 5 teaching assistantships (averaging $18,301 per year) were awarded; fellowships and career-related internships or fieldwork also available. Financial award applicants required to submit FAFSA. *Faculty research:* Electron linear acceleration, x-ray and imaging. *Unit head:* Dr. Aris Christou, Professor and Chair, 301-405-5208, Fax: 301-314-9601, E-mail: christou@umd.edu. *Application contact:* Dr. Charles A. Caramello, Dean of Graduate School, 301-405-0358, Fax: 301-314-9305.

The University of Tennessee, Graduate School, College of Engineering, Department of Chemical Engineering, Knoxville, TN 37996. Offers chemical engineering (MS, PhD); reliability and maintainability engineering (MS); MS/MBA. Part-time programs available. *Faculty:* 23 full-time (3 women). *Students:* 47 full-time (12 women), 2 part-time (1 woman); includes 6 minority (2 American Indian or Alaska Native, non-Hispanic/Latino; 3 Asian, non-Hispanic/Latino; 1 Hispanic/Latino), 23 international. Average age 26. 129 applicants, 12% accepted, 13 enrolled. In 2011, 5 master's, 2 doctorates awarded. *Degree requirements:* For master's, thesis or alternative; for doctorate, comprehensive exam, thesis/dissertation. *Entrance requirements:* For master's, GRE General Test (for MS students pursuing research thesis), minimum GPA of 2.7 (for U.S. degree holders), 3.0 (for international degree holders); for doctorate, College requires GRE General Test for all PhD candidates, minimum GPA of 3.0 on previous graduate course work. Additional exam requirements/recommendations for international students: Required—TOEFL (minimum score 550 paper-based; 213 computer-based). *Application deadline:* For fall admission, 2/1 priority date for domestic students, 2/1 for international students; for spring admission, 6/15 for domestic and international students. Applications are processed on a rolling basis. Application fee: $35. Electronic applications accepted. *Expenses:* Tuition, state resident: full-time $8332; part-time $464 per credit hour. Tuition, nonresident: full-time $25,174; part-time $1400 per credit hour. *Required fees:* $1162; $56 per credit hour. Tuition and fees vary according to program. *Financial support:* In 2011–12, 43 students received support, including 31 research assistantships with full tuition reimbursements available (averaging $21,863 per year), 12 teaching assistantships with full tuition reimbursements available (averaging $20,357 per year); fellowships, career-related internships or fieldwork, Federal Work-Study, institutionally sponsored loans, health care benefits, and unspecified assistantships also available. Financial award application deadline: 2/1; financial award applicants required to submit FAFSA. *Faculty research:* Bio-fuels; engineering of soft, functional and structural materials; fuel cells and energy storage devices; molecular and cellular bioengineering; molecular modeling and simulations. *Total annual research expenditures:* $4 million. *Unit head:* Dr. Bamin Khomami, Head, 865-974-2421, Fax: 865-974-7076, E-mail: bkhomami@utk.edu. *Application contact:* Dr. Paul Frymier, Graduate Program Coordinator, 865-974-4961, Fax: 865-974-7076, E-mail: pdf@utk.edu. Web site: http://www.engr.utk.edu/cbe/.

The University of Tennessee, Graduate School, College of Engineering, Department of Electrical Engineering and Computer Science, Knoxville, TN 37996. Offers computer engineering (MS, PhD); computer science (MS, PhD); electrical engineering (MS, PhD); reliability and maintainability engineering (MS); MS/MBA. Part-time programs available. *Faculty:* 36 full-time (6 women), 3 part-time/adjunct (2 women). *Students:* 181 full-time (33 women), 29 part-time (3 women); includes 8 minority (1 Black or African American, non-Hispanic/Latino; 1 American Indian or Alaska Native, non-Hispanic/Latino; 5 Asian, non-Hispanic/Latino; 1 Hispanic/Latino), 124 international. Average age 29. 677 applicants, 11% accepted, 52 enrolled. In 2011, 36 master's, 10 doctorates awarded. *Degree requirements:* For master's, thesis or alternative; for doctorate, comprehensive exam, thesis/dissertation. *Entrance requirements:* For master's, GRE General Test (for MS students pursuing research thesis), minimum GPA of 2.7 (for U.S. degree holders), 3.0 (for international degree holders); 3 references; personal statement; for doctorate, College requires GRE General Test for all PhD candidates, minimum GPA of 3.0 on previous graduate course work; 3 references; personal statement. Additional exam requirements/recommendations for international students: Required—TOEFL (minimum score 550 paper-based; 213 computer-based). *Application deadline:* For fall admission, 2/1 priority date for domestic students, 2/1 for international students; for spring admission, 6/15 for domestic and international students. Applications are processed on a rolling basis. Application fee: $35. Electronic applications accepted. *Expenses:* Tuition, state resident: full-time $8332; part-time $464 per credit hour. Tuition, nonresident: full-time $25,174; part-time $1400 per credit hour. *Required fees:* $1162; $56 per credit hour. Tuition and fees vary according to program. *Financial support:* In 2011–12, 183 students received support, including 13 fellowships with full tuition reimbursements available (averaging $12,312 per year), 88 research assistantships with full tuition reimbursements available (averaging $21,689 per year), 71 teaching assistantships with full tuition reimbursements available (averaging $16,292 per year); career-related internships or fieldwork, Federal Work-Study, institutionally sponsored loans, health care benefits, and unspecified assistantships also available. Financial award application deadline: 2/1; financial award applicants required to submit FAFSA. *Faculty research:* Artificial intelligence and visualization; microelectronics, mixed-signal electronics, VLSI, embedded systems; scientific and distributed computing; computer vision, robotics, and image processing; power electronics, power systems, communications. *Total annual research expenditures:* $12.4 million. *Unit head:* Dr. Kevin Tomsovic, Head, 865-974-3461, Fax: 865-974-5483, E-mail: tomsovic@eecs.utk.edu. *Application contact:* Dr. Lynne E. Parker, Associate Head, 865-974-4394, Fax: 865-974-5483, E-mail: parker@eecs.utk.edu. Web site: http://www.eecs.utk.edu.

The University of Tennessee, Graduate School, College of Engineering, Department of Industrial and Information Engineering, Knoxville, TN 37966. Offers engineering management (MS); industrial engineering (MS, PhD); reliability and maintainability engineering (MS); MS/MBA. Part-time programs available. Postbaccalaureate distance learning degree programs offered (minimal on-campus study). *Faculty:* 7 full-time (1 woman), 14 part-time/adjunct (1 woman). *Students:* 51 full-time (11 women), 64 part-time (21 women); includes 21 minority (11 Black or African American, non-Hispanic/Latino; 1 American Indian or Alaska Native, non-Hispanic/Latino; 7 Asian, non-Hispanic/Latino; 1 Hispanic/Latino; 1 Native Hawaiian or other Pacific Islander, non-Hispanic/Latino), 27 international. Average age 28. 119 applicants, 50% accepted, 47 enrolled. In 2011, 13 master's, 4 doctorates awarded. *Degree requirements:* For master's, thesis or alternative; for doctorate, comprehensive exam, thesis/dissertation. *Entrance requirements:* For master's, GRE General Test (for MS students pursuing research thesis), minimum GPA of 2.7 (for U.S. degree holders), 3.0 (for international degree holders); for doctorate, College requires GRE General Test for all PhD candidates, minimum GPA of 3.0 on previous graduate course work. Additional exam requirements/recommendations for international students: Required—TOEFL (minimum score 550 paper-based; 213 computer-based). *Application deadline:* For fall admission, 2/1 priority date for domestic students, 2/1 for international students; for spring admission, 6/15 for domestic and international students. Applications are processed on a rolling basis. Application fee: $35. Electronic applications accepted. *Expenses:* Tuition, state resident: full-time $8332; part-time $464 per credit hour. Tuition, nonresident: full-time $25,174; part-time $1400 per credit hour. *Required fees:* $1162; $56 per credit hour. Tuition and fees vary according to program. *Financial support:* In 2011–12, 27 students received support, including 13 research assistantships with full tuition reimbursements available (averaging $17,355 per year), 10 teaching assistantships with full tuition reimbursements available (averaging $16,985 per year); career-related internships or fieldwork, Federal Work-Study, institutionally sponsored loans, health care benefits, and unspecified assistantships also available. Financial award application deadline: 2/1; financial award applicants required to submit FAFSA. *Faculty research:* Defense-oriented supply chain modeling; dependability and reliability of large computer networks; design of lean, reliable systems; new product development; operations research in the automotive industry. *Total annual research expenditures:* $800,000. *Unit head:* Dr. Rapinder Sawhney, Department Head, 865-974-3333, Fax: 865-974-0588, E-mail: sawhney@utk.edu. *Application contact:* Dr. Denise Jackson, Graduate Representative, 865-946-3248, E-mail: djackson@utk.edu. Web site: http://www.engr.utk.edu/ie/.

The University of Tennessee, Graduate School, College of Engineering, Department of Materials Science and Engineering, Knoxville, TN 37996-2200. Offers materials science and engineering (MS, PhD); polymer engineering (MS, PhD); reliability and maintainability engineering (MS); MS/MBA. Part-time programs available. *Faculty:* 35 full-time (4 women), 11 part-time/adjunct (3 women). *Students:* 84 full-time (18 women), 11 part-time (0 women); includes 10 minority (4 Black or African American, non-Hispanic/Latino; 2 Asian, non-Hispanic/Latino; 4 Hispanic/Latino), 56 international. Average age 28. 235 applicants, 11% accepted, 20 enrolled. In 2011, 8 master's, 9 doctorates awarded. *Degree requirements:* For master's, thesis or alternative; for doctorate, comprehensive exam, thesis/dissertation. *Entrance requirements:* For master's, GRE General Test (for MS students pursuing research thesis), minimum GPA of 2.7 (for U.S. degree holders), 3.0 (for international degree holders); 3 references; for doctorate, College requires GRE General Test for all PhD candidates, minimum GPA of 3.0 on previous graduate course work; 3 references. Additional exam requirements/recommendations for international students: Required—TOEFL (minimum score 550 paper-based; 213 computer-based). *Application deadline:* For fall admission, 2/1 priority date for domestic students, 2/1 for international students; for spring admission, 6/15 for domestic and international students. Applications are processed on a rolling basis. Application fee: $35. Electronic applications accepted. *Expenses:* Tuition, state resident: full-time $8332; part-time $464 per credit hour. Tuition, nonresident: full-time $25,174; part-time $1400 per credit hour. *Required fees:* $1162; $56 per credit hour. Tuition and fees vary according to program. *Financial support:* In 2011–12, 80 students received support, including 3 fellowships with full tuition reimbursements available (averaging $8,892 per year), 64 research assistantships with full tuition reimbursements available (averaging $20,396 per year), 7 teaching assistantships with full tuition reimbursements available (averaging $18,471 per year); career-related internships or fieldwork, Federal Work-Study, institutionally sponsored loans, health care benefits, and unspecified assistantships also available. Financial award application deadline: 2/1; financial award applicants required to submit FAFSA. *Faculty research:* Biomaterials; functional materials electronic, magnetic and optical; high temperature materials; mechanical behavior of materials; neutron materials science. *Total annual research expenditures:* $7.9 million. *Unit head:* Dr. Kurt Sickafus, Head, 865-974-4858, Fax: 865-974-4115, E-mail: kurt@utk.edu. *Application contact:* Dr. Roberto S. Benson, Associate Head, 865-974-5347, Fax: 865-974-4115, E-mail: rbenson1@utk.edu. Web site: http://www.engr.utk.edu/mse.

The University of Tennessee, Graduate School, College of Engineering, Department of Nuclear and Radiological Engineering, Program in Reliability and Maintainability Engineering, Knoxville, TN 37996. Offers MS. *Students:* 2 full-time, 12 part-time (1 woman), 2 international. Average age 30. 2 applicants, 50% accepted, 1 enrolled. In 2011, 5 master's awarded. *Degree requirements:* For master's, thesis or alternative. *Entrance requirements:* For master's, GRE General Test (for MS students pursuing research thesis), minimum GPA of 2.7 (for U.S. degree holders), 3.0 (for international degree holders). Additional exam requirements/recommendations for international students: Required—TOEFL (minimum score 550 paper-based; 213 computer-based). *Application deadline:* For fall admission, 2/1 priority date for domestic students, 2/1 for international students; for spring admission, 6/15 for domestic and international students. Applications are processed on a rolling basis. Application fee: $35. Electronic applications accepted. *Expenses:* Tuition, state resident: full-time $8332; part-time $464 per credit hour. Tuition, nonresident: full-time $25,174; part-time $1400 per credit hour. *Required fees:* $1162; $56 per credit hour. Tuition and fees vary according to program. *Financial support:* Career-related internships or fieldwork, Federal Work-Study, institutionally sponsored loans, health care benefits, and unspecified assistantships available. Financial award application deadline: 2/1; financial award applicants required to submit FAFSA. *Unit head:* Dr. J. Wesley Hines, Head, 865-974-2525, Fax: 865-974-0668, E-mail: jhines2@utk.edu. *Application contact:* Dr. Masood Parang, Associate Dean of Student Affairs, 865-974-2454, Fax: 865-974-9871, E-mail: mparang@utk.edu. Web site: http://www.engr.utk.edu/rme/.

Safety Engineering

Embry-Riddle Aeronautical University–Prescott, Program in Safety Science, Prescott, AZ 86301-3720. Offers MSSS. *Faculty:* 4 full-time (0 women), 1 (woman) part-time/adjunct. *Students:* 45 full-time (9 women), 6 part-time (2 women); includes 4 minority (1 Black or African American, non-Hispanic/Latino; 1 Asian, non-Hispanic/Latino; 2 Hispanic/Latino), 8 international. Average age 29. 34 applicants, 68% accepted, 13 enrolled. In 2011, 15 master's awarded. *Degree requirements:* For master's, thesis (for some programs). *Entrance requirements:* Additional exam requirements/recommendations for international students: Required—TOEFL (minimum score 550 paper-based; 213 computer-based; 79 iBT). *Application deadline:* For fall admission, 6/1 priority date for domestic students, 6/1 for international students; for spring admission, 11/1 priority date for domestic students, 11/1 for international students. Applications are processed on a rolling basis. Application fee: $50. Electronic applications accepted. *Expenses: Tuition:* Full-time $14,340; part-time $1195 per credit hour. *Financial support:* In 2011–12, 18 students received support, including 6 research assistantships with full and partial tuition reimbursements available (averaging $1,225 per year); career-related internships or fieldwork, Federal Work-Study, and unspecified assistantships also available. Support available to part-time students. Financial award application deadline: 4/15; financial award applicants required to submit FAFSA. *Faculty research:* Service quality in aviation, engineering psychology, accident investigation and analysis, occupational safety/biomechanics, crash management/response/survivability. *Unit head:* Dr. Gary Northam, Dean, College of Aviation, 928-777-3964, Fax: 928-777-6958. *Application contact:* Bryan Dougherty, Director, Admissions, 928-777-6993, E-mail: bryan.dougherty@erau.edu.

Indiana University Bloomington, School of Health, Physical Education and Recreation, Department of Applied Health Science, Bloomington, IN 47405-7000. Offers biostatistics (MPH); environmental health (MPH, PhD); epidemiology (MPH, PhD); health behavior (PhD); health promotion (MS); human development/family studies (MS); nutrition science (MS); public health administration (MPH); safety management (MS); school and college health programs (MS); social, behavioral and community health (MPH). *Accreditation:* CEPH (one or more programs are accredited). *Faculty:* 24 full-time (12 women). *Students:* 169 full-time (126 women), 25 part-time (17 women); includes 56 minority (39 Black or African American, non-Hispanic/Latino; 2 American Indian or Alaska Native, non-Hispanic/Latino; 4 Asian, non-Hispanic/Latino; 9 Hispanic/Latino; 2 Two or more races, non-Hispanic/Latino), 29 international. Average age 30. 170 applicants, 74% accepted, 79 enrolled. In 2011, 52 master's, 9 doctorates awarded. *Degree requirements:* For master's, thesis optional; for doctorate, thesis/dissertation. *Entrance requirements:* For master's, GRE (MS in nutrition science), 3 recommendations; for doctorate, GRE, 3 recommendations. Additional exam requirements/recommendations for international students: Required—TOEFL (minimum score 550 paper-based; 213 computer-based; 79 iBT). *Application deadline:* For fall admission, 4/30 priority date for domestic students, 12/1 for international students; for spring admission, 11/15 priority date for domestic students, 9/1 for international students. Application fee: $55 ($65 for international students). *Financial support:* Fellowships, research assistantships with full and partial tuition reimbursements, teaching assistantships with full and partial tuition reimbursements, career-related internships or fieldwork, Federal Work-Study, institutionally sponsored loans, scholarships/grants, tuition waivers (partial), and fee remissions available. Financial award application deadline: 3/1. *Faculty research:* Cancer education, HIV/AIDS and drug education, public health, parent-child interactions, safety education. *Total annual research expenditures:* $2.8 million. *Unit head:* Dr. David K. Lohrmann, Chair, 812-856-5101, Fax: 812-855-3936, E-mail: dlohrman@indiana.edu. *Application contact:* Dr. Susan Middlestadt, Associate Professor and Graduate Coordinator, 812-856-5768, Fax: 812-855-3936, E-mail: semiddle@indiana.edu. Web site: http://www.indiana.edu/~aphealth/.

Murray State University, College of Health Sciences and Human Services, Program in Occupational Safety and Health, Murray, KY 42071. Offers environmental science (MS); industrial hygiene (MS); safety management (MS). *Accreditation:* ABET. Part-time programs available. *Degree requirements:* For master's, comprehensive exam, thesis optional, professional internship. Electronic applications accepted. *Faculty research:* Light effects on plant growth, ergonomics, toxic effects of pets' pesticides, traffic safety.

National University, Academic Affairs, School of Engineering, Technology and Media, Department of Applied Engineering, La Jolla, CA 92037-1011. Offers engineering management (MS); environmental engineering (MS); homeland security and safety engineering (MS); project management (Certificate); security and safety engineering (Certificate); sustainability management (MS); wireless communications (MS). Part-time and evening/weekend programs available. Postbaccalaureate distance learning degree programs offered (no on-campus study). *Degree requirements:* For master's, thesis. *Entrance requirements:* For master's, interview, minimum GPA of 2.5. Additional exam requirements/recommendations for international students: Required—TOEFL (minimum score 550 paper-based; 213 computer-based; 79 iBT), IELTS (minimum score 6). *Application deadline:* Applications are processed on a rolling basis. Application fee: $60 ($65 for international students). Electronic applications accepted. *Financial support:* Career-related internships or fieldwork, institutionally sponsored loans, scholarships/grants, and tuition waivers (partial) available. Support available to part-time students. Financial award application deadline: 6/30; financial award applicants required to submit FAFSA. *Unit head:* Dr. Shekar Viswanathan, Chair and Associate Professor, 858-309-3416, Fax: 858-309-3420, E-mail: sviswana@nu.edu. *Application contact:* Dominick Giovanniello, Associate Regional Dean, 800-NAT-UNIV, Fax: 858-541-7792, E-mail: dgiovann@nu.edu. Web site: http://www.nu.edu/OurPrograms/SchoolOfEngineeringAndTechnology/AppliedEngineering.html.

New Jersey Institute of Technology, Office of Graduate Studies, Newark College of Engineering, Department of Mechanical Engineering, Program in Occupational Safety and Health Engineering, Newark, NJ 07102. Offers MS. Part-time and evening/weekend programs available. *Students:* 7 full-time (3 women), 6 part-time (3 women); includes 7 minority (2 Black or African American, non-Hispanic/Latino; 3 Asian, non-Hispanic/Latino; 2 Hispanic/Latino), 1 international. Average age 33. 16 applicants, 50%

accepted, 4 enrolled. In 2011, 4 master's awarded. *Degree requirements:* For master's, thesis or alternative. *Entrance requirements:* For master's, GRE General Test. Additional exam requirements/recommendations for international students: Required—TOEFL (minimum score 550 paper-based; 213 computer-based; 79 iBT). *Application deadline:* For fall admission, 6/1 priority date for domestic students, 5/1 for international students; for spring admission, 11/15 priority date for domestic students, 11/15 for international students. Applications are processed on a rolling basis. Application fee: $65. Electronic applications accepted. *Expenses:* Tuition, state resident: full-time $7980; part-time $867 per credit. Tuition, nonresident: full-time $11,336; part-time $1196 per credit. *Required fees:* $230 per credit. *Financial support:* Fellowships with full and partial tuition reimbursements, research assistantships with full and partial tuition reimbursements, teaching assistantships with full and partial tuition reimbursements, career-related internships or fieldwork, Federal Work-Study, institutionally sponsored loans, and unspecified assistantships available. Financial award application deadline: 1/15. *Faculty research:* Human factors engineering, manufacturing systems, materials, manufacturing automation and computer integration. *Unit head:* Dr. Rajpal Sodhi, Interim Chair, 973-596-3362, E-mail: rajpal.s.sodhi@njit.edu. *Application contact:* Kathryn Kelly, Director of Admissions, 973-596-3300, Fax: 973-596-3461, E-mail: admissions@njit.edu.

Rochester Institute of Technology, Graduate Enrollment Services, College of Applied Science and Technology, School of Engineering Technology, Department of Civil Engineering Technology, Environmental Management and Safety, Program in Environmental Health and Safety Management, Rochester, NY 14623-5603. Offers MS. Part-time programs available. Postbaccalaureate distance learning degree programs offered (no on-campus study). *Students:* 16 full-time (3 women), 37 part-time (14 women); includes 7 minority (2 Black or African American, non-Hispanic/Latino; 1 American Indian or Alaska Native, non-Hispanic/Latino; 4 Asian, non-Hispanic/Latino), 14 international. Average age 29. 42 applicants, 38% accepted, 10 enrolled. In 2011, 21 degrees awarded. *Degree requirements:* For master's, thesis or project. *Entrance requirements:* Additional exam requirements/recommendations for international students: Required—TOEFL (minimum score 550 paper-based; 213 computer-based; 79 iBT) or IELTS (minimum score 6). *Application deadline:* Applications are processed on a rolling basis. Application fee: $50. Electronic applications accepted. *Expenses: Tuition:* Full-time $34,659; part-time $963 per credit hour. *Required fees:* $228; $76 per quarter. *Faculty research:* Design, implementation and effectiveness of integrated environmental health and safety management systems in industry. *Unit head:* Joseph Rosenbeck, Graduate Program Director, 585-475-6469, E-mail: jmrcem@rit.edu. *Application contact:* Diane Ellison, Assistant Vice President, Graduate Enrollment Services, 585-475-2229, Fax: 585-475-7164, E-mail: gradinfo@rit.edu. Web site: http://www.rit.edu/cast/cetems/ms-in-environmental-health-and-safety-management.php.

The University of Alabama at Birmingham, School of Engineering, Program in Engineering, Birmingham, AL 35294. Offers advanced safety engineering and management (M Eng); construction engineering management (M Eng); information engineering and management (M Eng). *Expenses:* Tuition, state resident: full-time $5922; part-time $309 per hour. Tuition, nonresident: full-time $13,428; part-time $726 per hour. Tuition and fees vary according to program. *Unit head:* Dr. Melinda Lalor, Dean, 205-934-8410, E-mail: mlalor@uab.edu. Web site: http://www.uab.edu/engineering/degrees-cert/master-of-engineering.

University of Minnesota, Duluth, Graduate School, Swenson College of Science and Engineering, Department of Mechanical and Industrial Engineering, Duluth, MN 55812-2496. Offers engineering management (MSEM); environmental health and safety (MEHS). Part-time and evening/weekend programs available. Postbaccalaureate distance learning degree programs offered (no on-campus study). *Degree requirements:* For master's, comprehensive exam, thesis or alternative, capstone design project (MSEM), field project (MEHS). *Entrance requirements:* For master's, GRE (MEHS), interview (MEHS), letters of recommendation. Additional exam requirements/recommendations for international students: Required—TOEFL (minimum score 550 paper-based; 213 computer-based). *Faculty research:* Transportation, ergonomics, toxicology, supply chain management, automation and robotics.

University of Southern California, Graduate School, Viterbi School of Engineering, Daniel J. Epstein Department of Industrial and Systems Engineering, Los Angeles, CA 90089. Offers digital supply chain management (MS); engineering management (MS); engineering technology communication (Graduate Certificate); health systems operations (Graduate Certificate); industrial and systems engineering (MS, PhD, Engr); manufacturing engineering (MS); operations research engineering (MS); optimization and supply chain management (Graduate Certificate); product development engineering (MS); safety systems and security (MS); systems architecting and engineering (MS, Graduate Certificate); systems safety and security (Graduate Certificate); transportation systems (Graduate Certificate); MS/MBA. Part-time and evening/weekend programs available. Postbaccalaureate distance learning degree programs offered (no on-campus study). Terminal master's awarded for partial completion of doctoral program. *Degree requirements:* For master's, thesis optional; for doctorate, thesis/dissertation. *Entrance requirements:* For master's and doctorate, GRE General Test. Additional exam requirements/recommendations for international students: Recommended—TOEFL. Electronic applications accepted. *Faculty research:* Health systems, music cognition and retrieval, transportation and logistics, manufacturing and automation, engineering systems design, risk and economic analysis.

West Virginia University, College of Engineering and Mineral Resources, Department of Industrial and Management Systems Engineering, Program in Safety Management, Morgantown, WV 26506. Offers MS. *Accreditation:* ABET. *Degree requirements:* For master's, comprehensive exam, thesis optional. *Entrance requirements:* For master's, minimum GPA of 3.0 for regular admission; 2.75 for provisional. Additional exam requirements/recommendations for international students: Required—TOEFL (minimum score 550 paper-based; 213 computer-based; 80 iBT). Electronic applications accepted.

Systems Engineering

Air Force Institute of Technology, Graduate School of Engineering and Management, Department of Aeronautics and Astronautics, Dayton, OH 45433-7765. Offers aeronautical engineering (MS, PhD); astronautical engineering (MS, PhD); materials science (MS, PhD); space operations (MS); systems engineering (MS, PhD). *Accreditation:* ABET (one or more programs are accredited). Part-time programs available. *Degree requirements:* For master's, thesis; for doctorate, thesis/dissertation. *Entrance requirements:* For master's and doctorate, GRE General Test, minimum GPA of 3.0, U.S. citizenship. *Faculty research:* Computational fluid dynamics, experimental aerodynamics, computational structural mechanics, experimental structural mechanics, aircraft and spacecraft stability and control.

The American University of Athens, School of Graduate Studies, Athens, Greece. Offers biomedical sciences (MS); business (MBA); business communication (MA); computer sciences (MS); engineering and applied sciences (MS); politics and policy making (MA); systems engineering (MS); telecommunications (MS). *Entrance requirements:* For master's, resume, 2 recommendation letters. Additional exam requirements/recommendations for international students: Required—TOEFL (minimum score 550 paper-based; 213 computer-based). *Faculty research:* Nanotechnology, environmental sciences, rock mechanics, human skin studies, Monte Carlo algorithms and software.

Arizona State University, Ira A. Fulton School of Engineering, ASU Engineering Online Programs, Tempe, AZ 85287. Offers construction (MS); embedded systems (M Eng); enterprise systems innovation and management (MSE); modeling and simulation (M Eng); quality and reliability engineering (M Eng); software engineering (MSE); systems engineering (M Eng).

Auburn University, Graduate School, Ginn College of Engineering, Department of Industrial and Systems Engineering, Auburn University, AL 36849. Offers MISE, MS, PhD, Graduate Certificate. Part-time programs available. *Faculty:* 8 full-time (1 woman), 3 part-time/adjunct (0 women). *Students:* 79 full-time (21 women), 45 part-time (12 women); includes 15 minority (10 Black or African American, non-Hispanic/Latino; 1 American Indian or Alaska Native, non-Hispanic/Latino; 2 Asian, non-Hispanic/Latino; 2 Hispanic/Latino), 68 international. Average age 29. 154 applicants, 80% accepted, 30 enrolled. In 2011, 46 master's, 5 doctorates awarded. *Degree requirements:* For master's, thesis (MS); for doctorate, thesis/dissertation. *Entrance requirements:* For master's and doctorate, GRE General Test. *Application deadline:* For fall admission, 7/7 for domestic students; for spring admission, 11/24 for domestic students. Applications are processed on a rolling basis. Application fee: $50 ($60 for international students). *Expenses:* Tuition, state resident: full-time $7290; part-time $405 per credit hour. Tuition, nonresident: full-time $21,870; part-time $1215 per credit hour. *International tuition:* $22,000 full-time. *Required fees:* $1402. *Financial support:* Fellowships, research assistantships, teaching assistantships, and Federal Work-Study available. Support available to part-time students. Financial award application deadline: 3/15; financial award applicants required to submit FAFSA. *Unit head:* Dr. Jorge Valenzuela, Chair, 334-844-1400. *Application contact:* Dr. George Flowers, Dean of the Graduate School, 334-844-2125. Web site: http://www.eng.auburn.edu/department/ie.

Boston University, College of Engineering, Division of Systems Engineering, Boston, MA 02215. Offers M Eng, MS, PhD. Part-time programs available. *Students:* 36 full-time (8 women), 4 part-time (0 women), 31 international. Average age 26. 133 applicants, 15% accepted, 14 enrolled. In 2011, 5 master's, 8 doctorates awarded. Terminal master's awarded for partial completion of doctoral program. *Degree requirements:* For master's, thesis (for some programs); for doctorate, comprehensive exam, thesis/dissertation. *Entrance requirements:* For master's and doctorate, GRE General Test. Additional exam requirements/recommendations for international students: Required—TOEFL (minimum score 550 paper-based; 213 computer-based; 84 iBT), IELTS (minimum score 6.5). *Application deadline:* For fall admission, 3/15 for domestic and international students; for spring admission, 10/1 for domestic and international students. Application fee: $70. Electronic applications accepted. *Expenses:* Tuition: Full-time $40,848; part-time $1276 per credit hour. *Required fees:* $572; $286 per semester. *Financial support:* In 2011–12, 29 students received support, including 7 fellowships with full tuition reimbursements available (averaging $28,950 per year), 17 research assistantships with full tuition reimbursements available (averaging $19,300 per year), 3 teaching assistantships with full tuition reimbursements available (averaging $19,300 per year); career-related internships or fieldwork, Federal Work-Study, institutionally sponsored loans, scholarships/grants, traineeships, health care benefits, and tuition waivers (full and partial) also available. Financial award application deadline: 1/15; financial award applicants required to submit FAFSA. *Faculty research:* Communication, network, sensing, and information systems; control systems, automation, and robotics; discrete event, queuing, hybrid, and complex systems; optimization and algorithms; production, service, distribution, and energy systems. *Unit head:* Dr. Christos Cassandras, Division Head, 617-353-7154, Fax: 617-353-5548, E-mail: cgc@bu.edu. *Application contact:* Stephen Doherty, Director of Graduate Programs, 617-353-9760, Fax: 617-353-0259, E-mail: enggrad@bu.edu. Web site: http://www.bu.edu/se/.

California Institute of Technology, Division of Engineering and Applied Science, Option in Control and Dynamical Systems, Pasadena, CA 91125-0001. Offers MS, PhD. *Degree requirements:* For doctorate, thesis/dissertation. *Faculty research:* Robustness, multivariable and nonlinear systems, optimal control, decentralized control, modeling and system identification for robust control.

California State University, Fullerton, Graduate Studies, College of Engineering and Computer Science, Department of Electrical Engineering, Fullerton, CA 92834-9480. Offers electrical engineering (MS); systems engineering (MS). Part-time programs available. *Students:* 52 full-time (12 women), 89 part-time (18 women); includes 46 minority (3 Black or African American, non-Hispanic/Latino; 37 Asian, non-Hispanic/Latino; 5 Hispanic/Latino; 1 Two or more races, non-Hispanic/Latino), 62 international. Average age 27. 264 applicants, 75% accepted, 35 enrolled. In 2011, 67 master's awarded. *Degree requirements:* For master's, comprehensive exam, project or thesis. *Entrance requirements:* For master's, GRE General Test, GRE Subject Test, minimum undergraduate GPA of 2.5, 3.0 graduate. Application fee: $55. *Financial support:* Career-related internships or fieldwork, Federal Work-Study, institutionally sponsored loans, and scholarships/grants available. Support available to part-time students. Financial award application deadline: 3/1; financial award applicants required to submit FAFSA. *Unit head:* Dr. Mostafa Shiva, Chair, 657-278-3013. *Application contact:* Admissions/Applications, 657-278-2371.

California State University, Northridge, Graduate Studies, College of Engineering and Computer Science, Department of Manufacturing Systems Engineering and Management, Northridge, CA 91330. Offers engineering automation (MS); engineering management (MS); manufacturing systems engineering (MS); materials engineering (MS). Postbaccalaureate distance learning degree programs offered. *Entrance requirements:* For master's, GRE (if cumulative undergraduate GPA less than 3.0).

Carleton University, Faculty of Graduate Studies, Faculty of Engineering and Design, Ottawa-Carleton Institute for Electrical Engineering, Department of Systems and Computer Engineering, Ottawa, ON K1S 5B6, Canada. Offers electrical engineering (MA Sc, PhD); information and systems science (M Sc); technology innovation management (M Eng, MA Sc). PhD program offered jointly with University of Ottawa. *Degree requirements:* For master's, thesis optional. *Entrance requirements:* For master's, honors degree. Additional exam requirements/recommendations for international students: Required—TOEFL. *Faculty research:* Design manufacturing management; network design, protocols, and performance; software engineering; wireless and satellite communications.

Carnegie Mellon University, Carnegie Institute of Technology, Information Networking Institute, Pittsburgh, PA 15213. Offers information networking (MS); information security technology and management (MS); information technology - information security (MS); information technology - mobility (MS); information technology - software management (MS). *Degree requirements:* For master's, thesis optional. *Entrance requirements:* For master's, GRE General Test, bachelor's degree in computer science, computer engineering, or electrical engineering, or related technology degree; programming skills (C/C++ fluency for some programs). Additional exam requirements/recommendations for international students: Required—TOEFL. *Faculty research:* Computer forensics and incident response; dependable systems, embedded systems, mobile systems, and sensor networks; computer and information networks, network and information security, human and socio-economic factors in secure system design; wireless sensor networks, survivable embedded systems, signal processing/compression; strategic management, international strategic management, group dynamics and decision-making structures, simulated competitive environments.

Case Western Reserve University, School of Graduate Studies, Case School of Engineering, Department of Electrical Engineering and Computer Science, Cleveland, OH 44106. Offers computer engineering (MS, PhD); computing and information sciences (MS, PhD); electrical engineering (MS, PhD); systems and control engineering (MS, PhD). Part-time and evening/weekend programs available. Postbaccalaureate distance learning degree programs offered (minimal on-campus study). *Faculty:* 33 full-time (3 women). *Students:* 188 full-time (34 women), 22 part-time (4 women); includes 6 minority (3 Black or African American, non-Hispanic/Latino; 3 Asian, non-Hispanic/Latino), 132 international. In 2011, 30 master's, 22 doctorates awarded. Terminal master's awarded for partial completion of doctoral program. *Degree requirements:* For master's, thesis; for doctorate, thesis/dissertation, qualifying exam, teaching experience. *Entrance requirements:* For master's and doctorate, GRE General Test. Additional exam requirements/recommendations for international students: Required—TOEFL. *Application deadline:* For fall admission, 2/1 for domestic students; for spring admission, 11/1 for domestic students. Applications are processed on a rolling basis. Application fee: $50. *Financial support:* Fellowships with full and partial tuition reimbursements, research assistantships with full and partial tuition reimbursements, teaching assistantships, career-related internships or fieldwork, Federal Work-Study, and institutionally sponsored loans available. Support available to part-time students. Financial award application deadline: 3/1; financial award applicants required to submit FAFSA. *Faculty research:* Applied artificial intelligence, automation, computer-aided design and testing of digital systems. *Total annual research expenditures:* $6 million. *Unit head:* Dr. Michael Branicky, Department Chair, 216-368-6888, E-mail: branicky@case.edu. *Application contact:* David Easler, Student Affairs Coordinator, 216-368-4080, Fax: 216-368-2801, E-mail: david.easler@case.edu. Web site: http://eecs.cwru.edu/.

Colorado School of Mines, Graduate School, Division of Engineering, Golden, CO 80401-1887. Offers engineering systems (ME, MS, PhD). Part-time programs available. *Faculty:* 39 full-time (5 women), 25 part-time/adjunct (7 women). *Students:* 179 full-time (26 women), 45 part-time (5 women); includes 32 minority (5 Black or African American, non-Hispanic/Latino; 2 American Indian or Alaska Native, non-Hispanic/Latino; 5 Asian, non-Hispanic/Latino; 17 Hispanic/Latino; 3 Two or more races, non-Hispanic/Latino), 42 international. Average age 28. 279 applicants, 69% accepted, 72 enrolled. In 2011, 108 master's, 13 doctorates awarded. *Degree requirements:* For master's, thesis (for some programs); for doctorate, one foreign language, comprehensive exam, thesis/dissertation. *Entrance requirements:* For master's and doctorate, GRE General Test. Additional exam requirements/recommendations for international students: Required—TOEFL (minimum score 550 paper-based; 213 computer-based; 80 iBT). *Application deadline:* For fall admission, 1/15 priority date for domestic students, 1/15 for international students; for spring admission, 10/15 priority date for domestic students, 10/15 for international students. Application fee: $50 ($70 for international students). Electronic applications accepted. *Expenses:* Tuition, state resident: full-time $12,585; part-time $699 per credit. Tuition, nonresident: full-time $27,270; part-time $1516 per credit. *Required fees:* $1864.20; $670 per semester. *Financial support:* In 2011–12, 89 students received support, including 15 fellowships with full tuition reimbursements available (averaging $20,000 per year), 54 research assistantships with full tuition reimbursements available (averaging $20,000 per year), 20 teaching assistantships with full tuition reimbursements available (averaging $20,000 per year); scholarships/grants, health care benefits, and unspecified assistantships also available. Financial award application deadline: 1/15; financial award applicants required to submit FAFSA. *Faculty research:* Geotechnical engineering, offshore mechanics, analytical design, process simulation, health monitoring. *Total annual research expenditures:* $2.9 million. *Unit head:* Dr. Kevin Moore, Director, 303-273-3899, Fax: 303-273-3602, E-mail: kmoore@mines.edu. *Application contact:* Sara Perna, Administrative Assistant, 303-384-2394, Fax: 303-273-3602, E-mail: sperna@mines.edu. Web site: http://cecs.mines.edu.

Colorado State University–Pueblo, College of Education, Engineering and Professional Studies, Department of Engineering, Pueblo, CO 81001-4901. Offers industrial and systems engineering (MS). *Degree requirements:* For master's, thesis optional. *Entrance requirements:* For master's, GRE General Test. Additional exam requirements/recommendations for international students: Required—TOEFL (minimum score 500 paper-based). *Faculty research:* Nanotechnology, applied operations, research transportation, decision analysis.

Colorado Technical University Colorado Springs, Graduate Studies, Program in Systems Engineering, Colorado Springs, CO 80907-3896. Offers MS.

Colorado Technical University Denver South, Program in Systems Engineering, Aurora, CO 80014. Offers MS.

Concordia University, School of Graduate Studies, Faculty of Engineering and Computer Science, Concordia Institute for Information Systems Engineering (CIISE), Montréal, QC H3G 1M8, Canada. Offers 3D graphics and game development (Certificate); information systems security (M Eng, MA Sc); quality systems engineering (M Eng, MA Sc); service engineering and network management (Certificate).

Cornell University, Graduate School, Graduate Fields of Engineering, Field of Systems Engineering, Ithaca, NY 14853-0001. Offers M Eng. *Faculty:* 29 full-time (2 women). *Students:* 111 full-time (25 women); includes 28 minority (3 Black or African American, non-Hispanic/Latino; 16 Asian, non-Hispanic/Latino; 9 Hispanic/Latino), 21 international. Average age 25. 113 applicants, 71% accepted, 65 enrolled. In 2011, 54 master's awarded. *Degree requirements:* For master's, thesis. *Entrance requirements:* For master's, GRE General Test. Additional exam requirements/recommendations for international students: Required—TOEFL (minimum score 600 paper-based; 250 computer-based; 77 iBT). *Application deadline:* For fall admission, 2/1 priority date for domestic students. Application fee: $95. *Financial support:* In 2011–12, 2 fellowships with full and partial tuition reimbursements, 1 research assistantship with full and partial tuition reimbursement were awarded; teaching assistantships with full and partial tuition reimbursements, institutionally sponsored loans, scholarships/grants, health care benefits, tuition waivers (full and partial), and unspecified assistantships also available. Financial award applicants required to submit FAFSA. *Faculty research:* Space systems, systems engineering of mechanical and aerospace systems, multi-echelon inventory theory, math modeling of complex systems, chain supply integration. *Unit head:* Director of Graduate Studies, 607-255-8998, Fax: 607-255-9004, E-mail: systemseng@cornell.edu. *Application contact:* Graduate Field Assistant, 607-255-8998, Fax: 607-255-9004, E-mail: systemseng@cornell.edu. Web site: http://www.gradschool.cornell.edu/fields.php?id-19&a-2.

Embry-Riddle Aeronautical University–Daytona, Daytona Beach Campus Graduate Program, Department of Human Factors and Systems, Daytona Beach, FL 32114-3900. Offers human factors engineering (MSHFS); systems engineering (MSHFS). Part-time and evening/weekend programs available. *Faculty:* 6 full-time (1 woman). *Students:* 39 full-time (14 women), 18 part-time (8 women); includes 11 minority (1 Black or African American, non-Hispanic/Latino; 1 American Indian or Alaska Native, non-Hispanic/Latino; 1 Asian, non-Hispanic/Latino; 7 Hispanic/Latino; 1 Two or more races, non-Hispanic/Latino), 4 international. Average age 27. 40 applicants, 68% accepted, 10 enrolled. In 2011, 12 master's awarded. *Degree requirements:* For master's, thesis, practicum, qualifying oral exam. *Entrance requirements:* For master's, minimum GPA of 2.5. Additional exam requirements/recommendations for international students: Required—TOEFL (minimum score 550 paper-based; 213 computer-based; 79 iBT). *Application deadline:* For fall admission, 6/1 priority date for domestic students, 6/1 for international students; for spring admission, 11/1 priority date for domestic students, 10/1 for international students. Applications are processed on a rolling basis. Application fee: $50. Electronic applications accepted. *Expenses: Tuition:* Full-time $14,340; part-time $1195 per credit hour. *Financial support:* In 2011–12, 14 students received support, including 4 research assistantships with full and partial tuition reimbursements available (averaging $4,738 per year); teaching assistantships with full and partial tuition reimbursements available, career-related internships or fieldwork, and unspecified assistantships also available. Financial award application deadline: 4/15; financial award applicants required to submit FAFSA. *Faculty research:* Color discrimination on computer displays, human-machine interfaces, cognitive assessment, performance enhancement, integration of advanced training technologies into live military training, unmanned aerial systems, human performance assessment, fatigue management, impairment prediction models, shift settings, circadian technology, countermeasures, human factors analysis and classification system, medical errors, general aviation errors, commercial helicopter operational errors, team errors. *Total annual research expenditures:* $256,585. *Unit head:* Dr. Shawn Doherty, Graduate Program Coordinator, 386-226-6249, E-mail: shawn.doherty@erau.edu. *Application contact:* Flavia Carreiro, Assistant Director, International and Graduate Admissions, 800-388-3728, Fax: 386-226-7070, E-mail: graduate.admissions@erau.edu.

Embry-Riddle Aeronautical University–Worldwide, Worldwide Headquarters - Graduate Degrees and Programs, Program in Systems Engineering, Daytona Beach, FL 32114-3900. Offers M Sys E. Part-time and evening/weekend programs available. *Faculty:* 2 full-time (0 women), 4 part-time/adjunct (1 woman). *Students:* 1 (woman) full-time, 13 part-time (1 woman). Average age 41. 18 applicants, 61% accepted, 7 enrolled. *Entrance requirements:* Additional exam requirements/recommendations for international students: Required—TOEFL (minimum score 550 paper-based; 213 computer-based; 79 iBT). *Application deadline:* Applications are processed on a rolling basis. Application fee: $50. Electronic applications accepted. *Expenses: Tuition:* Part-time $395 per credit hour. Tuition and fees vary according to degree level and program. *Faculty research:* Quantifying uncertainty in expert judgments, efficient engineering organizations. *Unit head:* Dr. Bruce Conway, Department Chair, 757-369-3683, E-mail: bruce.conway@erau.edu. *Application contact:* Linda Dammer, Director of Admissions, 386-226-6396 Ext. 1, Fax: 386-226-6984, E-mail: worldwide@erau.edu. Web site: http://worldwide.erau.edu/degrees/graduate/systems-engineering/index.html.

Florida Institute of Technology, Graduate Programs, College of Engineering, Engineering Systems Department, Melbourne, FL 32901-6975. Offers engineering management (MS); systems engineering (MS, PhD). Part-time and evening/weekend programs available. *Faculty:* 5 full-time (0 women). *Students:* 29 full-time (11 women), 71 part-time (16 women); includes 13 minority (6 Black or African American, non-Hispanic/Latino; 3 Asian, non-Hispanic/Latino; 3 Hispanic/Latino; 1 Two or more races, non-Hispanic/Latino), 29 international. Average age 33. 120 applicants, 63% accepted, 32 enrolled. In 2011, 38 master's awarded. *Degree requirements:* For master's, comprehensive exam (for some programs), thesis optional, portfolio of competencies and summary of career relevance. *Entrance requirements:* For master's, GRE General Test (if GPA less than 3.0), minimum GPA of 3.0, 2 letters of recommendation, resume, bachelor's degree in engineering from ABET-accredited program, statement of objectives. Additional exam requirements/recommendations for international students: Required—TOEFL (minimum score 550 paper-based; 213 computer-based; 79 iBT). *Application deadline:* For fall admission, 4/1 for international students; for spring admission, 9/30 for international students. Applications are processed on a rolling basis. Electronic applications accepted. *Expenses: Tuition:* Full-time $19,620; part-time $1090 per credit hour. Tuition and fees vary according to campus/location. *Financial support:* In 2011–12, 3 research assistantships with full and partial tuition reimbursements (averaging $9,999 per year) were awarded; career-related internships or fieldwork, institutionally sponsored loans, unspecified assistantships, and tuition remissions also available. Support available to part-time students. Financial award application deadline: 3/1; financial award applicants required to submit FAFSA. *Faculty research:* System/software engineering, simulation and analytical modeling, project management, multimedia tools, quality. *Unit head:* Dr. Muzaffar A. Shaikh, Department Head, 321-674-7345, Fax: 321-674-7136, E-mail: mshaikh@fit.edu. *Application contact:* Cheryl A.

Brown, Associate Director of Graduate Admissions, 321-674-7581, Fax: 321-723-9468, E-mail: cbrown@fit.edu. Web site: http://coe.fit.edu/se/.

George Mason University, Volgenau School of Engineering, Department of Civil, Environmental, and Infrastructure Engineering, Fairfax, VA 22030. Offers civil and infrastructure engineering (MS, PhD); civil infrastructure and security engineering (Certificate); leading technical enterprises (Certificate); sustainability and the environment (Certificate); water resources engineering (Certificate). *Faculty:* 9 full-time (3 women), 22 part-time/adjunct (3 women). *Students:* 26 full-time (9 women), 59 part-time (14 women); includes 18 minority (5 Black or African American, non-Hispanic/Latino; 5 Asian, non-Hispanic/Latino; 7 Hispanic/Latino; 1 Two or more races, non-Hispanic/Latino), 10 international. Average age 31. 73 applicants, 63% accepted, 29 enrolled. In 2011, 16 master's, 7 other advanced degrees awarded. *Degree requirements:* For master's, thesis (for some programs), 30 credits, departmental seminars; for doctorate, thesis/dissertation, qualifying exams. *Entrance requirements:* For master's, GRE, photocopy of passport; 2 official college transcripts; resume; official bank statement; proof of financial support; expanded goals statement; self-evaluation form; BS in engineering or other related science; 3 letters of recommendation; for doctorate, GRE (for those who received degree outside of the U.S.), photocopy of passport; 2 official college transcripts; resume; official bank statement; proof of financial support; expanded goals statement; self-evaluation form; baccalaureate degree in engineering or related science; master's degree (preferred); 3 letters of recommendation; for Certificate, BS in related field; photocopy of passport; 2 official college transcripts; resume; official bank statement; proof of financial support; expanded goals statement; self evaluation form; 3 letters of recommendation. Additional exam requirements/recommendations for international students: Required—TOEFL (minimum score 575 paper-based; 230 computer-based; 88 iBT), IELTS, Pearson Test of English. *Application deadline:* For fall admission, 1/15 priority date for domestic students; for spring admission, 8/1 priority date for domestic students. Application fee: $65 ($80 for international students). Electronic applications accepted. *Expenses:* Tuition, state resident: full-time $8750; part-time $364.58 per credit. Tuition, nonresident: full-time $24,092; part-time $1003.83 per credit. *Required fees:* $2514; $104.75 per credit. *Financial support:* In 2011–12, 17 students received support, including 3 fellowships (averaging $18,000 per year), 2 research assistantships with full and partial tuition reimbursements available (averaging $17,893 per year), 12 teaching assistantships with full and partial tuition reimbursements available (averaging $8,884 per year); career-related internships or fieldwork, Federal Work-Study, scholarships/grants, unspecified assistantships, and health care benefits (full-time research or teaching assistantship recipients) also available. Support available to part-time students. Financial award application deadline: 3/1; financial award applicants required to submit FAFSA. *Faculty research:* Evolutionary design, infrastructure security, intelligent transportation systems, national transportation networks, water quality modeling. *Total annual research expenditures:* $655,402. *Unit head:* Dr. Deborah J. Goodings, Chair, 703-993-1675, Fax: 703-993-9790, E-mail: goodings@gmu.edu. *Application contact:* Nicole Jerome, Administrative Assistant, 703-993-1675, Fax: 703-993-9790, E-mail: njerome@gmu.edu. Web site: http://civil.gmu.edu/.

George Mason University, Volgenau School of Engineering, Department of Systems Engineering and Operations Research, Fairfax, VA 22030. Offers architecture-based systems integration (Certificate); command, control, communication, computing and intelligence (Certificate); computational modeling (Certificate); discovery, design and innovation (Certificate); military operations research (Certificate); operations research (MS); systems engineering (MS); systems engineering analysis and architecture (Certificate); systems engineering and operations research (PhD); systems engineering of software intensive systems (Certificate). MS programs offered jointly with Old Dominion University, University of Virginia, Virginia Commonwealth University, and Virginia Polytechnic Institute and State University. *Faculty:* 16 full-time (4 women), 15 part-time/adjunct (4 women). *Students:* 42 full-time (5 women), 153 part-time (31 women); includes 46 minority (5 Black or African American, non-Hispanic/Latino; 2 American Indian or Alaska Native, non-Hispanic/Latino; 27 Asian, non-Hispanic/Latino; 11 Hispanic/Latino; 1 Two or more races, non-Hispanic/Latino), 13 international. Average age 32. 124 applicants, 74% accepted, 51 enrolled. In 2011, 50 master's, 1 doctorate, 11 other advanced degrees awarded. *Degree requirements:* For master's, thesis optional; for doctorate, comprehensive exam, thesis/dissertation, qualifying exams. *Entrance requirements:* For master's, GRE General Test, BS in related field; minimum GPA of 3.0; 3 letters of recommendation; 2 official transcripts; expanded goals statement; proof of financial support; photocopy of passport; official bank statement; multivariable calculus, applied probability, statistics and a computer language course; self evaluation form; for doctorate, GRE, MS with minimum GPA of 3.5; BS with minimum GPA of 3.0 in systems or operational research; 2 official transcripts; 3 letters of recommendation; resume; expanded goals statement; self evaluation form; photocopy of passport; official bank statement; proof of financial support; for Certificate, personal goals statement; 2 official transcripts; self-evaluation form; 1 letter of recommendation; resume; official bank statement; photocopy of passport; proof of financial support; baccalaureate degree in related field. Additional exam requirements/recommendations for international students: Required—TOEFL (minimum score 575 paper-based; 230 computer-based; 88 iBT), IELTS, Pearson Test of English. *Application deadline:* For fall admission, 1/15 priority date for domestic students; for spring admission, 8/15 priority date for domestic students. Application fee: $65 ($80 for international students). Electronic applications accepted. *Expenses:* Tuition, state resident: full-time $8750; part-time $364.58 per credit. Tuition, nonresident: full-time $24,092; part-time $1003.83 per credit. *Required fees:* $2514; $104.75 per credit. *Financial support:* In 2011–12, 12 students received support, including 7 research assistantships with full and partial tuition reimbursements available (averaging $15,028 per year), 5 teaching assistantships with full and partial tuition reimbursements available (averaging $12,474 per year); career-related internships or fieldwork, Federal Work-Study, scholarships/grants, unspecified assistantships, and health care benefits (full-time research or teaching assistantship recipients) also available. Support available to part-time students. Financial award application deadline: 3/1; financial award applicants required to submit FAFSA. *Faculty research:* Requirements engineering, signal processing, systems architecture, data fusion. *Total annual research expenditures:* $1.5 million. *Unit head:* Dr. Ariela Sofer, Chair, 703-993-1692, Fax: 703-993-1521, E-mail: asofer@gmu.edu. *Application contact:* Josefine Wiecks, Administrative Assistant, 703-993-1785, Fax: 703-993-1521, E-mail: jwiecks@gmu.edu. Web site: http://seor.gmu.edu.

The George Washington University, School of Engineering and Applied Science, Department of Engineering Management and Systems Engineering, Washington, DC 20052. Offers MS, D Sc, App Sc, Engr, Graduate Certificate. Part-time and evening/weekend programs available. *Faculty:* 16 full-time (2 women), 19 part-time/adjunct (5 women). *Students:* 121 full-time (40 women), 1,004 part-time (260 women); includes 243 minority (129 Black or African American, non-Hispanic/Latino; 3 American Indian or Alaska Native, non-Hispanic/Latino; 66 Asian, non-Hispanic/Latino; 36 Hispanic/Latino; 3 Native Hawaiian or other Pacific Islander, non-Hispanic/Latino; 6 Two or more races, non-Hispanic/Latino), 106 international. Average age 35. 482 applicants, 89% accepted, 271 enrolled. In 2011, 394 master's, 22 doctorates, 236 other advanced degrees awarded. *Degree requirements:* For master's, thesis optional; for doctorate, one foreign language, thesis/dissertation, final and qualifying exams, submission of articles; for other advanced degree, professional project. *Entrance requirements:* For master's, appropriate bachelor's degree, minimum GPA of 2.7, second semester calculus; for doctorate, appropriate master's degree, minimum GPA of 3.5, 2 letters of recommendation; for other advanced degree, appropriate master's degree, minimum GPA of 3.4. Additional exam requirements/recommendations for international students: Required—TOEFL or The George Washington University English as a Foreign Language Test. *Application deadline:* For fall admission, 3/1 for domestic students; for spring admission, 10/1 for domestic students. Applications are processed on a rolling basis. Application fee: $75. *Financial support:* In 2011–12, 35 students received support. Fellowships with tuition reimbursements available, research assistantships, teaching assistantships with tuition reimbursements available, career-related internships or fieldwork, and institutionally sponsored loans available. Financial award application deadline: 3/1; financial award applicants required to submit FAFSA. *Faculty research:* Artificial intelligence and expert systems, human factors engineering and systems analysis. *Total annual research expenditures:* $421,800. *Unit head:* Dr. Thomas Mazzuchi, Chair, 202-994-7424, Fax: 202-994-0245, E-mail: mazzu@gwu.edu. *Application contact:* Adina Lav, Marketing, Recruiting and Admissions, 202-994-5827, Fax: 202-994-0909, E-mail: engineering@gwu.edu. Web site: http://www.emse.gwu.edu/.

Georgia Institute of Technology, Graduate Studies and Research, College of Engineering, School of Industrial and Systems Engineering, Program in Industrial and Systems Engineering, Atlanta, GA 30332-0001. Offers algorithms, combinatorics, and optimization (PhD); industrial and systems engineering (PhD); industrial engineering (MS, MSIE); statistics (MS Stat). Part-time programs available. Terminal master's awarded for partial completion of doctoral program. *Degree requirements:* For master's, thesis optional; for doctorate, thesis/dissertation. *Entrance requirements:* For master's and doctorate, GRE General Test, minimum GPA of 3.0. Additional exam requirements/recommendations for international students: Required—TOEFL. Electronic applications accepted. *Faculty research:* Computer-integrated manufacturing systems, materials handling systems, production and distribution.

Harrisburg University of Science and Technology, Program in Information Systems Engineering and Management, Harrisburg, PA 17101. Offers digital government specialization (MS); digital health specialization (MS); entrepreneurship specialization (MS). Part-time programs available. *Degree requirements:* For master's, comprehensive exam, thesis optional. *Entrance requirements:* For master's, baccalaureate degree. Additional exam requirements/recommendations for international students: Required—TOEFL (minimum score 520 paper-based; 200 computer-based; 80 iBT). Electronic applications accepted.

Indiana University–Purdue University Fort Wayne, College of Engineering, Technology, and Computer Science, Department of Engineering, Fort Wayne, IN 46805-1499. Offers computer engineering (MSE); electrical engineering (MSE); mechanical engineering (MSE); systems engineering (MSE). Part-time programs available. *Faculty:* 21 full-time (0 women), 2 part-time/adjunct (0 women). *Students:* 6 full-time (0 women), 29 part-time (5 women); includes 3 minority (2 Asian, non-Hispanic/Latino; 1 Hispanic/Latino), 3 international. Average age 28. 26 applicants, 96% accepted, 17 enrolled. In 2011, 16 master's awarded. *Entrance requirements:* For master's, minimum GPA of 3.0, bachelor's degree in engineering discipline. Additional exam requirements/recommendations for international students: Required—TOEFL (minimum score 550 paper-based; 213 computer-based; 77 iBT); Recommended—TWE. *Application deadline:* For fall admission, 7/15 priority date for domestic students, 5/15 for international students; for spring admission, 12/1 priority date for domestic students, 10/15 for international students. Applications are processed on a rolling basis. Application fee: $55 ($60 for international students). Electronic applications accepted. *Financial support:* In 2011–12, 7 research assistantships with partial tuition reimbursements (averaging $12,930 per year), 3 teaching assistantships with partial tuition reimbursements (averaging $12,930 per year) were awarded. Financial award application deadline: 3/1; financial award applicants required to submit FAFSA. *Faculty research:* Thermal science, robot prototypes, worm-scanning strategies. *Total annual research expenditures:* $185,757. *Unit head:* Dr. Donald Mueller, Chair, 260-481-5707, Fax: 260-481-6281, E-mail: mueller@engr.ipfw.edu. *Application contact:* Dr. Carlos Pomalaza-Raez, Program Director/Professor, 260-481-6353, Fax: 260-481-5734, E-mail: carlos-pomalaza-raez@purdue.edu. Web site: http://www.ipfw.edu/engr.

Instituto Tecnológico y de Estudios Superiores de Monterrey, Campus Chihuahua, Graduate Programs, Chihuahua, Mexico. Offers computer systems engineering (Ingeniero); electrical engineering (Ingeniero); electromechanical engineering (Ingeniero); electronic engineering (Ingeniero); engineering administration (MEA); industrial engineering (MIE, Ingeniero); international trade (MIT); mechanical engineering (Ingeniero).

Instituto Tecnológico y de Estudios Superiores de Monterrey, Campus Monterrey, Graduate and Research Division, Programs in Engineering, Monterrey, Mexico. Offers applied statistics (M Eng); artificial intelligence (PhD); automation engineering (M Eng); chemical engineering (M Eng); civil engineering (M Eng); electrical engineering (M Eng); electronic engineering (M Eng); environmental engineering (M Eng); industrial engineering (M Eng, PhD); manufacturing engineering (M Eng); mechanical engineering (M Eng); systems and quality engineering (M Eng). M Eng program offered jointly with University of Waterloo; PhD in industrial engineering with Texas A&M University. Part-time and evening/weekend programs available. Terminal master's awarded for partial completion of doctoral program. *Degree requirements:* For master's, one foreign language, thesis; for doctorate, one foreign language, thesis/dissertation. *Entrance requirements:* For master's, EXADEP; for doctorate, GRE, master's degree in related field. Additional exam requirements/recommendations for international students: Required—TOEFL. *Faculty research:* Flexible manufacturing cells, materials, statistical methods, environmental prevention, control and evaluation.

Iowa State University of Science and Technology, Program in Systems Engineering, Ames, IA 50011. Offers M Eng. *Entrance requirements:* Additional exam requirements/recommendations for international students: Required—TOEFL (minimum score 550 paper-based; 79 iBT), IELTS (minimum score 6.5). *Application deadline:* Applications are processed on a rolling basis. Application fee: $40 ($90 for international students). Electronic applications accepted. *Unit head:* Douglas D. Gemmill, Director of Graduate Education, 515-294-8731, Fax: 515-294-3524, E-mail: n2ddg@iastate.edu. *Application contact:* Douglas D. Gemmill, Information Contact, 515-294-8731, Fax: 515-294-3524, E-mail: grad_admissions@iastate.edu. Web site: http://www.imse.iastate.edu/graduate-program/.

The Johns Hopkins University, Engineering Program for Professionals, Part-time Program in Systems Engineering, Baltimore, MD 21218-2699. Offers MS, Graduate Certificate, Post-Master's Certificate. Part-time and evening/weekend programs available. Postbaccalaureate distance learning degree programs offered (no on-campus study). Electronic applications accepted.

Lehigh University, P.C. Rossin College of Engineering and Applied Science, Department of Industrial and Systems Engineering, Bethlehem, PA 18015. Offers analytical finance (MS); healthcare systems engineering (M Eng); industrial and systems engineering (M Eng, MS); industrial engineering (PhD); management science and engineering (M Eng, MS); MBA/E. Part-time programs available. Postbaccalaureate distance learning degree programs offered (no on-campus study). *Faculty:* 14 full-time (2 women). *Students:* 73 full-time (28 women), 12 part-time (3 women); includes 2 minority (both Black or African American, non-Hispanic/Latino), 70 international. Average age 27. 275 applicants, 25% accepted, 20 enrolled. In 2011, 28 master's, 2 doctorates awarded. *Degree requirements:* For master's, thesis (MS); project (M Eng); for doctorate, comprehensive exam, thesis/dissertation. *Entrance requirements:* For master's and doctorate, GRE General Test. Additional exam requirements/recommendations for international students: Required—TOEFL (minimum score 550 paper-based; 213 computer-based; 79 iBT). *Application deadline:* For fall admission, 7/15 for domestic and international students; for spring admission, 12/1 for domestic and international students. Applications are processed on a rolling basis. Application fee: $75. Electronic applications accepted. *Financial support:* In 2011–12, 36 students received support, including 3 fellowships with full tuition reimbursements available (averaging $17,460 per year), 16 research assistantships with full tuition reimbursements available (averaging $15,300 per year), 11 teaching assistantships with full tuition reimbursements available (averaging $18,360 per year); career-related internships or fieldwork, scholarships/grants, tuition waivers, and unspecified assistantships also available. Financial award application deadline: 1/15. *Faculty research:* Optimization, mathematical programming; logistics and supply chain, stochastic processes and simulation; computational optimization and high performance computing; financial engineering and robust optimization. *Total annual research expenditures:* $1.5 million. *Unit head:* Dr. Tamas Terlaky, Chair, 610-758-4050, Fax: 610-758-4886, E-mail: terlaky@lehigh.edu. *Application contact:* Rita Frey, Graduate Coordinator, 610-758-4051, Fax: 610-758-4886, E-mail: ise@lehigh.edu. Web site: http://www.lehigh.edu/ise.

Lehigh University, P.C. Rossin College of Engineering and Applied Science, Program in Manufacturing Systems Engineering, Bethlehem, PA 18015. Offers MS, MBA/E. Part-time and evening/weekend programs available. Postbaccalaureate distance learning degree programs offered (no on-campus study). *Faculty:* 1 full-time (0 women). *Students:* 27 part-time (10 women); includes 3 minority (1 Asian, non-Hispanic/Latino; 2 Hispanic/Latino). Average age 35. 38 applicants, 26% accepted, 9 enrolled. In 2011, 5 degrees awarded. *Degree requirements:* For master's, comprehensive exam, project or thesis. *Entrance requirements:* For master's, GRE General Test, minimum GPA of 2.75. Additional exam requirements/recommendations for international students: Required—TOEFL (minimum score 620 paper-based; 260 computer-based; 85 iBT). *Application deadline:* For fall admission, 7/15 for domestic and international students; for spring admission, 12/1 for domestic and international students. Applications are processed on a rolling basis. Application fee: $75. Electronic applications accepted. *Faculty research:* Manufacturing systems design, development, and implementation; accounting and management; agile/lean systems; supply chain issues; sustainable systems design; product design. *Unit head:* Dr. Keith M. Gardiner, Director, 610-758-5070, Fax: 610-758-6527, E-mail: kg03@lehigh.edu. *Application contact:* Carolyn C. Jones, Graduate Coordinator, 610-758-5157, Fax: 610-758-6527, E-mail: ccj1@lehigh.edu. Web site: http://www.lehigh.edu/~inmse/gradprogram/.

Loyola Marymount University, College of Business Administration, MBA/MS Program in Systems Engineering, Los Angeles, CA 90045. Offers MBA/MS. Part-time programs available. *Faculty:* 42 full-time (13 women), 11 part-time/adjunct (2 women). *Students:* 11 full-time (1 woman), 3 part-time (0 women); includes 7 minority (2 Black or African American, non-Hispanic/Latino; 2 Asian, non-Hispanic/Latino; 2 Hispanic/Latino; 1 Native Hawaiian or other Pacific Islander, non-Hispanic/Latino). Average age 32. 5 applicants, 60% accepted, 3 enrolled. *Entrance requirements:* Additional exam requirements/recommendations for international students: Required—TOEFL (minimum score 600 paper-based; 250 computer-based; 100 iBT). *Application deadline:* For fall admission, 7/15 for domestic students; for spring admission, 12/15 for domestic students. Application fee: $50. Electronic applications accepted. *Expenses:* Contact institution. *Financial support:* In 2011–12, 6 students received support. Career-related internships or fieldwork, institutionally sponsored loans, scholarships/grants, and unspecified assistantships available. Financial award application deadline: 6/30; financial award applicants required to submit FAFSA. *Unit head:* Dr. Dennis Draper, Dean, 310-338-7504, E-mail: ddraper@lmu.edu. *Application contact:* Chake H. Kouyoumjian, Associate Dean of the Graduate Division, 310-338-2721, E-mail: kouyoum@lmu.edu. Web site: http://cse.lmu.edu/programs/Systems_Engineering/selp.htm.

Loyola Marymount University, College of Science and Engineering, Department of Systems Engineering and Engineering Management, Program in System Engineering Leadership, Los Angeles, CA 90045-2659. Offers MS, MS/MBA. *Faculty:* 2 full-time (0 women), 3 part-time/adjunct (1 woman). *Students:* 11 full-time (1 woman), 3 part-time (0 women); includes 7 minority (2 Black or African American, non-Hispanic/Latino; 2 Asian, non-Hispanic/Latino; 2 Hispanic/Latino; 1 Native Hawaiian or other Pacific Islander, non-Hispanic/Latino). Average age 32. 5 applicants, 60% accepted, 3 enrolled. In 2011, 5 master's awarded. *Degree requirements:* For master's, thesis. *Entrance requirements:* For master's, GMAT, must be admitted to both business and engineering schools. Additional exam requirements/recommendations for international students: Required—TOEFL (minimum score 550 paper-based; 213 computer-based; 80 iBT). *Application deadline:* For fall admission, 7/15 for domestic students; for spring admission, 12/15 for domestic students. Applications are processed on a rolling basis. Application fee: $50. Electronic applications accepted. *Financial support:* In 2011–12, 6 students received support. Scholarships/grants and unspecified assistantships available. Support available to part-time students. Financial award application deadline: 6/1; financial award applicants required to submit FAFSA. *Unit head:* Dr. Frederick S. Brown, Graduate Director, 310-338-7878, E-mail: fbrown@lmu.edu. *Application contact:* Chake H. Kouyoumjian, Associate Dean for Graduate Studies, 310-338-2721, E-mail: ckouyoum@lmu.edu. Web site: http://cse.lmu.edu/programs/Systems_Engineering/selp.htm.

Loyola Marymount University, College of Science and Engineering, Department of Systems Engineering and Engineering Management, Program in Systems Engineering, Los Angeles, CA 90045. Offers MS. *Faculty:* 2 full-time (0 women), 3 part-time/adjunct (1 woman). *Students:* 18 full-time (3 women), 11 part-time (2 women); includes 19 minority (5 Black or African American, non-Hispanic/Latino; 5 Asian, non-Hispanic/Latino; 7 Hispanic/Latino; 2 Two or more races, non-Hispanic/Latino), 7 international. Average age 31. 18 applicants, 83% accepted, 9 enrolled. In 2011, 8 master's awarded. *Degree requirements:* For master's, thesis. *Entrance requirements:* For master's, personal statement, resume, letters of recommendation. Additional exam requirements/recommendations for international students: Required—TOEFL (minimum score 550 paper-based; 213 computer-based; 80 iBT). *Application deadline:* For fall admission, 7/15 for domestic students; for spring admission, 12/15 for domestic students. Applications are processed on a rolling basis. Application fee: $50. Electronic applications accepted. *Financial support:* In 2011–12, 11 students received support. Scholarships/grants and unspecified assistantships available. Support available to part-time students. Financial award applicants required to submit FAFSA. *Unit head:* Dr. Frederick S. Brown, Program Director, 310-338-7878, E-mail: fbrown@lmu.edu. *Application contact:* Chake H. Kouyoumjian, Associate Dean of Graduate Studies, 310-338-2721, E-mail: graduate@lmu.edu. Web site: http://cse.lmu.edu/about/graduateeducation/systemsengineering.htm.

Massachusetts Institute of Technology, School of Engineering, Engineering Systems Division, Cambridge, MA 02139. Offers engineering and management (SM); engineering systems (SM, PhD); logistics (M Eng); technology and policy (SM); technology, management and policy (PhD); SM/MBA. *Faculty:* 22 full-time (7 women). *Students:* 296 full-time (88 women); includes 36 minority (3 Black or African American, non-Hispanic/Latino; 22 Asian, non-Hispanic/Latino; 6 Hispanic/Latino; 5 Two or more races, non-Hispanic/Latino), 132 international. Average age 31. 909 applicants, 26% accepted, 181 enrolled. In 2011, 143 master's, 13 doctorates awarded. *Degree requirements:* For master's, thesis; for doctorate, comprehensive exam, thesis/dissertation. *Entrance requirements:* For master's, GRE General Test (or GMAT for some programs); for doctorate, GRE General Test. Additional exam requirements/recommendations for international students: Required—IELTS (minimum score 7.5). Application fee: $75. Electronic applications accepted. *Expenses:* Contact institution. *Financial support:* In 2011–12, 223 students received support, including 44 fellowships (averaging $30,600 per year), 96 research assistantships (averaging $29,000 per year), 16 teaching assistantships (averaging $29,800 per year); career-related internships or fieldwork, Federal Work-Study, institutionally sponsored loans, scholarships/grants, health care benefits, and unspecified assistantships also available. *Faculty research:* Critical infrastructures, extended enterprises, energy and sustainability, health care delivery, humans and technology, uncertainty and dynamics, design and implementation, networks and flows, policy and standards. *Total annual research expenditures:* $13.7 million. *Unit head:* Prof. Joseph M. Sussman, Interim Director, 617-253-1764, E-mail: esdinquiries@mit.edu. *Application contact:* Graduate Admissions, 617-253-1182, E-mail: esdgrad@mit.edu. Web site: http://esd.mit.edu/.

Mississippi State University, Bagley College of Engineering, Department of Industrial and Systems Engineering, Mississippi State, MS 39762. Offers industrial and systems engineering (PhD); industrial engineering (MS). Part-time programs available. Postbaccalaureate distance learning degree programs offered (no on-campus study). *Faculty:* 8 full-time (3 women), 1 part-time/adjunct (0 women). *Students:* 30 full-time (9 women), 55 part-time (9 women); includes 19 minority (10 Black or African American, non-Hispanic/Latino; 5 Asian, non-Hispanic/Latino; 4 Hispanic/Latino), 20 international. Average age 34. 80 applicants, 35% accepted, 16 enrolled. In 2011, 8 master's, 4 doctorates awarded. *Degree requirements:* For master's, thesis (for some programs), comprehensive oral or written exam; for doctorate, thesis/dissertation, candidacy exam. *Entrance requirements:* For master's, GRE General Test, minimum GPA of 3.0; for doctorate, GRE General Test, minimum GPA of 3.3. Additional exam requirements/recommendations for international students: Required—TOEFL (minimum score 550 paper-based; 213 computer-based; 79 iBT); Recommended—IELTS (minimum score 6.5). *Application deadline:* For fall admission, 7/1 for domestic students, 5/1 for international students; for spring admission, 11/1 for domestic students, 9/1 for international students. Applications are processed on a rolling basis. Application fee: $40. *Expenses:* Tuition, state resident: full-time $5805; part-time $322.50 per credit hour. Tuition, nonresident: full-time $14,670; part-time $815 per credit hour. *Financial support:* In 2011–12, 15 research assistantships with full tuition reimbursements (averaging $15,051 per year), 6 teaching assistantships with full tuition reimbursements (averaging $12,230 per year) were awarded; Federal Work-Study, institutionally sponsored loans, and unspecified assistantships also available. Financial award application deadline: 4/1; financial award applicants required to submit FAFSA. *Faculty research:* Operations research, ergonomics, production systems, management systems, transportation. *Unit head:* Dr. John Usher, Professor/Interim Head/Graduate Coordinator, 662-325-7624, Fax: 662-325-7618, E-mail: usher@ise.msstate.edu. Web site: http://www.ie.msstate.edu/.

Missouri University of Science and Technology, Graduate School, Department of Engineering Management and Systems Engineering, Rolla, MO 65409. Offers engineering management (MS, DE, PhD); manufacturing engineering (M Eng, MS); systems engineering (MS, PhD). *Degree requirements:* For master's, thesis optional; for doctorate, comprehensive exam. *Entrance requirements:* For master's, GRE (minimum score 1150 verbal and quantitative, 4.5 writing); for doctorate, GRE (minimum score: 1100 verbal and quantitative, 3.5 writing). Additional exam requirements/recommendations for international students: Required—TOEFL (minimum score 580 paper-based; 213 computer-based). *Faculty research:* Management of technology, industrial engineering, manufacturing engineering, packaging engineering, quality engineering.

Naval Postgraduate School, Departments and Academic Groups, Department of Systems Engineering, Monterey, CA 93943. Offers engineering systems (MS); product development (MS); systems engineering (MS, PhD, Certificate); systems engineering analysis (MS, PhD); systems engineering management (MS, PhD). Program only open to commissioned officers of the United States and friendly nations and selected United States federal civilian employees. Part-time programs available. *Faculty:* 32 full-time (6 women), 3 part-time/adjunct (2 women). *Students:* 399 full-time (63 women), 49 part-time (7 women); includes 109 minority (22 Black or African American, non-Hispanic/Latino; 47 Asian, non-Hispanic/Latino; 40 Hispanic/Latino), 4 international. Average age 42. In 2011, 162 master's awarded. *Degree requirements:* For master's, thesis (for some programs), internal project, capstone project, or research/dissertation paper (for some programs); for doctorate, thesis/dissertation (for some programs), internal project, capstone project, or research/dissertation paper (for some programs). *Faculty research:* Net-centric enterprise systems/services, artificial intelligence (AI) systems engineering, unconventional weapons of mass destruction, complex systems engineering, risk-benefit analysis. *Total annual research expenditures:* $7.6 million. *Unit head:* Dr. Philip Durkee, Dean, 831-656-2517, E-mail: durkee@nps.edu. Web site: http://www.nps.edu/Academics/Schools/GSEAS/Departments/SE/.

New Jersey Institute of Technology, Office of Graduate Studies, Newark College of Engineering, Department of Civil and Environmental Engineering, Program in Critical Infrastructure Systems, Newark, NJ 07102. Offers MS. *Students:* 2 full-time (1 woman), 1 part-time; includes 2 minority (both Asian, non-Hispanic/Latino). Average age 30. 7 applicants, 86% accepted, 1 enrolled. In 2011, 2 master's awarded. *Entrance requirements:* Additional exam requirements/recommendations for international students: Required—TOEFL (minimum score 550 paper-based; 213 computer-based; 79 iBT). *Application deadline:* For fall admission, 6/1 priority date for domestic students, 5/1 for international students; for spring admission, 11/15 priority date for domestic students, 11/15 for international students. Applications are processed on a rolling basis. Application fee: $65. Electronic applications accepted. *Expenses:* Tuition, state resident: full-time $7980; part-time $867 per credit. Tuition, nonresident: full-time $11,336; part-time $1196 per credit. *Required fees:* $230 per credit. *Financial support:* Application deadline: 1/15. *Unit head:* Dr. Taha F. Marhaba, Chair, 973-642-4599, E-mail: marhaba@njit.edu. *Application contact:* Kathryn Kelly, Director of Admissions, 973-596-3300, Fax: 973-596-3461, E-mail: admissions@njit.edu. Web site: http://civil.njit.edu/academics/graduate/ms-infrastructuresystems.php.

New Mexico Institute of Mining and Technology, Graduate Studies, Program in Engineering Science in Mechanics, Socorro, NM 87801. Offers explosives engineering (MS); fluid and thermal sciences (MS); mechatronics systems engineering (MS); solid mechanics (MS). *Faculty:* 5 full-time (0 women). *Students:* 26 full-time (1 woman), 19 part-time (1 woman); includes 13 minority (1 American Indian or Alaska Native, non-Hispanic/Latino; 1 Asian, non-Hispanic/Latino; 11 Hispanic/Latino). Average age 27. 21 applicants, 67% accepted, 11 enrolled. In 2011, 6 master's awarded. *Degree requirements:* For master's, thesis (for some programs). *Entrance requirements:* For master's, GRE General Test. Additional exam requirements/recommendations for international students: Required—TOEFL (minimum score 540 paper-based; 207 computer-based). *Application deadline:* For fall admission, 3/1 priority date for domestic students; for spring admission, 6/1 for domestic students. Applications are processed on a rolling basis. Application fee: $16 ($30 for international students). *Expenses:* Tuition, state resident: full-time $4849; part-time $269.41 per credit hour. Tuition, nonresident: full-time $16,041; part-time $891.15 per credit hour. *Required fees:* $622; $65 per credit hour. $20 per semester. Part-time tuition and fees vary according to course load. *Financial support:* In 2011–12, 9 research assistantships (averaging $18,997 per year), 5 teaching assistantships with full and partial tuition reimbursements (averaging $14,615 per year) were awarded; fellowships, Federal Work-Study, institutionally sponsored loans, and unspecified assistantships also available. Financial award application deadline: 3/1; financial award applicants required to submit CSS PROFILE or FAFSA. *Faculty research:* Vibrations, fluid-structure interactions. *Unit head:* Dr. Warren Ostergren, Chair, 575-835-5693, E-mail: warreno@nmt.edu. *Application contact:* Dr. Lorie Liebrock, Dean of Graduate Studies, 575-835-5513, Fax: 575-835-5476, E-mail: graduate@nmt.edu. Web site: http://infohost.nmt.edu/~mecheng/grad_programs.xml.

New Mexico State University, Graduate School, College of Engineering, Department of Industrial Engineering, Las Cruces, NM 88003-8001. Offers industrial engineering (MSIE, PhD); systems engineering (Graduate Certificate). Part-time and evening/weekend programs available. Postbaccalaureate distance learning degree programs offered (no on-campus study). *Faculty:* 6 full-time (2 women). *Students:* 45 full-time (11 women), 90 part-time (25 women); includes 41 minority (7 Black or African American, non-Hispanic/Latino; 1 American Indian or Alaska Native, non-Hispanic/Latino; 2 Asian, non-Hispanic/Latino; 29 Hispanic/Latino; 2 Two or more races, non-Hispanic/Latino), 25 international. Average age 31. 58 applicants, 76% accepted, 39 enrolled. In 2011, 41 master's, 2 doctorates, 6 other advanced degrees awarded. *Degree requirements:* For master's, thesis optional; for doctorate, comprehensive exam, thesis/dissertation. *Entrance requirements:* For doctorate, qualifying exam. Additional exam requirements/recommendations for international students: Required—TOEFL (minimum score 550 paper-based; 79 iBT), IELTS (minimum score 6.5). *Application deadline:* For fall admission, 7/1 priority date for domestic students, 3/1 for international students; for spring admission, 11/1 for domestic students, 10/1 for international students. Applications are processed on a rolling basis. Application fee: $40 ($50 for international students). Electronic applications accepted. *Expenses:* Tuition, state resident: full-time $5004; part-time $208.50 per credit. Tuition, nonresident: full-time $17,446; part-time $726.90 per credit. *Financial support:* In 2011–12, 2 fellowships (averaging $37,852 per year), 6 research assistantships (averaging $12,804 per year), 8 teaching assistantships (averaging $20,231 per year) were awarded; career-related internships or fieldwork, Federal Work-Study, health care benefits, and unspecified assistantships also available. Financial award application deadline: 3/1. *Faculty research:* Optimization, healthcare systems, manufacturing engineering, systems engineering. *Unit head:* Dr. Edward Pines, Head, 575-646-4923, Fax: 575-646-2976, E-mail: epines@nmsu.edu. *Application contact:* Sarah Deyoe, Department Secretary, 575-646-4923, Fax: 575-646-2976, E-mail: sdeyoe@nmsu.edu. Web site: http://ie.nmsu.edu.

North Carolina Agricultural and Technical State University, School of Graduate Studies, College of Engineering, Department of Industrial and Systems Engineering, Greensboro, NC 27411. Offers industrial engineering (MSIE, PhD). Part-time programs available. *Degree requirements:* For master's, thesis, project; for doctorate, thesis/dissertation. *Entrance requirements:* For master's, GRE General Test (recommended); for doctorate, GRE General Test, degree in engineering, BS in industrial engineering from ABET-accredited program with minimum cumulative credit point average of 3.7 or MS in discipline related to industrial engineering from college or university recognized by a regional or general accrediting agency with minimum cumulative GPA of 3.3. Additional exam requirements/recommendations for international students: Required—TOEFL (minimum score 550 paper-based; 213 computer-based; 79 iBT). *Faculty research:* Human-machine systems engineering, management systems engineering, operations research and systems analysis, production systems engineering.

Oakland University, Graduate Study and Lifelong Learning, School of Engineering and Computer Science, Department of Computer Science and Engineering, Rochester, MI 48309-4401. Offers computer science (MS); embedded systems (MS); information systems engineering (MS); software engineering (MS). Part-time and evening/weekend programs available. *Entrance requirements:* For master's, minimum GPA of 3.0 for unconditional admission. Electronic applications accepted. *Expenses:* Contact institution. *Faculty research:* Cyber security, 3D imaging of neurochemicals in rat brains.

Oakland University, Graduate Study and Lifelong Learning, School of Engineering and Computer Science, Department of Industrial and Systems Engineering, Program in Systems Engineering, Rochester, MI 48309-4401. Offers MS, PhD. *Degree requirements:* For doctorate, thesis/dissertation. *Entrance requirements:* For master's and doctorate, minimum GPA of 3.0 for unconditional admission. Additional exam requirements/recommendations for international students: Required—TOEFL (minimum score 550 paper-based; 213 computer-based). Electronic applications accepted. *Expenses:* Contact institution.

The Ohio State University, Graduate School, College of Engineering, Program in Industrial and Systems Engineering, Columbus, OH 43210. Offers industrial and systems engineering (MS, PhD); welding engineering (MS, MWE, PhD). *Faculty:* 20. *Students:* 66 full-time (22 women), 34 part-time (8 women); includes 6 minority (1 Black or African American, non-Hispanic/Latino; 3 Asian, non-Hispanic/Latino; 1 Hispanic/Latino; 1 Two or more races, non-Hispanic/Latino), 57 international. Average age 28. In 2011, 12 master's, 6 doctorates awarded. *Degree requirements:* For master's, thesis optional; for doctorate, thesis/dissertation. *Entrance requirements:* For master's and doctorate, GRE General Test. Additional exam requirements/recommendations for international students: Required—Michigan English Language Assessment Battery (minimum score 82); Recommended—TOEFL (minimum score 600 paper-based; 250 computer-based; 79 iBT). *Application deadline:* For fall admission, 8/15 priority date for domestic students, 11/1 for international students; for winter admission, 12/1 priority date for domestic students, 7/1 for international students; for spring admission, 3/1 priority date for domestic students, 2/1 for international students. Applications are processed on a rolling basis. Application fee: $40 ($50 for international students). Electronic applications accepted. *Expenses:* Tuition, state resident: full-time $11,400. Tuition, nonresident: full-time $28,125. Tuition and fees vary according to course load, degree level, campus/location and program. *Financial support:* Fellowships, research assistantships, teaching assistantships, career-related internships or fieldwork, Federal Work-Study, institutionally sponsored loans, and unspecified assistantships available. Support available to part-time students. *Unit head:* Dr. Philip J. Smith, Interim Department Chair, 614-292-4120, E-mail: smith.131@osu.edu. *Application contact:* Dr. Jerald Brevik, Graduate Studies Chair, 614-292-0177, Fax: 614-292-7852, E-mail: brevik.1@osu.edu. Web site: http://ise.osu.edu/.

Ohio University, Graduate College, Russ College of Engineering and Technology, Department of Industrial and Systems Engineering, Athens, OH 45701-2979. Offers M Eng Mgt, MS. Part-time and evening/weekend programs available. *Students:* 50 full-time (16 women), 23 part-time (5 women); includes 8 minority (3 Black or African American, non-Hispanic/Latino; 1 Asian, non-Hispanic/Latino; 3 Hispanic/Latino; 1 Two or more races, non-Hispanic/Latino), 14 international. 67 applicants, 57% accepted, 29 enrolled. In 2011, 26 master's awarded. *Degree requirements:* For master's, comprehensive exam (for some programs), thesis optional, research project. *Entrance requirements:* For master's, GRE General Test. Additional exam requirements/recommendations for international students: Required—TOEFL (minimum score 550 paper-based; 80 iBT) or IELTS (minimum score 6.5). *Application deadline:* For fall admission, 3/1 priority date for domestic students, 3/1 for international students; for winter admission, 9/1 priority date for domestic students, 9/1 for international students; for spring admission, 1/1 priority date for domestic students, 1/1 for international students. Applications are processed on a rolling basis. Application fee: $50 ($55 for international students). Electronic applications accepted. *Financial support:* In 2011–12, research assistantships with full tuition reimbursements (averaging $9,000 per year) were awarded; Federal Work-Study, institutionally sponsored loans, tuition waivers (full), and unspecified assistantships also available. Financial award application deadline: 2/15; financial award applicants required to submit FAFSA. *Faculty research:* Software systems integration, human factors and ergonomics. *Total annual research expenditures:* $350,000. *Unit head:* Dr. Robert P. Judd, Chairman, 740-593-0106, Fax: 740-593-0778, E-mail: judd@ohio.edu. *Application contact:* Dr. Gursel Suer, Graduate Chairman, 740-593-1542, Fax: 740-593-0778, E-mail: suer@ohio.edu. Web site: http://www.ohio.edu/industrial/.

Old Dominion University, Frank Batten College of Engineering and Technology, Program in Engineering Management and Systems Engineering, Norfolk, VA 23529. Offers D Eng. Part-time and evening/weekend programs available. Postbaccalaureate distance learning degree programs offered (no on-campus study). *Faculty:* 14 full-time (3 women), 9 part-time/adjunct (1 woman). *Students:* 4 full-time (1 woman), 11 part-time (2 women); includes 4 minority (1 Black or African American, non-Hispanic/Latino; 3 Hispanic/Latino). Average age 42. 3 applicants, 67% accepted, 2 enrolled. *Degree requirements:* For doctorate, thesis/dissertation, candidacy exam, project. *Entrance requirements:* For doctorate, GRE, resume, letters of recommendation, minimum GPA of 3.0, interview. Additional exam requirements/recommendations for international students: Required—TOEFL (minimum score 550 paper-based; 213 computer-based; 79 iBT). *Application deadline:* For fall admission, 6/1 priority date for domestic students, 4/15 for international students; for spring admission, 11/1 priority date for domestic students, 2/1 for international students. Applications are processed on a rolling basis. Application fee: $50. Electronic applications accepted. *Expenses:* Tuition, state resident: full-time $9096; part-time $379 per credit. Tuition, nonresident: full-time $23,064; part-time $961 per credit. *Required fees:* $127 per semester. One-time fee: $50. *Financial support:* In 2011–12, research assistantships with full and partial tuition reimbursements (averaging $20,000 per year), teaching assistantships with full and partial tuition reimbursements (averaging $20,000 per year) were awarded; fellowships, career-related internships or fieldwork, and tuition waivers also available. Support available to part-time students. Financial award application deadline: 2/15; financial award applicants required to submit FAFSA. *Faculty research:* Project management, systems engineering, modeling and simulation, virtual collaboration environments, multidisciplinary designs. *Total annual research expenditures:* $3.2 million. *Unit head:* Dr. Resit Unal, Department Chair, 757-683-4558, Fax: 757-683-5640, E-mail: enmagpd@odu.edu. *Application contact:* Dr. Ariel Pinto, Graduate Program Director, 757-683-4218, Fax: 757-683-5640, E-mail: enmagpd@odu.edu. Web site: http://eng.odu.edu/enma/.

Old Dominion University, Frank Batten College of Engineering and Technology, Program in Systems Engineering, Norfolk, VA 23529. Offers ME. Part-time and evening/weekend programs available. Postbaccalaureate distance learning degree programs offered (no on-campus study). *Faculty:* 14 full-time (3 women), 9 part-time/adjunct (1 woman). *Students:* 6 full-time (0 women), 31 part-time (7 women); includes 11 minority (5 Black or African American, non-Hispanic/Latino; 2 Asian, non-Hispanic/Latino; 3 Hispanic/Latino; 1 Two or more races, non-Hispanic/Latino), 2 international. Average age 34. 16 applicants, 81% accepted, 11 enrolled. In 2011, 11 master's awarded. *Degree requirements:* For master's, comprehensive exam, project. *Entrance requirements:* For master's, GRE, minimum GPA of 3.0. Additional exam requirements/recommendations for international students: Required—TOEFL (minimum score 550 paper-based; 213 computer-based; 79 iBT). *Application deadline:* For fall admission, 6/1 priority date for domestic students, 4/15 for international students; for spring admission, 11/1 priority date for domestic students, 2/1 for international students. Applications are processed on a rolling basis. Application fee: $50. Electronic applications accepted. *Expenses:* Tuition, state resident: full-time $9096; part-time $379 per credit. Tuition, nonresident: full-time $23,064; part-time $961 per credit. *Required fees:* $127 per semester. One-time fee: $50. *Financial support:* In 2011–12, research assistantships with partial tuition reimbursements (averaging $20,000 per year), teaching assistantships with partial tuition reimbursements (averaging $20,000 per year) were awarded; fellowships, career-related internships or fieldwork, scholarships/grants, and tuition waivers (partial) also available. Support available to part-time students. Financial award application deadline: 2/15; financial award applicants required to submit FAFSA. *Faculty research:* System of systems engineering, complex systems, optimization. *Total annual research expenditures:* $3.2 million. *Unit head:* Dr. Resit Unal, Chair, 757-683-4558, Fax: 757-683-5640, E-mail: enmagpd@odu.edu. *Application contact:* Dr. Ariel Pinto, Graduate Program Director, 757-683-4218, Fax: 757-683-5640, E-mail: enmagpd@odu.edu. Web site: http://eng.odu.edu/enma/academics/systemsengr.shtml.

Oregon State University, Graduate School, College of Engineering, School of Mechanical, Industrial, and Manufacturing Engineering, Corvallis, OR 97331. Offers human systems engineering (MS, PhD); industrial engineering (MS, PhD); information systems engineering (MS, PhD); manufacturing engineering (M Engr); manufacturing systems engineering (MS, PhD); materials science (MAIS, MS, PhD); mechanical engineering (MS, PhD); nano/micro fabrication (MS, PhD). Part-time programs available. Postbaccalaureate distance learning degree programs offered (minimal on-campus study). *Degree requirements:* For master's, thesis or alternative; for doctorate, thesis/dissertation. *Entrance requirements:* For master's, placement exam, minimum GPA of 3.0 in last 90 hours of course work; for doctorate, GRE, placement exam, minimum GPA of 3.0 in last 90 hours of course work. Additional exam requirements/recommendations for international students: Required—TOEFL (minimum score 550 paper-based; 213 computer-based). *Faculty research:* Computer-integrated manufacturing, human factors, robotics, decision support systems, simulation modeling and analysis.

Penn State Great Valley, Graduate Studies, Engineering Division, Malvern, PA 19355-1488. Offers engineering management (MEM); information science (MS); software engineering (MSE); systems engineering (M Eng). Postbaccalaureate distance learning degree programs offered (no on-campus study). *Unit head:* Dr. James A. Nemes, Interim Director, Academic Affairs, 610-648-3335 Ext. 610, Fax: 648-648-3377, E-mail: jan16@psu.edu. *Application contact:* 610-648-3242, Fax: 610-889-1334. Web site: http://www.sgps.psu.edu/Level3.aspx?id=662.

Polytechnic Institute of New York University, Department of Electrical and Computer Engineering, Major in Systems Engineering, Brooklyn, NY 11201-2990. Offers MS. Part-time and evening/weekend programs available. *Students:* 9 full-time (3 women), 4 part-time (2 women); includes 4 minority (2 Black or African American, non-Hispanic/Latino; 2 Asian, non-Hispanic/Latino), 6 international. Average age 26. 16 applicants, 50% accepted, 3 enrolled. In 2011, 2 master's awarded. *Degree requirements:* For master's, comprehensive exam (for some programs), thesis (for some programs). *Entrance requirements:* For master's, BS in electrical engineering. Additional exam requirements/recommendations for international students: Required—TOEFL (minimum score 550 paper-based; 213 computer-based; 80 iBT); Recommended—IELTS (minimum score 6.5). *Application deadline:* For fall admission, 7/31 priority date for domestic students, 4/30 for international students; for spring admission, 12/31 priority date for domestic students, 11/30 for international students. Applications are processed on a rolling basis. Application fee: $75. Electronic applications accepted. *Expenses: Tuition:* Full-time $22,464; part-time $1248 per credit. *Required fees:* $501 per semester. *Financial support:* Fellowships, research assistantships, teaching assistantships, institutionally sponsored loans, scholarships/grants, and unspecified assistantships available. Support available to part-time students. Financial award applicants required to submit FAFSA. *Unit head:* Dr. Jonathan Chao, Head, 718-860-3478, Fax: 718-260-3302, E-mail: chao@poly.edu. *Application contact:* JeanCarlo Bonilla, Director, Graduate Enrollment Management, 718-260-3182, Fax: 718-260-3624.

Polytechnic Institute of NYU, Long Island Graduate Center, Graduate Programs, Department of Computer Science and Engineering, Melville, NY 11747. Offers computer science (MS); information systems engineering (MS). Part-time and evening/weekend programs available. *Faculty:* 5 part-time/adjunct (0 women). *Students:* 2 full-time, 2 part-time; includes 2 minority (1 Black or African American, non-Hispanic/Latino; 1 Asian, non-Hispanic/Latino). Average age 32. 10 applicants, 60% accepted, 4 enrolled. In 2011, 7 master's awarded. *Degree requirements:* For master's, comprehensive exam (for some programs), thesis (for some programs). *Entrance requirements:* Additional exam requirements/recommendations for international students: Required—TOEFL (minimum score 550 paper-based; 213 computer-based; 80 iBT); Recommended—IELTS (minimum score 6.5). *Application deadline:* For fall admission, 7/31 priority date for domestic students, 4/30 for international students; for spring admission, 12/31 priority date for domestic students, 11/30 for international students. Applications are processed on a rolling basis. Application fee: $75. Electronic applications accepted. *Financial support:* In 2011–12, 36 fellowships (averaging $2,037 per year) were awarded; institutionally sponsored loans, scholarships/grants, and unspecified assistantships also available. Support available to part-time students. Financial award applicants required to submit FAFSA. *Faculty research:* Ultra-wideband electromagnetics, high resolution space-time signal, medical image compression, microwave-plasma interaction. *Unit head:* Dr. Keith W. Ross, Department Head, 718-260-3859, E-mail: ross@poly.edu. *Application contact:* JeanCarlo Bonilla, Director of Graduate Enrollment Management, 718-260-3182, Fax: 718-260-3624, E-mail: gradinfo@poly.edu.

Polytechnic Institute of NYU, Long Island Graduate Center, Graduate Programs, Department of Electrical and Computer Engineering, Program in Systems Engineering, Melville, NY 11747. Offers MS. Part-time and evening/weekend programs available. *Students:* 1 full-time (0 women), 1 part-time (0 women); includes 1 minority (Black or African American, non-Hispanic/Latino), 1 international. Average age 30. 3 applicants, 67% accepted, 2 enrolled. In 2011, 1 master's awarded. *Degree requirements:* For master's, comprehensive exam (for some programs), thesis (for some programs). *Entrance requirements:* Additional exam requirements/recommendations for international students: Required—TOEFL (minimum score 550 paper-based; 213 computer-based; 80 iBT); Recommended—IELTS (minimum score 6.5). *Application deadline:* For fall admission, 7/31 priority date for domestic students, 4/30 for international students; for spring admission, 12/31 priority date for domestic students, 11/30 for international students. Applications are processed on a rolling basis. Application fee: $75. Electronic applications accepted. *Financial support:* Institutionally sponsored loans, scholarships/grants, and unspecified assistantships available. Support available to part-time students. *Unit head:* Dr. Jonathan Chao, Department Head, 718-260-3302, E-mail: chao@poly.edu. *Application contact:* JeanCarlo Bonilla, Director of Graduate Enrollment Management, 718-260-3182, Fax: 718-260-3624, E-mail: gradinfo@poly.edu.

Portland State University, Graduate Studies, Maseeh College of Engineering and Computer Science, Program in Systems Engineering, Portland, OR 97207-0751. Offers systems engineering (M Eng); systems engineering fundamentals (Certificate). Postbaccalaureate distance learning degree programs offered (no on-campus study). *Degree requirements:* For master's, internship/project. *Entrance requirements:* For master's, 3 years of engineering experience, bachelor's degree in engineering, minimum undergraduate GPA of 3.0 in upper division courses. Additional exam requirements/recommendations for international students: Required—TOEFL (minimum score 550 paper-based; 213 computer-based).

Regis University, College for Professional Studies, School of Computer and Information Sciences, Denver, CO 80221-1099. Offers database administration with Oracle (Certificate); database development (Certificate); database technologies (M Sc); enterprise Java software development (Certificate); enterprise resource planning (Certificate); executive information technologies (Certificate); information assurance (M Sc, Certificate); information technology management (M Sc); software engineering

(M Sc, Certificate); software engineering and database technologies (M Sc); storage area networks (Certificate); systems engineering (M Sc, Certificate). Offered at Boulder Campus, Northwest Denver Campus, Southeast Denver Campus, Fort Collins Campus, Colorado Springs Campus, and Broomfield Campus. Part-time and evening/weekend programs available. Postbaccalaureate distance learning degree programs offered (no on-campus study). *Degree requirements:* For master's, thesis, final research project. *Entrance requirements:* For master's, 2 years of related experience, resume, interview; for Certificate, 2 years of related experience, resumé. Additional exam requirements/recommendations for international students: Required—TOEFL (minimum score 213 computer-based), TWE (minimum score 5) or university-based test. Electronic applications accepted. *Expenses:* Contact institution. *Faculty research:* Secure Virtual Laboratory Architecture, Joint IA project with W2C06 Institute, Information Policy, OLTP and OLAP Technologies, knowledge management, software architectures.

Rensselaer Polytechnic Institute, Graduate School, School of Engineering, Program in Computer and Systems Engineering, Troy, NY 12180-3590. Offers M Eng, MS, PhD. Part-time programs available. Terminal master's awarded for partial completion of doctoral program. *Degree requirements:* For master's, thesis (for some programs); for doctorate, thesis/dissertation. *Entrance requirements:* For master's, GRE; for doctorate, GRE, qualifying exam, candidacy exam. Additional exam requirements/recommendations for international students: Required—TOEFL (minimum score 570 paper-based; 89 iBT). Electronic applications accepted. *Faculty research:* Multimedia via ATM, mobile robotics, thermophotovoltaic devices, microelectronic interconnections, agile manufacturing.

Rensselaer Polytechnic Institute, Graduate School, School of Engineering, Program in Decision Sciences and Engineering Systems, Troy, NY 12180-3590. Offers industrial and systems engineering (PhD). Part-time programs available. Terminal master's awarded for partial completion of doctoral program. *Degree requirements:* For doctorate, thesis/dissertation. *Entrance requirements:* For doctorate, GRE General Test (minimum score 550 verbal). Additional exam requirements/recommendations for international students: Required—TOEFL (minimum score 570 paper-based). Electronic applications accepted. *Faculty research:* Decision support systems, simulation and modeling, statistical methods/computing, operations research, supply chain logistics.

Rensselaer Polytechnic Institute, Graduate School, School of Engineering, Program in Systems Engineering and Technology Management, Troy, NY 12180-3590. Offers M Eng. Part-time programs available. *Degree requirements:* For master's, thesis (for some programs). *Entrance requirements:* For master's, GRE General Test (minimum score 550 Verbal). Additional exam requirements/recommendations for international students: Required—TOEFL (minimum score 570 paper-based). Electronic applications accepted. *Faculty research:* Decision support systems, simulation and modeling, statistical methods/computing, operations research, supply chain logistics.

Rochester Institute of Technology, Graduate Enrollment Services, Kate Gleason College of Engineering, Department of Industrial and Systems Engineering, Rochester, NY 14623-5603. Offers engineering management (ME); industrial engineering (ME, MS); manufacturing engineering (ME, MS); systems engineering (ME). Part-time programs available. *Students:* 58 full-time (13 women), 31 part-time (13 women); includes 3 minority (1 Black or African American, non-Hispanic/Latino; 1 Asian, non-Hispanic/Latino; 1 Hispanic/Latino), 59 international. Average age 25. 231 applicants, 44% accepted, 34 enrolled. In 2011, 49 degrees awarded. *Degree requirements:* For master's, internship. *Entrance requirements:* For master's, GRE, minimum GPA of 3.0. Additional exam requirements/recommendations for international students: Required—TOEFL (minimum score 570 paper-based; 230 computer-based; 88 iBT) or IELTS (minimum score 6.5). *Application deadline:* For fall admission, 2/15 priority date for domestic students, 2/15 for international students. Applications are processed on a rolling basis. Application fee: $50. *Expenses: Tuition:* Full-time $34,659; part-time $963 per credit hour. *Required fees:* $228; $76 per quarter. *Financial support:* Research assistantships with partial tuition reimbursements, teaching assistantships with partial tuition reimbursements, career-related internships or fieldwork, institutionally sponsored loans, scholarships/grants, tuition waivers (partial), and unspecified assistantships available. Support available to part-time students. Financial award applicants required to submit FAFSA. *Faculty research:* Operations; manufacturing systems and sustainable product design; product development and design robustness; lean manufacturing; ergonomics/human factors; simulation, systems engineering; rapid prototyping, rapid manufacturing. *Unit head:* Dr. Scott E. Grasman, Interim Department Head, 585-475-2598, E-mail: scott.grasman@rit.edu. *Application contact:* Diane Ellison, Assistant Vice President, Graduate Enrollment Services, 585-475-2229, Fax: 585-475-7164, E-mail: gradinfo@rit.edu.

Rochester Institute of Technology, Graduate Enrollment Services, Kate Gleason College of Engineering, Department of Microsystems Engineering, Rochester, NY 14623-5603. Offers PhD. Part-time programs available. *Students:* 29 full-time (7 women), 9 part-time (0 women); includes 3 minority (1 Black or African American, non-Hispanic/Latino; 1 American Indian or Alaska Native, non-Hispanic/Latino; 1 Asian, non-Hispanic/Latino), 17 international. Average age 30. 34 applicants, 26% accepted, 7 enrolled. In 2011, 11 degrees awarded. *Degree requirements:* For doctorate, comprehensive exam, thesis/dissertation. *Entrance requirements:* For doctorate, GRE. Additional exam requirements/recommendations for international students: Required—TOEFL (minimum score 570 paper-based; 230 computer-based; 88 iBT) or IELTS (minimum score 6.5). *Application deadline:* For fall admission, 2/15 priority date for domestic students, 2/15 for international students. Application fee: $50. *Expenses: Tuition:* Full-time $34,659; part-time $963 per credit hour. *Required fees:* $228; $76 per quarter. *Financial support:* Fellowships with full tuition reimbursements, research assistantships with partial tuition reimbursements, teaching assistantships with partial tuition reimbursements, career-related internships or fieldwork, institutionally sponsored loans, scholarships/grants, health care benefits, and unspecified assistantships available. Support available to part-time students. Financial award applicants required to submit FAFSA. *Faculty research:* Scaling-driven nanoelectronics, MEMS (micro-electro-mechanical systems); photonics and nanophotonics imaging, communications, and sensing research; photovoltaics research in silicon, organic, and stacked solar cells and thermovoltaics; microfluids research on the behavior, control, and manipulation of fluids at the micro-scale. *Unit head:* Dr. Bruce Smith, Director, 585-475-2058, Fax: 585-475-6879, E-mail: bwsemc@rit.edu. *Application contact:* Diane Ellison, Assistant Vice President, Graduate Enrollment Services, 585-475-2229, Fax: 585-475-7164, E-mail: gradinfo@rit.edu.

Rochester Institute of Technology, Graduate Enrollment Services, Kate Gleason College of Engineering, Program in Product Development, Rochester, NY 14623-5603. Offers MS. Part-time and evening/weekend programs available. *Students:* 1 full-time (0 women), 43 part-time (2 women); includes 5 minority (1 Black or African American, non-Hispanic/Latino; 3 Asian, non-Hispanic/Latino; 1 Hispanic/Latino). Average age 38. 18 applicants, 89% accepted, 16 enrolled. In 2011, 12 degrees awarded. *Degree requirements:* For master's, capstone project. *Entrance requirements:* For master's,

undergraduate degree in engineering or related field, minimum GPA of 3.0, 5 years experience in product development. Additional exam requirements/recommendations for international students: Required—TOEFL (minimum score 570 paper-based; 230 computer-based; 88 iBT) or IELTS (minimum score 6.5). *Application deadline:* For fall admission, 2/15 priority date for domestic students, 2/15 for international students. Application fee: $50. *Expenses:* Contact institution. *Financial support:* Applicants required to submit FAFSA. *Faculty research:* Platform element dynamics in a multi-product development environment, applying self-organizing principles to product development in a globally-distributed environment, collaborative design and development to accelerate durable goods design and manufacturing. *Unit head:* Christine Fisher, Graduate Program Director, 585-475-7971, Fax: 585-475-4080, E-mail: mpdmail@rit.edu. *Application contact:* Diane Ellison, Assistant Vice President, Graduate Enrollment Services, 585-475-2229, Fax: 585-475-7164, E-mail: gradinfo@rit.edu. Web site: http://www.rit.edu/kgcoe/mpd/.

Rutgers, The State University of New Jersey, New Brunswick, Graduate School-New Brunswick, Department of Industrial and Systems Engineering, Piscataway, NJ 08854-8097. Offers industrial and systems engineering (MS, PhD); information technology (MS); manufacturing systems engineering (MS); quality and reliability engineering (MS). Part-time and evening/weekend programs available. Terminal master's awarded for partial completion of doctoral program. *Degree requirements:* For master's, thesis or alternative, seminar; for doctorate, comprehensive exam, thesis/dissertation. *Entrance requirements:* For master's and doctorate, GRE General Test. Additional exam requirements/recommendations for international students: Required—TOEFL. *Faculty research:* Production and manufacturing systems, quality and reliability engineering, systems engineering and aviation safety.

San Jose State University, Graduate Studies and Research, Charles W. Davidson College of Engineering, Department of Industrial and Systems Engineering, San Jose, CA 95192-0001. Offers industrial and systems engineering (MS). Part-time programs available. *Degree requirements:* For master's, comprehensive exam. Electronic applications accepted.

Southern Methodist University, Bobby B. Lyle School of Engineering, Department of Engineering Management, Information, and Systems, Dallas, TX 75275. Offers applied science (MS); engineering management (MSEM, DE); information engineering and management (MSIEM); operations research (MS, PhD); systems engineering (MS, PhD). Part-time and evening/weekend programs available. Postbaccalaureate distance learning degree programs offered. Terminal master's awarded for partial completion of doctoral program. *Degree requirements:* For master's, thesis optional; for doctorate, thesis/dissertation, oral and written qualifying exams. *Entrance requirements:* For master's, minimum GPA of 3.0 in last 2 years; bachelor's degree in engineering, mathematics, sciences, or technical area; for doctorate, GRE General Test (operations research, engineering management), bachelor's degree in related field. Additional exam requirements/recommendations for international students: Required—TOEFL. *Faculty research:* Telecommunications, decision systems, information engineering, operations research, software.

Southern Polytechnic State University, School of Engineering, Department of Mechanical and Systems Engineering, Marietta, GA 30060-2896. Offers systems engineering (MS). Part-time and evening/weekend programs available. Postbaccalaureate distance learning degree programs offered (no on-campus study). *Faculty:* 3 full-time (1 woman), 2 part-time/adjunct (0 women). *Students:* 3 full-time (0 women), 49 part-time (9 women); includes 17 minority (10 Black or African American, non-Hispanic/Latino; 4 Asian, non-Hispanic/Latino; 2 Hispanic/Latino; 1 Two or more races, non-Hispanic/Latino), 3 international. Average age 39. 19 applicants, 84% accepted, 12 enrolled. In 2011, 13 master's, 1 other advanced degree awarded. *Degree requirements:* For master's, thesis optional. *Entrance requirements:* For master's, GRE. Additional exam requirements/recommendations for international students: Required—TOEFL (minimum score 550 paper-based; 213 computer-based; 79 iBT), IELTS (minimum score 6.5). *Application deadline:* For fall admission, 7/1 priority date for domestic students, 5/1 for international students; for spring admission, 11/1 priority date for domestic students, 9/1 for international students. Applications are processed on a rolling basis. Application fee: $50. Electronic applications accepted. *Expenses: Tuition,* state resident: full-time $2592; part-time $216 per semester hour. Tuition, nonresident: full-time $9408; part-time $784 per semester hour. *Required fees:* $698 per term. *Faculty research:* Supply chain and logistics reliability, maintainability system analysis, design optimization, engineering education. *Unit head:* Dr. Renee Butler, Department Chair, 678-915-5414, Fax: 678-915-5527, E-mail: rbutler@spsu.edu. *Application contact:* Nikki Palamiotis, Director of Graduate Studies, 678-915-4276, Fax: 678-915-7292, E-mail: npalamio@spsu.edu. Web site: http://www.spsu.edu/systemseng/graduate_programs/index.htm.

Stevens Institute of Technology, Graduate School, School of Systems and Enterprises, Program in Systems Engineering, Hoboken, NJ 07030. Offers agile systems and enterprises (Certificate); systems and supportability engineering (Certificate); systems engineering (M Eng, PhD); systems engineering management (Certificate).

Stony Brook University, State University of New York, Graduate School, College of Engineering and Applied Sciences, Department of Computer Science, Program in Information Systems Engineering, Stony Brook, NY 11794. Offers MS.

Syracuse University, L. C. Smith College of Engineering and Computer Science, Program in Systems Assurance, Syracuse, NY 13244. Offers CAS. *Entrance requirements:* For degree, GRE General Test. *Expenses: Tuition:* Part-time $1206 per credit. *Application contact:* Kathleen Joyce, Assistant Dean, 314-443-2219, E-mail: topgrads@syr.edu. Web site: http://lcs.syr.edu.

Texas Tech University, Graduate School, Edward E. Whitacre Jr. College of Engineering, Department of Industrial Engineering, Lubbock, TX 79409. Offers industrial engineering (MSIE, PhD); systems and engineering management (MSSEM, PhD). Part-time programs available. Postbaccalaureate distance learning degree programs offered (minimal on-campus study). *Faculty:* 13 full-time (2 women), 2 part-time/adjunct (1 woman). *Students:* 66 full-time (13 women), 47 part-time (7 women); includes 12 minority (3 Black or African American, non-Hispanic/Latino; 1 Asian, non-Hispanic/Latino; 7 Hispanic/Latino; 1 Two or more races, non-Hispanic/Latino), 57 international. Average age 31. 201 applicants, 50% accepted, 22 enrolled. In 2011, 28 master's, 9 doctorates awarded. *Degree requirements:* For master's, thesis or alternative; for doctorate, thesis/dissertation. *Entrance requirements:* For master's, GRE General Test; for doctorate, GRE General Test, MS. Additional exam requirements/recommendations for international students: Required—TOEFL (minimum score 550 paper-based; 213 computer-based; 79 iBT). *Application deadline:* For fall admission, 6/1 priority date for domestic students, 1/15 for international students; for spring admission, 9/1 priority date for domestic students, 6/15 for international students. Applications are processed on a rolling basis. Application fee: $50 ($75 for international students). Electronic applications accepted. *Expenses:* Tuition, state resident: full-time $5899; part-time $245.80 per credit hour. Tuition, nonresident: full-time $13,411; part-time $558.80 per credit hour. *Required fees:* $2680.60; $86.50 per credit hour. $920.30 per semester. *Financial support:* In 2011–12, 32 students received support. Application deadline: 4/15; applicants required to submit FAFSA. *Faculty research:* Knowledge and engineering management, environmentally conscious manufacturing, biomechanical simulation, aviation security, supply chain management. *Total annual research expenditures:* $924,834. *Unit head:* Dr. Pat Patterson, Chair, 806-742-3543, Fax: 806-742-3411, E-mail: pat.patterson@ttu.edu. *Application contact:* Dr. Mario Beruvides, Professor, 806-742-3543, Fax: 806-742-3411, E-mail: mario.beruvides@ttu.edu. Web site: http://www.ie.ttu.edu/.

The University of Alabama in Huntsville, School of Graduate Studies, College of Engineering, Department of Industrial and Systems Engineering and Engineering Management, Huntsville, AL 35899. Offers industrial and systems engineering (MSE, PhD); industrial engineering (MSE, PhD); operations research (MSOR); systems engineering (MSE). Part-time and evening/weekend programs available. Postbaccalaureate distance learning degree programs offered (minimal on-campus study). *Faculty:* 9 full-time (2 women), 3 part-time/adjunct (1 woman). *Students:* 13 full-time (7 women), 147 part-time (39 women); includes 25 minority (14 Black or African American, non-Hispanic/Latino; 3 American Indian or Alaska Native, non-Hispanic/Latino; 4 Asian, non-Hispanic/Latino; 3 Hispanic/Latino; 1 Two or more races, non-Hispanic/Latino), 4 international. Average age 35. 98 applicants, 56% accepted, 32 enrolled. In 2011, 23 master's, 5 doctorates awarded. *Degree requirements:* For master's, comprehensive exam, thesis or alternative, oral and written exams; for doctorate, comprehensive exam, thesis/dissertation, oral and written exams. *Entrance requirements:* For master's and doctorate, GRE General Test, minimum GPA of 3.0. Additional exam requirements/recommendations for international students: Required—TOEFL (minimum score 500 paper-based; 173 computer-based; 62 iBT). *Application deadline:* For fall admission, 7/15 for domestic students, 4/1 for international students; for spring admission, 11/30 for domestic students, 9/1 for international students. Applications are processed on a rolling basis. Application fee: $40 ($50 for international students). Electronic applications accepted. *Expenses:* Tuition, state resident: full-time $7830; part-time $473.50 per credit. Tuition, nonresident: full-time $18,748; part-time $1128.33 per credit. Tuition and fees vary according to course load and program. *Financial support:* In 2011–12, 8 students received support, including 2 research assistantships with full tuition reimbursements available (averaging $6,784 per year), 5 teaching assistantships with full tuition reimbursements available (averaging $12,080 per year); career-related internships or fieldwork, Federal Work-Study, institutionally sponsored loans, scholarships/grants, health care benefits, and unspecified assistantships also available. Support available to part-time students. Financial award application deadline: 4/1; financial award applicants required to submit FAFSA. *Faculty research:* Engineering management, systems engineering, manufacturing, logistics, simulation. *Total annual research expenditures:* $8.4 million. *Unit head:* Dr. James Swain, Chair, 256-824-6749, Fax: 256-824-6733, E-mail: jswain@ise.uah.edu. *Application contact:* Kim Gray, Graduate Studies Admissions Coordinator, 256-824-6002, Fax: 256-824-6405, E-mail: deangrad@uah.edu. Web site: http://www.uah.edu/eng/departments/iseem/welcome.

University of Alberta, Faculty of Graduate Studies and Research, Department of Electrical and Computer Engineering, Edmonton, AB T6G 2E1, Canada. Offers communications (M Eng, M Sc, PhD); computer engineering (M Eng, M Sc, PhD); electromagnetics (M Eng, M Sc, PhD); nanotechnology and microdevices (M Eng, M Sc, PhD); power/power electronics (M Eng, M Sc, PhD); systems (M Eng, M Sc, PhD). Terminal master's awarded for partial completion of doctoral program. *Degree requirements:* For master's, thesis; for doctorate, thesis/dissertation. *Entrance requirements:* Additional exam requirements/recommendations for international students: Required—TOEFL. Electronic applications accepted. *Faculty research:* Controls, communications, microelectronics, electromagnetics.

The University of Arizona, College of Engineering, Department of Systems and Industrial Engineering, Program in Systems and Industrial Engineering, Tucson, AZ 85721. Offers MS, PhD. Postbaccalaureate distance learning degree programs offered. *Faculty:* 7 full-time (1 woman). *Students:* 29 full-time (5 women), 1 part-time (0 women), all international. Average age 27. 24 applicants, 75% accepted, 6 enrolled. In 2011, 3 doctorates awarded. *Degree requirements:* For doctorate, thesis/dissertation. *Entrance requirements:* For master's, GRE General Test (minimum score: 500 Verbal, 700 Quantitative), 3 letters of recommendation, letter of intent; for doctorate, GRE General Test (minimum score: 500 Verbal, 750 Quantitative), 3 letters of recommendation, letter of intent. Additional exam requirements/recommendations for international students: Required—TOEFL (minimum score 575 paper-based; 233 computer-based; 80 iBT). *Application deadline:* For fall admission, 6/1 for domestic students, 12/1 for international students; for spring admission, 9/1 for domestic students, 6/1 for international students. Applications are processed on a rolling basis. Application fee: $75. Electronic applications accepted. *Expenses:* Tuition, state resident: full-time $10,840. Tuition, nonresident: full-time $25,802. *Financial support:* Tuition waivers (full) and unspecified assistantships available. *Faculty research:* Optimization, systems theory, logistics, transportation, embedded systems. *Unit head:* Dr. K. Larry Head, Head, 520-621-6551, E-mail: larry@sie.arizona.edu. *Application contact:* Linda Cramer, Graduate Secretary, 520-626-4644, Fax: 520-621-6555, E-mail: gradapp@sie.arizona.edu. Web site: http://www.sie.arizona.edu.

The University of Arizona, College of Engineering, Department of Systems and Industrial Engineering, Program in Systems Engineering, Tucson, AZ 85721. Offers MS, PhD. Part-time programs available. *Faculty:* 7 full-time (1 woman). *Students:* 7 full-time (2 women), 6 part-time (0 women); includes 5 minority (1 Asian, non-Hispanic/Latino; 3 Hispanic/Latino; 1 Two or more races, non-Hispanic/Latino). Average age 29. 20 applicants, 60% accepted, 9 enrolled. In 2011, 13 master's awarded. *Entrance requirements:* For master's, GRE General Test (minimum score: 500 Verbal, 700 Quantitative), 3 letters of recommendation, letter of intent; for doctorate, GRE General Test (minimum score: 500 Verbal, 750 Quantitative), minimum GPA of 3.5, 3 letters of recommendation, letter of intent. Additional exam requirements/recommendations for international students: Required—TOEFL (minimum score 575 paper-based; 233 computer-based; 80 iBT). *Application deadline:* For fall admission, 6/1 for domestic students, 12/1 for international students; for spring admission, 10/1 for domestic students, 6/1 for international students. Applications are processed on a rolling basis. Application fee: $75. Electronic applications accepted. *Expenses:* Tuition, state resident: full-time $10,840. Tuition, nonresident: full-time $25,802. *Financial support:* Institutionally sponsored loans, scholarships/grants, and unspecified assistantships available. *Faculty research:* Man/machine systems, optimal control, algorithmic probability. *Unit head:* Dr. K. Larry Head, Head, 520-621-6551, E-mail: larry@sie.arizona.edu. *Application contact:* Linda Cramer, Graduate Secretary, 520-626-4644, Fax: 520-621-6555, E-mail: gradapp@sie.arizona.edu. Web site: http://www.sie.arizona.edu.

University of Arkansas at Little Rock, Graduate School, George W. Donaghey College of Engineering and Information Technology, Department of Systems Engineering, Little Rock, AR 72204-1099. Offers Graduate Certificate.

University of Central Florida, College of Engineering and Computer Science, Department of Industrial Engineering and Management Systems, Orlando, FL 32816. Offers applied operations research (Certificate); design for usability (Certificate); engineering management (PSM); industrial engineering (MSIE, PhD); industrial engineering and management systems (MS); industrial ergonomics and safety (Certificate); project engineering (Certificate); quality assurance (Certificate); systems engineering (Certificate); systems simulation for engineers (Certificate); training simulation (Certificate). Part-time and evening/weekend programs available. *Faculty:* 18 full-time (4 women), 5 part-time/adjunct (1 woman). *Students:* 105 full-time (27 women), 151 part-time (47 women); includes 84 minority (20 Black or African American, non-Hispanic/Latino; 1 American Indian or Alaska Native, non-Hispanic/Latino; 20 Asian, non-Hispanic/Latino; 37 Hispanic/Latino; 1 Native Hawaiian or other Pacific Islander, non-Hispanic/Latino; 5 Two or more races, non-Hispanic/Latino), 52 international. Average age 32. 199 applicants, 79% accepted, 75 enrolled. In 2011, 83 master's, 11 doctorates, 40 other advanced degrees awarded. *Degree requirements:* For master's, thesis; for doctorate, thesis/dissertation, departmental qualifying exam, candidacy exam. *Entrance requirements:* For master's, GRE General Test, minimum GPA of 3.0 in last 60 hours of course work; for doctorate, minimum GPA of 3.5 in last 60 hours of course work. Additional exam requirements/recommendations for international students: Required—TOEFL. *Application deadline:* For fall admission, 7/15 priority date for domestic students; for spring admission, 12/1 priority date for domestic students. Application fee: $30. Electronic applications accepted. *Expenses:* Tuition, state resident: part-time $277.08 per credit hour. Tuition, nonresident: part-time $277.08 per credit hour. Part-time tuition and fees vary according to degree level and program. *Financial support:* In 2011–12, 19 students received support, including 8 fellowships with partial tuition reimbursements available (averaging $3,500 per year), 10 research assistantships with partial tuition reimbursements available (averaging $11,100 per year), 6 teaching assistantships with partial tuition reimbursements available (averaging $12,300 per year); career-related internships or fieldwork, Federal Work-Study, institutionally sponsored loans, tuition waivers (partial), and unspecified assistantships also available. Financial award application deadline: 3/1; financial award applicants required to submit FAFSA. *Unit head:* Dr. Waldemar Karwowski, Chair, 407-823-2204, E-mail: wkar@ucf.edu. *Application contact:* Barbara Rodriguez, Director, Admissions and Registration, 407-823-2766, Fax: 407-823-6442, E-mail: gradadmissions@ucf.edu. Web site: http://iems.ucf.edu/.

University of Denver, School of Engineering and Computer Science, Department of Computer Science, Denver, CO 80208. Offers computer science (MS, PhD); computer science systems engineering (MS). Part-time programs available. *Faculty:* 10 full-time (2 women), 3 part-time/adjunct (1 woman). *Students:* 2 full-time (1 woman), 58 part-time (10 women); includes 8 minority (1 Black or African American, non-Hispanic/Latino; 4 Asian, non-Hispanic/Latino; 3 Hispanic/Latino), 14 international. Average age 33. 61 applicants, 70% accepted, 16 enrolled. In 2011, 32 master's, 1 doctorate awarded. *Median time to degree:* Of those who began their doctoral program in fall 2003, 100% received their degree in 8 years or less. *Degree requirements:* For doctorate, variable foreign language requirement, comprehensive exam, thesis/dissertation, reading competency in two languages, modern typesetting system, or additional coursework. *Entrance requirements:* For master's and doctorate, GRE General Test, personal statement, three letters of recommendation. Additional exam requirements/recommendations for international students: Required—TOEFL (minimum score 550 paper-based; 80 iBT). *Application deadline:* Applications are processed on a rolling basis. Application fee: $60. Electronic applications accepted. *Financial support:* In 2011–12, 27 students received support, including 1 research assistantship with full and partial tuition reimbursement available (averaging $18,300 per year), 9 teaching assistantships with full and partial tuition reimbursements available (averaging $14,911 per year); career-related internships or fieldwork, Federal Work-Study, institutionally sponsored loans, scholarships/grants, and unspecified assistantships also available. Financial award application deadline: 2/15; financial award applicants required to submit FAFSA. *Faculty research:* Gaming, UML designs, STAMP. *Unit head:* Dr. Ramakrishna Thurimella, Chair, 303-871-3329, E-mail: ramki@cs.du.edu. *Application contact:* Information Contact, 303-871-2458, E-mail: info@cs.du.edu. Web site: http://www.du.edu/cs.

University of Florida, Graduate School, College of Engineering, Department of Industrial and Systems Engineering, Gainesville, FL 32611. Offers ME, MS, PhD, Engr. Part-time and evening/weekend programs available. Postbaccalaureate distance learning degree programs offered (minimal on-campus study). Terminal master's awarded for partial completion of doctoral program. *Degree requirements:* For master's, thesis (for some programs); for doctorate, comprehensive exam (for some programs), thesis/dissertation (for some programs). *Entrance requirements:* For master's and doctorate, GRE General Test, minimum GPA of 3.0; for Engr, GRE General Test. Additional exam requirements/recommendations for international students: Required—TOEFL (minimum score 550 paper-based; 213 computer-based; 80 iBT), IELTS (minimum score 6). Electronic applications accepted. *Faculty research:* Operations research; financial engineering; logistics and supply chain management; energy, healthcare, and transportation applications of operations research.

University of Houston–Clear Lake, School of Science and Computer Engineering, Program in System Engineering, Houston, TX 77058-1098. Offers MS. *Entrance requirements:* Additional exam requirements/recommendations for international students: Required—TOEFL (minimum score 550 paper-based; 213 computer-based).

University of Illinois at Urbana–Champaign, Graduate College, College of Engineering, Department of Industrial and Enterprise Systems Engineering, Champaign, IL 61820. Offers industrial engineering (MS, PhD); systems and entrepreneurial engineering (MS, PhD); MBA/MS. *Faculty:* 18 full-time (5 women). *Students:* 42 full-time (12 women), 20 part-time (8 women); includes 3 minority (1 Black or African American, non-Hispanic/Latino; 1 Asian, non-Hispanic/Latino; 1 Hispanic/Latino), 48 international. 233 applicants, 14% accepted, 14 enrolled. In 2011, 14 master's, 7 doctorates awarded. *Entrance requirements:* For master's and doctorate, GRE, minimum GPA of 3.25. Additional exam requirements/recommendations for international students: Required—TOEFL (minimum score 613 paper-based; 257 computer-based; 103 iBT) or IELTS (minimum score 7). *Application deadline:* Applications are processed on a rolling basis. Application fee: $75 ($90 for international students). Electronic applications accepted. *Financial support:* In 2011–12, 7 fellowships, 43 research assistantships, 49 teaching assistantships were awarded; tuition waivers (full and partial) also available. *Unit head:* Jong-Shi Pang, Head, 217-244-5703, Fax: 217-244-5705, E-mail: jspang@illinois.edu. *Application contact:* Michelle Holly Tipsword, Graduate Programs Specialist, 217-333-2730, Fax: 217-244-5705, E-mail: tippy6@illinois.edu. Web site: http://www.iese.illinois.edu.

University of Maryland, Baltimore County, Graduate School, Program in Systems Engineering, Baltimore, MD 21250. Offers MS, Postbaccalaureate Certificate. Part-time programs available. *Students:* 4 full-time (1 woman), 35 part-time (2 women); includes 12 minority (5 Black or African American, non-Hispanic/Latino; 4 Asian, non-Hispanic/Latino; 2 Hispanic/Latino; 1 Two or more races, non-Hispanic/Latino), 1 international. Average age 35. 28 applicants, 79% accepted, 12 enrolled. In 2011, 8 master's, 7 other advanced degrees awarded. *Degree requirements:* For master's, comprehensive exam (for some programs), thesis optional. *Entrance requirements:* For master's, BS in engineering or information technology with minimum GPA of 3.0. Additional exam requirements/recommendations for international students: Required—TOEFL (minimum score 550 paper-based; 213 computer-based; 80 iBT). *Application deadline:* For fall admission, 7/1 for domestic and international students; for spring admission, 12/1 for domestic and international students. Applications are processed on a rolling basis. Application fee: $70. Electronic applications accepted. *Financial support:* In 2011–12, 1 fellowship (averaging $17,000 per year) was awarded; career-related internships or fieldwork, Federal Work-Study, scholarships/grants, health care benefits, tuition waivers (partial), and unspecified assistantships also available. Support available to part-time students. Financial award application deadline: 6/30; financial award applicants required to submit FAFSA. *Faculty research:* Systems architecture design, modeling and simulation, design and risk analysis, system integrations test, management and engineering projects. *Unit head:* Dr. Gary Carter, Professor and Chair, 410-455-3500, Fax: 410-455-3969, E-mail: carter@cs.umbc.edu. *Application contact:* Dr. Ted M. Foster, Professor of Practice/Assistant Dean/Director, 410-455-1564, Fax: 410-455-3559, E-mail: tfoster@umbc.edu. Web site: http://www.umbc.edu/gradschool/gradcatalog/programs/sys_eng.html.

University of Maryland, College Park, Academic Affairs, A. James Clark School of Engineering, Department of Continuing and Distance Learning in Engineering, College Park, MD 20742. Offers engineering (M Eng), including aerospace engineering, chemical engineering, civil engineering, electrical engineering, engineering, fire protection engineering, materials science and engineering, mechanical engineering, reliability engineering, systems engineering. *Faculty:* 3 full-time (0 women), 8 part-time/adjunct (0 women). *Students:* 75 full-time (24 women), 418 part-time (81 women); includes 154 minority (62 Black or African American, non-Hispanic/Latino; 64 Asian, non-Hispanic/Latino; 23 Hispanic/Latino; 5 Two or more races, non-Hispanic/Latino), 67 international. 447 applicants, 52% accepted, 154 enrolled. In 2011, 155 master's awarded. *Application deadline:* For fall admission, 8/15 for domestic students, 2/1 for international students; for spring admission, 1/10 for domestic students, 8/1 for international students. Applications are processed on a rolling basis. Application fee: $75. Electronic applications accepted. *Expenses: Tuition, area resident:* Part-time $525 per credit hour. Tuition, state resident: part-time $525 per credit hour. Tuition, nonresident: part-time $1131 per credit hour. *Required fees:* $386.31 per term. Tuition and fees vary according to program. *Financial support:* In 2011–12, 3 research assistantships (averaging $21,498 per year), 13 teaching assistantships (averaging $16,889 per year) were awarded. *Unit head:* Dr. Darryll Pines, Dean, 301-405-8539, E-mail: pines@umd.edu. *Application contact:* Dr. Charles A. Caramello, Dean of the Graduate School, 301-405-0358, Fax: 301-314-9305.

University of Maryland, College Park, Academic Affairs, A. James Clark School of Engineering, Systems Engineering Program, College Park, MD 20742. Offers M Eng, MS. Part-time and evening/weekend programs available. *Faculty:* 81 full-time (15 women), 12 part-time/adjunct (4 women). *Students:* 11 full-time (2 women), 6 part-time (3 women); includes 5 minority (1 Black or African American, non-Hispanic/Latino; 4 Asian, non-Hispanic/Latino), 6 international. 37 applicants, 22% accepted, 3 enrolled. *Degree requirements:* For master's, thesis optional. *Entrance requirements:* For master's, GRE General Test, minimum GPA of 3.0. *Application deadline:* For fall admission, 3/15 for domestic students, 2/1 for international students. Applications are processed on a rolling basis. Application fee: $75. Electronic applications accepted. *Expenses: Tuition, area resident:* Part-time $525 per credit hour. Tuition, state resident: part-time $525 per credit hour. Tuition, nonresident: part-time $1131 per credit hour. *Required fees:* $386.31 per term. Tuition and fees vary according to program. *Financial support:* In 2011–12, 1 fellowship with full tuition reimbursement (averaging $33,935 per year), 4 research assistantships with tuition reimbursements (averaging $16,657 per year), 1 teaching assistantship with tuition reimbursement (averaging $22,570 per year) were awarded; Federal Work-Study and scholarships/grants also available. Support available to part-time students. Financial award applicants required to submit FAFSA. *Faculty research:* Automation, computer, information, manufacturing, and process systems. *Total annual research expenditures:* $12.3 million. *Unit head:* Dr. Reza Ghodssi, Director, 301-405-8158, Fax: 301-314-9920, E-mail: ghodssi@umd.edu. *Application contact:* Dean of Graduate School, 301-405-0358, Fax: 301-314-9305.

University of Michigan–Dearborn, College of Engineering and Computer Science, Department of Industrial and Manufacturing Systems Engineering, Dearborn, MI 48128-1491. Offers program and project management (MS); MBA/MSE. Part-time and evening/weekend programs available. *Faculty:* 13 full-time (0 women), 3 part-time/adjunct (0 women). *Students:* 18 full-time (6 women), 147 part-time (32 women); includes 49 minority (7 Black or African American, non-Hispanic/Latino; 1 American Indian or Alaska Native, non-Hispanic/Latino; 34 Asian, non-Hispanic/Latino; 7 Hispanic/Latino), 20 international. Average age 31. 98 applicants, 51% accepted, 45 enrolled. In 2011, 38 master's awarded. *Degree requirements:* For master's, thesis optional. *Entrance requirements:* For master's, bachelor's degree in applied mathematics, computer science, engineering, or physical science; minimum GPA of 3.0. Additional exam requirements/recommendations for international students: Required—TOEFL (minimum score 560 paper-based; 220 computer-based; 84 iBT). *Application deadline:* For fall admission, 8/1 priority date for domestic students, 4/1 for international students; for winter admission, 12/1 priority date for domestic students, 8/1 for international students; for spring admission, 4/1 for domestic students, 12/1 for international students. Applications are processed on a rolling basis. Application fee: $60. *Financial support:* Fellowships, research assistantships, teaching assistantships, and Federal Work-Study available. Financial award application deadline: 4/1; financial award applicants required to submit FAFSA. *Faculty research:* Health care systems, data and knowledge management, human factors engineering, machine diagnostics, precision machining. *Unit head:* Dr. Armen Zakarian, Chair, 313-593-5361, Fax: 313-593-3692, E-mail: zakarian@umd.umich.edu. *Application contact:* Joey W. Woods, Graduate Program Assistant, 313-593-5361, Fax: 313-593-3692, E-mail: jwwoods@umd.umich.edu. Web site: http://www.engin.umd.umich.edu/IMSE/.

University of Michigan–Dearborn, College of Engineering and Computer Science, Interdisciplinary Programs, PhD Program in Information Systems Engineering, Dearborn, MI 48128-1491. Offers PhD. Part-time and evening/weekend programs available. *Faculty:* 1 full-time (0 women). *Students:* 12 full-time (1 woman), 5 part-time (0 women), 12 international. Average age 32. 2 applicants, 100% accepted, 1 enrolled. *Degree requirements:* For doctorate, thesis/dissertation. *Entrance requirements:* For doctorate, GRE. Additional exam requirements/recommendations for international students: Required—TOEFL (minimum score 560 paper-based; 220 computer-based; 84 iBT). *Application deadline:* For fall admission, 1/15 priority date for domestic students, 1/15 for international students; for winter admission, 4/15 priority date for domestic students, 4/15 for international students. Applications are processed on a rolling basis. Application fee: $60. Electronic applications accepted. *Financial support:* In 2011–12, 1 research assistantship (averaging $26,500 per year) was awarded; scholarships/grants and unspecified assistantships also available. Financial award applicants required to submit FAFSA. *Unit head:* Dr. Pankaj K. Mallick, Director/Professor, 313-593-5119, Fax: 313-593-5386, E-mail: pkm@umich.edu. *Application contact:* Sherry Boyd, Intermediate Administrative Assistant, 313-593-5582, Fax: 313-593-5386, E-mail: idpgrad@umd.umich.edu. Web site: http://www.engin.umd.umich.edu/IDP/phd_ise/.

University of Minnesota, Twin Cities Campus, College of Science and Engineering, Technological Leadership Institute, Program in Infrastructure Systems Engineering, Minneapolis, MN 55455-0213. Offers MSISE. Evening/weekend programs available. *Faculty:* 3 full-time (0 women), 5 part-time/adjunct (0 women). *Students:* 19 full-time (6 women); includes 5 minority (1 Black or African American, non-Hispanic/Latino; 1 American Indian or Alaska Native, non-Hispanic/Latino; 2 Asian, non-Hispanic/Latino; 1 Hispanic/Latino), 1 international. *Degree requirements:* For master's, capstone project. *Entrance requirements:* For master's, minimum of one year of work experience in related field, undergraduate degree in civil engineering or related field, minimum GPA of 3.0. Additional exam requirements/recommendations for international students: Required—TOEFL (minimum score 580 paper-based; 240 computer-based; 90 iBT). *Application deadline:* For spring admission, 10/15 priority date for domestic students. Applications are processed on a rolling basis. Application fee: $75 ($95 for international students). Electronic applications accepted. *Expenses:* Contact institution. *Financial support:* Fellowships, institutionally sponsored loans, and scholarships/grants available. Financial award applicants required to submit FAFSA. *Faculty research:* Water distribution, pavement maintenance and management, traffic management systems, infrastructure systems maintenance and management. *Application contact:* ISE Program, E-mail: tliss@umn.edu. Web site: http://tli.umn.edu.

University of Nebraska at Omaha, Graduate Studies, College of Information Science and Technology, Department of Computer Science, Omaha, NE 68182. Offers artificial intelligence (Certificate); communication networks (Certificate); computer science (MA, MS); systems architecture (Certificate). Part-time and evening/weekend programs available. *Faculty:* 15 full-time (2 women). *Students:* 33 full-time (2 women), 53 part-time (5 women); includes 7 minority (2 Black or African American, non-Hispanic/Latino; 5 Asian, non-Hispanic/Latino), 31 international. Average age 30. 65 applicants, 51% accepted, 20 enrolled. In 2011, 22 master's, 2 other advanced degrees awarded. *Degree requirements:* For master's, comprehensive exam, thesis (for some programs). *Entrance requirements:* For master's, GRE General Test, minimum GPA of 3.0, course work in computer science, resume. Additional exam requirements/recommendations for international students: Required—TOEFL (minimum score 500 paper-based; 173 computer-based; 61 iBT). *Application deadline:* For fall admission, 7/1 priority date for domestic students; for spring admission, 11/1 priority date for domestic students. Applications are processed on a rolling basis. Application fee: $45. Electronic applications accepted. *Financial support:* In 2011–12, 9 students received support, including 9 research assistantships with tuition reimbursements available; teaching assistantships with tuition reimbursements available, Federal Work-Study, institutionally sponsored loans, scholarships/grants, tuition waivers (full), and unspecified assistantships also available. Support available to part-time students. Financial award application deadline: 3/1; financial award applicants required to submit FAFSA. *Unit head:* Dr. Qiuming Zhu, Chairperson, 402-554-2423. *Application contact:* Carla Frakes, Information Contact, 402-554-2423.

University of New Haven, Graduate School, Tagliatela College of Engineering, Program in Computer and Information Science, West Haven, CT 06516-1916. Offers computer science (MS, Certificate), including advanced applications (MS), computer programming (Certificate), computer systems (MS), database and information systems (MS), network systems (MS), software engineering and development (MS). Part-time and evening/weekend programs available. *Students:* 53 full-time (16 women), 32 part-time (7 women); includes 4 minority (1 Black or African American, non-Hispanic/Latino; 1 Asian, non-Hispanic/Latino; 2 Hispanic/Latino), 69 international. 133 applicants, 98% accepted, 23 enrolled. In 2011, 19 master's, 1 other advanced degree awarded. *Degree requirements:* For master's, thesis or alternative. *Entrance requirements:* Additional exam requirements/recommendations for international students: Required—TOEFL (minimum score 520 paper-based; 190 computer-based; 70 iBT); Recommended—IELTS (minimum score 5.5). *Application deadline:* For fall admission, 5/31 for international students; for winter admission, 10/15 for international students; for spring admission, 1/15 for international students. Applications are processed on a rolling basis. Application fee: $50. Electronic applications accepted. *Expenses: Tuition:* Part-time $750 per credit. *Financial support:* Research assistantships with partial tuition reimbursements, teaching assistantships with partial tuition reimbursements, career-related internships or fieldwork, Federal Work-Study, scholarships/grants, tuition waivers, and unspecified assistantships available. Support available to part-time students. Financial award applicants required to submit FAFSA. *Unit head:* Dr. David Eggert, Coordinator, 203-932-7097, E-mail: deggert@newhaven.edu. *Application contact:* Eloise Gormley, Director of Graduate Admissions, 203-932-7449, Fax: 203-932-7137, E-mail: gradinfo@newhaven.edu. Web site: http://www.newhaven.edu/9591/.

The University of North Carolina at Charlotte, Graduate School, The William States Lee College of Engineering, Department of Civil and Environmental Engineering, Charlotte, NC 28223-0001. Offers civil engineering (MSCE); infrastructure and environmental systems (PhD), including infrastructure and environmental systems design. Part-time and evening/weekend programs available. *Faculty:* 20 full-time (2 women). *Students:* 57 full-time (12 women), 41 part-time (10 women); includes 15 minority (3 Black or African American, non-Hispanic/Latino; 2 American Indian or Alaska Native, non-Hispanic/Latino; 3 Asian, non-Hispanic/Latino; 6 Hispanic/Latino; 1 Two or more races, non-Hispanic/Latino), 34 international. Average age 29. 56 applicants, 73% accepted, 24 enrolled. In 2011, 20 master's, 4 doctorates awarded. Terminal master's awarded for partial completion of doctoral program. *Degree requirements:* For master's, thesis or project. *Entrance requirements:* For master's, GRE General Test, minimum GPA of 3.0 in undergraduate major, 2.75 overall. Additional exam requirements/recommendations for international students: Required—TOEFL (minimum score 550 paper-based; 220 computer-based; 83 iBT). *Application deadline:* For fall admission, 7/1 for domestic students, 5/1 for international students; for spring admission, 11/1 for domestic students, 10/1 for international students. Applications are processed on a rolling basis. Application fee: $65 ($75 for international students). Electronic applications accepted. *Expenses:* Tuition, state resident: full-time $3689. Tuition, nonresident: full-time $15,226. *Required fees:* $2198. Tuition and fees vary according to course load and program. *Financial support:* In 2011–12, 44 students received support, including 2 fellowships (averaging $23,547 per year), 25 research assistantships (averaging $5,581 per year), 17 teaching assistantships (averaging $5,679 per year); career-related internships or fieldwork, Federal Work-Study, institutionally sponsored loans, and scholarships/grants also available. Support available to part-time students. Financial award application deadline: 4/1; financial award applicants required to submit FAFSA. *Faculty research:* Structural composite materials, storm water systems, natural and man-made disaster reduction engineering, older drivers and nighttime driving, soil contamination and transport. *Total annual research expenditures:* $1.3 million. *Unit head:* Dr. David T. Young, Chair, 704-687-4175, Fax: 704-687-6953, E-mail: dyoung@.uncc.edu. *Application contact:* Kathy B. Giddings, Director of Graduate Admissions, 704-687-5503, Fax: 704-687-3279, E-mail: gradadm@uncc.edu. Web site: http://cee.uncc.edu/.

University of Pennsylvania, School of Engineering and Applied Science, Department of Electrical and Systems Engineering, Philadelphia, PA 19104. Offers MSE, PhD. Part-time programs available. *Faculty:* 27 full-time (2 women), 5 part-time/adjunct (0 women). *Students:* 199 full-time (49 women), 38 part-time (5 women); includes 16 minority (1 Black or African American, non-Hispanic/Latino; 14 Asian, non-Hispanic/Latino; 1 Two or more races, non-Hispanic/Latino), 182 international. 1,027 applicants, 30% accepted, 134 enrolled. In 2011, 69 master's, 9 doctorates awarded. Terminal master's awarded for partial completion of doctoral program. *Degree requirements:* For master's, thesis optional; for doctorate, comprehensive exam, thesis/dissertation. *Entrance requirements:* For master's and doctorate, GRE General Test. Additional exam requirements/recommendations for international students: Required—TOEFL. *Application deadline:* For fall admission, 6/1 priority date for domestic students, 5/1 for international students; for spring admission, 11/1 priority date for domestic students, 10/1 for international students. Applications are processed on a rolling basis. Application fee: $70. Electronic applications accepted. *Expenses: Tuition:* Full-time $26,660; part-time $4944 per course. *Required fees:* $2318; $291 per course. Tuition and fees vary according to course load, degree level and program. *Financial support:* Fellowships, research assistantships, teaching assistantships, institutionally sponsored loans, scholarships/grants, traineeships, health care benefits, and unspecified assistantships available. *Faculty research:* Electro-optics, microwave and millimeter-wave optics, solid-state and chemical electronics, electromagnetic propagation, telecommunications. *Unit head:* Eduardo D. Glandt, Dean, 215-898-7244, Fax: 215-573-2018, E-mail: seasdean@seas.upenn.edu. *Application contact:* Nichole Wood, Graduate Coordinator, 215-898-9390, E-mail: woodn@seas.upenn.edu. Web site: http://www.seas.upenn.edu/

University of Regina, Faculty of Graduate Studies and Research, Faculty of Engineering and Applied Science, Program in Industrial Systems Engineering, Regina, SK S4S 0A2, Canada. Offers M Eng, MA Sc, PhD. Part-time programs available. *Faculty:* 13 full-time (2 women). *Students:* 47 full-time (8 women), 5 part-time (0 women). 72 applicants, 38% accepted. In 2011, 8 master's, 1 doctorate awarded. *Degree requirements:* For master's, thesis (for some programs); for doctorate, thesis/dissertation. *Entrance requirements:* For doctorate, master's degree. Additional exam requirements/recommendations for international students: Required—TOEFL (minimum score 550 paper-based; 80 iBT), IELTS (minimum score 6.5). *Application deadline:* For fall admission, 3/31 for domestic and international students; for winter admission, 7/31 for domestic and international students; for spring admission, 11/30 for domestic and international students. Applications are processed on a rolling basis. Application fee: $100. *Financial support:* In 2011–12, 4 fellowships (averaging $6,500 per year), 1 research assistantship (averaging $5,500 per year), 6 teaching assistantships (averaging $2,298 per year) were awarded; career-related internships or fieldwork and scholarships/grants also available. Financial award application deadline: 6/15. *Faculty research:* Stochastic systems simulation, metallurgy of welding, computer-aided engineering, finite element method of engineering systems, manufacturing systems. *Unit head:* Dr. Raphael Idem, Associate Dean, Research and Graduate Studies, 306-337-2696, E-mail: raphael.idem@uregina.ca. *Application contact:* Dr. Andy Aroonwilas, Graduate Program Coordinator, 306-337-2469, Fax: 306-585-4855, E-mail: adisorn.aroonwilas@uregina.ca.

University of Regina, Faculty of Graduate Studies and Research, Faculty of Engineering and Applied Science, Program in Petroleum Systems Engineering, Regina, SK S4S 0A2, Canada. Offers M Eng, MA Sc, PhD. Part-time programs available. *Faculty:* 7 full-time (1 woman). *Students:* 44 full-time (11 women), 3 part-time (0 women). 110 applicants, 13% accepted. In 2011, 5 master's, 1 doctorate awarded. *Degree requirements:* For master's, thesis; for doctorate, thesis/dissertation. *Entrance requirements:* Additional exam requirements/recommendations for international students: Required—TOEFL (minimum score 550 paper-based; 80 iBT), IELTS (minimum score 6.5). *Application deadline:* For fall admission, 3/31 for domestic and international students; for winter admission, 7/31 for domestic and international students; for spring admission, 11/30 for domestic and international students. Application fee: $100. Electronic applications accepted. *Financial support:* In 2011–12, 6 fellowships (averaging $6,500 per year), 2 research assistantships (averaging $17,250 per year), 12 teaching assistantships (averaging $2,298 per year) were awarded; career-related internships or fieldwork and scholarships/grants also available. Financial award application deadline: 6/15. *Faculty research:* Enhanced oil recovery, production engineering, reservoir engineering, surface thermodynamics, geostatistics. *Unit head:* Dr. Raphael Idem, Associate Dean, Research and Graduate Studies, 306-337-3287, Fax: 306-585-4855, E-mail: raphael.idem@uregina.ca. *Application contact:* Dr. Farshid Torabi, Graduate Program Coordinator, 306-337-3287, Fax: 306-585-4855, E-mail: farshid.torabi@uregina.ca.

University of Regina, Faculty of Graduate Studies and Research, Faculty of Engineering and Applied Science, Program in Process Systems Engineering, Regina, SK S4S 0A2, Canada. Offers M Eng, MA Sc, PhD. Part-time programs available. *Faculty:* 1 full-time (0 women). *Students:* 10 full-time (5 women), 5 part-time (0 women). 36 applicants, 28% accepted. In 2011, 2 degrees awarded. *Degree requirements:* For master's, thesis (for some programs); for doctorate, thesis/dissertation. *Entrance requirements:* Additional exam requirements/recommendations for international students: Required—TOEFL (minimum score 550 paper-based; 80 iBT), IELTS (minimum score 6.5). *Application deadline:* For fall admission, 3/31 for domestic and international students; for winter admission, 7/31 for domestic and international students; for spring admission, 11/30 for domestic and international students. Application fee: $100. Electronic applications accepted. *Financial support:* In 2011–12, 4 fellowships (averaging $6,500 per year), 1 teaching assistantship (averaging $2,298 per year) were awarded; research assistantships, career-related internships or fieldwork, and scholarships/grants also available. Financial award application deadline: 6/15. *Faculty research:* Membrane separation technologies, advanced reaction engineering, advanced transport phenomena, advanced heat transfer, advanced mass transfer. *Unit head:* Dr. Raphael Idem, Associate Dean, Research and Graduate Studies, 306-585-4470, Fax: 306-585-4855, E-mail: raphael.idem@uregina.ca.

Application contact: Dr. David deMontigny, Graduate Program Coordinator, 306-337-2277, Fax: 306-585-4855, E-mail: david.demontigny@uregina.ca.

University of St. Thomas, Graduate Studies, School of Engineering, St. Paul, MN 55105-1096. Offers manufacturing engineering and operations (MS); mechanical engineering (MS); medical device development (Certificate); regulatory science (MS); software engineering (MS); software management (MS); software systems (MSS); systems engineering (MS); technology management (MS). *Accreditation:* ABET (one or more programs are accredited). *Students:* 8 full-time, 210 part-time (38 women); includes 47 minority (22 Black or African American, non-Hispanic/Latino; 4 Asian, non-Hispanic/Latino; 6 Hispanic/Latino; 1 Native Hawaiian or other Pacific Islander, non-Hispanic/Latino; 14 Two or more races, non-Hispanic/Latino), 14 international. Average age 33. *Entrance requirements:* For master's, resume, official transcripts. Additional exam requirements/recommendations for international students: Required—TOEFL (minimum score 550 paper-based). *Application deadline:* For fall admission, 8/1 priority date for domestic students; for spring admission, 1/1 priority date for domestic students. Applications are processed on a rolling basis. Application fee: $30. Electronic applications accepted. *Expenses:* Contact institution. *Financial support:* Fellowships, research assistantships, institutionally sponsored loans, and scholarships/grants available. Support available to part-time students. Financial award application deadline: 4/1; financial award applicants required to submit FAFSA. *Unit head:* Don Weinkauf, Dean, 651-962-5760, Fax: 651-962-6419, E-mail: dhweinkauf@stthomas.edu. *Application contact:* Joyce A. Taylor, Graduate Programs Coordinator, 651-962-5756, Fax: 651-962-6419, E-mail: jataylor1@stthomas.edu.

University of Southern California, Graduate School, Viterbi School of Engineering, Daniel J. Epstein Department of Industrial and Systems Engineering, Los Angeles, CA 90089. Offers digital supply chain management (MS); engineering management (MS); engineering technology communication (Graduate Certificate); health systems operations (Graduate Certificate); industrial and systems engineering (MS, PhD, Engr); manufacturing engineering (MS); operations research engineering (MS); optimization and supply chain management (Graduate Certificate); product development engineering (MS); safety systems and security (MS); systems architecting and engineering (MS, Graduate Certificate); systems safety and security (Graduate Certificate); transportation systems (Graduate Certificate); MS/MBA. Part-time and evening/weekend programs available. Postbaccalaureate distance learning degree programs offered (no on-campus study). Terminal master's awarded for partial completion of doctoral program. *Degree requirements:* For master's, thesis optional; for doctorate, thesis/dissertation. *Entrance requirements:* For master's and doctorate, GRE General Test. Additional exam requirements/recommendations for international students: Recommended—TOEFL. Electronic applications accepted. *Faculty research:* Health systems, music cognition and retrieval, transportation and logistics, manufacturing and automation, engineering systems design, risk and economic analysis.

The University of Texas at Arlington, Graduate School, College of Engineering, Department of Industrial and Manufacturing Systems Engineering, Program in Systems Engineering, Arlington, TX 76019. Offers MS. *Students:* 25 part-time (4 women); includes 8 minority (3 Black or African American, non-Hispanic/Latino; 1 Asian, non-Hispanic/Latino; 4 Hispanic/Latino). 19 applicants, 79% accepted, 6 enrolled. In 2011, 4 degrees awarded. *Unit head:* Dr. Donald H. Liles, Chair, 817-272-3092, Fax: 817-272-3406, E-mail: dliles@uta.edu. *Application contact:* Dr. Sheik Imrhan, Graduate Advisor, 817-272-3167, Fax: 817-272-3406, E-mail: imrhan@uta.edu.

The University of Texas at Dallas, Erik Jonsson School of Engineering and Computer Science, Department of Electrical Engineering, Richardson, TX 75080. Offers computer engineering (MS, PhD); electrical engineering (MSEE, PhD); systems engineering and management (MS); telecommunications (MSTE, PhD). Part-time and evening/weekend programs available. *Faculty:* 44 full-time (2 women), 4 part-time/adjunct (0 women). *Students:* 510 full-time (108 women), 279 part-time (53 women); includes 110 minority (17 Black or African American, non-Hispanic/Latino; 65 Asian, non-Hispanic/Latino; 25 Hispanic/Latino; 3 Two or more races, non-Hispanic/Latino), 555 international. Average age 27. 1,933 applicants, 42% accepted, 265 enrolled. In 2011, 168 master's, 30 doctorates awarded. *Degree requirements:* For master's, thesis or major design project; for doctorate, thesis/dissertation. *Entrance requirements:* For master's, GRE General Test, minimum GPA of 3.0 in related bachelor's degree; for doctorate, GRE General Test, minimum GPA of 3.5. Additional exam requirements/recommendations for international students: Required—TOEFL (minimum score 550 paper-based; 215 computer-based). *Application deadline:* For fall admission, 7/15 for domestic students, 5/1 for international students; for spring admission, 11/15 for domestic students, 9/1 for international students. Applications are processed on a rolling basis. Application fee: $50 ($100 for international students). Electronic applications accepted. *Expenses:* Tuition, state resident: full-time $11,170; part-time $620.56 per credit hour. Tuition, nonresident: full-time $20,212; part-time $1122.89 per credit hour. *Financial support:* In 2011–12, 224 students received support, including 132 research assistantships with partial tuition reimbursements available (averaging $21,532 per year), 47 teaching assistantships with partial tuition reimbursements available (averaging $14,850 per year); fellowships with partial tuition reimbursements available, Federal Work-Study, institutionally sponsored loans, scholarships/grants, unspecified assistantships, and cooperative positions also available. Support available to part-time students. Financial award application deadline: 4/30; financial award applicants required to submit FAFSA. *Faculty research:* Semiconductor device manufacturing, photonics devices and systems, signal processing and language technology, nano-fabrication, energy efficient digital systems. *Unit head:* Dr. John H. L. Hansen, Department Head, 972-883-6755, Fax: 972-883-2710, E-mail: john.hansen@utdallas.edu. *Application contact:* Kathy Gribble, Graduate Program Coordinator, 972-883-2649, Fax: 972-883-2710, E-mail: gradecs@utdallas.edu. Web site: http://www.ee.utdallas.edu.

The University of Texas at Dallas, Erik Jonsson School of Engineering and Computer Science, Department of Mechanical Engineering, Richardson, TX 75080. Offers mechanical systems engineering (MSME); microelectromechanical systems (MSME). Part-time and evening/weekend programs available. *Faculty:* 9 full-time (1 woman). *Students:* 23 full-time (3 women), 5 part-time (1 woman); includes 3 minority (1 Asian, non-Hispanic/Latino; 1 Hispanic/Latino; 1 Two or more races, non-Hispanic/Latino), 10 international. Average age 29. 92 applicants, 39% accepted, 13 enrolled. *Degree requirements:* For master's, thesis or major design project. *Entrance requirements:* For master's, GRE General Test, minimum GPA of 3.0 in related bachelor's degree. Additional exam requirements/recommendations for international students: Required—TOEFL (minimum score 550 paper-based; 215 computer-based). *Application deadline:* For fall admission, 7/15 for domestic students, 5/1 for international students; for spring admission, 11/15 for domestic students, 9/1 for international students. Applications are processed on a rolling basis. Application fee: $50 ($100 for international students). Electronic applications accepted. *Expenses:* Tuition, state resident: full-time $11,170; part-time $620.56 per credit hour. Tuition, nonresident: full-time $20,212; part-time $1122.89 per credit hour. *Financial support:* In 2011–12, 13 students received support, including 2 research assistantships with partial tuition reimbursements available (averaging $19,800 per year), 7 teaching assistantships with partial tuition reimbursements available (averaging $14,829 per year); career-related internships or fieldwork, Federal Work-Study, institutionally sponsored loans, scholarships/grants, and unspecified assistantships also available. Support available to part-time students. Financial award application deadline: 4/30; financial award applicants required to submit FAFSA. *Faculty research:* Nano-materials and nano-electronic devices, biomedical devices, nonlinear systems and controls, semiconductor and oxide surfaces, flexible electronics. *Unit head:* Dr. Mario Rotea, Department Head, 972-883-2720, Fax: 972-883-2813, E-mail: rotea@utdallas.edu. *Application contact:* Dr. Hongbing Lu, Associate Department Head, 972-883-4647, Fax: 972-883-2813, E-mail: gradecs@utdallas.edu. Web site: http://me.utdallas.edu.

The University of Texas at El Paso, Graduate School, College of Engineering, Department of Industrial Engineering, El Paso, TX 79968-0001. Offers industrial engineering (MS); manufacturing engineering (MS); systems engineering (MS, Certificate). Part-time and evening/weekend programs available. *Students:* 107 (28 women); includes 60 minority (2 Black or African American, non-Hispanic/Latino; 1 Asian, non-Hispanic/Latino; 57 Hispanic/Latino), 44 international. Average age 34. 56 applicants, 91% accepted, 43 enrolled. In 2011, 27 master's awarded. *Degree requirements:* For master's, thesis optional. *Entrance requirements:* For master's, GRE General Test, minimum GPA of 3.0 in major. Additional exam requirements/recommendations for international students: Required—TOEFL. *Application deadline:* For fall admission, 7/1 priority date for domestic students, 3/1 for international students; for spring admission, 11/1 priority date for domestic students, 9/1 for international students. Applications are processed on a rolling basis. Application fee: $15 ($65 for international students). Electronic applications accepted. *Financial support:* In 2011–12, research assistantships with partial tuition reimbursements (averaging $21,125 per year), teaching assistantships with partial tuition reimbursements (averaging $16,900 per year) were awarded; fellowships with partial tuition reimbursements, Federal Work-Study, institutionally sponsored loans, scholarships/grants, and tuition waivers (partial) also available. Financial award application deadline: 3/15; financial award applicants required to submit FAFSA. *Faculty research:* Computer vision, automated inspection, simulation and modeling. *Unit head:* Dr. Rafael S. Gutierrez, Chair, 915-747-5450, Fax: 915-747-5019, E-mail: rsgutier@utep.edu. *Application contact:* Dr. Benjamin Flores, Interim Dean of the Graduate School, 915-747-5491, Fax: 915-747-5788, E-mail: bflores@utep.edu.

The University of Texas–Pan American, College of Engineering and Computer Science, Department of Manufacturing Engineering, Edinburg, TX 78539. Offers engineering management (MS); manufacturing engineering (MS); systems engineering (MS). Tuition and fees vary according to course load, program and student level. *Unit head:* Dr. Rajiv Nambiar, Dean, 956-665-7056, E-mail: nambiar@utpa.edu. Web site: http://portal.utpa.edu/portal/page/portal/utpa_main/daa_home/cose_home/manu_home.

University of Virginia, School of Engineering and Applied Science, Department of Systems and Information Engineering, Charlottesville, VA 22903. Offers ME, MS, PhD, ME/MBA. Postbaccalaureate distance learning degree programs offered (no on-campus study). *Faculty:* 18 full-time (1 woman). *Students:* 69 full-time (16 women), 10 part-time (2 women); includes 13 minority (3 Black or African American, non-Hispanic/Latino; 3 Asian, non-Hispanic/Latino; 4 Hispanic/Latino; 3 Two or more races, non-Hispanic/Latino), 26 international. Average age 29. 131 applicants, 18% accepted, 18 enrolled. In 2011, 52 master's, 5 doctorates awarded. *Degree requirements:* For master's, comprehensive exam (for some programs); for doctorate, comprehensive exam, thesis/dissertation. *Entrance requirements:* For master's, GRE General Test, 3 letters of recommendation; for doctorate, GRE General Test, 3 letters of recommendation; essay. Additional exam requirements/recommendations for international students: Required—TOEFL (minimum score 650 paper-based; 250 computer-based; 90 iBT), IELTS (minimum score 7). *Application deadline:* For fall admission, 8/1 for domestic students, 4/1 for international students; for winter admission, 12/1 for domestic students, 8/1 for international students; for spring admission, 5/1 for domestic students, 1/1 for international students. Applications are processed on a rolling basis. Application fee: $60. Electronic applications accepted. *Financial support:* Fellowships, research assistantships, and teaching assistantships available. Financial award application deadline: 1/15; financial award applicants required to submit FAFSA. *Faculty research:* Systems integration, human factors, computational statistics and simulation, risk and decision analysis, optimization and control. *Unit head:* Barry Horowitz, Chair, 434-924-5393, Fax: 434-982-2972, E-mail: bh8e@virginia.edu. *Application contact:* Departmental Office, 434-924-5393, Fax: 434-982-2972, E-mail: siegradadministration@virginia.edu. Web site: http://www.sys.virginia.edu/.

University of Waterloo, Graduate Studies, Faculty of Engineering, Department of Systems Design Engineering, Waterloo, ON N2L 3G1, Canada. Offers M Eng, MA Sc, PhD. Part-time programs available. *Degree requirements:* For master's, research project or thesis; for doctorate, comprehensive exam, thesis/dissertation. *Entrance requirements:* For master's, honors degree, minimum B average, resumé; for doctorate, master's degree, minimum A- average. Additional exam requirements/recommendations for international students: Required—TOEFL, TWE. Electronic applications accepted. *Faculty research:* Ergonomics, human factors and biomedical engineering, modeling and simulation, pattern analysis, machine intelligence and robotics.

University of Wisconsin–Madison, Graduate School, College of Engineering, Department of Industrial and Systems Engineering, Madison, WI 53706. Offers MS, PhD. Part-time programs available. *Faculty:* 21 full-time (6 women), 12 part-time/adjunct (4 women). *Students:* 99 full-time (32 women), 20 part-time (7 women); includes 12 minority (8 Black or African American, non-Hispanic/Latino; 1 American Indian or Alaska Native, non-Hispanic/Latino; 2 Asian, non-Hispanic/Latino; 1 Hispanic/Latino), 83 international. Average age 27. 500 applicants, 11% accepted, 39 enrolled. In 2011, 71 master's, 11 doctorates awarded. Terminal master's awarded for partial completion of doctoral program. *Degree requirements:* For master's, thesis optional; for doctorate, comprehensive exam, thesis/dissertation. *Entrance requirements:* For master's, GRE General Test, minimum GPA of 3.0, BS in engineering or equivalent, course work in computer programming and statistics; for doctorate, GRE General Test, minimum GPA of 3.0. Additional exam requirements/recommendations for international students: Required—IELTS (minimum score 6); Recommended—TOEFL (minimum score 550 paper-based; 213 computer-based; 80 iBT). *Application deadline:* For fall admission, 2/1 priority date for domestic students, 2/1 for international students; for spring admission, 10/1 priority date for domestic students, 10/1 for international students. Application fee: $56. Electronic applications accepted. *Expenses:* Tuition, state resident: full-time $10,296; part-time $643.51 per credit. Tuition, nonresident: full-time $24,054; part-time $1503.40 per credit. *Required fees:* $70.06 per credit. Tuition and fees vary according to course load, campus/location, program and reciprocity agreements. *Financial support:* In 2011–12, 87 students received support, including fellowships with full tuition reimbursements available (averaging $21,760 per year), 46 research assistantships with full tuition reimbursements available (averaging $40,800 per year), 8 teaching assistantships with full tuition reimbursements available (averaging $28,175 per year); career-related internships or fieldwork, Federal Work-Study, institutionally sponsored loans, scholarships/grants, traineeships, health care benefits, and unspecified assistantships also available. *Faculty research:* Human factors and ergonomics, manufacturing and production systems, health systems engineering, decision science/operations research, quality engineering. *Total annual research expenditures:* $10.2 million. *Unit head:* Dr. Vicki M. Bier, Chair, 608-262-2064, Fax: 608-262-8454, E-mail: bier@engr.wisc.edu. *Application contact:* Staci Rubenzer, Graduate Admissions Coordinator, 608-890-2248, Fax: 608-890-2204, E-mail: srubenzer@engr.wisc.edu. Web site: http://www.engr.wisc.edu/ie/.

Virginia Polytechnic Institute and State University, Graduate School, College of Engineering, Department of Civil and Environmental Engineering, Blacksburg, VA 24061. Offers civil engineering (M Eng, MS, PhD); civil infrastructure systems (Certificate); environmental engineering (MS); environmental sciences and engineering (MS); transportation systems engineering (Certificate); treatment process engineering (Certificate); urban hydrology and stormwater management (Certificate); water quality management (Certificate). *Accreditation:* ABET (one or more programs are accredited). *Degree requirements:* For master's, comprehensive exam (for some programs), thesis (for some programs); for doctorate, comprehensive exam (for some programs), thesis/dissertation (for some programs). *Entrance requirements:* For master's and doctorate, GRE. Additional exam requirements/recommendations for international students: Required—TOEFL (minimum score 550 paper-based; 213 computer-based). *Application deadline:* For fall admission, 7/1 for domestic and international students; for spring admission, 12/1 for domestic and international students. Applications are processed on a rolling basis. Application fee: $65. Electronic applications accepted. *Expenses:* Tuition, state resident: full-time $10,048; part-time $558.25 per credit hour. Tuition, nonresident: full-time $19,497; part-time $1083.25 per credit hour. *Required fees:* $405 per semester. Tuition and fees vary according to course load, campus/location and program. *Financial support:* Fellowships with full tuition reimbursements, research assistantships with full tuition reimbursements, teaching assistantships with full tuition reimbursements, career-related internships or fieldwork, Federal Work-Study, scholarships/grants, health care benefits, and unspecified assistantships available. Financial award application deadline: 1/15. *Faculty research:* Construction, environmental geotechnical hydrosystems, structures and transportation engineering. *Unit head:* Dr. Sam Easterling, Unit Head, 540-231-5143, Fax: 540-231-7532, E-mail: seaster@vt.edu. *Application contact:* Marc Widdowson, Information Contact, 540-231-7153, Fax: 540-231-7532, E-mail: mwiddows@vt.edu. Web site: http://www.cee.vt.edu/.

Virginia Polytechnic Institute and State University, Graduate School, College of Engineering, Department of Industrial and Systems Engineering, Blacksburg, VA 24061. Offers human-system integration (Certificate); industrial and systems engineering (MEA, MS, PhD). *Degree requirements:* For master's, comprehensive exam (for some programs), thesis (for some programs); for doctorate, comprehensive exam (for some programs), thesis/dissertation (for some programs). *Entrance requirements:* For master's and doctorate, GRE. Additional exam requirements/recommendations for international students: Required—TOEFL (minimum score 550 paper-based; 213 computer-based). *Application deadline:* For fall admission, 7/1 for domestic and international students; for spring admission, 12/1 for domestic and international students. Applications are processed on a rolling basis. Application fee: $65. Electronic applications accepted. *Expenses:* Tuition, state resident: full-time $10,048; part-time $558.25 per credit hour. Tuition, nonresident: full-time $19,497; part-time $1083.25 per credit hour. *Required fees:* $405 per semester. Tuition and fees vary according to course load, campus/location and program. *Financial support:* Fellowships with full tuition reimbursements, research assistantships with full tuition reimbursements, teaching assistantships with full tuition reimbursements, career-related internships or fieldwork, Federal Work-Study, scholarships/grants, health care benefits, and unspecified assistantships available. Financial award application deadline: 1/15. *Unit head:* Dr. Gaylon D. Taylor, Unit Head, 540-231-4771, Fax: 540-231-3322, E-mail: taylorgd@vt.edu. *Application contact:* Jaime Camelio, Information Contact, 540-231-8976, Fax: 540-231-3322, E-mail: jcamelio@vt.edu. Web site: http://ise.vt.edu/.

Virginia Polytechnic Institute and State University, VT Online, Blacksburg, VA 24061. Offers advanced transportation systems (Certificate); aerospace engineering (MS); agricultural and life sciences (MSLFS); business information systems (Graduate Certificate); career and technical education (MS); civil engineering (MS); computer engineering (M Eng, MS); decision support systems (Graduate Certificate); eLearning leadership (MA); electrical engineering (M Eng, MS); engineering administration (MEA); environmental engineering (Certificate); environmental politics and policy (Graduate Certificate); environmental sciences and engineering (MS); foundations of political analysis (Graduate Certificate); health product risk management (Graduate Certificate); industrial and systems engineering (MS); information policy and society (Graduate Certificate); information security (Graduate Certificate); information technology (MIT); instructional technology (MA); integrative STEM education (MA Ed); liberal arts (Graduate Certificate); life sciences: health product risk management (MS); natural resources (MNR, Graduate Certificate); networking (Graduate Certificate); nonprofit and nongovernmental organization management (Graduate Certificate); ocean engineering (MS); political science (MA); security studies (Graduate Certificate); software development (Graduate Certificate). *Expenses:* Tuition, state resident: full-time $10,048; part-time $558.25 per credit hour. Tuition, nonresident: full-time $19,497; part-time $1083.25 per credit hour. *Required fees:* $405 per semester. Tuition and fees vary according to course load, campus/location and program. *Application contact:* Graduate School Applications General Assistance, 540-231-8636, Fax: 540-231-2039, E-mail: gradappl@vt.edu. Web site: http://www.vto.vt.edu/.

Wayne State University, College of Engineering, Department of Industrial and Manufacturing Engineering, Detroit, MI 48202. Offers engineering management (MS, Certificate); industrial engineering (MS, PhD); manufacturing engineering (MS); systems engineering (Certificate). *Students:* 46 full-time (13 women), 87 part-time (21 women); includes 27 minority (12 Black or African American, non-Hispanic/Latino; 11 Asian, non-Hispanic/Latino; 3 Hispanic/Latino; 1 Two or more races, non-Hispanic/Latino), 37 international. Average age 34. 167 applicants, 40% accepted, 15 enrolled. In 2011, 45 master's, 2 doctorates awarded. *Degree requirements:* For master's, thesis optional; for doctorate, thesis/dissertation. *Entrance requirements:* For master's, minimum upper-division undergraduate GPA of 2.8, bachelor's degree in engineering from ABET-accredited institution (or other discipline with strong analytical base); for doctorate, MS in industrial engineering or operations research with minimum graduate GPA of 3.5; for Certificate, GRE (if institution not ABET-accredited). Additional exam requirements/recommendations for international students: Required—TOEFL (minimum score 550 paper-based; 213 computer-based), Michigan English Language Assessment Battery (minimum score 85). GRE; Recommended—TWE (minimum score 5.5). *Application deadline:* For fall admission, 6/1 priority date for domestic students, 5/1 for international students; for winter admission, 10/1 priority date for domestic students, 9/1 for international students; for spring admission, 2/1 priority date for domestic students, 1/1 for international students. Applications are processed on a rolling basis. Application fee:

$50. Electronic applications accepted. *Expenses:* Tuition, state resident: part-time $512.85 per credit. Tuition, nonresident: part-time $1132.65 per credit. *Required fees:* $26.60 per credit. $199.65 per semester. Tuition and fees vary according to course load and program. *Financial support:* In 2011–12, 20 students received support, including 2 fellowships with tuition reimbursements available (averaging $13,708 per year), 10 research assistantships with tuition reimbursements available (averaging $18,141 per year), 9 teaching assistantships with tuition reimbursements available (averaging $17,835 per year); career-related internships or fieldwork, scholarships/grants, health care benefits, tuition waivers (full), and unspecified assistantships also available. *Faculty research:* Robust design and quality and reliability engineering; Six Sigma; globalization of engineering and manufacturing management and collaborative products development; intelligent engineering and lean, flexible and computer-integrated manufacturing systems; human factors engineering and performance; supply chain management. *Total annual research expenditures:* $1.2 million. *Unit head:* Dr. Kyuoung-Yun Kim, Graduate Program Director, 313-577-4396, E-mail: kykim@eng.wayne.edu. *Application contact:* Gail Evans, Academic Advisor, 313-577-2660, E-mail: ac3913@wayne.edu. Web site: http://ise.wayne.edu/.

Western International University, Graduate Programs in Business, Master of Science Program in Information System Engineering, Phoenix, AZ 85021-2718. Offers MS. Part-time and evening/weekend programs available. Postbaccalaureate distance learning degree programs offered (no on-campus study). *Entrance requirements:* For master's, minimum GPA of 2.75. Additional exam requirements/recommendations for international students: Required—TOEFL (minimum score 550 paper-based; 213 computer-based; 79 iBT), TWE (minimum score 5), or IELTS. Electronic applications accepted.

Section 15
Management of Engineering and Technology

This section contains a directory of institutions offering graduate work in management of engineering and technology. Additional information about programs listed in the directory but not augmented by an in-depth entry may be obtained by writing directly to the dean of a graduate school or chair of a department at the address given in the directory.

For programs offering related work, in the other guides in this series:

Graduate Programs in the Humanities, Arts & Social Sciences

See *Applied Arts and Design, Architecture, Economics,* and *Sociology, Anthropology, and Archaeology*

Graduate Programs in the Biological/Biomedical Sciences & Health-Related Medical Professions

See *Biophysics (Radiation Biology); Ecology, Environmental Biology, and Evolutionary Biology;* and *Health Services (Health Services Management and Hospital Administration)*

Graduate Programs in Business, Education, Information Studies, Law & Social Work

See *Business Administration and Management* and *Law*

CONTENTS

Program Directories

Construction Management

The American University in Dubai, Master in Business Administration Program, Dubai, United Arab Emirates. Offers general (MBA); healthcare management (MBA); international finance (MBA); international marketing (MBA); management of construction enterprises (MBA). Part-time and evening/weekend programs available. *Degree requirements:* For master's, thesis optional. *Entrance requirements:* For master's, GMAT, Interview. Additional exam requirements/recommendations for international students: Required—TOEFL (minimum score 550 paper-based; 213 computer-based; 79 iBT). Electronic applications accepted.

Arizona State University, Ira A. Fulton School of Engineering, ASU Engineering Online Programs, Tempe, AZ 85287. Offers construction (MS); embedded systems (M Eng); enterprise systems innovation and management (MSE); modeling and simulation (M Eng); quality and reliability engineering (M Eng); software engineering (MSE); systems engineering (M Eng).

Arizona State University, Ira A. Fulton School of Engineering, Del E. Webb School of Construction, Tempe, AZ 85287-5306. Offers civil, environmental and sustainable engineering (MS, MSE, PhD); construction (MS, MSE, PhD); construction engineering (MSE). Part-time and evening/weekend programs available. Postbaccalaureate distance learning degree programs offered (minimal on-campus study). Terminal master's awarded for partial completion of doctoral program. *Degree requirements:* For master's, thesis optional, comprehensive exams (MSE); interactive Program of Study (iPOS) submitted before completing 50 percent of required credit hours; for doctorate, comprehensive exam, thesis/dissertation, interactive Program of Study (iPOS) submitted before completing 50 percent of required credit hours. *Entrance requirements:* For master's, GRE, minimum GPA of 3.0 or equivalent in last 2 years of work leading to bachelor's degree; for doctorate, GRE, minimum GPA of 3.0 in last 2 years of work leading to bachelor's degree, 3.2 in all graduate-level coursework with master's degree; 3 letters of recommendation; resume/curriculum vitae; letter of intent; thesis (if applicable); statement of research interests. Additional exam requirements/ recommendations for international students: Required—TOEFL (minimum score 80 iBT), TOEFL, IELTS, or Pearson Test of English. Electronic applications accepted. *Expenses:* Contact institution. *Faculty research:* Water purification, transportation (safety and materials), construction management, environmental biotechnology, environmental nanotechnology, earth systems engineering and management, SMART innovations, project performance metrics, and underground infrastructure.

Auburn University, Graduate School, College of Architecture, Design, and Construction, Department of Building Science, Auburn University, AL 36849. Offers building construction (MBC); construction management (MBC). *Faculty:* 15 full-time (0 women), 1 (woman) part-time/adjunct. *Students:* 10 full-time (0 women), 21 part-time (5 women); includes 3 minority (all Black or African American, non-Hispanic/Latino), 1 international. Average age 30. 36 applicants, 67% accepted, 24 enrolled. In 2011, 31 master's awarded. *Entrance requirements:* For master's, GRE General Test. *Application deadline:* For fall admission, 7/7 for domestic students; for spring admission, 11/24 for domestic students. Applications are processed on a rolling basis. Application fee: $50 ($60 for international students). Electronic applications accepted. *Expenses:* Tuition, state resident: full-time $7290; part-time $405 per credit hour. Tuition, nonresident: full-time $21,870; part-time $1215 per credit hour. *International tuition:* $22,000 full-time. *Required fees:* $1402. *Financial support:* Application deadline: 3/15; applicants required to submit FAFSA. *Unit head:* Dr. Richard Burt, Head, 334-844-5260. *Application contact:* Dr. George Flowers, Dean of the Graduate School, 334-844-2125. Web site: http://www.bsc.auburn.edu/.

Bowling Green State University, Graduate College, College of Technology, Department of Technology Systems, Bowling Green, OH 43403. Offers construction management (MIT); manufacturing technology (MIT). Part-time programs available. *Degree requirements:* For master's, thesis or alternative. *Entrance requirements:* For master's, GRE General Test. Additional exam requirements/recommendations for international students: Required—TOEFL. Electronic applications accepted.

Brigham Young University, Graduate Studies, Ira A. Fulton College of Engineering and Technology, School of Technology, Provo, UT 84602-1001. Offers construction management (MS); information technology (MS); manufacturing systems (MS); technology and engineering education (MS). *Faculty:* 26 full-time (0 women). *Students:* 25 full-time (2 women), 9 part-time (3 women); includes 3 minority (1 Asian, non-Hispanic/Latino; 2 Hispanic/Latino), 5 international. Average age 25. 27 applicants, 59% accepted, 14 enrolled. In 2011, 12 master's awarded. *Degree requirements:* For master's, thesis. *Entrance requirements:* For master's, GRE General Test; GMAT or GRE (for construction management emphasis), minimum GPA of 3.0 in last 60 hours of course work. Additional exam requirements/recommendations for international students: Required—TOEFL (minimum score 580 paper-based; 237 computer-based; 85 iBT). *Application deadline:* For fall admission, 2/15 for domestic and international students; for winter admission, 9/15 for domestic and international students; for spring admission, 2/15 for domestic and international students. Application fee: $50. Electronic applications accepted. *Expenses: Tuition:* Full-time $5760; part-time $320 per credit. Tuition and fees vary according to student's religious affiliation. *Financial support:* In 2011–12, 34 students received support, including 11 research assistantships (averaging $3,506 per year), 7 teaching assistantships (averaging $3,254 per year); scholarships/grants also available. *Faculty research:* Information assurance and security, computerized systems in CM, pedagogy in technology and engineering, manufacturing planning. *Total annual research expenditures:* $220,300. *Unit head:* Val D. Hawks, Director, 801-422-6300, Fax: 801-422-0490, E-mail: hawksv@byu.edu. *Application contact:* Barry M. Lunt, Graduate Coordinator, 801-422-2264, Fax: 801-422-0490, E-mail: ralowe@byu.edu. Web site: http://www.et.byu.edu/sot/.

California State University, East Bay, Office of Academic Programs and Graduate Studies, College of Science, Engineering Department, Program in Construction Management, Hayward, CA 94542-3000. Offers MS. *Faculty:* 1 full-time, 1 part-time/ adjunct. *Students:* 8 full-time (1 woman), 49 part-time (15 women); includes 21 minority (3 Black or African American, non-Hispanic/Latino; 7 Asian, non-Hispanic/Latino; 10 Hispanic/Latino; 1 Two or more races, non-Hispanic/Latino), 6 international. Average age 34. 44 applicants, 80% accepted, 24 enrolled. In 2011, 1 master's awarded. *Degree requirements:* For master's, comprehensive exam (for some programs), research project or exam. *Entrance requirements:* For master's, GRE or GMAT, baccalaureate degree from accredited university with minimum overall GPA of 2.5; relevant work experience; college algebra and trigonometry or equivalent level math courses; personal statement; resume; two letters of recommendation. Additional exam requirements/ recommendations for international students: Required—TOEFL (minimum score 550 paper-based; 213 computer-based; 79 iBT). *Application deadline:* For fall admission, 6/ 30 for domestic and international students. Applications are processed on a rolling basis. Application fee: $55. Electronic applications accepted. *Expenses:* Tuition, state resident: full-time $6738; part-time $1302 per quarter. Tuition, nonresident: full-time $12,690; part-time $2294 per quarter. *Required fees:* $449 per quarter. Tuition and fees vary according to degree level, program and reciprocity agreements. *Financial support:* Federal Work-Study and institutionally sponsored loans available. Support available to part-time students. Financial award application deadline: 3/2; financial award applicants required to submit FAFSA. *Faculty research:* Construction management. *Unit head:* Dr. Saeid Motavalli, Department Chair/Graduate Advisor, 510-885-2654, Fax: 510-885-2678, E-mail: saeid.motavalli@csueastbay.edu. Web site: http://www20.csueastbay.edu/csci/departments/engineering/.

Carnegie Mellon University, College of Fine Arts, School of Architecture, Pittsburgh, PA 15213-3891. Offers architectural engineering construction management (M Sc); architecture (MSA); architecture, engineering, and construction management (PhD); building performance and diagnostics (M Sc, PhD); computational design (M Sc, PhD); sustainable design (M Sc); urban design (M Sc). Terminal master's awarded for partial completion of doctoral program. *Degree requirements:* For doctorate, thesis/ dissertation. *Entrance requirements:* For master's and doctorate, GRE General Test. Additional exam requirements/recommendations for international students: Required— TOEFL.

Central Connecticut State University, School of Graduate Studies, School of Technology, Department of Manufacturing and Construction Management, New Britain, CT 06050-4010. Offers construction management (MS, Certificate); lean manufacturing and Six Sigma (Certificate); supply chain and logistics (Certificate); technology management (MS). Part-time and evening/weekend programs available. *Faculty:* 18 full-time (4 women), 26 part-time/adjunct (2 women). *Students:* 23 full-time (5 women), 89 part-time (22 women); includes 18 minority (10 Black or African American, non-Hispanic/ Latino; 7 Asian, non-Hispanic/Latino; 1 Hispanic/Latino), 7 international. Average age 36. 68 applicants, 78% accepted, 39 enrolled. In 2011, 25 master's, 1 other advanced degree awarded. *Degree requirements:* For master's, comprehensive exam, thesis or alternative; for Certificate, qualifying exam. *Entrance requirements:* For master's, minimum undergraduate GPA of 2.7. Additional exam requirements/recommendations for international students: Required—TOEFL (minimum score 550 paper-based; 213 computer-based). *Application deadline:* For fall admission, 6/1 for domestic students, 5/ 1 for international students; for spring admission, 11/1 for domestic and international students. Applications are processed on a rolling basis. Application fee: $50. Electronic applications accepted. *Expenses: Tuition,* area resident: Full-time $5137; part-time $482 per credit. Tuition, state resident: full-time $7707; part-time $494 per credit. Tuition, nonresident: full-time $14,311; part-time $494 per credit. *Required fees:* $3865. One-time fee: $62 part-time. *Financial support:* In 2011–12, 9 students received support, including 7 research assistantships; career-related internships or fieldwork, Federal Work-Study, scholarships/grants, and unspecified assistantships also available. Support available to part-time students. Financial award application deadline: 4/15; financial award applicants required to submit FAFSA. *Faculty research:* All aspects of middle management, technical supervision in the workplace. *Unit head:* Dr. Jacob Kovel, Chair, 860-832-1830, E-mail: kovelj@ccsu.edu. *Application contact:* Patricia Gardner, Associate Director of Graduate Studies, 860-832-2350, Fax: 860-832-2352, E-mail: graduateadmissions@ccsu.edu. Web site: http://www.ccsu.edu/page.cfm?p=6497.

Clemson University, Graduate School, College of Architecture, Arts, and Humanities, Department of Construction Science and Management, Clemson, SC 29634. Offers MCSM. Part-time programs available. *Faculty:* 5 full-time (2 women). *Students:* 13 full-time (2 women), 5 part-time (0 women), 54 international. Average age 29. 324 applicants, 4% accepted, 6 enrolled. In 2011, 5 master's awarded. *Degree requirements:* For master's, thesis optional. *Entrance requirements:* For master's, GRE General Test, one year of construction experience, current resume. Additional exam requirements/recommendations for international students: Required—TOEFL. *Application deadline:* For fall admission, 2/1 for domestic students, 4/15 for international students; for spring admission, 10/1 for domestic students, 9/15 for international students. Application fee: $70 ($80 for international students). Electronic applications accepted. *Financial support:* In 2011–12, 8 students received support, including 7 teaching assistantships with partial tuition reimbursements available (averaging $4,000 per year); career-related internships or fieldwork, institutionally sponsored loans, scholarships/grants, health care benefits, and unspecified assistantships also available. Support available to part-time students. Financial award applicants required to submit FAFSA. *Faculty research:* Construction best practices, productivity improvement, women's issues in construction, construction project management. *Total annual research expenditures:* $2,451. *Unit head:* Roger Liska, Chair, 864-656-0181, Fax: 864-656-0204, E-mail: riggor@clemson.edu. *Application contact:* Roger Liska, 864-656-0181, Fax: 864-656-0204, E-mail: riggor@clemson.edu. Web site: http://www.clemson.edu/caah/csm/.

Colorado State University, Graduate School, College of Applied Human Sciences, Department of Construction Management, Fort Collins, CO 80523-1584. Offers MS. Part-time and evening/weekend programs available. *Faculty:* 11 full-time (4 women). *Students:* 15 full-time (3 women), 27 part-time (5 women); includes 2 minority (1 Black or African American, non-Hispanic/Latino; 1 Two or more races, non-Hispanic/Latino), 3 international. Average age 35. 29 applicants, 86% accepted, 9 enrolled. In 2011, 20 master's awarded. *Degree requirements:* For master's, thesis optional, professional paper, article for journal or proceedings with faculty advisor. *Entrance requirements:* For master's, GRE, BA/BS from accredited institution, minimum GPA of 3.0. Additional exam requirements/recommendations for international students: Required—TOEFL (minimum score 550 paper-based; 213 computer-based; 80 iBT). *Application deadline:* For fall admission, 2/15 for domestic and international students. Application fee: $50. Electronic applications accepted. *Expenses:* Tuition, state resident: full-time $7992. Tuition, nonresident: full-time $19,592. *Required fees:* $1735; $58 per credit. *Financial support:* In 2011–12, 10 students received support, including 3 research assistantships (averaging $6,446 per year), 7 teaching assistantships with full tuition reimbursements available (averaging $14,566 per year); fellowships, scholarships/grants, and unspecified assistantships also available. Financial award application deadline: 3/1; financial award applicants required to submit FAFSA. *Faculty research:* Sustainable construction management, construction materials science, information technology and transfer, renewable energy systems, Internet project management. *Total annual research expenditures:* $91,821. *Unit head:* Dr. Mostafa M. Khattab, Interim Head, 970-491-6808, Fax: 970-491-2473, E-mail: mostafa.khattab@colostate.edu. *Application contact:* Kristen Haller, Graduate Program Advisor, 970-491-7355, Fax: 970-491-2473, E-mail: kristen.haller@colostate.edu. Web site: http://www.cm.cahs.colostate.edu/.

Columbia University, The Fu Foundation School of Engineering and Applied Science, Department of Civil Engineering and Engineering Mechanics, New York, NY 10027. Offers civil engineering (MS, Eng Sc D, PhD, Engr); construction engineering and management (MS); engineering mechanics (MS, Eng Sc D, PhD, Engr). Part-time programs available. Postbaccalaureate distance learning degree programs offered (no on-campus study). *Faculty:* 15 full-time (1 woman), 24 part-time/adjunct (2 women). *Students:* 119 full-time (27 women), 56 part-time (20 women); includes 36 minority (3

Black or African American, non-Hispanic/Latino; 15 Asian, non-Hispanic/Latino; 3 Hispanic/Latino; 15 Two or more races, non-Hispanic/Latino), 93 international. Average age 28. 302 applicants, 36% accepted, 69 enrolled. In 2011, 61 master's, 4 doctorates, 2 other advanced degrees awarded. Terminal master's awarded for partial completion of doctoral program. *Degree requirements:* For doctorate, thesis/dissertation, qualifying exam. *Entrance requirements:* For master's, doctorate, and Engr, GRE General Test. Additional exam requirements/recommendations for international students: Required—TOEFL, IELTS. *Application deadline:* For fall admission, 12/1 priority date for domestic students, 12/1 for international students; for spring admission, 10/1 priority date for domestic students, 10/1 for international students. Application fee: $95. Electronic applications accepted. *Financial support:* In 2011–12, 39 students received support, including 11 fellowships with full tuition reimbursements available (averaging $25,386 per year), 16 research assistantships with full tuition reimbursements available (averaging $31,128 per year), 10 teaching assistantships with full tuition reimbursements available (averaging $31,128 per year); traineeships, health care benefits, and tuition waivers also available. Financial award application deadline: 12/1; financial award applicants required to submit FAFSA. *Faculty research:* Structural dynamics, structural health and monitoring, fatigue and fracture mechanics, geo-enviornmental engineering, multiscale science and engineering. *Unit head:* Dr. Raimondo Betti, Professor and Department Chairman, 212-854-6388, E-mail: betti@civil.columbia.edu. *Application contact:* Dr. Rene B. Testa, Professor, 212-854-6383, Fax: 212-854-6267, E-mail: testa@civil.columbia.edu. Web site: http://www.civil.columbia.edu/.

Columbia University, School of Continuing Education, Program in Construction Administration, New York, NY 10027. Offers MS. Part-time and evening/weekend programs available. *Degree requirements:* For master's, minimum GPA of 3.0 or internship. *Entrance requirements:* For master's, bachelor's degree, minimum GPA of 3.0. Additional exam requirements/recommendations for international students: Recommended—TOEFL. Electronic applications accepted.

Drexel University, Goodwin College of Professional Studies, School of Technology and Professional Studies, Philadelphia, PA 19104-2875. Offers construction management (MS); engineering technology (MS); food science (MS); hospitality management (MS); professional studies: creativity studies (MS); professional studies: e-learning leadership (MS); professional studies: homeland security management (MS); project management (MS); property management (MS); sport management (MS). Postbaccalaureate distance learning degree programs offered.

Eastern Michigan University, Graduate School, College of Technology, School of Engineering Technology, Program in Construction Management, Ypsilanti, MI 48197. Offers MS. Part-time and evening/weekend programs available. Postbaccalaureate distance learning degree programs offered (minimal on-campus study). *Students:* 13 full-time (1 woman), 16 part-time (4 women); includes 7 minority (all Black or African American, non-Hispanic/Latino), 5 international. Average age 33. 34 applicants, 59% accepted, 8 enrolled. In 2011, 11 degrees awarded. *Entrance requirements:* Additional exam requirements/recommendations for international students: Required—TOEFL. *Application deadline:* Applications are processed on a rolling basis. Application fee: $35. *Expenses:* Tuition, state resident: full-time $10,367; part-time $432 per credit hour. Tuition, nonresident: full-time $20,435; part-time $851 per credit hour. *Required fees:* $39 per credit hour. $46 per semester. One-time fee: $100. Tuition and fees vary according to course level, degree level and reciprocity agreements. *Financial support:* Fellowships, research assistantships with full tuition reimbursements, teaching assistantships with full tuition reimbursements, career-related internships or fieldwork, Federal Work-Study, institutionally sponsored loans, scholarships/grants, tuition waivers (partial), and unspecified assistantships available. Support available to part-time students. Financial award applicants required to submit FAFSA. *Unit head:* Dr. James Stein, Program Coordinator, 734-487-1940, Fax: 734-487-8755, E-mail: jstein@emich.edu. *Application contact:* Graduate Admissions, 734-487-2400, Fax: 734-487-6559, E-mail: graduate.admissions@emich.edu.

Florida International University, College of Engineering and Computing, Department of Construction Management, Miami, FL 33175. Offers MS. Part-time and evening/weekend programs available. *Degree requirements:* For master's, thesis optional. *Entrance requirements:* For master's, minimum GPA of 3.0 in upper-level course work. Additional exam requirements/recommendations for international students: Required—TOEFL (minimum score 550 paper-based; 80 iBT). Electronic applications accepted. *Faculty research:* Information technology, construction organizations, contracts and partnerships in construction, construction education, concrete technology.

Harrisburg University of Science and Technology, Program in Project Management, Harrisburg, PA 17101. Offers construction services (MS); governmental services (MS); information technology (MS). Part-time and evening/weekend programs available. *Entrance requirements:* For master's, BS, BBA. Additional exam requirements/recommendations for international students: Required—TOEFL (minimum score 520 paper-based; 200 computer-based; 80 iBT). Electronic applications accepted.

Illinois Institute of Technology, Graduate College, Armour College of Engineering, Department of Civil, Architectural and Environmental Engineering, Chicago, IL 60616-3793. Offers architectural engineering (M Arch E); civil engineering (MS, PhD), including architectural engineeering (MS), construction engineering and management (MS), geoenvironmental engineering (MS), geotechnical engineering (MS), structural engineering (MS), transportation engineering (MS); construction engineering and management (MCEM); environmental engineering (M Env E, PhD); geoenvironmental engineering (M Geoenv E); geotechnical engineering (MGE); public works (MPW); structural engineering (MSE); transportation engineering (M Trans E). Part-time and evening/weekend programs available. Postbaccalaureate distance learning degree programs offered (minimal on-campus study). Terminal master's awarded for partial completion of doctoral program. *Degree requirements:* For master's, thesis (for some programs); for doctorate, comprehensive exam, thesis/dissertation. *Entrance requirements:* For master's, GRE General Test (minimum score 900 Quantitative and Verbal, 2.5 Analytical Writing), minimum undergraduate GPA of 3.0; for doctorate, GRE General Test (minimum score 1000 Quantitative and Verbal, 3.0 Analytical Writing), minimum undergraduate GPA of 3.0. Additional exam requirements/recommendations for international students: Required—TOEFL (minimum score 523 paper-based; 70 iBT); Recommended—IELTS (minimum score 5.5). Electronic applications accepted. *Faculty research:* Structural, architectural, geotechnical and geoenvironmental engineering; construction engineering and management; transportation engineering; environmental engineering and public works.

Indiana University–Purdue University Fort Wayne, College of Engineering, Technology, and Computer Science, Program in Technology, Fort Wayne, IN 46805-1499. Offers facilities and construction management (MS); industrial technology/manufacturing (MS); information technology/advanced computer applications (MS). Part-time programs available. *Faculty:* 14 full-time (5 women). *Students:* 1 full-time (0 women), 18 part-time (1 woman); includes 3 minority (1 Black or African American, non-Hispanic/Latino; 1 Asian, non-Hispanic/Latino; 1 Hispanic/Latino), 3 international. Average age 32. 9 applicants, 100% accepted, 7 enrolled. In 2011, 5 master's awarded. *Entrance requirements:* For master's, minimum GPA of 3.0. Additional exam requirements/recommendations for international students: Required—TOEFL (minimum score 550 paper-based; 213 computer-based; 77 iBT), TWE. *Application deadline:* For fall admission, 7/15 for domestic students, 5/15 for international students; for spring admission, 12/1 for domestic students, 10/15 for international students. Applications are processed on a rolling basis. Application fee: $55 ($60 for international students). Electronic applications accepted. *Financial support:* Career-related internships or fieldwork, scholarships/grants, and unspecified assistantships available. Support available to part-time students. Financial award application deadline: 3/1; financial award applicants required to submit FAFSA. *Unit head:* Dr. Max Yen, Dean, 260-481-6839, Fax: 260-481-5734, E-mail: yens@ipfw.edu. *Application contact:* Dr. Gary Steffen, Chair, 260-481-6344, Fax: 260-481-5734, E-mail: steffen@ipfw.edu. Web site: http://www.ipfw.edu/etcs.

Instituto Tecnologico de Santo Domingo, Graduate School, Area of Engineering, Santo Domingo, Dominican Republic. Offers construction administration (MS, Certificate); data telecommunications (M Eng, MS, Certificate); industrial engineering (M Eng, Certificate); industrial management (M Mgmt); information technology (Certificate); maintenance engineering (M Eng); occupational hazard prevention (M Mgmt); production management (Certificate); quantitative methods (Certificate); sanitary and environmental engineering (M Eng); structural engineering (M Eng); systems engineering and electronic data processing (Certificate); transportation (Certificate).

Marquette University, Graduate School, College of Engineering, Department of Civil and Environmental Engineering, Milwaukee, WI 53201-1881. Offers construction and public works management (MS, PhD); construction engineering and management (Certificate); environmental/water resources engineering (MS, PhD); structural design (Certificate); structural/geotechnical engineering (MS, PhD); transportation planning and engineering (MS, PhD); waste and wastewater treatment processes (Certificate). Part-time and evening/weekend programs available. *Faculty:* 13 full-time (0 women), 5 part-time/adjunct (0 women). *Students:* 26 full-time (5 women), 11 part-time (0 women); includes 2 minority (1 Black or African American, non-Hispanic/Latino; 1 Asian, non-Hispanic/Latino), 12 international. Average age 27. 74 applicants, 62% accepted, 9 enrolled. In 2011, 6 master's, 3 doctorates awarded. Terminal master's awarded for partial completion of doctoral program. *Degree requirements:* For master's, comprehensive exam (for some programs), thesis or alternative; for doctorate, thesis/dissertation. *Entrance requirements:* For master's, GRE General Test (recommended), minimum GPA of 3.0, official transcripts from all current and previous colleges/universities except Marquette, three letters of recommendation; for doctorate, GRE General Test, minimum GPA of 3.0, official transcripts from all current and previous colleges/universities except Marquette, three letters of recommendation, brief statement of purpose, submission of any English language publications authored by applicant (strongly recommended). Additional exam requirements/recommendations for international students: Required—TOEFL (minimum score 530 paper-based; 78 computer-based). *Application deadline:* For fall admission, 6/1 priority date for domestic students. Applications are processed on a rolling basis. Application fee: $50. Electronic applications accepted. *Expenses: Tuition:* Full-time $17,010; part-time $945 per credit hour. Tuition and fees vary according to program. *Financial support:* In 2011–12, 21 students received support, including 6 fellowships with partial tuition reimbursements available (averaging $9,177 per year), 1 research assistantship with full tuition reimbursement available (averaging $13,745 per year), 7 teaching assistantships with full tuition reimbursements available (averaging $13,902 per year); scholarships/grants, health care benefits, tuition waivers (partial), and unspecified assistantships also available. Support available to part-time students. Financial award application deadline: 2/15. *Faculty research:* Highway safety, highway performance, and intelligent transportation systems; surface mount technology; watershed management. *Total annual research expenditures:* $826,608. *Unit head:* Dr. Thomas Wenzel, Chair, 414-288-7030, Fax: 414-288-7521, E-mail: thomas.wenzel@marquette.edu. *Application contact:* Dr. Stephen M. Heinrich, Director of Graduate Studies, 414-288-5466, E-mail: stephen.heinrich@marquette.edu. Web site: http://www.marquette.edu/engineering/pages/AllYouNeed/Civil_Environmental/civil.html.

Michigan State University, The Graduate School, College of Agriculture and Natural Resources and College of Social Science, School of Planning, Design and Construction, East Lansing, MI 48824. Offers construction management (MS, PhD); environmental design (MA); interior design and facilities management (MA); international planning studies (MIPS); urban and regional planning (MURP). *Degree requirements:* For master's, thesis or alternative. *Entrance requirements:* Additional exam requirements/recommendations for international students: Required—TOEFL. Electronic applications accepted.

Missouri State University, Graduate College, College of Business Administration, Department of Technology and Construction Management, Springfield, MO 65897. Offers MS. Part-time programs available. *Faculty:* 6 full-time (1 woman). *Students:* 21 full-time (5 women), 39 part-time (13 women); includes 11 minority (3 Black or African American, non-Hispanic/Latino; 2 American Indian or Alaska Native, non-Hispanic/Latino; 1 Asian, non-Hispanic/Latino; 2 Hispanic/Latino; 3 Two or more races, non-Hispanic/Latino), 5 international. Average age 34. 37 applicants, 89% accepted, 19 enrolled. In 2011, 19 master's awarded. *Degree requirements:* For master's, thesis or alternative. *Entrance requirements:* For master's, GRE or GMAT, minimum GPA of 2.75. Additional exam requirements/recommendations for international students: Required—TOEFL (minimum score 550 paper-based; 213 computer-based; 79 iBT). *Application deadline:* For fall admission, 7/20 for domestic students, 5/1 for international students; for spring admission, 12/20 for domestic students, 9/1 for international students. Applications are processed on a rolling basis. Application fee: $35 ($50 for international students). Electronic applications accepted. *Expenses:* Tuition, state resident: full-time $4086; part-time $227 per credit hour. Tuition, nonresident: full-time $8172; part-time $454 per credit hour. *Required fees:* $275 per semester. Tuition and fees vary according to course load, campus/location and program. *Financial support:* Federal Work-Study, institutionally sponsored loans, scholarships/grants, and unspecified assistantships available. Financial award application deadline: 3/31; financial award applicants required to submit FAFSA. *Unit head:* Dr. Shawn Strong, Head, 417-836-5121, Fax: 417-836-8556, E-mail: indmgt@missouristate.edu. *Application contact:* Dr. R. Neal Callahan, Director, 417-836-5160, Fax: 417-836-8556, E-mail: nealcallahan@missouristate.edu. Web site: http://tcm.missouristate.edu/.

New York University, School of Continuing and Professional Studies, Schack Institute of Real Estate, Program in Construction Management, New York, NY 10012-1019. Offers MS, Advanced Certificate. Part-time and evening/weekend programs available. *Faculty:* 5 full-time (1 woman), 23 part-time/adjunct (2 women). *Students:* 16 full-time (5 women), 72 part-time (15 women); includes 6 minority (3 Black or African American, non-Hispanic/Latino; 1 Asian, non-Hispanic/Latino; 2 Hispanic/Latino), 8 international.

Average age 33. 73 applicants, 66% accepted, 30 enrolled. In 2011, 36 master's awarded. *Degree requirements:* For master's, capstone project. *Entrance requirements:* For master's, GRE/GMAT only upon request, relevant professional work, internship or volunteer experience. Additional exam requirements/recommendations for international students: Required—TOEFL (minimum score 600 paper-based; 250 computer-based; 100 iBT), IELTS (minimum score 7). *Application deadline:* For fall admission, 2/1 priority date for domestic students, 2/1 for international students; for spring admission, 10/15 priority date for domestic students, 8/15 for international students. Applications are processed on a rolling basis. Application fee: $150. Electronic applications accepted. *Financial support:* In 2011–12, 47 students received support, including 45 fellowships (averaging $1,992 per year); scholarships/grants also available. Financial award application deadline: 3/1; financial award applicants required to submit FAFSA. *Unit head:* Rosemary Scanlon, Divisional Dean. *Application contact:* Office of Admissions, 212-998-7100, E-mail: scps.gradadmissions@nyu.edu. Web site: http://www.scps.nyu.edu/areas-of-study/real-estate/graduate-programs/.

North Carolina Agricultural and Technical State University, School of Graduate Studies, School of Technology, Department of Construction Management and Occupational Safety and Health, Greensboro, NC 27411. Offers construction management (MSTM); environmental and occupational safety (MSTM); occupational safety and health (MSTM).

North Dakota State University, College of Graduate and Interdisciplinary Studies, College of Engineering and Architecture, Department of Construction Management and Engineering, Fargo, ND 58108. Offers construction management (MS). *Faculty:* 4 full-time (0 women), 2 part-time/adjunct (0 women). *Students:* 14 full-time (2 women), 26 part-time (5 women); includes 4 minority (1 Black or African American, non-Hispanic/Latino; 1 Asian, non-Hispanic/Latino; 1 Hispanic/Latino; 1 Native Hawaiian or other Pacific Islander, non-Hispanic/Latino), 16 international. 13 applicants, 31% accepted, 1 enrolled. In 2011, 5 master's awarded. *Entrance requirements:* Additional exam requirements/recommendations for international students: Required—TOEFL (minimum score 525 paper-based; 197 computer-based; 71 iBT). *Application deadline:* For fall admission, 5/1 for international students; for spring admission, 8/1 for international students. Applications are processed on a rolling basis. Application fee: $35. Electronic applications accepted. *Unit head:* Dr. Charles McIntyre, Chair, 701-231-7879, Fax: 701-231-7431, E-mail: charles.mcintyre@ndsu.edu. *Application contact:* Dr. David A. Wittrock, Dean, 701-231-7033, Fax: 701-231-6524.

Norwich University, College of Graduate and Continuing Studies, Master of Civil Engineering Program, Northfield, VT 05663. Offers construction management (MCE); environmental water resources (MCE); geo-technical (MCE); structural (MCE). Evening/weekend programs available. *Faculty:* 12 part-time/adjunct (1 woman). *Students:* 88 full-time (23 women); includes 15 minority (8 Black or African American, non-Hispanic/Latino; 1 American Indian or Alaska Native, non-Hispanic/Latino; 4 Asian, non-Hispanic/Latino; 2 Hispanic/Latino). Average age 33. In 2011, 44 master's awarded. *Entrance requirements:* For master's, minimum GPA of 2.75. Additional exam requirements/recommendations for international students: Required—TOEFL (minimum score 550 paper-based; 213 computer-based; 83 iBT). *Application deadline:* For fall admission, 8/10 for domestic and international students; for spring admission, 2/6 for domestic and international students. Applications are processed on a rolling basis. Application fee: $50. Electronic applications accepted. *Expenses: Tuition:* Full-time $16,174. *Required fees:* $2130. Full-time tuition and fees vary according to program. *Financial support:* In 2011–12, 5 students received support. Scholarships/grants available. Financial award applicants required to submit FAFSA. *Unit head:* Dr. Thomas Descoteaux, Program Director, 802-485-2730, Fax: 802-485-2533, E-mail: tdescote@norwich.edu. *Application contact:* Rija Ramahatra, Associate Program Director, 802-485-2892, Fax: 802-485-2533, E-mail: ramahatr@norwich.edu. Web site: http://mce.norwich.edu.

Philadelphia University, College of Architecture and the Built Environment, Program in Construction Management, Philadelphia, PA 19144. Offers MS.

Polytechnic Institute of New York University, Department of Civil Engineering, Major in Construction Management, Brooklyn, NY 11201-2990. Offers MS. *Students:* 28 full-time (9 women), 65 part-time (16 women); includes 28 minority (14 Black or African American, non-Hispanic/Latino; 9 Asian, non-Hispanic/Latino; 5 Hispanic/Latino), 22 international. Average age 30. 97 applicants, 52% accepted, 29 enrolled. In 2011, 44 degrees awarded. *Degree requirements:* For master's, comprehensive exam (for some programs), thesis (for some programs). *Entrance requirements:* Additional exam requirements/recommendations for international students: Required—TOEFL (minimum score 550 paper-based; 213 computer-based; 80 iBT); Recommended—IELTS (minimum score 6.5). *Application deadline:* For fall admission, 7/31 priority date for domestic students, 4/30 for international students; for spring admission, 12/31 priority date for domestic students, 10/30 for international students. Applications are processed on a rolling basis. Application fee: $75. Electronic applications accepted. *Expenses: Tuition:* Full-time $22,464; part-time $1248 per credit. *Required fees:* $501 per semester. *Financial support:* Institutionally sponsored loans, scholarships/grants, and unspecified assistantships available. Support available to part-time students. *Unit head:* Dr. Lawrence Chiarelli, Head, 718-260-4040, Fax: 718-260-3433, E-mail: lchiarel@poly.edu. *Application contact:* JeanCarlo Bonilla, Director, Graduate Enrollment Management, 718-260-3182, Fax: 718-260-3624, E-mail: gradinfo@poly.edu.

Polytechnic Institute of New York University, Department of Technology Management, Brooklyn, NY 11201-2990. Offers construction management (Advanced Certificate); electronic business management (Advanced Certificate); entrepreneurship (Advanced Certificate); human resources management (Advanced Certificate); information management (Advanced Certificate); management (MS); management of technology (MS); organizational behavior (MS, Advanced Certificate); project management (Advanced Certificate); technology management (MBA, PhD, Advanced Certificate); telecommunications and information management (MS); telecommunications management (Advanced Certificate). Part-time and evening/weekend programs available. *Faculty:* 6 full-time (1 woman), 32 part-time/adjunct (4 women). *Students:* 185 full-time (84 women), 94 part-time (41 women); includes 56 minority (15 Black or African American, non-Hispanic/Latino; 31 Asian, non-Hispanic/Latino; 10 Hispanic/Latino), 143 international. Average age 30. 467 applicants, 48% accepted, 123 enrolled. In 2011, 174 master's, 1 doctorate awarded. *Degree requirements:* For master's, comprehensive exam (for some programs), thesis (for some programs); for doctorate, comprehensive exam, thesis/dissertation. *Entrance requirements:* For master's, GMAT, minimum B average in undergraduate course work. Additional exam requirements/recommendations for international students: Required—TOEFL (minimum score 550 paper-based; 213 computer-based; 80 iBT); Recommended—IELTS (minimum score 6.5). *Application deadline:* For fall admission, 7/31 priority date for domestic students, 4/30 for international students; for spring admission, 12/31 priority date for domestic students, 11/30 for international students. Applications are processed on a rolling basis. Application fee: $75. Electronic applications accepted. *Expenses: Tuition:* Full-time $22,464; part-time $1248 per credit.

Required fees: $501 per semester. *Financial support:* In 2011–12, 1 fellowship (averaging $26,400 per year) was awarded; research assistantships, teaching assistantships, institutionally sponsored loans, scholarships/grants, and unspecified assistantships also available. Support available to part-time students. *Unit head:* Prof. Bharadwaj Rao, Head, 718-260-3617, Fax: 718-260-3874, E-mail: brao@poly.edu. *Application contact:* JeanCarlo Bonilla, Director of Graduate Enrollment Management, 718-260-3182, Fax: 718-260-3624, E-mail: gradinfo@poly.edu. Web site: http://www.managementdept.poly.edu.

Polytechnic Institute of NYU, Long Island Graduate Center, Graduate Programs, Department of Civil Engineering, Major in Construction Management, Melville, NY 11747. Offers MS. Part-time and evening/weekend programs available. *Students:* 4 part-time (2 women). Average age 29. 10 applicants, 100% accepted, 4 enrolled. *Entrance requirements:* Additional exam requirements/recommendations for international students: Required—TOEFL (minimum score 550 paper-based; 213 computer-based; 80 iBT); Recommended—IELTS (minimum score 6.5). *Application deadline:* For fall admission, 7/31 priority date for domestic students, 4/30 for international students; for spring admission, 12/31 priority date for domestic students, 11/30 for international students. Applications are processed on a rolling basis. Application fee: $75. Electronic applications accepted. *Financial support:* Institutionally sponsored loans, scholarships/grants, and unspecified assistantships available. Support available to part-time students. *Unit head:* Dr. Lawrence Chiarelli, Department Head, 718-260-4040, E-mail: lchiarel@duke.poly.edu. *Application contact:* JeanCarlo Bonilla, Director of Graduate Enrollment Management, 718-260-3182, Fax: 718-260-3624, E-mail: gradinfo@poly.edu.

Polytechnic Institute of NYU, Westchester Graduate Center, Graduate Programs, Department of Civil Engineering, Hawthorne, NY 10532-1507. Offers construction management (MS). *Students:* 17 part-time (2 women); includes 4 minority (1 Black or African American, non-Hispanic/Latino; 1 Asian, non-Hispanic/Latino; 2 Hispanic/Latino). 15 applicants, 67% accepted, 5 enrolled. *Application contact:* JeanCarlo Bonilla, Director of Graduate Enrollment Management, 718-260-3182, Fax: 718-260-3624, E-mail: gradinfo@poly.edu.

Polytechnic University of Puerto Rico, Miami Campus, Graduate School, Miami, FL 33166. Offers accounting (MBA); business administration (MBA); construction management (MEM); environmental management (MEM); finance (MBA); human resources management (MBA); logistics and supply chain management (MBA); management of international enterprises (MBA); manufacturing management (MEM); marketing management (MBA); project management (MBA). Part-time and evening/weekend programs available. Postbaccalaureate distance learning degree programs offered (no on-campus study). *Entrance requirements:* For master's, minimum GPA of 3.0. Electronic applications accepted.

Polytechnic University of Puerto Rico, Orlando Campus, Graduate School, Winter Park, FL 32792. Offers accounting (MBA); business administration (MBA); construction management (MEM); engineering management (MEM); environmental management (MEM); finance (MBA); human resources management (MBA); management of international enterprises (MBA); management of technology (MBA); manufacturing management (MEM). Part-time and evening/weekend programs available. Postbaccalaureate distance learning degree programs offered (no on-campus study). *Entrance requirements:* For master's, minimum GPA of 3.0. Additional exam requirements/recommendations for international students: Recommended—TOEFL. Electronic applications accepted.

Roger Williams University, School of Engineering, Computing and Construction Management, Bristol, RI 02809. Offers construction management (MSCM).

Rowan University, Graduate School, College of Engineering, Department of Civil and Environmental Engineering, Program in Construction Management, Glassboro, NJ 08028-1701. Offers MS. *Entrance requirements:* For master's, GRE General Test. Additional exam requirements/recommendations for international students: Required—TOEFL. Electronic applications accepted.

South Dakota School of Mines and Technology, Graduate Division, Program in Construction Management, Rapid City, SD 57701-3995. Offers MS.

Southern Polytechnic State University, School of Architecture and Construction Management, Department of Construction Management, Marietta, GA 30060-2896. Offers MS. Part-time and evening/weekend programs available. *Faculty:* 8 full-time (1 woman), 1 part-time/adjunct (0 women). *Students:* 26 full-time (4 women), 9 part-time (3 women); includes 12 minority (9 Black or African American, non-Hispanic/Latino; 3 Hispanic/Latino), 4 international. Average age 33. 23 applicants, 78% accepted, 14 enrolled. In 2011, 8 master's awarded. *Degree requirements:* For master's, comprehensive exam, thesis or alternative. *Entrance requirements:* For master's, GMAT or GRE, 3 reference forms, minimum GPA of 2.75. Additional exam requirements/recommendations for international students: Required—TOEFL (minimum score 550 paper-based; 213 computer-based; 79 iBT), IELTS (minimum score 6.5). *Application deadline:* For fall admission, 7/1 priority date for domestic students, 5/1 for international students; for spring admission, 11/1 priority date for domestic students, 9/1 for international students. Applications are processed on a rolling basis. Application fee: $50. Electronic applications accepted. *Expenses:* Tuition, state resident: full-time $2592; part-time $216 per semester hour. Tuition, nonresident: full-time $9408; part-time $784 per semester hour. *Required fees:* $698 per term. *Financial support:* Research assistantships with tuition reimbursements, career-related internships or fieldwork, scholarships/grants, and unspecified assistantships available. Support available to part-time students. Financial award application deadline: 5/1; financial award applicants required to submit FAFSA. *Faculty research:* Environmental construction and green building techniques, risk management, bidding strategies in construction, construction worker safety, building automation and performance measurements. *Total annual research expenditures:* $30,100. *Unit head:* Dr. Khalid M. Siddiqi, Chair, 678-915-7221, Fax: 678-915-4966, E-mail: ksiddiqi@spsu.edu. *Application contact:* Nikki Palamiotis, Director of Graduate Studies, 678-915-4276, Fax: 678-915-7292, E-mail: npalamio@spsu.edu. Web site: http://www.spsu.edu/constmgmt/index.htm.

State University of New York College of Environmental Science and Forestry, Department of Sustainable Construction Management and Engineering, Syracuse, NY 13210-2779. Offers construction management (MPS, MS, PhD); engineered wood products and structures (MPS, MS, PhD); sustainable construction (MPS, MS, PhD); tropical timbers (MPS, MS, PhD); wood anatomy and ultrastructure (MPS, MS, PhD); wood science and technology (MPS, MS, PhD); wood treatments (MPS, MS, PhD). *Degree requirements:* For master's, thesis (for some programs); for doctorate, comprehensive exam, thesis/dissertation. *Entrance requirements:* For master's and doctorate, GRE General Test, minimum GPA of 3.0. Additional exam requirements/recommendations for international students: Required—TOEFL (minimum score 550 paper-based; 213 computer-based; 80 iBT), IELTS (minimum score 6). *Application* *deadline:* For fall admission, 2/1 priority date for domestic students, 2/1 for international students; for spring admission, 11/1 priority date for domestic students, 11/1 for international students. Applications are processed on a rolling basis. Application fee: $60. *Expenses:* Tuition, state resident: full-time $8870; part-time $370 per credit hour. Tuition, nonresident: full-time $15,160; part-time $632 per credit hour. *Required fees:* $60; $370 per credit hour. $350 per semester. One-time fee: $85. *Financial support:* Fellowships with full tuition reimbursements, research assistantships with full tuition reimbursements, teaching assistantships with full tuition reimbursements, career-related internships or fieldwork, Federal Work-Study, institutionally sponsored loans, scholarships/grants, health care benefits, and unspecified assistantships available. Financial award application deadline: 6/30; financial award applicants required to submit FAFSA. *Total annual research expenditures:* $160,385. *Unit head:* Dr. Susan E. Anagnost, Chair, 315-470-6880, Fax: 315-470-6879, E-mail: seanagno@esf.edu. *Application contact:* Dr. Dudley J. Raynal, Dean, Instruction and Graduate Studies, 315-470-6599, Fax: 315-470-6879, E-mail: esfgrad@esf.edu. Web site: http://www.esf.edu/scme/.

Stevens Institute of Technology, Graduate School, Charles V. Schaefer Jr. School of Engineering, Department of Civil, Environmental, and Ocean Engineering, Program in Construction Management, Hoboken, NJ 07030. Offers construction accounting/estimating (Certificate); construction engineering (Certificate); construction law/disputes (Certificate); construction management (MS); construction/quality management (Certificate). *Degree requirements:* For master's, thesis optional. *Entrance requirements:* For master's, GMAT, GRE General Test. Additional exam requirements/recommendations for international students: Required—TOEFL. Electronic applications accepted.

Texas A&M University, College of Architecture, Department of Construction Science, College Station, TX 77843. Offers construction management (MS). *Faculty:* 16. *Students:* 39 full-time (15 women), 8 part-time (1 woman); includes 6 minority (1 Black or African American, non-Hispanic/Latino; 4 Hispanic/Latino; 1 Two or more races, non-Hispanic/Latino), 24 international. Average age 30. In 2011, 34 master's awarded. *Degree requirements:* For master's, comprehensive exam. *Entrance requirements:* For master's, GRE General Test. Additional exam requirements/recommendations for international students: Required—TOEFL. *Application deadline:* For fall admission, 4/1 priority date for domestic students; for winter admission, 1/1 priority date for domestic students; for spring admission, 9/1 priority date for domestic students. Applications are processed on a rolling basis. Application fee: $50 ($75 for international students). Electronic applications accepted. *Expenses:* Tuition, state resident: full-time $5437; part-time $226.55 per credit hour. Tuition, nonresident: full-time $12,949; part-time $539.55 per credit hour. *Required fees:* $2741. *Financial support:* In 2011–12, fellowships with partial tuition reimbursements (averaging $1,000 per year), research assistantships with partial tuition reimbursements (averaging $9,000 per year), teaching assistantships with partial tuition reimbursements (averaging $9,000 per year) were awarded. Financial award application deadline: 4/1; financial award applicants required to submit FAFSA. *Faculty research:* Fire safety, housing foundations, construction project management, quality management. *Unit head:* Dr. Joe Horlen, Head, 979-458-3477, E-mail: jhorlen@tamu.edu. *Application contact:* Graduate Admissions, 979-458-0427, E-mail: admissions@tamu.edu. Web site: http://cosc.arch.tamu.edu/.

Texas A&M University, College of Engineering, Zachry Department of Civil Engineering, College Station, TX 77843. Offers coastal and ocean engineering (M Eng, MS, D Eng, PhD); construction engineering and management (M Eng, MS, D Eng, PhD); environmental engineering (M Eng, MS, D Eng, PhD); geotechnical engineering (M Eng, MS, D Eng, PhD); materials engineering (M Eng, MS, D Eng, PhD); structural engineering (M Eng, MS, D Eng, PhD); transportation engineering (M Eng, MS, D Eng, PhD); water resources engineering (M Eng, MS, D Eng, PhD). Part-time programs available. *Faculty:* 57. *Students:* 361 full-time (76 women), 46 part-time (8 women); includes 41 minority (3 Black or African American, non-Hispanic/Latino; 16 Asian, non-Hispanic/Latino; 21 Hispanic/Latino; 1 Two or more races, non-Hispanic/Latino), 247 international. Average age 29. In 2011, 123 master's, 27 doctorates awarded. *Degree requirements:* For master's, thesis (MS); for doctorate, dissertation (PhD), internship (D Eng). *Entrance requirements:* For master's and doctorate, GRE General Test. Additional exam requirements/recommendations for international students: Required—TOEFL. *Application deadline:* Applications are processed on a rolling basis. Application fee: $50 ($75 for international students). Electronic applications accepted. *Expenses:* Tuition, state resident: full-time $5437; part-time $226.55 per credit hour. Tuition, nonresident: full-time $12,949; part-time $539.55 per credit hour. *Required fees:* $2741. *Financial support:* In 2011–12, fellowships (averaging $4,500 per year), research assistantships (averaging $14,000 per year), teaching assistantships (averaging $14,400 per year) were awarded; career-related internships or fieldwork and institutionally sponsored loans also available. Financial award application deadline: 4/15; financial award applicants required to submit FAFSA. *Unit head:* Dr. John Niedzwecki, Head, 979-845-3858, E-mail: j-niedzwecki@tamu.edu. *Application contact:* Graduate Advisor, 979-845-7435, Fax: 979-845-6156, E-mail: info@civil.tamu.edu. Web site: https://www.civil.tamu.edu/.

Universidad de las Américas–Puebla, Division of Graduate Studies, School of Engineering, Program in Construction Management, Puebla, Mexico. Offers M Adm. Part-time and evening/weekend programs available. *Degree requirements:* For master's, one foreign language, thesis. *Faculty research:* Building structures, budget, project management.

University of Alaska Fairbanks, College of Engineering and Mines, Department of Civil and Environmental Engineering, Fairbanks, AK 99775-5900. Offers arctic engineering (MS, PhD); civil engineering (MCE, MS, PhD); construction management (Graduate Certificate); engineering (PhD); engineering and science management (MS, PhD), including engineering management, science management (MS); environmental engineering (MS, PhD), including engineering (PhD), environmental engineering (MS); environmental quality science (MS), including environmental contaminants, environmental quality science, environmental science and management, water supply and waste treatment. Part-time programs available. *Faculty:* 11 full-time (2 women). *Students:* 25 full-time (12 women), 16 part-time (6 women); includes 4 minority (1 Black or African American, non-Hispanic/Latino; 1 American Indian or Alaska Native, non-Hispanic/Latino; 1 Asian, non-Hispanic/Latino; 1 Two or more races, non-Hispanic/Latino), 13 international. Average age 32. 21 applicants, 62% accepted, 8 enrolled. In 2011, 10 master's, 1 doctorate awarded. Terminal master's awarded for partial completion of doctoral program. *Degree requirements:* For master's, comprehensive exam, thesis or alternative; for doctorate, comprehensive exam, thesis/dissertation, oral exam, oral defense. *Entrance requirements:* For doctorate, GRE General Test. Additional exam requirements/recommendations for international students: Required—TOEFL (minimum score 550 paper-based; 213 computer-based; 80 iBT). *Application deadline:* For fall admission, 6/1 for domestic students, 3/1 for international students; for spring admission, 10/15 for domestic students, 9/1 for international students. Applications are processed on a rolling basis. Application fee: $60. Electronic applications accepted. *Expenses:* Tuition, state resident: full-time $6696; part-time $372 per credit. Tuition, nonresident: full-time $13,680; part-time $760 per credit. Tuition and fees vary according to course load and reciprocity agreements. *Financial support:* In 2011–12, 12 research assistantships with tuition reimbursements (averaging $12,027 per year), 6 teaching assistantships with tuition reimbursements (averaging $6,390 per year) were awarded; fellowships with tuition reimbursements, career-related internships or fieldwork, Federal Work-Study, scholarships/grants, health care benefits, and unspecified assistantships also available. Support available to part-time students. Financial award application deadline: 7/1; financial award applicants required to submit FAFSA. *Faculty research:* Soils, structures, culvert thawing with solar power, pavement drainage, contaminant hydrogeology. *Unit head:* Dr. David Barnes, Department Chair, 907-474-7241, Fax: 907-474-6087, E-mail: fycee@uaf.edu. *Application contact:* Mike Earnest, Director of Admissions, 907-474-7500, Fax: 907-474-5379, E-mail: admissions@uaf.edu. Web site: http://www.alaska.edu/uaf/cem/cee/.

University of Arkansas at Little Rock, Graduate School, College of Business Administration, Little Rock, AR 72204-1099. Offers accountancy (M Acc, Graduate Certificate); business administration (MBA); construction management (Graduate Certificate); management (Graduate Certificate); management information system (MIS); management information systems (Graduate Certificate); management information systems leadership (Graduate Certificate); taxation (MS, Graduate Certificate). *Accreditation:* AACSB. Part-time and evening/weekend programs available. *Entrance requirements:* For master's, GMAT, minimum undergraduate GPA of 2.7. Additional exam requirements/recommendations for international students: Required—TOEFL (minimum score 525 paper-based; 195 computer-based).

University of California, Berkeley, UC Berkeley Extension, Certificate Programs in Engineering, Construction and Facilities Management, Berkeley, CA 94720-1500. Offers construction management (Certificate); HVAC (Certificate); integrated circuit design and techniques (online) (Certificate). Postbaccalaureate distance learning degree programs offered.

University of Denver, Daniels College of Business, Franklin L. Burns School of Real Estate and Construction Management, Denver, CO 80208. Offers construction management (IMBA, MS); real estate (IMBA, MBA, MS). Part-time and evening/weekend programs available. *Faculty:* 7 full-time (0 women). *Students:* 24 full-time (3 women), 61 part-time (14 women); includes 9 minority (2 Black or African American, non-Hispanic/Latino; 1 Asian, non-Hispanic/Latino; 3 Hispanic/Latino; 3 Two or more races, non-Hispanic/Latino), 16 international. Average age 33. 84 applicants, 85% accepted, 42 enrolled. In 2011, 64 degrees awarded. *Entrance requirements:* For master's, GRE General Test or GMAT, essay, two letters of recommendation. Additional exam requirements/recommendations for international students: Required—TOEFL (minimum score 570 paper-based; 88 iBT). *Application deadline:* For fall admission, 11/15 priority date for domestic students; for spring admission, 10/15 priority date for domestic students. Applications are processed on a rolling basis. Application fee: $100. Electronic applications accepted. *Financial support:* In 2011–12, 2 teaching assistantships with full and partial tuition reimbursements (averaging $1,987 per year) were awarded; career-related internships or fieldwork, Federal Work-Study, institutionally sponsored loans, scholarships/grants, and unspecified assistantships also available. Support available to part-time students. Financial award application deadline: 2/15; financial award applicants required to submit FAFSA. *Unit head:* Dr. Mark Levine, Director, 303-871-2142, E-mail: mark.levine@du.edu. *Application contact:* Victoria Chen, Graduate Admissions Manager, 303-871-3826, E-mail: victoria.chen@du.edu. Web site: http://www.daniels.du.edu/schoolsdepartments/realestate/.

University of Florida, Graduate School, College of Design, Construction and Planning, M. E. Rinker, Sr. School of Building Construction, Gainesville, FL 32611. Offers building construction (MBC, MSBC); international construction management (MICM). Part-time programs available. *Faculty:* 15 full-time (2 women). *Students:* 34 full-time (13 women), 11 part-time (2 women); includes 7 minority (2 Asian, non-Hispanic/Latino; 5 Hispanic/Latino), 4 international. Average age 29. 66 applicants, 73% accepted, 19 enrolled. In 2011, 58 master's awarded. *Degree requirements:* For master's, thesis. *Entrance requirements:* For master's, GRE General Test, minimum GPA of 3.0. Additional exam requirements/recommendations for international students: Required—TOEFL (minimum score 550 paper-based; 213 computer-based; 80 iBT), IELTS (minimum score 6). *Application deadline:* Applications are processed on a rolling basis. Application fee: $30. Electronic applications accepted. *Financial support:* Research assistantships with full tuition reimbursements, teaching assistantships with full tuition reimbursements, career-related internships or fieldwork, and unspecified assistantships available. Financial award applicants required to submit FAFSA. *Faculty research:* Safety, affordable housing, construction management, environmental issues, sustainable construction. *Unit head:* Dr. Abdol R. Chini, Director, 352-273-1165, Fax: 352-392-9606, E-mail: chini@ufl.edu. *Application contact:* Dr. Ian Flood, Coordinator of PhD Program, 352-273-1159, Fax: 352-392-7266, E-mail: flood@ufl.edu. Web site: http://www.bcn.ufl.edu/.

University of Houston, College of Technology, Department of Engineering Technology, Houston, TX 77204. Offers construction management (MS); engineering technology (MS); network communications (M Tech). Part-time programs available. *Degree requirements:* For master's, project or thesis (most programs). *Entrance requirements:* For master's, GRE. Additional exam requirements/recommendations for international students: Required—TOEFL (minimum score 550 paper-based; 79 iBT). Electronic applications accepted.

The University of Kansas, Graduate Studies, School of Engineering, Program in Construction Management, Lawrence, KS 66045. Offers MCM. Part-time and evening/weekend programs available. *Faculty:* 3 full-time (0 women). *Students:* 1 (woman) full-time, 6 part-time (1 woman); includes 1 minority (Asian, non-Hispanic/Latino), 1 international. Average age 31. 13 applicants, 31% accepted, 2 enrolled. *Degree requirements:* For master's, thesis or alternative, exam. *Entrance requirements:* For master's, GRE. Additional exam requirements/recommendations for international students: Required—TOEFL. *Application deadline:* For fall admission, 7/1 priority date for domestic students, 3/1 for international students; for spring admission, 12/1 priority date for domestic students, 8/15 for international students. Applications are processed on a rolling basis. Application fee: $55 ($65 for international students). Electronic applications accepted. Tuition and fees vary according to course load, campus/location, program and reciprocity agreements. *Financial support:* Career-related internships or fieldwork available. Financial award application deadline: 2/7. *Faculty research:* Construction engineering, construction management. *Unit head:* Craig D. Adams, Chair, 785-864-2700, Fax: 785-864-5631, E-mail: adamscd@ku.edu. *Application contact:* Bruce M. McEnroe, Graduate Advisor, 785-864-2925, Fax: 785-864-2925, E-mail: mcenroe@ku.edu. Web site: http://www.ceae.ku.edu/.

University of Nevada, Las Vegas, Graduate College, Howard R. Hughes College of Engineering, Department of Construction Management, Las Vegas, NV 89154-4054. Offers MS. *Faculty:* 3 full-time (0 women). *Students:* 4 full-time (1 woman), 9 part-time (1 woman); includes 3 minority (2 Hispanic/Latino; 1 Two or more races, non-Hispanic/

Latino), 5 international. Average age 30. 8 applicants, 88% accepted, 1 enrolled. In 2011, 7 master's awarded. *Entrance requirements:* Additional exam requirements/recommendations for international students: Required—TOEFL (minimum score 550 paper-based; 213 computer-based; 80 iBT), IELTS (minimum score 7). *Application deadline:* For fall admission, 6/15 priority date for domestic students, 5/1 for international students; for spring admission, 11/15 priority date for domestic students, 10/1 for international students. Applications are processed on a rolling basis. Application fee: $60 ($95 for international students). Electronic applications accepted. *Financial support:* In 2011–12, 5 students received support, including 2 research assistantships with partial tuition reimbursements available (averaging $7,500 per year), 3 teaching assistantships with partial tuition reimbursements available (averaging $9,375 per year); institutionally sponsored loans, scholarships/grants, health care benefits, and unspecified assistantships also available. Financial award application deadline: 3/1. *Faculty research:* Sustainable construction, construction safety, infrastructure project performance, construction education, construction performance improvement. *Unit head:* Dr. David Ashley, Director/Associate Professor, 702-895-4040, Fax: 702-895-4966, E-mail: david.b.ashley@unlv.edu. *Application contact:* Graduate College Admissions Evaluator, 702-895-3320, Fax: 702-895-4180, E-mail: gradcollege@unlv.edu. Web site: http://www.cem.egr.unlv.edu/index.html.

University of New Mexico, Graduate School, School of Engineering, Department of Civil Engineering, Program in Construction Management, Albuquerque, NM 87131-2039. Offers MCM. Part-time programs available. *Students:* 2 full-time (0 women), 5 part-time (1 woman); includes 3 minority (all American Indian or Alaska Native, non-Hispanic/Latino). Average age 40. 5 applicants, 60% accepted, 2 enrolled. In 2011, 3 degrees awarded. *Degree requirements:* For master's, comprehensive exam, thesis optional. *Entrance requirements:* For master's, GMAT (minimum score 500), minimum GPA of 3.0; courses in statistics, elements of calculus, engineering economy, and construction contracting. Additional exam requirements/recommendations for international students: Required—TOEFL (minimum score 550 paper-based; 213 computer-based; 79 iBT). *Application deadline:* For fall admission, 7/15 for domestic students, 3/1 for international students; for spring admission, 11/10 for domestic students, 8/1 for international students. Applications are processed on a rolling basis. Application fee: $50. Electronic applications accepted. *Financial support:* In 2011–12, 2 students received support. Scholarships/grants, health care benefits, and unspecified assistantships available. Support available to part-time students. Financial award application deadline: 3/1; financial award applicants required to submit FAFSA. *Faculty research:* Applied industry research and training, integration of the design/construction continuum, leadership in project management, life-cycle costing, production management and productivity management, project delivery methods, sustainable asset management, sustainable design and construction. *Total annual research expenditures:* $3 million. *Unit head:* Dr. John C. Stormont, Chair, 505-277-2722, Fax: 505-277-1988, E-mail: jcstorm@unm.edu. *Application contact:* Josie Gibson, Professional Academic Advisor, 505-277-2722, Fax: 505-277-1988, E-mail: civil@unm.edu. Web site: http://civil.unm.edu.

University of North Florida, Coggin College of Business, MBA Program, Jacksonville, FL 32224. Offers accounting (MBA); construction management (MBA); e-commerce (MBA); economics (MBA); finance (MBA); human resource management (MBA); international business (MBA); logistics (MBA); management applications (MBA). *Accreditation:* AACSB. Part-time and evening/weekend programs available. *Faculty:* 19 full-time (6 women), 1 part-time/adjunct (0 women). *Students:* 145 full-time (57 women), 277 part-time (108 women); includes 67 minority (19 Black or African American, non-Hispanic/Latino; 21 Asian, non-Hispanic/Latino; 20 Hispanic/Latino; 7 Two or more races, non-Hispanic/Latino), 34 international. Average age 29. 200 applicants, 48% accepted, 70 enrolled. In 2011, 153 master's awarded. *Entrance requirements:* For master's, GMAT or GRE, U.S. bachelor's degree from regionally-accredited university or equivalent foreign degree. Additional exam requirements/recommendations for international students: Required—TOEFL (minimum score 550 paper-based; 213 computer-based; 79 iBT). *Application deadline:* For fall admission, 7/1 priority date for domestic students, 5/1 for international students; for spring admission, 11/1 priority date for domestic students, 10/1 for international students. Applications are processed on a rolling basis. Application fee: $30. *Expenses:* Tuition, state resident: full-time $8793; part-time $366.38 per credit hour. Tuition, nonresident: full-time $23,502; part-time $979.24 per credit hour. *Required fees:* $1384; $57.66 per credit hour. Tuition and fees vary according to course load and program. *Financial support:* In 2011–12, 55 students received support, including 1 teaching assistantship (averaging $5,333 per year); research assistantships, Federal Work-Study, and tuition waivers (partial) also available. Support available to part-time students. Financial award application deadline: 4/1; financial award applicants required to submit FAFSA. *Faculty research:* Performance measures, costing, and inventory issues in logistics and supply chain management; inter-organizational systems; international management and marketing practices; e-commerce; organizational learning and socialization processes. *Total annual research expenditures:* $7,686. *Unit head:* Dr. C. Bruce Kavan, Chair, 904-620-2780, Fax: 904-620-2832. *Application contact:* Cheryl Campbell, Graduate Advisor, 904-620-2575, Fax: 904-620-2832, E-mail: ccampbell@unf.edu. Web site: http://www.unf.edu/coggin/academics/graduate/mba.aspx.

University of Oklahoma, College of Architecture, Division of Construction Science, Norman, OK 73019. Offers construction administration (MS). Part-time and evening/weekend programs available. *Faculty:* 2 full-time (1 woman), 1 part-time/adjunct (0 women). *Students:* 14 full-time (5 women), 9 part-time (2 women); includes 7 minority (1 American Indian or Alaska Native, non-Hispanic/Latino; 5 Hispanic/Latino; 1 Two or more races, non-Hispanic/Latino), 3 international. Average age 30. 17 applicants, 65% accepted, 8 enrolled. In 2011, 10 degrees awarded. *Degree requirements:* For master's, thesis or alternative, portfolio, project. *Entrance requirements:* For master's, GRE General Test, portfolio. Additional exam requirements/recommendations for international students: Required—TOEFL (minimum score 600 paper-based; 79 iBT). *Application deadline:* For fall admission, 4/1 priority date for domestic students, 3/1 for international students. Applications are processed on a rolling basis. Application fee: $40 ($90 for international students). Electronic applications accepted. *Expenses:* Tuition, state resident: full-time $4087; part-time $170.30 per credit hour. Tuition, nonresident: full-time $14,875; part-time $619.80 per credit hour. *Required fees:* $2659; $100.25 per credit hour. Tuition and fees vary according to course load and degree level. *Financial support:* In 2011–12, 6 students received support, including 3 teaching assistantships with partial tuition reimbursements available (averaging $14,025 per year); career-related internships or fieldwork, scholarships/grants, tuition waivers (partial), and unspecified assistantships also available. Support available to part-time students. Financial award applicants required to submit FAFSA. *Faculty research:* Online education, highway construction, lean construction, Hispanic construction worker design/safety, online instructional design. *Unit head:* Kenneth Robson, Director, 405-325-6404, Fax: 405-325-7558, E-mail: krobson@ou.edu. *Application contact:* Richard C.

Ryan, Professor, 405-325-3976, Fax: 405-325-7558, E-mail: rryan@ou.edu. Web site: http://cns.ou.edu/.

University of Southern California, Graduate School, Viterbi School of Engineering, Sonny Astani Department of Civil Engineering, Los Angeles, CA 90089. Offers applied mechanics (MS); civil engineering (MS, PhD); computer-aided engineering (ME, Graduate Certificate); construction management (MCM); engineering technology commercialization (Graduate Certificate); environmental engineering (MS, PhD); environmental quality management (ME); structural design (ME); sustainable cities (Graduate Certificate); transportation systems (MS, Graduate Certificate); water and waste management (MS). Part-time and evening/weekend programs available. Terminal master's awarded for partial completion of doctoral program. *Degree requirements:* For master's, thesis optional; for doctorate, thesis/dissertation. *Entrance requirements:* For master's and doctorate, GRE General Test. Additional exam requirements/recommendations for international students: Recommended—TOEFL. Electronic applications accepted. *Faculty research:* Geotechnical engineering, transportation engineering, structural engineering, construction management, environmental engineering, water resources.

The University of Texas at El Paso, Graduate School, College of Engineering, Department of Civil Engineering, El Paso, TX 79968-0001. Offers civil engineering (MS, PhD); construction management (MS, Certificate); environmental engineering (MEENE, MSENE). Part-time and evening/weekend programs available. *Students:* 106 (25 women); includes 55 minority (2 Asian, non-Hispanic/Latino; 53 Hispanic/Latino), 44 international. Average age 34. 71 applicants, 86% accepted, 47 enrolled. In 2011, 22 master's awarded. *Degree requirements:* For master's, thesis optional. *Entrance requirements:* For master's, GRE General Test, minimum GPA of 3.0. Additional exam requirements/recommendations for international students: Required—TOEFL. *Application deadline:* For fall admission, 7/1 priority date for domestic students, 3/1 for international students; for spring admission, 11/1 priority date for domestic students, 9/1 for international students. Applications are processed on a rolling basis. Application fee: $15 ($65 for international students). Electronic applications accepted. *Financial support:* In 2011–12, research assistantships with partial tuition reimbursements (averaging $21,125 per year), teaching assistantships with partial tuition reimbursements (averaging $16,900 per year) were awarded; fellowships with partial tuition reimbursements, career-related internships or fieldwork, Federal Work-Study, institutionally sponsored loans, scholarships/grants, tuition waivers (partial), and stipends also available. Financial award application deadline: 3/15; financial award applicants required to submit FAFSA. *Faculty research:* On-site wastewater treatment systems, wastewater reuse, disinfection by-product control, water resources, membrane filtration. *Unit head:* Wen-Whai Li, Chair, 915-747-5464, E-mail: wli@utep.edu. *Application contact:* Dr. Benjamin Flores, Interim Dean of the Graduate School, 915-747-5491, Fax: 915-747-5788, E-mail: bflores@utep.edu. Web site: http://ce.utep.edu/.

The University of Texas at San Antonio, College of Business, Department of Finance, San Antonio, TX 78249-0617. Offers business (MBA), including finance; construction science and management (MS); finance (MS). Part-time and evening/weekend programs available. *Faculty:* 8 full-time (1 woman), 1 part-time/adjunct (0 women). *Students:* 37 full-time (16 women), 48 part-time (7 women); includes 27 minority (4 Black or African American, non-Hispanic/Latino; 3 Asian, non-Hispanic/Latino; 19 Hispanic/Latino; 1 Two or more races, non-Hispanic/Latino), 15 international. Average age 28. 77 applicants, 51% accepted, 23 enrolled. In 2011, 20 master's awarded. *Degree requirements:* For master's, comprehensive exam, thesis or alternative, 33 semester credit hours. *Entrance requirements:* For master's, GMAT or GRE. Additional exam requirements/recommendations for international students: Required—TOEFL (minimum score 500 paper-based; 61 iBT), IELTS (minimum score 5). *Application deadline:* For fall admission, 7/1 for domestic students, 4/1 for international students; for spring admission, 11/1 for domestic students, 9/1 for international students. Applications are processed on a rolling basis. Application fee: $45 ($85 for international students). Electronic applications accepted. *Expenses:* Tuition, state resident: full-time $3148; part-time $2176 per semester. Tuition, nonresident: full-time $8782; part-time $5932 per semester. *Required fees:* $719 per semester. *Financial support:* In 2011–12, 12 students received support, including research assistantships (averaging $10,000 per year), teaching assistantships (averaging $10,000 per year). *Faculty research:* Corporate finance, governance, capital structure, compensations, venture capital, restructuring, bankruptcy, international finance, market interrelationships, pricing, options and futures, micro-structure, somparative corporate studies, interest rate, instruments and strategies. *Total annual research expenditures:* $5,000. *Unit head:* Dr. Lalatendu Misra, Chair, 210-458-6315, Fax: 210-458-6320, E-mail: kfairchild@utsa.edu. *Application contact:* Katherine Pope, Graduate Advisor of Record, 210-458-7316, Fax: 210-458-7316, E-mail: katherine.pope@utsa.edu.

University of Washington, Graduate School, College of Built Environments, Department of Construction Management, Seattle, WA 98195. Offers MSCM. Part-time and evening/weekend programs available. *Degree requirements:* For master's, thesis or alternative. *Entrance requirements:* For master's, GRE General Test, minimum GPA of 3.0. Additional exam requirements/recommendations for international students: Required—TOEFL. Electronic applications accepted. *Faculty research:* Business practices, delivery methods, materials, productivity.

Wentworth Institute of Technology, Construction Management Program, Boston, MA 02115-5998. Offers MS. Part-time and evening/weekend programs available. *Faculty:* 10 full-time (3 women), 5 part-time/adjunct (2 women). *Students:* 48 part-time (11 women); includes 5 minority (3 Black or African American, non-Hispanic/Latino; 1 Asian, non-Hispanic/Latino; 1 Hispanic/Latino). Average age 33. 47 applicants, 51% accepted, 22 enrolled. *Degree requirements:* For master's, thesis optional. *Entrance requirements:* For master's, GRE or GMAT. Additional exam requirements/recommendations for international students: Required—TOEFL (minimum score 525 paper-based; 197 computer-based). *Application deadline:* For fall admission, 5/1 for domestic and international students. Applications are processed on a rolling basis. Application fee: $50. Electronic applications accepted. *Expenses: Tuition:* Full-time $31,200; part-time $1130 per credit. *Financial support:* Loans available. Financial award application deadline: 5/1; financial award applicants required to submit FAFSA. *Unit head:* E. Scott Sumner, Director, 617-989-4259, Fax: 617-989-4399, E-mail: sumnere@wit.edu. *Application contact:* Ashley Roberts, Associate Director of Admissions for Continuing Education, 617-989-4651, Fax: 617-989-4399, E-mail: robertsa2@wit.edu. Web site: http://www.wit.edu/ccev/mscm/.

Western Carolina University, Graduate School, Kimmel School of Construction Management and Technology, Department of Construction Management, Cullowhee, NC 28723. Offers MCM. Part-time and evening/weekend programs available. Postbaccalaureate distance learning degree programs offered. *Students:* 3 full-time (0 women), 21 part-time (2 women); includes 5 minority (3 Black or African American, non-Hispanic/Latino; 1 American Indian or Alaska Native, non-Hispanic/Latino; 1 Asian, non-Hispanic/Latino), 1 international. Average age 37. 22 applicants, 95% accepted, 16 enrolled. In 2011, 14 master's awarded. *Entrance requirements:* For master's, GRE or GMAT, appropriate undergraduate degree, resume, letters of recommendation, work experience. Additional exam requirements/recommendations for international students: Required—TOEFL (minimum score 550 paper-based; 270 computer-based; 79 iBT). *Application deadline:* For fall admission, 5/1 priority date for domestic students. Application fee: $50. *Expenses:* Tuition, state resident: full-time $3348. Tuition, nonresident: full-time $12,933. *Required fees:* $3155. *Financial support:* Fellowships, research assistantships with full and partial tuition reimbursements, teaching assistantships with full and partial tuition reimbursements, career-related internships or fieldwork, institutionally sponsored loans, traineeships, and unspecified assistantships available. Financial award application deadline: 3/31; financial award applicants required to submit FAFSA. *Faculty research:* Hazardous waste management, energy management and conservation, engineering materials, refrigeration and air conditioning systems. *Unit head:* Dr. Michael Smith, Head, 828-227-3697, Fax: 828-227-7838, E-mail: mesmith@email.wcu.edu. *Application contact:* Admissions Specialist for Construction Management, 828-227-7398, Fax: 828-227-7480, E-mail: gradsch@email.wcu.edu. Web site: http://cm.wcu.edu.

Western Michigan University, Graduate College, College of Engineering and Applied Sciences, Department of Civil and Construction Engineering, Kalamazoo, MI 49008. Offers civil engineering (MS), including construction engineering and management, structural engineering, transportation engineering. *Entrance requirements:* For master's, minimum GPA of 3.0.

Worcester Polytechnic Institute, Graduate Studies and Research, Department of Civil and Environmental Engineering, Worcester, MA 01609-2280. Offers civil and environmental engineering (Advanced Certificate, Graduate Certificate); civil engineering (ME, MS, PhD); construction project management (MS); environmental

engineering (MS); master builder environmental engineering (M Eng). Part-time and evening/weekend programs available. Postbaccalaureate distance learning degree programs offered (no on-campus study). *Faculty:* 12 full-time (1 woman), 2 part-time/adjunct (0 women). *Students:* 28 full-time (9 women), 49 part-time (14 women); includes 7 minority (1 Black or African American, non-Hispanic/Latino; 1 American Indian or Alaska Native, non-Hispanic/Latino; 2 Asian, non-Hispanic/Latino; 1 Hispanic/Latino; 2 Two or more races, non-Hispanic/Latino), 17 international. 144 applicants, 44% accepted, 28 enrolled. In 2011, 26 master's, 1 doctorate awarded. *Degree requirements:* For master's, thesis optional; for doctorate, comprehensive exam, thesis/dissertation. *Entrance requirements:* For master's and doctorate, GRE (recommended), 3 letters of recommendation. Additional exam requirements/recommendations for international students: Required—TOEFL (minimum score 563 paper-based; 223 computer-based; 84 iBT), IELTS (minimum score 7). *Application deadline:* For fall admission, 1/1 priority date for domestic students, 1/1 for international students; for spring admission, 10/1 priority date for domestic students, 10/1 for international students. Applications are processed on a rolling basis. Application fee: $70. Electronic applications accepted. *Financial support:* Research assistantships, teaching assistantships, career-related internships or fieldwork, institutionally sponsored loans, scholarships/grants, and unspecified assistantships available. Financial award application deadline: 1/1; financial award applicants required to submit FAFSA. *Faculty research:* Pavement engineering and highway materials, analysis and design of structural systems and smart structures, design-construction integration, water resources and physical and chemical treatment processes, energy and sustainability. *Unit head:* Dr. Tahar El-Korchi, Interim Head, 508-831-5530, Fax: 508-831-5808, E-mail: tek@wpi.edu. *Application contact:* Dr. Paul Mathisen, Graduate Coordinator, 508-831-5530, Fax: 508-831-5808, E-mail: mathisen@wpi.edu. Web site: http://www.wpi.edu/Academics/Depts/CEE/.

Energy Management and Policy

Franklin Pierce University, Graduate Studies, Rindge, NH 03461-0060. Offers curriculum and instruction (M Ed); emerging network technologies (Graduate Certificate); energy and sustainability studies (MBA); health administration (MBA, Graduate Certificate); human resource management (MBA, Graduate Certificate); information technology (MBA); information technology management (MS); leadership (MBA, DA); nursing (MS); physical therapy (DPT); physician assistant studies (MPAS); special education (M Ed); sports management (MBA). *Accreditation:* APTA. Part-time programs available. Postbaccalaureate distance learning degree programs offered (no on-campus study). *Degree requirements:* For master's, concentrated original research projects; student teaching; fieldwork and/or internship; leadership project; PRAXIS I and II (for M Ed); for doctorate, concentrated original research projects, clinical fieldwork and/or internship, leadership project. *Entrance requirements:* For master's, minimum GPA of 2.5, 3 letters of recommendation; competencies in accounting, economics, statistics, and computer skills through life experience or undergraduate coursework (for MBA); certification/e-portfolio, minimum C grade in all education courses (for M Ed); license to practice as RN (for, MS in nursing); for doctorate, GRE, BA/BS, 3 letters of recommendation, personal mission statement, interview, writing sample, minimum cumulative GPA of 2.8, master's degree (for DA); 80 hours of observation/work in PT settings, completion of anatomy, chemistry, physics, and statistics, minimum GPA of 3.0 (for DPT). Additional exam requirements/recommendations for international students: Required—TOEFL (minimum score 550 paper-based; 195 computer-based; 61 iBT). Electronic applications accepted. *Faculty research:* Evidence-based practice in sports physical therapy, human resource management in economic crisis, leadership in nursing, innovation in sports facility management, differentiated learning and understanding by design.

Holy Names University, Graduate Division, Department of Business, Oakland, CA 94619-1699. Offers energy and environment management (MBA); finance (MBA); management and leadership (MBA); marketing (MBA); sports management (MBA). Part-time and evening/weekend programs available. *Entrance requirements:* For master's, minimum undergraduate GPA of 2.6 overall, 3.0 in major. Additional exam requirements/recommendations for international students: Required—TOEFL (minimum score 550 paper-based; 213 computer-based; 80 iBT). *Faculty research:* Business ethics, sustainable economics, accounting models, cross-cultural management, diversity in organizations.

Indiana University Bloomington, School of Public and Environmental Affairs, Environmental Science Programs, Bloomington, IN 47405. Offers applied ecology (MSES); energy (MSES); environmental chemistry, toxicology, and risk assessment (MSES); environmental science (PhD); specialized environmental science (MSES); water resources (MSES); JD/MSES; MSES/MPA; MSES/MS. Part-time programs available. *Faculty:* 80 full-time (30 women), 102 part-time/adjunct (43 women). *Students:* 142 full-time, 6 part-time; includes 8 minority (2 Black or African American, non-Hispanic/Latino; 5 Asian, non-Hispanic/Latino; 1 Hispanic/Latino), 18 international. Average age 24. 152 applicants, 57 enrolled. In 2011, 58 master's, 2 doctorates awarded. Terminal master's awarded for partial completion of doctoral program. *Degree requirements:* For master's, core classes; capstone or thesis; internship; for doctorate, comprehensive exam, thesis/dissertation. *Entrance requirements:* For master's, GRE General Test or GMAT, official transcripts, 3 letters of recommendation, resume, personal statement; for doctorate, GRE General Test or LSAT, official transcripts, 3 letters of recommendation, resume or curriculum vitae, statement of purpose. Additional exam requirements/recommendations for international students: Required—TOEFL (minimum score 600 paper-based; 96 iBT); Recommended—IELTS (minimum score 7). *Application deadline:* For fall admission, 2/1 priority date for domestic students, 12/1 for international students. Applications are processed on a rolling basis. Application fee: $55 ($65 for international students). Electronic applications accepted. *Financial support:* Fellowships with partial tuition reimbursements, research assistantships with partial tuition reimbursements, teaching assistantships with partial tuition reimbursements, career-related internships or fieldwork, Federal Work-Study, scholarships/grants, health care benefits, unspecified assistantships, and Service Corps programs available. Financial award application deadline: 2/1; financial award applicants required to submit FAFSA. *Faculty research:* Applied ecology, bio-geo chemistry, toxicology, wetlands ecology, environmental microbiology, forest ecology, environmental chemistry. *Unit head:* Jennifer J. Forney, Director, Graduate Student Services, 812-855-9485, Fax: 812-856-3665, E-mail: speampo@indiana.edu. *Application contact:* Admissions Assistant, 812-855-2840, Fax: 812-856-3665, E-mail: speaapps@indiana.edu. Web site: http://www.indiana.edu/~spea/prospective_students/masters/.

Indiana University Bloomington, School of Public and Environmental Affairs, Public Affairs Programs, Bloomington, IN 47405. Offers comparative and international affairs (MPA); economic development (MPA); energy (MPA); environmental policy (PhD); environmental policy and natural resource management (MPA); hazardous materials management (Certificate); information systems (MPA); international development (MPA); local government management (MPA); nonprofit management (MPA, Certificate); policy analysis (MPA); public budgeting and financial management (Certificate); public finance (PhD); public financial administration (MPA); public management (MPA, PhD, Certificate); public policy analysis (PhD); social entrepreneurship (Certificate); specialized public affairs (MPA); sustainability and sustainable development (MPA); JD/MPA; MPA/MA; MPA/MIS; MPA/MLS; MSES/MPA. *Accreditation:* NASPAA (one or more programs are accredited). Part-time programs available. *Faculty:* 80 full-time (30 women), 102 part-time/adjunct (43 women). *Students:* 338 full-time, 30 part-time; includes 27 minority (7 Black or African American, non-Hispanic/Latino; 2 American Indian or Alaska Native, non-Hispanic/Latino; 10 Asian, non-Hispanic/Latino; 8 Hispanic/Latino), 56 international. Average age 24. 501 applicants, 148 enrolled. In 2011, 172 master's, 7 doctorates awarded. *Degree requirements:* For master's, core classes, capstone, internship; for doctorate, comprehensive exam, thesis/dissertation. *Entrance requirements:* For master's, GRE General Test or GMAT, official transcripts, 3 letters of recommendation, resume, personal statement; for doctorate, GRE General Test or LSAT, official transcripts, 3 letters of recommendation, resume or curriculum vitae, statement of purpose. Additional exam requirements/recommendations for international students: Required—TOEFL (minimum score 600 paper-based; 96 iBT); Recommended—IELTS (minimum score 7). *Application deadline:* For fall admission, 2/1 priority date for domestic students, 12/1 for international students. Applications are processed on a rolling basis. Application fee: $55 ($65 for international students). Electronic applications accepted. *Financial support:* Fellowships with partial tuition reimbursements, research assistantships with partial tuition reimbursements, teaching assistantships with partial tuition reimbursements, career-related internships or fieldwork, Federal Work-Study, scholarships/grants, health care benefits, unspecified assistantships, and Service Corps programs available. Financial award application deadline: 2/1; financial award applicants required to submit FAFSA. *Faculty research:* Comparative and international affairs, environmental policy and resource management, policy analysis, public finance, public management, urban management, nonprofit management, energy policy, social policy, public finance. *Unit head:* Jennifer Forney, Director of Graduate Student Services, 812-855-9485, Fax: 812-856-3665, E-mail: speampo@indiana.edu. *Application contact:* Admissions Assistant, 812-855-2840, E-mail: speaapps@indiana.edu. Web site: http://www.indiana.edu/~spea/prospective_students/masters/.

Instituto Tecnologico de Santo Domingo, Graduate School, Area of Basic And Environmental Sciences, Santo Domingo, Dominican Republic. Offers environmental science (M En S), including environmental education, environmental management, marine resources, natural resources management; mathematics (MS, PhD); renewable energy technology (MS, Certificate).

New York Institute of Technology, Graduate Division, School of Engineering and Computing Sciences, Program in Energy Management, Old Westbury, NY 11568-8000. Offers energy management (MS); energy technology (Advanced Certificate); environmental management (Advanced Certificate); facilities management (Advanced Certificate). Part-time and evening/weekend programs available. Postbaccalaureate distance learning degree programs offered. *Students:* 48 full-time (8 women), 97 part-time (17 women); includes 32 minority (11 Black or African American, non-Hispanic/Latino; 1 American Indian or Alaska Native, non-Hispanic/Latino; 4 Asian, non-Hispanic/Latino; 15 Hispanic/Latino; 1 Two or more races, non-Hispanic/Latino), 31 international. Average age 32. In 2011, 53 master's, 28 other advanced degrees awarded. *Degree requirements:* For master's, comprehensive exam, thesis or alternative. *Entrance requirements:* For master's, minimum QPA of 2.85. Additional exam requirements/recommendations for international students: Required—TOEFL (minimum score 550 paper-based; 213 computer-based). *Application deadline:* For fall admission, 7/1 priority date for domestic students; for spring admission, 12/1 priority date for domestic students. Applications are processed on a rolling basis. Application fee: $50. Electronic applications accepted. *Expenses:* Tuition: Part-time $930 per credit hour. *Financial support:* Fellowships, research assistantships with partial tuition reimbursements, institutionally sponsored loans, tuition waivers (full and partial), and unspecified assistantships available. Support available to part-time students. Financial award applicants required to submit FAFSA. *Unit head:* Dr. Robert Amundsen, Department Chair, 516-686-7578, E-mail: ramundse@nyit.edu. *Application contact:* Dr. Jacquelyn

Nealon, Vice President for Enrollment Services, 516-686-7925, Fax: 516-686-7597, E-mail: jnealon@nyit.edu.

Oklahoma City University, Meinders School of Business, Program in Energy Management, Oklahoma City, OK 73106-1402. Offers MS. *Expenses: Tuition:* Full-time $16,848; part-time $936 per credit hour. *Required fees:* $2070; $115 per credit hour. One-time fee: $300. *Unit head:* Dr. Steve Agee, Dean, 405-208-5275, Fax: 405-208-5008, E-mail: sagee@okcu.edu. *Application contact:* Michelle Cook, Director, Admission, 800-633-7242, Fax: 405-208-5356, E-mail: gadmissions@okcu.edu.

Santa Clara University, School of Engineering, Program in Electrical Engineering, Santa Clara, CA 95053. Offers analog circuit design (Certificate); ASIC design and test (Certificate); digital signal processing (Certificate); electrical engineering (MS, PhD, Engineer); fundamentals of electrical engineering (Certificate); microwave and antennas (Certificate); renewable energy (Certificate). Part-time and evening/weekend programs available. *Students:* 46 full-time (11 women), 93 part-time (14 women); includes 48 minority (2 Black or African American, non-Hispanic/Latino; 43 Asian, non-Hispanic/Latino; 2 Hispanic/Latino; 1 Native Hawaiian or other Pacific Islander, non-Hispanic/Latino), 47 international. Average age 32. 128 applicants, 46% accepted, 30 enrolled. In 2011, 59 master's, 5 doctorates, 7 other advanced degrees awarded. *Degree requirements:* For master's, thesis (for some programs); for doctorate, thesis/dissertation; for other advanced degree, thesis. *Entrance requirements:* For master's, GRE, transcript; for doctorate, GRE, master's degree or equivalent; for other advanced degree, master's degree, published paper. Additional exam requirements/recommendations for international students: Required—TOEFL (minimum score 550 paper-based; 213 computer-based; 79 iBT). *Application deadline:* For fall admission, 8/12 for domestic students, 7/15 for international students; for winter admission, 10/28 for domestic students, 9/23 for international students; for spring admission, 2/25 for domestic students, 1/21 for international students. Applications are processed on a rolling basis. Application fee: $60. Electronic applications accepted. *Expenses:* Contact institution. *Financial support:* Research assistantships and teaching assistantships available. Financial award application deadline: 3/2; financial award applicants required to submit FAFSA. *Faculty research:* Thermal and electrical nanoscale transport (TENT). *Unit head:* Dr. Alex Zecevic, Associate Dean for Graduate Studies, 408-554-2394, E-mail: azecevic@scu.edu. *Application contact:* Stacey Tinker, Director of Enrollment Management, 408-554-4748, Fax: 408-554-4323, E-mail: stinker@scu.edu.

Université du Québec, Institut National de la Recherche Scientifique, Graduate Programs, Research Center - Energy, Materials and Telecommunications, Québec, QC G1K 9A9, Canada. Offers energy and materials science (M Sc, PhD); telecommunications (M Sc, PhD). Programs given in French; PhD programs offered jointly with Université du Québec à Trois-Rivières. Part-time programs available. *Faculty:* 39. *Students:* 175 full-time (71 women), 19 part-time (4 women), 107 international. Average age 32. In 2011, 12 master's, 17 doctorates awarded. *Degree requirements:* For master's, thesis optional; for doctorate, thesis/dissertation. *Entrance requirements:* For master's, appropriate bachelor's degree, proficiency in French; for doctorate, appropriate master's degree, proficiency in French. *Application deadline:* For fall admission, 3/30 for domestic and international students; for winter admission, 11/1 for domestic and international students; for spring admission, 3/1 for domestic and international students. Application fee: $45. *Financial support:* In 2011–12, 141 students received support, including fellowships (averaging $16,500 per year); research assistantships also available. *Faculty research:* New energy sources, plasmas, fusion. *Unit head:* Frederico Rosei, Director, 450-228-6905, E-mail: rosei@emt.inrs.ca. *Application contact:* Yvonne Boisvert, Registrar, 418-654-3861, Fax: 418-654-3858, E-mail: registrariat@adm.inrs.ca. Web site: http://www.inrs.ca/english/research-centres/energie-materiaux-telecommunications-research-centre.

University of California, Berkeley, Graduate Division, Group in Energy and Resources, Berkeley, CA 94720-1500. Offers MA, MS, PhD. *Degree requirements:* For master's, project or thesis; for doctorate, one foreign language, thesis/dissertation, qualifying exam. *Entrance requirements:* For master's and doctorate, GRE General Test, minimum GPA of 3.0, 3 letters of recommendation. *Faculty research:* Technical, economic, environmental, and institutional aspects of energy conservation in residential and commercial buildings; international patterns of energy use; renewable energy sources; assessment of valuation of energy and environmental resources pricing.

University of Colorado Denver, Business School, Program in Global Energy Management, Denver, CO 80217. Offers MS. Postbaccalaureate distance learning degree programs offered (minimal on-campus study). *Students:* 59 full-time (15 women); includes 6 minority (1 Black or African American, non-Hispanic/Latino; 1 Asian, non-Hispanic/Latino; 4 Hispanic/Latino), 2 international. Average age 34. 27 applicants, 93% accepted, 17 enrolled. In 2011, 53 master's awarded. *Degree requirements:* For master's, 36 semester credit hours. *Entrance requirements:* For master's, GMAT if less than three years of experience in the energy industry and no undergraduate degree in energy sciences or engineering, minimum of 5 years' experience in energy industry. Additional exam requirements/recommendations for international students: Required—TOEFL (minimum score 525 paper-based; 71 iBT). *Application deadline:* For fall admission, 6/1 for domestic and international students; for winter admission, 12/1 for domestic and international students. Application fee: $50 ($75 for international students). Electronic applications accepted. *Expenses:* Contact institution. *Financial support:* Application deadline: 4/1; applicants required to submit FAFSA. *Unit head:* Wayne Cascio, Chair in Global Leadership Management, 303-315-8434, E-mail: wayne.cascio@ucdenver.edu. *Application contact:* Shelly Townley, Admissions Coordinator, 303-315-8202, Fax: 303-556-5904, E-mail: shelly.townley@ucdenver.edu. Web site: http://www.ucdenver.edu/academics/colleges/business/degrees/ms/gem/Pages/Overview.aspx.

University of Delaware, Center for Energy and Environmental Policy, Newark, DE 19716. Offers energy and environmental policy (MA, MEEP, PhD); urban affairs and public policy (PhD), including technology, environment, and society. *Degree requirements:* For master's, analytical paper or thesis; for doctorate, comprehensive exam, thesis/dissertation. *Entrance requirements:* For master's, GRE General Test, minimum GPA of 3.0; for doctorate, GRE General Test, minimum GPA of 3.5. Additional exam requirements/recommendations for international students: Required—TOEFL. Electronic applications accepted. *Faculty research:* Sustainable development, renewable energy, climate change, environmental policy, environmental justice, disaster policy.

University of Denver, University College, Denver, CO 80208. Offers arts and culture (MLS, Certificate), including art, literature, and culture, arts development and program management (Certificate), creative writing; environmental policy and management (MAS, Certificate), including energy and sustainability (Certificate), environmental assessment of nuclear power (Certificate), environmental health and safety (Certificate), environmental management, natural resource management (Certificate); geographic information systems (MAS, Certificate); global affairs (MLS, Certificate), including translation studies, world history and culture; healthcare leadership (MPH, Certificate), including healthcare policy, law, and ethics, medical and healthcare information technologies, strategic management of healthcare; information and communications technology (MCIS, Certificate), including database design and administration (Certificate), geographic information systems (MCIS), information security systems security (Certificate), information systems security (MCIS), project management (MCIS, MPS, Certificate), software design and administration (Certificate), software design and programming (MCIS), technology management, telecommunications technology (MCIS), Web design and development; leadership and organizations (MPS, Certificate), including human capital in organizations, philanthropic leadership, project management (MCIS, MPS, Certificate), strategic innovation and change; organizational and professional communication (MPS, Certificate), including alternative dispute resolution, organizational communication, organizational development and training, public relations and marketing; security management (MAS, Certificate), including emergency planning and response, information security (MAS), organizational security; strategic human resource management (MPS, Certificate), including global human resources (MPS), human resource management and development (MPS). Part-time and evening/weekend programs available. Postbaccalaureate distance learning degree programs offered (no on-campus study). *Faculty:* 204 part-time/adjunct (80 women). *Students:* 56 full-time (26 women), 1,096 part-time (647 women); includes 196 minority (81 Black or African American, non-Hispanic/Latino; 7 American Indian or Alaska Native, non-Hispanic/Latino; 30 Asian, non-Hispanic/Latino; 66 Hispanic/Latino; 3 Native Hawaiian or other Pacific Islander, non-Hispanic/Latino; 9 Two or more races, non-Hispanic/Latino), 76 international. Average age 36. 572 applicants, 95% accepted, 410 enrolled. In 2011, 404 master's, 123 other advanced degrees awarded. *Degree requirements:* For master's, capstone project. *Entrance requirements:* For master's, two letters of recommendation, personal statement, resume. Additional exam requirements/recommendations for international students: Required—TOEFL (minimum score 550 paper-based; 80 iBT). *Application deadline:* For fall admission, 7/20 priority date for domestic students, 6/8 for international students; for winter admission, 10/26 priority date for domestic students, 9/14 for international students; for spring admission, 2/1 priority date for domestic students, 12/14 for international students. Applications are processed on a rolling basis. Application fee: $75. Electronic applications accepted. *Expenses:* Contact institution. *Financial support:* Applicants required to submit FAFSA. *Unit head:* Dr. James Davis, Dean, 303-871-2291, Fax: 303-871-4047, E-mail: jdavis@du.edu. *Application contact:* Information Contact, 303-871-3155, Fax: 303-871-4047, E-mail: ucolinfo@du.edu. Web site: http://www.universitycollege.du.edu/.

University of Illinois at Urbana–Champaign, Graduate College, College of Agricultural, Consumer and Environmental Sciences, Program in Bioenergy, Champaign, IL 61820. Offers MS. Applications are only accepted for the fall semester. *Students:* 11 full-time (2 women), 1 part-time (0 women); includes 1 minority (Asian, non-Hispanic/Latino), 1 international. 15 applicants, 73% accepted, 6 enrolled. In 2011, 6 master's awarded. *Degree requirements:* For master's, internship. *Entrance requirements:* For master's, GRE, baccalaureate degree in recognized field of biological, physical, agricultural, socio-economic or engineering science. Additional exam requirements/recommendations for international students: Required—TOEFL (minimum score 590 paper-based; 243 computer-based). Application fee: $75 ($90 for international students). Electronic applications accepted. *Unit head:* Hans Blaschek, Director, 217-244-9270, E-mail: blascheck@illinois.edu. *Application contact:* Gregory S. Harman, Admissions Support Staff, 217-244-4637. Web site: http://www.bioenergy.illinois.edu/.

University of Phoenix–Bay Area Campus, School of Business, San Jose, CA 95134-1805. Offers accountancy (MS); accounting (MBA); business administration (MBA, DBA); energy management (MBA); global management (MBA); health care management (MBA); human resource management (MBA); human resources management (MM); management (MM); marketing (MBA); organizational leadership (DM); project management (MBA); public administration (MPA); technology management (MBA). Evening/weekend programs available. Postbaccalaureate distance learning degree programs offered (no on-campus study). *Degree requirements:* For master's, thesis (for some programs). *Entrance requirements:* For master's, minimum undergraduate GPA of 3.0, 3 years of work experience. Additional exam requirements/recommendations for international students: Required—TOEFL (minimum score 550 paper-based; 213 computer-based; 79 iBT). Electronic applications accepted.

University of Phoenix–Online Campus, School of Business, Phoenix, AZ 85034-7209. Offers accountancy (MS); accounting (MBA); business administration (MBA); energy management (MBA); global management (MBA); health care management (MBA); human resource management (MBA); human resources management (MM); international (MM); management (MM); marketing (MBA, Graduate Certificate); organizational management (MA); project management (MBA, Graduate Certificate); public administration (MBA, MM, MPA); technology management (MBA). Evening/weekend programs available. Postbaccalaureate distance learning degree programs offered. *Students:* 18,883 full-time (11,868 women); includes 6,302 minority (4,182 Black or African American, non-Hispanic/Latino; 121 American Indian or Alaska Native, non-Hispanic/Latino; 478 Asian, non-Hispanic/Latino; 1,252 Hispanic/Latino; 121 Native Hawaiian or other Pacific Islander, non-Hispanic/Latino; 148 Two or more races, non-Hispanic/Latino), 1,000 international. Average age 37. *Entrance requirements:* Additional exam requirements/recommendations for international students: Required—TOEFL, TOEIC (Test of English as an International Communication), Berlitz Online English Proficiency Exam, PTE (Pearson Test of English), or IELTS. *Application deadline:* Applications are processed on a rolling basis. Application fee: $45. Electronic applications accepted. *Expenses: Tuition:* Full-time $17,160. *Required fees:* $920. One-time fee: $45 full-time. Full-time tuition and fees vary according to course load, degree level, campus/location and program. *Financial support:* Scholarships/grants available. Financial award applicants required to submit FAFSA. *Application contact:* 866-766-0766. Web site: http://www.phoenix.edu/colleges_divisions/business.html.

University of Phoenix–Phoenix Main Campus, School of Business, Tempe, AZ 85282-2371. Offers accounting (MBA, MS); business administration (MBA); energy management (MBA); global management (MBA); health care management (MBA); human resource management (MBA); management (MM); marketing (MBA); project management (MBA); public administration (MPA); technology management (MBA). Evening/weekend programs available. Postbaccalaureate distance learning degree programs offered. *Students:* 1,151 full-time (531 women); includes 310 minority (99 Black or African American, non-Hispanic/Latino; 10 American Indian or Alaska Native, non-Hispanic/Latino; 39 Asian, non-Hispanic/Latino; 130 Hispanic/Latino; 15 Native Hawaiian or other Pacific Islander, non-Hispanic/Latino; 17 Two or more races, non-Hispanic/Latino), 63 international. Average age 34. *Entrance requirements:* Additional exam requirements/recommendations for international students: Required—TOEFL, TOEIC (Test of English as an International Communication), Berlitz Online English Proficiency Exam, PTE (Pearson Test of English), or IELTS. *Application deadline:* Applications are processed on a rolling basis. Application fee: $45. Electronic applications accepted. *Expenses:* Contact institution. *Financial support:* Scholarships/

grants available. Financial award applicants required to submit FAFSA. *Application contact:* 866-766-0766. Web site: http://www.phoenix.edu/colleges_divisions/business.html.

University of Phoenix–Puerto Rico Campus, School of Business, Guaynabo, PR 00968. Offers accounting (MBA); energy management (MBA); global management (MBA); human resource management (MBA); marketing (MBA); project management (MBA); small business administration (MBA). Evening/weekend programs available. *Degree requirements:* For master's, thesis (for some programs). *Entrance requirements:* For master's, minimum undergraduate GPA of 3.0, 3 years work experience. Additional exam requirements/recommendations for international students: Required—TOEFL (minimum score 550 paper-based; 213 computer-based; 79 iBT). Electronic applications accepted.

University of Phoenix–Southern California Campus, School of Business, Costa Mesa, CA 92626. Offers accounting (MIS); business administration (MBA); energy management (MBA); global management (MBA); health care management (MBA); human resource management (MBA); management (MM); marketing (MBA); project management (MBA); public administration (MPA); technology management (MBA). Evening/weekend programs available. Postbaccalaureate distance learning degree programs offered. *Students:* 699 full-time (341 women); includes 318 minority (124 Black or African American, non-Hispanic/Latino; 4 American Indian or Alaska Native, non-Hispanic/Latino; 44 Asian, non-Hispanic/Latino; 124 Hispanic/Latino; 15 Native Hawaiian or other Pacific Islander, non-Hispanic/Latino; 7 Two or more races, non-Hispanic/Latino), 29 international. Average age 38. *Entrance requirements:* Additional exam requirements/recommendations for international students: Required—TOEFL, TOEIC (Test of English as an International Communication), Berlitz Online English Proficiency Exam, PTE (Pearson Test of English), or IELTS. *Application deadline:* Applications are processed on a rolling basis. Application fee: $45. Electronic applications accepted. *Expenses:* Contact institution. *Financial support:* Scholarships/grants available. Financial award applicants required to submit FAFSA. *Application contact:* 866-766-0766. Web site: http://www.phoenix.edu/colleges_divisions/business.html.

University of Rochester, Hajim School of Engineering and Applied Sciences, Center for Entrepreneurship, Rochester, NY 14627-0360. Offers technical entrepreneurship and management (TEAM) (MS), including biomedical engineering, chemical engineering, computer science, electrical and computer engineering, energy and the environment, materials science, mechanical engineering, optics. *Faculty:* 61 full-time (8 women), 5 part-time/adjunct (1 woman). *Students:* 18 full-time (5 women), 3 part-time (1 woman); includes 4 minority (1 Asian, non-Hispanic/Latino; 3 Hispanic/Latino), 12 international. Average age 23. 134 applicants, 48% accepted, 21 enrolled. *Degree requirements:* For master's, comprehensive exam. *Entrance requirements:* For master's, GRE or GMAT, technical concentration of interest, 3 letters of recommendation, personal statement, official transcript. Additional exam requirements/recommendations for international students: Required—TOEFL or IELTS. *Application deadline:* For fall admission, 2/1 for domestic and international students. Applications are processed on a rolling basis. Application fee: $60. Electronic applications accepted. *Expenses: Tuition:* Full-time $41,040. *Financial support:* Career-related internships or fieldwork and scholarships/grants available. Financial award application deadline: 2/1.

Faculty research: High efficiency solar cells, macromolecular self-assembly, digital signal processing, memory hierarchy management, molecular and physical mechanisms in cell migration. *Unit head:* Duncan T. Moore, Vice Provost for Entrepreneurship, 585-275-5248, Fax: 585-473-6745, E-mail: moore@optics.rochester.edu. *Application contact:* Andrea M. Galati, Executive Director, 585-276-3407, Fax: 585-276-2357, E-mail: andrea.galati@rochester.edu. Web site: http://www.rochester.edu/team.

University of Tulsa, Graduate School, Collins College of Business, Master of Business Administration Program, Tulsa, OK 74104-3189. Offers accounting (MBA); business administration (MBA); energy management (MBA); finance (MBA); international business (MBA); management information systems (MBA); taxation (MBA); JD/MBA; MBA/MSCS; MBA/MSF. *Accreditation:* AACSB. Part-time and evening/weekend programs available. *Faculty:* 32 full-time (6 women). *Students:* 56 full-time (29 women), 28 part-time (7 women); includes 7 minority (1 Black or African American, non-Hispanic/Latino; 2 American Indian or Alaska Native, non-Hispanic/Latino; 2 Asian, non-Hispanic/Latino; 2 Hispanic/Latino), 16 international. Average age 26. 70 applicants, 67% accepted, 29 enrolled. In 2011, 35 master's awarded. *Entrance requirements:* For master's, GMAT. Additional exam requirements/recommendations for international students: Required—TOEFL (minimum score 577 paper-based; 233 computer-based; 91 iBT), IELTS (minimum score 6.5). *Application deadline:* Applications are processed on a rolling basis. Application fee: $40. Electronic applications accepted. *Expenses: Tuition:* Full-time $17,748; part-time $986 per hour. *Required fees:* $5 per contact hour. $75 per semester. Tuition and fees vary according to program. *Financial support:* In 2011–12, 30 students received support, including 30 teaching assistantships (averaging $11,044 per year); fellowships, research assistantships, career-related internships or fieldwork, institutionally sponsored loans, scholarships/grants, health care benefits, tuition waivers (full and partial), and unspecified assistantships also available. Support available to part-time students. Financial award application deadline: 2/1; financial award applicants required to submit FAFSA. *Faculty research:* Accounting, energy management, finance, international business, management information systems, taxation. *Unit head:* Dr. Linda Nichols, Associate Dean of the Collins College of Business, 918-631-2242, Fax: 918-631-2142, E-mail: linda-nichols@utulsa.edu. *Application contact:* Information Contact, 918-631-2242, E-mail: graduate-business@utulsa.edu. Web site: http://www.cba.utulsa.edu/.

University of Washington, Graduate School, College of the Environment, School of Forest Resources, Seattle, WA 98195. Offers bioresource science and engineering (MS, PhD); environmental horticulture (MEH); environmental horticulture and urban forestry (MS, PhD); forest ecology (MS, PhD); forest management (MFR); forest soils (MS, PhD); forest systems and bioenergy (MS, PhD); restoration ecology (MS, PhD); social sciences (MS, PhD); sustainable resource management (MS, PhD); wildlife science (MS, PhD); MFR/MAIS; MPA/MS. *Accreditation:* SAF. *Degree requirements:* For master's, thesis (for some programs); for doctorate, comprehensive exam (for some programs), thesis/dissertation. *Entrance requirements:* For master's and doctorate, GRE, minimum GPA of 3.0. Additional exam requirements/recommendations for international students: Required—TOEFL. Electronic applications accepted. *Faculty research:* Ecosystem analysis, silviculture and forest protection, paper science and engineering, environmental horticulture and urban forestry, natural resource policy and economics.

Engineering Management

Air Force Institute of Technology, Graduate School of Engineering and Management, Department of Systems and Engineering Management, Dayton, OH 45433-7765. Offers cost analysis (MS); environmental and engineering management (MS); environmental engineering science (MS); information resource/systems management (MS). *Accreditation:* ABET. Part-time programs available. *Degree requirements:* For master's, thesis. *Entrance requirements:* For master's, GRE, GMAT, minimum GPA of 3.0.

American University of Beirut, Graduate Programs, Faculty of Engineering and Architecture, Beirut, Lebanon. Offers applied energy (MME); civil engineering (ME, PhD); electrical and computer engineering (ME, PhD); engineering management (MEM); environmental and water resources (ME); environmental and water resources engineering (PhD); environmental technology (MSES); mechanical engineering (ME, PhD); urban design (MUD); urban planning and policy (MUP). Part-time programs available. *Faculty:* 53 full-time (8 women), 10 part-time/adjunct (2 women). *Students:* 290 full-time (101 women), 59 part-time (18 women). Average age 25. 336 applicants, 80% accepted, 83 enrolled. In 2011, 72 master's, 5 doctorates awarded. *Degree requirements:* For master's, one foreign language, comprehensive exam, thesis (for some programs); for doctorate, one foreign language, comprehensive exam, thesis/dissertation, publications. *Entrance requirements:* For master's, GRE (for electrical and computer engineering), letters of recommendation; for doctorate, GRE, letters of recommendation, master's degree, transcripts, curriculum vitae, interview. Additional exam requirements/recommendations for international students: Required—TOEFL (minimum score 600 paper-based; 250 computer-based; 100 iBT), IELTS (minimum score 7.5). *Application deadline:* For fall admission, 2/5 priority date for domestic students, 2/5 for international students; for spring admission, 11/1 priority date for domestic students, 11/1 for international students. Applications are processed on a rolling basis. Application fee: $50. Electronic applications accepted. *Expenses: Tuition:* Full-time $12,780; part-time $710 per credit. *Required fees:* $528; $528 per credit. Tuition and fees vary according to course load and program. *Financial support:* In 2011–12, 9 fellowships with full tuition reimbursements (averaging $24,800 per year), 33 research assistantships with full tuition reimbursements (averaging $24,800 per year), 74 teaching assistantships with full tuition reimbursements (averaging $9,800 per year) were awarded; career-related internships or fieldwork, institutionally sponsored loans, scholarships/grants, health care benefits, and unspecified assistantships also available. *Total annual research expenditures:* $1.1 million. *Unit head:* Prof. Makram T. Suidan, Dean, 961-135-0000 Ext. 3400, Fax: 961-174-4462, E-mail: msuidan@aub.edu.lb. *Application contact:* Dr. Salim Kanaan, Director, Admissions Office, 961-135-0000 Ext. 2594, Fax: 961-175-0775, E-mail: sk00@aub.edu.lb. Web site: http://staff.aub.edu.lb/~webfea.

Arkansas State University, Graduate School, College of Engineering, Jonesboro, State University, AR 72467. Offers MEM. Part-time programs available. *Faculty:* 7 full-time (0 women). *Students:* 5 full-time (0 women), 15 part-time (1 woman); includes 2 minority (1 Black or African American, non-Hispanic/Latino; 1 Asian, non-Hispanic/Latino), 15 international. Average age 26. 24 applicants, 79% accepted, 10 enrolled. In 2011, 6 master's awarded. *Degree requirements:* For master's, comprehensive exam.

Entrance requirements: For master's, GRE, appropriate bachelor's degree, official transcript, letters of recommendation, resume, immunization records. Additional exam requirements/recommendations for international students: Required—TOEFL (minimum score 550 paper-based; 213 computer-based; 79 iBT), IELTS (minimum score 6), PTE: Pearson Test of English Academic (minimum score 56). *Application deadline:* For fall admission, 6/1 for domestic and international students; for spring admission, 10/15 for domestic and international students. Applications are processed on a rolling basis. Application fee: $30 ($40 for international students). Electronic applications accepted. *Expenses:* Contact institution. *Financial support:* In 2011–12, 4 students received support. Career-related internships or fieldwork, scholarships/grants, and unspecified assistantships available. Financial award application deadline: 7/1; financial award applicants required to submit FAFSA. *Unit head:* Dr. David Beasley, Dean, 870-972-2088, Fax: 870-972-3539, E-mail: dbbeasley@astate.edu. *Application contact:* Dr. Andrew Sustich, Dean of the Graduate School, 870-972-3029, Fax: 870-972-3857, E-mail: sustich@astate.edu. Web site: http://www.astate.edu/engr/.

California Maritime Academy, Graduate Studies, Vallejo, CA 94590. Offers transportation and engineering management (MS). Postbaccalaureate distance learning degree programs offered (no on-campus study). *Degree requirements:* For master's, capstone course.

California National University for Advanced Studies, College of Quality and Engineering Management, Northridge, CA 91325. Offers MEM. Part-time programs available. *Entrance requirements:* For master's, minimum GPA of 3.0.

California State Polytechnic University, Pomona, Academic Affairs, College of Engineering, Program in Engineering Management, Pomona, CA 91768-2557. Offers MS. *Students:* 5 full-time (2 women), 25 part-time (4 women); includes 13 minority (1 Black or African American, non-Hispanic/Latino; 6 Asian, non-Hispanic/Latino; 6 Hispanic/Latino), 3 international. Average age 32. 35 applicants, 49% accepted, 8 enrolled. In 2011, 14 master's awarded. *Degree requirements:* For master's, thesis or project. *Application deadline:* Applications are processed on a rolling basis. Application fee: $55. Electronic applications accepted. *Expenses:* Tuition, state resident: full-time $6738. Tuition, nonresident: full-time $12,300. *Required fees:* $657. Tuition and fees vary according to course load and program. *Unit head:* Dr. Abdul B. Sadat, Chair/Graduate Coordinator, 909-869-2555, E-mail: absadat@csupomona.edu. *Application contact:* Dr. Kamran Abedini, Graduate Coordinator, 909-869-2569, E-mail: kabedini@csupomona.edu. Web site: http://www.csupomona.edu/~ime/msem.htm.

California State University, East Bay, Office of Academic Programs and Graduate Studies, College of Science, Engineering Department, Program in Engineering Management, Hayward, CA 94542-3000. Offers MS. *Faculty:* 5 full-time (2 women), 1 part-time/adjunct. *Students:* 14 full-time (6 women), 26 part-time (7 women); includes 8 minority (1 Black or African American, non-Hispanic/Latino; 3 Asian, non-Hispanic/Latino; 4 Hispanic/Latino), 21 international. Average age 31. 74 applicants, 55% accepted, 17 enrolled. In 2011, 17 master's awarded. *Degree requirements:* For master's, comprehensive exam (for some programs), research project or exam. *Entrance requirements:* For master's, GRE or GMAT, minimum GPA of 2.5; personal statement, two letters of recommendation, resume; college algebra/trigonometry or equivalent. Additional exam requirements/recommendations for international students: Required—TOEFL (minimum score 550 paper-based; 213 computer-based). *Application deadline:* For fall admission, 6/30 for domestic and international students. Application fee: $55. Electronic applications accepted. *Expenses:* Tuition, state resident: full-time $6738; part-time $1302 per quarter. Tuition, nonresident: full-time $12,690; part-time $2294 per quarter. *Required fees:* $449 per quarter. Tuition and fees vary according to degree level, program and reciprocity agreements. *Financial support:* Federal Work-Study and institutionally sponsored loans available. Support available to part-time students. Financial award application deadline: 3/2; financial award applicants required to submit FAFSA. *Unit head:* Dr. Saeid Motavalli, Department Chair/Graduate Advisor, 510-885-2654, Fax: 510-885-2678, E-mail: saeid.motavalli@csueastbay.edu. Web site: http://www20.csueastbay.edu/csci/departments/engineering/.

California State University, Long Beach, Graduate Studies, College of Engineering, Department of Mechanical and Aerospace Engineering, Long Beach, CA 90840. Offers aerospace engineering (MSAE); engineering and industrial applied mathematics (PhD); interdisciplinary engineering (MSE); management engineering (MSE); mechanical engineering (MSME). Part-time programs available. *Faculty:* 11 full-time (3 women), 6 part-time/adjunct (0 women). *Students:* 35 full-time (3 women), 54 part-time (4 women); includes 45 minority (1 Black or African American, non-Hispanic/Latino; 2 American Indian or Alaska Native, non-Hispanic/Latino; 17 Asian, non-Hispanic/Latino; 22 Hispanic/Latino; 3 Two or more races, non-Hispanic/Latino), 9 international. Average age 28. 142 applicants, 51% accepted, 26 enrolled. In 2011, 38 master's awarded. *Entrance requirements:* Additional exam requirements/recommendations for international students: Required—TOEFL. *Application deadline:* For fall admission, 7/1 for domestic students. Application fee: $55. Electronic applications accepted. *Financial support:* Career-related internships or fieldwork, Federal Work-Study, institutionally sponsored loans, scholarships/grants, and unspecified assistantships available. Financial award application deadline: 3/2. *Faculty research:* Unsteady turbulent flows, solar energy, energy conversion, CAD/CAM, computer-assisted instruction. *Unit head:* Dr. Hamid Hefazi, Chair, 562-985-1502, Fax: 562-985-1564, E-mail: hefazi@csulb.edu. *Application contact:* Dr. Hamid Rahai, Graduate Advisor, 562-985-5132, Fax: 562-985-4408, E-mail: rahai@csulb.edu.

California State University, Northridge, Graduate Studies, College of Engineering and Computer Science, Department of Manufacturing Systems Engineering and Management, Northridge, CA 91330. Offers engineering automation (MS); engineering management (MS); manufacturing systems engineering (MS); materials engineering (MS). Postbaccalaureate distance learning degree programs offered. *Entrance requirements:* For master's, GRE (if cumulative undergraduate GPA less than 3.0).

Case Western Reserve University, School of Graduate Studies, Case School of Engineering, The Institute for Management and Engineering, Cleveland, OH 44106. Offers MEM. *Students:* 30 full-time (7 women); includes 4 minority (2 Asian, non-Hispanic/Latino; 1 Hispanic/Latino; 1 Two or more races, non-Hispanic/Latino), 4 international. In 2011, 24 master's awarded. *Entrance requirements:* Additional exam requirements/recommendations for international students: Required—TOEFL (minimum score 100 computer-based), IELTS (minimum score 7.5). *Application deadline:* For fall admission, 5/1 for domestic students, 2/1 for international students. *Financial support:* In 2011–12, 29 fellowships (averaging $17,830 per year) were awarded; scholarships/grants also available. *Total annual research expenditures:* $309,183. *Unit head:* Suzette Williamson, Executive Director, 216-368-0598, Fax: 216-368-0144, E-mail: sxwll@cwru.edu. *Application contact:* Ramona David, Program Assistant, 216-368-0596, Fax: 216-368-0144, E-mail: rxd47@cwru.edu. Web site: http://www.mem.case.edu.

The Catholic University of America, School of Engineering, Program in Engineering Management, Washington, DC 20064. Offers MSE, Certificate. Part-time programs available. *Faculty:* 6 part-time/adjunct (0 women). *Students:* 23 full-time (11 women), 34 part-time (11 women); includes 6 minority (2 Black or African American, non-Hispanic/Latino; 1 Asian, non-Hispanic/Latino; 3 Hispanic/Latino), 26 international. Average age 30. 62 applicants, 63% accepted, 26 enrolled. In 2011, 18 degrees awarded. *Degree requirements:* For master's, thesis optional. *Entrance requirements:* For master's and Certificate, statement of purpose, official copies of academic transcripts, three letters of recommendation. Additional exam requirements/recommendations for international students: Required—TOEFL (minimum score 580 paper-based; 237 computer-based). *Application deadline:* For fall admission, 8/1 priority date for domestic students, 7/15 for international students; for spring admission, 12/1 priority date for domestic students, 10/15 for international students. Applications are processed on a rolling basis. Application fee: $55. Electronic applications accepted. *Expenses:* Contact institution. *Financial support:* Fellowships, research assistantships, teaching assistantships, Federal Work-Study, scholarships/grants, tuition waivers (full and partial), and unspecified assistantships available. Financial award application deadline: 2/1; financial award applicants required to submit FAFSA. *Faculty research:* Engineering management and organization, project and systems engineering management, technology management. *Unit head:* Jeffrey E. Giangiuli, Director, 202-319-5191, Fax: 202-319-6860, E-mail: giangiuli@cua.edu. *Application contact:* Andrew Woodall, Director of Graduate Admissions, 202-319-5057, Fax: 202-319-6533, E-mail: cua-admissions@cua.edu. Web site: http://engrmgmt.cua.edu/.

The Citadel, The Military College of South Carolina, Citadel Graduate College, Department of Civil Engineering, Charleston, SC 29409. Offers technical project management (MS). Part-time and evening/weekend programs available. *Faculty:* 2 full-time, 3 part-time/adjunct. *Students:* 4 full-time (1 woman), 30 part-time (9 women); includes 4 minority (3 Black or African American, non-Hispanic/Latino; 1 Hispanic/Latino). Average age 37. In 2011, 8 master's awarded. *Entrance requirements:* For master's, GRE or GMAT, evidence of a minimum of one year of professional experience, or permission from department head; two letters of reference; resume detailing previous work. Additional exam requirements/recommendations for international students: Required—TOEFL (minimum score 550 paper-based; 213 computer-based; 79 iBT). *Application deadline:* For fall admission, 8/1 priority date for domestic students. Applications are processed on a rolling basis. Application fee: $30. Electronic applications accepted. *Expenses: Tuition, area resident:* Part-time $501 per credit hour. Tuition, state resident: part-time $501 per credit hour. Tuition, nonresident: part-time $824 per credit hour. *Required fees:* $40 per term. One-time fee: $30. *Financial support:* Health care benefits available. Support available to part-time students. Financial award application deadline: 7/1; financial award applicants required to submit FAFSA. *Unit head:* Dr. Kenneth P. Brannan, Department Head, 843-953-5007, Fax: 843-953-6328, E-mail: ken.brannan@citadel.edu. *Application contact:* Maj. Keith Plemmons, Program Director, 843-953-7677, Fax: 843-953-6328, E-mail: keith.plemmons@citadel.edu. Web site: http://www.citadel.edu/pmgt/.

Clarkson University, Graduate School, School of Business, Program in Engineering and Global Operations Management, Potsdam, NY 13699. Offers MS. Part-time and evening/weekend programs available. Postbaccalaureate distance learning degree programs offered (minimal on-campus study). *Students:* 19 part-time (5 women); includes 2 minority (both Hispanic/Latino). Average age 42. 9 applicants, 78% accepted, 3 enrolled. In 2011, 15 master's awarded. *Entrance requirements:* For master's, GMAT or GRE, transcripts of all college coursework, resume, personal statement, three letters of recommendation. Additional exam requirements/recommendations for international students: Required—TOEFL (minimum score 550 paper-based; 213 computer-based; 80 iBT), IELTS (minimum score 6.5), TSE required for some. *Application deadline:* For fall admission, 1/30 priority date for domestic students, 1/30 for international students; for spring admission, 9/1 priority date for domestic students, 9/1 for international students. Applications are processed on a rolling basis. Application fee: $25 ($35 for international students). Electronic applications accepted. *Expenses: Tuition:* Full-time $14,376; part-time $1198 per credit hour. *Required fees:* $295 per semester. *Financial support:* Scholarships/grants available. *Faculty research:* Global supply chain management, business to business marketing, operations strategy, engineering economics process control. *Unit head:* Dr. Boris Jukic, Director, 315-268-6613, Fax: 315-268-3810, E-mail: bjukic@clarkson.edu. *Application contact:* Karen Fuhr, Assistant to the Graduate Director, 315-268-6613, Fax: 315-268-3810, E-mail: fuhrk@clarkson.edu. Web site: http://www.clarkson.edu/business/graduate/egom/.

Colorado School of Mines, Graduate School, Division of Economics and Business, Golden, CO 80401-1887. Offers engineering and technology management (MS); mineral economics (MS, PhD). Part-time programs available. *Faculty:* 10 full-time (2 women), 6 part-time/adjunct (2 women). *Students:* 118 full-time (18 women), 19 part-time (4 women); includes 14 minority (1 Black or African American, non-Hispanic/Latino; 2 American Indian or Alaska Native, non-Hispanic/Latino; 2 Asian, non-Hispanic/Latino; 7 Hispanic/Latino; 2 Two or more races, non-Hispanic/Latino), 29 international. Average age 29. 177 applicants, 64% accepted, 59 enrolled. In 2011, 53 master's, 3 doctorates awarded. *Degree requirements:* For master's, thesis (for some programs); for doctorate, comprehensive exam, thesis/dissertation. *Entrance requirements:* For master's and doctorate, GRE General Test. Additional exam requirements/recommendations for international students: Required—TOEFL (minimum score 550 paper-based; 213 computer-based; 80 iBT). *Application deadline:* For fall admission, 1/15 priority date for domestic students, 1/15 for international students; for spring admission, 10/15 priority date for domestic students, 10/15 for international students. Application fee: $50 ($70 for international students). Electronic applications accepted. *Expenses:* Tuition, state resident: full-time $12,585; part-time $699 per credit. Tuition, nonresident: full-time $27,270; part-time $1516 per credit. *Required fees:* $1864.20; $670 per semester. *Financial support:* In 2011–12, 37 students received support, including 4 fellowships with full tuition reimbursements available (averaging $20,000 per year), 16 research assistantships with full tuition reimbursements available (averaging $20,000 per year), 17 teaching assistantships with full tuition reimbursements available (averaging $20,000 per year); scholarships/grants, health care benefits, and unspecified assistantships also available. Financial award application deadline: 1/15; financial award applicants required to submit FAFSA. *Faculty research:* International trade, resource and environmental economics, energy economics, operations research. *Total annual research expenditures:* $140,148. *Unit head:* Dr. Rod Eggert, Director, 303-273-3981, Fax: 303-273-3416, E-mail: reggert@mines.edu. *Application contact:* Kathleen A. Feighny, Administrative Faculty, 303-273-3979, Fax: 303-273-3416, E-mail: kfeighny@mines.edu. Web site: http://econbus.mines.edu.

Cornell University, Graduate School, Graduate Fields of Engineering, Field of Civil and Environmental Engineering, Ithaca, NY 14853-0001. Offers engineering management (M Eng, MS, PhD); environmental engineering (M Eng, MS, PhD); environmental fluid mechanics and hydrology (M Eng, MS, PhD); environmental systems engineering (M Eng, MS, PhD); geotechnical engineering (M Eng, MS, PhD); remote sensing (M Eng, MS, PhD); structural engineering (M Eng, MS, PhD); structural mechanics (M Eng, MS); transportation engineering (MS, PhD); transportation systems engineering (M Eng); water resource systems (M Eng, MS, PhD). *Faculty:* 39 full-time (4 women). *Students:* 143 full-time (49 women); includes 20 minority (6 Black or African American, non-Hispanic/Latino; 1 American Indian or Alaska Native, non-Hispanic/Latino; 9 Asian, non-Hispanic/Latino; 4 Hispanic/Latino), 72 international. Average age 25. 574 applicants, 47% accepted, 100 enrolled. In 2011, 88 master's, 13 doctorates awarded. Terminal master's awarded for partial completion of doctoral program. *Degree requirements:* For master's, thesis (MS); for doctorate, comprehensive exam, thesis/dissertation. *Entrance requirements:* For master's and doctorate, GRE General Test (recommended), 2 letters of recommendation. Additional exam requirements/recommendations for international students: Required—TOEFL (minimum score 600 paper-based; 250 computer-based; 77 iBT). *Application deadline:* For fall admission, 1/15 priority date for domestic students; for spring admission, 10/15 for domestic students. Application fee: $95. Electronic applications accepted. *Financial support:* In 2011–12, 50 students received support, including 20 fellowships with full tuition reimbursements available, 27 research assistantships with full tuition reimbursements available, 17 teaching assistantships with full tuition reimbursements available; institutionally sponsored loans, scholarships/grants, health care benefits, tuition waivers (full and partial), and unspecified assistantships also available. Financial award applicants required to submit FAFSA. *Faculty research:* Environmental engineering, geotechnical engineering, remote sensing, environmental fluid mechanics and hydrology, structural engineering. *Unit head:* Director of Graduate Studies, 607-255-7560, Fax: 607-255-9004. *Application contact:* Graduate Field Assistant, 607-255-7560, Fax: 607-255-9004, E-mail: cee_grad@cornell.edu. Web site: http://www.gradschool.cornell.edu/fields.php?id-27&a-2.

Dallas Baptist University, College of Business, Business Administration Program, Dallas, TX 75211-9299. Offers accounting (MBA); business communication (MBA); conflict resolution management (MBA); entrepreneurship (MBA); finance (MBA); health care management (MBA); international business (MBA); leading the non-profit organization (MBA); management (MBA); management information systems (MBA); marketing (MBA); project management (MBA); technology and engineering management (MBA). *Accreditation:* ACBSP. Part-time and evening/weekend programs available. *Entrance requirements:* For master's, GMAT, minimum GPA of 3.0. Additional exam requirements/recommendations for international students: Required—TOEFL, IELTS. *Application deadline:* Applications are processed on a rolling basis. Application fee: $25. Electronic applications accepted. *Expenses: Tuition:* Full-time $12,060; part-time $670 per credit hour. *Required fees:* $100; $50 per semester. *Financial support:* Federal Work-Study, institutionally sponsored loans, scholarships/grants, and tuition waivers (full and partial) available. Support available to part-time students. Financial award applicants required to submit FAFSA. *Faculty research:* Sports management, services marketing, retailing, strategic management, financial planning/investments. *Unit head:* Dr. Sandra .S. Reid, Director, 214-333-5280, Fax: 214-333-5293, E-mail: graduate@dbu.edu. *Application contact:* Kit P. Montgomery, Director of Graduate Programs, 214-333-5242, Fax: 214-333-5579, E-mail: graduate@dbu.edu. Web site: http://www3.dbu.edu/graduate/mba.asp.

Dartmouth College, Thayer School of Engineering, Program in Engineering Management, Hanover, NH 03755. Offers MEM, MBA/MEM. *Degree requirements:* For master's, design experience. *Entrance requirements:* For master's, GRE General Test. Additional exam requirements/recommendations for international students: Required—TOEFL. *Application deadline:* For fall admission, 1/1 priority date for domestic students. Applications are processed on a rolling basis. Application fee: $45. *Financial support:* Fellowships, teaching assistantships, career-related internships or fieldwork, Federal Work-Study, institutionally sponsored loans, and tuition waivers (full and partial) available. Financial award application deadline: 1/15; financial award applicants required to submit CSS PROFILE. *Unit head:* Dr. Joseph J. Helbie, Dean, 603-646-2238, Fax: 603-646-2580, E-mail: joseph.j.helbie@dartmouth.edu. *Application contact:* Candace S. Potter, Graduate Admissions Administrator, 603-646-3844, Fax: 603-646-1620, E-mail: candace.potter@dartmouth.edu. Web site: http://engineering.dartmouth.edu/.

Drexel University, College of Engineering, Program in Engineering Management, Philadelphia, PA 19104-2875. Offers MS, Certificate. Part-time and evening/weekend programs available. Postbaccalaureate distance learning degree programs offered (no on-campus study). *Degree requirements:* For master's, thesis optional. *Entrance requirements:* For master's, minimum GPA of 3.0. Additional exam requirements/recommendations for international students: Required—TOEFL. Electronic applications accepted. *Faculty research:* Quality, operations research and management, ergonomics, applied statistics.

Duke University, Graduate School, Pratt School of Engineering, Distributed Master of Engineering Management Program (d-MEMP), durham, NC 27708-0271. Offers MEM. Part-time and evening/weekend programs available. Postbaccalaureate distance learning degree programs offered (minimal on-campus study). *Entrance requirements:* For master's, GRE General Test, resume, 3 letters of recommendation, statement of purpose. Additional exam requirements/recommendations for international students: Required—TOEFL. Electronic applications accepted. *Expenses:* Contact institution. *Faculty research:* Entrepreneurship, innovation and product development, project management, operations and supply chain management, financial engineering.

Duke University, Graduate School, Pratt School of Engineering, Master of Engineering Management Program, Durham, NC 27708-0271. Offers MEM. Part-time programs available. Postbaccalaureate distance learning degree programs offered. *Entrance requirements:* For master's, GRE General Test, resume, 3 letters of recommendation, statement of purpose. Additional exam requirements/recommendations for international students: Required—TOEFL. Electronic applications accepted. *Expenses:* Contact institution. *Faculty research:* Entrepreneurship, innovation and product development, project management, operations and supply chain management, financial engineering.

Eastern Michigan University, Graduate School, College of Technology, School of Engineering Technology, Program in Engineering Management, Ypsilanti, MI 48197. Offers MS. Part-time and evening/weekend programs available. Postbaccalaureate distance learning degree programs offered (minimal on-campus study). *Students:* 14 full-time (3 women), 86 part-time (14 women); includes 15 minority (6 Black or African American, non-Hispanic/Latino; 5 Asian, non-Hispanic/Latino; 4 Hispanic/Latino), 15 international. Average age 33. 58 applicants, 59% accepted, 15 enrolled. In 2011, 30 degrees awarded. *Entrance requirements:* Additional exam requirements/recommendations for international students: Required—TOEFL. *Application deadline:* Applications are processed on a rolling basis. Application fee: $35. *Expenses:* Tuition, state resident: full-time $10,367; part-time $432 per credit hour. Tuition, nonresident: full-time $20,435; part-time $851 per credit hour. *Required fees:* $39 per credit hour. $46 per semester. One-time fee: $100. Tuition and fees vary according to course level, degree level and reciprocity agreements. *Financial support:* Fellowships, research assistantships with full tuition reimbursements, teaching assistantships with full tuition reimbursements, career-related internships or fieldwork, Federal Work-Study, institutionally sponsored loans, scholarships/grants, tuition waivers (partial), and unspecified assistantships available. Support available to part-time students. Financial award applicants required to submit FAFSA. *Unit head:* Dr. Muhammad Ahmad, Program Coordinator, 734-487-2040, Fax: 734-487-8755, E-mail: mahmed@emich.edu. *Application contact:* Graduate Admissions, 734-487-2400, Fax: 734-487-6559, E-mail: graduate.admissions@emich.edu.

Florida Institute of Technology, Graduate Programs, College of Engineering, Engineering Systems Department, Melbourne, FL 32901-6975. Offers engineering management (MS); systems engineering (MS, PhD). Part-time and evening/weekend programs available. *Faculty:* 5 full-time (0 women). *Students:* 29 full-time (11 women), 71 part-time (16 women); includes 13 minority (6 Black or African American, non-Hispanic/Latino; 3 Asian, non-Hispanic/Latino; 3 Hispanic/Latino; 1 Two or more races, non-Hispanic/Latino), 29 international. Average age 33. 120 applicants, 63% accepted, 32 enrolled. In 2011, 38 master's awarded. *Degree requirements:* For master's, comprehensive exam (for some programs), thesis optional, portfolio of competencies and summary of career relevance. *Entrance requirements:* For master's, GRE General Test (if GPA less than 3.0), minimum GPA of 3.0, 2 letters of recommendation, resume, bachelor's degree in engineering from ABET-accredited program, statement of objectives. Additional exam requirements/recommendations for international students: Required—TOEFL (minimum score 550 paper-based; 213 computer-based; 79 iBT). *Application deadline:* For fall admission, 4/1 for international students; for spring admission, 9/30 for international students. Applications are processed on a rolling basis. Electronic applications accepted. *Expenses: Tuition:* Full-time $19,620; part-time $1090 per credit hour. Tuition and fees vary according to campus/location. *Financial support:* In 2011–12, 3 research assistantships with full and partial tuition reimbursements (averaging $9,999 per year) were awarded; career-related internships or fieldwork, institutionally sponsored loans, unspecified assistantships, and tuition remissions also available. Support available to part-time students. Financial award application deadline: 3/1; financial award applicants required to submit FAFSA. *Faculty research:* System/software engineering, simulation and analytical modeling, project management, multimedia tools, quality. *Unit head:* Dr. Muzaffar A. Shaikh, Department Head, 321-674-7345, Fax: 321-674-7136, E-mail: mshaikh@fit.edu. *Application contact:* Cheryl A. Brown, Associate Director of Graduate Admissions, 321-674-7581, Fax: 321-723-9468, E-mail: cbrown@fit.edu. Web site: http://coe.fit.edu/se/.

Florida Institute of Technology, Graduate Programs, Extended Studies Division, Melbourne, FL 32901-6975. Offers acquisition and contract management (MS); aerospace engineering (MS); business administration (MBA); computer information systems (MS); computer science (MS); electrical engineering (MS); engineering management (MS); human resources management (MS); logistics management (MS), including humanitarian and disaster relief logistics; management (MS), including acquisition and contract management, e-business, human resources management, information systems, logistics management, management, transportation management; material acquisition management (MS); mechanical engineering (MS); operations research (MS); project management (MS), including information systems, operations research; public administration (MPA); quality management (MS); software engineering

(MS); space systems (MS); space systems management (MS); supply chain management (MS); systems management (MS), including information systems, operations research. Part-time and evening/weekend programs available. Postbaccalaureate distance learning degree programs offered (no on-campus study). *Faculty:* 9 full-time (2 women), 105 part-time/adjunct (24 women). *Students:* 113 full-time (52 women), 1,150 part-time (484 women); includes 496 minority (332 Black or African American, non-Hispanic/Latino; 11 American Indian or Alaska Native, non-Hispanic/Latino; 42 Asian, non-Hispanic/Latino; 71 Hispanic/Latino; 2 Native Hawaiian or other Pacific Islander, non-Hispanic/Latino; 38 Two or more races, non-Hispanic/Latino), 11 international. Average age 35. 568 applicants, 56% accepted, 296 enrolled. In 2011, 471 master's awarded. *Degree requirements:* For master's, comprehensive exam (for some programs), capstone course. *Entrance requirements:* For master's, GMAT or resume showing 8 years of supervised experience, minimum GPA of 3.0, 2 letters of recommendation, resume. Additional exam requirements/recommendations for international students: Required—TOEFL (minimum score 550 paper-based; 213 computer-based; 79 iBT). *Application deadline:* For fall admission, 4/1 for international students; for spring admission, 9/30 for international students. Applications are processed on a rolling basis. Application fee: $0. Electronic applications accepted. *Expenses:* Contact institution. *Financial support:* Application deadline: 3/1; applicants required to submit FAFSA. *Unit head:* Dr. Theodore R. Richardson, III, Senior Associate Dean, 321-674-8123, Fax: 321-674-7597, E-mail: trichardson@fit.edu. *Application contact:* Carolyn Farrior, Director of Graduate Admissions, Online Learning and Off-Campus Programs, 321-674-7118, Fax: 321-674-8216, E-mail: cfarrior@fit.edu. Web site: http://es.fit.edu.

Gannon University, School of Graduate Studies, College of Engineering and Business, School of Engineering and Computer Science, Program in Engineering Management, Erie, PA 16541-0001. Offers MSEM. Part-time and evening/weekend programs available. Postbaccalaureate distance learning degree programs offered (no on-campus study). *Students:* 18 full-time (0 women), 8 part-time (2 women); includes 1 minority (Asian, non-Hispanic/Latino), 16 international. Average age 27. 87 applicants, 74% accepted, 5 enrolled. In 2011, 12 master's awarded. *Degree requirements:* For master's, comprehensive exam, thesis. *Entrance requirements:* For master's, GRE or GMAT, bachelor's degree in engineering, minimum QPA of 2.5. Additional exam requirements/recommendations for international students: Required—TOEFL (minimum score 79 iBT). *Application deadline:* Applications are processed on a rolling basis. Application fee: $25. Electronic applications accepted. *Financial·support:* Scholarships/grants available. Financial award application deadline: 7/1; financial award applicants required to submit FAFSA. *Unit head:* Dr. Scott Steinbrink, Chair, 814-871-5302, E-mail: steinbri001@gannon.edu. *Application contact:* Kara Morgan, Director of Graduate Admissions, 814-871-5831, Fax: 814-871-5827, E-mail: graduate@gannon.edu.

The George Washington University, School of Engineering and Applied Science, Department of Engineering Management and Systems Engineering, Washington, DC 20052. Offers MS, D Sc, App Sc, Engr, Graduate Certificate. Part-time and evening/weekend programs available. *Faculty:* 16 full-time (2 women), 19 part-time/adjunct (5 women). *Students:* 121 full-time (40 women), 1,004 part-time (260 women); includes 243 minority (129 Black or African American, non-Hispanic/Latino; 3 American Indian or Alaska Native, non-Hispanic/Latino; 66 Asian, non-Hispanic/Latino; 36 Hispanic/Latino; 3 Native Hawaiian or other Pacific Islander, non-Hispanic/Latino; 6 Two or more races, non-Hispanic/Latino), 106 international. Average age 35. 482 applicants, 89% accepted, 271 enrolled. In 2011, 394 master's, 22 doctorates, 236 other advanced degrees awarded. *Degree requirements:* For master's, thesis optional; for doctorate, one foreign language, thesis/dissertation, final and qualifying exams, submission of articles; for other advanced degree, professional project. *Entrance requirements:* For master's, appropriate bachelor's degree, minimum GPA of 2.7, second semester calculus; for doctorate, appropriate master's degree, minimum GPA of 3.5, 2 letters of recommendation; for other advanced degree, appropriate master's degree, minimum GPA of 3.4. Additional exam requirements/recommendations for international students: Required—TOEFL or The George Washington University English as a Foreign Language Test. *Application deadline:* For fall admission, 3/1 for domestic students; for spring admission, 10/1 for domestic students. Applications are processed on a rolling basis. Application fee: $75. *Financial support:* In 2011–12, 35 students received support. Fellowships with tuition reimbursements available, research assistantships, teaching assistantships with tuition reimbursements available, career-related internships or fieldwork, and institutionally sponsored loans available. Financial award application deadline: 3/1; financial award applicants required to submit FAFSA. *Faculty research:* Artificial intelligence and expert systems, human factors engineering and systems analysis. *Total annual research expenditures:* $421,800. *Unit head:* Dr. Thomas Mazzuchi, Chair, 202-994-7424, Fax: 202-994-0245, E-mail: mazzu@gwu.edu. *Application contact:* Adina Lav, Marketing, Recruiting and Admissions, 202-994-5827, Fax: 202-994-0909, E-mail: engineering@gwu.edu. Web site: http://www.emse.gwu.edu/.

Instituto Tecnológico y de Estudios Superiores de Monterrey, Campus Chihuahua, Graduate Programs, Chihuahua, Mexico. Offers computer systems engineering (Ingeniero); electrical engineering (Ingeniero); electromechanical engineering (Ingeniero); electronic engineering (Ingeniero); engineering administration (MEA); industrial engineering (MIE, Ingeniero); international trade (MIT); mechanical engineering (Ingeniero).

International Technological University, Program in Engineering Management, Santa Clara, CA 95050. Offers MEM.

The Johns Hopkins University, Whiting School of Engineering, Program in Engineering Management, Baltimore, MD 21218-2699. Offers biomaterials (MSEM); communications science (MSEM); computer science (MSEM); fluid mechanics (MSEM); materials science and engineering (MSEM); mechanical engineering (MSEM); mechanics and materials (MSEM); nano-biotechnology (MSEM); nanomaterials and nanotechnology (MSEM); probability and statistics (MSEM); smart product and device design (MSEM); systems analysis, management and environmental policy (MSEM). *Entrance requirements:* For master's, GRE, 3 letters of recommendation, resume. Additional exam requirements/recommendations for international students: Required—TOEFL (minimum score 600 paper-based; 250 computer-based; 100 iBT) or IELTS (minimum score 7). Electronic applications accepted.

Kansas State University, Graduate School, College of Engineering, Department of Industrial and Manufacturing Systems Engineering, Manhattan, KS 66506. Offers engineering management (MEM); industrial engineering (MS, PhD); operations research (MS). Part-time programs available. Postbaccalaureate distance learning degree programs offered. *Faculty:* 12 full-time (3 women), 4 part-time/adjunct (1 woman). *Students:* 43 full-time (11 women), 57 part-time (14 women); includes 8 minority (1 Black or African American, non-Hispanic/Latino; 1 Asian, non-Hispanic/Latino; 2 Hispanic/Latino; 4 Two or more races, non-Hispanic/Latino), 34 international. Average age 29. 94 applicants, 46% accepted, 14 enrolled. In 2011, 21 master's, 3 doctorates awarded.

Degree requirements: For master's, thesis or alternative; for doctorate, thesis/dissertation. *Entrance requirements:* For master's, GRE General Test (minimum 750 [old version], 159 [new format] on Quantitative portion of exam), bachelor's degree in engineering, mathematics, or physical science; for doctorate, GRE General Test (minimum 770 [old version], 164 [new format] on Quantitative portion of exam), master's degree in engineering or industrial manufacturing. Additional exam requirements/recommendations for international students: Required—TOEFL (minimum score 550 paper-based; 79 iBT) or IELTS (minimum score 6.5). *Application deadline:* For fall admission, 6/1 priority date for domestic students, 2/1 for international students; for spring admission, 11/1 priority date for domestic students, 8/1 for international students. Applications are processed on a rolling basis. Application fee: $40 ($55 for international students). Electronic applications accepted. *Financial support:* In 2011–12, 15 research assistantships (averaging $12,412 per year), 1 teaching assistantship with full tuition reimbursement (averaging $12,000 per year) were awarded; Federal Work-Study, institutionally sponsored loans, and scholarships/grants also available. Support available to part-time students. Financial award application deadline: 3/1; financial award applicants required to submit FAFSA. *Faculty research:* Industrial engineering, ergonomics, healthcare systems engineering, manufacturing processes, operations research, engineering management. *Total annual research expenditures:* $645,655. *Unit head:* Bradley Kramer, Head, 785-532-5606, Fax: 785-532-3738, E-mail: bradleyk@ksu.edu. *Application contact:* David Ben-Arieh, Chair of Graduate Committee, 785-532-5606, Fax: 785-532-3738, E-mail: imse@ksu.edu. Web site: http://imse.ksu.edu/.

Kettering University, Graduate School, Department of Business, Flint, MI 48504. Offers MBA, MS. *Accreditation:* ACBSP. Part-time and evening/weekend programs available. Postbaccalaureate distance learning degree programs offered (no on-campus study). *Faculty:* 11 full-time (3 women), 7 part-time/adjunct (0 women). *Students:* 9 full-time (1 woman), 270 part-time (83 women); includes 73 minority (46 Black or African American, non-Hispanic/Latino; 1 American Indian or Alaska Native, non-Hispanic/Latino; 7 Asian, non-Hispanic/Latino; 19 Hispanic/Latino), 20 international. Average age 33. 106 applicants, 83% accepted, 50 enrolled. In 2011, 98 master's awarded. *Entrance requirements:* Additional exam requirements/recommendations for international students: Required—TOEFL (minimum score 550 paper-based; 213 computer-based; 79 iBT). *Application deadline:* For fall admission, 9/15 for domestic students, 6/15 for international students; for winter admission, 12/15 for domestic students, 9/15 for international students; for spring admission, 3/15 for domestic students, 12/15 for international students. Applications are processed on a rolling basis. Electronic applications accepted. *Expenses: Tuition:* Full-time $11,456; part-time $716 per credit hour. *Financial support:* In 2011–12, 24 students received support, including fellowships with full tuition reimbursements available (averaging $13,000 per year), research assistantships with full tuition reimbursements available (averaging $13,000 per year), teaching assistantships with full tuition reimbursements available (averaging $13,000 per year); Federal Work-Study, scholarships/grants, and tuition waivers (partial) also available. Support available to part-time students. Financial award application deadline: 7/15. *Faculty research:* Entrepreneurship. *Total annual research expenditures:* $151,000. *Unit head:* Dr. W. L. Scheller, Department Head, 810-762-7974, Fax: 810-762-9944, E-mail: wschelle@kettering.edu. *Application contact:* Bonnie Switzer, Admissions Representative, 810-762-7953, Fax: 810-762-9935, E-mail: bswitzer@kettering.edu.

Lamar University, College of Graduate Studies, College of Engineering, Department of Industrial Engineering, Beaumont, TX 77710. Offers engineering management (MEM); industrial engineering (ME, MES, DE). *Faculty:* 8 full-time (0 women). *Students:* 27 full-time (4 women), 10 part-time (3 women); includes 5 minority (1 Black or African American, non-Hispanic/Latino; 2 Asian, non-Hispanic/Latino; 2 Hispanic/Latino), 30 international. Average age 28. 39 applicants, 79% accepted, 8 enrolled. In 2011, 24 master's, 2 doctorates awarded. *Degree requirements:* For doctorate, thesis/dissertation. *Entrance requirements:* For master's and doctorate, GRE General Test. Additional exam requirements/recommendations for international students: Required—TOEFL. *Application deadline:* For fall admission, 5/15 priority date for domestic students; for spring admission, 10/1 priority date for domestic students. Applications are processed on a rolling basis. Application fee: $25 ($50 for international students). *Expenses:* Tuition, state resident: full-time $5430; part-time $272 per credit hour. Tuition, nonresident: full-time $11,540; part-time $577 per credit hour. *Required fees:* $1916. *Financial support:* In 2011–12, 2 fellowships (averaging $6,000 per year), 4 research assistantships (averaging $1,000 per year), 2 teaching assistantships (averaging $4,500 per year) were awarded. Financial award application deadline: 4/1. *Faculty research:* Process simulation, total quality management, ergonomics and safety, scheduling. *Unit head:* Dr. Victor Zaloom, Chair, 409-880-8804, Fax: 409-880-8121. *Application contact:* Dr. Hsing-Wei Chu, Professor, 409-880-8804, Fax: 409-880-8121. Web site: http://dept.lamar.edu/industrial/.

Lawrence Technological University, College of Engineering, Southfield, MI 48075-1058. Offers architectural engineering (MS); automotive engineering (MS); civil engineering (MA, MS); construction engineering management (MA); electrical and computer engineering (MS); engineering management (MEM); industrial engineering (MS); manufacturing systems (ME, DE); mechanical engineering (MS, DE); mechatronic systems engineering (MS). Part-time and evening/weekend programs available. *Faculty:* 25 full-time (4 women), 20 part-time/adjunct (1 woman). *Students:* 8 full-time (0 women), 332 part-time (52 women); includes 58 minority (21 Black or African American, non-Hispanic/Latino; 1 American Indian or Alaska Native, non-Hispanic/Latino; 32 Asian, non-Hispanic/Latino; 2 Hispanic/Latino; 2 Two or more races, non-Hispanic/Latino), 84 international. Average age 32. 652 applicants, 44% accepted, 70 enrolled. In 2011, 127 master's, 2 doctorates awarded. *Degree requirements:* For master's, thesis (for some programs). *Entrance requirements:* Additional exam requirements/recommendations for international students: Required—TOEFL (minimum score 550 paper-based; 213 computer-based; 79 iBT). *Application deadline:* For fall admission, 7/27 priority date for domestic students, 5/23 for international students; for spring admission, 11/15 priority date for domestic students, 11/15 for international students. Applications are processed on a rolling basis. Application fee: $50. Electronic applications accepted. *Financial support:* In 2011–12, 68 students received support, including 6 research assistantships (averaging $8,078 per year); Federal Work-Study and institutionally sponsored loans also available. Support available to part-time students. Financial award application deadline: 4/1; financial award applicants required to submit FAFSA. *Faculty research:* Advanced composite materials in bridges, strengthening existing bridges with carbon and glass fiber sheets, development of drive shafts using composite materials. *Unit head:* Dr. Nabil Grace, Dean, 248-204-2500, Fax: 248-204-2509, E-mail: engrdean@ltu.edu. *Application contact:* Jane Rohrback, Director of Admissions, 248-204-3160, Fax: 248-204-2228, E-mail: admissions@ltu.edu. Web site: http://www.ltu.edu/engineering/index.asp.

Lehigh University, P.C. Rossin College of Engineering and Applied Science, Department of Industrial and Systems Engineering, Bethlehem, PA 18015. Offers analytical finance (MS); healthcare systems engineering (M Eng); industrial and systems engineering (M Eng, MS); industrial engineering (PhD); management science and engineering (M Eng, MS); MBA/E. Part-time programs available. Postbaccalaureate distance learning degree programs offered (no on-campus study). *Faculty:* 14 full-time (2 women). *Students:* 73 full-time (28 women), 12 part-time (3 women); includes 2 minority (both Black or African American, non-Hispanic/Latino), 70 international. Average age 27. 275 applicants, 25% accepted, 20 enrolled. In 2011, 28 master's, 2 doctorates awarded. *Degree requirements:* For master's, thesis (MS); project (M Eng); for doctorate, comprehensive exam, thesis/dissertation. *Entrance requirements:* For master's and doctorate, GRE General Test. Additional exam requirements/recommendations for international students: Required—TOEFL (minimum score 550 paper-based; 213 computer-based; 79 iBT). *Application deadline:* For fall admission, 7/15 for domestic and international students; for spring admission, 12/1 for domestic and international students. Applications are processed on a rolling basis. Application fee: $75. Electronic applications accepted. *Financial support:* In 2011–12, 36 students received support, including 3 fellowships with full tuition reimbursements available (averaging $17,460 per year), 16 research assistantships with full tuition reimbursements available (averaging $15,300 per year), 11 teaching assistantships with full tuition reimbursements available (averaging $18,360 per year); career-related internships or fieldwork, scholarships/grants, tuition waivers, and unspecified assistantships also available. Financial award application deadline: 1/15. *Faculty research:* Optimization, mathematical programming; logistics and supply chain, stochastic processes and simulation; computational optimization and high performance computing; financial engineering and robust optimization. *Total annual research expenditures:* $1.5 million. *Unit head:* Dr. Tamas Terlaky, Chair, 610-758-4050, Fax: 610-758-4886, E-mail: terlaky@lehigh.edu. *Application contact:* Rita Frey, Graduate Coordinator, 610-758-4051, Fax: 610-758-4886, E-mail: ise@lehigh.edu. Web site: http://www.lehigh.edu/ise.

Long Island University–C. W. Post Campus, College of Information and Computer Science, Department of Computer Science/Management Engineering, Brookville, NY 11548-1300. Offers information systems (MS); information technology education (MS); management engineering (MS). Part-time and evening/weekend programs available. *Degree requirements:* For master's, comprehensive exam, thesis or alternative. *Entrance requirements:* For master's, bachelor's degree in science, mathematics, or engineering; minimum GPA of 2.5. Additional exam requirements/recommendations for international students: Required—TOEFL (minimum score 500 paper-based; 173 computer-based). Electronic applications accepted. *Faculty research:* Inductive music learning, re-engineering business process, technology and ethics.

Loyola Marymount University, College of Science and Engineering, Department of Systems Engineering and Engineering Management, Program in System Engineering Leadership, Los Angeles, CA 90045-2659. Offers MS, MS/MBA. *Faculty:* 2 full-time (0 women), 3 part-time/adjunct (1 woman). *Students:* 11 full-time (1 woman), 3 part-time (0 women); includes 7 minority (2 Black or African American, non-Hispanic/Latino; 2 Asian, non-Hispanic/Latino; 2 Hispanic/Latino; 1 Native Hawaiian or other Pacific Islander, non-Hispanic/Latino). Average age 32. 5 applicants, 60% accepted, 3 enrolled. In 2011, 5 master's awarded. *Degree requirements:* For master's, thesis. *Entrance requirements:* For master's, GMAT, must be admitted to both business and engineering schools. Additional exam requirements/recommendations for international students: Required—TOEFL (minimum score 550 paper-based; 213 computer-based; 80 iBT). *Application deadline:* For fall admission, 7/15 for domestic students; for spring admission, 12/15 for domestic students. Applications are processed on a rolling basis. Application fee: $50. Electronic applications accepted. *Financial support:* In 2011–12, 6 students received support. Scholarships/grants and unspecified assistantships available. Support available to part-time students. Financial award application deadline: 6/1; financial award applicants required to submit FAFSA. *Unit head:* Dr. Frederick S. Brown, Graduate Director, 310-338-7878, E-mail: fbrown@lmu.edu. *Application contact:* Chake H. Kouyoumjian, Associate Dean for Graduate Studies, 310-338-2721, E-mail: ckouyoum@lmu.edu. Web site: http://cse.lmu.edu/programs/Systems_Engineering/selp.htm.

Marquette University, Graduate School, College of Engineering, Department of Mechanical Engineering, Milwaukee, WI 53201-1881. Offers engineering innovation (Certificate); engineering management (MSEM); mechanical engineering (MS, PhD); new product and process development (Certificate). Part-time and evening/weekend programs available. *Faculty:* 16 full-time (1 woman), 2 part-time/adjunct (0 women). *Students:* 21 full-time (3 women), 35 part-time (5 women); includes 4 minority (1 Asian, non-Hispanic/Latino; 3 Hispanic/Latino), 18 international. Average age 29. 66 applicants, 56% accepted, 13 enrolled. In 2011, 19 master's, 2 doctorates, 2 other advanced degrees awarded. Terminal master's awarded for partial completion of doctoral program. *Degree requirements:* For master's, comprehensive exam, thesis (for some programs); for doctorate, comprehensive exam, thesis/dissertation, qualifying exam. *Entrance requirements:* For master's, GRE General Test, minimum GPA of 3.0, official transcripts from all current and previous colleges/universities except Marquette, three letters of recommendation; for doctorate, GRE General Test, minimum GPA of 3.0, official transcripts from all current and previous colleges/universities except Marquette, three letters of recommendation, statement of purpose, copies of any published work. Additional exam requirements/recommendations for international students: Required—TOEFL (minimum score 530 paper-based; 78 computer-based). *Application deadline:* For fall admission, 8/1 priority date for domestic students; for spring admission, 1/1 priority date for domestic students. Applications are processed on a rolling basis. Application fee: $50. Electronic applications accepted. *Expenses: Tuition:* Full-time $17,010; part-time $945 per credit hour. Tuition and fees vary according to program. *Financial support:* In 2011–12, 12 students received support, including 1 research assistantship with full tuition reimbursement available (averaging $13,745 per year), 9 teaching assistantships with full tuition reimbursements available (averaging $13,867 per year); fellowships, scholarships/grants, tuition waivers (partial), and unspecified assistantships also available. Support available to part-time students. Financial award application deadline: 2/15. *Faculty research:* Computer-integrated manufacturing, energy conversion, simulation modeling and optimization, applied mechanics, metallurgy. *Total annual research expenditures:* $595,179. *Unit head:* Dr. Kyle Kim, Chair, 414-288-7259, Fax: 414-288-7790, E-mail: kyle.kim@marquette.edu. *Application contact:* Dr. James Rice, Director of Graduate Studies, 414-288-5405, Fax: 414-288-7790, E-mail: nicholas.nigro@marquette.edu. Web site: http://www.marquette.edu/engineering/mechanical/grad.shtml.

Marquette University, Graduate School, College of Professional Studies, Milwaukee, WI 53201-1881. Offers criminal justice administration (MLS); dispute resolution (MDR, MLS); engineering (MLS); health care administration (MLS); law enforcement leadership and management (Certificate); leadership studies (Certificate); non-profit sector (MLS); public service (MAPS, MLS); sports leadership (MLS). Part-time and evening/weekend programs available. Postbaccalaureate distance learning degree programs offered (no on-campus study). *Faculty:* 9 full-time (8 women), 10 part-time/adjunct (5 women).

Students: 26 full-time (13 women), 142 part-time (90 women); includes 29 minority (19 Black or African American, non-Hispanic/Latino; 1 American Indian or Alaska Native, non-Hispanic/Latino; 3 Asian, non-Hispanic/Latino; 5 Hispanic/Latino; 1 Two or more races, non-Hispanic/Latino), 3 international. Average age 37. 88 applicants, 78% accepted, 36 enrolled. In 2011, 36 master's, 29 Certificates awarded. *Degree requirements:* For master's, comprehensive exam (for some programs). *Entrance requirements:* For master's, GRE General Test (preferred), GMAT, or LSAT, official transcripts from all current and previous colleges/universities except Marquette, three letters of recommendation, statement of purpose. Additional exam requirements/recommendations for international students: Required—TOEFL. *Application deadline:* Applications are processed on a rolling basis. Application fee: $50. Electronic applications accepted. *Expenses: Tuition:* Full-time $17,010; part-time $945 per credit hour. Tuition and fees vary according to program. *Financial support:* In 2011–12, 9 students received support, including 8 fellowships with full tuition reimbursements available (averaging $16,247 per year). Financial award application deadline: 2/15. *Unit head:* Dr. Johnette Caulfield, Adjunct Assistant Professor/Director, 414-288-5556, E-mail: jay.caulfield@marquette.edu. *Application contact:* Craig Pierce; Assistant Director for Recruitment, 414-288-5740, Fax: 414-288-1902, E-mail: craig.pierce@marquette.edu.

Marshall University, Academic Affairs Division, College of Information Technology and Engineering, Weisberg Division of Engineering and Computer Science, Huntington, WV 25755. Offers engineering (MSE); information systems (MS). Part-time and evening/weekend programs available. *Faculty:* 10 full-time (1 woman), 3 part-time/adjunct (1 woman). *Students:* 15 full-time (3 women), 45 part-time (8 women); includes 5 minority (3 Black or African American, non-Hispanic/Latino; 2 Asian, non-Hispanic/Latino), 7 international. Average age 32. In 2011, 23 master's awarded. *Degree requirements:* For master's, final project, oral exam. *Entrance requirements:* For master's, GMAT or GRE General Test, minimum undergraduate GPA of 2.75. Application fee: $40. *Financial support:* Tuition waivers (full) available. Support available to part-time students. Financial award application deadline: 8/1; financial award applicants required to submit FAFSA. *Unit head:* Dr. Bill Pierson, Chair, 304-696-2695, E-mail: pierson@marshall.edu. *Application contact:* Information Contact, 304-746-1900, Fax: 304-746-1902, E-mail: services@marshall.edu. Web site: http://www.marshall.edu/cite/.

Massachusetts Institute of Technology, School of Engineering, Engineering Systems Division, Cambridge, MA 02139. Offers engineering and management (SM); engineering systems (SM, PhD); logistics (M Eng); technology and policy (SM); technology, management and policy (PhD); SM/MBA. *Faculty:* 22 full-time (7 women). *Students:* 296 full-time (88 women); includes 36 minority (3 Black or African American, non-Hispanic/Latino; 22 Asian, non-Hispanic/Latino; 6 Hispanic/Latino; 5 Two or more races, non-Hispanic/Latino), 132 international. Average age 31. 909 applicants, 26% accepted, 181 enrolled. In 2011, 143 master's, 13 doctorates awarded. *Degree requirements:* For master's, thesis; for doctorate, comprehensive exam, thesis/dissertation. *Entrance requirements:* For master's, GRE General Test (or GMAT for some programs); for doctorate, GRE General Test. Additional exam requirements/recommendations for international students: Required—IELTS (minimum score 7.5). Application fee: $75. Electronic applications accepted. *Expenses:* Contact institution. *Financial support:* In 2011–12, 223 students received support, including 44 fellowships (averaging $30,600 per year), 96 research assistantships (averaging $29,000 per year), 16 teaching assistantships (averaging $29,800 per year); career-related internships or fieldwork, Federal Work-Study, institutionally sponsored loans, scholarships/grants, health care benefits, and unspecified assistantships also available. *Faculty research:* Critical infrastructures, extended enterprises, energy and sustainability, health care delivery, humans and technology, uncertainty and dynamics, design and implementation, networks and flows, policy and standards. *Total annual research expenditures:* $13.7 million. *Unit head:* Prof. Joseph M. Sussman, Interim Director, 617-253-1764, E-mail: esdinquiries@mit.edu. *Application contact:* Graduate Admissions, 617-253-1182, E-mail: esdgrad@mit.edu. Web site: http://esd.mit.edu/.

McNeese State University, Doré School of Graduate Studies, College of Engineering and Engineering Technology, Lake Charles, LA 70609. Offers chemical engineering (M Eng); civil engineering (M Eng); electrical engineering (M Eng); engineering management (M Eng); mechanical engineering (M Eng); pump reliability engineering (Postbaccalaureate Certificate). Part-time and evening/weekend programs available. *Faculty:* 13 full-time (1 woman). *Students:* 21 full-time (4 women), 18 part-time (5 women); includes 5 minority (4 Black or African American, non-Hispanic/Latino; 1 American Indian or Alaska Native, non-Hispanic/Latino), 23 international. In 2011, 28 master's awarded. *Degree requirements:* For master's, thesis or alternative. *Entrance requirements:* For master's, GRE, minimum undergraduate GPA of 3.0. Additional exam requirements/recommendations for international students: Required—TOEFL (minimum score 560 paper-based; 220 computer-based; 83 iBT). *Application deadline:* For fall admission, 5/15 priority date for domestic students, 5/15 for international students; for spring admission, 10/15 priority date for domestic students, 10/15 for international students. Applications are processed on a rolling basis. Application fee: $20 ($30 for international students). *Expenses:* Tuition, state resident: part-time $519 per credit hour. Tuition and fees vary according to course load. *Financial support:* Federal Work-Study available. Support available to part-time students. Financial award application deadline: 5/1. *Unit head:* Dr. Nikos Kiritsis, Dean, 337-475-5875, Fax: 337-475-5237, E-mail: nikosk@mcneese.edu. *Application contact:* Dr. George F. Mead, Jr., Interim Dean of Dore' School of Graduate Studies, 337-475-5396, Fax: 337-475-5397, E-mail: admissions@mcneese.edu.

Mercer University, Graduate Studies, Macon Campus, School of Engineering, Macon, GA 31207-0003. Offers biomedical engineering (MSE); computer engineering (MSE); electrical engineering (MSE); engineering management (MSE); environmental engineering (MSE); environmental systems (MS); mechanical engineering (MSE); software engineering (MSE); software systems (MS); technical communications management (MS); technical management (MS). Part-time and evening/weekend programs available. Postbaccalaureate distance learning degree programs offered (no on-campus study). *Faculty:* 17 full-time (3 women), 1 part-time/adjunct (0 women). *Students:* 12 full-time (3 women), 113 part-time (28 women); includes 23 minority (13 Black or African American, non-Hispanic/Latino; 9 Asian, non-Hispanic/Latino; 1 Hispanic/Latino). Average age 31. In 2011, 44 master's awarded. *Degree requirements:* For master's, thesis or alternative. *Entrance requirements:* For master's, minimum undergraduate GPA of 3.0. Additional exam requirements/recommendations for international students: Required—TOEFL. *Application deadline:* For fall admission, 7/1 for domestic students; for spring admission, 11/15 for domestic students. Applications are processed on a rolling basis. Application fee: $35 ($50 for international students). Electronic applications accepted. *Expenses:* Contact institution. *Financial support:* Federal Work-Study available. *Unit head:* Dr. Wade H. Shaw, Dean, 478-301-2459, Fax: 478-301-5593, E-mail: shaw_wh@mercer.edu. *Application contact:* Greg Lofton, Graduate Program Coordinator, 478-301-5480, Fax: 478-301-5434, E-mail: lofton_g@mercer.edu. Web site: http://engineering.mercer.edu/.

Milwaukee School of Engineering, Rader School of Business, Program in Engineering Management, Milwaukee, WI 53202-3109. Offers MS. Part-time and evening/weekend programs available. *Faculty:* 3 full-time (2 women), 6 part-time/adjunct (1 woman). *Students:* 5 full-time (1 woman), 69 part-time (11 women); includes 8 minority (2 Black or African American, non-Hispanic/Latino; 4 Asian, non-Hispanic/Latino; 2 Hispanic/Latino), 5 international. Average age 27. 38 applicants, 53% accepted, 14 enrolled. In 2011, 37 master's awarded. *Degree requirements:* For master's, thesis, thesis defense or capstone project. *Entrance requirements:* For master's, GRE General Test or GMAT, BS in engineering, science, management or related field, 2 letters of recommendation. Additional exam requirements/recommendations for international students: Required—TOEFL (minimum score 79 iBT) or IELTS. *Application deadline:* Applications are processed on a rolling basis. Application fee: $0. Electronic applications accepted. Application fee is waived when completed online. *Expenses: Tuition:* Full-time $17,550; part-time $650 per credit hour. *Financial support:* In 2011–12, 12 students received support, including 2 research assistantships (averaging $15,000 per year). Financial award applicants required to submit FAFSA. *Faculty research:* Operations, project management, quality marketing. *Unit head:* Dr. Kathy Faggiani, Director, 414-277-2711, Fax: 414-277-7279, E-mail: faggiani@msoe.com. *Application contact:* Katie Gassenhuber, Graduate Program Associate, 800-321-6763, Fax: 414-277-7208, E-mail: gassenhuber@msoe.edu.

Missouri University of Science and Technology, Graduate School, Department of Engineering Management and Systems Engineering, Rolla, MO 65409. Offers engineering management (MS, DE, PhD); manufacturing engineering (M Eng, MS); systems engineering (MS, PhD). *Degree requirements:* For master's, thesis optional; for doctorate, comprehensive exam. *Entrance requirements:* For master's, GRE (minimum score 1150 verbal and quantitative, 4.5 writing); for doctorate, GRE (minimum score: 1100 verbal and quantitative, 3.5 writing). Additional exam requirements/recommendations for international students: Required—TOEFL (minimum score 580 paper-based; 213 computer-based). *Faculty research:* Management of technology, industrial engineering, manufacturing engineering, packaging engineering, quality engineering.

National University, Academic Affairs, School of Engineering, Technology and Media, Department of Applied Engineering, La Jolla, CA 92037-1011. Offers engineering management (MS); environmental engineering (MS); homeland security and safety engineering (MS); project management (Certificate); security and safety engineering (Certificate); sustainability management (MS); wireless communications (MS). Part-time and evening/weekend programs available. Postbaccalaureate distance learning degree programs offered (no on-campus study). *Degree requirements:* For master's, thesis. *Entrance requirements:* For master's, interview, minimum GPA of 2.5. Additional exam requirements/recommendations for international students: Required—TOEFL (minimum score 550 paper-based; 213 computer-based; 79 iBT), IELTS (minimum score 6). *Application deadline:* Applications are processed on a rolling basis. Application fee: $60 ($65 for international students). Electronic applications accepted. *Financial support:* Career-related internships or fieldwork, institutionally sponsored loans, scholarships/grants, and tuition waivers (partial) available. Support available to part-time students. Financial award application deadline: 6/30; financial award applicants required to submit FAFSA. *Unit head:* Dr. Shekar Viswanathan, Chair and Associate Professor, 858-309-3416, Fax: 858-309-3420, E-mail: sviswana@nu.edu. *Application contact:* Dominick Giovanniello, Associate Regional Dean, 800-NAT-UNIV, Fax: 858-541-7792, E-mail: dgiovann@nu.edu. Web site: http://www.nu.edu/OurPrograms/SchoolOfEngineeringAndTechnology/AppliedEngineering.html.

Naval Postgraduate School, Departments and Academic Groups, Department of Systems Engineering, Monterey, CA 93943. Offers engineering systems (MS); product development (MS); systems engineering (MS, PhD, Certificate); systems engineering analysis (MS, PhD); systems engineering management (MS, PhD). Program only open to commissioned officers of the United States and friendly nations and selected United States federal civilian employees. Part-time programs available. *Faculty:* 32 full-time (6 women), 3 part-time/adjunct (2 women). *Students:* 399 full-time (63 women), 49 part-time (7 women); includes 109 minority (22 Black or African American, non-Hispanic/Latino; 47 Asian, non-Hispanic/Latino; 40 Hispanic/Latino), 4 international. Average age 42. In 2011, 162 master's awarded. *Degree requirements:* For master's, thesis (for some programs), internal project, capstone project, or research/dissertation paper (for some programs); for doctorate, thesis/dissertation (for some programs), internal project, capstone project, or research/dissertation paper (for some programs). *Faculty research:* Net-centric enterprise systems/services, artificial intelligence (AI) systems engineering, unconventional weapons of mass destruction, complex systems engineering, risk-benefit analysis. *Total annual research expenditures:* $7.6 million. *Unit head:* Dr. Philip Durkee, Dean, 831-656-2517, E-mail: durkee@nps.edu. Web site: http://www.nps.edu/Academics/Schools/GSEAS/Departments/SE/.

New Jersey Institute of Technology, Office of Graduate Studies, Newark College of Engineering, Department of Mechanical Engineering, Program in Engineering Management, Newark, NJ 07102. Offers MS. Part-time and evening/weekend programs available. *Students:* 57 full-time (14 women), 167 part-time (55 women); includes 75 minority (19 Black or African American, non-Hispanic/Latino; 20 Asian, non-Hispanic/Latino; 35 Hispanic/Latino; 1 Two or more races, non-Hispanic/Latino), 95 international. Average age 30. 241 applicants, 72% accepted, 96 enrolled. In 2011, 104 master's awarded. *Degree requirements:* For master's, thesis or alternative. *Entrance requirements:* For master's, GRE General Test. Additional exam requirements/recommendations for international students: Required—TOEFL (minimum score 550 paper-based; 213 computer-based; 79 iBT). *Application deadline:* For fall admission, 6/1 priority date for domestic students, 5/1 for international students; for spring admission, 11/15 priority date for domestic students, 11/15 for international students. Applications are processed on a rolling basis. Application fee: $65. Electronic applications accepted. *Expenses:* Tuition, state resident: full-time $7980; part-time $867 per credit. Tuition, nonresident: full-time $11,336; part-time $1196 per credit. *Required fees:* $230 per credit. *Financial support:* Fellowships with full and partial tuition reimbursements, research assistantships with full and partial tuition reimbursements, teaching assistantships with full and partial tuition reimbursements, career-related internships or fieldwork, Federal Work-Study, institutionally sponsored loans, and unspecified assistantships available. Financial award application deadline: 1/15. *Unit head:* Dr. Rajpal Sodhi, Interim Chair, 973-596-3362, E-mail: rajpal.s.sodhi@njit.edu. *Application contact:* Kathryn Kelly, Director of Admissions, 973-596-3300, Fax: 973-596-3461, E-mail: admissions@njit.edu.

New Mexico Institute of Mining and Technology, Graduate Studies, Department of Management, Socorro, NM 87801. Offers engineering management (MEM). Part-time programs available. *Faculty:* 4 full-time (1 woman), 4 part-time/adjunct (2 women). *Students:* 6 full-time (1 woman), 10 part-time (2 women); includes 7 minority (1 American Indian or Alaska Native, non-Hispanic/Latino; 1 Asian, non-Hispanic/Latino; 5 Hispanic/Latino). Average age 32. 9 applicants, 33% accepted, 3 enrolled. In 2011, 4 master's awarded. *Expenses:* Tuition, state resident: full-time $4849; part-time $269.41

per credit hour. Tuition, nonresident: full-time $16,041; part-time $891.15 per credit hour. *Required fees:* $622; $65 per credit hour. $20 per semester. Part-time tuition and fees vary according to course load. *Financial support:* In 2011–12, 1 research assistantship (averaging $20,218 per year) was awarded; teaching assistantships also available. *Unit head:* Dr. Peter Anselmo, Chair, 575-835-5438, E-mail: anselmo@nmt.edu. *Application contact:* Dr. Lorie Liebrock, Dean of Graduate Studies, 575-835-5513, Fax: 575-835-5476, E-mail: graduate@nmt.edu. Web site: http://management.nmt.edu/.

Northeastern University, College of Engineering, Department of Mechanical, Industrial, and Manufacturing Engineering, Boston, MA 02115-5096. Offers engineering management (MS); industrial engineering (MS, PhD); mechanical engineering (MS, PhD); operations research (MS). Part-time programs available. *Faculty:* 34 full-time, 7 part-time/adjunct. *Students:* 297 full-time (70 women), 103 part-time (20 women). 616 applicants, 77% accepted, 140 enrolled. In 2011, 107 master's, 5 doctorates awarded. *Degree requirements:* For master's, thesis (for some programs); for doctorate, thesis/dissertation, departmental qualifying exam. *Entrance requirements:* For master's and doctorate, GRE General Test. Additional exam requirements/recommendations for international students: Required—TOEFL (minimum score 550 paper-based; 213 computer-based; 80 iBT). *Application deadline:* For fall admission, 1/15 priority date for domestic students, 1/15 for international students; for spring admission, 11/1 priority date for domestic students. Applications are processed on a rolling basis. Application fee: $50. Electronic applications accepted. *Financial support:* In 2011–12, 79 students received support, including 50 research assistantships with full tuition reimbursements available (averaging $18,325 per year), 33 teaching assistantships with full tuition reimbursements available (averaging $18,325 per year); fellowships with full tuition reimbursements available, career-related internships or fieldwork, Federal Work-Study, scholarships/grants, health care benefits, and unspecified assistantships also available. Support available to part-time students. Financial award application deadline: 1/15; financial award applicants required to submit FAFSA. *Faculty research:* Dry sliding instabilities, droplet deposition, combustion, manufacturing systems, nano-manufacturing, advanced materials processing, bio-nano robotics, burning speed measurement, virtual environments. *Unit head:* Dr. Hameed Metghalchi, Chairman, 617-373-2973, Fax: 617-373-2921. *Application contact:* Jeffery Hengel, Admissions Specialist, 617-373-2711, Fax: 617-373-2501, E-mail: grad-eng@coe.neu.edu.

Northwestern University, McCormick School of Engineering and Applied Science, Department of Industrial Engineering and Management Sciences, Master's in Engineering Management Program, Evanston, IL 60208. Offers MEM. Part-time and evening/weekend programs available. *Faculty:* 9 full-time (0 women), 8 part-time/adjunct (1 woman). *Students:* 129 full-time (30 women), 44 part-time (12 women); includes 44 minority (8 Black or African American, non-Hispanic/Latino; 27 Asian, non-Hispanic/Latino; 9 Hispanic/Latino), 50 international. Average age 34. 299 applicants, 36% accepted, 79 enrolled. In 2011, 83 master's awarded. *Entrance requirements:* For master's, 3 years of work experience. Additional exam requirements/recommendations for international students: Required—TOEFL (minimum score 550 paper-based; 213 computer-based; 80 iBT), IELTS (minimum score 7). *Application deadline:* For fall admission, 8/15 priority date for domestic students, 7/1 for international students; for winter admission, 11/15 priority date for domestic students, 11/1 for international students; for spring admission, 2/15 priority date for domestic students, 2/1 for international students. Applications are processed on a rolling basis. Application fee: $50. Electronic applications accepted. *Expenses:* Contact institution. *Financial support:* Institutionally sponsored loans available. Financial award application deadline: 12/31; financial award applicants required to submit FAFSA. *Faculty research:* Supply chain and operations management, design and innovation, project and process management. *Unit head:* Dr. Bruce Ankenman, Director, 847-491-5674, Fax: 847-491-5980, E-mail: ankenman@northwestern.edu. *Application contact:* Susan Fox, Associate Director, 847-491-5584, Fax: 847-491-5980, E-mail: s-fox@northwestern.edu. Web site: http://www.mem.northwestern.edu/program/.

Northwestern University, McCormick School of Engineering and Applied Science, MMM Program, Evanston, IL 60208. Offers MBA/MEM. *Unit head:* Dr. Julio Ottino, Dean, 847-491-3558, Fax: 847-491-5220, E-mail: jm-ottino@northwestern.edu. *Application contact:* Dr. Bruce Alan Lindvall, Assistant Dean for Graduate Studies, 847-491-4547, Fax: 847-491-5341, E-mail: b-lindvall@northwestern.edu. Web site: http://www.mmm.northwestern.edu/.

Oakland University, Graduate Study and Lifelong Learning, School of Engineering and Computer Science, Department of Industrial and Systems Engineering, Program in Engineering Management, Rochester, MI 48309-4401. Offers MS. *Entrance requirements:* Additional exam requirements/recommendations for international students: Required—TOEFL (minimum score 550 paper-based; 213 computer-based). Electronic applications accepted. *Expenses:* Contact institution.

Old Dominion University, Frank Batten College of Engineering and Technology, Program in Engineering Management, Norfolk, VA 23529. Offers MEM, MS, PhD. Part-time and evening/weekend programs available. Postbaccalaureate distance learning degree programs offered (no on-campus study). *Faculty:* 14 full-time (3 women), 9 part-time/adjunct (1 woman). *Students:* 30 full-time (12 women), 307 part-time (59 women); includes 70 minority (40 Black or African American, non-Hispanic/Latino; 10 Asian, non-Hispanic/Latino; 14 Hispanic/Latino; 2 Native Hawaiian or other Pacific Islander, non-Hispanic/Latino; 4 Two or more races, non-Hispanic/Latino), 30 international. Average age 33. 176 applicants, 78% accepted, 107 enrolled. In 2011, 87 master's, 10 doctorates awarded. *Degree requirements:* For master's, comprehensive exam, thesis optional, project; for doctorate, thesis/dissertation, candidacy exam. *Entrance requirements:* For master's, GRE, minimum GPA of 3.0; for doctorate, GRE, resume, letters of recommendation, minimum GPA of 3.0. Additional exam requirements/recommendations for international students: Required—TOEFL (minimum score 550 paper-based; 213 computer-based; 79 iBT). *Application deadline:* For fall admission, 6/1 priority date for domestic students, 4/15 for international students; for spring admission, 11/1 priority date for domestic students, 2/1 for international students. Applications are processed on a rolling basis. Application fee: $50. Electronic applications accepted. *Expenses:* Tuition, state resident: full-time $9096; part-time $379 per credit. Tuition, nonresident: full-time $23,064; part-time $961 per credit. *Required fees:* $127 per semester. One-time fee: $50. *Financial support:* In 2011–12, research assistantships with full and partial tuition reimbursements (averaging $20,000 per year), teaching assistantships with full and partial tuition reimbursements (averaging $20,000 per year) were awarded; fellowships, career-related internships or fieldwork, scholarships/grants, and tuition waivers (partial) also available. Support available to part-time students. Financial award application deadline: 2/15; financial award applicants required to submit FAFSA. *Faculty research:* Project management, systems engineering, modeling and simulation, virtual collaborative environments, multidisciplinary designs. *Total annual research expenditures:* $3.2 million. *Unit head:* Dr. Resit Unal, Chair, 757-683-4558, Fax: 757-683-5640, E-mail: runal@odu.edu. *Application contact:* Dr. Ariel Pinto, Graduate Program Director, 757-683-4218, Fax: 757-683-5640, E-mail: enmagpd@odu.edu. Web site: http://eng.odu.edu/enma/.

Old Dominion University, Frank Batten College of Engineering and Technology, Program in Engineering Management and Systems Engineering, Norfolk, VA 23529. Offers D Eng. Part-time and evening/weekend programs available. Postbaccalaureate distance learning degree programs offered (no on-campus study). *Faculty:* 14 full-time (3 women), 9 part-time/adjunct (1 woman). *Students:* 4 full-time (1 woman), 11 part-time (2 women); includes 4 minority (1 Black or African American, non-Hispanic/Latino; 3 Hispanic/Latino). Average age 42. 3 applicants, 67% accepted, 2 enrolled. *Degree requirements:* For doctorate, thesis/dissertation, candidacy exam, project. *Entrance requirements:* For doctorate, GRE, resume, letters of recommendation, minimum GPA of 3.0, interview. Additional exam requirements/recommendations for international students: Required—TOEFL (minimum score 550 paper-based; 213 computer-based; 79 iBT). *Application deadline:* For fall admission, 6/1 priority date for domestic students, 4/15 for international students; for spring admission, 11/1 priority date for domestic students, 2/1 for international students. Applications are processed on a rolling basis. Application fee: $50. Electronic applications accepted. *Expenses:* Tuition, state resident: full-time $9096; part-time $379 per credit. Tuition, nonresident: full-time $23,064; part-time $961 per credit. *Required fees:* $127 per semester. One-time fee: $50. *Financial support:* In 2011–12, research assistantships with full and partial tuition reimbursements (averaging $20,000 per year), teaching assistantships with full and partial tuition reimbursements (averaging $20,000 per year) were awarded; fellowships, career-related internships or fieldwork, and tuition waivers also available. Support available to part-time students. Financial award application deadline: 2/15; financial award applicants required to submit FAFSA. *Faculty research:* Project management, systems engineering, modeling and simulation, virtual collaboration environments, multidisciplinary designs. *Total annual research expenditures:* $3.2 million. *Unit head:* Dr. Resit Unal, Department Chair, 757-683-4558, Fax: 757-683-5640, E-mail: enmagpd@odu.edu. *Application contact:* Dr. Ariel Pinto, Graduate Program Director, 757-683-4218, Fax: 757-683-5640, E-mail: enmagpd@odu.edu. Web site: http://eng.odu.edu/enma/.

Penn State Great Valley, Graduate Studies, Engineering Division, Malvern, PA 19355-1488. Offers engineering management (MEM); information science (MS); software engineering (MSE); systems engineering (M Eng). Postbaccalaureate distance learning degree programs offered (no on-campus study). *Unit head:* Dr. James A. Nemes, Interim Director, Academic Affairs, 610-648-3335 Ext. 610, Fax: 648-648-3377, E-mail: jan16@psu.edu. *Application contact:* 610-648-3242, Fax: 610-889-1334. Web site: http://www.sgps.psu.edu/Level3.aspx?id=662.

Penn State Harrisburg, Graduate School, School of Science, Engineering and Technology, Middletown, PA 17057-4898. Offers computer science (MS); electrical engineering (M Eng, MS); engineering management (MPS); engineering science (M Eng); environmental engineering (M Eng); environmental pollution control (MEPC, MS). Part-time and evening/weekend programs available. *Unit head:* Dr. Jerry F. Shoup, Interim Director, 717-948-6352, E-mail: jfs1@psu.edu. *Application contact:* Robert Coffman, Director of Admissions, 717-948-6250, Fax: 717-948-6325, E-mail: ric1@psu.edu. Web site: http://harrisburg.psu.edu/science-engineering-technology.

Point Park University, School of Arts and Sciences, Department of Natural Science and Engineering Technology, Pittsburgh, PA 15222-1984. Offers engineering management (MS); environmental studies (MS). Part-time and evening/weekend programs available. *Faculty:* 4 full-time, 4 part-time/adjunct. *Students:* 14 full-time (7 women), 19 part-time (6 women); includes 4 minority (2 Black or African American, non-Hispanic/Latino; 2 Two or more races, non-Hispanic/Latino), 6 international. Average age 35. 53 applicants, 60% accepted, 14 enrolled. In 2011, 15 master's awarded. *Degree requirements:* For master's, comprehensive exam (for some programs), thesis or alternative. *Entrance requirements:* For master's, minimum QPA of 2.75, 2 letters of recommendation, minimum B average in engineering technology or a related field, official undergraduate transcript, statement of intent, resume. Additional exam requirements/recommendations for international students: Required—TOEFL. *Application deadline:* Applications are processed on a rolling basis. Application fee: $30. Electronic applications accepted. *Expenses: Tuition:* Full-time $13,050; part-time $725 per credit. *Required fees:* $720; $40 per credit. *Financial support:* In 2011–12, 15 students received support, including 2 teaching assistantships with full tuition reimbursements available (averaging $6,400 per year); scholarships/grants also available. Financial award application deadline: 4/15; financial award applicants required to submit FAFSA. *Unit head:* Dr. Mark Farrell, Chair, 412-392-3879, Fax: 421-392-3962, E-mail: mfarrell@pointpark.edu. *Application contact:* Jennifer Sellman, Recruiter/Counselor, 412-392-4794, Fax: 412-392-6164, E-mail: jseelman@pointpark.edu.

Polytechnic University of Puerto Rico, Graduate School, Hato Rey, PR 00919. Offers business administration (MBA), including computer information systems, general management, management of information systems, management of international enterprises; civil engineering (ME, MS); computer engineering (ME, MS); computer science (MCS, MS); electrical engineering (ME, MS); engineering management (MEM); environmental management (MEM); landscape architecture (M Land Arch); manufacturing competitiveness (MMC, MS); manufacturing engineering (ME, MS); mechanical engineering (M Mech E). Part-time and evening/weekend programs available. *Entrance requirements:* For master's, 3 letters of recommendation.

Polytechnic University of Puerto Rico, Orlando Campus, Graduate School, Winter Park, FL 32792. Offers accounting (MBA); business administration (MBA); construction management (MEM); engineering management (MEM); environmental management (MEM); finance (MBA); human resources management (MBA); management of international enterprises (MBA); management of technology (MBA); manufacturing management (MEM). Part-time and evening/weekend programs available. Postbaccalaureate distance learning degree programs offered (no on-campus study). *Entrance requirements:* For master's, minimum GPA of 3.0. Additional exam requirements/recommendations for international students: Recommended—TOEFL. Electronic applications accepted.

Portland State University, Graduate Studies, Maseeh College of Engineering and Computer Science, Department of Civil and Environmental Engineering, Portland, OR 97207-0751. Offers civil and environmental engineering (M Eng, MS, PhD); civil and environmental engineering management (M Eng); environmental sciences and resources (PhD); systems science (PhD). Part-time and evening/weekend programs available. *Degree requirements:* For master's, thesis or alternative, oral exam; for doctorate, one foreign language, thesis/dissertation, oral and written exams. *Entrance requirements:* For master's, minimum GPA of 3.0 in upper-division course work, BS in civil engineering or allied field; for doctorate, GRE General Test, GRE Subject Test, minimum GPA of 3.0 in upper-division course work, master's in civil and environmental engineering, 2 years full-time graduate work beyond master's degree. Additional exam requirements/recommendations for international students: Required—TOEFL (minimum score 550 paper-based; 213 computer-based). *Faculty research:* Structures, water resources, geotechnical engineering, environmental engineering, transportation.

Portland State University, Graduate Studies, Maseeh College of Engineering and Computer Science, Department of Engineering and Technology Management, Portland, OR 97207-0751. Offers engineering and technology management (M Eng); engineering management (MS); manufacturing engineering (ME); manufacturing management (M Eng); systems science/engineering management (PhD); MS/MBA; MS/MS. Part-time and evening/weekend programs available. *Degree requirements:* For master's, thesis optional; for doctorate, one foreign language, thesis/dissertation, oral and written exams. *Entrance requirements:* For master's, minimum GPA of 3.0 in upper-division course work, BS in civil engineering; for doctorate, GRE General Test, GRE Subject Test, minimum GPA of 3.0 in upper-division course work. Additional exam requirements/recommendations for international students: Required—TOEFL (minimum score 550 paper-based; 213 computer-based). *Faculty research:* Scheduling, hierarchical decision modeling, operations research, knowledge-based information systems.

Portland State University, Graduate Studies, Systems Science Program, Portland, OR 97207-0751. Offers computational intelligence (Certificate); computer modeling and simulation (Certificate); systems science (MS); systems science/anthropology (PhD); systems science/business administration (PhD); systems science/civil engineering (PhD); systems science/economics (PhD); systems science/engineering management (PhD); systems science/general (PhD); systems science/mathematical sciences (PhD); systems science/mechanical engineering (PhD); systems science/psychology (PhD); systems science/sociology (PhD). *Degree requirements:* For doctorate, variable foreign language requirement, thesis/dissertation. *Entrance requirements:* For master's, 2 letters of recommendation; for doctorate, GMAT, GRE General Test, minimum undergraduate GPA of 3.0. Additional exam requirements/recommendations for international students: Required—TOEFL. *Faculty research:* Systems theory and methodology, artificial intelligence neural networks, information theory, nonlinear dynamics/chaos, modeling and simulation.

Rensselaer Polytechnic Institute, Graduate School, Lally School of Management and Technology, Troy, NY 12180-3590. Offers business (MBA); financial engineering and risk analysis (MS); management (MS, PhD); technology, commercialization, and entrepreneurship (MS). *Accreditation:* AACSB. Part-time and evening/weekend programs available. *Degree requirements:* For doctorate, thesis/dissertation. *Entrance requirements:* For master's, GMAT, 2 letters of recommendation, resume; for doctorate, GMAT or GRE General Test, 2 letters of recommendation. Additional exam requirements/recommendations for international students: Required—TOEFL (minimum score 600 paper-based; 250 computer-based; 100 iBT); Recommended—IELTS (minimum score 7). Electronic applications accepted. *Faculty research:* Technological entrepreneurship, operations management, new product development and marketing, finance and financial engineering and risk analytics, information systems.

Robert Morris University, Graduate Studies, School of Engineering, Mathematics and Science, Moon Township, PA 15108-1189. Offers engineering management (MS). Part-time and evening/weekend programs available. *Faculty:* 3 full-time (0 women). *Students:* 30 part-time (0 women); includes 2 minority (1 Black or African American, non-Hispanic/Latino; 1 American Indian or Alaska Native, non-Hispanic/Latino), 9 international. *Entrance requirements:* For master's, letters of recommendation. Additional exam requirements/recommendations for international students: Required—TOEFL (minimum score 550 paper-based; 213 computer-based; 79 iBT). *Application deadline:* For fall admission, 7/1 priority date for domestic students, 7/1 for international students; for spring admission, 11/1 priority date for domestic students, 11/1 for international students. Applications are processed on a rolling basis. Application fee: $35. Electronic applications accepted. *Expenses:* Contact institution. *Financial support:* Federal Work-Study, institutionally sponsored loans, and unspecified assistantships available. Financial award application deadline: 5/1; financial award applicants required to submit FAFSA. *Unit head:* Dr. Maria V. Kalevitch, Dean, 412-397-4020, Fax: 412-397-2472, E-mail: kalevitch@rmu.edu. *Application contact:* Deborah Roach, Assistant Dean, Graduate Admissions, 412-397-5200, Fax: 412-397-2425, E-mail: graduateadmissions@rmu.edu. Web site: http://www.rmu.edu/web/cms/schools/sems/.

Rochester Institute of Technology, Graduate Enrollment Services, Kate Gleason College of Engineering, Department of Industrial and Systems Engineering, Rochester, NY 14623-5603. Offers engineering management (ME); industrial engineering (ME, MS); manufacturing engineering (ME, MS); systems engineering (ME). Part-time programs available. *Students:* 58 full-time (13 women), 31 part-time (13 women); includes 3 minority (1 Black or African American, non-Hispanic/Latino; 1 Asian, non-Hispanic/Latino; 1 Hispanic/Latino), 59 international. Average age 25. 231 applicants, 44% accepted, 34 enrolled. In 2011, 49 degrees awarded. *Degree requirements:* For master's, internship. *Entrance requirements:* For master's, GRE, minimum GPA of 3.0. Additional exam requirements/recommendations for international students: Required—TOEFL (minimum score 570 paper-based; 230 computer-based; 88 iBT) or IELTS (minimum score 6.5). *Application deadline:* For fall admission, 2/15 priority date for domestic students, 2/15 for international students. Applications are processed on a rolling basis. Application fee: $50. *Expenses: Tuition:* Full-time $34,659; part-time $963 per credit hour. *Required fees:* $228; $76 per quarter. *Financial support:* Research assistantships with partial tuition reimbursements, teaching assistantships with partial tuition reimbursements, career-related internships or fieldwork, institutionally sponsored loans, scholarships/grants, tuition waivers (partial), and unspecified assistantships available. Support available to part-time students. Financial award applicants required to submit FAFSA. *Faculty research:* Operations; manufacturing systems and sustainable product design; product development and design robustness; lean manufacturing; ergonomics/human factors; simulation, systems engineering; rapid prototyping, rapid manufacturing. *Unit head:* Dr. Scott E. Grasman, Interim Department Head, 585-475-2598, E-mail: scott.grasman@rit.edu. *Application contact:* Diane Ellison, Assistant Vice President, Graduate Enrollment Services, 585-475-2229, Fax: 585-475-7164, E-mail: gradinfo@rit.edu.

Rochester Institute of Technology, Graduate Enrollment Services, Kate Gleason College of Engineering, Program in Product Development, Rochester, NY 14623-5603. Offers MS. Part-time and evening/weekend programs available. *Students:* 1 full-time (0 women), 43 part-time (2 women); includes 5 minority (1 Black or African American, non-Hispanic/Latino; 3 Asian, non-Hispanic/Latino; 1 Hispanic/Latino). Average age 38. 18 applicants, 89% accepted, 16 enrolled. In 2011, 12 degrees awarded. *Degree requirements:* For master's, capstone project. *Entrance requirements:* For master's, undergraduate degree in engineering or related field, minimum GPA of 3.0, 5 years experience in product development. Additional exam requirements/recommendations for international students: Required—TOEFL (minimum score 570 paper-based; 230 computer-based; 88 iBT) or IELTS (minimum score 6.5). *Application deadline:* For fall admission, 2/15 priority date for domestic students, 2/15 for international students. Application fee: $50. *Expenses:* Contact institution. *Financial support:* Applicants required to submit FAFSA. *Faculty research:* Platform element dynamics in a multi-product development environment, applying self-organizing principles to product development in a globally-distributed environment, collaborative design and development to accelerate durable goods design and manufacturing. *Unit head:* Christine Fisher, Graduate Program Director, 585-475-7971, Fax: 585-475-4080, E-mail: mpdmail@rit.edu. *Application contact:* Diane Ellison, Assistant Vice President, Graduate Enrollment Services, 585-475-2229, Fax: 585-475-7164, E-mail: gradinfo@rit.edu. Web site: http://www.rit.edu/kgcoe/mpd/.

Rose-Hulman Institute of Technology, Faculty of Engineering and Applied Sciences, Department of Engineering Management, Terre Haute, IN 47803-3999. Offers MS. Part-time and evening/weekend programs available. Postbaccalaureate distance learning degree programs offered (minimal on-campus study). *Faculty:* 3 full-time (0 women), 3 part-time/adjunct (1 woman). *Students:* 17 full-time (5 women), 19 part-time (5 women); includes 1 minority (Black or African American, non-Hispanic/Latino), 11 international. Average age 25. 25 applicants, 100% accepted, 20 enrolled. In 2011, 32 master's awarded. *Degree requirements:* For master's, integrated project. *Entrance requirements:* For master's, GRE, minimum GPA of 3.0. Additional exam requirements/recommendations for international students: Required—TOEFL (minimum score 580 paper-based; 237 computer-based; 92 iBT). *Application deadline:* For fall admission, 2/1 priority date for domestic students. Applications are processed on a rolling basis. Application fee: $0. *Expenses: Tuition:* Full-time $37,197; part-time $1085 per credit hour. *Financial support:* In 2011–12, 13 students received support. Fellowships with full and partial tuition reimbursements available available. *Faculty research:* Entrepreneurship, management of technology, manufacturing systems, project management, technology forecasting. *Unit head:* Dr. Craig Downing, Interim Chairman, 812-877-8822, Fax: 812-877-8878, E-mail: craig.downing@rose-hulman.edu. *Application contact:* Dr. Daniel J. Moore, Associate Dean of the Faculty, 812-877-8110, Fax: 812-877-8061, E-mail: daniel.j.moore@rose-hulman.edu. Web site: http://www.rose-hulman.edu/Class/EngMgmt/HTML/index.htm.

Rowan University, Graduate School, College of Engineering, Program in Engineering Management, Glassboro, NJ 08028-1701. Offers MEM. Part-time and evening/weekend programs available. *Degree requirements:* For master's, thesis. *Entrance requirements:* For master's, GRE General Test. Additional exam requirements/recommendations for international students: Required—TOEFL. Electronic applications accepted.

St. Cloud State University, School of Graduate Studies, College of Science and Engineering, Program in Engineering Management, St. Cloud, MN 56301-4498. Offers MEM. *Degree requirements:* For master's, thesis or alternative. *Entrance requirements:* For master's, GRE General Test, minimum GPA of 2.75. Additional exam requirements/recommendations for international students: Required—Michigan English Language Assessment Battery; Recommended—TOEFL (minimum score 550 paper-based; 213 computer-based), IELTS (minimum score 6.5). Electronic applications accepted.

Saint Martin's University, Graduate Programs, Program in Engineering Management, Lacey, WA 98503. Offers M Eng Mgt. Part-time and evening/weekend programs available. *Faculty:* 1 full-time (0 women), 1 part-time/adjunct (0 women). *Students:* 8 full-time (1 woman), 5 part-time (0 women), 4 international. Average age 30. 9 applicants, 89% accepted, 7 enrolled. In 2011, 4 master's awarded. *Degree requirements:* For master's, comprehensive exam (for some programs), thesis optional. *Entrance requirements:* For master's, minimum GPA of 2.8 or professional engineer license. Additional exam requirements/recommendations for international students: Required—TOEFL (minimum score 525 paper-based). *Application deadline:* For fall admission, 8/1 priority date for domestic students, 8/1 for international students; for spring admission, 12/1 priority date for domestic students, 12/1 for international students. Applications are processed on a rolling basis. Application fee: $35. *Expenses: Tuition:* Part-time $910 per credit hour. Tuition and fees vary according to course level, campus/location and program. *Financial support:* In 2011–12, 3 students received support. Fellowships, research assistantships, and Federal Work-Study available. Support available to part-time students. Financial award application deadline: 3/1; financial award applicants required to submit FAFSA. *Faculty research:* Highway safety management, transportation, hydraulics, database structure. *Unit head:* Bill Phillips, Director, 360-438-4320, Fax: 560-438-4522, E-mail: bphillips@stmartin.edu. *Application contact:* Hopie Lopez, Administrative Assistant, 360-438-4320, Fax: 360-438-4548, E-mail: hlopez@stmartin.edu. Web site: http://www.stmartin.edu/engineering/mem.

St. Mary's University, Graduate School, Department of Engineering, Program in Engineering Systems Management, San Antonio, TX 78228-8507. Offers MS. Part-time programs available. Postbaccalaureate distance learning degree programs offered (no on-campus study). *Degree requirements:* For master's, comprehensive exam. *Entrance requirements:* For master's, GRE or GMAT. Additional exam requirements/recommendations for international students: Required—TOEFL (minimum score 550 paper-based; 213 computer-based; 80 iBT). Electronic applications accepted.

St. Mary's University, Graduate School, Department of Engineering, Program in Industrial Engineering, San Antonio, TX 78228-8507. Offers engineering computer applications (MS); engineering management (MS); industrial engineering (MS); operations research (MS); JD/MS. Part-time programs available. *Degree requirements:* For master's, comprehensive exam. *Entrance requirements:* For master's, GRE General Test, BS in science or engineering, minimum GPA of 3.0. Additional exam requirements/recommendations for international students: Required—TOEFL (minimum score 550 paper-based; 213 computer-based; 80 iBT). Electronic applications accepted. *Faculty research:* Robotics, artificial intelligence, manufacturing engineering.

Santa Clara University, School of Engineering, Program in Engineering Management, Santa Clara, CA 95053. Offers MS. Part-time and evening/weekend programs available. *Students:* 54 full-time (15 women), 158 part-time (29 women); includes 83 minority (3 Black or African American, non-Hispanic/Latino; 66 Asian, non-Hispanic/Latino; 10 Hispanic/Latino; 2 Native Hawaiian or other Pacific Islander, non-Hispanic/Latino; 2 Two or more races, non-Hispanic/Latino), 69 international. Average age 30. 106 applicants, 53% accepted, 32 enrolled. In 2011, 113 degrees awarded. *Degree requirements:* For master's, thesis (for some programs). *Entrance requirements:* For master's, GRE, transcript. Additional exam requirements/recommendations for international students: Required—TOEFL (minimum score 550 paper-based; 213 computer-based; 79 iBT). *Application deadline:* For fall admission, 8/12 for domestic students, 7/15 for international students; for winter admission, 10/28 for domestic students, 9/23 for international students; for spring admission, 2/25 for domestic students, 1/21 for international students. Applications are processed on a rolling basis. Application fee: $60. Electronic applications accepted. *Expenses:* Contact institution. *Financial support:* Research assistantships and teaching assistantships available. Financial award application deadline: 3/2; financial award applicants required to submit FAFSA. *Unit head:* Dr. Alex Zecevic, Associate Dean for Graduate Studies, 408-554-2394, E-mail: azecevic@scu.edu. *Application contact:* Stacey Tinker, Director of Enrollment Management, 408-554-4748, Fax: 408-554-4323, E-mail: stinker@scu.edu.

South Dakota School of Mines and Technology, Graduate Division, Program in Engineering Management, Rapid City, SD 57701-3995. Offers MS. Program offered jointly with The University of South Dakota. Part-time programs available. *Entrance requirements:* For master's, GMAT. Additional exam requirements/recommendations for international students: Required—TOEFL, TWE. Electronic applications accepted.

Southern Methodist University, Bobby B. Lyle School of Engineering, Department of Engineering Management, Information, and Systems, Dallas, TX 75275. Offers applied science (MS); engineering management (MSEM, DE); information engineering and management (MSIEM); operations research (MS, PhD); systems engineering (MS, PhD). Part-time and evening/weekend programs available. Postbaccalaureate distance learning degree programs offered. Terminal master's awarded for partial completion of doctoral program. *Degree requirements:* For master's, thesis optional; for doctorate, thesis/dissertation, oral and written qualifying exams. *Entrance requirements:* For master's, minimum GPA of 3.0 in last 2 years; bachelor's degree in engineering, mathematics, sciences, or technical area; for doctorate, GRE General Test (operations research, engineering management), bachelor's degree in related field. Additional exam requirements/recommendations for international students: Required—TOEFL. *Faculty research:* Telecommunications, decision systems, information engineering, operations research, software.

Stanford University, School of Engineering, Department of Management Science and Engineering, Stanford, CA 94305-9991. Offers management science and engineering (MS, PhD). Terminal master's awarded for partial completion of doctoral program. *Degree requirements:* For doctorate, thesis/dissertation, qualification procedure. *Entrance requirements:* For master's and doctorate, GRE General Test. Additional exam requirements/recommendations for international students: Required—TOEFL. Electronic applications accepted. *Expenses: Tuition:* Full-time $40,050; part-time $890 per credit.

Stevens Institute of Technology, Graduate School, School of Systems and Enterprises, Program in Engineering Management, Hoboken, NJ 07030. Offers M Eng, PhD.

Stevens Institute of Technology, Graduate School, Wesley J. Howe School of Technology Management, Program in Business Administration, Hoboken, NJ 07030. Offers engineering management (MBA); financial engineering (MBA); information management (MBA); information technology in financial services (MBA); information technology in the pharmaceutical industry (MBA); information technology outsourcing (MBA); pharmaceutical management (MBA); project management (MBA); technology management (MBA); telecommunications management (MBA).

Syracuse University, L. C. Smith College of Engineering and Computer Science, Program in Engineering Management, Syracuse, NY 13244. Offers MS. Part-time and evening/weekend programs available. *Students:* 61 full-time (26 women), 17 part-time (1 woman); includes 2 minority (1 Asian, non-Hispanic/Latino; 1 Hispanic/Latino), 60 international. Average age 25. 134 applicants, 44% accepted, 28 enrolled. In 2011, 46 degrees awarded. *Entrance requirements:* Additional exam requirements/recommendations for international students: Required—TOEFL (minimum score 100 iBT). *Application deadline:* For fall admission, 7/1 priority date for domestic students, 6/1 for international students. Applications are processed on a rolling basis. Application fee: $75. Electronic applications accepted. *Expenses: Tuition:* Part-time $1206 per credit. *Financial support:* Fellowships with full tuition reimbursements, research assistantships with full and partial tuition reimbursements, teaching assistantships with full and partial tuition reimbursements, and tuition waivers (partial) available. Financial award application deadline: 1/1. *Unit head:* Fred Carranti, Program Director, 315-443-4346. *Application contact:* Kathy Datthyn-Madigan, Information Contact, 315-443-4367, E-mail: kjdatthy@syr.edu. Web site: http://lcs.syr.edu/.

Texas Tech University, Graduate School, Edward E. Whitacre Jr. College of Engineering, Department of Industrial Engineering, Lubbock, TX 79409. Offers industrial engineering (MSIE, PhD); systems and engineering management (MSSEM, PhD). Part-time programs available. Postbaccalaureate distance learning degree programs offered (minimal on-campus study). *Faculty:* 13 full-time (2 women), 2 part-time/adjunct (1 woman). *Students:* 66 full-time (13 women), 47 part-time (7 women); includes 12 minority (3 Black or African American, non-Hispanic/Latino; 1 Asian, non-Hispanic/Latino; 7 Hispanic/Latino; 1 Two or more races, non-Hispanic/Latino), 57 international. Average age 31. 201 applicants, 50% accepted, 22 enrolled. In 2011, 28 master's, 9 doctorates awarded. *Degree requirements:* For master's, thesis or alternative; for doctorate, thesis/dissertation. *Entrance requirements:* For master's, GRE General Test; for doctorate, GRE General Test, MS. Additional exam requirements/recommendations for international students: Required—TOEFL (minimum score 550 paper-based; 213 computer-based; 79 iBT). *Application deadline:* For fall admission, 6/1 priority date for domestic students, 1/15 for international students; for spring admission, 9/1 priority date for domestic students, 6/15 for international students. Applications are processed on a rolling basis. Application fee: $50 ($75 for international students). Electronic applications accepted. *Expenses: Tuition,* state resident: full-time $5899; part-time $245.80 per credit hour. Tuition, nonresident: full-time $13,411; part-time $558.80 per credit hour. *Required fees:* $2680.60; $86.50 per credit hour. $920.30 per semester. *Financial support:* In 2011–12, 32 students received support. Application deadline: 4/15; applicants required to submit FAFSA. *Faculty research:* Knowledge and engineering management, environmentally conscious manufacturing, biomechanical simulation, aviation security, supply chain management. *Total annual research expenditures:* $924,834. *Unit head:* Dr. Pat Patterson, Chair, 806-742-3543, Fax: 806-742-3411, E-mail: pat.patterson@ttu.edu. *Application contact:* Dr. Mario Beruvides, Professor, 806-742-3543, Fax: 806-742-3411, E-mail: mario.beruvides@ttu.edu. Web site: http://www.ie.ttu.edu/.

Tufts University, School of Engineering, Gordon Institute, Medford, MA 02155. Offers MSEM. Part-time programs available. *Faculty:* 9 part-time/adjunct. *Students:* 176 (39 women); includes 21 minority (3 Black or African American, non-Hispanic/Latino; 2 American Indian or Alaska Native, non-Hispanic/Latino; 12 Asian, non-Hispanic/Latino; 4 Hispanic/Latino), 9 international. 94 applicants, 74% accepted, 59 enrolled. In 2011, 29 master's awarded. *Entrance requirements:* Additional exam requirements/recommendations for international students: Required—TOEFL (minimum score 550 paper-based; 213 computer-based; 80 iBT). *Application deadline:* For fall admission, 3/15 priority date for domestic students. Applications are processed on a rolling basis. Application fee: $75. Electronic applications accepted. *Expenses:* Contact institution. *Faculty research:* Engineering management, engineering leadership. *Unit head:* Dr. Robert Hannemann, Director, 617-627-3111, Fax: 617-627-3180, E-mail: tgi@tufts.edu. *Application contact:* Information Contact, 617-628-5000, E-mail: tgi@tufts.edu. Web site: http://gordon.tufts.edu/.

Union Graduate College, School of Engineering and Computer Science, Schenectady, NY 12308-3107. Offers computer science (MS); electrical engineering (MS); engineering and management systems (MS); mechanical engineering (MS). Part-time and evening/weekend programs available. *Faculty:* 3 full-time (0 women), 20 part-time/adjunct (2 women). *Students:* 13 full-time (1 woman), 103 part-time (13 women); includes 15 minority (2 Black or African American, non-Hispanic/Latino; 6 Asian, non-Hispanic/

Latino; 6 Hispanic/Latino; 1 Two or more races, non-Hispanic/Latino), 3 international. Average age 28. 62 applicants, 69% accepted, 38 enrolled. In 2011, 29 master's awarded. *Degree requirements:* For master's, capstone course. *Entrance requirements:* For master's, minimum GPA of 3.0, letters of recommendation. Additional exam requirements/recommendations for international students: Required—TOEFL (minimum score 550 paper-based; 213 computer-based). *Application deadline:* Applications are processed on a rolling basis. Application fee: $60. Electronic applications accepted. *Expenses:* Contact institution. *Financial support:* In 2011–12, 2 students received support. Research assistantships, Federal Work-Study, scholarships/grants, health care benefits, and tuition waivers (full and partial) available. Support available to part-time students. Financial award applicants required to submit FAFSA. *Unit head:* Robert Kozik, Dean, 515-631-9881, Fax: 518-631-9902, E-mail: kozikr@union.edu. *Application contact:* Diane Trzaskos, Coordinator, Admissions, 518-631-9837, Fax: 518-631-9901, E-mail: trzaskod@uniongraduatecollege.edu.

Université de Sherbrooke, Faculty of Engineering, Programs in Engineering Management, Sherbrooke, QC J1K 2R1, Canada. Offers M Eng, Diploma. Part-time and evening/weekend programs available. *Entrance requirements:* For master's and Diploma, bachelor's degree in engineering, 1 year of practical experience. Electronic applications accepted.

The University of Akron, Graduate School, College of Engineering, Program in Engineering (Management Specialization), Akron, OH 44325. Offers MS. *Students:* 3 full-time (0 women), 10 part-time (2 women); includes 2 minority (both Asian, non-Hispanic/Latino), 2 international. Average age 27. 16 applicants, 56% accepted, 6 enrolled. In 2011, 3 master's awarded. *Degree requirements:* For master's, engineering report. *Entrance requirements:* For master's, GRE, minimum GPA of 2.75, two letters of recommendation, statement of purpose, resume. Additional exam requirements/recommendations for international students: Required—TOEFL (minimum score 550 paper-based; 213 computer-based; 79 iBT). *Application deadline:* Applications are processed on a rolling basis. Application fee: $30 ($40 for international students). Electronic applications accepted. *Expenses:* Tuition, state resident: full-time $7038; part-time $391 per credit hour. Tuition, nonresident: full-time $12,051; part-time $670 per credit hour. *Required fees:* $1274; $34 per credit hour. *Unit head:* Dr. Subramaniya Hariharan, Coordinator, 330-972-6580, E-mail: hari@uakron.edu. *Application contact:* Dr. Craig Menzemer, Associate Dean, 330-972-5536, E-mail: ccmenze@uakron.edu.

University of Alaska Anchorage, School of Engineering, Program in Engineering Management, Anchorage, AK 99508. Offers MS. Part-time and evening/weekend programs available. *Degree requirements:* For master's, comprehensive exam (for some programs), thesis optional. *Entrance requirements:* For master's, BS in engineering or science, work experience in engineering or science. Additional exam requirements/recommendations for international students: Required—TOEFL (minimum score 550 paper-based; 213 computer-based). *Faculty research:* Engineering economy, long-range forecasting, multicriteria design making, project management process and training.

University of Alaska Anchorage, School of Engineering, Program in Science Management, Anchorage, AK 99508. Offers MS. Part-time and evening/weekend programs available. *Degree requirements:* For master's, comprehensive exam (for some programs), thesis (for some programs). *Entrance requirements:* For master's, GRE General Test, BS in engineering or scientific field. Additional exam requirements/recommendations for international students: Required—TOEFL (minimum score 550 paper-based; 213 computer-based). *Faculty research:* Engineering economy, long-range forecasting, multicriteria decision making, project management process and training.

University of Alaska Fairbanks, College of Engineering and Mines, Department of Civil and Environmental Engineering, Engineering and Science Management Program, Fairbanks, AK 99775. Offers engineering management (MS, PhD); science management (MS). Part-time programs available. *Students:* 1 full-time (0 women), 1 part-time (0 women), 1 international. Average age 30. 3 applicants, 33% accepted, 0 enrolled. In 2011, 2 master's awarded. *Degree requirements:* For master's, comprehensive exam, thesis or alternative, oral exam; for doctorate, comprehensive exam, thesis/dissertation, oral exam, oral defense. *Entrance requirements:* For doctorate, GRE General Test. Additional exam requirements/recommendations for international students: Required—TOEFL (minimum score 550 paper-based; 213 computer-based; 80 iBT). *Application deadline:* For fall admission, 6/1 for domestic students, 3/1 for international students; for spring admission, 10/15 for domestic students, 9/1 for international students. Applications are processed on a rolling basis. Application fee: $60. Electronic applications accepted. *Expenses:* Tuition, state resident: full-time $6696; part-time $372 per credit. Tuition, nonresident: full-time $13,680; part-time $760 per credit. Tuition and fees vary according to course load and reciprocity agreements. *Financial support:* In 2011–12, 1 teaching assistantship (averaging $7,302 per year) was awarded; fellowships, research assistantships, career-related internships or fieldwork, Federal Work-Study, scholarships/grants, health care benefits, and unspecified assistantships also available. Support available to part-time students. Financial award application deadline: 7/1; financial award applicants required to submit FAFSA. *Faculty research:* Traffic studies, decision analysis, application of optimization, transportation safety. *Unit head:* Dr. Robert A. Perkins, Program Coordinator, 907-474-7694, Fax: 907-474-6087, E-mail: raperkins@alaska.edu. *Application contact:* Mike Earnest, Director of Admissions, 907-474-7500, Fax: 907-474-5379, E-mail: admissions@uaf.edu. Web site: http://cem.uaf.edu/cee/.

University of Alberta, Faculty of Graduate Studies and Research, Department of Mechanical Engineering, Edmonton, AB T6G 2E1, Canada. Offers engineering management (M Eng); mechanical engineering (M Eng, M Sc, PhD); MBA/M Eng. Part-time programs available. *Degree requirements:* For master's, thesis; for doctorate, thesis/dissertation. *Entrance requirements:* For master's and doctorate, minimum GPA of 7.0 on a 9.0 scale. Additional exam requirements/recommendations for international students: Required—TOEFL (minimum score 580 paper-based; 237 computer-based). *Faculty research:* Combustion and environmental issues, advanced materials, computational fluid dynamics, biomedical, acoustics and vibrations.

University of California, Berkeley, Graduate Division, College of Engineering, Department of Civil and Environmental Engineering, Berkeley, CA 94720-1500. Offers engineering and project management (M Eng, MS, D Eng, PhD); environmental engineering (M Eng, MS, D Eng, PhD); geoengineering (M Eng, MS, D Eng, PhD); structural engineering, mechanics and materials (M Eng, MS, D Eng, PhD); transportation engineering (M Eng, MS, D Eng, PhD); M Arch/MS; MCP/MS; MPP/MS. *Degree requirements:* For master's, comprehensive exam or thesis (MS); for doctorate, thesis/dissertation, qualifying exam. *Entrance requirements:* For master's, GRE General Test, minimum GPA of 3.0, 3 letters of recommendation; for doctorate, GRE General Test, minimum GPA of 3.5, 3 letters of recommendation. Additional exam requirements/recommendations for international students: Required—TOEFL (minimum score 570 paper-based; 230 computer-based). Electronic applications accepted.

University of Central Florida, College of Engineering and Computer Science, Department of Industrial Engineering and Management Systems, Orlando, FL 32816. Offers applied operations research (Certificate); design for usability (Certificate); engineering management (PSM); industrial engineering (MSIE, PhD); industrial engineering and management systems (MS); industrial ergonomics and safety (Certificate); project engineering (Certificate); quality assurance (Certificate); systems engineering (Certificate); systems simulation for engineers (Certificate); training simulation (Certificate). Part-time and evening/weekend programs available. *Faculty:* 18 full-time (4 women), 5 part-time/adjunct (1 woman). *Students:* 105 full-time (27 women), 151 part-time (47 women); includes 84 minority (20 Black or African American, non-Hispanic/Latino; 1 American Indian or Alaska Native, non-Hispanic/Latino; 20 Asian, non-Hispanic/Latino; 37 Hispanic/Latino; 1 Native Hawaiian or other Pacific Islander, non-Hispanic/Latino; 5 Two or more races, non-Hispanic/Latino), 52 international. Average age 32. 199 applicants, 79% accepted, 75 enrolled. In 2011, 83 master's, 11 doctorates, 40 other advanced degrees awarded. *Degree requirements:* For master's, thesis; for doctorate, thesis/dissertation, departmental qualifying exam, candidacy exam. *Entrance requirements:* For master's, GRE General Test, minimum GPA of 3.0 in last 60 hours of course work; for doctorate, minimum GPA of 3.5 in last 60 hours of course work. Additional exam requirements/recommendations for international students: Required—TOEFL. *Application deadline:* For fall admission, 7/15 priority date for domestic students; for spring admission, 12/1 priority date for domestic students. Application fee: $30. Electronic applications accepted. *Expenses:* Tuition, state resident: part-time $277.08 per credit hour. Tuition, nonresident: part-time $277.08 per credit hour. Part-time tuition and fees vary according to degree level and program. *Financial support:* In 2011–12, 19 students received support, including 8 fellowships with partial tuition reimbursements available (averaging $3,500 per year), 10 research assistantships with partial tuition reimbursements available (averaging $11,100 per year), 6 teaching assistantships with partial tuition reimbursements available (averaging $12,300 per year); career-related internships or fieldwork, Federal Work-Study, institutionally sponsored loans, tuition waivers (partial), and unspecified assistantships also available. Financial award application deadline: 3/1; financial award applicants required to submit FAFSA. *Unit head:* Dr. Waldemar Karwowski, Chair, 407-823-2204, E-mail: wkar@ucf.edu. *Application contact:* Barbara Rodriguez, Director, Admissions and Registration, 407-823-2766, Fax: 407-823-6442, E-mail: gradadmissions@ucf.edu. Web site: http://iems.ucf.edu/.

University of Colorado at Colorado Springs, College of Engineering and Applied Science, Department of Mechanical and Aerospace Engineering, Colorado Springs, CO 80933-7150. Offers engineering management (ME); information operations (ME); manufacturing (ME); mechanical engineering (MS); software engineering (ME); space operations (ME); space systems (MS). Part-time and evening/weekend programs available. *Faculty:* 11 full-time (2 women). *Students:* 48 full-time (14 women), 44 part-time (11 women); includes 15 minority (3 Black or African American, non-Hispanic/Latino; 6 Asian, non-Hispanic/Latino; 5 Hispanic/Latino; 1 Two or more races, non-Hispanic/Latino), 3 international. Average age 33. 40 applicants, 60% accepted, 13 enrolled. In 2011, 31 degrees awarded. *Degree requirements:* For master's, thesis optional. *Entrance requirements:* For master's, GRE General Test, bachelor's degree in engineering or related degree, minimum GPA of 3.0. Additional exam requirements/recommendations for international students: Required—TOEFL (minimum score 550 paper-based; 213 computer-based; 79 iBT). *Application deadline:* For fall admission, 3/1 for domestic and international students; for spring admission, 10/1 for domestic and international students. Applications are processed on a rolling basis. Application fee: $60 ($75 for international students). *Expenses:* Tuition, state resident: part-time $660 per credit hour. Tuition, nonresident: part-time $1133 per credit hour. Tuition and fees vary according to degree level, program and student level. *Financial support:* In 2011–12, 5 students received support. Federal Work-Study and scholarships/grants available. Support available to part-time students. Financial award application deadline: 3/1; financial award applicants required to submit FAFSA. *Faculty research:* Neural networks, artificial intelligence, robust control, space operations, space propulsion. *Total annual research expenditures:* $163,405. *Unit head:* Rebecca Webb, Director, 719-255-3581, Fax: 719-255-3674, E-mail: rwebb@uccs.edu. *Application contact:* Siew Nylund, Academic Adviser, 719-255-3243, Fax: 719-255-3589, E-mail: snylund@eas.uccs.edu. Web site: http://eas.uccs.edu/mae/.

University of Colorado Boulder, Graduate School, College of Engineering and Applied Science, Engineering Management Program, Boulder, CO 80309. Offers operations and logistics (ME); quality and process (ME); research and development (ME). *Students:* 46 full-time (11 women), 80 part-time (30 women); includes 22 minority (2 Black or African American, non-Hispanic/Latino; 1 American Indian or Alaska Native, non-Hispanic/Latino; 11 Asian, non-Hispanic/Latino; 7 Hispanic/Latino; 1 Two or more races, non-Hispanic/Latino), 12 international. Average age 34. 39 applicants, 74% accepted, 21 enrolled. In 2011, 32 master's awarded. *Entrance requirements:* For master's, minimum undergraduate GPA of 3.0. *Application deadline:* For fall admission, 2/15 for domestic students, 12/1 for international students; for spring admission, 8/15 for domestic students, 5/1 for international students. Application fee: $50 ($60 for international students). Electronic applications accepted. *Financial support:* In 2011–12, 5 students received support, including 2 fellowships (averaging $4,250 per year), 1 research assistantship with full and partial tuition reimbursement available (averaging $11,842 per year), 1 teaching assistantship with full and partial tuition reimbursement available (averaging $7,280 per year); institutionally sponsored loans, scholarships/grants, health care benefits, and unspecified assistantships also available. *Faculty research:* Quality and process, research and development, operations and logistics. *Total annual research expenditures:* $2,907. *Application contact:* E-mail: cuemp@colorado.edu. Web site: http://emp.colorado.edu.

University of Dayton, Department of Engineering Management and Systems, Dayton, OH 45469-1300. Offers engineering management (MSEM); management science (MSMS). Part-time and evening/weekend programs available. Postbaccalaureate distance learning degree programs offered (no on-campus study). *Faculty:* 4 full-time (0 women), 5 part-time/adjunct (0 women). *Students:* 66 full-time (15 women), 36 part-time (8 women); includes 15 minority (11 Black or African American, non-Hispanic/Latino; 2 Asian, non-Hispanic/Latino; 2 Hispanic/Latino), 25 international. Average age 31. 89 applicants, 56% accepted, 22 enrolled. In 2011, 37 master's awarded. *Degree requirements:* For master's, thesis, 7 core courses /5 electives (for MSEM); 4 core courses/8 electives (for MSMS). *Entrance requirements:* For master's, bachelor's degree. Additional exam requirements/recommendations for international students: Required—TOEFL (minimum score 550 paper-based; 213 computer-based; 80 iBT). *Application deadline:* For fall admission, 8/1 for domestic students, 3/1 for international students; for winter admission, 7/1 for international students; for spring admission, 1/1 for international students. Applications are processed on a rolling basis. Application fee: $0. Electronic applications accepted. *Expenses: Tuition:* Full-time $8400; part-time $700 per credit hour. *Required fees:* $25 per semester. Tuition and fees vary according to degree level. *Financial support:* Applicants required to submit FAFSA. *Faculty research:*

OPS research, simulation, reliability. *Total annual research expenditures:* $70,621. *Unit head:* Dr. Patrick Sweeney, Chair, 937-229-2238, E-mail: psweeney1@udayton.edu. *Application contact:* Dr. Patrick Sweeney, Chair, 937-229-2238, E-mail: psweeney1@udayton.edu.

University of Denver, School of Engineering and Computer Science, Department of Mechanical and Materials Engineering, Denver, CO 80208. Offers bioengineering (MS); engineering (MS, PhD); engineering/management (MS); interdisciplinary engineering (PhD); materials science (MS, PhD); mechanical engineering (MS, PhD); nanoscale science and engineering (MS, PhD). Part-time programs available. *Faculty:* 10 full-time (2 women), 1 part-time/adjunct (0 women). *Students:* 1 (woman) full-time, 25 part-time (5 women); includes 1 minority (Asian, non-Hispanic/Latino), 9 international. Average age 30. 69 applicants, 67% accepted, 11 enrolled. In 2011, 6 degrees awarded. Terminal master's awarded for partial completion of doctoral program. *Degree requirements:* For master's, thesis or alternative; for doctorate, comprehensive exam, thesis/dissertation. *Entrance requirements:* For master's, GRE General Test, essay/personal statement, three letters of recommendation; for doctorate, GRE General Test, essay/personal statement, three letters of recommendation, curriculum vitae. Additional exam requirements/recommendations for international students: Required—TOEFL (minimum score 550 paper-based; 80 iBT). *Application deadline:* Applications are processed on a rolling basis. Application fee: $60. Electronic applications accepted. *Financial support:* In 2011–12, 14 students received support, including 8 research assistantships with full and partial tuition reimbursements available (averaging $15,631 per year), 7 teaching assistantships with full and partial tuition reimbursements available (averaging $13,943 per year); Federal Work-Study, health care benefits, and unspecified assistantships also available. Financial award application deadline: 2/15; financial award applicants required to submit FAFSA. *Faculty research:* Aerosols, biomechanics, composite materials, photo optics, drug delivery. *Total annual research expenditures:* $818,288. *Unit head:* Dr. Matt Gordon, Chair, 303-871-3580, Fax: 303-871-4450, E-mail: matthew.gordon@du.edu. *Application contact:* Renee Carvalho, Assistant to the Chair, 303-871-2107, Fax: 303-871-4450, E-mail: renee.carvalho@du.edu. Web site: http://www.mme.du.edu/.

University of Detroit Mercy, College of Engineering and Science, Program in Engineering Management, Detroit, MI 48221. Offers M Eng Mgt. Evening/weekend programs available. *Degree requirements:* For master's, thesis or alternative.

University of Idaho, College of Graduate Studies, College of Engineering, Department of Civil Engineering, Program in Engineering Management, Moscow, ID 83844-2282. Offers M Engr. *Students:* 1 full-time, 33 part-time. Average age 35. In 2011, 14 master's awarded. *Application deadline:* Applications are processed on a rolling basis. Application fee: $60. Electronic applications accepted. *Expenses:* Tuition, state resident: full-time $3874; part-time $334 per credit hour. Tuition, nonresident: full-time $16,394; part-time $861 per credit hour. *Required fees:* $2808; $99 per credit hour. Tuition and fees vary according to program. *Financial support:* Applicants required to submit FAFSA. *Unit head:* Dr. Richard J. Nielsen, Department Chair. *Application contact:* Erick Larson, Director of Graduate Admissions, 208-885-4723, E-mail: gadms@uidaho.edu. Web site: http://www.uidaho.edu/engr/engineeringmanagement.

The University of Kansas, Graduate Studies, School of Engineering, Program in Engineering Management, Overland Park, KS 66213. Offers MS. Part-time and evening/weekend programs available. Postbaccalaureate distance learning degree programs offered (no on-campus study). *Faculty:* 3 full-time (1 woman), 10 part-time/adjunct (1 woman). *Students:* 7 full-time (2 women), 135 part-time (18 women); includes 25 minority (8 Black or African American, non-Hispanic/Latino; 12 Asian, non-Hispanic/Latino; 5 Hispanic/Latino), 24 international. Average age 34. 37 applicants, 76% accepted, 21 enrolled. In 2011, 29 master's awarded. *Degree requirements:* For master's, exam. *Entrance requirements:* For master's, minimum GPA of 3.0, 2 years of industrial experience. Additional exam requirements/recommendations for international students: Required—TOEFL (minimum score 600 paper-based; 250 computer-based; 100 iBT). *Application deadline:* Applications are processed on a rolling basis. Application fee: $55 ($65 for international students). Electronic applications accepted. Tuition and fees vary according to course load, campus/location, program and reciprocity agreements. *Faculty research:* Project management, systems analysis, high performance teams, manufacturing systems, strategic analysis. *Unit head:* Herbert R. Tuttle, Director, 913-897-8561, Fax: 913-897-8682, E-mail: emgt@ku.edu. *Application contact:* Parveen Mozaffar, Academic Services Coordinator, 913-897-8560, Fax: 913-897-8682, E-mail: emgt@ku.edu. Web site: http://emgt.ku.edu/.

University of Louisiana at Lafayette, College of Engineering, Department of Engineering and Technology Management, Lafayette, LA 70504. Offers MSET. Part-time and evening/weekend programs available. *Degree requirements:* For master's, comprehensive exam, thesis or alternative. *Entrance requirements:* For master's, GRE General Test, minimum GPA of 2.85. Additional exam requirements/recommendations for international students: Required—TOEFL (minimum score 550 paper-based; 213 computer-based). Electronic applications accepted. *Faculty research:* Mathematical programming, production management forecasting.

University of Louisville, J. B. Speed School of Engineering, Department of Industrial Engineering, Louisville, KY 40292-0001. Offers engineering management (M Eng); industrial engineering (M Eng, MS, PhD); logistics and distribution (Certificate). *Accreditation:* ABET (one or more programs are accredited). Part-time programs available. *Faculty:* 10 full-time (1 woman). *Students:* 42 full-time (13 women), 11 part-time (6 women); includes 5 minority (4 Black or African American, non-Hispanic/Latino; 1 Hispanic/Latino), 21 international. Average age 28. 52 applicants, 33% accepted, 11 enrolled. In 2011, 43 master's, 3 doctorates awarded. Terminal master's awarded for partial completion of doctoral program. *Degree requirements:* For master's, comprehensive exam (for some programs), thesis or alternative; for doctorate, comprehensive exam, thesis/dissertation, minimum GPA of 3.0. *Entrance requirements:* For master's and doctorate, GRE General Test. Additional exam requirements/recommendations for international students: Required—TOEFL (minimum score 550 paper-based; 213 computer-based; 80 iBT), IELTS (minimum score 6.5). *Application deadline:* For fall admission, 5/1 priority date for domestic students, 5/1 for international students; for spring admission, 11/1 priority date for domestic students, 11/1 for international students. Applications are processed on a rolling basis. Application fee: $50. Electronic applications accepted. *Expenses:* Tuition, state resident: full-time $9692; part-time $539 per credit hour. Tuition, nonresident: full-time $20,168; part-time $1121 per credit hour. Tuition and fees vary according to program and reciprocity agreements. *Financial support:* In 2011–12, 15 students received support, including 7 fellowships with full tuition reimbursements available (averaging $20,000 per year), 2 research assistantships with full tuition reimbursements available (averaging $20,000 per year), 6 teaching assistantships with full tuition reimbursements available (averaging $20,000 per year). Financial award application deadline: 1/25; financial award applicants required to submit FAFSA. *Faculty research:* Optimization, computer simulation, logistics and distribution, ergonomics and human factors, advanced manufacturing process. *Total annual research expenditures:* $748,000. *Unit head:* Dr. John S. Usher, Chair, 502-852-6342, Fax: 502-852-5633, E-mail: usher@louisville.edu. *Application contact:* Dr. Michael Day, Associate Dean, 502-852-6195, Fax: 502-852-7294, E-mail: day@louisville.edu. Web site: http://www.louisville.edu/speed/industrial/.

The University of Manchester, School of Mechanical, Aerospace and Civil Engineering, Manchester, United Kingdom. Offers advanced manufacturing technology (M Ent); aerospace engineering (M Phil, M Sc, PhD); civil engineering (M Phil, M Sc, PhD); environmental engineering (M Phil, PhD); management of projects (M Phil, M Sc, PhD); mechanical engineering (M Phil, M Sc, PhD); mechanical engineering design (M Ent); nuclear engineering (M Phil, D Eng, PhD).

University of Maryland, Baltimore County, Graduate School, Program in Engineering Management, Baltimore, MD 21250. Offers MS, Postbaccalaureate Certificate. Part-time programs available. *Students:* 15 full-time (5 women), 67 part-time (17 women); includes 27 minority (17 Black or African American, non-Hispanic/Latino; 1 American Indian or Alaska Native, non-Hispanic/Latino; 5 Asian, non-Hispanic/Latino; 3 Hispanic/Latino; 1 Two or more races, non-Hispanic/Latino), 11 international. Average age 32. 63 applicants, 84% accepted, 23 enrolled. In 2011, 28 master's, 17 other advanced degrees awarded. *Degree requirements:* For master's, comprehensive exam (for some programs), thesis optional. *Entrance requirements:* For master's, BS in engineering or information technology with minimum GPA of 3.0. Additional exam requirements/recommendations for international students: Required—TOEFL (minimum score 550 paper-based; 213 computer-based; 80 iBT). *Application deadline:* For fall admission, 7/1 for domestic and international students; for spring admission, 12/1 for domestic and international students. Applications are processed on a rolling basis. Application fee: $70. Electronic applications accepted. *Financial support:* Career-related internships or fieldwork, Federal Work-Study, scholarships/grants, health care benefits, and unspecified assistantships available. Support available to part-time students. Financial award application deadline: 6/30; financial award applicants required to submit FAFSA. *Faculty research:* Regulatory engineering, environmental engineering, systems engineering, advanced manufacturing, chemical engineering. *Unit head:* Dr. Gary Carter, Professor and Chair, 410-455-3500, Fax: 410-455-3969, E-mail: carter@cs.umbc.edu. *Application contact:* Dr. Ted M. Foster, Professor of Practice/Assistant Dean/Director, 410-455-1564, Fax: 410-455-3559, E-mail: tfoster@umbc.edu.

University of Massachusetts Amherst, Graduate School, Interdisciplinary Programs, Dual Degree Program in Business Administration and Industrial Engineering, Amherst, MA 01003. Offers MBA/MSIE. Part-time programs available. *Entrance requirements:* Additional exam requirements/recommendations for international students: Required—TOEFL (minimum score 600 paper-based; 250 computer-based; 100 iBT), IELTS (minimum score 7). *Application deadline:* For fall admission, 1/15 for domestic and international students. Applications are processed on a rolling basis. Application fee: $50 ($65 for international students). Electronic applications accepted. Tuition and fees vary according to course load, campus/location and program. *Financial support:* Career-related internships or fieldwork, Federal Work-Study, scholarships/grants, traineeships, health care benefits, tuition waivers (full), and unspecified assistantships available. Support available to part-time students. *Unit head:* Dr. David P. Schmidt, Graduate Program Director, 413-545-3827, Fax: 413-545-1027. *Application contact:* Lindsay DeSantis, Interim Supervisor of Admissions, 413-545-0722, Fax: 413-577-0010, E-mail: gradadm@grad.umass.edu. Web site: http://www-new.ecs.umass.edu/degrees#MBA.

University of Massachusetts Amherst, Graduate School, Interdisciplinary Programs, Dual Degree Program in Business Administration and Mechanical Engineering, Amherst, MA 01003. Offers MSME/MBA. Part-time programs available. *Students:* 1 full-time (0 women); minority (Two or more races, non-Hispanic/Latino). Average age 26. 1 applicant, 0% accepted, 0 enrolled. *Entrance requirements:* Additional exam requirements/recommendations for international students: Required—TOEFL (minimum score 600 paper-based; 250 computer-based; 100 iBT), IELTS (minimum score 7). *Application deadline:* For fall admission, 1/15 for domestic and international students. Applications are processed on a rolling basis. Application fee: $50 ($65 for international students). Electronic applications accepted. Tuition and fees vary according to course load, campus/location and program. *Financial support:* Career-related internships or fieldwork, Federal Work-Study, scholarships/grants, traineeships, health care benefits, tuition waivers (full), and unspecified assistantships available. Support available to part-time students. *Unit head:* Dr. David P. Schmidt, Graduate Program Director, 413-545-3827, Fax: 413-545-1027. *Application contact:* Lindsay DeSantis, Interim Supervisor of Admissions, 413-545-0722, Fax: 413-577-0010, E-mail: gradadm@grad.umass.edu. Web site: http://www-new.ecs.umass.edu/degrees#MBA.

University of Minnesota, Duluth, Graduate School, Swenson College of Science and Engineering, Department of Mechanical and Industrial Engineering, Duluth, MN 55812-2496. Offers engineering management (MSEM); environmental health and safety (MEHS). Part-time and evening/weekend programs available. Postbaccalaureate distance learning degree programs offered (no on-campus study). *Degree requirements:* For master's, comprehensive exam, thesis or alternative, capstone design project (MSEM), field project (MEHS). *Entrance requirements:* For master's, GRE (MEHS), interview (MEHS), letters of recommendation. Additional exam requirements/recommendations for international students: Required—TOEFL (minimum score 550 paper-based; 213 computer-based). *Faculty research:* Transportation, ergonomics, toxicology, supply chain management, automation and robotics.

University of Nebraska–Lincoln, Graduate College, College of Engineering, Department of Industrial and Management Systems Engineering, Lincoln, NE 68588. Offers engineering management (M Eng); industrial and management systems engineering (MS, PhD); manufacturing systems engineering (MS). Postbaccalaureate distance learning degree programs offered. *Degree requirements:* For master's, thesis optional; for doctorate, comprehensive exam, thesis/dissertation. *Entrance requirements:* For master's and doctorate, GRE. Additional exam requirements/recommendations for international students: Required—TOEFL (minimum score 525 paper-based; 195 computer-based). Electronic applications accepted. *Faculty research:* Ergonomics, occupational safety, quality control, industrial packaging, facility design.

University of New Brunswick Fredericton, School of Graduate Studies, Faculty of Business Administration, Fredericton, NB E3B 5A3, Canada. Offers business administration (MBA); engineering management (MBA); entrepreneurship (MBA); sports and recreation management (MBA); MBA/LL B. Part-time programs available. *Faculty:* 23 full-time (3 women), 5 part-time/adjunct (2 women). *Students:* 50 full-time (10 women), 27 part-time (12 women). In 2011, 46 master's awarded. *Degree requirements:* For master's, thesis optional. *Entrance requirements:* For master's, GMAT (minimum score 550), minimum GPA of 3.0; 3-5 years work experience. Additional exam requirements/recommendations for international students: Required—TOEFL (minimum score 580 paper-based; 92 iBT) or IELTS (minimum score 7). *Application deadline:* For fall admission, 3/1 priority date for domestic students. Applications are processed on a rolling basis. Application fee: $50 Canadian dollars. *Financial support:* In 2011–12, 7

fellowships, 1 research assistantship (averaging $4,500 per year), 17 teaching assistantships (averaging $2,250 per year) were awarded. *Faculty research:* Accounting and auditing practices, human resource management, the non-profit sector, marketing, strategic management, entrepreneurship, investment practices, supply chain management, operations management. *Unit head:* Judy Roy, Director of Graduate Studies, 506-458-7307, Fax: 506-453-3561, E-mail: jroy@unb.ca. *Application contact:* Marilyn Davis, Acting Graduate Secretary, 506-453-4766, Fax: 506-453-3561, E-mail: mbacontact@unb.ca. Web site: http://www.business.unbf.ca.

University of New Haven, Graduate School, Tagliatela College of Engineering, Program in Engineering and Operations Management, West Haven, CT 06516-1916. Offers MS. *Students:* 3 full-time (1 woman), 38 part-time (4 women); includes 6 minority (3 Black or African American, non-Hispanic/Latino; 3 Asian, non-Hispanic/Latino), 3 international. 30 applicants, 97% accepted, 14 enrolled. *Entrance requirements:* For master's, five or more years' experience in a supervisory role in engineering, technical staff support, engineering or systems management, project management, systems engineering, manufacturing, logistics, industrial engineering, military operations, or quality assurance. Additional exam requirements/recommendations for international students: Required—TOEFL (minimum score 520 paper-based; 190 computer-based; 70 iBT); Recommended—IELTS (minimum score 5.5). *Application deadline:* For fall admission, 5/31 for international students; for winter admission, 10/15 for international students; for spring admission, 1/15 for international students. Application fee: $50. *Expenses:* Tuition: Part-time $750 per credit. *Unit head:* Dr. John Sarris, Chair, 203-932-7146. *Application contact:* Eloise Gormley, Director of Graduate Admissions, 203-932-7449, Fax: 203-932-7137, E-mail: gradinfo@newhaven.edu. Web site: http://www.newhaven.edu/88389/.

University of New Orleans, Graduate School, College of Engineering, Program in Engineering Management, New Orleans, LA 70148. Offers MS, Certificate. *Degree requirements:* For master's, thesis optional. *Entrance requirements:* For master's, GRE General Test, minimum GPA of 3.0. Additional exam requirements/recommendations for international students: Required—TOEFL (minimum score 550 paper-based; 213 computer-based; 79 iBT). Electronic applications accepted.

University of Oklahoma, College of Engineering, School of Industrial Engineering, Norman, OK 73019. Offers industrial engineering (MS, PhD), including engineering management (MS), general (MS). Part-time programs available. *Faculty:* 14 full-time (4 women). *Students:* 40 full-time (15 women), 31 part-time (10 women); includes 13 minority (4 Black or African American, non-Hispanic/Latino; 1 American Indian or Alaska Native, non-Hispanic/Latino; 3 Asian, non-Hispanic/Latino; 2 Hispanic/Latino; 3 Two or more races, non-Hispanic/Latino), 32 international. Average age 30. 88 applicants, 76% accepted, 31 enrolled. In 2011, 20 master's, 3 doctorates awarded. *Degree requirements:* For master's, comprehensive exam, thesis (for some programs); for doctorate, thesis/dissertation, qualifying exam. *Entrance requirements:* For master's and doctorate, GRE, minimum GPA of 3.0, 3 letters of reference, resume or curriculum vitae. Additional exam requirements/recommendations for international students: Required—TOEFL (minimum score 550 paper-based; 79 iBT). *Application deadline:* For fall admission, 6/1 priority date for domestic students, 3/1 for international students; for spring admission, 11/1 for domestic students, 9/1 for international students. Applications are processed on a rolling basis. Application fee: $40 ($90 for international students). Electronic applications accepted. *Expenses:* Tuition, state resident: full-time $4087; part-time $170.30 per credit hour. Tuition, nonresident: full-time $14,875; part-time $619.80 per credit hour. *Required fees:* $2659; $100.25 per credit hour. Tuition and fees vary according to course load and degree level. *Financial support:* In 2011–12, 44 students received support, including 18 research assistantships with partial tuition reimbursements available (averaging $13,795 per year), 4 teaching assistantships with partial tuition reimbursements available (averaging $11,335 per year); scholarships/grants and unspecified assistantships also available. Financial award applicants required to submit FAFSA. *Faculty research:* Computational optimization, logistics and supply chain management, human factors, design and manufacturing, systems modeling, engineering education. *Total annual research expenditures:* $2.1 million. *Unit head:* Dr. Randa Shehab, Director, 405-325-3721, Fax: 405-325-7555, E-mail: rlshehab@ou.edu. *Application contact:* Amy J. Piper, Student Services Coordinator, 405-325-3721, Fax: 405-325-7555, E-mail: ajpiper@ou.edu. Web site: http://www.ou.edu/coe/ie.

University of Ottawa, Faculty of Graduate and Postdoctoral Studies, Faculty of Engineering, Engineering Management Program, Ottawa, ON K1N 6N5, Canada. Offers engineering management (M Eng); information technology (Certificate); project management (Certificate). *Degree requirements:* For master's, thesis or alternative. *Entrance requirements:* For master's and Certificate, honors degree or equivalent, minimum B average. Electronic applications accepted.

University of St. Thomas, Graduate Studies, School of Engineering, St. Paul, MN 55105-1096. Offers manufacturing engineering and operations (MS); mechanical engineering (MS); medical device development (Certificate); regulatory science (MS); software engineering (MS); software management (MS); software systems (MSS); systems engineering (MS); technology management (MS). *Accreditation:* ABET (one or more programs are accredited). *Students:* 8 full-time, 210 part-time (38 women); includes 47 minority (22 Black or African American, non-Hispanic/Latino; 4 Asian, non-Hispanic/Latino; 6 Hispanic/Latino; 1 Native Hawaiian or other Pacific Islander, non-Hispanic/Latino; 14 Two or more races, non-Hispanic/Latino), 14 international. Average age 33. *Entrance requirements:* For master's, resume, official transcripts. Additional exam requirements/recommendations for international students: Required—TOEFL (minimum score 550 paper-based). *Application deadline:* For fall admission, 8/1 priority date for domestic students; for spring admission, 1/1 priority date for domestic students. Applications are processed on a rolling basis. Application fee: $30. Electronic applications accepted. *Expenses:* Contact institution. *Financial support:* Fellowships, research assistantships, institutionally sponsored loans, and scholarships/grants available. Support available to part-time students. Financial award application deadline: 4/1; financial award applicants required to submit FAFSA. *Unit head:* Don Weinkauf, Dean, 651-962-5760, Fax: 651-962-6419, E-mail: dhweinkauf@stthomas.edu. *Application contact:* Joyce A. Taylor, Graduate Programs Coordinator, 651-962-5756, Fax: 651-962-6419, E-mail: jataylor1@stthomas.edu.

University of Southern California, Graduate School, Viterbi School of Engineering, Daniel J. Epstein Department of Industrial and Systems Engineering, Los Angeles, CA 90089. Offers digital supply chain management (MS); engineering management (MS); engineering technology communication (Graduate Certificate); health systems operations (Graduate Certificate); industrial and systems engineering (MS, PhD, Engr); manufacturing engineering (MS); operations research engineering (MS); optimization and supply chain management (Graduate Certificate); product development engineering (MS); safety systems and security (MS); systems architecting and engineering (MS, Graduate Certificate); systems safety and security (Graduate Certificate); transportation systems (Graduate Certificate); MS/MBA. Part-time and evening/weekend programs available. Postbaccalaureate distance learning degree programs offered (no on-campus study). Terminal master's awarded for partial completion of doctoral program. *Degree requirements:* For master's, thesis optional; for doctorate, thesis/dissertation. *Entrance requirements:* For master's and doctorate, GRE General Test. Additional exam requirements/recommendations for international students: Recommended—TOEFL. Electronic applications accepted. *Faculty research:* Health systems, music cognition and retrieval, transportation and logistics, manufacturing and automation, engineering systems design, risk and economic analysis.

University of Southern California, Graduate School, Viterbi School of Engineering, Department of Aerospace and Mechanical Engineering, Los Angeles, CA 90089. Offers aerospace and mechanical engineering: computational fluid and solid mechanics (MS); aerospace and mechanical engineering: dynamics and control (MS); aerospace engineering (MS, PhD, Engr), including aerospace engineering (PhD, Engr); green technologies (MS); mechanical engineering (MS, PhD, Engr), including mechanical engineering (PhD, Engr); product development engineering (MS). Part-time and evening/weekend programs available. Postbaccalaureate distance learning degree programs offered (no on-campus study). Terminal master's awarded for partial completion of doctoral program. *Degree requirements:* For master's, thesis optional; for doctorate, thesis/dissertation. *Entrance requirements:* For master's, doctorate, and Engr, GRE General Test. Additional exam requirements/recommendations for international students: Recommended—TOEFL. Electronic applications accepted. *Faculty research:* Mechanics and materials, aerodynamics of air/ground vehicles, gas dynamics, aerosols, astronautics and space science, geophysical and microgravity flows, planetary physics, power MEMs and MEMS vacuum pumps, heat transfer and combustion.

University of South Florida, Graduate School, College of Engineering, Department of Industrial and Management Systems Engineering, Tampa, FL 33620-9951. Offers engineering management (MSEM, MSIE); engineering science (PhD); industrial engineering (MIE, MSIE, PhD). Part-time programs available. Postbaccalaureate distance learning degree programs offered (minimal on-campus study). *Faculty:* 11 full-time (3 women), 10 part-time/adjunct (2 women). *Students:* 61 full-time (14 women), 64 part-time (18 women); includes 32 minority (5 Black or African American, non-Hispanic/Latino; 2 Asian, non-Hispanic/Latino; 24 Hispanic/Latino; 1 Two or more races, non-Hispanic/Latino), 40 international. Average age 31. 124 applicants, 44% accepted, 20 enrolled. In 2011, 46 master's, 4 doctorates awarded. Terminal master's awarded for partial completion of doctoral program. *Degree requirements:* For master's, comprehensive exam, thesis (for some programs); for doctorate, comprehensive exam, thesis/dissertation, 2 tools of research as specified by dissertation committee. *Entrance requirements:* For master's, GRE, minimum GPA of 3.0 in last 60 hours of coursework, three letters of recommendation; one letter of recommendation, BS in engineering, and resume (for MSEM in engineering management); for doctorate, GRE, minimum GPA of 3.0 in last 60 hours of coursework, three letters of recommendation, statement of purpose. Additional exam requirements/recommendations for international students: Required—TOEFL (minimum score 550 paper-based; 213 computer-based; 79 iBT) or IELTS (minimum score 6.5). *Application deadline:* For fall admission, 2/15 for domestic students, 1/2 for international students; for spring admission, 10/15 for domestic students, 6/1 for international students. Application fee: $30. Electronic applications accepted. *Financial support:* In 2011–12, 31 students received support, including 20 research assistantships with partial tuition reimbursements available (averaging $16,748 per year), 11 teaching assistantships with partial tuition reimbursements available (averaging $15,000 per year); tuition waivers (partial) also available. Financial award applicants required to submit FAFSA. *Faculty research:* Bio-health engineering, engineering health care systems, energy markets, nanotechnology and nanomanufacturing, transportation and logistics, innovation in education. *Total annual research expenditures:* $501,470. *Unit head:* Dr. Jose Zayas-Castro, Chair, 813-974-2269, Fax: 813-974-5953, E-mail: josezaya@usf.edu. *Application contact:* Dr. Ali Yalcin, Program Coordinator, 813-974-5590, Fax: 813-974-5953, E-mail: ayalcin@usf.edu. Web site: http://imse.eng.usf.edu.

The University of Tennessee, Graduate School, College of Engineering, Department of Industrial and Information Engineering, Knoxville, TN 37966. Offers engineering management (MS); industrial engineering (MS, PhD); reliability and maintainability engineering (MS); MS/MBA. Part-time programs available. Postbaccalaureate distance learning degree programs offered (minimal on-campus study). *Faculty:* 7 full-time (1 woman), 14 part-time/adjunct (1 woman). *Students:* 51 full-time (11 women), 64 part-time (21 women); includes 21 minority (11 Black or African American, non-Hispanic/Latino; 1 American Indian or Alaska Native, non-Hispanic/Latino; 7 Asian, non-Hispanic/Latino; 1 Hispanic/Latino; 1 Native Hawaiian or other Pacific Islander, non-Hispanic/Latino), 27 international. Average age 28. 119 applicants, 50% accepted, 47 enrolled. In 2011, 13 master's, 4 doctorates awarded. *Degree requirements:* For master's, thesis or alternative; for doctorate, comprehensive exam, thesis/dissertation. *Entrance requirements:* For master's, GRE General Test (for MS students pursuing research thesis), minimum GPA of 2.7 (for U.S. degree holders), 3.0 (for international degree holders); for doctorate, College requires GRE General Test for all PhD candidates, minimum GPA of 3.0 on previous graduate course work. Additional exam requirements/recommendations for international students: Required—TOEFL (minimum score 550 paper-based; 213 computer-based). *Application deadline:* For fall admission, 2/1 priority date for domestic students, 2/1 for international students; for spring admission, 6/15 for domestic and international students. Applications are processed on a rolling basis. Application fee: $35. Electronic applications accepted. *Expenses:* Tuition, state resident: full-time $8332; part-time $464 per credit hour. Tuition, nonresident: full-time $25,174; part-time $1400 per credit hour. *Required fees:* $1162; $56 per credit hour. Tuition and fees vary according to program. *Financial support:* In 2011–12, 27 students received support, including 13 research assistantships with full tuition reimbursements available (averaging $17,355 per year), 10 teaching assistantships with full tuition reimbursements available (averaging $16,985 per year); career-related internships or fieldwork, Federal Work-Study, institutionally sponsored loans, health care benefits, and unspecified assistantships also available. Financial award application deadline: 2/1; financial award applicants required to submit FAFSA. *Faculty research:* Defense-oriented supply chain modeling; dependability and reliability of large computer networks; design of lean, reliable systems; new product development; operations research in the automotive industry. *Total annual research expenditures:* $800,000. *Unit head:* Dr. Rapinder Sawhney, Department Head, 865-974-3333, Fax: 865-974-0588, E-mail: sawhney@utk.edu. *Application contact:* Dr. Denise Jackson, Graduate Representative, 865-946-3248, E-mail: djackson@utk.edu. Web site: http://www.engr.utk.edu/ie/.

The University of Tennessee at Chattanooga, Graduate School, College of Engineering and Computer Science, Program in Engineering Management, Chattanooga, TN 37403. Offers engineering management (MS); fundamentals of engineering management (Graduate Certificate); power systems management (Graduate Certificate); project and value management (Graduate Certificate); quality management (Graduate Certificate). Postbaccalaureate distance learning degree programs offered (no on-campus study). *Faculty:* 5 full-time (1 woman), 2 part-time/adjunct (1 woman). *Students:* 14 full-time (2 women), 72 part-time (14 women); includes 17 minority (13 Black or African American, non-Hispanic/Latino; 2 Asian, non-Hispanic/Latino; 2 Hispanic/Latino). Average age 32. 52 applicants, 52% accepted, 14 enrolled. In 2011, 37 master's, 4 other advanced degrees awarded. *Degree requirements:* For master's, thesis. *Entrance requirements:* For master's, GRE General Test, letters of recommendation; minimum undergraduate GPA of 2.5 overall or 3.0 in senior year. Additional exam requirements/recommendations for international students: Required—TOEFL (minimum score 550 paper-based; 213 computer-based; 79 iBT), IELTS (minimum score 6). *Application deadline:* For fall admission, 8/1 priority date for domestic students, 6/1 for international students; for spring admission, 12/1 priority date for domestic students, 10/1 for international students. Applications are processed on a rolling basis. Application fee: $35. Electronic applications accepted. *Expenses:* Tuition, state resident: full-time $6472; part-time $359 per credit hour. Tuition, nonresident: full-time $20,006; part-time $1111 per credit hour. *Required fees:* $1320; $160 per credit hour. *Financial support:* Career-related internships or fieldwork, scholarships/grants, and unspecified assistantships available. Support available to part-time students. Financial award applicants required to submit FAFSA. *Faculty research:* Plant layout design, lean manufacturing, six sigma, value management, product development. *Unit head:* Dr. Neslihan Alp, Director, 423-425-4032, Fax: 423-425-5229, E-mail: neslihan-alp@utc.edu. *Application contact:* Dr. Jerald Ainsworth, Dean of Graduate Studies, 423-425-4478, Fax: 423-425-5223, E-mail: jerald-ainsworth@utc.edu. Web site: http://www.utc.edu/Departments/engrcs/engm/index.php.

The University of Tennessee Space Institute, Graduate Programs, Program in Industrial Engineering (Engineering Management), Tullahoma, TN 37388-9700. Offers engineering management (MS, PhD). Part-time programs available. Postbaccalaureate distance learning degree programs offered (no on-campus study). *Faculty:* 1 full-time (0 women), 2 part-time/adjunct (1 woman). *Students:* 22 full-time (2 women), 50 part-time (18 women); includes 16 minority (9 Black or African American, non-Hispanic/Latino; 1 American Indian or Alaska Native, non-Hispanic/Latino; 4 Asian, non-Hispanic/Latino; 1 Hispanic/Latino; 1 Two or more races, non-Hispanic/Latino). 60 applicants, 50% accepted, 25 enrolled. In 2011, 9 degrees awarded. *Degree requirements:* For master's, thesis (for some programs). *Entrance requirements:* Additional exam requirements/recommendations for international students: Required—TOEFL (minimum score 550 paper-based; 213 computer-based), IELTS (minimum score 6.5). *Application deadline:* For fall admission, 2/1 for international students; for spring admission, 6/15 for international students. Applications are processed on a rolling basis. Application fee: $35. Electronic applications accepted. *Financial support:* In 2011–12, 2 research assistantships with full tuition reimbursements (averaging $19,768 per year) were awarded; fellowships, career-related internships or fieldwork, Federal Work-Study, institutionally sponsored loans, health care benefits, tuition waivers (full and partial), and unspecified assistantships also available. Financial award applicants required to submit FAFSA. *Unit head:* Dr. Greg Sedrick, Degree Program Chairman, 931-393-7293, Fax: 931-393-7201, E-mail: gsedrick@utsi.edu. *Application contact:* Dee Merriman, Coordinator III, 931-393-7213, Fax: 931-393-7211, E-mail: dmerrima@utsi.edu. Web site: http://www.utsi.edu/academics/iieandem/.

The University of Texas at Arlington, Graduate School, College of Engineering, Department of Industrial and Manufacturing Systems Engineering, Program in Engineering Management, Arlington, TX 76019. Offers MS. Part-time and evening/weekend programs available. Postbaccalaureate distance learning degree programs offered (minimal on-campus study). *Students:* 25 full-time (8 women), 16 part-time (3 women); includes 7 minority (1 Black or African American, non-Hispanic/Latino; 1 Asian, non-Hispanic/Latino; 5 Hispanic/Latino), 27 international. 76 applicants, 72% accepted, 13 enrolled. In 2011, 17 degrees awarded. *Degree requirements:* For master's, comprehensive exam, thesis optional. *Entrance requirements:* For master's, GRE, 3 years of full-time work experience, minimum GPA of 3.0. Additional exam requirements/recommendations for international students: Required—TOEFL (minimum score 550 paper-based; 213 computer-based). *Application deadline:* For fall admission, 6/6 for domestic students, 4/4 for international students; for spring admission, 10/15 for domestic students, 9/5 for international students. Application fee: $35 ($50 for international students). *Financial support:* Fellowships, research assistantships, teaching assistantships, career-related internships or fieldwork, Federal Work-Study, institutionally sponsored loans, scholarships/grants, and unspecified assistantships available. Financial award application deadline: 6/1; financial award applicants required to submit FAFSA. *Unit head:* Dr. Donald H. Liles, Chair, 817-272-3092, Fax: 817-272-3406, E-mail: dliles@uta.edu. *Application contact:* Dr. Donald H. Liles, Chair, 817-272-3092, Fax: 817-272-3092, E-mail: dliles@uta.edu. Web site: http://ie.uta.edu/.

The University of Texas–Pan American, College of Engineering and Computer Science, Department of Manufacturing Engineering, Edinburg, TX 78539. Offers engineering management (MS); manufacturing engineering (MS); systems engineering (MS). Tuition and fees vary according to course load, program and student level. *Unit head:* Dr. Rajiv Nambiar, Dean, 956-665-7056, E-mail: nambiar@utpa.edu. Web site: http://portal.utpa.edu/portal/page/portal/utpa_main/daa_home/cose_home/manu_home.

University of Waterloo, Graduate Studies, Faculty of Engineering, Department of Management Sciences, Waterloo, ON N2L 3G1, Canada. Offers applied operations research (MA Sc, MMS, PhD); information systems (MA Sc, MMS, PhD); management of technology (MA Sc, MMS, PhD). Part-time programs available. Postbaccalaureate distance learning degree programs offered (no on-campus study). *Degree requirements:* For master's, research paper or thesis; for doctorate, comprehensive exam, thesis/dissertation. *Entrance requirements:* For master's, GMAT or GRE, honors degree, minimum B average, resume; for doctorate, GMAT or GRE, master's degree, minimum A- average, resumé. Additional exam requirements/recommendations for international students: Required—TOEFL, TWE. *Faculty research:* Operations research, manufacturing systems, scheduling, information systems.

University of Wisconsin–Milwaukee, Graduate School, College of Engineering and Applied Science, Program in Engineering, Milwaukee, WI 53201-0413. Offers civil engineering (MS); electrical and computer engineering (MS); energy engineering (Certificate); engineering (PhD); engineering management (MS); engineering mechanics (MS); ergonomics (Certificate); industrial and management engineering (MS); manufacturing engineering (MS); materials engineering (MS); mechanical engineering (MS); MUP/MS. Part-time programs available. *Faculty:* 41 full-time (5 women), 2 part-time/adjunct (0 women). *Students:* 170 full-time (33 women), 101 part-time (18 women); includes 30 minority (6 Black or African American, non-Hispanic/Latino; 15 Asian, non-Hispanic/Latino; 2 Hispanic/Latino; 7 Two or more races, non-Hispanic/Latino), 153 international. Average age 30. 170 applicants, 56% accepted, 48 enrolled. In 2011, 47 master's, 12 doctorates awarded. *Degree requirements:* For master's, comprehensive exam (for some programs), thesis or alternative; for doctorate, comprehensive exam, thesis/dissertation, internship. *Entrance requirements:* For master's, GRE, minimum GPA of 2.75; for doctorate, GRE, minimum GPA of 3.5. Additional exam requirements/recommendations for international students: Required—TOEFL (minimum score 550 paper-based; 79 iBT), IELTS (minimum score 6.5). *Application deadline:* For fall admission, 1/1 priority date for domestic students; for spring admission, 9/1 for domestic students. Applications are processed on a rolling basis. Application fee: $56 ($96 for international students). One-time fee: $506.10 full-time. Tuition and fees vary according to course load and reciprocity agreements. *Financial support:* In 2011–12, 3 fellowships, 55 research assistantships, 77 teaching assistantships were awarded; career-related internships or fieldwork, Federal Work-Study, unspecified assistantships, and project assistantships also available. Support available to part-time students. Financial award application deadline: 4/15. *Total annual research expenditures:* $10.3 million. *Unit head:* David Yu, Representative, 414-229-6169, E-mail: yu@uwm.edu. *Application contact:* Betty Warras, General Information Contact, 414-229-6169, Fax: 414-229-6967, E-mail: bwarras@uwm.edu. Web site: http://www.wum.edu/CEAS/.

Valparaiso University, Graduate School, College of Business Administration, Valparaiso, IN 46383. Offers business administration (MBA); engineering management (MEM); management (Certificate); JD/MBA; MSN/MBA. *Accreditation:* AACSB. Part-time and evening/weekend programs available. Postbaccalaureate distance learning degree programs offered (minimal on-campus study). *Faculty:* 18 part-time/adjunct (6 women). *Students:* 14 full-time (3 women), 49 part-time (22 women); includes 11 minority (5 Black or African American, non-Hispanic/Latino; 1 Asian, non-Hispanic/Latino; 2 Hispanic/Latino; 3 Two or more races, non-Hispanic/Latino), 4 international. Average age 34. In 2011, 31 master's, 5 other advanced degrees awarded. *Entrance requirements:* For master's, GMAT, GRE, minimum GPA of 3.0. Additional exam requirements/recommendations for international students: Required—TOEFL (minimum score 550 paper-based; 213 computer-based; 80 iBT). *Application deadline:* Applications are processed on a rolling basis. Application fee: $30 ($50 for international students). Electronic applications accepted. *Expenses:* Contact institution. *Financial support:* Available to part-time students. Applicants required to submit FAFSA. *Unit head:* Bruce MacLean, Director of Graduate Programs in Management, 219-465-7952, Fax: 219-464-5789, E-mail: bruce.maclean@valpo.edu. *Application contact:* Cindy Scanlan, Assistant Director of Graduate Programs in Management, 219-465-7952, Fax: 219-464-5789, E-mail: cindy.scanlan@valpo.edu. Web site: http://valpo.edu/mba.

Virginia Polytechnic Institute and State University, VT Online, Blacksburg, VA 24061. Offers advanced transportation systems (Certificate); aerospace engineering (MS); agricultural and life sciences (MSLFS); business information systems (Graduate Certificate); career and technical education (MS); civil engineering (MS); computer engineering (M Eng, MS); decision support systems (Graduate Certificate); eLearning leadership (MA); electrical engineering (M Eng, MS); engineering administration (MEA); environmental engineering (Certificate); environmental politics and policy (Graduate Certificate); environmental sciences and engineering (MS); foundations of political analysis (Graduate Certificate); health product risk management (Graduate Certificate); industrial and systems engineering (MS); information policy and society (Graduate Certificate); information security (Graduate Certificate); information technology (MIT); instructional technology (MA); integrative STEM education (MA Ed); liberal arts (Graduate Certificate); life sciences: health product risk management (MS); natural resources (MNR, Graduate Certificate); networking (Graduate Certificate); nonprofit and nongovernmental organization management (Graduate Certificate); ocean engineering (MS); political science (MA); security studies (Graduate Certificate); software development (Graduate Certificate). *Expenses:* Tuition, state resident: full-time $10,048; part-time $558.25 per credit hour. Tuition, nonresident: full-time $19,497; part-time $1083.25 per credit hour. *Required fees:* $405 per semester. Tuition and fees vary according to course load, campus/location and program. *Application contact:* Graduate School Applications General Assistance, 540-231-8636, Fax: 540-231-2039, E-mail: gradappl@vt.edu. Web site: http://www.vto.vt.edu/.

Washington State University Spokane, Graduate Programs, Program in Engineering Management, Spokane, WA 99210. Offers METM. *Faculty:* 6. In 2011, 3 master's awarded. *Degree requirements:* For master's, comprehensive exam (for some programs), thesis (for some programs), project. *Entrance requirements:* For master's, GMAT, minimum GPA of 3.0, 3 letters of recommendation, resume. *Application deadline:* For fall admission, 1/10 priority date for domestic students, 1/10 for international students; for spring admission, 7/1 priority date for domestic students, 7/1 for international students. Application fee: $75. *Financial support:* Application deadline: 4/1. *Faculty research:* Operations research for decision analysis quality control and liability, analytical techniques to formulating decisions. *Unit head:* Dr. Hal Rumsey, Program Director, 509-358-7936, E-mail: rumsey@wsu.edu. *Application contact:* Graduate School Admissions, 800-GRADWSU, Fax: 509-335-1949, E-mail: gradsch@wsu.edu.

Wayne State University, College of Engineering, Department of Industrial and Manufacturing Engineering, Program in Engineering Management, Detroit, MI 48202. Offers MS, Certificate. *Students:* 14 full-time (4 women), 44 part-time (9 women); includes 10 minority (4 Black or African American, non-Hispanic/Latino; 3 Asian, non-Hispanic/Latino; 2 Hispanic/Latino; 1 Two or more races, non-Hispanic/Latino), 3 international. Average age 35. 25 applicants, 24% accepted, 3 enrolled. In 2011, 16 master's awarded. *Degree requirements:* For master's, thesis optional. *Entrance requirements:* For master's, GRE (if baccalaureate is not from ABET-accredited institution), minimum undergraduate upper-division GPA of 2.8; 3 years experience as engineer or technical leader; for Certificate, GRE (if baccalaureate is not from ABET-

accredited institution), minimum undergraduate upper-division GPA of 3.0; 1 year of experience as engineer or technical leader. Additional exam requirements/recommendations for international students: Required—TOEFL (minimum score 550 paper-based; 213 computer-based); Recommended—TWE (minimum score 5.5). *Application deadline:* For fall admission, 6/1 priority date for domestic students, 5/1 for international students; for winter admission, 10/1 priority date for domestic students, 9/1 for international students; for spring admission, 2/1 priority date for domestic students, 1/1 for international students. Applications are processed on a rolling basis. Application fee: $50. Electronic applications accepted. *Expenses:* Tuition, state resident: part-time $512.85 per credit. Tuition, nonresident: part-time $1132.65 per credit. *Required fees:* $26.60 per credit. $199.65 per semester. Tuition and fees vary according to course load and program. *Financial support:* In 2011–12, 20 students received support. Fellowships with tuition reimbursements available, research assistantships with tuition reimbursements available, teaching assistantships with tuition reimbursements available, career-related internships or fieldwork, scholarships/grants, and unspecified assistantships available. Support available to part-time students. *Faculty research:* Technology and change management, quality/reliability, manufacturing systems/infrastructure. *Unit head:* Dr. Leslie Monplaisir, Chair, 313-577-1645, E-mail: ad5365@wayne.edu. *Application contact:* Dr. Kenneth Chelst, Director, 313-577-3857, E-mail: aa1276@wayne.edu. Web site: http://ise.wayne.edu/.

Webster University, College of Arts and Sciences, Department of Biological Sciences, Program in Professional Science Management and Leadership, St. Louis, MO 63119-3194. Offers MA. *Entrance requirements:* Additional exam requirements/recommendations for international students: Required—TOEFL. *Expenses:* Tuition: Full-time $10,890; part-time $605 per credit hour. Tuition and fees vary according to campus/location and program.

Western Michigan University, Graduate College, College of Engineering and Applied Sciences, Department of Industrial and Manufacturing Engineering, Program in Engineering Management, Kalamazoo, MI 49008. Offers MS. *Entrance requirements:* For master's, minimum GPA of 3.0.

Western New England University, College of Engineering, Master's Program in Engineering Management, Springfield, MA 01119. Offers business and engineering information systems (MSEM); general engineering management (MSEM); production and manufacturing systems (MSEM); quality engineering (MSEM). Evening/weekend programs available. Postbaccalaureate distance learning degree programs offered (no on-campus study). *Students:* 36 part-time (7 women); includes 6 minority (1 Asian, non-Hispanic/Latino; 5 Hispanic/Latino), 1 international. *Degree requirements:* For master's, thesis optional. *Unit head:* Dr. S. Hossein Cheraghi, Dean, 413-782-1272, E-mail: cheraghi@wnec.edu. *Application contact:* Matt Fox, Director of Recruiting and Marketing for Adult Learners, 413-782-1517, Fax: 413-782-1777, E-mail: study@wnec.edu.

Western New England University, College of Engineering, PhD Program in Engineering Management, Springfield, MA 01119. Offers PhD. Evening/weekend programs available. *Unit head:* Dr. S. Hossein Cheraghi, Dean, 413-782-1272, E-mail: cheraghi@wnec.edu. *Application contact:* Matt Fox, Director of Recruiting and Marketing for Adult Learners, 413-782-1517, Fax: 413-782-1777, E-mail: study@wnec.edu.

Wichita State University, Graduate School, College of Engineering, Department of Industrial and Manufacturing Engineering, Wichita, KS 67260. Offers engineering management (MEM); industrial engineering (MS, PhD). Part-time programs available. In 2011, 37 master's, 3 doctorates awarded. *Entrance requirements:* Additional exam requirements/recommendations for international students: Required—TOEFL. *Expenses:* Tuition, state resident: full-time $4746; part-time $263.65 per credit. Tuition, nonresident: full-time $11,669; part-time $648.30 per credit. *Financial support:* Teaching assistantships available. *Unit head:* Dr. Krishna Krishnan, Chair, 316-978-3425, Fax: 316-978-3742, E-mail: krishna.krishnan@wichita.edu. *Application contact:* Carrie C. Henderson, Admissions Coordinator, 316-978-3095, Fax: 316-978-3253, E-mail: carrie.henderson@wichita.edu. Web site: http://www.wichita.edu/.

Widener University, Graduate Programs in Engineering, Program in Engineering Management, Chester, PA 19013-5792. Offers M Eng. Part-time and evening/weekend programs available. *Degree requirements:* For master's, thesis optional.

Wilkes University, College of Graduate and Professional Studies, College of Science and Engineering, Division of Engineering and Physics, Wilkes-Barre, PA 18766-0002. Offers electrical engineering (MSEE); engineering management (MS); mechanical engineering (MS). Part-time programs available. *Students:* 27 full-time (2 women), 26 part-time (4 women); includes 2 minority (both Asian, non-Hispanic/Latino), 19 international. Average age 30. In 2011, 11 master's awarded. *Entrance requirements:* For master's, GRE General Test. Additional exam requirements/recommendations for international students: Required—TOEFL (minimum score 550 paper-based; 213 computer-based; 79 iBT). *Application deadline:* Applications are processed on a rolling basis. Application fee: $45 ($65 for international students). Electronic applications accepted. *Financial support:* Federal Work-Study and unspecified assistantships available. Financial award application deadline: 3/1; financial award applicants required to submit FAFSA. *Unit head:* Dr. Rodney Ridley, Director, 570-408-4824, Fax: 570-408-7846, E-mail: rodney.ridley@wilkes.edu. *Application contact:* Erin Sutzko, Director of Extended Learning, 570-408-4253, Fax: 570-408-7846, E-mail: erin.sutzko@wilkes.edu. Web site: http://www.wilkes.edu/pages/387.asp.

Ergonomics and Human Factors

Arizona State University, College of Technology and Innovation, Department of Technology Management, Mesa, AZ 85212. Offers technology (aviation management and human factors) (MS); technology (environmental technology management) (MS); technology (global technology and development) (MS); technology (graphic information technology) (MS); technology (management of technology) (MS). Part-time and evening/weekend programs available. Postbaccalaureate distance learning degree programs offered (minimal on-campus study). *Degree requirements:* For master's, thesis or applied project and oral defense; interactive Program of Study (iPOS) submitted before completing 50 percent of required credit hours. *Entrance requirements:* For master's, GRE, minimum GPA of 3.0 or equivalent in last 2 years of work leading to bachelor's degree. Additional exam requirements/recommendations for international students: Required—TOEFL (minimum score 83 iBT), TOEFL, IELTS, or Pearson Test of English. Electronic applications accepted. *Faculty research:* Digital imaging, digital publishing, Internet development/e-commerce, information aviation human factors, pilot selection, databases, multimedia, commercial digital photography, digital workflow, computer graphics modeling and animation, information design, sociotechnology, visual and

technical literacy, environmental management, quality management, project management, industrial ethics, hazardous materials, environmental chemistry.

Bentley University, McCallum Graduate School of Business, Program in Human Factors in Information Design, Waltham, MA 02452-4705. Offers MSHFID. Part-time and evening/weekend programs available. Postbaccalaureate distance learning degree programs offered (minimal on-campus study). *Entrance requirements:* For master's, GMAT or GRE General Test. Additional exam requirements/recommendations for international students: Required—TOEFL (minimum score 600 paper-based; 250 computer-based; 100 iBT) or IELTS (minimum score 7). Electronic applications accepted. *Faculty research:* Usability engineering, ethnography, human-computer interaction, project management, user experience.

California State University, Long Beach, Graduate Studies, College of Liberal Arts, Department of Psychology, Long Beach, CA 90840. Offers human factors (MS); industrial/organizational psychology (MS); psychology (MA). Part-time and evening/weekend programs available. *Faculty:* 19 full-time (5 women), 2 part-time/adjunct (1 woman). *Students:* 46 full-time (29 women), 21 part-time (11 women); includes 27 minority (3 Black or African American, non-Hispanic/Latino; 10 Asian, non-Hispanic/Latino; 11 Hispanic/Latino; 3 Two or more races, non-Hispanic/Latino), 1 international. Average age 26. 225 applicants, 13% accepted, 27 enrolled. In 2011, 21 master's awarded. *Degree requirements:* For master's, comprehensive exam, thesis. *Entrance requirements:* For master's, GRE General Test, GRE Subject Test. *Application deadline:* For fall admission, 3/1 for domestic students. Applications are processed on a rolling basis. Application fee: $55. Electronic applications accepted. *Financial support:* Federal Work-Study, institutionally sponsored loans, and scholarships/grants available. Financial award application deadline: 3/2. *Faculty research:* Physiological psychology, social and personality psychology, community-clinical psychology, industrial-organizational psychology, developmental psychology. *Unit head:* Dr. Kenneth Green, Chair, 562-985-5049, Fax: 562-985-8004, E-mail: kgreen@csulb.edu. *Application contact:* Dr. Mark Wiley, Associate Dean, 562-985-5381, Fax: 562-985-2463, E-mail: mwiley@csulb.edu.

California State University, Northridge, Graduate Studies, College of Social and Behavioral Sciences, Department of Psychology, Northridge, CA 91330. Offers clinical psychology (MA); general-experimental psychology (MA); human factors and applied experimental psychology (MA). *Degree requirements:* For master's, thesis. *Entrance requirements:* For master's, GRE General Test, GRE Subject Test, minimum GPA of 3.0, letters of recommendation. Additional exam requirements/recommendations for international students: Required—TOEFL.

The Catholic University of America, School of Arts and Sciences, Department of Psychology, Washington, DC 20064. Offers applied experimental psychology (PhD); clinical psychology (PhD); general psychology (MA); human factors (MA); MA/JD. *Accreditation:* APA (one or more programs are accredited). Part-time programs available. *Faculty:* 13 full-time (6 women), 6 part-time/adjunct (2 women). *Students:* 35 full-time (28 women), 33 part-time (23 women); includes 13 minority (3 Black or African American, non-Hispanic/Latino; 3 Asian, non-Hispanic/Latino; 6 Hispanic/Latino; 1 Two or more races, non-Hispanic/Latino). Average age 28. 219 applicants, 24% accepted, 19 enrolled. In 2011, 20 master's, 8 doctorates awarded. *Degree requirements:* For master's, comprehensive exam, thesis (for some programs); for doctorate, comprehensive exam, thesis/dissertation. *Entrance requirements:* For master's, GRE General Test, statement of purpose, official copies of academic transcripts, three letters of recommendation; for doctorate, GRE General Test, GRE Subject Test, statement of purpose, official copies of academic transcripts, three letters of recommendation. Additional exam requirements/recommendations for international students: Required—TOEFL (minimum score 580 paper-based; 237 computer-based). *Application deadline:* For fall admission, 8/1 priority date for domestic students, 7/15 for international students; for spring admission, 12/1 priority date for domestic students, 10/15 for international students. Applications are processed on a rolling basis. Application fee: $55. Electronic applications accepted. *Expenses: Tuition:* Full-time $35,260; part-time $1380 per credit. *Required fees:* $80; $40 per semester hour. One-time fee: $425. *Financial support:* Fellowships, research assistantships, teaching assistantships, Federal Work-Study, scholarships/grants, tuition waivers (full and partial), and unspecified assistantships available. Financial award application deadline: 2/1; financial award applicants required to submit FAFSA. *Faculty research:* Clinical psychology, applied cognitive science, psychopathology, cognitive neuroscience, psychotherapy. *Total annual research expenditures:* $557,439. *Unit head:* Dr. Marc M. Sebrechts, Chair, 202-319-5750, Fax: 202-319-6263, E-mail: sebrechts@cua.edu. *Application contact:* Andrew Woodall, Director of Graduate Admissions, 202-319-5057, Fax: 202-319-6533, E-mail: cua-admissions@cua.edu. Web site: http://psychology.cua.edu/.

Clemson University, Graduate School, College of Business and Behavioral Science, Department of Psychology, Program in Human Factors Psychology, Clemson, SC 29634. Offers PhD. *Students:* 14 full-time (7 women); includes 1 minority (Two or more races, non-Hispanic/Latino). Average age 30. 40 applicants, 13% accepted, 2 enrolled. *Degree requirements:* For doctorate, thesis/dissertation. *Entrance requirements:* For doctorate, GRE General Test. Additional exam requirements/recommendations for international students: Required—TOEFL. *Application deadline:* For fall admission, 1/15 for domestic students. Applications are processed on a rolling basis. Application fee: $70 ($80 for international students). Electronic applications accepted. *Expenses:* Contact institution. *Financial support:* In 2011–12, 13 students received support, including 2 fellowships with full and partial tuition reimbursements available (averaging $7,500 per year), 3 research assistantships with partial tuition reimbursements available (averaging $8,467 per year), 14 teaching assistantships with partial tuition reimbursements available (averaging $11,114 per year); career-related internships or fieldwork, institutionally sponsored loans, scholarships/grants, health care benefits, and unspecified assistantships also available. Support available to part-time students. *Faculty research:* Transportation safety, human factors in health care, human-computer interaction, ergonomics, vision and visual performance. *Unit head:* Dr. Patrick Raymark, Chair, 864-656-4715, Fax: 864-656-0358, E-mail: praymar@clemson.edu. *Application contact:* Dr. Lee Gugerty, 864-656-4467, Fax: 864-656-0358, E-mail: gugerty@clemson.edu. Web site: http://www.clemson.edu/psych.

Cornell University, Graduate School, Graduate Fields of Human Ecology, Field of Design and Environmental Analysis, Ithaca, NY 14853. Offers applied research in human-environment relations (MS); facilities planning and management (MS); housing and design (MS); human factors and ergonomics (MS); human-environment relations (MS); interior design (MA, MPS). *Faculty:* 15 full-time (6 women). *Students:* 22 full-time (18 women); includes 6 minority (1 Black or African American, non-Hispanic/Latino; 4 Asian, non-Hispanic/Latino; 1 Hispanic/Latino), 7 international. Average age 26. 61 applicants, 33% accepted, 13 enrolled. In 2011, 12 master's awarded. *Degree requirements:* For master's, thesis. *Entrance requirements:* For master's, GRE General Test, portfolio or slides of recent work; bachelor's degree in interior design, architecture or related design discipline; 2 letters of recommendation. Additional exam requirements/recommendations for international students: Required—TOEFL (minimum score 600 paper-based; 250 computer-based; 105 iBT). *Application deadline:* For fall admission, 2/1 priority date for domestic students. Application fee: $95. Electronic applications accepted. *Financial support:* In 2011–12, 13 students received support, including 1 fellowship with full tuition reimbursement available, 2 research assistantships with full tuition reimbursements available, 9 teaching assistantships with full tuition reimbursements available; institutionally sponsored loans, scholarships/grants, health care benefits, tuition waivers (full and partial), and unspecified assistantships also available. Financial award applicants required to submit FAFSA. *Faculty research:* Facility planning and management, environmental psychology, housing, interior design, ergonomics and human factors. *Unit head:* Director of Graduate Studies, 607-255-2168, Fax: 607-255-0305. *Application contact:* Graduate Field Assistant, 607-255-2168, Fax: 607-255-0305, E-mail: deagrad@cornell.edu. Web site: http://www.gradschool.cornell.edu/fields.php?id-77&a-2.

Embry-Riddle Aeronautical University–Daytona, Daytona Beach Campus Graduate Program, Department of Human Factors and Systems, Daytona Beach, FL 32114-3900. Offers human factors engineering (MSHFS); systems engineering (MSHFS). Part-time and evening/weekend programs available. *Faculty:* 6 full-time (1 woman). *Students:* 39 full-time (14 women), 18 part-time (8 women); includes 11 minority (1 Black or African American, non-Hispanic/Latino; 1 American Indian or Alaska Native, non-Hispanic/Latino; 1 Asian, non-Hispanic/Latino; 7 Hispanic/Latino; 1 Two or more races, non-Hispanic/Latino), 4 international. Average age 27. 40 applicants, 68% accepted, 10 enrolled. In 2011, 12 master's awarded. *Degree requirements:* For master's, thesis, practicum, qualifying oral exam. *Entrance requirements:* For master's, minimum GPA of 2.5. Additional exam requirements/recommendations for international students: Required—TOEFL (minimum score 550 paper-based; 213 computer-based; 79 iBT). *Application deadline:* For fall admission, 6/1 priority date for domestic students, 6/1 for international students; for spring admission, 11/1 priority date for domestic students, 10/1 for international students. Applications are processed on a rolling basis. Application fee: $50. Electronic applications accepted. *Expenses: Tuition:* Full-time $14,340; part-time $1195 per credit hour. *Financial support:* In 2011–12, 14 students received support, including 4 research assistantships with full and partial tuition reimbursements available (averaging $4,738 per year); teaching assistantships with full and partial tuition reimbursements available, career-related internships or fieldwork, and unspecified assistantships also available. Financial award application deadline: 4/15; financial award applicants required to submit FAFSA. *Faculty research:* Color discrimination on computer displays, human-machine interfaces, cognitive assessment, performance enhancement, integration of advanced training technologies into live military training, unmanned aerial systems, human performance assessment, fatigue management, impairment prediction models, shift settings, circadian technology, countermeasures, human factors analysis and classification system, medical errors, general aviation errors, commercial helicopter operational errors, team errors. *Total annual research expenditures:* $256,585. *Unit head:* Dr. Shawn Doherty, Graduate Program Coordinator, 386-226-6249, E-mail: shawn.doherty@erau.edu. *Application contact:* Flavia Carreiro, Assistant Director, International and Graduate Admissions, 800-388-3728, Fax: 386-226-7070, E-mail: graduate.admissions@erau.edu.

Florida Institute of Technology, Graduate Programs, College of Aeronautics, Melbourne, FL 32901-6975. Offers airport development and management (MSA); applied aviation safety option (MSA); aviation human factors (MS); human factors in aeronautics (MS). Part-time and evening/weekend programs available. *Faculty:* 5 full-time (0 women), 2 part-time/adjunct (0 women). *Students:* 27 full-time (6 women), 18 part-time (7 women); includes 6 minority (4 Black or African American, non-Hispanic/Latino; 1 Asian, non-Hispanic/Latino; 1 Hispanic/Latino), 12 international. Average age 26. 70 applicants, 76% accepted, 29 enrolled. In 2011, 14 master's awarded. *Degree requirements:* For master's, thesis (for some programs). *Entrance requirements:* For master's, GRE, minimum GPA of 3.0, 3 letters of recommendation, resume, statement of objectives. Additional exam requirements/recommendations for international students: Required—TOEFL (minimum score 550 paper-based; 213 computer-based; 79 iBT). *Application deadline:* For fall admission, 4/1 for international students; for spring admission, 9/30 for international students. Applications are processed on a rolling basis. Electronic applications accepted. *Expenses: Tuition:* Full-time $19,620; part-time $1090 per credit hour. Tuition and fees vary according to campus/location. *Financial support:* In 2011–12, 1 research assistantship with full and partial tuition reimbursement (averaging $2,000 per year) was awarded; career-related internships or fieldwork, institutionally sponsored loans, tuition waivers (partial), and tuition remissions also available. Support available to part-time students. Financial award application deadline: 3/1; financial award applicants required to submit FAFSA. *Faculty research:* Aircraft cockpit design, medical human factors, operating room human factors, hypobaric chamber operations and effects, aviation professional education. *Total annual research expenditures:* $4.5 million. *Unit head:* Dr. Kenneth P. Stackpoole, Dean, 321-674-8971, Fax: 321-674-7368, E-mail: kenStackpoole@fit.edu. *Application contact:* Cheryl A. Brown, Associate Director of Graduate Admissions, 321-674-7581, Fax: 321-723-9468, E-mail: cbrown@fit.edu. Web site: http://coa.fit.edu.

Florida Institute of Technology, Graduate Programs, College of Engineering, Program in Human-Centered Design, Melbourne, FL 32901-6975. Offers PhD. Part-time and evening/weekend programs available. *Faculty:* 1 full-time (0 women). *Students:* 1 (woman) part-time. Average age 47. 3 applicants, 67% accepted, 1 enrolled. *Degree requirements:* For doctorate, comprehensive exam, thesis/dissertation, publication in journal. *Entrance requirements:* For doctorate, GRE, master's degree with minimum cumulative GPA of 3.2; transcripts; three letters of recommendation; statement of objectives. Additional exam requirements/recommendations for international students: Required—TOEFL (minimum score 550 paper-based; 213 computer-based; 79 iBT). *Application deadline:* For fall admission, 4/1 for international students; for spring admission, 9/30 for international students. Applications are processed on a rolling basis. Electronic applications accepted. *Expenses: Tuition:* Full-time $19,620; part-time $1090 per credit hour. Tuition and fees vary according to campus/location. *Financial support:* Research assistantships with full and partial tuition reimbursements, career-related internships or fieldwork, institutionally sponsored loans, tuition waivers (partial), unspecified assistantships, and tuition remissions available. Support available to part-time students. Financial award application deadline: 3/1; financial award applicants required to submit FAFSA. *Faculty research:* Cognitive engineering, advanced interaction media, complexity analysis in human-centered design, life-critical systems, human-centered organization design and management, modeling and simulation. *Unit head:* Dr. Guy Boy, Interim Dean, 321-674-7631, Fax: 321-984-8461, E-mail: gboy@fit.edu. *Application contact:* Cheryl A. Brown, Associate Director of Graduate Admissions, 321-674-7581, Fax: 321-723-9468, E-mail: cbrown@fit.edu. Web site: http://research.fit.edu/hcdi/.

Georgia Institute of Technology, Graduate Studies and Research, College of Computing, Atlanta, GA 30332-0001. Offers algorithms, combinatorics, and optimization (PhD); computational science and engineering (MS, PhD); computer science (MS, MSCS, PhD); human computer interaction (MSHCI); human-centered computing (PhD); information security (MS). Part-time programs available. Postbaccalaureate distance learning degree programs offered. Terminal master's awarded for partial completion of doctoral program. *Degree requirements:* For master's, thesis optional; for doctorate, comprehensive exam, thesis/dissertation. *Entrance requirements:* For master's, GRE General Test, GRE Subject Test, minimum GPA of 3.0; for doctorate, GRE General Test, GRE Subject Test, minimum GPA of 3.3. Additional exam requirements/recommendations for international students: Required—TOEFL. *Faculty research:* Computer systems, graphics, intelligent systems and artificial intelligence, networks and telecommunications, software engineering.

Georgia Institute of Technology, Graduate Studies and Research, College of Sciences, School of Psychology, Atlanta, GA 30332-0001. Offers human computer interaction (MSHCI); psychology (MS, MS Psy, PhD), including engineering psychology (PhD), experimental psychology (PhD), industrial/organizational psychology (PhD). Terminal master's awarded for partial completion of doctoral program. *Degree requirements:* For master's, thesis; for doctorate, thesis/dissertation. *Entrance requirements:* For master's and doctorate, GRE General Test, GRE Subject Test, minimum GPA of 3.0. Additional exam requirements/recommendations for international students: Required—TOEFL. Electronic applications accepted. *Faculty research:* Experimental, industrial-organizational, and engineering psychology; cognitive aging and processes; leadership; human factors.

Indiana University Bloomington, School of Health, Physical Education and Recreation, Department of Kinesiology, Bloomington, IN 47405-7000. Offers adapted physical education (MS); applied sport science (MS); athletic administration/sport management (MS); athletic training (MS); biomechanics (MS); ergonomics (MS); exercise physiology (MS); human performance (PhD), including adapted physical education, biomechanics, exercise physiology, motor learning/control, sport management; motor learning/control (MS); physical activity, fitness and wellness (MS). Part-time programs available. *Faculty:* 28 full-time (11 women). *Students:* 150 full-time (59 women), 22 part-time (9 women); includes 20 minority (12 Black or African American, non-Hispanic/Latino; 1 American Indian or Alaska Native, non-Hispanic/Latino; 1 Asian, non-Hispanic/Latino; 4 Hispanic/Latino; 2 Two or more races, non-Hispanic/Latino), 33 international. Average age 28. 211 applicants, 60% accepted, 62 enrolled. In 2011, 67 master's, 7 doctorates awarded. Terminal master's awarded for partial completion of doctoral program. *Degree requirements:* For master's, thesis optional; for doctorate, variable foreign language requirement, thesis/dissertation. *Entrance requirements:* For master's, GRE General Test, minimum GPA of 2.8; for doctorate, GRE General Test, minimum graduate GPA of 3.5, undergraduate 3.0. *Application deadline:* For fall admission, 1/1 for international students; for spring admission, 9/1 for international students. Applications are processed on a rolling basis. Application fee: $55 ($65 for international students). *Financial support:* Fellowships, research assistantships with full tuition reimbursements, teaching assistantships with full tuition reimbursements, career-related internships or fieldwork, Federal Work-Study, institutionally sponsored loans, scholarships/grants, tuition waivers (partial), and fee remissions available. Financial award application deadline: 3/1. *Faculty research:* Exercise physiology and biochemistry, sports biomechanics, human motor control, adaptation of fitness and exercise to special populations. *Unit head:* Dr. David M. Koceja, Chairperson, 812-855-5523, Fax: 812-855-3193, E-mail: koceja@indiana.edu. *Application contact:* Kristine M. Wasson, Administrative Assistant for Graduate Studies, 812-855-5523, Fax: 812-855-3193, E-mail: ktanksle@indiana.edu. Web site: http://www.indiana.edu/~kines/.

Michigan Technological University, Graduate School, College of Sciences and Arts, Department of Cognitive and Learning Sciences, Houghton, MI 49931. Offers applied cognitive science and human factors (PhD); applied science education (MS). *Faculty:* 12 full-time (4 women), 3 part-time/adjunct (0 women). *Students:* 12 full-time (7 women), 21 part-time (13 women); includes 4 minority (2 American Indian or Alaska Native, non-Hispanic/Latino; 1 Asian, non-Hispanic/Latino; 1 Hispanic/Latino), 3 international. Average age 38. 26 applicants, 31% accepted, 6 enrolled. In 2011, 3 master's awarded. *Degree requirements:* For master's, comprehensive exam (for some programs), thesis (for some programs); for doctorate, comprehensive exam, thesis/dissertation. *Entrance requirements:* For master's and doctorate, GRE (recommended minimum score of 310 [1200 old version]), statement of purpose, official transcripts, 3 letters of recommendation, bachelor's/master's degree in a field related to cognitive science, human factors, or ergonomics, minimum GPA of 3.5 (recommended), resume/curriculum vitae, writing sample (preferably related to the field of interest). Additional exam requirements/recommendations for international students: Required—TOEFL (minimum score 79 iBT) or IELTS. *Application deadline:* For fall admission, 2/15 for domestic and international students. Applications are processed on a rolling basis. Electronic applications accepted. *Expenses:* Tuition, state resident: full-time $12,636; part-time $702 per credit. Tuition, nonresident: full-time $12,636; part-time $702 per credit. *Required fees:* $226; $226 per year. *Financial support:* In 2011–12, 15 students received support, including 1 fellowship with full tuition reimbursement available (averaging $6,065 per year), 4 research assistantships with full tuition reimbursements available (averaging $6,065 per year), teaching assistantships (averaging $6,065 per year). Financial award applicants required to submit FAFSA. *Faculty research:* Cognitive engineering and decision-making, human-centered design, individual differences in human performance. *Total annual research expenditures:* $167,794. *Unit head:* Dr. Bradley H. Baltensperger, Chair, 906-487-2460, Fax: 906-487-2468, E-mail: brad@mtu.edu. *Application contact:* Carol T. Wingerson, Senior Staff Assistant, 906-487-2327, Fax: 906-487-2463, E-mail: gradadms@mtu.edu. Web site: http://cls.mtu.edu/.

Missouri Western State University, Program in Applied Science, St. Joseph, MO 64507-2294. Offers chemistry (MAS); engineering technology management (MAS); human factors and usability testing (MAS); information technology management (MAS). Part-time programs available. *Application deadline:* For fall admission, 7/15 for domestic and international students; for spring admission, 10/1 for domestic and international students. Electronic applications accepted. *Expenses:* Tuition, state resident: full-time $4697; part-time $261 per credit hour. Tuition, nonresident: full-time $9355; part-time $520 per credit hour. *Required fees:* $343; $19.10 per credit hour. $30 per semester. Tuition and fees vary according to course load. *Application contact:* Dr. Brian C. Cronk, Dean of the Graduate School, 816-271-4394, E-mail: graduate@missouriwestern.edu.

New York University, Graduate School of Arts and Science, Department of Environmental Medicine, New York, NY 10012-1019. Offers environmental health sciences (MS, PhD), including biostatistics (PhD), environmental hygiene (MS), epidemiology (PhD), ergonomics and biomechanics (PhD), exposure assessment and health effects (PhD), molecular toxicology/carcinogenesis (PhD), toxicology. Part-time programs available. *Faculty:* 26 full-time (7 women). *Students:* 62 full-time (43 women), 9 part-time (4 women); includes 12 minority (2 Black or African American, non-Hispanic/Latino; 3 Asian, non-Hispanic/Latino; 7 Hispanic/Latino), 27 international. Average age 30. 70 applicants, 56% accepted, 26 enrolled. In 2011, 9 master's, 8 doctorates awarded. Terminal master's awarded for partial completion of doctoral program. *Degree requirements:* For master's, thesis or alternative; for doctorate, one foreign language, thesis/dissertation, oral and written exams. *Entrance requirements:* For master's and doctorate, GRE General Test, GRE Subject Test, minimum GPA of 3.0; bachelor's degree in biological, physical, or engineering science. Additional exam requirements/recommendations for international students: Required—TOEFL. *Application deadline:* For fall admission, 12/12 for domestic and international students. Application fee: $90. *Financial support:* Fellowships with tuition reimbursements, teaching assistantships with tuition reimbursements, career-related internships or fieldwork, Federal Work-Study, institutionally sponsored loans, and health care benefits available. Financial award application deadline: 12/12; financial award applicants required to submit FAFSA. *Unit head:* Dr. Max Costa, Chair, 845-731-3661, Fax: 845-351-4510, E-mail: ehs@env.med.nyu.edu. *Application contact:* Dr. Jerome J. Solomon, Director of Graduate Studies, 845-731-3661, Fax: 845-351-4510, E-mail: ehs@env.med.nyu.edu. Web site: http://environmental-medicine.med.nyu.edu/.

North Carolina State University, Graduate School, College of Humanities and Social Sciences, Department of Psychology, Raleigh, NC 27695. Offers developmental psychology (PhD); ergonomics and experimental psychology (PhD); industrial/organizational psychology (PhD); psychology in the public interest (PhD); school psychology (PhD). *Accreditation:* APA. *Degree requirements:* For doctorate, comprehensive exam, thesis/dissertation. *Entrance requirements:* For doctorate, GRE General Test, GRE Subject Test (industrial/organizational psychology), MAT (recommended), minimum GPA of 3.0 in major. Electronic applications accepted. *Faculty research:* Cognitive and social development (human factors, families, the workplace, community issues and health, aging).

Old Dominion University, College of Sciences, Doctoral Program in Psychology, Norfolk, VA 23529. Offers applied experimental psychology (PhD); human factors psychology (PhD); industrial/organizational psychology (PhD). *Faculty:* 20 full-time (9 women). *Students:* 35 full-time (19 women), 8 part-time (6 women); includes 2 minority (both Hispanic/Latino), 4 international. Average age 28. 61 applicants, 28% accepted, 10 enrolled. In 2011, 5 doctorates awarded. *Degree requirements:* For doctorate, thesis/dissertation, candidacy exam. *Entrance requirements:* For doctorate, GRE General Test, GRE Subject Test, 3 recommendation letters. Additional exam requirements/recommendations for international students: Required—TOEFL. *Application deadline:* For winter admission, 1/5 for domestic and international students. Application fee: $50. Electronic applications accepted. *Expenses:* Tuition, state resident: full-time $9096; part-time $379 per credit. Tuition, nonresident: full-time $23,064; part-time $961 per credit. *Required fees:* $127 per semester. One-time fee: $50. *Financial support:* In 2011–12, 33 students received support, including 4 fellowships with full tuition reimbursements available (averaging $18,000 per year), 4 research assistantships with full tuition reimbursements available (averaging $12,000 per year), 25 teaching assistantships with full tuition reimbursements available (averaging $12,000 per year). Financial award application deadline: 1/15. *Faculty research:* Human factors, industrial psychology, organizational psychology, applied experimental (health, developmental, quantitative). *Total annual research expenditures:* $978,563. *Unit head:* Dr. Bryan E. Porter, Graduate Program Director, 757-683-4458, Fax: 757-683-5087, E-mail: bporter@odu.edu. *Application contact:* William Heffelfinger, Director of Graduate Admissions, 757-683-5554, Fax: 757-683-3255, E-mail: gradadmit@odu.edu. Web site: http://sci.odu.edu/psychology/.

Purdue University, Graduate School, College of Health and Human Sciences, School of Health Sciences, West Lafayette, IN 47907. Offers health physics (MS, PhD); medical physics (MS, PhD); occupational and environmental health science (MS, PhD), including aerosol deposition and lung disease, ergonomics, exposure and risk assessment, indoor air quality and bioaerosols (PhD), liver/lung toxicology; occupational and environmental health science (PhD), including indoor air quality and bioaerosols; radiation biology (PhD); toxicology (PhD); MS/PhD. Part-time programs available. *Faculty:* 10 full-time (3 women), 24 part-time/adjunct (3 women). *Students:* 24 full-time (9 women), 7 part-time (2 women); includes 2 minority (both Asian, non-Hispanic/Latino), 13 international. Average age 30. 49 applicants, 37% accepted, 7 enrolled. In 2011, 18 master's, 5 doctorates awarded. *Degree requirements:* For master's, thesis optional; for doctorate, one foreign language, thesis/dissertation. *Entrance requirements:* For master's and doctorate, GRE General Test, minimum undergraduate GPA of 3.0 or equivalent. Additional exam requirements/recommendations for international students: Required—TOEFL (minimum score 550 computer-based; 77 iBT); Recommended—TWE. *Application deadline:* For fall admission, 5/15 for domestic and international students; for spring admission, 10/15 for domestic and international students. Applications are processed on a rolling basis. Application fee: $60 ($75 for international students). Electronic applications accepted. *Financial support:* In 2011–12, fellowships with tuition reimbursements (averaging $14,400 per year), research assistantships with tuition reimbursements (averaging $12,000 per year), teaching assistantships with tuition reimbursements (averaging $12,000 per year) were awarded; career-related internships or fieldwork and traineeships also available. Support available to part-time students. Financial award applicants required to submit FAFSA. *Faculty research:* Environmental toxicology, industrial hygiene, radiation dosimetry. *Unit head:* Dr. Wei Zheng, Head, 765-494-1419, E-mail: wz18@purdue.edu. *Application contact:* Jennifer S. Franklin, Graduate Contact, 765-494-0248, E-mail: jfranklin@purdue.edu. Web site: http://www.healthsciences.purdue.edu/.

Tufts University, School of Engineering, Department of Mechanical Engineering, Medford, MA 02155. Offers bioengineering (ME, MS), including bioinformatics (ME), biomechanical systems and devices, signals and systems (ME); human factors (MS); mechanical engineering (ME, MS, PhD). Part-time programs available. *Faculty:* 13 full-time, 5 part-time/adjunct. *Students:* 83 full-time (22 women); includes 13 minority (2 Black or African American, non-Hispanic/Latino; 2 American Indian or Alaska Native, non-Hispanic/Latino; 7 Asian, non-Hispanic/Latino; 2 Hispanic/Latino), 14 international. Average age 27. 126 applicants, 46% accepted, 28 enrolled. In 2011, 21 degrees awarded. Terminal master's awarded for partial completion of doctoral program. *Degree requirements:* For master's, thesis; for doctorate, thesis/dissertation. *Entrance requirements:* For master's and doctorate, GRE General Test. Additional exam requirements/recommendations for international students: Required—TOEFL (minimum score 550 paper-based; 213 computer-based; 80 iBT). *Application deadline:* For fall admission, 1/15 priority date for domestic students, 12/15 for international students; for spring admission, 10/15 for domestic students, 9/15 for international students. Applications are processed on a rolling basis. Application fee: $75. Electronic applications accepted. *Expenses: Tuition:* Full-time $41,208; part-time $1030 per credit hour. Full-time tuition and fees vary according to degree level, program and student level. Part-time tuition and fees vary according to course load. *Financial support:* Fellowships with full tuition reimbursements, research assistantships with full and partial tuition reimbursements, teaching assistantships with full and partial tuition reimbursements, Federal Work-Study, scholarships/grants, tuition waivers (partial), and unspecified assistantships available. Financial award application deadline: 1/15; financial award applicants required to submit FAFSA. *Faculty research:* Applied mechanics, biomaterials, controls/robotics, design/systems, human factors. *Unit head:* Dr. Robert Hannemann, Acting Department Chair, 617-627-3239, Fax: 617-627-3058. *Application contact:* Lorin Polidora, Department Administrator, 617-627-3239, E-mail: meinfo@tufts.edu. Web site: http://engineering.tufts.edu/me.

Université de Montréal, Faculty of Medicine, Programs in Ergonomics, Montréal, QC H3C 3J7, Canada. Offers occupational therapy (DESS). Program offered jointly with École Polytechnique de Montréal.

Université du Québec à Montréal, Graduate Programs, Program in Ergonomics in Occupational Health and Safety, Montréal, QC H3C 3P8, Canada. Offers Diploma. Part-time programs available. *Entrance requirements:* For degree, appropriate bachelor's degree or equivalent, proficiency in French.

The University of Alabama, Graduate School, College of Human Environmental Sciences, Program in Human Environmental Science, Tuscaloosa, AL 35487. Offers family financial planning and counseling (MS); interactive technology (MS); quality management (MS); restaurant and meeting management (MS); rural community health (MS); sport management (MS). *Faculty:* 1 full-time (0 women). *Students:* 80 full-time (53 women), 93 part-time (55 women); includes 51 minority (42 Black or African American, non-Hispanic/Latino; 3 American Indian or Alaska Native, non-Hispanic/Latino; 3 Hispanic/Latino; 3 Two or more races, non-Hispanic/Latino), 1 international. Average age 33. 118 applicants, 79% accepted, 75 enrolled. In 2011, 83 degrees awarded. *Degree requirements:* For master's, comprehensive exam. *Entrance requirements:* For master's, GRE (for some specializations), minimum GPA of 3.0. Additional exam requirements/recommendations for international students: Required—TOEFL. *Application deadline:* Applications are processed on a rolling basis. Application fee: $50 ($60 for international students). Electronic applications accepted. *Expenses:* Tuition, state resident: full-time $8600. Tuition, nonresident: full-time $21,900. *Faculty research:* Hospitality management, sports medicine education, technology and education. *Unit head:* Dr. Milla D. Boschung, Dean, 205-348-6250, Fax: 205-348-1786, E-mail: mboschun@ches.ua.edu. *Application contact:* Dr. Stuart Usdan, Associate Dean, 205-348-6150, Fax: 205-348-3789, E-mail: susdan@ches.ua.edu.

University of Central Florida, College of Engineering and Computer Science, Department of Industrial Engineering and Management Systems, Orlando, FL 32816. Offers applied operations research (Certificate); design for usability (Certificate); engineering management (PSM); industrial engineering (MSIE, PhD); industrial engineering and management systems (MS); industrial ergonomics and safety (Certificate); project engineering (Certificate); quality assurance (Certificate); systems engineering (Certificate); systems simulation for engineers (Certificate); training simulation (Certificate). Part-time and evening/weekend programs available. *Faculty:* 18 full-time (4 women), 5 part-time/adjunct (1 woman). *Students:* 105 full-time (27 women), 151 part-time (47 women); includes 84 minority (20 Black or African American, non-Hispanic/Latino; 1 American Indian or Alaska Native, non-Hispanic/Latino; 20 Asian, non-Hispanic/Latino; 37 Hispanic/Latino; 1 Native Hawaiian or other Pacific Islander, non-Hispanic/Latino; 5 Two or more races, non-Hispanic/Latino), 52 international. Average age 32. 199 applicants, 79% accepted, 75 enrolled. In 2011, 83 master's, 11 doctorates, 40 other advanced degrees awarded. *Degree requirements:* For master's, thesis; for doctorate, thesis/dissertation, departmental qualifying exam, candidacy exam. *Entrance requirements:* For master's, GRE General Test, minimum GPA of 3.0 in last 60 hours of course work; for doctorate, minimum GPA of 3.5 in last 60 hours of course work. Additional exam requirements/recommendations for international students: Required—TOEFL. *Application deadline:* For fall admission, 7/15 priority date for domestic students; for spring admission, 12/1 priority date for domestic students. Application fee: $30. Electronic applications accepted. *Expenses:* Tuition, state resident: part-time $277.08 per credit hour. Tuition, nonresident: part-time $277.08 per credit hour. Part-time tuition and fees vary according to degree level and program. *Financial support:* In 2011–12, 19 students received support, including 8 fellowships with partial tuition reimbursements available (averaging $3,500 per year), 10 research assistantships with partial tuition reimbursements available (averaging $11,100 per year), 6 teaching assistantships with partial tuition reimbursements available (averaging $12,300 per year); career-related internships or fieldwork, Federal Work-Study, institutionally sponsored loans, tuition waivers (partial), and unspecified assistantships also available. Financial award application deadline: 3/1; financial award applicants required to submit FAFSA. *Unit head:* Dr. Waldemar Karwowski, Chair, 407-823-2204, E-mail: wkar@ucf.edu. *Application contact:* Barbara Rodriguez, Director, Admissions and Registration, 407-823-2766, Fax: 407-823-6442, E-mail: gradadmissions@ucf.edu. Web site: http://iems.ucf.edu/.

University of Cincinnati, Graduate School, College of Medicine, Graduate Programs in Biomedical Sciences, Department of Environmental Health, Cincinnati, OH 45221. Offers environmental and industrial hygiene (MS, PhD); environmental and occupational medicine (MS); environmental genetics and molecular toxicology (MS, PhD); epidemiology and biostatistics (MS, PhD); occupational safety and ergonomics (MS, PhD). *Accreditation:* ABET (one or more programs are accredited). Terminal master's awarded for partial completion of doctoral program. *Degree requirements:* For master's, thesis; for doctorate, thesis/dissertation, qualifying exam. *Entrance requirements:* For master's, GRE General Test, bachelor's degree in science; for doctorate, GRE General Test. Additional exam requirements/recommendations for international students: Required—TOEFL (minimum score 600 paper-based; 250 computer-based; 100 iBT). Electronic applications accepted. *Faculty research:* Carcinogens and mutagenesis, pulmonary studies, reproduction and development.

University of Illinois at Urbana–Champaign, Institute of Aviation, Champaign, IL 61820. Offers human factors (MS). *Students:* 1 full-time (0 women). 10 applicants, 0% accepted, 0 enrolled. In 2011, 5 master's awarded. *Entrance requirements:* For master's, GRE, minimum undergraduate GPA of 3.0 for last 60 hours. Additional exam requirements/recommendations for international students: Required—TOEFL. *Application deadline:* Applications are processed on a rolling basis. Application fee: $75 ($90 for international students). Electronic applications accepted. *Financial support:* Fellowships, research assistantships, teaching assistantships, and tuition waivers (full and partial) available. *Unit head:* Tom Emanuel, Acting Head, 217-244-8972, E-mail: emanuel@illinois.edu. *Application contact:* Peter Vlach, Information Systems Specialist, 217-265-9456, E-mail: pvlach@illinois.edu. Web site: http://www.aviation.illinois.edu.

The University of Iowa, Graduate College, College of Engineering, Department of Industrial Engineering, Iowa City, IA 52242-1316. Offers engineering design and manufacturing (MS, PhD); ergonomics (MS, PhD); information and engineering management (MS, PhD); operations research (MS, PhD); quality engineering (MS, PhD). *Faculty:* 7 full-time (0 women). *Students:* 21 full-time (6 women); includes 2 minority (1 Black or African American, non-Hispanic/Latino; 1 Asian, non-Hispanic/Latino), 14 international. Average age 27. 69 applicants, 13% accepted, 5 enrolled. In 2011, 8 master's, 6 doctorates awarded. *Degree requirements:* For master's, thesis optional, exam; for doctorate, comprehensive exam, thesis/dissertation, final defense exam. *Entrance requirements:* For master's and doctorate, GRE General Test. Additional exam requirements/recommendations for international students: Required— TOEFL (minimum score 550 paper-based; 213 computer-based; 81 iBT). *Application deadline:* For fall admission, 7/15 for domestic students, 4/15 for international students; for spring admission, 12/1 for domestic students, 10/1 for international students. Applications are processed on a rolling basis. Application fee: $60 ($100 for international students). Electronic applications accepted. *Financial support:* In 2011–12, 5 fellowships with partial tuition reimbursements (averaging $30,450 per year), 17 research assistantships with partial tuition reimbursements (averaging $20,000 per

year), 5 teaching assistantships with partial tuition reimbursements (averaging $16,630 per year) were awarded; career-related internships or fieldwork, scholarships/grants, and unspecified assistantships also available. Support available to part-time students. Financial award applicants required to submit FAFSA. *Faculty research:* Operations research, informatics, human factors engineering, manufacturing systems, human-machine interaction. *Total annual research expenditures:* $4.6 million. *Unit head:* Dr. Andrew Kusiak, Department Executive Officer, 319-335-5934, Fax: 319-335-5669, E-mail: andrew-kusiak@uiowa.edu. *Application contact:* Andrea Flaherty, Academic Program Specialist, 319-335-5939, Fax: 319-335-5669, E-mail: indeng@engineering.uiowa.edu. Web site: http://www.mie.engineering.uiowa.edu/.

University of Massachusetts Lowell, School of Health and Environment, Department of Work Environment, Lowell, MA 01854-2881. Offers cleaner production and pollution prevention (MS, Sc D); environmental risk assessment (Certificate); epidemiology (MS, Sc D); ergonomics and safety (MS, Sc D); identification and control of ergonomic hazards (Certificate); job stress and healthy job redesign (Certificate); occupational and environmental hygiene (MS, Sc D); radiological health physics and general work environment protection (Certificate); work environment policy (MS, Sc D). *Accreditation:* ABET (one or more programs are accredited). Part-time programs available. Terminal master's awarded for partial completion of doctoral program. *Degree requirements:* For master's, thesis optional; for doctorate, thesis/dissertation. *Entrance requirements:* For master's and doctorate, GRE General Test. Additional exam requirements/recommendations for international students: Required—TOEFL.

University of Miami, Graduate School, College of Engineering, Department of Industrial Engineering, Program in Occupational Ergonomics and Safety, Coral Gables, FL 33124. Offers environmental health and safety (MS); occupational ergonomics and safety (MSOES). Part-time programs available. *Degree requirements:* For master's, thesis optional. *Entrance requirements:* For master's, GRE General Test, minimum GPA of 3.0. Additional exam requirements/recommendations for international students: Required—TOEFL (minimum score 550 paper-based; 213 computer-based). Electronic applications accepted. *Faculty research:* Noise, heat stress, water pollution.

University of Wisconsin–Milwaukee, Graduate School, College of Engineering and Applied Science, Program in Engineering, Milwaukee, WI 53201-0413. Offers civil engineering (MS); electrical and computer engineering (MS); energy engineering (Certificate); engineering (PhD); engineering management (MS); engineering mechanics (MS); ergonomics (Certificate); industrial and management engineering (MS); manufacturing engineering (MS); materials engineering (MS); mechanical engineering (MS); MUP/MS. Part-time programs available. *Faculty:* 41 full-time (5 women), 2 part-time/adjunct (0 women). *Students:* 170 full-time (33 women), 101 part-time (18 women); includes 30 minority (6 Black or African American, non-Hispanic/Latino; 15 Asian, non-Hispanic/Latino; 2 Hispanic/Latino; 7 Two or more races, non-Hispanic/Latino), 153 international. Average age 30. 170 applicants, 56% accepted, 48 enrolled. In 2011, 47 master's, 12 doctorates awarded. *Degree requirements:* For master's, comprehensive exam (for some programs), thesis or alternative; for doctorate, comprehensive exam, thesis/dissertation, internship. *Entrance requirements:* For master's, GRE, minimum GPA of 2.75; for doctorate, GRE, minimum GPA of 3.5. Additional exam requirements/recommendations for international students: Required—TOEFL (minimum score 550 paper-based; 79 iBT), IELTS (minimum score 6.5). *Application deadline:* For fall admission, 1/1 priority date for domestic students; for spring admission, 9/1 for domestic students. Applications are processed on a rolling basis. Application fee: $56 ($96 for international students). One-time fee: $506.10 full-time. Tuition and fees vary according to course load and reciprocity agreements. *Financial support:* In 2011–12, 3 fellowships, 55 research assistantships, 77 teaching assistantships were awarded; career-related internships or fieldwork, Federal Work-Study, unspecified assistantships, and project assistantships also available. Support available to part-time students. Financial award application deadline: 4/15. *Total annual research expenditures:* $10.3 million. *Unit head:* David Yu, Representative, 414-229-6169, E-mail: yu@uwm.edu. *Application contact:* Betty Warras, General Information Contact, 414-229-6169, Fax: 414-229-6967, E-mail: bwarras@uwm.edu. Web site: http://www.wum.edu/CEAS/.

University of Wisconsin–Milwaukee, Graduate School, College of Health Sciences, Department of Occupational Science and Technology, Milwaukee, WI 53201-0413. Offers ergonomics (Certificate); occupational therapy (MS); therapeutic recreation (Certificate). *Accreditation:* AOTA. *Faculty:* 11 full-time (6 women), 1 (woman) part-time/adjunct. *Students:* 36 full-time (30 women), 11 part-time (7 women), 3 international. Average age 30. 16 applicants, 31% accepted, 0 enrolled. In 2011, 29 degrees awarded. *Degree requirements:* For master's, thesis or alternative. *Entrance requirements:* Additional exam requirements/recommendations for international students: Required—TOEFL (minimum score 550 paper-based; 79 iBT), IELTS (minimum score 6.5). *Application deadline:* For fall admission, 1/1 priority date for domestic students; for spring admission, 9/1 for domestic students. Applications are processed on a rolling basis. Application fee: $45 ($75 for international students). One-time fee: $506.10 full-time. Tuition and fees vary according to course load and reciprocity agreements. *Financial support:* Fellowships, research assistantships, teaching assistantships, and unspecified assistantships available. Support available to part-time students. Financial award application deadline: 4/15. *Total annual research expenditures:* $21,103. *Unit head:* Carol Haertlein Sells, Department Chair, 414-229-6933, E-mail: chaert@uwm.edu. *Application contact:* Roger O. Smith, General Information Contact, 414-229-6697, Fax: 414-229-6697, E-mail: smithro@uwm.edu. Web site: http://www4.uwm.edu/chs/academics/occupational_therapy/.

Wright State University, School of Graduate Studies, College of Engineering and Computer Science, Programs in Engineering, Program in Biomedical and Human Factors Engineering, Dayton, OH 45435. Offers biomedical engineering (MSE); human factors engineering (MSE). Part-time programs available. *Degree requirements:* For master's, thesis or course option alternative. *Entrance requirements:* Additional exam requirements/recommendations for international students: Required—TOEFL. *Faculty research:* Medical imaging, functional electrical stimulation, implantable aids, man-machine interfaces, expert systems.

Wright State University, School of Graduate Studies, College of Science and Mathematics, Department of Psychology, Program in Human Factors and Industrial/Organizational Psychology, Dayton, OH 45435. Offers MS, PhD. *Degree requirements:* For master's, thesis; for doctorate, thesis/dissertation.

Management of Technology

Air Force Institute of Technology, Graduate School of Engineering and Management, Department of Operational Sciences, Dayton, OH 45433-7765. Offers logistics management (MS); operations research (MS, PhD); space operations (MS). Part-time programs available. *Degree requirements:* For master's, thesis; for doctorate, thesis/dissertation. *Entrance requirements:* For doctorate, GRE General Test, minimum GPA of 3.0, U.S. citizenship. *Faculty research:* Optimization, simulation, combat modeling and analysis, reliability and maintainability, resource scheduling.

Arizona State University, College of Technology and Innovation, Department of Technology Management, Mesa, AZ 85212. Offers technology (aviation management and human factors) (MS); technology (environmental technology management) (MS); technology (global technology and development) (MS); technology (graphic information technology) (MS); technology (management of technology) (MS). Part-time and evening/weekend programs available. Postbaccalaureate distance learning degree programs offered (minimal on-campus study). *Degree requirements:* For master's, thesis or applied project and oral defense; interactive Program of Study (iPOS) submitted before completing 50 percent of required credit hours. *Entrance requirements:* For master's, GRE, minimum GPA of 3.0 or equivalent in last 2 years of work leading to bachelor's degree. Additional exam requirements/recommendations for international students: Required—TOEFL (minimum score 83 iBT), TOEFL, IELTS, or Pearson Test of English. Electronic applications accepted. *Faculty research:* Digital imaging, digital publishing, Internet development/e-commerce, information aviation human factors, pilot selection, databases, multimedia, commercial digital photography, digital workflow, computer graphics modeling and animation, information design, sociotechnology, visual and technical literacy, environmental management, quality management, project management, industrial ethics, hazardous materials, environmental chemistry.

Athabasca University, Centre for Innovative Management, St. Albert, AB T8N 1B4, Canada. Offers business administration (MBA); information technology management (MBA), including policing concentration; management (GDM); project management (MBA, GDM). Part-time and evening/weekend programs available. Postbaccalaureate distance learning degree programs offered (no on-campus study). *Degree requirements:* For master's, thesis or alternative, applied project. *Entrance requirements:* For master's, 3-8 years of managerial experience, 3 years with undergraduate degree, 5 years managerial experience with professional designation, 8-10 years management experience (on exception). Electronic applications accepted. *Expenses:* Contact institution. *Faculty research:* Human resources, project management, operations research, information technology management, corporate stewardship, energy management.

Boston University, Metropolitan College, Department of Administrative Sciences, Boston, MA 02215. Offers banking and financial management (MSM); business continuity in emergency management (MSM); economics development and tourism management (MSAS); electronic commerce, systems, and technology (MSAS); financial economics (MSAS); innovation and technology (MSAS); insurance management (MSM); international market management (MSM); multinational commerce (MSAS); project management (MSM). *Accreditation:* AACSB. Part-time and evening/weekend programs available. Postbaccalaureate distance learning degree programs offered (no on-campus study). *Faculty:* 14 full-time (2 women), 21 part-time/adjunct (2 women). *Students:* 151 full-time (75 women), 106 part-time (51 women); includes 27 minority (6 Black or African American, non-Hispanic/Latino; 14 Asian, non-Hispanic/Latino; 7 Hispanic/Latino), 173 international. Average age 28. 500 applicants, 65% accepted, 194 enrolled. In 2011, 154 master's awarded. *Degree requirements:* For master's, thesis optional. *Entrance requirements:* For master's, 1 year of work experience, minimum GPA of 3.0. Additional exam requirements/recommendations for international students: Required—TOEFL (minimum score 560 paper-based; 220 computer-based; 84 iBT). *Application deadline:* Applications are processed on a rolling basis. Application fee: $70. Electronic applications accepted. *Expenses: Tuition:* Full-time $40,848; part-time $1276 per credit hour. *Required fees:* $572; $286 per semester. *Financial support:* In 2011–12, 15 students received support, including 7 research assistantships (averaging $10,000 per year); career-related internships or fieldwork, Federal Work-Study, and unspecified assistantships also available. *Faculty research:* International business, innovative process. *Unit head:* Dr. Kip Becker, Chairman, 617-353-3016, E-mail: adminsc@bu.edu. *Application contact:* Lucille Dicker, Administrative Sciences Department, 617-353-3016, E-mail: adminsc@bu.edu. Web site: http://www.bu.edu/met/programs/.

California Lutheran University, Graduate Studies, School of Management, Thousand Oaks, CA 91360-2787. Offers business (IMBA); computer science (MS); econometrics (MBA); economics (MS); entrepreneurship (MBA, Certificate); finance (MBA, Certificate); financial planning (MBA, Certificate); information systems and technology (MS); information technology management (MBA, Certificate); international business (MBA, Certificate); management and organization behavior (MBA); management and organizational behavior (Certificate); marketing (MBA, Certificate); microeconomics (MBA); nonprofit and social enterprise (MBA). Part-time and evening/weekend programs available. Postbaccalaureate distance learning degree programs offered (no on-campus study). *Entrance requirements:* For master's, GMAT, interview, minimum GPA of 3.0. *Expenses:* Contact institution.

California State University, Los Angeles, Graduate Studies, College of Engineering, Computer Science, and Technology, Department of Technology, Los Angeles, CA 90032-8530. Offers industrial and technical studies (MA). Part-time and evening/weekend programs available. *Faculty:* 2 part-time/adjunct (0 women). *Students:* 11 full-time (2 women), 12 part-time (0 women); includes 12 minority (2 Black or African American, non-Hispanic/Latino; 2 Asian, non-Hispanic/Latino; 8 Hispanic/Latino), 6 international. Average age 33. 22 applicants, 64% accepted, 7 enrolled. In 2011, 10 master's awarded. *Entrance requirements:* For master's, minimum GPA of 2.5. Additional exam requirements/recommendations for international students: Required—TOEFL (minimum score 550 paper-based). *Application deadline:* For fall admission, 5/1 for domestic and international students. Applications are processed on a rolling basis. Application fee: $55. *Expenses:* Tuition, state resident: full-time $8225. *Financial support:* Federal Work-Study available. Support available to part-time students. Financial award application deadline: 3/1. *Unit head:* Dr. Keith Mew, Chair, 323-343-4550, Fax: 323-343-4571, E-mail: kmew@calstatela.edu. *Application contact:* Dr. Karin Brown, Acting Associate Dean of Graduate Studies, 323-343-3820, Fax: 323-343-5653, E-mail: kbrown5@calstatela.edu. Web site: http://www.calstatela.edu/academic/ecst/tech/.

Cambridge College, School of Management, Cambridge, MA 02138-5304. Offers business negotiation and conflict resolution (M Mgt); general business (M Mgt); health care informatics (M Mgt); health care management (M Mgt); leadership in human and organizational dynamics (M Mgt); non-profit and public organization management (M Mgt); small business development (M Mgt); technology management (M Mgt). Part-time and evening/weekend programs available. *Degree requirements:* For master's, thesis, seminars. *Entrance requirements:* For master's, resume, 2 professional references. Additional exam requirements/recommendations for international students: Required—TOEFL (minimum score 550 paper-based; 213 computer-based; 79 iBT); Recommended—IELTS (minimum score 6). Electronic applications accepted. *Expenses:* Contact institution. *Faculty research:* Negotiation, mediation and conflict resolution; leadership; management of diverse organizations; case studies and simulation methodologies for management education, digital as a second language: social networking for digital immigrants, non-profit and public management.

Capella University, School of Business and Technology, Minneapolis, MN 55402. Offers accounting (MBA), including system design and programming; business (Certificate), including human resource management (MS, PhD, Certificate), information technology management (MS, PhD, Certificate), leadership (MBA, MS, PhD, Certificate); finance (MBA); general business (MBA); health care management (MBA); information technology (MS, Certificate), including general information technology (MS), information security, network architecture and design (MS), professional projects management (Certificate), project management and leadership (MS), system design and development (MS),); information technology management (MBA); marketing (MBA); organization and management (MBA, MS, PhD), including general business (PhD), general organization and management (MBA, MS), human resource management (MS, PhD, Certificate), information technology management (MS, PhD, Certificate), leadership (MBA, MS, PhD, Certificate); project management (MBA). Part-time and evening/weekend programs available. Postbaccalaureate distance learning degree programs offered (minimal on-campus study). Terminal master's awarded for partial completion of doctoral program. *Degree requirements:* For master's, thesis optional, integrative project; for doctorate, comprehensive exam, thesis/dissertation. *Entrance requirements:* Additional exam requirements/recommendations for international students: Required—TOEFL (minimum score 550 paper-based; 213 computer-based), TWE (minimum score 4). Electronic applications accepted. *Faculty research:* Business policies: strategic, corporate, and financial management; interplay of technological, organizational and social change.

Carleton University, Faculty of Graduate Studies, Faculty of Engineering and Design, Ottawa-Carleton Institute for Electrical Engineering, Department of Systems and Computer Engineering, Program in Technology Innovation Management, Ottawa, ON K1S 5B6, Canada. Offers M Eng, MA Sc. *Degree requirements:* For master's, thesis optional. *Entrance requirements:* For master's, honors degree. Additional exam requirements/recommendations for international students: Required—TOEFL.

Carlow University, School of Management, MBA Program, Pittsburgh, PA 15213-3165. Offers business administration (MBA); innovation management (MBA); technology management (MBA). Part-time and evening/weekend programs available. Postbaccalaureate distance learning degree programs offered (no on-campus study). *Students:* 84 full-time (70 women), 24 part-time (17 women); includes 25 minority (22 Black or African American, non-Hispanic/Latino; 3 Hispanic/Latino). Average age 32. 138 applicants, 44% accepted, 46 enrolled. In 2011, 38 master's awarded. *Entrance requirements:* For master's, minimum undergraduate GPA of 3.0; essay; resume; transcripts; two recommendations. Additional exam requirements/recommendations for international students: Required—TOEFL (minimum score 550 paper-based; 213 computer-based). *Application deadline:* Applications are processed on a rolling basis. Application fee: $20. Electronic applications accepted. Application fee is waived when completed online. *Expenses: Tuition:* Full-time $10,290; part-time $686 per credit. Tuition and fees vary according to course load, degree level and program. *Unit head:* Dr. Enrique Mu, Director, MBA Program, 412-578-8729, Fax: 412-587-6367, E-mail: muex@carlow.edu. *Application contact:* Jo Danhires, Administrative Assistant, Admissions, 412-578-6088, Fax: 412-578-6321, E-mail: gradstudies@carlow.edu. Web site: http://gradstudies.carlow.edu/management/mba.html.

Carnegie Mellon University, Mellon College of Science, Department of Chemistry, Pittsburgh, PA 15213-3891. Offers biotechnology and management (MS); chemistry (PhD), including bioinorganic, bioorganic, organic and materials, biophysics and spectroscopy, computational and theoretical, polymer; colloids, polymers and surfaces (MS). Part-time programs available. Terminal master's awarded for partial completion of doctoral program. *Degree requirements:* For doctorate, thesis/dissertation, departmental qualifying and oral exams, teaching experience. *Entrance requirements:* For master's, GRE General Test; for doctorate, GRE General Test, GRE Subject Test. Additional exam requirements/recommendations for international students: Required—TOEFL. Electronic applications accepted. *Faculty research:* Physical and theoretical chemistry, chemical synthesis, biophysical/bioinorganic chemistry.

Central Connecticut State University, School of Graduate Studies, School of Technology, Department of Manufacturing and Construction Management, New Britain, CT 06050-4010. Offers construction management (MS, Certificate); lean manufacturing and Six Sigma (Certificate); supply chain and logistics (Certificate); technology management (MS). Part-time and evening/weekend programs available. *Faculty:* 18 full-time (4 women), 26 part-time/adjunct (2 women). *Students:* 23 full-time (5 women), 89 part-time (22 women); includes 18 minority (10 Black or African American, non-Hispanic/Latino; 7 Asian, non-Hispanic/Latino; 1 Hispanic/Latino), 7 international. Average age 36. 68 applicants, 78% accepted, 39 enrolled. In 2011, 25 master's, 1 other advanced degree awarded. *Degree requirements:* For master's, comprehensive exam, thesis or alternative; for Certificate, qualifying exam. *Entrance requirements:* For master's, minimum undergraduate GPA of 2.7. Additional exam requirements/recommendations for international students: Required—TOEFL (minimum score 550 paper-based; 213 computer-based). *Application deadline:* For fall admission, 6/1 for domestic students, 5/1 for international students; for spring admission, 11/1 for domestic and international students. Applications are processed on a rolling basis. Application fee: $50. Electronic applications accepted. *Expenses: Tuition, area resident:* Full-time $5137; part-time $482 per credit. Tuition, state resident: full-time $7707; part-time $494 per credit. Tuition, nonresident: full-time $14,311; part-time $494 per credit. *Required fees:* $3865. One-time fee: $62 part-time. *Financial support:* In 2011–12, 9 students received support, including 7 research assistantships; career-related internships or fieldwork, Federal Work-Study, scholarships/grants, and unspecified assistantships also available. Support available to part-time students. Financial award application deadline: 4/15; financial award applicants required to submit FAFSA. *Faculty research:* All aspects of middle management, technical supervision in the workplace. *Unit head:* Dr. Jacob Kovel, Chair, 860-832-1830, E-mail: kovelj@ccsu.edu. *Application contact:* Patricia Gardner,

Associate Director of Graduate Studies, 860-832-2350, Fax: 860-832-2352, E-mail: graduateadmissions@ccsu.edu. Web site: http://www.ccsu.edu/page.cfm?p=6497.

Champlain College, Graduate Studies, Burlington, VT 05402-0670. Offers business (MBA); digital forensic management (MS); education (M Ed); emergent media (MFA); health care management (MS); law (MS); managing innovation and information technology (MS); mediation and applied conflict studies (MS). Part-time programs available. Postbaccalaureate distance learning degree programs offered (no on-campus study). *Faculty:* 11 full-time (1 woman), 26 part-time/adjunct (11 women). *Students:* 328 full-time (213 women), 66 part-time (36 women); includes 17 minority (11 Black or African American, non-Hispanic/Latino; 1 Asian, non-Hispanic/Latino; 4 Hispanic/Latino; 1 Two or more races, non-Hispanic/Latino). Average age 37. 132 applicants, 90% accepted, 102 enrolled. In 2011, 8 master's awarded. *Degree requirements:* For master's, capstone project. *Entrance requirements:* Additional exam requirements/recommendations for international students: Required—TOEFL. *Application deadline:* For fall admission, 8/1 priority date for domestic students, 8/1 for international students; for spring admission, 1/1 priority date for domestic students, 1/1 for international students. Applications are processed on a rolling basis. Application fee: $50. Electronic applications accepted. *Expenses: Tuition:* Part-time $746 per credit. Tuition and fees vary according to program. *Financial support:* Applicants required to submit FAFSA. *Unit head:* Dr. Donald Haggerty, Associate Provost, 802-865-6403, Fax: 802-865-6447. *Application contact:* Jon Walsh, Assistant Vice President, Graduate Admission, 800-570-5858, E-mail: walsh@champlain.edu. Web site: http://www.champlain.edu/master/.

City University of Seattle, Graduate Division, School of Management, Bellevue, WA 98005. Offers accounting (Certificate); change leadership (MBA, Certificate); computer systems (MS); finance (Certificate); financial management (MBA); general management (MBA); general management-Europe (MBA); global marketing (MBA); human resources management (Certificate); individualized study (MBA); information security (MS); information systems (MBA); leadership (MA); marketing (MBA, Certificate); project management (MBA, MS, Certificate); sustainable business (Certificate); technology management (MBA, Certificate). Part-time and evening/weekend programs available. Postbaccalaureate distance learning degree programs offered (no on-campus study). *Faculty:* 6 full-time (2 women), 95 part-time/adjunct (33 women). *Students:* 397 full-time (193 women), 283 part-time (137 women); includes 127 minority (67 Black or African American, non-Hispanic/Latino; 5 American Indian or Alaska Native, non-Hispanic/Latino; 33 Asian, non-Hispanic/Latino; 15 Hispanic/Latino; 1 Native Hawaiian or other Pacific Islander, non-Hispanic/Latino; 6 Two or more races, non-Hispanic/Latino), 117 international. Average age 36. 151 applicants, 100% accepted, 151 enrolled. In 2011, 369 master's, 32 other advanced degrees awarded. *Degree requirements:* For master's, comprehensive exam (for some programs), thesis (for some programs). *Entrance requirements:* Additional exam requirements/recommendations for international students: Required—TOEFL (minimum score 567 paper-based; 227 computer-based; 87 iBT); Recommended—IELTS. *Application deadline:* For fall admission, 9/1 for international students; for winter admission, 12/1 for international students; for spring admission, 3/1 for international students. Applications are processed on a rolling basis. Application fee: $50. Electronic applications accepted. *Financial support:* Federal Work-Study and scholarships/grants available. Support available to part-time students. Financial award applicants required to submit FAFSA. *Unit head:* Dr. Kurt Kirstein, Dean, 425-637-1010 Ext. 5456, Fax: 425-709-5363, E-mail: kdkirstein@cityu.edu. *Application contact:* Alysa Borelli, Director, Recruiting, 888-422-4898, Fax: 425-709-5363, E-mail: info@cityu.edu. Web site: http://www.cityu.edu/programs/som/index.aspx.

Coleman University, Program in Business and Technology Management, San Diego, CA 92123. Offers MS. Evening/weekend programs available. Postbaccalaureate distance learning degree programs offered (no on-campus study). *Entrance requirements:* For master's, bachelor's degree, minimum GPA of 3.0. Additional exam requirements/recommendations for international students: Required—TOEFL (minimum score 500 paper-based; 173 computer-based).

Colorado School of Mines, Graduate School, Division of Economics and Business, Golden, CO 80401-1887. Offers engineering and technology management (MS); mineral economics (MS, PhD). Part-time programs available. *Faculty:* 10 full-time (2 women), 6 part-time/adjunct (2 women). *Students:* 118 full-time (18 women), 19 part-time (4 women); includes 14 minority (1 Black or African American, non-Hispanic/Latino; 2 American Indian or Alaska Native, non-Hispanic/Latino; 2 Asian, non-Hispanic/Latino; 7 Hispanic/Latino; 2 Two or more races, non-Hispanic/Latino), 29 international. Average age 29. 177 applicants, 64% accepted, 59 enrolled. In 2011, 53 master's, 3 doctorates awarded. *Degree requirements:* For master's, thesis (for some programs); for doctorate, comprehensive exam, thesis/dissertation. *Entrance requirements:* For master's and doctorate, GRE General Test. Additional exam requirements/recommendations for international students: Required—TOEFL (minimum score 550 paper-based; 213 computer-based; 80 iBT). *Application deadline:* For fall admission, 1/15 priority date for domestic students, 1/15 for international students; for spring admission, 10/15 priority date for domestic students, 10/15 for international students. Application fee: $50 ($70 for international students). Electronic applications accepted. *Expenses:* Tuition, state resident: full-time $12,585; part-time $699 per credit. Tuition, nonresident: full-time $27,270; part-time $1516 per credit. *Required fees:* $1864.20; $670 per semester. *Financial support:* In 2011–12, 37 students received support, including 4 fellowships with full tuition reimbursements available (averaging $20,000 per year), 16 research assistantships with full tuition reimbursements available (averaging $20,000 per year), 17 teaching assistantships with full tuition reimbursements available (averaging $20,000 per year); scholarships/grants, health care benefits, and unspecified assistantships also available. Financial award application deadline: 1/15; financial award applicants required to submit FAFSA. *Faculty research:* International trade, resource and environmental economics, energy economics, operations research. *Total annual research expenditures:* $140,148. *Unit head:* Dr. Rod Eggert, Director, 303-273-3981, Fax: 303-273-3416, E-mail: reggert@mines.edu. *Application contact:* Kathleen A. Feighny, Administrative Faculty, 303-273-3979, Fax: 303-273-3416, E-mail: kfeighny@mines.edu. Web site: http://econbus.mines.edu.

Colorado Technical University Colorado Springs, Graduate Studies, Program in Management, Colorado Springs, CO 80907-3896. Offers accounting (MBA, MSA); business administration (MBA); finance (MBA); human resources management (MBA); logistics/supply chain management (MBA); management (DM); marketing (MBA); mediation and dispute resolution (MBA); operations management (MBA); project management (MBA); technology management (MBA). Part-time and evening/weekend programs available. Postbaccalaureate distance learning degree programs offered. *Degree requirements:* For master's, thesis or alternative; for doctorate, thesis/dissertation. *Entrance requirements:* For doctorate, minimum graduate GPA of 3.0, 5 years of related work experience. *Faculty research:* Sexual harassment, performance evaluation, critical thinking.

Colorado Technical University Denver South, Programs in Business Administration and Management, Aurora, CO 80014. Offers accounting (MBA); business administration (MBA); business administration and management (EMBA); finance (MBA); human resource management (MBA); marketing (MBA); mediation and dispute resolution (MBA); operations management (MBA); project management (MBA); technology management (MBA). Part-time and evening/weekend programs available. *Degree requirements:* For master's, thesis or alternative. *Entrance requirements:* For master's, minimum undergraduate GPA of 3.0, resume.

Colorado Technical University Sioux Falls, Programs in Business Administration and Management, Sioux Falls, SD 57108. Offers business administration (MBA); business management (MSM); health science management (MSM); human resources management (MSM); information technology (MSM); organizational leadership (MSM); project management (MBA); technology management (MBA). Evening/weekend programs available. *Degree requirements:* For master's, thesis optional. *Entrance requirements:* For master's, minimum 2 years work experience, resume.

Columbia University, School of Continuing Education, Program in Technology Management, New York, NY 10027. Offers Exec MS. Part-time and evening/weekend programs available. *Entrance requirements:* For master's, minimum undergraduate GPA of 3.0. Additional exam requirements/recommendations for international students: Required—American Language Program placement test. Electronic applications accepted. *Faculty research:* Information systems, management.

Dallas Baptist University, College of Business, Business Administration Program, Dallas, TX 75211-9299. Offers accounting (MBA); business communication (MBA); conflict resolution management (MBA); entrepreneurship (MBA); finance (MBA); health care management (MBA); international business (MBA); leading the non-profit organization (MBA); management (MBA); management information systems (MBA); marketing (MBA); project management (MBA); technology and engineering management (MBA). *Accreditation:* ACBSP. Part-time and evening/weekend programs available. *Entrance requirements:* For master's, GMAT, minimum GPA of 3.0. Additional exam requirements/recommendations for international students: Required—TOEFL, IELTS. *Application deadline:* Applications are processed on a rolling basis. Application fee: $25. Electronic applications accepted. *Expenses: Tuition:* Full-time $12,060; part-time $670 per credit hour. *Required fees:* $100; $50 per semester. *Financial support:* Federal Work-Study, institutionally sponsored loans, scholarships/grants, and tuition waivers (full and partial) available. Support available to part-time students. Financial award applicants required to submit FAFSA. *Faculty research:* Sports management, services marketing, retailing, strategic management, financial planning/investments. *Unit head:* Dr. Sandra S. Reid, Director, 214-333-5280, Fax: 214-333-5293, E-mail: graduate@dbu.edu. *Application contact:* Kit P. Montgomery, Director of Graduate Programs, 214-333-5242, Fax: 214-333-5579, E-mail: graduate@dbu.edu. Web site: http://www3.dbu.edu/graduate/mba.asp.

DePaul University, College of Computing and Digital Media, Chicago, IL 60604. Offers animation (MA, MFA); applied technology (MS); business information technology (MS); cinema (MFA); cinema production (MS); computational finance (MS); computer and information sciences (PhD); computer game development (MS); computer graphics and motion technology (MS); computer information and network security (MS); computer science (MS); e-commerce technology (MS); human-computer interaction (MS); information systems (MS); information technology (MA); information technology project management (MS); network engineering and management (MS); predictive analytics (MS); screenwriting (MFA); software engineering (MS); JD/MA; JD/MS. Part-time and evening/weekend programs available. Postbaccalaureate distance learning degree programs offered (no on-campus study). *Faculty:* 64 full-time (16 women), 44 part-time/adjunct (5 women). *Students:* 969 full-time (250 women), 936 part-time (231 women); includes 566 minority (204 Black or African American, non-Hispanic/Latino; 3 American Indian or Alaska Native, non-Hispanic/Latino; 166 Asian, non-Hispanic/Latino; 135 Hispanic/Latino; 7 Native Hawaiian or other Pacific Islander, non-Hispanic/Latino; 51 Two or more races, non-Hispanic/Latino), 282 international. Average age 32. 1,040 applicants, 65% accepted, 324 enrolled. In 2011, 478 master's, 4 doctorates awarded. *Degree requirements:* For master's, thesis (for some programs); for doctorate, comprehensive exam, thesis/dissertation. *Entrance requirements:* For master's, GRE or GMAT (MS in computational finance only), bachelor's degree, resume (MS in predictive analytics only), IT experience (MS in information technology project management only), portfolio review (all MFA programs and MA in animation); for doctorate, GRE, master's degree in computer science. Additional exam requirements/recommendations for international students: Required—TOEFL (minimum score 550 paper-based; 213 computer-based; 80 iBT), IELTS (minimum score 6.5), Pearson Test of English (minimum score 53). *Application deadline:* For fall admission, 8/1 priority date for domestic students, 6/1 for international students; for winter admission, 12/1 priority date for domestic students, 10/1 for international students; for spring admission, 3/1 priority date for domestic students, 1/1 for international students. Applications are processed on a rolling basis. Application fee: $25. Electronic applications accepted. *Expenses:* Contact institution. *Financial support:* In 2011–12, 56 students received support, including 3 fellowships with full tuition reimbursements available (averaging $30,000 per year), 3 research assistantships with full and partial tuition reimbursements available (averaging $22,833 per year), 50 teaching assistantships (averaging $6,194 per year); Federal Work-Study, scholarships/grants, tuition waivers (full and partial), and unspecified assistantships also available. Support available to part-time students. Financial award application deadline: 4/30. *Faculty research:* Data mining, theoretical computer science, gaming, security, animation and film. *Total annual research expenditures:* $3.9 million. *Unit head:* Elly Kafritsas-Wessels, Senior Administrative Assistant, 312-362-5816, Fax: 312-362-5185, E-mail: ekafrits@cdm.depaul.edu. *Application contact:* James Parker, Director of Graduate Admission, 312-362-8714, Fax: 312-362-5179, E-mail: jparke29@cdm.depaul.edu. Web site: http://cdm.depaul.edu.

East Carolina University, Graduate School, College of Technology and Computer Science, Department of Technology Systems, Greenville, NC 27858-4353. Offers computer network professional (Certificate); industrial technology (MS), including computer networking management, digital communications, industrial distribution and logistics, information security, manufacturing, performance improvement, quality systems; information assurance (Certificate); Lean Six Sigma Black Belt (Certificate); occupational safety (MS); technology management (PhD); Website developer (Certificate). *Entrance requirements:* For master's and Certificate, GRE General Test or MAT, minimum GPA of 2.5; for doctorate, GRE General Test, related work experience. *Application deadline:* For fall admission, 6/1 priority date for domestic students. Applications are processed on a rolling basis. Application fee: $50. *Expenses:* Tuition, state resident: full-time $3557; part-time $444.63 per semester hour. Tuition, nonresident: full-time $14,351; part-time $1793.88 per semester hour. *Required fees:* $2016; $252 per semester hour. Part-time tuition and fees vary according to course load, campus/location and program. *Financial support:* Application deadline: 6/1. *Unit head:* Dr. Tijjani Mohammed, Interim Chair, 252-328-9668, E-mail: mohammedt@ecu.edu. Web site: http://www.ecu.edu/cs-tecs/techsystems/.

Management of Technology

Eastern Michigan University, Graduate School, College of Technology, Program in Technology, Ypsilanti, MI 48197. Offers PhD. Part-time and evening/weekend programs available. *Students:* 2 full-time (both women), 60 part-time (19 women); includes 10 minority (6 Black or African American, non-Hispanic/Latino; 1 Asian, non-Hispanic/Latino; 3 Hispanic/Latino), 15 international. Average age 41. 41 applicants, 22% accepted, 5 enrolled. In 2011, 9 doctorates awarded. *Degree requirements:* For doctorate, comprehensive exam, thesis/dissertation. *Entrance requirements:* For doctorate, GRE. Additional exam requirements/recommendations for international students: Required—TOEFL. *Application deadline:* For fall admission, 2/15 for domestic and international students; for winter admission, 10/15 for domestic and international students. Applications are processed on a rolling basis. Application fee: $35. *Expenses:* Tuition, state resident: full-time $10,367; part-time $432 per credit hour. Tuition, nonresident: full-time $20,435; part-time $851 per credit hour. *Required fees:* $39 per credit hour. $46 per semester. One-time fee: $100. Tuition and fees vary according to course level, degree level and reciprocity agreements. *Financial support:* Fellowships, research assistantships with full and partial tuition reimbursements, teaching assistantships with full and partial tuition reimbursements, career-related internships or fieldwork, Federal Work-Study, institutionally sponsored loans, scholarships/grants, tuition waivers (partial), and unspecified assistantships available. Support available to part-time students. Financial award applicants required to submit FAFSA. *Unit head:* Dr. Morell Boone, Dean, 734-487-0354, Fax: 734-487-0843, E-mail: mboone@emich.edu. *Application contact:* Graduate Admissions, 734-487-2400, Fax: 734-487-6559, E-mail: graduate.admissions@emich.edu.

École Polytechnique de Montréal, Graduate Programs, Department of Mathematics and Industrial Engineering, Montréal, QC H3C 3A7, Canada. Offers ergonomy (M Eng, M Sc A, DESS); mathematical method in CA engineering (M Eng, M Sc A, PhD); operational research (M Eng, M Sc A, PhD); production (M Eng, M Sc A); technology management (M Eng, M Sc A). DESS program offered jointly with HEC Montreal and Université de Montréal. Part-time programs available. *Degree requirements:* For master's, one foreign language, thesis. *Entrance requirements:* For master's, minimum GPA of 2.75. *Faculty research:* Use of computers in organizations.

Embry-Riddle Aeronautical University–Worldwide, Worldwide Headquarters - Graduate Degrees and Programs, Program in Technical Management, Daytona Beach, FL 32114-3900. Offers MSTM, MSTM/MBAA. Part-time and evening/weekend programs available. Postbaccalaureate distance learning degree programs offered. *Faculty:* 4 full-time (1 woman), 50 part-time/adjunct (15 women). *Students:* 21 full-time (2 women), 40 part-time (6 women); includes 18 minority (7 Black or African American, non-Hispanic/Latino; 1 Asian, non-Hispanic/Latino; 9 Hispanic/Latino; 1 Two or more races, non-Hispanic/Latino), 1 international. Average age 39. 14 applicants, 36% accepted, 3 enrolled. In 2011, 71 master's awarded. *Degree requirements:* For master's, thesis (for some programs). *Entrance requirements:* For master's, GMAT. *Application deadline:* Applications are processed on a rolling basis. Application fee: $50. Electronic applications accepted. *Expenses: Tuition:* Part-time $395 per credit hour. Tuition and fees vary according to degree level and program. *Financial support:* In 2011–12, 6 students received support. Applicants required to submit FAFSA. *Unit head:* Dr. Kees Rietsema, Chair, 602-904-1285, E-mail: rietsd37@erau.edu. *Application contact:* Linda Dammer, Director of Admissions, 386-226-6396 Ext. 1, Fax: 386-226-6984, E-mail: worldwide@erau.edu.

Excelsior College, School of Business and Technology, Albany, NY 12203-5159. Offers business administration (MBA); cybersecurity (MS); cybersecurity management (MBA, Graduate Certificate); human performance technology (MBA); information security (MBA); leadership (MBA); technology management (MBA). Part-time and evening/weekend programs available. Postbaccalaureate distance learning degree programs offered (no on-campus study).

Fairfield University, School of Engineering, Fairfield, CT 06824-5195. Offers electrical and computer engineering (MS); management of technology (MS); mechanical engineering (MS); software engineering (MS). Part-time and evening/weekend programs available. *Faculty:* 10 full-time (2 women), 11 part-time/adjunct. *Students:* 44 full-time (15 women), 86 part-time (22 women); includes 19 minority (4 Black or African American, non-Hispanic/Latino; 8 Asian, non-Hispanic/Latino; 4 Hispanic/Latino; 1 Native Hawaiian or other Pacific Islander, non-Hispanic/Latino; 2 Two or more races, non-Hispanic/Latino), 21 international. Average age 34. 100 applicants, 76% accepted, 27 enrolled. In 2011, 38 master's awarded. *Degree requirements:* For master's, thesis, capstone course. *Entrance requirements:* For master's, interview, minimum GPA of 2.8, resume, 2 recommendations. Additional exam requirements/recommendations for international students: Required—TOEFL (minimum score 550 paper-based; 213 computer-based; 80 iBT)or IELTS (minimum score 6.5). *Application deadline:* For fall admission, 5/15 for international students; for spring admission, 10/15 for international students. Applications are processed on a rolling basis. Application fee: $60. Electronic applications accepted. *Expenses:* Contact institution. *Financial support:* In 2011–12, 50 students received support. Scholarships/grants and unspecified assistantships available. Financial award applicants required to submit FAFSA. *Faculty research:* Vehicle dynamics, image processing, multimedia in instruction, thermal packaging, character recognition, photovoltaics and nanotechnology, Web technology. *Unit head:* Dr. Jack Beal, Dean, 203-254-4000 Ext. 4147, Fax: 203-254-4013, E-mail: jwbeal@fairfield.edu. *Application contact:* Marianne Gumpper, Director of Graduate and Continuing Studies Admission, 203-254-4184, Fax: 203-254-4073, E-mail: gradadmis@fairfield.edu. Web site: http://www.fairfield.edu/soe/soe_grad_1.html.

Fairleigh Dickinson University, College at Florham, Silberman College of Business, Departments of Management, Marketing, and Entrepreneurial Studies, Program in Management, Madison, NJ 07940-1099. Offers evolving technology (Certificate); management (MBA); MBA/MA.

Florida Institute of Technology, Graduate Programs, Nathan M. Bisk College of Business, Online Programs, Melbourne, FL 32901-6975. Offers accounting (MBA); accounting and finance (MBA); business administration (MBA); finance (MBA); healthcare management (MBA); information technology (MS); information technology cybersecurity (MS); information technology management (MBA); international business (MBA); Internet marketing (MBA); management (MBA); marketing (MBA); project management (MBA). Part-time and evening/weekend programs available. Postbaccalaureate distance learning degree programs offered (no on-campus study). *Faculty:* 47 part-time/adjunct (15 women). *Students:* 8 full-time (4 women), 1,122 part-time (547 women); includes 418 minority (271 Black or African American, non-Hispanic/Latino; 5 American Indian or Alaska Native, non-Hispanic/Latino; 55 Asian, non-Hispanic/Latino; 81 Hispanic/Latino; 6 Native Hawaiian or other Pacific Islander, non-Hispanic/Latino), 23 international. Average age 36. In 2011, 329 master's awarded. *Entrance requirements:* For master's, GMAT or resume showing 8 years of supervised experience, 2 letters of recommendation, resume, competency in math past college algebra. Additional exam requirements/recommendations for international students: Required—TOEFL (minimum score 550 paper-based; 213 computer-based; 79 iBT). *Application deadline:* For fall admission, 4/1 for international students; for spring admission, 9/30 for international students. Applications are processed on a rolling basis. Electronic applications accepted. *Expenses:* Contact institution. *Financial support:* Available to part-time students. Application deadline: 3/1; applicants required to submit FAFSA. *Unit head:* Dr. Mary S. Bonhomme, Dean, Florida Tech Online/Associate Provost for Online Learning, 321-674-8202, Fax: 321-674-8216, E-mail: bonhomme@fit.edu. *Application contact:* Carolyn Farrior, Director of Graduate Admissions, Online Learning and Off-Campus Programs, 321-674-7118, Fax: 321-674-8216, E-mail: cfarrior@fit.edu. Web site: http://online.fit.edu.

George Mason University, School of Management, Program in Technology Management, Fairfax, VA 22030. Offers MS. *Faculty:* 8 full-time (1 woman), 2 part-time/adjunct. *Students:* 20 full-time (2 women); includes 8 minority (3 Black or African American, non-Hispanic/Latino; 5 Asian, non-Hispanic/Latino), 1 international. Average age 38. 55 applicants, 78% accepted, 20 enrolled. In 2011, 78 degrees awarded. *Entrance requirements:* For master's, GMAT/GRE, resume; official transcripts; 2 professional letters of recommendation; professional essay; expanded goals statement; interview. Additional exam requirements/recommendations for international students: Required—TOEFL (minimum score 570 paper-based; 230 computer-based; 88 iBT), IELTS, Pearson Test of English. *Application deadline:* For spring admission, 10/1 priority date for domestic students. Application fee: $65 ($80 for international students). Electronic applications accepted. *Expenses:* Contact institution. *Financial support:* In 2011–12, 1 student received support, including 1 research assistantship with full and partial tuition reimbursement available (averaging $18,285 per year). Financial award application deadline: 3/1; financial award applicants required to submit FAFSA. *Faculty research:* Leadership careers in technology-oriented businesses, achieving success in the technology marketplace, emphasizing technology leadership and management, technology innovation, commercialization, methods and approaches of systems thinking. *Unit head:* J. P. Auffret, Director, 703-993-5641, Fax: 703-993-1778, E-mail: jauffret@gmu.edu. *Application contact:* Clodagh Bassett, Assistant Director, 703-993-1792, Fax: 703-993-1778, E-mail: cbassett@gmu.edu. Web site: http://som.gmu.edu/DegreePrograms/MSTM.

George Mason University, School of Public Policy, Program in Public Policy, Arlington, VA 22201. Offers MPP, PhD. *Faculty:* 54 full-time (18 women), 20 part-time/adjunct (8 women). *Students:* 163 full-time (84 women), 358 part-time (179 women); includes 99 minority (36 Black or African American, non-Hispanic/Latino; 30 Asian, non-Hispanic/Latino; 27 Hispanic/Latino; 6 Two or more races, non-Hispanic/Latino), 55 international. Average age 31. 475 applicants, 63% accepted, 135 enrolled. In 2011, 132 master's, 12 doctorates awarded. *Degree requirements:* For master's, thesis or alternative; for doctorate, comprehensive exam, thesis/dissertation. *Entrance requirements:* For master's, GRE/GMAT (for students seeking merit-based scholarships), bachelor's degree with minimum GPA of 3.0, current resume, 2 letters of recommendation, expanded goals statement, 2 copies of official transcripts; for doctorate, GMAT or GRE General Test, master's degree with minimum GPA of 3.0; current resume; expanded goals statement; 2 official copies of transcripts; writing sample. Additional exam requirements/recommendations for international students: Required—TOEFL (minimum score 575 paper-based; 230 computer-based; 88 iBT), IELTS, Pearson Test of English. *Application deadline:* For fall admission, 6/1 priority date for domestic students; 5/1 for international students; for spring admission, 12/1 priority date for domestic students, 11/1 for international students. Applications are processed on a rolling basis. Application fee: $65 ($80 for international students). Electronic applications accepted. *Expenses:* Contact institution. *Financial support:* In 2011–12, 41 students received support, including 1 fellowship with full tuition reimbursement available (averaging $18,000 per year), 40 research assistantships with full and partial tuition reimbursements available (averaging $17,652 per year), 1 teaching assistantship with full and partial tuition reimbursement available (averaging $11,058 per year); career-related internships or fieldwork, Federal Work-Study, scholarships/grants, unspecified assistantships, and health care benefits (full-time research or teaching assistantship recipients) also available. Support available to part-time students. Financial award application deadline: 3/1; financial award applicants required to submit FAFSA. *Unit head:* Jeremy Mayer, Director, 703-703-8223, Fax: 703-993-8215, E-mail: jmayer4@gmu.edu. *Application contact:* Tennille Haegele, Director, Graduate Admissions, 703-993—8099, Fax: 703-993-4876, E-mail: spp@gmu.edu. Web site: http://policy.gmu.edu/Home/AcademicProfessionalPrograms/MastersPrograms/PublicPolicy/tabid/105/Default.aspx.

The George Washington University, School of Business, Department of Information Systems and Technology Management, Washington, DC 20052. Offers information and decision systems (PhD); information systems (MSIST); information systems development (MSIST); information systems management (MBA); information systems project management (MSIST); management information systems (MSIST); management of science, technology, and innovation (MBA, PhD). Programs also offered in Ashburn and Arlington, VA. Part-time and evening/weekend programs available. *Faculty:* 12 full-time (4 women), 5 part-time/adjunct (2 women). *Students:* 111 full-time (37 women), 144 part-time (47 women); includes 87 minority (36 Black or African American, non-Hispanic/Latino; 1 American Indian or Alaska Native, non-Hispanic/Latino; 30 Asian, non-Hispanic/Latino; 19 Hispanic/Latino; 1 Two or more races, non-Hispanic/Latino), 45 international. Average age 33. 231 applicants, 72% accepted, 93 enrolled. In 2011, 86 master's, 3 doctorates awarded. *Entrance requirements:* For master's, GMAT. Additional exam requirements/recommendations for international students: Required—TOEFL. *Application deadline:* For fall admission, 4/1 priority date for domestic students; for spring admission, 10/1 for domestic students. Applications are processed on a rolling basis. Application fee: $75. *Financial support:* In 2011–12, 35 students received support. Fellowships, teaching assistantships, career-related internships or fieldwork, Federal Work-Study, institutionally sponsored loans, and tuition waivers available. Financial award application deadline: 4/1. *Faculty research:* Expert systems, decision support systems. *Unit head:* Richard G. Donnelly, Chair, 202-994-4364, E-mail: rgd@gwu.edu. *Application contact:* Kristin Williams, Assistant Vice President for Graduate and Special Enrollment Management, 202-994-0467, Fax: 202-994-0371, E-mail: ksw@gwu.edu.

Georgia Institute of Technology, Graduate Studies and Research, College of Management, Program in Business Administration, Atlanta, GA 30332-0001. Offers accounting (MBA); e-commerce (Certificate); engineering entrepreneurship (MBA); entrepreneurship (Certificate); finance (MBA); information technology management (MBA); international business (MBA, Certificate); management of technology (Certificate); marketing (MBA); operations management (MBA); organizational behavior (MBA); strategic management (MBA). *Accreditation:* AACSB.

Georgia Institute of Technology, Graduate Studies and Research, College of Management, Program in Management of Technology, Atlanta, GA 30332-0001. Offers EMBA. Part-time and evening/weekend programs available. *Degree requirements:* For master's, study abroad. *Entrance requirements:* For master's, GMAT, 5 years of professional work experience. Additional exam requirements/recommendations for international students: Required—TOEFL. Electronic applications accepted. *Expenses:*

Contact institution. *Faculty research:* Innovation management, technology analysis, operations management.

Golden Gate University, Ageno School of Business, San Francisco, CA 94105-2968. Offers accounting (MBA); business administration (EMBA, MBA, PMBA, DBA); finance (MBA, MS, Certificate); financial planning (MS, Certificate); healthcare information systems (Certificate); human resource management (MBA, MS); human resources management (Certificate); information systems (MS); information technology (MBA); information technology management (Certificate); integrated marketing and communications (MS, Certificate); international business (MBA); management (MBA); marketing (MBA, MS, Certificate); operations supply chain management (Certificate); psychology (MA, Certificate); public administration (EMPA); public relations (MS, Certificate); technical market analysis (Certificate); JD/MBA. Part-time and evening/weekend programs available. *Faculty:* 19 full-time (6 women), 241 part-time/adjunct (72 women). *Students:* 397 full-time (230 women), 779 part-time (432 women); includes 376 minority (105 Black or African American, non-Hispanic/Latino; 5 American Indian or Alaska Native, non-Hispanic/Latino; 161 Asian, non-Hispanic/Latino; 77 Hispanic/Latino; 12 Native Hawaiian or other Pacific Islander, non-Hispanic/Latino; 16 Two or more races, non-Hispanic/Latino), 265 international. Average age 34. 871 applicants, 64% accepted, 271 enrolled. In 2011, 550 master's, 13 doctorates awarded. *Degree requirements:* For doctorate, thesis/dissertation, qualifying examination. *Entrance requirements:* For master's, GMAT (MBA), minimum GPA of 2.5 (MS). Additional exam requirements/recommendations for international students: Required—TOEFL (minimum score 550 paper-based; 213 computer-based; 79 iBT). *Application deadline:* For fall admission, 5/15 for domestic and international students; for winter admission, 1/15 for domestic and international students; for spring admission, 9/15 for domestic and international students. Applications are processed on a rolling basis. Application fee: $70 ($110 for international students). Electronic applications accepted. *Expenses:* Contact institution. *Financial support:* Career-related internships or fieldwork, Federal Work-Study, institutionally sponsored loans, and scholarships/grants available. Support available to part-time students. Financial award applicants required to submit FAFSA. *Unit head:* Dr. Paul Fouts, Dean, 415-442-7026, Fax: 415-442-6579. *Application contact:* Angela Melero, Enrollment Services, 415-442-7800, Fax: 415-442-7807, E-mail: info@ggu.edu. Web site: http://www.ggu.edu/programs/business-and-management.

Harding University, Paul R. Carter College of Business Administration, Searcy, AR 72149-0001. Offers health care management (MBA); information technology management (MBA); international business (MBA); leadership and organizational management (MBA). *Accreditation:* ACBSP. Part-time and evening/weekend programs available. Postbaccalaureate distance learning degree programs offered (no on-campus study). *Faculty:* 30 part-time/adjunct (6 women). *Students:* 60 full-time (25 women), 140 part-time (63 women); includes 33 minority (26 Black or African American, non-Hispanic/Latino; 1 American Indian or Alaska Native, non-Hispanic/Latino; 3 Asian, non-Hispanic/Latino; 1 Hispanic/Latino; 2 Two or more races, non-Hispanic/Latino), 24 international. Average age 30. 65 applicants, 98% accepted, 64 enrolled. In 2011, 120 master's awarded. *Degree requirements:* For master's, portfolio. *Entrance requirements:* For master's, GMAT (minimum score of 500) or GRE (minimum score of 300), minimum GPA of 3.0, 2 letters of recommendation, resume, 3 essays, all official transcripts. Additional exam requirements/recommendations for international students: Required—TOEFL (minimum score 550 paper-based; 213 computer-based; 79 iBT). *Application deadline:* For fall admission, 8/1 priority date for domestic students, 8/1 for international students; for spring admission, 12/1 priority date for domestic students, 12/1 for international students. Applications are processed on a rolling basis. Application fee: $40. *Expenses: Tuition:* Full-time $10,512; part-time $584 per credit hour. *Required fees:* $500; $25 per credit hour. Tuition and fees vary according to course load, degree level and program. *Financial support:* In 2011–12, 19 students received support. Unspecified assistantships available. Financial award application deadline: 7/30; financial award applicants required to submit FAFSA. *Unit head:* Glen Metheny, Director of Graduate Studies, 501-279-5851, Fax: 501-279-4805, E-mail: gmetheny@harding.edu. *Application contact:* Melanie Kiihnl, Recruiting Manager/Director of Marketing, 501-279-4523, Fax: 501-279-4805, E-mail: mba@harding.edu. Web site: http://www.harding.edu/mba.

Harrisburg University of Science and Technology, Program in Project Management, Harrisburg, PA 17101. Offers construction services (MS); governmental services (MS); information technology (MS). Part-time and evening/weekend programs available. *Entrance requirements:* For master's, BS, BBA. Additional exam requirements/recommendations for international students: Required—TOEFL (minimum score 520 paper-based; 200 computer-based; 80 iBT). Electronic applications accepted.

Harvard University, Graduate School of Arts and Sciences, Program in Information, Technology and Management, Cambridge, MA 02138. Offers PhD. *Expenses: Tuition:* Full-time $36,304. *Required fees:* $1186. Full-time tuition and fees vary according to program.

Harvard University, Harvard Business School, Doctoral Programs in Management, Boston, MA 02163. Offers accounting and management (DBA); business economics (PhD); health policy management (PhD); management (DBA); marketing (DBA); organizational behavior (PhD); science, technology and management (PhD); strategy (DBA); technology and operations management (DBA). *Degree requirements:* For doctorate, comprehensive exam (for some programs), thesis/dissertation. *Entrance requirements:* For doctorate, GRE General Test or GMAT. Additional exam requirements/recommendations for international students: Required—TOEFL. *Expenses: Tuition:* Full-time $36,304. *Required fees:* $1186. Full-time tuition and fees vary according to program.

Herzing University Online, Program in Business Administration, Milwaukee, WI 53203. Offers accounting (MBA); business administration (MBA); business management (MBA); healthcare management (MBA); human resources (MBA); marketing (MBA); project management (MBA); technology management (MBA). Postbaccalaureate distance learning degree programs offered (no on-campus study).

Idaho State University, Office of Graduate Studies, College of Technology, Department of Human Resource Training and Development, Pocatello, ID 83209-8380. Offers MTD. Part-time and evening/weekend programs available. *Degree requirements:* For master's, comprehensive exam, thesis optional, statistical procedures. *Entrance requirements:* For master's, GRE or MAT, minimum GPA of 3.0 in upper-division courses. Additional exam requirements/recommendations for international students: Required—TOEFL (minimum score 550 paper-based; 213 computer-based; 80 iBT). Electronic applications accepted. *Faculty research:* Learning styles, instructional methodology, leadership administration.

Illinois State University, Graduate School, College of Applied Science and Technology, Department of Technology, Normal, IL 61790-2200. Offers MS. *Degree requirements:* For master's, thesis or alternative. *Entrance requirements:* For master's, GRE General Test, minimum GPA of 2.8. *Faculty research:* National Center for Engineering and Technology Education, Illinois Manufacturing Extension Center Field Office hosting, model for the professional development of K-12 technology education teachers, Illinois State University Illinois Mathermatics and Science Partnership, Illinois University council for career and technical education.

Indiana State University, College of Graduate and Professional Studies, Program in Technology Management, Terre Haute, IN 47809. Offers PhD. Postbaccalaureate distance learning degree programs offered (minimal on-campus study). *Degree requirements:* For doctorate, thesis/dissertation. *Entrance requirements:* For doctorate, GRE or GMAT, minimum graduate GPA of 3.5, 6000 hours of occupational experience. Electronic applications accepted. *Faculty research:* Production management, quality control, human resource development, construction project management, lean manufacturing.

Instituto Centroamericano de Administración de Empresas, Graduate Programs, La Garita, Costa Rica. Offers agribusiness management (MIAM); business administration (EMBA); finance (MBA); real estate management (MGREM); sustainable development (MBA); technology (MBA). *Degree requirements:* For master's, comprehensive exam, essay. *Entrance requirements:* For master's, GMAT or GRE General Test, fluency in Spanish, interview, letters of recommendation, minimum 1 year of work experience. Additional exam requirements/recommendations for international students: Recommended—TOEFL. Electronic applications accepted. *Faculty research:* Competitiveness, production.

Instituto Tecnológico y de Estudios Superiores de Monterrey, Campus Central de Veracruz, Graduate Programs, Córdoba, Mexico. Offers administration (MA); administration of information technologies (MTI); computer sciences (MCC); education (MEE); educational institution administration (MAD); educational technology (MTE); electronic commerce (MCE); finance (MAF); humanistic studies (MEH); international business for Latin America (MNL); marketing (MMT); science (MCP); technology management (MTT). Part-time and evening/weekend programs available. Postbaccalaureate distance learning degree programs offered (minimal on-campus study). *Degree requirements:* For master's, thesis (for some programs). *Entrance requirements:* For master's, PAEP College Board. Electronic applications accepted.

Instituto Tecnológico y de Estudios Superiores de Monterrey, Campus Cuernavaca, Programs in Information Science, Temixco, Mexico. Offers administration of information technology (MATI); computer science (MCC, DCC); information technology (MTI).

Instituto Tecnológico y de Estudios Superiores de Monterrey, Campus Irapuato, Graduate Programs, Irapuato, Mexico. Offers administration (MBA); administration of information technology (MAIT); administration of telecommunications (MAT); architecture (M Arch); computer science (MCS); education (M Ed); educational administration (MEA); educational innovation and technology (DEIT); educational technology (MET); electronic commerce (MBA); environmental administration and planning (MEAP); environmental systems (MES); finances (MBA); humanistic studies (MHS); international management for Latin American executives (MIMLAE); library and information science (MLIS); manufacturing quality management (MMQM); marketing research (MBA).

Iona College, Hagan School of Business, Department of Information Systems, New Rochelle, NY 10801-1890. Offers MBA, PMC. Part-time and evening/weekend programs available. *Faculty:* 5 full-time (0 women), 3 part-time/adjunct (0 women). *Students:* 4 full-time (1 woman), 25 part-time (11 women); includes 7 minority (6 Black or African American, non-Hispanic/Latino; 1 Asian, non-Hispanic/Latino). Average age 30. 4 applicants, 100% accepted, 4 enrolled. In 2011, 10 master's awarded. *Entrance requirements:* For master's, GMAT, 2 letters of recommendation; for PMC, GMAT. Additional exam requirements/recommendations for international students: Required—TOEFL (minimum score 550 paper-based; 213 computer-based; 80 iBT). *Application deadline:* For fall admission, 8/15 priority date for domestic students, 8/1 for international students; for winter admission, 11/15 priority date for domestic students, 11/1 for international students; for spring admission, 2/15 priority date for domestic students, 2/1 for international students. Applications are processed on a rolling basis. Application fee: $50. Electronic applications accepted. *Expenses:* Contact institution. *Financial support:* Scholarships/grants, tuition waivers (partial), and unspecified assistantships available. Support available to part-time students. Financial award application deadline: 4/15; financial award applicants required to submit FAFSA. *Faculty research:* Fuzzy sets, risk management, computer security, competence set analysis, investment strategies. *Unit head:* Dr. Robert Richardson, Chairman, 914-637-7726, E-mail: rrichardson@iona.edu. *Application contact:* Ben Fan, Director of MBA Admissions, 914-633-2289, Fax: 914-637-2708, E-mail: sfan@iona.edu. Web site: http://www.iona.edu.hagan/.

The Johns Hopkins University, Engineering Program for Professionals, Part-time Program in Technical Management, Baltimore, MD 21218-2699. Offers MS, Graduate Certificate, Post-Master's Certificate. Part-time and evening/weekend programs available. Electronic applications accepted.

Jones International University, School of Business, Centennial, CO 80112. Offers accounting (MBA); business communication (MABC); entrepreneurship (MABC, MBA); finance (MBA); global enterprise management (MBA); health care management (MBA); information security management (MBA); information technology management (MBA); leadership and influence (MABC); leading the customer-driven organization (MABC); negotiation and conflict management (MBA); project management (MABC, MBA). Program only offered online. Part-time and evening/weekend programs available. Postbaccalaureate distance learning degree programs offered (no on-campus study). *Degree requirements:* For master's, capstone project. *Entrance requirements:* For master's, minimum cumulative GPA of 2.5. Additional exam requirements/recommendations for international students: Recommended—TOEFL (minimum score 550 paper-based; 213 computer-based). Electronic applications accepted.

Kansas State University, Graduate School, College of Technology and Aviation, Salina, KS 67401. Offers MT. *Faculty:* 2 full-time (0 women). *Students:* 1 full-time (0 women), 1 part-time (0 women); includes 1 minority (Black or African American, non-Hispanic/Latino). Average age 37. 2 applicants, 100% accepted, 2 enrolled. *Entrance requirements:* For master's, GRE. Additional exam requirements/recommendations for international students: Required—TOEFL (minimum score 550 paper-based; 79 iBT), IELTS (minimum score 6.5), TWE, or PTE. *Application deadline:* For fall admission, 3/1 for domestic students, 1/1 for international students; for spring admission, 10/1 for domestic students, 8/1 for international students. Application fee: $40 ($55 for international students). Electronic applications accepted. *Total annual research expenditures:* $1.1 million. *Unit head:* Dennis Kuhlman, Dean, 785-826-2601, E-mail: dkuhlman@ksu.edu. *Application contact:* Dr. Patricia E. Ackerman, Graduate Program Director, 785-826-2904, E-mail: salgrad@k-state.edu. Web site: http://www.salina.k-state.edu/masterdegree/.

La Salle University, School of Arts and Sciences, Program in Information Technology Leadership, Philadelphia, PA 19141-1199. Offers MS.

Lawrence Technological University, College of Management, Southfield, MI 48075-1058. Offers business administration (MBA, DBA); business administration international (MBA); global leadership and management (MS); global operations and project management (MS); information systems (MS); information technology (DM); operations management (MS). *Accreditation:* ACBSP. Part-time and evening/weekend programs available. *Faculty:* 12 full-time (6 women), 39 part-time/adjunct (11 women). *Students:* 10 full-time (4 women), 518 part-time (228 women); includes 183 minority (123 Black or African American, non-Hispanic/Latino; 2 American Indian or Alaska Native, non-Hispanic/Latino; 44 Asian, non-Hispanic/Latino; 11 Hispanic/Latino; 3 Two or more races, non-Hispanic/Latino), 50 international. Average age 36. 420 applicants, 45% accepted, 97 enrolled. In 2011, 177 master's, 14 doctorates awarded. *Degree requirements:* For master's, thesis (for some programs). *Entrance requirements:* For master's, GMAT. Additional exam requirements/recommendations for international students: Required—TOEFL (minimum score 550 paper-based; 213 computer-based; 79 iBT). *Application deadline:* For fall admission, 7/27 priority date for domestic students, 5/23 for international students; for spring admission, 11/15 priority date for domestic students, 11/15 for international students. Applications are processed on a rolling basis. Application fee: $50. Electronic applications accepted. *Financial support:* In 2011–12, 122 students received support. Federal Work-Study and institutionally sponsored loans available. Support available to part-time students. Financial award application deadline: 4/1; financial award applicants required to submit FAFSA. *Unit head:* Dr. Alan McCord, Interim Dean, 248-204-3050, E-mail: mgtdean@ltu.edu. *Application contact:* Jane Rohrback, Director of Admissions, 248-204-3160, Fax: 248-204-2228, E-mail: admissions@ltu.edu. Web site: http://www.ltu.edu/management/index.asp.

Lewis University, College of Business, Graduate School of Management, Program in Business Administration, Romeoville, IL 60446. Offers accounting (MBA); custom elective option (MBA); e-business (MBA); finance (MBA); healthcare management (MBA); human resources management (MBA); information security (MBA); international business (MBA); management information systems (MBA); marketing (MBA); project management (MBA); technology and operations management (MBA). Part-time and evening/weekend programs available. *Students:* 112 full-time (60 women), 232 part-time (118 women); includes 104 minority (62 Black or African American, non-Hispanic/Latino; 1 American Indian or Alaska Native, non-Hispanic/Latino; 7 Asian, non-Hispanic/Latino; 33 Hispanic/Latino; 1 Native Hawaiian or other Pacific Islander, non-Hispanic/Latino), 9 international. Average age 28. In 2011, 99 master's awarded. *Entrance requirements:* For master's, interview, bachelor's degree, resume, 2 recommendations. Additional exam requirements/recommendations for international students: Required—TOEFL (minimum score 550 paper-based; 213 computer-based). *Application deadline:* For fall admission, 8/15 priority date for domestic students, 5/1 for international students; for spring admission, 11/15 for international students. Applications are processed on a rolling basis. Application fee: $40. Electronic applications accepted. *Financial support:* Career-related internships or fieldwork, Federal Work-Study, scholarships/grants, and unspecified assistantships available. Financial award application deadline: 5/1; financial award applicants required to submit FAFSA. *Unit head:* Dr. Maureen Culleeney, Academic Program Director, 815-838-0500 Ext. 5631, E-mail: culleema@lewisu.edu. *Application contact:* Michele Ryan, Director of Admission, 815-838-0500 Ext. 5384, E-mail: gsm@lewisu.edu.

Marist College, Graduate Programs, School of Computer Science and Mathematics, Poughkeepsie, NY 12601-1387. Offers computer science/software development (MS); information systems (MS, Adv C); technology management (MS). Part-time and evening/weekend programs available. Postbaccalaureate distance learning degree programs offered (minimal on-campus study). *Entrance requirements:* For master's, resume. Additional exam requirements/recommendations for international students: Required—TOEFL (minimum score 550 paper-based; 213 computer-based; 80 iBT); Recommended—IELTS (minimum score 6.5). Electronic applications accepted. *Faculty research:* Data quality, artificial intelligence, imaging, analysis of algorithms, distributed systems and applications.

Marist College, Graduate Programs, School of Management and School of Computer Science and Mathematics, Program in Technology Management, Poughkeepsie, NY 12601-1387. Offers MS. Part-time and evening/weekend programs available. Postbaccalaureate distance learning degree programs offered (minimal on-campus study). *Entrance requirements:* For master's, GMAT or GRE, minimum undergraduate GPA of 3.0, 2 letters of recommendation, resume, professional experience. Additional exam requirements/recommendations for international students: Required—TOEFL (minimum score 550 paper-based; 213 computer-based; 80 iBT); Recommended—IELTS (minimum score 6.5). Electronic applications accepted.

Marquette University, Graduate School, College of Engineering, Department of Biomedical Engineering, Milwaukee, WI 53201-1881. Offers biocomputing (ME); bioimaging (ME); bioinstrumentation (ME); bioinstrumentation/computers (MS, PhD); biomechanics (ME); biomechanics/biomaterials (MS, PhD); biorehabilitation (ME); functional imaging (PhD); healthcare technologies management (MS); rehabilitation bioengineering (PhD); systems physiology (MS, PhD). Part-time and evening/weekend programs available. *Faculty:* 15 full-time (5 women), 5 part-time/adjunct (2 women). *Students:* 39 full-time (13 women), 24 part-time (7 women); includes 8 minority (5 Asian, non-Hispanic/Latino; 1 Hispanic/Latino; 1 Native Hawaiian or other Pacific Islander, non-Hispanic/Latino; 1 Two or more races, non-Hispanic/Latino), 13 international. Average age 28. 86 applicants, 35% accepted, 14 enrolled. In 2011, 19 master's, 5 doctorates awarded. Terminal master's awarded for partial completion of doctoral program. *Degree requirements:* For master's, comprehensive exam, thesis; for doctorate, comprehensive exam, thesis/dissertation, dissertation defense, qualifying exam. *Entrance requirements:* For master's, GRE General Test, minimum GPA of 3.0, official transcripts from all current and previous colleges/universities except Marquette, three letters of recommendation, brief statement of purpose that includes proposed area of research specialization, interview with program director (for ME), one year of post-baccalaureate professional work experience; for doctorate, GRE General Test, minimum GPA of 3.0, official transcripts from all current and previous colleges/universities except Marquette, three letters of recommendation, brief statement of purpose that includes proposed area of research specialization. Additional exam requirements/recommendations for international students: Required—TOEFL (minimum score 530 paper-based; 78 computer-based). *Application deadline:* For fall admission, 2/15 priority date for domestic students; for spring admission, 11/15 priority date for domestic students. Applications are processed on a rolling basis. Application fee: $50. Electronic applications accepted. *Expenses:* Tuition: Full-time $17,010; part-time $945 per credit hour. Tuition and fees vary according to program. *Financial support:* In 2011–12, 8 students received support, including 2 research assistantships with full tuition reimbursements available (averaging $20,134 per year), 6 teaching assistantships with full tuition reimbursements available; fellowships, scholarships/grants, health care benefits, tuition waivers (partial), and unspecified assistantships also available. Support available to part-time students. Financial award application deadline: 2/15. *Faculty*

research: Cell and organ physiology, signal processing, gait analysis, orthopedic rehabilitation engineering, telemedicine. *Total annual research expenditures:* $2 million. *Unit head:* Dr. Kristina Ropella, Chair, 414-288-3375, Fax: 414-288-7938, E-mail: kristina.ropella@marquette.edu. *Application contact:* Craig Pierce, Assistant Dean of the Graduate School, 414-288-5740, Fax: 414-288-1902, E-mail: craig.pierce@marquette.edu. Web site: http://www.marquette.edu/engineering/biomedical/.

Marshall University, Academic Affairs Division, College of Information Technology and Engineering, Division of Applied Science and Technology, Program in Technology Management, Huntington, WV 25755. Offers MS. Part-time and evening/weekend programs available. *Students:* 25 full-time (5 women), 36 part-time (9 women); includes 7 minority (6 Black or African American, non-Hispanic/Latino; 1 Asian, non-Hispanic/Latino), 17 international. Average age 34. In 2011, 15 master's awarded. *Degree requirements:* For master's, final project, oral exam. *Entrance requirements:* For master's, GRE General Test or GMAT, minimum undergraduate GPA of 2.5. Application fee: $40. *Financial support:* Tuition waivers (full) available. Support available to part-time students. Financial award application deadline: 8/1; financial award applicants required to submit FAFSA. *Unit head:* Dr. Tracy Christofero, Program Coordinator, 304-746-2078, E-mail: christofero@marshall.edu. *Application contact:* Information Contact, 304-746-1900, Fax: 304-746-1902, E-mail: services@marshall.edu. Web site: http://www.marshall.edu/cite/.

Mercer University, Graduate Studies, Macon Campus, School of Engineering, Macon, GA 31207-0003. Offers biomedical engineering (MSE); computer engineering (MSE); electrical engineering (MSE); engineering management (MSE); environmental engineering (MSE); environmental systems (MS); mechanical engineering (MSE); software engineering (MSE); software systems (MS); technical communications management (MS); technical management (MS). Part-time and evening/weekend programs available. Postbaccalaureate distance learning degree programs offered (no on-campus study). *Faculty:* 17 full-time (3 women), 1 part-time/adjunct (0 women). *Students:* 12 full-time (3 women), 113 part-time (28 women); includes 23 minority (13 Black or African American, non-Hispanic/Latino; 9 Asian, non-Hispanic/Latino; 1 Hispanic/Latino). Average age 31. In 2011, 44 master's awarded. *Degree requirements:* For master's, thesis or alternative. *Entrance requirements:* For master's, minimum undergraduate GPA of 3.0. Additional exam requirements/recommendations for international students: Required—TOEFL. *Application deadline:* For fall admission, 7/1 for domestic students; for spring admission, 11/15 for domestic students. Applications are processed on a rolling basis. Application fee: $35 ($50 for international students). Electronic applications accepted. *Expenses:* Contact institution. *Financial support:* Federal Work-Study available. *Unit head:* Dr. Wade H. Shaw, Dean, 478-301-2459, Fax: 478-301-5593, E-mail: shaw_wh@mercer.edu. *Application contact:* Greg Lofton, Graduate Program Coordinator, 478-301-5480, Fax: 478-301-5434, E-mail: lofton_g@mercer.edu. Web site: http://engineering.mercer.edu/.

Murray State University, College of Science, Engineering and Technology, Program in Management of Technology, Murray, KY 42071. Offers MS. Part-time and evening/weekend programs available. *Degree requirements:* For master's, comprehensive exam. *Entrance requirements:* Additional exam requirements/recommendations for international students: Required—TOEFL (computer-based 273) or IELTS. *Faculty research:* Environmental, hydrology, groundworks.

New Jersey Institute of Technology, Office of Graduate Studies, College of Computing Science, Department of Information Technology, Program in Information Technology Administration and Security, Newark, NJ 07102. Offers MS. *Students:* 29 full-time (6 women), 56 part-time (6 women); includes 48 minority (11 Black or African American, non-Hispanic/Latino; 17 Asian, non-Hispanic/Latino; 20 Hispanic/Latino), 7 international. Average age 30. 82 applicants, 68% accepted, 35 enrolled. In 2011, 17 master's awarded. *Entrance requirements:* Additional exam requirements/recommendations for international students: Required—TOEFL (minimum score 550 paper-based; 213 computer-based; 79 iBT). *Application deadline:* For fall admission, 6/1 priority date for domestic students, 5/1 for international students; for spring admission, 11/15 priority date for domestic students, 11/15 for international students. Applications are processed on a rolling basis. Application fee: $65. Electronic applications accepted. *Expenses:* Tuition, state resident: full-time $7980; part-time $867 per credit. Tuition, nonresident: full-time $11,336; part-time $1196 per credit. *Required fees:* $230 per credit. *Financial support:* Application deadline: 1/15. *Unit head:* Dr. Narain Gehani, Dean, 973-542-5488, Fax: 973-596-5777, E-mail: narain.gehani@njit.edu. *Application contact:* Kathryn Kelly, Director of Admissions, 973-596-3300, Fax: 973-596-3461, E-mail: admissions@njit.edu.

New Jersey Institute of Technology, Office of Graduate Studies, School of Management, Program in Management of Technology, Newark, NJ 07102. Offers MS. Part-time and evening/weekend programs available. *Students:* 9 full-time (4 women), 26 part-time (3 women); includes 15 minority (4 Black or African American, non-Hispanic/Latino; 8 Asian, non-Hispanic/Latino; 3 Hispanic/Latino), 11 international. Average age 34. Terminal master's awarded for partial completion of doctoral program. *Degree requirements:* For master's, thesis optional. *Entrance requirements:* For master's, GMAT. Additional exam requirements/recommendations for international students: Required—TOEFL (minimum score 550 paper-based; 213 computer-based; 79 iBT). *Application deadline:* For fall admission, 6/1 priority date for domestic students, 5/1 for international students; for spring admission, 11/15 priority date for domestic students, 11/15 for international students. Applications are processed on a rolling basis. Application fee: $65. Electronic applications accepted. *Expenses:* Tuition, state resident: full-time $7980; part-time $867 per credit. Tuition, nonresident: full-time $11,336; part-time $1196 per credit. *Required fees:* $230 per credit. *Financial support:* Fellowships with full and partial tuition reimbursements, research assistantships with full and partial tuition reimbursements, teaching assistantships with full and partial tuition reimbursements, career-related internships or fieldwork, Federal Work-Study, institutionally sponsored loans, and unspecified assistantships available. Financial award application deadline: 1/15; financial award applicants required to submit FAFSA. *Unit head:* Dr. Robert English, Chair, 973-596-3224, Fax: 973-596-3074, E-mail: robert.english@njit.edu. *Application contact:* Kathryn Kelly, Director of Admissions, 973-596-3300, Fax: 973-596-3461, E-mail: admissions@njit.edu.

North Carolina Agricultural and Technical State University, School of Graduate Studies, School of Technology, Department of Manufacturing Systems, Greensboro, NC 27411. Offers manufacturing (MSTM). Part-time and evening/weekend programs available. *Degree requirements:* For master's, comprehensive exam, thesis or alternative, qualifying exam. *Entrance requirements:* For master's, GRE General Test, minimum GPA of 3.0.

North Carolina State University, Graduate School, College of Textiles, Program in Textile Technology Management, Raleigh, NC 27695. Offers PhD. *Degree requirements:* For doctorate, one foreign language, thesis/dissertation, cumulative exams. *Entrance requirements:* For doctorate, GRE or GMAT. Electronic applications accepted. *Faculty research:* Niche markets, supply chain, globalization, logistics.

Northern Kentucky University, Office of Graduate Programs, College of Informatics, Program in Computer Information Technology, Highland Heights, KY 41099. Offers MSCIT. Part-time and evening/weekend programs available. *Faculty:* 11 full-time (3 women), 1 part-time/adjunct. *Students:* 13 full-time (5 women), 42 part-time (13 women); includes 6 minority (3 Black or African American, non-Hispanic/Latino; 2 Asian, non-Hispanic/Latino; 1 Hispanic/Latino), 2 international. Average age 34. 35 applicants, 57% accepted, 14 enrolled. In 2011, 1 master's awarded. *Degree requirements:* For master's, thesis optional. *Entrance requirements:* For master's, GRE, minimum GPA of 2.5, computer science or related undergraduate degree, letter of intent, resume. Additional exam requirements/recommendations for international students: Required—TOEFL (minimum score 550 paper-based; 213 computer-based; 79 iBT); Recommended—IELTS (minimum score 6.5). *Application deadline:* For fall admission, 8/1 for domestic students, 6/1 for international students; for spring admission, 12/1 for domestic students, 10/1 for international students. Applications are processed on a rolling basis. Application fee: $40. Electronic applications accepted. *Expenses:* Tuition, state resident: full-time $7614; part-time $423 per credit hour. Tuition, nonresident: full-time $13,104; part-time $728 per credit hour. Tuition and fees vary according to degree level and reciprocity agreements. *Financial support:* Scholarships/grants and unspecified assistantships available. Financial award applicants required to submit FAFSA. *Faculty research:* Data privacy, software security, database security, mobile and wireless networks, network security. *Unit head:* Dr. Traian Marius Truta, Coordinator, 859-572-7551, E-mail: trutat1@nku.edu. *Application contact:* Dr. Peg Griffin, Director of Graduate Programs, 859-572-6934, Fax: 859-572-6670, E-mail: griffinp@nku.edu. Web site: http://informatics.nku.edu/csc/mscit/.

Old Dominion University, College of Business and Public Administration, MBA Program, Norfolk, VA 23529. Offers business and economic forecasting (MBA); financial analysis and valuation (MBA); information technology and enterprise integration (MBA); international business (MBA); maritime and port management (MBA); public administration (MBA). *Accreditation:* AACSB. Part-time and evening/weekend programs available. *Faculty:* 66 full-time (15 women), 6 part-time/adjunct (1 woman). *Students:* 69 full-time (21 women), 230 part-time (85 women); includes 49 minority (22 Black or African American, non-Hispanic/Latino; 1 American Indian or Alaska Native, non-Hispanic/Latino; 10 Asian, non-Hispanic/Latino; 3 Hispanic/Latino; 1 Native Hawaiian or other Pacific Islander, non-Hispanic/Latino; 12 Two or more races, non-Hispanic/Latino), 19 international. Average age 31. 177 applicants, 43% accepted, 53 enrolled. In 2011, 115 master's awarded. *Entrance requirements:* For master's, GMAT, GRE, letter of reference, resume, coursework in calculus, essay. Additional exam requirements/recommendations for international students: Required—TOEFL (minimum score 550 paper-based; 213 computer-based; 80 iBT). *Application deadline:* For fall admission, 6/1 priority date for domestic students, 4/15 for international students; for spring admission, 11/1 priority date for domestic students, 10/1 for international students. Applications are processed on a rolling basis. Application fee: $75. Electronic applications accepted. *Expenses:* Tuition, state resident: full-time $9096; part-time $379 per credit. Tuition, nonresident: full-time $23,064; part-time $961 per credit. *Required fees:* $127 per semester. One-time fee: $50. *Financial support:* In 2011–12, 44 students received support, including 90 research assistantships with partial tuition reimbursements available (averaging $8,900 per year); career-related internships or fieldwork, scholarships/grants, and unspecified assistantships also available. Support available to part-time students. Financial award application deadline: 2/15; financial award applicants required to submit FAFSA. *Faculty research:* International business, buyer behavior, financial markets, strategy, operations research, maritime and transportation economics. *Unit head:* Dr. Larry Filer, Graduate Program Director, 757-683-3585, Fax: 757-683-5750, E-mail: mbainfo@odu.edu. *Application contact:* Shanna Wood, MBA Program Manager, 757-683-3585, Fax: 757-683-5750, E-mail: mbainfo@odu.edu. Web site: http://bpa.odu.edu/mba/.

Pacific Lutheran University, Division of Graduate Studies, School of Business, Tacoma, WA 98447. Offers business administration (MBA), including technology and innovation management. *Accreditation:* AACSB. Part-time and evening/weekend programs available. *Faculty:* 13 full-time (6 women), 2 part-time/adjunct (1 woman). *Students:* 37 full-time (15 women), 30 part-time (9 women); includes 12 minority (4 Black or African American, non-Hispanic/Latino; 1 American Indian or Alaska Native, non-Hispanic/Latino; 2 Asian, non-Hispanic/Latino; 1 Hispanic/Latino; 4 Two or more races, non-Hispanic/Latino), 11 international. Average age 33. In 2011, 31 master's awarded. *Entrance requirements:* For master's, GMAT. Additional exam requirements/recommendations for international students: Required—TOEFL (minimum score 550 paper-based; 213 computer-based). *Application deadline:* Applications are processed on a rolling basis. Application fee: $40. *Expenses: Tuition:* Part-time $915 per semester hour. *Financial support:* Fellowships, career-related internships or fieldwork, Federal Work-Study, scholarships/grants, and unspecified assistantships available. Financial award application deadline: 3/1. *Unit head:* Dr. James Brock, Dean, School of Business, 253-535-7251, Fax: 253-535-8723, E-mail: plumba@plu.edu. *Application contact:* Theresa Ramos, Director, MBA Program, 253-535-7330, Fax: 253-535-8723, E-mail: plumba@plu.edu. Web site: http://www.plu.edu/mba/.

Pacific States University, College of Business, Los Angeles, CA 90006. Offers accounting (MBA); finance (MBA); international business (MBA, DBA); management of information technology (MBA); real estate management (MBA). Part-time and evening/weekend programs available. Postbaccalauréate distance learning degree programs offered (no on-campus study). *Faculty:* 6 full-time (2 women), 14 part-time/adjunct (0 women). *Students:* 157 full-time (70 women); includes 13 minority (2 Black or African American, non-Hispanic/Latino; 8 Asian, non-Hispanic/Latino; 3 Native Hawaiian or other Pacific Islander, non-Hispanic/Latino), 140 international. Average age 31. 42 applicants, 83% accepted, 33 enrolled. *Degree requirements:* For doctorate, comprehensive exam, thesis/dissertation. *Entrance requirements:* For master's, minimum undergraduate GPA of 2.5 during last 90 hours of course work. Additional exam requirements/recommendations for international students: Required—TOEFL (minimum score 133 computer-based; 45 iBT), IELTS (minimum score 4.5). *Application deadline:* For fall admission, 8/15 priority date for domestic students; for winter admission, 10/15 priority date for domestic students; for spring admission, 1/15 priority date for domestic students. Applications are processed on a rolling basis. Application fee: $100. *Expenses: Tuition:* Full-time $11,040; part-time $345 per credit hour. *Required fees:* $150 per quarter. *Financial support:* Scholarships/grants available. Financial award applicants required to submit FAFSA. *Application contact:* Zolzaya Enkhbayar, Interim Registrar, 323-731-2383, Fax: 323-731-7276, E-mail: registrar@psuca.edu.

Polytechnic Institute of New York University, Department of Finance and Risk Engineering, Brooklyn, NY 11201-2990. Offers financial engineering (MS, Advanced Certificate), including capital markets (MS), computational finance (MS), financial technology (MS); financial technology management (Advanced Certificate); organizational behavior (Advanced Certificate); risk management (Advanced Certificate); technology management (Advanced Certificate). Part-time and evening/weekend programs available. *Faculty:* 6 full-time (2 women), 23 part-time/adjunct (5 women). *Students:* 149 full-time (49 women), 44 part-time (8 women); includes 30 minority (6 Black or African American, non-Hispanic/Latino; 22 Asian, non-Hispanic/Latino; 2 Hispanic/Latino), 135 international. Average age 27. 515 applicants, 36% accepted, 102 enrolled. In 2011, 95 degrees awarded. *Degree requirements:* For master's, comprehensive exam (for some programs), thesis (for some programs). *Entrance requirements:* For master's, GMAT, minimum B average in undergraduate course work. Additional exam requirements/recommendations for international students: Required—TOEFL (minimum score 550 paper-based; 213 computer-based; 80 iBT); Recommended—IELTS (minimum score 6.5). *Application deadline:* For fall admission, 7/31 priority date for domestic students, 4/30 for international students; for spring admission, 12/31 priority date for domestic students, 11/30 for international students. Applications are processed on a rolling basis. Application fee: $75. Electronic applications accepted. *Expenses: Tuition:* Full-time $22,464; part-time $1248 per credit. *Required fees:* $501 per semester. *Financial support:* Institutionally sponsored loans, scholarships/grants, and unspecified assistantships available. Support available to part-time students. Financial award applicants required to submit FAFSA. *Unit head:* Prof. Charles S. Tapiero, Academic Director, 718-260-3653, Fax: 718-260-3874, E-mail: ctapiero@poly.edu. *Application contact:* JeanCarlo Bonilla, Director, Graduate Enrollment Management, 718-260-3182, Fax: 718-260-3624.

Polytechnic Institute of New York University, Department of Technology Management, Major in Management of Technology, Brooklyn, NY 11201-2990. Offers MS. *Students:* 33 full-time (14 women), 12 part-time (4 women); includes 8 minority (2 Black or African American, non-Hispanic/Latino; 5 Asian, non-Hispanic/Latino; 1 Hispanic/Latino), 19 international. Average age 30. 133 applicants, 65% accepted, 45 enrolled. In 2011, 31 master's awarded. *Degree requirements:* For master's, comprehensive exam (for some programs), thesis (for some programs). *Entrance requirements:* For master's, GMAT, minimum B average in undergraduate course work. Additional exam requirements/recommendations for international students: Required—TOEFL (minimum score 550 paper-based; 213 computer-based; 80 iBT); Recommended—IELTS (minimum score 6.5). *Application deadline:* For fall admission, 7/31 priority date for domestic students, 4/30 for international students; for spring admission, 12/31 priority date for domestic students, 11/30 for international students. Applications are processed on a rolling basis. Application fee: $75. Electronic applications accepted. *Expenses: Tuition:* Full-time $22,464; part-time $1248 per credit. *Required fees:* $501 per semester. *Financial support:* Institutionally sponsored loans, scholarships/grants, and unspecified assistantships available. Support available to part-time students. Financial award applicants required to submit FAFSA. *Unit head:* Prof. Bharadwaj Rao, Head, 718-260-3617, Fax: 718-260-3874, E-mail: brao@poly.edu. *Application contact:* JeanCarlo Bonilla, Director of Graduate Enrollment Management, 718-260-3182, Fax: 718-260-3624, E-mail: gradinfo@poly.edu.

Polytechnic Institute of New York University, Department of Technology Management, Major in Technology Management, Brooklyn, NY 11201-2990. Offers MBA, PhD. *Students:* 1 (woman) full-time, 4 part-time (1 woman); includes 1 minority (Hispanic/Latino), 2 international. Average age 35. 21 applicants, 14% accepted, 1 enrolled. In 2011, 1 degree awarded. *Entrance requirements:* Additional exam requirements/recommendations for international students: Required—TOEFL (minimum score 550 paper-based; 213 computer-based; 80 iBT); Recommended—IELTS (minimum score 6.5). *Application deadline:* For fall admission, 7/31 priority date for domestic students, 4/30 for international students; for spring admission, 12/31 priority date for domestic students, 11/30 for international students. Applications are processed on a rolling basis. Application fee: $75. Electronic applications accepted. *Expenses: Tuition:* Full-time $22,464; part-time $1248 per credit. *Required fees:* $501 per semester. *Financial support:* Institutionally sponsored loans, scholarships/grants, and unspecified assistantships available. Support available to part-time students. *Unit head:* Bharadwaj Rao, Head, 718-260-3617, Fax: 718-260-3874, E-mail: brao@poly.edu. *Application contact:* JeanCarlo Bonilla, Director, Graduate Enrollment Management, 718-260-3182, Fax: 718-260-3624, E-mail: gradinfo@poly.edu.

Polytechnic Institute of NYU, Long Island Graduate Center, Graduate Programs, Department of Technology Management, Major in Management, Melville, NY 11747. Offers MS. Part-time and evening/weekend programs available. *Faculty:* 3 part-time/adjunct (0 women). *Students:* Average age 39. In 2011, 1 master's awarded. *Degree requirements:* For master's, comprehensive exam (for some programs), thesis (for some programs). *Entrance requirements:* Additional exam requirements/recommendations for international students: Required—TOEFL (minimum score 550 paper-based; 213 computer-based; 80 iBT); Recommended—IELTS (minimum score 6.5). *Application deadline:* For fall admission, 7/31 priority date for domestic students, 4/30 for international students; for spring admission, 12/31 priority date for domestic students, 11/30 for international students. Applications are processed on a rolling basis. Application fee: $75. Electronic applications accepted. *Financial support:* Institutionally sponsored loans, scholarships/grants, and unspecified assistantships available. Support available to part-time students. Financial award applicants required to submit FAFSA. *Unit head:* Dr. Bharadwaj Rao, Department Head, 718-260-3617, E-mail: brao@poly.edu. *Application contact:* JeanCarlo Bonilla, Director of Graduate Enrollment Management, 718-260-3182, Fax: 718-260-3624, E-mail: gradinfo@poly.edu.

Polytechnic Institute of NYU, Long Island Graduate Center, Graduate Programs, Department of Technology Management, Major in Management of Technology, Melville, NY 11747. Offers MS. Part-time and evening/weekend programs available. *Students:* 2 part-time (0 women). Average age 37. 2 applicants, 100% accepted, 2 enrolled. *Entrance requirements:* Additional exam requirements/recommendations for international students: Required—TOEFL (minimum score 550 paper-based; 213 computer-based; 80 iBT); Recommended—IELTS (minimum score 6.5). *Application deadline:* For fall admission, 7/31 priority date for domestic students, 4/30 for international students; for spring admission, 12/31 priority date for domestic students, 11/30 for international students. Applications are processed on a rolling basis. Application fee: $75. Electronic applications accepted. *Financial support:* Institutionally sponsored loans, scholarships/grants, and unspecified assistantships available. Support available to part-time students. *Unit head:* Dr. Bharadwaj Rao, Department Head, 718-260-3617, E-mail: brao@poly.edu. *Application contact:* JeanCarlo Bonilla, Director of Graduate Enrollment Management, 718-260-3182, Fax: 718-260-3624, E-mail: gradinfo@poly.edu. Web site: http://www.poly.edu/academics/programs/management-technology-ms.

Polytechnic Institute of NYU, Westchester Graduate Center, Graduate Programs, Department of Technology Management, Major in Management, Hawthorne, NY 10532-1507. Offers MS. Part-time and evening/weekend programs available. *Faculty:* 5 part-time/adjunct (1 woman). In 2011, 2 master's awarded. *Degree requirements:* For master's, comprehensive exam (for some programs), thesis (for some programs). *Entrance requirements:* Additional exam requirements/recommendations for international students: Required—TOEFL (minimum score 550 paper-based; 213 computer-based; 80 iBT); Recommended—IELTS (minimum score 6.5). *Application* *deadline:* For fall admission, 7/31 priority date for domestic students, 4/30 for international students; for spring admission, 12/31 priority date for domestic students, 11/30 for international students. Applications are processed on a rolling basis. Application fee: $75. Electronic applications accepted. *Financial support:* Institutionally sponsored loans, scholarships/grants, and unspecified assistantships available. Support available to part-time students. *Unit head:* Dr. Bharadwaj Rao, Department Head, 718-260-3617, E-mail: brao@poly.edu. *Application contact:* JeanCarlo Bonilla, Director of Graduate Enrollment Management, 718-260-3182, Fax: 718-260-3624, E-mail: gradinfo@poly.edu.

Polytechnic Institute of NYU, Westchester Graduate Center, Graduate Programs, Department of Technology Management, Major in Management of Technology, Hawthorne, NY 10532-1507. Offers MS. *Students:* Average age 35. In 2011, 1 master's awarded. *Entrance requirements:* Additional exam requirements/recommendations for international students: Required—TOEFL (minimum score 550 paper-based; 213 computer-based; 80 iBT); Recommended—IELTS (minimum score 6.5). *Application deadline:* For fall admission, 7/31 priority date for domestic students, 4/30 for international students; for spring admission, 12/31 priority date for domestic students, 11/30 for international students. Applications are processed on a rolling basis. Application fee: $75. Electronic applications accepted. *Financial support:* Institutionally sponsored loans, scholarships/grants, and unspecified assistantships available. Support available to part-time students. *Unit head:* Dr. Bharadwaj Rao, Department Head, 718-260-3617, E-mail: brao@poly.edu. *Application contact:* JeanCarlo Bonilla, Director of Graduate Enrollment Management, 718-260-3182, Fax: 718-260-3624, E-mail: gradinfo@poly.edu.

Polytechnic University of Puerto Rico, Graduate School, Hato Rey, PR 00919. Offers business administration (MBA), including computer information systems, general management, management of information systems, management of international enterprises; civil engineering (ME, MS); computer engineering (ME, MS); computer science (MCS, MS); electrical engineering (ME, MS); engineering management (MEM); environmental management (MEM); landscape architecture (M Land Arch); manufacturing competitiveness (MMC, MS); manufacturing engineering (ME, MS); mechanical engineering (M Mech E). Part-time and evening/weekend programs available. *Entrance requirements:* For master's, 3 letters of recommendation.

Polytechnic University of Puerto Rico, Orlando Campus, Graduate School, Winter Park, FL 32792. Offers accounting (MBA); business administration (MBA); construction management (MEM); engineering management (MEM); environmental management (MEM); finance (MBA); human resources management (MBA); management of international enterprises (MBA); management of technology (MBA); manufacturing management (MEM). Part-time and evening/weekend programs available. Postbaccalaureate distance learning degree programs offered (no on-campus study). *Entrance requirements:* For master's, minimum GPA of 3.0. Additional exam requirements/recommendations for international students: Recommended—TOEFL. Electronic applications accepted.

Portland State University, Graduate Studies, Maseeh College of Engineering and Computer Science, Department of Engineering and Technology Management, Portland, OR 97207-0751. Offers engineering and technology management (M Eng); engineering management (MS); manufacturing engineering (ME); manufacturing management (M Eng); systems science/engineering management (PhD); MS/MBA; MS/MS. Part-time and evening/weekend programs available. *Degree requirements:* For master's, thesis optional; for doctorate, one foreign language, thesis/dissertation, oral and written exams. *Entrance requirements:* For master's, minimum GPA of 3.0 in upper-division course work, BS in civil engineering; for doctorate, GRE General Test, GRE Subject Test, minimum GPA of 3.0 in upper-division course work. Additional exam requirements/recommendations for international students: Required—TOEFL (minimum score 550 paper-based; 213 computer-based). *Faculty research:* Scheduling, hierarchical decision modeling, operations research, knowledge-based information systems.

Regis University, College for Professional Studies, School of Management, Denver, CO 80221-1099. Offers accounting (MS, Certificate); executive international management (Certificate); executive leadership (Certificate); executive project management (Certificate); finance and accounting (MBA); general business administration (MBA); health care management (MBA); human resource management and leadership (MSOL); information technology leadership and management (MSOL); international business (MBA); marketing (MBA); operations management (MBA); organizational leadership and management (MSOL); project leadership and management (MSOL); project management (Certificate); strategic business management (Certificate); strategic human resource management (Certificate); strategic management (MBA). Offered at Colorado Springs Campus, Northwest Denver Campus, Southeast Denver Campus, Fort Collins Campus, Broomfield Campus, Henderson (Nevada) Campus, and Summerlin (Nevada) Campus and online. Part-time and evening/weekend programs available. Postbaccalaureate distance learning degree programs offered (no on-campus study). *Degree requirements:* For master's, thesis optional, capstone project. *Entrance requirements:* For master's, GMAT or essays, interview, 2 years of full-time business work experience, resume; for Certificate, GMAT. Additional exam requirements/recommendations for international students: Required—TOEFL, TWE (minimum score 5) or university-based test. Electronic applications accepted. *Faculty research:* Impact of information technology on small business regulation of accounting, international project financing, mineral development, delivery of healthcare to rural indigenous communities.

Rollins College, Crummer Graduate School of Business, Winter Park, FL 32789-4499. Offers entrepreneurship (MBA); finance (MBA); international business (MBA); management (MBA); marketing (MBA); operations and technology management (MBA). *Accreditation:* AACSB. Part-time and evening/weekend programs available. Postbaccalaureate distance learning degree programs offered (minimal on-campus study). *Faculty:* 23 full-time (3 women), 6 part-time/adjunct (4 women). *Students:* 257 full-time (95 women), 121 part-time (39 women); includes 75 minority (12 Black or African American, non-Hispanic/Latino; 1 American Indian or Alaska Native, non-Hispanic/Latino; 20 Asian, non-Hispanic/Latino; 39 Hispanic/Latino; 3 Two or more races, non-Hispanic/Latino), 27 international. Average age 28. 363 applicants, 44% accepted, 100 enrolled. In 2011, 213 master's awarded. *Degree requirements:* For master's, minimum GPA of 2.85. *Entrance requirements:* For master's, GMAT or GRE, official transcripts, two letters of recommendation, essay, current resume/curriculum vitae, interview. Additional exam requirements/recommendations for international students: Required—TOEFL (minimum score 100 iBT) or IELTS (minimum score 7). *Application deadline:* Applications are processed on a rolling basis. Application fee: $50. Electronic applications accepted. *Expenses:* Contact institution. *Financial support:* In 2011–12, 258 students received support. Federal Work-Study and scholarships/grants available. Support available to part-time students. Financial award applicants required to submit FAFSA. *Faculty research:* Sustainability, world financial markets, international business, market research, strategic marketing. *Unit head:* Dr. Craig M. McAllaster,

Dean, 407-646-2249, Fax: 407-646-1550, E-mail: cmcallaster@rollins.edu. *Application contact:* Eva Gauthier Oleksiw, Admissions Coordinator, 407-646-2405, Fax: 407-646-1550, E-mail: mbaadmissions@rollins.edu. Web site: http://www.rollins.edu/mba/.

Rutgers, The State University of New Jersey, Newark, Rutgers Business School–Newark and New Brunswick, Doctoral Programs in Management, Newark, NJ 07102. Offers accounting (PhD); accounting information systems (PhD); economics (PhD); finance (PhD); individualized study (PhD); information technology (PhD); international business (PhD); management science (PhD); marketing science (PhD); organizational management (PhD); science, technology and management (PhD); supply chain management (PhD). *Degree requirements:* For doctorate, comprehensive exam, thesis/dissertation. *Entrance requirements:* For doctorate, GRE or GMAT. Additional exam requirements/recommendations for international students: Required—TOEFL (minimum score 550 paper-based; 213 computer-based; 79 iBT). Electronic applications accepted.

St. Ambrose University, College of Business, Program in Information Technology Management, Davenport, IA 52803-2898. Offers MSITM. Part-time programs available. *Faculty:* 4 full-time (0 women). *Students:* 6 full-time (0 women), 16 part-time (8 women); includes 1 minority (Black or African American, non-Hispanic/Latino), 5 international. Average age 32. 15 applicants, 93% accepted, 8 enrolled. In 2011, 2 master's awarded. *Degree requirements:* For master's, thesis (for some programs), practica. *Entrance requirements:* For master's, GRE or GMAT, minimum GPA of 2.8. Additional exam requirements/recommendations for international students: Required—TOEFL. *Application deadline:* For fall admission, 8/15 priority date for domestic students; for winter admission, 12/15 priority date for domestic students; for spring admission, 1/1 priority date for domestic students. Applications are processed on a rolling basis. Application fee: $25. Electronic applications accepted. *Expenses: Tuition:* Full-time $13,770; part-time $765 per credit hour. *Required fees:* $60 per semester. Tuition and fees vary according to degree level, program and reciprocity agreements. *Financial support:* In 2011–12, 5 students received support. Research assistantships with partial tuition reimbursements available, career-related internships or fieldwork, scholarships/grants, and unspecified assistantships available. Financial award application deadline: 3/15; financial award applicants required to submit FAFSA. *Unit head:* Kenneth R. Grenier, Director, 563-333-6173, Fax: 563-333-6268, E-mail: grenierkennethr@sau.edu. *Application contact:* Deborah K. Bennett, Administrative Assistant, 563-333-6266, Fax: 563-333-6268, E-mail: bennettdeborahk@sau.edu. Web site: http://web.sau.edu/msitm/

Santa Clara University, Leavey School of Business, Program in Business Administration, Santa Clara, CA 95053. Offers accounting (MBA); entrepreneurship (MBA); executive business administration (EMBA); finance (MBA); food and agribusiness (MBA); international business (MBA); leading people and organizations (MBA); managing technology and innovation (MBA); marketing management (MBA); supply chain management (MBA). *Accreditation:* AACSB. Part-time and evening/weekend programs available. *Students:* 196 full-time (80 women), 669 part-time (224 women); includes 302 minority (12 Black or African American, non-Hispanic/Latino; 246 Asian, non-Hispanic/Latino; 35 Hispanic/Latino; 6 Native Hawaiian or other Pacific Islander, non-Hispanic/Latino; 3 Two or more races, non-Hispanic/Latino), 186 international. Average age 32. 365 applicants, 74% accepted, 199 enrolled. In 2011, 366 degrees awarded. *Degree requirements:* For master's, thesis or alternative. *Entrance requirements:* For master's, GMAT, GRE. Additional exam requirements/recommendations for international students: Required—TOEFL (minimum score 600 paper-based; 250 computer-based; 100 iBT). *Application deadline:* For fall admission, 6/1 for domestic and international students; for spring admission, 1/19 for domestic students, 1/17 for international students. Applications are processed on a rolling basis. Application fee: $75 ($100 for International students). Electronic applications accepted. *Expenses:* Contact institution. *Financial support:* In 2011–12, 350 students received support. Fellowships with partial tuition reimbursements available, research assistantships with partial tuition reimbursements available, career-related internships or fieldwork, Federal Work-Study, institutionally sponsored loans, scholarships/grants, health care benefits, and unspecified assistantships available. Support available to part-time students. Financial award application deadline: 6/1; financial award applicants required to submit FAFSA. *Unit head:* Elizabeth B. Ford, Senior Assistant Dean, 408-554-2752, Fax: 408-554-4571, E-mail: eford@scu.edu. *Application contact:* Tammy Fox, Assistant Director, Graduate Business Admissions, 408-554-7858, E-mail: tkfox@scu.edu.

Seton Hall University, Stillman School of Business, Programs in Business Administration, South Orange, NJ 07079-2697. Offers accounting (MBA); finance (MBA); information technology management (MBA); international business (MBA); management (MBA); marketing (MBA); sport management (MBA); supply chain management (MBA). Part-time and evening/weekend programs available. *Faculty:* 37 full-time (9 women), 19 part-time/adjunct (1 woman). *Students:* 166 full-time (65 women), 284 part-time (131 women); includes 113 minority (21 Black or African American, non-Hispanic/Latino; 81 Asian, non-Hispanic/Latino; 9 Hispanic/Latino; 2 Native Hawaiian or other Pacific Islander, non-Hispanic/Latino). Average age 29. 459 applicants, 59% accepted, 208 enrolled. In 2011, 210 master's awarded. *Degree requirements:* For master's, 20 hours of community service (Social Responsibility Project). *Entrance requirements:* For master's, GMAT, GRE or CPA, advanced degree from AACSB institution, MS in a business discipline, professional degree (MD, JD, PhD, DVM, DDS, etc.), minimum undergraduate GPA of 3.0. Additional exam requirements/recommendations for international students: Required—TOEFL (minimum score 102 iBT), IELTS or Pearson Test of English (PTE). *Application deadline:* For fall admission, 5/31 priority date for domestic students, 3/31 for international students; for spring admission, 10/31 priority date for domestic students, 9/30 for international students. Applications are processed on a rolling basis. Application fee: $75. Electronic applications accepted. *Expenses: Tuition:* Part-time $1033 per credit hour. *Required fees:* $85 per semester. *Financial support:* In 2011–12, research assistantships with full tuition reimbursements (averaging $35,610 per year) were awarded; career-related internships or fieldwork, Federal Work-Study, scholarships/grants, and unspecified assistantships also available. Support available to part-time students. Financial award application deadline: 6/30; financial award applicants required to submit FAFSA. *Faculty research:* Financial, hedge funds, international business, legal issues, disclosure and branding. *Unit head:* Dr. Joyce A. Strawser, Dean, 973-761-9013, Fax: 973-761-9217, E-mail: joyce.strawser@shu.edu. *Application contact:* Catherine Bianchi, Director of Graduate Admissions, 973-761-9262, Fax: 973-761-9208, E-mail: catherine.bianchi@shu.edu. Web site: http://www.shu.edu/academics/business.

Simon Fraser University, Graduate Studies, Faculty of Business Administration, Burnaby, BC V5A 1S6, Canada. Offers business administration (EMBA, PhD); financial management (MA); general business (MBA); global asset and wealth management (MBA); management of technology/biotechnology (MBA); MBA/MRM. *Accreditation:* AACSB. Postbaccalaureate distance learning degree programs offered. *Degree requirements:* For master's, thesis or written project. *Entrance requirements:* For master's, minimum GPA of 3.0. Additional exam requirements/recommendations for international students: Required—TOEFL. *Expenses:* Contact institution. *Faculty research:* Leadership, marketing and technology, wealth management.

South Dakota School of Mines and Technology, Graduate Division, Program in Engineering Management, Rapid City, SD 57701-3995. Offers MS. Program offered jointly with The University of South Dakota. Part-time programs available. *Entrance requirements:* For master's, GMAT. Additional exam requirements/recommendations for international students: Required—TOEFL, TWE. Electronic applications accepted.

Southeast Missouri State University, School of Graduate Studies, Department of Industrial and Engineering Technology, Cape Girardeau, MO 63701-4799. Offers technology management (MS). Part-time programs available. Postbaccalaureate distance learning degree programs offered (no on-campus study). *Faculty:* 13 full-time (1 woman), 1 part-time/adjunct (0 women). *Students:* 50 full-time (14 women), 39 part-time (6 women); includes 3 minority (1 Black or African American, non-Hispanic/Latino; 1 Hispanic/Latino; 1 Two or more races, non-Hispanic/Latino), 56 international. Average age 26. 79 applicants, 87% accepted, 18 enrolled. In 2011, 14 master's awarded. *Degree requirements:* For master's, comprehensive exam (for some programs), thesis (for some programs), thesis and oral exam, or comprehensive exam and research project. *Entrance requirements:* For master's, minimum undergraduate GPA of 2.75; baccalaureate degree in industrial/engineering technology, engineering, industrial/technical education or related field with course work or significant background in industrial safety, quality control, and supervision. Additional exam requirements/recommendations for international students: Required—TOEFL (minimum score 550 paper-based; 213 computer-based; 79 iBT); Recommended—IELTS (minimum score 6). *Application deadline:* For fall admission, 8/1 for domestic students, 7/1 for international students; for spring admission, 11/21 for domestic students, 11/1 for international students. Applications are processed on a rolling basis. Application fee: $30 ($40 for international students). Electronic applications accepted. *Expenses:* Tuition, state resident: full-time $4896; part-time $272 per credit hour. Tuition, nonresident: full-time $8649; part-time $480.50 per credit hour. *Financial support:* In 2011–12, 57 students received support, including 8 teaching assistantships with full tuition reimbursements available (averaging $7,600 per year); career-related internships or fieldwork, Federal Work-Study, scholarships/grants, tuition waivers (full), and unspecified assistantships also available. Financial award application deadline: 6/30; financial award applicants required to submit FAFSA. *Faculty research:* Cybersecurity, energy conservation, supply chain management, lean manufacturing, graphic communications. *Unit head:* Dr. Doug Koch, Interim Chairperson, 573-651-2104, Fax: 573-986-6174, E-mail: dskoch@semo.edu. *Application contact:* Alisa Aleen McFerron, Assistant Director of Admissions for Operations, 573-651-5937, Fax: 573-651-5936, E-mail: amcferron@semo.edu. Web site: http://www.semo.edu/iet/.

State University of New York Institute of Technology, Program in Business Administration in Technology Management, Utica, NY 13504-3050. Offers technology management (MBA). *Entrance requirements:* For master's, GMAT, minimum GPA of 3.0. Additional exam requirements/recommendations for international students: Required—TOEFL (minimum score 550 paper-based; 213 computer-based). *Faculty research:* Technology management, writing schools, leadership, new products.

Stevens Institute of Technology, Graduate School, Wesley J. Howe School of Technology Management, Doctoral Program in Technology Management, Hoboken, NJ 07030. Offers information management (PhD); technology management (PhD); telecommunications management (PhD). Part-time and evening/weekend programs available. Postbaccalaureate distance learning degree programs offered (minimal on-campus study). *Entrance requirements:* Additional exam requirements/recommendations for international students: Required—TOEFL. Electronic applications accepted.

Stevens Institute of Technology, Graduate School, Wesley J. Howe School of Technology Management, Program in Business Administration for Experienced Professionals, Hoboken, NJ 07030. Offers technology management (EMBA).

Stevens Institute of Technology, Graduate School, Wesley J. Howe School of Technology Management, Program in Management, Hoboken, NJ 07030. Offers general management (MS); global innovation management (MS); human resource management (MS); information management (MS); project management (MS); technology commercialization (MS); technology management (MS). Part-time programs available. *Degree requirements:* For master's, thesis optional. *Entrance requirements:* For master's, GMAT, GRE General Test. Additional exam requirements/recommendations for international students: Required—TOEFL. Electronic applications accepted. *Faculty research:* Industrial economics.

Stevens Institute of Technology, Graduate School, Wesley J. Howe School of Technology Management, Program in Technology Management for Experienced Professionals, Hoboken, NJ 07030. Offers EMTM, MS, Certificate. Part-time and evening/weekend programs available. Postbaccalaureate distance learning degree programs offered. *Entrance requirements:* For master's, GMAT, GRE General Test. Additional exam requirements/recommendations for international students: Required—TOEFL. Electronic applications accepted. *Expenses:* Contact institution.

Stevens Institute of Technology, Graduate School, Wesley J. Howe School of Technology Management, Program in Telecommunications Management, Hoboken, NJ 07030. Offers business (MS); global innovation management (MS); management of wireless networks (MS); online security, technology and business (MS); project management (MS); technical management (MS); telecommunications management (PhD, Certificate). *Degree requirements:* For master's, thesis optional; for doctorate, thesis/dissertation. *Entrance requirements:* For master's and doctorate, GMAT, GRE General Test. Additional exam requirements/recommendations for international students: Required—TOEFL. Electronic applications accepted.

Stevenson University, Program in Business and Technology Management, Stevenson, MD 21153. Offers MS. *Degree requirements:* For master's, capstone course.

Stony Brook University, State University of New York, Graduate School, College of Business, Program in Technology Management, Stony Brook, NY 11794. Offers MS. Program conducted mostly in Korea. Evening/weekend programs available. Postbaccalaureate distance learning degree programs offered. *Entrance requirements:* For master's, GMAT or GRE General Test, 3 years of work experience, minimum GPA of 3.0, letters of recommendation. Additional exam requirements/recommendations for international students: Required—TOEFL (minimum score 550 paper-based; 213 computer-based).

Stony Brook University, State University of New York, Graduate School, College of Engineering and Applied Sciences, Department of Technology and Society, Program in Global Operations Management, Stony Brook, NY 11794. Offers MS. Postbaccalaureate distance learning degree programs offered. Electronic applications accepted.

Teachers College, Columbia University, Graduate Faculty of Education, Department of Math, Science and Technology, Program in Technology Specialist, New York, NY 10027-6696. Offers MA. *Unit head:* Dr. Ellen Meier, Program Coordinator, 212-678-3829, E-mail: ebm15@columbia.edu. *Application contact:* Deanna Ghozati, Admissions Contact, 212-678-3710.

Texas A&M University–Commerce, Graduate School, College of Science, Engineering and Agriculture, Department of Engineering and Technology, Commerce, TX 75429-3011. Offers technology management (MS).

Texas State University–San Marcos, Graduate School, College of Science and Engineering, Department of Engineering Technology, San Marcos, TX 78666. Offers industrial technology (MST). Part-time and evening/weekend programs available. *Faculty:* 11 full-time (0 women). *Students:* 21 full-time (3 women), 17 part-time (1 woman); includes 9 minority (2 Black or African American, non-Hispanic/Latino; 1 Asian, non-Hispanic/Latino; 5 Hispanic/Latino; 1 Two or more races, non-Hispanic/Latino), 7 international. Average age 31. 23 applicants, 43% accepted, 4 enrolled. In 2011, 15 master's awarded. *Degree requirements:* For master's, comprehensive exam, thesis optional. *Entrance requirements:* For master's, minimum GPA of 2.75 in last 60 hours of undergraduate work. Additional exam requirements/recommendations for international students: Required—TOEFL (minimum score 550 paper-based; 213 computer-based; 78 iBT). *Application deadline:* For fall admission, 6/15 priority date for domestic students, 6/1 for international students; for spring admission, 10/15 priority date for domestic students, 10/1 for international students. Applications are processed on a rolling basis. Application fee: $40 ($90 for international students). Electronic applications accepted. *Expenses:* Tuition, state resident: full-time $6408; part-time $3204 per semester. Tuition, nonresident: full-time $14,832; part-time $7416 per semester. *Required fees:* $1824; $912 per semester. Tuition and fees vary according to course load. *Financial support:* In 2011–12, 9 students received support, including 3 research assistantships (averaging $16,002 per year), 8 teaching assistantships (averaging $10,341 per year); career-related internships or fieldwork, Federal Work-Study, institutionally sponsored loans, scholarships/grants, health care benefits, and unspecified assistantships also available. Support available to part-time students. Financial award application deadline: 4/1; financial award applicants required to submit FAFSA. *Faculty research:* SOKKIA Total Station, attack of concrete, microsurfacing, measurement science. *Total annual research expenditures:* $182,448. *Unit head:* Dr. Andy Batey, Interim Chair, 512-245-2137, Fax: 512-245-3052, E-mail: ab08@txstate.edu. *Application contact:* Dr. Andy Batey, Graduate Adviser, 512-245-2137, Fax: 512-245-3052, E-mail: ab08@txstate.edu. Web site: http://www.txstate.edu/technology/.

Trevecca Nazarene University, College of Lifelong Learning, Graduate Business Programs, Nashville, TN 37210-2877. Offers business administration (MBA); information technology (MBA); management (MSM). Evening/weekend programs available. *Faculty:* 9 full-time (1 woman). *Students:* 40 full-time (20 women), 49 part-time (24 women); includes 25 minority (22 Black or African American, non-Hispanic/Latino; 1 Asian, non-Hispanic/Latino; 1 Hispanic/Latino; 1 Two or more races, non-Hispanic/Latino). Average age 35. In 2011, 43 master's awarded. *Entrance requirements:* For master's, GMAT, proficiency exam (quantitative skills), minimum GPA of 2.5, resume, employer letter of recommendation, 2 letters of recommendation, written business analysis. Additional exam requirements/recommendations for international students: Required—TOEFL (minimum score 550 paper-based; 213 computer-based). *Application deadline:* Applications are processed on a rolling basis. Application fee: $25. *Expenses:* Contact institution. *Financial support:* Applicants required to submit FAFSA. *Unit head:* Dr. Ed Anthony, Director of Graduate and Professional Programs (School of Business), 615-248-1529, Fax: 615-248-1700, E-mail: management@trevecca.edu. *Application contact:* Marcus Lackey, Enrollment Manager, 615-248-1427, E-mail: cll@trevecca.edu.

University at Albany, State University of New York, School of Business, Department of Information Technology Management, Albany, NY 12222-0001. Offers MBA. *Degree requirements:* For master's, field study project. *Entrance requirements:* For master's, GMAT. Additional exam requirements/recommendations for international students: Required—TOEFL (minimum score 550 paper-based; 213 computer-based). Electronic applications accepted. *Faculty research:* Data quality, expert systems, collaborative technology, expert information systems.

University of Advancing Technology, Master of Science Program in Technology, Tempe, AZ 85283-1042. Offers advancing computer science (MS); emerging technologies (MS); game production and management (MS); information assurance (MS); technology leadership (MS). *Degree requirements:* For master's, project or thesis. *Entrance requirements:* Additional exam requirements/recommendations for international students: Required—TOEFL (minimum score 550 paper-based). Electronic applications accepted. *Faculty research:* Artificial intelligence, fractals, organizational management.

The University of Akron, Graduate School, College of Business Administration, Department of Management, Program in Management of Technology, Akron, OH 44325. Offers MBA. *Students:* 1 full-time (0 women), 10 part-time (1 woman); includes 1 minority (Black or African American, non-Hispanic/Latino). Average age 30. 5 applicants, 40% accepted, 2 enrolled. *Entrance requirements:* For master's, GMAT, minimum GPA of 2.75, two letters of recommendation, statement of purpose, resume. Additional exam requirements/recommendations for international students: Required—TOEFL (minimum score 550 paper-based; 213 computer-based; 79 iBT). *Application deadline:* For fall admission, 7/15 for domestic and international students; for spring admission, 11/15 for domestic and international students. Application fee: $30 ($40 for international students). Electronic applications accepted. *Expenses:* Tuition, state resident: full-time $7038; part-time $391 per credit hour. Tuition, nonresident: full-time $12,051; part-time $670 per credit hour. *Required fees:* $1274; $34 per credit hour. *Unit head:* Head. *Application contact:* Dr. Susan Hanlon, Director of Graduate Business Programs, 330-972-7043, Fax: 330-972-6588, E-mail: shanlon@uakron.edu.

The University of Alabama in Huntsville, School of Graduate Studies, College of Business Administration, Department of Management and Marketing, Huntsville, AL 35899. Offers federal contract procurement (Certificate); management (MBA), including acquisition management, entrepreneurship, federal contract accounting, finance, human resource management, logistics and supply chain management, marketing, project management; supply chain management (Certificate); technology and innovation management (Certificate). *Accreditation:* AACSB. Part-time and evening/weekend programs available. *Faculty:* 11 full-time (2 women), 3 part-time/adjunct (0 women). *Students:* 52 full-time (25 women), 145 part-time (68 women); includes 28 minority (14 Black or African American, non-Hispanic/Latino; 4 American Indian or Alaska Native, non-Hispanic/Latino; 7 Asian, non-Hispanic/Latino; 2 Hispanic/Latino; 1 Two or more races, non-Hispanic/Latino), 15 international. Average age 31. 103 applicants, 73% accepted, 65 enrolled. In 2011, 76 master's awarded. *Degree requirements:* For master's, comprehensive exam, thesis or alternative. *Entrance requirements:* For master's, GMAT (minimum score 500), minimum AACSB index of 1080. Additional exam requirements/recommendations for international students: Required—TOEFL (minimum score 550 paper-based; 213 computer-based; 62 iBT). *Application deadline:* For fall admission, 8/1 for domestic students, 4/1 for international students; for spring admission, 12/1 for domestic students, 9/1 for international students. Applications are processed on a rolling basis. Application fee: $40 ($50 for international students). Electronic applications accepted. *Expenses:* Tuition, state resident: full-time $7830; part-time $473.50 per credit. Tuition, nonresident: full-time $18,748; part-time $1128.33 per credit. Tuition and fees vary according to course load and program. *Financial support:* In 2011–12, 12 students received support, including 7 research assistantships with full tuition reimbursements available (averaging $9,829 per year), 4 teaching assistantships with full tuition reimbursements available (averaging $8,000 per year); career-related internships or fieldwork, Federal Work-Study, institutionally sponsored loans, scholarships/grants, health care benefits, and unspecified assistantships also available. Support available to part-time students. Financial award application deadline: 4/1; financial award applicants required to submit FAFSA. *Faculty research:* Strategic human resources, corporate governance, cross-function integration and the management of research and development, determinants of team performance. *Total annual research expenditures:* $3.4 million. *Unit head:* Dr. Cynthia Gramm, Chair, 256-824-6913, Fax: 256-824-6328, E-mail: cynthia.gramm@uah.edu. *Application contact:* Jennifer Pettitt, Director of Graduate Programs, 256-824-6681, Fax: 256-824-7571, E-mail: jennifer.pettitt@uah.edu.

University of Arkansas at Little Rock, Graduate School, College of Business Administration, Little Rock, AR 72204-1099. Offers accountancy (M Acc, Graduate Certificate); business administration (MBA); construction management (Graduate Certificate); management (Graduate Certificate); management information system (MIS); management information systems (Graduate Certificate); management information systems leadership (Graduate Certificate); taxation (MS, Graduate Certificate). *Accreditation:* AACSB. Part-time and evening/weekend programs available. *Entrance requirements:* For master's, GMAT, minimum undergraduate GPA of 2.7. Additional exam requirements/recommendations for international students: Required—TOEFL (minimum score 525 paper-based; 195 computer-based).

University of Bridgeport, School of Engineering, Department of Technology Management, Bridgeport, CT 06604. Offers MS. *Faculty:* 3 full-time (2 women), 11 part-time/adjunct (0 women). *Students:* 98 full-time (27 women), 35 part-time (13 women); includes 5 minority (1 Asian, non-Hispanic/Latino; 1 Hispanic/Latino; 3 Two or more races, non-Hispanic/Latino), 126 international. Average age 27. 211 applicants, 61% accepted, 19 enrolled. In 2011, 94 master's awarded. *Degree requirements:* For master's, thesis optional. *Entrance requirements:* Additional exam requirements/recommendations for international students: Recommended—TOEFL (minimum score 550 paper-based; 213 computer-based; 80 iBT), IELTS (minimum score 6.5). *Application deadline:* For fall admission, 8/1 priority date for domestic students, 8/1 for international students; for spring admission, 12/1 priority date for domestic students, 12/1 for international students. Applications are processed on a rolling basis. Application fee: $50. Electronic applications accepted. *Expenses: Tuition:* Full-time $22,880; part-time $700 per credit. *Required fees:* $1870; $95 per semester. Tuition and fees vary according to course load and program. *Financial support:* In 2011–12, 20 students received support. Fellowships, research assistantships, teaching assistantships, career-related internships or fieldwork, Federal Work-Study, institutionally sponsored loans, and tuition waivers (partial) available. Support available to part-time students. Financial award application deadline: 6/1; financial award applicants required to submit FAFSA. *Faculty research:* CAD/CAM. *Unit head:* Dr. Gad Selig, Director, 203-576-4870, Fax: 203-576-4750, E-mail: gadselig@bridgeport.edu. *Application contact:* Karissa Peckham, Dean of Admissions, 203-576-4552, Fax: 203-576-4941, E-mail: admit@bridgeport.edu.

University of California, Santa Cruz, Division of Graduate Studies, Jack Baskin School of Engineering, Department of Technology and Information Management, Santa Cruz, CA 95064. Offers MS, PhD. Terminal master's awarded for partial completion of doctoral program. *Degree requirements:* For master's, thesis, 2 seminars; for doctorate, thesis/dissertation, 2 seminars. *Entrance requirements:* For master's and doctorate, GRE General Test; GRE Subject Test preferably in computer science, engineering, physics, or mathematics (highly recommended), minimum GPA of 3.5. Additional exam requirements/recommendations for international students: Required—TOEFL (minimum score 570 paper-based; 230 computer-based; 89 iBT); Recommended—IELTS (minimum score 8). Electronic applications accepted. *Faculty research:* Integration of information systems, technology, and business management.

University of Central Missouri, The Graduate School, College of Science and Technology, Warrensburg, MO 64093. Offers applied mathematics (MS); aviation safety (MS); biology (MS); computer science (MS); environmental studies (MA); industrial management (MS); mathematics (MS); technology (MS); technology management (PhD). PhD is offered jointly with Indiana State University. Part-time programs available. Postbaccalaureate distance learning degree programs offered. *Entrance requirements:* Additional exam requirements/recommendations for international students: Required—TOEFL (minimum score 550 paper-based; 79 computer-based). Electronic applications accepted.

University of Colorado Denver, Business School, Master of Business Administration Program, Denver, CO 80217. Offers business intelligence (MBA); business strategy (MBA); business to business marketing (MBA); business to consumer marketing (MBA); change management (MBA); corporate financial management (MBA); enterprise technology management (MBA); entrepreneurship (MBA); health administration (MBA), including financial management, health administration, health information technologies, international health management and policy; human resources management (MBA); investment management (MBA); managing for sustainability (MBA); services management (MBA); sports and entertainment management (MBA). *Accreditation:* AACSB. Part-time and evening/weekend programs available. Postbaccalaureate distance learning degree programs offered (no on-campus study). *Students:* 784 full-time (306 women), 203 part-time (81 women); includes 135 minority (18 Black or African American, non-Hispanic/Latino; 5 American Indian or Alaska Native, non-Hispanic/Latino; 50 Asian, non-Hispanic/Latino; 58 Hispanic/Latino; 4 Two or more races, non-Hispanic/Latino), 38 international. Average age 31. 433 applicants, 76% accepted, 212 enrolled. In 2011, 326 master's awarded. *Degree requirements:* For master's, 48 semester hours, including 30 of core courses, 3 in international business, and 15 in electives from over 50 other graduate business courses. *Entrance requirements:* For master's, GMAT, resume, official transcripts, essay, two letters of recommendation, financial statements (for international applicants). Additional exam requirements/recommendations for international students: Required—TOEFL (minimum score 560 paper-based; 197 computer-based; 83 iBT). *Application deadline:* For fall admission, 4/15 priority date for domestic students, 3/15 for international students; for spring admission, 10/15 priority date for domestic students, 10/1 for international students. Applications are processed on a rolling basis. Application fee: $50 ($75 for international students). Electronic applications accepted. *Expenses:* Contact institution. *Financial support:* Scholarships/grants available. Support available to part-time students. Financial award application deadline: 4/1; financial award applicants required to submit FAFSA. *Faculty research:* Marketing, management, entrepreneurship, finance, health administration. *Unit head:* Elizabeth Cooperman, Professor of Finance and Managing for Sustainability/MBA Program Director, 303-315-8422, E-mail: elizabeth.cooperman@ucdenver.edu. *Application contact:* Shelly Townley, Admissions Director, Graduate Programs, 303-315-8202, E-mail: shelly.townley@ucdenver.edu. Web site: http://www.ucdenver.edu/academics/colleges/business/degrees/ms/accounting/Pages/Accounting.aspx.

University of Colorado Denver, Business School, Program in Information Systems, Denver, CO 80217. Offers accounting and information systems audit and control (PhD); business intelligence (MS); enterprise technology management (MS); geographic information systems (MS); health information technology management (MS); web and mobile computing (MS). Part-time and evening/weekend programs available. Postbaccalaureate distance learning degree programs offered (no on-campus study). *Students:* 53 full-time (17 women), 34 part-time (5 women); includes 13 minority (1 Black or African American, non-Hispanic/Latino; 9 Asian, non-Hispanic/Latino; 3 Hispanic/Latino), 11 international. Average age 34. 36 applicants, 61% accepted, 12 enrolled. In 2011, 16 master's awarded. *Degree requirements:* For master's, 30 credit hours. *Entrance requirements:* For master's, GMAT, resume, essay, two letters of recommendation, financial statements (for international applicants). Additional exam requirements/recommendations for international students: Required—TOEFL (minimum score 525 paper-based; 197 computer-based; 71 iBT). *Application deadline:* For fall admission, 4/15 priority date for domestic students, 3/15 for international students; for spring admission, 10/15 priority date for domestic students, 10/1 for international students. Applications are processed on a rolling basis. Application fee: $50 ($75 for international students). Electronic applications accepted. *Expenses:* Contact institution. *Financial support:* Federal Work-Study and scholarships/grants available. Support available to part-time students. Financial award application deadline: 4/1; financial award applicants required to submit FAFSA. *Faculty research:* Human-computer interaction, expert systems, database management, electronic commerce, object-oriented software development. *Unit head:* Dr. Jahangir Karimi, Director of Information Systems Programs, 303-315-8430, E-mail: jahangir.karimi@ucdenver.edu. *Application contact:* Shelly Townley, Admissions Director, Graduate Programs, 303-315-8202, E-mail: shelly.townley@ucdenver.edu. Web site: http://ucdenver.edu/academics/colleges/business/degrees/ms/IS/Pages/Information-Systems.aspx.

University of Dallas, Graduate School of Management, Irving, TX 75062-4736. Offers accounting (MBA, MM, MS); business management (MBA, MM); corporate finance (MBA, MM); financial services (MBA); global business (MBA, MM); health services management (MBA, MM); human resource management (MBA, MM); information assurance (MBA, MM, MS); information technology (MBA, MM, MS); information technology service management (MBA, MM, MS); marketing management (MBA, MM); organization development (MBA, MM); project management (MBA, MM); sports and entertainment management (MBA, MM); strategic leadership (MBA, MM); supply chain management (MBA); supply chain management and market logistics (MM). *Accreditation:* ACBSP. Part-time and evening/weekend programs available. Postbaccalaureate distance learning degree programs offered (no on-campus study). *Entrance requirements:* Additional exam requirements/recommendations for international students: Required—TOEFL. Electronic applications accepted. *Expenses:* Contact institution.

University of Delaware, Alfred Lerner College of Business and Economics, Department of Accounting and Management Information Systems and Department of Electrical and Computer Engineering, Program in Information Systems and Technology Management, Newark, DE 19716. Offers MS. Part-time and evening/weekend programs available. *Entrance requirements:* For master's, GRE or GMAT, 2 letters of recommendation, resume, minimum GPA of 2.75. Additional exam requirements/recommendations for international students: Required—TOEFL (minimum score 600 paper-based; 250 computer-based). *Faculty research:* Security, developer trust, XML.

University of Denver, University College, Denver, CO 80208. Offers arts and culture (MLS, Certificate), including art, literature, and culture, arts development and program management (Certificate), creative writing; environmental policy and management (MAS, Certificate), including energy and sustainability (Certificate), environmental assessment of nuclear power (Certificate), environmental health and safety (Certificate), environmental management, natural resource management (Certificate); geographic information systems (MAS, Certificate); global affairs (MLS, Certificate), including translation studies, world history and culture; healthcare leadership (MPH, Certificate), including healthcare policy, law, and ethics, medical and healthcare information technologies, strategic management of healthcare; information and communications technology (MCIS, Certificate), including database design and administration (Certificate), geographic information systems (MCIS), information security systems security (Certificate), information systems security (MCIS), project management (MCIS, MPS, Certificate), software design and administration (Certificate), software design and programming (MCIS), technology management, telecommunications technology (MCIS), Web design and development; leadership and organizations (MPS, Certificate), including human capital in organizations, philanthropic leadership, project management (MCIS, MPS, Certificate), strategic innovation and change; organizational and professional communication (MPS, Certificate), including alternative dispute resolution, organizational communication, organizational development and training, public relations and marketing; security management (MAS, Certificate), including emergency planning and response, information security (MAS), organizational security; strategic human resource management (MPS, Certificate), including global human resources (MPS), human resource management and development (MPS). Part-time and evening/weekend programs available. Postbaccalaureate distance learning degree programs offered (no on-campus study). *Faculty:* 204 part-time/adjunct (80 women). *Students:* 56 full-time (26 women), 1,096 part-time (647 women); includes 196 minority (81 Black or African American, non-Hispanic/Latino; 7 American Indian or Alaska Native, non-Hispanic/Latino; 30 Asian, non-Hispanic/Latino; 66 Hispanic/Latino; 3 Native Hawaiian or other Pacific Islander, non-Hispanic/Latino; 9 Two or more races, non-Hispanic/Latino), 76 international. Average age 36. 572 applicants, 95% accepted, 410 enrolled. In 2011, 404 master's, 123 other advanced degrees awarded. *Degree requirements:* For master's, capstone project. *Entrance requirements:* For master's, two letters of recommendation, personal statement, resume. Additional exam requirements/recommendations for international students: Required—TOEFL (minimum score 550 paper-based; 80 iBT). *Application deadline:* For fall admission, 7/20 priority date for domestic students, 6/8 for international students; for winter admission, 10/26 priority date for domestic students, 9/14 for international students; for spring admission, 2/1 priority date for domestic students, 12/14 for international students. Applications are processed on a rolling basis. Application fee: $75. Electronic applications accepted. *Expenses:* Contact institution. *Financial support:* Applicants required to submit FAFSA. *Unit head:* Dr. James Davis, Dean, 303-871-2291, Fax: 303-871-4047, E-mail: jdavis@du.edu. *Application contact:* Information Contact, 303-871-3155, Fax: 303-871-4047, E-mail: ucolinfo@du.edu. Web site: http://www.universitycollege.du.edu/.

University of Idaho, College of Graduate Studies, College of Engineering, Department of Engineering, Moscow, ID 83844-1011. Offers environmental engineering (M Engr, MS); nuclear engineering (M Engr, MS, PhD); technology management (MS). *Faculty:* 3 full-time, 2 part-time/adjunct. *Students:* 17 full-time, 34 part-time. Average age 35. In 2011, 1 master's awarded. *Application deadline:* Applications are processed on a rolling basis. Application fee: $60. Electronic applications accepted. *Expenses:* Tuition, state resident: full-time $3874; part-time $334 per credit hour. Tuition, nonresident: full-time $16,394; part-time $861 per credit hour. *Required fees:* $2808; $99 per credit hour. Tuition and fees vary according to program. *Financial support:* Applicants required to submit FAFSA. *Unit head:* Dr. Larry Stauffer, Interim Dean, 208-885-6579. *Application contact:* Erick Larson, Director of Graduate Admissions, 208-885-4723, E-mail: gadms@uidaho.edu. Web site: http://www.uidaho.edu/engr/.

University of Illinois at Urbana–Champaign, Graduate College, College of Agricultural, Consumer and Environmental Sciences, Department of Agricultural and Biological Engineering, Champaign, IL 61820. Offers agricultural and biological engineering (MS, PhD); technical systems management (MS, PSM). *Faculty:* 19 full-time (2 women). *Students:* 59 full-time (15 women), 9 part-time (3 women); includes 7 minority (1 Black or African American, non-Hispanic/Latino; 1 Asian, non-Hispanic/Latino; 2 Hispanic/Latino; 3 Two or more races, non-Hispanic/Latino), 47 international. 66 applicants, 41% accepted, 22 enrolled. In 2011, 10 master's, 5 doctorates awarded. *Entrance requirements:* For master's and doctorate, minimum GPA of 3.0. Additional exam requirements/recommendations for international students: Required—TOEFL (minimum score 570 paper-based; 230 computer-based; 88 iBT) or IELTS (minimum score 6.5). *Application deadline:* Applications are processed on a rolling basis. Application fee: $75 ($90 for international students). Electronic applications accepted. *Financial support:* In 2011–12, 16 fellowships, 47 research assistantships, 19 teaching assistantships were awarded; tuition waivers (full and partial) also available. *Unit head:* Kuan Chong Ting, Head, 217-333-3570, Fax: 217-244-0323, E-mail: kcting@illinois.edu. *Application contact:* Mary Schultze, Office Manager, 217-333-5423, Fax: 217-244-0323, E-mail: mlschltz@illinois.edu. Web site: http://abe.illinois.edu.

University of Illinois at Urbana–Champaign, Graduate College, College of Business, Department of Business Administration, Champaign, IL 61820. Offers business administration (MS, PhD); technology management (MS). *Accreditation:* AACSB. *Faculty:* 42 full-time (6 women), 8 part-time/adjunct (3 women). *Students:* 117 full-time (42 women), 7 part-time (1 woman); includes 6 minority (2 Black or African American, non-Hispanic/Latino; 3 Asian, non-Hispanic/Latino; 1 Two or more races, non-Hispanic/Latino), 99 international. 391 applicants, 31% accepted, 74 enrolled. In 2011, 49 master's, 8 doctorates awarded. *Entrance requirements:* For master's, minimum GPA of 3.0; for doctorate, GMAT or GRE, minimum GPA of 3.0. Additional exam requirements/recommendations for international students: Required—TOEFL (minimum score 550 paper-based; 231 computer-based; 79 iBT) or IELTS (6.5). *Application deadline:* Applications are processed on a rolling basis. Application fee: $75 ($90 for international students). Electronic applications accepted. *Expenses:* Contact institution. *Financial support:* In 2011–12, 28 fellowships, 34 research assistantships, 12 teaching assistantships were awarded; tuition waivers (full and partial) also available. *Unit head:* William J. Qualls, Interim Head, 217-265-0794, Fax: 217-244-7969, E-mail: wqualls@illinois.edu. *Application contact:* J. E. Miller, Coordinator of Graduate Programs, 217-244-8002, Fax: 217-244-7969, E-mail: j-miller@illinois.edu. Web site: http://www.business.illinois.edu/ba/.

University of Maryland University College, Graduate School of Management and Technology, Master of Science in Technology Management Program, Adelphi, MD 20783. Offers MS, Certificate. Program held entirely online. Part-time and evening/weekend programs available. Postbaccalaureate distance learning degree programs offered (no on-campus study). *Students:* 10 full-time (4 women), 514 part-time (233 women); includes 279 minority (215 Black or African American, non-Hispanic/Latino; 27 Asian, non-Hispanic/Latino; 32 Hispanic/Latino; 5 Two or more races, non-Hispanic/Latino), 10 international. Average age 38. 144 applicants, 100% accepted, 69 enrolled. In 2011, 158 master's, 74 other advanced degrees awarded. *Degree requirements:* For master's, thesis or alternative, capstone course. *Application deadline:* Applications are processed on a rolling basis. Application fee: $50. Electronic applications accepted. *Financial support:* Federal Work-Study and scholarships/grants available. Support available to part-time students. Financial award application deadline: 6/1; financial award applicants required to submit FAFSA. *Unit head:* Dr. Joyce Shirazi, Chair, Information and Technology Systems, 240-684-2400, Fax: 240-684-2401, E-mail: jshirazi@umuc.edu. *Application contact:* Coordinator, Graduate Admissions, 800-888-8682, Fax: 240-684-2151, E-mail: newgrad@umuc.edu. Web site: http://www.umuc.edu/grad/tman.shtml.

University of Miami, Graduate School, College of Engineering, Department of Industrial Engineering, Coral Gables, FL 33124. Offers ergonomics (PhD); industrial engineering (MSIE, PhD); management of technology (MS); occupational ergonomics and safety (MS, MSOES), including environmental health and safety (MS), occupational ergonomics and safety (MSOES); MBA/MSIE. Part-time programs available. *Degree requirements:* For master's, thesis (for some programs); for doctorate, comprehensive exam, thesis/dissertation. *Entrance requirements:* For master's and doctorate, GRE General Test, minimum GPA of 3.0. Additional exam requirements/recommendations for international students: Required—TOEFL (minimum score 550 paper-based; 213 computer-based). *Faculty research:* Logistics, supply chain management, industrial applications of biomechanics and ergonomics, technology management, back pain, aging, operations research, manufacturing, safety, human reliability, energy assessment.

University of Minnesota, Twin Cities Campus, College of Science and Engineering, Technological Leadership Institute, Program in Management of Technology, Minneapolis, MN 55455-0213. Offers MSMOT. Evening/weekend programs available. *Faculty:* 1 full-time (0 women), 13 part-time/adjunct (0 women). *Students:* 57 (13 women); includes 15 minority (5 Black or African American, non-Hispanic/Latino; 2 American Indian or Alaska Native, non-Hispanic/Latino; 7 Asian, non-Hispanic/Latino; 1 Hispanic/Latino), 5 international. Average age 34. *Degree requirements:* For master's, thesis, capstone project. *Entrance requirements:* For master's, 5 years of work experience in high-tech company, preferably in Twin Cities area; demonstrated technological leadership ability. Additional exam requirements/recommendations for international students: Required—TOEFL (minimum score 580 paper-based; 240 computer-based; 90 iBT). *Application deadline:* For fall admission, 6/15 priority date for domestic students, 5/1 for international students. Applications are processed on a rolling basis. Application fee: $75 ($95 for international students). Electronic applications accepted. *Expenses:* Contact institution. *Financial support:* Fellowships, institutionally sponsored loans, and scholarships/grants available. Financial award application deadline: 7/15; financial award applicants required to submit FAFSA. *Faculty research:* Operations management, strategic management, technology foresight, marketing, business analysis. *Unit head:* Dr. Massoud Amin, Director, 612-624-5747, Fax: 612-624-

7510. *Application contact:* MOT Program, E-mail: mot@umn.edu. Web site: http://tli.umn.edu.

University of New Hampshire, Graduate School, Whittemore School of Business and Economics, Department of Business Administration, Program in Management of Technology, Durham, NH 03824. Offers MS. Part-time programs available. *Students:* 4 full-time (0 women), 2 part-time (1 woman); includes 1 minority (Hispanic/Latino). Average age 40. 8 applicants, 25% accepted, 2 enrolled. *Entrance requirements:* Additional exam requirements/recommendations for international students: Required—TOEFL (minimum score 550 paper-based; 213 computer-based; 80 iBT); Recommended—IELTS (minimum score 6.5). *Application deadline:* For fall admission, 6/1 for domestic students, 4/1 for international students; for spring admission, 12/1 for domestic students. Application fee: $65. *Expenses:* Tuition, state resident: full-time $12,360; part-time $687 per credit hour. Tuition, nonresident: full-time $25,680; part-time $1058 per credit hour. International tuition: $29,550 full-time. *Required fees:* $1666; $833 per course. $416.50 per semester. Tuition and fees vary according to course load and degree level. *Financial support:* Fellowships, research assistantships, and teaching assistantships available. *Unit head:* Christine Shea, Chairperson, 603-862-3316. *Application contact:* Holly Hurwitch, Administrative Assistant, 603-862-0277, E-mail: management.technology@unh.edu. Web site: http://www.wsbe.unh.edu/master-science-management-technology-ms-mot.

University of New Mexico, Robert O. Anderson Graduate School of Management, Department of Finance, International, Technology and Entrepreneurship, Albuquerque, NM 87131-1221. Offers finance (MBA); international management (MBA); international management in Latin America (MBA); management of technology (MBA). Part-time and evening/weekend programs available. *Faculty:* 14 full-time (2 women), 17 part-time/adjunct (4 women). In 2011, 53 master's awarded. *Degree requirements:* For master's, minimum GPA of 3.0. *Entrance requirements:* For master's, GMAT or GRE. Additional exam requirements/recommendations for international students: Required—TOEFL (minimum score 550 paper-based; 213 computer-based; 79 iBT). *Application deadline:* For fall admission, 4/1 priority date for domestic students, 4/1 for international students; for spring admission, 10/1 priority date for domestic students, 10/1 for international students. Applications are processed on a rolling basis. Application fee: $50. Electronic applications accepted. *Financial support:* Fellowships, research assistantships, career-related internships or fieldwork, Federal Work-Study, scholarships/grants, and unspecified assistantships available. Support available to part-time students. Financial award application deadline: 6/1. *Faculty research:* Corporate finance, investments, management in Latin America, management of technology, entrepreneurship. *Unit head:* Dr. Leslie Boni, Chair, 505-277-6471, Fax: 505-277-7108. *Application contact:* Megan Conner, Director, Student Services, 505-277-3290, Fax: 505-277-8436, E-mail: mconner@mgt.unm.edu.

The University of North Carolina at Charlotte, Graduate School, Belk College of Business, Department of Business Information Systems and Operation Management, Charlotte, NC 28223-0001. Offers information and technology management (MBA); supply chain management (MBA). *Faculty:* 14 full-time (5 women). *Expenses:* Tuition, state resident: full-time $3689. Tuition, nonresident: full-time $15,226. *Required fees:* $2198. Tuition and fees vary according to course load and program. *Unit head:* Dr. Joe Mazzola, Interim Dean, 704-687-7577, Fax: 704-687-4014, E-mail: jmazzola@uncc.edu. *Application contact:* Kathy B. Giddings, Director of Graduate Admissions, 704-687-5503, Fax: 704-687-3279, E-mail: gradadm@uncc.edu. Web site: http://belkcollege.uncc.edu/about-college/departments/bisom.

University of North Dakota, Graduate School, College of Business and Public Administration, Department of Technology, Grand Forks, ND 58202. Offers MSIT. Part-time programs available. *Degree requirements:* For master's, comprehensive exam (for some programs), thesis optional. *Entrance requirements:* For master's, minimum GPA of 2.75. Additional exam requirements/recommendations for international students: Required—TOEFL (minimum score 550 paper-based; 213 computer-based; 79 iBT), IELTS (minimum score 6.5). Electronic applications accepted.

University of Pennsylvania, School of Engineering and Applied Science, Executive Master's in Technology Management Program, Philadelphia, PA 19104. Offers EMBA. Program offered jointly with The Wharton School. Part-time and evening/weekend programs available. *Students:* 1 full-time (0 women), 80 part-time (11 women); includes 30 minority (5 Black or African American, non-Hispanic/Latino; 19 Asian, non-Hispanic/Latino; 5 Hispanic/Latino; 1 Native Hawaiian or other Pacific Islander, non-Hispanic/Latino), 5 international. 2 applicants, 0% accepted, 0 enrolled. In 2011, 32 degrees awarded. *Application deadline:* For fall admission, 4/1 priority date for domestic students. Application fee: $70. *Expenses: Tuition:* Full-time $26,660; part-time $4944 per course. *Required fees:* $2318; $291 per course. Tuition and fees vary according to course load, degree level and program. *Unit head:* Eduardo D. Glandt, Dean, 215-898-7244, Fax: 215-573-2018, E-mail: seasdean@seas.upenn.edu. *Application contact:* 215-898-2897, E-mail: emtm-admissions@emtm.upenn.edu. Web site: http://www.seas.upenn.edu.

University of Phoenix–Atlanta Campus, College of Information Systems and Technology, Sandy Springs, GA 30350-4153. Offers information systems (MIS); technology management (MBA). Evening/weekend programs available. *Degree requirements:* For master's, thesis (for some programs). *Entrance requirements:* For master's, 3 years of work experience, minimum undergraduate GPA of 3.0. Additional exam requirements/recommendations for international students: Required—TOEFL (minimum score 550 paper-based; 213 computer-based; 79 iBT). Electronic applications accepted.

University of Phoenix–Augusta Campus, College of Information Systems and Technology, Augusta, GA 30909-4583. Offers information systems (MIS); technology management (MBA).

University of Phoenix–Austin Campus, College of Information Systems and Technology, Austin, TX 78759. Offers information systems (MIS); technology management (MBA).

University of Phoenix–Bay Area Campus, School of Business, San Jose, CA 95134-1805. Offers accountancy (MS); accounting (MBA); business administration (MBA, DBA); energy management (MBA); global management (MBA); health care management (MBA); human resource management (MBA); human resources management (MM); management (MM); marketing (MBA); organizational leadership (DM); project management (MBA); public administration (MPA); technology management (MBA). Evening/weekend programs available. Postbaccalaureate distance learning degree programs offered (no on-campus study). *Degree requirements:* For master's, thesis (for some programs). *Entrance requirements:* For master's, minimum undergraduate GPA of 3.0, 3 years of work experience. Additional exam requirements/recommendations for international students: Required—TOEFL (minimum score 550 paper-based; 213 computer-based; 79 iBT). Electronic applications accepted.

Management of Technology

University of Phoenix–Birmingham Campus, College of Information Systems and Technology, Birmingham, AL 35244. Offers information systems (MIS); technology management (MBA).

University of Phoenix–Boston Campus, College of Information Systems and Technology, Braintree, MA 02184-4949. Offers technology management (MBA). Evening/weekend programs available. *Degree requirements:* For master's, thesis (for some programs). *Entrance requirements:* For master's, minimum GPA of 3.0, 3 years of work experience. Additional exam requirements/recommendations for international students: Required—TOEFL (minimum score 550 paper-based; 213 computer-based; 79 iBT). Electronic applications accepted.

University of Phoenix–Central Florida Campus, College of Information Systems and Technology, Maitland, FL 32751-7057. Offers management (MIS); technology management (MBA). Evening/weekend programs available. *Degree requirements:* For master's, thesis (for some programs). *Entrance requirements:* For master's, minimum undergraduate GPA of 3.0, 3 years work experience. Additional exam requirements/recommendations for international students: Required—TOEFL (minimum score 550 paper-based; 213 computer-based; 79 iBT). Electronic applications accepted.

University of Phoenix–Central Massachusetts Campus, College of Information Systems and Technology, Westborough, MA 01581-3906. Offers technology management (MBA). Evening/weekend programs available. *Degree requirements:* For master's, thesis (for some programs). *Entrance requirements:* For master's, minimum undergraduate GPA of 3.0, 3 years of work experience. Additional exam requirements/recommendations for international students: Required—TOEFL (minimum score 550 paper-based; 213 computer-based; 79 iBT). Electronic applications accepted.

University of Phoenix–Central Valley Campus, College of Information Systems and Technology, Fresno, CA 93720-1562. Offers information systems (MIS); technology management (MBA).

University of Phoenix–Charlotte Campus, College of Information Systems and Technology, Charlotte, NC 28273-3409. Offers information systems (MIS); information systems management (MISM); technology management (MBA). Evening/weekend programs available. *Degree requirements:* For master's, thesis (for some programs). *Entrance requirements:* For master's, minimum undergraduate GPA of 3.0, 3 years work experience. Additional exam requirements/recommendations for international students: Required—TOEFL (minimum score 550 paper-based; 213 computer-based; 79 iBT). Electronic applications accepted.

University of Phoenix–Chattanooga Campus, College of Information Systems and Technology, Chattanooga, TN 37421-3707. Offers information systems (MIS); technology management (MBA). Postbaccalaureate distance learning degree programs offered.

University of Phoenix–Cheyenne Campus, College of Information Systems and Technology, Cheyenne, WY 82009. Offers information systems (MIS); technology management (MBA).

University of Phoenix–Chicago Campus, College of Information Systems and Technology, Schaumburg, IL 60173-4399. Offers e-business (MBA); information systems (MIS); management (MM); technology management (MBA). Evening/weekend programs available. *Degree requirements:* For master's, thesis (for some programs). *Entrance requirements:* For master's, 3 years of work experience, minimum undergraduate GPA of 3.0. Additional exam requirements/recommendations for international students: Required—TOEFL (minimum score 550 paper-based; 213 computer-based; 79 iBT). Electronic applications accepted.

University of Phoenix–Cincinnati Campus, College of Information Systems and Technology, West Chester, OH 45069-4875. Offers electronic business (MBA); information systems (MIS); technology management (MBA). Evening/weekend programs available. Postbaccalaureate distance learning degree programs offered. *Degree requirements:* For master's, thesis (for some programs). *Entrance requirements:* For master's, minimum undergraduate GPA of 2.5, 3 years of work experience. Additional exam requirements/recommendations for international students: Required—TOEFL (minimum score 550 paper-based; 213 computer-based; 79 iBT). Electronic applications accepted.

University of Phoenix–Cleveland Campus, College of Information Systems and Technology, Independence, OH 44131-2194. Offers information management (MIS); technology management (MBA). Evening/weekend programs available. Postbaccalaureate distance learning degree programs offered (no on-campus study). *Degree requirements:* For master's, thesis (for some programs). *Entrance requirements:* For master's, minimum undergraduate GPA of 3.0, 3 years of work experience. Additional exam requirements/recommendations for international students: Required—TOEFL (minimum score 550 paper-based; 213 computer-based; 79 iBT). Electronic applications accepted.

University of Phoenix–Columbia Campus, College of Information Systems and Technology, Columbia, SC 29223. Offers technology management (MBA).

University of Phoenix–Columbus Georgia Campus, College of Information Systems and Technology, Columbus, GA 31904-6321. Offers e-business (MBA); information systems (MIS); technology management (MBA). Evening/weekend programs available. Postbaccalaureate distance learning degree programs offered. *Degree requirements:* For master's, thesis (for some programs). *Entrance requirements:* For master's, minimum undergraduate GPA of 3.0, 3 years of work experience. Additional exam requirements/recommendations for international students: Required—TOEFL (minimum score 550 paper-based; 213 computer-based; 79 iBT). Electronic applications accepted.

University of Phoenix–Columbus Ohio Campus, College of Information Systems and Technology, Columbus, OH 43240-4032. Offers information systems (MIS); technology management (MBA). Postbaccalaureate distance learning degree programs offered.

University of Phoenix–Dallas Campus, College of Information Systems and Technology, Dallas, TX 75251-2009. Offers e-business (MBA); information systems (MIS); technology management (MBA). Evening/weekend programs available. *Degree requirements:* For master's, thesis (for some programs). *Entrance requirements:* For master's, minimum undergraduate GPA of 3.0, 3 years of work experience. Additional exam requirements/recommendations for international students: Required—TOEFL (minimum score 550 paper-based; 213 computer-based; 79 iBT). Electronic applications accepted.

University of Phoenix–Denver Campus, College of Information Systems and Technology, Lone Tree, CO 80124-5453. Offers e-business (MBA); management (MIS); technology management (MBA). Evening/weekend programs available. Postbaccalaureate distance learning degree programs offered. *Degree requirements:* For master's, thesis (for some programs). *Entrance requirements:* For master's, minimum undergraduate GPA of 3.0, 3 years of work experience. Additional exam requirements/recommendations for international students: Required—TOEFL (minimum score 550 paper-based; 213 computer-based; 79 iBT). Electronic applications accepted.

University of Phoenix–Des Moines Campus, College of Information Systems and Technology, Des Moines, IA 50266. Offers information systems (MIS); technology management (MBA). Postbaccalaureate distance learning degree programs offered.

University of Phoenix–Eastern Washington Campus, College of Information Systems and Technology, Spokane Valley, WA 99212-2531. Offers technology management (MBA).

University of Phoenix–Harrisburg Campus, College of Information Systems and Technology, Harrisburg, PA 17112. Offers information systems (MIS); technology management (MBA). Postbaccalaureate distance learning degree programs offered.

University of Phoenix–Hawaii Campus, College of Information Systems and Technology, Honolulu, HI 96813-4317. Offers information systems (MIS); technology management (MBA). Evening/weekend programs available. *Degree requirements:* For master's, thesis (for some programs). *Entrance requirements:* For master's, minimum undergraduate GPA of 3.0, 3 years of work experience. Additional exam requirements/recommendations for international students: Required—TOEFL (minimum score 550 paper-based; 213 computer-based; 79 iBT). Electronic applications accepted.

University of Phoenix–Houston Campus, College of Information Systems and Technology, Houston, TX 77079-2004. Offers e-business (MBA); information systems (MIS); technology management (MBA). Evening/weekend programs available. Postbaccalaureate distance learning degree programs offered. *Degree requirements:* For master's, comprehensive exam (for some programs), thesis. *Entrance requirements:* For master's, minimum undergraduate GPA of 3.0, 3 years of work experience. Additional exam requirements/recommendations for international students: Required—TOEFL (minimum score 550 paper-based; 213 computer-based; 79 iBT). Electronic applications accepted.

University of Phoenix–Idaho Campus, College of Information Systems and Technology, Meridian, ID 83642-5114. Offers information systems (MIS); technology management (MBA). Evening/weekend programs available. *Degree requirements:* For master's, thesis (for some programs). *Entrance requirements:* For master's, minimum undergraduate GPA of 3.0, 3 years of work experience. Additional exam requirements/recommendations for international students: Required—TOEFL (minimum score 550 paper-based; 213 computer-based). Electronic applications accepted.

University of Phoenix–Indianapolis Campus, College of Information Systems and Technology, Indianapolis, IN 46250-932. Offers information systems (MIS); technology management (MBA). Evening/weekend programs available. *Degree requirements:* For master's, thesis (for some programs). *Entrance requirements:* For master's, minimum undergraduate GPA of 3.0, 3 years of work experience. Additional exam requirements/recommendations for international students: Required—TOEFL (minimum score 550 paper-based; 213 computer-based). Electronic applications accepted.

University of Phoenix–Jersey City Campus, College of Information Systems and Technology, Jersey City, NJ 07310. Offers information systems (MIS); technology management (MBA). Postbaccalaureate distance learning degree programs offered.

University of Phoenix–Kansas City Campus, College of Information Systems and Technology, Kansas City, MO 64131-4517. Offers management (MIS); technology management (MBA). Evening/weekend programs available. *Degree requirements:* For master's, thesis (for some programs). *Entrance requirements:* For master's, minimum undergraduate GPA of 3.0, 3 years of work experience. Additional exam requirements/recommendations for international students: Required—TOEFL (minimum score 550 paper-based; 213 computer-based). Electronic applications accepted.

University of Phoenix–Las Vegas Campus, College of Information Systems and Technology, Las Vegas, NV 89128. Offers information systems (MIS); technology management (MBA). Evening/weekend programs available. *Degree requirements:* For master's, thesis (for some programs). *Entrance requirements:* For master's, minimum undergraduate GPA of 3.0, 3 years of work experience. Additional exam requirements/recommendations for international students: Required—TOEFL (minimum score 550 paper-based; 213 computer-based; 79 iBT). Electronic applications accepted.

University of Phoenix–Louisiana Campus, College of Information Systems and Technology, Metairie, LA 70001-2082. Offers information systems/management (MIS); technology management (MBA). Evening/weekend programs available. *Degree requirements:* For master's, thesis (for some programs). *Entrance requirements:* For master's, minimum undergraduate GPA of 3.0, 3 years work experience. Additional exam requirements/recommendations for international students: Required—TOEFL (minimum score 550 paper-based; 213 computer-based). Electronic applications accepted.

University of Phoenix–Madison Campus, College of Information Systems and Technology, Madison, WI 53718-2416. Offers information systems (MIS); management (MIS); technology management (MBA).

University of Phoenix–Maryland Campus, School of Business, Columbia, MD 21045-5424. Offers global management (MBA); technology management (MBA). Evening/weekend programs available. Postbaccalaureate distance learning degree programs offered. *Students:* 121 full-time (58 women); includes 65 minority (59 Black or African American, non-Hispanic/Latino; 3 Asian, non-Hispanic/Latino; 1 Hispanic/Latino; 2 Two or more races, non-Hispanic/Latino), 3 international. Average age 41. *Entrance requirements:* Additional exam requirements/recommendations for international students: Required—TOEFL, TOEIC (Test of English as an International Communication), Berlitz Online English Proficiency Exam, PTE (Pearson Test of English), or IELTS. *Application deadline:* Applications are processed on a rolling basis. Application fee: $45. Electronic applications accepted. *Expenses: Tuition:* Full-time $17,098. *Required fees:* $915. One-time fee: $45 full-time. Full-time tuition and fees vary according to course load, campus/location and program. *Financial support:* Scholarships/grants available. Financial award applicants required to submit FAFSA. *Application contact:* 866-766-0766. Web site: http://www.phoenix.edu/colleges_divisions/business.html.

University of Phoenix–Memphis Campus, College of Information Systems and Technology, Cordova, TN 38018. Offers information systems (MIS); technology management (MBA).

University of Phoenix–Minneapolis/St. Louis Park Campus, College of Information Systems and Technology, St. Louis Park, MN 55426. Offers technology management (MBA).

University of Phoenix–Nashville Campus, College of Information Systems and Technology, Nashville, TN 37214-5048. Offers technology management (MBA). Evening/weekend programs available. *Degree requirements:* For master's, thesis (for some programs). *Entrance requirements:* For master's, 3 years of work experience, minimum undergraduate GPA of 3.0. Additional exam requirements/recommendations for international students: Required—TOEFL (minimum score 550 paper-based; 213 computer-based; 79 iBT). Electronic applications accepted.

University of Phoenix–New Mexico Campus, College of Information Systems and Technology, Albuquerque, NM 87113-1570. Offers e-business (MBA); information systems (MS); technology management (MBA). Evening/weekend programs available. *Degree requirements:* For master's, thesis (for some programs). *Entrance requirements:* For master's, minimum undergraduate GPA of 3.0, 3 years of work experience. Additional exam requirements/recommendations for international students: Required—TOEFL (minimum score 550 paper-based; 213 computer-based; 79 iBT). Electronic applications accepted.

University of Phoenix–Northern Nevada Campus, College of Information Systems and Technology, Reno, NV 89521-5862. Offers information systems (MIS); technology management (MBA).

University of Phoenix–Northwest Arkansas Campus, College of Information Systems and Technology, Rogers, AR 72756-9615. Offers information systems (MIS); technology management (MBA).

University of Phoenix–Oklahoma City Campus, College of Information Systems and Technology, Oklahoma City, OK 73116-8244. Offers e-business (MBA); technology management (MBA). Evening/weekend programs available. *Degree requirements:* For master's, thesis (for some programs). *Entrance requirements:* For master's, minimum undergraduate GPA of 3.0, 3 years of work experience. Additional exam requirements/recommendations for international students: Required—TOEFL (minimum score 550 paper-based; 213 computer-based; 79 iBT). Electronic applications accepted.

University of Phoenix–Omaha Campus, College of Information Systems and Technology, Omaha, NE 68154-5240. Offers information systems (MIS); technology management (MBA).

University of Phoenix–Online Campus, School of Business, Phoenix, AZ 85034-7209. Offers accountancy (MS); accounting (MBA); business administration (MBA); energy management (MBA); global management (MBA); health care management (MBA); human resource management (MBA); human resources management (MM); international (MM); management (MM); marketing (MBA, Graduate Certificate); organizational management (MA); project management (MBA, Graduate Certificate); public administration (MBA, MM, MPA); technology management (MBA). Evening/weekend programs available. Postbaccalaureate distance learning degree programs offered. *Students:* 18,883 full-time (11,868 women); includes 6,302 minority (4,182 Black or African American, non-Hispanic/Latino; 121 American Indian or Alaska Native, non-Hispanic/Latino; 478 Asian, non-Hispanic/Latino; 1,252 Hispanic/Latino; 121 Native Hawaiian or other Pacific Islander, non-Hispanic/Latino; 148 Two or more races, non-Hispanic/Latino), 1,000 international. Average age 37. *Entrance requirements:* Additional exam requirements/recommendations for international students: Required—TOEFL, TOEIC (Test of English as an International Communication), Berlitz Online English Proficiency Exam, PTE (Pearson Test of English), or IELTS. *Application deadline:* Applications are processed on a rolling basis. Application fee: $45. Electronic applications accepted. *Expenses: Tuition:* Full-time $17,160. *Required fees:* $920. One-time fee: $45 full-time. Full-time tuition and fees vary according to course load, degree level, campus/location and program. *Financial support:* Scholarships/grants available. Financial award applicants required to submit FAFSA. *Application contact:* 866-766-0766. Web site: http://www.phoenix.edu/colleges_divisions/business.html.

University of Phoenix–Oregon Campus, College of Information Systems and Technology, Tigard, OR 97223. Offers information systems (MIS); technology management (MBA). Evening/weekend programs available. *Degree requirements:* For master's, thesis (for some programs). *Entrance requirements:* For master's, minimum undergraduate GPA of 2.5, 3 years work experience. Additional exam requirements/recommendations for international students: Required—TOEFL (minimum score 550 paper-based; 213 computer-based; 79 iBT). Electronic applications accepted.

University of Phoenix–Philadelphia Campus, College of Information Systems and Technology, Wayne, PA 19087-2121. Offers information systems (MIS); technology management (MBA). Evening/weekend programs available. *Degree requirements:* For master's, thesis (for some programs). *Entrance requirements:* For master's, 3 years of work experience, minimum undergraduate GPA of 3.0. Additional exam requirements/recommendations for international students: Required—TOEFL (minimum score 550 paper-based; 213 computer-based; 79 iBT). Electronic applications accepted.

University of Phoenix–Phoenix Main Campus, School of Business, Tempe, AZ 85282-2371. Offers accounting (MBA, MS); business administration (MBA); energy management (MBA); global management (MBA); health care management (MBA); human resource management (MBA); management (MM); marketing (MBA); project management (MBA); public administration (MPA); technology management (MBA). Evening/weekend programs available. Postbaccalaureate distance learning degree programs offered. *Students:* 1,151 full-time (531 women); includes 310 minority (99 Black or African American, non-Hispanic/Latino; 10 American Indian or Alaska Native, non-Hispanic/Latino; 39 Asian, non-Hispanic/Latino; 130 Hispanic/Latino; 15 Native Hawaiian or other Pacific Islander, non-Hispanic/Latino; 17 Two or more races, non-Hispanic/Latino), 63 international. Average age 34. *Entrance requirements:* Additional exam requirements/recommendations for international students: Required—TOEFL, TOEIC (Test of English as an International Communication), Berlitz Online English Proficiency Exam, PTE (Pearson Test of English), or IELTS. *Application deadline:* Applications are processed on a rolling basis. Application fee: $45. Electronic applications accepted. *Expenses:* Contact institution. *Financial support:* Scholarships/grants available. Financial award applicants required to submit FAFSA. *Application contact:* 866-766-0766. Web site: http://www.phoenix.edu/colleges_divisions/business.html.

University of Phoenix–Pittsburgh Campus, College of Information Systems and Technology, Pittsburgh, PA 15276. Offers e-business (MBA); information systems (MIS); technology management (MBA). Evening/weekend programs available. *Degree requirements:* For master's, thesis (for some programs). *Entrance requirements:* For master's, minimum undergraduate GPA of 3.0, 3 years work experience. Additional exam requirements/recommendations for international students: Required—TOEFL (minimum score 550 paper-based; 213 computer-based; 79 iBT). Electronic applications accepted.

University of Phoenix–Puerto Rico Campus, College of Information Systems and Technology, Guaynabo, PR 00968. Offers technology management (MBA). Evening/weekend programs available. *Degree requirements:* For master's, thesis (for some programs). *Entrance requirements:* For master's, minimum undergraduate GPA of 3.0, 3 years of work experience. Additional exam requirements/recommendations for international students: Required—TOEFL (minimum score 550 paper-based; 213 computer-based; 79 iBT). Electronic applications accepted.

University of Phoenix–Raleigh Campus, College of Information Systems and Technology, Raleigh, NC 27606. Offers information systems and technology (MIS); management (MIS); technology management (MBA).

University of Phoenix–Richmond Campus, College of Information Systems and Technology, Richmond, VA 23230. Offers information systems (MIS); technology management (MBA). Evening/weekend programs available. *Degree requirements:* For master's, thesis (for some programs). *Entrance requirements:* For master's, minimum undergraduate GPA of 3.0, 3 years work experience. Additional exam requirements/recommendations for international students: Required—TOEFL (minimum score 500 paper-based; 213 computer-based; 79 iBT). Electronic applications accepted.

University of Phoenix–Sacramento Valley Campus, College of Information Systems and Technology, Sacramento, CA 95833-3632. Offers management (MIS); technology management (MBA). Evening/weekend programs available. *Degree requirements:* For master's, thesis (for some programs). *Entrance requirements:* For master's, minimum undergraduate GPA of 3.0, 3 years work experience. Additional exam requirements/recommendations for international students: Required—TOEFL (minimum score 550 paper-based; 213 computer-based; 79 iBT). Electronic applications accepted.

University of Phoenix–San Antonio Campus, College of Information Systems and Technology, San Antonio, TX 78230. Offers information systems (MIS); technology management (MBA).

University of Phoenix–San Diego Campus, College of Information Systems and Technology, San Diego, CA 92123. Offers management (MIS); technology management (MBA). Evening/weekend programs available. *Degree requirements:* For master's, thesis (for some programs). *Entrance requirements:* For master's, minimum undergraduate GPA of 3.0, 3 years work experience. Additional exam requirements/recommendations for international students: Required—TOEFL (minimum score 550 paper-based; 213 computer-based; 79 iBT). Electronic applications accepted.

University of Phoenix–Savannah Campus, College of Information Systems and Technology, Savannah, GA 31405-7400. Offers information systems and technology (MIS); technology management (MBA).

University of Phoenix–Southern Arizona Campus, College of Information Systems and Technology, Tucson, AZ 85711. Offers information systems (MIS); technology management (MBA). Evening/weekend programs available. *Degree requirements:* For master's, thesis (for some programs). *Entrance requirements:* For master's, minimum undergraduate GPA of 3.0, 3 years of work experience. Additional exam requirements/recommendations for international students: Required—TOEFL (minimum score 550 paper-based; 213 computer-based; 79 iBT). Electronic applications accepted.

University of Phoenix–Southern California Campus, School of Business, Costa Mesa, CA 92626. Offers accounting (MIS); business administration (MBA); energy management (MBA); global management (MBA); health care management (MBA); human resource management (MBA); management (MM); marketing (MBA); project management (MBA); public administration (MPA); technology management (MBA). Evening/weekend programs available. Postbaccalaureate distance learning degree programs offered. *Students:* 699 full-time (341 women); includes 318 minority (124 Black or African American, non-Hispanic/Latino; 4 American Indian or Alaska Native, non-Hispanic/Latino; 44 Asian, non-Hispanic/Latino; 124 Hispanic/Latino; 15 Native Hawaiian or other Pacific Islander, non-Hispanic/Latino; 7 Two or more races, non-Hispanic/Latino), 29 international. Average age 38. *Entrance requirements:* Additional exam requirements/recommendations for international students: Required—TOEFL, TOEIC (Test of English as an International Communication), Berlitz Online English Proficiency Exam, PTE (Pearson Test of English), or IELTS. *Application deadline:* Applications are processed on a rolling basis. Application fee: $45. Electronic applications accepted. *Expenses:* Contact institution. *Financial support:* Scholarships/grants available. Financial award applicants required to submit FAFSA. *Application contact:* 866-766-0766. Web site: http://www.phoenix.edu/colleges_divisions/business.html.

University of Phoenix–Southern Colorado Campus, College of Information Systems and Technology, Colorado Springs, CO 80919-2335. Offers technology management (MBA). Evening/weekend programs available. *Degree requirements:* For master's, thesis (for some programs). *Entrance requirements:* For master's, minimum undergraduate GPA of 3.0, 3 years of work experience. Additional exam requirements/recommendations for international students: Required—TOEFL (minimum score 550 paper-based; 213 computer-based; 79 iBT). Electronic applications accepted.

University of Phoenix–Springfield Campus, College of Information Systems and Technology, Springfield, MO 65804-7211. Offers information systems (MIS); technology management (MBA).

University of Phoenix–Tulsa Campus, College of Information Systems and Technology, Tulsa, OK 74134-1412. Offers information systems and technology (MIS); technology management (MBA).

University of Phoenix–Utah Campus, School of Business, Salt Lake City, UT 84123-4617. Offers accounting (MBA); business administration (MBA); global management (MBA); human resource management (MBA, MM); management (MM); marketing (MBA); technology management (MBA). Evening/weekend programs available. *Degree requirements:* For master's, thesis (for some programs). *Entrance requirements:* For master's, minimum undergraduate GPA of 3.0, 3 years of work experience. Additional exam requirements/recommendations for international students: Required—TOEFL (minimum score 550 paper-based; 213 computer-based; 79 iBT). Electronic applications accepted.

University of Phoenix–Vancouver Campus, John Sperling School of Business, College of Information Systems and Technology, Burnaby, BC V5C 6G9, Canada. Offers technology management (MBA). Evening/weekend programs available. *Degree requirements:* For master's, thesis (for some programs). *Entrance requirements:* For master's, minimum undergraduate GPA of 3.0, 3 years of work experience. Additional exam requirements/recommendations for international students: Required—TOEFL (minimum score 550 paper-based; 213 computer-based; 79 iBT). Electronic applications accepted.

University of Phoenix–West Florida Campus, College of Information Systems and Technology, Temple Terrace, FL 33637. Offers information systems (MIS); technology management (MBA). Evening/weekend programs available. *Degree requirements:* For master's, thesis (for some programs). *Entrance requirements:* For master's, minimum undergraduate GPA of 3.0, 3 years work experience. Additional exam requirements/recommendations for international students: Required—TOEFL (minimum score 550 paper-based; 213 computer-based; 79 iBT). Electronic applications accepted.

University of Portland, Dr. Robert B. Pamplin, Jr. School of Business, Portland, OR 97203-5798. Offers business administration (MBA); entrepreneurship (MBA); finance (MBA, MS); health care management (MBA); marketing (MBA); nonprofit management (EMBA); operations and technology management (MBA); sustainability (MBA).

Accreditation: AACSB. Part-time and evening/weekend programs available. *Faculty:* 13 full-time (1 woman), 8 part-time/adjunct (1 woman). *Students:* 50 full-time (13 women), 90 part-time (41 women); includes 19 minority (1 Black or African American, non-Hispanic/Latino; 1 American Indian or Alaska Native, non-Hispanic/Latino; 8 Asian, non-Hispanic/Latino; 5 Hispanic/Latino; 2 Native Hawaiian or other Pacific Islander, non-Hispanic/Latino; 2 Two or more races, non-Hispanic/Latino), 18 international. Average age 31. In 2011, 54 master's awarded. *Entrance requirements:* For master's, GMAT, minimum GPA of 3.0, resume, 2 letters of recommendation. Additional exam requirements/recommendations for international students: Required—TOEFL (minimum score 570 paper-based; 89 iBT), IELTS (minimum score 7). *Application deadline:* For fall admission, 7/15 priority date for domestic students, 7/15 for international students; for spring admission, 12/15 priority date for domestic students, 12/15 for international students. Applications are processed on a rolling basis. Application fee: $50. *Expenses:* Contact institution. *Financial support:* Federal Work-Study, scholarships/grants, and tuition waivers (partial) available. Support available to part-time students. Financial award application deadline: 3/1; financial award applicants required to submit FAFSA. *Unit head:* Dr. Howard Feldman, Associate Dean, 503-943-7224, E-mail: feldman@up.edu. *Application contact:* Melissa McCarthy, Academic Specialist, 503-943-7225, E-mail: mccarthy@up.edu. Web site: http://business.up.edu/.

University of St. Thomas, Graduate Studies, School of Engineering, St. Paul, MN 55105-1096. Offers manufacturing engineering and operations (MS); mechanical engineering (MS); medical device development (Certificate); regulatory science (MS); software engineering (MS); software management (MS); software systems (MSS); systems engineering (MS); technology management (MS). *Accreditation:* ABET (one or more programs are accredited). *Students:* 8 full-time, 210 part-time (38 women); includes 47 minority (22 Black or African American, non-Hispanic/Latino; 4 Asian, non-Hispanic/Latino; 6 Hispanic/Latino; 1 Native Hawaiian or other Pacific Islander, non-Hispanic/Latino; 14 Two or more races, non-Hispanic/Latino), 14 international. Average age 33. *Entrance requirements:* For master's, resume, official transcripts. Additional exam requirements/recommendations for international students: Required—TOEFL (minimum score 550 paper-based). *Application deadline:* For fall admission, 8/1 priority date for domestic students; for spring admission, 1/1 priority date for domestic students. Applications are processed on a rolling basis. Application fee: $30. Electronic applications accepted. *Expenses:* Contact institution. *Financial support:* Fellowships, research assistantships, institutionally sponsored loans, and scholarships/grants available. Support available to part-time students. Financial award application deadline: 4/1; financial award applicants required to submit FAFSA. *Unit head:* Don Weinkauf, Dean, 651-962-5760, Fax: 651-962-6419, E-mail: dhweinkauf@stthomas.edu. *Application contact:* Joyce A. Taylor, Graduate Programs Coordinator, 651-962-5756, Fax: 651-962-6419, E-mail: jataylor1@stthomas.edu.

The University of Texas at San Antonio, College of Business, Department of Information Systems and Cyber Security, San Antonio, TX 78249-0617. Offers business (MBA); business administration (PhD); information technology (MSIT); management of technology (MSMOT). Part-time and evening/weekend programs available. *Faculty:* 11 full-time (3 women), 5 part-time/adjunct (1 woman). *Students:* 23 full-time (7 women), 73 part-time (13 women); includes 41 minority (3 Black or African American, non-Hispanic/Latino; 5 Asian, non-Hispanic/Latino; 30 Hispanic/Latino; 1 Native Hawaiian or other Pacific Islander, non-Hispanic/Latino; 2 Two or more races, non-Hispanic/Latino), 4 international. Average age 31. 50 applicants, 40% accepted, 13 enrolled. In 2011, 41 master's awarded. *Degree requirements:* For master's, thesis or alternative; for doctorate, comprehensive exam, thesis/dissertation. *Entrance requirements:* For master's, GMAT, bachelor's degree with 18 credit hours in the field of study or another appropriate field of study, statement of purpose; for doctorate, GMAT or GRE, resume or curriculum vitae, three letters of recommendation from academic or professional sources familiar with the applicant's background. Additional exam requirements/recommendations for international students: Required—TOEFL (minimum score 500 paper-based; 61 iBT), IELTS (minimum score 5). *Application deadline:* For fall admission, 7/1 for domestic students, 4/1 for international students; for spring admission, 11/1 for domestic students, 9/1 for international students. Applications are processed on a rolling basis. Application fee: $45 ($85 for international students). Electronic applications accepted. *Expenses:* Tuition, state resident: full-time $3148; part-time $2176 per semester. Tuition, nonresident: full-time $8782; part-time $5932 per semester. *Required fees:* $719 per semester. *Financial support:* In 2011–12, 23 students received support, including 10 fellowships (averaging $22,000 per year), research assistantships (averaging $10,000 per year), teaching assistantships (averaging $10,000 per year); scholarships/grants, health care benefits, and unspecified assistantships also available. *Faculty research:* economics of information systems, information security, digital forensics, information systems strategy, adoption and diffusion. *Total annual research expenditures:* $300,000. *Unit head:* Dr. Jan Clark, Chair, 210-458-5244, Fax: 210-458-6305, E-mail: jan.clark@utsa.edu. *Application contact:* Katherine Pope, Graduate Advisor of Record, 210-458-7316, Fax: 210-458-4398, E-mail: katherine.pope@utsa.edu.

The University of Texas at San Antonio, College of Business, General Business Program, San Antonio, TX 78249-0617. Offers business (MBA); business administration (PhD), including accounting, business administration, finance, information technology, management and organization studies, marketing; information systems (MBA); international business (MBA); management accounting (MBA); management of technology (MBA); marketing management (MBA); taxation (MBA). *Students:* 170 full-time (52 women), 120 part-time (49 women); includes 90 minority (14 Black or African American, non-Hispanic/Latino; 2 American Indian or Alaska Native, non-Hispanic/Latino; 15 Asian, non-Hispanic/Latino; 55 Hispanic/Latino; 1 Native Hawaiian or other Pacific Islander, non-Hispanic/Latino; 3 Two or more races, non-Hispanic/Latino), 37 international. Average age 32. 395 applicants, 45% accepted, 133 enrolled. In 2011, 95 master's, 8 doctorates awarded. *Entrance requirements:* Additional exam requirements/recommendations for international students: Required—TOEFL (minimum score 500 paper-based; 61 iBT), IELTS (minimum score 5). *Application deadline:* For fall admission, 7/1 for domestic students, 4/1 for international students; for spring admission, 11/1 for domestic students, 9/1 for international students. Application fee: $45 ($85 for international students). *Expenses:* Tuition, state resident: full-time $3148; part-time $2176 per semester. Tuition, nonresident: full-time $8782; part-time $5932 per semester. *Required fees:* $719 per semester. *Financial support:* In 2011–12, fellowships (averaging $22,000 per year), research assistantships (averaging $10,000 per year), teaching assistantships (averaging $10,000 per year) were awarded. *Unit head:* Dr. Lynda Y. de la Vinna, Dean, 210-458-4317, Fax: 210-458-4308, E-mail: lynda.delavina@utsa.edu. *Application contact:* Katherine Pope, Director of Graduate Student Services, 210-458-7316, Fax: 210-458-4398, E-mail: katherine.pope@utsa.edu. Web site: http://business.utsa.edu.

University of Toronto, Faculty of Medicine, Program in Management of Innovation, Toronto, ON M5S 1A1, Canada. Offers MMI. *Entrance requirements:* For master's, GMAT, minimum B+ average, 2 reference letters, resume/curriculum vitae. Additional

exam requirements/recommendations for international students: Required—TOEFL (minimum score 580 paper-based; 93 iBT), TWE (minimum score 5). Electronic applications accepted.

University of Washington, Graduate School, Michael G. Foster School of Business, Seattle, WA 98195-3233. Offers auditing and assurance (MP Acc); business (PhD); business administration (evening) (MBA); business administration (full-time) (MBA); executive business administration (MBA); global business administration (MBA); global executive business administration (MBA); taxation (MP Acc); technology management (MBA); JD/MBA; MBA/MAIS; MBA/MHA. *Accreditation:* AACSB. Part-time programs available. *Faculty:* 100 full-time (28 women), 55 part-time/adjunct (22 women). *Students:* 385 full-time (116 women), 483 part-time (118 women); includes 183 minority (16 Black or African American, non-Hispanic/Latino; 2 American Indian or Alaska Native, non-Hispanic/Latino; 133 Asian, non-Hispanic/Latino; 25 Hispanic/Latino; 2 Native Hawaiian or other Pacific Islander, non-Hispanic/Latino; 5 Two or more races, non-Hispanic/Latino), 178 international. Average age 32. 1,367 applicants, 76% accepted, 868 enrolled. In 2011, 458 master's, 12 doctorates awarded. Terminal master's awarded for partial completion of doctoral program. *Degree requirements:* For doctorate, comprehensive exam, thesis/dissertation. *Entrance requirements:* For master's, GMAT; for doctorate, GMAT, GRE. Additional exam requirements/recommendations for international students: Required—TOEFL (minimum score 600 paper-based; 250 computer-based; 100 iBT). *Application deadline:* For fall admission, 3/15 for domestic students, 1/20 for international students. Application fee: $75. Electronic applications accepted. *Expenses:* Contact institution. *Financial support:* Fellowships with partial tuition reimbursements, research assistantships with partial tuition reimbursements, teaching assistantships with partial tuition reimbursements, Federal Work-Study, institutionally sponsored loans, and scholarships/grants available. Financial award application deadline: 2/28; financial award applicants required to submit FAFSA. *Faculty research:* Finance, marketing, organizational behavior, information technology, strategy. *Unit head:* Dr. James Jiambalvo, Dean, 206-543-4750. *Application contact:* Erin Ernst, Assistant Director of Admissions, 206-543-4661, Fax: 206-616-7351, E-mail: mba@u.washington.edu. Web site: http://www.foster.washington.edu/mba.

University of Waterloo, Graduate Studies, Centre for Business, Entrepreneurship and Technology, Waterloo, ON N2L 3G1, Canada. Offers MBET. *Entrance requirements:* For master's, honors degree. Additional exam requirements/recommendations for international students: Required—TOEFL (minimum score 550 paper-based; 213 computer-based), TWE. Electronic applications accepted.

University of Waterloo, Graduate Studies, Faculty of Engineering, Department of Management Sciences, Waterloo, ON N2L 3G1, Canada. Offers applied operations research (MA Sc, MMS, PhD); information systems (MA Sc, MMS, PhD); management of technology (MA Sc, MMS, PhD). Part-time programs available. Postbaccalaureate distance learning degree programs offered (no on-campus study). *Degree requirements:* For master's, research paper or thesis; for doctorate, comprehensive exam, thesis/dissertation. *Entrance requirements:* For master's, GMAT or GRE, honors degree, minimum B average, resume; for doctorate, GMAT or GRE, master's degree, minimum A- average, resumé. Additional exam requirements/recommendations for international students: Required—TOEFL, TWE. *Faculty research:* Operations research, manufacturing systems, scheduling, information systems.

University of Wisconsin–Madison, Graduate School, Wisconsin School of Business, Wisconsin Full-Time MBA Program, Madison, WI 53706-1380. Offers applied security analysis (MBA); arts administration (MBA); brand and product management (MBA); corporate finance and investment banking (MBA); marketing research (MBA); operations and technology management (MBA); real estate (MBA); risk management and insurance (MBA); strategic human resource management (MBA); supply chain management (MBA). *Faculty:* 32 full-time (6 women), 27 part-time/adjunct (7 women). *Students:* 228 full-time (75 women); includes 53 minority (16 Black or African American, non-Hispanic/Latino; 25 Asian, non-Hispanic/Latino; 10 Hispanic/Latino; 2 Native Hawaiian or other Pacific Islander, non-Hispanic/Latino), 28 international. Average age 28. 509 applicants, 30% accepted, 111 enrolled. In 2011, 120 master's awarded. *Degree requirements:* For master's, thesis (for arts administration). *Entrance requirements:* For master's, GMAT, bachelor's or equivalent degree, 2 years of work experience, letters of recommendation. Additional exam requirements/recommendations for international students: Required—TOEFL (minimum score 600 paper-based; 250 computer-based; 100 iBT), IELTS. *Application deadline:* For fall admission, 11/4 for domestic and international students; for winter admission, 2/3 for domestic and international students; for spring admission, 4/27 for domestic and international students. Applications are processed on a rolling basis. Application fee: $56. Electronic applications accepted. *Expenses:* Tuition, state resident: full-time $10,296; part-time $643.51 per credit. Tuition, nonresident: full-time $24,054; part-time $1503.40 per credit. *Required fees:* $70.06 per credit. Tuition and fees vary according to course load, campus/location, program and reciprocity agreements. *Financial support:* In 2011–12, 176 students received support, including 20 fellowships with full and partial tuition reimbursements available (averaging $18,756 per year), 128 research assistantships with full tuition reimbursements available (averaging $25,185 per year), 28 teaching assistantships with full tuition reimbursements available (averaging $25,097 per year); scholarships/grants, health care benefits, and unspecified assistantships also available. Financial award application deadline: 4/27; financial award applicants required to submit FAFSA. *Faculty research:* Market consequences of International Financial Reporting Standards (IFRS), inter-firm relationships and strategic partnerships, application of Bayesian statistical methods and applied probability models to understanding individuals' behaviors in the context of customer relationship management (CRM) applications, liquidity provision and the structure of financial markets, strategic management of global startups. *Unit head:* Dr. Larry "Chip" W. Hunter, Associate Dean of Master's Programs, 608-265-3494, Fax: 608-265-4192, E-mail: lhunter@bus.wisc.edu. *Application contact:* Maria Reis, Assistant Director of MBA Marketing and Recruiting, 608-262-4000, Fax: 608-265-4192, E-mail: mreis@bus.wisc.edu. Web site: http://www.bus.wisc.edu/mba.

University of Wisconsin–Stout, Graduate School, College of Technology, Engineering, and Management, Program in Technology Management, Menomonie, WI 54751. Offers MS. Part-time programs available. *Degree requirements:* For master's, thesis. *Entrance requirements:* For master's, minimum GPA of 2.75. Additional exam requirements/recommendations for international students: Required—TOEFL (minimum score 500 paper-based; 173 computer-based; 61 iBT). Electronic applications accepted. *Faculty research:* Miniature engines, solid modeling, packaging, lean manufacturing, supply chain management.

University of Wisconsin–Whitewater, School of Graduate Studies, College of Business and Economics, Program in Business Administration, Whitewater, WI 53190-1790. Offers finance (MBA); human resource management (MBA); information technology management (MBA); international business (MBA); management (MBA); marketing (MBA); operations and supply chain management (MBA). *Accreditation:*

AACSB. Part-time and evening/weekend programs available. Postbaccalaureate distance learning degree programs offered (no on-campus study). *Students:* 170 full-time (53 women), 538 part-time (213 women); includes 130 minority (28 Black or African American, non-Hispanic/Latino; 87 Asian, non-Hispanic/Latino; 15 Hispanic/Latino). Average age 31. 448 applicants, 33% accepted, 120 enrolled. In 2011, 304 master's awarded. *Entrance requirements:* For master's, GMAT or GRE, minimum AACSB index of 1000, minimum GPA of 2.75. Additional exam requirements/recommendations for international students: Required—TOEFL (minimum score 550 paper-based; 213 computer-based; 80 iBT), IELTS (minimum score 6). *Application deadline:* For fall admission, 7/15 for domestic and international students; for spring admission, 12/1 for domestic and international students. Applications are processed on a rolling basis. Application fee: $56. Electronic applications accepted. *Expenses:* Tuition, state resident: full-time $4088. Tuition, nonresident: full-time $8817. Tuition and fees vary according to program. *Financial support:* In 2011–12, research assistantships (averaging $7,245 per year) were awarded; Federal Work-Study, unspecified assistantships, and out-of-state fee waivers also available. Support available to part-time students. Financial award application deadline: 3/15; financial award applicants required to submit FAFSA. *Faculty research:* Interface between social institutions and individual behavior, technology and innovation management, occupational mental health, workplace deviance and workplace romance. *Unit head:* Dr. John Chenoweth, Associate Dean, 262-472-1945, Fax: 262-472-4863, E-mail: chenowej@uww.edu.

Walden University, Graduate Programs, School of Management, Minneapolis, MN 55401. Offers accounting (MS, DBA), including accounting for the professional (MS), CPA (MS), self-designed (MS); accounting and management (MS), including accounting for strategic managers, self-designed; accounting for managers (MBA); advanced project management (Post-Graduate Certificate); applied project management (Post-Graduate Certificate); corporate finance (MBA); entrepreneurship (MBA, DBA); finance (DBA); global management (MS); global supply chain management (DBA); healthcare management (MBA, DBA); healthcare system improvement (MBA); human resource management (MBA, MS, PhD), including functional human resource management (MS), integrating functional and strategic human resource management (MS), organizational strategy (MS); information systems management (DBA); international business (MBA, DBA); leadership (MBA, MS, DBA), including entrepreneurship (MS), general management (MS), human resources leadership (MS), innovation and technology (MS), leader development (MS), leading sustainability (MS), project management (MS), self-designed (MS); management (MS), including healthcare management; managers as leaders (MS); marketing (MBA, DBA); project management (MBA, MS, DBA); research strategies (MS); risk management (MBA); self-designed (MBA, DBA, PhD); social impact management (DBA); strategies for sustainability (MBA); strategy and operations (MS); sustainable management (MS); technology (MBA); technology entrepreneurship (DBA); technology management (MS). Part-time and evening/weekend programs available. Postbaccalaureate distance learning degree programs offered (minimal on-campus study). *Faculty:* 32 full-time (14 women), 275 part-time/adjunct (98 women). *Students:* 3,962 full-time (2,095 women), 1,557 part-time (959 women); includes 3,003 minority (2,510 Black or African American, non-Hispanic/Latino; 25 American Indian or Alaska Native, non-Hispanic/Latino; 140 Asian, non-Hispanic/Latino; 240 Hispanic/Latino; 9 Native Hawaiian or other Pacific Islander, non-Hispanic/Latino; 79 Two or more races, non-Hispanic/Latino), 395 international. Average age 41. In 2011, 586 master's, 87 doctorates, 4 other advanced degrees awarded. *Degree requirements:* For doctorate, thesis/dissertation (for some programs), residency. *Entrance requirements:* For master's, bachelor's degree or equivalent in related field; minimum GPA of 2.5; official transcripts; goal statement; access to computer and Internet; for doctorate, master's degree or equivalent in related field; minimum GPA of 3.0; 3 years of related professional/academic experience (preferred). Additional exam requirements/ recommendations for international students: Required—TOEFL (minimum score 550

paper-based; 213 computer-based), IELTS (minimum score 6.5), Michigan English Language Assessment Battery (minimum score 82). *Application deadline:* Applications are processed on a rolling basis. Application fee: $50. Electronic applications accepted. *Financial support:* Federal Work-Study, scholarships/grants, unspecified assistantships, and family tuition reduction, active duty/veteran tuition reduction, group tuition reduction, interest-free payment plans, employee tuition reduction available. Support available to part-time students. Financial award applicants required to submit FAFSA. *Unit head:* Dr. William Schulz, III, Associate Dean, 800-925-3368. *Application contact:* Jennifer Hall, Vice President of Enrollment Management, 866-4-WALDEN, E-mail: info@waldenu.edu. Web site: http://www.waldenu.edu/Colleges-and-Schools/College-of-Management-and-Technology.htm.

Western Kentucky University, Graduate Studies, Ogden College of Science and Engineering, Department of Architectural and Manufacturing Sciences, Bowling Green, KY 42101. Offers technology management (MS).

Westminster College, The Bill and Vieve Gore School of Business, Salt Lake City, UT 84105-3697. Offers accountancy (M Acc); business administration (MBA, Certificate); technology management (MBATM). *Accreditation:* ACBSP. Part-time and evening/weekend programs available. Postbaccalaureate distance learning degree programs offered (minimal on-campus study). *Faculty:* 24 full-time (7 women), 19 part-time/adjunct (3 women). *Students:* 153 full-time (45 women), 241 part-time (79 women); includes 27 minority (1 Black or African American, non-Hispanic/Latino; 16 Asian, non-Hispanic/Latino; 10 Hispanic/Latino), 1 international. Average age 33. 502 applicants, 38% accepted, 111 enrolled. In 2011, 182 master's, 37 other advanced degrees awarded. *Degree requirements:* For master's, international trip, minimum grade of C in all classes. *Entrance requirements:* For master's, GMAT, 2 professional recommendations, employer letter of support, personal resume, essay questions, official transcripts. Additional exam requirements/recommendations for international students: Required—TOEFL (minimum score 600 paper-based; 250 computer-based; 100 iBT), IELTS (minimum score 7). *Application deadline:* Applications are processed on a rolling basis. Application fee: $50. Electronic applications accepted. *Expenses:* Contact institution. *Financial support:* In 2011–12, 22 students received support. Career-related internships or fieldwork and tuition reimbursement, tuition remission available. Support available to part-time students. Financial award applicants required to submit FAFSA. *Faculty research:* Innovation and entrepreneurship, business strategy and change, financial analysis and capital budgeting, leadership development, knowledge management. *Unit head:* Dr. Jin Wang, Dean, Gore School of Business, 801-832-2600, Fax: 801-832-3106, E-mail: jwang@westminstercollege.edu. *Application contact:* Dr. Gary Daynes, Vice President for Strategic Outreach and Enrollment, 801-832-2200, Fax: 801-832-3101, E-mail: admission@westminstercollege.edu.
Web site: http://www.westminstercollege.edu/mba/.

Wilfrid Laurier University, Faculty of Graduate and Postdoctoral Studies, School of Business and Economics, Department of Business, Waterloo, ON N2L 3C5, Canada. Offers accounting (PhD); finance (M Fin); financial economics (PhD); marketing (PhD); operations and supply chain management (PhD); organizational behavior and human resource management (M Sc); organizational behaviour and human resource management (PhD); supply chain management (M Sc); technology management (EMTM). Part-time and evening/weekend programs available. *Degree requirements:* For master's, thesis optional; for doctorate, comprehensive exam, thesis/dissertation. *Entrance requirements:* For master's, GMAT, 4-year honors degree with minimum B+ average; for doctorate, GMAT, master's degree, minimum B+ average. Additional exam requirements/recommendations for international students: Required—TOEFL (minimum score 89 iBT). Electronic applications accepted. *Faculty research:* Financial economics, management and organizational behavior, operations and supply chain management.

Operations Research

Air Force Institute of Technology, Graduate School of Engineering and Management, Department of Operational Sciences, Dayton, OH 45433-7765. Offers logistics management (MS); operations research (MS, PhD); space operations (MS). Part-time programs available. *Degree requirements:* For master's, thesis; for doctorate, thesis/dissertation. *Entrance requirements:* For doctorate, GRE General Test, minimum GPA of 3.0, U.S. citizenship. *Faculty research:* Optimization, simulation, combat modeling and analysis, reliability and maintainability, resource scheduling.

Bowling Green State University, Graduate College, College of Arts and Sciences, Department of Computer Science, Bowling Green, OH 43403. Offers computer science (MS), including operations research, parallel and distributed computing, software engineering. Part-time programs available. *Degree requirements:* For master's, thesis or alternative. *Entrance requirements:* For master's, GRE General Test. Additional exam requirements/recommendations for international students: Required—TOEFL. Electronic applications accepted. *Faculty research:* Artificial intelligence, real time and concurrent programming languages, behavioral aspects of computing, network protocols.

Carnegie Mellon University, Tepper School of Business, Program in Operations Research, Pittsburgh, PA 15213-3891. Offers PhD. *Degree requirements:* For doctorate, thesis/dissertation. *Entrance requirements:* For doctorate, GMAT or GRE General Test.

Case Western Reserve University, Weatherhead School of Management, Department of Operations, Management Program, Cleveland, OH 44106. Offers operations research (MSM); supply chain (MSM); MBA/MSM. *Accreditation:* AACSB. Part-time and evening/weekend programs available. *Entrance requirements:* For master's, GMAT or GRE, 3 letters of recommendation, resume. Additional exam requirements/recommendations for international students: Required—TOEFL (minimum score 600 paper-based; 250 computer-based). *Faculty research:* Supply chain management, operations management, operations/finance interface optimization, scheduling.

Claremont Graduate University, Graduate Programs, School of Mathematical Sciences, Claremont, CA 91711-6160. Offers computational and systems biology (PhD); computational mathematics and numerical analysis (MA, MS); computational science (PhD); engineering and industrial applied mathematics (PhD); mathematics (PhD); operations research and statistics (MA, MS); physical applied mathematics (MA, MS); pure mathematics (MA, MS); scientific computing (MA, MS); systems and control theory (MA, MS). Part-time programs available. *Faculty:* 6 full-time (0 women), 1 part-time/adjunct (0 women). *Students:* 52 full-time (16 women), 24 part-time (9 women); includes 25 minority (3 Black or African American, non-Hispanic/Latino; 10 Asian, non-Hispanic/

Latino; 11 Hispanic/Latino; 1 Two or more races, non-Hispanic/Latino), 17 international. Average age 33. In 2011, 15 master's, 3 doctorates awarded. Terminal master's awarded for partial completion of doctoral program. *Entrance requirements:* For master's and doctorate, GRE General Test. Additional exam requirements/recommendations for international students: Required—TOEFL (minimum score 550 paper-based; 213 computer-based; 80 iBT). *Application deadline:* For fall admission, 2/1 priority date for domestic students. Applications are processed on a rolling basis. Application fee: $60. Electronic applications accepted. *Expenses:* Tuition: Full-time $36,374; part-time $1581 per unit. *Required fees:* $165 per semester. *Financial support:* Fellowships, research assistantships, Federal Work-Study, institutionally sponsored loans, scholarships/grants, and tuition waivers (full and partial) available. Support available to part-time students. Financial award application deadline: 2/15; financial award applicants required to submit FAFSA. *Unit head:* Ellis Cumberbatch, Dean, 909-607-3369, Fax: 909-607-8261, E-mail: ellis.cumberbatch@cgu.edu. *Application contact:* Susan Townzen, Program Coordinator, 909-621-8080, Fax: 909-607-8261, E-mail: susan.n.townzen@cgu.edu. Web site: http://www.cgu.edu/pages/168.asp.

Clemson University, Graduate School, College of Engineering and Science, Department of Mathematical Sciences, Clemson, SC 29634. Offers applied and pure mathematics (MS, PhD); computational mathematics (MS, PhD); operations research (MS, PhD); statistics (MS, PhD). Part-time programs available. *Faculty:* 46 full-time (13 women), 10 part-time/adjunct (5 women). *Students:* 119 full-time (50 women), 6 part-time (4 women); includes 5 minority (2 Black or African American, non-Hispanic/Latino; 2 American Indian or Alaska Native, non-Hispanic/Latino; 1 Two or more races, non-Hispanic/Latino), 40 international. Average age 27. 133 applicants, 75% accepted, 31 enrolled. In 2011, 23 master's, 6 doctorates awarded. *Degree requirements:* For master's, thesis optional, final project; for doctorate, thesis/dissertation, qualifying exams. *Entrance requirements:* For master's and doctorate, GRE General Test. Additional exam requirements/recommendations for international students: Required—TOEFL. *Application deadline:* For fall admission, 1/15 priority date for domestic students, 1/15 for international students; for spring admission, 10/1 priority date for domestic students, 9/15 for international students. Applications are processed on a rolling basis. Application fee: $70 ($80 for international students). Electronic applications accepted. *Financial support:* In 2011–12, 113 students received support, including 1 fellowship with full and partial tuition reimbursement available (averaging $10,000 per year), 9 research assistantships with partial tuition reimbursements available (averaging $18,373 per year), 104 teaching assistantships with partial tuition reimbursements available (averaging $17,869 per year); career-related internships or fieldwork, institutionally sponsored loans, scholarships/grants, health care benefits, and unspecified assistantships also available. Support available to part-time students. Financial award application deadline: 4/15. *Faculty research:* Applied and computational analysis, cryptography, discrete mathematics, optimization, statistics. *Total annual research expenditures:* $780,865. *Unit head:* Dr. Robert L. Taylor, Chair, 864-656-5240, Fax: 864-656-5230, E-mail: rtaylo2@clemson.edu. *Application contact:* Dr. K. B. Kulasekera, Graduate Coordinator, 864-656-5231, Fax: 864-656-5230, E-mail: kk@clemson.edu. Web site: http://www.clemson.edu/ces/departments/math/index.html.

The College of William and Mary, Faculty of Arts and Sciences, Department of Computer Science, Program in Computational Operations Research, Williamsburg, VA 23187-8795. Offers computer science (MS), including operations research. Part-time programs available. *Faculty:* 9 full-time (2 women), 2 part-time/adjunct (1 woman). *Students:* 20 full-time (5 women); includes 2 minority (both Black or African American, non-Hispanic/Latino), 4 international. Average age 26. *Degree requirements:* For master's, research project. *Entrance requirements:* For master's, GRE General Test, minimum GPA of 2.5. Additional exam requirements/recommendations for international students: Required—TOEFL. *Application deadline:* For fall admission, 3/1 priority date for domestic students, 3/15 for international students; for spring admission, 11/1 for domestic and international students. Applications are processed on a rolling basis. Application fee: $45. Electronic applications accepted. *Expenses:* Tuition, state resident: full-time $6400; part-time $365 per credit hour. Tuition, nonresident: full-time $19,720; part-time $985 per credit hour. *Required fees:* $4562. *Financial support:* In 2011–12, 13 students received support, including 6 fellowships (averaging $9,000 per year), 7 teaching assistantships with full tuition reimbursements available (averaging $11,500 per year); scholarships/grants, tuition waivers (full), and unspecified assistantships also available. Financial award application deadline: 3/1; financial award applicants required to submit FAFSA. *Faculty research:* Metaheuristics, reliability, optimization, statistics, networks. *Unit head:* Dr. Rex Kincaid, Professor, 757-221-2038, Fax: 757-221-1717, E-mail: rrkinc@math.wm.edu. *Application contact:* Vanessa Godwin, Administrative Director, 757-221-3455, Fax: 757-221-1717, E-mail: cor@cs.wm.edu. Web site: http://www.wm.edu/computerscience/grad/.

Columbia University, The Fu Foundation School of Engineering and Applied Science, Department of Industrial Engineering and Operations Research, New York, NY 10027. Offers financial engineering (MS); industrial engineering (Engr); industrial engineering and operations research (MS, Eng Sc D, PhD); MS/MBA. Part-time and evening/weekend programs available. Postbaccalaureate distance learning degree programs offered (no on-campus study). *Faculty:* 22 full-time (3 women), 27 part-time/adjunct (2 women). *Students:* 344 full-time (99 women), 205 part-time (54 women); includes 34 minority (28 Asian, non-Hispanic/Latino; 2 Hispanic/Latino; 1 Native Hawaiian or other Pacific Islander, non-Hispanic/Latino; 3 Two or more races, non-Hispanic/Latino), 460 international. Average age 26. 2,041 applicants, 19% accepted, 311 enrolled. In 2011, 229 master's, 6 doctorates, 1 other advanced degree awarded. *Degree requirements:* For doctorate, thesis/dissertation, oral and written qualifying exams. *Entrance requirements:* For master's, doctorate, and Engr, GRE General Test. Additional exam requirements/recommendations for international students: Required—TOEFL, IELTS. *Application deadline:* For fall admission, 12/1 priority date for domestic students, 12/1 for international students; for spring admission, 10/1 priority date for domestic students, 10/1 for international students. Application fee: $95. Electronic applications accepted. *Financial support:* In 2011–12, 44 students received support, including 2 fellowships with full tuition reimbursements available (averaging $35,968 per year), 22 research assistantships with full tuition reimbursements available (averaging $31,380 per year), 20 teaching assistantships with full tuition reimbursements available (averaging $31,380 per year); career-related internships or fieldwork and health care benefits also available. Financial award application deadline: 12/1; financial award applicants required to submit FAFSA. *Faculty research:* Applied probability and optimization; financial engineering, modeling risk including credit risk and systemic risk, asset allocation, portfolio execution, behavioral finance, agent-based model in finance; revenue management; management and optimization of service systems, call centers, capacity allocation in healthcare systems, inventory control for vaccines; energy, smart grids, demand shaping, managing renewable energy sources, energy-aware scheduling. *Unit head:* Dr. Cliff S. Stein, Professor and Department Chairman, 212-854-5238, Fax: 212-854-8103, E-mail: cliff@ieor.columbia.edu. *Application contact:* Adina Berrios Brooks, Student Affairs Manager, 212-854-1934, Fax: 212-854-8103, E-mail: admit@ieor.columbia.edu. Web site: http://www.ieor.columbia.edu/.

Cornell University, Graduate School, Graduate Fields of Engineering, Field of Operations Research and Information Engineering, Ithaca, NY 14853. Offers applied probability and statistics (PhD); manufacturing systems engineering (PhD); mathematical programming (PhD); operations research and industrial engineering (M Eng). *Faculty:* 38 full-time (6 women). *Students:* 172 full-time (47 women); includes 25 minority (2 Black or African American, non-Hispanic/Latino; 19 Asian, non-Hispanic/Latino; 4 Hispanic/Latino), 120 international. Average age 24. 1,070 applicants, 24% accepted, 106 enrolled. In 2011, 93 master's, 6 doctorates awarded. *Degree requirements:* For doctorate, comprehensive exam, thesis/dissertation. *Entrance requirements:* For master's and doctorate, GRE General Test, 3 letters of recommendation. Additional exam requirements/recommendations for international students: Required—TOEFL (minimum score 600 paper-based; 250 computer-based; 100 iBT). *Application deadline:* For fall admission, 12/15 for domestic students. Application fee: $95. Electronic applications accepted. *Financial support:* In 2011–12, 44 students received support, including 11 fellowships with full tuition reimbursements available, 13 research assistantships with full tuition reimbursements available, 19 teaching assistantships with full tuition reimbursements available; institutionally sponsored loans, scholarships/grants, health care benefits, tuition waivers (full and partial), and unspecified assistantships also available. Financial award applicants required to submit FAFSA. *Faculty research:* Mathematical programming and combinatorial optimization, statistics, stochastic processes, mathematical finance, simulation, manufacturing, e-commerce. *Unit head:* Director of Graduate Studies, 607-255-9128, Fax: 607-255-9129. *Application contact:* Graduate Field Assistant, 607-255-9128, Fax: 607-255-9129, E-mail: orie@cornell.edu. Web site: http://www.gradschool.cornell.edu/fields.php?id-35&a-2.

École Polytechnique de Montréal, Graduate Programs, Department of Mathematics and Industrial Engineering, Montréal, QC H3C 3A7, Canada. Offers ergonomy (M Eng, M Sc A, DESS); mathematical method in CA engineering (M Eng, M Sc A, PhD); operational research (M Eng, M Sc A, PhD); production (M Eng, M Sc A); technology management (M Eng, M Sc A). DESS program offered jointly with HEC Montreal and Université de Montréal. Part-time programs available. *Degree requirements:* For master's, one foreign language, thesis. *Entrance requirements:* For master's, minimum GPA of 2.75. *Faculty research:* Use of computers in organizations.

Florida Institute of Technology, Graduate Programs, College of Science, Department of Mathematical Sciences, Melbourne, FL 32901-6975. Offers applied mathematics (MS, PhD); operations research (MS, PhD). Part-time and evening/weekend programs available. *Faculty:* 11 full-time (2 women). *Students:* 31 full-time (12 women), 10 part-time (2 women); includes 5 minority (3 Black or African American, non-Hispanic/Latino; 1 Asian, non-Hispanic/Latino; 1 Hispanic/Latino), 20 international. Average age 32. 82 applicants, 61% accepted, 17 enrolled. In 2011, 8 master's, 5 doctorates awarded. *Degree requirements:* For master's, comprehensive exam (for some programs), thesis optional; for doctorate, comprehensive exam, thesis/dissertation, preliminary exam. *Entrance requirements:* For master's, minimum GPA of 3.0, computer programming literacy; for doctorate, minimum GPA of 3.2, resume, 3 letters of recommendation, statement of objectives. Additional exam requirements/recommendations for international students: Required—TOEFL (minimum score 550 paper-based; 213 computer-based; 79 iBT). *Application deadline:* For fall admission, 4/1 for international students; for spring admission, 9/30 for international students. Applications are processed on a rolling basis. Application fee: $0. Electronic applications accepted. *Expenses:* Tuition: Full-time $19,620; part-time $1090 per credit hour. Tuition and fees vary according to campus/location. *Financial support:* In 2011–12, 17 teaching assistantships with full and partial tuition reimbursements (averaging $7,586 per year) were awarded; research assistantships, career-related internships or fieldwork, institutionally sponsored loans, tuition waivers (partial), unspecified assistantships, and tuition remissions also available. Support available to part-time students. Financial award application deadline: 3/1; financial award applicants required to submit FAFSA. *Faculty research:* Real analysis, numerical analysis, statistics, data analysis, combinatorics, artificial intelligence, simulation. *Total annual research expenditures:* $58,346. *Unit head:* Dr. Semen Koksal, Department Head, 321-674-8765, Fax: 321-674-7412, E-mail: skoksal@fit.edu. *Application contact:* Cheryl A. Brown, Associate Director of Graduate Admissions, 321-674-7581, Fax: 321-723-9468, E-mail: cbrown@fit.edu. Web site: http://cos.fit.edu/math/.

Florida Institute of Technology, Graduate Programs, Extended Studies Division, Melbourne, FL 32901-6975. Offers acquisition and contract management (MS); aerospace engineering (MS); business administration (MBA); computer information systems (MS); computer science (MS); electrical engineering (MS); engineering management (MS); human resources management (MS); logistics management (MS), including humanitarian and disaster relief logistics; management (MS), including acquisition and contract management, e-business, human resources management, information systems, logistics management, management, transportation management; material acquisition management (MS); mechanical engineering (MS); operations research (MS); project management (MS), including information systems, operations research; public administration (MPA); quality management (MS); software engineering (MS); space systems (MS); space systems management (MS); supply chain management (MS); systems management (MS), including information systems, operations research. Part-time and evening/weekend programs available. Postbaccalaureate distance learning degree programs offered (no on-campus study). *Faculty:* 9 full-time (2 women), 105 part-time/adjunct (24 women). *Students:* 113 full-time (52 women), 1,150 part-time (484 women); includes 496 minority (332 Black or African American, non-Hispanic/Latino; 11 American Indian or Alaska Native, non-Hispanic/Latino; 42 Asian, non-Hispanic/Latino; 71 Hispanic/Latino; 2 Native Hawaiian or other Pacific Islander, non-Hispanic/Latino; 38 Two or more races, non-Hispanic/Latino), 11 international. Average age 35. 568 applicants, 56% accepted, 296 enrolled. In 2011, 471 master's awarded. *Degree requirements:* For master's, comprehensive exam (for some programs), capstone course. *Entrance requirements:* For master's, GMAT or resume showing 8 years of supervised experience, minimum GPA of 3.0, 2 letters of recommendation, resume. Additional exam requirements/recommendations for international students: Required—TOEFL (minimum score 550 paper-based; 213 computer-based; 79 iBT). *Application deadline:* For fall admission, 4/1 for international students; for spring admission, 9/30 for international students. Applications are processed on a rolling basis. Application fee: $0. Electronic applications accepted. *Expenses:* Contact institution. *Financial support:* Application deadline: 3/1; applicants required to submit FAFSA. *Unit head:* Dr. Theodore R. Richardson, III, Senior Associate Dean, 321-674-8123, Fax: 321-674-7597, E-mail: trichardson@fit.edu. *Application contact:* Carolyn Farrior, Director of Graduate Admissions, Online Learning and Off-Campus Programs, 321-674-7118, Fax: 321-674-8216, E-mail: cfarrior@fit.edu. Web site: http://es.fit.edu.

George Mason University, Volgenau School of Engineering, Department of Systems Engineering and Operations Research, Fairfax, VA 22030. Offers architecture-based systems integration (Certificate); command, control, communication, computing and intelligence (Certificate); computational modeling (Certificate); discovery, design and innovation (Certificate); military operations research (Certificate); operations research (MS); systems engineering (MS); systems engineering analysis and architecture (Certificate); systems engineering and operations research (PhD); systems engineering of software intensive systems (Certificate). MS programs offered jointly with Old Dominion University, University of Virginia, Virginia Commonwealth University, and Virginia Polytechnic Institute and State University. *Faculty:* 16 full-time (4 women), 15 part-time/adjunct (4 women). *Students:* 42 full-time (5 women), 153 part-time (31 women); includes 46 minority (5 Black or African American, non-Hispanic/Latino; 2 American Indian or Alaska Native, non-Hispanic/Latino; 27 Asian, non-Hispanic/Latino; 11 Hispanic/Latino; 1 Two or more races, non-Hispanic/Latino), 13 international. Average age 32. 124 applicants, 74% accepted, 51 enrolled. In 2011, 50 master's, 1 doctorate, 11 other advanced degrees awarded. *Degree requirements:* For master's, thesis optional; for doctorate, comprehensive exam, thesis/dissertation, qualifying exams. *Entrance requirements:* For master's, GRE General Test, BS in related field; minimum GPA of 3.0; 3 letters of recommendation; 2 official transcripts; expanded goals statement; proof of financial support; photocopy of passport; official bank statement; multivariable calculus, applied probability, statistics and a computer language course; self evaluation form; for doctorate, GRE, MS with minimum GPA of 3.5; BS with minimum GPA of 3.0 in systems or operational research; 2 official transcripts; 3 letters of recommendation; resume; expanded goals statement; self evaluation form; photocopy of passport; official bank statement; proof of financial support; for Certificate, personal goals statement; 2 official transcripts; self-evaluation form; 1 letter of recommendation; resume; official bank statement; photocopy of passport; proof of financial support; baccalaureate degree in related field. Additional exam requirements/recommendations for international students: Required—TOEFL (minimum score 575 paper-based; 230 computer-based; 88 iBT), IELTS, Pearson Test of English. *Application deadline:* For fall admission, 1/15 priority date for domestic students; for spring admission, 8/15 priority date for domestic students. Application fee: $65 ($80 for international students). Electronic applications accepted. *Expenses:* Tuition, state resident: full-time $8750; part-time $364.58 per credit. Tuition, nonresident: full-time $24,092; part-time $1003.83 per credit. *Required fees:* $2514; $104.75 per credit. *Financial support:* In 2011–12, 12 students received support, including 7 research assistantships with full and partial tuition reimbursements available (averaging $15,028 per year), 5 teaching assistantships with full and partial tuition reimbursements available (averaging $12,474 per year); career-related internships or fieldwork, Federal Work-Study, scholarships/grants, unspecified assistantships, and health care benefits (full-time research or teaching assistantship recipients) also available. Support available to part-time students. Financial award application deadline: 3/1; financial award applicants required to submit FAFSA. *Faculty research:* Requirements engineering, signal processing, systems architecture, data fusion. *Total annual research expenditures:* $1.5 million. *Unit head:* Dr. Ariela Sofer, Chair, 703-993-1692, Fax: 703-993-1521, E-mail: asofer@gmu.edu. *Application contact:* Josefine Wiecks, Administrative Assistant, 703-993-1785, Fax: 703-993-1521, E-mail: jwiecks@gmu.edu. Web site: http://seor.gmu.edu.

Georgia Institute of Technology, Graduate Studies and Research, College of Engineering, School of Industrial and Systems Engineering, Program in Operations Research, Atlanta, GA 30332-0001. Offers MSOR, PhD. Part-time programs available. *Entrance requirements:* For master's, GRE General Test, minimum GPA of 3.0. Additional exam requirements/recommendations for international students: Required—TOEFL. Electronic applications accepted. *Faculty research:* Linear and nonlinear deterministic models in operations research, mathematical statistics, design of experiments.

Georgia State University, J. Mack Robinson College of Business, Department of Managerial Sciences, Atlanta, GA 30302-3083. Offers business analysis (MBA, MS); decision sciences (PhD); entrepreneurship (MBA); human resources management (MBA, MS); management (MBA, PhD); operations management (MBA, MS); organization change (MS); personnel employee relations (PhD); strategic management (PhD). *Accreditation:* AACSB. Part-time and evening/weekend programs available. *Degree requirements:* For doctorate, thesis/dissertation. *Entrance requirements:* For master's and doctorate, GMAT. Additional exam requirements/recommendations for international students: Required—TOEFL (minimum score 610 paper-based; 255 computer-based; 101 iBT). Electronic applications accepted. *Faculty research:* Abusive supervision, entrepreneurship, time series and neural networks, organizational controls, inventory control systems.

HEC Montreal, School of Business Administration, Master of Science Programs in Administration, Program in Business Analytics, Montréal, QC H3T 2A7, Canada. Offers M Sc. Part-time programs available. *Students:* 9 full-time (4 women). 2 applicants, 50% accepted, 1 enrolled. In 2011, 1 master's awarded. *Degree requirements:* For master's, one foreign language, thesis. *Entrance requirements:* For master's, Test de francais international (TFI) with minimum score of 850 (for those who have never studied in French), BBA, undergraduate degree in another field, degree deemed equivalent by program director and minimum GPA of 3.0 on 4.3 scale. *Application deadline:* For fall admission, 3/15 for domestic and international students; for winter admission, 9/15 for domestic and international students. Application fee: $80. Electronic applications accepted. Application fee is waived when completed online. *Expenses:* Contact institution. *Financial support:* Research assistantships, teaching assistantships, and scholarships/grants available. Financial award application deadline: 9/2. *Unit head:* Claude Laurin, Director, 514-340-6485, Fax: 514-340-6880, E-mail: claude.laurin@hec.ca. *Application contact:* Virginie Lefebvre, Administrative Director, 514-340-6112, Fax: 514-340-6411, E-mail: virginie.lefebvre@hec.ca. Web site: http://www.hec.ca/en/programs_training/msc/options/business_analytics/index.html.

Idaho State University, Office of Graduate Studies, College of Science and Engineering, Mechanical Engineering Department, Pocatello, ID 83209-8060. Offers measurement and control engineering (MS); mechanical engineering (MS). Part-time programs available. *Degree requirements:* For master's, comprehensive exam (for some programs), 2 semesters of seminar; thesis or project. *Entrance requirements:* For master's, GRE. Additional exam requirements/recommendations for international students: Required—TOEFL (minimum score 550 paper-based; 213 computer-based; 80 iBT). Electronic applications accepted. *Faculty research:* Modeling and identification of biomedical systems, intelligent systems and adaptive control, active flow control of turbo machinery, validation of advanced computational codes for thermal fluid interactions, development of methodologies for the assessment of passive safety system performance in advanced reactors, alternative energy research (wind, solar, hydrogen).

Indiana University–Purdue University Fort Wayne, College of Arts and Sciences, Department of Mathematical Sciences, Fort Wayne, IN 46805-1499. Offers applied mathematics (MS); applied statistics (Certificate); mathematics (MS); operations research (MS); teaching (MAT). Part-time and evening/weekend programs available. *Faculty:* 20 full-time (5 women). *Students:* 1 full-time (0 women), 16 part-time (3 women). Average age 32. 6 applicants, 100% accepted, 3 enrolled. In 2011, 8 master's, 2 other advanced degrees awarded. *Entrance requirements:* For master's, minimum GPA of 3.0, major or minor in mathematics, three letters of recommendation. Additional exam requirements/recommendations for international students: Required—TOEFL (minimum score 550 paper-based; 213 computer-based; 77 iBT); Recommended—TWE. *Application deadline:* For fall admission, 8/1 priority date for domestic students, 7/1 for international students; for spring admission, 12/1 for domestic students, 10/1 for international students. Applications are processed on a rolling basis. Application fee: $55 ($60 for international students). Electronic applications accepted. *Financial support:* In 2011–12, 6 teaching assistantships with partial tuition reimbursements (averaging $12,930 per year) were awarded; scholarships/grants and unspecified assistantships also available. Support available to part-time students. Financial award application deadline: 3/1; financial award applicants required to submit FAFSA. *Faculty research:* Brick factory problem, CR singularities, carleman orthogonal polynomials. *Unit head:* Dr. David A. Legg, Chair, 260-481-6222, Fax: 260-481-0155, E-mail: legg@ipfw.edu. *Application contact:* Dr. W. Douglas Weakley, Director of Graduate Studies, 260-481-6233, Fax: 260-481-0155, E-mail: weakley@ipfw.edu. Web site: http://www.ipfw.edu/math/.

Iowa State University of Science and Technology, Department of Industrial and Manufacturing Systems Engineering, Ames, IA 50011. Offers industrial engineering (M Eng, MS, PhD); operations research (MS); systems engineering (M Eng). *Degree requirements:* For master's, thesis or alternative; for doctorate, thesis/dissertation. *Entrance requirements:* For master's and doctorate, GRE General Test. Additional exam requirements/recommendations for international students: Required—TOEFL (minimum score 550 paper-based; 79 iBT), IELTS (minimum score 6.5). *Application deadline:* For fall admission, 1/15 for international students; for spring admission, 7/15 for international students. Application fee: $40 ($90 for international students). Electronic applications accepted. *Faculty research:* Economic modeling, valuation techniques, robotics, digital controls, systems reliability. *Unit head:* Dr. Sarah Ryan, Director of Graduate Education, 515-294-0129, Fax: 515-294-3524, E-mail: bushore@iastate.edu. *Application contact:* Lori Bushore, Director of Graduate Studies, 515-294-0129, Fax: 515-294-3524, E-mail: bushore@iastate.edu. Web site: http://www.imse.iastate.edu.

The Johns Hopkins University, Whiting School of Engineering, Department of Applied Mathematics and Statistics, Baltimore, MD 21218-2699. Offers computational medicine (PhD); discrete mathematics (MA, MSE, PhD); financial mathematics (MSE); operations research/optimization/decision science (MA, MSE, PhD); statistics/probability/stochastic

processes (MA, MSE, PhD). Terminal master's awarded for partial completion of doctoral program. *Degree requirements:* For master's, thesis (for some programs); for doctorate, thesis/dissertation, oral exam, introductory exam. *Entrance requirements:* For master's and doctorate, GRE General Test, GRE Subject Test. Additional exam requirements/recommendations for international students: Required—TOEFL (minimum score 600 paper-based; 250 computer-based; 100 iBT). Electronic applications accepted. *Faculty research:* Discrete mathematics, probability, statistics, optimization and operations research, scientific computation, financial mathematics.

Kansas State University, Graduate School, College of Engineering, Department of Industrial and Manufacturing Systems Engineering, Manhattan, KS 66506. Offers engineering management (MEM); industrial engineering (MS, PhD); operations research (MS). Part-time programs available. Postbaccalaureate distance learning degree programs offered. *Faculty:* 12 full-time (3 women), 4 part-time/adjunct (1 woman). *Students:* 43 full-time (11 women), 57 part-time (14 women); includes 8 minority (1 Black or African American, non-Hispanic/Latino; 1 Asian, non-Hispanic/Latino; 2 Hispanic/Latino; 4 Two or more races, non-Hispanic/Latino), 34 international. Average age 29. 94 applicants, 46% accepted, 14 enrolled. In 2011, 21 master's, 3 doctorates awarded. *Degree requirements:* For master's, thesis or alternative; for doctorate, thesis/dissertation. *Entrance requirements:* For master's, GRE General Test (minimum 750 [old version], 159 [new format] on Quantitative portion of exam), bachelor's degree in engineering, mathematics, or physical science; for doctorate, GRE General Test (minimum 770 [old version], 164 [new format] on Quantitative portion of exam), master's degree in engineering or industrial manufacturing. Additional exam requirements/recommendations for international students: Required—TOEFL (minimum score 550 paper-based; 79 iBT) or IELTS (minimum score 6.5). *Application deadline:* For fall admission, 6/1 priority date for domestic students, 2/1 for international students; for spring admission, 11/1 priority date for domestic students, 8/1 for international students. Applications are processed on a rolling basis. Application fee: $40 ($55 for international students). Electronic applications accepted. *Financial support:* In 2011–12, 15 research assistantships (averaging $12,412 per year), 1 teaching assistantship with full tuition reimbursement (averaging $12,000 per year) were awarded; Federal Work-Study, institutionally sponsored loans, and scholarships/grants also available. Support available to part-time students. Financial award application deadline: 3/1; financial award applicants required to submit FAFSA. *Faculty research:* Industrial engineering, ergonomics, healthcare systems engineering, manufacturing processes, operations research, engineering management. *Total annual research expenditures:* $645,655. *Unit head:* Bradley Kramer, Head, 785-532-5606, Fax: 785-532-3738, E-mail: bradleyk@ksu.edu. *Application contact:* David Ben-Arieh, Chair of Graduate Committee, 785-532-5606, Fax: 785-532-3738, E-mail: imse@ksu.edu. Web site: http://imse.ksu.edu/.

Massachusetts Institute of Technology, Operations Research Center, Cambridge, MA 02139. Offers SM, PhD. *Faculty:* 46 full-time (9 women), 1 part-time/adjunct (0 women). *Students:* 54 full-time (12 women); includes 4 minority (3 Asian, non-Hispanic/Latino; 1 Hispanic/Latino), 29 international. Average age 26. 245 applicants, 13% accepted, 14 enrolled. In 2011, 5 master's, 10 doctorates awarded. Terminal master's awarded for partial completion of doctoral program. *Degree requirements:* For master's, thesis; for doctorate, comprehensive exam, thesis/dissertation. *Entrance requirements:* For master's and doctorate, GRE General Test. Additional exam requirements/recommendations for international students: Required—TOEFL (minimum score 600 paper-based; 250 computer-based; 100 iBT), IELTS (minimum score 7). *Application deadline:* For fall admission, 12/15 for domestic and international students. Application fee: $75. Electronic applications accepted. *Expenses: Tuition:* Full-time $40,460; part-time $630 per credit hour. *Required fees:* $272. *Financial support:* In 2011–12, 49 students received support, including 10 fellowships (averaging $28,700 per year), 31 research assistantships (averaging $29,800 per year), 9 teaching assistantships (averaging $31,600 per year); Federal Work-Study, institutionally sponsored loans, scholarships/grants, health care benefits, and unspecified assistantships also available. Financial award application deadline: 12/15. *Faculty research:* Probability, mathematical programming, statistics, stochastic processes, business analytics. *Unit head:* Dr. Dimitris J. Bertsimas, Co-Director, 617-253-3601, Fax: 617-258-9214, E-mail: orc-www@mit.edu. *Application contact:* Laura A. Rose, Graduate Admissions Coordinator, 617-253-9303, Fax: 617-258-9214, E-mail: lrose@mit.edu. Web site: http://web.mit.edu/orc/www/.

Naval Postgraduate School, Departments and Academic Groups, Department of Operations Research, Monterey, CA 93943. Offers applied science (MS), including operations research; cost estimating analysis (MS); human systems integration (MS); operations research (MS, PhD); systems analysis (MS). Program only open to commissioned officers of the United States and friendly nations and selected United States federal civilian employees. Part-time programs available. *Faculty:* 38 full-time (11 women), 12 part-time/adjunct (3 women). *Students:* 142 full-time (21 women), 137 part-time (30 women); includes 66 minority (19 Black or African American, non-Hispanic/Latino; 3 American Indian or Alaska Native, non-Hispanic/Latino; 27 Asian, non-Hispanic/Latino; 17 Hispanic/Latino), 18 international. Average age 41. In 2011, 97 master's, 2 doctorates awarded. *Degree requirements:* For master's, thesis (for some programs); for doctorate, thesis/dissertation. *Faculty research:* Next generation network science, performance analysis of ground solider mobile ad-hoc networks, irregular warfare methods and tools, human social cultural behavior modeling, large-scale optimization. *Total annual research expenditures:* $6.7 million. *Unit head:* Prof. Robert Dell, Chairman, 831-656-2853, E-mail: dell@nps.edu. Web site: http://nps.edu/Academics/Schools/GSOIS/Departments/OR/index.html.

Naval Postgraduate School, Departments and Academic Groups, Undersea Warfare Academic Group, Monterey, CA 93943. Offers applied mathematics (MS); applied physics (MS); applied science (MS), including acoustics, operations research, physical oceanography, signal processing; electrical engineering (MS); engineering acoustics (MS, PhD); engineering science (MS), including electrical engineering, mechanical engineering; mechanical engineer (ME); mechanical engineering (MS, MSME); meteorology (MS); operations research (MS); physical oceanography (MS). Program only open to commissioned officers of the United States and friendly nations and selected United States federal civilian employees. Part-time programs available. *Students:* 2 full-time, both international. Average age 36. *Degree requirements:* For master's, thesis. *Faculty research:* Unmanned/autonomous vehicles, sea mines and countermeasures, submarine warfare in the twentieth and twenty-first centuries. *Unit head:* Dr. Clyde Scandrett, Academic Group Chairman, 831-656-2027. Web site: http://www.nps.edu/Academics/Schools/GSEAS/Departments/USW/USW-Index.html.

New Mexico Institute of Mining and Technology, Graduate Studies, Department of Mathematics, Socorro, NM 87801. Offers applied and industrial mathematics (PhD); industrial mathematics (MS); mathematics (MS); operations research and statistics (MS). *Faculty:* 11 full-time (0 women), 2 part-time/adjunct (1 woman). *Students:* 15 full-time (3 women), 1 part-time (0 women); includes 6 minority (1 Black or African American, non-Hispanic/Latino; 4 Asian, non-Hispanic/Latino; 1 Two or more races, non-Hispanic/Latino), 1 international. Average age 32. 13 applicants, 77% accepted, 6 enrolled. In 2011, 6 degrees awarded. *Degree requirements:* For master's, thesis optional; for doctorate, thesis/dissertation. *Entrance requirements:* For master's, GRE General Test. Additional exam requirements/recommendations for international students: Required—TOEFL (minimum score 540 paper-based; 207 computer-based). *Application deadline:* For fall admission, 3/1 priority date for domestic students; for spring admission, 6/1 for domestic students. Applications are processed on a rolling basis. Application fee: $16 ($30 for international students). *Expenses:* Tuition, state resident: full-time $4849; part-time $269.41 per credit hour. Tuition, nonresident: full-time $16,041; part-time $891.15 per credit hour. *Required fees:* $622; $65 per credit hour. $20 per semester. Part-time tuition and fees vary according to course load. *Financial support:* In 2011–12, 2 research assistantships (averaging $19,516 per year), 13 teaching assistantships with full and partial tuition reimbursements (averaging $34,112 per year) were awarded; fellowships, Federal Work-Study, and institutionally sponsored loans also available. Financial award application deadline: 3/1; financial award applicants required to submit CSS PROFILE or FAFSA. *Faculty research:* Applied mathematics, differential equations, industrial mathematics, numerical analysis, stochastic processes. *Unit head:* Dr. Anwar Hossain, Chairman, 575-835-5135, Fax: 575-835-5366, E-mail: hossain@nmt.edu. *Application contact:* Dr. Lorie Liebrock, Dean of Graduate Studies, 575-835-5513, Fax: 575-835-5476, E-mail: graduate@nmt.edu. Web site: http://www.nmt.edu/~math/.

North Carolina State University, Graduate School, College of Engineering and College of Physical and Mathematical Sciences, Program in Operations Research, Raleigh, NC 27695. Offers MOR, MS, PhD. Part-time programs available. *Degree requirements:* For master's, thesis (for some programs), thesis (MS); for doctorate, thesis/dissertation, comprehensive oral and written exams. *Entrance requirements:* For master's, GRE General Test, minimum GPA of 2.7; for doctorate, GRE General Test, minimum GPA of 3.0. Additional exam requirements/recommendations for international students: Required—TOEFL. Electronic applications accepted. *Faculty research:* Queuing analysis, simulation, inventory theory, supply chain management, mathematical programming.

North Carolina State University, Graduate School, Poole College of Management, Institute for Advanced Analytics, Raleigh, NC 27695. Offers analytics (MS). *Entrance requirements:* For master's, GRE General Test. Additional exam requirements/recommendations for international students: Required—TOEFL. Electronic applications accepted.

North Dakota State University, College of Graduate and Interdisciplinary Studies, College of Science and Mathematics, Department of Computer Science, Fargo, ND 58108. Offers computer science (MS, PhD); operations research (MS); software engineering (MS, PhD, Certificate). Part-time programs available. *Faculty:* 15 full-time (5 women). *Students:* 99 full-time (16 women), 123 part-time (33 women); includes 9 minority (1 Black or African American, non-Hispanic/Latino; 1 American Indian or Alaska Native, non-Hispanic/Latino; 4 Asian, non-Hispanic/Latino; 1 Hispanic/Latino; 2 Two or more races, non-Hispanic/Latino), 178 international. Average age 24. 146 applicants, 57% accepted, 23 enrolled. In 2011, 28 master's, 6 doctorates, 1 other advanced degree awarded. *Degree requirements:* For master's, comprehensive exam, thesis optional; for doctorate, thesis/dissertation, qualifying exam. *Entrance requirements:* For master's, minimum GPA of 3.0, BS in computer science or related field; for doctorate, minimum GPA of 3.25, MS in computer science or related field. Additional exam requirements/recommendations for international students: Required—TOEFL (minimum score 550 paper-based; 213 computer-based; 79 iBT). *Application deadline:* For fall admission, 3/31 priority date for domestic students. Applications are processed on a rolling basis. Application fee: $35. Electronic applications accepted. *Financial support:* In 2011–12, 37 research assistantships with full tuition reimbursements (averaging $10,000 per year), 17 teaching assistantships with full tuition reimbursements (averaging $4,500 per year) were awarded; career-related internships or fieldwork, Federal Work-Study, institutionally sponsored loans, and tuition waivers (full) also available. Financial award application deadline: 4/15. *Faculty research:* Networking, software engineering, artificial intelligence, database, programming languages. *Unit head:* Dr. Brian Slator, Head, 701-231-8562, Fax: 701-231-8255. *Application contact:* Dr. Ken R. Nygard, Graduate Coordinator, 701-231-9460, Fax: 701-231-8255, E-mail: kendall.nygard@ndsu.edu. Web site: http://www.cs.ndsu.nodak.edu/.

Northeastern University, College of Engineering, Department of Mechanical, Industrial, and Manufacturing Engineering, Boston, MA 02115-5096. Offers engineering management (MS); industrial engineering (MS, PhD); mechanical engineering (MS, PhD); operations research (MS). Part-time programs available. *Faculty:* 34 full-time, 7 part-time/adjunct. *Students:* 297 full-time (70 women), 103 part-time (20 women). 616 applicants, 77% accepted, 140 enrolled. In 2011, 107 master's, 5 doctorates awarded. *Degree requirements:* For master's, thesis (for some programs); for doctorate, thesis/ dissertation, departmental qualifying exam. *Entrance requirements:* For master's and doctorate, GRE General Test. Additional exam requirements/recommendations for international students: Required—TOEFL (minimum score 550 paper-based; 213 computer-based; 80 iBT). *Application deadline:* For fall admission, 1/15 priority date for domestic students, 1/15 for international students; for spring admission, 11/1 priority date for domestic students. Applications are processed on a rolling basis. Application fee: $50. Electronic applications accepted. *Financial support:* In 2011–12, 79 students received support, including 50 research assistantships with full tuition reimbursements available (averaging $18,325 per year), 33 teaching assistantships with full tuition reimbursements available (averaging $18,325 per year); fellowships with full tuition reimbursements available, career-related internships or fieldwork, Federal Work-Study, scholarships/grants, health care benefits, and unspecified assistantships also available. Support available to part-time students. Financial award application deadline: 1/15; financial award applicants required to submit FAFSA. *Faculty research:* Dry sliding instabilities, droplet deposition, combustion, manufacturing systems, nano-manufacturing, advanced materials processing, bio-nano robotics, burning speed measurement, virtual environments. *Unit head:* Dr. Hameed Metghalchi, Chairman, 617-373-2973, Fax: 617-373-2921. *Application contact:* Jeffery Hengel, Admissions Specialist, 617-373-2711, Fax: 617-373-2501, E-mail: grad-eng@coe.neu.edu.

Northeastern University, College of Science, Department of Mathematics, Boston, MA 02115-5096. Offers applied mathematics (MS); mathematics (MS, PhD); operations research (MSOR). Part-time and evening/weekend programs available. *Faculty:* 39 full-time, 15 part-time/adjunct. *Students:* 52 full-time, 3 part-time. 164 applicants, 58% accepted, 14 enrolled. In 2011, 6 master's, 7 doctorates awarded. *Degree requirements:* For master's, thesis (for some programs); for doctorate, thesis/dissertation, qualifying exams. *Entrance requirements:* For master's and doctorate, GRE Subject Test, GRE General Test. Additional exam requirements/recommendations for international students: Required—TOEFL. *Application deadline:* For fall admission, 2/1 priority date for domestic students, 2/1 for international students. Applications are processed on a rolling basis. Application fee: $50. Electronic applications accepted. *Financial support:* In 2011–12, 26 teaching assistantships with tuition reimbursements (averaging $17,345

per year) were awarded; research assistantships with tuition reimbursements, Federal Work-Study, institutionally sponsored loans, tuition waivers (full and partial), and unspecified assistantships also available. Financial award application deadline: 3/1; financial award applicants required to submit FAFSA. *Faculty research:* Algebra and singularities, combinatorics, topology, probability and statistics, geometric analysis and partial differential equations. *Unit head:* Dr. Jerzy Weyman, Graduate Coordinator, 617-373-5513, Fax: 617-373-5658, E-mail: j.weyman@neu.edu. *Application contact:* Jo-Anne Dickinson, Admissions Contact, 617-373-5990, Fax: 617-373-7281, E-mail: gsas@neu.edu. Web site: http://www.math.neu.edu/.

The Ohio State University, Graduate School, Max M. Fisher College of Business, Program in Business Operational Excellence, Columbus, OH 43210. Offers MBOE. Postbaccalaureate distance learning degree programs offered (minimal on-campus study). *Faculty:* 30. *Students:* 35 full-time (9 women); includes 3 minority (1 Black or African American, non-Hispanic/Latino; 2 Asian, non-Hispanic/Latino), 2 international. Average age 43. In 2011, 22 master's awarded. *Entrance requirements:* For master's, GMAT if undergraduate GPA is below a 3.0, bachelor's degree from accredited university (all disciplines are welcome); at least 3-5 years of successful work experience in which managing processes are part of the job; recommendation by an executive sponsor. Additional exam requirements/recommendations for international students: Required—TOEFL (minimum score 550 paper-based; 250 computer-based; 79 iBT), Michigan English Language Assessment Battery (minimum score 82). *Expenses:* Tuition, state resident: full-time $11,400. Tuition, nonresident: full-time $28,125. Tuition and fees vary according to course load, degree level, campus/location and program. *Unit head:* Christine A. Poon, Dean, 614-292-2666, E-mail: poon.36@osu.edu. *Application contact:* Graduate Admissions, 614-292-6031, Fax: 614-292-3656, E-mail: gradadmissions@osu.edu. Web site: http://fisher.osu.edu/mboe.

Oregon State University, Graduate School, College of Science, Department of Statistics, Corvallis, OR 97331. Offers operations research (MA, MS); statistics (MA, MS, PhD). Part-time programs available. *Degree requirements:* For master's, consulting experience; for doctorate, thesis/dissertation, consulting experience. *Entrance requirements:* For master's and doctorate, minimum GPA of 3.0 in last 90 hours. Additional exam requirements/recommendations for international students: Required—TOEFL. *Faculty research:* Analysis of enumerative data, nonparametric statistics, asymptotics, experimental design, generalized regression models, linear model theory, reliability theory, survival analysis, wildlife and general survey methodology.

Princeton University, Graduate School, School of Engineering and Applied Science, Department of Operations Research and Financial Engineering, Princeton, NJ 08544-1019. Offers M Eng, MSE, PhD. Terminal master's awarded for partial completion of doctoral program. *Degree requirements:* For master's, thesis (MSE); for doctorate, thesis/dissertation, general exam. *Entrance requirements:* For master's and doctorate, GRE General Test, official transcript(s), 3 letters of recommendation, personal statement. Additional exam requirements/recommendations for international students: Required—TOEFL. Electronic applications accepted. *Faculty research:* Applied and computational mathematics; financial mathematics; optimization, queuing theory, and machine learning; statistics and stochastic analysis; transportation and logistics.

Rutgers, The State University of New Jersey, New Brunswick, Graduate School-New Brunswick, Program in Operations Research, Piscataway, NJ 08854-8097. Offers PhD. Part-time programs available. *Degree requirements:* For doctorate, comprehensive exam, thesis/dissertation, qualifying exam. *Entrance requirements:* For doctorate, GRE General Test, GRE Subject Test. Electronic applications accepted. *Faculty research:* Mathematical programming, combinatorial optimization, graph theory, stochastic modeling, queuing theory.

St. Mary's University, Graduate School, Department of Engineering, Program in Industrial Engineering, San Antonio, TX 78228-8507. Offers engineering computer applications (MS); engineering management (MS); industrial engineering (MS); operations research (MS); JD/MS. Part-time programs available. *Degree requirements:* For master's, comprehensive exam. *Entrance requirements:* For master's, GRE General Test, BS in science or engineering, minimum GPA of 3.0. Additional exam requirements/recommendations for international students: Required—TOEFL (minimum score 550 paper-based; 213 computer-based; 80 iBT). Electronic applications accepted. *Faculty research:* Robotics, artificial intelligence, manufacturing engineering.

Southern Illinois University Edwardsville, Graduate School, College of Arts and Sciences, Department of Mathematics and Statistics, Edwardsville, IL 62026. Offers mathematics (MS), including computational mathematics, postsecondary mathematics education, pure math, statistics and operations research. Part-time programs available. *Faculty:* 19 full-time (5 women). *Students:* 13 full-time (2 women), 30 part-time (17 women); includes 2 minority (both Black or African American, non-Hispanic/Latino), 12 international. 34 applicants, 47% accepted. In 2011, 14 master's awarded. *Degree requirements:* For master's, thesis (for some programs), research paper/project. *Entrance requirements:* Additional exam requirements/recommendations for international students: Required—TOEFL (minimum score 550 paper-based; 213 computer-based; 79 iBT), IELTS (minimum score 6.5). *Application deadline:* For fall admission, 7/22 for domestic students, 6/1 for international students; for spring admission, 12/9 for domestic students, 10/1 for international students. Applications are processed on a rolling basis. Application fee: $30. Electronic applications accepted. Tuition and fees vary according to course load and program. *Financial support:* In 2011–12, 3 research assistantships with full tuition reimbursements (averaging $9,927 per year), 22 teaching assistantships with full tuition reimbursements (averaging $9,927 per year) were awarded; fellowships with full tuition reimbursements, institutionally sponsored loans, scholarships/grants, and unspecified assistantships also available. Financial award application deadline: 3/1; financial award applicants required to submit FAFSA. *Unit head:* Dr. Krzysztof Jarosz, Chair, 618-650-2354, E-mail: kjarosz@ siue.edu. *Application contact:* Dr. Adam Weyhaupt, Director, 618-650-2220, E-mail: aweyhau@siue.edu. Web site: http://www.siue.edu/artsandsciences/math/.

Southern Methodist University, Bobby B. Lyle School of Engineering, Department of Engineering Management, Information, and Systems, Dallas, TX 75275. Offers applied science (MS); engineering management (MSEM, DE); information engineering and management (MSIEM); operations research (MS, PhD); systems engineering (MS, PhD). Part-time and evening/weekend programs available. Postbaccalaureate distance learning degree programs offered. Terminal master's awarded for partial completion of doctoral program. *Degree requirements:* For master's, thesis optional; for doctorate, thesis/dissertation, oral and written qualifying exams. *Entrance requirements:* For master's, minimum GPA of 3.0 in last 2 years; bachelor's degree in engineering, mathematics, sciences, or technical area; for doctorate, GRE General Test (operations research, engineering management), bachelor's degree in related field. Additional exam requirements/recommendations for international students: Required—TOEFL. *Faculty research:* Telecommunications, decision systems, information engineering, operations research, software.

The University of Alabama in Huntsville, School of Graduate Studies, College of Engineering, Department of Industrial and Systems Engineering and Engineering Management, Huntsville, AL 35899. Offers industrial and systems engineering (MSE, PhD); industrial engineering (MSE, PhD); operations research (MSOR); systems engineering (MSE). Part-time and evening/weekend programs available. Postbaccalaureate distance learning degree programs offered (minimal on-campus study). *Faculty:* 9 full-time (2 women), 3 part-time/adjunct (1 woman). *Students:* 13 full-time (7 women), 147 part-time (39 women); includes 25 minority (14 Black or African American, non-Hispanic/Latino; 3 American Indian or Alaska Native, non-Hispanic/Latino; 4 Asian, non-Hispanic/Latino; 3 Hispanic/Latino; 1 Two or more races, non-Hispanic/Latino), 4 international. Average age 35. 98 applicants, 56% accepted, 32 enrolled. In 2011, 23 master's, 5 doctorates awarded. *Degree requirements:* For master's, comprehensive exam, thesis or alternative, oral and written exams; for doctorate, comprehensive exam, thesis/dissertation, oral and written exams. *Entrance requirements:* For master's and doctorate, GRE General Test, minimum GPA of 3.0. Additional exam requirements/recommendations for international students: Required—TOEFL (minimum score 500 paper-based; 173 computer-based; 62 iBT). *Application deadline:* For fall admission, 7/15 for domestic students, 4/1 for international students; for spring admission, 11/30 for domestic students, 9/1 for international students. Applications are processed on a rolling basis. Application fee: $40 ($50 for international students). Electronic applications accepted. *Expenses:* Tuition, state resident: full-time $7830; part-time $473.50 per credit. Tuition, nonresident: full-time $18,748; part-time $1128.33 per credit. Tuition and fees vary according to course load and program. *Financial support:* In 2011–12, 8 students received support, including 2 research assistantships with full tuition reimbursements available (averaging $6,784 per year), 5 teaching assistantships with full tuition reimbursements available (averaging $12,080 per year); career-related internships or fieldwork, Federal Work-Study, institutionally sponsored loans, scholarships/grants, health care benefits, and unspecified assistantships also available. Support available to part-time students. Financial award application deadline: 4/1; financial award applicants required to submit FAFSA. *Faculty research:* Engineering management, systems engineering, manufacturing, logistics, simulation. *Total annual research expenditures:* $8.4 million. *Unit head:* Dr. James Swain, Chair, 256-824-6749, Fax: 256-824-6733, E-mail: jswain@ise.uah.edu. *Application contact:* Kim Gray, Graduate Studies Admissions Coordinator, 256-824-6002, Fax: 256-824-6405, E-mail: deangrad@uah.edu. Web site: http://www.uah.edu/eng/departments/iseem/welcome.

University of Arkansas, Graduate School, College of Engineering, Department of Industrial Engineering, Fayetteville, AR 72701-1201. Offers industrial engineering (MSE, MSIE, PhD); operations management (MS); operations research (MSE, MSOR). *Faculty:* 10 full-time (1 woman), 26 part-time/adjunct (1 woman). *Students:* 57 full-time (20 women), 483 part-time (118 women); includes 108 minority (64 Black or African American, non-Hispanic/Latino; 6 American Indian or Alaska Native, non-Hispanic/Latino; 13 Asian, non-Hispanic/Latino; 15 Hispanic/Latino; 1 Native Hawaiian or other Pacific Islander, non-Hispanic/Latino; 9 Two or more races, non-Hispanic/Latino), 49 international. 198 applicants, 83% accepted. In 2011, 191 master's awarded. *Degree requirements:* For master's, thesis optional; for doctorate, one foreign language, thesis/dissertation. *Application deadline:* For fall admission, 4/1 for international students; for spring admission, 10/1 for international students. Applications are processed on a rolling basis. Application fee: $40 ($50 for international students). Electronic applications accepted. *Financial support:* In 2011–12, 34 research assistantships were awarded; fellowships, teaching assistantships, career-related internships or fieldwork, and Federal Work-Study also available. Support available to part-time students. Financial award application deadline: 4/1; financial award applicants required to submit FAFSA. *Unit head:* Dr. Kim Needy, Departmental Chair, 479-575-3157, Fax: 479-575-8431, E-mail: kneedy@uark.edu. *Application contact:* Dr. Justin Chimka, Graduate Coordinator, 479-575-6756, E-mail: jchimka@uark.edu. Web site: http://www.ineg.uark.edu.

The University of British Columbia, Sauder School of Business, Master of Management in Operations Research, Vancouver, BC V6T 1Z1, Canada. Offers MM. *Degree requirements:* For master's, course work and industry project. *Entrance requirements:* For master's, GMAT or GRE, strong quantitative or analytical background, bachelor's degree or recognized equivalent from an accredited university-level institution, minimum of B+ average in undergraduate upper-level course work. Additional exam requirements/recommendations for international students: Required—TOEFL, IELTS or Michigan English Language Assessment Battery. Electronic applications accepted. *Expenses:* Contact institution. *Faculty research:* Operations and Logistics.

University of California, Berkeley, Graduate Division, College of Engineering, Department of Industrial Engineering and Operations Research, Berkeley, CA 94720-1500. Offers M Eng, MS, D Eng, PhD. *Degree requirements:* For master's, comprehensive exam or thesis (MS); for doctorate, thesis/dissertation, qualifying exam. *Entrance requirements:* For master's and doctorate, GRE General Test, minimum GPA of 3.0, 3 letters of recommendation. *Faculty research:* Mathematical programming, robotics and manufacturing, linear and nonlinear optimization, production planning and scheduling, queuing theory.

University of Central Florida, College of Engineering and Computer Science, Department of Industrial Engineering and Management Systems, Orlando, FL 32816. Offers applied operations research (Certificate); design for usability (Certificate); engineering management (PSM); industrial engineering (MSIE, PhD); industrial engineering and management systems (MS); industrial ergonomics and safety (Certificate); project engineering (Certificate); quality assurance (Certificate); systems engineering (Certificate); systems simulation for engineers (Certificate); training simulation (Certificate). Part-time and evening/weekend programs available. *Faculty:* 18 full-time (4 women), 5 part-time/adjunct (1 woman). *Students:* 105 full-time (27 women), 151 part-time (47 women); includes 84 minority (20 Black or African American, non-Hispanic/Latino; 1 American Indian or Alaska Native, non-Hispanic/Latino; 20 Asian, non-Hispanic/Latino; 37 Hispanic/Latino; 1 Native Hawaiian or other Pacific Islander, non-Hispanic/Latino; 5 Two or more races, non-Hispanic/Latino), 52 international. Average age 32. 199 applicants, 79% accepted, 75 enrolled. In 2011, 83 master's, 11 doctorates, 40 other advanced degrees awarded. *Degree requirements:* For master's, thesis; for doctorate, thesis/dissertation, departmental qualifying exam, candidacy exam. *Entrance requirements:* For master's, GRE General Test, minimum GPA of 3.0 in last 60 hours of course work; for doctorate, minimum GPA of 3.5 in last 60 hours of course work. Additional exam requirements/recommendations for international students: Required—TOEFL. *Application deadline:* For fall admission, 7/15 priority date for domestic students; for spring admission, 12/1 priority date for domestic students. Application fee: $30. Electronic applications accepted. *Expenses:* Tuition, state resident: part-time $277.08 per credit hour. Tuition, nonresident: part-time $277.08 per credit hour. Part-time tuition and fees vary according to degree level and program. *Financial support:* In 2011–12, 19 students received support, including 8 fellowships with partial tuition reimbursements available (averaging $3,500 per year), 10 research assistantships with partial tuition reimbursements available (averaging $11,100 per year), 6 teaching assistantships with partial tuition reimbursements available (averaging $12,300 per year); career-related internships or fieldwork, Federal Work-Study, institutionally sponsored loans, tuition waivers (partial), and unspecified assistantships also available. Financial award application deadline: 3/1; financial award applicants required to submit FAFSA. *Unit head:* Dr. Waldemar Karwowski, Chair, 407-823-2204, E-mail: wkar@ucf.edu. *Application contact:* Barbara Rodriguez, Director, Admissions and Registration, 407-823-2766, Fax: 407-823-6442, E-mail: gradadmissions@ucf.edu. Web site: http://iems.ucf.edu/.

University of Colorado Boulder, Graduate School, College of Engineering and Applied Science, Engineering Management Program, Boulder, CO 80309. Offers operations and logistics (ME); quality and process (ME); research and development (ME). *Students:* 46 full-time (11 women), 80 part-time (30 women); includes 22 minority (2 Black or African American, non-Hispanic/Latino; 1 American Indian or Alaska Native, non-Hispanic/Latino; 11 Asian, non-Hispanic/Latino; 7 Hispanic/Latino; 1 Two or more races, non-Hispanic/Latino), 12 international. Average age 34. 39 applicants, 74% accepted, 21 enrolled. In 2011, 32 master's awarded. *Entrance requirements:* For master's, minimum undergraduate GPA of 3.0. *Application deadline:* For fall admission, 2/15 for domestic students, 12/1 for international students; for spring admission, 8/15 for domestic students, 5/1 for international students. Application fee: $50 ($60 for international students). Electronic applications accepted. *Financial support:* In 2011–12, 5 students received support, including 2 fellowships (averaging $4,250 per year), 1 research assistantship with full and partial tuition reimbursement available (averaging $11,842 per year), 1 teaching assistantship with full and partial tuition reimbursement available (averaging $7,280 per year); institutionally sponsored loans, scholarships/grants, health care benefits, and unspecified assistantships also available. *Faculty research:* Quality and process, research and development, operations and logistics. *Total annual research expenditures:* $2,907. *Application contact:* E-mail: cuemp@colorado.edu. Web site: http://emp.colorado.edu.

University of Colorado Denver, College of Liberal Arts and Sciences, Department of Mathematical and Statistical Sciences, Denver, CO 80217. Offers applied mathematics (MS, PhD), including applied mathematics, applied probability (MS), applied statistics (MS), computational biology, computational mathematics (PhD), discrete mathematics, finite geometry (PhD), mathematics education (PhD), mathematics of engineering and science (MS), numerical analysis, operations research (MS), optimization and operations research (PhD), probability (PhD), statistics (PhD). Part-time programs available. *Faculty:* 26 full-time (4 women), 2 part-time/adjunct (1 woman). *Students:* 44 full-time (14 women), 14 part-time (5 women); includes 6 minority (4 Asian, non-Hispanic/Latino; 2 Hispanic/Latino), 10 international. Average age 33. 66 applicants, 79% accepted, 17 enrolled. In 2011, 6 master's, 6 doctorates awarded. *Degree requirements:* For master's, comprehensive exam, thesis optional, 30 hours of course work with minimum GPA of 3.0; for doctorate, comprehensive exam, thesis/dissertation. *Entrance requirements:* For master's and doctorate, GRE General Test; GRE Subject Test in math (recommended), 30 hours of course work in mathematics (24 of which must be upper-division mathematics), minimum GPA of 3.0. Additional exam requirements/recommendations for international students: Required—TOEFL (minimum score 525 paper-based; 192 computer-based; 71 iBT). *Application deadline:* For fall admission, 4/1 for domestic students, 3/1 for international students; for spring admission, 11/1 for domestic students, 10/1 for international students. Application fee: $50 ($75 for international students). Electronic applications accepted. *Financial support:* Fellowships with partial tuition reimbursements, research assistantships with full tuition reimbursements, teaching assistantships with full tuition reimbursements, Federal Work-Study, scholarships/grants, and unspecified assistantships available. Financial award application deadline: 4/1; financial award applicants required to submit FAFSA. *Faculty research:* Computational mathematics, computational biology, discrete mathematics and geometry, probability and statistics, optimization. *Unit head:* Dr. Stephen Billups, Graduate Chair, 303-556-4814, E-mail: stephen.billups@ucdenver.edu. *Application contact:* Lisa Herbert, Graduate Program Assistant, 303-556-2341, E-mail: lisa.herbert@ucdenver.edu. Web site: http://www.ucdenver.edu/academics/colleges/CLAS/Departments/math/Pages/MathStats.aspx.

University of Delaware, College of Agriculture and Natural Resources, Department of Food and Resource Economics, Operations Research Program, Newark, DE 19716. Offers MS. Part-time programs available. *Degree requirements:* For master's, thesis, oral exam. *Entrance requirements:* For master's, GRE General Test, 3 letters of recommendation, program language/s, engineering calculus. Additional exam requirements/recommendations for international students: Required—TOEFL. Electronic applications accepted. *Faculty research:* Simulation and modeling-production scheduling and optimization, agricultural production and resource economics, transportation engineering, statistical quality control.

University of Illinois at Chicago, Graduate College, College of Engineering, Department of Mechanical and Industrial Engineering, Program in Industrial Engineering and Operations Research, Chicago, IL 60607-7128. Offers PhD. Part-time programs available. *Degree requirements:* For doctorate, thesis/dissertation. *Entrance requirements:* For doctorate, GRE General Test, minimum GPA of 2.75. Additional exam requirements/recommendations for international students: Required—TOEFL. Electronic applications accepted.

The University of Iowa, Graduate College, College of Engineering, Department of Industrial Engineering, Iowa City, IA 52242-1316. Offers engineering design and manufacturing (MS, PhD); ergonomics (MS, PhD); information and engineering management (MS, PhD); operations research (MS, PhD); quality engineering (MS, PhD). *Faculty:* 7 full-time (0 women). *Students:* 21 full-time (6 women); includes 2 minority (1 Black or African American, non-Hispanic/Latino; 1 Asian, non-Hispanic/Latino), 14 international. Average age 27. 69 applicants, 13% accepted, 5 enrolled. In 2011, 8 master's, 6 doctorates awarded. *Degree requirements:* For master's, thesis optional, exam; for doctorate, comprehensive exam, thesis/dissertation, final defense exam. *Entrance requirements:* For master's and doctorate, GRE General Test. Additional exam requirements/recommendations for international students: Required—TOEFL (minimum score 550 paper-based; 213 computer-based; 81 iBT). *Application deadline:* For fall admission, 7/15 for domestic students, 4/15 for international students; for spring admission, 12/1 for domestic students, 10/1 for international students. Applications are processed on a rolling basis. Application fee: $60 ($100 for international students). Electronic applications accepted. *Financial support:* In 2011–12, 5 fellowships with partial tuition reimbursements (averaging $30,450 per year), 17 research assistantships with partial tuition reimbursements (averaging $20,000 per year), 5 teaching assistantships with partial tuition reimbursements (averaging $16,630 per year) were awarded; career-related internships or fieldwork, scholarships/grants, and unspecified assistantships also available. Support available to part-time students. Financial award applicants required to submit FAFSA. *Faculty research:* Operations research, informatics, human factors engineering, manufacturing systems, human-machine interaction. *Total annual research expenditures:* $4.6 million. *Unit head:* Dr.

Andrew Kusiak, Department Executive Officer, 319-335-5934, Fax: 319-335-5669, E-mail: andrew-kusiak@uiowa.edu. *Application contact:* Andrea Flaherty, Academic Program Specialist, 319-335-5939, Fax: 319-335-5669, E-mail: indeng@engineering.uiowa.edu. Web site: http://www.mie.engineering.uiowa.edu/.

University of Massachusetts Amherst, Graduate School, College of Engineering, Department of Mechanical and Industrial Engineering, Amherst, MA 01003. Offers industrial engineering and operations research (MS, PhD); mechanical engineering (MSME, PhD). Part-time programs available. *Faculty:* 36 full-time (3 women). *Students:* 103 full-time (26 women), 14 part-time (3 women); includes 10 minority (2 Black or African American, non-Hispanic/Latino; 4 Asian, non-Hispanic/Latino; 3 Hispanic/Latino; 1 Native Hawaiian or other Pacific Islander, non-Hispanic/Latino), 60 international. Average age 28. 350 applicants, 32% accepted, 29 enrolled. In 2011, 16 master's, 4 doctorates awarded. Terminal master's awarded for partial completion of doctoral program. *Degree requirements:* For master's, thesis or alternative; for doctorate, comprehensive exam, thesis/dissertation. *Entrance requirements:* For master's and doctorate, GRE General Test. Additional exam requirements/recommendations for international students: Required—TOEFL (minimum score 550 paper-based; 213 computer-based; 80 iBT), IELTS (minimum score 6.5). *Application deadline:* For fall admission, 1/15 for domestic and international students; for spring admission, 10/1 for domestic and international students. Applications are processed on a rolling basis. Application fee: $50 ($65 for international students). Electronic applications accepted. Tuition and fees vary according to course load, campus/location and program. *Financial support:* Fellowships with full and partial tuition reimbursements, research assistantships with full tuition reimbursements, teaching assistantships with full tuition reimbursements, career-related internships or fieldwork, Federal Work-Study, scholarships/grants, traineeships, health care benefits, tuition waivers (full and partial), and unspecified assistantships available. Support available to part-time students. Financial award application deadline: 1/15. *Unit head:* Dr. David P. Schmidt, Graduate Program Director, 413-545-3827, Fax: 413-545-1027. *Application contact:* Lindsay DeSantis, Interim Supervisor of Admissions, 413-545-0722, Fax: 413-577-0100, E-mail: gradadm@grad.umass.edu. Web site: http://mie.umass.edu/.

University of Michigan, College of Engineering, Department of Industrial and Operations Engineering, Ann Arbor, MI 48109. Offers MS, MSE, PhD, MBA/MS, MBA/MSE. *Accreditation:* ABET. Part-time programs available. *Students:* 210 full-time (71 women), 2 part-time (0 women). 534 applicants, 42% accepted, 92 enrolled. In 2011, 79 master's, 8 doctorates awarded. Terminal master's awarded for partial completion of doctoral program. *Degree requirements:* For doctorate, oral defense of dissertation, preliminary exams, qualifying exam. *Entrance requirements:* For master's, GRE General Test, minimum GPA of 3.2; for doctorate, GRE General Test, minimum GPA of 3.5. Additional exam requirements/recommendations for international students: Required—TOEFL. *Application deadline:* Applications are processed on a rolling basis. Application fee: $65 ($75 for international students). Electronic applications accepted. *Financial support:* In 2011–12, 71 students received support. Fellowships, research assistantships, teaching assistantships, Federal Work-Study, institutionally sponsored loans, scholarships/grants, traineeships, health care benefits, and unspecified assistantships available. Financial award applicants required to submit FAFSA. *Faculty research:* Production/distribution/logistics, financial engineering and enterprise systems, ergonomics (physical and cognitive), stochastic processes, linear and nonlinear optimization, operations research. *Unit head:* Mark Daskin, Chair, 734-764-9422, Fax: 734-764-3451, E-mail: msdaskin@umich.edu. *Application contact:* Matt Irelan, Graduate Student Advisor/Program Coordinator, 734-764-6480, Fax: 734-764-3451, E-mail: mirelan@umich.edu. Web site: http://ioe.engin.umich.edu/.

The University of North Carolina at Chapel Hill, Graduate School, College of Arts and Sciences, Department of Operations Research, Chapel Hill, NC 27599. Offers MS, PhD. *Degree requirements:* For master's, comprehensive exam; for doctorate, comprehensive exam, thesis/dissertation. *Entrance requirements:* For master's and doctorate, GRE General Test, minimum GPA of 3.0.

University of Southern California, Graduate School, Viterbi School of Engineering, Daniel J. Epstein Department of Industrial and Systems Engineering, Los Angeles, CA 90089. Offers digital supply chain management (MS); engineering management (MS); engineering technology communication (Graduate Certificate); health systems operations (Graduate Certificate); industrial and systems engineering (MS, PhD, Engr); manufacturing engineering (MS); operations research engineering (MS); optimization and supply chain management (Graduate Certificate); product development engineering (MS); safety systems and security (MS); systems architecting and engineering (MS, Graduate Certificate); systems safety and security (Graduate Certificate); transportation systems (Graduate Certificate); MS/MBA. Part-time and evening/weekend programs available. Postbaccalaureate distance learning degree programs offered (no on-campus study). Terminal master's awarded for partial completion of doctoral program. *Degree requirements:* For master's, thesis optional; for doctorate, thesis/dissertation. *Entrance requirements:* For master's and doctorate, GRE General Test. Additional exam requirements/recommendations for international students: Recommended—TOEFL. Electronic applications accepted. *Faculty research:* Health systems, music cognition and retrieval, transportation and logistics, manufacturing and automation, engineering systems design, risk and economic analysis.

The University of Texas at Austin, Graduate School, Cockrell School of Engineering, Department of Mechanical Engineering, Program in Operations Research and Industrial Engineering, Austin, TX 78712-1111. Offers MS, PhD. *Entrance requirements:* For master's and doctorate, GRE General Test. Additional exam requirements/recommendations for international students: Required—TOEFL. Application fee: $50 ($75 for international students). *Financial support:* Fellowships, research assistantships, and teaching assistantships available. Financial award application deadline: 2/1. *Unit head:* David Morton, Program Coordinator, 512-471-4104, Fax: 512-471-8727, E-mail: morton@mail.utexas.edu. *Application contact:* John J. Hasenbein, Graduate Advisor, 512-471-3079, Fax: 512-471-1494, E-mail: jhas@mail.utexas.edu. Web site: http://www.me.utexas.edu/areas/orie/.

University of Waterloo, Graduate Studies, Faculty of Engineering, Department of Management Sciences, Waterloo, ON N2L 3G1, Canada. Offers applied operations research (MA Sc, MMS, PhD); information systems (MA Sc, MMS, PhD); management of technology (MA Sc, MMS, PhD). Part-time programs available. Postbaccalaureate distance learning degree programs offered (no on-campus study). *Degree requirements:* For master's, research paper or thesis; for doctorate, comprehensive exam, thesis/dissertation. *Entrance requirements:* For master's, GMAT or GRE, honors degree, minimum B average, resume; for doctorate, GMAT or GRE, master's degree, minimum A- average, resumé. Additional exam requirements/recommendations for international students: Required—TOEFL, TWE. *Faculty research:* Operations research, manufacturing systems, scheduling, information systems.

Virginia Commonwealth University, Graduate School, College of Humanities and Sciences, Department of Statistical Sciences and Operations Research, Richmond, VA 23284-9005. Offers operations research (MS); statistics (MS); systems modeling and analysis (PhD). *Students:* 20 applicants, 70% accepted, 11 enrolled. *Entrance requirements:* For master's, GRE General Test, 30 undergraduate credits in mathematics, statistics, or operations research, including calculus I and II, multivariate calculus, linear algebra, probability and statistics. Additional exam requirements/recommendations for international students: Required—TOEFL (minimum score 600 paper-based; 250 computer-based; 100 iBT); Recommended—IELTS (minimum score 6.5). *Application deadline:* For fall admission, 3/1 for domestic students; for spring admission, 10/15 for domestic students. Applications are processed on a rolling basis. Application fee: $50. Electronic applications accepted. *Expenses:* Tuition, state resident: full-time $9133; part-time $507 per credit. Tuition, nonresident: full-time $18,777; part-time $1043 per credit. *Required fees:* $77 per credit. Tuition and fees vary according to degree level, campus/location, program and student level. *Unit head:* Dr. D'Arcy P. Mays, Chair, 804-828-1301 Ext. 151, E-mail: jemays@vcu.edu. *Application contact:* Dr. Edward L. Boone, Director, 804-828-4637, E-mail: elboone@VCU.edu. Web site: http://www.stat.vcu.edu/.

Technology and Public Policy

Arizona State University, College of Liberal Arts and Sciences, Program in Science and Technology Policy, Tempe, AZ 85287-6505. Offers PSM. Fall admission only. *Degree requirements:* For master's, thesis or alternative, internship, applied project, interactive Program of Study (iPOS) submitted before completing 50 percent of required credit hours. *Entrance requirements:* For master's, GRE, bachelor's degree (or equivalent) or graduate degree from regionally-accredited college or university or of recognized standing; minimum GPA of 3.0 or equivalent in last 2 years of work leading to bachelor's degree; 3 letters of recommendation; personal statement; current resume. Additional exam requirements/recommendations for international students: Required—TOEFL (minimum score 80 iBT), TOEFL, IELTS, or Pearson Test of English. Electronic applications accepted. *Expenses:* Contact institution.

Carnegie Mellon University, Carnegie Institute of Technology, Department of Civil and Environmental Engineering, Pittsburgh, PA 15213. Offers advanced infrastructure systems (MS, PhD); civil and environmental engineering (MS, PhD); civil and environmental engineering/engineering and public policy (PhD); civil engineering (MS, PhD); computational mechanics (MS, PhD); environmental engineering (MS, PhD); environmental management and science (MS, PhD). Part-time programs available. *Faculty:* 22 full-time (4 women), 24 part-time/adjunct (5 women). *Students:* 147 full-time (64 women), 7 part-time (0 women); includes 13 minority (5 Black or African American, non-Hispanic/Latino; 6 Asian, non-Hispanic/Latino; 2 Hispanic/Latino), 101 international. Average age 26. 487 applicants, 55% accepted, 80 enrolled. In 2011, 84 master's, 12 doctorates awarded. Terminal master's awarded for partial completion of doctoral program. *Degree requirements:* For master's, thesis optional; for doctorate, comprehensive exam, thesis/dissertation, two-part qualifying exam, public defense of dissertation. *Entrance requirements:* For master's and doctorate, GRE General Test. Additional exam requirements/recommendations for international students: Required—TOEFL (minimum score 84 iBT). *Application deadline:* For fall admission, 1/15 priority date for domestic students, 1/15 for international students; for spring admission, 9/30 priority date for domestic students, 9/30 for international students. Application fee: $65. Electronic applications accepted. *Financial support:* In 2011–12, 108 students received support, including 26 fellowships with full and partial tuition reimbursements available (averaging $2,087 per year), 35 research assistantships with full and partial tuition reimbursements available (averaging $2,094 per year); tuition waivers (partial), unspecified assistantships, and service assistantships also available. Financial award application deadline: 1/15. *Faculty research:* Advanced infrastructure systems; environmental engineering science and management; mechanics, materials, and computing; green design; global sustainable construction. *Total annual research expenditures:* $4.9 million. *Unit head:* Dr. James H. Garrett, Jr., Head, 412-268-2941, Fax: 412-268-7813, E-mail: garrett@cmu.edu. *Application contact:* Maxine A. Leffard, Director of the Graduate Program, 412-268-5673, Fax: 412-268-7813, E-mail: ce-admissions@andrew.cmu.edu. Web site: http://www.ce.cmu.edu/.

Carnegie Mellon University, Carnegie Institute of Technology, Department of Engineering and Public Policy, Pittsburgh, PA 15213-3891. Offers PhD. *Degree requirements:* For doctorate, thesis/dissertation. *Entrance requirements:* For doctorate, GRE General Test, BS in physical sciences or engineering. Additional exam requirements/recommendations for international students: Required—TOEFL. *Faculty research:* Issues in energy and environmental policy, IT and telecommunications policy, risk analysis and communication, management of technological innovation, security and engineered civil systems.

Eastern Michigan University, Graduate School, College of Technology, School of Technology Studies, Program in Technology Studies, Ypsilanti, MI 48197. Offers interdisciplinary technology (MLS); technology studies (MS). Part-time and evening/weekend programs available. Postbaccalaureate distance learning degree programs offered (minimal on-campus study). *Students:* 11 full-time (2 women), 95 part-time (23 women); includes 18 minority (11 Black or African American, non-Hispanic/Latino; 1 American Indian or Alaska Native, non-Hispanic/Latino; 4 Asian, non-Hispanic/Latino; 1 Hispanic/Latino; 1 Two or more races, non-Hispanic/Latino), 4 international. Average age 35. 64 applicants, 67% accepted, 23 enrolled. In 2011, 34 degrees awarded. *Degree requirements:* For master's, thesis optional. *Entrance requirements:* For master's, GRE General Test, minimum GPA of 2.6. Additional exam requirements/recommendations for international students: Required—TOEFL. *Application deadline:* Applications are processed on a rolling basis. Application fee: $35. *Expenses:* Tuition, state resident: full-time $10,367; part-time $432 per credit hour. Tuition, nonresident: full-time $20,435; part-time $851 per credit hour. *Required fees:* $39 per credit hour. $46 per semester. One-time fee: $100. Tuition and fees vary according to course level, degree level and reciprocity agreements. *Financial support:* Fellowships, research assistantships with full tuition reimbursements, teaching assistantships with full tuition reimbursements, career-related internships or fieldwork, Federal Work-Study, institutionally sponsored loans, scholarships/grants, tuition waivers (partial), and unspecified assistantships available. Support available to part-time students. Financial award applicants required to submit FAFSA. *Unit head:* Dr. Denise Pilato, Program Coordinator, 734-487-1161, Fax: 734-487-7690, E-mail: denise.pilato@emich.edu. *Application contact:* Graduate Admissions, 734-487-2400, Fax: 734-487-6559, E-mail: graduate.admissions@emich.edu.

The George Washington University, Elliott School of International Affairs, Program in International Science and Technology Policy, Washington, DC 20052. Offers MA, JD/MA. Part-time and evening/weekend programs available. *Students:* 19 full-time (6 women), 16 part-time (5 women); includes 5 minority (2 Asian, non-Hispanic/Latino; 3 Hispanic/Latino), 2 international. Average age 29. 30 applicants, 93% accepted, 10 enrolled. In 2011, 21 master's awarded. *Degree requirements:* For master's, one foreign language, capstone project. *Entrance requirements:* For master's, GRE General Test. Additional exam requirements/recommendations for international students: Required—TOEFL. *Application deadline:* For fall admission, 2/1 for domestic students; for spring admission, 10/1 for domestic students. Application fee: $75. Electronic applications accepted. *Financial support:* In 2011–12, 15 students received support. Fellowships with tuition reimbursements available, research assistantships with tuition reimbursements available, career-related internships or fieldwork, Federal Work-Study, institutionally sponsored loans, and tuition waivers (full and partial) available. Financial award application deadline: 1/15; financial award applicants required to submit FAFSA. *Faculty research:* Science policy, space policy, risk assessment, technology transfer, energy policy. *Unit head:* Dr. Nicholas Vonortas, Director, 202-994-6458, E-mail: vonortas@gwu.edu. *Application contact:* Jeff V. Miles, Director of Graduate Admissions, 202-994-7050, Fax: 202-994-9537, E-mail: esiagrad@gwu.edu. Web site: http://www.gwu.edu/~elliott/academics/grad/istp/.

Massachusetts Institute of Technology, School of Engineering, Engineering Systems Division, Cambridge, MA 02139. Offers engineering and management (SM); engineering systems (SM, PhD); logistics (M Eng); technology and policy (SM); technology, management and policy (PhD); SM/MBA. *Faculty:* 22 full-time (7 women). *Students:* 296 full-time (88 women); includes 36 minority (3 Black or African American, non-Hispanic/Latino; 22 Asian, non-Hispanic/Latino; 6 Hispanic/Latino; 5 Two or more races, non-Hispanic/Latino), 132 international. Average age 31. 909 applicants, 26% accepted, 181 enrolled. In 2011, 143 master's, 13 doctorates awarded. *Degree requirements:* For master's, thesis; for doctorate, comprehensive exam, thesis/dissertation. *Entrance requirements:* For master's, GRE General Test (or GMAT for some programs); for doctorate, GRE General Test. Additional exam requirements/recommendations for international students: Required—IELTS (minimum score 7.5). Application fee: $75. Electronic applications accepted. *Expenses:* Contact institution. *Financial support:* In 2011–12, 223 students received support, including 44 fellowships (averaging $30,600 per year), 96 research assistantships (averaging $29,000 per year), 16 teaching assistantships (averaging $29,800 per year); career-related internships or fieldwork, Federal Work-Study, institutionally sponsored loans, scholarships/grants, health care benefits, and unspecified assistantships also available. *Faculty research:* Critical infrastructures, extended enterprises, energy and sustainability, health care delivery, humans and technology, uncertainty and dynamics, design and implementation, networks and flows, policy and standards. *Total annual research expenditures:* $13.7 million. *Unit head:* Prof. Joseph M. Sussman, Interim Director, 617-253-1764, E-mail: esdinquiries@mit.edu. *Application contact:* Graduate Admissions, 617-253-1182, E-mail: esdgrad@mit.edu. Web site: http://esd.mit.edu/.

Massachusetts Institute of Technology, School of Humanities, Arts, and Social Sciences, Program in Science, Technology, and Society, Cambridge, MA 02139. Offers history, anthropology, and science, technology and society (PhD). *Faculty:* 12 full-time (5 women). *Students:* 26 full-time (20 women); includes 5 minority (1 Black or African American, non-Hispanic/Latino; 1 American Indian or Alaska Native, non-Hispanic/Latino; 2 Asian, non-Hispanic/Latino; 1 Two or more races, non-Hispanic/Latino), 7 international. Average age 31. 130 applicants, 9% accepted, 6 enrolled. In 2011, 6 doctorates awarded. *Degree requirements:* For doctorate, comprehensive exam, thesis/dissertation. *Entrance requirements:* For doctorate, GRE General Test. Additional exam requirements/recommendations for international students: Required—TOEFL (minimum score 577 paper-based; 233 computer-based; 90 iBT), IELTS (minimum score 7). *Application deadline:* For fall admission, 1/1 for domestic and international students. Application fee: $75. Electronic applications accepted. *Expenses:* Tuition: Full-time $40,460; part-time $630 per credit hour. *Required fees:* $272. *Financial support:* In 2011–12, 26 students received support, including 17 fellowships (averaging $30,400 per year), 1 research assistantship (averaging $31,500 per year), 5 teaching assistantships (averaging $32,300 per year); Federal Work-Study, institutionally sponsored loans, scholarships/grants, health care benefits, and unspecified assistantships also available. *Faculty research:* History of science; history of technology; sociology of science and technology; anthropology of science and technology; science, technology, and society; humans and automation. *Total annual research expenditures:* $315,000. *Unit head:* Prof. David Kaiser, Director, 617-253-4062, Fax: 617-258-8118, E-mail: stsprogram@mit.edu. *Application contact:* Academic Administrator, 617-253-9759, Fax: 617-258-8118, E-mail: hasts@mit.edu. Web site: http://web.mit.edu/sts/.

Rensselaer Polytechnic Institute, Graduate School, School of Humanities, Arts, and Social Sciences, Program in Science and Technology Studies, Troy, NY 12180-3590. Offers design studies (MS, PhD); policy studies (MS, PhD); science studies (MS, PhD); sustainability studies (MS, PhD); technology studies (MS, PhD). Terminal master's awarded for partial completion of doctoral program. *Degree requirements:* For master's, thesis (for some programs); for doctorate, comprehensive exam, thesis/dissertation. *Entrance requirements:* For master's and doctorate, GRE General Test. Additional exam requirements/recommendations for international students: Required—TOEFL (minimum score 600 paper-based; 250 computer-based). Electronic applications accepted. *Faculty research:* Communities and technology, social dimensions of IT and biotechnology, ethics and policy, design.

Rochester Institute of Technology, Graduate Enrollment Services, College of Liberal Arts, Department of Science, Technology and Society/Public Policy, Rochester, NY 14623-5603. Offers science, technology and public policy (MS). Part-time programs available. *Students:* 8 full-time (3 women), 6 part-time (2 women); includes 1 minority (Asian, non-Hispanic/Latino). Average age 28. 9 applicants, 44% accepted, 1 enrolled. In 2011, 3 degrees awarded. *Degree requirements:* For master's, thesis. *Entrance requirements:* For master's, GRE General Test, minimum GPA of 3.0. Additional exam

requirements/recommendations for international students: Required—TOEFL (minimum score 570 paper-based; 230 computer-based; 88 iBT) or IELTS (minimum score 6.5). *Application deadline:* For fall admission, 2/15 priority date for domestic students, 2/15 for international students; for winter admission, 11/1 for domestic and international students; for spring admission, 2/1 for domestic and international students. Applications are processed on a rolling basis. Application fee: $50. Electronic applications accepted. *Expenses:* Tuition: Full-time $34,659; part-time $963 per credit hour. *Required fees:* $228; $76 per quarter. *Financial support:* Research assistantships with partial tuition reimbursements, teaching assistantships with partial tuition reimbursements, career-related internships or fieldwork, scholarships/grants, and unspecified assistantships available. Support available to part-time students. Financial award applicants required to submit FAFSA. *Faculty research:* Environmental policy, information and communications policy, energy policy, biotechnology policy . *Unit head:* Dr. Franz Foltz, Graduate Program Director, 585-475-5368, Fax: 585-475-2510, E-mail: franz.foltz@rit.edu. *Application contact:* Diane Ellison, Assistant Vice President, Graduate Enrollment Services, 585-475-2229, Fax: 585-475-7164, E-mail: gradinfo@rit.edu. Web site: http://www.rit.edu/cla/publicpolicy/.

St. Cloud State University, School of Graduate Studies, College of Science and Engineering, Department of Environmental and Technological Studies, St. Cloud, MN 56301-4498. Offers MS. *Degree requirements:* For master's, thesis or alternative. *Entrance requirements:* For master's, minimum GPA of 2.75. Additional exam requirements/recommendations for international students: Required—TOEFL (minimum score 550 paper-based; 213 computer-based), Michigan English Language Assessment Battery; Recommended—IELTS (minimum score 6.5). Electronic applications accepted.

Stony Brook University, State University of New York, Graduate School, College of Engineering and Applied Sciences, Department of Technology and Society, Program in Technology, Policy, and Innovation, Stony Brook, NY 11794-3760. Offers PhD. *Degree requirements:* For doctorate, comprehensive exam, thesis/dissertation. *Entrance requirements:* For doctorate, GRE General Test, minimum undergraduate GPA of 3.0. Additional exam requirements/recommendations for international students: Required—TOEFL.

University of Minnesota, Twin Cities Campus, Graduate School, Hubert H. Humphrey School of Public Affairs, Program in Science, Technology, and Environmental Policy, Minneapolis, MN 55455-0213. Offers MS, JD/MS. Part-time programs available. *Degree requirements:* For master's, thesis. *Entrance requirements:* For master's, GRE General Test, undergraduate training in the biological or physical sciences or engineering, minimum undergraduate GPA of 3.0. Additional exam requirements/recommendations for international students: Required—TOEFL (minimum score 600 paper-based; 250 computer-based; 100 iBT). Electronic applications accepted. *Faculty research:* Economics, history, philosophy, and politics of science and technology; organization and management of science and technology.

University of South Africa, College of Human Sciences, Pretoria, South Africa. Offers adult education (M Ed); African languages (MA, PhD); African politics (MA, PhD); Afrikaans (MA, PhD); ancient history (MA, PhD); ancient Near Eastern studies (MA, PhD); anthropology (MA, PhD); applied linguistics (MA); Arabic (MA, PhD); archaeology (MA); art history (MA); Biblical archaeology (MA); Biblical studies (M Th, D Th, PhD); Christian spirituality (M Th, D Th); church history (M Th, D Th); classical studies (MA, PhD); clinical psychology (MA); communication (MA, PhD); comparative education (M Ed, Ed D); consulting psychology (D Admin, D Com, PhD); curriculum studies (M Ed, Ed D); development studies (M Admin, MA, D Admin, PhD); didactics (M Ed, Ed D); education (M Tech); education management (M Ed, Ed D); educational psychology (M Ed); English (MA); environmental education (M Ed); French (MA, PhD); German (MA, PhD); Greek (MA); guidance and counseling (M Ed); health studies (MA, PhD), including health sciences education (MA), health services management (MA), medical and surgical nursing science (critical care general) (MA), midwifery and neonatal nursing science (MA), trauma and emergency care (MA); history (MA, PhD); history of education (Ed D); inclusive education (M Ed, Ed D); information and communications technology policy and regulation (MA); information science (MA, MIS, PhD); international politics (MA, PhD); Islamic studies (MA, PhD); Italian (MA, PhD); Judaica (MA, PhD); linguistics (MA, PhD); mathematical education (M Ed); mathematics education (MA); missiology (M Th, D Th); modern Hebrew (MA, PhD); musicology (MA, MMus, D Mus, PhD); natural science education (M Ed); New Testament (M Th, D Th); Old Testament (D Th); pastoral therapy (M Th, D Th); philosophy (MA); philosophy of education (M Ed, Ed D); politics (MA, PhD); Portuguese (MA, PhD); practical theology (M Th, D Th); psychology (MA, MS, PhD); psychology of education (M Ed, Ed D); public health (MA); religious studies (MA, D Th, PhD); Romance languages (MA); Russian (MA, PhD); Semitic languages (MA, PhD); social behavior studies in HIV/AIDS (MA); social science (mental health) (MA); social science in development studies (MA); social science in psychology (MA); social science in social work (MA); social science in sociology (MA); social work (MSW, DSW, PhD); socio-education (M Ed, Ed D); sociolinguistics (MA); sociology (MA, PhD); Spanish (MA, PhD); systematic theology (M Th, D Th); TESOL (teaching English to speakers of other languages) (MA); theological ethics (M Th, D Th); theory of literature (MA, PhD); urban ministries (D Th); urban ministry (M Th).

The University of Texas at Austin, Graduate School, McCombs School of Business, Program in Technology Commercialization, Austin, TX 78712-1111. Offers MS. Twelve-month program, beginning in May, with classes held every other Friday and Saturday. Evening/weekend programs available. Postbaccalaureate distance learning degree programs offered (no on-campus study). *Degree requirements:* For master's, year-long global teaming project. *Entrance requirements:* For master's, GRE General Test or GMAT. Additional exam requirements/recommendations for international students: Required—TOEFL (minimum score 550 paper-based; 213 computer-based; 79 iBT). *Application deadline:* For spring admission, 2/1 priority date for domestic students, 2/1 for international students. Applications are processed on a rolling basis. Application fee: $50 ($75 for international students). Electronic applications accepted. *Expenses:* Contact institution. *Financial support:* Institutionally sponsored loans and scholarships/grants available. Financial award application deadline: 2/15; financial award applicants required to submit FAFSA. *Faculty research:* Technology transfer; entrepreneurship; commercialization; research, development and innovation. *Unit head:* Dr. Gary M. Cadenhead, Director, 512-471-2227, Fax: 512-475-8903, E-mail: gary.cadenhead@mccombs.utexas.edu. *Application contact:* Marketing Coordinator, 512-475-8900, Fax: 512-475-8903, E-mail: mstc@ic2.utexas.edu. Web site: http://www.ic2.utexas.edu/mstc.

Section 16
Materials Sciences and Engineering

This section contains a directory of institutions offering graduate work in materials sciences and engineering, followed by an in-depth entry submitted by an institution that chose to prepare a detailed program description. Additional information about programs listed in the directory but not augmented by an in-depth entry may be obtained by writing directly to the dean of a graduate school or chair of a department at the address given in the directory.

For programs offering related work, see also in this book *Agricultural Engineering and Bioengineering, Biomedical Engineering and Biotechnology, Engineering and Applied Sciences,* and *Geological, Mineral/Mining, and Petroleum Engineering.* In another guide in this series:

Graduate Programs in the Physical Sciences, Mathematics, Agricultural Sciences, the Environment & Natural Resources
See *Chemistry* and *Geosciences*

CONTENTS

Program Directories

Display and Close-Up

Ceramic Sciences and Engineering

Alfred University, Graduate School, New York State College of Ceramics, School of Engineering, Alfred, NY 14802-1205. Offers biomedical materials engineering science (MS); ceramic engineering (MS); ceramics (PhD); electrical engineering (MS); glass science (MS, PhD); materials science and engineering (MS, PhD); mechanical engineering (MS). *Degree requirements:* For master's, thesis; for doctorate, thesis/dissertation. *Entrance requirements:* Additional exam requirements/recommendations for international students: Required—TOEFL (minimum score 590 paper-based; 243 computer-based). Electronic applications accepted. *Expenses:* Contact institution. *Faculty research:* Fine-particle technology, x-ray diffraction, superconductivity, electronic materials.

Missouri University of Science and Technology, Graduate School, Department of Materials Science and Engineering, Rolla, MO 65409. Offers ceramic engineering (MS, DE, PhD); metallurgical engineering (MS, PhD). *Degree requirements:* For master's, thesis optional; for doctorate, comprehensive exam. *Entrance requirements:* For master's, GRE (minimum combined score 1100, 600 verbal, 3.5 writing); for doctorate, GRE (minimum score: quantitative 600, writing 3.5). Additional exam requirements/recommendations for international students: Required—TOEFL (minimum score 570 paper-based; 230 computer-based).

Rensselaer Polytechnic Institute, Graduate School, School of Engineering, Program in Materials Science and Engineering, Troy, NY 12180. Offers ceramics and glass science (M Eng, MS, PhD); composites (M Eng, MS, PhD); electronic materials (M Eng, MS, PhD); metallurgy (M Eng, MS, PhD); polymers (M Eng, MS, PhD). Part-time programs available. Terminal master's awarded for partial completion of doctoral program. *Degree requirements:* For master's, thesis; for doctorate, comprehensive exam, thesis/dissertation. *Entrance requirements:* For master's and doctorate, GRE. Additional exam requirements/recommendations for international students: Required—TOEFL (minimum score 570 paper-based; 230 computer-based; 100 iBT). Electronic applications accepted. *Faculty research:* Materials processing, nanostructural materials, materials for microelectronics, composite materials, computational materials.

University of Washington, Graduate School, College of Engineering, Department of Materials Science and Engineering, Seattle, WA 98195-2120. Offers ceramic engineering (PhD); materials science and engineering (MS, MSE, PhD); materials science and engineering and nanotechnology (PhD). Part-time programs available. *Faculty:* 23 full-time (5 women), 1 part-time/adjunct (0 women). *Students:* 53 full-time (16 women), 9 part-time (2 women); includes 11 minority (1 Black or African American, non-Hispanic/Latino; 1 American Indian or Alaska Native, non-Hispanic/Latino; 6 Asian, non-Hispanic/Latino; 3 Hispanic/Latino), 20 international. Average age 30. 291 applicants, 9% accepted, 9 enrolled. In 2011, 4 master's, 8 doctorates awarded. *Degree requirements:* For master's, comprehensive exam, thesis optional; for doctorate, comprehensive exam, thesis/dissertation, qualifying evaluation, general and final exams. *Entrance requirements:* For master's and doctorate, GRE General Test, minimum GPA of 3.0. Additional exam requirements/recommendations for international students: Required—TOEFL (minimum score 580 paper-based; 237 computer-based; 92 iBT); Recommended—IELTS (minimum score 7). *Application deadline:* For fall admission, 1/15 priority date for domestic students, 12/15 for international students. Applications are processed on a rolling basis. Application fee: $75. Electronic applications accepted. *Expenses:* Contact institution. *Financial support:* In 2011–12, 51 students received support, including 4 fellowships with full tuition reimbursements available (averaging $16,200 per year), 36 research assistantships with full tuition reimbursements available (averaging $16,416 per year), 8 teaching assistantships with full tuition reimbursements available (averaging $16,416 per year); career-related internships or fieldwork, Federal Work-Study, institutionally sponsored loans, scholarships/grants, health care benefits, unspecified assistantships, and stipend supplements also available. Financial award application deadline: 1/15; financial award applicants required to submit FAFSA. *Faculty research:* Biomimetics and biomaterials; electronic, optical and magnetic materials; eco-materials and materials for energy applications; ceramics, metals, composites, and polymers. *Total annual research expenditures:* $7.4 million. *Unit head:* Dr. Alex Jen, Professor/Chair, 206-543-2600, Fax: 206-543-3100, E-mail: ajen@uw.edu. *Application contact:* Kathleen A. Elkins, Academic Counselor, 206-616-6581, Fax: 206-543-3100, E-mail: kelkins@uw.edu. Web site: http://depts.washington.edu/mse/.

Electronic Materials

Colorado School of Mines, Graduate School, Department of Metallurgical and Materials Engineering, Golden, CO 80401-1887. Offers materials science (MS, PhD); metallurgical and materials engineering (ME, MS, PhD). Part-time programs available. *Faculty:* 34 full-time (2 women), 6 part-time/adjunct (0 women). *Students:* 74 full-time (14 women), 6 part-time (0 women); includes 7 minority (1 American Indian or Alaska Native, non-Hispanic/Latino; 2 Asian, non-Hispanic/Latino; 3 Hispanic/Latino; 1 Two or more races, non-Hispanic/Latino), 22 international. Average age 26. 124 applicants, 27% accepted, 31 enrolled. In 2011, 19 master's, 5 doctorates awarded. *Degree requirements:* For master's, thesis (for some programs); for doctorate, comprehensive exam, thesis/dissertation. *Entrance requirements:* For master's and doctorate, GRE General Test. Additional exam requirements/recommendations for international students: Required—TOEFL (minimum score 550 paper-based; 213 computer-based; 80 iBT). *Application deadline:* For fall admission, 1/15 priority date for domestic students, 1/15 for international students; for spring admission, 10/15 priority date for domestic students, 10/15 for international students. Application fee: $50 ($70 for international students). Electronic applications accepted. *Expenses:* Tuition, state resident: full-time $12,585; part-time $699 per credit. Tuition, nonresident: full-time $27,270; part-time $1516 per credit. *Required fees:* $1864.20; $670 per semester. *Financial support:* In 2011–12, 53 students received support, including 5 fellowships with full tuition reimbursements available (averaging $20,000 per year), 39 research assistantships with full tuition reimbursements available (averaging $20,000 per year), 9 teaching assistantships with full tuition reimbursements available (averaging $20,000 per year); scholarships/grants, health care benefits, and unspecified assistantships also available. Financial award application deadline: 1/15; financial award applicants required to submit FAFSA. *Total annual research expenditures:* $6.7 million. *Unit head:* Dr. Michael Kaufman, Interim Head, 303-273-8009, Fax: 303-273-3795, E-mail: mkaufman@mines.edu. *Application contact:* Susan Ballantype, Program Assistant, 303-273-3660, Fax: 303-273-3795, E-mail: susan.ballantyne@is.mines.edu. Web site: http://metallurgy.mines.edu.

Northwestern University, McCormick School of Engineering and Applied Science, Department of Electrical Engineering and Computer Science and Department of Materials Science and Engineering, Program in Electronic Materials, Evanston, IL 60208. Offers MS, PhD, Certificate. Part-time programs available. Terminal master's awarded for partial completion of doctoral program. *Degree requirements:* For master's, thesis; for doctorate, comprehensive exam, thesis/dissertation. *Faculty research:* Electronic optical magnetic materials and devices.

Princeton University, Princeton Institute for the Science and Technology of Materials (PRISM), Princeton, NJ 08544-1019. Offers materials (PhD).

University of Arkansas, Graduate School, Interdisciplinary Program in Microelectronics and Photonics, Fayetteville, AR 72701-1201. Offers MS, PhD. *Students:* 7 full-time (0 women), 39 part-time (5 women); includes 6 minority (4 Black or African American, non-Hispanic/Latino; 2 Asian, non-Hispanic/Latino), 19 international. In 2011, 4 master's, 4 doctorates awarded. *Degree requirements:* For doctorate, thesis/dissertation. *Application deadline:* For fall admission, 4/1 for international students; for spring admission, 10/1 for international students. Applications are processed on a rolling basis. Application fee: $40 ($50 for international students). Electronic applications accepted. *Financial support:* In 2011–12, 25 research assistantships, 4 teaching assistantships were awarded; fellowships with tuition reimbursements also available. Financial award application deadline: 4/1; financial award applicants required to submit FAFSA. *Unit head:* Dr. Ken Vickers, Head, 479-575-2875, Fax: 479-575-4580, E-mail: vickers@uark.edu. *Application contact:* Graduate Admissions, 479-575-6246, Fax: 479-575-5908, E-mail: gradinfo@uark.edu. Web site: http://microep.uark.edu.

Materials Engineering

Arizona State University, Ira A. Fulton School of Engineering, Department of Mechanical and Aerospace Engineering, Tempe, AZ 85281. Offers aerospace engineering (MS, MSE, PhD); chemical engineering (MS, MSE, PhD); materials science and engineering (MS, PhD); mechanical engineering (MS, MSE, PhD). Part-time and evening/weekend programs available. Postbaccalaureate distance learning degree programs offered (minimal on-campus study). Terminal master's awarded for partial completion of doctoral program. *Degree requirements:* For master's, thesis and oral defense (MS); applied project or comprehensive exam (MSE); interactive Program of Study (iPOS) submitted before completing 50 percent of required credit hours; for doctorate, comprehensive exam, thesis/dissertation, interactive Program of Study (iPOS) submitted before completing 50 percent of required credit hours. *Entrance requirements:* For master's, GRE, minimum GPA of 3.0 or equivalent in last 2 years of work leading to bachelor's degree; for doctorate, GRE, minimum GPA of 3.0 in last 2 years of work leading to bachelor's degree. Additional exam requirements/recommendations for international students: Required—TOEFL (minimum score 80 iBT), TOEFL, IELTS, or Pearson Test of English. Electronic applications accepted. *Expenses:* Contact institution. *Faculty research:* Electronic materials and packaging, materials for energy (batteries), adaptive/intelligent materials and structures, multiscale fluid mechanics, membranes, therapeutics and bioseparations, flexible structures, nanostructured materials, and micro/nano transport.

Auburn University, Graduate School, Ginn College of Engineering, Department of Mechanical Engineering, Program in Materials Engineering, Auburn University, AL 36849. Offers M Mtl E, MS, PhD. *Faculty:* 29 full-time (0 women), 2 part-time/adjunct (0 women). *Students:* 17 full-time (7 women), 26 part-time (8 women); includes 2 minority (1 Black or African American, non-Hispanic/Latino; 1 Hispanic/Latino), 24 international. Average age 28. 46 applicants, 70% accepted, 10 enrolled. In 2011, 3 master's, 6 doctorates awarded. *Degree requirements:* For master's, thesis (MS), oral exam; for doctorate, one foreign language, thesis/dissertation. *Entrance requirements:* For master's and doctorate, GRE General Test. *Application deadline:* For fall admission, 7/7 for domestic students; for spring admission, 11/24 for domestic students. Applications are processed on a rolling basis. Application fee: $50 ($60 for international students). Electronic applications accepted. *Expenses:* Tuition, state resident: full-time $7290; part-time $405 per credit hour. Tuition, nonresident: full-time $21,870; part-time $1215 per credit hour. *International tuition:* $22,000 full-time. *Required fees:* $1402. *Financial support:* Fellowships, research assistantships, teaching assistantships, and Federal Work-Study available. Support available to part-time students. Financial award application deadline: 3/15; financial award applicants required to submit FAFSA. *Faculty research:* Smart materials. *Unit head:* Dr. Bryan Chin, Head, 334-844-3322. *Application contact:* Dr. George Flowers, Dean of the Graduate School, 334-844-2125.

Boise State University, Graduate College, College of Engineering, Department of Materials Science and Engineering, Boise, ID 83725-0399. Offers M Engr, MS.

Boston University, College of Engineering, Division of Materials Science and Engineering, Boston, MA 02215. Offers M Eng, MS, PhD. Part-time programs available. *Students:* 40 full-time (11 women); includes 5 minority (3 Asian, non-Hispanic/Latino; 2 Hispanic/Latino), 23 international. Average age 25. 92 applicants, 26% accepted, 13 enrolled. In 2011, 5 degrees awarded. Terminal master's awarded for partial completion of doctoral program. *Degree requirements:* For master's, thesis (for some programs); for doctorate, comprehensive exam, thesis/dissertation. *Entrance requirements:* For master's and doctorate, GRE General Test. Additional exam requirements/recommendations for international students: Required—TOEFL (minimum score 550 paper-based; 213 computer-based; 84 iBT), IELTS (minimum score 6.5). *Application deadline:* For fall admission, 3/15 for domestic and international students; for spring admission, 10/1 for domestic and international students. Application fee: $70. Electronic applications accepted. *Expenses:* Tuition: Full-time $40,848; part-time $1276 per credit hour. *Required fees:* $572; $286 per semester. *Financial support:* In 2011–12, 23 students received support, including 2 fellowships with full tuition reimbursements available (averaging $28,950 per year), 15 research assistantships with full tuition reimbursements available (averaging $19,300 per year), 4 teaching assistantships with full tuition reimbursements available (averaging $19,300 per year); career-related internships or fieldwork, Federal Work-Study, institutionally sponsored loans, scholarships/grants, traineeships, health care benefits, and tuition waivers also available. Financial award application deadline: 1/15; financial award applicants required to submit FAFSA. *Faculty research:* Biomaterials, electronic and photonic materials, materials for energy and environment, nanomaterials. *Unit head:* Dr. David Bishop, Division Head, 617-353-8899, Fax: 617-353-5548, E-mail: djb1@bu.edu. *Application contact:* Stephen Doherty, Director of Graduate Programs, 617-353-9760, Fax: 617-353-0259, E-mail: enggrad@bu.edu. Web site: http://www.bu.edu/mse/.

California State University, Northridge, Graduate Studies, College of Engineering and Computer Science, Department of Manufacturing Systems Engineering and Management, Northridge, CA 91330. Offers engineering automation (MS); engineering management (MS); manufacturing systems engineering (MS); materials engineering (MS). Postbaccalaureate distance learning degree programs offered. *Entrance requirements:* For master's, GRE (if cumulative undergraduate GPA less than 3.0).

Carleton University, Faculty of Graduate Studies, Faculty of Engineering and Design, Department of Mechanical and Aerospace Engineering, Ottawa, ON K1S 5B6, Canada. Offers aerospace engineering (M Eng, MA Sc, PhD); materials engineering (M Eng, MA Sc); mechanical engineering (M Eng, MA Sc, PhD). *Degree requirements:* For master's, thesis optional; for doctorate, thesis/dissertation. *Entrance requirements:* For master's, honors degree; for doctorate, MA Sc or M Eng. Additional exam requirements/recommendations for international students: Required—TOEFL. *Faculty research:* Thermal fluids engineering, heat transfer, vehicle engineering.

Carnegie Mellon University, Carnegie Institute of Technology, Department of Materials Science and Engineering, Pittsburgh, PA 15213-3891. Offers MS, PhD. Part-time programs available. Terminal master's awarded for partial completion of doctoral program. *Degree requirements:* For master's, exam; for doctorate, thesis/dissertation, qualifying exam. *Entrance requirements:* For master's and doctorate, GRE General Test. Additional exam requirements/recommendations for international students: Required—TOEFL. *Faculty research:* Materials characterization, process metallurgy, high strength alloys, growth kinetics, ceramics.

Case Western Reserve University, School of Graduate Studies, Case School of Engineering, Department of Materials Science and Engineering, Cleveland, OH 44106. Offers materials science and engineering (MS, PhD). Part-time programs available. Postbaccalaureate distance learning degree programs offered (no on-campus study). *Faculty:* 11 full-time (0 women). *Students:* 35 full-time (11 women), 5 part-time (1 woman); includes 2 minority (both Asian, non-Hispanic/Latino), 29 international. In 2011, 9 master's, 8 doctorates awarded. Terminal master's awarded for partial completion of doctoral program. *Degree requirements:* For master's, thesis (for some programs); for doctorate, thesis/dissertation, qualifying exam, teaching experience. *Entrance requirements:* For master's and doctorate, GRE General Test. Additional exam requirements/recommendations for international students: Required—TOEFL. *Application deadline:* For fall admission, 2/15 priority date for domestic students; for spring admission, 9/15 for domestic students. Applications are processed on a rolling basis. Application fee: $50. *Financial support:* Fellowships with full and partial tuition reimbursements, research assistantships with full and partial tuition reimbursements, and teaching assistantships available. Financial award application deadline: 4/30; financial award applicants required to submit FAFSA. *Faculty research:* Surface hardening of steels and other alloys, chemistry and structure of surfaces, microstructural and mechanical property characterization, materials for energy applications, thermodynamics and kinetics of materials, performance and reliability of materials. *Total annual research expenditures:* $3.7 million. *Unit head:* Dr. James D. McGuffin-Cawley, Department Chair, 216-368-6482, Fax: 216-368-4224, E-mail: emse.info@case.edu. *Application contact:* Theresa Claytor, Student Affairs Coordinator, 216-368-8555, Fax: 216-368-8555, E-mail: esme.info@case.edu. Web site: http://dmseg5.case.edu.

The Catholic University of America, School of Engineering, Department of Materials Science and Engineering, Washington, DC 20064. Offers MS. Part-time programs available. *Students:* 1 full-time (0 women), 1 part-time (0 women); includes 1 minority (Black or African American, non-Hispanic/Latino). Average age 27. 1 applicant, 100% accepted, 1 enrolled. *Degree requirements:* For master's, thesis optional. *Entrance requirements:* For master's, GRE (minimum score 1250), minimum GPA of 3.0, statement of purpose, official copies of academic transcripts. Additional exam requirements/recommendations for international students: Required—TOEFL (minimum score 580 paper-based; 237 computer-based). *Application deadline:* For fall admission, 8/1 for domestic students, 7/15 for international students; for spring admission, 12/1 for domestic students, 10/15 for international students. Applications are processed on a rolling basis. Application fee: $55. Electronic applications accepted. *Expenses: Tuition:* Full-time $35,260; part-time $1380 per credit. *Required fees:* $80; $40 per semester hour. One-time fee: $425. *Financial support:* Fellowships, research assistantships, teaching assistantships, Federal Work-Study, scholarships/grants, tuition waivers (full and partial), and unspecified assistantships available. Financial award application deadline: 2/1; financial award applicants required to submit FAFSA. *Faculty research:* Nanotechnology, biomaterials, magnetic and optical materials, glass, ceramics, and metallurgy processing and instrumentation . *Unit head:* Dr. Biprodas Dutta, Director, 202-319-5535, Fax: 202-319-4469, E-mail: duttab@cua.edu. *Application contact:* Andrew Woodall, Director of Graduate Admissions, 202-319-5057, Fax: 202-319-6533, E-mail: cua-admissions@cua.edu. Web site: http://materialsscience.cua.edu/.

Clarkson University, Graduate School, Wallace H. Coulter School of Engineering, Program in Materials Science and Engineering, Potsdam, NY 13699. Offers PhD. Part-time programs available. *Students:* 2 full-time (both women), 1 international. Average age 26. 20 applicants, 70% accepted, 0 enrolled. *Degree requirements:* For doctorate, comprehensive exam, thesis/dissertation, departmental qualifying exam. *Entrance requirements:* For doctorate, GRE, transcripts of all college coursework, resume, personal statement, three letters of recommendation. Additional exam requirements/recommendations for international students: Required—TOEFL (minimum score 550 paper-based; 213 computer-based; 80 iBT), IELTS (minimum score 6.5). *Application*

deadline: For fall admission, 1/30 priority date for domestic students, 1/30 for international students; for spring admission, 9/1 priority date for domestic students, 9/1 for international students. Applications are processed on a rolling basis. Application fee: $25 ($35 for international students). Electronic applications accepted. *Expenses: Tuition:* Full-time $14,376; part-time $1198 per credit hour. *Required fees:* $295 per semester. *Financial support:* In 2011–12, 2 students received support, including fellowships with full tuition reimbursements available (averaging $21,999 per year), 2 research assistantships with full tuition reimbursements available (averaging $21,999 per year), 1 teaching assistantship with full tuition reimbursement available (averaging $21,999 per year); scholarships/grants, tuition waivers (partial), and unspecified assistantships also available. *Unit head:* Dr. Ian I. Suni, Chair, 315-268-4471, Fax: 315-268-6654, E-mail: isuni@clarkson.edu. *Application contact:* Kelly Sharlow, Assistant to the Dean, 315-268-7929, Fax: 315-268-4494, E-mail: ksharlow@clarkson.edu. Web site: http://www.clarkson.edu/engineering/graduate/mat_sci_eng_phd/.

Clemson University, Graduate School, College of Engineering and Science, School of Materials Science and Engineering, Clemson, SC 29634. Offers MS, PhD. Part-time programs available. *Faculty:* 15 full-time (2 women), 7 part-time/adjunct (0 women). *Students:* 58 full-time (18 women), 8 part-time (3 women); includes 3 minority (1 Asian, non-Hispanic/Latino; 2 Two or more races, non-Hispanic/Latino), 35 international. Average age 27. 126 applicants, 19% accepted, 15 enrolled. In 2011, 6 master's, 2 doctorates awarded. Terminal master's awarded for partial completion of doctoral program. *Degree requirements:* For master's, thesis; for doctorate, comprehensive exam, thesis/dissertation. *Entrance requirements:* For master's and doctorate, GRE General Test. Additional exam requirements/recommendations for international students: Required—TOEFL. *Application deadline:* For fall admission, 2/1 for domestic students; for spring admission, 9/1 for domestic students. Applications are processed on a rolling basis. Application fee: $70 ($80 for international students). Electronic applications accepted. *Financial support:* In 2011–12, 54 students received support, including 4 fellowships with full and partial tuition reimbursements available (averaging $4,250 per year), 37 research assistantships with partial tuition reimbursements available (averaging $19,998 per year), 17 teaching assistantships with partial tuition reimbursements available (averaging $14,118 per year); career-related internships or fieldwork, institutionally sponsored loans, scholarships/grants, health care benefits, and unspecified assistantships also available. Support available to part-time students. Financial award applicants required to submit FAFSA. *Total annual research expenditures:* $3.1 million. *Unit head:* Dr. Kathleen Richardson, Chair and Director of the School of Materials Science and Engineering, 864-656-3311, Fax: 864-656-5973, E-mail: richar3@clemson.edu. *Application contact:* Dr. Gary C. Lickfield, Graduate Program Coordinator, 864-656-5964, Fax: 864-656-5973, E-mail: lgary@clemson.edu. Web site: http://www.clemson.edu/mse/.

Colorado School of Mines, Graduate School, Department of Metallurgical and Materials Engineering, Golden, CO 80401-1887. Offers materials science (MS, PhD); metallurgical and materials engineering (ME, MS, PhD). Part-time programs available. *Faculty:* 34 full-time (2 women), 6 part-time/adjunct (0 women). *Students:* 74 full-time (14 women), 6 part-time (0 women); includes 7 minority (1 American Indian or Alaska Native, non-Hispanic/Latino; 2 Asian, non-Hispanic/Latino; 3 Hispanic/Latino; 1 Two or more races, non-Hispanic/Latino), 22 international. Average age 26. 124 applicants, 27% accepted, 31 enrolled. In 2011, 19 master's, 5 doctorates awarded. *Degree requirements:* For master's, thesis (for some programs); for doctorate, comprehensive exam, thesis/dissertation. *Entrance requirements:* For master's and doctorate, GRE General Test. Additional exam requirements/recommendations for international students: Required—TOEFL (minimum score 550 paper-based; 213 computer-based; 80 iBT). *Application deadline:* For fall admission, 1/15 priority date for domestic students, 1/15 for international students; for spring admission, 10/15 priority date for domestic students, 10/15 for international students. Application fee: $50 ($70 for international students). Electronic applications accepted. *Expenses:* Tuition, state resident: full-time $12,585; part-time $699 per credit. Tuition, nonresident: full-time $27,270; part-time $1516 per credit. *Required fees:* $1864.20; $670 per semester. *Financial support:* In 2011–12, 53 students received support, including 5 fellowships with full tuition reimbursements available (averaging $20,000 per year), 39 research assistantships with full tuition reimbursements available (averaging $20,000 per year), 9 teaching assistantships with full tuition reimbursements available (averaging $20,000 per year); scholarships/grants, health care benefits, and unspecified assistantships also available. Financial award application deadline: 1/15; financial award applicants required to submit FAFSA. *Total annual research expenditures:* $6.7 million. *Unit head:* Dr. Michael Kaufman, Interim Head, 303-273-3009, Fax: 303-273-3795, E-mail: mkaufman@mines.edu. *Application contact:* Susan Ballantype, Program Assistant, 303-273-3660, Fax: 303-273-3795, E-mail: susan.ballantyne@is.mines.edu. Web site: http://metallurgy.mines.edu/.

Columbia University, The Fu Foundation School of Engineering and Applied Science, Department of Applied Physics and Applied Mathematics, New York, NY 10027. Offers applied physics (Eng Sc D); applied physics and applied mathematics (MS, PhD, Engr); materials science and engineering (MS, Eng Sc D, PhD); medical physics (MS). Part-time programs available. Postbaccalaureate distance learning degree programs offered (no on-campus study). *Faculty:* 32 full-time (2 women), 23 part-time/adjunct (2 women). *Students:* 98 full-time (22 women), 38 part-time (10 women); includes 19 minority (14 Asian, non-Hispanic/Latino; 1 Hispanic/Latino; 4 Two or more races, non-Hispanic/Latino), 50 international. Average age 28. 371 applicants, 18% accepted, 41 enrolled. In 2011, 57 master's, 18 doctorates awarded. Terminal master's awarded for partial completion of doctoral program. *Degree requirements:* For master's, comprehensive exam; for doctorate, thesis/dissertation, qualifying exam. *Entrance requirements:* For master's, GRE General Test, GRE Subject Test (strongly recommended); for doctorate, GRE General Test, GRE Subject Test (applied physics); for Engr, GRE General Test. Additional exam requirements/recommendations for international students: Required—TOEFL, IELTS. *Application deadline:* For fall admission, 12/1 priority date for domestic students, 12/1 for international students; for spring admission, 10/1 priority date for domestic students, 10/1 for international students. Application fee: $95. Electronic applications accepted. *Financial support:* In 2011–12, 71 students received support, including 2 fellowships with full tuition reimbursements available (averaging $31,140 per year), 55 research assistantships with full tuition reimbursements available (averaging $31,133 per year), 16 teaching assistantships with full tuition reimbursements available (averaging $31,133 per year); health care benefits also available. Financial award application deadline: 12/1; financial award applicants required to submit FAFSA. *Faculty research:* Plasma physics and fusion energy; optical and laser physics; atmospheric, oceanic and earth physics; applied mathematics; solid state science and processing of materials, their properties, and their structure; medical physics. *Unit head:* Dr. Ismail C. Noyan, Professor and Department Chairman, 212-854-8919, E-mail: icn2@columbia.edu. *Application contact:* Montserrat Fernandez-Pinkley, Student Services Coordinator, 212-854-4457, Fax: 212-854-8257, E-mail: mf2157@columbia.edu. Web site: http://www.apam.columbia.edu/.

Materials Engineering

Cornell University, Graduate School, Graduate Fields of Engineering, Field of Materials Science and Engineering, Ithaca, NY 14853. Offers materials engineering (M Eng, PhD); materials science (M Eng, PhD). *Faculty:* 46 full-time (5 women). *Students:* 76 full-time (26 women); includes 14 minority (3 Black or African American, non-Hispanic/Latino; 10 Asian, non-Hispanic/Latino; 1 Hispanic/Latino), 38 international. Average age 26. 403 applicants, 20% accepted, 33 enrolled. In 2011, 24 master's, 6 doctorates awarded. *Degree requirements:* For doctorate, comprehensive exam, thesis/dissertation. *Entrance requirements:* For master's and doctorate, GRE General Test, 3 letters of recommendation. Additional exam requirements/recommendations for international students: Required—TOEFL (minimum score 550 paper-based; 213 computer-based; 77 iBT). *Application deadline:* For fall admission, 1/15 priority date for domestic students. Application fee: $95. Electronic applications accepted. *Financial support:* In 2011–12, 48 students received support, including 17 fellowships with full tuition reimbursements available, 31 research assistantships with full tuition reimbursements available, 8 teaching assistantships with full tuition reimbursements available; institutionally sponsored loans, scholarships/grants, health care benefits, tuition waivers (full and partial), and unspecified assistantships also available. Financial award applicants required to submit FAFSA. *Faculty research:* Ceramics, complex fluids, glass, metals, polymers semiconductors. *Unit head:* Director of Graduate Studies, 607-255-9159, Fax: 607-255-2365. *Application contact:* Graduate Field Assistant, 607-255-9159, Fax: 607-255-2365, E-mail: matsci@cornell.edu. Web site: http://www.gradschool.cornell.edu/fields.php?id-31&a-2.

Dalhousie University, Faculty of Engineering, Department of Materials Engineering, Halifax, NS B3H 1Z1, Canada. Offers M Eng, MA Sc, PhD. *Degree requirements:* For master's, thesis; for doctorate, thesis/dissertation. *Entrance requirements:* Additional exam requirements/recommendations for international students: Required—TOEFL, IELTS, CANTEST, CAEL, or Michigan English Language Assessment Battery. Electronic applications accepted. *Faculty research:* Ceramic and metal matrix composites, electron microscopy, electrolysis in molten salt, fracture mechanics, electronic materials.

Dartmouth College, Thayer School of Engineering, Program in Materials Sciences and Engineering, Hanover, NH 03755. Offers MS, PhD. *Degree requirements:* For master's, thesis; for doctorate, thesis/dissertation, candidacy oral exam. *Entrance requirements:* For master's and doctorate, GRE General Test. *Application deadline:* For fall admission, 1/1 priority date for domestic students. Application fee: $45. *Financial support:* Fellowships, research assistantships, teaching assistantships, career-related internships or fieldwork, Federal Work-Study, institutionally sponsored loans, and tuition waivers (full and partial) available. Financial award application deadline: 1/15. *Faculty research:* Electronic and magnetic materials, microstructural evolution, biomaterials and nanostructures, laser-material interactions, nano composites. *Total annual research expenditures:* $2.4 million. *Unit head:* Dr. Joseph J. Helbie, Dean, 603-646-2238, Fax: 603-646-2580, E-mail: joseph.j.helbie@dartmouth.edu. *Application contact:* Candace S. Potter, Graduate Admissions Administrator, 603-646-3844, Fax: 603-646-1620, E-mail: candace.potter@dartmouth.edu. Web site: http://engineering.dartmouth.edu/.

Drexel University, College of Engineering, Department of Materials Engineering, Philadelphia, PA 19104-2875. Offers MS, PhD. Part-time and evening/weekend programs available. Terminal master's awarded for partial completion of doctoral program. *Degree requirements:* For master's, thesis or alternative; for doctorate, thesis/dissertation. *Entrance requirements:* For master's, minimum GPA of 3.0; for doctorate, minimum GPA of 3.0, MS. Additional exam requirements/recommendations for international students: Required—TOEFL. Electronic applications accepted. *Faculty research:* Composite science; polymer and biomedical engineering; solidification; near net shape processing, including powder metallurgy.

Duke University, Graduate School, Pratt School of Engineering, Master of Engineering Program, Durham, NC 27708-0271. Offers biomedical engineering (M Eng); civil engineering (M Eng); electrical and computer engineering (M Eng); environmental engineering (M Eng); materials science and engineering (M Eng); mechanical engineering (M Eng); photonics and optical sciences (M Eng). Part-time programs available. *Entrance requirements:* For master's, GRE General Test, resume, 3 letters of recommendation, statement of purpose. Additional exam requirements/recommendations for international students: Required—TOEFL. *Expenses: Tuition:* Full-time $40,720. *Required fees:* $3107.

Florida International University, College of Engineering and Computing, Department of Mechanical and Materials Engineering, Materials Science and Engineering Program, Miami, FL 33175. Offers MS, PhD. Part-time and evening/weekend programs available. Terminal master's awarded for partial completion of doctoral program. *Degree requirements:* For master's, thesis or alternative; for doctorate, comprehensive exam, thesis/dissertation. *Entrance requirements:* For master's, GRE, 3 letters of recommendation, minimum undergraduate GPA of 3.0 in upper-level course work; for doctorate, GRE, minimum GPA of 3.0, 3 letters of recommendation, letter of intent. Additional exam requirements/recommendations for international students: Required—TOEFL (minimum score 550 paper-based; 80 iBT). Electronic applications accepted.

Florida State University, The Graduate School, Materials Science and Engineering Program, Tallahassee, FL 32310. Offers computational materials science and mechanics (MS); functional materials (MS); materials science and engineering (PhD); nanoscale materials, composite materials, and interfaces (MS); polymers and bio-inspired materials (MS). MS not open to international students. *Faculty:* 23 full-time (3 women). *Students:* 10 full-time (2 women); includes 1 minority (Hispanic/Latino), 5 international. Average age 24. 13 applicants, 23% accepted, 3 enrolled. In 2011, 3 master's awarded. Terminal master's awarded for partial completion of doctoral program. *Degree requirements:* For master's, thesis; for doctorate, comprehensive exam, thesis/dissertation. *Entrance requirements:* For master's and doctorate, GRE General Test (minimum old version score 1100 Verbal and Quantitative; 55th percentile Verbal, 75th percentile Quantitative in new format), minimum GPA of 3.0, 3 letters of recommendation. Additional exam requirements/recommendations for international students: Required—TOEFL (minimum score 80 iBT). *Application deadline:* For fall admission, 7/1 for domestic students, 5/1 for international students; for spring admission, 11/1 for domestic students, 9/1 for international students. Applications are processed on a rolling basis. Application fee: $25. Electronic applications accepted. *Expenses:* Tuition, state resident: full-time $9474; part-time $350.88 per credit hour. Tuition, nonresident: full-time $16,236; part-time $601.34 per credit hour. *Required fees:* $630 per semester. One-time fee: $20. Tuition and fees vary according to course load and campus/location. *Financial support:* In 2011–12, 10 students received support, including 1 fellowship with full tuition reimbursement available (averaging $30,526 per year), 7 research assistantships with full tuition reimbursements available (averaging $20,700 per year), 1 teaching assistantship with full tuition reimbursement available (averaging $20,880 per year); partial payment of required health insurance also available. Financial award application deadline: 1/15. *Faculty research:* Magnetism and magnetic materials, composites, superconductors, polymers, computations, nanotechnology. *Unit head:* Prof. Eric Hellstrom, Director, 850-645-7489, Fax: 850-645-7754, E-mail: hellstrom@asc.magnet.fsu.edu. *Application contact:* Judy Gardner, Admissions Coordinator, 850-645-8980, Fax: 850-645-9123, E-mail: gardner@eng.fsu.edu. Web site: http://materials.fsu.edu.

Georgia Institute of Technology, Graduate Studies and Research, College of Engineering, School of Materials Science and Engineering, Atlanta, GA 30332-0001. Offers biomedical engineering (MS Bio E); materials science and engineering (MS, PhD); polymers (MS Poly). Terminal master's awarded for partial completion of doctoral program. *Degree requirements:* For master's, thesis (for some programs); for doctorate, comprehensive exam, thesis/dissertation. *Entrance requirements:* For master's and doctorate, GRE General Test. Additional exam requirements/recommendations for international students: Required—TOEFL (minimum score 620 paper-based; 260 computer-based). Electronic applications accepted. *Faculty research:* Nanomaterials, biomaterials, computational materials science, mechanical behavior, advanced engineering materials.

Illinois Institute of Technology, Graduate College, Armour College of Engineering, Department of Mechanical, Materials and Aerospace Engineering, Chicago, IL 60616-3793. Offers manufacturing engineering (MME, MS); materials science and engineering (MMME, MS, PhD); mechanical and aerospace engineering (MMAE, MS, PhD), including economics (MS), energy (MS), environment (MS). Part-time and evening/weekend programs available. Postbaccalaureate distance learning degree programs offered (minimal on-campus study). Terminal master's awarded for partial completion of doctoral program. *Degree requirements:* For master's, comprehensive exam (for some programs), thesis (for some programs); for doctorate, comprehensive exam, thesis/dissertation. *Entrance requirements:* For master's and doctorate, GRE General Test (minimum score 1000 Quantitative and Verbal, 3.0 Analytical Writing), minimum undergraduate GPA of 3.0. Additional exam requirements/recommendations for international students: Required—TOEFL (minimum score 523 paper-based; 70 iBT); Recommended—IELTS (minimum score 5.5). Electronic applications accepted. *Faculty research:* Fluid dynamics, metallurgical and materials engineering, solids and structures, computational mechanics, theoretical mechanics.

Instituto Tecnológico y de Estudios Superiores de Monterrey, Campus Estado de México, Professional and Graduate Division, Estado de Mexico, Mexico. Offers administration of information technologies (MITA); architecture (M Arch); business administration (GMBA, MBA); computer sciences (MCS, PhD); education (M Ed); educational institution administration (MAD); educational technology and innovation (PhD); electronic commerce (MEC); environmental systems (MS); finance (MAF); humanistic studies (MHS); information sciences and knowledge management (MISKM); information systems (MS); manufacturing systems (MS); marketing (MEM); quality systems and productivity (MS); science and materials engineering (PhD); telecommunications management (MTM). Part-time programs available. Postbaccalaureate distance learning degree programs offered (minimal on-campus study). *Degree requirements:* For master's, one foreign language, thesis (for some programs); for doctorate, one foreign language, thesis/dissertation. *Entrance requirements:* For master's, E-PAEP 500, interview; for doctorate, E-PAEP 500, research proposal. Additional exam requirements/recommendations for international students: Required—TOEFL (minimum score 550 paper-based). *Faculty research:* Surface treatments by plasmas, mechanical properties, robotics, graphical computing, mechatronics security protocols.

Iowa State University of Science and Technology, Department of Materials Science and Engineering, Ames, IA 50011. Offers MS, PhD. *Entrance requirements:* For master's and doctorate, GRE General Test. Additional exam requirements/recommendations for international students: Required—TOEFL (minimum score 550 paper-based; 79 iBT), IELTS (minimum score 6.5). *Application deadline:* For fall admission, 1/15 priority date for domestic students, 1/15 for international students; for spring admission, 8/15 priority date for domestic students, 8/15 for international students. Application fee: $40 ($90 for international students). Electronic applications accepted. *Financial support:* Teaching assistantships, scholarships/grants, health care benefits, and unspecified assistantships available. *Unit head:* Dr. Vitaliji Pecharsky, Director of Graduate Education, 515-294-1224, Fax: 515-204-5444, E-mail: gradmse@iastate.edu. *Application contact:* Carla Harris, Director of Graduate Education, 515-294-1224, Fax: 515-294-5444, E-mail: gradmse@iastate.edu. Web site: http://www.mse.iastate.edu.

The Johns Hopkins University, Engineering Program for Professionals, Part-time Program in Materials Science and Engineering, Baltimore, MD 21218-2699. Offers M Mat SE, MSE. Part-time and evening/weekend programs available. Electronic applications accepted.

The Johns Hopkins University, Whiting School of Engineering, Department of Materials Science and Engineering, Baltimore, MD 21218-2699. Offers M Mat SE, MSE, PhD. Part-time and evening/weekend programs available. Terminal master's awarded for partial completion of doctoral program. *Degree requirements:* For master's, thesis, oral exam; for doctorate, thesis/dissertation, oral exam, thesis defense. *Entrance requirements:* For master's and doctorate, GRE General Test. Additional exam requirements/recommendations for international students: Required—TOEFL (minimum score 600 paper-based; 250 computer-based). Electronic applications accepted. *Faculty research:* Thin films, nanomaterials, biomaterials, materials characterization, electronic materials.

The Johns Hopkins University, Whiting School of Engineering, Program in Engineering Management, Baltimore, MD 21218-2699. Offers biomaterials (MSEM); communications science (MSEM); computer science (MSEM); fluid mechanics (MSEM); materials science and engineering (MSEM); mechanical engineering (MSEM); mechanics and materials (MSEM); nano-biotechnology (MSEM); nanomaterials and nanotechnology (MSEM); probability and statistics (MSEM); smart product and device design (MSEM); systems analysis, management and environmental policy (MSEM). *Entrance requirements:* For master's, GRE, 3 letters of recommendation, resume. Additional exam requirements/recommendations for international students: Required—TOEFL (minimum score 600 paper-based; 250 computer-based; 100 iBT) or IELTS (minimum score 7). Electronic applications accepted.

Lehigh University, P.C. Rossin College of Engineering and Applied Science, Department of Materials Science and Engineering, Bethlehem, PA 18015. Offers materials science and engineering (M Eng, MS, PhD); photonics (MS); polymer science/engineering (M Eng, MS, PhD); MBA/E. Part-time programs available. *Faculty:* 13 full-time (3 women), 1 part-time/adjunct (0 women). *Students:* 28 full-time (6 women), 6 part-time (1 woman); includes 2 minority (both Asian, non-Hispanic/Latino), 14 international.

Average age 26. 321 applicants, 2% accepted, 6 enrolled. In 2011, 2 master's, 2 doctorates awarded. *Degree requirements:* For master's, thesis; for doctorate, comprehensive exam, thesis/dissertation. *Entrance requirements:* For master's and doctorate, GRE General Test, minimum GPA of 3.0. Additional exam requirements/recommendations for international students: Required—TOEFL (minimum score 487 paper-based; 216 computer-based; 85 iBT). *Application deadline:* For fall admission, 1/15 priority date for domestic students, 1/15 for international students; for spring admission, 12/1 priority date for domestic students, 12/1 for international students. Applications are processed on a rolling basis. Application fee: $75. Electronic applications accepted. *Financial support:* In 2011–12, 29 students received support, including 3 fellowships with full and partial tuition reimbursements available (averaging $22,400 per year), 25 research assistantships with full tuition reimbursements available (averaging $22,449 per year), 13 teaching assistantships with partial tuition reimbursements available (averaging $17,512 per year); career-related internships or fieldwork, Federal Work-Study, institutionally sponsored loans, scholarships/grants, and unspecified assistantships also available. Support available to part-time students. Financial award application deadline: 1/15. *Faculty research:* Metals, ceramics, crystals, polymers, fatigue crack propagation. *Total annual research expenditures:* $4.1 million. *Unit head:* Dr. Helen Chan, Chairperson, 610-758-5554, Fax: 610-758-4244, E-mail: hmc0@lehigh.edu. *Application contact:* Anne Marie Lobley, Graduate Administrative Coordinator, 610-758-4222, Fax: 610-758-4244, E-mail: amme@lehigh.edu. Web site: http://www.lehigh.edu/~inmatsci/.

Massachusetts Institute of Technology, School of Engineering, Department of Civil and Environmental Engineering, Cambridge, MA 02139. Offers biological oceanography (PhD, Sc D); chemical oceanography (PhD, Sc D); civil and environmental engineering (PhD, Sc D); civil and environmental systems (PhD, Sc D); civil engineering (PhD, Sc D, CE); coastal engineering (PhD, Sc D); construction engineering and management (PhD, Sc D); environmental and water quality engineering (M Eng); environmental biology (PhD, Sc D); environmental chemistry (PhD, Sc D); environmental engineering (PhD, Sc D); environmental fluid mechanics (PhD, Sc D); environmental science and engineering (SM); geotechnical and geoenvironmental engineering (PhD, Sc D); geotechnology (M Eng); high-performance structures (M Eng); hydrology (PhD, Sc D); information technology (PhD, Sc D); mechanics (SM); oceanographic engineering (PhD, Sc D); structures and materials (PhD, Sc D); transportation (M Eng, PhD, Sc D); SM/MBA. *Faculty:* 35 full-time (6 women), 1 part-time/adjunct (0 women). *Students:* 216 full-time (80 women); includes 30 minority (4 Black or African American, non-Hispanic/Latino; 13 Asian, non-Hispanic/Latino; 8 Hispanic/Latino; 5 Two or more races, non-Hispanic/Latino), 110 international. Average age 27. 589 applicants, 26% accepted, 91 enrolled. In 2011, 62 master's, 14 doctorates awarded. *Degree requirements:* For master's and CE, thesis; for doctorate, comprehensive exam, thesis/dissertation. *Entrance requirements:* For master's and doctorate, GRE General Test. Additional exam requirements/recommendations for international students: Required—TOEFL (minimum score 577 paper-based; 233 computer-based; 90 iBT), IELTS (minimum score 7). *Application deadline:* For fall admission, 12/15 for domestic and international students. Application fee: $75. Electronic applications accepted. *Expenses: Tuition:* Full-time $40,460; part-time $630 per credit hour. *Required fees:* $272. *Financial support:* In 2011–12, 180 students received support, including 51 fellowships (averaging $30,800 per year), 110 research assistantships (averaging $29,500 per year), 19 teaching assistantships (averaging $29,500 per year); career-related internships or fieldwork, Federal Work-Study, institutionally sponsored loans, scholarships/grants, health care benefits, and unspecified assistantships also available. *Faculty research:* Environmental chemistry, environmental fluid mechanics and coastal engineering, environmental microbiology, geotechnical engineering and geomechanics, hydrology and hydroclimatology, infrastructure systems, mechanics of materials and structures, transportation systems. *Total annual research expenditures:* $17.7 million. *Unit head:* Prof. Andrew Whittle, Head, 617-253-7101. *Application contact:* Patricia Glidden, Graduate Admissions Coordinator, 617-253-7119, Fax: 617-258-6775, E-mail: cee-admissions@mit.edu. Web site: http://cee.mit.edu/.

Massachusetts Institute of Technology, School of Engineering, Department of Materials Science and Engineering, Cambridge, MA 02139. Offers archaeological materials (PhD, Sc D); materials engineering (Mat E); materials science and engineering (SM, PhD, Sc D). *Faculty:* 32 full-time (9 women). *Students:* 193 full-time (48 women); includes 33 minority (2 Black or African American, non-Hispanic/Latino; 20 Asian, non-Hispanic/Latino; 8 Hispanic/Latino; 3 Two or more races, non-Hispanic/Latino), 110 international. Average age 26. 384 applicants, 15% accepted, 35 enrolled. In 2011, 35 master's, 32 doctorates awarded. Terminal master's awarded for partial completion of doctoral program. *Degree requirements:* For master's, thesis; for doctorate, comprehensive exam, thesis/dissertation. *Entrance requirements:* For master's and doctorate, GRE General Test. Additional exam requirements/recommendations for international students: Required—IELTS (minimum score 7). *Application deadline:* For fall admission, 12/15 for domestic and international students. Application fee: $75. Electronic applications accepted. *Expenses: Tuition:* Full-time $40,460; part-time $630 per credit hour. *Required fees:* $272. *Financial support:* In 2011–12, 179 students received support, including 47 fellowships (averaging $35,400 per year), 129 research assistantships (averaging $29,700 per year), 6 teaching assistantships (averaging $32,300 per year); career-related internships or fieldwork, Federal Work-Study, institutionally sponsored loans, scholarships/grants, traineeships, health care benefits, and unspecified assistantships also available. *Faculty research:* Thermodynamics and kinetics of materials; structure, processing and properties of materials: metals, ceramics, semiconductors, polymers, biomaterials; electronic, structural and biological applications and devices; computational materials science; materials in energy, medicine, nanotechnology and the environment. *Total annual research expenditures:* $29.6 million. *Unit head:* Prof. Christopher Schuh, Head, 617-253-3300, Fax: 617-252-1775. *Application contact:* Angelita Mireles, Academic Administrator, 617-253-3302, E-mail: dmse-admissions@mit.edu. Web site: http://dmse.mit.edu.

McGill University, Faculty of Graduate and Postdoctoral Studies, Faculty of Engineering, Department of Civil Engineering and Applied Mechanics, Montréal, QC H3A 2T5, Canada. Offers environmental engineering (M Eng, M Sc, PhD); fluid mechanics (M Sc); fluid mechanics and hydraulic engineering (M Eng, PhD); materials engineering (M Eng, PhD); rehabilitation of urban infrastructure (M Eng, PhD); soil behavior (M Eng, PhD); soil mechanics and foundations (M Eng, PhD); structures and structural mechanics (M Eng, PhD); water resources (M Sc); water resources engineering (M Eng, PhD).

McGill University, Faculty of Graduate and Postdoctoral Studies, Faculty of Engineering, Department of Mining and Materials Engineering, Montréal, QC H3A 2T5, Canada. Offers materials engineering (M Eng, PhD); mining engineering (M Eng, M Sc, PhD, Diploma).

McMaster University, School of Graduate Studies, Faculty of Engineering, Department of Materials Science and Engineering, Hamilton, ON L8S 4M2, Canada. Offers materials engineering (M Eng, MA Sc, PhD); materials science (M Eng, PhD). *Degree requirements:* For master's, thesis; for doctorate, comprehensive exam, thesis/dissertation. *Entrance requirements:* Additional exam requirements/recommendations for international students: Required—TOEFL (minimum score 550 paper-based; 213 computer-based). *Faculty research:* Localized corrosion of metals and alloys, electron microscopy, polymer synthesis and characterization, polymer reaction kinetics and engineering, polymer process modeling.

Michigan State University, The Graduate School, College of Engineering, Department of Chemical Engineering and Materials Science, East Lansing, MI 48824. Offers chemical engineering (MS, PhD); materials science and engineering (MS, PhD). *Entrance requirements:* Additional exam requirements/recommendations for international students: Required—TOEFL. Electronic applications accepted.

Michigan Technological University, Graduate School, College of Engineering, Department of Materials Science and Engineering, Houghton, MI 49931. Offers MS, PhD. Part-time programs available. *Faculty:* 18 full-time (2 women), 7 part-time/adjunct (0 women). *Students:* 27 full-time (7 women), 6 part-time (2 women); includes 3 minority (2 Asian, non-Hispanic/Latino; 1 Hispanic/Latino), 16 international. Average age 28. 205 applicants, 4% accepted, 6 enrolled. In 2011, 3 master's, 2 doctorates awarded. Terminal master's awarded for partial completion of doctoral program. *Degree requirements:* For master's, comprehensive exam (for some programs), thesis (for some programs); for doctorate, comprehensive exam, thesis/dissertation. *Entrance requirements:* For master's and doctorate, GRE (domestic students from ABET-accredited programs exempt), statement of purpose, official transcripts, 3 letters of recommendation. Additional exam requirements/recommendations for international students: Required—TOEFL (minimum score 79 iBT) or IELTS. *Application deadline:* For fall admission, 1/1 for domestic and international students. Applications are processed on a rolling basis. Electronic applications accepted. *Expenses:* Contact institution. *Financial support:* In 2011–12, 29 students received support, including 1 fellowship with full tuition reimbursement available (averaging $6,065 per year), 21 research assistantships with full tuition reimbursements available (averaging $6,065 per year), 1 teaching assistantship with full tuition reimbursement available (averaging $6,065 per year); career-related internships or fieldwork, Federal Work-Study, scholarships/grants, health care benefits, tuition waivers (partial), unspecified assistantships, and cooperative program also available. Financial award applicants required to submit FAFSA. *Faculty research:* Structure/property/processing relationships, microstructural characterization, alloy design, electronic/magnetic/photonic materials, materials and manufacturing processes. *Total annual research expenditures:* $1.3 million. *Unit head:* Dr. Stephen L. Kampe, Department Chair, 906-487-2630, Fax: 906-487-2934, E-mail: kampe@mtu.edu. *Application contact:* Beth R. Ruohonen, Departmental Coordinator, 906-487-4326, Fax: 906-487-2934, E-mail: beth@mtu.edu. Web site: http://www.mtu.edu/materials/.

New Jersey Institute of Technology, Office of Graduate Studies, Program in Materials Science and Engineering, Newark, NJ 07102. Offers MS, PhD. Part-time and evening/weekend programs available. *Students:* 29 full-time (5 women), 9 part-time (2 women); includes 10 minority (1 Black or African American, non-Hispanic/Latino; 7 Asian, non-Hispanic/Latino; 2 Hispanic/Latino), 22 international. Average age 30. 107 applicants, 79% accepted, 9 enrolled. In 2011, 4 doctorates awarded. Terminal master's awarded for partial completion of doctoral program. *Degree requirements:* For master's, thesis; for doctorate, thesis/dissertation. *Entrance requirements:* For master's, GRE General Test; for doctorate, GRE General Test, minimum graduate GPA of 3.5. Additional exam requirements/recommendations for international students: Required—TOEFL (minimum score 550 paper-based; 213 computer-based; 79 iBT). *Application deadline:* For fall admission, 6/1 priority date for domestic students, 5/1 for international students; for spring admission, 11/15 for domestic and international students. Applications are processed on a rolling basis. Application fee: $65. Electronic applications accepted. *Expenses:* Tuition, state resident: full-time $7980; part-time $867 per credit. Tuition, nonresident: full-time $11,336; part-time $1196 per credit. *Required fees:* $230 per credit. *Financial support:* Fellowships with full and partial tuition reimbursements, research assistantships with full and partial tuition reimbursements, teaching assistantships with full and partial tuition reimbursements, career-related internships or fieldwork, Federal Work-Study, institutionally sponsored loans, and unspecified assistantships available. Financial award application deadline: 1/15. *Unit head:* Dr. Marino Xanthos, Associate Provost, 973-596-3462, E-mail: marinos.xanthos@njit.edu. *Application contact:* Kathryn Kelly, Director of Admissions, 973-596-3300, Fax: 973-596-3461, E-mail: admissions@njit.edu.

New Mexico Institute of Mining and Technology, Graduate Studies, Department of Materials Engineering, Socorro, NM 87801. Offers MS, PhD. *Faculty:* 8 full-time (2 women), 6 part-time/adjunct (1 woman). *Students:* 14 full-time (3 women), 15 part-time (5 women); includes 10 minority (2 Black or African American, non-Hispanic/Latino; 2 Asian, non-Hispanic/Latino; 5 Hispanic/Latino; 1 Two or more races, non-Hispanic/Latino), 1 international. Average age 31. 19 applicants, 68% accepted, 6 enrolled. In 2011, 11 master's, 1 doctorate awarded. *Degree requirements:* For master's, thesis; for doctorate, thesis/dissertation. *Entrance requirements:* For master's, GRE General Test; for doctorate, GRE General Test, GRE Subject Test. Additional exam requirements/recommendations for international students: Required—TOEFL (minimum score 540 paper-based; 207 computer-based). *Application deadline:* For fall admission, 3/1 priority date for domestic students; for spring admission, 6/1 for domestic students. Applications are processed on a rolling basis. Application fee: $16 ($30 for international students). *Expenses:* Tuition, state resident: full-time $4849; part-time $269.41 per credit hour. Tuition, nonresident: full-time $16,041; part-time $891.15 per credit hour. *Required fees:* $622; $65 per credit hour. $20 per semester. Part-time tuition and fees vary according to course load. *Financial support:* In 2011–12, 5 research assistantships (averaging $19,131 per year), 5 teaching assistantships with full and partial tuition reimbursements (averaging $9,560 per year) were awarded; fellowships, Federal Work-Study, institutionally sponsored loans, and unspecified assistantships also available. Financial award application deadline: 3/1; financial award applicants required to submit CSS PROFILE or FAFSA. *Faculty research:* Thin films, ceramics, damage studies from radiation, corrosion shock. *Unit head:* Dr. Bhaskar Majumdar, Chair, 575-835-5152, E-mail: majumdar@nmt.edu. *Application contact:* Dr. Lorie Liebrock, Dean of Graduate Studies, 575-835-5513, Fax: 575-835-5476, E-mail: graduate@nmt.edu. Web site: http://www.nmt.edu/~mtls/.

North Carolina State University, Graduate School, College of Engineering, Department of Materials Science and Engineering, Raleigh, NC 27695. Offers MMSE, MS, PhD. PhD offered jointly with The University of North Carolina at Charlotte. *Degree requirements:* For master's, thesis; for doctorate, thesis/dissertation. Electronic applications accepted. *Faculty research:* Processing and properties of wide band gap semiconductors, ferroelectric thin-film materials, ductility of nanocrystalline materials, computational materials science, defects in silicon-based devices.

Northwestern University, McCormick School of Engineering and Applied Science, Department of Materials Science and Engineering, Evanston, IL 60208. Offers integrated computational materials engineering (Certificate); materials science and engineering (MS, PhD). Admissions and degrees offered through The Graduate School. Part-time programs available. *Faculty:* 25 full-time (6 women), 1 (woman) part-time/ adjunct. *Students:* 200 full-time (60 women), 5 part-time (1 woman); includes 37 minority (2 Black or African American, non-Hispanic/Latino; 24 Asian, non-Hispanic/Latino; 8 Hispanic/Latino; 3 Two or more races, non-Hispanic/Latino), 85 international. Average age 26. In 2011, 17 master's, 22 doctorates awarded. Terminal master's awarded for partial completion of doctoral program. *Degree requirements:* For master's, thesis, oral thesis defense; for doctorate, comprehensive exam, thesis/dissertation, oral defense of dissertation, preliminary evaluation, qualifying exam. *Entrance requirements:* For master's and doctorate, GRE General Test. Additional exam requirements/ recommendations for international students: Required—TOEFL (minimum score 577 paper-based, 233 computer-based; 90 iBT) or IELTS (minimum score 7). *Application deadline:* For fall admission, 12/31 for domestic and international students. Application fee: $75. Electronic applications accepted. *Financial support:* Fellowships with full tuition reimbursements, research assistantships with full tuition reimbursements, teaching assistantships with full tuition reimbursements, career-related internships or fieldwork, institutionally sponsored loans, health care benefits, and unspecified assistantships available. Financial award application deadline: 1/15; financial award applicants required to submit FAFSA. *Faculty research:* Biomaterials, cement, ceramics, composites, electrical properties, electron and ion microscopy, energy, materials design, materials processing, materials theory, mechanical properties, metals, molecular synthesis, nanomaterials, optical properties, phase transformation, polymers, scattering and diffraction, self-assembly, semiconductors, surfaces and interfaces, thin films. *Total annual research expenditures:* $23.5 million. *Unit head:* Dr. Michael Bedzyk, Chair, 847-491-3570, Fax: 847-491-7820, E-mail: bedzyk@northwestern.edu. *Application contact:* Dr. Chris Wolverton, Admissions Officer, 847-497-0593, Fax: 847-491-7820, E-mail: c-wolverton@northwestern.edu. Web site: http://www.matsci.northwestern.edu/.

The Ohio State University, Graduate School, College of Engineering, Department of Materials Science and Engineering, Columbus, OH 43210. Offers materials science and engineering (MS, PhD); welding engineering (MS, MWE, PhD). *Faculty:* 34. *Students:* 70 full-time (10 women), 45 part-time (13 women); includes 6 minority (3 Asian, non-Hispanic/Latino; 3 Hispanic/Latino), 56 international. Average age 27. In 2011, 14 master's, 10 doctorates awarded. *Degree requirements:* For master's, thesis; for doctorate, thesis/dissertation. *Entrance requirements:* For master's and doctorate, GRE (for graduates of foreign universities and holders of non-engineering degrees). Additional exam requirements/recommendations for international students: Required— Michigan English Language Assessment Battery (minimum score 82); Recommended—TOEFL (minimum score 600 paper-based; 250 computer-based; 79 iBT). *Application deadline:* For fall admission, 8/15 priority date for domestic students, 7/ 1 for international students; for winter admission, 12/1 priority date for domestic students, 11/1 for international students; for spring admission, 3/1 priority date for domestic students, 2/1 for international students. Applications are processed on a rolling basis. Application fee: $40 ($50 for international students). Electronic applications accepted. *Expenses:* Tuition, state resident: full-time $11,400. Tuition, nonresident: full-time $28,125. Tuition and fees vary according to course load, degree level, campus/ location and program. *Financial support:* In 2011–12, fellowships (averaging $43,000 per year), research assistantships (averaging $40,700 per year) were awarded; teaching assistantships, career-related internships or fieldwork, scholarships/grants, and unspecified assistantships also available. *Faculty research:* Computational materials modeling, biomaterials, metallurgy, ceramics, advanced alloys/composites. *Total annual research expenditures:* $10 million. *Unit head:* Rudolph G. Buchheit, Chair, 614-292-6085, Fax: 614-292-1357, E-mail: buchheit.8@osu.edu. *Application contact:* Mark Cooper, Graduate Studies Coordinator, 614-292-7280, Fax: 614-292-1357, E-mail: cooper.73@osu.edu. Web site: http://mse.osu.edu/.

Penn State University Park, Graduate School, College of Earth and Mineral Sciences, Department of Materials Science and Engineering, State College, University Park, PA 16802-1503. Offers MS, PhD. *Unit head:* Dr. William E. Easterling, III, Dean, 814-865-6546, Fax: 814-863-7708, E-mail: wee2@psu.edu. *Application contact:* Cynthia E. Nicosia, Director of Graduate Enrollment Services, 814-865-1834, E-mail: cey1@ psu.edu. Web site: http://www.matse.psu.edu/.

Purdue University, College of Engineering, School of Materials Engineering, West Lafayette, IN 47907. Offers MSMSE, PhD. Part-time programs available. *Entrance requirements:* For master's and doctorate, minimum GPA of 3.0. Additional exam requirements/recommendations for international students: Required—TOEFL (minimum score 550 paper-based; 213 computer-based; 77 iBT); Recommended—TWE. Electronic applications accepted. *Faculty research:* Electronic behavior, mechanical behavior, thermodynamics, kinetics, phase transformations.

Rensselaer Polytechnic Institute, Graduate School, School of Engineering, Program in Materials Science and Engineering, Troy, NY 12180. Offers ceramics and glass science (M Eng, MS, PhD); composites (M Eng, MS, PhD); electronic materials (M Eng, MS, PhD); metallurgy (M Eng, MS, PhD); polymers (M Eng, MS, PhD). Part-time programs available. Terminal master's awarded for partial completion of doctoral program. *Degree requirements:* For master's, thesis; for doctorate, comprehensive exam, thesis/dissertation. *Entrance requirements:* For master's and doctorate, GRE. Additional exam requirements/recommendations for international students: Required— TOEFL (minimum score 570 paper-based; 230 computer-based; 100 iBT). Electronic applications accepted. *Faculty research:* Materials processing, nanostructural materials, materials for microelectronics, composite materials, computational materials.

Rochester Institute of Technology, Graduate Enrollment Services, College of Science, Center for Materials Science and Engineering, Rochester, NY 14623-5603. Offers MS. Part-time and evening/weekend programs available. *Students:* 16 full-time (4 women), 5 part-time (1 woman); includes 2 minority (both Asian, non-Hispanic/Latino), 9 international. Average age 26. 27 applicants, 70% accepted, 7 enrolled. In 2011, 8 degrees awarded. *Degree requirements:* For master's, thesis or project. *Entrance requirements:* For master's, GRE (recommended), minimum GPA of 3.0. Additional exam requirements/recommendations for international students: Required—TOEFL (minimum score 575 paper-based; 233 computer-based; 90 iBT) or IELTS (minimum score 6.5). *Application deadline:* For fall admission, 2/15 priority date for domestic students, 2/15 for international students; for winter admission, 11/1 for domestic students, 10/1 for international students; for spring admission, 2/1 for domestic students, 1/1 for international students. Applications are processed on a rolling basis. Application fee: $50. Electronic applications accepted. *Expenses: Tuition:* Full-time $34,659; part-

time $963 per credit hour. *Required fees:* $228; $76 per quarter. *Financial support:* Research assistantships with partial tuition reimbursements, teaching assistantships with partial tuition reimbursements, career-related internships or fieldwork, scholarships/ grants, tuition waivers (partial), and unspecified assistantships available. Support available to part-time students. Financial award application deadline: 7/29; financial award applicants required to submit FAFSA. *Faculty research:* VUV modification of polymers, stress and morphology of sputtered copper films, MRI applications to materials problems. *Unit head:* Dr. K. S. V. Santhanam, Graduate Program Director, 585-475-2920, Fax: 585-475-2800, E-mail: ksssch@rit.edu. *Application contact:* Diane Ellison, Assistant Vice President, Graduate Enrollment Services, 585-475-2229, Fax: 585-475-7164, E-mail: gradinfo@rit.edu. Web site: http://www.rit.edu/cos/cmse/.

Rutgers, The State University of New Jersey, New Brunswick, Graduate School-New Brunswick, Program in Materials Science and Engineering, Piscataway, NJ 08854-8097. Offers MS, PhD. Part-time programs available. *Degree requirements:* For master's, thesis; for doctorate, comprehensive exam, thesis/dissertation. *Entrance requirements:* For master's and doctorate, GRE General Test. Additional exam requirements/recommendations for international students: Recommended—TOEFL. Electronic applications accepted. *Faculty research:* Ceramic processing, nanostructured materials, electrical and structural ceramics, fiber optics.

San Jose State University, Graduate Studies and Research, Charles W. Davidson College of Engineering, Department of Chemical and Materials Engineering, Program in Materials Engineering, San Jose, CA 95192-0001. Offers MS. Part-time programs available. *Degree requirements:* For master's, thesis or alternative. *Entrance requirements:* For master's, GRE. Additional exam requirements/recommendations for international students: Required—TOEFL. Electronic applications accepted. *Faculty research:* Electronic materials, thin films, electron microscopy, fiber composites, polymeric materials.

Santa Clara University, School of Engineering, Program in Mechanical Engineering, Santa Clara, CA 95053. Offers controls (Certificate); dynamics (Certificate); materials engineering (Certificate); mechanical design analysis (Certificate); mechanical engineering (MS, PhD, Engineer); mechatronics systems engineering (Certificate); technology jump-start (Certificate); thermofluids (Certificate). Part-time and evening/ weekend programs available. *Students:* 36 full-time (5 women), 68 part-time (11 women); includes 42 minority (33 Asian, non-Hispanic/Latino; 9 Hispanic/Latino), 16 international. Average age 27. 109 applicants, 56% accepted, 36 enrolled. In 2011, 33 master's, 1 doctorate, 1 other advanced degree awarded. *Degree requirements:* For master's, thesis (for some programs); for doctorate, thesis/dissertation; for other advanced degree, thesis. *Entrance requirements:* For master's, GRE, transcript; for doctorate, GRE, master's degree or equivalent; for other advanced degree, master's degree, published paper. Additional exam requirements/recommendations for international students: Required—TOEFL (minimum score 550 paper-based; 213 computer-based; 79 iBT). *Application deadline:* For fall admission, 8/12 for domestic students, 7/15 for international students; for winter admission, 10/28 for domestic students, 9/23 for international students; for spring admission, 2/25 for domestic students, 1/21 for international students. Applications are processed on a rolling basis. Application fee: $60. Electronic applications accepted. *Expenses:* Contact institution. *Financial support:* Research assistantships and teaching assistantships available. Financial award application deadline: 3/2; financial award applicants required to submit FAFSA. *Faculty research:* Development of small satellite design, tests and operations technology. *Unit head:* Dr. Alex Zecevic, Associate Dean for Graduate Studies, 408-554-2394, E-mail: azecevic@scu.edu. *Application contact:* Stacey Tinker, Director of Admissions, Graduate Engineering, 408-554-4748, Fax: 408-554-4323, E-mail: stinker@scu.edu.

South Dakota School of Mines and Technology, Graduate Division, Doctoral Program in Materials Engineering and Science, Rapid City, SD 57701-3995. Offers PhD. Part-time programs available. *Degree requirements:* For doctorate, thesis/dissertation. *Entrance requirements:* For doctorate, GRE General Test, minimum graduate GPA of 3.0, 3 letters of recommendation. Additional exam requirements/recommendations for international students: Required—TOEFL, TWE. Electronic applications accepted. *Faculty research:* Thermophysical properties of solids, development of multiphase materials and composites, concrete technology, electronic polymer materials.

South Dakota School of Mines and Technology, Graduate Division, Master's Program in Materials Engineering and Science, Rapid City, SD 57701-3995. Offers MS. *Entrance requirements:* For master's, GRE General Test. Additional exam requirements/ recommendations for international students: Required—TOEFL, TWE. Electronic applications accepted.

Stanford University, School of Engineering, Department of Materials Science and Engineering, Stanford, CA 94305-9991. Offers MS, PhD, Eng. Terminal master's awarded for partial completion of doctoral program. *Degree requirements:* For doctorate, thesis/dissertation; for Eng, thesis. *Entrance requirements:* For master's, doctorate, and Eng, GRE General Test. Additional exam requirements/recommendations for international students: Required—TOEFL. Electronic applications accepted. *Expenses: Tuition:* Full-time $40,050; part-time $890 per credit.

State University of New York at Binghamton, Graduate School, Thomas J. Watson School of Engineering and Applied Science and School of Arts and Sciences, Materials Science and Engineering Program, Binghamton, NY 13902-6000. Offers MS, PhD. *Faculty:* 3 full-time (0 women). *Students:* 16 full-time (8 women), 26 part-time (8 women); includes 1 minority (Native Hawaiian or other Pacific Islander, non-Hispanic/ Latino), 34 international. Average age 29. 23 applicants, 30% accepted, 6 enrolled. In 2011, 3 master's, 7 doctorates awarded. Application fee: $60. *Financial support:* In 2011–12, 27 students received support, including 18 research assistantships with full tuition reimbursements available (averaging $16,500 per year), 8 teaching assistantships with full tuition reimbursements available (averaging $16,500 per year); career-related internships or fieldwork, Federal Work-Study, institutionally sponsored loans, scholarships/grants, health care benefits, tuition waivers (full and partial), and unspecified assistantships also available. Financial award application deadline: 2/15; financial award applicants required to submit FAFSA. *Unit head:* Dr. Stanley Whittingham, Director, 607-777-4623, E-mail: stanwhit@binghamton.edu. *Application contact:* Catherine Smith, Recruiting and Admissions Coordinator, 607-777-2151, Fax: 607-777-2501, E-mail: cmsmith@binghamton.edu. Web site: http:// materials.binghamton.edu/materials/.

Stevens Institute of Technology, Graduate School, Charles V. Schaefer Jr. School of Engineering, Department of Chemical Engineering and Materials Science, Program in Materials Science, Hoboken, NJ 07030. Offers M Eng, PhD.

Stony Brook University, State University of New York, Graduate School, College of Engineering and Applied Sciences, Department of Materials Science and Engineering,

Stony Brook, NY 11794. Offers MS, PhD. *Degree requirements:* For master's, thesis or alternative; for doctorate, comprehensive exam, thesis/dissertation. *Entrance requirements:* For master's and doctorate, GRE General Test, minimum undergraduate GPA of 3.0. Additional exam requirements/recommendations for international students: Required—TOEFL. *Faculty research:* Electronic materials, biomaterials, synchrotron topography.

Texas A&M University, College of Engineering, Zachry Department of Civil Engineering, College Station, TX 77843. Offers coastal and ocean engineering (M Eng, MS, D Eng, PhD); construction engineering and management (M Eng, MS, D Eng, PhD); environmental engineering (M Eng, MS, D Eng, PhD); geotechnical engineering (M Eng, MS, D Eng, PhD); materials engineering (M Eng, MS, D Eng, PhD); structural engineering (M Eng, MS, D Eng, PhD); transportation engineering (M Eng, MS, D Eng, PhD); water resources engineering (M Eng, MS, D Eng, PhD). Part-time programs available. *Faculty:* 57. *Students:* 361 full-time (76 women), 46 part-time (8 women); includes 41 minority (3 Black or African American, non-Hispanic/Latino; 16 Asian, non-Hispanic/Latino; 21 Hispanic/Latino; 1 Two or more races, non-Hispanic/Latino), 247 international. Average age 29. In 2011, 123 master's, 27 doctorates awarded. *Degree requirements:* For master's, thesis (MS); for doctorate, dissertation (PhD), internship (D Eng). *Entrance requirements:* For master's and doctorate, GRE General Test. Additional exam requirements/recommendations for international students: Required—TOEFL. *Application deadline:* Applications are processed on a rolling basis. Application fee: $50 ($75 for international students). Electronic applications accepted. *Expenses:* Tuition, state resident: full-time $5437; part-time $226.55 per credit hour. Tuition, nonresident: full-time $12,949; part-time $539.55 per credit hour. *Required fees:* $2741. *Financial support:* In 2011–12, fellowships (averaging $4,500 per year), research assistantships (averaging $14,000 per year), teaching assistantships (averaging $14,400 per year) were awarded; career-related internships or fieldwork and institutionally sponsored loans also available. Financial award application deadline: 4/15; financial award applicants required to submit FAFSA. *Unit head:* Dr. John Niedzwecki, Head, 979-845-3858, E-mail: j-niedzwecki@tamu.edu. *Application contact:* Graduate Advisor, 979-845-7435, Fax: 979-845-6156, E-mail: info@civil.tamu.edu. Web site: https://www.civil.tamu.edu/.

Texas State University–San Marcos, Graduate School, College of Science and Engineering, Ingram School of Engineering, Program in Materials Science, Engineering, and Commercialization, San Marcos, TX 78666. Offers PhD. *Degree requirements:* For doctorate, comprehensive exam, thesis/dissertation. *Entrance requirements:* For doctorate, GRE (preferred minimum score of 1150 verbal and quantitative combined), two degrees with one advanced with minimum GPA of 3.5 in graduate work; statement of history and goals; 3 letters outlining skills and potential in the MSEC field, current curriculum vitae or resume, interview with core doctoral faculty conducted either by phone, Internet or face-to-face. Additional exam requirements/recommendations for international students: Required—TOEFL (minimum score 550 paper-based; 78 iBT). *Application deadline:* For fall admission, 6/15 for domestic students, 6/1 for international students; for spring admission, 11/30 for domestic students, 10/1 for international students. Application fee: $40 ($90 for international students). Electronic applications accepted. *Expenses:* Tuition, state resident: full-time $6408; part-time $3204 per semester. Tuition, nonresident: full-time $14,832; part-time $7416 per semester. *Required fees:* $1824; $912 per semester. Tuition and fees vary according to course load. *Unit head:* Dr. Thomas Myers, Director, 512-245-1839, E-mail: tm33@txstate.edu. *Application contact:* Dr. J. Michael Willoughby, Dean of Graduate School, 512-245-2581, Fax: 512-245-8365, E-mail: gradcollege@txstate.edu.

Tuskegee University, Graduate Programs, College of Engineering, Architecture and Physical Sciences, Program in Material Science and Engineering, Tuskegee, AL 36088. Offers PhD. *Students:* 12 full-time (4 women), 1 part-time (0 women); includes 9 minority (all Black or African American, non-Hispanic/Latino), 2 international. Average age 30. 5 applicants, 20% accepted, 1 enrolled. *Entrance requirements:* Additional exam requirements/recommendations for international students: Required—TOEFL (minimum score 500 paper-based; 69 computer-based). *Application deadline:* For fall admission, 7/15 for domestic students. Applications are processed on a rolling basis. Application fee: $25 ($35 for international students). *Expenses: Tuition:* Full-time $17,070; part-time $705 per credit hour. *Financial support:* Application deadline: 4/15. *Unit head:* Dr. Shaik Jeelani, Head, 334-727-8375. *Application contact:* Dr. Robert L. Laney, Jr., Vice President/Director of Admissions and Enrollment Management, 334-727-8580, Fax: 334-727-5750, E-mail: planey@tuskegee.edu.

The University of Alabama, Graduate School, College of Engineering, Department of Metallurgical and Materials Engineering, Tuscaloosa, AL 35487. Offers MS Met E, PhD. PhD offered jointly with The University of Alabama at Birmingham. *Faculty:* 9 full-time (2 women). *Students:* 23 full-time (2 women), 3 part-time (1 woman); includes 2 minority (1 Black or African American, non-Hispanic/Latino; 1 Asian, non-Hispanic/Latino), 13 international. Average age 26. 23 applicants, 57% accepted, 7 enrolled. In 2011, 8 master's, 1 doctorate awarded. *Median time to degree:* Of those who began their doctoral program in fall 2003, 100% received their degree in 8 years or less. *Degree requirements:* For master's, thesis or alternative; for doctorate, thesis/dissertation. *Entrance requirements:* For master's, GRE General Test, minimum GPA of 3.0 in last 60 hours; for doctorate, GRE General Test, minimum graduate GPA of 3.0, graduate degree. Additional exam requirements/recommendations for international students: Required—TOEFL (minimum score 550 paper-based; 213 computer-based). *Application deadline:* For fall admission, 7/1 priority date for domestic students. Applications are processed on a rolling basis. Application fee: $50 ($60 for international students). Electronic applications accepted. *Expenses:* Tuition, state resident: full-time $8600. Tuition, nonresident: full-time $21,900. *Financial support:* In 2011–12, 3 fellowships (averaging $15,000 per year), 14 research assistantships (averaging $14,700 per year), 6 teaching assistantships (averaging $12,250 per year) were awarded; Federal Work-Study and unspecified assistantships also available. *Faculty research:* Thermodynamics, molten metals processing, casting and solidification, mechanical properties of materials, thin films and nanostructures, electrochemistry, corrosion and alloy development. *Total annual research expenditures:* $1.6 million. *Unit head:* Dr. Ramana G. Reddy, Head/Professor, 205-348-4246, Fax: 205-348-2164. *Application contact:* Dr. Su Gupta, Associate Professor, 205-348-4272, Fax: 205-348-2164, E-mail: sgupta@eng.ua.edu. Web site: http://www.eng.ua.edu/~mtedept/.

The University of Alabama at Birmingham, School of Engineering, Program in Materials Engineering, Birmingham, AL 35294. Offers MS Mt E, PhD. PhD offered jointly with The University of Alabama (Tuscaloosa). *Degree requirements:* For master's, comprehensive exam, project/thesis; for doctorate, comprehensive exam, thesis/dissertation. *Entrance requirements:* For master's and doctorate, GRE General Test. *Application deadline:* Applications are processed on a rolling basis. Application fee: $35 ($60 for international students). Electronic applications accepted. *Expenses:* Tuition, state resident: full-time $5922; part-time $309 per hour. Tuition, nonresident: full-time $13,428; part-time $726 per hour. Tuition and fees vary according to program. *Financial support:* Fellowships with full and partial tuition reimbursements, research assistantships with full tuition reimbursements, career-related internships or fieldwork, Federal Work-Study, and institutionally sponsored loans available. Support available to part-time students. *Faculty research:* Casting metallurgy, microgravity solidification, thin film techniques, ceramics/glass processing, biomedical materials processing. *Unit head:* Dr. J. Barry Andrews, Chair, 205-934-8460, Fax: 205-934-8485, E-mail: barry@uab.edu. *Application contact:* Julie Bryant, Director of Graduate Admissions, 205-934-8227, Fax: 205-934-8413, E-mail: jbryant@uab.edu.

Web site: http://www.uab.edu/engineering/departments-research/mse/grad#Master%20of%20Science%20in%20Civil%20Engineering%20%28M.S.C.E.%29%20Program%20Requirement.

University of Alberta, Faculty of Graduate Studies and Research, Department of Chemical and Materials Engineering, Edmonton, AB T6G 2E1, Canada. Offers chemical engineering (M Eng, M Sc, PhD); materials engineering (M Eng, M Sc, PhD); process control (M Eng, M Sc, PhD); welding (M Eng). Part-time programs available. Postbaccalaureate distance learning degree programs offered (minimal on-campus study). Terminal master's awarded for partial completion of doctoral program. *Degree requirements:* For master's, thesis; for doctorate, thesis/dissertation. *Faculty research:* Advanced materials and polymers, catalytic and reaction engineering, mineral processing, physical metallurgy, fluid mechanics.

The University of Arizona, College of Engineering, Department of Materials Science and Engineering, Tucson, AZ 85721. Offers MS, PhD. Part-time programs available. *Faculty:* 9 full-time (2 women), 3 part-time/adjunct (1 woman). *Students:* 39 full-time (13 women), 10 part-time (5 women); includes 12 minority (1 Black or African American, non-Hispanic/Latino; 2 Asian, non-Hispanic/Latino; 6 Hispanic/Latino; 3 Two or more races, non-Hispanic/Latino), 17 international. Average age 29. 82 applicants, 20% accepted, 6 enrolled. In 2011, 8 master's, 7 doctorates awarded. *Degree requirements:* For master's, thesis (for some programs); for doctorate, comprehensive exam, thesis/dissertation. *Entrance requirements:* For master's and doctorate, GRE General Test, 3 letters of recommendation, statement of purpose. Additional exam requirements/recommendations for international students: Required—TOEFL (minimum score 550 paper-based; 213 computer-based). *Application deadline:* Applications are processed on a rolling basis. Application fee: $75. Electronic applications accepted. *Expenses:* Tuition, state resident: full-time $10,840. Tuition, nonresident: full-time $25,802. *Financial support:* In 2011–12, 22 research assistantships with full tuition reimbursements (averaging $23,789 per year), 1 teaching assistantship with full tuition reimbursement (averaging $23,586 per year) were awarded; institutionally sponsored loans, scholarships/grants, health care benefits, tuition waivers (full), and unspecified assistantships also available. Financial award application deadline: 12/31. *Faculty research:* High-technology ceramics, optical materials, electronic materials, chemical metallurgy, science of materials. *Total annual research expenditures:* $1.9 million. *Unit head:* Dr. Pierre Deymier, Head, 520-621-6080, Fax: 520-621-8059, E-mail: deymier@email.arizona.edu. *Application contact:* Information Contact, 520-626-6762, Fax: 520-621-8059, E-mail: msed@email.arizona.edu. Web site: http://www.mse.arizona.edu/.

The University of British Columbia, Faculty of Applied Science, Department of Materials Engineering, Vancouver, BC V6T 1Z1, Canada. Offers materials and metallurgy (M Sc, PhD); metals and materials engineering (MA Sc, PhD). *Degree requirements:* For master's, comprehensive exam, thesis; for doctorate, comprehensive exam, thesis/dissertation. *Entrance requirements:* Additional exam requirements/recommendations for international students: Required—TOEFL (minimum score 560 paper-based; 220 computer-based; 83 iBT). Electronic applications accepted. *Faculty research:* Electroslag melting, mathematical modeling, solidification and hydrometallurgy.

University of California, Berkeley, Graduate Division, College of Engineering, Department of Materials Science and Engineering, Berkeley, CA 94720-1500. Offers engineering (M Eng, MS, D Eng, PhD); engineering science (M Eng, MS, PhD). *Degree requirements:* For master's, comprehensive exam or thesis (MS); for doctorate, comprehensive exam, thesis/dissertation, qualifying exam. *Entrance requirements:* For master's and doctorate, GRE General Test, minimum GPA of 3.0, 3 letters of recommendation. Additional exam requirements/recommendations for international students: Required—TOEFL (minimum score 230 computer-based). *Faculty research:* Ceramics, biomaterials, structural, electronic, magnetic and optical materials.

University of California, Davis, College of Engineering, Program in Materials Science and Engineering, Davis, CA 95616. Offers MS, PhD. Terminal master's awarded for partial completion of doctoral program. *Degree requirements:* For master's, comprehensive exam (for some programs), thesis (for some programs); for doctorate, comprehensive exam, thesis/dissertation. *Entrance requirements:* Additional exam requirements/recommendations for international students: Required—TOEFL (minimum score 550 paper-based; 213 computer-based).

University of California, Irvine, School of Engineering, Department of Chemical Engineering and Materials Science, Irvine, CA 92697. Offers chemical and biochemical engineering (MS, PhD); materials science and engineering (MS, PhD). Part-time programs available. *Students:* 84 full-time (29 women), 2 part-time (0 women); includes 23 minority (1 American Indian or Alaska Native, non-Hispanic/Latino; 19 Asian, non-Hispanic/Latino; 2 Hispanic/Latino; 1 Native Hawaiian or other Pacific Islander, non-Hispanic/Latino), 37 international. Average age 27. 343 applicants, 22% accepted, 22 enrolled. In 2011, 17 master's, 4 doctorates awarded. Terminal master's awarded for partial completion of doctoral program. *Degree requirements:* For doctorate, thesis/dissertation. *Entrance requirements:* For master's and doctorate, GRE General Test, minimum GPA of 3.0, 3 letters of recommendation. Additional exam requirements/recommendations for international students: Required—TOEFL (minimum score 550 paper-based; 213 computer-based). *Application deadline:* For fall admission, 1/15 priority date for domestic students, 1/15 for international students. Applications are processed on a rolling basis. Application fee: $80 ($100 for international students). Electronic applications accepted. *Financial support:* Fellowships with tuition reimbursements, research assistantships with full tuition reimbursements, teaching assistantships with tuition reimbursements, institutionally sponsored loans, traineeships, health care benefits, and unspecified assistantships available. Financial award application deadline: 3/1; financial award applicants required to submit FAFSA. *Faculty research:* Molecular biotechnology, nano-bio-materials, biophotonics, synthesis, superplasticity and mechanical behavior, characterization of advanced and nanostructural materials. *Unit head:* Prof. Albert Yee, Chair, 949-824-7320, Fax: 949-824-2541, E-mail: albert.yee@uci.edu. *Application contact:* Grace Hai-Chin Chau, Academic Program and Graduate Admission Coordinator, 949-824-3887, Fax: 949-824-2541, E-mail: chaug@uci.edu. Web site: http://www.eng.uci.edu/dept/chems.

Materials Engineering

University of California, Irvine, School of Engineering, Program in Materials Engineering and Manufacturing Technology, Irvine, CA 92697. Offers engineering (MS, PhD). Part-time programs available. *Students:* 14 full-time (5 women), 4 part-time (2 women); includes 4 minority (all Asian, non-Hispanic/Latino), 11 international. Average age 28. 12 applicants, 50% accepted, 4 enrolled. In 2011, 2 master's, 5 doctorates awarded. *Entrance requirements:* For master's and doctorate, GRE General Test, 3 letters of recommendation, minimum GPA of 3.0. Additional exam requirements/recommendations for international students: Required—TOEFL (minimum score 550 paper-based; 213 computer-based). *Application deadline:* For fall admission, 1/15 priority date for domestic students, 1/15 for international students. Applications are processed on a rolling basis. Application fee: $80 ($100 for international students). Electronic applications accepted. *Financial support:* Fellowships with tuition reimbursements, research assistantships with full tuition reimbursements, teaching assistantships with tuition reimbursements, institutionally sponsored loans, traineeships, health care benefits, and unspecified assistantships available. Financial award application deadline: 3/1; financial award applicants required to submit FAFSA. *Faculty research:* Advanced materials, microelectronic and photonic devices and packaging, biomedical devices, MEMS, thin film materials, nanotechnology. *Unit head:* Dr. Andrew Asher Shapiro, Associate Adjunct Professor, 949-393-7311, Fax: 949-824-5055, E-mail: aashapir@uci.edu. *Application contact:* Jean Harmony Bennett, Academic Counselor, 949-824-6475, Fax: 949-824-3440, E-mail: jean.bennett@uci.edu. Web site: http://www.eng.uci.edu/.

University of California, Los Angeles, Graduate Division, Henry Samueli School of Engineering and Applied Science, Department of Materials Science and Engineering, Los Angeles, CA 90095-1595. Offers MS, PhD. *Faculty:* 12 full-time (2 women), 2 part-time/adjunct (0 women). *Students:* 106 full-time (19 women); includes 20 minority (2 Black or African American, non-Hispanic/Latino; 13 Asian, non-Hispanic/Latino; 4 Hispanic/Latino; 1 Two or more races, non-Hispanic/Latino), 64 international. 220 applicants, 49% accepted, 31 enrolled. In 2011, 20 master's, 8 doctorates awarded. *Degree requirements:* For master's, comprehensive exam or thesis; for doctorate, thesis/dissertation, qualifying exams. *Entrance requirements:* For master's, GRE General Test, minimum GPA of 3.0; for doctorate, GRE General Test, minimum GPA of 3.25. Additional exam requirements/recommendations for international students: Required—TOEFL (minimum score 560 paper-based; 220 computer-based; 87 iBT). *Application deadline:* For fall admission, 12/15 for domestic and international students. Application fee: $80 ($100 for international students). Electronic applications accepted. *Financial support:* In 2011–12, 42 fellowships, 302 research assistantships, 33 teaching assistantships were awarded; Federal Work-Study, institutionally sponsored loans, and tuition waivers (full and partial) also available. Financial award application deadline: 1/15; financial award applicants required to submit FAFSA. *Faculty research:* Ceramics and ceramic processing, electronic and optical materials, structural materials. *Total annual research expenditures:* $7.2 million. *Unit head:* Dr. Jenn-Ming Yang, Chair, 310-825-2758, E-mail: jyang@seas.ucla.edu. *Application contact:* Patti Barrera, Student Affairs Officer, 310-825-8916, Fax: 310-206-7353, E-mail: patti@ea.ucla.edu. Web site: http://www.ms.ucla.edu.

University of California, Riverside, Graduate Division, Graduate Materials Science and Engineering Program, Riverside, CA 92521. Offers MS, PhD. *Entrance requirements:* For master's and doctorate, GRE. Additional exam requirements/recommendations for international students: Required—TOEFL (minimum score 550 paper-based; 213 computer-based; 80 iBT). Electronic applications accepted.

University of California, Santa Barbara, Graduate Division, College of Engineering, Department of Materials, Santa Barbara, CA 93106-5050. Offers MS, PhD, MS/PhD. *Faculty:* 27 full-time (2 women), 6 part-time/adjunct (0 women). *Students:* 132 full-time (26 women); includes 35 minority (2 Black or African American, non-Hispanic/Latino; 27 Asian, non-Hispanic/Latino; 2 Hispanic/Latino; 4 Two or more races, non-Hispanic/Latino), 22 international. Average age 26. 316 applicants, 24% accepted, 32 enrolled. In 2011, 6 master's, 6 doctorates awarded. Terminal master's awarded for partial completion of doctoral program. *Median time to degree:* Of those who began their doctoral program in fall 2003, 99% received their degree in 8 years or less. *Degree requirements:* For doctorate, comprehensive exam, thesis/dissertation. *Entrance requirements:* For master's and doctorate, GRE General Test. Additional exam requirements/recommendations for international students: Required—TOEFL (minimum score 600 paper-based; 100 iBT), IELTS (minimum score 7). *Application deadline:* For fall admission, 1/7 priority date for domestic students, 1/7 for international students; for winter admission, 11/1 priority date for domestic students, 11/1 for international students; for spring admission, 1/1 priority date for domestic students, 1/1 for international students. Application fee: $80 ($100 for international students). Electronic applications accepted. *Expenses:* Tuition, state resident: full-time $12,192. Tuition, nonresident: full-time $27,294. *Required fees:* $764.13. *Financial support:* In 2011–12, 12 students received support, including 45 fellowships with full and partial tuition reimbursements available (averaging $19,654 per year), 70 research assistantships with full and partial tuition reimbursements available (averaging $28,000 per year), 24 teaching assistantships with partial tuition reimbursements available (averaging $2,885 per year); career-related internships or fieldwork, scholarships/grants, tuition waivers (full), and unspecified assistantships also available. Financial award application deadline: 3/2; financial award applicants required to submit FAFSA. *Faculty research:* Electronic and photonic materials, inorganic materials, macromolecular and biomolecular materials, structural materials. *Unit head:* Dr. Tresa M. Pollock, Chair and Professor, 805-893-4362, Fax: 805-893-8486, E-mail: speck@mrl.ucsb.edu. *Application contact:* Oura Neak, Graduate Program Assistant, 805-893-4601, Fax: 805-893-8486, E-mail: mtrl-applications@engineering.ucsb.edu. Web site: http://www.materials.ucsb.edu/.

University of Central Florida, College of Engineering and Computer Science, Department of Mechanical, Materials, and Aerospace Engineering, Program in Materials Science and Engineering, Orlando, FL 32816. Offers MSMSE, PhD. *Students:* 46 full-time (10 women), 16 part-time (8 women); includes 9 minority (1 Black or African American, non-Hispanic/Latino; 1 American Indian or Alaska Native, non-Hispanic/Latino; 2 Asian, non-Hispanic/Latino; 5 Hispanic/Latino), 31 international. Average age 29. 53 applicants, 70% accepted, 17 enrolled. In 2011, 11 master's, 6 doctorates awarded. *Degree requirements:* For master's, thesis or alternative; for doctorate, thesis/dissertation, candidacy exam, departmental qualifying exam. *Application deadline:* For fall admission, 7/15 priority date for domestic students; for spring admission, 12/1 priority date for domestic students. Application fee: $30. Electronic applications accepted. *Expenses:* Tuition, state resident: part-time $277.08 per credit hour. Tuition, nonresident: part-time $277.08 per credit hour. Part-time tuition and fees vary according to degree level and program. *Financial support:* In 2011–12, 31 students received support, including 9 fellowships (averaging $1,900 per year), 27 research assistantships (averaging $10,500 per year), 5 teaching assistantships (averaging $8,900 per year). *Unit head:* Dr. Suhada Jayasuriya, Chair, 407-823-5792, Fax: 407-823-0208, E-mail: suhada@ucf.edu. *Application contact:* Barbara Rodriguez, Director, Admissions and Registration, 407-823-2766, Fax: 407-823-6442, E-mail: gradadmissions@ucf.edu. Web site: http://mmae.ucf.edu/.

University of Cincinnati, Graduate School, College of Engineering and Applied Science, Department of Chemical and Materials Engineering, Program in Materials Science and Engineering, Cincinnati, OH 45221. Offers MS, PhD. Evening/weekend programs available. *Degree requirements:* For master's, thesis optional; for doctorate, one foreign language, comprehensive exam, thesis/dissertation, oral English proficiency exam. *Entrance requirements:* For master's and doctorate, GRE General Test, BS in related field, minimum undergraduate GPA of 3.0. Additional exam requirements/recommendations for international students: Required—TOEFL. Electronic applications accepted. *Faculty research:* Polymer characterization, surface analysis, and adhesion; mechanical behavior of high-temperature materials; composites; electrochemistry of materials.

University of Connecticut, Graduate School, School of Engineering, Department of Metallurgy and Materials Engineering, Storrs, CT 06269. Offers MS, PhD. Terminal master's awarded for partial completion of doctoral program. *Degree requirements:* For master's, comprehensive exam, thesis or alternative; for doctorate, thesis/dissertation. *Entrance requirements:* For master's and doctorate, GRE General Test, GRE Subject Test. Additional exam requirements/recommendations for international students: Required—TOEFL (minimum score 550 paper-based; 213 computer-based). Electronic applications accepted. *Faculty research:* Microsegregation and coarsening, fatigue crack, electron-dislocation interaction.

University of Dayton, Department of Materials Engineering, Dayton, OH 45469-1300. Offers MS Mat E, DE, PhD. Part-time and evening/weekend programs available. *Faculty:* 6 full-time (0 women), 5 part-time/adjunct (0 women). *Students:* 58 full-time (17 women), 10 part-time (5 women); includes 9 minority (4 Black or African American, non-Hispanic/Latino; 1 Asian, non-Hispanic/Latino; 4 Hispanic/Latino), 30 international. Average age 29. 91 applicants, 65% accepted, 28 enrolled. In 2011, 17 master's, 1 doctorate awarded. *Degree requirements:* For master's, thesis optional; for doctorate, variable foreign language requirement, thesis/dissertation, departmental qualifying exam. *Entrance requirements:* Additional exam requirements/recommendations for international students: Required—TOEFL (minimum score 550 paper-based; 213 computer-based; 80 iBT). *Application deadline:* For fall admission, 8/1 for domestic students, 3/1 for international students; for winter admission, 7/1 for international students; for spring admission, 1/1 for international students. Applications are processed on a rolling basis. Application fee: $0 ($50 for international students). Electronic applications accepted. *Expenses:* *Tuition:* Full-time $8400; part-time $700 per credit hour. *Required fees:* $25 per semester. Tuition and fees vary according to degree level. *Financial support:* In 2011–12, 1 fellowship with full tuition reimbursement (averaging $27,500 per year), 10 research assistantships with full tuition reimbursements (averaging $19,055 per year) were awarded. Financial award applicants required to submit FAFSA. *Faculty research:* Ultra-fine microstructure by rapid hot-compaction of Armstrong-process titanium powder, diffusion during synthesis of titanium alloys by means of power metallurgy. *Total annual research expenditures:* $37,397. *Unit head:* Dr. Daniel Eylon, Director, 937-229-2679, E-mail: deylon@udayton.edu. *Application contact:* Dr. Daniel Eylon, Director, 937-229-2679, E-mail: deylon@udayton.edu.

University of Delaware, College of Engineering, Department of Materials Science and Engineering, Newark, DE 19716. Offers MMSE, PhD. Terminal master's awarded for partial completion of doctoral program. *Degree requirements:* For master's, thesis; for doctorate, thesis/dissertation. *Entrance requirements:* For master's and doctorate, GRE General Test, 3 letters of recommendation, minimum GPA of 3.2. Additional exam requirements/recommendations for international students: Required—TOEFL. Electronic applications accepted. *Faculty research:* Thin films and self assembly, drug delivery and tissue engineering, biomaterials and nanocomposites, semiconductor and oxide interfaces, electronic and magnetic materials.

University of Denver, School of Engineering and Computer Science, Department of Mechanical and Materials Engineering, Denver, CO 80208. Offers bioengineering (MS); engineering (MS, PhD); engineering/management (MS); interdisciplinary engineering (PhD); materials science (MS, PhD); mechanical engineering (MS, PhD); nanoscale science and engineering (MS, PhD). Part-time programs available. *Faculty:* 10 full-time (2 women), 1 part-time/adjunct (0 women). *Students:* 1 (woman) full-time, 25 part-time (5 women); includes 1 minority (Asian, non-Hispanic/Latino), 9 international. Average age 30. 69 applicants, 67% accepted, 11 enrolled. In 2011, 6 degrees awarded. Terminal master's awarded for partial completion of doctoral program. *Degree requirements:* For master's, thesis or alternative; for doctorate, comprehensive exam, thesis/dissertation. *Entrance requirements:* For master's, GRE General Test, essay/personal statement, three letters of recommendation; for doctorate, GRE General Test, essay/personal statement, three letters of recommendation, curriculum vitae. Additional exam requirements/recommendations for international students: Required—TOEFL (minimum score 550 paper-based; 80 iBT). *Application deadline:* Applications are processed on a rolling basis. Application fee: $60. Electronic applications accepted. *Financial support:* In 2011–12, 14 students received support, including 8 research assistantships with full and partial tuition reimbursements available (averaging $15,631 per year), 7 teaching assistantships with full and partial tuition reimbursements available (averaging $13,943 per year); Federal Work-Study, health care benefits, and unspecified assistantships also available. Financial award application deadline: 2/15; financial award applicants required to submit FAFSA. *Faculty research:* Aerosols, biomechanics, composite materials, photo optics, drug delivery. *Total annual research expenditures:* $818,288. *Unit head:* Dr. Matt Gordon, Chair, 303-871-3580, Fax: 303-871-4450, E-mail: matthew.gordon@du.edu. *Application contact:* Renee Carvalho, Assistant to the Chair, 303-871-2107, Fax: 303-871-4450, E-mail: renee.carvalho@du.edu. Web site: http://www.mme.du.edu.

University of Florida, Graduate School, College of Engineering, Department of Materials Science and Engineering, Gainesville, FL 32611. Offers ME, MS, PhD, Engr, JD/MS. Part-time programs available. Terminal master's awarded for partial completion of doctoral program. *Degree requirements:* For master's, comprehensive exam, thesis; for doctorate, comprehensive exam, thesis/dissertation; for Engr, thesis optional. *Entrance requirements:* For master's and doctorate, GRE General Test, minimum GPA of 3.0; for Engr, GRE General Test. Additional exam requirements/recommendations for international students: Required—TOEFL (minimum score 550 paper-based; 213 computer-based; 80 iBT), IELTS (minimum score 6). Electronic applications accepted. *Faculty research:* Polymeric system, biomaterials and biomimetics; inorganic and organic electronic materials; functional ceramic materials for energy systems and microelectronic applications; advanced metallic systems for aerospace, transportation and biological applications; nuclear materials.

University of Illinois at Chicago, Graduate College, College of Engineering, Department of Civil and Materials Engineering, Chicago, IL 60607-7128. Offers civil engineering (MS, PhD); materials engineering (MS, PhD). Evening/weekend programs available. *Degree requirements:* For master's, thesis (for some programs); for doctorate, thesis/dissertation, preliminary and qualifying exams. *Entrance requirements:* For master's and doctorate, GRE General Test, minimum GPA of 3.0. Additional exam requirements/recommendations for international students: Required—TOEFL. Electronic applications accepted. *Faculty research:* Transportation and geotechnical engineering, damage and anisotropic behavior, steel processing.

University of Illinois at Urbana–Champaign, Graduate College, College of Engineering, Department of Materials Science and Engineering, Champaign, IL 61820. Offers MS, PhD, MS/MBA, PhD/MBA. *Faculty:* 23 full-time (3 women), 4 part-time/adjunct (0 women). *Students:* 158 full-time (37 women), 10 part-time (2 women); includes 22 minority (1 American Indian or Alaska Native, non-Hispanic/Latino; 14 Asian, non-Hispanic/Latino; 3 Hispanic/Latino; 4 Two or more races, non-Hispanic/Latino), 90 international. 432 applicants, 25% accepted, 47 enrolled. In 2011, 11 master's, 28 doctorates awarded. *Entrance requirements:* For master's and doctorate, GRE, minimum GPA of 3.0. Additional exam requirements/recommendations for international students: Required—TOEFL (minimum score 613 paper-based; 257 computer-based; 103 iBT) or IELTS (minimum score 7). *Application deadline:* Applications are processed on a rolling basis. Application fee: $75 ($90 for international students). Electronic applications accepted. *Financial support:* In 2011–12, 20 fellowships, 153 research assistantships, 14 teaching assistantships were awarded; tuition waivers (full and partial) also available. *Unit head:* David G. Cahill, Head, 217-333-6753, Fax: 217-244-1631, E-mail: d-cahill@illinois.edu. *Application contact:* Michelle L. Malloch, Office Support Associate, 217-333-8517, Fax: 217-333-2736, E-mail: malloch@illinois.edu. Web site: http://www.matse.illinois.edu/.

University of Maryland, College Park, Academic Affairs, A. James Clark School of Engineering, Department of Continuing and Distance Learning in Engineering, College Park, MD 20742. Offers engineering (M Eng), including aerospace engineering, chemical engineering, civil engineering, electrical engineering, engineering, fire protection engineering, materials science and engineering, mechanical engineering, reliability engineering, systems engineering. *Faculty:* 3 full-time (0 women), 8 part-time/adjunct (0 women). *Students:* 75 full-time (24 women), 418 part-time (81 women); includes 154 minority (62 Black or African American, non-Hispanic/Latino; 64 Asian, non-Hispanic/Latino; 23 Hispanic/Latino; 5 Two or more races, non-Hispanic/Latino), 67 international. 447 applicants, 52% accepted, 154 enrolled. In 2011, 155 master's awarded. *Application deadline:* For fall admission, 8/15 for domestic students, 2/1 for international students; for spring admission, 1/10 for domestic students, 8/1 for international students. Applications are processed on a rolling basis. Application fee: $75. Electronic applications accepted. *Expenses: Tuition, area resident:* Part-time $525 per credit hour. Tuition, state resident: part-time $525 per credit hour. Tuition, nonresident: part-time $1131 per credit hour. *Required fees:* $386.31 per term. Tuition and fees vary according to program. *Financial support:* In 2011–12, 3 research assistantships (averaging $21,498 per year), 13 teaching assistantships (averaging $16,889 per year) were awarded. *Unit head:* Dr. Darryll Pines, Dean, 301-405-8539, E-mail: pines@umd.edu. *Application contact:* Dr. Charles A. Caramello, Dean of the Graduate School, 301-405-0358, Fax: 301-314-9305.

University of Maryland, College Park, Academic Affairs, A. James Clark School of Engineering, Department of Materials Science and Engineering, Materials Science and Engineering Program, College Park, MD 20742. Offers MS, PhD. Part-time and evening/weekend programs available. Postbaccalaureate distance learning degree programs offered. *Students:* 60 full-time (14 women), 5 part-time (2 women); includes 11 minority (3 Black or African American, non-Hispanic/Latino; 4 Asian, non-Hispanic/Latino; 3 Hispanic/Latino; 1 Two or more races, non-Hispanic/Latino), 19 international. 189 applicants, 22% accepted, 13 enrolled. In 2011, 6 master's, 6 doctorates awarded. *Degree requirements:* For master's, comprehensive exam, thesis optional, research paper; for doctorate, thesis/dissertation, oral exam. *Entrance requirements:* For master's and doctorate, GRE General Test, minimum B+ average in undergraduate course work. Additional exam requirements/recommendations for international students: Required—TOEFL. *Application deadline:* For fall admission, 1/15 for domestic and international students; for spring admission, 6/1 for domestic and international students. Applications are processed on a rolling basis. Application fee: $75. Electronic applications accepted. *Expenses: Tuition, area resident:* Part-time $525 per credit hour. Tuition, state resident: part-time $525 per credit hour. Tuition, nonresident: part-time $1131 per credit hour. *Required fees:* $386.31 per term. Tuition and fees vary according to program. *Financial support:* In 2011–12, 4 fellowships with full and partial tuition reimbursements (averaging $58,774 per year), 42 research assistantships (averaging $24,011 per year), 8 teaching assistantships (averaging $25,981 per year) were awarded. Financial award applicants required to submit FAFSA. *Unit head:* Robert Briber, Chair, 301-405-7313, E-mail: rbriber@umd.edu. *Application contact:* Dr. Charles A. Caramello, Dean of Graduate School, 301-405-0358, Fax: 301-314-9305, E-mail: ccaramel@umd.edu.

University of Maryland, College Park, Academic Affairs, A. James Clark School of Engineering, Department of Mechanical Engineering, College Park, MD 20742. Offers electronic packaging and reliability (MS, PhD); manufacturing and design (MS, PhD); mechanics and materials (MS, PhD); reliability engineering (M Eng, MS, PhD); thermal and fluid sciences (MS, PhD). Part-time and evening/weekend programs available. Postbaccalaureate distance learning degree programs offered. *Faculty:* 88 full-time (8 women), 20 part-time/adjunct. *Students:* 240 full-time (36 women), 72 part-time (6 women); includes 54 minority (14 Black or African American, non-Hispanic/Latino; 2 American Indian or Alaska Native, non-Hispanic/Latino; 23 Asian, non-Hispanic/Latino; 11 Hispanic/Latino; 4 Two or more races, non-Hispanic/Latino), 145 international. 457 applicants, 19% accepted, 61 enrolled. In 2011, 35 master's, 29 doctorates awarded. *Degree requirements:* For master's, thesis optional; for doctorate, thesis/dissertation, qualifying exam. *Entrance requirements:* For master's, GRE General Test, 3 letters of recommendation; for doctorate, GRE General Test, minimum GPA of 3.0. Additional exam requirements/recommendations for international students: Required—TOEFL. *Application deadline:* For fall admission, 5/15 for domestic students, 2/1 for international students; for spring admission, 10/15 for domestic students, 6/1 for international students. Applications are processed on a rolling basis. Application fee: $75. Electronic applications accepted. *Expenses: Tuition, area resident:* Part-time $525 per credit hour. Tuition, state resident: part-time $525 per credit hour. Tuition, nonresident: part-time $1131 per credit hour. *Required fees:* $386.31 per term. Tuition and fees vary according to program. *Financial support:* In 2011–12, 7 fellowships with full and partial tuition reimbursements (averaging $24,003 per year), 166 research assistantships (averaging $23,766 per year), 17 teaching assistantships (averaging $17,967 per year) were awarded; Federal Work-Study and scholarships/grants also available. Support available to part-time students. Financial award applicants required to submit FAFSA. *Faculty research:* Injection molding, electronic packaging, fluid mechanics, product engineering. *Total annual research expenditures:* $19 million. *Unit head:* Dr. B. Balachandran, Chair, 301-405-5309, E-mail: balab@umd.edu. *Application contact:* Dr. Charles A. Caramello, Graduate Director, 301-405-0358, Fax: 301-314-9305, E-mail: ccaramel@umd.edu.

University of Massachusetts Lowell, College of Engineering, Department of Plastics Engineering, Lowell, MA 01854-2881. Offers elastomers (Graduate Certificate); medical plastics design and manufacturing (Graduate Certificate); plastics design (Graduate Certificate); plastics engineering (MS Eng, D Eng, PhD), including coatings and adhesives (MS Eng), plastics materials (MS Eng), plastics processing (MS Eng), product design (MS Eng); plastics engineering fundamentals (Graduate Certificate); plastics materials (Graduate Certificate); plastics processing (Graduate Certificate); polymer science/plastics engineering (PhD). Part-time programs available. Terminal master's awarded for partial completion of doctoral program. *Degree requirements:* For master's, thesis optional; for doctorate, comprehensive exam, thesis/dissertation. *Entrance requirements:* For master's and doctorate, GRE General Test. Additional exam requirements/recommendations for international students: Required—TOEFL.

University of Michigan, College of Engineering, Department of Materials Science and Engineering, Ann Arbor, MI 48109. Offers MS, PhD. Part-time programs available. *Students:* 153 full-time (42 women), 3 part-time (0 women). 525 applicants, 25% accepted, 52 enrolled. In 2011, 12 master's, 19 doctorates awarded. *Degree requirements:* For master's, thesis, oral defense of thesis; for doctorate, thesis/dissertation, oral defense of dissertation, written exam. *Entrance requirements:* For master's, GRE General Test, minimum GPA of 3.0 in related field; for doctorate, GRE General Test, minimum GPA of 3.0 in related field, master's degree. Additional exam requirements/recommendations for international students: Required—TOEFL. *Application deadline:* Applications are processed on a rolling basis. Application fee: $65 ($75 for international students). Electronic applications accepted. *Financial support:* Fellowships, research assistantships, and teaching assistantships available. Financial award applicants required to submit FAFSA. *Faculty research:* Soft materials (polymers, biomaterials), computational materials science, structural materials, electronic and optical materials, nanocomposite materials. *Unit head:* Peter Green, Department Chair, 734-763-2445, Fax: 734-763-4788. *Application contact:* Renee Hilgendorf, Graduate Program Coordinator, 734-763-9790, Fax: 734-763-4788, E-mail: reneeh@umich.edu. Web site: http://msewww.engin.umich.edu/.

See Display on page 522 and Close-Up on page 533.

University of Minnesota, Twin Cities Campus, College of Science and Engineering, Department of Chemical Engineering and Materials Science, Program in Materials Science and Engineering, Minneapolis, MN 55455-0132. Offers M Mat SE, MS Mat SE, PhD. Part-time programs available. *Students:* 68 (13 women); includes 4 minority (3 Asian, non-Hispanic/Latino; 1 Hispanic/Latino), 35 international. Terminal master's awarded for partial completion of doctoral program. *Degree requirements:* For master's, thesis; for doctorate, thesis/dissertation. *Entrance requirements:* For master's and doctorate, GRE General Test. Additional exam requirements/recommendations for international students: Required—TOEFL. *Application deadline:* For fall admission, 1/1 for domestic and international students. Applications are processed on a rolling basis. Application fee: $75 ($95 for international students). Electronic applications accepted. *Financial support:* Fellowships, research assistantships, and teaching assistantships available. *Faculty research:* Ceramics and metals; coating processes and interfacial engineering; crystal growth and design; polymers; electronic, photonic and magnetic materials . *Application contact:* Graduate Programs in Chemical Engineering and Materials Science, E-mail: cemsgrad@umn.edu. Web site: http://www.cems.umn.edu/.

University of Nebraska–Lincoln, Graduate College, College of Engineering, Department of Mechanical and Materials Engineering, Lincoln, NE 68588. Offers engineering mechanics (MS, PhD); materials engineering (PhD); mechanical engineering (MS, PhD), including materials science engineering (MS), metallurgical engineering (MS). *Degree requirements:* For master's, thesis optional; for doctorate, comprehensive exam, thesis/dissertation. *Entrance requirements:* For master's and doctorate, GRE General Test. Additional exam requirements/recommendations for international students: Required—TOEFL (minimum score 550 paper-based; 213 computer-based). Electronic applications accepted. *Faculty research:* Robotics for planetary exploration, vehicle crashworthiness, transient heat conduction, laser beam/particle interactions.

University of Nevada, Las Vegas, Graduate College, Howard R. Hughes College of Engineering, Department of Mechanical Engineering, Las Vegas, NV 89154-4027. Offers aerospace engineering (MS); biomedical engineering (MS); materials and nuclear engineering (MS); mechanical engineering (MSE, PhD). Part-time programs available. *Faculty:* 14 full-time (0 women), 19 part-time/adjunct (1 woman). *Students:* 14 full-time (2 women), 40 part-time (8 women); includes 12 minority (1 Black or African American, non-Hispanic/Latino; 4 Asian, non-Hispanic/Latino; 3 Hispanic/Latino; 1 Native Hawaiian or other Pacific Islander, non-Hispanic/Latino; 3 Two or more races, non-Hispanic/Latino), 13 international. Average age 31. 31 applicants, 74% accepted, 8 enrolled. In 2011, 18 master's, 3 doctorates awarded. *Degree requirements:* For master's, comprehensive exam, thesis (for some programs), project; for doctorate, comprehensive exam, thesis/dissertation. *Entrance requirements:* For master's and doctorate, GRE General Test. Additional exam requirements/recommendations for international students: Required—TOEFL (minimum score 550 paper-based; 213 computer-based; 80 iBT), IELTS (minimum score 7). *Application deadline:* For fall admission, 8/1 priority date for domestic students, 5/1 for international students; for spring admission, 12/1 priority date for domestic students, 10/1 for international students. Applications are processed on a rolling basis. Application fee: $60 ($95 for international students). Electronic applications accepted. *Financial support:* In 2011–12, 29 students received support, including 14 research assistantships with partial tuition reimbursements available (averaging $9,415 per year), 15 teaching assistantships with partial tuition reimbursements available (averaging $10,934 per year); institutionally sponsored loans, scholarships/grants, health care benefits, and unspecified assistantships also available. Financial award application deadline: 3/1. *Faculty research:* Dynamics and control systems; energy systems including renewable and nuclear; computational fluid and solid mechanics; structures, materials and manufacturing; vibrations and acoustics. *Total annual research expenditures:* $2.9 million. *Unit head:* Dr. Woosoon Yim, Chair/Professor, 702-895-0956, Fax: 702-895-3936, E-mail: wy@me.unlv.edu. *Application contact:* Graduate College Admissions Evaluator, 702-895-3320, Fax: 702-895-4180, E-mail: gradcollege@unlv.edu. Web site: http://www.me.unlv.edu/.

University of Nevada, Reno, Graduate School, College of Engineering, Department of Chemical and Materials Engineering, Program in Materials Science and Engineering, Reno, NV 89557. Offers MS, PhD. Terminal master's awarded for partial completion of doctoral program. *Degree requirements:* For master's, thesis; for doctorate, one foreign language, thesis/dissertation. *Entrance requirements:* For master's, minimum GPA of 2.75; for doctorate, GRE, minimum GPA of 3.0. Additional exam requirements/

recommendations for international students: Required—TOEFL (minimum score 500 paper-based; 173 computer-based; 61 iBT), IELTS (minimum score 6). Electronic applications accepted. *Faculty research:* Hydrometallurgy, applied surface chemistry, mineral processing, mineral bioprocessing, ceramics.

University of Pennsylvania, School of Engineering and Applied Science, Department of Materials Science and Engineering, Philadelphia, PA 19104. Offers MSE, PhD, MSE/MBA. Part-time programs available. *Faculty:* 14 full-time (3 women), 2 part-time/adjunct (0 women). *Students:* 115 full-time (35 women), 11 part-time (5 women); includes 9 minority (8 Asian, non-Hispanic/Latino; 1 Hispanic/Latino), 94 international. 444 applicants, 30% accepted, 66 enrolled. In 2011, 32 master's, 6 doctorates awarded. Terminal master's awarded for partial completion of doctoral program. *Degree requirements:* For master's, thesis; for doctorate, thesis/dissertation. *Entrance requirements:* Additional exam requirements/recommendations for international students: Required—TOEFL. *Application deadline:* For fall admission, 6/1 priority date for domestic students, 5/1 for international students; for spring admission, 11/1 priority date for domestic students, 10/1 for international students. Applications are processed on a rolling basis. Application fee: $70. Electronic applications accepted. *Expenses: Tuition:* Full-time $26,660; part-time $4944 per course. *Required fees:* $2318; $291 per course. Tuition and fees vary according to course load, degree level and program. *Financial support:* Fellowships, research assistantships, teaching assistantships, institutionally sponsored loans, scholarships/grants, traineeships, health care benefits, and unspecified assistantships available. *Faculty research:* Advanced metallic, ceramic, and polymeric materials for device applications; micromechanics and structure of interfaces; thin film electronic materials; physics and chemistry of solids. *Unit head:* Eduardo D. Glandt, Dean, 215-898-7244, Fax: 215-573-2018, E-mail: seasdean@seas.upenn.edu. *Application contact:* Irene Clements, Graduate Coordinator, 215-898-8337, E-mail: ipc@lrsm.upenn.edu. Web site: http://www.mse.seas.upenn.edu/.

University of Southern California, Graduate School, Viterbi School of Engineering, Mork Family Department of Chemical Engineering and Materials Science, Los Angeles, CA 90089. Offers chemical engineering (MS, PhD, Engr); materials engineering (MS); materials science (MS, PhD, Engr); petroleum engineering (MS, PhD, Engr); smart oilfield technologies (MS, Graduate Certificate). Terminal master's awarded for partial completion of doctoral program. *Degree requirements:* For master's, thesis optional; for doctorate, thesis/dissertation. *Entrance requirements:* For master's and doctorate, GRE General Test. Additional exam requirements/recommendations for international students: Recommended—TOEFL. Electronic applications accepted. *Expenses:* Contact institution. *Faculty research:* Heterogeneous materials and porous media, statistical mechanics, molecular simulation, polymer science and engineering, advanced materials, reaction engineering and catalysis, membrane processes and separation, biochemical engineering, cell culture, bioreactor modeling, petroleum engineering.

The University of Tennessee, Graduate School, College of Engineering, Department of Materials Science and Engineering, Program in Materials Science and Engineering, Knoxville, TN 37996. Offers MS, PhD. *Faculty:* 29 full-time (3 women), 11 part-time/adjunct (3 women). *Students:* 76 full-time (17 women), 10 part-time (0 women); includes 9 minority (3 Black or African American, non-Hispanic/Latino; 2 Asian, non-Hispanic/Latino; 4 Hispanic/Latino), 53 international. Average age 29. 179 applicants, 14% accepted, 18 enrolled. In 2011, 7 master's, 9 doctorates awarded. *Degree requirements:* For master's, thesis or alternative; for doctorate, comprehensive exam, thesis/dissertation. *Entrance requirements:* For master's, GRE General Test (for MS students pursuing research thesis), minimum GPA of 2.7 (for U.S. degree holders), 3.0 (for international degree holders); 3 references; for doctorate, College requires GRE General Test for all PhD candidates, minimum GPA of 3.0 on previous graduate course work; 3 references. Additional exam requirements/recommendations for international students: Required—TOEFL (minimum score 550 paper-based; 213 computer-based). *Application deadline:* For fall admission, 2/1 priority date for domestic students, 2/1 for international students; for spring admission, 6/15 for domestic and international students. Applications are processed on a rolling basis. Application fee: $35. Electronic applications accepted. *Expenses:* Tuition, state resident: full-time $8332; part-time $464 per credit hour. Tuition, nonresident: full-time $25,174; part-time $1400 per credit hour. *Required fees:* $1162; $56 per credit hour. Tuition and fees vary according to program. *Financial support:* In 2011–12, 72 students received support, including 3 fellowships with full tuition reimbursements available (averaging $8,892 per year), 58 research assistantships with full tuition reimbursements available (averaging $20,400 per year), 6 teaching assistantships with full tuition reimbursements available (averaging $18,650 per year); career-related internships or fieldwork, Federal Work-Study, institutionally sponsored loans, health care benefits, and unspecified assistantships also available. Financial award application deadline: 2/1; financial award applicants required to submit FAFSA. *Faculty research:* Biomaterials; functional materials electronic, magnetic and optical; high temperature materials; mechanical behavior of materials; neutron materials science. *Unit head:* Dr. Kurt Sickafus, Head, 865-974-4858, Fax: 865-974-4115, E-mail: kurt@utk.edu. *Application contact:* Dr. Roberto S. Benson, Associate Head, 865-974-5347, Fax: 865-974-4115, E-mail: rbenson1@utk.edu. Web site: http://www.engr.utk.edu/mse.

The University of Tennessee Space Institute, Graduate Programs, Program in Materials Science and Engineering, Tullahoma, TN 37388-9700. Offers MS. *Faculty:* 3 full-time (0 women). *Students:* 1 full-time (0 women), 1 part-time (0 women), 1 international. 4 applicants, 25% accepted, 0 enrolled. In 2011, 3 degrees awarded. *Entrance requirements:* Additional exam requirements/recommendations for international students: Required—TOEFL (minimum score 550 paper-based; 213 computer-based; 80 iBT), IELTS (minimum score 6.5). *Application deadline:* For fall admission, 2/1 for international students; for spring admission, 6/15 for international students. Applications are processed on a rolling basis. Application fee: $35. Electronic applications accepted. *Financial support:* In 2011–12, 2 research assistantships with full tuition reimbursements (averaging $17,791 per year) were awarded; fellowships, career-related internships or fieldwork, Federal Work-Study, institutionally sponsored loans, health care benefits, tuition waivers (full and partial), and unspecified assistantships also available. *Unit head:* Dr. William Hofmeister, Degree Program Chairman, 931-393-7466, Fax: 931-393-7437, E-mail: whofmeis@utsi.edu. *Application contact:* Dee Merriman, Coordinator III, 931-393-7213, Fax: 931-393-7211, E-mail: dmerrima@utsi.edu. Web site: http://www.utsi.edu/academics/MSE/index.htm.

The University of Texas at Arlington, Graduate School, College of Engineering, Department of Materials Science and Engineering, Arlington, TX 76019. Offers M Engr, MS, PhD. *Faculty:* 8 full-time (0 women). *Students:* 45 full-time (13 women), 13 part-time (3 women); includes 4 minority (1 Black or African American, non-Hispanic/Latino; 3 Asian, non-Hispanic/Latino), 48 international. 33 applicants, 61% accepted, 11 enrolled. In 2011, 21 master's, 5 doctorates awarded. Terminal master's awarded for partial completion of doctoral program. *Degree requirements:* For master's, comprehensive exam (for some programs), thesis optional; for doctorate, comprehensive exam, thesis/

dissertation optional. *Entrance requirements:* For master's, GRE General Test, minimum GPA of 3.0; for doctorate, GRE General Test, minimum GPA of 3.5. Additional exam requirements/recommendations for international students: Required—TOEFL (minimum score 550 paper-based; 213 computer-based; 79 iBT), IELTS. *Application deadline:* For fall admission, 6/1 for domestic students, 4/1 for international students; for spring admission, 10/15 for domestic students, 9/15 for international students. Applications are processed on a rolling basis. Application fee: $35 ($50 for international students). *Financial support:* In 2011–12, 27 students received support, including 4 fellowships (averaging $1,000 per year), 10 research assistantships (averaging $16,000 per year), 13 teaching assistantships (averaging $16,000 per year); scholarships/grants and unspecified assistantships also available. Financial award application deadline: 6/1; financial award applicants required to submit FAFSA. *Faculty research:* Electronic materials, conductive polymer, composites biomaterial, structural materials. *Total annual research expenditures:* $400,000. *Unit head:* Dr. Efstathios I. Meletis, Chair, 817-272-2398 Ext. 2559, Fax: 817-272-2538, E-mail: meletis@uta.edu. *Application contact:* Dr. Choong-Un Kim, Graduate Adviser, 817-272-5497, Fax: 817-272-2538, E-mail: choongun@uta.edu. Web site: http://www.uta.edu/mse.

The University of Texas at Austin, Graduate School, Cockrell School of Engineering, Program in Materials Science and Engineering, Austin, TX 78712-1111. Offers MS, PhD. Part-time programs available. *Degree requirements:* For master's, thesis (for some programs); for doctorate, thesis/dissertation. *Entrance requirements:* For master's and doctorate, GRE General Test. Additional exam requirements/recommendations for international students: Required—TOEFL (minimum score 550 paper-based; 213 computer-based). *Application deadline:* For fall admission, 1/2 priority date for domestic students, 1/2 for international students; for spring admission, 10/1 for domestic and international students. Applications are processed on a rolling basis. Application fee: $50 ($75 for international students). Electronic applications accepted. *Financial support:* Fellowships with full tuition reimbursements, research assistantships with full tuition reimbursements, teaching assistantships with full tuition reimbursements, career-related internships or fieldwork, and institutionally sponsored loans available. Financial award application deadline: 1/1; financial award applicants required to submit FAFSA. *Unit head:* Donald R. Paul, Director, Texas Materials Institute, 512-471-5392, Fax: 512-471-0542, E-mail: drp@che.utexas.edu. *Application contact:* Rebecca Christian, Graduate Coordinator, 512-471-1504, Fax: 512-475-8482, E-mail: rjchristian@mail.utexas.edu. Web site: http://www.tmi.utexas.edu.

The University of Texas at Dallas, Erik Jonsson School of Engineering and Computer Science, Department of Materials Science and Engineering, Richardson, TX 75080. Offers MS, PhD. Part-time and evening/weekend programs available. *Faculty:* 14 full-time (3 women), 1 part-time/adjunct (0 women). *Students:* 58 full-time (14 women), 9 part-time (3 women); includes 11 minority (2 Black or African American, non-Hispanic/Latino; 2 Asian, non-Hispanic/Latino; 6 Hispanic/Latino; 1 Two or more races, non-Hispanic/Latino), 43 international. Average age 29. 94 applicants, 40% accepted, 17 enrolled. In 2011, 9 master's, 3 doctorates awarded. *Degree requirements:* For master's, thesis or major design project; for doctorate, thesis/dissertation. *Entrance requirements:* For master's, GRE General Test, minimum GPA of 3.0 in related bachelor's degree; for doctorate, GRE General Test, minimum GPA of 3.5. Additional exam requirements/recommendations for international students: Required—TOEFL (minimum score 550 paper-based; 215 computer-based). *Application deadline:* For fall admission, 7/15 for domestic students, 5/1 for international students; for spring admission, 11/15 for domestic students, 9/1 for international students. Applications are processed on a rolling basis. Application fee: $50 ($100 for international students). Electronic applications accepted. *Expenses:* Tuition, state resident: full-time $11,170; part-time $620.56 per credit hour. Tuition, nonresident: full-time $20,212; part-time $1122.89 per credit hour. *Financial support:* In 2011–12, 49 students received support, including 1 fellowship (averaging $30,000 per year), 54 research assistantships with partial tuition reimbursements available (averaging $23,638 per year), 1 teaching assistantship with partial tuition reimbursement available (averaging $15,300 per year); career-related internships or fieldwork, Federal Work-Study, institutionally sponsored loans, scholarships/grants, and unspecified assistantships also available. Support available to part-time students. Financial award application deadline: 4/30; financial award applicants required to submit FAFSA. *Faculty research:* Graphene-based semiconducting materials, neuro-inspired computational paradigms, electronic materials with emphasis on dielectrics, energy harvesting (photovoltaics, Li-ion batteries), biosensors and H2 storage materials. *Unit head:* Dr. Yves Chabal, Department Head, 972-883-5751, Fax: 972-883-5725, E-mail: chabal@utdallas.edu. *Application contact:* Diane Griffith, Graduate Admissions Coordinator, 972-883-6748, Fax: 972-883-5725, E-mail: gradecs@utdallas.edu. Web site: http://mse.utdallas.edu/.

The University of Texas at El Paso, Graduate School, College of Engineering, Department of Metallurgical and Materials Engineering, El Paso, TX 79968-0001. Offers materials science and engineering (PhD); metallurgical and materials engineering (MS). Part-time and evening/weekend programs available. *Students:* 16 (8 women); includes 12 minority (all Hispanic/Latino), 2 international. Average age 34. 10 applicants, 80% accepted, 5 enrolled. *Degree requirements:* For master's, thesis. *Entrance requirements:* For master's, GRE General Test. Additional exam requirements/recommendations for international students: Required—TOEFL. *Application deadline:* For fall admission, 7/1 priority date for domestic students, 3/1 for international students; for spring admission, 11/1 priority date for domestic students, 9/1 for international students. Applications are processed on a rolling basis. Application fee: $15 ($65 for international students). Electronic applications accepted. *Financial support:* In 2011–12, research assistantships with partial tuition reimbursements (averaging $21,125 per year), teaching assistantships with partial tuition reimbursements (averaging $16,900 per year) were awarded; fellowships with partial tuition reimbursements, career-related internships or fieldwork, Federal Work-Study, institutionally sponsored loans, scholarships/grants, and tuition waivers (partial) also available. Financial award application deadline: 3/15; financial award applicants required to submit FAFSA. *Unit head:* Dr. Lawrence E. Murr, Chairperson, 915-747-5468, Fax: 915-747-8036, E-mail: fekberg@utep.edu. *Application contact:* Dr. Benjamin Flores, Interim Dean of the Graduate School, 915-747-5491, Fax: 915-747-5788, E-mail: bflores@utep.edu.

The University of Texas at El Paso, Graduate School, Interdisciplinary Program in Materials Science and Engineering, El Paso, TX 79968-0001. Offers PhD. Part-time and evening/weekend programs available. *Students:* 26 (13 women); includes 12 minority (1 Black or African American, non-Hispanic/Latino; 1 Asian, non-Hispanic/Latino; 9 Hispanic/Latino; 1 Two or more races, non-Hispanic/Latino), 13 international. Average age 34. In 2011, 4 doctorates awarded. *Degree requirements:* For doctorate, thesis/dissertation. *Entrance requirements:* For doctorate, GRE, letters of recommendation. Additional exam requirements/recommendations for international students: Required—TOEFL; Recommended—IELTS. *Application deadline:* For fall admission, 8/1 priority date for domestic students, 3/1 for international students; for spring admission, 11/1 priority date for domestic students, 9/3 for international students. Applications are processed on a rolling basis. Application fee: $45 ($80 for international students). Electronic applications accepted. *Financial support:* In 2011–12, research assistantships with partial tuition reimbursements (averaging $22,500 per year), teaching assistantships with partial tuition reimbursements (averaging $1,800 per year) were awarded; fellowships with partial tuition reimbursements, institutionally sponsored loans, scholarships/grants, health care benefits, tuition waivers (partial), and unspecified assistantships also available. Support available to part-time students. Financial award application deadline: 3/15; financial award applicants required to submit FAFSA. *Unit head:* Dr. Lawrence E. Murr, Director, 915-747-8002, Fax: 915-747-8036, E-mail: fekberg@utep.edu. *Application contact:* Dr. Benjamin Flores, Interim Dean of the Graduate School, 915-747-5491, Fax: 915-747-5788, E-mail: bflores@utep.edu.

The University of Texas at San Antonio, College of Engineering, Department of Electrical and Computer Engineering, San Antonio, TX 78249-0617. Offers computer engineering (MS); electrical engineering (MSEE, PhD); materials engineering (MS). Part-time programs available. *Faculty:* 21 full-time (3 women), 2 part-time/adjunct (0 women). *Students:* 111 full-time (34 women), 56 part-time (11 women); includes 32 minority (6 Black or African American, non-Hispanic/Latino; 4 Asian, non-Hispanic/Latino; 19 Hispanic/Latino; 3 Two or more races, non-Hispanic/Latino), 106 international. Average age 28. 228 applicants, 67% accepted, 47 enrolled. In 2011, 33 master's, 4 doctorates awarded. Terminal master's awarded for partial completion of doctoral program. *Degree requirements:* For master's, comprehensive exam, thesis (for some programs); for doctorate, comprehensive exam, thesis/dissertation. *Entrance requirements:* For master's, GRE General Test, bachelor's degree in electrical or computer engineering from ABET-accredited institution of higher education or related field; minimum GPA of 3.0 on the last 60 semester credit hours of undergraduate studies; for doctorate, GRE General Test, master's degree or minimum GPA of 3.3 in last 60 semester credit hours of undergraduate level coursework in electrical engineering; statement of purpose. Additional exam requirements/recommendations for international students: Required—TOEFL (minimum score 550 paper-based; 79 iBT), IELTS (minimum score 6.5). *Application deadline:* For fall admission, 7/1 for domestic students, 4/1 for international students; for spring admission, 11/1 for domestic students, 9/1 for international students. Applications are processed on a rolling basis. Application fee: $45 ($85 for international students). Electronic applications accepted. *Expenses:* Tuition, state resident: full-time $3148; part-time $2176 per semester. Tuition, nonresident: full-time $8782; part-time $5932 per semester. *Required fees:* $719 per semester. *Financial support:* In 2011–12, 60 students received support, including 11 fellowships (averaging $24,500 per year), 26 research assistantships (averaging $21,653 per year), 11 teaching assistantships (averaging $15,200 per year); unspecified assistantships and Valero Residency Fellowships, travel grants also available. Financial award application deadline: 3/31. *Faculty research:* Computer engineering, digital signal processing, systems and controls, communications, electronics materials and devices, electric power engineering. *Unit head:* Dr. Ruyan Guo, Interim Department Chair, 210-458-7057/7076, Fax: 210-458-5947, E-mail: electrical.engineering@utsa.edu. *Application contact:* Dr. Chunjiang Qian, Graduate Advisor of Record, 210-458-5587, Fax: 210-458-5947, E-mail: graduate.ece@utsa.edu. Web site: http://ece.utsa.edu/.

University of Toronto, School of Graduate Studies, Faculty of Applied Science and Engineering, Department of Materials Science and Engineering, Toronto, ON M5S 1A1, Canada. Offers M Eng, MA Sc, PhD. Part-time programs available. *Degree requirements:* For master's, thesis (for some programs), oral presentation/thesis defense (MA Sc), qualifying exam; for doctorate, thesis/dissertation. *Entrance requirements:* For master's, BA Sc or B Sc in materials science and engineering, 2 letters of reference; for doctorate, MA Sc or equivalent, 2 letters of reference, minimum B+ average in last 2 years. Additional exam requirements/recommendations for international students: Required—TOEFL (minimum score 580 paper-based), TWE (minimum score 4). Electronic applications accepted.

University of Utah, Graduate School, College of Engineering, Department of Materials Science and Engineering, Salt Lake City, UT 84112. Offers MS, PhD. *Faculty:* 8 full-time (1 woman), 2 part-time/adjunct (0 women). *Students:* 33 full-time (4 women), 9 part-time (1 woman); includes 1 minority (Asian, non-Hispanic/Latino), 24 international. Average age 29. 87 applicants, 14% accepted, 9 enrolled. In 2011, 3 master's, 3 doctorates awarded. Terminal master's awarded for partial completion of doctoral program. *Median time to degree:* Of those who began their doctoral program in fall 2003, 50% received their degree in 8 years or less. *Degree requirements:* For master's, thesis; for doctorate, thesis/dissertation, exam. *Entrance requirements:* For master's and doctorate, GRE General Test, minimum GPA of 3.0. Additional exam requirements/recommendations for international students: Required—TOEFL (minimum score 570 paper-based; 230 computer-based; 88 iBT), IELTS (minimum score 7). *Application deadline:* For fall admission, 1/15 for domestic students, 12/15 for international students. Applications are processed on a rolling basis. Application fee: $55 ($65 for international students). Electronic applications accepted. *Expenses:* Contact institution. *Financial support:* In 2011–12, 3 students received support, including 2 fellowships (averaging $30,000 per year), 27 research assistantships (averaging $22,000 per year); career-related internships or fieldwork and Federal Work-Study also available. Financial award application deadline: 2/5; financial award applicants required to submit FAFSA. *Faculty research:* Solid oxide fuel cells, computational nanostructures, computational polymers, biomaterials, electronic materials, nanomaterials, renewable energy materials. *Total annual research expenditures:* $3.7 million. *Unit head:* Dr. Feng Liu, Chair, 801-581-6863, Fax: 801-581-4816, E-mail: fliu@eng.utah.edu. *Application contact:* Ashley Quimby, Academic Program Specialist, 801-581-6863, Fax: 801-581-4816, E-mail: ashley.quimby@utah.edu. Web site: http://www.mse.utah.edu/.

University of Washington, Graduate School, College of Engineering, Department of Materials Science and Engineering, Seattle, WA 98195-2120. Offers ceramic engineering (PhD); materials science and engineering (MS, MSE, PhD); materials science and engineering and nanotechnology (PhD). Part-time programs available. *Faculty:* 23 full-time (5 women), 1 part-time/adjunct (0 women). *Students:* 53 full-time (16 women), 9 part-time (2 women); includes 11 minority (1 Black or African American, non-Hispanic/Latino; 1 American Indian or Alaska Native, non-Hispanic/Latino; 6 Asian, non-Hispanic/Latino; 3 Hispanic/Latino), 20 international. Average age 30. 291 applicants, 9% accepted, 9 enrolled. In 2011, 4 master's, 8 doctorates awarded. *Degree requirements:* For master's, comprehensive exam, thesis optional; for doctorate, comprehensive exam, thesis/dissertation, qualifying evaluation, general and final exams. *Entrance requirements:* For master's and doctorate, GRE General Test, minimum GPA of 3.0. Additional exam requirements/recommendations for international students: Required—TOEFL (minimum score 580 paper-based; 237 computer-based; 92 iBT); Recommended—IELTS (minimum score 7). *Application deadline:* For fall admission, 1/15 priority date for domestic students, 12/15 for international students. Applications are processed on a rolling basis. Application fee: $75. Electronic applications accepted. *Expenses:* Contact institution. *Financial support:* In 2011–12, 51 students received support, including 4 fellowships with full tuition reimbursements available (averaging $16,200 per year), 36 research assistantships with full tuition reimbursements available (averaging $16,416 per year), 8 teaching assistantships with full tuition reimbursements available (averaging $16,416 per year); career-related internships or fieldwork, Federal Work-Study, institutionally sponsored loans, scholarships/grants, health care benefits, unspecified assistantships, and stipend supplements also available. Financial award application deadline: 1/15; financial award applicants required to submit FAFSA. *Faculty research:* Biomimetics and biomaterials; electronic, optical and magnetic materials; eco-materials and materials for energy applications; ceramics, metals, composites, and polymers. *Total annual research expenditures:* $7.4 million. *Unit head:* Dr. Alex Jen, Professor/Chair, 206-543-2600, Fax: 206-543-3100, E-mail: ajen@uw.edu. *Application contact:* Kathleen A. Elkins, Academic Counselor, 206-616-6581, Fax: 206-543-3100, E-mail: kelkins@uw.edu. Web site: http://depts.washington.edu/mse/.

The University of Western Ontario, Faculty of Graduate Studies, Physical Sciences Division, Faculty of Engineering, London, ON N6A 5B8, Canada. Offers chemical and biochemical engineering (ME Sc, PhD); civil and environmental engineering (M Eng, ME Sc, PhD); electrical and computer engineering (M Eng, ME Sc, PhD); mechanical and materials engineering (M Eng, ME Sc, PhD). Part-time programs available. Terminal master's awarded for partial completion of doctoral program. *Degree requirements:* For master's, thesis; for doctorate, thesis/dissertation. *Entrance requirements:* For master's, minimum B average; for doctorate, minimum B+ average. *Faculty research:* Wind, geotechnical, chemical reactor engineering, applied electrostatics, biochemical engineering.

University of Windsor, Faculty of Graduate Studies, Faculty of Engineering, Department of Mechanical, Automotive, and Materials Engineering, Windsor, ON N9B 3P4, Canada. Offers engineering materials (M Eng, MA Sc, PhD); mechanical engineering (M Eng, MA Sc, PhD). Part-time programs available. *Degree requirements:* For master's, thesis; for doctorate, comprehensive exam, thesis/dissertation. *Entrance requirements:* For master's, minimum B average; for doctorate, master's degree, minimum B average. Additional exam requirements/recommendations for international students: Required—TOEFL (minimum score 600 paper-based; 250 computer-based). Electronic applications accepted. *Faculty research:* Thermofluids, applied mechanics, materials engineering.

University of Wisconsin–Madison, Graduate School, College of Engineering, Department of Materials Science and Engineering, Madison, WI 53706-1380. Offers materials engineering (MS, PhD). Part-time programs available. *Faculty:* 20 full-time (4 women). *Students:* 7 full-time (3 women); includes 5 minority (all Asian, non-Hispanic/Latino). Average age 25. 156 applicants, 2% accepted, 3 enrolled. Terminal master's awarded for partial completion of doctoral program. *Degree requirements:* For master's, thesis; for doctorate, comprehensive exam, thesis/dissertation. *Entrance requirements:* For master's and doctorate, GRE General Test. Additional exam requirements/recommendations for international students: Required—TOEFL (minimum score 580 paper-based; 237 computer-based). *Application deadline:* For fall admission, 1/1 priority date for domestic students, 1/1 for international students; for spring admission, 10/15 priority date for domestic students, 10/15 for international students. Applications are processed on a rolling basis. Application fee: $9. Electronic applications accepted. *Expenses:* Tuition, state resident: full-time $10,296; part-time $643.51 per credit. Tuition, nonresident: full-time $24,054; part-time $1503.40 per credit. *Required fees:* $70.06 per credit. Tuition and fees vary according to course load, campus/location, program and reciprocity agreements. *Financial support:* In 2011–12, 1 fellowship with tuition reimbursement (averaging $20,760 per year), 4 research assistantships with tuition reimbursements (averaging $20,184 per year), 1 teaching assistantship with tuition reimbursement (averaging $10,200 per year) were awarded. Financial award application deadline: 1/15. *Faculty research:* Materials characterization, electronic materials, metallurgy, computational materials science, nanotechnology. *Total annual research expenditures:* $16.3 million. *Unit head:* Dr. Donald S. Stone, Chair, 608-262-8791, Fax: 608-262-8353, E-mail: mat_engr@engr.wisc.edu. *Application contact:* Lynn J. Neis, University Services Program Associate, 608-262-3732, Fax: 608-262-8353, E-mail: lynn@engr.wisc.edu. Web site: http://www.engr.wisc.edu/mse/.

University of Wisconsin–Milwaukee, Graduate School, College of Engineering and Applied Science, Program in Engineering, Milwaukee, WI 53201-0413. Offers civil engineering (MS); electrical and computer engineering (MS); energy engineering (Certificate); engineering (PhD); engineering management (MS); engineering mechanics (MS); ergonomics (Certificate); industrial and management engineering (MS); manufacturing engineering (MS); materials engineering (MS); mechanical engineering (MS); MUP/MS. Part-time programs available. *Faculty:* 41 full-time (5 women), 2 part-time/adjunct (0 women). *Students:* 170 full-time (33 women), 101 part-time (18 women); includes 30 minority (6 Black or African American, non-Hispanic/Latino; 15 Asian, non-Hispanic/Latino; 2 Hispanic/Latino; 7 Two or more races, non-Hispanic/Latino), 153 international. Average age 30. 170 applicants, 56% accepted, 48 enrolled. In 2011, 47 master's, 12 doctorates awarded. *Degree requirements:* For master's, comprehensive exam (for some programs), thesis or alternative; for doctorate, comprehensive exam, thesis/dissertation, internship. *Entrance requirements:* For master's, GRE, minimum GPA of 2.75; for doctorate, GRE, minimum GPA of 3.5. Additional exam requirements/recommendations for international students: Required—TOEFL (minimum score 550 paper-based; 79 iBT), IELTS (minimum score 6.5). *Application deadline:* For fall admission, 1/1 priority date for domestic students; for spring admission, 9/1 for domestic students. Applications are processed on a rolling basis. Application fee: $56 ($96 for international students). One-time fee: $506.10 full-time. Tuition and fees vary according to course load and reciprocity agreements. *Financial support:* In 2011–12, 3 fellowships, 55 research assistantships, 77 teaching assistantships were awarded; career-related internships or fieldwork, Federal Work-Study, unspecified assistantships, and project assistantships also available. Support available to part-time students. Financial award application deadline: 4/15. *Total annual research expenditures:* $10.3 million. *Unit head:* David Yu, Representative, 414-229-6169, E-mail: yu@uwm.edu. *Application contact:* Betty Warras, General Information Contact, 414-229-6169, Fax: 414-229-6967, E-mail: bwarras@uwm.edu. Web site: http://www.wum.edu/CEAS/.

Virginia Polytechnic Institute and State University, Graduate School, College of Engineering, Department of Materials Science and Engineering, Blacksburg, VA 24061. Offers M Eng, MS, PhD. *Degree requirements:* For master's, comprehensive exam (for some programs), thesis (for some programs); for doctorate, comprehensive exam (for some programs), thesis/dissertation (for some programs). *Entrance requirements:* For master's and doctorate, GRE. Additional exam requirements/recommendations for international students: Required—TOEFL (minimum score 550 paper-based; 213 computer-based). *Application deadline:* For fall admission, 7/1 for domestic and international students; for spring admission, 12/1 for domestic and international students. Applications are processed on a rolling basis. Application fee: $65. Electronic applications accepted. *Expenses:* Tuition, state resident: full-time $10,048; part-time

$558.25 per credit hour. Tuition, nonresident: full-time $19,497; part-time $1083.25 per credit hour. *Required fees:* $405 per semester. Tuition and fees vary according to course load, campus/location and program. *Financial support:* Fellowships with full tuition reimbursements, research assistantships with full tuition reimbursements, teaching assistantships with full tuition reimbursements, career-related internships or fieldwork, Federal Work-Study, scholarships/grants, health care benefits, and unspecified assistantships available. Financial award application deadline: 1/15. *Unit head:* Dr. David E. Clark, Unit Head, 540-231-6640, Fax: 540-231-8819, E-mail: dclark@vt.edu. *Application contact:* Gary Pickrell, Information Contact, 540-231-3504, Fax: 540-231-8919, E-mail: pickrell@vt.edu. Web site: http://www.mse.vt.edu/.

Washington State University, Graduate School, College of Engineering and Architecture, School of Mechanical and Materials Engineering, Program in Material Science Engineering, Pullman, WA 99164. Offers MS. *Faculty:* 29. *Students:* 54 full-time (15 women), 9 part-time (2 women); includes 4 minority (1 Black or African American, non-Hispanic/Latino; 1 American Indian or Alaska Native, non-Hispanic/Latino; 1 Asian, non-Hispanic/Latino; 1 Hispanic/Latino), 40 international. Average age 26. 67 applicants, 28% accepted, 16 enrolled. In 2011, 11 master's awarded. *Degree requirements:* For master's, comprehensive exam (for some programs), thesis. *Entrance requirements:* For master's, GRE, statement of purpose, three letters of recommendation, transcripts. Additional exam requirements/recommendations for international students: Required—TOEFL, IELTS. *Application deadline:* For fall admission, 1/10 for domestic and international students; for spring admission, 7/1 for domestic and international students. Applications are processed on a rolling basis. Application fee: $75. Electronic applications accepted. *Financial support:* In 2011–12, fellowships (averaging $2,500 per year), research assistantships with tuition reimbursements (averaging $13,917 per year) were awarded. Financial award application deadline: 2/10. *Total annual research expenditures:* $2.2 million. *Unit head:* Dr. Matthew McCluskey, Chair, 509-335-5356, Fax: 509-335-4662, E-mail: mattmcc@wsu.edu. *Application contact:* Graduate School Admissions, 800-GRADWSU, Fax: 509-335-1949, E-mail: gradsch@wsu.edu.

Wayne State University, College of Engineering, Department of Chemical Engineering and Materials Science, Program in Materials Science and Engineering, Detroit, MI 48202. Offers materials science and engineering (MS, PhD); polymer engineering (Certificate). Part-time programs available. *Students:* 12 full-time (4 women); includes 1 minority (Black or African American, non-Hispanic/Latino), 10 international. Average age 27. 39 applicants, 41% accepted, 3 enrolled. In 2011, 3 master's awarded. Terminal master's awarded for partial completion of doctoral program. *Degree requirements:* For master's, thesis optional; for doctorate, thesis/dissertation. *Entrance requirements:* For master's, GRE (if applying for financial support), recommendations; resume; for doctorate, GRE (if applying for financial support), recommendations; resume, personal statement. Additional exam requirements/recommendations for international students: Required—TOEFL (minimum score 550 paper-based; 213 computer-based); Recommended—TWE (minimum score 5.5). *Application deadline:* For fall admission, 6/1 priority date for domestic students, 5/1 for international students; for winter admission, 10/1 priority date for domestic students, 9/1 for international students; for spring admission, 2/1 priority date for domestic students, 1/1 for international students. Applications are processed on a rolling basis. Application fee: $50. Electronic applications accepted. *Expenses:* Tuition, state resident: part-time $512.85 per credit. Tuition, nonresident: part-time $1132.65 per credit. *Required fees:* $26.60 per credit. $199.65 per semester. Tuition and fees vary according to course load and program. *Financial support:* In 2011–12, 9 students received support. Fellowships with tuition reimbursements available, research assistantships with tuition reimbursements available, teaching assistantships with tuition reimbursements available, scholarships/grants, health care benefits, and unspecified assistantships available. Support available to part-time students. Financial award application deadline: 2/15. *Faculty research:* Polymer science, rheology, fatigue in metals, metal matrix composites, ceramics. *Unit head:* Dr. Charles Manke, Chair, 313-577-3849, Fax: 313-577-3810, E-mail: cmanke@eng.wayne.edu. *Application contact:* Dr. Yinlun Huang, Graduate Program Director, 313-577-3771, E-mail: yhuang@eng.wayne.edu. Web site: http://cheme.eng.wayne.edu/ChE.

Worcester Polytechnic Institute, Graduate Studies and Research, Department of Mechanical Engineering, Program in Materials Science and Engineering, Worcester, MA 01609-2280. Offers MS, PhD. Part-time and evening/weekend programs available. *Faculty:* 1 full-time (0 women). *Students:* 39 full-time (15 women), 22 part-time (6 women); includes 6 minority (1 Black or African American, non-Hispanic/Latino; 5 Hispanic/Latino), 47 international. 131 applicants, 85% accepted, 36 enrolled. In 2011, 14 master's, 1 doctorate awarded. *Degree requirements:* For master's, thesis; for doctorate, comprehensive exam, thesis/dissertation. *Entrance requirements:* For master's and doctorate, GRE (recommended), 3 letters of recommendation. Additional exam requirements/recommendations for international students: Required—TOEFL (minimum score 563 paper-based; 223 computer-based; 84 iBT), IELTS (minimum score 7), GRE. *Application deadline:* For fall admission, 1/1 priority date for domestic students, 1/1 for international students; for spring admission, 10/1 priority date for domestic students, 10/1 for international students. Applications are processed on a rolling basis. Application fee: $70. Electronic applications accepted. *Financial support:* Research assistantships, teaching assistantships, career-related internships or fieldwork, institutionally sponsored loans, scholarships/grants, and unspecified assistantships available. Financial award application deadline: 1/1; financial award applicants required to submit FAFSA. *Faculty research:* Metals processing, nanomaterials, reliability analysis, surface metrology, biopolymers. *Unit head:* Dr. Richard D. Sisson, Jr., Director, 508-831-5633, Fax: 508-831-5178, E-mail: sisson@wpi.edu. *Application contact:* Rita Shilansky, Graduate Secretary, 508-831-5633, Fax: 508-831-5178, E-mail: rita@wpi.edu. Web site: http://www.wpi.edu/academics/me/grad-mse.html?/index.html.

Wright State University, School of Graduate Studies, College of Engineering and Computer Science, Programs in Engineering, Program in Mechanical and Materials Engineering, Dayton, OH 45435. Offers materials science and engineering (MSE); mechanical engineering (MSE). *Degree requirements:* For master's, thesis or course option alternative. *Entrance requirements:* Additional exam requirements/recommendations for international students: Required—TOEFL.

Materials Sciences

Air Force Institute of Technology, Graduate School of Engineering and Management, Department of Aeronautics and Astronautics, Dayton, OH 45433-7765. Offers aeronautical engineering (MS, PhD); astronautical engineering (MS, PhD); materials science (MS, PhD); space operations (MS); systems engineering (MS, PhD). *Accreditation:* ABET (one or more programs are accredited). Part-time programs available. *Degree requirements:* For master's, thesis; for doctorate, thesis/dissertation. *Entrance requirements:* For master's and doctorate, GRE General Test, minimum GPA of 3.0, U.S. citizenship. *Faculty research:* Computational fluid dynamics, experimental aerodynamics, computational structural mechanics, experimental structural mechanics, aircraft and spacecraft stability and control.

Air Force Institute of Technology, Graduate School of Engineering and Management, Department of Engineering Physics, Dayton, OH 45433-7765. Offers applied physics (MS, PhD); electro-optics (MS, PhD); materials science (PhD); nuclear engineering (MS, PhD); space physics (MS). Part-time programs available. *Degree requirements:* For master's, thesis; for doctorate, thesis/dissertation. *Entrance requirements:* For master's and doctorate, GRE General Test, minimum GPA of 3.0, U.S. citizenship. *Faculty research:* High-energy lasers, space physics, nuclear weapon effects, semiconductor physics.

Alabama Agricultural and Mechanical University, School of Graduate Studies, School of Arts and Sciences, Department of Physics, Huntsville, AL 35811. Offers physics (MS, PhD), including applied physics (PhD), materials science (PhD), optics/lasers (PhD). Part-time and evening/weekend programs available. *Degree requirements:* For doctorate, thesis/dissertation. *Entrance requirements:* For master's and doctorate, GRE General Test. Additional exam requirements/recommendations for international students: Required—TOEFL (minimum score 500 paper-based; 173 computer-based; 61 iBT). Electronic applications accepted.

Alfred University, Graduate School, New York State College of Ceramics, School of Engineering, Alfred, NY 14802-1205. Offers biomedical materials engineering science (MS); ceramic engineering (MS); ceramics (PhD); electrical engineering (MS); glass science (MS, PhD); materials science and engineering (MS, PhD); mechanical engineering (MS). *Degree requirements:* For master's, thesis; for doctorate, thesis/dissertation. *Entrance requirements:* Additional exam requirements/recommendations for international students: Required—TOEFL (minimum score 590 paper-based; 243 computer-based). Electronic applications accepted. *Expenses:* Contact institution. *Faculty research:* Fine-particle technology, x-ray diffraction, superconductivity, electronic materials.

Arizona State University, Ira A. Fulton School of Engineering, Department of Mechanical and Aerospace Engineering, Tempe, AZ 85281. Offers aerospace engineering (MS, MSE, PhD); chemical engineering (MS, MSE, PhD); materials science and engineering (MS, PhD); mechanical engineering (MS, MSE, PhD). Part-time and evening/weekend programs available. Postbaccalaureate distance learning degree programs offered (minimal on-campus study). Terminal master's awarded for partial completion of doctoral program. *Degree requirements:* For master's, thesis and oral defense (MS); applied project or comprehensive exam (MSE); interactive Program of Study (iPOS) submitted before completing 50 percent of required credit hours; for doctorate, comprehensive exam, thesis/dissertation, interactive Program of Study (iPOS) submitted before completing 50 percent of required credit hours. *Entrance requirements:* For master's, GRE, minimum GPA of 3.0 or equivalent in last 2 years of work leading to bachelor's degree; for doctorate, GRE, minimum GPA of 3.0 in last 2 years of work leading to bachelor's degree. Additional exam requirements/recommendations for international students: Required—TOEFL (minimum score 80 iBT), TOEFL, IELTS, or Pearson Test of English. Electronic applications accepted. *Expenses:* Contact institution. *Faculty research:* Electronic materials and packaging, materials for energy (batteries), adaptive/intelligent materials and structures, multiscale fluid mechanics, membranes, therapeutics and bioseparations, flexible structures, nanostructured materials, and micro/nano transport.

Boston University, College of Engineering, Division of Materials Science and Engineering, Boston, MA 02215. Offers M Eng, MS, PhD. Part-time programs available. *Students:* 40 full-time (11 women); includes 5 minority (3 Asian, non-Hispanic/Latino; 2 Hispanic/Latino), 23 international. Average age 25. 92 applicants, 26% accepted, 13 enrolled. In 2011, 5 degrees awarded. Terminal master's awarded for partial completion of doctoral program. *Degree requirements:* For master's, thesis (for some programs); for doctorate, comprehensive exam, thesis/dissertation. *Entrance requirements:* For master's and doctorate, GRE General Test. Additional exam requirements/recommendations for international students: Required—TOEFL (minimum score 550 paper-based; 213 computer-based; 84 iBT), IELTS (minimum score 6.5). *Application deadline:* For fall admission, 3/15 for domestic and international students; for spring admission, 10/1 for domestic and international students. Application fee: $70. Electronic applications accepted. *Expenses: Tuition:* Full-time $40,848; part-time $1276 per credit hour. *Required fees:* $572; $286 per semester. *Financial support:* In 2011–12, 23 students received support, including 2 fellowships with full tuition reimbursements available (averaging $28,950 per year), 15 research assistantships with full tuition reimbursements available (averaging $19,300 per year), 4 teaching assistantships with full tuition reimbursements available (averaging $19,300 per year); career-related internships or fieldwork, Federal Work-Study, institutionally sponsored loans, scholarships/grants, traineeships, health care benefits, and tuition waivers also available. Financial award application deadline: 1/15; financial award applicants required to submit FAFSA. *Faculty research:* Biomaterials, electronic and photonic materials, materials for energy and environment, nanomaterials. *Unit head:* Dr. David Bishop, Division Head, 617-353-8899, Fax: 617-353-5548, E-mail: djb1@bu.edu. *Application contact:* Stephen Doherty, Director of Graduate Programs, 617-353-9760, Fax: 617-353-0259, E-mail: enggrad@bu.edu. Web site: http://www.bu.edu/mse/.

Brown University, Graduate School, Division of Engineering, Program in Materials Science and Engineering, Providence, RI 02912. Offers Sc M, PhD. *Degree requirements:* For doctorate, thesis/dissertation, preliminary exam.

California Institute of Technology, Division of Engineering and Applied Science, Option in Materials Science, Pasadena, CA 91125-0001. Offers MS, PhD. *Degree requirements:* For doctorate, thesis/dissertation. *Faculty research:* Mechanical properties, physical properties, kinetics of phase transformations, metastable phases, transmission electron microscopy.

Carnegie Mellon University, Carnegie Institute of Technology, Department of Materials Science and Engineering, Pittsburgh, PA 15213-3891. Offers MS, PhD. Part-time programs available. Terminal master's awarded for partial completion of doctoral program. *Degree requirements:* For master's, exam; for doctorate, thesis/dissertation, qualifying exam. *Entrance requirements:* For master's and doctorate, GRE General Test. Additional exam requirements/recommendations for international students: Required—TOEFL. *Faculty research:* Materials characterization, process metallurgy, high strength alloys, growth kinetics, ceramics.

Case Western Reserve University, School of Graduate Studies, Case School of Engineering, Department of Materials Science and Engineering, Cleveland, OH 44106. Offers materials science and engineering (MS, PhD). Part-time programs available. Postbaccalaureate distance learning degree programs offered (no on-campus study). *Faculty:* 11 full-time (0 women). *Students:* 35 full-time (11 women), 5 part-time (1 woman); includes 2 minority (both Asian, non-Hispanic/Latino), 29 international. In 2011, 9 master's, 8 doctorates awarded. Terminal master's awarded for partial completion of doctoral program. *Degree requirements:* For master's, thesis (for some programs); for doctorate, thesis/dissertation, qualifying exam, teaching experience. *Entrance requirements:* For master's and doctorate, GRE General Test. Additional exam requirements/recommendations for international students: Required—TOEFL. *Application deadline:* For fall admission, 2/15 priority date for domestic students; for spring admission, 9/15 for domestic students. Applications are processed on a rolling basis. Application fee: $50. *Financial support:* Fellowships with full and partial tuition reimbursements, research assistantships with full and partial tuition reimbursements, and teaching assistantships available. Financial award application deadline: 4/30; financial award applicants required to submit FAFSA. *Faculty research:* Surface hardening of steels and other alloys, chemistry and structure of surfaces, microstructural and mechanical property characterization, materials for energy applications, thermodynamics and kinetics of materials, performance and reliability of materials. *Total annual research expenditures:* $3.7 million. *Unit head:* Dr. James D. McGuffin-Cawley, Department Chair, 216-368-6482, Fax: 216-368-4224, E-mail: emse.info@case.edu. *Application contact:* Theresa Claytor, Student Affairs Coordinator, 216-368-8555, Fax: 216-368-8555, E-mail: esme.info@case.edu. Web site: http://dmseg5.case.edu.

The Catholic University of America, School of Engineering, Department of Materials Science and Engineering, Washington, DC 20064. Offers MS. Part-time programs available. *Students:* 1 full-time (0 women), 1 part-time (0 women); includes 1 minority (Black or African American, non-Hispanic/Latino). Average age 27. 1 applicant, 100% accepted, 1 enrolled. *Degree requirements:* For master's, thesis optional. *Entrance requirements:* For master's, GRE (minimum score 1250), minimum GPA of 3.0, statement of purpose, official copies of academic transcripts. Additional exam requirements/recommendations for international students: Required—TOEFL (minimum score 580 paper-based; 237 computer-based). *Application deadline:* For fall admission, 8/1 for domestic students, 7/15 for international students; for spring admission, 12/1 for domestic students, 10/15 for international students. Applications are processed on a rolling basis. Application fee: $55. Electronic applications accepted. *Expenses: Tuition:* Full-time $35,260; part-time $1380 per credit. *Required fees:* $80; $40 per semester hour. One-time fee: $425. *Financial support:* Fellowships, research assistantships, teaching assistantships, Federal Work-Study, scholarships/grants, tuition waivers (full and partial), and unspecified assistantships available. Financial award application deadline: 2/1; financial award applicants required to submit FAFSA. *Faculty research:* Nanotechnology, biomaterials, magnetic and optical materials, glass, ceramics, and metallurgy processing and instrumentation . *Unit head:* Dr. Biprodas Dutta, Director, 202-319-5535, Fax: 202-319-4469, E-mail: duttab@cua.edu. *Application contact:* Andrew Woodall, Director of Graduate Admissions, 202-319-5057, Fax: 202-319-6533, E-mail: cua-admissions@cua.edu. Web site: http://materialsscience.cua.edu/.

Central Michigan University, College of Graduate Studies, College of Science and Technology, Department of Physics, Program in the Science of Advanced Materials, Mount Pleasant, MI 48859. Offers PhD. *Degree requirements:* For doctorate, comprehensive exam, thesis/dissertation. *Entrance requirements:* For doctorate, GRE. Electronic applications accepted. *Faculty research:* Electronic properties of nanomaterials, polymers for energy and for environmental applications, inorganic materials synthesis, magnetic properties from first-principles, and nano devices for biomedical applications and environmental remediation.

Clarkson University, Graduate School, Wallace H. Coulter School of Engineering, Program in Materials Science and Engineering, Potsdam, NY 13699. Offers PhD. Part-time programs available. *Students:* 2 full-time (both women), 1 international. Average age 26. 20 applicants, 70% accepted, 0 enrolled. *Degree requirements:* For doctorate, comprehensive exam, thesis/dissertation, departmental qualifying exam. *Entrance requirements:* For doctorate, GRE, transcripts of all college coursework, resume, personal statement, three letters of recommendation. Additional exam requirements/recommendations for international students: Required—TOEFL (minimum score 550 paper-based; 213 computer-based; 80 iBT), IELTS (minimum score 6.5). *Application deadline:* For fall admission, 1/30 priority date for domestic students, 1/30 for international students; for spring admission, 9/1 priority date for domestic students, 9/1 for international students. Applications are processed on a rolling basis. Application fee: $25 ($35 for international students). Electronic applications accepted. *Expenses: Tuition:* Full-time $14,376; part-time $1198 per credit hour. *Required fees:* $295 per semester. *Financial support:* In 2011–12, 2 students received support, including fellowships with full tuition reimbursements available (averaging $21,999 per year), 2 research assistantships with full tuition reimbursements available (averaging $21,999 per year), 1 teaching assistantship with full tuition reimbursement available (averaging $21,999 per year); scholarships/grants, tuition waivers (partial), and unspecified assistantships also available. *Unit head:* Dr. Ian I. Suni, Chair, 315-268-4471, Fax: 315-268-6654, E-mail: isuni@clarkson.edu. *Application contact:* Kelly Sharlow, Assistant to the Dean, 315-268-7929, Fax: 315-268-4494, E-mail: ksharlow@clarkson.edu. Web site: http://www.clarkson.edu/engineering/graduate/mat_sci_eng_phd/.

Clemson University, Graduate School, College of Engineering and Science, School of Materials Science and Engineering, Clemson, SC 29634. Offers MS, PhD. Part-time programs available. *Faculty:* 15 full-time (2 women), 7 part-time/adjunct (0 women). *Students:* 58 full-time (18 women), 8 part-time (3 women); includes 3 minority (1 Asian, non-Hispanic/Latino; 2 Two or more races, non-Hispanic/Latino), 35 international. Average age 27. 126 applicants, 19% accepted, 15 enrolled. In 2011, 6 master's, 2 doctorates awarded. Terminal master's awarded for partial completion of doctoral program. *Degree requirements:* For master's, thesis; for doctorate, comprehensive exam, thesis/dissertation. *Entrance requirements:* For master's and doctorate, GRE General Test. Additional exam requirements/recommendations for international students: Required—TOEFL. *Application deadline:* For fall admission, 2/1 for domestic students; for spring admission, 9/1 for domestic students. Applications are processed on a rolling basis. Application fee: $70 ($80 for international students). Electronic applications accepted. *Financial support:* In 2011–12, 54 students received support, including 4 fellowships with full and partial tuition reimbursements available (averaging $4,250 per year), 37 research assistantships with partial tuition reimbursements available (averaging $19,998 per year), 17 teaching assistantships with partial tuition reimbursements available (averaging $14,118 per year); career-related internships or fieldwork, institutionally sponsored loans, scholarships/grants, health care benefits, and unspecified assistantships also available. Support available to part-time students. Financial award applicants required to submit FAFSA. *Total annual research expenditures:* $3.1 million. *Unit head:* Dr. Kathleen Richardson, Chair and Director of the School of Materials Science and Engineering, 864-656-3311, Fax: 864-656-5973, E-mail: richar3@clemson.edu. *Application contact:* Dr. Gary C. Lickfield, Graduate Program Coordinator, 864-656-5964, Fax: 864-656-5973, E-mail: lgary@clemson.edu. Web site: http://www.clemson.edu/mse/.

Colorado School of Mines, Graduate School, Department of Metallurgical and Materials Engineering, Golden, CO 80401-1887. Offers materials science (MS, PhD); metallurgical and materials engineering (ME, MS, PhD). Part-time programs available. *Faculty:* 34 full-time (2 women), 6 part-time/adjunct (0 women). *Students:* 74 full-time (14 women), 6 part-time (0 women); includes 7 minority (1 American Indian or Alaska Native, non-Hispanic/Latino; 2 Asian, non-Hispanic/Latino; 3 Hispanic/Latino; 1 Two or more races, non-Hispanic/Latino), 22 international. Average age 26. 124 applicants, 27% accepted, 31 enrolled. In 2011, 19 master's, 5 doctorates awarded. *Degree requirements:* For master's, thesis (for some programs); for doctorate, comprehensive exam, thesis/dissertation. *Entrance requirements:* For master's and doctorate, GRE General Test. Additional exam requirements/recommendations for international students: Required—TOEFL (minimum score 550 paper-based; 213 computer-based; 80 iBT). *Application deadline:* For fall admission, 1/15 priority date for domestic students, 1/15 for international students; for spring admission, 10/15 priority date for domestic students, 10/15 for international students. Application fee: $50 ($70 for international students). Electronic applications accepted. *Expenses:* Tuition, state resident: full-time $12,585; part-time $699 per credit. Tuition, nonresident: full-time $27,270; part-time $1516 per credit. *Required fees:* $1864.20; $670 per semester. *Financial support:* In 2011–12, 53 students received support, including 5 fellowships with full tuition reimbursements available (averaging $20,000 per year), 39 research assistantships with full tuition reimbursements available (averaging $20,000 per year), 9 teaching assistantships with full tuition reimbursements available (averaging $20,000 per year); scholarships/grants, health care benefits, and unspecified assistantships also available. Financial award application deadline: 1/15; financial award applicants required to submit FAFSA. *Total annual research expenditures:* $6.7 million. *Unit head:* Dr. Michael Kaufman, Interim Head, 303-273-3009, Fax: 303-273-3795, E-mail: mkaufman@mines.edu. *Application contact:* Susan Ballantype, Program Assistant, 303-273-3660, Fax: 303-273-3795, E-mail: susan.ballantyne@is.mines.edu. Web site: http://metallurgy.mines.edu.

Colorado School of Mines, Graduate School, Program in Materials Science, Golden, CO 80401-1887. Offers MS, PhD. Part-time programs available. *Students:* 57 full-time (15 women), 4 part-time (2 women); includes 5 minority (2 Asian, non-Hispanic/Latino; 3 Hispanic/Latino), 21 international. Average age 29. 94 applicants, 27% accepted, 13 enrolled. In 2011, 12 master's, 6 doctorates awarded. *Degree requirements:* For master's, thesis (for some programs); for doctorate, comprehensive exam, thesis/dissertation. *Entrance requirements:* For master's and doctorate, GRE General Test. Additional exam requirements/recommendations for international students: Required—TOEFL (minimum score 550 paper-based; 213 computer-based; 80 iBT). *Application deadline:* For fall admission, 1/15 priority date for domestic students, 1/15 for international students; for spring admission, 10/15 priority date for domestic students, 10/15 for international students. Application fee: $50 ($70 for international students). Electronic applications accepted. *Expenses:* Tuition, state resident: full-time $12,585; part-time $699 per credit. Tuition, nonresident: full-time $27,270; part-time $1516 per credit. *Required fees:* $1864.20; $670 per semester. *Financial support:* In 2011–12, 56 students received support, including 4 fellowships with full tuition reimbursements available (averaging $20,000 per year), 52 research assistantships with full tuition reimbursements available (averaging $20,000 per year), teaching assistantships with full tuition reimbursements available (averaging $20,000 per year); scholarships/grants, health care benefits, and unspecified assistantships also available. Financial award application deadline: 1/15; financial award applicants required to submit FAFSA. *Faculty research:* Ceramics processing, solar and electronic materials, optical properties of surfaces and interfaces, materials synthesis, metal and alloy processing. *Unit head:* Dr. Michael Kaufman, Interim Department Head, 303-273-3009, Fax: 303-273-3795, E-mail: mkaufman@mines.edu. *Application contact:* Susan Ballantyne, Program Assistant, 303-273-3660, Fax: 303-273-3795, E-mail: susan.ballantyne@is.mines.edu. Web site: http://materials.mines.edu.

Columbia University, The Fu Foundation School of Engineering and Applied Science, Department of Applied Physics and Applied Mathematics, New York, NY 10027. Offers applied physics (Eng Sc D); applied physics and applied mathematics (MS, PhD, Engr); materials science and engineering (MS, Eng Sc D, PhD); medical physics (MS). Part-time programs available. Postbaccalaureate distance learning degree programs offered (no on-campus study). *Faculty:* 32 full-time (2 women), 23 part-time/adjunct (2 women). *Students:* 98 full-time (22 women), 38 part-time (10 women); includes 19 minority (14 Asian, non-Hispanic/Latino; 1 Hispanic/Latino; 4 Two or more races, non-Hispanic/Latino), 50 international. Average age 28. 371 applicants, 18% accepted, 41 enrolled. In 2011, 57 master's, 18 doctorates awarded. Terminal master's awarded for partial completion of doctoral program. *Degree requirements:* For master's, comprehensive exam; for doctorate, thesis/dissertation, qualifying exam. *Entrance requirements:* For master's, GRE General Test, GRE Subject Test (strongly recommended); for doctorate, GRE General Test, GRE Subject Test (applied physics); for Engr, GRE General Test. Additional exam requirements/recommendations for international students: Required—TOEFL, IELTS. *Application deadline:* For fall admission, 12/1 priority date for domestic students, 12/1 for international students; for spring admission, 10/1 priority date for domestic students, 10/1 for international students. Application fee: $95. Electronic applications accepted. *Financial support:* In 2011–12, 71 students received support, including 2 fellowships with full tuition reimbursements available (averaging $31,140 per year), 55 research assistantships with full tuition reimbursements available (averaging $31,133 per year), 16 teaching assistantships with full tuition reimbursements available (averaging $31,133 per year); health care benefits also available. Financial award application deadline: 12/1; financial award applicants required to submit FAFSA. *Faculty research:* Plasma physics and fusion energy; optical and laser physics; atmospheric, oceanic and earth physics; applied mathematics; solid state science and processing of materials, their properties, and their structure; medical physics. *Unit head:* Dr. Ismail C. Noyan, Professor and Department Chairman, 212-854-8919, E-mail: icn2@

columbia.edu. *Application contact:* Montserrat Fernandez-Pinkley, Student Services Coordinator, 212-854-4457, Fax: 212-854-8257, E-mail: mf2157@columbia.edu. Web site: http://www.apam.columbia.edu/.

Cornell University, Graduate School, Graduate Fields of Engineering, Field of Materials Science and Engineering, Ithaca, NY 14853. Offers materials engineering (M Eng, PhD); materials science (M Eng, PhD). *Faculty:* 46 full-time (5 women). *Students:* 76 full-time (26 women); includes 14 minority (3 Black or African American, non-Hispanic/Latino; 10 Asian, non-Hispanic/Latino; 1 Hispanic/Latino), 38 international. Average age 26. 403 applicants, 20% accepted, 33 enrolled. In 2011, 24 master's, 6 doctorates awarded. *Degree requirements:* For doctorate, comprehensive exam, thesis/dissertation. *Entrance requirements:* For master's and doctorate, GRE General Test, 3 letters of recommendation. Additional exam requirements/recommendations for international students: Required—TOEFL (minimum score 550 paper-based; 213 computer-based; 77 iBT). *Application deadline:* For fall admission, 1/15 priority date for domestic students. Application fee: $95. Electronic applications accepted. *Financial support:* In 2011–12, 48 students received support, including 17 fellowships with full tuition reimbursements available, 31 research assistantships with full tuition reimbursements available, 8 teaching assistantships with full tuition reimbursements available; institutionally sponsored loans, scholarships/grants, health care benefits, tuition waivers (full and partial), and unspecified assistantships also available. Financial award applicants required to submit FAFSA. *Faculty research:* Ceramics, complex fluids, glass, metals, polymers semiconductors. *Unit head:* Director of Graduate Studies, 607-255-9159, Fax: 607-255-2365. *Application contact:* Graduate Field Assistant, 607-255-9159, Fax: 607-255-2365, E-mail: matsci@cornell.edu. Web site: http://www.gradschool.cornell.edu/fields.php?id-31&a-2.

Dartmouth College, Thayer School of Engineering, Program in Materials Sciences and Engineering, Hanover, NH 03755. Offers MS, PhD. *Degree requirements:* For master's, thesis; for doctorate, thesis/dissertation, candidacy oral exam. *Entrance requirements:* For master's and doctorate, GRE General Test. *Application deadline:* For fall admission, 1/1 priority date for domestic students. Application fee: $45. *Financial support:* Fellowships, research assistantships, teaching assistantships, career-related internships or fieldwork, Federal Work-Study, institutionally sponsored loans, and tuition waivers (full and partial) available. Financial award application deadline: 1/15. *Faculty research:* Electronic and magnetic materials, microstructural evolution, biomaterials and nanostructures, laser-material interactions, nano composites. *Total annual research expenditures:* $2.4 million. *Unit head:* Dr. Joseph J. Helbie, Dean, 603-646-2238, Fax: 603-646-2580, E-mail: joseph.j.helbie@dartmouth.edu. *Application contact:* Candace S. Potter, Graduate Admissions Administrator, 603-646-3844, Fax: 603-646-1620, E-mail: candace.potter@dartmouth.edu. Web site: http://engineering.dartmouth.edu/.

Duke University, Graduate School, Pratt School of Engineering, Department of Mechanical Engineering and Materials Science, Durham, NC 27708. Offers materials science (MS, PhD); mechanical engineering (MS, PhD); JD/MS. Part-time programs available. Terminal master's awarded for partial completion of doctoral program. *Degree requirements:* For master's, thesis optional; for doctorate, thesis/dissertation. *Entrance requirements:* For master's and doctorate, GRE General Test. Additional exam requirements/recommendations for international students: Required—TOEFL (minimum score 550 paper-based; 213 computer-based; 83 iBT), IELTS (minimum score 7). Electronic applications accepted. *Expenses: Tuition:* Full-time $40,720. *Required fees:* $3107.

Duke University, Graduate School, Pratt School of Engineering, Master of Engineering Program, Durham, NC 27708-0271. Offers biomedical engineering (M Eng); civil engineering (M Eng); electrical and computer engineering (M Eng); environmental engineering (M Eng); materials science and engineering (M Eng); mechanical engineering (M Eng); photonics and optical sciences (M Eng). Part-time programs available. *Entrance requirements:* For master's, GRE General Test, resume, 3 letters of recommendation, statement of purpose. Additional exam requirements/recommendations for international students: Required—TOEFL. *Expenses: Tuition:* Full-time $40,720. *Required fees:* $3107.

Florida International University, College of Engineering and Computing, Department of Mechanical and Materials Engineering, Materials Science and Engineering Program, Miami, FL 33175. Offers MS, PhD. Part-time and evening/weekend programs available. Terminal master's awarded for partial completion of doctoral program. *Degree requirements:* For master's, thesis or alternative; for doctorate, comprehensive exam, thesis/dissertation. *Entrance requirements:* For master's, GRE, 3 letters of recommendation, minimum undergraduate GPA of 3.0 in upper-level course work; for doctorate, GRE, minimum GPA of 3.0, 3 letters of recommendation, letter of intent. Additional exam requirements/recommendations for international students: Required—TOEFL (minimum score 550 paper-based; 80 iBT). Electronic applications accepted.

Florida State University, The Graduate School, College of Arts and Sciences, Department of Chemistry and Biochemistry, Tallahassee, FL 32306-4390. Offers analytical chemistry (MS, PhD); biochemistry (MS, PhD); inorganic chemistry (MS, PhD); materials chemistry (PhD); organic chemistry (MS, PhD); physical chemistry (MS, PhD). *Faculty:* 35 full-time (5 women), 1 (woman) part-time/adjunct. *Students:* 138 full-time (52 women), 8 part-time (1 woman); includes 14 minority (6 Black or African American, non-Hispanic/Latino; 3 Asian, non-Hispanic/Latino; 2 Hispanic/Latino; 3 Two or more races, non-Hispanic/Latino), 63 international. Average age 25. 147 applicants, 40% accepted, 28 enrolled. In 2011, 10 master's, 24 doctorates awarded. Terminal master's awarded for partial completion of doctoral program. *Median time to degree:* Of those who began their doctoral program in fall 2003, 58% received their degree in 8 years or less. *Degree requirements:* For master's, comprehensive exam (for some programs), thesis (for some programs); for doctorate, comprehensive exam (for some programs), thesis/dissertation. *Entrance requirements:* For master's and doctorate, GRE General Test, minimum B average in undergraduate course work. Additional exam requirements/recommendations for international students: Required—TOEFL (minimum score 550 paper-based; 213 computer-based; 80 iBT). *Application deadline:* For fall admission, 12/15 priority date for domestic students, 12/15 for international students; for spring admission, 9/15 for domestic and international students. Applications are processed on a rolling basis. Application fee: $30. Electronic applications accepted. *Expenses:* Contact institution. *Financial support:* In 2011–12, 140 students received support, including fellowships with full tuition reimbursements available (averaging $20,000 per year), 50 research assistantships with full tuition reimbursements available (averaging $20,000 per year), 100 teaching assistantships with full tuition reimbursements available (averaging $20,000 per year). Financial award application deadline: 12/15; financial award applicants required to submit FAFSA. *Faculty research:* Materials synthesis including polymers, natural products; catalysis, NMR; mass spectrometry; optical spectroscopy, scattering techniques, computational chemistry, separation technology; nanostructured materials including metallic, semiconducting and

magnetic nanocrystals; nanoscience interfaced with biology; supramolecular materials for solar energy conversion. *Total annual research expenditures:* $9.9 million. *Unit head:* Dr. Timothy Logan, Chairman, 850-644-1244, Fax: 850-644-8281, E-mail: gradinfo@chem.fsu.edu. *Application contact:* Dr. Michael Shatruk, Chair, Graduate Admissions Committee, 888-525-9286, Fax: 850-644-0465, E-mail: gradinfo@chem.fsu.edu. Web site: http://www.chem.fsu.edu/.

Florida State University, The Graduate School, College of Arts and Sciences, Department of Scientific Computing, Tallahassee, FL 32306-4120. Offers computational science (MS, PSM, PhD), including atmospheric science (PhD), biochemistry (PhD), biological science (PhD), computational molecular biology/bioinformatics (PSM), computational science (PhD), geological science (PhD), materials science (PhD), physics (PhD). Part-time programs available. *Faculty:* 14 full-time (2 women). *Students:* 32 full-time (6 women), 3 part-time (0 women); includes 13 minority (1 Black or African American, non-Hispanic/Latino; 11 Asian, non-Hispanic/Latino; 1 Hispanic/Latino), 13 international. Average age 28. 29 applicants, 41% accepted, 9 enrolled. In 2011, 14 master's, 3 doctorates awarded. Terminal master's awarded for partial completion of doctoral program. *Degree requirements:* For master's, thesis (for some programs); for doctorate, comprehensive exam, thesis/dissertation. *Entrance requirements:* For master's and doctorate, GRE General Test, knowledge of at least one object-oriented computing language, 3 letters of recommendations. Additional exam requirements/recommendations for international students: Required—TOEFL (minimum score 550 paper-based; 80 iBT). *Application deadline:* For fall admission, 1/15 for domestic and international students. Application fee: $30. Electronic applications accepted. *Expenses:* Tuition, state resident: full-time $9474; part-time $350.88 per credit hour. Tuition, nonresident: full-time $16,236; part-time $601.34 per credit hour. *Required fees:* $630 per semester. One-time fee: $20. Tuition and fees vary according to course load and campus/location. *Financial support:* In 2011–12, 32 students received support, including 12 research assistantships with full tuition reimbursements available (averaging $20,000 per year), 18 teaching assistantships with full tuition reimbursements available (averaging $20,000 per year); unspecified assistantships also available. Financial award application deadline: 4/15. *Faculty research:* Morphometrics, mathematical and systems biology, mining proteomic and metabolic data, computational materials research at Scientific Computing, advanced 4-D Var Data-Assimilation methods in dynamic meteorology and oceanography, computational fluid dynamics, astrophysics. *Unit head:* Dr. Sam Huckaba, Interim Dean, 850-644-1081. *Application contact:* Maribel Amwake, Graduate Academic Coordinator, 850-644-0143, Fax: 850-644-0098, E-mail: mamwake@fsu.edu. Web site: http://www.sc.fsu.edu.

Florida State University, The Graduate School, Materials Science and Engineering Program, Tallahassee, FL 32310. Offers computational materials science and mechanics (MS); functional materials (MS); materials science and engineering (PhD); nanoscale materials, composite materials, and interfaces (MS); polymers and bio-inspired materials (MS). MS not open to international students. *Faculty:* 23 full-time (3 women). *Students:* 10 full-time (2 women); includes 1 minority (Hispanic/Latino), 5 international. Average age 24. 13 applicants, 23% accepted, 3 enrolled. In 2011, 3 master's awarded. Terminal master's awarded for partial completion of doctoral program. *Degree requirements:* For master's, thesis; for doctorate, comprehensive exam, thesis/dissertation. *Entrance requirements:* For master's and doctorate, GRE General Test (minimum old version score 1100 Verbal and Quantitative; 55th percentile Verbal, 75th percentile Quantitative in new format), minimum GPA of 3.0, 3 letters of recommendation. Additional exam requirements/recommendations for international students: Required—TOEFL (minimum score 80 iBT). *Application deadline:* For fall admission, 7/1 for domestic students, 5/1 for international students; for spring admission, 11/1 for domestic students, 9/1 for international students. Applications are processed on a rolling basis. Application fee: $25. Electronic applications accepted. *Expenses:* Tuition, state resident: full-time $9474; part-time $350.88 per credit hour. Tuition, nonresident: full-time $16,236; part-time $601.34 per credit hour. *Required fees:* $630 per semester. One-time fee: $20. Tuition and fees vary according to course load and campus/location. *Financial support:* In 2011–12, 10 students received support, including 1 fellowship with full tuition reimbursement available (averaging $30,526 per year), 7 research assistantships with full tuition reimbursements available (averaging $20,700 per year), 1 teaching assistantship with full tuition reimbursement available (averaging $20,880 per year); partial payment of required health insurance also available. Financial award application deadline: 1/15. *Faculty research:* Magnetism and magnetic materials, composites, superconductors, polymers, computations, nanotechnology. *Unit head:* Prof. Eric Hellstrom, Director, 850-645-7489, Fax: 850-645-7754, E-mail: hellstrom@asc.magnet.fsu.edu. *Application contact:* Judy Gardner, Admissions Coordinator, 850-645-8980, Fax: 850-645-9123, E-mail: gardner@eng.fsu.edu. Web site: http://materials.fsu.edu.

Georgetown University, Graduate School of Arts and Sciences, Department of Chemistry, Washington, DC 20057. Offers analytical chemistry (PhD); biochemistry (PhD); computational chemistry (PhD); inorganic chemistry (PhD); materials chemistry (PhD); organic chemistry (PhD); physical chemistry (PhD); theoretical chemistry (PhD). Terminal master's awarded for partial completion of doctoral program. *Degree requirements:* For doctorate, comprehensive exam, thesis/dissertation. *Entrance requirements:* For doctorate, GRE General Test. Additional exam requirements/recommendations for international students: Required—TOEFL.

The George Washington University, Columbian College of Arts and Sciences, Department of Chemistry, Washington, DC 20052. Offers analytical chemistry (MS, PhD); inorganic chemistry (MS, PhD); materials science (MS, PhD); organic chemistry (MS, PhD); physical chemistry (MS, PhD). Part-time and evening/weekend programs available. *Faculty:* 16 full-time (5 women), 5 part-time/adjunct (2 women). *Students:* 22 full-time (10 women), 10 part-time (7 women); includes 4 minority (3 Asian, non-Hispanic/Latino; 1 Hispanic/Latino), 7 international. Average age 27. 55 applicants, 42% accepted, 8 enrolled. In 2011, 4 master's, 3 doctorates awarded. Terminal master's awarded for partial completion of doctoral program. *Degree requirements:* For master's, comprehensive exam, thesis or alternative; for doctorate, thesis/dissertation, general exam. *Entrance requirements:* For master's and doctorate, GRE General Test, interview, minimum GPA of 3.0. Additional exam requirements/recommendations for international students: Required—TOEFL (minimum score 550 paper-based; 213 computer-based; 80 iBT). *Application deadline:* For fall admission, 1/15 priority date for domestic students, 1/15 for international students; for spring admission, 9/1 priority date for domestic students, 9/1 for international students. Applications are processed on a rolling basis. Application fee: $75. Electronic applications accepted. *Financial support:* In 2011–12, 27 students received support. Fellowships with tuition reimbursements available, research assistantships, teaching assistantships with tuition reimbursements available, Federal Work-Study, and tuition waivers available. Financial award application deadline: 1/15. *Unit head:* Dr. Michael King, Chair, 202-994-6488. *Application contact:* Information Contact, 202-994-6121, E-mail: gwchem@gwu.edu. Web site: http://www.gwu.edu/~gwchem/.

Illinois Institute of Technology, Graduate College, Armour College of Engineering, Department of Mechanical, Materials and Aerospace Engineering, Chicago, IL 60616-3793. Offers manufacturing engineering (MME, MS); materials science and engineering (MMME, MS, PhD); mechanical and aerospace engineering (MMAE, MS, PhD), including economics (MS), energy (MS), environment (MS). Part-time and evening/weekend programs available. Postbaccalaureate distance learning degree programs offered (minimal on-campus study). Terminal master's awarded for partial completion of doctoral program. *Degree requirements:* For master's, comprehensive exam (for some programs), thesis (for some programs); for doctorate, comprehensive exam, thesis/dissertation. *Entrance requirements:* For master's and doctorate, GRE General Test (minimum score 1000 Quantitative and Verbal, 3.0 Analytical Writing), minimum undergraduate GPA of 3.0. Additional exam requirements/recommendations for international students: Required—TOEFL (minimum score 523 paper-based; 70 iBT); Recommended—IELTS (minimum score 5.5). Electronic applications accepted. *Faculty research:* Fluid dynamics, metallurgical and materials engineering, solids and structures, computational mechanics, theoretical mechanics.

Illinois Institute of Technology, Graduate College, College of Science and Letters, Department of Biological, Chemical and Physical Sciences, Chemistry Division, Chicago, IL 60616. Offers analytical chemistry (M Ch); chemistry (M Chem, MS, PhD); materials and chemical synthesis (M Ch). Part-time and evening/weekend programs available. Postbaccalaureate distance learning degree programs offered (no on-campus study). Terminal master's awarded for partial completion of doctoral program. *Degree requirements:* For master's, comprehensive exam, thesis (for some programs); for doctorate, comprehensive exam, thesis/dissertation. *Entrance requirements:* For master's, GRE General Test (minimum score 1000 Quantitative and Verbal, 2.5 Analytical Writing), minimum undergraduate GPA of 3.0; for doctorate, GRE General Test (minimum score 1100 Quantitative and Verbal, 3.0 Analytical Writing), GRE Subject Test, minimum undergraduate GPA of 3.0. Additional exam requirements/recommendations for international students: Required—TOEFL (minimum score 523 paper-based; 213 computer-based; 70 iBT); Recommended—IELTS. Electronic applications accepted. *Faculty research:* Synthesis and analysis of inorganic nanoparticles; synthetic and mechanistic organic chemistry; synthesis of penicillin-related compounds; design, synthesis and property studies of nanomaterials for applications in chemical sensing, energy storage and biomedical usage; scanning probe microscopy.

Indiana University Bloomington, University Graduate School, College of Arts and Sciences, Department of Chemistry, Bloomington, IN 47405. Offers analytical chemistry (PhD); chemical biology chemistry (PhD); chemistry (MAT); inorganic chemistry (PhD); materials chemistry (PhD); organic chemistry (PhD); physical chemistry (PhD). *Faculty:* 42 full-time (4 women). *Students:* 200 full-time (82 women), 3 part-time (0 women); includes 18 minority (7 Black or African American, non-Hispanic/Latino; 8 Asian, non-Hispanic/Latino; 1 Hispanic/Latino; 1 Native Hawaiian or other Pacific Islander, non-Hispanic/Latino; 1 Two or more races, non-Hispanic/Latino), 63 international. Average age 27. 290 applicants, 49% accepted, 46 enrolled. In 2011, 11 master's, 20 doctorates awarded. Terminal master's awarded for partial completion of doctoral program. *Median time to degree:* Of those who began their doctoral program in fall 2003, 49% received their degree in 8 years or less. *Degree requirements:* For master's, thesis; for doctorate, thesis/dissertation. *Entrance requirements:* For master's and doctorate, GRE General Test, GRE Subject Test. Additional exam requirements/recommendations for international students: Required—TOEFL. *Application deadline:* For fall admission, 1/15 priority date for domestic students, 12/15 for international students. Applications are processed on a rolling basis. Application fee: $55 ($65 for international students). *Financial support:* In 2011–12, 200 students received support, including 10 fellowships with full tuition reimbursements available, 76 research assistantships with full tuition reimbursements available, 111 teaching assistantships with full tuition reimbursements available; Federal Work-Study and institutionally sponsored loans also available. *Faculty research:* Synthesis of complex natural products, organic reaction mechanisms, organic electrochemistry, transitive-metal chemistry, solid-state and surface chemistry. *Total annual research expenditures:* $7.7 million. *Unit head:* David Giedroc, Chairperson, 812-855-6239, E-mail: chemchair@indiana.edu. *Application contact:* Daniel Mindiola, Director of Graduate Admissions, 812-855-2069, Fax: 812-855-8385, E-mail: mindiola@indiana.edu. Web site: http://www.chem.indiana.edu/.

Instituto Tecnológico y de Estudios Superiores de Monterrey, Campus Estado de México, Professional and Graduate Division, Estado de Mexico, Mexico. Offers administration of information technologies (MITA); architecture (M Arch); business administration (GMBA, MBA); computer sciences (MCS, PhD); education (M Ed); educational institution administration (MAD); educational technology and innovation (PhD); electronic commerce (MEC); environmental systems (MS); finance (MAF); humanistic studies (MHS); information sciences and knowledge management (MISKM); information systems (MS); manufacturing systems (MS); marketing (MEM); quality systems and productivity (MS); science and materials engineering (PhD); telecommunications management (MTM). Part-time programs available. Postbaccalaureate distance learning degree programs offered (minimal on-campus study). *Degree requirements:* For master's, one foreign language, thesis (for some programs); for doctorate, one foreign language, thesis/dissertation. *Entrance requirements:* For master's, E-PAEP 500, interview; for doctorate, E-PAEP 500, research proposal. Additional exam requirements/recommendations for international students: Required—TOEFL (minimum score 550 paper-based). *Faculty research:* Surface treatments by plasmas, mechanical properties, robotics, graphical computing, mechatronics security protocols.

Iowa State University of Science and Technology, Department of Materials Science and Engineering, Ames, IA 50011. Offers MS, PhD. *Entrance requirements:* For master's and doctorate, GRE General Test. Additional exam requirements/recommendations for international students: Required—TOEFL (minimum score 550 paper-based; 79 iBT), IELTS (minimum score 6.5). *Application deadline:* For fall admission, 1/15 priority date for domestic students, 1/15 for international students; for spring admission, 8/15 priority date for domestic students, 8/15 for international students. Application fee: $40 ($90 for international students). Electronic applications accepted. *Financial support:* Teaching assistantships, scholarships/grants, health care benefits, and unspecified assistantships available. *Unit head:* Dr. Vitaliji Pecharsky, Director of Graduate Education, 515-294-1224, Fax: 515-204-5444, E-mail: gradmse@iastate.edu. *Application contact:* Carla Harris, Director of Graduate Education, 515-294-1224, Fax: 515-294-5444, E-mail: gradmse@iastate.edu. Web site: http://www.mse.iastate.edu.

Jackson State University, Graduate School, College of Science, Engineering and Technology, Department of Technology, Jackson, MS 39217. Offers hazardous materials management (MS); technology education (MS Ed). Part-time and evening/weekend programs available. *Degree requirements:* For master's, comprehensive exam, thesis or alternative. *Entrance requirements:* For master's, GRE General Test. Additional exam requirements/recommendations for international students: Required—TOEFL (minimum score 520 paper-based; 195 computer-based; 67 iBT).

The Johns Hopkins University, Engineering Program for Professionals, Part-time Program in Materials Science and Engineering, Baltimore, MD 21218-2699. Offers M Mat SE, MSE. Part-time and evening/weekend programs available. Electronic applications accepted.

The Johns Hopkins University, Whiting School of Engineering, Department of Materials Science and Engineering, Baltimore, MD 21218-2699. Offers M Mat SE, MSE, PhD. Part-time and evening/weekend programs available. Terminal master's awarded for partial completion of doctoral program. *Degree requirements:* For master's, thesis, oral exam; for doctorate, thesis/dissertation, oral exam, thesis defense. *Entrance requirements:* For master's and doctorate, GRE General Test. Additional exam requirements/recommendations for international students: Required—TOEFL (minimum score 600 paper-based; 250 computer-based). Electronic applications accepted. *Faculty research:* Thin films, nanomaterials, biomaterials, materials characterization, electronic materials.

The Johns Hopkins University, Whiting School of Engineering, Program in Engineering Management, Baltimore, MD 21218-2699. Offers biomaterials (MSEM); communications science (MSEM); computer science (MSEM); fluid mechanics (MSEM); materials science and engineering (MSEM); mechanical engineering (MSEM); mechanics and materials (MSEM); nano-biotechnology (MSEM); nanomaterials and nanotechnology (MSEM); probability and statistics (MSEM); smart product and device design (MSEM); systems analysis, management and environmental policy (MSEM). *Entrance requirements:* For master's, GRE, 3 letters of recommendation, resume. Additional exam requirements/recommendations for international students: Required—TOEFL (minimum score 600 paper-based; 250 computer-based; 100 iBT) or IELTS (minimum score 7). Electronic applications accepted.

Lehigh University, P.C. Rossin College of Engineering and Applied Science, Department of Materials Science and Engineering, Bethlehem, PA 18015. Offers materials science and engineering (M Eng, MS, PhD); photonics (MS); polymer science/engineering (M Eng, MS, PhD); MBA/E. Part-time programs available. *Faculty:* 13 full-time (3 women), 1 part-time/adjunct (0 women). *Students:* 28 full-time (6 women), 6 part-time (1 woman); includes 2 minority (both Asian, non-Hispanic/Latino), 14 international. Average age 26. 321 applicants, 2% accepted, 6 enrolled. In 2011, 2 master's, 2 doctorates awarded. *Degree requirements:* For master's, thesis; for doctorate, comprehensive exam, thesis/dissertation. *Entrance requirements:* For master's and doctorate, GRE General Test, minimum GPA of 3.0. Additional exam requirements/recommendations for international students: Required—TOEFL (minimum score 487 paper-based; 216 computer-based; 85 iBT). *Application deadline:* For fall admission, 1/15 priority date for domestic students, 1/15 for international students; for spring admission, 12/1 priority date for domestic students, 12/1 for international students. Applications are processed on a rolling basis. Application fee: $75. Electronic applications accepted. *Financial support:* In 2011–12, 29 students received support, including 3 fellowships with full and partial tuition reimbursements available (averaging $22,400 per year), 25 research assistantships with full tuition reimbursements available (averaging $22,449 per year), 13 teaching assistantships with partial tuition reimbursements available (averaging $17,512 per year); career-related internships or fieldwork, Federal Work-Study, institutionally sponsored loans, scholarships/grants, and unspecified assistantships also available. Support available to part-time students. Financial award application deadline: 1/15. *Faculty research:* Metals, ceramics, crystals, polymers, fatigue crack propagation. *Total annual research expenditures:* $4.1 million. *Unit head:* Dr. Helen Chan, Chairperson, 610-758-5554, Fax: 610-758-4244, E-mail: hmc0@lehigh.edu. *Application contact:* Anne Marie Lobley, Graduate Administrative Coordinator, 610-758-4222, Fax: 610-758-4244, E-mail: amme@lehigh.edu. Web site: http://www.lehigh.edu/~inmatsci/.

Massachusetts Institute of Technology, School of Engineering, Department of Materials Science and Engineering, Cambridge, MA 02139. Offers archaeological materials (PhD, Sc D); materials engineering (Mat E); materials science and engineering (SM, PhD, Sc D). *Faculty:* 32 full-time (9 women). *Students:* 193 full-time (48 women); includes 33 minority (2 Black or African American, non-Hispanic/Latino; 20 Asian, non-Hispanic/Latino; 8 Hispanic/Latino; 3 Two or more races, non-Hispanic/Latino), 110 international. Average age 26. 384 applicants, 15% accepted, 35 enrolled. In 2011, 35 master's, 32 doctorates awarded. Terminal master's awarded for partial completion of doctoral program. *Degree requirements:* For master's, thesis; for doctorate, comprehensive exam, thesis/dissertation. *Entrance requirements:* For master's and doctorate, GRE General Test. Additional exam requirements/recommendations for international students: Required—IELTS (minimum score 7). *Application deadline:* For fall admission, 12/15 for domestic and international students. Application fee: $75. Electronic applications accepted. *Expenses: Tuition:* Full-time $40,460; part-time $630 per credit hour. *Required fees:* $272. *Financial support:* In 2011–12, 179 students received support, including 47 fellowships (averaging $35,400 per year), 129 research assistantships (averaging $29,700 per year), 6 teaching assistantships (averaging $32,300 per year); career-related internships or fieldwork, Federal Work-Study, institutionally sponsored loans, scholarships/grants, traineeships, health care benefits, and unspecified assistantships also available. *Faculty research:* Thermodynamics and kinetics of materials; structure, processing and properties of materials: metals, ceramics, semiconductors, polymers, biomaterials; electronic, structural and biological applications and devices; computational materials science; materials in energy, medicine, nanotechnology and the environment. *Total annual research expenditures:* $29.6 million. *Unit head:* Prof. Christopher Schuh, Head, 617-253-3300, Fax: 617-252-1775. *Application contact:* Angelita Mireles, Academic Administrator, 617-253-3302, E-mail: dmse-admissions@mit.edu. Web site: http://dmse.mit.edu.

McMaster University, School of Graduate Studies, Faculty of Engineering, Department of Materials Science and Engineering, Hamilton, ON L8S 4M2, Canada. Offers materials engineering (M Eng, MA Sc, PhD); materials science (M Eng, PhD). *Degree requirements:* For master's, thesis; for doctorate, comprehensive exam, thesis/dissertation. *Entrance requirements:* Additional exam requirements/recommendations for international students: Required—TOEFL (minimum score 550 paper-based; 213 computer-based). *Faculty research:* Localized corrosion of metals and alloys, electron microscopy, polymer synthesis and characterization, polymer reaction kinetics and engineering, polymer process modeling.

Michigan State University, The Graduate School, College of Engineering, Department of Chemical Engineering and Materials Science, East Lansing, MI 48824. Offers chemical engineering (MS, PhD); materials science and engineering (MS, PhD). *Entrance requirements:* Additional exam requirements/recommendations for international students: Required—TOEFL. Electronic applications accepted.

Materials Sciences

Missouri State University, Graduate College, College of Natural and Applied Sciences, Department of Physics, Astronomy, and Materials Science, Springfield, MO 65897. Offers materials science (MS); physics, astronomy, and materials science (MNAS); secondary education (MS Ed), including physics. Part-time programs available. *Faculty:* 13 full-time (0 women). *Students:* 9 full-time (1 woman), 4 part-time (1 woman); includes 2 minority (1 Black or African American, non-Hispanic/Latino; 1 Hispanic/Latino), 8 international. Average age 29. 7 applicants, 100% accepted, 6 enrolled. In 2011, 6 master's awarded. *Degree requirements:* For master's, comprehensive exam, thesis. *Entrance requirements:* For master's, GRE (MS, MNAS), minimum undergraduate GPA of 3.0 (MS and MNAS), 9-12 teaching certification (MS Ed). Additional exam requirements/recommendations for international students: Required—TOEFL (minimum score 550 paper-based; 213 computer-based; 79 iBT). *Application deadline:* For fall admission, 7/20 priority date for domestic students, 5/1 for international students; for spring admission, 12/20 priority date for domestic students, 9/1 for international students. Applications are processed on a rolling basis. Application fee: $35 ($50 for international students). Electronic applications accepted. *Expenses:* Tuition, state resident: full-time $4086; part-time $227 per credit hour. Tuition, nonresident: full-time $8172; part-time $454 per credit hour. *Required fees:* $275 per semester. Tuition and fees vary according to course load, campus/location and program. *Financial support:* In 2011–12, 3 teaching assistantships with full tuition reimbursements (averaging $9,730 per year) were awarded; Federal Work-Study, institutionally sponsored loans, scholarships/grants, and unspecified assistantships also available. Financial award application deadline: 3/31; financial award applicants required to submit FAFSA. *Faculty research:* Nanocomposites, ferroelectricity, infrared focal plane array sensors, biosensors, pulsating stars. *Unit head:* Dr. David Cornelison, Head, 417-836-5131, Fax: 417-836-6226, E-mail: physics@missouristate.edu. *Application contact:* Misty Stewart, Coordinator of Admissions and Recruitment, 417-836-6079, Fax: 417-836-6200, E-mail: mistystewart@missouristate.edu. Web site: http://physics.missouristate.edu/.

New Jersey Institute of Technology, Office of Graduate Studies, Program in Materials Science and Engineering, Newark, NJ 07102. Offers MS, PhD. Part-time and evening/weekend programs available. *Students:* 29 full-time (5 women), 9 part-time (2 women); includes 10 minority (1 Black or African American, non-Hispanic/Latino; 7 Asian, non-Hispanic/Latino; 2 Hispanic/Latino), 22 international. Average age 30. 107 applicants, 79% accepted, 9 enrolled. In 2011, 4 doctorates awarded. Terminal master's awarded for partial completion of doctoral program. *Degree requirements:* For master's, thesis; for doctorate, thesis/dissertation. *Entrance requirements:* For master's, GRE General Test; for doctorate, GRE General Test, minimum graduate GPA of 3.5. Additional exam requirements/recommendations for international students: Required—TOEFL (minimum score 550 paper-based; 213 computer-based; 79 iBT). *Application deadline:* For fall admission, 6/1 priority date for domestic students, 5/1 for international students; for spring admission, 11/15 for domestic and international students. Applications are processed on a rolling basis. Application fee: $65. Electronic applications accepted. *Expenses:* Tuition, state resident: full-time $7980; part-time $867 per credit. Tuition, nonresident: full-time $11,336; part-time $1196 per credit. *Required fees:* $230 per credit. *Financial support:* Fellowships with full and partial tuition reimbursements, research assistantships with full and partial tuition reimbursements, teaching assistantships with full and partial tuition reimbursements, career-related internships or fieldwork, Federal Work-Study, institutionally sponsored loans, and unspecified assistantships available. Financial award application deadline: 1/15. *Unit head:* Dr. Marino Xanthos, Associate Provost, 973-596-3462, E-mail: marinos.xanthos@njit.edu. *Application contact:* Kathryn Kelly, Director of Admissions, 973-596-3300, Fax: 973-596-3461, E-mail: admissions@njit.edu.

Norfolk State University, School of Graduate Studies, School of Science and Technology, Department of Chemistry, Norfolk, VA 23504. Offers materials science (MS). *Entrance requirements:* Additional exam requirements/recommendations for international students: Required—TOEFL (minimum score 500 paper-based).

North Carolina State University, Graduate School, College of Engineering, Department of Materials Science and Engineering, Raleigh, NC 27695. Offers MMSE, MS, PhD. PhD offered jointly with The University of North Carolina at Charlotte. *Degree requirements:* For master's, thesis; for doctorate, thesis/dissertation. Electronic applications accepted. *Faculty research:* Processing and properties of wide band gap semiconductors, ferroelectric thin-film materials, ductility of nanocrystalline materials, computational materials science, defects in silicon-based devices.

North Dakota State University, College of Graduate and Interdisciplinary Studies, Interdisciplinary Program in Materials and Nanotechnology, Fargo, ND 58108. Offers PhD. *Students:* 13 full-time (2 women), 3 part-time (0 women), 12 international. 12 applicants, 42% accepted, 3 enrolled. *Entrance requirements:* For doctorate, GRE General Test. Additional exam requirements/recommendations for international students: Required—TOEFL (minimum score 525 paper-based; 197 computer-based; 71 iBT). *Application deadline:* For fall admission, 5/1 for international students; for spring admission, 8/1 for international students. Application fee: $35. *Unit head:* Dr. Erik Hobbe, Director, 701-231-7049, E-mail: erik.hobbie@ndsu.edu. *Application contact:* Sonya Goergen, Marketing, Recruitment, and Public Relations Coordinator, 701-231-7033, Fax: 701-231-6524.

Northwestern University, McCormick School of Engineering and Applied Science, Department of Civil and Environmental Engineering, Evanston, IL 60208-3109. Offers environmental engineering and science (MS, PhD); geotechnical engineering (MS, PhD); mechanics of materials and solids (MS, PhD); project management (MS, PhD); structural engineering and materials (MS, PhD); theoretical and applied mechanics (MS, PhD), including fluid mechanics, solid mechanics; transportation systems analysis and planning (MS, PhD). MS and PhD admissions and degrees offered through The Graduate School. Part-time programs available. Terminal master's awarded for partial completion of doctoral program. *Degree requirements:* For master's, thesis (for some programs); for doctorate, thesis/dissertation. *Entrance requirements:* For master's and doctorate, GRE General Test, minimum 2 letters of recommendation, transcripts from all academic institutions attended. Additional exam requirements/recommendations for international students: Required—TOEFL (minimum score 600 paper-based; 250 computer-based; 100 iBT), IELTS (minimum score 7). Electronic applications accepted. *Faculty research:* Environmental engineering and science, geotechnics, mechanics of materials and solids, structural engineering and materials, transportation systems analysis and planning.

Northwestern University, McCormick School of Engineering and Applied Science, Department of Materials Science and Engineering, Evanston, IL 60208. Offers integrated computational materials engineering (Certificate); materials science and engineering (MS, PhD). Admissions and degrees offered through The Graduate School. Part-time programs available. *Faculty:* 25 full-time (6 women), 1 (woman) part-time/adjunct. *Students:* 200 full-time (60 women), 5 part-time (1 woman); includes 37 minority (2 Black or African American, non-Hispanic/Latino; 24 Asian, non-Hispanic/Latino; 8 Hispanic/Latino; 3 Two or more races, non-Hispanic/Latino), 85 international. Average age 26. In 2011, 17 master's, 22 doctorates awarded. Terminal master's awarded for partial completion of doctoral program. *Degree requirements:* For master's, thesis, oral thesis defense; for doctorate, comprehensive exam, thesis/dissertation, oral defense of dissertation, preliminary evaluation, qualifying exam. *Entrance requirements:* For master's and doctorate, GRE General Test. Additional exam requirements/recommendations for international students: Required—TOEFL (minimum score 577 paper-based, 233 computer-based, 90 iBT) or IELTS (minimum score 7). *Application deadline:* For fall admission, 12/31 for domestic and international students. Application fee: $75. Electronic applications accepted. *Financial support:* Fellowships with full tuition reimbursements, research assistantships with full tuition reimbursements, teaching assistantships with full tuition reimbursements, career-related internships or fieldwork, institutionally sponsored loans, health care benefits, and unspecified assistantships available. Financial award application deadline: 1/15; financial award applicants required to submit FAFSA. *Faculty research:* Biomaterials, cement, ceramics, composites, electrical properties, electron and ion microscopy, energy, materials design, materials processing, materials theory, mechanical properties, metals, molecular synthesis, nanomaterials, optical properties, phase transformation, polymers, scattering and diffraction, self-assembly, semiconductors, surfaces and interfaces, thin films. *Total annual research expenditures:* $23.5 million. *Unit head:* Dr. Michael Bedzyk, Chair, 847-491-3570, Fax: 847-491-7820, E-mail: bedzyk@northwestern.edu. *Application contact:* Dr. Chris Wolverton, Admissions Officer, 847-497-0593, Fax: 847-491-7820, E-mail: c-wolverton@northwestern.edu. Web site: http://www.matsci.northwestern.edu/.

The Ohio State University, Graduate School, College of Engineering, Department of Materials Science and Engineering, Columbus, OH 43210. Offers materials science and engineering (MS, PhD); welding engineering (MS, MWE, PhD). *Faculty:* 34. *Students:* 70 full-time (10 women), 45 part-time (13 women); includes 6 minority (3 Asian, non-Hispanic/Latino; 3 Hispanic/Latino), 56 international. Average age 27. In 2011, 14 master's, 10 doctorates awarded. *Degree requirements:* For master's, thesis; for doctorate, thesis/dissertation. *Entrance requirements:* For master's and doctorate, GRE (for graduates of foreign universities and holders of non-engineering degrees). Additional exam requirements/recommendations for international students: Required—Michigan English Language Assessment Battery (minimum score 82); Recommended—TOEFL (minimum score 600 paper-based; 250 computer-based; 79 iBT). *Application deadline:* For fall admission, 8/15 priority date for domestic students, 7/1 for international students; for winter admission, 12/1 priority date for domestic students, 11/1 for international students; for spring admission, 3/1 priority date for domestic students, 2/1 for international students. Applications are processed on a rolling basis. Application fee: $40 ($50 for international students). Electronic applications accepted. *Expenses:* Tuition, state resident: full-time $11,400. Tuition, nonresident: full-time $28,125. Tuition and fees vary according to course load, degree level, campus/location and program. *Financial support:* In 2011–12, fellowships (averaging $43,000 per year), research assistantships (averaging $40,700 per year) were awarded; teaching assistantships, career-related internships or fieldwork, scholarships/grants, and unspecified assistantships also available. *Faculty research:* Computational materials modeling, biomaterials, metallurgy, ceramics, advanced alloys/composites. *Total annual research expenditures:* $10 million. *Unit head:* Rudolph G. Buchheit, Chair, 614-292-6085, Fax: 614-292-1357, E-mail: buchheit.8@osu.edu. *Application contact:* Mark Cooper, Graduate Studies Coordinator, 614-292-7280, Fax: 614-292-1357, E-mail: cooper.73@osu.edu. Web site: http://mse.osu.edu/.

Oregon State University, Graduate School, College of Engineering, School of Mechanical, Industrial, and Manufacturing Engineering, Program in Materials Science, Corvallis, OR 97331. Offers MAIS, MS, PhD. *Degree requirements:* For master's, thesis or alternative. *Entrance requirements:* For master's, GRE General Test, minimum GPA of 3.0 in last 90 hours of course work. Additional exam requirements/recommendations for international students: Required—TOEFL (minimum score 550 paper-based; 213 computer-based).

Penn State University Park, Graduate School, College of Earth and Mineral Sciences, Department of Materials Science and Engineering, State College, University Park, PA 16802-1503. Offers MS, PhD. *Unit head:* Dr. William E. Easterling, III, Dean, 814-865-6546, Fax: 814-863-7708, E-mail: wee2@psu.edu. *Application contact:* Cynthia E. Nicosia, Director of Graduate Enrollment Services, 814-865-1834, E-mail: cey1@psu.edu. Web site: http://www.matse.psu.edu/.

Princeton University, Princeton Institute for the Science and Technology of Materials (PRISM), Princeton, NJ 08544-1019. Offers materials (PhD).

Rensselaer Polytechnic Institute, Graduate School, School of Engineering, Program in Materials Science and Engineering, Troy, NY 12180. Offers ceramics and glass science (M Eng, MS, PhD); composites (M Eng, MS, PhD); electronic materials (M Eng, MS, PhD); metallurgy (M Eng, MS, PhD); polymers (M Eng, MS, PhD). Part-time programs available. Terminal master's awarded for partial completion of doctoral program. *Degree requirements:* For master's, thesis; for doctorate, comprehensive exam, thesis/dissertation. *Entrance requirements:* For master's and doctorate, GRE. Additional exam requirements/recommendations for international students: Required—TOEFL (minimum score 570 paper-based; 230 computer-based; 100 iBT). Electronic applications accepted. *Faculty research:* Materials processing, nanostructural materials, materials for microelectronics, composite materials, computational materials.

Rice University, Graduate Programs, George R. Brown School of Engineering, Department of Mechanical Engineering and Materials Science, Houston, TX 77251-1892. Offers materials science (MMS, MS, PhD); mechanical engineering (MME, MS, PhD); MBA/ME. Part-time programs available. Terminal master's awarded for partial completion of doctoral program. *Degree requirements:* For master's, comprehensive exam, thesis; for doctorate, comprehensive exam, thesis/dissertation. *Entrance requirements:* For master's and doctorate, GRE General Test, minimum GPA of 3.0. Additional exam requirements/recommendations for international students: Required—TOEFL (minimum score 600 paper-based; 250 computer-based; 90 iBT), IELTS (minimum score 7). Electronic applications accepted. *Faculty research:* Heat transfer, biomedical engineering, fluid dynamics, aero-astronautics, control systems/robotics, materials science.

Rochester Institute of Technology, Graduate Enrollment Services, College of Science, Center for Materials Science and Engineering, Rochester, NY 14623-5603. Offers MS. Part-time and evening/weekend programs available. *Students:* 16 full-time (4 women), 5 part-time (1 woman); includes 2 minority (both Asian, non-Hispanic/Latino), 9 international. Average age 26. 27 applicants, 70% accepted, 7 enrolled. In 2011, 8 degrees awarded. *Degree requirements:* For master's, thesis or project. *Entrance requirements:* For master's, GRE (recommended), minimum GPA of 3.0. Additional exam requirements/recommendations for international students: Required—TOEFL (minimum score 575 paper-based; 233 computer-based; 90 iBT) or IELTS (minimum score 6.5). *Application deadline:* For fall admission, 2/15 priority date for domestic students, 2/15 for international students; for winter admission, 11/1 for domestic students, 10/1 for international students; for spring admission, 2/1 for domestic students, 1/1 for international students. Applications are processed on a rolling basis. Application fee: $50. Electronic applications accepted. *Expenses: Tuition:* Full-time $34,659; part-time $963 per credit hour. *Required fees:* $228; $76 per quarter. *Financial support:* Research assistantships with partial tuition reimbursements, teaching assistantships with partial tuition reimbursements, career-related internships or fieldwork, scholarships/grants, tuition waivers (partial), and unspecified assistantships available. Support available to part-time students. Financial award application deadline: 7/29; financial award applicants required to submit FAFSA. *Faculty research:* VUV modification of polymers, stress and morphology of sputtered copper films, MRI applications to materials problems. *Unit head:* Dr. K. S. V. Santhanam, Graduate Program Director, 585-475-2920, Fax: 585-475-2800, E-mail: ksssch@rit.edu. *Application contact:* Diane Ellison, Assistant Vice President, Graduate Enrollment Services, 585-475-2229, Fax: 585-475-7164, E-mail: gradinfo@rit.edu. Web site: http://www.rit.edu/cos/cmse/.

Royal Military College of Canada, Division of Graduate Studies and Research, Engineering Division, Program in Chemical and Materials Science, Kingston, ON K7K 7B4, Canada. Offers M Sc, PhD. *Degree requirements:* For master's, thesis; for doctorate, comprehensive exam, thesis/dissertation. *Entrance requirements:* For master's, honours degree with second-class standing; for doctorate, master's degree. Electronic applications accepted.

Rutgers, The State University of New Jersey, New Brunswick, Graduate School-New Brunswick, Program in Materials Science and Engineering, Piscataway, NJ 08854-8097. Offers MS, PhD. Part-time programs available. *Degree requirements:* For master's, thesis; for doctorate, comprehensive exam, thesis/dissertation. *Entrance requirements:* For master's and doctorate, GRE General Test. Additional exam requirements/recommendations for international students: Recommended—TOEFL. Electronic applications accepted. *Faculty research:* Ceramic processing, nanostructured materials, electrical and structural ceramics, fiber optics.

School of the Art Institute of Chicago, Graduate Division, Department of Fiber and Material Studies, Chicago, IL 60603-3103. Offers MFA. *Accreditation:* NASAD. *Entrance requirements:* Additional exam requirements/recommendations for international students: Required—TOEFL, IELTS.

South Dakota School of Mines and Technology, Graduate Division, Doctoral Program in Materials Engineering and Science, Rapid City, SD 57701-3995. Offers PhD. Part-time programs available. *Degree requirements:* For doctorate, thesis/dissertation. *Entrance requirements:* For doctorate, GRE General Test, minimum graduate GPA of 3.0, 3 letters of recommendation. Additional exam requirements/recommendations for international students: Required—TOEFL, TWE. Electronic applications accepted. *Faculty research:* Thermophysical properties of solids, development of multiphase materials and composites, concrete technology, electronic polymer materials.

South Dakota School of Mines and Technology, Graduate Division, Master's Program in Materials Engineering and Science, Rapid City, SD 57701-3995. Offers MS. *Entrance requirements:* For master's, GRE General Test. Additional exam requirements/recommendations for international students: Required—TOEFL, TWE. Electronic applications accepted.

Stanford University, School of Engineering, Department of Materials Science and Engineering, Stanford, CA 94305-9991. Offers MS, PhD, Eng. Terminal master's awarded for partial completion of doctoral program. *Degree requirements:* For doctorate, thesis/dissertation; for Eng, thesis. *Entrance requirements:* For master's, doctorate, and Eng, GRE General Test. Additional exam requirements/recommendations for international students: Required—TOEFL. Electronic applications accepted. *Expenses: Tuition:* Full-time $40,050; part-time $890 per credit.

State University of New York at Binghamton, Graduate School, Thomas J. Watson School of Engineering and Applied Science and School of Arts and Sciences, Materials Science and Engineering Program, Binghamton, NY 13902-6000. Offers MS, PhD. *Faculty:* 3 full-time (0 women). *Students:* 16 full-time (8 women), 26 part-time (8 women); includes 1 minority (Native Hawaiian or other Pacific Islander, non-Hispanic/Latino), 34 international. Average age 29. 23 applicants, 30% accepted, 6 enrolled. In 2011, 3 master's, 7 doctorates awarded. Application fee: $60. *Financial support:* In 2011–12, 27 students received support, including 18 research assistantships with full tuition reimbursements available (averaging $16,500 per year), 8 teaching assistantships with full tuition reimbursements available (averaging $16,500 per year); career-related internships or fieldwork, Federal Work-Study, institutionally sponsored loans, scholarships/grants, health care benefits, tuition waivers (full and partial), and unspecified assistantships also available. Financial award application deadline: 2/15; financial award applicants required to submit FAFSA. *Unit head:* Dr. Stanley Whittingham, Director, 607-777-4623, E-mail: stanwhit@binghamton.edu. *Application contact:* Catherine Smith, Recruiting and Admissions Coordinator, 607-777-2151, Fax: 607-777-2501, E-mail: cmsmith@binghamton.edu. Web site: http://materials.binghamton.edu/materials/.

State University of New York College of Environmental Science and Forestry, Department of Paper and Bioprocess Engineering, Syracuse, NY 13210-2779. Offers biomaterials engineering (MS, PhD); bioprocess engineering (MPS, MS, PhD); paper science and engineering (MPS, MS, PhD); sustainable engineering management (MPS). *Degree requirements:* For master's, thesis; for doctorate, comprehensive exam, thesis/dissertation. *Entrance requirements:* For master's and doctorate, GRE General Test, minimum GPA of 3.0. Additional exam requirements/recommendations for international students: Required—TOEFL (minimum score 550 paper-based; 213 computer-based; 80 iBT), IELTS (minimum score 6). *Application deadline:* For fall admission, 2/1 priority date for domestic students, 2/1 for international students; for spring admission, 11/1 priority date for domestic students, 11/1 for international students. Applications are processed on a rolling basis. Application fee: $60. *Expenses:* Tuition, state resident: full-time $8870; part-time $370 per credit hour. Tuition, nonresident: full-time $15,160; part-time $632 per credit hour. *Required fees:* $60; $370 per credit hour. $350 per semester. One-time fee: $85. *Financial support:* Fellowships with full tuition reimbursements, research assistantships with full tuition reimbursements, teaching assistantships with full tuition reimbursements, career-related internships or fieldwork, Federal Work-Study, institutionally sponsored loans, scholarships/grants, health care benefits, and unspecified assistantships available. Support available to part-time students. Financial award application deadline: 6/30; financial award applicants required to submit FAFSA. *Total annual research expenditures:* $604,516. *Unit head:* Dr. Gary M. Scott, Chair, 315-470-6501, Fax: 315-470-6945, E-mail: gscott@esf.edu. *Application contact:* Dr. Dudley J. Raynal, Dean, Instruction and Graduate Studies, 315-

470-6599, Fax: 315-470-6978, E-mail: esfgrad@esf.edu. Web site: http://www.esf.edu/pbe/.

Stony Brook University, State University of New York, Graduate School, College of Engineering and Applied Sciences, Department of Materials Science and Engineering, Stony Brook, NY 11794. Offers MS, PhD. *Degree requirements:* For master's, thesis or alternative; for doctorate, comprehensive exam, thesis/dissertation. *Entrance requirements:* For master's and doctorate, GRE General Test, minimum undergraduate GPA of 3.0. Additional exam requirements/recommendations for international students: Required—TOEFL. *Faculty research:* Electronic materials, biomaterials, synchrotron topography.

Texas State University–San Marcos, Graduate School, College of Science and Engineering, Ingram School of Engineering, Program in Materials Science, Engineering, and Commercialization, San Marcos, TX 78666. Offers PhD. *Degree requirements:* For doctorate, comprehensive exam, thesis/dissertation. *Entrance requirements:* For doctorate, GRE (preferred minimum score of 1150 verbal and quantitative combined), two degrees with one advanced with minimum GPA of 3.5 in graduate work; statement of history and goals; 3 letters outlining skills and potential in the MSEC field; current curriculum vitae or resume, interview with core doctoral faculty conducted either by phone, Internet or face-to-face. Additional exam requirements/recommendations for international students: Required—TOEFL (minimum score 550 paper-based; 78 iBT). *Application deadline:* For fall admission, 6/15 for domestic students, 6/1 for international students; for spring admission, 11/30 for domestic students, 10/1 for international students. Application fee: $40 ($90 for international students). Electronic applications accepted. *Expenses:* Tuition, state resident: full-time $6408; part-time $3204 per semester. Tuition, nonresident: full-time $14,832; part-time $7416 per semester. *Required fees:* $1824; $912 per semester. Tuition and fees vary according to course load. *Unit head:* Dr. Thomas Myers, Director, 512-245-1839, E-mail: tm33@txstate.edu. *Application contact:* Dr. J. Michael Willoughby, Dean of Graduate School, 512-245-2581, Fax: 512-245-8365, E-mail: gradcollege@txstate.edu.

Texas State University–San Marcos, Graduate School, College of Science and Engineering, Program in Material Physics, San Marcos, TX 78666. Offers MS. *Faculty:* 7 full-time (0 women), 2 part-time/adjunct (1 woman). *Students:* 2 full-time (0 women), 2 part-time (0 women); includes 1 minority (Hispanic/Latino), 2 international. Average age 30. 4 applicants, 25% accepted, 0 enrolled. *Degree requirements:* For master's, comprehensive exam, thesis. *Entrance requirements:* For master's, minimum GPA of 2.75 on junior- and senior-level physics courses or 2.5 and GRE (preferred minimum score of 900 verbal and quantitative). Additional exam requirements/recommendations for international students: Required—TOEFL (minimum score 550 paper-based; 213 computer-based; 78 iBT). *Application deadline:* For fall admission, 6/15 for domestic students, 6/1 for international students; for spring admission, 10/15 for domestic students, 10/1 for international students. Applications are processed on a rolling basis. Application fee: $40 ($90 for international students). Electronic applications accepted. *Expenses:* Tuition, state resident: full-time $6408; part-time $3204 per semester. Tuition, nonresident: full-time $14,832; part-time $7416 per semester. *Required fees:* $1824; $912 per semester. Tuition and fees vary according to course load. *Financial support:* In 2011–12, 2 students received support, including 2 teaching assistantships (averaging $10,152 per year); research assistantships, Federal Work-Study, institutionally sponsored loans, scholarships/grants, health care benefits, and unspecified assistantships also available. Support available to part-time students. Financial award application deadline: 4/1; financial award applicants required to submit FAFSA. *Faculty research:* Micropower chip plan, uniflow SE bypass, high performance FET, growth of expitaxial, layer superlattices, geteronintegration. *Total annual research expenditures:* $383,881. *Unit head:* Dr. David Donnelly, Graduate Advisor, 512-245-2131, E-mail: donnelly@txstate.edu. *Application contact:* Dr. J. Michael Willoughby, Dean of Graduate School, 512-245-2581, Fax: 512-245-8365, E-mail: gradcollege@txstate.edu. Web site: http://www.mse.txstate.edu/.

Trent University, Graduate Studies, Program in Materials Science, Peterborough, ON K9J 7B8, Canada. Offers M Sc.

Université du Québec, Institut National de la Recherche Scientifique, Graduate Programs, Research Center - Energy, Materials and Telecommunications, Québec, QC G1K 9A9, Canada. Offers energy and materials science (M Sc, PhD); telecommunications (M Sc, PhD). Programs given in French; PhD programs offered jointly with Université du Québec à Trois-Rivières. Part-time programs available. *Faculty:* 39. *Students:* 175 full-time (71 women), 19 part-time (4 women), 107 international. Average age 32. In 2011, 12 master's, 17 doctorates awarded. *Degree requirements:* For master's, thesis optional; for doctorate, thesis/dissertation. *Entrance requirements:* For master's, appropriate bachelor's degree, proficiency in French; for doctorate, appropriate master's degree, proficiency in French. *Application deadline:* For fall admission, 3/30 for domestic and international students; for winter admission, 11/1 for domestic and international students; for spring admission, 3/1 for domestic and international students. Application fee: $45. *Financial support:* In 2011–12, 141 students received support, including fellowships (averaging $16,500 per year); research assistantships also available. *Faculty research:* New energy sources, plasmas, fusion. *Unit head:* Frederico Rosei, Director, 450-228-6905, E-mail: rosei@emt.inrs.ca. *Application contact:* Yvonne Boisvert, Registrar, 418-654-3861, Fax: 418-654-3858, E-mail: registrariat@adm.inrs.ca. Web site: http://www.inrs.ca/english/research-centres/energie-materiaux-telecommunications-research-centre.

University at Buffalo, the State University of New York, Graduate School, School of Dental Medicine, Graduate Programs in Dental Medicine, Department of Oral Diagnostic Sciences, Buffalo, NY 14260. Offers biomaterials (MS). Part-time programs available. *Degree requirements:* For master's, thesis. *Entrance requirements:* Additional exam requirements/recommendations for international students: Required—TOEFL (minimum score 79 iBT). Electronic applications accepted. *Faculty research:* Bioengineering, surface science, bioadhesion, regulatory sterilization.

The University of Alabama, Graduate School, College of Engineering and College of Arts and Sciences, Tri-Campus Materials Science PhD Program, Tuscaloosa, AL 35487. Offers PhD. Program offered jointly with The University of Alabama at Birmingham, The University of Alabama in Huntsville. *Students:* 14 full-time (1 woman); includes 3 minority (all Black or African American, non-Hispanic/Latino), 9 international. Average age 26. 18 applicants, 33% accepted, 5 enrolled. In 2011, 1 degree awarded. *Median time to degree:* Of those who began their doctoral program in fall 2003, 100% received their degree in 8 years or less. *Degree requirements:* For doctorate, comprehensive exam, thesis/dissertation. *Entrance requirements:* For doctorate, GRE General Test. Additional exam requirements/recommendations for international students: Required—TOEFL (minimum score 550 paper-based; 213 computer-based). *Application deadline:* For fall admission, 2/28 priority date for domestic students, 2/28 for international students; for spring admission, 10/30 priority date for domestic students, 9/30 for international students. Applications are processed on a rolling basis. Application fee: $50 ($60 for international students). Electronic applications accepted. *Expenses:* Tuition, state resident: full-time $8600. Tuition, nonresident: full-time $21,900. *Financial support:* In 2011–12, 4 research assistantships with full tuition reimbursements (averaging $19,500 per year) were awarded; career-related internships or fieldwork and unspecified assistantships also available. Financial award application deadline: 2/28. *Faculty research:* Magnetic multilayers, metals casting, molecular electronics, conducting polymers, metals physics, electrodeposition. *Unit head:* Prof. Garry Warren, Campus Coordinator, 205-348-4337, E-mail: gwarren@coe.eng.ua.edu. *Application contact:* Dr. David A. Francko, Dean, 205-348-8280, Fax: 205-348-0400, E-mail: dfrancko@ua.edu.

The University of Alabama at Birmingham, School of Engineering, Joint Materials Science PhD Program, Birmingham, AL 35294. Offers PhD. Program offered jointly with The University of Alabama (Tuscaloosa), The University of Alabama in Huntsville. *Degree requirements:* For doctorate, thesis/dissertation. *Entrance requirements:* For doctorate, GRE General Test. *Expenses:* Tuition, state resident: full-time $5922; part-time $309 per hour. Tuition, nonresident: full-time $13,428; part-time $726 per hour. Tuition and fees vary according to program. *Financial support:* Fellowships with full and partial tuition reimbursements, research assistantships with full tuition reimbursements, career-related internships or fieldwork, Federal Work-Study, and institutionally sponsored loans available. Support available to part-time students. Financial award application deadline: 4/1. *Faculty research:* Biocompatibility studies with biomaterials, microgravity solidification of proteins and metals, analysis of microelectronic materials, thin film analysis using TEM. *Unit head:* Dr. J. Barry Andrews, Chair, 205-934-8460, Fax: 205-934-8485, E-mail: barry@uab.edu. Web site: http://www.uab.edu/engineering/departments-research/mse/grad#Master%20of%20Science%20in%20Civil%20Engineering%20%28M.S.C.E.%29%20Program%20Requirement.

The University of Alabama in Huntsville, School of Graduate Studies, Interdisciplinary Studies, Interdisciplinary Program in Materials Science, Huntsville, AL 35899. Offers MS, PhD. PhD offered jointly with The University of Alabama and The University of Alabama at Birmingham. Part-time and evening/weekend programs available. *Faculty:* 12 full-time (1 woman). *Students:* 5 full-time (1 woman), 3 part-time (2 women); includes 2 minority (both Black or African American, non-Hispanic/Latino), 3 international. Average age 34. 15 applicants, 27% accepted, 2 enrolled. *Degree requirements:* For master's, comprehensive exam, thesis or alternative, oral and written exams; for doctorate, comprehensive exam, thesis/dissertation, oral and written exams. *Entrance requirements:* For master's, GRE General Test, minimum GPA of 3.0; for doctorate, GRE General Test, bachelor's degree in engineering or physical science, minimum GPA of 3.0. Additional exam requirements/recommendations for international students: Required—TOEFL (minimum score 500 paper-based; 173 computer-based; 62 iBT). *Application deadline:* For fall admission, 7/15 for domestic students, 4/1 for international students; for spring admission, 11/30 for domestic students, 9/1 for international students. Applications are processed on a rolling basis: Application fee: $40 ($50 for international students). Electronic applications accepted. *Expenses:* Tuition, state resident: full-time $7830; part-time $473.50 per credit. Tuition, nonresident: full-time $18,748; part-time $1128.33 per credit. Tuition and fees vary according to course load and program. *Financial support:* In 2011–12, 4 students received support, including 4 teaching assistantships with full and partial tuition reimbursements available (averaging $11,115 per year); career-related internships or fieldwork, Federal Work-Study, institutionally sponsored loans, scholarships/grants, health care benefits, and unspecified assistantships also available. Support available to part-time students. Financial award application deadline: 4/1; financial award applicants required to submit FAFSA. *Faculty research:* Materials structure and properties; materials processing; mechanical behavior; macromolecular materials; electronic, optical, and magnetic materials. *Unit head:* Dr. Michael Banish, Coordinator, 256-824-6810, Fax: 256-824-6349, E-mail: banishm@uah.edu. *Application contact:* Kim Gray, Graduate Studies Admissions Coordinator, 256-824-6002, Fax: 256-824-6405, E-mail: deangrad@uah.edu. Web site: http://matsci.uah.edu.

The University of Arizona, College of Engineering, Department of Materials Science and Engineering, Tucson, AZ 85721. Offers MS, PhD. Part-time programs available. *Faculty:* 9 full-time (2 women), 3 part-time/adjunct (1 woman). *Students:* 39 full-time (13 women), 10 part-time (5 women); includes 12 minority (1 Black or African American, non-Hispanic/Latino; 2 Asian, non-Hispanic/Latino; 6 Hispanic/Latino; 3 Two or more races, non-Hispanic/Latino), 17 international. Average age 29. 82 applicants, 20% accepted, 6 enrolled. In 2011, 8 master's, 7 doctorates awarded. *Degree requirements:* For master's, thesis (for some programs); for doctorate, comprehensive exam, thesis/dissertation. *Entrance requirements:* For master's and doctorate, GRE General Test, 3 letters of recommendation, statement of purpose. Additional exam requirements/recommendations for international students: Required—TOEFL (minimum score 550 paper-based; 213 computer-based). *Application deadline:* Applications are processed on a rolling basis. Application fee: $75. Electronic applications accepted. *Expenses:* Tuition, state resident: full-time $10,840. Tuition, nonresident: full-time $25,802. *Financial support:* In 2011–12, 22 research assistantships with full tuition reimbursements (averaging $23,789 per year), 1 teaching assistantship with full tuition reimbursement (averaging $23,586 per year) were awarded; institutionally sponsored loans, scholarships/grants, health care benefits, tuition waivers (full), and unspecified assistantships also available. Financial award application deadline: 12/31. *Faculty research:* High-technology ceramics, optical materials, electronic materials, chemical metallurgy, science of materials. *Total annual research expenditures:* $1.9 million. *Unit head:* Dr. Pierre Deymier, Head, 520-621-6080, Fax: 520-621-8059, E-mail: deymier@email.arizona.edu. *Application contact:* Information Contact, 520-626-6762, Fax: 520-621-8059, E-mail: msed@email.arizona.edu. Web site: http://www.mse.arizona.edu/.

The University of British Columbia, Faculty of Applied Science, Department of Materials Engineering, Vancouver, BC V6T 1Z1, Canada. Offers materials and metallurgy (M Sc, PhD); metals and materials engineering (MA Sc, PhD). *Degree requirements:* For master's, comprehensive exam, thesis; for doctorate, comprehensive exam, thesis/dissertation. *Entrance requirements:* Additional exam requirements/recommendations for international students: Required—TOEFL (minimum score 560 paper-based; 220 computer-based; 83 iBT). Electronic applications accepted. *Faculty research:* Electroslag melting, mathematical modeling, solidification and hydrometallurgy.

University of California, Berkeley, Graduate Division, College of Engineering, Department of Materials Science and Engineering, Berkeley, CA 94720-1500. Offers engineering (M Eng, MS, D Eng, PhD); engineering science (M Eng, MS, PhD). *Degree requirements:* For master's, comprehensive exam or thesis (MS); for doctorate, comprehensive exam, thesis/dissertation, qualifying exam. *Entrance requirements:* For master's and doctorate, GRE General Test, minimum GPA of 3.0, 3 letters of

recommendation. Additional exam requirements/recommendations for international students: Required—TOEFL (minimum score 230 computer-based). *Faculty research:* Ceramics, biomaterials, structural, electronic, magnetic and optical materials.

University of California, Davis, College of Engineering, Program in Materials Science and Engineering, Davis, CA 95616. Offers MS, PhD. Terminal master's awarded for partial completion of doctoral program. *Degree requirements:* For master's, comprehensive exam (for some programs), thesis (for some programs); for doctorate, comprehensive exam, thesis/dissertation. *Entrance requirements:* Additional exam requirements/recommendations for international students: Required—TOEFL (minimum score 550 paper-based; 213 computer-based).

University of California, Irvine, School of Engineering, Department of Chemical Engineering and Materials Science, Irvine, CA 92697. Offers chemical and biochemical engineering (MS, PhD); materials science and engineering (MS, PhD). Part-time programs available. *Students:* 84 full-time (29 women), 2 part-time (0 women); includes 23 minority (1 American Indian or Alaska Native, non-Hispanic/Latino; 19 Asian, non-Hispanic/Latino; 2 Hispanic/Latino; 1 Native Hawaiian or other Pacific Islander, non-Hispanic/Latino), 37 international. Average age 27. 343 applicants, 22% accepted, 22 enrolled. In 2011, 17 master's, 4 doctorates awarded. Terminal master's awarded for partial completion of doctoral program. *Degree requirements:* For doctorate, thesis/dissertation. *Entrance requirements:* For master's and doctorate, GRE General Test, minimum GPA of 3.0, 3 letters of recommendation. Additional exam requirements/recommendations for international students: Required—TOEFL (minimum score 550 paper-based; 213 computer-based). *Application deadline:* For fall admission, 1/15 priority date for domestic students, 1/15 for international students. Applications are processed on a rolling basis. Application fee: $80 ($100 for international students). Electronic applications accepted. *Financial support:* Fellowships with tuition reimbursements, research assistantships with full tuition reimbursements, teaching assistantships with tuition reimbursements, institutionally sponsored loans, traineeships, health care benefits, and unspecified assistantships available. Financial award application deadline: 3/1; financial award applicants required to submit FAFSA. *Faculty research:* Molecular biotechnology, nano-bio-materials, biophotonics, synthesis, superplasticity and mechanical behavior, characterization of advanced and nanostructural materials. *Unit head:* Prof. Albert Yee, Chair, 949-824-7320, Fax: 949-824-2541, E-mail: albert.yee@uci.edu. *Application contact:* Grace Hai-Chin Chau, Academic Program and Graduate Admission Coordinator, 949-824-3887, Fax: 949-824-2541, E-mail: chaug@uci.edu. Web site: http://www.eng.uci.edu/dept/chems.

University of California, Irvine, School of Physical Sciences, Department of Chemistry and Department of Physics and Astronomy, Program in Chemical and Materials Physics (CHAMP), Irvine, CA 92697. Offers MS, PhD. *Students:* 60 full-time (15 women), 2 part-time (1 woman); includes 16 minority (1 American Indian or Alaska Native, non-Hispanic/Latino; 9 Asian, non-Hispanic/Latino; 5 Hispanic/Latino; 1 Two or more races, non-Hispanic/Latino), 9 international. Average age 27. 38 applicants, 32% accepted, 7 enrolled. In 2011, 5 master's, 7 doctorates awarded. *Degree requirements:* For doctorate, thesis/dissertation. *Entrance requirements:* For master's and doctorate, GRE General Test, GRE Subject Test, minimum GPA of 3.0. *Application deadline:* For fall admission, 1/15 priority date for domestic students, 1/15 for international students. Applications are processed on a rolling basis. Application fee: $80 ($100 for international students). Electronic applications accepted. *Financial support:* Fellowships, research assistantships with full tuition reimbursements, teaching assistantships, institutionally sponsored loans, traineeships, health care benefits, and unspecified assistantships available. Financial award application deadline: 3/1; financial award applicants required to submit FAFSA. *Unit head:* Craig Martens, Co-Director, 949-824-5141, E-mail: cmartens@uci.edu. *Application contact:* Philip Collins, Advisor, 949-824-9961, E-mail: collinsp@uci.edu.

University of California, Los Angeles, Graduate Division, Henry Samueli School of Engineering and Applied Science, Department of Materials Science and Engineering, Los Angeles, CA 90095-1595. Offers MS, PhD. *Faculty:* 12 full-time (2 women), 2 part-time/adjunct (0 women). *Students:* 106 full-time (19 women); includes 20 minority (2 Black or African American, non-Hispanic/Latino; 13 Asian, non-Hispanic/Latino; 4 Hispanic/Latino; 1 Two or more races, non-Hispanic/Latino), 64 international. 220 applicants, 49% accepted, 31 enrolled. In 2011, 20 master's, 8 doctorates awarded. *Degree requirements:* For master's, comprehensive exam or thesis; for doctorate, thesis/dissertation, qualifying exams. *Entrance requirements:* For master's, GRE General Test, minimum GPA of 3.0; for doctorate, GRE General Test, minimum GPA of 3.25. Additional exam requirements/recommendations for international students: Required—TOEFL (minimum score 560 paper-based; 220 computer-based; 87 iBT). *Application deadline:* For fall admission, 12/15 for domestic and international students. Application fee: $80 ($100 for international students). Electronic applications accepted. *Financial support:* In 2011–12, 42 fellowships, 302 research assistantships, 33 teaching assistantships were awarded; Federal Work-Study, institutionally sponsored loans, and tuition waivers (full and partial) also available. Financial award application deadline: 1/15; financial award applicants required to submit FAFSA. *Faculty research:* Ceramics and ceramic processing, electronic and optical materials, structural materials. *Total annual research expenditures:* $7.2 million. *Unit head:* Dr. Jenn-Ming Yang, Chair, 310-825-2758, E-mail: jyang@seas.ucla.edu. *Application contact:* Patti Barrera, Student Affairs Officer, 310-825-8916, Fax: 310-206-7353, E-mail: patti@ea.ucla.edu. Web site: http://www.ms.ucla.edu.

University of California, Riverside, Graduate Division, Graduate Materials Science and Engineering Program, Riverside, CA 92521. Offers MS, PhD. *Entrance requirements:* For master's and doctorate, GRE. Additional exam requirements/recommendations for international students: Required—TOEFL (minimum score 550 paper-based; 213 computer-based; 80 iBT). Electronic applications accepted.

University of California, San Diego, Office of Graduate Studies, Materials Science and Engineering Program, La Jolla, CA 92093. Offers MS, PhD. *Degree requirements:* For doctorate, thesis/dissertation. *Entrance requirements:* For master's and doctorate, GRE General Test, minimum GPA of 3.0. Additional exam requirements/recommendations for international students: Required—TOEFL. Electronic applications accepted.

University of California, Santa Barbara, Graduate Division, College of Engineering, Department of Materials, Santa Barbara, CA 93106-5050. Offers MS, PhD, MS/PhD. *Faculty:* 27 full-time (2 women), 6 part-time/adjunct (0 women). *Students:* 132 full-time (26 women); includes 35 minority (2 Black or African American, non-Hispanic/Latino; 27 Asian, non-Hispanic/Latino; 2 Hispanic/Latino; 4 Two or more races, non-Hispanic/Latino), 22 international. Average age 26. 316 applicants, 24% accepted, 32 enrolled. In 2011, 6 master's, 6 doctorates awarded. Terminal master's awarded for partial completion of doctoral program. *Median time to degree:* Of those who began their doctoral program in fall 2003, 99% received their degree in 8 years or less. *Degree requirements:* For doctorate, comprehensive exam, thesis/dissertation. *Entrance* *requirements:* For master's and doctorate, GRE General Test. Additional exam requirements/recommendations for international students: Required—TOEFL (minimum score 600 paper-based; 100 iBT), IELTS (minimum score 7). *Application deadline:* For fall admission, 1/7 priority date for domestic students, 1/7 for international students; for winter admission, 11/1 priority date for domestic students, 11/1 for international students; for spring admission, 1/1 priority date for domestic students, 1/1 for international students. Application fee: $80 ($100 for international students). Electronic applications accepted. *Expenses:* Tuition, state resident: full-time $12,192. Tuition, nonresident: full-time $27,294. *Required fees:* $764.13. *Financial support:* In 2011–12, 12 students received support, including 45 fellowships with full and partial tuition reimbursements available (averaging $19,654 per year), 70 research assistantships with full and partial tuition reimbursements available (averaging $28,000 per year), 24 teaching assistantships with partial tuition reimbursements available (averaging $2,885 per year); career-related internships or fieldwork, scholarships/grants, tuition waivers (full), and unspecified assistantships also available. Financial award application deadline: 3/2; financial award applicants required to submit FAFSA. *Faculty research:* Electronic and photonic materials, inorganic materials, macromolecular and biomolecular materials, structural materials. *Unit head:* Dr. Tresa M. Pollock, Chair and Professor, 805-893-4362, Fax: 805-893-8486, E-mail: speck@mrl.ucsb.edu. *Application contact:* Oura Neak, Graduate Program Assistant, 805-893-4601, Fax: 805-893-8486, E-mail: mtrl-applications@engineering.ucsb.edu. Web site: http://www.materials.ucsb.edu/.

University of Central Florida, College of Engineering and Computer Science, Department of Mechanical, Materials, and Aerospace Engineering, Program in Materials Science and Engineering, Orlando, FL 32816. Offers MSMSE, PhD. *Students:* 46 full-time (10 women), 16 part-time (8 women); includes 9 minority (1 Black or African American, non-Hispanic/Latino; 1 American Indian or Alaska Native, non-Hispanic/Latino; 2 Asian, non-Hispanic/Latino; 5 Hispanic/Latino), 31 international. Average age 29. 53 applicants, 70% accepted, 17 enrolled. In 2011, 11 master's, 6 doctorates awarded. *Degree requirements:* For master's, thesis or alternative; for doctorate, thesis/dissertation, candidacy exam, departmental qualifying exam. *Application deadline:* For fall admission, 7/15 priority date for domestic students; for spring admission, 12/1 priority date for domestic students. Application fee: $30. Electronic applications accepted. *Expenses:* Tuition, state resident: part-time $277.08 per credit hour. Tuition, nonresident: part-time $277.08 per credit hour. Part-time tuition and fees vary according to degree level and program. *Financial support:* In 2011–12, 31 students received support, including 9 fellowships (averaging $1,900 per year), 27 research assistantships (averaging $10,500 per year), 5 teaching assistantships (averaging $8,900 per year). *Unit head:* Dr. Suhada Jayasuriya, Chair, 407-823-5792, Fax: 407-823-0208, E-mail: suhada@ucf.edu. *Application contact:* Barbara Rodriguez, Director, Admissions and Registration, 407-823-2766, Fax: 407-823-6442, E-mail: gradadmissions@ucf.edu. Web site: http://mmae.ucf.edu/.

University of Cincinnati, Graduate School, College of Engineering and Applied Science, Department of Chemical and Materials Engineering, Program in Materials Science and Engineering, Cincinnati, OH 45221. Offers MS, PhD. Evening/weekend programs available. *Degree requirements:* For master's, thesis optional; for doctorate, one foreign language, comprehensive exam, thesis/dissertation, oral English proficiency exam. *Entrance requirements:* For master's and doctorate, GRE General Test, BS in related field, minimum undergraduate GPA of 3.0. Additional exam requirements/recommendations for international students: Required—TOEFL. Electronic applications accepted. *Faculty research:* Polymer characterization, surface analysis, and adhesion; mechanical behavior of high-temperature materials; composites; electrochemistry of materials.

University of Connecticut, Graduate School, School of Engineering, Department of Chemical, Materials and Biomolecular Engineering, Field of Materials Science and Engineering, Storrs, CT 06269. Offers MS, PhD. Terminal master's awarded for partial completion of doctoral program. *Degree requirements:* For master's, comprehensive exam; for doctorate, thesis/dissertation. *Entrance requirements:* For master's and doctorate, GRE General Test, GRE Subject Test. Additional exam requirements/recommendations for international students: Required—TOEFL (minimum score 550 paper-based; 213 computer-based). Electronic applications accepted.

University of Connecticut, Institute of Materials Science, Storrs, CT 06269. Offers MS, PhD.

University of Delaware, College of Engineering, Department of Materials Science and Engineering, Newark, DE 19716. Offers MMSE, PhD. Terminal master's awarded for partial completion of doctoral program. *Degree requirements:* For master's, thesis; for doctorate, thesis/dissertation. *Entrance requirements:* For master's and doctorate, GRE General Test, 3 letters of recommendation, minimum GPA of 3.2. Additional exam requirements/recommendations for international students: Required—TOEFL. Electronic applications accepted. *Faculty research:* Thin films and self assembly, drug delivery and tissue engineering, biomaterials and nanocomposites, semiconductor and oxide interfaces, electronic and magnetic materials.

University of Denver, School of Engineering and Computer Science, Department of Mechanical and Materials Engineering, Denver, CO 80208. Offers bioengineering (MS); engineering (MS, PhD); engineering/management (MS); interdisciplinary engineering (PhD); materials science (MS, PhD); mechanical engineering (MS, PhD); nanoscale science and engineering (MS, PhD). Part-time programs available. *Faculty:* 10 full-time (2 women), 1 part-time/adjunct (0 women). *Students:* 1 (woman) full-time, 25 part-time (5 women); includes 1 minority (Asian, non-Hispanic/Latino), 9 international. Average age 30. 69 applicants, 67% accepted, 11 enrolled. In 2011, 6 degrees awarded. Terminal master's awarded for partial completion of doctoral program. *Degree requirements:* For master's, thesis or alternative; for doctorate, comprehensive exam, thesis/dissertation. *Entrance requirements:* For master's, GRE General Test, essay/personal statement, three letters of recommendation; for doctorate, GRE General Test, essay/personal statement, three letters of recommendation, curriculum vitae. Additional exam requirements/recommendations for international students: Required—TOEFL (minimum score 550 paper-based; 80 iBT). *Application deadline:* Applications are processed on a rolling basis. Application fee: $60. Electronic applications accepted. *Financial support:* In 2011–12, 14 students received support, including 8 research assistantships with full and partial tuition reimbursements available (averaging $15,631 per year), 7 teaching assistantships with full and partial tuition reimbursements available (averaging $13,943 per year); Federal Work-Study, health care benefits, and unspecified assistantships also available. Financial award application deadline: 2/15; financial award applicants required to submit FAFSA. *Faculty research:* Aerosols, biomechanics, composite materials, photo optics, drug delivery. *Total annual research expenditures:* $818,288. *Unit head:* Dr. Matt Gordon, Chair, 303-871-3580, Fax: 303-871-4450, E-mail: matthew.gordon@du.edu. *Application contact:* Renee Carvalho, Assistant to the Chair, 303-871-2107, Fax: 303-871-4450, E-mail: renee.carvalho@du.edu. Web site: http://www.mme.du.edu.

University of Florida, Graduate School, College of Engineering, Department of Materials Science and Engineering, Gainesville, FL 32611. Offers ME, MS, PhD, Engr, JD/MS. Part-time programs available. Terminal master's awarded for partial completion of doctoral program. *Degree requirements:* For master's, comprehensive exam, thesis; for doctorate, comprehensive exam, thesis/dissertation; for Engr, thesis optional. *Entrance requirements:* For master's and doctorate, GRE General Test, minimum GPA of 3.0; for Engr, GRE General Test. Additional exam requirements/recommendations for international students: Required—TOEFL (minimum score 550 paper-based; 213 computer-based; 80 iBT), IELTS (minimum score 6). Electronic applications accepted. *Faculty research:* Polymeric system, biomaterials and biomimetics; inorganic and organic electronic materials; functional ceramic materials for energy systems and microelectronic applications; advanced metallic systems for aerospace, transportation and biological applications; nuclear materials.

University of Idaho, College of Graduate Studies, College of Engineering, Department of Chemical and Materials Engineering, Moscow, ID 83844-3024. Offers chemical engineering (MS, PhD); materials science and engineering (MS, PhD), including materials science and engineering, metallurgical engineering (MS); metallurgy (MS). *Faculty:* 10 full-time. *Students:* 16 full-time, 10 part-time. Average age 33. In 2011, 6 master's awarded. *Degree requirements:* For master's, thesis; for doctorate, one foreign language, thesis/dissertation. *Entrance requirements:* For master's, GRE, minimum GPA of 2.8; for doctorate, GRE, minimum undergraduate GPA of 2.8, 3.0 graduate. *Application deadline:* For fall admission, 8/1 for domestic students; for spring admission, 12/15 for domestic students. Applications are processed on a rolling basis. Application fee: $60. Electronic applications accepted. *Expenses:* Tuition, state resident: full-time $3874; part-time $334 per credit hour. Tuition, nonresident: full-time $16,394; part-time $861 per credit hour. *Required fees:* $2808; $99 per credit hour. Tuition and fees vary according to program. *Financial support:* Fellowships, research assistantships, and teaching assistantships available. Financial award applicants required to submit FAFSA. *Faculty research:* Geothermal energy utilization, alcohol production from agriculture waste material, energy conservation in pulp and paper mills. *Unit head:* Dr. Wudneh Admassu, 208-885-7572, E-mail: gailb@uidaho.edu. *Application contact:* Erick Larson, Director of Graduate Admissions, 208-885-4723, E-mail: gadms@uidaho.edu. Web site: http://www.uidaho.edu/engr/cme/about/materials.

University of Illinois at Urbana–Champaign, Graduate College, College of Engineering, Department of Materials Science and Engineering, Champaign, IL 61820. Offers MS, PhD, MS/MBA, PhD/MBA. *Faculty:* 23 full-time (3 women), 4 part-time/adjunct (0 women). *Students:* 158 full-time (37 women), 10 part-time (2 women); includes 22 minority (1 American Indian or Alaska Native, non-Hispanic/Latino; 14 Asian, non-Hispanic/Latino; 3 Hispanic/Latino; 4 Two or more races, non-Hispanic/Latino), 90 international. 432 applicants, 25% accepted, 47 enrolled. In 2011, 11 master's, 28 doctorates awarded. *Entrance requirements:* For master's and doctorate, GRE, minimum GPA of 3.0. Additional exam requirements/recommendations for international students: Required—TOEFL (minimum score 613 paper-based; 257 computer-based; 103 iBT) or IELTS (minimum score 7). *Application deadline:* Applications are processed on a rolling basis. Application fee: $75 ($90 for international students). Electronic applications accepted. *Financial support:* In 2011–12, 20 fellowships, 153 research assistantships, 14 teaching assistantships were awarded; tuition waivers (full and partial) also available. *Unit head:* David G. Cahill, Head, 217-333-6753, Fax: 217-244-1631, E-mail: d-cahill@illinois.edu. *Application contact:* Michelle L. Malloch, Office Support Associate, 217-333-8517, Fax: 217-333-2736, E-mail: malloch@illinois.edu. Web site: http://www.matse.illinois.edu/.

University of Kentucky, Graduate School, College of Engineering, Program in Materials Science, Lexington, KY 40506-0032. Offers materials science and engineering (MSMAE, PhD). *Degree requirements:* For master's, comprehensive exam, thesis optional; for doctorate, comprehensive exam, thesis/dissertation. *Entrance requirements:* For master's, GRE General Test, minimum undergraduate GPA of 2.75; for doctorate, GRE General Test, minimum undergraduate GPA of 3.0. Additional exam requirements/recommendations for international students: Required—TOEFL (minimum score 550 paper-based; 213 computer-based). Electronic applications accepted. *Faculty research:* Physical and mechanical metallurgy, computational material engineering, polymers and composites, high-temperature ceramics, powder metallurgy.

The University of Manchester, School of Chemistry, Manchester, United Kingdom. Offers biological chemistry (PhD); chemistry (M Ent, M Phil, M Sc, D Ent, PhD); inorganic chemistry (PhD); materials chemistry (PhD); nanoscience (PhD); nuclear fission (PhD); organic chemistry (PhD); physical chemistry (PhD); theoretical chemistry (PhD).

The University of Manchester, School of Materials, Manchester, United Kingdom. Offers advanced aerospace materials engineering (M Sc); advanced metallic systems (PhD); biomedical materials (M Phil, M Sc, PhD); ceramics and glass (M Phil, M Sc, PhD); composite materials (M Sc, PhD); corrosion and protection (M Phil, M Sc, PhD); materials (M Phil, PhD); metallic materials (M Phil, M Sc, PhD); nanostructural materials (M Phil, M Sc, PhD); paper science (M Phil, M Sc, PhD); polymer science and engineering (M Phil, M Sc, PhD); technical textiles (M Sc); textile design, fashion and management (M Phil, M Sc, PhD); textile science and technology (M Phil, M Sc, PhD); textiles (M Phil, PhD); textiles and fashion (M Ent).

University of Maryland, College Park, Academic Affairs, A. James Clark School of Engineering, Department of Continuing and Distance Learning in Engineering, College Park, MD 20742. Offers engineering (M Eng), including aerospace engineering, chemical engineering, civil engineering, electrical engineering, engineering, fire protection engineering, materials science and engineering, mechanical engineering, reliability engineering, systems engineering. *Faculty:* 3 full-time (0 women), 8 part-time/adjunct (0 women). *Students:* 75 full-time (24 women), 418 part-time (81 women); includes 154 minority (62 Black or African American, non-Hispanic/Latino; 64 Asian, non-Hispanic/Latino; 23 Hispanic/Latino; 5 Two or more races, non-Hispanic/Latino), 67 international. 447 applicants, 52% accepted, 154 enrolled. In 2011, 155 master's awarded. *Application deadline:* For fall admission, 8/15 for domestic students, 2/1 for international students; for spring admission, 1/10 for domestic students, 8/1 for international students. Applications are processed on a rolling basis. Application fee: $75. Electronic applications accepted. *Expenses: Tuition, area resident:* Part-time $525 per credit hour. Tuition, state resident: part-time $525 per credit hour. Tuition, nonresident: part-time $1131 per credit hour. *Required fees:* $386.31 per term. Tuition and fees vary according to program. *Financial support:* In 2011–12, 3 research assistantships (averaging $21,498 per year), 13 teaching assistantships (averaging $16,889 per year) were awarded. *Unit head:* Dr. Darryll Pines, Dean, 301-405-8539,

E-mail: pines@umd.edu. *Application contact:* Dr. Charles A. Caramello, Dean of the Graduate School, 301-405-0358, Fax: 301-314-9305.

University of Maryland, College Park, Academic Affairs, A. James Clark School of Engineering, Department of Materials Science and Engineering, Materials Science and Engineering Program, College Park, MD 20742. Offers MS, PhD. Part-time and evening/weekend programs available. Postbaccalaureate distance learning degree programs offered. *Students:* 60 full-time (14 women), 5 part-time (2 women); includes 11 minority (3 Black or African American, non-Hispanic/Latino; 4 Asian, non-Hispanic/Latino; 3 Hispanic/Latino; 1 Two or more races, non-Hispanic/Latino), 19 international. 189 applicants, 22% accepted, 13 enrolled. In 2011, 6 master's, 6 doctorates awarded. *Degree requirements:* For master's, comprehensive exam, thesis optional, research paper; for doctorate, thesis/dissertation, oral exam. *Entrance requirements:* For master's and doctorate, GRE General Test, minimum B+ average in undergraduate course work. Additional exam requirements/recommendations for international students: Required—TOEFL. *Application deadline:* For fall admission, 1/15 for domestic and international students; for spring admission, 6/1 for domestic and international students. Applications are processed on a rolling basis. Application fee: $75. Electronic applications accepted. *Expenses: Tuition, area resident:* Part-time $525 per credit hour. *Tuition, state resident:* part-time $525 per credit hour. *Tuition, nonresident:* part-time $1131 per credit hour. *Required fees:* $386.31 per term. Tuition and fees vary according to program. *Financial support:* In 2011–12, 4 fellowships with full and partial tuition reimbursements (averaging $58,774 per year), 42 research assistantships (averaging $24,011 per year), 8 teaching assistantships (averaging $25,981 per year) were awarded. Financial award applicants required to submit FAFSA. *Unit head:* Robert Briber, Chair, 301-405-7313, E-mail: rbriber@umd.edu. *Application contact:* Dr. Charles A. Caramello, Dean of Graduate School, 301-405-0358, Fax: 301-314-9305, E-mail: ccaramel@umd.edu.

University of Michigan, College of Engineering, Department of Materials Science and Engineering, Ann Arbor, MI 48109. Offers MS, PhD. Part-time programs available. *Students:* 153 full-time (42 women), 3 part-time (0 women). 525 applicants, 25% accepted, 52 enrolled. In 2011, 12 master's, 19 doctorates awarded. *Degree requirements:* For master's, thesis, oral defense of thesis; for doctorate, thesis/dissertation, oral defense of dissertation, written exam. *Entrance requirements:* For master's, GRE General Test, minimum GPA of 3.0 in related field; for doctorate, GRE General Test, minimum GPA of 3.0 in related field, master's degree. Additional exam requirements/recommendations for international students: Required—TOEFL. *Application deadline:* Applications are processed on a rolling basis. Application fee: $65 ($75 for international students). Electronic applications accepted. *Financial support:* Fellowships, research assistantships, and teaching assistantships available. Financial award applicants required to submit FAFSA. *Faculty research:* Soft materials (polymers, biomaterials), computational materials science, structural materials, electronic and optical materials, nanocomposite materials. *Unit head:* Peter Green, Department Chair, 734-763-2445, Fax: 734-763-4788. *Application contact:* Renee Hilgendorf, Graduate Program Coordinator, 734-763-9790, Fax: 734-763-4788, E-mail: reneeh@umich.edu. Web site: http://msewww.engin.umich.edu/.

See Display below and Close-Up on page 533.

University of Minnesota, Twin Cities Campus, College of Science and Engineering, Department of Chemical Engineering and Materials Science, Program in Materials Science and Engineering, Minneapolis, MN 55455-0132. Offers M Mat SE, MS Mat SE, PhD. Part-time programs available. *Students:* 68 (13 women); includes 4 minority (3 Asian, non-Hispanic/Latino; 1 Hispanic/Latino), 35 international. Terminal master's awarded for partial completion of doctoral program. *Degree requirements:* For master's, thesis; for doctorate, thesis/dissertation. *Entrance requirements:* For master's and doctorate, GRE General Test. Additional exam requirements/recommendations for international students: Required—TOEFL. *Application deadline:* For fall admission, 1/1 for domestic and international students. Applications are processed on a rolling basis. Application fee: $75 ($95 for international students). Electronic applications accepted. *Financial support:* Fellowships, research assistantships, and teaching assistantships available. *Faculty research:* Ceramics and metals; coating processes and interfacial engineering; crystal growth and design; polymers; electronic, photonic and magnetic materials . *Application contact:* Graduate Programs in Chemical Engineering and Materials Science, E-mail: cemsgrad@umn.edu. Web site: http://www.cems.umn.edu/.

University of Nebraska–Lincoln, Graduate College, College of Arts and Sciences, Department of Chemistry, Lincoln, NE 68588. Offers analytical chemistry (PhD); biochemistry (PhD); chemistry (MS); inorganic chemistry (PhD); materials chemistry (PhD); organic chemistry (PhD); physical chemistry (PhD). *Degree requirements:* For master's, one foreign language, thesis optional, departmental qualifying exam; for doctorate, one foreign language, comprehensive exam, thesis/dissertation, departmental qualifying exams. *Entrance requirements:* For master's and doctorate, GRE. Additional exam requirements/recommendations for international students: Required—TOEFL (minimum score 550 paper-based; 213 computer-based). Electronic applications accepted. *Faculty research:* Bioorganic and bioinorganic chemistry, biophysical and bioanalytical chemistry, structure-function of DNA and proteins, organometallics, mass spectrometry.

University of New Brunswick Fredericton, School of Graduate Studies, Faculty of Engineering, Department of Civil Engineering, Fredericton, NB E3B 5A3, Canada. Offers construction engineering and management (M Eng, M Sc E, PhD); environmental engineering (M Eng, M Sc E, PhD); environmental studies (M Eng); geotechnical engineering (M Eng, M Sc E, PhD); groundwater/hydrology (M Eng, M Sc E, PhD); materials (M Eng, M Sc E, PhD); pavements (M Eng, M Sc E, PhD); structures (M Eng, M Sc E, PhD); transportation (M Eng, M Sc E, PhD). Part-time programs available. *Faculty:* 13 full-time (1 woman), 7 part-time/adjunct (1 woman). *Students:* 31 full-time (7 women), 17 part-time (2 women). In 2011, 11 master's, 2 doctorates awarded. *Degree requirements:* For master's, thesis, proposal; for doctorate, comprehensive exam, thesis/dissertation, qualifying exam; proposal; 27 credit hours of courses. *Entrance requirements:* For master's, minimum GPA of 3.0; B Sc E in civil engineering or related engineering degree; for doctorate, minimum GPA of 3.0; graduate degree in engineering or applied science. Additional exam requirements/recommendations for international students: Required—TWE (minimum score 4), TOEFL (minimum score 580 paper-based; 237 computer-based) or IELTS (minimum score 7.5). *Application deadline:* For fall admission, 5/1 priority date for domestic students; for winter admission, 11/1 priority date for domestic students. Applications are processed on a rolling basis. Application fee: $50 Canadian dollars. *Financial support:* In 2011–12, 14 fellowships, 30 research assistantships (averaging $7,000 per year), 42 teaching assistantships (averaging $2,000 per year) were awarded; career-related internships or fieldwork and scholarships/grants also available. *Faculty research:* Construction engineering and management; materials and infrastructure renewal; highway and pavement research; structures and solid mechanics; geotechnical, soil; structure interaction; transportation and planning; environment, solid waste management. *Unit head:* Dr. Eric Hildebrand, Director of Graduate Studies, 506-453-5113, Fax: 506-453-3568, E-mail: edh@unb.ca.

Application contact: Joyce Moore, Graduate Secretary, 506-452-6127, Fax: 506-453-3568, E-mail: civil-grad@unb.ca. Web site: http://www.unbf.ca/eng/civil/.

University of New Hampshire, Graduate School, College of Engineering and Physical Sciences, Program in Materials Science, Durham, NH 03824. Offers MS, PhD. *Faculty:* 3 full-time (0 women). *Students:* 10 full-time (5 women), 1 part-time (0 women); includes 1 minority (Two or more races, non-Hispanic/Latino), 9 international. Average age 27. 36 applicants, 42% accepted, 1 enrolled. In 2011, 2 doctorates awarded. *Degree requirements:* For master's, thesis or alternative. *Entrance requirements:* For master's, GRE. Additional exam requirements/recommendations for international students: Required—TOEFL (minimum score 550 paper-based; 213 computer-based; 80 iBT). *Application deadline:* For fall admission, 4/1 priority date for domestic students, 4/1 for international students. Applications are processed on a rolling basis. Application fee: $65. Electronic applications accepted. *Expenses:* Tuition, state resident: full-time $12,360; part-time $687 per credit hour. Tuition, nonresident: full-time $25,680; part-time $1058 per credit hour. *International tuition:* $29,550 full-time. *Required fees:* $1666; $833 per course. $416.50 per semester. Tuition and fees vary according to course load and degree level. *Financial support:* In 2011–12, 10 students received support, including 1 fellowship, 5 research assistantships, 4 teaching assistantships; Federal Work-Study, scholarships/grants, and tuition waivers (full and partial) also available. Support available to part-time students. Financial award application deadline: 2/15. *Unit head:* Dr. Glenn Miller, Chairperson, 603-862-2456. *Application contact:* Katie Makem-Boucher, Administrative Assistant, 603-862-2669, E-mail: materials.science@unh.edu. Web site: http://www.unh.edu/materials-science/.

The University of North Carolina at Chapel Hill, Graduate School, College of Arts and Sciences, Curriculum in Applied Sciences and Engineering, Chapel Hill, NC 27599. Offers materials science (MS, PhD). Terminal master's awarded for partial completion of doctoral program. *Degree requirements:* For doctorate, thesis/dissertation. *Entrance requirements:* For master's, GRE General Test, minimum GPA of 3.0; for doctorate, GRE General Test. Electronic applications accepted. *Faculty research:* Scanning tunneling microscopy, magnetic resonance, carbon nanotubes, thin films, biomaterials, nano-materials, nanotechnology, polymeric materials, electronic and optic materials, tissue engineering.

University of North Texas, Toulouse Graduate School, College of Engineering, Department of Materials Science and Engineering, Denton, TX 76203. Offers MS, PhD. Part-time programs available. *Degree requirements:* For master's, comprehensive exam, thesis optional; for doctorate, thesis/dissertation. *Entrance requirements:* For master's and doctorate, GRE General Test. Additional exam requirements/recommendations for international students: Recommended—TOEFL (minimum score 550 paper-based; 213 computer-based). Electronic applications accepted. *Expenses:* Tuition, state resident: part-time $100 per credit hour. Tuition, nonresident: part-time $413 per credit hour. *Faculty research:* Polymers, electronic materials, ceramics, metals, nanomaterials.

University of Pennsylvania, School of Engineering and Applied Science, Department of Materials Science and Engineering, Philadelphia, PA 19104. Offers MSE, PhD, MSE/MBA. Part-time programs available. *Faculty:* 14 full-time (3 women), 2 part-time/adjunct (0 women). *Students:* 115 full-time (35 women), 11 part-time (5 women); includes 9 minority (8 Asian, non-Hispanic/Latino; 1 Hispanic/Latino), 94 international. 444 applicants, 30% accepted, 66 enrolled. In 2011, 32 master's, 6 doctorates awarded. Terminal master's awarded for partial completion of doctoral program. *Degree requirements:* For master's, thesis; for doctorate, thesis/dissertation. *Entrance requirements:* Additional exam requirements/recommendations for international students: Required—TOEFL. *Application deadline:* For fall admission, 6/1 priority date for domestic students, 5/1 for international students; for spring admission, 11/1 priority date for domestic students, 10/1 for international students. Applications are processed on a rolling basis. Application fee: $70. Electronic applications accepted. *Expenses: Tuition:* Full-time $26,660; part-time $4944 per course. *Required fees:* $2318; $291 per course. Tuition and fees vary according to course load, degree level and program. *Financial support:* Fellowships, research assistantships, teaching assistantships, institutionally sponsored loans, scholarships/grants, traineeships, health care benefits, and unspecified assistantships available. *Faculty research:* Advanced metallic, ceramic, and polymeric materials for device applications; micromechanics and structure of interfaces; thin film electronic materials; physics and chemistry of solids. *Unit head:* Eduardo D. Glandt, Dean, 215-898-7244, Fax: 215-573-2018, E-mail: seasdean@seas.upenn.edu. *Application contact:* Irene Clements, Graduate Coordinator, 215-898-8337, E-mail: ipc@lrsm.upenn.edu. Web site: http://www.mse.seas.upenn.edu/.

University of Pittsburgh, Swanson School of Engineering, Department of Mechanical Engineering and Materials Science, Pittsburgh, PA 15260. Offers MSME, PhD. Part-time programs available. Postbaccalaureate distance learning degree programs offered. *Faculty:* 27 full-time (4 women), 41 part-time/adjunct (3 women). *Students:* 102 full-time (17 women), 150 part-time (26 women); includes 14 minority (5 Black or African American, non-Hispanic/Latino; 1 American Indian or Alaska Native, non-Hispanic/Latino; 7 Asian, non-Hispanic/Latino; 1 Hispanic/Latino), 60 international. 445 applicants, 33% accepted, 67 enrolled. In 2011, 40 master's, 6 doctorates awarded. Terminal master's awarded for partial completion of doctoral program. *Degree requirements:* For master's, thesis optional; for doctorate, comprehensive exam, thesis/dissertation, final oral exams. *Entrance requirements:* For master's and doctorate, minimum QPA of 3.0. Additional exam requirements/recommendations for international students: Required—TOEFL (minimum score 550 paper-based; 230 computer-based). *Application deadline:* For fall admission, 3/1 priority date for domestic students; for spring admission, 7/1 priority date for domestic students. Applications are processed on a rolling basis. Application fee: $50. Electronic applications accepted. *Expenses:* Tuition, state resident: full-time $18,774; part-time $760 per credit. Tuition, nonresident: full-time $30,736; part-time $1258 per credit. *Required fees:* $740; $200 per term. Tuition and fees vary according to program. *Financial support:* In 2011–12, 83 students received support, including 5 fellowships with full tuition reimbursements available (averaging $27,432 per year), 47 research assistantships with full tuition reimbursements available (averaging $22,680 per year), 31 teaching assistantships with full tuition reimbursements available (averaging $24,144 per year); scholarships/grants and tuition waivers (full and partial) also available. Financial award application deadline: 4/15. *Faculty research:* Smart materials and structure solid mechanics, computational fluid dynamics, multiphase bio-fluid dynamics, mechanical vibration analysis. *Total annual research expenditures:* $6.7 million. *Unit head:* Dr. Minking K. Chyu, Chairman, 412-624-9784, Fax: 412-624-4846. *Application contact:* Dr. Qing-Ming Wamg, Graduate Coordinator, 412-624-4885, Fax: 412-624-4846, E-mail: qiw4@pitt.edu. Web site: http://www.engineering.pitt.edu/MEMS/.

University of Rochester, Hajim School of Engineering and Applied Sciences, Center for Entrepreneurship, Rochester, NY 14627-0360. Offers technical entrepreneurship and management (TEAM) (MS), including biomedical engineering, chemical engineering, computer science, electrical and computer engineering, energy and the environment, materials science, mechanical engineering, optics. *Faculty:* 61 full-time (8 women), 5 part-time/adjunct (1 woman). *Students:* 18 full-time (5 women), 3 part-time (1 woman); includes 4 minority (1 Asian, non-Hispanic/Latino; 3 Hispanic/Latino), 12 international. Average age 23. 134 applicants, 48% accepted, 21 enrolled. *Degree requirements:* For master's, comprehensive exam. *Entrance requirements:* For master's, GRE or GMAT, technical concentration of interest, 3 letters of recommendation, personal statement, official transcript. Additional exam requirements/recommendations for international students: Required—TOEFL or IELTS. *Application deadline:* For fall admission, 2/1 for domestic and international students. Applications are processed on a rolling basis. Application fee: $60. Electronic applications accepted. *Expenses: Tuition:* Full-time $41,040. *Financial support:* Career-related internships or fieldwork and scholarships/grants available. Financial award application deadline: 2/1. *Faculty research:* High efficiency solar cells, macromolecular self-assembly, digital signal processing, memory hierarchy management, molecular and physical mechanisms in cell migration. *Unit head:* Duncan T. Moore, Vice Provost for Entrepreneurship, 585-275-5248, Fax: 585-473-6745, E-mail: moore@optics.rochester.edu. *Application contact:* Andrea M. Galati, Executive Director, 585-276-3407, Fax: 585-276-2357, E-mail: andrea.galati@rochester.edu. Web site: http://www.rochester.edu/team.

University of Rochester, Hajim School of Engineering and Applied Sciences, Program in Materials Science, Rochester, NY 14627. Offers MS, PhD. *Students:* 38 full-time (15 women), 2 part-time (0 women); includes 1 minority (Hispanic/Latino), 31 international. 86 applicants, 43% accepted, 16 enrolled. In 2011, 8 master's, 4 doctorates awarded. Terminal master's awarded for partial completion of doctoral program. *Degree requirements:* For master's, comprehensive exam, thesis optional; for doctorate, thesis/dissertation, preliminary and qualifying exams. *Entrance requirements:* For master's and doctorate, GRE. Additional exam requirements/recommendations for international students: Required—TOEFL. *Application deadline:* For fall admission, 2/1 for domestic students. *Expenses: Tuition:* Full-time $41,040. *Financial support:* Fellowships, research assistantships, teaching assistantships, and tuition waivers (full and partial) available. Financial award application deadline: 2/1. *Unit head:* Dr. Todd D. Krauss, Director, 585-275-5093. Web site: http://www.rochester.edu/college/matsci/.

University of Southern California, Graduate School, Viterbi School of Engineering, Mork Family Department of Chemical Engineering and Materials Science, Los Angeles, CA 90089. Offers chemical engineering (MS, PhD, Engr); materials engineering (MS); materials science (MS, PhD, Engr); petroleum engineering (MS, PhD, Engr); smart oilfield technologies (MS, Graduate Certificate). Terminal master's awarded for partial completion of doctoral program. *Degree requirements:* For master's, thesis optional; for doctorate, thesis/dissertation. *Entrance requirements:* For master's and doctorate, GRE General Test. Additional exam requirements/recommendations for international students: Recommended—TOEFL. Electronic applications accepted. *Expenses:* Contact institution. *Faculty research:* Heterogeneous materials and porous media, statistical mechanics, molecular simulation, polymer science and engineering, advanced materials, reaction engineering and catalysis, membrane processes and separation, biochemical engineering, cell culture, bioreactor modeling, petroleum engineering.

The University of Tennessee, Graduate School, College of Engineering, Department of Materials Science and Engineering, Program in Materials Science and Engineering, Knoxville, TN 37996. Offers MS, PhD. *Faculty:* 29 full-time (3 women), 11 part-time/adjunct (3 women). *Students:* 76 full-time (17 women), 10 part-time (0 women); includes 9 minority (3 Black or African American, non-Hispanic/Latino; 2 Asian, non-Hispanic/Latino; 4 Hispanic/Latino), 53 international. Average age 29. 179 applicants, 14% accepted, 18 enrolled. In 2011, 7 master's, 9 doctorates awarded. *Degree requirements:* For master's, thesis or alternative; for doctorate, comprehensive exam, thesis/dissertation. *Entrance requirements:* For master's, GRE General Test (for MS students pursuing research thesis), minimum GPA of 2.7 (for U.S. degree holders), 3.0 (for international degree holders); 3 references; for doctorate, College requires GRE General Test for all PhD candidates, minimum GPA of 3.0 on previous graduate course work; 3 references. Additional exam requirements/recommendations for international students: Required—TOEFL (minimum score 550 paper-based; 213 computer-based). *Application deadline:* For fall admission, 2/1 priority date for domestic students, 2/1 for international students; for spring admission, 6/15 for domestic and international students. Applications are processed on a rolling basis. Application fee: $35. Electronic applications accepted. *Expenses:* Tuition, state resident: full-time $8332; part-time $464 per credit hour. Tuition, nonresident: full-time $25,174; part-time $1400 per credit hour. *Required fees:* $1162; $56 per credit hour. Tuition and fees vary according to program. *Financial support:* In 2011–12, 72 students received support, including 3 fellowships with full tuition reimbursements available (averaging $8,892 per year), 58 research assistantships with full tuition reimbursements available (averaging $20,400 per year), 6 teaching assistantships with full tuition reimbursements available (averaging $18,650 per year); career-related internships or fieldwork, Federal Work-Study, institutionally sponsored loans, health care benefits, and unspecified assistantships also available. Financial award application deadline: 2/1; financial award applicants required to submit FAFSA. *Faculty research:* Biomaterials; functional materials electronic, magnetic and optical; high temperature materials; mechanical behavior of materials; neutron materials science. *Unit head:* Dr. Kurt Sickafus, Head, 865-974-4858, Fax: 865-974-4115, E-mail: kurt@utk.edu. *Application contact:* Dr. Roberto S. Benson, Associate Head, 865-974-5347, Fax: 865-974-4115, E-mail: rbenson1@utk.edu. Web site: http://www.engr.utk.edu/mse.

The University of Tennessee Space Institute, Graduate Programs, Program in Materials Science and Engineering, Tullahoma, TN 37388-9700. Offers MS. *Faculty:* 3 full-time (0 women). *Students:* 1 full-time (0 women), 1 part-time (0 women), 1 international. 4 applicants, 25% accepted, 0 enrolled. In 2011, 3 degrees awarded. *Entrance requirements:* Additional exam requirements/recommendations for international students: Required—TOEFL (minimum score 550 paper-based; 213 computer-based; 80 iBT), IELTS (minimum score 6.5). *Application deadline:* For fall admission, 2/1 for international students; for spring admission, 6/15 for international students. Applications are processed on a rolling basis. Application fee: $35. Electronic applications accepted. *Financial support:* In 2011–12, 2 research assistantships with full tuition reimbursements (averaging $17,791 per year) were awarded; fellowships, career-related internships or fieldwork, Federal Work-Study, institutionally sponsored loans, health care benefits, tuition waivers (full and partial), and unspecified assistantships also available. *Unit head:* Dr. William Hofmeister, Degree Program Chairman, 931-393-7466, Fax: 931-393-7437, E-mail: whofmeis@utsi.edu. *Application contact:* Dee Merriman, Coordinator III, 931-393-7213, Fax: 931-393-7211, E-mail: dmerrima@utsi.edu. Web site: http://www.utsi.edu/academics/MSE/index.htm.

The University of Texas at Arlington, Graduate School, College of Engineering, Department of Materials Science and Engineering, Arlington, TX 76019. Offers M Engr,

MS, PhD. *Faculty:* 8 full-time (0 women). *Students:* 45 full-time (13 women), 13 part-time (3 women); includes 4 minority (1 Black or African American, non-Hispanic/Latino; 3 Asian, non-Hispanic/Latino), 48 international. 33 applicants, 61% accepted, 11 enrolled. In 2011, 21 master's, 5 doctorates awarded. Terminal master's awarded for partial completion of doctoral program. *Degree requirements:* For master's, comprehensive exam (for some programs), thesis optional; for doctorate, comprehensive exam, thesis/dissertation optional. *Entrance requirements:* For master's, GRE General Test, minimum GPA of 3.0; for doctorate, GRE General Test, minimum GPA of 3.5. Additional exam requirements/recommendations for international students: Required—TOEFL (minimum score 550 paper-based; 213 computer-based; 79 iBT), IELTS. *Application deadline:* For fall admission, 6/1 for domestic students, 4/1 for international students; for spring admission, 10/15 for domestic students, 9/15 for international students. Applications are processed on a rolling basis. Application fee: $35 ($50 for international students). *Financial support:* In 2011–12, 27 students received support, including 4 fellowships (averaging $1,000 per year), 10 research assistantships (averaging $16,000 per year), 13 teaching assistantships (averaging $16,000 per year); scholarships/grants and unspecified assistantships also available. Financial award application deadline: 6/1; financial award applicants required to submit FAFSA. *Faculty research:* Electronic materials, conductive polymer, composites biomaterial, structural materials. *Total annual research expenditures:* $400,000. *Unit head:* Dr. Efstathios I. Meletis, Chair, 817-272-2398 Ext. 2559, Fax: 817-272-2538, E-mail: meletis@uta.edu. *Application contact:* Dr. Choong-Un Kim, Graduate Adviser, 817-272-5497, Fax: 817-272-2538, E-mail: choongun@uta.edu. Web site: http://www.uta.edu/mse.

The University of Texas at Austin, Graduate School, Cockrell School of Engineering, Program in Materials Science and Engineering, Austin, TX 78712-1111. Offers MS, PhD. Part-time programs available. *Degree requirements:* For master's, thesis (for some programs); for doctorate, thesis/dissertation. *Entrance requirements:* For master's and doctorate, GRE General Test. Additional exam requirements/recommendations for international students: Required—TOEFL (minimum score 550 paper-based; 213 computer-based). *Application deadline:* For fall admission, 1/2 priority date for domestic students, 1/2 for international students; for spring admission, 10/1 for domestic and international students. Applications are processed on a rolling basis. Application fee: $50 ($75 for international students). Electronic applications accepted. *Financial support:* Fellowships with full tuition reimbursements, research assistantships with full tuition reimbursements, teaching assistantships with full tuition reimbursements, career-related internships or fieldwork, and institutionally sponsored loans available. Financial award application deadline: 1/1; financial award applicants required to submit FAFSA. *Unit head:* Donald R. Paul, Director, Texas Materials Institute, 512-471-5392, Fax: 512-471-0542, E-mail: drp@che.utexas.edu. *Application contact:* Rebecca Christian, Graduate Coordinator, 512-471-1504, Fax: 512-475-8482, E-mail: rjchristian@mail.utexas.edu. Web site: http://www.tmi.utexas.edu/.

The University of Texas at Dallas, Erik Jonsson School of Engineering and Computer Science, Department of Materials Science and Engineering, Richardson, TX 75080. Offers MS, PhD. Part-time and evening/weekend programs available. *Faculty:* 14 full-time (3 women), 1 part-time/adjunct (0 women). *Students:* 58 full-time (14 women), 9 part-time (3 women); includes 11 minority (2 Black or African American, non-Hispanic/Latino; 2 Asian, non-Hispanic/Latino; 6 Hispanic/Latino; 1 Two or more races, non-Hispanic/Latino), 43 international. Average age 29. 94 applicants, 40% accepted, 17 enrolled. In 2011, 9 master's, 3 doctorates awarded. *Degree requirements:* For master's, thesis or major design project; for doctorate, thesis/dissertation. *Entrance requirements:* For master's, GRE General Test, minimum GPA of 3.0 in related bachelor's degree; for doctorate, GRE General Test, minimum GPA of 3.5. Additional exam requirements/recommendations for international students: Required—TOEFL (minimum score 550 paper-based; 215 computer-based). *Application deadline:* For fall admission, 7/15 for domestic students, 5/1 for international students; for spring admission, 11/15 for domestic students, 9/1 for international students. Applications are processed on a rolling basis. Application fee: $50 ($100 for international students). Electronic applications accepted. *Expenses:* Tuition, state resident: full-time $11,170; part-time $620.56 per credit hour. Tuition, nonresident: full-time $20,212; part-time $1122.89 per credit hour. *Financial support:* In 2011–12, 49 students received support, including 1 fellowship (averaging $30,000 per year), 54 research assistantships with partial tuition reimbursements available (averaging $23,638 per year), 1 teaching assistantship with partial tuition reimbursement available (averaging $15,300 per year); career-related internships or fieldwork, Federal Work-Study, institutionally sponsored loans, scholarships/grants, and unspecified assistantships also available. Support available to part-time students. Financial award application deadline: 4/30; financial award applicants required to submit FAFSA. *Faculty research:* Graphene-based semiconducting materials, neuro-inspired computational paradigms, electronic materials with emphasis on dielectrics, energy harvesting (photovoltaics, Li-ion batteries), biosensors and H2 storage materials. *Unit head:* Dr. Yves Chabal, Department Head, 972-883-5751, Fax: 972-883-5725, E-mail: chabal@utdallas.edu. *Application contact:* Diane Griffith, Graduate Admissions Coordinator, 972-883-6748, Fax: 972-883-5725, E-mail: gradecs@utdallas.edu. Web site: http://mse.utdallas.edu/.

The University of Texas at El Paso, Graduate School, College of Engineering, Department of Metallurgical and Materials Engineering, El Paso, TX 79968-0001. Offers materials science and engineering (PhD); metallurgical and materials engineering (MS). Part-time and evening/weekend programs available. *Students:* 16 (8 women); includes 12 minority (all Hispanic/Latino), 2 international. Average age 34. 10 applicants, 80% accepted, 5 enrolled. *Degree requirements:* For master's, thesis. *Entrance requirements:* For master's, GRE General Test. Additional exam requirements/recommendations for international students: Required—TOEFL. *Application deadline:* For fall admission, 7/1 priority date for domestic students, 3/1 for international students; for spring admission, 11/1 priority date for domestic students, 9/1 for international students. Applications are processed on a rolling basis. Application fee: $15 ($65 for international students). Electronic applications accepted. *Financial support:* In 2011–12, research assistantships with partial tuition reimbursements (averaging $21,125 per year), teaching assistantships with partial tuition reimbursements (averaging $16,900 per year) were awarded; fellowships with partial tuition reimbursements, career-related internships or fieldwork, Federal Work-Study, institutionally sponsored loans, scholarships/grants, and tuition waivers (partial) also available. Financial award application deadline: 3/15; financial award applicants required to submit FAFSA. *Unit head:* Dr. Lawrence E. Murr, Chairperson, 915-747-5468, Fax: 915-747-8036, E-mail: fekberg@utep.edu. *Application contact:* Dr. Benjamin Flores, Interim Dean of the Graduate School, 915-747-5491, Fax: 915-747-5788, E-mail: bflores@utep.edu.

The University of Texas at El Paso, Graduate School, Interdisciplinary Program in Materials Science and Engineering, El Paso, TX 79968-0001. Offers PhD. Part-time and evening/weekend programs available. *Students:* 26 (13 women); includes 12 minority (1 Black or African American, non-Hispanic/Latino; 1 Asian, non-Hispanic/Latino; 9 Hispanic/Latino; 1 Two or more races, non-Hispanic/Latino), 13 international. Average age 34. In 2011, 4 doctorates awarded. *Degree requirements:* For doctorate, thesis/dissertation. *Entrance requirements:* For doctorate, GRE, letters of recommendation. Additional exam requirements/recommendations for international students: Required—TOEFL; Recommended—IELTS. *Application deadline:* For fall admission, 8/1 priority date for domestic students, 3/1 for international students; for spring admission, 11/1 priority date for domestic students, 9/3 for international students. Applications are processed on a rolling basis. Application fee: $45 ($80 for international students). Electronic applications accepted. *Financial support:* In 2011–12, research assistantships with partial tuition reimbursements (averaging $22,500 per year), teaching assistantships with partial tuition reimbursements (averaging $1,800 per year) were awarded; fellowships with partial tuition reimbursements, institutionally sponsored loans, scholarships/grants, health care benefits, tuition waivers (partial), and unspecified assistantships also available. Support available to part-time students. Financial award application deadline: 3/15; financial award applicants required to submit FAFSA. *Unit head:* Dr. Lawrence E. Murr, Director, 915-747-8002, Fax: 915-747-8036, E-mail: fekberg@utep.edu. *Application contact:* Dr. Benjamin Flores, Interim Dean of the Graduate School, 915-747-5491, Fax: 915-747-5788, E-mail: bflores@utep.edu.

The University of Toledo, College of Graduate Studies, College of Natural Sciences and Mathematics, Department of Physics and Astronomy, Toledo, OH 43606-3390. Offers physics (MS, PhD), including astrophysics (PhD), materials science (PhD), medical physics (PhD). *Faculty:* 26. *Students:* 65 full-time (13 women), 3 part-time (0 women); includes 1 minority (Asian, non-Hispanic/Latino), 24 international. Average age 29. 94 applicants, 15% accepted, 13 enrolled. In 2011, 2 master's, 8 doctorates awarded. *Degree requirements:* For master's, thesis; for doctorate, thesis/dissertation, departmental qualifying exam. *Entrance requirements:* For master's and doctorate, GRE General Test, GRE Subject Test, minimum cumulative point-hour ratio of 2.7 for all previous academic work, three letters of recommendation, statement of purpose, transcripts from all prior institutions attended. Additional exam requirements/recommendations for international students: Required—TOEFL (minimum score 550 paper-based; 213 computer-based; 80 iBT), IELTS (minimum score 6.5). *Application deadline:* For fall admission, 1/15 priority date for domestic students, 1/15 for international students. Applications are processed on a rolling basis. Application fee: $45 ($75 for international students). Electronic applications accepted. *Financial support:* In 2011–12, 47 research assistantships with full and partial tuition reimbursements (averaging $17,484 per year), 22 teaching assistantships with full and partial tuition reimbursements (averaging $19,131 per year) were awarded; Federal Work-Study, institutionally sponsored loans, scholarships/grants, tuition waivers (full), and unspecified assistantships also available. Support available to part-time students. *Faculty research:* Atomic physics, solid-state physics, materials science, astrophysics. *Unit head:* Dr. Lawrence Anderson-Huang, Chair, 419-530-7257, E-mail: lawrence.anderson@utoledo.edu. *Application contact:* Graduate School Office, 419-530-4723, Fax: 419-537-4724, E-mail: grdsch@utnet.utoledo.edu. Web site: http://www.utoledo.edu/nsm/.

University of Toronto, School of Graduate Studies, Faculty of Applied Science and Engineering, Department of Materials Science and Engineering, Toronto, ON M5S 1A1, Canada. Offers M Eng, MA Sc, PhD. Part-time programs available. *Degree requirements:* For master's, thesis (for some programs), oral presentation/thesis defense (MA Sc), qualifying exam; for doctorate, thesis/dissertation. *Entrance requirements:* For master's, BA Sc or B Sc in materials science and engineering, 2 letters of reference; for doctorate, MA Sc or equivalent, 2 letters of reference, minimum B+ average in last 2 years. Additional exam requirements/recommendations for international students: Required—TOEFL (minimum score 580 paper-based), TWE (minimum score 4). Electronic applications accepted.

University of Utah, Graduate School, College of Engineering, Department of Materials Science and Engineering, Salt Lake City, UT 84112. Offers MS, PhD. *Faculty:* 8 full-time (1 woman), 2 part-time/adjunct (0 women). *Students:* 33 full-time (4 women), 9 part-time (1 woman); includes 1 minority (Asian, non-Hispanic/Latino), 24 international. Average age 29. 87 applicants, 14% accepted, 9 enrolled. In 2011, 3 master's, 3 doctorates awarded. Terminal master's awarded for partial completion of doctoral program. *Median time to degree:* Of those who began their doctoral program in fall 2003, 50% received their degree in 8 years or less. *Degree requirements:* For master's, thesis; for doctorate, thesis/dissertation, exam. *Entrance requirements:* For master's and doctorate, GRE General Test, minimum GPA of 3.0. Additional exam requirements/recommendations for international students: Required—TOEFL (minimum score 570 paper-based; 230 computer-based; 88 iBT), IELTS (minimum score 7). *Application deadline:* For fall admission, 1/15 for domestic students, 12/15 for international students. Applications are processed on a rolling basis. Application fee: $55 ($65 for international students). Electronic applications accepted. *Expenses:* Contact institution. *Financial support:* In 2011–12, 3 students received support, including 2 fellowships (averaging $30,000 per year), 27 research assistantships (averaging $22,000 per year); career-related internships or fieldwork and Federal Work-Study also available. Financial award application deadline: 2/5; financial award applicants required to submit FAFSA. *Faculty research:* Solid oxide fuel cells, computational nanostructures, computational polymers, biomaterials, electronic materials, nanomaterials, renewable energy materials. *Total annual research expenditures:* $3.7 million. *Unit head:* Dr. Feng Liu, Chair, 801-581-6863, Fax: 801-581-4816, E-mail: fliu@eng.utah.edu. *Application contact:* Ashley Quimby, Academic Program Specialist, 801-581-6863, Fax: 801-581-4816, E-mail: ashley.quimby@utah.edu. Web site: http://www.mse.utah.edu/.

University of Vermont, Graduate College, College of Engineering and Mathematics, Program in Materials Science, Burlington, VT 05405. Offers MS, PhD. *Students:* 8 (3 women), 4 international. 21 applicants, 10% accepted, 1 enrolled. In 2011, 1 master's, 3 doctorates awarded. *Degree requirements:* For master's, thesis or alternative; for doctorate, thesis/dissertation. *Entrance requirements:* For master's and doctorate, GRE General Test. Additional exam requirements/recommendations for international students: Required—TOEFL (minimum score 550 paper-based; 213 computer-based; 80 iBT). *Application deadline:* For fall admission, 4/1 priority date for domestic students, 4/1 for international students. Applications are processed on a rolling basis. Application fee: $40. Electronic applications accepted. *Financial support:* Research assistantships and teaching assistantships available. Financial award application deadline: 3/1. *Unit head:* Bernard Cole, Interim Dean, 802-656-2644. *Application contact:* Randall Headrick, Coordinator, 802-656-2644.

University of Virginia, School of Engineering and Applied Science, Department of Materials Science and Engineering, Charlottesville, VA 22903. Offers materials science (MMSE, MS, PhD). Part-time programs available. Postbaccalaureate distance learning degree programs offered (no on-campus study). *Faculty:* 23 full-time (2 women). *Students:* 44 full-time (14 women), 1 part-time (0 women); includes 7 minority (3 Black or African American, non-Hispanic/Latino; 3 Asian, non-Hispanic/Latino; 1 Hispanic/Latino), 12 international. Average age 26. 114 applicants, 22% accepted, 13 enrolled. In

2011, 11 master's, 9 doctorates awarded. Terminal master's awarded for partial completion of doctoral program. *Degree requirements:* For master's, comprehensive exam, thesis (for some programs); for doctorate, comprehensive exam, thesis/dissertation. *Entrance requirements:* For master's and doctorate, GRE General Test, three recommendations. Additional exam requirements/recommendations for international students: Required—TOEFL. *Application deadline:* For fall admission, 1/15 for domestic and international students. Applications are processed on a rolling basis. Application fee: $60. Electronic applications accepted. *Financial support:* Fellowships, research assistantships, and teaching assistantships available. Financial award application deadline: 1/15; financial award applicants required to submit FAFSA. *Faculty research:* Environmental effects on material behavior, electronic materials, metals, polymers, tribology. *Unit head:* William C. Johnson, Chair, 434-982-5641, Fax: 434-982-5660, E-mail: wcj2c@virginia.edu. *Application contact:* Kathryn C. Thornton, Assistant Dean for Graduate Programs, 434-924-3897, Fax: 434-982-2214, E-mail: seas-grad-admission@cs.virginia.edu. Web site: http://www.virginia.edu/ms/.

University of Washington, Graduate School, College of Engineering, Department of Materials Science and Engineering, Seattle, WA 98195-2120. Offers ceramic engineering (PhD); materials science and engineering (MS, MSE, PhD); materials science and engineering and nanotechnology (PhD). Part-time programs available. *Faculty:* 23 full-time (5 women), 1 part-time/adjunct (0 women). *Students:* 53 full-time (16 women), 9 part-time (2 women); includes 11 minority (1 Black or African American, non-Hispanic/Latino; 1 American Indian or Alaska Native, non-Hispanic/Latino; 6 Asian, non-Hispanic/Latino; 3 Hispanic/Latino), 20 international. Average age 30. 291 applicants, 9% accepted, 9 enrolled. In 2011, 4 master's, 8 doctorates awarded. *Degree requirements:* For master's, comprehensive exam, thesis optional; for doctorate, comprehensive exam, thesis/dissertation, qualifying evaluation, general and final exams. *Entrance requirements:* For master's and doctorate, GRE General Test, minimum GPA of 3.0. Additional exam requirements/recommendations for international students: Required—TOEFL (minimum score 580 paper-based; 237 computer-based; 92 iBT); Recommended—IELTS (minimum score 7). *Application deadline:* For fall admission, 1/15 priority date for domestic students, 12/15 for international students. Applications are processed on a rolling basis. Application fee: $75. Electronic applications accepted. *Expenses:* Contact institution. *Financial support:* In 2011–12, 51 students received support, including 4 fellowships with full tuition reimbursements available (averaging $16,200 per year), 36 research assistantships with full tuition reimbursements available (averaging $16,416 per year), 8 teaching assistantships with full tuition reimbursements available (averaging $16,416 per year); career-related internships or fieldwork, Federal Work-Study, institutionally sponsored loans, scholarships/grants, health care benefits, unspecified assistantships, and stipend supplements also available. Financial award application deadline: 1/15; financial award applicants required to submit FAFSA. *Faculty research:* Biomimetics and biomaterials; electronic, optical and magnetic materials; eco-materials and materials for energy applications; ceramics, metals, composites, and polymers. *Total annual research expenditures:* $7.4 million. *Unit head:* Dr. Alex Jen, Professor/Chair, 206-543-2600, Fax: 206-543-3100, E-mail: ajen@uw.edu. *Application contact:* Kathleen A. Elkins, Academic Counselor, 206-616-6581, Fax: 206-543-3100, E-mail: kelkins@uw.edu. Web site: http://depts.washington.edu/mse/.

University of Wisconsin–Madison, Graduate School, College of Engineering, Materials Science Program, Madison, WI 53704. Offers MS, PhD. Part-time programs available. *Faculty:* 76 full-time (15 women). *Students:* 85 full-time (20 women); includes 39 minority (1 Black or African American, non-Hispanic/Latino; 1 American Indian or Alaska Native, non-Hispanic/Latino; 29 Asian, non-Hispanic/Latino; 8 Hispanic/Latino). Average age 29. 387 applicants, 10% accepted, 16 enrolled. In 2011, 11 master's, 3 doctorates awarded. Terminal master's awarded for partial completion of doctoral program. *Degree requirements:* For master's, thesis or alternative; for doctorate, comprehensive exam, thesis/dissertation. *Entrance requirements:* For master's and doctorate, GRE General Test. Additional exam requirements/recommendations for international students: Required—TOEFL (minimum score 550 paper-based; 213 computer-based; 80 iBT). *Application deadline:* For fall admission, 4/1 for domestic and international students; for spring admission, 10/1 for domestic and international students. Applications are processed on a rolling basis. Application fee: $56. Electronic applications accepted. *Expenses:* Tuition, state resident: full-time $10,296; part-time $643.51 per credit. Tuition, nonresident: full-time $24,054; part-time $1503.40 per credit. *Required fees:* $70.06 per credit. Tuition and fees vary according to course load, campus/location, program and reciprocity agreements. *Financial support:* In 2011–12, 11 fellowships with full tuition reimbursements (averaging $22,440 per year), 73 research assistantships with full tuition reimbursements (averaging $20,400 per year), 1 teaching assistantship with tuition reimbursement (averaging $28,175 per year) were awarded; traineeships, health care benefits, and unspecified assistantships also available. Financial award application deadline: 1/15. *Faculty research:* Electronic materials, polymers and biomaterials, nanotechnology and nanoscience, structural and mechanical materials, magnetic and superconducting materials, ceramics, metals, computational and theoretical modeling of materials, photonics and optical materials, materials for energy or environmental technology. *Unit head:* Ray Vanderby, Director, 608-265-3032, Fax: 608-262-8353, E-mail: matsciad@engr.wisc.edu. *Application contact:* Diana J. Rhoads, University Services Program Associate, 608-263-1795, Fax: 608-262-8353, E-mail: rhoads@engr.wisc.edu. Web site: http://www.engr.wisc.edu/interd/msp/.

Vanderbilt University, School of Engineering, Interdisciplinary Program in Materials Science, Nashville, TN 37240-1001. Offers M Eng, MS, PhD. Part-time programs available. *Faculty:* 43 full-time (6 women), 2 part-time/adjunct (0 women). *Students:* 31 full-time (14 women); includes 5 minority (all Black or African American, non-Hispanic/Latino), 10 international. Average age 26. 135 applicants, 7% accepted, 6 enrolled. In 2011, 8 degrees awarded. Terminal master's awarded for partial completion of doctoral program. *Degree requirements:* For master's, thesis; for doctorate, thesis/dissertation. *Entrance requirements:* For master's and doctorate, GRE General Test. *Application deadline:* For fall admission, 1/15 for domestic students; for spring admission, 11/1 for domestic students. Application fee: $0. Electronic applications accepted. *Financial support:* In 2011–12, fellowships with tuition reimbursements (averaging $30,000 per year), 6 research assistantships with tuition reimbursements (averaging $26,084 per year), teaching assistantships with tuition reimbursements (averaging $18,000 per year) were awarded; institutionally sponsored loans and tuition waivers (partial) also available. Support available to part-time students. Financial award application deadline: 1/15. *Faculty research:* Nanostructure materials, materials physics, surface and interface science, materials synthesis, biomaterials. *Unit head:* Dr. D. Greg Walker, Director, 615-343-6959, Fax: 615-343-6687, E-mail: greg.walker@vanderbilt.edu. *Application contact:* Sarah R. Satterwhite, Administrative Assistant, 615-343-6868, Fax: 615-322-3202, E-mail: sarah.m.ross@vanderbilt.edu. Web site: http://www.ims.vanderbilt.edu/.

Virginia Polytechnic Institute and State University, Graduate School, College of Engineering, Department of Materials Science and Engineering, Blacksburg, VA 24061.

Offers M Eng, MS, PhD. *Degree requirements:* For master's, comprehensive exam (for some programs), thesis (for some programs); for doctorate, comprehensive exam (for some programs), thesis/dissertation (for some programs). *Entrance requirements:* For master's and doctorate, GRE. Additional exam requirements/recommendations for international students: Required—TOEFL (minimum score 550 paper-based; 213 computer-based). *Application deadline:* For fall admission, 7/1 for domestic and international students; for spring admission, 12/1 for domestic and international students. Applications are processed on a rolling basis. Application fee: $65. Electronic applications accepted. *Expenses:* Tuition, state resident: full-time $10,048; part-time $558.25 per credit hour. Tuition, nonresident: full-time $19,497; part-time $1083.25 per credit hour. *Required fees:* $405 per semester. Tuition and fees vary according to course load, campus/location and program. *Financial support:* Fellowships with full tuition reimbursements, research assistantships with full tuition reimbursements, teaching assistantships with full tuition reimbursements, career-related internships or fieldwork, Federal Work-Study, scholarships/grants, health care benefits, and unspecified assistantships available. Financial award application deadline: 1/15. *Unit head:* Dr. David E. Clark, Unit Head, 540-231-6640, Fax: 540-231-8819, E-mail: dclark@vt.edu. *Application contact:* Gary Pickrell, Information Contact, 540-231-3504, Fax: 540-231-8919, E-mail: pickrell@vt.edu. Web site: http://www.mse.vt.edu/.

Washington State University, Graduate School, College of Engineering and Architecture, School of Mechanical and Materials Engineering, Program in Material Science Engineering, Pullman, WA 99164. Offers MS. *Faculty:* 29. *Students:* 54 full-time (15 women), 9 part-time (2 women); includes 4 minority (1 Black or African American, non-Hispanic/Latino; 1 American Indian or Alaska Native, non-Hispanic/Latino; 1 Asian, non-Hispanic/Latino; 1 Hispanic/Latino), 40 international. Average age 26. 67 applicants, 28% accepted, 16 enrolled. In 2011, 11 master's awarded. *Degree requirements:* For master's, comprehensive exam (for some programs), thesis. *Entrance requirements:* For master's, GRE, statement of purpose, three letters of recommendation, transcripts. Additional exam requirements/recommendations for international students: Required—TOEFL, IELTS. *Application deadline:* For fall admission, 1/10 for domestic and international students; for spring admission, 7/1 for domestic and international students. Applications are processed on a rolling basis. Application fee: $75. Electronic applications accepted. *Financial support:* In 2011–12, fellowships (averaging $2,500 per year), research assistantships with tuition reimbursements (averaging $13,917 per year) were awarded. Financial award application deadline: 2/10. *Total annual research expenditures:* $2.2 million. *Unit head:* Dr. Matthew McCluskey, Chair, 509-335-5356, Fax: 509-335-4662, E-mail: mattmcc@wsu.edu. *Application contact:* Graduate School Admissions, 800-GRADWSU, Fax: 509-335-1949, E-mail: gradsch@wsu.edu.

Wayne State University, College of Engineering, Department of Chemical Engineering and Materials Science, Program in Materials Science and Engineering, Detroit, MI 48202. Offers materials science and engineering (MS, PhD); polymer engineering (Certificate). Part-time programs available. *Students:* 12 full-time (4 women); includes 1 minority (Black or African American, non-Hispanic/Latino), 10 international. Average age 27. 39 applicants, 41% accepted, 3 enrolled. In 2011, 3 master's awarded. Terminal master's awarded for partial completion of doctoral program. *Degree requirements:* For master's, thesis optional; for doctorate, thesis/dissertation. *Entrance requirements:* For master's, GRE (if applying for financial support), recommendations; resume; for doctorate, GRE (if applying for financial support), recommendations; resume, personal statement. Additional exam requirements/recommendations for international students: Required—TOEFL (minimum score 550 paper-based; 213 computer-based); Recommended—TWE (minimum score 5.5). *Application deadline:* For fall admission, 6/1 priority date for domestic students, 5/1 for international students; for winter admission, 10/1 priority date for domestic students, 9/1 for international students; for spring admission, 2/1 priority date for domestic students, 1/1 for international students. Applications are processed on a rolling basis. Application fee: $50. Electronic applications accepted. *Expenses:* Tuition, state resident: part-time $512.85 per credit. Tuition, nonresident: part-time $1132.65 per credit. *Required fees:* $26.60 per credit. $199.65 per semester. Tuition and fees vary according to course load and program. *Financial support:* In 2011–12, 9 students received support. Fellowships with tuition reimbursements available, research assistantships with tuition reimbursements available, teaching assistantships with tuition reimbursements available, scholarships/grants, health care benefits, and unspecified assistantships available. Support available to part-time students. Financial award application deadline: 2/15. *Faculty research:* Polymer science, rheology, fatigue in metals, metal matrix composites, ceramics. *Unit head:* Dr. Charles Manke, Chair, 313-577-3849, Fax: 313-577-3810, E-mail: cmanke@eng.wayne.edu. *Application contact:* Dr. Yinlun Huang, Graduate Program Director, 313-577-3771, E-mail: yhuang@eng.wayne.edu. Web site: http://cheme.eng.wayne.edu/ChE.

Worcester Polytechnic Institute, Graduate Studies and Research, Department of Mechanical Engineering, Program in Materials Process Engineering, Worcester, MA 01609-2280. Offers MS. Part-time and evening/weekend programs available. *Students:* 1 full-time (0 women), 6 part-time (4 women), 2 international. 4 applicants, 100% accepted, 1 enrolled. *Degree requirements:* For master's, thesis optional. *Entrance requirements:* For master's, GRE (recommended), 3 letters of recommendation. Additional exam requirements/recommendations for international students: Required—TOEFL (minimum score 563 paper-based; 223 computer-based; 84 iBT), GRE. *Application deadline:* For fall admission, 1/1 priority date for domestic students, 1/1 for international students; for spring admission, 10/1 priority date for domestic students, 10/1 for international students. Applications are processed on a rolling basis. Application fee: $70. Electronic applications accepted. *Financial support:* Research assistantships and teaching assistantships available. Financial award application deadline: 1/1; financial award applicants required to submit FAFSA. *Unit head:* Dr. Richard D. Sisson, Jr., Director, 508-831-5633, Fax: 508-831-5178, E-mail: sisson@wpi.edu. *Application contact:* Rita Shilansky, Graduate Secretary, 508-831-5633, Fax: 508-831-5178, E-mail: rita@wpi.edu.

Worcester Polytechnic Institute, Graduate Studies and Research, Department of Mechanical Engineering, Program in Materials Science and Engineering, Worcester, MA 01609-2280. Offers MS, PhD. Part-time and evening/weekend programs available. *Faculty:* 1 full-time (0 women). *Students:* 39 full-time (15 women), 22 part-time (6 women); includes 6 minority (1 Black or African American, non-Hispanic/Latino; 5 Hispanic/Latino), 47 international. 131 applicants, 85% accepted, 36 enrolled. In 2011, 14 master's, 1 doctorate awarded. *Degree requirements:* For master's, thesis; for doctorate, comprehensive exam, thesis/dissertation. *Entrance requirements:* For master's and doctorate, GRE (recommended), 3 letters of recommendation. Additional exam requirements/recommendations for international students: Required—TOEFL (minimum score 563 paper-based; 223 computer-based; 84 iBT), IELTS (minimum score 7), GRE. *Application deadline:* For fall admission, 1/1 priority date for domestic students, 1/1 for international students; for spring admission, 10/1 priority date for domestic students, 10/1 for international students. Applications are processed on a rolling basis. Application fee: $70. Electronic applications accepted. *Financial support:* Research assistantships, teaching assistantships, career-related internships or fieldwork, institutionally sponsored loans, scholarships/grants, and unspecified assistantships available. Financial award application deadline: 1/1; financial award applicants required to submit FAFSA. *Faculty research:* Metals processing, nanomaterials, reliability analysis, surface metrology, biopolymers. *Unit head:* Dr. Richard D. Sisson, Jr., Director, 508-831-5633, Fax: 508-831-5178, E-mail: sisson@wpi.edu. *Application contact:* Rita Shilansky, Graduate Secretary, 508-831-5633, Fax:

508-831-5178, E-mail: rita@wpi.edu. Web site: http://www.wpi.edu/academics/me/grad-mse.html?/index.html.

Wright State University, School of Graduate Studies, College of Engineering and Computer Science, Programs in Engineering, Program in Mechanical and Materials Engineering, Dayton, OH 45435. Offers materials science and engineering (MSE); mechanical engineering (MSE). *Degree requirements:* For master's, thesis or course option alternative. *Entrance requirements:* Additional exam requirements/recommendations for international students: Required—TOEFL.

Metallurgical Engineering and Metallurgy

Colorado School of Mines, Graduate School, Department of Metallurgical and Materials Engineering, Golden, CO 80401-1887. Offers materials science (MS, PhD); metallurgical and materials engineering (ME, MS, PhD). Part-time programs available. *Faculty:* 34 full-time (2 women), 6 part-time/adjunct (0 women). *Students:* 74 full-time (14 women), 6 part-time (0 women); includes 7 minority (1 American Indian or Alaska Native, non-Hispanic/Latino; 2 Asian, non-Hispanic/Latino; 3 Hispanic/Latino; 1 Two or more races, non-Hispanic/Latino), 22 international. Average age 26. 124 applicants, 27% accepted, 31 enrolled. In 2011, 19 master's, 5 doctorates awarded. *Degree requirements:* For master's, thesis (for some programs); for doctorate, comprehensive exam, thesis/dissertation. *Entrance requirements:* For master's and doctorate, GRE General Test. Additional exam requirements/recommendations for international students: Required—TOEFL (minimum score 550 paper-based; 213 computer-based; 80 iBT). *Application deadline:* For fall admission, 1/15 priority date for domestic students, 1/15 for international students; for spring admission, 10/15 priority date for domestic students, 10/15 for international students. Application fee: $50 ($70 for international students). Electronic applications accepted. *Expenses:* Tuition, state resident: full-time $12,585; part-time $699 per credit. Tuition, nonresident: full-time $27,270; part-time $1516 per credit. *Required fees:* $1864.20; $670 per semester. *Financial support:* In 2011–12, 53 students received support, including 5 fellowships with full tuition reimbursements available (averaging $20,000 per year), 39 research assistantships with full tuition reimbursements available (averaging $20,000 per year), 9 teaching assistantships with full tuition reimbursements available (averaging $20,000 per year); scholarships/grants, health care benefits, and unspecified assistantships also available. Financial award application deadline: 1/15; financial award applicants required to submit FAFSA. *Total annual research expenditures:* $6.7 million. *Unit head:* Dr. Michael Kaufman, Interim Head, 303-273-3009, Fax: 303-273-3795, E-mail: mkaufman@mines.edu. *Application contact:* Susan Ballantype, Program Assistant, 303-273-3660, Fax: 303-273-3795, E-mail: susan.ballantyne@is.mines.edu. Web site: http://metallurgy.mines.edu.

Columbia University, The Fu Foundation School of Engineering and Applied Science, Department of Earth and Environmental Engineering, New York, NY 10027. Offers earth and environmental engineering (MS, Eng Sc D, PhD); metallurgical engineering (Engr); mining engineering (Engr); MS/MBA. Part-time programs available. Postbaccalaureate distance learning degree programs offered (minimal on-campus study). *Faculty:* 13 full-time (1 woman), 6 part-time/adjunct (0 women). *Students:* 48 full-time (17 women), 15 part-time (8 women); includes 6 minority (3 Asian, non-Hispanic/Latino; 3 Two or more races, non-Hispanic/Latino), 32 international. Average age 30. 171 applicants, 15% accepted, 14 enrolled. In 2011, 16 master's, 4 doctorates awarded. Terminal master's awarded for partial completion of doctoral program. *Degree requirements:* For master's, thesis; for doctorate, thesis/dissertation, qualifying exam. *Entrance requirements:* For master's, doctorate, and Engr, GRE General Test. Additional exam requirements/recommendations for international students: Required—TOEFL, IELTS. *Application deadline:* For fall admission, 12/1 priority date for domestic students, 12/1 for international students; for spring admission, 10/1 priority date for domestic students, 10/1 for international students. Application fee: $95. Electronic applications accepted. *Financial support:* In 2011–12, 39 students received support, including 6 fellowships with full and partial tuition reimbursements available (averaging $16,478 per year), 26 research assistantships with full tuition reimbursements available (averaging $27,733 per year), 7 teaching assistantships with full tuition reimbursements available (averaging $22,500 per year); health care benefits and unspecified assistantships also available. Financial award application deadline: 12/1; financial award applicants required to submit FAFSA. *Faculty research:* Sustainable energy and materials, waste to energy, water resources and climate risks, environmental health engineering, life cycle analysis. *Unit head:* Dr. Klaus S. Lackner, Professor of Geophysics/Chairman, 212-854-0304, Fax: 212-854-7081, E-mail: kl2010@columbia.edu. *Application contact:* Gary Hill, Administrative Assistant, 212-854-2905, Fax: 212-854-7081, E-mail: gh2206@columbia.edu. Web site: http://www.eee.columbia.edu/.

Michigan Technological University, Graduate School, College of Engineering, Department of Materials Science and Engineering, Houghton, MI 49931. Offers MS, PhD. Part-time programs available. *Faculty:* 18 full-time (2 women), 7 part-time/adjunct (0 women). *Students:* 27 full-time (7 women), 6 part-time (2 women); includes 3 minority (2 Asian, non-Hispanic/Latino; 1 Hispanic/Latino), 16 international. Average age 28. 205 applicants, 4% accepted, 6 enrolled. In 2011, 3 master's, 2 doctorates awarded. Terminal master's awarded for partial completion of doctoral program. *Degree requirements:* For master's, comprehensive exam (for some programs), thesis (for some programs); for doctorate, comprehensive exam, thesis/dissertation. *Entrance requirements:* For master's and doctorate, GRE (domestic students from ABET-accredited programs exempt), statement of purpose, official transcripts, 3 letters of recommendation. Additional exam requirements/recommendations for international students: Required—TOEFL (minimum score 79 iBT) or IELTS. *Application deadline:* For fall admission, 1/1 for domestic and international students. Applications are processed on a rolling basis. Electronic applications accepted. *Expenses:* Contact institution. *Financial support:* In 2011–12, 29 students received support, including 1 fellowship with full tuition reimbursement available (averaging $6,065 per year), 21 research assistantships with full tuition reimbursements available (averaging $6,065 per year), 1 teaching assistantship with full tuition reimbursement available (averaging $6,065 per year); career-related internships or fieldwork, Federal Work-Study, scholarships/grants, health care benefits, tuition waivers (partial), unspecified assistantships, and cooperative program also available. Financial award applicants required to submit FAFSA. *Faculty research:* Structure/property/processing relationships, microstructural characterization, alloy design, electronic/magnetic/photonic materials, materials and manufacturing processes. *Total annual research expenditures:* $1.3 million. *Unit head:* Dr. Stephen L. Kampe, Department Chair, 906-487-2630, Fax: 906-487-2934, E-mail: kampe@mtu.edu. *Application contact:* Beth R.

Ruohonen, Departmental Coordinator, 906-487-4326, Fax: 906-487-2934, E-mail: beth@mtu.edu. Web site: http://www.mtu.edu/materials/.

Missouri University of Science and Technology, Graduate School, Department of Materials Science and Engineering, Rolla, MO 65409. Offers ceramic engineering (MS, DE, PhD); metallurgical engineering (MS, PhD). *Degree requirements:* For master's, thesis optional; for doctorate, comprehensive exam. *Entrance requirements:* For master's, GRE (minimum combined score 1100, 600 verbal, 3.5 writing); for doctorate, GRE (minimum score: quantitative 600, writing 3.5). Additional exam requirements/recommendations for international students: Required—TOEFL (minimum score 570 paper-based; 230 computer-based).

Montana Tech of The University of Montana, Graduate School, Metallurgical/Mineral Processing Engineering Programs, Butte, MT 59701-8997. Offers MS. Part-time programs available. *Faculty:* 6 full-time (0 women). *Students:* 3 full-time (1 woman), 1 (woman) part-time. 5 applicants, 40% accepted, 1 enrolled. In 2011, 3 master's awarded. *Degree requirements:* For master's, comprehensive exam (for some programs), thesis optional. *Entrance requirements:* For master's, GRE General Test, minimum GPA of 3.0. Additional exam requirements/recommendations for international students: Required—TOEFL (minimum score 525 paper-based; 195 computer-based; 71 iBT). *Application deadline:* For fall admission, 4/1 priority date for domestic students, 3/1 for international students; for spring admission, 10/1 priority date for domestic students, 7/1 for international students. Applications are processed on a rolling basis. Application fee: $30. Electronic applications accepted. *Financial support:* In 2011–12, 4 students received support, including 2 teaching assistantships with partial tuition reimbursements available (averaging $5,000 per year); research assistantships with partial tuition reimbursements available, career-related internships or fieldwork, tuition waivers (full and partial), and unspecified assistantships also available. Financial award application deadline: 4/1; financial award applicants required to submit FAFSA. *Faculty research:* Stabilizing hazardous waste, decontamination of metals by melt refining, ultraviolet enhancement of stabilization reactions, extractive metallurgy, fuel cells. *Unit head:* Dr. Courtney Young, Department Head, 406-496-4158, Fax: 406-496-4664, E-mail: cyoung@mtech.edu. *Application contact:* Fred Sullivan, Administrator, Graduate School, 406-496-4304, Fax: 406-496-4710, E-mail: fsullivan@mtech.edu. Web site: http://www.mtech.edu/academics/gradschool/degreeprograms/degrees-metallurgical.htm.

The Ohio State University, Graduate School, College of Engineering, Department of Materials Science and Engineering, Program in Welding Engineering, Columbus, OH 43210. Offers MS, MWE, PhD. *Faculty:* 34. *Students:* 22 full-time (4 women), 16 part-time (2 women); includes 4 minority (2 Black or African American, non-Hispanic/Latino; 1 Asian, non-Hispanic/Latino; 1 Two or more races, non-Hispanic/Latino), 10 international. Average age 28. In 2011, 6 master's, 1 doctorate awarded. *Degree requirements:* For master's, thesis optional; for doctorate, thesis/dissertation. *Entrance requirements:* For master's and doctorate, GRE General Test or engineering degree. Additional exam requirements/recommendations for international students: Required—Michigan English Language Assessment Battery (minimum score 82); Recommended—TOEFL (minimum score 600 paper-based; 250 computer-based; 79 iBT). *Application deadline:* For fall admission, 8/15 priority date for domestic students, 7/1 for international students; for winter admission, 12/1 priority date for domestic students, 11/1 for international students; for spring admission, 3/1 priority date for domestic students, 2/1 for international students. Applications are processed on a rolling basis. Application fee: $40 ($50 for international students). Electronic applications accepted. *Expenses:* Tuition, state resident: full-time $11,400. Tuition, nonresident: full-time $28,125. Tuition and fees vary according to course load, degree level, campus/location and program. *Financial support:* Fellowships, research assistantships, teaching assistantships, Federal Work-Study, and institutionally sponsored loans available. Support available to part-time students. *Unit head:* Avaraham Benatar, Graduate Studies Committee Chair, 614-292-1390, E-mail: benatar.1@osu.edu. *Application contact:* Mark Cooper, Graduate Studies Coordinator, 614-292-7280, Fax: 614-292-1537, E-mail: cooper.73@osu.edu. Web site: http://engineering.osu.edu/graduate/welding.

The Ohio State University, Graduate School, College of Engineering, Program in Industrial and Systems Engineering, Columbus, OH 43210. Offers industrial and systems engineering (MS, PhD); welding engineering (MS, MWE, PhD). *Faculty:* 20. *Students:* 66 full-time (22 women), 34 part-time (8 women); includes 6 minority (1 Black or African American, non-Hispanic/Latino; 3 Asian, non-Hispanic/Latino; 1 Hispanic/Latino; 1 Two or more races, non-Hispanic/Latino), 57 international. Average age 28. In 2011, 12 master's, 6 doctorates awarded. *Degree requirements:* For master's, thesis optional; for doctorate, thesis/dissertation. *Entrance requirements:* For master's and doctorate, GRE General Test. Additional exam requirements/recommendations for international students: Required—Michigan English Language Assessment Battery (minimum score 82); Recommended—TOEFL (minimum score 600 paper-based; 250 computer-based; 79 iBT). *Application deadline:* For fall admission, 8/15 priority date for domestic students, 11/1 for international students; for winter admission, 12/1 priority date for domestic students, 7/1 for international students; for spring admission, 3/1 priority date for domestic students, 2/1 for international students. Applications are processed on a rolling basis. Application fee: $40 ($50 for international students). Electronic applications accepted. *Expenses:* Tuition, state resident: full-time $11,400. Tuition, nonresident: full-time $28,125. Tuition and fees vary according to course load, degree level, campus/location and program. *Financial support:* Fellowships, research assistantships, teaching assistantships, career-related internships or fieldwork, Federal Work-Study, institutionally sponsored loans, and unspecified assistantships available. Support available to part-time students. *Unit head:* Dr. Philip J. Smith, Interim

Department Chair, 614-292-4120, E-mail: smith.131@osu.edu. *Application contact:* Dr. Jerald Brevik, Graduate Studies Chair, 614-292-0177, Fax: 614-292-7852, E-mail: brevik.1@osu.edu. Web site: http://ise.osu.edu/.

Rensselaer Polytechnic Institute, Graduate School, School of Engineering, Program in Materials Science and Engineering, Troy, NY 12180. Offers ceramics and glass science (M Eng, MS, PhD); composites (M Eng, MS, PhD); electronic materials (M Eng, MS, PhD); metallurgy (M Eng, MS, PhD); polymers (M Eng, MS, PhD). Part-time programs available. Terminal master's awarded for partial completion of doctoral program. *Degree requirements:* For master's, thesis; for doctorate, comprehensive exam, thesis/dissertation. *Entrance requirements:* For master's and doctorate, GRE. Additional exam requirements/recommendations for international students: Required—TOEFL (minimum score 570 paper-based; 230 computer-based; 100 iBT). Electronic applications accepted. *Faculty research:* Materials processing, nanostructural materials, materials for microelectronics, composite materials, computational materials.

Université Laval, Faculty of Sciences and Engineering, Department of Mining, Metallurgical and Materials Engineering, Programs in Metallurgical Engineering, Québec, QC G1K 7P4, Canada. Offers M Sc, PhD. Terminal master's awarded for partial completion of doctoral program. *Degree requirements:* For master's, thesis; for doctorate, comprehensive exam, thesis/dissertation. *Entrance requirements:* For master's and doctorate, knowledge of French and English. Electronic applications accepted.

The University of Alabama, Graduate School, College of Engineering, Department of Metallurgical and Materials Engineering, Tuscaloosa, AL 35487. Offers MS Met E, PhD. PhD offered jointly with The University of Alabama at Birmingham. *Faculty:* 9 full-time (2 women). *Students:* 23 full-time (2 women), 3 part-time (1 woman); includes 2 minority (1 Black or African American, non-Hispanic/Latino; 1 Asian, non-Hispanic/Latino), 13 international. Average age 26. 23 applicants, 57% accepted, 7 enrolled. In 2011, 8 master's, 1 doctorate awarded. *Median time to degree:* Of those who began their doctoral program in fall 2003, 100% received their degree in 8 years or less. *Degree requirements:* For master's, thesis or alternative; for doctorate, thesis/dissertation. *Entrance requirements:* For master's, GRE General Test, minimum GPA of 3.0 in last 60 hours; for doctorate, GRE General Test, minimum graduate GPA of 3.0, graduate degree. Additional exam requirements/recommendations for international students: Required—TOEFL (minimum score 550 paper-based; 213 computer-based). *Application deadline:* For fall admission, 7/1 priority date for domestic students. Applications are processed on a rolling basis. Application fee: $50 ($60 for international students). Electronic applications accepted. *Expenses:* Tuition, state resident: full-time $8600. Tuition, nonresident: full-time $21,900. *Financial support:* In 2011–12, 3 fellowships (averaging $15,000 per year), 14 research assistantships (averaging $14,700 per year), 6 teaching assistantships (averaging $12,250 per year) were awarded; Federal Work-Study and unspecified assistantships also available. *Faculty research:* Thermodynamics, molten metals processing, casting and solidification, mechanical properties of materials, thin films and nanostructures, electrochemistry, corrosion and alloy development. *Total annual research expenditures:* $1.6 million. *Unit head:* Dr. Ramana G. Reddy, Head/Professor, 205-348-4246, Fax: 205-348-2164. *Application contact:* Dr. Su Gupta, Associate Professor, 205-348-4272, Fax: 205-348-2164, E-mail: sgupta@eng.ua.edu. Web site: http://www.eng.ua.edu/~mtedept/.

The University of British Columbia, Faculty of Applied Science, Department of Materials Engineering, Vancouver, BC V6T 1Z1, Canada. Offers materials and metallurgy (M Sc, PhD); metals and materials engineering (MA Sc, PhD). *Degree requirements:* For master's, comprehensive exam, thesis; for doctorate, comprehensive exam, thesis/dissertation. *Entrance requirements:* Additional exam requirements/recommendations for international students: Required—TOEFL (minimum score 560 paper-based; 220 computer-based; 83 iBT). Electronic applications accepted. *Faculty research:* Electroslag melting, mathematical modeling, solidification and hydrometallurgy.

University of Connecticut, Graduate School, School of Engineering, Department of Metallurgy and Materials Engineering, Storrs, CT 06269. Offers MS, PhD. Terminal master's awarded for partial completion of doctoral program. *Degree requirements:* For master's, comprehensive exam, thesis or alternative; for doctorate, thesis/dissertation. *Entrance requirements:* For master's and doctorate, GRE General Test, GRE Subject Test. Additional exam requirements/recommendations for international students: Required—TOEFL (minimum score 550 paper-based; 213 computer-based). Electronic applications accepted. *Faculty research:* Microsegregation and coarsening, fatigue crack, electron-dislocation interaction.

University of Idaho, College of Graduate Studies, College of Engineering, Department of Chemical and Materials Engineering, Moscow, ID 83844-3024. Offers chemical engineering (MS, PhD); materials science and engineering (MS, PhD), including materials science and engineering, metallurgical engineering (MS); metallurgy (MS). *Faculty:* 10 full-time. *Students:* 16 full-time, 10 part-time. Average age 33. In 2011, 6 master's awarded. *Degree requirements:* For master's, thesis; for doctorate, one foreign language, thesis/dissertation. *Entrance requirements:* For master's, GRE, minimum GPA of 2.8; for doctorate, GRE, minimum undergraduate GPA of 2.8, 3.0 graduate. *Application deadline:* For fall admission, 8/1 for domestic students; for spring admission, 12/15 for domestic students. Applications are processed on a rolling basis. Application fee: $60. Electronic applications accepted. *Expenses:* Tuition, state resident: full-time $3874; part-time $334 per credit hour. Tuition, nonresident: full-time $16,394; part-time $861 per credit hour. *Required fees:* $2808; $99 per credit hour. Tuition and fees vary according to program. *Financial support:* Fellowships, research assistantships, and teaching assistantships available. Financial award applicants required to submit FAFSA. *Faculty research:* Geothermal energy utilization, alcohol production from agriculture waste material, energy conservation in pulp and paper mills. *Unit head:* Dr. Wudneh

Admassu, 208-885-7572, E-mail: gailb@uidaho.edu. *Application contact:* Erick Larson, Director of Graduate Admissions, 208-885-4723, E-mail: gadms@uidaho.edu. Web site: http://www.uidaho.edu/engr/cme/about/materials.

The University of Manchester, School of Materials, Manchester, United Kingdom. Offers advanced aerospace materials engineering (M Sc); advanced metallic systems (PhD); biomedical materials (M Phil, M Sc, PhD); ceramics and glass (M Phil, M Sc, PhD); composite materials (M Sc, PhD); corrosion and protection (M Phil, M Sc, PhD); materials (M Phil, PhD); metallic materials (M Phil, M Sc, PhD); nanostructural materials (M Phil, M Sc, PhD); paper science (M Phil, M Sc, PhD); polymer science and engineering (M Phil, M Sc, PhD); technical textiles (M Sc); textile design, fashion and management (M Phil, M Sc, PhD); textile science and technology (M Phil, M Sc, PhD); textiles (M Phil, PhD); textiles and fashion (M Ent).

University of Nebraska–Lincoln, Graduate College, College of Engineering, Department of Mechanical and Materials Engineering, Lincoln, NE 68588. Offers engineering mechanics (MS, PhD); materials engineering (PhD); mechanical engineering (MS, PhD), including materials science engineering (MS), metallurgical engineering (MS). *Degree requirements:* For master's, thesis optional; for doctorate, comprehensive exam, thesis/dissertation. *Entrance requirements:* For master's and doctorate, GRE General Test. Additional exam requirements/recommendations for international students: Required—TOEFL (minimum score 550 paper-based; 213 computer-based). Electronic applications accepted. *Faculty research:* Robotics for planetary exploration, vehicle crashworthiness, transient heat conduction, laser beam/particle interactions.

University of Nevada, Reno, Graduate School, College of Engineering, Department of Chemical and Materials Engineering, Program in Materials Science and Engineering, Reno, NV 89557. Offers MS, PhD. Terminal master's awarded for partial completion of doctoral program. *Degree requirements:* For master's, thesis; for doctorate, one foreign language, thesis/dissertation. *Entrance requirements:* For master's, minimum GPA of 2.75; for doctorate, GRE, minimum GPA of 3.0. Additional exam requirements/recommendations for international students: Required—TOEFL (minimum score 500 paper-based; 173 computer-based; 61 iBT), IELTS (minimum score 6). Electronic applications accepted. *Faculty research:* Hydrometallurgy, applied surface chemistry, mineral processing, mineral bioprocessing, ceramics.

The University of Texas at El Paso, Graduate School, College of Engineering, Department of Metallurgical and Materials Engineering, El Paso, TX 79968-0001. Offers materials science and engineering (PhD); metallurgical and materials engineering (MS). Part-time and evening/weekend programs available. *Students:* 16 (8 women); includes 12 minority (all Hispanic/Latino), 2 international. Average age 34. 10 applicants, 80% accepted, 5 enrolled. *Degree requirements:* For master's, thesis. *Entrance requirements:* For master's, GRE General Test. Additional exam requirements/recommendations for international students: Required—TOEFL. *Application deadline:* For fall admission, 7/1 priority date for domestic students, 3/1 for international students; for spring admission, 11/1 priority date for domestic students, 9/1 for international students. Applications are processed on a rolling basis. Application fee: $15 ($65 for international students). Electronic applications accepted. *Financial support:* In 2011–12, research assistantships with partial tuition reimbursements (averaging $21,125 per year), teaching assistantships with partial tuition reimbursements (averaging $16,900 per year) were awarded; fellowships with partial tuition reimbursements, career-related internships or fieldwork, Federal Work-Study, institutionally sponsored loans, scholarships/grants, and tuition waivers (partial) also available. Financial award application deadline: 3/15; financial award applicants required to submit FAFSA. *Unit head:* Dr. Lawrence E. Murr, Chairperson, 915-747-5468, Fax: 915-747-8036, E-mail: fekberg@utep.edu. *Application contact:* Dr. Benjamin Flores, Interim Dean of the Graduate School, 915-747-5491, Fax: 915-747-5788, E-mail: bflores@utep.edu.

University of Utah, Graduate School, College of Mines and Earth Sciences, Department of Metallurgical Engineering, Salt Lake City, UT 84112. Offers ME, MS, PhD. Part-time programs available. *Faculty:* 9 full-time (0 women), 2 part-time/adjunct (0 women). *Students:* 43 full-time (11 women), 6 part-time (2 women); includes 4 minority (3 Asian, non-Hispanic/Latino; 1 Hispanic/Latino), 38 international. Average age 28. 31 applicants, 61% accepted, 7 enrolled. In 2011, 3 master's, 7 doctorates awarded. Terminal master's awarded for partial completion of doctoral program. *Median time to degree:* Of those who began their doctoral program in fall 2003, 100% received their degree in 8 years or less. *Degree requirements:* For master's, thesis; for doctorate, comprehensive exam, thesis/dissertation. *Entrance requirements:* For master's and doctorate, GRE General Test, minimum GPA of 3.0. Additional exam requirements/recommendations for international students: Required—TOEFL (minimum score 71 iBT), TOEFL (minimum score 530 paper-based; 197 computer-based) or IELTS (minimum score 5.5). *Application deadline:* For fall admission, 4/1 for domestic students, 2/1 for international students; for spring admission, 11/1 priority date for domestic students, 9/1 for international students. Applications are processed on a rolling basis. Application fee: $55 ($65 for international students). Electronic applications accepted. *Financial support:* In 2011–12, 1 student received support, including 2 fellowships with full and partial tuition reimbursements available (averaging $16,500 per year), 46 research assistantships with full and partial tuition reimbursements available (averaging $17,266 per year); institutionally sponsored loans also available. Financial award application deadline: 2/15; financial award applicants required to submit FAFSA. *Faculty research:* Physical metallurgy, mathematical modeling, mineral processing, chemical metallurgy nanoscience and technology. *Total annual research expenditures:* $2.9 million. *Unit head:* Dr. Jan D. Miller, Chair, 801-581-5160, Fax: 801-581-4937, E-mail: jan.miller@utah.edu. *Application contact:* Evelyn Wells, Department Assistant, 801-581-6386, Fax: 801-581-4937, E-mail: evelyn.wells@utah.edu. Web site: http://www.metallurgy.utah.edu/.

Polymer Science and Engineering

Auburn University, Graduate School, Ginn College of Engineering, Department of Polymer and Fiber Engineering, Auburn University, AL 36849. Offers MS, PhD. *Faculty:* 8 full-time (2 women). *Students:* 9 full-time (3 women), 6 part-time (1 woman); includes 1 minority (American Indian or Alaska Native, non-Hispanic/Latino), 9 international. Average age 25. 41 applicants, 61% accepted, 3 enrolled. In 2011, 7 master's, 5 doctorates awarded. *Degree requirements:* For master's, thesis optional. *Expenses:*

Tuition, state resident: full-time $7290; part-time $405 per credit hour. Tuition, nonresident: full-time $21,870; part-time $1215 per credit hour. *International tuition:* $22,000 full-time. *Required fees:* $1402. *Financial support:* Unspecified assistantships available. *Unit head:* Peter Schwartz, Head, 334-844-5452. *Application contact:* Dr. George Flowers, Dean of the Graduate School, 334-844-2125. Web site: http://www.eng.auburn.edu/programs/pfen/programs/grad/index.html.

Polymer Science and Engineering

California Polytechnic State University, San Luis Obispo, College of Science and Mathematics, Department of Chemistry and Biochemistry, San Luis Obispo, CA 93407. Offers polymers and coating science (MS). Part-time programs available. *Faculty:* 1 full-time (0 women). *Students:* 2 full-time (1 woman), 3 part-time (0 women); includes 2 minority (both Asian, non-Hispanic/Latino). Average age 24. 5 applicants, 40% accepted, 1 enrolled. In 2011, 3 master's awarded. *Degree requirements:* For master's, comprehensive exam (for some programs), thesis (for some programs), comprehensive oral exam. *Entrance requirements:* For master's, minimum GPA of 2.5 in last 90 quarter units of course work. Additional exam requirements/recommendations for international students: Required—TOEFL (minimum score 550 paper-based; 213 computer-based) or IELTS (minimum score 6). *Application deadline:* For fall admission, 7/1 for domestic students, 11/30 for international students; for winter admission, 11/1 for domestic students, 6/30 for international students; for spring admission, 2/1 for domestic students. Applications are processed on a rolling basis. Application fee: $55. Electronic applications accepted. *Expenses:* Tuition, state resident: full-time $6738. Tuition, nonresident: full-time $17,898. *Required fees:* $2449. *Financial support:* Fellowships, research assistantships, career-related internships or fieldwork, Federal Work-Study, and scholarships/grants available. Support available to part-time students. Financial award application deadline: 3/2; financial award applicants required to submit FAFSA. *Faculty research:* Polymer physical chemistry and analysis, polymer synthesis, coatings formulation. *Unit head:* Dr. Ray Fernando, Graduate Coordinator, 805-756-2395, Fax: 805-756-5500, E-mail: rhfernan@calpoly.edu. *Application contact:* Dr. James Maraviglia, Associate Vice Provost for Marketing and Enrollment Development, 805-756-2311, Fax: 805-756-5400, E-mail: admissions@calpoly.edu. Web site: http://polymerscoatings.calpoly.edu/graduate.htm.

Carnegie Mellon University, Carnegie Institute of Technology, Department of Chemical Engineering and Department of Chemistry, Program in Colloids, Polymers and Surfaces, Pittsburgh, PA 15213-3891. Offers MS. Part-time and evening/weekend programs available. *Entrance requirements:* For master's, GRE General Test, GRE Subject Test. Additional exam requirements/recommendations for international students: Required—TOEFL. *Faculty research:* Surface phenomena, polymer rheology, solubilization phenomena, colloid transport phenomena, polymer synthesis.

Carnegie Mellon University, Mellon College of Science, Department of Chemistry, Pittsburgh, PA 15213-3891. Offers biotechnology and management (MS); chemistry (PhD), including bioinorganic, bioorganic, organic and materials, biophysics and spectroscopy, computational and theoretical, polymer; colloids, polymers and surfaces (MS). Part-time programs available. Terminal master's awarded for partial completion of doctoral program. *Degree requirements:* For doctorate, thesis/dissertation, departmental qualifying and oral exams, teaching experience. *Entrance requirements:* For master's, GRE General Test; for doctorate, GRE General Test, GRE Subject Test. Additional exam requirements/recommendations for international students: Required—TOEFL. Electronic applications accepted. *Faculty research:* Physical and theoretical chemistry, chemical synthesis, biophysical/bioinorganic chemistry.

Case Western Reserve University, School of Graduate Studies, Case School of Engineering, Department of Macromolecular Science and Engineering, Cleveland, OH 44106. Offers MS, PhD, MD/PhD. Part-time programs available. *Faculty:* 12 full-time (2 women). *Students:* 54 full-time (17 women), 1 (woman) part-time; includes 5 minority (1 Black or African American, non-Hispanic/Latino; 2 Asian, non-Hispanic/Latino; 1 Hispanic/Latino; 1 Two or more races, non-Hispanic/Latino), 30 international. In 2011, 13 degrees awarded. Terminal master's awarded for partial completion of doctoral program. *Degree requirements:* For master's, thesis; for doctorate, thesis/dissertation, qualifying exam, teaching experience. *Entrance requirements:* For master's and doctorate, GRE General Test. Additional exam requirements/recommendations for international students: Required—TOEFL. *Application deadline:* For fall admission, 2/28 priority date for domestic students; for spring admission, 10/1 priority date for domestic students. Applications are processed on a rolling basis. Application fee: $50. *Financial support:* Fellowships with full tuition reimbursements, research assistantships with full and partial tuition reimbursements, and teaching assistantships available. Financial award applicants required to submit FAFSA. *Faculty research:* Synthesis and molecular design; processing, modeling and simulation, structure-property relationships. *Total annual research expenditures:* $6.4 million. *Unit head:* Dr. David Schiraldi, Department Chair, 216-368-4243, Fax: 216-368-4202, E-mail: das44@case.edu. *Application contact:* Theresa Claytor, Student Affairs Coordinator, 216-368-8555, Fax: 216-368-8555, E-mail: theresa.claytor@case.edu. Web site: http://polymers.case.edu.

Cornell University, Graduate School, Graduate Fields of Engineering, Field of Chemical Engineering, Ithaca, NY 14853-0001. Offers advanced materials processing (M Eng, MS, PhD); applied mathematics and computational methods (M Eng, MS, PhD); biochemical engineering (M Eng, MS, PhD); chemical reaction engineering (M Eng, MS, PhD); classical and statistical thermodynamics (M Eng, MS, PhD); fluid dynamics, rheology and biorheology (M Eng, MS, PhD); heat and mass transfer (M Eng, MS, PhD); kinetics and catalysis (M Eng, MS, PhD); polymers (M Eng, MS, PhD); surface science (M Eng, MS, PhD). *Faculty:* 29 full-time (2 women). *Students:* 106 full-time (30 women); includes 21 minority (3 Black or African American, non-Hispanic/Latino; 14 Asian, non-Hispanic/Latino; 4 Hispanic/Latino), 46 international. Average age 25. 379 applicants, 35% accepted, 53 enrolled. In 2011, 50 master's, 8 doctorates awarded. *Degree requirements:* For master's, thesis (MS); for doctorate, comprehensive exam, thesis/dissertation. *Entrance requirements:* For master's and doctorate, GRE General Test, 2 letters of recommendation. Additional exam requirements/recommendations for international students: Required—TOEFL (minimum score 600 paper-based; 237 computer-based; 77 iBT). *Application deadline:* For fall admission, 1/15 priority date for domestic students. Application fee: $95. Electronic applications accepted. *Financial support:* In 2011–12, 67 students received support, including 24 fellowships with full tuition reimbursements available, 44 research assistantships with full tuition reimbursements available, 5 teaching assistantships with full tuition reimbursements available; institutionally sponsored loans, scholarships/grants, health care benefits, tuition waivers (full and partial), and unspecified assistantships also available. Financial award applicants required to submit FAFSA. *Faculty research:* Biochemical, biomedical and metabolic engineering; fluid and polymer dynamics; surface science and chemical kinetics; electronics materials; microchemical systems and nanotechnology. *Unit head:* Director of Graduate Studies, 607-255-4550. *Application contact:* Graduate Field Assistant, 607-255-4550, E-mail: dgs@cheme.cornell.edu. Web site: http://www.gradschool.cornell.edu/fields.php?id-25&a-2.

Cornell University, Graduate School, Graduate Fields of Human Ecology, Field of Textiles, Ithaca, NY 14853. Offers apparel design (MA, MPS); fiber science (MS, PhD); polymer science (MS, PhD); textile science (MS, PhD). *Faculty:* 23 full-time (9 women). *Students:* 19 full-time (14 women); includes 2 minority (1 Black or African American, non-Hispanic/Latino; 1 Asian, non-Hispanic/Latino), 10 international. Average age 26. 37 applicants, 32% accepted, 8 enrolled. In 2011, 1 master's, 1 doctorate awarded. *Degree requirements:* For master's, thesis (MA, MS), project paper (MPS); for doctorate, comprehensive exam, thesis/dissertation. *Entrance requirements:* For master's, GRE General Test, 2 letters of recommendation, portfolio (functional apparel design); for doctorate, GRE General Test, 2 letters of recommendation. Additional exam requirements/recommendations for international students: Required—TOEFL (minimum score 600 paper-based; 250 computer-based; 77 iBT). *Application deadline:* For fall admission, 3/1 for domestic students; for spring admission, 10/1 for domestic students. Application fee: $95. Electronic applications accepted. *Financial support:* In 2011–12, 19 students received support, including 3 fellowships with full tuition reimbursements available, 3 research assistantships with full tuition reimbursements available, 7 teaching assistantships with full tuition reimbursements available; institutionally sponsored loans, scholarships/grants, health care benefits, tuition waivers (full and partial), and unspecified assistantships also available. Financial award applicants required to submit FAFSA. *Faculty research:* Apparel design, consumption, mass customization, 3-D body scanning. *Unit head:* Director of Graduate Studies, 607-255-3151, Fax: 607-255-1093. *Application contact:* Graduate Field Assistant, 607-255-3151, Fax: 607-255-1093, E-mail: textiles_grad@cornell.edu. Web site: http://www.gradschool.cornell.edu/fields.php?id-95&a-2.

DePaul University, College of Science and Health, Department of Chemistry, Chicago, IL 60614. Offers biochemistry (MS); chemistry (MS); polymer chemistry and coatings technology (MS). Part-time and evening/weekend programs available. *Faculty:* 13 full-time (7 women), 4 part-time/adjunct (1 woman). *Students:* 11 full-time (6 women), 3 part-time (2 women); includes 5 minority (1 Asian, non-Hispanic/Latino; 3 Hispanic/Latino; 1 Two or more races, non-Hispanic/Latino), 1 international. Average age 26. 6 applicants, 100% accepted, 4 enrolled. In 2011, 2 master's awarded. *Degree requirements:* For master's, thesis (for some programs), oral exam (for select programs). *Entrance requirements:* For master's, GRE Subject Test (chemistry), GRE General Test, BS in chemistry or equivalent. Additional exam requirements/recommendations for international students: Required—TOEFL (minimum score 590 paper-based; 243 computer-based). *Application deadline:* For fall admission, 7/15 for domestic students, 5/1 for international students; for winter admission, 11/15 for domestic students, 9/1 for international students; for spring admission, 2/15 for domestic students, 12/1 for international students. Applications are processed on a rolling basis. Application fee: $40. Electronic applications accepted. *Financial support:* In 2011–12, 4 students received support, including 6 teaching assistantships with partial tuition reimbursements available (averaging $9,000 per year). Financial award application deadline: 6/1. *Faculty research:* Computational chemistry, organic synthesis, inorganic synthesis, polymer synthesis, biochemistry. *Total annual research expenditures:* $30,000. *Unit head:* Dr. Richard F. Niedziela, Chair, 773-325-7307, Fax: 773-325-7421, E-mail: rniedzie@condor.depaul.edu. *Application contact:* Dr. Matthew Dintzner, Director of Graduate Studies, 773-325-4726, Fax: 773-325-7421, E-mail: mdintzne@depaul.edu. Web site: http://chemistry.depaul.edu.

Eastern Michigan University, Graduate School, College of Technology, School of Engineering Technology, Program in Polymers and Coatings Technology, Ypsilanti, MI 48197. Offers polymer technology (MS). Part-time and evening/weekend programs available. Postbaccalaureate distance learning degree programs offered (minimal on-campus study). *Students:* 3 full-time (1 woman), 11 part-time (3 women); includes 3 minority (all Asian, non-Hispanic/Latino), 3 international. Average age 32. 21 applicants, 57% accepted, 5 enrolled. In 2011, 8 degrees awarded. *Degree requirements:* For master's, thesis optional. *Entrance requirements:* For master's, GRE General Test, BS in chemistry, minimum GPA of 2.6. Additional exam requirements/recommendations for international students: Required—TOEFL. *Application deadline:* Applications are processed on a rolling basis. Application fee: $35. *Expenses:* Tuition, state resident: full-time $10,367; part-time $432 per credit hour. Tuition, nonresident: full-time $20,435; part-time $851 per credit hour. *Required fees:* $39 per credit hour. $46 per semester. One-time fee: $100. Tuition and fees vary according to course level, degree level and reciprocity agreements. *Financial support:* Fellowships, research assistantships with full tuition reimbursements, teaching assistantships with full tuition reimbursements, career-related internships or fieldwork, Federal Work-Study, institutionally sponsored loans, scholarships/grants, tuition waivers (partial), and unspecified assistantships available. Support available to part-time students. Financial award applicants required to submit FAFSA. *Unit head:* Dr. Jamil Baghdachi, Program Coordinator, 734-487-3192, Fax: 734-487-8755, E-mail: jamil.baghdachi@emich.edu. *Application contact:* Graduate Admissions, 734-487-2400, Fax: 734-487-6559, E-mail: graduate.admissions@emich.edu.

Florida State University, The Graduate School, Materials Science and Engineering Program, Tallahassee, FL 32310. Offers computational materials science and mechanics (MS); functional materials (MS); materials science and engineering (PhD); nanoscale materials, composite materials, and interfaces (MS); polymers and bio-inspired materials (MS). MS not open to international students. *Faculty:* 23 full-time (3 women). *Students:* 10 full-time (2 women); includes 1 minority (Hispanic/Latino), 5 international. Average age 24. 13 applicants, 23% accepted, 3 enrolled. In 2011, 3 master's awarded. Terminal master's awarded for partial completion of doctoral program. *Degree requirements:* For master's, thesis; for doctorate, comprehensive exam, thesis/dissertation. *Entrance requirements:* For master's and doctorate, GRE General Test (minimum old version score 1100 Verbal and Quantitative; 55th percentile Verbal, 75th percentile Quantitative in new format), minimum GPA of 3.0, 3 letters of recommendation. Additional exam requirements/recommendations for international students: Required—TOEFL (minimum score 80 iBT). *Application deadline:* For fall admission, 7/1 for domestic students, 5/1 for international students; for spring admission, 11/1 for domestic students, 9/1 for international students. Applications are processed on a rolling basis. Application fee: $25. Electronic applications accepted. *Expenses:* Tuition, state resident: full-time $9474; part-time $350.88 per credit hour. Tuition, nonresident: full-time $16,236; part-time $601.34 per credit hour. *Required fees:* $630 per semester. One-time fee: $20. Tuition and fees vary according to course load and campus/location. *Financial support:* In 2011–12, 10 students received support, including 1 fellowship with full tuition reimbursement available (averaging $30,526 per year), 7 research assistantships with full tuition reimbursements available (averaging $20,700 per year), 1 teaching assistantship with full tuition reimbursement available (averaging $20,880 per year); partial payment of required health insurance also available. Financial award application deadline: 1/15. *Faculty research:* Magnetism and magnetic materials, composites, superconductors, polymers, computations, nanotechnology. *Unit head:* Prof. Eric Hellstrom, Director, 850-645-7489, Fax: 850-645-7754, E-mail: hellstrom@asc.magnet.fsu.edu. *Application contact:* Judy Gardner, Admissions Coordinator, 850-645-8980, Fax: 850-645-9123, E-mail: gardner@eng.fsu.edu. Web site: http://materials.fsu.edu.

Georgia Institute of Technology, Graduate Studies and Research, College of Engineering, Multidisciplinary Program in Polymers, Atlanta, GA 30332-0001. Offers MS Poly. *Degree requirements:* For master's, thesis. *Entrance requirements:* For master's, minimum GPA of 2.7. Additional exam requirements/recommendations for international students: Required—TOEFL.

Georgia Institute of Technology, Graduate Studies and Research, College of Engineering, School of Polymer, Textile, and Fiber Engineering, Atlanta, GA 30332-0001. Offers polymer, textile and fiber engineering (MS, PhD); polymers (MS Poly). *Degree requirements:* For master's, thesis (for some programs); for doctorate, comprehensive exam, thesis/dissertation. *Entrance requirements:* For master's, GRE, minimum GPA of 2.7; for doctorate, GRE, minimum GPA of 3.0. Additional exam requirements/recommendations for international students: Required—TOEFL (minimum score 550 paper-based; 213 computer-based). Electronic applications accepted. *Faculty research:* Energy conservation, environmental control, engineered fibrous structures, polymer synthesis and degradation, high performance organic-carbon-ceramic fibers.

Lehigh University, College of Arts and Sciences, Department of Physics, Bethlehem, PA 18015. Offers photonics (MS); physics (MS, PhD); polymer science (MS, PhD). Part-time programs available. *Faculty:* 17 full-time (1 woman). *Students:* 42 full-time (14 women), 1 part-time (0 women), 21 international. Average age 26. 84 applicants, 10% accepted, 8 enrolled. In 2011, 9 master's, 9 doctorates awarded. *Degree requirements:* For doctorate, comprehensive exam, thesis/dissertation. *Entrance requirements:* For master's and doctorate, GRE General Test. Additional exam requirements/recommendations for international students: Required—TOEFL (minimum score 213 computer-based; 79 iBT). *Application deadline:* For fall admission, 2/15 priority date for domestic students, 2/15 for international students. Applications are processed on a rolling basis. Application fee: $75. Electronic applications accepted. *Financial support:* In 2011–12, 42 students received support, including 3 fellowships with full tuition reimbursements available (averaging $26,000 per year), 14 research assistantships with full tuition reimbursements available (averaging $24,770 per year), 25 teaching assistantships with full tuition reimbursements available (averaging $24,770 per year); career-related internships or fieldwork, Federal Work-Study, institutionally sponsored loans, scholarships/grants, tuition waivers (full and partial), and unspecified assistantships also available. Support available to part-time students. Financial award application deadline: 1/15. *Faculty research:* Condensed matter physics; atomic, molecular and optical physics; plasma physics; nonlinear optics and photonics; astronomy and astrophysics. *Total annual research expenditures:* $2.5 million. *Unit head:* Dr. Volkmar Dierolf, Chair, 610-758-3915, Fax: 610-758-5730, E-mail: vod2@lehigh.edu. *Application contact:* Dr. Dimitrios Vavylonis, Graduate Admissions Officer, 610-758-3724, Fax: 610-758-5730, E-mail: div206@lehigh.edu. Web site: http://www.physics.lehigh.edu/.

Lehigh University, P.C. Rossin College of Engineering and Applied Science and College of Arts and Sciences, Center for Polymer Science and Engineering, Bethlehem, PA 18015. Offers M Eng, MS, PhD. Part-time and evening/weekend programs available. Postbaccalaureate distance learning degree programs offered (no on-campus study). *Students:* 4 full-time (1 woman), 8 part-time (2 women); includes 1 minority (Hispanic/Latino), 3 international. Average age 34. 4 applicants, 0% accepted, 0 enrolled. In 2011, 1 master's, 2 doctorates awarded. Terminal master's awarded for partial completion of doctoral program. *Degree requirements:* For master's, thesis (for some programs); for doctorate, thesis/dissertation. *Entrance requirements:* For master's and doctorate, GRE General Test. Additional exam requirements/recommendations for international students: Required—TOEFL (minimum score 487 paper-based; 216 computer-based; 85 iBT). *Application deadline:* For fall admission, 7/15 for domestic students, 1/15 for international students; for spring admission, 12/1 for domestic and international students. Applications are processed on a rolling basis. Application fee: $75. Electronic applications accepted. *Financial support:* In 2011–12, 3 students received support, including 2 research assistantships (averaging $23,380 per year), 1 teaching assistantship (averaging $25,092 per year). Financial award application deadline: 1/15. *Faculty research:* Polymer colloids, polymer coatings, blends and composites, polymer interfaces, emulsion polymer. *Unit head:* Dr. Raymond A. Pearson, Director, 610-758-3857, Fax: 610-758-3526, E-mail: rp02@lehigh.edu. *Application contact:* James E. Roberts, Chair, Polymer Education Committee, 610-758-4841, Fax: 610-758-6536, E-mail: jer1@lehigh.edu. Web site: http://fp2.cc.lehigh.edu/inpolctr/cpse_home_page.htm.

Lehigh University, P.C. Rossin College of Engineering and Applied Science, Department of Materials Science and Engineering, Bethlehem, PA 18015. Offers materials science and engineering (M Eng, MS, PhD); photonics (MS); polymer science/engineering (M Eng, MS, PhD); MBA/E. Part-time programs available. *Faculty:* 13 full-time (3 women), 1 part-time/adjunct (0 women). *Students:* 28 full-time (6 women), 6 part-time (1 woman); includes 2 minority (both Asian, non-Hispanic/Latino), 14 international. Average age 26. 321 applicants, 2% accepted, 6 enrolled. In 2011, 2 master's, 2 doctorates awarded. *Degree requirements:* For master's, thesis; for doctorate, comprehensive exam, thesis/dissertation. *Entrance requirements:* For master's and doctorate, GRE General Test, minimum GPA of 3.0. Additional exam requirements/recommendations for international students: Required—TOEFL (minimum score 487 paper-based; 216 computer-based; 85 iBT). *Application deadline:* For fall admission, 1/15 priority date for domestic students, 1/15 for international students; for spring admission, 12/1 priority date for domestic students, 12/1 for international students. Applications are processed on a rolling basis. Application fee: $75. Electronic applications accepted. *Financial support:* In 2011–12, 29 students received support, including 3 fellowships with full and partial tuition reimbursements available (averaging $22,400 per year), 25 research assistantships with full tuition reimbursements available (averaging $22,449 per year), 13 teaching assistantships with partial tuition reimbursements available (averaging $17,512 per year); career-related internships or fieldwork, Federal Work-Study, institutionally sponsored loans, scholarships/grants, and unspecified assistantships also available. Support available to part-time students. Financial award application deadline: 1/15. *Faculty research:* Metals, ceramics, crystals, polymers, fatigue crack propagation. *Total annual research expenditures:* $4.1 million. *Unit head:* Dr. Helen Chan, Chairperson, 610-758-5554, Fax: 610-758-4244, E-mail: hmc0@lehigh.edu. *Application contact:* Anne Marie Lobley, Graduate Administrative Coordinator, 610-758-4222, Fax: 610-758-4244, E-mail: amme@lehigh.edu. Web site: http://www.lehigh.edu/~inmatsci/.

Lehigh University, P.C. Rossin College of Engineering and Applied Science, Department of Mechanical Engineering and Mechanics, Bethlehem, PA 18015. Offers computational engineering and mechanics (MS, PhD); mechanical engineering (M Eng, MS, PhD, MBA/E); polymer science/engineering (M Eng, MS, PhD, MBA/E); MBA/E. Part-time and evening/weekend programs available. Postbaccalaureate distance learning degree programs offered. *Faculty:* 24 full-time (0 women). *Students:* 113 full-time (12 women), 30 part-time (3 women); includes 6 minority (3 Black or African American, non-Hispanic/Latino; 2 Asian, non-Hispanic/Latino; 1 Hispanic/Latino), 79 international. Average age 26. 298 applicants, 50% accepted, 37 enrolled. In 2011, 35 master's, 6 doctorates awarded. Terminal master's awarded for partial completion of doctoral program. *Degree requirements:* For master's, thesis; for doctorate, thesis/dissertation, general exam. *Entrance requirements:* Additional exam requirements/recommendations for international students: Required—TOEFL (minimum score 550 paper-based; 213 computer-based; 79 iBT). *Application deadline:* For fall admission, 7/15 for domestic and international students; for spring admission, 12/1 for domestic and international students. Applications are processed on a rolling basis. Application fee: $75. Electronic applications accepted. *Financial support:* In 2011–12, 47 students received support, including 5 fellowships with full and partial tuition reimbursements available (averaging $24,480 per year), 24 research assistantships with full and partial tuition reimbursements available (averaging $20,700 per year), 12 teaching assistantships with full and partial tuition reimbursements available (averaging $25,092 per year); unspecified assistantships and dean's doctoral assistantships also available. Financial award application deadline: 1/15. *Faculty research:* Thermofluids, dynamic systems, CAD/CAM, computational mechanics, solid mechanics. *Total annual research expenditures:* $3.5 million. *Unit head:* Dr. D. Gary Harlow, Chairman, 610-758-4102, Fax: 610-758-6224, E-mail: dgh0@lehigh.edu. *Application contact:* Jo Ann M. Casciano, Graduate Coordinator, 610-758-4107, Fax: 610-758-6224, E-mail: jmc4@lehigh.edu. Web site: http://www.lehigh.edu/~inmem/.

North Carolina State University, Graduate School, College of Textiles, Program in Fiber and Polymer Science, Raleigh, NC 27695. Offers PhD. *Degree requirements:* For doctorate, one foreign language, thesis/dissertation, cumulative exams. *Entrance requirements:* For doctorate, GRE. Electronic applications accepted. *Faculty research:* Polymer science, fiber mechanics, medical textiles, nanotechnology.

North Dakota State University, College of Graduate and Interdisciplinary Studies, College of Science and Mathematics, Department of Coatings and Polymeric Materials, Fargo, ND 58108. Offers MS, PhD. Part-time programs available. *Faculty:* 4 full-time (1 woman), 1 part-time/adjunct (0 women). *Students:* 16 full-time (6 women), 7 part-time (1 woman); includes 2 minority (both Asian, non-Hispanic/Latino), 16 international. 16 applicants, 6% accepted, 0 enrolled. In 2011, 2 master's, 6 doctorates awarded. Terminal master's awarded for partial completion of doctoral program. *Degree requirements:* For master's, thesis, cumulative exams; for doctorate, comprehensive exam, thesis/dissertation, cumulative exams. *Entrance requirements:* For master's and doctorate, BS in chemistry or chemical engineering, minimum GPA of 3.0. Additional exam requirements/recommendations for international students: Required—TOEFL (minimum score 550 paper-based; 213 computer-based). *Application deadline:* For fall admission, 4/15 priority date for domestic students. Applications are processed on a rolling basis. Application fee: $35. Electronic applications accepted. *Financial support:* Fellowships, research assistantships with full tuition reimbursements, teaching assistantships with full tuition reimbursements, Federal Work-Study, institutionally sponsored loans, scholarships/grants, health care benefits, and tuition waivers (full) available. Support available to part-time students. Financial award application deadline: 3/15. *Faculty research:* Nanomaterials, combinatorial materials science. *Unit head:* Dr. Dean C. Webster, Chair, 701-231-8709, Fax: 701-231-8439, E-mail: dean.webster@ndsu.edu. Web site: http://cpm.ndsu.nodak.edu/.

Polytechnic Institute of New York University, Department of Chemical and Biological Engineering, Major in Polymer Science and Engineering, Brooklyn, NY 11201-2990. Offers MS. *Degree requirements:* For master's, comprehensive exam (for some programs), thesis (for some programs). *Entrance requirements:* Additional exam requirements/recommendations for international students: Required—TOEFL (minimum score 550 paper-based; 213 computer-based; 80 iBT); Recommended—IELTS (minimum score 6.5). *Application deadline:* For fall admission, 7/31 priority date for domestic students, 4/30 for international students; for spring admission, 12/31 priority date for domestic students, 10/30 for international students. Applications are processed on a rolling basis. Application fee: $75. Electronic applications accepted. *Expenses: Tuition:* Full-time $22,464; part-time $1248 per credit. *Required fees:* $501 per semester. *Unit head:* Dr. Walter Zurawsky, Department Head, 718-260-3600. *Application contact:* JeanCarlo Bonilla, Director, Graduate Enrollment Management, 718-260-3182, Fax: 718-260-3624.

Rensselaer Polytechnic Institute, Graduate School, School of Engineering, Program in Materials Science and Engineering, Troy, NY 12180. Offers ceramics and glass science (M Eng, MS, PhD); composites (M Eng, MS, PhD); electronic materials (M Eng, MS, PhD); metallurgy (M Eng, MS, PhD); polymers (M Eng, MS, PhD). Part-time programs available. Terminal master's awarded for partial completion of doctoral program. *Degree requirements:* For master's, thesis; for doctorate, comprehensive exam, thesis/dissertation. *Entrance requirements:* For master's and doctorate, GRE. Additional exam requirements/recommendations for international students: Required—TOEFL (minimum score 570 paper-based; 230 computer-based; 100 iBT). Electronic applications accepted. *Faculty research:* Materials processing, nanostructural materials, materials for microelectronics, composite materials, computational materials.

Stevens Institute of Technology, Graduate School, Charles V. Schaefer Jr. School of Engineering, Department of Chemistry, Chemical Biology and Biomedical Engineering, Hoboken, NJ 07030. Offers analytical chemistry (PhD, Certificate); bioinformatics (PhD, Certificate); biomedical chemistry (Certificate); biomedical engineering (M Eng, Certificate); chemical biology (MS, PhD, Certificate); chemical physiology (Certificate); chemistry (MS, PhD); organic chemistry (PhD); physical chemistry (PhD); polymer chemistry (PhD, Certificate). Part-time and evening/weekend programs available. Postbaccalaureate distance learning degree programs offered (no on-campus study). Terminal master's awarded for partial completion of doctoral program. *Degree requirements:* For master's, thesis or alternative; for doctorate, one foreign language, thesis/dissertation; for Certificate, project or thesis. *Entrance requirements:* Additional exam requirements/recommendations for international students: Required—TOEFL. Electronic applications accepted. *Faculty research:* Biochemical reaction engineering, polymerization engineering, reactor design, biochemical process control and synthesis.

The University of Akron, Graduate School, College of Engineering, Program in Engineering (Polymer Specialization), Akron, OH 44325. Offers MS. *Students:* 4 applicants, 0% accepted, 0 enrolled. *Degree requirements:* For master's, thesis. *Entrance requirements:* For master's, GRE, minimum GPA of 2.75, three letters of recommendation, statement of purpose, resume. Additional exam requirements/recommendations for international students: Required—TOEFL (minimum score 550 paper-based; 213 computer-based; 79 iBT). *Application deadline:* Applications are processed on a rolling basis. Application fee: $30 ($40 for international students). Electronic applications accepted. *Expenses:* Tuition, state resident: full-time $7038; part-time $391 per credit hour. Tuition, nonresident: full-time $12,051; part-time $670 per credit hour. *Required fees:* $1274; $34 per credit hour. *Unit head:* Dr. Subramaniya Hariharan, Coordinator, 330-972-6580, E-mail: hari@uakron.edu. *Application contact:* Director of Graduate Studies.

Polymer Science and Engineering

The University of Akron, Graduate School, College of Polymer Science and Polymer Engineering, Department of Polymer Engineering, Akron, OH 44325. Offers MS, PhD. Part-time and evening/weekend programs available. *Faculty:* 14 full-time (0 women), 2 part-time/adjunct (1 woman). *Students:* 101 full-time (32 women), 7 part-time (0 women); includes 4 minority (2 Black or African American, non-Hispanic/Latino; 1 Asian, non-Hispanic/Latino; 1 Hispanic/Latino), 89 international. Average age 26. 153 applicants, 37% accepted, 41 enrolled. In 2011, 3 master's, 8 doctorates awarded. *Degree requirements:* For master's, thesis, basic engineering exam; for doctorate, one foreign language, thesis/dissertation, candidacy exam. *Entrance requirements:* For master's and doctorate, GRE, bachelor's degree in engineering or physical science, minimum GPA of 2.75 (3.0 in last two years), three letters of recommendation. Additional exam requirements/recommendations for international students: Required—TOEFL (minimum score 550 paper-based; 213 computer-based; 79 iBT). *Application deadline:* For fall admission, 1/15 priority date for domestic students, 1/15 for international students. Application fee: $30 ($40 for international students). Electronic applications accepted. *Expenses:* Tuition, state resident: full-time $7038; part-time $391 per credit hour. Tuition, nonresident: full-time $12,051; part-time $670 per credit hour. *Required fees:* $1274; $34 per credit hour. *Financial support:* In 2011–12, 82 research assistantships with full tuition reimbursements were awarded; unspecified assistantships also available. *Faculty research:* Processing and properties of multi-functional polymeric materials, nanomaterials and nanocomposites, micro and nano-scale materials processing, novel self-assembled polymeric materials for energy applications, coating materials and coating technology. *Unit head:* Dr. Robert Weiss, Chair, 330-972-2581, E-mail: rweiss@uakron.edu. *Application contact:* Sarah Thorley, Coordinator of Academic Program, 330-972-8845, E-mail: sarah3@uakron.edu. Web site: http://www.poly-eng.uakron.edu/.

The University of Akron, Graduate School, College of Polymer Science and Polymer Engineering, Department of Polymer Science, Akron, OH 44325. Offers MS, PhD. Part-time and evening/weekend programs available. *Faculty:* 16 full-time (3 women), 3 part-time/adjunct (0 women). *Students:* 124 full-time (38 women), 14 part-time (9 women); includes 8 minority (3 Black or African American, non-Hispanic/Latino; 5 Asian, non-Hispanic/Latino), 101 international. Average age 27. 210 applicants, 25% accepted, 53 enrolled. In 2011, 3 master's, 17 doctorates awarded. Terminal master's awarded for partial completion of doctoral program. *Degree requirements:* For master's, thesis; for doctorate, one foreign language, thesis/dissertation, cumulative exam, seminars. *Entrance requirements:* For master's and doctorate, GRE, minimum GPA of 3.0, three letters of recommendation, statement of purpose. Additional exam requirements/recommendations for international students: Required—TOEFL (minimum score 550 paper-based; 213 computer-based; 79 iBT). *Application deadline:* For fall admission, 12/1 priority date for domestic students, 12/15 for international students. Application fee: $30 ($40 for international students). Electronic applications accepted. *Expenses:* Tuition, state resident: full-time $7038; part-time $391 per credit hour. Tuition, nonresident: full-time $12,051; part-time $670 per credit hour. *Required fees:* $1274; $34 per credit hour. *Financial support:* In 2011–12, 87 research assistantships with full tuition reimbursements were awarded; fellowships and scholarships/grants also available. *Faculty research:* Synthesis of polymers, structure of polymers, physical properties of polymers, engineering and technological properties of polymers, elastomers. *Total annual research expenditures:* $3.9 million. *Unit head:* Dr. Ali Dhinojwala, Chair, 330-972-6246, E-mail: ali4@uakron.edu. *Application contact:* Melissa Bowman, Coordinator, Academic Programs, 330-972-7532, E-mail: mb8@uakron.edu. Web site: http://www2.uakron.edu/cpspe/DPS/.

University of Connecticut, Institute of Materials Science, Polymer Program, Storrs, CT 06269-3136. Offers polymer science and engineering (MS, PhD). Part-time programs available. Terminal master's awarded for partial completion of doctoral program. *Degree requirements:* For master's, thesis (for some programs); for doctorate, one foreign language, comprehensive exam, thesis/dissertation. *Entrance requirements:* For master's and doctorate, GRE General Test. Additional exam requirements/recommendations for international students: Required—TOEFL (minimum score 550 paper-based; 213 computer-based; 80 iBT), IELTS (minimum score 6.5). Electronic applications accepted. *Faculty research:* Nanomaterials and nanotechnology, biomaterials and sensors, synthesis, electronic/photonic materials, solar cells and fuel cells, structure and function of proteins, biodegradable polymers, molecular simulations, drug targeting and delivery.

The University of Manchester, School of Materials, Manchester, United Kingdom. Offers advanced aerospace materials engineering (M Sc); advanced metallic systems (PhD); biomedical materials (M Phil, M Sc, PhD); ceramics and glass (M Phil, M Sc, PhD); composite materials (M Sc, PhD); corrosion and protection (M Phil, M Sc, PhD); materials (M Phil, PhD); metallic materials (M Phil, M Sc, PhD); nanostructural materials (M Phil, M Sc, PhD); paper science (M Phil, M Sc, PhD); polymer science and engineering (M Phil, M Sc, PhD); technical textiles (M Sc); textile design, fashion and management (M Phil, M Sc, PhD); textile science and technology (M Phil, M Sc, PhD); textiles (M Phil, PhD); textiles and fashion (M Ent).

University of Massachusetts Amherst, Graduate School, College of Natural Sciences, Department of Polymer Science and Engineering, Amherst, MA 01003. Offers MS, PhD. *Faculty:* 17 full-time (1 woman). *Students:* 106 full-time (37 women), 7 part-time (4 women); includes 7 minority (4 Asian, non-Hispanic/Latino; 2 Hispanic/Latino; 1 Two or more races, non-Hispanic/Latino), 55 international. Average age 26. 270 applicants, 13% accepted, 15 enrolled. In 2011, 16 master's, 14 doctorates awarded. Terminal master's awarded for partial completion of doctoral program. *Degree requirements:* For master's, thesis or alternative; for doctorate, comprehensive exam, thesis/dissertation. *Entrance requirements:* For master's and doctorate, GRE General Test. Additional exam requirements/recommendations for international students: Required—TOEFL (minimum score 550 paper-based; 213 computer-based; 80 iBT), IELTS (minimum score 6.5). *Application deadline:* For fall admission, 1/2 for domestic and international students. Applications are processed on a rolling basis. Application fee: $50 ($65 for international students). Electronic applications accepted. Tuition and fees vary according to course load, campus/location and program. *Financial support:* Fellowships with full and partial tuition reimbursements, research assistantships with full and partial tuition reimbursements, teaching assistantships with full and partial tuition reimbursements, career-related internships or fieldwork, Federal Work-Study, scholarships/grants, traineeships, health care benefits, tuition waivers (partial), and unspecified assistantships available. Support available to part-time students. Financial award application deadline: 1/2. *Unit head:* Dr. Gregory Tew, Graduate Program Director, 413-577-9120, Fax: 413-545-0082. *Application contact:* Lindsay DeSantis, Interim Supervisor of Admissions, 413-545-0722, Fax: 413-577-0010, E-mail: gradadm@grad.umass.edu. Web site: http://www.pse.umass.edu/.

University of Massachusetts Lowell, College of Engineering, Department of Plastics Engineering, Lowell, MA 01854-2881. Offers elastomers (Graduate Certificate); medical plastics design and manufacturing (Graduate Certificate); plastics design (Graduate Certificate); plastics engineering (MS Eng, D Eng, PhD), including coatings and adhesives (MS Eng), plastics materials (MS Eng), plastics processing (MS Eng), product design (MS Eng); plastics engineering fundamentals (Graduate Certificate); plastics materials (Graduate Certificate); plastics processing (Graduate Certificate); polymer science/plastics engineering (PhD). Part-time programs available. Terminal master's awarded for partial completion of doctoral program. *Degree requirements:* For master's, thesis optional; for doctorate, comprehensive exam, thesis/dissertation. *Entrance requirements:* For master's and doctorate, GRE General Test. Additional exam requirements/recommendations for international students: Required—TOEFL.

University of Massachusetts Lowell, College of Sciences, Department of Chemistry, Program in Polymer Science, Lowell, MA 01854-2881. Offers MS. *Degree requirements:* For master's, thesis. *Entrance requirements:* For master's, GRE General Test. Electronic applications accepted.

University of Missouri–Kansas City, College of Arts and Sciences, Department of Chemistry, Kansas City, MO 64110-2499. Offers analytical chemistry (MS, PhD); inorganic chemistry (MS, PhD); organic chemistry (MS, PhD); physical chemistry (MS, PhD); polymer chemistry (MS, PhD). PhD (interdisciplinary) offered through the School of Graduate Studies. Part-time and evening/weekend programs available. *Faculty:* 16 full-time (3 women), 1 part-time/adjunct (0 women). *Students:* 1 (woman) part-time; minority (Black or African American, non-Hispanic/Latino). Average age 30. 28 applicants, 32% accepted, 0 enrolled. In 2011, 2 degrees awarded. *Degree requirements:* For master's, thesis (for some programs); for doctorate, thesis/dissertation. *Entrance requirements:* For master's, equivalent of American Chemical Society approved bachelor's degree in chemistry; for doctorate, GRE General Test, equivalent of American Chemical Society approved bachelor's degree in chemistry. Additional exam requirements/recommendations for international students: Required—TOEFL (minimum score 550 paper-based; 213 computer-based; 80 iBT), TWE. *Application deadline:* For fall admission, 4/15 for domestic and international students; for spring admission, 10/15 for domestic and international students. Applications are processed on a rolling basis. Application fee: $45 ($50 for international students). Electronic applications accepted. *Expenses:* Tuition, state resident: full-time $5798; part-time $322.10 per credit hour. Tuition, nonresident: full-time $14,969; part-time $831.60 per credit hour. *Required fees:* $93.51 per credit hour. *Financial support:* In 2011–12, 9 research assistantships with partial tuition reimbursements (averaging $19,119 per year), 14 teaching assistantships with partial tuition reimbursements (averaging $17,187 per year) were awarded; Federal Work-Study, institutionally sponsored loans, and scholarships/grants also available. Support available to part-time students. Financial award application deadline: 3/1; financial award applicants required to submit FAFSA. *Faculty research:* Molecular spectroscopy, characterization and synthesis of materials and compounds, computational chemistry, natural products, drug delivery systems and anti-tumor agents. *Unit head:* Dr. Kathleen V. Kilway, Chair, 816-235-2289, Fax: 816-235-5502. *Application contact:* Graduate Recruiting Committee, 816-235-2272, Fax: 816-235-5502, E-mail: umkc-chemdept@umkc.edu. Web site: http://cas.umkc.edu/chem/.

University of Southern Mississippi, Graduate School, College of Science and Technology, School of Polymers and High Performance Materials, Hattiesburg, MS 39406-0001. Offers polymer science (MS); polymer science and engineering (MS, PhD), including polymer science and engineering (PhD), sports and high performance materials. *Faculty:* 14 full-time (1 woman), 1 part-time/adjunct (0 women). *Students:* 68 full-time (22 women), 13 part-time (3 women); includes 2 minority (both Asian, non-Hispanic/Latino), 18 international. Average age 28. 89 applicants, 28% accepted, 19 enrolled. In 2011, 4 master's, 9 doctorates awarded. Terminal master's awarded for partial completion of doctoral program. *Degree requirements:* For master's, comprehensive exam, thesis; for doctorate, comprehensive exam, thesis/dissertation, original proposal. *Entrance requirements:* For master's, GRE General Test, minimum GPA of 2.75; for doctorate, GRE General Test, minimum GPA of 3.5. Additional exam requirements/recommendations for international students: Required—TOEFL, IELTS. *Application deadline:* For fall admission, 3/1 priority date for domestic students, 3/1 for international students. Applications are processed on a rolling basis. Application fee: $50. Electronic applications accepted. *Financial support:* In 2011–12, 60 research assistantships with full tuition reimbursements (averaging $20,000 per year), 15 teaching assistantships with full tuition reimbursements (averaging $10,000 per year) were awarded; fellowships, Federal Work-Study, scholarships/grants, health care benefits, and unspecified assistantships also available. Financial award application deadline: 3/15; financial award applicants required to submit FAFSA. *Faculty research:* Water-soluble polymers; polymer composites; coatings; solid-state, laser-initiated polymerization. *Unit head:* Dr. Robert Lochhead, Chair, 601-266-4868, Fax: 601-266-6178. *Application contact:* Dr. Brett Calhoun, Director, Graduate Studies, 601-266-4868. Web site: http://www.usm.edu/graduateschool/table.php.

University of South Florida, Graduate School, College of Arts and Sciences, Department of Chemistry, Tampa, FL 33620-9951. Offers analytical chemistry (MS, PhD); biochemistry (MS, PhD); computational chemistry (MS, PhD); environmental chemistry (MS, PhD); inorganic chemistry (MS, PhD); organic chemistry (MS); physical chemistry (MS, PhD); polymer chemistry (PhD). Part-time programs available. *Faculty:* 25 full-time (4 women), 9 part-time/adjunct (1 woman). *Students:* 118 full-time (46 women), 14 part-time (7 women); includes 28 minority (8 Black or African American, non-Hispanic/Latino; 11 Asian, non-Hispanic/Latino; 9 Hispanic/Latino), 58 international. Average age 29. 127 applicants, 31% accepted, 19 enrolled. In 2011, 3 master's, 16 doctorates awarded. Terminal master's awarded for partial completion of doctoral program. *Degree requirements:* For master's, comprehensive exam, thesis (for some programs); for doctorate, comprehensive exam, thesis/dissertation. *Entrance requirements:* For master's and doctorate, GRE General Test, minimum GPA of 3.0. Additional exam requirements/recommendations for international students: Required—TOEFL (minimum score 550 paper-based; 213 computer-based; 79 iBT) or IELTS (minimum score 6.5). *Application deadline:* For fall admission, 2/15 priority date for domestic students, 1/2 for international students; for spring admission, 10/1 priority date for domestic students, 6/1 for international students. Applications are processed on a rolling basis. Application fee: $30. Electronic applications accepted. *Financial support:* In 2011–12, 136 students received support, including 28 research assistantships with tuition reimbursements available (averaging $15,020 per year), 108 teaching assistantships with tuition reimbursements available (averaging $15,164 per year); unspecified assistantships also available. Financial award application deadline: 6/30. *Faculty research:* Synthesis, bio-organic chemistry, bioinorganic chemistry, environmental chemistry, NMR. *Total annual research expenditures:* $3.1 million. *Unit head:* Dr. Randy Larsen, Chairperson, 813-974-4129, Fax: 813-974-3203, E-mail: rlarsen@cas.usf.edu. *Application contact:* Patricia Muisener, Director, 813-974-1730, Fax: 813-974-3203, E-mail: muisener@cas.usf.edu. Web site: http://chemistry.usf.edu/.

The University of Tennessee, Graduate School, College of Engineering, Department of Materials Science and Engineering, Program in Polymer Engineering, Knoxville, TN 37996. Offers MS, PhD. *Faculty:* 6 full-time (1 woman). *Students:* 8 full-time (1 woman), 1 part-time (0 women); includes 1 minority (Black or African American, non-Hispanic/Latino), 3 international. Average age 27. 56 applicants, 4% accepted, 2 enrolled. In 2011, 1 degree awarded. *Degree requirements:* For master's, thesis or alternative; for doctorate, comprehensive exam, thesis/dissertation. *Entrance requirements:* For master's, GRE General Test (for MS students pursuing research thesis), minimum GPA of 2.7 (for U.S. degree holders), 3.0 (for international degree holders); 3 references; for doctorate, College requires GRE General Test for all PhD candidates, minimum GPA of 3.0 on previous graduate course work; 3 references. Additional exam requirements/recommendations for international students: Required—TOEFL (minimum score 550 paper-based; 213 computer-based). *Application deadline:* For fall admission, 2/1 priority date for domestic students, 2/1 for international students; for spring admission, 6/15 for domestic and international students. Applications are processed on a rolling basis. Application fee: $35. Electronic applications accepted. *Expenses:* Tuition, state resident: full-time $8332; part-time $464 per credit hour. Tuition, nonresident: full-time $25,174; part-time $1400 per credit hour. *Required fees:* $1162; $56 per credit hour. Tuition and fees vary according to program. *Financial support:* In 2011–12, 8 students received support, including 6 research assistantships with full tuition reimbursements available (averaging $20,360 per year), 1 teaching assistantship with full tuition reimbursement available (averaging $17,400 per year); fellowships with full tuition reimbursements available, career-related internships or fieldwork, Federal Work-Study, institutionally sponsored loans, health care benefits, and unspecified assistantships also available. Financial award application deadline: 2/1; financial award applicants required to submit FAFSA. *Faculty research:* Polymer chemistry, processing, and characterization. *Unit head:* Dr. Kurt Sickafus, Head, 865-974-4858, Fax: 865-974-4115, E-mail: kurt@utk.edu. *Application contact:* Dr. Roberto S. Benson, Associate Head, 865-974-5347, Fax: 865-974-4115, E-mail: rbenson1@utk.edu. Web site: http://www.engr.utk.edu/mse.

University of Wisconsin–Madison, Graduate School, College of Engineering, Department of Mechanical Engineering, Madison, WI 53706-1380. Offers energy systems (ME); engine systems (ME); mechanical engineering (MS, PhD); polymers (ME). Part-time programs available. Postbaccalaureate distance learning degree programs offered (no on-campus study). *Faculty:* 33 full-time (3 women), 1 part-time/adjunct (0 women). *Students:* 191 full-time (17 women), 18 part-time (1 woman); includes 23 minority (1 Black or African American, non-Hispanic/Latino; 1 American Indian or Alaska Native, non-Hispanic/Latino; 10 Asian, non-Hispanic/Latino; 10 Hispanic/Latino; 1 Native Hawaiian or other Pacific Islander, non-Hispanic/Latino). Average age 25. 615 applicants, 19% accepted, 46 enrolled. In 2011, 56 master's, 16 doctorates awarded. Terminal master's awarded for partial completion of doctoral program. *Degree requirements:* For master's, thesis optional; for doctorate, thesis/dissertation, qualifying exam, preliminary exam. *Entrance requirements:* For master's, GRE, BS in mechanical engineering or related field, minimum GPA of 3.0 in last 60 hours of course work; for doctorate, GRE, BS in mechanical engineering or related field, minimum undergraduate GPA of 3.0 in last 60 hours of course work. Additional exam requirements/recommendations for international students: Required—TOEFL (minimum score 550 paper-based; 213 computer-based; 80 iBT). *Application deadline:* For fall admission, 5/1 for domestic students, 6/1 for international students; for spring admission, 11/30 for domestic students, 10/1 for international students. Applications are processed on a rolling basis. Application fee: $56. Electronic applications accepted. *Expenses:* Tuition, state resident: full-time $10,296; part-time $643.51 per credit. Tuition, nonresident: full-time $24,054; part-time $1503.40 per credit. *Required fees:* $70.06 per credit. Tuition and fees vary according to course load, campus/location, program and reciprocity agreements. *Financial support:* In 2011–12, 168 students received support, including 11 fellowships with full tuition reimbursements available (averaging $22,224 per year), 121 research assistantships with full tuition reimbursements available (averaging $19,596 per year), 37 teaching assistantships with full tuition reimbursements available (averaging $8,595 per year); career-related internships or fieldwork, institutionally sponsored loans, scholarships/grants, traineeships, health care benefits, and unspecified assistantships also available. *Faculty research:* Design and manufacturing, materials processing, combustion, energy systems nanotechnology. *Total annual research expenditures:* $10 million. *Unit head:* Roxann L. Engelstad, Chair, 608-262-5745, Fax: 608-265-2316, E-mail: engelsta@engr.wisc.edu. *Application contact:* 608-262-2433, Fax: 608-262-5134, E-mail: gradadmiss@mail.bascom.wisc.edu. Web site: http://www.engr.wisc.edu/me/.

Wayne State University, College of Engineering, Department of Chemical Engineering and Materials Science, Program in Materials Science and Engineering, Detroit, MI 48202. Offers materials science and engineering (MS, PhD); polymer engineering (Certificate). Part-time programs available. *Students:* 12 full-time (4 women); includes 1 minority (Black or African American, non-Hispanic/Latino), 10 international. Average age 27. 39 applicants, 41% accepted, 3 enrolled. In 2011, 3 master's awarded. Terminal master's awarded for partial completion of doctoral program. *Degree requirements:* For master's, thesis optional; for doctorate, thesis/dissertation. *Entrance requirements:* For master's, GRE (if applying for financial support), recommendations; resume; for doctorate, GRE (if applying for financial support), recommendations; resume, personal statement. Additional exam requirements/recommendations for international students: Required—TOEFL (minimum score 550 paper-based; 213 computer-based); Recommended—TWE (minimum score 5.5). *Application deadline:* For fall admission, 6/1 priority date for domestic students, 5/1 for international students; for winter admission, 10/1 priority date for domestic students, 9/1 for international students; for spring admission, 2/1 priority date for domestic students, 1/1 for international students. Applications are processed on a rolling basis. Application fee: $50. Electronic applications accepted. *Expenses:* Tuition, state resident: part-time $512.85 per credit. Tuition, nonresident: part-time $1132.65 per credit. *Required fees:* $26.60 per credit. $199.65 per semester. Tuition and fees vary according to course load and program. *Financial support:* In 2011–12, 9 students received support. Fellowships with tuition reimbursements available, research assistantships with tuition reimbursements available, teaching assistantships with tuition reimbursements available, scholarships/grants, health care benefits, and unspecified assistantships available. Support available to part-time students. Financial award application deadline: 2/15. *Faculty research:* Polymer science, rheology, fatigue in metals, metal matrix composites, ceramics. *Unit head:* Dr. Charles Manke, Chair, 313-577-3849, Fax: 313-577-3810, E-mail: cmanke@eng.wayne.edu. *Application contact:* Dr. Yinlun Huang, Graduate Program Director, 313-577-3771, E-mail: yhuang@eng.wayne.edu. Web site: http://cheme.eng.wayne.edu/ChE.

UNIVERSITY OF MICHIGAN

College of Engineering
Department of Materials Science and Engineering

MICHIGAN ENGINEERING

UNIVERSITY of MICHIGAN ■ COLLEGE of ENGINEERING

Programs of Study

The Department of Materials Science and Engineering offers Master of Science in Engineering (M.S.E.) and Ph.D. programs leading to degrees in materials science and engineering. Students may emphasize work in various materials categories or phenomena, although the Department encourages a broad graduate educational experience. Course offerings include basic materials courses in structure of materials, thermodynamics, diffusion, phase transformations, mechanical behavior, and materials characterization. Courses also exist in many areas of special interest, such as corrosion, composites, deformation processing, and failure analysis. The M.S.E. degree, typically completed in one to two years, requires 30 credit hours of graduate study. A research project of up to 6 credit hours or a master's thesis of 9–11 credit hours is included within this total and often forms the basis for the student's Ph.D. written examination. The Ph.D. degree, usually completed in four to five years beyond the B.S. degree, requires 18 credit hours of courses beyond the M.S.E. degree, passing grades on a written examination based on advanced undergraduate and graduate-level course material, a research-based oral examination, satisfactory completion of research, and defense of the doctoral dissertation. A precandidate must complete at least 18 credit hours of graded graduate course work registered as a Rackham student while in residence on the Ann Arbor campus. Master's students must complete at least one-half of the minimum required credit hours on the home campus. Each student is also required to complete one teaching assignment prior to the completion of the Ph.D. degree.

Faculty interests are diverse (see the reverse of this page) and fall into five main categories: inorganic materials, organic and biomaterials, electronic materials, structural materials, and computational materials science. Many additional research activities exist in collaboration with other departments and graduate programs.

Research Facilities

The Department occupies approximately 50,000 square feet, primarily in the H. H. Dow Building, but also in the adjacent G. G. Brown Building and the nearby Space Research and Gerstacker Buildings. Research facilities include world-class laboratories for electron microscopy and X-ray diffraction, ion-beam characterization and modification of materials, thin-film deposition, and solid-state device research. Modern instrumentation is added regularly. The Electron Microbeam Analysis Laboratory (EMAL) is a user facility that provides a broad spectrum of analytical equipment for the microstructural and microchemical characterization of materials. The facility includes two dual-beam focused ion beam (FIB) systems; four scanning electron microscopes (SEM); two environmental SEMs; three transmission electron microscopes (TEM) equipped with STEM, XEDS, and EELS; one X-ray photoelectron spectroscopy (XPS) system; and two atomic force microscopes (AFM). The J. D. Hanawalt X-ray Diffraction Laboratory offers several Rigaku, Phillips, and Siemens X-ray diffractometers. The Michigan Ion Beam Laboratory includes facilities for Rutherford backscattering spectrometry, ion channeling, nuclear reaction analysis, elastic recoil detection, and ion implantation for most of the elements of the periodic table, over a wide energy range. The Lurie Nanofabrication Facility offers complete capabilities for the fabrication and characterization of solid-state materials, devices, and circuits using silicon and compound semiconductors, and organic materials.

Financial Aid

Qualified applicants are eligible for fellowships and teaching or research assistantships that paid stipends of up to $26,553 per calendar year in 2011–12 plus tuition remission and some fringe benefits. Students funded by faculty advisers as research assistants work on research problems that are appropriate for their thesis topic. Teaching and research assistantships carry certain defined responsibilities that are adjusted to the needs of the student and the Department.

Cost of Study

The 2011–12 tuition fee for full-time students was $10,630 per term for Michigan residents and $20,003 per term for nonresidents.

Living and Housing Costs

A residence hall contract for room and board for the 2011–12 fall and winter terms ranged in cost from $9242 for a double to $12,530 for a single. Family housing units cost from $845 per month for an unfurnished one-bedroom unit to $1241 per month for a furnished three-bedroom unit. Prices include all utilities except telephone.

Many graduate students live in privately owned off-campus housing, which varies in expense depending on its proximity to the University. Food costs and local restaurant prices are typical of those in smaller cities in the Midwest.

Student Group

The Department has 144 full-time graduate students and 1 part-time student from local industry and research laboratories. Approximately 60 percent of the students are from the United States, and 40 percent are from abroad. Most students receive financial aid from the Department. The Department also has about 140 undergraduate students. The College of Engineering currently enrolls 8,800 students in twelve engineering departments/divisions and more than sixty engineering fields of study. The current total student enrollment on the Ann Arbor campus is approximately 42,000. The student-based Michigan Materials Society is very active.

Location

Ann Arbor is a cultural and cosmopolitan community of approximately 105,000 about 40 miles west of Detroit in southeastern Michigan. Ann Arbor offers world-class orchestras, dance companies, dramatic artists, and musical performers throughout the year. The internationally renowned May Festival of classical music and the Ann Arbor Folk Festival are held annually. Ann Arbor art fairs attract 500,000 patrons from across the nation every July. Recreational facilities are extensive, both on campus and throughout the community.

The University and The College

The University of Michigan, one of the nation's most distinguished state universities, is internationally recognized in all of its schools and colleges. The 6,400 faculty members and 42,000 students work in a modern environment that includes more than 275 research units. Michigan consistently ranks as a national leader in total research expenditures. The College of Engineering, of which the Department is a part, awards about 1,250 B.S., 1,030 M.S., and 250 Ph.D. degrees annually. There are more than 400 faculty members, 500 supporting staff members, 91 research faculty, and more than 65,000 alumni. Many of the programs in the College are rated among the ten best in the nation, and the College itself is often ranked among the top five engineering schools and colleges.

Applying

Applications are accepted for either the fall (September) or winter (January) terms; however, most students are admitted in the fall term. Applications for fall admission should be received by December 15 if financial support is required. Additional information on admission may be obtained from the Department or from the Horace H. Rackham School of Graduate Studies.

Correspondence and Information

Graduate Program Office
Department of Materials Science and Engineering
College of Engineering
University of Michigan
Ann Arbor, Michigan 48109-2136
Phone: 734-763-9790
Web site: http:// www.mse.engin.umich.edu

Horace H. Rackham School of Graduate Studies
Mail Office
University of Michigan
Ann Arbor, Michigan 48109

THE FACULTY AND THEIR RESEARCH

John Allison, Professor of Materials Science and Engineering, Ph.D., Carnegie-Mellon, 1982. Understanding the inter-relationships between processing, microstructure and properties in advanced metallic materials and the utilization of this knowledge to engineer metallic materials for use in engineering applications.

Michael Atzmon, Professor of Materials Science and Engineering and Nuclear Engineering and Radiological Sciences; Ph.D., Caltech, 1985. Phase transformations and mechanical behavior of nonequilibrium metal alloys.

Akram Boukai, Assistant Professor of Materials Science and Engineering; Ph.D., Caltech, 2008. Growth and characterization of nanomaterials for energy and electronic applications.

Samantha Daly, Assistant Professor of Materials Science and Engineering; Ph.D., Caltech, 2007. Multi-scale material characterization, with application to active materials, high temperature ceramics.

Rodney C. Ewing, Professor of Materials Science and Engineering, Geological Sciences and Nuclear Engineering and Radiological Sciences; Ph.D., Stanford, 1974. Radiation effects in complex ceramics and minerals, crystal chemistry of actinides, nuclear materials.

Steven Forrest, Professor of Materials Science and Engineering, Electrical Engineering and Computer Science, Physics, and Vice President for Research; Ph.D., Michigan, 1979. Theory, growth, and characterization of organic and III-V semiconductors for optoelectronic device applications.

Amit K. Ghosh, Professor of Materials Science and Engineering and Mechanical Engineering; Ph.D., MIT, 1972. Superplasticity, deformation processing, advanced metallic materials, composites and laminates, friction stir processing.

University of Michigan

Sharon C. Glotzer, Professor of Materials Science and Engineering, Chemical Engineering, and Physics; Ph.D., Boston University, 1993. Soft materials, polymers, dense liquids, glasses, colloids, and liquid crystals.

Rachel S. Goldman, Professor of Materials Science and Engineering, Electrical Engineering and Computer Science, and Physics; Ph.D., California, San Diego, 1995. Atomic-scale design of electronic materials; strain relaxation, alloy formation, and diffusion; correlations between microstructure and electronic and optical properties of semiconductor films, nanostructures, and heterostructures.

Peter Green, Professor and Chair of Materials Science and Engineering; Ph.D., Cornell, 1985. Polymer physics, oxide glasses, nanocomposites, thin films.

John W. Halloran, Professor of Materials Science and Engineering; Ph.D., MIT, 1977. Ceramics, rapid prototyping, electromagnetic materials, fuel cells, hydrogen and carbon.

J. Wayne Jones, Professor of Materials Science and Engineering; Ph.D., Vanderbilt, 1977. Fatigue of structural alloys for transportation and energy systems. Lightweight alloys.

John Kieffer, Professor of Materials Science and Engineering; Ph.D., Clausthal (Germany), 1985. Molecular design of materials for energy, photonics, and structural applications.

Jinsang Kim, Associate Professor of Materials Science and Engineering and Chemical Engineering; Ph.D., MIT, 2001. Functional polymers for biomedical and optoelectronic applications..

Emmanouil Kioupakis, Assistant Professor of Materials Science and Engineering; Ph.D., Berkeley, 2008. Computational study of novel materials for energy applications.

Nicholas Kotov, Professor of Materials Science and Engineering and Chemical Engineering; Ph.D., Moscow State, 1990. Applications of nanostructured materials to biology and medicine, self-organization of nanocolloidal systems.

Joerg Lahann, Professor of Materials Science and Engineering; Ph.D., RWTH Aachen, 1998. Designer surfaces, advanced polymers, biomimetic materials, microfluidic devices, engineered cellular microenvironments, nanoscale self-assembly.

Richard M. Laine, Professor of Materials Science and Engineering, Macromolecular Science and Engineering, and Chemistry; Ph.D., USC, 1973. Inorganic and organometallic precursors, materials chemistry, catalysis.

Victor Li, Professor of Materials Science and Engineering and Civil and Environmental Engineering; Ph.D., Brown, 1981. Fiber reinforced cementitious composites, micromechanics, self-healing design, sustainable material development.

Brian Love, Professor of Materials Science and Engineering; Ph.D., SMU, 1990. Photopolymerization, chemorheology, tissue engineering, proteins as polymers.

Peter Ma, Professor of Materials Science and Engineering; Ph.D., Rutgers. Polymeric biomaterials.

John F. Mansfield, Associate Research Scientist; Ph.D., Bristol (England), 1983. Analytical electron microscopy of metals, semiconductors, and superconductors.

Emmanuelle Marquis, Assistant Professor of Materials Science and Engineering; Ph.D. Northwestern, 2002. Microstructure evolution, atomic scale characterization.

Jyotirmoy Mazumder, Professor of Materials Science and Engineering and Mechanical Engineering; Ph.D., Imperial College (London), 1978. Laser-aided manufacturing, atom to application for nonequilibrium synthesis, mathematical modeling, spectroscopic and optical diagnostics of laser materials interaction.

Joanna Mirecki Millunchick, Professor of Materials Science and Engineering; Ph.D., Northwestern, 1995. Growth and characterization of thin films, directed self-assembly, and nanomanufacturing.

Xiaoqing Pan, Professor of Materials Science and Engineering and Director of EMAL; Ph.D., Saarlandes (Germany), 1991. High-resolution electron microscopy, structural-property relationships of materials interfaces, thin-film growth and characterization.

Pierre Ferdinand P. Poudeu, Assistant Professor of Materials Science and Engineering; Ph.D., Dresden University of Technology, 2004. Design, synthesis, and evaluation of solid-state inorganic materials with the goal to (1) discover new materials with significantly useful technological applications combining multiple interesting physical properties and (2) to understand and control the interplay between coexisting functionalities.

Pramod Reddy, Assistant Professor of Materials Science and Engineering and Mechanical Engineering; Ph.D., Berkeley, 2007. Nanoscale charge and energy transport, thermoelectric devices, microscale heat transfer, organic photovoltaics, scanning probe microscopy and optics.

Richard E. Robertson, Professor of Materials Science and Engineering and Macromolecular Science and Engineering; Ph.D., Caltech, 1960. Polymer structure, molecular dynamics and fracture, fiber composite properties, composite design and manufacturing.

Anne Marie Sastry, Professor of Materials Science and Engineering and Mechanical Engineering; Ph.D., Cornell, 1994. Battery design, biomaterials, disordered microstructures, nanomanufacturing.

Max Shtein, Associate Professor of Materials Science and Engineering; Ph.D., Princeton, 2004. Optoelectronic materials and devices; thin-film processing; energy.

John Smith, Research Professor; Ph.D., Ohio State. Computer simulation and theory of solid surfaces, adhesion, electronic properties, magnetic properties, chemisorption and machining.

Kai Sun, Associate Research Scientist; Ph.D., Dalian (China), 1998. Characterization of materials by analytical electron microscopy, scanning electron microscopy, atomic force microscopy, X-ray photoelectron spectroscopy techniques.

Katsuyo Thornton, Associate Professor of Materials Science and Engineering; Ph.D., Chicago, 1997. Computational materials science, nano- and microstructures, materials for energy.

Michael D. Thouless, Professor of Materials Science and Engineering and Mechanical Engineering and Applied Mechanics; Ph.D., Berkeley, 1984. Mechanics of materials and interfaces; physics of adhesion and fracture.

Anish Tuteja, Assistant Professor of Materials Science and Engineering; Ph.D., Michigan State, 2006. Surface and interfacial science; functional polymer nanocomposites.

Anton Van der Ven, Associate Professor of Materials Science and Engineering; Ph.D., MIT, 2000. Electronic structure methods (density functional theory), with techniques from statistical mechanics to calculate thermodynamic and kinetic properties of new materials.

Lumin Wang, Professor of Materials Science and Engineering and Nuclear Engineering and Radiological Sciences, and Director of Electron Microbeam Analysis Laboratory, Ph.D., Wisconsin–Madison, 1988. Radiation effects, Ion-beam processing of nanostructured materials, transmission electron microscopy.

Gary S. Was, Professor of Materials Science and Engineering, and Nuclear Engineering and Radiological Sciences; Sc.D., MIT, 1980. Ion-solid interactions, radiation effects, stress corrosion cracking, hydrogen embrittlement.

Steven M. Yalisove, Professor; Ph.D., Pennsylvania, 1986. Ultrafast laser/material interaction; atomic scale assembly and characterization.

Students working in the Van Vlack undergraduate lab.

The Lurie Carillon Tower on North Campus.

Section 17
Mechanical Engineering and Mechanics

This section contains a directory of institutions offering graduate work in mechanical engineering and mechanics. Additional information about programs listed in the directory but not augmented by an in-depth entry may be obtained by writing directly to the dean of a graduate school or chair of a department at the address given in the directory.

For programs offering related work, see also in this book *Engineering and Applied Sciences, Management of Engineering and Technology,* and *Materials Sciences and Engineering.* In another guide in this series:

Graduate Programs in the Physical Sciences, Mathematics, Agricultural Sciences, the Environment & Natural Resources
See *Geosciences* and *Physics*

CONTENTS

Program Directories

Mechanical Engineering

Alfred University, Graduate School, New York State College of Ceramics, School of Engineering, Alfred, NY 14802-1205. Offers biomedical materials engineering science (MS); ceramic engineering (MS); ceramics (PhD); electrical engineering (MS); glass science (MS, PhD); materials science and engineering (MS, PhD); mechanical engineering (MS). *Degree requirements:* For master's, thesis; for doctorate, thesis/dissertation. *Entrance requirements:* Additional exam requirements/recommendations for international students: Required—TOEFL (minimum score 590 paper-based; 243 computer-based). Electronic applications accepted. *Expenses:* Contact institution. *Faculty research:* Fine-particle technology, x-ray diffraction, superconductivity, electronic materials.

The American University in Cairo, School of Sciences and Engineering, Department of Mechanical Engineering, Cairo, Egypt. Offers mechanical engineering (MS); product development and systems management (M Eng). *Expenses: Tuition:* Part-time $932 per credit hour. Tuition and fees vary according to course load, degree level and program. *Unit head:* Dr. Salah El-Haggar, Chair, 20-2-2615-3065, E-mail: elhaggar@aucegypt.edu. *Application contact:* Wesley Clark, Director of North American Admissions and Financial Aid, 212-646-810-9433 Ext. 4547, E-mail: wclark@aucnyo.edu. Web site: http://www.aucegypt.edu/sse/meng/.

American University of Beirut, Graduate Programs, Faculty of Engineering and Architecture, Beirut, Lebanon. Offers applied energy (MME); civil engineering (ME, PhD); electrical and computer engineering (ME, PhD); engineering management (MEM); environmental and water resources (ME); environmental and water resources engineering (PhD); environmental technology (MSES); mechanical engineering (ME, PhD); urban design (MUD); urban planning and policy (MUP). Part-time programs available. *Faculty:* 53 full-time (8 women), 10 part-time/adjunct (2 women). *Students:* 290 full-time (101 women), 59 part-time (18 women). Average age 25. 336 applicants, 80% accepted, 83 enrolled. In 2011, 72 master's, 5 doctorates awarded. *Degree requirements:* For master's, one foreign language, comprehensive exam, thesis (for some programs); for doctorate, one foreign language, comprehensive exam, thesis/dissertation, publications. *Entrance requirements:* For master's, GRE (for electrical and computer engineering), letters of recommendation; for doctorate, GRE, letters of recommendation, master's degree, transcripts, curriculum vitae, interview. Additional exam requirements/recommendations for international students: Required—TOEFL (minimum score 600 paper-based; 250 computer-based; 100 iBT), IELTS (minimum score 7.5). *Application deadline:* For fall admission, 2/5 priority date for domestic students, 2/5 for international students; for spring admission, 11/1 priority date for domestic students, 11/1 for international students. Applications are processed on a rolling basis. Application fee: $50. Electronic applications accepted. *Expenses: Tuition:* Full-time $12,780; part-time $710 per credit. *Required fees:* $528; $528 per credit. Tuition and fees vary according to course load and program. *Financial support:* In 2011–12, 9 fellowships with full tuition reimbursements (averaging $24,800 per year), 33 research assistantships with full tuition reimbursements (averaging $24,800 per year), 74 teaching assistantships with full tuition reimbursements (averaging $9,800 per year) were awarded; career-related internships or fieldwork, institutionally sponsored loans, scholarships/grants, health care benefits, and unspecified assistantships also available. *Total annual research expenditures:* $1.1 million. *Unit head:* Prof. Makram T. Suidan, Dean, 961-135-0000 Ext. 3400, Fax: 961-174-4462, E-mail: msuidan@aub.edu.lb. *Application contact:* Dr. Salim Kanaan, Director, Admissions Office, 961-135-0000 Ext. 2594, Fax: 961-175-0775, E-mail: sk00@aub.edu.lb. Web site: http://staff.aub.edu.lb/~webfea.

American University of Sharjah, Graduate Programs, Sharjah, United Arab Emirates. Offers business (EMBA, GEMPA, MBA); chemical engineering (MS Ch E); civil engineering (MSCE); computer engineering (MS); electrical engineering (MSEE); mechanical engineering (MSME); mechatronics engineering (MS); public administration (MPA); teaching English to speakers of other languages (MA); translation and interpreting (MA); urban planning (MUP). Part-time and evening/weekend programs available. *Entrance requirements:* For master's, GMAT (MBA). Additional exam requirements/recommendations for international students: Required—TOEFL (minimum score 550 paper-based; 213 computer-based; 80 iBT), TWE (minimum score 5). Electronic applications accepted. *Faculty research:* Chemical engineering, civil engineering, computer engineering, electrical engineering, linguistics, translation.

Arizona State University, College of Technology and Innovation, Department of Engineering Technology, Mesa, AZ 85212. Offers technology (alternative energy technologies) (MS); technology (electronic systems engineering technology) (MS); technology (integrated electronic systems) (MS); technology (manufacturing engineering technology) (MS). Part-time and evening/weekend programs available. *Degree requirements:* For master's, thesis or applied project and oral defense, final examination, interactive Program of Study (iPOS) submitted before completing 50 percent of required credit hours. *Entrance requirements:* For master's, bachelor's degree with minimum of 30 credit hours or equivalent in a technology area including course work applicable to the concentration being sought and minimum of 16 credit hours of math and science; industrial experience beyond bachelor's degree (recommended). Additional exam requirements/recommendations for international students: Required—TOEFL (minimum score 83 iBT), TOEFL, IELTS, or Pearson Test of English. Electronic applications accepted. *Faculty research:* Manufacturing modeling and simulation &ITsmart&RO and composite materials, optimization of turbine engines, machinability and manufacturing processes design, fuel cells and other alternative energy sources.

Arizona State University, Ira A. Fulton School of Engineering, Department of Mechanical and Aerospace Engineering, Tempe, AZ 85281. Offers aerospace engineering (MS, MSE, PhD); chemical engineering (MS, MSE, PhD); materials science and engineering (MS, PhD); mechanical engineering (MS, MSE, PhD). Part-time and evening/weekend programs available. Postbaccalaureate distance learning degree programs offered (minimal on-campus study). Terminal master's awarded for partial completion of doctoral program. *Degree requirements:* For master's, thesis and oral defense (MS); applied project or comprehensive exam (MSE); interactive Program of Study (iPOS) submitted before completing 50 percent of required credit hours; for doctorate, comprehensive exam, thesis/dissertation, interactive Program of Study (iPOS) submitted before completing 50 percent of required credit hours. *Entrance requirements:* For master's, GRE, minimum GPA of 3.0 or equivalent in last 2 years of work leading to bachelor's degree; for doctorate, GRE, minimum GPA of 3.0 in last 2 years of work leading to bachelor's degree. Additional exam requirements/recommendations for international students: Required—TOEFL (minimum score 80 iBT), TOEFL, IELTS, or Pearson Test of English. Electronic applications accepted. *Expenses:* Contact institution. *Faculty research:* Electronic materials and packaging, materials for energy (batteries), adaptive/intelligent materials and structures, multiscale fluid mechanics, membranes, therapeutics and bioseparations, flexible structures, nanostructured materials, and micro/nano transport.

Auburn University, Graduate School, Ginn College of Engineering, Department of Mechanical Engineering, Auburn University, AL 36849. Offers materials engineering (M Mtl E, MS, PhD); mechanical engineering (MME, MS, PhD). Part-time programs available. *Faculty:* 29 full-time (0 women), 2 part-time/adjunct (0 women). *Students:* 40 full-time (5 women), 64 part-time (4 women); includes 6 minority (2 Black or African American, non-Hispanic/Latino; 3 Asian, non-Hispanic/Latino; 1 Hispanic/Latino), 56 international. Average age 28. 151 applicants, 73% accepted, 21 enrolled. In 2011, 29 master's, 8 doctorates awarded. *Degree requirements:* For master's, thesis (for some programs); for doctorate, one foreign language, thesis/dissertation. *Entrance requirements:* For master's and doctorate, GRE General Test. *Application deadline:* For fall admission, 7/7 for domestic students; for spring admission, 11/24 for domestic students. Applications are processed on a rolling basis. Application fee: $50 ($60 for international students). *Expenses:* Tuition, state resident: full-time $7290; part-time $405 per credit hour. Tuition, nonresident: full-time $21,870; part-time $1215 per credit hour. *International tuition:* $22,000 full-time. *Required fees:* $1402. *Financial support:* Fellowships, research assistantships, teaching assistantships, and Federal Work-Study available. Support available to part-time students. Financial award application deadline: 3/15; financial award applicants required to submit FAFSA. *Faculty research:* Engineering mechanics, experimental mechanics, engineering design, engineering acoustics, engineering optics. *Unit head:* Dr. Jeff Suhling, Chair, 334-844-3332. *Application contact:* Dr. George Flowers, Dean of the Graduate School, 334-844-2125. Web site: http://www.eng.auburn.edu/department/me/.

Baylor University, Graduate School, School of Engineering and Computer Science, Department of Engineering, Waco, TX 76798. Offers biomedical engineering (MSBE); electrical and computer engineering (MSECE, PhD); engineering (ME); mechanical engineering (MSME). *Faculty:* 14 full-time (1 woman). *Students:* 25 full-time (2 women), 7 part-time (1 woman); includes 6 minority (2 Black or African American, non-Hispanic/Latino; 1 Asian, non-Hispanic/Latino; 1 Hispanic/Latino; 2 Two or more races, non-Hispanic/Latino), 6 international. In 2011, 19 master's awarded. *Unit head:* Dr. Mike Thompson, Graduate Director, 254-710-4188. *Application contact:* Linda Keer, Administrative Assistant, 254-710-4188, Fax: 254-710-3870, E-mail: linda_kerr@baylor.edu. Web site: http://www.ecs.baylor.edu/engineering.

Boise State University, Graduate College, College of Engineering, Department of Mechanical and Biomedical Engineering, Boise, ID 83725-0399. Offers mechanical engineering (M Engr, MS). Part-time and evening/weekend programs available. *Degree requirements:* For master's, thesis. *Entrance requirements:* For master's, GRE General Test, minimum GPA of 3.0. Additional exam requirements/recommendations for international students: Required—TOEFL. Electronic applications accepted.

Boston University, College of Engineering, Department of Mechanical Engineering, Boston, MA 02215. Offers global manufacturing (MS); manufacturing engineering (M Eng, MS); mechanical engineering (M Eng, MS, PhD); MS/MBA. Part-time programs available. Postbaccalaureate distance learning degree programs offered (no on-campus study). *Faculty:* 38 full-time (5 women), 1 part-time/adjunct (0 women). *Students:* 109 full-time (13 women), 19 part-time (8 women); includes 15 minority (2 Black or African American, non-Hispanic/Latino; 6 Asian, non-Hispanic/Latino; 3 Hispanic/Latino; 4 Two or more races, non-Hispanic/Latino), 58 international. Average age 26. 298 applicants, 21% accepted, 30 enrolled. In 2011, 45 master's, 13 doctorates awarded. Terminal master's awarded for partial completion of doctoral program. *Degree requirements:* For master's, thesis (for some programs); for doctorate, comprehensive exam, thesis/dissertation. *Entrance requirements:* For master's and doctorate, GRE General Test. Additional exam requirements/recommendations for international students: Required—TOEFL (minimum score 550 paper-based; 213 computer-based; 84 iBT), IELTS (minimum score 6.5). *Application deadline:* For fall admission, 3/15 for domestic and international students; for spring admission, 10/1 for domestic and international students. Application fee: $70. Electronic applications accepted. *Expenses: Tuition:* Full-time $40,848; part-time $1276 per credit hour. *Required fees:* $572; $286 per semester. *Financial support:* In 2011–12, 81 students received support, including 13 fellowships with full tuition reimbursements available (averaging $28,950 per year), 41 research assistantships with full tuition reimbursements available (averaging $19,300 per year), 19 teaching assistantships with full tuition reimbursements available (averaging $19,300 per year); career-related internships or fieldwork, Federal Work-Study, institutionally sponsored loans, scholarships/grants, health care benefits, and tuition waivers (full and partial) also available. Financial award application deadline: 1/15; financial award applicants required to submit FAFSA. *Faculty research:* Acoustics, ultrasound, and vibrations; biomechanics; dynamics, control, and robotics; energy and thermofluid sciences; MEMS and nanotechnology. *Total annual research expenditures:* $11 million. *Unit head:* Dr. Ronald A. Roy, Chairman, 617-353-2814, Fax: 617-353-5866, E-mail: ronroy@bu.edu. *Application contact:* Stephen Doherty, Director of Graduate Programs, 617-353-9760, Fax: 617-353-0259, E-mail: enggrad@bu.edu. Web site: http://www.bu.edu/me/.

Bradley University, Graduate School, College of Engineering and Technology, Department of Mechanical Engineering, Peoria, IL 61625-0002. Offers MSME. Part-time and evening/weekend programs available. *Degree requirements:* For master's, comprehensive exam, thesis optional. *Entrance requirements:* For master's, minimum GPA of 3.0. Additional exam requirements/recommendations for international students: Required—TOEFL (minimum score 550 paper-based; 213 computer-based; 79 iBT). *Faculty research:* Ground-coupled heat pumps, robotic end-effectors, power plant optimization.

Brigham Young University, Graduate Studies, Ira A. Fulton College of Engineering and Technology, Department of Mechanical Engineering, Provo, UT 84602. Offers MS, PhD. *Faculty:* 27 full-time (1 woman), 1 part-time/adjunct (0 women). *Students:* 117 full-time (3 women), 6 part-time (2 women); includes 4 minority (1 American Indian or Alaska Native, non-Hispanic/Latino; 1 Asian, non-Hispanic/Latino; 2 Hispanic/Latino), 3 international. Average age 26. 69 applicants, 80% accepted, 34 enrolled. In 2011, 41 master's, 7 doctorates awarded. Terminal master's awarded for partial completion of doctoral program. *Degree requirements:* For master's, thesis; for doctorate, comprehensive exam, thesis/dissertation. *Entrance requirements:* For master's and doctorate, GRE General Test, minimum GPA of 3.0 in last 60 hours of upper-division course work. Additional exam requirements/recommendations for international students: Required—TOEFL (minimum score 580 paper-based; 85 iBTwith minimum 22 speaking; 21 listening, reading, writing), IELTS (minimum score 7). *Application deadline:* For fall admission, 1/15 for domestic and international students; for winter admission, 9/15 for domestic and international students; for spring admission, 1/15 for domestic and international students. Application fee: $50. Electronic applications accepted. Full-time tuition for non-LDS students: $11,520 per year; $640 per credit. *Expenses: Tuition:* Full-time $5760; part-time $320 per credit. Tuition and fees vary according to student's religious affiliation. *Financial support:* In 2011–12, 6 students received support, including 15 fellowships with full tuition reimbursements available (averaging $4,800 per year), 18 research assistantships with full tuition reimbursements available (averaging $5,526 per year), 12 teaching assistantships with full and partial tuition reimbursements available (averaging $2,613 per year); scholarships/grants and unspecified assistantships also available. Financial award application deadline: 3/1; financial award applicants required to submit FAFSA. *Faculty research:* Combustion, composite materials, advanced design methods and optimization, electronics heat transfer, acoustic noise controls and robotics. *Total annual research expenditures:* $3.5 million. *Unit head:* Dr. Timothy W. McLain, Chair, 801-422-2625, Fax: 801-422-0516, E-mail: tmclaine@et.byu.edu. *Application contact:* Miriam Busch, Graduate Advisor, 801-422-2624, Fax: 801-422-0516, E-mail: mbusch@byu.edu. Web site: http://me.byu.edu/.

Brown University, Graduate School, Division of Engineering, Program in Mechanics of Solids, Providence, RI 02912. Offers Sc M, PhD. *Degree requirements:* For doctorate, thesis/dissertation, preliminary exam.

Bucknell University, Graduate Studies, College of Engineering, Department of Mechanical Engineering, Lewisburg, PA 17837. Offers MSME. Part-time programs available. *Faculty:* 12 full-time (3 women). *Students:* 3 full-time (0 women), 1 part-time (0 women). 3 applicants, 67% accepted, 1 enrolled. In 2011, 5 master's awarded. *Degree requirements:* For master's, thesis. *Entrance requirements:* For master's, GRE General Test, minimum GPA of 3.0. Additional exam requirements/recommendations for international students: Required—TOEFL (minimum score 600 paper-based). *Application deadline:* For fall admission, 2/1 priority date for domestic students, 1/1 for international students. Application fee: $25. *Financial support:* In 2011–12, 3 students received support, including 3 research assistantships with full tuition reimbursements available (averaging $28,000 per year); unspecified assistantships also available. Financial award application deadline: 2/1. *Faculty research:* Heat pump performance, microprocessors in heat engine testing, computer-aided design. *Unit head:* Dr. M. Laura Bewninati, Chair, 570-577-3193. *Application contact:* Gretchen H. Fegley, Coordinator, 570-577-3655, Fax: 570-577-3760, E-mail: gfegley@bucknell.edu. Web site: http://www.bucknell.edu/mechanicalengineering.

California Institute of Technology, Division of Engineering and Applied Science, Option in Mechanical Engineering, Pasadena, CA 91125-0001. Offers MS, PhD, Engr. *Degree requirements:* For doctorate, thesis/dissertation. *Faculty research:* Design, mechanics, thermal and fluids engineering, jet propulsion.

California Polytechnic State University, San Luis Obispo, College of Engineering, Department of Mechanical Engineering, San Luis Obispo, CA 93407. Offers MS. Part-time programs available. *Faculty:* 2 full-time (0 women). *Students:* 33 full-time (3 women), 9 part-time (0 women); includes 9 minority (3 Asian, non-Hispanic/Latino; 6 Hispanic/Latino), 3 international. Average age 25. 26 applicants, 69% accepted, 9 enrolled. In 2011, 35 master's awarded. *Degree requirements:* For master's, comprehensive exam (for some programs), thesis (for some programs). *Entrance requirements:* For master's, GRE, minimum GPA of 3.0 in last 90 quarter units of course work, 3 letters of recommendation. Additional exam requirements/recommendations for international students: Required—TOEFL (minimum score 550 paper-based; 213 computer-based) or IELTS (minimum score 6). *Application deadline:* For fall admission, 12/1 for domestic students, 11/30 for international students. Applications are processed on a rolling basis. Application fee: $55. Electronic applications accepted. *Expenses:* Tuition, state resident: full-time $6738. Tuition, nonresident: full-time $17,898. *Required fees:* $2449. *Financial support:* Fellowships, research assistantships, teaching assistantships, career-related internships or fieldwork, Federal Work-Study, and scholarships/grants available. Support available to part-time students. Financial award application deadline: 3/2; financial award applicants required to submit FAFSA. *Faculty research:* Mechatronics, robotics, thermosciences, mechanics and stress analysis, composite materials. *Unit head:* Dr. Saeed Niku, Graduate Coordinator, 805-756-1376, Fax: 805-756-1137, E-mail: sniku@calpoly.edu. *Application contact:* Dr. James Maraviglia, Associate Vice Provost for Marketing and Enrollment Development, 805-756-2311, Fax: 805-756-5400, E-mail: admissions@calpoly.edu. Web site: http://me.calpoly.edu.

California State Polytechnic University, Pomona, Academic Affairs, College of Engineering, Program in Mechanical Engineering, Pomona, CA 91768-2557. Offers MS. *Students:* 3 full-time (0 women), 43 part-time (7 women); includes 24 minority (13 Asian, non-Hispanic/Latino; 8 Hispanic/Latino; 3 Two or more races, non-Hispanic/Latino), 4 international. Average age 32. 62 applicants, 37% accepted, 10 enrolled. In 2011, 10 master's awarded. *Application deadline:* Applications are processed on a rolling basis. Application fee: $55. Electronic applications accepted. *Expenses:* Tuition, state resident: full-time $6738. Tuition, nonresident: full-time $12,300. *Required fees:* $657. Tuition and fees vary according to course load and program. *Unit head:* Dr. Parham Piroozan, Graduate Coordinator, 909-869-2597, E-mail: ppiroozan@csupomona.edu. *Application contact:* Deborah L. Brandon, Executive Director, Admissions and Outreach, 909-869-3427, Fax: 909-869-5315, E-mail: dlbrandon@csupomona.edu. Web site: http://www.csupomona.edu/~me.

California State University, Fresno, Division of Graduate Studies, College of Engineering and Computer Science, Program in Mechanical Engineering, Fresno, CA 93740-8027. Offers MS. Offered at Edwards Air Force Base. Part-time programs available. *Degree requirements:* For master's, thesis or alternative. *Entrance requirements:* For master's, GRE General Test, minimum GPA of 2.7. Additional exam requirements/recommendations for international students: Required—TOEFL. Electronic applications accepted. *Faculty research:* Flowmeter calibration, digital camera calibration.

California State University, Fullerton, Graduate Studies, College of Engineering and Computer Science, Department of Mechanical Engineering, Fullerton, CA 92834-9480. Offers MS. Part-time programs available. *Students:* 17 full-time (2 women), 37 part-time (4 women); includes 23 minority (1 Black or African American, non-Hispanic/Latino; 14 Asian, non-Hispanic/Latino; 6 Hispanic/Latino; 2 Two or more races, non-Hispanic/Latino), 19 international. Average age 27. 111 applicants, 50% accepted, 18 enrolled. In 2011, 21 master's awarded. *Degree requirements:* For master's, comprehensive exam, project or thesis. *Entrance requirements:* For master's, minimum undergraduate GPA of 2.5. Application fee: $55. *Financial support:* Career-related internships or fieldwork, Federal Work-Study, institutionally sponsored loans, and scholarships/grants available. Support available to part-time students. Financial award application deadline: 3/1; financial award applicants required to submit FAFSA. *Unit head:* Dr. Hossein Moini, Chair, 657-278-4304. *Application contact:* Admissions/Applications, 657-278-2371.

California State University, Long Beach, Graduate Studies, College of Engineering, Department of Mechanical and Aerospace Engineering, Long Beach, CA 90840. Offers aerospace engineering (MSAE); engineering and industrial applied mathematics (PhD); interdisciplinary engineering (MSE); management engineering (MSE); mechanical engineering (MSME). Part-time programs available. *Faculty:* 11 full-time (3 women), 6 part-time/adjunct (0 women). *Students:* 35 full-time (3 women), 54 part-time (4 women); includes 45 minority (1 Black or African American, non-Hispanic/Latino; 2 American Indian or Alaska Native, non-Hispanic/Latino; 17 Asian, non-Hispanic/Latino; 22 Hispanic/Latino; 3 Two or more races, non-Hispanic/Latino), 9 international. Average age 28. 142 applicants, 51% accepted, 26 enrolled. In 2011, 38 master's awarded. *Entrance requirements:* Additional exam requirements/recommendations for international students: Required—TOEFL. *Application deadline:* For fall admission, 7/1 for domestic students. Application fee: $55. Electronic applications accepted. *Financial support:* Career-related internships or fieldwork, Federal Work-Study, institutionally sponsored loans, scholarships/grants, and unspecified assistantships available. Financial award application deadline: 3/2. *Faculty research:* Unsteady turbulent flows, solar energy, energy conversion, CAD/CAM, computer-assisted instruction. *Unit head:* Dr. Hamid Hefazi, Chair, 562-985-1502, Fax: 562-985-1564, E-mail: hefazi@csulb.edu. *Application contact:* Dr. Hamid Rahai, Graduate Advisor, 562-985-5132, Fax: 562-985-4408, E-mail: rahai@csulb.edu.

California State University, Los Angeles, Graduate Studies, College of Engineering, Computer Science, and Technology, Department of Mechanical Engineering, Los Angeles, CA 90032-8530. Offers MS. Part-time and evening/weekend programs available. *Faculty:* 4 full-time (0 women), 1 part-time/adjunct (0 women). *Students:* 15 full-time (3 women), 37 part-time (4 women); includes 26 minority (2 Black or African American, non-Hispanic/Latino; 9 Asian, non-Hispanic/Latino; 14 Hispanic/Latino; 1 Two or more races, non-Hispanic/Latino), 16 international. Average age 28. 65 applicants, 52% accepted, 14 enrolled. In 2011, 38 master's awarded. *Degree requirements:* For master's, comprehensive exam or thesis. *Entrance requirements:* For master's, minimum GPA of 2.75. Additional exam requirements/recommendations for international students: Required—TOEFL (minimum score 550 paper-based). *Application deadline:* For fall admission, 5/1 for domestic and international students. Applications are processed on a rolling basis. Application fee: $55. Electronic applications accepted. *Expenses:* Tuition, state resident: full-time $8225. *Financial support:* Federal Work-Study available. Support available to part-time students. Financial award application deadline: 3/1. *Faculty research:* Mechanical design, thermal systems, solar-powered vehicle. *Unit head:* Dr. Darrell Guillaume, Chair, 323-343-4490, Fax: 323-343-5004, E-mail: dguilla@calstatela.edu. *Application contact:* Dr. Karin Brown, Acting Associate Dean of Graduate Studies, 323-343-3820, Fax: 323-343-5653, E-mail: kbrown5@calstatela.edu. Web site: http://www.calstatela.edu/academic/ecst/me/.

California State University, Northridge, Graduate Studies, College of Engineering and Computer Science, Department of Mechanical Engineering, Northridge, CA 91330. Offers MS. Part-time and evening/weekend programs available. *Degree requirements:* For master's, thesis or project. *Entrance requirements:* Additional exam requirements/recommendations for international students: Required—TOEFL.

California State University, Sacramento, Office of Graduate Studies, College of Engineering and Computer Science, Department of Mechanical Engineering, Sacramento, CA 95819-6031. Offers MS. Evening/weekend programs available. *Faculty:* 11 full-time (3 women), 10 part-time/adjunct (2 women). *Students:* 30 full-time, 28 part-time; includes 19 minority (3 Black or African American, non-Hispanic/Latino; 4 Asian, non-Hispanic/Latino; 8 Hispanic/Latino; 3 Native Hawaiian or other Pacific Islander, non-Hispanic/Latino; 1 Two or more races, non-Hispanic/Latino), 4 international. Average age 29. 48 applicants, 71% accepted, 23 enrolled. In 2011, 16 master's awarded. *Entrance requirements:* Additional exam requirements/recommendations for international students: Required—TOEFL. *Application deadline:* For fall admission, 3/1 for domestic and international students; for spring admission, 9/15 for domestic students, 9/30 for international students. Applications are processed on a rolling basis. Application fee: $55. Electronic applications accepted. *Financial support:* Research assistantships, teaching assistantships, career-related internships or fieldwork, and Federal Work-Study available. Support available to part-time students. Financial award application deadline: 3/1; financial award applicants required to submit FAFSA. *Unit head:* Robin Bandy, Chair, 916-278-6625, Fax: 916-278-7713, E-mail: bandyr@ecs.csus.edu. *Application contact:* Jose Martinez, Outreach and Graduate Diversity Coordinator, 916-278-6470, Fax: 916-278-5669, E-mail: martinj@skymail.csus.edu. Web site: http://www.ecs.csus.edu/wcm/me.

Carleton University, Faculty of Graduate Studies, Faculty of Engineering and Design, Department of Mechanical and Aerospace Engineering, Ottawa, ON K1S 5B6, Canada. Offers aerospace engineering (M Eng, MA Sc, PhD); materials engineering (M Eng, MA Sc); mechanical engineering (M Eng, MA Sc, PhD). *Degree requirements:* For master's, thesis optional; for doctorate, thesis/dissertation. *Entrance requirements:* For master's, honors degree; for doctorate, MA Sc or M Eng. Additional exam requirements/recommendations for international students: Required—TOEFL. *Faculty research:* Thermal fluids engineering, heat transfer, vehicle engineering.

Carnegie Mellon University, Carnegie Institute of Technology, Department of Mechanical Engineering, Pittsburgh, PA 15213-3891. Offers MS, PhD. Part-time and evening/weekend programs available. Terminal master's awarded for partial completion of doctoral program. *Degree requirements:* For master's, thesis (for some programs); for doctorate, thesis/dissertation (for some programs), qualifying exam. *Entrance requirements:* For master's and doctorate, GRE General Test. Additional exam requirements/recommendations for international students: Required—TOEFL. *Faculty research:* Combustion, design, fluid, and thermal sciences; computational fluid dynamics; energy and environment; solid mechanics; systems and controls; materials and manufacturing.

Case Western Reserve University, School of Graduate Studies, Case School of Engineering, Department of Mechanical and Aerospace Engineering, Cleveland, OH 44106. Offers MS, PhD, MD/PhD. Part-time programs available. Postbaccalaureate distance learning degree programs offered (no on-campus study). *Faculty:* 13 full-time (3 women). *Students:* 58 full-time (4 women), 16 part-time (4 women); includes 12 minority (4 Black or African American, non-Hispanic/Latino; 6 Asian, non-Hispanic/Latino; 2 Two or more races, non-Hispanic/Latino), 29 international. In 2011, 13 master's, 8 doctorates awarded. *Degree requirements:* For master's, thesis (for some programs); for doctorate, thesis/dissertation, qualifying exam, teaching experience. *Entrance requirements:* For master's and doctorate, GRE General Test. Additional exam requirements/recommendations for international students: Required—TOEFL. *Application deadline:* For fall admission, 7/1 priority date for domestic students. Applications are processed on a rolling basis. Application fee: $50. *Financial support:* Fellowships with full and partial tuition reimbursements, research assistantships with full and partial tuition reimbursements, teaching assistantships, institutionally sponsored loans, and tuition waivers (full and partial) available. Financial award application deadline: 3/1; financial award applicants required to submit FAFSA. *Faculty research:* Musculoskeletal biomechanics, combustion diagnostics and computation, mechanical behavior of advanced materials and nanostructures, biorobotics. *Total annual research expenditures:* $6.2 million. *Unit head:* Dr. Iwan Alexander, Department Chair, 216-368-6045, Fax: 216-368-6445, E-mail: ida2@case.edu. *Application contact:* Carla Wilson, Student Affairs Coordinator, 216-368-4580, Fax: 216-368-3007, E-mail: cxw75@case.edu. Web site: http://www.engineering.case.edu/emae.

Mechanical Engineering

The Catholic University of America, School of Engineering, Department of Mechanical Engineering, Washington, DC 20064. Offers MME, MSE, PhD. Part-time programs available. *Faculty:* 7 full-time (0 women), 5 part-time/adjunct (0 women). *Students:* 5 full-time (0 women), 18 part-time (3 women); includes 3 minority (2 Black or African American, non-Hispanic/Latino; 1 Asian, non-Hispanic/Latino), 5 international. Average age 29. 28 applicants, 68% accepted, 8 enrolled. In 2011, 8 master's, 1 doctorate awarded. *Degree requirements:* For master's, thesis (for some programs); for doctorate, comprehensive exam, thesis/dissertation, oral exams. *Entrance requirements:* For master's and doctorate, statement of purpose, official copies of academic transcripts, three letters of recommendation. Additional exam requirements/recommendations for international students: Required—TOEFL (minimum score 580 paper-based; 237 computer-based). *Application deadline:* For fall admission, 8/1 priority date for domestic students, 7/15 for international students; for spring admission, 12/1 priority date for domestic students, 10/15 for international students. Applications are processed on a rolling basis. Application fee: $55. Electronic applications accepted. *Expenses:* Contact institution. *Financial support:* Fellowships, research assistantships, teaching assistantships, Federal Work-Study, scholarships/grants, tuition waivers (full and partial), and unspecified assistantships available. Financial award application deadline: 2/1; financial award applicants required to submit FAFSA. *Faculty research:* Fluid mechanics, dynamics, acoustics, computational mechanics, solar winds. *Total annual research expenditures:* $699,310. *Unit head:* Dr. Sen Nieh, Chair, 202-319-5170, Fax: 202-319-5173, E-mail: nieh@cua.edu. *Application contact:* Andrew Woodall, Director of Graduate Admissions, 202-319-5057, Fax: 202-319-6533, E-mail: cua-admissions@cua.edu. Web site: http://mechanical.cua.edu/.

City College of the City University of New York, Graduate School, Grove School of Engineering, Department of Mechanical Engineering, New York, NY 10031-9198. Offers ME, MS, PhD. PhD program offered jointly with Graduate School and University Center of the City University of New York. Part-time programs available. *Degree requirements:* For master's, thesis optional; for doctorate, one foreign language, comprehensive exam, thesis/dissertation. *Entrance requirements:* For master's and doctorate, GRE General Test. Additional exam requirements/recommendations for international students: Required—TOEFL (minimum score 500 paper-based; 173 computer-based). *Faculty research:* Bio-heat and mass transfer, bone mechanics, fracture mechanics, heat transfer in computer parts, mechanisms design.

Clarkson University, Graduate School, Wallace H. Coulter School of Engineering, Department of Mechanical and Aeronautical Engineering, Potsdam, NY 13699. Offers mechanical engineering (ME, MS, PhD). Part-time programs available. *Faculty:* 24 full-time (3 women), 2 part-time/adjunct (1 woman). *Students:* 65 full-time (5 women); includes 6 minority (2 Black or African American, non-Hispanic/Latino; 1 Asian, non-Hispanic/Latino; 3 Hispanic/Latino), 24 international. Average age 26. 93 applicants, 81% accepted, 18 enrolled. In 2011, 13 master's, 4 doctorates awarded. Terminal master's awarded for partial completion of doctoral program. *Degree requirements:* For master's, thesis; for doctorate, comprehensive exam, thesis/dissertation, departmental qualifying exam. *Entrance requirements:* For master's and doctorate, GRE, transcripts of all college coursework, resume, personal statement, three letters of recommendation. Additional exam requirements/recommendations for international students: Required—TOEFL (minimum score 550 paper-based; 213 computer-based; 80 iBT), IELTS (minimum score 6.5). *Application deadline:* For fall admission, 1/30 priority date for domestic students, 1/30 for international students; for spring admission, 9/1 priority date for domestic students, 9/1 for international students. Applications are processed on a rolling basis. Application fee: $25 ($35 for international students). Electronic applications accepted. *Expenses: Tuition:* Full-time $14,376; part-time $1198 per credit hour. *Required fees:* $295 per semester. *Financial support:* In 2011–12, 59 students received support, including 2 fellowships with full tuition reimbursements available (averaging $21,999 per year), 29 research assistantships with full tuition reimbursements available (averaging $21,999 per year), 30 teaching assistantships with full tuition reimbursements available (averaging $21,999 per year); scholarships/grants, tuition waivers (partial), and unspecified assistantships also available. *Faculty research:* Gas turbines, concrete feasibility, aerosol generation, diesel emissions, prosthesis project. *Total annual research expenditures:* $1.9 million. *Unit head:* Dr. Daryush Aidun, Chair, 315-268-6586, Fax: 315-268-6695, E-mail: daidun@clarkson.edu. *Application contact:* Kelly Sharlow, Assistant to the Dean, 315-268-7929, Fax: 315-268-4494, E-mail: ksharlow@clarkson.edu. Web site: http://www.clarkson.edu/mae/.

Clemson University, Graduate School, College of Engineering and Science, Department of Mechanical Engineering, Clemson, SC 29634. Offers MS, PhD. *Faculty:* 30 full-time (1 woman), 2 part-time/adjunct (0 women). *Students:* 139 full-time (18 women), 14 part-time (2 women); includes 5 minority (4 Asian, non-Hispanic/Latino; 1 Two or more races, non-Hispanic/Latino), 106 international. Average age 26. 251 applicants, 66% accepted, 56 enrolled. In 2011, 59 master's, 19 doctorates awarded. *Degree requirements:* For master's, thesis; for doctorate, thesis/dissertation. *Entrance requirements:* For master's and doctorate, GRE General Test. Additional exam requirements/recommendations for international students: Required—TOEFL. *Application deadline:* For fall admission, 6/1 for domestic students. Applications are processed on a rolling basis. Application fee: $70 ($80 for international students). Electronic applications accepted. *Expenses:* Contact institution. *Financial support:* In 2011–12, 107 students received support, including 1 fellowship with partial tuition reimbursement available (averaging $20,000 per year), 57 research assistantships with partial tuition reimbursements available (averaging $14,827 per year), 56 teaching assistantships with partial tuition reimbursements available (averaging $9,354 per year); career-related internships or fieldwork, institutionally sponsored loans, scholarships/grants, health care benefits, and unspecified assistantships also available. Support available to part-time students. Financial award applicants required to submit FAFSA. *Faculty research:* Thermal sciences, fluid mechanics, automated manufacturing and robotics, materials engineering. *Total annual research expenditures:* $2.6 million. *Unit head:* Dr. Donald Beasley, Chair, 864-656-5622, Fax: 864-656-4435, E-mail: debsl@exchange.clemson.edu. *Application contact:* Dr. Richard Miller, Coordinator, 864-656-6248, Fax: 864-656-4435, E-mail: rm@clemson.edu. Web site: http://www.ces.clemson.edu/me/.

Cleveland State University, College of Graduate Studies, Fenn College of Engineering, Department of Civil and Environmental Engineering, Cleveland, OH 44115. Offers accelerated program civil engineering (MS); accelerated program environmental engineering (MS); civil engineering (MS, D Eng); engineering mechanics (MS); environmental engineering (MS). Part-time and evening/weekend programs available. *Faculty:* 8 full-time (2 women). *Students:* 10 full-time (2 women), 38 part-time (7 women); includes 4 minority (1 Black or African American, non-Hispanic/Latino; 1 American Indian or Alaska Native, non-Hispanic/Latino; 2 Asian, non-Hispanic/Latino), 14 international. Average age 29. 81 applicants, 64% accepted, 11 enrolled. In 2011, 25 master's, 1 doctorate awarded. *Degree requirements:* For master's, project or thesis; for doctorate, comprehensive exam, thesis/dissertation, candidacy and qualifying exams. *Entrance requirements:* For master's, GRE General Test, GRE Subject Test, minimum GPA of 2.75; for doctorate, GRE General Test, GRE Subject Test, minimum GPA of 3.25. Additional exam requirements/recommendations for international students: Required—TOEFL (minimum score 525 paper-based; 197 computer-based). *Application deadline:* For fall admission, 7/15 priority date for domestic students. Applications are processed on a rolling basis. Application fee: $30. *Expenses:* Tuition, state resident: full-time $6416; part-time $494 per credit hour. Tuition, nonresident: full-time $12,074; part-time $929 per credit hour. *Financial support:* In 2011–12, 9 research assistantships with full and partial tuition reimbursements (averaging $3,920 per year) were awarded; teaching assistantships with tuition reimbursements, career-related internships or fieldwork, scholarships/grants, and unspecified assistantships also available. Financial award application deadline: 9/1. *Faculty research:* Solid-waste disposal, constitutive modeling, transportation, safety engineering. *Total annual research expenditures:* $800,000. *Unit head:* Dr. Stephen F. Duffy, Chairperson, 216-687-3874, Fax: 216-687-9280, E-mail: p.bosela@csuohio.edu. *Application contact:* Deborah L. Brown, Interim Assistant Director, Graduate Admissions, 216-523-7572, Fax: 216-687-9214, E-mail: d.l.brown@csuohio.edu. Web site: http://www.csuohio.edu/engineering/civil.

Cleveland State University, College of Graduate Studies, Fenn College of Engineering, Department of Mechanical Engineering, Cleveland, OH 44115. Offers MS, D Eng. Part-time programs available. *Faculty:* 8 full-time (0 women). *Students:* 5 full-time (0 women), 52 part-time (14 women); includes 2 minority (1 Black or African American, non-Hispanic/Latino; 1 Hispanic/Latino), 28 international. Average age 28. 91 applicants, 54% accepted, 12 enrolled. In 2011, 19 master's awarded. *Degree requirements:* For master's, project or thesis; for doctorate, thesis/dissertation, candidacy and qualifying exams. *Entrance requirements:* For master's, GRE General Test, minimum GPA of 3.0; for doctorate, GRE General Test, minimum GPA of 3.25. Additional exam requirements/recommendations for international students: Required—TOEFL (minimum score 525 paper-based; 197 computer-based). *Application deadline:* For fall admission, 7/15 priority date for domestic students; for spring admission, 12/15 priority date for domestic students. Applications are processed on a rolling basis. Application fee: $30. *Expenses:* Tuition, state resident: full-time $6416; part-time $494 per credit hour. Tuition, nonresident: full-time $12,074; part-time $929 per credit hour. *Financial support:* In 2011–12, 22 students received support, including 9 research assistantships with full and partial tuition reimbursements available (averaging $3,480 per year); teaching assistantships with partial tuition reimbursements available, career-related internships or fieldwork, Federal Work-Study, institutionally sponsored loans, and unspecified assistantships also available. Support available to part-time students. *Faculty research:* Fluid piezoelectric sensors, laser-optical inspection simulation of forging and forming processes, multiphase flow and heat transfer, turbulent flows. *Unit head:* Dr. William J. Atherton, Interim Chair, 216-687-2595, Fax: 216-687-5375, E-mail: w.atherton@csuohio.edu. *Application contact:* Deborah L. Brown, Interim Assistant Director, Graduate Admissions, 216-523-7572, Fax: 216-687-9214, E-mail: d.l.brown@csuohio.edu. Web site: http://www.csuohio.edu/mce/.

Colorado State University, Graduate School, College of Engineering, Department of Mechanical Engineering, Fort Collins, CO 80523-1374. Offers ME, MS, PhD. Part-time and evening/weekend programs available. Postbaccalaureate distance learning degree programs offered (no on-campus study). *Faculty:* 17 full-time (2 women), 1 part-time/adjunct (0 women). *Students:* 34 full-time (7 women), 71 part-time (5 women); includes 10 minority (3 Asian, non-Hispanic/Latino; 5 Hispanic/Latino; 1 Native Hawaiian or other Pacific Islander, non-Hispanic/Latino; 1 Two or more races, non-Hispanic/Latino), 27 international. Average age 29. 118 applicants, 19% accepted, 14 enrolled. In 2011, 19 master's, 6 doctorates awarded. Terminal master's awarded for partial completion of doctoral program. *Degree requirements:* For master's, comprehensive exam, thesis, oral exam; for doctorate, comprehensive exam, thesis/dissertation, preliminary exams, diagnostic exams, defense as final exam. *Entrance requirements:* For master's, GRE General Test (minimum score 1200 verbal and quantitative, 4.5 analytical), minimum GPA of 3.0, BS/BA from ABET-accredited institution, 3 letters of recommendation, curriculum vitae/resume; for doctorate, GRE General Test (minimum score of 1200 on Verbal and Quantitative sections and 4.5 on the Analytical section), minimum GPA of 3.0, 3 letters of recommendation, curriculum vitae, department application, statement of purpose, resume. Additional exam requirements/recommendations for international students: Required—TOEFL (minimum score 550 paper-based; 213 computer-based; 80 iBT). *Application deadline:* For fall admission, 1/15 priority date for domestic students, 1/15 for international students; for spring admission, 4/1 priority date for domestic students, 4/1 for international students. Application fee: $50. Electronic applications accepted. *Expenses:* Contact institution. *Financial support:* In 2011–12, 57 students received support, including 4 fellowships (averaging $16,052 per year), 37 research assistantships with tuition reimbursements available (averaging $13,784 per year), 16 teaching assistantships with tuition reimbursements available (averaging $11,931 per year); Federal Work-Study and scholarships/grants also available. Financial award application deadline: 1/15; financial award applicants required to submit FAFSA. *Faculty research:* Advanced materials processing and plasma engineering, energy conversion, dynamic and industrial systems, motorsport engineering, bioengineering. *Total annual research expenditures:* $4.8 million. *Unit head:* Dr. Susan P. James, Head, 970-491-6559, Fax: 970-491-3827, E-mail: susan.james@colostate.edu. *Application contact:* Karen Mueller, Graduate Coordinator, 970-491-3872, Fax: 970-491-3827, E-mail: karen.mueller@colostate.edu. Web site: http://www.engr.colostate.edu/me/.

Columbia University, The Fu Foundation School of Engineering and Applied Science, Department of Mechanical Engineering, New York, NY 10027. Offers MS, Eng Sc D, PhD, Engr. PhD offered through the Graduate School of Arts and Sciences. Part-time programs available. Postbaccalaureate distance learning degree programs offered (no on-campus study). *Faculty:* 13 full-time (1 woman), 11 part-time/adjunct (1 woman). *Students:* 131 full-time (21 women), 46 part-time (7 women); includes 21 minority (4 Black or African American, non-Hispanic/Latino; 11 Asian, non-Hispanic/Latino; 1 Hispanic/Latino; 5 Two or more races, non-Hispanic/Latino), 110 international. Average age 27. 419 applicants, 33% accepted, 63 enrolled. In 2011, 66 master's, 7 doctorates awarded. *Degree requirements:* For doctorate, thesis/dissertation, qualifying exam. *Entrance requirements:* For master's, GRE General Test, minimum GPA of 3.3; for doctorate and Engr, GRE General Test. Additional exam requirements/recommendations for international students: Required—TOEFL, IELTS. *Application deadline:* For fall admission, 12/1 priority date for domestic students, 12/1 for international students; for spring admission, 10/1 priority date for domestic students, 10/1 for international students. Application fee: $95. Electronic applications accepted. *Financial support:* In 2011–12, 63 students received support, including 2 fellowships with full tuition reimbursements available (averaging $37,000 per year), 45 research assistantships with full tuition reimbursements available (averaging $31,133 per year), 16 teaching assistantships with full tuition reimbursements available (averaging $31,133 per year). Financial award application deadline: 12/1; financial award applicants required to submit FAFSA. *Faculty research:* Musculoskeletal biomechanics; nanomechanics, nanomaterials and nanofabrication; manufacturing; optical nanostructure; biofludic micro systems. *Unit head:* Dr. Gerard A. Ateshian, Professor and Department Chair, 212-854-8602, Fax: 212-854-3304, E-mail: ateshian@columbia.edu. *Application contact:* Sandra Morris, Administrator, 212-854-6269, Fax: 212-854-3304, E-mail: swm16@columbia.edu. Web site: http://www.me.columbia.edu.

Concordia University, School of Graduate Studies, Faculty of Engineering and Computer Science, Department of Mechanical and Industrial Engineering, Montréal, QC H3G 1M8, Canada. Offers composites (M Eng); industrial engineering (M Eng, MA Sc); mechanical engineering (M Eng, MA Sc, PhD, Certificate); software systems for industrial engineering (Certificate). M Eng in composites program offered jointly with École Polytechnique de Montréal. *Degree requirements:* For master's, variable foreign language requirement, thesis or alternative; for doctorate, comprehensive exam, thesis/dissertation. *Faculty research:* Mechanical systems, fluid control systems, thermofluids engineering and robotics, industrial control systems.

Cooper Union for the Advancement of Science and Art, Albert Nerken School of Engineering, New York, NY 10003-7120. Offers chemical engineering (ME); civil engineering (ME); electrical engineering (ME); mechanical engineering (ME). Part-time programs available. *Faculty:* 27 full-time (1 woman), 15 part-time/adjunct (2 women). *Students:* 39 full-time (10 women), 17 part-time (3 women); includes 18 minority (1 Black or African American, non-Hispanic/Latino; 1 American Indian or Alaska Native, non-Hispanic/Latino; 15 Asian, non-Hispanic/Latino; 1 Hispanic/Latino), 11 international. *Degree requirements:* For master's, thesis. *Entrance requirements:* For master's, GRE, BE, minimum GPA of 3.5. Additional exam requirements/recommendations for international students: Required—TOEFL (minimum score 600 paper-based; 250 computer-based; 100 iBT). *Application deadline:* For fall admission, 2/15 for domestic and international students. Application fee: $65. *Expenses: Tuition:* Full-time $37,500. *Required fees:* $825 per semester. *Financial support:* Fellowships with full tuition reimbursements, career-related internships or fieldwork, Federal Work-Study, tuition waivers (full), and full-tuition scholarships for all admitted students available. Support available to part-time students. Financial award application deadline: 5/1; financial award applicants required to submit CSS PROFILE or FAFSA. *Faculty research:* Civil infrastructure, imaging and sensing technology, biomedical engineering, encryption technology, process engineering. *Unit head:* Dr. Simon Ben-Avi, Acting Dean, 212-353-4286, E-mail: benavi@cooper.edu. *Application contact:* Student Contact, 212-353-4120, E-mail: admissions@cooper.edu. Web site: http://cooper.edu/engineering.

Cornell University, Graduate School, Graduate Fields of Engineering, Field of Mechanical Engineering, Ithaca, NY 14853-0001. Offers biomechanical engineering (M Eng, MS, PhD); combustion (M Eng, MS, PhD); energy and power systems (M Eng, MS, PhD); fluid mechanics (M Eng, MS, PhD); heat transfer (M Eng, MS, PhD); materials and manufacturing engineering (M Eng, MS, PhD); mechanical systems and design (M Eng, MS, PhD); multiphase flows (M Eng, MS, PhD). *Faculty:* 57 full-time (7 women). *Students:* 158 full-time (39 women); includes 32 minority (5 Black or African American, non-Hispanic/Latino; 19 Asian, non-Hispanic/Latino; 8 Hispanic/Latino), 47 international. Average age 24. 581 applicants, 25% accepted, 81 enrolled. In 2011, 60 master's, 3 doctorates awarded. Terminal master's awarded for partial completion of doctoral program. *Degree requirements:* For master's, project (M Eng), thesis (MS); for doctorate, one foreign language, comprehensive exam, thesis/dissertation, 2 semesters of teaching experience. *Entrance requirements:* For master's and doctorate, GRE General Test, 3 letters of recommendation. Additional exam requirements/recommendations for international students: Required—TOEFL (minimum score 550 paper-based; 213 computer-based; 77 iBT). *Application deadline:* For fall admission, 1/15 for domestic students; for spring admission, 11/1 for domestic students. Application fee: $95. Electronic applications accepted. *Financial support:* In 2011–12, 47 students received support, including 27 fellowships with full tuition reimbursements available, 58 research assistantships with full tuition reimbursements available, 19 teaching assistantships with full tuition reimbursements available; institutionally sponsored loans, scholarships/grants, health care benefits, tuition waivers (full and partial), and unspecified assistantships also available. Financial award applicants required to submit FAFSA. *Faculty research:* Combustion and heat transfer, fluid mechanics and CFD, system dynamics and control, biomechanics, manufacturing. *Unit head:* Director of Graduate Studies, 607-255-5250. *Application contact:* Graduate Field Assistant, 607-255-5250, E-mail: maegrad@cornell.edu. Web site: http://www.gradschool.cornell.edu/fields.php?id-33&a-2.

Dalhousie University, Faculty of Engineering, Department of Mechanical Engineering, Halifax, NS B3J 2X4, Canada. Offers M Eng, MA Sc, PhD. *Degree requirements:* For master's, thesis; for doctorate, thesis/dissertation. *Entrance requirements:* Additional exam requirements/recommendations for international students: Required—TOEFL, IELTS, CANTEST, CAEL, or Michigan English Language Assessment Battery. Electronic applications accepted. *Faculty research:* Fluid dynamics and energy, system dynamics, naval architecture, MEMS, space structures.

Dartmouth College, Thayer School of Engineering, Program in Mechanical Engineering, Hanover, NH 03755. Offers MS, PhD. *Degree requirements:* For master's, thesis; for doctorate, thesis/dissertation, candidacy oral exam. *Entrance requirements:* For master's and doctorate, GRE General Test. *Application deadline:* For fall admission, 1/1 priority date for domestic students. Application fee: $45. *Financial support:* Fellowships, research assistantships, teaching assistantships, career-related internships or fieldwork, Federal Work-Study, institutionally sponsored loans, and tuition waivers (full and partial) available. Financial award application deadline: 1/15. *Faculty research:* Tribology, dynamics and control systems, thermal science and energy conversion, fluid mechanics and multi-phase flow, mobile robots. *Total annual research expenditures:* $379,814. *Unit head:* Dr. Joseph J. Helbie, Dean, 603-646-2238, Fax: 603-646-2580, E-mail: joseph.j.helbie@dartmouth.edu. *Application contact:* Candace S. Potter, Graduate Admissions Administrator, 603-646-3844, Fax: 603-646-1620, E-mail: candace.potter@dartmouth.edu. Web site: http://engineering.dartmouth.edu/.

Drexel University, College of Engineering, Department of Mechanical Engineering and Mechanics, Philadelphia, PA 19104-2875. Offers mechanical engineering (MS, PhD). Part-time and evening/weekend programs available. Terminal master's awarded for partial completion of doctoral program. *Degree requirements:* For master's, thesis optional; for doctorate, thesis/dissertation. *Entrance requirements:* For master's, minimum GPA of 3.0, BS in engineering or science; for doctorate, minimum GPA of 3.5, MS in engineering or science. Additional exam requirements/recommendations for international students: Required—TOEFL. Electronic applications accepted. *Faculty research:* Composites, dynamic systems and control, combustion and fuels, biomechanics, mechanics and thermal fluid sciences.

Duke University, Graduate School, Pratt School of Engineering, Department of Mechanical Engineering and Materials Science, Durham, NC 27708. Offers materials science (MS, PhD); mechanical engineering (MS, PhD); JD/MS. Part-time programs available. Terminal master's awarded for partial completion of doctoral program. *Degree requirements:* For master's, thesis optional; for doctorate, thesis/dissertation. *Entrance requirements:* For master's and doctorate, GRE General Test. Additional exam requirements/recommendations for international students: Required—TOEFL (minimum score 550 paper-based; 213 computer-based; 83 iBT), IELTS (minimum score 7). Electronic applications accepted. *Expenses: Tuition:* Full-time $40,720. *Required fees:* $3107.

Duke University, Graduate School, Pratt School of Engineering, Master of Engineering Program, Durham, NC 27708-0271. Offers biomedical engineering (M Eng); civil engineering (M Eng); electrical and computer engineering (M Eng); environmental engineering (M Eng); materials science and engineering (M Eng); mechanical engineering (M Eng); photonics and optical sciences (M Eng). Part-time programs available. *Entrance requirements:* For master's, GRE General Test, resume, 3 letters of recommendation, statement of purpose. Additional exam requirements/recommendations for international students: Required—TOEFL. *Expenses: Tuition:* Full-time $40,720. *Required fees:* $3107.

École Polytechnique de Montréal, Graduate Programs, Department of Mechanical Engineering, Montréal, QC H3C 3A7, Canada. Offers aerothermics (M Eng, M Sc A, PhD); applied mechanics (M Eng, M Sc A, PhD); tool design (M Eng, M Sc A, PhD). Part-time and evening/weekend programs available. *Degree requirements:* For master's, one foreign language, thesis; for doctorate, one foreign language, thesis/dissertation. *Entrance requirements:* For master's, minimum GPA of 2.75; for doctorate, minimum GPA of 3.0. *Faculty research:* Noise control and vibration, fatigue and creep, aerodynamics, composite materials, biomechanics, robotics.

Embry-Riddle Aeronautical University–Daytona, Daytona Beach Campus Graduate Program, Department of Mechanical, Civil and Engineering Sciences, Daytona Beach, FL 32114-3900. Offers MSME. *Faculty:* 8 full-time (1 woman). *Students:* 51 full-time (11 women), 6 part-time (2 women); includes 14 minority (3 Black or African American, non-Hispanic/Latino; 6 Asian, non-Hispanic/Latino; 4 Hispanic/Latino; 1 Two or more races, non-Hispanic/Latino), 15 international. Average age 24. 45 applicants, 89% accepted, 20 enrolled. In 2011, 11 master's awarded. *Degree requirements:* For master's, thesis optional. *Entrance requirements:* Additional exam requirements/recommendations for international students: Required—TOEFL (minimum score 550 paper-based; 213 computer-based; 79 iBT). *Application deadline:* For fall admission, 6/1 priority date for domestic students, 6/1 for international students; for spring admission, 11/1 priority date for domestic students, 10/1 for international students. Applications are processed on a rolling basis. Application fee: $50. Electronic applications accepted. *Expenses: Tuition:* Full-time $14,340; part-time $1195 per credit hour. *Financial support:* In 2011–12, 25 students received support, including 12 research assistantships (averaging $3,491 per year), 2 teaching assistantships (averaging $3,491 per year). Financial award applicants required to submit FAFSA. *Faculty research:* Scramjet Engine simulation, PHLEX marine turbines, fuel slosh research in microgravity, remote airport lighting systems. *Unit head:* Dr. Charles Reinholtz, Department Chair, 386-323-8848, E-mail: charles.reinholtz@erau.edu. *Application contact:* Flavia Carreiro, Assistant Director, International and Graduate Admissions, 800-388-3728, Fax: 386-226-7070, E-mail: graduate.admissions@erau.edu. Web site: http://daytonabeach.erau.edu/coe/degrees/graduate-degrees/mechanical-engineering/index.html.

Fairfield University, School of Engineering, Fairfield, CT 06824-5195. Offers electrical and computer engineering (MS); management of technology (MS); mechanical engineering (MS); software engineering (MS). Part-time and evening/weekend programs available. *Faculty:* 10 full-time (2 women), 11 part-time/adjunct. *Students:* 44 full-time (15 women), 86 part-time (22 women); includes 19 minority (4 Black or African American, non-Hispanic/Latino; 8 Asian, non-Hispanic/Latino; 4 Hispanic/Latino; 1 Native Hawaiian or other Pacific Islander, non-Hispanic/Latino; 2 Two or more races, non-Hispanic/Latino), 21 international. Average age 34. 100 applicants, 76% accepted, 27 enrolled. In 2011, 38 master's awarded. *Degree requirements:* For master's, thesis, capstone course. *Entrance requirements:* For master's, interview, minimum GPA of 2.8, resume, 2 recommendations. Additional exam requirements/recommendations for international students: Required—TOEFL (minimum score 550 paper-based; 213 computer-based; 80 iBT)or IELTS (minimum score 6.5). *Application deadline:* For fall admission, 5/15 for international students; for spring admission, 10/15 for international students. Applications are processed on a rolling basis. Application fee: $60. Electronic applications accepted. *Expenses:* Contact institution. *Financial support:* In 2011–12, 50 students received support. Scholarships/grants and unspecified assistantships available. Financial award applicants required to submit FAFSA. *Faculty research:* Vehicle dynamics, image processing, multimedia in instruction, thermal packaging, character recognition, photovoltaics and nanotechnology, Web technology. *Unit head:* Dr. Jack Beal, Dean, 203-254-4000 Ext. 4147, Fax: 203-254-4013, E-mail: jwbeal@fairfield.edu. *Application contact:* Marianne Gumpper, Director of Graduate and Continuing Studies Admission, 203-254-4184, Fax: 203-254-4073, E-mail: gradadmis@fairfield.edu. Web site: http://www.fairfield.edu/soe/soe_grad_1.html.

Florida Agricultural and Mechanical University, Division of Graduate Studies, Research, and Continuing Education, FAMU-FSU College of Engineering, Department of Mechanical Engineering, Tallahassee, FL 32307-3200. Offers MS, PhD. *Degree requirements:* For master's, thesis optional; for doctorate, comprehensive exam, thesis/dissertation. *Entrance requirements:* For master's, GRE General Test, minimum GPA of 3.0. Additional exam requirements/recommendations for international students: Required—TOEFL (minimum score 550 paper-based; 213 computer-based). *Faculty research:* Fluid mechanical and heat transfer, thermodynamics, dynamics and controls, mechanics and materials.

Florida Atlantic University, College of Engineering and Computer Science, Department of Ocean and Mechanical Engineering, Boca Raton, FL 33431-0991. Offers mechanical engineering (MS, PhD); ocean engineering (MS, PhD). Part-time and evening/weekend programs available. *Faculty:* 20 full-time (0 women), 2 part-time/adjunct (0 women). *Students:* 39 full-time (9 women), 34 part-time (6 women); includes 15 minority (5 Black or African American, non-Hispanic/Latino; 1 American Indian or Alaska Native, non-Hispanic/Latino; 9 Hispanic/Latino), 18 international. Average age 29. 63 applicants, 48% accepted, 12 enrolled. In 2011, 36 master's, 1 doctorate awarded. Terminal master's awarded for partial completion of doctoral program. *Degree requirements:* For master's, thesis (for some programs); for doctorate, comprehensive exam, thesis/dissertation, qualifying exam. *Entrance requirements:* For master's and doctorate, GRE General Test, minimum GPA of 3.0. Additional exam requirements/recommendations for international students: Required—TOEFL. *Application deadline:* For fall admission, 7/1 priority date for domestic students, 2/15 for international students; for spring admission, 11/1 for domestic students, 7/15 for international students. Applications are processed on a rolling basis. Application fee: $30. *Expenses: Tuition, area resident:* Part-time $343.02 per credit hour. Tuition, state resident: full-time $8232. Tuition, nonresident: full-time $23,931; part-time $997.14 per credit hour. *Financial support:* In 2011–12, research assistantships (averaging $15,000 per year) were awarded; career-related internships or fieldwork, Federal Work-Study, scholarships/grants, and unspecified assistantships also available. Financial award application deadline: 1/10; financial award applicants required to submit FAFSA. *Faculty research:* Marine materials and corrosion, ocean structures, marine vehicles, acoustics and vibrations, hydrodynamics, coastal engineering. *Unit head:* Dr. Javad Hashemi, Chair, 561-297-3430, E-mail: jhashemi@fau.edu. *Application contact:* Joanna Arlington, Manager, Graduate Admissions, 561-297-2428, Fax: 561-297-2117, E-mail: arlingto@fau.edu. Web site: http://www.ome.fau.edu/.

Florida Institute of Technology, Graduate Programs, College of Engineering, Mechanical and Aerospace Engineering Department, Melbourne, FL 32901-6975. Offers aerospace engineering (MS, PhD); mechanical engineering (MS, PhD). Part-time programs available. *Faculty:* 9 full-time (0 women). *Students:* 59 full-time (8 women), 36 part-time (4 women); includes 7 minority (1 Black or African American, non-Hispanic/Latino; 2 Asian, non-Hispanic/Latino; 4 Hispanic/Latino), 50 international. Average age 27. 259 applicants, 61% accepted, 44 enrolled. In 2011, 27 master's, 1 doctorate awarded. Terminal master's awarded for partial completion of doctoral program. *Degree requirements:* For master's, comprehensive exam (for some programs), thesis optional; for doctorate, comprehensive exam, thesis/dissertation, oral section of written exam, complete program of significant original research. *Entrance requirements:* For master's, GRE General Test, minimum GPA of 3.0, bachelor's degree from an ABET-accredited program, transcripts; for doctorate, GRE General Test, 3 letters of recommendation, minimum GPA of 3.2, resume, statement of objectives. Additional exam requirements/recommendations for international students: Required—TOEFL (minimum score 550 paper-based; 213 computer-based; 79 iBT). *Application deadline:* For fall admission, 4/1 for international students; for spring admission, 9/30 for international students. Applications are processed on a rolling basis. Application fee: $0. Electronic applications accepted. *Expenses:* Tuition: Full-time $19,620; part-time $1090 per credit hour. Tuition and fees vary according to campus/location. *Financial support:* In 2011–12, 6 research assistantships with full and partial tuition reimbursements (averaging $4,472 per year), 12 teaching assistantships with full and partial tuition reimbursements (averaging $3,893 per year) were awarded; career-related internships or fieldwork, institutionally sponsored loans, tuition waivers (partial), unspecified assistantships, and tuition remissions also available. Support available to part-time students. Financial award application deadline: 3/1; financial award applicants required to submit FAFSA. *Faculty research:* Dynamic systems, robotics, and controls; structures, solid mechanics, and materials; thermal-fluid sciences, optical tomography, composite/recycled materials. *Total annual research expenditures:* $733,898. *Unit head:* Dr. Pei-feng Hsu, Department Head, 321-674-8092, Fax: 321-674-8813, E-mail: phsu@fit.edu. *Application contact:* Cheryl A. Brown, Associate Director of Graduate Admissions, 321-674-7581, Fax: 321-723-9468, E-mail: cbrown@fit.edu. Web site: http://coe.fit.edu/mae/.

Florida Institute of Technology, Graduate Programs, Extended Studies Division, Melbourne, FL 32901-6975. Offers acquisition and contract management (MS); aerospace engineering (MS); business administration (MBA); computer information systems (MS); computer science (MS); electrical engineering (MS); engineering management (MS); human resources management (MS); logistics management (MS), including humanitarian and disaster relief logistics; management (MS), including acquisition and contract management, e-business, human resources management, information systems, logistics management, management, transportation management; material acquisition management (MS); mechanical engineering (MS); operations research (MS); project management (MS), including information systems, operations research; public administration (MPA); quality management (MS); software engineering (MS); space systems (MS); space systems management (MS); supply chain management (MS); systems management (MS), including information systems, operations research. Part-time and evening/weekend programs available. Postbaccalaureate distance learning degree programs offered (no on-campus study). *Faculty:* 9 full-time (2 women), 105 part-time/adjunct (24 women). *Students:* 113 full-time (52 women), 1,150 part-time (484 women); includes 496 minority (332 Black or African American, non-Hispanic/Latino; 11 American Indian or Alaska Native, non-Hispanic/Latino; 42 Asian, non-Hispanic/Latino; 71 Hispanic/Latino; 2 Native Hawaiian or other Pacific Islander, non-Hispanic/Latino; 38 Two or more races, non-Hispanic/Latino), 11 international. Average age 35. 568 applicants, 56% accepted, 296 enrolled. In 2011, 471 master's awarded. *Degree requirements:* For master's, comprehensive exam (for some programs), capstone course. *Entrance requirements:* For master's, GMAT or resume showing 8 years of supervised experience, minimum GPA of 3.0, 2 letters of recommendation, resume. Additional exam requirements/recommendations for international students: Required—TOEFL (minimum score 550 paper-based; 213 computer-based; 79 iBT). *Application deadline:* For fall admission, 4/1 for international students; for spring admission, 9/30 for international students. Applications are processed on a rolling basis. Application fee: $0. Electronic applications accepted. *Expenses:* Contact institution. *Financial support:* Application deadline: 3/1; applicants required to submit FAFSA. *Unit head:* Dr. Theodore R. Richardson, III, Senior Associate Dean, 321-674-8123, Fax: 321-674-7597, E-mail: trichardson@fit.edu. *Application contact:* Carolyn Farrior, Director of Graduate Admissions, Online Learning and Off-Campus Programs, 321-674-7118, Fax: 321-674-8216, E-mail: cfarrior@fit.edu. Web site: http://es.fit.edu.

Florida International University, College of Engineering and Computing, Department of Mechanical and Materials Engineering, Mechanical Engineering Program, Miami, FL 33175. Offers MS, PhD. Part-time and evening/weekend programs available. Terminal master's awarded for partial completion of doctoral program. *Degree requirements:* For master's, thesis or alternative; for doctorate, comprehensive exam, thesis/dissertation. *Entrance requirements:* For master's, minimum undergraduate GPA of 3.0 in upper level coursework, letters of recommendation, letter of intent; for doctorate, GRE, minimum undergraduate GPA of 3.0, 3 letters of recommendation, letter of intent. Additional exam requirements/recommendations for international students: Required—TOEFL (minimum score 550 paper-based; 80 iBT). Electronic applications accepted.

Florida State University, The Graduate School, FAMU-FSU College of Engineering, Department of Mechanical Engineering, Tallahassee, FL 32310-6046. Offers mechanical engineering (MS, PhD); sustainable energy (MS). Part-time programs available. *Faculty:* 17 full-time (1 woman), 4 part-time/adjunct (0 women). *Students:* 72 full-time (12 women); includes 8 minority (5 Black or African American, non-Hispanic/Latino; 3 Hispanic/Latino), 25 international. 113 applicants, 72% accepted, 15 enrolled. In 2011, 18 master's, 9 doctorates awarded. Terminal master's awarded for partial completion of doctoral program. *Degree requirements:* For master's, thesis optional; for doctorate, thesis/dissertation, 45 credit hours (21 coursework, 24 research). *Entrance requirements:* For master's and doctorate, GRE General Test (minimum scores: Verbal 150, Quantitative 155), minimum GPA of 3.0, official transcripts, resume, personal statement, 3 letters of recommendation. Additional exam requirements/recommendations for international students: Required—TOEFL (minimum score 550 paper-based; 213 computer-based; 80 iBT), IELTS (minimum score 6.5), Michigan English Language Assessment Battery (minimum score 77). *Application deadline:* For fall admission, 5/1 for domestic and international students; for spring admission, 10/1 for domestic and international students. Applications are processed on a rolling basis. Application fee: $30. Electronic applications accepted. *Expenses:* Tuition, state resident: full-time $9474; part-time $350.88 per credit hour. Tuition, nonresident: full-

time $16,236; part-time $601.34 per credit hour. *Required fees:* $630 per semester. One-time fee: $20. Tuition and fees vary according to course load and campus/location. *Financial support:* In 2011–12, fellowships with full tuition reimbursements (averaging $30,000 per year), 55 research assistantships with full tuition reimbursements (averaging $20,000 per year), 11 teaching assistantships with full tuition reimbursements (averaging $20,000 per year) were awarded; career-related internships or fieldwork, institutionally sponsored loans, scholarships/grants, health care benefits, tuition waivers (partial), and unspecified assistantships also available. Support available to part-time students. Financial award applicants required to submit FAFSA. *Faculty research:* Aero-propulsion, superconductivity, smart materials, nano-materials, intelligent robotic systems, robotic locomotion, sustainable energy. *Total annual research expenditures:* $5 million. *Unit head:* Dr. Emmanuel Collins, Chair, 850-410-6373, Fax: 850-410-6337, E-mail: ecollins@eng.fsu.edu. *Application contact:* George Green, Coordinator of Graduate Studies, 850-410-6196, Fax: 850-410-6337, E-mail: ggreen@admin.fsu.edu. Web site: http://www.eng.fsu.edu/me/.

Gannon University, School of Graduate Studies, College of Engineering and Business, School of Engineering and Computer Science, Program in Mechanical Engineering, Erie, PA 16541-0001. Offers MSME. Part-time and evening/weekend programs available. *Students:* 28 full-time (1 woman), 13 part-time (4 women); includes 1 minority (Asian, non-Hispanic/Latino), 22 international. Average age 25. 141 applicants, 77% accepted, 7 enrolled. In 2011, 15 master's awarded. *Degree requirements:* For master's, comprehensive exam, thesis or project. *Entrance requirements:* For master's, GRE or GMAT, bachelor's degree in mechanical engineering, minimum QPA of 2.5. Additional exam requirements/recommendations for international students: Required—TOEFL (minimum score 79 iBT). *Application deadline:* Applications are processed on a rolling basis. Application fee: $25. Electronic applications accepted. *Financial support:* Career-related internships or fieldwork, scholarships/grants, traineeships, and unspecified assistantships available. Financial award application deadline: 7/1; financial award applicants required to submit FAFSA. *Unit head:* Dr. Scott Steinbrink, Chair, 814-871-5302, E-mail: steinbri001@gannon.edu. *Application contact:* Kara Morgan, Director of Graduate Admissions, 814-871-5831, Fax: 814-871-5827, E-mail: graduate@gannon.edu.

The George Washington University, School of Engineering and Applied Science, Department of Mechanical and Aerospace Engineering, Washington, DC 20052. Offers MS, D Sc, App Sc, Engr, Graduate Certificate. Part-time and evening/weekend programs available. *Faculty:* 17 full-time (1 woman), 13 part-time/adjunct (2 women). *Students:* 51 full-time (13 women), 37 part-time (5 women); includes 17 minority (7 Black or African American, non-Hispanic/Latino; 1 American Indian or Alaska Native, non-Hispanic/Latino; 4 Asian, non-Hispanic/Latino; 4 Hispanic/Latino; 1 Two or more races, non-Hispanic/Latino), 28 international. Average age 29. 123 applicants, 77% accepted, 25 enrolled. In 2011, 16 master's, 6 doctorates, 1 other advanced degree awarded. *Degree requirements:* For master's, thesis optional; for doctorate, thesis/dissertation, final and qualifying exams. *Entrance requirements:* For master's, appropriate bachelor's degree, minimum GPA of 3.0; for doctorate, GRE (if highest earned degree is BS), appropriate bachelor's or master's degree, minimum GPA of 3.4; for other advanced degree, appropriate master's degree, minimum GPA of 3.0. Additional exam requirements/recommendations for international students: Required—TOEFL or The George Washington University English as a Foreign Language Test. *Application deadline:* For fall admission, 3/1 priority date for domestic students; for spring admission, 10/1 for domestic students. Applications are processed on a rolling basis. Application fee: $75. *Financial support:* In 2011–12, 51 students received support. Fellowships with tuition reimbursements available, research assistantships, teaching assistantships with tuition reimbursements available, career-related internships or fieldwork, and institutionally sponsored loans available. Financial award application deadline: 3/1; financial award applicants required to submit FAFSA. *Unit head:* Dr. Michael Plesniak, Chairman, 202-994-6749, E-mail: maeng@gwu.edu. *Application contact:* Adina Lav, Marketing, Recruiting and Admissions, 202-994-5827, Fax: 202-994-0909, E-mail: engineering@gwu.edu. Web site: http://www.mae.gwu.edu/.

Georgia Institute of Technology, Graduate Studies and Research, College of Engineering, George W. Woodruff School of Mechanical Engineering, Program in Mechanical Engineering, Atlanta, GA 30332-0001. Offers biomedical engineering (MS Bio E); mechanical engineering (MS, MSME, PhD). Part-time programs available. Postbaccalaureate distance learning degree programs offered (no on-campus study). Terminal master's awarded for partial completion of doctoral program. *Degree requirements:* For master's, thesis optional; for doctorate, comprehensive exam, thesis/dissertation. *Entrance requirements:* For master's and doctorate, GRE General Test, minimum GPA of 3.0. Additional exam requirements/recommendations for international students: Required—TOEFL. Electronic applications accepted. *Faculty research:* Automation and mechatronics; computer-aided engineering and design; micro-electronic mechanical systems; heat transfer, combustion and energy systems; fluid mechanics.

Georgia Southern University, Jack N. Averitt College of Graduate Studies, Allen E. Paulson College of Science and Technology, Department of Mechanical and Electrical Engineering Technology, Statesboro, GA 30460. Offers M Tech, MSAE, Certificate. Part-time and evening/weekend programs available. *Students:* 38 full-time (4 women), 19 part-time (3 women); includes 19 minority (11 Black or African American, non-Hispanic/Latino; 1 Asian, non-Hispanic/Latino; 4 Hispanic/Latino; 3 Two or more races, non-Hispanic/Latino), 5 international. Average age 27. 30 applicants, 90% accepted, 21 enrolled. In 2011, 14 master's awarded. *Degree requirements:* For master's, comprehensive exam, thesis optional. *Entrance requirements:* For master's, GRE. Additional exam requirements/recommendations for international students: Required—TOEFL (minimum score 550 paper-based; 213 computer-based; 80 iBT). *Application deadline:* For fall admission, 3/1 priority date for domestic students, 3/1 for international students; for spring admission, 10/1 priority date for domestic students, 10/1 for international students. Applications are processed on a rolling basis. Application fee: $50. Electronic applications accepted. *Expenses:* Tuition, state resident: full-time $6300; part-time $263 per semester hour. Tuition, nonresident: full-time $25,174; part-time $1049 per semester hour. *Required fees:* $1872. *Financial support:* In 2011–12, 23 students received support, including 4 research assistantships with partial tuition reimbursements available (averaging $7,200 per year); tuition waivers (partial) and unspecified assistantships also available. Financial award application deadline: 4/15; financial award applicants required to submit FAFSA. *Faculty research:* Interdisciplinary research in computational mechanics, experimental and computational biofuel combustion and tribology, mechatronics and control, thermomechanical and thermofluid finite element modeling, information technology. *Total annual research expenditures:* $458,293. *Unit head:* Dr. Mohammad S. Davoud, Chair, 912-478-0540, Fax: 912-478-1455, E-mail: mdavoud@georgiasouthern.edu. *Application contact:* Amanda Gilliland, Coordinator for Graduate Student Recruitment, 912-478-5384, Fax: 912-478-0740, E-mail: gradadmissions@georgiasouthern.edu.

Graduate School and University Center of the City University of New York, Graduate Studies, Program in Engineering, New York, NY 10016-4039. Offers biomedical engineering (PhD); chemical engineering (PhD); civil engineering (PhD); electrical engineering (PhD); mechanical engineering (PhD). *Degree requirements:* For doctorate, thesis/dissertation. *Entrance requirements:* For doctorate, GRE General Test. Additional exam requirements/recommendations for international students: Required—TOEFL. Electronic applications accepted.

Grand Valley State University, Padnos College of Engineering and Computing, School of Engineering, Allendale, MI 49401-9403. Offers electrical and computer engineering (MSE); manufacturing operations (MSE); mechanical engineering (MSE); product design and manufacturing engineering (MSE). Part-time and evening/weekend programs available. *Degree requirements:* For master's, project or thesis. *Entrance requirements:* For master's, engineering degree, minimum GPA of 3.0. Additional exam requirements/recommendations for international students: Required—TOEFL. Electronic applications accepted. *Faculty research:* Digital signal processing, computer aided design, computer aided manufacturing, manufacturing simulation, biomechanics, product design.

Howard University, College of Engineering, Architecture, and Computer Sciences, School of Engineering and Computer Science, Department of Mechanical Engineering, Washington, DC 20059-0002. Offers M Eng, PhD. *Degree requirements:* For master's, comprehensive exam, thesis; for doctorate, one foreign language, comprehensive exam, thesis/dissertation, 2 terms of residency. *Entrance requirements:* For master's and doctorate, GRE General Test, minimum GPA of 3.0. Additional exam requirements/recommendations for international students: Required—TOEFL (minimum score 213 computer-based). Electronic applications accepted. *Faculty research:* The dynamics and control of large flexible space structures, optimization of space structures.

Idaho State University, Office of Graduate Studies, College of Science and Engineering, Mechanical Engineering Department, Pocatello, ID 83209-8060. Offers measurement and control engineering (MS); mechanical engineering (MS). Part-time programs available. *Degree requirements:* For master's, comprehensive exam (for some programs), 2 semesters of seminar; thesis or project. *Entrance requirements:* For master's, GRE. Additional exam requirements/recommendations for international students: Required—TOEFL (minimum score 550 paper-based; 213 computer-based; 80 iBT). Electronic applications accepted. *Faculty research:* Modeling and identification of biomedical systems, intelligent systems and adaptive control, active flow control of turbo machinery, validation of advanced computational codes for thermal fluid interactions, development of methodologies for the assessment of passive safety system performance in advanced reactors, alternative energy research (wind, solar, hydrogen).

Illinois Institute of Technology, Graduate College, Armour College of Engineering, Department of Mechanical, Materials and Aerospace Engineering, Chicago, IL 60616-3793. Offers manufacturing engineering (MME, MS); materials science and engineering (MMME, MS, PhD); mechanical and aerospace engineering (MMAE, MS, PhD), including economics (MS), energy (MS), environment (MS). Part-time and evening/weekend programs available. Postbaccalaureate distance learning degree programs offered (minimal on-campus study). Terminal master's awarded for partial completion of doctoral program. *Degree requirements:* For master's, comprehensive exam (for some programs), thesis (for some programs); for doctorate, comprehensive exam, thesis/dissertation. *Entrance requirements:* For master's and doctorate, GRE General Test (minimum score 1000 Quantitative and Verbal, 3.0 Analytical Writing), minimum undergraduate GPA of 3.0. Additional exam requirements/recommendations for international students: Required—TOEFL (minimum score 523 paper-based; 70 iBT); Recommended—IELTS (minimum score 5.5). Electronic applications accepted. *Faculty research:* Fluid dynamics, metallurgical and materials engineering, solids and structures, computational mechanics, theoretical mechanics.

Indiana University–Purdue University Fort Wayne, College of Engineering, Technology, and Computer Science, Department of Engineering, Fort Wayne, IN 46805-1499. Offers computer engineering (MSE); electrical engineering (MSE); mechanical engineering (MSE); systems engineering (MSE). Part-time programs available. *Faculty:* 21 full-time (0 women), 2 part-time/adjunct (0 women). *Students:* 6 full-time (0 women), 29 part-time (5 women); includes 3 minority (2 Asian, non-Hispanic/Latino; 1 Hispanic/Latino), 3 international. Average age 28. 26 applicants, 96% accepted, 17 enrolled. In 2011, 16 master's awarded. *Entrance requirements:* For master's, minimum GPA of 3.0, bachelor's degree in engineering discipline. Additional exam requirements/recommendations for international students: Required—TOEFL (minimum score 550 paper-based; 213 computer-based; 77 iBT); Recommended—TWE. *Application deadline:* For fall admission, 7/15 priority date for domestic students, 5/15 for international students; for spring admission, 12/1 priority date for domestic students, 10/15 for international students. Applications are processed on a rolling basis. Application fee: $55 ($60 for international students). Electronic applications accepted. *Financial support:* In 2011–12, 7 research assistantships with partial tuition reimbursements (averaging $12,930 per year), 3 teaching assistantships with partial tuition reimbursements (averaging $12,930 per year) were awarded. Financial award application deadline: 3/1; financial award applicants required to submit FAFSA. *Faculty research:* Thermal science, robot prototypes, worm-scanning strategies. *Total annual research expenditures:* $185,757. *Unit head:* Dr. Donald Mueller, Chair, 260-481-5707, Fax: 260-481-6281, E-mail: mueller@engr.ipfw.edu. *Application contact:* Dr. Carlos Pomalaza-Raez, Program Director/Professor, 260-481-6353, Fax: 260-481-5734, E-mail: carlos-pomalaza-raez@purdue.edu. Web site: http://www.ipfw.edu/engr.

Indiana University–Purdue University Indianapolis, School of Engineering and Technology, Department of Mechanical Engineering, Indianapolis, IN 46202-2896. Offers biomedical engineering (MS Bm E); computer-aided mechanical engineering (Certificate); mechanical engineering (MSME, PhD). Part-time programs available. *Students:* 25 full-time (2 women), 49 part-time (7 women); includes 5 minority (1 Black or African American, non-Hispanic/Latino; 2 Asian, non-Hispanic/Latino; 2 Hispanic/Latino), 32 international. Average age 28. 84 applicants, 55% accepted, 25 enrolled. In 2011, 19 master's, 1 other advanced degree awarded. *Degree requirements:* For master's, thesis optional. *Entrance requirements:* For master's, GRE. Additional exam requirements/recommendations for international students: Required—TOEFL. *Application deadline:* For fall admission, 7/1 for domestic students. Application fee: $55 ($65 for international students). *Financial support:* Fellowships with tuition reimbursements, research assistantships with full and partial tuition reimbursements, and tuition waivers (full and partial) available. Financial award application deadline: 3/1. *Faculty research:* Computational fluid dynamics, heat transfer, finite-element methods, composites, biomechanics. *Unit head:* Dr. Hasan Akay, Chairman, 317-274-9717, Fax: 317-274-9744. *Application contact:* Valerie Diemer, Graduate Program, 317-278-4960, Fax: 317-278-1671, E-mail: grad@engr.iupui.edu. Web site: http://www.engr.iupui.edu/me/.

Instituto Tecnológico y de Estudios Superiores de Monterrey, Campus Chihuahua, Graduate Programs, Chihuahua, Mexico. Offers computer systems engineering (Ingeniero); electrical engineering (Ingeniero); electromechanical engineering (Ingeniero); electronic engineering (Ingeniero); engineering administration (MEA); industrial engineering (MIE, Ingeniero); international trade (MIT); mechanical engineering (Ingeniero).

Instituto Tecnológico y de Estudios Superiores de Monterrey, Campus Monterrey, Graduate and Research Division, Programs in Engineering, Monterrey, Mexico. Offers applied statistics (M Eng); artificial intelligence (PhD); automation engineering (M Eng); chemical engineering (M Eng); civil engineering (M Eng); electrical engineering (M Eng); electronic engineering (M Eng); environmental engineering (M Eng); industrial engineering (M Eng, PhD); manufacturing engineering (M Eng); mechanical engineering (M Eng); systems and quality engineering (M Eng). M Eng program offered jointly with University of Waterloo; PhD in industrial engineering with Texas A&M University. Part-time and evening/weekend programs available. Terminal master's awarded for partial completion of doctoral program. *Degree requirements:* For master's, one foreign language, thesis; for doctorate, one foreign language, thesis/dissertation. *Entrance requirements:* For master's, EXADEP; for doctorate, GRE, master's degree in related field. Additional exam requirements/recommendations for international students: Required—TOEFL. *Faculty research:* Flexible manufacturing cells, materials, statistical methods, environmental prevention, control and evaluation.

Iowa State University of Science and Technology, Department of Mechanical Engineering, Ames, IA 50011. Offers mechanical engineering (M Eng, MS, PhD); systems engineering (M Eng). *Degree requirements:* For master's, thesis or alternative; for doctorate, thesis/dissertation. *Entrance requirements:* For master's and doctorate, GRE General Test, resume. Additional exam requirements/recommendations for international students: Required—TOEFL (minimum score 570 paper-based; 79 iBT), IELTS (minimum score 6.5). *Application deadline:* For fall admission, 1/10 priority date for domestic students, 1/10 for international students; for spring admission, 8/10 priority date for domestic students, 8/10 for international students. Application fee: $40 ($90 for international students). Electronic applications accepted. *Unit head:* Dr. Pranav Shrotriya, Director of Graduate Education, 515-294-0838, Fax: 515-294-6960, E-mail: megradinfo@iastate.edu. *Application contact:* Amy Carver, Director of Graduate Education, 515-294-0838, Fax: 515-294-6960, E-mail: megradinfo@iastate.edu. Web site: http://www.me.iastate.edu/graduate-program/.

The Johns Hopkins University, Engineering Program for Professionals, Part-time Program in Mechanical Engineering, Baltimore, MD 21218-2699. Offers MME. Part-time and evening/weekend programs available. Electronic applications accepted.

The Johns Hopkins University, Whiting School of Engineering, Department of Mechanical Engineering, Baltimore, MD 21218-2681. Offers MSE, PhD. Terminal master's awarded for partial completion of doctoral program. *Degree requirements:* For master's, thesis (for some programs); for doctorate, comprehensive exam, thesis/dissertation, oral exam. *Entrance requirements:* For master's and doctorate, GRE General Test. Additional exam requirements/recommendations for international students: Required—TOEFL or IELTS. Electronic applications accepted. *Faculty research:* Microscale/nanoscale science and engineering, computational engineering, aerospace and marine systems, robotics and human-machine interaction, energy and the environment, mechanics and materials.

The Johns Hopkins University, Whiting School of Engineering, Program in Engineering Management, Baltimore, MD 21218-2699. Offers biomaterials (MSEM); communications science (MSEM); computer science (MSEM); fluid mechanics (MSEM); materials science and engineering (MSEM); mechanical engineering (MSEM); mechanics and materials (MSEM); nano-biotechnology (MSEM); nanomaterials and nanotechnology (MSEM); probability and statistics (MSEM); smart product and device design (MSEM); systems analysis, management and environmental policy (MSEM). *Entrance requirements:* For master's, GRE, 3 letters of recommendation, resume. Additional exam requirements/recommendations for international students: Required—TOEFL (minimum score 600 paper-based; 250 computer-based; 100 iBT) or IELTS (minimum score 7). Electronic applications accepted.

Kansas State University, Graduate School, College of Engineering, Department of Mechanical and Nuclear Engineering, Manhattan, KS 66506. Offers mechanical engineering (MS, PhD); nuclear engineering (MS, PhD). *Faculty:* 18 full-time (2 women), 2 part-time/adjunct (0 women). *Students:* 42 full-time (8 women), 22 part-time (3 women); includes 2 minority (1 Black or African American, non-Hispanic/Latino; 1 Two or more races, non-Hispanic/Latino), 24 international. Average age 29. 97 applicants, 29% accepted, 9 enrolled. In 2011, 22 master's, 6 doctorates awarded. *Degree requirements:* For master's, thesis or alternative; for doctorate, comprehensive exam, thesis/dissertation. *Entrance requirements:* For master's, GRE General Test, minimum GPA of 3.0 in physics, mathematics, and chemistry; for doctorate, GRE General Test, master's degree in mechanical engineering. Additional exam requirements/recommendations for international students: Required—TOEFL. *Application deadline:* For fall admission, 2/1 priority date for domestic students, 2/1 for international students; for spring admission, 7/1 priority date for domestic students, 8/1 for international students. Applications are processed on a rolling basis. Application fee: $40 ($55 for international students). Electronic applications accepted. *Financial support:* In 2011–12, 33 research assistantships (averaging $19,839 per year), 5 teaching assistantships with full and partial tuition reimbursements (averaging $14,400 per year) were awarded; career-related internships or fieldwork, institutionally sponsored loans, and scholarships/grants also available. Support available to part-time students. Financial award application deadline: 3/1; financial award applicants required to submit FAFSA. *Faculty research:* Radiation detection and protection, heat and mass transfer, machine design, control systems, nuclear reactor physics and engineering. *Total annual research expenditures:* $3.6 million. *Unit head:* Donald Fenton, Head, 785-532-2321, Fax: 785-532-7057, E-mail: fenton@ksu.edu. *Application contact:* Steve Eckels, Director, 785-532-2283, Fax: 785-532-7057, E-mail: grad@mne.ksu.edu. Web site: http://www.mne.ksu.edu/.

Kettering University, Graduate School, Mechanical Engineering Department, Flint, MI 48504. Offers engineering (MS). Part-time and evening/weekend programs available. Postbaccalaureate distance learning degree programs offered (no on-campus study). *Faculty:* 6 full-time (0 women). *Students:* 1 full-time (0 women), 28 part-time (3 women); includes 4 minority (3 Asian, non-Hispanic/Latino; 1 Hispanic/Latino), 8 international. Average age 28. 47 applicants, 68% accepted, 12 enrolled. In 2011, 15 master's awarded. *Degree requirements:* For master's, thesis optional. *Entrance requirements:* Additional exam requirements/recommendations for international students: Required—TOEFL (minimum score 550 paper-based; 213 computer-based; 79 iBT). *Application deadline:* For fall admission, 9/15 for domestic students, 6/15 for international students; for winter admission, 12/15 for domestic students, 9/15 for international students; for spring admission, 3/15 for domestic students, 12/15 for international students. Applications are processed on a rolling basis. Electronic applications accepted. *Expenses: Tuition:* Full-time $11,456; part-time $716 per credit hour. *Financial support:* In 2011–12, 6 students received support, including fellowships with full tuition reimbursements available (averaging $13,000 per year), research assistantships with full tuition reimbursements available (averaging $13,000 per year), teaching assistantships with full tuition reimbursements available (averaging $13,000 per year); Federal Work-Study, scholarships/grants, and tuition waivers (partial) also available. Support available to part-time students. Financial award application deadline: 7/15; financial award applicants required to submit CSS PROFILE or FAFSA. *Faculty research:* Fuel cells, chemical agents, crash safety, bio-gas, sustainable energy, biomechanical. *Total annual research expenditures:* $3.7 million. *Unit head:* Dr. Craig Hoff, Department Head, 810-762-9856, Fax: 810-762-7860, E-mail: choff@kettering.edu. *Application contact:* Bonnie Switzer, Graduate Admissions Officer, 810-762-7953, Fax: 810-762-9935, E-mail: bswitzer@kettering.edu. Web site: http://www.kettering.edu/.

Lamar University, College of Graduate Studies, College of Engineering, Department of Mechanical Engineering, Beaumont, TX 77710. Offers ME, MES, DE. Part-time programs available. *Faculty:* 6 full-time (1 woman). *Students:* 29 full-time (0 women), 25 part-time (3 women); includes 2 minority (1 Black or African American, non-Hispanic/Latino; 1 Asian, non-Hispanic/Latino), 50 international. Average age 25. 47 applicants, 83% accepted, 4 enrolled. In 2011, 51 master's awarded. Terminal master's awarded for partial completion of doctoral program. *Degree requirements:* For master's, comprehensive exam (for some programs), thesis (for some programs); for doctorate, thesis/dissertation. *Entrance requirements:* For master's and doctorate, GRE General Test. Additional exam requirements/recommendations for international students: Required—TOEFL. *Application deadline:* For fall admission, 5/15 priority date for domestic students; for spring admission, 10/1 priority date for domestic students. Applications are processed on a rolling basis. Application fee: $25 ($50 for international students). *Expenses:* Tuition, state resident: full-time $5430; part-time $272 per credit hour. Tuition, nonresident: full-time $11,540; part-time $577 per credit hour. *Required fees:* $1916. *Financial support:* In 2011–12, 2 fellowships (averaging $7,200 per year), 4 research assistantships, 5 teaching assistantships were awarded; tuition waivers (partial) also available. Financial award application deadline: 4/1. *Faculty research:* Materials combustion, mechanical and multiphysics study in micro-electronics, structural instability/reliability, mechanics of micro electronics. *Unit head:* Dr. Malur N. Srinivasan, Chair, 409-880-8094, Fax: 409-880-8121, E-mail: srinivasmn@hal.lamar.edu. *Application contact:* Dr. James L. Thomas, Director of Recruitment, 409-880-7870, Fax: 409-880-8121, E-mail: thomasjl@hal.lamar.edu.

Lawrence Technological University, College of Engineering, Southfield, MI 48075-1058. Offers architectural engineering (MS); automotive engineering (MS); civil engineering (MA, MS); construction engineering management (MA); electrical and computer engineering (MS); engineering management (MEM); industrial engineering (MS); manufacturing systems (ME, DE); mechanical engineering (MS, DE); mechatronic systems engineering (MS). Part-time and evening/weekend programs available. *Faculty:* 25 full-time (4 women), 20 part-time/adjunct (1 woman). *Students:* 8 full-time (0 women), 332 part-time (52 women); includes 58 minority (21 Black or African American, non-Hispanic/Latino; 1 American Indian or Alaska Native, non-Hispanic/Latino; 32 Asian, non-Hispanic/Latino; 2 Hispanic/Latino; 2 Two or more races, non-Hispanic/Latino), 84 international. Average age 32. 652 applicants, 44% accepted, 70 enrolled. In 2011, 127 master's, 2 doctorates awarded. *Degree requirements:* For master's, thesis (for some programs). *Entrance requirements:* Additional exam requirements/recommendations for international students: Required—TOEFL (minimum score 550 paper-based; 213 computer-based; 79 iBT). *Application deadline:* For fall admission, 7/27 priority date for domestic students, 5/23 for international students; for spring admission, 11/15 priority date for domestic students, 11/15 for international students. Applications are processed on a rolling basis. Application fee: $50. Electronic applications accepted. *Financial support:* In 2011–12, 68 students received support, including 6 research assistantships (averaging $8,078 per year); Federal Work-Study and institutionally sponsored loans also available. Support available to part-time students. Financial award application deadline: 4/1; financial award applicants required to submit FAFSA. *Faculty research:* Advanced composite materials in bridges, strengthening existing bridges with carbon and glass fiber sheets, development of drive shafts using composite materials. *Unit head:* Dr. Nabil Grace, Dean, 248-204-2500, Fax: 248-204-2509, E-mail: engrdean@ltu.edu. *Application contact:* Jane Rohrback, Director of Admissions, 248-204-3160, Fax: 248-204-2228, E-mail: admissions@ltu.edu. Web site: http://www.ltu.edu/engineering/index.asp.

Lehigh University, P.C. Rossin College of Engineering and Applied Science, Department of Mechanical Engineering and Mechanics, Bethlehem, PA 18015. Offers computational engineering and mechanics (MS, PhD); mechanical engineering (M Eng, MS, PhD, MBA/E); polymer science/engineering (M Eng, MS, PhD, MBA/E); MBA/E. Part-time and evening/weekend programs available. Postbaccalaureate distance learning degree programs offered. *Faculty:* 24 full-time (0 women). *Students:* 113 full-time (12 women), 30 part-time (3 women); includes 6 minority (3 Black or African American, non-Hispanic/Latino; 2 Asian, non-Hispanic/Latino; 1 Hispanic/Latino), 79 international. Average age 26. 298 applicants, 50% accepted, 37 enrolled. In 2011, 35 master's, 6 doctorates awarded. Terminal master's awarded for partial completion of doctoral program. *Degree requirements:* For master's, thesis; for doctorate, thesis/dissertation, general exam. *Entrance requirements:* Additional exam requirements/recommendations for international students: Required—TOEFL (minimum score 550 paper-based; 213 computer-based; 79 iBT). *Application deadline:* For fall admission, 7/15 for domestic and international students; for spring admission, 12/1 for domestic and international students. Applications are processed on a rolling basis. Application fee: $75. Electronic applications accepted. *Financial support:* In 2011–12, 47 students received support, including 5 fellowships with full and partial tuition reimbursements available (averaging $24,480 per year), 24 research assistantships with full and partial tuition reimbursements available (averaging $20,700 per year), 12 teaching assistantships with full and partial tuition reimbursements available (averaging $25,092 per year); unspecified assistantships and dean's doctoral assistantships also available. Financial award application deadline: 1/15. *Faculty research:* Thermofluids, dynamic systems, CAD/CAM, computational mechanics, solid mechanics. *Total annual research expenditures:* $3.5 million. *Unit head:* Dr. D. Gary Harlow, Chairman, 610-758-4102, Fax: 610-758-6224, E-mail: dgh0@lehigh.edu. *Application contact:* Jo Ann M. Casciano, Graduate Coordinator, 610-758-4107, Fax: 610-758-6224, E-mail: jmc4@lehigh.edu. Web site: http://www.lehigh.edu/~inmem/.

Louisiana State University and Agricultural and Mechanical College, Graduate School, College of Engineering, Department of Mechanical Engineering, Baton Rouge, LA 70803. Offers MSME, PhD. Part-time programs available. *Faculty:* 27 full-time (1 woman). *Students:* 100 full-time (9 women), 8 part-time (0 women); includes 5 minority (2 Black or African American, non-Hispanic/Latino; 1 Asian, non-Hispanic/Latino; 2 Hispanic/Latino), 78 international. Average age 28. 94 applicants, 61% accepted, 16 enrolled. In 2011, 7 master's, 8 doctorates awarded. Terminal master's awarded for partial completion of doctoral program. *Degree requirements:* For master's, thesis; for doctorate, thesis/dissertation. *Entrance requirements:* For master's and doctorate, GRE General Test, minimum GPA of 3.0. Additional exam requirements/recommendations for international students: Required—TOEFL (minimum score 550 paper-based; 213 computer-based; 79 iBT) or IELTS (minimum score 6.5). *Application deadline:* For fall admission, 1/25 priority date for domestic students, 2/15 for international students; for spring admission, 10/15 for international students. Applications are processed on a rolling basis. Application fee: $50 ($70 for international students). Electronic applications accepted. *Financial support:* In 2011–12, 94 students received support, including 14 fellowships with full and partial tuition reimbursements available (averaging $13,406 per year), 69 research assistantships with partial tuition reimbursements available (averaging $18,362 per year), 23 teaching assistantships with partial tuition reimbursements available (averaging $13,696 per year); Federal Work-Study, institutionally sponsored loans, health care benefits, tuition waivers (full and partial), and unspecified assistantships also available. Financial award applicants required to submit FAFSA. *Faculty research:* Computer-aided design, thermal and fluid sciences materials engineering, fluid mechanics, combustion and microsystems engineering. *Total annual research expenditures:* $2.2 million. *Unit head:* Dr. Dimitris Nikitopoulos, Chair, 225-578-5900, E-mail: medimi@egateway.lsu.edu. *Application contact:* Dr. Eyassu Woldesenbet, Graduate Adviser, 225-578-5900, Fax: 225-578-5924, E-mail: woldesen@me.lsu.edu. Web site: http://me.lsu.edu/.

Louisiana Tech University, Graduate School, College of Engineering and Science, Department of Mechanical Engineering, Ruston, LA 71272. Offers MS, PhD. Part-time programs available. Terminal master's awarded for partial completion of doctoral program. *Degree requirements:* For master's, thesis; for doctorate, thesis/dissertation. *Entrance requirements:* For master's, GRE General Test, minimum GPA of 3.0 in last 60 hours; for doctorate, minimum graduate GPA of 3.25 (with MS) or GRE General Test. Additional exam requirements/recommendations for international students: Required—TOEFL. *Faculty research:* Engineering management, facilities planning, thermodynamics, automated manufacturing, micromanufacturing.

Loyola Marymount University, College of Science and Engineering, Department of Mechanical Engineering, Program in Mechanical Engineering, Los Angeles, CA 90045-2659. Offers MSE. *Faculty:* 6 full-time (0 women), 1 part-time/adjunct (0 women). *Students:* 10 full-time (4 women), 2 part-time (0 women); includes 5 minority (2 Asian, non-Hispanic/Latino; 3 Hispanic/Latino), 1 international. Average age 29. 5 applicants, 100% accepted, 4 enrolled. In 2011, 6 master's awarded. *Degree requirements:* For master's, thesis or alternative. *Entrance requirements:* For master's, letters of recommendation, personal statement. Additional exam requirements/recommendations for international students: Required—TOEFL (minimum score 550 paper-based; 213 computer-based; 80 iBT). *Application deadline:* Applications are processed on a rolling basis. Application fee: $50. Electronic applications accepted. *Financial support:* In 2011–12, 6 students received support. Federal Work-Study, scholarships/grants, and laboratory assistantships available. Support available to part-time students. Financial award application deadline: 6/1; financial award applicants required to submit FAFSA. *Total annual research expenditures:* $2 million. *Unit head:* Dr. Matthew T. Siniawski, Graduate Director, 310-338-5849, E-mail: matthew.siniawski@lmu.edu. *Application contact:* Chake H. Kouyoumjian, Associate Dean of the Graduate Division, 310-338-2721, E-mail: ckouyoum@lmu.edu. Web site: http://cse.lmu.edu/departments/mechanicalengineering/Graduate_Program.htm.

Manhattan College, Graduate Division, School of Engineering, Program in Mechanical Engineering, Riverdale, NY 10471. Offers MS. Part-time and evening/weekend programs available. *Faculty:* 8 full-time (1 woman), 3 part-time/adjunct (0 women). *Students:* 8 full-time (2 women), 16 part-time (1 woman); includes 4 minority (2 Black or African American, non-Hispanic/Latino; 2 Hispanic/Latino). Average age 26. 24 applicants, 100% accepted, 18 enrolled. In 2011, 7 master's awarded. *Degree requirements:* For master's, thesis optional. *Entrance requirements:* For master's, GRE (recommended), minimum GPA of 3.0. Additional exam requirements/recommendations for international students: Required—TOEFL (minimum score 550 paper-based; 213 computer-based; 80 iBT), IELTS (minimum score 6). *Application deadline:* For fall admission, 8/10 priority date for domestic students, 8/10 for international students; for spring admission, 1/7 for domestic and international students. Applications are processed on a rolling basis. Application fee: $50. *Expenses: Tuition:* Full-time $14,850; part-time $825 per credit. *Required fees:* $390; $150. *Financial support:* In 2011–12, 8 students received support, including 8 teaching assistantships with partial tuition reimbursements available (averaging $4,000 per year); unspecified assistantships also available. Financial award application deadline: 2/1. *Faculty research:* Thermal analysis of rocket thrust chambers, quality of wood, biomechanics/structural analysis of cacti, orthodontic research. *Unit head:* Dr. Bahman Litkouhi, Director, Graduate Program, 718-862-7927, Fax: 718-862-7163, E-mail: mechdept@manhattan.edu. *Application contact:* Kathy Balaj, Information Contact, 718-862-7145, Fax: 718-862-7163, E-mail: kathy.balaj@manhattan.edu. Web site: http://www.engineering.manhattan.edu.

Marquette University, Graduate School, College of Engineering, Department of Mechanical Engineering, Milwaukee, WI 53201-1881. Offers engineering innovation (Certificate); engineering management (MSEM); mechanical engineering (MS, PhD); new product and process development (Certificate). Part-time and evening/weekend programs available. *Faculty:* 16 full-time (1 woman), 2 part-time/adjunct (0 women). *Students:* 21 full-time (3 women), 35 part-time (5 women); includes 4 minority (1 Asian, non-Hispanic/Latino; 3 Hispanic/Latino), 18 international. Average age 29. 66 applicants, 56% accepted, 13 enrolled. In 2011, 19 master's, 2 doctorates, 2 other advanced degrees awarded. Terminal master's awarded for partial completion of doctoral program. *Degree requirements:* For master's, comprehensive exam, thesis (for some programs); for doctorate, comprehensive exam, thesis/dissertation, qualifying exam. *Entrance requirements:* For master's, GRE General Test, minimum GPA of 3.0, official transcripts from all current and previous colleges/universities except Marquette, three letters of recommendation; for doctorate, GRE General Test, minimum GPA of 3.0, official transcripts from all current and previous colleges/universities except Marquette, three letters of recommendation, statement of purpose, copies of any published work. Additional exam requirements/recommendations for international students: Required—TOEFL (minimum score 530 paper-based; 78 computer-based). *Application deadline:* For fall admission, 8/1 priority date for domestic students; for spring admission, 1/1 priority date for domestic students. Applications are processed on a rolling basis. Application fee: $50. Electronic applications accepted. *Expenses: Tuition:* Full-time $17,010; part-time $945 per credit hour. Tuition and fees vary according to program. *Financial support:* In 2011–12, 12 students received support, including 1 research assistantship with full tuition reimbursement available (averaging $13,745 per year), 9 teaching assistantships with full tuition reimbursements available (averaging $13,867 per year); fellowships, scholarships/grants, tuition waivers (partial), and unspecified assistantships also available. Support available to part-time students. Financial award application deadline: 2/15. *Faculty research:* Computer-integrated manufacturing, energy conversion, simulation modeling and optimization, applied mechanics, metallurgy. *Total annual research expenditures:* $595,179. *Unit head:* Dr. Kyle Kim, Chair, 414-288-7259, Fax: 414-288-7790, E-mail: kyle.kim@marquette.edu. *Application contact:* Dr. James Rice, Director of Graduate Studies, 414-288-5405, Fax: 414-288-

7790, E-mail: nicholas.nigro@marquette.edu. Web site: http://www.marquette.edu/engineering/mechanical/grad.shtml.

Massachusetts Institute of Technology, School of Engineering, Department of Mechanical Engineering, Cambridge, MA 02139. Offers manufacturing (M Eng); mechanical engineering (SM, PhD, Sc D, Mech E); naval architecture and marine engineering (SM, PhD, Sc D); naval engineering (Naval E); ocean engineering (SM, PhD, Sc D), including); oceanographic engineering (SM, PhD, Sc D); SM/MBA. *Faculty:* 68 full-time (8 women). *Students:* 540 full-time (111 women), 1 part-time (0 women); includes 98 minority (9 Black or African American, non-Hispanic/Latino; 1 American Indian or Alaska Native, non-Hispanic/Latino; 52 Asian, non-Hispanic/Latino; 29 Hispanic/Latino; 7 Two or more races, non-Hispanic/Latino), 220 international. Average age 26. 881 applicants, 27% accepted, 142 enrolled. In 2011, 123 master's, 56 doctorates, 11 other advanced degrees awarded. Terminal master's awarded for partial completion of doctoral program. *Degree requirements:* For master's and other advanced degree, thesis; for doctorate, comprehensive exam, thesis/dissertation. *Entrance requirements:* For master's, doctorate, and other advanced degree, GRE General Test. Additional exam requirements/recommendations for international students: Required—IELTS (minimum score 7). *Application deadline:* For fall admission, 12/15 for domestic and international students. Application fee: $75. Electronic applications accepted. *Expenses:* Tuition: Full-time $40,460; part-time $630 per credit hour. *Required fees:* $272. *Financial support:* In 2011–12, 447 students received support, including 95 fellowships (averaging $30,800 per year), 318 research assistantships (averaging $29,200 per year), 45 teaching assistantships (averaging $33,000 per year); career-related internships or fieldwork, Federal Work-Study, institutionally sponsored loans, scholarships/grants, health care benefits, and unspecified assistantships also available. *Faculty research:* Mechanics: modeling, experimentation and computation; design, manufacturing, and product development; controls, instrumentation, and robotics; energy science and engineering; ocean science and engineering; bioengineering; micro and nano engineering. *Total annual research expenditures:* $50.9 million. *Unit head:* Prof. Mary C. Boyce, Head, 617-253-2201, Fax: 617-258-6156, E-mail: mehq@mit.edu. *Application contact:* Graduate Office, 617-253-2291, Fax: 617-258-5802, E-mail: megradoffice@mit.edu. Web site: http://meche.mit.edu.

McGill University, Faculty of Graduate and Postdoctoral Studies, Faculty of Engineering, Department of Mechanical Engineering, Montréal, QC H3A 2T5, Canada. Offers aerospace (M Eng); manufacturing management (MMM); mechanical engineering (M Eng, M Sc, PhD).

McMaster University, School of Graduate Studies, Faculty of Engineering, Department of Mechanical Engineering, Hamilton, ON L8S 4M2, Canada. Offers M Eng, MA Sc, PhD. M Eng degree offered as part of the Advanced Design and Manufacturing Institute (ADMI) group collaboration with the University of Toronto, University of Western Ontario, and University of Waterloo. *Degree requirements:* For master's, thesis; for doctorate, comprehensive exam, thesis/dissertation. *Entrance requirements:* Additional exam requirements/recommendations for international students: Required—TOEFL (minimum score 550 paper-based; 213 computer-based). *Faculty research:* Manufacturing engineering, dimensional metrology, micro-fluidics, multi-phase flow and heat transfer, process modeling simulation.

McNeese State University, Doré School of Graduate Studies, College of Engineering and Engineering Technology, Lake Charles, LA 70609. Offers chemical engineering (M Eng); civil engineering (M Eng); electrical engineering (M Eng); engineering management (M Eng); mechanical engineering (M Eng); pump reliability engineering (Postbaccalaureate Certificate). Part-time and evening/weekend programs available. *Faculty:* 13 full-time (1 woman). *Students:* 21 full-time (4 women), 18 part-time (5 women); includes 5 minority (4 Black or African American, non-Hispanic/Latino; 1 American Indian or Alaska Native, non-Hispanic/Latino), 23 international. In 2011, 28 master's awarded. *Degree requirements:* For master's, thesis or alternative. *Entrance requirements:* For master's, GRE, minimum undergraduate GPA of 3.0. Additional exam requirements/recommendations for international students: Required—TOEFL (minimum score 560 paper-based; 220 computer-based; 83 iBT). *Application deadline:* For fall admission, 5/15 priority date for domestic students, 5/15 for international students; for spring admission, 10/15 priority date for domestic students, 10/15 for international students. Applications are processed on a rolling basis. Application fee: $20 ($30 for international students). *Expenses:* Tuition, state resident: part-time $519 per credit hour. Tuition and fees vary according to course load. *Financial support:* Federal Work-Study available. Support available to part-time students. Financial award application deadline: 5/1. *Unit head:* Dr. Nikos Kiritsis, Dean, 337-475-5875, Fax: 337-475-5237, E-mail: nikosk@mcneese.edu. *Application contact:* Dr. George F. Mead, Jr., Interim Dean of Dore' School of Graduate Studies, 337-475-5396, Fax: 337-475-5397, E-mail: admissions@mcneese.edu.

Memorial University of Newfoundland, School of Graduate Studies, Faculty of Engineering and Applied Science, St. John's, NL A1C 5S7, Canada. Offers civil engineering (M Eng, PhD); electrical and computer engineering (M Eng, PhD); mechanical engineering (M Eng, PhD); ocean and naval architecture engineering (M Eng, PhD). Part-time programs available. *Degree requirements:* For master's, thesis; for doctorate, comprehensive exam, thesis/dissertation, oral thesis defense. *Entrance requirements:* For master's, 2nd class degree; for doctorate, master's degree in engineering. Electronic applications accepted. *Faculty research:* Engineering analysis, environmental and hydrotechnical studies, manufacturing and robotics, mechanics, structures and materials.

Mercer University, Graduate Studies, Macon Campus, School of Engineering, Macon, GA 31207-0003. Offers biomedical engineering (MSE); computer engineering (MSE); electrical engineering (MSE); engineering management (MSE); environmental engineering (MSE); environmental systems (MS); mechanical engineering (MSE); software engineering (MSE); software systems (MS); technical communications management (MS); technical management (MS). Part-time and evening/weekend programs available. Postbaccalaureate distance learning degree programs offered (no on-campus study). *Faculty:* 17 full-time (3 women), 1 part-time/adjunct (0 women). *Students:* 12 full-time (3 women), 113 part-time (28 women); includes 23 minority (13 Black or African American, non-Hispanic/Latino; 9 Asian, non-Hispanic/Latino; 1 Hispanic/Latino). Average age 31. In 2011, 44 master's awarded. *Degree requirements:* For master's, thesis or alternative. *Entrance requirements:* For master's, minimum undergraduate GPA of 3.0. Additional exam requirements/recommendations for international students: Required—TOEFL. *Application deadline:* For fall admission, 7/1 for domestic students; for spring admission, 11/15 for domestic students. Applications are processed on a rolling basis. Application fee: $35 ($50 for international students). Electronic applications accepted. *Expenses:* Contact institution. *Financial support:* Federal Work-Study available. *Unit head:* Dr. Wade H. Shaw, Dean, 478-301-2459, Fax: 478-301-5593, E-mail: shaw_wh@mercer.edu. *Application contact:* Greg Lofton, Graduate Program Coordinator, 478-301-5480, Fax: 478-301-5434, E-mail: lofton_g@mercer.edu. Web site: http://engineering.mercer.edu/.

Michigan State University, The Graduate School, College of Engineering, Department of Mechanical Engineering, East Lansing, MI 48824. Offers engineering mechanics (MS, PhD); mechanical engineering (MS, PhD). *Entrance requirements:* For master's, GRE General Test. Additional exam requirements/recommendations for international students: Required—TOEFL. Electronic applications accepted.

Michigan Technological University, Graduate School, College of Engineering, Department of Mechanical Engineering-Engineering Mechanics, Houghton, MI 49931. Offers engineering mechanics (MS); hybrid electric drive vehicle engineering (Graduate Certificate); mechanical engineering (MS, PhD). Part-time programs available. Postbaccalaureate distance learning degree programs offered (minimal on-campus study). *Faculty:* 55 full-time (6 women), 21 part-time/adjunct (1 woman). *Students:* 246 full-time (18 women), 57 part-time (9 women); includes 10 minority (2 Black or African American, non-Hispanic/Latino; 2 Asian, non-Hispanic/Latino; 6 Hispanic/Latino), 203 international. Average age 26. 567 applicants, 64% accepted, 109 enrolled. In 2011, 78 master's, 12 doctorates, 1 other advanced degree awarded. Terminal master's awarded for partial completion of doctoral program. *Degree requirements:* For master's, comprehensive exam (for some programs), thesis (for some programs); for doctorate, comprehensive exam, thesis/dissertation. *Entrance requirements:* For master's, GRE, statement of purpose, official transcripts, 3 letters of recommendation; for doctorate, GRE, MS (preferred), statement of purpose, official transcripts, 3 letters of recommendation. Additional exam requirements/recommendations for international students: Required—TOEFL (minimum score 79 iBT) or IELTS. *Application deadline:* Applications are processed on a rolling basis. Electronic applications accepted. *Expenses:* Contact institution. *Financial support:* In 2011–12, 202 students received support, including 4 fellowships with full tuition reimbursements available (averaging $6,065 per year), 55 research assistantships with full tuition reimbursements available (averaging $6,065 per year), 24 teaching assistantships with full tuition reimbursements available (averaging $6,065 per year); career-related internships or fieldwork, Federal Work-Study, scholarships/grants, health care benefits, tuition waivers (partial), unspecified assistantships, and cooperative program also available. Financial award applicants required to submit FAFSA. *Faculty research:* Design and dynamic systems, energy-thermofluids, manufacturing, solid mechanics, sustainability. *Total annual research expenditures:* $4.3 million. *Unit head:* Dr. William W. Predebon, Chair, 906-487-2551, Fax: 906-487-2822, E-mail: wwpredeb@mtu.edu. *Application contact:* JoAnne Stimac, Senior Staff Assistant, 906-487-2327, Fax: 906-487-2463, E-mail: jstimac@mtu.edu. Web site: http://www.mtu.edu/mechanical/.

Mississippi State University, Bagley College of Engineering, Department of Mechanical Engineering, Mississippi State, MS 39762. Offers engineering (PhD), including mechanical engineering; mechanical engineering (MS). Part-time programs available. Postbaccalaureate distance learning degree programs offered (minimal on-campus study). *Faculty:* 21 full-time (2 women), 1 part-time/adjunct (0 women). *Students:* 74 full-time (12 women), 9 part-time (2 women); includes 11 minority (8 Black or African American, non-Hispanic/Latino; 1 Asian, non-Hispanic/Latino; 2 Hispanic/Latino), 22 international. Average age 26. 136 applicants, 24% accepted, 24 enrolled. In 2011, 10 master's, 6 doctorates awarded. *Degree requirements:* For master's, thesis optional, oral exam; for doctorate, thesis/dissertation, qualifying exam, preliminary exam, dissertation defense. *Entrance requirements:* For master's and doctorate, GRE General Test, minimum GPA of 2.75. Additional exam requirements/recommendations for international students: Required—TOEFL (minimum score 550 paper-based; 213 computer-based; 79 iBT); Recommended—IELTS (minimum score 6.5). *Application deadline:* For fall admission, 7/1 for domestic students, 5/1 for international students; for spring admission, 11/1 for domestic students, 9/1 for international students. Applications are processed on a rolling basis. Application fee: $40. Electronic applications accepted. *Expenses:* Tuition, state resident: full-time $5805; part-time $322.50 per credit hour. Tuition, nonresident: full-time $14,670; part-time $815 per credit hour. *Financial support:* In 2011–12, 29 research assistantships with full tuition reimbursements (averaging $14,504 per year), 1 teaching assistantship with full tuition reimbursement (averaging $13,500 per year) were awarded; career-related internships or fieldwork, Federal Work-Study, institutionally sponsored loans, scholarships/grants, and unspecified assistantships also available. Financial award application deadline: 4/1; financial award applicants required to submit FAFSA. *Faculty research:* Fatigue and fracture, heat transfer, fluid dynamics, manufacturing systems, materials. *Total annual research expenditures:* $13 million. *Unit head:* Dr. Steve Daniewicz, Professor/Head/Graduate Coordinator, 662-325-7322, Fax: 662-325-7223, E-mail: daniewicz@me.msstate.edu. Web site: http://www.me.msstate.edu/.

Missouri University of Science and Technology, Graduate School, Department of Mechanical and Aerospace Engineering, Rolla, MO 65409. Offers aerospace engineering (MS, PhD); mechanical engineering (MS, DE, PhD). Part-time and evening/weekend programs available. Terminal master's awarded for partial completion of doctoral program. *Degree requirements:* For master's, thesis optional; for doctorate, comprehensive exam, thesis/dissertation. *Entrance requirements:* For master's, GRE General Test (minimum score 1100 verbal and quantitative, writing 3.5), minimum GPA of 3.0; for doctorate, GRE General Test (minimum score: verbal and quantitative 1100, writing 3.5), minimum GPA of 3.5. Additional exam requirements/recommendations for international students: Required—TOEFL. Electronic applications accepted. *Faculty research:* Dynamics and controls, acoustics, computational fluid dynamics, space mechanics, hypersonics.

Montana State University, College of Graduate Studies, College of Engineering, Department of Mechanical and Industrial Engineering, Bozeman, MT 59717. Offers engineering (PhD), including industrial engineering, mechanical engineering; industrial and management engineering (MS); mechanical engineering (MS). Part-time programs available. *Degree requirements:* For master's, comprehensive exam, thesis, oral exams; for doctorate, comprehensive exam, thesis/dissertation, qualifying exam. *Entrance requirements:* For master's, GRE, official transcript, minimum GPA of 3.0, demonstrated potential for success, statement of goals, three letters of recommendation, proof of funds affidavit; for doctorate, minimum undergraduate GPA of 3.0, 3.2 graduate; three letters of recommendation; statement of objectives. Additional exam requirements/recommendations for international students: Required—TOEFL or IELTS. Electronic applications accepted. *Faculty research:* Human factors engineering, energy, design and manufacture, systems modeling, materials and structures, measurement systems.

Naval Postgraduate School, Departments and Academic Groups, Department of Mechanical and Aerospace Engineering, Monterey, CA 93943. Offers astronautical engineer (AstE); astronautical engineering (MS); engineering science (MS), including astronautical engineering, mechanical engineering; mechanical and aerospace engineering (PhD); mechanical engineering (MS). Program only open to commissioned officers of the United States and friendly nations and selected United States federal civilian employees. *Accreditation:* ABET (one or more programs are accredited). Part-time programs available. Postbaccalaureate distance learning degree programs offered. *Faculty:* 30 full-time (3 women), 2 part-time/adjunct (1 woman). *Students:* 81 full-time (10 women), 88 part-time (3 women); includes 16 minority (5 Black or African American, non-Hispanic/Latino; 1 American Indian or Alaska Native, non-Hispanic/Latino; 3 Asian, non-Hispanic/Latino; 7 Hispanic/Latino), 14 international. Average age 35. In 2011, 29 master's, 7 other advanced degrees awarded. *Degree requirements:* For master's, thesis (for some programs), capstone or research/dissertation paper (for some programs); for doctorate, thesis/dissertation; for AstE, thesis. *Faculty research:* Sensors and actuators, new materials and methods, mechanics of materials, laser and material interaction, energy harvesting and storage. *Total annual research expenditures:* $8.2 million. *Unit head:* Prof. Knox Millsaps, Department Chairman, 831-656-3382, E-mail: millsaps@nps.edu. Web site: http://www.nps.edu/Academics/GSEAS/MAE/Index.asp.

Naval Postgraduate School, Departments and Academic Groups, Space Systems Academic Group, Monterey, CA 93943. Offers applied physics (MS); astronautical engineering (MS); computer science (MS); electrical engineering (MS); mechanical engineering (MS); space systems (Engr); space systems operations (MS). Program only open to commissioned officers of the United States and friendly nations and selected United States federal civilian employees. Part-time programs available. *Faculty:* 5 full-time, 5 part-time/adjunct (2 women). *Students:* 37 full-time (2 women), 14 part-time; includes 11 minority (5 Black or African American, non-Hispanic/Latino; 2 Asian, non-Hispanic/Latino; 4 Hispanic/Latino), 1 international. Average age 33. In 2011, 20 master's awarded. *Degree requirements:* For master's and Engr, thesis; for doctorate, thesis/dissertation. *Faculty research:* Militaryapplications for space; space reconnaissance and remote sensing; radiation-hardened electronics for space; design, construction and operations of small satellites; satellite communications systems. *Total annual research expenditures:* $2 million. *Unit head:* Dr. Rudy Panholzer, Chairman, 831-656-2154. Web site: http://www.nps.edu/Academics/Schools/GSEAS/Departments/SpaceSystems/.

Naval Postgraduate School, Departments and Academic Groups, Undersea Warfare Academic Group, Monterey, CA 93943. Offers applied mathematics (MS); applied physics (MS); applied science (MS), including acoustics, operations research, physical oceanography, signal processing; electrical engineering (MS); engineering acoustics (MS, PhD); engineering science (MS), including electrical engineering, mechanical engineering; mechanical engineer (ME); mechanical engineering (MS, MSME); meteorology (MS); operations research (MS); physical oceanography (MS). Program only open to commissioned officers of the United States and friendly nations and selected United States federal civilian employees. Part-time programs available. *Students:* 2 full-time, both international. Average age 36. *Degree requirements:* For master's, thesis. *Faculty research:* Unmanned/autonomous vehicles, sea mines and countermeasures, submarine warfare in the twentieth and twenty-first centuries. *Unit head:* Dr. Clyde Scandrett, Academic Group Chairman, 831-656-2027. Web site: http://www.nps.edu/Academics/Schools/GSEAS/Departments/USW/USW-Index.html.

New Jersey Institute of Technology, Office of Graduate Studies, Newark College of Engineering, Department of Mechanical Engineering, Program in Mechanical Engineering, Newark, NJ 07102. Offers MS, PhD. *Students:* 64 full-time (3 women), 35 part-time (2 women); includes 27 minority (3 Black or African American, non-Hispanic/Latino; 13 Asian, non-Hispanic/Latino; 11 Hispanic/Latino), 49 international. Average age 27. 268 applicants, 64% accepted, 40 enrolled. In 2011, 42 master's, 2 doctorates awarded. *Entrance requirements:* For doctorate, GRE General Test, minimum graduate GPA of 3.5. Additional exam requirements/recommendations for international students: Required—TOEFL (minimum score 550 paper-based; 213 computer-based; 79 iBT). *Application deadline:* For fall admission, 6/1 priority date for domestic students, 5/1 for international students; for spring admission, 11/15 priority date for domestic students, 11/15 for international students. Applications are processed on a rolling basis. Application fee: $65. Electronic applications accepted. *Expenses:* Tuition, state resident: full-time $7980; part-time $867 per credit. Tuition, nonresident: full-time $11,336; part-time $1196 per credit. *Required fees:* $230 per credit. *Financial support:* Application deadline: 1/15. *Unit head:* Dr. Rajpal S. Sodhi, Interim Chair, 973-596-3333, E-mail: rajpal.s.sodhi@njit.edu. *Application contact:* Kathryn Kelly, Director of Admissions, 973-596-3300, Fax: 973-596-3461, E-mail: admissions@njit.edu.

New Mexico Institute of Mining and Technology, Graduate Studies, Program in Engineering Science in Mechanics, Socorro, NM 87801. Offers explosives engineering (MS); fluid and thermal sciences (MS); mechatronics systems engineering (MS); solid mechanics (MS). *Faculty:* 5 full-time (0 women). *Students:* 26 full-time (1 woman), 19 part-time (1 woman); includes 13 minority (1 American Indian or Alaska Native, non-Hispanic/Latino; 1 Asian, non-Hispanic/Latino; 11 Hispanic/Latino). Average age 27. 21 applicants, 67% accepted, 11 enrolled. In 2011, 6 master's awarded. *Degree requirements:* For master's, thesis (for some programs). *Entrance requirements:* For master's, GRE General Test. Additional exam requirements/recommendations for international students: Required—TOEFL (minimum score 540 paper-based; 207 computer-based). *Application deadline:* For fall admission, 3/1 priority date for domestic students; for spring admission, 6/1 for domestic students. Applications are processed on a rolling basis. Application fee: $16 ($30 for international students). *Expenses:* Tuition, state resident: full-time $4849; part-time $269.41 per credit hour. Tuition, nonresident: full-time $16,041; part-time $891.15 per credit hour. *Required fees:* $622; $65 per credit hour. $20 per semester. Part-time tuition and fees vary according to course load. *Financial support:* In 2011–12, 9 research assistantships (averaging $18,997 per year), 5 teaching assistantships with full and partial tuition reimbursements (averaging $14,615 per year) were awarded; fellowships, Federal Work-Study, institutionally sponsored loans, and unspecified assistantships also available. Financial award application deadline: 3/1; financial award applicants required to submit CSS PROFILE or FAFSA. *Faculty research:* Vibrations, fluid-structure interactions. *Unit head:* Dr. Warren Ostergren, Chair, 575-835-5693, E-mail: warreno@nmt.edu. *Application contact:* Dr. Lorie Liebrock, Dean of Graduate Studies, 575-835-5513, Fax: 575-835-5476, E-mail: graduate@nmt.edu. Web site: http://infohost.nmt.edu/~mecheng/grad_programs.xml.

New Mexico State University, Graduate School, College of Engineering, Department of Mechanical Engineering, Las Cruces, NM 88003-8001. Offers MSME, PhD. Postbaccalaureate distance learning degree programs offered (no on-campus study). *Faculty:* 17 full-time (1 woman), 1 part-time/adjunct (0 women). *Students:* 47 full-time (5 women), 6 part-time (1 woman); includes 12 minority (all Hispanic/Latino), 25 international. Average age 28. 33 applicants, 67% accepted, 7 enrolled. In 2011, 13 master's, 4 doctorates awarded. *Degree requirements:* For master's, thesis (for some programs); for doctorate, thesis/dissertation, 2 research tools. *Entrance requirements:* For master's, minimum GPA of 3.0; for doctorate, qualifying exam, minimum GPA of 3.0. Additional exam requirements/recommendations for international students: Required—TOEFL (minimum score 550 paper-based; 79 iBT), IELTS (minimum score 6.5). *Application deadline:* For fall admission, 7/1 priority date for domestic students; for spring admission, 11/1 for domestic students. Applications are processed on a rolling basis. Application fee: $40 ($50 for international students). Electronic applications accepted. *Expenses:* Tuition, state resident: full-time $5004; part-time $208.50 per credit. Tuition, nonresident: full-time $17,446; part-time $726.90 per credit. *Financial support:* In 2011–12, 4 fellowships with partial tuition reimbursements (averaging $2,866 per year), 18 research assistantships with partial tuition reimbursements

(averaging $19,871 per year), 17 teaching assistantships with partial tuition reimbursements (averaging $19,959 per year) were awarded; career-related internships or fieldwork, Federal Work-Study, scholarships/grants, and health care benefits also available. Support available to part-time students. Financial award application deadline: 3/1. *Faculty research:* Computational mechanics; robotics; CAD/CAM; control, dynamics, and solid mechanics; interconnection engineering; heat transfer; composites. *Unit head:* Dr. Thomas Burton, Head, 575-646-3501, Fax: 575-646-6111, E-mail: tdburton@nmsu.edu. *Application contact:* Coordinator, 575-646-2736, Fax: 575-646-7721, E-mail: gradinfo@nmsu.edu. Web site: http://mae.nmsu.edu/.

North Carolina Agricultural and Technical State University, School of Graduate Studies, College of Engineering, Department of Mechanical Engineering, Greensboro, NC 27411. Offers MSME, PhD. Part-time programs available. *Degree requirements:* For master's, thesis, qualifying exam, thesis defense; for doctorate, thesis/dissertation. *Entrance requirements:* For master's, BS in mechanical engineering from accredited institution with minimum overall GPA of 3.0; for doctorate, GRE, MS in mechanical engineering or closely-related field with minimum GPA of 3.3. *Faculty research:* Composites, smart materials and sensors, mechanical systems modeling and finite element analysis, computational fluid dynamics and engine research, design and manufacturing.

North Carolina State University, Graduate School, College of Engineering, Department of Mechanical and Aerospace Engineering, Program in Mechanical Engineering, Raleigh, NC 27695. Offers MS, PhD. Part-time programs available. Postbaccalaureate distance learning degree programs offered (no on-campus study). *Degree requirements:* For master's, thesis optional, oral exam; for doctorate, thesis/dissertation, oral and preliminary exams. *Entrance requirements:* For master's and doctorate, GRE General Test. Additional exam requirements/recommendations for international students: Required—TOEFL (minimum score 550 paper-based; 213 computer-based). Electronic applications accepted. *Faculty research:* Vibration and control, fluid dynamics, thermal sciences, structures and materials, aerodynamics acoustics.

North Dakota State University, College of Graduate and Interdisciplinary Studies, College of Engineering and Architecture, Department of Mechanical Engineering and Applied Mechanics, Fargo, ND 58108. Offers MS, PhD. Part-time programs available. *Faculty:* 16 full-time (3 women). *Students:* 30 full-time (7 women), 19 part-time (1 woman); includes 2 minority (both Asian, non-Hispanic/Latino), 27 international. Average age 28. 36 applicants, 56% accepted, 4 enrolled. In 2011, 7 master's, 1 doctorate awarded. *Degree requirements:* For master's, thesis; for doctorate, comprehensive exam, thesis/dissertation. *Entrance requirements:* For master's and doctorate, minimum GPA of 3.0. Additional exam requirements/recommendations for international students: Required—TOEFL (minimum score 550 paper-based). *Application deadline:* For fall admission, 2/15 priority date for domestic students; for spring admission, 9/15 priority date for domestic students. Applications are processed on a rolling basis. Application fee: $35. Electronic applications accepted. *Financial support:* In 2011–12, 20 students received support, including research assistantships with full tuition reimbursements available (averaging $9,000 per year), teaching assistantships with full tuition reimbursements available (averaging $9,000 per year); career-related internships or fieldwork, Federal Work-Study, and institutionally sponsored loans also available. Financial award application deadline: 2/15. *Faculty research:* Thermodynamics, finite element analysis, automotive systems, robotics, nanotechnology. *Unit head:* Dr. Alan Kallmeyer, Chair, 701-231-8836, Fax: 701-231-8913, E-mail: alan.kallmeyer@ndsu.edu. *Application contact:* Dr. Ghodrat Karami, Graduate Coordinator, 701-231-8671, Fax: 701-231-8913, E-mail: g.karami@ndsu.edu. Web site: http://www.ndsu.nodak.edu/me/.

Northeastern University, College of Engineering, Department of Mechanical, Industrial, and Manufacturing Engineering, Boston, MA 02115-5096. Offers engineering management (MS); industrial engineering (MS, PhD); mechanical engineering (MS, PhD); operations research (MS). Part-time programs available. *Faculty:* 34 full-time, 7 part-time/adjunct. *Students:* 297 full-time (70 women), 103 part-time (20 women). 616 applicants, 77% accepted, 140 enrolled. In 2011, 107 master's, 5 doctorates awarded. *Degree requirements:* For master's, thesis (for some programs); for doctorate, thesis/dissertation, departmental qualifying exam. *Entrance requirements:* For master's and doctorate, GRE General Test. Additional exam requirements/recommendations for international students: Required—TOEFL (minimum score 550 paper-based; 213 computer-based; 80 iBT). *Application deadline:* For fall admission, 1/15 priority date for domestic students, 1/15 for international students; for spring admission, 11/1 priority date for domestic students. Applications are processed on a rolling basis. Application fee: $50. Electronic applications accepted. *Financial support:* In 2011–12, 79 students received support, including 50 research assistantships with full tuition reimbursements available (averaging $18,325 per year), 33 teaching assistantships with full tuition reimbursements available (averaging $18,325 per year); fellowships with full tuition reimbursements available, career-related internships or fieldwork, Federal Work-Study, scholarships/grants, health care benefits, and unspecified assistantships also available. Support available to part-time students. Financial award application deadline: 1/15; financial award applicants required to submit FAFSA. *Faculty research:* Dry sliding instabilities, droplet deposition, combustion, manufacturing systems, nano-manufacturing, advanced materials processing, bio-nano robotics, burning speed measurement, virtual environments. *Unit head:* Dr. Hameed Metghalchi, Chairman, 617-373-2973, Fax: 617-373-2921. *Application contact:* Jeffery Hengel, Admissions Specialist, 617-373-2711, Fax: 617-373-2501, E-mail: grad-eng@coe.neu.edu.

Northern Arizona University, Graduate College, College of Engineering, Forestry and Natural Sciences, Programs in Engineering, Flagstaff , AZ 86011. Offers civil and environmental engineering (M Eng); civil engineering (MSE); computer science (MSE); electrical engineering (M Eng, MSE); engineering (M Eng, MSE); environmental engineering (M Eng, MSE); mechanical engineering (M Eng, MSE). Part-time programs available. Postbaccalaureate distance learning degree programs offered (no on-campus study). *Faculty:* 42 full-time (10 women). *Students:* 15 full-time (1 woman), 12 part-time (1 woman); includes 2 minority (both Hispanic/Latino), 6 international. Average age 28. 29 applicants, 52% accepted, 8 enrolled. In 2011, 15 degrees awarded. *Degree requirements:* For master's, thesis. *Entrance requirements:* For master's, GRE General Test. Additional exam requirements/recommendations for international students: Required—TOEFL (minimum score 550 paper-based; 213 computer-based; 80 iBT), IELTS (minimum score 7). *Application deadline:* For fall admission, 3/1 priority date for domestic students, 3/1 for international students; for spring admission, 9/15 priority date for domestic students, 9/15 for international students. Applications are processed on a rolling basis. Application fee: $65. Electronic applications accepted. *Expenses:* Tuition, state resident: full-time $7190; part-time $355 per credit hour. Tuition, nonresident: full-time $18,092; part-time $1005 per credit hour. *Required fees:* $818; $328 per semester. *Financial support:* In 2011–12, 3 research assistantships with partial tuition reimbursements (averaging $14,541 per year), 12 teaching assistantships with partial tuition reimbursements (averaging $12,863 per year) were awarded; career-related internships or fieldwork, Federal Work-Study, scholarships/grants, health care benefits, and unspecified assistantships also available. Financial award applicants required to submit FAFSA. *Unit head:* Dr. Ernesto Penado, Chair, 928-523-9453, Fax: 928-523-2300, E-mail: ernesto.penado@nau.edu. *Application contact:* Natasha Kypfer, Program Coordinator, 928-523-1447, Fax: 928-523-2300, E-mail: egrmasters@nau.edu. Web site: http://nau.edu/CEFNS/Engineering/.

Northern Illinois University, Graduate School, College of Engineering and Engineering Technology, Department of Mechanical Engineering, De Kalb, IL 60115-2854. Offers MS. Part-time programs available. *Faculty:* 9 full-time (0 women). *Students:* 19 full-time (0 women), 32 part-time (4 women); includes 4 minority (2 Hispanic/Latino; 2 Two or more races, non-Hispanic/Latino), 36 international. Average age 24. 64 applicants, 53% accepted, 15 enrolled. In 2011, 30 master's awarded. *Degree requirements:* For master's, comprehensive exam, thesis optional. *Entrance requirements:* For master's, GRE General Test, minimum GPA of 2.75. Additional exam requirements/recommendations for international students: Required—TOEFL (minimum score 550 paper-based; 213 computer-based). *Application deadline:* For fall admission, 6/1 for domestic students, 5/1 for international students; for spring admission, 11/1 for domestic students, 10/1 for international students. Applications are processed on a rolling basis. Application fee: $40. Electronic applications accepted. *Financial support:* In 2011–12, 8 research assistantships with full tuition reimbursements, 17 teaching assistantships with full tuition reimbursements were awarded; fellowships with full tuition reimbursements, Federal Work-Study, scholarships/grants, tuition waivers (full), and staff assistantships also available. Support available to part-time students. Financial award applicants required to submit FAFSA. *Faculty research:* Robotics, nonlinear dynamic systems, piezo mechanics, quartz resonators, sheet metal forming. *Unit head:* Dr. Simon Song, Chair, 815-753-9970, Fax: 815-753-0416, E-mail: smsong@ceet.niu.edu. *Application contact:* Graduate School Office, 815-753-0395, E-mail: gradsch@niu.edu. Web site: http://www.ceet.niu.edu/depts/me/.

Northwestern University, McCormick School of Engineering and Applied Science, Department of Mechanical Engineering, Evanston, IL 60208. Offers MS, PhD. MS and PhD offered through the Graduate School. Part-time programs available. *Faculty:* 24 full-time (5 women). *Students:* 129 full-time (21 women); includes 16 minority (2 Black or African American, non-Hispanic/Latino; 8 Asian, non-Hispanic/Latino; 3 Hispanic/Latino; 3 Two or more races, non-Hispanic/Latino), 69 international. Average age 26. 473 applicants, 14% accepted, 31 enrolled. In 2011, 19 master's, 11 doctorates awarded. Terminal master's awarded for partial completion of doctoral program. *Degree requirements:* For master's, thesis optional; for doctorate, comprehensive exam, thesis/dissertation. *Entrance requirements:* For master's and doctorate, GRE General Test. Additional exam requirements/recommendations for international students: Required—TOEFL (minimum score 577 paper-based, 233 computer-based, 90 iBT) or IELTS. *Application deadline:* For fall admission, 12/31 for domestic and international students. Application fee: $75. Electronic applications accepted. *Financial support:* Fellowships with full tuition reimbursements, research assistantships with partial tuition reimbursements, teaching assistantships with full tuition reimbursements, career-related internships or fieldwork, institutionally sponsored loans, health care benefits, and unspecified assistantships available. Financial award application deadline: 1/15; financial award applicants required to submit FAFSA. *Faculty research:* Experimental, theoretical and computational mechanics of materials; fluid mechanics; manufacturing processes; robotics and control; micro-electromechanical systems and nanotechnology. *Total annual research expenditures:* $8.2 million. *Unit head:* Dr. Cate Brinson, Chair, 847-467-2347, Fax: 847-491-3915, E-mail: cbrinson@northwestern.edu. *Application contact:* Dr. Jian Cao, Admission Officer, 847-467-1032, Fax: 847-491-3915, E-mail: jcao@northwestern.edu. Web site: http://www.mech.northwestern.edu/web/index.php.

Oakland University, Graduate Study and Lifelong Learning, School of Engineering and Computer Science, Department of Mechanical Engineering, Rochester, MI 48309-4401. Offers MS, PhD. Part-time and evening/weekend programs available. *Entrance requirements:* For master's, minimum GPA of 3.0 for unconditional admission. Additional exam requirements/recommendations for international students: Required—TOEFL (minimum score 550 paper-based; 213 computer-based). Electronic applications accepted. *Expenses:* Contact institution. *Faculty research:* Efficient reliability-based design optimization and robust design methods, mechanical loading and Bunc, automotive research, industrial mentorship.

The Ohio State University, Graduate School, College of Engineering, Department of Mechanical and Aerospace Engineering, Columbus, OH 43210. Offers mechanical engineering (MS, PhD); nuclear engineering (MS, PhD). *Faculty:* 47. *Students:* 239 full-time (36 women), 117 part-time (13 women); includes 16 minority (4 Black or African American, non-Hispanic/Latino; 5 Asian, non-Hispanic/Latino; 6 Hispanic/Latino; 1 Two or more races, non-Hispanic/Latino), 125 international. Average age 27. In 2011, 56 master's, 21 doctorates awarded. *Degree requirements:* For doctorate, thesis/dissertation. *Entrance requirements:* For master's, GRE General Test or U.S. engineering degree with minimum GPA of 3.3; for doctorate, GRE General Test or U.S. engineering degree with minimum GPA of 3.75. Additional exam requirements/recommendations for international students: Required—Michigan English Language Assessment Battery (minimum score 82); Recommended—TOEFL (minimum score 600 paper-based; 250 computer-based; 79 iBT). *Application deadline:* For fall admission, 8/15 priority date for domestic students, 7/1 for international students; for winter admission, 12/1 priority date for domestic students, 11/1 for international students; for spring admission, 3/1 priority date for domestic students, 2/1 for international students. Applications are processed on a rolling basis. Application fee: $40 ($50 for international students). Electronic applications accepted. *Expenses:* Tuition, state resident: full-time $11,400. Tuition, nonresident: full-time $28,125. Tuition and fees vary according to course load, degree level, campus/location and program. *Financial support:* Fellowships, research assistantships, teaching assistantships, career-related internships or fieldwork, Federal Work-Study, institutionally sponsored loans, and unspecified assistantships available. Support available to part-time students. *Unit head:* Krishnaswamy Srinivasan, Chair, 614-292-0503, E-mail: srinivasan.3@osu.edu. *Application contact:* Janeen Sands, Graduate Programs Coordinator, 614-247-6605, Fax: 614-292-3656, E-mail: sands.3@osu.edu. Web site: http://mae.osu.edu/.

Ohio University, Graduate College, Russ College of Engineering and Technology, Department of Mechanical Engineering, Athens, OH 45701-2979. Offers biomedical engineering (MS); mechanical engineering (MS), including CAD/CAM, design, energy, manufacturing, materials, robotics, thermofluids. Part-time programs available. *Students:* 23 full-time (2 women), 4 part-time (0 women); includes 2 minority (1 Black or African American, non-Hispanic/Latino; 1 Two or more races, non-Hispanic/Latino), 10 international. 52 applicants, 23% accepted, 7 enrolled. In 2011, 8 master's awarded. *Degree requirements:* For master's, comprehensive exam (for some programs), thesis. *Entrance requirements:* For master's, GRE, BS in engineering or science, minimum GPA of 2.8. Additional exam requirements/recommendations for international students: Required—TOEFL (minimum score 550 paper-based; 80 iBT) or IELTS (minimum score 6.5). *Application deadline:* For fall admission, 2/15 priority date for domestic students, 2/

15 for international students. Applications are processed on a rolling basis. Application fee: $50 ($55 for international students). Electronic applications accepted. *Financial support:* In 2011–12, research assistantships with tuition reimbursements (averaging $14,000 per year), teaching assistantships with tuition reimbursements (averaging $14,000 per year) were awarded; career-related internships or fieldwork, Federal Work-Study, institutionally sponsored loans, tuition waivers (full and partial), and unspecified assistantships also available. Financial award application deadline: 2/15; financial award applicants required to submit FAFSA. *Faculty research:* Biomedical, energy and the environment, materials and manufacturing, bioengineering. *Unit head:* Dr. Greg Kremer, Chairman, 740-593-1561, Fax: 740-593-0476, E-mail: kremer@bobcat.ent.ohiou.edu. *Application contact:* Dr. Frank F. Kraft, Graduate Chairman, 740-597-1478, Fax: 740-593-0476, E-mail: kraft@ohio.edu. Web site: http://www.ohio.edu/mechanical.

Ohio University, Graduate College, Russ College of Engineering and Technology, Program in Mechanical and Systems Engineering, Athens, OH 45701-2979. Offers industrial engineering (PhD); mechanical engineering (PhD). *Students:* 14 full-time (2 women), 2 part-time (1 woman), 13 international. 18 applicants, 6% accepted, 1 enrolled. In 2011, 2 doctorates awarded. *Degree requirements:* For doctorate, comprehensive exam, thesis/dissertation. *Entrance requirements:* For doctorate, GRE General Test, MS in engineering or related field. Additional exam requirements/recommendations for international students: Required—TOEFL (minimum score 550 paper-based; 80 iBT) or IELTS (minimum score 6.5). *Application deadline:* For fall admission, 3/15 priority date for domestic students, 3/15 for international students. Applications are processed on a rolling basis. Application fee: $50 ($55 for international students). Electronic applications accepted. *Financial support:* In 2011–12, 4 research assistantships with full tuition reimbursements (averaging $14,000 per year) were awarded; Federal Work-Study, institutionally sponsored loans, and unspecified assistantships also available. Financial award application deadline: 3/15; financial award applicants required to submit FAFSA. *Faculty research:* Material processing, expert systems, environmental geotechnical manufacturing, thermal systems, robotics. *Total annual research expenditures:* $1.8 million. *Unit head:* Dr. Shawn Ostermann, Associate Dean, 740-593-1482, Fax: 740-593-0659, E-mail: ostermann@ohio.edu. *Application contact:* Dr. Shawn Ostermann, Associate Dean, 740-593-1482, Fax: 740-593-0659, E-mail: ostermann@ohio.edu. Web site: http://www.ohio.edu/engineering/msephd/.

Oklahoma State University, College of Engineering, Architecture and Technology, School of Mechanical and Aerospace Engineering, Stillwater, OK 74078. Offers mechanical and aerospace engineering (MS, PhD); mechanical engineering (MS, PhD). Postbaccalaureate distance learning degree programs offered. *Faculty:* 28 full-time (1 woman). *Students:* 77 full-time (8 women), 81 part-time (12 women); includes 3 minority (1 Asian, non-Hispanic/Latino; 2 Two or more races, non-Hispanic/Latino), 113 international. Average age 26. 274 applicants, 23% accepted, 33 enrolled. In 2011, 53 master's, 6 doctorates awarded. *Degree requirements:* For master's, thesis or alternative; for doctorate, comprehensive exam, thesis/dissertation. *Entrance requirements:* For master's and doctorate, GRE or GMAT. Additional exam requirements/recommendations for international students: Required—TOEFL (minimum score 550 paper-based; 79 iBT). *Application deadline:* For fall admission, 3/1 for international students; for spring admission, 8/1 for international students. Applications are processed on a rolling basis. Application fee: $40 ($75 for international students). Electronic applications accepted. *Expenses:* Tuition, state resident: full-time $4044; part-time $168.50 per credit hour. Tuition, nonresident: full-time $16,008; part-time $667 per credit hour. *Required fees:* $2122; $88.45 per credit hour. One-time fee: $50. Tuition and fees vary according to course load and campus/location. *Financial support:* In 2011–12, 90 research assistantships (averaging $11,744 per year), 59 teaching assistantships (averaging $8,282 per year) were awarded; career-related internships or fieldwork, Federal Work-Study, scholarships/grants, health care benefits, tuition waivers (partial), and unspecified assistantships also available. Support available to part-time students. Financial award application deadline: 3/1; financial award applicants required to submit FAFSA. *Unit head:* Dr. Lawrence L. Hoberock, Head, 405-744-5900, Fax: 405-744-7873. *Application contact:* Dr. Sheryl Tucker, Dean, 405-744-7099, Fax: 405-744-0355, E-mail: grad-i@okstate.edu. Web site: http://www.mae.okstate.edu.

Old Dominion University, Frank Batten College of Engineering and Technology, Program in Mechanical Engineering, Norfolk, VA 23529. Offers ME, MS, D Eng, PhD. Part-time and evening/weekend programs available. Postbaccalaureate distance learning degree programs offered (no on-campus study). *Faculty:* 24 full-time (2 women). *Students:* 29 full-time (3 women), 39 part-time (6 women); includes 13 minority (2 Black or African American, non-Hispanic/Latino; 5 Asian, non-Hispanic/Latino; 4 Hispanic/Latino; 2 Two or more races, non-Hispanic/Latino), 26 international. Average age 29. 50 applicants, 76% accepted, 7 enrolled. In 2011, 16 master's, 1 doctorate awarded. *Degree requirements:* For master's, comprehensive exam, thesis optional; for doctorate, thesis/dissertation, candidacy exam. *Entrance requirements:* For master's, GRE, minimum GPA of 3.0; for doctorate, GRE, minimum GPA of 3.5. Additional exam requirements/recommendations for international students: Required—TOEFL (minimum score 550 paper-based; 213 computer-based). *Application deadline:* For fall admission, 6/1 for domestic students, 2/15 for international students; for spring admission, 11/1 for domestic students, 10/1 for international students. Applications are processed on a rolling basis. Application fee: $50. Electronic applications accepted. *Expenses:* Tuition, state resident: full-time $9096; part-time $379 per credit. Tuition, nonresident: full-time $23,064; part-time $961 per credit. *Required fees:* $127 per semester. One-time fee: $50. *Financial support:* In 2011–12, 12 students received support, including 5 fellowships with partial tuition reimbursements available (averaging $16,000 per year), 11 research assistantships with partial tuition reimbursements available (averaging $15,000 per year), 15 teaching assistantships with partial tuition reimbursements available (averaging $6,400 per year); career-related internships or fieldwork, institutionally sponsored loans, scholarships/grants, and unspecified assistantships also available. Financial award application deadline: 2/15; financial award applicants required to submit FAFSA. *Faculty research:* Computational applied mechanics, manufacturing, experimental stress analysis, systems dynamics and control, mechanical design. *Total annual research expenditures:* $975,887. *Unit head:* Dr. Jen-Kuang Huang, Chair, 757-683-3734, Fax: 757-683-5344, E-mail: jhuang@odu.edu. *Application contact:* Dr. Gene Hou, Graduate Program Director, 757-683-3728, Fax: 757-683-5344, E-mail: megpd@odu.edu. Web site: http://eng.odu.edu/mae.

Oregon State University, Graduate School, College of Engineering, School of Mechanical, Industrial, and Manufacturing Engineering, Corvallis, OR 97331. Offers human systems engineering (MS, PhD); industrial engineering (MS, PhD); information systems engineering (MS, PhD); manufacturing engineering (M Engr); manufacturing systems engineering (MS, PhD); materials science (MAIS, MS, PhD); mechanical engineering (MS, PhD); nano/micro fabrication (MS, PhD). Part-time programs available. Postbaccalaureate distance learning degree programs offered (minimal on-campus study). *Degree requirements:* For master's, thesis or alternative; for doctorate, thesis/dissertation. *Entrance requirements:* For master's, placement exam, minimum GPA of 3.0 in last 90 hours of course work; for doctorate, GRE, placement exam, minimum GPA of 3.0 in last 90 hours of course work. Additional exam requirements/recommendations for international students: Required—TOEFL (minimum score 550 paper-based; 213 computer-based). *Faculty research:* Computer-integrated manufacturing, human factors, robotics, decision support systems, simulation modeling and analysis.

Penn State University Park, Graduate School, College of Engineering, Department of Mechanical and Nuclear Engineering, State College, University Park, PA 16802-1503. Offers mechanical engineering (MS, PhD); nuclear engineering (M Eng, MS, PhD). *Faculty research:* Reactor safety, radiation damage, advanced controls, radiation instrumentation, computational methods. *Unit head:* Dr. David N. Wormley, Dean, 814-865-7537, Fax: 814-865-8767, E-mail: dnw2@engr.psu.edu. *Application contact:* Cynthia E. Nicosia, Director, Graduate Enrollment Services, 814-865-1834, E-mail: cey1@psu.edu. Web site: http://www.mne.psu.edu.

Polytechnic Institute of New York University, Department of Mechanical and Aerospace Engineering, Major in Mechanical Engineering, Brooklyn, NY 11201-2990. Offers MS, PhD. Part-time and evening/weekend programs available. *Students:* 40 full-time (5 women), 27 part-time (5 women); includes 15 minority (2 Black or African American, non-Hispanic/Latino; 10 Asian, non-Hispanic/Latino; 3 Hispanic/Latino), 32 international. Average age 25. 208 applicants, 36% accepted, 28 enrolled. In 2011, 16 master's, 3 doctorates awarded. *Degree requirements:* For master's, comprehensive exam (for some programs), thesis (for some programs); for doctorate, comprehensive exam, thesis/dissertation. *Entrance requirements:* For master's, BE or BS in engineering, physics, chemistry, mathematical sciences, or biological sciences or MBA. Additional exam requirements/recommendations for international students: Required—TOEFL (minimum score 550 paper-based; 213 computer-based; 80 iBT); Recommended—IELTS (minimum score 6.5). *Application deadline:* For fall admission, 7/31 priority date for domestic students, 4/30 for international students; for spring admission, 12/31 priority date for domestic students, 11/30 for international students. Applications are processed on a rolling basis. Application fee: $75. Electronic applications accepted. *Expenses: Tuition:* Full-time $22,464; part-time $1248 per credit. *Required fees:* $501 per semester. *Financial support:* Institutionally sponsored loans, scholarships/grants, and unspecified assistantships available. Support available to part-time students. Financial award applicants required to submit FAFSA. *Unit head:* Dr. George Vradis, Head, 718-260-3875, Fax: 718-260-3532, E-mail: gvradis@poly.edu. *Application contact:* JeanCarlo Bonilla, Director of Graduate Enrollment Management, 718-260-3182, Fax: 718-260-3624, E-mail: gradinfo@poly.edu.

Polytechnic Institute of NYU, Long Island Graduate Center, Graduate Programs, Department of Mechanical and Aerospace Engineering, Melville, NY 11747. Offers aeronautics and astronautics (MS); industrial engineering (MS); manufacturing engineering (MS); mechanical engineering (MS). Part-time and evening/weekend programs available. *Students:* 1 full-time (0 women). Average age 28. In 2011, 2 master's awarded. *Degree requirements:* For master's, comprehensive exam (for some programs), thesis (for some programs). *Entrance requirements:* Additional exam requirements/recommendations for international students: Required—TOEFL (minimum score 550 paper-based; 213 computer-based; 80 iBT); Recommended—IELTS (minimum score 6.5). *Application deadline:* For fall admission, 7/31 priority date for domestic students, 4/30 for international students; for spring admission, 12/31 priority date for domestic students, 11/30 for international students. Applications are processed on a rolling basis. Application fee: $75. Electronic applications accepted. *Financial support:* In 2011–12, 16 fellowships with tuition reimbursements (averaging $1,394 per year) were awarded; research assistantships with tuition reimbursements, institutionally sponsored loans, scholarships/grants, and unspecified assistantships also available. Support available to part-time students. Financial award applicants required to submit FAFSA. *Faculty research:* UV filter, fuel efficient hydrodynamic containment for gas core fission, turbulent boundary layer research. *Unit head:* Dr. George Vradis, Department Head, 718-260-3875, E-mail: gvradis@duke.poly.edu. *Application contact:* JeanCarlo Bonilla, Director of Graduate Enrollment Management, 718-260-3182, Fax: 718-260-3624, E-mail: gradinfo@poly.edu.

Polytechnic University of Puerto Rico, Graduate School, Hato Rey, PR 00919. Offers business administration (MBA), including computer information systems, general management, management of information systems, management of international enterprises; civil engineering (ME, MS); computer engineering (ME, MS); computer science (MCS, MS); electrical engineering (ME, MS); engineering management (MEM); environmental management (MEM); landscape architecture (M Land Arch); manufacturing competitiveness (MMC, MS); manufacturing engineering (ME, MS); mechanical engineering (M Mech E). Part-time and evening/weekend programs available. *Entrance requirements:* For master's, 3 letters of recommendation.

Portland State University, Graduate Studies, Maseeh College of Engineering and Computer Science, Department of Mechanical Engineering, Portland, OR 97207-0751. Offers M Eng, MS, PhD. Part-time and evening/weekend programs available. *Degree requirements:* For master's, thesis or alternative; for doctorate, one foreign language, thesis/dissertation, oral and written exams. *Entrance requirements:* For master's, minimum GPA of 3.0 in upper-division course work, BS in mechanical engineering or allied field; for doctorate, GRE General Test, GRE Subject Test, minimum GPA of 3.0 in upper-division course work. Additional exam requirements/recommendations for international students: Required—TOEFL (minimum score 550 paper-based; 213 computer-based). *Faculty research:* Mechanical system modeling, indoor air quality, manufacturing process, computational fluid dynamics, building science.

Portland State University, Graduate Studies, Systems Science Program, Portland, OR 97207-0751. Offers computational intelligence (Certificate); computer modeling and simulation (Certificate); systems science (MS); systems science/anthropology (PhD); systems science/business administration (PhD); systems science/civil engineering (PhD); systems science/economics (PhD); systems science/engineering management (PhD); systems science/general (PhD); systems science/mathematical sciences (PhD); systems science/mechanical engineering (PhD); systems science/psychology (PhD); systems science/sociology (PhD). *Degree requirements:* For doctorate, variable foreign language requirement, thesis/dissertation. *Entrance requirements:* For master's, 2 letters of recommendation; for doctorate, GMAT, GRE General Test, minimum undergraduate GPA of 3.0. Additional exam requirements/recommendations for international students: Required—TOEFL. *Faculty research:* Systems theory and methodology, artificial intelligence neural networks, information theory, nonlinear dynamics/chaos, modeling and simulation.

Princeton University, Graduate School, School of Engineering and Applied Science, Department of Mechanical and Aerospace Engineering, Princeton, NJ 08544. Offers M Eng, MSE, PhD. Terminal master's awarded for partial completion of doctoral program. *Degree requirements:* For master's, thesis (MSE); for doctorate, thesis/dissertation, general exam. *Entrance requirements:* For master's, GRE General Test, 3 letters of recommendation; for doctorate, GRE General Test, official transcript(s), 3 letters of recommendation, personal statement. Additional exam requirements/

recommendations for international students: Required—TOEFL. Electronic applications accepted. *Faculty research:* Bioengineering and bio-mechanics; combustion, energy conversion, and climate; fluid mechanics, dynamics, and control systems; lasers and applied physics; materials and mechanical systems.

Purdue University, College of Engineering, School of Mechanical Engineering, West Lafayette, IN 47907-2088. Offers MS, MSE, MSME, PhD, Certificate. MS and PhD degree programs in biomedical engineering offered jointly with School of Electrical and Computer Engineering and School of Chemical Engineering. Part-time programs available. Postbaccalaureate distance learning degree programs offered (no on-campus study). *Entrance requirements:* For master's and doctorate, GRE General Test, minimum GPA of 3.2. Additional exam requirements/recommendations for international students: Required—TOEFL (minimum score 575 paper-based; 233 computer-based; 77 iBT); Recommended—TWE. Electronic applications accepted. *Faculty research:* Design, manufacturing, thermal/fluid sciences, mechanics, electromechanical systems.

Purdue University Calumet, Graduate Studies Office, School of Engineering, Mathematics, and Science, Department of Engineering, Hammond, IN 46323-2094. Offers computer engineering (MSE); electrical engineering (MSE); engineering (MS); mechanical engineering (MSE). Evening/weekend programs available. *Entrance requirements:* Additional exam requirements/recommendations for international students: Required—TOEFL.

Queen's University at Kingston, School of Graduate Studies and Research, Faculty of Applied Science, Department of Mechanical and Materials Engineering, Kingston, ON K7L 3N6, Canada. Offers M Eng, M Sc, M Sc Eng, PhD. Part-time programs available. *Degree requirements:* For master's, thesis optional; for doctorate, comprehensive exam, thesis/dissertation. *Entrance requirements:* Additional exam requirements/recommendations for international students: Required—TOEFL. Electronic applications accepted. *Faculty research:* Dynamics and control systems, manufacturing and design, materials and engineering, heat transferring fluid dynamics, energy systems and combustion.

Rensselaer at Hartford, Department of Engineering, Program in Mechanical Engineering, Hartford, CT 06120-2991. Offers ME, MS. Part-time and evening/weekend programs available. *Degree requirements:* For master's, thesis optional. *Entrance requirements:* For master's, GRE. Additional exam requirements/recommendations for international students: Required—TOEFL (minimum score 600 paper-based; 250 computer-based; 100 iBT).

Rensselaer Polytechnic Institute, Graduate School, School of Engineering, Program in Mechanical Engineering, Troy, NY 12180-3590. Offers M Eng, MS, PhD. Part-time programs available. Postbaccalaureate distance learning degree programs offered. *Degree requirements:* For master's, thesis (for some programs); for doctorate, thesis/dissertation. *Entrance requirements:* For master's and doctorate, GRE. Additional exam requirements/recommendations for international students: Required—TOEFL (minimum score 600 paper-based; 250 computer-based; 100 iBT). Electronic applications accepted. *Faculty research:* Tribology, advanced composite materials, energy and combustion systems, computer-aided and optimal design, manufacturing.

Rice University, Graduate Programs, George R. Brown School of Engineering, Department of Mechanical Engineering and Materials Science, Houston, TX 77251-1892. Offers materials science (MMS, MS, PhD); mechanical engineering (MME, MS, PhD); MBA/ME. Part-time programs available. Terminal master's awarded for partial completion of doctoral program. *Degree requirements:* For master's, comprehensive exam, thesis; for doctorate, comprehensive exam, thesis/dissertation. *Entrance requirements:* For master's and doctorate, GRE General Test, minimum GPA of 3.0. Additional exam requirements/recommendations for international students: Required—TOEFL (minimum score 600 paper-based; 250 computer-based; 90 iBT), IELTS (minimum score 7). Electronic applications accepted. *Faculty research:* Heat transfer, biomedical engineering, fluid dynamics, aero-astronautics, control systems/robotics, materials science.

Rochester Institute of Technology, Graduate Enrollment Services, College of Applied Science and Technology, School of Engineering Technology, Department of Electrical, Computer and Telecommunications Engineering Technology, Rochester, NY 14623-5603. Offers facility management (MS); manufacturing and mechanical systems integration (MS); telecommunications engineering technology (MS). Part-time and evening/weekend programs available. Postbaccalaureate distance learning degree programs offered (no on-campus study). *Students:* 54 full-time (13 women), 34 part-time (6 women); includes 7 minority (4 Black or African American, non-Hispanic/Latino; 1 Asian, non-Hispanic/Latino; 1 Hispanic/Latino; 1 Two or more races, non-Hispanic/Latino), 70 international. Average age 26. 154 applicants, 55% accepted, 32 enrolled. In 2011, 24 master's awarded. *Degree requirements:* For master's, thesis. *Entrance requirements:* For master's, GRE, minimum GPA of 3.0. Additional exam requirements/recommendations for international students: Required—TOEFL (minimum score 550 paper-based; 213 computer-based; 79 iBT) or IELTS (minimum score 6.5). *Application deadline:* For fall admission, 2/15 priority date for domestic students, 2/15 for international students; for winter admission, 11/1 for domestic and international students; for spring admission, 2/1 for domestic and international students. Applications are processed on a rolling basis. Application fee: $50. Electronic applications accepted. *Expenses: Tuition:* Full-time $34,659; part-time $963 per credit hour. *Required fees:* $228; $76 per quarter. *Financial support:* Research assistantships with partial tuition reimbursements, teaching assistantships with partial tuition reimbursements, career-related internships or fieldwork, and unspecified assistantships available. Support available to part-time students. Financial award application deadline: 2/15; financial award applicants required to submit FAFSA. *Faculty research:* Fiber optic networks, next generation networks, project management. *Unit head:* Michael Eastman, Department Chair, 585-475-7787, Fax: 585-475-2178, E-mail: mgeiee@rit.edu. *Application contact:* Diane Ellison, Assistant Vice President, Graduate Enrollment Services, 585-475-2229, Fax: 585-475-7164, E-mail: gradinfo@rit.edu. Web site: http://www.rit.edu/cast/ectet/.

Rochester Institute of Technology, Graduate Enrollment Services, College of Applied Science and Technology, School of Engineering Technology, Department of Manufacturing and Mechanical Engineering Technology/Packaging Science, Program in Manufacturing and Mechanical Systems Integration, Rochester, NY 14623-5603. Offers MS. Part-time and evening/weekend programs available. *Students:* 13 full-time (3 women), 13 part-time (0 women), 8 international. Average age 25. 18 applicants, 67% accepted, 8 enrolled. In 2011, 10 master's awarded. *Degree requirements:* For master's, thesis. *Entrance requirements:* For master's, GRE, minimum GPA of 3.0. Additional exam requirements/recommendations for international students: Required—TOEFL (minimum score 550 paper-based; 213 computer-based; 79 iBT) or IELTS (minimum score 6.5). *Application deadline:* For fall admission, 2/15 priority date for domestic students, 2/15 for international students; for winter admission, 11/1 for domestic and international students; for spring admission, 2/1 for domestic and international students. Applications are processed on a rolling basis. Application fee: $50. Electronic applications accepted. *Expenses: Tuition:* Full-time $34,659; part-time $963 per credit hour. *Required fees:* $228; $76 per quarter. *Financial support:* Research assistantships with partial tuition reimbursements, teaching assistantships with partial tuition reimbursements, career-related internships or fieldwork, scholarships/grants, and unspecified assistantships available. Support available to part-time students. Financial award application deadline: 2/15; financial award applicants required to submit FAFSA. *Faculty research:* Biodegradable plastics, health physics, nuclear engineering technology, solidworks, automotive engineering, compression strength, protective package development. *Unit head:* Dr. S. Manian Ramkumar, Graduate Program Director, 585-475-6081, Fax: 585-475-5227, E-mail: smrmet@rit.edu. *Application contact:* Diane Ellison, Assistant Vice President, Graduate Enrollment Services, 585-475-2229, Fax: 585-475-7164, E-mail: gradinfo@rit.edu. Web site: http://www.rit.edu/cast/mmetps/ms-in-manufacturing-and-mechanical-systems-integration.php.

Rochester Institute of Technology, Graduate Enrollment Services, Kate Gleason College of Engineering, Department of Mechanical Engineering, Rochester, NY 14623-5603. Offers ME, MS. Part-time programs available. *Students:* 47 full-time (3 women), 40 part-time (1 woman); includes 3 minority (2 Asian, non-Hispanic/Latino; 1 Hispanic/Latino), 24 international. Average age 26. 155 applicants, 60% accepted, 21 enrolled. In 2011, 55 master's awarded. *Degree requirements:* For master's, thesis optional. *Entrance requirements:* For master's, GRE, minimum GPA of 3.0. Additional exam requirements/recommendations for international students: Required—TOEFL (minimum score 570 paper-based; 230 computer-based; 88 iBT) or IELTS (minimum score 6.5). *Application deadline:* For fall admission, 2/15 priority date for domestic students, 2/15 for international students; for winter admission, 10/15 for domestic and international students; for spring admission, 2/1 for domestic and international students. Applications are processed on a rolling basis. Application fee: $50. Electronic applications accepted. *Expenses: Tuition:* Full-time $34,659; part-time $963 per credit hour. *Required fees:* $228; $76 per quarter. *Financial support:* Research assistantships with partial tuition reimbursements, teaching assistantships with partial tuition reimbursements, career-related internships or fieldwork, institutionally sponsored loans, scholarships/grants, and unspecified assistantships available. Support available to part-time students. Financial award applicants required to submit FAFSA. *Faculty research:* Aerospace systems, unmanned aircraft design, fabrication and testing, automotive systems, assistive device technologies, artificial organ engineering, biomedical device engineering, microscale heat and mass transfer, thermoelectric energy, energy systems for developing countries. *Unit head:* Dr. Edward Hensel, Department Head, 585-475-5181, Fax: 585-475-7710, E-mail: echeme@rit.edu. *Application contact:* Diane Ellison, Assistant Vice President, Graduate Enrollment Services, 585-475-2229, Fax: 585-475-7164, E-mail: gradinfo@rit.edu. Web site: http://www.rit.edu/kgcoe/mechanical/.

Rose-Hulman Institute of Technology, Faculty of Engineering and Applied Sciences, Department of Mechanical Engineering, Terre Haute, IN 47803-3999. Offers MS. Part-time programs available. Postbaccalaureate distance learning degree programs offered (minimal on-campus study). *Faculty:* 24 full-time (3 women). *Students:* 10 full-time (0 women), 4 part-time (0 women); includes 1 minority (Asian, non-Hispanic/Latino), 3 international. Average age 23. 9 applicants, 100% accepted, 6 enrolled. In 2011, 4 master's awarded. *Degree requirements:* For master's, thesis. *Entrance requirements:* For master's, GRE, minimum GPA of 3.0. Additional exam requirements/recommendations for international students: Required—TOEFL (minimum score 580 paper-based; 237 computer-based; 92 iBT). *Application deadline:* For fall admission, 2/1 priority date for domestic students. Applications are processed on a rolling basis. Application fee: $0. *Expenses: Tuition:* Full-time $37,197; part-time $1085 per credit hour. *Financial support:* In 2011–12, 9 students received support. Fellowships with full and partial tuition reimbursements available, research assistantships with full and partial tuition reimbursements available, institutionally sponsored loans, scholarships/grants, and tuition waivers (full and partial) available. *Faculty research:* Dynamics of large flexible space structures, finite-element analysis, system simulation and optimization, mechanical design, fracture mechanics and fatigue. *Total annual research expenditures:* $104,801. *Unit head:* Dr. David J. Purdy, Chairman, 812-877-8320, Fax: 812-877-3198. *Application contact:* Dr. Daniel J. Moore, Associate Dean of the Faculty, 812-877-8110, Fax: 812-877-8061, E-mail: daniel.j.moore@rose-hulman.edu. Web site: http://www.rose-hulman.edu/me/.

Rowan University, Graduate School, College of Engineering, Department of Mechanical Engineering, Glassboro, NJ 08028-1701. Offers MS. Part-time and evening/weekend programs available. *Entrance requirements:* For master's, GRE General Test. Additional exam requirements/recommendations for international students: Required—TOEFL. Electronic applications accepted.

Royal Military College of Canada, Division of Graduate Studies and Research, Engineering Division, Department of Mechanical Engineering, Kingston, ON K7K 7B4, Canada. Offers M Eng, MA Sc, PhD. *Degree requirements:* For master's, thesis; for doctorate, comprehensive exam, thesis/dissertation. *Entrance requirements:* For master's, honours degree with second-class standing; for doctorate, master's degree. Electronic applications accepted.

Rutgers, The State University of New Jersey, New Brunswick, Graduate School-New Brunswick, Program in Mechanical and Aerospace Engineering, Piscataway, NJ 08854-8097. Offers design and control (MS, PhD); fluid mechanics (MS, PhD); solid mechanics (MS, PhD); thermal sciences (MS, PhD). Part-time and evening/weekend programs available. *Degree requirements:* For master's, thesis (for some programs); for doctorate, thesis/dissertation. *Entrance requirements:* For master's, GRE General Test, BS in mechanical/aerospace engineering or related field; for doctorate, GRE General Test, MS in mechanical/aerospace engineering or related field. Additional exam requirements/recommendations for international students: Required—TOEFL. Electronic applications accepted. *Faculty research:* Combustion, propulsion, thermal transport, crystal plasticity, optimization, fabrication, nanoidentation.

St. Cloud State University, School of Graduate Studies, College of Science and Engineering, Program in Mechanical Engineering, St. Cloud, MN 56301-4498. Offers MS. *Degree requirements:* For master's, thesis or alternative. *Entrance requirements:* For master's, GRE General Test, minimum GPA of 2.75. Additional exam requirements/recommendations for international students: Required—Michigan English Language Assessment Battery; Recommended—TOEFL (minimum score 550 paper-based; 213 computer-based), IELTS (minimum score 6.5). Electronic applications accepted.

San Diego State University, Graduate and Research Affairs, College of Engineering, Department of Mechanical Engineering, San Diego, CA 92182. Offers engineering sciences and applied mechanics (PhD); manufacture and design (MS); mechanical engineering (MS). PhD offered jointly with University of California, San Diego and Department of Aerospace Engineering and Engineering Mechanics. Evening/weekend programs available. *Degree requirements:* For master's, comprehensive exam (for some programs), thesis (for some programs); for doctorate, thesis/dissertation. *Entrance requirements:* For master's, GRE General Test; for doctorate, GRE, 3 letters of recommendation. Additional exam requirements/recommendations for international students: Required—TOEFL. Electronic applications accepted. *Faculty research:* Energy analysis and diagnosis, seawater pump design, space-related research.

San Jose State University, Graduate Studies and Research, Charles W. Davidson College of Engineering, Department of Mechanical and Aerospace Engineering, Program in Mechanical Engineering, San Jose, CA 95192-0001. Offers MS. Part-time programs available. *Degree requirements:* For master's, thesis optional. *Entrance requirements:* For master's, GRE. Additional exam requirements/recommendations for international students: Required—TOEFL. Electronic applications accepted. *Faculty research:* Gas dynamics, mechanics/vibrations, heat transfer, structural analysis, two-phase fluid flow.

Santa Clara University, School of Engineering, Program in Mechanical Engineering, Santa Clara, CA 95053. Offers controls (Certificate); dynamics (Certificate); materials engineering (Certificate); mechanical design analysis (Certificate); mechanical engineering (MS, PhD, Engineer); mechatronics systems engineering (Certificate); technology jump-start (Certificate); thermofluids (Certificate). Part-time and evening/weekend programs available. *Students:* 36 full-time (5 women), 68 part-time (11 women); includes 42 minority (33 Asian, non-Hispanic/Latino; 9 Hispanic/Latino), 16 international. Average age 27. 109 applicants, 56% accepted, 36 enrolled. In 2011, 33 master's, 1 doctorate, 1 other advanced degree awarded. *Degree requirements:* For master's, thesis (for some programs); for doctorate, thesis/dissertation; for other advanced degree, thesis. *Entrance requirements:* For master's, GRE, transcript; for doctorate, GRE, master's degree or equivalent; for other advanced degree, master's degree, published paper. Additional exam requirements/recommendations for international students: Required—TOEFL (minimum score 550 paper-based; 213 computer-based; 79 iBT). *Application deadline:* For fall admission, 8/12 for domestic students, 7/15 for international students; for winter admission, 10/28 for domestic students, 9/23 for international students; for spring admission, 2/25 for domestic students, 1/21 for international students. Applications are processed on a rolling basis. Application fee: $60. Electronic applications accepted. *Expenses:* Contact institution. *Financial support:* Research assistantships and teaching assistantships available. Financial award application deadline: 3/2; financial award applicants required to submit FAFSA. *Faculty research:* Development of small satellite design, tests and operations technology. *Unit head:* Dr. Alex Zecevic, Associate Dean for Graduate Studies, 408-554-2394, E-mail: azecevic@scu.edu. *Application contact:* Stacey Tinker, Director of Admissions, Graduate Engineering, 408-554-4748, Fax: 408-554-4323, E-mail: stinker@scu.edu.

South Carolina State University, School of Graduate Studies, Department of Civil and Mechanical Engineering Technology and Nuclear Engineering, Orangeburg, SC 29117-0001. Offers transportation (MS). Part-time and evening/weekend programs available. *Faculty:* 2 full-time (0 women), 3 part-time/adjunct (1 woman). *Students:* 19 full-time (6 women), 3 part-time (1 woman); includes 20 minority (19 Black or African American, non-Hispanic/Latino; 1 Hispanic/Latino), 2 international. Average age 28. 12 applicants, 83% accepted, 5 enrolled. In 2011, 3 master's awarded. *Degree requirements:* For master's, comprehensive exam, thesis, departmental qualifying exam. *Entrance requirements:* For master's, GRE. Additional exam requirements/recommendations for international students: Recommended—TOEFL. *Application deadline:* For fall admission, 6/15 for domestic and international students; for spring admission, 11/1 for domestic and international students. Application fee: $25. Electronic applications accepted. *Expenses:* Tuition, state resident: full-time $8688; part-time $514 per credit hour. Tuition, nonresident: full-time $17,600; part-time $1009 per credit hour. *Required fees:* $570. *Financial support:* In 2011–12, 6 fellowships (averaging $5,150 per year) were awarded; research assistantships, career-related internships or fieldwork, Federal Work-Study, institutionally sponsored loans, and unspecified assistantships also available. Financial award application deadline: 6/1. *Faculty research:* Societal competence, relationship of parent-child interaction to adult, rehabilitation evaluation, vocation, language assessment of rural children. *Unit head:* Dr. Stanley Ihekweazu, Chair, 803-536-7117, Fax: 803-516-4607, E-mail: sihekweazu@scsu.edu. *Application contact:* Annette Hazzard-Jones, Program Coordinator II, 803-536-8809, Fax: 803-536-8812, E-mail: zs_ahazzard@scsu.edu. Web site: http://www.scsu.edu/schoolofgraduatestudies.aspx.

South Dakota School of Mines and Technology, Graduate Division, Department of Mechanical Engineering, Rapid City, SD 57701-3995. Offers MS, PhD. Part-time programs available. *Entrance requirements:* Additional exam requirements/recommendations for international students: Required—TOEFL, TWE. Electronic applications accepted. *Faculty research:* Advanced composite materials, robotics, computer-integrated manufacturing, enhanced heat transfer, dynamic systems controls.

South Dakota State University, Graduate School, College of Engineering, Department of Mechanical Engineering, Brookings, SD 57007. Offers engineering (MS). Part-time programs available. *Degree requirements:* For master's, thesis (for some programs), oral exam. *Entrance requirements:* Additional exam requirements/recommendations for international students: Required—TOEFL (minimum score 525 paper-based; 197 computer-based; 71 iBT). *Faculty research:* Thermo-fluid science, solid mechanics and dynamics, industrial and quality control engineering, bioenergy.

Southern Illinois University Carbondale, Graduate School, College of Engineering, Department of Mechanical Engineering and Energy Processes, Carbondale, IL 62901-4701. Offers MS. *Faculty:* 16 full-time (0 women), 1 part-time/adjunct (0 women). *Students:* 12 full-time (1 woman), 21 part-time (3 women); includes 3 minority (2 Black or African American, non-Hispanic/Latino; 1 Hispanic/Latino), 12 international. Average age 23. 42 applicants, 31% accepted, 7 enrolled. In 2011, 17 master's awarded. *Degree requirements:* For master's, comprehensive exam, thesis or alternative. *Entrance requirements:* For master's, GRE General Test, minimum GPA of 2.7. Additional exam requirements/recommendations for international students: Required—TOEFL. *Application deadline:* For fall admission, 1/31 for domestic students. Applications are processed on a rolling basis. Application fee: $20. *Financial support:* Fellowships with full tuition reimbursements, research assistantships with full tuition reimbursements, teaching assistantships with full tuition reimbursements, Federal Work-Study, and institutionally sponsored loans available. Support available to part-time students. *Faculty research:* Coal conversion and processing, combustion, materials science and engineering, mechanical system dynamics. *Total annual research expenditures:* $1.4 million. *Unit head:* Dr. Dale Wittmer, Chair, 618-453-7010, E-mail: wittmer@engr.siu.edu. *Application contact:* Judi L. Cockrum, Administrative Clerk, 618-453-7015, E-mail: judi@engr.siu.edu.

Southern Illinois University Edwardsville, Graduate School, School of Engineering, Department of Mechanical and Industrial Engineering, Program in Mechanical Engineering, Edwardsville, IL 62026-0001. Offers MS. Part-time programs available. *Students:* 18 full-time (2 women), 24 part-time (7 women); includes 3 minority (all Black or African American, non-Hispanic/Latino), 24 international. 46 applicants, 63% accepted. In 2011, 7 master's awarded. *Degree requirements:* For master's, comprehensive exam (for some programs), thesis (for some programs). *Entrance* *requirements:* Additional exam requirements/recommendations for international students: Required—TOEFL (minimum score 550 paper-based; 213 computer-based; 79 iBT), IELTS (minimum score 6.5). *Application deadline:* For fall admission, 7/22 for domestic students, 6/1 for international students; for spring admission, 12/9 for domestic students, 10/1 for international students. Applications are processed on a rolling basis. Application fee: $30. Electronic applications accepted. Tuition and fees vary according to course load and program. *Financial support:* In 2011–12, 4 research assistantships with full tuition reimbursements (averaging $9,927 per year), 15 teaching assistantships with full tuition reimbursements (averaging $9,927 per year) were awarded; fellowships with tuition reimbursements, institutionally sponsored loans, scholarships/grants, and unspecified assistantships also available. Financial award application deadline: 3/1; financial award applicants required to submit FAFSA. *Unit head:* Dr. Kegin Gu, Chair, 618-650-3389, E-mail: kgu@siue.edu. *Application contact:* Dr. Terry Yan, Program Director, 618-650-3463, E-mail: xyan@siue.edu. Web site: http://www.siue.edu/ENGINEER/ME/.

Southern Methodist University, Bobby B. Lyle School of Engineering, Department of Mechanical Engineering, Dallas, TX 75205. Offers electronic and optical packaging (MS); manufacturing systems management (MS); mechanical engineering (MSME, PhD). Part-time and evening/weekend programs available. Postbaccalaureate distance learning degree programs offered (no on-campus study). Terminal master's awarded for partial completion of doctoral program. *Degree requirements:* For master's, thesis optional; for doctorate, thesis/dissertation, oral and written qualifying exams, oral final exam. *Entrance requirements:* For master's, GRE General Test, minimum GPA of 3.0 in last 2 years; bachelor's degree in engineering, mathematics, or sciences; for doctorate, preliminary counseling exam, minimum graduate GPA of 3.0, bachelor's degree in related field. Additional exam requirements/recommendations for international students: Required—TOEFL. *Faculty research:* Design, systems, and controls; thermal and fluid sciences.

Stanford University, School of Engineering, Department of Mechanical Engineering, Stanford, CA 94305-9991. Offers biomechanical engineering (MS); mechanical engineering (MS, PhD, Eng); product design (MS). *Degree requirements:* For doctorate, thesis/dissertation; for Eng, thesis. *Entrance requirements:* For master's, GRE General Test, undergraduate degree in engineering, math or sciences; for doctorate and Eng, GRE General Test, MS in engineering, math or sciences. Additional exam requirements/recommendations for international students: Required—TOEFL. *Expenses: Tuition:* Full-time $40,050; part-time $890 per credit.

State University of New York at Binghamton, Graduate School, Thomas J. Watson School of Engineering and Applied Science, Department of Mechanical Engineering, Binghamton, NY 13902-6000. Offers M Eng, MS, PhD. Part-time and evening/weekend programs available. *Faculty:* 17 full-time (0 women), 3 part-time/adjunct (0 women). *Students:* 66 full-time (4 women), 33 part-time (2 women); includes 6 minority (2 Asian, non-Hispanic/Latino; 4 Native Hawaiian or other Pacific Islander, non-Hispanic/Latino), 49 international. Average age 26. 88 applicants, 64% accepted, 32 enrolled. In 2011, 22 master's, 4 doctorates awarded. *Degree requirements:* For master's, thesis or alternative; for doctorate, thesis/dissertation. *Entrance requirements:* For master's and doctorate, GRE General Test, GRE Subject Test. Additional exam requirements/recommendations for international students: Required—TOEFL. *Application deadline:* For fall admission, 4/15 priority date for domestic students, 1/15 for international students; for spring admission, 11/1 for domestic students, 10/1 for international students. Applications are processed on a rolling basis. Application fee: $60. Electronic applications accepted. *Financial support:* In 2011–12, 48 students received support, including 29 research assistantships with full tuition reimbursements available (averaging $16,500 per year), 15 teaching assistantships with full tuition reimbursements available (averaging $16,500 per year); fellowships with full tuition reimbursements available, career-related internships or fieldwork, Federal Work-Study, institutionally sponsored loans, scholarships/grants, health care benefits, tuition waivers (full), and unspecified assistantships also available. Financial award application deadline: 2/15; financial award applicants required to submit FAFSA. *Unit head:* Dr. James M. Pitarresi, Chairperson, 607-777-4037, E-mail: jmp@binghamton.edu. *Application contact:* Catherine Smith, Recruiting and Admissions Coordinator, 607-777-2151, Fax: 607-777-2501, E-mail: cmsmith@binghamton.edu.

Stevens Institute of Technology, Graduate School, Charles V. Schaefer Jr. School of Engineering, Department of Mechanical Engineering, Hoboken, NJ 07030. Offers advanced manufacturing (Certificate); air pollution technology (Certificate); computational fluid mechanics and heat transfer (Certificate); design and production management (Certificate); integrated product development (M Eng), including armament engineering, computer and electrical engineering, manufacturing technologies, systems reliability and design; mechanical engineering (M Eng, PhD), including manufacturing systems (M Eng), pharmaceutical manufacturing systems (M Eng), product design (M Eng), thermal engineering (M Eng); pharmaceutical manufacturing (M Eng, MS, Certificate); power generation (Certificate); product architecture and engineering (M Eng); robotics and control (Certificate); structural analysis and design (Certificate); vibration and noise control (Certificate). Part-time and evening/weekend programs available. Terminal master's awarded for partial completion of doctoral program. *Degree requirements:* For master's, thesis optional; for doctorate, variable foreign language requirement, thesis/dissertation; for Certificate, project or thesis. *Entrance requirements:* Additional exam requirements/recommendations for international students: Required—TOEFL. Electronic applications accepted. *Faculty research:* Acoustics, incineration, CAD/CAM, computational fluid dynamics and heat transfer, robotics.

Stony Brook University, State University of New York, Graduate School, College of Engineering and Applied Sciences, Department of Mechanical Engineering, Stony Brook, NY 11794. Offers MS, PhD. Evening/weekend programs available. *Degree requirements:* For master's, thesis or alternative; for doctorate, comprehensive exam, thesis/dissertation. *Entrance requirements:* For master's, GRE General Test, minimum GPA of 3.0; for doctorate, GRE General Test, minimum GPA of 3.5. Additional exam requirements/recommendations for international students: Required—TOEFL. *Faculty research:* Atmospheric sciences, thermal fluid sciences, solid mechanics.

Syracuse University, L. C. Smith College of Engineering and Computer Science, Program in Mechanical and Aerospace Engineering, Syracuse, NY 13244. Offers MS, PhD. *Students:* 112 full-time (19 women), 12 part-time (1 woman); includes 4 minority (1 Black or African American, non-Hispanic/Latino; 2 Asian, non-Hispanic/Latino; 1 Hispanic/Latino), 100 international. Average age 25. 213 applicants, 46% accepted, 49 enrolled. In 2011, 28 master's, 7 doctorates awarded. *Degree requirements:* For master's, project or thesis; for doctorate, thesis/dissertation. *Entrance requirements:* For master's and doctorate, GRE General Test. Additional exam requirements/recommendations for international students: Required—TOEFL (minimum score 100 iBT). *Application deadline:* For fall admission, 7/1 priority date for domestic students, 6/1 for international students. Applications are processed on a rolling basis. Application fee: $75. Electronic applications accepted. *Expenses: Tuition:* Part-time $1206 per credit.

Financial support: Fellowships with full tuition reimbursements, research assistantships with full and partial tuition reimbursements, teaching assistantships with full and partial tuition reimbursements, scholarships/grants, and tuition waivers (partial) available. Financial award application deadline: 1/1. *Faculty research:* Solid mechanics and materials, fluid mechanics, thermal sciences, controls and robotics. *Unit head:* Dr. Achille Messac, Chair, 315-443-2341, Fax: 315-443-9099, E-mail: messac@syr.edu. *Application contact:* Kathy Datthyn-Madigan, Information Contact, 315-443-4367, E-mail: kjdatthy@syr.edu. Web site: http://www.ecs.syr.edu/academic/mechaero_engineering/.

Temple University, College of Engineering, Department of Mechanical Engineering, Philadelphia, PA 19122-6096. Offers MSE. Part-time and evening/weekend programs available. *Faculty:* 11 full-time (3 women). *Students:* 7 full-time (1 woman), 5 part-time (1 woman); includes 2 minority (both Asian, non-Hispanic/Latino), 5 international. Average age 25. 21 applicants, 71% accepted, 6 enrolled. In 2011, 10 master's awarded. *Degree requirements:* For master's, thesis optional. *Entrance requirements:* For master's, GRE General Test, minimum GPA of 3.0. Additional exam requirements/recommendations for international students: Required—TOEFL (minimum score 550 paper-based; 213 computer-based; 79 iBT). *Application deadline:* For fall admission, 7/1 priority date for domestic students, 12/15 for international students; for spring admission, 11/1 priority date for domestic students, 8/1 for international students. Applications are processed on a rolling basis. Application fee: $50. Electronic applications accepted. *Expenses:* Tuition, state resident: full-time $12,366; part-time $687 per credit hour. Tuition, nonresident: full-time $17,298; part-time $961 per credit hour. *Required fees:* $590; $213 per year. *Financial support:* In 2011–12, 1 research assistantship with full tuition reimbursement, 8 teaching assistantships with full tuition reimbursements were awarded; fellowships and Federal Work-Study also available. Financial award application deadline: 1/15; financial award applicants required to submit FAFSA. *Faculty research:* Rapid solidification by melt spinning, microfracture analysis of dental materials, failure detection methods. *Unit head:* Dr. Mohammad Kiani, Chair, 215-204-4644, Fax: 215-204-4956, E-mail: mkiani@temple.edu. *Application contact:* Tara Schumacher, Coordinator of Outreach, 215-204-6575, Fax: 215-204-8781, E-mail: tara.schumacher@temple.edu. Web site: http://www.temple.edu/engineering/mechanical.

Tennessee Technological University, Graduate School, College of Engineering, Department of Mechanical Engineering, Cookeville, TN 38505. Offers MS. Part-time programs available. *Faculty:* 25 full-time (2 women). *Students:* 8 full-time (0 women), 15 part-time (0 women); includes 3 minority (1 Black or African American, non-Hispanic/Latino; 2 Asian, non-Hispanic/Latino), 3 international. Average age 28. 43 applicants, 35% accepted, 6 enrolled. In 2011, 9 master's awarded. *Degree requirements:* For master's, thesis. *Entrance requirements:* For master's, GRE. Additional exam requirements/recommendations for international students: Required—TOEFL (minimum score 550 paper-based; 79 iBT), IELTS (minimum score 5.5), PTE Academic. *Application deadline:* For fall admission, 8/1 for domestic students, 5/1 for international students; for spring admission, 12/1 for domestic students, 10/1 for international students. Application fee: $25 ($30 for international students). Electronic applications accepted. *Expenses:* Tuition, state resident: full-time $8094; part-time $422 per credit hour. Tuition, nonresident: full-time $20,574; part-time $1046 per credit hour. *Financial support:* In 2011–12, fellowships (averaging $8,000 per year), 20 research assistantships (averaging $8,190 per year), 8 teaching assistantships (averaging $6,711 per year) were awarded. Financial award application deadline: 4/1. *Faculty research:* Energy-related systems, design, acoustics and acoustical systems. *Unit head:* Dr. Darrell A. Hoy, Interim Chairperson, 931-372-3254, Fax: 931-372-6340, E-mail: dhoy@tntech.edu. *Application contact:* Shelia K. Kendrick, Coordinator of Graduate Admissions, 931-372-3808, Fax: 931-372-3497, E-mail: skendrick@tntech.edu.

Texas A&M University, College of Engineering, Department of Mechanical Engineering, College Station, TX 77843. Offers M Eng, MS, D Eng, PhD. *Faculty:* 57. *Students:* 400 full-time (83 women), 54 part-time (10 women); includes 53 minority (8 Black or African American, non-Hispanic/Latino; 1 American Indian or Alaska Native, non-Hispanic/Latino; 17 Asian, non-Hispanic/Latino; 23 Hispanic/Latino; 4 Two or more races, non-Hispanic/Latino), 288 international. Average age 24. In 2011, 115 master's, 22 doctorates awarded. *Degree requirements:* For master's, thesis (MS); for doctorate, dissertation (PhD). *Entrance requirements:* For master's, GRE General Test, minimum undergraduate GPA of 3.0; for doctorate, GRE General Test, minimum graduate GPA of 3.5. Additional exam requirements/recommendations for international students: Required—TOEFL (minimum score 570 paper-based). *Application deadline:* For fall admission, 2/1 priority date for domestic students; for spring admission, 11/1 for domestic students. Applications are processed on a rolling basis. Application fee: $50 ($75 for international students). Electronic applications accepted. *Expenses:* Tuition, state resident: full-time $5437; part-time $226.55 per credit hour. Tuition, nonresident: full-time $12,949; part-time $539.55 per credit hour. *Required fees:* $2741. *Financial support:* In 2011–12, fellowships with partial tuition reimbursements (averaging $5,000 per year), research assistantships with partial tuition reimbursements (averaging $14,000 per year), teaching assistantships (averaging $14,000 per year) were awarded; institutionally sponsored loans also available. Financial award application deadline: 3/1; financial award applicants required to submit FAFSA. *Faculty research:* Thermal/fluid sciences, materials/manufacturing and controls systems. *Unit head:* Dr. Jerald A. Caton, Head, 979-845-4705, E-mail: jcaton@tamu.edu. *Application contact:* Missy Cornett, Senior Academic Advisor I, 979-845-1270, Fax: 979-845-3081, E-mail: mcornett@tamu.edu. Web site: http://www.mengr.tamu.edu/.

Texas A&M University–Kingsville, College of Graduate Studies, College of Engineering, Department of Mechanical and Industrial Engineering, Program in Mechanical Engineering, Kingsville, TX 78363. Offers ME, MS. *Degree requirements:* For master's, comprehensive exam, thesis or alternative. *Entrance requirements:* For master's, GRE General Test, minimum GPA of 3.0. Additional exam requirements/recommendations for international students: Required—TOEFL. *Faculty research:* Intelligent systems and controls; neural networks and fuzzy logic; robotics and automation; biomass, cogeneration, and enhanced heat transfer.

Texas Tech University, Graduate School, Edward E. Whitacre Jr. College of Engineering, Department of Mechanical Engineering, Lubbock, TX 79409. Offers MSME, PhD. Part-time programs available. *Faculty:* 27 full-time (3 women), 1 part-time/adjunct (0 women). *Students:* 87 full-time (8 women), 25 part-time (1 woman); includes 12 minority (2 Black or African American, non-Hispanic/Latino; 4 Asian, non-Hispanic/Latino; 6 Hispanic/Latino), 51 international. Average age 29. 136 applicants, 35% accepted, 17 enrolled. In 2011, 12 master's, 3 doctorates awarded. *Degree requirements:* For master's, thesis or alternative; for doctorate, thesis/dissertation. *Entrance requirements:* For master's and doctorate, GRE General Test, minimum GPA of 3.0, 3 letters of recommendation, statement of purpose. Additional exam requirements/recommendations for international students: Required—TOEFL (minimum score 550 paper-based; 213 computer-based; 79 iBT). *Application deadline:* For fall admission, 6/1 priority date for domestic students, 1/15 for international students; for spring admission, 9/1 priority date for domestic students, 6/15 for international students. Applications are processed on a rolling basis. Application fee: $50 ($75 for international students). Electronic applications accepted. *Expenses:* Tuition, state resident: full-time $5899; part-time $245.80 per credit hour. Tuition, nonresident: full-time $13,411; part-time $558.80 per credit hour. *Required fees:* $2680.60; $86.50 per credit hour. $920.30 per semester. *Financial support:* In 2011–12, 59 students received support. Application deadline: 4/15; applicants required to submit FAFSA. *Faculty research:* Dynamics and control, wind energy, materials and mechanics, experimental and computational fluid mechanics, bioengineering. *Total annual research expenditures:* $1.6 million. *Unit head:* Dr. Jharna Chaudhuri, Chair, 806-742-3563, Fax: 806-742-3540, E-mail: jharna.chandhuri@ttu.edu. *Application contact:* Dr. Sira P. Parameswaran, Graduate Advisor, 806-742-3563 Ext. 247, Fax: 806-742-3540, E-mail: sira.parameswaran@ttu.edu. Web site: http://www.me.ttu.edu/.

Trine University, Allen School of Engineering and Technology, Angola, IN 46703-1764. Offers civil engineering (ME); mechanical engineering (ME). Part-time and evening/weekend programs available. *Degree requirements:* For master's, comprehensive exam, thesis. *Faculty research:* CAD, computer aided MFG, computer numerical control, parametric modeling, megatronics.

Tufts University, School of Engineering, Department of Mechanical Engineering, Medford, MA 02155. Offers bioengineering (ME, MS), including bioinformatics (ME), biomechanical systems and devices, signals and systems (ME); human factors (MS); mechanical engineering (ME, MS, PhD). Part-time programs available. *Faculty:* 13 full-time, 5 part-time/adjunct. *Students:* 83 full-time (22 women); includes 13 minority (2 Black or African American, non-Hispanic/Latino; 2 American Indian or Alaska Native, non-Hispanic/Latino; 7 Asian, non-Hispanic/Latino; 2 Hispanic/Latino), 14 international. Average age 27. 126 applicants, 46% accepted, 28 enrolled. In 2011, 21 degrees awarded. Terminal master's awarded for partial completion of doctoral program. *Degree requirements:* For master's, thesis; for doctorate, thesis/dissertation. *Entrance requirements:* For master's and doctorate, GRE General Test. Additional exam requirements/recommendations for international students: Required—TOEFL (minimum score 550 paper-based; 213 computer-based; 80 iBT). *Application deadline:* For fall admission, 1/15 priority date for domestic students, 12/15 for international students; for spring admission, 10/15 for domestic students, 9/15 for international students. Applications are processed on a rolling basis. Application fee: $75. Electronic applications accepted. *Expenses: Tuition:* Full-time $41,208; part-time $1030 per credit hour. Full-time tuition and fees vary according to degree level, program and student level. Part-time tuition and fees vary according to course load. *Financial support:* Fellowships with full tuition reimbursements, research assistantships with full and partial tuition reimbursements, teaching assistantships with full and partial tuition reimbursements, Federal Work-Study, scholarships/grants, tuition waivers (partial), and unspecified assistantships available. Financial award application deadline: 1/15; financial award applicants required to submit FAFSA. *Faculty research:* Applied mechanics, biomaterials, controls/robotics, design/systems, human factors. *Unit head:* Dr. Robert Hannemann, Acting Department Chair, 617-627-3239, Fax: 617-627-3058. *Application contact:* Lorin Polidora, Department Administrator, 617-627-3239, E-mail: meinfo@tufts.edu. Web site: http://engineering.tufts.edu/me.

Tuskegee University, Graduate Programs, College of Engineering, Architecture and Physical Sciences, Department of Mechanical Engineering, Tuskegee, AL 36088. Offers MSME. *Faculty:* 11 full-time (0 women). *Students:* 13 full-time (6 women), 1 part-time (0 women); includes 3 minority (all Black or African American, non-Hispanic/Latino), 10 international. Average age 29. In 2011, 12 master's awarded. *Degree requirements:* For master's, thesis or alternative. *Entrance requirements:* For master's, GRE General Test, GRE Subject Test. Additional exam requirements/recommendations for international students: Required—TOEFL (minimum score 500 paper-based; 69 computer-based). *Application deadline:* For fall admission, 7/15 for domestic students. Applications are processed on a rolling basis. Application fee: $25 ($35 for international students). *Expenses: Tuition:* Full-time $17,070; part-time $705 per credit hour. *Financial support:* Fellowships, research assistantships, teaching assistantships, career-related internships or fieldwork, Federal Work-Study, and institutionally sponsored loans available. Support available to part-time students. Financial award application deadline: 4/15. *Faculty research:* Superalloys, fatigue and surface machinery, energy management, solar energy. *Unit head:* Dr. Pradosh Ray, Head, 334-727-8989. *Application contact:* Dr. Robert L. Laney, Jr., Vice President/Director of Admissions and Enrollment Management, 334-727-8580, Fax: 334-727-5750, E-mail: planey@tuskegee.edu.

Union Graduate College, School of Engineering and Computer Science, Schenectady, NY 12308-3107. Offers computer science (MS); electrical engineering (MS); engineering and management systems (MS); mechanical engineering (MS). Part-time and evening/weekend programs available. *Faculty:* 3 full-time (0 women), 20 part-time/adjunct (2 women). *Students:* 13 full-time (1 woman), 103 part-time (13 women); includes 15 minority (2 Black or African American, non-Hispanic/Latino; 6 Asian, non-Hispanic/Latino; 6 Hispanic/Latino; 1 Two or more races, non-Hispanic/Latino), 3 international. Average age 28. 62 applicants, 69% accepted, 38 enrolled. In 2011, 29 master's awarded. *Degree requirements:* For master's, capstone course. *Entrance requirements:* For master's, minimum GPA of 3.0, letters of recommendation. Additional exam requirements/recommendations for international students: Required—TOEFL (minimum score 550 paper-based; 213 computer-based). *Application deadline:* Applications are processed on a rolling basis. Application fee: $60. Electronic applications accepted. *Expenses:* Contact institution. *Financial support:* In 2011–12, 2 students received support. Research assistantships, Federal Work-Study, scholarships/grants, health care benefits, and tuition waivers (full and partial) available. Support available to part-time students. Financial award applicants required to submit FAFSA. *Unit head:* Robert Kozik, Dean, 515-631-9881, Fax: 518-631-9902, E-mail: kozikr@union.edu. *Application contact:* Diane Trzaskos, Coordinator, Admissions, 518-631-9837, Fax: 518-631-9901, E-mail: trzaskod@uniongraduatecollege.edu.

Université de Moncton, Faculty of Engineering, Program in Mechanical Engineering, Moncton, NB E1A 3E9, Canada. Offers M Sc A. *Degree requirements:* For master's, thesis, proficiency in French. *Faculty research:* Composite materials, thermal energy systems, control systems, fluid mechanics and heat transfer, CAD/CAM and robotics.

Université de Sherbrooke, Faculty of Engineering, Department of Mechanical Engineering, Sherbrooke, QC J1K 2R1, Canada. Offers M Sc A, PhD. *Degree requirements:* For master's, one foreign language, thesis; for doctorate, comprehensive exam, thesis/dissertation. *Entrance requirements:* For master's, bachelor's degree in engineering or equivalent; for doctorate, master's degree in engineering or equivalent. Electronic applications accepted. *Faculty research:* Acoustics, aerodynamics, vehicle dynamics, composite materials, heat transfer.

Université Laval, Faculty of Sciences and Engineering, Department of Mechanical Engineering, Programs in Mechanical Engineering, Québec, QC G1K 7P4, Canada. Offers M Sc, PhD. Part-time programs available. Terminal master's awarded for partial completion of doctoral program. *Degree requirements:* For master's, thesis; for doctorate, comprehensive exam, thesis/dissertation. *Entrance requirements:* For master's and doctorate, knowledge of French. Electronic applications accepted.

University at Buffalo, the State University of New York, Graduate School, School of Engineering and Applied Sciences, Department of Mechanical and Aerospace Engineering, Buffalo, NY 14260. Offers aerospace engineering (MS, PhD); mechanical engineering (MS, PhD). Part-time programs available. *Faculty:* 28 full-time (4 women), 8 part-time/adjunct (0 women). *Students:* 164 full-time (16 women), 53 part-time (4 women); includes 10 minority (3 Black or African American, non-Hispanic/Latino; 1 American Indian or Alaska Native, non-Hispanic/Latino; 3 Asian, non-Hispanic/Latino; 3 Hispanic/Latino), 114 international. Average age 26. 842 applicants, 8% accepted, 63 enrolled. In 2011, 92 master's, 7 doctorates awarded. Terminal master's awarded for partial completion of doctoral program. *Degree requirements:* For master's, comprehensive exam, project or thesis; for doctorate, thesis/dissertation. *Entrance requirements:* For master's and doctorate, GRE General Test, GRE Subject Test. Additional exam requirements/recommendations for international students: Required—TOEFL (minimum score 79 iBT). *Application deadline:* For fall admission, 1/15 for domestic and international students; for spring admission, 9/15 for domestic and international students. Applications are processed on a rolling basis. Application fee: $75. *Financial support:* In 2011–12, 73 students received support, including 3 fellowships with full tuition reimbursements available (averaging $28,900 per year), 24 research assistantships with full tuition reimbursements available (averaging $26,000 per year), 31 teaching assistantships with full tuition reimbursements available (averaging $20,900 per year); Federal Work-Study, institutionally sponsored loans, tuition waivers (partial), and unspecified assistantships also available. Financial award application deadline: 1/15; financial award applicants required to submit FAFSA. *Faculty research:* Fluid and thermal sciences, systems and design, mechanics and materials. *Total annual research expenditures:* $4.6 million. *Unit head:* Dr. Gary Dargush, Chair, 716-645-2593, Fax: 716-645-2883, E-mail: gdargush@buffalo.edu. *Application contact:* Dr. John Crassidis, Director of Graduate Studies, 716-645-1426, Fax: 716-645-3875, E-mail: johnc@.buffalo.edu. Web site: http://www.mae.buffalo.edu/.

The University of Akron, Graduate School, College of Engineering, Department of Mechanical Engineering, Akron, OH 44325. Offers MS, PhD. Part-time and evening/weekend programs available. *Faculty:* 24 full-time (1 woman), 7 part-time/adjunct (0 women). *Students:* 60 full-time (11 women), 33 part-time (5 women); includes 2 minority (both Asian, non-Hispanic/Latino), 47 international. Average age 29. 74 applicants, 68% accepted, 15 enrolled. In 2011, 6 master's, 4 doctorates awarded. Terminal master's awarded for partial completion of doctoral program. *Degree requirements:* For master's, thesis optional; for doctorate, one foreign language, thesis/dissertation, candidacy exam, qualifying exam. *Entrance requirements:* For master's, GRE, minimum GPA of 2.75, baccalaureate degree in engineering, three letters of recommendation, statement of purpose, resume; for doctorate, GRE, minimum GPA of 3.0 with bachelor's degree, 3.5 with master's degree; three letters of recommendation, statement of purpose, resume. Additional exam requirements/recommendations for international students: Required—TOEFL (minimum score 550 paper-based; 213 computer-based; 79 iBT). *Application deadline:* Applications are processed on a rolling basis. Application fee: $30 ($40 for international students). Electronic applications accepted. *Expenses:* Tuition, state resident: full-time $7038; part-time $391 per credit hour. Tuition, nonresident: full-time $12,051; part-time $670 per credit hour. *Required fees:* $1274; $34 per credit hour. *Financial support:* In 2011–12, 19 research assistantships with full tuition reimbursements, 33 teaching assistantships with full tuition reimbursements were awarded. *Faculty research:* Materials science, tribology and lubrication, vibration and dynamic analysis, solid mechanics, MEMS and NEMS, bio-mechanics. *Total annual research expenditures:* $1.3 million. *Unit head:* Dr. Celal Batur, Chair, 330-972-7367, E-mail: batur@uakron.edu. *Application contact:* Dr. Craig Menzemer, Associate Dean, 330-972-5536, E-mail: ccmenze@uakron.edu. Web site: http://www.uakron.edu/engineering/ME/.

The University of Alabama, Graduate School, College of Engineering, Department of Mechanical Engineering, Tuscaloosa, AL 35487. Offers MS, PhD. Part-time programs available. *Faculty:* 19 full-time (2 women). *Students:* 57 full-time (4 women), 7 part-time (1 woman); includes 5 minority (2 Black or African American, non-Hispanic/Latino; 2 Asian, non-Hispanic/Latino; 1 Hispanic/Latino), 21 international. Average age 26. 71 applicants, 44% accepted, 17 enrolled. In 2011, 21 master's, 5 doctorates awarded. Terminal master's awarded for partial completion of doctoral program. *Median time to degree:* Of those who began their doctoral program in fall 2003, 100% received their degree in 8 years or less. *Degree requirements:* For master's, comprehensive exam, thesis (for some programs); for doctorate, comprehensive exam, thesis/dissertation. *Entrance requirements:* For master's, GRE General Test (waived for ABET accredited engineering degree), minimum GPA of 3.0; for doctorate, GRE General Test (waived for ABET-accredited engineering degree), minimum GPA of 3.0 with MS, 3.3 without MS. Additional exam requirements/recommendations for international students: Required—TOEFL (minimum score 600 paper-based). *Application deadline:* For fall admission, 7/1 priority date for domestic students, 1/15 for international students; for spring admission, 11/1 priority date for domestic students, 6/1 for international students. Applications are processed on a rolling basis. Application fee: $50 ($60 for international students). Electronic applications accepted. *Expenses:* Tuition, state resident: full-time $8600. Tuition, nonresident: full-time $21,900. *Financial support:* In 2011–12, 32 students received support, including 5 fellowships with full tuition reimbursements available (averaging $15,000 per year), 14 research assistantships with full tuition reimbursements available (averaging $15,000 per year), 13 teaching assistantships with full tuition reimbursements available (averaging $12,000 per year); career-related internships or fieldwork and unspecified assistantships also available. Financial award application deadline: 3/30. *Faculty research:* Thermal/fluids, robotics, numerical modeling, energy conservation, energy and combustion systems, internal combustion engines, manufacturing, vehicular systems, solid mechanics and materials. *Total annual research expenditures:* $2.7 million. *Unit head:* Dr. Robert P. Taylor, Head and Professor, 205-348-4078, Fax: 205-348-6419, E-mail: btaylor2@eng.ua.edu. *Application contact:* Dr. Will Schreiber, Coordinator and Professor, 205-348-1650, Fax: 205-348-6419, E-mail: wschreiber@eng.ua.edu. Web site: http://www.me.ua.edu.

The University of Alabama at Birmingham, School of Engineering, Program in Mechanical Engineering, Birmingham, AL 35294. Offers MSME. *Expenses:* Tuition, state resident: full-time $5922; part-time $309 per hour. Tuition, nonresident: full-time $13,428; part-time $726 per hour. Tuition and fees vary according to program. *Unit head:* Dr. Bharat K. Soni, Chair, 205-934-8460. *Application contact:* Julie Bryant, Director of Graduate Admissions, 205-934-8227, Fax: 205-934-8413, E-mail: jbryant@uab.edu. Web site: http://www.uab.edu/engineering/departments-research/me/graduate#Master%20of%20Science%20in%20Civil%20Engineering%20%28M.S.C.E.%29%20Program%20Requirem.

The University of Alabama in Huntsville, School of Graduate Studies, College of Engineering, Department of Mechanical and Aerospace Engineering, Huntsville, AL

35899. Offers aerospace engineering (MSE), including aerospace engineering, missile systems engineering, rotorcraft systems engineering; aerospace systems engineering (MS, PhD); mechanical engineering (MSE, PhD). Part-time and evening/weekend programs available. *Faculty:* 19 full-time (0 women), 6 part-time/adjunct (0 women). *Students:* 62 full-time (10 women), 120 part-time (18 women); includes 17 minority (6 Black or African American, non-Hispanic/Latino; 1 American Indian or Alaska Native, non-Hispanic/Latino; 6 Asian, non-Hispanic/Latino; 4 Hispanic/Latino), 16 international. Average age 30. 124 applicants, 62% accepted, 52 enrolled. In 2011, 41 master's, 2 doctorates awarded. *Degree requirements:* For master's, comprehensive exam, thesis or alternative, oral and written exams; for doctorate, comprehensive exam, thesis/dissertation, oral and written exams. *Entrance requirements:* For master's, GRE General Test, BSE, minimum GPA of 3.0; for doctorate, GRE General Test, minimum GPA of 3.0. Additional exam requirements/recommendations for international students: Required—TOEFL (minimum score 500 paper-based; 173 computer-based; 62 iBT). *Application deadline:* For fall admission, 7/15 for domestic students, 4/1 for international students; for spring admission, 1/30 for domestic students, 9/1 for international students. Applications are processed on a rolling basis. Application fee: $40 ($50 for international students). Electronic applications accepted. *Expenses:* Tuition, state resident: full-time $7830; part-time $473.50 per credit. Tuition, nonresident: full-time $18,748; part-time $1128.33 per credit. Tuition and fees vary according to course load and program. *Financial support:* In 2011–12, 46 students received support, including 29 research assistantships with full tuition reimbursements available (averaging $12,881 per year), 17 teaching assistantships with full tuition reimbursements available (averaging $11,141 per year); career-related internships or fieldwork, Federal Work-Study, institutionally sponsored loans, scholarships/grants, health care benefits, and unspecified assistantships also available. Support available to part-time students. Financial award application deadline: 4/1; financial award applicants required to submit FAFSA. *Faculty research:* Combustion, fluid dynamics, materials and structures, propulsion, laser diagnostics. *Total annual research expenditures:* $19.7 million. *Unit head:* Dr. Keith Hollingsworth, Chair, 256-824-6154, Fax: 256-824-6758, E-mail: keith.hollingsworth@uah.edu. *Application contact:* Kim Gray, Graduate Studies Admissions Coordinator, 256-824-6002, Fax: 256-824-6405, E-mail: deangrad@uah.edu. Web site: http://www.mae.uah.edu/graduate.shtml.

University of Alaska Fairbanks, College of Engineering and Mines, Department of Mechanical Engineering, Fairbanks, AK 99775-5905. Offers engineering (PhD); mechanical engineering (MS). Part-time programs available. *Faculty:* 7 full-time (0 women). *Students:* 14 full-time (4 women), 4 part-time (1 woman); includes 4 minority (1 Black or African American, non-Hispanic/Latino; 2 Asian, non-Hispanic/Latino; 1 Two or more races, non-Hispanic/Latino), 6 international. Average age 28. 16 applicants, 19% accepted, 3 enrolled. In 2011, 6 degrees awarded. Terminal master's awarded for partial completion of doctoral program. *Degree requirements:* For master's, comprehensive exam, thesis or alternative; for doctorate, comprehensive exam, thesis/dissertation, oral exam, oral defense. *Entrance requirements:* For master's and doctorate, GRE General Test. Additional exam requirements/recommendations for international students: Required—TOEFL (minimum score 550 paper-based; 213 computer-based; 80 iBT). *Application deadline:* For fall admission, 6/1 for domestic students, 3/1 for international students; for spring admission, 10/15 for domestic students, 9/1 for international students. Applications are processed on a rolling basis. Application fee: $60. Electronic applications accepted. *Expenses:* Tuition, state resident: full-time $6696; part-time $372 per credit. Tuition, nonresident: full-time $13,680; part-time $760 per credit. Tuition and fees vary according to course load and reciprocity agreements. *Financial support:* In 2011–12, 6 research assistantships with tuition reimbursements (averaging $14,327 per year), 5 teaching assistantships with tuition reimbursements (averaging $7,302 per year) were awarded; fellowships with tuition reimbursements, career-related internships or fieldwork, Federal Work-Study, scholarships/grants, health care benefits, and unspecified assistantships also available. Support available to part-time students. Financial award application deadline: 7/1; financial award applicants required to submit FAFSA. *Faculty research:* Cold regions engineering, fluid mechanics, heat transfer, energy systems, indoor air quality. *Unit head:* Dr. Jonah Lee, Department Chair, 907-474-7136, Fax: 907-474-6141, E-mail: fymech@uaf.edu. *Application contact:* Mike Earnest, Director of Admissions, 907-474-7500, Fax: 907-474-5379, E-mail: admissions@uaf.edu. Web site: http://cem.uaf.edu/me/.

University of Alberta, Faculty of Graduate Studies and Research, Department of Mechanical Engineering, Edmonton, AB T6G 2E1, Canada. Offers engineering management (M Eng); mechanical engineering (M Eng, M Sc, PhD); MBA/M Eng. Part-time programs available. *Degree requirements:* For master's, thesis; for doctorate, thesis/dissertation. *Entrance requirements:* For master's and doctorate, minimum GPA of 7.0 on a 9.0 scale. Additional exam requirements/recommendations for international students: Required—TOEFL (minimum score 580 paper-based; 237 computer-based). *Faculty research:* Combustion and environmental issues, advanced materials, computational fluid dynamics, biomedical, acoustics and vibrations.

The University of Arizona, College of Engineering, Department of Aerospace and Mechanical Engineering, Program in Mechanical Engineering, Tucson, AZ 85721. Offers MS, PhD. Part-time programs available. *Faculty:* 20 full-time, 2 part-time/adjunct. *Students:* 58 full-time (10 women), 9 part-time (0 women); includes 3 minority (all Hispanic/Latino), 46 international. Average age 27. 64 applicants, 69% accepted, 16 enrolled. In 2011, 8 master's, 8 doctorates awarded. *Degree requirements:* For master's, thesis or alternative; for doctorate, one foreign language, thesis/dissertation. *Entrance requirements:* For master's and doctorate, GRE General Test, minimum GPA of 3.25, 3 letters of recommendation, statement of purpose. Additional exam requirements/recommendations for international students: Required—TOEFL (minimum score 550 paper-based; 213 computer-based; 79 iBT). *Application deadline:* For fall admission, 6/1 for domestic students, 12/1 for international students; for spring admission, 10/1 for domestic students, 6/1 for international students. Applications are processed on a rolling basis. Application fee: $75. Electronic applications accepted. *Expenses:* Tuition, state resident: full-time $10,840. Tuition, nonresident: full-time $25,802. *Financial support:* Research assistantships, teaching assistantships, and unspecified assistantships available. *Faculty research:* Fluid mechanics, structures, computer-aided design, stability and control, probabilistic design. *Unit head:* Dr. Ara Arabyan, Interim Department Head, 520-621-2116, Fax: 520-621-8191, E-mail: arabyan@email.arizona.edu. *Application contact:* Barbara Heefner, Graduate Secretary, 520-621-4692, Fax: 520-621-8191, E-mail: heefner@email.arizona.edu. Web site: http://www.ame.arizona.edu/.

University of Arkansas, Graduate School, College of Engineering, Department of Mechanical Engineering, Fayetteville, AR 72701-1201. Offers MSE, MSME, PhD. Part-time programs available. Postbaccalaureate distance learning degree programs offered. *Students:* 12 full-time (0 women), 21 part-time (3 women); includes 5 minority (2 Black or African American, non-Hispanic/Latino; 2 Asian, non-Hispanic/Latino; 1 Two or more races, non-Hispanic/Latino), 16 international. 40 applicants, 65% accepted. In 2011, 11 master's awarded. *Degree requirements:* For master's, thesis optional; for doctorate, one foreign language, thesis/dissertation. *Application deadline:* For fall admission, 4/1 for international students; for spring admission, 10/1 for international students. Applications are processed on a rolling basis. Application fee: $40 ($50 for international students). Electronic applications accepted. *Financial support:* In 2011–12, 16 research assistantships, 1 teaching assistantship were awarded; fellowships, career-related internships or fieldwork, and Federal Work-Study also available. Support available to part-time students. Financial award application deadline: 4/1; financial award applicants required to submit FAFSA. *Unit head:* Dr. James Leylek, Departmental Chair, 479-575-4153, Fax: 479-575-6982, E-mail: jleylek@uark.edu. *Application contact:* Dr. Rick Couvillion, Graduate Coordinator, 479-575-4155, E-mail: rjc@uark.edu. Web site: http://www.meeg.uark.edu.

University of Bridgeport, School of Engineering, Department of Mechanical Engineering, Bridgeport, CT 06604. Offers MS. *Faculty:* 2 full-time (1 woman), 2 part-time/adjunct (0 women). *Students:* 39 full-time (2 women), 29 part-time (1 woman); includes 3 minority (all Asian, non-Hispanic/Latino), 63 international. Average age 26. 150 applicants, 65% accepted, 6 enrolled. In 2011, 66 master's awarded. *Degree requirements:* For master's, thesis optional. *Entrance requirements:* Additional exam requirements/recommendations for international students: Recommended—TOEFL (minimum score 550 paper-based; 213 computer-based; 80 iBT), IELTS (minimum score 6.5). *Application deadline:* For fall admission, 8/1 priority date for domestic students, 8/1 for international students; for spring admission, 12/1 priority date for domestic students, 12/1 for international students. Applications are processed on a rolling basis. Application fee: $50. Electronic applications accepted. *Expenses: Tuition:* Full-time $22,880; part-time $700 per credit. *Required fees:* $1870; $95 per semester. Tuition and fees vary according to course load and program. *Financial support:* In 2011–12, 10 students received support. Fellowships, research assistantships, teaching assistantships, career-related internships or fieldwork, Federal Work-Study, institutionally sponsored loans, and tuition waivers (partial) available. Support available to part-time students. Financial award application deadline: 6/1; financial award applicants required to submit FAFSA. *Faculty research:* Residual stress in composite material resins, helicopter composite structure and dynamic components, water spray cooling, heat transfer. *Unit head:* Dr. Jani Macari pallis, Chairperson, 203-576-4579, Fax: 203-576-4750, E-mail: jpallis@bridgeport.edu. *Application contact:* Karissa Peckham, Dean of Admissions, 203-576-4552, Fax: 203-576-4941, E-mail: admit@bridgeport.edu.

The University of British Columbia, Faculty of Applied Science, Program in Mechanical Engineering, Vancouver, BC V6T 1Z1, Canada. Offers M Eng, MA Sc, PhD. *Degree requirements:* For master's, thesis; for doctorate, comprehensive exam, thesis/dissertation, 33 credits beyond bachelor's degree. *Entrance requirements:* For master's, bachelor's degree, minimum B+ average; for doctorate, master's degree, minimum B+ average. Additional exam requirements/recommendations for international students: Required—TOEFL (minimum score 580 paper-based; 237 computer-based; 93 iBT), IELTS (minimum score 6.5); Recommended—TWE. Electronic applications accepted. *Faculty research:* Applied mechanics, manufacturing, robotics and controls, thermodynamics and combustion, fluid/aerodynamics, acoustics.

University of Calgary, Faculty of Graduate Studies, Schulich School of Engineering, Department of Mechanical and Manufacturing Engineering, Calgary, AB T2N 1N4, Canada. Offers M Eng, M Sc, PhD. *Degree requirements:* For master's, thesis (for some programs); for doctorate, thesis/dissertation, candidacy exam. *Entrance requirements:* For master's, minimum GPA of 3.0; for doctorate, minimum GPA of 3.3. Additional exam requirements/recommendations for international students: Required—TOEFL (minimum score 550 paper-based; 213 computer-based), IELTS (minimum score 7). *Faculty research:* Thermofluids, solid mechanics, materials, biomechanics, manufacturing.

University of California, Berkeley, Graduate Division, College of Engineering, Department of Mechanical Engineering, Berkeley, CA 94720-1500. Offers M Eng, MS, D Eng, PhD. *Degree requirements:* For master's, comprehensive exam or thesis (MS); for doctorate, thesis/dissertation, preliminary and qualifying exams. *Entrance requirements:* For master's and doctorate, GRE General Test, minimum GPA of 3.0, 3 letters of recommendation. Additional exam requirements/recommendations for international students: Required—TOEFL.

University of California, Davis, College of Engineering, Program in Mechanical and Aeronautical Engineering, Davis, CA 95616. Offers aeronautical engineering (M Engr, MS, D Engr, PhD, Certificate); mechanical engineering (M Engr, MS, D Engr, PhD, Certificate); M Engr/MBA. *Degree requirements:* For master's, comprehensive exam (for some programs), thesis (for some programs); for doctorate, thesis/dissertation. *Entrance requirements:* For master's and doctorate, GRE General Test, minimum GPA of 3.0. Additional exam requirements/recommendations for international students: Required—TOEFL (minimum score 550 paper-based; 213 computer-based). Electronic applications accepted.

University of California, Irvine, School of Engineering, Department of Mechanical and Aerospace Engineering, Irvine, CA 92697. Offers MS, PhD. Part-time programs available. *Students:* 111 full-time (16 women), 6 part-time (0 women); includes 31 minority (18 Asian, non-Hispanic/Latino; 11 Hispanic/Latino; 2 Two or more races, non-Hispanic/Latino), 49 international. Average age 27. 448 applicants, 25% accepted, 30 enrolled. In 2011, 36 master's, 14 doctorates awarded. Terminal master's awarded for partial completion of doctoral program. *Degree requirements:* For doctorate, thesis/dissertation. *Entrance requirements:* For master's and doctorate, GRE General Test, minimum GPA of 3.0, 3 letters of recommendation. Additional exam requirements/recommendations for international students: Required—TOEFL (minimum score 550 paper-based; 213 computer-based). *Application deadline:* For fall admission, 1/15 priority date for domestic students, 1/15 for international students. Applications are processed on a rolling basis. Application fee: $80 ($100 for international students). Electronic applications accepted. *Financial support:* Fellowships with tuition reimbursements, research assistantships with full tuition reimbursements, teaching assistantships with tuition reimbursements, institutionally sponsored loans, traineeships, health care benefits, and unspecified assistantships available. Financial award application deadline: 3/1; financial award applicants required to submit FAFSA. *Faculty research:* Thermal and fluid sciences, combustion and propulsion, control systems, robotics, lightweight structures. *Unit head:* Prof. Derek Dunn-Rankin, Chair, 949-824-8745, Fax: 949-824-8585, E-mail: ddunnran@uci.edu. *Application contact:* Lousie Yeager, Graduate Coordinator, 949-824-7984, Fax: 949-824-8585, E-mail: lyeager@uci.edu. Web site: http://mae.eng.uci.edu/.

University of California, Los Angeles, Graduate Division, Henry Samueli School of Engineering and Applied Science, Department of Mechanical and Aerospace Engineering, Program in Mechanical Engineering, Los Angeles, CA 90095-1597. Offers MS, PhD. *Faculty:* 29 full-time (2 women), 6 part-time/adjunct. *Students:* 208 full-time (35 women); includes 74 minority (3 Black or African American, non-Hispanic/Latino; 53 Asian, non-Hispanic/Latino; 14 Hispanic/Latino; 4 Two or more races, non-Hispanic/Latino), 73 international. 477 applicants, 43% accepted, 86 enrolled. In 2011, 69 master's, 20 doctorates awarded. *Degree requirements:* For master's, comprehensive exam or thesis; for doctorate, thesis/dissertation, qualifying exams. *Entrance requirements:* For master's, GRE General Test, minimum GPA of 3.0; for doctorate, GRE General Test, minimum GPA of 3.25. Additional exam requirements/recommendations for international students: Required—TOEFL (minimum score 560 paper-based; 87 iBT). *Application deadline:* For fall admission, 12/15 for domestic and international students; for winter admission, 10/1 for domestic students; for spring admission, 12/31 for domestic students. Application fee: $80 ($100 for international students). Electronic applications accepted. *Financial support:* In 2011–12, 126 fellowships, 273 research assistantships, 93 teaching assistantships were awarded; Federal Work-Study, institutionally sponsored loans, and tuition waivers (full and partial) also available. Financial award application deadline: 1/5; financial award applicants required to submit FAFSA. *Faculty research:* Dynamics, fluid mechanics, heat and mass transfer, manufacturing and design, nanoelectromechanical/microelectromechanical systems (NEMS/MEMS), structural and solid mechanics, systems and control. *Total annual research expenditures:* $15 million. *Unit head:* Dr. Tsu-Chin Tsao, Chair, 310-206-2819, E-mail: ttsao@seas.ucla.edu. *Application contact:* Angie Castillo, Student Affairs Officer, 310-825-7793, Fax: 310-206-4830, E-mail: angie@ea.ucla.edu. Web site: http://www.mae.ucla.edu/.

University of California, Merced, Division of Graduate Studies, School of Natural Sciences, Merced, CA 95343. Offers applied mathematics (MS, PhD); biological engineering and small-scale technologies (MS, PhD); environmental systems (MS, PhD); mechanical engineering and applied mechanics (MS, PhD); physics and chemistry (PhD); quantitative and systems biology (MS, PhD). *Unit head:* Dr. Samuel J. Traina, Dean, 209-228-4723, Fax: 209-228-6906, E-mail: grad.dean@ucmerced.edu. *Application contact:* Tsu Ya, Graduate Admissions and Academic Services Manager, 209-228-4723, Fax: 209-228-6906, E-mail: tya@ucmerced.edu.

University of California, Riverside, Graduate Division, Department of Mechanical Engineering, Riverside, CA 92521. Offers MS, PhD. Part-time programs available. Terminal master's awarded for partial completion of doctoral program. *Degree requirements:* For master's, comprehensive exam or thesis, seminar in mechanical engineering; for doctorate, comprehensive exam, thesis/dissertation, seminar in mechanical engineering. *Entrance requirements:* Additional exam requirements/recommendations for international students: Required—TOEFL (minimum score 550 paper-based; 213 computer-based; 80 iBT). *Faculty research:* Advanced robotics and machine design, air quality modeling group, computational fluid dynamics, computational mechanics and materials, biomaterials and nanotechnology laboratory.

University of California, San Diego, Office of Graduate Studies, Department of Mechanical and Aerospace Engineering, Program in Mechanical Engineering, La Jolla, CA 92093. Offers MS, PhD. Part-time programs available. *Degree requirements:* For master's, comprehensive exam or thesis; for doctorate, thesis/dissertation, qualifying exam. *Entrance requirements:* For master's and doctorate, GRE General Test, minimum GPA of 3.0. Additional exam requirements/recommendations for international students: Required—TOEFL. Electronic applications accepted. *Faculty research:* Combustion engineering, environmental mechanics, magnetic recording, materials processing, computational fluid dynamics.

University of California, Santa Barbara, Graduate Division, College of Engineering, Department of Mechanical Engineering, Santa Barbara, CA 93106-5070. Offers computational science and engineering (MS, PhD); mechanical engineering (MS, PhD); MS/PhD. *Faculty:* 28 full-time (4 women), 8 part-time/adjunct (3 women). *Students:* 80 full-time (9 women); includes 10 minority (1 Black or African American, non-Hispanic/Latino; 7 Asian, non-Hispanic/Latino; 2 Hispanic/Latino), 28 international. Average age 27. 279 applicants, 19% accepted, 19 enrolled. In 2011, 7 master's, 8 doctorates awarded. *Median time to degree:* Of those who began their doctoral program in fall 2003, 100% received their degree in 8 years or less. *Degree requirements:* For master's, thesis; for doctorate, comprehensive exam, thesis/dissertation. *Entrance requirements:* For master's and doctorate, GRE. Additional exam requirements/recommendations for international students: Required—TOEFL (minimum score 550 paper-based; 213 computer-based; 80 iBT), IELTS (minimum score 7). *Application deadline:* For fall admission, 12/15 for domestic and international students. Application fee: $80 ($100 for international students). Electronic applications accepted. *Expenses:* Tuition, state resident: full-time $12,192. Tuition, nonresident: full-time $27,294. *Required fees:* $764.13. *Financial support:* In 2011–12, 72 students received support, including 7 fellowships with full and partial tuition reimbursements available (averaging $22,000 per year), 27 research assistantships with full and partial tuition reimbursements available (averaging $19,099 per year), 24 teaching assistantships with full and partial tuition reimbursements available (averaging $17,308 per year); scholarships/grants, health care benefits, tuition waivers (full and partial), and unspecified assistantships also available. Financial award application deadline: 12/15; financial award applicants required to submit FAFSA. *Faculty research:* Micro/nanoscale technology; computational science and engineering; dynamics systems, controls and robotics; thermofluid sciences; solid mechanics, materials, and structures. *Total annual research expenditures:* $5.7 million. *Unit head:* Dr. Kimberly Turner, Chair, 805-893-8080, Fax: 805-893-8651, E-mail: turner@engineering.ucsb.edu. *Application contact:* Laura L. Reynolds, Staff Graduate Program Advisor, 805-893-2239, Fax: 805-893-8651, E-mail: megrad@engineering.ucsb.edu. Web site: http://www.me.ucsb.edu/.

University of Central Florida, College of Engineering and Computer Science, Department of Mechanical, Materials, and Aerospace Engineering, Program in Mechanical Engineering, Orlando, FL 32816. Offers mechanical engineering (MSME, PhD). *Students:* 98 full-time (17 women), 67 part-time (3 women); includes 32 minority (5 Black or African American, non-Hispanic/Latino; 6 Asian, non-Hispanic/Latino; 19 Hispanic/Latino; 2 Two or more races, non-Hispanic/Latino), 48 international. Average age 27. 113 applicants, 65% accepted, 37 enrolled. In 2011, 27 master's, 6 doctorates awarded. *Degree requirements:* For master's, thesis or alternative; for doctorate, thesis/dissertation, candidacy exam, departmental qualifying exam. *Application deadline:* For fall admission, 7/15 priority date for domestic students; for spring admission, 12/1 priority date for domestic students. Electronic applications accepted. *Expenses:* Tuition, state resident: part-time $277.08 per credit hour. Tuition, nonresident: part-time $277.08 per credit hour. Part-time tuition and fees vary according to degree level and program. *Financial support:* In 2011–12, 56 students received support, including 13 fellowships (averaging $8,700 per year), 24 research assistantships (averaging $7,800 per year), 38 teaching assistantships (averaging $10,800 per year); career-related internships or fieldwork, institutionally sponsored loans, scholarships/grants, tuition waivers (partial), and unspecified assistantships also available. *Unit head:* Dr. Suhada Jayasuriya, Chair, 407-823-5792, Fax: 407-823-0208, E-mail: suhada@ucf.edu. *Application contact:* Barbara Rodriguez, Director, Admissions and Registration, 407-823-2766, Fax: 407-823-6442, E-mail: gradadmissions@ucf.edu. Web site: http://mmae.ucf.edu/.

University of Cincinnati, Graduate School, College of Engineering and Applied Science, Department of Mechanical, Industrial and Nuclear Engineering, Program in Mechanical Engineering, Cincinnati, OH 45221. Offers MS, PhD. Evening/weekend programs available. Terminal master's awarded for partial completion of doctoral program. *Degree requirements:* For master's, oral exam or thesis defense; for doctorate, variable foreign language requirement, thesis/dissertation. *Entrance requirements:* For master's and doctorate, GRE General Test. Additional exam requirements/recommendations for international students: Required—TOEFL (minimum score 575 paper-based; 233 computer-based). Electronic applications accepted. *Faculty research:* Signature analysis, structural analysis, energy, design, robotics.

University of Colorado at Colorado Springs, College of Engineering and Applied Science, Department of Mechanical and Aerospace Engineering, Colorado Springs, CO 80933-7150. Offers engineering management (ME); information operations (ME); manufacturing (ME); mechanical engineering (MS); software engineering (ME); space operations (ME); space systems (MS). Part-time and evening/weekend programs available. *Faculty:* 11 full-time (2 women). *Students:* 48 full-time (14 women), 44 part-time (11 women); includes 15 minority (3 Black or African American, non-Hispanic/Latino; 6 Asian, non-Hispanic/Latino; 5 Hispanic/Latino; 1 Two or more races, non-Hispanic/Latino), 3 international. Average age 33. 40 applicants, 60% accepted, 13 enrolled. In 2011, 31 degrees awarded. *Degree requirements:* For master's, thesis optional. *Entrance requirements:* For master's, GRE General Test, bachelor's degree in engineering or related degree, minimum GPA of 3.0. Additional exam requirements/recommendations for international students: Required—TOEFL (minimum score 550 paper-based; 213 computer-based; 79 iBT). *Application deadline:* For fall admission, 3/1 for domestic and international students; for spring admission, 10/1 for domestic and international students. Applications are processed on a rolling basis. Application fee: $60 ($75 for international students). *Expenses:* Tuition, state resident: part-time $660 per credit hour. Tuition, nonresident: part-time $1133 per credit hour. Tuition and fees vary according to degree level, program and student level. *Financial support:* In 2011–12, 5 students received support. Federal Work-Study and scholarships/grants available. Support available to part-time students. Financial award application deadline: 3/1; financial award applicants required to submit FAFSA. *Faculty research:* Neural networks, artificial intelligence, robust control, space operations, space propulsion. *Total annual research expenditures:* $163,405. *Unit head:* Rebecca Webb, Director, 719-255-3581, Fax: 719-255-3674, E-mail: rwebb@uccs.edu. *Application contact:* Siew Nylund, Academic Adviser, 719-255-3243, Fax: 719-255-3589, E-mail: snylund@eas.uccs.edu. Web site: http://eas.uccs.edu/mae/.

University of Colorado Boulder, Graduate School, College of Engineering and Applied Science, Department of Mechanical Engineering, Boulder, CO 80309. Offers ME, MS, PhD. *Faculty:* 23 full-time (5 women). *Students:* 178 full-time (33 women), 29 part-time (4 women); includes 25 minority (2 Black or African American, non-Hispanic/Latino; 2 American Indian or Alaska Native, non-Hispanic/Latino; 11 Asian, non-Hispanic/Latino; 6 Hispanic/Latino; 4 Two or more races, non-Hispanic/Latino), 55 international. Average age 26. 297 applicants, 51% accepted, 41 enrolled. In 2011, 66 master's, 10 doctorates awarded. Terminal master's awarded for partial completion of doctoral program. *Degree requirements:* For master's, comprehensive exam, thesis optional; for doctorate, comprehensive exam, thesis/dissertation, final and preliminary exams. *Entrance requirements:* For master's and doctorate, minimum undergraduate GPA of 3.0. Additional exam requirements/recommendations for international students: Required—TOEFL. *Application deadline:* For fall admission, 1/15 priority date for domestic students, 12/1 for international students; for spring admission, 10/15 for domestic students, 9/1 for international students. Applications are processed on a rolling basis. Application fee: $50 ($60 for international students). Electronic applications accepted. *Financial support:* In 2011–12, 174 students received support, including 84 fellowships (averaging $5,126 per year), 59 research assistantships with full and partial tuition reimbursements available (averaging $23,631 per year), 19 teaching assistantships with full and partial tuition reimbursements available (averaging $20,629 per year); institutionally sponsored loans, scholarships/grants, health care benefits, and unspecified assistantships also available. Financial award application deadline: 1/15; financial award applicants required to submit FAFSA. *Faculty research:* Thermal science, fluid mechanics, solid mechanics, materials science, interactive design and manufacturing. *Total annual research expenditures:* $8.6 million. *Application contact:* E-mail: megrad@colorado.edu. Web site: http://www.colorado.edu/mechanical/.

University of Colorado Denver, College of Engineering and Applied Science, Department of Bioengineering, Aurora, CO 80045-2560. Offers bioengineering (PhD); clinical application (PhD); clinical imaging (MS); commercialization of medical technologies (MS, PhD); device design and entrepreneurship (MS); research (MS). Part-time programs available. *Faculty:* 3 full-time (1 woman). *Students:* 38 full-time (13 women), 1 part-time; includes 7 minority (3 Black or African American, non-Hispanic/Latino; 2 Asian, non-Hispanic/Latino; 1 Hispanic/Latino; 1 Two or more races, non-Hispanic/Latino), 2 international. Average age 27. 56 applicants, 48% accepted, 24 enrolled. Terminal master's awarded for partial completion of doctoral program. *Degree requirements:* For master's, thesis or alternative, 30 credit hours; for doctorate, comprehensive exam, thesis/dissertation, 36 credit hours of classwork (18 core, 18 elective), additional 30 hours of thesis work, three formal examinations, approval of dissertations. *Entrance requirements:* For master's and doctorate, GRE, transcripts, three letters of recommendation, resume, statement of purpose. Additional exam requirements/recommendations for international students: Required—TOEFL (minimum score 550 paper-based; 213 computer-based; 79 iBT), TOEFL (minimum score 600 paper-based; 250 computer-based; 100 iBT) for Ph D. *Application deadline:* For fall admission, 2/15 for domestic students. Application fee: $50. Electronic applications accepted. *Expenses:* Contact institution. *Financial support:* Fellowships, research assistantships, teaching assistantships, and Federal Work-Study available. Financial award application deadline: 4/1; financial award applicants required to submit FAFSA. *Faculty research:* Imaging and biophotonics, cardiovascular biomechanics and hemodynamics, orthopedic biomechanics, ophthalmology, neuroscience engineering, diabetes, surgery and urological sciences. *Unit head:* Dr. Robin Shandas, Chair, 303-724-4196, E-mail: robin.shandas@ucdenver.edu. *Application contact:* Graduate School Admissions, 303-556-2704, E-mail: admissions@ucdenver.edu. Web site: http://bioengineering.ucdenver.edu/.

University of Colorado Denver, College of Engineering and Applied Science, Department of Mechanical Engineering, Denver, CO 80217. Offers mechanical engineering (MS); mechanics (MS); thermal sciences (MS). Part-time and evening/weekend programs available. *Faculty:* 8 full-time (0 women), 2 part-time/adjunct (both women). *Students:* 25 full-time (4 women), 19 part-time (3 women); includes 9 minority (3 Black or African American, non-Hispanic/Latino; 4 Asian, non-Hispanic/Latino; 2 Hispanic/Latino), 10 international. Average age 30. 25 applicants, 68% accepted, 5 enrolled. In 2011, 12 master's awarded. *Degree requirements:* For master's, comprehensive exam, thesis or alternative, 30 credit hours, project or thesis. *Entrance requirements:* For master's, GRE. Additional exam requirements/recommendations for international students: Required—TOEFL (minimum score 525 paper-based; 197 computer-based). *Application deadline:* For fall admission, 7/15 for domestic students;

for spring admission, 11/15 for domestic students. Applications are processed on a rolling basis. Application fee: $50 ($75 for international students). Electronic applications accepted. *Expenses:* Contact institution. *Financial support:* Research assistantships, teaching assistantships, career-related internships or fieldwork, and Federal Work-Study available. Financial award application deadline: 4/1; financial award applicants required to submit FAFSA. *Faculty research:* Applied and computational mechanics, bioengineering, energy systems, tribology, micro/mesofluidics and biomechanics, vehicle dynamics. *Unit head:* Dr. Sam Welch, Chair, 303-556-8488, Fax: 303-556-6371, E-mail: sam.welch@ucdenver.edu. *Application contact:* Catherine McCoy, Program Assistant, 303-556-8516, E-mail: catherine.mccoy@ucdenver.edu. Web site: http://www.ucdenver.edu/academics/colleges/Engineering/Programs/Mechanical-Engineering/Pages/MechanicalEngineering.aspx.

University of Colorado Denver, College of Engineering and Applied Science, Master of Engineering Program, Denver, CO 80217-3364. Offers civil engineering (M Eng), including civil engineering, geographic information systems, transportation systems; electrical engineering (M Eng); mechanical engineering (M Eng). Part-time programs available. *Students:* 21 full-time (9 women), 30 part-time (7 women); includes 5 minority (2 Black or African American, non-Hispanic/Latino; 1 Asian, non-Hispanic/Latino; 2 Hispanic/Latino), 1 international. Average age 34. 13 applicants, 69% accepted, 8 enrolled. In 2011, 19 master's awarded. *Degree requirements:* For master's, comprehensive exam, thesis, 27 credit hours of course work, 3 credit hours of report or thesis work. *Entrance requirements:* For master's, GRE (for those with GPA below 2.75), transcripts, references, statement of purpose. Additional exam requirements/recommendations for international students: Required—TOEFL (minimum score 525 paper-based; 197 computer-based; 71 iBT). *Application deadline:* For fall admission, 7/15 for domestic students, 6/15 for international students; for spring admission, 12/1 for domestic students, 11/1 for international students. Applications are processed on a rolling basis. Application fee: $50 ($75 for international students). Electronic applications accepted. *Expenses:* Contact institution. *Financial support:* Federal Work-Study and scholarships/grants available. Financial award application deadline: 4/1; financial award applicants required to submit FAFSA. *Faculty research:* Civil, electrical and mechanical engineering. *Unit head:* 303-556-2870, Fax: 303-556-2511, E-mail: engineering@ucdenver.edu. *Application contact:* Graduate School Admissions, 303-556-2704, E-mail: admissions@ucdenver.edu. Web site: http://ucdenver.edu/academics/colleges/Engineering/admissions/Masters/Pages/MastersAdmissions.aspx.

University of Connecticut, Graduate School, School of Engineering, Department of Mechanical Engineering, Storrs, CT 06269. Offers MS, PhD. Terminal master's awarded for partial completion of doctoral program. *Degree requirements:* For master's, comprehensive exam, thesis or alternative; for doctorate, thesis/dissertation. *Entrance requirements:* For master's and doctorate, GRE General Test, GRE Subject Test. Additional exam requirements/recommendations for international students: Required—TOEFL (minimum score 550 paper-based; 213 computer-based). Electronic applications accepted. *Faculty research:* Design, applied mechanics, dynamics and control, energy and thermal sciences, manufacturing.

University of Dayton, Department of Mechanical and Aerospace Engineering, Dayton, OH 45469-1300. Offers aerospace engineering (MSAE, DE, PhD); mechanical engineering (MSME, DE, PhD); renewable and clean energy (MS). Part-time programs available. Postbaccalaureate distance learning degree programs offered (no on-campus study). *Faculty:* 16 full-time (2 women), 11 part-time/adjunct (1 woman). *Students:* 150 full-time (22 women), 28 part-time (6 women); includes 15 minority (7 Black or African American, non-Hispanic/Latino; 3 Asian, non-Hispanic/Latino; 5 Hispanic/Latino), 77 international. Average age 27. 177 applicants, 63% accepted, 55 enrolled. In 2011, 66 master's, 4 doctorates awarded. Terminal master's awarded for partial completion of doctoral program. *Degree requirements:* For master's, thesis optional; for doctorate, variable foreign language requirement, thesis/dissertation, departmental qualifying exam. *Entrance requirements:* Additional exam requirements/recommendations for international students: Required—TOEFL (minimum score 550 paper-based; 213 computer-based; 80 iBT). *Application deadline:* For fall admission, 8/1 priority date for domestic students, 6/1 for international students; for winter admission, 9/1 for international students; for spring admission, 3/1 for international students. Applications are processed on a rolling basis. Application fee: $0. Electronic applications accepted. *Expenses: Tuition:* Full-time $8400; part-time $700 per credit hour. *Required fees:* $25 per semester. Tuition and fees vary according to degree level. *Financial support:* In 2011–12, 25 students received support, including 29 research assistantships with full tuition reimbursements available (averaging $11,000 per year), 7 teaching assistantships with full tuition reimbursements available (averaging $9,100 per year). Financial award applicants required to submit FAFSA. *Faculty research:* Jet engine combustion, surface coating friction and wear, aircraft thermal management, aerospace fuels, energy efficient buildings, energy efficient manufacturing, renewable energy. *Total annual research expenditures:* $1.2 million. *Unit head:* Dr. Kelly Kissock, Chair, 937-229-2999, Fax: 937-229-4766, E-mail: kelly.kissock@udayton.edu. *Application contact:* Dr. Vinod Jain, Graduate Program Director, 937-229-2992, Fax: 937-229-4766, E-mail: vinod.jain@notes.udayton.edu. Web site: http://www.udayton.edu/engineering/mechanical_and_aerospace/.

University of Delaware, College of Engineering, Department of Mechanical Engineering, Newark, DE 19716. Offers MEM, MSME, PhD. Part-time programs available. Terminal master's awarded for partial completion of doctoral program. *Degree requirements:* For master's, thesis (for some programs); for doctorate, thesis/dissertation. *Entrance requirements:* For master's and doctorate, GRE General Test. Additional exam requirements/recommendations for international students: Required—TOEFL (minimum score 600 paper-based; 250 computer-based). Electronic applications accepted. *Faculty research:* Biomedical engineering, clean energy, composites and nanotechnology, robotics and controls, fluid mechanics.

University of Denver, School of Engineering and Computer Science, Department of Mechanical and Materials Engineering, Denver, CO 80208. Offers bioengineering (MS); engineering (MS, PhD); engineering/management (MS); interdisciplinary engineering (PhD); materials science (MS, PhD); mechanical engineering (MS, PhD); nanoscale science and engineering (MS, PhD). Part-time programs available. *Faculty:* 10 full-time (2 women), 1 part-time/adjunct (0 women). *Students:* 1 (woman) full-time, 25 part-time (5 women); includes 1 minority (Asian, non-Hispanic/Latino), 9 international. Average age 30. 69 applicants, 67% accepted, 11 enrolled. In 2011, 6 degrees awarded. Terminal master's awarded for partial completion of doctoral program. *Degree requirements:* For master's, thesis or alternative; for doctorate, comprehensive exam, thesis/dissertation. *Entrance requirements:* For master's, GRE General Test, essay/personal statement, three letters of recommendation; for doctorate, GRE General Test, essay/personal statement, three letters of recommendation, curriculum vitae. Additional exam requirements/recommendations for international students: Required—TOEFL (minimum score 550 paper-based; 80 iBT). *Application deadline:* Applications are processed on a rolling basis. Application fee: $60. Electronic applications accepted. *Financial support:* In 2011–12, 14 students received support, including 8 research

assistantships with full and partial tuition reimbursements available (averaging $15,631 per year), 7 teaching assistantships with full and partial tuition reimbursements available (averaging $13,943 per year); Federal Work-Study, health care benefits, and unspecified assistantships also available. Financial award application deadline: 2/15; financial award applicants required to submit FAFSA. *Faculty research:* Aerosols, biomechanics, composite materials, photo optics, drug delivery. *Total annual research expenditures:* $818,288. *Unit head:* Dr. Matt Gordon, Chair, 303-871-3580, Fax: 303-871-4450, E-mail: matthew.gordon@du.edu. *Application contact:* Renee Carvalho, Assistant to the Chair, 303-871-2107, Fax: 303-871-4450, E-mail: renee.carvalho@du.edu. Web site: http://www.mme.du.edu.

University of Detroit Mercy, College of Engineering and Science, Department of Mechanical Engineering, Detroit, MI 48221. Offers mechanical engineering (ME, DE). Evening/weekend programs available. *Degree requirements:* For doctorate, thesis/dissertation. *Faculty research:* CAD/CAM.

University of Florida, Graduate School, College of Engineering, Department of Mechanical and Aerospace Engineering, Gainesville, FL 32611. Offers aerospace engineering (ME, MS, PhD, Engr); mechanical engineering (ME, MS, PhD, Engr). Part-time programs available. *Degree requirements:* For master's, thesis (for some programs); for doctorate, comprehensive exam, thesis/dissertation; for Engr, thesis. *Entrance requirements:* For master's and doctorate, GRE General Test, minimum GPA of 3.0; for Engr, GRE General Test. Additional exam requirements/recommendations for international students: Required—TOEFL (minimum score 550 paper-based; 213 computer-based; 80 iBT), IELTS (minimum score 6). Electronic applications accepted. *Faculty research:* Thermal sciences, design, controls and robotics, manufacturing, energy transport and utilization.

University of Hawaii at Manoa, Graduate Division, College of Engineering, Department of Mechanical Engineering, Honolulu, HI 96822. Offers MS, PhD. Part-time programs available. *Degree requirements:* For master's, comprehensive exam, thesis; for doctorate, comprehensive exam, thesis/dissertation. *Entrance requirements:* For master's and doctorate, GRE General Test. Additional exam requirements/recommendations for international students: Required—TOEFL (minimum score 550 paper-based; 213 computer-based; 79 iBT), IELTS (minimum score 5). *Faculty research:* Materials and manufacturing; mechanics, systems and control; thermal and fluid sciences.

University of Houston, Cullen College of Engineering, Department of Mechanical Engineering, Houston, TX 77204. Offers MME, MSME, PhD. Part-time programs available. Terminal master's awarded for partial completion of doctoral program. *Degree requirements:* For master's, thesis (for some programs); for doctorate, thesis/dissertation, departmental qualifying exam. *Entrance requirements:* For master's and doctorate, GRE General Test. Additional exam requirements/recommendations for international students: Required—TOEFL.

University of Illinois at Chicago, Graduate College, College of Engineering, Department of Mechanical and Industrial Engineering, Chicago, IL 60607-7128. Offers energy engineering (MEE); industrial engineering (MS); industrial engineering and operations research (PhD); mechanical engineering (MS, PhD), including fluids engineering, mechanical analysis and design, thermomechanical and power engineering. Part-time programs available. *Degree requirements:* For doctorate, thesis/dissertation. *Entrance requirements:* For master's and doctorate, GRE General Test, minimum GPA of 2.75. Additional exam requirements/recommendations for international students: Required—TOEFL. Electronic applications accepted.

University of Illinois at Urbana–Champaign, Graduate College, College of Engineering, Department of Mechanical Science and Engineering, Champaign, IL 61820. Offers mechanical engineering (MS, PhD); theoretical and applied mechanics (MS, PhD); MS/MBA. *Faculty:* 52 full-time (5 women), 2 part-time/adjunct (0 women). *Students:* 323 full-time (42 women), 35 part-time (5 women); includes 30 minority (16 Asian, non-Hispanic/Latino; 12 Hispanic/Latino; 2 Two or more races, non-Hispanic/Latino), 211 international. 807 applicants, 26% accepted, 75 enrolled. In 2011, 90 master's, 31 doctorates awarded. Terminal master's awarded for partial completion of doctoral program. *Entrance requirements:* For master's, GRE General Test, minimum GPA of 3.25; for doctorate, GRE General Test, minimum GPA of 3.5. Additional exam requirements/recommendations for international students: Required—TOEFL (minimum score 613 paper-based; 257 computer-based; 103 iBT). *Application deadline:* Applications are processed on a rolling basis. Application fee: $75 ($90 for international students). Electronic applications accepted. *Financial support:* In 2011–12, 44 fellowships, 244 research assistantships, 109 teaching assistantships were awarded; tuition waivers (full and partial) also available. *Faculty research:* Combustion and propulsion, design methodology, dynamic systems and controls, energy transfer, materials behavior and processing, manufacturing systems operations, management. *Unit head:* Placid Mathew Ferreira, Head, 217-333-0639, Fax: 217-244-6534, E-mail: pferreir@illinois.edu. *Application contact:* Katrina Hagler, Graduate Admissions Coordinator, 217-244-3416, Fax: 217-244-6534, E-mail: kkappes2@illinois.edu. Web site: http://mechse.illinois.edu.

The University of Iowa, Graduate College, College of Engineering, Department of Mechanical Engineering, Iowa City, IA 52242-1316. Offers MS, PhD. *Faculty:* 13 full-time (1 woman), 1 part-time/adjunct (0 women). *Students:* 59 full-time (8 women); includes 2 minority (1 Black or African American, non-Hispanic/Latino; 1 Hispanic/Latino), 36 international. Average age 28. 90 applicants, 19% accepted, 12 enrolled. In 2011, 13 master's, 2 doctorates awarded. *Degree requirements:* For master's, oral exam or thesis; for doctorate, comprehensive exam, thesis/dissertation. *Entrance requirements:* For master's and doctorate, GRE. Additional exam requirements/recommendations for international students: Required—TOEFL (minimum score 550 paper-based; 213 computer-based; 81 iBT). *Application deadline:* For fall admission, 7/15 for domestic students, 4/15 for international students; for spring admission, 12/1 for domestic students, 10/1 for international students. Applications are processed on a rolling basis. Application fee: $60 ($100 for international students). Electronic applications accepted. *Financial support:* In 2011–12, 46 research assistantships with partial tuition reimbursements (averaging $21,930 per year), 19 teaching assistantships with partial tuition reimbursements (averaging $16,575 per year) were awarded; fellowships with partial tuition reimbursements, traineeships, and unspecified assistantships also available. Financial award applicants required to submit FAFSA. *Faculty research:* Computer simulation methodology, biomechanics, dynamics, solid mechanics, fluid dynamics. *Total annual research expenditures:* $9.3 million. *Unit head:* Dr. Andrew Kusiak, Departmental Executive Officer, 319-335-5934, Fax: 319-335-5669, E-mail: andrew-kusiak@uiowa.edu. *Application contact:* Andrea Flaherty, Academic Program Specialist, 319-335-5668, Fax: 319-335-5669, E-mail: mech_eng@engineering.uiowa.edu. Web site: http://www.mie.engineering.uiowa.edu/.

The University of Kansas, Graduate Studies, School of Engineering, Department of Mechanical Engineering, Lawrence, KS 66045. Offers MS, DE, PhD. Part-time programs available. *Faculty:* 17 full-time (4 women). *Students:* 45 full-time (8 women),

10 part-time (1 woman); includes 3 minority (1 Asian, non-Hispanic/Latino; 1 Hispanic/Latino; 1 Two or more races, non-Hispanic/Latino), 19 international. Average age 26. 70 applicants, 31% accepted, 14 enrolled. In 2011, 9 master's, 3 doctorates awarded. *Degree requirements:* For master's, thesis or alternative, exam; for doctorate, comprehensive exam, thesis/dissertation. *Entrance requirements:* For master's, minimum GPA of 3.0; for doctorate, minimum GPA of 3.5. Additional exam requirements/recommendations for international students: Required—TOEFL. *Application deadline:* For fall admission, 6/1 priority date for domestic students, 3/31 for international students; for spring admission, 11/1 priority date for domestic students, 9/30 for international students. Applications are processed on a rolling basis. Application fee: $55 ($65 for international students). Electronic applications accepted. Tuition and fees vary according to course load, campus/location, program and reciprocity agreements. *Financial support:* Fellowships with full and partial tuition reimbursements, research assistantships with full and partial tuition reimbursements, teaching assistantships with full and partial tuition reimbursements, and career-related internships or fieldwork available. Financial award application deadline: 5/15. *Faculty research:* Heat transfer, energy analysis, computer-aided design, biomedical engineering, computational mathematics. *Unit head:* Ronald Dougherty, Chair, 785-864-3181, E-mail: kume@ku.edu. *Application contact:* Glen Marotz, Associate Dean, 785-864-2941, Fax: 785-864-5445, E-mail: gama@ku.edu.

University of Kentucky, Graduate School, College of Engineering, Program in Mechanical Engineering, Lexington, KY 40506-0032. Offers MSME, PhD. *Degree requirements:* For master's, comprehensive exam, thesis optional; for doctorate, comprehensive exam, thesis/dissertation. *Entrance requirements:* For master's, GRE General Test, minimum undergraduate GPA of 2.75; for doctorate, GRE General Test, minimum undergraduate GPA of 3.0. Additional exam requirements/recommendations for international students: Required—TOEFL (minimum score 550 paper-based; 213 computer-based). Electronic applications accepted. *Faculty research:* Combustion, computational fluid dynamics, design and systems, manufacturing, thermal and fluid sciences.

University of Louisiana at Lafayette, College of Engineering, Department of Mechanical Engineering, Lafayette, LA 70504. Offers MSE. Evening/weekend programs available. *Degree requirements:* For master's, comprehensive exam, thesis or alternative. *Entrance requirements:* For master's, GRE General Test, BS in mechanical engineering, minimum GPA of 2.85. Additional exam requirements/recommendations for international students: Required—TOEFL (minimum score 550 paper-based; 213 computer-based). Electronic applications accepted. *Faculty research:* CAD/CAM, machine design and vibration, thermal science.

University of Louisville, J. B. Speed School of Engineering, Department of Mechanical Engineering, Louisville, KY 40292-0001. Offers M Eng, MS, PhD. *Accreditation:* ABET (one or more programs are accredited). Part-time programs available. *Faculty:* 17 full-time (2 women). *Students:* 71 full-time (5 women), 22 part-time (1 woman); includes 10 minority (1 Black or African American, non-Hispanic/Latino; 1 American Indian or Alaska Native, non-Hispanic/Latino; 2 Asian, non-Hispanic/Latino; 4 Hispanic/Latino; 2 Two or more races, non-Hispanic/Latino), 12 international. Average age 28. 35 applicants, 63% accepted, 12 enrolled. In 2011, 48 master's, 2 doctorates awarded. Terminal master's awarded for partial completion of doctoral program. *Median time to degree:* Of those who began their doctoral program in fall 2003, 50% received their degree in 8 years or less. *Degree requirements:* For master's, comprehensive exam (for some programs), thesis or alternative; for doctorate, comprehensive exam, thesis/dissertation, minimum GPA of 3.0. *Entrance requirements:* For master's and doctorate, GRE General Test. Additional exam requirements/recommendations for international students: Required—TOEFL (minimum score 550 paper-based; 213 computer-based; 80 iBT), IELTS (minimum score 6.5). *Application deadline:* For fall admission, 5/1 priority date for domestic students, 5/1 for international students; for spring admission, 11/1 priority date for domestic students, 11/1 for international students. Applications are processed on a rolling basis. Application fee: $50. Electronic applications accepted. *Expenses:* Tuition, state resident: full-time $9692; part-time $539 per credit hour. Tuition, nonresident: full-time $20,168; part-time $1121 per credit hour. Tuition and fees vary according to program and reciprocity agreements. *Financial support:* In 2011–12, 16 students received support, including 1 fellowship with full tuition reimbursement available (averaging $22,000 per year), 4 research assistantships with full tuition reimbursements available (averaging $22,500 per year), 11 teaching assistantships with full tuition reimbursements available (averaging $20,000 per year). Financial award application deadline: 1/25; financial award applicants required to submit FAFSA. *Faculty research:* Aerospace and automotive engineering, air pollution control, biomechanics and rehabilitation engineering, computer-aided design, micro and nanotechnology. *Total annual research expenditures:* $1.3 million. *Unit head:* Dr. Glen Prater, Jr., Chair, 502-852-6331, Fax: 502-852-6053, E-mail: gprater@louisville.edu. *Application contact:* Dr. Michael Day, Associate Dean, 502-852-6195, Fax: 502-852-7294, E-mail: day@louisville.edu. Web site: http://www.louisville.edu/speed/mechanical.

University of Maine, Graduate School, College of Engineering, Department of Mechanical Engineering, Orono, ME 04469. Offers MS, PhD. *Faculty:* 12 full-time (0 women), 7 part-time/adjunct (1 woman). *Students:* 21 full-time (3 women), 12 part-time (3 women), 14 international. Average age 31. 32 applicants, 53% accepted, 11 enrolled. In 2011, 2 master's, 1 doctorate awarded. *Degree requirements:* For master's, thesis (for some programs). *Entrance requirements:* For master's and doctorate, GRE General Test. Additional exam requirements/recommendations for international students: Required—TOEFL. *Application deadline:* For fall admission, 2/1 priority date for domestic students. Applications are processed on a rolling basis. Application fee: $65. Electronic applications accepted. *Expenses:* Tuition, state resident: full-time $5016. Tuition, nonresident: full-time $14,424. *Financial support:* In 2011–12, 1 fellowship with full tuition reimbursement (averaging $25,000 per year), 18 research assistantships with full tuition reimbursements (averaging $15,380 per year), 2 teaching assistantships with full tuition reimbursements (averaging $13,600 per year) were awarded; Federal Work-Study and tuition waivers (full and partial) also available. Financial award application deadline: 3/1. *Faculty research:* Higher order beam and plate theories, dynamic response of structural systems, heat transfer in window systems, forced convection heat transfer in gas turbine passages, effect of parallel space heating systems on utility load management. *Total annual research expenditures:* $361,584. *Unit head:* Dr. Moshen Shahinpoor, Chair, 207-581-2120, Fax: 207-581-2379. *Application contact:* Scott G. Delcourt, Associate Dean of the Graduate School, 207-581-3291, Fax: 207-581-3232, E-mail: graduate@maine.edu. Web site: http://www2.umaine.edu/graduate/.

The University of Manchester, School of Mechanical, Aerospace and Civil Engineering, Manchester, United Kingdom. Offers advanced manufacturing technology (M Ent); aerospace engineering (M Phil, M Sc, PhD); civil engineering (M Phil, M Sc, PhD); environmental engineering (M Phil, PhD); management of projects (M Phil, M Sc, PhD); mechanical engineering (M Phil, M Sc, PhD); mechanical engineering design (M Ent); nuclear engineering (M Phil, D Eng, PhD).

University of Manitoba, Faculty of Graduate Studies, Faculty of Engineering, Department of Mechanical and Manufacturing Engineering, Winnipeg, MB R3T 2N2, Canada. Offers M Eng, M Sc, PhD. *Degree requirements:* For master's, thesis; for doctorate, thesis/dissertation.

University of Maryland, Baltimore County, Graduate School, College of Engineering and Information Technology, Department of Mechanical Engineering, Baltimore, MD 21250. Offers computational thermal/fluid dynamics (Postbaccalaureate Certificate); mechanical engineering (MS, PhD); mechatronics (Postbaccalaureate Certificate). Part-time programs available. *Faculty:* 14 full-time (3 women), 2 part-time/adjunct (0 women). *Students:* 53 full-time (9 women), 29 part-time (3 women); includes 15 minority (6 Black or African American, non-Hispanic/Latino; 3 Asian, non-Hispanic/Latino; 5 Hispanic/Latino; 1 Two or more races, non-Hispanic/Latino), 28 international. Average age 36. 59 applicants, 64% accepted, 15 enrolled. In 2011, 10 master's, 6 doctorates, 2 other advanced degrees awarded. *Degree requirements:* For master's, comprehensive exam (for some programs), thesis (for some programs); for doctorate, comprehensive exam, thesis/dissertation. *Entrance requirements:* For master's, GRE General Test, minimum GPA of 3.0; for doctorate, GRE General Test, minimum overall GPA of 3.3; bachelor's degree in mechanical, aerospace, civil, industrial, or chemical engineering. Additional exam requirements/recommendations for international students: Required—TOEFL (minimum score 550 paper-based; 250 computer-based; 80 iBT). *Application deadline:* For fall admission, 6/1 for domestic students, 1/1 for international students; for spring admission, 11/1 for domestic students, 6/1 for international students. Applications are processed on a rolling basis. Application fee: $70. Electronic applications accepted. *Financial support:* In 2011–12, 9 fellowships with full tuition reimbursements (averaging $15,000 per year), 14 research assistantships with full tuition reimbursements (averaging $20,000 per year), 16 teaching assistantships with full tuition reimbursements (averaging $17,000 per year) were awarded; career-related internships or fieldwork, Federal Work-Study, scholarships/grants, health care benefits, tuition waivers (partial), and unspecified assistantships also available. Support available to part-time students. Financial award application deadline: 6/30; financial award applicants required to submit FAFSA. *Faculty research:* Mechanics and materials, thermal/fluids sciences, design-manufacturing systems, bio-mechanics biomaterials, engineering education (STEM). *Total annual research expenditures:* $1.5 million. *Unit head:* Dr. Charles Eggleton, Professor and Acting Chair, 410-455-3334, Fax: 410-455-1052, E-mail: eggleton@umbc.edu. *Application contact:* Chuck Smithson, Program Management Specialist, 410-455-3357, Fax: 410-455-1052, E-mail: csmithso@umbc.edu. Web site: http://www.me.umbc.edu/.

University of Maryland, College Park, Academic Affairs, A. James Clark School of Engineering, Department of Continuing and Distance Learning in Engineering, College Park, MD 20742. Offers engineering (M Eng), including aerospace engineering, chemical engineering, civil engineering, electrical engineering, engineering, fire protection engineering, materials science and engineering, mechanical engineering, reliability engineering, systems engineering. *Faculty:* 3 full-time (0 women), 8 part-time/adjunct (0 women). *Students:* 75 full-time (24 women), 418 part-time (81 women); includes 154 minority (62 Black or African American, non-Hispanic/Latino; 64 Asian, non-Hispanic/Latino; 23 Hispanic/Latino; 5 Two or more races, non-Hispanic/Latino), 67 international. 447 applicants, 52% accepted, 154 enrolled. In 2011, 155 master's awarded. *Application deadline:* For fall admission, 8/15 for domestic students, 2/1 for international students; for spring admission, 1/10 for domestic students, 8/1 for international students. Applications are processed on a rolling basis. Application fee: $75. Electronic applications accepted. *Expenses: Tuition, area resident:* Part-time $525 per credit hour. Tuition, state resident: part-time $525 per credit hour. Tuition, nonresident: part-time $1131 per credit hour. *Required fees:* $386.31 per term. Tuition and fees vary according to program. *Financial support:* In 2011–12, 3 research assistantships (averaging $21,498 per year), 13 teaching assistantships (averaging $16,889 per year) were awarded. *Unit head:* Dr. Darryll Pines, Dean, 301-405-8539, E-mail: pines@umd.edu. *Application contact:* Dr. Charles A. Caramello, Dean of the Graduate School, 301-405-0358, Fax: 301-314-9305.

University of Maryland, College Park, Academic Affairs, A. James Clark School of Engineering, Department of Mechanical Engineering, College Park, MD 20742. Offers electronic packaging and reliability (MS, PhD); manufacturing and design (MS, PhD); mechanics and materials (MS, PhD); reliability engineering (M Eng, MS, PhD); thermal and fluid sciences (MS, PhD). Part-time and evening/weekend programs available. Postbaccalaureate distance learning degree programs offered. *Faculty:* 88 full-time (8 women), 20 part-time/adjunct. *Students:* 240 full-time (36 women), 72 part-time (6 women); includes 54 minority (14 Black or African American, non-Hispanic/Latino; 2 American Indian or Alaska Native, non-Hispanic/Latino; 23 Asian, non-Hispanic/Latino; 11 Hispanic/Latino; 4 Two or more races, non-Hispanic/Latino), 145 international. 457 applicants, 19% accepted, 61 enrolled. In 2011, 35 master's, 29 doctorates awarded. *Degree requirements:* For master's, thesis optional; for doctorate, thesis/dissertation, qualifying exam. *Entrance requirements:* For master's, GRE General Test, 3 letters of recommendation; for doctorate, GRE General Test, minimum GPA of 3.0. Additional exam requirements/recommendations for international students: Required—TOEFL. *Application deadline:* For fall admission, 5/15 for domestic students, 2/1 for international students; for spring admission, 10/15 for domestic students, 6/1 for international students. Applications are processed on a rolling basis. Application fee: $75. Electronic applications accepted. *Expenses: Tuition, area resident:* Part-time $525 per credit hour. Tuition, state resident: part-time $525 per credit hour. Tuition, nonresident: part-time $1131 per credit hour. *Required fees:* $386.31 per term. Tuition and fees vary according to program. *Financial support:* In 2011–12, 7 fellowships with full and partial tuition reimbursements (averaging $24,003 per year), 166 research assistantships (averaging $23,766 per year), 17 teaching assistantships (averaging $17,967 per year) were awarded; Federal Work-Study and scholarships/grants also available. Support available to part-time students. Financial award applicants required to submit FAFSA. *Faculty research:* Injection molding, electronic packaging, fluid mechanics, product engineering. *Total annual research expenditures:* $19 million. *Unit head:* Dr. B. Balachandran, Chair, 301-405-5309, E-mail: balab@umd.edu. *Application contact:* Dr. Charles A. Caramello, Graduate Director, 301-405-0358, Fax: 301-314-9305, E-mail: ccaramel@umd.edu.

University of Massachusetts Amherst, Graduate School, College of Engineering, Department of Mechanical and Industrial Engineering, Amherst, MA 01003. Offers industrial engineering and operations research (MS, PhD); mechanical engineering (MSME, PhD). Part-time programs available. *Faculty:* 36 full-time (3 women). *Students:* 103 full-time (26 women), 14 part-time (3 women); includes 10 minority (2 Black or African American, non-Hispanic/Latino; 4 Asian, non-Hispanic/Latino; 3 Hispanic/Latino; 1 Native Hawaiian or other Pacific Islander, non-Hispanic/Latino), 60 international. Average age 28. 350 applicants, 32% accepted, 29 enrolled. In 2011, 16 master's, 4 doctorates awarded. Terminal master's awarded for partial completion of doctoral program. *Degree requirements:* For master's, thesis or alternative; for doctorate, comprehensive exam, thesis/dissertation. *Entrance requirements:* For master's and doctorate, GRE General Test. Additional exam requirements/recommendations for international students: Required—TOEFL (minimum score 550 paper-based; 213 computer-based; 80 iBT), IELTS (minimum score 6.5). *Application deadline:* For fall admission, 1/15 for domestic and international students; for spring admission, 10/1 for domestic and international students. Applications are processed on a rolling basis. Application fee: $50 ($65 for international students). Electronic applications accepted. Tuition and fees vary according to course load, campus/location and program. *Financial support:* Fellowships with full and partial tuition reimbursements, research assistantships with full tuition reimbursements, teaching assistantships with full tuition reimbursements, career-related internships or fieldwork, Federal Work-Study, scholarships/grants, traineeships, health care benefits, tuition waivers (full and partial), and unspecified assistantships available. Support available to part-time students. Financial award application deadline: 1/15. *Unit head:* Dr. David P. Schmidt, Graduate Program Director, 413-545-3827, Fax: 413-545-1027. *Application contact:* Lindsay DeSantis, Interim Supervisor of Admissions, 413-545-0722, Fax: 413-577-0100, E-mail: gradadm@grad.umass.edu. Web site: http://mie.umass.edu/.

University of Massachusetts Amherst, Graduate School, Interdisciplinary Programs, Dual Degree Program in Business Administration and Mechanical Engineering, Amherst, MA 01003. Offers MSME/MBA. Part-time programs available. *Students:* 1 full-time (0 women); minority (Two or more races, non-Hispanic/Latino). Average age 26. 1 applicant, 0% accepted, 0 enrolled. *Entrance requirements:* Additional exam requirements/recommendations for international students: Required—TOEFL (minimum score 600 paper-based; 250 computer-based; 100 iBT), IELTS (minimum score 7). *Application deadline:* For fall admission, 1/15 for domestic and international students. Applications are processed on a rolling basis. Application fee: $50 ($65 for international students). Electronic applications accepted. Tuition and fees vary according to course load, campus/location and program. *Financial support:* Career-related internships or fieldwork, Federal Work-Study, scholarships/grants, traineeships, health care benefits, tuition waivers (full), and unspecified assistantships available. Support available to part-time students. *Unit head:* Dr. David P. Schmidt, Graduate Program Director, 413-545-3827, Fax: 413-545-1027. *Application contact:* Lindsay DeSantis, Interim Supervisor of Admissions, 413-545-0722, Fax: 413-577-0010, E-mail: gradadm@grad.umass.edu. Web site: http://www-new.ecs.umass.edu/degrees#MBA.

University of Massachusetts Dartmouth, Graduate School, College of Engineering, Program in Mechanical Engineering, North Dartmouth, MA 02747-2300. Offers MS. Part-time programs available. *Faculty:* 11 full-time (1 woman), 1 (woman) part-time/adjunct. *Students:* 11 full-time (2 women), 24 part-time (3 women), 14 international. Average age 28. 16 applicants, 63% accepted, 6 enrolled. In 2011, 8 degrees awarded. *Degree requirements:* For master's, thesis or alternative. *Entrance requirements:* For master's, GRE General Test, minimum undergraduate GPA of 3.0, 3 letters of recommendation, resume, statement of intent. Additional exam requirements/recommendations for international students: Required—TOEFL (minimum score 533 paper-based; 200 computer-based; 72 iBT). *Application deadline:* For fall admission, 2/15 priority date for domestic students, 1/15 for international students; for spring admission, 11/15 priority date for domestic students, 10/15 for international students. Applications are processed on a rolling basis. Application fee: $40 ($60 for international students). Electronic applications accepted. *Expenses:* Tuition, state resident: full-time $2071; part-time $86.29 per credit. Tuition, nonresident: full-time $8099; part-time $337.46 per credit. *Required fees:* $438.58 per credit. Part-time tuition and fees vary according to class time, course load, degree level and reciprocity agreements. *Financial support:* In 2011–12, 9 research assistantships with full tuition reimbursements (averaging $9,858 per year), 8 teaching assistantships with full tuition reimbursements (averaging $7,000 per year) were awarded; Federal Work-Study and unspecified assistantships also available. Support available to part-time students. Financial award application deadline: 3/1. *Faculty research:* Biofluid mechanics, universal design, heat and mass transfer, computer simulation, volcanic flows . *Total annual research expenditures:* $468,493. *Unit head:* Dr. John Rice, Graduate Program Director, 508-999-8498, E-mail: jrice@umassd.edu. *Application contact:* Elan Turcotte-Shamski, Graduate Admissions Officer, 508-999-8604, Fax: 508-999-8183, E-mail: graduate@umassd.edu. Web site: http://www.umassd.edu/engineering/mne/graduate/welcome.cfm.

University of Massachusetts Lowell, College of Engineering, Department of Mechanical Engineering, Lowell, MA 01854-2881. Offers MS Eng, D Eng, PhD. Part-time programs available. *Degree requirements:* For master's, thesis or alternative; for doctorate, 2 foreign languages, comprehensive exam, thesis/dissertation. *Entrance requirements:* For master's and doctorate, GRE General Test. Additional exam requirements/recommendations for international students: Required—TOEFL (minimum score 560 paper-based; 215 computer-based). Electronic applications accepted. *Faculty research:* Composites, heat transfer.

University of Memphis, Graduate School, Herff College of Engineering, Department of Mechanical Engineering, Memphis, TN 38152. Offers design and mechanical engineering (MS); energy systems (MS); industrial engineering (MS); mechanical engineering (PhD); mechanical systems (MS); power systems (MS). Part-time programs available. Terminal master's awarded for partial completion of doctoral program. *Degree requirements:* For master's, comprehensive exam, thesis; for doctorate, comprehensive exam, thesis/dissertation. *Entrance requirements:* For master's, GRE General Test, BS in mechanical engineering, minimum undergraduate GPA of 3.0. *Faculty research:* Computational fluid dynamics, computational mechanics, integrated design, nondestructive testing, operations research.

University of Miami, Graduate School, College of Engineering, Department of Mechanical and Aerospace Engineering, Coral Gables, FL 33124. Offers MSME, PhD. Part-time programs available. *Degree requirements:* For master's, thesis (for some programs); for doctorate, comprehensive exam, thesis/dissertation. *Entrance requirements:* For master's and doctorate, GRE General Test, minimum GPA of 3.0. Additional exam requirements/recommendations for international students: Required—TOEFL (minimum score 550 paper-based; 213 computer-based). Electronic applications accepted. *Faculty research:* Internal combustion engines, heat transfer, hydrogen energy, controls, fuel cells.

University of Michigan, College of Engineering, Department of Mechanical Engineering, Ann Arbor, MI 48109. Offers MSE, PhD. Part-time programs available. *Students:* 443 full-time (63 women), 8 part-time (2 women). 1,411 applicants, 20% accepted, 130 enrolled. In 2011, 120 master's, 47 doctorates awarded. Terminal master's awarded for partial completion of doctoral program. *Degree requirements:* For master's, thesis optional; for doctorate, thesis/dissertation, oral defense of dissertation, preliminary and qualifying exams. *Entrance requirements:* For master's, GRE General Test, undergraduate degree in same or relevant field; for doctorate, GRE General Test. Additional exam requirements/recommendations for international students: Required—TOEFL (minimum score 560 paper-based; 220 computer-based). *Application deadline:* Applications are processed on a rolling basis. Application fee: $65 ($75 for international students). Electronic applications accepted. *Financial support:* Fellowships, research assistantships, teaching assistantships, institutionally sponsored loans, health care benefits, tuition waivers (full), and unspecified assistantships available. *Faculty research:* Design and manufacturing, systems and controls, combustion and heat transfer, materials and solid mechanics, dynamics and vibrations, biosystems, fluid mechanics, microsystems, environmental sustainabilities. *Unit head:* Kon-Well Wang, Department Chair, 734-764-8464, E-mail: kwwang@umich.edu. *Application contact:* Cynthia Quann-White, Graduate Admissions and Program Coordinator, 734-763-9223, Fax: 734-647-7303, E-mail: me.grad.application@umich.edu. Web site: http://me.engin.umich.edu/.

University of Michigan–Dearborn, College of Engineering and Computer Science, Department of Mechanical Engineering, Dearborn, MI 48128. Offers MSE. Part-time and evening/weekend programs available. Postbaccalaureate distance learning degree programs offered (no on-campus study). *Faculty:* 19 full-time (2 women), 6 part-time/adjunct (1 woman). *Students:* 16 full-time (0 women), 62 part-time (10 women); includes 18 minority (3 Black or African American, non-Hispanic/Latino; 11 Asian, non-Hispanic/Latino; 2 Hispanic/Latino; 2 Two or more races, non-Hispanic/Latino), 10 international. Average age 28. 73 applicants, 68% accepted, 31 enrolled. In 2011, 18 master's awarded. *Degree requirements:* For master's, thesis optional. *Entrance requirements:* For master's, BS/BSE in mechanical engineering and/or applied mathematics, minimum GPA of 3.0 or equivalent. Additional exam requirements/recommendations for international students: Required—TOEFL (minimum score 560 paper-based; 220 computer-based; 84 iBT), IELTS, or Michigan English Language Assessment Battery (MELAB). *Application deadline:* For fall admission, 7/1 priority date for domestic students, 4/1 for international students; for winter admission, 11/1 priority date for domestic students, 8/1 for international students; for spring admission, 3/1 priority date for domestic students, 12/1 for international students. Applications are processed on a rolling basis. Application fee: $60. Electronic applications accepted. *Financial support:* In 2011–12, 5 students received support, including 2 research assistantships with full tuition reimbursements available (averaging $14,700 per year), 2 teaching assistantships (averaging $3,400 per year); Federal Work-Study, scholarships/grants, health care benefits, and unspecified assistantships also available. Financial award application deadline: 4/1; financial award applicants required to submit FAFSA. *Faculty research:* Combustion, fatigue, fracture/damage mechanics, noise and vibration, vehicle climate control. *Unit head:* Dr. Ben Q. Li, Chair, 313-593-5241, Fax: 313-593-3851, E-mail: benqli@umich.edu. *Application contact:* Rebekah S. Awood, Graduate Secretary, 313-593-5241, Fax: 313-593-3851, E-mail: rsdew@umd.umich.edu. Web site: http://www.engin.umd.umich.edu/ME/.

University of Minnesota, Twin Cities Campus, College of Science and Engineering, Department of Mechanical Engineering, Minneapolis, MN 55455-0213. Offers MSME, PhD. Part-time programs available. *Faculty:* 37 full-time (4 women). *Students:* 271 (40 women); includes 15 minority (1 Black or African American, non-Hispanic/Latino; 1 American Indian or Alaska Native, non-Hispanic/Latino; 11 Asian, non-Hispanic/Latino; 2 Hispanic/Latino), 104 international. *Degree requirements:* For doctorate, thesis/dissertation. *Entrance requirements:* For master's, GRE General Test, minimum GPA of 3.0; for doctorate, GRE General Test. Additional exam requirements/recommendations for international students: Required—TOEFL. *Application deadline:* For fall admission, 12/15 for domestic and international students. Applications are processed on a rolling basis. Application fee: $75 ($95 for international students). Electronic applications accepted. *Financial support:* Fellowships, research assistantships, and teaching assistantships available. *Faculty research:* Particle technology, solar energy, controls, heat transfer, fluid power, plasmas, medical devices, bioengineering, nanotechnology, intelligent vehicles. *Application contact:* Director of Graduate Studies, E-mail: dgs@me.umn.edu. Web site: http://www.me.umn.edu/.

University of Missouri, Graduate School, College of Engineering, Department of Mechanical and Aerospace Engineering, Columbia, MO 65211. Offers MS, PhD. *Faculty:* 22 full-time (0 women), 1 part-time/adjunct (0 women). *Students:* 60 full-time (3 women), 27 part-time (4 women); includes 5 minority (1 Black or African American, non-Hispanic/Latino; 1 Asian, non-Hispanic/Latino; 1 Hispanic/Latino; 2 Two or more races, non-Hispanic/Latino), 42 international. Average age 26. 125 applicants, 42% accepted, 23 enrolled. In 2011, 11 master's, 7 doctorates awarded. *Degree requirements:* For master's, thesis; for doctorate, one foreign language, thesis/dissertation. *Entrance requirements:* For master's and doctorate, GRE General Test, minimum GPA of 3.0. Additional exam requirements/recommendations for international students: Required—TOEFL (minimum score 500 paper-based; 173 computer-based; 61 iBT). *Application deadline:* Applications are processed on a rolling basis. Application fee: $55 ($75 for international students). *Expenses:* Tuition, state resident: full-time $5881. Tuition, nonresident: full-time $15,183. *Required fees:* $952. Tuition and fees vary according to campus/location and program. *Financial support:* Fellowships, research assistantships, teaching assistantships, and institutionally sponsored loans available. *Faculty research:* Dynamics and Control, design and manufacturing, materials and solids and thermal and fluid science engineering. *Unit head:* Dr. Roberta Tzou, Department Chair, E-mail: tzour@missouri.edu. *Application contact:* Melanie Gerlach, 573-882-2085, E-mail: gerlachm@missouri.edu. Web site: http://engineering.missouri.edu/mae/.

University of Missouri–Kansas City, School of Computing and Engineering, Kansas City, MO 64110-2499. Offers civil engineering (MS); computer and electrical engineering (PhD); computer science (MS), including bioinformatics, software engineering, telecommunications networking; computer science and informatics (PhD); computing (PhD); electrical engineering (MS); engineering (PhD); mechanical engineering (MS); telecommunications (PhD). PhD (interdisciplinary) offered through the School of Graduate Studies. Part-time programs available. *Faculty:* 36 full-time (6 women), 27 part-time/adjunct (3 women). *Students:* 155 full-time (44 women), 136 part-time (24 women); includes 19 minority (4 Black or African American, non-Hispanic/Latino; 7 Asian, non-Hispanic/Latino; 6 Hispanic/Latino; 2 Two or more races, non-Hispanic/Latino), 201 international. Average age 26. 455 applicants, 46% accepted, 96 enrolled. In 2011, 194 degrees awarded. *Degree requirements:* For doctorate, thesis/dissertation. *Entrance requirements:* For master's, GRE General Test, minimum GPA of 3.0, 3 letters of recommendation from professors; for doctorate, GRE General Test, minimum GPA of 3.5. Additional exam requirements/recommendations for international students: Required—TOEFL (minimum score 550 paper-based; 213 computer-based; 80 iBT). *Application deadline:* For fall admission, 1/15 priority date for domestic students, 1/15 for international students. Applications are processed on a rolling basis. Application fee: $45 ($50 for international students). *Expenses:* Tuition, state resident: full-time $5798; part-time $322.10 per credit hour. Tuition, nonresident: full-time $14,969; part-time $831.60 per credit hour. *Required fees:* $93.51 per credit hour. *Financial support:* In 2011–12, 47 research assistantships with partial tuition reimbursements (averaging $13,190 per year), 10 teaching assistantships with partial tuition reimbursements (averaging $9,815 per year) were awarded; career-related internships or fieldwork, Federal Work-Study, scholarships/grants, tuition waivers (partial), and unspecified assistantships also available. Support available to part-time students. Financial award application deadline: 3/1; financial award applicants required to submit FAFSA. *Faculty research:* Algorithms, bioinformatics and medical informatics, biomechanics/

biomaterials, civil engineering materials, networking and telecommunications, thermal science. *Unit head:* Dr. Kevin Z. Truman, Dean, 816-235-2399, Fax: 816-235-5159. *Application contact:* 816-235-2399, Fax: 816-235-5159. Web site: http://sce.umkc.edu/.

University of Nebraska–Lincoln, Graduate College, College of Engineering, Department of Mechanical and Materials Engineering, Lincoln, NE 68588. Offers engineering mechanics (MS, PhD); materials engineering (PhD); mechanical engineering (MS, PhD), including materials science engineering (MS), metallurgical engineering (MS). *Degree requirements:* For master's, thesis optional; for doctorate, comprehensive exam, thesis/dissertation. *Entrance requirements:* For master's and doctorate, GRE General Test. Additional exam requirements/recommendations for international students: Required—TOEFL (minimum score 550 paper-based; 213 computer-based). Electronic applications accepted. *Faculty research:* Robotics for planetary exploration, vehicle crashworthiness, transient heat conduction, laser beam/particle interactions.

University of Nevada, Las Vegas, Graduate College, Howard R. Hughes College of Engineering, Department of Mechanical Engineering, Las Vegas, NV 89154-4027. Offers aerospace engineering (MS); biomedical engineering (MS); materials and nuclear engineering (MS); mechanical engineering (MSE, PhD). Part-time programs available. *Faculty:* 14 full-time (0 women), 19 part-time/adjunct (1 woman). *Students:* 14 full-time (2 women), 40 part-time (8 women); includes 12 minority (1 Black or African American, non-Hispanic/Latino; 4 Asian, non-Hispanic/Latino; 3 Hispanic/Latino; 1 Native Hawaiian or other Pacific Islander, non-Hispanic/Latino; 3 Two or more races, non-Hispanic/Latino), 13 international. Average age 31. 31 applicants, 74% accepted, 8 enrolled. In 2011, 18 master's, 3 doctorates awarded. *Degree requirements:* For master's, comprehensive exam, thesis (for some programs), project; for doctorate, comprehensive exam, thesis/dissertation. *Entrance requirements:* For master's and doctorate, GRE General Test. Additional exam requirements/recommendations for international students: Required—TOEFL (minimum score 550 paper-based; 213 computer-based; 80 iBT), IELTS (minimum score 7). *Application deadline:* For fall admission, 8/1 priority date for domestic students, 5/1 for international students; for spring admission, 12/1 priority date for domestic students, 10/1 for international students. Applications are processed on a rolling basis. Application fee: $60 ($95 for international students). Electronic applications accepted. *Financial support:* In 2011–12, 29 students received support, including 14 research assistantships with partial tuition reimbursements available (averaging $9,415 per year), 15 teaching assistantships with partial tuition reimbursements available (averaging $10,934 per year); institutionally sponsored loans, scholarships/grants, health care benefits, and unspecified assistantships also available. Financial award application deadline: 3/1. *Faculty research:* Dynamics and control systems; energy systems including renewable and nuclear; computational fluid and solid mechanics; structures, materials and manufacturing; vibrations and acoustics. *Total annual research expenditures:* $2.9 million. *Unit head:* Dr. Woosoon Yim, Chair/Professor, 702-895-0956, Fax: 702-895-3936, E-mail: wy@me.unlv.edu. *Application contact:* Graduate College Admissions Evaluator, 702-895-3320, Fax: 702-895-4180, E-mail: gradcollege@unlv.edu. Web site: http://www.me.unlv.edu/.

University of Nevada, Reno, Graduate School, College of Engineering, Department of Mechanical Engineering, Reno, NV 89557. Offers MS, PhD. Terminal master's awarded for partial completion of doctoral program. *Degree requirements:* For master's, thesis optional; for doctorate, thesis/dissertation. *Entrance requirements:* For master's, GRE General Test, minimum GPA of 2.75; for doctorate, GRE General Test, minimum GPA of 3.0. Additional exam requirements/recommendations for international students: Required—TOEFL (minimum score 500 paper-based; 173 computer-based; 61 iBT), IELTS (minimum score 6). Electronic applications accepted. *Faculty research:* Composite, solid, fluid, thermal, and smart materials.

University of New Brunswick Fredericton, School of Graduate Studies, Faculty of Engineering, Department of Mechanical Engineering, Fredericton, NB E3B 5A3, Canada. Offers applied mechanics (M Eng, M Sc E, PhD); mechanical engineering (M Eng, M Sc E, PhD). Part-time programs available. *Faculty:* 14 full-time (1 woman), 2 part-time/adjunct (0 women). *Students:* 47 full-time (4 women), 7 part-time (0 women). In 2011, 8 master's, 3 doctorates awarded. *Degree requirements:* For master's, thesis; for doctorate, comprehensive exam, thesis/dissertation, qualifying exam. *Entrance requirements:* For master's, minimum GPA of 3.0; B Sc E; for doctorate, minimum GPA of 3.0; M Sc E. Additional exam requirements/recommendations for international students: Required—TOEFL (minimum score 550 paper-based), IELTS, TWE (minimum score 4). *Application deadline:* For fall admission, 3/1 priority date for domestic students. Applications are processed on a rolling basis. Application fee: $50 Canadian dollars. *Financial support:* In 2011–12, 104 fellowships, 31 research assistantships, 54 teaching assistantships were awarded. *Faculty research:* Analysis of gross motor activities as a means of assessing upper limb prosthesis, distance determination algorithms and their applications, void nucleation in automotive aluminum alloy, robot kinematics, micromechanics, analysis of human walking, plastic injection molding, green nanotechnology, mechatronics, fatigue assessment of structures, ocean renewable energy. *Unit head:* Dr. Zengtao Chen, Director of Graduate Studies, 506-458-7784, Fax: 506-453-5025, E-mail: ztchen@unb.ca. *Application contact:* Wanda Wyman, Graduate Secretary, 506-458-7742, Fax: 506-453-5025, E-mail: wanda.wyman@unb.ca. Web site: http://www.unbf.ca/eng/me.

University of New Hampshire, Graduate School, College of Engineering and Physical Sciences, Department of Mechanical Engineering, Durham, NH 03824. Offers mechanical engineering (MS, PhD); systems design (PhD). Part-time programs available. *Faculty:* 14 full-time (1 woman). *Students:* 29 full-time (3 women), 24 part-time (0 women); includes 2 minority (1 Black or African American, non-Hispanic/Latino; 1 Two or more races, non-Hispanic/Latino), 13 international. Average age 25. 50 applicants, 68% accepted, 18 enrolled. In 2011, 15 master's, 2 doctorates awarded. *Degree requirements:* For master's, thesis or alternative; for doctorate, thesis/dissertation. *Entrance requirements:* For master's and doctorate, GRE. Additional exam requirements/recommendations for international students: Required—TOEFL (minimum score 550 paper-based; 213 computer-based; 80 iBT). *Application deadline:* For fall admission, 4/1 priority date for domestic students, 4/1 for international students; for spring admission, 12/1 for domestic students. Applications are processed on a rolling basis. Application fee: $65. Electronic applications accepted. *Expenses:* Tuition, state resident: full-time $12,360; part-time $687 per credit hour. Tuition, nonresident: full-time $25,680; part-time $1058 per credit hour. *International tuition:* $29,550 full-time. *Required fees:* $1666; $833 per course. $416.50 per semester. Tuition and fees vary according to course load and degree level. *Financial support:* In 2011–12, 36 students received support, including 2 fellowships, 16 research assistantships, 17 teaching assistantships; Federal Work-Study, scholarships/grants, and tuition waivers (full and partial) also available. Support available to part-time students. Financial award application deadline: 2/15. *Faculty research:* Solid mechanics, dynamics, materials science, dynamic systems, automatic control. *Unit head:* Dr. Todd Gross, Chairperson, 603-862-2445. *Application contact:* Tracey Harvey, Administrative Assistant, 603-862-

1353, E-mail: mechanical.engineering@unh.edu. Web site: http://www.unh.edu/mechanical-engineering/.

University of New Haven, Graduate School, Tagliatela College of Engineering, Program in Mechanical Engineering, West Haven, CT 06516-1916. Offers MS. Part-time and evening/weekend programs available. *Students:* 12 full-time, 9 part-time; includes 2 minority (both Asian, non-Hispanic/Latino), 14 international. 3 applicants, 100% accepted, 2 enrolled. In 2011, 10 master's awarded. *Degree requirements:* For master's, thesis. *Entrance requirements:* Additional exam requirements/recommendations for international students: Required—TOEFL (minimum score 520 paper-based; 190 computer-based; 70 iBT); Recommended—IELTS (minimum score 5.5). *Application deadline:* For fall admission, 5/31 for international students; for winter admission, 10/15 for international students; for spring admission, 1/15 for international students. Applications are processed on a rolling basis. Application fee: $50. Electronic applications accepted. *Expenses: Tuition:* Part-time $750 per credit. *Financial support:* Research assistantships with partial tuition reimbursements, teaching assistantships with partial tuition reimbursements, career-related internships or fieldwork, Federal Work-Study, scholarships/grants, tuition waivers, and unspecified assistantships available. Support available to part-time students. Financial award applicants required to submit FAFSA. *Unit head:* Dr. Stephen Ross, Coordinator, 203-932-7408. *Application contact:* Eloise Gormley, Director of Graduate Admissions, 203-932-7449, Fax: 203-932-7137, E-mail: gradinfo@newhaven.edu. Web site: http://www.newhaven.edu/9596/

University of New Mexico, Graduate School, School of Engineering, Department of Mechanical Engineering, Albuquerque, NM 87131-2039. Offers MS, PhD. Part-time programs available. *Faculty:* 15 full-time (1 woman), 1 part-time/adjunct (0 women). *Students:* 30 full-time (1 woman), 46 part-time (7 women); includes 20 minority (1 American Indian or Alaska Native, non-Hispanic/Latino; 1 Asian, non-Hispanic/Latino; 18 Hispanic/Latino), 3 international. Average age 29. 57 applicants, 51% accepted, 24 enrolled. In 2011, 13 master's, 3 doctorates awarded. *Degree requirements:* For master's, thesis optional; for doctorate, comprehensive exam, thesis/dissertation. *Entrance requirements:* For master's and doctorate, GRE. Additional exam requirements/recommendations for international students: Required—TOEFL (minimum score 550 paper-based; 210 computer-based; 80 iBT). *Application deadline:* For fall admission, 7/30 for domestic students, 3/1 for international students; for spring admission, 11/30 for domestic students, 8/1 for international students. Applications are processed on a rolling basis. Application fee: $50. Electronic applications accepted. *Financial support:* In 2011–12, 49 students received support, including 1 fellowship (averaging $10,000 per year), 33 research assistantships with full and partial tuition reimbursements available (averaging $15,740 per year), 13 teaching assistantships with full and partial tuition reimbursements available (averaging $7,066 per year); scholarships/grants, health care benefits, and unspecified assistantships also available. Financial award application deadline: 3/1; financial award applicants required to submit FAFSA. *Faculty research:* Engineering mechanics and materials (including solid mechanics and materials science), mechanical sciences and engineering (including dynamic systems, controls and robotics), thermal sciences and engineering. *Total annual research expenditures:* $811,981. *Unit head:* Dr. Chris Hall, Chairperson, 505-277-1325, Fax: 505-277-1571, E-mail: cdhall@unm.edu. *Application contact:* Dr. Yu-Lin Shen, Director of Graduate Programs, 505-277-6286, Fax: 505-277-1571, E-mail: shenyl@unm.edu. Web site: http://megrad.unm.edu/.

University of New Orleans, Graduate School, College of Engineering, Concentration in Mechanical Engineering, New Orleans, LA 70148. Offers MS. *Degree requirements:* For master's, thesis optional. *Entrance requirements:* For master's, GRE General Test, minimum GPA of 3.0. Additional exam requirements/recommendations for international students: Required—TOEFL (minimum score 550 paper-based; 213 computer-based; 79 iBT). Electronic applications accepted. *Faculty research:* Two-phase flow instabilities, thermal-hydrodynamic modeling, solar energy, heat transfer from sprays, boundary integral techniques in mechanics.

The University of North Carolina at Charlotte, Graduate School, The William States Lee College of Engineering, Department of Mechanical Engineering and Engineering Science, Charlotte, NC 28223-0001. Offers engineering (MS); mechanical engineering (MSE, MSME, PhD). Evening/weekend programs available. *Faculty:* 33 full-time (3 women). *Students:* 62 full-time (6 women), 36 part-time (4 women); includes 5 minority (3 Black or African American, non-Hispanic/Latino; 1 Asian, non-Hispanic/Latino; 1 Hispanic/Latino), 57 international. Average age 27. 128 applicants, 59% accepted, 22 enrolled. In 2011, 18 master's, 2 doctorates awarded. Terminal master's awarded for partial completion of doctoral program. *Degree requirements:* For master's, thesis; for doctorate, thesis/dissertation. *Entrance requirements:* For master's, GRE General Test, minimum GPA of 3.0 in undergraduate major, 2.75 overall; for doctorate, GRE General Test, 3 letters of reference from faculty or professionals. Additional exam requirements/recommendations for international students: Required—TOEFL (minimum score 557 paper-based; 220 computer-based; 83 iBT). *Application deadline:* For fall admission, 7/1 for domestic students, 5/1 for international students; for spring admission, 11/1 for domestic students, 10/1 for international students. Applications are processed on a rolling basis. Application fee: $65 ($75 for international students). Electronic applications accepted. *Expenses:* Tuition, state resident: full-time $3689. Tuition, nonresident: full-time $15,226. *Required fees:* $2198. Tuition and fees vary according to course load and program. *Financial support:* In 2011–12, 54 students received support, including 2 fellowships (averaging $46,500 per year), 31 research assistantships (averaging $11,031 per year), 21 teaching assistantships (averaging $6,726 per year); career-related internships or fieldwork, Federal Work-Study, institutionally sponsored loans, scholarships/grants, and unspecified assistantships also available. Support available to part-time students. Financial award application deadline: 4/1; financial award applicants required to submit FAFSA. *Faculty research:* Precision metrology, bioengineering/cell preservation, computational mechanics/computational modeling, materials processing, precision design. *Total annual research expenditures:* $2.1 million. *Unit head:* Dr. Scott Smith, Chair, 704-687-8350, Fax: 704-687-8345, E-mail: kssmith@uncc.edu. *Application contact:* Kathy B. Giddings, Director of Graduate Admissions, 704-687-5503, Fax: 704-687-3279, E-mail: gradadm@uncc.edu.

University of North Dakota, Graduate School, School of Engineering and Mines, Department of Mechanical Engineering, Grand Forks, ND 58202. Offers M Engr, MS. Part-time programs available. *Degree requirements:* For master's, comprehensive exam, thesis or alternative. *Entrance requirements:* For master's, GRE General Test, minimum GPA of 3.0 (MS), 2.5 (M Engr). Additional exam requirements/recommendations for international students: Required—TOEFL (minimum score 550 paper-based; 213 computer-based; 79 iBT), IELTS (minimum score 6.5). Electronic applications accepted. *Faculty research:* Energy conversion, dynamics, control, manufacturing processes with special emphasis on machining, stress vibration analysis.

University of North Florida, College of Computing, Engineering, and Construction, School of Engineering, Jacksonville, FL 32224. Offers MSCE, MSEE, MSME. Part-time programs available. *Faculty:* 20 full-time (1 woman). *Students:* 6 full-time (2 women), 35 part-time (6 women); includes 9 minority (1 Black or African American, non-Hispanic/Latino; 3 Asian, non-Hispanic/Latino; 4 Hispanic/Latino; 1 Two or more races, non-Hispanic/Latino), 6 international. Average age 29. 33 applicants, 58% accepted, 6 enrolled. In 2011, 7 master's awarded. *Application deadline:* For fall admission, 7/1 for domestic students, 5/1 for international students; for spring admission, 11/1 for domestic students, 10/1 for international students. Application fee: $30. *Expenses:* Tuition, state resident: full-time $8793; part-time $366.38 per credit hour. Tuition, nonresident: full-time $23,502; part-time $979.24 per credit hour. *Required fees:* $1384; $57.66 per credit hour. Tuition and fees vary according to course load and program. *Financial support:* In 2011–12, 16 students received support, including 14 research assistantships (averaging $3,428 per year), 1 teaching assistantship (averaging $1,600 per year); Federal Work-Study, scholarships/grants, tuition waivers, and unspecified assistantships also available. Financial award application deadline: 4/1; financial award applicants required to submit FAFSA. *Total annual research expenditures:* $5 million. *Unit head:* Gerald Merckel, Associate Dean, 904-620-1390, E-mail: gmerckel@unf.edu. *Application contact:* Lillith Richardson, Assistant Director, The Graduate School, 904-320-1360, Fax: 904-620-1362, E-mail: graduateschool@unf.edu. Web site: http://www.unf.edu/ccec/engineering/.

University of Notre Dame, Graduate School, College of Engineering, Department of Aerospace and Mechanical Engineering, Notre Dame, IN 46556. Offers aerospace and mechanical engineering (M Eng, PhD); aerospace engineering (MS Aero E); mechanical engineering (MEME, MSME). Terminal master's awarded for partial completion of doctoral program. *Degree requirements:* For master's, comprehensive exam, thesis or alternative; for doctorate, thesis/dissertation, candidacy exam. *Entrance requirements:* For master's and doctorate, GRE General Test. Additional exam requirements/recommendations for international students: Required—TOEFL (minimum score 600 paper-based; 250 computer-based; 80 iBT). Electronic applications accepted. *Faculty research:* Aerodynamics/fluid dynamics, design and manufacturing, controls/robotics, solid mechanics or biomechanics/biomaterials.

University of Oklahoma, College of Engineering, School of Aerospace and Mechanical Engineering, Program in Mechanical Engineering, Norman, OK 73019. Offers mechanical engineering (MS, PhD), including combustion, controls, fluid mechanics, general, heat transfer, solid mechanics. Part-time programs available. *Students:* 48 full-time (1 woman), 22 part-time (1 woman); includes 12 minority (1 Black or African American, non-Hispanic/Latino; 2 American Indian or Alaska Native, non-Hispanic/Latino; 5 Asian, non-Hispanic/Latino; 3 Hispanic/Latino; 1 Two or more races, non-Hispanic/Latino), 32 international. Average age 27. 67 applicants, 45% accepted, 22 enrolled. In 2011, 18 degrees awarded. *Degree requirements:* For master's, comprehensive exam, thesis or alternative; for doctorate, comprehensive exam, thesis/dissertation optional, combined general and qualifying exam. *Entrance requirements:* For master's, GRE General Test, BS in engineering or physical sciences; for doctorate, GRE General Test, MS in mechanical engineering or equivalent. Additional exam requirements/recommendations for international students: Required—TOEFL (minimum score 600 paper-based; 100 iBT). *Application deadline:* For fall admission, 6/1 priority date for domestic students, 3/1 for international students; for spring admission, 11/1 for domestic students, 9/1 for international students. Applications are processed on a rolling basis. Application fee: $40 ($90 for international students). Electronic applications accepted. *Expenses:* Tuition, state resident: full-time $4087; part-time $170.30 per credit hour. Tuition, nonresident: full-time $14,875; part-time $619.80 per credit hour. *Required fees:* $2659; $100.25 per credit hour. Tuition and fees vary according to course load and degree level. *Financial support:* In 2011–12, 52 students received support. Unspecified assistantships available. Financial award applicants required to submit FAFSA. *Faculty research:* Design and analysis of complex systems, computer-aided design and manufacturing, thermal/fluid systems design and analysis, alternative fuels, engineering education. *Unit head:* Farrokh Mistree, Director, 405-325-5011, Fax: 405-325-1088, E-mail: farrokh.mistree@ou.edu. *Application contact:* Dr. Peter Attar, Graduate Liaison, Fax: 405-325-1088, E-mail: peter.attar@ou.edu. Web site: http://www.ame.ou.edu.

University of Ottawa, Faculty of Graduate and Postdoctoral Studies, Faculty of Engineering, Ottawa-Carleton Institute for Mechanical and Aerospace Engineering, Ottawa, ON K1N 6N5, Canada. Offers M Eng, MA Sc, PhD. MA Sc, M Eng, PhD offered jointly with Carleton University. *Degree requirements:* For master's, thesis or alternative; for doctorate, thesis/dissertation, seminar series, qualifying exam. *Entrance requirements:* For master's, honors degree or equivalent, minimum B average; for doctorate, master's degree, minimum B+ average. Electronic applications accepted. *Faculty research:* Fluid mechanics-heat transfer, solid mechanics, design, manufacturing and control.

University of Pennsylvania, School of Engineering and Applied Science, Department of Mechanical Engineering and Applied Mechanics, Philadelphia, PA 19104. Offers applied mechanics (MSE, PhD); mechanical engineering (MSE, PhD). Part-time programs available. *Faculty:* 28 full-time (4 women), 9 part-time/adjunct (0 women). *Students:* 138 full-time (19 women), 33 part-time (5 women); includes 20 minority (8 Black or African American, non-Hispanic/Latino; 11 Asian, non-Hispanic/Latino; 1 Hispanic/Latino), 90 international. 599 applicants, 34% accepted, 94 enrolled. In 2011, 44 master's, 5 doctorates awarded. *Degree requirements:* For master's, thesis optional; for doctorate, thesis/dissertation. *Entrance requirements:* Additional exam requirements/recommendations for international students: Required—TOEFL. *Application deadline:* For fall admission, 1/2 priority date for domestic students. Applications are processed on a rolling basis. Application fee: $70. Electronic applications accepted. *Expenses: Tuition:* Full-time $26,660; part-time $4944 per course. *Required fees:* $2318; $291 per course. Tuition and fees vary according to course load, degree level and program. *Financial support:* Fellowships, research assistantships, teaching assistantships, institutionally sponsored loans, scholarships/grants, traineeships, health care benefits, and unspecified assistantships available. *Faculty research:* Heat transfer, fluid mechanics, energy conversion, solid mechanics, dynamics of mechanisms and robots. *Unit head:* Eduardo D. Glandt, Dean, 215-898-7244, Fax: 215-573-2018, E-mail: seasdean@seas.upenn.edu. *Application contact:* 215-898-4825, E-mail: meam@seas.upenn.edu. Web site: http://www.seas.upenn.edu/meam/.

University of Pittsburgh, Swanson School of Engineering, Department of Mechanical Engineering and Materials Science, Pittsburgh, PA 15260. Offers MSME, PhD. Part-time programs available. Postbaccalaureate distance learning degree programs offered. *Faculty:* 27 full-time (4 women), 41 part-time/adjunct (3 women). *Students:* 102 full-time (17 women), 150 part-time (26 women); includes 14 minority (5 Black or African American, non-Hispanic/Latino; 1 American Indian or Alaska Native, non-Hispanic/Latino; 7 Asian, non-Hispanic/Latino; 1 Hispanic/Latino), 60 international. 445 applicants, 33% accepted, 67 enrolled. In 2011, 40 master's, 6 doctorates awarded. Terminal master's awarded for partial completion of doctoral program. *Degree requirements:* For master's, thesis optional; for doctorate, comprehensive exam, thesis/dissertation, final oral exams. *Entrance requirements:* For master's and doctorate, minimum QPA of 3.0. Additional exam requirements/recommendations for international students: Required—TOEFL (minimum score 550 paper-based; 230 computer-based). *Application deadline:* For fall admission, 3/1 priority date for domestic students; for spring admission, 7/1 priority date for domestic students. Applications are processed on a rolling basis. Application fee: $50. Electronic applications accepted. *Expenses:* Tuition, state resident: full-time $18,774; part-time $760 per credit. Tuition, nonresident: full-time $30,736; part-time $1258 per credit. *Required fees:* $740; $200 per term. Tuition and fees vary according to program. *Financial support:* In 2011–12, 83 students received support, including 5 fellowships with full tuition reimbursements available (averaging $27,432 per year), 47 research assistantships with full tuition reimbursements available (averaging $22,680 per year), 31 teaching assistantships with full tuition reimbursements available (averaging $24,144 per year); scholarships/grants and tuition waivers (full and partial) also available. Financial award application deadline: 4/15. *Faculty research:* Smart materials and structure solid mechanics, computational fluid dynamics, multiphase bio-fluid dynamics, mechanical vibration analysis. *Total annual research expenditures:* $6.7 million. *Unit head:* Dr. Minking K. Chyu, Chairman, 412-624-9784, Fax: 412-624-4846. *Application contact:* Dr. Qing-Ming Wamg, Graduate Coordinator, 412-624-4885, Fax: 412-624-4846, E-mail: qiw4@pitt.edu. Web site: http://www.engineering.pitt.edu/MEMS/.

University of Puerto Rico, Mayagüez Campus, Graduate Studies, College of Engineering, Department of Mechanical Engineering, Mayagüez, PR 00681-9000. Offers ME, MS. Part-time programs available. *Students:* 57 full-time (11 women), 13 part-time (1 woman); includes 57 minority (all Hispanic/Latino), 13 international. 24 applicants, 67% accepted, 12 enrolled. In 2011, 10 master's awarded. *Degree requirements:* For master's, comprehensive exam, thesis. *Entrance requirements:* For master's, BS in mechanical engineering or the equivalent; minimum GPA of 2.75, 3.0 in field of specialty. Additional exam requirements/recommendations for international students: Required—TOEFL. *Application deadline:* For fall admission, 2/15 for domestic and international students; for spring admission, 9/15 for domestic and international students. Applications are processed on a rolling basis. Application fee: $25. Tuition and fees vary according to course level and course load. *Financial support:* In 2011–12, 26 students received support, including 11 research assistantships (averaging $15,000 per year), 15 teaching assistantships (averaging $8,500 per year); Federal Work-Study and institutionally sponsored loans also available. *Faculty research:* Metallurgy, hybrid vehicles, manufacturing, thermal and fluid sciences, HVAC. *Total annual research expenditures:* $1.2 million. *Unit head:* Dr. Gustavo Gutierrez, Director, 787-832-4040 Ext. 2496, Fax: 787-265-3817, E-mail: jorgegustavo.gutierrez@upr.edu. *Application contact:* Yolanda Perez, Graduate Program Secretary, 787-832-4040 Ext. 3659, Fax: 787-265-3817, E-mail: yolanda.perez4@upr.edu. Web site: http://www.me.uprm.edu.

University of Rochester, Hajim School of Engineering and Applied Sciences, Center for Entrepreneurship, Rochester, NY 14627-0360. Offers technical entrepreneurship and management (TEAM) (MS), including biomedical engineering, chemical engineering, computer science, electrical and computer engineering, energy and the environment, materials science, mechanical engineering, optics. *Faculty:* 61 full-time (8 women), 5 part-time/adjunct (1 woman). *Students:* 18 full-time (5 women), 3 part-time (1 woman); includes 4 minority (1 Asian, non-Hispanic/Latino; 3 Hispanic/Latino), 12 international. Average age 23. 134 applicants, 48% accepted, 21 enrolled. *Degree requirements:* For master's, comprehensive exam. *Entrance requirements:* For master's, GRE or GMAT, technical concentration of interest, 3 letters of recommendation, personal statement, official transcript. Additional exam requirements/recommendations for international students: Required—TOEFL or IELTS. *Application deadline:* For fall admission, 2/1 for domestic and international students. Applications are processed on a rolling basis. Application fee: $60. Electronic applications accepted. *Expenses: Tuition:* Full-time $41,040. *Financial support:* Career-related internships or fieldwork and scholarships/grants available. Financial award application deadline: 2/1. *Faculty research:* High efficiency solar cells, macromolecular self-assembly, digital signal processing, memory hierarchy management, molecular and physical mechanisms in cell migration. *Unit head:* Duncan T. Moore, Vice Provost for Entrepreneurship, 585-275-5248, Fax: 585-473-6745, E-mail: moore@optics.rochester.edu. *Application contact:* Andrea M. Galati, Executive Director, 585-276-3407, Fax: 585-276-2357, E-mail: andrea.galati@rochester.edu. Web site: http://www.rochester.edu/team.

University of Rochester, Hajim School of Engineering and Applied Sciences, Department of Mechanical Engineering, Rochester, NY 14627. Offers MS, PhD. Part-time programs available. *Faculty:* 15 full-time (1 woman). *Students:* 25 full-time (4 women), 1 part-time (0 women); includes 4 minority (3 Asian, non-Hispanic/Latino; 1 Hispanic/Latino), 11 international. 97 applicants, 30% accepted, 9 enrolled. In 2011, 15 master's, 3 doctorates awarded. Terminal master's awarded for partial completion of doctoral program. *Degree requirements:* For master's, comprehensive exam, thesis optional; for doctorate, thesis/dissertation, preliminary and qualifying exams. *Entrance requirements:* For master's and doctorate, GRE. Additional exam requirements/recommendations for international students: Required—TOEFL. *Application deadline:* For fall admission, 2/1 for domestic students. Application fee: $60. *Expenses: Tuition:* Full-time $41,040. *Financial support:* Fellowships, research assistantships, teaching assistantships, and tuition waivers (full and partial) available. Financial award application deadline: 2/1. *Faculty research:* Applied mechanics, biomechanics, fusion/plasma, materials science. *Unit head:* John C. Lambropoulos, Chair, 585-275-4070. *Application contact:* Graduate Program Advisor/Coordinator, 585-275-2849. Web site: http://www.me.rochester.edu/graduate/index.html.

University of St. Thomas, Graduate Studies, School of Engineering, St. Paul, MN 55105-1096. Offers manufacturing engineering and operations (MS); mechanical engineering (MS); medical device development (Certificate); regulatory science (MS); software engineering (MS); software management (MS); software systems (MSS); systems engineering (MS); technology management (MS). *Accreditation:* ABET (one or more programs are accredited). *Students:* 8 full-time, 210 part-time (38 women); includes 47 minority (22 Black or African American, non-Hispanic/Latino; 4 Asian, non-Hispanic/Latino; 6 Hispanic/Latino; 1 Native Hawaiian or other Pacific Islander, non-Hispanic/Latino; 14 Two or more races, non-Hispanic/Latino), 14 international. Average age 33. *Entrance requirements:* For master's, resume, official transcripts. Additional exam requirements/recommendations for international students: Required—TOEFL (minimum score 550 paper-based). *Application deadline:* For fall admission, 8/1 priority date for domestic students; for spring admission, 1/1 priority date for domestic students. Applications are processed on a rolling basis. Application fee: $30. Electronic applications accepted. *Expenses:* Contact institution. *Financial support:* Fellowships, research assistantships, institutionally sponsored loans, and scholarships/grants available. Support available to part-time students. Financial award application deadline: 4/1; financial award applicants required to submit FAFSA. *Unit head:* Don Weinkauf, Dean, 651-962-5760, Fax: 651-962-6419, E-mail: dhweinkauf@stthomas.edu. *Application contact:* Joyce A. Taylor, Graduate Programs Coordinator, 651-962-5756, Fax: 651-962-6419, E-mail: jataylor1@stthomas.edu.

University of Saskatchewan, College of Graduate Studies and Research, College of Engineering, Department of Mechanical Engineering, Saskatoon, SK S7N 5A2, Canada. Offers M Sc, PhD. *Degree requirements:* For master's, thesis (for some programs); for doctorate, thesis/dissertation. *Entrance requirements:* For master's and doctorate, GRE. Additional exam requirements/recommendations for international students: Required—TOEFL.

University of South Alabama, Graduate School, College of Engineering, Department of Mechanical Engineering, Mobile, AL 36688-0002. Offers MSME. *Faculty:* 6 full-time (2 women). *Students:* 14 full-time (3 women), 4 part-time (0 women); includes 3 minority (1 Asian, non-Hispanic/Latino; 2 Hispanic/Latino), 5 international. 19 applicants, 63% accepted, 5 enrolled. In 2011, 7 master's awarded. *Degree requirements:* For master's, project or thesis. *Entrance requirements:* For master's, GRE General Test, BS in engineering, minimum GPA of 3.0. *Application deadline:* For fall admission, 7/15 priority date for domestic students, 6/15 for international students; for spring admission, 12/1 priority date for domestic students, 11/1 for international students. Applications are processed on a rolling basis. Application fee: $35. *Expenses:* Tuition, state resident: full-time $7968; part-time $332 per credit hour. Tuition, nonresident: full-time $15,936; part-time $664 per credit hour. *Financial support:* Research assistantships, career-related internships or fieldwork, and institutionally sponsored loans available. Support available to part-time students. Financial award application deadline: 4/1. *Unit head:* Dr. David Nelson, Chair, 251-460-6168. *Application contact:* Dr. B. Keith Harrison, Director of Graduate Studies, 251-460-6160. Web site: http://www.southalabama.edu/engineering/mechanical.

University of South Carolina, The Graduate School, College of Engineering and Computing, Department of Mechanical Engineering, Columbia, SC 29208. Offers ME, MS, PhD. Part-time and evening/weekend programs available. Postbaccalaureate distance learning degree programs offered. *Degree requirements:* For master's, thesis (for some programs); for doctorate, thesis/dissertation. *Entrance requirements:* For master's and doctorate, GRE General Test. Additional exam requirements/recommendations for international students: Required—TOEFL (minimum score 600 paper-based; 250 computer-based). Electronic applications accepted. *Faculty research:* Heat exchangers, computer vision measurements in solid mechanics and biomechanics, robot dynamics and control.

University of Southern California, Graduate School, Viterbi School of Engineering, Department of Aerospace and Mechanical Engineering, Los Angeles, CA 90089. Offers aerospace and mechanical engineering: computational fluid and solid mechanics (MS); aerospace and mechanical engineering: dynamics and control (MS); aerospace engineering (MS, PhD, Engr), including aerospace engineering (PhD, Engr); green technologies (MS); mechanical engineering (MS, PhD, Engr), including mechanical engineering (PhD, Engr); product development engineering (MS). Part-time and evening/weekend programs available. Postbaccalaureate distance learning degree programs offered (no on-campus study). Terminal master's awarded for partial completion of doctoral program. *Degree requirements:* For master's, thesis optional; for doctorate, thesis/dissertation. *Entrance requirements:* For master's, doctorate, and Engr, GRE General Test. Additional exam requirements/recommendations for international students: Recommended—TOEFL. Electronic applications accepted. *Faculty research:* Mechanics and materials, aerodynamics of air/ground vehicles, gas dynamics, aerosols, astronautics and space science, geophysical and microgravity flows, planetary physics, power MEMs and MEMS vacuum pumps, heat transfer and combustion.

University of South Florida, Graduate School, College of Engineering, Department of Mechanical Engineering, Tampa, FL 33620-9951. Offers ME, MME, MSES, MSME, PhD. Part-time programs available. *Faculty:* 16 full-time (1 woman), 2 part-time/adjunct (0 women). *Students:* 70 full-time (11 women), 19 part-time (0 women); includes 19 minority (3 Black or African American, non-Hispanic/Latino; 7 Asian, non-Hispanic/Latino; 8 Hispanic/Latino; 1 Two or more races, non-Hispanic/Latino), 39 international. Average age 28. 86 applicants, 62% accepted, 17 enrolled. In 2011, 29 master's, 3 doctorates awarded. Terminal master's awarded for partial completion of doctoral program. *Degree requirements:* For master's, comprehensive exam, thesis or alternative; for doctorate, comprehensive exam, thesis/dissertation, 2 tools of research as specified by dissertation committee. *Entrance requirements:* For master's and doctorate, GRE, minimum GPA of 3.0 in last 60 hours of coursework. Additional exam requirements/recommendations for international students: Required—TOEFL (minimum score 550 paper-based; 213 computer-based; 79 iBT) or IELTS (minimum score 6.5). *Application deadline:* For fall admission, 2/15 for domestic students, 1/2 for international students; for spring admission, 10/15 for domestic students, 6/1 for international students. Application fee: $30. Electronic applications accepted. *Financial support:* In 2011–12, 64 students received support, including 42 research assistantships with tuition reimbursements available (averaging $12,819 per year), 22 teaching assistantships with partial tuition reimbursements available (averaging $14,017 per year). Financial award applicants required to submit FAFSA. *Faculty research:* Robot sensors, rehabilitation engineering, mechatronics, vibrations, composites. *Total annual research expenditures:* $3.4 million. *Unit head:* Dr. Rajiv Dubey, Chair, 813-974-5619, Fax: 813-974-5094, E-mail: dubey@usf.edu. *Application contact:* Dr. Muhammad Rahman, Program Director, 813-974-5625, Fax: 813-974-3539, E-mail: rahman@usf.edu. Web site: http://www.me.eng.usf.edu/.

The University of Tennessee, Graduate School, College of Engineering, Department of Mechanical, Aerospace and Biomedical Engineering, Program in Mechanical Engineering, Knoxville, TN 37996. Offers MS, PhD, MS/MBA. Part-time programs available. Postbaccalaureate distance learning degree programs offered (minimal on-campus study). *Faculty:* 14 full-time (0 women), 7 part-time/adjunct (0 women). *Students:* 50 full-time (2 women), 29 part-time (1 woman); includes 3 minority (1 Black or African American, non-Hispanic/Latino; 2 Asian, non-Hispanic/Latino), 21 international. Average age 30. 123 applicants, 53% accepted, 25 enrolled. In 2011, 25 master's, 1 doctorate awarded. *Degree requirements:* For master's, thesis or alternative; for doctorate, comprehensive exam, thesis/dissertation. *Entrance requirements:* For master's, GRE General Test (for MS students pursuing research thesis), minimum GPA of 2.7 (for U.S. degree holders), 3.0 (for international degree holders); 3 references; statement of purpose; for doctorate, College requires GRE General Test for all PhD candidates, minimum GPA of 3.0 on previous graduate course work; 3 references; statement of purpose. Additional exam requirements/recommendations for international students: Required—TOEFL (minimum score 550 paper-based; 213 computer-based). *Application deadline:* For fall admission, 2/1 priority date for domestic students, 2/1 for international students; for spring admission, 6/15 for domestic and international students. Applications are processed on a rolling basis. Application fee: $35. Electronic applications accepted. *Expenses:* Tuition, state resident: full-time $8332; part-time $464 per credit hour. Tuition, nonresident: full-time $25,174; part-time $1400 per credit hour. *Required fees:* $1162; $56 per credit hour. Tuition and fees vary according to program. *Financial support:* In 2011–12, 45 students received support, including 20 research assistantships with full tuition reimbursements available (averaging $18,920 per year), 16 teaching assistantships with full tuition reimbursements available (averaging $17,754 per year); fellowships with full tuition reimbursements available, career-related internships or fieldwork, Federal Work-Study, institutionally sponsored loans, health care benefits, and unspecified assistantships also available. Financial award application deadline: 2/1; financial award applicants required to submit FAFSA. *Faculty research:* Automotive systems and technology; combustion and emissions; alternative fuels; electromechanical actuators; nanomechanics, nanomaterials, and nanotechnology. *Unit head:* Dr. William Hamel, Head, 865-974-5115, Fax: 865-974-5274, E-mail: whamel@utk.edu. *Application contact:* Dr. Gary V. Smith, Associate Head, 865-974-5271, Fax: 865-974-5274, E-mail: gvsmith@utk.edu. Web site: http://www.engr.utk.edu/mabe.

The University of Tennessee at Chattanooga, Graduate School, College of Engineering and Computer Science, Program in Engineering, Chattanooga, TN 37403. Offers chemical engineering (MS Engr); civil engineering (MS Engr); computational engineering (MS Engr); electrical engineering (MS Engr); industrial engineering (MS Engr); mechanical engineering (MS Engr). Part-time and evening/weekend programs available. *Faculty:* 27 full-time (3 women), 3 part-time/adjunct (1 woman). *Students:* 40 full-time (7 women), 41 part-time (11 women); includes 23 minority (10 Black or African American, non-Hispanic/Latino; 1 American Indian or Alaska Native, non-Hispanic/Latino; 6 Asian, non-Hispanic/Latino; 4 Hispanic/Latino; 2 Two or more races, non-Hispanic/Latino), 20 international. Average age 28. 89 applicants, 53% accepted, 29 enrolled. In 2011, 8 master's awarded. *Degree requirements:* For master's, comprehensive exam, thesis or alternative, engineering project. *Entrance requirements:* For master's, GRE General Test, minimum undergraduate GPA of 2.5 or 3.0 in last 30 hours of coursework. Additional exam requirements/recommendations for international students: Required—TOEFL (minimum score 550 paper-based; 213 computer-based; 79 iBT), IELTS (minimum score 6). *Application deadline:* For fall admission, 8/1 priority date for domestic students, 6/1 for international students; for spring admission, 12/1 priority date for domestic students, 10/1 for international students. Applications are processed on a rolling basis. Application fee: $35. Electronic applications accepted. *Expenses:* Tuition, state resident: full-time $6472; part-time $359 per credit hour. Tuition, nonresident: full-time $20,006; part-time $1111 per credit hour. *Required fees:* $1320; $160 per credit hour. *Financial support:* Career-related internships or fieldwork, scholarships/grants, and unspecified assistantships available. Support available to part-time students. *Faculty research:* Quality control and reliability engineering, financial management, thermal science, energy conservation, structural analysis. *Total annual research expenditures:* $3.5 million. *Unit head:* Dr. Neslihan Alp, Director, 423-425-4032, Fax: 423-425-5229, E-mail: neslihan-alp@utc.edu. *Application contact:* Dr. Jerald Ainsworth, Dean of Graduate Studies, 423-425-4478, Fax: 423-425-5223, E-mail: jerald-ainsworth@utc.edu. Web site: http://www.utc.edu/Departments/engrcs/ms_engr.php.

The University of Tennessee Space Institute, Graduate Programs, Program in Mechanical Engineering, Tullahoma, TN 37388-9700. Offers MS, PhD. Part-time programs available. *Faculty:* 8 full-time (1 woman), 8 part-time/adjunct (0 women). *Students:* 5 full-time (1 woman), 20 part-time (1 woman); includes 1 minority (Asian, non-Hispanic/Latino), 3 international. 9 applicants, 33% accepted, 1 enrolled. In 2011, 6 degrees awarded. Terminal master's awarded for partial completion of doctoral program. *Degree requirements:* For master's, thesis (for some programs); for doctorate, one foreign language, thesis/dissertation. *Entrance requirements:* For master's and doctorate, GRE General Test. Additional exam requirements/recommendations for international students: Required—TOEFL (minimum score 550 paper-based; 213 computer-based), IELTS (minimum score 6.5). *Application deadline:* For fall admission, 2/1 for international students; for spring admission, 6/15 for international students. Applications are processed on a rolling basis. Application fee: $35. Electronic applications accepted. *Financial support:* In 2011–12, 5 research assistantships with full tuition reimbursements (averaging $17,791 per year) were awarded; fellowships, career-related internships or fieldwork, Federal Work-Study, institutionally sponsored loans, health care benefits, tuition waivers (full and partial), and unspecified assistantships also available. Financial award applicants required to submit FAFSA. *Unit head:* Dr. Trevor Moeller, Degree Program Chairman, 931-393-7351, Fax: 931-393-7437, E-mail: tmoeller@utsi.edu. *Application contact:* Dee Merriman, Coordinator III, 931-393-7213, Fax: 931-393-7211, E-mail: dmerrima@utsi.edu. Web site: http://www.utsi.edu/academics/MABE/.

The University of Texas at Arlington, Graduate School, College of Engineering, Department of Mechanical and Aerospace Engineering, Program in Mechanical Engineering, Arlington, TX 76019. Offers M Engr, MS, PhD. Part-time and evening/weekend programs available. Postbaccalaureate distance learning degree programs offered (minimal on-campus study). *Students:* 131 full-time (9 women), 52 part-time (6 women); includes 19 minority (3 Black or African American, non-Hispanic/Latino; 4 Asian, non-Hispanic/Latino; 12 Hispanic/Latino), 138 international. 228 applicants, 77% accepted, 39 enrolled. In 2011, 33 master's, 6 doctorates awarded. Terminal master's awarded for partial completion of doctoral program. *Degree requirements:* For master's, thesis optional; for doctorate, comprehensive exam, thesis/dissertation. *Entrance requirements:* For master's and doctorate, GRE General Test, minimum GPA of 3.0. Additional exam requirements/recommendations for international students: Required—TOEFL (minimum score 550 paper-based; 213 computer-based). *Application deadline:* For fall admission, 6/1 for domestic students, 4/1 for international students; for spring admission, 10/5 for domestic students, 9/15 for international students. Applications are processed on a rolling basis. Application fee: $50 ($70 for international students). *Financial support:* In 2011–12, 61 students received support, including 1 fellowship with partial tuition reimbursement available (averaging $1,000 per year), 10 research assistantships with partial tuition reimbursements available (averaging $13,500 per year), 20 teaching assistantships with partial tuition reimbursements available (averaging $14,400 per year); institutionally sponsored loans, scholarships/grants, health care benefits, and unspecified assistantships also available. Financial award application deadline: 6/1; financial award applicants required to submit FAFSA. *Unit head:* Dr. Erian Armanios, Chair, 817-272-2603, Fax: 817-272-5010, E-mail: armanios@uta.edu. *Application contact:* Dr. Albert Tong, Graduate Advisor, 817-272-2297, Fax: 817-272-2952, E-mail: tong@uta.edu. Web site: http://www.mae.uta.edu/.

The University of Texas at Austin, Graduate School, Cockrell School of Engineering, Department of Mechanical Engineering, Austin, TX 78712-1111. Offers mechanical engineering (MS, PhD); operations research and industrial engineering (MS, PhD); MBA/MSE; MP Aff/MSE. *Entrance requirements:* For master's and doctorate, GRE General Test. Additional exam requirements/recommendations for international students: Required—TOEFL. Application fee: $50 ($75 for international students). *Financial support:* Fellowships, research assistantships, and teaching assistantships available. Financial award application deadline: 2/1. *Unit head:* Dr. Joseph J. Beaman, Jr., Chairman, 512-471-3058, Fax: 512-232-7917, E-mail: jbeaman@mail.utexas.edu. *Application contact:* Prabhu P. Khalsa, Graduate Advisor, 512-232-2702, Fax: 512-471-8727, E-mail: prabhu.khalsa@me.utexas.edu. Web site: http://www.me.utexas.edu/.

The University of Texas at Dallas, Erik Jonsson School of Engineering and Computer Science, Department of Mechanical Engineering, Richardson, TX 75080. Offers mechanical systems engineering (MSME); microelectromechanical systems (MSME). Part-time and evening/weekend programs available. *Faculty:* 9 full-time (1 woman). *Students:* 23 full-time (3 women), 5 part-time (1 woman); includes 3 minority (1 Asian, non-Hispanic/Latino; 1 Hispanic/Latino; 1 Two or more races, non-Hispanic/Latino), 10 international. Average age 29. 92 applicants, 39% accepted, 13 enrolled. *Degree requirements:* For master's, thesis or major design project. *Entrance requirements:* For master's, GRE General Test, minimum GPA of 3.0 in related bachelor's degree. Additional exam requirements/recommendations for international students: Required—TOEFL (minimum score 550 paper-based; 215 computer-based). *Application deadline:* For fall admission, 7/15 for domestic students, 5/1 for international students; for spring admission, 11/15 for domestic students, 9/1 for international students. Applications are processed on a rolling basis. Application fee: $50 ($100 for international students). Electronic applications accepted. *Expenses:* Tuition, state resident: full-time $11,170; part-time $620.56 per credit hour. Tuition, nonresident: full-time $20,212; part-time $1122.89 per credit hour. *Financial support:* In 2011–12, 13 students received support, including 2 research assistantships with partial tuition reimbursements available (averaging $19,800 per year), 7 teaching assistantships with partial tuition reimbursements available (averaging $14,829 per year); career-related internships or fieldwork, Federal Work-Study, institutionally sponsored loans, scholarships/grants, and unspecified assistantships also available. Support available to part-time students. Financial award application deadline: 4/30; financial award applicants required to submit FAFSA. *Faculty research:* Nano-materials and nano-electronic devices, biomedical devices, nonlinear systems and controls, semiconductor and oxide surfaces, flexible electronics. *Unit head:* Dr. Mario Rotea, Department Head, 972-883-2720, Fax: 972-883-2813, E-mail: rotea@utdallas.edu. *Application contact:* Dr. Hongbing Lu, Associate Department Head, 972-883-4647, Fax: 972-883-2813, E-mail: gradecs@utdallas.edu. Web site: http://me.utdallas.edu.

The University of Texas at El Paso, Graduate School, College of Engineering, Department of Mechanical Engineering, El Paso, TX 79968-0001. Offers MS. Part-time and evening/weekend programs available. *Students:* 64 (5 women); includes 37 minority (2 Asian, non-Hispanic/Latino; 35 Hispanic/Latino), 23 international. Average age 34. 29 applicants, 45% accepted, 9 enrolled. In 2011, 9 master's awarded. *Degree requirements:* For master's, thesis optional. *Entrance requirements:* For master's, GRE, minimum GPA of 3.0, letter of reference. Additional exam requirements/recommendations for international students: Required—TOEFL; Recommended—IELTS. *Application deadline:* For fall admission, 8/1 priority date for domestic students, 3/1 for international students; for spring admission, 11/1 priority date for domestic students, 9/1 for international students. Applications are processed on a rolling basis. Application fee: $45 ($80 for international students). Electronic applications accepted. *Financial support:* In 2011–12, research assistantships with partial tuition reimbursements (averaging $21,125 per year), teaching assistantships with partial tuition reimbursements (averaging $16,900 per year) were awarded; fellowships with partial tuition reimbursements, institutionally sponsored loans, scholarships/grants, health care benefits, tuition waivers (partial), and unspecified assistantships also available. Support available to part-time students. Financial award application deadline: 3/15; financial award applicants required to submit FAFSA. *Unit head:* Dr. Louis Everett, Chair, 915-747-5450 Ext. 7987, Fax: 915-747-5019, E-mail: leverett@utep.edu. *Application contact:* Dr. Benjamin Flores, Interim Dean of the Graduate School, 915-747-5491, Fax: 915-747-5788, E-mail: bflores@utep.edu.

The University of Texas at San Antonio, College of Engineering, Department of Mechanical Engineering, San Antonio, TX 78249-0617. Offers advanced manufacturing and enterprise engineering (MS); mechanical engineering (MSME, PhD). Part-time and evening/weekend programs available. *Faculty:* 14 full-time (1 woman), 4 part-time/adjunct (0 women). *Students:* 37 full-time (4 women), 38 part-time (3 women); includes 21 minority (4 Asian, non-Hispanic/Latino; 14 Hispanic/Latino; 3 Two or more races, non-Hispanic/Latino), 32 international. Average age 27. 98 applicants, 69% accepted, 29 enrolled. In 2011, 24 master's awarded. Terminal master's awarded for partial completion of doctoral program. *Degree requirements:* For master's, comprehensive exam (for some programs), thesis; for doctorate, comprehensive exam (for some programs), thesis/dissertation, oral and written qualifying exams, dissertation proposal. *Entrance requirements:* For master's, GRE General Test, bachelor's degree in mechanical engineering or related field from accredited institution of higher education; for doctorate, GRE, master's degree in mechanical engineering or exceptionally outstanding undergraduate record in mechanical engineering or related field. Additional exam requirements/recommendations for international students: Required—TOEFL (minimum score 500 paper-based; 61 iBT), IELTS (minimum score 5). *Application deadline:* For fall admission, 7/1 for domestic students, 4/1 for international students; for spring admission, 11/1 for domestic students, 9/1 for international students. Application fee: $45 ($85 for international students). *Expenses:* Tuition, state resident: full-time $3148; part-time $2176 per semester. Tuition, nonresident: full-time $8782; part-time $5932 per semester. *Required fees:* $719 per semester. *Financial support:* In 2011–12, 33 students received support, including 4 fellowships, 16 research assistantships, 34 teaching assistantships; scholarships/grants and unspecified assistantships also available. Financial award application deadline: 3/31. *Faculty research:* Mechanics of materials, biomechanics and bioengineering, manufacturing and engineering enterprise, mechanical systems and design, thermal and fluid systems. *Unit head:* Dr. Harry R. Millwater, Department Chair, 210-458-4481, Fax: 210-458-6504, E-mail: harry.millwater@utsa.edu. *Application contact:* Dr. Xiaodu Wang, Assistant Dean of the Graduate School, 210-458-5565, Fax: 210-458-5565, E-mail: xiaodu.wang@utsa.edu.

The University of Texas at Tyler, College of Engineering and Computer Science, Department of Mechanical Engineering, Tyler, TX 75799-0001. Offers MS. Part-time and evening/weekend programs available. *Degree requirements:* For master's, engineering project. *Entrance requirements:* For master's, GRE or GMAT, bachelor's degree in engineering. *Faculty research:* Mechatronics vibration analysis, fluid dynamics, electronics and instrumentation, manufacturing processes, optics, computational fluid dynamics, signal processing, high voltage related studies, real time systems, semiconductors.

The University of Texas–Pan American, College of Engineering and Computer Science, Department of Mechanical Engineering, Edinburg, TX 78539. Offers MS. Tuition and fees vary according to course load, program and student level. *Unit head:* Dr. Constantine Tarawneh, Program Director, 956-665-2607, E-mail: tarawneh@utpa.edu.

The University of Toledo, College of Graduate Studies, College of Engineering, Department of Mechanical, Industrial, and Manufacturing Engineering, Toledo, OH 43606-3390. Offers industrial engineering (MS, PhD); mechanical engineering (MS, PhD). Part-time programs available. Postbaccalaureate distance learning degree programs offered (minimal on-campus study). *Degree requirements:* For master's, thesis optional; for doctorate, thesis/dissertation, qualifying exam. *Entrance requirements:* For master's, GRE General Test, minimum GPA of 3.0; for doctorate, GRE General Test, minimum GPA of 3.3. Additional exam requirements/

recommendations for international students: Required—TOEFL (minimum score 550 paper-based; 213 computer-based; 80 iBT). Electronic applications accepted. *Faculty research:* Computational and experimental thermal sciences, manufacturing process and systems, mechanics, materials, design, quality and management engineering systems.

University of Toronto, School of Graduate Studies, Faculty of Applied Science and Engineering, Department of Mechanical and Industrial Engineering, Toronto, ON M5S 1A1, Canada. Offers M Eng, MA Sc, PhD. Part-time programs available. *Degree requirements:* For master's, thesis (for some programs), oral exam/thesis defense (MA Sc); for doctorate, thesis/dissertation, thesis defense, qualifying examination. *Entrance requirements:* For master's, GRE (recommended), minimum B+ average in last 2 years of undergraduate study, 2 letters of reference, resume, Canadian citizenship or permanent residency (M Eng); for doctorate, GRE (recommended), minimum B+ average, 2 letters of reference, resume. Additional exam requirements/recommendations for international students: Required—TOEFL (580 paper-based, 237 computer-based), Michigan English Language Assessment Battery (85), IELTS (7) or COPE (4). Electronic applications accepted.

University of Tulsa, Graduate School, College of Engineering and Natural Sciences, Department of Mechanical Engineering, Tulsa, OK 74104-3189. Offers ME, MSE, PhD. Part-time programs available. *Faculty:* 9 full-time (0 women). *Students:* 21 full-time (2 women), 17 part-time (3 women); includes 1 minority (Asian, non-Hispanic/Latino), 19 international. Average age 28. 32 applicants, 63% accepted, 9 enrolled. In 2011, 9 master's, 3 doctorates awarded. Terminal master's awarded for partial completion of doctoral program. *Degree requirements:* For master's, thesis (MSE); for doctorate, thesis/dissertation. *Entrance requirements:* For master's and doctorate, GRE General Test. Additional exam requirements/recommendations for international students: Required—TOEFL (minimum score 550 paper-based; 213 computer-based; 80 iBT), IELTS (minimum score 6). *Application deadline:* Applications are processed on a rolling basis. Application fee: $40. Electronic applications accepted. *Expenses: Tuition:* Full-time $17,748; part-time $986 per hour. *Required fees:* $5 per contact hour. $75 per semester. Tuition and fees vary according to program. *Financial support:* In 2011–12, 34 students received support, including 6 fellowships with full and partial tuition reimbursements available (averaging $1,312 per year), 31 research assistantships with full and partial tuition reimbursements available (averaging $8,960 per year), 12 teaching assistantships with full and partial tuition reimbursements available (averaging $6,016 per year); career-related internships or fieldwork, Federal Work-Study, scholarships/grants, health care benefits, tuition waivers (full and partial), and unspecified assistantships also available. Support available to part-time students. Financial award application deadline: 2/1; financial award applicants required to submit FAFSA. *Faculty research:* Erosion and corrosion, solid mechanics, composite material, computational fluid dynamics, coiled tubing mechanics. *Total annual research expenditures:* $3.5 million. *Unit head:* Dr. John Henshaw, Chairperson, 918-631-3002, Fax: 918-631-2397, E-mail: john-henshaw@utulsa.edu. *Application contact:* Dr. Siamack A. Shirazi, Adviser, 918-631-3001, Fax: 918-631-2397, E-mail: grad@utulsa.edu. Web site: http://www.me.utulsa.edu/.

University of Utah, Graduate School, College of Engineering, Department of Mechanical Engineering, Salt Lake City, UT 84112. Offers M Phil, MS, PhD. Part-time programs available. *Faculty:* 28 full-time (5 women), 3 part-time/adjunct (0 women). *Students:* 134 full-time (10 women), 78 part-time (3 women); includes 16 minority (2 Black or African American, non-Hispanic/Latino; 1 American Indian or Alaska Native, non-Hispanic/Latino; 8 Asian, non-Hispanic/Latino; 4 Hispanic/Latino; 1 Two or more races, non-Hispanic/Latino), 47 international. Average age 29. 192 applicants, 54% accepted, 52 enrolled. In 2011, 63 master's, 6 doctorates awarded. Terminal master's awarded for partial completion of doctoral program. *Median time to degree:* Of those who began their doctoral program in fall 2003, 86% received their degree in 8 years or less. *Degree requirements:* For master's, comprehensive exam (for some programs), thesis (for some programs); for doctorate, comprehensive exam, thesis/dissertation, qualifying exam. *Entrance requirements:* For master's and doctorate, GRE General Test, minimum GPA of 3.0, statement of purpose, 3 letters of recommendation, curriculum vitae/resume, transcripts. Additional exam requirements/recommendations for international students: Required—TOEFL (minimum score 590 paper-based; 243 computer-based; 96 iBT). *Application deadline:* For fall admission, 1/15 priority date for domestic students, 12/1 for international students; for spring admission, 10/1 priority date for domestic students. Application fee: $55 ($65 for international students). Electronic applications accepted. *Expenses:* Contact institution. *Financial support:* In 2011–12, 110 students received support, including 16 fellowships with full tuition reimbursements available (averaging $25,457 per year), 96 research assistantships with full and partial tuition reimbursements available (averaging $13,125 per year), 107 teaching assistantships with full and partial tuition reimbursements available (averaging $12,500 per year); institutionally sponsored loans, traineeships, health care benefits, and unspecified assistantships also available. Financial award application deadline: 1/15; financial award applicants required to submit FAFSA. *Faculty research:* Thermal science and energy systems, robotics, design and fatigue, automated manufacturing, ergonomics and safety. *Total annual research expenditures:* $2.9 million. *Unit head:* Dr. Timothy Ameel, Chair, 801-585-9730, Fax: 801-585-9826, E-mail: ameel@mech.utah.edu. *Application contact:* Dr. A. K. Balaji, Director of Graduate Studies, 801-587-7772, Fax: 801-585-9826, E-mail: balaji@mech.utah.edu. Web site: http://www.mech.utah.edu/.

University of Vermont, Graduate College, College of Engineering and Mathematics, Department of Mechanical Engineering, Burlington, VT 05405. Offers MS, PhD. *Students:* 29 (6 women); includes 2 minority (1 Black or African American, non-Hispanic/Latino; 1 Asian, non-Hispanic/Latino), 6 international. 27 applicants, 67% accepted, 4 enrolled. In 2011, 5 master's, 1 doctorate awarded. *Degree requirements:* For master's, thesis; for doctorate, thesis/dissertation. *Entrance requirements:* For master's and doctorate, GRE General Test. Additional exam requirements/recommendations for international students: Required—TOEFL (minimum score 550 paper-based; 213 computer-based; 80 iBT). *Application deadline:* For fall admission, 2/1 priority date for domestic students, 2/1 for international students. Applications are processed on a rolling basis. Application fee: $40. Electronic applications accepted. *Financial support:* Fellowships, research assistantships, and teaching assistantships available. Financial award application deadline: 3/1. *Unit head:* James Burgmeier, Chair, 802-656-3333. *Application contact:* Prof. Frederic Sansoz, Coordinator, 802-656-3333.

University of Victoria, Faculty of Graduate Studies, Faculty of Engineering, Department of Mechanical Engineering, Victoria, BC V8W 2Y2, Canada. Offers M Eng, MA Sc, PhD. Part-time programs available. *Degree requirements:* For master's, thesis (for some programs); for doctorate, thesis/dissertation, candidacy exam. *Entrance requirements:* For master's, minimum B average in undergraduate course work. Additional exam requirements/recommendations for international students: Required—TOEFL (minimum score 575 paper-based; 233 computer-based), IELTS (minimum score 7). Electronic applications accepted. *Faculty research:* CAD/CAM, energy systems, cryofuels, fuel cell technology, computational mechanics.

University of Virginia, School of Engineering and Applied Science, Department of Mechanical and Aerospace Engineering, Charlottesville, VA 22903. Offers ME, MS, PhD. Postbaccalaureate distance learning degree programs offered (no on-campus study). *Faculty:* 20 full-time (2 women), 2 part-time/adjunct (1 woman). *Students:* 77 full-time (9 women), 8 part-time (1 woman); includes 4 minority (all Asian, non-Hispanic/Latino), 24 international. Average age 27. 191 applicants, 18% accepted, 21 enrolled. In 2011, 19 master's, 12 doctorates awarded. *Degree requirements:* For master's, thesis (MS); for doctorate, comprehensive exam, thesis/dissertation. *Entrance requirements:* For master's and doctorate, GRE General Test, 3 letters of recommendation. Additional exam requirements/recommendations for international students: Required—TOEFL (minimum score 650 paper-based; 250 computer-based; 90 iBT), IELTS (minimum score 7). *Application deadline:* For fall admission, 8/1 for domestic students, 4/1 for international students; for winter admission, 12/1 for domestic students, 8/1 for international students; for spring admission, 5/1 for domestic students, 1/1 for international students. Applications are processed on a rolling basis. Application fee: $60. Electronic applications accepted. *Financial support:* Fellowships, research assistantships, and teaching assistantships available. Financial award application deadline: 1/15; financial award applicants required to submit FAFSA. *Faculty research:* Solid mechanics, dynamical systems and control, thermofluids. *Unit head:* Hossein Haj-Hariri, Chair, 434-924-7424, Fax: 434-982-2037, E-mail: mae-adm@virginia.edu. *Application contact:* Graduate Secretary, 434-924-7425, Fax: 434-982-2037, E-mail: mae-adm@virginia.edu. Web site: http://www.mae.virginia.edu/.

University of Washington, Graduate School, College of Engineering, Department of Mechanical Engineering, Seattle, WA 98195-2600. Offers MS, MSE, MSME, PhD. Part-time programs available. Postbaccalaureate distance learning degree programs offered (minimal on-campus study). *Faculty:* 42 full-time (5 women), 12 part-time/adjunct (1 woman). *Students:* 110 full-time (20 women), 72 part-time (9 women); includes 32 minority (2 Black or African American, non-Hispanic/Latino; 2 American Indian or Alaska Native, non-Hispanic/Latino; 20 Asian, non-Hispanic/Latino; 8 Hispanic/Latino), 49 international. Average age 24. 360 applicants, 45% accepted, 47 enrolled. In 2011, 58 master's, 11 doctorates awarded. *Degree requirements:* For master's, thesis optional; for doctorate, comprehensive exam, thesis/dissertation, qualifying, general, and final exams. *Entrance requirements:* For master's, GRE General Test (minimum scores: 450 Verbal, 650 Quantitative, and 4.0 Analytical Writing), minimum GPA of 3.0 (overall undergraduate GPA of 3.2 preferred); letters of recommendation; statement of purpose; for doctorate, GRE General Test (minimum scores: 450 Verbal, 650 Quantitative, and 4.0 Analytical Writing), minimum GPA of 3.0 (overall undergraduate GPA of 3.2, graduate 3.5 preferred); letters of recommendation; statement of purpose. Additional exam requirements/recommendations for international students: Required—TOEFL (minimum score 580 paper-based; 237 computer-based; 92 iBT). *Application deadline:* For fall admission, 1/15 priority date for domestic students, 1/15 for international students; for winter admission, 11/1 for domestic students, 9/1 for international students; for spring admission, 2/1 for domestic students, 1/1 for international students. Applications are processed on a rolling basis. Application fee: $75. Electronic applications accepted. *Expenses:* Contact institution. *Financial support:* In 2011–12, 124 students received support, including 16 fellowships with partial tuition reimbursements available (averaging $23,409 per year), 81 research assistantships with full tuition reimbursements available (averaging $17,316 per year), 23 teaching assistantships with full tuition reimbursements available (averaging $14,769 per year); Federal Work-Study and health care benefits also available. Financial award application deadline: 1/15; financial award applicants required to submit FAFSA. *Faculty research:* Environmentally sensitive energy conversion; health systems and biotechnology; mechatronics; advanced materials, structures and manufacturing. *Total annual research expenditures:* $8.9 million. *Unit head:* Dr. Per Reinhall, Professor/Chair, 206-543-5090, Fax: 206-685-8047, E-mail: reinhall@u.washington.edu. *Application contact:* Maria Tovar Hopper, Graduate Academic Adviser, 206-543-7963, Fax: 206-685-8047, E-mail: mariah3@u.washington.edu. Web site: http://www.me.washington.edu.

University of Waterloo, Graduate Studies, Faculty of Engineering, Department of Mechanical and Mechatronics Engineering, Waterloo, ON N2L 3G1, Canada. Offers mechanical engineering (M Eng, MA Sc, PhD); mechanical engineering design and manufacturing (M Eng). Part-time and evening/weekend programs available. *Degree requirements:* For master's, research paper or thesis; for doctorate, comprehensive exam, thesis/dissertation. *Entrance requirements:* For master's, honors degree, minimum B average, resume; for doctorate, master's degree, minimum A- average, resumé. Additional exam requirements/recommendations for international students: Required—TOEFL (minimum score 550 paper-based; 213 computer-based), TWE (minimum score 4). Electronic applications accepted. *Faculty research:* Fluid mechanics, thermal engineering, solid mechanics, automation and control, materials engineering.

The University of Western Ontario, Faculty of Graduate Studies, Physical Sciences Division, Faculty of Engineering, London, ON N6A 5B8, Canada. Offers chemical and biochemical engineering (ME Sc, PhD); civil and environmental engineering (M Eng, ME Sc, PhD); electrical and computer engineering (M Eng, ME Sc, PhD); mechanical and materials engineering (M Eng, ME Sc, PhD). Part-time programs available. Terminal master's awarded for partial completion of doctoral program. *Degree requirements:* For master's, thesis; for doctorate, thesis/dissertation. *Entrance requirements:* For master's, minimum B average; for doctorate, minimum B+ average. *Faculty research:* Wind, geotechnical, chemical reactor engineering, applied electrostatics, biochemical engineering.

University of Windsor, Faculty of Graduate Studies, Faculty of Engineering, Department of Mechanical, Automotive, and Materials Engineering, Windsor, ON N9B 3P4, Canada. Offers engineering materials (M Eng, MA Sc, PhD); mechanical engineering (M Eng, MA Sc, PhD). Part-time programs available. *Degree requirements:* For master's, thesis; for doctorate, comprehensive exam, thesis/dissertation. *Entrance requirements:* For master's, minimum B average; for doctorate, master's degree, minimum B average. Additional exam requirements/recommendations for international students: Required—TOEFL (minimum score 600 paper-based; 250 computer-based). Electronic applications accepted. *Faculty research:* Thermofluids, applied mechanics, materials engineering.

University of Wisconsin–Madison, Graduate School, College of Engineering, Department of Mechanical Engineering, Madison, WI 53706-1380. Offers energy systems (ME); engine systems (ME); mechanical engineering (MS, PhD); polymers (ME). Part-time programs available. Postbaccalaureate distance learning degree programs offered (no on-campus study). *Faculty:* 33 full-time (3 women), 1 part-time/adjunct (0 women). *Students:* 191 full-time (17 women), 18 part-time (1 woman); includes 23 minority (1 Black or African American, non-Hispanic/Latino; 1 American Indian or Alaska Native, non-Hispanic/Latino; 10 Asian, non-Hispanic/Latino; 10

Hispanic/Latino; 1 Native Hawaiian or other Pacific Islander, non-Hispanic/Latino). Average age 25. 615 applicants, 19% accepted, 46 enrolled. In 2011, 56 master's, 16 doctorates awarded. Terminal master's awarded for partial completion of doctoral program. *Degree requirements:* For master's, thesis optional; for doctorate, thesis/dissertation, qualifying exam, preliminary exam. *Entrance requirements:* For master's, GRE, BS in mechanical engineering or related field, minimum GPA of 3.0 in last 60 hours of course work; for doctorate, GRE, BS in mechanical engineering or related field, minimum undergraduate GPA of 3.0 in last 60 hours of course work. Additional exam requirements/recommendations for international students: Required—TOEFL (minimum score 550 paper-based; 213 computer-based; 80 iBT). *Application deadline:* For fall admission, 5/1 for domestic students, 6/1 for international students; for spring admission, 11/30 for domestic students, 10/1 for international students. Applications are processed on a rolling basis. Application fee: $56. Electronic applications accepted. *Expenses:* Tuition, state resident: full-time $10,296; part-time $643.51 per credit. Tuition, nonresident: full-time $24,054; part-time $1503.40 per credit. *Required fees:* $70.06 per credit. Tuition and fees vary according to course load, campus/location, program and reciprocity agreements. *Financial support:* In 2011–12, 168 students received support, including 11 fellowships with full tuition reimbursements available (averaging $22,224 per year), 121 research assistantships with full tuition reimbursements available (averaging $19,596 per year), 37 teaching assistantships with full tuition reimbursements available (averaging $8,595 per year); career-related internships or fieldwork, institutionally sponsored loans, scholarships/grants, traineeships, health care benefits, and unspecified assistantships also available. *Faculty research:* Design and manufacturing, materials processing, combustion, energy systems nanotechnology. *Total annual research expenditures:* $10 million. *Unit head:* Roxann L. Engelstad, Chair, 608-262-5745, Fax: 608-265-2316, E-mail: engelsta@engr.wisc.edu. *Application contact:* 608-262-2433, Fax: 608-262-5134, E-mail: gradadmiss@mail.bascom.wisc.edu. Web site: http://www.engr.wisc.edu/me/.

University of Wisconsin–Milwaukee, Graduate School, College of Engineering and Applied Science, Program in Engineering, Milwaukee, WI 53201-0413. Offers civil engineering (MS); electrical and computer engineering (MS); energy engineering (Certificate); engineering (PhD); engineering management (MS); engineering mechanics (MS); ergonomics (Certificate); industrial and management engineering (MS); manufacturing engineering (MS); materials engineering (MS); mechanical engineering (MS); MUP/MS. Part-time programs available. *Faculty:* 41 full-time (5 women), 2 part-time/adjunct (0 women). *Students:* 170 full-time (33 women), 101 part-time (18 women); includes 30 minority (6 Black or African American, non-Hispanic/Latino; 15 Asian, non-Hispanic/Latino; 2 Hispanic/Latino; 7 Two or more races, non-Hispanic/Latino), 153 international. Average age 30. 170 applicants, 56% accepted, 48 enrolled. In 2011, 47 master's, 12 doctorates awarded. *Degree requirements:* For master's, comprehensive exam (for some programs), thesis or alternative; for doctorate, comprehensive exam, thesis/dissertation, internship. *Entrance requirements:* For master's, GRE, minimum GPA of 2.75; for doctorate, GRE, minimum GPA of 3.5. Additional exam requirements/recommendations for international students: Required—TOEFL (minimum score 550 paper-based; 79 iBT), IELTS (minimum score 6.5). *Application deadline:* For fall admission, 1/1 priority date for domestic students; for spring admission, 9/1 for domestic students. Applications are processed on a rolling basis. Application fee: $56 ($96 for international students). One-time fee: $506.10 full-time. Tuition and fees vary according to course load and reciprocity agreements. *Financial support:* In 2011–12, 3 fellowships, 55 research assistantships, 77 teaching assistantships were awarded; career-related internships or fieldwork, Federal Work-Study, unspecified assistantships, and project assistantships also available. Support available to part-time students. Financial award application deadline: 4/15. *Total annual research expenditures:* $10.3 million. *Unit head:* David Yu, Representative, 414-229-6169, E-mail: yu@uwm.edu. *Application contact:* Betty Warras, General Information Contact, 414-229-6169, Fax: 414-229-6967, E-mail: bwarras@uwm.edu. Web site: http://www.wum.edu/CEAS/.

University of Wyoming, College of Engineering and Applied Sciences, Department of Mechanical Engineering, Laramie, WY 82070. Offers MS, PhD. Terminal master's awarded for partial completion of doctoral program. *Degree requirements:* For master's, thesis; for doctorate, thesis/dissertation. *Entrance requirements:* For master's, GRE General Test (minimum score 900), minimum GPA of 3.0; for doctorate, GRE General Test (minimum score: 1000), minimum GPA of 3.0. Additional exam requirements/recommendations for international students: Required—TOEFL (minimum score 550 paper-based; 215 computer-based). Electronic applications accepted. *Faculty research:* Composite materials, thermal and fluid sciences, continuum mechanics, material science.

Utah State University, School of Graduate Studies, College of Engineering, Department of Mechanical and Aerospace Engineering, Logan, UT 84322. Offers aerospace engineering (MS, PhD); mechanical engineering (ME, MS, PhD). Terminal master's awarded for partial completion of doctoral program. *Degree requirements:* For master's, thesis (for some programs); for doctorate, thesis/dissertation. *Entrance requirements:* For master's, GRE General Test, minimum GPA of 3.0; for doctorate, GRE General Test, minimum GPA of 3.3. Additional exam requirements/recommendations for international students: Required—TOEFL. *Faculty research:* In-space instruments, cryogenic cooling, thermal science, space structures, composite materials.

Vanderbilt University, School of Engineering, Department of Mechanical Engineering, Nashville, TN 37240-1001. Offers M Eng, MS, PhD. MS and PhD offered through the Graduate School. Part-time programs available. *Faculty:* 16 full-time (1 woman). *Students:* 59 full-time (8 women); includes 4 minority (1 Black or African American, non-Hispanic/Latino; 2 Asian, non-Hispanic/Latino; 1 Hispanic/Latino), 19 international. Average age 27. 279 applicants, 6% accepted, 10 enrolled. In 2011, 6 master's, 8 doctorates awarded. Terminal master's awarded for partial completion of doctoral program. *Degree requirements:* For master's, comprehensive exam, thesis; for doctorate, comprehensive exam, thesis/dissertation. *Entrance requirements:* For master's and doctorate, GRE General Test. Additional exam requirements/recommendations for international students: Required—TOEFL (minimum score 550 paper-based; 220 computer-based); Recommended—TWE (minimum score 4). *Application deadline:* For fall admission, 1/15 for domestic students; for spring admission, 11/1 for domestic students. Applications are processed on a rolling basis. Application fee: $0. Electronic applications accepted. *Financial support:* In 2011–12, 7 fellowships with full tuition reimbursements (averaging $27,480 per year), 33 research assistantships with full tuition reimbursements (averaging $26,532 per year), 13 teaching assistantships with full tuition reimbursements (averaging $24,540 per year) were awarded; institutionally sponsored loans, health care benefits, and tuition waivers (full) also available. Support available to part-time students. Financial award application deadline: 1/15. *Faculty research:* Active noise and vibration control, robotics, mesoscale and microscale energy conversions, laser diagnostics, combustion. *Total annual research expenditures:* $3.1 million. *Unit head:* Dr. Robert W. Pitz, Chair, 615-322-2413, Fax: 615-343-6687, E-mail: robert.w.pitz@vanderbilt.edu. *Application contact:* Dr.

Nilanjan Sarkar, Director of Graduate Studies, 615-343-7219, Fax: 615-343-6687, E-mail: nilanjan.sarkar@vanderbilt.edu. Web site: http://frontweb.vuse.vanderbilt.edu/me/.

Villanova University, College of Engineering, Department of Electrical and Computer Engineering, Program in Electrical Engineering, Villanova, PA 19085-1699. Offers electric power systems (Certificate); electrical engineering (MSEE); electro mechanical systems (Certificate); high frequency systems (Certificate); intelligent control systems (Certificate); wireless and digital communications (Certificate). Part-time and evening/weekend programs available. *Degree requirements:* For master's, thesis optional. *Entrance requirements:* For master's, GRE General Test (for applicants with degrees from foreign universities), BEE, minimum GPA of 3.0. Additional exam requirements/recommendations for international students: Required—TOEFL (minimum score 600 paper-based; 250 computer-based; 100 iBT). *Expenses: Tuition:* Part-time $675 per credit. Part-time tuition and fees vary according to degree level and program. *Faculty research:* Signal processing, communications, antennas, devices.

Villanova University, College of Engineering, Department of Mechanical Engineering, Villanova, PA 19085-1699. Offers electro-mechanical systems (Certificate); machinery dynamics (Certificate); mechanical engineering (MSME); nonlinear dynamics and control (Certificate); thermofluid systems (Certificate). Part-time and evening/weekend programs available. Postbaccalaureate distance learning degree programs offered (no on-campus study). *Degree requirements:* For master's, thesis optional. *Entrance requirements:* For master's, GRE General Test (for applicants with degrees from foreign universities), BME, minimum GPA of 3.0. Additional exam requirements/recommendations for international students: Required—TOEFL (minimum score 600 paper-based; 250 computer-based; 100 iBT). Electronic applications accepted. *Expenses: Tuition:* Part-time $675 per credit. Part-time tuition and fees vary according to degree level and program. *Faculty research:* Composite materials, power plant systems, fluid mechanics, automated manufacturing, dynamic analysis.

Virginia Commonwealth University, Graduate School, School of Engineering, Department of Mechanical Engineering, Richmond, VA 23284-9005. Offers MS, PhD. *Entrance requirements:* For master's and doctorate, GRE. Additional exam requirements/recommendations for international students: Required—TOEFL (minimum score 600 paper-based; 250 computer-based; 100 iBT). Electronic applications accepted. *Expenses:* Tuition, state resident: full-time $9133; part-time $507 per credit. Tuition, nonresident: full-time $18,777; part-time $1043 per credit. *Required fees:* $77 per credit. Tuition and fees vary according to degree level, campus/location, program and student level.

Virginia Polytechnic Institute and State University, Graduate School, College of Engineering, Department of Mechanical Engineering, Blacksburg, VA 24061. Offers M Eng, MS, PhD. *Degree requirements:* For master's, comprehensive exam (for some programs), thesis (for some programs); for doctorate, comprehensive exam (for some programs), thesis/dissertation (for some programs). *Entrance requirements:* For master's and doctorate, GRE. Additional exam requirements/recommendations for international students: Required—TOEFL (minimum score 550 paper-based; 213 computer-based). *Application deadline:* For fall admission, 7/1 for domestic and international students; for spring admission, 12/1 for domestic and international students. Applications are processed on a rolling basis. Application fee: $65. Electronic applications accepted. *Expenses:* Tuition, state resident: full-time $10,048; part-time $558.25 per credit hour. Tuition, nonresident: full-time $19,497; part-time $1083.25 per credit hour. *Required fees:* $405 per semester. Tuition and fees vary according to course load, campus/location and program. *Financial support:* Fellowships with full tuition reimbursements, research assistantships with full tuition reimbursements, teaching assistantships with full tuition reimbursements, career-related internships or fieldwork, Federal Work-Study, scholarships/grants, health care benefits, and unspecified assistantships available. Financial award application deadline: 1/15. *Faculty research:* Turbomachinery, CAD/CAM, thermofluid sciences, controls, mechanical system dynamics. *Unit head:* Dr. Kenneth S. Ball, Unit Head, 540-231-6661, Fax: 540-231-9100, E-mail: ball@vt.edu. *Application contact:* Mary Kasarda, Information Contact, 540-231-8552, Fax: 540-231-9100, E-mail: maryk@vt.edu. Web site: http://www.me.vt.edu/.

Washington State University, Graduate School, College of Engineering and Architecture, School of Mechanical and Materials Engineering, Program in Mechanical Engineering, Pullman, WA 99164. Offers MS, PhD. Part-time programs available. *Faculty:* 32. *Students:* 68 full-time (10 women), 28 part-time (7 women); includes 10 minority (2 Black or African American, non-Hispanic/Latino; 3 Asian, non-Hispanic/Latino; 5 Hispanic/Latino), 44 international. Average age 27. 152 applicants, 20% accepted, 16 enrolled. In 2011, 11 master's, 4 doctorates awarded. Terminal master's awarded for partial completion of doctoral program. *Degree requirements:* For master's, comprehensive exam (for some programs), thesis (for some programs), oral exam; for doctorate, comprehensive exam, thesis/dissertation, oral exam, qualifying exam. *Entrance requirements:* For master's, GRE (recommended), minimum GPA of 3.0, resume, 3 letters of recommendation with evaluation forms, student interest profile; for doctorate, minimum GPA of 3.4, resume, 3 letters of recommendation with evaluation forms, student interest profile. Additional exam requirements/recommendations for international students: Required—TOEFL, IELTS. *Application deadline:* For fall admission, 1/10 priority date for domestic students, 1/10 for international students; for spring admission, 7/1 priority date for domestic students, 7/1 for international students. Applications are processed on a rolling basis. Application fee: $75. Electronic applications accepted. *Financial support:* In 2011–12, 38 students received support, including 3 fellowships (averaging $3,252 per year), 19 research assistantships with full tuition reimbursements available (averaging $13,917 per year), 15 teaching assistantships with full tuition reimbursements available (averaging $13,056 per year); career-related internships or fieldwork, Federal Work-Study, institutionally sponsored loans, scholarships/grants, health care benefits, and unspecified assistantships also available. Financial award application deadline: 4/1; financial award applicants required to submit FAFSA. *Faculty research:* Thermal and fluid sciences, solid mechanics, manufacturing, MEMS, computer-aided design. *Total annual research expenditures:* $2.2 million. *Unit head:* Dr. Hussein M. Zbib, Director, 509-335-8654, Fax: 509-335-4662, E-mail: director@mme.wsu.edu. *Application contact:* Graduate School Admissions, 800-GRADWSU, Fax: 509-335-1949, E-mail: gradsch@wsu.edu. Web site: http://www.mme.wsu.edu/.

Washington State University Tri-Cities, Graduate Programs, College of Engineering and Architecture, Richland, WA 99352-1671. Offers computer science (MS, PhD); electrical engineering (MS, PhD); mechanical engineering (MS, PhD). Part-time programs available. *Faculty:* 28. *Students:* 20 full-time (5 women), 37 part-time (10 women); includes 6 minority (1 Black or African American, non-Hispanic/Latino; 2 Asian, non-Hispanic/Latino; 1 Hispanic/Latino; 2 Two or more races, non-Hispanic/Latino), 4 international. Average age 27. 27 applicants, 33% accepted, 6 enrolled. *Degree requirements:* For master's, comprehensive exam, thesis (for some programs); for

doctorate, comprehensive exam, thesis/dissertation, oral exam. *Entrance requirements:* For master's and doctorate, GRE, minimum GPA of 3.0, 3 letters of recommendation. Additional exam requirements/recommendations for international students: Required—TOEFL (minimum score 550 paper-based; 213 computer-based). *Application deadline:* For fall admission, 1/10 priority date for domestic students, 1/10 for international students; for spring admission, 7/1 priority date for domestic students, 7/1 for international students. Application fee: $75. *Financial support:* Application deadline: 3/1. *Faculty research:* Positive ion track structure, biological systems computer simulations. *Unit head:* Dr. Ali Saberi, Chair, 509-372-7178, E-mail: sidra@eecs.wsu.edu. *Application contact:* Dr. Scott Hudson, Associate Director, 509-372-7254, Fax: 509-335-1949, E-mail: hudson@tricity.wsu.edu. Web site: http://cea.tricity.wsu.edu/.

Washington State University Vancouver, Graduate Programs, School of Engineering and Computer Science, Vancouver, WA 98686. Offers computer science (MS); mechanical engineering (MS). Part-time programs available. *Faculty:* 9. *Students:* 22 full-time (2 women), 5 part-time (1 woman); includes 2 minority (both Asian, non-Hispanic/Latino), 10 international. Average age 29. 48 applicants, 33% accepted, 13 enrolled. *Degree requirements:* For master's, comprehensive exam (for some programs), thesis, research project. *Entrance requirements:* For master's, minimum GPA of 3.0, 3 letters of recommendation with evaluation forms, resume. Additional exam requirements/recommendations for international students: Required—TOEFL (minimum score 550 paper-based). *Application deadline:* For fall admission, 1/10 priority date for domestic students, 1/10 for international students; for spring admission, 7/1 priority date for domestic students, 7/1 for international students. Applications are processed on a rolling basis. Application fee: $75. *Financial support:* In 2011–12, research assistantships with full tuition reimbursements (averaging $14,634 per year), teaching assistantships with full tuition reimbursements (averaging $13,383 per year) were awarded; health care benefits and unspecified assistantships also available. Financial award application deadline: 2/15. *Faculty research:* Software design, artificial intelligence, sensor networks, robotics, nanotechnology. *Total annual research expenditures:* $3.4 million. *Unit head:* Dr. Hakan Gurocak, Director, 360-546-9637, Fax: 360-546-9438, E-mail: hgurocak@vancouver.wsu.edu. *Application contact:* Peggy Moore, Academic Coordinator, 360-546-9638, Fax: 360-546-9438, E-mail: moorep@vancouver.wsu.edu. Web site: http://ecs.vancouver.wsu.edu/.

Washington University in St. Louis, School of Engineering and Applied Science, Department of Mechanical, Aerospace and Structural Engineering, St. Louis, MO 63130-4899. Offers MS, D Sc, PhD. Part-time programs available. Terminal master's awarded for partial completion of doctoral program. *Degree requirements:* For master's, thesis optional; for doctorate, thesis/dissertation optional. *Entrance requirements:* For master's, GRE; for doctorate, GRE General Test, departmental qualifying exam. *Faculty research:* Aerosols science and technology, applied mechanics, biomechanics and biomedical engineering, design, dynamic systems, combustion science, composite materials, materials science.

Wayne State University, College of Engineering, Department of Mechanical Engineering, Detroit, MI 48202. Offers MS, PhD. *Students:* 88 full-time (11 women), 29 part-time (1 woman); includes 14 minority (3 Black or African American, non-Hispanic/Latino; 10 Asian, non-Hispanic/Latino; 1 Two or more races, non-Hispanic/Latino), 73 international. Average age 30. 185 applicants, 47% accepted, 27 enrolled. In 2011, 54 master's, 4 doctorates awarded. *Degree requirements:* For master's, thesis optional; for doctorate, thesis/dissertation. *Entrance requirements:* For master's, GRE (if BS is not from ABET-accredited university), minimum undergraduate GPA of 3.0; for doctorate, GRE, minimum graduate or undergraduate upper-division GPA of 3.5, undergraduate major of substantial work in doctoral field. Additional exam requirements/recommendations for international students: Required—TOEFL (minimum score 550 paper-based; 213 computer-based); Recommended—TWE (minimum score 5.5). *Application deadline:* For fall admission, 6/1 priority date for domestic students, 5/1 for international students; for winter admission, 10/1 priority date for domestic students, 9/1 for international students; for spring admission, 2/1 priority date for domestic students, 1/1 for international students. Applications are processed on a rolling basis. Application fee: $50. Electronic applications accepted. *Expenses:* Tuition, state resident: part-time $512.85 per credit. Tuition, nonresident: part-time $1132.65 per credit. *Required fees:* $26.60 per credit. $199.65 per semester. Tuition and fees vary according to course load and program. *Financial support:* In 2011–12, 35 students received support, including 7 fellowships with tuition reimbursements available (averaging $14,331 per year), 15 research assistantships with tuition reimbursements available (averaging $18,983 per year), 11 teaching assistantships with tuition reimbursements available (averaging $17,391 per year); career-related internships or fieldwork, Federal Work-Study, scholarships/grants, health care benefits, tuition waivers (full and partial), and unspecified assistantships also available. Financial award application deadline: 2/28. *Faculty research:* Acoustics and vibrations/noise control, engine combustion and emission controls, advanced materials and structures, computational fluid mechanics, material processing and manufacturing. *Total annual research expenditures:* $2 million. *Unit head:* Dr. Walter Bryzik, Chair, 313-577-5135, E-mail: wbryzik@eng.wayne.edu. *Application contact:* Dr. Trilochan Singh, Director of Graduate Studies, 313-577-3843, E-mail: tsing@eng.wayne.edu. Web site: http://www.eng.wayne.edu/page.php?id=4845.

Western Michigan University, Graduate College, College of Engineering and Applied Sciences, Department of Mechanical and Aeronautical Engineering, Kalamazoo, MI 49008. Offers mechanical engineering (MSE, PhD). Part-time programs available. *Degree requirements:* For master's, thesis optional; for doctorate, thesis/dissertation, oral exam. *Entrance requirements:* For master's, minimum GPA of 3.0; for doctorate, GRE General Test, minimum GPA of 3.0. *Faculty research:* Computational fluid dynamics, manufacturing process designs, composite materials, thermal fluid flow, experimental stress analysis.

Western New England University, College of Engineering, Department of Mechanical Engineering, Springfield, MA 01119. Offers MSE. Part-time and evening/weekend programs available. *Students:* 2 part-time (0 women). In 2011, 1 master's awarded. *Degree requirements:* For master's, comprehensive exam, thesis optional. *Entrance requirements:* For master's, GRE, bachelor's degree in engineering or related field. *Application deadline:* Applications are processed on a rolling basis. Application fee: $30. *Financial support:* Available to part-time students. Application deadline: 4/1; applicants required to submit FAFSA. *Faculty research:* Low-loss fluid mixing, flow separation delay and alleviation, high-lift airfoils, ejector research, compact heat exchangers. *Unit head:* Dr. Said Dini, Chair, 413-782-1272, E-mail: sdini@wne.edu. *Application contact:* Douglas Kenyon, Assistant Vice President, Graduate Studies and Continuing Education, 413-782-1249, Fax: 413-782-1779, E-mail: learn@wne.edu. Web site: http://www1.wne.edu/continuinged/.

West Virginia University, College of Engineering and Mineral Resources, Department of Mechanical and Aerospace Engineering, Program in Mechanical Engineering, Morgantown, WV 26506. Offers MSME, PhD. Part-time programs available. Terminal master's awarded for partial completion of doctoral program. *Degree requirements:* For master's, thesis; for doctorate, comprehensive exam, thesis/dissertation, qualifying exam, proposal and defense. *Entrance requirements:* For master's and doctorate, GRE Subject Test, minimum GPA of 3.0, 3 references. Additional exam requirements/ recommendations for international students: Required—TOEFL. *Faculty research:* Thermal sciences, material sciences, automatic controls, mechanical/structure design.

Wichita State University, Graduate School, College of Engineering, Department of Mechanical Engineering, Wichita, KS 67260. Offers MS, PhD. Part-time programs available. *Expenses:* Tuition, state resident: full-time $4746; part-time $263.65 per credit. Tuition, nonresident: full-time $11,669; part-time $648.30 per credit. *Unit head:* Dr. David Koert, Chair, 316-978-3402, Fax: 316-978-3236, E-mail: david.koert@wichita.edu. *Application contact:* Dr. T. S. Ravigururajan, Graduate Coordinator, 316-978-3402, E-mail: ts.ravi@wichita.edu. Web site: http://www.wichita.edu/.

Widener University, Graduate Programs in Engineering, Program in Mechanical Engineering, Chester, PA 19013-5792. Offers M Eng. Part-time and evening/weekend programs available. *Degree requirements:* For master's, thesis optional. *Faculty research:* Computational fluid mechanics, thermal and solar engineering, energy conversion, composite materials, solid mechanics.

Wilkes University, College of Graduate and Professional Studies, College of Science and Engineering, Division of Engineering and Physics, Wilkes-Barre, PA 18766-0002. Offers electrical engineering (MSEE); engineering management (MS); mechanical engineering (MS). Part-time programs available. *Students:* 27 full-time (2 women), 26 part-time (4 women); includes 2 minority (both Asian, non-Hispanic/Latino), 19 international. Average age 30. In 2011, 11 master's awarded. *Entrance requirements:* For master's, GRE General Test. Additional exam requirements/recommendations for international students: Required—TOEFL (minimum score 550 paper-based; 213 computer-based; 79 iBT). *Application deadline:* Applications are processed on a rolling basis. Application fee: $45 ($65 for international students). Electronic applications accepted. *Financial support:* Federal Work-Study and unspecified assistantships available. Financial award application deadline: 3/1; financial award applicants required to submit FAFSA. *Unit head:* Dr. Rodney Ridley, Director, 570-408-4824, Fax: 570-408-7846, E-mail: rodney.ridley@wilkes.edu. *Application contact:* Erin Sutzko, Director of Extended Learning, 570-408-4253, Fax: 570-408-7846, E-mail: erin.sutzko@wilkes.edu. Web site: http://www.wilkes.edu/pages/387.asp.

Worcester Polytechnic Institute, Graduate Studies and Research, Department of Mechanical Engineering, Worcester, MA 01609-2280. Offers manufacturing engineering (MS, PhD); materials process engineering (MS); materials science and engineering (MS, PhD); mechanical engineering (MS, PhD, Graduate Certificate). Part-time and evening/weekend programs available. Postbaccalaureate distance learning degree programs offered (minimal on-campus study). *Faculty:* 24 full-time (3 women), 4 part-time/adjunct (1 woman). *Students:* 60 full-time (11 women), 97 part-time (15 women); includes 14 minority (1 Black or African American, non-Hispanic/Latino; 6 Asian, non-Hispanic/Latino; 4 Hispanic/Latino; 3 Two or more races, non-Hispanic/Latino), 46 international. 336 applicants, 81% accepted, 103 enrolled. In 2011, 61 master's, 1 doctorate awarded. *Degree requirements:* For master's, thesis optional; for doctorate,

comprehensive exam, thesis/dissertation. *Entrance requirements:* For master's, GRE (recommended), BS in mechanical engineering or related field, 3 letters of recommendation; for doctorate, GRE (recommended), MS in mechanical engineering or related field, 3 letters of recommendation, statement of purpose. Additional exam requirements/recommendations for international students: Required—TOEFL (minimum score 563 paper-based; 223 computer-based; 84 iBT), IELTS (minimum score 7). *Application deadline:* For fall admission, 1/1 priority date for domestic students, 1/1 for international students; for spring admission, 10/1 priority date for domestic students, 10/1 for international students. Applications are processed on a rolling basis. Application fee: $70. Electronic applications accepted. *Financial support:* Research assistantships, teaching assistantships, career-related internships or fieldwork, institutionally sponsored loans, scholarships/grants, and unspecified assistantships available. Financial award application deadline: 1/1; financial award applicants required to submit FAFSA. *Faculty research:* Theoretical, numerical and experimental work in rarefied gas and plasma dynamics; electric propulsion; multiphase flows; rotating flows; turbomachinery; fluid-structure interactions; structural analysis; nonlinear dynamics and control; cooperative control in network systems; random vibrations; biomechanics and biomaterials; mesh generation for biomedical imaging; robotics and biorobotics; materials processing; mechanics of granular materials; laser holography; MEMS; computer-aided engineering. *Unit head:* Dr. Jamal Yagoobi, Interim Head, 508-831-5556, Fax: 508-831-5680, E-mail: jyagoobi@wpi.edu. *Application contact:* Dr. Mark Richman, Graduate Coordinator, 508-831-5556, Fax: 508-831-5680, E-mail: mrichman@wpi.edu. Web site: http://www.me.wpi.edu/.

Wright State University, School of Graduate Studies, College of Engineering and Computer Science, Programs in Engineering, Program in Mechanical and Materials Engineering, Dayton, OH 45435. Offers materials science and engineering (MSE); mechanical engineering (MSE). *Degree requirements:* For master's, thesis or course option alternative. *Entrance requirements:* Additional exam requirements/recommendations for international students: Required—TOEFL.

Yale University, Graduate School of Arts and Sciences, School of Engineering and Applied Science, Department of Mechanical Engineering, New Haven, CT 06520. Offers MS, PhD. Terminal master's awarded for partial completion of doctoral program. *Degree requirements:* For doctorate, thesis/dissertation, exam. *Entrance requirements:* For master's and doctorate, GRE General Test. Additional exam requirements/recommendations for international students: Required—TOEFL. *Faculty research:* Mechanics of fluids, mechanics of solids/material science.

Youngstown State University, Graduate School, College of Science, Technology, Engineering and Mathematics, Department of Mechanical Engineering, Youngstown, OH 44555-0001. Offers MSE. Part-time and evening/weekend programs available. *Degree requirements:* For master's, thesis optional. *Entrance requirements:* For master's, minimum GPA of 2.75 in field. Additional exam requirements/recommendations for international students: Required—TOEFL. *Faculty research:* Kinematics and dynamics of machines, computational and experimental heat transfer, machine controls and mechanical design.

Mechanics

Brown University, Graduate School, Division of Engineering, Program in Mechanics of Solids, Providence, RI 02912. Offers Sc M, PhD. *Degree requirements:* For doctorate, thesis/dissertation, preliminary exam.

California Institute of Technology, Division of Engineering and Applied Science, Option in Applied Mechanics, Pasadena, CA 91125-0001. Offers MS, PhD. *Degree requirements:* For doctorate, thesis/dissertation. *Faculty research:* Elasticity, mechanics of quasi-static and dynamic fracture, dynamics and mechanical vibrations, stability and control.

California State University, Fullerton, Graduate Studies, College of Engineering and Computer Science, Department of Civil Engineering and Engineering Mechanics, Fullerton, CA 92834-9480. Offers MS. Part-time programs available. *Students:* 96 full-time (20 women), 78 part-time (21 women); includes 87 minority (6 Black or African American, non-Hispanic/Latino; 48 Asian, non-Hispanic/Latino; 27 Hispanic/Latino; 6 Two or more races, non-Hispanic/Latino), 27 international. Average age 29. 213 applicants, 64% accepted, 68 enrolled. In 2011, 59 master's awarded. *Degree requirements:* For master's, comprehensive exam, project or thesis. *Entrance requirements:* For master's, minimum undergraduate GPA of 2.5. Application fee: $55. *Financial support:* Career-related internships or fieldwork, Federal Work-Study, institutionally sponsored loans, and scholarships/grants available. Support available to part-time students. Financial award application deadline: 3/1; financial award applicants required to submit FAFSA. *Faculty research:* Soil-structure interaction, finite-element analysis, computer-aided analysis and design. *Unit head:* Dr. Pinaki Chakrabarti, Chair, 657-278-3016. *Application contact:* Admissions/Applications, 657-278-2371.

Carnegie Mellon University, Carnegie Institute of Technology, Department of Civil and Environmental Engineering, Pittsburgh, PA 15213. Offers advanced infrastructure systems (MS, PhD); civil and environmental engineering (MS, PhD); civil and environmental engineering/engineering and public policy (PhD); civil engineering (MS, PhD); computational mechanics (MS, PhD); environmental engineering (MS, PhD); environmental management and science (MS, PhD). Part-time programs available. *Faculty:* 22 full-time (4 women), 24 part-time/adjunct (5 women). *Students:* 147 full-time (64 women), 7 part-time (0 women); includes 13 minority (5 Black or African American, non-Hispanic/Latino; 6 Asian, non-Hispanic/Latino; 2 Hispanic/Latino), 101 international. Average age 26. 487 applicants, 55% accepted, 80 enrolled. In 2011, 84 master's, 12 doctorates awarded. Terminal master's awarded for partial completion of doctoral program. *Degree requirements:* For master's, thesis optional; for doctorate, comprehensive exam, thesis/dissertation, two-part qualifying exam, public defense of dissertation. *Entrance requirements:* For master's and doctorate, GRE General Test. Additional exam requirements/recommendations for international students: Required—TOEFL (minimum score 84 iBT). *Application deadline:* For fall admission, 1/15 priority date for domestic students, 1/15 for international students; for spring admission, 9/30 priority date for domestic students, 9/30 for international students. Application fee: $65. Electronic applications accepted. *Financial support:* In 2011–12, 108 students received support, including 26 fellowships with full and partial tuition reimbursements available (averaging $2,087 per year), 35 research assistantships with full and partial tuition reimbursements available (averaging $2,094 per year); tuition waivers (partial), unspecified assistantships, and service assistantships also available. Financial award

application deadline: 1/15. *Faculty research:* Advanced infrastructure systems; environmental engineering science and management; mechanics, materials, and computing; green design; global sustainable construction. *Total annual research expenditures:* $4.9 million. *Unit head:* Dr. James H. Garrett, Jr., Head, 412-268-2941, Fax: 412-268-7813, E-mail: garrett@cmu.edu. *Application contact:* Maxine A. Leffard, Director of the Graduate Program, 412-268-5673, Fax: 412-268-7813, E-mail: ce-admissions@andrew.cmu.edu. Web site: http://www.ce.cmu.edu/.

Columbia University, The Fu Foundation School of Engineering and Applied Science, Department of Civil Engineering and Engineering Mechanics, New York, NY 10027. Offers civil engineering (MS, Eng Sc D, PhD, Engr); construction engineering and management (MS); engineering mechanics (MS, Eng Sc D, PhD, Engr). Part-time programs available. Postbaccalaureate distance learning degree programs offered (no on-campus study). *Faculty:* 15 full-time (1 woman), 24 part-time/adjunct (2 women). *Students:* 119 full-time (27 women), 56 part-time (20 women); includes 36 minority (3 Black or African American, non-Hispanic/Latino; 15 Asian, non-Hispanic/Latino; 3 Hispanic/Latino; 15 Two or more races, non-Hispanic/Latino), 93 international. Average age 28. 302 applicants, 36% accepted, 69 enrolled. In 2011, 61 master's, 4 doctorates, 2 other advanced degrees awarded. Terminal master's awarded for partial completion of doctoral program. *Degree requirements:* For doctorate, thesis/dissertation, qualifying exam. *Entrance requirements:* For master's, doctorate, and Engr, GRE General Test. Additional exam requirements/recommendations for international students: Required—TOEFL, IELTS. *Application deadline:* For fall admission, 12/1 priority date for domestic students, 12/1 for international students; for spring admission, 10/1 priority date for domestic students, 10/1 for international students. Application fee: $95. Electronic applications accepted. *Financial support:* In 2011–12, 39 students received support, including 11 fellowships with full tuition reimbursements available (averaging $25,386 per year), 16 research assistantships with full tuition reimbursements available (averaging $31,128 per year), 10 teaching assistantships with full tuition reimbursements available (averaging $31,128 per year); traineeships, health care benefits, and tuition waivers also available. Financial award application deadline: 12/1; financial award applicants required to submit FAFSA. *Faculty research:* Structural dynamics, structural health and monitoring, fatigue and fracture mechanics, geo-enviornmental engineering, multiscale science and engineering. *Unit head:* Dr. Raimondo Betti, Professor and Department Chairman, 212-854-6388, E-mail: betti@civil.columbia.edu. *Application contact:* Dr. Rene B. Testa, Professor, 212-854-6383, Fax: 212-854-6267, E-mail: testa@civil.columbia.edu. Web site: http://www.civil.columbia.edu/.

Cornell University, Graduate School, Graduate Fields of Engineering, Field of Theoretical and Applied Mechanics, Ithaca, NY 14853-0001. Offers advanced composites and structures (M Eng); dynamics and space mechanics (MS, PhD); fluid mechanics (MS, PhD); mechanics of materials (MS, PhD); solid mechanics (MS, PhD). *Faculty:* 23 full-time (1 woman). *Students:* 24 full-time (6 women), 15 international. Average age 26. 33 applicants, 3% accepted, 1 enrolled. In 2011, 3 master's, 3 doctorates awarded. *Degree requirements:* For master's, thesis (MS); for doctorate, one foreign language, comprehensive exam, thesis/dissertation, teaching experience. *Entrance requirements:* For master's and doctorate, GRE General Test, 3 letters of recommendation. Additional exam requirements/recommendations for international students: Required—TOEFL (minimum score 600 paper-based; 237 computer-based; 77 iBT). *Application deadline:* For fall admission, 1/15 for domestic students. Application fee: $95. Electronic applications accepted. *Financial support:* In 2011–12, 5 fellowships with full tuition reimbursements, 6 research assistantships with full tuition reimbursements, 13 teaching assistantships with full tuition reimbursements were awarded; institutionally sponsored loans, scholarships/grants, health care benefits, and unspecified assistantships also available. *Faculty research:* Biomathematics, bio-fluids, animal locomotion; non-linear dynamics, celestial mechanics, control; mechanics of materials, computational mechanics; experimental mechanics; non-linear elasticity, granular materials, phase transitions. *Unit head:* Director of Graduate Studies, 607-255-5062, Fax: 607-255-2011. *Application contact:* Graduate Field Assistant, 607-255-5062, Fax: 607-255-2011, E-mail: tam_grad@cornell.edu. Web site: http://www.gradschool.cornell.edu/fields.php?id-37&a-2.

Drexel University, College of Engineering, Department of Mechanical Engineering and Mechanics, Philadelphia, PA 19104-2875. Offers mechanical engineering (MS, PhD). Part-time and evening/weekend programs available. Terminal master's awarded for partial completion of doctoral program. *Degree requirements:* For master's, thesis optional; for doctorate, thesis/dissertation. *Entrance requirements:* For master's, minimum GPA of 3.0, BS in engineering or science; for doctorate, minimum GPA of 3.5, MS in engineering or science. Additional exam requirements/recommendations for international students: Required—TOEFL. Electronic applications accepted. *Faculty research:* Composites, dynamic systems and control, combustion and fuels, biomechanics, mechanics and thermal fluid sciences.

École Polytechnique de Montréal, Graduate Programs, Department of Mechanical Engineering, Montréal, QC H3C 3A7, Canada. Offers aerothermics (M Eng, M Sc A, PhD); applied mechanics (M Eng, M Sc A, PhD); tool design (M Eng, M Sc A, PhD). Part-time and evening/weekend programs available. *Degree requirements:* For master's, one foreign language, thesis; for doctorate, one foreign language, thesis/dissertation. *Entrance requirements:* For master's, minimum GPA of 2.75; for doctorate, minimum GPA of 3.0. *Faculty research:* Noise control and vibration, fatigue and creep, aerodynamics, composite materials, biomechanics, robotics.

Georgia Institute of Technology, Graduate Studies and Research, College of Engineering, School of Civil and Environmental Engineering, Program in Engineering Science and Mechanics, Atlanta, GA 30332-0001. Offers MS, MSESM, PhD. Part-time programs available. Terminal master's awarded for partial completion of doctoral program. *Degree requirements:* For doctorate, thesis/dissertation. *Entrance requirements:* For master's, GRE; for doctorate, GRE, minimum GPA of 3.2. Additional exam requirements/recommendations for international students: Required—TOEFL. *Faculty research:* Bioengineering, structural mechanics, solid mechanics, dynamics.

Iowa State University of Science and Technology, Program in Engineering Mechanics, Ames, IA 50011-2271. Offers M Eng, MS, PhD. *Entrance requirements:* For master's and doctorate, GRE. Additional exam requirements/recommendations for international students: Required—TOEFL (minimum score 550 paper-based; 80 iBT), IELTS (minimum score 6.5). *Application deadline:* For fall admission, 1/1 for domestic students; for spring admission, 9/1 for domestic students. Electronic applications accepted. *Unit head:* Zhi Wang, Director of Graduate Education, 515-294-9669, Fax: 515-294-3262, E-mail: aere-info@iastate.edu. *Application contact:* Gayle Fay, Application Contact, 515-294-9669, Fax: 515-294-3262, E-mail: aere-info@iastate.edu. Web site: http://www.aere.iastate.edu.

The Johns Hopkins University, Whiting School of Engineering, Program in Engineering Management, Baltimore, MD 21218-2699. Offers biomaterials (MSEM); communications science (MSEM); computer science (MSEM); fluid mechanics (MSEM); materials science and engineering (MSEM); mechanical engineering (MSEM); mechanics and materials (MSEM); nano-biotechnology (MSEM); nanomaterials and nanotechnology (MSEM); probability and statistics (MSEM); smart product and device design (MSEM); systems analysis, management and environmental policy (MSEM). *Entrance requirements:* For master's, GRE, 3 letters of recommendation, resume. Additional exam requirements/recommendations for international students: Required—TOEFL (minimum score 600 paper-based; 250 computer-based; 100 iBT) or IELTS (minimum score 7). Electronic applications accepted.

Lehigh University, P.C. Rossin College of Engineering and Applied Science, Department of Mechanical Engineering and Mechanics, Bethlehem, PA 18015. Offers computational engineering and mechanics (MS, PhD); mechanical engineering (M Eng, MS, PhD, MBA/E); polymer science/engineering (M Eng, MS, PhD, MBA/E); MBA/E. Part-time and evening/weekend programs available. Postbaccalaureate distance learning degree programs offered. *Faculty:* 24 full-time (0 women). *Students:* 113 full-time (12 women), 30 part-time (3 women); includes 6 minority (3 Black or African American, non-Hispanic/Latino; 2 Asian, non-Hispanic/Latino; 1 Hispanic/Latino), 79 international. Average age 26. 298 applicants, 50% accepted, 37 enrolled. In 2011, 35 master's, 6 doctorates awarded. Terminal master's awarded for partial completion of doctoral program. *Degree requirements:* For master's, thesis; for doctorate, thesis/dissertation, general exam. *Entrance requirements:* Additional exam requirements/recommendations for international students: Required—TOEFL (minimum score 550 paper-based; 213 computer-based; 79 iBT). *Application deadline:* For fall admission, 7/15 for domestic and international students; for spring admission, 12/1 for domestic and international students. Applications are processed on a rolling basis. Application fee: $75. Electronic applications accepted. *Financial support:* In 2011–12, 47 students received support, including 5 fellowships with full and partial tuition reimbursements available (averaging $24,480 per year), 24 research assistantships with full and partial tuition reimbursements available (averaging $20,700 per year), 12 teaching assistantships with full and partial tuition reimbursements available (averaging $25,092 per year); unspecified assistantships and dean's doctoral assistantships also available. Financial award application deadline: 1/15. *Faculty research:* Thermofluids, dynamic systems, CAD/CAM, computational mechanics, solid mechanics. *Total annual research expenditures:* $3.5 million. *Unit head:* Dr. D. Gary Harlow, Chairman, 610-758-4102, Fax: 610-758-6224, E-mail: dgh0@lehigh.edu. *Application contact:* Jo Ann M. Casciano, Graduate Coordinator, 610-758-4107, Fax: 610-758-6224, E-mail: jmc4@lehigh.edu. Web site: http://www.lehigh.edu/~inmem/.

Louisiana State University and Agricultural and Mechanical College, Graduate School, College of Engineering, Department of Civil and Environmental Engineering, Baton Rouge, LA 70803. Offers environmental engineering (MSCE, PhD); geotechnical engineering (MSCE, PhD); structural engineering and mechanics (MSCE, PhD); transportation engineering (MSCE, PhD); water resources (MSCE, PhD). Part-time programs available. *Faculty:* 25 full-time (2 women). *Students:* 90 full-time (23 women), 34 part-time (8 women); includes 11 minority (4 Black or African American, non-Hispanic/Latino; 1 American Indian or Alaska Native, non-Hispanic/Latino; 4 Asian, non-Hispanic/Latino; 2 Hispanic/Latino), 73 international. Average age 30. 106 applicants, 67% accepted, 25 enrolled. In 2011, 32 master's, 4 doctorates awarded. *Degree requirements:* For master's, thesis optional; for doctorate, one foreign language, thesis/dissertation. *Entrance requirements:* For master's and doctorate, GRE General Test, minimum GPA of 3.0. Additional exam requirements/recommendations for international students: Required—TOEFL (minimum score 550 paper-based; 213 computer-based; 79 iBT) or IELTS (minimum score 6.5). *Application deadline:* For fall admission, 1/25 priority date for domestic students, 5/15 for international students; for spring admission, 10/15 for international students. Applications are processed on a rolling basis. Application fee: $50 ($70 for international students). Electronic applications accepted. *Financial support:* In 2011–12, 91 students received support, including 3 fellowships with full and partial tuition reimbursements available (averaging $18,050 per year), 72 research assistantships with full and partial tuition reimbursements available (averaging $15,942 per year), 6 teaching assistantships with full and partial tuition reimbursements available (averaging $12,469 per year); career-related internships or fieldwork, institutionally sponsored loans, scholarships/grants, and health care benefits also available. Financial award application deadline: 3/1; financial award applicants required to submit FAFSA. *Faculty research:* Mechanics and structures, environmental, geotechnical transportation, water resources. *Total annual research expenditures:* $3 million. *Unit head:* Dr. George Z. Voyiadjis, Chair/Professor, 225-578-8668, Fax: 225-578-9176, E-mail: voyaidjis@lsu.edu. *Application contact:* Dr. Clinton Willson, Professor, 225-578-8672, E-mail: cwillson@lsu.edu. Web site: http://www.cee.lsu.edu/.

Massachusetts Institute of Technology, School of Engineering, Department of Civil and Environmental Engineering, Cambridge, MA 02139. Offers biological oceanography (PhD, Sc D); chemical oceanography (PhD, Sc D); civil and environmental engineering (PhD, Sc D); civil and environmental systems (PhD, Sc D); civil engineering (PhD, Sc D, CE); coastal engineering (PhD, Sc D); construction engineering and management (PhD, Sc D); environmental and water quality engineering (M Eng); environmental biology (PhD, Sc D); environmental chemistry (PhD, Sc D); environmental engineering (PhD, Sc D); environmental fluid mechanics (PhD, Sc D); environmental science and engineering (SM); geotechnical and geoenvironmental engineering (PhD, Sc D); geotechnology (M Eng); high-performance structures (M Eng); hydrology (PhD, Sc D); information technology (PhD, Sc D); mechanics (SM); oceanographic engineering (PhD, Sc D); structures and materials (PhD, Sc D); transportation (M Eng, PhD, Sc D); SM/MBA. *Faculty:* 35 full-time (6 women), 1 part-time/adjunct (0 women). *Students:* 216 full-time (80 women); includes 30 minority (4 Black or African American, non-Hispanic/Latino; 13 Asian, non-Hispanic/Latino; 8 Hispanic/Latino; 5 Two or more races, non-Hispanic/Latino), 110 international. Average age 27. 589 applicants, 26% accepted, 91 enrolled. In 2011, 62 master's, 14 doctorates awarded. *Degree requirements:* For master's and CE, thesis; for doctorate, comprehensive exam, thesis/dissertation. *Entrance requirements:* For master's and doctorate, GRE General Test. Additional exam requirements/recommendations for international students: Required—TOEFL (minimum score 577 paper-based; 233 computer-based; 90 iBT), IELTS (minimum score 7). *Application deadline:* For fall admission, 12/15 for domestic and international students. Application fee: $75. Electronic applications accepted. *Expenses: Tuition:* Full-time $40,460; part-time $630 per credit hour. *Required fees:* $272. *Financial support:* In 2011–12, 180 students received support, including 51 fellowships (averaging $30,800 per year), 110 research assistantships (averaging $29,500 per year), 19 teaching assistantships (averaging $29,500 per year); career-related internships or fieldwork, Federal Work-Study, institutionally sponsored loans, scholarships/grants, health care benefits, and unspecified assistantships also available. *Faculty research:* Environmental chemistry, environmental fluid mechanics and coastal engineering, environmental microbiology, geotechnical engineering and geomechanics, hydrology and hydroclimatology, infrastructure systems, mechanics of materials and structures, transportation systems. *Total annual research expenditures:* $17.7 million. *Unit head:* Prof. Andrew Whittle, Head, 617-253-7101. *Application contact:* Patricia Glidden, Graduate Admissions Coordinator, 617-253-7119, Fax: 617-258-6775, E-mail: cee-admissions@mit.edu. Web site: http://cee.mit.edu/.

McGill University, Faculty of Graduate and Postdoctoral Studies, Faculty of Engineering, Department of Civil Engineering and Applied Mechanics, Montréal, QC H3A 2T5, Canada. Offers environmental engineering (M Eng, M Sc, PhD); fluid mechanics (M Sc); fluid mechanics and hydraulic engineering (M Eng, PhD); materials engineering (M Eng, PhD); rehabilitation of urban infrastructure (M Eng, PhD); soil behavior (M Eng, PhD); soil mechanics and foundations (M Eng, PhD); structures and structural mechanics (M Eng, PhD); water resources (M Sc); water resources engineering (M Eng, PhD).

Michigan State University, The Graduate School, College of Engineering, Department of Mechanical Engineering, East Lansing, MI 48824. Offers engineering mechanics (MS, PhD); mechanical engineering (MS, PhD). *Entrance requirements:* For master's, GRE General Test. Additional exam requirements/recommendations for international students: Required—TOEFL. Electronic applications accepted.

Michigan Technological University, Graduate School, College of Engineering, Department of Mechanical Engineering-Engineering Mechanics, Houghton, MI 49931. Offers engineering mechanics (MS); hybrid electric drive vehicle engineering (Graduate Certificate); mechanical engineering (MS, PhD). Part-time programs available. Postbaccalaureate distance learning degree programs offered (minimal on-campus study). *Faculty:* 55 full-time (6 women), 21 part-time/adjunct (1 woman). *Students:* 246 full-time (18 women), 57 part-time (9 women); includes 10 minority (2 Black or African American, non-Hispanic/Latino; 2 Asian, non-Hispanic/Latino; 6 Hispanic/Latino), 203 international. Average age 26. 567 applicants, 64% accepted, 109 enrolled. In 2011, 78 master's, 12 doctorates, 1 other advanced degree awarded. Terminal master's awarded for partial completion of doctoral program. *Degree requirements:* For master's, comprehensive exam (for some programs), thesis (for some programs); for doctorate, comprehensive exam, thesis/dissertation. *Entrance requirements:* For master's, GRE, statement of purpose, official transcripts, 3 letters of recommendation; for doctorate, GRE, MS (preferred), statement of purpose, official transcripts, 3 letters of recommendation. Additional exam requirements/recommendations for international students: Required—TOEFL (minimum score 79 iBT) or IELTS. *Application deadline:* Applications are processed on a rolling basis. Electronic applications accepted. *Expenses:* Contact institution. *Financial support:* In 2011–12, 202 students received support, including 4 fellowships with full tuition reimbursements available (averaging $6,065 per year), 55 research assistantships with full tuition reimbursements available (averaging $6,065 per year), 24 teaching assistantships with full tuition reimbursements available (averaging $6,065 per year); career-related internships or fieldwork, Federal Work-Study, scholarships/grants, health care benefits, tuition waivers (partial), unspecified assistantships, and cooperative program also available. Financial award applicants required to submit FAFSA. *Faculty research:* Design and dynamic systems, energy-thermofluids, manufacturing, solid mechanics, sustainability. *Total annual research expenditures:* $4.3 million. *Unit head:* Dr. William W. Predebon, Chair, 906-487-2551, Fax: 906-487-2822, E-mail: wwpredeb@mtu.edu. *Application contact:* JoAnne Stimac, Senior Staff Assistant, 906-487-2327, Fax: 906-487-2463, E-mail: jstimac@mtu.edu. Web site: http://www.mtu.edu/mechanical/.

Missouri University of Science and Technology, Graduate School, Department of Civil, Architectural, and Environmental Engineering, Rolla, MO 65409. Offers civil engineering (MS, DE, PhD); construction engineering (MS, DE, PhD); environmental engineering (MS); fluid mechanics (MS, DE, PhD); geotechnical engineering (MS, DE, PhD); hydrology and hydraulic engineering (MS, DE, PhD). Part-time and evening/weekend programs available. Terminal master's awarded for partial completion of doctoral program. *Degree requirements:* For master's, thesis optional; for doctorate, comprehensive exam, thesis/dissertation. *Entrance requirements:* For master's, GRE General Test (minimum combined score 1100), minimum GPA of 3.0; for doctorate, GRE General Test (minimum score: verbal and quantitative 400, writing 3.5), minimum GPA of 3.0. Additional exam requirements/recommendations for international students: Required—TOEFL. Electronic applications accepted. *Faculty research:* Earthquake engineering, structural optimization and control systems, structural health monitoring/damage detection, soil-structure interaction, soil mechanics and foundation engineering.

Montana State University, College of Graduate Studies, College of Engineering, Department of Civil Engineering, Bozeman, MT 59717. Offers civil engineering (MS); construction engineering management (MCEM); engineering (PhD), including applied mechanics option, civil engineering option. Part-time programs available. *Degree requirements:* For master's, comprehensive exam, thesis (for some programs); for doctorate, comprehensive exam, thesis/dissertation. *Entrance requirements:* For master's and doctorate, GRE General Test. Additional exam requirements/recommendations for international students: Required—TOEFL (minimum score 550 paper-based; 213 computer-based). Electronic applications accepted. *Faculty research:* Snow and ice mechanics, biofilm engineering, transportation, structural and geo materials, water resources.

New Mexico Institute of Mining and Technology, Graduate Studies, Program in Engineering Science in Mechanics, Socorro, NM 87801. Offers explosives engineering (MS); fluid and thermal sciences (MS); mechatronics systems engineering (MS); solid mechanics (MS). *Faculty:* 5 full-time (0 women). *Students:* 26 full-time (1 woman), 19 part-time (1 woman); includes 13 minority (1 American Indian or Alaska Native, non-Hispanic/Latino; 1 Asian, non-Hispanic/Latino; 11 Hispanic/Latino). Average age 27. 21 applicants, 67% accepted, 11 enrolled. In 2011, 6 master's awarded. *Degree requirements:* For master's, thesis (for some programs). *Entrance requirements:* For master's, GRE General Test. Additional exam requirements/recommendations for international students: Required—TOEFL (minimum score 540 paper-based; 207 computer-based). *Application deadline:* For fall admission, 3/1 priority date for domestic students; for spring admission, 6/1 for domestic students. Applications are processed on a rolling basis. Application fee: $16 ($30 for international students). *Expenses:* Tuition, state resident: full-time $4849; part-time $269.41 per credit hour. Tuition, nonresident: full-time $16,041; part-time $891.15 per credit hour. *Required fees:* $622; $65 per credit hour. $20 per semester. Part-time tuition and fees vary according to course load. *Financial support:* In 2011–12, 9 research assistantships (averaging $18,997 per year), 5 teaching assistantships with full and partial tuition reimbursements (averaging $14,615 per year) were awarded; fellowships, Federal Work-Study, institutionally sponsored loans, and unspecified assistantships also available. Financial award application deadline: 3/1; financial award applicants required to submit CSS PROFILE or FAFSA. *Faculty research:* Vibrations, fluid-structure interactions. *Unit head:* Dr. Warren Ostergren, Chair, 575-835-5693, E-mail: warreno@nmt.edu. *Application contact:* Dr. Lorie Liebrock, Dean of Graduate Studies, 575-835-5513, Fax: 575-835-5476, E-mail: graduate@nmt.edu. Web site: http://infohost.nmt.edu/~mecheng/grad_programs.xml.

North Dakota State University, College of Graduate and Interdisciplinary Studies, College of Engineering and Architecture, Department of Mechanical Engineering and Applied Mechanics, Fargo, ND 58108. Offers MS, PhD. Part-time programs available. *Faculty:* 16 full-time (3 women). *Students:* 30 full-time (7 women), 19 part-time (1 woman); includes 2 minority (both Asian, non-Hispanic/Latino), 27 international. Average age 28. 36 applicants, 56% accepted, 4 enrolled. In 2011, 7 master's, 1 doctorate awarded. *Degree requirements:* For master's, thesis; for doctorate, comprehensive exam, thesis/dissertation. *Entrance requirements:* For master's and doctorate, minimum GPA of 3.0. Additional exam requirements/recommendations for international students: Required—TOEFL (minimum score 550 paper-based). *Application deadline:* For fall admission, 2/15 priority date for domestic students; for spring admission, 9/15 priority date for domestic students. Applications are processed on a rolling basis. Application fee: $35. Electronic applications accepted. *Financial support:* In 2011–12, 20 students received support, including research assistantships with full tuition reimbursements available (averaging $9,000 per year), teaching assistantships with full tuition reimbursements available (averaging $9,000 per year); career-related internships or fieldwork, Federal Work-Study, and institutionally sponsored loans also available. Financial award application deadline: 2/15. *Faculty research:* Thermodynamics, finite element analysis, automotive systems, robotics, nanotechnology. *Unit head:* Dr. Alan Kallmeyer, Chair, 701-231-8836, Fax: 701-231-8913, E-mail: alan.kallmeyer@ndsu.edu. *Application contact:* Dr. Ghodrat Karami, Graduate Coordinator, 701-231-8671, Fax: 701-231-8913, E-mail: g.karami@ndsu.edu. Web site: http://www.ndsu.nodak.edu/me/.

Northwestern University, McCormick School of Engineering and Applied Science, Department of Civil and Environmental Engineering, Program in Theoretical and Applied Mechanics, Evanston, IL 60208. Offers fluid mechanics (MS, PhD); solid mechanics (MS, PhD). Admissions and degrees offered through The Graduate School. Terminal master's awarded for partial completion of doctoral program. *Degree requirements:* For master's, thesis; for doctorate, thesis/dissertation. *Entrance requirements:* For master's, GRE General Test, minimum 2 letters of recommendation; for doctorate, GRE General Test, minimum 2 letters of recommendation, transcripts from all academic institutions attended. Additional exam requirements/recommendations for international students: Required—TOEFL (minimum score 600 paper-based; 250 computer-based; 100 iBT), IELTS (minimum score 7), TOEFL (Iternet-based) speaking score of 26. Electronic applications accepted. *Faculty research:* Composite materials, computational mechanics, fracture and damage mechanics, geophysics, nondestructive evaluation.

Ohio University, Graduate College, Russ College of Engineering and Technology, Department of Civil Engineering, Athens, OH 45701-2979. Offers civil engineering (PhD); construction (MS); environmental (MS); geotechnical and geoenvironmental (MS); mechanics (MS); structures (MS); transportation (MS); water resources and structures (MS). Part-time programs available. *Students:* 32 full-time (6 women), 7 part-time (2 women); includes 3 minority (1 Hispanic/Latino; 2 Two or more races, non-Hispanic/Latino), 13 international. 52 applicants, 52% accepted, 4 enrolled. In 2011, 10 degrees awarded. *Degree requirements:* For master's, comprehensive exam (for some programs), thesis or alternative; for doctorate, comprehensive exam, thesis/dissertation. *Entrance requirements:* For master's, GRE General Test, minimum GPA of 3.0, 3 letters of recommendation; for doctorate, GRE General Test. Additional exam requirements/recommendations for international students: Required—TOEFL (minimum score 550 paper-based; 80 iBT) or IELTS (minimum score 6.5). *Application deadline:* For fall admission, 5/1 priority date for domestic students, 2/1 for international students; for winter admission, 8/1 priority date for domestic students, 4/1 for international students; for spring admission, 2/1 priority date for domestic students, 7/1 for international students. Applications are processed on a rolling basis. Application fee: $50 ($55 for international students). Electronic applications accepted. *Financial support:* Research assistantships with full tuition reimbursements, teaching assistantships with full tuition reimbursements, Federal Work-Study, institutionally sponsored loans, scholarships/grants, and unspecified assistantships available. Financial award application deadline: 3/15; financial award applicants required to submit FAFSA. *Faculty research:* Noise abatement, materials and environment, highway infrastructure, subsurface investigation (pavements, pipes, bridges). *Unit head:* Dr. Gayle F. Mitchell, Chair, 740-593-0430, Fax: 740-593-0625, E-mail: mitchelg@ohio.edu. *Application contact:* Dr. Shad M. Sargand, Graduate Chair, 740-593-1465, Fax: 740-593-0625, E-mail: sargand@ohio.edu. Web site: http://www.ohio.edu/civil/.

Penn State University Park, Graduate School, College of Engineering, Department of Engineering Science and Mechanics, State College, University Park, PA 16802-1503. Offers engineering mechanics (M Eng, MS); engineering science (M Eng, MS); engineering science and mechanics (PhD). *Unit head:* Dr. David N. Wormley, Dean, 814-865-7537, Fax: 814-865-8767, E-mail: dnw2@engr.psu.edu. *Application contact:* Cynthia E. Nicosia, Director, Graduate Enrollment Services, 814-865-1834, E-mail: cey1@psu.edu. Web site: http://www.esm.psu.edu.

Rutgers, The State University of New Jersey, New Brunswick, Graduate School-New Brunswick, Program in Mechanics, Piscataway, NJ 08854-8097. Offers MS, PhD. Part-time programs available. Terminal master's awarded for partial completion of doctoral program. *Degree requirements:* For master's, thesis optional, qualifying exam; for doctorate, thesis/dissertation, qualifying exam. *Entrance requirements:* For master's and doctorate, GRE General Test, GRE Subject Test (recommended). Additional exam requirements/recommendations for international students: Required—TOEFL. Electronic applications accepted. *Faculty research:* Continuum mechanics, constitutive theory, thermodynamics, visolasticity, liquid crystal theory.

San Diego State University, Graduate and Research Affairs, College of Engineering, Department of Aerospace Engineering and Engineering Mechanics, San Diego, CA 92182. Offers aerospace engineering (MS); engineering mechanics (MS); engineering sciences and applied mechanics (PhD); flight dynamics (MS); fluid dynamics (MS). PhD offered jointly with University of California, San Diego and Department of Mechanical Engineering. Terminal master's awarded for partial completion of doctoral program. *Degree requirements:* For master's, comprehensive exam (for some programs), thesis (for some programs); for doctorate, thesis/dissertation. *Entrance requirements:* For master's, GRE General Test; for doctorate, GRE, 3 letters of recommendation. Additional exam requirements/recommendations for international students: Required—TOEFL. Electronic applications accepted. *Faculty research:* Organized structures in post-stall flow over wings/three dimensional separated flow, airfoil growth effect, probabilities, structural mechanics.

Southern Illinois University Carbondale, Graduate School, College of Engineering, Department of Civil and Environmental Engineering, Carbondale, IL 62901-4701. Offers civil engineering (MS). *Faculty:* 10 full-time (1 woman). *Students:* 19 full-time (4 women), 21 part-time (2 women); includes 1 minority (Black or African American, non-Hispanic/Latino), 22 international. Average age 26. 38 applicants, 37% accepted, 9 enrolled. In 2011, 7 master's awarded. *Degree requirements:* For master's, comprehensive exam, thesis. *Entrance requirements:* For master's, minimum GPA of 2.7. Additional exam requirements/recommendations for international students: Required—TOEFL. *Application deadline:* Applications are processed on a rolling basis. Application fee: $20. *Financial support:* In 2011–12, 21 students received support, including 5 research assistantships with full tuition reimbursements available, 9 teaching assistantships with full tuition reimbursements available; fellowships with full tuition reimbursements available, Federal Work-Study, institutionally sponsored loans, and tuition waivers (full) also available. Support available to part-time students. Financial award application deadline: 7/1. *Faculty research:* Composite materials, wastewater treatment, solid waste disposal, slurry transport, geotechnical engineering. *Total annual research expenditures:* $230,856. *Unit head:* Dr. Lizette Chevalier, Interim Chair, 618-453-7815, E-mail: cheval@engr.siu.edu. *Application contact:* Steve Rogers, Administrative Clerk, 618-536-2368, E-mail: nihil@siu.edu. Web site: http://civil.engr.siu.edu/civil/.

Southern Illinois University Carbondale, Graduate School, College of Engineering, Program in Engineering Science, Carbondale, IL 62901-4701. Offers electrical systems (PhD); fossil energy (PhD); mechanics (PhD). *Faculty:* 55 full-time (3 women), 3 part-time/adjunct (0 women). *Students:* 12 full-time (1 woman), 34 part-time (7 women); includes 5 minority (2 Black or African American, non-Hispanic/Latino; 3 Asian, non-Hispanic/Latino), 28 international. 22 applicants, 55% accepted, 7 enrolled. In 2011, 3 doctorates awarded. *Degree requirements:* For doctorate, thesis/dissertation. *Entrance requirements:* For doctorate, GRE General Test, minimum GPA of 3.5. Additional exam requirements/recommendations for international students: Required—TOEFL. Application fee: $20. *Financial support:* In 2011–12, 13 students received support. Fellowships with full tuition reimbursements available, research assistantships with full tuition reimbursements available, teaching assistantships with full tuition reimbursements available, Federal Work-Study, institutionally sponsored loans, and tuition waivers (full) available. Support available to part-time students. *Unit head:* Dr. Josh Nicklow, Associate Dean, 618-453-7746, Fax: 618-453-4235. *Application contact:* Anna Maria Alms, Student Contact, 618-453-4321, Fax: 618-453-4235, E-mail: amalms@siu.edu.

The University of Alabama, Graduate School, College of Engineering, Department of Aerospace Engineering and Mechanics, Tuscaloosa, AL 35487. Offers aerospace engineering (MAE); engineering science and mechanics (MES, PhD). Part-time programs available. Postbaccalaureate distance learning degree programs offered (no on-campus study). *Faculty:* 14 full-time (1 woman). *Students:* 22 full-time (4 women), 33 part-time (7 women); includes 3 minority (all Hispanic/Latino), 13 international. Average age 29. 41 applicants, 73% accepted, 15 enrolled. In 2011, 14 degrees awarded. Terminal master's awarded for partial completion of doctoral program. *Degree requirements:* For master's, comprehensive exam (for some programs), thesis (for some programs); for doctorate, comprehensive exam, thesis/dissertation, 1-year residency. *Entrance requirements:* For master's and doctorate, GRE, minimum undergraduate GPA of 3.0. Additional exam requirements/recommendations for international students: Required—TOEFL (minimum score 550 paper-based). *Application deadline:* For fall admission, 7/1 priority date for domestic students, 1/15 for international students; for spring admission, 11/1 priority date for domestic students, 6/1 for international students. Applications are processed on a rolling basis. Application fee: $50 ($60 for international students). Electronic applications accepted. *Expenses:* Tuition, state resident: full-time $8600. Tuition, nonresident: full-time $21,900. *Financial support:* In 2011–12, 18 students received support, including fellowships with full tuition reimbursements available (averaging $20,000 per year), research assistantships with full tuition reimbursements available (averaging $18,375 per year), teaching assistantships with full tuition reimbursements available (averaging $18,375 per year); Federal Work-Study, institutionally sponsored loans, scholarships/grants, health care benefits, and unspecified assistantships also available. Financial award application deadline: 2/15. *Faculty research:* Intelligent computer systems, genetic algorithms, neural networks, impact and penetration mechanics, spacecraft dynamics and controls. *Total annual research expenditures:* $1.5 million. *Unit head:* Dr. Stanley E. Jones, Interim Head/ Professor, 205-348-7242, Fax: 205-348-7240, E-mail: sejones@eng.ua.edu. *Application contact:* Dr. John E. Jackson, Professor, 205-348-7306, Fax: 208-348-7240, E-mail: johnjackson@eng.ua.edu. Web site: http://aem.eng.ua.edu/.

The University of Arizona, College of Engineering, Department of Civil Engineering and Engineering Mechanics, Tucson, AZ 85721. Offers civil engineering (MS, PhD); engineering mechanics (MS, PhD). Part-time programs available. *Faculty:* 10 full-time (1 woman). *Students:* 53 full-time (12 women), 17 part-time (0 women); includes 13 minority (2 Black or African American, non-Hispanic/Latino; 1 Asian, non-Hispanic/ Latino; 4 Hispanic/Latino; 6 Two or more races, non-Hispanic/Latino), 31 international. Average age 29. 74 applicants, 46% accepted, 7 enrolled. In 2011, 9 master's, 4 doctorates awarded. *Degree requirements:* For master's, thesis; for doctorate, thesis/ dissertation, departmental qualifying exam. *Entrance requirements:* For master's, GRE General Test, 3 letters of recommendation, statement of purpose; for doctorate, GRE General Test, minimum GPA of 3.5, 3 letters of recommendation, statement of purpose. Additional exam requirements/recommendations for international students: Required—TOEFL (minimum score 550 paper-based; 213 computer-based; 79 iBT). *Application deadline:* For fall admission, 6/1 for domestic students, 12/1 for international students; for spring admission, 10/1 for domestic students, 6/1 for international students. Applications are processed on a rolling basis. Application fee: $75. Electronic applications accepted. *Expenses:* Tuition, state resident: full-time $10,840. Tuition, nonresident: full-time $25,802. *Financial support:* In 2011–12, 26 research assistantships with full tuition reimbursements (averaging $23,586 per year), 11 teaching assistantships with full tuition reimbursements (averaging $23,586 per year) were awarded; institutionally sponsored loans, scholarships/grants, health care benefits, tuition waivers (partial), and unspecified assistantships also available. Financial award application deadline: 4/1. *Faculty research:* Constitutive modeling, rehabilitation of structures, groundwater, earthquake engineering, hazardous waste treatment. *Total annual research expenditures:* $1.1 million. *Unit head:* Kevin E. Lansey, Department Head, 520-621-6564, E-mail: lansey@engr.arizona.edu. *Application contact:* Graduate Coordinator, 520-621-2266, Fax: 520-621-2550, E-mail: ceemg@engr.arizona.edu. Web site: http://civil.arizona.edu/cms/.

University of California, Berkeley, Graduate Division, College of Engineering, Department of Civil and Environmental Engineering, Berkeley, CA 94720-1500. Offers engineering and project management (M Eng, MS, D Eng, PhD); environmental engineering (M Eng, MS, D Eng, PhD); geoengineering (M Eng, MS, D Eng, PhD); structural engineering, mechanics and materials (M Eng, MS, D Eng, PhD); transportation engineering (M Eng, MS, D Eng, PhD); M Arch/MS; MCP/MS; MPP/MS. *Degree requirements:* For master's, comprehensive exam or thesis (MS); for doctorate, thesis/dissertation, qualifying exam. *Entrance requirements:* For master's, GRE General Test, minimum GPA of 3.0, 3 letters of recommendation; for doctorate, GRE General Test, minimum GPA of 3.5, 3 letters of recommendation. Additional exam requirements/ recommendations for international students: Required—TOEFL (minimum score 570 paper-based; 230 computer-based). Electronic applications accepted.

University of California, Merced, Division of Graduate Studies, School of Natural Sciences, Merced, CA 95343. Offers applied mathematics (MS, PhD); biological engineering and small-scale technologies (MS, PhD); environmental systems (MS, PhD); mechanical engineering and applied mechanics (MS, PhD); physics and chemistry (PhD); quantitative and systems biology (MS, PhD). *Unit head:* Dr. Samuel J. Traina, Dean, 209-228-4723, Fax: 209-228-6906, E-mail: grad.dean@ucmerced.edu. *Application contact:* Tsu Ya, Graduate Admissions and Academic Services Manager, 209-228-4723, Fax: 209-228-6906, E-mail: tya@ucmerced.edu.

University of California, San Diego, Office of Graduate Studies, Department of Mechanical and Aerospace Engineering, Program in Applied Mechanics, La Jolla, CA 92093. Offers MS, PhD. PhD offered jointly with San Diego State University. Part-time programs available. *Degree requirements:* For master's, comprehensive exam or thesis; for doctorate, thesis/dissertation, qualifying exam. *Entrance requirements:* For master's and doctorate, GRE General Test, minimum GPA of 3.0. Additional exam requirements/ recommendations for international students: Required—TOEFL. Electronic applications accepted. *Faculty research:* Combustion engineering, environmental mechanics, magnetic recording, materials processing, computational fluid dynamics.

University of Cincinnati, Graduate School, College of Engineering and Applied Science, Department of Aerospace Engineering and Engineering Mechanics, Cincinnati, OH 45221. Offers MS, PhD. Part-time programs available. Terminal master's awarded for partial completion of doctoral program. *Degree requirements:* For master's, project or thesis; for doctorate, thesis/dissertation. *Entrance requirements:* For master's and doctorate, GRE General Test. Additional exam requirements/recommendations for international students: Required—TOEFL (minimum score 550 paper-based; 213 computer-based). Electronic applications accepted. *Faculty research:* Computational fluid mechanics/propulsion, large space structures, dynamics and guidance of VTOL vehicles.

University of Colorado Denver, College of Engineering and Applied Science, Department of Mechanical Engineering, Denver, CO 80217. Offers mechanical engineering (MS); mechanics (MS); thermal sciences (MS). Part-time and evening/ weekend programs available. *Faculty:* 8 full-time (0 women), 2 part-time/adjunct (both women). *Students:* 25 full-time (4 women), 19 part-time (3 women); includes 9 minority (3 Black or African American, non-Hispanic/Latino; 4 Asian, non-Hispanic/Latino; 2 Hispanic/Latino), 10 international. Average age 30. 25 applicants, 68% accepted, 5 enrolled. In 2011, 12 master's awarded. *Degree requirements:* For master's, comprehensive exam, thesis or alternative, 30 credit hours, project or thesis. *Entrance requirements:* For master's, GRE. Additional exam requirements/recommendations for international students: Required—TOEFL (minimum score 525 paper-based; 197 computer-based). *Application deadline:* For fall admission, 7/15 for domestic students; for spring admission, 11/15 for domestic students. Applications are processed on a rolling basis. Application fee: $50 ($75 for international students). Electronic applications accepted. *Expenses:* Contact institution. *Financial support:* Research assistantships, teaching assistantships, career-related internships or fieldwork, and Federal Work-Study available. Financial award application deadline: 4/1; financial award applicants required to submit FAFSA. *Faculty research:* Applied and computational mechanics, bioengineering, energy systems, tribology, micro/mesofluidics and biomechanics, vehicle dynamics. *Unit head:* Dr. Sam Welch, Chair, 303-556-8488, Fax: 303-556-6371, E-mail: sam.welch@ucdenver.edu. *Application contact:* Catherine McCoy, Program Assistant, 303-556-8516, E-mail: catherine.mccoy@ucdenver.edu. Web site: http:// www.ucdenver.edu/academics/colleges/Engineering/Programs/Mechanical-Engineering/Pages/MechanicalEngineering.aspx.

University of Dayton, Department of Civil and Environmental Engineering and Engineering Mechanics, Dayton, OH 45469-1300. Offers engineering mechanics (MSEM); environmental engineering (MSCE); geotechnical engineering (MSCE); structural engineering (MSCE); transportation engineering (MSCE); water resources engineering (MSCE). Part-time programs available. *Faculty:* 7 full-time (2 women), 2 part-time/adjunct (0 women). *Students:* 16 full-time (4 women), 9 part-time (4 women); includes 1 minority (Asian, non-Hispanic/Latino), 13 international. Average age 27. 53 applicants, 38% accepted, 5 enrolled. In 2011, 7 degrees awarded. *Degree requirements:* For master's, thesis optional. *Entrance requirements:* For master's, minimum GPA of 3.0 in undergraduate work. Additional exam requirements/ recommendations for international students: Required—TOEFL (minimum score 550 paper-based; 213 computer-based; 80 iBT). *Application deadline:* For fall admission, 8/1 for domestic students, 3/1 for international students; for winter admission, 7/1 for international students; for spring admission, 1/1 for international students. Applications are processed on a rolling basis. Application fee: $0 ($50 for international students). Electronic applications accepted. *Expenses: Tuition:* Full-time $8400; part-time $700 per credit hour. *Required fees:* $25 per semester. Tuition and fees vary according to degree level. *Financial support:* Research assistantships available. Financial award applicants required to submit FAFSA. *Faculty research:* Physical modeling of hydraulic systems, finite element methods, mechanics of composite materials, transportation systems safety, biological treatment processes. *Total annual research expenditures:* $200,000. *Unit head:* Dr. Donald V. Chase, Chair, 937-229-3847, Fax: 937-229-3491, E-mail: dchase1@udayton.edu. *Application contact:* Dr. Donald Chase, Chair, 937-229-3847, Fax: 937-229-3491, E-mail: dchase1@udayton.edu. Web site: http://www.udayton.edu/ engineering/civil.

University of Illinois at Urbana–Champaign, Graduate College, College of Engineering, Department of Mechanical Science and Engineering, Champaign, IL 61820. Offers mechanical engineering (MS, PhD); theoretical and applied mechanics (MS, PhD); MS/MBA. *Faculty:* 52 full-time (5 women), 2 part-time/adjunct (0 women). *Students:* 323 full-time (42 women), 35 part-time (5 women); includes 30 minority (16 Asian, non-Hispanic/Latino; 12 Hispanic/Latino; 2 Two or more races, non-Hispanic/ Latino), 211 international. 807 applicants, 26% accepted, 75 enrolled. In 2011, 90 master's, 31 doctorates awarded. Terminal master's awarded for partial completion of doctoral program. *Entrance requirements:* For master's, GRE General Test, minimum GPA of 3.25; for doctorate, GRE General Test, minimum GPA of 3.5. Additional exam requirements/recommendations for international students: Required—TOEFL (minimum score 613 paper-based; 257 computer-based; 103 iBT). *Application deadline:* Applications are processed on a rolling basis. Application fee: $75 ($90 for international students). Electronic applications accepted. *Financial support:* In 2011–12, 44 fellowships, 244 research assistantships, 109 teaching assistantships were awarded; tuition waivers (full and partial) also available. *Faculty research:* Combustion and propulsion, design methodology, dynamic systems and controls, energy transfer, materials behavior and processing, manufacturing systems operations, management. *Unit head:* Placid Mathew Ferreira, Head, 217-333-0639, Fax: 217-244-6534, E-mail: pferreir@illinois.edu. *Application contact:* Katrina Hagler, Graduate Admissions Coordinator, 217-244-3416, Fax: 217-244-6534, E-mail: kkappes2@illinois.edu. Web site: http://mechse.illinois.edu.

University of Maryland, College Park, Academic Affairs, A. James Clark School of Engineering, Department of Mechanical Engineering, College Park, MD 20742. Offers electronic packaging and reliability (MS, PhD); manufacturing and design (MS, PhD); mechanics and materials (MS, PhD); reliability engineering (M Eng, MS, PhD); thermal and fluid sciences (MS, PhD). Part-time and evening/weekend programs available. Postbaccalaureate distance learning degree programs offered. *Faculty:* 88 full-time (8 women), 20 part-time/adjunct. *Students:* 240 full-time (36 women), 72 part-time (6 women); includes 54 minority (14 Black or African American, non-Hispanic/Latino; 2 American Indian or Alaska Native, non-Hispanic/Latino; 23 Asian, non-Hispanic/Latino; 11 Hispanic/Latino; 4 Two or more races, non-Hispanic/Latino), 145 international. 457 applicants, 19% accepted, 61 enrolled. In 2011, 35 master's, 29 doctorates awarded. *Degree requirements:* For master's, thesis optional; for doctorate, thesis/dissertation, qualifying exam. *Entrance requirements:* For master's, GRE General Test, 3 letters of recommendation; for doctorate, GRE General Test, minimum GPA of 3.0. Additional exam requirements/recommendations for international students: Required—TOEFL. *Application deadline:* For fall admission, 5/15 for domestic students, 2/1 for international students; for spring admission, 10/15 for domestic students, 6/1 for international students. Applications are processed on a rolling basis. Application fee: $75. Electronic applications accepted. *Expenses: Tuition, area resident:* Part-time $525 per credit hour. Tuition, state resident: part-time $525 per credit hour. Tuition, nonresident: part-time $1131 per credit hour. *Required fees:* $386.31 per term. Tuition and fees vary according to program. *Financial support:* In 2011–12, 7 fellowships with full and partial tuition reimbursements (averaging $24,003 per year), 166 research assistantships (averaging $23,766 per year), 17 teaching assistantships (averaging $17,967 per year) were awarded; Federal Work-Study and scholarships/grants also available. Support available to part-time students. Financial award applicants required to submit FAFSA. *Faculty research:* Injection molding, electronic packaging, fluid mechanics, product engineering. *Total annual research expenditures:* $19 million. *Unit head:* Dr. B. Balachandran, Chair, 301-405-5309, E-mail: balab@umd.edu. *Application contact:* Dr. Charles A. Caramello, Graduate Director, 301-405-0358, Fax: 301-314-9305, E-mail: ccaramel@umd.edu.

University of Massachusetts Amherst, Graduate School, College of Engineering, Department of Civil and Environmental Engineering, Amherst, MA 01003. Offers civil engineering (MSCE, PhD); environmental and water resources (MSCE); geotechnical (MSCE); structural engineering and mechanics (MSCE); transportation (MSCE). *Accreditation:* ABET (one or more programs are accredited). Part-time programs available. *Faculty:* 28 full-time (7 women). *Students:* 91 full-time (30 women), 11 part-time (0 women); includes 13 minority (3 Black or African American, non-Hispanic/Latino; 5 Asian, non-Hispanic/Latino; 4 Hispanic/Latino; 1 Two or more races, non-Hispanic/ Latino), 29 international. Average age 27. 293 applicants, 53% accepted, 40 enrolled. In 2011, 38 master's, 1 doctorate awarded. Terminal master's awarded for partial completion of doctoral program. *Degree requirements:* For master's, thesis or alternative; for doctorate, comprehensive exam, thesis/dissertation. *Entrance requirements:* For master's and doctorate, GRE General Test. Additional exam requirements/recommendations for international students: Required—TOEFL (minimum score 550 paper-based; 213 computer-based; 80 iBT), IELTS (minimum score 6.5). *Application deadline:* For fall admission, 2/1 for domestic and international students; for spring admission, 10/1 for domestic and international students. Applications are processed on a rolling basis. Application fee: $50 ($65 for international students). Electronic applications accepted. Tuition and fees vary according to course load, campus/location and program. *Financial support:* In 2011–12, 1 fellowship with full tuition reimbursement (averaging $1,000 per year), 74 research assistantships with full tuition reimbursements (averaging $15,151 per year), 6 teaching assistantships with full tuition reimbursements (averaging $15,151 per year) were awarded; career-related internships or fieldwork, Federal Work-Study, scholarships/grants, traineeships, health care benefits, tuition waivers, and unspecified assistantships also available. Support available to part-time students. Financial award application deadline: 2/1; financial award applicants required to submit FAFSA. *Unit head:* Dr. Sanjay Arwade, Graduate Program Director, 413-545-0686, Fax: 413-545-2840. *Application contact:* Lindsay DeSantis, Interim Supervisor of Admissions, 413-545-0722, Fax: 413-577-0100, E-mail: gradadm@grad.umass.edu. Web site: http://cee.umass.edu/.

University of Massachusetts Lowell, College of Sciences, Department of Physics and Applied Physics, Program in Applied Physics, Lowell, MA 01854-2881. Offers applied mechanics (PhD); applied physics (MS, PhD), including optical sciences (MS). Terminal master's awarded for partial completion of doctoral program. *Degree requirements:* For master's, thesis; for doctorate, 2 foreign languages, thesis/dissertation. *Entrance requirements:* For master's, GRE General Test, 3 letters of reference; for doctorate, GRE General Test, transcripts, 3 letters of reference. Additional exam requirements/recommendations for international students: Required—TOEFL.

University of Minnesota, Twin Cities Campus, College of Science and Engineering, Department of Aerospace Engineering and Mechanics, Minneapolis, MN 55455-0213. Offers aerospace engineering (M Aero E); aerospace engineering and mechanics (MS, PhD). Part-time programs available. *Degree requirements:* For doctorate, thesis/dissertation. *Entrance requirements:* Additional exam requirements/recommendations for international students: Required—TOEFL (minimum score 550 paper-based; 213 computer-based). Electronic applications accepted. *Faculty research:* Fluid mechanics, solid and continuum fluid mechanics, computational mechanics, aerospace systems.

University of Nebraska–Lincoln, Graduate College, College of Engineering, Department of Engineering Mechanics, Lincoln, NE 68588. Offers MS, PhD. *Degree requirements:* For master's, thesis optional; for doctorate, comprehensive exam, thesis/dissertation. *Entrance requirements:* For master's and doctorate, GRE. Additional exam requirements/recommendations for international students: Required—TOEFL (minimum score 550 paper-based; 213 computer-based). Electronic applications accepted. *Faculty research:* Polymer mechanics, piezoelectric materials, meshless methods, smart materials, fracture mechanics.

University of New Brunswick Fredericton, School of Graduate Studies, Faculty of Engineering, Department of Mechanical Engineering, Fredericton, NB E3B 5A3, Canada. Offers applied mechanics (M Eng, M Sc E, PhD); mechanical engineering (M Eng, M Sc E, PhD). Part-time programs available. *Faculty:* 14 full-time (1 woman), 2 part-time/adjunct (0 women). *Students:* 47 full-time (4 women), 7 part-time (0 women). In 2011, 8 master's, 3 doctorates awarded. *Degree requirements:* For master's, thesis; for doctorate, comprehensive exam, thesis/dissertation, qualifying exam. *Entrance requirements:* For master's, minimum GPA of 3.0; B Sc E; for doctorate, minimum GPA of 3.0; M Sc E. Additional exam requirements/recommendations for international students: Required—TOEFL (minimum score 550 paper-based), IELTS, TWE (minimum score 4). *Application deadline:* For fall admission, 3/1 priority date for domestic students. Applications are processed on a rolling basis. Application fee: $50 Canadian dollars. *Financial support:* In 2011–12, 104 fellowships, 31 research assistantships, 54 teaching assistantships were awarded. *Faculty research:* Analysis of gross motor activities as a means of assessing upper limb prosthesis, distance determination algorithms and their applications, void nucleation in automotive aluminum alloy, robot kinematics, micromechanics, analysis of human walking, plastic injection molding, green nanotechnology, mechatronics, fatigue assessment of structures, ocean renewable energy. *Unit head:* Dr. Zengtao Chen, Director of Graduate Studies, 506-458-7784, Fax: 506-453-5025, E-mail: ztchen@unb.ca. *Application contact:* Wanda Wyman, Graduate Secretary, 506-458-7742, Fax: 506-453-5025, E-mail: wanda.wyman@unb.ca. Web site: http://www.unbf.ca/eng/me.

University of Pennsylvania, School of Engineering and Applied Science, Department of Mechanical Engineering and Applied Mechanics, Philadelphia, PA 19104. Offers applied mechanics (MSE, PhD); mechanical engineering (MSE, PhD). Part-time programs available. *Faculty:* 28 full-time (4 women), 9 part-time/adjunct (0 women). *Students:* 138 full-time (19 women), 33 part-time (5 women); includes 20 minority (8 Black or African American, non-Hispanic/Latino; 11 Asian, non-Hispanic/Latino; 1 Hispanic/Latino), 90 international. 599 applicants, 34% accepted, 94 enrolled. In 2011, 44 master's, 5 doctorates awarded. *Degree requirements:* For master's, thesis optional; for doctorate, thesis/dissertation. *Entrance requirements:* Additional exam requirements/recommendations for international students: Required—TOEFL. *Application deadline:* For fall admission, 1/2 priority date for domestic students. Applications are processed on a rolling basis. Application fee: $70. Electronic applications accepted. *Expenses: Tuition:* Full-time $26,660; part-time $4944 per course. *Required fees:* $2318; $291 per course. Tuition and fees vary according to course load, degree level and program. *Financial support:* Fellowships, research assistantships, teaching assistantships, institutionally sponsored loans, scholarships/grants, traineeships, health care benefits, and unspecified assistantships available. *Faculty research:* Heat transfer, fluid mechanics, energy conversion, solid mechanics, dynamics of mechanisms and robots. *Unit head:* Eduardo D. Glandt, Dean, 215-898-7244, Fax: 215-573-2018, E-mail: seasdean@seas.upenn.edu. *Application contact:* 215-898-4825, E-mail: meam@seas.upenn.edu. Web site: http://www.seas.upenn.edu/meam/.

University of Southern California, Graduate School, Viterbi School of Engineering, Sonny Astani Department of Civil Engineering, Los Angeles, CA 90089. Offers applied mechanics (MS); civil engineering (MS, PhD); computer-aided engineering (ME, Graduate Certificate); construction management (MCM); engineering technology commercialization (Graduate Certificate); environmental engineering (MS, PhD); environmental quality management (ME); structural design (ME); sustainable cities (Graduate Certificate); transportation systems (MS, Graduate Certificate); water and waste management (MS). Part-time and evening/weekend programs available. Terminal master's awarded for partial completion of doctoral program. *Degree requirements:* For master's, thesis optional; for doctorate, thesis/dissertation. *Entrance requirements:* For master's and doctorate, GRE General Test. Additional exam requirements/recommendations for international students: Recommended—TOEFL. Electronic applications accepted. *Faculty research:* Geotechnical engineering, transportation engineering, structural engineering, construction management, environmental engineering, water resources.

The University of Tennessee Space Institute, Graduate Programs, Program in Engineering Sciences and Mechanics, Tullahoma, TN 37388-9700. Offers engineering sciences (MS, PhD); mechanics (MS, PhD). Part-time programs available. *Faculty:* 8 full-time (1 woman), 8 part-time/adjunct (0 women). *Students:* 6 full-time (2 women), 1 part-time (0 women); includes 2 minority (1 Black or African American, non-Hispanic/Latino; 1 Asian, non-Hispanic/Latino), 1 international. 3 applicants, 100% accepted, 3 enrolled. In 2011, 3 degrees awarded. *Degree requirements:* For master's, thesis (for

some programs); for doctorate, one foreign language, thesis/dissertation. *Entrance requirements:* Additional exam requirements/recommendations for international students: Required—TOEFL (minimum score 550 paper-based; 213 computer-based), IELTS (minimum score 6.5). *Application deadline:* For fall admission, 2/1 for international students; for spring admission, 6/15 for international students. Applications are processed on a rolling basis. Application fee: $35. Electronic applications accepted. *Financial support:* In 2011–12, 2 fellowships with full and partial tuition reimbursements (averaging $1,850 per year), 3 research assistantships with full tuition reimbursements (averaging $17,791 per year) were awarded; career-related internships or fieldwork, Federal Work-Study, institutionally sponsored loans, health care benefits, tuition waivers (full and partial), and unspecified assistantships also available. Financial award applicants required to submit FAFSA. *Unit head:* Dr. Trevor Meller, Degree Program Chairman, 931-393-7351, Fax: 931-393-7437, E-mail: tmoeller@utsi.edu. *Application contact:* Dee Merriman, Coordinator III, 931-393-7213, Fax: 931-393-7211, E-mail: dmerrima@utsi.edu. Web site: http://www.utsi.edu/academics/MABE/.

The University of Texas at Austin, Graduate School, Cockrell School of Engineering, Department of Aerospace Engineering and Engineering Mechanics, Program in Engineering Mechanics, Austin, TX 78712-1111. Offers MS, PhD. *Degree requirements:* For doctorate, one foreign language, thesis/dissertation, qualifying exam. *Entrance requirements:* For master's and doctorate, GRE General Test. *Application deadline:* For fall admission, 1/15 priority date for domestic students; for spring admission, 10/1 priority date for domestic students. Applications are processed on a rolling basis. Application fee: $50 ($75 for international students). *Financial support:* Fellowships, research assistantships with tuition reimbursements, and teaching assistantships with tuition reimbursements available. Financial award application deadline: 2/1. *Unit head:* Dr. Philip L. Varghese, Chair, 512-471-7593, E-mail: varghese@mail.utexas.edu. *Application contact:* Tina Woods, Graduate Coordinator, 512-471-7595, E-mail: twoods@mail.utexas.edu. Web site: http://www.ae.utexas.edu/graduate-programs/em.

University of Wisconsin–Madison, Graduate School, College of Engineering, Department of Engineering Physics, Madison, WI 53706. Offers engineering mechanics (MS, PhD); nuclear engineering and engineering physics (MS, PhD). Part-time programs available. Postbaccalaureate distance learning degree programs offered (minimal on-campus study). *Faculty:* 20 full-time (0 women), 9 part-time/adjunct (4 women). *Students:* 102 full-time (11 women), 16 part-time (1 woman); includes 12 minority (3 Black or African American, non-Hispanic/Latino; 1 American Indian or Alaska Native, non-Hispanic/Latino; 1 Asian, non-Hispanic/Latino; 7 Hispanic/Latino), 18 international. Average age 25. 198 applicants, 37% accepted, 38 enrolled. In 2011, 43 master's, 8 doctorates awarded. Terminal master's awarded for partial completion of doctoral program. *Degree requirements:* For master's, thesis optional; for doctorate, thesis/dissertation. *Entrance requirements:* For master's and doctorate, GRE General Test, minimum GPA of 3.0 in last 60 hours, appropriate bachelor's degree. Additional exam requirements/recommendations for international students: Required—TOEFL (minimum score 600 paper-based; 245 computer-based). *Application deadline:* For fall admission, 1/15 priority date for domestic students, 1/15 for international students. Applications are processed on a rolling basis. Application fee: $56. Electronic applications accepted. *Expenses:* Tuition, state resident: full-time $10,296; part-time $643.51 per credit. Tuition, nonresident: full-time $24,054; part-time $1503.40 per credit. *Required fees:* $70.06 per credit. Tuition and fees vary according to course load, campus/location, program and reciprocity agreements. *Financial support:* In 2011–12, 106 students received support, including 20 fellowships with full tuition reimbursements available (averaging $25,000 per year), 76 research assistantships with full tuition reimbursements available (averaging $20,400 per year), 10 teaching assistantships with full tuition reimbursements available (averaging $12,633 per year); career-related internships or fieldwork, Federal Work-Study, institutionally sponsored loans, and unspecified assistantships also available. Support available to part-time students. Financial award application deadline: 1/15. *Faculty research:* Fission reactor engineering and safety, plasma physics and fusion technology, plasma processing and ion implantation, nanotechnology, engineering mechanics and astronautics. *Total annual research expenditures:* $18.8 million. *Unit head:* Dr. James P. Blanchard, Chair, 608-263-0391, Fax: 608-263-7451, E-mail: blanchard@engr.wisc.edu. *Application contact:* Betsy A. Wood, Graduate Coordinator, 608-263-7038, Fax: 608-263-7451, E-mail: bwood@engr.wisc.edu. Web site: http://www.engr.wisc.edu/ep/.

University of Wisconsin–Milwaukee, Graduate School, College of Engineering and Applied Science, Program in Engineering, Milwaukee, WI 53201-0413. Offers civil engineering (MS); electrical and computer engineering (MS); energy engineering (Certificate); engineering (PhD); engineering management (MS); engineering mechanics (MS); ergonomics (Certificate); industrial and management engineering (MS); manufacturing engineering (MS); materials engineering (MS); mechanical engineering (MS); MUP/MS. Part-time programs available. *Faculty:* 41 full-time (5 women), 2 part-time/adjunct (0 women). *Students:* 170 full-time (33 women), 101 part-time (18 women); includes 30 minority (6 Black or African American, non-Hispanic/Latino; 15 Asian, non-Hispanic/Latino; 2 Hispanic/Latino; 7 Two or more races, non-Hispanic/Latino), 153 international. Average age 30. 170 applicants, 56% accepted, 48 enrolled. In 2011, 47 master's, 12 doctorates awarded. *Degree requirements:* For master's, comprehensive exam (for some programs), thesis or alternative; for doctorate, comprehensive exam, thesis/dissertation, internship. *Entrance requirements:* For master's, GRE, minimum GPA of 2.75; for doctorate, GRE, minimum GPA of 3.5. Additional exam requirements/recommendations for international students: Required—TOEFL (minimum score 550 paper-based; 79 iBT), IELTS (minimum score 6.5). *Application deadline:* For fall admission, 1/1 priority date for domestic students; for spring admission, 9/1 for domestic students. Applications are processed on a rolling basis. Application fee: $56 ($96 for international students). One-time fee: $506.10 full-time. Tuition and fees vary according to course load and reciprocity agreements. *Financial support:* In 2011–12, 3 fellowships, 55 research assistantships, 77 teaching assistantships were awarded; career-related internships or fieldwork, Federal Work-Study, unspecified assistantships, and project assistantships also available. Support available to part-time students. Financial award application deadline: 4/15. *Total annual research expenditures:* $10.3 million. *Unit head:* David Yu, Representative, 414-229-6169, E-mail: yu@uwm.edu. *Application contact:* Betty Warras, General Information Contact, 414-229-6169, Fax: 414-229-6967, E-mail: bwarras@uwm.edu. Web site: http://www.wum.edu/CEAS/.

Virginia Polytechnic Institute and State University, Graduate School, College of Engineering, Department of Engineering Science and Mechanics, Blacksburg, VA 24061. Offers computational engineering science and mechanics (Certificate); engineering mechanics (M Eng, MS, PhD). Part-time programs available. Terminal master's awarded for partial completion of doctoral program. *Degree requirements:* For master's, thesis optional, 21-30 credit hours; for doctorate, comprehensive exam, thesis/dissertation, 45 credit hours. *Entrance requirements:* For master's and doctorate, GRE General Test. Additional exam requirements/recommendations for international students: Required—TOEFL (minimum score 550 paper-based; 213 computer-based). *Application deadline:* For fall admission, 7/1 for domestic and international students; for spring admission, 12/1 for domestic and international students. Applications are processed on a rolling basis. Application fee: $65. Electronic applications accepted. *Expenses:* Tuition, state resident: full-time $10,048; part-time $558.25 per credit hour. Tuition, nonresident: full-time $19,497; part-time $1083.25 per credit hour. *Required fees:* $405 per semester. Tuition and fees vary according to course load, campus/location and program. *Financial support:* Fellowships with tuition reimbursements, research assistantships with full tuition reimbursements, teaching assistantships with full tuition reimbursements, career-related internships or fieldwork, Federal Work-Study, scholarships/grants, health care benefits, and unspecified assistantships available.

Financial award application deadline: 12/31. *Faculty research:* Solid mechanics and materials, fluid mechanics, dynamics and vibrations, composite materials, computational mechanics and finite element methods. *Unit head:* Dr. Ishwar K. Puri, Professor/Head, 540-231-3243, Fax: 540-231-4574, E-mail: ikpuri@vt.edu. *Application contact:* Lisa L. Smith, Information Contact, 540-231-4935, Fax: 540-231-4574, E-mail: lisas@vt.edu. Web site: http://www.esm.vt.edu/esm.html.

Section 18
Ocean Engineering

This section contains a directory of institutions offering graduate work in ocean engineering. Additional information about programs listed in the directory but not augmented by an in-depth entry may be obtained by writing directly to the dean of a graduate school or chair of a department at the address given in the directory.

For programs offering related work, see also in this book *Civil and Environmental Engineering* and *Engineering and Applied Sciences*. In the other guides in this series:

Graduate Programs in the Biological/Biomedical Sciences & Health-Related Medical Professions
See *Marine Biology*

Graduate Programs in the Physical Sciences, Mathematics, Agricultural Sciences, the Environment & Natural Resources
See *Environmental Sciences and Management* and *Marine Sciences and Oceanography*

CONTENTS

Program Directory

Ocean Engineering

Florida Atlantic University, College of Engineering and Computer Science, Department of Ocean and Mechanical Engineering, Boca Raton, FL 33431-0991. Offers mechanical engineering (MS, PhD); ocean engineering (MS, PhD). Part-time and evening/weekend programs available. *Faculty:* 20 full-time (0 women), 2 part-time/adjunct (0 women). *Students:* 39 full-time (9 women), 34 part-time (6 women); includes 15 minority (5 Black or African American, non-Hispanic/Latino; 1 American Indian or Alaska Native, non-Hispanic/Latino; 9 Hispanic/Latino), 18 international. Average age 29. 63 applicants, 48% accepted, 12 enrolled. In 2011, 36 master's, 1 doctorate awarded. Terminal master's awarded for partial completion of doctoral program. *Degree requirements:* For master's, thesis (for some programs); for doctorate, comprehensive exam, thesis/dissertation, qualifying exam. *Entrance requirements:* For master's and doctorate, GRE General Test, minimum GPA of 3.0. Additional exam requirements/recommendations for international students: Required—TOEFL. *Application deadline:* For fall admission, 7/1 priority date for domestic students, 2/15 for international students; for spring admission, 11/1 for domestic students, 7/15 for international students. Applications are processed on a rolling basis. Application fee: $30. *Expenses: Tuition, area resident:* Part-time $343.02 per credit hour. Tuition, state resident: full-time $8232. Tuition, nonresident: full-time $23,931; part-time $997.14 per credit hour. *Financial support:* In 2011–12, research assistantships (averaging $15,000 per year) were awarded; career-related internships or fieldwork, Federal Work-Study, scholarships/grants, and unspecified assistantships also available. Financial award application deadline: 1/10; financial award applicants required to submit FAFSA. *Faculty research:* Marine materials and corrosion, ocean structures, marine vehicles, acoustics and vibrations, hydrodynamics, coastal engineering. *Unit head:* Dr. Javad Hashemi, Chair, 561-297-3430, E-mail: jhashemi@fau.edu. *Application contact:* Joanna Arlington, Manager, Graduate Admissions, 561-297-2428, Fax: 561-297-2117, E-mail: arlingto@fau.edu. Web site: http://www.ome.fau.edu/.

Florida Institute of Technology, Graduate Programs, College of Engineering, Department of Marine and Environmental Systems, Program in Ocean Engineering, Melbourne, FL 32901-6975. Offers MS, PhD. Part-time programs available. *Faculty:* 11 full-time (0 women), 3 part-time/adjunct (0 women). *Students:* 23 full-time (4 women), 10 part-time (3 women); includes 3 minority (1 American Indian or Alaska Native, non-Hispanic/Latino; 1 Asian, non-Hispanic/Latino; 1 Hispanic/Latino), 9 international. Average age 27. 52 applicants, 69% accepted, 13 enrolled. In 2011, 4 master's awarded. *Degree requirements:* For master's, comprehensive exam (for some programs), thesis (for some programs); for doctorate, comprehensive exam, thesis/dissertation. *Entrance requirements:* For master's, GRE General Test, minimum GPA of 3.0, 3 letters of recommendation, resume, transcripts, statement of objectives; for doctorate, GRE General Test, minimum GPA of 3.3, resume, 3 letters of recommendation, statement of objectives, on-campus interview (highly recommended). Additional exam requirements/recommendations for international students: Required—TOEFL (minimum score 550 paper-based; 213 computer-based; 79 iBT). *Application deadline:* Applications are processed on a rolling basis. Application fee: $0. Electronic applications accepted. *Expenses: Tuition:* Full-time $19,620; part-time $1090 per credit hour. Tuition and fees vary according to campus/location. *Financial support:* Career-related internships or fieldwork, institutionally sponsored loans, tuition waivers (partial), unspecified assistantships, and tuition remissions available. Support available to part-time students. Financial award application deadline: 3/1; financial award applicants required to submit FAFSA. *Faculty research:* Underwater technology, materials and structures, coastal processes and engineering, marine vehicles and ocean systems, naval architecture. *Total annual research expenditures:* $1.6 million. *Unit head:* Dr. George Maul, Department Head, 321-674-7453, Fax: 321-674-7212, E-mail: gmaul@fit.edu. *Application contact:* Cheryl A. Brown, Associate Director of Graduate Admission, 321-674-7581, Fax: 321-723-9468, E-mail: cbrown@fit.edu. Web site: http://coe.fit.edu/dmes/.

Massachusetts Institute of Technology, School of Engineering, Department of Mechanical Engineering, Cambridge, MA 02139. Offers manufacturing (M Eng); mechanical engineering (SM, PhD, Sc D, Mech E); naval architecture and marine engineering (SM, PhD, Sc D); naval engineering (Naval E); ocean engineering (SM, PhD, Sc D), including); oceanographic engineering (SM, PhD, Sc D); SM/MBA. *Faculty:* 68 full-time (8 women). *Students:* 540 full-time (111 women), 1 part-time (0 women); includes 98 minority (9 Black or African American, non-Hispanic/Latino; 1 American Indian or Alaska Native, non-Hispanic/Latino; 52 Asian, non-Hispanic/Latino; 29 Hispanic/Latino; 7 Two or more races, non-Hispanic/Latino), 220 international. Average age 26. 881 applicants, 27% accepted, 142 enrolled. In 2011, 123 master's, 56 doctorates, 11 other advanced degrees awarded. Terminal master's awarded for partial completion of doctoral program. *Degree requirements:* For master's and other advanced degree, thesis; for doctorate, comprehensive exam, thesis/dissertation. *Entrance requirements:* For master's, doctorate, and other advanced degree, GRE General Test. Additional exam requirements/recommendations for international students: Required—IELTS (minimum score 7). *Application deadline:* For fall admission, 12/15 for domestic and international students. Application fee: $75. Electronic applications accepted. *Expenses: Tuition:* Full-time $40,460; part-time $630 per credit hour. *Required fees:* $272. *Financial support:* In 2011–12, 447 students received support, including 95 fellowships (averaging $30,800 per year), 318 research assistantships (averaging $29,200 per year), 45 teaching assistantships (averaging $33,000 per year); career-related internships or fieldwork, Federal Work-Study, institutionally sponsored loans, scholarships/grants, health care benefits, and unspecified assistantships also available. *Faculty research:* Mechanics: modeling, experimentation and computation; design, manufacturing, and product development; controls, instrumentation, and robotics; energy science and engineering; ocean science and engineering; bioengineering; micro and nano engineering. *Total annual research expenditures:* $50.9 million. *Unit head:* Prof. Mary C. Boyce, Head, 617-253-2201, Fax: 617-258-6156, E-mail: mehq@mit.edu. *Application contact:* Graduate Office, 617-253-2291, Fax: 617-258-5802, E-mail: me-gradoffice@mit.edu. Web site: http://meche.mit.edu.

Memorial University of Newfoundland, School of Graduate Studies, Faculty of Engineering and Applied Science, St. John's, NL A1C 5S7, Canada. Offers civil engineering (M Eng, PhD); electrical and computer engineering (M Eng, PhD); mechanical engineering (M Eng, PhD); ocean and naval architecture engineering (M Eng, PhD). Part-time programs available. *Degree requirements:* For master's, thesis; for doctorate, comprehensive exam, thesis/dissertation, oral thesis defense. *Entrance requirements:* For master's, 2nd class degree; for doctorate, master's degree in engineering. Electronic applications accepted. *Faculty research:* Engineering analysis, environmental and hydrotechnical studies, manufacturing and robotics, mechanics, structures and materials.

Oregon State University, Graduate School, College of Engineering, School of Civil and Construction Engineering, Program in Coastal and Ocean Engineering, Corvallis, OR 97331. Offers M Oc E, MS, PhD. Part-time programs available. *Degree requirements:* For master's, thesis or alternative. *Entrance requirements:* For master's, GRE General Test, minimum GPA of 3.0 in last 90 hours. Additional exam requirements/recommendations for international students: Required—TOEFL. *Faculty research:* Beach erosion and coastal protection, loads on sea-based structures, ocean wave mechanics, wave forces on structures, breakwater behavior.

Princeton University, Graduate School, Department of Geosciences, Princeton, NJ 08544-1019. Offers atmospheric and oceanic sciences (PhD); geosciences (PhD); ocean sciences and marine biology (PhD). *Degree requirements:* For doctorate, one foreign language, thesis/dissertation. *Entrance requirements:* For doctorate, GRE General Test. Additional exam requirements/recommendations for international students: Required—TOEFL (minimum score 600 paper-based; 250 computer-based). Electronic applications accepted. *Faculty research:* Biogeochemistry, climate science, earth history, regional geology and tectonics, solid–earth geophysics.

Stevens Institute of Technology, Graduate School, Charles V. Schaefer Jr. School of Engineering, Department of Civil, Environmental, and Ocean Engineering, Program in Ocean Engineering, Hoboken, NJ 07030. Offers M Eng, PhD. *Degree requirements:* For master's, thesis optional; for doctorate, variable foreign language requirement, thesis/dissertation. *Entrance requirements:* For doctorate, GRE. Additional exam requirements/recommendations for international students: Required—TOEFL. Electronic applications accepted. *Faculty research:* Estuarine oceanography, hydrodynamic and environmental processes, wave/ship interaction.

Texas A&M University, College of Engineering, Zachry Department of Civil Engineering, College Station, TX 77843. Offers coastal and ocean engineering (M Eng, MS, D Eng, PhD); construction engineering and management (M Eng, MS, D Eng, PhD); environmental engineering (M Eng, MS, D Eng, PhD); geotechnical engineering (M Eng, MS, D Eng, PhD); materials engineering (M Eng, MS, D Eng, PhD); structural engineering (M Eng, MS, D Eng, PhD); transportation engineering (M Eng, MS, D Eng, PhD); water resources engineering (M Eng, MS, D Eng, PhD). Part-time programs available. *Faculty:* 57. *Students:* 361 full-time (76 women), 46 part-time (8 women); includes 41 minority (3 Black or African American, non-Hispanic/Latino; 16 Asian, non-Hispanic/Latino; 21 Hispanic/Latino; 1 Two or more races, non-Hispanic/Latino), 247 international. Average age 29. In 2011, 123 master's, 27 doctorates awarded. *Degree requirements:* For master's, thesis (MS); for doctorate, dissertation (PhD), internship (D Eng). *Entrance requirements:* For master's and doctorate, GRE General Test. Additional exam requirements/recommendations for international students: Required—TOEFL. *Application deadline:* Applications are processed on a rolling basis. Application fee: $50 ($75 for international students). Electronic applications accepted. *Expenses:* Tuition, state resident: full-time $5437; part-time $226.55 per credit hour. Tuition, nonresident: full-time $12,949; part-time $539.55 per credit hour. *Required fees:* $2741. *Financial support:* In 2011–12, fellowships (averaging $4,500 per year), research assistantships (averaging $14,000 per year), teaching assistantships (averaging $14,400 per year) were awarded; career-related internships or fieldwork and institutionally sponsored loans also available. Financial award application deadline: 4/15; financial award applicants required to submit FAFSA. *Unit head:* Dr. John Niedzwecki, Head, 979-845-3858, E-mail: j-niedzwecki@tamu.edu. *Application contact:* Graduate Advisor, 979-845-7435, Fax: 979-845-6156, E-mail: info@civil.tamu.edu. Web site: https://www.civil.tamu.edu/.

University of Alaska Anchorage, School of Engineering, Program in Civil Engineering, Anchorage, AK 99508. Offers civil engineering (MCE, MS); port and coastal engineering (Certificate). Part-time and evening/weekend programs available. *Degree requirements:* For master's, thesis (for some programs). *Entrance requirements:* For master's, bachelor's degree in engineering. Additional exam requirements/recommendations for international students: Required—TOEFL (minimum score 550 paper-based; 213 computer-based). *Faculty research:* Structural engineering, engineering education, astronomical observations related to engineering.

University of California, San Diego, Office of Graduate Studies, Department of Electrical and Computer Engineering, La Jolla, CA 92093. Offers applied ocean science (MS, PhD); applied physics (MS, PhD); communication theory and systems (MS, PhD); computer engineering (MS, PhD); electrical engineering (M Eng); electronic circuits and systems (MS, PhD); intelligent systems, robotics and control (MS, PhD); photonics (MS, PhD); signal and image processing (MS, PhD). MS only offered to students who have been admitted to the PhD program. *Entrance requirements:* For master's and doctorate, GRE General Test. Electronic applications accepted.

University of California, San Diego, Office of Graduate Studies, Department of Mechanical and Aerospace Engineering, Program in Applied Ocean Science, La Jolla, CA 92093. Offers MS, PhD. Part-time programs available. *Degree requirements:* For master's, comprehensive exam or thesis; for doctorate, thesis/dissertation, qualifying exam. *Entrance requirements:* For master's and doctorate, GRE General Test, minimum GPA of 3.0. Additional exam requirements/recommendations for international students: Required—TOEFL. Electronic applications accepted.

University of Delaware, College of Earth, Ocean, and Environment, School of Marine Science and Policy, Newark, DE 19716. Offers marine policy (MMP); marine studies (MS, PhD), including marine biosciences, oceanography, physical ocean science and engineering; oceanography (PhD).

University of Delaware, College of Engineering, Department of Civil and Environmental Engineering, Newark, DE 19716. Offers environmental engineering (MAS, MCE, PhD); geotechnical engineering (MAS, MCE, PhD); ocean engineering (MAS, MCE, PhD); structural engineering (MAS, MCE, PhD); transportation engineering (MAS, MCE, PhD); water resource engineering (MAS, MCE, PhD). Part-time programs available. Terminal master's awarded for partial completion of doctoral program. *Degree requirements:* For master's, thesis; for doctorate, thesis/dissertation. *Entrance requirements:* For master's and doctorate, GRE General Test. Additional exam requirements/recommendations for international students: Required—TOEFL. Electronic applications accepted. *Faculty research:* Structural engineering and mechanics; transportation engineering; ocean engineering; soil mechanics and foundation; water resources and environmental engineering.

University of Florida, Graduate School, College of Engineering, Department of Civil and Coastal Engineering, Gainesville, FL 32611. Offers civil engineering (MCE, MS, PhD, Engr); coastal and oceanographic engineering (ME, MS, PhD, Engr). Part-time programs available. Postbaccalaureate distance learning degree programs offered (no on-campus study). Terminal master's awarded for partial completion of doctoral program. *Degree requirements:* For master's, thesis (for some programs); for doctorate, comprehensive exam, thesis/dissertation. *Entrance requirements:* For master's and doctorate, GRE General Test, minimum GPA of 3.0. Additional exam requirements/recommendations for international students: Required—TOEFL (minimum score 550 paper-based; 213 computer-based; 80 iBT), IELTS (minimum score 6). Electronic applications accepted. *Faculty research:* Traffic congestion mitigation, wind mitigation, sustainable infrastructure materials, improved sensors for in situ measurements, storm surge modeling.

University of Hawaii at Manoa, Graduate Division, School of Ocean and Earth Science and Technology, Department of Ocean and Resources Engineering, Honolulu, HI 96822. Offers MS, PhD. *Accreditation:* ABET (one or more programs are accredited). Part-time programs available. *Degree requirements:* For master's, thesis optional; exams; for doctorate, comprehensive exam, thesis/dissertation, exams. *Entrance requirements:* For master's and doctorate, GRE General Test. Additional exam requirements/recommendations for international students: Required—TOEFL (minimum score 560 paper-based; 220 computer-based; 83 iBT), IELTS (minimum score 5). *Faculty research:* Coastal and harbor engineering, near shore environmental ocean engineering, marine structures/naval architecture.

University of Maine, Graduate School, Interdisciplinary Doctoral Program, Orono, ME 04469. Offers communication (PhD); functional genomics (PhD); mass communication (PhD); ocean engineering (PhD). Part-time and evening/weekend programs available. *Students:* 21 full-time (11 women), 22 part-time (16 women); includes 2 minority (both Asian, non-Hispanic/Latino), 3 international. Average age 38. 25 applicants, 32% accepted, 6 enrolled. In 2011, 6 degrees awarded. *Degree requirements:* For doctorate, comprehensive exam, thesis/dissertation. *Entrance requirements:* For doctorate, GRE General Test. Additional exam requirements/recommendations for international students: Required—TOEFL. *Application deadline:* For fall admission, 4/1 for domestic students; for spring admission, 11/1 for domestic students. Applications are processed on a rolling basis. Application fee: $65. Electronic applications accepted. *Expenses:* Tuition, state resident: full-time $5016. Tuition, nonresident: full-time $14,424. *Unit head:* Scott G. Delcourt, Associate Dean of the Graduate School, 207-581-3291, Fax: 207-581-3232, E-mail: graduate@maine.edu. *Application contact:* Scott G. Delcourt, Associate Dean of the Graduate School, 207-581-3291, Fax: 207-581-3232, E-mail: graduate@maine.edu. Web site: http://www2.umaine.edu/graduate/.

University of Michigan, College of Engineering, Department of Naval Architecture and Marine Engineering, Ann Arbor, MI 48109. Offers concurrent marine design (M Eng); naval architecture and marine engineering (MS, MSE, PhD, Mar Eng, Nav Arch); MBA/MSE. Part-time programs available. *Students:* 90 full-time (14 women), 3 part-time (0 women). 117 applicants, 59% accepted, 43 enrolled. In 2011, 38 master's, 3 doctorates awarded. Terminal master's awarded for partial completion of doctoral program. *Degree requirements:* For master's, thesis (for some programs); for doctorate, comprehensive exam, thesis/dissertation, oral defense of dissertation, preliminary exams (written and oral); for other advanced degree, comprehensive exam, thesis, oral defense of thesis. *Entrance requirements:* For doctorate, GRE General Test, master's degree; for other advanced degree, GRE General Test. Additional exam requirements/recommendations for international students: Required—TOEFL (minimum score 560 paper-based; 220 computer-based). *Application deadline:* Applications are processed on a rolling basis. Application fee: $65 ($75 for international students). Electronic applications accepted. *Financial support:* Fellowships, research assistantships, teaching assistantships, career-related internships or fieldwork, Federal Work-Study, institutionally sponsored loans, scholarships/grants, and unspecified assistantships available. *Faculty research:* System and structural reliability, design and analysis of offshore structures and vehicles, marine systems design, remote sensing of ship wakes and sea surfaces, marine hydrodynamics, nonlinear seakeeping analysis. *Unit head:* Dr. Steven Ceccio, Chair, 734-936-7636, Fax: 734-936-8820, E-mail: kdrake@engin.umich.edu. *Application contact:* Nathalie Fiveland, Unit Administrator, 734-936-0566, Fax: 734-936-8820, E-mail: fiveland@umich.edu. Web site: http://www.engin.umich.edu/dept/name.

University of New Hampshire, Graduate School, College of Engineering and Physical Sciences, Program in Ocean Engineering, Durham, NH 03824. Offers ocean engineering (MS, PhD); ocean mapping (MS, Postbaccalaureate Certificate). *Faculty:* 13 full-time (1 woman). *Students:* 19 full-time (5 women), 6 part-time (0 women); includes 2 minority (1 Hispanic/Latino; 1 Two or more races, non-Hispanic/Latino), 15 international. Average age 31. 29 applicants, 86% accepted, 13 enrolled. In 2011, 2 master's, 1 doctorate, 6 other advanced degrees awarded. *Degree requirements:* For master's, thesis. *Entrance requirements:* Additional exam requirements/recommendations for international students: Required—TOEFL (minimum score 550 paper-based; 213 computer-based; 80 iBT). *Application deadline:* For fall admission, 4/1 priority date for domestic students; for spring admission, 12/1 for domestic students. Applications are processed on a rolling basis. Application fee: $65. Electronic applications accepted. *Expenses:* Tuition, state resident: full-time $12,360; part-time $687 per credit hour. Tuition, nonresident: full-time $25,680; part-time $1058 per credit hour. *International*

tuition: $29,550 full-time. *Required fees:* $1666; $833 per course. $416.50 per semester. Tuition and fees vary according to course load and degree level. *Financial support:* In 2011–12, 18 students received support, including 13 research assistantships, 1 teaching assistantship; fellowships, Federal Work-Study, scholarships/grants, and tuition waivers (full and partial) also available. Support available to part-time students. Financial award application deadline: 2/15. *Unit head:* Dr. Kenneth Baldwin, Chairperson, 603-862-1898. *Application contact:* Jennifer Bedsole, Information Contact, 603-862-0672, E-mail: ocean.engineering@unh.edu. Web site: http://www.unh.edu/oe/.

University of Rhode Island, Graduate School, College of Engineering, Department of Ocean Engineering, Narragansett, RI 02882. Offers MS, PhD. Part-time programs available. *Faculty:* 10 full-time (2 women), 1 part-time/adjunct (0 women). *Students:* 25 full-time (6 women), 13 part-time (4 women); includes 1 minority (Asian, non-Hispanic/Latino), 5 international. In 2011, 8 master's, 1 doctorate awarded. *Degree requirements:* For master's, comprehensive exam (for some programs), thesis optional; for doctorate, comprehensive exam, thesis/dissertation. *Entrance requirements:* For master's and doctorate, 2 letters of recommendation. Additional exam requirements/recommendations for international students: Required—TOEFL (minimum score 550 paper-based; 213 computer-based). *Application deadline:* For fall admission, 7/15 for domestic students, 2/1 for international students; for spring admission, 11/15 for domestic students, 7/15 for international students. Application fee: $65. Electronic applications accepted. *Expenses:* Tuition, state resident: full-time $10,432; part-time $580 per credit hour. Tuition, nonresident: full-time $23,130; part-time $1285 per credit hour. *Required fees:* $1362; $36 per credit hour. $35 per semester. One-time fee: $130. *Financial support:* In 2011–12, 4 research assistantships with full and partial tuition reimbursements (averaging $8,181 per year), 3 teaching assistantships with full and partial tuition reimbursements (averaging $13,894 per year) were awarded. Financial award application deadline: 2/1; financial award applicants required to submit FAFSA. *Faculty research:* Tele-presence technology for high bandwidth ship-to-shore link, wave-induced sediment transport, tsunami impact, geohazards, acoustical oceanography, underwater vehicle mechanical and control system design, deep sea drilling. *Unit head:* Dr. Christopher H. Baxter, Chairman, 401-874-6575, Fax: 401-874-6837, E-mail: baxter@oce.uri.edu. *Application contact:* Dr. Christopher Baxter, Associate Professor, 401-874-6575, Fax: 401-874-6837, E-mail: baxter@oce.uri.edu. Web site: http://www.oce.uri.edu/.

Virginia Polytechnic Institute and State University, VT Online, Blacksburg, VA 24061. Offers advanced transportation systems (Certificate); aerospace engineering (MS); agricultural and life sciences (MSLFS); business information systems (Graduate Certificate); career and technical education (MS); civil engineering (MS); computer engineering (M Eng, MS); decision support systems (Graduate Certificate); eLearning leadership (MA); electrical engineering (M Eng, MS); engineering administration (MEA); environmental engineering (Certificate); environmental politics and policy (Graduate Certificate); environmental sciences and engineering (MS); foundations of political analysis (Graduate Certificate); health product risk management (Graduate Certificate); industrial and systems engineering (MS); information policy and society (Graduate Certificate); information security (Graduate Certificate); information technology (MIT); instructional technology (MA); integrative STEM education (MA Ed); liberal arts (Graduate Certificate); life sciences: health product risk management (MS); natural resources (MNR, Graduate Certificate); networking (Graduate Certificate); nonprofit and nongovernmental organization management (Graduate Certificate); ocean engineering (MS); political science (MS); security studies (Graduate Certificate); software development (Graduate Certificate). *Expenses:* Tuition, state resident: full-time $10,048; part-time $558.25 per credit hour. Tuition, nonresident: full-time $19,497; part-time $1083.25 per credit hour. *Required fees:* $405 per semester. Tuition and fees vary according to course load, campus/location and program. *Application contact:* Graduate School Applications General Assistance, 540-231-8636, Fax: 540-231-2039, E-mail: gradappl@vt.edu. Web site: http://www.vto.vt.edu/.

Woods Hole Oceanographic Institution, MIT/WHOI Joint Program in Oceanography/Applied Ocean Science and Engineering, Woods Hole, MA 02543-1541. Offers applied ocean science and engineering (PhD); biological oceanography (PhD); chemical oceanography (PhD); marine geology and geophysics (PhD); physical oceanography (PhD). Program offered jointly with Massachusetts Institute of Technology. *Degree requirements:* For doctorate, thesis/dissertation. *Entrance requirements:* For doctorate, GRE General Test, GRE Subject Test. Additional exam requirements/recommendations for international students: Required—TOEFL. Electronic applications accepted.

Section 19
Paper and Textile Engineering

This section contains a directory of institutions offering graduate work in paper and textile engineering. Additional information about programs listed in the directory but not augmented by an in-depth entry may be obtained by writing directly to the dean of a graduate school or chair of a department at the address given in the directory.

For programs offering related work, see also in this book *Engineering and Applied Sciences* and *Materials Sciences and Engineering.* In another guide in this series:

Graduate Programs in the Humanities, Arts & Social Sciences
See *Family and Consumer Sciences (Clothing and Textiles)*

CONTENTS

Program Directories

Paper and Pulp Engineering

Miami University, School of Engineering and Applied Science, Department of Chemical and Paper Engineering, Oxford, OH 45056. Offers MS. *Students:* 10 full-time (4 women), 1 part-time (0 women), 9 international. Average age 24. In 2011, 5 master's awarded. *Entrance requirements:* For master's, GRE General Test, minimum undergraduate GPA of 3.0 during previous 2 years or 2.75 overall. Additional exam requirements/recommendations for international students: Required—TOEFL. *Application deadline:* For fall admission, 3/1 for domestic and international students. Application fee: $50. *Expenses:* Tuition, state resident: full-time $12,023; part-time $501 per credit hour. Tuition, nonresident: full-time $26,554; part-time $1107 per credit hour. *Required fees:* $528. *Financial support:* Fellowships, research assistantships, teaching assistantships, Federal Work-Study, health care benefits, tuition waivers (full), and unspecified assistantships available. Financial award application deadline: 3/1. *Unit head:* Dr. Shashi Lalvani, Chair, 513-529-0763, Fax: 513-529-0761, E-mail: lalvansb@muohio.edu. *Application contact:* Chemical and Paper Engineering Department, 513-529-0760, Fax: 513-529-0761, E-mail: seasgrad@muohio.edu. Web site: http://www.eas.muohio.edu/departments/pce/.

North Carolina State University, Graduate School, College of Natural Resources, Department of Wood and Paper Science, Raleigh, NC 27695. Offers MS, MWPS, PhD. Postbaccalaureate distance learning degree programs offered. *Degree requirements:* For master's, thesis optional; for doctorate, thesis/dissertation. *Entrance requirements:* For master's and doctorate, GRE General Test. Additional exam requirements/recommendations for international students: Required—TOEFL. Electronic applications accepted. *Faculty research:* Pulping, bleaching, recycling, papermaking, drying of wood.

Oregon State University, Graduate School, College of Forestry, Department of Wood Science and Engineering, Corvallis, OR 97331. Offers forest products (MAIS, MF, MS, PhD); wood science and technology (MF, MS, PhD). *Accreditation:* SAF (one or more programs are accredited). Part-time programs available. *Degree requirements:* For master's, thesis (for some programs); for doctorate, thesis/dissertation. *Entrance requirements:* For master's and doctorate, GRE General Test, minimum GPA of 3.0 in last 90 hours. Additional exam requirements/recommendations for international students: Required—TOEFL. *Faculty research:* Biodeterioration and preservation, timber engineering, process engineering and control, composite materials science, anatomy, chemistry and physical properties.

State University of New York College of Environmental Science and Forestry, Department of Paper and Bioprocess Engineering, Syracuse, NY 13210-2779. Offers biomaterials engineering (MS, PhD); bioprocess engineering (MPS, MS, PhD); paper science and engineering (MPS, MS, PhD); sustainable engineering management (MPS). *Degree requirements:* For master's, thesis; for doctorate, comprehensive exam, thesis/dissertation. *Entrance requirements:* For master's and doctorate, GRE General Test, minimum GPA of 3.0. Additional exam requirements/recommendations for international students: Required—TOEFL (minimum score 550 paper-based; 213 computer-based; 80 iBT), IELTS (minimum score 6). *Application deadline:* For fall admission, 2/1 priority date for domestic students, 2/1 for international students; for spring admission, 11/1 priority date for domestic students, 11/1 for international students. Applications are processed on a rolling basis. Application fee: $60. *Expenses:* Tuition, state resident: full-time $8870; part-time $370 per credit hour. Tuition, nonresident: full-time $15,160; part-time $632 per credit hour. *Required fees:* $60; $370 per credit hour. $350 per semester. One-time fee: $85. *Financial support:* Fellowships with full tuition reimbursements, research assistantships with full tuition reimbursements, teaching assistantships with full tuition reimbursements, career-related internships or fieldwork, Federal Work-Study, institutionally sponsored loans, scholarships/grants, health care benefits, and unspecified assistantships available. Support available to part-time students. Financial award application deadline: 6/30; financial award applicants required to submit FAFSA. *Total annual research expenditures:* $604,516. *Unit head:* Dr. Gary M. Scott, Chair, 315-470-6501, Fax: 315-470-6945, E-mail: gscott@esf.edu. *Application contact:* Dr. Dudley J. Raynal, Dean, Instruction and Graduate Studies, 315-470-6599, Fax: 315-470-6978, E-mail: esfgrad@esf.edu. Web site: http://www.esf.edu/pbe/.

The University of Manchester, School of Materials, Manchester, United Kingdom. Offers advanced aerospace materials engineering (M Sc); advanced metallic systems (PhD); biomedical materials (M Phil, M Sc, PhD); ceramics and glass (M Phil, M Sc, PhD); composite materials (M Sc, PhD); corrosion and protection (M Phil, M Sc, PhD); materials (M Phil, PhD); metallic materials (M Phil, M Sc, PhD); nanostructural materials (M Phil, M Sc, PhD); paper science (M Phil, M Sc, PhD); polymer science and engineering (M Phil, M Sc, PhD); technical textiles (M Sc); textile design, fashion and management (M Phil, M Sc, PhD); textile science and technology (M Phil, M Sc, PhD); textiles (M Phil, PhD); textiles and fashion (M Ent).

Western Michigan University, Graduate College, College of Engineering and Applied Sciences, Department of Paper Engineering, Chemical Engineering, and Imaging, Kalamazoo, MI 49008. Offers paper and imaging science and engineering (MS, PhD). *Degree requirements:* For master's, thesis optional; for doctorate, one foreign language, comprehensive exam, thesis/dissertation. *Entrance requirements:* For master's, minimum GPA of 3.0. *Faculty research:* Fiber recycling, paper machine wet end operations, paper coating.

Textile Sciences and Engineering

Auburn University, Graduate School, Interdepartmental Programs, Interdepartmental Program in Integrated Textile and Apparel Sciences, Auburn University, AL 36849. Offers PhD. *Faculty:* 23 full-time (16 women), 1 (woman) part-time/adjunct. *Students:* 12 full-time (5 women), 12 part-time (9 women); includes 3 minority (1 Black or African American, non-Hispanic/Latino; 2 Asian, non-Hispanic/Latino), 16 international. Average age 29. 33 applicants, 55% accepted, 2 enrolled. In 2011, 3 doctorates awarded. *Application deadline:* For fall admission, 7/7 for domestic students; for spring admission, 11/24 for domestic students. Applications are processed on a rolling basis. Application fee: $50 ($60 for international students). *Expenses:* Tuition, state resident: full-time $7290; part-time $405 per credit hour. Tuition, nonresident: full-time $21,870; part-time $1215 per credit hour. *International tuition:* $22,000 full-time. *Required fees:* $1402. *Financial support:* Research assistantships and Federal Work-Study available. Support available to part-time students. Financial award application deadline: 3/15; financial award applicants required to submit FAFSA. *Faculty research:* Design and utilization of textile products, engineering and technology of textile production, textile material science, textile chemistry, use of resources. *Unit head:* Dr. Carol Warfield, Jr., Graduate Program Officer, 334-844-1329, E-mail: royalb@eng.auburn.edu. *Application contact:* Dr. George Flowers, Dean of the Graduate School, 334-844-2125. Web site: http://humsci.auburn.edu/cahs/phd-itas.php.

Cornell University, Graduate School, Graduate Fields of Human Ecology, Field of Textiles, Ithaca, NY 14853. Offers apparel design (MA, MPS); fiber science (MS, PhD); polymer science (MS, PhD); textile science (MS, PhD). *Faculty:* 23 full-time (9 women). *Students:* 19 full-time (14 women); includes 2 minority (1 Black or African American, non-Hispanic/Latino; 1 Asian, non-Hispanic/Latino), 10 international. Average age 26. 37 applicants, 32% accepted, 8 enrolled. In 2011, 1 master's, 1 doctorate awarded. *Degree requirements:* For master's, thesis (MA, MS), project paper (MPS); for doctorate, comprehensive exam, thesis/dissertation. *Entrance requirements:* For master's, GRE General Test, 2 letters of recommendation, portfolio (functional apparel design); for doctorate, GRE General Test, 2 letters of recommendation. Additional exam requirements/recommendations for international students: Required—TOEFL (minimum score 600 paper-based; 250 computer-based; 77 iBT). *Application deadline:* For fall admission, 3/1 for domestic students; for spring admission, 10/1 for domestic students. Application fee: $95. Electronic applications accepted. *Financial support:* In 2011–12, 19 students received support, including 3 fellowships with full tuition reimbursements available, 3 research assistantships with full tuition reimbursements available, 7 teaching assistantships with full tuition reimbursements available; institutionally sponsored loans, scholarships/grants, health care benefits, tuition waivers (full and partial), and unspecified assistantships also available. Financial award applicants required to submit FAFSA. *Faculty research:* Apparel design, consumption, mass customization, 3-D body scanning. *Unit head:* Director of Graduate Studies, 607-255-3151, Fax: 607-255-1093. *Application contact:* Graduate Field Assistant, 607-255-3151, Fax: 607-255-1093, E-mail: textiles_grad@cornell.edu. Web site: http://www.gradschool.cornell.edu/fields.php?id-95&a-2.

Georgia Institute of Technology, Graduate Studies and Research, College of Engineering, School of Polymer, Textile, and Fiber Engineering, Atlanta, GA 30332-0001. Offers polymer, textile and fiber engineering (MS, PhD); polymers (MS Poly). *Degree requirements:* For master's, thesis (for some programs); for doctorate, comprehensive exam, thesis/dissertation. *Entrance requirements:* For master's, GRE, minimum GPA of 2.7; for doctorate, GRE, minimum GPA of 3.0. Additional exam requirements/recommendations for international students: Required—TOEFL (minimum score 550 paper-based; 213 computer-based). Electronic applications accepted. *Faculty research:* Energy conservation, environmental control, engineered fibrous structures, polymer synthesis and degradation, high performance organic-carbon-ceramic fibers.

North Carolina State University, Graduate School, College of Textiles, Department of Textile and Apparel Technology and Management, Raleigh, NC 27695. Offers MS, MT. *Degree requirements:* For master's, thesis optional. *Entrance requirements:* For master's, GRE. Electronic applications accepted. *Faculty research:* Textile and apparel products and processes, management systems, nonwovens, process simulation, structure design and analysis.

North Carolina State University, Graduate School, College of Textiles, Department of Textile Engineering, Chemistry, and Science, Program in Textile Chemistry, Raleigh, NC 27695. Offers MS. *Degree requirements:* For master's, thesis optional. *Entrance requirements:* For master's, GRE. Electronic applications accepted. *Faculty research:* Color science, polymer science, dye chemistry, fiber formation, wet processing technology.

North Carolina State University, Graduate School, College of Textiles, Department of Textile Engineering, Chemistry, and Science, Program in Textile Engineering, Raleigh, NC 27695. Offers MS. *Degree requirements:* For master's, thesis optional. *Entrance requirements:* For master's, GRE. Electronic applications accepted. *Faculty research:* Electro-mechanical design, inventory and supply chain control, textile composites, biomedical textile appliations, pollution prevention.

North Carolina State University, Graduate School, College of Textiles, Program in Fiber and Polymer Science, Raleigh, NC 27695. Offers PhD. *Degree requirements:* For doctorate, one foreign language, thesis/dissertation, cumulative exams. *Entrance requirements:* For doctorate, GRE. Electronic applications accepted. *Faculty research:* Polymer science, fiber mechanics, medical textiles, nanotechnology.

Philadelphia University, School of Design and Engineering, Program in Textile Engineering, Philadelphia, PA 19144. Offers MS, PhD. Part-time programs available. *Entrance requirements:* For master's, GRE, minimum GPA of 2.8; for doctorate, master's degree. Additional exam requirements/recommendations for international students: Required—TOEFL (minimum score 550 paper-based; 213 computer-based; 79 iBT). Electronic applications accepted.

University of Massachusetts Dartmouth, Graduate School, College of Engineering, Department of Materials and Textiles, North Dartmouth, MA 02747-2300. Offers textile chemistry (MS); textile technology (MS). Part-time programs available. *Faculty:* 5 full-time (0 women). *Students:* 3 full-time (0 women), 3 part-time (1 woman); includes 1 minority (Hispanic/Latino), 4 international. Average age 29. 9 applicants, 78% accepted, 6 enrolled. In 2011, 6 degrees awarded. *Degree requirements:* For master's, thesis. *Entrance requirements:* For master's, GRE General Test, 3 letters of recommendation, resume, statement of intent. Additional exam requirements/recommendations for international students: Required—TOEFL (minimum score 533 paper-based; 200 computer-based; 72 iBT). *Application deadline:* For fall admission, 2/15 priority date for domestic students, 1/15 for international students; for spring admission, 11/15 priority date for domestic students, 10/15 for international students. Applications are processed on a rolling basis. Application fee: $40 ($60 for international students). Electronic applications accepted. *Expenses:* Tuition, state resident: full-time $2071; part-time $86.29 per credit. Tuition, nonresident: full-time $8099; part-time $337.46 per credit. *Required fees:* $438.58 per credit. Part-time tuition and fees vary according to class time, course load, degree level and reciprocity agreements. *Financial support:* In 2011–12, 1 teaching assistantship with partial tuition reimbursement (averaging $6,250 per year) was awarded; research assistantships and Federal Work-Study also available. Support available to part-time students. Financial award application deadline: 3/1; financial award applicants required to submit FAFSA. *Faculty research:* Flock fundamentals, nanofibers, bio-active fabrics, high stress elastic materials, nano-engineered fire resistant composite fibers. *Total annual research expenditures:* $419,598. *Unit head:* Dr. Qinguo Fan, Graduate Program Director, 508-999-9147, Fax: 508-999-9139, E-mail: qfan@umassd.edu. *Application contact:* Elan Turcotte-Shamski, Graduate Admissions Officer, 508-999-8604, Fax: 508-999-8183, E-mail: graduate@umassd.edu. Web site: http://www.umassd.edu/engineering/mtx/graduate/.

The University of Texas at Austin, Graduate School, College of Natural Sciences, School of Human Ecology, Program in Textile and Apparel Technology, Austin, TX 78712-1111. Offers MS. *Unit head:* Sheldon Ekland-Olson, Department Head, 512-232-5879, Fax: 512-471-5630, E-mail: seo@mail.utexas.edu. Web site: http://he.utexas.edu/txa/graduate-program.

Section 20
Telecommunications

This section contains a directory of institutions offering graduate work in tele-communications. Additional information about programs listed in the directory but not augmented by an in-depth entry may be obtained by writing directly to the dean of a graduate school or chair of a department at the address given in the directory.

For programs offering related work, see also in this book *Computer Science and Information Technology* and *Engineering and Applied Sciences*. In the other guides in this series:

Graduate Programs in the Humanities, Arts & Social Sciences
See *Communication and Media*
Graduate Programs in Business, Education, Information Studies, Law & Social Work
See *Business Administration and Management*

CONTENTS

Program Directories

Telecommunications

The American University of Athens, School of Graduate Studies, Athens, Greece. Offers biomedical sciences (MS); business (MBA); business communication (MA); computer sciences (MS); engineering and applied sciences (MS); politics and policy making (MA); systems engineering (MS); telecommunications (MS). *Entrance requirements:* For master's, resume, 2 recommendation letters. Additional exam requirements/recommendations for international students: Required—TOEFL (minimum score 550 paper-based; 213 computer-based). *Faculty research:* Nanotechnology, environmental sciences, rock mechanics, human skin studies, Monte Carlo algorithms and software.

Ball State University, Graduate School, College of Communication, Information, and Media, Department of Telecommunications, Muncie, IN 47306-1099. Offers digital storytelling (MA). *Faculty:* 13 full-time (3 women). *Students:* 18 full-time (2 women), 11 part-time (3 women); includes 5 minority (1 Black or African American, non-Hispanic/Latino; 3 Hispanic/Latino; 1 Two or more races, non-Hispanic/Latino), 1 international. 16 applicants, 81% accepted, 8 enrolled. In 2011, 15 master's awarded. Application fee: $50. Tuition and fees vary according to program and reciprocity agreements. *Financial support:* In 2011–12, 23 students received support, including 20 teaching assistantships with full tuition reimbursements available (averaging $7,944 per year). *Unit head:* Timothy Pollard, Chairperson, 765-285-1480, Fax: 765-285-9278, E-mail: tpollard@bsu.edu. *Application contact:* Dr. Robert Morris, Associate Provost for Research and Dean of the Graduate School, 765-285-4723, Fax: 765-285-1328, E-mail: rmorris@bsu.edu. Web site: http://www.bsu.edu/tcom/.

Boston University, Metropolitan College, Department of Computer Science, Boston, MA 02215. Offers computer information systems (MS), including computer networks, database management and business intelligence, health informatics, IT project management, security, Web application development; computer science (MS), including computer networks, security; telecommunications (MS), including security. Evening/weekend programs available. Postbaccalaureate distance learning degree programs offered. *Faculty:* 12 full-time (2 women), 28 part-time/adjunct (2 women). *Students:* 25 full-time (6 women), 732 part-time (167 women); includes 208 minority (51 Black or African American, non-Hispanic/Latino; 1 American Indian or Alaska Native, non-Hispanic/Latino; 104 Asian, non-Hispanic/Latino; 43 Hispanic/Latino; 1 Native Hawaiian or other Pacific Islander, non-Hispanic/Latino; 8 Two or more races, non-Hispanic/Latino), 86 international. Average age 35. 260 applicants, 67% accepted, 143 enrolled. In 2011, 143 master's awarded. *Degree requirements:* For master's, thesis optional. *Entrance requirements:* For master's, 3 letters of recommendation, professional resume. Additional exam requirements/recommendations for international students: Required—TOEFL (minimum score 550 paper-based; 213 computer-based; 80 iBT). *Application deadline:* For fall admission, 6/1 for international students; for spring admission, 10/1 for international students. Applications are processed on a rolling basis. Application fee: $70. Electronic applications accepted. *Expenses: Tuition:* Full-time $40,848; part-time $1276 per credit hour. *Required fees:* $572; $286 per semester. *Financial support:* In 2011–12, 9 research assistantships (averaging $5,000 per year) were awarded; career-related internships or fieldwork and unspecified assistantships also available. Support available to part-time students. Financial award applicants required to submit FAFSA. *Faculty research:* Medical informatics, Web technologies, telecom and networks, security and forensics, software engineering, programming languages, multimedia and AI, information systems and IT project management. *Unit head:* Dr. Lubomir Chitkushev, Chairman, 617-353-2566, Fax: 617-353-2367, E-mail: csinfo@bu.edu. *Application contact:* Kim Richards, Program Coordinator, 617-353-2566, Fax: 617-353-2367, E-mail: kimrich@bu.edu. Web site: http://www.bu.edu/csmet/.

California Miramar University, Program in Telecommunications Management, San Diego, CA 92126. Offers MST.

Claremont Graduate University, Graduate Programs, School of Information Systems and Technology, Claremont, CA 91711-6160. Offers electronic commerce (MS, PhD); health information management (MS); information systems (Certificate); knowledge management (MS, PhD); systems development (MS, PhD); telecommunications and networking (MS, PhD); MBA/MS. Part-time programs available. *Faculty:* 7 full-time (1 woman), 1 part-time/adjunct (0 women). *Students:* 68 full-time (20 women), 26 part-time (10 women); includes 31 minority (5 Black or African American, non-Hispanic/Latino; 14 Asian, non-Hispanic/Latino; 9 Hispanic/Latino; 1 Native Hawaiian or other Pacific Islander, non-Hispanic/Latino; 2 Two or more races, non-Hispanic/Latino), 31 international. Average age 37. In 2011, 16 master's, 5 doctorates awarded. *Degree requirements:* For doctorate, comprehensive exam, thesis/dissertation, portfolio. *Entrance requirements:* For master's and doctorate, GMAT, GRE General Test. Additional exam requirements/recommendations for international students: Required—TOEFL (minimum score 550 paper-based; 213 computer-based; 80 iBT). *Application deadline:* For fall admission, 2/1 priority date for domestic students. Applications are processed on a rolling basis. Application fee: $60. Electronic applications accepted. *Expenses: Tuition:* Full-time $36,374; part-time $1581 per unit. *Required fees:* $165 per semester. *Financial support:* Fellowships, research assistantships, teaching assistantships, Federal Work-Study, institutionally sponsored loans, and scholarships/grants available. Support available to part-time students. Financial award application deadline: 2/15; financial award applicants required to submit FAFSA. *Faculty research:* GPSS, man-machine interaction, organizational aspects of computing, implementation of information systems, information systems practice. *Unit head:* Tom Horan, Dean, 909-607-9302, Fax: 909-621-8564, E-mail: tom.horan@cgu.edu. *Application contact:* Anondah Saide, Program Coordinator, 909-607-6006, E-mail: anonda.saide@cgu.edu. Web site: http://www.cgu.edu/pages/153.asp.

Drexel University, College of Engineering, Department of Electrical and Computer Engineering, Program in Telecommunications Engineering, Philadelphia, PA 19104-2875. Offers MSEE. *Entrance requirements:* For master's, BS in electrical engineering or physics, minimum GPA of 3.0. Additional exam requirements/recommendations for international students: Required—TOEFL. Electronic applications accepted.

Florida International University, College of Engineering and Computing, Department of Electrical and Computer Engineering, Miami, FL 33175. Offers computer engineering (MS); electrical engineering (MS, PhD); telecommunications and networking (MS). Part-time and evening/weekend programs available. Terminal master's awarded for partial completion of doctoral program. *Degree requirements:* For master's, thesis optional; for doctorate, comprehensive exam, thesis/dissertation. *Entrance requirements:* For master's, minimum undergraduate GPA of 3.0 in upper-level coursework, resume, letters of recommendation, letter of intent; for doctorate, GRE General Test, minimum graduate GPA of 3.3, resume, letters of recommendation, letter of intent. Additional exam requirements/recommendations for international students: Required—TOEFL (minimum score 550 paper-based; 80 iBT). Electronic applications accepted.

Florida International University, College of Engineering and Computing, School of Computing and Information Sciences, Program in Telecommunications and Networking, Miami, FL 33175. Offers MS. Part-time and evening/weekend programs available.

Entrance requirements: For master's, minimum undergraduate GPA of 3.0 in upper-level coursework. Additional exam requirements/recommendations for international students: Required—TOEFL (minimum score 550 paper-based; 80 iBT). Electronic applications accepted. *Faculty research:* Wireless networks and mobile computing, high-performance routers and switches, network-centric middleware components, distributed systems, networked databases.

Franklin Pierce University, Graduate Studies, Rindge, NH 03461-0060. Offers curriculum and instruction (M Ed); emerging network technologies (Graduate Certificate); energy and sustainability studies (MBA); health administration (MBA, Graduate Certificate); human resource management (MBA, Graduate Certificate); information technology (MBA); information technology management (MS); leadership (MBA, DA); nursing (MS); physical therapy (DPT); physician assistant studies (MPAS); special education (M Ed); sports management (MBA). *Accreditation:* APTA. Part-time programs available. Postbaccalaureate distance learning degree programs offered (no on-campus study). *Degree requirements:* For master's, concentrated original research projects; student teaching; fieldwork and/or internship; leadership project; PRAXIS I and II (for M Ed); for, doctorate, concentrated original research projects, clinical fieldwork and/or internship, leadership project. *Entrance requirements:* For master's, minimum GPA of 2.5, 3 letters of recommendation; competencies in accounting, economics, statistics, and computer skills through life experience or undergraduate coursework (for MBA); certification/e-portfolio, minimum C grade in all education courses (for M Ed); license to practice as RN (for MS in nursing); for doctorate, GRE, BA/BS, 3 letters of recommendation, personal mission statement, interview, writing sample, minimum cumulative GPA of 2.8, master's degree (for DA); 80 hours of observation/work in PT settings, completion of anatomy, chemistry, physics, and statistics, minimum GPA of 3.0 (for DPT). Additional exam requirements/recommendations for international students: Required—TOEFL (minimum score 550 paper-based; 195 computer-based; 61 iBT). Electronic applications accepted. *Faculty research:* Evidence-based practice in sports physical therapy, human resource management in economic crisis, leadership in nursing, innovation in sports facility management, differentiated learning and understanding by design.

George Mason University, Volgenau School of Engineering, Department of Electrical and Computer Engineering, Fairfax, VA 22030. Offers advanced networking protocols for telecommunications (Certificate); communications and networking (Certificate); computer engineering (MS); computer forensics (MS); electrical and computer engineering (PhD); electrical engineering (MS); network technology and applications (Certificate); networks, system integration and testing (Certificate); signal processing (Certificate); telecommunications (MS); telecommunications forensics and security (Certificate); wireless communication (Certificate). MS program offered jointly with Old Dominion University, University of Virginia, Virginia Commonwealth University, and Virginia Polytechnic Institute and State University. *Faculty:* 29 full-time (4 women), 36 part-time/adjunct (2 women). *Students:* 162 full-time (49 women), 284 part-time (52 women); includes 101 minority (30 Black or African American, non-Hispanic/Latino; 1 American Indian or Alaska Native, non-Hispanic/Latino; 47 Asian, non-Hispanic/Latino; 19 Hispanic/Latino; 1 Native Hawaiian or other Pacific Islander, non-Hispanic/Latino; 3 Two or more races, non-Hispanic/Latino), 169 international. Average age 30. 478 applicants, 68% accepted, 106 enrolled. In 2011, 129 master's, 5 doctorates, 45 other advanced degrees awarded. *Degree requirements:* For master's, thesis optional; for doctorate, comprehensive exam, thesis or scholarly paper. *Entrance requirements:* For master's, GRE, personal goals statement; 2 official copies of transcripts; self-evaluation form; 3 letters of recommendation; resume; official bank statement; photocopy of passport; proof of financial support; for doctorate, GRE (waived for GMU electrical and computer engineering master's graduates with minimum GPA of 3.0), personal goals statement; 2 official copies of transcripts; self-evaluation form; 3 letters of recommendation; resume; official bank statement; photocopy of passport; proof of financial support. Additional exam requirements/recommendations for international students: Required—TOEFL (minimum score 575 paper-based; 230 computer-based; 88 iBT), IELTS, Pearson Test of English. *Application deadline:* For fall admission, 1/15 priority date for domestic students; for spring admission, 8/15 priority date for domestic students. Applications are processed on a rolling basis. Application fee: $65 ($80 for international students). Electronic applications accepted. *Expenses:* Tuition, state resident: full-time $8750; part-time $364.58 per credit. Tuition, nonresident: full-time $24,092; part-time $1003.83 per credit. *Required fees:* $2514; $104.75 per credit. *Financial support:* In 2011–12, 77 students received support, including 3 fellowships with full tuition reimbursements available (averaging $18,000 per year), 24 research assistantships with full and partial tuition reimbursements available (averaging $15,736 per year), 50 teaching assistantships with full and partial tuition reimbursements available (averaging $10,961 per year); career-related internships or fieldwork, Federal Work-Study, scholarships/grants, unspecified assistantships, and health care benefits (full-time research or teaching assistantship recipients) also available. Support available to part-time students. Financial award application deadline: 3/1; financial award applicants required to submit FAFSA. *Faculty research:* Communication networks, signal processing, system failure diagnosis, multiprocessors, material processing using microwave energy. *Total annual research expenditures:* $4.4 million. *Unit head:* Dr. Andre Manitius, Chairperson, 703-993-1569, Fax: 703-993-1601, E-mail: amanitiu@gmu.edu. *Application contact:* Jammie Chang, Academic Program Coordinator, 703-993-1523, Fax: 703-993-1601, E-mail: jchangn@gmu.edu. Web site: http://ece.gmu.edu/#.

The George Washington University, School of Engineering and Applied Science, Department of Electrical and Computer Engineering, Washington, DC 20052. Offers electrical and computer engineering (MS, D Sc); telecommunication and computers (MS). Part-time and evening/weekend programs available. *Faculty:* 24 full-time (2 women), 9 part-time/adjunct (0 women). *Students:* 131 full-time (25 women), 101 part-time (14 women); includes 40 minority (16 Black or African American, non-Hispanic/Latino; 18 Asian, non-Hispanic/Latino; 5 Hispanic/Latino; 1 Native Hawaiian or other Pacific Islander, non-Hispanic/Latino), 136 international. Average age 29. 362 applicants, 86% accepted, 68 enrolled. In 2011, 78 master's, 12 doctorates awarded. *Degree requirements:* For master's, thesis optional; for doctorate, comprehensive exam, thesis/dissertation, dissertation defense, qualifying exam. *Entrance requirements:* For master's, appropriate bachelor's degree, minimum GPA of 3.0; for doctorate, GRE (if highest earned degree is BS), appropriate bachelor's or master's degree, minimum GPA of 3.3. Additional exam requirements/recommendations for international students: Required—TOEFL or The George Washington University English as a Foreign Language Test. *Application deadline:* For fall admission, 3/1 priority date for domestic students; for spring admission, 10/1 for domestic students. Applications are processed on a rolling basis. Application fee: $75. *Financial support:* In 2011–12, 39 students received support. Fellowships with tuition reimbursements available, research assistantships, teaching assistantships with tuition reimbursements available, career-related internships or fieldwork, and institutionally sponsored loans available. Financial award application deadline: 3/1; financial award applicants required to submit FAFSA. *Faculty research:* Computer graphics, multimedia systems. *Unit head:* Can E. Korman, Chair, 202-994-4952, E-mail: korman@gwu.edu. *Application contact:* Adina Lav, Marketing, Recruiting and Admissions, 202-994-5827, Fax: 202-994-0909, E-mail: engineering@gwu.edu. Web site: http://www.ece.gwu.edu/.

Illinois Institute of Technology, Graduate College, Armour College of Engineering, Department of Electrical and Computer Engineering, Chicago, IL 60616-3793. Offers biomedical imaging and signals (MBMI); computer engineering (MS, PhD); electrical and computer engineering (MECE); electrical engineering (MS, PhD); electricity markets (MEM); network engineering (MNE); power engineering (MPE); telecommunications and software engineering (MTSE); VLSI and microelectronics (MVM). Part-time and evening/weekend programs available. Postbaccalaureate distance learning degree programs offered (minimal on-campus study). Terminal master's awarded for partial completion of doctoral program. *Degree requirements:* For master's, comprehensive exam (for some programs), thesis (for some programs); for doctorate, comprehensive exam, thesis/dissertation. *Entrance requirements:* For master's and doctorate, GRE General Test (minimum score 1100 Quantitative and Verbal, 3.5 Analytical Writing), minimum undergraduate GPA of 3.0. Additional exam requirements/recommendations for international students: Required—TOEFL (minimum score 523 paper-based; 70 iBT); Recommended—IELTS (minimum score 5.5). Electronic applications accepted. *Faculty research:* Communication systems, computer systems and micro-electronics, electromagnetics and electronics, power and control systems, signal and image processing.

Illinois Institute of Technology, Graduate College, College of Science and Letters, Department of Computer Science, Chicago, IL 60616-3793. Offers business (MCS); computer networking and telecommunications (MCS); computer science (MCS, MS, PhD); information systems (MCS); software engineering (MCS); teaching (MST). Part-time and evening/weekend programs available. Postbaccalaureate distance learning degree programs offered (no on-campus study). Terminal master's awarded for partial completion of doctoral program. *Degree requirements:* For master's, thesis optional; for doctorate, comprehensive exam, thesis/dissertation. *Entrance requirements:* For master's, GRE General Test (minimum scores: 1000 Quantitative and Verbal, 3.0 Analytical Writing), minimum undergraduate GPA of 3.0; for doctorate, GRE General Test (minimum scores: 1100 Quantitative and Verbal, 3.5 Analytical Writing), minimum undergraduate GPA of 3.0. Additional exam requirements/recommendations for international students: Required—TOEFL (minimum score 523 paper-based; 70 iBT). Electronic applications accepted. *Faculty research:* Algorithms, data structures, artificial intelligences, computer architecture, computer graphics, computer networking and telecommunications.

Indiana University Bloomington, University Graduate School, College of Arts and Sciences, Department of Telecommunications, Program in Telecommunications, Bloomington, IN 47405-7000. Offers MA, MS. *Faculty:* 17 full-time (5 women). *Students:* 25 full-time (14 women), 5 part-time (2 women); includes 5 minority (1 Black or African American, non-Hispanic/Latino; 1 American Indian or Alaska Native, non-Hispanic/Latino; 1 Asian, non-Hispanic/Latino; 1 Hispanic/Latino; 1 Two or more races, non-Hispanic/Latino), 12 international. Average age 28. 38 applicants, 47% accepted, 13 enrolled. In 2011, 16 master's awarded. *Degree requirements:* For master's, comprehensive exam (for some programs), thesis (for some programs). *Entrance requirements:* For master's, GRE General Test. Additional exam requirements/recommendations for international students: Required—TOEFL (minimum score 600 paper-based; 250 computer-based; 100 iBT). *Application deadline:* For fall admission, 1/15 priority date for domestic students, 12/1 for international students. Applications are processed on a rolling basis. Application fee: $55 ($65 for international students). Electronic applications accepted. *Financial support:* Application deadline: 1/15. *Faculty research:* Media management, media psychology, telecommunications law and policy, media processes and effects, media design and production (e.g., video games, virtual worlds, documentary, multi-media art). *Unit head:* Tamera Theodore, Graduate Program Administrator, 812-855-2017, E-mail: ttheodor@indiana.edu. *Application contact:* Graduate Secretary. Web site: http://www.indiana.edu/~telecom/index.shtml.

Instituto Tecnologico de Santo Domingo, Graduate School, Area of Engineering, Santo Domingo, Dominican Republic. Offers construction administration (MS, Certificate); data telecommunications (M Eng, MS, Certificate); industrial engineering (M Eng, Certificate); industrial management (M Mgmt); information technology (Certificate); maintenance engineering (M Eng); occupational hazard prevention (M Mgmt); production management (Certificate); quantitative methods (Certificate); sanitary and environmental engineering (M Eng); structural engineering (M Eng); systems engineering and electronic data processing (Certificate); transportation (Certificate).

The Johns Hopkins University, Engineering Program for Professionals, Part-Time Program in Computer Science, Baltimore, MD 21218-2699. Offers bioinformatics (MS); computer science (MS, Post-Master's Certificate); telecommunications and networking (MS). Part-time and evening/weekend programs available. Postbaccalaureate distance learning degree programs offered (no on-campus study). Electronic applications accepted.

Michigan State University, The Graduate School, College of Communication Arts and Sciences, Department of Telecommunication, Information Studies, and Media, East Lansing, MI 48824. Offers digital media arts and technology (MA); information and telecommunication management (MA); information, policy and society (MA); serious game design (MA). *Entrance requirements:* Additional exam requirements/recommendations for international students: Required—TOEFL. Electronic applications accepted.

National University, Academic Affairs, School of Engineering, Technology and Media, Department of Applied Engineering, La Jolla, CA 92037-1011. Offers engineering management (MS); environmental engineering (MS); homeland security and safety engineering (MS); project management (Certificate); security and safety engineering (Certificate); sustainability management (MS); wireless communications (MS). Part-time and evening/weekend programs available. Postbaccalaureate distance learning degree programs offered (no on-campus study). *Degree requirements:* For master's, thesis. *Entrance requirements:* For master's, interview, minimum GPA of 2.5. Additional exam requirements/recommendations for international students: Required—TOEFL (minimum score 550 paper-based; 213 computer-based; 79 iBT), IELTS (minimum score 6). *Application deadline:* Applications are processed on a rolling basis. Application fee: $60 ($65 for international students). Electronic applications accepted. *Financial support:* Career-related internships or fieldwork, institutionally sponsored loans, scholarships/grants, and tuition waivers (partial) available. Support available to part-time students. Financial award application deadline: 6/30; financial award applicants required to submit FAFSA. *Unit head:* Dr. Shekar Viswanathan, Chair and Associate Professor, 858-309-3416, Fax: 858-309-3420, E-mail: sviswana@nu.edu. *Application contact:* Dominick Giovanniello, Associate Regional Dean, 800-NAT-UNIV, Fax: 858-541-7792, E-mail: dgiovann@nu.edu. Web site: http://www.nu.edu/OurPrograms/SchoolOfEngineeringAndTechnology/AppliedEngineering.html.

New Jersey Institute of Technology, Office of Graduate Studies, Newark College of Engineering, Department of Electrical and Computer Engineering, Program in Telecommunications, Newark, NJ 07102. Offers MS. *Students:* 21 full-time (5 women), 3 part-time (0 women); includes 2 minority (1 Black or African American, non-Hispanic/Latino; 1 Asian, non-Hispanic/Latino), 21 international. Average age 26. 126 applicants, 68% accepted, 7 enrolled. In 2011, 15 master's awarded. *Degree requirements:* For master's, thesis or project. *Entrance requirements:* Additional exam requirements/recommendations for international students: Required—TOEFL (minimum score 550 paper-based; 213 computer-based; 79 iBT). *Application deadline:* For fall admission, 6/1 priority date for domestic students, 5/1 for international students; for spring admission, 11/15 priority date for domestic students, 11/15 for international students. Applications are processed on a rolling basis. Application fee: $65. Electronic applications accepted. *Expenses:* Tuition, state resident: full-time $7980; part-time $867 per credit. Tuition, nonresident: full-time $11,336; part-time $1196 per credit. *Required fees:* $230 per credit. *Financial support:* Application deadline: 1/15. *Unit head:* Dr. Leonid Tsybeskov, Chair, 973-596-6594, E-mail: leonid.tsybeskov@njit.edu. *Application contact:* Kathryn Kelly, Director of Admissions, 973-596-3300, Fax: 973-596-3461, E-mail: admissions@njit.edu. Web site: http://ece.njit.edu/academics/graduate/ms-telecom.php.

Ohio University, Graduate College, Scripps College of Communication, J. Warren McClure School of Information and Telecommunication Systems, Athens, OH 45701-2979. Offers MCTP. Part-time programs available. *Students:* 11 full-time (1 woman), 5 part-time (2 women); includes 1 minority (Asian, non-Hispanic/Latino), 8 international. 23 applicants, 57% accepted, 8 enrolled. In 2011, 11 master's awarded. *Degree requirements:* For master's, comprehensive exam (for some programs), thesis (for some programs). *Entrance requirements:* For master's, GRE or GMAT, minimum cumulative GPA of 3.0. Additional exam requirements/recommendations for international students: Required—TOEFL (minimum score 550 paper-based; 80 iBT) or IELTS (minimum score 6.5). *Application deadline:* For fall admission, 2/1 priority date for domestic students, 12/15 for international students. Applications are processed on a rolling basis. Application fee: $50 ($55 for international students). Electronic applications accepted. *Financial support:* Research assistantships with full and partial tuition reimbursements, institutionally sponsored loans, and unspecified assistantships available. Financial award application deadline: 2/1; financial award applicants required to submit FAFSA. *Faculty research:* Voice and data networks, with special emphasis on the interaction of technology and policy issues in the successful design, deployment, and operation of complex networks and information systems. *Total annual research expenditures:* $200,000. *Unit head:* Philip D. Campbell, Associate Professor and Director, 740-593-4907, Fax: 740-593-4889, E-mail: campbell@ohio.edu. *Application contact:* Dr. Andy Snow, Professor and Associate Director for Graduate Studies, 740-593-0421, Fax: 740-593-4889, E-mail: snowa@ohio.edu. Web site: http://www.ohio.edu/mcclure/.

Pace University, Seidenberg School of Computer Science and Information Systems, New York, NY 10038. Offers computer communications and networks (Certificate); computer science (MS); computing studies (DPS); information systems (MS); Internet technologies for e-commerce (Certificate); Internet technology (MS); object-oriented programming (Certificate); security and information assurance (Certificate); software development and engineering (MS); telecommunications (MS, Certificate). Part-time and evening/weekend programs available. *Students:* 82 full-time (19 women), 356 part-time (99 women); includes 175 minority (64 Black or African American, non-Hispanic/Latino; 1 American Indian or Alaska Native, non-Hispanic/Latino; 59 Asian, non-Hispanic/Latino; 47 Hispanic/Latino; 4 Two or more races, non-Hispanic/Latino), 72 international. Average age 37. 304 applicants, 67% accepted, 92 enrolled. In 2011, 136 master's, 9 doctorates, 32 other advanced degrees awarded. *Entrance requirements:* For master's, GRE General Test. Additional exam requirements/recommendations for international students: Required—TOEFL. *Application deadline:* For fall admission, 7/31 priority date for domestic students; for spring admission, 11/30 for domestic students. Applications are processed on a rolling basis. Application fee: $70. Electronic applications accepted. *Expenses:* Contact institution. *Financial support:* Research assistantships and career-related internships or fieldwork available. Support available to part-time students. Financial award applicants required to submit FAFSA. *Unit head:* Dr. Constance Knapp, Interim Dean, 914-773-3750, Fax: 914-773-3533, E-mail: cknapp@pace.edu. *Application contact:* Susan Ford-Goldschein, Director of Graduate Admissions, 914-422-4283, Fax: 914-422-4287, E-mail: gradwp@pace.edu. Web site: http://www.pace.edu/.

Polytechnic Institute of New York University, Department of Electrical and Computer Engineering, Major in Telecommunication Networks, Brooklyn, NY 11201-2990. Offers MS. Part-time and evening/weekend programs available. *Students:* 35 full-time (7 women), 21 part-time (4 women); includes 6 minority (3 Asian, non-Hispanic/Latino; 3 Hispanic/Latino), 43 international. 123 applicants, 45% accepted, 14 enrolled. In 2011, 21 master's awarded. *Degree requirements:* For master's, comprehensive exam (for some programs), thesis (for some programs). *Entrance requirements:* For master's, BS in electrical engineering. Additional exam requirements/recommendations for international students: Required—TOEFL (minimum score 550 paper-based; 213 computer-based; 80 iBT); Recommended—IELTS (minimum score 6.5). *Application deadline:* For fall admission, 7/31 priority date for domestic students, 4/30 for international students; for spring admission, 12/31 priority date for domestic students, 11/30 for international students. Applications are processed on a rolling basis. Application fee: $75. Electronic applications accepted. *Expenses: Tuition:* Full-time $22,464; part-time $1248 per credit. *Required fees:* $501 per semester. *Financial support:* Fellowships, research assistantships, teaching assistantships, institutionally sponsored loans, scholarships/grants, and unspecified assistantships available. Support available to part-time students. Financial award applicants required to submit FAFSA. *Unit head:* Dr. Jonathan Chao, Head, 718-260-3478, Fax: 718-260-3302, E-mail: chao@poly.edu. *Application contact:* JeanCarlo Bonilla, Director, Graduate Enrollment Management, 718-260-3182, Fax: 718-260-3624.

Polytechnic Institute of NYU, Long Island Graduate Center, Graduate Programs, Department of Electrical and Computer Engineering, Major in Telecommunication Networks, Melville, NY 11747. Offers MS. Part-time and evening/weekend programs available. In 2011, 1 master's awarded. *Degree requirements:* For master's, comprehensive exam (for some programs), thesis (for some programs). *Entrance requirements:* Additional exam requirements/recommendations for international students: Required—TOEFL (minimum score 550 paper-based; 213 computer-based; 80 iBT); Recommended—IELTS (minimum score 6.5). *Application deadline:* For fall admission, 7/31 priority date for domestic students, 4/30 for international students; for spring admission, 12/31 priority date for domestic students, 11/30 for international students. Applications are processed on a rolling basis. Application fee: $75. Electronic applications accepted. *Financial support:* Institutionally sponsored loans, scholarships/grants, and unspecified assistantships available. Support available to part-time students. Financial award applicants required to submit FAFSA. *Unit head:* Dr. Jonathan Chao,

Department Head, 718-260-3302, E-mail: chao@poly.edu. *Application contact:* JeanCarlo Bonilla, Director of Graduate Enrollment Management, 718-260-3182, Fax: 718-260-3624, E-mail: gradinfo@poly.edu.

Polytechnic Institute of NYU, Westchester Graduate Center, Graduate Programs, Department of Electrical and Computer Engineering, Major in Telecommunication Networks, Hawthorne, NY 10532-1507. Offers MS. Part-time and evening/weekend programs available. *Students:* Average age 32. In 2011, 2 master's awarded. *Degree requirements:* For master's, thesis (for some programs). *Entrance requirements:* Additional exam requirements/recommendations for international students: Required— TOEFL (minimum score 550 paper-based; 213 computer-based; 80 iBT); Recommended—IELTS (minimum score 6.5). *Application deadline:* For fall admission, 7/31 priority date for domestic students, 4/30 for international students; for spring admission, 12/31 priority date for domestic students, 11/30 for international students. Applications are processed on a rolling basis. Application fee: $75. Electronic applications accepted. *Financial support:* Institutionally sponsored loans, scholarships/ grants, and unspecified assistantships available. Support available to part-time students. *Unit head:* Dr. Jonathan Chao, Department Head, 718-260-3302, E-mail: chao@ poly.edu. *Application contact:* JeanCarlo Bonilla, Director of Graduate Enrollment Management, 718-260-3182, Fax: 718-260-3624, E-mail: gradinfo@poly.edu.

Rochester Institute of Technology, Graduate Enrollment Services, College of Applied Science and Technology, School of Engineering Technology, Department of Electrical, Computer and Telecommunications Engineering Technology, Rochester, NY 14623- 5603. Offers facility management (MS); manufacturing and mechanical systems integration (MS); telecommunications engineering technology (MS). Part-time and evening/weekend programs available. Postbaccalaureate distance learning degree programs offered (no on-campus study). *Students:* 54 full-time (13 women), 34 part-time (6 women); includes 7 minority (4 Black or African American, non-Hispanic/Latino; 1 Asian, non-Hispanic/Latino; 1 Hispanic/Latino; 1 Two or more races, non-Hispanic/ Latino), 70 international. Average age 26. 154 applicants, 55% accepted, 32 enrolled. In 2011, 24 master's awarded. *Degree requirements:* For master's, thesis. *Entrance requirements:* For master's, GRE, minimum GPA of 3.0. Additional exam requirements/ recommendations for international students: Required—TOEFL (minimum score 550 paper-based; 213 computer-based; 79 iBT) or IELTS (minimum score 6.5). *Application deadline:* For fall admission, 2/15 priority date for domestic students, 2/15 for international students; for winter admission, 11/1 for domestic and international students; for spring admission, 2/1 for domestic and international students. Applications are processed on a rolling basis. Application fee: $50. Electronic applications accepted. *Expenses: Tuition:* Full-time $34,659; part-time $963 per credit hour. *Required fees:* $228; $76 per quarter. *Financial support:* Research assistantships with partial tuition reimbursements, teaching assistantships with partial tuition reimbursements, career-related internships or fieldwork, and unspecified assistantships available. Support available to part-time students. Financial award application deadline: 2/15; financial award applicants required to submit FAFSA. *Faculty research:* Fiber optic networks, next generation networks, project management. *Unit head:* Michael Eastman, Department Chair, 585-475-7787, Fax: 585-475-2178, E-mail: mgeiee@rit.edu. *Application contact:* Diane Ellison, Assistant Vice President, Graduate Enrollment Services, 585-475-2229, Fax: 585-475-7164, E-mail: gradinfo@rit.edu. Web site: http:// www.rit.edu/cast/ectet/.

Roosevelt University, Graduate Division, College of Arts and Sciences, Department of Computer Science and Telecommunications, Program in Telecommunications, Chicago, IL 60605. Offers MST. Part-time and evening/weekend programs available. *Entrance requirements:* For master's, GRE. *Faculty research:* Coding theory, mathematical models, network design, simulation models.

Saint Mary's University of Minnesota, Schools of Graduate and Professional Programs, Graduate School of Business and Technology, Information Technology Management Program, Winona, MN 55987-1399. Offers MS. *Unit head:* Paula Justich, Director, 612-728-5165, E-mail: pjustich@smumn.edu. *Application contact:* Yasin Alsaidi, Director of Admissions for Graduate and Professional Programs, 612-728-5207, Fax: 612-728-5121, E-mail: yalsaidi@smumn.edu. Web site: http://www.smumn.edu/ graduate-home/areas-of-study/graduate-school-of-business-technology/ms-in-information-technology-management.

Southern Methodist University, Bobby B. Lyle School of Engineering, Department of Electrical Engineering, Dallas, TX 75275-0338. Offers electrical engineering (MSEE, PhD); telecommunications (MS). Part-time and evening/weekend programs available. Postbaccalaureate distance learning degree programs offered (no on-campus study). Terminal master's awarded for partial completion of doctoral program. *Degree requirements:* For master's, thesis optional; for doctorate, thesis/dissertation, oral and written qualifying exams, oral final exam. *Entrance requirements:* For master's, GRE General Test, minimum GPA of 3.0 in last 2 years; bachelor's degree in engineering, mathematics, or sciences; for doctorate, preliminary counseling exam, minimum GPA of 3.0, bachelor's degree in related field. Additional exam requirements/recommendations for international students: Required—TOEFL. Electronic applications accepted. *Faculty research:* Mobile communications, optical communications, digital signal processing, photonics.

State University of New York Institute of Technology, Program in Telecommunications, Utica, NY 13504-3050. Offers MS. Part-time and evening/ weekend programs available. *Degree requirements:* For master's, thesis, project or capstone. *Entrance requirements:* For master's, GRE General Test, minimum GPA of 3.0, letters of recommendation (3). Additional exam requirements/recommendations for international students: Required—TOEFL (minimum score 550 paper-based; 213 computer-based). *Faculty research:* Network design/simulation/management, wireless telecommunication systems, international telecommunications policy and management, information assurance, disaster recovery.

Stevens Institute of Technology, Graduate School, Wesley J. Howe School of Technology Management, Program in Telecommunications Management, Hoboken, NJ 07030. Offers business (MS); global innovation management (MS); management of wireless networks (MS); online security, technology and business (MS); project management (MS); technical management (MS); telecommunications management (PhD, Certificate). *Degree requirements:* For master's, thesis optional; for doctorate, thesis/dissertation. *Entrance requirements:* For master's and doctorate, GMAT, GRE General Test. Additional exam requirements/recommendations for international students: Required—TOEFL. Electronic applications accepted.

Stratford University, School of Graduate Studies, Falls Church, VA 22043. Offers accounting (MS); business administration (IMBA, MBA); enterprise business management (MS); entrepreneurial management (MS); information assurance (MS); information systems (MS); software engineering (MS); telecommunications (MS). Part-time and evening/weekend programs available. Postbaccalaureate distance learning degree programs offered (no on-campus study). *Degree requirements:* For master's, comprehensive exam, capstone project. *Entrance requirements:* For master's, GRE or

GMAT, baccalaureate degree. Additional exam requirements/recommendations for international students: Required—TOEFL (minimum score 213 computer-based, 79 iBT) or IELTS (6.5). Electronic applications accepted.

Syracuse University, School of Information Studies, Program in Telecommunications and Network Management, Syracuse, NY 13244. Offers MS, MS/CAS. Part-time and evening/weekend programs available. Postbaccalaureate distance learning degree programs offered (minimal on-campus study). *Students:* 45 full-time (10 women), 25 part-time (6 women); includes 12 minority (3 Black or African American, non-Hispanic/ Latino; 4 Asian, non-Hispanic/Latino; 5 Hispanic/Latino), 38 international. Average age 29. 78 applicants, 68% accepted, 28 enrolled. In 2011, 30 degrees awarded. *Degree requirements:* For master's, internship or research project. *Entrance requirements:* For master's, GRE General Test. Additional exam requirements/recommendations for international students: Required—TOEFL (minimum score 100 iBT). *Application deadline:* For fall admission, 2/1 priority date for domestic students, 2/1 for international students; for spring admission, 10/15 priority date for domestic students, 10/15 for international students. Applications are processed on a rolling basis. Application fee: $75. Electronic applications accepted. *Expenses: Tuition:* Part-time $1206 per credit. *Financial support:* Fellowships with full tuition reimbursements, research assistantships with partial tuition reimbursements, teaching assistantships with partial tuition reimbursements, career-related internships or fieldwork, and Federal Work-Study available. Financial award application deadline: 1/1. *Faculty research:* Multimedia, information resources management. *Unit head:* Prof. Martha Garcia-Marillo, Director, 315-443-2911, Fax: 315-443-6886, E-mail: mgarciam@syr.edu. *Application contact:* Susan Corieri, Director of Enrollment Management, 315-443-2575, E-mail: ischool@ syr.edu. Web site: http://ischool.syr.edu/.

Universidad del Turabo, Graduate Programs, School of Engineering, Program in Telecommunication and Network Administration, Gurabo, PR 00778-3030. Offers MS. *Students:* 18 full-time (0 women), 16 part-time (1 woman); includes 28 minority (all Hispanic/Latino). Average age 32. 25 applicants, 72% accepted, 15 enrolled. In 2011, 8 master's awarded. *Unit head:* David Mendez, Head, 787-743-7979. *Application contact:* Virginia Gonzalez, Admissions Officer, 787-746-3009.

Université du Québec, Institut National de la Recherche Scientifique, Graduate Programs, Research Center - Energy, Materials and Telecommunications, Québec, QC G1K 9A9, Canada. Offers energy and materials science (M Sc, PhD); telecommunications (M Sc, PhD). Programs given in French; PhD programs offered jointly with Université du Québec à Trois-Rivières. Part-time programs available. *Faculty:* 39. *Students:* 175 full-time (71 women), 19 part-time (4 women), 107 international. Average age 32. In 2011, 12 master's, 17 doctorates awarded. *Degree requirements:* For master's, thesis optional; for doctorate, thesis/dissertation. *Entrance requirements:* For master's, appropriate bachelor's degree, proficiency in French; for doctorate, appropriate master's degree, proficiency in French. *Application deadline:* For fall admission, 3/30 for domestic and international students; for winter admission, 11/1 for domestic and international students; for spring admission, 3/1 for domestic and international students. Application fee: $45. *Financial support:* In 2011–12, 141 students received support, including fellowships (averaging $16,500 per year); research assistantships also available. *Faculty research:* New energy sources, plasmas, fusion. *Unit head:* Frederico Rosei, Director, 450-228-6905, E-mail: rosei@emt.inrs.ca. *Application contact:* Yvonne Boisvert, Registrar, 418-654-3861, Fax: 418-654-3858, E-mail: registrariat@adm.inrs.ca. Web site: http://www.inrs.ca/english/research-centres/ energie-materiaux-telecommunications-research-centre.

University of Alberta, Faculty of Graduate Studies and Research, Department of Electrical and Computer Engineering, Edmonton, AB T6G 2E1, Canada. Offers communications (M Eng, M Sc, PhD); computer engineering (M Eng, M Sc, PhD); electromagnetics (M Eng, M Sc, PhD); nanotechnology and microdevices (M Eng, M Sc, PhD); power/power electronics (M Eng, M Sc, PhD); systems (M Eng, M Sc, PhD). Terminal master's awarded for partial completion of doctoral program. *Degree requirements:* For master's, thesis; for doctorate, thesis/dissertation. *Entrance requirements:* Additional exam requirements/recommendations for international students: Required—TOEFL. Electronic applications accepted. *Faculty research:* Controls, communications, microelectronics, electromagnetics.

University of Arkansas, Graduate School, College of Engineering, Department of Electrical Engineering, Fayetteville, AR 72701-1201. Offers electrical engineering (MSEE, PhD); telecommunications engineering (MS Tc E). *Students:* 14 full-time (3 women), 65 part-time (7 women); includes 5 minority (4 Black or African American, non-Hispanic/Latino; 1 Asian, non-Hispanic/Latino), 47 international. In 2011, 12 master's awarded. *Degree requirements:* For master's, thesis optional; for doctorate, one foreign language, thesis/dissertation. *Entrance requirements:* For master's and doctorate, GRE General Test. *Application deadline:* For fall admission, 4/1 for international students; for spring admission, 10/1 for international students. Applications are processed on a rolling basis. Application fee: $40 ($50 for international students). Electronic applications accepted. *Financial support:* In 2011–12, 48 research assistantships, 8 teaching assistantships were awarded; fellowships with tuition reimbursements, career-related internships or fieldwork, and Federal Work-Study also available. Support available to part-time students. Financial award application deadline: 4/1; financial award applicants required to submit FAFSA. *Unit head:* Dr. Juan Balda, Department Chair, 479-575-3005, Fax: 479-575-7967, E-mail: jbalda@uark.edu. *Application contact:* Dr. Randy Brown, Graduate Coordinator, 479-575-6581, E-mail: rlb02@uark.edu. Web site: http:// www.eleg.uark.edu/.

University of California, San Diego, Office of Graduate Studies, Department of Electrical and Computer Engineering, La Jolla, CA 92093. Offers applied ocean science (MS, PhD); applied physics (MS, PhD); communication theory and systems (MS, PhD); computer engineering (MS, PhD); electrical engineering (M Eng); electronic circuits and systems (MS, PhD); intelligent systems, robotics and control (MS, PhD); photonics (MS, PhD); signal and image processing (MS, PhD). MS only offered to students who have been admitted to the PhD program. *Entrance requirements:* For master's and doctorate, GRE General Test. Electronic applications accepted.

University of California, Santa Cruz, Division of Graduate Studies, Jack Baskin School of Engineering, Program in Computer Engineering, Santa Cruz, CA 95064. Offers computer engineering (MS, PhD); network engineering (MS). Part-time programs available. Terminal master's awarded for partial completion of doctoral program. *Degree requirements:* For master's, thesis; for doctorate, comprehensive exam, thesis/ dissertation, oral qualifying exams. *Entrance requirements:* For master's and doctorate, GRE General Test, GRE Subject Test. Additional exam requirements/recommendations for international students: Required—TOEFL (minimum score 570 paper-based; 230 computer-based; 89 iBT); Recommended—IELTS (minimum score 8). Electronic applications accepted. *Faculty research:* Computer-aided design of digital systems, networks, robotics and control, sensing and interaction.

University of Colorado Boulder, Graduate School, College of Engineering and Applied Science, Interdisciplinary Telecommunications Program, Boulder, CO 80309. Offers

MS, JD/MS, MBA/MS. *Students:* 88 full-time (11 women), 28 part-time (2 women); includes 6 minority (3 Asian, non-Hispanic/Latino; 3 Hispanic/Latino), 72 international. Average age 29. 166 applicants, 56% accepted, 34 enrolled. In 2011, 46 master's awarded. Terminal master's awarded for partial completion of doctoral program. *Degree requirements:* For master's, comprehensive exam, thesis or alternative. *Entrance requirements:* For master's, minimum undergraduate GPA of 3.0. *Application deadline:* For fall admission, 6/15 priority date for domestic students, 3/15 for international students; for spring admission, 11/1 for domestic students, 10/1 for international students. Applications are processed on a rolling basis. Application fee: $50 ($60 for international students). Electronic applications accepted. *Financial support:* In 2011–12, 16 students received support, including 20 fellowships (averaging $11,969 per year), 1 research assistantship with full and partial tuition reimbursement available (averaging $11,842 per year), 2 teaching assistantships with full and partial tuition reimbursements available (averaging $5,893 per year); institutionally sponsored loans, scholarships/grants, health care benefits, and unspecified assistantships also available. Financial award applicants required to submit FAFSA. *Faculty research:* Technology, planning, and management of telecommunications systems. *Total annual research expenditures:* $35,450. *Application contact:* E-mail: itp@colorado.edu. Web site: http://itp.colorado.edu/.

University of Denver, University College, Denver, CO 80208. Offers arts and culture (MLS, Certificate), including art, literature, and culture, arts development and program management (Certificate), creative writing; environmental policy and management (MAS, Certificate), including energy and sustainability (Certificate), environmental assessment of nuclear power (Certificate), environmental health and safety (Certificate), environmental management, natural resource management (Certificate); geographic information systems (MAS, Certificate); global affairs (MLS, Certificate), including translation studies, world history and culture; healthcare leadership (MPH, Certificate), including healthcare policy, law, and ethics, medical and healthcare information technologies, strategic management of healthcare; information and communications technology (MCIS, Certificate), including database design and administration (Certificate), geographic information systems (MCIS), information security systems security (Certificate), information systems security (MCIS), project management (MCIS, MPS, Certificate), software design and administration (Certificate), software design and programming (MCIS), technology management, telecommunications technology (MCIS), Web design and development; leadership and organizations (MPS, Certificate), including human capital in organizations, philanthropic leadership, project management (MCIS, MPS, Certificate), strategic innovation and change; organizational and professional communication (MPS, Certificate), including alternative dispute resolution, organizational communication, organizational development and training, public relations and marketing; security management (MAS, Certificate), including emergency planning and response, information security (MAS), organizational security; strategic human resource management (MPS, Certificate), including global human resources (MPS), human resource management and development (MPS). Part-time and evening/weekend programs available. Postbaccalaureate distance learning degree programs offered (no on-campus study). *Faculty:* 204 part-time/adjunct (80 women). *Students:* 56 full-time (26 women), 1,096 part-time (647 women); includes 196 minority (81 Black or African American, non-Hispanic/Latino; 7 American Indian or Alaska Native, non-Hispanic/Latino; 30 Asian, non-Hispanic/Latino; 66 Hispanic/Latino; 3 Native Hawaiian or other Pacific Islander, non-Hispanic/Latino; 9 Two or more races, non-Hispanic/Latino), 76 international. Average age 36. 572 applicants, 95% accepted, 410 enrolled. In 2011, 404 master's, 123 other advanced degrees awarded. *Degree requirements:* For master's, capstone project. *Entrance requirements:* For master's, two letters of recommendation, personal statement, resume. Additional exam requirements/recommendations for international students: Required—TOEFL (minimum score 550 paper-based; 80 iBT). *Application deadline:* For fall admission, 7/20 priority date for domestic students, 6/8 for international students; for winter admission, 10/26 priority date for domestic students, 9/14 for international students; for spring admission, 2/1 priority date for domestic students, 12/14 for international students. Applications are processed on a rolling basis. Application fee: $75. Electronic applications accepted. *Expenses:* Contact institution. *Financial support:* Applicants required to submit FAFSA. *Unit head:* Dr. James Davis, Dean, 303-871-2291, Fax: 303-871-4047, E-mail: jdavis@du.edu. *Application contact:* Information Contact, 303-871-3155, Fax: 303-871-4047, E-mail: ucolinfo@du.edu. Web site: http://www.universitycollege.du.edu/.

University of Hawaii at Manoa, Graduate Division, College of Social Sciences, School of Communications, Program in Telecommunication and Information Resource Management, Honolulu, HI 96822. Offers Graduate Certificate. Part-time programs available. *Entrance requirements:* Additional exam requirements/recommendations for international students: Required—TOEFL (minimum score 500 paper-based; 173 computer-based; 61 iBT), IELTS (minimum score 5).

University of Houston, College of Technology, Department of Engineering Technology, Houston, TX 77204. Offers construction management (MS); engineering technology (MS); network communications (M Tech). Part-time programs available. *Degree requirements:* For master's, project or thesis (most programs). *Entrance requirements:* For master's, GRE. Additional exam requirements/recommendations for international students: Required—TOEFL (minimum score 550 paper-based; 79 iBT). Electronic applications accepted.

University of Louisiana at Lafayette, College of Engineering, Department of Electrical and Computer Engineering, Program in Telecommunications, Lafayette, LA 70504. Offers MSTC. *Degree requirements:* For master's, thesis or alternative. *Entrance requirements:* For master's, GRE General Test, minimum GPA of 2.75. Additional exam requirements/recommendations for international students: Required—TOEFL (minimum score 550 paper-based; 213 computer-based). Electronic applications accepted.

University of Maryland, College Park, Academic Affairs, A. James Clark School of Engineering, Department of Electrical and Computer Engineering, Program in Telecommunications, College Park, MD 20742. Offers MS. Part-time and evening/weekend programs available. *Students:* 207 full-time (55 women), 27 part-time (4 women); includes 22 minority (6 Black or African American, non-Hispanic/Latino; 10 Asian, non-Hispanic/Latino; 6 Hispanic/Latino), 199 international. 489 applicants, 58% accepted, 135 enrolled. In 2011, 57 master's awarded. *Degree requirements:* For master's, thesis or alternative. *Entrance requirements:* For master's, GRE General Test, minimum GPA of 3.0, professional experience. Additional exam requirements/recommendations for international students: Required—TOEFL. *Application deadline:* For fall admission, 5/1 for domestic students, 2/1 for international students. Applications are processed on a rolling basis. Application fee: $75. Electronic applications accepted. *Expenses: Tuition, area resident:* Part-time $525 per credit hour. Tuition, state resident: part-time $525 per credit hour. Tuition, nonresident: part-time $1131 per credit hour. *Required fees:* $386.31 per term. Tuition and fees vary according to program. *Financial support:* In 2011–12, 2 fellowships with full and partial tuition reimbursements (averaging $17,500 per year), 7 research assistantships (averaging $17,386 per year), 26 teaching assistantships (averaging $15,917 per year) were awarded. Financial award applicants required to submit FAFSA. *Unit head:* Dr. Zoltan Safar, Director, 301-405-5779, E-mail: zsafar@umd.edu. *Application contact:* Charles A. Caramello, Dean of Graduate School, 301-405-0358, Fax: 301-314-9305, E-mail: ccaramel@umd.edu.

University of Massachusetts Dartmouth, Graduate School, College of Engineering, Department of Electrical and Computer Engineering, North Dartmouth, MA 02747-2300. Offers acoustics (Postbaccalaureate Certificate); communications (Postbaccalaureate Certificate); computer engineering (MS, PhD); computer systems engineering (Postbaccalaureate Certificate); digital signal processing (Postbaccalaureate Certificate); electrical engineering (MS, PhD); electrical engineering systems (Postbaccalaureate Certificate). Part-time programs available. *Faculty:* 15 full-time (3 women), 4 part-time/adjunct (1 woman). *Students:* 37 full-time (5 women), 52 part-time (8 women); includes 9 minority (2 Black or African American, non-Hispanic/Latino; 2 Asian, non-Hispanic/Latino; 1 Hispanic/Latino; 4 Two or more races, non-Hispanic/Latino), 45 international. Average age 29. 83 applicants, 93% accepted, 26 enrolled. In 2011, 17 master's, 1 doctorate awarded. *Degree requirements:* For master's, culminating project or thesis; for doctorate, comprehensive exam, thesis/dissertation. *Entrance requirements:* For master's, GRE, minimum undergraduate GPA of 3.0, 3 letters of recommendation, statement of intent, resume; for doctorate, GRE, 3 letters of recommendation, resume, statement of intent; for Postbaccalaureate Certificate, 3 letters of recommendation, resume, statement of intent. Additional exam requirements/recommendations for international students: Required—TOEFL (minimum score 533 paper-based; 200 computer-based; 72 iBT). *Application deadline:* For fall admission, 2/15 priority date for domestic students, 1/15 for international students; for spring admission, 11/1 priority date for domestic students, 10/1 for international students. Applications are processed on a rolling basis. Application fee: $40 ($60 for international students). Electronic applications accepted. *Expenses:* Tuition, state resident: full-time $2071; part-time $86.29 per credit. Tuition, nonresident: full-time $8099; part-time $337.46 per credit. *Required fees:* $438.58 per credit. Part-time tuition and fees vary according to class time, course load, degree level and reciprocity agreements. *Financial support:* In 2011–12, 10 research assistantships with full tuition reimbursements (averaging $12,720 per year), 14 teaching assistantships with full tuition reimbursements (averaging $10,385 per year) were awarded; fellowships, Federal Work-Study, and unspecified assistantships also available. Support available to part-time students. Financial award application deadline: 3/1; financial award applicants required to submit FAFSA. *Faculty research:* Speech acoustics, marine applications, signals and systems, applied electromagnetics, intelligent agency. *Total annual research expenditures:* $921,048. *Unit head:* Dr. Karen Payton, Graduate Program Director, 508-999-8434, Fax: 508-999-8489, E-mail: kpayton@umassd.edu. *Application contact:* Elan Turcotte-Shamski, Graduate Admissions Officer, 508-999-8604, Fax: 508-999-8183, E-mail: graduate@umassd.edu. Web site: http://www.umassd.edu/engineering/ece/graduate/welcome.cfm.

University of Missouri–Kansas City, School of Computing and Engineering, Kansas City, MO 64110-2499. Offers civil engineering (MS); computer and electrical engineering (PhD); computer science (MS), including bioinformatics, software engineering, telecommunications networking; computer science and informatics (PhD); computing (PhD); electrical engineering (MS); engineering (PhD); mechanical engineering (MS); telecommunications (PhD). PhD (interdisciplinary) offered through the School of Graduate Studies. Part-time programs available. *Faculty:* 36 full-time (6 women), 27 part-time/adjunct (3 women). *Students:* 155 full-time (44 women), 136 part-time (24 women); includes 19 minority (4 Black or African American, non-Hispanic/Latino; 7 Asian, non-Hispanic/Latino; 6 Hispanic/Latino; 2 Two or more races, non-Hispanic/Latino), 201 international. Average age 26. 455 applicants, 46% accepted, 96 enrolled. In 2011, 194 degrees awarded. *Degree requirements:* For doctorate, thesis/dissertation. *Entrance requirements:* For master's, GRE General Test, minimum GPA of 3.0, 3 letters of recommendation from professors; for doctorate, GRE General Test, minimum GPA of 3.5. Additional exam requirements/recommendations for international students: Required—TOEFL (minimum score 550 paper-based; 213 computer-based; 80 iBT). *Application deadline:* For fall admission, 1/15 priority date for domestic students, 1/15 for international students. Applications are processed on a rolling basis. Application fee: $45 ($50 for international students). *Expenses:* Tuition, state resident: full-time $5798; part-time $322.10 per credit hour. Tuition, nonresident: full-time $14,969; part-time $831.60 per credit hour. *Required fees:* $93.51 per credit hour. *Financial support:* In 2011–12, 47 research assistantships with partial tuition reimbursements (averaging $13,190 per year), 10 teaching assistantships with partial tuition reimbursements (averaging $9,815 per year) were awarded; career-related internships or fieldwork, Federal Work-Study, scholarships/grants, tuition waivers (partial), and unspecified assistantships also available. Support available to part-time students. Financial award application deadline: 3/1; financial award applicants required to submit FAFSA. *Faculty research:* Algorithms, bioinformatics and medical informatics, biomechanics/biomaterials, civil engineering materials, networking and telecommunications, thermal science. *Unit head:* Dr. Kevin Z. Truman, Dean, 816-235-2399, Fax: 816-235-5159. *Application contact:* 816-235-2399, Fax: 816-235-5159. Web site: http://sce.umkc.edu/.

University of Oklahoma, College of Engineering, Department of Electrical and Computer Engineering, Program in Telecommunications Engineering, Tulsa, OK 74135. Offers MS. Part-time programs available. *Students:* 9 full-time (5 women), 5 part-time (2 women), 13 international. Average age 24. 20 applicants, 95% accepted, 8 enrolled. In 2011, 2 degrees awarded. *Entrance requirements:* Additional exam requirements/recommendations for international students: Required—TOEFL (minimum score 550 paper-based; 79 iBT). *Application deadline:* For fall admission, 4/1 for domestic students, 3/1 for international students; for spring admission, 11/1 for domestic students, 9/1 for international students. Application fee: $40 ($90 for international students). Electronic applications accepted. *Expenses:* Tuition, state resident: full-time $4087; part-time $170.30 per credit hour. Tuition, nonresident: full-time $14,875; part-time $619.80 per credit hour. *Required fees:* $2659; $100.25 per credit hour. Tuition and fees vary according to course load and degree level. *Financial support:* In 2011–12, 6 students received support. Career-related internships or fieldwork, scholarships/grants, health care benefits, tuition waivers (partial), and unspecified assistantships available. *Faculty research:* Optical communications and networks, wireless communications and networking, telecommunications security, photonic systems, information theory. *Unit head:* Dr. James Sluss, Director, 405-325-4721, Fax: 405-325-7066, E-mail: sluss@ou.edu. *Application contact:* Pramode Verma, Director/Graduate Liaison, 918-660-3236, Fax: 918-660-3238, E-mail: pverma@ou.edu. Web site: http://tcom.ou.edu.

University of Pennsylvania, School of Engineering and Applied Science, Telecommunications and Networking Program, Philadelphia, PA 19104. Offers MSE. Part-time programs available. *Students:* 64 full-time (18 women), 6 part-time (2 women); includes 4 minority (1 Black or African American, non-Hispanic/Latino; 3 Asian, non-Hispanic/Latino), 65 international. 247 applicants, 42% accepted, 43 enrolled. In 2011, 34 master's awarded. *Application deadline:* For fall admission, 6/1 for domestic students, 5/1 for international students; for spring admission, 11/1 for domestic students, 10/1 for international students. Application fee: $70. Electronic applications accepted.

Expenses: *Tuition:* Full-time $26,660; part-time $4944 per course. *Required fees:* $2318; $291 per course. Tuition and fees vary according to course load, degree level and program. *Unit head:* Eduardo D. Glandt, Dean, 215-898-7244, Fax: 215-573-2018, E-mail: seasdean@seas.upenn.edu. *Application contact:* 215-898-0696, E-mail: tcom@seas.upenn.edu. Web site: http://www.seas.upenn.edu/profprog/tcom//.

University of Pittsburgh, School of Information Sciences, Telecommunications and Networking Program, Pittsburgh, PA 15260. Offers MST, PhD, Certificate. Part-time and evening/weekend programs available. *Faculty:* 6 full-time (0 women), 1 part-time/adjunct (0 women). *Students:* 37 full-time (11 women), 15 part-time (2 women); includes 3 minority (1 Black or African American, non-Hispanic/Latino; 2 Asian, non-Hispanic/Latino), 36 international. 63 applicants, 86% accepted, 15 enrolled. In 2011, 21 master's, 1 doctorate, 1 other advanced degree awarded. *Degree requirements:* For master's, thesis optional; for doctorate, comprehensive exam, thesis/dissertation. *Entrance requirements:* For master's, GRE General Test, undergraduate degree with minimum GPA of 3.0; previous course work in computer programming, calculus, and probability; for doctorate, GRE, master's degree; minimum GPA of 3.3; course work in computer programming (2 languages), differential and integral calculus, and probability and statistics; for Certificate, MSIS, MST from accredited university. Additional exam requirements/recommendations for international students: Required—TOEFL (minimum score 550 paper-based; 0 computer-based; 80 iBT). *Application deadline:* For fall admission, 1/15 priority date for domestic students, 1/15 for international students; for winter admission, 9/15 priority date for domestic students, 6/15 for international students; for spring admission, 1/15 priority date for domestic students, 12/15 for international students. Applications are processed on a rolling basis. Application fee: $50. Electronic applications accepted. *Expenses:* Contact institution. *Financial support:* Fellowships with full and partial tuition reimbursements, research assistantships with full and partial tuition reimbursements, teaching assistantships, career-related internships or fieldwork, scholarships/grants, health care benefits, tuition waivers (full and partial), and unspecified assistantships available. Financial award application deadline: 1/15; financial award applicants required to submit FAFSA. *Faculty research:* Telecommunication systems, telecommunications policy, network design and management, wireless information systems, network security. *Unit head:* Dr. David Tipper, Program Chair, 412-624-9421, Fax: 412-624-2788, E-mail: tipper@tele.pitt.edu. *Application contact:* Shabana Reza, Student Recruiting Coordinator, 412-624-3988, Fax: 412-624-5231, E-mail: teleinq@sis.pitt.edu. Web site: http://www.ischool.pitt.edu/tele/.

University of Southern California, Graduate School, Viterbi School of Engineering, Daniel J. Epstein Department of Industrial and Systems Engineering, Los Angeles, CA 90089. Offers digital supply chain management (MS); engineering management (MS); engineering technology communication (Graduate Certificate); health systems operations (Graduate Certificate); industrial and systems engineering (MS, PhD, Engr); manufacturing engineering (MS); operations research engineering (MS); optimization and supply chain management (Graduate Certificate); product development engineering (MS); safety systems and security (MS); systems architecting and engineering (MS, Graduate Certificate); systems safety and security (Graduate Certificate); transportation systems (Graduate Certificate); MS/MBA. Part-time and evening/weekend programs available. Postbaccalaureate distance learning degree programs offered (no on-campus study). Terminal master's awarded for partial completion of doctoral program. *Degree requirements:* For master's, thesis optional; for doctorate, thesis/dissertation. *Entrance requirements:* For master's and doctorate, GRE General Test. Additional exam requirements/recommendations for international students: Recommended—TOEFL. Electronic applications accepted. *Faculty research:* Health systems, music cognition and retrieval, transportation and logistics, manufacturing and automation, engineering systems design, risk and economic analysis.

University of Southern California, Graduate School, Viterbi School of Engineering, Ming Hsieh Department of Electrical Engineering, Los Angeles, CA 90089. Offers computer engineering (MS, PhD); electric power (MS); electrical engineering (MS, PhD, Engr); engineering technology commercialization (Graduate Certificate); multimedia and creative technologies (MS); telecommunications (MS); VLSI design (MS); wireless health technology (MS). Part-time programs available. Postbaccalaureate distance learning degree programs offered (no on-campus study). Terminal master's awarded for partial completion of doctoral program. *Degree requirements:* For master's, thesis optional; for doctorate, thesis/dissertation. *Entrance requirements:* For master's and doctorate, GRE General Test. Additional exam requirements/recommendations for international students: Recommended—TOEFL. Electronic applications accepted. *Faculty research:* Communications, computer engineering and networks, control systems, integrated circuits and systems, electromagnetics and energy conversion, micro electro-mechanical systems and nanotechnology, photonics and quantum electronics, plasma research, signal and image processing.

The University of Texas at Dallas, Erik Jonsson School of Engineering and Computer Science, Department of Electrical Engineering, Richardson, TX 75080. Offers computer engineering (MS, PhD); electrical engineering (MSEE, PhD); systems engineering and management (MS); telecommunications (MSTE, PhD). Part-time and evening/weekend programs available. *Faculty:* 44 full-time (2 women), 4 part-time/adjunct (0 women). *Students:* 510 full-time (108 women), 279 part-time (53 women); includes 110 minority (17 Black or African American, non-Hispanic/Latino; 65 Asian, non-Hispanic/Latino; 25 Hispanic/Latino; 3 Two or more races, non-Hispanic/Latino), 555 international. Average age 27. 1,933 applicants, 42% accepted, 265 enrolled. In 2011, 168 master's, 30 doctorates awarded. *Degree requirements:* For master's, thesis or major design project; for doctorate, thesis/dissertation. *Entrance requirements:* For master's, GRE General Test, minimum GPA of 3.0 in related bachelor's degree; for doctorate, GRE General Test, minimum GPA of 3.5. Additional exam requirements/recommendations for international students: Required—TOEFL (minimum score 550 paper-based; 215 computer-based). *Application deadline:* For fall admission, 7/15 for domestic students, 5/1 for international students; for spring admission, 11/15 for domestic students, 9/1 for international students. Applications are processed on a rolling basis. Application fee: $50 ($100 for international students). Electronic applications accepted. *Expenses:* Tuition, state resident: full-time $11,170; part-time $620.56 per credit hour. Tuition, nonresident: full-time $20,212; part-time $1122.89 per credit hour. *Financial support:* In 2011–12, 224 students received support, including 132 research assistantships with partial tuition reimbursements available (averaging $21,532 per year), 47 teaching assistantships with partial tuition reimbursements available (averaging $14,850 per year); fellowships with partial tuition reimbursements available, Federal Work-Study, institutionally sponsored loans, scholarships/grants, unspecified assistantships, and cooperative positions also available. Support available to part-time students. Financial award application deadline: 4/30; financial award applicants required to submit FAFSA. *Faculty research:* Semiconductor device manufacturing, photonics devices and systems, signal processing and language technology, nano-fabrication, energy efficient digital systems. *Unit head:* Dr. John H. L. Hansen, Department Head, 972-883-6755, Fax: 972-883-2710, E-mail: john.hansen@utdallas.edu. *Application contact:* Kathy Gribble, Graduate Program Coordinator, 972-883-2649, Fax: 972-883-2710, E-mail: gradecs@utdallas.edu. Web site: http://www.ee.utdallas.edu.

Widener University, Graduate Programs in Engineering, Program Telecommunications Engineering, Chester, PA 19013-5792. Offers M Eng. Part-time and evening/weekend programs available. *Degree requirements:* For master's, thesis optional. *Faculty research:* Signal and image processing, electromagnetics, telecommunications and computer network.

Telecommunications Management

Alaska Pacific University, Graduate Programs, Business Administration Department, Programs in Information and Communication Technology, Anchorage, AK 99508-4672. Offers MBAICT. Part-time and evening/weekend programs available. *Degree requirements:* For master's, capstone course. *Entrance requirements:* For master's, GMAT or GRE General Test, minimum GPA of 3.0.

Boston University, Metropolitan College, Department of Computer Science, Boston, MA 02215. Offers computer information systems (MS), including computer networks, database management and business intelligence, health informatics, IT project management, security, Web application development; computer science (MS), including computer networks, security; telecommunications (MS), including security. Evening/weekend programs available. Postbaccalaureate distance learning degree programs offered. *Faculty:* 12 full-time (2 women), 28 part-time/adjunct (2 women). *Students:* 25 full-time (6 women), 732 part-time (167 women); includes 208 minority (51 Black or African American, non-Hispanic/Latino; 1 American Indian or Alaska Native, non-Hispanic/Latino; 104 Asian, non-Hispanic/Latino; 43 Hispanic/Latino; 1 Native Hawaiian or other Pacific Islander, non-Hispanic/Latino; 8 Two or more races, non-Hispanic/Latino), 86 international. Average age 35. 260 applicants, 67% accepted, 143 enrolled. In 2011, 143 master's awarded. *Degree requirements:* For master's, thesis optional. *Entrance requirements:* For master's, 3 letters of recommendation, professional resume. Additional exam requirements/recommendations for international students: Required—TOEFL (minimum score 550 paper-based; 213 computer-based; 80 iBT). *Application deadline:* For fall admission, 6/1 for international students; for spring admission, 10/1 for international students. Applications are processed on a rolling basis. Application fee: $70. Electronic applications accepted. *Expenses:* *Tuition:* Full-time $40,848; part-time $1276 per credit hour. *Required fees:* $572; $286 per semester. *Financial support:* In 2011–12, 9 research assistantships (averaging $5,000 per year) were awarded; career-related internships or fieldwork and unspecified assistantships also available. Support available to part-time students. Financial award applicants required to submit FAFSA. *Faculty research:* Medical informatics, Web technologies, telecom and networks, security and forensics, software engineering, programming languages, multimedia and AI, information systems and IT project management. *Unit head:* Dr. Lubomir Chitkushev, Chairman, 617-353-2566, Fax: 617-353-2367, E-mail: csinfo@bu.edu. *Application contact:* Kim Richards, Program Coordinator, 617-353-2566, Fax: 617-353-2367, E-mail: kimrich@bu.edu. Web site: http://www.bu.edu/csmet/.

California Miramar University, Program in Telecommunications Management, San Diego, CA 92126. Offers MST.

Capitol College, Graduate Programs, Laurel, MD 20708-9759. Offers business administration (MBA); computer science (MS); electrical engineering (MS); information and telecommunications systems management (MS); information architecture (MS); network security (MS). Part-time and evening/weekend programs available. Postbaccalaureate distance learning degree programs offered (no on-campus study). *Entrance requirements:* For master's, minimum GPA of 3.0. Electronic applications accepted.

Carnegie Mellon University, Carnegie Institute of Technology, Information Networking Institute, Pittsburgh, PA 15213. Offers information networking (MS); information security technology and management (MS); information technology - information security (MS); information technology - mobility (MS); information technology - software management (MS). *Degree requirements:* For master's, thesis optional. *Entrance requirements:* For master's, GRE General Test, bachelor's degree in computer science, computer engineering, or electrical engineering, or related technology degree; programming skills (C/C++ fluency for some programs). Additional exam requirements/recommendations for international students: Required—TOEFL. *Faculty research:* Computer forensics and incident response; dependable systems, embedded systems, mobile systems, and sensor networks; computer and information networks, network and information security, human and socio-economic factors in secure system design; wireless sensor networks, survivable embedded systems, signal processing/compression; strategic management, international strategic management, group dynamics and decision-making structures, simulated competitive environments.

Concordia University, School of Graduate Studies, Faculty of Engineering and Computer Science, Concordia Institute for Information Systems Engineering (CIISE), Montréal, QC H3G 1M8, Canada. Offers 3D graphics and game development (Certificate); information systems security (M Eng, MA Sc); quality systems engineering (M Eng, MA Sc); service engineering and network management (Certificate).

George Mason University, Volgenau School of Engineering, Department of Electrical and Computer Engineering, Fairfax, VA 22030. Offers advanced networking protocols for telecommunications (Certificate); communications and networking (Certificate); computer engineering (MS); computer forensics (MS); electrical and computer engineering (PhD); electrical engineering (MS); network technology and applications (Certificate); networks, system integration and testing (Certificate); signal processing (Certificate); telecommunications (MS); telecommunications forensics and security (Certificate); wireless communication (Certificate). MS program offered jointly with Old Dominion University, University of Virginia, Virginia Commonwealth University, and Virginia Polytechnic Institute and State University. *Faculty:* 29 full-time (4 women), 36 part-time/adjunct (2 women). *Students:* 162 full-time (49 women), 284 part-time (52 women); includes 101 minority (30 Black or African American, non-Hispanic/Latino; 1 American Indian or Alaska Native, non-Hispanic/Latino; 47 Asian, non-Hispanic/Latino; 19 Hispanic/Latino; 1 Native Hawaiian or other Pacific Islander, non-Hispanic/Latino; 3 Two or more races, non-Hispanic/Latino), 169 international. Average age 30. 478 applicants, 68% accepted, 106 enrolled. In 2011, 129 master's, 5 doctorates, 45 other advanced degrees awarded. *Degree requirements:* For master's, thesis optional; for doctorate, comprehensive exam, thesis or scholarly paper. *Entrance requirements:* For master's, GRE, personal goals statement; 2 official copies of transcripts; self-evaluation form; 3 letters of recommendation; resume; official bank statement; photocopy of passport; proof of financial support; for doctorate, GRE (waived for GMU electrical and computer engineering master's graduates with minimum GPA of 3.0), personal goals statement; 2 official copies of transcripts; self-evaluation form; 3 letters of recommendation; resume; official bank statement; photocopy of passport; proof of financial support. Additional exam requirements/recommendations for international students: Required—TOEFL (minimum score 575 paper-based; 230 computer-based; 88 iBT), IELTS, Pearson Test of English. *Application deadline:* For fall admission, 1/15 priority date for domestic students; for spring admission, 8/15 priority date for domestic students. Applications are processed on a rolling basis. Application fee: $65 ($80 for international students). Electronic applications accepted. *Expenses:* Tuition, state resident: full-time $8750; part-time $364.58 per credit. Tuition, nonresident: full-time $24,092; part-time $1003.83 per credit. *Required fees:* $2514; $104.75 per credit. *Financial support:* In 2011–12, 77 students received support, including 3 fellowships with full tuition reimbursements available (averaging $18,000 per year), 24 research assistantships with full and partial tuition reimbursements available (averaging $15,736 per year), 50 teaching assistantships with full and partial tuition reimbursements available (averaging $10,961 per year); career-related internships or fieldwork, Federal Work-Study, scholarships/grants, unspecified assistantships, and health care benefits (full-time research or teaching assistantship recipients) also available. Support available to part-time students. Financial award application deadline: 3/1; financial award applicants required to submit FAFSA. *Faculty research:* Communication networks, signal processing, system failure diagnosis, multiprocessors, material processing using microwave energy. *Total annual research expenditures:* $4.4 million. *Unit head:* Dr. Andre Manitius, Chairperson, 703-993-1569, Fax: 703-993-1601, E-mail: amanitiu@gmu.edu. *Application contact:* Jammie Chang, Academic Program Coordinator, 703-993-1523, Fax: 703-993-1601, E-mail: jchangn@gmu.edu. Web site: http://ece.gmu.edu/#.

Hawai`i Pacific University, College of Business Administration, Program in Information Systems, Honolulu, HI 96813. Offers knowledge management (MSIS); software engineering (MSIS); telecommunications security (MSIS). Part-time and evening/weekend programs available. *Faculty:* 9 full-time (2 women), 3 part-time/adjunct (1 woman). *Students:* 46 full-time (7 women), 51 part-time (9 women); includes 64 minority (6 Black or African American, non-Hispanic/Latino; 29 Asian, non-Hispanic/Latino; 10 Hispanic/Latino; 2 Native Hawaiian or other Pacific Islander, non-Hispanic/Latino; 17 Two or more races, non-Hispanic/Latino). Average age 32. 52 applicants, 83% accepted, 23 enrolled. In 2011, 52 master's awarded. *Expenses:* Tuition: Full-time $13,230; part-time $735 per credit. Tuition and fees vary according to course load and program. *Financial support:* In 2011–12, 12 students received support. Career-related internships or fieldwork, Federal Work-Study, scholarships/grants, tuition waivers, and unspecified assistantships available. *Unit head:* Dr. Gordon Jones, Dean, 808-544-1181, Fax: 808-544-0247, E-mail: gjones@hpu.edu. *Application contact:* Chad Schempp, Director of Graduate Admissions, 808-543-8035, Fax: 808-544-0280, E-mail: graduate@hpu.edu.

Instituto Tecnológico y de Estudios Superiores de Monterrey, Campus Ciudad de México, School of Design, Engineering and Architecture, Ciudad de Mexico, Mexico. Offers management (MA); telecommunications (MA). Part-time and evening/weekend programs available. Postbaccalaureate distance learning degree programs offered (minimal on-campus study). *Faculty research:* Telecommunications; informatics; technology development; computer systems.

Instituto Tecnológico y de Estudios Superiores de Monterrey, Campus Ciudad Obregón, Program in Administration of Telecommunications, Ciudad Obregón, Mexico. Offers MAT.

Instituto Tecnológico y de Estudios Superiores de Monterrey, Campus Estado de México, Professional and Graduate Division, Estado de Mexico, Mexico. Offers administration of information technologies (MITA); architecture (M Arch); business administration (GMBA, MBA); computer sciences (MCS, PhD); education (M Ed); educational institution administration (MAD); educational technology and innovation (PhD); electronic commerce (MEC); environmental systems (MS); finance (MAF); humanistic studies (MHS); information sciences and knowledge management (MISKM); information systems (MS); manufacturing systems (MS); marketing (MEM); quality systems and productivity (MS); science and materials engineering (PhD); telecommunications management (MTM). Part-time programs available. Postbaccalaureate distance learning degree programs offered (minimal on-campus study). *Degree requirements:* For master's, one foreign language, thesis (for some programs); for doctorate, one foreign language, thesis/dissertation. *Entrance requirements:* For master's, E-PAEP 500, interview; for doctorate, E-PAEP 500, research proposal. Additional exam requirements/recommendations for international students: Required—TOEFL (minimum score 550 paper-based). *Faculty research:* Surface treatments by plasmas, mechanical properties, robotics, graphical computing, mechatronics security protocols.

Instituto Tecnológico y de Estudios Superiores de Monterrey, Campus Irapuato, Graduate Programs, Irapuato, Mexico. Offers administration (MBA); administration of information technology (MAIT); administration of telecommunications (MAT); architecture (M Arch); computer science (MCS); education (M Ed); educational administration (MEA); educational innovation and technology (DEIT); educational technology (MET); electronic commerce (MBA); environmental administration and planning (MEAP); environmental systems (MES); finances (MBA); humanistic studies (MHS); international management for Latin American executives (MIMLAE); library and information science (MLIS); manufacturing quality management (MMQM); marketing research (MBA).

Morgan State University, School of Graduate Studies, College of Liberal Arts, Department of Telecommunications Management, Baltimore, MD 21251. Offers MS. *Degree requirements:* For master's, comprehensive exam. *Entrance requirements:* For master's, GRE. Additional exam requirements/recommendations for international students: Required—TOEFL (minimum score 550 paper-based; 213 computer-based).

Murray State University, College of Business and Public Affairs, Program in Telecommunications Systems Management, Murray, KY 42071. Offers MS. *Entrance requirements:* For master's, GMAT or GRE. Additional exam requirements/recommendations for international students: Required—TOEFL (minimum score 213

computer-based). *Faculty research:* Network security, emergency management communications, network economies.

Northeastern University, College of Engineering, Program in Telecommunication Systems Management, Boston, MA 02115-5096. Offers MS. Part-time programs available. *Students:* 82 full-time, 3 part-time. Average age 25. 124 applicants, 81% accepted, 19 enrolled. In 2011, 57 master's awarded. *Entrance requirements:* For master's, GRE General Test. Additional exam requirements/recommendations for international students: Required—TOEFL (minimum score 550 paper-based; 213 computer-based). *Application deadline:* For fall admission, 1/15 for domestic and international students. Applications are processed on a rolling basis. Application fee: $50. Electronic applications accepted. *Financial support:* In 2011–12, 2 students received support, including 1 fellowship (averaging $18,325 per year), 1 research assistantship (averaging $18,325 per year); teaching assistantships, career-related internships or fieldwork, Federal Work-Study, scholarships/grants, health care benefits, tuition waivers, and unspecified assistantships also available. Support available to part-time students. Financial award application deadline: 1/15; financial award applicants required to submit FAFSA. *Faculty research:* Information theory, wireless grids, IP telephony architecture. *Unit head:* Dr. Peter O'Reilly, Director, 617-373-5548, Fax: 617-373-2501. *Application contact:* Stephen L. Gibson, Associate Director, 617-373-2711, Fax: 617-373-2501, E-mail: grad-eng@coe.neu.edu.

Oklahoma State University, Spears School of Business, Department of Management Science and Information Systems, Stillwater, OK 74078. Offers management information systems (MS); management science and information systems (PhD); telecommunications management (MS). Part-time programs available. Postbaccalaureate distance learning degree programs offered. *Faculty:* 17 full-time (3 women), 2 part-time/adjunct (0 women). *Students:* 57 full-time (12 women), 75 part-time (9 women); includes 10 minority (3 Black or African American, non-Hispanic/Latino; 3 American Indian or Alaska Native, non-Hispanic/Latino; 1 Asian, non-Hispanic/Latino; 2 Hispanic/Latino; 1 Two or more races, non-Hispanic/Latino), 54 international. Average age 30. 280 applicants, 37% accepted, 50 enrolled. In 2011, 60 degrees awarded. *Degree requirements:* For master's, thesis or alternative; for doctorate, comprehensive exam, thesis/dissertation. *Entrance requirements:* For master's and doctorate, GRE or GMAT. Additional exam requirements/recommendations for international students: Required—TOEFL (minimum score 550 paper-based; 79 iBT). *Application deadline:* For fall admission, 3/1 for international students; for spring admission, 8/1 for international students. Applications are processed on a rolling basis. Application fee: $40 ($75 for international students). Electronic applications accepted. *Expenses:* Tuition, state resident: full-time $4044; part-time $168.50 per credit hour. Tuition, nonresident: full-time $16,008; part-time $667 per credit hour. *Required fees:* $2122; $88.45 per credit hour. One-time fee: $50. Tuition and fees vary according to course load and campus/location. *Financial support:* In 2011–12, 1 research assistantship (averaging $4,200 per year), 12 teaching assistantships (averaging $13,083 per year) were awarded; career-related internships or fieldwork, Federal Work-Study, scholarships/grants, health care benefits, tuition waivers (partial), and unspecified assistantships also available. Support available to part-time students. Financial award application deadline: 3/1; financial award applicants required to submit FAFSA. *Unit head:* Dr. Rick Wilson, Head, 405-744-3551, Fax: 405-744-5180. *Application contact:* Dr. Sheryl Tucker, Dean, 405-744-7099, Fax: 405-744-0355, E-mail: grad-i@okstate.edu. Web site: http://spears.okstate.edu/msis.

Polytechnic Institute of New York University, Department of Technology Management, Major in Telecommunications and Information Management, Brooklyn, NY 11201-2990. Offers MS. *Students:* 1 part-time (0 women). Average age 34. 1 applicant, 0% accepted, 0 enrolled. *Degree requirements:* For master's, comprehensive exam (for some programs), thesis (for some programs). *Entrance requirements:* For master's, GMAT, minimum B average in undergraduate course work. Additional exam requirements/recommendations for international students: Required—TOEFL (minimum score 550 paper-based; 213 computer-based; 80 iBT); Recommended—IELTS (minimum score 6.5). *Application deadline:* For fall admission, 7/31 priority date for domestic students, 4/30 for international students; for spring admission, 12/31 priority date for domestic students, 11/30 for international students. Applications are processed on a rolling basis. Application fee: $75. Electronic applications accepted. *Expenses:* Tuition: Full-time $22,464; part-time $1248 per credit. *Required fees:* $501 per semester. *Financial support:* Institutionally sponsored loans, scholarships/grants, and unspecified assistantships available. Support available to part-time students. Financial award applicants required to submit FAFSA. *Unit head:* Prof. Bharadwaj Rao, Head, 718-260-3617, Fax: 718-260-3874, E-mail: ro@poly.edu. *Application contact:* JeanCarlo Bonilla, Director of Graduate Enrollment Management, 718-260-3182, Fax: 718-260-3624, E-mail: gradinfo@poly.edu.

San Diego State University, Graduate and Research Affairs, College of Professional Studies and Fine Arts, School of Communication, San Diego, CA 92182. Offers advertising and public relations (MA); critical-cultural studies (MA); interaction studies (MA); intercultural and international studies (MA); new media studies (MA); news and information studies (MA); telecommunications and media management (MA). *Degree requirements:* For master's, thesis. *Entrance requirements:* For master's, GRE General Test, 3 letters of recommendation. Additional exam requirements/recommendations for international students: Required—TOEFL. Electronic applications accepted.

Stevens Institute of Technology, Graduate School, Wesley J. Howe School of Technology Management, Doctoral Program in Technology Management, Hoboken, NJ 07030. Offers information management (PhD); technology management (PhD); telecommunications management (PhD). Part-time and evening/weekend programs available. Postbaccalaureate distance learning degree programs offered (minimal on-campus study). *Entrance requirements:* Additional exam requirements/recommendations for international students: Required—TOEFL. Electronic applications accepted.

Stevens Institute of Technology, Graduate School, Wesley J. Howe School of Technology Management, Program in Business Administration, Hoboken, NJ 07030. Offers engineering management (MBA); financial engineering (MBA); information management (MBA); information technology in financial services (MBA); information technology in the pharmaceutical industry (MBA); information technology outsourcing (MBA); pharmaceutical management (MBA); project management (MBA); technology management (MBA); telecommunications management (MBA).

Stevens Institute of Technology, Graduate School, Wesley J. Howe School of Technology Management, Program in Information Systems, Hoboken, NJ 07030. Offers computer science (MS); e-commerce (MS); enterprise systems (MS); entrepreneurial information technology (MS); information architecture (MS); information management (MS, Certificate); information security (MS); information technology in financial services industry (MS); information technology in the pharmaceutical industry (MS); information technology outsourcing management (MS); project management (MS, Certificate); software engineering (MS); telecommunications (MS). *Degree requirements:* For master's, thesis optional. *Entrance requirements:* For master's, GMAT, GRE General Test. Additional exam requirements/recommendations for international students: Required—TOEFL. Electronic applications accepted.

Stevens Institute of Technology, Graduate School, Wesley J. Howe School of Technology Management, Program in Telecommunications Management, Hoboken, NJ 07030. Offers business (MS); global innovation management (MS); management of wireless networks (MS); online security, technology and business (MS); project management (MS); technical management (MS); telecommunications management (PhD, Certificate). *Degree requirements:* For master's, thesis optional; for doctorate, thesis/dissertation. *Entrance requirements:* For master's and doctorate, GMAT, GRE General Test. Additional exam requirements/recommendations for international students: Required—TOEFL. Electronic applications accepted.

Strayer University, Graduate Studies, Washington, DC 20005-2603. Offers accounting (MS); acquisition (MBA); business administration (MBA); communications technology (MS); educational management (M Ed); finance (MBA); health services administration (MHSA); hospitality and tourism management (MBA); human resource management (MBA); information systems (MS), including computer security management, decision support system management, enterprise resource management, network management, software engineering management, systems development management; management (MBA); management information systems (MS); marketing (MBA); professional accounting (MS), including accounting information systems, controllership, taxation; public administration (MPA); supply chain management (MBA); technology in education (M Ed). Programs also offered at campus locations in Birmingham, AL; Chamblee, GA; Cobb County, GA; Morrow, GA; White Marsh, MD; Charleston, SC; Columbia, SC; Greensboro, NC; Greenville, SC; Lexington, KY; Louisville, KY; Nashville, TN; North Raleigh, NC; Washington, DC. Part-time and evening/weekend programs available. Postbaccalaureate distance learning degree programs offered (minimal on-campus study). *Degree requirements:* For master's, thesis. *Entrance requirements:* For master's, GMAT, GRE General Test, bachelor's degree from an accredited college or university, minimum undergraduate GPA of 2.75. Electronic applications accepted.

Syracuse University, School of Information Studies, Program in Information Systems and Telecommunications Management, Syracuse, NY 13244. Offers CAS. Part-time and evening/weekend programs available. Postbaccalaureate distance learning degree programs offered. *Students:* 2 full-time (0 women), 15 part-time (5 women); includes 2 minority (1 Black or African American, non-Hispanic/Latino; 1 Hispanic/Latino), 3 international. Average age 33. 16 applicants, 75% accepted, 8 enrolled. In 2011, 11 degrees awarded. *Entrance requirements:* Additional exam requirements/recommendations for international students: Required—TOEFL (minimum score 100 iBT). *Application deadline:* For fall admission, 2/1 priority date for domestic students, 2/1 for international students; for spring admission, 10/15 priority date for domestic students, 10/15 for international students. Applications are processed on a rolling basis. Application fee: $75. Electronic applications accepted. *Expenses: Tuition:* Part-time $1206 per credit. *Financial support:* Fellowships with full tuition reimbursements, research assistantships with partial tuition reimbursements, and teaching assistantships with partial tuition reimbursements available. Financial award application deadline: 1/1; financial award applicants required to submit FAFSA. *Unit head:* David Dischiave, Director, 315-443-4681, Fax: 315-443-6886, E-mail: ddischia@syr.edu. *Application contact:* Susan Corieri, Director of Enrollment Management, 315-443-2575, E-mail: ischool@syr.edu. Web site: http://ischool.syr.edu/.

Syracuse University, School of Information Studies, Program in Telecommunications and Network Management, Syracuse, NY 13244. Offers MS, MS/CAS. Part-time and evening/weekend programs available. Postbaccalaureate distance learning degree programs offered (minimal on-campus study). *Students:* 45 full-time (10 women), 25 part-time (6 women); includes 12 minority (3 Black or African American, non-Hispanic/Latino; 4 Asian, non-Hispanic/Latino; 5 Hispanic/Latino), 38 international. Average age 29. 78 applicants, 68% accepted, 28 enrolled. In 2011, 30 degrees awarded. *Degree requirements:* For master's, internship or research project. *Entrance requirements:* For master's, GRE General Test. Additional exam requirements/recommendations for international students: Required—TOEFL (minimum score 100 iBT). *Application deadline:* For fall admission, 2/1 priority date for domestic students, 2/1 for international students; for spring admission, 10/15 priority date for domestic students, 10/15 for international students. Applications are processed on a rolling basis. Application fee: $75. Electronic applications accepted. *Expenses: Tuition:* Part-time $1206 per credit. *Financial support:* Fellowships with full tuition reimbursements, research assistantships with partial tuition reimbursements, teaching assistantships with partial tuition reimbursements, career-related internships or fieldwork, and Federal Work-Study available. Financial award application deadline: 1/1. *Faculty research:* Multimedia, information resources management. *Unit head:* Prof. Martha Garcia-Marillo, Director, 315-443-2911, Fax: 315-443-6886, E-mail: mgarciam@syr.edu. *Application contact:* Susan Corieri, Director of Enrollment Management, 315-443-2575, E-mail: ischool@syr.edu. Web site: http://ischool.syr.edu/.

University of Colorado Boulder, Graduate School, College of Engineering and Applied Science, Interdisciplinary Telecommunications Program, Boulder, CO 80309. Offers MS, JD/MS, MBA/MS. *Students:* 88 full-time (11 women), 28 part-time (2 women); includes 6 minority (3 Asian, non-Hispanic/Latino; 3 Hispanic/Latino), 72 international. Average age 29. 166 applicants, 56% accepted, 34 enrolled. In 2011, 46 master's awarded. Terminal master's awarded for partial completion of doctoral program. *Degree requirements:* For master's, comprehensive exam, thesis or alternative. *Entrance requirements:* For master's, minimum undergraduate GPA of 3.0. *Application deadline:* For fall admission, 6/15 priority date for domestic students, 3/15 for international students; for spring admission, 11/1 for domestic students, 10/1 for international students. Applications are processed on a rolling basis. Application fee: $50 ($60 for international students). Electronic applications accepted. *Financial support:* In 2011–12, 16 students received support, including 20 fellowships (averaging $11,969 per year), 1 research assistantship with full and partial tuition reimbursement available (averaging $11,842 per year), 2 teaching assistantships with full and partial tuition reimbursements available (averaging $5,893 per year); institutionally sponsored loans, scholarships/grants, health care benefits, and unspecified assistantships also available. Financial award applicants required to submit FAFSA. *Faculty research:* Technology, planning, and management of telecommunications systems. *Total annual research expenditures:* $35,450. *Application contact:* E-mail: itp@colorado.edu. Web site: http://itp.colorado.edu/.

University of New Haven, Graduate School, School of Business, Program in Business Administration, West Haven, CT 06516-1916. Offers accounting (MBA, Certificate), including CPA (MBA); business management (Certificate); business policy and strategy (MBA); finance (MBA), including CFA; global marketing (MBA); human resource management (Certificate); human resources management (MBA); international business (Certificate); marketing (Certificate); sports management (MBA); telecommunications management (Certificate); MBA/MPA. Part-time and evening/weekend programs

available. *Students:* 215 full-time (106 women), 182 part-time (87 women); includes 73 minority (38 Black or African American, non-Hispanic/Latino; 2 American Indian or Alaska Native, non-Hispanic/Latino; 22 Asian, non-Hispanic/Latino; 11 Hispanic/Latino), 129 international. 179 applicants, 97% accepted, 93 enrolled. In 2011, 197 master's, 28 other advanced degrees awarded. *Degree requirements:* For master's, thesis or alternative. *Entrance requirements:* For master's, GMAT. Additional exam requirements/recommendations for international students: Required—TOEFL (minimum score 520 paper-based; 190 computer-based; 70 iBT), IELTS (minimum score 5.5). *Application deadline:* For fall admission, 5/31 for international students; for winter admission, 10/15 for international students; for spring admission, 1/15 for international students. Applications are processed on a rolling basis. Application fee: $50. Electronic applications accepted. *Expenses:* Contact institution. *Financial support:* Research assistantships with partial tuition reimbursements, teaching assistantships with partial tuition reimbursements, Federal Work-Study, scholarships/grants, health care benefits, tuition waivers, and unspecified assistantships available. Support available to part-time students. Financial award applicants required to submit FAFSA. *Unit head:* Charles Coleman, Chairman, 203-932-7375. *Application contact:* Eloise Gormley, Director of Graduate Admissions, 203-932-7449, Fax: 203-932-7137, E-mail: gradinfo@newhaven.edu. Web site: http://www.newhaven.edu/7433/.

University of Pennsylvania, School of Engineering and Applied Science, Telecommunications and Networking Program, Philadelphia, PA 19104. Offers MSE. Part-time programs available. *Students:* 64 full-time (18 women), 6 part-time (2 women); includes 4 minority (1 Black or African American, non-Hispanic/Latino; 3 Asian, non-Hispanic/Latino), 65 international. 247 applicants, 42% accepted, 43 enrolled. In 2011, 34 master's awarded. *Application deadline:* For fall admission, 6/1 for domestic students, 5/1 for international students; for spring admission, 11/1 for domestic students, 10/1 for international students. Application fee: $70. Electronic applications accepted. *Expenses: Tuition:* Full-time $26,660; part-time $4944 per course. *Required fees:* $2318; $291 per course. Tuition and fees vary according to course load, degree level and program. *Unit head:* Eduardo D. Glandt, Dean, 215-898-7244, Fax: 215-573-2018, E-mail: seasdean@seas.upenn.edu. *Application contact:* 215-898-0696, E-mail: tcom@seas.upenn.edu. Web site: http://www.seas.upenn.edu/profprog/tcom//.

University of San Francisco, School of Management, Masagung Graduate School of Management, Program in Business Administration, San Francisco, CA 94117-1080. Offers business economics (MBA); e-business (MBA); entrepreneurship (MBA); finance (MBA); international business (MBA); management (MBA); marketing (MBA); telecommunications management and policy (MBA); JD/MBA; MSN/MBA. *Accreditation:* AACSB. *Faculty:* 18 full-time (4 women), 18 part-time/adjunct (9 women). *Students:* 247 full-time (122 women), 9 part-time (3 women); includes 85 minority (5 Black or African American, non-Hispanic/Latino; 55 Asian, non-Hispanic/Latino; 16 Hispanic/Latino; 1 Native Hawaiian or other Pacific Islander, non-Hispanic/Latino; 8 Two or more races, non-Hispanic/Latino), 38 international. Average age 29. 552 applicants, 55% accepted, 99 enrolled. In 2011, 173 master's awarded. *Entrance requirements:* For master's, GMAT, minimum undergraduate GPA of 3.2. Additional exam requirements/recommendations for international students: Required—TOEFL. *Application deadline:* For fall admission, 7/1 priority date for domestic students; for spring admission, 11/30 for domestic students. Applications are processed on a rolling basis. Application fee: $55 ($65 for international students). *Expenses: Tuition:* Full-time $20,070; part-time $1115 per unit. Tuition and fees vary according to course load, campus/location and program. *Financial support:* In 2011–12, 33 students received support. Fellowships available. Financial award application deadline: 3/2; financial award applicants required to submit FAFSA. *Faculty research:* International financial markets, technology transfer licensing, international marketing, strategic planning. *Total annual research expenditures:* $50,000. *Unit head:* Kelly Brookes, Director, 415-422-2221, Fax: 415-422-6315. *Application contact:* Director, MBA Program, 415-422-2221, Fax: 415-422-6315, E-mail: mba@usfca.edu.

University of South Africa, College of Human Sciences, Pretoria, South Africa. Offers adult education (M Ed); African languages (MA, PhD); African politics (MA, PhD); Afrikaans (MA, PhD); ancient history (MA, PhD); ancient Near Eastern studies (MA, PhD); anthropology (MA, PhD); applied linguistics (MA); Arabic (MA, PhD); archaeology (MA); art history (MA); Biblical archaeology (MA); Biblical studies (M Th, D Th, PhD); Christian spirituality (M Th, D Th); church history (M Th, D Th); classical studies (MA, PhD); clinical psychology (MA); communication (MA, PhD); comparative education (M Ed, Ed D); consulting psychology (D Admin, D Com, PhD); curriculum studies (M Ed, Ed D); development studies (M Admin, MA, D Admin, PhD); didactics (M Ed, Ed D); education (M Tech); education management (M Ed, Ed D); educational psychology (M Ed); English (MA); environmental education (M Ed); French (MA, PhD); German (MA, PhD); Greek (MA); guidance and counseling (M Ed); health studies (MA, PhD), including health sciences education (MA), health services management (MA), medical and surgical nursing science (critical care general) (MA), midwifery and neonatal nursing science (MA), trauma and emergency care (MA); history (MA, PhD); history of education (Ed D); inclusive education (M Ed, Ed D); information and communications technology policy and regulation (MA); information science (MA, MIS, PhD); international politics (MA, PhD); Islamic studies (MA, PhD); Italian (MA, PhD); Judaica (MA, PhD); linguistics (MA, PhD); mathematical education (M Ed); mathematics education (MA); missiology (M Th, D Th); modern Hebrew (MA, PhD); musicology (MA, MMus, D Mus, PhD); natural science education (M Ed); New Testament (M Th, D Th); Old Testament (D Th); pastoral therapy (M Th, D Th); philosophy (MA); philosophy of education (M Ed, Ed D); politics (MA, PhD); Portuguese (MA, PhD); practical theology (M Th, D Th); psychology (MA, MS, PhD); psychology of education (M Ed, Ed D); public health (MA); religious studies (MA, D Th, PhD); Romance languages (MA); Russian (MA, PhD); Semitic languages (MA, PhD); social behavior studies in HIV/AIDS (MA); social science (mental health) (MA); social science in development studies (MA); social science in psychology (MA); social science in social work (MA); social science in sociology (MA); social work (MSW, DSW, PhD); socio-education (M Ed, Ed D); sociolinguistics (MA); sociology (MA, PhD); Spanish (MA, PhD); systematic theology (M Th, D Th); TESOL (teaching English to speakers of other languages) (MA); theological ethics (M Th, D Th); theory of literature (MA, PhD); urban ministries (D Th); urban ministry (M Th).

University of Wisconsin–Stout, Graduate School, College of Technology, Engineering, and Management, Program in Information and Communication Technologies, Menomonie , WI 54751. Offers MS. Part-time programs available. Postbaccalaureate distance learning degree programs offered (minimal on-campus study). *Degree requirements:* For master's, thesis. *Entrance requirements:* For master's, minimum GPA of 2.75. Additional exam requirements/recommendations for international students: Required—TOEFL (minimum score 500 paper-based; 173 computer-based; 61 iBT). Electronic applications accepted.

Webster University, George Herbert Walker School of Business and Technology, Department of Business, St. Louis, MO 63119-3194. Offers business (MA); business and organizational security management (MBA); computer resources and information management (MBA); environmental management (MBA); finance (MA, MBA); health services management (MBA); human resources development (MBA); human resources management (MBA); international business (MA, MBA); management and leadership (MBA); marketing (MBA); procurement and acquisitions management (MBA); telecommunications management (MBA). *Accreditation:* ACBSP. Part-time and evening/weekend programs available. Postbaccalaureate distance learning degree programs offered (no on-campus study). *Degree requirements:* For master's, comprehensive exam (for some programs), thesis (for some programs). *Entrance requirements:* Additional exam requirements/recommendations for international students: Required—TOEFL. *Expenses: Tuition:* Full-time $10,890; part-time $605 per credit hour. Tuition and fees vary according to campus/location and program.

Webster University, George Herbert Walker School of Business and Technology, Department of Management, St. Louis, MO 63119-3194. Offers business and organizational security management (MA); computer resources and information management (MA); environmental management (MS); government contracting (Certificate); health care management (MA); health services management (MA); human resources development (MA); human resources management (MA); management (DM); management and leadership (MA); marketing (MA); nonprofit management (Certificate); procurement and acquisitions management (MA); public administration (MA); quality management (MA); space systems operations management (MS); telecommunications management (MA). *Accreditation:* ACBSP. Part-time and evening/weekend programs available. Postbaccalaureate distance learning degree programs offered (no on-campus study). *Degree requirements:* For master's, thesis (for some programs); for doctorate, thesis/dissertation, written exam. *Entrance requirements:* For doctorate, GMAT, 3 years of work experience, MBA. Additional exam requirements/recommendations for international students: Required—TOEFL. *Expenses: Tuition:* Full-time $10,890; part-time $605 per credit hour. Tuition and fees vary according to campus/location and program.

APPENDIXES

Institutional Changes
Since the 2012 Edition

Following is an alphabetical listing of institutions that have recently closed, merged with other institutions, or changed their names or status. In the case of a name change, the former name appears first, followed by the new name.

Adams State College (Alamosa, CO): name changed to Adams State University

Andrew Jackson University (Birmingham, AL): name changed to New Charter University

The Art Institute of Atlanta (Atlanta, GA): no longer offers graduate degrees

The Art Institute of Boston at Lesley University (Boston, MA): merged into a single entry for Lesley University (Cambridge, MA)

The Art Institute of California–San Francisco (San Francisco, CA): name changed to The Art Institute of California, a college of Argosy University, San Francisco

Atlantic Union College (South Lancaster, MA): currently not accepting applications

Babel University School of Translation (Honolulu, HI): name changed to Babel University Professional School of Translation

Baldwin-Wallace College (Berea, OH): name changed to Baldwin Wallace University

Baltimore International College (Baltimore, MD): name changed to Stratford University

Bethany University (Scotts Valley, CA): closed

Bethesda Christian University (Anaheim, CA): name changed to Bethesda University of California

Broadview University (West Jordan, UT): name changed to Broadview University–West Jordan

City of Hope National Medical Center/Beckman Research Institute (Duarte, CA): name changed to Irell & Manella Graduate School of Biological Sciences

City University of New York School of Law at Queens College (Flushing, NY): name changed to City University of New York School of Law

Cleveland Chiropractic College–Los Angeles Campus (Los Angeles, CA): closed

College of Notre Dame of Maryland (Baltimore, MD): name changed to Notre Dame of Maryland University

College of the Humanities and Sciences, Harrison Middleton University (Tempe, AZ): name changed to Harrison Middleton University

Colorado Technical University Denver (Greenwood Village, CO): name changed to Colorado Technical University Denver South

Concordia University (Ann Arbor, MI): name changed to Concordia University Ann Arbor

Cornell University, Joan and Sanford I. Weill Medical College and Graduate School of Medical Sciences (New York, NY): name changed to Weill Cornell Medical College

Daniel Webster College–Portsmouth Campus (Portsmouth, NH): closed

Edward Via Virginia College of Osteopathic Medicine (Blacksburg, VA): name changed to Edward Via College of Osteopahtic Medicine–Virginia Campus

Evangelical Theological Seminary (Myerstown, PA): name changed to Evangelical Seminary

Everest University (Lakeland, FL): no longer offers graduate degrees

Faith Evangelical Lutheran Seminary (Tacoma, WA): name changed to Faith Evangelical College & Seminary

Franklin Pierce Law Center (Concord, NH): name changed to University of New Hampshire School of Law

Frontier School of Midwifery and Family Nursing (Hyden, KY): name changed to Frontier Nursing University

Globe University (Woodbury, MN): name changed to Globe University–Woodbury

Harding University Graduate School of Religion (Memphis, TN): name changed to Harding School of Theology

Kol Yaakov Torah Center (Monsey, NY): closed

Long Island University at Riverhead (Riverhead, NY): name changed to Long Island University–Riverhead

Long Island University, Brentwood Campus (Brentwood, NY): name changed to Long Island University–Brentwood Campus

Long Island University, Brooklyn Campus (Brooklyn, NY): name changed to Long Island University–Brooklyn Campus

Long Island University, C.W. Post Campus (Brookville, NY): name changed to Long Island University–C. W. Post Campus

Long Island University, Rockland Graduate Campus (Orangeburg, NY): name changed to Long Island University–Hudson at Rockland

Long Island University, Westchester Graduate Campus (Purchase, NY): name changed to Long Island University–Hudson at Westchester

Lourdes College (Sylvania, OH): name changed to Lourdes University

Lutheran Theological Seminary (Saskatoon, SK, Canada): name changed to Lutheran Theological Seminary Saskatoon

Mars Hill Graduate School (Seattle, WA): name changed to The Seattle School of Theology and Psychology

Mesa State College (Grand Junction, CO): name changed to Colorado Mesa University

Michigan Theological Seminary (Plymouth, MI): name changed to Moody Theological Seminary–Michigan

Midwest University (Wentzville, MO): no longer accredited by agency recognized by USDE or CHEA

National Defense Intelligence College (Washington, DC): name changed to National Intelligence University

National-Louis University (Chicago, IL): name changed to National Louis University

National Theatre Conservatory (Denver, CO): closed

The New School: A University (New York, NY): name changed to The New School

Northeastern Ohio Universities Colleges of Medicine and Pharmacy (Rootstown, OH): name changed to Northeastern Ohio Medical University

Northwest Baptist Seminary (Tacoma, WA): name changed to Corban University School of Ministry

Northwood University (Midland, MI): name changed to Northwood University, Michigan Campus

OGI School of Science & Engineering at Oregon Health & Science University (Beaverton, OR): merged into a single entry for Oregon Health & Science University (Portland, OR) by request from the institution

Parker College of Chiropractic (Dallas, TX): name changed to Parker University

Philadelphia Biblical University (Langhorne, PA): name changed to Cairn University

Piedmont Baptist College and Graduate School (Winston-Salem, NC): name changed to Piedmont International University

Pikeville College (Pikeville, KY): name changed to University of Pikeville

Polytechnic Institute of NYU (Brooklyn, NY): name changed to Polytechnic Institute of New York University

Ponce School of Medicine (Ponce, PR): name changed to Ponce School of Medicine & Health Sciences

Rivier College (Nashua, NH): name changed to Rivier University

Saint Bernard's School of Theology and Ministry (Rochester, NY): name changed to St. Bernard's School of Theology and Ministry

St. Charles Borromeo Seminary, Overbrook (Wynnewood, PA): name changed to Saint Charles Borromeo Seminary, Overbrook

Saint Francis Seminary (St. Francis, WI): name changed to Saint Francis de Sales Seminary

Saint Joseph College (West Hartford, CT): name changed to University of Saint Joseph

Saint Vincent de Paul Regional Seminary (Boynton Beach, FL): name changed to St. Vincent de Paul Regional Seminary

Schiller International University (London, United Kingdom): closed

Silver Lake College (Manitowoc, WI): name changed to Silver Lake College of the Holy Family

Trinity (Washington) University (Washington, DC): name changed to Trinity Washington University

TUI University (Cypress, CA): name changed to Trident University International

University of Phoenix (Phoenix, AZ): name changed to University of Phoenix–Online Campus

University of Phoenix–Phoenix Campus (Phoenix, AZ): name changed to University of Phoenix–Phoenix Main Campus

The University of Tennessee–Oak Ridge National Laboratory Graduate School of Genome Science and Technology (Oak Ridge, TN): name changed to The University of Tennessee–Oak Ridge National Laboratory

The University of Texas Southwestern Medical Center at Dallas (Dallas, TX): name changed to The University of Texas Southwestern Medical Center

University of Trinity College (Toronto, ON, Canada): name changed to Trinity College

Washington Theological Union (Washington, DC): closed

West Virginia University Institute of Technology (Montgomery, WV): no longer offers graduate degrees.

Abbreviations Used in the Guides

The following list includes abbreviations of degree names used in the profiles in the 2013 edition of the guides. Because some degrees (e.g., Doctor of Education) can be abbreviated in more than one way (e.g., D.Ed. or Ed.D.), and because the abbreviations used in the guides reflect the preferences of the individual colleges and universities, the list may include two or more abbreviations for a single degree.

DEGREES

A Mus D	Doctor of Musical Arts
AC	Advanced Certificate
AD	Artist's Diploma
	Doctor of Arts
ADP	Artist's Diploma
Adv C	Advanced Certificate
Adv M	Advanced Master
AGC	Advanced Graduate Certificate
AGSC	Advanced Graduate Specialist Certificate
ALM	Master of Liberal Arts
AM	Master of Arts
AMBA	Accelerated Master of Business Administration
	Aviation Master of Business Administration
AMRS	Master of Arts in Religious Studies
APC	Advanced Professional Certificate
APMPH	Advanced Professional Master of Public Health
App Sc	Applied Scientist
App Sc D	Doctor of Applied Science
AstE	Astronautical Engineer
Au D	Doctor of Audiology
B Th	Bachelor of Theology
CAES	Certificate of Advanced Educational Specialization
CAGS	Certificate of Advanced Graduate Studies
CAL	Certificate in Applied Linguistics
CALS	Certificate of Advanced Liberal Studies
CAMS	Certificate of Advanced Management Studies
CAPS	Certificate of Advanced Professional Studies
CAS	Certificate of Advanced Studies
CASPA	Certificate of Advanced Study in Public Administration
CASR	Certificate in Advanced Social Research
CATS	Certificate of Achievement in Theological Studies
CBHS	Certificate in Basic Health Sciences
CBS	Graduate Certificate in Biblical Studies
CCJA	Certificate in Criminal Justice Administration
CCSA	Certificate in Catholic School Administration
CCTS	Certificate in Clinical and Translational Science
CE	Civil Engineer
CEM	Certificate of Environmental Management
CET	Certificate in Educational Technologies
CGS	Certificate of Graduate Studies
Ch E	Chemical Engineer
CM	Certificate in Management
CMH	Certificate in Medical Humanities
CMM	Master of Church Ministries
CMS	Certificate in Ministerial Studies
CNM	Certificate in Nonprofit Management
CPASF	Certificate Program for Advanced Study in Finance
CPC	Certificate in Professional Counseling
	Certificate in Publication and Communication
CPH	Certificate in Public Health
CPM	Certificate in Public Management
CPS	Certificate of Professional Studies
CScD	Doctor of Clinical Science
CSD	Certificate in Spiritual Direction
CSS	Certificate of Special Studies
CTS	Certificate of Theological Studies
CURP	Certificate in Urban and Regional Planning
D Admin	Doctor of Administration
D Arch	Doctor of Architecture
D Be	Doctor in Bioethics
D Com	Doctor of Commerce
D Couns	Doctor of Counseling
D Div	Doctor of Divinity
D Ed	Doctor of Education
D Ed Min	Doctor of Educational Ministry
D Eng	Doctor of Engineering
D Engr	Doctor of Engineering
D Ent	Doctor of Enterprise
D Env	Doctor of Environment
D Law	Doctor of Law
D Litt	Doctor of Letters
D Med Sc	Doctor of Medical Science
D Min	Doctor of Ministry
D Miss	Doctor of Missiology
D Mus	Doctor of Music
D Mus A	Doctor of Musical Arts
D Phil	Doctor of Philosophy
D Prof	Doctor of Professional Studies
D Ps	Doctor of Psychology
D Sc	Doctor of Science
D Sc D	Doctor of Science in Dentistry
D Sc IS	Doctor of Science in Information Systems
D Sc PA	Doctor of Science in Physician Assistant Studies
D Th	Doctor of Theology
D Th P	Doctor of Practical Theology
DA	Doctor of Accounting
	Doctor of Arts
DA Ed	Doctor of Arts in Education
DAH	Doctor of Arts in Humanities
DAOM	Doctorate in Acupuncture and Oriental Medicine
DAT	Doctorate of Athletic Training
DATH	Doctorate of Art Therapy
DBA	Doctor of Business Administration
DBH	Doctor of Behavioral Health
DBL	Doctor of Business Leadership
DBS	Doctor of Buddhist Studies
DC	Doctor of Chiropractic
DCC	Doctor of Computer Science
DCD	Doctor of Communications Design
DCL	Doctor of Civil Law
	Doctor of Comparative Law
DCM	Doctor of Church Music
DCN	Doctor of Clinical Nutrition
DCS	Doctor of Computer Science
DDN	Dipllf.me du Droit Notarial
DDS	Doctor of Dental Surgery
DE	Doctor of Education
	Doctor of Engineering
DED	Doctor of Economic Development
DEIT	Doctor of Educational Innovation and Technology
DEL	Doctor of Executive Leadership
DEM	Doctor of Educational Ministry
DEPD	Dipllf.me IfEtudes Splfecialislfees
DES	Doctor of Engineering Science
DESS	Dipllf.me IfEtudes Suplferieures Splfecialislfees
DFA	Doctor of Fine Arts
DGP	Diploma in Graduate and Professional Studies
DH Ed	Doctor of Health Education
DH Sc	Doctor of Health Sciences
DHA	Doctor of Health Administration
DHCE	Doctor of Health Care Ethics
DHL	Doctor of Hebrew Letters
	Doctor of Hebrew Literature
DHS	Doctor of Health Science
DHSc	Doctor of Health Science
Dip CS	Diploma in Christian Studies
DIT	Doctor of Industrial Technology
DJ Ed	Doctor of Jewish Education
DJS	Doctor of Jewish Studies
DLS	Doctor of Liberal Studies
DM	Doctor of Management
	Doctor of Music
DMA	Doctor of Musical Arts
DMD	Doctor of Dental Medicine
DME	Doctor of Music Education
DMEd	Doctor of Music Education
DMFT	Doctor of Marital and Family Therapy
DMH	Doctor of Medical Humanities
DML	Doctor of Modern Languages
DMP	Doctorate in Medical Physics
DMPNA	Doctor of Management Practice in Nurse Anesthesia

DN Sc	Doctor of Nursing Science	JCL	Licentiate in Canon Law
DNAP	Doctor of Nurse Anesthesia Practice	JD	Juris Doctor
DNP	Doctor of Nursing Practice	JSD	Doctor of Juridical Science
DNP-A	Doctor of Nursing PracticeAnesthesia		Doctor of Jurisprudence
DNS	Doctor of Nursing Science		Doctor of the Science of Law
DO	Doctor of Osteopathy	JSM	Master of Science of Law
DOT	Doctor of Occupational Therapy	L Th	Licenciate in Theology
DPA	Doctor of Public Administration	LL B	Bachelor of Laws
DPC	Doctor of Pastoral Counseling	LL CM	Master of Laws in Comparative Law
DPDS	Doctor of Planning and Development Studies	LL D	Doctor of Laws
DPH	Doctor of Public Health	LL M	Master of Laws
DPM	Doctor of Plant Medicine	LL M in Tax	Master of Laws in Taxation
	Doctor of Podiatric Medicine	LL M CL	Master of Laws (Common Law)
DPPD	Doctor of Policy, Planning, and Development	M Ac	Master of Accountancy
DPS	Doctor of Professional Studies		Master of Accounting
DPT	Doctor of Physical Therapy		Master of Acupuncture
DPTSc	Doctor of Physical Therapy Science	M Ac OM	Master of Acupuncture and Oriental Medicine
Dr DES	Doctor of Design	M Acc	Master of Accountancy
Dr NP	Doctor of Nursing Practice		Master of Accounting
Dr PH	Doctor of Public Health	M Acct	Master of Accountancy
Dr Sc PT	Doctor of Science in Physical Therapy		Master of Accounting
DRSc	Doctor of Regulatory Science	M Accy	Master of Accountancy
DS	Doctor of Science	M Actg	Master of Accounting
DS Sc	Doctor of Social Science	M Acy	Master of Accountancy
DSJS	Doctor of Science in Jewish Studies	M Ad	Master of Administration
DSL	Doctor of Strategic Leadership	M Ad Ed	Master of Adult Education
DSW	Doctor of Social Work	M Adm	Master of Administration
DTL	Doctor of Talmudic Law	M Adm Mgt	Master of Administrative Management
DV Sc	Doctor of Veterinary Science	M Admin	Master of Administration
DVM	Doctor of Veterinary Medicine	M ADU	Master of Architectural Design and Urbanism
DWS	Doctor of Worship Studies	M Adv	Master of Advertising
EAA	Engineer in Aeronautics and Astronautics	M Aero E	Master of Aerospace Engineering
EASPh D	Engineering and Applied Science Doctor of Philosophy	M AEST	Master of Applied Environmental Science and Technology
ECS	Engineer in Computer Science	M Ag	Master of Agriculture
Ed D	Doctor of Education	M Ag Ed	Master of Agricultural Education
Ed DCT	Doctor of Education in College Teaching	M Agr	Master of Agriculture
Ed L D	Doctor of Education Leadership	M Anesth Ed	Master of Anesthesiology Education
Ed M	Master of Education	M App Comp Sc	Master of Applied Computer Science
Ed S	Specialist in Education	M App St	Master of Applied Statistics
Ed Sp	Specialist in Education	M Appl Stat	Master of Applied Statistics
EDB	Executive Doctorate in Business	M Aq	Master of Aquaculture
EDM	Executive Doctorate in Management	M Arc	Master of Architecture
EE	Electrical Engineer	M Arch	Master of Architecture
EJD	Executive Juris Doctor	M Arch I	Master of Architecture I
EMBA	Executive Master of Business Administration	M Arch II	Master of Architecture II
EMFA	Executive Master of Forensic Accounting	M Arch E	Master of Architectural Engineering
EMHA	Executive Master of Health Administration	M Arch H	Master of Architectural History
EMIB	Executive Master of International Business	M Bioethics	Master in Bioethics
EML	Executive Master of Leadership	M Biomath	Master of Biomathematics
EMPA	Executive Master of Public Administration	M Ch	Master of Chemistry
EMS	Executive Master of Science	M Ch E	Master of Chemical Engineering
EMTM	Executive Master of Technology Management	M Chem	Master of Chemistry
Eng	Engineer	M Cl D	Master of Clinical Dentistry
Eng Sc D	Doctor of Engineering Science	M Cl Sc	Master of Clinical Science
Engr	Engineer	M Comp	Master of Computing
Ex Doc	Executive Doctor of Pharmacy	M Comp Sc	Master of Computer Science
Exec Ed D	Executive Doctor of Education	M Coun	Master of Counseling
Exec MBA	Executive Master of Business Administration	M Dent	Master of Dentistry
Exec MPA	Executive Master of Public Administration	M Dent Sc	Master of Dental Sciences
Exec MPH	Executive Master of Public Health	M Des	Master of Design
Exec MS	Executive Master of Science	M Des S	Master of Design Studies
G Dip	Graduate Diploma	M Div	Master of Divinity
GBC	Graduate Business Certificate	M Ec	Master of Economics
GCE	Graduate Certificate in Education	M Econ	Master of Economics
GDM	Graduate Diploma in Management	M Ed	Master of Education
GDPA	Graduate Diploma in Public Administration	M Ed T	Master of Education in Teaching
GDRE	Graduate Diploma in Religious Education	M En	Master of Engineering
GEMBA	Global Executive Master of Business Administration		Master of Environmental Science
		M En S	Master of Environmental Sciences
GEMPA	Gulf Executive Master of Public Administration	M Eng	Master of Engineering
GM Acc	Graduate Master of Accountancy	M Eng Mgt	Master of Engineering Management
GMBA	Global Master of Business Administration	M Engr	Master of Engineering
GP LL M	Global Professional Master of Laws	M Ent	Master of Enterprise
GPD	Graduate Performance Diploma	M Env	Master of Environment
GSS	Graduate Special Certificate for Students in Special Situations	M Env Des	Master of Environmental Design
		M Env E	Master of Environmental Engineering
IEMBA	International Executive Master of Business Administration	M Env Sc	Master of Environmental Science
		M Fin	Master of Finance
IM Acc	Integrated Master of Accountancy	M Geo E	Master of Geological Engineering
IMA	Interdisciplinary Master of Arts	M Geoenv E	Master of Geoenvironmental Engineering
IMBA	International Master of Business Administration	M Geog	Master of Geography
IMES	International Master's in Environmental Studies	M Hum	Master of Humanities
Ingeniero	Engineer	M Hum Svcs	Master of Human Services
JCD	Doctor of Canon Law	M IBD	Master of Integrated Building Delivery

M IDST	Master's in Interdisciplinary Studies	MAAA	Master of Arts in Arts Administration
M Kin	Master of Kinesiology	MAAAP	Master of Arts Administration and Policy
M Land Arch	Master of Landscape Architecture	MAAE	Master of Arts in Art Education
M Litt	Master of Letters	MAAT	Master of Arts in Applied Theology
M Mat SE	Master of Material Science and Engineering		Master of Arts in Art Therapy
M Math	Master of Mathematics	MAB	Master of Agribusiness
M Mech E	Master of Mechanical Engineering	MABC	Master of Arts in Biblical Counseling
M Med Sc	Master of Medical Science		Master of Arts in Business Communication
M Mgmt	Master of Management	MABE	Master of Arts in Bible Exposition
M Mgt	Master of Management	MABL	Master of Arts in Biblical Languages
M Min	Master of Ministries	MABM	Master of Agribusiness Management
M Mtl E	Master of Materials Engineering	MABMH	bioethics and medical humanities
M Mu	Master of Music	MABS	Master of Arts in Biblical Studies
M Mus	Master of Music	MABT	Master of Arts in Bible Teaching
M Mus Ed	Master of Music Education	MAC	Master of Accountancy
M Music	Master of Music		Master of Accounting
M Nat Sci	Master of Natural Science		Master of Arts in Communication
M Oc E	Master of Oceanographic Engineering		Master of Arts in Counseling
M Pet E	Master of Petroleum Engineering	MACC	Master of Arts in Christian Counseling
M Pharm	Master of Pharmacy		Master of Arts in Clinical Counseling
M Phil	Master of Philosophy	MACCM	Master of Arts in Church and Community
M Phil F	Master of Philosophical Foundations		Ministry
M Pl	Master of Planning	MACCT	Master of Accounting
M Plan	Master of Planning	MACD	Master of Arts in Christian Doctrine
M Pol	Master of Political Science	MACE	Master of Arts in Christian Education
M Pr Met	Master of Professional Meteorology	MACFM	Master of Arts in Children's and Family Ministry
M Prob S	Master of Probability and Statistics	MACH	Master of Arts in Church History
M Psych	Master of Psychology	MACI	Master of Arts in Curriculum and Instruction
M Pub	Master of Publishing	MACIS	Master of Accounting and Information Systems
M Rel	Master of Religion	MACJ	Master of Arts in Criminal Justice
M Sc	Master of Science	MACL	Master of Arts in Christian Leadership
M Sc A	Master of Science (Applied)	MACM	Master of Arts in Christian Ministries
M Sc AC	Master of Science in Applied Computing		Master of Arts in Christian Ministry
M Sc AHN	Master of Science in Applied Human Nutrition		Master of Arts in Church Music
M Sc BMC	Master of Science in Biomedical		Master of Arts in Counseling Ministries
	Communications	MACN	Master of Arts in Counseling
M Sc CS	Master of Science in Computer Science	MACO	Master of Arts in Counseling
M Sc E	Master of Science in Engineering	MAcOM	Master of Acupuncture and Oriental Medicine
M Sc Eng	Master of Science in Engineering	MACP	Master of Arts in Christian Practice
M Sc Engr	Master of Science in Engineering		Master of Arts in Counseling Psychology
M Sc F	Master of Science in Forestry	MACS	Master of Applied Computer Science
M Sc FE	Master of Science in Forest Engineering		Master of Arts in Catholic Studies
M Sc Geogr	Master of Science in Geography		Master of Arts in Christian Studies
M Sc N	Master of Science in Nursing	MACSE	Master of Arts in Christian School Education
M Sc OT	Master of Science in Occupational Therapy	MACT	Master of Arts in Christian Thought
M Sc P	Master of Science in Planning		Master of Arts in Communications and
M Sc Pl	Master of Science in Planning		Technology
M Sc PT	Master of Science in Physical Therapy	MAD	Master in Educational Institution Administration
M Sc T	Master of Science in Teaching		Master of Art and Design
M SEM	Master of Sustainable Environmental	MAD-Crit	Master of Arts in Design Criticism
	Management	MADR	Master of Arts in Dispute Resolution
M Serv Soc	Master of Social Service	MADS	Master of Animal and Dairy Science
M Soc	Master of Sociology		Master of Applied Disability Studies
M Sp Ed	Master of Special Education	MAE	Master of Aerospace Engineering
M Stat	Master of Statistics		Master of Agricultural Economics
M Sys E	Master of Systems Engineering		Master of Agricultural Education
M Sys Sc	Master of Systems Science		Master of Architectural Engineering
M Tax	Master of Taxation		Master of Art Education
M Tech	Master of Technology		Master of Arts in Education
M Th	Master of Theology		Master of Arts in English
M Tox	Master of Toxicology	MAEd	Master of Arts Education
M Trans E	Master of Transportation Engineering	MAEL	Master of Arts in Educational Leadership
M Urb	Master of Urban Planning	MAEM	Master of Arts in Educational Ministries
M Vet Sc	Master of Veterinary Science	MAEN	Master of Arts in English
MA	Master of Accounting	MAEP	Master of Arts in Economic Policy
	Master of Administration	MAES	Master of Arts in Environmental Sciences
	Master of Arts	MAET	Master of Arts in English Teaching
MA Comm	Master of Arts in Communication	MAF	Master of Arts in Finance
MA Ed	Master of Arts in Education	MAFE	Master of Arts in Financial Economics
MA Ed Ad	Master of Arts in Educational Administration	MAFLL	Master of Arts in Foreign Language and
MA Ext	Master of Agricultural Extension		Literature
MA Islamic	Master of Arts in Islamic Studies	MAFM	Master of Accounting and Financial
MA Min	Master of Arts in Ministry		Management
MA Miss	Master of Arts in Missiology	MAFS	Master of Arts in Family Studies
MA Past St	Master of Arts in Pastoral Studies	MAG	Master of Applied Geography
MA Ph	Master of Arts in Philosophy	MAGU	Master of Urban Analysis and Management
MA Psych	Master of Arts in Psychology	MAH	Master of Arts in Humanities
MA Sc	Master of Applied Science	MAHA	Master of Arts in Humanitarian Assistance
MA Sp	Master of Arts (Spirituality)		Master of Arts in Humanitarian Studies
MA Th	Master of Arts in Theology	MAHCM	Master of Arts in Health Care Mission
MA-R	Master of Arts (Research)	MAHG	Master of American History and Government
MAA	Master of Administrative Arts	MAHL	Master of Arts in Hebrew Letters
	Master of Applied Anthropology	MAHN	Master of Applied Human Nutrition
	Master of Applied Arts	MAHSR	Master of Applied Health Services Research
	Master of Arts in Administration	MAIA	Master of Arts in International Administration

MAIB	Master of Arts in International Affairs
	Master of Arts in International Business
MAIDM	Master of Arts in Interior Design and Merchandising
MAIH	Master of Arts in Interdisciplinary Humanities
MAIOP	Master of Arts in Industrial/Organizational Psychology
MAIPCR	Master of Arts in International Peace and Conflict Management
MAIS	Master of Arts in Intercultural Studies
	Master of Arts in Interdisciplinary Studies
	Master of Arts in International Studies
MAIT	Master of Administration in Information Technology
	Master of Applied Information Technology
MAJ	Master of Arts in Journalism
MAJ Ed	Master of Arts in Jewish Education
MAJCS	Master of Arts in Jewish Communal Service
MAJE	Master of Arts in Jewish Education
MAJPS	Master of Arts in Jewish Professional Studies
MAJS	Master of Arts in Jewish Studies
MAL	Master in Agricultural Leadership
MALA	Master of Arts in Liberal Arts
MALD	Master of Arts in Law and Diplomacy
MALER	Master of Arts in Labor and Employment Relations
MALM	Master of Arts in Leadership Evangelical Mobilization
MALP	Master of Arts in Language Pedagogy
MALPS	Master of Arts in Liberal and Professional Studies
MALS	Master of Arts in Liberal Studies
MAM	Master of Acquisition Management
	Master of Agriculture and Management
	Master of Applied Mathematics
	Master of Arts in Ministry
	Master of Arts Management
	Master of Avian Medicine
MAMB	Master of Applied Molecular Biology
MAMC	Master of Arts in Mass Communication
	Master of Arts in Ministry and Culture
	Master of Arts in Ministry for a Multicultural Church
	Master of Arts in Missional Christianity
MAME	Master of Arts in Missions/Evangelism
MAMFC	Master of Arts in Marriage and Family Counseling
MAMFCC	Master of Arts in Marriage, Family, and Child Counseling
MAMFT	Master of Arts in Marriage and Family Therapy
MAMHC	Master of Arts in Mental Health Counseling
MAMI	Master of Arts in Missions
MAMS	Master of Applied Mathematical Sciences
	Master of Arts in Ministerial Studies
	Master of Arts in Ministry and Spirituality
MAMT	Master of Arts in Mathematics Teaching
MAN	Master of Applied Nutrition
MANT	Master of Arts in New Testament
MAOL	Master of Arts in Organizational Leadership
MAOM	Master of Acupuncture and Oriental Medicine
	Master of Arts in Organizational Management
MAOT	Master of Arts in Old Testament
MAP	Master of Applied Psychology
	Master of Arts in Planning
	Master of Psychology
	Master of Public Administration
MAP Min	Master of Arts in Pastoral Ministry
MAPA	Master of Arts in Public Administration
MAPC	Master of Arts in Pastoral Counseling
	Master of Arts in Professional Counseling
MAPE	Master of Arts in Political Economy
MAPM	Master of Arts in Pastoral Ministry
	Master of Arts in Pastoral Music
	Master of Arts in Practical Ministry
MAPP	Master of Arts in Public Policy
MAPPS	Master of Arts in Asia Pacific Policy Studies
MAPS	Master of Arts in Pastoral Counseling/Spiritual Formation
	Master of Arts in Pastoral Studies
	Master of Arts in Public Service
MAPT	Master of Practical Theology
MAPW	Master of Arts in Professional Writing
MAR	Master of Arts in Reading
	Master of Arts in Religion
Mar Eng	Marine Engineer

MARC	Master of Arts in Rehabilitation Counseling
MARE	Master of Arts in Religious Education
MARL	Master of Arts in Religious Leadership
MARS	Master of Arts in Religious Studies
MAS	Master of Accounting Science
	Master of Actuarial Science
	Master of Administrative Science
	Master of Advanced Study
	Master of Aeronautical Science
	Master of American Studies
	Master of Applied Science
	Master of Applied Statistics
	Master of Archival Studies
MASA	Master of Advanced Studies in Architecture
MASD	Master of Arts in Spiritual Direction
MASE	Master of Arts in Special Education
MASF	Master of Arts in Spiritual Formation
MASJ	Master of Arts in Systems of Justice
MASLA	Master of Advanced Studies in Landscape Architecture
MASM	Master of Aging Services Management
	Master of Arts in Specialized Ministries
MASP	Master of Applied Social Psychology
	Master of Arts in School Psychology
MASPAA	Master of Arts in Sports and Athletic Administration
MASS	Master of Applied Social Science
	Master of Arts in Social Science
MAST	Master of Arts in Science Teaching
MASW	Master of Aboriginal Social Work
MAT	Master of Arts in Teaching
	Master of Arts in Theology
	Master of Athletic Training
	Master's in Administration of Telecommunications
Mat E	Materials Engineer
MATCM	Master of Acupuncture and Traditional Chinese Medicine
MATDE	Master of Arts in Theology, Development, and Evangelism
MATDR	Master of Territorial Management and Regional Development
MATE	Master of Arts for the Teaching of English
MATESL	Master of Arts in Teaching English as a Second Language
MATESOL	Master of Arts in Teaching English to Speakers of Other Languages
MATF	Master of Arts in Teaching English as a Foreign Language/Intercultural Studies
MATFL	Master of Arts in Teaching Foreign Language
MATH	Master of Arts in Therapy
MATI	Master of Administration of Information Technology
MATL	Master of Arts in Teacher Leadership
	Master of Arts in Teaching of Languages
	Master of Arts in Transformational Leadership
MATM	Master of Arts in Teaching of Mathematics
MATS	Master of Arts in Theological Studies
	Master of Arts in Transforming Spirituality
MATSL	Master of Arts in Teaching a Second Language
MAUA	Master of Arts in Urban Affairs
MAUD	Master of Arts in Urban Design
MAURP	Master of Arts in Urban and Regional Planning
MAWSHP	Master of Arts in Worship
MAYM	Master of Arts in Youth Ministry
MB	Master of Bioinformatics
	Master of Biology
MBA	Master of Business Administration
MBA-AM	Master of Business Administration in Aviation Management
MBA-EP	Master of Business AdministrationNExperienced Professionals
MBA/MGPS	Master of Business Administration/Master of Global Policy Studies
MBAA	Master of Business Administration in Aviation
MBAE	Master of Biological and Agricultural Engineering
	Master of Biosystems and Agricultural Engineering
MBAH	Master of Business Administration in Health
MBAi	Master of Business AdministrationNInternational
MBAICT	Master of Business Administration in Information and Communication Technology

MBATM	Master of Business Administration in Technology Management
MBC	Master of Building Construction
MBE	Master of Bilingual Education
	Master of Bioengineering
	Master of Bioethics
	Master of Biological Engineering
	Master of Biomedical Engineering
	Master of Business and Engineering
	Master of Business Economics
	Master of Business Education
MBEE	Master in Biotechnology Enterprise and Entrepreneurship
MBET	Master of Business, Entrepreneurship and Technology
MBIOT	Master of Biotechnology
MBiotech	Master of Biotechnology
MBL	Master of Business Law
	Master of Business Leadership
MBLE	Master in Business Logistics Engineering
MBMI	Master of Biomedical Imaging and Signals
MBMSE	Master of Business Management and Software Engineering
MBOE	Master of Business Operational Excellence
MBS	Master of Biblical Studies
	Master of Biological Science
	Master of Biomedical Sciences
	Master of Bioscience
	Master of Building Science
	Master of Business and Science
MBST	Master of Biostatistics
MBT	Master of Biblical and Theological Studies
	Master of Biomedical Technology
	Master of Biotechnology
	Master of Business Taxation
MC	Master of Communication
	Master of Counseling
	Master of Cybersecurity
MC Ed	Master of Continuing Education
MC Sc	Master of Computer Science
MCA	Master of Arts in Applied Criminology
	Master of Commercial Aviation
MCAM	Master of Computational and Applied Mathematics
MCC	Master of Computer Science
MCCS	Master of Crop and Soil Sciences
MCD	Master of Communications Disorders
	Master of Community Development
MCE	Master in Electronic Commerce
	Master of Christian Education
	Master of Civil Engineering
	Master of Control Engineering
MCEM	Master of Construction Engineering Management
MCH	Master of Chemical Engineering
MCHE	Master of Chemical Engineering
MCIS	Master of Communication and Information Studies
	Master of Computer and Information Science
	Master of Computer Information Systems
MCIT	Master of Computer and Information Technology
MCJ	Master of Criminal Justice
MCJA	Master of Criminal Justice Administration
MCL	Master in Communication Leadership
	Master of Canon Law
	Master of Comparative Law
MCM	Master of Christian Ministry
	Master of Church Music
	Master of City Management
	Master of Communication Management
	Master of Community Medicine
	Master of Construction Management
	Master of Contract Management
	Master of Corporate Media
MCMP	Master of City and Metropolitan Planning
MCMS	Master of Clinical Medical Science
MCN	Master of Clinical Nutrition
MCOL	Master of Arts in Community and Organizational Leadership
MCP	Master of City Planning
	Master of Community Planning
	Master of Counseling Psychology
	Master of Cytopathology Practice

	Master of Science in Quality Systems and Productivity
MCPC	Master of Arts in Chaplaincy and Pastoral Care
MCPD	Master of Community Planning and Development
MCR	Master in Clinical Research
MCRP	Master of City and Regional Planning
MCRS	Master of City and Regional Studies
MCS	Master of Christian Studies
	Master of Clinical Science
	Master of Combined Sciences
	Master of Communication Studies
	Master of Computer Science
	Master of Consumer Science
MCSE	Master of Computer Science and Engineering
MCSL	Master of Catholic School Leadership
MCSM	Master of Construction Science/Management
MCST	Master of Science in Computer Science and Information Technology
MCTP	Master of Communication Technology and Policy
MCTS	Master of Clinical and Translational Science
MCVS	Master of Cardiovascular Science
MD	Doctor of Medicine
MDA	Master of Development Administration
	Master of Dietetic Administration
MDB	Master of Design-Build
MDE	Master of Developmental Economics
	Master of Distance Education
	Master of the Education of the Deaf
MDH	Master of Dental Hygiene
MDM	Master of Design Methods
	Master of Digital Media
MDP	Master in Sustainable Development Practice
	Master of Development Practice
MDR	Master of Dispute Resolution
MDS	Master of Dental Surgery
	Master of Design Studies
ME	Master of Education
	Master of Engineering
	Master of Entrepreneurship
	Master of Evangelism
ME Sc	Master of Engineering Science
MEA	Master of Educational Administration
	Master of Engineering Administration
MEAP	Master of Environmental Administration and Planning
MEBT	Master in Electronic Business Technologies
MEC	Master of Electronic Commerce
MECE	Master of Electrical and Computer Engineering
Mech E	Mechanical Engineer
MED	Master of Education of the Deaf
MEDS	Master of Environmental Design Studies
MEE	Master in Education
	Master of Electrical Engineering
	Master of Energy Engineering
	Master of Environmental Engineering
MEEM	Master of Environmental Engineering and Management
MEENE	Master of Engineering in Environmental Engineering
MEEP	Master of Environmental and Energy Policy
MEERM	Master of Earth and Environmental Resource Management
MEH	Master in Humanistic Studies
	Master of Environmental Horticulture
MEHP	Master of Education in the Health Professions
MEHS	Master of Environmental Health and Safety
MEIM	Master of Entertainment Industry Management
MEL	Master of Educational Leadership
	Master of English Literature
MELP	Master of Environmental Law and Policy
MEM	Master of Ecosystem Management
	Master of Electricity Markets
	Master of Engineering Management
	Master of Environmental Management
	Master of Marketing
MEME	Master of Engineering in Manufacturing Engineering
	Master of Engineering in Mechanical Engineering
MENG	Master of Arts in English
MENVEGR	Master of Environmental Engineering
MEP	Master of Engineering Physics
MEPC	Master of Environmental Pollution Control

MEPD	Master of EducationNProfessional Development
	Master of Environmental Planning and Design
MER	Master of Employment Relations
MERE	Master of Entrepreneurial Real Estate
MES	Master of Education and Science
	Master of Engineering Science
	Master of Environment and Sustainability
	Master of Environmental Science
	Master of Environmental Studies
	Master of Environmental Systems
	Master of Special Education
MESM	Master of Environmental Science and Management
MET	Master of Educational Technology
	Master of Engineering Technology
	Master of Entertainment Technology
	Master of Environmental Toxicology
METM	Master of Engineering and Technology Management
MEVE	Master of Environmental Engineering
MF	Master of Finance
	Master of Forestry
MFA	Master of Fine Arts
MFAM	Master in Food Animal Medicine
MFAS	Master of Fisheries and Aquatic Science
MFAW	Master of Fine Arts in Writing
MFC	Master of Forest Conservation
MFCS	Master of Family and Consumer Sciences
MFE	Master of Financial Economics
	Master of Financial Engineering
	Master of Forest Engineering
MFG	Master of Functional Genomics
MFHD	Master of Family and Human Development
MFM	Master of Financial Management
	Master of Financial Mathematics
MFMS	Master's in Food Microbiology and Safety
MFPE	Master of Food Process Engineering
MFR	Master of Forest Resources
MFRC	Master of Forest Resources and Conservation
MFS	Master of Food Science
	Master of Forensic Sciences
	Master of Forest Science
	Master of Forest Studies
	Master of French Studies
MFST	Master of Food Safety and Technology
MFT	Master of Family Therapy
	Master of Food Technology
MFWB	Master of Fishery and Wildlife Biology
MFWCB	Master of Fish, Wildlife and Conservation Biology
MFWS	Master of Fisheries and Wildlife Sciences
MFYCS	Master of Family, Youth and Community Sciences
MG	Master of Genetics
MGA	Master of Global Affairs
	Master of Governmental Administration
MGC	Master of Genetic Counseling
MGD	Master of Graphic Design
MGE	Master of Geotechnical Engineering
MGEM	Master of Global Entrepreneurship and Management
MGIS	Master of Geographic Information Science
	Master of Geographic Information Systems
MGM	Master of Global Management
MGP	Master of Gestion de Projet
MGPS	Master of Global Policy Studies
MGPS/MA	Master of Global Policy Studies/Master of Arts
MGPS/MPH	Master of Global Policy Studies/Master of Public Health
MGREM	Master of Global Real Estate Management
MGS	Master of Gerontological Studies
	Master of Global Studies
MH	Master of Humanities
MH Ed	Master of Health Education
MH Sc	Master of Health Sciences
MHA	Master of Health Administration
	Master of Healthcare Administration
	Master of Hospital Administration
	Master of Hospitality Administration
MHAD	Master of Health Administration
MHB	Master of Human Behavior
MHCA	Master of Health Care Administration
MHCI	Master of Health Care Informatics
	Master of Human-Computer Interaction

MHCL	Master of Health Care Leadership
MHE	Master of Health Education
	Master of Human Ecology
MHE Ed	Master of Home Economics Education
MHEA	Master of Higher Education Administration
MHHS	Master of Health and Human Services
MHI	Master of Health Informatics
	Master of Healthcare Innovation
MHIIM	Master of Health Informatics and Information Management
MHIS	Master of Health Information Systems
MHK	Master of Human Kinetics
MHL	Master of Hebrew Literature
MHM	Master of Healthcare Management
MHMS	Master of Health Management Systems
MHP	Master of Health Physics
	Master of Heritage Preservation
	Master of Historic Preservation
MHPA	Master of Heath Policy and Administration
MHPE	Master of Health Professions Education
MHR	Master of Human Resources
MHRD	Master in Human Resource Development
MHRIR	Master of Human Resources and Industrial Relations
MHRLR	Master of Human Resources and Labor Relations
MHRM	Master of Human Resources Management
MHS	Master of Health Science
	Master of Health Sciences
	Master of Health Studies
	Master of Hispanic Studies
	Master of Human Services
	Master of Humanistic Studies
MHSA	Master of Health Services Administration
MHSM	Master of Health Systems Management
MI	Master of Information
	Master of Instruction
MI Arch	Master of Interior Architecture
MIA	Master of Interior Architecture
	Master of International Affairs
MIAA	Master of International Affairs and Administration
MIAM	Master of International Agribusiness Management
MIAPD	Master of Interior Architecture and Product Design
MIB	Master of International Business
MIBA	Master of International Business Administration
MICM	Master of International Construction Management
MID	Master of Industrial Design
	Master of Industrial Distribution
	Master of Interior Design
	Master of International Development
MIDC	Master of Integrated Design and Construction
MIE	Master of Industrial Engineering
MIH	Master of Integrative Health
MIHTM	Master of International Hospitality and Tourism Management
MIJ	Master of International Journalism
MILR	Master of Industrial and Labor Relations
MiM	Master in Management
MIM	Master of Industrial Management
	Master of Information Management
	Master of International Management
MIMLAE	Master of International Management for Latin American Executives
MIMS	Master of Information Management and Systems
	Master of Integrated Manufacturing Systems
MIP	Master of Infrastructure Planning
	Master of Intellectual Property
	Master of International Policy
MIPA	Master of International Public Affairs
MIPER	Master of International Political Economy of Resources
MIPP	Master of International Policy and Practice
	Master of International Public Policy
MIPS	Master of International Planning Studies
MIR	Master of Industrial Relations
	Master of International Relations
MIRHR	Master of Industrial Relations and Human Resources
MIS	Master of Industrial Statistics
	Master of Information Science

	Master of Information Systems	MMF	Master of Mathematical Finance
	Master of Integrated Science	MMFT	Master of Marriage and Family Therapy
	Master of Interdisciplinary Studies	MMG	Master of Management
	Master of International Service	MMH	Master of Management in Hospitality
	Master of International Studies		Master of Medical Humanities
MISE	Master of Industrial and Systems Engineering	MMI	Master of Management of Innovation
MISKM	Master of Information Sciences and Knowledge Management	MMIS	Master of Management Information Systems
MISM	Master of Information Systems Management	MMM	Master of Manufacturing Management
MIT	Master in Teaching		Master of Marine Management
	Master of Industrial Technology		Master of Medical Management
	Master of Information Technology	MMME	Master of Metallurgical and Materials Engineering
	Master of Initial Teaching	MMP	Master of Management Practice
	Master of International Trade		Master of Marine Policy
	Master of Internet Technology		Master of Medical Physics
MITA	Master of Information Technology Administration		Master of Music Performance
MITM	Master of Information Technology and Management	MMPA	Master of Management and Professional Accounting
MITO	Master of Industrial Technology and Operations	MMQM	Master of Manufacturing Quality Management
MJ	Master of Journalism	MMR	Master of Marketing Research
	Master of Jurisprudence	MMRM	Master of Marine Resources Management
MJ Ed	Master of Jewish Education	MMS	Master of Management Science
MJA	Master of Justice Administration		Master of Management Studies
MJM	Master of Justice Management		Master of Manufacturing Systems
MJS	Master of Judicial Studies		Master of Marine Studies
	Master of Juridical Science		Master of Materials Science
MKM	Master of Knowledge Management		Master of Medical Science
ML	Master of Latin		Master of Medieval Studies
ML Arch	Master of Landscape Architecture	MMSE	Master of Manufacturing Systems Engineering
MLA	Master of Landscape Architecture		Multidisciplinary Master of Science in Engineering
	Master of Liberal Arts	MMSM	Master of Music in Sacred Music
MLAS	Master of Laboratory Animal Science	MMT	Master in Marketing
	Master of Liberal Arts and Sciences		Master of Music Teaching
MLAUD	Master of Landscape Architecture in Urban Development		Master of Music Therapy
MLD	Master of Leadership Development		Master's in Marketing Technology
MLE	Master of Applied Linguistics and Exegesis	MMus	Master of Music
MLER	Master of Labor and Employment Relations	MN	Master of Nursing
MLHR	Master of Labor and Human Resources		Master of Nutrition
MLI Sc	Master of Library and Information Science	MN NP	Master of Nursing in Nurse Practitioner
MLIS	Master of Library and Information Science	MNA	Master of Nonprofit Administration
	Master of Library and Information Studies		Master of Nurse Anesthesia
MLM	Master of Library Media	MNAL	Master of Nonprofit Administration and Leadership
MLRHR	Master of Labor Relations and Human Resources	MNAS	Master of Natural and Applied Science
MLS	Master of Leadership Studies	MNCM	Master of Network and Communications Management
	Master of Legal Studies	MNE	Master of Network Engineering
	Master of Liberal Studies		Master of Nuclear Engineering
	Master of Library Science	MNL	Master in International Business for Latin America
	Master of Life Sciences	MNM	Master of Nonprofit Management
MLSP	Master of Law and Social Policy	MNO	Master of Nonprofit Organization
MLT	Master of Language Technologies	MNPL	Master of Not-for-Profit Leadership
MLTCA	Master of Long Term Care Administration	MNpS	Master of Nonprofit Studies
MM	Master of Management	MNR	Master of Natural Resources
	Master of Ministry	MNRES	Master of Natural Resources and Environmental Studies
	Master of Missiology		
	Master of Music	MNRM	Master of Natural Resource Management
MM Ed	Master of Music Education	MNRS	Master of Natural Resource Stewardship
MM Sc	Master of Medical Science	MNS	Master of Natural Science
MM St	Master of Museum Studies	MO	Master of Oceanography
MMA	Master of Marine Affairs	MOD	Master of Organizational Development
	Master of Media Arts	MOGS	Master of Oil and Gas Studies
	Master of Musical Arts	MOH	Master of Occupational Health
MMAE	Master of Mechanical and Aerospace Engineering	MOL	Master of Organizational Leadership
MMAL	Master of Maritime Administration and Logistics	MOM	Master of Oriental Medicine
		MOR	Master of Operations Research
MMAS	Master of Military Art and Science	MOT	Master of Occupational Therapy
MMB	Master of Microbial Biotechnology	MP	Master of Physiology
MMBA	Managerial Master of Business Administration		Master of Planning
MMC	Master of Manufacturing Competitiveness	MP Ac	Master of Professional Accountancy
	Master of Mass Communications	MP Acc	Master of Professional Accountancy
	Master of Music Conducting		Master of Professional Accounting
MMCM	Master of Music in Church Music		Master of Public Accounting
MMCSS	Master of Mathematical Computational and Statistical Sciences	MP Aff	Master of Public Affairs
		MP Aff/MPH	Master of Public Affairs/Master of Public Health
MME	Master of Manufacturing Engineering	MP Th	Master of Pastoral Theology
	Master of Mathematics Education	MPA	Master of Physician Assistant
	Master of Mathematics for Educators		Master of Professional Accountancy
	Master of Mechanical Engineering		Master of Professional Accounting
	Master of Medical Engineering		Master of Public Administration
	Master of Mining Engineering		Master of Public Affairs
	Master of Music Education	MPAC	Master of Professional Accounting

MPAID	Master of Public Administration and International Development
MPAP	Master of Physician Assistant Practice
	Master of Public Affairs and Politics
MPAS	Master of Physician Assistant Science
	Master of Physician Assistant Studies
MPC	Master of Pastoral Counseling
	Master of Professional Communication
	Master of Professional Counseling
MPCU	Master of Planning in Civic Urbanism
MPD	Master of Product Development
	Master of Public Diplomacy
MPDS	Master of Planning and Development Studies
MPE	Master of Physical Education
	Master of Power Engineering
MPEM	Master of Project Engineering and Management
MPH	Master of Public Health
MPHE	Master of Public Health Education
MPHTM	Master of Public Health and Tropical Medicine
MPI	Master of Product Innovation
MPIA	Master in International Affairs
	Master of Public and International Affairs
MPM	Master of Pastoral Ministry
	Master of Pest Management
	Master of Policy Management
	Master of Practical Ministries
	Master of Project Management
	Master of Public Management
MPNA	Master of Public and Nonprofit Administration
MPO	Master of Prosthetics and Orthotics
MPOD	Master of Positive Organizational Development
MPP	Master of Public Policy
MPPA	Master of Public Policy Administration
	Master of Public Policy and Administration
MPPAL	Master of Public Policy, Administration and Law
MPPM	Master of Public and Private Management
	Master of Public Policy and Management
MPPPM	Master of Plant Protection and Pest Management
MPRTM	Master of Parks, Recreation, and Tourism Management
MPS	Master of Pastoral Studies
	Master of Perfusion Science
	Master of Planning Studies
	Master of Political Science
	Master of Preservation Studies
	Master of Professional Studies
	Master of Public Service
MPSA	Master of Public Service Administration
MPSRE	Master of Professional Studies in Real Estate
MPT	Master of Pastoral Theology
	Master of Physical Therapy
	Master of Practical Theology
MPVM	Master of Preventive Veterinary Medicine
MPW	Master of Professional Writing
	Master of Public Works
MQM	Master of Quality Management
MQS	Master of Quality Systems
MR	Master of Recreation
	Master of Retailing
MRA	Master in Research Administration
MRC	Master of Rehabilitation Counseling
MRCP	Master of Regional and City Planning
	Master of Regional and Community Planning
MRD	Master of Rural Development
MRE	Master of Real Estate
	Master of Religious Education
MRED	Master of Real Estate Development
MREM	Master of Resource and Environmental Management
MRLS	Master of Resources Law Studies
MRM	Master of Resources Management
MRP	Master of Regional Planning
MRS	Master of Religious Studies
MRSc	Master of Rehabilitation Science
MS	Master of Science
MS Cmp E	Master of Science in Computer Engineering
MS Kin	Master of Science in Kinesiology
MS Acct	Master of Science in Accounting
MS Accy	Master of Science in Accountancy
MS Aero E	Master of Science in Aerospace Engineering
MS Ag	Master of Science in Agriculture
MS Arch	Master of Science in Architecture
MS Arch St	Master of Science in Architectural Studies

MS Bio E	Master of Science in Bioengineering
	Master of Science in Biomedical Engineering
MS Bm E	Master of Science in Biomedical Engineering
MS Ch E	Master of Science in Chemical Engineering
MS Chem	Master of Science in Chemistry
MS Cp E	Master of Science in Computer Engineering
MS Eco	Master of Science in Economics
MS Econ	Master of Science in Economics
MS Ed	Master of Science in Education
MS El	Master of Science in Educational Leadership and Administration
MS En E	Master of Science in Environmental Engineering
MS Eng	Master of Science in Engineering
MS Engr	Master of Science in Engineering
MS Env E	Master of Science in Environmental Engineering
MS Exp Surg	Master of Science in Experimental Surgery
MS Int A	Master of Science in International Affairs
MS Mat E	Master of Science in Materials Engineering
MS Mat SE	Master of Science in Material Science and Engineering
MS Met E	Master of Science in Metallurgical Engineering
MS Mgt	Master of Science in Management
MS Min	Master of Science in Mining
MS Min E	Master of Science in Mining Engineering
MS Mt E	Master of Science in Materials Engineering
MS Otal	Master of Science in Otalrynology
MS Pet E	Master of Science in Petroleum Engineering
MS Phys	Master of Science in Physics
MS Poly	Master of Science in Polymers
MS Psy	Master of Science in Psychology
MS Pub P	Master of Science in Public Policy
MS Sc	Master of Science in Social Science
MS Sp Ed	Master of Science in Special Education
MS Stat	Master of Science in Statistics
MS Surg	Master of Science in Surgery
MS Tax	Master of Science in Taxation
MS Tc E	Master of Science in Telecommunications Engineering
MS-R	Master of Science (Research)
MS/CAGS	Master of Science/Certificate of Advanced Graduate Studies
MSA	Master of School Administration
	Master of Science Administration
	Master of Science in Accountancy
	Master of Science in Accounting
	Master of Science in Administration
	Master of Science in Aeronautics
	Master of Science in Agriculture
	Master of Science in Anesthesia
	Master of Science in Architecture
	Master of Science in Aviation
	Master of Sports Administration
MSA Phy	Master of Science in Applied Physics
MSAA	Master of Science in Astronautics and Aeronautics
MSAAE	Master of Science in Aeronautical and Astronautical Engineering
MSABE	Master of Science in Agricultural and Biological Engineering
MSAC	Master of Science in Acupuncture
MSACC	Master of Science in Accounting
MSAE	Master of Science in Aeronautical Engineering
	Master of Science in Aerospace Engineering
	Master of Science in Applied Economics
	Master of Science in Applied Engineering
	Master of Science in Architectural Engineering
MSAH	Master of Science in Allied Health
MSAL	Master of Sport Administration and Leadership
MSAM	Master of Science in Applied Mathematics
MSANR	Master of Science in Agriculture and Natural Resources Systems Management
MSAPM	Master of Security Analysis and Portfolio Management
MSAS	Master of Science in Applied Statistics
	Master of Science in Architectural Studies
MSAT	Master of Science in Accounting and Taxation
	Master of Science in Advanced Technology
	Master of Science in Athletic Training
MSB	Master of Science in Bible
	Master of Science in Biotechnology
	Master of Science in Business
	Master of Sustainable Business
MSBA	Master of Science in Business Administration

	Master of Science in Business Analysis
MSBAE	Master of Science in Biological and Agricultural Engineering
	Master of Science in Biosystems and Agricultural Engineering
MSBC	Master of Science in Building Construction
MSBCB	bioinformatics and computational biology
MSBE	Master of Science in Biological Engineering
	Master of Science in Biomedical Engineering
MSBENG	Master of Science in Bioengineering
MSBIT	Master of Science in Business Information Technology
MSBM	Master of Sport Business Management
MSBME	Master of Science in Biomedical Engineering
MSBMS	Master of Science in Basic Medical Science
MSBS	Master of Science in Biomedical Sciences
MSC	Master of Science in Commerce
	Master of Science in Communication
	Master of Science in Computers
	Master of Science in Counseling
	Master of Science in Criminology
MSCC	Master of Science in Christian Counseling
	Master of Science in Community Counseling
MSCD	Master of Science in Communication Disorders
	Master of Science in Community Development
MSCE	Master of Science in Civil Engineering
	Master of Science in Clinical Epidemiology
	Master of Science in Computer Engineering
	Master of Science in Continuing Education
MSCEE	Master of Science in Civil and Environmental Engineering
MSCF	Master of Science in Computational Finance
MSCH	Master of Science in Chemical Engineering
MSChE	Master of Science in Chemical Engineering
MSCI	Master of Science in Clinical Investigation
	Master of Science in Curriculum and Instruction
MSCIS	Master of Science in Computer and Information Systems
	Master of Science in Computer Information Science
	Master of Science in Computer Information Systems
MSCIT	Master of Science in Computer Information Technology
MSCJ	Master of Science in Criminal Justice
MSCJA	Master of Science in Criminal Justice Administration
MSCJS	Master of Science in Crime and Justice Studies
MSCLS	Master of Science in Clinical Laboratory Studies
MSCM	Master of Science in Church Management
	Master of Science in Conflict Management
	Master of Science in Construction Management
MScM	Master of Science in Management
MSCM	Master of Supply Chain Management
MSCNU	Master of Science in Clinical Nutrition
MSCP	Master of Science in Clinical Psychology
	Master of Science in Community Psychology
	Master of Science in Computer Engineering
	Master of Science in Counseling Psychology
MSCPE	Master of Science in Computer Engineering
MSCPharm	Master of Science in Pharmacy
MSCPI	Master in Strategic Planning for Critical Infrastructures
MSCR	Master of Science in Clinical Research
MSCRP	Master of Science in City and Regional Planning
	Master of Science in Community and Regional Planning
MSCRP/MP Aff	Master of Science in Community and Regional Planning/Master of Public Affairs
MSCRP/MSSD	Master of Science in Community and Regional Planning/Master of Science in Sustainable Design
MSCRP/MSUD	Master of Science in Community and Regional Planning/Masters of Science in Urban Design
MSCS	Master of Science in Clinical Science
	Master of Science in Computer Science
MSCSD	Master of Science in Communication Sciences and Disorders
MSCSE	Master of Science in Computer Science and Engineering

MSCTE	Master of Science in Career and Technical Education
MSD	Master of Science in Dentistry
	Master of Science in Design
	Master of Science in Dietetics
MSE	Master of Science Education
	Master of Science in Economics
	Master of Science in Education
	Master of Science in Engineering
	Master of Science in Engineering Management
	Master of Software Engineering
	Master of Special Education
	Master of Structural Engineering
MSECE	Master of Science in Electrical and Computer Engineering
MSED	Master of Sustainable Economic Development
MSEE	Master of Science in Electrical Engineering
	Master of Science in Environmental Engineering
MSEH	Master of Science in Environmental Health
MSEL	Master of Science in Educational Leadership
MSEM	Master of Science in Engineering Management
	Master of Science in Engineering Mechanics
	Master of Science in Environmental Management
MSENE	Master of Science in Environmental Engineering
MSEO	Master of Science in Electro-Optics
MSEP	Master of Science in Economic Policy
MSEPA	Master of Science in Economics and Policy Analysis
MSES	Master of Science in Embedded Software Engineering
	Master of Science in Engineering Science
	Master of Science in Environmental Science
	Master of Science in Environmental Studies
MSESM	Master of Science in Engineering Science and Mechanics
MSET	Master of Science in Educational Technology
	Master of Science in Engineering Technology
MSEV	Master of Science in Environmental Engineering
MSEVH	Master of Science in Environmental Health and Safety
MSF	Master of Science in Finance
	Master of Science in Forestry
	Master of Spiritual Formation
MSFA	Master of Science in Financial Analysis
MSFAM	Master of Science in Family Studies
MSFCS	Master of Science in Family and Consumer Science
MSFE	Master of Science in Financial Engineering
MSFOR	Master of Science in Forestry
MSFP	Master of Science in Financial Planning
MSFS	Master of Science in Financial Sciences
	Master of Science in Forensic Science
MSFSB	Master of Science in Financial Services and Banking
MSFT	Master of Science in Family Therapy
MSGC	Master of Science in Genetic Counseling
MSH	Master of Science in Health
	Master of Science in Hospice
MSHA	Master of Science in Health Administration
MSHCA	Master of Science in Health Care Administration
MSHCI	Master of Science in Human Computer Interaction
MSHCPM	Master of Science in Health Care Policy and Management
MSHE	Master of Science in Health Education
MSHES	Master of Science in Human Environmental Sciences
MSHFID	Master of Science in Human Factors in Information Design
MSHFS	Master of Science in Human Factors and Systems
MSHI	Master of Science in Health Informatics
MSHP	Master of Science in Health Professions
	Master of Science in Health Promotion
MSHR	Master of Science in Human Resources
MSHRL	Master of Science in Human Resource Leadership
MSHRM	Master of Science in Human Resource Management

MSHROD	Master of Science in Human Resources and Organizational Development
MSHS	Master of Science in Health Science
	Master of Science in Health Services
	Master of Science in Health Systems
	Master of Science in Homeland Security
MSHT	Master of Science in History of Technology
MSI	Master of Science in Information
	Master of Science in Instruction
	Master of System Integration
MSIA	Master of Science in Industrial Administration
	Master of Science in Information Assurance and Computer Security
MSIB	Master of Science in International Business
MSIDM	Master of Science in Interior Design and Merchandising
MSIDT	Master of Science in Information Design and Technology
MSIE	Master of Science in Industrial Engineering
	Master of Science in International Economics
MSIEM	Master of Science in Information Engineering and Management
MSIID	Master of Science in Information and Instructional Design
MSIM	Master of Science in Information Management
	Master of Science in International Management
MSIMC	Master of Science in Integrated Marketing Communications
MSIR	Master of Science in Industrial Relations
MSIS	Master of Science in Information Science
	Master of Science in Information Studies
	Master of Science in Information Systems
	Master of Science in Interdisciplinary Studies
MSIS/MA	Master of Science in Information Studies/ Master of Arts
MSISE	Master of Science in Infrastructure Systems Engineering
MSISM	Master of Science in Information Systems Management
MSISPM	Master of Science in Information Security Policy and Management
MSIST	Master of Science in Information Systems Technology
MSIT	Master of Science in Industrial Technology
	Master of Science in Information Technology
	Master of Science in Instructional Technology
MSITM	Master of Science in Information Technology Management
MSJ	Master of Science in Journalism
	Master of Science in Jurisprudence
MSJC	Master of Social Justice and Criminology
MSJE	Master of Science in Jewish Education
MSJFP	Master of Science in Juvenile Forensic Psychology
MSJJ	Master of Science in Juvenile Justice
MSJPS	Master of Science in Justice and Public Safety
MSJS	Master of Science in Jewish Studies
MSK	Master of Science in Kinesiology
MSL	Master of School Leadership
	Master of Science in Leadership
	Master of Science in Limnology
	Master of Strategic Leadership
	Master of Studies in Law
MSLA	Master of Science in Landscape Architecture
	Master of Science in Legal Administration
MSLD	Master of Science in Land Development
MSLFS	Master of Science in Life Sciences
MSLP	Master of Speech-Language Pathology
MSLS	Master of Science in Library Science
MSLSCM	Master of Science in Logistics and Supply Chain Management
MSLT	Master of Second Language Teaching
MSM	Master of Sacred Ministry
	Master of Sacred Music
	Master of School Mathematics
	Master of Science in Management
	Master of Science in Organization Management
	Master of Security Management
MSMA	Master of Science in Marketing Analysis
MSMAE	Master of Science in Materials Engineering
MSMC	Master of Science in Mass Communications
MSME	Master of Science in Mathematics Education
	Master of Science in Mechanical Engineering

MSMFE	Master of Science in Manufacturing Engineering
MSMFT	Master of Science in Marriage and Family Therapy
MSMIS	Master of Science in Management Information Systems
MSMIT	Master of Science in Management and Information Technology
MSMLS	Master of Science in Medical Laboratory Science
MSMOT	Master of Science in Management of Technology
MSMS	Master of Science in Management Science
	Master of Science in Medical Sciences
MSMSE	Master of Science in Manufacturing Systems Engineering
	Master of Science in Material Science and Engineering
	Master of Science in Mathematics and Science Education
MSMT	Master of Science in Management and Technology
MSMus	Master of Sacred Music
MSN	Master of Science in Nursing
MSN-R	Master of Science in Nursing (Research)
MSNA	Master of Science in Nurse Anesthesia
MSNE	Master of Science in Nuclear Engineering
MSNED	Master of Science in Nurse Education
MSNM	Master of Science in Nonprofit Management
MSNS	Master of Science in Natural Science
	Master of Science in Nutritional Science
MSOD	Master of Science in Organizational Development
MSOEE	Master of Science in Outdoor and Environmental Education
MSOES	Master of Science in Occupational Ergonomics and Safety
MSOH	Master of Science in Occupational Health
MSOL	Master of Science in Organizational Leadership
MSOM	Master of Science in Operations Management
	Master of Science in Oriental Medicine
MSOR	Master of Science in Operations Research
MSOT	Master of Science in Occupational Technology
	Master of Science in Occupational Therapy
MSP	Master of Science in Pharmacy
	Master of Science in Planning
	Master of Science in Psychology
	Master of Speech Pathology
MSPA	Master of Science in Physician Assistant
	Master of Science in Professional Accountancy
MSPAS	Master of Science in Physician Assistant Studies
MSPC	Master of Science in Professional Communications
	Master of Science in Professional Counseling
MSPE	Master of Science in Petroleum Engineering
MSPG	Master of Science in Psychology
MSPH	Master of Science in Public Health
MSPHR	Master of Science in Pharmacy
MSPM	Master of Science in Professional Management
	Master of Science in Project Management
MSPNGE	Master of Science in Petroleum and Natural Gas Engineering
MSPS	Master of Science in Pharmaceutical Science
	Master of Science in Political Science
	Master of Science in Psychological Services
MSPT	Master of Science in Physical Therapy
MSpVM	Master of Specialized Veterinary Medicine
MSR	Master of Science in Radiology
	Master of Science in Reading
MSRA	Master of Science in Recreation Administration
MSRC	Master of Science in Resource Conservation
MSRE	Master of Science in Real Estate
	Master of Science in Religious Education
MSRED	Master of Science in Real Estate Development
MSRLS	Master of Science in Recreation and Leisure Studies
MSRMP	Master of Science in Radiological Medical Physics
MSRS	Master of Science in Rehabilitation Science
MSS	Master of Science in Software
	Master of Security Studies
	Master of Social Science
	Master of Social Services

	Master of Software Systems	MUA	Master of Urban Affairs
	Master of Sports Science	MUCD	Master of Urban and Community Design
	Master of Strategic Studies	MUD	Master of Urban Design
MSSA	Master of Science in Social Administration	MUDS	Master of Urban Design Studies
MSSCP	Master of Science in Science Content and Process	MUEP	Master of Urban and Environmental Planning
MSSD	Master of Science in Sustainable Design	MUP	Master of Urban Planning
MSSE	Master of Science in Software Engineering	MUPDD	Master of Urban Planning, Design, and Development
	Master of Science in Space Education	MUPP	Master of Urban Planning and Policy
	Master of Science in Special Education	MUPRED	Master of Urban Planning and Real Estate Development
MSSEM	Master of Science in Systems and Engineering Management	MURP	Master of Urban and Regional Planning
MSSI	Master of Science in Security Informatics		Master of Urban and Rural Planning
	Master of Science in Strategic Intelligence	MURPL	Master of Urban and Regional Planning
MSSL	Master of Science in School Leadership	MUS	Master of Urban Studies
	Master of Science in Strategic Leadership	MUSA	Master of Urban Spatial Analytics
MSSLP	Master of Science in Speech-Language Pathology	MVM	Master of VLSI and Microelectronics
		MVP	Master of Voice Pedagogy
MSSM	Master of Science in Sports Medicine	MVPH	Master of Veterinary Public Health
MSSP	Master of Science in Social Policy	MVS	Master of Visual Studies
MSSPA	Master of Science in Student Personnel Administration	MWC	Master of Wildlife Conservation
		MWE	Master in Welding Engineering
MSSS	Master of Science in Safety Science	MWPS	Master of Wood and Paper Science
	Master of Science in Systems Science	MWR	Master of Water Resources
MSST	Master of Science in Security Technologies	MWS	Master of Women's Studies
MSSW	Master of Science in Social Work		Master of Worship Studies
MSSWE	Master of Science in Software Engineering	MZS	Master of Zoological Science
MST	Master of Science and Technology	Nav Arch	Naval Architecture
	Master of Science in Taxation	Naval E	Naval Engineer
	Master of Science in Teaching	ND	Doctor of Naturopathic Medicine
	Master of Science in Technology	NE	Nuclear Engineer
	Master of Science in Telecommunications	Nuc E	Nuclear Engineer
	Master of Science Teaching	OD	Doctor of Optometry
MSTC	Master of Science in Technical Communication	OTD	Doctor of Occupational Therapy
	Master of Science in Telecommunications	PBME	Professional Master of Biomedical Engineering
MSTCM	Master of Science in Traditional Chinese Medicine	PC	Performer's Certificate
		PD	Professional Diploma
MSTE	Master of Science in Telecommunications Engineering	PGC	Post-Graduate Certificate
		PGD	Postgraduate Diploma
	Master of Science in Transportation Engineering	Ph L	Licentiate of Philosophy
		Pharm D	Doctor of Pharmacy
MSTM	Master of Science in Technical Management	PhD	Doctor of Philosophy
	Master of Science in Technology Management	PhD Otal	Doctor of Philosophy in Otalrynology
	Master of Science in Transfusion Medicine	PhD Surg	Doctor of Philosophy in Surgery
MSTOM	Master of Science in Traditional Oriental Medicine	PhDEE	Doctor of Philosophy in Electrical Engineering
		PMBA	Professional Master of Business Administration
MSUD	Master of Science in Urban Design	PMC	Post Master Certificate
MSW	Master of Social Work	PMD	Post-Master's Diploma
MSWE	Master of Software Engineering	PMS	Professional Master of Science
MSWREE	Master of Science in Water Resources and Environmental Engineering		Professional Master's
		Post-Doctoral MS	Post-Doctoral Master of Science
MSX	Master of Science in Exercise Science	Post-MSN Certificate	Post-Master of Science in Nursing Certificate
MT	Master of Taxation	PPDPT	Postprofessional Doctor of Physical Therapy
	Master of Teaching	Pro-MS	Professional Science Master's
	Master of Technology	PSM	Professional Master of Science
	Master of Textiles		Professional Science Master's
MTA	Master of Tax Accounting	Psy D	Doctor of Psychology
	Master of Teaching Arts	Psy M	Master of Psychology
	Master of Tourism Administration	Psy S	Specialist in Psychology
MTCM	Master of Traditional Chinese Medicine	Psya D	Doctor of Psychoanalysis
MTD	Master of Training and Development	Rh D	Doctor of Rehabilitation
MTE	Master in Educational Technology	S Psy S	Specialist in Psychological Services
MTESOL	Master in Teaching English to Speakers of Other Languages	Sc D	Doctor of Science
		Sc M	Master of Science
MTHM	Master of Tourism and Hospitality Management	SCCT	Specialist in Community College Teaching
MTI	Master of Information Technology	ScDPT	Doctor of Physical Therapy Science
MTIM	Master of Trust and Investment Management	SD	Doctor of Science
MTL	Master of Talmudic Law		Specialist Degree
MTM	Master of Technology Management	SJD	Doctor of Juridical Science
	Master of Telecommunications Management	SLPD	Doctor of Speech-Language Pathology
	Master of the Teaching of Mathematics	SM	Master of Science
MTMH	Master of Tropical Medicine and Hygiene	SM Arch S	Master of Science in Architectural Studies
MTOM	Master of Traditional Oriental Medicine	SMACT	Master of Science in Art, Culture and Technology
MTP	Master of Transpersonal Psychology		
MTPC	Master of Technical and Professional Communication	SMBT	Master of Science in Building Technology
		SP	Specialist Degree
MTR	Master of Translational Research	Sp C	Specialist in Counseling
MTS	Master of Theatre Studies	Sp Ed	Specialist in Education
	Master of Theological Studies	Sp LIS	Specialist in Library and Information Science
MTSC	Master of Technical and Scientific Communication	SPA	Specialist in Arts
		SPCM	Specialist in Church Music
MTSE	Master of Telecommunications and Software Engineering	Spec	Specialist's Certificate
		Spec M	Specialist in Music
MTT	Master in Technology Management	SPEM	Specialist in Educational Ministries
MTX	Master of Taxation	Spt	Specialist Degree

ABBREVIATIONS USED IN THE GUIDES

SPTH	Specialist in Theology	Th D	Doctor of Theology
SSP	Specialist in School Psychology	Th M	Master of Theology
STB	Bachelor of Sacred Theology	VMD	Doctor of Veterinary Medicine
STD	Doctor of Sacred Theology	WEMBA	Weekend Executive Master of Business Administration
STL	Licentiate of Sacred Theology		
STM	Master of Sacred Theology	XMA	Executive Master of Arts
TDPT	Transitional Doctor of Physical Therapy		

INDEXES

Displays and Close-Ups

Directories and Subject Areas

Following is an alphabetical listing of directories and subject areas. Also listed are cross-references for subject area names not used in the directory structure of the guides, for example, "City and Regional Planning (*see* Urban and Regional Planning)."

Graduate Programs in the Humanities, Arts & Social Sciences

Addictions/Substance Abuse Counseling
Administration (*see* Arts Administration; Public Administration)
African-American Studies
African Languages and Literatures (*see* African Studies)
African Studies
Agribusiness (*see* Agricultural Economics and Agribusiness)
Agricultural Economics and Agribusiness
Alcohol Abuse Counseling (*see* Addictions/Substance Abuse Counseling)
American Indian/Native American Studies
American Studies
Anthropology
Applied Arts and Design—General
Applied Behavior Analysis
Applied Economics
Applied History (*see* Public History)
Applied Psychology
Applied Social Research
Arabic (*see* Near and Middle Eastern Languages)
Arab Studies (*see* Near and Middle Eastern Studies)
Archaeology
Architectural History
Architecture
Archives Administration (*see* Public History)
Area and Cultural Studies (*see* African-American Studies; African Studies; American Indian/Native American Studies; American Studies; Asian-American Studies; Asian Studies; Canadian Studies; Cultural Studies; East European and Russian Studies; Ethnic Studies; Folklore; Gender Studies; Hispanic Studies; Holocaust Studies; Jewish Studies; Latin American Studies; Near and Middle Eastern Studies; Northern Studies; Pacific Area/ Pacific Rim Studies; Western European Studies; Women's Studies)
Art/Fine Arts
Art History
Arts Administration
Arts Journalism
Art Therapy
Asian-American Studies
Asian Languages
Asian Studies
Behavioral Sciences (*see* Psychology)
Bible Studies (*see* Religion; Theology)
Biological Anthropology
Black Studies (*see* African-American Studies)
Broadcasting (*see* Communication; Film, Television, and Video Production)
Broadcast Journalism
Building Science
Canadian Studies
Celtic Languages
Ceramics (*see* Art/Fine Arts)
Child and Family Studies
Child Development
Chinese
Chinese Studies (*see* Asian Languages; Asian Studies)
Christian Studies (*see* Missions and Missiology; Religion; Theology)
Cinema (*see* Film, Television, and Video Production)
City and Regional Planning (*see* Urban and Regional Planning)
Classical Languages and Literatures (*see* Classics)
Classics
Clinical Psychology
Clothing and Textiles
Cognitive Psychology (*see* Psychology—General; Cognitive Sciences)
Cognitive Sciences
Communication—General
Community Affairs (*see* Urban and Regional Planning; Urban Studies)
Community Planning (*see* Architecture; Environmental Design; Urban and Regional Planning; Urban Design; Urban Studies)
Community Psychology (*see* Social Psychology)
Comparative and Interdisciplinary Arts
Comparative Literature

Composition (*see* Music)
Computer Art and Design
Conflict Resolution and Mediation/Peace Studies
Consumer Economics
Corporate and Organizational Communication
Corrections (*see* Criminal Justice and Criminology)
Counseling (*see* Counseling Psychology; Pastoral Ministry and Counseling)
Counseling Psychology
Crafts (*see* Art/Fine Arts)
Creative Arts Therapies (*see* Art Therapy; Therapies—Dance, Drama, and Music)
Criminal Justice and Criminology
Cultural Anthropology
Cultural Studies
Dance
Decorative Arts
Demography and Population Studies
Design (*see* Applied Arts and Design; Architecture; Art/Fine Arts; Environmental Design; Graphic Design; Industrial Design; Interior Design; Textile Design; Urban Design)
Developmental Psychology
Diplomacy (*see* International Affairs)
Disability Studies
Drama Therapy (*see* Therapies—Dance, Drama, and Music)
Dramatic Arts (*see* Theater)
Drawing (*see* Art/Fine Arts)
Drug Abuse Counseling (*see* Addictions/Substance Abuse Counseling)
Drug and Alcohol Abuse Counseling (*see* Addictions/Substance Abuse Counseling)
East Asian Studies (*see* Asian Studies)
East European and Russian Studies
Economic Development
Economics
Educational Theater (*see* Theater; Therapies—Dance, Drama, and Music)
Emergency Management
English
Environmental Design
Ethics
Ethnic Studies
Ethnomusicology (*see* Music)
Experimental Psychology
Family and Consumer Sciences—General
Family Studies (*see* Child and Family Studies)
Family Therapy (*see* Child and Family Studies; Clinical Psychology; Counseling Psychology; Marriage and Family Therapy)
Filmmaking (*see* Film, Television, and Video Production)
Film Studies (*see* Film, Television, and Video Production)
Film, Television, and Video Production
Film, Television, and Video Theory and Criticism
Fine Arts (*see* Art/Fine Arts)
Folklore
Foreign Languages (*see* specific language)
Foreign Service (*see* International Affairs; International Development)
Forensic Psychology
Forensic Sciences
Forensics (*see* Speech and Interpersonal Communication)
French
Gender Studies
General Studies (*see* Liberal Studies)
Genetic Counseling
Geographic Information Systems
Geography
German
Gerontology
Graphic Design
Greek (*see* Classics)
Health Communication
Health Psychology
Hebrew (*see* Near and Middle Eastern Languages)
Hebrew Studies (*see* Jewish Studies)
Hispanic and Latin American Languages
Hispanic Studies
Historic Preservation
History
History of Art (*see* Art History)
History of Medicine
History of Science and Technology

Holocaust and Genocide Studies
Home Economics (*see* Family and Consumer Sciences—General)
Homeland Security
Household Economics, Sciences, and Management (*see* Family and
   Consumer Sciences—General)
Human Development
Humanities
Illustration
Industrial and Labor Relations
Industrial and Organizational Psychology
Industrial Design
Interdisciplinary Studies
Interior Design
International Affairs
International Development
International Economics
International Service (*see* International Affairs; International Development)
International Trade Policy
Internet and Interactive Multimedia
Interpersonal Communication (*see* Speech and Interpersonal
   Communication)
Interpretation (*see* Translation and Interpretation)
Islamic Studies (*see* Near and Middle Eastern Studies; Religion)
Italian
Japanese
Japanese Studies (*see* Asian Languages; Asian Studies; Japanese)
Jewelry (*see* Art/Fine Arts)
Jewish Studies
Journalism
Judaic Studies (*see* Jewish Studies; Religion)
Labor Relations (*see* Industrial and Labor Relations)
Landscape Architecture
Latin American Studies
Latin (*see* Classics)
Law Enforcement (*see* Criminal Justice and Criminology)
Liberal Studies
Lighting Design
Linguistics
Literature (*see* Classics; Comparative Literature; specific language)
Marriage and Family Therapy
Mass Communication
Media Studies
Medical Illustration
Medieval and Renaissance Studies
Metalsmithing (*see* Art/Fine Arts)
Middle Eastern Studies (*see* Near and Middle Eastern Studies)
Military and Defense Studies
Mineral Economics
Ministry (*see* Pastoral Ministry and Counseling; Theology)
Missions and Missiology
Motion Pictures (*see* Film, Television, and Video Production)
Museum Studies
Music
Musicology (*see* Music)
Music Therapy (*see* Therapies—Dance, Drama, and Music)
National Security
Native American Studies (*see* American Indian/Native American Studies)
Near and Middle Eastern Languages
Near and Middle Eastern Studies
Near Environment (*see* Family and Consumer Sciences)
Northern Studies
Organizational Psychology (*see* Industrial and Organizational Psychology)
Oriental Languages (*see* Asian Languages)
Oriental Studies (*see* Asian Studies)
Pacific Area/Pacific Rim Studies Painting (*see* Art/Fine Arts)
Pastoral Ministry and Counseling
Philanthropic Studies
Philosophy
Photography
Playwriting (*see* Theater; Writing)
Policy Studies (*see* Public Policy)
Political Science
Population Studies (*see* Demography and Population Studies)
Portuguese
Printmaking (*see* Art/Fine Arts)
Product Design (*see* Industrial Design)
Psychoanalysis and Psychotherapy Psychology—General
Public Administration
Public Affairs
Public History
Public Policy
Public Speaking (*see* Mass Communication; Rhetoric; Speech and
   Interpersonal Communication)
Publishing

Regional Planning (*see* Architecture; Urban and Regional Planning; Urban
   Design; Urban Studies)
Rehabilitation Counseling
Religion
Renaissance Studies (*see* Medieval and Renaissance Studies)
Rhetoric
Romance Languages
Romance Literatures (*see* Romance Languages)
Rural Planning and Studies
Rural Sociology
Russian
Scandinavian Languages
School Psychology
Sculpture (*see* Art/Fine Arts)
Security Administration (*see* Criminal Justice and Criminology)
Slavic Languages
Slavic Studies (*see* East European and Russian Studies; Slavic
   Languages)
Social Psychology
Social Sciences
Sociology
Southeast Asian Studies (*see* Asian Studies)
Soviet Studies (*see* East European and Russian Studies; Russian)
Spanish
Speech and Interpersonal Communication
Sport Psychology
Studio Art (*see* Art/Fine Arts)
Substance Abuse Counseling (*see* Addictions/Substance Abuse
   Counseling)
Survey Methodology
Sustainable Development
Technical Communication
Technical Writing
Telecommunications (*see* Film, Television, and Video Production)
Television (*see* Film, Television, and Video Production)
Textile Design
Textiles (*see* Clothing and Textiles; Textile Design)
Thanatology
Theater
Theater Arts (*see* Theater)
Theology
Therapies—Dance, Drama, and Music
Translation and Interpretation
Transpersonal and Humanistic Psychology
Urban and Regional Planning
Urban Design
Urban Planning (*see* Architecture; Urban and Regional Planning; Urban
   Design; Urban Studies)
Urban Studies
Video (*see* Film, Television, and Video Production)
Visual Arts (*see* Applied Arts and Design; Art/Fine Arts; Film, Television,
   and Video Production; Graphic Design; Illustration; Photography)
Western European Studies
Women's Studies
World Wide Web (*see* Internet and Interactive Multimedia)
Writing

Graduate Programs in the Biological/ Biomedical Sciences & Health Related/ Medical Professions

Acupuncture and Oriental Medicine
Acute Care/Critical Care Nursing Administration (*see* Health Services
   Management and Hospital Administration; Nursing and Healthcare
   Administration; Pharmaceutical Administration)
Adult Nursing
Advanced Practice Nursing (*see* Family Nurse Practitioner Studies)
Allied Health—General
Allied Health Professions (*see* Clinical Laboratory Sciences/Medical
   Technology; Clinical Research; Communication Disorders; Dental
   Hygiene; Emergency Medical Services; Occupational Therapy; Physical
   Therapy; Physician Assistant Studies; Rehabilitation Sciences)
Allopathic Medicine
Anatomy
Anesthesiologist Assistant Studies
Animal Behavior
Bacteriology
Behavioral Sciences (*see* Biopsychology; Neuroscience; Zoology)
Biochemistry
Bioethics
Biological and Biomedical Sciences—General Biological Chemistry (*see*
   Biochemistry)

Biological Oceanography (*see* Marine Biology)
Biophysics
Biopsychology
Botany
Breeding (*see* Botany; Plant Biology; Genetics)
Cancer Biology/Oncology
Cardiovascular Sciences
Cell Biology
Cellular Physiology (*see* Cell Biology; Physiology)
Child-Care Nursing (*see* Maternal and Child/Neonatal Nursing)
Chiropractic
Clinical Laboratory Sciences/Medical Technology
Clinical Research
Community Health
Community Health Nursing
Computational Biology
Conservation (*see* Conservation Biology; Environmental Biology)
Conservation Biology
Crop Sciences (*see* Botany; Plant Biology)
Cytology (*see* Cell Biology)
Dental and Oral Surgery (*see* Oral and Dental Sciences)
Dental Assistant Studies (*see* Dental Hygiene)
Dental Hygiene
Dental Services (*see* Dental Hygiene)
Dentistry
Developmental Biology Dietetics (*see* Nutrition)
Ecology
Embryology (*see* Developmental Biology)
Emergency Medical Services
Endocrinology (*see* Physiology)
Entomology
Environmental Biology
Environmental and Occupational Health
Epidemiology
Evolutionary Biology
Family Nurse Practitioner Studies
Foods (*see* Nutrition)
Forensic Nursing
Genetics
Genomic Sciences
Gerontological Nursing
Health Physics/Radiological Health
Health Promotion
Health-Related Professions (*see* individual allied health professions)
Health Services Management and Hospital Administration
Health Services Research
Histology (*see* Anatomy; Cell Biology)
HIV/AIDS Nursing
Hospice Nursing
Hospital Administration (*see* Health Services Management and Hospital Administration)
Human Genetics
Immunology
Industrial Hygiene
Infectious Diseases
International Health
Laboratory Medicine (*see* Clinical Laboratory Sciences/Medical Technology; Immunology; Microbiology; Pathology)
Life Sciences (*see* Biological and Biomedical Sciences)
Marine Biology
Maternal and Child Health
Maternal and Child/Neonatal Nursing
Medical Imaging
Medical Microbiology
Medical Nursing (*see* Medical/Surgical Nursing)
Medical Physics
Medical/Surgical Nursing
Medical Technology (*see* Clinical Laboratory Sciences/Medical Technology)
Medical Sciences (*see* Biological and Biomedical Sciences)
Medical Science Training Programs (*see* Biological and Biomedical Sciences)
Medicinal and Pharmaceutical Chemistry
Medicinal Chemistry (*see* Medicinal and Pharmaceutical Chemistry)
Medicine (*see* Allopathic Medicine; Naturopathic Medicine; Osteopathic Medicine; Podiatric Medicine)
Microbiology
Midwifery (*see* Nurse Midwifery)
Molecular Biology
Molecular Biophysics
Molecular Genetics
Molecular Medicine
Molecular Pathogenesis
Molecular Pathology
Molecular Pharmacology
Molecular Physiology

Molecular Toxicology
Naturopathic Medicine
Neural Sciences (*see* Biopsychology; Neurobiology; Neuroscience)
Neurobiology
Neuroendocrinology (*see* Biopsychology; Neurobiology; Neuroscience; Physiology)
Neuropharmacology (*see* Biopsychology; Neurobiology; Neuroscience; Pharmacology)
Neurophysiology (*see* Biopsychology; Neurobiology; Neuroscience; Physiology)
Neuroscience
Nuclear Medical Technology (*see* Clinical Laboratory Sciences/ Medical Technology)
Nurse Anesthesia
Nurse Midwifery
Nurse Practitioner Studies (*see* Family Nurse Practitioner Studies)
Nursing Administration (*see* Nursing and Healthcare Administration)
Nursing and Healthcare Administration
Nursing Education
Nursing—General
Nursing Informatics
Nutrition
Occupational Health (*see* Environmental and Occupational Health; Occupational Health Nursing)
Occupational Health Nursing
Occupational Therapy
Oncology (*see* Cancer Biology/Oncology)
Oncology Nursing
Optometry
Oral and Dental Sciences
Oral Biology (*see* Oral and Dental Sciences)
Oral Pathology (*see* Oral and Dental Sciences)
Organismal Biology (*see* Biological and Biomedical Sciences; Zoology)
Oriental Medicine and Acupuncture (*see* Acupuncture and Oriental Medicine)
Orthodontics (*see* Oral and Dental Sciences)
Osteopathic Medicine
Parasitology
Pathobiology
Pathology
Pediatric Nursing
Pedontics (*see* Oral and Dental Sciences)
Perfusion
Pharmaceutical Administration
Pharmaceutical Chemistry (*see* Medicinal and Pharmaceutical Chemistry)
Pharmaceutical Sciences
Pharmacology
Pharmacy
Photobiology of Cells and Organelles (*see* Botany; Cell Biology; Plant Biology)
Physical Therapy
Physician Assistant Studies
Physiological Optics (*see* Vision Sciences)
Podiatric Medicine
Preventive Medicine (*see* Community Health and Public Health)
Physiological Optics (*see* Physiology)
Physiology
Plant Biology
Plant Molecular Biology
Plant Pathology
Plant Physiology
Pomology (*see* Botany; Plant Biology)
Psychiatric Nursing
Public Health—General
Public Health Nursing (*see* Community Health Nursing)
Psychiatric Nursing
Psychobiology (*see* Biopsychology)
Psychopharmacology (*see* Biopsychology; Neuroscience; Pharmacology)
Radiation Biology
Radiological Health (*see* Health Physics/Radiological Health)
Rehabilitation Nursing
Rehabilitation Sciences
Rehabilitation Therapy (*see* Physical Therapy)
Reproductive Biology
School Nursing
Sociobiology (*see* Evolutionary Biology)
Structural Biology
Surgical Nursing (*see* Medical/Surgical Nursing)
Systems Biology
Teratology
Therapeutics
Theoretical Biology (*see* Biological and Biomedical Sciences)
Therapeutics (*see* Pharmaceutical Sciences; Pharmacology; Pharmacy)
Toxicology

Transcultural Nursing
Translational Biology
Tropical Medicine (*see* Parasitology)
Veterinary Medicine
Veterinary Sciences
Virology
Vision Sciences
Wildlife Biology (*see* Zoology)
Women's Health Nursing
Zoology

Graduate Programs in the Physical Sciences, Mathematics, Agricultural Sciences, the Environment & Natural Resources

Acoustics
Agricultural Sciences
Agronomy and Soil Sciences
Analytical Chemistry
Animal Sciences
Applied Mathematics
Applied Physics
Applied Statistics
Aquaculture
Astronomy
Astrophysical Sciences (*see* Astrophysics; Atmospheric Sciences; Meteorology; Planetary and Space Sciences)
Astrophysics
Atmospheric Sciences
Biological Oceanography (*see* Marine Affairs; Marine Sciences; Oceanography)
Biomathematics
Biometry
Biostatistics
Chemical Physics
Chemistry
Computational Sciences
Condensed Matter Physics
Dairy Science (*see* Animal Sciences)
Earth Sciences (*see* Geosciences)
Environmental Management and Policy
Environmental Sciences
Environmental Studies (*see* Environmental Management and Policy)
Experimental Statistics (*see* Statistics)
Fish, Game, and Wildlife Management
Food Science and Technology
Forestry
General Science (*see* specific topics)
Geochemistry
Geodetic Sciences
Geological Engineering (*see* Geology)
Geological Sciences (*see* Geology)
Geology
Geophysical Fluid Dynamics (*see* Geophysics)
Geophysics
Geosciences
Horticulture
Hydrogeology
Hydrology
Inorganic Chemistry
Limnology
Marine Affairs
Marine Geology
Marine Sciences
Marine Studies (*see* Marine Affairs; Marine Geology; Marine Sciences; Oceanography)
Mathematical and Computational Finance
Mathematical Physics
Mathematical Statistics (*see* Applied Statistics; Statistics)
Mathematics
Meteorology
Mineralogy
Natural Resource Management (*see* Environmental Management and Policy; Natural Resources)
Natural Resources
Nuclear Physics (*see* Physics)
Ocean Engineering (*see* Marine Affairs; Marine Geology; Marine Sciences; Oceanography)
Oceanography
Optical Sciences

Optical Technologies (*see* Optical Sciences)
Optics (*see* Applied Physics; Optical Sciences; Physics)
Organic Chemistry
Paleontology
Paper Chemistry (*see* Chemistry)
Photonics
Physical Chemistry
Physics
Planetary and Space Sciences
Plant Sciences
Plasma Physics
Poultry Science (*see* Animal Sciences)
Radiological Physics (*see* Physics)
Range Management (*see* Range Science)
Range Science
Resource Management (*see* Environmental Management and Policy; Natural Resources)
Solid-Earth Sciences (*see* Geosciences)
Space Sciences (*see* Planetary and Space Sciences)
Statistics
Theoretical Chemistry
Theoretical Physics
Viticulture and Enology
Water Resources

Graduate Programs in Engineering & Applied Sciences

Aeronautical Engineering (*see* Aerospace/Aeronautical Engineering)
Aerospace/Aeronautical Engineering
Aerospace Studies (*see* Aerospace/Aeronautical Engineering)
Agricultural Engineering
Applied Mechanics (*see* Mechanics)
Applied Science and Technology
Architectural Engineering
Artificial Intelligence/Robotics
Astronautical Engineering (*see* Aerospace/Aeronautical Engineering)
Automotive Engineering
Aviation
Biochemical Engineering
Bioengineering Bioinformatics
Biological Engineering (*see* Bioengineering)
Biomedical Engineering
Biosystems Engineering
Biotechnology
Ceramic Engineering (*see* Ceramic Sciences and Engineering)
Ceramic Sciences and Engineering
Ceramics (*see* Ceramic Sciences and Engineering)
Chemical Engineering
Civil Engineering
Computer and Information Systems Security
Computer Engineering
Computer Science
Computing Technology (*see* Computer Science)
Construction Engineering
Construction Management
Database Systems
Electrical Engineering
Electronic Materials
Electronics Engineering (*see* Electrical Engineering)
Energy and Power Engineering
Energy Management and Policy
Engineering and Applied Sciences
Engineering and Public Affairs (*see* Technology and Public Policy)
Engineering and Public Policy (*see* Energy Management and Policy; Technology and Public Policy)
Engineering Design
Engineering Management
Engineering Mechanics (*see* Mechanics)
Engineering Metallurgy (*see* Metallurgical Engineering and Metallurgy)
Engineering Physics
Environmental Design (*see* Environmental Engineering)
Environmental Engineering
Ergonomics and Human Factors
Financial Engineering
Fire Protection Engineering
Food Engineering (*see* Agricultural Engineering)
Game Design and Development
Gas Engineering (*see* Petroleum Engineering)
Geological Engineering
Geophysics Engineering (*see* Geological Engineering)
Geotechnical Engineering
Hazardous Materials Management

Health Informatics
Health Systems (*see* Safety Engineering; Systems Engineering)
Highway Engineering (*see* Transportation and Highway Engineering)
Human-Computer Interaction
Human Factors (*see* Ergonomics and Human Factors)
Hydraulics
Hydrology (*see* Water Resources Engineering)
Industrial Engineering (*see* Industrial/Management Engineering)
Industrial/Management Engineering
Information Science
Internet Engineering
Macromolecular Science (*see* Polymer Science and Engineering)
Management Engineering (*see* Engineering Management; Industrial/
   Management Engineering)
Management of Technology
Manufacturing Engineering
Marine Engineering (*see* Civil Engineering)
Materials Engineering
Materials Sciences
Mechanical Engineering
Mechanics
Medical Informatics
Metallurgical Engineering and Metallurgy
Metallurgy (*see* Metallurgical Engineering and Metallurgy)
Mineral/Mining Engineering
Modeling and Simulation
Nanotechnology
Nuclear Engineering
Ocean Engineering
Operations Research
Paper and Pulp Engineering
Petroleum Engineering
Pharmaceutical Engineering
Plastics Engineering (*see* Polymer Science and Engineering)
Polymer Science and Engineering
Public Policy (*see* Energy Management and Policy; Technology and Public
   Policy)
Reliability Engineering
Robotics (*see* Artificial Intelligence/Robotics)
Safety Engineering
Software Engineering
Solid-State Sciences (*see* Materials Sciences)
Structural Engineering
Surveying Science and Engineering
Systems Analysis (*see* Systems Engineering)
Systems Engineering
Systems Science
Technology and Public Policy
Telecommunications
Telecommunications Management
Textile Sciences and Engineering
Textiles (*see* Textile Sciences and Engineering)
Transportation and Highway Engineering
Urban Systems Engineering (*see* Systems Engineering)
Waste Management (*see* Hazardous Materials Management)
Water Resources Engineering

Graduate Programs in Business, Education, Information Studies, Law & Social Work

Accounting
Actuarial Science
Adult Education
Advertising and Public Relations
Agricultural Education
Alcohol Abuse Counseling (*see* Counselor Education)
Archival Management and Studies
Art Education
Athletics Administration (*see* Kinesiology and Movement Studies)
Athletic Training and Sports Medicine
Audiology (*see* Communication Disorders)
Aviation Management
Banking (*see* Finance and Banking)
Business Administration and Management—General
Business Education
Communication Disorders
Community College Education
Computer Education
Continuing Education (*see* Adult Education)
Counseling (*see* Counselor Education)
Counselor Education

Curriculum and Instruction
Developmental Education
Distance Education Development
Drug Abuse Counseling (*see* Counselor Education)
Early Childhood Education
Educational Leadership and Administration
Educational Measurement and Evaluation
Educational Media/Instructional Technology
Educational Policy
Educational Psychology
Education—General
Education of the Blind (*see* Special Education)
Education of the Deaf (*see* Special Education)
Education of the Gifted
Education of the Hearing Impaired (*see* Special Education)
Education of the Learning Disabled (*see* Special Education)
Education of the Mentally Retarded (*see* Special Education)
Education of the Physically Handicapped (*see* Special Education)
Education of Students with Severe/Multiple Disabilities
Education of the Visually Handicapped (*see* Special Education)
Electronic Commerce
Elementary Education
English as a Second Language
English Education
Entertainment Management
Entrepreneurship
Environmental Education
Environmental Law
Exercise and Sports Science
Exercise Physiology (*see* Kinesiology and Movement Studies)
Facilities and Entertainment Management
Finance and Banking
Food Services Management (*see* Hospitality Management)
Foreign Languages Education
Foundations and Philosophy of Education
Guidance and Counseling (*see* Counselor Education)
Health Education
Health Law
Hearing Sciences (*see* Communication Disorders)
Higher Education
Home Economics Education
Hospitality Management
Hotel Management (*see* Travel and Tourism)
Human Resources Development
Human Resources Management
Human Services
Industrial Administration (*see* Industrial and Manufacturing Management)
Industrial and Manufacturing Management
Industrial Education (*see* Vocational and Technical Education)
Information Studies
Instructional Technology (*see* Educational Media/Instructional Technology)
Insurance
Intellectual Property Law
International and Comparative Education
International Business
International Commerce (*see* International Business)
International Economics (*see* International Business)
International Trade (*see* International Business)
Investment and Securities (*see* Business Administration and
   Management; Finance and Banking; Investment Management)
Investment Management
Junior College Education (*see* Community College Education)
Kinesiology and Movement Studies
Law
Legal and Justice Studies
Leisure Services (*see* Recreation and Park Management)
Leisure Studies
Library Science
Logistics
Management (*see* Business Administration and Management)
Management Information Systems
Management Strategy and Policy
Marketing
Marketing Research
Mathematics Education
Middle School Education
Movement Studies (*see* Kinesiology and Movement Studies)
Multilingual and Multicultural Education
Museum Education
Music Education
Nonprofit Management
Nursery School Education (*see* Early Childhood Education)
Occupational Education (*see* Vocational and Technical Education)
Organizational Behavior
Organizational Management

Parks Administration (*see* Recreation and Park Management)
Personnel (*see* Human Resources Development; Human Resources Management; Organizational Behavior; Organizational Management; Student Affairs)
Philosophy of Education (*see* Foundations and Philosophy of Education)
Physical Education
Project Management
Public Relations (*see* Advertising and Public Relations)
Quality Management
Quantitative Analysis
Reading Education
Real Estate
Recreation and Park Management
Recreation Therapy (*see* Recreation and Park Management)
Religious Education
Remedial Education (*see* Special Education)
Restaurant Administration (*see* Hospitality Management)
Science Education
Secondary Education
Social Sciences Education
Social Studies Education (*see* Social Sciences Education)
Social Work
Special Education

Speech-Language Pathology and Audiology (*see* Communication Disorders)
Sports Management
Sports Medicine (*see* Athletic Training and Sports Medicine)
Sports Psychology and Sociology (*see* Kinesiology and Movement Studies)
Student Affairs
Substance Abuse Counseling (*see* Counselor Education)
Supply Chain Management
Sustainability Management
Systems Management (*see* Management Information Systems)
Taxation
Teacher Education (*see* specific subject areas)
Teaching English as a Second Language (*see* English as a Second Language)
Technical Education (*see* Vocational and Technical Education)
Transportation Management
Travel and Tourism
Urban Education
Vocational and Technical Education
Vocational Counseling (*see* Counselor Education)

Directories and Subject Areas in This Book